Reference Guide to

WORLD LITERATURE

THIRD EDITION

VOLUME 1

ST. JAMES REFERENCE GUIDES

American Literature

English Literature, 3 vols.

French Literature, 2 vols.

Holocaust Literature

Short Fiction

World Literature, 2 vols.

Reference Guide to

WORLD
LITERATURE

THIRD EDITION

Volume 1
AUTHORS

EDITORS
SARA PENDERGAST
and
TOM PENDERGAST

St J
**ST. JAMES
PRESS**

THOMSON

GALE

Detroit • New York • San Diego • San Francisco • Cleveland • New Haven, Conn. • Waterville, Maine • London • Munich

Reference Guide to World Literature, 3rd edition

Sara and Tom Pendergast

Project Editor
Kristin Hart

Editorial
Erin Bealmear, Joann Cerrito, Jim Craddock, Stephen Cusack, Miranda H. Ferrara, Peter

M. Gareffa, Margaret Mazurkiewicz, Carol A. Schwartz, Christine Tomassini, Michael J. Tyrkus

Manufacturing
Rhonda Williams

LIBRARY OF CONGRESS CATALOG NUMBER

Reference guide to world literature / editors, Sara Pendergast, Tom Pendergast.— 3rd ed.
    p. cm.
Includes bibliographical references and index.
    ISBN 1-55862-490-2 (hardcover : set) — ISBN 1-55862-491-0 (v. 1) — ISBN 1-55862-492-9 (v. 2)
    1. Literature—History and criticism. I. Pendergast, Sara. II. Pendergast, Tom.
  PN524.R44 2003 v. 1
  809—dc21

2002015410

This title is also available as an e-book.
ISBN: 1-55862-534-8 (set)
Contact your Gale sales representative for ordering information.

ISBN: 1-55862-490-2

Printed in the United States of America
10 9 8 7 6 5 4 3 2 1

CONTENTS

EDITOR'S NOTE

You are holding in your hands the third edition of the *Reference Guide to World Literature*, the second edition of which was published in 1995 and was itself an updated and expanded edition of *Great Foreign Language Writers*, published in 1984. Expanding on the coverage of these earlier works, the present edition contains some 1100 entries, divided nearly evenly between entries on writers and literary works. The scope of the *Reference Guide* spans recorded history and reaches up to the present.

The Reference Guide to World Literature contains two distinct types of entries: those covering the work of an author and those covering a literary work. Each author entry begins with a biographical summary of the subject and includes details (where known) of the author's birth, education and training, military service, family, career, awards, honors, and honorary degrees. Then follows a selected list of publications by the author, and a selected list of bibliographical and critical works about the author. Finally, each author entry contains a signed critical essay which assesses the author's work, reputation, and influence. Each entry on a literary work contains a brief header indicating the author and date of creation and a signed critical essay. In the case that the author of the literary work is unknown, an introductory section provides information about the known circumstances of the work's creation and a brief listing of critical studies about the work.

The publications section of the author entries attempts to account for all separately published books by the author, including translations into English. Broadsheets, single sermons and lectures, minor pamphlets, exhibition catalogs, etc., are omitted. Dates refer to the first publication in book form unless indicated otherwise; we have attempted to list the actual year of publication, which is sometimes different from the date given on the title page. Reprints of works including facsimile editions are generally not listed unless they involve a revision of the title. Titles are given in modern spelling and are often in ''short'' form. They are always in italic, except for those that are literal (i.e. non-published) translations, which appear in square brackets. The publication list may contain some or all of the following categories:

Collections: This contains a selection of ''standard'' editions, including the most recent collection of the complete works and of the individual genres (verse, plays, fiction, etc.). For those collections published after the author's death, only those that have some editorial authority are cited.

Fiction: Where it is not made apparent by the title, collections of short fiction are indicated by the inclusion of ''stories'' in parentheses after the title.

Verse: This includes collections and individual poems that were published in book form, listed chronologically by date of publication.

Plays: This includes original plays, adaptations, and other works for the stage (libretti, ballet scenarios, etc.). Dates for both publication and production are given. Titles are arranged chronologically by date of first performance or date of first publication, whichever is earliest. Published English translations are listed, but not those of individual productions.

Screenplays/Television Plays/Radio Plays: These categories include original works and adaptations for these media, listed by date of release or first broadcast.

Other: This includes publications that do not fit readily into the above categories, principally miscellanies and nonfiction writing, such as journalism, essays, theoretical works, travel writing, memoirs, letters, etc.

A separate section contains selected works about the author. This section may contain one or both of the following categories:

Bibliography: This includes published works relating to primary and secondary literature. General bibliographies of literary periods, genres, or counties, etc., are rarely listed.

Critical Studies: This includes critical works and biographies of the subject, listed in chronological order of publication. This section concentrates on book-length studies in English published after 1945, although in a few cases selected earlier material is cited. Where there is a noticeable scarcity of critical works in English, publications written in the subject's own language are included. On occasion articles, usually written in English, have also been listed.

This book concludes with a Title Index to the publications lists. This contains titles of all works listed in the fiction, verse, and plays sections of each entry including titles in the writer's original language and English translations, as well as selected important works of nonfiction.

ACKNOWLEDGMENTS

A reference work such as this is the product of many hands. Our thanks begin with Steven Serafin, whose guiding hand in selecting advisers and entries and whose expertise with the languages represented in this collection were indispensable. We would like to thank our advisers for their skill and expertise in selecting suitable entrants to include in this edition. Thanks also to the authors of the entries; many of these authors are the acknowledged authorities on their subject, and their expertise and acumen can be clearly seen in their thoughtful introductions to each of the subjects. We would like to thank our copyeditors, Jennifer Wallace and Michael Najjar, as well as our contacts/friends Kristin Hart and Peter Gareffa at St. James Press. Finally, we would like to thank all those at St. James Press whose names we do not know, but who help turn the electronic files that we work with into the reality that you hold today.

INTRODUCTION

In his letters dating from the second century AD, the Roman orator and statesman Pliny the Younger wrote of finding solace in poetry as a means to embrace the uncertainties of life and to accept, albeit reluctantly, the inevitability of death. "Literature," he said, "is both my joy and my comfort: it can add to every happiness and there is no sorrow it cannot console." The poet took refuge in his work and sought to communicate to others the depth of his emotion and the expanse of his intellect. It is through literature that we embrace our potential and acknowledge our limitations, and it was undoubtedly this presence of mind and spirit that forged the first attempts at literary expression and that continues in our own time to define the essence and value of artistic endeavor.

The growth and development of literature is most often viewed as a reflection of history, mapping the evolution of human culture and serving in its earliest renderings as either documentation or eulogy: to record for posterity or to sing praise and exaltation. It was a task assigned to the scribe not the artist, but in time the purpose and practice of literature would evolve in form and meaning to where the telling of the tale became as important as the tale itself. The nature of literature broadened in scope and objective to provide entertainment as well as instruction. As a result, the reader found pleasure in literature as the imagination unfolded in stories of gods and monsters, the death of kings, and the making of legend. If we believe as posited by philosopher Bernard Berenson that literature is "the autobiography of humanity," then we come to better know ourselves by knowing those who came before us and those with whom we share our existence. In effect, literature becomes a means to examine and to understand the differences, as well as the similarities, among peoples, languages, and societies. It serves to engage our expectation, to enrich our sensibilities, and to elevate our perception of self-awareness and identity.

Designed as a complement to the St. James Reference Guides to American and British literatures, the third edition of the *Reference Guide to World Literature* represents a comprehensive and authoritative survey to literatures written in languages other than English from the earliest known manuscripts to the works of present-day writers of international stature. Merging East and West, the ancient with the contemporary, the *Reference Guide* provides a broad spectrum of world literature extending from the anonymous prose and verse of the *Vedas*, the sacred texts of Hinduism, originating in the third millennium BC, to the ancient Sumerian epic of *Gilgamesh*; from the Hebrew texts of the Old Testament to *The Iliad* of Homer; from the Golden Age of Greek drama to the Indian folk epic the *Mahābhārata*; from the *Confessions* of St. Augustine to the classical poetry of the Tang dynasty; from *The Conference of the Birds* by the Persian poet Farid al-Din Attār to *The Divine Comedy* by Dante Alighiera; from *The Praise of Folly* by Desiderius Erasmus to *Don Quixote* by Miguel de Cervantes; from Molière's *Don Juan* to Goethe's *Faust*; from realism and naturalism to the advent of modernism; from existentialism to the theater of the absurd; from postmodernism to the literature of the new millennium.

The present edition provides expanded coverage of literatures in less represented languages, the primary focus being Arabic, Chinese, and Japanese, as well as previously unrepresented languages including Albanian, Estonian, Indonesian, Kurdish, and Thai. Writers from the Arab world added to the edition include the pre-Islamic poet Imru' al-Qays, the poetess al-Khansā', the classical poet al-Mutanabbī, the Andalusian poet Ibn Khafājah, and the Sufi poets Ibn al-Fārid and Ibn al-'Arabī and contemporary authors such as the Iranian novelist and short-story writer Jalal Al-e Ahmad, the Egyptian short-story writer and dramatist Yūsuf Idrīs, and the Syrian-Lebanese poet Adūnīs. Chinese authors include the Ming dynasty dramatist Tang Xianzu, the novelist Ding Ling, and dramatist, novelist, and Nobel laureate Gao Xingjian. Japanese authors include poets Miyazawa Kenji, Hagiwara Sakutaro, and Nishiwaki Junzaburo and novelists Lao She, Shimazaki Toson, Shiga Naoya, Ibuse Masuji, and Abe Kobo.

Authors writing in previously unrepresented languages include the Albanian novelist and poet Ismail Kadaré, the Estonian poet Jaan Kaplinski and the poet and novelist Jaan Kross, the Indonesian novelist Pramoedya Ananta Toer and the poet Chairil Anwar, the Kurdish poet Abdulla Goran, and the Thai novelist Siburapha. Authors from previously underrepresented literatures include East and Central European writers such as the dramatist Václav Havel, the novelist Ivan Klíma, and the novelist Milan Kundera, writing in Czech; the short-story writer and poet Tadeusz Borowski, and the poet and dramatist Tadeusz Różewicz, writing in Polish; francophone and lusophone writers from North, East, and West Africa including the Moroccan novelist and poet Tahar Ben Jelloun and the novelist Abdelkebir Khatibi, the Tunisian novelist Albert Memmi, and the Ivorian novelist Ahmadou Kourouma, writing in French, and Mozambican poet José Craveirinha, writing in Portuguese.

This edition is also noteworthy for its expanded coverage of contemporary women writers, including the Lebanese novelist Evelyne Accad, the Algerian novelist Assia Djebar, and the Canadian poet and novelist Nicole Brossard, writing in French; the Chilean novelist Isabel Allende, the Nicaraguan poet and novelist Gioconda Belli, and the Argentinian novelist Luisa Valenzuela, writing in Spanish; the Polish poet and Nobel laureate Wisława Szymborska; the Indian novelist Qurratulain Hyder, writing in Urdu; the

Italian novelist Francesca Duranti; the Russian novelist Tatyana Tolstaya; the Japanese novelist Tsushima Yuko; and the Chinese short-story writer and novelist Li Ang. Within the context of the social and political transformation from the postwar twentieth century to the present, the increasing representation and contribution of women on an international basis has redefined the scope and dimension of world literature. Other major contemporary authors include the Martinican novelist Patrick Chamoiseau, writing in French; the Hungarian novelist and short-story writer Péter Esterházy, the Danish novelist Peter Høeg; the Chinese poet Bei Dao and the novelists Mo Yan and Su Tong; and the Japanese novelist Murakami Haruki.

Literature in the new millennium is complex as it is convoluted, informed by diverse and elements: postmodernism, multiculturalism, and global diaspora. Yet it is the voice of Pliny the Younger that resonates to remind us of the true essence of literary endeavor: to bring joy and comfort; to provide inspiration and understanding; to justify our being; and to bear witness on the times in which we live. As noted by author Salman Rushdie, ''Literature is where I go to explore the highest and lowest places in human society and in the human spirit, where I hope to find not absolute truth but the truth of the tale, of the imagination and of the heart.''

—Steven R. Serafin
Hunter College of the City University of New York

ADVISERS

Roger Allen
University of Pennsylvania

Alison Bailey
University of London

Christopher Cairns
University College, Wales

Marvin Carlson
CUNY, New York

Ruby Cohn
University of California, Davis

Bogdan Czaykowski
University of British Columbia

James Diggle
Queen's College, Cambridge

David William Foster
Arizona State University

Michael Freeman
University of Leicester

Janet Garton
University of East Anglia, Norwich

Howard Goldblatt
University of Notre Dame

Theo Hermans
University College, London

Hosea Hirata
Tufts University

Peter Hutchinson
Trinity Hall, Cambridge

R.S. McGregor
University of Cambridge

A.B. McMillin
University of London

David O'Connell
Georgia State University

P.A. Odber de Baubeta
University of Birmingham

Jerzy Peterkiewicz
London

Christopher R. Pike
University of Keele

Girdar Rathi
New Delhi

Sven H. Rossel
University of Vienna

Steven Serafin
Hunter College, CUNY, New York

G. Singh
formerly of Queen's
University, Belfast

Peter Skrine
University of Bristol

Daniel Weissbort
University of Iowa

CONTRIBUTORS

Donald Adamson
Peter F. Ainsworth
Robin Aizlewood
Ahmed Ali
Margrethe Alexandroni
Hans Christian Andersen
J.K. Anderson
D.J. Andrews
Alireza Anushiravani
Brigitte Edith Zapp Archibald
A. James Arnold
William Arrowsmith
B. Ashbrook
Keith Aspley
Stuart Atkins
Howard Atkinson
Harry Aveling
Peter Avery

K.P. Bahadur
Ehrhard Bahr
D.R. Shackleton Bailey
David M. Bain
Barry Baldwin
Aida A. Bamia
Alan F. Bance
Gabrielle Barfoot
John Barsby
Peter I. Barta
Susan Bassnett
Edward Batley
Roderick Beaton
Janine Beichman
David Bell
Ian A. Bell
Thomas G. Bergin
Alan Best
Binghong Lu
Sandra Blane
Elizabeth Bobrick
Joan Booth
Paul W. Borgeson, Jr.
Patrick Brady
Denis Brass
Gerard J. Brault
S.H. Braund
Peter Broome
Michael Brophy
Catherine Savage Brosman
Gordon Brotherston
Jennifer Brown
Penny Brown
Dorothy Bryson
A.W. Bulloch
Alan Bullock
B. Burns

J.M. Buscall

Alessandro Cancian
Francisco Carenas
Steven D. Carter
Anthony J. Cascardi
Remo Catani
Philip Cavendish
Mary Ann Caws
Andrea C. Cervi
C. Chadwick
Roland A. Champagne
Linda H. Chance
Tom Cheeseman
Ying-Ying Chein
Diana Chlebek
Erik C. Christensen
Mirna Cicioni
John R. Clark
Stephen Clark
Shirley Clarke
David Coad
Michael Collie
Desmond J. Conacher
David Constantine
Ray Cooke
Thomas L. Cooksey
Neil Cornwell
C.D.N. Costa
Sally McMullen (Croft)
Carmen Cross
G.P. Cubbin
Jan Čulík
James M. Curtis
G.F. Cushing
Edmund Cusick
Adam Czerniawski
Lóránt Czigány

James N. Davidson
Catherine Davies
Santiago Daydi-Tolson
René de Costa
Alan Deighton
John Dickie
Sheila J. Dickson
C.E.J. Dolamore
Ken Dowden
Sam Driver
John Dunkley
Osman Durrani

Gwynne Edwards
Stanislaw Eile
Sarah Ekdawi
Robert Elsie

Herman Ermolaev
Jo Evans

Michael Falchikov
Nancy Kanach Fehsenfeld
Jane Fenoulhet
Alvaro Fernández-Bravo
Bruno Ferraro
John Fletcher
John L. Flood
A.P. Foulkes
Wallace Fowlie
Frank J. Frost
Barbara P. Fulks
Michael A. Fuller

David Gascoyne
John Gatt-Rutter
Tina Gianoulis
Margaret Gibson
Robert Gibson
Mary E. Giles
Donald Gilman
Nahum N. Glatzer
John Gledson
Gary Godfrey
Ingeborg M. Goesll
Marketa Goetz-Stankiewicz
Janet N. Gold
Sander M. Goldberg
George Gömöri
D.C.R.A. Goonetilleke
Colin Graham
Peter J. Graves
Roger Green
R.P.H. Green
Claire E. Gruzelier
Albert E. Gurganus

Oscar A. Haac
David T. Haberly
Brigid Haines
Igor Hájek
David M. Halperin
P.T. Harries
Nigel Harris
Patricia Harry
John Hart
Thomas R. Hart
E.C. Hawkesworth
Ronald Hayman
Patrick Heenan
John Hibberd
James Higgins
David Hill
Sabine Hillen

Ian Hilton
Hosea Hirata
Keith Hitchins
Leighton Hodson
Th. Emil Homerin
Edward Waters Hood
Louise Hopkins
Thomas K. Hubbard
Lothar Huber
William M. Hutchins
Lois Boe Hyslop

Margaret C. Ives

David Jackson
Tony James
Regina Janes
D.E. Jenkinson
Lewis Jillings
Jeffrey Johnson
D. Mervyn Jones
Roger Jones
W. Glyn Jones

Bożena Karwowska
Brian Keith-Smith
Hanaa Kilany
Rachel Killick
J.H. King
Peter King
Robert Kirsner
W.J.S. Kirton
Charles Klopp
A.V. Knowles
Wulf Koepke
Jack Kolbert
Kathleen L. Komar
Linn Bratteteig Konrad
David Konstan
Myrto Konstantarakos
Charles Kwong

F.J. Lamport
Jordan Lancaster
Pierre J. Lapaire
David H.J. Larmour
Rex W. Last
Dan Latimer
Renate Latimer
John Lee
Mabel Lee
André Lefevere
Harry Levin
Silvano Levy
Virginia L. Lewis
Dian Li
Emanuele Licastro
Sylvia Li-Chun Lin
Maria Manuel Lisboa
Heather Lloyd

Rosemary Lloyd
Ladislaus Löb
Rosa Lombardi
Jacqueline Long
Dagmar C.G. Lorenz
Andrea Loselle
Gregory L. Lucente
David S. Luft
Torborg Lundell
Christopher Lupke

J.F. Marfany
Gaetana Marrone
Heitor Martins
David Maskell
Eve Mason
Haydn Mason
Derek Maus
Gita May
Jane McAdoo
E.A. McCobb
Patrick McCarthy
A. McDermott
David McDuff
Richard J.A. McGregor
Martin L. McLaughlin
Alexander G. McKay
Keith McMahon
Arnold McMillin
Rory McTurk
Gordon McVay
A.J. Meech
Siegfried Mews
Vasa D. Mihailovich
Michael J. Mikós
Gary B. Miles
Paul Allen Miller
Kristina Milnor
Earl Miner
John Douglas Minyard
Masao Miyoshi
Matthew Mizenko
Edward Moran
Nicole Mosher
Warren Motte
Anna Lydia Motto
Vanna Motta
Kenneth Muir
Brian Murdoch
S.M. Murk-Jansen
Brian Murphy
Walter Musolino

William E. Naff
Susan Napier
Frank J. Nisetich
Paul Norlen

R.J. Oakley
Jeanne A. Ojala

Tom O'Neill
Dayna Oscherwitz

Seija Paddon
Cecil Parrott
Alan K.G. Paterson
Georgina Paul
D. Keith Peacock
Noel A. Peacock
Roger Pearson
Janet Pérez
Elli Philokyprou
Donald Peter Alexander Pirie
David Platton
Gordon Pocock
Beth Pollack
Valentina Polukhina
Charles A. Porter
Oralia Preble-Niemi
Michael P. Predmore
Nicole Prunster
Joseph Pucci
Judith Purver
Dušan Puvačić

Olga Ragusa
Ana M. Ranero
Judy Rawson
J.H. Reid
Robert Reid
John H. Reilly
Barbara Reynolds
Hugh Ridley
Norma Rinsler
Colin Riordan
Michael Robinson
Philip E.J. Robinson
David Rock
Eamonn Rodgers
Margaret Rogister
Michele Valerie Ronnick
Hugh Rorrison
Wendy Rosslyn
John Rothenberg
Andrew Rothwell
Donald Roy
Lisa M. Ruch
R.B. Rutherford

William Merritt Sale, III
Thomas Salumets
Jeffrey L. Sammons
N.K. Sandars
L. Natalie Sandomirsky
Gerlinde Ulm Sanford
Hélène N. Sanko
Kumiko Sato
Barbara Saunders
Barry P. Scherr
Gerd K. Schneider

Thomas Schnellbächer
Irene Scobbie
Mary Scott
Edward Seidensticker
Dorothy S. Severin
Sabina Sharkey
Jocelyn Sharlet
Ruth Sharman
Barnett Shaw
David Shaw
Faiza W. Shereen
Emi Shimokawa
Shoichi Saeki
David Sices
Tony Simoes da Silva
John D. Simons
Colin Smethurst
Christopher Smith
Natalie Smith
Sarah Cox Smith
David Smyth
J. Kelly Sowards
Ronald Speirs
James Russell Stamm
Noel Stanley
Roy Starrs
Paul Starkey
C.C. Stathatos
Susan Isabel Stein
Carl Steiner
R.H. Stephenson
Eric Sterling
Mary E. Stewart

Alexander Stillmark
Elisabeth C. Stopp
Ian C. Storey
Matthew Strecher
Sarah Strong
J.R. Stubbs
Arrigo V. Subiotto
Mary Sugar
Henry W. Sullivan
Helena Szépe
Elzbieta Szoka

John E. Tailby
Myron Taylor
Anna-Marie Taylor
Philip Thody
David Thomas
Judith Thurman
Shawkat M. Toorawa
Robert M. Torrance
Tamara Trojanowska
Andrew T. Tsubaki

Sabine Vanacker
Rolf Venner
Hugo J. Verani
Maïr Verthuy
Robert Vilain
Pascale Voilley

Frank W. Walbank
Bruce Walker

Albert H. Wallace
George Walsh
J. Michael Walton
Edward Wasiolek
Bruce Watson
Shawncey J. Webb
David Welsh
Alfred D. White
Sally A. White-Wallis
Kenneth S. Whitton
Juliet Wigmore
Faith Wigzell
Mark Williams
Rhys Williams
Jason Wilson
Jerry Phillips Winfield
Michael Winkler
A.J. Woodman
M.J. Woods
Tim Woods
James B. Woodward
A. Colin Wright
Barbara Wright
Elizabeth Wright

Xiaobin Yang
John D. Yohannan
Howard T. Young
Robin Young

Magdalena J. Zaborowska
G. Zanker
Jeanne Morgan Zarucchi

ALPHABETICAL LIST OF WRITERS AND WORKS

Ihara Saikaku
Gyula Illyés
   "A Sentence For Tyranny"
Eugène Ionesco
   The Bald Prima Donna
   Rhinoceros
Ishigaki Rin
Max Jacob
Alfred Jarry
   Ubu Rex
Johannes V. Jensen
St. Jerome
Journey to the West
Juan Ramón Jiménez
   Platero and I
St. John of the Cross
Uwe Johnson
Sor Juana Inés de la Cruz
Ernst Jünger
Juvenal
   Satire 10
Kabīr
Ismail Kadare
Franz Kafka
   The Castle
   The Metamorphosis
   The Trial
Georg Kaiser
   The Gas Trilogy: The Coral (Die
     Koralle), Gas I, GasII
Kalevala
Kālidāsa
   The Cloud Messenger
   Śakuntalā
Jaan Kaplinski
Kawabata Yasunari
   Snow Country
Nikos Kazantzakis
   The Last Temptation
Gottfried Keller
Kenkō
Abdelkebir Khatibi
Velimir Khlebnikov
   "Incantation by Laughter"
Søren Kierkegaard
Danilo Kiš
Heinrich von Kleist
   The Broken Jug
   Michael Kohlhaas
   The Prince of Homburg
Ivan Klíma
Friedrich Gottlieb Klopstock
Jan Kochanowski
Ahmadou Kourouma
Zygmunt Krasiński
Miroslav Krleža
Jaan Kross
Maria Kuncewicz
Milan Kundera

Jean de La Fontaine
   Fables
François La Rochefoucauld
   Maxims
Choderlos de Laclos
   Les Liaisons dangereuses
Madame de Lafayette
Jules Laforgue
   The Last Poems
Pär Lagerkvist
Selma Lagerlöf
   Gösta Berling's Saga
Alphonse de Lamartine
Giuseppe Tomasi di Lampedusa
Lao She
   Rickshaw Boy
Compte de Lautréamont
Halldór Laxness
Lazarillo de Tormes
Jakob Michael Reinhold Lenz
   The Tutor
Siegfried Lenz
   The German Lesson
Giacomo Leopardi
   "The Broom"
   "The Infinite"
   "To Himself"
Mikhail Lermontov
   A Hero Of Our Time
Alain-René Lesage
Gotthold Ephraim Lessing
   Minna Von Barnhelm
   Nathan The Wise
Carlo Levi
   Christ Stopped at Eboli
Primo Levi
   The Periodic Table
José Lezama Lima
Li Ang
Li Bai
   "Hard is the Road to Shu"
   "Invitation to Wine"
Väinö Linna
Clarice Lispector
The Little Clay Cart
Livy
Ivar Lo-Johansson
Lu Xun
Lucan
Lucian
Lucretius
Martin Luther
   "Ein Feste Burg"
The Mabinogion
Antonio Machado
Joaquim Maria Machado de Assis
   Dom Casmurro
   The Posthumous Memoirs of
     Braz Cubas

Niccolò Machiavelli
   The Mandrake
   The Prince
Maurice Maeterlinck
   The Blue Bird
   The Intruder
Mahābhārata
Naguib Mahfouz
Vladimir Maiakovskii
   About This
   The Bedbug
   Cloud in Trousers
Stéphane Mallarmé
   L'Après-midi d'un faune
   Un coup de dés jamais n'abolira
     le Hasard
   Hérodiade
   Ses purs ongles très haut dédiant
     leur onyx
André Malraux
   Man's Fate
Osip Mandel'shtam
Heinrich Manh
   The Blue Angel
Thomas Mann
   Buddenbrooks: The Decline of
     a Family
   Confessions of Felix Krull,
     Confidence Man
   Death in Venice
   Doctor Faustus
   The Magic Mountain
Alessandro Manzoni
   The Betrothed
Leopoldo Marechal
Marguerite de Navarre
Marie de France
   Guigamor
Marivaux
   The False Confessions
   The Game of Love and Chance
   A Matter of Dispute
José Martí
Martial
   "Epigrams"
Roger Martin Du Gard
Masaoka Shiki
Guy de Maupassant
   "L'Abandonné"
   "The Necklace"
   Pierre and Jean
François Mauriac
   Thérèse
Albert Memmi
   The Pillar of Salt
Menander
   The Grouch
Prosper Mérimée
Pietro Metastasio
Conrad Ferdinand Meyer

Henri Michaux
Adam Mickiewicz
   Pan Tadeusz
Czesław Miłosz
Mīrā Bāī
Mishima Yukio
Gabriela Mistral
Miyazawa Kenji
Mo Yan
Molière
   The Conceited Young Ladies
   Don Juan
   The Hypochondriac
   The Misanthrope
   The Miser
   Tartuffe
Ferenc Molnár
Michel de Montaigne
   "Apology for Raymond Sebond"
   "On the Power of the
     Imagination"
   "On Vanity"
Eugenio Montale
   Cuttlefish Bones
   "The Storm"
Elsa Morante
   House of Liars
Alberto Moravia
   The Time of Indifference
Ōgai Mori
Eduard Mörike
Multatuli
Murakami Haruki
Murasaki Shikibu
Robert Musil
   The Man Without Qualities
   Young Törless
Alfred de Musset
   Lorenzaccio
Natsume Sōseki
Pablo Neruda
   "Arte Poética"
   Tentativa del hombre infinito
Gérard de Nerval
Johann Nepomuk Nestroy
Nibelungenlied
Friedrich Nietzsche
   The Birth of Tragedy
   Thus Spoke Zarathustra
Martinus Nijhoff
Nishiwaki Junzaburō
Njáls Saga
Cees Nooteboom
Cyprian Kamil Norwid
Novalis
   Hymns to the Night
Ōe Kenzaburō
Yuri Olesha
   Envy

Omar Khayyam
   The Rubaiyat
On the Sublime
Paul van Ostaijen
Ovid
   The Art of Love
   Loves
   Metamorphoses
Amos Oz
Marcel Pagnol
Kostes Palamas
Emilia Pardo Bazán
Blaise Pascal
Pier Paolo Pasolini
Boris Pasternak
   Doctor Zhivago
Cesare Pavese
   The Moon and the Bonfires
Milorad Pavić
Miodrag Pavlović
Octavio Paz
   Sun Stone
Georges Perec
   Life A User's Manual
Ramón Pérez de Ayala
Benito Pérez Galdós
Charles Perrault
Persius
Fernando Pessoa
Sándor Petőfi
Petrarch
   "Sonnet 90"
Petronius
Boris Pil'niak
Pindar
   Olympian One
   Pythian Odes Four and Five
Luigi Pirandello
   Henry IV
   *Six Characters in Search of
     an Author*
Plato
   Phaedrus
   The Republic
   The Symposium
Plautus
   Amphitryo
   The Brothers Menaechmus
   The Pot of Gold
Plutarch
   Lives of Lysander and Sulla
The Poetic *Edda*
Polybius
Francis Ponge
   The Voice of Things
Vasko Popa
Vasco Pratolini
Jacques Prévert
Abbé Prévost
   Manon Lescaut

Sextus Propertius
Marcel Proust
   Against Sainte-Beuve
   Remembrance of Things Past
Aurelius Clemens Prudentius
Bolesław Prus
Manuel Puig
   Kiss of the Spider Woman
Aleksandr Pushkin
   The Bronze Horseman
   Eugene Onegin
Salvatore Quasimodo
Rachel de Queiroz
Raymond Queneau
   The Blue Flowers
   Zazie
Quintilian
François Rabelais
   Gargantua and *Pantagruel*
Jean Racine
   Athalie
   Bajazet
   Bérénice
   Phaedra
Raymond Radiguet
   The Devil in the Flesh
Miklós Radnóti
Rāmāyaṇa
Erich Maria Remarque
   All Quiet on the Western Front
Rendra
Rainer Maria Rilke
   Seventh *Duino Elegy*
   Sonnets to Orpheus
Arthur Rimbaud
   "Alchimie du verbe"
   "Le Bateau ivre"
   "Fleurs"
Yannis Ritsos
Alain Robbe-Grillet
   In the Labyrinth
   The Voyeur
Nélson Rodrigues
Fernando de Rojas
Romain Rolland
The Romance of the Rose
Pièrre de Ronsard
   "Hymn to Autumn"
   "Ode to Michel de l'Hospital"
   "Quand vous serez bien
     vieille . . ."
Edmond Rostand
   Cyrano De Bergerac
Joseph Roth
   The Radetzky March
Jean-Jacques Rousseau
   The Confessions
   Emile
   The Reveries of a Solitary
   The Social Contract

Claude Roy
Gabrielle Roy
Tadeusz Różewicz
Juan Rulfo
Jalalu'd-Din Muhammad Rumi
Ruzzante [or Ruzante]
Umberto Saba
Hans Sachs
   The Wandering Scholar in
     Paradise
Nelly Sachs
Marquis de Sade
   Justine
Shaikh Muslih-al-Din Sa'di
   Rose Garden
Juan José Saer
Saigyō
Antoine de Saint-Exupéry
   Night Flight
Saint-John Perse
   Seamarks
Sallust
George Sand
   Lélia
Jacopo Sannazaro
Sappho
   Fragment 1 ["Address to
     Aphrodite"]
   Fragment 31 ["Declaration of
     Love for a Young Girl"]
Nathalie Sarraute
   Tropisms
Jean-Paul Sartre
   The Age Of Reason
   The Flies
   Nausea
   No Exit
Paul Scarron
Friedrich von Schiller
   Don-Carlos
   Mary Stuart
   Ode to Joy
   Wallenstein
   William Tell
August Wilhelm and Friedrich von
   Schlegel
Arthur Schnitzler
   Professor Bernhardi
   La Ronde
Bruno Schulz
Leonardo Sciascia
Eugène Scribe
George Seferis
   Mythistorima
Ramón J. Sender
Seneca
   Oedipus
   Thyestes
Shiga Naoya
Shimazaki Haruki

Mikhail Sholokhov
Siburapha
Henryk Sienkiewicz
Angelos Sikelianos
   "The Sacred Way"
Ignazio Silone
   Bread and Wine
   Fontamara
Georges Simenon
Antonio Skármeta
Juliusz Słowacki
Edith Södergran
Sasha Sokolov
   A School for Fools
Aleksandr Solzhenitsyn
   Cancer Ward
   One Day in the Life of Ivan
     Denisovich
The Song of Roland
Sophocles
   Ajax
   Antigone
   Electra
   Oedipus at Colonus
   Oedipus the King
   Philoctetes
   Women of Trachis
Madame de Staël
Gaspara Stampa
Stendhal
   The Charterhouse of Parma
   Scarlet and Black
Carl Sternheim
Adalbert Stifter
   "Abdias"
   Indian Summer
   "Rock Crystal"
Theodor Storm
   Immensee
   The White Horseman
August Strindberg
   The Ghost Sonata
   Miss Julie
Snorri Sturluson
   The Prose *Edda*
   The Saga of King Óláf the Saint
Su Shi
Su Tong
   Rice
Suetonius
Sūrdās
Italo Svevo
   Confessions of Zeno
Wisława Szymborska
Tacitus
   Annals
Rabindranath Tagore
The Tale of the Campaign Of Igor
Tang Xianzu
   The Peony Pavilion

Tanizaki Jun'ichiro
   Some Prefer Nettles
Tao Qian
Torquato Tasso
   Aminta
   Jerusalem Delivered
Tawfiq al-Hakim
Terence
   The Brothers
   The Eunuch
   Phormio
Theocritus
   "Idyll" I
   "Idyll" IV
   "Idyll" VII
Theophrastus
   Characters
The Thousand and One Nights
Thucydides
Albius Tibillus
Ludwig Tieck
Tirso de Molina
   The Trickster of Seville
Pramoedya Ananta Toer
   The Fugitive
Ernst Toller
Tatyana Tolstaya
Lev Tolstoi
   Anna Karenina
   The Death Of Ivan Ilyich
   The Kreutzer Sonata
   War And Peace
Miguel Torga
Georg Trakl
   "Grodek"
Iurii Trifonov
Tsushima Yuko
Marina Tsvetaeva
Gosvami Tulsīdās
Ivan Turgenev
   Fathers and Sons
   First Love
   A Month in the Country
Miguel de Unamuno
   The Christ of Velazquez
   Mist
Sigrid Undset
   Kristin Lavransdatter
Giuseppe Ungaretti
   "Sirens"
Upanishads
Honoré d'Urfé
Luisa Valenzuela
Paul Valéry
   "Le Cimetière marin"
   "La Jeune Parque"
Ramón del Valle-Inclán
César Vallejo
   "Considerando en frio"
   "The Eternal Dice"

CHRONOLOGICAL LIST OF WRITERS

fl. 8th century BC(?)	Homer
fl. c. 700 BC	Hesiod
c. 612 BC– ?	Sappho
c. 570 BC–c. 475 BC	Anacreon
525/524 BC–456 BC	Aeschylus
518/522 BC–438/446 BC	Pindar
c. 496 BC–406 BC	Sophocles
484 BC–420 BC	Herodotus
480/485 BC–c. 406 BC	Euripides
c. 460 BC–c. 399 BC	Thucydides
c. 450 BC–c. 385 BC	Aristophanes
c. 431 BC–c. 354 BC	Xenophon
c. 429 BC–347 BC	Plato
384 BC–322 BC	Aristotle
384 BC–322 BC	Demosthenes
c. 370 BC–c. 287 BC	Theophrastus
c. 342 BC–c. 295 BC	Menander
c. 300 BC– ?	Theocritus
c. 254 BC–c. 184 BC	Plautus
fl. 250 BC	Apollonius
fl. 250 BC	Callimachus
239 BC–169 BC	Ennius
c. 200 BC–c. 118 BC	Polybius
c. 190 BC–159 BC	Terence
106 BC–43 BC	Cicero
c. 100 BC–44 BC	Caesar
c. 99 BC–c. 55 BC	Lucretius
86 BC–35 BC	Sallust
c. 84 BC–c. 54 BC	Catullus
70 BC–19 BC	Virgil
65 BC–8 BC	Horace
64/59 BC–AD 12/17	Livy
c. 57 BC–19/18 BC	Tibullus
57/50 BC–c. 16 BC	Propertius
43 BC–AD 17	Ovid
c. 4 BC–AD 65	Seneca
c. AD 30–c. AD 104	Martial
AD 34–AD 62	Persius
c. AD 35–c. AD 100	Quintilian
AD 39–AD 65	Lucan
c. AD 46–c. AD 120	Plutarch
AD 50–AD 130	Juvenal
c. AD 56–c. AD 116	Tacitus
d. AD 66	Petronius
c. AD 69–AD 160	Suetonius
c. AD 120–after AD 180	Lucian
AD 121–AD 180	Aurelius
c. AD 123–after 163 AD	Apuleius
2nd/3rd century AD	Longus
c. AD 310–c. AD 395	Ausonius
fl. late 4th century AD	Claudian
c. AD 347–AD 420	St. Jerome
AD 348–AD 405	Prudentius
AD 354–AD 430	St. Augustine
AD 365–427	Tao Qian
fl. c. AD 400	Kālidāsa
c. AD 480–AD 524	Boethius
c. 497–545	Imru Al-Qays
c. 575–646	Al-Khansa'
701/705–762	Li Bai
712–770	Du Fu
772–846	Bai Juyi
c. 915–965	Al-Mutanabbi
c. 935–c. 1020	Abu'l Qāsim Ferdowsi
c. 978– ?	Murasaki Shikibu
1037–1101	Su Shi
1048–1131	Omar Khayyam
1054–1122	Al-Hariri
c. 1058–1139	Ibn Khafajah
c. 1118–1190	Saigyo
c. 1130–1220/1231	Farid al-Din Attār
1160–1210/1220	Hartmann von Aue
c. 1165–1240	Ibn Al-'Arabi
fl. c. 1170	Chrétien de Troyes
c. 1170–c. 1230	Walther von der Vogelweide
1179–1241	Snorri Sturluson
c. 1181–1235	Ibn Al-Farid
fl. late 12th century	Marie de France
fl. 1195–1220	Wolfram von Eschenbach
fl. c. 1200	Gottfried von Strassburg
1207–1273	Jalalu'd-Din Rumi
1209–1292	Muslih-al-Din Sa'di
fl. c. 1250	Hadewijch
c. 1255–1300	Guido Cavalcanti
1265–1321	Dante Alighieri
c. 1283–1352	Kenko
c. 1300(?)–1377	Guillaume de Machaut
1304–1374	Petrarch
1313–1375	Giovanni Boccaccio
1325/26–1389/90	Shams al-Din Muhammad Hafiz
c. 1337– ?	Jean Froissart
1363–1443	Zeami
c. 1365–c. 1430	Christine de Pizan
c. 1430– ?	François Villon
1456–1530	Jacopo Sannazaro
1457–1521	Sebastian Brant
c. 1465–c. 1536	Gil Vicente
1467–1536	Desiderius Erasmus
1469–1527	Niccolò Machiavelli
1470–1520	Bernardo Dovizi da Bibbiena
1470–1547	Pietro Bembo
1474–1533	Ludovico Ariosto
1478/c. 1530–1583/1610	Sūrdās
1478–1529	Baldassarre Castiglione
1483–1546	Martin Luther
1483(?)–1553	François Rabelais
1492–1547	Vittoria Colonna
1492–1549	Marguerite de Navarre
1492–1556	Pietro Aretino
1494–1576	Hans Sachs
c. 1495–1542	Ruzzante
1498–1546/47	Mīrā Bāī

d. 1518	Kabīr	1770–1843	Friedrich Hölderlin
1522–1566	Joachim Du Bellay	1772–1801	Novalis
c. 1524–1554	Gaspara Stampa	1772–1829	Friedrich von Schlegel
1524/25–1580	Luís de Camões	1773–1853	Ludwig Tieck
1524–1585	Pierre de Ronsard	1775(?)–1831	Caroline de la Motte Fouqué
1530–1584	Jan Kochanowski	1776–1822	E.T.A. Hoffmann
1532–1623	Tulsīdās	1777–1811	Heinrich von Kleist
1533–1592	Michel de Montaigne	1777–1843	Friedrich de la Motte Fouqué
1544–1595	Torquato Tasso	1778–1842	Clemens Brentano
1548–1600	Giordano Bruno	1781–1838	Adelbert von Chamisso
1550–1616	Tang Xianzu	1783–1842	Stendhal
1567(?)–1625	Honoré d'Urfé	1785–1859	Bettina von Arnim
1568–1639	Tommaso Campanella	1785–1863	Jacob Grimm
1581–1647	Pieter Corneliszoon Hooft	1785–1873	Alessandro Manzoni
1585–1618	Gerbrandt Bredero	1786–1859	Wilhelm Grimm
1587–1679	Joost van den Vondel	1788–1857	Joseph von Eichendorff
1596–1687	Constantijn Huygens	1790–1869	Alphonse de Larmartine
1606–1684	Pierre Corneille	1791–1861	Eugène Scribe
1610–1660	Paul Scarron	1791–1872	Franz Grillparzer
1613–1680	François La Rochefoucauld	1795–1829	Aleksandr Griboedov
1616–1664	Andreas Gryphius	1797–1848	Annette von Droste-Hülshoff
1619–1655	Cyrano de Bergerac	1797–1854	Jeremias Gotthelf
1620–1664	Count Miklós Zrínyi	1797–1856	Heinrich Heine
1621–1695	Jean de La Fontaine	1797–1863	Alfred de Vigny
1622–1673	Molière	1797–1869	Asadullāh Khān Ghālib
1622–1676	Hans Jakob Christoffel von Grimmelshausen	1798–1837	Giacomo Leopardi
		1798–1855	Adam Mickiewicz
1623–1662	Blaise Pascal	1799–1837	Aleksandr Pushkin
1628–1703	Charles Perrault	1799–1850	Honoré de Balzac
1634–1693	Madame de Lafayette	1800–1855	Mihály Vörösmarty
1636–1711	Nicolas Boileau	1801–1836	Christian Dietrich Grabbe
1639–1699	Jean Racine	1801–1862	Johann Nepomuk Nestroy
1642–1693	Ihara Saikaku	1802–1870	Alexandre Dumas *père*
1644–1694	Bashō	1802–1885	Victor Hugo
1651–1695	Sor Juana Inés de la Cruz	1803–1870	Prosper Mérimée
1653–1725	Chikamatsu Monzaemon	1803–1899	Guido Gezelle
1668–1747	Alain-René Lesage	1804–1875	Eduard Mörike
1684–1754	Ludvig Holberg	1804–1876	George Sand
1688–1763	Marivaux	1805–1868	Adalbert Stifter
1694–1778	Voltaire	1805–1875	Hans Christian Andersen
1697–1763	Abbé Prévost	1808–1855	Gérard de Nerval
1698–1782	Pietro Metastasio	1809–1849	Juliusz Slowacki
1707–1793	Carlo Goldoni	1809–1852	Nikolai Gogol'
1712–1778	Jean-Jacques Rousseau	1810–1857	Alfred de Musset
1713–1784	Denis Diderot	1811–1872	Théophile Gautier
1724–1803	Friedrich Gottlieb Klopstock	1812–1859	Zygmunt Krasiński
1729–1781	Gotthold Ephraim Lessing	1812–1891	Ivan Goncharov
1732–1799	Beaumarchais	1813–1837	Georg Büchner
1733–1813	Christoph Martin Wieland	c. 1813–1855	Søren Kierkegaard
1740–1814	Marquis de Sade	1813–1863	Friedrich Hebbel
1741–1803	Choderlos de Laclos	1813–1871	Baron Jószef Eötvös
1745–1792	Denis Fonvizin	1814–1841	Mikhail Lermontov
1749–1803	Vittorio Alfieri	1817–1888	Theodor Storm
1749–1832	Johann Wolfgang von Goethe	1818–1883	Ivan Turgenev
1751–1792	Jakob Michael Reinhold Lenz	1819–1890	Gottfried Keller
1756–1831	Willem Bilderdijk	1819–1898	Theodor Fontane
1759–1805	Friedrich von Schiller	1820–1881	Multatuli
1766–1817	Madame de Staël	1821–1867	Charles Baudelaire
1767–1845	August Wilhelm von Schlegel	1821–1880	Gustave Flaubert
1768–1848	Chateaubriand	1821–1881	Fedor Dostoevskii

c. 1821–1883	Cyprian Kamil Norwid	1872–1943	Shimazaki Toson
1822–1896	Edmond Goncourt	1873–1907	Alfred Jarry
1823–1849	Sándor Petöfi	1873–1950	Johannes V. Jensen
1824–1895	Alexandre Dumas *fils*	1873–1935	Henri Barbusse
1825–1898	Conrad Ferdinand Meyer	1873–1954	Colette
1828–1905	Jules Verne	1874–1929	Hugo von Hofmannsthal
1828–1906	Henrik Ibsen	1875–1926	Rainer Maria Rilke
1828–1910	Lev Tolstoi	1875–1955	Thomas Mann
1830–1870	Jules Goncourt	1876–1944	Max Jacob
1832–1910	Bjørnstjerne Bjørnson	1877–1962	Hermann Hesse
1834–1886	José Hernández	1878–1942	Carl Sternheim
1835–1907	Giosuè Carducci	1878–1942	Yosano Akiko
1839–1908	Joaquim Maria Machado de Assis	1878–1945	Georg Kaiser
1840–1902	Émile Zola	1878–1952	Ferenc Molnár
1840–1922	Giovanni Verga	1878–1957	Alfred Döblin
1842–1898	Stéphane Mallarmé	1880–1918	Guillaume Apollinaire
1844–1896	Paul Verlaine	1880–1921	Aleksandr Blok
1844–1900	Friedrich Nietzsche	1880–1934	Andrei Belyi
1844–1924	Anatole France	1880–1942	Robert Musil
1845–1900	José Maria de Eça de Queirós	1881–1936	Lu Xun
1846–1870	Comte de Lautréamont	1881–1958	Roger Martin du Gard
1846–1916	Henryk Sienkiewicz	1882–1949	Sigrid Undset
1847–1912	Bolesław Prus	1883–1923	Jaroslav Hašek
1848–1907	Joris-Karl Huysmans	1883–1924	Franz Kafka
1849–1912	August Strindberg	1883–1957	Nikos Kazantzakis
1850–1893	Guy de Maupassant	1883–1957	Umberto Saba
1853–1995	José Martí	1883–1971	Shiga Naoya
1854–1891	Arthur Rimbaud	1884–1937	Evgenii Zamiatin
1858–1940	Selma Lagerlöf	1884–1951	Angelo Sikelianos
1859–1943	Kostes Palamas	1885–1922	Velimir Khlebnikov
1859–1952	Knut Hamsun	1885–1939	Stanisław Witkiewicz
1860–1887	Jules Laforgue	1885–1962	Isak Dinesen
1860–1904	Anton Chekhov	1885–1970	François Mauriac
1861–1928	Italo Svevo	1886–1914	Alain-Fournier
1861–1941	Rabindranath Tagore	1886–1942	Hagiwara Sakutaro
1862–1921	Georges Feydeau	1886–1951	Hermann Broch
1862–1922	Mori Ogai	1886–1956	Gottfried Benn
1862–1931	Arthur Schnitzler	1886–1965	Tanizaki Jun'ichiro
1862–1944	Jean Giraudoux	1887–1914	Georg Trakl
1862–1946	Gerhart Hauptmann	1887–1961	Blaise Cendrars
1862–1949	Maurice Maeterlinck	1887–1975	Saint-John Perse
1863–1923	Louis Couperus	1888–1935	Fernando Pessoa
1863–1933	C. P. Cavafy	1888–1948	Georges Bernanos
1863–1938	Gabriele D'Annunzio	1888–1970	S.Y. Agnon
1864–1918	Frank Wedekind	1888–1970	Giuseppe Ungaretti
1866–1944	Romain Rolland	1889–1957	Gabriela Mistral
1867–1902	Masaoka Shiki	1889–1963	Jean Cocteau
1867–1916	Rubén Darío	1889–1966	Anna Akhmatova
1867–1916	Natsume Sōseki	1889–1984	Henri Michaux
1867–1936	Luigi Pirandello	1890–1938	Karel Čapek
1868–1918	Edmond Rostand	1890–1945	Franz Werfel
1868–1936	Maksim Gor'kii	1890–1960	Boris Pasternak
1868–1955	Paul Claudel	1891–1938	Osip Mandel'shtam
1869–1907	Stanisław Wyspiański	1891–1940	Mikhail Bulgakov
1869–1951	André Gide	1891–1950	Ivan Goll
1870–1953	Ivan Bunin	1891–1970	Nelly Sachs
1871–1922	Marcel Proust	1891–1974	Pär Lagerkvist
1871–1936	Grazia Deledda	1892–1923	Edith Södergran
1871–1945	Paul Valéry	1892–1927	Akutagawa Ryunosuke
1871–1950	Heinrich Mann	1892–1938	César Vallejo

1892–1941	Marina Tsvetaeva	1902–1998	Halldór Laxness
1892–1942	Bruno Schulz	1903–1923	Raymond Radiguet
1892–1953	Ugo Betti	1903–1976	Raymond Queneau
1892–1975	Ivo Andrić	1903–1987	Marguerite Yourcenar
1893–1930	Vladimir Maiakovskii	1903–1989	Georges Simenon
1893–1939	Ernst Toller	1904–1962	Abdulla Goran
1893–1945	Mario de Andrade	1904–1969	Witold Gombrowicz
1893–1981	Miroslav Krleža	1904–1973	Pablo Neruda
1894–1938	Boris Pil'niak	1904–1980	Alejo Carpentier
1894–1939	Joseph Roth	1905–1974	Siburapha
1894–1941(?)	Isaak Babel	1905–1980	Jean-Paul Sartre
1894–1961	Louis-Ferdinand Céline	1905–1984	Mikhail Sholokhov
1894–1982	Nishiwaki Junzaburo	1905–1994	Elias Canetti
1895–1925	Sergei Esenin	1906–1972	Dino Buzzati
1895–1952	Paul Éluard	1906–1989	Samuel Beckett
1895–1958	Mikhail Mikhailovich Zoshchenko	1907–1968	Ding Ling
1895–1960	Iurii Olesha	1907–1972	Gnter Eich
1895–1970	Jean Giono	1907–1986	Mircea Eliade
1895–1974	Marcel Pagnol	1907–1988	René Char
1895–1989	Maria Kuncewicz	1907–1990	Alberto Moravia
1895–1998	Ernst Jünger	1907–1995	Miguel Torga
1896–1928	Paul van Ostaijen	1908–1950	Cesare Pavese
1896–1933	Miyazawa Kenji	1908–1966	Elio Vittorini
1896–1948	Antonin Artaud	1908–1967	João Guimarães Rosa
1896–1953	Martinus Nijhoff	1908–1970	Arthur Adamov
1896–1957	Giuseppe Tomasi di Lampedusa	1908–1986	Simone de Beauvoir
1896–1966	André Breton	1909–1944	Miklós Radnóti
1896–1966	Heimito von Doderer	1909–1945	Robert Brasillach
1896–1977	Carl Zuckmayer	1909–1948	Dazai Osamu
1896–1981	Eugenio Montale	1909–1981	Demetrio Aguilera Malta
1897–1970	Tarjei Vesaas	1909–1983	Jerzy Andrzejewski
1897–1982	Louis Aragon	1909–1983	Gabrielle Roy
1898–1956	Bertolt Brecht	1909–1990	Yannis Ritsos
1898–1970	Erich Maria Remarque	1909–1994	Eugène Ionesco
1898–1971	Simon Vestdijk	1910–1976	José Lezama Lima
1898–1987	Tawfiq al-Hakim	1910–1986	Jean Genet
1898–1993	Ibuse Masuji	1910–1987	Jean Anhouilh
1899–1966	Lao She	1910–	Rachel de Queiroz
1899–1972	Kawabata Yasunari	1911–1942	Xiao Hong
1899–1974	Miguel Ángel Asturias	1911–1969	José Mariá Arguedas
1899–1986	Jorge Luis Borges	1911–1986	Fritz Hochwälder
1899–1988	Francis Ponge	1911–1991	Max Frisch
1900–1944	Antoine de Saint-Exupéry	1911–1996	Odysseus Elytis
1900–1970	Leopoldo Marechal	1911–	Naguib Mahfouz
1900–1971	George Seferis	1911–	Czesław Miłosz
1900–1977	Jacques Prévert	1912–1980	Nélson Rodrigues
1900–1978	Ignazio Silone	1912–1985	Elsa Morante
1900–1984	Eduardo De Filippo	1912–2001	Jorge Amado
1900–1987	Gilberto Freyre	1913–1960	Albert Camus
1900–1991	William Heinesen	1913–1989	Sándor Weöres
1900–1999	Nathalie Sarraute	1913–1991	Vasco Pratolini
1901–1938	Ödön von Horváth	1914–1984	Julio Cortázar
1901–1968	Salvatore Quasimodo	1914–1996	Marguerite Duras
1901–1976	André Malraux	1914–1998	Octavio Paz
1901–1990	Ivar Lo-Johansson	1915–1997	Claude Roy
1902–1967	Marcel Aymé	1916–1982	Peter Weiss
1902–1975	Carlo Levi	1916–1991	Natalia Ginzburg
1902–1983	Gyula Illyés	1916–2000	Giorgio Bassani
1902–1987	Carlos Drummond de Andrade	1917–1965	Johannes Bobrowski
1902–1989	Nicolás Guillén	1917–1985	Heinrich Böll

1917–1987	Carlo Cassola	1929–	Christa Wolf
1918–1986	Juan Rulfo	1930–	Adonis
1918–	Aleksandr Solzhenitsyn	1931–1989	Thomas Bernhard
1919–1987	Primo Levi	1931–	Ivan Klíma
1920–1959	Boris Vian	1932–1990	Manuel Puig
1920–1970	Paul Celan	1932–	Umberto Eco
1920–1992	Väinö Linna	1933–	Evgenii Evtushenko
1920–	Ishigaki Rin	1933–	Cees Nooteboom
1920–	Jaan Kross	1934–1984	Uwe Johnson
1920–	Albert Memmi	1935–1989	Danilo Kiš
1921–	Tadeusz Różewicz	1935–	Manlio Argueta
1921–1989	Leonardo Sciascia	1935–	Francesca Duranti
1921–1990	Friedrich Dürrenmatt	1935–	Ōe Kenzaburō
1922–1949	Chairil Anwar	1935–	Rendra
1922–1951	Tadeusz Borowski	1936–1982	Georges Perec
1922–1975	Pier Paolo Pasolini	1936–	Assia Djebar
1922–1991	Vasko Popa	1936–	Vaclav Havel
1922–	José Craveirinha	1936–	Ismail Kadare
1922–	Alain Robbe-Grillet	1936–	Mario Vargas Llosa
1923–1969	Jalal Âl-e Ahmad	1936–	A. B. Yehoshua
1923–1985	Italo Calvino	1937–	Juan José Saer
1923–1998	Miroslav Holub	1938–	Abdelkebir Khatibi
1923–1996	Endō Shūsaku	1938–	Luisa Valenzuela
1923–	Wislawa Szymborska	1939–	Huang Chunming
1924–1986	Vasil Bykaw	1939–	Amos Oz
1924–1993	Abe Kōbō	1940–1996	Iosif Brodskii
1925–1970	Mishima Yukio	1940–	Gao Xingjian
1925–1974	Rosario Castellanos	1940–	Antonio Skármeta
1925–1977	Clarice Lispector	1941–	Jaan Kaplinski
1925–1981	Iurii Trifonov	1942–	Isabel Allende
1925–	Ernesto Cardenal	1942–	Dev Virahsawmy
1925–	Pramoedya Ananta Toer	1943–1990	Reinaldo Arenas
1926–1973	Ingeborg Bachmann	1943–	Evelyne Accad
1926–	René Depestre	1943–	Nicole Brossard
1926–	Siegfried Lenz	1943–	Sasha Sokolov
1927–1991	Yusuf Idris	1944–	Tahar Ben Jelloun
1927–	Günter Grass	1947–	Tsushima Yuko
1927–	Qurratulain Hyder	1948–	Gioconda Belli
1927–	Ahmadou Kourouma	1949–	Bei Dao
1928–	Carlos Fuentes	1949–	Murakami Haruki
1928–	Gabriel García Márquez	1950–	Péter Esterházy
1928–	Edouard Glissant	1951–	Tatyana Tolstaya
1928–	Miodrag Pavlović	1952–	Li Ang
1928–	Elie Wiesel	1953–	Patrick Chamoiseau
1929–	Hugo Claus	1957–	Peter Høeg
1929–	Milan Kundera	1963–	Dorothea Rosa Herilany
1929–	Milorad Pavić	1963–	Su Tong

ALPHABETICAL LIST OF WORKS

"L'Abandonné," story by Guy de Maupassant, 1884

"Abdias," story by Adalbert Stifter, 1843

About This, poem by Vladimir Maiakovskii, 1923

The Aeneid, poem by Virgil, 1st century BC

Aetia, poem by Callimachus, 3rd century BC

Against Sainte-Beuve, prose by Marcel Proust, 1954

The Age of Reason, novel by Jean-Paul Sartre, 1945

Ajax, play by Sophocles, before 441 BC(?)

"Alchemy of the Word," poem by Arthur Rimbaud, 1873

All Quiet on the Western Front, novel by Erich Maria Remarque, 1929

Aminta, play by Torquato Tasso, 1573

Andreas, fiction by Hugo von Hofmannsthal, 1930 (written 1912–13)

"L'Angoisse," poem by Paul Verlaine, 1866

Amphitryo, play by Plautus, 2nd century BC

Andorra, play by Max Frisch, 1961

Anna Karenina, novel by Lev Tolstoi, 1875–77

Annals, prose by Tacitus, early 2nd century AD

Antigone, play by Jean Anhouilh, 1944

Antigone, play by Sophocles, c. 441 BC(?)

"Apology for Raymond Sebond," prose by Michel de Montaigne, 1570

"L'Après-midi d'un faune," poem by Stéphane Mallarmé, 1876

Around the World in Eighty Days, novel by Jules Verne, 1873

"Art," poem by Théophile Gautier, 1856

The Art of Love, poem by Ovid, 1st century BC/1st century AD

The Art of Poetry, poem by Nicolas Boileau, 1674

"Art poétique," poem by Paul Verlaine, 1874

"Arte poética," poem by Pablo Neruda, 1935

Ashes and Diamonds, novel by Jerzy Andrzejewski, 1948

L'Assommoir, novel by Émile Zola, 1877

Athalie, play by Jean Racine, 1691

Aucassin and Nicolette (Anon), romance, 13th century

Auto-da-Fé, novel by Elias Canetti, 1936

Auto da Barca do Inferno, Auto da Barca do Purgatorio, Auto da Barca da Gloria, plays by Gil Vicente, 1517, 1518, 1519

Baal, play by Bertolt Brecht, 1922

Bajazet, play by Jean Racine, 1672

The Balcony, play by Jean Genet, 1956

The Bald Prima Donna, play by Eugène Ionesco, 1950

"Ballade des dames du temps jadis," poem by François Villon, 1489 (written c. 1460?)

"Ballade des pendus," poem by François Villon, 1489

The Barber of Seville, play by Beaumarchais, 1775

"Le Bateau ivre," poem by Arthur Rimbaud, 1871

The Bedbug, play by Vladimir Maiakovskii, 1929

Before the Storm, novel by Theodor Fontane, 1878

Berenice, play by Jean Racine, 1670

Berlin Alexanderplatz, novel by Alfred Döblin, 1929

The Betrothed, novel by Alessandro Manzoni, 1827

The Bible, anonymous verse and prose, c. 900 BC onwards

The Birds, play by Aristophanes, 414 BC

The Birth of Tragedy, prose by Friedrich Nietzsche, 1872

Blood Wedding, play by Federico García Lorca, 1933

The Blue Angel, novel by Heinrich Mann, 1905

The Blue Bird, play by Maurice Maeterlinck, 1909

Blue Flowers, novel by Raymond Queneau, 1965

The Book of the City of Ladies, prose by Christine de Pizan, 1405

Brand, play by Henrik Ibsen, 1865

"Bread and Wine," poem by Friedrich Hölderlin, 1806 (written 1800–01)

Bread and Wine, novel by Ignazio Silone, 1937

The Bridge on the Drina, novel by Ivo Andrić, 1945

The Broken Jug, play by Heinrich von Kleist, 1808

The Bronze Horseman, poem by Aleksandr Pushkin, written 1833

"The Broom," poem by Giacomo Leopardi, 1845

The Brothers, play by Terence, 160 BC

The Brothers Karamazov, novel by Fedor Dostoevskii, 1880

The Brothers Menaechmus, play by Plautus, 2nd century BC

Buddenbrooks, novel by Thomas Mann, 1900

Camille, novel by Alexandre Dumas *fils*, 1848

Cancer Ward, novel by Aleksandr Solzhenitsyn, 1968

Candide, novella by Voltaire, 1759

The Castle, novel by Franz Kafka, 1926 (written 1922)

The Caucasian Chalk Circle, play by Bertolt Brecht, 1948

"Le Chanson du mal-aime," poem by Guillaume Apollinaire, 1913

Characters, prose by Theophrastus, c. 319 BC

The Charterhouse of Parma, novel by Stendhal, 1839

Chatterton, play by Alfred de Vigny, 1835

Chéri, novel by Colette, 1920

The Cherry Orchard, play by Anton Chekhov, 1904

The Christ of Velazquez, poem by Miguel de Unamuno, 1920

Christ Stopped at Eboli, novel by Carlo Levi, 1945

The Cid, play by Pierre Corneille, 1636–37

"Le Cimetière marin," poem by Paul Valéry, 1920

The City of God, prose by St Augustine, 5th century

Cloud in Trousers, poem by Vladimir Maiakovskii, 1915

The Cloud Messenger, poem by Kālidāsa, 5th century

The Clouds, play by Aristophanes, 423 BC

The Colloquies, prose by Desiderius Erasmus, 1518

The Comic Theatre, play by Carlo Goldoni, 1750

The Conceited Young Ladies, play by Molière, 1659

The Conference of the Birds, poem by Farid al-Din Attār, c. 1177

The Confessions, prose by Jean-Jacques Rousseau, 1781

Confessions, Book I, prose by St. Augustine, 4th century

Confessions of Felix Krull, Confidence Man, novel by Thomas Mann, 1922 (complete 1954)

Confessions of Zeno, novel by Italo Svevo, 1923

"Considerando en frio," poem by César Vallejo, 1939

The Consolation of Philosophy, prose by Boethius, early 6th century

Conversation in Sicily, novel by Elio Vittorini, 1939

La cortigiana, play by Pietro Aretino, 1534

The Counterfeiters, novel by André Gide, 1926

"Un Coup de dés jamais n'abolira le hasard," poem by Stéphane Mallarmé, 1914 (written 1897)

Cousin Bette, novel by Honoré de Balzac, 1847

Le Crève-coeur, poems by Louis Aragon, 1941

Crime and Punishment, novel by Fedor Dostoevskii, 1867

Cupid and Psyche, story by Apuleius, c. 180

Cuttlefish Bones, poems by Eugenio Montale, 1925

Cyrano de Bergerac, play by Edmond Rostand, 1897

Danton's Death, play by Georg Bchner, 1835 (complete version 1850)

Daphnis and Chloe, poem by Longus, 2nd/3rd century

Dead Souls, novel by Nikolai Gogol', 1842

In the Labyrinth, novel by Alain Robbe-Grillet, 1959

"Incantation by Laughter," poem by Velimir Khlebnikov, 1909

Indian Summer, novel by Adalbert Stifter, 1857

The Infernal Machine, play by Jean Cocteau, 1934

"The Infinite," poem by Giacomo Leopardi, 1819

The Insect Play, play by Karel Čapek, 1921

The Intruder, play by Maurice Maeterlinck, 1890

The Investigation, play by Peter Weiss, 1965

"Invitation to Wine," poem by Li Bai, 752

Ion, play by Euripides, c. 421–13 BC

Jacques the Fatalist, novel by Denis Diderot, 1796

Jerusalem Delivered, poem by Torquato Tasso, 1580

"La Jeune Parque," poem by Paul Valéry, 1917 (written 1912–17)

The Jew's Beech Tree, novella by Annette von Droste-Hülshoff, 1851

Journey to the End of the Night, novel by Louis-Ferdinand Céline, 1932

Journey to the West, anonymous novel, 11/12th century

Justice Without Revenge, play by Lope de Vega Carpio, 1632

Justine, novel by Marquis de Sade, 1791

Kalevala, anonymous poem, origins date to early 1st century AD

The Kingdom of This World, novel by Alejo Carpentier, 1947

Kiss of the Spider Woman, novel by Manuel Puig, 1976

The Kreutzer Sonata, novella by Lev Tolstoi, 1891

Kristin Lavransdatter, novels by Sigrid Undset, 1920–22

The Lady with a Dog, story by Anton Chekhov, written 1899

Lancelot, poem by Chrétien de Troyes, written c. 1170

The Last Poems, poems by Jules Laforgue, 1890

The Last Temptation, novel by Nikos Kazantzakis, 1955

Lazarillo de Tormes, anonymous novel, 1554

Les Liaisons Dangereuses, novel by Choderlos de Laclos, 1782

Life: A User's Manual, novel by Georges Perece, 1978

Life Is a Dream, play by Pedro Calderón de la Barca, 1623

The Life of Galileo, play by Bertolt Brecht, 1943

The Lime Works, novel by Thomas Bernhard, 1970

The Little Clay Cart, anonymous play, 1st century AD(?)

Lives of Lysander and Sulla, prose by Plutarch, 1st/2nd century AD

Lorenzaccio, play by Alfred de Musset, 1834

The Lost Honor of Katharina Blum, novel by Heinrich Böll, 1974

Lost Illusions, novel by Honoré de Balzac, 1837–43

The Lost Steps, novel by Alejo Carpentier, 1953

Love in the Time of Cholera, novel by Gabriel García Márquez, 1985

Loves, poem by Ovid, late 1st century BC

The Lower Depths, play by Maksim Gor'kii, 1902

The Lulu Plays, plays by Frank Wedekind, 1895–1904

The Lusiads, poem by Luís de Camões, 1572

Lysistrata, play by Aristophanes, 411 BC

Mad Love, prose by André Breton, 1937

Madame Bovary, novel by Gustave Flaubert, 1857

The Madwoman of Chaillot, play by Jean Giraudoux, 1945

The Magic Mountain, novel by Thomas Mann, 1924

Mahābhārata, epic poem attributed to Vyāsa, 1st millennium BC/AD

The Maids, play by Jean Genet, 1947

The Man Without Qualities, novel by Robert Musil, 1930–43

The Mandarins, novel by Simone de Beauvoir, 1954

The Mandrake, play by Niccolò Machiavelli, 1524

Manon Lescaut, novel by Abbé Prévost, 1733

Man's Fate, novel by André Malraux, 1933

Marat/Sade, play by Peter Weiss, 1964

Maria Magdalena, play by Friedrich Hebbel, 1844

Mary Stuart, play by Friedrich von Schiller, 1800

The Master and Margarita, novel by Mikhail Bulgakov, 1966

The Master Builder, play by Henrik Ibsen, 1892

Master Don Gesualdo, novel by Giovanni Verga, 1889

A Matter of Dispute, play by Marivaux, 1744

Maxims, prose by La Rouchefoucauld, 1665–78

Medea, play by Euripides, 431 BC

Meditations, prose by Aurelius, c. 170

Memoirs, prose by Chateaubriand, 1849–50

Memoirs of a Good-for-Nothing, novella by Joseph von Eichendorff, 1826

Memoirs of Hadrian, novel by Marguerite Yourcenar, 1951

Metamorphoses, poem by Ovid, 1st century BC/1st century AD

The Metamorphosis, novella by Franz Kafka, 1915

"Mía," poem by Rubén Darío, 1896

Michael Kohlhaas, story by Heinrich von Kleist, 1810

Military Servitude and Grandeur, stories by Alfred de Vigny, 1835

Minna von Barnhelm, play by Gotthold Ephraim Lessing, 1767

The Minor, play by Denis Fonvizin, 1782

The Misanthrope, play by Molière, 1666

The Miser, play by Molière, 1668

Les Misérables, novel by Victor Hugo, 1862

Miss Julie, play by August Strindberg, 1888

Mist, novel by Miguel de Unamuno, 1914

Mr. Mani, novel by A.B. Yehoshua, 1989

The Mistress of the Inn, play by Carlo Goldoni, 1753

Molloy, Malone Dies, The Unnamable, novels by Samuel Beckett, 1951–53

A Month in the Country, play by Ivan Turgenev, 1869

The Moon and the Bonfires, novel by Cesare Pavese, 1950

The Mosella, poem by Ausonius, c. 371

"Moses," poem by Alfred de Vigny, 1826 (written 1822)

Mother Courage and Her Children, play by Bertolt Brecht, 1941

Mythistorima, poem by George Seferis, 1935

Name of the Rose, novel by Umberto Eco, 1980

Nathan the Wise, play by Gotthold Ephraim Lessing, 1779

Nausea, novel by Jean-Paul Sartre, 1938

"The Necklace," story by Guy de Maupassant, 1884

The New Life, poems by Dante Alighieri, 1295

Nibelungenlied, poem, c. 1200

Night Flight, novel by Antoine de Saint-Exupéry, 1931

The Ninth Tale of the Fifth Day of *The Decameron*, story by Giovanni Boccaccio, c. 1350

Njáls saga, anonymous prose, 13th century

No Exit, play by Jean-Paul Sartre, 1944

Notes from the Underground, prose by Fedor Dostoevskii, 1864

Oblomov, novel by Ivan Goncharov, 1859

Ode to Charles Fourier, poem by André Breton, 1947

Ode to Joy, poem by Friedrich von Schiller, written 1785

"Ode to Michel de l'Hospital," poem by Pierre de Ronsard, 1552

Odes Book I, Poem 5, poem by Horace, 1st century BC

Odes Book IV, Poem 7, poem by Horace, 1st century BC

The Odyssey, poem by Homer, c. 720 BC

Oedipus, play by Seneca, c. 48 BC

Oedipus at Colonus, play by Sophocles, 401 BC

Oedipus the King, play by Sophocles, after 430 BC

Old Goriot, novel by Honoré de Balzac, 1835

Olympian One, poem by Pindar, c. 476 BC(?)

On Old Age, prose by Cicero, 44 BC

On the Commonwealth, prose by Cicero, c. 51 BC

On the Crown, prose by Demosthenes, 330 BC

"On the Power of the Imagination," prose by Michel de Montaigne, 1588

On the Sublime, anonymous poem, late 1st century AD

"On Vanity," prose by Michel de Montaigne, 1588

One Day in the Life of Ivan Denisovich, novella by Aleksandr Solzhenitsyn, 1962

One Hundred Years of Solitude, novel by Gabriel García Márquez, 1967

The Ordeal, novel by Vasil Bykaw, 1970

The Oresteia, play by Aeschylus, 458 BC

Orestes, play by Euripides, 408 BC

Orlando Furioso, poem by Ludovico Ariosto, 1515

The Outsider, novel by Albert Camus, 1942

"Palau," poem by Gottfried Benn, 1922

Paris Peasant, prose poem by Louis Aragon, 1926

A Part of Speech, poems by Iosif Brodskii, 1977

Parzival, poem by Wolfram von Eschenbach, written c. 1200–10

Pascual Duarte's Family, novel by Camilo José Cela, 1942

Peasant Tales, stories by Bjørnstjerne Bjørnson, 1856?

Peer Gynt, play by Henrik Ibsen, 1867

The Peony Pavilion, novel by Tang Xianzu, 1598

Peribáñez and the Comendador of Ocaña, play by Lope de Vega Carpio, 1608

The Periodic Table, stories by Primo Levi, 1975

The Persians, play by Aeschylus, 472 BC

Peter Schlemihl, novella by Adelbert von Chamisso, 1814

Petersburg, novel by Andrei Belyi, 1916

Phaedra, play by Jean Racine, 1677

Phaedrus, prose by Plato, 5th/4th century BC

Philoctetes, play by Sophocles, 409 BC

The Philosophical Dictionary, prose by Voltaire, 1764

Phormio, play by Terence, 161 BC

The Physicists, play by Friedrich Dürrenmatt, 1962

Pierre and Jean, novella by Guy de Maupassant, 1888

The Pillar of Salt, novel by Albert Memmi, 1953

The Plague, novel by Albert Camus, 1947

Plagued by the West, novel by Jalal Âl-e Ahmad, 1962

Platero and I, poem by Juan Ramón Jiménez, 1914

"Il pleure dans mon coeur . . . ," poem by Paul Verlaine, 1874

Poem 85, poem by Catullus, 1st century BC

Poem on the Disaster of Lisbon, poem by Voltaire, 1756

Poem without a Hero, poem by Anna Akhmatova, 1963

The Poetic Art, poem by Horace, late 1st century BC

The Poetic *Edda*, anonymous poems, 13th century

The Posthumous Memoirs of Braz Cubas, novel by Joaquim Maria Machado de Assis, 1880

The Pot of Gold, play by Plautus, 2nd century BC

The Praise of Folly, prose by Desiderius Erasmus, 1511

The President, novel by Miguel Ángel Asturias, 1946

The Prince, prose by Niccolò Machiavelli, 1513

The Prince of Homburg, play by Heinrich von Kleist, 1821

Professor Bernhardi, play by Arthur Schnitzler, 1912

Professeur Taranne, play by Arthur Adamov, 1953

Prometheus Bound, play by Aeschylus, c. 466–59 BC

The Prose *Edda*, prose by Snorri Sturluson, 13th century

Pythian Odes Four and Five, poems by Pindar, c. 462 BC(?)

"Quand vous serez bien vieille . . . ," poem by Pierre de Ronsard, 1578 (written 1572)

The Radetzky March, novel by Joseph Roth, 1932

"Rain in the Pine Forest," poem by Gabriele D'Annunzio, 1903

Rāmāyana, poem attributed to Vālmīki, 1st/2nd century

The Rape of Proserpine, poem by Claudian, c. 400

Red Cavalry, stories by Isaak Babel, 1926

Remembrance of Things Past, novel by Marcel Proust, 1913–27

René, prose by Chateaubriand, 1802

The Republic, prose by Plato, 5th/4th century BC

Requiem, poem cycle by Anna Akhmatova, 1963

The Reveries of a Solitary, prose by Jean-Jacques Rousseau, 1782

Rhinoceros, play by Eugène Ionesco, 1959

Rice, novel by Su Tong, 1991

Rickshaw Boy, novel by Lao She, 1937

"Rock Crystal," story by Adalbert Stifter, 1853

The Romance of the Rose (de Lorris and Meung), poem, c. 1225–70

La Ronde, play by Arthur Schnitzler, 1900

Rose Garden, prose and verse by Sa'di, 1258

Ruba'iyat, poems by Omar Khayyam, 11/12th century

"The Sacred Way," poem by Angelos Sikelianos, 1935

The Saga of King Óláf the Saint, prose by Snorri Sturluson, 12th/13th century

Śakuntalā, poem by Kālidāsa, 5th century

The Satin Slipper, play by Paul Claudel, 1928–29

Satire 10, poem by Juvenal, 1st/2nd century AD

Saul, play by Vittorio Alfieri, 1782

Scarlet and Black, novel by Stendhal, 1830

A School for Fools, novel by Sasha Sokolov, 1976

The Seagull, play by Anton Chekhov, 1896

Seamarks, poem by Saint-John Perse, 1957

The Second Sex, prose by Simone de Beauvoir, 1949

"A Sentence for Tyranny," poem by Gyula Illyés, 1956

Sentimental Education, novel by Gustave Flaubert, 1869

"Ses purs ongles trés haut dédiant leur onyx," poem by Stéphane Mallarmé, 1887

The Seven Against Thebes, play by Aeschylus, 467 BC

Seventh Duino Elegy, poem by Rainer Maria Rilke, 1923

The Ship of Fools, poem by Sebastian Brant, 1494

Siddhartha, novel by Hermann Hesse, 1922

Silence, novel by Endō Shūsaku, 1966

"A Simple Heart," story by Gustave Flaubert, 1877

"Sirens," poem by Giuseppe Ungaretti, 1933

Six Characters in Search of an Author, play by Luigi Pirandello, 1921

The Sleepwalkers, novels by Hermann Broch, 1931–32

Snow Country, novel by Kawabata Yasunari, 1937

"The Snow Queen," story by Hans Christian Andersen, 1845

The Social Contract, prose by Jean-Jacques Rousseau, 1762

Some Prefer Nettles, novel by Tanizaki Jun'ichiro, 1928

The Song of Roland, poem, c. 1100

"Sonnet 90," poem by Petrarch, before 1356

Sonnets to Orpheus, poems by Rainer Maria Rilke, 1923

"Spleen," poems by Charles Baudelaire, 1861

Spring Awakening, play by Frank Wedekind, 1891

Steppenwolf, novel by Hermann Hesse, 1927

"The Storm," poem by Eugenio Montale, 1941

The Story of Just Caspar and Fair Annie, novella by Clemens Brentano, 1817

Die Strudlhofstiege, novel by Heimito von Doderer, 1951

The Sufferings of Young Werther, novel by Johann Wolfgang von Goethe, 1774

Sun Stone, poem by Octavio Paz, 1957

The Suppliant Maidens, play by Aeschylus, c. 463 BC

The Symposium, prose by Plato, 4th century BC

The Tale of the Campaign of Igor, anonymous poem, c. 1185

Tales from the Vienna Woods, play by Ödön von Horváth, 1931

Tartuffe, play by Molière, 1664

CHRONOLOGICAL LIST OF WORKS

Vedas, anonymous prose and verse, c. 3000–c. 500 BC

Epic of Gilgamesh, anonymous poem cycle, early 2nd millennium BC

The Bible, anonymous verse and prose, c. 900 BC onwards

Upanishads, anonymous prose and verse, c. 800–c. 500 BC

The Iliad, poem by Homer, c. 750 BC

The Odyssey, poem by Homer, c. 720 BC

Fragment 1 ["Address to Aphrodite"], poem by Sappho, 7th century BC

Fragment 31 ["Declaration of Love for a Young Girl"], poem by Sappho, 7th century BC

The City of God, prose by St Augustine, 5th century

Olympian One, poem by Pindar, c. 476 BC(?)

The Persians, play by Aeschylus, 472 BC

The Seven Against Thebes, play by Aeschylus, 467 BC

Prometheus Bound, play by Aeschylus, c. 466–59 BC

The Suppliant Maidens, play by Aeschylus, c. 463 BC

Pythian Odes Four and Five, poems by Pindar, c. 462 BC(?)

The Oresteia, play by Aeschylus, 458 BC

Ajax, play by Sophocles, before 441 BC(?)

Antigone, play by Sophocles, c. 441 BC(?)

Medea, play by Euripides, 431 BC

Women of Trachis, play by Sophocles, c. 430–20 BC

Oedipus the King, play by Sophocles, after 430 BC

Hippolytus, play by Euripides, 428 BC

The Clouds, play by Aristophanes, 423 BC

Electra, play by Euripides, c. 422–16 BC

Ion, play by Euripides, c. 421–13 BC

Electra, play by Sophocles, c. 418–10 BC(?)

The Trojan Women, play by Euripides, 415 BC

The Birds, play by Aristophanes, 414 BC

Lysistrata, play by Aristophanes, 411 BC

Philoctetes, play by Sophocles, 409 BC

Orestes, play by Euripides, 408 BC

The Frogs, play by Aristophanes, 405 BC

Oedipus at Colonus, play by Sophocles, 401 BC

Phaedrus, prose by Plato, 5th/4th century BC

The Republic, prose by Plato, 5th/4th century BC

The Symposium, prose by Plato, 4th century BC

On the Crown, prose by Demosthenes, 330 BC

Characters, prose by Theophrastus, c. 319 BC

The Grouch, play by Menander, 316 BC

Aetia, poem by Callimachus, 3rd century BC

Hecale, poem by Callimachus, 3rd century BC

Idyll I, poem by Theocritus, c. 270s BC

Idyll IV, poem by Theocritus, c. 270s BC

Idyll VII, poem by Theocritus, c. 270s BC

Amphitryo, play by Plautus, 2nd century BC

The Brothers Menaechmus, play by Plautus, 2nd century BC

The Pot of Gold, play by Plautus, 2nd century BC

The Eunuch, play by Terence, 161 BC

Phormio, play by Terence, 161 BC

The Brothers, play by Terence, 160 BC

The Aeneid, poem by Virgil, 1st century BC

Epigrams, poems by Martial, 1st century BC

Georgics, poem by Virgil, 1st century BC

Odes Book I, Poem 5, poem by Horace, 1st century BC

Odes Book IV, Poem 7, poem by Horace, 1st century BC

Poem 85, poem by Catullus, 1st century BC

Three Poems: 2, 63, and 76, poems by Catullus, 1st century BC

In Defence of Marcus Caelius Rufus, prose by Cicero, 56 BC

On the Commonwealth, prose by Cicero, c. 51 BC

Oedipus, play by Seneca, c. 48 BC

Thyestes, play by Seneca, c. 48 BC

On Old Age, prose by Cicero, 44 BC

Loves, poem by Ovid, late 1st century BC

The Poetic Art, poem by Horace, late 1st century BC

Mahābhārata, epic poem attributed to Vyāsa, 1st millennium BC/AD

The Art of Love, poem by Ovid, 1st century BC/1st century AD

Metamorphoses, poem by Ovid, 1st century BC/1st century AD

Kalevala, anonymous poem, origins date to early 1st century AD

The Little Clay Cart, anonymous play, 1st century AD(?)

On the Sublime, anonymous poem, late 1st century AD

Rāmāyana, poem attributed to Vālmīki, 1st/2nd century

Lives of Lysander and Sulla, prose by Plutarch, 1st/2nd century AD

Satire 10, poem by Juvenal, 1st/2nd century AD

Annals, prose by Tacitus, early 2nd century AD

Meditations, prose by Aurelius, c. 170

Cupid and Psyche, story by Apuleius, c. 180

Daphnis and Chloe, poem by Longus, 2nd/3rd century

Confessions, Book I, prose by St. Augustine, 4th century

The Mosella, poem by Ausonius, c. 371

The Cloud Messenger, poem by Kālidāsa, 5th century

Śakuntalā, poem by Kālidāsa, 5th century

The Rape of Proserpine, poem by Claudian, c. 400

The Consolation of Philosophy, prose by Boethius, early 6th century

"Hard Is the Road to Shu," poem by Li Bai, c. 744

"Invitation to Wine," poem by Li Bai, 752

The Thousand and One Nights, anonymous stories, 9th century

Journey to the West, anonymous novel, 11/12th century

Ruba'iyat, poems by Omar Khayyam, 11/12th century

The Song of Roland, poem, c. 1100

Erec and Énide, poem by Chrétien de Troyes, written c. 1170

Lancelot, poem by Chrétien de Troyes, written c. 1170

The Conference of the Birds, poem by Farid al-Din Attār, c. 1177

The Tale of the Campaign of Igor, anonymous poem, c. 1185

Guigamor, poem by Marie de France, late 12th century

The Saga of King Óláf the Saint, prose by Snorri Sturluson, 12th/13th century

Aucassin and Nicolette (Anon), romance, 13th century

Egils saga, anonymous prose, 13th century

Njáls saga, anonymous prose, 13th century

The Poetic *Edda*, anonymous poems, 13th century

The Prose *Edda*, prose by Snorri Sturluson, 13th century

Nibelungenlied, poem, c. 1200

Parzival, poem by Wolfram von Eschenbach, written c. 1200–10

Willehalm, unfinished poem by Wolfram von Eschenbach, written c. 1210–12

Titurel, poetic fragment by Wolfram von Eschenbach, written c. 1212–20

The Romance of the Rose (de Lorris and Meung), poem, c. 1225–70

Rose Garden, prose and verse by Sa'di, 1258

The New Life, poems by Dante Alighieri, 1295

Water Margin, anonymous novel, 14th century

The Divine Comedy, poem by Dante Alighieri, 1321 The Ninth Tale of the Fifth Day of *The Decameron*, story by Giovanni Boccaccio, c. 1350

"Sonnet 90," poem by Petrarch, before 1356

The Book of the City of Ladies, prose by Christine de Pizan, 1405

"Ballade des dames du temps jadis," poem by François Villon, 1489 (written c. 1460?)

"Ballade des pendus," poem by François Villon, 1489

The Ship of Fools, poem by Sebastian Brant, 1494

The Praise of Folly, prose by Desiderius Erasmus, 1511

The Prince, prose by Niccolò Machiavelli, 1513

Orlando Furioso, poem by Ludovico Ariosto, 1515

Auto da Barca do Inferno, Auto da Barca do Purgatorio, Auto da Barca da Gloria, plays by Gil Vicente, 1517, 1518, 1519

The Colloquies, prose by Desiderius Erasmus, 1518

Farsa de Inês Pereira, play by Gil Vicente, 1523

The Mandrake, play by Niccolò Machiavelli, 1524

"Ein feste Burg," hymn by Martin Luther, 1531 (written 1528?)

Gargantua and *Pantagruel*, novels by François Rabelais, 1532–34(?)

La cortigiana, play by Pietro Aretino, 1534

The Wandering Scholar in Paradise, play by Hans Sachs, written 1550

"Ode to Michel de l'Hospital," poem by Pierre de Ronsard, 1552

Lazarillo de Tormes, anonymous novel, 1554

"Heureux qui, comme Ulysse, a fait un beau voyage," poem by Joachim Du Bellay, 1558

"Hymn to Autumn," poem by Pierre de Ronsard, 1563

"Apology for Raymond Sebond," prose by Michel de Montaigne, 1570

The Lusiads, poem by Luís de Camões, 1572

Aminta, play by Torquato Tasso, 1573

"Quand vous serez bien vieille . . . ," poem by Pierre de Ronsard, 1578 (written 1572)

Jerusalem Delivered, poem by Torquato Tasso, 1580

"On the Power of the Imagination," prose by Michel de Montaigne, 1588

"On Vanity," prose by Michel de Montaigne, 1588

The Peony Pavilion, novel by Tang Xianzu, 1598

Peribáñez and the Comendador of Ocaña, play by Lope de Vega Carpio, 1608

Don Quixote, novel by Miguel de Cervantes, 1615

Fuenteovejuna, play by Lope de Vega Carpio, 1619

Life Is a Dream, play by Pedro Calderón de la Barca, 1623

The Trickster of Seville, play by Tirso de Molina, 1625

Justice Without Revenge, play by Lope de Vega Carpio, 1632

The Great Stage of the World, play by Pedro Calderón de la Barca, c. 1635

The Theatrical Illusion, play by Pierre Corneille, 1635–36

The Cid, play by Pierre Corneille, 1636–37

Voyages to the Moon and the Sun, novels by Cyrano de Bergerac, 1657–62

The Conceited Young Ladies, play by Molière, 1659

Tartuffe, play by Molière, 1664

Don Juan, play by Molière, 1665

Maxims, prose by La Rouchefoucauld, 1665–78

The Misanthrope, play by Molière, 1666

The Miser, play by Molière, 1668

Berenice, play by Jean Racine, 1670

Bajazet, play by Jean Racine, 1672

The Hypochondriac, play by Molière, 1673

The Art of Poetry, poem by Nicolas Boileau, 1674

Phaedra, play by Jean Racine, 1677

Fables, stories by Jean de La Fontaine, 1688–89

Athalie, play by Jean Racine, 1691

The Game of Love and Chance, play by Marivaux, 1730

Manon Lescaut, novel by Abbé Prévost, 1733

The False Confessions, play by Marivaux, 1737

A Matter of Dispute, play by Marivaux, 1744

Zadig, novella by Voltaire, 1748

The Dream of the Red Chamber, novel by Cao Xueqin, mid-18th century

The Comic Theatre, play by Carlo Goldoni, 1750

The Mistress of the Inn, play by Carlo Goldoni, 1753

Poem on the Disaster of Lisbon, poem by Voltaire, 1756

The Test of Virtue, play by Denis Diderot, 1757

Candide, novella by Voltaire, 1759

Emile, fiction by Jean-Jacques Rousseau, 1762

The Social Contract, prose by Jean-Jacques Rousseau, 1762

The Philosophical Dictionary, prose by Voltaire, 1764

Minna von Barnhelm, play by Gotthold Ephraim Lessing, 1767

Goetz of Berlichingen, play by Johann Wolfgang von Goethe, 1773

The Sufferings of Young Werther, novel by Johann Wolfgang von Goethe, 1774

The Tutor, play by Jakob Michael Reinhold Lenz, 1774

The Barber of Seville, play by Beaumarchais, 1775

Nathan the Wise, play by Gotthold Ephraim Lessing, 1779

The Confessions, prose by Jean-Jacques Rousseau, 1781

Les Liaisons Dangereuses, novel by Choderlos de Laclos, 1782

The Minor, play by Denis Fonvizin, 1782

The Reveries of a Solitary, prose by Jean-Jacques Rousseau, 1782

Saul, play by Vittorio Alfieri, 1782

Ode to Joy, poem by Friedrich von Schiller, written 1785

Don Carlos, play by Friedrich von Schiller, 1787

Torquato Tasso, play by Johann Wolfgang von Goethe, 1790

Justine, novel by Marquis de Sade, 1791

Wilhelm Meister's Apprenticeship, novel by Johann Wolfgang von Goethe, 1795–96

Jacques the Fatalist, novel by Denis Diderot, 1796

Wallenstein, plays by Friedrich von Schiller, 1798–99

Hymns to the Night, poems by Novalis, 1800

Mary Stuart, play by Friedrich von Schiller, 1800

René, prose by Chateaubriand, 1802

William Tell, play by Friedrich von Schiller, 1804

"Bread and Wine," poem by Friedrich Hlderlin , 1806 (written 1800–01)

The Broken Jug, play by Heinrich von Kleist, 1808

Faust, play by Johann Wolfgang von Goethe: part I, 1808; part II, 1832

Elective Affinities, novel by Johann Wolfgang von Goethe, 1809

Michael Kohlhaas, story by Heinrich von Kleist, 1810

"Hansel and Gretel," story by Jacob and Wilhelm Grimm, 1812

Peter Schlemihl, novella by Adelbert von Chamisso, 1814

The Devil's Elixirs, novel by E.T.A. Hoffmann, 1815–16

The Story of Just Caspar and Fair Annie, novella by Clemens Brentano, 1817

"The Infinite," poem by Giacomo Leopardi, 1819

The Prince of Homburg, play by Heinrich von Kleist, 1821

"Homecoming," 20, poem by Heinrich Heine, 1824

Memoirs of a Good-for-Nothing, novella by Joseph von Eichendorff, 1826

"Moses," poem by Alfred de Vigny, 1826 (written 1822)

The Betrothed, novel by Alessandro Manzoni, 1827

Scarlet and Black, novel by Stendhal, 1830

Eugene Onegin, poem by Aleksandr Pushkin, 1831

Death in Venice, novella by Thomas Mann, 1912
The Gods Are Athirst, novel by Anatole France, 1912
Professor Bernhardi, play by Arthur Schnitzler, 1912
"Le Chanson du mal-aime," poem by Guillaume Apollinaire, 1913
The Wanderer, novel by Alain-Fournier, 1913
"Zone," poem by Guillaume Apollinaire, 1913
Remembrance of Things Past, novel by Marcel Proust, 1913–27
"Un Coup de dés jamais n'abolira le hasard," poem by Stéphane Mallarmé, 1914 (written 1897)
Mist, novel by Miguel de Unamuno, 1914
Platero and I, poem by Juan Ramón Jiménez, 1914
Cloud in Trousers, poem by Vladimir Maiakovskii, 1915
The Gentleman from San Francisco, novella by Ivan Bunin, 1915
"Grodek," poem by Georg Trakl, 1915
The Metamorphosis, novella by Franz Kafka, 1915
Petersburg, novel by Andrei Belyi, 1916
Under Fire, novel by Henri Barbusse, 1916
"La Jeune Parque," poem by Paul Valéry, 1917 (written 1912–17)
The Gas Trilogy, plays by Georg Kaiser, 1917–20
The Twelve, poem by Aleksandr Blok, 1918
"The Eternal Dice," poem by César Vallejo, 1919
Chéri, novel by Colette, 1920
The Christ of Velazquez, poem by Miguel de Unamuno, 1920
"Le Cimetière marin," poem by Paul Valéry, 1920
Kristin Lavransdatter, novels by Sigrid Undset, 1920–22
Confessions of Felix Krull, Confidence Man, novel by Thomas Mann, 1922 (complete 1954)
The Difficult Man, play by Hugo von Hofmannsthal, 1921
Henry IV, play by Luigi Pirandello, 1921
The Insect Play, play by Karel Čapek, 1921
Six Characters in Search of an Author, play by Luigi Pirandello, 1921
The Good Soldier Švejk and His Fortunes in the World War, novel by Jaroslav Hašek, 1921–23
Baal, play by Bertolt Brecht, 1922
"Palau," poem by Gottfried Benn, 1922
Siddhartha, novel by Hermann Hesse, 1922
About This, poem by Vladimir Maiakovskii, 1923
Confessions of Zeno, novel by Italo Svevo, 1923
The Devil in the Flesh, novel by Raymond Radiguet, 1923
Seventh Duino Elegy, poem by Rainer Maria Rilke, 1923
Sonnets to Orpheus, poems by Rainer Maria Rilke, 1923
The Magic Mountain, novel by Thomas Mann, 1924
We, novel by Evgenii Zamiatin, 1924
Cuttlefish Bones, poems by Eugenio Montale, 1925
The Tower, play by Hugo von Hofmannsthal, 1925
The Trial, novel by Franz Kafka, 1925 (written 1914–15)
The Castle, novel by Franz Kafka, 1926 (written 1922)
The Counterfeiters, novel by André Gide, 1926
Paris Peasant, prose poem by Louis Aragon, 1926
Red Cavalry, stories by Isaak Babel, 1926
Tentativa del hombre infinito, poem by Pablo Neruda, 1926
Envy, novel by Iurii Olesha, 1927
Steppenwolf, novel by Hermann Hesse, 1927
Thérèse, novel by François Mauriac, 1927
Some Prefer Nettles, novel by Tanizaki Jun'ichiro, 1928
The Threepenny Opera, play by Bertolt Brecht, 1928
"You the Only One," poem by Paul Éluard, 1928
The Satin Slipper, play by Paul Claudel, 1928–29
All Quiet on the Western Front, novel by Erich Maria Remarque, 1929
The Bedbug, play by Vladimir Maiakovskii, 1929

Berlin Alexanderplatz, novel by Alfred Döblin, 1929
The Holy Terrors, novel by Jean Cocteau, 1929
The Time of Indifference, novel by Alberto Moravia, 1929
The White Guard, novel by Mikhail Bulgakov, 1929
Andreas, fiction by Hugo von Hofmannsthal, 1930 (written 1912–13)
Fontamara, novel by Ignazio Silone, 1930
The Man Without Qualities, novel by Robert Musil, 1930–43
Free Union, poem by André Breton, 1931
Night Flight, novel by Antoine de Saint-Exupéry, 1931
Tales from the Vienna Woods, play by Ödön von Horváth, 1931
The Sleepwalkers, novels by Hermann Broch, 1931–32
Journey to the End of the Night, novel by Louis-Ferdinand Céline, 1932
The Radetzky March, novel by Joseph Roth, 1932
Blood Wedding, play by Federico García Lorca, 1933
Man's Fate, novel by André Malraux, 1933
"Sirens," poem by Giuseppe Ungaretti, 1933
The Infernal Machine, play by Jean Cocteau, 1934
Yerma, play by Federico García Lorca, 1934
"Arte poética," poem by Pablo Neruda, 1935
Mythistorima, poem by George Seferis, 1935
"The Sacred Way," poem by Angelos Sikelianos, 1935
Tiger at the Gates, play by Jean Giraudoux, 1935
Auto-da-Fé, novel by Elias Canetti, 1936
Bread and Wine, novel by Ignazio Silone, 1937
Ferdydurke, novel by Witold Gombrowicz, 1937
Mad Love, prose by André Breton, 1937
Rickshaw Boy, novel by Lao She, 1937
Snow Country, novel by Kawabata Yasunari, 1937
Nausea, novel by Jean-Paul Sartre, 1938
The Theatre and Its Double, prose by Antonin Artaud, 1938
"Considerando en frio," poem by César Vallejo, 1939
Conversation in Sicily, novel by Elio Vittorini, 1939
Tropisms, prose by Nathalie Sarraute, 1939
Le Crève-coeur, poems by Louis Aragon, 1941
Mother Courage and Her Children, play by Bertolt Brecht, 1941
"The Storm," poem by Eugenio Montale, 1941
"Death and the Compass," story by Jorge Luis Borges, 1942
The Outsider, novel by Albert Camus, 1942
Pascual Duarte's Family, novel by Camilo Jos´ Cela, 1942
The Voice of Things, poems by Francis Ponge, 1942
The Flies, play by Jean-Paul Sartre, 1943
The Glass Bead Game, novel by Hermann Hesse, 1943
The Good Person of Szechwan, play by Bertolt Brecht, 1943
The Life of Galileo, play by Bertolt Brecht, 1943
Antigone, play by Jean Anhouilh, 1944
No Exit, play by Jean-Paul Sartre, 1944
The Age of Reason, novel by Jean-Paul Sartre, 1945
The Bridge on the Drina, novel by Ivo Andrić, 1945
Christ Stopped at Eboli, novel by Carlo Levi, 1945
The Death of Virgil, novel by Hermann Broch, 1945
The House of Bernarda Alba, play by Federico García Lorca, 1945
The Madwoman of Chaillot, play by Jean Giraudoux, 1945
Filumena Marturano, play by Eduardo De Filippo, 1946
The President, novel by Miguel Ángel Asturias, 1946
Doctor Faustus, novel by Thomas Mann, 1947
The Kingdom of This World, novel by Alejo Carpentier, 1947
The Maids, play by Jean Genet, 1947
Ode to Charles Fourier, poem by André Breton, 1947
The Plague, novel by Albert Camus, 1947
Ashes and Diamonds, novel by Jerzy Andrzejewski, 1948

The Caucasian Chalk Circle, play by Bertolt Brecht, 1948
The Fire Raisers, play by Max Frisch, 1948
House of Liars, novel by Elsa Morante, 1948
The Second Sex, prose by Simone de Beauvoir, 1949
The Bald Prima Donna, play by Eugène Ionesco, 1950
The Fugitive, novel by Pramoedya Ananta Toer, 1950
The Moon and the Bonfires, novel by Cesare Pavese, 1950
Die Strudlhofstiege, novel by Heimito von Doderer, 1951
The Hussar on the Roof, novel by Jean Giono, 1951
Memoirs of Hadrian, novel by Marguerite Yourcenar, 1951
Molloy, Malone Dies, The Unnamable, novels by Samuel Beckett, 1951–53
"Death Fugue," poem by Paul Celan, 1952 (written 1948)
Waiting for Godot, play by Samuel Beckett, 1952
The Lost Steps, novel by Alejo Carpentier, 1953
The Pillar of Salt, novel by Albert Memmi, 1953
Professeur Taranne, play by Arthur Adamov, 1953
Against Sainte-Beuve, prose by Marcel Proust, 1954
I'm Not Stiller, play by Max Frisch, 1954
The Mandarins, novel by Simone de Beauvoir, 1954
The Last Temptation, novel by Nikos Kazantzakis, 1955
The Voyeur, novel by Alain Robbe-Grillet, 1955
The Balcony, play by Jean Genet, 1956
The Fall, novel by Albert Camus, 1956
"A Sentence for Tyranny," poem by Gyula Illyés, 1956
The Visit, play by Friedrich Dürrenmatt, 1956
Doctor Zhivago, novel by Boris Pasternak, 1957
Endgame, play by Samuel Beckett, 1957
Seamarks, poem by Saint-John Perse, 1957
Sun Stone, poem by Octavio Paz, 1957
Deep Rivers, novel by José Mariá Arguedas, 1958
In the Labyrinth, novel by Alain Robbe-Grillet, 1959
Rhinoceros, play by Eugène Ionesco, 1959
The Tin Drum, novel by Günter Grass, 1959

Zazie, novel by Raymond Queneau, 1959
Andorra, play by Max Frisch, 1961
Voices in the Evening, novel by Natalia Ginzburg, 1961
One Day in the Life of Ivan Denisovich, novella by Aleksandr Solzhenitsyn, 1962
The Physicists, play by Friedrich Dürrenmatt, 1962
Plagued by the West, novel by Jalal Âl-e Ahmad, 1962
Woman in the Dunes, novel by Abe Kōbō, 1962
Poem without a Hero, poem by Anna Akhmatova, 1963
Requiem, poem cycle by Anna Akhmatova, 1963
Marat/Sade, play by Peter Weiss, 1964
Blue Flowers, novel by Raymond Queneau, 1965
The Investigation, play by Peter Weiss, 1965
The Master and Margarita, novel by Mikhail Bulgakov, 1966
Silence, novel by Endō Shūsaku, 1966
One Hundred Years of Solitude, novel by Gabriel García Márquez, 1967
Cancer Ward, novel by Aleksandr Solzhenitsyn, 1968
The German Lesson, novel by Seigfried Lenz, 1968
The Lime Works, novel by Thomas Bernhard, 1970
The Ordeal, novel by Vasil Bykaw, 1970
Group Portrait with Lady, novel by Heinrich Böll, 1971
The Lost Honor of Katharina Blum, novel by Heinrich Böll, 1974
The Periodic Table, stories by Primo Levi, 1975
Kiss of the Spider Woman, novel by Manuel Puig, 1976
A School for Fools, novel by Sasha Sokolov, 1976
A Part of Speech, poems by Iosif Brodskii, 1977
Life: A User's Manual, novel by Georges Perece, 1978
If on a Winter's Night a Traveller, novel by Italo Calvino, 1979
Name of the Rose, novel by Umberto Eco, 1980
The House of the Spirits, novel by Isabel Allende, 1982
Fantasia: An Algerian Cavalcade, novel by Assia Djebar, 1985
Love in the Time of Cholera, novel by Gabriel García Márquez, 1985
Mr. Mani, novel by A.B. Yehoshua, 1989
Rice, novel by Su Tong, 1991

Reference Guide to

WORLD LITERATURE

THIRD EDITION

VOLUME 1

A

ABE Kōbō

Born: Abe Kimifusa in Tokyo, Japan, 7 March 1924. **Education:** Chiyoda Elementary School, Mukden, Manchuria (now Shen-yang, Liaoning Province, China), 1930–36; interrupted by a spell at a local elementary school in his father's home town of Takasu, Hokkaido, Japan, 1931–32; Second Middle School, Mukden, 1936–40; Seijō High School, Tokyo, 1940–43; interrupted for several months at the end of 1940 when he returned to Mukden after contracting pneumonia during a school military drill; began to study medicine at Tokyo Imperial University (now Tokyo University) in 1940, interrupting his course in 1944 to join his parents in Mukden having been given time off after faking a diagnosis; graduated March 1948 after repatriation at the end of 1946 but never practiced as a doctor. **Family:** Married Yamada Machiko (pseudonym Abe Machi, graphic artist), 1947; one daughter. **Career:** Co-founder of Seiki (The Century), an interest group for authors and journalists, c. 1947; Executive Committee of the New Japan Literature Association, 1955–61?; maintained his own theater troupe, the Abe Kōbō Studio, 1973–79. **Awards:** Postwar Literature prize for "Akai mayu" ("The Red Cocoon"), 1951; Akutagawa prize for literature for "S. Karuma-shi no hanzai," 1951; Kishida Drama prize for *Yūrei wa koko ni iru*, 1958; Yomiuri Literature prize (fiction) for *Suna no onna*, 1962; Tanizaki Jun'ichirō prize for literature for *Tomodachi*, 1967; Yomiuri Literature prize (drama) for *Midoriiro no sutokkingu*, 1974; Honorary doctorate from Columbia University, New York, 1975. **Member:** Japan Communist Party, 1951?–1962, later expelled. **Died:** Tokyo, 22 January 1993, of heart failure.

PUBLICATIONS

Collections

Abe Kōbō gikyoku zenshū (collected plays). 1970.
Abe Kōbō zensakuhin (collected works). 15 vols., 1972–73.
Abe Kōbō zenshū (complete works). 29 vols., 1997–2000.
Three Plays by Kōbō Abe, translated by Donald Keene. 1993.

Fiction

Owarishi michi no shirube ni [To Mark the End of the Road]. 1948; revised 1967.
"Dendorokakariya." 1949; as "Dendrocacalia," translated by Juliet Winters Carpenter, in *Beyond the Curve*. 1991.
Kabe: S. Karuma-shi no hanzai [Walls: The Crime of S. Karma] (short stories). 1951; "Akai mayu," translated as "Red Cocoon" by John Nathan, 1966; "Mahō no chōku" translated as "The Magic Chalk" by Alison Kibrick, 1982; "S. Karuma-shi no hanzai" translated as "The Crime of S. Karma" by Juliet Winters Carpenter, in *Beyond the Curve*, 1991; "Kōzui" translated as "The Flood" by Lane Dunlop, 1989.
"Shijin no shōgai." 1951; as "The Life of a Poet," translated by Juliet Winters Carpenter, in *Beyond the Curve*, 1991.

R 62 no hatsumei [The Invention of R 62] (short stories). 1954; "Shinda musume ga utatta" translated as "Song of a Dead Girl" by Stuart A. Harrington, 1986.
"Yume no heishi." 1955; as "The Dream Soldier," translated by Andrew Horvat, in *Four Stories*, 1973.
Daiyon kanpyōki. 1959; as *Inter Ice Age 4*, translated by E. Dale Saunders, 1970.
Suna no onna. 1962; as *The Woman in the Dunes*, translated by E. Dale Saunders, 1964.
Tanin no kao. 1964; as *The Face of Another*, translated by E. Dale Saunders, 1966.
Moetsukita chizu. 1967; as *The Ruined Map*, translated by E. Dale Saunders, 1969.
Hako otoko (with photographs by the author). 1973; as *The Box Man*, translated by E. Dale Saunders, 1974.
Four Stories by Abe Kobo. 1973; translated by Andrew Horvat.
Mikkai. 1977; as *Secret Rendezvous*, translated by Juliet Winters Carpenter, 1980.
Hakobune Sakuramaru (with photographs by the author). 1984; as *The Ark Sakura*, translated by Juliet Winters Carpenter, 1988.
Beyond the Curve and Other Stories, translated by Juliet Winters Carpenter. 1991.
Kangarū nōto. 1991; as *Kangaroo Notebook*, translated by Maryellen Toman Mori, 1996.
Tobu otoko [The Flying Man]. 1994.

Plays

Seifuku (produced 1955). 1954; as *Uniform*, translated by Noah S. Brannen, 1979.
Doreigari [Slave Hunt] (produced 1955). 1955.
Yūrei wa koko ni iru (produced 1958). 1958; revised 1970; directed by the author, 1975; as *The Ghost is Here,* translated by Donald Keene, in *Three Plays*, 1993.
Kawaii onna [Pretty Woman] (musical; music by Mayuzumi Toshirō; produced 1959). 1959.
Omae ni mo tsumi ga aru (produced 1965). 1965; as "You, Too, Are Guilty," translated by Ted. T. Takaya, 1979.
Tomodachi (produced 1967). 1967; revised and produced 1974, directed by the author; as *Friends*, translated by Donald Keene, 1969; adapted for cinema as *Friends*, Japan/Sweden, 1988, directed by Kjell-Åke Andersson.
Bō ni natta otoko (produced 1969). 1969; as *The Man Who Turned into a Stick*, translated by Donald Keene, 1977; "Toki no gake" translated as "The Cliff of Time" by Andrew Horvat, in *Four Stories*, 1973; also adapted as a 16 mm film directed by the author, 1971.
Mihitsu no koi (produced 1971). 1971; as *Involuntary Homicide*, translated by Donald Keene, in *Three Plays*, 1993.
Gaido bukku [Guide Book] (produced 1971). 1971; directed by the author.
Annainin, [Guide Book II or The Tour Guide]. 1976; directed by the author.
Suichū toshi [Guide Book III or The City in the Water]. 1977; directed by the author.

S. Karuma-shi no hanzai [Guide Book IV]. 1978; directed by the author.

Ai no megane wa irogarasu [Love is like Tinted Spectacles] (produced 1973). 1973; directed by the author.

Midoriiro no sutokkingu (produced 1974). 1974; directed by the author; as *Green Stockings,* translated by Donald Keene, in *Three Plays,* 1993.

Imēji no Tenrankai [An Exhibition of Pictures] (produced 1977). 1977; directed by the author, synthesizer music composed by the author.

Hitosarai [An Exhibition of Pictures II or The Abduction] (produced 1978). 1978; directed by the author.

Kozō wa shinda [An Exhibition of Pictures III or The Baby Elephant is Dead] (produced 1979). 1979; directed by the author, synthesizer music composed by the author.

Screenplays: *Kabe atsuki heya* [Rooms with Thick Walls], 1954; *Otoshiana* [Pitfalls], 1962; *Suna no onna,* 1964; *Tanin no kao,* 1966; *Moetsukita chizu,* 1968.

Radio Plays: *Mimi* [The Ear], 1956; *Kuchi* [The Mouth], 1957; *Kitchu kutchu ketchu* (children's radio series), 1957; *Chanpion* [The Champion] (radio play/sound collage; together with the composer Takemitsu Toru). 1962.

Television Plays: *Ningen sokkuri* [Almost Human], 1959; *Shijin no shōgai* [The Life of a Poet], 1959; *Mokugekisha* [The Eye Witness], 1965.

Verse

Mumei shishū [Poems without Names]. 1947; published and printed by the author.

Essays

Mōjū no kokoro ni keisanki no te o [With the Heart of a Beast and a Hand like a Calculating Machine]. 1956.

Tōō o yuku [Through Eastern Europe]. 1956.

Sabaku no shisō [The Philosophy of the Desert]. 1964.

"Uchi naru henkyō." 1971; as "The Frontier Within," translated by Andrew Horvat, 1975.

Warau tsuki [The Laughing Moon]. 1975.

Toshi e no kairo [Closing the Circuit with the City] (essays, interviews, and photographs). 1980.

Shini-isogu kujiratachi [Whales in a Hurry to Die] (essays, interviews, and photographs). 1986.

Other

Editor, *Gendai geijutsu* [Contemporary Art] (magazine). 1960–1961.

*

Critical Studies: *Abe Kōbō* by T. Takano, 1951, revised 1979; *Metaphors of Alienation: The Fiction of Abe, Beckett and Kafka* (dissertation) by W. J. Currie, 1973, published 1975; "Abe Kobo and Symbols of Absurdity" by P. Williams, in *Studies on Japanese Culture,* Japan P.E.N. Club, edited by S. Ota and R. Fukuda, 1973; *Meiro no shōsetsuron* [Study of a Labyrinthine Novel] by T. Hiraoka, 1974; *Hanada Kiyoteru to Abe Kōbō* [Hanada Kiyoteru and Abe

Kōbō] by N. Okaniwa, 1980; "Metamorphosis in Abe Kobo's Works" by F. Yamamoto, in *Journal of the Association of Teachers of Japanese,* vol. 15, November, 1980; "Skinless" by A. Dworkin, in *Intercourse,* 1987; "Abe Kōbō und der Nouveau Roman" by I. Hijiya-Kirschnereit, in *Was heißt: Japanische Literatur verstehen?,* 1990; "Self, Place and Body in 'The Woman in the Dunes': A Comparative Study of the Novel and the Film" by W. Dissanayake, in *Literary Relations East and West: Selected Essays,* edited by J. Toyama and N. Ochner, 1990; *Le sanatorium des malades du temps. Temps, attente et fiction, autour de Julien Gracq, Dino Buzzati, Thomas Mann, Kôbô Abé* by E. Faye, 1996; "The Woman in the Dunes" by J. Whittier Treat, in *Masterworks of Asian Literature in Comparative Perspective: A Guide for Teaching,* edited by B. Stoler Miller, 1994; *Abe Kōbō: An Exploration of His Prose, Drama, and Theatre* by T. Iles, 2000.

*   *   *

Abe Kōbō is a leading representative of a postwar modernism comparable to the Theater of the Absurd, the French *nouveau roman,* or Latin American magical realism. His work not only found an echo in the capitalist West; he was also published in socialist countries, helped by his communist background and the thaw under Khrushchev. Central to his reputation both in Japan and abroad is the novel *Suna no onna (The Woman in the Dunes).* The fact that this work undoubtedly marks a watershed in Abe's career, however, should not obscure how multi-faceted a writer he was.

Abe writes in analytical language fond of technical vocabulary, often conveyed by overly rational narrators whose discourse veers off at an obsessive tangent to reality. His style avowedly owes much to both Franz Kafka and Edgar Allan Poe, while the way in which he combines and modulates his images is indebted to surrealism, in which he was keenly interested from the late 1940s. At the very beginning of his career, before coming into contact with avant-garde artists in post-war Tokyo, Abe was strongly influenced by existentialist philosophy and the work of the poet Rainer Maria Rilke and in the 1950s by Marxist teachings on materialism and historical change. But as his essays reveal, his world view also drew consciously on the technical details of sciences from calculus to neurology.

In theoretical texts of the 1960s, Abe explains how he sees language as the motor of history: It has a liberating effect, but also an alienating one, since it places a screen between human perception and material things. This alienation results in the creation of ghosts as things that exist in language only, later of alchemy, and ultimately science. Only the irony of artistic fiction ("ghost stories without a belief in ghosts") can reveal the screen of language for what it is— science cannot. All his heterogeneous influences are built into Abe's model of the world as if it were a machine that its inventor spends his life modifying.

After his contact with surrealism, Abe began using image puns to illustrate the power of language over people. A good example is "S. Karuma-shi no hanzai" ("The Crime of S. Karma"), in which the protagonist arrives at work to find his place taken by his business card. The power of language is depicted in a less allegorical mode in the play *Yūrei wa koko ni iru (The Ghost Is Here),* whose effective main character is a dead man existing only as a space on the stage, but around whom a lucrative industry develops.

Progressing from surrealism in the course of the 1950s, Abe became interested in science fiction for its power to speculate realistically about changes in the world (the anti-realistic collages of his earlier stories can only work allegorically). In fact, he wrote the first science fiction novel in Japanese, *Daiyon kanpyōki* (*Inter Ice Age 4*), in which a computer sets about manipulating human evolution. Although *Inter Ice Age 4* has aged better than most of the genre science fiction of its day, it, like Abe's earlier allegorical stories, failed to appeal to a wide audience. The first of his novels to do this is *The Woman in the Dunes*, which pictures a society that can be seen as existing alongside the everyday familiar to the readers, but which still conveys a science fiction-like "sense of wonder."

It should not be forgotten, however, that Abe's most formative artistic years in the 1950s were also his most politically radical. Among the reasons for this radicalization, which was not Abe's alone, were the soon disappointed high hopes for social change and equality after the end of World War II. Moreover, most older writers and critics, including those on the left, favored realistic documentary literature. Abe was among the radical artists who responded by finding a sense of purpose in political radicalism. But when the factions of the dominant New Japan Literature Association were reconciled in 1955, Abe was voted into the Executive Committee and proved a diplomatic mediator between the 'realist' and the 'formalist' factions. Marxist theory and leftwing organizations formed his social and historical consciousness in the 1950s by giving it a practical and theoretical frame. The result was a sharpened sense of historical perspective and a feel for the cultural differences between the classes.

After his expulsion from the Communist Party in 1962 following a communist writers' initiative protesting against undemocratic practices by the party leaders, Abe also withdrew from active participation in mass organizations. He now preferred to rely on the wider though more anonymous spread of literature through the growing mass media culture. This perceived retreat from class solidarity was taken amiss by some of his former companions.

Abe was, however, an avowed believer in community. The theater gave him a respite from the isolation of writing, and he maintained his contacts with the workers' theater after 1962. What characterized his work in both areas was an insistence, running counter to the mainstream of serious literature, that the person appearing in the work of art (the character, or the narrative voice) must be distinguished from the person of the author. The novel *Tanin no kao* (*The Face of Another*) describes what can result when one tries to force the two together. In this piece, the first person narrator makes a new face for himself after the original is disfigured, only to become trapped in the superimposed personality of the mask. He ends as an outsider full of hatred for society.

Though Abe left it to his protagonists to cultivate such hatred, he himself became increasingly withdrawn and pessimistic, especially after his theater group broke up in 1979. While the theater was at the center of his work in the 1970s, he produced two more remarkable novels with striking spatial relationships in *Hako otoko* (*The Box Man*) and *Mikkai* (*Secret Rendezvous*). His one novel of the 1980s, *Hakobune Sakuramaru* (*The Ark Sakura*), is full of original ideas, but lacks the same poignancy.

More successful was his last novel, *Kangarū nōto* (*Kangaroo Notebook*), in which the narrator travels on a hospital bed down a sewer to "Hell Valley Hot Spring," passing through a succession of dreams within dreams. It ends with a newspaper clipping about the discovery of an unidentified corpse in a disused railway station. The book was called autobiographical in the publisher's blurb, but it is more properly seen as an illustration of authorship, or even of the human condition in general, showing it to be as melancholy as it is humorous. The human subject is driven from each existence to the next deeper level, his alienation and isolation increasing each time, and dies before arrival.

—Thomas Schnellbächer

See the essay on *The Woman in the Dunes*.

ACCAD, Evelyne

Born: Beirut, Lebanon, 10 October 1943; daughter of a Lebanese father and Swiss mother; naturalized U.S. citizen, 1972. **Education:** Primary and secondary education in Beirut, Beirut College for Women (then Beirut University College, now Lebanese American University), A.A., 1965; Anderson College, Anderson, Indiana, B.A. in English Literature, 1967; Ball State University, Muncie, Indiana, M.A. in French, 1968; Indiana University, Bloomington, Ph.D. in Comparative Literature, 1973. **Family:** Divorced from husband; living with her long-term companion. **Career:** Taught French at Anderson College, Anderson, Indiana, 1967–68, and both English and French at International College, Beirut, Lebanon, 1968–70. Worked at University of Illinois at Urbana-Champaign as assistant professor, 1974–79, and associate professor from 1979–88. Taught at Beirut University College, 1984, and visiting professor at Northwestern University, 1991. She continues her work at the University of Illinois at the African Center, Women's Studies Center, French Department, Comparative Literature Department, the Honors Program and Center for Middle East Studies. Taught in Beirut, Lebanon on a Fulbright Scholarship, 2002. Lives in the United States. **Awards:** Florence Howard award, Women's Caucus for the Modern Languages Association, 1975; Special Recognition award, Illinois Arts Council, 1979; International Educator's award, Delta Kappa Gamma, 1979; Fulbright award, Tunisia, 1983–85; Social Science Research Council grant, 1987–88; Prix France-Liban, Association des Écrivans de Langue Française, 1993; American Institute for Maghrebi Studies grant, 1995; Prix Phénix de literature, 2001; Fulbright award, Lebanon, 2002. **Member:** Coordination Internationale des Chercheurs sur les Litteratures Maghrebines, Conseil International d'Études Francophones, Expert Witness International, Modern Language Association of America, National Women's Studies Association, Middle East Studies Association, African Literature Association, American Association of Teachers of French, African Studies Association, American Institute for Maghribi Studies, Arab American University Graduates, Arab Women Solidarity Association, Radius of Arab-American Writers, Association des Écrivains de Langue Française, Société des Auteurs, Compositeurs, et Editeurs de Musique, Women's Caucus for the Modern Language Association, North Eastern Modern Language Association, Foundation Noureddine Aba, Coalition against Trafficking in Women, Delta Kappa Gamma.

PUBLICATIONS

Fiction and Critical Studies

Veil of Shame: The Role of Women in the Modern Fiction of North Africa and the Arab World. 1978.
L'Excisee. 1982 and 1992; as *The Excised*, translated by David K. Bruner, 1989 and 1994.

Contemporary Arab Women Writers and Poets, with Rose Ghurayyeb. 1986.

Coquelicot du massacre (with a cassette of songs). 1988.

Sexuality and War: Literary Masks of the Middle East. 1990; as *Des femmes, des homes et la guerre: Fiction et réalité au Proche-Orient*, 1993.

Blessures des mots: journal de Tunisie. 1993; as *Wounding Words: A Woman's Journal in Tunisia*, translated by Cynthia T. Hahn, 1996.

Voyages en Cancer. 2000; as *The Wounded Breast: Intimate Journeys Through Cancer*, 2001.

Other

Les filles de Tahar Haddad (play). Adaptation of *Blessures des mots*, in conjunction with women of the feminist movement Accad met in Tunisia while on a Fulbright scholarship, 1995.

Translator, *Montjoie Palestine!; or, Last Year in Jerusalem*, dramatic poem by Noureddine Aba. 1980.

*

Critical Studies: "Sexuality and War: Literary Masks of the Middle East" by Mona Fayad, in *College Literature*, vol. 19, no. 3, 1992; "Wounding Words" by Saadi A. Simawe, in *Arab Studies Quarterly*, vol. 21, issue 4; "A Poetics of Pain: Evelyne Accad's Critical and Fictional World" by Ruth A. Hottell, in *World Literature Today*, vol. 71 no. 3; *Postcolonial Representation: Women, Literature, Identity* by Francoise Lionnet, 1995.

*   *   *

Evelyne Accad was first published during the 1970s, when the sexual revolution was in full swing, giving American women unprecedented rights in relation to their bodies, careers, and social roles. In contrast, the status of women in most Arab and North African countries during the 1970s did not change, and grew worse in some cases, as authoritarian dictators took over post-colonial governments. Accad's youth in Beirut, Lebanon was restricted by the patriarchal social ties of Arab society; bonds that she broke by moving to the United States in 1965 and becoming a naturalized citizen. Her literature gives all Arab women a voice, and a greater chance to live free from male oppression. The issue of women's rights in the Arab world gained national prominence after the 11 September 2001 terrorist attacks perpetrated by Islamic extremists in the United States, and the subsequent attacks on the Taliban in Afghanistan. The position of women in Islamic societies was well advertised by American propagandists who sought to spur the United States into military action. If Accad's novels gain popularity from American attempts to understand Islamic culture, so much the better. Accad gives a unique first-hand account of the sexual politics found in Arab and North African countries.

Accad's novels turn personal experiences into engaging social treatises, shedding light on complex political and social issues. Themes that surface in her works include the relationship between men and women, the social effects of war, the tolerance (or intolerance) of difference, and responsibility for the environment. Arab and North African women are shown as the victims of societies that attempt to hide, shame, and destroy all that is feminine. War in Lebanon and other countries is seen as an activity propagated by men, to the detriment of women, as reflected in Accad's images of raped cities violently bombed and conquered. The female body is also the scene of man's war with nature, to tame and dominate; but Accad reminds us that it is also man's duty to tend to the environment and the female body. Accad renders the conflicts between men and women, cultures, and ideologies into poignant accounts of personal suffering and triumph.

In *Veil of Shame* Accad revisits the female oppression that she endured during her upbringing in Lebanon, by evaluating the role of women in North African and Arab culture and literature. This novel of literary criticism reflects Accad's scholarly background, while emphasizing the utility of unconventional literary genres such as poetry and the personal memoir. The practice of female circumcision in Arab society is examined in *L'Excisee (The Excised)*, with the story of one woman's physical and psychological domination by men. Although the main character is unable to speak out against her aggressors, she escapes and is exiled, or "excised" from her own country. Civil war in Beirut, Lebanon (1975–90), and the ways in which the victims of this war deal with pain, are described in *Coquelicot du massacre*. The female protagonist, Nour, is overwhelmed by the suffering city of Beirut, but she is able to overcome her pain with hope. *Sexuality and War* is a political treatise on the use of nationalism and war to oppress women in Lebanon and other countries. Accad's theory that men's violence (and thus war) stems from the fear and loathing of women is supported by the criticism and interpretation of several Arab authors. Female authors Hanan al-Shaykh, Etel Adnan, and Andree Chedid are compared to male writers Tawfiq Yusuf Awwad, Halim Barakat, and Elias Khoury. All authors, regardless of sex, admit that war is damaging to society as a whole, but does much greater ill to women than to men. After *Sexuality and War* Accad wrote a more personal account of sexual politics, *Blessures des mots (Wounding Words)*, a story loosely based on Accad's stay as a Fulbright scholar in Tunisia. The protagonist travels to Tunisia in order to study and advocate feminism, but is dismayed to find a society mired in patriarchic Islamic tradition.

The main character, Hayate, attempts to understand the gap that has formed between men and women in Tunisian society. Her story is told in a way that highlights communication differences between genders. The novel is interspersed with emotional poems and scholarly observations; feminine and masculine literary genres that are balanced with the medium that is prose. *Wounding Words* was also turned into a play by women of the Tunisian feminist movement in 1995, called *Les filles de Tahar Haddad*, performed in Tunisia and accompanied by Accad's own songs. Poems, songs, and speeches often supplement Accad's writings. This multidisciplinary approach is likewise enhanced by her mastery of several languages: French, English, and Arabic. Accad's multicultural background allows her to explain Arab and North African cultures to Western minds, while it has also given her the ability to transcend her cultural and gender-based biases to entertain a worldview.

In 1994 Accad started chemotherapy to treat breast cancer. Her struggles with this disease are chronicled in *Voyages en Cancer (The Wounded Breast)*; on the cover is a picture of the defiant author with bald head and naked chest. Her hair has fallen out due to the chemotherapy, and she is missing one breast due to a mastectomy. The novel contains the poems and personal investigations of cancer that she undertook while she was sick, and recovering from therapy. Accad draws a strong link between man's abuse of nature, and the abuse of the female body with environmental chemicals and pre-scribed drugs, which she blames for causing her illness. Her mastectomy is reminiscent of the fabled Amazons, who cut off their breasts in order to become more effective in battle. However, it is not a war that Accad proposes, rather a reevaluation of the social and cultural attitudes that bring about violence, particularly against women. Male dominance has not only crippled *women* in patriarchic Arab societies; it has also tipped the balance of power in the *whole* of these societies, making war and intolerance commonplace. Accad suggests through her many novels, poems, songs, and critical works that oppressed women should leave their abusers, and return with reinforcements to help those who are still in need.

—Mary Sugar

ADAMOV, Arthur

Born: Baku, Azerbaijan, 23 August 1908; lived abroad after 1912. **Education:** Educated at Rosset School, Geneva; lycée, Mainz, Germany, 1922–24; Lycée Lakanal, Paris, 1924–27. **Family:** Married Jacqueline Trehet in 1961. **Career:** Translator and writer in Paris; editor of the review, *Discontinuité* in late 1920s and *L'Heure Nouvelle*, 1945–47; increasingly involved in left-wing politics during the 1950s; visiting lecturer, Cornell University, Ithaca, New York, 1964. co-signatory of the "Manifeste des 121" opposing the war in Algeria, 1960; visiting lecturer, Cornell University, Ithaca, New York, 1964. **Died:** Suicide, 15 March 1970.

PUBLICATIONS

Plays

L'Arbitre aux mains vides (produced 1928).

Mains blanches (produced 1928).

La Mort de Danton, from the play by Georg Büchner (produced 1948). 1953.

L'Invasion (produced 1950). With *La Parodie*, 1950; as *The Invasion*, translated by Peter Doan, 1968.

La Parodie (produced 1952). With *L'Invasion*, 1950.

La grande et la petite manoeuvre (produced 1950). 1951.

Tous contre tous (produced 1953). In *Théâtre 1*, 1953.

Le Professeur Taranne (produced 1953). 1953; as *Professor Taranne*, translated by Albert Bermel, in *Four Modern Comedies*, 1960, and by Peter Meyer, in *Two Plays*, 1962.

Le Sens de la marche (produced 1953). In *Théâtre 2*, 1955.

Comme nous avons été (produced 1954). In *La Nouvelle Revue Française*, 1, 1953; as *As We Were*, in *Evergreen Review*, 1(4), 1957.

Théâtre I–4. 1953–68.

La Cruche cassée, from the play by Heinrich von Kleist (produced 1954). In *Théâtre populaire*, 1954.

Edward II, from the play by Christopher Marlowe (produced 1954).

Le Ping-Pong (produced 1955). In *Théâtre 2*, 1955; as *Ping Pong*, translated by Richard Howard, 1959; also translated by Derek Prouse, in *Two Plays*, 1962.

Les Retrouvailles. In *Théâtre2*, 1955.

Le Pélican, from the play by August Strindberg (produced 1956). In *Théâtre populaire*, 17, 1956.

Les Ennemis, from the play by Maksim Gor'kii (produced 1965). In *Théâtre populaire*, 27, 1957.

Paolo Paoli (produced 1957). 1957; as *Paolo Paoli*, translated by Geoffrey Brereton, 1959.

Le Revizor, from the play by Nikolai Gogol' (produced 1967). 1958.

Vassa Geleznova, from the play by Maksim Gor'kii (produced 1959). 1958.

Le Père, from the play by August Strindberg. 1958.

Les Petits Bourgeois, from the play by Maksim Gor'kii (produced 1959). 1958.

Les Âmes mortes, from the novel by Nikolai Gogol' (produced 1960). 1960.

Le Printemps 71 (produced 1962). 1961.

La Sonate des spectres, with C.G. Björström, from the play by August Strindberg (produced 1962).

La Politique des restes (produced 1963). In *Théâtre 3*, 1966.

Sainte Europe. In *Théâtre3*. 1966.

M. Le Modéré (produced 1968). In *Théâtre 4*, 1968.

Off Limits (produced 1969). 1969.

La Grande Muraille, from the play by Max Frisch (produced 1969). 1969.

Si l'été revenait (produced 1972). 1970.

Radio Plays: *La Logeuse*, 1950; *Polly*, 1951; *L'Éternel Mari*, 1952; *Le Potier politicien*, 1952; *L'Agence universelle*, 1953; *Lady Macbeth au village*, 1953; *Parallèlement*, 1954; *Les Âmes mortes*, 1955; *Raillerie, satire, ironie et signification plus profonde*, 1957; *L'Autre Rive*, 1959;*Le Temps vivant*, 1963; *En fiacre*, 1963; *Finita la commedia*, 1964; *Du matin à minuit*, 1966; *Theatre radiophonique*, 5 CDs, 1997.

Television Plays: *La Parole est au prophète*, with Bernard Hecht, 1952; *Tous contre tous*, 1956; *Les Trois Soeurs*, 1958; *Le Manteau*, 1966; *Une femme douce*, 1970; *La Mort de Danton*, 1970; *La Cigale*, 1970; *Vassa Geleznova*, 1971.

Other

L'Aveu (autobiography). 1946; enlarged edition as *Je . . . ils. . .* , 1969; translated in part as *Endless Humiliations*, in *Evergreen Review*, 2(8), 1959.

Auguste Strindberg, dramaturge, with Maurice Gravier. 1955.

Théâtre de société. 1958.

Ici et maintenant (essays). 1964.

L'Homme et l'enfant (autobiography). 1968; as *Man and Child*, translated by Jo Levy. 1992.

Editor, *Le Commune de Paris*. 1959.

Translator, *Le Moi et l'inconscient*, by C.G. Jung. 1938.

Translator, with Marie Geringer, *Le Livre de la pauvreté et de la mort*, by Rainer Maria Rilke. 1941.

Translator, *Crime et châtiment*, by Fedor Dostoevskii. 1956.

Translator, *Les Âmes mortes*, by Nikolai Gogol'. 1956, first part; both parts, 1964.

Translator, *La Mère*, by Maksim Gor'kii. 1958.

Translator, *Théâtre*, by Anton Chekhov. 1958.

Translator, *Oblomov*, by Ivan Goncharov. 1959.

Translator, *Cinq récits*, by Nikolai Gogol'. 1961.

Translator, with Claude Sebisch, *Le Théâtre politique*, by Erwin Piscator. 1962.

Translator, *Ivanov; La mouette,* by Anton Chekhov, revised and edited by Michel Cadot, 1996.

*

Bibliography: *Adamov* by David Bradby, 1975.

Critical Studies: *Regards sur le théâtre de Adamov* by Samia Assad Chahine, 1961; *Arthur Adamov* by John H. Reilly, 1974; *The Theatre of Arthur Adamov* by John J. McCann, 1975; *Lectures d'Adamov: Actes du colloque international, Würzburg, 1981,* 1983; *Lecture d'Adamov* by Elizabeth Hervic, 1984; *Langage et corps, fantasme dans le théâtre des années cinquante: Ionesco, Beckett, Adamov* by Marie-Claude Hubert, 1987; *Le théâtre de dérision: Beckett, Ionesco, Adamov* by Emmanuel C. Jacquart, 1998; *Typologie des Zweiakters: Mit Einer Untersuchung der Funktion zweiaktiger Strukturen im Theater Arthur Adamovs* by Susanne Hartwig, 2000.

* * *

When Arthur Adamov first began writing for the French stage in the late 1940s and early 1950s, he was considered, along with Samuel Beckett and Eugène Ionesco, one of the most promising dramatists of the burgeoning movement of the theatre of the absurd. Similar to these two playwrights, Adamov wanted to free himself from the normal constraints of dramatic construction, eliminating the traditional concepts of characterization, action, and even time and place, if need be.

He differed from Beckett and Ionesco, however, to the extent that he used the stage as a means of expressing the enormous fears and obsessions that plagued him. For Adamov, the theatre became a personal cry of anguish, a form of catharsis, a way of attempting to liberate himself from his private demons. Essentially, the Russian-born playwright revealed his feelings of injustice and his sense of persecution and victimization in his works. In his early play, *La Parodie* [The Parody], the dramatist communicated the solitude and futility of living. The two central characters are the victims of life's horrors: the one, identified only by the initial ''N,'' is crushed by a car, his body swept away by the sanitation department; the other, The Employee, ends up in prison, blind, both events spelling out the absurd uselessness of life, which was a reflection of Adamov's state of mind at the time of writing. In one of his most successful works, *Le Professeur Taranne* (*Professor Taranne*), based on a dream Adamov had, Professor Taranne finds himself in a nightmarish situation in which he has been accused by some children of indecent exposure on a beach. By the end of the play, unable to convince anyone of his innocence, he slowly begins to undress, thereby performing the very act with which he had been charged. *Professor Taranne* is a fairly direct translation of the author's most personal fears, dictated by the subconscious. To that extent, it is an honest expression of a soul in torment. This work is probably Adamov's most powerful play, making a highly trenchant statement about humankind at the mercy of fate and expressing more than any other of his dramas the playwright's deep sense of sadness.

At this stage in his writing, Adamov's expression of his personal visions of terror had much in common with the Surrealist movement as well as with the theories of the theatre of cruelty espoused by Antonin Artaud. During the 1950s, however, Adamov took an unusual step—he rejected all of his previous theatre: ''I already saw in the

'avant-garde' an easy escape, a diversion from the real problems, the words 'absurd theatre' already irritated me. Life was not absurd—only difficult, very difficult.'' Having achieved some limited control of his personal obsessions, he was now able to develop his political and social concerns. Much of his drama of that period, like *Paolo Paoli* and *Le Printemps 71* [Spring 71], has strongly Marxist overtones and reflected the alienation effect experienced in the works of Brecht. Another important play of this genre, (and considered by some to be his most successful work) is *Le Ping-Pong* (*Ping Pong*). This is a delicately balanced presentation of the futility of all human action contrasted with the effects on the individual of the capitalist system. Adamov examines two men's obsession with a simple pinball machine and the disastrous results when they are swept up into the capitalist world of big business. On the one hand, the result is a visual representation of the tragedy of life's wastefulness. Yet the play is also a study of the workings of society, a recognition of its defects, and an exploration of ways of improvement. This new thrust of Adamov's writing stressed that the direction of a person's life was more often dictated by the economic forces surrounding him/her than by the strength of the will.

Yet, finally, while Adamov may have planned to write politically committed theatre, he was basically still dealing with the sense of victimization and injustice that had always pursued him. Probably because of this, his theatre, while often highly acclaimed, never went on to achieve the popularity with the public of the works of Beckett or Ionesco—it was too private, too personal to attain universal appeal. Interestingly enough, Adamov's most successful writing may have been one of his earliest works, *L'Aveu* (*Endless Humiliations*). Written between 1938 and 1943, it is a series of ruthlessly honest journals in which the writer recounted directly the difficulties of existence. In the journals, the most personal form of expression, Adamov may have found his best means of communication.

—John H. Reilly

See the essay on *Professor Taranne.*

ADONIS

Also known as Adunis; Ali Ahmad Esber; Ali Ahmad Sa'id. **Born:** Ali Ahmad Esber in Qassabin, Syria, in 1930. **Education:** Attended school in Qassabin (in Arabic), and Tarsus, 1943–47 (where he learned French); Lycée in Latakia, 1947–49; studied philosophy at Damascus University, 1950–54; in Paris on French government scholarship, 1960–61; St. Joseph University, Beirut, Ph.D., 1973. **Military Service:** 1954–55, including 6 months in prison for political activities in the Syrian National Socialist Party. **Family:** Married Khalida Sa'id, née Saleh in 1956; two daughters. **Career:** In Beirut: freelance journalist, 1954–; ran journal *Shi'r,* which he founded with Yusuf al-Khal, 1957–68; worked for journal *Lisan al-Hal,* 1965–67; revived short-lived journal *Afaq,* 1968; founded and ran journal *Mawaqif,* 1968–94; professor at Lebanese University, 1971–85; thesis supervisor, St. Joseph University, 1971–85. Visiting professor, Damascus University, 1976; associate professor, Sorbonne Nouvelle (Censier-Paris III), France, 1980–81; visiting professor, Georgetown University, 1985; permanent Arab League delegate to UNESCO,

Paris, 1986–89; associate professor, University of Geneva, 1989–95; Senior Fellow, Princeton University, New Jersey, 1996–97; Fellow, Wissenschaftskolleg, Berlin, 1998–99. Lives in Courbevoie, France. **Awards:** Prix des Amis du Livre, Beirut, 1968; Syria-Lebanon award of the International Poetry Forum, Pittsburgh, 1971; National Poetry prize, Lebanon, 1974; Officier des Arts et des Lettres, France, 1984; Grand Prix des Bienniales Internationales de la Poésie, Liège, Belgium, 1986; Prix Jean Malrieu 'Etranger,' Marseille, 1991; Feronia-Cita di Fiamo prize, Rome, 1993; Nazim Hikmet prize, Istanbul, 1994; Prix Méditerranée-Etranger, Paris, 1995; Prix du Forum culturel libanais, Paris, 1995; Nonino International prize for literature, Udine, Italy, 1997; Commandeur de l'Ordre des Arts et des Lettres, France, 1997; Struga International Poetry Festival Golden Crown, Macedonia, 1998; Lerici-Pea prize, Italy, 2000.

PUBLICATIONS

Collections

Diwan Adunis. 2 vols., 1971; reissued as *al-A'mal al-shi'riyya al-kamila* (also *al-Athar al-kamila: shi'r*), 1985; revised, enlarged, definitive edition, as *al-A'mal al-shi'riyya al-kamila.* 3 vols., 1996.

Poetry

Qalat al-ard. 1952; revised, 1954.
Qasa'id ula. 1957; revised, as *Qasa'id ula, 1929–1955: siyagha niha'iyya.* 1988.
Awraq fi al-rih. 1958; as *Awraq fi mahabb al-rih,* 1971; revised, as *Awraq fi al-rih (1955–1960): siyagha niha'iyya,* 1988; selection in *An Anthology of Modern Arabic Poetry,* translated by Mounah A. Khouri and Hamid Algar, 1974.
Aghani Mihyar al-Dimashqi. 1961, revised, 1988; selection in *Modern Poetry of the Arab World,* translated by Abdullah al-Udhari, 1986; selection in *Modern Arabic Poetry,* edited by Salma Khadra Jayyusi, 1987.
Kitab al-Tahawwulat wa al-hijra fi aqalim al-nahar wa al-layl. 1965; revised as *Kitab al-Tahawwulat wa al-hijra fi aqalim al-nahar wa al-layl: siyagha niha'iyya,* 1988; selection in *The Blood of Adonis, transpositions of selected poems of Adonis (Ali Ahmed Said),* 1971; enlarged and expanded as *Transformations of the Lover,* 1983; revised as *The Pages of Day and Night,* 1994, all translated by Samuel Hazo, Mirène Ghossein and Kamal Boullata.
Al-Masrah wa al-maraya. 1968; revised as *Al-Masrah wa al-maraya (1965–1967): siyagha niha'iyya,* 1988; as *Mirrors,* translated by Abdullah al-Udhari, 1976; selection in *When the Words Burn,* translated by John M. Asfour, 1992.
Waqt bayna al-ramad wa al-ward. 1970; enlarged, 1972; reissued as *Hadha huwa ismi,* 1980; revised as *Hadha huwa ismi: siyagha niha'iyya,* 1988; as *A Time between Ashes and Roses,* translated by Shawkat M. Toorawa, 2003.
Mufrad bi-sighat al-jam'. 1975; revised as *Mufrad bi-sighat al-jam': siyagha niha'iyya,* 1988; selection in *Modern Arab Poets,* translated by Issa J. Boullata, 1978.
Kitab al-qasa'id al-khams taliha al-Mutabaqat wa al-awa'il. 1979; revised as *al-Mutabaqat wa-al-awa'il: siyagha niha'iyya,* 1988; selections as *Beginnings,* translated by Kamal Boullata and Mirène Ghossein, 1992; selection in *Victims of a Map: Mahmud Darwish, Samih al-Qasim, Adonis,* translated by Abdullah al-Udhari, 1994.

Kitab al-hisar. 1985; selections in *If Only the Sea Could Sleep: Love Poems,* translated by Kamal Abu Deeb, 1988.
Shahwa tataqaddam fi khara'it al-madda. 1987.
Ihtifa'an bi al-ashya' al-wadiha al-ghamida. 1988.
Abjadiyya thaniyya. 1994.
Fihris li-a'mal al-rih. 1998.
Al-Mahd: li fi turab al-Yaman 'irqun ma. 2001.
Al-Kitab: ams al-makan al-an. Makhtutah tunsabu ila al-Mutanabbi. 2 vols., 1995, 1998.

Other

Muqaddima li al-shi'r al-'arabi. 1971.
Zaman al-shi'r. 1972; selections as *La prière et l'épee: essais sur la culture arabe,* translated by Leila Khatib and Anne Wade Minkowski, 1993.
Al-Thabit wa al-mutahawwil: bahth fi al-ibda' wa al-ittiba' 'inda al-'arab. 3 vols., 1974, 1977, 1978; revised and enlarged in 4 vols., 1994.
Fatiha li-nihayat al-qarn: bayanat min ajl thaqafa 'arabiyya jadida. 1980; revised and enlarged, 1998.
Al-shi'riyya al-'arabiyya. 1985; as *An Introduction to Arab Poetics,* translated by Catherine Cobham, 1990.
Siyasat al-shi'r: dirasah fi al-shi'riyya al-'arabiyya al-mu'asira. 1985.
Kalam al-bidayat. 1989.
Al-Sufiyya wa al-suriyaliyya. 1992.
Al-Nass al-qur'ani wa afaq al-kitaba. 1993.
Ha-anta, ayyuha al-waqt: sira shi'riyya thaqafiyya. 1993.
Al-Nizam wa-al-kalam. 1993.
Hiwar ma'a Adunis: al-tufula, al-shi'r, al-manfa. 2000.
Editor, *Mukhtarat min shi'r Yusuf al-Khal.* 1962; as *Qasa'id mukhtara,* 1964.
Editor, *Diwan al-shi'r al-'arabi.* 3 vols., 1964–68.
Editor, *Mukhtarat min shi'r al-Sayyab.* 1967; as *Badr Shakir al-Sayyab: qasa'id,* 1978.
Editor with Khalida Sa'id, *Mukhtarat min al-Kawakibi.* 1982.
Editor with Khalida Sa'id, *Mukhtarat min shi'r Ahmad Shawqi.* 1982.
Editor with Khalida Sa'id, *Mukhtarat min al-Imam Muhammad 'Abduh.* 1983.
Editor with Khalida Sa'id, *Mukhtarat min Muhammad Rashid Rida.* 1983.
Editor with Khalida Sa'id, *Mukhtarat min Jamil Sidqi al-Zahawi.* 1983.
Editor with Khalida Sa'id, *Mukhtarat min al-Shaykh al-Imam Muhammad ibn 'Abd al-Wahhab.* 1983.
Translator, *Théâtre complet,* 6 vols., by Georges Schéhadé. 1972–75; vol. 1 revised, 2000.
Translator, *Eloges, La Gloire des rois, Anabase, Exil, Pluies, Poèmes à l'étrangère, Amers,* by Saint-John Perse, 2 vols. 1976, 1977.
Translator, *La Thébaïde ou les Frères ennemis,* Phèdre, by Jean Racine. 1972, 1975; revised 1979.
Translator, *L'Oeuvre complète,* by Yves Bonnefoy. 1986.
Translator with Anne Wade Minkowski, selections from *al-Luzumiyyat,* by al-Ma'arri, as Rets d'éternité. 1988.
Translator with Anne Wade Minkowski, *al-Mawakib,* by Kahlil Gibran, as *Le livre des processions.* 1998.
With others, *al-Islam wa al-hadathah.* 1990.
With others, *al-Bayanat.* 1995.

*

Bibliography: In *Chronique des branches*, translated by Anne Wade Minkowski, 1991; in *Adonis. Un poète dans le monde d'aujoud'hui, 1950–2000*, 2000.

Critical Studies: *A Critical Introduction to Modern Arabic Poetry* by M.M. Badawi, 1975; "The perplexity of the all-knowing: A study of Adonis" by Kamal Abu Deeb, in *Mundius Artium*, vol.10, 1977; "Adonis: Revolt in Modern Arabic Poetics" by Issa J. Boullata, in *Edebiyat*, vol. 2, 1977; *Trends and Movements in Modern Arabic Poetry*, by Salma K. Jayyusi, 1977; "Myth and Symbol in the Poetry of Adunis and Yusuf al-Khal" by Joseph Zeidan, in *Journal of Arabic Literature*, vol. 10, 1979; "An Analytical Study of the Adonisian Poem" (unpublished thesis) by Ali Ahmad al-Shar', 1982; "Modernity: a Study of Adunis' theory and poetry" (unpublished thesis) by Mohammad Mohmoud Khazali, 1983; "The Complex Poem in New Arabic Poetry 1950–1985" (unpublished thesis) by Nayef Khaled El-Hasan, 1985; "The Metamorphic Vision: The Poetics of Time and History in the Works of Adunis ('Ali Ahmad Sa'id)" (unpublished thesis) by Teirab Ash Shareef, 1986; "The Poetic Theories of the Leading Poet-Critics of Arabic New Poetry" (unpublished thesis) by Ahmed Salih al-Tami, 1987; *Reading Adonis* by Dennis Lee, 1987; "A Critique of Adonis's Perspectives on Arabic Literature and Culture" in *Studies in Contemporary Arabic Poetry and Criticism* by Mounah A. Khouri, 1987; "Making Mihyar: The Familiarization of Adunis's Knight of Strange Works" by Adnan Haydar, in *Literature East & West*, vol. 4, 1988; "Criticism and the Heritage: Adonis as Advocate of a New Arab Culture" by Mounah Khouri, in *Arab Civilization: Challenges and Responses*, edited by George N. Atiyeh and Ibrahim M. Oweiss, 1988; "A critical translation of *Waqt bayna al-ramad wa al-ward*" (unpublished thesis) by Shawkat M. Toorawa, 1989; special issue of *Détours d'écriture* edited by Noël Blandin, 1991; "Introduction" to *When the Words Burn. An Anthology of Modern Arabic Poetry: 1945–1987* by John M. Asfour, 1992; "La symbolique du bien et du mal dans la poésie d'Adonis" by Krystyna Skarzynska-Bochenska, in *Rocznik Orientalistyczny*, vol. 48, 1992; *The Poetics of T. S. Eliot and Adunis* by Atef Faddul, 1993; "Upon One Double String: The Metaphysical Element in Adunis' Poetry" by Terri deYoung, in *al-Arabiyya*, vol. 27, 1994; "A Study of Elegy for al-Hallaj by Adunis" by Reuven Snir, in *Journal of Arabic Literature*, vol. 25, 1994; "Walt Whitman in Adonis' Manhattan: Some Thoughts on *A Grave for New York*" by Shawkat M. Toorawa, in *Periodica Islamica*, vol. 6, 1996; 'Adonis' by Stefan Weidner, in *Kritisches Lexicon zur fremdsprachigen Gegenwartsliteratur*, vol. 41, 1996; "Adunis" in *Encyclopedia of Arabic Literature*, edited by Julie Meisami and Paul Starkey, by Kamal Abu Deeb, 1998; "Whitman and Lebanon's Adonis" by Roger Asselineau and Ed Folsom, in *Walt Whitman Quarterly Review*, vol. 15, 1998; "Ishmael Must Be Sacrificed: Adunis and the Quest for a New God" by As'ad Khairallah, in *Myths, Historical Archetypes and Symbolic Figures in Arabic Literature: Towards a New Hermeneutic Approach*, edited by Angelika Neuwirth, 1999; "A Guardian of Change? The Poetry of Adunis between Hermeticism and Commitment" by Stefan Weidner, in *Conscious Voices. Concepts of Writing in the Middle East*, edited by Stephan Guth et al., 1999; *Adonis le visionnaire: essai et anthologie* by Michel Camus, 2000; *Adonis. Un poète dans le monde d'aujoud'hui, 1950–2000*, edited by Institut du monde arabe, 2000; "Adonis et la poésie arabe moderne" by Muhammad Jamal Barout, in *Adonis: Un poète dans le monde d'aujoud'hui, 1950–2000*, edited by Institut du monde arabe, 2000; "Adunis" by Paul Starkey, in *Encyclopedia of Literary Translation into English*, edited by Olive Classe, 2000.

* * *

Adonis is the most significant Arab poet of the 20th century. His enormously influential modernist poetic output is rivaled by the quality and impact of his cultural criticism, of his translations from French into Arabic and vice versa, of his critical editions of other poets' works, and of half a century of grappling with and contributing to the Arabic literary tradition. Adonis has twice been a Nobel prize finalist, and is still, in his seventies, a prolific and major presence on the Arabic and international literary scenes.

Ali Ahmad Esber was born in an 'Alawite family in Qassabin, a remote mountain village of Syria. His father, a farmer and prayer leader, instructed his son in theology and in classical poetry which the boy memorized effortlessly. At the age of 13, Ali was rewarded by the new Syrian president with a scholarship for a poem he declaimed to him. Thus began Adonis' instruction in French, though he continued to write in Arabic. His first poem to appear in print (1947) was under the nom de plume, Adonis, that of the Near Eastern divinity of fertility, harvest and renewal—this is the name he has used since. The death and rebirth represented by the god Adonis would become, and remain, central to Adonis' poetic vision of transformation and renewal (*tajdid*), advocated and actualized in free verse, and in "new poetry" (*al-shi'r al-jadid*). The closing sentiment of his 1998 revision of a 1980 collection of essays, *Fatiha li-nihayat al-qarn* [Introduction to the Century's Endings], reads: "Let this book's new edition, then, be a hand extended toward the many other hands which are igniting the flames of transformation."

Adonis' first publication, *Qalat al-ard* [The Earth Said], appeared in his final undergraduate year at the University of Damascus, where he studied philosophy and where he developed an enthusiasm for French authors, directly and also through his reading of Arabic poets such as Ilyas Abu Shabaka, who greatly appreciated Baudelaire, and Sa'id 'Aql, who admired Mallarmé. Adonis' conscription in the Syrian army and the several months he spent in jail for political activities, in particular for support of the Ba'athist party of Antun Sa'ada, would impel him to leave for Beirut in 1956 with his future wife, literary critic Khalida Saleh. Adonis would not return to Syria, but the influence of Sa'ada would remain. Not only did Adonis develop political and social beliefs in the company of Sa'ada but it was Sa'ada who made Adonis acutely aware of the importance of myth and history to literature, something he would discover in Eliot too. In 1957, Adonis published *Qasa'id ula* [First Poems] and that same year founded, with the Lebanese poet, critic and translator Yusuf al-Khal, the poetry journal *Shi'r* [Poetry], which for two decades would be the leading avant-garde forum for Arabic letters. Adonis kept company with, and published, countless poets, including Badr Shakir al-Sayyab, Fadwa Tuqan, Nazik al-Mala'ika, Michel Trad, and of course al-Khal; Adonis later edited selections of the poetry of al-Sayyab and al-Khal.

In spite of the quality and volume of the journal *Shi'r*'s output, and the publication of *Awraq fi al-rih* [Leaves in the Wind], which reveals the poet's early attempts to fuse the Arabic and French literary traditions, it was the year 1961 that would propel Adonis's career. He spent 1960–61 in Paris where he met Aragon, Prévert, Michaux and others, and would begin there the collection many critics (including Adonis himself) consider one of his finest and most important, *Aghani Mihyar al-Dimashqi* [The Songs of Mihyar of Damascus]. In

Aghani, Adonis sought new flames from old fires, sought to rekindle language from the stuff of the Arabic and Islamic heritage. In 1961 Adonis also delivered a paper at a conference in Rome in which he indicted the past, and famously asserted that ''it is an essential task of poetry to be prophecy and vision, to break through closed horizons in order to emerge onto a wider world,'' and in which he downplayed the *Nahda*, the 19th century Arab renaissance, calling it ''nothing but new ornamentation in old colors, a continuation of a traditional cycle in which no breach was effected, no window opened,'' but exempting the *Mahjar* writers who emigrated to the Americas, such as Amin Rihani, and Kahlil Gibran, whom he admired. Not content merely to observe this as a critic, Adonis spent the sixties revisiting the canon in his three-volume *Diwan al-shi'r al-'arabi* [Anthology of Arabic Poetry]. In the early eighties, with his wife's collaboration, Adonis edited six volumes of poetry and prose by Nahda writers.

In the 1970s Adonis published prolifically. The introspective triad of poems in *Waqt bayna al-ramad wa al-ward* (*A Time between Ashes and Roses*) addressed the issues of Arab defeat and defeatism, occasioned by the losses of 1967 Arab-Israeli War; called into question the opposition East/West by appropriating Whitman and the American modernist tradition; and by attempting to fashion a new poetic language. The often inscrutable ideas and poetry of *Mufrad bi-sighat al-jam'* [Singular in the Form of Plural], which would find echoes later in *Abjadiyya thaniya* [A Second Alphabet], earned Adonis the reputation for abstruseness and opacity. But he did not only write poetry: his doctoral thesis, *al-Thabit wa al-mutahawwil* [The Fixed and the Moving], written at St. Joseph University in Beirut where he taught for 15 years, and translations of important Francophone writers also appeared. In the former Adonis engaged in a controversial and wide-ranging analysis of what he deemed the stifling effect of Islam's theologies of political and artistic control. This is not to say that Adonis' writing is not informed by a profound knowledge of Islam; indeed, he has a special affection for its esoteric and mystical dimensions. It comes as no surprise, therefore, to find 'Ali, the first Shi'ite Imam, a recurring persona in Adonis' poetry. Present also is the 10th century author and mystic al-Niffari, the title of whose *Kitab al-Mawaqif wa al-mukhatabat* [The Book of Spiritual Stations and Addresses] was the inspiration for *Mawaqif*, the influential cultural and literary journal founded by Adonis in 1968.

In the 1980s and 1990s, Adonis continued to publish poetry, criticism, editions, and translations. He left war-torn Beirut for Paris, serving at UNESCO and teaching in France and Switzerland. The poems of *Shahwa tataqaddam fi khara'it al-madda* [A Desire Advancing in the Maps of Matter] and other collections take up many of the early questions, questions that Adonis tackled also in such essays as *al-Shi'riyya al-'arabiyya* (*An Introduction to Arab Poetics*), the first prose volume by Adonis to be translated into English. In 1988, Adonis edited and reissued definitive editions of his early collections, and followed these with *al-Sufiyya wa al-suriyaliyya* [Sufism and Surrealism], in which he attempted to show that Islamic mysticism and European surrealism share similar sources. His study *al-Nass al-qur'ani wa afaq al-kitaba* [The Quranic Text and the Horizons of Writing] set the stage for a poetic enterprise of considerable daring, *al-Kitab* [The Book], which, as its subtitle shows, he 'attributes' to the formidable 10th century poet al-Mutanabbi (*Ams al-makan al-an. Makhtutah tunsabu ila al-Mutanabbi*). In 1993 Adonis produced his first autobographical work. In 2000 the Institut du monde arabe in Paris, long a friend of Adonis' poetry and art, organized a retrospective exhibition of his work. In the intervening years Adonis received distinguished poetry prizes and fellowships all over the world. Adonis

has not put down the pen and is not likely to: a new poetry collection appeared in 2001.

—Shawkat M. Toorawa

AESCHYLUS

Born: Eleusis, Greece, 525 or 524 BC. **Military Service:** Fought in the Battle of Marathon, 490 BC, and probably at Artemisium and Salamis, 480 BC. **Career:** Wrote possibly over 90 plays; also acted in his plays; visited Sicily to produce plays for Hieron I of Syracuse, soon after the foundation of the city of Aetna, 476 BC, and again in 456 BC. **Awards:** Won his first playwriting prize in 484 BC, 12 subsequent prizes, some posthumously. **Died:** 456 BC.

PUBLICATIONS

Collections

[Works], edited by Martin West. 1990; also edited by Ulrich von Wilamowitz-Moellendorff, 1914, Gilbert Murray, 1937, and Denys L. Page, 1972; translated by H.W. Smyth [Loeb Edition; bilingual], 2 vols., 1922–26; also translated by Richmond Lattimore, David Grene, and S.G. Benardete, in *Complete Greek Tragedies* series, edited by Lattimore, 2 vols., 1953–56; Frederic Raphael and Kenneth McLeish, in *Plays 1–2*, 2 vols., 1991; translated by David R. Slavitt, and edited by Slavitt and Palmer Bovie, 2 vols., 1998–99.
Fragments, edited by S. Radt. 1985.

Plays

Persae (produced 472 BC). Edited by H.D. Broadhead, 1960; as *The Persians*, translated by S.G. Benardete, in *Complete Greek Tragedies*, 1956; also translated by Anthony J. Podlecki, 1970; Janet Lembke and C.J. Herington, 1981; as *The Persians*, adapted by Roberta Auletta, 1993.
Septem contra Thebas (produced 467 BC). Edited by G.O. Hutchinson, 1985; as *The Seven Against Thebes*, translated by David Grene, in *Complete Greek Tragedies*, 1956; also translated by Peter Arnott, 1968; Christopher M. Dawson, 1970; Anthony Hecht and Helen H. Bacon, 1974.
Prometheus Vinctus (attributed) (produced c. 466–59 BC). Edited by Mark Griffith, 1983; as *Prometheus Bound*, translated by Rex Warner, 1947; also translated by David Grene, in *Complete Greek Tragedies*, 1956; Warren B. Anderson, 1963; Paul Roche, 1964; Michael Townsend, 1966; Peter Arnott, 1968; James Scully and C.J. Herington, 1975.
Supplices (produced c. 463 BC). Edited by H. Johansen and E.W. Whittle, 1980; as *The Suppliant Maidens*, translated by S.G. Benardete, in *Complete Greek Tragedies*, 1956; as *The Suppliants*, translated by Philip Vellacott, 1961; also translated by Janet Lembke, 1975; Peter Burian, 1991.
Oresteia (trilogy; produced 458 BC). Edited by George Thomson, 1966; as *The Oresteia*, translated by Richmond Lattimore, in *Complete Greek Tragedies*, 1953; also translated by Philip Vellacott, 1956; Michael Townsend, 1966; Hugh Lloyd-Jones, 1970; Douglas Young, 1974; Robert Fagles, 1976; Robert Lowell, 1978; Tony

Harrison, 1981; David Grene and Wendy Doniger O'Flaherty, 1989; Peter Meineck, 1998; as *The Orestes Plays*, translated by Paul Roche, 1962; as *The House of Atreus*, translated by John Lewin, 1966; as *The Oresteia of Aeschylus*, translated by Edward Wright Haile, 1994; adapted by Ted Hughes, 1999.

Agamemnon, edited by Eduard Fraenkel (includes prose translation). 1950; also edited by John Dewar Denniston and Denys L. Page, 1957, and Raymond Postgate, 1969; numerous translations, including by Louis MacNeice, 1936; Anthony Holden, 1969; Hugh Lloyd-Jones, 1970; D.W. Myatt, 1993.

Choephoroi, edited by A.F. Garvie. 1986; also edited by A. Bowen, 1986; as *The Libation Bearers*, translated by Hugh Lloyd-Jones, 1970.

Eumenides, edited by Alan H. Sommerstein. 1989; edited and translated by Anthony J. Podlecki, 1989; as *The Eumenides* (*The Furies*), translated by Gilbert Murray, 1925; as *The Eumenides*, translated by Hugh Lloyd-Jones, 1970.

*

Critical Studies: *Aeschylus, The Creator of Tragedy* by Gilbert Murray, 1940; *Aeschylus and Athens: Study in the Social Origins of Drama* by George Thomson, 1941; *Aeschylus in His Style: Study in the Social Origins of Drama* by W.B. Stanford, 1942; *Aeschylus: New Texts and Old Problems* by E. Fraenkel, 1943; *The Style of Aeschylus* by F.R. Earp, 1948; *The Harmony of Aeschylus* by E.T. Owen, 1952; *Pindar and Aeschylus* by J.H. Finley, 1955; *A Commentary on the Surviving Plays of Aeschylus* by H.J. Rose, 2 vols., 1957–58; *Collation and Investigation of the Manuscripts of Aeschylus* by R.D. Dawe, 1964; *Image and Idea of the Agamemnon of Aeschylus*, 1964, and *The Oresteia: A Study in Language and Structure*, 1971, both by Anne Lebeck; *The Political Background of Aeschylean Tragedy* by A.J. Podlecki, 1966; *Aeschylus Supplices: Play and Trilogy* by A.F. Garvie, 1969; *The Author of Prometheus Bound*, 1970, and *Aeschylus*, 1986, both by C.J. Herington; *Studies on the Seven Against Thebes of Aeschylus* by H.D. Cameron, 1971; *Aeschylus: A Collection of Critical Essays* edited by Marsh H. McCall, Jr, 1972; *Aeschylus: Playwright Educator* by R.H. Beck, 1975; *Aeschylean Metaphors for Intellectual Activity* by D. Sansome, 1975; *Aeschylean Drama* by Michael Gagarin, 1976; *The Authenticity of Prometheus Bound* by Mark Griffith, 1977; *The Stagecraft of Aeschylus* by Oliver Taplin, 1977; *Dramatic Art in Aeschylus' Seven Against Thebes* by William G. Thalmann, 1978; *Aeschylus: Prometheus Bound: A Literary Commentary*, 1980, and *Aeschylus: Oresteia: A Literary Commentary*, 1987, both by Desmond J. Conacher; *The Phoenician Presence in The Seven Against Thebes* by Roland F. Perkins, 1980; *Problem and Spectacle: Studies in the Oresteia* by William Whallon, 1980; *The Early Printed Editions (1518–1664) of Aeschylus: A Chapter in the History of Classical Scholarship* by J.A. Gruys, 1981; *Tradition and Dramatic Form in the Persians of Aeschylus* by Ann N. Michelini, 1982; *The Art of Aeschylus* by Thomas G. Rosenmeyer, 1982; *Under the Sign of the Shield: Semiotics and Aeschylus' Seven Against Thebes* by Froma I. Zeillin, 1982; *Studies in Aeschylus* by R.P. Winnington-Ingram, 1983; *Language, Sexuality and Narrative: The Oresteia*, 1984, and *Aeschylus, The Oresteia*, 1992, both by Simon Goldhill; *Apollo and His Oracle in the Oresteia* by Deborah H. Roberts, 1984; *Musical Design in Aeschylean Theater* by William C. Scott, 1984; *The Logic of Tragedy: Moral and Integrity in Aeschylus' Oresteia*, 1984, and *An English Reader's Guide to Aeschylus' Oresteia*, 1991, both by Philip Vellacott; *The Oresteia: Iconographic and Narrative Tradition* by A.J.N.W. Prag, 1985; *Studies in Aeschylus* by Martin West, 1991; *Aeschylus: The Earlier Plays and Related Studies* by D.J. Conacher, 1996; *Aeschylean Tragedy* by Alan H. Sommerstein, 1996; *The Political Background of Aeschylean Tragedy* by Anthony J. Podlecki, 1999; *The Emptiness of Asia: Aeschylus' "Persians" and the History of the Fifth Century* by Thomas Harrison, 2000.

* * *

Aeschylus was the first of the three famous poets (Sophocles and Euripides are the other two) who, from antiquity onwards, have been celebrated as the great tragic dramatists of ancient Greece. In accordance with the conventions of the tragic festivals at Athens, Aeschylus based most of his plays on ancient myths, dating back to the Mycenaean Age at the dawn of Greek civilization; however, like the other Greek tragic poets, he invested this legendary (and, occasionally, historical) material with new, often contemporary, meanings of his own. Whether from choice or because of a convention of early Greek tragedy, Aeschylus composed most of his tragedies in the form of connected trilogies. (Three tragedies, not necessarily related in subject matter, followed by a semi-comic satyr-play, remained the normal requirement for those competing in the tragic festivals throughout the classical period.) A brief survey of his extant plays will illustrate the wide-ranging material of his themes (theological, ethical, and, in the loftiest sense of the term, political), most of which are well suited, by the grandeur of their dramatic conceptions, to the trilogic form of composition.

Persae (*The Persians*), Aeschylus' earliest extant tragedy (and the earliest Greek tragedy which we possess), is exceptional in that it is *not* part of a connected trilogy. It is of particular interest also because it is the only extant Greek tragedy based on historical, not mythological, material. *The Persians* is, however, by no means merely "dramatized history." Rather, in his treatment of the recent defeat of the Persian despot Xerxes and his Persian fleet by the Athenians at Salamis, Aeschylus "mythologizes" history to present a striking illustration of the tragic theme of *koros, hubris, atê*: excessive confidence in wealth and power, leading to an act of outrage (in this case, that of Xerxes overstepping the divinely ordained limits of his rule), which brings down the swift retribution of the gods. To present his material in tragic rather than in "historical" terms, the poet takes certain bold liberties with the factual material and employs typically Aeschylean touches of symbolism (such as the striking image of "the yoke of the sea," constraining the great sea-god Poseidon, for Xerxes' bridge of boats across "the sacred Hellespont") to stress the overreaching ambition of the Persian King.

In *Septem contra Thebas* (*The Seven Against Thebes*) Aeschylus brings to a tragic conclusion (the lost plays *Laius* and *Oedipus* were the preceding plays of this trilogy) the treatment of another of his favourite themes: the working out of a family curse, inevitably fulfilled by the gods through the "free" decisions of one of its doomed heroic victims.

In the *Oresteia* (*The Oresteia*), Aeschylus' only extant trilogy, the poet combines, in magnificent fashion, both of the above two themes, that of a family curse and that of divine vengeance for a deed of hubristic outrage. In the first play, *Agamemnon*, Agamemnon suffers (by the murderous hand of his queen, Clytemnestra) both for the outrageous deed of his father, Atreus, against the children of his brother Thyestes, and for his own sacrifice ("impious, unholy and polluting," however "necessitous") of his daughter, Iphigenia, in order to obtain favourable winds for his great assault on Troy. In the trilogy sequel, *Choephoroi* (*The Libation Bearers*), Orestes and Electra, loyal children of King Agamemnon, continue the sequence of "blood for blood" by murdering, at the god Apollo's command, the usurpers, Clytemnestra (their mother) and her paramour, Aegisthus. Only in the third play, the *Eumenides* (*The Furies*), is the curse on the family, and the attendant blood feud, resolved. In this play, Orestes takes refuge from Clytemnestra's avenging Furies (the chorus in the play), first at Apollo's Oracle at Delphi and then at Athens. Here the goddess Athena institutes a human court of justice (the Areopagus, which was a celebrated Athenian institution of some political importance in Aeschylus' time), in which Orestes (and all homicides thereafter) will be tried. Orestes is acquitted by Athena's casting vote and the Chorus of Furies, exactors of the old "blood-for-blood justice," are persuaded by Athena, daughter of Olympian Zeus, to become beneficent, though still awe-inspiring, guardians, supporting the new order of justice which Athena has instituted.

This brief review of *The Oresteia* highlights another feature of Aeschylean thought and dramatic structure which some scholars (most notably C.J. Herington in "The Last Phase," *Arion 4*, 1965) believe was typical of the trilogies (the Danaid and the Prometheus trilogies as well as the *Oresteia*) composed in the final period of the poet's career. Thus, in the Danaid trilogy (only the first play of which, *Supplices* [*The Suppliant Maidens*], survives) a violent sequence of forced marriage and murderous requital appears to have been "resolved" by the decision of one bride (out of the 50 sworn to slay their violent suitors) who chooses love instead of further bloodshed. As in *The Furies*, a goddess (in this case Aphrodite, as a fragment of the final play reveals) appears as a champion of this fruitful resolution.

Finally, the Prometheus trilogy seems to have presented a comparable sequence of tragic action leading to a positive finale. *Prometheus Vinctus* (*Prometheus Bound*) was probably the first play in the trilogy; we have only fragmentary knowledge of *Prometheus Unbound* and *Pyrphoros* (*Prometheus the Firebearer*), and the Aeschylean authorship of even the extant *Prometheus Bound* has been doubted by some scholars (see especially Mark Griffith, *The Authenticity of Prometheus Bound* and Martin West, *Studies in Aeschylus*). This time the struggle is between Prometheus, divine champion of men, bestower of fire and all the human arts, and Zeus, man's would-be destroyer, here presented as a harsh and tyrannical new god, only recently established as lord of the Universe. That Zeus, the god of power and order, needs Promethean intelligence and foresight is established on the literal level by the fact that only Prometheus has the secret knowledge which can prevent Zeus falling from power. That intelligence and foresight are unavailing when suppressed by power, as demonstrated by the noble martyrdom of the enchained Prometheus, whose heroic defiance ends (in the finale of *Prometheus Bound*) in his further punishment in the lowest depths of Tartaros. Again the fragments of the trilogy (and other external evidence) suffice to indicate its probable denouement. Prometheus and Zeus are ultimately reconciled by their mutual needs. Zeus, saved by Prometheus' foreknowledge, continues to reign supreme over a less troubled universe, and Prometheus, his "cause" now vindicated, is re-established, under Zeus, as the bestower of the civilizing gift of fire (hence the third title, *Prometheus the Firebearer*) to men. Once again, if this symbolic interpretation of the evidence be sound, we find that the sequence of suffering presented in the trilogy ends in a triumphant resolution.

In this brief survey of the extant themes of Aeschylean tragedy, it has not been possible to do justice to the impressive dramatic structure of his plays and to the grandeur of his choral odes which,

particularly in *The Oresteia*, are an integral part of that structure. While it is true, as Aristotle believed, that the plot is the soul of tragedy, in Aeschylus' plays the plots are simple, both "action" and "characterization" being kept to the minimum necessary to expound, in compelling dramatic form, the recurrent and meaningful patterns of tragic experience.

—Desmond J. Conacher

See the essays on *The Oresteia*, *The Persians*, *Prometheus Bound*, *The Seven Against Thebes*, and *The Suppliant Maidens*.

AGNON, S. Y.

Born: Shmuel Yosef Halesi Czaczkes in Buczacz, Galicia, Austro-Hungarian Empire (now in Poland), 17 July 1888. **Education:** Educated at private schools; Baron Hirsch School. **Family:** Married Esther Marx in 1919; one daughter and one son. **Career:** Lived in Palestine, 1907–13: first secretary of Jewish Court in Jaffa, and secretary of the National Jewish Council; lecturer and tutor in Germany, 1913–24; in Palestine again from 1924. Fellow, Bar Ilan University. **Awards:** Bialik prize, 1934, 1954; Hakhnasat Kala, 1937; Ussishkin prize, 1950; Israel prize, 1954, 1958; Nobel prize for literature, 1966. D.H.L.: Jewish Theological Seminary of America, 1936; Ph.D.: Hebrew University, Jerusalem, 1959. President, Mekitzei Nirdamim, 1950. **Member:** Hebrew Language Academy. **Died:** 17 February 1970.

PUBLICATIONS

Fiction

VeHayah he'Akov leMishor. 1919.
Giv'at haChol [The Hill of Sand]. 1920.
Besod Yesharim [Among the Pious]. 1921.
MeChamat haMetsik [From the Wrath of the Oppressor]. 1921.
Al Kapot haMan'ul [Upon the Handles of the Lock]. 1922.
Polin [Poland]. 1925.
Ma'aseh rabi Gadi'el haTinok [The Tale of Little Reb Gadiel]. 1925.
Sipur haShanin haTovot. 1927.
Agadat haSofer [The Tale of the Scribe]. 1929.
Kol Sipurav [Collected Fiction]. 11 vols., 1931–52; revised edition
    (includes additional volume *Al Kapot HaMan'ul*), 8 vols., 1952–62.
Hakhnasath Kallah. 2 vols., 1931; as *The Bridal Canopy*, translated
    by I.M. Lask, 1937.
Me'Az ume'Atah [From Then and from Now]. 1931.
Sipurey Ahavim [Love Stories]. 1931.
Sipur Pashut. 1935; as *A Simple Story*, translated by Hillel Halkin,
    1985.
BeShuva uveNachat [In Peace and Tranquillity]. 1935.
Kovets sipurim. 1937.
Ore'ah Nata Lalun. 1939; as *A Guest for the Night*, translated by
    Misha Louvish, 1968.
Elu va'Elu [These and Those]. 1941.
Temol Shilshom [The Day Before Yesterday]. 1945; in part as *Kelev
    Chutsot*, 1950.
Samuch veNireh [Never and Apparent]. 1950.
Ad Heinah [Until Now]. 1952.

Bilvav Yamim. 1935; as *In the Heart of the Seas*, translated by I.M. Lask, 1948.

Sefer, Sofer veSipur [Book, Scribe, Tale]. 1938.

Shevu'at Emunim. 1943; as *The Betrothed*, translated by Walter Lever, in *Two Tales*, 1966.

Sipurim veAgadot. 1944.

Tehilla (in English). 1956.

Two Tales: The Betrothed, Edo and Enam, translated by Walter Lever. 1966.

Selected Stories (in Hebrew), edited by Samuel Leiter. 1970.

Twenty-One Stories, edited by Nahum N. Glatzer, various translators. 1970; as *Selection*, 1977.

Shirah [Song]. 1971; as *Shira*, translated by Zeva Shapiro, 1989.

Pitchey Dvarim [Opening Remarks]. 1977.

A Dwelling Place of My People: Sixteen Stories of the Chassidim, translated by J. Weinberg and H. Russell. 1983.

Takhrikh shel sipurim (stories), edited by Emunah Yaron. 1984.

A Book That Was Lost and Other Stories, edited with introductions by Alan Mintz and Anne Golomb Hoffman, 1995

Other

Me'Atsmi el Atsmi [From Me to Me]. 1976.

Esterlain yekirati: mikhatavim 684–691 (1924–1931) (letters). 1983.

Kurzweil, Agnon, Greenberg (letters), edited by L. Dabby-Goury. 1987.

Sipure haBest. 1987.

Agnon's Alef bet: Poems, translated by Robert Friend, 1998.

Editor, with Ahron Eliasberg, *Das Buch von den polnischen Juden*. 1916.

Editor, *Yamim Nora'im*. 1937; as *Days of Awe, Being a Treasury of Traditions, Legends, and Learned Commentaries . . . ,* translated by I.M. Lask, 1948.

Editor, *Atem re'item*. 1959; as *Present at Sinai: The Giving of the Law*, translated by Michael Swirsky, 1994.

Editor, *Sifrehem shel Tsadikim*. 1961.

*

Bibliography: *S.Y. Agnon: Eine Bibliographic seiner Werke* by Werner Martin, 1980.

Critical Studies: *Nostalgia and Nightmare: A Study in the Fiction of S.Y. Agnon* (includes bibliography) by Arnold J. Band, 1968; *The Fiction of S.Y. Agnon* by Baruch Hochman, 1970; *A Study of the Evolution of S.Y. Agnon's Style* by Joseph Kaspi, 1972; *Agnon* by Harold Fisch, 1975; *Shay Agnon's World of Mystery and Allegory* by Israel Rosenberg, 1978; *At the Handles of the Lock: Themes in the Fiction of S.Y. Agnon* by David Aberbach, 1984; *Character and Context: Studies in the Fiction of Abramovilsh, Brenner and Agnon* by Jeffrey Fleck, 1984; *The Triple Cord: Agnon, Hamsun, Strindberg: Where Scandinavian and Hebrew Literature Meet* by Yain Mazor, 1987; *S.Y. Agnon: Texts and Contexts in English Translation* edited by Leon I. Yudkin, 1988; *S.Y. Agnon: A Revolutionary Traditionalist* by Gershon Shaked, translated by Jeffrey M. Green, 1989; *Between Exile and Return: S.Y. Agnon and the Drama of Writing* by Anne G. Hoffman, 1991; *Agnon's Art of Indirection: Uncovering Latent Content in the Fiction of S.Y. Agnon* by N. Ben-Dov, 1993; *Tradition and Trauma: Studies in the Fiction of S.Y. Agnon* edited by David Patterson and Glenda Abrahamson, 1994; *Ghetto, Shtetl, or Polis?:*

The Jewish Community in the Writings of Karl Emil Franzos, Sholom Aleichem, and Shemuel Yosef Agnon by Miriam Roshwald, 1997; *The Centrifugal Novel: S.Y. Agnon's Poetics of Composition* by Stephen Katz, 1999. *Translating Israel: Contemporary Hebrew Literature and its Reception in America* by Alan L. Mintz, 2001.

*   *   *

S.Y. Agnon was a man of two worlds: the world of his ancestors' Judaic tradition and the realm of modernity. Some literary critics attempt to point to a harmony of the two, while others insist on the radical difference and inconsistency between them.

The province of tradition comprised the daily prayers and the celebration of the Sabbath, the lighting of the candles by the mother with its songs, hymns, special food, and parental blessings; the feasts such as the Passover, celebrating the Exodus from Egypt; Yom Kippur, the most holy Day of Atonement, a fast day and a season of forgiveness; the rabbi's home, the synagogue, and the House of Study; the spirit of neighbourliness and mutual help; the occasions of birth, circumcision, marriage, and death. The learned men were honoured and the youth encouraged to emulate them. The language of everyday was Yiddish, a mixture of Hebrew, German, and Polish (or Russian), while Hebrew was reserved for prayer and the sacred texts; God was exalted for his majesty and goodness and the Messiah expected to redeem Israel and the world.

Agnon grew up in this world. Though the 19-year-old left his native Buczacz, Galicia, in 1907, the memories of the "old home" were strong and vivid enough to sustain his creative imagination for years to come. He portrays this culture in the novel *Hakhnasath Kallah* (*The Bridal Canopy*) and the short story "Agadat ha-Sofer" [The Tale of the Scribe]. Agnon was aware of the breakdown of this culture; thus a tragic element enters both the novels and the short stories: in "The Tale of the Scribe" both the humble and saintly scribe and his pious, chaste wife, as well as the sacred scroll, perish in a conflagration.

Answering some critics' contention that Agnon adheres to a style patterned after the Jewish folk-tale and the homiletic mode of the ancient Midrash, he wrote a series of pieces in a strictly modern, expressionistic form. Here the laws of cause and effect do not apply; for example, the narrator in one story attends a memorial service for an important person, and returning home he finds that person waiting for him. Agnon made it clear that he was not confined to any one style; moreover, he chose his particular mode because he believed it to be most readily and universally understood by the Hebrew reader. The stories are evidence that the writer was indeed a man of the Western world and that the problems of the Jewish people and those of the world at large meet and cross.

—Nahum N. Glatzer

AGUILERA MALTA, Demetrio

Born: Guayaquil, Ecuador, 24 May, 1909. **Education:** Elementary studies in the Colegio de San José and the Escuela Municipal Nelson Mateus; high school in the Colegio Vicente Rocafuerte; studied law for two years at the University of Guayas, in Guayaquil at the same time attending art classes at the School of Fine Arts. **Family:** Married 1) a Panamanian in 1932 (divorced), two daughters; 2) Mexican writer and diplomat Velia Márquez Inclán in 1957, three children. **Career:** Writer, playwright, journalist, director of the Museo Nacional and Assistant Secretary of Education; professor of literature at the Rocafuerte Institute; printer; manufacturer of candy; worked at the Pan American Union in Washington, D.C., 1946–48; secretary to the Embassador of Ecuador in Chile, 1948; writer in Residence or Visiting Professor at several U.S. universities and at universities in Guatemala, México and Brazil; Cultural attaché in Argentina, Brazil, Chile, México and Uruguay; Minister of Culture, appointed Embassador to México in 1980; Aguilera Malta contributed about two thousand articles and stories to newspapers and magazines; he also wrote and produced three films. **Awards:** Gold medal at the Reunion of Latin American Writers in Guyaquil, 1971; Eugenio Espejo prize, most distinguished literary prize given in Ecuador, 1981. **Member:** Latin American Community of Writers, Pan American Union. **Died:** Mexico City, 29 December, 1981; suffered from diabetes and blindness, fell in his home sustaining a head injury and did not recover consciousness.

PUBLICATIONS

Collections

Teatro completo, 1970.

Plays

España leal: Tragedia en un prologo y tres actos, el último dividido en tres cuadros. 1938.
Campeonatomania. 1939.
Carbón. 1939.
El sátiro encadenado. 1939.
Lázaro. 1941.
Sangre azul (three-act). With Willis Knapp Jones, 1946; as *Blue Blood*, translated by the authors, 1948.
Dos comedias fáciles. 1950, includes *Sangre azul* and *El pirata fantasma*.
No bastan los átomos. 1955.
Dientes blancos. 1955 and 1956; as *White Teeth: A Play in One Act*, translated by Robert Losada, Jr., 1956.
El tigre: Pieza en un acto dividido en tres cuadros. 1955/1956.
Honorarios. 1957.
Trilogía ecuatoriana: Teatro breve (contains *Dientes blancos*, *Honorarios*, and *El tigre*). 1959.
Infierno negro: Pieza en dos actos. 1967; as *Black Hell*, translated by Elizabeth Lowe, 1977.
Fantoche. 1970.
Muerte, S.A.—La muerte es un gran negocio. 1970.
Una mujer para cada acto. 1970.

Fiction

Los que se van (short story), with Enrique Gil Gilbert and Joaquín Gallegos Lara. 1930.
Don Goyo. 1933; as *Don Goyo*, translated by John Brushwood and Carolyn Brushwood, 1980.
Canal Zone: Los yanquis en Panama. 1935.

¡Madrid!: Reportaje novelado de una retaguardia heroica. 1936/1937.
La isla virgen. 1942.
Una cruz en la Sierra Maestra. 1960.
La caballeresa del sol: El gran amor de Bolivar. 1964; as *Manuela, la caballeresa del sol*, translated by Willis Knapp Jones, foreword by J. Cary Davis, 1967.
El Quijote de El Dorado: Orellana y el Río de las Amazonas. 1964.
Un nuevo mar para el rey: Balboa, Anayansi, y el Océano Pacífico. 1965.
Hechos y leyendas de nuestra América: Relatos hispanoamericanos (short story). 1975.
Siete lunas y siete serpientes. 1970; as *Seven Moons and Seven Serpents*, translated by Gregory Rabassa, 1979.
El secuestro del general. 1973; as *Babelandia*, translated by Peter G. Earle, illustrated by George Bartko, 1985.
Jaguar. 1977.
Réquiem para el diablo. 1978.
Una pelota, un sueño y diez centavos. 1988, published posthumously.

*

Bibliography: De Andrea, Pedro Frank. "Demetrio Aguilera Malta: bibliografía." *Boletín de la Comunidad Latinoamericano de Escritores* 5, September 1969.

Critical Studies: "The 'Episodios Americanos' of Aguilera Malta" by J. Davis, in *Foreign Language Quarterly*, 9, 1970; *La narrativa de Aguilera Malta* by María E. Valverde, 1979; "The Apocalyptic Tropics of Aguilera Malta" by Luis A. Díez, in *Latin American Theatre Review*, 10, Spring-Summer 1982; "Demetrio Aguilera Malta" in *Spanish American Authors of the Twentieth Century*, edited by Angle Flores, 1992; "Demetrio Aguilera Malta" by Robert Scott in, *Encyclopedia of World Literature*, 2nd Edition, 1999; *Demetrio Aguilera Malta and Social Justice: The Tertiary Phase of Epic Tradition in Latin American Literature* by Clemintine Christos Rabassa, 1980; "The Antichrist-Figure in Three Latin American Novels" by William L. Siemens, in *The Power of Myth in Literature and Film*, 1980; "Absurdity, Hyperbole and the Grotesque in Demetrio Aguilera's Last Novel, *Requiem para el diablo*" by Michael C. Waag, in *SECOLAS* Annals 20, March 1989.

*   *   *

Demetrio Aguilera Malta championed the Ecuadorian working poor, illustrating the injustices they endured in his social realist novels with his passionate writing. One of the earliest writers to use elements of magic realism, he intersected quotidian activities with supernatural elements. Aguilera Malta was an adventurer and lived a nomadic existence, which is reflected directly in his short stories, novels, and plays. Much of his writing is culturally specific to Ecuador and to the region of Guayaquil. Yet, he is able to transcend national boundaries and utilize his literary works to exemplify social injustice.

His first work published in conjunction with two other young Ecuadorian coastal writers, Enrique Gil Gilbert and Joaquín Gallegos Lara is a collection of twenty-four short stories entitled *Los que se van* [Those Who Got Away]. This work initiated a new trend and era in Ecuadorian and Spanish American literature, combining social realism with psychoanalysis. The language is crude and violent, and makes use of local slang, portraying the hardships and physical violence the *cholos* (mixed blooded or mestizos) endured. Literary critics found the book shocking, but the reading public enthusiastically reveled in the story's lack of traditionalism and its break with 19th-century pretensions. Aguilera Malta together with his two collaborators from *Los que se van* and with José de la Cuadra and Alfredo Pareja Diezcanseco came to be known as the "Grupo de Guayaquil."

Don Goyo and *La isla virgen* [The Virgin Island] are two early works dealing with life of the coastal Ecuadorian cholos, living at the mouth of the Guayas River, the area where the author grew up and which heavily influenced his formation and writing. *Don Goyo* depicts the *cholo* in his native or natural environment but at the same time imbues it with magical qualities. He included such techniques as talking trees and axes that think, listen and converse as examples of his early usage as an initiator of magic realism. The central character is the centenarian Don Goyo; he is attuned to the surrounding natural environment, and his disappearance leads to his people's enslavement by the white men. In *La isla virgen*, Don Nestor is juxtaposed with Don Goyo from the preceding novel, by the fact that he exploits nature.

In response to the occupation of the Canal Zone by the U.S. military and the Civil War in Spain, he produced the historical biographical novels *Canal Zone* and *¡Madrid!: Reportaje novelado de una retaguardia heroica* [Madrid: A Fictional Account of a Heroic Rearguard], published in Barcelona in 1936. *Canal Zone* tackles the topic of racial discrimination by the United States against the black workers building the canal. After publication of this work, Aguilera Malta was unable to enter the United States for several years. *¡Madrid!* echoes his loyalist affiliation as he also wrote propaganda for the Republican government.

One of his best known novels, *La isla virgen*, dramatized the life of the cholos, highlighting their customs, folklore, and the influence nature had on their culture through the use of techniques gleaned from his work in theatre and movies. After moving to Mexico in 1955, he returned to the novel and began a series of historical biographical novels under the rubric of *Historias americanos*. The series included *La caballeresca del sol*, a treatment of Simón Bolivar's lover; *El Quijote de El Dorado* dealing with the Amazon region and Orellano; and *Un nuevo mar para el rey* [A New Sea for the King], a treatment of the discovery of the Pacific Ocean by Balboa. These works present no new narrative techniques and treat the topics in a traditional manner.

In the 1970s and 1980s, Aguilera Malta's works were deeply influenced by the Latin American New Novel: *Siete lunas y siete serpientes* (*Seven Moons and Seven Serpents*); *El secuestro del general* [The Kidnapping of the General]; *Jaguar*; *Réquiem para el diablo*; and *Una pelota, un sueño y diez centavos* [A Ball, a Dream, and Ten Cents]. *Siete lunas y siete serpientes* marks a return to the region of the Guayas River; with its cholos and island milieu, he included elements of magic realism. Regionalism becomes allegory here in the form of good versus evil. The depiction of evil is seen in the characters represented by traditional Latin American figures of power such as the military, politicians, the oligarchy, the institution of the church. According to Robert Scott, they face the forces of good represented by true "Christianity, scientific enlightenment, and nostalgia for a lost paradise. . . "

While known more as a novelist outside his country, Aguilera Malta is possibly Ecuador's best known playwright and his theatrical works represent many of the same themes as his novels. The first play staged by Aguilera Malta was a propaganda piece titled *España leal*,

produced shortly after his return from the Spanish Civil War. *Lázaro* is a tragedy about a schoolteacher who was forced to abandon the classroom because of lack of funding and how he wastes his time trying to survive economically. *Dientes blancos* (*White Teeth*) denounces the racial discrimination he witnessed as a reporter in Panama and the Canal Zone. The same theme appears in *Infierno Negro* [Black Hell]. Perhaps his best-known play, as it is his most anthologized, is *El tigre*. The play is based on an incident in his novel *La isla virgen*. It fuses an explicit use of symbols while at the same time rejecting any attempt to reconstruct external reality. It deals with the primitive life of a group of cane cutters on the Guayas River, particularly one unfortunate worker, Aguayo, fixated on being eaten by a jaguar. The supervisor dismisses Aguayo's fears as irrational but the other two workers vacillate between the practical and the mythical interpretation for their colleague's fear.

The significance of Aguilera Malta's contributions may lie in his earlier works. However, one of his later novels, *Siete lunas y siete serpientes*, is particularly important as it recuperates his earlier techniques and completes the circle returning to his own literary roots. Aguilera Malta's social and political message is not only important for Ecuador but for Latin America in general.

—Beth Pollack

AKHMATOVA, Anna

Born: Anna Andreievna Gorenko in Bolshoi Fontan, near Odessa, Ukraine, 23 June 1889. **Education:** Educated at girls' gymnasium, Tsarskoe Selo; Smolnyi Institute, St. Petersburg; Fundukleevskaia gymnasium, 1906, and law school, 1907, both Kiev. **Family:** Married 1) Nikolai S. Gumilev in 1910 (divorced 1918), one son, the writer Lev Gumilev; 2) Vladimir Shileiko in 1918 (separated 1920, divorced 1928); 3) Nikolai N. Punin (died 1953). **Career:** Associated with the Acmeist movement whose members included Gumilev, Mandel'shtam, *q.v.*, Gorodetskii, Narbut, and Zenkevich; worked as a librarian, Institute of Agronomy, Petrograd, 1920; banned from publishing her poetry, 1925–40; lived in Leningrad, evacuated to Moscow, 1941, then to Tashkent; returned to Leningrad, 1945; expelled from Union of Soviet Writers, 1946. **Awards:** Taormina prize, 1964. D.Litt.: Oxford University, 1965. **Died:** 5 March 1966.

PUBLICATIONS

Collections

Sochineniia [Works], edited by Gleb Struve and Boris Filippov. 2 vols., 1965–68.
Selected Poems, edited by Walter Arndt, translated by Robin Kemball and Carl R. Proffer. 1976.
Stikhi i proza [Poems and Prose] (selections), edited by B.G. Druian. 1977.
Stikhi, perepiska, vospominaniia, ikonografiia [Poems, Correspondence, Reminiscences, Iconography], edited by Ellendea Proffer. 1977.
Sochineniia [Works], edited by V.A. Chernykh. 2 vols., 1986.

The Complete Poems, edited by Roberta Reeder, translated by Judith Hemschemeyer. 2 vols., 1990; revised edition, 1 vol., 1992.

Selected Poems of Anna Akhmatova, translated by Judith Hemschemeyer, 2000.

Verse

Vecher [Evening]. 1912.

Chetki [The Rosary]. 1914.

Belaia staia [The White Flock]. 1917.

Skrizhal sbornik [Ecstasy Collection]. 1921.

Podorozhnik [Plantain]. 1921.

Anno Domini MCMXXI. 1922; enlarged edition, 1923.

Forty-Seven Love Poems, translated by Natalie Duddington. 1927.

Stikhi [Poems]. 1940.

Iz shesti knig [From Six Books]. 1940.

Izbrannoe [Selection]. 1943.

Izbrannye stikhi [Selected Poems]. 1946.

Stikhotvoreniia 1909–1945 [Poetry]. 1946.

Stikhotvoreniia 1909–1957 [Poetry], edited by A.A. Surkov. 1958; revised edition, 1965.

Stikhotvoreniia 1909–1960 [Poetry]. 1961.

50 Stikhotvorenii [50 Poems]. 1963.

Rekviem: Tsikl stikhotvorenii. 1963; as *Requiem*, with *Poem Without a Hero*, translated by D.M. Thomas, 1976.

Beg vremeni [The Flight of Time]. 1965.

Selected Poems, translated by Richard McKane. 1969; revised edition 1989.

Poems (bilingual edition), edited and translated by Stanley Kunitz and Max Hayward. 1973.

Tale Without a Hero and Twenty-Two Poems, edited and translated by Jeanne van der Eng-Liedmeier and Kees Verheul. 1973.

Way of All the Earth, translated by D.M. Thomas. 1979.

Poems (selection), translated by Lyn Coffin. 1983.

Three Russian Women Poets (with Bella Akhmadulina and Marina Tsvetaeva), edited and translated by Mary Maddock. 1983.

Twenty Poems, translated by Jane Kenyon and Vera Sandomirsky Dunham. 1985.

You Will Hear Thunder, translated by D.M. Thomas, 1985.

Selected Early Love Lyrics (bilingual edition), translated by Jessie Davies. 1988.

Poem Without a Hero and Selected Poems, translated by Lenore Mayhew and William McNaughton. 1989.

Evening: Poems 1912 (bilingual edition), translated by Jessie Davies. 1990.

A Stranger to Heaven and Earth: Poems, edited and translated by Judith Hemschemeyer. 1993.

Other

Conversations with Akhmatova 1:1938–1941, edited by Lydia Chukovskaya. 1989.

Anna Akhmatova: My Half Century: Selected Prose, translated by Ronald Meyer. 1992.

The Akhmatova Journals, 1938–1941, by Lydia Chukoskaya, translated by Milena Michalski and Sylva Rubashova. 1993.

Anna Akhmatova and Her Circle, compilation and notes by Konstantin Polivanov, translated by Patricia Beriozkina, 1994.

Translator, *Koreiskaya klassicheskaya poeziya* [Korean Classical Poetry], edited by A.A. Kholodovich. 1956.

Translator, with Vera Potapova, *Lirika drevnego Egipta* [Ancient Egyptian Lyrics]. 1965.

Translator, *Golosa poetov* [Voices of the Poets]. 1965.

Translator, *Klassicheskaia poeziia vostoka* [Classical Poetry of the East]. 1969.

*

Bibliography: *Anna Akhmatova in English: A Bibliography 1889–1986–1989* by Garth M. Terry, 1989.

Critical Studies: *The Theme of Time in the Poetry of Anna Axmatova* by Kees Verheul, 1971; *Anna Akhmatova* by Sam Driver, 1972; *Anna Akhmatova: A Poetic Pilgrimage* by Amanda Haight, 1976; *Akhmatova's Petersburg* by Sharon Leiter, 1983; *The Prince, the Fool and the Nunnery: The Religious Theme in the Early Poetry of Anna Akhmatova* by Wendy Rosslyn, 1984, *The Speech of Unknown Eyes: Akhmatova's Readers on Her Poetry* edited by Rosslyn, 2 vols., 1990, and *Remembering Anna Akhmatova* by Anatoli Naiman, translated by Rosslyn, 1991; *The Poetry of Anna Akhmatova: A Conquest of Time and Space* by Sonia Ketchian, 1986; *Anna of All the Russias: The Life of Anna Akhmatova* by Jessie Davies, 1988, and *Memoirs of Anna Akhmatova's Years, 1944–1950* by Sophie Kazimirovna Ostrovskaya, translated by Davies, 1988; *Anna Akhmatova and Russian Culture of the Beginning of the Twentieth Century: Papers of the Moscow Conference 1989* by V.N. Toporov, 1989; Anna Akhmatova issue of *Soviet Literature*, 6, 1989; *In a Shattered Mirror: The Later Poetry of Anna Akhmatova* by Susan Amert, 1992; *Anna Akhmatova: Poet and Prophet* by Roberta Reeder, 1994; *A Concordance to the Poetry of Anna Akhmatova,* edited and compiled by Tatiana Patera, 1995; *Anna Akhmatova: Her Poetry* by David N. Wells, 1996; *The Guest from the Future: Anna Achmatova and Isaiah Berlin,* by György Dalos, translated by Antony Wood, 1998.

* * *

Anna Akhmatova occupies a position unique in the history of modern Russian poetry. An established poet before the revolution, she continued her active creative life well into the mid-1960s, and after the death of Pasternak, Akhmatova was the last remaining major link with what had been one of the great ages of Russian poetry.

Her early career was closely associated with Acmeism, a poetic movement which defined itself in opposition to Russian symbolism, stressing craftsmanship in poetry and affirming the significance of this phenomenal world in contradistinction to the abstract ''Other World'' of the Symbolists. Akhmatova's early work was perceived as exemplary for the new movement, and achieved a remarkable popular and critical success. The reading public welcomed the clarity, accessibility, and almost conversational style of her brief, fragile love lyrics, especially after the mystifications and abstractions of the Symbolists. The critics recognized and appreciated Akhmatova's innovations, her technical accomplishment, and the extraordinary compactness of her verse. By the publication of her fifth book in 1922, an ''Akhmatova style'' in Russian poetry was widely recognized.

As a matter of conscious artistic choice, Akhmatova limited her early themes in large part to love, to poetry, and to her homeland. Settings for the predominant love theme are typically drawn from what has traditionally been thought of as the woman's world: home, interiors, garden, details of decor, and dress. Simple enough in themselves, the images evolve in sum into a complex symbolic system. The otherwise spare and laconic poems are enriched, moreover, by a matrix of images drawn from Russia's cultural history: folk motifs, the old patriarchal life, Orthodoxy, the great cities of Russia. Related to this matrix, and just below the surface of the worldly love lyrics, are the old Orthodox themes of conscience and remorse, sin and retribution, repentance and self-abnegation. It is such themes that developed in the later major works to an extraordinary power and dignity.

Although Akhmatova maintained a remarkable stylistic consistency throughout her career, it was as early as 1924 that her beloved friend and fellow-poet Mandel'shtam noted a "sharp break" in Akhmatova's work: "The voice of self-abnegation grows stronger in Akhmatova's poetry, and at present her poetry approaches becoming one of the symbols of the greatness of Russia." Mandel'shtam's words were prophetic for Akhmatova's longer works like *Rekviem* (*Requiem*), *Poema bez geroia* (*Poem Without a Hero*), and the "Northern Elegies."

In the dark years of official disfavour and persecution that followed her former husband's execution, Akhmatova continued to write, but except for a brief respite during World War II she was not permitted to publish any original poetry. Many of her poems were lost in those tragic years; during the worst of them, many were burned by the poet herself. For a long time, Akhmatova did not dare even to set new poems to paper: the more important ones were committed to memory by her friends and thus preserved.

As works from this period began to appear in the 1950s, it was clear that Akhmatova had undergone an amazing growth and development. The poet emerges as a preserver and continuator of a poetic culture older and broader than the one of her current reality. In the longer works, the poet stands also as conscience and judge for a society suffering under the cataclysms of wars and revolution. *Requiem* is an epic lament for a Russia in the grip of the Stalinist Terror. *Poem Without a Hero* is a retrospective of Akhmatova's own world from Petersburg in 1913 to the nightmare of World War II and beyond. It is her judgement on an age and also her retribution for her own suffering. By the time she added the last touches to the poem in 1962, Akhmatova had become for Russian poetry the very symbol of moral rectitude and artistic integrity in the face of intolerable personal hardship and official persecution. Along with some of the shorter poems, these masterworks stand as tribute to one of the great Russian poets of the 20th century.

—Sam Driver

See the essays on *Poem Without a Hero* and *Requiem*.

AKUTAGAWA Ryūnosuke

Born: Niihara Ryūnosuke in Tokyo, Japan, 1 March 1892; adopted by uncle and given the family name Akutagawa. **Education:** Educated at Tokyo Imperial University, 1913–16, degree in English. **Family:** Married Tsukamoto Fumi in 1918; three sons. **Career:** Member of literary staff, *Shinshichō* [New Thought Tides], university magazine, 1914, 1916–17; English teacher, Naval Engineering College, Yokosuka, 1916–19; literary staff member, *Osaka Mainichi* *Shimbun* newspaper, 1919; travelled through China and Korea for *Osaka Mainichi*, March-July 1921. Addicted to opium by 1926. **Died:** (suicide) 24 July 1927.

PUBLICATIONS

Collections

Shū [Selected Works], edited by Nakamura Shin'ichirō. 1928; 2 vols., 1953.
Zenshū [Collected Works]. 10 vols., 1934–35; 20 vols., 1954–57; 8 vols., 1964–65; 11 vols., 1967–69; 9 vols., 1971.
Sakuhin shū [Collection of Pieces], edited by Hori Tatsuo, Kuzumaki Yoshitoshi, and Akutagawa Hiroshi. 1949.
Bungaku tokuhon [Literary Reader], edited by Yoshida Seiichi. 1955.
Ōchōmono zenshū. 2 vols., 1960.
Miteikō shū [Unfinished Works], edited by Kuzumaki Yoshitoshi. 1968.
Jihitsu miteikō zuho [Projects for Unfinished Works in His Own Hand], edited by Tsunoda Chūzō. 1971.
The Essential Akutagawa: Rashomon, Hell Screen, Cogwheels, A Fool's Life and Other Short Fiction, edited by Seiji M. Lippit, 1999.

Fiction

"Rōnen" [Old Age]. 1914.
"Rashōmon." 1915; as "Rashomon," translated by Takashi Kojima, in *Rashomon and Other Stories*, 1952; also translated by Glenn W. Shaw, 1964.
"Hana." 1916; as "The Nose," translated by Glenn W. Shaw, 1930; also translated by Dorothy Britton, 1987.
"Imogayu." 1916; as "Yam Gruel," translated by Takashi Kojima, 1952.
"Hankechi." 1916; as "Handkerchief," translated by Glenn W. Shaw, 1930.
"Gesaku zammai" [A Life of Frivolous Writing]. 1917.
"Tabako to akuma" [Tobacco and the Devil]. 1917.
"Jigokuhen." 1918; as "Hell Screen," translated by W.H.H. Norman, in *Hell Screen ("Jigokuhen") and Other Stories*, 1948; translated as *Hell Screen*, 1987.
"Hōkyōjin no shi." 1918; as "The Martyr," translated by Takashi Kojima, 1952.
"Kumo no ito." 1918; as "The Spider's Thread," translated by Glenn W. Shaw, 1930; also translated by Dorothy Britton, 1987.
"Kesa to Moritō." 1918; as "Kesa and Morito," translated by Takashi Kojima, 1952.
"Kare no shō" [Withered Fields]. 1918.
"Kairaishi" [The Puppeteer]. 1919.
"Mikan" [Tangerines]. 1919.
"Kage dōro" [Street of Shadows]. 1920.
"Yabu no naka." 1921; as "In a Grove," translated by Takashi Kojima, 1952.
"Yarai no hana" [Flowers from the Night Before]. 1921.
"Torokko." 1922; as "Flatcar," translated by Richard N. McKinnon, in *The Heart Is Alone*, 1957.
"Ikkai no tsuchi." 1924; as "A Clod of Earth," translated by Richard N. McKinnon, in *The Heart Is Alone*, 1957.

"Daidōji shinsuke no Hansei" [The Early Life of Daidoji Shinsuke].
1924.

"Genkaku sanbō" [Genkaku's Villa]. 1927.

Kappa. 1927; as *Kappa,* translated by Seuchi Shiojiri, 1947; also
translated by Geoffrey Bownas, 1970.

Tales Grotesque and Curious, translated by Glenn W. Shaw. 1930.

Hell Screen ("Jigokuhen") and Other Stories, translated by W.H.H.
Norman. 1948.

Rashomon and Other Stories, translated by Takashi Kojima. 1952.

Japanese Short Stories, translated by Takashi Kojima. 1961; revised
edition, 1962.

Exotic Japanese Stories, translated by Takashi Kojima and John
McVittie. 1964.

The Spider's Thread and Other Stories, translated by Dorothy Britton.
1987.

Verse

Kushū [Poems]. 1976.

Other

Toshishun. 1920; as *Tu Tzu-chün,* translated by Sasaki Takamasa,
1944; revised edition, 1951; as *Tu Tze-chun,* translated by Dorothy
Britton, 1965.

Shina-yuki [Notes on a Chinese Journey]. 1925.

Ume, uma, uguisu [Plum, Horse, Nightingale]. 1926.

Tenkibo [Death Register]. 1926.

Bungeiteki na, amari ni bungeiteki na [Literary, All Too Literary].
1927.

Yūwaku [Temptation] and *Asakusa Kōen* [Asakusa Park] (unproduced
film scripts). 1927.

Shinkirō [Mirage]. 1927.

Aru ahō no isshō. 1927; as *A Fool's Life,* translated by Will Petersen,
1970.

Haguruma. 1930; as *Cogwheels,* translated by Cid Corman, 1987.

The Three Treasures (stories for children), translated by Sasaki
Takamasa. 1944; revised edition, 1951.

Shuju no kotoba (essays). 1968.

Hell Screen, Cogwheels, and A Fool's Life, translated by Takashi
Kojima, Cid Corman, Susumu Kamaike, and Will Petersen. 1987.

*

Bibliography: in *Akutagawa: An Introduction* by Beongcheon Yu,
1972; in *The Search for Authenticity in Modern Japanese Literature*
by Hisaaki Yamaouchi, 1978.

Critical Studies: *Akutagawa,* edited and translated by Akio Inoue,
1961; "Akutagawa: The Literature of Defeatism" by T. Arima, in
The Failure of Freedom, 1969; "Akutagawa and the Negative Ideal"
by Howard Hibbert, in *Personality in Japanese History,* edited by
Albert Craig and Donald Shively, 1970; *Akutagawa: An Introduction*
by Beongcheon Yu, 1972; in *Modern Japanese Writers* by Makoto
Ueda, 1976; "From Tale to Short Story: Akutagawa's *Toshishun* and
Its Chinese Origins" and "The Plot Controversy between Tanizaki
and Akutagawa," in *Reality and Fiction in Modern Japanese Litera-
ture* by Noriko Mizuta Lippit, 1980; "Akutagawa Ryunosuke" by
Donald Keene, in *Dawn to the West: Japanese Literature of the
Modern Era: Fiction,* 1984.

*   *   *

Akutagawa Ryūnosuke's reputation as a purveyor of grotesque
and exotic narratives, suggested by the titles of two collections of his
stories in English, has been reinforced, not only by the film *Rashōmon,*
which Kurosawa Akira based on two of Akutagawa's stories—
"Rashōmon" and "Yabu no naka" ("In a Grove")—but also by
reference to the facts of his often unhappy life, ending in a suicide
which, committed at the early age of 35 and leaving three small boys
in his wife's care, was shocking even in a country where suicide is
traditionally regarded with less dismay than in most other cultures.

However, there is more to Akutagawa's work than the morbidness
that all this may suggest. The range of his interests and of the genres
he wrote in was unusually broad. His thoughtful essays on the
literature of East and West from which he drew general inspiration
and specific ideas and images; his stories for children; his reflections
on his journey through China and Korea in 1921—none of these
deserves to be overshadowed, as they often have been, either by the
more popular stories or by "Haguruma" ("Cogwheels"), "Aru ahō
no isshō" ("A Fool's Life"), and the other harrowing autobiographical texts of his final months. Nor are the stories as simple as the
conventional labels would indicate. The "grotesque" stories are
vivid explorations of extreme situations and their psychological
effects, rather than merely exercises in making the reader shudder.
Yoshihide in "Jigokuhen" ("Hell Screen"), continuing painting the
fires of Hell even as his daughter burns, is more than just another
image of the obsessive artist, though he is that too. He is also a father
maddened by grief, whose predicament is so convincingly evoked
that the horror of the situation comes to seem understandable.
Rashomon stands out among all the many Japanese fictions about
Kyoto as a depiction of the ancient capital at its lowest ebb, desolated
by war and deserted by most of its population, with a resonance which
the course of Japan's history since Akutagawa's death has accidentally enhanced. As for his "exotic" stories, such as "Kumo no ito"
("The Spider's Thread"), based on Buddhist eschatology, or "Kare
no shō" [Withered Fields], depicting the disciples of the 17th-century
poet Bashō, these reflect the depth of his knowledge of history and of
religion, though it should be stressed that he was neither didactic nor
romantic about either of these interests. The best of the many stories
which fit neither of these all-too-convenient labels is perhaps "Mikan"
[Tangerines], a deft exercise in social observation and psychological
insight, in which one simple action transforms the narrator's view of
the apparently stupid girl sharing his train compartment.

But the masterpiece among Akutagawa's fictions is the novella
Kappa, which transcends all labels. There are obvious comparisons to
be made between its hero's journey to the land of the *kappa,* the
legendary sprites or gnomes that live in Japanese rivers, and the
travels of Jonathan Swift's character Lemuel Gulliver. Both are
presented in first-person narratives which use imaginary countries to
imply critical observations of the authors' own societies; both travellers eventually overcome their initial confusion and mystification
about the strange creatures they observe to conclude that human
beings are in many ways even stranger. Yet the differences are also
telling. Gulliver visits several different societies, takes part in their
activities as far as he can, and returns home at last wiser, perhaps more
cynical. Akutagawa's hero, a patient in a mental hospital rather than a
prosperous sea-captain, is a passive observer of only one society,
which turns out to be all too much like his own, and what he learns
from the final poem of his dead *kappa* friend Tok supplies a kind of

wisdom he would rather not have had. It is as though the misanthropy which marks Gulliver's visit to the land of the Houyhnhnms, the wise and virtuous talking horses, had been extended to a general revulsion from human and non-human creatures alike, since all alike lack wisdom and virtue. For Gulliver, if not perhaps for himself, Swift the Christian was able to find solace and a kind of resolution; Akutagawa, who killed himself some months after finishing *Kappa*, was at the end of his tether. Thus the difficulties that *Kappa* presents, for both Japanese and non-Japanese readers, are not so much stylistic or intellectual—it is a deceptively simple tale, simply told—as emotional. Without any overt use of horrific imagery its cumulative effect is nonetheless not for the squeamish.

In the end, then, Akutagawa's enduring position as one of the most popular and influential of modern Japanese writers rests on the sheer variety of his subject matter, handled in a lucid and elegant prose style, particularly on his use of Chinese and Japanese themes familiar to generations of his compatriots. But the significance of his work also lies in his efforts to assimilate the impact of Western technology, values, and, not least, literary forms. Before him Natsume Sōseki, of whom Akutagawa considered himself a disciple, had made his own peace between his heritage as a scholar of Chinese traditions and his career as an English teacher and newspaper contributor (jobs which did not exist for earlier Japanese writers, and which Akutagawa also took). In later years Tanizaki Junichirō, with whom he debated literary principles in *Bungeiteki na, amari ni bungeiteki na* [Literary, All Too Literary], would embrace in turn extreme "Westernization" and the revival of native tradition, finding means of self-expression within both, at least partly by inheriting and extending Akutagawa's tendencies toward grotesquerie. It is a matter for great regret that Akutagawa's frequently expressed self-disgust should have overwhelmed the intelligence and passion that are the mark of almost all his writings.

—Patrick Heenan

ALAIN-FOURNIER

Born: Henri Alban Fournier in La Chapelle d'Angillon, France, 3 October 1886. **Education:** Educated at the Lycée Voltaire, Paris, 1898–1901, lycée in Brest 1901–03; lycée in Bourges, 1902–03, baccalauréat, 1903; Lycée Lakanal, Paris. **Military Service:** Served in the French cavalry and infantry 1907–09, 1911, 1913–14; second lieutenant. **Career:** Secretary and translator for wallpaper factory, London, 1905; journalist, *Paris Journal*, 1910–12, *L'Intransigeant*, Paris, 1912–14. Tutor of French to T.S. Eliot; secretary to Claude Casimir Périer, 1912. **Died:** (killed in action) 22 September 1914.

PUBLICATIONS

Fiction

Le Grand Meaulnes. 1913; as *The Wanderer*, translated by Françoise Delisle, 1928; as *The Lost Domain*, translated by Frank Davison, 1959; also translated by Sandra Morris, 1966; as *The Wanderer; or, the End of Youth*, translated by Lowell Bair, 1971; as *Le Grand*

Meaulnes: The Land of the Lost Content, translated by Katherine Vivian, 1979.

Miracles (stories). 1924.

Colombe Blanchet (unfinished), edited by Gabriella Manca. 1990.

Other

Jacques Rivière et Alain-Fournier: Correspondance 1905–1914. 4 vols., 1926–28; revised edition, edited by Isabelle Rivière, 2 vols., 1948; also edited by Alain Rivière and P. de Gaulmun, 1991.

Lettres au Petit B. . . . 1930; revised and enlarged edition, 1986.

Lettres d'Alain-Fournier à sa famille 1905–1914. 1930; enlarged editions 1940, 1949, 1986.

Alain-Fournier–Madame Simone, Correspondance 1912–1914, edited by Claude Sicard, 1992.

Charles Péguy et Alain-Fournier: Correspondance 1910–1914, edited by Yves Rey-Herme. 1973; revised edition, 1990.

Miracles: Poèmes et proses. 1986.

La Peinture, le coeur et l'esprit: Correspondance inédite (1907–1924), with André Lhote and Jacques Rivière, edited by Alain Rivière, Jean-Georges Morgenthaler, and Françoise Garcia. 1986.

Towards the Lost Domain: Letters from London 1905, edited and translated by W.J. Strachan. 1986.

Chroniques et critiques, edited by André Guyon. 1991.

"Le Corps de la Femme" et Quelques Lettres d'Alain-Fournier et Jacques Rivière by Pascale McGarry, 1998.

*

Critical Studies: *Images d'Alain-Fournier*, 1938, and *Vie et passion d'Alain-Fournier*, 1963, both by Isabelle Rivière; *The Quest of Alain-Fournier*, 1953, revised edition as *The Land Without a Name: Alain-Fournier and His World*, 1975, and *Le Grand Meaulnes*, 1986, both by Robert Gibson; *Portrait of a Symbolist Hero: An Existential Study Based on the Work of Alain-Fournier* by Robert Champigny, 1954; *Alain-Fournier et le Grand Meaulnes* by Jean-Marie Delettrez, 1954; *A Critical Commentary on Alain-Fournier's "Le Grand Meaulnes"* by Marian G. Jones, 1968; *Alain-Fournier: Sa vie et "Le Grand Meaulnes"* by Jean Loize, 1968; *Alain-Fournier: A Brief Life 1886–1914* by David Arkell, 1986; *Le Grand Meaulnes: Images et documents* edited by Daniel Leuwers, 1986; *Alain-Fournier* by Stephen Gurney, 1987; *Alain-Fournier: Les Chemins d'Une Vie: Guide Biographique Illustré* by Alain Rivière, 1994; *L'énigme Alain-Fournier 1914–1991* by Alain Denizot and Jean Louis, 2000.

* * *

Although Alain-Fournier's fame seems likely to rest on *Le Grand Meaulnes* (*The Wanderer*), his only completed novel, he does not deserve to be seen simply as a one-book author. In his tragically foreshortened life, he produced a number of poems and short stories as well as an impressive array of letters and newspaper articles. All this material has now been published and occupies several hundred closely printed pages.

None of the 12 poems he completed was published in his lifetime. The first was written in August 1904 and the last in August 1906. They are nearly all in free verse form and bear the clear imprint of the great enthusiasms of his later teens: Francis Jammes, Jules Laforgue and *Pelléas et Mélisande*. Their principal interest is that they already include some of the dominant motifs of his later writing; a pair of sweethearts in a peaceful country setting, the cooing of doves, the notes of a distant piano, an elusive girl who is loved in vain. The most accomplished of these poems, "A travers les étés. . . ," written in August 1905, was the first attempt to transpose into polished form his impressions of the brief encounter two months previously with Yvonne de Quièvrecourt; it was eventually to become the centrepiece of the fancy dress party at the lost domain in *The Wanderer*.

The first of his writings ever to appear in print was "Le Corps de la Femme," completed in September 1907, just before the author began his two years of compulsory Army service, and published in *La Grande Revue* two months later. It is a series of vignettes expressing his youthful ideal of womanhood, composed as a deliberate counter to Pierre Lous, who sang the praises of the female nude and wrote captions for pornographic "art-studies," Alain-Fournier argued that French women would remain loyal to their gender and to the traditions of their country only if they kept clothed and remained remote. His next contribution to this subject, "La Femme empoisonnée," completed 18 months later, reveals the effect of army service on his youthful ideals: the woman of the title, once the pure girl who sets schoolboy hearts a-flutter, is now the garrison whore riddled with the pox.

From 1909 onwards, the consequences of lost innocence became Alain-Fournier's abiding concern. While he continued to yearn for the inaccessible aristocratic Yvonne, he embarked on a series of short-lived love-affairs with lower-class women, the legacy of which was invariably self-disgust. Loss of purity, he came to believe, squandered his hopes of happiness and directly threatened the child-like sense of wonderment that he felt was crucial to his art. Variations on this theme are to be found in the short stories in *Miracles* and in the earliest attempts he made to write a novel where his version of the Land of Lost Contentment is simply called *le pays sans nom* (the land without a name): in *The Wanderer*, finally completed in 1913 after all manner of false starts, this becomes the "Lost Domain" which Meaulnes is convinced he has no right to re-enter because he is no longer innocent. The theme was also to have been of central importance to Alain-Fournier's second novel, *Colombe Blanchet*, only a few fragments of which were ever written. Set like all his fiction against a rural background, its characters were to have been young schoolteachers rather than schoolboys in their teens. The projected epigraph was a quotation from the *Imitation of Christ*: "I seek a pure heart and there I will take my rest."

While Alain-Fournier's poetry and fiction remain deeply rooted in his rural past, his prolific correspondence and numerous newspaper articles have a spectacularly wider range. The first of his published letters, written to his parents in 1898, lists his examination successes at the end of his first term at his Paris lycée; the last, sent to his beloved sister in September 1914, is from the battlefield of the Marne. Between these two dates, he wrote scores of letters, many positively voluminous, to his closest relatives, to school-friends, and eventually, as he began to make his way in the literary world, to such fellow-writers as Gide, Jacques Copeau, Jammes, and T.S. Eliot, who was, for a brief while in 1910–11, his private pupil. By some way the most important correspondence is that with Jacques Rivière, his closest friend and eventually his brother-in-law. Circumstances separated them for four years and they exchanged long letters in which they described and analyzed for each other their evolving thoughts and feelings and their impressions of the world around them. Alain-Fournier builds up a detailed picture of the London scene in 1905 and

records vivid impressions of his army service which played so significant a part in both his sentimental education and his literary apprenticeship. Especially revealing is the record of their latest discoveries in the worlds of literature, music, and painting, where they respond with infectious enthusiasm yet analyze and evaluate with admirable perceptiveness.

Their appetite remained insatiable to the end. While Rivière went on to become secretary then editor-in-chief of *La Nouvelle Revue Française*, Alain-Fournier became a literary critic and gossip-columnist for a variety of newspapers and journals. By its very nature, much of this work was ephemeral, but it remains impressive for its wealth of judicious comment and the sheer breadth of its range. Taken together with his many letters, it constitutes an invaluable chronicle of that inordinately rich decade in the cultural life of Paris which preceded World War I.

—Robert Gibson

See the essay on *The Wanderer*.

ALBERTI, Rafael (Merello)

Born: Puerto de Santa María, near Cádiz, Spain, 16 December 1902. **Education:** Educated at the Jesuit Colegio de San Luis Gonzaga, Puerto de Santa María, 1912–17; studied painting in Madrid, 1917, and lived at the Residencia de Estudiantes. **Family:** Married María Teresa León c. 1930; one daughter. **Career:** Worked as an impressionist and cubist painter until 1923; suffered from tuberculosis, 1923–24; co-founder, with his wife, *Octubre* magazine, 1934; director, Museo Romántico, Madrid, from 1936; co-founder and co-director, *El Mono Azul*, 1936–38; supported Republican government during Spanish Civil War (1936–39): co-founder, 1936, then secretary, Alliance of Anti-Fascist Intellectuals; subsequently joined the Communist Party; after the War, went into self-imposed exile: in Paris, 1939–40, Buenos Aires, 1940–63, and Rome, 1963–77; returned to Spain, 1977; elected deputy for the province of Cádiz, 1977. Lives in Barcelona. **Awards:** National literature prize, 1925; Lenin prize, 1965; Etna-Taormina prize, 1975; Strega prize, 1976; Kristo Botev de Bulgaria prize, 1980; National Theatre prize, 1981; Pedro Salinas prize, 1981; Cervantes prize, 1983. Honorary doctorates: University of Toulouse, 1982; University of Cádiz, 1985. Commandeur de l'Ordre des Arts et des Lettres (France), 1982. **Died:** 28 October 1999, Puerto de Santa María, Spain.

PUBLICATIONS

Verse

Marinero en tierra. 1925; edited by José Luis Tejada, 1987.
La amante: Canciones. 1926.
El alba del alhelí. 1927.
Sobre los ángeles. 1929; as *Concerning the Angels*, translated by Geoffrey Connell, 1967.
Cal y canto. 1929.
Consignas. 1933.

Un fantasma recorre Europa. 1933; as *A Spectre Is Haunting Europe: Poems of Revolutionary Spain,* translated by Ira Jan Wallach and Angel Flores, 1936.

Poesía 1924–1930. 1934.

Verte y no verte. 1934.

13 bandas y 48 estrellas. 1936.

Poesía 1924–1937. 1938.

Poesía 1924–1938. 1940.

Entre el clavel y la espada 1939–1940. 1941.

Vida bilingüe de un refugiado español en Francia. 1942.

Antología poética 1924–1940. 1942.

Pleamar 1942–1944. 1944.

Selected Poems, translated by Lloyd Mallan. 1944.

A la pintura: Cantata de la línea y del color. 1945; revised editions, 1948 and 1953; as *A la pintura,* translated by Ben Belitt, 1972.

Antología poética 1924–1944. 1945; revised edition, 1959.

Poesía 1924–1944. 1946.

El ceñidor de Venus desceñido. 1947.

Coplas de Juan Panadero (Libro I). 1949.

Buenos Aires en tinta china, edited by Attilio Rossi. 1951.

Retornos de lo vivo lejano 1948–1952. 1952; revised edition, 1972.

Ora marítima. 1953.

Baladas y canciones del Paraná. 1954.

Diez liricografías. 1954.

María Carmen Portela. 1956.

Sonríe China, with María Teresa León, illustrated by Alberti. 1958.

Cal y canto; Sobre los ángeles; Sermones y moradas. 1959.

El otoño otra vez. 1960.

Los viejos olivos. 1960.

Poesías completas. 1961.

Diez sonetos romanos. 1964.

Abierto a todas horas 1960–1963. 1964.

El poeta en la calle: Poesía civil 1931–1965. 1966.

Selected Poems, edited and translated by Ben Belitt. 1966.

Poemas de amor. 1967.

Balada de la bicicleta con alas. 1967.

Roma, peligro para caminantes 1964–1967. 1968.

Libro del mar, edited by Aitana Alberti. 1968.

Poesía anteriores a Marinero en tierra 1920–1923. 1969.

Los ocho nombres de Picasso, y No digo más que lo que no digo 1966–1970. 1970; *Los ochos nombres de Picasso* as *The Eight Names of Picasso,* translated by Gabriel Berns and David Shapiro, 1992.

Canciones del alto valle del Aniene, y otros versos y prosas 1967–1972. 1972.

Poesía 1924–1967, edited by Aitana Alberti. 1972.

The Owl's Insomnia: Poems (selection), edited and translated by Mark Strand. 1973.

Poemas del destierro y de la espera, edited by J. Corredor-Matheos. 1976.

Poesía. 1976.

Coplas de Juan Panadero 1949–1977; Vida bilingüe de un refugiado español en Francia 1939–1940. 1977; *Coplas de Juan Panadero* as *Poética de Juan Panadero,* 1987.

Poesía 1924–1977. 1977.

Sobre los ángeles; Sermones y morales; Yo era tonto y lo que he visto ha hecho dos tontos. 1977.

Poemas anteriores a Marinero en tierra; Marinero en tierra; La amante; Dos estampidas reales; El alba del ahelí. 1978.

Los cinco destacagados. 1978.

Signos del día; La primavera de los muebles. 1978.

El matador: Poemas escénicos 1961–1965. 1979.

Fustigada luz (1972–1978). 1980.

Canto de siempre. 1980.

101 sonetos (1924–1975). 1980.

Antología, edited by Jerónimo Pablo González Martín. 1980.

The Other Shore: 100 Poems, edited by Kosrof Chantikian, translated by José A. Elgorriaga and Paul Martin. 1981.

Versos sueltos de cada día: Primer y segundo cuadernos chinos (1979–1982). 1982.

X a X: Una correspondencia en verso (inedita) Roma—Madrid, with José Bergamín. 1982.

Robert Motherwell, el Negro, illustrated by Robert Motherwell. 1983.

Antología poética, edited by Natalia Calamaí. 1983.

Todo el mar. 1986.

Los hijos del drago, y otros poemas. 1986.

Golfo de sombras. 1986.

Retornos de un isla dichosa, y otros poemas. 1987.

Cuatro canciones. 1987.

Accidente: Poemas del hospital. 1987.

Canciones para Altair. 1989.

Antología comentada, edited by María Asunción Mateo. 2 vols., 1990.

Noventa poemas. 1992.

Plays

El hombre deshabitado (produced 1931). 1930; edited by Gregorio Torres Nebrera, with *Noche de guerra en el Museo del Prado,* 1991.

Santa Casilda (produced 1931).

Fermín Galán (produced 1931). 1931.

La pájara pinta (produced 1931?). 1964; in *Lope de Vega y la poesía contemporánea,* 1964.

Bazar de la providencia (produced 1934). In *Dos farsas revolucionarios,* 1934.

Dos farsas revolucionarios: Bazar de la providencia (negocio); Farsa de los Reyes Magos. 1934.

El enamorado y la muerte (produced 1936). In *Revista de Occidente,* 128, 1973.

Los salvadores de España (produced 1936). In *Cuadernos Hispanoamericanos,* 485–486, 1990.

De un momento a otro (produced 1938). 1937; edited by Gregorio Torres Nebrera, with *El adefesio,* 1992.

Radio Sevilla (produced 1937). In *Teatro de urgencia,* 1938.

Numancia, from the play by Cervantes (produced 1937; revised version produced 1943). 1937; as *La destrucción de Numancia,* 1975.

Cantata de los héroes y la fraternidad de los pueblos (produced 1938). 1938.

El ladrón de niños, from a play by Jules Supervielle (produced 1943).

El adefesio (produced 1944). 1944; edited by Gregorio Torres Nebrera, with *De un momento a otro,* 1992.

Farsa del licenciado Pathelin, from an anonymous French play (produced 1944). 1970.

El trébol florido (produced 1966). In *Teatro,* 1950.

Teatro (includes *El hombre deshabitado; El trébol florido; La gallarda*). 1950; enlarged edition (includes *El adefesio*), 1959.

Noche de guerra en el Museo del Prado (produced 1975). 1956; edited by Gregorio Torres Nebrera, with *El hombre deshabitado*, 1991; as *Night and War in the Prado Museum*, translated by Lemuel Johnson, in *Modern Spanish Theatre*, edited by Michael Benedikt and George E. Wellwarth, 1968.

Las picardías de Scapin, from a play by Molière (produced 1958).

El testamento de la rosa (produced 1962). In *Poemas escénicos*, 1962.

Poemas escénicos (dramatic poems). 1962.

La Lozana andaluza, from a work by Francisco Delicado (produced 1980). In *Teatro 2*, 1964.

Teatro 2 (includes *La Lozana andaluza; De un momento a otro; Noche de guerra en el Museo del Prado*). 1964.

El despertar a quien duerme, from a play by Lope de Vega (produced 1978). In *Primer Acto*, 178, 1975.

Screenplay: *La dama duende*, with María Teresa León, 1944.

Fiction

Selectiones: Relatos y prosa. 1980.

Prosas. 1980.

Prosas Encontradas, compilation and prologue by Robert Marrast, 2000.

Other

La poesía popular en la lírica española contemporánea. 1933.

Nuestra diaria palabra. 1936.

Defensa de Catalunya. 1937.

El poeta en la España de 1931. 1942.

La arboleda perdida, y otras prosas. 1942; revised edition, 1959; as *The Lost Grove: Autobiography of a Spanish Poet in Exile*, edited and translated by Gabriel Berns, 1976.

Eh, los toros!, illustrated by Luis Seoane. 1942.

Imagen primera de Rafael Alberti (1940–1944). 1945.

Suma taurina: Verso, prosa, teatro, illustrated by Alberti, edited by Rafael Montesinos. 1963.

Lope de Vega y la poesía contemporánea (includes the play *La pájara pinta*). 1964.

Prosas encontradas 1924–1942, edited by Robert Marrast. 1970.

A Year of Picasso's Paintings. 1971.

Obras completas. 7 vols., 1972–88.

Picasso, el rayo que no cesa. 1975.

Maravillas con variaciones acrósticas en el jardín de Miró. 1975.

Teatro de agitación política, with others. 1976.

Cuaderno de Rute (1925): Un libro inédito. 1977.

Conversaciones con Rafael Alberti, with José Miguel Velloso. 1977.

Picasso (catologue), with others. 1977.

El poeta en la calle; De un momento a otro; Vida bilingüe de un refugiado español en Francia (poetry and plays). 1978.

Lo que conté y dije de Picasso. 1981.

Aire, que me lleva el aire (for children). 1981.

Federico García Lorca, poeta y amigo. 1984.

Otra Andalucía, with Julio Anguita. 1986.

A una verdad: Luis Cernuda, with others. 1988.

Obra completa, edited by Luis García Montero. 7 vols., 1988–.

La palabra y el signo. 1989.

The Bullfighter Sánchez Mejías as Elegized by Lorca, Alberti, and Diego, with verse translations and afterword by Carl W. Cobb, 1993.

Editor, *Églogas y fábulas castellanas.* 2 vols., 1944.

Editor, *Romancero general de la guerra española.* 1944.

Editor, with Guillermo de Torre, *Antología poética 1918–1936*, by Federico García Lorca. 1957.

Editor, *Poesías*, by Lope de Vega. 1965.

Editor, *Antología poética: Antonio Machado, Juan Ramón Jiménez, Federico García Lorca.* 1970.

Editor, *Antología poética*, by Pablo Neruda. 1982.

Editor and Translator, *Doinas y baladas populares rumanas.* 1964.

Translator, *Visages*, by Gloria Alcorta. 1951.

Translator, *Homenaje a la pintura*, by Robert Motherwell. 1991.

*

Critical Studies: *Rafael Alberti's Sobre los ángeles: Four Major Themes* by Cyril Brian Morris, 1966; *El mundo poético de Rafael Alberti* by Solita Salinas de Marichal, 1968: *Rafael Alberti* by Ignacio Delogue, 1972; *Rafael Alberti: Prosas encontradas 1924–1942* by Robert Marrast, 1973 (second edition); *Sobre Alberti* by Manuel Bayo, 1975; *Rafael Alberti* edited by Manuel Durán Gili, 1975; *The Theatre of Rafael Alberti* by Louise B. Popkin, 1975; *La poesía de Rafael Alberti* by Ricardo Senabre, 1977; *Rafael Alberti* by Jerónimo Pablo González Martín, 1978; *The Poetry of Rafael Alberti: A Visual Approach* by Robert C. Manteiga, 1978; *El dilema de la nostalgia en la poesía de Rafael Alberti* by Barbara Dale May, 1978; Alberti issue of *Malahat Review*, July 1978; *Revolution and Tradition: The Poetry of Rafael Alberti* by Pieter Wesseling, 1981; *El teatro de Rafael Alberti* by Giorgio Torres Nebrera, 1982; *Rafael Alberti: El escritor y la crítica* by Manuel Durán, 1984; *La poesía de Rafael Alberti* by Antonio Jimenez Millan, 1984; *Dramatists in Perspective: Spanish Theatre in the Twentieth Century* by Gwynne Edwards, 1985; *Multiple Spaces: The Poetry of Rafael Alberti* by Salvador Jiménez Fajardo, 1985; *Rafael Alberti: Poesía del destierro* by Concha Argente del Castillo, 1986; *Rafael Alberti's Poetry of the Thirties: The Poet's Public Voice* by Judith Nantell, 1986; *Antología comentada de Rafael Alberti* edited by María Asunción Mateo, 2 vols., 1990; *Inquietud y nostalgia: La poesía de Rafael Alberti* by Kurt Spang, 1990; *Rafael Alberti: Arte y poesía de vanguardia* by Pedro Guerrero Ruiz, 1991; *Lorca, Alberti, and the Theater of Popular Poetry* by Sandra Robertson, 1992; *The Crucified Mind: Rafael Alberti and the Surrealist Ethos in Spain* by Robert Harvard, 2001.

* * *

Rafael Alberti's theatre and poetry can be separated only with difficulty, for numerous areas of thematic and stylistic similarity exist. Not only does his first attempt at theatre, *La pájara pinta* [The Painted Bird], written in the *guiñolesque* (puppet) tradition, parallel early poetic works, but the surrealism of his poetry collection *Sobre los ángeles* (*Concerning the Angels*), echoes in the imagery of his play of the same period, *El hombre deshabitado* [The Uninhabited Man]. Several of his Civil War plays repeat the titles and themes of poetry collections produced during the conflict (1936–39), while the later play *Noche de guerra en el Museo del Prado* (*Night and War in the Prado Museum*) connects directly to *A la pintura* [To Painting], poetry written in exile and devoted to his cherished avocation.

Alberti is considered primarily a poet, and his fame rests on his lyrics; yet his plays have been performed by numerous troupes since Franco's death: he is not an insignificant dramatist. His plays are largely historical, and their political—even propagandist—intent dominates his "urgent theatre" (including *Bazar de la providencia* [Bazaar of Providence], *Farsa de los Reyes Magos* [Farce of the Three Kings], *Los salvadores de España* [Saviours of Spain], *Radio Sevilla* [Radio Seville], and *Cantata de los héroes y de la fraternidad de los pueblos* [Song of Heroes and Fraternity Among Peoples]). Because the propagandist content, resulting from war-time urgency, is less overt in *Night and War in the Prado Museum*, this play (influenced by Bertolt Brecht both in its staging conventions—it has a play within the play—and its intent) exemplifies his best political theatre. Recalling the Nationalist bombardment of Madrid, the play depicts efforts of Republican militia and partisans to save national treasures. Characters from Goya's paintings are brought to life to join contemporary patriots in their struggle. Political ideology is essentially absent in earlier plays such as *Fermín Galán*, and is not the major thrust of the plays *De un momento a otro* [From One Moment to the Next], *El trébol florido* [The Flowering Clover], *La gallarda* [The Graceful Woman], or *El adefesio* [The Ridiculous Gentleman]. *La Lozana andaluza* [The Attractive Andalusian Woman] is based on the 1528 picaresque novel by Francisco Delicado.

As one of the more versatile and prolific poets of the Generation of 1927 (which included equally famous contemporaries such as Federico García Lorca, Vicente Aleixandre, and Luis Cernuda), Alberti evolves similarly to those colleagues who survived the Civil War, from early post-romanticism through the baroque, neo-Gongorine mode for which the generation first became known, through subsequent vanguardist experimentation, and then to war-influenced political commitment and engagement. Despite relatively facile initial success with his first three collections, *Marinero en tierra* [Landlocked Sailor], *La amante* [The Lover], and *El alba del alhelí* [Dawn of the Gillyflower], rooted in Spain's popular oral balladry tradition, Alberti consciously incorporated generational innovations in his own verse. Thus a more stylized, baroque poetry appears in *Cal y canto* [Whitewash and Song], whose later poems reflect influences of the Ultraist movement. *Concerning the Angels* (written during a personal crisis) is Alberti's most surrealist work.

The *engagé* ideological nature of his 1930s poetry intensifies from the transitional civil elegy, "Con los zapatos puestos tengo que morir" [I Must Die with My Shoes On] through *Consignas* [Watchword], *Un fantasma recorre Europe* (*A Spectre Is Haunting Europe*), and *13 bandas y 48 estrellas* [13 Bars and 48 Stripes], culminating in *El poeta en la calle* [The Poet in the Street], "omances de la guerra de España" [Spanish War Ballads], and *De un momento a otro* [From One Moment to the Next]. Reflections of exile appear in *Vida bilingüe de un refugiado español en Francia* [The Bilingual Life of a Spanish Refugee in France] and collections written in Argentina: *Entre el clavel y la espada* [Between the Carnation and the Sword]; *Pleamar* [High Tide]; *Retornos de lo vivo lejano* [Songs of a Vivid Past], re-creating some especially significant moments in the poet's life; *Buenos Aires en tinta china* [Buenos Aires in Indian Ink]; and "Poemas de Punta del Este" [Poems from Punta del Este]. Alberti's leftist political connections motivate a continuing vein of Marxist ideology in much of his exile poetry, notably in *Coplas de Juan Panadero* [Ditties of Juan the Baker] and "La primavera de los pueblos" [Springtime of the Peoples]. *Sonríe China* [China Smiles], done in collaboration with his wife, María Teresa León, followed a visit to China.

Alberti's best poetry from Argentina celebrates his paternity and love for his daughter, born in exile, in *Pleamar*, and *Baladas y canciones del Paraná* [Songs and Ballads of the Paraná River]. In Italy, Alberti's political fervour slowly waned, and other emphases appear in *Poemas de amor* [Love Poems], *Roma, peligro para caminantes* [Rome, Danger for Pedestrians], *Los ocho nombres de Picasso* (*The Eight Names of Picasso*), and *Canciones del alto valle del Aniene* [Songs of the Upper Aniene Valley]. *El matador: Poemas escénicos* [The Matador: Scenic Poems] reveals that the bullfight continues to fascinate Alberti just as when he wrote his early elegy on the death of Ignacio Sánchez Mejías, "Verte y no verte" [To See You and Not See You].

The partisan nature of Alberti's political poetry makes it difficult to read or judge impartially, and certain critics have dismissed it as tendentious and overly propagandist. Some of his verse is excessively allegorical, yet it contains unique rhetorical and metrical innovations and many expressive images, particularly in *Entre el clavel y la espada*, his most creative political expression. The best-known, most frequently studied and anthologized of Alberti's poems are in his first four collections. The childlike perspective and notes of fantasy with which the poet re-creates his native fishing village in *Marinero en tierra* make it a mythical paradise, and here, as in *La amante*, the poet's great love for the sea imbues his lines with lyric passion.

Nevertheless, the darkly serious, subjective poems of *Concerning the Angels* are considered by many his greatest achievement. Through contrasts (of good and evil, light and dark) and antithetical images, Alberti portrays his emotional crisis in an oneiric landscape of air and fire. Another critical favourite, *El alba del alhelí*, recreates popular customs, myths, and beliefs of Andalusia, expressing rural traditions, joys, and sufferings through popular metric forms drawn from oral culture. The unpretentious early works have proven to be the most widely known and enduring aspects of Alberti's work.

—Janet Pérez

ÂL-E AHMAD, Jalâl

Born: Tehran, February 1923. **Education:** Finished his preliminary and high education in Tehran (*Dâr al-Fonûn*); Faculty of Letters, Theran Teachers' College, 1943–1946. **Family:** Married the writer Sîmîn Dâneshvar in 1950. **Career:** Studied English and French on his own and used his competence in translating major western works into Persian and carrying out research in sociology, anthropology and dialectology of some remote areas of Iran, 1956–1960. Worked as a teacher throughout his life; was actively involved in the *Tûdeh* ("People"), the local communist party, and was editor of its publications, *Mardom* and *Rahbar*, 1944–1947; Joined in the founding of the *Hezb-e zahmatkeshân* ("Toilers' Party"), 1950; supported the nationalist government of Muhammad Mosaddeq, 1951–1953; served as unofficial spokesman for the 1950s and 1960s dissident intelligentsia, and edited its two publications, *Nîrû-ye sevvom* ("Third force") and *'Elm o zendegî* ("Science and life"); composed many travel journals and village studies; his *Chahâr Ka'be* ("Four Ka'bas"), including accounts of his journeys to the U.S.S.R., United States,

Europe, and Israel, remains unpublished; in the last part of life, he tried to restore a nationalist government that would return Iran to independence. **Died:** In a village in Gilan region, 9 September 1969; according to his wife, poisoned by Shah's agents. He was buried near the Fîrûzâbâdî mosque at Shahr-e Rey, Tehran.

PUBLICATIONS

Collections of Short Stories

Dîd o bâzdîd. 1945.
Az ranj ke mîbarîm. 1947.
Se-târ. 1948; translated in *Iranian Society; An Anthology of Writings by Jalal Al-e Ahmad*, edited by Michael C. Hillman, 1982.
Zan-e ziyâdî. 1952.
Panj dastân. 1974.

Novels and Novelettes

Sargozâsht-e kandûhâ.1956.
Modîr-e madrase. 1958; as *The School Principal*, translated by John Newton, 1974.
Nûn wa'l-qalam. 1961; as *By the Pen*, translated by M. R. Ghanooparvar, 1988.
Sang-î bar gûr-î. 1964; as *A Gravestone*, 1991.
Nefrîn-e zamîn. 1967.

Essays

Haft maqâle. 1955.
Se maqâle-ye dîgar. 1960.
Gharbzadegî. 1960; as *Plagued by the West*, translated by Paul Sprachman, 1982; as *Weststruckness*, translated by John Green and Ahmad Alizadeh, 1982 (2nd ed. 1997); as *Occidentosis: A Plague from the West*, translated by R. Campbell, 1984.
Arziyâbî-e shetâbzâde. 1964.
Yek châh va do châle va masalan sarh-e ahwâlât. 1969.
Dar khedmat va khiyânat-e roushanfekrân. 1964–68.
Kârnâme-ye se sâle. 1968.
Esrâ'îl 'âmel-e emperyâlîsm. 1978.

Other

Khas-î dar mîqât. 1966.
Ourazân. 1956.
Tât-neshînhâ-ye bolûk-e Zahrâ. 1958.
Dorr-e yatîm-e Khalîj: Jazîre-ye Khârg. 1960.
Translator, *Qomârbâz (Igrok)*, by Fëdor Dostoevskij, from French.
Translator, *Bigâne (L'Etranger)*, by Albert Camus; with A. Khebrâzâde.
Translator, *Sû'e tafâhom (Le Malentendu)*, by Albert Camus.
Translator, *Bâzgasht az Shouravî (Retour d'U.R.S.S.)*, by A. Gide.
Translator, *Mâ'edahâ-ye zamînî (Les nourritures terrestres)*, by A. Gide, with P. Dâryûsh.
Translator, *Dasthâ-ye âlûde (Les mains sales)*, by J. P. Sartre.
Translator, *'Obûr az khatt (Über die Linie)*, by Ernst Jünger, with M. Hûman. 1966.
Translator, *Kargadan (Le rhinoceros)*, by E. Ionesco.

Translator, *Teshnegî o gorosnegî (La soif et la faim)*, by E. Ionesco; completed by M. Hezârkhânî. 1976.

*

Critical Studies: *Human Values in the Works of Two Persian Writers*, in *Correspondence d'Orient*, by G. R. Sabri-Tabrizi, 1970; *The Modern Literary Idiom*, in *Iran Faces the Seventies*, by E. Yarshater, 1971; *Âl-e Ahmad Fictional Legacy*, in *Iranian Studies*, 9/4, by M. Hillman, 1976; *Âl-e Ahmad, Jalâl*, in *Encyclopædia Iranica*, by J. W. Clinton, 1985. *Gecshichte und Entwicklung der modern persischen Literatur*, 1964; *Jalâl Âl-e Ahmad, écrivain iranien d'aujourd'hui*, in *Mélanges de l'Institut dominicain d'u Caire*, by G. Jourdain Monnot, 1967. *Qesse-nevîsî*, by R. Barâhenî, 1969.

* * *

Jalâl Âl-e Ahmad is one of the most eminent figures of contemporary Persian literature, basically a fiction writer, but nevertheless an equally important ideologue of modern Iran. Being very talented, energetic, and passionately interested in the fate of his nation's culture and political future, he played a decisive role in shaping the mind and actions of an entire generation of young intellectuals. In many respects he is a literary precursor of Dr. 'Alî Sharî'atî who couldn't surpass Âl-e Ahmad in literary excellence.

Jalâl Âl-e Ahmad's typical telegraphic prose, revealing both arrogance and impatience even in syntax and rhythm, became a pattern for many Iranian young aspiring writers. He impressed the audience as one who knew the troubles and had the remedy for the problems of his country; critics termed him the "wide-awake conscience" of Iran.

Âl-e Ahmad published writings fill more than twenty volumes and include, not to mention the works of fiction for which he is most admired, travel journals, translations, village studies, essays, and reviews. His first published story, *Ziyârat* [The Pilgrimage], appeared in the March 21st (*nourûz*, the Iranian New Year's Day) issue of *Sokhan* in 1945. An immediate critical success, it was republished at the end of the same year in his first published collection of stories, *Dîd o bâzdîd* [The Exchange of Visits]. His anti-religious stance in those stories marked his complete break with Islam and his family background (he belonged to a family of strong religious traditions). Three more collections of stories followed in the next seven years: *Az ranj ke mîbarîm* [From Our Suffering], *Se-târ* [The Sitar] and *Zan-e ziyâdî* [The Superfluous Woman], respectively in 1947, 1948, and 1952. His stories are detailed sketches from the ordinary events of daily life; one of his critics likens him to a photographer who can convey the whole complex emotional universe of ordinary people by the careful arrangement of ordinary snapshots (B. Alavi, *Gecshichte*, pp.221–23). Âl-e Ahmad turned to the composition of longer works in 1954, and in 1958 published his most celebrated novel, *Modîr-e madrase* [The School Principal]; these novelettes have more extended plots than the earlier short stories, but share with them a taste for incident, an emphasis on colloquial and idiomatic language, and an understated style of characterisation of the psychological and emotional depths of the individuals portrayed. The themes of Âl-e Ahmad fiction are diverse; prominent among them, however, are the superstitious beliefs of the common people, recorded in people's own language; excess of the clergy in their exploitation of the visible advantages of religion; and intrusion of western ideas into Iranian traditional ideology.

But the fame of Al-e Ahmad increased considerably with his most widely known work of non-fiction, *Gharbzadegî* (a Persian compound word whose meaning is approximately "weststruckness" or "occidentosis"). This work has more the quality of polemic than of reasoned historical argument, and gives voice to the widespread belief that Iranian culture is endangered by the forces for change now at work within it. The importance of Âl-e Ahmad's work was rediscovered by the Islamic intelligentsia during the 1979 Revolution when his anthropological research in remote areas of rural Iran helped to bolster his re-evaluation of Islam.

The two elements of Jalâl Âl-e Ahmad's work that appear to have made the greatest impression on his younger contemporaries are his deep sense of social commitment and his prose style. He was well read in such modern French writers as Camus, Sartre and Céline, but was also a careful student of Persian literature, both classical and modern. From this various sources he elaborated a powerful and idiomatic style, that is a vivid representation of colloquial speech and yet as richly suggestive as classical prose.

See the essay on *Plagued by the West*.

ALEIXANDRE (MERLO), Vicente

Born: Seville, Spain, 26 April 1898, Family moved to Malaga, 1900, and to Madrid, 1909. **Education:** Educated at the Colegio Teresiano, Madrid, 1909–13; entered Central School of Commerce and the University of Madrid (Faculty of Law), 1914, licence in law and diploma in business administration, both 1919. **Career:** Lecturer in mercantile law, Central School of Commerce, Madrid, 1919–22; worked for Andalusian Railroads, 1921–25: had to retire on grounds of ill health, 1925; staff member, *La Semana Financiera* magazine; full-time writer from 1925; suffered serious illness, 1936–39. **Awards:** National literature prize, 1933; Spanish Academy prize, 1934; Critics prize, 1963, 1969, 1975; Nobel prize for literature, 1977. Honorary fellow, Professors of Spanish Association (USA). Grand Cross of Order of Carlos III, 1977. **Member:** Royal Spanish Academy, 1949, Hispanic Society of America, and Monde Latin Academy, Paris. Corresponding member, Arts Academy, Malaga, and Sciences and Arts Academy, Puerto Rico. **Died:** 13 December 1984.

PUBLICATIONS

Verse

Ámbito. 1928.
Espadas como labios. 1932; edited by José Luis Cano, with *La destrucción o El amor*, 1972.
Pasión de la tierra. 1935; revised edition, 1946; edited by Luis Antonio de Villena, 1976, and by Gabriele Morelli, 1987.
La destrucción o el amor. 1935; edited by Jose Luis Cano, with *Espadas como labios*, 1972; as *Destruction of Love*, in *Destruction of Love and Other Poems*, translated by S. Kessler, 1977.
Sombra del paraíso. 1944; edited by Leopoldo de Luis, 1976; selection as *Poemas paradisíacos*, 1952, edited by Jose Luis

Cano, 1977; as *Shadow of Paradise*, translated by Hugh A. Harter (bilingual edition), 1987.
Mundo a solas 1934–1936. 1950.
Nacimiento último. 1953.
Historia del corazón. 1954.
Mis poemas mejores. 1956; revised editions, 1966, 1968, 1976.
Poesías completas. 1960.
Poemas amorosos. 1960; revised edition, 1970.
Antigua casa madrileña. 1961.
Picasso, edited by A. Caffarena Such. 1961.
En un vasto dominio. 1962.
Presencias. 1965.
Retratos con nombre. 1965.
Dos vidas. 1967.
Poemas de la consumación. 1968.
Poemas varios. 1968.
Poesía superrealista. 1971.
Antología del mar y la noche, edited by J. Lostale. 1971.
Sonido de la guerra. 1972.
Arguijo: Obra poética. 1972.
Diálogos del conocimiento. 1974.
Antología total, edited by Pere Gimferrer. 1975.
Antología poética, edited by Leopoldo de Luis. 1977.
Twenty Poems (bilingual edition), translated by Robert Bly and Lewis Hyde. 1977.
A Longing for the Light: Selected Poems, edited and translated by Lewis Hyde. 1979.
The Crackling Sun: Selected Poems, translated by Louis M. Bourne. 1981.
A Bird of Paper, translated by Willis Barnstone and David Garrison. 1982.
Primeros poemas. 1985.
Nuevos poemas varios, edited by Irma Emiliozzi and Alejandro Duque Amuseo. 1987.
Vicente Aleixandre para niños, edited by Leopoldo de Luis. 1988.
En gran noche: Últimos poemas, edited by Carlos Bousoño and Alejandro Duque Amusco. 1991.

Other

En la vida del poeta: El amor y la poesía. 1950.
El niño ciego de Vázquez Díaz. 1954.
Algunos caracteres de la nueva poesía española. 1955.
Los encuentros. 1958; enlarged edition, edited by José Luis Cano, 1985.
Obras completas. 1968; revised edition, 2 vols., 1977–78.
Epistolario, edited by José Luis Cano, 1986.
Prosas recobradas, edited by Alejandro Duque Amusco. 1987.
Miré los muros: Textos inéditos y olvidados. 1991.
Antología esencial. 1993.
Album: Versos de Juventud: Vicente Aleixandre, Dámaso Alonso y Otros, edition, prologue and notes by Alenjandro Duque Amusco y María-Jesús Velo García, 1993.

*

Critical Studies: *La poesía de Vicente Aleixandre* by Carlos Bousoño, 1950, revised editions, 1968, 1977; *Vicente Aleixandre* by Leopoldo de Luis, 1970, revised edition as *Vida y obra de Vicente Aleixandre*, 1978; *Vicente Aleixandre* (in English) by Kessel Schwartz, 1970; *La* *poesía superrealista de Vicente Aleixandre* by Hernán Galilea, 1971; "The Spiritualization of Matter in the Poetry of Vicente Aleixandre" by Louis M. Bourne, in *Revista de Letras*, 22, 1974; *Tres poetas a la luz de la metáfora: Salinas, Aleixandre y Guillén* by Vicente Cabrera, 1975, and *Critical Views on Vicente Aleixandre's Poetry* (includes translations) edited by Cabrera and Harriet Boyar, 1979; *Vicente Aleixandre* edited by José Luis Cano, 1977; *Conocer: Vicente Aleixandre y su obra* by Antonio Colinas, 1977; *La poesía de Vicente Aleixandre* (*formacion y evolución*) by Vicente Granados, 1977; *La palabra poética de Vicente Aleixandre* by D. Puccini, 1979; *Vicente Aleixandre: A Critical Appraisal* edited by Santiago Daydí-Tolson, 1981; *Vicente Aleixandre* by J.O. Jiménez, 1981; *Vicente Aleixandre's Stream of Lyric Consciousness* by Daniel Murphy, 2001.

* * *

Educated in strict religious private schools, Vicente Aleixandre had no contact with poetry until a chance acquaintance with the future poetry critic Dámaso Alonso, in the summer of 1917, initiated him into it, via the latter's enthusiasm for Rubén Darío. Aleixandre read Antonio Machado and Juan Ramón Jiménez, under whose influence he wrote his first lyrics (never published). The modernist sensibility was foreign to him, but Gustavo Adolfo Bécquer and the Romantics were to be lasting influences, as were the mystic poets, especially St. John of the Cross.

Fearing an adverse reception, he kept his poetic activity secret until some poems composed in isolated convalescence in the Guadarrama Mountains were read by friends, who published them in Ortega y Gasset's prestigious *Revista de Occidente* under the title "Número" [Number], reflecting the "dehumanized" vogue of poetry of the day. Aleixandre's association with other poets of the Generation of 1927 dates from this time: friendships were initiated with Gerardo Diego, Jorge Guillén, Luis Cernuda, Frederico García Lorca, and Miguel Hernández (and he had met Rafael Alberti at an art exhibition in 1922). Aleixandre participated in the group's homage to the baroque poet Góngora in 1927, and with these colleagues he subsequently moved toward vanguardism.

His first collection, *Ámbito* [Ambit], like "pure poetry" of that time, sought the geometric ideal of its practitioners whose poems were conceived as polyhedrons. None the less, *Ámbito* was typical of Aleixandre, in its symbols of sea and night (which recur throughout his work) and in its irrational, elusive imagery. Insistent chiaroscuro and visions of cosmic love convey the poet's attempts to fuse with the universe. The surrealistic prose poems of *Pasión de la tierra* [Passion of the Earth] reflect Aleixandre's discovery of Freud (he read the Spanish translation of *The Interpretation of Dreams* in 1928). *Pasión de la tierra* has been considered one of the key works of Spanish surrealism, despite the author's denials of such descriptions. In 1971, Aleixandre published an anthology entitled *Poesía superrealista*, seemingly accepting the label at last. Spanish surrealism is an unorthodox variant, also called "super-realism," "hyper-realism," and even "neo-Romanticism." While some critics consider it an offshoot of French surrealism, others find its origins in the painters Goya and Solana, and the "grotesque" plays (*esperpentos*) of Valle-Inclán. Vanguardism in Spain in the late 1920s was not exclusively surrealist, nor were there collective surrealist manifestos, although Aleixandre is reputed to have planned one together with Luis Cernuda and Emilio Prados. Irrationalism and a search for new techniques stand in lieu of common norms, formulated doctrines, and the desire to scandalize.

Like most other Spanish writers classed as surrealist (Lorca, Cernuda, Alberti), Aleixandre is unorthodox, rejecting "automatic writing," but suppressing logical control via elimination of nexus. He employs normal punctuation in *Pasión de la tierra*, but not in *Espadas como labios* [Swords like Lips] which juxtaposes love and death, offering glimpses of an irrational, erotic pantheism in which Thanatos and Eros are interchangeable.

La destrucción o el amor (*Destruction of Love*), won the National literature prize in 1933, and for many represents the zenith of Aleixandre's surrealism. Its exuberant vitalism, directly linked to his illness and successful fight for life, depicts unleashed cosmic forces in a mysterious universe, where nature is simultaneously destroyed and created, and where the inanimate triumphs over the living. Filled with images of light and darkness, the volume has an internal logic resulting from its amorous unity showing love as an all-consuming force.

The pessimistic *Mundo a solas* [World Alone], written shortly after the death of his mother, abounds in telluric beings and powers, expressing a passionate striving towards love, but not exempt from cruelty and morbidity. *Sombra del paraíso* (*Shadow of Paradise*), a book of light and clarity, masterful chiaroscuro, and experimental metaphors, depicts a purified pre-human world of beauty and innocence. The atmosphere is Mediterranean, pantheistic, mythic, with the major theme being the poet's lost paradise of infancy and childhood in Mélaga.

Aleixandre describes his works as being illuminated by varicoloured lights—black in *Pasión*, red in *Destruction of Love*, brighter colours in *Mundo a solas*, and, in *Shadow of Paradise*, the white glare of midday. In *Nacimiento último* [Final Birth], a transitional work closing his cosmic cycle, light becomes diaphanous, transparent. Aleixandre's development from the surrealistic prose poems of *Pasión de la tierra* to the stark vision of death in *Nacimiento último* becomes, metaphorically, a drama of progressive enlightenment or illumination. The final stage of this progression is *Historia del corazón* [History of the Heart], with its gamut of light and shade, a turning point emphasizing historical existence, human joys, and sorrows, in a temporal rather than cosmic universe. Considered Aleixandre's masterpiece by most critics, *Historia del corazón* marks man's emergence from the background of the poetry to assume the role of protagonist in the poet's post-war historical and social preoccupations.

En un vasto dominio [In a Vast Domain] unites the human and the cosmic elements through love, its title reflecting the presence of the collectivity. *Poemas de ta consumación* [Poems of Consummation] explores the epistemological preoccupations of the ageing poet, who meditates on knowledge, doubt, hope, youth, and old age, as he approaches death. *Diálogos del conocimiento* [Dialogues of Knowledge], Aleixandre's final collection, published when the poet was 76, introduces several speakers whose monologues contrast sensuality and meditation and juxtapose intuitive, existential, idealistic, cynical, and transcendental views.

Social poetry in Spain during the 1950s and 1960s was essentially political, an implied indictment of the ideology perpetuating social injustice—poetry of protest. Aleixandre's treatment of existential material is far removed from sociopolitical criticism and the manner of a sociological casebook to which much poetry of these years descended. His final poetry is less exuberant in its imagery, more restrained and reflective, without being totally purged of surrealistic elements. His last works do not merely repeat the forms of earlier ones, but evolve toward greater sobriety and thoughtfulness—poetry of the intellect and intuition, poetry as epistemology, meditations upon the metaphysical, rendered in a manner somewhere between that of the philosopher and the mystic.

—Janet Pérez

ALFIERI, Vittorio

Born: Asti, Italy, 16 January 1749. **Education:** Educated at Royal Academy, Turin, 1759–66. **Military Service:** Served as an ensign, 1766 (resigned commission, 1774). **Career:** Travelled extensively in Europe, 1767–72; began lifelong relationship with Luisa Stolberg, Countess of Albany, 1777; fled from revolutionary Paris with the Countess, 1792, settled in Florence; left Florence during the French occupation. **Died:** 8 October 1803.

PUBLICATIONS

Collections

Opere postume. 13 vols., 1804.
Opere, edited by Francesco Maggini. 1926–33.
Opere, edited by Luigi Fassò and others. 35 vols., 1951–.
Opere I, edited by Mario Fabini and Arnaldo DiBenedetto. 1977.
Antologia Poetica, 1993.

Plays

Tragedie. 3 vols., 1783–85, enlarged edition, 1789.
Tragedie. 6 vols., 1787–89; edited by U. Brilli, 1961.
The Tragedies, translated by Charles Lloyd. 4 vols., 1815; revised edition, edited by E.A. Bowring, 2 vols., 1876; with introduction by Sergio Romagnoli, 1993.
Commedie, edited by Simona Costa. 1990.

Verse

L'America libera: Odi. 1784; as *Ode to America's Independence,* translated by Adolph Caso (bilingual edition), 1976.
Parigi sbastigliata. 1789.
Rime. 1789.
L'Etruria vendicata. 1800.

Other

La virtù sconosciuta: Dialogo. 1786.
Della tirannide. 1789; as *Of Tyranny,* translated by Julius A. Molinaro and Beatrice Corrigan, 1960.
Del principe e delle lettere. 1795; edited by Luigi Rosso, 1943; as *The Prince and Letters,* translated by Julius A. Molinaro and Beatrice Corrigan, 1972.
Il misogallo: prose e rime. 1799.
Vita. 1806; as *Memoirs,* translated anonymously, 1810, revised edition, by E.R. Vincent, 1961; as *The Autobiography of Vittorio Alfieri,* translated by C. Edwards Lester, 1845, and by Henry McAnally, 1949; as *Life of Vittorio Alfieri,* 1877.
Mirandomi in Appannato Specchio, 1994.
Translator, *Panegirico a Trajano,* by Pliny. 1787.
Translator, [Works], by Sallust. 1826.

*

Bibliography: *Bibliografia di Vittorio Alfieri* by G. Bustico, 3rd edition, 1927; *La critica alfieriana* by W. Binni, 1951.

Critical Studies: *Vittorio Alfieri: Forerunner of Italian Nationalism* by Gaudens Megaro, 1930; *Alfieri: A Biography* by Charles R.D. Miller, 1936; *Ritratto dell'Alfieri* by Mario Fubini, 1967; *Saggi alfieriani* by Walter Binni, 1969; *Studi e ricerche sulla genesi e le fonti delle commedie alfieriane* by Giuseppe Santarelli, 1971; *Alfieri comico* by V. Placella, 1973; *Studi alfieriani vecchi e nuovi* by Carmine Mensi, 1974; *Gli affetti nella tragedia di Vittorio Alfieri* by Pino Mensi, 1974; *Vittorio Alfieri* by Guido Nicastro, 1974; *Di Vittorio Alfieri e della tragedia* by F. Portinari, 1976; *Il messaggio poetico dell'Alfieri: La natura del limite tragico* by Mario Travato, 1978; *Vittorio Alfieri* (in English) by Franco Betti, 1984; *Vittorio Alfieri e la cultura piemontese fra illuminismo e rivoluzione* edited by Giovanna Ioli, 1985; *Lo Stile e l'Idea: Elaborazione dei Trattati Alfierani* by Guido Santato, 1994; *Studi Alfieriani* by Walter Binni, 1995; *L'altro Alfieri: Politica e Letteratura Nelle Satire* by Giulio Carnazzi, 1996; *Il Nano e il Gigante e Altri Studi Alfieriani* by Massimo Manghi, 1998; *Tra Mito e Palinodia: Itinerari Alfieriani* by Guido Santato, 1999; *Vittorio Alfieri e le Sue Tragedie* by Pietro Seddio, 1999.

* * *

"A truly remarkable individual," Vittorio Alfieri was called by his contemporary Alessandro Verri, a judgement anyone will concur in who reads the *Vita* (*Memoirs*) without being waylaid, as earlier critics were, by doubts as to their reliability. From 1775, after having spent six restless years in intellectually stimulating European travels and three years in frivolous aristocratic pursuits in Turin, Alfieri turned to literature, and henceforth his life was intensely and singlemindedly devoted to his studies and his writing. His major public objective was to give Italy tragedy, the genre it lacked almost completely and which had recently been brought to new splendour in France. To achieve this he had to master a language which, as a French-speaker since birth, was virtually foreign to him. The project came to fruition in 19 tragedies (23, if the first one, rejected by him, and the so-called posthumous ones are added), their range, according to George Steiner, "an index to the romantic imagination." The style he forged for himself was unique, a radical departure from the melodious, often sing-song verses for which Italian lyric poetry, thanks to the *Arcadia* and Metastasio, was famous. "Mi trovan duro? . . . Taccia ho d'oscuro?" ("They find me difficult/harsh? . . . I have the reputation of being obscure?"), he asked in an epigram dated 30 July 1783, harbinger of his repeated efforts at self-clarification.

Alfieri's tragedies have been classified variously: chronologically by periods, treated as Greek, Roman, and modern; by themes, as tragedies of love, freedom, royal ambition, familial affections, and inner struggle; or again, as those in which fate predominates, those built on the contrast between liberty and servitude, and those in which the tyrant triumphs over his victims. But no doubt the best comprehensive commentary on his work—which he approaches both diachronically and synchronically—is his own self-exegesis: in his answer written to the critic Calsabigi in 1783, in his "Parere dell'autore su le presenti tragedie" [The Author's Opinions on the Present Tragedies] prepared for the 1789 Paris edition, repeatedly in the *Memoirs,* and indirectly but forcefully in *Del principe e delle lettere* (*The Prince and Letters*). What distinguishes Alfieri's perception of his originality is his self-knowledge: his grounding of the impulse that led him to tragedy in his passionate reaction to great deeds (such as those recorded in Plutarch's *Lives*) and his desire to emulate them in the only arena—art—in which he felt his times gave him freedom to act; and secondly, his intimate understanding of the stubborn determination needed to vanquish the difficulties of a genre which he conceived of as exceptionally concentrated and concise, making no allowances for even such normal procedures in drama as the use of secondary characters and episodic actions. Basing himself on the distinctions of classical theories of rhetoric between *inventio, dispositio*, and *elocutio* (the selection of a subject, its distribution into its component parts or acts and scenes, its expression, which in his case meant turning it into verses), he detailed the various stages through which each of his tragedies passed, incidentally leaving an analysis of composition, a blueprint for the construction of a text, which continues to be valid even today. The unity he achieves is not given; it is arrived at. But in a circular movement that goes back to the moment of "inspiration"—the *impulso naturale*, the *bollore di cuore e di mente* (the natural impulse, the excitement of heart and mind), so eloquently described in *The Prince and Letters*—he ends up by giving its due to the inescapable coherence of content and form in great art.

From the point of view of *inventio* (or originality), Alfieri thought of his tragedies as falling into two groups: the few "new" ones (on subjects never before treated in tragic form) and the majority, in which he strove to "make something new out of something old." Among the first group are two of his recognized masterpieces, *Saul* and *Mirra*, both of which depart from the model most frequently associated with Alfieri, the unmasker of arbitrary power and its trappings as analysed in the treatise *Della tirannide* (*Of Tyranny*). In the dramatization of the struggle between the aged Biblical king and the young David, in which the accent falls on the human rather than regal destiny of the "tyrant" condemned to fearful solitude, even the usual norms of neo-classical tragedy are broken by the insertion into the text of David's songs (passages that remind us that Alfieri was also a great lyric poet, in the tradition of Petrarch). In his retelling on stage of Ovid's story of the incestuous love of Mirra for her father, Alfieri defies the rules of *bienséance* and creates a work of the utmost dramatic tension as the hapless protagonist—no more than a young girl—is again and again on the verge of revealing a secret (to which the spectator who knows his classics is privy), whose ultimate telling spells self-imposed death.

—Olga Ragusa

See the essay on *Saul*.

AL-HARIRI, al-Qasim ibn 'Ali Abu Muhammad al-Basri

Born: Mashan, near Basra, Iraq, in 446 ᴀʜ/1054 ᴄᴇ. **Family:** One known son, 'Abd Allah. **Career:** Oversaw the date palm plantation that he inherited in Mashan; held a position in the intelligence branch of the central government of the Caliphate in Basra; and studied, taught, and wrote literary and grammatical works in Basra and Baghdad; his most famous work, *al-Maqamat*, was allegedly composed for Anushirwan ibn Khalid, minister to the Caliph al-Mustarshid. **Died:** 516 ᴀʜ/1122 ᴄᴇ in Basra, Iraq.

Pᴜʙʟɪᴄᴀᴛɪᴏɴꜱ

Fiction

Al-Maqamat (a linked series of stories in rhymed prose). c. 504 ᴀʜ/ 1110 ᴄᴇ; as *The Assemblies of al-Hariri*, translated by Amina Shah, 1980.

Verse

Diwan al-Hariri (collection of poetry), not extant. c. 516 ᴀʜ/1122 ᴄᴇ
Mulhat al-I'rab (a grammatical treatise in verse). c. 516 ᴀʜ/1122 ᴄᴇ

Other

Rasa'il (letters), not extant. c. 516 ᴀʜ/1122 ᴄᴇ
Durrat al-Ghawwas fi awham al-khawass (a grammatical treatise in prose). c. 516 ᴀʜ/1122 ᴄᴇ

*

Critical Studies: *Al-Maqamah* by Shawqi Dayf, 1954; *Les Seances: Recits et codes culturels chez Hamadhani et Hariri* by Abdelfattah Kilito, 1983;; *Ra'y fi al-maqamat* by Abd al-Rahman Yaghi, 1985; *al-Ghaib: Dirasah fi maqamah lil-Hariri* by Abdelfattah Kilito, 1987; *Fann al-maqamah bayna al-Badi' wa-al-Hariri wa-al-Suyuti* by Ahmad Amin Mustafa, 1991.

* * *

Al-Hariri is without a doubt best known for *al-Maqamat* (*The Assemblies of al-Hariri*), a linked series of comic stories written in rhymed prose. *Al-Maqamat* is the name of a literary genre that is first attributed to al-Hariri's predecessor, al-Hamadhani, who also wrote in Arabic (d. 398 ᴀʜ/1008 ᴄᴇ). Although al-Hariri pays homage to al-Hamadhani in his introduction to *The Assemblies of al-Hariri*, it was al-Hariri's contribution to the genre that became the model for its further development over the centuries.

While the narrative structure of the *maqamah* genre varies from author to author, in al-Hariri's case, each of the fifty stories is related by a narrator named al-Harith ibn Hammam and portrays the mischievous adventures of a lowly but eloquent character named Abu Zayd al-Saruji. Each story takes place in, and is named for, a different city of the Islamic world. The series of stories is further linked by the parallel between the first and last stories. In the first story, al-Harith witnesses Abu Zayd pretend to be an itinerant preacher in order to collect money and follows him home, only to find that he is served a lavish meal accompanied by wine, although Islamic law prohibits the drinking of alcohol. In the final story, al-Harith witnesses Abu Zayd pretend to be an itinerant preacher once again, but this time Abu Zayd repents for his mischievous ways before a large crowd in a mosque.

Al-Hariri's fame is due not only to his skillful presentation of the *maqamah* genre, but also to the newness of this genre and its importance in the development of the Arabic literary tradition. Other examples of written narrative fiction, such as animal fables and transmitted stories, were in circulation at the time. However, the *maqamah* as conceived first by al-Hamadhani and then by al-Hariri was perhaps the first example of written narrative that was openly presented as fiction rather than factual transmission. The newness of this idea of fiction is evident from biographies of al-Hariri that attempt to explain who Abu Zayd really was, although al-Hariri himself explains that he is a fictional character.

Perhaps in order to protect himself and his work in this anti-fiction literary environment, al-Hariri also suggests in his introduction that these stories, though fictional, are didactic, and thus morally acceptable and relevant to real life. The final story, in which the phony preacher repents, perhaps bears out this assertion of didactic significance. It is as if al-Hariri implies that eloquence, however refined and persuasive, is worthless without the good intention of honesty.

Although al-Hariri's role in the development of classical Arabic fiction is important to the history of Arabic literature, al-Hariri's contemporaries were much more interested in his carefully crafted style. Credit is given to his predecessor al-Hamadhani for inventing the genre of linked stories in rhymed prose, but al-Hariri is generally considered to be the superior master of style. Combining narrative fiction with verse, sermons, letters, grammatical points, and riddles in a smoothly flowing rhymed prose, al-Hariri's series of stories were considered a masterpiece of style and refined entertainment. This emphasis on style displays the relationship between al-Hariri's series of linked stories and his two grammatical works, one in prose about common mistakes (*Durrat al-Ghawwas*) and another in verse designed to introduce students to grammatical concepts (*Mulhat al-I'rab*).

The genre of linked narratives in rhymed prose, and the example of al-Hariri in particular, was widely imitated throughout the Arabic-speaking world for centuries, down to the beginning of the twentieth century and the emergence of modern forms of prose. His ornate style is still appreciated as a masterpiece of classical literature, but is no longer imitated by modern prose writers. However, the question of fiction associated with the genre of linked stories, and al-Hariri and al-Hamadhani in particular, has taken on a new significance in modern Arabic literature. Many critics reject the idea that narrative fiction in Arabic is exclusively imported from the West. They assert that classical forms of fiction, especially the orally transmitted *Thousand and One Nights* and the written genre of linked stories in rhymed prose known as the *maqamah*, constitute an Arabic fiction tradition that is independent of Western influence. Thus while al-Hariri had to defend his series of stories from accusations that they were unacceptable because of their fictional status, that same fictional status has become a source of pride for modern Arab critics.

—Jocelyn Sharlet

AL-KHANSA'

Name means "snub-nosed" or "the gazelle." **Born:** Tamadir bint Amr bin al-Harith b. al-Sharid b. Mudar, c. 575 AD, from the tribe Sulaym and the clan al-Sharid. **Family:** Married 1) her cousin Rawaha b. Abd al-'Aziyy al-Salmi; 2) Murdas Bin Abi 'Amer; four children. **Career:** Mukhadrama poetess who lived prior to and after the revelation of Islam; converted to Islam, 629 AD. **Died:** 646 AD.

PUBLICATIONS

Collections

Diwan al Khansa, translated from the text of Karim Bustani by Arthur Wormhoudt. 1973; as *Selections from the Diwan of al Khansa*, translated and commented on by Arthur Wormhoudt, 1973.

*

Critical Studies: *Commentaires sur le Diwan d'al-Khansâ*, 1896, as *Moi, poète et femme d'Arabie*, translated into French by Anissa Boumediène, 1987. *The Mute Immortals Speak: Pre-Islamic Poetry and the Poetics of Ritual* by Suzanne Pinckney Stetkevych, 1993.

* * *

Al-Khansa' is the most celebrated poetess of eulogy (*marthiyya*) in Arabic literature. Nineteenth-century Arab critics assigned al-Khansa' to secondary status in the hierarchy of Arab poets, yet she perfected the inherited forms and themes of traditional elegies by adding new expressions, emotions, and imagery. Her elegies about her brothers and children demonstrate a marked shift in emotions and imageries from previous elegies. Her eulogy for her two brothers—a blood brother Mu'awiya and a half-brother Sakhr, both killed in skirmishes with rival neighboring tribes—are characterized by their pagan metaphors and brought her much fame. After Mu'awiya's death in a raid, al-Khansa' beseeched Sakhr to take vengeance on the offending tribe. Sakhr successfully defeated the tribe and killed his brother's murderers, but he was fatally wounded in the battle. Al-khansa's focus on Sakhr in her elegies could be attributed to his generosity, for he shared his wealth with his sister on multiple occasions when her husband had squandered his money on gambling. Sakhr had suffered for a year before he died. The poems al-Khansa' wrote during that year and the elegies she wrote after his death are some of the finest elegies in Arabic literature.

Similar to her predecessor poets, al-Khansa' created an anecdotal narratives about Sakhr in which she lamented the deceased's integrity, gallantry, munificence, and justice. But to temper her strong and tender expression of perpetual grief, a grief evinced by a constant stream of tears which badly affected her eyes, she introduced new universal themes such as patience, mishaps that befall man, man's struggle with his fate, and, his ultimate surrender to God's will. Prophet Muhammad commended her themes on death and accepting God's will. Al-Khansa's poetry is characterized by the splendor of her language, genuine compassion for her brothers, beautiful sensory and pagan metaphors and similes, an economy of words, and musical rhymes, as this extract from one of her elegies for Sakhr demonstrates:

> Verily, Sakhr if you have made my eyes shed tears
> You long brought me mirth
> I had tears for you among wailing women
> I had the most reason to be the one wailing
> I incited you on the battle
> When you were alive
> But who can avert the invincible death
> Though (they say) weeping over the killed is improper
> I think crying for you is the best of the pleasant deeds.

Al-Khansa' demonstrated the excellence of her poetry and word choice in poetic competitions at the 'Ukaz market, a bazaar in the city of Mecca where, in addition to trading, Arab poets held poetry contests prior to the revelation of Islam in Mecca in 610 AD. She outwitted the prominent poet of her time, Hassan bin Thabit, in her depiction of Arab self-esteem. Well-esteemed poets such as the pre-Islamic poet al-Nabigh al-Dhubyaani asserted that no poet could match al-Khansa', and the Umayyad poet Bashshar b. Burd reported that she was better than the best poets. Arab critics considered her poetry to be paramount to the *mu'allaqat*, the fine poems that were posted on the Ka'ba, the holy place in Mecca.

Al-Khansa's life was a chain of wounds that never healed, for she lost not only her brothers, but also her four sons years later in the Qadisiyya battle in 635 AD. Though al-Khansa' exhorted her brother and children to fight for different objectives, her verses now lacked pagan imageries, less shedding of tears, and she stopped lamenting the blind twist of fate. Her suffering from the loss of her sons was more serene and congruent with the Islam that she embraced in 629. Upon hearing of their death, she reported, ''Who dies, if Islam lives?'' When the second caliph 'Umar b. al-Khattab went to offer his condolences for the deaths of her sons, al-Khansa' replied, ''Congratulate me commander of the faithful, for I'm the mother of the martyrs.'' In one of her later poems she writes:

My sons I carried you with pain and raised you with care
You have fallen today for the cause of Islam
Who says you are dead
You are very much alive
And alive with honor
I feel proud to be the mother of martyrs

Al-Khansa's poetry is compiled in *Tabaqat al-Shu'ara'* by Ibn Sallam, *al-Aghani* by al-Asfahani, and *al-'I'jaz wa al-'Ijaz* by al-Tha'alibi among many anthologies of Arabic literature. Al-Khansa's profound anguish for her brothers enriched the elegies with expansive imagery and strong emotions, and her poetry was an exquisite model for poets to come.

—Hanaa Kilany

AL-MUTANABBI, Ahmad ibn al-Husayn Abu al-Tayyib al-Ju'fi al-Kindi

Born: Kufa, Iraq, in 303 AH/915 CE. **Education:** Educated in Kufa, Iraq, and Syria. **Family:** One known son, Muhassad. **Career:** Worked as a minor panegyrist in Baghdad; led a political and religious Bedouin revolt in Syria and was imprisoned in 322 AH/933 CE; worked as a panegyrist for the Hamdanid ruler Sayf al-Dawlah in Aleppo, Syria, beginning 337 AH/948 CE; fled the Hamdanid court and worked as a panegyrist for the Ikhshidid ruler Kafur in Fustat, Egypt, then fled the Ikhshidid court and worked as a panegyrist for the Buwayhid ruler Adud al-Dawlah in Shiraz, Iran, beginning 354 AH/965 CE. **Died:** Killed when his party was attacked as he returned from Iran to Iraq in 354 AH/965 CE

PUBLICATIONS

Collections

Diwan al-Mutanabbi (poems), c. 354 AH/965 CE; *Poems of al-Mutanabbi*, translated by A. J. Arberry, 1967.

*

Critical Studies: *Un poete arabe du IVe siecle de l'Hegire (Xe siecle de J.-C.): Abou t-Tayyib al-Motanabbi* by Regis Blachere, 1935; *Dhikra Abi al-Tayyib ba'd alf 'am* by 'Abd al-Wahhab 'Azzam, 1936; *Ma'a al-Mutanabbi* by Taha Husayn, 1936; *al-Mutanabbi* by Mahmud Muhammad Shakir, 1977; *al-Harb wa-al-furusiyah fi shi'r Abi al-Tayyib al-Mutanabbi* by Husni Khidr Said; *Mimiyat al-Mutanabbi: majallat al-ibda' wa-tabi'at al-mu'alajah* by Mayy Yusuf Khulayyif; *The Composition of Mutanabbi's Panegyrics to Sayf al-Dawla* by Andras Hamori, 1992; *al-Badi' fi shi'r al-Mutanabbi* by Munir Sultan, 1993.

*   *   *

Al-Mutanabbi is the last of the four great panegyric poets in classical Arabic literature of the Islamic period. Because lyric genres, and panegyric poetry in particular, were among the most important literary forms of this period, al-Mutanabbi is considered to be a major figure in the classical Arabic heritage. His place in the tradition is the result of his innovative yet carefully crafted poetic language and his vivid portrayal of members of the elite and major events. The lyric genre used by al-Mutanabbi is known as the qasidah, a metered, monorhyme poem of about 20–100 bipartite verses.

Like many renowned Arab poets of this period, al-Mutanabbi is said to have gained his command of poetic language from time spent in the desert with pastoral Arab tribes. Whether or not this is literally true, it is certain that this theme in biographies of al-Mutanabbi emphasizes his position in a tradition that traces its roots back to the Arab tribes of pre-Islamic Arabia. Another reflection of al-Mutanabbi's position in the Arab poetic tradition is the range of commentaries on his poetry in general and on the difficult passages in particular, ranging from the eleventh century commentator al-Wahidi to the twentieth century commentator al-Barquqi. Finally, the large number of classical polemical works that praise, blame, and analyze al-Mutanabbi's poetry, such as the works of Ibn Waki' and al-Sahib ibn 'Abbad, display his importance in debates about the roles of mannerism, intertextuality, and innovation in the poetic tradition. Al-Mutanabbi's role in these debates echoes that of his predecessor Abu Tammam (d. 231 AH/850 CE), whose mannerist style appears to have influenced al-Mutanabbi's own approach to convention and innovation.

Although al-Mutanabbi praised a number of patrons over the course of his career, he is best known for his bold and heroic portrayals of the Hamdanid ruler Sayf al-Dawlah of Aleppo, Syria. Sayf al-Dawlah's numerous military campaigns on the nearby border with Byzantium provided ample material for panegyric. Perhaps the most famous of his panegyrics to Sayf al-Dawlah is his poem composed on the occasion of the siege of al-Hadath. His vivid use of figurative language and rhetorical devices contributes to the coherence of the poem and dramatizes the event that it depicts. Al-Mutanabbi's panegyrics are noteworthy for their frequent departure from the convention of beginning with a description of a love affair, instead beginning with gnomic statements and moving quickly to the serious events of the poem. Some biographers have linked his penchant for gnomic statements to his early exposure to and participation in Isma'ili movements, which is said to be the source of his nickname al-Mutanabbi, ''the one who claims to be a prophet.''

Like most panegyric poets of this period, al-Mutanabbi included invective and elegy in his repertoire, usually as a component of patronage relationships. His invectives against Kafur, the Ikhshidid ruler of Fustat, Egypt (near Cairo), which he composed as their patronage relationship deteriorated, are particularly well known. While problematic patronage relationships were not uncommon in this period, al-Mutanabbi's break with Sayf al-Dawlah and his subsequent break with Kafur indicate his power in court life and the tensions that it brought to his relationships. As for elegy, al-Mutanabbi's graceful poems in honor of Sayf al-Dawlah's mother, as well as a poem for his own grandmother, show that his abilities were not limited to the heroic mode of battle and court life.

Al-Mutanabbi's position as one of the four great panegyrists of the Islamic period has remained relatively stable throughout the intervening centuries and down to the present day. His place in school and university study of Arabic literature, as well as the constant stream of books and articles about him in Arabic and other languages, is testimony to his lasting impact on the Arabic literary tradition.

—Jocelyn Sharlet

AL-QAYS, Imru'

Also known as Imru' al-Qais, Imr al-Qays, Imru' al-Qays. **Born:** Probably in Yemen, c. AD 497. **Education:** Introduced to poetry by his uncle al-Muhalhil, his mother's younger brother; also self-taught. **Family:** Married a woman named Jundhub while in exile; one known daughter although it is unclear whether Jundhub is her mother. **Career:** Exiled twice by his father for his love of poetry; wandered the deserts of the Arabian Peninsula with companions singing, drinking, and reciting poetry; later returned to avenge his father's death. **Died:** c. AD 542, under mysterious circumstances but most likely from the bubonic plague.

PUBLICATIONS

Verse

The Diwan of Imr al Qais ibn Hujr ibn Kinda ibn Qahtan (contains commentary and Arabic texts). 1974; translated by Arthur Wormhoudt.

"The Wandering King" in *The Seven Odes: The First Chapter in Arabic Literature* by A.J. Arberry. 1957.

*

Critical Studies: *Imrulkais of Kinda, Poet Circa A.D. 500–535: The Poems, The Life, The Background* by Charles Greville Tuetey, 1977; "The Last Days of Imru' Al-Qays: Anatolia" by Irfan Shahid and "Imru' Al-Qays Praises the Prophet" by Julie Scott Meisami in *Tradition and Modernity in Arabic Literature*, edited by Issa J. Boullata and Terri DeYoung, 1997; "Regicide and Retribution: The Mu'allaqah of Imru' al-Qays" in *The Mute Immortals Speak: Pre-Islamic Poetry and the Poetics of Ritual* by Suzanne Pinckney Stetkevych, 1993; "Imru' al-Kays b. Hudjr" in *Encyclopaedia of Islam*, 1999.

*   *   *

Imru' al-Qays is considered by many Arabic literary scholars to be poet *par exellence* of the pre-Islamic period. The testimony to this

epithet is his famous *mu'allaqa*, or "Suspended Ode," which was written in *qasīda* form and composed during the sixth century AD. This literary masterpiece, only one of seven of his works to have survived, is without a doubt the most influential poem in Arabic literature not only for its premature fascinations but also for its aesthetic qualities and innovative imagery, which has served as a model for later generations of Arab poets, especially those who lived during the 'Abbāsid period (c. 750–1258 AD). Although poetry was the genre of choice for the pre-Islamic poets, only vestiges remain due to the fact that the means of transmission was strictly oral; it was not until the end of the eighth century AD that great pains were taken to collect, record, and edit this massive body of work.

Imru' al-Qays, also known as "al-Malik al-Dillīl," which can be translated as either the "Vagabond King" or the "Errant King," is believed to have been the youngest son of Hujr, reportedly the last king of Kindah, an influential South Arabian tribe who achieved prominence in the Arabian Peninsula in the fifth and sixth centuries AD. Sources mention that he was banished because he had been enamored of his cousin Fatima and had supposedly composed erotic poetry about her. Thus began perhaps the most famous chapter in Arabic literature and certainly in pre-Islamic poetry: the wayward, and oftentimes scandalous, adventures of Imru' al-Qays. After his banishment from his father's kingdom, he spent his days roaming the length and breadth of the Arabian Peninsula with a band of companions, drinking, reciting poetry, and enjoying the company of women. It was during this time, it is said, that he had learned of his father's murder while he was playing backgammon with a companion. At first, he paid no attention to the messenger, and, according to A. J. Arberry, it was only after he inquired further about his father's murder that he is said to have exclaimed, "He left me to rot when I was a boy, and now that I am a man he has loaded me with his blood." It was then that he vowed to avenge his father's death. These circumstances in Imru' al-Qays's early life provide the context for his famous *mu'allaqa*.

Imru' al-Qays's *mu'allaqa* is based on the *qasīda*, usually translated into English as "ode." This complex literary form possesses a rigid structure, and al-Qays's masterpiece consists of at least 60 couplets. Also, the poet must strictly adhere to a chosen meter, as well as follow an identical rhyme. In addition, the *qasīda* is composed of a tripartite structure: a beginning, middle, and an end. Due to this compact organization, the *qasīda* utilizes metaphor to a large extent rather than mere description in order to convey meaning.

The events in Imru' al-Qays's *mu'allaqa* revolve around two main themes: premature sexuality and the vowing of vengeance for his murdered father. In the opening section, known as the *nasīb*, we see the poet stopping at a deserted desert encampment remembering his youthful, and often scandalous, encounters with various women of his tribe. Several scholars, among them Suzanne Pinckney Stetkevych, believe that these events of this extended *nasīb*, which is longer than the traditional *nasīb*, are illustrative of the poet's "arrested development" into manhood. As Stetkevych observes, "whereas mature men are consoled or diverted from the foolish infatuations of their youth, [Imru' al-Qays's] heart remains bound to puerile passion." There are numerous other indications of Imru al-Qays's arrested development both in his real life and in his *mu'allaqa*, which in the latter takes a metaphoric form. Two examples from his poetry that demonstrate a lack of maturity are his cavalier reaction to his father's murder and the slaughtering of his camel for maidens who, instead of cooking the raw meat and consuming it, prefer simply to play with it.

The famous storm scene, reproduced in part below from quatrains 71–72, *The Mute Immortals Speak*, introduces the second major event of Imru' al-Qays's *mu'allaqa*. Since it occurs in the text where there is traditionally a battle fought and also is a fairly common metaphor in pre-Islamic poetry, it is very probable that the storm is symbolic of an engagement to have been fought in revenge for his father's murder:

> O friend, do you see the lightning?
> There is its flash—
> Like two hands shining in a high-crowned
> cumulus!
> Its flashing illumining the sky, or like
> the sudden flare of a monk's lamp
> When, tilting it, he soaks with oil
> the tightly twisted wick.

By including the storm scene, Imru' al-Qays, in effect, elevates his *qasīda* from the earthly level to that of the cosmic. Or in Stetkevych's words, "a military triumph has given way to a poetic one."

Imru' al-Qays is thought to have died in 542 AD, just a quarter of a century before the advent of Islam in the Arabian Peninsula. However, the cause of his death remains a mystery. Legend has it that he met his untimely end by wearing a poisoned robe given to him by the Emperor Justinian after having apparently seduced his daughter. However, Arabic literary scholars dismiss this account as fictitious, as history reports that Justinian was childless. It is more likely that he died of the bubonic plague, which is known to have occurred during the reign of Justinian in Ancyra (modern Ankara, the capital of Turkey) and was buried there.

—Carmen Cross

ALIGHIERI, Dante

Born: Florence, in 1265, probably late May. **Education:** Details of his education are conjectural, but he was raised as a gentleman and was an avid student of philosophy and poetry. **Military Service:** Served in the Florentine army cavalry in campaign against Arezzo, 1289; fought in battle of Campaldino. **Family:** Married Gemma di Maretto Donati in 1294 (affianced 1283), three sons and one daughter. **Career:** Met Beatrice Portinari, 1274 (died 1290); friend of Guido Cavalcanti, *q.v.*, from 1283, and associated with group of *dolce stil nuovo* poets around him; involved in Florentine civic affairs: served on people's council, 1295–96, and other councils, 1296 and 1297, and diplomatic missions to San Gimignano, 1300; one of the six priors governing Florence, 1300; in charge of road works in Florence (probably in preparation for a siege), 1301; while on a mission to Pope Boniface VIII in Rome in 1301 his party (the Whites) was defeated in Florence and he was exiled: sought refuge at courts of various Ghibelline lords in northern Italy: in San Godenzo in 1302, Forlì, 1303, and Verona, 1303; broke with other White exiles, 1304, and probably went to the university town of Bologna; agent in court of Franceschino Malaspina in the Lunigiana, 1306; in Lucca, c. 1306–08; strong supporter of the Holy Roman Empire, Henry VII of Luxemburg, 1309–13 (probably wrote *De monarchia* at this time); in Lucca, c. 1314–16; refused conditional amnesty from Florence, 1316; at court of Can Grande della Scala in Verona, 1317, and court of Guido Novello da Polento in Ravenna, c. 1317–21: sent by Guido on diplomatic mission to Venice, 1321. **Died:** 14 September 1321.

PUBLICATIONS

Collections

The Latin Works, translated by A.G. Ferrers Howell and P.H. Wicksteed. 1904.
Opere, edited by Michele Barbi and others. 2 vols., 1921–22; 2nd edition, 1960.
The Portable Dante, edited by Paolo Milano. 1947; revised edition, 1978.
Selected Works. 1972.
Opere, edited by Fredi Chiapelli. 6th edition, 1974.
Opere minore, edited by Domenico de Robertis and Gianfranco Contini. 1979–84.
Tutti le Opere. 1981.

Verse

Commedia, edited by Natalino Sapegno. 1957, also edited by Giorgio Petrocchi, 4 vols., 1966–67, and by Umberto Bosco and Giovanni Reggio, 1979; edited (with translation) by Charles S. Singleton, 6 vols., 1970–75; translated by Henry Boyd, 3 vols., 1802; numerous subsequent translations as *The Divine Comedy,* including by H.W. Longfellow, 3 vols., 1867; Laurence Binyon, 1933–46; L.G. White, 1948; Dorothy L. Savers and Barbara Reynolds, 3 vols., 1949–62; John Ciardi, 1954–70; G.L. Bickersteth, 1955; John D. Sinclair, 3 vols., 1961; Kenneth Mackenzie, 1979; C.H. Sisson, 1980; Allen Mandelbaum, 3 vols., 1980–84; Robert Pinsky, 1994; Mark Musa, 1995; Peter Dale, 1996; Elio Zappulla, 1998; as *Dante's Inferno: Translations by Twenty Contemporary Poets,* edited by Daniel Halpern, 1993; translated into prose by Charles Eliot Norton, 3 vols., 1891–92; also by J. Carlyle, T. Okey, and P.H. Wicksteed, 3 vols., 1899–1901; as *The Vision,* translated by Henry, Francis Cary, 3 vols., 1814; as *Presenting Paradise: Dante's Paradiso: Translation and Commentary* by James Torrens, 1993; as *Inferno III,* translated by Patrick Creagh and Robert Hollander, 1993; as *Hell,* translated by Steve Ellis, 1994; as *Cantos from Dante's Inferno,* translated by Armand Schwerner, 2000; as *Purgatorio,* translated by W.S. Merwin, 2000.
La vita nuova, edited by Michele Barbi. 1932, also in *Opere*, 1960, also edited by Domenico De Robertis, 1980; translated by Dante Gabriel Rossetti, in *The Early Italian Poets,* 1861; also translated by Mark Musa, 1957, revised edition, 1973; Barbara Reynolds, 1969; as *The New Life,* translated by William S. Anderson, 1964.
Eclogae latinae, edited by E. Pistelli, in *Opere.* 1960; translated by P.H. Wicksteed, 1902; also translated by W. Brewer, 1927.
Rime, edited by D. Mattalia. 1943, also edited by Gianfranco Contini, 2nd edition, 1946, and by Michele Barbi and F. Maggini, 1956; as *Il Canzoniere*, edited by G. Zonta, 1921; translated by Patrick S. Diehl, 1979.
Lyric Poetry, edited by Kenelm Foster and Patrick Boyde. 2 vols., 1967.
Eighteen Poems, translated by Anthony Conran. 1975.

Other

De vulgari eloquentia, edited by A. Marigo, revised edition, edited by P.G. Ricci. 1957, and by Pier Vincenzo Mengaldo, 1968; translated by A.G. Ferrers Howell, 1890; also translated by P.H. Wicksteed, in *Latin Works*, 1904; as *Literature in the Vernacular,* translated by Sally Purcell, 1981; translated by Steven Botterill, 1996.

De monarchia, edited by E. Rostagno, in *Opere*. 1960, also edited by P.G. Ricci, 1965, and by Bruno Nardi, in *Opere Minori*, 1979; translated by A.G. Ferrers Howell, 1890; as *Monarchy, and Three Political Letters*, translated by Donald Nicholl and Colin Hardie, 1954; as *On World-Government*, edited and translated by H.W. Schneider, 1957; as *Monarchy*, translated by Prue Shaw, 1996; as *Dante's Monarchia*, translated with commentary by Richard Kay, 1998.

Epistolae: The Letters, translated by P.H. Wicksteed. 1902; edited and translated by Paget Toynbee, 1920; revised edition, edited by Colin Hardie, 1966.

Questio de aqua et de terra, edited by E. Pistelli, in *Opere*. 1960; translated by P.H. Wicksteed, 1902, and in *Latin Works*, 1904.

Il convivio, edited by G. Busnelli and G. Vandelli. 1964, and by M. Simonelli, 1966; as *The Banquet*, translated by P.H. Wicksteed, 1903; also translated by William W. Jackson, 1909; Christopher Ryan, 1989; Richard H. Lansing, 1990.

De situ, edited by V. Biagi. 1907, and by G. Padoan, 1968.

Literary Criticism, edited by Robert S. Haller. 1973.

The Stone Beloved (selections). 1986.

The Fiore and the Detto d'amore: A Late 13th-century Italian Translation of the Roman de la Rose, Attributable to Dante, translated by Santa Casciani and Christopher Kleinhenz. 2000.

*

Critical Studies: *Studies in Dante* edited by Edward Moore, 4 vols., 1896–1917, reprinted 1968; *Dante's Ten Heavens: A Study of the Paradiso* by Edmund Garratt Gardner, 1904; *In Patriam: An Exposition of Dante's Paradiso* by John S. Carroll, 1911; *Dante and Aquinas* by P.H. Wicksteed, 1913; *Dante: Essays in Commemoration, 1321–1921*, 1921; *Symbolism in Medieval Thought and Its Consummation in the Divine Comedy* by H.F. Dunbar, 1929; *Essays on the Vita Nuova*, 1929, and *The Lady Philosophy in the Convivio*, 1938, both by James E. Shaw; *Medieval Culture: An Introduction to Dante and His Times* by Karl Vossler, translated by William Cranston Lawton, 2 vols., 1929; *Dante the Philosopher* by Étienne Gilson, translated by David Moore, 1948; *An Essay on the Vita Nuova*, 1949, in *Dante Studies, 1–2*, 1954–58, *Journey to Beatrice*, 1958, and *Dante's Commedia: Elements of Structure*, 1977, all by Charles S. Singleton; *A Handbook to Dante Studies* by Umberto Cosmo, translated by David Moore, 1950; *Dante as a Political Thinker* by A. Passerin d'Entrèves, 1952; *Dante's Drama of the Mind: A Modern Reading of the Purgatorio*, 1953, *Dante*, 1966, and *Trope and Allegory: Themes Common to Dante and Shakespeare*, 1977, all by Francis Fergusson; *Life of Dante* by Michele Barbi, translated by P. Ruggiers, 1954; *Introductory Papers on Dante*, 1954, and *Further Papers on Dante*, 1957, both by Dorothy L. Sayers; *Dante and the Idea of Rome*, 1957, and *Dante's Italy and Other Essays*, 1984, both by Charles T. Davis; *Dante and the Early Astronomers* by Mary A. Orr (2nd edition) 1957; *Structure and Thought in the Paradiso*, 1958, and *Medieval Cultural Tradition in Dante's Comedy*, 1960, both by Joseph Mazzeo; *The Ladder of Vision: A Study of Dante's Comedy* by Irma Brandeis, 1960, and *Discussions of the Divine Comedy* edited by Brandeis, 1961; *Dante, Poet of the Secular World* by Erich Auerbach, translated by Ralph Manheim, 1961; *Essays on Dante*, 1964, and *Dante's Vita Nuova*, 1973, both by Mark Musa; *Dante* by Thomas G. Bergin, 1965, as *An Approach to Dante*, 1965, and *From Time to*

Eternity: Essays on Dante's Divine Comedy edited by Bergin, 1967; *Dante: A Collection of Critical Essays* edited by John Freccero, 1965, and *Dante: The Poetics of Conversion* by Freccero, 1986; *The Mind of Dante* edited by U. Limentani, 1965; *Dante Alighieri: His Life and Works*, 1965, and *A Dictionary of Proper Names and Notable Matters in the Works of Dante*, 1968, both by Paget Toynbee; *Events and Their Afterlife: The Dialectics of Christian Typology in the Bible and Dante* by A.C. Charity, 1966; *Dante and His World* by T.C. Chubb, 1966; *Enciclopedia dantesca*, 5 vols., 1970–75; *Dante's Style in His Lyric Poetry*, 1971, *Dante Philomythes and Philosopher: Man in the Cosmos*, 1981, and *Perception and Passion in Dante's Comedy*, 1993, all by Patrick Boyde; *The Greatness of Dante Alighieri* by Herbert William Smith, 1974; *Dante's Epic Journeys* by David Thompson, 1974; *Companion to the Divine Comedy: Commentary* by C.H. Grandgent, 1975; *Dark Wood to White Rose* by Helen M. Luke, 1975; *Woman, Earthly and Divine, in the Comedy of Dante* by Marianne Shapiro, 1975; *The Two Dantes, and Other Studies* by Kenelm Foster, 1977, and *Cambridge Readings in Dante's Comedy* edited by Foster and Patrick Boyde, 1981; *Dante Commentaries*, 1977, and *Dante Soundings: Eight Literary and Historical Essays*, 1981, both edited by David Nolan; *Dante's Paradiso and the Limitations of Modern Criticism: A Study of Style and Poetic Theory*, 1978, *Dante: The Divine Comedy*, 1987, and *Dante's Inferno, Difficulty and Dead Poetry*, 1987, all by Robin Kirkpatrick; *The Discipline of the Mountain: Dante's Purgatorio in a Nuclear World* by Daniel Berrigan, 1979; *Essays on Dante's Philosophy of History*, 1979, and *Dante's Journey of Sanctification*, 1990, both by Antonio C. Mastrobuono; *Dante, Poet of the Desert: History and Allegory in the Divine Comedy* by Giuseppe Mazzotta, 1979, and *Critical Essays on Dante* edited by Mazzotta, 1991; *Dante Alighieri* by Ricardo J. Quinones, 1979; *Dante the Maker* by William Anderson, 1980; *The World of Dante: Essays on Dante and His Times* edited by Cecil Grayson, 1980; *Studies in Dante* by Robert Hollander, 1980; *Dante* by George Holmes, 1980; *Shadowy Prefaces: Conversion and Writing in the Divine Comedy* by James Thomas Chiampi, 1981; *Irenic Apocalypse: Some Uses of Apolcalyptic in Dante, Petrarch and Rabelais* by Dennis Costa, 1981: *A Reading of Dante's Inferno* by Wallace Fowlie, 1981; *The Figure of Dante: An Essay on the Vita Nuova* by Jerome Nazzaro, 1981; *Dante and the Roman de la Rose: An Investigation into the Vernacular Narrative Context of the Commedia* by Earl Jeffrey Richards, 1981; *Dante in the Twentieth Century* edited by Adolph Caso, 1982; *Confessions of Sin and Love in the Middle Ages: Dante's Commedia and St. Augustine's Confessions* by Shirley J. Paolini, 1982; *Dante's Incarnation of the Trinity* by Paul Priest, 1982; *Essays on Dante* by Karl Witte, 1982; *The Door of Purgatory: A Study of Multiple Symbolism in Dante's Purgatorio*, 1983, and *Dante's Griffin and the History of the World: A Study of the Earthly Paradise*, 1989, both by Peter Armour; *Dante's Angelic Intelligences: Their Importance in the Cosmos and in Pre-Christian Religion* by Stephen Bemrose, 1983; *Dante, Petrarch, Boccaccio: Studies in the Italian Trecento in Honor of Charles S. Singleton* edited by Aldo S. Bernardo and Anthony L. Pelligrini, 1983; *Dante in America: The First Two Centuries* edited by A. Bartlett Giamatti, 1983; *Dante, Chaucer and the Currency of the Word: Money, Images and Reference in Late Medieval Poetry* by Richard A. Shoaf, 1983; *Dante's Poets: Texuality and Truth in the Comedy*, 1984, and *The Undivine Comedy: Detheologizing Dante*, 1992, both by Teodolinda Barolini; *Dante's Fearful Art of Justice* by Anthony K. Cassell, 1984; *Pilgrim in Love: An Introduction to Dante and His Spirituality*, 1984, and *Dante: Layman, Prophet, Mystic*, 1989, both by James J. Collins; *The*

Political Vision of the Divine Comedy, 1984, and Dante's Beatrice: Priest of an Androgynous God, 1992, both by Joan M. Ferrante; Chaucer and Dante: A Revaluation by Howard H. Schess, 1984; The Symbolic Rose in Dante's Paradiso by Giuseppe C. Di Scipio, 1984; Aesthetic Ideas in Dante: "Etterno Piacer," 1984, and Dante: Lyric Poet and Philosopher: An Introduction to the Minor Works, 1990, both by J.F. Took; The Political Ideas in the Divine Comedy by Stewart Farnell, 1985; Dante Comparisons edited by Eric Haywood and Barry Jones, 1985, and Dante Readings edited by Haywood, 1986; Dante's Poetry of Dreams by Dino S. Cervigni, 1986; Dante and Medieval Latin Traditions by Peter Dronke, 1986; The Reader's Companion to Dante's Divine Comedy by Angelo A. De Gennaro, 1986; The Transfiguration of History at the Center of Dante's Paradise by Jeffrey T. Schnapp, 1986; Dante: Numerological Studies by John J. Guzzardo, 1987; Dante's Poems: An Essay on History and Origins by J.M.W. Hill, 1987; The Pilgrim and the Book: A Study of Dante, Langland and Chaucer by Julia Bolton Holloway, 1987; Dante and the Empire by Donna M. Mancusi-Ungaro, 1987; Mary in the Writings of Dante by Max Saint, 1987; Dante: The Critical Heritage 1314(?)–1870 edited by Michael Caesar, 1988; The Body of Beatrice by Robert Pogue Harrison, 1988; Dante and Difference: Writing in the Commedia by Jeremy Tambling, 1988; The Divine Comedy: Tracing God's Art by Marguerite Mills Chiarenza, 1989; A Study of the Theology and the Imagery of Dante's Divina Commedia: Sensory Perception, Reason and Free Will by Sharon Harwood-Gordon, 1989; On the Defence of the Comedy of Dante by Giacopo Mazzoni, translated by R.L. Montgomery, 1989; The Influence of Dante on Medieval Dream Visions by Roberta L. Payne, 1989; Dante Studies in the Age of Vico by Domenico Pietropaolo, 1989; Time and the Crystal: Studies in Dante's Rime Petrose by Robert M. Durling and Ronald L. Martinez, 1990; Dante and the Medieval Other World by Alison Morgan, 1990; Eternal Feminines: Three Theological Allegories in Dante's Paradiso by Jaroslav Pelikan, 1990; Dante, edited by Harold Bloom, 1991; Dante's Burning Sands: Some New Perspectives by Francesca Guerra D'Antoni, 1991; Dante as Dramatist: Myth of the Early, Paradise and Tragic Vision in the Divine Comedy by Franco Masciandaro, 1991; Word and Drama in Dante: Essays on the Divina Commedia by John C. Barnes and Jennifer Petrie, 1992; Dante and the Bible: An Introduction by Daniel H. Higgins, 1992; Cambridge Companion to Dante edited by Rachel Jacoff, 1993; Commentary and Ideology: Dante in the Renaissance by Deborah Parker, 1993; Dante and the Mystical Tradition: Bernard of Clairvaux in the Commedia by Steven Botterill, 1994; Dante's Christian Astrology by Richard Kay, 1994; The Circle of Our Vision: Dante's Presence in English Romantic Poetry by Ralph Pite, 1994; Mismapping the Underworld: Daring and Error in Dante's Comedy by John Kleiner, 1994; Dante and the Middle Ages: Literary and Historical Essays, edited by John C. Barnes and Cormac Ó Cuilleanáin, 1995; Dante Now: Current Trends in Dante Studies, edited by Theodore J. Cachey, Jr., 1995; Sense Perception in Dante's Commedia by Edward G. Miller, 1996; Dante's Political Purgatory by John A. Scott, 1996; Dante's Interpretive Journey by William Franke, 1996; Images of the Journey in Dante's Divine Comedy by Charles H. Taylor and Patricia Finley, 1997; Dante and Governance, edited by John Woodhouse, 1997; Dante: Contemporary Perspectives, edited by Amilcare A. Iannucci, 1997; The Metaphysics of Reading Underlying Dante's Commedia: The Ingegno by Paul Arvisu, 1998; Dante and the Victorians by Alison Milbank, 1998; Lectura Dantis: Inferno, edited by Allen Mandelbaum, Anthony Oldcorn, and Charles Ross, 1998; Dante and the Knot of Body and Soul by Marianne Shapiro,

1998; Dante Alighieri: Divine Comedy, Divine Spirituality by Robert Royal, 1999; The Design in the Wax: The Structure of the Divine Comedy and Its Meaning by Marc Cogan, 1999; Dante's Testaments: Essays in Scriptural Imagination by Peter S. Hawkins, 1999; Dante, edited and introduced by Jeremy Tambling, 1999; Dante's Aesthetics of Being by Warren Ginsberg, 1999; Human Vices and Human Worth in Dante's Comedy by Patrick Boyde, 2000; Sound and Structure in the Divine Comedy by David Robey, 2000; Divine Dialectic: Dante's Incarnational Poetry by Guy P. Raffa, 2000; The Dante Encyclopedia, edited by Richard Lansing, 2000; A New Life of Dante by Stephen Bemrose, 2000; Reading Dante's Stars by Alison Cornish, 2000; Formulas of Repetition in Dante's Commedia: Signposted Journeys Across Textual Space by Lloyd Howard, 2001; Dante by R.W.B. Lewis, 2001; Dante: A Life in Works by Robert Hollander, 2001.

* * *

The city in which Dante Alighieri was born and where he spent the first 38 years of his life was in his time already an important cultural centre as well as the focus of conflicting political forces having cast off its feudal allegiance it was a self-governing community, administered by its own citizens under the direction of a prosperous bourgeoisie. Although Dante's father was not a prominent figure in the life of the city (he was perhaps a money lender) the poet claimed to be descended from the aristocracy and he was in his youth sufficiently well off to enable him to study painting, music, and letters (according to Boccaccio) and, it seems likely, to spend a year at the University of Bologna. Florence already possessed a literary tradition; Dante readily acknowledged his indebtedness to Brunetto Latini, author of the allegorizing Tesoretto, and to the poet Guido Cavalcanti (slightly older than Dante) who had brought a speculative element into the love lyric of the Provençal tradition. Dante's literary production in fact begins with lyrics in the Cavalcanti style. Dante's first notable work, however, was La vita nuova (The New Life), an account of his idealistic love for Beatrice Portinari, composed after her death. It is a carefully constructed composition of unique and original character: prose is interspersed with verse, serving to provide a narrative line between the lyrics and also to illuminate their meaning by exegesis of a scholastic tone. The combination of realism and suggestion of hidden meanings as well as the calculated design of the little book give the reader a foretaste of the Commedia (The Divine Comedy).

The poet's immersion in politics following the death of Beatrice and his subsequent banishment and disillusionment altered the course of both his reading and his writing: he turned from the quasi-mystic devotion to Beatrice (and Revelation) to the study of philosophy. This shift is documented in Il Convivio (The Banquet), a long, digressive work, dealing with philosophical, ethical, and even political matters, revealing a new area of study: Aristotle, Boethius, and Virgil are authorities of recurrent reference. As in The New Life, prose is used to explicate poems but in The Banquet the prose element is far greater. Another area of his studies after his exile is disclosed by De vulgari eloquentia (Literature in the Vernacular), written in Latin, a pioneering exercise in linguistic studies in which the author attempts to define the characteristics of true Italian speech. The all but obsessive interest in political matters, a natural concomitant of his exile, is the motivation for his De monarchia (Monarchy) and his impassioned Epistolae (The Letters). These Latin items of his canon were composed in all likelihood in the years of Henry VII's effort to reassert Imperial supremacy in Italy and probably when the writing of The Divine Comedy was already in progress.

For his "minor works" alone—all original and significant—Dante would be accounted a major figure in Italian—and even European—literary history, but it is *The Divine Comedy* which has given him a unique and enduring pre-eminence. In the context of the times it is surprising that a work of such epic dimensions should not have been written in Latin—and, according to Boccaccio, Dante at first thought of using that tongue. The choice of the vernacular for his masterpiece was of crucial importance in the development of Italian literature, but the greatness of the work makes even such a determinant role merely incidental.

The prestige of the poem has long endured. Through the centuries immediately following its composition it maintained its eminence and survived through the less appreciative climate of the 17th and 18th centuries, gathering new vitality in the 19th and growing in popularity and esteem over the past 200 years. The scope of its attraction has been uniquely vast, rivalling that of the Homeric poems; through the years it has consistently won wide readership and critical attention in all nations of the old world and the new. It has charmed the "man in the street" and fascinated intellectuals. For the English-speaking world, one eloquent statistic may be cited: there have been no fewer than 47 translations of the poem into English (not counting partial versions) and more are in the course of preparation.

There are many reasons for such persistent vitality just as there are many facets and levels of meaning in the work itself. For Dante, according to his letter to Can Grande, the literal substance of the poem is simply an account of the state of souls after death, with allegorical implications below the surface. But the mode of depiction is not simply expositional; it is cast in narrative form. And it is a story compellingly told, in which the protagonist, the author himself, describes his pilgrimage through the Christian realms of the after-life, Hell, Purgatory, and Heaven. These are kingdoms of fancy, to be sure, in which the author is free to invent backgrounds, scenes, and events. But these kingdoms are populated by characters drawn not from inventive fancy but from the narrator's own acquaintance, whether in experience or in his readings, and they are set forth with convincing realism. The essential ingredients for assuring the reader's interest—movement, suspense, recognition—are present from beginning to end as the pilgrim-narrator moves from one circle of Hell, one terrace of Purgatory, or one circling Heaven to another with surprises for himself and his reader at every passage. In all of these realms the wayfarer has a companion and guide (Virgil or Beatrice) to instruct and advise him but with the tactical function also of giving life to the narrative through dialogue, more effective than simple narrational exposition in providing dramatic movement. No writer of fiction has planned his art with greater care or shrewdness. But *The Divine Comedy* is more than fiction. The characters, including the narrator, have suggestive symbolic dimensions, allusive and often challengingly ambiguous. As the story unrolls the reader becomes aware that the realms of fancy or theological postulate are also provinces of the world we live in, depicted with a perception fortified by learning and a commitment born of faith and hope. It is our world that we recognize behind the veil, with all its faltering waywardness, penitential meditation, and yearning for salvation and exaltation. The wayfarer too is not simply a 14th-century Florentine exile; he is Everyman, and he speaks for all of us. We are his fellow pilgrims *sub specie aeternitatis*.

The substance of the poem is given strength and beauty by rare technical artistry. *The Divine Comedy* is a masterful design, with carefully planned and harmonious proportions: all of the *cantiche* are of approximately the same length, and the dimensions of each canto also bear witness to the "fren dell'arte." *Terza rima* itself, with its

syllogistic construction and its subliminal trinitarian implications, has also the practical uses of linkage and invitation to memorization. The poet makes skilful use, too, of such devices as alliteration, assonance, and even deft repetition. His imagery is remarkable for its variety—animals, plants, trees, and flowers mingle with historical allusions and numerological and mathematical figures in the embroidery of the poem. Some of these are lost in translation but a good translation—and there have been many such—can convey much of this accidental charm into another tongue.

So many, rich, and varied are the threads of which the cloth of *The Divine Comedy* is woven that the nature of the work defies simple definition. It has been called "a personal epic": it is assuredly a confessional autobiography. It is likewise a patient and lucid exposition of orthodox dogma and an encyclopedia as well. At the same time it may be seen as a great love poem, for Beatrice is the motivation and the goal of the pilgrimage; furthermore each great division ends with the same word, suggesting a vast "canzone" of three great stanzas. Or we may see the *Comedy* as a "synthesis of medieval learning," which, at least incidentally, it is. But it is also a synthesis of the aspirations, sensibilities, and ultimate destiny of mankind. It is, most deeply, a statement of affirmation, set forth in terms of a certain time and place and contingent circumstance but valid for all times. Matter, manner, and message are blended not only with exceptional craftsmanship but with commitment and conviction. Aesthetically irresistible, the story of the extra-terrestrial pilgrimage is also on a deeper level reassuring and inspirational.

—Thomas G. Bergin

See the essays on *The Divine Comedy* and *The New Life*.

ALLENDE, Isabel

Born: Lima, Perú, 2 August 1942. Niece and goddaughter of former Chilean President Salvador Allende who died in the military takeover in 1973. **Education:** Graduated from a private high school in Santiago, Chile, 1959. **Family:** Married 1) Miguel Frías, 1962 (divorced, 1987), one daughter (deceased) and one son; 2) William Gordon, 1988; one stepson. **Career:** Secretary, United Nations Food and Agricultural Organization, Santiago, Chile, 1959–65; worked as a journalist, editor and advice columnist for the magazine *Paula* from 1967–74; interviewer for Channel 13/Channel 7 television station 1970–75; worked on movie newsreels, 1973–75; administrator, Colegio Marroco, Caracas, Venezuela, 1979–82; guest teacher, Montclair State College, New Jersey, 1985, and University of Virginia, 1988; Gildersleeve Lecturer, Barnard College, New York, 1988; taught creative writing at the University of California, Berkeley, 1989. Lives in San Rafael, California. **Awards:** Best Novel of the Year, Chile, 1983; "Panorama Literario," Chile, 1983; Author of the Year, Germany, 1984; Book of the Year, Germany, 1984; "Grand Prix d'Evasion," France, 1984; "Radio Televisión Belga: Point de Mire," Belguim, 1985; Colima Literary prize, México, 1986; "XV Premio Internazionale I Migliori Dell'Anno," Italy, 1987; Book of the Year, Switzerland, 1987; *Library Journal*'s Best Book, United States, 1988; Before Columbus Foundation award, United States, 1988; Best Novel, México, 1985; Author of the Year, Germany, 1986; Freedom to Write Pen Club, United States, 1991;"XLI Bancarella," Italy,

1993; Independent Foreign Fiction, England, 1993; Brandeis University Major Book Collection, USA 1993; "Feminist of the Year award," The Feminist Majority Foundation, United States, 1994; "Condecoración Gabriela Mistral," Chile, 1994; "Critics Choice," United States, 1996; "Books to Remember," American Library Association, United States, 1996; "Books to Remember," The New York Public Library; "Malaparte" Amici di Capri, Italy, 1998; "Donna Citta Di Roma," Italy, 1998; "Dorothy and Lilian Gish prize for Excellence in the Arts," United States, 1998; "Sara Lee Foundation," United States, 1998. Professor of Literature Honoris Causae, University of Chile, 1991; Doctor of Letters at SUNY, United States, 1991; Doctor of Humane Letters at Florida Atlantic University, United States, 1996. **Member:** Academy of Arts and Sciences, Puerto Rico, 1995; "Academia de la Lengua," Chile, 1989.

PUBLICATIONS

Fiction

Civilice a su troglodita: Los impertinentes de Isabel Allende (humor). 1974.
La casa de los espíritus (novel). 1982; as *The House of the Spirits* by Magda Bogin, 1985.
La gorda de porcelana (juvenile literature). 1983.
De amor y de sombra (novel). 1984; as *Of Love and Shadows* by Margaret Sayers Peden, 1987.
Eva Luna (novel). 1987; as *Eva Luna* by Margaret Sayers Peden, 1988.
Cuentos de Eva Luna (short stories). 1989; as *The Stories of Eva Luna* by Margaret Sayers Peden, 1991.
El plan infinito (novel). 1991; as *The Infinite Plan* by Margaret Sayers Peden, 1993.
Afrodita: Recetas, cuentos y otros afrodisiacos. 1997; as *Aphrodite: A Memoir of the Senses* by Margaret Sayers Peden, 1998.
Hija de la fortuna (novel). 1999.
Retrato en sepia (novel). 2001.

Other

Paula (memoirs/ autobiography). 1994; translated by Margaret Sayers Peden, 1995

*

Critical Studies: "Entrevista a Isabel Allende/Interview with Isabel Allende" by Marjorie Agosín, translated by Cola Franzen in, *Imagine* vol. 1, no. 2, Winter, 1984; *Narrative Magic in the Fiction of Isabel Allende* by Patricia Hart, 1989; "A Passage to Andorgyny: Isabel Allende's *La casa de los espíritus*" by Linda Gould Levine, in *In the Feminine Mode: Essays on Hispanic Women Writers*, edited by Noel Valis and Carol Maier, 1990; *Isabel Allende*, in *Spanish American Women Writers: A Bio-bibliographical Source Book* by Linda Gould Levine, edited by Diane Marting, 1990; *Critical Approaches to Isabel Allende's Novels*, edited by Sonia Riquelme Rojas and Edna Aguirre Rehbein, 1991.

*   *   *

Isabel Allende is one of the most widely read Latin American women authors, her work having been translated into some thirty

languages. A great deal of Isabel Allende's appeal to international readers is the images she presents of Chile and Latin America. She portrays it as a dichotomy and a world of radical differences with rich and poor, military coups, revolutionary governments, passionate women and men, women with magical powers and men who can be monsters, where there exits poets alongside of torturers and there exist enthralling storytellers. After the military coup of 1973, Allende and her family moved to Venezuela. While in Venezuela, she wrote her first novel *La casa de los espíritus* (*The House of the Spirits*). The theme of exile is present in *Eva Luna, De amor y de sombra* (*Of Love and Shadows*), *Daughter of Fortune*, and the autobiographical *Paula* besides *The House of the Spirits*.

Her second novel, *Of Love and Shadows* also takes place in an unnamed Latin American country, which is of course Chile under the military dictatorship of General Pinochet. It details the coming of age of a young upper class journalist who develops a political consciousness, as she realizes things are not what they seem on the surface. She and her photographer lover investigate a boarded up mine discovering "disappeared" buried there. Afterwards, they are forced to flee the country. The novel is suspenseful as the personal dramas reveal themselves and take shape. She skillfully maintains the tension and terror inherent in life under a military dictatorship while at the same time developing the love story between the journalist and her photographer. The novel is based, in part, on events that took place at Lonquén mine. Here as she does in *The House of the Spirits*, Allende constructs fiction on the base of historical reality, which is the story of Latin American politics and its effects on the lives of her people.

Her next works are *Eva Luna* and *Cuentos de Eva Luna* (*The Stories of Eva Luna*) where the theme of dictatorship is not directly visible although, they are imbued with revolutionary politics. *Eva Luna* is set in Venezuela and like her previous novels recounts the life of the protagonist. It is a coming of age novel, with a picaresque element as Eva encounters and becomes friends with a variety of people: Huberto Naranjo, a future guerrilla fighter; Halabí, a Turkish merchant; Mimí the transsexual; and Elvira, who is a surrogate grandmother. Each contributes to Eva's development as a storyteller. Allende weaves together the personal story of the illegitimate orphan, Eva Luna, who becomes a scriptwriter and storyteller with that of Rolf Carlé, a filmmaker and Austrian immigrant, who carries the burden of his father having been a Nazi, both of whom come of age in this novel. *The Stories of Eva Luna* are twenty-three short stories whose theme centers around love, supposedly written by Eva Luna during the previous novel.

Again taking a page from her life, *El plan infinito* (*The Infinite Plan*) is based on the life of William Gordon (who is today her husband) and is set in the western United States and explores the drug culture, Viet Nam and the trauma of war. *Paula* is more autobiographical than other works as she narrates her daughter's death. Like *The House of the Spirits*, it too began as a letter to her daughter. This work rises above the sentimentality of a memoir. After the death of Paula, Allende was unable to write until she thought of the delights of food and came up with *Afrodita: Recetas, cuentos y otros afrodisiacos* (*Aphrodite: A Memoir of the Senses*), which is both a cookbook and a playful memoir.

The story of Eliza Sommers is told in *Daughter of Fortune* when a young Chilean women travels to California during the Gold Rush in search of love. Here again we see the theme of exile. Eliza is left on the doorstep of Jeremy Sommers at birth. His sister Rose and brother John convince him to keep the child who grows up between two worlds—Rose's liberal lifestyle and the housekeeper Mamá Fresia who teaches her about herbs and cooking. Joaquín Andieta awakens Eliza's adolescent passions; he leaves for San Francisco and with the help of Mamá Fresia, Eliza sets sail for California too. Once in California, the novel recounts Eliza's adventures. *Daughter of Fortune* reiterates many of the characteristics of Allende's previous novels, beginning with the strong female characters. Both Rose and Eliza break and trespass on traditional roles and own their own destinies. Also evident is the use of national myths but not through a military coup—rather by way of the role Chileans played in the Gold Rush, thereby they are exiled from their homeland and are marginalized. Allende admitted that this book is pure fiction and is the one that least deals with her.

Considered in part a magic realist, Allende is also part of the Latin American feminist awakening, working with the themes of feminism, politics, and writing as an art. Allende is not passive but passionate about politics, history, and her society. The majority of her protagonists are marginalized and/or exiled from their home country. She continues to prove her capacity and capability as an engaging writer who weaves intriguing stories of high intensity in a concise and straightforward way. Isabel Allende's novels depict strong female characters that possess paranormal characteristics *á la* magical realism. Her female protagonists are able to function successfully in reality when dictated by events such as social injustice. Her male characters are sensitive revolutionaries engaged in political intrigue and social issues. Critics have pointed out and noted as a distraction that an overriding theme is the search for the one perfect male partner to complete, as many of her novels can be viewed as sentimental love stories. Nevertheless, there is intrinsic entertainment in a good love story, particularly when it is combined with well-formed prose intertwined and permeated with history, politics, and a dash of the unknown. As many readers are unfamiliar with Latin America, this is a way to make the message more palatable. Isabel Allende may be one of a handful of Latin American women who have garnered recognition outside the academic community and become well known to the general reading public.

—Beth Pollack

See the essay on *The House of the Spirits*.

AMADO (DE FARIA), Jorge (Leal)

Born: Ferradas, Itabuna, Bahia, Brazil, 10 August 1912. **Education:** Educated at the Jesuit Colégio Antônio Vieira, Salvador, 1923–26; entered the Ginásio Ipiranga, Salvador, 1926; Faculty of Law, Federal University, Rio de Janeiro, 1931–35, diploma in law 1935. **Family:** Married 1) Matilde Garcia Roas in 1933 (separated 1944), one daughter; 2) Zélia Gattai in 1945, one son and one daughter. **Career:** Reporter, *Diário da Bahia*, 1927, and contributor, *A Luva, Samba, Meridiano, A Semana, O Momento, O Jornal, Diário de Notícias, A Gazeta de Notícias*, and *O Correiro do Povo*, 1927–30; moved to Rio de Janeiro, 1930; editor, *Revista Rio Magazine*, 1933; worked for José Olímpio, publishers, from 1934; editor, *A Manhã* the publication of the opposition Aliança Nacional Libertadora [National Freedom Alliance]; co-editor, Centro de Cultura Moderna's *Movimento*, 1934–35; imprisoned for suspected involvement in coup attempt,

1935, and his books banned, 1938–43; travelled to Mexico and the USA, 1937; editor, *Dom Casmurro*, 1938–39, and contributor, *Diretrizes*, 1939; lived mainly in Argentina, 1941–42; returned to Brazil, 1942, and was re-arrested and confined to the Bahia region; contributor, "Diário da Guerra" column for *O Imparcial*, from 1943; editor, *Hoje*, São Paulo, 1945; after the fall of Getúlio Vargas's regime (1930–45), elected Communist deputy for the São Paulo region, 1945, until the Party again declared illegal in 1947; went into exile: in Paris, 1947–49, Scandinavia and Eastern Europe, 1949–50, and Prague, 1950–51; travelled to China and Mongolia, 1952; returned to Brazil, 1952; founder, *Para Todos*, Rio de Janeiro, and its editor, 1956–58; travelled to Cuba and Mexico, 1962; settled in Salvador, 1963; visited Canada and USA 1971: writer in residence, Pennsylvania State University; lived in London, 1976. Delegate, first Brazilian Writers Congress, 1945; vice-president, Brazilian Union, 1954; co-organizer, first Festival of Brazilian Writing, 1960. **Awards:** Graça Aranha Foundation prize; Stalin peace prize, 1951; National literary prize, 1958; Gulbenkian prize (Portugal), 1971; Italian Latin-American Institute prize, 1976; Nonnino literary prize (Italy), 1983; Neruda prize, 1989; Volterra prize (Italy), 1989; Sino del Duca prize (Paris), 1990; Mediterranean prize, 1990. **Member:** Brazilian Academy, since 1961; corresponding member, East German Academy of Science and Letters. Commander, Légion d'honneur, 1984. **Died:** 6 August 2001, in Salvador, Brazil.

PUBLICATIONS

Fiction

Lenita, with Dias da Costa and Edison Carneiro. 1930.
O país do carnaval. 1932.
Cacau. 1933.
Suor. 1934; translated as *Sweat*, 1937.
Jubiabá. 1935; as *Jubiabá*, translated by Margaret A. Neves, 1984.
Mar morto. 1936; as *Sea of Death*, translated by Gregory Rabassa, 1984.
Capitães de areia. 1937; as *Captains of the Sands*, translated by Gregory Rabassa, 1988.
Terras do sem fim. 1942; as *The Violent Land*, translated by Samuel Putnam, 1945; revised editions, 1965 and 1989.
São Jorge dos Ilhéus. 1944.
Seara vermelha. 1946.
Os subterrâneos da liberdade: Os asperos tempos, Agonia da noite, A luz no túnel. 3 vols., 1954.
Gabriela, cravo e canela. 1958; as *Gabriela, Clove and Cinnamon*, translated by William L. Grossman and James L. Taylor, 1962.
Os velhos marinheiros: Duas hisódrias de cais de Bahia (includes *A morte e a morte de Quincas Berro d'Água*). 1961; *A morte e a morte de Quincas Berro d'Água* published separately, 1978; as *Home Is the Sailor*, translated by Harriet de Onís, 1964; as *The Two Deaths of Quincas Wateryell*, translated by Barbara Shelby, 1965.
Os pastores da noite. 1964; as *Shepherds of the Night*, translated by Harriet de Onís, 1966.
Dona Flor e seus dois maridos. 1966; as *Dona Flor and Her Two Husbands*, translated by Harriet de Onís, 1969.
Tenda dos milagres. 1969; as *Tent of Miracles*, translated by Barbara Shelby, 1971.
Tereza Batista, cansada de guerra. 1972; as *Tereza Batista, Home from the Wars*, translated by Barbara Shelby, 1975.

O gato malhado e a andorinha sinhá (for children). 1976; as *The Swallow and the Tomcat: A Love Story*, translated by Barbara Shelby Merello, 1982.

Tieta do Agreste, pastora de cabras. 1977; as *Tieta the Goat Girl*, translated by Barbara Shelby Merello, 1979.

Farda, fardão, camisola de dormir: Fábula para acender uma esperança. 1979; as *Pen, Sword, Camisole: A Fable to Kindle a Hope*, translated by Helen R. Lane, 1985.

Tocaia grande: a face obscura. 1984; as *Showdown*, translated by Gregory Rabassa, 1988.

O sumiço da santa: Uma história de feitiçaria: Romance baiano. 1988; as *The Golden Harvest*, translated by Clifford E. Landers, 1992.

A descoberta da América pelos turcos ou come do o árabe Jamil Bichara, desbravador de florestas, de visita á cidade de Itabuna para dar abasto ao corpo, ali lhe ofereceram fartura e casamento ou ainda os esponsais de Adma. 1992.

The War of the Saints, translated by Gregory Rabassa, 1993.

Suor: Romance, 1998.

Verse

A estrada do mar. 1938.

Plays

O amor de Castro Alves. 1947; as *O amor do soldado*, 1958.

Other

ABC de Castro Alves (biography). 1941.

Vida de Luis Carlos Prestes, o cavaleiro da esperança (biography). 1942; as *O Cavaleiro da Esperança*, 1945.

Obras. 17 vols., 1944–67.

Bahia de todos os santos: Guia das ruas e dos mistérios da cidade do Salvador (travel writing). 1945.

Homens e coisas do partido comunista (political writings). 1946.

O mundo da paz (travel writing). 1951.

Obras ilustradas. 19 vols., 1961–72.

O mistério dos MMM, with others. 1962.

Bahia boa terra Bahia, with Carybé and Flávia Damm. 1967,

Iconografia dos deuses africanos no Candomblé da Bahia, with Pierre Verger and Waldeloir Rego. 1980.

O menino Grapiúna (memoirs). 1982.

A cidade de Bahia, with Carybé, photographs by Mario Cravo Neto. 1984.

Terra mágica da Bahia, with Alain Draeger. 1984.

A bola e o goleiro (for children). 1984.

Navegação de cabotagem. 1992.

*

Bibliography: *Brazilian Literature: A Research Guide* by David William Foster and Walter Rela, 1990.

Critical Studies: *Brazil's New Novel: Four Northeastern Masters* by Fred P. Ellison, 1954; *Escritores Brasileiros Contemporâneos* by Renard Perez, 1960; *Jorge Amado: Vida e obra* (includes bibliography) by Miécio Táti, 1961; "Poetry and Progress in Jorge Amado's *Gabriela, cravo e canela*" by Richard A. Mazzara, in *Hispania*, 46, 1963; "The Five Faces of Love in Jorge Amado's Bahian Novels" by Gregory Rabassa, in *Revista de Letras*, 1963; *Gabriela: seu cravo e sua canela*, 1964, *Os mistérios de vida e os mistérios de Dona Flor*, 1972, *O barroco e o maravilhoso no romance de Jorge Amado*, 1973, and *A contraprova de Tereza, Favo-de-Mel*, 1973, all by Juarez da Gama Batista; "Narrative Focus in Jorge Amado's Story of Vasco Moscoso Aragão" by Judith Bernard, in *Romance Notes*, 8, 1966; "Afro-Brazilian Cults in the Novels of Jorge Amado" by Russell G. Hamilton, in *Hispania*, 50(2), 1967; "The 'New' Jorge Amado" by Elizabeth Schlomann Lowe, in *Luso-Brazilian Review*, 6, 1969; *Criaturas de Jorge Amado* by Paulo Tavares, 1969; "Allegory in Two Works of Jorge Amado" and "Moral Dilemma in Jorge Amado's *Dona Flor e seus dois maridos*" both in *Romance Notes*, 13, 1971, and "Duality in Jorge Amado's *The Two Deaths of Quincas Wateryell*" in *Studies in Short Fiction*, 15, 1978, all by Malcolm Noel Silverman; "The Preservation of African Culture in Brazilian Literature: The Novels of Jorge Amado" by Maria Luísa Nunes, in *Luso-Brazilian Review*, 10, 1973; "Popular Poetry in the Novels of Jorge Amado" by Nancy T. Baden, in *Journal of Latin American Lore*, 2(1), 1976; "The *Malandro*, or Rogue Figure, in the Fiction of Jorge Amado" in *Mester*, 6, 1976, and "Double Perspective in Two Works of Jorge Amado" in *Estudios Iberoamericanos*, 4, 1978, both by Bobby J. Chamberlain; "Jorge Amado, Jorge Desprezado" by Jon S. Vincent, in *Luso-Brazilian Review*, 15 (supplement), 1978; *Jorge Amado: Política e literatura* by Alfredo Wagner Berno de Almeida, 1979; "The Problem of the Unreliable Narrator in Jorge Amado's *Tenda dos milagres*" in *Romance Quarterly*, 30, 1983, and "Structural Ambiguity in Jorge Amado's *A morte e a morte de Quincas Berro d'Água*" in *Hispania*, 67, 1984, both by Earl E. Fitz; "The Guys and Dolls of Jorge Amado" by L. Clark Keating, in *Hispania*, 66, 1983; "Jorge Amado: Morals and Marvels" by Daphne Patai, in her *Myth and Ideology in Contemporary Brazilian Fiction*, 1983; "Jorge Amado: Populism and Prejudice" by David Brookshaw, in *Race and Color in Brazilian Literature*, 1986; *Jorge Amado: Retrato Incompleto*, 1993; *Jorge Amado: Ricette Narrative*, 1994; *Blackness: Culture, Ideology and Discourse: A Comparative Study* by Femi Abodunrin, 1996; *Jorge Amado: New Critical Essays*, edited by Keith H. Brower, Earl E. Fitz, and Enrique Martinez-Vidal, 2001.

*   *   *

Jorge Amado is described rightly as Brazil's best-known novelist. An exceedingly prolific writer whose work spanned seven decades, Amado began writing in 1930 and published his first novel, *O país do carnaval* [Carnival Country] in 1932; in 1992, the year of his 80th birthday, he published a volume of memoirs, *Navegação de cabotagem* [Coastwise Shipping], and a novella, *A descoberta da América pelos turcos ou de como o árabe Jamil Bichara, desbravador de florestas, de visita à cidade de Itabuna para dar abasto ao corpo, ali lhe ofereceram fartura e casamento ou ainda os esponsais de Adma* [America's Discovery by the Turks, or How the Arab Jamil Bichara, Clearer of Forests, on a Visit to the City of Itabuna to Fortify His Body, Was Offered Abundance and Marriage, or Even the Marriage Vows of Adma], destined to mark the quincentenary of Christopher

Columbus's discovery of America. His works have been translated into some 40 languages, adapted for film, and serialized for television. There is some disagreement among critics about the "literariness" of his work, but this has affected neither his popularity nor, indeed, his immense readability. Several controversies surround his literary output, and critical opinion is divided as to whether or not his early novels are little more than crude exposées of sociopolitical conditions driven by left-wing ideology, whether he is sexist in his attitude to women, and whether his works, regardless of how well-intentioned, enshrine and perpetrate racist attitudes.

Amado made his literary debut as an exponent of the Northeastern novel, and the greater part of his work has retained this regional bias. Few of his novels do not have as their geographical setting Salvador, capital of Bahia, or the cacao-producing region of Northeastern Brazil.

It is usual to separate Amado's work into two main phases. The first, stemming from a strong ideological commitment to depict the Northeastern reality as faithfully as possible, begins with *O país do carnaval* and ends with *Capitães da areia* (*Captains of the Sands*). In these novels he chooses as his subject-matter some of the typical motifs of the Northeast: the drought and its effects on the inhabitants of the region; the plight of the hired plantation workers, and the urban poor; the situation of the black man in Brazil. His later works, from *Terras do sem fim* (*The Violent Land*) onwards, are characterized by a greater preoccupation with style and technique, incorporating elements of lyricism, humour, irony, and what some critics have tagged "magical socialism."

Any attempt to evaluate Amado's writing must inevitably lead to the conclusion that his major achievement is the group of novels that constitute his "cacao cycle." In *Cacau*, the situation in the Northeast is interpreted very much in terms of the class struggle. Although this work is not an aesthetic success, it introduces the themes that find a fuller, more artistic expression years later in *The Violent Land*, a "tropical western" considered by many to be Amado's best work. It deals with the conquest of the land, when ruthless men cleared the jungle to plant cacao, then fought for political control over their empires. *The Violent Land* focuses on the bloodthirsty struggle between two such planters, Colonel Horácio Silveira and Juca Badaró. The emphasis is on epic deeds rather than denunciation of social evils, and the main protagonist of the novel is the land itself.

São Jorge dos Ilhéus [St. George of the Islanders] continues the story told in *The Violent Land*, with more political content than its predecessor. It chronicles the transition from the pioneering days to the emergence of a new ruling class, the exporters, who employ different means to conquer the land. Whereas Amado views the pioneers with mingled affection and respect, it is clear that he feels a profound antipathy for the new order.

Gabriela, cravo e canela (*Gabriela, Clove and Cinnamon*) takes as its subject the city of Ilhéus during the period 1925 to 1926. This is very much a work of Amado's maturity, and romanticism and humour take precedence over social and political comment. The background of the novel is one of social change, with an ongoing conflict between defenders of the *status quo* and those who desire progress. Against the backdrop is narrated the love story of Nacib, the son of immigrants, and Gabriela, the picaresque *mulata* who comes out of the backlands to fuel male fantasies.

In 1984 Amado returned to the early days of the cacao region in *Tocaia grande: a face obscura* (*Showdown*), whose tone is predominantly nostalgic.

In his later works, Amado becomes increasingly interested in the art of story-telling, introducing elements of fantasy and popular culture into his novels. He is particularly interested in presenting strong female protagonists who symbolize for him the struggle against exploitation—the most notable being Tereza Batista in *Tereza Batista, cansada de guerra* (*Tereza Batista, Home from the Wars*) and Tieta in *Tieta do Agreste* (*Tieta the Goat Girl*)—and showing how they overcome adversity by using their sexuality as a weapon. However, as feminist critics have pointed out, the author is not advocating a radical change in the situation of women; rather he tends to emphasize the traditional stereotype of women as dependent on men for emotional and financial security.

The importance of Afro-Brazilian elements in Amado's work should not be overlooked—for instance, in *Jubiabá*, *Gabriela, Clove and Cinnamon*, and *Tenda dos milagres* (*Tent of Miracles*). In the numerous interviews he has given over the years, Amado has always insisted that Brazilian society, just as Brazilian Portuguese, must be understood as the product of the intermingling of various cultures, religions, and traditions. Thus he makes much of the religious syncretism to be found in the Northeast. It has, however, been suggested that his novels also reinforce white myths about the Afro-Brazilian containing what might be perceived as elements of prejudice.

Amado selects very specific aspects of the Brazilian social reality, focusing on the poor and disadvantaged, on blacks and women, as well as the rich and powerful. He might almost be described as the Master of the Brazilian picaresque, concentrating on the marginal elements of society and recounting their adventures with evident gusto, for instance, the escapades of Vadinho in *Dona Flor e seus dois maridos* (*Dona Flor and Her Two Husbands*), or the eponymous Quincas Berro d'Água (*The Two Deaths of Quincas Wateryell*).

Amado's writing derives much of its vigour from oral narrative tradition and his subject matter is unashamedly popular and picturesque. His overall achievement has been to write with exuberance and affection about the region and society he knows best. He will be remembered above all for his rich and creative use of the Brazilian idiom and for the essentially Brazilian characters he has created.

—P.A. Odber de Baubeta

ANACREON

Born: Teos, Ionia, Asia Minor, c. 570 BC. **Career:** When the Persians invaded in about 540 BC, left for Thrace, where he helped compatriots found the Greek colony of Abdera; tutor to the son of the tyrant Polycrates at Samos; after Polycrates' fall, invited to Athens by Hipparchus, son of the tyrant Pisistratus; may have gone to Thessaly after the assassination of Hipparchus in 514 BC. Honoured by statue on Acropolis. **Died:** c. 475 BC.

PUBLICATIONS

Verse

[Works], edited by T. Bergk, in *Poetae lyrici Graeci*, vol. 3, 1843, and in *Anthologia lyrica*, 1854; also edited by Valentino Rose, 1868,

B. Gentile, 1948, and M.L. West, 1984; selections in *Poetae Melici Graeci* (with commentary), edited by Denys Page, 1962, *Supplementum Lyricis Graecis*, 1974, and in *Greek Lyric Poetry* (with commentary), edited by David A. Campbell, 1982.

Anacreon Done into English, translated by Francis Willis, Thomas Wood, Abraham Cowley, and John Oldham. 1683, reprinted 1923.

The Odes, translated by Thomas Moore. 1800; also translated by Erastus Richardson, 1928.

The Anacreonta, translated by P.M. Pope. 1955.

*

Critical Studies: *Anacréon et les poèmes anacréontiques*, edited by A. Delbaille, 1891, reprinted 1970; *Sappho und Simonides* by U. von Wilamowitz-Moellendorff, 1913; *Anacreon* (in Italian) by B. Gentili, 1958; *Greek Lyric Poetry* by C.M. Bowra, 1961; *The Poetics of Imitation: Anacreon and the Anacreontic Tradition* (with Greek and Latin texts) by Patricia A. Rosenmeyer, 1992; *Anaqcreon Redivivus: A Study of Anacreontic Translation in Mid-sixteenth-century France* by John O'Brien, 1995; *Greek Lyric Poetry: A Commentary on Selected Larger Pieces: Alcman, Stesichorus, Sappho, Alceaus, Ibycus, Anacreon, Simonides, Bacchylides, Pindar, Sophocles, Euripides* by G.O. Hutchinson, 2001.

* * *

Anacreon composed various kinds of poetry, including iambics, elegies, epigrams, and choral maiden-songs, but he is most celebrated for his short lyric pieces. The setting for many poems is the aristocratic symposium, where wine and witty conversation flowed freely. Anacreon wrote mainly in the metre known as the "anacreontic" (anaclastic ionic dimeter) or in a mixture of glyconic and pherecratean rhythms; his poetry represents the peak of technical skill in the Greek monodic tradition. The careful choice and deft positioning of words create a concise and symmetrical perfection of expression, as exemplified by poem 395:

My temples are already grey and my head white;
Graceful youth is no longer with me, my teeth are old,
And of sweet life no long time is now left:
So often I weep, terrified of Tartarus,
For the chasm of Hades is dreadful, and the road down is
Painful; and, for certain, he who goes down does not return.

Epithets and colours are judiciously chosen: the spear is "tearful" and Eros is "melting," while nymphs are "blue eyed," Eros is "golden-haired" throwing a "purple" ball, and Persuasion shines "silver." Effective metaphors are found, such as the "crown" of the city, referring to its walls, and also images, such as the leap from the Leucadian rock, "into the grey wave, drunk with love."

The subject matter of Anacreon's lyrics is typical of the genre: love, wine, the onset of old age, and death. He generally eschews certain other topics, such as politics and warfare, which were so popular with poets like Alcaeus. In eleg. fragment 1, he makes clear his preference:

I do not like the man who, while drinking wine near a full
    mixing-bowl,
Speaks of strife and tearful war,
But whoever, by combining the shining gifts of the Muses and
    Aphrodite,
Recalls the lovely good cheer.

Personal invective in the tradition of Archilochus is represented by poem 388, which ridicules a certain Artemon, who used to go about in filthy clothes and hang around with whores: now he travels in a lady's carriage, holding an ivory parasol. This piece indicates that Anacreon was well able to compose in the barbed style.

In the poems and fragments which survive, the poet is particularly concerned with the bittersweet experience of love with both boys and girls, as in poem 360:

O boy with the girlish look,
I am after you, but you do not notice,
Unaware that you hold
The reins of my soul.

Several poems are addressed to Eros, the god of love, who is variously depicted as a boxer, a smith, and a dice-player (with dice called Madness and Confusion). In Anacreon's verses, Eros is often a violent and disruptive force, envisaged as a personal opponent, who toys with and abuses his victims. Yet at the same time there is a general lightness of tone in the description of these little love affairs, befitting their sophisticated symposiastic context. Thus, even though the poet often names the objects of his passion, such as Cleoboulus, there is a sense that the romance is inevitably fleeting, and all part of the delightful intoxication induced by the "honey-sweet wine." After Eros, the deity most frequently mentioned is, appropriately enough, Dionysus.

Fragment 347 comes from a poem which appears to have been a not entirely serious lament for the lost locks of Smerdis, who has come back from the barber looking less beautiful than before:

Now you are bald and your hair,
Having fallen into rough hands,
Has flown down all at once
Into the black dust,

Having miserably fallen upon
the cut of the iron;
and I am worn away with anguish. . . .

Anacreon's verses, then, are not simply frivolous, but lack the personal intensity of, say, Sappho. Their tone is usually ironic, which creates a distancing effect. Here, the cutting of a youth's hair provokes an exaggerated and amusing reaction in his lover. The almost tragic tone of the lament sits incongruously with such a trivial event. Yet the falling of the severed hair into the black dust is symbolic of death, and the "iron" suggests not only the barber's blade, but also the sword of war. The cutting of the young man's hair represents a rite of passage, and momentarily takes us away from the carefree atmosphere of the banquet to the harsh world of daily life and its conflicts. For the young Greek male, warfare was almost as inevitable as death itself. It is this co-existence of the light and the dark, of the comic and the serious, which gives Anacreon's poetry its peculiar charm and which led to numerous imitations. Sixty of these are collected in a 10th-century manuscript of the Palatine Anthology and are known as the *Anacreonta*. None of the imitations is likely to be earlier than the Hellenistic period; while falling short of the original in linguistic virtuosity and versification, they are not without charm, and testify to the distinctive contribution of Anacreon to the Greek poetic tradition.

—David H. J. Larmour

ANDERSEN, Hans Christian

Born: Odense, Denmark, 2 April 1805. **Education:** Educated at schools in Odense to age 14; alone in Copenhagen, 1819–22, and patronized by various benefactors: loosely associated with the singing and dancing schools at Royal Theatre, 1819–22; attended Slagelse Latin school, 1822–26, and Elsinore grammar school, 1826–27; tutored in Copenhagen by L.C. Müller, 1827–28; completed *examen artium*, 1828. **Career:** Freelance writer from 1828: royal grant for travel, 1833, 1834, and pension from Frederik VI, 1838; granted title of professor, 1851; privy councillor, 1874. **Member:** Knight of Red Eagle (Prussia), 1845; Order of the Dannebrog, 1846; Knight of the Northern Star (Sweden), 1848; Order of the White Falcon (Weimar), 1848. **Died:** 4 August 1875.

PUBLICATIONS

Collections

Samlede skrifter [Collected Writings]. 33 vols., 1853–79; 2nd edition, 15 vols., 1876–80.
Romaner og rejseskildringer [Novels and Travel Notes], edited by H. Topsøe-Jensen. 7 vols., 1941–44.
Fairy Tales, edited by Svend Larsen, translated by R.P. Keigwin. 4 vols., 1951–40.
Complete Fairy Tales and Stories, translated by Erik Haugaard. 1974.
Samlede eventyr og historier [Collected Tales and Stories], edited by Erik Dal. 5 vols., 1975.

Fiction

Improvisatoren. 1835; as *The Improvisatore; or, Life in Italy*, translated by Mary Howitt, 1845.
Eventyr: Fortalt for børn [Fairy Tales for Children]. 6 vols., 1835–42; *Nye Eventyr* [New Fairy Tales], 4 vols., 1843–47; edited by Erik Dal and Erling Nielsen, 1963—; numerous subsequent translations.
O.T. 1836; as *O.T.; or, Life in Denmark*, translated by Mary Howitt, with *Only a Fiddler*, 1845.
Kun en Spillemand. 1837; as *Only a Fiddler*, translated by Mary Howitt, with *O. T.*, 1845.
Billedbog uden billeder. 2 vols., 1838–40; as *Picture Book Without Pictures*, translated by Hanby Crump, 1856; as *Tales the Moon Can Tell*, translated by R.P. Keigwin, 1955.

Eventyr og historier [Tales and Stories]. 1839; *Nye Eventyr og Historier*, 6 vols., 1858–67; edited by Hans Brix and Anker Jensen, 5 vols., 1918–20.
De to baronesser. 1848; as *The Two Baronesses*, translated by Charles Beckwith Lohmeyer, 1848.
A Poet's Day Dreams (selected tales). 1853.
At være eller ikke være. 1857; as *To Be, or Not to Be?* translated by Mrs. Bushby, 1857.
Later Tales, translated by Caroline Peachey. 1869.
Lykke-Peer. 1870: as *Lucky Peer*, translated by Horace E. Scudder, 1871.

Verse

Digte [Poems]. 1830.
Samlede digte [Collected Poems]. 1833.
Seven Poems, translated by R.P. Keigwin. 1955.
Udvalgte digte [Selected Poems]. 1975.
Brothers, Very Far Away: and Other Poems, translated by Paula Hostrup-Jessen, 1991.

Plays

Kjærlighed paa Nicolai Taarn [Love on St. Nicholas Tower] (produced 1829). 1829.
Skibet, from a play by Scribe. 1831.
Bruden fra Lammermoor, music by Ivar Bredal, from the novel *The Bride of Lammermoor* by Scott (produced 1832). 1832.
Ravnen [The Raven], music by J.P.E. Hartmann, from a play by Gozzi (produced 1832). 1832.
Agnete og Havmanden [Agnete and the Merman], music by Nils V. Gade, from Andersen's poem (produced 1833). 1834.
Festen paa Kenilworth [The Festival at Kenilworth], music by C.E.F. Weyse, from the novel *Kenilworth* by Scott (produced 1836).
Skilles og mødes [Parting and Meeting] (produced 1836). In *Det Kongelige Theaters Repertoire*, n.d.
Den Usynlige paa Sprogø [The Invisible Man on Sprogø] (produced 1839).
Mulatten [The Mulatto], from a story by Fanny Reybaud (produced 1840). 1840.
Mikkels Kjærligheds historier i Paris [Mikkel's Parisian Love Stories] (produced 1840).
Maurerpigen [The Moorish Girl] (produced 1840), 1840.
En comedie i det grønne [Country Comedy], from a play by Dorvigny (produced 1840).
Fuglen i pæretræet [The Bird in the Pear Tree] (produced 1842).
Kongen drømmer [Dreams of the King] (produced 1844), 1844.
Dronningen paa 16 aar [The 16-Year-Old Queen], from a play by Bayard. 1844.
Lykkens blomst [The Blossom of Happiness] (produced 1845). 1847.
Den nye barselstue [The New Maternity Ward] (produced 1845). 1850.
Herr Rasmussen (produced 1846). Edited by E. Agerholm, 1913.
Liden Kirsten [Little Kirsten], music by J.P.E. Hartmann, from the story by Andersen (produced 1846). 1847.
Kunstens dannevirke [The Bulwark of Art] (produced 1848). 1848.
En nat i Roskilde [A Night in Roskilde], from a play by C. Warin and C.E. Lefevre (produced 1848). 1850.
Brylluppet ved Como-Søen [The Wedding at Lake Como], music by Franz Gläser, from a novel by Manzoni (produced 1849). 1849.

Meer end perler og guld [More Than Pearls and Gold], from a play by
Ferdinand Raimund (produced 1849). 1849.

Ole Lukøie [Old Shuteye] (produced 1850). 1850.

Hyldemoer [Mother Elder] (produced 1851). 1851.

Nøkken [The Nix], music by Franz Gläser (produced 1853). 1853.

Paa Langebro [On the Bridge] (produced 1864).

Han er ikke født [He Is Not Well-Born] (produced 1864). 1864.

Da Spanierne var her [When the Spaniards Were Here] (produced
1865). 1865.

Other

Ungdoms-forsøg [Youthful Attempts]. 1822.

Fodreise fra Holmens Canal til Østpynten af Amager i 1828 og 1829
[A Walking Trip from Holmen's Canal to Amager]. 1829.

Skyggebilleder af en Reise til Harzen. 1831; as *Rambles in the
Romantic Regions of the Harz Mountains*, translated by Charles
Beckwith Lohmeyer, 1848.

En digters bazar. 1842; as *A Poet's Bazaar*, translated by Charles
Beckwith Lohmeyer, 1846; as *A Visit to Germany, Italy and
Malta*, translated by Grace Thornton, 1987.

Das Märchen meines Lebens ohne Dichtung (in collected German
edition). 1847; as *The True Story of My Life*, translated by Mary
Howitt, 1847; as *Mit eget eventyr uden digtning*, edited by H.
Topsøe-Jensen, 1942.

I Sverrig. 1851; as *Pictures of Sweden*, translated by Charles Beckwith
Lohmeyer, 1851; as *In Sweden*, translated by K.R.K. MacKenzie,
1852.

Mit livs eventyr. 1855; revised editions, 1859, 1877; edited by H.
Topsøe-Jensen, 1951; as *The Story of My Life*, translated by D.
Spillan, 1871; as *The Fairy Tale of My Life*, translated by W. Glyn
Jones, 1954; in part as *The Mermaid Man*, translated by Maurice
Michael, 1955.

I Spanien. 1863; as *In Spain, and A Visit to Portugal*, translated by
Mrs. Bushby, 1864; as *A Visit to Spain*, edited and translated by
Grace Thornton. 1975.

Collected Writings. 10 vols., 1870–71.

Breve, edited by C.S.A. Bille and N. Bøgh. 2 vols., 1878.

*Briefwechsel mit dem Grossherzog Carl Alexander von Sachsen-
Weimar-Eisenach*, edited by Emil Jonas. 1887.

*Correspondence with the Late Grand-Duke of Saxe-Weimar, Charles
Dickens, etc.*, edited by Frederick Crawford. 1891.

Optegnelsesbog, edited by Julius Clausen. 1926.

Breve til Therese og Martin R. Henriques 1860–75 (correspondence),
edited by H. Topsøe-Jensen. 1932.

Brevveksling med Edvard og Henriette Collin (correspondence),
edited by H. Topsøe-Jensen. 6 vols., 1933–37.

*Brevveksling med Jonas Collin den Ældre og andre Medlemmer af
det Collinske Hus* (correspondence), edited by H. Topsøe-Jensen.
3 vols., 1945–48.

Romerske Dagbøger [Roman Diaries], edited by Paul V. Rubow and
H. Topsøe-Jensen. 1947.

Brevveksling (correspondence), with Horace E. Scudder, edited by
Jean Hersholt. 1948; as *The Andersen-Scudder Letters*, translated
by Waldemar Westergaard, 1949.

Reise fra Kjøbenhavn til Rhinen [Travels from Copenhagen to the
Rhine], edited by H. Topsøe-Jensen. 1955.

Brevveksling (correspondence), with Henriette Wulff, edited by H.
Topsøe-Jensen. 3 vols., 1959–60.

Breve til Mathias Weber (correspondence), edited by Arne Portman.
1961.

Levnedsbog 1805–1831 [The Book of Life], edited by H. Topsøe-
Jensen. 1962.

Et besøg i Portugal 1866, edited by Pout Høybye. 1968; as A *Visit to
Portugal 1866*, translated by Grace Thornton, 1972.

Skuggebilleder, edited by H. Topsøe-Jensen. 1968.

Breve til Carl B. Lorck (correspondence), edited by H. Tøpsoe-
Jensen. 1969.

Dagbøger 1825–75, edited by Kåre Olsen and H. Tøpsoe-Jensen. 12
vols., 1971–76; as *Diaries*, edited and translated by Patricia
Conroy and Sven H. Rossel, 1989.

Tegninger til Otto Zinck [Drawings for Otto Zinck], edited by Kjeld
Heltoft. 2 vols., 1972.

Rom dagbogsnotater og tegninger [Diary and Drawings from Rome],
edited by H. Topsøe-Jensen. 1980.

Album, edited by Kåre Olsen and others. 3 vols., 1980.

Hans Christian Andersen on Copenhagen, edited by Johan de Mylius,
1997.

The Red Shoes, retold and illustrated by Barbara Bazilian, 1997.

The Ugly Duckling, adapted and illustrated by Jerry Pinkney, 1999.

The Little Match Girl, adapted and illustrated by Jerry Pinkney, 1999.

*The Dinosaur's New Clothes: A Retelling of the Hans Christian
Andersen Tale* by Diane Goode, 1999.

*

Bibliography: *Andersen bibliografi 1822–1875* by B.F. Nielsen,
1942; *Andersen litteraturen 1875–1968* by Aage Jørgensen, 1970,
supplement, 1973; *H.C. Andersen-litteraturen 1969–1994: en
bibliografi* by Aage Jørgensen, 1995.

Critical Studies: *Hans Christian Andersen: His Life and Work* edited
by Svend Dahl and H. Topsøe-Jensen, 1955; *Hans Christian Andersen: A Biography* by Fredrick Böök, 1962; *Hans Christian Andersen
and the Romantic Theatre* by Frederick J. Marker, 1971; *Hans
Christian Andersen and His World* by Reginald Spink, 1972; *Hans
Christian Andersen: The Story of His Life and Work, 1805–75* by
Elias Bredsdorff, 1975; *Hans Christian Andersen* by Bo Grønbech,
1980; ''Andersen's Love'' by Peter Brask and Turid Sverre, in *The
Nordic Mind: Current Trends in Scandinavian Literary Criticism*
edited by Frank E. Andersen and John Weinstock, 1986; *H.C.
Andersen og Thalia* by Hans Christian Andersen, 1992; *Hans Chris-
tian Andersen: Danish Writer and Citizen of the World* edited by Sven
Hakon Rossel, 1996; *Hans Christian Andersen: The Fan Dancer* by
Alison Prince, 1998; *Hans Christian Andersen: The Life of a Storyteller* by Jackie Wullschlager, 2000.

*   *   *

The fame of Hans Christian Andersen—H.C. Andersen to his
fellow countrymen and Hans Andersen to countless readers outside
Denmark—is founded on paradox. Although he was—and is—a very
distinctly Danish author, he was anything but parochial. Well-read,
well-informed about the cultural and scientific developments of his
time, and well-travelled—some of Andersen's travel-books still
deserve attention, e.g., *En digters bazar* (*A Poet's Bazaar*)—he made

a name for himself both in his own country and internationally as a novelist during his own lifetime. And yet, as the physicist H.C. Ørsted told a sceptical Andersen, if his novels made him famous, his fairy-tales would make him immortal.

Andersen's first love was the theatre, but in spite of his many works for the stage—of which *Mulatten* [The Mulatto] was the most significant—he was more at home in the free form of the novel than in the conventionally more disciplined forms of lyric and drama. His first novel, *Improvisatoren* (*The Improvisatore*), soon became popular abroad because of its perceptive descriptions of the colourful Italian life and landscapes. Like much of Andersen's work, including the fairy-tales, it had its roots in his own experience, and aspects of his own childhood among the lower classes formed part of the next two novels, *O.T.* and *Kun en Spillemand* (*Only a Fiddler*). He described his life directly in his autobiography, *Mit livs eventyr* (*The Fairy Tale of My Life*).

If the novel had given him greater freedom, it was only in the shorter form of the fairy-tale, which did not demand control of long plots or complex characterization, that he found his true medium. Andersen's first tales were published in 1835. That they gave him a reputation as a children's writer is no coincidence: the earliest among his 156 tales were written for children, and until 1843 his published collections carried the subtitle ''Told for Children.'' As he gained confidence and increasingly wrote original stories—in fact only a minority, e.g., ''Fyrtøjet'' (''The Tinder Box''), 1835, derive from traditional folk-tales—he abandoned that subtitle and increasingly addressed himself to a grown-up audience. Stories like ''Historien om en Moder'' (''Story of a Mother,'' 1848) can be understood but not fully appreciated by children. Andersen's great achievement was to develop the form of the folk-tale into original, mature art in a way which has not been surpassed, and he did so partly by creating a new literary language which was essentially that of spoken narration, free of abstractions, concrete and deceptively simple. His best tales reveal his keen sense of observation of human behaviour and his deep understanding of the major issues of human existence, told with humour and sympathy.

—Hans Christian Andersen

See the essays on ''The Emperor's New Clothes'' and ''The Snow Queen.''

ANDRADE, Carlos Drummond de

Born: Itabira do Mato Dentro, Minas Gerais, Brazil, 31 October 1902. **Education:** Educated at Arnaldo College, Belo Horizonte, 1910–13; forced to return home because of poor health, where he was educated privately; Jesuit Anchieta College, Novo Friburgo, 1916–18 (expelled); studied pharmacy 1923–24, qualified 1925, but never practised. **Family:** Married Dolores Dutra de Morais in 1925; one daughter. **Career:** Journalist, Belo Horizonte and Rio de Janeiro, 1920–22; co-founding editor of the magazine, *A Revista*, 1925: closed after three issues; teacher of geography and Portuguese, Itabira, 1926; worked on newspapers *Diário de Minas*, 1926–29, and *Minas Gerais*,

1929, both Belo Horizonte; civil servant from 1928: chief secretary to minister of education, Rio de Janeiro, 1934–45 (resigned); briefly co-editor, *Tribuna Popular*, 1945; worked for Office of the National Historical and Artistic Heritage, 1945–62. Visited Buenos Aires, 1950 and 1953. Contributor to several newspapers and journals, including *Correio de Manhã* and *Jornal de Brasil*, 1963–84. **Awards:** Brasília prize for literature (refused), 1975; National Walmap prize for literature, 1975. **Died:** 17 August 1987.

PUBLICATIONS

Collection

Obra poética. 8 vols., 1989.

Verse

Alguma poesia. 1930.
Brejo das almas. 1934.
Sentimento do mundo. 1940.
José. 1942.
Poesias. 1942.
A rosa do povo. 1945.
Novos poemas. 1948.
Poesia até agora (includes *Novos poemas*). 1948.
Claro enigma. 1951.
Viola de bolso. 1952.
Fazendeiro do ar e Poesia até agora. 1954.
A vida passada a limpo. 1959.
Antologia poetica. 1962.
Lição de coisas. 1962.
In the Middle of the Road (selected poems), translated by John Nist. 1965.
José e outros. 1967.
Boitempo; A falta que ama. 1968.
Reunião (includes all collections published 1930–62, except *Viola de Bolso*). 1969.
As impurezas do branco. 1973.
Menino antigo—Boitempo II. 1973.
Poesia completa e prosa. 1973.
Souvenir of the Ancient World, translated by Mark Strand. 1976.
Discurso de primavera. 1977; enlarged edition, 1978.
O marginal Clorindo gato e a visita. 1978.
Esquecer para lembrar—Boitempo III. 1979.
A paixão medida. 1980.
The Minus Sign: A Selection from the Poetic Anthology, translated by Virginia de Araújo. 1981.
Nova reunião. 2 vols., 1983.
Corpo. 1984.
Amar ds aprende amando. 1985.
Travelling in the Family, edited by Thomas Colchie and Mark Strand, translated by Colchie, Strand, Elizabeth Bishop, and Gregory Rabassa, 1987.
Poesia errante, derrames líricos. 1988.
Farewell. 1996.

Fiction

O gerente (stories). 1945.
Contos de aprendiz (stories). 1951.

Other

Confissões de Minas. 1944.
Passeios na Ilha (articles and essays). 1952.
Fala, Amendoeira. 1957.
A bolsa e a vida (includes verse). 1962.
Rio de Janeiro em prosa e verso, with Manuel Bandeira. 1965.
Cadeiro de balanço (articles). 1966.
Obra completa. 1967.
Caminhos de João Brandão (includes verse). 1970.
O poder ultrajovem (includes verse). 1972.
De notícias o não notícias farz-se a crônica, histórias, diálogos, diragações. 1974.
Os dias lindos: crônicas. 1977.
Contos plausíveis. 1981.
Boca de Luar. 1984.
História de dois amores (for children). 1985.
O observador no escritório (diary). 1985.
Moça deitada na grama (chronicles). 1987.
Auto-retrato e outras crônicas (articles), edited by Fernando Py. 1989.
O avesso das coisas: aforismos. 1989.
Translator, *Uma gota de veneno*, by François Mauriac. 1943.
Translator, *As relações perigosas*, by Choderlos de Laclos. 1947.
Translator, *A fugitiva*, by Proust. 1956.
Translator, *Artimanhas de Scapino* by Molière. 1962.

*

Bibliography: *Bibliografia comentader de Carlos Drummond de Andrade (1918–1930)* by Fernando Py, 1980.

Critical Studies: "Conscience of Brazil: Carlos Drummond de Andrade," in *Américas*, 15(1), 1963, and *The Modernist Movement in Brazil*, 1967, both by John Nist; *Lira e antilira: Mário, Drummond, Cabral* by Luiz Costa Lima, 1968; *A rima na poesia de Carlos Drummond de Andrade* by Hélcio Martins, 1968; "Inquietudes na Poesia de Drummond" by Antônio Cândido, in his *Vários Escritos*, 1970; *Drummond: A Estilística da Repetição* by Gilberto Mendonça Teles, 1970; *Carlos Drummond de Andrade* (biography) by Assis Brasil, 1971; *A Astúcia da Mímese: Ensaios sobre lírica*, 1975, and *Verso universo em Drummond*, 1975, both by José Guilherme Merquior; *Terra e família na poesia de Carlos Drummond de Andrade* by Joaquim Francisco Coelho, 1973; *Poetas modernos de Brasil, 4. Carlos Drummond de Andrade* by Silviano Santiago, 1976; *Coleção fortuna crítica, 1. Carlos Drummond de Andrade* edited by Sônia Brayner, 1977; *Drummond: Uma poética do risco* by Iumna Maria Simon, 1978; *A dramaticidade na poesia de Drummond* by Donaldo Schuler, 1979; *Drummond o "Gauche" no tempo*, 1972, and *Carlos Drummond de Andrade: análise da obra*, 1980, both by Affonso Romano de Sant'Anna; *Poesia e poética de Carlos Drummond de Andrade* by John Gledson, 1981; "The Precarious Self: Carlos Drummond de Andrade's *Brejo das Almas*," in *Hispania*, 65, 1, 1982, and *The Unquiet Self: Self and Society in the Poetry of Carlos Drummond de Andrade*, 1984, both by Ricardo da Silveira Lobo Sternberg; *Os Sapatos de Orfeu: Biografia de Carlos Drummond de Andrade* by José Maria Cançado, 1993; *Confidência Mineira: O Amor na Poesia de Carlos Drummond de Andrade* by Mirella Vieira Lima, 1995; *Carlos Drummond de Andrade* by Francisco Achcar, 2000.

* * *

In the middle of the road there was a stone
there was a stone in the middle of the road
there was a stone
in the middle of the road there was a stone.
I shall never forget this event
in the life of my tired eyes.
I shall never forget that in the middle of the road
there was a stone
there was a stone in the middle of the road
in the middle of the road there was a stone

(translated by John Nist)

If Carlos Drummond de Andrade were still alive he might well feel irritated at being reminded that the above poem, "No meio do caminho" ("In the Middle of the Road"), remains his best known, and in a sense, most celebrated, poem. It was certainly, along with "Ode ao burguês" [Ode to the Bourgeois] by Mário de Andrade, the greatest *succès de scandale* created by the Brazilian Modernist Movement in the 1920s. It is but one of the 56 poems that comprise Drummond's (he liked to be know by his mother's family name) first collection that he did not publish until the age of 28. At first sight it looks like yet another of those *poemas-piadas* (joke-poems) with which the cheerfully irreverent Modernists either delighted or scandalized their public. Less charitably, one critic described this poem as the work of a man who had turned into a parrot.

The poem, like many more in *Alguma poesia* and the collections that followed it, *Brejo das almas* [Marsh of the Souls], *Sentimento do mundo* [Sentiment of the World], *José*, and *A rosa do povo* [The People's Rose], is the *reductio ad absurdam* of the peculiarly drummondian poetic process whereby poetry is distilled from the banal. Contemplation of the stone is a metaphor for life that is senselessly circular, returning one ceaselessly to the blank contingency of matter. Repetition, in the poem, as in life, reigns supreme. In another early poem Drummond writes: "Planet, planet, vast planet/if I had been christened Janet/it'd be a rhyme, much less a start./ Planet, planet, vast planet/But so much vaster is my heart." In the same poem, Drummond creates the concept of the *gauche*: "Go, Carlos! Be *gauche* in life". The poet's fallible subjectivity will always torment him. He, the subject, confronts the ineffability of the object. His mission is to achieve an equilibrium between these two. The timid poet from the exterior of Minas Gerais would confront and interpret existence. Poetry is provoked out of a desperate search for this equilibrium over some 60 years of poetic creation.

The poetic stance of the *gauche*, the awkward, left-handed, marginalized outsider *avant la lettre*, was Drummond's response to the riddle of existence. In one of his rare prose poems, entitled "O enigma," composed some 20 years later, he confronts again the image of an irreducible and incomprehensible object in the road, but it is not a stone; it is an "enigma," an "enormous thing." There are stones, but these are, presumably, human beings on the road of life. The mysterious form stands in their path; it paralyses them forever. Of course, as the poet observes, if the enigma could be interpreted it would no longer be an enigma. It is a projection of man's own imagination and his contradictions. The stones bewail their lot:

Oh! what good is intelligence . . . We were intelligent, and yet, to ponder on the threat is not to remove it; that only creates it. Oh! what good is sensitivity—sob the stones. We were sensitive, and the gift of compassion rebounds upon us, when we thought to show it to less favoured species.

"O enigma" is the final poem in *Novos poemas* [New Poems], and like his most celebrated volume, *A rosa do povo* [The People's Rose], was a product of the 1940s in which Drummond did attain some kind of equilibrium between the utterly unreliable self, or subject, and the equally unknowable world of things. In "A flor e a náusea" he portrays himself as defeated prisoner of society and oppressed by tedium; and yet in the "river of steel" that is the busy street, a flower is born: "It is ugly. But it is a flower. It has made its way through the asphalt, the tedium, the loathing and the hate." The flower, traditional symbol of life and hope, joins with the very visual image of the *gauche* in the figure of Charlie Chaplin, another obscure marginal—but with the power, as Drummond portrays him in the final poem of *A rosa do povo*, entitled "Canto ao homem ao povo Charlie Chaplin" [Song of the Man of the People Charlie Chaplin], to bring a form of redemption to the oppressed: "and they speak as well, the flowers that you love so dearly when they are trodden underfoot."

This is a humane poetry of love; but despite the strong vein of eroticism in the early volumes—Drummond's very last collection was an entire set of erotic poems—and the strong theme of human solidarity that informs the poetry of the 1940s, love is seen, in the present tense, as a sad game, and in retrospect, as an aching nostalgia for the passing of all that, with hindsight, one might still hold dear. Like the Modernist Movement which in his youth inspired him, Drummond seeks to forge an identity for Brazil, but in doing so creates a tragic vision of his destiny in the historical continuum that is Brazil. If the *modernistas* reached out into the four corners of their vast country to seize, spatially, the totality of their nation, Drummond's mission turned out to be more temporal. He chose to plunge into the past, the past he knew, that of rural Minas Gerais, in order to articulate his own destiny as well as that of Brazil. In the process, he universalized his poetic drama: by evoking the past, he hoped to explain the present. It is a painful process that may be doomed to failure. His supreme myth plucked out of past time is his birthplace, Itabira: "Itabira is just a photograph on the wall./But how it makes me suffer!" It is above all the poet's lucidity, honesty, and struggle for truth that makes him suffer in the course of his odyssey through the past and present of Minas Gerais. The great church clock in the poem "O relógio" [The Clock] in the collection *Boitempo* [Ox-time] symbolizes Drummond's fate as the poet from Minas whose function is to bear witness, record and interpret Brazil, past, present, and future. But the poet in his old age has travelled far not only in terms of longevity but also in terms of ontological and poetic investigation. The poetry, of *Boitempo* and beyond seeks profound acceptance and disengagement, yet always within the unspoken pact forged with the phenomenological and spiritual world in his most overtly philosophical collection, *Claro enigma* [Clear Enigma]. Minas Gerais means "General Mines," seen as a landscape of untold mineral wealth since the discovery in the 18th century of silver, gold, diamonds, and later, iron ore in vast quantities. This wealth built the now decaying baroque cities of Minas. Drummond meditates in "Os bens e o sangue" [The Gods and the Blood] on the wealth of which he has been disinherited and the blood he has inherited.

As he contemplates the family archive, his ancestors seem to address him across the decades and acknowledge his role in the continuum: "You are our natural seed and we fructify. you,/we are your explanation, your simplest virtue. . . /For it was only right that one of us should deny us the better to serve us." Thus does

Drummond fulfil a destiny, tragic in its resignation. In another poem from *Claro enigma*, "Morte das casas de Ouro Preto" [Death of the Houses of Ouro Preto], the rain falls endlessly on the decaying mansions of the once fabulous city. Water in Drummond is flux, passing time, destruction, and eternity. Now it is no longer a matter of change but of the absorption of man-made structures into the timeless pathos of Minas, back into the soil of Minas in order to complete the cycle: "May the beams of today body forth into trees!/May the dust on them be again the dust of the highways!".

For all his intermittent engagement with the theme of love, with the problems of urban society and with politics, Drummond is, ultimately, a great existential poet; perhaps the greatest that America has produced.

—R.J. Oakley

ANDRADE, Mário (Raul) de

Born: São Paulo, Brazil, 9 October 1893. **Education:** Educated at Escola de Nossa Senhora do Carmo, São Paulo, 1905–09; Alvares Penteado Commerical School, São Paulo, 1910; studied piano at the Musical and Dramatic Conservatory, São Paulo, 1911, degree 1917. **Career:** Involved in avant-garde artistic circles in the 1920s: co-organizer, the Modern Art Week at the Teatro Municipal, São Paulo, 1922; professor of the history of music and aesthetics, São Paulo Conservatory, 1925; contributor, "Taxi" column for *Diário Nacional*, from 1928; worked for the Ministry of Education's schools' music reform programme, 1930; co-founder, with Paulo Duarte, and director, Municipal Department of Culture, São Paulo, 1934–37: founded the Municipal Library, the Department of National Heritage, the journal *Revista do Arquivo Municipal de São Paulo*, and São Paulo's Ethnography and Folklore Society (and its first president); moved to Rio de Janeiro, 1937; director, Federal University Institute of Arts, Rio de Janeiro, 1938–40, and held the chair of philosophy and history of art; headed the *Enciclopédia Brasileira* project for the National Book Institute, 1939; made anthropological research trips to northern Brazil, under commission from the Department of National Heritage, 1941. Organizer, first National Language Congress, 1937; co-founder, Brazilian Society of Writers, 1942. **Member:** São Paulo Academy of Letters. **Died:** 25 February 1945.

PUBLICATIONS

Collections

Obras completas. 24 vols., 1960–91.
   1. *Obra imatura.*
   2. *Poesias completas.*
   3. *Amar, verbo intransitivo.*
   4. *Macunaíma.*
   5. *Os contos de Belazarte.*
   6. *Ensaio sobre a musica brasileira.*
   7. *Música doce música.*
   8. *Pequena história da música.*
   9. *Namoros com a medicina.*
   10. *Aspectos da literatura brasileira.*

11. *Aspectos da música brasileira.*
12. *Aspectos das artes plásticas no Brasil.*
13. *Música de feitiçaria no Brasil.*
14. *O baile das quatro artes.*
15. *Os filhos da Candinha.*
16. *O padre Jesuíno de Monte Carmelo*
17. *Contos novos.*
18. *Danças dramáticas do Brasil.*
19. *Modinhas imperiais.*
20. *O empalhador de Passarinho.*
21. *Quatro Pessoas.*
22. *Dicionário musical brasileiro.*
23. *Vida de cantador.*
24. *Cartas de Mário de Andrade a Luís da Câmara Cascudo.*

Obras [50th Anniversary of Modern Art Week Edition]. 15 vols., 1972.
Poesias completas, edited by Diléa Zanotto Manfio. 1987.

Verse

Há uma gota de sangue em cada poema (as Mário Sobral). 1917.
Paulicéia desvairada. 1926; as *Hallucinated City* (bilingual edition), edited and translated by Jack E. Tomlins, 1968.
Clã do Jabuti. 1927.
Remate de Males. 1930.
Lira paulistana. 1946.

Fiction

Primeiro andar (stories). 1926.
Amar, verbo intransitivo. 1927; edited by Telê Porto Ancona Lopez, 1982; as *Fräulein*, translated by Margaret Richardson Hollingsworth, 1933.
Macunaíma. 1928; edited by Telê Porto Ancona Lopez, 1978; as *Macunaíma*, translated by Edward Arthur Goodland, 1984.
Belazarte. 1934.
Contos novos. 1947.

Other

A escrava que não é isaura. 1925.
Compêndio de história da música. 1929; revised edition, as *Pequena história da música*, 1942.
Modinhas imperiais. 1930.
Música, doce música. 1933.
O Aleijadinho e Álvares de Azevedo. 1935.
A música e a canção populares no Brasil. 1936.
Namoros com a medicina. 1939.
A expressão musical dos Estados Unidos. 1940.
Música do Brasil. 1941.
O movimento modernista. 1942.
Aspectos de literatura brasileira. 1943.
O baile das quatro artes. 1943.
Os filhos da Candinha. 1943.
O Empalhador de Passarinho. 1944(?).
Cartas de Mário Andrade a Manuel Bandeira. 1958.
Danças dramáticas do Brasil. 3 vols., 1959.
Música de feitiçaria do Brasil. 1963.
Setenta e uma cartas de Mário de Andrade. 1963.
Aspectos das artes plásticas no Brasil. 1965.

Mário de Andrade escreve a Alceu, Meyer e outros, edited by Lygia Fernandes. 1968.
Itinerário: cartas a Alphonsus de Guimaraens filho. 1974.
Táxi e crônicas no Diário Nacional. 1976.
O turista aprendiz (diaries), edited by Telê Porto Ancona Lopez. 1976.
O banquete. 1977.
A lição do Amigo: cartas de Mário de Andrade a Carlos Drummond de Andrade. 1982.
Correspondente contumaz 1925–1944 (letters to Pedro Naval), edited by Fernando da Rocha Peres. 1982.
Cartas: Mário de Andrade, Oneyda Alvarenga. 1983.
Entrevistas e depoimentos, edited by Telê Porto Ancona Lopez, 1983.
Cartas de Mário de Andrade a Álvaro Lins. 1983.
Os cocos, edited by Oneyda Alvarenga. 1984.
Cartas de Mário de Andrade a Prudente de Moraes, edited by Georgina Koifman. 1985.
Miguel de Andrade por el mismo, edited by Paulo Duarte. 1985.
Dicionário musical brasileiro, edited by Oneyda Alvarenga and Flávia Camargo Toni. 1989.
Cartas de Trabalho: Correspondência com Rodrigo Mello Franco de Andrade (1936–1945). 1989.
A lição do guru: cartas a Guilherme Figueiredo, 1937–1945. 1989.
Querida Henriqueta: cartas de Mário de Andrade a Henriqueta Lisboa, edited by Lauro Palú. 1991.
Será o benedito! Artigos publicados no suplemento em rotogravura de O Estado de S. Paulo, edited by Telê Porto Ancona Lopez. 1992.

*

Bibliography: *Mário de Andrade: Bibliografia sobre a sua obra* (*Revista do Libro* supplement) by António Simões dos Reis, 1960; *Brazilian Literature: A Research Guide* by David William Foster and Walter Rela, 1990.

Critical Studies: *Lição de Mário de Andrade* by Lêdo Ivo, 1952; *Mário de Andrade* by Fernando Mendes de Almeida, 1962; "Some Formal Types in the Poetry of Mário de Andrade" by David William Foster, in *Luso-Brazilian Review*, December 1965; *The Modernist Movement in Brazil: A Literary Study* by John Nist, 1967; "The Literary Criticism of Mário de Andrade" by Thomas R. Hart, in *Disciplines of Criticism: Essays in Literary Theory, Interpretation, and History* edited by Peter Demetz and others, 1968; *Roteiro de Macunaíma* by M. Cavalcanti Proença, 1969; *Poesia e prosa de Mário de Andrade* by João Pacheco, 1970; *Morfología de Macunaíma* by Haroldo de Campos, 1973; *Roteiro de Macuníama* by M. Cavalcanti Proença, 1977; *Política e poesia em Mário de Andrade* by Joan Dassin, 1978; "Macunaíma as Brazilian Hero", in *Latin American Literary Review*, 1978, and *Literatura e Cinema: Macunaíma: do modernismo na literatura ao cinema novo*, 1982, both by Randal Johnson; *Mário de Andrade e a revolução da linguagem* by José Maria Barbosa Gomes, 1979; "*Preguiça* and Power: Mário de Andrade's *Macunaíma*" by Renata R. Mautner, in *Luso-Brazilian Review*, Summer 1984; *Mário de Andrade: Hoje* edited by Carlos E.O. Berriel, 1990; *A presença do povo na cultura brasileira: ensaio sobre o pensamento de Mário de Andrade e Paulo Friere* by Vivian

Schelling, 1991; *Modernisme brésilien et négritude antillaise: Mario de Andrade et Aimé Césaire* by Maria de Lourdes Teodoro, 1999; *Mário de Andrade: the Creative Works* by José I. Suárez and Jack E. Tomlins, 2000; *Correspondência Mario de Andrade and Manuel Banderia*, with introduction by Marcos Antonio de Moraes, 2000.

* * *

To call Mário de Andrade the creator of Brazilian modernism is an oversimplification, but if Oswald de Andrade, fellow poet and novelist, was its catalyst and presiding genius, Mário was surely the doyen, supreme symbol, and principal ideologue of that iconoclastic and brilliant artistic movement that burst upon the Brazilian cultural scene in 1922, changing forever the aesthetic landscape of Brazil. Andrade also distinguished himself in more, and disparate, fields than any other single individual among the talented generation of writers and artists that included the sculptor Brecheret, the composer Villa Lobos and the important poets Oswald de Andrade, Manuel Bandeira, and Carlos Drummond de Andrade.

Born in São Paulo in 1893, Andrade first studied sciences, but entered the São Paulo Conservatory of Musical and Dramatic Art in 1911, graduating in 1917 with the piano as his special subject. His musical background and a lifelong passion for folklore and the plastic arts caused him to make a mark early in his writing career as journalist, critic, and essayist. His writings on music, painting and folklore, especially that of his native Brazil, run to many volumes; but he was to make his mark most spectacularly as writer of lyric poetry and prose fiction. At the time of World War I, the predominant fashion in Brazilian poetry was that of a polite symbolism and Parnassianism. Andrade's first volume, *Há uma gota de sangue em cada poema* [There Is a Drop of Blood in Every Poem] betrays the Parnassian influence but it contains, too, the unmistakeable rebelliousness and innovatory drive of all his imaginative *oeuvre*. He was destined to spearhead the artistic revolution of *modernismo* that was inspired by the Symbolist and Expressionist currents abroad in Europe in the last decades of the 19th century and the first two decades of the 20th. In formal terms, this meant experimentation with free verse, a broadening of terms of reference with regard to the possible thematics of poetry, and an impulse to embrace, artistically, the whole of lived experience—all the phenomena of early 20th-century life; hence the inordinate impact on Andrade and his artistic comrades-in-arms of Marinetti's Futurist Manifesto published in Paris in 1909. The age of speed and of the machine would fuel the imagination of the Brazilian Modernist movement in its heroic phase. Indeed, Andrade and his friends were called "futurists" in the months leading up to the São Paulo Modern Art Week they organized in February 1922. Andrade had written most of his second and most famous book of poetry, *Paulicéia desvairada* (*Hallucinated City*)—referring to São Paulo—in 1920, but it had been quoted extensively in the press and widely disseminated by members of the group, so that the poetry of the man whom Oswald de Andrade had hailed in a famous article as "my Futurist poet" was predictably greeted with boos and catcalls of the massed opponents of *modernismo* who crowded the hall in February of that year to hear it recited. The impact of this aggressive, anti-bourgeois poetry has a very rough English parallel in the reception accorded to the poetry of T.S. Eliot up to and including *The Waste Land*, although *Hallucinated City* and the febrile

urban poetry that was to follow it was far more uneven in quality; but just as Eliot found himself the poet of London, so Andrade became in the 1920s the quintessential urban poet of São Paulo.

The collections of poetry that Andrade published later in the 1920s and in the 1930s add to the iconoclasm, the humour and the irreverence a wealth of allusion to Brazilian myth and folklore. At its worst, this poetry is undisciplined and structured in a wayward fashion. This ill-discipline is redeemed by the humour, the by now typically Modernist incorporation into lyric poetry of the rhythms and lexis of colloquial speech—the language of the street—and by the pervasive, gentle lyricism. In "Momento" (1937) he writes:

> The wind cuts people in two
> Only a desire for clarity buoys up the world. . .
> The sun shines. The rain rains. And the gale
> Scatters in the blue the trombones of the clouds.
> Nobody gets to be one in this city.
> The doves cling to the skyscrapers, comes the rain.
> Comes the cold. And comes the anguish . . . It is this
>   violent wind
> That bursts out of the gorges of the human soil
> Demanding sky, peace and a little spring.

Andrade was to earn considerable critical acclaim within Brazil for his prose fiction. Few Brazilians have written better short stories, but it is his novel, *Macunaíma*, that has brought him most enduring, and international, celebrity as a storyteller. *Macunaíma* ("The Hero Without Character" is a translation of its subtitle) is a surrealistic fantasy in which Andrade draws on his compendious folkloric research in order to weave a coherent fiction that is, at the same time, also a compendium of Brazil itself. Here, he demonstrates his lifelong contention that popular forms of expression are legitimate material for the elaboration of high art—a cornerstone of Brazilian Modernist ideology. Thus are Brazil and its culture rescued from its European and colonialist past. Yet, the protagonist has no character because of his colonial status. The 20-year-old, magical Amazonian chief whose hilarious passage along with his brothers Jiguê and Maanape through the society and the streets of São Paulo is wide-eyed and innocent. Macunaíma, the hero, exhibits all of the vices and virtues Andrade saw in his countryman together with an unformed character: only when Brazil comes of age, Andrade declared, will she emancipate herself from Europe and acquire a character. The setting of the opening chapters is Amazonian, but the novel is by no means regionalist. Macunaíma's magical journeys quarter the length and breadth of Brazil from the island of Marajó in the mouth of the Amazon to Rio Grande in the far south. In the course of these peregrinations Macunaíma experiences extreme suffering and extreme joy. At the close of his journeying he is in a state of profound disenchantment. The Brazilian gods take pity and transform him into a new constellation of stars—the Great Bear, in the midst of which "he broods alone in the vast expanse of heaven."

Andrade succeeded, as perhaps only Lima Barreto among Brazilian writers before his time did, in viewing Brazil and its people through entirely Brazilian eyes. This capacity, he felt, was the true legacy of Brazilian modernism. Barreto had opined that in Brazil "the desert encircles the city." Andrade, urban poet, expressed eloquently his awareness of the difficulty of this pan-Brazilian enterprise, the dilemma of the mutually alienated Brazils, in his "Dois poemas Acreanos" [Two Poems Concerning Acre]:

Brazilian rubber-tapper,
In the gloom of the forest
Rubber-tapper, sleep.
Striking the chord of love I sleep.
How incredibly hard this is!
I want to sing but cannot,
I want to feel and I don't feel
The Brazilian word
That will make you sleep. . .
Rubber-tapper, sleep. . .

—R.J. Oakley

ANDRIĆ, Ivo

Born: Trávnik, Bosnia (then in the Austro-Hungarian Empire), 9 October 1892. **Education:** Educated at schools in Višegrad and Sarajevo, 1898–1912; University of Zagreb, 1912; Vienna University, 1913; Jagiellonian University, Cracow, 1914; Graz University, Ph.D. 1923. **Military Service:** Served in the army, 1917. **Family:** Married Milica Babić in 1959 (died 1968). **Career:** Served in the Yugoslav diplomatic service, 1920–41, in the Vatican (Rome), Geneva, Madrid, Bucharest, Trieste, Graz, Belgrade, Marseilles, Paris, Brussels, and as Ambassador to Germany, Berlin; full-time writer, 1941–49; representative of Bosnia, Yugoslav parliament, 1949–55. Co-founder and member of the editorial board, *Književni jug* [The Literary South], 1918–19. President, Federation of Writers of Yugoslavia, 1946–51. **Awards:** Yugoslav Government prize, 1956; Nobel prize for literature, 1961; Vuk prize (Serbia), 1972. Red Cross medal, 1936; Légion d'honneur (France), 1937; Order of the Supreme Commander of Resurgent Poland, 1937; Order of St. Sava, first class (Yugoslavia), 1938. Honorary doctorate: University of Cracow, 1964. **Member:** of Mlada Bosna [Young Bosnia] and interned for three years during World War I; Member, Serbian Academy; honorary member, Bosnian Academy, 1970. **Died:** 13 March 1975.

PUBLICATIONS

Collection

Sabrana djela [Collected Works], edited by Risto Trifković and others. 17 vols., 1984.

Fiction

Pripovetke [Stories]. 3 vols., 1924–36.
Gospodjica. 1945; as *The Woman from Sarajevo*, translated by Joseph Hitrec, 1965.
Travnička hronika. 1945; as *Bosnian Story*, translated by Kenneth Johnstone, 1958; as *Bosnian Chronicle*, translated by Joseph Hitrec, 1963; as *The Days of the Consuls*, translated by Celia Hawkesworth and Bogdan Rakić, 1992.
Na Drini ćuprija. 1945; as *The Bridge on the Drina*, translated by Lovett Edwards, 1959.

Priča o vezirovom slonu. 1948; as *The Vizier's Elephant: Three Novellas*, translated by Drenka Willen, 1962.
Nove pripovetke [New Stories]. 1949.
Priča o kmetu Simanu [The Tale of the Peasant Simon]. 1950.
Novele [Short Stories]. 1951.
Pod Grabićem: Pripovetke o životu bosanskog sela [Under the Elm: Stories of Life in a Bosnian Village]. 1952.
Prokleta avlija. 1954; as *Devil's Yard*, translated by Kenneth Johnstone, 1962; as *The Damned Yard*, translated by Celia Hawkesworth, in *The Damned Yard and Other Stories*, 1992.
Panorama: Pripovetke [Panorama: Stories] (for children). 1958.
Izbor [Selection]. 1961.
Ljubav u kasabi [Love in a Market Town]. 1963.
Anikina vremena [Anika's Times] (stories). 1967.
The Pasha's Concubine and Other Tales, translated by Joseph Hitrec. 1968.
Kula i druge pripovetke (for children). 1970.
The Damned Yard and Other Stories, translated by Celia Hawkesworth. 1992.

Verse

Ex ponto. 1918.
Nemiri [Anxieties]. 1919.

Other

Lica [Faces]. 1960.
Goya. 1972.
Letters, edited and translated by Želimir Juričić. 1984.
The Development of Spiritual Life under the Turks, edited by Želimir B. Juričić and J.F. Loud. 1990.
Conversation with Goya, Signs, Bridges, translated by Celia Hawkesworth and Andrew Harvey. 1992.
Diplomatski spisi [Diplomatic Papers]. 1992.
Three Stories About Bosnia: 1908, 1946, 1992/Leo Tolstoy, Ivo Andrić, Rajko Dolecek, translated by Margot and Bosko Milosavljevic, 1995.
Literature, History, and Postcolonial Cultural Identity in Africa and the Balkans: the Search for a Usable Past in Farah, Ngugi, Krleza, and Andrić by Dubravka Juraga, 1996.

*

Bibliography: *Andrić: Bibliografija dela, prevoda, i literature 1911–1970*, 1974; in *A Comprehensive Bibliography of Yugoslav Literature in English, 1953–1980* by Vasa D. Mihailovich and Mateja Matejić, 1984, supplements, 1988, 1992.

Critical Studies: "The French in *The Chronicle of Travnik*" by Ante Kadić, in *California Slavic Studies*, 1, 1960; "The Work of Ivo Andrić" by E.D. Goy, in *Slavonic and East European Review*, 41, 1963; "The Later Stories of Ivo Andrić" by Thomas Eekman, in *Slavonic and East European Review*, 48, 1970; "Ivo Andrić and the Quintessence of Time" by Nicholas Moracevich, in *Slavic and East European Journal*, 16(3), 1972; *Ivo Andrić: Bridge Between East and West* by Celia Hawkesworth, 1984; *Ivo Andrić: Proceedings of a Symposium Held at the School of Slavonic and East European Studies 10–12 July 1984*, 1985; "Ivo Andrić and World Literature" by Milan V. Dimić, in *Canadian Slavonic Papers*, 27(3), 1985; *The Man and* the Artist: Essays on Ivo Andrić, 1986, and "Andrić's Berlin Writings: Between the Two Sirens," in Russian, Croatian and Serbian, Czech and Slovak, Polish Literature, 30(1), 1991, both by Želimir B. Juričić "Ivo Andrić and the Swing to Infinity," in Scottish Slavonic Review, 6, 1986, and "The Short Stories of Ivo Andrić: Autobiography and the Chain of Proof", in Slavonic and East European Review, 67(1), 1989, both by Felicity Rosslyn; "Narrator and Narrative in Andrić's Prokleta avlija" by Anita Lekić-Trbojević, in Serbian Studies, 4(3), 1987; "Some Rhetorical Aspects of the Novel The Bridge on the Drina" by Vladimir Miličić, in Serbian Studies 4(3), 1987; "Ivo Andrić's Historical Thought" by Predrag Palavestra, in Reflets d'histoire européenne dans l'oeuvre d'Ivo Andrić edited by Dragan Nedeljković, 1987; Ivo Andrić: A Writer's Life by Radovan Popović, 1988; "The Echoes of the Second World War" by Dušan Puvačić, in Serbian Studies, 4(4), 1988; Ivo Andrić: A Critical Biography by Vanita Singh Mukerji, 1991; "Ivo Andrić: A Yugoslav Career" by Hans-Peter Stoffel, in New Zealand Slavonic Journal, 1992; Ivo Andrić Revisited: the Bridge Still Stands, edited by Wayne S. Vucinich, 1995.

* * *

The work for which Ivo Andrić is probably best known outside Bosnia is Na Drini ćuprija (The Bridge on the Drina), a chronicle of the life of the small Bosnian town of Višegrad over several centuries. This rich fusion of legend and history is given shape by the central symbol of the bridge, linking East and West, past and future, and instilling in the townspeople a sense of harmony and the endurance of life despite individual transience.

The major part of Andrić's fiction—five novels and six volumes of short stories—is set in his native Bosnia and informed by a detailed knowledge of this region of the Balkans under Ottoman and, later, Habsburg rule. This precise setting in time and space is an essential feature of Andrić's work, but it has proved an obstacle to his reception in some countries, despite the fact that he has been extensively translated. There has been a tendency not to look beyond the "exotic" setting in this "remote" corner of Europe. Andrić focuses his attention on Bosnia because it represents a particularly varied concentration of cultures: an indigenous population of both Catholic and Orthodox Christians, a large Muslim community, Jews, and gypsies. Bosnia also represents a crossroads between East and West, visited by Ottoman dignitaries and European merchants, diplomats, and administrators. It serves consequently as a microcosm of both the variety of human life and the arbitrary divisions and antagonisms between men.

A detailed exploration of this clash of cultures is offered by Travnička hronika (Bosnian Story or The Days of the Consuls) in which the French and Austrian consuls and the Turkish vizier confront and, when international politics permit, console each other in this harsh and hostile land. Andrić exploits this setting to reveal universal patterns of behaviour and experience, drawing on legend, myth, archetype, and symbol. The complement of the symbol of the bridge in Andrić's work is that of its opposite, the prison, suggesting all the constraints which compel an individual to seek some way out of the fundamental laws of human existence. The image is most fully developed in the short novel, or novella, Prokleta avlija (Devil's Yard or The Damned Yard), in which the prison inmates "escape" by telling stories. It is perhaps in the shorter prose forms that Andrić excels and the best of his stories offer a vivid, intensely suggestive and often disturbing image or anecdote, rich in meanings and associations.

Andrić also wrote verse intermittently throughout his life. More characteristic, however, are his prose reflections, jottings prompted by experiences of all kinds. Selections of these were published posthumously in his collected works as Znakovi pored puta [Signs by the Roadside] and Sveske [Notebooks], providing insight into the fine and subtle mind of this otherwise very private man. Parallels may be drawn between Andrić's work and that of Thomas Mann, Joseph Conrad, and Henry James. He was an avid reader and himself spoke of a sense of affinity with a wide variety of writers from Camus and Goethe to Marcus Aurelius.

—E.C. Hawkesworth

See the essay on The Bridge on the Drina.

ANDRZEJEWSKI, Jerzy

Born: Warsaw, Poland, 19 August 1909. **Education:** Educated at a gymnasium in Warsaw 1919–27; University in Warsaw, 1927–31. **Family:** Married Maria Abgarowicz. **Career:** Took part in underground cultural work in Warsaw during World War II. Writer from 1932; editor of literature section of weekly Prosto z mostu, 1935–37; after the war moved to Cracow: chair of the Cracow Division of Polish Writers Union, 1946–47; involved in social work in Szczecin, 1948–52; joined Polish Communist Party, 1949; editor-in-chief of weekly Przegld kulturalny [Cultural Review], 1952–54; His book Apelacja (The Appeal) was banned in Poland, 1968. **Awards:** Polish Academy of Literature Young Writers prize, 1939; Cracow prize, 1946; Odrodzenie award, 1948; Order of the Banner of Labour (1st Class), 1949; Polish Readers prize, 1959, 1964, and 1965; Złoty Kłos award, 1965. **Member:** Polish parliament, 1952–56: resigned his Party membership in protest when the government banned a new literary magazine, 1957. **Died:** 19 April 1983.

PUBLICATIONS

Fiction

Drogi nieuniknione [Inescapable Ways] (stories). 1936.
Ład Serca [Peace of Mind]. 1938.
Wielki tydzień [Holy Week] (novella). 1943.
Noc [Night] (stories). 1945.
Popiół i diament. 1948; as Ashes and Diamonds, translated by D.F. Welsh, 1962.
Wojna skuteczna [An Effective War]. 1953.
Złoty lis [The Golden Fox] (story). 1955.
Ciemności kryją ziemię [Darkness Covers the Earth]. 1957; as The Inquisitors, also translated by Konrad Syrop, 1960.
Bramy Raju. 1958; as The Gates of Paradise, translated by James Kirkup, 1962.
Niby gaj: Opowiadania 1939–58 [As if the Grove] (stories). 1959.
Idzie skaczc po górach. 1963; as A Sitter for a Satyr, translated by Celina Wieniewska, 1964; as He Cometh Leaping upon the Mountains, translated by Wieniewska, 1965.
Apelacja. 1968; as The Appeal, translated by Celina Wieniewska, 1971.

Teraz na ciebie zagłada [Now Annihilation Is Coming upon You]. 1976.
Już prawnie nic [Already Next to Nothing]. 1979.
Miazga [Pulp]. 1979.
Nowe opowiadania [New Tales]. 1980.
Nikt [Nobody] (novella). 1983.
Intermezzo, i inne opowiadania. 1986.

Plays

Święto Winkelrida [Winkelreid's Day], with J. Zagorski. 1957.
Prometheus. 1972.

Screenplays: *Popiół i diament*, with Andrzej Wajda, 1958; *Niewinni Czarodzieje* (collaborator), 1959.

Other

Aby pokój zwyciężył [May Peace Win]. 1950.
Wyznania i rozmyślania pisarza [Confessions and Thoughts of a Writer]. 1950.
O człowieku radzieckim [About the Russian Man]. 1951.
Ludzie i zdarzenia [People and Events]. 1952.
Partia i twórczość pisarza [The Party and Writer's Works]. 1952.
Książka dla Marcina [The Book for Martin: Reminiscences]. 1954.
Gra z cieniem (diary). 1987.
Z dnia na dzień: Dziennik literacki 1972–1979 (newspaper articles). 2 vols., 1988.
Listy [Letters], with Andrzej Fiett. 1991.

*

Critical Studies: *Andrzejewski* by Wacław Sadkowski, translated by Krystyna Cękalska, 1975; *Jerzy Andrzejewskis Roman "Ciemności kryj ziemię" und die Darstellung der Spanischen Inquisition in Werken der fiktionalen Literatur* by Jürgen Schreiber, 1981; *Andrzejewski* by Anna Synoradzka, 1997.

* * *

Jerzy Andrzejewski is one of the best Polish novelists of the 20th century. It would be difficult, however, to pin down his literary masterwork. He has left a number of novels and short stories of challenging content and skilful narration. Following various narrative styles of modern times that reflect the meanders of his intellectual search and formal experiments, and being, in turn, a Catholic, a Communist, and an outspoken dissident, Andrzejewski defies easy classifications. It appears, however, that the impact of Conradian solipsism, apart from his Marxist phase, influenced him until the last days.

Joseph Conrad's principle that there is no escape from the prison of the self and that, consequently, one is unable to communicate with others, thus living in solitude and despondency, forms the basis for Andrzejewski's first collection of short stories *Drogi nieuniknione* [Inescapable Ways]. The best account of anxieties caused by such a situation was the novel *Ład Serca* [Peace of Mind], in the mould of Georges Bernanos's Catholic fiction. Its extraordinary setting in a secluded Belarussian village, surrounded by forests, exudes the atmosphere of symbolic darkness and unavoidable fate. The story of a parish priest, tormented by a guilty conscience, and the misfortunes of

his forlorn flock, represents a world of feeble mortals, where God seems far away, His grace scarce, while evil is on the rampage. Christian ideas of love and repentance are eventually engulfed by despair over the absence of justice and moral order. This kind of pessimism dominates the war fiction, the short stories published in Andrzejewski's first post-war volume *Noc* [Night], and in later collections. The symbolic "night" reveals a similar distress, magnified only by a much more ruthless background, where fighting intensifies inborn human wickedness and increases hatred and isolation. The portrayed events polarize between unrestricted killing and preposterous patriotic gestures of sham conspirators.

At the end of World War II Conradian solitude was suspended in favour of a growing belief in the power of collective efforts. In the final, reworked version of the novella *Wielki tydzień* [Holy Week], one of the underground soldiers advocates a united front of all freedom fighters. According to the writer's own confession, he was looking for a "magic circle of a well-ordered world" and eventually found it in Marxism. As a result, he published his controversial novel about the first days of the Polish People's Republic, *Popiół i diament* (*Ashes and Diamonds*), subsequently filmed by Andrzej Wajda. The biased picture of the non-Communist Home Army and staunch support for the party line secured official recognition, and over 25 editions were printed. Nevertheless Andrzejewski's traditional categories of human loneliness in the world of conflict between good and evil have simply been adjusted to new, Marxist-inspired views on history and progress. The unequivocal condemnation of the recent past and those hostile to communism resulted from that approach.

Andrzejewski's fairly brief links with communism were reflected in political articles and in the unsuccessful satirical novel *Wojna skuteczna* [An Effective War]. The publication of *Ciemności kryją ziemię* (*The Inquisitors*) marked a fundamental rejection of any political system that upholds the supremacy of ideology over personal freedom. Accordingly, the portrayal of the Inquisition in medieval Spain can be understood as an allegory, referring above all to Stalinism. In this account, absolute power destroys individual conscience and human loyalty, transforming even committed idealists into the blind instruments of terror. Similar scepticism about the human values of any dogma guided Andrzejewski's experimental short narrative, *Bramy Raju* (*The Gates of Paradise*), where several confessions follow each other without any full stops. In this story the authentic pilgrimage to Jerusalem by French youngsters is described as a mundane affair, whose participants are motivated not by divine love but by adolescent sensuality and carnal desires. The worst, however, is their leader, an idealist, whose erroneous belief in Jerusalem's golden gates to paradise makes him unwittingly a false prophet, deluding others.

Idzie skacząc po górach (*He Cometh Leaping upon the Mountains*), set in contemporary France, can be regarded as a pastiche of various narrative styles, including the stream of consciousness, still fashionable at that time. Its portrayal of French writers and artists contains satirical undertones, condemning what amounts to the commercially oriented and relatively decadent western civilization. The author's irony embraces his own narrative commentaries, where various intellectual trends such as psychoanalysis and anthropology are taunted.

Apelacja (*The Appeal*), published in the West and subsequently banned in Poland, aims at the simplicity of confession, articulated by a "little man" whose obvious mediocrity accounts for the impression of documentary truth. A former officer of the "people's militia" and a party *apparatchik*, he eventually finds himself in a mental hospital, persecuted by the Kafkaesque nightmare of being constantly spied upon by secret agents. Once an autocratic and suspicious administrator himself, he can be regarded as a victim of his own standards, but his naive faith in the party, which has survived all ups and downs, shifts responsibility mostly upon the system and its destructive potential.

Andrzejewski's last novel, *Miazga* [Pulp], planned first as a portrayal of the Polish cultural and political élite, eventually turned into an experimental attempt to lay open the author's growing doubts about storytelling and moral commitment. Its crumbled form questions the reliability of fiction by giving two parallel accounts of the same event; blends invented stories with documents (the author's diary) and quasi-documents (the "biographies" of Poles); and includes short stories written by the main character, which were published a year later under Andrzejewski's own name, in *Nowe opowiadania* [New Tales]. The Conradian prison of the self eventually inhibits all attempts to say anything more than personal truth: "the writer narrates and asks questions. Nothing more."

The novella *Nikt* [Nobody] is Andrzejewski's final expression of disillusionment and bitterness. This openly personal retelling of the story of ageing Odysseus contains nothing but scepticism about the power of love and the human search for truth. The fear of death, distressing the Homeric hero, is superseded only by his own legend, that is, by his fictitious *alter ego*.

—Stanislaw Eile

See the essay on *Ashes and Diamonds*.

ANNUNZIO, Gabriele d'

See D'ANNUNZIO, Gabriele

ANOUILH, Jean (Marie Lucien Pierre)

Born: Cérisole, Bordeaux, France, 23 June 1910. **Education:** Educated at École Colbert, Bordeaux; Collège Chaptal; studied law at the Sorbonne, Paris, 1928–29. **Military Service:** Served during the 1930s. **Family:** Married 1) the actress Monelle Valentin in 1931 (divorced 1953), one daughter; 2) Nicole Lançon in 1953, two daughters and one son. **Career:** Publicity and gag writer for films, and advertising copywriter for Publicité Damour, Paris, 2 years; secretary, Louis Jouvet's Comédie des Champs-Elysées, Paris, 1931–32; assistant to the director Georges Pitoëff; full-time writer; also a film director. **Awards:** Grand prize of the French Cinema, 1949; Tony award (United States), 1955; New York Drama Critics Circle award, 1957; Cino del Duca prize, 1970; French Drama Critics award, 1970; Paris Critics prize, 1971. **Died:** 3 October 1987.

PUBLICATIONS

Plays

L'Hermine (produced 1932). 1934; as *The Ermine*, translated by Miriam John, in *Plays of the Year*, 13, 1956; also translated by John, in *Five Plays* (I), 1958.
La Mandarine (produced 1933).

Y'avait un prisonnier (produced 1935). In *La Petite Illustration*, 1935.
Le Voyageur sans bagage (produced 1937). In *Pièces noires*, 1942; edited by Diane W. Birckbichler, 1973; as *Traveller Without Luggage*, translated by John Whiting, 1959; also translated by Whiting, in *Seven Plays*, 1967; Lucienne Hill, 1959.
La Sauvage (produced 1938). 1938; as *The Restless Heart*, translated by Lucienne Hill, 1957; also translated by Hill, in *Five Plays* (II), 1959.
Le Bal des voleurs (produced 1938). 1938; as *Thieves' Carnival*, translated by Lucienne Hill, 1952; also translated by Hill, in *Seven Plays*, 1967.
Léocadia (produced 1940). In *Pièces roses*, 1942; edited by Bettina L. Knapp and Alba Della Fazia, 1965; as *Time Remembered*, translated by Patricia Moyes, 1955; also in *Five Plays* (II), 1959; as *Léocadia*, translated by Timberlake Wertenbaker, in *Five Plays*, 1987.
Marie-Jeanne; ou, La Fille du peuple, from a play by Dennery and Mallain (produced 1940).
Le Rendez-vous de Senlis (produced 1941). In *Pièces roses*, 1942; as *Dinner with the Family*, translated by Edward O. Marsh, 1958.
Eurydice (produced 1942). In *Pièces noires*, 1942; edited by E. Freeman, with *Médée*, 1984; as *Point of Departure*, translated by Kitty Black, 1951; as *Legend of Lovers*, translated by Black, 1952; as *Eurydice*, translated by Black, in *Five Plays* (I), 1958.
Pièces roses (includes *Le Bal des voleurs; Le Rendez-vous de Senlis; Léocadia*). 1942; enlarged edition (includes *Humulus le muet*), 1958.
Pièces noires (includes *L'Hermine; La Sauvage; Le Voyageur sans bagage; Eurydice*). 1942.
Antigone, from the play by Sophocles (produced 1944). 1946; edited by W.M. Landers, 1954; also edited by R. Laubreaux, 1965, and J. Monférier, 1968; as *Antigone*, translated and adapted by Lewis Galantière, 1946; also translated by Lothian Small, with *Eurydice*, 1951; in *Five Plays* (I), 1958; Barbara Bray, in *Five Plays*, 1987.
Roméo et Jeannette (produced 1946). In *Nouvelles pièces noires*, 1946; as *Romeo and Jeannette*, translated by Miriam John, in *Five Plays* (I), 1958.
Nouvelles pièces noires (includes *Jézabel; Antigone; Roméo et Jeannette; Médée*). 1946.
Médée (produced 1953). In *Nouvelles pièces noires*, 1946; as *Medea*, translated by Lothian Small, in *Plays of the Year*, 15, 1956; as *Medea: A "Black" Play*, translated by Luce and Arthur Klein 1957; also translated by Klein and Klein, in *Seven Plays*, 1967.
L'Invitation au château (produced 1947). 1948; as *Ring Round the Moon*, translated by Christopher Fry, 1950.
Ardèle; ou, La Marguerite (produced 1948). 1949; as *Ardele*, translated by Lucienne Hill, 1951; also translated by Hill, in *Five Plays* (II), 1959.
Les Demoiselles de la nuit (ballet scenario; produced 1948).
Épisode de la vie d'un auteur (produced 1948). With *La Belle Vie*, 1980; as *Episode in the Life of an Author*, translated by Miriam John, in *Seven Plays*, 1967.
Humulus le muet, with Jean Aurenche (produced 1948). N.d; as *Humulus the Mute*, translated by Michael Benedikt, in *Modern French Theatre*, 1964.
La Répétition; ou, L'Amour puni (produced 1950). 1950; as *The Rehearsal*, translated by Pamela Hansford Johnson and Kitty Black, in *Five Plays* (I), 1958; also translated by Jeremy Sams, 1991.

Colombe (produced 1951). In *Pièces brillantes*, 1951; as *Colombe*, translated by Denis Cannan, 1952; as *Mademoiselle Colombe*, in *Five Plays* (II), 1959.

Monsieur Vincent (screenplay), with Jean Bernard Luc. 1951.

Pièces brillantes (includes *L'Invitation au château; Colombe; La Répétition; Cécile*). 1951.

Cécile; ou, L'École des pères (produced 1954). In *Pièces brillantes*, 1951; as *Cecile; or, The School for Fathers*, translated by Luce and Arthur Klein, in *From the Modern Repertoire*, 3, edited by Eric Bentley, 1956; also translated by Klein and Klein, in *Seven Plays*, 1967.

La Valse des toréadors (produced 1952) 1952; as *Waltz of the Toreadors*, translated by Lucienne Hill in *Plays of the Year*, 8, 1953; revised translation by Hill, in *Five Plays*, 1987.

La Nuit des rois, from the play by Shakespeare (produced 1961). In *Trois comédies*, 1952.

Le Loup (ballet scenario), with Georges Neveux. 1953.

L'Alouette (produced 1953). 1953; edited by Merlin Thomas and Simon Lee, 1956; as *The Lark*, translated by Christopher Fry, 1955; in *Five Plays* (II), 1959; translated by Fry, in *Five Plays*, 1987.

Ornifle; ou, Le Courant d'air (produced 1955). 1956; as *Ornifle*, translated by Lucienne Hill, 1970; as *It's Later Than You Think*, translated by Hill, 1970.

Il est important d'être aimé, with Claude Vincent, from the play by Oscar Wilde (produced 1964). In *L'Avant-scène*, 101, 1955.

Pauvre Bitos; ou, Le Dîner de têtes (produced 1956). In *Pièces grinçantes*, 1956; as *Poor Bitos*, translated by Lucienne Hill, 1964; revised translation by Hill, in *Five Plays*, 1987.

Pièces grinçantes (includes *Ardèle; La Valse des torèadors; Ornifle; Pauvre Bitos*). 1956.

Five Plays (I) (includes *Antigone; Eurydice; The Ermine; The Rehearsal; Romeo and Jeannette*), translated by Miriam John, Lucienne Hill, Lewis Galantière, and Kitty Black. 1958.

Five Plays (II) (includes *The Restless Heart; Time Remembered; Ardele; Mademoiselle Colombe; The Lark*), translated by Lucienne Hill, Patricia Moyes, Louis Kronenberger, and Lilian Hellman. 1959.

L'Hurluberlu; ou, Le Réactionnaire amoureux (produced 1959). 1959; as *The Fighting Cock*, translated and adapted by Lucienne Hill, 1960.

Becket; ou, L'Honneur de Dieu (produced 1959). 1959; as *Becket; or, The Honor of God*, translated by Lucienne Hill, 1961.

Madame de. . . (in English, produced 1959). 1959.

La Petite Molière, with Roland Laudenback (produced 1959). In *L'Avant-scène*, 1959.

Le Songe du critique (produced 1960). In *L'Avant-scène*, 143, 1959.

Pièces costumées (includes *L'Alouette; Becket; La Foire d'empoigne*). 1960.

La Foire d'empoigne (produced 1962). In *Pièces costumées*, 1960; as *Catch as Catch Can*, translated by Lucienne Hill, in *Seven Plays*, 1967.

Tartuffe, from the play by Molière (produced 1960). In *L'Avant-scène*, 1961.

La Grotte (produced 1961). 1961; as *The Cavern*, translated by Lucienne Hill, 1966.

Victor; ou, Les Enfants au pouvoir, from the play by Roger Vitrac (produced 1962). In *L'Avant-scène*, 1962.

L'Amant complaisant, with Nicole Anouilh, from the play by Graham Greene (produced 1962). 1962.

L'Orchestre (produced 1962). 1970; as *The Orchestra*, translated by Miriam John, in *Seven Plays*, 1967; published separately, 1975.

Richard III, from the play by Shakespeare (produced 1964). N.d.

L'Ordalie; ou, La Petite Catherine de Heilbronn, from a story by Heinrich von Kleist (produced 1966). In *L'Avant-scène*, 1967.

Collected Plays. 2 vols., 1966–67.

Seven Plays (includes *Thieves' Carnival; Medea; Cecile; or, The School for Fathers; Traveller Without Luggage; The Orchestra; Episode in the Life of an Author; Catch as Catch Can*), translated by John Whiting, Luce and Arthur Klein, Miriam John, and Lucienne Hill. 1967.

Le Boulanger, la boulangère, et le petit mitron (produced 1968), 1969.

Théâtre complet. 9 vols., 1968.

Cher Antoine; ou, L'Amour raté (produced 1969). 1969; as *Dear Antoine; or, The Love That Failed*, translated by Lucienne Hill, 1971.

Le Théâtre; ou, La Vie comme elle est (produced 1970).

Ne Réveillez pas Madame (produced 1970). 1970.

Les Poissons rouges; ou, Mon père, ce héros (produced 1970). 1970.

Nouvelles pièces grinçantes (includes *L'Hurluberlu; La Grotte; L'Orchestre; Le Boulanger, la boulangère, et le petit mitron; Les Poissons rouges*). 1970.

Tu étais si gentil quand tu étais petit (produced 1971). 1972.

Le Directeur de l'Opéra (produced 1973). 1972; as *The Director of the Opera*, translated by Lucienne Hill, 1973.

Pièces baroques (includes *Chef Antoine; Ne Réveillez pas Madame; Le Directeur de l'Opéra*). 1974.

Monsieur Barnett (produced 1974). In *L'Avant-scène*, 559, 1975.

L'Arrestation (produced 1975). 1975; as *The Arrest*, translated by Lucienne Hill, 1978.

Le Scénario (produced 1976). 1976.

Chers Zoizeaux (produced 1976). 1977.

Pièces secrètes (includes *Tu étais si gentil quand tu étais petit; L'Arrestation; Le Scénario*). 1977.

Vive Henri IV. 1977.

La Culotte (produced 1978). 1978.

La Belle Vie (television play), with *Épisode de la vie d'un auteur*. 1980.

Le Nombril (produced 1981). 1981; as *Number One*, translated by Michael Frayn, 1984.

Pièces farceuses (includes *Chers Zoiseaux; La Culotte; Épisode de la vie d'un auteur; Le Nombril*). 1984.

Oedipe; ou, Le Roi boiteux, from the play by Sophocles. 1986.

Thomas More; ou, L'Homme libre (screenplay). 1987.

Five Plays (includes *Antigone; Léocadia; The Lark; Poor Bitos; The Waltz of the Toreadors*), translated by Barbara Bray, Timberlake Wertenbaker, Christopher Fry, and Lucienne Hill. 1987.

Plays 2 (includes *The Rehearsal; Becket; Eurydice; The Orchestra*). 1992.

Vive Henri IV!, ou, La Galigaï, 2000.

Screenplays: *Les Déyourdis de la onzième*, with Jean Aurenche, 1936; *Vous n'avez rien à déclarer*, with Jean Aurenche, 1937; *Les Otages*, with Jean Aurenche, 1939; *Cavalcade d'amour*, 1939; *Le Voyageur sans bagage (Identity Unknown)*, with Jean Aurenche, 1944; *Monsieur Vincent*, with Jean Bernard Luc, 1947; *Anna Karenina*, with Julien Duvivier and Guy Morgan, 1948; *Pattes blanches*, with Jean Bernard Luc, 1949; *Caroline chérie*, 1951; *Deux sous de violettes*, with Monelle Valentin, 1951; *Le Rideau rouge*, 1952; *Le*

Chevalier de la nuit, 1953; *La Mort de belle (The Passion of Slow Fire),* 1961; *La Ronde,* 1964; *A Time for Loving,* 1972.

Television Plays: *Le Jeune Homme et le lion,* 1976; *La Belle Vie,* 1979.

Other

Michel-Marie Poulain, with Pierre Imbourg and André Warnod. 1953.
Fables. 1962.
Robert Brasillach et la génération perdue, with others. 1987.
La Vicomtesse d'Eristal n'a pas reçu son balai mécanique: souvenirs d'un jeune homme (autobiography). 1987.

*

Bibliography: *Jean Anouilh: An Annotated Bibliography* by Kathleen White Kelley, 1973.

Critical Studies: *Anouilh* by Marguerite Archer, 1951; *Jean Anouilh: Poet of Pierrot and Pantaloon* by Edward O. Marsh, 1953; *The World of Jean Anouilh* by Leonard C. Pronko, 1961; *Anouilh: A Study of Theatrics* by John Harvey, 1964; *Anouilh: La Peine de vivre* by Clément Borgal, 1966; *Jean Anouilh* by Philip Thody, 1968; *Anouilh* by Alba della Fazia Amoia, 1969; *Jean Anouilh: Textes d'Anouilh, points de vue critiques, témoignages, chronologie, bibliographie, illustrations* by Paul Ginestier, 1969; *"Antigone": Analyse critique* by Etienne Frois, 1972; *Théâtre d'Anouilh* by Bernard Beugnot, 1973; *Jean Anouilh: Stages in Rebellion* by Branko Lenski, 1975; *La Pureté dans le théâtre de Jean Anouilh* by André F. Rombout, 1975; *Le Théâtre de Jean Anouilh* by Jacques Vier, 1976; *Anouilh, littérature et politique* by Élie de Comminges, 1977; *Jean Anouilh* by Lewis W. Falb, 1977; *Lecture d'Anouilh: Textes et réflexions critiques* by Benito d'Ajetti, 1978; *Jean Anouilh: Les Problèmes de l'existence dans un théâtre de marionettes* by Thérèse Malachy, 1978; *The Theatre of Jean Anouilh* by H.G. McIntyre, 1981; *Anouilh: Antigone* by W.D. Howarth, 1983; *Jean Anouilh: Life, Work, and Criticism* by Christopher Smith, 1985; *Pour Saluer Jean Anouilh* by Christophe Mercier, 1995.

* * *

After two early plays, *L'Hermine (The Ermine)* and *Y'avait un prisonnier,* considered promising but not extremely successful, Jean Anouilh achieved his real breakthrough, artistically and financially, with *Le Voyageur sans bagage (Traveller Without Luggage),* and later seasons in Paris almost always included a new Anouilh work, many subsequently revived in England and America. These three works, along with the contemporary *Jézabel,* and *La Sauvage (The Restless Heart),* were characterized by their author as *pièces noires* ("black plays"), in contrast to three other works of the same period, *Le Bal des voleurs (Thieves' Carnival), Le Rendez-vous de Senlis (Dinner with the Family)* and *Léocadia (Time Remembered),* which he designated *pièces roses* ("rose plays"). A common theme of these plays is shared by Anouilh with the pioneers of modern realistic drama, especially Ibsen—the burden of the environment and especially of the past on a protagonist seeking a happier, freer existence. Although neither type of play takes an ultimately optimistic position, the "black plays" generally demonstrate the hopelessness of this dream, while the "rose plays" allow their protagonists at least a temporary happiness, often through an escape into a world of make-believe.

During the 1940s Anouilh, while maintaining his complex tonality and deft dramatic technique, turned from contemporary to mythical, classic, and historic subjects and to themes more closely related to the concerns of such writers as Sartre and Camus. Now the past was regarded as only part of the contingent circumstances of existence against which the independent spirit of the protagonist must define itself. The best-known play of this group is *Antigone,* which established Anouilh as a leading dramatist, not only because of the power with which he drew the classic confrontation between the uncompromising Antigone and the politically expedient Creon, but because French theatre-goers under the occupation read the play as a contemporary political parable. The immediate post-war plays *Roméo et Jeannette (Romeo and Jeannette)* and *Médée (Medea)* similarly focused upon protagonists who refused to strike a bargain with the world of compromise. Much the same spirit infuses Anouilh's Joan of Arc story *L'Alouette (The Lark),* the success of which rivalled that of *Antigone.*

With the exception of *The Lark,* Anouilh's plays of the late 1940s and the 1950s depict a darker and crueller universe, where his heroic protagonists give way to more common souls who have in one way or another accepted life as it is—simply and unquestioningly, as victims, or calculatedly and manipulatively. Anouilh divided his plays of this period into *pièces brillantes* ("brilliant plays") and *pièces grinçantes* ("grating plays"). The "brilliance" of the first group, *L'Invitation au château (Ring Round the Moon), Cécile, La Répétition; ou, L'Amour puni (The Rehearsal),* and *Colombe,* comes from their elegant, aristocratic settings and from their polished, witty language, often reminiscent of the sparkle of Marivaux (indeed it is a Marivaux play that is being rehearsed in *The Rehearsal*). The pain and cruelty of life and the inevitability of death are still present, but these can be put aside at least temporarily by the pleasures of living for the moment, often developed in specifically theatrical metaphors. A darker tone and a more bitter humour mark the "grating plays," *Ardèle, La Valse des toréadors (Waltz of the Toreadors), Ornifle, Pauvre Bitos; ou, Le Dîner de têtes (Poor Bitos),* and *L'Hurluberlu; ou, Le Réactionnaire amoureux (The Fighting Cock).* Here, as in the "brilliant plays," the idealistic young lovers of Anouilh's early works have been replaced by middle-aged characters, all too aware of the disillusion of passing time.

Becket, a major international success, depicts another historical martyr, Thomas à Becket, and *La Foire d'empoigne (Catch as Catch Can)* pits a cynical and gross Napoleon against a noble but ineffective Louis XVIII. These, along with *The Lark,* were characterized by Anouilh as his *pièces costumées* ("costume plays"), although they share not only historical "costumed" settings, but also an idealistic protagonist seeking a moral path in a world of corruption and manipulation. In each case the quest ends in death and apparent defeat, but the hero leaves the history of his struggle as an example and inspiration for others, and so the forces of nobility achieve at least a qualified affirmation.

Anouilh's final period begins with *La Grotte (The Cavern).* It is a Pirandellian work, whose central character is a frustrated author and whose action concerns the tensions of a play he has been unable to write. Anouilh felt his subsequent plays took a new direction, but this is more a matter of emphasis than of actual new concerns. The interrelationship of theatre and life is a theme recurrent throughout his *oeuvre,* but it takes on a special prominence in these late works, whose central figures are most often dramatists or theatre directors. Family relationships and the tensions of private life, another long-time concern, are also central in the late plays. In a number of them a special relationship exists between theatre and family, suggesting, as Maeterlinck argued in "The Tragedy in Everyday Life," that the inner drama of everyday interpersonal relationships is more profound and more important than the traditional heightened action of "theatre." Antoine, the playwright-protagonist of *Cher Antoine; ou, L'Amour raté* (*Dear Antoine; or, The Love That Failed*), advocates an attention to such *pièces secrètes* ("secret dramas")—the title of an Anouilh collection.

In the last plays, concluding with *Le Nombril* (*Number One*), the author, however successful and honoured, becomes ever more isolated from friends and family, who simultaneously blame him for all their misfortunes and feed upon his success. Anouilh's dark view of the human condition here reaches its final expression. His young heroes are constrained by the past and by social circumstances; the more mature protagonists of the "grating plays" suffered more personal unhappiness from their own ageing and in their human relationships. The artists of the final plays, with death close upon them, find that even the closest relationships are tainted by selfishness and greed, and offer as consolation only whatever appreciation artist and audience may derive from a sensitive awareness of life's "secret drama."

—Marvin Carlson

See the essay on *Antigone*.

ANWAR, Chairil

Born: Medan, North Sumatra, 26 July 1922. **Education:** Dutch schools for indigenous Indonesians in Medan, HIS (primary) and MULO (junior high school). **Family:** Married to Hapsah, 1946 (divorced late 1948); one daughter. **Career:** Abandoned secondary education after moving to Jakarta with his mother in 1940; followed a bohemian lifestyle, reading widely, and mixing with many strata of society; worked fitfully as the literary editor of "Gelanggang" (the literary supplement for the magazine *Siasat*), 1948–49, and *Gema Suasana*, 1949. **Died:** 28 April 1949, in Jakarta, from a combination of diseases (typhoid, syphilis, pneumonia, and tuberculosis).

PUBLICATIONS

Collections

Aku ini Bintang Jalang. 1986.
Derai-derai Cemara. 1999.
The Complete Poetry and Prose of Chairil Anwar by Burton Raffel. 1970; republished as *The Voice of the Night.* 1993.

Verse

Kerikil Tajam, dan Yang Terampas dan yang Putus. 1949.
Deru Campur Debu. 1949.
Tiga Menguak Takdir, with Asrul Sani and Rivai Apin. 1950.

*

Critical Studies: *Chairil Anwar, Pelopor Angkatan 45* by H.B. Jassin, 1956; *Chairil Anwar: The Poet and His Language* by Boen Sri Oemarjati, 1972; *The Development of Modern Indonesian Poetry* by Burton Raffel, 1967.

*   *   *

For many Indonesians, Chairil Anwar has come to be seen as the truly representative artistic figure. Dead at the age of 26 from a truly appalling combination of diseases, he stands out as someone who was completely dedicated to the creative life and to whom no one and nothing else mattered. Although he wrote only about 70 poems, it is agreed that this small number of works utterly transformed the nature of poetry in the Indonesian language.

Prior to World War II, Indonesian poetry used the quatrain form which had been dominant in traditional writing for some four centuries. As "modern writers," prewar Indonesian poets were heavily influenced by the themes of late European romanticism: the idea of art as the outcome of sudden inspiration, nature as a realm of intense beauty, and melancholy as the appropriate attitude for one who long suffered the loss of happiness.

Chairil Anwar introduced the use of a free verse form, in which every word carried maximum impact. His stanzas could range from one line to as many as 30. He wrote honestly about his own experiences and fought vigorously to be free from the traditional conventions of the genre.

Perhaps his best known poem is "Aku," which uses the first person pronoun of power, the "I" which speaks down to others. The poem begins with the recognition: "When my time comes / I know no one will mourn for me / Not even you." (Some texts insist: "I want no one to mourn for me."). Quickly he admits to being "a wild beast / cast out from its herd." Although he admits to feeling intense pain, he insists that he will "endure in a rage," fighting and kicking, until all sense of suffering has gone. The poem concludes with the heavily rhythmical line: "*Aku mau hidup seribu taun lagi!*" or "I want to live for a thousand years!"

In some poems, Anwar treats others with this same arrogance. In "Penerimaan" ("Acceptance"), he begins with an apparent show of generosity: "If you want, I'll take you back again / With all my heart." The return of his lover, however, actually means little to the narrator: "I will still be alone." He can condemn her for her unfaithfulness, "I know you are not what you were before," but still insist that she meet his gaze. After repeating the opening lines, the poem concludes in utter selfishness: "I won't even share my mirror with you."

At other times, it becomes clear that this apparent disdain was a mask for a fear of personal intimacy. "Sia-Sia" ("Futile"), describes a day spent with a woman who has come to give herself to him when neither was able to approach the other. "Damn you, my heart!" it ends in rage. "You would not let yourself love! / May you be shredded by the silence."

This contradictory violence and fear even extends to Anwar's depiction of God. God comes to Anwar in the poem "Di Mesjid," ("In the Mosque") after Anwar has shouted at Him to show Himself. Although God burns in his heart, Anwar struggles to extinguish Him, "Kneeling, sweating, like a horse which will not be ridden." The empty space of the mosque and Anwar's own heart are like "an arena,'' in which they fight. Neither wins. Instead, they destroy each other: ''One abusing, the other mad.'' Who is which, the poem does not say.

As the Japanese occupation of Indonesia (1942–45) turned into the War of Independence (1945–49), Anwar occasionally wrote patriotic poems. ''Come, Sukarno, my friend, give me your hand,'' he cried out in ''Persetujuan dengan Bung Karno'' (''An Agreement with Bung Karno,'' 1948). He also sometimes plagiarized poems, including Archibald MacLeish's ''The Young Dead Soldiers'' and Willem Elschott's ''Tot den Arme,'' simply so that he could buy medicine.

But the approach of death made itself heard above the confusion of love, the emptiness of night, and the refusal of divine comfort. In what was one of his very last poems, ''Derai-derai Cemara'' (''The Whispering Pines''), Anwar concluded:

Life is only the postponement of death,
As we grow further isolated from our high school loves,
And we learn that there is nothing more to be said,
Before we finally surrender ourselves to the dark.

Anwar's own life is often evaluated in the words of one of his earliest poems: ''Once to have meaning / And after that, to die.'' Anwar's poetry, in its honesty, its depth of self-exploration, and its directness of expression, continues to be extremely meaningful for all Indonesians who know and value their own literature.

—Harry Aveling

APOLLINAIRE, Guillaume

Born: Guillaume Apollinaris de Kostrowitzky in Rome, Italy, 26 August 1880. **Education:** Educated in Monte Carlo, Cannes, and Nice, until 1897. **Military Service:** Served in World War I, 1914–16: invalided out. **Family:** Married Jacqueline Kolb in 1918. **Career:** Moved to the Ardennes, 1899; began using name Apollinaire, 1901; tutor in Germany, 1901–02; freelance writer and critic in Paris; editor, *Le Festin d'Ésope*, 1903, and *La Revue Immoraliste*; helped organize cubist room at Salon des Indépendants, 1911, and wrote manifesto on Futurism; imprisoned briefly on suspicion of art theft, 1911; art critic, *Le Petit Bleu*, 1912; editor, *Les Soirées de Paris*, 1912–14. **Died:** 9 November 1918.

PUBLICATIONS

Collections

Selected Writings, edited and translated by Roger Shattuck. 1950.
Oeuvres poétiques, edited by Michel Décaudin and Marcel Adéma. 1956.
Oeuvres complètes, edited by Michel Décaudin. 4 vols., 1965–66.
Oeuvres en prose, edited by Michel Décaudin. 1977.
Oeuvres. 5 vols., 1983–84.
Oeuvres en prose complètes, edited by Pierre Caizergues and Michel Décaudin. 1993.

Verse

Le Bestiaire; ou, Cortege d'Orphée. 1911; translated as *Le Bestiaire*, 1977; as *Bestiary; or, the Parade of Orpheus*, translated by Pepe Karmel and Lauren Shakley, 1980.
Alcools: Poèmes 1898–1913. 1913; edited by Tristan Tzara, 1953, and Garnet Rees, 1975; as *Alcools*, translated by William Meredith, 1964, also translated by Anne Hyde Greet, 1965.
Case d'armons. 1915.
Vitam impendere amori. 1917.
Calligrammes: Poèmes de la paix et de la guerre 1913–1916. 1918; as *Calligrammes: Poems of Peace and War (1913–1916)*, translated by Anne Hyde Greet (bilingual edition), 1980.
Le Cortège priapique. 1925.
Julie; ou, La Rose. 1927.
Le Condor et le morpion. 1931.
Ombre de mon amour. 1947; revised edition, as *Poèmes à Lou*, 1955.
Le Guetteur mélancolique. 1952.
Tendre comme le souvenir. 1952.
Selected Poems (bilingual edition), edited and translated by Oliver Bernard. 1965, enlarged edition, 1986.
Alcools: Poems, translated by Donald Revell, 1995.

Plays

Les Mamelles de Tirésias (produced 1917). 1918.
Couleur du temps (produced 1918). 1949.
Casanova. 1952.
La Température, with André Salmon (produced 1975). In *Oeuvres en prose*, 1977.
A Quelle Heure un train partira-t-il pour Paris?. 1982.

Fiction

Les Exploits d'un jeune Don Juan. 1907; as *The Exploits of a Young Don Juan*, translated by Alex Lykiard, 1986.
Les Onze Mille Verges. 1907; as *The Debauched Hospodar*, translated by Arcan Mole, 1953; as *Les Onze Mille Verges; or, the Amorous Adventures of Prince Mony Vibescu*, translated by Nina Rootes, 1976.
L'Enchanteur pourrissant. 1909.
L'Hérésiarque et cie. 1910; selection, as *Contes choisis*, 1922; as *The Heresiarch and Company*, translated by Rémy Inglis Hall, 1965; as *The Wandering Jew and Other Stories*, 1965.
La Fin de Babylone. 1914.
Les Trois Don Juan. 1915.
Le Poète assassiné. 1916; edited by Michel Décaudin, 1959; as *The Poet Assassinated*, translated by Matthew Josephson, 1923; also translated by Ron Padgett, 1968.
La Femme assise: Chronique de France et d'Amérique. 1920.
Les Épingles: Contes. 1928.
Que faire?. 1950.
Three Pre-surrealist Plays, translated with an introduction and notes by Maya Slater, 1997.
Lettres à Guillaume Apollinaire, 1904–1918 by Ricciotto Canudo, 1999.

Other

Méditations esthétiques: Les Peintres cubistes. 1913; edited by Leroy C. Breunig and J.-Cl. Chevalier, 1965; as *The Cubist Painters:*

Aesthetic Meditations 1913, translated by Lionel Abel, 1944; revised editions, 1949, 1962.

Le Flâneur des deux rives. 1918.

Il y a. 1925.

Anecdotiques. 1926.

Contemporains pittoresques. 1929.

Oeuvres érotiques completes (verse and prose). 3 vols., 1934.

L'Esprit nouveau et les poètes. 1946.

Lettres à sa marraine. 1948.

Chroniques d'art, 1902–1918, edited by Leroy C. Breunig. 1961; as *Apollinaire On Art: Essays and Reviews*, translated by Susan Suliman. 1972.

Correspondance, with André Level, edited by Brigitte Level. 1976.

Petites flâneries d'art, edited by Pierre Caizergues. 1980.

Correspondance avec son frère et sa mère, edited by Gilbert Boudar and Michel Décaudin, 1987.

Correspondance, with Jean Cocteau, edited by Pierre Caizergues and Michel Décaudin. 1991.

Journal intime: 1898–1918, edited by Michel Décaudin. 1991.

Editor, *Chronique des grands siècles de la France*. 1912.

*

Critical Studies: *Apollinaire* by Marcel Adéma, 1954; *The Evolution of Apollinaire's Poetics, 1901–1914* by Francis J. Carmody, 1963; *Apollinaire, Poet among Painters* by Francis Steegmuller, 1963, reprinted 1985; *Apollinaire* by Margaret Davies, 1964; *Apollinaire* by Scott Bates, 1967, revised edition, 1989; *Apollinaire* by Leroy C. Breunig, 1969; *The Drama of Self in Apollinaire's Alcools* by Richard Howard Stamelman, 1975; *Guillaume Apollinaire* by Roger Little, 1976; *Guillaume Apollinaire as an Art Critic* by Harry E. Buckley, 1981; *The Creative Vision of Apollinaire: A Study of Imagination* by David Berry, 1982; *Apollinaire: Catalyst for Primitivism, Picabia and Duchamps* by Katia Samaltanos, 1984; *Alfred Jarry and Guillaume Apollinaire* by Claude Schumacher, 1984; *Reading Apollinaire: Theories of Poetic Language* by Timothy Mathews, 1987; *Apollinaire, Visual Poetry, and Art Criticism* by William Bohn, 1993; *Poetry and Painting: Baudelaire, Mallarmé, Apollinaire, and their Painter Friends* by Alan Bowness, 1994; *Apollinaire and the International Avant-garde* by William Bohn, 1997.

* * *

Guillaume Apollinaire's culture was eclectic. He preferred the Latin of the mystics to that of Virgil, heretical theologians to St. Thomas, Italian storytellers of the Renaissance to Dante, The Kabbala to the Bible. In contrast to his learning, his heart was simple and limpid. At the publication of *Alcools* in 1913, Georges Duhamel called Apollinaire a pedlar with the mingled characteristics of a Levantine Jew, a South American, a Polish gentleman, and an Italian porter. To these roles might be added that of the innocent hero, part braggart, part simpleton, who discovered in war the brotherhood of man, and revealed to his many friends one of the truly noble, truly good souls of his age.

His poetry is composed of influences, readings, memories, echoes of many poets, from Villon to Verlaine and Jarry. But his voice is also bare and personal. The story of his life was the effort he made to guard secrets and mysteries, and to create for his friends and his public a character whom they would love and yet not know too intimately. The

buffoonery of his character, his endless anecdotes and pranks, permitted him to conceal or disguise the nostalgia and sadness and even perhaps the tragedy of his life. But the poetry of Apollinaire is not mask and deceit. It is fantasy in the deepest sense of the word. It is lawful fantasy: its images rightfully conceal and communicate at the same time the emotions he had experienced.

His poetic fantasy was, first, that of revolt, by which he always remained precious and close to the Surrealists. He broke with the familiar patterns of thought, with the poetic clichés and literariness of the Parnassians and Symbolists, and with the familiar units and rules of syntax. His poetry comes together in a great freedom of composition, as if he allowed the images and emotions to compose themselves. In his poetry, phantoms, wanderers, mythic characters bearing sonorous names, appear and disappear as do the laws of syntax and prosody.

It was appropriate that Apollinaire, coming after the highly self-conscious and studied literary school of Symbolism, would, in rebellion against such artifice, seek to return to the most primitive sources of lyricism. His adventure, if we were to extract such a subject from his work, would closely resemble Gide's adventure: the lessons on freedom and gratuitousness and individual morality, which were being formulated at the same time. Apollinaire thus prolongs the lesson of Rimbaud and Mallarmé, in considering poetic activity as a secret means of knowledge, self-knowledge and world-knowledge.

All the opposites are joined and harmonized in his poetry: fire and water, day and night, the bookish and the popular, the libertine and the sorrowing lover. All the myths are in his verses, in close company with pure inventions. He called upon his immediate knowledge of cities and ports, of unscrupulous *voyous* and popular songs, in order to speak in his tone of prophet and discoverer. His universe is one of chance and naïvety, of a certain childlike candour which the Surrealists would later try to reconstruct. He was the first to use a facile exoticism and eroticism which today is found in American films and jazz music. But in his most facile songs, as in "Le Musicien de Saint-Merry," he is able to generate a delicate irony from the shifts in tone.

There is a record of Apollinaire's voice reciting "Le Pont Mirabeau," which contains his most persistent theme—the passing and change of sentiments, and the poet's own stability:

Vienne la nuit sonne l'heure
Les jours s'en vont je demeure

The chance meetings in the world and their dissolutions bear relationship with the chance meetings of words in a poem. Apollinaire is first a poet of regret, of delicate nostalgia, and then, in a very mysterious way, he is the poet of resurrection and exaltation. His memory of the dead makes them into constant presences. "Vendémiaire," the long poem that ends *Alcools*, is a striking evocation of Paris and of all the myths of poetic preservation, of Orpheus and of Icarus who tried to possess the world. The wine of the universe brought contentment to "oceans animals plants cities destinies and singing stars." The poem also contains accents of sorrow and Apollinaire's familiar reference to the sadness of children with their salt tears that taste of the ocean. But it is at the same time a poem on hope and one of the most stirring of the century.

The contrast between Apollinaire's erudition, nourished on pornography, magic, popular literature, encyclopedias, and his total simplicity as a song writer, explains to some degree the profound irony pervading all of his poetry. His appearance, at the beginning of the 20th century, coincided with many new aesthetic preoccupations to which he brought his own inventiveness and speculative inquiry. His work joined with that of Max Jacob, Picasso, Braque, Derain, and Matisse in a series of fantasies and works of art that have gone far in shaping modern sensitivity. A farcical festive air presided over many of the modes of art that were given the names of cubism, fauvism, Negro art, cosmopolitanism, erotology. Apollinaire himself was responsible for the term "surrealism." He literally became a prophet in his support of aesthetic innovations that were to become the accepted forms of the future. His articles on painting place him second to Baudelaire among the aestheticians of modern France.

The lesson Apollinaire teaches about poetry is the most important in France since Rimbaud's. ("La Chanson du mal-aimé" has become for our age what "Le Lac" and "Tristesse d'Olympio" were for the 19th century.) His poetry does not try to fathom the supernatural, but simply to state the incomprehensibility of the ordinary and the commonplace. Every human expression he saw became sphinx-like for him, and every word he overheard resembled a sibyl's utterance. Nascent language it would seem to be, as the poet, performing his earliest role of demiurge, calls the world to be born again by naming it.

—Wallace Fowlie

See the essays on "La Chanson du mal-aimé" and "Zone."

APOLLONIUS OF RHODES

Born: Apollonius Rhodius in Alexandria, Egypt, possibly c. 295 BC. Active during first half of 3rd century BC, and possibly later. **Education:** Studied under Callimachus, *q.v.*: said to have quarrelled with Callimachus and retired to Rhodes, but evidence for this is unreliable. **Career:** Held post of director (*prostates*) of the Museum Library at Alexandria, possibly c. 260–247 BC; tutor to Ptolemy III Euergetes. In addition to various poems, of which only the *Argonautica* survives, wrote scholarly works on Homer, Hesiod, and Archilochus, now lost. **Died:** c. 215 BC.

PUBLICATIONS

Verse

Argonautica, edited by H. Fränkel. 1961; also edited by F. Vian (includes French translation), 3 vols., 1974–81; Book III edited by R.L. Hunter, 1989; as *The Tale of the Argonauts*, translated by A.S. Way, 1901; as *Argonautica*, translated by R.C. Seaton (prose), 1912; also translated by Charles E. MacBean, 1976; as *The Voyage of the Argo*, translated by E.V. Rieu (prose), 1959; as *Jason and the Golden Fleece (The Argonautica)*, translated by Richard Hunter, 1993; as *The Argonautika*, translated by Peter Green, 1997.

*

Critical Studies: *Hellenistic Poetry* by A. Körte, 1929; *Echoes and Imitations of Early Epic in Apollonius Rhodius*, 1981, *Index verborum in Apollonium Rhodius*, 1983, and *Studies in the Third Book of Apollonius Rhodius' Argonautica*, 1983, all by Malcolm Campbell; *Epic and Romance in the Argonautica of Apollonius* by C.R. Beye, 1982;

Landscape in the Argonautica of Apollonius Rhodius by Mary Frances Williams, 1991; *The Best of the Argonauts: The Redefinition of the Epic Hero in Book 1 of Apollonius's Argonautica* by James J. Clauss, 1993; *The Argonautica of Apollonius* by Richard Hunter, 1993.

* * *

The only work of Apollonius which survives is the epic *Argonautica*, written in hexameters, the traditional epic metre, with the high archaic language and style of the Homeric poems. After the *Iliad* and *Odyssey* the *Argonautica* is the most important epic from the ancient Greek world, and it was soon recognized as such; Virgil's *Aeneid* was profoundly influenced by it (behind Virgil's Dido, for instance, stand Apollonius' Hypsipyle and Medea). Early history of the work is uncertain. The Greek biographical tradition (which usually contains much palpably fictitious material) reports that the *Argonautica* was at first badly received in Alexandria and suggests that Apollonius was at odds with his "teacher" Callimachus, the most important scholar and poet of the Hellenistic period, who radically changed the course of Greek poetry, but only amid great controversy; to what extent the *Argonautica* was considered by Apollonius' contemporaries more traditional than avant-garde is no longer known, but there are many cross-references between the poems of Callimachus and the *Argonautica*, and Apollonius' poem is thoroughly modernistic in tone and style.

Superficially the *Argonautica* would seem to be an orthodox work aiming for a place in the mainstream tradition of heroic epic (though of literate, not oral, composition), and it has often been so regarded; modern critics who view it in this way generally contrast the *Argonautica* with what they see as the straightforward heroic world of the Homeric poems and conclude that Apollonius' work is an interesting failure. However, the *Iliad* and *Odyssey* are far from simplistic in outlook, and recent scholarship on Hellenistic poetry suggests that the *Argonautica* is a complex and original poem which successfully reworked the old epic form and reflects the troubled and introspective mentality of 3rd-century BC Alexandria.

The *Argonautica* can appear to be an episodic, disjointed work with many characteristically Hellenistic "travelogue" features (it touches often on matters of ethnography, geography, anthropology, etc.); but in fact the poem is remarkably whole. The work's perspective is established not through narrative directness, or through imagery or symbolism, but by a process of reversal often thought of as "irony" in the 20th century: the familiar is taken for granted and suppressed in favour of the less familiar, and what is important is most often expressed indirectly and at a secondary level. The result can be enigmatic but genuinely disturbing, and an effective way of conveying a pessimistic vision of a fragile and fragmented world. First, the story of the voyage of Jason and the Argonauts to Colchis in the distant parts of the Black Sea to capture the Golden Fleece, and of the difficult but crucial passion of the local princess Medea for Jason, was an ancient one, and Apollonius assumes that his audience does not need to have it retold in all its details; Jason's subsequent abandonment of Medea, for example, is nowhere recounted openly (the poem even ends just before the Argonauts reach home), but the whole poem broods on the issues of commitment, trust, and deception. Secondly, Apollonius takes for granted a familiarity with the two monumental epics preceding his own, and, by using the *Iliad* and *Odyssey* as "archetypal" reference points against which the Argonauts and their various encounters are juxtaposed and interpreted, he creates a multiplicity of dimensions and a kind of commentary to his *Argonautica*;

thus Medea does not appear until Book III (the poem consists of four long "books"), but the most substantial episode of Book I, the Argonauts' visit to the strange island of Lemnos with its all-female population, turns out to be diagnostic for Colchis. Although Jason's affair with the Lemnian queen Hypsipyle seems idle and inconsequential on the surface of the narrative, once Apollonius' references to Homer are recognized and Hypsipyle is considered as a figure reminiscent of Nausicaa and Circe, and Jason as an Odysseus or even Agamemnon, the real issues of ambivalence, pressure of circumstance, and expedient compromise begin to emerge. These are the issues underlying the whole poem, whether in the exotic account of the outward journey of Books I and II, the pathology of Medea's awful passion and conflict in Book III, or the alienated return home through the strange, semimythical half-real world of the Adriatic and north Africa in Book IV.

—A.W. Bulloch

APULEIUS, Lucius

Born: Madaura, province of Africa (now M'Daourouch, Algeria), c. AD 123–25. **Education:** Educated in Carthage, Athens, and Rome. **Family:** Married Aemilia Pudentilla; possibly had a son called Faustinus. **Career:** Lived in Oea (now Tripoli) where he married; acquitted of a charge of magic at nearby Sabratha; later lived in Carthage, where his success in public speaking led to various honours, including a statue and the important priesthood of Asclepius. **Died:** later than AD 163 (probably much later).

PUBLICATIONS

Collection

[Works], edited by Rudolph Helm and P. Thomas. 3 vols., 1907–31.

Fiction

Metamorphoses, edited by D.S. Robertson. 3 vols., 1940–45; also edited by Rudolph Helm, 1955, and C. Giarratano, revised by P. Frassinetti, 1960; edited and translated by J. Arthur Hanson [Loeb Edition], 2 vols., 1989; as *The Golden Ass*, translated by William Adlington, 1566, reprinted 1967, revised by Stephen Gaselee [Loeb Edition], 1915, also revised by Harry C. Schnur, 1962; also translated by Thomas Taylor, 1822; H.E. Butler, 2 vols., 1910; Jack Lindsay, 1932; Robert Graves, 1950; P.G. Walsh, 1994; as *The Isis-Book*, translated by J. Gwyn Griffiths, 1975; in part as *Cupid and Psyche*, edited and translated by E.J. Kenny, 1990; commentaries by A. Scobie (Book I), 1975, R.T. van der Paardt (Book III), 1971, B.L. Hijmans, Jr and others (Book IV), 1977, (Book VI and VII), 1981, (Book VIII), 1985, and J.G. Griffiths (Book XI), 1975; translated with introduction and explanatory notes by P.G. Walsh, 1994.

Other

Apologia, Florida, edited (with French translation) by P. Vallette. 2nd edition, 1960; as *The Apologia and Florida*, translated by H.E. Butler, 1909.

Philosophica (includes *De deo Socratis*; *De dogmate Platonis*; *De Mundo*), edited (with French translation) by J. Beaujeu. 1973.

*

Bibliography: *Ad Apulei Madaurensis Metamorphoseon librum primum commentarius Exegeticus* by Margaretha Molt (dissertation, Groningen), 1938; "The Scholarship on Apuleius since 1938" by Carl C. Schlam, in *Classical World*, 64, 1971.

Critical Studies: *Apuleius and His Influence* by E.H. Haight, 1927; *The Ancient Romances* by B.E. Perry, 1967; *Aspects of the Ancient Romance and Its Heritage: Essays on Apuleius, Petronius, and the Greek Romances* by Alexander Scobie, 1969; *The Roman Novel: The "Satyricon" of Petronius and the "Metamorphoses" of Apuleius* by P.G. Walsh, 1970; *Cupid and Psyche: Apuleius and the Monuments*, 1972, and *The Metamorphoses of Apuleius: On Making an Ass of Oneself*, 1992, both by Carl C. Schlam; *Amor and Psyche: The Psychic Development of the Feminine: A Commentary on the Tale by Apuleius* by Erich Neuman, 1973; *Aspects of the Golden Ass* edited by B.L. Hijmans, Jr. and R. Th. van der Paardt, 1978; *Apuleius and the Golden Ass* by James Tatum, 1979; *Shakespeare's Favourite Novel: A Study of the Golden Ass as a Prime Source* by J.J.M. Tobin, 1984; *Auctor and Actor: A Narratological Reading of Apuleius' Golden Ass* by John J. Winkler, 1985; *Unity in Diversity: A Study of Apuleius' Metamorphoses* by Paula James, 1987; *The Metamorphoses of Apuleius* by Judith K. Krabbe, 1989; *The Golden Ass of Apuleius: The Liberation of the Feminine in Man* by Marie-Louise von Franz, revised edition, 1992; *Metamorphosis of Language in Apuleius: A Study of Allusion in the Novel* by Ellen D. Finkelpearl, 1998; *The Religious Dreamworld of Apuleius' Metamorphoses: Recovering a Forgotten Hermeneutic* by James Gollnick, 1999; *Apuleius: A Latin Sophist* by S.J. Harrison, 2000; *Tales Within Tales: Apuleius Through Time*, edited by Constance S. Wright and Julia Bolton Holloway, 2000.

*   *   *

Apuleius is best understood as a performer. He regularly gave public speeches before the large crowds they attracted in his age, and his written work too reflects a concern to use style and knowledge to capture and maintain an audience's attention.

The *Florida*, a collection of the most "florid" parts of his public speeches, displays a man supremely confident before his admiring audience. He speaks with authority on a multitude of subjects, from Alexander the Great to parrots, though usually in a philosophical or cultural key. His style is as luxuriant as his subjects: in defiance of the careful, if at times precious, styles of the Golden and Silver Ages of Latin literature before him, his own style overflows with archaism, colloquialism, neologism, particularly if it will add to the rhythm, balance, music, or patterning. His style not only exemplifies the new tendencies of the age, but pushes them to an extreme.

Public speakers such as Apuleius considered they had a duty to educate, and some fulfilled this duty through a sort of popularizing philosophy. Apuleius had pretensions to being a Platonist philosopher, and there survive works ascribed to him which expound the philosophy of Plato as understood in his time. Most Apuleian is the energetic showpiece *De deo Socratis* [On the God of Socrates], which analyses the way in which an intermediary spirit connects us with God and which, for instance, memorably depicts the human condition in 19 successive epithets. Otherwise, these philosophical works are more disappointing and sometimes simply translate minor Greek works, although the translations seem to have proved useful to Greekless readers, if one may judge by the example of St Augustine.

Once, Apuleius *needed* to deliver a speech, to defend himself against the charge of winning the rich widow Pudentilla's affections by magic. The *Apologia* (or *On Magic*) is the only surviving classical Latin law-court speech not by Cicero, and, at least in its published form, displays the style of the *Florida* and a wicked sense of humour that we meet again in his novel.

The *Metamorphoses*, or *The Golden Ass* as it is generally known, is Apuleius' sole surviving novel (novels were in any case rare, late, and unprestigious in Greek and Roman literature), and is what Apuleius is best known for today. He takes a Greek short story and lengthens it to five times its original size by inserting stories (unlikely to be his own invention), thus making a Latin novel of some 250 modern pages. The Greek tale told how Lucius, dabbling in magic, was accidentally turned into an ass and underwent various adventures before being restored. Apuleius enriches the simple style of the original, producing something not easily translated into modern English. The inserted stories—of magic, brigands, and adultery—are related with verve and humour. Apuleius is interested too in psychological portrayal, though not in psychological development current in the modern novel; rather, the mind is as promising a subject for a description as is a brigands' camp or a god's garden.

The longest inserted tale, the celebrated story of *Cupid and Psyche*, is different. Its magical tone stands in stark contrast to the rumbustiousness of most of the novel. It adds, too, problems of interpretation: it is like a folk-tale, and thought by many to *be* a folk-tale; but it is difficult to deny some connection with the Platonic doctrine that Soul (*Psyche*) reaches its divine target through an intermediary spirit, Love (*Cupid*). The ending of the novel too, where Apuleius' hero is saved by initiation in the rites of the Egyptian goddess Isis, is thought by some to be a mere show of seriousness to finish, but by others to be the climax of a novel all along about the dangers of worldly vices.

We know nothing of the initial reception of the novel; and something of our assessment must depend on the precise interpretation adopted. But the extraordinary energy of the work is undeniable, as is the success of the frame-and-insertion structure in maintaining an unflagging interest. It displays many contrasts, from the flippant to the gruesome, from realism to make-believe, from bawdiness to extravagant piety. In character development it has the limitations of all ancient novels and most ancient thought. Its style has offended purists, but may be more validly criticized for unrelievedly trying too hard. Apuleius seems self-indulgent, but, more accurately, is preoccupied with dazzling his audience, an aim in which, as a professional, he generally succeeds.

—Ken Dowden

See the essay on *Cupid and Psyche*.

ARAGON, Louis

Born: Paris, France, 3 October 1897. **Education:** Educated at the Lycée Saint-Pierre, Neuilly, 1908–14; studied medicine, University of Paris, 1916–17. **Military Service:** Served in the French army,

medical auxiliary, 1918; medical corps, 1939–40, captured by the Nazis, escaped; active with the French Resistance, 1940–45: Croix de Guerre, 1918. **Family:** Married the writer Elsa Kagan Triolet in 1939 (died 1970). **Career:** Co-founding editor, with André Breton and Philippe Soupault, *Littérature*, 1919–24; active advocate of Dada, 1921–24, moved towards Surrealism from late 1920s; joined the Communist Party, 1927; attempted suicide, 1928; travelled to the Soviet Union, with his wife, November 1930; attended Revolutionary Writers Congress, Kharkov, publicly rejected Surrealism, 1931; lived in the Soviet Union, 1932–33; reporter and columnist, *L'Humanité*, 1933–34, member of the editorial board, *Commune*, 1933–36, both Paris; representative, 1st Congress of Soviet Writers, Moscow, 1934; organizer, 1st Congress of Writers in Defense of Culture, Paris, 1935; returned to the Soviet Union, June-December 1936; founding editor, *Ce Soir*, Paris, 1937–39 (publication banned 1939) and 1944–46; editor, *Les Lettres françaises*, 1953–72. **Awards:** Renaudot prize, 1936; Lenin Peace prize, USSR, 1957. Order of October Revolution, USSR, 1972; Order of People's Friendship, USSR, 1977; Chevalier, Légion d'honneur, 1981. **Died:** 24 December 1982.

PUBLICATIONS

Collections

Oeuvres romanesques croisées d'Elsa Triolet et Aragon, edited by Robert Laffont. 42 vols., 1964–74.
Oeuvre poétique. 15 vols., 1974–81.
Poésie. 1980.

Fiction

Anicet; ou, Le Panorama. 1921.
Les Aventures de Télémaque. 1922; as *The Adventures of Telemachus*, translated and with an introduction by Renee Riese Hubert and Judd D. Hubert, 1997.
Le Con d'Irène (as Albert de Routisie). 1928; as *Irène*, 1968; as *Irene*, translated by Lowell Bair, 1970; as *Irene's Cunt*, translated by Alexis Lykiard, 1996.
Les Plaisirs de la capitale. 1923.
Le Monde réel:
    Les Cloches de Bâle. 1934; as *The Bells of Basel*, translated by Haakon M. Chevalier, 1936.
    Les Beaux Quartiers. 1936; as *Residential Quarter*, translated by Haakon M. Chevalier, 1936.
    Les Voyageurs de l'impériale. 1942; as *The Century Was Young*, translated by Hannah Josephson, 1941; as *Passengers of Destiny*, translated by Josephson, 1947.
    Aurélien. 1944; as *Aurélien*, translated by Eithne Wilkins, 1946.
Servitude et grandeur des Français: Scènes des années terribles (stories). 1945.
Trois contes (stories). 1945.
Les Communistes. 1949–51; revised edition, 4 vols., 1966.
La Semaine sainte. 1958; as *Holy Week*, translated by Haakon M. Chevalier, 1961.
La Mise à mort. 1965.
Shakespeare (stories), illustrated by Picasso. 1965; as *Shakespeare*, translated by Bernard Frechtman, 1965.
Blanche ou l'oubli. 1967.

Henri Matisse. 2 vols., 1971; as *Henri Matisse*, translated by Jean Stewart, 1972.
Théâtre/Roman. 1974.
Le Mentir vrai (stories). 1980.
La Défense de l'infini (includes *Les Aventures de Jean-Foutre La Bite*). 1986.

Verse

Feu de joie. 1920.
Le Mouvement perpétual. 1926.
La Grande gaîté. 1929.
Persécuté persécuteur. 1931.
Front Rouge. 1931; as *The Red Front*, translated by E.E. Cummings, 1933.
Hourra l'Oural. 1934.
Le Crève-coeur. 1941; part translated in *Aragon: Poet of the French Resistance*, edited by Malcolm Cowley and Hannah Josephson, 1945.
Cantique à Elsa. 1941.
Brocéliande. 1942.
Les Yeux d'Elsa. 1942.
En français dans le texte. 1943.
Le Musée Grévin (as François La Colère). 1943.
Poèmes français. 1943.
France, écoute. 1944.
Le Crève-coeur et Les Yeux d'Elsa. 1944.
Neuf chansons interdites, 1942–1944. 1945.
En étrange pays dans mon pays lui-même (includes *En français dans le texte*; *Brocéliande*; *De l'exactitude historique en poésie*). 1945.
La Diane française. 1945.
Le Nouveau Crève-coeur. 1948.
Les Yeux et la mémoire. 1954.
Mes caravanes et autres poèmes. 1954.
Le Roman inachevé. 1956; as *The Unfinished Romance*, 1956.
Elsa. 1959.
Choix de poèmes. 1959.
Poésies: Anthologie, 1917–1960. 1960.
Les Poètes. 1960; revised edition, 1968 and 1976.
Le Fou d'Elsa. 1963.
Il ne m'est Paris que d'Elsa (anthology). 1964; revised edition, 1975.
Le Voyage de Hollande. 1964.
Élégie à Pablo Neruda. 1966.
Les Chambres. 1969.
Élégie à Romano, with Hamid Foulâdvind. 1980.
Les Adieux: poèmes. 1981.
Les Adieux et autres poèmes. 1982.

Plays

L'Armoire à glace un beau soir. 1924; as *The Mirror-Wardrobe One Fine Evening*, translated by Michael Benedikt, in *Modern French Theater*, edited by Benedikt and George E. Wellwarth, 1964.
Au pied du mur. 1924.
Le trésor des Jésuites. 1929.

Other

Le Libertinage (essays; includes play). 1924. as *The Libertine*, translated by Jo Levy, 1987.

Le Paysan de Paris (essays). 1926; as *Nightwalker*, translated by Frederick Brown, 1970; as *Paris Peasant*, translated by Simon Taylor Watson, 1971.
Traité du style. 1928.
La Peinture au défi. 1930.
Pour un réalisme socialiste. 1935.
Le Crime contre l'esprit, par le témoin des martyrs. 1942.
Les Bons Voisins (as Arnaud de saint Roman). 1943.
En français dans le texte. 1943.
"Matisse-en-France". 1943.
Je vous salue ma France. 1944.
Saint-Pol-Roux, ou l'espoir. 1945.
Servitude et grandeur des Français. 1945
L'Homme communiste. 2 vols., 1946–53.
Apologie du luxe. 1946.
Chroniques du bel canto. 1947.
La Culture et les hommes. 1947.
La Lumière et la Paix. 1950.
Hugo, poète réaliste. 1952.
L'Exemple de Courbet. 1952.
La Vrai Liberté de la culture, réduire notre train de mort pour accroître notre train de vie. 1952.
Les Egmont d'aujourd'hui s'appellent André Stil. 1952.
Le Neveu de Monsieur Duval. 1953.
Journal d'une poésie nationale. 1954.
La Lumière de Stendhal. 1954.
Les Yeux et la mémoire. 1954.
Littératures soviétiques. 1955.
Entretiens sur le Musée de Dresde, with Jean Cocteau. 1957; as *Conversations on the Dresden Gallery*, 1982.
J'abats mon jeu (essays). 1959.
Histoire parallèle des États-Unis et de l'URSS, with André Maurois. 4 vols., 1962; revised edition as *Les Deux Géants: Histoire des États-Unis et de l'URSS de 1917 à nos jours*, 5 vols., 1962–64; translated in part as *A History of the USSR: From Lenin to Krushchev*, by Patrick O'Brian, 1964.
Entretiens avec Francis Crémieux. 1964.
Les Collages. 1965.
Aragon parle avec Dominique Arban. 1968.
Fernand Séguin rencontre Louis Aragon. 1969.
Je n'ai jamais appris à écrire; ou, Les Incipits. 1969.
Comme je vous en donne l'exemple. 1974.
Vie de Charlot: Charles Spencer Chaplin, ses films et son temps, with Georges Sadoul. 1978.
Écrits sur l'art moderne (essays), edited by Jean Ristat. 1981.
Réflexions sur Rimbaud. 1983.
Pour expliquer ce que j'étais (journal). 1989.
Une vague de rêves. 1990.
Editor, *Avez-vous lu Victor Hugo?*. 1952.
Editor, *Introduction aux littératures soviétiques: Contes et nouvelles*. 1956.
Editor, *Elsa Triolet choisie par Aragon*. 1960.
Translator, *La Chasse au snark*, by Lewis Carroll. 1928.
Translator, *Fraternity*, by Stephen Spender. 1939.
Translator, *Cinq Sonnets de Pêtrarque*. 1947.
Translator, with A. Dimitriev, *Djamilia*, by Tchinghiz Aitmatov. 1959.

*

Bibliography: *Louis Aragon: Essai de bibliographie* by Crispin Geoghegan, 1979–80; *Louis Aragon: Bibliographie analytique* by Marie Lemaître, 1983.

Critical Studies: *Aragon: Poet of the French Resistance* (includes translations from *Le Crève-coeur*) edited by Malcolm Cowley and Hannah Josephson, 1945, as *Aragon: Poet of the Resurgent France*, 1946; *Aragon* by Hubert Juin, 1960; *Aragon: Romancier* by Pierre Lescure, 1960; *L'Itinéraire d'Aragon* by Roger Garaudy, 1961; *Aragon* by Georges Raillard, 1964; *Malraux, Sartre and Aragon as Political Novelists* by Catherine H. Savage, 1964; *Aragon, prosateur surréaliste* by Yvette Gendine, 1966; *Aragon: Le Réalisme de l'amour*, 1966; *The Poetry of Dada and Surrealism: Aragon, Breton, Tzara, Éluard and Desnos* by Mary Ann Caws, 1970; *Louis Aragon* by Lucille F. Becker, 1971; *Aragon* by Bernard Lecherbonnier, 1971; *La Résistance et ses poètes* by Pierre Seghers, 1974; *Aragon: Une vie à changer* by Pierre Daix, 1975; *Un nouveau cadavre: Aragon* by Paul Morelle, 1984; *Aragon: The Resistance Poems* by M. Adereth, 1985; *Aragon romancier: d'Anicet à Aurélien* by Jacqueline Lévi-Valensi, 1989; *Socialist Realism in Louis Aragon's Le monde réel* by Angela Kimyongür, 1995.

*   *   *

One of the most considerable French writers of the mid-20th century, Louis Aragon produced a large and varied body of work that is representative of the political aspirations and artistic orientations of the intellectuals of his age. From an early age he was a committed Marxist, although he did not always toe the Moscow line, and, like Jean-Paul Sartre, to quote another very notable instance, he was always ready to turn to journalism as well as to literature in order to express and communicate his ideas.

On return from service in the army medical corps during World War I, Aragon joined with André Breton and Philippe Soupault to found the magazine *Littérature* for avant-garde poetry. Its original tendency was Dadaist, in accord with the negative spirit born of the despair of the war years and disgust with bourgeois aesthetic values. Before long, however, Aragon and Breton, who had both studied medicine and had an interest in psychiatry, abandoned Dadaism in favour of surrealism, which combined an abiding concern with the operation of the unconscious with marked left-wing political concerns.

In 1921, a year after publishing *Feu de joie* [Bonfire], his first collection of verse, Aragon brought out the first of his major prose works, *Anicet; ou, Le Panorama* [Anicet; or, The Panorama Novel]. Though the very title challenges the surrealist tenet that the traditional novel was a spent force, Aragon uses his narrative very freely, borrowing some distancing techniques developed in the 18th century by Voltaire and Diderot to depict a poet, the eponymous Anicet. Anicet's education has left him emotionally parched, and the novel is essentially an account of his discovery of the significance of love that culminates in admission to a clandestine cult devoted to a female symbol of modern beauty. This was followed by *Les Adventures de Télémaque* (*The Adventures of Telemachus*). The title is taken from the classic 17th-century educational novel by Fénelon, Archbishop of Cambrai, and in a radical re-interpretation of the original, Aragon explores the theme of personal freedom. Published in 1926, *Le Paysan de Paris* (*Paris Peasant*), with a striking oxymoronic title that points to a relationship with the artificially constructed environment as close and intimate as the one that peasants are traditionally

supposed to have with the soil they till, is generally regarded as Aragon's most important single contribution to surrealism because of the way in which it displays how the quotidian can be transformed magically by the free imagination of the passer-by. The most famous section is the presentation of the arcade called "The Passage de l'Opéra." Though Aragon attacked established classics and orthodox contemporary writers such as Mauriac and Gide in his *Traité du style* [Treatise on Style], he also revealed that he was beginning to lose sympathy with surrealism in what was for him a time of personal crisis that he resolved partially by taking up a firmer political stance, especially after a visit to Russia.

As well as becoming a journalist, working for the French Communist newspaper *L'Humanité*, founding *Ce Soir*, and visiting Spain in 1937 to support Spanish intellectuals, Aragon wrote *Les Cloches de Bâle* (*The Bells of Basel*), which was followed by *Les Beaux Quartiers* (*Residential Quarter*), *Les Voyageurs de l'impériale* (*The Century Was Young*) and *Aurélien*. They form a series of novels under the global title of *Le Monde réel* [The Real World] that present, from a Marxist perspective, a historically-based and at times autobiographical picture of the struggles of the French bourgeoisie to maintain its position in the face of working-class challenges. In the course of World War II, during which he was associated with the Resistance, and in the turbulent post-war period, Aragon turned increasingly towards journalism and political writing. *Les Communistes* is devoted primarily to extolling the role played by women in the evolution of communism in France. The style owes a great deal to documentary techniques, and the characterization is shallow, being determined largely by class and circumstance.

If *Les Communistes* appeared to support the view that the novel was not a form that really appealed to Aragon, *La Semaine sainte* (*Holy Week*) seemed to rebut it. Set against a familiar background of stirring historical events as Napoleon returns from exile in Elba to eject the restored monarchy of Louis XVIII, and reclaim the imperial crown, the novel centres on the painter Théodore Géricault and what might be called his political education as he witnesses people's responses to the crisis.

In addition to his prose, Aragon wrote a great deal of verse, and the poetry he wrote in later life is particularly admired. The poetry inspired by his love for his companion, Elsa Triolet, a Russian-born novelist and journalist whom he had first met in 1928, struck a particular responsive chord. As well as choosing themes with a wide appeal, Aragon was able to mix tradition forms and innovatory techniques in his versification that found a receptive audience.

—Christopher Smith

See the essays on *Le Crève-coeur* and *Paris Peasant*.

ARENAS, Reinaldo

Born: Oriente Province, Cuba, 16 July 1943. **Education:** Studied agricultural accountancy at a vocational secondary school and the University of Havana, 1959–1962; also studied philosophy and literature without completing his degree. **Military Service:** Spent 1958 in the ranks of Fidel Castro's revolutionary movement. **Career:** Briefly worked in agricultural accounting at a farm in rural Oriente Province before beginning higher studies in Havana; began writing in the early 1960s and started working at the National Library in Havana in 1963; later became an editor for the Cuban Book Institute and a contributor to literary magazines such as *Unión* and *La Gaceta de Cuba*. Persecuted for his homosexuality and for publishing abroad without official permission, he was in and out of prison and forced work camps from the early to mid-1970s. After leaving Cuba in 1980, he settled in New York where he wrote and published prodigiously for the next decade. **Awards:** Honorable mention, Concurso Nacional de Novela (Cuba) for *Celestino antes del alba*, 1965; Prix Medici Etranger (France) for the best novel by a foreign author for *Celestino antes del alba*, 1969. **Died:** Terminally ill with AIDS, he took his life on 7 December 1990.

PUBLICATIONS

Collections

Mona and Other Tales. 2001; selected and translated by Dolores M. Koch.

Fiction

Celestino antes del alba. 1967; as *Singing from the Well*, translated by Andrew Hurley, 1987.
El mundo alucinante. 1969; as *Hallucinations*, translated by Gordon Brotherson, 1971.
La Vieja Rosa. 1980; as *Old Rosa*, translated by Ann Tashi Slater and Andrew Hurley, 1989.
Otra vez el mar. 1982; as *Farewell to the Sea*, translated by Andrew Hurley, 1986.
Cantando en el pozo. 1982; as *Singing from the Well*, translated by Andrew Hurley, 1987.
El Palacio de las Blanquísimas Mofetas. 1983; as *The Palace of the White Skunks*, translated by Andrew Hurley, 1990.
Arturo, la estrella más brillante. 1984; as *The Brightest Star*, translated by Andrew Hurley, 1989.
La loma del ángel. 1987; as *Graveyard of Angels*, translated by Alfred MacAdam, 1987.
El portero. 1988; as *The Doorman*, translated by Dolores Koch, 1991.
Viaje a La Habana [Journey to Havana]. 1990.
El color del verano. 1991; as *Color of Summer, or, the New Garden of Earthly Delights*, translated by Andrew Hurley, 2000.
El asalto. 1991; as *The Assault*, translated by Andrew Hurley, 1994.

Verse

El central. 1981; as *El Central: A Cuban Sugar Mill*, translated by Anthony Kerrigan, 1984.
Voluntad de vivir manifestándose. 1989.
Leprosorio [Leprosarium]. 1990.

Plays

Persecución: cinco piezas de teatro experimental. 1996.

Other

Necesidad de libertad. 1986.
Un plebiscito a Fidel Castro. 1990.
Final de un cuento. 1991.
Antes que anochezca (autobiography). 1992; as *Before Night Falls*, translated by Dolores Koch, 1993.

*

Bibliography: "Critical Monographs, Dissertations, and Critical Essays about Reinaldo Arenas" by David William Foster, in *Cuban Literature: A Research Guide* by David William Foster, 1985.

Critical Studies: *La textualidad de Reinaldo Arenas* by Eduardo Béjar, 1987; *Conversación con Reinaldo Arenas* by Francisco Soto, 1990; *El desamparado humor de Reinaldo Arenas* by Roberto Valero, 1991; *Reinaldo Arenas: The Pentagonia* by Francisco Soto, 1994; *Reinaldo Arenas: recuerdo y presencia* edited by Reinaldo Sánchez, 1994; *Reinaldo Arenas* by Francisco Soto, 1998; *Reinaldo Arenas: una apreciación política* by Adolfo Cacheiro, 2000.

*   *   *

Reinaldo Arenas is the most widely read and highly acclaimed writer to emerge from post-revolutionary Cuba and is viewed as one of the most original and controversial voices in twentieth century Latin American literature. Although mainly known as a novelist, Arenas also produced a considerable amount of poetry, drama, short fiction, essays, and, of course, his celebrated autobiography *Antes que anochezca* (*Before Night Falls*), which was made into a major motion picture in 2000.

In addition to the fame brought by his writing, Arenas's quasi-mythical status in twentieth century Latin American literature is due to his remarkable life story and his status as a symbol of the Cuban revolution's repression of dissident voices. Born in the remote Cuban countryside and raised in dire poverty among illiterate *campesinos*, Arenas joined Fidel Castro's revolutionary movement and was awarded for his service with scholarships. As a free-thinking homosexual writer, however, Arenas soon fell into disfavor with the regime and became a "non-person" in Cuba even while enjoying great literary success abroad. In the early to mid-1970s, he was imprisoned and sent to forced labor camps on several occasions. By virtue of a bureaucratic oversight, Arenas managed to escape from Cuba with the 1980 Mariel boatlift and spent the remaining ten years of his life in exile.

Arenas's first and only novel to be published in Cuba, *Celestino antes del alba* (*Singing from the Well*), is the first in a series of five books that the author called his *pentagonía*. These highly poetic novels can be understood as a sort of homosexual *bildungsroman*, or story of personal development, contained within a metaphor of twentieth century Cuban history. These texts are highly autobiographical and are meant to challenge the rigid norms of social realism that dominated the country's literary production as the revolution became more dogmatic. *Singing from the Well* is the story of a child who uses his imagination to overcome the poverty and oppression of his childhood. Although this novel does not explicitly deal with homosexuality, its themes of creative rebelliousness and denunciation of intolerance are emblematic of Arenas's entire oeuvre. With its lack of a traditional plot, its non-linear timeline, and its nameless narrator-protagonist, the novel typifies Arenas's rejection of literary conventions. The distinctions between narrator, writer, and character are blurred in this text, a tendency that continues to manifest itself in Arenas's later work. As the Cuban government became more repressive in the late 1960s, this novel came to be viewed as subversive and Arenas was forbidden to publish in Cuba.

In the second novel of the series, *El Palacio de las Blanquísimas Mofetas* (*The Palace of the White Skunks*), the protagonist of *Singing from the Well* is reincarnated as Fortunato, a rebellious adolescent with homosexual tendencies living in the chaotic pre-Revolutionary period. This novel showcases Arenas's nonconformity in its use of multiple narrative voices and its rejection of the predominant tendency among Cuban novelists of the era to portray the revolution as an unquestionably positive event that changed Cuba for the better. The third installment, *Otra vez al mar* (*Farewell to the Sea*) continues the story of Fortunato as the adult Héctor, a homosexual who lives on the margins of revolutionary Cuban society as a tortured dissident. *El color del verano* (*Color of Summer*) is the fourth novel in the series and takes place in Cuba in the summer of 1999, during the 50th year of the dictator Fifo's repressive regime. The first person narrative voice in this text is split among Gabriel, Reinaldo, and the Gloomy Skunk, a parody of the Catholic Holy Trinity. The text revolves around the exploits of a myriad of characters that engage in subversive adventures in preparation for celebrating the dictator's anniversary. *El asalto* (*The Assault*) is the final installment in the *pentagonía*. In a vein reminiscent of George Orwell's *1984*, this book presents a futuristic version of Cuban society in which totalitarianism has been allowed to foster unchallenged. Despite the many clear references to Cuban society in these books, they can also be read on a more universal level as parables on the effects of intolerance and the importance of free self-expression.

Arenas's writing became more explicitly autobiographical with the posthumous publication of his autobiography *Before Night Falls*. Arenas dictated his life story, which he had begun to write many years earlier in the treetops of Havana's Lenin Park as a fugitive from the Cuban police, into a tape recorder while suffering from the advanced stages of AIDS. This text has been hailed as a landmark in Latin American literature because of its open and frank treatment of the life story and erotic adventures of a homosexual writer. This book, like the novels of the *pentagonía*, is clearly critical of the Cuban regime and cries out for the need to respect individual freedoms.

Most prominent among Arenas's short fiction is *Viaje a La Habana* [Journey to Havana], a collection of three novellas that are unified thematically around the idea of the homosexual's search for liberation from society's oppression.

Although much of Arenas's prose writing is characterized by its highly lyrical style, he also wrote more traditional verse such as the extensive poem *El central* (*El Central: A Cuban Sugar Mill*), which later came to form part of a poetic trilogy titled *Leprosorio* [Leprosarium]. This series of poems, which represent Cuban history from the Spanish conquest to the present, is Arenas's most blatantly politicized text. These are compositions full of rage directed at the atrocities committed against marginalized subjects—from African slaves to homosexual dissidents—throughout 500 years of Cuban history.

Since his death in 1990, Arenas's body of work has become increasingly popular and there is now general agreement among critics regarding his status as one of the most daring, creative, and rebellious writers in the history of Latin American letters.

—Stephen J. Clark

ARETINO, Pietro

Born: Arezzo, Florentine Republic (now in Italy), 20 April 1492. **Education:** Studied poetry and painting in Perugia. **Family:** Had two daughters, the first by Caterina Sandella. **Career:** Moved to Perugia, 1508; First poetry published, 1512; moved to Rome, 1517, under protection of Agostino Chigi, and entered political and artistic circles; under protection of Pope Leo X and the Medici, wrote lampoons and "pasquinades" against influential and powerful contemporaries, often gaining their enmity; fled Rome on the election of Pope Adrian VI, 1522, whom he had satirized; returned to Rome on election of Giulio de' Medici as Pope Clement VII, 1523; following assault by servants of a Curia official, left Rome again, and finally settled in Venice, 1527. **Died:** 21 October 1556.

PUBLICATIONS

Collections

Teatro, edited by Nunzio Macarrone. 2 vols., 1914.
Works, translated by Samuel Putnam. 2 vols., 1926.
Poesie, edited by Gaetano Sborselli. 2 vols., 1930–34.
Tutte le comedie, edited by G.B. Sanctis. 1968.
Teatro, edited by Giorgio Petrocchi. 1971.

Fiction

Ragionamenti, edited by Dario Carraroli. 2 vols., 1914; edited by Giovanni Aquilecchia, 1980; as *The Ragionamenti: The Lives of Nuns; The Lives of Married Women; The Lives of Courtesans*, edited and translated by Peter Stafford, 1971.
    Ragionamento della Nanna e della Antonia. 1534; as *The Lives of Nuns*, in *Works*, 1926; also translated in *The Ragionamenti*, 1971.
    Dialogo nel quale la Nanna insegna a la Pippa. 1536; as *The Lives of Married Women*, in *Works*, 1926; also translated in *The Ragionamenti*, 1971.
    Ragionamento de le corti. 1538; edited by Guido Batteli, 1914; as *The Lives of Courtesans*, in *Works*, 1926; also translated in *The Ragionamenti*, 1971.
Le carte parlanti. 1543; edited by F. Campi, 1926.
A Dialogue of Dying Well, translated by Richard Verstagen. 1603.
Sei giornate: Ragionamento della Nanna e della Antonia; Dialogo nel quale la Nanna insegna a la Pippa, edited by Giovanni Aquilecchia. 1969.
Aretino's Dialogues, translated by Raymond Rosenthal. 1972.
Sei giornate, edited by Guide Davico Bonino. 1975.
Il romanzo della ruffiana, edited by G.B. De Sanctis. 1977.

Verse

Opera nova del fecundissimo Giovane Pietro Pictore Arentino zoe strambotti sonetti capitoli epistole barzellette ed una desperata. 1512.
Marfisa. 1532.
Stanze in lode di Madonna Angela Sirena. 1537.
Sonetti lussuriosi e pasquinate (selection), edited by M.B. Sirolesi. 1980.
Sonnets, translated by Oscar Wilde. N.d.

Plays

Il marescalco (produced 1526/27). 1533; as *The Stablemaster*, translated by George Bull, in *Five Italian Renaissance Comedies*, edited by Bruce Penman, 1978; as *The Marescalco*, translated by Leonard G. Sbrocchi and J. Douglas Campbell, 1986.

La cortigiana (produced 1537). 1534 (edited version); in full, edited by Giuliano Innamorati, 1970.

La Talanta (produced 1542). 1542; as *Talanta*, translated by Christopher Cairns, in *Three Renaissance Comedies*, edited by Cairns, 1991.

Lo ipocrito (produced 1545). 1542.

L'Orazia. 1546.

Il filosofo. 1546.

Other

La Passione di Giesu. 1534.

I Sette Salmi della penitenzia di David. 1535; as *A Paraphrase upon the Seven Penitential Psalms*, translated by Robert Persons, 1635.

Tre libri de la Humanità di Cristo. 1535.

Lettere. 6 vols., 1537–57; edited by Fausto Nicolini, 2 vols., 1913–16, and by Francesco Flora and A. Del Vito, 1960; selections as *Lettere scelte*, edited by Guido Battelli, 1913, and as *Lettere sull'arte*, edited by E. Camesasca, 3 vols., 1957–60; selections translated by Thomas Caldecot Chubb, as *The Letters*, 1967, and by George Bull, as *Selected Letters*, 1976.

Il Genesi. 3 vols., 1538.

Vita di Maria Vergine. 1539.

Vita di Caterina vergine e martire. 1540; edited by Flavia Santin, 1978.

Orlandino. 1540.

Vita di san Tommaso signor D'Aquino. 1543; edited by Flavia Santin, 1978.

Prose sacre, edited by Ettore Allodoli. 1926.

*

Critical Studies: *Pietro Aretino e le sue opere* by C. Bertani, 1901; *Le commedie di Pietro Aretino* by U. Fresco, 1901; *Pietro Aretino: The Scourge of Princes* by Edward Hutton, 1922; *L'Aretino: Le cause della sua potenza e della sua fortuna* by A. Del Vito, 1939; *Pietro Aretino* by Giorgio Petrocchi, 1948; *Pietro Aretino: Studio e note critiche* by Giuliano Innamorati, 1957; *Progetto corporativo e autonomia dell'arte in Pietro Aretino* by Giovanni Falaschi, 1977; *Le voci dell'istrione: Pietro Arentino e la dissoluzione del teatro* by Giulio Ferroni, 1977; *L'Aretino* by Cesare Marchi, 1980; *Pietro Aretino and the Republic of Venice: Researches on Aretino and His Circle in Venice, 1527–1556*, 1985, "Aretino's Comedies and the Italian 'Erasmian' Connection in Shakespeare and Jonson," in *Theatre of the English and Italian Renaissance* edited by J.R. Mulryne and M. Shrewsbury, 1991, and "Aretino's *Talanta* (1542) and the Influence of Vasari," in *Italian Renaissance Festivals and Their European Influence* edited by Mulryne and Shrewsbury, 1992, all by Christopher Cairns; "Rhetoric and Drama: Monologues and Set Speeches in Aretino's Comedies" by Richard Adams, in *The Languages of Literature in Renaissance Italy* edited by Peter Hainsworth and others, 1988; *Periegesi aretiniane, testi, schede e note biografiche intorno a Pietro Aretino* (includes texts) by Angelo Romano, 1991; *Aretino Dead or Alive: A 500th Birthday Tribute* by W.A. Caswell, 1992; *The Sixteen Pleasures* by Robert Hellenga, 1994; *Titian's Portraits Through Aretino's Lens* by Luba Freedman, 1995.

* * *

Pietro Aretino is known chiefly for his plays (five comedies, one tragedy), dialogues, including the *Dialogues on Courts and Cards*, and the publication of his letters to the rich and famous. From 1538 he was the first to publish his own letters in the vulgar tongue (i.e. not in Latin). Six letter books were to follow until 1557 (one posthumously) constituting a rich vein of information on the customs of the times, as well as a valuable register of the current movements of artists and the creation of artworks. Aretino was on friendly terms with many of the greatest artists working in Venice, including Titian and Tintoretto. Representing the glitter and the license of the Renaissance, he also experienced the Catholic Reformation, and its censure of his sonnets written to accompany the *Sedici modi* (a book of sexual postures) by Marcantonio Raimondi, after designs by Giulio Romano, and his *Ragionamenti* or *Sei giornate* [Dialogues Between Whores]. For these activities, Aretino was classified by figures of the English Renaissance, such as Thomas Nashe and Ben Jonson, as the representative of Italian private or domestic vice, to parallel Machiavelli as the representative of Italian public vice (in politics).

Aretino was born in Arezzo in 1492 and of humble stock. He seems to have had early experience as a painter: he was described as Pietro *pictore* Aretino in his first anthology of youthful poems, the *Opera nova*. An aspiring courtier at the papal court of Pope Leo X and in the household of Agostino Chigi, the papal banker who was also the patron of Raphael, Aretino's first comedy, written in 1525, was *La cortigiana* [The Courtesan], a satirical exposé of conditions for the courtier in Rome (it was later revised for publication in Venice to include references to his new Venetian patrons). Aretino was also notorious for the *pasquinate* (libellous satirical poems lampooning both prominent members of the papal court and candidates for the papal conclave), which were traditionally affixed to the statue of Pasquino in Rome.

When the election of Pope Adrian VI and the repercussions from the *Sedici modi* made Rome too dangerous for him, Aretino moved to the camp of the condottiere Captain Giovanni dalle Bande Nere, and thence to the Gonzaga Court of Mantua, where the second comedy, *Il marescalco* (*The Stablemaster*) was composed. This satirized (while implicitly accepting) the subservient status of a courtier obliged to marry at his master's bidding in spite of his clearly homosexual proclivities. In Venice, in 1527, Aretino had at last found a permanently safe haven. Protected by the Doge Andrea Gritti, and fêted by artists and writers alike, he began a life of writing and self-publicity, using the nascent Venetian printing press. A wide variety of works flowed from his pen in the following years, including revised versions of the first two comedies in 1533–34; works of religious orientation in deference to the growing influence of Catholic reformist currents; and the above-mentioned *Sei giornate* in 1534–36. With the arrival of Nicolò Franco—colleague, later enemy, and sometime secretary—in Venice and with Venetian bookshops full of the fashion for Erasmus's Latin letters, the idea was born to publish his own letters in Italian. Part literature, part journalism, the first collection of these saw the light of day in 1537, going through some ten editions within the year. Quite apart from any literary merit, this success was due partly to the novelty of the enterprise. Profits for the author consisted of both rewards from the published letters' recipients (both fictional and actual) and payments for his silence. Further religious works followed, with the lives of three saints in 1540, encouraging the author's hopes for possible church preferment, and two more comedies, *Lo ipocrito* [The Hypocrite] and *La Talanta* (*Talanta*) in 1542. The latter was produced in Venice that year in a celebrated performance against a perspective set of Roman monuments by Giorgio Vasari, author of the *Lives of the Artists*. *Talanta* marked a return to the traditional unities for Aretino's comedy and contained what can be interpreted as early examples of *commedia dell'arte* stereotypes. Aretino himself complained in a letter that his actors had exceeded their brief in using plebeian accents. This play highlighted the Venice-versus-Rome polemic, as well as featuring a tour of the set in the script. *Lo ipocrito* was written in the same year, and launched a literary character, the religious pedant, possibly derived from Aretino's own society, but which has had a long history culminating in Molière's *Tartuffe*.

The last comedy, *Il filosofo* [The Philosopher], satirizing the pretensions to authority of philosophers, was published in 1546. Aretino's only tragedy, *L'Orazia*, of the same year, is now highly regarded as a distinguished example of this 16th-century genre. By 1545, his prestige and notoriety was such that he enjoyed the friendship, or respect, of most of the crowned heads of Europe, and made a celebrated ride to Peschiera in the company of the Emperor Charles V. Predictably within a year of his death, in 1556, the whole of Aretino's literary production was on the Catholic Index, although the publication of his comedies and dialogues in London in the 1580s, in Italian, must doubtless have done as much to propagate his reputation in Europe as the earlier *succès de scandale* of the *Sei giornate* and the *Sedici modi*. The subject of vituperation and prejudice on moral and religious grounds for centuries, Aretino's works are only now being treated as subjects for serious literary study.

—Christopher Cairns

See the essay on *La cortigiana*.

ARGUEDAS, José María (Altamirano)

Born: Andahuaylas, Apurímac region, Peru, 18 January 1911. **Education:** Educated at Colegio Miguel Grau de los Padres Mercedarios, Abancay, 1924–25; Colegio San Luis Gonzaga, Ica, 1926–27; Colegio Santa Isabel, Huancayo, 1928–30; Colegio de Mercedarios, Lima, 1929–30; studied literature and anthropology at San Marcos University, Lima, 1931–32 (university closed by authorities, 1932), 1935–37, 1947–50, degree 1957, doctorate 1963. **Family:** Married 1) Celia Bustamante in 1939 (divorced 1966); 2) Sybila Arredondo in 1967. **Career:** Lived in San Juan de Lucanas, 1917–24. Worked for the Peruvian postal service, Lima, 1932–37; co-founder and co-editor, *Palabra*, 1936; imprisoned for involvement in demonstrations against the insurrection in Spain, 1937–38; teacher of Spanish and geography, Colegio Nacional Mateo Pumacahua, Sicuani, 1939, and continued as secondary school teacher until 1946; lived in Mexico, 1940–42; returned to Lima, 1942, and worked with government commission for education reforms; teacher, 1942–47, Colegio Alfonso Ugarte and Colegio Guadalupe, both Lima, and the Instituto Pedagógico, Varones, 1950–53; suffered nervous breakdown, 1943; curator-general, 1947–50, then director, 1950–53, Ministry of Education Department of Folklore and Fine Art, Lima; travelled to Chile, 1951; director, Museum of Peruvian Culture Institute of Ethnological Studies, 1953; travelled to Spain, 1957–58; professor of Quechua and ethnic studies, San Marcos University, 1958–63, and later lectured at the Agrarian University, 1962–66; director, Institute of Contemporary Arts, Lima, 1961; director, Casa de la Cultura, 1963–64; director, Museum of the

Republic (Museum of National History), Lima, 1964–66; founder, *Cultura y Pueblo*, 1964; visited the United States, 1965; attempted suicide by overdose of barbiturates, 1966; visited Cuba, 1968. **Awards:** Javier Prado prize, 1958; Ricardo Palma prize, 1959, 1962; William Faulkner Foundation certificate of merit, 1963; Inca Garcilaso de la Vega prize, 1968. **Died:** (suicide) 2 December 1969.

PUBLICATIONS

Collection

Obras completas. 5 vols., 1983.

Fiction

Agua (stories). 1935.
Runa yu pay. 1939.
Yawar fiesta. 1941; revised and corrected edition, 1958; as *Yawar Fiesta*, translated by Frances Horning Barraclough, 1985.
Diamantes y pedernales (includes "Diamantes y pedernales," "Orovilca," and the stories of *Agua*). 1954.
Todas las sangres. 1954.
Los ríos profundos. 1958; edited by William Rowe, 1973; as *Deep Rivers*, translated by Frances Horning Barraclough, 1978.
El sexto. 1961.
La agonía de Rasu-Ñiti. 1962.
Amor mundo y otros cuentos (includes "La agonía de Rasu-Ñiti" and the stories of *Agua*). 1967; enlarged edition, 1972.
Amor mundo y todos los cuentos. 1967.
El zorro de arriba y el zorro de abajo (unfinished), edited by Eve Marie Fell. 1971; enlarged edition, 1990.
El forastero y otros cuentos (includes "El barranco," "Orovilca," "Hijo solo"). 1972.
Cuentos olvidados, edited by José Luis Rouillon. 1973.
Relatos completos, edited by Jorge Lafforgue. 1975; revised edition, 1977.
Breve antología didáctica (stories). 1986.
Diamantes y pedernales; La agonía de Rasu-Ñiti; El sueño del pongo; Cuentos olvidados; Taller. 1986.
Relatos completos. 1987.

Other (including Quechua works)

Canto Kechwa (songs in Spanish and Quechua). 1938; translated in *The Singing Mountaineers*, 1957.
Cuzco. 1947.
Canciones y cuentos del pueblo quechua, with Jorge A. Lira. 1949; translated in *The Singing Mountaineers*, 1957.
Cuentos mágico-realistas y canciones de fiestas tradicionales en el valle del Mantaro. 1953.
Apu Inca Atawallpaman: Elegía quechua anónima (Spanish and Quechua), edited by José M.B. Farfán. 1955.
The Singing Mountaineers: Songs and Tales of the Quechua People, edited and translated by Ruth Stephen. 1957.
Estudio etnográfico de la Feria de Huancayo. 1957.
Ollantay: Cantos y narraciones quechuas, with César Miró and Salazar Bondy. 1957.
El arte popular religioso y la cultura mestiza. 1958.
Kunturpa munaskkan sipasmanta/De la amante del Cóndor (Quechua and Spanish), with Jorge A. Lira. 1961.

Tupac Amaru Kamaq taytanchisman: Haylli-taki/A nuestro padre creador Tupac Amaru: Himno-canción (Quechua and Spanish). 1962.

El sueño del pongo: Cuento quechua; Pongo mosqoynin: Qatqa runapa willaskusqan (Spanish and Quechua). 1965.

Dioses y hombres de Huarochirí (Spanish and Quechua). 1966.

Notas sobre la cultura latinoamericana y su destino, with Francisco Miró Quesada and Fernando de Szyszlo. 1966.

Las comunidades de España y del Perú. 1968.

El sueño del pongo; Canciones quechuas tradicionales, with recording. 1969.

Temblar/Katatay (Spanish and Quechua). 1972; edited by Sybila de Arguedas, 1984.

Páginas escogidas, edited by E.A. Westphalen. 1972.

Formación de una cultura nacional indoamericana. 1975; edited by Ángel Rama, 1981.

Señores e indios: Acerca de la cultura quechua (journalism), edited by Ángel Rama. 1976.

Temblar; El sueño del pongo; Katatay; Pongo mosqoynin (Spanish and Quechua). 1976.

Evolución de las comunidades indígenas: Dos estudios sobre Huancayo. 1977.

Nosotros los maestros (selection), edited by Wilfredo Kapsoli. 1986.

Indios, mestizos y señores (journalism), edited by Sybila de Arguedas. 1989.

Editor, with Francisco Izquierdo Ríos, *Mitos, leyendas y cuentos peruanos* (Quechua miscellany). 1947.

Editor, *Poesía quechua.* 1966.

*

Bibliography: "Bibliografía de José María Arguedas" by William Rowe, in *Revista Peruana de Cultura*, 13–14, 1970; "José María Arguedas" in *Peruvian Literature: A Bibliography of Secondary Sources* by David William Foster, 1981.

Critical Studies: *La multitud y el paisaje peruanos en los relatos de José María Arguedas*, 1939, and *José María Arguedas: Etapas de su vida*, 1972, both by Moises Arroyo Posadas; "The Quechua World of José María Arguedas," in *Hispania*, 45, 1962, and *The Modern Short Story in Peru*, 1966, both by Earl M. Aldrich; *Arguedas: Un sentimiento trágico de la vida* by César Levano, 1969; *El tema de la violencia en Yawar fiesta* by François Borricaud, 1970; *José María Arguedas y la nueva novela indígena del Perú* edited by Julio V. Flores, 1970; "The Literary Progression of José María Arguedas" by Phyllis Rodríguez-Peralta, in *Hispania*, 55(2), 1972; *Los universos narrativos de José María Arguedas* by Antonio Cornejo Polar, 1973; *La experiencia americana de José María Arguedas* by Gladys C. Marín, 1973; *José María Arguedas: El nuevo rostro del indio, una estructura míticopoética* by Antonio Urello, 1974; *Recopilación de textos sobre José María Arguedas*, 1976; "The Foxes in José María Arguedas's Last Novel" by F. Mitchell, Jr, in *Hispania*, 61, 1978; *José María Arguedas: Entre sapos y halcones* by Mario Vargas Llosa, 1978; *Mito e ideología en la obra de José María Arguedas* by William Rowe, 1979; *Cultura popular andina y forma novelesca: Zorros y danzantes en la última novela de Arguedas* by Martin Lienhard, 1982, enlarged edition, 1990; *Arguedas: Mito, historia y religión; Entre las calandrias* by Pedro Trigo and Gustavo Gutierrez, 1982; *Arguedas; o, La utopía de la lengua* by Alberto Escobar, 1984; "Arguedas the Innovator: Yawar fiesta and Tupac Amaru" by T.K. Lewis, in *Discurso Literario*,

3(1), 1985; *Mythological Consciousness and the Future: José María Arguedas* by Claudette Kemper Columbus, 1986; *El modo épico en José María Arguedas* by Vincent Spina, 1986; *José María Arguedas y el mito de la salvación por la cultura* by Silverio Muñoz, 1987; *Estudios sobre José María Arguedas y Vargas Llosa* by F.J. Carranza Romero, 1989; *De Yawar fiesta a El zorro de arriba y el zorro de abajo* by C. Vildoso Chirinos, 1989; *José María Arguedas, del pensamiento dialéctico al pensamiento trágico, Historia de una utopía* by Roland Forgues, 1989; *La utopía arcaica: José María Arguedas y las ficciones del indigenismo* by Mario Vargas Llosa, 1996; *José María Arguedas: Reconsiderations for Latin American Cultural Studies*, edited by Ciro A. Sandoval and Sandra M. Boschetto-Sandoval, 1998.

*   *   *

José María Arguedas ranks as one of Peru's two leading novelists, the other being Mario Vargas Llosa. However, while Vargas Llosa belongs to the Western mainstream, Arguedas wrote as a spokesman of the indigenous Quechua-speaking Andean world, setting out to correct the distorted, stereotyped image of the native presented by earlier fiction. While his own portrayal of the native is still the view of an outsider, being the work of a non-native writing for a non-native public, it offers a deeper insight into the native people's mentality than anything published hitherto. The basis of the native people's culture, we are shown, is a magical-religious view of the world that regards the earth not merely as something to be conquered and exploited, but as a single cosmic order animated by supernatural forces and linked in a universal harmony.

In his early fiction Arguedas's success in communicating that world view was restricted by his continuing reliance on a conventional realist manner, but from *Los ríos profundos* (*Deep Rivers*) onwards he evolved a more effective lyrical style akin to that of the Mexican, Juan Rulfo. Artistically, too, he was faced with the problem of translating into the alien medium of Spanish the sensibility of a people who express themselves in Quechua. His initial solution was to modify Spanish in such a way as to incorporate the basic features of Quechua syntax and thus reproduce something of the special character of native speech; but these experiments were only partially successful and subsequently he opted for a correct Spanish skilfully manipulated to convey Andean thought-patterns.

The context of Arguedas's fiction is the semi-feudal socioeconomic order that prevailed in the Andean highlands from the Spanish Conquest until recent times. However, while earlier writers had simplistically depicted a black-and-white confrontation between oppressive white landowners and a downtrodden native peasantry, Arguedas presents a much more complex picture of Andean society. *Yawar fiesta* highlights the social tensions within the various racial groups. It also challenges the conventional image of abject, defeated natives by emphasizing the resilience that has enabled the native peoples to survive centuries of oppression. Indeed, oppression is seen to have actually strengthened their culture, for it is by clinging to their traditional ways and refusing to be absorbed into the Western order that they have retained their pride and sense of identity. Furthermore, Arguedas demonstrates that centuries of co-existence have brought about a process of transculturation and that, if the whites dominate socially and economically, it is the native influence that predominates culturally, pervading the outlook of the whites despite their assumptions of cultural superiority. This paradoxical situation is encapsulated in the festival around which the novel revolves, a bullfight which simultaneously re-enacts racial hostilities and binds the whole community together in a common enthusiasm.

Most of Arguedas's novels are very much social in character in that they attempt to convey an overview of Andean society. However, another important strand in his work draws on his personal experience to depict the clash of Peru's two main cultures at an individual level, by focusing on the predicament of a young boy torn between the two. Thus, the child protagonist of the stories of *Agua* [Water] rejects the cruelty and injustice of the white landowning society into which he was born, and identifies emotionally with the native people among whom he was brought up and whose culture affords him the comfort denied him by his own kind, but he can never escape the fact that he is different. Likewise, the protagonist of *Deep Rivers* is cut off from the beloved native world of his childhood when he is sent to a Church-run school to receive the education that will equip him to take his place in white society. In the oppressive atmosphere of the school he finds himself completely alienated, and his faith in native culture is undermined by its seeming ineffectiveness in the world of the whites; but, in a triumphal climax, that faith is restored as the downtrodden native peoples assert the validity of their culture by challenging the dominant social order and forcing it to accede to their demands. This autobiographical element was to resurface more directly in Arguedas's last, uncompleted novel *El zorro de arriba y el zorro de abajo* [The Fox of Above and the Fox of Below], where the narrative is interspersed with sections of diary recording the crisis that led him to commit suicide.

Arguedas's work also explores the impact of change on traditional Andean society. In *Yawar fiesta* we see the region emerge from its centuries-old isolation, progress being symbolized by a government decree banning non-professional bullfights; but the novel highlights the paradox that the very modernity that promises to liberate the native peoples also threatens to destroy their culture and thereby their existence as a separate group. *Todas las sangres* [All Bloods] reflects the political and economic changes that had been taking place in Peru since the mid-1950s. The most optimistic of Arguedas's novels, it portrays the break-up of the traditional semi-feudal order and the emergence of the newly mobilized native peasantry as a political force, and expresses confidence in the ability of Quechua culture to adapt to a modern industrial society without losing its distinctive identity. Subsequently, Arguedas was to become disillusioned as the country embarked on an uncontrolled process of capitalist development that brought with it a depopulation of the countryside and the erosion of traditional ways of life. *El zorro de arriba y el zorro de abajo* paints a horrific picture of this new reality, epitomized by the coastal boom-town of Chimbote. Nonetheless, a positive note is maintained by the pervasive presence of the Quechua culture of the Andean migrants, and it is implied that out of the melting-pot that is present-day coastal Peru there will emerge a new national culture for the native peoples.

—James Higgins

See the essay on *Deep Rivers*.

ARGUETA, Manlio

Born: San Miguel, El Salvador, 24 November 1935. **Education:** Doctorate in Law and Social Sciences at the University of El Salvador. **Career:** Lived in exile in Costa Rica, where he taught at the Universidad de Costa Rica and directed Editorial Universitaria Centroamericana, an important Central American publishing house, 1972–1993; since returning to El Salvador in 1993, he has held several posts at the University of El Salvador, including, director of the Office of Nacional and International Relations (1996–2000) and director of of the National Library of El Salvador (from 2000). **Awards:** "Rubén Darío" poetry prize, 1967; Unico Consejo Superior Universitario Centroamericano prize, 1969; Casa de las Américas novel prize, 1978.

PUBLICATIONS

Fiction

El valle de las hamacas. 1969.
Caperucita en la zona roja. 1978; as *Little Red Riding Hood in the Red Light District*, translated by Edward Waters Hood, 1998.
Un día en la vida. 1980; as *One Day of Life*, translated by Bill Brow, 1984.
Cuzcatlán donde bate la Mar del Sur. 1986; as *Cuzcatlán: Where the Southern Sea Beats*, translated by Clark Hansen, 1987.
Milagro de la Paz. 1994; as *A Place Called Milagro de la Paz*, translated by Michael B. Miller, 2000.
Siglo de O(g)ro. 2000.

Verse

Poemas. 1967.
De aquí en adelante. 1967.
En el costado de la luz. 1968.
Las bellas armas reales. 1979.

Other

El Salvador. 1990.

*

Critical Studies: "Manlio Argueta" by Ineke Phaf, in *Modern Latin American Authors*, vol. 145 of *The Dictionary of Literary Biography*; "Las novelas de Manio Argueta: La historia, cultura e identidad salvadoreñas," dissertation by Anna Lee Utech, 1993; "Argueta, Dalton y la crítica de la historia" by Silvia L. López, in *Cambios estéticos y nuevos proyectos culturales en Centroamérica*, edited by Amelia Mondragón, 1994; "Novela y testimonio en la obra narrativa de Manlio Argueta: el contrato autorial" by Nicasio Urbina, in *Cambios estéticos y nuevos proyectos culturales en Centroamérica*, edited by Amelia Mondragón, 1994; "Tragedia de la paz, *Milagro de la Paz*: la evolución literaria de Manlio Argueta," by Edward Waters Hood, in *Antípodas*, vol. 10, 1998.

*   *   *

Called the "Poet" by his friends, Manlio Argueta is best known for his testimonial-style novels that chronicle the violent recent history of El Salvador. His works denounce, in a very personal way, the social and political injustices and inequalities that have provoked and continue to cause civil strife and suffering in his homeland.

Argueta's first novels, *El valle de las hamacas* and *Caperucita en la zona roja* (*Little Red Riding Hood in the Red Light District*), present the social instability and political repression that reigned in El Salvador during the 1960s and 1970s. Stylistically, these are fragmented novels, with interior monologues and shifts in time and place. Their plots revolve around the problems faced by two couples: Rosaura and Raúl in *El valle de las hamacas*, and Alfonso and Hormiga (Ant) in *Little Red Riding Hood in the Red Light District*. Argueta's third and fourth novels, *Un día en la vida* (*One Day of Life*) and *Cuzcatlán donde bate la mar del sur* (*Cuzcatlán: Where the Southern Sea Beats*), reflect the increasing levels of political repression and social rebellion in El Salvador during the late 1970s and early 1980s. Here, Argueta explores the possibilities of the testimonial novel for giving voice to his peasant protagonists who are victims of right-wing repression. He has sought to document violence and civil rights abuses in his country so that they will not be forgotten or repeated. As a group, these novels can be characterized as an oral, popular history of modern El Salvador. According to critic Ineke Phaf, Argueta has succeeded in giving a historical dimension to El Salvador's civil strife within the context of the recent conflicts in Central America.

Argueta's more recent work has taken a autobiographical turn. *Milagro de la Paz* (*A Place Called Milagro de la Paz*), perhaps his best novel, presents the lives of three generations of women living under the same roof in Milagro de la Paz (Miracle of Peace), the popular San Miguel neighborhood where Manlio Argueta was born. Through the experiences of the members of one family, this novel presents what life has been like for many people in his country, who have sought to live normal lives in the midst of extreme political violence. The principal characters are Latina, her daughters, Magdalena and Crista, her grandson Juan Bautista, and Lluvia, an orphaned girl who arrives one day at her doorstep. The women, who earn their living by making clothing at home, rarely leave their house for fear of the "unknown ones" that are murdering people in their neighborhood. Besides Juan Bautista, whose presence in the novel is limited, there are two other marginal male characters: Chele Pintura, who helps the women maintain their house in exchange for meals; and Nicolás Moreira, a young neighbor. Magdalena, Latina's oldest daughter, falls in love with Nicolás and becomes pregnant. A short time later, Magdalena is murdered by the "unknown ones." His dreams shattered, Nicolás hangs himself in desperation. These tragic deaths create a tremendous vacuum in the lives of Latina and Crista. In an attempt to recover her loss, Crista seduces Chele Pintura with the hope of bringing a new life to the house. The birth of Juan Bautista does not alleviate the suffering and emptiness created by Magdalena's absence. One day Lluvia, a little girl who has lost her parents in the violence, arrives at their doorstep unannounced. Latina, Crista, and Juan Bautista accept her into their home and lives. This child, who Latina views as a reincarnation of her murdered daughter, provides the women with the love and hope they need to continue living in spite of the violence that surrounds them. Latina's grandson, Juan Bautista, who is too young to understand the events taking place around him, is based on the author's own experiences growing up in San Miguel surrounded by women.

With his most recent novel, *Siglo de O(g)ro* [Golden (ogre) Age], Argueta moves further towards autobiography. In fact, this text, described by the author as a "bio-no-vela circular" (Circular Bio Novela), can be considered the first book of Argueta's memoirs. Stylistically, the author weaves a multiplicity of diverse texts to form a unified whole. In all, the book consists of 111 fragments, including poetry, theatre, narrative, testimony, essay, and folk tales.

Argueta has produced an impressive and important body of work and continues to be a vigorous writer. His novels have been translated into English and several other languages, and he receives many invitations to speak at universities and literary gatherings around the world. Although his works narrate events in El Salvador, a small nation in Central America, they have universal appeal and have earned him a deserved international reputation as a major Central American voice.

—Edward Waters Hood

ARIOSTO, Ludovico

Born: Reggio Emilia, Ferrara territory (now in Italy), 8 September 1474. **Education:** Studied in the law faculty, University of Ferrara, 1489–94. **Family:** Married Alessandra Benucci Strozzi in late 1520s; two earlier illegitimate children, whom he recognized. **Career:** Took a court post during the political unrest of the 1490s; captain of the garrison, Canossa, 1502–03; courtier, diplomat, and writer in service of Cardinal Ippolito d'Este until 1517; in service of Alfonso d'Este, Duke of Ferrara, 1518–33; commissario of the Garfagnana, 1522–25. **Died:** 6 July 1533.

PUBLICATIONS

Collections

Le commedie, edited by Michele Catalano. 2 vols., 1933.
Opere minori, edited by Cesare Segre. 1954.
Commedie, edited by Cesare Segre. 1974.
The Comedies (includes *The Coffer* [prose and verse versions]; *The Pretenders*; *The Necromancer*; *Lena*; *The Students*), edited and translated by Edmond M. Beame and Leonard G. Sbrocchi. 1975.
Satire e lettere, edited by Cesare Segre. 1976.
Opere, edited by Adriano Seroni. 1981.

Verse

Orlando furioso. 1515 (40 cantos); revised version, 1521; 3rd edition, 1532 (46 cantos); additional *Cinque Canti* published in 1545 edition; edited by S. De Benedetti and Cesare Segre, 1960, edited by Segre, 1976, and by Emilio Bigi, 1982; as *Orlando Furioso*, translated by John Harington, 1591, and by William Stewart Rose, 2 vols., 1823–31; as *The Frenzy of Orlando*, translated by Barbara Reynolds, 2 vols., 1975–77; several prose translations including by A. Gilbert, 1954, and by Guido Waldman, 1974; as *Five Cantos*, translated by Alexander Sheers and David Quint, 1996.
Satire. 1534; edited by Cesare Segre, 1976; as *Seven Planets Governing Italy*, 1611; as *The Satires*, translated by Peter DeSa Wiggins, 1976.
The Satires, edited by R.B. Gottfried. 1977.

Plays

La cassaria (produced 1508). 1509; revised version, in verse (produced 1531), 1546; as *The Coffer*, in *The Comedies*, 1975.

I suppositi (produced 1509). 1509 or 1510; revised version, in verse, 1525; as *Supposers*, translated by George Gascoigne, 1566; as *The Pretenders*, in *The Comedies*, 1975.

La Lena (produced 1528). 1533 or 1536; edited by Guido Davico Bonino, 1976; as *Lena*, in *The Comedies*, 1975; as *La Lena*, in *Five Italian Renaissance Comedies*, edited by Bruce Penman, 1978.

Il negromante (produced 1529). 1535; as *The Necromancer*, in *The Comedies*, 1975.

La scolastica, completed by Gabriele Ariosto. 1547; as *The Students*, in *The Comedies*, 1975.

Other

Lettere, edited by A. Stella. 1965.
Lettera della Garfagnana, edited by Gianna Scalia. 1977.

*

Bibliography: *Ludovico Ariosto: An Annotated Bibliography of Criticism 1956–1980* by Robert J. Rodini and Salvatore Di Maria, 1984; ''Selected Bibliography of Ariosto Criticism 1980–87,'' by Robert J. Rodini, in *Modern Language Notes*, 1988.

Critical Studies: *The King of the Court Poets: A Study of the Work, Life, and Times of Ludovico Ariosto* by Edmund G. Gardner, 1906, reprinted 1969; *The Figure of the Poet in the Renaissance Epic* by R.M. Durling, 1965; *Ariosto: A Preface to the Orlando Furioso* by C.P. Brand, 1974; *Ludovico Ariosto* by Robert Griffin, 1974; *Names on the Trees: Ariosto into Art* by Rennsselaer W. Lee, 1977; *Ariosto and the Classical Simile* by Kristen Olson Murtaugh, 1980; *Figures in Ariosto's Tapestry: Character and Design in the Orlando Furioso* by Peter DeSa Wiggins, 1986; *Ariosto's Bitter Harmony: Crisis and Evasion in the Italian Renaissance* by Albert Russell Ascoli, 1987; *The Poetics of Ariosto* by Marianne Shapiro, 1988; *Cervantes and Ariosto* by Thomas R. Hart, 1989; *Proclaiming a Classic: The Canonization of Orlando Furioso* by Daniel Javitch, 1991; *Rinaldo: Character and Intertext in Ariosto and Tasso* by Michael Sherberg, 1993; *Humility's Deceit: Calvino Reading Ariosto Reading Calvino* by Wiley Feinstein, 1995; *The Orlando Furioso: A Stoic Comedy* by Clare Carroll, 1997; *Renaissance Transactions: Ariosto and Tasso*, edited by Valeria Finucci, 1999.

* * *

Ludovico Ariosto's masterpiece, *Orlando furioso*, is the culmination of a long tradition. Beginning in the 11th century with the Old French epic, *La Chanson de Roland* (*The Song of Roland*), it continued in Italy (as elsewhere) in a series of extravagant romances, both oral and written. The legends, relating to Charlemagne and his paladins in their defence of Christendom against the Muslims, became part of folklore, as may be seen in Sicily where puppet masters in Palermo still perform the stories and where the sides of donkey carts are painted with colourful scenes of the combats.

In the 15th century Luigi Pulci of Florence wrote an elaborate version of Roland's (Orlando's) adventures. This was *I Morgante*, a poem in rhymed octaves, much admired by Byron, who translated the first canto. Pulci was followed by Matteo Boiardo of Ferrara, who complicated the story still further with oriental elements and combined it with episodes and characters drawn from the Arthurian cycle.

Boiardo's poem, also in rhymed octaves, was entitled *Orlando innamorato* [Roland in Love]. In 1494, when the French invaded Italy, he felt unable to continue and laid down his pen. Violent events had irrupted into his world of fantasy and destroyed it.

A generation later Ariosto undertook to complete Boiardo's poem. The result was his *Orlando Furioso* [Roland Driven Mad by Love]. In Ariosto's hands chivalrous romance becomes romantic epic. To the themes of war, chivalry, and love, already in Boiardo, Ariosto added history, from mythological antiquity down to contemporary times, from the Fall of Troy to the Sack of Rome. The factual is rendered poetic; the poetic acquires the solemnity of historical fact. It is this which converts romance into epic. Epic also is the intensity with which Ariosto visualizes and communicates his world. His descriptions of beauty, chivalry, noble achievement, violence, and evil are on a scale that exceeds life. Yet the work is far from solemn throughout. The legacy of exuberant exaggeration, rollicking humour, suspense and wilful complexity, inherited from the conventions of the *cantastorie* (narrators who recited the tales in public), as well as from Pulci and Boiardo, enriches and varies the 46 cantos. Ariosto's octaves justly deserve the epithet of ''golden.''

To 16th-century critics *Orlando Furioso* appeared to lack unity, and the stories it contained were dismissed as unworthy of the attention of serious-minded men of letters. Ariosto has also been condemned for his adulation of the House of Este, the rulers of Ferrara and his patrons. Such criticisms, still voiced in modern times, can be answered. On the charge of adulation it can be said that Ariosto's praise of Ferrara and of the Estense dynasty was in the tradition of works of praise (*encomia*), which had the warrant of Aristotle and also of Erasmus, who held that the most efficacious way of correcting a prince was to present him, in the guise of flattery, with an ideal picture of himself. This may have been Ariosto's intention in those octaves in praise of Duke Alfonso and his brother, Cardinal Ippolito, to whom he dedicated the poem. But the praise was not all flattery. There was much to admire in the achievements of the Dukes of Ferrara and in the world of beauty they created. Furthermore, what Ariosto thought worthy of condemnation he condemned: the use of gunfire in battle, for instance (in which Duke Alfonso was a pioneer), and the neglect of poets by their patrons.

The charge of disunity in the *Orlando Furioso* is based on assumptions which are not relevant to the nature of Ariosto's art. The poem is composed not of homogeneous elements arranged with predictable symmetry, but of vastly disparate material, controlled and balanced with apparent nonchalance but, in reality, with subtle skill. Thematic unity resides in the concept of Europe as the civilizing force both of antiquity and of the newly extended Christian world. The contemporary danger of Turkish power is imaged in the menace of the Muslims in the time of Charlemagne; and Charles V, on his election as Emperor, may have been seen by Ariosto, as his poem progressed, to be a natural symbol of that other Charles, the 8th-century head of Christendom.

Ariosto takes up the story at the point where Agramante, king of the Moors, and Marsilio, the Saracen King of Spain, have invaded France. Orlando has escorted the Princess Angelica from the Far East to the Pyrenees and is at once caught up in the war. Angelica was introduced into the story by Boiardo to serve, with her dazzling beauty, as a distraction to Christian and Muslim knights alike. Orlando and his cousin, Rinaldo, both love her and their rivalry is a danger to the Christian side. Angelica, unmoved by the adoration she inspires, eventually falls in love with a wounded Moorish soldier, whom she nurses back to health and marries. The discovery of this causes Orlando to lose his wits and supernatural aid is required before he can be brought back to sanity.

In constructing this sequel to Boiardo's poem Ariosto had three main tasks: to bring the war to a close, to disentangle both Orlando and Rinaldo from their infatuation for Angelica, and to enable Rinaldo's sister, Bradamante, to marry a noble warrior, Ruggiero, who, though fighting for the Infidel, is, as he discovers, of Christian origin. From their union is destined to descend the illustrious line of the House of Este. All three tasks are accomplished and all the minor stories left unfinished by Boiardo are likewise brought to a conclusion. The *Orlando Furioso* is, however, far more than an appendix to the *Innamorato*. It is an original work in its own right, dazzling in the *bravura* of its execution.   .

Ariosto's other works include *capitoli* (burlesques), satires, and five comedies on the models of Plautus and Terence, whose plays were then fashionable in Ferrara. Ariosto had acted in the court theatre in his youth and during his last years he was director of theatrical entertainments. His *Orlando Furioso* is itself rather like a huge theatrical production, of which the author is also the stage-manager and propertyman.

—Barbara Reynolds

See the essay on *Orlando Furioso*.

ARISTOPHANES

Born: Athens, possibly c. 450 BC, possibly as late as 444 BC. **Career:** May have lived or owned property on Aigina. His first plays directed by others; *Hippeis* (*The Knights*, 424 BC) was his first production in his own name. Besides the 11 surviving comedies, 32 other titles are known (some possibly alternative titles; four probably spurious), and nearly 1,000 fragments survive. His son, Araros, produced his last two plays; all three of his sons are known to have written plays of their own. Served on the *boule* (the Athenian Senate) in the early 4th century BC. **Awards:** Won at least four prizes at the City Dionysia and Lenaia festivals. **Died:** c. 385 BC.

PUBLICATIONS

Collections

[Comedies], edited by F.W. Hall and W.M. Geldart. 2 vols., 1901–02; also edited by Johannes van Leeuwen, 11 vols., 1893–1906, and Victor Coulon (includes French translations), 5 vols., 1923–30; edited and translated by B.B. Rogers, 11 vols., 1902–15, and Alan H. Sommerstein (bilingual editions; with commentary), 8 vols., 1980–94; as *The Complete Plays*, edited by Moses Hadas, translated by Hadas, B.B. Rogers, R.H. Webb, and Jack Lindsay, 1962; also translated by David Barrett and Alan H. Sommerstein, 3 vols., 1964–77; Patric Dickinson, 2 vols., 1970; Kenneth McLeish, 3 vols., 1993–94.

Poetae comici graeci (includes the fragments of lost comedies), edited by R. Kassel and Colin Austin. 1983.

Aristophanes 1: Clouds, Wasps, Birds, translated with notes by Peter Meineck, 1998.

Plays

Acharnes (produced 425 BC). Edited by William W. Merry, 1880; also edited by W. Rennie, 1909; edited and translated by W.J.M. Starkie, 1909; as *The Acharnians*, translated by Douglass Parker, 1961; also translated by B.B. Rogers, in *The Complete Plays*, 1962; Jeffrey Henderson, 1991.

Hippeis (produced 424 BC). Edited by William W. Merry, 1887; as *The Knights*, edited by Robert A. Nell, 1901; translated by R.H. Webb, in *The Complete Plays*, 1962; also translated by David Barrett and Alan H. Sommerstein, 1978; Kenneth McLeish, 1979.

Nephelai (produced 423 BC, partially revised 419–17 BC; only the revision has survived). Edited by William W. Merry, 1879; also edited by K.J. Dover, 1968; as *The Clouds*, edited and translated by W.J.M. Starkie, 1911; translated by Patric Dickinson, 1957; also translated by William Arrowsmith, 1962; Moses Hadas, in *The Complete Plays*, 1962: Alan H. Sommerstein, 1973; Kenneth McLeish, 1979; James H. Mantinband, in *Four Plays*, 1983; commentary by Raymond K. Fisher, 1984; translated by Marie C. Marianetti, 1997; Thomas G. West and Grace Starry West, in *Four Texts on Socrates: Plato's Euthyphro, Apology and Crito and Aristophanes' Clouds*, 1998.

Sphekes (produced 422 BC). Edited by William W. Merry, 1893; also edited by Douglas M. MacDowell, 1970; as *The Wasps*, edited and translated by W.J.M. Starkie, 1897; translated by Douglass Parker, 1962; also translated by Moses Hadas, in *The Complete Plays*, 1962.

Eirene (produced 421 BC). Edited by William W. Merry, 1900; also edited by H. Sharpley, 1905, and Maurice Platnauer, 1964; as *The Peace*, translated by Doros Alastos, 1953; also translated by B.B. Rogers, in *The Complete Plays*, 1962; edited with introduction and commentary by S. Douglas Olson, 1998.

Ornithes (produced 414 BC). Edited by William W. Merry, 1889; also edited by T. Kock, revised by O. Sehröder, 1927, and N.V. Dunbar, 1994; as *The Birds*, translated by William Arrowsmith, 1961; also translated by Dudley Fitts, in *Four Comedies*, 1962; R.H. Webb, in *The Complete Plays*, 1962; Patric Dickinson, 1970; Kenneth McLeish, 1970; Alan H. Sommerstein, 1977; James H. Mantinband, in *Four Plays*, 1983; translated by Paul Muldoon with Richard Martin, 1999.

Lysistrate (produced 411 BC). Edited by U.von Wilamowitz-Möllendorff, 1927; also edited by Jeffrey Henderson, 1987; as *Lysistrata*, translated by Jack Lindsay, 1925, and in *The Complete Plays*, 1962; also translated by Charles T. Murphy, 1944; Donald Sutherland, 1961; Dudley Fitts, in *Four Comedies*, 1962; Douglass Parker, 1964; James H. Mantinband, in *Four Plays*, 1983; Jeffrey Henderson, 1988.

Thesmophoriazousai (produced 411 BC). As *Ladies' Day*, translated by Dudley Fitts, in *Four Comedies*, 1962; also translated by B.B. Rogers, in *The Complete Plays*, 1962; as *The Poet and the Women*, translated by David Barrett, 1964.

Batrachoi (produced 405 BC). Edited by William W. Merry, 1884; also edited by T.G. Tucker, 1906, L. Radermacher, 1954, W.B. Stanford, 1963, and Kenneth Dover, 1993; as *The Frogs*, translated by Gilbert Murray, 1908; also translated by Dudley Fitts, in *Four Comedies*, 1962; Richmond Lattimore, 1962; R.H. Webb, in

The Complete Plays, 1962; Patric Dickinson, 1970; Kenneth McLeish, 1970; James H. Mantinband, in *Four Plays*, 1983.

Ekklesiazousai (produced c. 392 BC). Edited by R.G. Ussher, 1973; as *Women in Parliament*, translated by Jack Lindsay, 1929, and in *The Complete Plays*, 1962; as *The Congresswomen*, translated by Douglass Parker, 1967; as *Women in Power*, translated by Kenneth McLeish, 1979.

Ploutos (produced 388 BC). As *Plutus*, translated by William Rann Kennedy, 1912; also translated by B.B. Rogers, in *The Complete Plays*, 1962; as *Wealth*, translated by Alan H. Sommerstein, 1978.

Four Comedies (includes *Lysistrata*; *The Frogs*; *The Birds*; *Ladies' Day*), translated by Dudley Fitts. 1962.

Four Plays (includes *The Birds*; *The Clouds*; *The Frogs*; *Lysistrata*), translated by James H. Mantinband. 1983.

Plays One, translated with introduction by Kenneth McLeish, 1993.

Plays Two, translated with introduction by Kenneth McLeish, 1993.

Three Plays by Aristophanes: Staging Women, translated and edited by Jeffrey Henderson, 1996.

Birds, Lysistrata, Assembly-women, Wealth: A New Verse Translation with Introduction and Notes by Stephen Halliwell, 1997.

*

Critical Studies: *Aristophanes: A Study* by Gilbert Murray, 1933; "Aristophanes and Politics" by A.W. Gomme, in *Classical Review*, 1938; *Incongruity in Aristophanes* by C.C. Jernigan, 1939; *The Art of Greek Comedy* by K. Lever, 1956; *The People of Aristophanes: A Sociology of Old Attic Comedy* by Victor Ehrenberg, 1962, revised edition, 1974; *Aristophanes: His Plays and His Influence* by L.E. Lord, 1963; *Aristophanes and the Comic Hero* by C.H. Whitman, 1964; *The Origin of Old Attic Comedy* by F.M. Cornford, 1968; *Twentieth Century Interpretations of the Frogs* edited by D.J. Littlefield, 1968; *Aristophanic Comedy* by K.J. Dover, 1972; "The Political Opinions of Aristophanes," Appendix XXIX of *The Origins of the Peloponnesian War* by G.E.M. de Ste. Croix, 1972; *The Living Aristophanes* by A. Solomos, 1974; *The Stage of Aristophanes* by C.W. Dearden, 1976; *Aristophanes* by R.G. Ussher, 1979; *Studies in the Manuscript Tradition of the Ranae of Aristophanes* by Charles N. Eberline, 1980; *The Theatre of Aristophanes* by Kenneth McLeish, 1980; *Aristophanes: Essays in Interpretation* edited by Jeffrey Henderson, 1981; *Aristophanic Poetry* by Carroll Moulton, 1981; *Aristophanes and Athenian Society of the Early Fourth Century BC* by E. David, 1984; "Comedy" by E. Handley, in *Cambridge History of Classical Literature*, vol. 1 edited by P. Easterling and B.M.W. Knox, 1985; *Aristophanes: Poet and Dramatist* by Rosemary M. Harriott, 1986; *Political Comedy in Aristophanes* by Malcolm Heath, 1987; *Aristophanes' Old-and-New Comedy* by Kenneth J. Reckford, 1987; *Cleon, Knights and Aristophanes' Politics* by Lowell Edmunds, 1988; *Aristophanes and His Theatre of the Absurd* by Paul Cartledge, 1990; *Politics and Persuasion in Aristophanes' Ecclesiazusae* by Kenneth S. Rothwell, 1990; *The Mask of Comedy: Aristophanes and the Intertextual Parabasis* by T.K. Hubbard, 1991; *Ancient Comedy: The War of the Generations* by D.F. Sutton, 1993; *Aristophanes and Women* by Laura K. Taaffe, 1993; *Comic Angels* by O. Taplin, 1993; *Aristophanes: Myth, Ritual and Comedy* by A.M. Bowie, 1994; *Aristophanes: An Author for the Stage* by C.F. Russo, 1994; *Beyond Aristophanes: Transition and Diversity in Greek Comedy*, edited by Gregory W. Dobrov, 1995; *Aristophanes and Athens: An Introduction to the Plays* by Douglas M. MacDowell, 1995; *Oxford Readings in Aristophanes*, edited by Erich Segal, 1996; *Pericles On Stage:*

Political Comedy in Aristophanes' Early Plays by Michael Vickers, 1997; *Dialect in Aristophanes: and the Politics of Language in Ancient Greek Literature* by Stephen Colvin, 1999; *The Rivals of Aristophanes: Studies in Athenian Old Comedy*, edited by David Harvey and John Wilkins, 2000; *Aristophanes and the Definition of Comedy* by M.S. Silk, 2000; *Venom in Verse: Aristophanes in Modern Greece* by Gonda A.H. Van Steen, 2000.

* * *

Aristophanes is the best-known (and only surviving) exponent of Old Comedy, an art form which, like its older sister Tragedy, was performed as part of the artistic competitions at the civic festivals at Athens in honour of Dionysus, god of drama. Old Comedy reached its highest point during the last third of the 5th century BC, the years of the age of Pericles and of the vigorous Athenian democracy. Old Comedy was very much a child of that democracy. In the very best sense of the word, Aristophanes' comedy was "political" (*polis* = city-state), as his plays are concerned essentially with the Athens of his day, supplying him with his inspiration, his themes and issues, his jokes, characters, and personalities. Firmly anchored in the social milieu of 5th-century Athens, his work exhibits a unique mixture of humours, ranging from political satire to obscenity and toilet humour, from sophisticated parody to slapstick, from utopian fantasy to personal abuse. His comedy is without parallel or successors in Western literature.

Aristophanes is neither a master of comic plot (the "comedy of errors" on which so much Western comedy depends) nor a creator of subtle interaction between characters. Rather the kernel of his comedy is the establishment of a fantastic idea, a grand scheme, the more outrageous the better, whose implementation and consequences form the action; "plot" is not a term useful in Aristophanic criticism. Examples include *Acharnes* (*The Acharnians*) where the hero (whose name means "Just City") makes his own personal peace treaty with the Spartan enemy, or *Lysistrate* (*Lysistrata*) in which the wives of Greece occupy the Athenian acropolis and embark on a "sex-strike" to force the men (successfully) to end the war. The *grande idée* is developed in a series of more or less formal structural features, e.g. *parodos*, the visually splendid entry of the chorus who provided either an on-stage audience or the opposition; *agon*, a formally constructed debate in which the great idea was contested or explained; *parabasis*, in which the chorus spoke directly to the audience, often for the comedian himself; and the *episodes*, a series of loosely connected scenes in which the consequences of the great idea are worked out. In his later plays Aristophanes begins to employ a freer use of the traditional forms; *Thesmophoriazousai* (*The Poet and the Women*), in particular, most resembles a later Western comedy.

Space does not allow for individual discussion of the comedies. In the 11 extant comedies we can see that all aspects of Athenian life were fair game for the comic poet. There are the so-called "peace plays," *The Acharnians*, *Eirene* (*The Peace*), and *Lysistrata*, from which it is clear that Aristophanes was not himself a pacifist, but an ardent opponent of the Peloponnesian War (431–04 BC). *The Acharnians*, with its unparalleled identification of the protagonist with the comic poet and its open hostility to Athens' war policy and its proponents, is worthy of special attention. *Hippeis* (*The Knights*) and *Sphekes* (*The Wasps*) are both largely concerned with politics and the demagogues, especially Kleon whose distinctive political style is subjected to a sweeping and at times coarse caricature in *The Knights*. *The Wasps*, a humorous satire on the jury system and Kleon's manipulation of it, features Philokleon, perhaps the most appealing rogue in ancient literature. Philosophy and drama form the themes of *Nephelai* (*The Clouds*) and *The Poet and the Women*, the former containing the infamous depiction of Socrates as a sophistic charlatan, which Plato tells us contributed to his condemnation in 399 BC. *Lysistrata*, *The Poet and the Women*, and *Ekklesiazousai* (*Women in Power*) make up the "women's plays"; the last portrays the seizure by women of the government at Athens and the institution of a communistic regime very much like Plato's ideal Republic. *Lysistrata*, with its themes of "Women's Liberation" and "Make love, not war!", has become the favourite of modern audiences.

Two plays, *Ornithes* (*The Birds*) and *Batrachoi* (*The Frogs*), stand out as Aristophanes' masterpieces. *The Birds* features two Athenians who flee the problems of life in Athens to take refuge among the birds. They join with them in founding the now famous city, Cloudcuckooland, and in the end displace the Olympian gods as the rulers of the universe. *The Frogs* shows Dionysus, god of drama, descending to the underworld to bring back Euripides, the recently deceased and controversial tragic poet. After some amusing adventures, Dionysus ends up judging a witty contest between Euripides and Aeschylus, the old master, in which Dionysus eventually judges Aeschylus the victor and brings him back to Athens "to save the city." Produced in the months preceding Athens' defeat, this comedy with its mingling of political, literary, and religious themes provides an elegant farewell to Athens' greatness.

Critical discussion has focused on the motives of the comedian. In a landmark article A.W. Gomme argued that no serious political or satirical purpose was to be found in Aristophanes; his *forté* was a brilliant, revolutionary comedy. De Ste. Croix argued in return that although creation of comedy was his first concern, a consistent and intentional political stance may be ascertained, that of a "conservative," but neither oligarchic nor radical democrat. His opposition to Kleon and the demagogues is clear, as is his hostility to the war with Sparta. Aristophanes is essentially a regressive; the final scenes of *The Knights* and *Lysistrata* make clear his affection for the glorious days of Athens of previous generations, the triumphs of the Persian Wars. Similarly, despite his obvious fondness for the modern and avant-garde Euripides, he chooses Aeschylus in the end. Technical ability yields to the moral purpose of art. Yet Aristophanes is no anti-intellectual; his caricature of Socrates is more humorous than satirical, and his appreciation of and affinity with Euripides are evident. He, like Socrates and Euripides, was *sophos* (smart) and *dexios* (clever). Likewise in the treatment of the real people made fun of in his plays (*to onomasti komodein*—to make fun of by name), commentators have been quick to detect a moral purpose behind the jokes, but here too comedy should take precedence over satire. Only with Kleon and the demagogues can we detect any real malice. For the most part we should regard Aristophanes as what he himself claimed to be, a superb creator of imaginative and fantastic comedy.

—Ian C. Storey

See the essays on *The Birds*, *The Clouds*, *The Frogs*, and *Lysistrata*.

ARISTOTLE

Born: Stagira, Macedonia, 384 BC. **Family:** Married Pythias, niece of the tyrant Hermeias; after Pythias' death, had a son by Herpyllis.

Career: Pupil, then teacher, in Plato's (*q.v.*) Academy, Athens, 367–47 BC; on Plato's death he left the city to live with other philosophers from the Academy, at Assos, in the Troad. After the murder of Hermeias he went to live and teach at Mytilene on Lesbos; tutor to the son of Philip II of Macedon, the future Alexander the Great, from c. 342 BC; returned to Athens in 335 BC and founded his own school of literature, science, and philosophy, the Lyceum, whose students were known as "peripatetics"; after death of Alexander the Great in 323 BC Aristotle was accused of impiety and retreated, leaving his school to Theophrastus, *q.v.*, in Chalcis, Euboea. **Died:** 322 BC.

PUBLICATIONS

Collections

[Works], edited by J.A. Smith and W.D. Ross. 12 vols., 1908–52; also edited by John L. Ackrill, 1962—, revised edition edited by Jonathan Barnes, 2 vols., 1984; translated by Thomas Taylor, 1812.

Aristotle, edited and translated by Harold P. Cooke. 23 vols., 1926–1997.

Works

De anima [On the Soul], edited by W.D. Ross. 1956; translated by Kenelm Foster and Silvester Humphries, 1951; Books II and III translated by D.W. Hamlyn, revised edition, 1993; as *Aristotle's De anima in Focus*, edited by Michael Durrant, 1993.

De arte poetica, edited by R. Kassel. 1965; as *Aristotle on the Art of Poetry*, translated by Ingram Bywater, 1920; as *Poetics*, translated by John Warrington, with *On Style* and *On the Sublime* by Demetrius, 1963; also translated by D.W. Lucas (with commentary), 1968; M.E. Hubbard, in *Ancient Literary Criticism*, 1972; L. Golden and O.B. Hardison, 2nd edition, 1981; James Hutton, 1982; Stephen Halliwell (with commentary), 1987; as *Aristotle on the Art of Fiction*, translated by L.J. Potts, 1968; as *Poetics*, translated with an introduction and notes by Malcolm Heath, 1996; as *Aristotle's Poetics*, translated and with a commentary by George Whalley, 1997; as *Poetics*, translated and introduced by Kenneth McLeish, 1999.

De coelo, as *On the Heavens* (bilingual edition), translated by W.K.C. Guthrie. 1939; as *Aristotle On the Heavens*, edited and translated by Stuart Leggat, 1995.

De generatione et corruptione, translated by C.J.F. Williams. 1982.

De generatione animalium, selections as *Generation of Animals*, translated by D.M. Balme, 1972, revised edition, 1992.

De incessu animalium, with *De motu animalium*, as *On the Movement and Progression of Animals*, translated by Anthony Preus. 1981.

De motu animalium, edited and translated by Martha C. Nussbaum. 1978; with *De incessu animalium*, as *On the Movement and Progression of Animals*, translated by Anthony Preus, 1981.

De partibus animalium, as *On the Parts of Animals*, translated by W. Ogle. 1882, reprinted 1987; as *Parts of Animals*, translated by D.M. Balme, 1972, revised edition, 1992.

De republica Atheniensium, as *The Constitution of Athens*, in *Aristotle and Xenophon on Democracy and Oligarchy*, edited and translated by John M. Moore. 1975; as *The Athenian Constitution*, translated by H. Rackham, 1935; also translated by P.J. Rhodes, 1984.

Ethica, as *Ethics*, translated by David Ross, 1925, revised by John L. Ackrill and J.O. Urmson, 1980; also translated by Hippocrates G. Apostle, 1975.

> *Nichomachean Ethics*, edited by G. Ramsauer (with commentary). 1878, reprinted 1987; translated by J.A.K. Thomson, 1953, revised edition, 1976; as *Nicomachean Ethics: Books VIII and IX*, translated with a commentary by Michael Pakaluk, 1998; as *Nicomachean Ethics: Books VIII and IX*, translated with a commentary by Michael Pakaluk, 1998.

> *Ethica Eudemia*, edited by R.R. Walzer and J.M. Mingay. 1991; as *Eudemian Ethics*, edited and translated by M. Woods (with commentary), 1982; translated by H. Rackham, 1935.

Historia animalium, edited and translated by D.M. Balme. 1991; translated by A.L. Peck, 1965.

Metaphysica, edited by W.D. Ross (with commentary). 2 vols., 1928; also edited by Werner Jaeger, 1957; as *Metaphysics*, translated by Hippocrates G. Apostle (with commentary), 1966; part as *Oeconomica and Magna moralia*, translated by G.C. Armstrong, 1935; part as *Metaphysics, Books Gamma, Delta and Epsilon*, translated by Christopher Kirwan, 1971; Books VII and VIII translated by David Bostock, 1994; as *Metaphysics: Book B and Book K 1–2*, translated with a commentary by Arthur Madigan, 1999.

On Fallacies, translated by Edward Poste. 1866, reprinted 1987.

Organon, edited by W.D. Ross. 1958; part as *Analytica priora et posteriora*, edited by W.D. Ross, 1964; part as *The Categories* and *On Interpretation*, translated by H.P. Cooke, 1938; part as *Prior Analytics*, translated by Hugh Tredennick, 1938; part as *Prior and Posterior Analytics*, translated by John Warrington, 1964; part as *Posterior Anatytics*, translated by J. Barnes, revised edition, 1993.

Parva naturalia, as *Aristotle on Memory*, edited and translated by Richard Sorabji. 1972.

Physica, as *Physics*, translated by P. Wicksteed and F. M. Cornford. 2 vols., 1929–34; Books I and II translated by William Charlton, 1970; as *Physics*, translated by Robin Waterfield, 1996; as *Aristotle: Physics Book VIII*, translated with a commentary by Daniel W. Graham, 1999.

Politica, edited by Johann Gottlob Schneider. 2 vols., 1809; also edited and translated by Stephen Everson, 1988; as *The Politics of Aristotle*, translated by Benjamin Jowett, 1895; as *The Politics*, translated by T.A. Sinclair, 1962, revised by Trevor J. Saunders, 1981; also translated by Carnes Lord, 1984; as *Politics: Books III and IV*, translated with introduction and comments by Richard Robinson, 1995; as *Politics: Books I and II*, translated with a commentary by Trevor J. Saunders, 1995; as *The Politics of Aristotle*, translated with introduction, analysis, and notes by Peter L. Phillips Simpson, 1997; as *Politics: Books VII and VIII*, translated with a commentary by Richard Kraut, 1997; as *Politics*, translated with introduction and notes by C.D.C. Reeve, 1998; as *Politics: Books V and VI*, translated with a commentary by David Keyt, 1999.

Rhetorica, as *The Rhetoric of Aristotle*, translated by Lane Cooper. 1932; as *On Rhetoric*, translated by George A. Kelly, 1991; as *The Art of Rhetoric*, translated by H.C. Lawson-Tancred, 1991.

Aristotle: Selections, translated with introduction, notes and glossary by Terence Irwin and Gail Fine. 1995.

De sommo, as *Aristotle on Sleep and Dreams: A Text and Translation with Introduction, Notes and Glossary*, edited by David Gallop. 1996.

Topics: Books I and VIII, translated with a commentary by Robin Smith. 1996.

*

Bibliography: *Aristotle: A Select Bibliography*, by Jonathan Barnes, Malcolm Schofield, and Richard Sorabji, 1977.

Critical Studies: *The Poetics of Aristotle* by Lane Cooper, 1924; *The Psychology of Aristotle* by Clarence Shute, 1941; *Aristotle's Theory of Poetry and Fine Art* by S.H. Butcher, 1951; *The Philosophy of Aristotle* by D.J. Allan, 1952; *Aristotle* by A.E. Taylor, 1955; *Aristotle's Poetics* by A. House, 1956; *Tragedy: Serious Drama in Relation to Aristotle's Poetics* by F.L. Lucas, 1957; *The Development of Aristotle's Thought* by W.D. Ross, 1957; *Aristotle's Theory of Poetry and Drama, with Chapters on Plato and Longinus* by P.S. Shastri, 1963; *New Essays on Plato and Aristotle* by Renford Bambrough, 1965; *Aristotle's Ethical Theory* by William F. Hardie, 1968; *Prelude to Aesthetics* by E. Schaper, 1968; *On Aristotle and Greek Tragedy* by J. Jones, 1971; *The Eudemian and Nichomachean Ethics: A Study in the Development of Aristotle's Thought* by C.J. Rowe, 1971; *Towards Greek Tragedy* by B. Vickers, 1973; *Aristotle on Emotion* by Will Fortenbaugh, 1975; *Aristotle* by John B. Morrall, 1977; *Word and Action* by B. Knox, 1979; *Essays on Aristotle's Ethics* edited by Amélie Oksenberg Rorty, 1980; *Aristotle the Philosopher* by John L. Ackrill, 1981; *Poetic and Legal Fiction in the Aristotelian Tradition* by Kathy Eden, 1986; *Plato and Aristotle on Poetry* by Gerald F. Else, 1986; *Aristotle's Poetics* by Stephen Halliwell, 1986; *The Fragility of Goodness* by Martha C. Nussbaum, 1986; *Aristotle's Two Systems* by Daniel W. Graham, 1987; *Substance, Form and Psyche: An Aristotelian Metaphysics* by Montgomery Furth, 1988; *Aristotle's First Principles* by Terence Irwin, 1988; *Ethics with Aristotle* by Sarah Broadie, 1991; *Aristotle and the Later Tradition* edited by Henry Blumenthal and Howard Robinson, 1991; *Aristotle on the Perfect Life* by Anthony Kenny, 1992; *Aristotle on Moral Responsibility: Character and Cause* by Susan Sauvé Meyer, 1993; *The Problems of a Political Animal: Community, Justice, and Conflict in Aristotelian Political Thought* by Bernard Yack, 1993; *On Ideas: Aristotle's Criticism of Plato's Theory of Forms* by Gail Fine, 1993; *Engendering Origins: Critical Feminist Readings in Plato and Aristotle*, edited by Bat-Ami Bar On, 1994; *Aristotle's Rhetoric: An Art of Character* by Eugene Garver, 1994; *Aristotle on the Goals and Exactness of Ethics* by Georgios Anagnostopoulos, 1994; *Substance and Separation in Aristotle* by Lynne Spellman, 1995; *Aristotle's Economic Thought* by Scott Meikle, 1995; *Nature, Justice, and Rights in Aristotle's Politics* by Fred D. Miller, Jr., 1995; *Aristotelian Explorations* by G.E.R. Lloyd, 1996; *Aristotle on Nature and Incomplete Substance* by Sheldon M. Cohen, 1996; *The Politics of Philosophy: A Commentary on Aristotle's Politics* by Michael Davis, 1996; *Aristotle's Philosophical Development: Problems and Prospects*, edited by William Wians, 1996; *Aristotle and After*, edited by Richard Sorabji, 1997; *Analysis and Science in Aristotle* by Patrick H. Byrne, 1997; *Aristotle on Perception* by Stephen Everson, 1997; *An Approach to Aristotle's Physics: With Particular Attention to the Role of His Manner of Writing* by David Bolotin, 1998; *The Order of Nature in Aristotle's Physics: Place and the Elements* by Helen S. Lang, 1998; *Feminist Interpretations of Aristotle*, edited by Cynthia A. Freeland, 1998; *Aristotle's Ethics: Critical Essays*, edited by Nancy Sherman, 1999; *Aristotle: Critical Assessments*, edited by Lloyd P. Gerson, 1999; *Action and Contemplation: Studies in the Moral and Political Thought of Aristotle*, edited by Robert C. Bartlett and Susan D. Collins, 1999; *Order in Multiplicity: Homonymy in the Philosophy of Aristotle* by Christopher Shields, 1999; *Aristotle and*

Contemporary Science, edited by Demetra Sfendoni-Mentzou, 2000; *Life's Form: Late Aristotelian Conception of the Soul* by Dennis Des Chene, 2000; *The Myth of Aristotle's Development and the Betrayal of Metaphysics* by Walter E. Wehrle, 2000; *Aristotle on Meaning and Essence* by David Charles, 2000; *Aristotle's Theory of the Unity of Science* by Malcolm Wilson, 2000; *Aristotle and Aristotelianism in Medieval Muslim, Jewish, and Christian Philosophy* by Husain Kassim, 2000; *Substantial Knowledge: Aristotle's Metaphysics* by C.D.C. Reeve, 2000; *Revaluing Ethics: Aristotle's Dialectical Pedagogy* by Thomas W. Smith, 2001; *Hypothetical Syllogistic and Stoic Logic* by Anthony Speca, 2001; *Essays on the Aristotelian Tradition* by Anthony Kenny, 2001; *Ontology and the Art of Tragedy: An Approach to Aristotle's Poetics* by Martha Husain, 2002.

* * *

Written by a philosopher and scientist who was not born until 20 years after the death of Sophocles and Euripides, *De arte poetica* (*Poetics*) is an unlikely candidate the founding document of European dramatic theory. In fact it has no rival, offering the earliest view of the origins and form of Greek tragedy as well as a theoretical and structural base for all subsequent serious drama.

This is unlikely to be what Aristotle had in mind when he first committed his comparison of epic and dramatic poetry to paper. The *Poetics* appears to be unfinished or, at least, unrevised, and is widely believed to be no more than lecture notes. A companion volume on comedy has failed to survive. In early life Aristotle had studied under Plato who, in the *Republic* and elsewhere, had rejected the claims of drama and theatre to a place in his ideal state. This world, according to Plato, is no more than a pale reflection of reality, which is itself a reflection of the pure Idea. Drama, by being an imitation of an imitation, is doubly suspect. The capacity of actors to transform themselves is equally dangerous, as is the tendency of an audience to become engaged by fiction or "lies."

Aristotle sets out in the *Poetics* to compare the forms of epic and dramatic poetry and justify both. The information he provides, intriguing as it is, about the history of the theatre in Athens, is incidental to the main argument. In the light of subsequent scholarship, theatrical, historical, and anthropological, there is no reason to accept all of Aristotle's beliefs as necessarily historically accurate. When he talks of tragedy and comedy as "at first improvised" (or "in an experimental stage"), or of tragedy "moving from trivial plots and comic diction, exchanging satiric method for solemnity only late," he offers little more than hearsay evidence of the first form of "tragedy" in Athens. On the other hand, his assertion that Aeschylus introduced a second actor and relegated the chorus in favour of dialogue appears to be borne out by the surviving plays of Aeschylus. Sophocles, according to Aristotle, "increased the number of actors to three and introduced *skenographia*" (scenic decoration). Tantalizingly, Aristotle offers no further indication of the physical conditions in the Athenian theatre.

Though his remarks on the early form of theatre in Athens are incomplete, it is as a theorist on tragic structure that Aristotle was most influential, and most misinterpreted. The three unities, of time, place, and action, were treated as rules for the proper writing of tragedy as late as the 19th century in France. Extant Greek tragedies by Aeschylus, Sophocles, and Euripides pay no more than incidental attention to the notion that a play should take place within a single day and in a fixed location. Whatever later critics chose to believe, Aristotle himself treats such things as no more than passing recommendations. The unity of action has more substance but seems to be a by-product of a dramatic form whose rhythm derives from a chorus which dances and sings an interlude between the dramatic scenes.

The most stimulating and widely known section of the *Poetics* includes the famous definition of tragedy which is at the heart of Aristotle's argument in favour of a therapeutic purpose to dramatic performance:

> Tragedy is the representation (*mimesis*) of an action which is worthy of concern (*spoudaios*), complete in itself and of some substance. Heightened in language, different aspects of which are in the various parts, it takes the form of action (*praxis*), not narrative, by creating pity and fear causing the purgation (*katharsis*) of such emotions.

The precise meaning has been argued over for centuries, but a further reference to the cathartic effect of music in his *Politica* (*Politics*) implies that Aristotle considers emotions, of which "pity" and "fear" are examples rather than the gamut, to be unhealthy if denied an outlet. Music and theatre allow for a *katharsis*, a purgation or exorcizing of these emotions, and thereby help to create emotional balance. That the main function of tragedy was to induce emotional response was to remain virtually unchallenged as a principle until Brecht in the 20th century asserted the need for a detachment of response on the part of the spectator if theatre was to show how the world could be changed.

Much of the rest of the *Poetics* is taken up with the comparison between epic and dramatic poetry. Aristotle divides tragedy into six elements, "plot, character, speech, thought, the visual and song," these in order of importance, and uses examples from a number of plays to identify the better and less satisfactory elements of plays with which he is familiar. In this he shows himself to be more familiar with Sophocles and Euripides than with Aeschylus, whose plays were less often revived in the 4th century BC. Sophocles' *Oedipus Tyrannus* proves to be his example of all that is best in drama.

For all the fascinating insights that the *Poetics* supplies, it serves better as a discussion document than as a playwriting manual it was never intended to be. Aristotle does not write as a theatre goer but as a theorist. His final conclusion that dramatic poetry is more satisfactory than epic may appear to allow for a performance dimension. His corresponding belief that tragedy may well be better enjoyed on the page than on the stage is a comment both on Aristotle and on the theatre of his period.

—J. Michael Walton

ARNIM, Bettina von

Born: Catharina Elisabetha Ludovica Magdalena Brentano in Frankfurt, Germany, 4 April 1785. Granddaughter of the writer Sophie von La Roche, sister of the writer Clemens Brentano, *q.v.* **Education:** Educated at a convent in Fritzlar, 1794–97, then in Offenbach, Frankfurt, and Marburg. **Family:** Married Ludwig Achim von Arnim in 1811 (died 1831); seven children. **Career:** Became a friend of

Goethe, whom she met in 1807; lived in Berlin from 1817; associated with Ludwig Tieck, the Grimm brothers, the Humboldt brothers, F.H. Jacobi, and F. Schleiermacher; acquainted also with Beethoven, Franz Liszt, and Hans Christian Andersen; began her literary career in the 1830s, after her husband's death. **Died:** 20 January 1859.

PUBLICATIONS

Collections

Geschichten der Bettina von Arnim (selection), edited by Karl Hans Strobl and Karl Wilhelm Fritsch. 1908.
Sämtliche Werke, edited by Waldemar Oehlke. 7 vols., 1920–22.
Werke und Briefe, edited by Gustav Konrad and Joachim Müller. 5 vols., 1959–63.
"Die Sehnsucht hat allemal Recht": Gedichte, Prosa, Briefe, edited by Gerhard Wolf. 1984.
Werke, edited by Heinz Härtl. 1986–.
Werke und Briefe, edited by Walter Schmitz and Sibylle von Steinsdorff. 1986–.
Bettina von Arnim: Ein Lesebuch, edited by Christa Bürger and Birgitt Diefenbach. 1987.

Fiction

Goethes Briefwechsel mit einem Kinde. Seinem Denkmal. 1835; as *Goethe's Correspondence with a Child: For His Monument*, translated in part by the author, 1837, Book 3 translated as *The Diary of a Child*, 1838; translated by Wallace Smith Murray, in *German Classics of the Nineteenth and Twentieth Centuries*, vol. 7, 1913.
Die Günderode. 1840; as *Miss Günderode*, translated (incomplete) by Margaret Fuller, 1842; as *Correspondence of Fräulein Günderode and Bettine von Arnim*, complete translation by Minna Wesselhöft and Margaret Fuller, 1861.
Clemens Brentanos Frühlingskranz aus Jugendbriefen ihm geflochten, wie er selbst schriftlich verlangte. 1844.
Ilius Pamphilius und die Ambrosia. 1847–48.
Drei Märchen. 1853.
Das Leben der Hochgräfin Gritta von Rattenzuhausebeiuns, with Gisela von Arnim, edited by Otto Mallon. 1926; as *The Life of High Countess Gritta von Ratsinourhouse*, translated with introduction by Lisa Ohm, 1999.

Other

Dédié à Spontini. 1843.
Dies Buch gehört dem König. 2 vols., 1843.
An die aufgelöste Preussische National-Versammlung. Stimmen aus Paris (political pamphlet). 1848; as *Polenbroschüre*, edited by Ursula Püschel, 1954.
Gespräche mit Daemonen. Des Königsbuches zweiter Band. 1852.
Sämtliche Schriften. 11 vols., 1853.
Bettine von Arnim und Friedrich Wilhelm IV (correspondence), edited by Ludwig Geiger. 1902.
Achim von Arnim und Bettina Brentano (correspondence), edited by Reinhold Steig. 1913.
Goethes Mutter in ihren Briefen und in den Erzählungen der Bettina Brentano, edited by Kate Tischendorf. 1914.

Bettinas Briefwechsel mit Goethe: auf Grund ihres handschriftlichen Nachlasses nebst zeitgenössischen Dokumenten über ihr perönliches Verhältnis zu Goethe, edited by Reinhold Steig, 1922; revised edition edited by Fritz Bergemann. 1927.
Bettina in ihren Briefen, edited by Hartmann Goertz. 1935.
Bettina von Arnim und Rudolf Baier (correspondence), edited by Kurt Gassen. 1937.
Die Andacht zum Menschenbild. Unbekannte Briefe von Bettine Brentano, (correspondence with Carl von Savigny), edited by Wilhelm Schellberg and Friedrich Fuchs. 1942.
Clemens und Bettina: Geschwisterbriefe, edited by Ina Seidel. 1948.
Du wunderliches Kind . . . Bettine und Goethe. Aus dem Briefwechsel zwischen Goethe und Bettine von Arnim, edited by Alfred Kantorowicz. 1950.
Goethes Briefwechsel mit einem Kinde: aus dem Briefwechsel zwischen Goethe und Bettina von Arnim, edited by Gustav Konrad. 1960.
Achim und Bettina in ihren Briefen: Briefwechsel Achim von Arnim und Bettina Brentano, edited by Werner Vordtriede. 2 vols., 1961.
Das Armenbuch, edited by Werner Vordtriede. 1969.
Der Briefwechsel zwischen Bettine Brentano und Max Prokop von Freyberg, edited by Sybille von Steinsdorff. 1972.
Der Briefwechsel Bettine von Arnims mit dem Brüdern Grimm 1838–1841, edited by Hartwig Schultz. 1985.
Bettine und Arnim, Briefe der Freundschaft und der Liebe, edited by Otto Betz and Veronika Straub. 2 vols., 1986–87.
". . . und mehr als einmal nachts im Thiergarten." Bettina von Arnim und Heinrich Bernhard Oppenheim. Briefe 1841–1849, edited by Ursula Püschel. 1990.
Editor, with Wilhelm Grimm and Karl August Varnhagen von Ense, *Sämmtliche Werke*, by Ludwig Achim von Arnim. 2 vols., 1853–56; revised edition, 21 vols., 1857; reprinted 1982.

*

Critical Studies: *Bettina: A Portrait* by Arthur Helps and Elizabeth Jane Howard, 1957; "The Reception in England and America of Bettina von Arnim's *Goethe's Correspondence with a Child*" by Hildegard Platzer Collins and Philip Allison Shelley, in *Anglo-German and American-German Crosscurrents*, (2), 1962; *Bettina von Arnim* by Hans von Arnim, 1963; *Bettina von Arnim. Romantik-Revolution-Utopie* by Ingeborg Drewitz, 1969; *Bettina von Arnim: Eine weibliche Sozialbibliographie aus dem 19. Jahrhundert* by Gisela Dischner, 1977; *An der Grenze einer neuen Welt: Bettina von Arnims Botschaft vom freien Geist* by Frieda Margarete Reuschle, 1977; *Steuerromantik: Rund um Bettina von Arnims Hundesteuerprozess* by Alfons Pausch, 1978; *Bettina von Arnim* by Gertrud Mander, 1982; *Bettina von Arnim: Eine Chronik: Daten und Zitate zu Leben und Werk*, edited by Heinz Härtl, 1984; *Bettina von Arnim: Ein Leben zwischen Tag und Traum* by Fritz Böttger, 1986; *Bettine von Arnim: Romantik und Sozialismus (1831–1859)* by Hartwig Schultz, Heinz Härtl, and Marie-Claire Hoock-Demarle, 1987; *Bettina von Arnim und Goethe: Topographie einer Beziehung als Beispiel weiblicher Emanzipation zu Beginn des 19. Jahrhunderts* by Birgit Weissenborn, 1987; *Bettine von Arnim and the Politics of Romantic Conversation* by Edith Waldstein, 1988; *Ordnung im Chaos: Studien zur Poetik der Bettine Brentano-von Arnim* by Ursula Liebertz-Grün, 1989; *Bettina Brentano-von Arnim: Gender and Politics*, edited by Elke P. Frederiksen and Katherine R. Goodman, 1995; *Bettine's Song: The Musical Voice of Bettine von Arnim, née Brentano*,

1785–1859 by Ann Willison Lemke, 1998; *Women of Letters: A Study of Self and Genre in the Personal Writing of Caroline Schlegel-Schelling, Rahel Levin Varnhagen, and Bettina von Arnim* by Margaretmary Daley, 1998.

* * *

One of the most remarkable and controversial figures of her generation, distinguished both by her striking personality and her multiple artistic gifts, Bettina von Arnim played a unique role in the political and intellectual life of her age. No German woman of letters has had a more profound effect on other artists: Beethoven esteemed her; Schumann and Brahms dedicated compositions to her; authors as diverse as Balzac, Immermann, and Rilke commemorated her in their novels; she gathered material for Goethe's autobiography and for the important collection of poetry by her husband and brother, *Des Knaben Wunderhorn* (*The Boy's Magic Horn*); she influenced Turgenev; and in recent times she has held a particular fascination for German women writers such as Sarah Kinsch, Ingeborg Drewitz, and Christa Wolf. While she is still most widely known for her cult of Goethe and her part in the reception of his work, her practical political concerns and her advocacy of disadvantaged social groups—Jews, the poor, victims of political persecution—are equally noteworthy.

Goethes Briefwechsel mit einem Kinde (*Goethe's Correspondence with a Child*), her first publication apart from minor items of verse and song settings, catapulted her on to the literary scene and became her most famous work both in Germany and abroad. Like three of her subsequent books—*Die Günderode* (*Miss Günderode*), *Clemens Brentanos Frühlingskranz* [Clemens Brentano's Spring Garland], and *Ilius Pamphilius und die Ambrosia*—it is an epistolary novel based on actual but heavily edited, altered, and supplemented letters, and hence occupies an ambivalent position between fact and fiction. Conceived as a literary monument to Goethe, it celebrates him as the quasi-divine incarnation of the spirit of poetry. The rapturous tone, cult of genius, and secularized religious vocabulary which characterize the novel were inspired in part by her reading of Goethe's works, notably *The Sufferings of Young Werther*, which reflects his attraction to her mother, Maximiliane, and letters that he had written to her grandmother, Sophie von La Roche, in the early 1770s. To these influences from Goethe's *Sturm und Drang* period must be added Arnim's personal acquaintance with his mother, whose reminiscences she had noted down and made available to Goethe as well as using them herself; the androgynous child-woman, Mignon, from his novel, *Wilhelm Meister's Apprenticeship* (1795–96), with whom Arnim identified; and the decisive significance for her of Romantic thought, in which the child embodies the original, innocent, paradisal relationship of humanity with the divine before the Fall. By casting herself in the role of the childmuse, Arnim evokes these associations and symbolizes her own spiritual rebirth through contact with the creative genius of Goethe.

On its appearance the *Correspondence* provoked a heated public debate, which had as much to do with the polarized political, religious, and cultural climate of contemporary Germany as with the merits of the book itself. Reactions ranged from moral outrage on the part of both Catholics and Protestants to the unqualified praise of Jacob Grimm, who declared that the book had no equal in the power of either its language or its thought, and the enthusiasm of the young

German writers, who saw it as an emancipatory tract and elevated Arnim to mythical status as an embodiment of the progressive *Zeitgeist*. By combining Romantic qualities with the apotheosis of Goethe—regarded in Germany as the embodiment of classicism—and patriotism with liberal attitudes, Arnim challenged the antithetical view of late 18th and early 19th-century German culture which was current in the mid-1830s and still colours perceptions of the period today. Although her translation of the *Correspondence* into English, which was intended to finance the Goethe memorial that she designed, proved a financial disaster, the book was well received in intellectual and artistic circles abroad, particularly in Russia, in France, and among the Transcendentalists in the USA. A partial Russian translation by Mikhail Bakunin appeared in 1838, an American edition in 1841, and a complete French translation in 1843.

Arnim's other major epistolary works, *Miss Günderode* and *Clemens Brentanos Frühlingskranz*, commemorate, respectively, her friend Karoline von Günderode, a writer who had taken her own life in 1806 at the age of 26, and her favourite brother, who died in 1842. Both the dedication of *Miss Günderode* to "the students" and the title of the "Spring Garland" have political connotations, reflecting Arnim's concern with the younger generation and with the projection of a forward-looking image of Romanticism in contrast to contemporary criticism of the movement as reactionary and narrowly denominational. Thus in the *Frühlingskranz* she stresses her brother's unorthodox youth rather than the conservative Catholicism of his later years, while in *Miss Günderode*, drawing upon the traditions of the Enlightenment, Goethe, and early Romanticism, in particular the thought of Schleiermacher, she undertakes a radical critique of orthodox Christianity and proposes a new religion based on the Romantic conception of divine love as the principle of creation.

Like the *Correspondence, Dies Buch gehört dem König* [This Book Belongs to the King] caused a sensation. A fictitious dialogue dedicated to King Frederick William IV of Prussia, it advocates, through the figure of Goethe's mother, a constitutional monarchy, social reforms, a free press, and extensive civil liberties. Crime is attributed to social deprivation; consequently, Arnim opposes the death penalty and pleads for prison reform and education for offenders. An appendix documents conditions in a Berlin slum. In 1844, Arnim planned a comprehensive documentary study of poverty, *Das Armenbuch* [Book of the Poor]. She collected "pauper lists" from all over Germany, especially Silesia, but was dissuaded from publication by the uprising of the Silesian weavers in June of that year (the extant documents were first published by Werner Vortriede in 1962). The appearance of her correspondence with her young friend Philipp Nathusius (*Ilius Pamphilius*), and the sequel to the "King's Book," *Gespräche mit Daemonen* [Conversations with Spirits], met with little response, though the latter provoked accusations of communism. She spent her final years editing and publishing her husband's collected works.

—Judith Purver

ARTAUD, Antonin (Marie Joseph)

Born: Marseilles, France, 4 September 1896. **Military Service:** Served in the French military: medical discharge, 1916. **Career:**

Suffered from meningitis, hospitalized frequently, 1915–20; moved to Paris, 1920; co-editor, *Demain*, 1920–21, and *Le Bilboquet*, 1923; actor and designer for Lugné-Poe, Charles Dullin, and Georges Pitoeff theatre companies, Paris, 1921–24; actor in films by Abel Gance, Carl Dreyer, and others, 1924–35; director, Bureau of Surrealist Research, 1925, and editor of 3rd issue of *La Révolution Surréaliste*, 1925; founder, with Roger Vitrac and Robert Aron, Théâtre Alfred Jarry, Paris, 1926, and Théâtre de la Cruauté 1933; lecturer on theatre, the Sorbonne, Paris, 1928, 1931, 1933; confined in various asylums, primarily in Rodez, 1937–46, Drawings exhibited: Loeb Gallery, 1947. **Awards:** Sainte-Beuve prize, 1948. **Died:** 4 March 1948.

PUBLICATIONS

Collections

Oeuvres complétes. 24 vols., 1956–81; revised edition, 1970–.
Artaud Anthology, edited by Jack Hirschman. 1965.
Collected Works, translated by Victor Corti. 4 vols., 1968–5.
Selected Writings, edited by Susan Sontag, translated by Helen Weaver. 1976.
Watchfiends & Rack Screams: Works from the Final Period, edited and translated by Clayton Eshleman with Bernard Bador, 1995.

Plays

Les Cenci (produced 1935). In *Oeuvres complètes*, 4, 1967; as *The Cenci*, translated by Simon Watson Taylor, 1969.
Pour en finir avec le jugement de Dieu. 1948; as *To Have Done with the Judgment of God*, translated by Helen Weaver, in *Selected Writings*, 1976.

Verse

Tric-trac du ciel 1923.
Artaud le mômo. 1947; as *Artaud the Momo*, translated by Clayton Eshlemen and Norman Glass, *1976.*
Ci-gît, précedé de la culture indienne. 1947.

Other

Le Pèse-nerfs. 1925; with *Fragments d'un journal d'enfer*, 1927.
L'Ombilic des limbes. 1927.
Correspondance, with Jacques Rivière. 1927.
L'Art et la mort. 1929.
Le Théâtre Alfred Jarry et l'hostilité public, with Roger Vitrac. 1930.
Le Théâtre de ta cruauté. 1933.
Héliogabale; ou, L'Anarehiste couronné. 1934.
Le Théâtre de Séraphin. 1936.
Les Nouvelles Révélations de l'être. 1937.
Le Théâtre et son double. 1938; also translated by Brian Singleton, 1998; as *The Theatre and Its Double*, translated by Mary Caroline Richards, 1958; also translated by Victor Corti, 1981.
D'un voyage au pays de Tarahumaras (essays and letters). 1945.
Lettres de Rodez, 1946.
Van Gogh, Le Suicidé de la société. 1947.
Supplément aux Lettres de Rodez suivi de Coleridge le traître. 1949.
Lettres contre la Cabbale. 1949.
Lettres à Jean-Louis Barrault. 1952.

La Vie et mort de Satan le feu. 1953; as *The Death of Satan and Other Mystical Writings*, translated by Alastair Hamilton and Victor Corti, 1974.
Les Tarahumaras (letters and essays). 1955; as *The Peyote Dance*, translated by Helen Weaver, 1976.
Galapagos, Les Îles du bout du monde (travel). 1955.
Autre chose que l'enfant beau. 1957.
Voici un endroit. 1958.
Mexico. 1962.
Lettres à Anaïs Nin. 1965.
Poète noir et autres textes/Black Poet and Other Texts, edited by Paul Zweig. 1966.
Lettres à Génica Athanasiou. 1969.
Nouveaux écrits de Rodez. 1977.
Lettres à Anie Besnard. 1977.
Artaud on Theatre, edited by Claude Schumacher. 1989.
Antonin Artaud's Alternate Genealogies: Self-portraits and Family Romances by John C. Stout, 1996.
Translator, *Le Moine,* by Matthew Gregory Lewis. 1931.
Translator, with Bernard Steele, *Crime passionnel,* by Ludwig Lewisohn. 1932.
Antonin Artaud: Works on Paper, edited by Margit Rowell, 1996.

*

Bibliography: in *Artaud et te théâtre* by Alan Virmaux, 1970.

Critical Studies: *The Dramatic Concept of Artaud* by Eric Sellin, 1968; *Antonin Artaud: Man of Vision* by Bettina L. Knapp, 1969; *Antonin Artaud: Poet Without Words* by Naomi Greene, 1970; *Antonin Artaud* by Jean-Louis Brau, 1971; *Antonin Artaud* by Martin Esslin, 1976; *Artaud's Theatre of Cruelty* by Alfred Bermel, 1977; *Artaud and After* by Ronald Hayman, 1977; *Antonin Artaud* by Julia F. Costich, 1978; *Antonin Artaud: Blows and Bombs* by Stephen Barber, 1993; *Artaud, Genet, Shange: The Absence of the Theatre of Cruelty* by Sean Carney, 1994; *Antonin Artaud and the Modern Theatre,* edited by Gene A. Plunka, 1994; *Artaud and the Gnostic Drama* by Jane Goodall, 1994; *Issues of Otherness and Identity in the Works of Izquierdo, Kahlo, Artaud, and Breton* by Gina McDaniel Tarver, 1996; *Artaud: The Screaming Body* by Stephen Barber, 1999.

*   *   *

Paradox envelops Antonin Artaud. The man who wished to de-emphasize words in theatre—''No more masterpieces!''—has written 24 volumes of words. A theatre prophet who valued performance far above theory, Artaud's productions were limited to a few sporadic efforts of his Alfred Jarry Theatre and 17 performances of *Les Cenci* [The Cenci] as an example of theatre of cruelty; in contrast, Gallimard publishers printed 100,000 copies of *Le Théâtre et son double* [The Theatre and Its Double], his 1938 collection of manifestos and letters which has had wide influence. A strikingly handsome film actor, Artaud drew self-portraits when he was ill and haggard. Plagued with illness all his life, Artaud undertook to cure what he saw as a sick civilization. After nine years of neglect in asylums, he became a cult figure in post-World War II Paris, during the last two years of his life. After his death, Artaud inspired two divergent movements: 1) the experimental theatre groups of the 1960s, particularly in the USA; 2) the "human science" intellectuals of that same decade, particularly in France.

Artaud's writing takes many forms—fiction, drama, essays, diatribes, production plans, poems, and letters that sometimes read like soliloquies to be declaimed. All his writing is seared by his flaming self-consciousness; he flaunted his suffering with inimitable intensity. Up until the time of his incarceration in 1937, Artaud espoused theatre as an instrument of civilizational catharsis, and he equates theatre with plague, alchemy, metaphysics, and cruelty—doubles all. At Rodez Asylum and later, however, his long poems and essays lacerate in order to scourge. With sound play, obscenity, neologisms, occult and fantastic reference, Artaud inveighs against Western materialism; as *poète maudit* he curses the familiar scenes of modern life. His passion—utterance and suffering—has inspired theatre practitioners like Jean-Louis Barrault, Roger Blin, Peter Brook; and thinkers like Gilles Deleuze, Jacques Derrida, and Susan Sontag. Less read than read about, Artaud is only recently being studied as a writer rather than as a martyr.

—Ruby Cohn

See the essay on *The Theatre and Its Double*.

ASSIS, Joaquim Maria Machado de

See MACHADO DE ASSIS, Joaquim Maria

ASTURIAS, Miguel Ángel

Born: Guatemala City, Guatemala, 19 October 1899. Family moved to Salamá fearing government persecution, 1903; returned to the capital, 1908. **Education:** Educated at schools in Guatemala City; abandoned studies in medicine, 1917; studied law at San Carlos University, Guatemala City, 1917–23, degree 1923; also helped found the People's University [Universidad Popular] of Guatemala, 1922, and the Association of University Students; studied anthropology under Georges Raymond, the Sorbonne, Paris, 1923–28. **Family:** Married 1) Clemencia Amado (separated 1946–47), two sons; 2) Blanca de Mora y Araujo in 1950, two sons. **Career:** Founder, *Tiempos Nuevos*, 1923; travelled to England, 1923; based in Paris, 1923–32, mixing study and journalism; travelled through Europe and the Middle East in the 1920s; returned to Guatemala, 1933, and worked as radio broadcaster (co-creator, "Diario del aire" series, 1937) and journalist, 1933–42; a deputy, Guatemalan National Congress, 1942; undertook diplomatic posts, 1945–54: cultural attaché, Mexico City, 1945–47, and Buenos Aires, 1947–53, minister-counsellor, Buenos Aires, 1951–52, Guatemalan ambassador, Paris, 1952–53, and San Salvador (El Salvador), 1953–54; exiled for his support of the left-wing leader Jacobo Árbenz Guzmán, 1954, and moved to Argentina; journalist, *El Nacional* (Venezuela), 1954–62; cultural exchange programme member, Columanum, Italy, 1962;

Guatemalan ambassador, Paris, 1966–70; spent last years in Madrid. **Awards:** Sylla Monsegur prize for translation, 1932; William Faulkner Foundation Latin American award, 1962; International Lenin Peace prize, 1966; Nobel prize for literature, 1967. **Died:** 9 June 1974.

PUBLICATIONS

Collection

Edición crítica de las obras completas, various editors. 24 vols., 1977–.

Fiction

El Señor Presidente. 1946; edited by Ricardo Navas Ruiz and Jean-Marie Saint-Lu, 1978; as *The President*, translated by Frances Partridge, 1963; as *El Señor Presidente*, translated by Partridge, 1964.

Hombres de maíz. 1949; edited by Gerald Martín, 1981 and 1992; as *Men of Maize*, translated by Martín, 1974; translated by Gerald Martin, 1993.

Viento fuerte. 1949; as *The Cyclone*, translated by Darwin Flakoll and Claribel Alegría, 1967; as *Strong Wind*, translated by Gregory Rabassa, 1968.

El Papa verde. 1954; as *The Green Pope*, translated by Gregory Rabassa, 1971.

Week-end en Guatemala (stories). 1956.

Los ojos de los enterrados. 1960; as *The Eyes of the Interred*, translated by Gregory Rabassa, 1973.

El alhajadito (novella). 1961; as *The Bejeweled Boy*, translated by Martin Shuttleworth, 1971.

Mulata de tal. 1963; as *Mulatta*, translated by Gregory Rabassa, 1967; as *The Mulatta and Mr. Fly*, translated by Rabassa, 1967.

El espejo de Lida Sal (stories). 1967; as *The Mirror of Lida Sal: Tales Based on Mayan Myths and Guatemalan Legends*, translated by Gilbert Alter-Gilbert, 1997.

Maladrón: Epopeya de los Andes verdes. 1969.

Novelas y cuentos de juventud, edited by Claude Couffon. 1971.

Viernes de Dolores. 1972; edited by Marcel Brion and others, 1978.

Tres obras (includes *Leyendas de Guatemala; El Alhajadito; El Señor Presidente*), edited by Giuseppe Bellini, 1977.

Verse

Émulo Lipolidón. 1935.

Sonetos. 1937.

Anoche, 10 de marzo de 1543. 1943.

Poesía: Sien de alondra. 1949; complete edition, 1954.

Ejercicios poéticos en forma de soneto sobre temas de Horacio. 1951.

Alto es el sur. 1952.

Bolívar. 1955.

Obras escogidas. 3 vols., 1955.

Nombre custodio, e Imagen pasajera. 1959.

Clarivigilia primaveral. 1965.

Sonetos de Italia. 1965.

Sonetos venecianos. 1973.

Tres de cuatro soles (prose poem), edited by Dorita Nouhaud. 1977.

Plays

Rayito de estrella (in verse). 1925.
Alclasán: famtomina (in verse). 1939.
Soluna: Comedia prodigiosa en dos jornadas y un final. 1955.
La audiencia de los confines: Crónica en tres andanzas. 1957.
Teatro: Chantaje; Dique seco; Soluna; La audiencia de los confines. 1964.
Juárez. 1972.

Other

Sociología guatemalteca: El problema social del indio. 1923; as *Guatemalan Sociology: The Social Problem of the Indian*, translated by Maureen Ahern, 1977.
La arquitectura de la vida nueva (essays and lectures). 1928.
Carta aérea a mis amigos de América. 1952.
Rumania, su nueva imagen. 1964.
Juan Girador. 1964.
Obras escogidas. 2 vols., 1964.
Torotumbo; La audiencia de los confines; Mensajes indios (selection). 1967.
Coloquio con Asturias, with Hugo Cerezo Dardón and others. 1968.
Latinoamérica y otros ensayos (essays). 1968.
Antología, edited by Pablo Palomina. 1968.
Asturias: Semblanza para el estudio de su vida y obra, con una selección de poemas y prosas. 1968.
Obras completas, introduced by José María Souviron. 3 vols., 1968.
Comiendo en Hungría (verse and illustrations), with Pablo Neruda. 1969; as *Sentimental Journey around the Hungarian Cuisine*, translated by Barna Balogh, 1969.
The Talking Machine (for children), translated by Beverly Koch. 1971.
El problema social del indio y otros textos, edited by Claude Couffon, 1971.
El novelista en la universidad. 1971.
América, fábula de fábulas y otros ensayos (essays). 1972.
Novela y novelista. reunión de Málaga, with others. 1972.
Mi mejor obra, 1973; as *Lo mejor de mi obra*, 1974.
Conversaciones con Asturias, with Luis López Álvarez. 1974.
Sinceridades (essays), edited by Epaminondas Quintana. 1980.
Actos de fe en Guatemala, photographs by Sara Facio and María Cristina Orive. 1980.
El hombre que lo tenía todo, todo, todo, illustrated by Jacqueline Duheme. 1981.
Viajes, ensayos y fantasías. 1981.
París 1922–1923: Periodismo y creación literaria (articles), edited by Amos Segala. 1988.
Cartas de amor, with Blanca de Moray Araujo, edited by Felipe Mellizo. 1989.
Editor, *Leyendas de Guatemala* (stories). 1930; enlarged edition, 1948; as *Leyendas*, 1960.
Editor, *Poesía precolombiana.* 1960.
Editor, *Páginas de Rubén Darío*, 1963.
Translator, with J. Manuel González de Mendoza, *Los dioses, los héroes y los hombres de Guatemala antigua; o, El libro del consejo, Popol vuh de los indios quichés.* 1927; revised edition as *Popol vuh, o, el libro del consejo de los indios quichés*, 1969.
Translator, with J. Manuel González de Mendoza, *Anales de los xahil de los indios cakchiqueles* by Georges Raynaud. 1928.
Translator, *Antología de la prosa rumana.* 1967.

*

Bibliography: *Miguel Ángel Asturias: Anticipo bibliografíco* by Pedro F. de Andrea, 1969; *Asturias: A Checklist of Works and Criticism* by R.E. Moore, 1979.

Critical Studies: *Miguel Ángel Asturias* by Atilio Jorge Castelpoggi, 1961; *Asturias* by Earl and Beverly Jones, 1967; *Miguel Ángel Asturias* by G.W. Lorenz, 1968; *Miguel Ángel Asturias; Semblanza para el estudio de su vida y obra* by Marta Pilón, 1968; *El carácter de la literatura y la novelística de Miguel Ángel Asturias* by Iber Verdugo, 1968; *La narrativa de Miguel Ángel Asturias*, 1969, *Il laberinto magico*, 1973, *Il mondo allucinante: Da Asturias a García Márquez*, 1976, and *De tiranos, héroes y brujos: Estudios sobre la obra de Miguel Ángel Asturias*, 1982, all by Giuseppe Bellini; *Artists and Writers in the Evolution of Latin America* edited by Edward D. Terry, 1969; *Asturias* by Richard Callan, 1970; *Homenaje a Miguel Ángel Asturias* edited by Helmy F. Giacoman, 1971; *Miguel Ángel Asturias: La función de lo ancestral en la obra literaria* by Eladia L. Hill, 1972; *Miguel Ángel Asturias* by J. Sáenz, 1973; *El Miguel Ángel Asturias que yo conocí* by J. Olivero, 1980; *Asturias y Neruda* by G. Tavani, 1985; "Tall Tales Made to Order: The Making of Myth in *Men of Maize* by Miguel Ángel Asturias," in *Modern Language Notes*, 101, 1986, "The Unifying Principle of *Men of Maize*," in *Modern Language Studies*, 16(2), 1986, and "The New American Idiom of Miguel Ángel Asturias," in *Hispanic Review*, 56(2), 1988, all by R. Prieto; *La problemática de la identidad en El Señor Presidente de Miguel Ángel Asturias* by T. Rodríguez, 1989; *Miguel Angel Asturias's Archeology of Return* by R. Prieto, 1993; *Assuming the Light: The Parisian Literary Apprenticeship of Miguel Angel Asturias* by Stephen Henighan, 1999; *The Sexual Woman in Latin American Literature: Dangerous Desires* by Diane E. Marting, 2001.

* * *

The poetry, drama, essays, and articles for which Miguel Ángel Asturias received the 1967 Nobel prize for literature demonstrate his preoccupation with social and political conditions in Latin America (especially Guatemala) and with the region's mythic past. Critical attention has generally focused on his fiction (novels and "legends"), unfortunately eclipsing his achievements in other genres. In an essay about his aesthetic principles, Asturias characterized his fiction as "realismo mágico" (magic realism), a term he coined to define writing which, while closely related to surrealism, depicts a uniquely Latin American, fictional ambience that bridges two realities—one being the everyday lives of characters who speak the language of the Guatemalan people and are involved with their social and political concerns, the other an imaginary realm immersed in dreams and hallucinations. The oneiric quality of his fictional worlds is achieved by juxtaposing Guatemalan folk traditions and myths from the Mayan sacred book (the *Popol vuh*) with everyday reality.

Asturias came to the attention of international literary circles with the publication of *Leyendas de Guatemala* [Legends of Guatemala], a collection of short fictional pieces described in Paul Valéry's preface as "poems-dreams-fantasies." He continued writing "legends" in this "magical" vein throughout his career, and they appear in two later collections, *Week-end en Guatemala* [Weekend in Guatemala] and *El espejo de Lida Sal* (*The Mirror Of Lida Sal*).

From his first novel, *El Señor Presidente* (*The President*), to his last, *Viernes de Dolores* [Good Friday], Asturias's novels are social and political, reflecting the reality of Guatemala's people, on the one hand, and oneiric, magical, and mythical on the other. *The President* combines these two qualities very effectively. The most immediate quality of this novel is its unvarnished realism in which torture, graft, and injustice are seen as part of everyday life in a military dictatorship and are depicted in ghastly detail. A surreal atmosphere is discernible from the novel's opening passage, a diabolical, jabberwockylike incantation: "Boom, bloom, alum-bright, Lucifer of alunite!" The "magical" ambience is achieved by the use of mythical motifs and poetic or incantational language. These provide a mesmerizing experience for the reader. Asturias's last novel is based on the student strike that occasioned his first exile. Its narrative is tinged with the humour and idealism of the young Asturias and the irony and disillusion of the man close to the end of his life.

Other novels with significant socio-political content include *Viento fuerte* (*Strong Wind*), *El Papa verde* (*The Green Pope*), and *Los ojos de los enterrados* (*The Eyes of the Interred*), a trio often referred to as the "Banana Trilogy." They enunciate a protest against the exploitation of Guatemala's agricultural resources by foreign interests. Asturias resists a temptation to tar all his fictional United States citizens with the same brush. In *Strong Wind*, for example, the American Lester Mead makes common cause with the plantation labourers against Tropical Banana Inc., a fictionalized United Fruit Company.

Other Asturias novels are less political and more mythical. His characters move in a magic-realist world, with one foot in the prosaic reality of Guatemala, the other in the magic of the *Popol vuh* and traditional folk beliefs. This group includes *Hombres de maíz* (*Men of Maize*), *Mulata de tal* (*The Mulatta and Mr. Fly*), *El alhajadito* (*The Bejeweled Boy*), and *Maladrón* [Evil Thief]. The duality of Asturias's novelistic reality may be identified most readily in *Men of Maize*, where he depicts the cultivation of corn for profit as a practice that leads to abuse of the land and disrespect for nature. Simultaneously, he creates a "magical" context that alludes to ancient myths, for his characters descend from the first Mayans whose flesh was created from corn by the gods of the *Popol vuh*. Guatemalan folk tradition is present in the form of his characters' *nahuales* (animal counterparts believed to protect individuals, and whose form may be assumed by their protégées in times of need).

Asturias's poetry, most of which is gathered in *Poesía: Sien de alondra* [The Lark's Brow], has received undeserved short shrift from critics. The early poems are completely traditional—with the sonnet his favourite form—and are subjective and personal in content; but, by the mid-1940s, his poetic themes are universal, and, to re-create Guatemala's ancient Mayan atmosphere and re-mythologize its reality, he uses the parallel constructions, repetitions, and onomatopoeia characteristic of pre-Columbian Indian poetry. This trend culminates in *Clarivigilia primaveral* [Springtime Bright-Vigil], a book-length poem in which Asturias creates a new "myth" about Latin American artist gods. In this poem as elsewhere, while not actually alluding to characters from ancient Mayan myth, he creates characters and events with a mythic quality of relevance to modern Guatemala.

Asturias's theatrical works explore the essence of Guatemalan reality in the same way that his works of fiction and poetry do. *La audiencia de los confines* [The Royal Tribunal of the Frontier] is a historical play dealing with the duplicity of Church and State at the time of Fray Bartolomé de las Casas's defence of the Indians. *Chantaje* [Blackmail] and *Dique seco* [Dry Dock] are plays of social criticism with touches of the absurd. *Soluna* [Sun-Moon], perhaps the best known of his plays, uses the magic-realism characteristic of his fiction. In it, a myth (when the sun and moon merge during an eclipse,

time accelerates, compressing years into moments) provides the solution to the protagonist's dilemma. Asturias's language in his plays is, as it is in other genres, essentially poetic. In fact, he inserts poetic passages in several of his plays. His three "fantomimas" (fantasy-mimes), however, are dramas entirely in verse. He returns to the poetic theatre tradition of the Spanish Golden Age, using traditional Spanish versification. Ironically, these characteristics accentuate a very 20th-century quality of his theatre: the aesthetic distance created by the use of neologisms, repetitions, onomatopoeia, and jabberwocky-like passages.

Asturias's writings in every genre captivate his readers, pulling them into the ancient, mythical ambience of Guatemala, thereby forcing them to reconsider everyday reality.

—Oralia Preble-Niemi

See the essay on *The President*.

ATTĀR, Farid al-Din Abu Hamid Mohammad

Born: Nishāpūr, Persia (now Iran), c. 1116–41. **Education:** Trained and practised as a pharmacist (*attār*) and as a physician; reputedly, travelled throughout the Muslim Middle East, India, and Turkestan; after retirement became a member of the Sufi sect, writing numerous poems and compiling biographies of Sufi saints (*Tazkerāt al-'Awliā*). Around 20 of the works attributed to him in the past are now thought to be spurious. According to tradition, killed during the Mongol invasion of Persia. **Died:** c. 1220–31.

PUBLICATIONS

Verse

Ilaāhi-nāma, edited by H. Ritter. 1940; as *Book of God*, translated by John Andrew Boyle, 1976.
Manteq al-Tayr, edited by S. Gowharin. 1964, as *The Conference of the Birds*, translated by C.S. Nott (from French), 1954; also translated by Afkam Darbandi and Dick Davis, 1984; abridged version, as *The Bird Parliament*, translated by Edward Fitzgerald, 1899; as *Persian Mysticism*, translated by R.P. Masani, 1981.

Other

Tazkerāt al-'Awliā [The Memoirs of the Saints] (biographies), edited by R.A. Nicholson. 2 vols., 1905–07; part as *Muslim Saints and Mystics*, translated by A.R. Arberry, 1965.
The Persian Mystics: Attār by Margaret Smith, 1995.

*

Bibliography: in *Persian Literature* by C.A. Storey, 1953.

Critical Studies: *The Persian Mystics: Attar* (includes translations) by Margaret Smith, 1932; *Attar: Concordance and Lexical Repertories of 1000 Lines* by Daniela Meneghini Correale, 1993.

* * *

Farid al-Din Abu Hamid Mohammad Attār of Nishāpūr, known as Farid al-Din Attār, was an eminent Islamic mystic (Sufi) and Persian poet who was born during the 12th century in Nishāpūr, in what is now northeast Iran. The word *attār* in Persian is derived from the word *atr* which literally means perfume; an *attār* is a perfume seller, and the word also refers to a pharmacist. Attār says that he composed some of his works in *dāru khāneh*, which in modern Persian means a pharmacy, and he was also familiar with the practice of medicine. There are references in his early works to the many patients he received every day in his pharmacy. Later in his life he gave up his job, became a Sufi, and lived in seclusion. It is during this later period that he produced his most significant works.

Attār travelled extensively and visited Egypt, Damascus, Turkistan, Mecca, and India in pursuit of knowledge. During these travels he met great Sufis of his time, and learned the stories he used in his later works. He was a prolific poet and writer who composed, according to his biographers, as many as 114 works. Although this figure seems exaggerated, Attār's contribution to Islamic mysticism is undeniable. To appreciate his works one has to be familiar with the basic doctrines of Islamic mysticism (Sufism), including the Unity of Being (*wahdat al-wujūd*) which, briefly, means that the created universe is a manifestation of the Divine Reality. This must not be confused with pantheism, because the Oneness of God is at the heart of this doctrine. The created, which is an image of the Creator, will not rest until it achieves the esoteric knowledge (*ma'refat*) necessary for experiencing mystical union with the Divine. The unique relationship between the spiritual master (*morād* or *shaikh*) and the disciple (*morid* or *sālek*) is another cornerstone of Sufism. During the spiritual journey, the disciple constantly seeks his master's clarification on the subtleties of the path and depends on him to resolve his problems.

Attār delineated the doctrines of Sufism delicately and in a simple language in books that are among his best works of poetry and prose. In *Asrār-nāma* [The Book of Secrets] the narrator admonished the reader to leave his worldly desires behind and start looking for the Divine Reality. It is similar to another of his books, *Manteq al-Tayr* (*The Conference of the Birds*) in urging man to embark upon the spiritual journey. However, unlike his other major poetical works which have one general frame story with several embedded stories, this poem has no frame. *Ilāhi-nāma* (*Book of God*) is a poetical dialogue between a king and his six sons who are in pursuit of worldly happiness. The king tries to prove to them the absurdity and vanity of their pursuit through anecdotes and examples.

The Conference of the Birds, completed in 1177, is considered Attār's greatest poetical work. This poem is an allegorical account of Islamic mysticism. The story is about the birds of the world who are looking for a king. The hoopoe, Solomon's special messenger to Belqays, the Queen of Sheba, assumes the role of the spiritual master and leads them to the royal court of the Simurgh, the king of the birds. Once the birds are confronted with the insurmountable difficulties of the journey, they come up with various excuses as to why it is impossible for them to undertake the journey. Their excuses express typical weaknesses of human beings on the path of spirituality but in bondage to material things. Through a series of questions and answers, the hoopoe finally succeeds in encouraging them to embark on the trip, narrating admonishing stories and thus expounding the doctrines of Sufism. The hoopoe explains the seven valleys that lead to the Simurgh's court: quest (*talab*), love (*ishq*), esoteric knowledge (*ma'refat*), independence (*isteghnā*), unity (*towhid*), bewilderment

(*hayrat*), poverty (*faqr*), and annihilation (*fanā*). These are the seven stages on the path of the seeker's spiritual journey which have to be completed before reaching the royal court. The path of spirituality is dangerous and difficult and not everyone can make it to the end. Only 30 birds reach the court of His Majesty. Finally, when they are admitted to His Presence, they see themselves in His Majesty's mirror. The 30 birds are the Simurgh (*si*: 30, *murgh*: bird), and their journey is a conceptualization of man's spiritual journey to the Divine Reality.

Tazkerāt al-'Awliā [The Memoirs of the Saints], Attār's most important prose work, is the hagiography of 96 Islamic saints and mystics. In this book Attār shows his high opinion of the Islamic saints and mystics whose sayings he considers next to the Qur'ān and hadith (the sayings of the Prophet) in their authoritative voice. Two mystics in whom Attār shows a great deal of interest are Mansur Hallāj (d. 922) and Bāyazid Bastāmi (d. 874), both of whom were executed for their heretical views by the orthodox theologians. In compiling this book, Attār used several sources on the life of Sufis available to him. His achievement is, however, in using these stories for expounding Sufi principles.

Attār chooses his characters from common people and animals. In his works we see people from all layers of society including dervishes, beggars, craftsmen, and merchants. He has no interest in the aristocratic class, and whenever he mentions the word "king," he refers to the Divine Being. As a mystic, Attār was never concerned with material gain and never sold his poetic genius to earthly rulers to make a living. As a true Sufi he believed only in the Celestial King whose love was the only moving force in the poet's life. Attār has a talent for putting the most complicated ideas into simple language, masterfully using allegories to express the inexpressible experience and to describe the indescribable.

—Alireza Anushiravani

See the essay on *The Conference of the Birds*.

AUGUSTINE, St.

Born: Aurelius Augustinus in Tagaste (now Souk Ahras, Algeria), 13 November AD 354. **Education:** Reared as a Christian; educated in Tagaste and Carthage. **Family:** Had a son by his concubine. **Career:** Taught rhetoric in Tagaste, one year, Carthage, eight years, in Rome, 383–84, and Milan, 384–86, where he met the bishop Ambrose; after a period of Manichaeism, turned to Neoplatonism; converted to Christianity, 386: baptized by Ambrose, 387; returned to Tagaste, 388; ordained as a priest in Hippo Regius (now Annada, Algeria), 391, and became its bishop, 396–430, where contended with Donatist schism, Pelagian heresy, and Vandal invasions. **Died:** 28 August AD 430.

PUBLICATIONS

Collections

[Works], in *Patrologia Latina*, edited by Jacques Paul Migne, vols. 32–47. 1844–64; translations in *A Library of Fathers of the Holy*

Catholic Church, edited by E.B. Pusey, 12 vols., 1840–57; *Library of Nicene and Post-Nicene Fathers*, edited by Marcus Dods, 15 vols., 1871–76, revised edition, as *A Select Library of the Nicene and Post-Nicene Fathers*, edited by Philip Schaff, vols. 1–8, 1886–88; *Ancient Christian Writers*, edited by Johannes Quasten and Joseph C. Plumpe, 9 vols., 1946–61; *The Fathers of the Church*, edited by Ludwig Schopp, R.J. Defervari, and others, 10 vols., 1947–63; *Library of Christian Classics*, edited by John Baillie, John T. McNeill, and Henry P. Van Dusen, vols. 6–8, 1953–55; and *The Works of St. Augustine*, edited by John E. Rotelle, 7 vols., to 1994.

Basic Writings, edited by Whitney J. Oates. 2 vols., 1948.

Selected Sermons, edited and translated by Quincy Howe. 1966.

An Augustine Reader, edited by John J. O'Meara. 1973.

Selected Writings, translated by Mary T. Clark. 1984.

Sermons, translated by Edmund Hill. 2 vols., 1990.

Augustine: Major Writings by Benedict J. Groeschel, 1995.

Political Writings, translated by Michael W. Tkacz and Douglas Kries, 1994.

The Political Writings of St. Augustine, edited with an introduction by Henry Paolucci, 1996.

Works

De civitate Dei, edited by B. Dombart. 1853, revised by A. Kalb, 1928–29; also edited by J.E.C. Welldon, 1924; edited and translated by George E. McCracken and William C. Greene [Loeb Edition], 7 vols., 1957–72; as *The City of God*, translated by John Healey, 1610, revised by R.V.G. Trasker, 2 vols., 1945; also translated by Marcus Dods and George Wilson, in *Library of Nicene and Post-Nicene Fathers*, 1872, reprinted 1950; translated in *The Fathers of the Church*, vols. 6–8, 1950–54; as *The City of God Against the Pagans*, edited and translated by R.W. Dyson, 1998.

Contra litteras Petiliani, as *Answers to Letters of Petilian*, translated by J.R. King, in *A Select Library of Nicene and Post-Nicene Fathers of the Christian Church*, vol. 4. 1887.

De baptismo, contra Donatistas, as *On Baptism, Against the Donatists*, translated by J.R. King, in *A Select Library of Nicene and Post-Nicene Fathers of the Christian Church*, vol. 4. 1887.

De natura et gratia, as *On Nature and Grace*, translated by Peter Holmes, in *A Selected Library of Nicene and Post-Nicene Fathers of the Christian Church*, vol. 5. 1888.

De gratia Christi et de peccato originali, as *On the Grace of Christ and on Original Sin*, translated by Peter Holmes, in *A Select Library of Nicene and Post-Nicene Fathers of the Christian Church*, vol. 5. 1888.

Tractatus in Joannis Evangelium, as *Homilies on the Gospel of John*, translated by H. Browne, in *A Select Library of Nicene and Post-Nicene Fathers of the Christian Church*, vol. 7. 1888; as *Tractates on the Gospel of John*, translated by John W. Retting. 1995.

Confessiones, edited by P. Knöll. 1909; also edited by M. Skutella, revised by H. Juergens and W. Schaub, 1969, also revised by James J. O'Donnell, 1992; as *The Confessions*, translated by Sir Tobie Matthew, 1624; also translated by William Watts, 1631; E.B. Pusey, 2 vols., 1838; Charles Bigg, 1898; F.J. Sheed, 1943; J.M. Lelen, 1952; R.S. Pine-Coffin, 1961; Rex Warner, 1963; E.M. Blaiklock, 1983; Henry Chadwick, 1991; James J. O'Donnell, 1992; J.G. Pilkington, 1993; as *Confessions: Books I–IV*, edited by Gillian Clark, 1995.

Soliloquia, as *The Soliloquies*, translated by Rose E. Cleveland. 1910; also translated by Thomas F. Gilligan, in *The Fathers of the Church*, vol. 5, 1948.

De doctrina Christiana, edited by H.J. Vogels. 1930; as *On Christian Doctrine*, translated by F.J. Shaw, in *A Select Library of Nicene and Post-Nicene Fathers of the Christian Church*, vol. 2, 1886; as *Augustine De doctrina Christiana*, edited and translated by R.P.H. Green, 1995.

De beata vita, edited by Michael Schmaus. 1931; as *The Happy Life*, edited and translated by Ludwig Schopp, 1939.

De libero arbitrio, as *On Free Will*, edited and translated by Francis E. Tourscher. 1937; also translated by Carroll Mason Sparrow, 1947; Anna S. Benjamin and L.H. Hackstaff, 1964; as *The Problem of Free Choice*, translated by Mark Pontifex, in *Ancient Christian Writers*, 1955; as *On Free Choice of the Will*, translated by Thomas Williams, 1993.

Regula, translated as *The Rule of St. Augustine*. 1942; also translated by Raymond Canning, 1984.

De Genesi ad literam [Literal Commentary on Genesis], edited and translated by John Hammond Taylor. 1948.

De sermone Domini in monte, as *Commentary on the Lord's Sermon on the Mount*, translated by Denis J. Kavanagh, in *The Fathers of the Church*, vol. 5. 1948.

De spiritu et littera, as *On Spirit and the Letter*, translated by Peter Holmes, in *Basic Writings*. 1948.

De vera religione, as *Of True Religion*, translated by J.H.S. Burleigh. 1953.

Tractatus in Epistolam Joannis ad Parthos, translated as *Ten Homilies on St. John's Epistle*, in *Library of Christian Classics*, vol. 8. 1955.

Enarrationes in Psalmos, translated as *On the Psalms*, in *Ancient Christian Writers*. 1960.

De trinitate, edited by M.F. Sciacca. 1973; as *On the Trinity*, translated by Arthur W. Haddan, in *A Select Library of Nicene and Post-Nicene Fathers of the Christian Church*, vol. 3, 1887; also translated by Stephen McKenna, in *The Fathers of the Church*, vol. 45, 1963.

Epistolae, edited by L. Carrozzi. 1974; translated as *Letters*, in *The Fathers of the Church*, 1947–63; as *Select Letters* [Loeb Edition], 1930.

De dialectica, edited by Jan Pinborg, translated by B. Darrell Jackson. 1975.

Contra academicos, as *Against the Academicians; The Teacher*, translated with introduction and notes by Peter King. 1995.

*

Bibliography: *Revue des études augustiniennes*, 1956–; *Répertoire bibliographique de saint Augustin 1950–1960* by T.J. van Bavel, 1963; *Fichier augustinien*, 4 vols., 1972; *Bibliographia Augustiniana* by Carl Andresen, 1973; *Augustinian Bibliography 1970–1980* by Terry L. Miethe, 1982.

Critical Studies: *St. Augustine's Philosophy of Beauty* by Emmanuel Chapman, 1939; *The City of God* by J.H.S. Burleigh, 1949; *A Companion to the Study of St. Augustine* edited by R.W. Battenhouse, 1955; *St. Augustine and His Influence Through the Ages* by H.I. Marrou, 1957; *The Christian Philosophy of St. Augustine* by Etienne Gilson, 1960; *St. Augustine the Bishop* by F. van der Meer, 1961; *St. Augustine of Hippo: Life and Controversies*, 1963, and *God's Decree and Man's Destiny: Studies on the Thought of Augustine of Hippo*,

1987, both by Gerald Bonner; *Augustine of Hippo*, 1967, and *Religion and Society in the Age of St. Augustine*, 1972, both by P.R.L. Brown; *St. Augustine's Confessions: The Odyssey of a Soul*, 1969, *Art and the Christian Intelligence in St. Augustine*, 1978, and *Imagination and Metaphysics in St. Augustine*, 1986, all by R.J. O'Connell; *Augustine: A Collection of Critical Essays* edited by R.A. Markus, 1972; *Augustine's De moribus ecclesiae catholicae: A Study of the Work, Its Composition and Its Sources* by John Kevin Coyle, 1978; *Augustine: A Wayward Genius* by David Bentley-Taylor, 1980; *The Problem of Self-Love in St. Augustine* by Oliver O'Donovan, 1980; *The Young Augustine: An Introduction to the "Confessions" of St. Augustine* by John J. O'Meara, 1980; *Augustine: His Life and Thought* by Warren Thomas Smith, 1980; *Political Theory as Public Confession: The Social and Political Thought of Augustine of Hippo* by Peter Dennis Bathory, 1981; *St. Augustine of Hippo* by Gabriel McDonagh, 1982; *Augustine* by Henry Chadwick, 1986; *The Reality of the Mind: Augustine's Philosophical Arguments for the Human Soul as a Spiritual Substance* by Ludger Höscher, 1986; *Augustine of Hippo and His Monastic Rule* by George Lawless, 1987; *Augustine's Philosophy of Mind* by Gerald J.P. O'Daly, 1987; *Original Sin in Augustine's Confessions* by Paul Rigby, 1987; *Christian Love and Just War: Moral Paradox and Political Life in St. Augustine and His Modern Interpreters* by William R. Stevenson, 1987; *Augustine* by Christopher Kirwan, 1989; *Augustine's Prayerful Ascent: An Essay on the Literary Form of the Confessions* by Robert McMahon, 1989; *Jerusalem and Babylon: A Study into Augustine's City of God and the Sources of His Doctrine of the Two Cities* by Johannes van Oort, 1991; *Augustine: Ancient Thought Baptized* by John M. Rist, 1994; *Saint Augustine the Bishop: A Book of Essays*, edited by Fannie LeMoine and Christopher Kleinhenz, 1994; *Sacred and Secular: Studies on Augustine and Latin Christianity* by R.A. Markus, 1994; *Augustine* by Mary T. Clark, 1994; *Augustine and the Arians: The Bishop of Hippo's Encounters with Ulfilan Arianism* by William A. Sumruld, 1994; *Augustine: His Thought in Context* by T. Kermit Scott, 1995; *Augustine's World: An Introduction to His Speculative Philosophy* by Donald X. Burt, 1996; *Love and Saint Augustine* by Hannah Arendt, 1996; *Church and Faith in the Patristic Tradition: Augustine, Pelagianism, and Early Christian Northumbria* by Gerald Bonner, 1996; *St. Augustine on Marriage and Sexuality*, edited by Elizabeth A. Clark, 1996; *The Shadows of Poetry: Vergil in the Mind of Augustine* by Sabine MacCormack, 1998; *Friendship and Society: An Introduction to Augustine's Practical Philosophy* by Donald X. Burt, 1999; *Saint Augustine* by Garry Wills, 1999; *Augustine in Iconography: History and Legend*, edited by Joseph C. Schnaubelt and Frederick Van Fleteren, 1999; *Augustine: The Scattered and Gathered Self* by Sandra Lee Dixon, 1999; *The Augustinian Tradition*, edited by Gareth B. Matthews, 1999; *Augustine of Hippo: A Biography* by Peter Brown, 2000; *Augustine: Christian Truth and Fractured Humanity* by Carol Harrison, 2000; *Augustine and Russian Orthodoxy: Russian Orthodox Theologians and Augustine of Hippo: A Twentieth Century Dialogue* by Myroslaw I. Tataryn, 2000; *The Cambridge Companion to Augustine*, edited by Eleonore Stump and Norman Kretzmann, 2001.

* * *

St. Augustine's works are characterized by their number and their variety. When he came to edit them at the end of his life he had 93 on his library shelves, not including vast numbers of letters and sermons as well as the numerous abandoned projects that littered his life. His writings chart the stages of his personal development, from ambitious young career-maker to international religious thinker and controversialist: he described himself as one who writes because he has made progress and who makes progress—by writing.

Augustine received the traditional late classical education in rhetoric, the influence of which is apparent in his love of sophisticated wordplay, paradox and contrast, vivid similes and verbal fireworks. His works show a precision in choice of words, a phenomenal memory for, and telling use of, both classical and scriptural quotations, and a mastery of dry irony and sarcasm. The abstract quality of his mind prevented him from dwelling on landscape or nature, but he was attracted by light, faces, music, and above all by the rhythms of speech. Augustine addressed in different capacities a diverse range of audiences and varied his style accordingly. Thus he composed the monumental and learned *De civitate Dei* (*The City of God*), with its expansive, orderly argumentation and sweeping periodic style; powerful, demagogic sermons with lapses into common parlance, the better to communicate with his congregation; letters to personal friends, officials of church and state, and a correspondence with St. Jerome notable for its tone of courteously veiled rancour; and outright ecclesiastical propaganda such as *De agone Christiano* (*On the Christian's Conflict*), written in deliberately simple Latin, and the literature attacking the Donatists, full of colloquialisms and popular jingles. Augustine was the only major Latin philosopher who never properly learned Greek, but he turned this seeming deficiency to advantage and ended by replacing the largely Greek culture of the contemporary church with his own works of scholarship, such as *De trinitate* (*On the Trinity*) and his commentary *De Genesi ad literam* [*On Genesis*]. Much of his philosophy was merely garnered from Cicero and translations of the Neo-Platonists, but with it Augustine transformed the shape of Latin Christianity.

Augustine's talents lie chiefly in self-justification and dialectic, and this is nowhere clearer than in *Confessiones* (*The Confessions*). This work, and the *Soliloquia* (*The Soliloquies*) preceding it, were startling innovations with their welding of classical and religious language and ideas and their ferocious self-analysis. *The Confessions* is not autobiography in the usual sense—Augustine wholly ignores such details as the number of his family, the name of the friend whose death caused him to flee to Carthage or of his faithful concubine who bore his son—rather it is an account of the emotional evolution of a relentless seeker after Truth and Perfection, an anatomy of the most well-documented conversion of antiquity. It is also the therapeutic self-reassessment of a man entering middle age and seeking to interpret his past from the viewpoint of a bishop of a provincial town on the frontiers of a collapsing empire. The public aspect of these preoccupations emerges in his polemical works against ecclesiastical opponents—Donatists, Pelagius, and Bishop Julian.

The climax of Augustine's career was the move outwards from himself and his community to address no less a task than the transformation of the secular pagan state. In *De doctrina Christiana* (*On Christian Doctrine*) he sought to strip the pagan gods and the empire itself of centuries of mystique. Finally, in *The City of God*, an outline for a theology of history depicting two cities—earthly and divine, of unbelief and of faith—Augustine exploited the resources given him by his education in the old tradition to transform it into a vehicle for the new.

—Claire E. Gruzelier

See the essays on *The City of God* and *Confessions*, Book I.

AURELIUS (ANTONINUS), Marcus

Born: Marcus Annius Verus in Rome, 26 April AD 121. **Family:** Married Annia Galeria Faustina in 145 (died 176); one daughter and one son. **Career:** Gained favour of Emperor Hadrian, who made him a Salian priest at age of 8, supervised his education, and arranged his marriage; adopted (as Marcus Aelius Aurelius Verus Caesar) by emperor designate Antoninus Pius in 138: quaestor in 139, consul with Antoninus Pius in 140, and also in 145 and 161; tribunicia potestas and proconsular imperium, the main formal powers of emperorship, conferred on him in 147; abandoned study of rhetoric about this time, and began study of philosophy; succeeded Antoninus Pius as emperor in 161, and elevated his fellow-consul for that year, Lucius Verus, to joint authority with himself (Verus died in 169); negotiated with German tribes in Aquileia, 168; fought the Marcomanni and Quadi, two Danube tribes, 170–74; visited Syria and Egypt to settle revolts, 175–76; raised his son Commodus to rank of Augustus, 177; fought the Marcomanni, 177–78. **Died:** 17 March AD 180.

PUBLICATIONS

Works

Meditations, edited by A.S.L. Farquharson. 2 vols., 1944 (includes translation); numerous subsequent translations including by C.R. Haines [Loeb Edition], 1930, G.M.A. Grube and Maxwell Staniforth, 1964, Roy Alan Lawes, 1984, Michael Chase, 1998.
Letters, edited by L. Pepe. 1957.
The Meditations and a Selection from the Letters of Marcus and Fronto, translated by A.S.L. Farquharson and R.B. Rutherford. 1989.

*

Critical Studies: *Marcus Aurelius: His Life and His World* by A.S.L. Farquharson, edited by D.A. Rees, 1951; *Marcus Aurelius: A Biography* by Anthony Birley, 1966, revised edition, 1987; *The Meditations of Marcus Aurelius: A Study* by R.B. Rutherford, 1989; *Logic and the Imperial Stoa* by Jonathan Barnes, 1997.

* * *

Marcus Aurelius' writings are unusual in the extant literature of the ancient world in being almost wholly personal documents, not intended for publication. He was a prolific letter writer, sometimes dispatching three notes to a friend in a single day, and there are about 200 letters still surviving. Many of these are preserved in the correspondence of Fronto, his tutor, for whom he shows great affection and concern. They date from between 139 and 166, when Fronto died, and shed passing illumination upon Marcus Aurelius' youthful enthusiasms, family concerns, and personal habits.

But his major work is that ''breviary for contemplatives'' which we call the *Meditations*, but should more correctly be translated (from the Greek) as *To Himself*. It consists of 12 books of unsystematic private reflections, addressed to himself in the second person like a dialogue, which lends itself to being sipped from time to time rather than drunk off in a draught. Historians concerned with facts are disappointed in their perusal of the *Meditations* since Marcus Aurelius makes little reference, except incidentally, to external events, and the books are consequently hard to date, beyond saying that they were largely written on campaign in the last ten years of his life. The present arrangement of the books is possibly not his own and certainly not chronological, since the first book, a summing up of all he owes to his family, friends, and associates, appears to have been written last. The manner of transmission is also uncertain—whether his notebooks were entrusted to his secretary's care or found among his papers after his death is not known—but there is little trace of organized editing since the work often progresses in a disconnected fashion from one topic to another and is full of repetitions and loose ends.

It is written in Greek, the language of upper-class, educated men. However, Marcus Aurelius abandoned rhetoric early in life, and his style, while being slightly old-fashioned and awkward, is plain and unadorned—an index of its private nature, but also of the character of the writer. He has a talent for epigrammatic brevity, and often resorts to quick enumeration of points as they occur to him, or even preserves straight lists of quotations from his reading of philosophers and poets. He has a quick eye for natural detail, such as the cracks in a loaf of baked bread or the way a sunbeam streams into a dark room, and his writing is full of brief, vivid similes showing an acute observation of the everyday scene like army surgeons' instruments, a fire burning a pile of rubbish, lotions and poultices for the sick, scuffling puppies, or fights in the arena. His comparisons are all drawn from war, dancing, wrestling, eating—the common occupations of life within his personal experience—and he employs certain predictable, recurring images: life as a road, time as a river, reason as a helmsman, the sphere as perfection.

Marcus Aurelius is not notable as an original thinker; he modestly considered scholarship and philosophy far above him. His attitude is mainly Stoic: a belief in calm acceptance of one's lot, a view of the world as a unified organism constantly changing and of the life spirit returning after death to the universal fire. But he read widely among different schools of philosophy and made his own choice influenced by his personal experience, transmuting pure Stoicism into an individual code for living, a code that in many ways prefigures Christianity.

The *Meditations* is a kind of spiritual last will and testament—the thoughts of an ill and ageing man aware of the increasing nearness of death and taking stock of what life has taught him: to accept himself, making a conscious effort to improve his failings, striving to assimilate the bad things that happen to good people as part of a universal plan of nature; to bear pain gracefully in the belief that there is a reason for suffering; to face the world with fortitude and his fellow man with understanding; to see man in his correct perspective in relation to the great universe as a transient piece of nothingness, so as to be able to accept approaching death as a small change and another of the processes of nature which is the universal lot of mankind.

Marcus Aurelius has often been accused of being a moral prig and a humbug, but it is obvious from his writings that he was a genuinely good man of sincere and sensitive character, conscious of his duties as emperor and military leader, who endured many personal griefs and public misfortunes and ended with a realistic, if melancholy, view of life—that one may not be rewarded for service or affection to others, but one does not cease to act according to personal canons of rightness because of this.

—Claire E. Gruzelier

See the essay on *Meditations*.

AUSONIUS, Decimus Magnus

Born: Burdigala (now Bordeaux, France) c. AD 310. **Education:** Educated in Burdigala and Tolosa (now Toulouse). **Family:** Married Lucana Sabina (died in childbirth); three children. **Career:** Taught grammar and rhetoric in Burdigala for 30 years; appointed tutor to Gratian, son of the Roman emperor Valentinian I: fought with both against the Alamanni, AD 368–69; on Gratian's accession, made prefect of Gaul and other provinces; consul by 379; retired to his Bordeaux estates after the murder of Gratian in 383. **Died:** c. AD 395.

PUBLICATIONS

Collections

[Works], edited by K. Schenkl. 2 vols., 1883, reprinted 1961; also edited by Rudolph S. Peiper, 1886, reprinted 1976, A. Pastorino, 1971, Sesto Prete, 1978, and R.P.H. Green, 1991; translated by Hugh G. Evelyn White [Loeb Edition], 2 vols., 1919–21.

Verse

Mosella, as *Die Mosella*, edited by Carl Hosius. 1894, 3rd edition, 1926; as *The Mosella*, translated by F.S. Flint, 1915; also translated by E.H. Blakeney, 1933.

*

Critical Studies: *Ausonius* by Evelyn Gurney, 1989; *Ausonius of Bordeaux: Genesis of a Gallic Aristocracy* by Hagith Sivan, 1993.

* * *

Ausonius of Bordeaux, a teacher of the Greek and Latin classics for some 40 years and after Gratian (his most famous pupil) became emperor, a powerful courtier for a further ten, is one of the most versatile and prolific writers of the 4th century AD. In his meticulous knowledge of the Latin classics, or the measured rhetoric of the speech that is his only surviving work in prose, the evidence of the schoolroom is seldom far away. However, his multifarious writings contain much that is refreshingly new. The range is very wide and is informed by a conviction that a wide variety of subjects were worthy of expression in verse. Most striking and appealing is his variety of intimately personal poetry: the poem on the birth of his new child, the *epicedion* (obituary) of his father, the poem of encouragement (*protrepticum*) to his grandson, and the poem about his inherited villa. Ausonius is not a profound thinker, nor does he probe deeply into his own feelings and experiences, least of all his experiences in political life. His 30 or so letters, for example, reveal little of substance. Where we see him faced with a real problem, such as the withdrawal of his favourite pupil Paulinus into monastic life, he adopts a distant style and takes refuge in the opacity of rhetoric, although it is clear that he saw no need to conceal his Christian beliefs. He wrote both Christian and pagan prayers, and, unusual for a man of this period, seems to have felt no tension between the old and the new.

His superficial experiences, whether as teacher, traveller, or family man, form the core of his poetry. He loves to record, to describe, and to enumerate. There is a poem on the leading cities of the Roman Empire, past and present—"Ordo Urbium Nobilium"; one on the emperors—"Caesares"—perhaps designed to extend into his own times; and there are fragments of one on the Roman consuls—"Fasti." A painting of Cupid in hell, which he saw in someone's dining room in Trier, was elaborated into the short poem "Cupido Cruciatus"; his masterpiece on the Moselle was also inspired by a prolonged stay in the area. His *Parentalia* is a series of recollections of departed relatives while his *Professores* commemorates deceased teachers and colleagues from the schools of Bordeaux and nearby towns. He appended to them a series of epitaphs of heroes and heroines from the Trojan War. Some of his more humble topics seem to derive if not from schoolroom diversions then from a schoolmaster's idea of fun. In the *Technopaegnion* all the lines end with a different monosyllable; the *Ludus Septem Sapientium* is a playlet in Plauto-Terentian form about the sayings of the Seven Sages: and the *Nuptial Cento* describes a wedding and the wedding-night by means of assorted lines and half-lines filched from Virgil. Ausonius is one of few poets to put mathematics into verse, and his miscellany of *Eclogues* is based to a large extent on pseudo-scientific material.

A lifelong student of the classics, Ausonius is adept at imitating and representing their forms and styles, and does so with taste and discrimination. After his *Epigrams*, perhaps his earliest work, and based on Greek models more than Roman ones, he tends to go his own way, weaving into his various poems passages in the style of epic, lyric, didactic, or satirical poetry, but seldom descending to pastiche. Particularly distinctive are his versified letters; part of a real correspondence, or two sequences in polymetric format, the *Daily Round*, an account of a typical day in his life, and *Bissula*, on a captive German girl who enthralled him. Both of these, though sadly curtailed in transmission, offer a succession of lively tableaux in changing metres. Even without them he would be one of ancient Rome's most metrically creative craftsmen.

Ausonius was a small-scale poet, with an outlook of limited depth, but one whose novelty of theme and originality of treatment combine to create a collection of surprises. His favoured register, certainly a constantly recurrent one, is a *humilitas* of style and tone which he sometimes exploits as a foil to his actual achievement but which is no doubt the way in which, for all his eminence, he wanted to be remembered. Nowhere is this clearer than in his preface to the general reader, a typical mix of modesty and pride. Just as the image of devoted family man and teacher, content with what he portrays as an average portion of worldly goods, makes a striking contrast with the external grandeur of his public career, so the unassuming tenor of much of Ausonius' verse is in marked antithesis to the love of the formal and spectacular which dominated the taste of his age.

—R.P.H. Green

See the essay on *The Mosella*.

AYALA, Ramón Pérez de

See PÉREZ DE AYALA, Ramón

AYMÉ, Marcel

Born: Joigny, France, 29 March 1902. **Education:** Educated at school in Dôle, 1910–19; Lycée Besançon, baccalauréat, 1919. **Military Service:** Served in the French army, 1922–23. **Family:** Married Marie-Antoinette Arnaud in 1927. **Career:** Lived in Germany, 1921–22; worked at a variety of jobs including reporter, clerk, translator, and film extra in Paris; wrote for various pro-German reviews during the Occupation, including *La Nouvelle Revue française*; visited the United States; contributed to *Collier's* magazine, New York, 1950. **Awards:** Prix de la Société des Gens de Lettres, 1926; Théophraste Renaudot prize, 1933. **Died:** 14 October 1967.

PUBLICATIONS

Collections

Oeuvres romanesques. 6 vols., 1977.
Oeuvres romanesques complètes, edited by Yves-Alain Favre. 1989.
[Novels and Stories]. 1991–.

Fiction

Brûdebois. 1926.
Aller retour. 1927.
Les Jumeaux du diable. 1928.
La Table-aux-crevés. 1929; as *The Hollow Field,* translated by Helen Waddell, 1933.
La Rue sans nom. 1930.
Le Vaurien. 1931.
Le Puits aux images (stories). 1932.
La Jument verte. 1933; as *The Green Mare,* translated by Norman Denny, 1955.
Les Contes du chat perché (stories; for children). 1934; as *The Wonderful Farm,* translated by Norman Denny, 1951.
Le Nain (stories). 1934.
Maison basse. 1935; as *The House of Men,* translated by Norman Denny, 1952.
Le Moulin de la Sourdine. 1936; as *The Secret Stream,* translated by Norman Denny, 1953.
Gustalin. 1937.
Derriére chez Martin (stories). 1938.
Le Boeuf clandestin. 1939.
La Belle Image. 1941; as *The Second Face,* translated by Norman Denny, 1951; as *The Grand Seduction,* translated by Denny, 1958.
Travelingue. 1941; as *The Miraculous Barber,* translated by Eric Sutton, 1950.
La Vouivre. 1943; as *The Fable and the Flesh,* translated by Eric Sutton, 1949.
Le Passe-muraille (stories). 1943; as *Across Paris and Other Stories,* translated by Norman Denny, 1950; as *The Walker-Through-Walls and Other Stories,* translated by Denny, 1950.
Traversée de Paris (stories). 1945.
Le Chemin des écoliers. 1946; as *The Transient Hour,* translated by Eric Sutton, 1948.
Le Vin de Paris (stories). 1947.
Uranus. 1948; as *The Barkeep of Blémont,* translated by Norman Denny, 1950; as *Fanfare in Blémont,* translated by Denny, 1950.
En arrière (stories). 1950.

Autres contes du chat perché (stories). 1950; as *Return to the Wonderful Farm,* translated by Norman Denny, 1954; as *The Magic Pictures: More About the Wonderful Farm,* translated by Denny, 1954.
Derniers contes du chat perché (stories). 1958.
Sorties de la ville et des champs. 1958.
Les Tiroirs de l'inconnu. 1960; as *The Conscience of Love,* translated by Norman Denny, 1962.
The Proverb and Other Stories, translated by Norman Denny. 1961.
Enjambées (stories). 1967.
L'Étrange, le merveilleux et le fantastique. 2 vols., 1983–84.
La Fille du shérif (stories), edited by Michel Lecureur. 1987.

Plays

Les Grandes Étapes, L'Image (produced 1933).
Vogue la galère (produced 1948). 1944.
Lucienne et le boucher. 1947.
Clérambard (produced 1950). 1950; as *Clérambard,* translated by Norman Denny, 1952.
La Tête des autres (produced 1952). 1952.
Les Quatre Vérités (produced 1954). 1954.
Les Sorcières de Salem, from a play by Arthur Miller. 1955.
Les Oiseaux de lune (produced 1955). 1956; as *Moonbirds,* translated by John Pauker, 1959.
La Mouche bleue (produced 1957). 1957.
Vu du pont, from a play by Arthur Miller. 1958.
Louisiane (produced 1961). 1961.
La Nuit de l'iguana, from a play by Tennessee Williams. 1962.
Les Maxibules (produced 1961). 1962.
Le Minotaure (produced 1966). With *Consommation* and *La Convention Belzébir,* 1967.
La Convention Belzébir (produced 1966). With *Le Minotaure* and *Consommation,* 1967.

Screenplays: *Le Club des soupirants,* 1936; *Madame et le mort* (adaptation by Aymé), 1942; *Désert vivant,* with others, 1954; *Papa, maman, la bonne et moi,* with others, 1954; *Papa, maman, ma femme et moi,* with others, 1955.

Other

Silhouette du scandale (essay). 1938.
Le Trou de la serrure (essays). 1946.
Le Confort intellectuel (essays). 1949.
Attente, Almanach du théâtre et du cinéma (autobiography). 1949.
Paris que j'aime, with Antoine Blondin, and Jean-Paul Clébert. 1956; as *The Paris I Love,* translated by Jean-Paul Clébert, 1963.
Images de l'amour. 1957.
L'Épuration et le délit d'opinion. 1968.
Marcel Aymé journaliste (articles), edited by M. Lecureur and Y.-A. Favre. 1988.
Du côté de chez Marianne: Chroniques 1933–1937, edited by Michel Lecureur. 1989.

*

Critical Studies: *Marcel Aymé ou, Le Paysan de Paris* by Jean Cathelin, 1958; *Marcel Aymé insolite* by Georges Robert and André Lioret, 1958; *Introduction à Aymé* by Pol Vandromme, 1960; *The Comic World of Marcel Aymé* by Dorothy Brodin, 1964; *Marcel*

Aymé et le merveilleux by Jean-Louis Dumont, 1970; *The Short Stories of Marcel Aymé*, 1980, and *Marcel Aymé*, 1987, both by Graham Lord; *Écriture et dérision: Le Comique dans l'oeuvre littéraire de Marcel Aymé* by Claude Dufresnoy, 1982; *L'Oeuvre de Marcel Aymé, de la quête du père au triomphe de l'écrivain* by Jean-Claude Veniel, 1990.

* * *

Marcel Aymé was born in 1902, in Joigny in the remote Jura region of France, the youngest of six children. Aymé's mother died when he was only two years old. His father placed the oldest children in boarding school and sent Marcel and his sister Suzanne to live with their maternal grandparents in the village of Villers-Robert near Dôle. He stayed there for six years and was then taken in by an aunt in Dôle. In later years he was always reluctant to talk much about his youth and childhood, but his philosophical attitudes in life (mainly characterized by sympathy for the underdog and a thirst for the truth underlying outward appearances) were shaped and formed during these early years. This experience of living in small towns and remote villages in close proximity to craftsmen and peasants would later have a strong influence on his work. What the sociologists call today ''la France profonde'' (the daily routine and belief system of provincial France which changes little over the decades as opposed to the instability and glitter of the Parisian spectacle), would become the stuff of much of his best work.

His first novel, *Brûlebois*, was followed by *La Table-auxcrevés* (*The Hollow Field*) and *La Jument verte* (*The Green Mare*). The action of each of these novels, set in his native Franche-Comté, portrays simple peasants and townspeople, republicans and clerics, humans and animals to convey his bittersweet view of life. These books use local linguistic terms and exploit regional folklore, including the marvellous and fantastic, to put across Aymé's essentially moderate conservative, commonsense view of life. *La Vouivre* (*The Fable and the Flesh*) is perhaps his best novel in this mode.

Aymé excelled in a number of different genres. Between 1926 and 1967, he wrote numerous novels and plays, three polemical essays and 83 short stories. He was also very active as a journalist throughout his career. Until 1944, the novel and short story were his preferred means of expression. But with the play *Vogue la galère*, written in the mid-1930s and published in 1944, his theatre career began. Astonishingly, Aymé never repeated himself. All of his works, especially the novels and plays, are quite different from each other.

In his novels, which dealt at first with rural people and then later with urban proletarians and sensitive political questions involving the politically potent Parisian bourgeoisie, Aymé sought to unmask hypocrisy, scandal, and the suppression of the truth. But when his novels showed how the Left could be as hypocritical as the Right, he began to find himself in trouble. His three novels of the 1930s and 1940s are unique in French literature and offer a revealing glimpse of what France was really like at this time. *Travelingue* (*The Miraculous Barber*), dealing with the era of the Popular Front, *Le Chemin des écoliers* (*The Transient Hour*), chronicling the early years of the Occupation, and *Uranus* (*The Barkeep of Blémont*), covering the end of the Occupation and Liberation, offer a view of these periods that is rich in complexity. Aymé's vision is a far cry from the simple-minded version presented in the press or, for that matter, by many academics. In the first of the three works Aymé sympathizes with the Left, but since he also applies the same moral yardstick in *The Barkeep of Blémont*, where he shows how the Communists and their Resistance friends simply replaced the Gestapo and the Wehrmacht after they came to power in 1944, he incurred the wrath of the politically powerful (*The Barkeep of Blémont* later became an internationally acclaimed film directed by Claude Béri in 1991). His essay *Silhouette du scandale*, published just before the war and generally overlooked at the time, can be read as an introduction to these novels. It lays bare the hypocrisy of successive governments of both Left and Right for the first 40 years of the century and is a masterpiece of understatement.

Since Aymé wrote and published in collaborationist newspapers during the war, the Comité National des Écrivains, largely dominated by Communists, resolved to settle accounts with him. Although he was not imprisoned, he was blacklisted. His fidelity to friends and personal courage were remarkable. He stood up for his friend Louis-Ferdinand Céline, as well as for the collaborationist writer Robert Brasillach, who was executed in February 1945 for having had incorrect political opinions during the war. Two years later, when Brasillach's brother-in-law, Maurice Bardèche, was censured for questioning the legality and fairness of the Nuremberg trials (*Nuremberg; ou, La Terre promise*, 1947), Aymé continued to support the principle that no writer should be punished for merely expressing an opinion. His voice was a lonely and courageous one at the time and, with the passage of time, we must admit largely a correct one. Aymé's courage in speaking out about the hypocrisy of the Left branded him as a voice of the Right. The tag has stuck with him ever since.

Aymé was unusually productive and successful as a short story writer. His 83 stories were published in seven main collections between 1932 and 1958, and he is widely recognized as one of the most important and versatile French short story writers of the 20th century. Like the novels, the stories treat rural and urban characters as well as the hypocrisy of the ruling classes. The style and tone of these pieces also vary widely, and include the use of dialectic terms and slang. Most successful of all are his children's stories built around the interaction of two little girls, Delphine and Marinette, with various representatives of the animal world.

After the war, a trip to the United States sponsored by *Collier's* magazine resulted in several stories that have never been studied seriously, but which reflect his reactions to American life and what Aymé took to be its materialism and hypocrisy (''Le Mendiant,'' ''Louisiane,'' ''La Mouche bleue'').

The first volume of the critical edition of Aymé's novels and stories appeared in the prestigious Éditions de la Pléiade in 1991. Inclusion in the Pléiade series is the highest practical form of recognition that a writer can receive in France. Serious research on his work will be possible in the years ahead. Certain stories, like ''Le Nouveau Passe-Muraille'' and the war-time trilogy, are truly masterpieces. He is one of the outstanding French fiction writers of the 20th century.

—David O'Connell

B

BABEL, Isaak (Emmanuilovich)

Born: Odessa, Ukraine, 13 July 1894. **Education:** Educated in Nikolaev; Nicholas I Commercial School, Odessa, 1905–11; Institute of Financial and Business Studies, Kiev, later in Saratov, 1911–15, graduated 1915. **Military Service:** Served in the army, 1917–18. **Family:** Married Evgeniia Gronfein in 1919, one daughter; also one daughter by Antonina Pirozhkova. **Career:** In St. Petersburg from 1918: worked on Gor'kii's, *q.v.*, magazine *Novaya Zhizn'* [New Life], 1918; editor, Ukrainian State Publishing House, 1919–20; news service correspondent with First Cavalry on the Polish campaign, 1920, and correspondent for *Tiflis* newspaper in Caucasus; in Moscow from 1923; secretary of the village soviet at Molodenovo, 1930; out of favour in the 1930s, and arrested, 1939; manuscripts confiscated, 1939. His exact fate remains unknown; probably shot soon after arrest. Posthumously cleared of charges against him, 1956. **Died:** (allegedly) 17 March 1941.

PUBLICATIONS

Collections

Collected Stories, edited and translated by Walter Morison. 1955.
Izbrannoe [Selected Works]. 1957; another edition, 1966.
Detstvo i drugie rasskazy [Childhood and Other Stories], edited by Efraim Sicher. 1979.
Izbrannye proizvedeniia [Selected Works]. 2 vols., 1988.
Sochineniia [Works], edited by A.N. Pirozhkova. 2 vols., 1990.
Collected Stories, translated by David McDuff. 1994.
The Complete Works of Isaak Babel, edited by Nathalie Babel, translated with notes by Peter Constantine. 2002.

Fiction

Rasskazy [Stories]. 1925.
Konarmiia (stories). 1926; revised edition, 1931; edited by C.D. Luck, 1994; as *Red Cavalry*, translated by N. Helstein, 1929; also translated by John Harland, 1929.
Bluzhdaiushchie zvezdy: Rasskaz dlia kino [Wandering Stars: A Cine-Story]. 1926.
Istoriia moei golubiatni [The Story of My Dovecote]. 1926.
Benia Krik: Kinopovest. 1926; as *Benia Krik: A Film-Novel*, translated by Ivor Montague and S.S. Nolbandov, 1935.
Korol' [The King]. 1926.
Odesskie rasskazy [Odessa Stories]. 1931.
Benya Krik, The Gangster, and Other Stories, edited by Avrahm Yarmolinsky. 1948.
Lyubka the Cossack and Other Stories, edited and translated by Andrew R. MacAndrew. 1963.
The Lonely Years 1925–29: Unpublished Stories and Private Correspondence, edited by Nathalie Babel, translated by Max Hayward and Andrew R. MacAndrew. 1964.
You Must Know Everything: Stories 1915–1937, edited by Nathalie Babel, translated by Max Hayward. 1969.

The Forgotten Prose, edited and translated by Nicholas Stroud. 1978; as *Zabytyi Babel*, 1979.

Plays

Zakat (produced 1927). 1928; as *Sunset*, translated by Raymond Rosenthal and Mirra Oinsburg, in *Noonday 3*, 1960.
Mariia (produced 1964). 1935; as *Marya*, translated by Michael Glenny and Harold Shukman, in *Three Soviet Plays*, edited by Glenny, 1966.

Other

1920 Diary, edited and with introduction and notes by Carol J. Avins, translated by H.T. Willetts. 1995.
At His Side: The Last Years of Isaac Babel by A.N. Pirozhkova, translated by Anne Frydman and Robert L. Busch. 1996.

*

Critical Studies: *The Art of Isaac Babel* by Patricia Carden, 1972; *Isaak Babel* by Richard W. Hallett, 1972; *Isaac Babel, Russian Master of the Short Story* by James E. Falen, 1974; *An Investigation of Composition and Theme in Babel's Literary Cycle "Konarmija"* by Ragna Grøngaard, 1979; *Isaac Babel's Red Cavalry* by Carol Luplow, 1982; *Metaphor in Babel's Short Stories* by Danuta Mendelsohn, 1982; "Art as Metaphor, Epiphany, and Aesthetic Statement: The Short Stories of Babel," in *Modern Language Review*, 1982, "The Road to a Red Cavalry: Myth and Mythology in the Works of Babel," in *Slavonic and East European Review*, 1982, and *Style and Structure in the Prose of Isaak Babel*, 1986, all by Efraim Sicher; *The Place of Space in Narration: A Semiotic Approach to the Problem of Literary Space, with an Analysis of the Role of Space in Isaak Babel's Konarmija* by J.J. von Baak, 1983; *Isaac Babel* by Milton Ehre, 1986; *Isaac Babel* edited by Harold Bloom, 1987: *The Field of Honour* by C.D. Luck, 1987; *Procedures of Montage in Isaak Babel's Red Cavalry* by Marc Schreurs, 1989; *Isaac Babel and His Film Work* by Jerry Heil, 1990; "A Poetic Inversion: The Non-Dialogic Aspect in Isaac Babel's *Red Cavalry*" by David K. Danow, in *Modern Language Review*, 86(4), 1991; *The Dionysian Art of Isaac Babel* by Robert Mann, 1994; *Red Calvary: A Critical Companion*, edited by Charles Rougle, 1996.

* * *

Isaak Babel is, along with Zamiatin and Olesha, an outstanding exponent of short prose of the decade or so in which, following 1917, modernist experimentation flourished in Soviet Russian fiction.

Babel's work is notable for its treatment of Jewish and revolutionary themes and for its cultivation of the "cycle" form: an open-ended series of short stories, linked by theme, character, setting, and imagery, with additions being made at will—e.g., that of "Argamak" (1931) to *Konarmiia* (*Red Cavalry*), 1926, with "The Kiss" (1937) and further (unwritten) stories possibly being intended for the same sequence.

Red Cavalry, Babel's best known work, deals by unusual techniques of snapshot and montage (Babel enjoyed close associations with the film industry) with the fortunes of Budenny's First Cavalry in the Polish campaign of 1920. A series of 35 "miniatures" examines the nature and ethics of personal and revolutionary violence, portraying a Jewish intellectual's quest for true fraternity amid Cossack fellow soldiers and assorted Jews, Poles, and peasants. Violence, sex, art, and nature are treated in rhythmic prose and striking images. Ambiguity, paradox and polarity, and the use of subsidiary narrators are key devices. Actions and perceptions are presented subjectively in an interplay of varied points of view underlined by use of metaphor; interpretations and judgements are left to the reader.

Other, less complete, main cycles ("definitively" ordered by Sicher in his 1979 edition) are set in the Jewish "Moldavanka" of Odessa. *Odesskie rasskazy* [Odessa Stories] features the exploits of Benia Krik (modelled on the real Mishka-Iaponchik), while the "early childhood" series, collected under the title *Istoriia moei golubiatni* [The Story of My Dovecote], concentrate on Jewish upbringing amid the pogroms of 1905.

The degree of overall unity varies, as much for biographical as for artistic reasons. *Red Cavalry*, with its clear time span and largely sequential plot development, can be viewed as an episodic modernist novel (Mendelson, 1982) or as "a 20th-century version of a Renaissance novella cycle" (Lowe, 1982). Important "independent" stories are "Line and Colour" (1923) and "Guy de Maupassant" (1932). However, the all-pervading presence of a purportedly autobiographical or obviously Babelian narrator suggests the possibility of considering Babel's short fictional *oeuvre* as a unit—a single collective "super-cycle."

Compression, to achieve a close organic unity of form and content, is the essence of Babel's compositional method. Plays and film scenarios apart, few of Babel's stories exceed ten pages. "A truly cautious master" (Mendelson), Babel re-worked his stories tirelessly, pruning every spare word, tightening paragraphing and punctuation. The resulting language is frequently called "a collision of styles"; words and their associations are foregrounded rather than the ideas behind them, while Babel's constant switches in modes of narrative discourse create a calculated role for the reader.

Babel was again neglected in the Soviet Union during the Brezhnev period, no edition of his works appearing after 1966. However, recent western studies (notably by Mendelson and Sicher) have advanced Babel criticism onto promising new ground, while the Gorbachev era supplied a two-volume "Selected Works" in 1988.

—Neil Cornwell

See the essay on *Red Cavalry*.

BACHMANN, Ingeborg

Born: Klagenfurt, Austria, 25 June 1926. Spent her childhood in Carinthia. **Education:** Educated at co-educational high school until 1938, girls' school, 1938–44; studied philosophy at Graz, Innsbruck, and Vienna universities, Ph.D. in philosophy 1950. **Family:** Lived with the composer, Hans Werner Henze, 1953–56; the writer, Max Frisch, *q.v.*, 1958–62. **Career:** Script writer and editor, Rot-Weiss-Rot radio station, Vienna, 1951–53; freelance writer in Ischia, Naples, Rome, and Munich, 1953–57, visited the United States in 1955; lived in Rome and Zurich, 1958–62, West Berlin, 1963–65, Rome, from 1965; visiting lecturer on poetics, Frankfurt University, 1959–60. **Awards:** Gruppe 47 prize, 1953; Culture Circle of German Industry literature award, 1955; Bremen prize, 1957; Association of German Critics literary award, 1961; Büchner prize, 1964; Great Austrian State prize, 1968; Wildgans prize, 1971. **Died:** 17 October 1973.

PUBLICATIONS

Collections

Werke, edited by Christine Koschel, Inge von Weidenbaum, and Clemens Münster. 4 vols., 1978.
Sämtliche Erzählungen. 1980.
Sämtliche Gedichte. 1983.
In the Storm of Roses: Selected Poems, edited and translated by Mark Anderson. 1986.
Selected Prose and Drama by Ingeborg Bachmann and Christa Wolf, edited by Patricia A. Herminghouse. 1998.

Verse

Die gestundete Zeit. 1953.
Anrufung des grossen Bären. 1956.
Gedichte: Eine Auswahl. 1966.
Die Gedichte. 1980.

Fiction

Das dreissigste Jahr (stories). 1961; revised edition 1966; as *The Thirtieth Year*, translated by Michael Bullock, 1964.
Malina. 1971; as *Malina*, translated by Philip Boehm, 1989.
Simultan (stories). 1972; as *Three Paths to the Lake*, translated by Mary Fran Gilbert, 1972.
Undine geht: Erzählungen. 1973; as "Undine Departs," translated by Cedric Hentschel, in *German Short Stories*, 1975.
Meisterzählungen. 1974.
Der Tag des Friedens. 1976.
Der Fall Franza. Requiem für Fanny Goldmann. 1979; as *The Book of Franza and Requiem for Fanny Goldmann*, translated with introduction by Peter Filkins, 1999.
Die Fähre. 1982.

Plays

Der Idiot, music by Hans Werner Henze (produced 1952). 1955.
Der gute Gott von Manhattan. 1958.
Der Prinz von Homburg (opera libretto), music by Hans Werner Henze, from the play by Heinrich von Kleist (produced 1960). 1960.
Der junge Lord (opera libretto), music by Hans Werner Henze (produced 1965). 1965; as *The Young Milord*, translated by Eugene Walter, 1967.

Die Hörspiele (radio plays; includes *Ein Geschäft mit Träumen; Die Zikaden; Der gute Gott von Manhattan*). 1976.

Radio Plays: *Ein Geschäft mit Träumen*, 1952; *Das Herrschaftshaus*, 1952; *Herrenhaus*, 1954; *Die Zikaden*, 1955; *Der gute Gott von Manhattan*, 1958.

Other

Jugend in einer österreichischen Stadt (memoir). 1961.
Gedichte, Erzählungen, Hörspiele, Essays. 1964.
Ein Ort für Zufälle. 1965.
Frankfurter Vorlesungen: Probleme zeitgenössischer Dichtung. 1980.
Die Wahrheit ist dem Menschen zumutbar: Essays, Reden, kleinere Schriften. 1981.
Das Honditschkreuz. 1983.
Wir müssen wahre Sätze finden: Gespräche und Interviews, edited by Christine Koschel and Inge von Weidenbaum. 1983.
Liebe: Dunkler Erdteil. Gedichte aus den Jahren 1942–1967. 1984.
Anrufung der grossen Dichterin (essays). 1984.
Translator, *Gedichte: italienisch und deutsch*, by Giuseppe Ungaretti. 1961.
Translator, with others, *Italienische Lyrik des 20. Jahrhunderts*, edited by Christine Wolter. 1971.
Translator, with others, *Freude der Schiffbrüche*, edited by Christine Wolter. 1977.

*

Bibliography: *Ingeborg Bachmann: Eine Bibliographie* by Otto Bareiss and Frauke Ohloff, 1978.

Critical Studies: *Ingeborg Bachmann: Die Auflösung der Figur in ihrem Roman Malina* by Ellen Summerfield, 1976; *Malina. Versuch einer Interpretation des Romans von Ingeborg Bachmann* by Robert Steiger, 1978; *Women Writers—The Divided Self: Analysis of Novels by Christa Wolf, Ingeborg Bachmann, Doris Lessing and Others* by Inta Ezergailis, 1982; *Der dunkle Schatten, dem ich schon seit Anfang folge. Ingeborg Bachmann. Vorschläge zu einer neuen Lektüre des Werks* edited by Hans Höller, 1982; *Ingeborg Bachmann* by Kurt Bartsch, 1988; *Ingeborg Bachmann* by Peter Beicken, 1988; *The Voice of History: An Exegesis of Selected Short Stories from Ingeborg Bachmann's Das dreissigste Jahr and Simultan from the Perspective of Austrian History* by Lisa de Serbine Bahrway, 1989; *Understanding Ingeborg Bachmann* by Karen R. Achberger, 1995; *Waking the Dead: Correspondences Between Walter Benjamin's Concept of Remembrance and Ingeborg Bachmann's Ways of Dying* by Karen Remmler, 1996; *Thunder Rumbling at My Heels: Tracing Ingeborg Bachmann*, edited and with introduction by Gudrun Brokoph-Mauch, 1998; *The Split Scene of Reading: Nietzsche/Derrida/Kafka/Bachmann* by Sabine I. Golz, 1998.

* * *

Ingeborg Bachmann first made her name as a poet with the collections *Die gestundete Zeit* [The Respite] and *Anrufung des grossen Bären* [Invocation of the Great Bear]. Her poems reveal discontent with present time and a utopian vision of a different world, often conveyed through metaphor or paradox; an awareness of the limitations imposed by language; and a sense of the precariousness of human existence, reflecting the influence of existentialism on her writing in the 1950s, as in the poem "The Respite":

> Do not look round
> Tie your shoelace
> Drive back the dogs.
> Throw the fishes into the sea.
> Put out the lupins!
> A harder time is coming.

(translated by Michael Hamburger)

In later years, Bachmann expounded her ideas mainly in prose fiction. Important themes are individual identity, possibilities for change, and the role of language. In the title story of the collection *Das dreissigste Jahr* (*The Thirtieth Year*), a man, in the year preceding his 30th birthday, decides it is time for a new departure. He relinquishes his home and his job and sets out to see the world and to find himself, realizing that this may be his last chance to make substantial changes to the pattern of his life. Eventually he returns, having realized, in Bachmann's famous formulation, that there can be "no new world without a new language." The insight that substantive change is not possible, together with a near escape from death, results in increased awareness of his own existence and in acceptance of life as it is. Reluctance to admit human imperfection, and the final acknowledgement of it, is also a theme of the story "Everything." A father attempts to prevent his son from acquiring a corrupt colloquial language, on the assumption that if the child developed his own language instead he would retain his original purity, innocence, and natural creativity. However, far from being innocent, his son contains the seeds of moral rottenness, as is conveyed metaphorically by his death caused by a brain tumour.

In most of these early stories the narrative centres on a male character, but there are two significant exceptions which address themselves specifically to women's predicament. "Undine geht" ("Undine Departs") reworks the myth of the water spirit Undine, who was permitted to join her male lover on land only if she accepted great physical suffering. Bachmann treats Undine's torment as a metaphor for women's suffering at the hands of men. In "A Step Towards Gomorrah," the problem of women's relations with men is made more explicit, when Charlotte, an artist, is presented with the possibility of experiencing new and different types of relationships. When a younger woman, Mara, attempts to lure her into a sexual relationship, Charlotte momentarily glimpses an alternative to her present problems and constraints. However, this possibility remains merely theoretical and the story ends, like other stories in the collection, in resignation.

In the novel *Malina*, the question of the identity of a woman artist becomes central and is presented in a narrative of great structural complexity. From a first-person perspective, the novel depicts a woman writer's struggle with various dimensions of patriarchal society. Her emotional life is elucidated through her relationship with her elusive lover, Ivan; her intellectual struggle is represented by the mysterious figure of Malina, her alter ego, with whom she shares her flat. The conflicting aspects represented by these two men are necessary to her survival as an artist. In the central section of the novel, entitled "The Third Man," another dimension is invoked, as the narrator experiences nightmares about her father—he appears in the guise of a Nazi doctor and mistreats her as one of his victims. The problem of the woman artist is thereby associated with the idea of oppression in a historical and social context. Finally, in a metaphorically suggestive ending, the narrator, abandoned by Ivan and maltreated by Malina and her ''father,'' disappears ''into the wall,'' as if transcending natural boundaries, but with little suggestion that this process leads in a more positive direction.

The later collection of stories *Simultan* (*Three Paths to the Lake*) depicts female figures from different facets of Viennese society. In the title story, Bachmann again takes up the problem of language and identity, now placed in a professional context. The central figure, Nadja, an interpreter, is estranged from her Viennese roots and her native language by her profession, which involves her constantly using other people's words and foreign languages, but rarely her own. This predicament acts as a metaphor for her crisis about her own identity, something which she partially succeeds in resolving when she takes a holiday with a fellow Viennese and is enabled to confront emotional issues in her own language. Her new insight is however achieved at considerable cost, as she is compelled to accept her professional and personal limitations. The wider perspective given by this analysis of professional life is also apparent in ''The Barking,'' in which a psychiatrist, Leo Jordan, appears to use professional authority and jargon as a means of refusing to face his own complicity regarding the Nazi past. This attitude towards society at large is reflected in Jordan's lack of responsibility towards his own family. Bachmann's critique emerges through the relationship which develops between his mother and his wife, who, though victims of his behaviour, also connive with it.

Apart from these major works, Bachmann left an unfinished novel, *Der Fall Franza* [Franza's Case], in which she attempts to relate the oppression of women by men to the processes underlying imperialism and fascism. The wide range of her writing also includes some successful radio plays broadcast in the 1950s. In partnership with the composer Hans Werner Henze, she wrote opera libretti, including *Der Prinz von Homburg*, from the play by Heinrich von Kleist. Her essays on literary and philosophical topics, collected after her death under the title *Die Wahrheit ist dem Menschen zumutbar* [Truth Can Be Expected], both shed light on her own writing and have been influential to other writers, notably the East German Christa Wolf.

—Juliet Wigmore

BAI JUYI

Also known as Po Chü-i. **Pseudonym:** Xiangshan. **Born:** Xinzheng, Henan province, China, in 772. **Education:** Passed provincial examinations in 799 and imperial examinations in 800; also received instruction at a Buddhist monastery. **Family:** Married. **Career:** Began career as an imperial official in Chang'an (the capital city), 801; moved to a minor county post, 806; passed State exams, and returned to Chang'an as official censor, 808; resided at Xiagui, in mourning for his mother, 811–14; exiled from Chang'an, after his criticism of official corruption, 815, but soon rehabilitated; recalled to Chang'an, 820, and was then appointed to various offical portfolios: Supervisor of Royal Documents, 820, Prefect of Hanzhou, 822, Prefect of Suzhou, 825, Chief Magistrate, Henan province, 831, and

Minister of Justice, 842; retired from official posts, 842. **Member:** Hanlin Literary Academy, 807. **Died:** 846.

PUBLICATIONS

Verse

Baishi Changqing ji [Collected Works]. Edited by Wang Liming (includes 2,900 poems), 1702; modern edition, 4 vols., 1979; as *Translations from Po Chü-i's Collected Works*, translated by Howard S. Levy, 4 vols., 1971–75; selections in: *170 Chinese Poems*, 1918, and *More Translations from the Chinese*, 1919, both translated by Arthur Waley (reissued together as *Chinese Poems*, 1946); *In the Jade Mountain*, translated by W. Bynner and Kiang Kang-hu, 1929; *The Everlasting Woe*, translated by Tai Jen, 1939; *The White Pony*, translated by R. Payne, 1949; *Gems of Chinese Literature*, translated by A. Giles, 1965; *The Selected Poems of Po Chü-i*, translated by David Hinton, 1999; *Po Chü-i: Selected Poems*, translated by Burton Watson, 2000.

Other

Po Chü-i as a Censor: His Memorials Presented to Emperor Hsientsung During the Years 808–810, translated by Eugene Feifel. 1961.

*

Critical Study: *The Life and Times of Po Chü-i* by Arthur Waley, 1949.

* * *

Poetry flourished during the Chinese Tang dynasty, and among 2,000 or so Tang poets, Bau Juyi enjoys world renown and ranks next to Du Fu and Li Bai.

Bai Juyi was born into a minor official's family and was a precocious boy. As he explained in a letter to his friend Yuan Zhen, he understood some written characters at the age of six or seven months and had mastered Chinese phonology when he was only nine years old. As a teenager he took to writing, and his poem ''The Grass on Ancient Plain,'' written around the age of 15, won him considerable fame. In his early days he moved from place to place with his father, who was transferred at the order of the Emperor. Bai Juyi's life spanned the reign of six emperors, and from childhood he witnessed the political upheaval and decline of the once strong and unified Tang Empire. At 12 he had to leave Central China for South China to seek refuge from the war. Here he tried unsuccessfully to win an official post through the civil examination but instead won fourth place in the highest imperial court examination at the age of 29 and was given a minor post in a county in 806. Disappointed as he was, it gave him opportunity to see the corruption of the Tang bureaucrats and the sufferings of the common people. During that short period he wrote well-known poems such as *Chang hen ge* (*The Everlasting Woe*) and ''Watching the Wheat-Reapers.'' He was summoned to Chang'an, the capital, in 807 and appointed, after further examinations, to various posts in the court. This gave him access to the Emperor and enabled him to experience at close quarters the political schemes and extravagant life at the palace. His duty was to give advice and present memorials to the Emperor, and he wrote into his poems what the memorials could not express in explicit terms. Most of these poems are included in what he called "satires": his satirical poems are exposés of the corruption and decadence of government officials. In his letter to Yuan Zhen he claimed, "When the influential nobles and Emperor's favourites at court heard my *Songs of Qin*, they changed their countenance, looking at one another; when the persons holding office heard my poem 'Delightful Garden,' they sighed; when the chiefs of the army heard my poem 'Lodged in Purple Tower Mountain Village,' they gnashed their teeth in hatred." His suggestion for redressing malpractice and corruption offended court officials and even the Emperor; consequently he lost favour and was banished from the capital on charges made up by his opponents. This was the turning point in his life and he asked to leave to avoid the conflicts among the bureaucrats, and he took up the governorship first in Hangzhou, and later in Suzhou. In later years he pursued a reclusive lifestyle until his death.

Bai Juyi was a prolific poet. His extant poems, about 3,000, outnumber the works of any other Tang poet. He classified his works as poems of satire, leisure, sentiment, and miscellaneous *lüshi* ("standard" poems with eight lines, each having five or seven characters, and with a strict tonal and rhyme pattern). However, this classification was not strictly observed. He attached great importance to content in poetry. His "New Yuefu Ballads" and "Songs of Qin" are representative of satirical poems which, as he put it, "aim at remedying social faults and prevailing wrongs." "The Charcoal-seller" describes the bitter life of a charcoal burner and exposes with fury the extortion of court officials: "A whole wagon of charcoal,/ more than a thousand catties! If the officials choose to take it away,/the woodman may not complain" (translated by Arthur Waley). "The Old Man with the Broken Arm" condemns the war imposed by Prime Minister Yang through the heartbreaking narrative of an old man who, at the age of 24, broke his arm with a huge stone in order to escape being conscripted. Among his poems of sentiment, "Chang hen ge" and "Piba xing" [Lute Song], the best-known of all his works, are facile in style and appealing in narrative. His leisure poems are lyric poetry written in his own style and tinged, sometimes, with Buddhism and Daoism. His miscellaneous *lüshi* account for about two-thirds of his poems, "The Grass on Ancient Plain" mentioned above being one of the representative works of this kind.

Bai was a poet of genius who inherited the legacy of classical Chinese literature and also learned from folk literature. On the other hand, he was creative and formed a distinctive style of his own. His language was plain, which helps to contribute much to his popularity. As he said in the aforementioned letter to Yuan Zhen, his poems were "inscribed on the walls of country schools, temples, inns, and travelling ships." And Yuan Zhen confirmed in the "Preface to Bai Juyi's Works" that Bai's poems were widely read and frequently on the lips of kings, princes, concubines, ladies, and grooms. His poems were circulated in Japan and Korea during his lifetime and are said to have been copied and read by the then Japanese king. Indeed, he has enjoyed high national as well as international renown to this day.

—Binghong Lu

BALZAC, Honoré de

Born: Tours, France, 20 May 1799. **Education:** Educated at pension Le Guay-Pinel, Tours, 1804–07; Collège de Vendome, 1807–13;

L'Institution Lepître, Paris, 1815; L'Institution Ganzer et Beuzelin, Paris, 1815–16; attended law lectures, the Sorbonne, Paris, baccalauréat of law 1819. **Family:** Married Mme. Hanska (Eve Rzewuska) in 1850. **Career:** Clerk for M. Guillonnet de Merville, 1816–18, and M. Passez, 1818–19; then writer, editor, magazine writer: obtained printer's license, 1826–28; owner, *La Chronique de Paris*, 1835–36; editor, *La Revue Parisienne*, 1840. President, Société des Gens de Lettres, 1839. **Awards:** Chevalier, Légion d'honneur, 1845. **Died:** 18 August 1850.

PUBLICATIONS

Collections

Oeuvres complètes, edited by Marcel Bouteron and Henri Longnon. 40 vols., 1912–40.
La Comédie humaine, edited by Marcel Bouteron. 11 vols., 1951–58; revised edition, edited by Pierre-George Castex and Pierre Citron, 1976–.
The Human Comedy, edited by George Saintsbury. 40 vols., 1895–98.
Works. 1901.

Fiction

L'Héritage de Birague, with Le Poitevin de Saint-Alme and Etienne Arago. 1822.
Jean-Louis; ou, La Fille trouvée, with Le Poitevin de Saint-Alme. 1822.
Clotilde de Lusignan; ou, Le beau juif. 1822.
Le Centenaire; ou, Les Deux Beringheld. 1822; as *Le Sorcier*, in *Oeuvres complètes de Horace de Saint-Aubin*, 1837.
Le Vicaire des Ardennes. 1822.
La Dernière Fée; ou, La Nouvelle Lampe merveilleuse. 1823.
Annette et le criminel. 1824.
Wann-Chlore. 1825; as *Jane la pâle*, in *Oeuvres complètes*, 1836.
Le Dernier Chouan; ou, Le Bretagne au 1800. 1829; revised edition, as *Les Chouans; ou, Le Bretagne en 1799*, 1834; as *Le Chouan*, 1838; as *The Chouans*, translated by George Saintsbury, 1890.
Mémoires pour servir à l'histoire de la révolution française, with Lheritier de l'Ain. 1829.
La Physiologie du mariage; ou, Méditations de philosophie éclectique. 1829; as *The Physiology of Marriage*, 1904; with introduction by Sharon Marcus, 1997.
Scènes de la vie privée. 1830; enlarged edition, 1832.
Le Peau de chagrin. 1831; edited by S. de Sasy, 1974; as *The Magic Skin*, 1888; as *The Wild Ass's Skin*, translated by Ellen Marriage, in *The Human Comedy*, 1895–98; as *The Heartless Woman*, translated by Owen Snell, 1945; as *The Fatal Skin*, translated by Cedar Paul, 1946.
Romans et contes philosophiques. 1831.
Contes bruns, with Philarète Chasles and Charles Rabou. 1832.
Les Salmigondis: Contes de toutes les couleurs. 1832; as *La Comtesse à deux maris*, in *Scènes de la vie privée*, 1835; as *Le Colonel Chabert*, in *Comédie humaine*, 1844; as *Colonel Chabert*, translated by Carol Cosman, 1997.
Les Cent Contes drôlatiques. 3 (of an intended 10) vols., 1832–37; *Quatrième dixain* (fragments), 1925; as *Contes drôlatiques*, translated by George R. Sims, 1874; as *Droll Stories*, translated anonymously, 1948; Alec Brown, 1958.
Nouveaux contes philosophiques. 1832.

Le Médecin de campagne. 1833; excerpt, as *Histoire de Napoléon*, 1833; edited by Patrick Barthier, 1974.

Études de moeurs au XIXe siècle. 12 vols., 1833–37; includes reprints and the following new works:

   La Fleur des pois. 1834.

   La Recherche de l'absolu. 1834; as *Balthazar; or, Science and Love*, translated by William Robson, 1859; as *The Alchemist*, 1861; as *The Quest of the Absolute*, translated by Ellen Marriage, in *The Human Comedy*, 1895–98; as *The Tragedy of a Genius*, translated by Henry Blanchamp, 1912.

   Eugénie Grandet. 1833; as *Eugenie Grandet*, translated anonymously, 1859; several subsequent translations including by E.K. Brown, with *Père Goriot*, 1950; Marion Ayton Crawford, 1955; Henry Reed, 1964; as *Eugénie Grandet*, translated by Sylvia Raphael, 1990.

   La Femme abandonnée. 1833.

   La Grenadière. 1833.

   L'Illustre Gaudissart. 1833.

   Les Marana. 1834.

   Histoire des treize. 1834–35; as *History of the Thirteen*, translated by Herbert J. Hunt, 1974; translated in part by Lady Knutsford, as *The Mystery of the Rue Soly*, 1894; *The Girl with the Golden Eyes*, translated by Ernest Dowson, 1896; *The Duchess of Langeais*, translated by D. Mitford, 1946.

   La Vieille Fille. 1837.

   Illusions perdues (part I: *Les Deux Poètes*). 1837.

Le Père Goriot. 1835; as *Daddy Goriot*, translated anonymously, 1860; as *Père Goriot*, translated 1886, and by E.K. Brown, with *Eugenie Grandet*, 1950; as *Old Goriot*, translated by Ellen Marriage, in *The Human Comedy*, 1895–98, and by Marion Ayton Crawford, 1951; as *Old Man Goriot*, translated by Joan Charles, 1949, and by Minot Sedgwick, 1950; as *Le Père Goriot*, translated by A.J. Krailsheimer, 1991; translated by Burton Raffel, 1994.

Le Livre mystique (includes *Louis Lambert* and *Séraphita*). 1835; translated as *Louis Lambert* and *Seraphita*, 2 vols., 1889.

Études philosophiques. 20 vols., 1835–40; includes reprints and the following new works:

   Un drame au bord de la mer. 1835.

   Melmoth réconcilié. 1836.

   L'Interdiction. 1836.

   La Messe de l'Athée. 1837.

   Facino cane. 1837.

   Les Martyrs ignorés. 1837.

   Le Secret des Ruggieri. 1837.

   L'Enfant maudit. 1837.

   Une passion dans le désert. 1837.

Le Lys dans la vallée. 1836; as *The Lily of the Valley*, translated by Lucienne Hill, 1891.

L'Excommuniée, with Auguste de Belloy, in *Oeuvres complètes de Horace de Saint-Aubin.* 1837.

La Femme supérieure. 1837; as *Les Employés*, 1865; as *Bureaucracy*, 1889; as *The Bureaucrats*, translated by Charles Foulkes, 1993.

Histoire de César Birotteau. 1838; as *History of the Grandeur and Downfall of Cesar Birotteau*, 1860; as *The Bankrupt*, translated by Frances Frenaye, 1959; as *Cesar Birotteau*, translated by Robin Buss, 1993; also translated by Graham Robb, 1994.

Le Femme supérieure, La Maison Nucingen, La Torpille. 1838.

Les Rivalités en province. 1838; as *Le Cabinet des antiques* (includes *Gamara*), 1839; as *The Jealousies of a Country Town*, in *The Human Comedy*, 1895–98.

Gambara; Adieu. 1839; translated as *Gambara*, in *The Human Comedy*, 1895–98.

Une fille d'Eve (includes *Massimilla Doni*). 1839; as *A Daughter of Eve* and *Massimilla Doni*, in *The Human Comedy*, 1895–98.

Un grand homme de province à Paris (Illusions perdues II). 1839; as *A Great Man of the Provinces in Paris*, 1893.

Béatrix; ou, Les Amours forcées. 1839; edited by Madeleine Fergeaud, 1979; as *Beatrix*, translated by Rosamund and Simon Harcourt-Smith, 1895.

Pierrette. 1840; translated as *Pierrette*, 1892.

Physiologie de l'employé. 1841.

Physiologie du rentier de Paris et de province, with Arnould Frémy. 1841.

Le Curé de village. 1841; as *The Country Parson*, translated anonymously, in *The Human Comedy*, 1895–98.

Oeuvres complètes: La Comédie humaine, 20 vols., 1842–53; includes reprints and the following new works:

   Albert Savarus. 1842; as *Albert Savarus*, translated by Ellen Marriage, 1892, and by Kathleen Raine, 1951.

   Autre étude de femme. 1842.

   Illusions perdues (part III). 1843; parts I and III translated as *Lost Illusions*, 1893.

   Esquisse d'homme d'affaires; Gaudissart II; Les Comédiens sans le savoir. 1846.

   Un épisode sous la terreur; L'Envers de l'histoire contemporain; Z; Marcas. 1846; *L'Envers. . .* translated as *Love*, 1893.

Ursule Mirouët. 1842; as *Ursula*, translated by Clara Bell, 1891; also translated by Donald Adamson, 1976.

Scènes de la vie privée et publique des animaux. 1842.

Mémoires de deux jeunes mariées. 1842; as *Memoirs of Two Young Married Women*, 1894; as *Two Young Birds*, translated anonymously, 1902.

Une ténébreuse affaire. 1842; edited by René Guise, 1973; as *The Gondreville Mystery*, 1898, also translated by Gerard Hopkins, 1958; as *A Murky Business*, translated by Herbert J. Hunt, 1972.

Les Deux Frères. 1842; as *Un ménage de garçon en province*, in *Comédie humaine*, 1843; as *La Rabouilleuse*, in *Oeuvres complètes*, 1912; edited by René Guise, 1972; as *The Two Brothers*, 1887; as *A Bachelor's Establishment*, in *The Human Comedy*, 1895–98; as *The Bachelor's House*, translated by Francis Frenaye, 1956; as *The Black Sheep*, translated by Donald Adamson, 1970.

Un début dans la vie (includes *La Fausse Maîtresse*). 1844.

Catherine de Médicis expliquée; Le Martyr calviniste. 1845; translated as *Catherine de' Medici*, 1894.

Honorine (includes *Un prince de la Bohème*). 1845.

Splendeurs et misères des courtisanes: Esther. 1845; as *A Harlot's Progress*, in *The Human Comedy*, 1895–98; as *A Harlot High and Low*, translated by Rayner Heppenstall, 1970.

La Lune de miel. 1845.

Petites misères de la vie conjugale. 1845–46; as *The Petty Annoyances of Married Life*, 1861.

Un drame dans les prisons. 1847.

Le Provincial à Paris (includes *Gillette, Le Rentier, El Verdugo*). 1847.

Les Parents pauvres (includes *La Cousine Bette* and *Le Cousin Pons*). 1847–48; as *Poor Relations*, translated by Philip Kent, 1880; as *Les Parents pauvres*, translated by James Waring, 1991; as *Cousin Pons*, 1886; as *Cousin Betty*, 1888; as *Cousin Bette*, translated by Kathleen Raine, 1948, and by Marion Ayton Crawford, 1965.

La Dernière Incarnation de Vautrin. 1848.

Le Député d'Arcis, completed by Charles Rabou. 1854; as *The Deputy of Arcis*, 1896.

Les Paysans, completed by Mme. Balzac. 1855; as *Sons of the Soil*, 1890; as *The Peasantry*, in *The Human Comedy*, 1895–98.

Les Petits Bourgeois, completed by Charles Rabou. 1856; as *The Lesser Bourgeoisie*, 1896; as *The Middle Classes*, 1898.

Sténie; ou, Les Erreurs philosophiques, edited by A. Prioult. 1936.

La Femme auteur et autres fragments inédits, edited by le Vicomte de Lovenjoul. 1950.

Mademoiselle du Vissard, edited by Pierre-George Castex. 1950.

Selected Short Stories. 1977.

Gillette; or, the Unknown Masterpiece, translated by Anthony Rudolf. 1988; as *The Unknown Masterpiece*, translated by Charles Hobson, 1993.

Plays

Vautrin (produced 1840). 1840; translated as *Vautrin*, in *Works*, 1901.

Les Ressources de Quinola (produced 1842). 1842; as *The Resources of Quinola*, in *Works*, 1901.

Paméla Giraud (produced 1843). 1843; translated as *Pamela Giraud*, in *Works*, 1901.

La Marâtre (produced 1848). 1848; as *The Stepmother*, in *Works*, 1901, also translated by Edith Saunders, 1951.

Le Faiseur (produced 1849). 1851; translated as *Mercadet*, in *Works*, 1901.

L'École des ménages, edited by le Vicomte de Lovenjoul (produced 1910). 1907.

Other

Du droit d'aînesse. 1824.

Histoire impartiale des Jésuites. 1824.

Code des gens honnêtes; ou, L'Art de ne pas être dupe des fripons. 1825.

Mémoires de Mme. la Duchesse d'Abrantes, with the duchess. vol. 1 only, 1831.

Maximes et pensées de Napoléon. 1838.

Traité de la vie élégante. 1853.

Lettres à l'étrangère (to Mme. Hanska). 4 vols., 1899–1950.

Cahiers balzaciens, edited by Marcel Bouteron. 8 vols., 1927–28.

Le Catéchisme social, edited by Bernard Guyon. 1933.

Traité de la prière, edited by Philippe Bertault. 1942.

Journaux à la mer, edited by Louis Jaffard. 1949.

Correspondance, edited by Roger Pierrot. 5 vols., 1960–68.

Editor, *Oeuvres complètes*, by La Fontaine. 1826.

Editor, *Oeuvres complètes*, by Molière. 1826.

*

Bibliography: *A Balzac Bibliography* and *Index* by W. Hobart Royce, 1929–30; *Bibliography of Balzac Criticism* by Mark W. Waggoner, 1990.

Critical Studies: *Balzac and the Novel* by Samuel G.A. Rogers, 1953; *Balzac: A Biography*, 1957, and *Balzac's Comédie Humaine*, 1959, both by Herbert J. Hunt; *Balzac the European* by Edward J. Oliver, 1959; *Balzac and the Human Comedie* by Philippe Bertault, translated by Richard Monges, 1963; *Prometheus: The Life of Balzac* by André Maurois, 1965; *Balzac: An Interpretation of the Comédie Humaine* by F.W.J. Hemmings, 1967; *The Hero as Failure: Balzac and the Rubempré Cycle* by Bernard N. Schilling, 1968; *Balzac* by V.S. Pritchett, 1973; *Balzac's Comedy of Words* by Martin Kanes, 1975; *Balzac's Recurring Characters* by Anthony Pugh, 1975; *Balzac Criticism in France (1850–1900): The Making of a Reputation*, 1976, *Balzac: La Cousine Bette*, 1980, and *Balzac: Old Goriot*, 1987, all by David Bellos; *Balzac: Fiction and Melodrama*, 1978, and *Order of Mimesis: Balzac, Hugo, Baudelaire, Flaubert*, 1988, both by Christopher Prendergast; *Honoré de Balzac* by Diana Festa-McCormack, 1979; *Unwrapping Balzac: A Reading of "La Peau de chagrin"* by Samuel Weber, 1979; *Balzac: Illusions Perdues* by Donald Adamson, 1981; *Balzac and His Reader* by Mary Susan McCarthy, 1982; *Balzac and the French Revolution* by Ronnie Butler, 1983; *Balzac, James and Realist Novel* by William W. Stone, 1983; *Balzac and the Drama of Perspective: The Narrator in Selected Works of La Comédie humaine* by Joan Dargan, 1985; *Family Plots: Balzac's Narrative Generations* by Janet L. Beizer, 1986; *Honoré de Balzac: Eugénie Grandet* by Arnold Saxton, 1987; *Realism and the Drama of Reference: Strategies of Representation in Balzac, Flaubert and James* by H. Meili Steele, 1988; *The Golden Scapegoat: Portrait of the Jews in the Novels of Balzac* by Frances Grodzinsky, 1989; *Evolution, Sacrifice and Narrative: Balzac, Zola and Faulkner* by Carol Colatrella, 1990; *Balzacian Montage: Configuring La Comédie humaine* by Allan H. Pasco, 1991; *Paratextuality in Balzac's La Peau de chagrin/The Wild Ass's Skin* by Jeri DeBois King, 1992; *Dissolute Characters: Irish Literary History through Balzac, Sheridan, Le Fanu, Yeats, and Bowen* by W.J. McCormack, 1993; *Honoré de Balzac* (in French) by Roger Pierrot, 1994; *Balzac* by Graham Robb, 1994; *Balzac*, edited and introduced by Michael Tilby, 1995; *The Poetics of Death: The Short Prose of Kleist and Balzac* by Beatrice Martina Guenther, 1996; *Pen vs. Paintbrush: Girodet, Balzac and the Myth of Pygmalion in Postrevolutionary France* by Alexandra K. Wettlaufer, 2001.

*   *   *

Honoré de Balzac's first sustained piece of writing was *Cromwell*, a stillborn historical tragedy in verse. Towards the end of his career he turned to drama once again, and it was probably not solely the need to raise some cash in a hurry that impelled him to do so. *La Marâtre* (*The Stepmother*), for instance, was well received by the critics in 1848, and after initial difficulties when first produced, the five-act melodrama *Vautrin* was a popular success at the Théâtre Porte-Saint-Martin. Yet though Balzac remained fascinated throughout his life by the drama of his age whose emphatic acting styles and tempestuous emotionality left their distinctive stamp on his style and imagination, it was not in the theatre that he was destined to make his mark. Instead we must look to his three sets of quasi-Rabelaisian *Contes drôlatiques* (*Droll Stories*), published between 1832 and 1837, and to his towering achievement, the teeming fictional world of *La Comédie humaine* (*The Human Comedy*), the creation of a lifetime devoted to writing, a work which though never carried through to completion encompasses upwards of 80 novels and tales.

The sheer scope of the enterprise is deeply impressive, even within the context of the enormous output of vast novels in the 19th century, and the audacity of transmuting the title of Dante's epic has been allowed to pass unchallenged, even though there are few obvious connections. A reliable census of Balzac's fictional world has established that it is peopled by over two thousand named characters. Nearly all are sharply individualized, by sex and, equally strongly, by social class, by temperament, appearance, mannerism, and speech habits. Many appear only fleetingly, but others are developed very fully, dominating the scene on occasion or else present as more or less shadowy background figures to events in which they do not play the primary role. A number of these characters, like some in Dickens and Dostoevskii, have made such an impact on the general consciousness that they have come to be regarded as having a status similar to that of historical personages, possessing individuality that seemingly transcends fiction. For a setting Balzac usually, though not exclusively, chose the period in French history just before the time at which he was writing. His characters stand before the backdrop of the French Revolution and the Empire, of the Restoration and the July Monarchy, an era of political turmoil and social upheaval that placed ordinary people under exceptional pressure and allowed unusual opportunities for outstanding individuals to develop their personalities to the full.

Balzac had a considerable number of major novels to his name before the grand concept of *The Human Comedy* dawned on him. *Les Chouans* (*The Chouans*) of 1829 reflected the current fashion for historical romance. That same year *La Physiologie du mariage* (*The Physiology of Marriage*) though not important in itself, marked the crucial decision to use the novel for the study of social conditions in relation to the individual. *Eugénie Grandet* and *Le Père Goriot*, two of Balzac's most popular novels, are evidence that he had indeed struck a rich vein, with observation and imagination combined in good proportion. But in the early 1830s he also began to perceive the possibility, indeed the necessity, of thinking not in terms of single novels but of sets of what he liked to think of as fictionalized studies of 19th-century French society. Slowly the idea crystallized, and in 1842 Balzac was ready to present his views, in somewhat oracular tones, in his famous Preface to *The Human Comedy*. In it he acknowledged his debt to Walter Scott who had raised the status of the novel by using it for the serious investigation of society in former times. The influences bearing on Balzac are not, however, just literary. He invokes the name of famous naturalists such as G.-L. Leclerc de Buffon and Geoffrey de Saint-Hilaire, and of mystical thinkers like Charles Bonnet, Emanuel Swedenborg, and L.-C. de Saint-Martin. What Balzac sought and found in their writings was some sort of corroboration of his intuitions of the unity of observed creation. In the rich variety of human life as he witnessed it there could, he believed, be perceived the working out of a single vital principle. His object became to present individual human beings as the products of the social forces bearing in on them just as biology was attempting to relate specialization and variation to environmental factors.

The pretension to using fiction as a tool for scientific analysis or even just demonstration is, of course, inadmissible, and despite Balzac's efforts to make his examination of society as comprehensive as possible and his mapping out *The Human Comedy* as "studies" of various aspects, the procedure inevitably lacks compelling experimental rigour. Though Balzac felt obliged to return to some of his earlier novels and make some changes, critics have, however, been ready to accept that the unifying vision emerged from the fiction, as a scientific observation might, and was not something deliberately imposed after the event. As early as 1834 Balzac had begun to employ the device of making the same character reappear in different novels, and the tendency to bring out patterns of continuity becomes more and more marked from then on. *The Human Comedy* is not a serial novel nor the chronicle of a family, but something more complex; it is a fictional world in which individual destinies may be best appreciated in wider perspectives. In his descriptions Balzac revealed himself as an observer of exceptional acumen. Yet to hail him primarily as a recorder of the life of his times is to diminish his achievement.

Though *The Human Comedy* represented a major step in the direction of Realism, Balzac is too much of a visionary to be thought of as a Realist. His prose style sometimes lacks elegance, and credibility is occasionally taxed by emotionality and improbability. These excesses are, it seems, inseparable from the vigour and vitality of his vision of human nature and the inescapable conflicts between the demonic forces that spur on mankind and the constraints of religion and the monarchy that alone may hold them in check.

Balzac's rank as a novelist was in question throughout his life. Only towards the end of the 19th century was it generally recognized that his importance, both as an observer and as an imaginative visionary, decisively outweighed a degree of clumsiness in execution and of coarseness in sensibility.

—Christopher Smith

See the essays on *Cousin Bette*, *Eugenie Grandet*, *Lost Illusions*, and *Le Père Goriot*.

BARBUSSE, Henri

Born: Asnières, France, 17 May 1873. **Education:** Educated at Collège Rollin, Paris; graduated 1895. **Military Service:** 1893–94; served in the French army infantry during World War I, invalided out, 1917: Croix de Guerre, 1915. **Career:** Worked in the civil service, Paris; contributor, *Petit Parisien* and *Echo de Paris*; founding editor, *Clarté*, 1917, and *Monde*, 1928; journalist and reviewer, *L'Humanité*, 1920s. **Awards:** Goncourt prize, 1917. **Member:** Involved in pacifist groups, Revue de la Paix and Paix par le Droit, 1903; founder member, Republican Association of War Veterans, 1917, and Clarté, 1919; member, Communist Party, 1923; president, Comité Mondial contre la Guerre et le Fascisme, 1933. **Died:** 30 August 1935.

PUBLICATIONS

Fiction

Les Suppliants. 1903.
L'Enfer. 1908; as *The Inferno*, translated by Edward O'Brien, 1913; as *Inferno*, translated by John Rodker, 1932; as *Hell*, translated by Robert Baldick, 1966.
Meissonier. 1911; as *Meissonier*, translated by Frederic Taber Cooper, 1912.
Nous autres. 1914; as *We Others: Stories of Fate, Love and Pity*, translated by Fitzwater Wray, 1918.
Le Feu: Journal d'une escouade. 1916; edited by Pierre Paraf, 1965; as *Under Fire: The Story of a Squad*, translated by Fitzwater Wray, 1917.
Clarté. 1919; as *Light*, translated by Fitzwater Wray, 1919.
L'Illusion. 1919.
Les Enchaînements. 2 vols., 1925; as *Chains*, translated by Stephen Haden Guest, 2 vols., 1925.

Verse

Pleureuses. 1895.

Other

La Lueur dans l'abîme. 1920.
Paroles d'un combattant: articles et discours. 1920.
Le Couteau entre les dents. 1921.
Quelques coins du coeur, illustrated by Frans Masereel. 1921.
Lettre aux intellectuels. 1921.
L'Étrangère. 1922.
Trois films: Force; L'Au-delà; Le Crieur. 1926.
Les Bourreaux. 1926.
Jésus. 1927; as *Jesus*, edited by Malcolm Cowley, translated by Solon Librescot, 1927.
Les Judas de Jésus. 1927.
Manifeste aux intellectuels. 1927.
Faits divers. 1928; as *And I Saw It Myself*, translated by Brian Rhys, 1928; as *Thus and Thus*, translated by Rhys, 1929.
Voici ce qu'on fait de la Géorgie. 1929.
Ce qui fut sera. 1930.
Élévation. 1930.
Russie. 1930; as *One Looks at Russia*, translated by Warre B. Wells, 1931.
J'accuse. 1932.
Zola. 1932; as *Zola*, translated by Mary Balairdie Green and Frederick C. Green, 1932.
Staline: Un monde nouveau vu à travers un homme. 1935; as *Stalin: A New World as Seen Through One Man*, translated by Vyvyan Holland, 1935.
Lettres de Henri Barbusse à sa femme 1914–1917. 1937.

*

Critical Studies: *Henri Barbusse, soldat de la paix* by A. Vidal, 1953; *Henri Barbusse: Sa marche vers la Clarté, son mouvement Clarté* by Vladimir Brett, 1963; *Communism and the French Intellectuals 1914–1960* by David Caute, 1964; *Three French Writers and the Great War: Studies in the Rise of Communism and Fascism* by Frank Field, 1975; *Les grands romans de la Guerre de 14–18*, with preface by François Rivière, 1994; *Henri Barbusse: écrivain combattant* by Jean Relinger, 1994; *Barbusse* by Philippe Baudorre, 1995.

* * *

Henri Barbusse was a writer and political activist at the centre of the preoccupation with Russian communism which characterized so many French intellectuals and artists in the early part of the 20th century. He began his career as a poet in the symbolist vein, wrote a naturalist novel *L'Enfer* (*The Inferno*), and then came the key novel *Le Feu: Journal d'une escouade* (*Under Fire: The Story of a Squad*), which won him the prestigious Goncourt prize. A further novel *Clarté* (*Light*), also the name of a political organization he co-founded, marked a movement on his part towards a strong political commitment to Marxism which culminated in the adulatory biography of Stalin.

When he first made the change from poetry to the novel in *The Inferno*, the move was fuelled by his sense of the helpless suffering of human beings in the face of the passions and ambitions that dominate them. In the novel, a man comes to Paris in order to work in a bank. Through a hole in the wall, he witnesses the actions of his neighbours and recognizes that there is no possibility that they can escape the futile suffering of existence. This bleak pessimism is both underpinned and, to some extent, transcended by his experiences of the war and the writing of *Under Fire*. As in Remarque's *All Quiet on the Western Front*, it is in the comradeship of the front line soldier that Barbusse sees some sense of meaning holding existence together, despite all the terrors of war.

The path which took him towards socialism, atheism, and humanism was greatly influenced by his experience of the horrors of World War I. Although he had symbolist beginnings, it was clear that, unlike the majority of those in that movement, he was not able to detach himself from awareness of and fellow feeling for the pain of others. *Under Fire* conveys not just a direct and uncompromising picture of the sufferings of the common soldiers in World War I, but also their political aspirations towards a world of equality and international brotherhood. As in much of his writing, political conviction rubbed shoulders uncomfortably with emotional commitment and narrative power. *Under Fire* in particular expresses this duality between creative writing and propaganda.

Barbusse was a genuine patriot, who saw in World War I a horror so great that it would purge humanity for ever of the lust for battle. He began to turn his attention more towards political activism in the movement Clarté, founded in 1919 and conceived as an international intellectual organization dedicated to peace. The committee that was to run Clarté contained a prestigious roll-call of names, among them Thomas Hardy, Georges Duhamel, Upton Sinclair, H.G. Wells, and Stefan Zweig. This left-wing movement had strong links with the French Communist Party (PCF), and it is typical of the contemporary relationships between the left wing in France and intellectuals that so many writers and thinkers joined its ranks. Despite his political views, though, Barbusse held off from joining the PCF until 1923, at the time when France occupied the Ruhr, an act opposed by the PCF. He then resolved to become an activist on behalf of socialism and internationalism. The concept of the nation state should be overcome by the brotherhood of man, by joining hands across political frontiers. He became convinced that Lenin was right in stating that imperialism and capitalism were responsible for military aggression. To overcome these twin evils, even the use of force was (ironically) justified.

In 1929, the worldwide financial collapse coupled with the rise of fascism underpinned even further Barbusse's communist convictions. He became increasingly pro-Soviet, and for a man who was not an unquestioning supporter of the party line, it was somewhat paradoxical to see in his biography of Stalin writing in unquestioningly glowing tones about the Soviet leader. His defence of Soviet communism was not so much an act of simple faith as a recognition on his part that it alone could act as a defence against fascism and the threat of yet another European war. In sum, Barbusse was a man of great conviction so convinced of the evils of capitalist society and the horrors of world war that it had spawned that he failed to see the even greater dangers of world communism.

—Rex Last

See the essay on *Under Fire: The Story of a Squad*.

BARCA, Pedro Calderón de la

See CALDERÓN DE LA BARCA, Pedro

BASHŌ

Born: Matsuo Munefusa at Ueno, near Kyoto, Japan, in 1644.
Career: In service to a local lord of samurai status, and studied poetry with him until the lord's death in 1666; then led an unsettled life: in Edo (now Tokyo) after 1672; lived in a recluse's hut near Edo from 1680, and took his name from banana (bashō) tree growing there, which he admired for its lack of practical utility: in Japan it produces no fruit and its leaves give no shade; his travels were described in verse and prose in journals and diaries; collections of his works appeared from 1684. **Died:** early Autumn 1694.

PUBLICATIONS

Collection

Zenshū [Complete Works], general editor Komiya Toyotaka. 10 vols., 1959–69.

Works

Oku no hosomichi. 1702; as *The Narrow Road to the Deep North*, translated by Nobuyuki Yuasa, in *The Narrow Road to the Deep North and Other Travel Sketches*, 1966; also translated by Earl Miner, in *Japanese Poetic Diaries*, 1969; as *The Narrow Road to the Deep North*, translated by Dorothy Britton, 1974; as *Narrow Road to the Interior*, translated by Sam Hamill, 1991; selections translated by Donald Keene, in *Anthology of Japanese Literature*, 1955; selections as *Back Roads to Far Towns*, translated by Cid Corman and Kamaike Susumu, 1968; as *Narrow Road to Oku*, translated by Donald Keene, 1996; as *Bashō's Narrow Road: Spring and Autumn Passages: Two Works*, translated by Hiroaki Sato.
Haiku (includes about 250 verses by Bashō), translated by R.H. Blyth. 4 vols., 1949–52.
"Bashō's Journey to Sarashina," translated by Donald Keene, in *Transactions of the Asiatic Society of Japan.* December 1957.
"Bashō's Journey of 1684," translated by Donald Keene, in *Asia Major.* December 1959.
A Darkening Sea: Poems of Bashō, translated by David Aylward. 1975.
The Monkey's Straw Raincoat and Other Poetry of the Bashō School, translated by Earl Miner and Hiroko Odagiri. 1981.
One Hundred Frogs, edited by Hiroaki Sato, various translators. 1983.
Traveler My Name, translated by Lucien Stryk. 1984.
On Love and Barley: Haiku of Bashō, translated by Lucien Stryk. 1985.

OTHER

The Essential Haiku: Versions of Bashō, Buson, and Issa, edited with introduction by Robert Haas, 1994.

*

Critical Studies: *An Introduction to Haiku*, by H.G. Henderson, 1958; *Zeami, Bashō, Yeats, Pound: A Study in Japanese and English Poetics*, 1965, *Bashō*, 1970, and *Bashō and His Interpreters: Selected Hokku with Commentary*, 1992, all by Makoto Ueda; "Bashō" by Earl Miner, in *Textual Analysis: Some Readers Reading* edited by Mary Ann Caws, 1986; "The Meaning of Bashō's *shigure*" by Ock Hee You, in *Transactions of the International Conference of Orientalists in Japan*, 33, 1988; *Traces of Dreams: Landscape, Cultural Memory, and the Poetry of Bashō* by Haruo Shirane, 1998; *Rediscovering Bashō: A 300th Anniversary Celebration*, edited by Stephen Henry Gill and C. Andrew Gerstle, 1999.

* * *

Bashō is recognized as one of Japan's greatest literary figures. He transformed haiku from a somewhat frivolous pastime into a serious art form and he remains to this day its greatest exponent. He was in addition a seminal critic and teacher. Though he himself produced only a few works of criticism, many of his critical opinions and comments are preserved in the voluminous notes and accounts of his pupils, particularly Mukai Kyorai and Hattori Doho. Such is the importance of his critical precepts and the example of his poetry that no writer of haiku from his time to the present has been able to escape his influence.

In Bashō's own day the haiku was regarded not as a form in itself but as the first stanza (the *hokku*) of a longer poem consisting of up to a hundred linked stanzas written by two or more poets taking turns. Much of Bashō's effort was given to this type of composition, known as *renku* or *haikai no renga*, and it was in this field that he showed his greatest superiority, for he was an unrivalled master at the subtleties of linking stanzas and controlling the changes of pace, mood, and theme, which are the essence of this extremely demanding form.

Bashō was also a skilled prose writer. He was as meticulous in his prose as in his verse and virtually forged a new style, in which he integrated prose and poetry to an extent never before achieved. In addition to his few critical commentaries, he produced *haibun*, which are short occasional essays written in the haiku spirit, and travel journals. His *Genjuan no ki* [Essay on the Unreal Dwelling] is a moving apologia for his life and is generally considered the finest *haibun* ever written. His travel journal *Oku no hosomichi* (*The Narrow Road to the Deep North*) is his most famous work and one of the masterpieces of Japanese literature, in which he displays his mastery of prose style together with a sure command of form and the highest skill at reshaping events into art.

Bashō's greatness lies not only in his technique but in the depth of his probing of life. To him art was a way of life, a search for religious truth, which was to be found in nature: and this search led to continuous development, giving his work a variety that can appeal to all types of reader. Following his move to Edo, his style changed from refined and often artificial wit to genuine humour in more mundane subjects; and on settling at his Bashō hermitage he continued this trend towards greater simplicity, objectivity, and description, creating a style of his own. The years of his wanderings saw his creative peak in the style of *sabi* ("loneliness"), in which nature, usually in its most insignificant forms, is shown quietly fulfilling its often bleak destiny. In his final years he turned to *karumi* ("lightness"), an obscure term that seems to imply a more contented attitude of acceptance and less tension within a poem. To some, this step was retrograde, but however it is judged, it shows Bashō developing and striving to the end to perfect his art in the light of his philosophy of life.

—P.T. Harries

BASSANI, Giorgio

Pseudonym: Used Giacomo Marchi for several years to avoid Nazi and Fascist persecution. **Born:** Bologna, Italy, 4 April 1916. **Education:** Educated at Liceo Ludovico Ariosto, Bologna; University of Bologna, from 1934, degree in literature. **Family:** Married Valeria Sinigallia in 1943, one son and one daughter. **Career:** Began antifascist activity in 1942: imprisoned briefly, 1943, and after release took part in the Resistance; lived in Ferrara until 1943, then in Rome; after World War II worked as scriptwriter and film dubbing editor; editor, *Botteghe Oscure, Rome*, 1948–60; co-editor, *Paragone*, Milan, 1953–55; editor, Feltrinelli, publishers, Milan, 1958–64; instructor in history of the theatre, Academy of Dramatic Art, Rome, 1957–68; vice-president, Radio Televisione Italiana, Rome, 1964–65. President, from 1966, and honorary president, Italia Nostra. **Awards:** Veillon prize, 1955; Strega prize, 1956; Viareggio prize, 1962; Campiello prize, 1969; Nelly Sachs prize, 1969; Bagutta prize, 1983. **Died:** 13 April 2000.

PUBLICATIONS

Fiction

Una città di pianura (as Giacomo Marchi). 1940.
La passeggiata prima di cena. 1953.
Gli ultimi anni di Clelia Trotti. 1955.
Il romanzo di Ferrara. 1974; revised edition, 1980.
   Cinque storie ferraresi. 1956; revised edition, as *Dentro le mura*, 1974; as *A Prospect of Ferrara*, translated by Isabel Quigly, 1962; as *Five Stories of Ferrara*, translated by William Weaver, 1971.
   Gli occhiali d'oro. 1958; with variants, 1970; as *The Gold-Rimmed Spectacles*, translated by Isabel Quigly, 1960; as *The Gold-Rimmed Eyeglasses*, translated by William Weaver, in *The Smell of Hay*, 1975.
   Il giardino dei Finzi-Contini. 1962; as *The Garden of the Finzi-Continis*, translated by Isabel Quigly, 1965; also translated by William Weaver, 1977.
   Dietro la porta. 1964; as *Behind the Door*, translated by William Weaver, 1973.
   L'airone. 1968; as *The Heron*, translated by William Weaver, 1970.
   L'odore del fieno (stories). 1972; as *The Smell of Hay* (includes *The Gold-Rimmed Eyeglasses*), translated by William Weaver, 1975.
Una notte del '43. 1960.
Le storie ferraresi (includes the five stories of *Cinque storie ferraresi*, *Gli occhiali d'oro*, and the stories "Il muro di cinta" and "In esilio"). 1960.
Due novelle. 1965.
Di là dal cuore. 1984.

Verse

Storie di poveri amanti e altri versi. 1945; enlarged edition, 1946.
Te lucis ante. 1947.
Un' altra libertà. 1952.
L'alba ai vetri: Poesie 1947–1950. 1963.

Epitaffio. 1974; parts translated in *Rolls Royce and Other Poems*, 1982.
In gran segreto. 1978; parts translated in *Rolls Royce and Other Poems*, 1982.
In rima e senza. 1982.
Rolls Royce and Other Poems (bilingual edition), edited and translated by Francesca Valente and others. 1982.

Plays

The Stranger's Hand (screenplay), with Guy Elmes and Graham Greene. 1954.

Screenplays: *The Stranger's Hand*, with Guy Elmes and Graham Greene, 1954.

Other

Le parole preparate e altri scritti di letteratura (essays). 1966.
Con Bassani verso Ferrara by Alberto Toni, 2001.

*

Critical Studies: *Bassani* by Giorgio Varanini, 1970; "The *Storie ferraresi* of Giorgio Bassani," in *Italica*, 49, 1972, and "Bassani's Ironic Mode," in Canadian Journal of Italian Studies, 1, 1978, both by Marianne Shapiro; "*The Garden of the Finzi-Continis*" by Stanley G. Eskin, in *Literature/Film Quarterly*, 1, 1973; "Mythical Dimensions of Micòl Finzi-Contini," in *Italica*, 51, 1974, "A Conversion to Death: Giorgio Bassani's *L'airone*," in *Canadian Journal of Italian Studies*, 1, 1978, and *Vengeance of the Victim: History and Symbol in Giorgio Bassani's Fiction*, 1986, all by Marilyn Schneider; "Transformation in Bassani's Garden," in *Modern Fiction Studies*, 21, 1975, "The Closed World of Giorgio Bassani," in *Italian Culture*, 3, 1981, "Exile in the Narrative Writings of Giorgio Bassani," in *Italian Culture*, 5, 1984, "Bassani: The Motivation of Language," in *Italica*, 62(2), 1985, *The Exile into Eternity: A Study of the Narrative Writings of Giorgio Bassani*, 1987, and "Bassani: The Guilt Beyond the Door," in *Gradiva*, 4(2[6]), 1988, all by Douglas Radcliff-Umstead; "Art and Death in Bassani's Poetry" by Stelio Cro, in *Canadian Journal of Italian Studies*, 1, 1978; *Invito all lettura di Bassani* by Massimo Grillandi, 1980; "Giorgio Bassani: The Record of a Confession" by Diego L. Bastianutti, in *Queen's Quarterly*, 88(4), 1981; *Le forme del sentimento: Prosa e poesie in Giorgio Bassani* by Anna Dolfi, 1981; "Insiders and Outsiders: Discourses of Oppression in Giorgio Bassani's *Gli occhiali d'oro*" by Mirna Cicioni, in *Italian Studies*, 41, 1986; "Visual Memory and the Nature of the Epitaph: Bassani's *Epitaffio*" by Linda Nemerow-Ulman, in *Italian Quarterly*, 27(106), 1986; "Narrated and Narrating I" in *Il giardino dei Finzi-Contini* by Harry Davis, in *Italian Studies*, 43, 1988; "The Structures of Silence: Re-reading Giorgio Bassani's *Gli occhiali d'oro*" by Lucienne Kroha, in *The Italianist*, 10, 1990; *Studi in onore Umberto Mariani: Da Verga a Calvino*, edited by Anthony G. Costantini and Franco Zangrilli, 2000.

* * *

All Giorgio Bassani's fiction is set in the northern Italian town of Ferrara in the years from the beginning of the 20th century to the late 1940s. He painstakingly revised his fictional writings twice, and finally published them as a whole under the comprehensive title *Il romanzo di Ferrara* [The Novel of Ferrara]. The town is a microcosm of Italian society, revisited in the light of memory by the first-person narrator of *Gli occhiali d'oro* (*The Gold-Rimmed Eyeglasses*), *Il giardino dei Finzi-Contini* (*The Garden of the Finzi-Continis*), and *Dietro la porta* (*Behind the Door*): a young middle-class Jew, who observes and judges the effects of history on social life and relationships between people divided by politics, sex, class, and, above all, race. Bassani's main focus is on the small Jewish community of Ferrara, which is represented as at first fully integrated with, and almost completely assimilated into, Gentile bourgeois—and later Fascist—society, only to face the shock, isolation, and despair of being labelled "other" and "undesirable" by the 1938 anti-semitic laws. In a 1964 interview Bassani defined himself as "the historian of the past," and 20 years later stated that he had been the first Italian writer to have written about Italian Jews within their historical and political context. The emphasis in all his writings on meticulous reconstruction of details—such as street names, trade names of watches, bicycles, and typewriters, and contemporary cultural references such as journal articles, popular films, and names of well-known public figures—can thus be interpreted as a desire to commit the past to memory as accurately as possible, because that past was irreparably lost with the Holocaust. This desire is fully consistent with the basic notion in Jewish culture that remembering the past is a religious duty for each Jew, and that temporal history is indissolubly connected with sacred history.

This historical perspective has a linguistic correlative in Bassani's writings in its "social indirect speech," where the narrator voices the collective opinions and judgements of the Ferrara bourgeoisie in its own vocabulary and phraseology. This "social indirect speech," however, like the community itself, is never fully homogenous: the narrator distances himself from it by expressing his own historical and moral judgements, and within the community individual characters attempt to formulate alternative political and social discourses.

The protagonists of the *Cinque storie ferraresi* (*Five Stories of Ferrara*) are individuals who are, at the same time, both part of the Ferrara community and isolated from it, physically and socially: they are enclosed behind windows and within cell-like rooms, locked within their historical and personal failures. A Jewish doctor marries outside his faith and his class; an old Socialist schoolteacher under house arrest fruitlessly attempts to convey her historical insights to a young middle-class Jew; an invalid refuses to give evidence against the Fascist murderers of 11 anti-Fascist and Jewish prisoners; and, most compelling of all, a Jew returns to Ferrara from Buchenwald and disappears again after trying unsuccessfully to make the town confront its historical responsibilities.

The Gold-Rimmed Eyeglasses, set in 1937, depicts conflicting discourses about integration and "outsiders." The heterosexual Jewish narrator tells the story of the gradual ostracism and destruction by the heterosexual bourgeoisie of a Gentile homosexual doctor who is driven to suicide, while his former Jewish friends, unable or unwilling to support him, begin to experience the alienation of the anti-semitic laws and to feel the shadow of their own destruction.

The title of *The Garden of the Finzi-Continis* displays both the self-imposed exile of the aristocratic Jewish family that lives within the garden's walls, and a temporary illusion of solidarity when its gates are opened up to the ostracized Jewish youth after the advent of the anti-semitic laws. Some of the characters (the 20-year-old narrator; his integrated, Fascist father; his friends Micòl and Alberto Finzi-Contini, and their elderly, scholarly father) do endeavour to define their identity in a multiplicity of Jewish discourses. However, none of

these discourses is presented as strong enough to oppose the dominant Fascist ideology. Significantly, the novel is pervaded by images of death, from the opening scene which links an Etruscan necropolis to the Jewish cemetery of Ferrara, to recurring references to cemeteries and literary references to silence and mourning.

In *Behind the Door*, set during 1929–30, the first-person narrator recounts his loss of innocence and trust at the age of 15, as a consequence of being ruthlessly betrayed by a Gentile classmate, and emphasizes the covert intolerance present in Ferrara long before the anti-semitic laws.

With *L'airone* (*The Heron*)—his last novel, set in 1947—Bassani returned to third-person narration. The protagonist, a wealthy Jew who has survived the war relatively unscathed, resolves to take his own life because of his hopeless disillusionment with the new social order, and his own lack of a cultural and personal identity. His spiritual emptiness is heightened by his isolation and alienation from what is left of the Jewish community, irreparably shattered by the war. Symbols of death also abound in this work: the protagonist identifies his pain and despair with those of a heron wounded by a hunting party, and his longing for peace away from life with a display of stuffed animals in a taxidermist's window.

The Ferrara Cycle also includes *L'odore del fieno* (*The Smell of Hay*), a series of separate stories which further develop characters or situations mentioned in the longer fiction works. Bassani's poetry—most of which has not been translated into English—moves from early reflections on his own Jewishness to later sarcastic observations on the cultural trends of the Italy of the 1970s. Significantly, many poems have an hourglass shape: although Bassani's major "historiography" project is now complete, all his writings share its historical dimension.

—Mirna Cicioni

BAUDELAIRE, Charles (Pierre)

Born: Paris, France, 9 April 1821. **Education:** Educated at Collège de Lyon, 1832–36; École Louis-le-Grand, Paris, 1836; expelled 1839; completed studies at Pension Levêque et Bailly, Paris, baccalauréat, 1839; law student, University of Paris, 1839–41. **Career:** Contracted syphilis and fell into debt; sent on a voyage to India by his parents, 1841, left the ship in Mauritius and returned to Paris; after 1842, was able to live on an inheritance from his father; art critic and translator; publication of *Les Fleurs du mal*, 1861, led to a trial for indecency, fined for offences against public morals and six poems were suppressed; moved to Brussels, 1864; returned to Paris, 1866; spent rest of his life in a sanatorium. **Died:** 31 August 1867.

PUBLICATIONS

Collections

Oeuvres complètes: Les Fleurs du mal; Curiosités esthétiques; L'Art romantique; Petits poèmes en prose, Les Paradis artificiels, La Fanfarlo, Le Jeune Enchanteur, foreword by Théophile Gautier. 4 vols., 1868–69; as *Artificial Paradises*, translated with introduction and notes by Stacy Diamond, 1996.

Oeuvres complètes, edited by Jacques Crépet and Claude Pichois. 19 vols., 1922–53.

Oeuvres complètes, edited by Claude Pichois. 2 vols., 1975–76.

Complete Verse (bilingual edition), edited and translated by Francis Scarfe. 2 vols., 1986–89.

The Painter of Modern Life and Other Essays, translated and edited by Jonathan Mayne, 1995.

Complete Poems, translated by Walter Martin, 1997.

Verse

Les Fleurs du mal. 1861; revised editions, 1861, 1868 (in *Oeuvres complètes*); as *The Flowers of Evil*, 1909; numerous subsequent translations including by George Dillon and Edna St. Vincent Millay, 1936; Geoffrey Wagner, 1946; Roy Campbell, 1952; W. Aggeler, 1954; Francis Scarfe (in prose), 1961; Florence Louie Friedman, 1966; Richard Howard, 1982; as *Poems of the Damned: Charles Baudelaire's Les Fleurs du mal—The Flowers of Evil*, translated by Ulick O'Connor, 1995.

Les Épaves. 1866.

Le Parnasse contemporain (includes "Les Nouvelles Fleurs du mal"). 1866.

Petits Poèmes en prose. 1869; as *Paris Spleen*, translated by Louise Varèse, 1869; as *Poems in Prose*, translated by Arthur Symons, 1905; as *Little Poems in Prose*, translated by Aleister Crowley, 1928; as *The Parisian Prowler*, translated by Edward K. Kaplan, 1989.

Vers retrouvés. 1929.

Selected Verse, translated by Francis Scarfe. 1961.

Flowers of Evil and Other Works, edited and translated by Wallace Fowlie. 1964.

Selected Poems, edited and translated by Joanna Richardson. 1975.

City Blues, translated by F.W.J. Hemmings. 1977.

Selected Poems, translated by John Goudge. 1979.

Spleen, translated by Elliot Ross. 1984.

The Prose Poems and La Fanfarlo, translated by Rosemary Lloyd. 1991.

Fiction

La Fanfarlo. In *Oeuvres complètes*, 1868–69; as *La Fanfarlo*, translated by Greg Boyd, 1986; also translated by Rosemary Lloyd, 1991.

Other

Salon de 1845. 1845; edited by André Ferran, 1933.

Salon de 1846. 1846; edited by David Kelley, 1975.

Théophile Gautier. 1859; edited by Philippe Terrier, 1985.

Les Paradis artificiels: Opium et haschisch. 1860.

Richard Wagner et Tannhäuser à Paris. 1861.

Le Peintre de la vie moderne. 1863.

L'Oeuvre et la vie d'Eugène Delacroix. 1863; as *Eugene Delacroix: His Life and Work*, translated by Joseph Bernstein, 1948.

Journaux intimes. 1920; as *Intimate Journals*, translated by Christopher Isherwood, 1930.

Selected Writings on Art and Artists, translated by P.E. Charvet. 1932.

Selected Critical Studies, edited by Douglas Parmée. 1949.

The Mirror of Art: Critical Studies, edited and translated by Jonathan Mayne. 1955.

Baudelaire: A Self-Portrait (selected letters), edited by Lois Boe and F.E. Hyslop. 1957.

Baudelaire as a Literary Critic (essays), edited and translated by Lois Boe and F.E. Hyslop. 1964.

The Painter of Modern Life and Other Essays, edited and translated by Jonathan Mayne. 1964.

Art in Paris 1845–1862: Salons and Other Exhibitions, edited and translated by Jonathan Mayne. 1965.

Edgar Allan Poe, sa vie et ses ouvrages, edited by W.T. Bandy. 1973.

Correspondance, edited by Claude Pichois and Jean Ziegler. 2 vols., 1973.

Selected Letters, edited by Rosemary Lloyd, 1986.

My Heart Laid Bare and Other Prose Writings, edited by Peter Quennell, translated by Norman Cameron. 1986.

Critique d'art; suivi de, Critique musicale (essays), edited by Claude Pichois. 1992.

Translator, *Histoires extraordinaires, Nouvelles histoires extraordinaires, Aventures d'Arthur Gordon Pym, Euréka, Histoires grotesques et sérieuses*, by Edgar Allan Poe. 5 vols., 1856–65.

*

Bibliography: *Baudelaire et la critique française 1868–1917* by A.E. Carter, 1936, supplemented by W.T. Bandy, 1953, and P.M. Trotman, 1971; *Baudelaire Criticism 1950–1967* by R.T. Cargo, 1968.

Critical Studies: *Baudelaire the Critic* by Margaret Gilman, 1943; *Baudelaire* by P. Mansell Jones, 1952; *Baudelaire: A Study of His Poetry* by Martin Turnell, 1953; *Baudelaire: Les Fleurs du Mal* by Alison Fairlie, 1960; *Baudelaire's Tragic Hero* by D.J. Mossop, 1961; *Baudelaire: A Collection of Critical Essays* edited by Henri Peyre, 1962; *Baudelaire* by M.A. Ruff, 1966; *Baudelaire and Nature*, 1969, *Collected Essays, 1953–1988*, 1990, and *Charles Pierre Baudelaire: Les Fleurs du mal*, 1992, all by F.W. Leakey; *Baudelaire as a Love Poet and Other Essays* edited by Lois Boe Hyslop, 1969, and *Baudelaire, Man of His Time* by Hyslop, 1980; *Baudelaire* (in English) by Enid Starkie, 1971; *Baudelaire: A Lyric Poet in the Era of High Capitalism* by Walter Benjamin, translated by Harry Zohn, 1973; *Baudelaire, Prince of Clouds* by Alex de Jonge, 1976; *Baudelaire and Freud* by Leo Bersani, 1977; *Charles Baudelaire* by A.E. Carter, 1977; *Baudelaire: A Fire to Conquer Darkness* by Nicole Ward Jouve, 1980; *Baudelaire's Literary Criticism* by Rosemary Lloyd, 1981; *Baudelaire the Damned: A Biography* by F.W.J. Hemmings, 1982; *Baudelaire, Mallarmé, Valéry: New Essays in Honour of Lloyd Austin* edited by Malcolm Bowie, Alison Fairlie, and Alison Finch, 1982; *Exploding Poetry: Baudelaire/Rimbaud* by Georges Poulet, 1984; *Baudelaire: La Fanfarlo and Le Spleen de Paris* by Barbara Wright and David H.T. Scott, 1984; *Baudelaire and Le Spleen de Paris* by J.A. Hiddleston, 1987; *Baudelaire in 1859: A Study of the Sources of Poetic Creativity*, 1988, and *Baudelaire and the Second Republic: Writing and Revolution*, 1991, both by Richard D.E. Burton; *Baudelaire and the Poetics of Craft* by Graham Chesters, 1988; *The Comical as Textual Practice in Les Fleurs du mal* by John W. MacInnes, 1988; *Narrative as Performance: The Baudelairean Experience* by Marie Maclean, 1988; *Baudelaire* by Claude Pichois, translated by Graham Robb, 1989; *A Poetics of Art Criticism: The Case of Baudelaire* by Timothy Raser, 1989; *Baudelaire's Prose Poems* by E. Kaplan, 1990; *Baudelaire's Argot plastique: Poetic Caricature and Modernism* by Ainslie Armstrong McLees, 1990; *Baudelaire and Intertextuality* by Margery A. Evans, 1992; *Baudelaire and Caricature: From the Comic to an Art of Modernity* by Michele

Hannoosh, 1992; *Baudelaire's Voyages: The Poet and His Painters* by Jeffrey Coven, 1993; *Baudelaire and Schizoanalysis: The Sociopoetics of Modernism* by Eugene W. Holland, 1993; *Baudelaire* by Joanna Richardson, 1994; *Poetry and Painting: Baudelaire, Mallarmé, Apollinaire, and their Painter Friends* by Alan Bowness, 1994; *Resonant Gaps: Between Baudelaire and Wagner* by Margaret Miner, 1995; *Baudelaire: Individualism, Dandyism and the Philosophy of History* by Bernard Howells, 1996; *Baudelaire in Russia* by Adrian Wanner, 1996; *Baudelaire: At the Limits and Beyond* by Nicolae Babuts, 1997; *The Integrative Vision: Poetry and the Visual Arts in Baudelaire, Rilke and MacDiarmid* by Tom Hubbard, 1997; *Poetry and Moral Dialectic: Baudelaire's "Secret Architecture"* by James R. Lawler, 1997; *Understanding Les fleurs du mal: Critical Readings*, edited by William J. Thompson, 1997; *Baudelaire and the Aesthetics of Bad Faith* by Susan Blood, 1997; *Virtuosity of the Nineteenth Century: Performing Music and Language in Heine, Liszt, and Baudelaire* by Susan Bernstein, 1998; *Baudelaire's Prose Poems: the Practice and Politics of Irony* by Sonya Stephens, 1999; *Baudelaire and the Art of Memory* by J.A. Hiddleston, 1999; *Translating Baudelaire* by Clive Scott, 2000; *Remnants of Song: Trauma and the Experience of Modernity in Charles Baudelaire and Paul Celan* by Ulrich Baer, 2000; *Baudelaire and the Poetics of Modernity*, edited by Patricia A. Ward, 2001.

*   *   *

Poet, critic, translator, Charles Baudelaire, though largely ignored in his own time, is today considered one of the literary giants of the 19th century. His translations of five volumes of Edgar Allan Poe's tales, in addition to his three essays on the American writer, are mainly responsible for Poe's fame in France and throughout Europe. His essays on art and literature and his article on Wagner make him one of the greatest critics of the 19th century. And finally his volume of verse *Les Fleurs du mal* (*The Flowers of Evil*) and his *Petits Poèmes en prose* (*Little Poems in Prose*) have earned him the title of our first modern poet as well as one of the finest of city poets.

Baudelaire is often called "the father of modern criticism" and "the first aesthetician of his age," not so much because of his value judgements of individual artists and writers as because of the ideas and principles he articulated. If his essays on art are usually considered superior to those on literature, it is mainly because demands of publishers often made it necessary for him to discuss a number of minor writers, while laws of censorship forced him to resort to irony, parody, and pastiche in order to express unpopular opinions.

Except during the Revolutionary period, when for a short time he adopted a more utilitarian conception of art, Baudelaire, like Flaubert, believed that the goal of art was beauty—beauty which, when "purified by art," could be derived from even ugliness, evil, and horror. That is why, in an unfinished epilogue intended for the second edition of *The Flowers of Evil*, he could say to the city of Paris: "You have given me your mud and I have turned it into gold."

Baudelaire's personal conception of beauty, as noted in his *Journaux intimes* (*Intimate Journals*), was much like that of Poe. Though he was obviously influenced by the American writer, even to the point of extensively plagiarizing him in his three Poe essays, recent investigation has proved that what he found in Poe's literary doctrine was a confirmation of his own poetic practice as well as an affirmation of aesthetic principles he had already espoused.

Like Poe, Baudelaire prefers a beauty tinged with melancholy, regret, and sadness. Like Poe also, he insists on the importance of the bizarre or strange—"an artless, unpremeditated, unconscious strangeness," as he wrote in his *Exposition universelle*. In his 1857 essay on Poe, he even agrees that "the principle of poetry is . . . human aspiration toward a superior beauty"—a definition less characteristic of his poetry than his observation that "every lyric poet by virtue of his nature inevitably effects a return to the lost Eden." In his verse, Baudelaire himself often made that return, whether to the Eden of his childhood or to that of tropical seas and skies and of happiness he had known with his dusky mistress.

With Delacroix, whose art he never ceased to glorify and whose opinions he frequently cited, Baudelaire believed that every age and every nation possesses its own particular beauty. In addition to its eternal or absolute element, all beauty, he maintained, must necessarily contain this particular or transitory element which, for him, was really synonymous with modernity. It was his emphasis on modernity—his call for "the heroism of modern life" and his belief that Parisian life was "rich in poetic and marvellous subjects"—that did much to change the course of both literature and painting and is often reflected in his own best verse.

Baudelaire was violently opposed to the servile imitation of nature as practised by the Realists. For him, as for Delacroix, nature was a dictionary whose hieroglyphics he sought to interpret. Imagination, the "queen of all faculties," alone permits the poet to discover in the vast storehouse of nature the symbols, analogies, and correspondences that can transform reality into the poet's own vision of reality.

Baudelaire's chief claim to fame is his volume of verse *The Flowers of Evil* in which can be seen a strange amalgam of old and new. Classic in its clarity, discipline, and reliance on traditional forms, Romantic in its subjectivity, its spirit of revolt, and its macabre elements, *The Flowers of Evil* is also considered a distant forerunner of Surrealism in its use of dreams, myths, and fantasies. Far more important, however, is the fact that, by its use of suggestion as opposed to description and narration, it anticipates Symbolism and opens the door to modern poetry.

The unifying theme running throughout the six sections of *The Flowers of Evil* is that of the human condition, of the conflict between good and evil, spleen and ideal, dream and reality. Obsessed with a belief in original sin and in the duality of man and using his own personal experiences as raw material, Baudelaire examined the spiritual problems of his age with a probing, almost brutal self-analysis. Unlike the Romantics, however, he saw himself not as unique but closely akin to the reader, whom he addresses in his introductory poem as "hypocritical reader, my counter-part, my brother."

One of Baudelaire's most important innovations is his use of correspondences. Although in his essays he speaks of the transcendental correspondences between the visible and invisible worlds, it is the synesthetic correspondences between colours, sounds, and perfumes that he employs in both his poetry and prose. Even more characteristic is his use of the correspondences between exterior nature and his own inner world. By finding symbols in outer reality that correspond to and suggest his inner thoughts and feelings, he often succeeds in creating what he himself called "a suggestive magic . . . containing the world exterior to the artist and the artist himself"— a suggestive magic leaving a "lacuna" to be filled by the reader. Such use of the symbol not only allowed him to exteriorize his idea or mood, by giving concrete form to the abstract, but also helped him achieve what he termed an "indispensable obscurity" that stops short of being hermetic.

Almost as important as his use of suggestion is Baudelaire's use of the cityscape to replace the nature description of the Romantics.

Although the city is never described, its sounds are heard almost everywhere, and its presence everywhere felt. Both *The Flowers of Evil* and the *Little Poems in Prose* are permeated with the omnipresence of the city, if only through choice of imagery or through implication.

In style, Baudelaire introduced a number of innovations that have since been adopted by most modern poets. As a result of his emphasis on suggestion, the image, no longer merely peripheral, often becomes the very essence of the poem. His tendency to introduce a prosaic or even crude image in the midst of an otherwise highly poetic style as well as his remarkable ability to treat sordid reality without losing poetic elevation have been widely imitated. Equally characteristic are his musical sonorities, his subtle and suggestive rhythms, his frequent use of monologue or dialogue to achieve dramatic effect, and his mingling of the grand manner with a quiet, subdued, and conversational tone.

—Lois Boe Hyslop

See the essays on "Spleen," "To the Reader," and "Windows."

BAZÁN, Emilia Pardo

See PARDO BAZÁN, Emilia

BEAUMARCHAIS

Born: Pierre-Augustin Caron, in Paris, France, 24 January 1732. **Education:** Educated at École des Métiers d'Alfort, for three years, to age 13, then apprenticed to his clockmaker father. **Family:** Married 1) Madeleine-Catherine Franquet in 1756 (died 1757); 2) Geneviève-Madeleine Warebled in 1768 (died 1770), one son (died in infancy); 3) Marie-Thérèse Willermawlas in 1786 (divorced 1794; remarried 1797), one daughter. **Career:** Clockmaker: his work recognized by Academy of Sciences, 1754, and popular at court; bought title of Clerk Controller in Royal Household, 1755; took name Beaumarchais from first wife's estate, 1757; also a harpist (improved the pedal system): gave lessons and organized concerts at court; bought title of Secrétaire du Roi, 1761 (and consequently ennobled, 1761), and Lt.-General of hunting in the Varenne du Louvre, 1761; visited Spain, 1764–66; involved in several spectacular court cases in 1770s; government agent, 1774–75, and responsible for aid to American insurgents, 1775; involved in founding the Bureau de Législation Dramatique (later Société des Auteurs et Compositeurs Dramatiques), 1777; arrested on suspicion of profiteering from arms, 1792, took refuge in London, but imprisoned for debt, 1792; released on payment of ransom, returned to France, 1793; left for Holland, on mission to buy arms; family imprisoned, 1794; exiled in Holland and Germany until 1796. **Died:** 17/18 May 1799.

PUBLICATIONS

Collections

Oeuvres complètes, edited by Édouard Fournier. 1876.

Théâtres, Lettres relatives à son théâtre, edited by Maurice Allem and Paul Courant. 1957.
Oeuvres complètes, edited by Albert Demazière. 1973.
Théâtre, edited by Jean-Pierre de Beaumarchais. 1980.
Oeuvres, edited by Pierre Lathomas. 1988.
The Barber of Seville; The Marriage of Figaro; The Guilty Mother: Three Plays, translated by Graham Anderson, 1993.
The Three Figaro Plays, translated with introduction and notes by David Edney, 2000.

Plays

Colin et Colette; Les Bottes de sept lieues; Les Députés de la Halle; Léandre Marchand d'Agnus; Jean Bête à la foire (farces: probably produced c. 1760–63). In *Théâtre*, 1957.
Eugénie (produced 1767). 1767; as *The School for Rakes*, translated by Elizabeth Griffith, 1769.
Les Deux Amis; ou, Le Négociant de Lyon (produced 1770). 1770; as *The Two Friends; or, the Liverpool Merchant*, translated by C.H. London, 1800.
Le Barbier de Séville; ou, La Precaution inutile (produced 1775). 1775; as *The Barber of Seville*, translated by Elizabeth Griffith, 1776; also translated by Arthur B. Myrick, 1905; W.R. Taylor, 1922; Stewart Robb, 1939; Wallace Fowlie, in *Classical French Drama*, 1962; Vincent Luciani, 1964; John Wood, 1966; as *Le Barbier de Séville*, edited with introduction and notes by Malcolm Cook; as *The Barber of Seville, or, The Futile Precaution: a New English Translation*, translated by Gilbert Pestureau, Ann Wakefield and Gavin Witt, 1997; as *The Barber of Seville*, translated and adapted by Bernard Sahlins, 1998.
La Folle Journée; ou, Le Mariage de Figaro (produced 1784). 1785; as *The Follies of a Day; or, The Marriage of Figaro*, translated by Thomas Holcroft, 1785; as *A Mad Day's Work; or, The Marriage of Figaro*, translated by Brodbury P. Ellis, 1961; as *The Marriage of Figaro*, edited by Malcolm Cook, 1992; translated by Vincent Luciani, 1964; also translated by John Wood, 1966; William Gaskill, in *Landmarks of French Classical Drama*, edited by David Bradby, 1991; as *The Marriage of Figaro*, translated and adapted by Bernard Sahlins, 1994.
Tarare, music by Antonio Salieri (produced 1787; revised version, produced 1790). 1790; translated as *Axur, King of Ormus*, 1813.
L'Autre Tartuffe; ou, La Mère coupable (produced 1792). 1794; as *Frailty and Hypocrisy*, translated by James Wild, 1804; as *A Mother's Guilt*, in *The Complete Figaro Plays*, 1983.

Other

Mémoires contre M. Goëzman. 1775.
Mémoires, edited by J. Ravenal. 4 vols., 1830.
Lettres inédites, edited by Gilbert Chinard. 1929.
Correspondance, edited by Brian N. Morton. 1969–.
For the Good of Mankind: Political Correspondence Relative to the American Revolution, edited and translated by Antoinette Shewmake. 1987.

*

Bibliography: *Bibliographie des oeuvres de Beaumarchais* by H. Cordier, 1883; *Beaumarchais: A Bibliography* by Brian N. Morton and Donald C. Spinelli, 1988.

Critical Studies: *Beaumarchais* by G. Lemaître, 1949; *The Comic Style of Beaumarchais* by J.B. Ratermanis and W.R. Irwin, 1961; *The Real Figaro: The Extraordinary Career of Caron de Beaumarchais* by Cynthia Cox, 1962; *Beaumarchais: Le Barbier de Seville* by Robert Niklaus, 1968; *A Critical Commentary on Beaumarchais's ''Le Mariage de Figaro''* by Anthony Pugh, 1968; *Beaumarchais* by Joseph Sungolowski, 1974; *Beaumarchais: The Man Who Was Figaro* by Frédéric Grendel, translated by Roger Greaves, 1977; ''Beaumarchais's Transformations'' by Jack Undank, in *Modern Language Notes*, 100(4), 1985; *Beaumarchais: The Barber of Seville* by John Dunkley, 1991; *Beaumarchais, ou, La Passion du Drame* by Béatrice Didier, 1994; *Beaumarchais, l'insolent* by Jean-Claude Brisville, 1996; *Le Langage Dramatique dans la Trilogie de Beaumarchais: Efficacité, Gaieté, Musicalité* by Sophie Lecarpentier, 1998; *Beaumarchais, l'aventure d'une Écriture* by Violaine Géraud, 1999; *Pierre-Augustin Caron de Beaumarchais* by Maurice Lever, 1999.

*   *   *

The creator of Figaro, perhaps the best known of all French fictional characters, was a highly successful businessman who smuggled arms to the American rebels of 1776, published a complete edition of the works of Voltaire between 1783 and 1790, and founded one of the first organizations to protect authors' rights, the *Société des Auteurs Dramatiques* (Society of Dramatic Authors), in 1777. The readiness of Figaro to defy his master Almaviva verbally in *Le Barbier de Séville* (*The Barber of Seville*) and to intrigue against him in *La Folle Journée; ou, Le Mariage de Figaro* (*The Marriage of Figaro*) was thus not the expression of any personal resentment on Beaumarchais's part towards a society which had not allowed him to prosper. It was much more the statement of a general need for the hierarchical, unjust, and inefficient society of the late 18th century to change so that other men of talent could more easily rise, as Beaumarchais himself had done, from being sons of clockmakers to becoming successful businessmen and even purchasing patents of nobility.

Both Beaumarchais's plays about Figaro have been turned into operas, the first by Rossini and the second by Mozart, and the musical genius of *Le Nozze de Figaro* inevitably makes a straight performance of the original play seem a little tame. Both plays are saved less by the plot, which is unoriginal in *The Barber of Seville* and not always easy to follow in *The Marriage of Figaro*, than by the character of Figaro himself, with his ready wit, verbal dexterity, and indomitable ingenuity. In this respect, he represents the archetypal Frenchman as the French would like to see themselves, mercifully free from the tendency to sentimental moralizing that makes its way into *The Marriage of Figaro* with the character of Marcelline, and which inspired other unperformable plays, such as *L'Autre Tartuffe; ou, La Mère coupable* (*A Mother's Guilt*). For Beaumarchais was also a man of his time in that he shared the opinion of Diderot about the need for serious plays that dealt in a serious manner with the sexual and other problems of the middle class. It is this rather than any Oedipal impulses that explains the presence of Marcelline as Figaro's mother in *The Marriage of Figaro*, and there is an interesting contrast with the lack of conviction which she carries for modern audiences and the much more genuine affection which links Figaro to Suzanne. In the history of the theatre, Beaumarchais stands as the first successful practitioner of a comic style deriving its appeal from rapidity of action, vivacity of dialogue, and complexity of intrigue. Sociologically, he provides a comment on his society by exploiting the paradox that it is the social inferior, Figaro, who far exceeds his official master, Almaviva, in wit and intelligence, and can thus be seen as an ancestor to the Jeeves/Bertie Wooster relationship in P.G. Wodehouse.

—Philip Thody

See the essay on *The Barber of Seville*.

BEAUVOIR, Simone (Lucie Ernestine Marie) de

Born: Paris, France, 9 January 1908. **Education:** Educated at Institut Normal Catholique Adeline-Désir, Paris, 1913–25; studied philosophy and literature at the Sorbonne, Paris, 1926; Institut Sainte-Marie, Neuilly-sur-Seine; École Normale Supérieure, Paris, agrégation in philosophy 1929. **Family:** Began lifelong relationship with the writer Jean-Paul Sartre, *q.v.*, in 1929. **Career:** Part-time teacher, Lycée Victor Duruy, Paris, 1929–31; philosophy teacher, Lycée Montgrand, Marseilles, 1931–32, Lycée Jeanne d'Arc, Rouen, 1932–36, Lycée Molière, Paris, 1936–39, and Lycée Camille-Sée and Lycée Henri IV, both Paris, 1939–43. Founding editor, with Sartre, *Les Temps Modernes*, Paris, from 1945. **Awards:** Goncourt prize, 1954; Jerusalem prize, 1975; Austrian State prize for European literature, 1978. Honorary LL.D.: Cambridge University. **Member:** Consultative Committee, Bibliothèque Nationale, 1969; president, Choisir, 1972; president, Ligue des Droits des Femmes, from 1974. **Died:** 4 April 1986.

PUBLICATIONS

Fiction

L'Invitée. 1943; as *She Came to Stay*, translated by Yvonne Moyse and Roger Senhouse, 1949.

Le Sang des autres. 1945; edited by John F. Davis, 1973; as *The Blood of Others*, translated by Yvonne Moyse and Roger Senhouse, 1948.

Tous les hommes sont mortels. 1946; as *All Men Are Mortal*, translated by Leonard M. Friedman, 1956.

Les Mandarins. 1954; as *The Mandarins*, translated by Leonard M. Friedman, 1957.

Les Belles Images. 1966; as *Les Belles Images*, translated by Patrick O'Brian, 1968.

La Femme rompue (includes *L'Âge de discrétion* and *Monologue*). 1968; as *The Woman Destroyed* (includes *The Age of Discretion* and *The Monologue*), translated by Patrick O'Brian, 1969.

Quand prime le spirituel (stories). 1979; as *When Things of the Spirit Come First: Five Early Tales*, translated by Patrick O'Brian, 1982.

Plays

Les Bouches inutiles (produced 1945). 1945; as *Who Shall Die?*, translated by Claude Francis and Fernande Gontier, 1983.

Other

Pyrrhus et Cinéas. 1944.

Pour une morale de l'ambiguïté. 1947; as *The Ethics of Ambiguity*, translated by Bernard Frechtman, 1948.

L'Amérique au jour le jour. 1948; as *America Day by Day*, translated by Patrick Dudley, 1952.

L'Existentialisme et la sagesse des nations. 1948.

Le Deuxième Sexe: Les Faits et les mythes and L'Expérience vécue. 2 vols., 1949; as *The Second Sex*, edited and translated by H.M. Parshley, 1953; vol. 1 as *A History of Sex*, 1961, and as *Nature of the Second Sex*, 1963.

Must We Burn de Sade?, translated by Annette Michelson, 1953, and in *The Marquis de Sade*, edited by Paul Dinnage, 1953.

Privilèges (includes *Faut-il brûler Sade?*; *La Pensée de droite aujourd'hui*; *Merleau-Ponty ou le pseudo-sartrism).* 1955.

La Longue Marche: Essai sur la Chine. 1957; as *The Long March*, translated by Austryn Wainhouse, 1958.

Mémoires d'une jeune fille rangée. 1958; as *Memoirs of a Dutiful Daughter*, translated by James Kirkup, 1959.

Brigitte Bardot and the Lolita Syndrome, translated by Bernard Frechtman, 1960.

La Force de l'âge. 1960; as *The Prime of Life*, translated by Peter Green, 1962.

Djamila Boupacha, with Gisèle Halimi. 1962; as *Djamila Boupacha*, translated by Peter Green, 1962.

La Force des choses. 1963; as *Force of Circumstance*, translated by Richard Howard, 1965.

Une Mort très douce. 1964; as *A Very Easy Death*, translated by Patrick O'Brian, 1966.

La Vieillesse. 1970; as *Old Age*, translated by Patrick O'Brian, 1972; as *The Coming of Age*, translated by O'Brian, 1972.

Toute compte fait. 1972; as *All Said and Done*, translated by Patrick O'Brian, 1974.

La Cérémonie des adieux. 1981; as *Adieux: A Farewell to Sartre*, translated by Patrick O'Brian, 1984.

Lettres à Sartre, edited by Sylvie Le Bon de Beauvoir. 2 vols., 1990; as *Letters to Sartre*, edited and translated by Quintin Hoare, 1991.

Journal de guerre: septembre 1939–janvier 1941, edited by Sylvie Le Bon de Beauvoir. 1990.

Plays by Women: Volume Ten, edited and introduced by Annie Castledine. 1994.

A Transatlantic Love Affair: Letters to Nelson Algren, translated, compiled, and annotated by Sylvie Le Bon de Beauvoir. 1998.

Editor, *Lettres au Castor et à quelques autres 1926–1939* and *1940–1963*, by Sartre, 2 vols., 1983; as *Witness to My Life: The Letters of Jean-Paul Sartre to Simone de Beauvoir 1926–1939* and *Quiet Moments in a War: The Letters of Jean-Paul Sartre to Simone de Beauvoir 1943–63*, translated by Lee Fahnestock and Norman MacAfee, 1993–94.

*

Bibliography: *Les Écrits de Simone de Beauvoir* by Claude Francis and Fernande Gontier, 1979; *Simone de Beauvoir: An Annotated Bibliography* by Jay Bennett and Gabriella Hochmann, 1989.

Critical Studies: *Simone de Beauvoir: Encounters with Death* by Elaine Marks, 1973, and *Critical Essays on Simone de Beauvoir* edited by Marks, 1987; *Simone de Beauvoir* by Robert D. Cottrell, 1975; *Simone de Beauvoir on Woman* by Jean Leighton, 1975; *Hearts*

and Minds: The Common Journey of Simone de Beauvoir and Jean-Paul Sartre by Axel Madsen, 1977; *Simone de Beauvoir* by Konrad Bieber, 1979; *Simone de Beauvoir: A Life of Freedom* by Carol Ascher, 1981; *Simone de Beauvoir and the Limits of Commitment* by Anne Whitmarsh, 1981; *Simone de Beauvoir: A Study of Her Writings* by Terry Keefe, 1983; *Understanding ''The Second Sex''* by Donald L. Hatcher, 1984; *After ''The Second Sex'': Conversations with Simone de Beauvoir* by Alice Schwarzer, translated by Marianne Howarth, 1984; *Simone de Beauvoir: A Feminist Mandarin* by Mary Evans, 1985; *Simone de Beauvoir* by Judith Okely, 1986; *The Novels of Simone de Beauvoir* by Elizabeth Fallaize, 1987; *Simone de Beauvoir: A Critical View* by Renee Winegarten, 1987; *Simone de Beauvoir: A Life, A Love Story* by Claude Francis and Fernande Gontier, translated by Lisa Nesselson, 1987; *Simone de Beauvoir* by Lisa Appignanesi, 1988; *Simone de Beauvoir* by Jane Heath, 1989; *Feminist Theory and Simone de Beauvoir* by Toril Moi, 1990; *Simone de Beauvoir: A Biography* by Deirdre Bair, 1990; *Simone de Beauvoir: The Woman and Her Work* by Margaret Crosland, 1992; *Simone de Beauvoir: The Making of an Intellectual Woman* by Toril Moi, 1994; *Simone de Beauvoir and Jean-Paul Sartre: The Remaking of a Twentieth-Century Legend* by Kate Fullbrook and Edward Fullbrook, 1994; *Feminist Interpretations of Simone de Beauvoir*, edited by Margaret A. Simons, 1995; *Simone de Beauvoir, Le sang des autres* by Alex Hughes, 1995; *Philosophy as Passion: The Thinking of Simone de Beauvoir* by Karen Vintges, 1996; *Sex and Existence: Simone de Beauvoir's The Second Sex* by Eva Lundgren-Gothlin, translated by Linda Schenck, 1996; *A Disgraceful Affair: Simone de Beauvoir, Jean-Paul Sartre, and Bianca Lamblin* by Bianca Lamblin, translated by Julie Plovnick, 1996; *Simone de Beauvoir* by Mary Evans, 1996; *Simone de Beauvoir: A Critical Introduction* by Edward Fullbrook and Kate Fullbrook, 1997; *Existentialism, Feminism, and Simone de Beauvoir* by Joseph Mahon, 1997; *The Philosophy of Simone de Beauvoir: Gendered Phenomenologies, Erotic Generosities* by Debra B. Bergoffen, 1997; *Simone de Beauvoir* by Terry Keefe, 1998; *Simone de Beauvoir: A Critical Reader*, edited by Elizabeth Fallaize, 1998; *Simone de Beauvoir's The Second Sex: New Interdisciplinary Essays*, edited by Ruth Evans, 1998; *Identity Without Selfhood: Simone de Beauvoir and Bisexuality* by Mariam Fraser, 1999; *Colette, Beauvoir, and Duras: Age and Women Writers* by Bethany Ladimer, 1999; *Simone de Beauvoir: Gender and Testimony* by Ursula Tidd, 1999; *Simone de Beauvoir Writing the Self: Philosophy Becomes Autobiography* by Jo-Ann Pilardi, 1999; *Contingent Loves: Simone de Beauvoir and Sexuality*, edited by Melanie C. Hawthorne, 2000; *The Existential Phenomenology of Simone de Beauvoir*, edited by Wendy O'Brien and Lester Embree, 2001; *The Bonds of Freedom: Simone de Beauvoir's Existential Ethics* by Kristana Arp, 2001; *Simone de Beauvoir: Philosophy and Feminism* by Nancy Bauer, 2001; *Simone de Beauvoir's Philosophy of Lived Experience: Literature and Metaphysics* by Eleanore Holveck, 2002.

* * *

Biographical criticism may be regarded in some quarters as an outmoded literary tool. However, exceptions seem to be made when discussing the work of French novelist, essayist, and thinker Simone de Beauvoir. As Toril Moi points out in *Feminist Theory and Simone de Beauvoir*, critical accounts of de Beauvoir's work regularly reduce her literary output to questions of personality, in a way that is not apparent (and would be regarded as unacceptable) in accounts of the work of contemporaries. More than almost any other woman writer, de Beauvoir has been subjected to accusations of bad faith, inauthentic experience, and compliance with masculine domination. This adverse reception has been particularly pronounced in her native France, among the second wave of feminist thinkers who emerged in the late 1960s, with more favourable appraisals coming from Britain and the United States.

Why this situation has developed with such a courageous writer can be difficult to understand. Moi locates the dismissal of de Beauvoir to the supplanting in France of her humanist and existentialist beliefs by other intellectual interests such as structuralism and post-structuralism, and to the dominant media image of the writer as a blue-stockinged, masculinized woman, an *ersatz* Sartre. This negative response, however, denies the achievement of de Beauvoir, whose literary output deserves continued interest and covers a lifetime of scrupulous thought. Although educated as a philosopher, de Beauvoir wrote only one full-length philosophical study, *Le Deuxième Sexe* (*The Second Sex*), her study of female identity, preferring to employ the literary forms of the novel, play, and autobiography to act as practical examples of her philosophical creed. In her fiction, she works through, and refines upon, ideas from Sartrian Existentialism, with problems relating to liberty, action, choice, responsibility, and the certainty of death prominent throughout. Although to some extent didactic, her work is no abstract demonstration, and her writing is further characterized by considerable incorporation of personal experience. However, such is the clarity and crispness of her expression, coupled with the continuing pertinence of many of her ideas, that it is possible to read her work without any knowledge of her philosophical tenets and biographical details.

De Beauvoir's first literary work to be published was *L'Invitée* (*She Came to Stay*), an account of how a couple's life is placed under scrutiny by the advent of a young girl from Rouen. This work investigates a theme prominent in de Beauvoir's work, that of jealousy. Françoise Miquel has had a happy relationship with the actor Pierre Labrousse for eight years. However, the pairing is threatened when Xavière Pagès comes into their life. To Françoise, Xavière represents a most unsuitable match for Pierre, and the novel ends in tragedy with Françoise murdering her rival. This tale of a *crime passionnel*, told from different viewpoints, goes beyond a realistic study of excessive jealousy, infidelity, and desire, though, as de Beauvoir also attempts to provide a concrete example of Sartre's concept of the Other (as outlined in *L'Être et le néant* [*Being and Nothingness*]), with Xavière's presence providing an extreme example of how an understanding between two people is tested by the intervention of a third.

On the whole, de Beauvoir's writings alternate between those that are locked into depicting personal relationships as such, and those that portray people's interaction within the context of historical and political events. Her only play, the overlooked *Les Bouches inutiles* (*Who Shall Die?*), adapts the Italian chronicles of Sismondi to examine the issues of political power and choice. The inhabitants of Vaucelles in Flanders have freed themselves from the tyranny of the Duke of Burgundy and have set up a representative government. But food is scarce, and the town's council must decide who is to die and who can live. The "useless mouths" of the title represent the weaker members of the community—women, the infirm, and children—who, in a reversal of humanitarian practice, are chosen to die.

With its vivid picture of French political life on the Left in the 1930s and during the early years of the war, *Le Sang des autres* (*The*

Blood of Others) also has a firmly realized political context. The head of a resistance group is waiting beside his lover who has been wounded in a rescue attempt sanctioned by him. As he waits for Hélène to die, Blomart has to decide whether to carry out political action on the following day. He muses upon his bourgeois upbringing, upon his rejection of his family's values, and upon his relationship with Hélène. In recalling his past, de Beauvoir's narrative moves from personal memories to a more objective evaluation of how Blomart was viewed by others. As in her other novels, the narrative structure of *The Blood of Others* is divided up between characters; here between the once self-centred but now politically-committed Hélène and the serious, guilt-obsessed Blomart. As in *She Came to Stay*, the issues raised here are those of interdependence, personal liberty, and responsibility, to which de Beauvoir adds questions of moral choice and commitment in times of personal and political crisis.

Tous les hommes sont mortels (*All Men Are Mortal*) stands out, rather as Sartre's *Les Jeux sont fairs* (*The Chips Are Down*), does in his *oeure*, as a departure from the consistent realism of her works. Here de Beauvoir explores the omnipotence of death by creating a love affair between a mortal woman, Régine, an actress who is terrified of death, and Fosca, who is immortal. Régine wishes to challenge Fosca's immortality by loving him more than any previous woman. Fosca recounts his life, and rather in the way that *The Second Sex* provided a broad historical sweep of a single issue (woman's identity as Other), she leads us through a questioning of justifiable political measures from the 13th century onwards.

Régine is death-haunted, self-centred, and ambitious, while Fosca is unable to die, altruistic, and in his immortality deprived of personal goals. The pairing of individuals with very different personae is a strategy used throughout de Beauvoir's work, and appears again in her longest and most accomplished novel, *Les Mandarins* (*The Mandarins*). In this expansive work, de Beauvoir returns to a contemporary setting, and drawing extensively upon her acquaintances and experience, she outlines the manners and mores of the Paris-based Left just after the Liberation. The debate begun in *The Blood of Others*, on commitment, responsibility to self and others, and the difficult ethical choices posed by political action, is continued in this stimulating and densely textured account of de Beauvoir's circle. Centred on the threat to the autonomy of a political magazine (not that remote from *Les Temps Modernes*, to which she contributed), this novelization of lived events contrasts the political behaviour of an enthusiastic and vital writer, Perron, with that of an older, more pragmatic and experienced political activist, Dubreuilh. A further perspective is provided by Anne Dubreuilh, who is a watchful and contained figure compared to the impulsive and active Henri.

De Beauvoir's next novel, *Les Belles Images*, recreates the codes and types of behaviour of a certain social group as acutely as *The Mandarins* does. This is much less of a *roman à clef* than previous works, as the milieu that de Beauvoir has chosen is that of the well-heeled elite who work in the media (*la grosse bourgeoisie technocratique*). Surrounded by expensive possessions, entertained by fashionable chatter, and preoccupied by getting on, the characters in *Les Belles Images* have affairs, take expensive holidays, and suffer under the stresses of late 20th-century affluence. *Les Belles Images* deals with the question of personal development, above all that of children. The book's main character Laurence, whose own mother is successful and domineering, is challenged by her daughter Catherine's awareness of poverty and misery outside their comfortable world. Forced to recall her own childhood and to reappraise her relations with her ambitious mother and her surprisingly self-centred father, Laurence undergoes a personal crisis.

Despite the fact that de Beauvoir elected not to be a mother, family life, in particular the effect of ageing on existing relationships, dominates this phase of her writing career, as is evident from her collection of short stories *La Femme rompue* (*The Woman Destroyed*), and her studies of old age, *Une Mort très douce* (*A Very Easy Death*), which deals with her mother's final illness, and *La Vieillesse* (*The Coming of Age*). In her three stories, de Beauvoir dissects the fears, failings, and personal stagnation of women who have reached a certain age. *L'Âge de discrétion* (*The Age of Discretion*) investigates how an elderly teacher has to come to terms with her son becoming another person from the one that she has nurtured and idealized. Unable to change or compromise, she rejects him and finds herself at odds with her husband's more phlegmatic attitude. *Monologue* is a powerful, first-person account of a woman consumed by self-destructive spleen and antagonism towards her family. Alone on New Year's Eve, Murielle, who has been rejected by two husbands, on account of her being held responsible for her daughter's suicide, rages madly against her lot. *The Woman Destroyed* is the strongest piece in the collection, and is a diary account of a middle-aged woman discovering her husband's infidelities. Monique has deceived herself into thinking she has the perfect marriage. Her husband's infatuation with what Monique considers to be a totally unsuitable woman, a glamorous and striving lawyer, leaves the distraught wife trapped within what remains of her marriage, unable to break free and create a life for herself.

The desire to seize what choices are possible, and to subject your own life to constant scrutiny, are the central impressions of de Beauvoir's four-part autobiography that runs alongside her fictional work. As with Anaïs Nin's journals, these volumes provide a fascinating account of intellectual and artistic life in Paris, here from 1914 to the 1960s. The first volume, *Mémoires d'une jeune fille rangée* (*Memoirs of a Dutiful Daughter*), investigates her own upbringing as a child of a Parisian middle-class family and her rejection of her family's religious and moral views. *La Force de l'âge* (*The Prime of Life*) evaluates her intellectual and personal development after leaving university and during the war years. *La Force des choses* (*Force of Circumstance*), the most pessimistic of her memoirs, delineates her life in the context of political events such as the liberation, the revelation of Nazi atrocities and the Algerian war of independence. *Toute compte fait* (*All Said and Done*), set in the 1960s, reveals de Beauvoir as more confident about her political involvement and socialist beliefs.

—Anna-Marie Taylor

See the essays on *The Mandarins* and *The Second Sex*.

BECKETT, Samuel (Barclay)

Born: Foxrock, near Dublin, Ireland, 13 April 1906. **Education:** Educated at Ida Elsner's Academy, Stillorgan; Earlsfort House preparatory school; Portora Royal School, County Fermanagh; Trinity College, Dublin (foundation scholar), B.A. in French and Italian 1927, M.A. 1931. **Family:** Married Suzanne Deschevaux-Dumesnil

in 1961 (died 1989). **Career:** French teacher, Campbell College, Belfast, 1928; lecturer in English, École Normale Supérieure, Paris, 1928–30; lecturer in French, Trinity College, Dublin, 1930–31; translator and writer in Paris in the 1920s and 1930s, and closely associated with James Joyce's circle; in Dublin and London, 1933–37; returned to Paris, 1937; joined French Resistance, 1940; fled to Roussillon in unoccupied France, where he remained 1942–45; worked at the Irish Red Cross Hospital, St. Lô, France, 1945; resumed literary activity in Paris after World War II; after 1945, published the majority of his work in both French and English versions. **Awards:** *Evening Standard* award, 1955; Obie award, 1958, 1960, 1962, 1964; Italia prize, 1959, International Publishers prize, 1961; Prix Filmcritice, 1965; Tours film prize, 1966; Nobel prize for literature, 1969; National Grand prize for theatre (France), 1975; New York Drama Critics Circle citation, 1984. D.Litt.: Dublin University, 1959. **Member:** German Academy of Art; Companion of Literature, Royal Society of Literature, 1984; Aosdána, 1986. **Died:** 22 December 1989.

PUBLICATIONS

Collection

The Complete Dramatic Works. 1986.

Plays

Le Kid, with Georges Pelorson (produced 1931).

En attendant Godot (produced 1953). 1952; as *Waiting for Godot: Tragicomedy*, translated by Beckett, 1954; as *Waiting for Godot: With a Revised Text*, edited with an introduction and notes by Dougald McMillan and James Knowlson, 1993.

Fin de partie: suivi de Acte sans paroles, music by John Beckett (produced 1957). 1957; as *Endgame*, edited by John Fletcher and Beryl S. Fletcher, 1970; as *Endgame: A Play in One Act; Followed by Act Without Words: A Mime for One Player*, translated by Beckett, 1958.

All That Fall (broadcast 1957; produced 1965). 1957; as *Tous ceux qui tombent*, translated by Beckett and Robert Pinget, 1957.

Krapp's Last Tape (produced 1958). With *Embers*, 1959; as *La Dernière Bande*, translated by Beckett and Pierre Leyris, 1960.

Embers (broadcast 1959). With *Krapp's Last Tape*, 1959; as *Cendres*, translated by Beckett and Robert Pinget, 1960.

Act Without Words II (produced 1960). In *Krapp's Last Tape and Other Dramatic Pieces*, 1960; as *Acte sans paroles II*, translated by Beckett, 1966.

La Manivelle/The Old Tune (bilingual edition), from the play by Robert Pinget. 1960; Beckett's text only (broadcast 1960), in *Plays 1*, by Pinget, 1963.

Krapp's Last Tape and Other Dramatic Pieces (includes *All That Fall; Embers; Act Without Words I and II*). 1960.

Happy Days (produced 1961). 1961; as *Oh, Les Beaux Jours*, translated by Beckett, 1963; bilingual edition, edited by James Knowlson, 1978.

Words and Music, music by John Beckett (broadcast 1962). In *Play and Two Short Pieces for Radio*, 1964; as *Paroles et Musique*, translated by Samuel Beckett, 1966.

Cascando, music by Marcel Milhalovici (broadcast in French 1963). In *Dramatische Dichtungen 1*, 1963; as *Cascando: A Radio Piece for Music and Voice*, translated by Beckett, in *Play and Two Short Pieces for Radio*, 1964.

Play (in German, as *Spiel*, produced 1963; as *Play*, produced 1964). In *Play and Two Short Pieces for Radio*, 1964; as *Comédie*, translated by Beckett, 1966.

Play and Two Short Pieces for Radio. 1964.

Eh Joe (televised 1966; produced 1978). In *Eh Joe and Other Writings*, 1967.

Va et vient: Dramaticule (in German as *Kommen und Gehen*, produced 1966; as *Va et vient*, produced 1966). 1966; as *Come and Go: Dramaticule*, translated by Beckett, 1967.

Eh Joe and Other Writings (includes *Acts Without Words II* and *Film*). 1967.

Cascando and Other Short Dramatic Pieces (includes *Words and Music; Eh Joe; Play; Come and Go; Film*). 1968.

Film (screenplay). 1969.

Breath (part of *Oh! Calcutta!* produced 1969). In *Breath and Other Shorts*, 1971.

Breath and Other Shorts (includes *Come and Go; Act Without Words I* and *II*; and the prose piece *From an Abandoned Work*). 1971.

Not I (produced 1972). 1973; as *Pas moi*, translated by Beckett, 1975.

Fragment de théâtre. 1974; as *Theatre I* and *II*, translated by Beckett, in *Ends and Odds*, 1976.

Ghost Trio (as *Tryst*, televised 1976). In *Ends and Odds*, 1976.

That Time (produced 1976). 1976; as *Cette fois*, translated by Beckett, 1978.

Footfalls (produced 1976). 1976; as *Pas*, translated by Beckett, 1977.

Ends and Odds: Eight New Dramatic Pieces (includes *Not I; That Time: Footfalls; Ghost Trio; Theatre I* and *II; Radio I* and *II*). 1976; as *Ends and Odds: Plays and Sketches* (includes *Not I; That Time; Footfalls; Ghost Trio; . . . but the clouds . . . ; Theatre I* and *II; Radio I* and *II*), 1977.

Rough for Radio (broadcast 1976). As *Radio II*, in *Ends and Odds*, 1976.

Theatre I and II (produced 1985). In *Ends and Odds*, 1976.

A Piece of Monologue (produced 1980). In *Rockaby and Other Short Pieces*, 1981.

Rockaby (produced 1981). In *Rockaby and Other Short Pieces*, 1981; as *Berceuse*, translated by Beckett, 1982.

Rockaby and Other Short Pieces. 1981.

Ohio Impromptu (produced 1981). In *Rockaby and Other Short Pieces*, 1981; as *Impromptu d'Ohio*, 1982.

Catastrophe (produced 1982). 1982; in *Collected Shorter Plays*, 1984.

Catastrophe et autres dramaticules: Cette fois, Solo, Berceuse, Impromptu d'Ohio (produced 1982). 1982; in *Collected Shorter Plays*, 1984.

Three Occasional Pieces (includes *A Piece of Monologue; Rockaby; Ohio Impromptu*). 1982.

Quad (as *Quadrat 1+2*, televised in German 1982: as *Quad*, televised 1982). In *Collected Shorter Plays*, 1984.

Nacht und Träume (televised 1983). In *Collected Shorter Plays*, 1984.

What Where (in German, as *Was Wo*, produced 1983; in English, produced 1983). In *Collected Shorter Plays*, 1984.

Collected Shorter Plays. 1984.

Ohio Impromptu, Catastrophe, and What Where. 1984.

The Shorter Plays, edited by S.E. Gontarski. 1992.

Eleuthéria, translated from the French by Barbara Wright, 1996.

Screenplays: *Film*, 1965.

Radio Plays: *All That Fall*, 1957; *Embers*, 1959, *The Old Tune*, from a play by Robert Pinget, 1960; *Words and Music*, 1962; *Cascando*, 1963; *Rough for Radio*, 1976.

Television Plays: *Eh Joe*, 1966; *Tryst*, 1976; *Shades* (*Ghost Trio, Not I, . . . but the clouds. . .*), 1977; *Quadrat 1+2*, 1982 (Germany); *Quad*, 1982; *Nacht und Träume*, 1983.

Fiction

More Pricks Than Kicks. 1934.

Murphy (in English). 1938; translated by Beckett and Alfred Péron, 1947.

Molloy (in French). 1951; translated by Beckett and Patrick Bowles, 1955.

Malone meurt. 1951; as *Malone Dies*, translated by Beckett, 1956.

L'Innommable. 1953: as *The Unnamable*, translated by Beckett, 1958.

Watt (in English). 1953; translated into French by Ludovic and Agnès Janvier in collaboration with Beckett, 1968.

Nouvelles et textes pour rien. 1955; as *Stories and Texts for Nothing*, translated by Beckett and Richard Seaver, 1967.

From an Abandoned Work, 1958; as *D'un ouvrage abandonné*, translated by Ludovic and Agnès Janvier in collaboration with Beckett, 1967.

Three Novels. 1959.

Molloy, Malone Dies, The Unnamable. 1960.

Comment c'est. 1961; as *How It Is*, translated by Beckett, 1964.

Imagination morte imaginez. 1965; as *Imagination Dead Imagine*, translated by Beckett, 1965.

Assez. 1966; as *Enough*, translated by Beckett, in *No's Knife*, 1967.

Bing (in French), 1966; as *Ping*, translated by Beckett, in *No's Knife*, 1967.

Têtes-Mortes (includes *D'Un Ouvrage Adandonné; Assez; Bing; Imagination morte imaginez*). 1967; translated by Beckett, in *No's Knife*, 1967.

No's Knife: Collected Shorter Prose 1945–66 (includes *Stories and Texts for Nothing; From an Abandoned Work; Enough; Imagination Dead Imagine; Ping*). 1967.

Dans le cylindre. 1967.

L'Issue. 1968.

Sans. 1969; as *Lessness*, translated by Beckett, 1970.

Mercier et Camier. 1970; as *Mercier and Camier*, translated by Beckett, 1974.

Séjour. 1970.

Premier Amour. 1970; as *First Love*, translated by Beckett, 1973; in *First Love and Other Novellas*, edited by Gerry Dukes, 2000.

Le Dépeupleur. 1971; as *The Lost Ones*, translated by Beckett, 1972.

The North. 1972.

Abandonné. 1972.

Au loin un oiseau. 1973.

First Love and Other Shorts. 1974.

Fizzles. 1976.

Pour finir encore et autres foirades. 1976; as *For to End Yet Again and Other Fizzles*, translated by Beckett, 1976.

All Strange Away. 1976.

Four Novellas (*First Love; The Expelled; The Calmative; The End*). 1977; as *The Expelled and Other Novellas*, 1980.

Six Residua. 1978.

Company. 1980.

Mal vu mat dit. 1981; as *Ill Seen Ill Said*, translated by Beckett, 1982; as *Samuel Beckett's Mal vu mal dit/Ill Seen Ill Said*, edited by Charles Krance, 1996.

Worstward Ho. 1983.

Stirrings Still. 1988.

Nohow On (includes *Company; Ill Seen Ill Said; Worstword Ho*). 1989.

Soubresauts. 1989.

Dream of Fair to Middling Women, edited by Eoin O'Brien and Edith Fournie. 1992.

Samuel Beckett: The Complete Short Prose, 1929–1989, edited with an introduction and notes by S.E. Gontarski, 1995.

Verse

Whoroscope. 1930.

Echo's Bones and Other Precipitates. 1935.

Gedichte (collected poems in English and French, with German translations). 1959.

Poems in English. 1961.

Poèmes. 1968.

Collected Poems in English and French. 1977; revised edition, as *Collected Poems 1930–1978*, 1984.

Mirlitonnades. 1978.

Other

"Dante . . . Bruno. Vico . . . Joyce," in *Our Exagmination Round His Factification for Incamination of Work in Progress.* 1929.

Proust. 1931; with *Three Dialogues with Georges Duthuit*, 1965.

Bram van Velde (in French), with Georges Duthuit and Jacques Putman. 1958; translated by Beckett and Olive Classe, 1960.

A Beckett Reader. 1967.

The Collected Works. 1970.

I Can't Go On: A Selection from the Work of Beckett, edited by Richard Seaver. 1976.

Disjecta: Miscellaneous Writings and a Dramatic Fragment, edited by Ruby Cohn. 1983.

Collected Shorter Prose 1945–1980. 1984.

Happy Days: The Production Notebook, edited by James Knowlson. 1985.

As the Story Was Told: Uncollected and Late Prose. 1990.

Krapp's Last Tape: Beckett's Theatrical Notebook, edited by James Knowlson. 1991.

The Theatrical Notebooks of Samuel Beckett, edited by Dougald McMillan, James Knowlson, and S.E. Gontarski. 4 vols., 1992.

Samuel Beckett: Photographs by John Minihan. 1995.

No Author Better Served: The Correspondence of Samuel Beckett and Alan Schneider, edited by Maurice Harmon. 1998.

Samuel Beckett: A Casebook, edited by Jennifer M. Jeffers. 1998.

Beckett's Dream Notebook, edited by John Pilling. 1999.

Translator, *Negro: An Anthology.* 1934; as *Beckett in Black and Red: The Translations for Nancy Cunard's Negro (1934)*, edited by Alan Warren Friedman. 2000.

Translator, *Anthology of Mexican Poetry*, edited by Octavio Paz. 1958.

Translator, *The Old Tune*, by Robert Pinget. 1960.

Translator, with others, *Selected Poems*, by Alain Bosquet. 1963.

Translator, *Zone*, by Guillaume Apollinaire. 1972.

Translator, *Drunken Boat*, by Arthur Rimbaud, edited by James Knowlson and Felix Leakey. 1977.

Translator, with others, *No Matter No Fact.* 1988.

*

Bibliography: *Samuel Beckett: His Works and His Critics: An Essay in Bibliography* by Raymond Federman and John Fletcher, 1970 (works to 1966); *Samuel Beckett: Checklist and Index of His Published Works 1967–76* by Robin John Davis, 1979; *Samuel Beckett: A Reference Guide* by Cathleen Culotta Andonian, 1988.

Critical Studies: *Samuel Beckett; A Critical Study*, 1961, revised edition, 1968, and *A Reader's Guide to Samuel Beckett*, 1973, both by Hugh Kenner; *Samuel Beckett: The Comic Gamut*, 1962, *Back to Beckett*, 1974, and *Just Play: Beckett's Theater*, 1980, all by Ruby Cohn, and *Samuel Beckett: A Collection of Criticism*, 1975, and *Waiting for Godot: A Casebook*, 1987, both edited by Cohn; *Samuel Beckett: The Language of Self* by Frederick J. Hoffman, 1962; *Beckett* by Richard N. Coe, 1964, retitled as *Samuel Beckett*, 1964; *The Novels of Samuel Beckett*, 1964, and *Samuel Beckett's Art*, 1967, both by John Fletcher, and *Beckett: A Study of His Plays* by Fletcher and John Spurling, 1972, revised edition as *Beckett the Playwright*, 1985; *Samuel Beckett* by William York Tindall, 1964; *Samuel Beckett: A Collection of Critical Essays* edited by Martin Esslin, 1965; *Journey to Chaos: Samuel Beckett's Early Fiction* by Raymond Federman, 1965; *Beckett at 60: A Festschrift* edited by John Calder, 1967; *Samuel Beckett's "Murphy": A Critical Excursion* by Robert Harrison, 1968; *Samuel Beckett* by Ronald Hayman, 1968, revised edition, 1980; *All I Can Manage More Than I Could: An Approach to the Plays of Samuel Beckett* by Alec Reid, 1968; *Twentieth Century Interpretations of "Endgame"* edited by Bell Gale Chevigny, 1969; *The Long Sonata of the Dead: A Study of Samuel Beckett* by Michael Robinson, 1969; *Samuel Beckett: A New Approach* by Guy C. Barnard, 1970; *Samuel Beckett Now: Critical Approaches to His Novels, Poetry, and Plays* edited by Melvin J. Friedman, 1970; *Samuel Beckett: Poet and Critic* by Lawrence E. Harvey, 1970; *Beckett: A Study of His Novels*, 1970, and *The Plays of Samuel Beckett*, 1972, both by Eugene Webb; *Samuel Beckett* by Francis Doherty, 1971; *The Shape of Chaos: An Interpretation of the Art of Samuel Beckett* by David Hesla, 1971; *Angels of Darkness: Dramatic Effect in Samuel Beckett* by Colin Duckworth, 1972; *The Fiction of Beckett: Form and Effect* by H. Porter Abbott, 1973; *Samuel Beckett* by A. Alvarez, 1973, revised edition, 1992; *Art and the Artist in the Works of Samuel Beckett* by Hannah Case Copeland, 1975; *Samuel Beckett's Dramatic Language* by James Eliopulos, 1975; *Beckett the Shape Changer* edited by Katharine J. Worth, 1975, and *Waiting for Godot and Happy Days* by Worth, 1990; *Condemned to Life: The World of Samuel Beckett* by Kenneth and Alice Hamilton, 1976; *Samuel Beckett* by John Pilling, 1976, and *The Cambridge Companion to Beckett* edited by Pilling, 1994; *Forme et signification dans le théâtre de Samuel Beckett* by Betty Rojtman, 1976; *Beckett and Broadcasting: A Study of the Works of Samuel Beckett for and in Radio and Television* by Clas Zilliacus, 1976; *Beckett's Happy Days: A Manuscript Study*, 1977, and *The Intent of Undoing in Samuel Beckett's Dramatic Texts*, 1985, both by S.E. Gontarski, and *On Beckett: Essays and Criticism*, 1986, and *The Beckett Studies Reader*, 1993, both edited by Gontarski, 1993; *Beckett/Beckett* by Vivian Mercier, 1977; *Samuel Beckett: A Biography* by Deirdre Bair, 1978; *A Student's Guide to the Plays of Samuel Beckett* by Beryl S. Fletcher,

1978, revised edition, with John Fletcher, 1985; *The Shape of Paradox: An Essay on Waiting for Godot* by Bert O. Slates, 1978; *The Samuel Beckett Manuscripts: A Critical Study* by Richard L. Admussen, 1979; *Samuel Beckett: The Critical Heritage* edited by Raymond Federmand and Lawrence Graver, 1979; *Beckett and Joyce: Friendship and Fiction* by Barbara Reich Gluck, 1979; *Frescoes of the Skull: The Later Prose and Drama of Samuel Beckett* edited by James Knowlson and John Pilling, 1979; *The Transformations of Godot* by Frederick Busi, 1980; *Waiting for Death: The Philosophical Significance of Beckett's En attendant Godot* by Ramona Cormier, 1980; *Samuel Beckett and the Voice of Species: A Study of the Prose Fiction* by Eric P. Levy, 1980; *Accommodating the Chaos: Samuel Beckett's Nonrelational Art* by J.E. Dearlove, 1982; *Abysmal Games in the Novels of Samuel Beckett* by Angela B. Moorjani, 1982; *Beckett's Real Silence* by Hélène L. Baldwin, 1983; *Samuel Beckett: Humanistic Perspectives* edited by Morris Beja, S.E. Gontarski, and Pierre Astier, 1983; *Samuel Beckett* by Charles Lyons, 1983; *Canters and Chronicles: The Use of Narrative in the Plays of Samuel Beckett and Harold Pinter* by Kristin Morrison, 1983; *Beckett's Theaters: Interpretations for Performance* by Sidney Homan, 1984; *The Development of Samuel Beckett's Fiction*, 1984, and *Innovation in Samuel Beckett's Fiction*, 1993, both by Rubin Rabinovitz; *Samuel Beckett and the Meaning of Being: A Study in Ontological Parable* by Lance St. John Butler, 1984, *Rethinking Beckett: A Collection of Critical Essays* edited by St. John Butler and Robin J. Davies, 1990, and *Critical Essays on Samuel Beckett* edited by St. John Butler, 1993; *Samuel Beckett: Modern Critical Views* edited by Harold Bloom, 1985; *Beckett on File* edited by Virginia Cooke, 1985; *Beckett at 80/ Beckett in Context* edited by Enoch Brater, 1986, and *Beyond Minimalism: Beckett's Late Style in the Theater*, 1987, and *Why Beckett*, 1989, both by Brater; *Samuel Beckett* by Linda Ben-Zvi, 1986, and *Women in Beckett: Performance and Critical Perspectives* edited by Ben-Zvi, 1990; *Understanding Beckett: A Study of Monologue and Gesture in the Works of Samuel Beckett* by Peter Gidal, 1986; *As No Other Dare Fail: For Samuel Beckett on His 80th Birthday*, 1986; *Beckett's New Worlds: Style in Metafiction* by Susan D. Brienza, 1987; *Beckett Translating/Translating Beckett* edited by Alan Warren Friedman, Charles Rossman, and Dina Sherzer, 1987; *The Broken Window: Beckett's Dramatic Perspective* by Jane Alison Hale, 1987; *Myth and Ritual in the Plays of Beckett* by Katherine H. Burkman, 1988; *Beckett: Repetition, Theory, and Text* by Stephen Connor, 1988; *Beckett and Babel: An Investigation into the Status of the Bilingual Work* by Brian T. Fitch, 1988; *Beckett's Critical Complicity: Carnival, Contestation and Tradition* by Sylvia Debevec Henning, 1988; *Beckett in the Theatre: The Author as Practical Playwright and Director 1: From Waiting for Godot to Krapp's Last Tape* by Douglas McMillan and Martha Fehsenfeld, 1988; *Theatre of Shadows: Beckett's Drama 1956–1976* by Rosemary Poutney, 1988; *The Humour of Beckett* by Valerie Topsfield, 1988; *Beckett and Zen: A Study of Dilemma in the Novels of Samuel Beckett* by Paul Foster, 1989; *Beckett: Waiting for Godot* by Lawrence Graver, 1989; *Beckett in Performance* by Jonathan Kalb, 1989; *Beckett* by Andrew K. Kennedy, 1989; *The World of Beckett* by Alan Astro, 1990; *Waiting for Godot: Form in Movement* by Thomas Couisneau, 1990; *Beckett's Fiction: In Different Words* by Leslie Hill, 1990; *Beckett's Self-Referential Drama* by Shimon Levy, 1990; *Unwording the World: Beckett's Prose Works after the Nobel Prize* by Carla Locatelli, 1990; *Paradox and Desire in Beckett's Fiction* by David Watson, 1990; *Early Beckett: Art and Allusion in More Pricks Than Kicks and Murphy* by Anthony Farrow, 1991; *Wandering and Home: Beckett's*

Metaphysical Narrative by Eyal Amiran, 1993; *Beckett's Dying Words: The Clarendon Lecture 1990* by Christopher Ricks, 1993; *Endgame: The Ashbin Play* by Arthur N. Athanason, 1993; *Women in Samuel Beckett's Prose and Drama: Her Own Other* by Mary Bryden, 1993; *Theatre on Trial: Samuel Beckett's Later Drama* by Anna McMullan, 1993; *Critical Essays on Samuel Beckett*, edited by Lance St. John Butler, 1993; *Directing Beckett*, edited by Lois Oppenheim, 1994; *The Drama in the Text: Beckett's Late Fiction* by Enoch Brater, 1994; *Beckett: the Irish Dimension* by Mary Junker, 1995; *Samuel Beckett and the End of Modernity* by Richard Begam, 1996; *Samuel Beckett: The Last Modernist* by Anthony Cronin, 1996; *Damned to Fame: The Life of Samuel Beckett* by James Knowlson, 1996; *Technique and Tradition in Beckett's Trilogy of Novels* by Gönöl Pultar, 1996; *Conversations With (and About) Beckett* by Mel Gussow, 1996; *The World of Samuel Beckett, 1906–1946* by Lois Gordon, 1996; *Beckett Before Godot* by John Pilling, 1997; *Samuel Beckett and Music*, edited by Mary Bryden, 1997; *Beckett and the Mythology of Psychoanalysis* by Phil Baker, 1997; *Samuel Beckett's Artistic Theory and Practice: Criticism, Drama, and Early Fiction* by James Acheson, 1997; *The Critical Response to Samuel Beckett*, edited by Cathleen Culotta Andonian, 1998; *Samuel Beckett and the Idea of God* by Mary Bryden, 1998; *Beckett and Poststructuralism* by Anthony Uhlmann, 1999; *Saying I No More: Subjectivity and Consciousness in the Prose of Samuel Beckett* by Daniel Katz, 1999; *Samuel Beckett's Theatre: Life Journeys* by Katharine Worth, 1999; *No-thing Is Left to Tell: Zen/Chaos Theory in the Dramatic Art of Samuel Beckett* by John Leeland and Kundert-Gibbs, 1999; *After the Final No: Samuel Beckett's Trilogy* by Thomas J. Cousineau, 1999; *The Complete Critical Guide to Samuel Beckett* by David Pattie, 2000; *Chronicles of Disorder: Samuel Beckett and the Cultural Politics of the Modern Novel* by David Weisberg, 2000; *Sails on the Herring Fleet: Essays on Beckett* by Herbert Blau, 2000; *Samuel Beckett*, edited and introduced by Jennifer Birkett and Kate Ince, 2000; *How It Was: a Memoir of Samuel Beckett* by Anne Atik, 2001; *The Philosophy of Samuel Beckett* by John Calder, 2001; *Interpreting Narrative in the Novels of Samuel Beckett* by Jonathan Boulter, 2001; *A Beckett Canon* by Ruby Cohn, 2001; *Engagement and Indifference: Beckett and the Political*, edited by Henry Sussman and Christopher Devenney, 2001.

* * *

Samuel Beckett has achieved recognition as a powerful creative writer working in both English and French. His prose fiction and drama are often startlingly innovative in form, and this break with tradition links him to the French new novelists, and to the theatre of the absurd. Like other writers of the 1950s and 1960s he moved away not only from realism and psychological presentation of character, but also from the limitations of rational sequence and plot. Beckett cannot be labelled however. He has a distinctive voice that places him outside all schools and categories. His best work combines a fiercely uncompromising struggle with essential questions and an awareness that there are no answers: the key word in his work is "perhaps." This awareness that his is "an art of failure" could lead to despair, and most of his characters are certainly living in a grimly purgatorial world, condemned to talk or write, in the forlorn hope of finding the words which will give them the right to silence, or simply to help pass the time of waiting, as in *En attendant Godot* (*Waiting for Godot*). What makes the works life-enhancing is the fact that the black vision of characters struggling to make sense of a cruel universe is coupled with a superb poetic feeling for language, and a brilliant, self-mocking sense of humour.

Beckett wrote *Watt*, his last major novel in English, in 1953, and the change to French clearly marks a change of direction, and the discovery of his mature style. During the earlier period he published some poetry, and his first successful novel, *Murphy*. This has a serious theme, as Murphy, a ''seedy solipsist,'' seeks to escape the outer world, and spend more time in his mind, ''in the dark, in the will-lessness,'' but his way of achieving this, by tying himself up naked in a rocking chair, typically undermines the seriousness. The novel works best as a brilliantly comic account of Murphy's battles with the everyday world he wishes to escape. *Murphy* is an odd novel, but it has characters, a plot, and a recognizable setting in London. Such traditional elements have been dropped in *Watt*, and the fiction in French confirms this new form.

The first major work in French is the trilogy: *Molloy, Malone meurt* (*Malone Dies*), and *L'Innommable* (*The Unnamable*). Molloy tells us at the beginning of his narrative that he is now in his mother's room, compelled to write stories, and aware of an inner voice which speaks ''of a world collapsing endlessly, a frozen world, under a faint untroubled sky.'' He tells the story of his journey, through a hostile world, towards his mother. His progress is marked by a steady physical deterioration, until he is finally crawling through a forest, with the aid of his crutches. This grim quest is constantly interrupted by comic digressions that Molloy uses to escape from his ''calvary with no hope of crucifixion.'' For the reader these episodes, such as the detailed account of how Molloy organizes his ''sucking stones,'' give the novel a defiantly comic vigour, in the face of suffering. There is also a black irony about the society through which the tramp-like Molloy journeys: ''Day is the time for lynching, for sleep is sacred.'' The second part of *Molloy* is narrated by Moran, who seems the opposite of Molloy, comfortably settled in a regular social and domestic routine, until he is sent on a mission to find Molloy. He is vaguely aware at the outset that the Molloy he has to find is within himself, and by the time he returns he has come to resemble his quarry. The novel can be interpreted, John Fletcher suggests, as ''an epic of the search for one's real self'' (*The Novels of Samuel Beckett*, 1964), and this is a central theme of the whole trilogy. *Malone Dies* focuses on the writer in his room, waiting to die, but hoping to tell the right story meanwhile. ''Words and images run riot in my head,'' he writes, but his stories are interrupted by comments on the decrepit, suffering body, whose pain is so bearable compared with that of the questing mind.

Malone wonders at times if he has not already died. The narrator of *The Unnamable* is simply a voice, not knowing whether he has died, or is waiting to be born. He is in a ''hell of stories,'' forced to go on speaking, but hoping to attain silence and peace. If he ever reaches that silence, however, he will not know it: ''in the silence you don't know.'' The final words of the desperate voice are: ''I can't go on, I'll go on.'' Beckett himself did go on, and in the best of his later works found completely new ways of pursuing the same concerns, often starting from the images of suffering and guilt in the trilogy. *Comment c'est* (*How It Is*) for instance, develops around the image of a muddy hell, in which torturer and victim endlessly exchange roles.

Beckett's plays explore the same themes as the novels, but in *Waiting for Godot* the two old tramps, waiting day after day for the mysterious Mr Godot to come, are given a comical human warmth towards each other that counterpoints the bleak hopelessness of their

waiting. The only people who do pass by the stretch of country road, with its solitary tree, are the brutal whip-cracking Pozzo and his slave, Lucky. Perhaps, it is hinted, Pozzo is Godot, and they have not recognized him. They hope that Godot will ''save'' them—he is the only reason for their suffering existence; but when the second act shows the same situation, with Pozzo now blind, and Lucky dumb, this hope seems futile, and Pozzo sums up the feeling of the play in the image ''they give birth astride of a grave.'' The best productions keep a balance between the comic games the tramps play, and the blackness they are trying to forget. *Fin de partie* (*Endgame*) is more inhuman. Hamm, blind and crippled, spends his days in a cell-like room with Clov, perhaps his son, and his parents, confined to dustbins. They are waiting, but only for the end, which may never come. They pass the time with wearisome routines, aware that what keeps them there is the dialogue. The later plays take the process of compression even further, using powerful theatrical images, which work despite the absence of action or plot. In *Happy Days* (*Oh, Les Beaux Jours*) Winnie is buried to the waist in the earth, and by Act II she has sunk to her neck. The contrast between her situation and her determinedly optimistic chatter is the basis for the play. In *Not I* (*Pas moi*) the character is physically reduced to a mouth, pouring out a stream of words in the hope that one day she will be allowed to fall silent.

Beckett's mastery, of form, the ''power of the text to claw,'' is an important element in his success, but so too is the fact that he struggles painfully, humorously, with questions which have always been central for the human spirit.

—John Rothenberg

See the essays on *Endgame*; *Molloy, Malone Dies, The Unnamable*; and *Waiting for Godot*.

BEI DAO

Born: Zhao Zhenkai in Beijing, 2 August 1949. **Education:** B.A., Chinese Language and Literature, the University Extension, Beijing, June 1983. **Family:** Divorced; one daughter. **Career:** Founding editor of *Jintian* [*Today*], 1978–80 and 1990–present; literary editor of *Xin guancha* [*New observation*], 1980–81; literary editor of *Zhongguo baodao* [*China report*], 1981–85; deputy editor-in-chief of *Guoji shitan* [*International poetry*], 1986–1987; visiting writer, International Writers' Program, University of Iowa, 1989; banished from China by the Chinese government, 1989 to 2001; visiting poet at European universities, 1989–1993; visiting poet or professor at American universities, 1994–present. Lives in Davis, California. **Awards:** May Fourth Literary prize from Beijing University, China, 1985; National award for Best Poetry Collection, China, 1988; Honorary member of the Swedish PEN, 1989; Tucholsky prize from the Swedish PEN, 1990; PEN American Center Freedom to Write award, 1990; Honorary member of the American Academy of Arts and Letters, 1996; Honorary member of the House of Poetry in Morocco, 1998; Guggenheim Fellow, 1998. **Member:** Chinese Writers Association, 1985; Advisory Board of PEN Foundation's Emergency Fund, 1992; Board of Directors of the Human Rights in China; Board of Directors of the International Parliament of Writers, 1995.

PUBLICATIONS

Collections

Bei Dao shixun (Selected poems of Bei Dao). 1985.
Bei Dao xunji (Selected works of Bei Dao). 2000.

Verse

Taiyangcheng zhaji; as *Notes From the City of Sun*, translated by Bonnie S. McDougall. 1983.
Guilai de moshengren [The Homecoming Stranger]. 1987.
Bayue de mengyouzhe; as *The August Sleepwalker*, translated by Bonnie S. McDougall. 1988.
Jiuxue; as *Old Snow*, translated by Bonnie S. McDougall and Chen Maiping. 1991.
Juli de xingshi; as *Forms of Distance*, translated by David Hinton. 1994.
Wuye geshou [Midnight singer]. 1995.
Lingdu yishang de fengjing; as *Landscape Over Zero*, translated by David Hinton with Yanbing Chen. 1996.
Shouye; as *Nightwatch*, translated by David Hinton. 1999.
Kaisuo; as *Unlock*, translated by Eliot Weinberger and Iona Man-Cheong. 2000.
Zai tianya; as *At the Sky's Edge*, translated by David Hinton. 2001.

Fiction

Bodong; as *Waves*, translated by Bonnie S. McDougall and Susette Ternent Cooke. 1987.

Other

Lan fangzi; as *Blue House*, translated by Theodore Huters and Fengying Ming. 2000.
Translator, *Bei Ou xiandai shi xuan* [Contemporary Scandinavian poetry]. 1987.

*

Critical Studies: "Bei Dao's Poetry: Revelation and Communication" by Bonnie S. McDougall, in *Modern Chinese Literature*, vol. 1, no. 2, 1985; "Zhao Zhenkai's Fiction: A Study in Cultural Alienation," in *Modern Chinese Literature*, vol. 1, no. 1, 1984; "Quest and Confrontation: The Poetic and Fictional Voices of Bei Dao/Zhao Zhenkai," in *Vägar till Kina: Göran Malmqvist 60 år, Orientaliska studier*, edited by Bert Edström et al., 1984; "A New Beginning for the Modernist Chinese Novel: Zhao Zhenkai's *Bodong*" by Philip Williams, in *Modern Chinese Literature*, vol. 5, no. 1, 1989; "What Is World Poetry?" by Stephen Owen, in *The New Republic*, 19 November 1990; "Ideology and Conflicts in Bei Dao's Poetry" by Dian Li, in *Modern Chinese Literature*, vol. 9, no. 2, 1996; "Translating Bei Dao: Translatability as Reading and Critique," in *Babel, the Official Journal of the International Federation of Translators*, vol. 44, no. 4, 1999.

*   *   *

Bei Dao has been writing poetry for over twenty years, and he is easily the best-known living Chinese poet in both China and the West today, although the reasons for his fame are very different. In China,

he is a memory, a literary giant of the 1980s whose path-breaking writings influenced a generation and sparked the democracy movement that helped accelerate the country's reform and openness. In the West, he is a reminder of China's repression and intolerance, a poetic enigma whose well-translated elliptical syntax and cryptic imagery represent a complex interior response to a hostile exterior world. Such different reactions toward Bei Dao underscore the transformation of the poet himself—from an uncompromising young rebel in pre-1989 China to a mellowing and meditative poetic voice in exile in the West.

Poetry almost happened to Bei Dao by accident. After high school, Bei Dao was sent to work as a construction worker in a Beijing suburb, where he started to write perhaps to fight boredom and a feeling of despair. By the end of the 1970s, China had just awakened from the nightmare of its Cultural Revolution and the oppressive Maoist ideology had lost much of its creditability. After years of overfeeding on the formulaic propaganda of socialist literature, the public, especially young readers, was ready for an alternative. Thus Bei Dao's personal pulse became that of a generation. Although, understandably, his writings paralleled the official poetry in the style of grandiosity and slogan-ism, they could not be more different in their messages. The significance of a simple statement such as "I—do—not—believe!" can only be grasped by those who must believe nothing else but Mao.

The central concern of Bei Dao's poetry at this time was a plea for the restoration of personal space and life's ordinariness against a general deprivation of humanity in China for the past decade. "I am no hero," he writes, "In an age without heroes / I just want to be a man." Being a man means, Bei Dao repeatedly clarifies, living a life of dignity and fulfillment without political consequences. Such apolitical ideas were given a political reading by both the student protesters of the 1980s and the Chinese government. When Bei Dao's influence spread from small circles of friends to many college campuses, the literary establishment launched a campaign against him and a like-minded group of young poets and maliciously labeled their works as "Misty Poetry," a label that Bei Dao would later gleefully embrace. The official hostility made Bei Dao famous but it ultimately led to his forced exile in 1989 following the Tian'anmen Student Protest.

"The exile of the word has begun," Bei Dao announced upon his arrival in Europe and immediately became the symbol of China's abortive democracy movement. He revived his short-lived journal *Jintian* [Today] and made it an important forum for the community of exiled Chinese writers and artists. As tragic as exile has been to his family life, Bei Dao has relished the unexpected freedom and the opportunity to work "the word" to attain the realm of pure poetry, a poetry of linguistic exactitude and aesthetic bliss. In terms of style and techniques, he has become a bolder experimentalist in truncated word-combinations and disjointed images. He has also reinvigorated his efforts to draw on classical Chinese poetry as well as his favorite Western poets such as Paul Celan and César Vallejo. Removed from familiar sensations and relationships, Bei Dao seizes the singularity of his life in exile and contextualizes his heightened sense of subjectivity in everything that is happening—be it an accidental mosquito bite, a Bach concert or a phone call home. In this mundaneness of life, however, an opponent always lurks, invisible and in some cases unnamable, working to undermine life's promise and fragment the self. It can be argued that exile is only an occasion for Bei Dao's profound sense of alienation and pessimism and that he also is reiterating a truth about modern life in general, a truth that is more powerful and long-lasting than a single political ideology. This is the very reason that Bei Dao deserves to be among the most potent voices in contemporary Chinese and world poetry.

—Dian Li

BELLI, Gioconda

Born: Managua, Nicaragua, 9 December 1948. **Education:** Graduated from the Royal School of Santa Isabel, Madrid, Spain, 1964; diploma in advertising and journalism, Charles Morris Price School, Philadelphia, PA, 1965; studied advertising management at INCAE, Harvard University's school of business administration in Central America; took courses in philosophy and literature at Georgetown University. **Family:** Married 1) Mariano A. Downing, 1967 (divorced 1976), two daughters; 2) Sergio de Castro, 1977 (divorced, 1979), one son; 3) Charles Castaldi, 1987, one daughter. **Career:** Worked in advertising and publicity, 1973–78; political-diplomatic commission, FSLN (Sandinista Liberation Front), 1978–79; director of communications and public relations, Ministry of Economic Planning, Sandinista government, 1979–82; international press liaison, FSLN, 1982–83; director of State Communications, 1984–86; resigned political appointments to become a full time writer, 1986. **Awards:** National University of Nicaragua poetry prize, 1972; Casa de las Americas poetry prize, 1978; Editors and Publishers Best Political Novel of the Year award, Friedrich Ebhert Foundation Book Sellers, for *The Inhabited Woman*, 1989; Anna Seghers prize, German Democratic Republic, 1989.

PUBLICATIONS

Collections

Amor insurrecto. 1985.
Poesía reunida. 1989.
El ojo de la mujer. 1991.
Sortilegio contra el frío. 1992.

Verse

Sobre la grama. 1972.
Línea de fuego. 1978.
Truenos y arco iris. 1982.
De la costilla de Eva. 1987, as *From Eve's Rib*, translated by Steven F. White, 1989.
Apogeo. 1997.

Fiction

La mujer habitada. 1988, as *The Inhabited Woman*, translated by Kathleen March, 1994.
Sofía de los presagios. 1990.
Waslala. 1996.

Other

El taller de las mariposas (for children). 1994.

El país bajo mi piel: memorias de amor y guerra (memoirs). 2001; translated by Gioconda Bellli and Kristina Cordero, 2001.

*

Critical Studies: "Gioconda Belli: The Erotic Politics of the Great Mother" by Kathleen March, in *Monographic Review*, vol. 6, 1990; "Gioconda Belli, novelista revolucionaria" by Maria Salgado, in *Monographic Review*, vol. 8, 1992; "La transformación de la mujer y la nación en la poesía comprometida de Gioconda Belli" by Pilar Moyano, in *Revista Canadiense de Estudios Hispánicos*, vol. 2, 1993; "Entradas a la historia: *La mujer habitada*" by Amy Kaminsky, in *Hispamérica*, vol. 67, 1994; "Gioconda Belli: The Magic and/of Eroticism" by Arturo Arias, in *The Postmodern in Latin and Latino American Cultural Narratives*, 1996; *Novels of Testimony and Resistance from Central America* by Linda Craft, 1997.

*   *   *

Gioconda Belli is one of contemporary Central America's best known writers and one of the few women writers from this region whose works have been translated and published in the United States and throughout Europe. Belli's literary career has from its beginning been intimately connected to her political life and the political life of her country, Nicaragua. The Sandinista revolution, which ousted the dictator Anastasio Somoza in 1979, gained widespread international attention in the 1970s and 1980s. The image of youthful Sandinista revolutionaries who were often poets, artists, and intellectuals, appealed to many and Gioconda Belli was one of the revolution's most articulate spokespersons. Belli joined the FSLN (Sandinista National Liberation Front) in 1970 and was in the underground resistance until 1975, when she had to flee the Somoza regime's secret police and go into exile. During her exile, she continued to be active in communications and logistic operations. When the Sandinistas came to power in 1979, she held various government positions, working primarily in communications, journalism, and public relations. Her profound commitment to the revolutionary ideal of working together to create a more just society is unquestionably at the heart of her writing, both poetry and fiction.

Her early poetry, particularly *Sobre la grama* [On the Grass], primarily celebrates heterosexual womanhood. Some of her recurring poetic themes include erotic pleasures, the beauty and satisfactions of all the stages of motherhood, and the irrepressible longing to live a full, creative, committed life. As her personal involvement in the revolution grew, her poetry reflected this experience. In subsequent books of poetry she continued to write sensual poems that celebrated physical love, but often the lover in these poems is a comrade in arms. Her lyric voice matured and evolved into that of a committed militant and revolutionary muse, a patriot who passionately loves her small, impoverished, tropical country and hopes her poems will inspire other Nicaraguans to dare to dream of and fight for a better life in a free and equitable society. In her book of poetry, *Apogeo* [Apogee], she celebrates mature womanhood in poems that are sensual and self-confident and that challenge stereotypes of older women.

Belli published her first novel, *La mujer habitada* (*The Inhabited Woman*), in 1988, shortly after she resigned her political appointments to become a full time writer. It is the story of a young, middle class woman who joins the underground resistance and struggles to define her role in it in the face of her lover's objections and her own middle class values and prejudices. Elements of magic and indigenous history and myth are woven into the plot and foreshadow her next novel, *Sofía de las presagios* [Sophie of the Omens], in which a young woman rebels against traditional society with the aid of a local medicine woman. Her last work of fiction to date, *Waslala*, is a futuristic novel that addresses the urgent issues of environmental destruction and the fate of small, impoverished nations. The protagonist is a young woman who travels in search of her mother, who had left home many years earlier to help found a utopian community in a remote part of the country. Her quest teaches her the value of having a vision of a better world and the beauty of living one's life committed to its realization. In 2001, Belli published the memoir *El país bajo mi piel: memorias de amor y Guerra*, an intimate retelling of the history of the Sandinista movement and her participation in the historic events it precipitated.

While it may be that Belli's early work was recognized because of her association with the Sandinista revolution, it is clear that she has transcended that label. Some of her contemporaries abandoned their writing or floundered in confusion or pessimism after the Sandinista electoral defeat and subsequent discrediting of the revolution, but Belli has kept her vision and her energy alive. All of her works since 1995 have been published in Nicaragua as well as abroad. Her writing has been translated into several languages, including Italian, German, Turkish, Greek, Dutch, Chinese, and Finnish. Since 1992 she has divided her time between Nicaragua and Los Angeles, California. While her writing continues to reflect and incorporate the realities of Nicaragua, the depth of her themes and the originality of her voice have justifiably earned her recognition as a writer of international stature.

—Janet N. Gold

BELYI, Andrei

Born: Boris Nikolaevich Bugaev in Moscow, Russia, 26 October 1880. **Education:** Educated at gymnasium, Polivanov, 1891–99; studied science, then philology, then philosophy, University of Moscow, 1899–1906. **Family:** Married 1) Asia Turgeneva, c. 1910 (separated 1914); 2) Klavdiia Vasil'eva in 1924; 3rd marriage in 1931. **Career:** Associate editor, *Scales*, 1907–09; associated with the publishers Musaget, 1909; travelled abroad, studying with Rudolf Steiner, 1910–16; lecturer in Moscow and St. Petersburg; in Berlin, 1921–23; editor, *Epopeia*, 1922–23. **Died:** 7/8 January 1934.

PUBLICATIONS

Collections

Stikhotvoreniia i poemy [Poetry and Narrative Verse], edited by T. Iu. Khmel'nitskaya. 1966.
Complete Short Stories, edited and translated by Ronald E. Peterson. 1979.
Stikhotvoreniia [Poetry], edited by John E. Malmstad. 3 vols., 1982–84.
Selected Essays, edited and translated by Steven Cassedy. 1985.
Sochineniia [Works], edited by V. Piskarev. 1990.

Verse

Zoloto v lazuri [Gold in Azure]. 1904.
Pepel [Ashes]. 1909; revised edition, 1929.
Urna [The Urn]. 1909.
Christos voskres [Christ Is Arisen]. 1918.
Pervoe svidanie. 1921; as *The First Encounter*, translated by Gerald Janeček, 1979.
Posle razluki: Berlinskii pesennik [After the Parting: A Berlin Songbook]. 1922.
Stikhi o Rossii [Poems about Russia]. 1922.
Vozvrashchen'e na rodinu [Returning Home]. 1922.
Stikhotvoreniia [Selected Poetry]. 1923.
Stikhotvoreniia [Selected Poetry]. 1940.

Fiction

Serebrianii golub'. 1909–10; as *The Silver Dove*, translated by George Reavey, 1974.
Peterburg. 1916; revised edition, 1922; as *St. Petersburg*, translated by John Cournos, 1959; complete version, as *Petersburg*, translated by R.A. Maguire and John E. Malmstad, 1978; as *Petersburg Nineteen Eighteen*, edited by Efraim Sicher, 1989; as *Petersburg: A Novel in Eight Chapters with a Prologue and an Epilogue*, translated by David McDuff, 1995.
Kotik Letaev. 1922; as *Kotik Letaev*, translated by Gerald Janeček, 1971.
Moskva. 1926.
Kreshchenyi kitaets. 1927; as *The Christened Chinaman*, translated by Thomas R. Beyer, 1991.
Maski [Masks]. 1932.

Other

Simfoniia (2-aia, dramaticheskaia). 1902; as *The Dramatic Symphony*, translated by Roger and Angela Keys, with *The Forms of Art*, 1986.
Severnaia simfoniia (1-aia, geroicheskaia) [Northern Symphony (First, Heroic)]. 1904.
Vozvrat: III-ia simfoniia. 1905; as *The Forms of Art*, translated by John Elsworth, with *The Dramatic Symphony*, 1986.
Kubok metelei: Chetvertaia simfoniia [A Golet of Blizzards: Fourth Symphony]. 1908.
Lug zelonyi [The Green Meadow]. 1910.
Simvolizm [Symbolism]. 1910.
Arabeski [Arabesques]. 1911.
Tragediia tvorchestva: Dostoevskii i Tolstoi [The Tragedy of an Oeuvre]. 1911.
Revoliutsiia i kul'tura [Revolution and Culture]. 1917.
Rudol'f Shteiner l Gete v mirovozzrenii sovremenosti [Rudolf Steiner and Goethe from a Contemporary Viewpoint]. 1917.
Na perevale [At the Divide]. 3 vols., 1918–20.
Korolevna i rytsari [The Princess and the Knights]. 1919.
Zapiski chudaka [Notes of an Eccentric]. 2 vols., 1922.
Glossolaliia: Poema o zvuke [Glossolalia: Poem about Sound]. 1922.
Putevye zametki: Sitsiliia i Tunis [Travel Notes: Sicily and Tunis]. 1922.
Poeziia slova: Pushkin, Tiutchev, Baratynskii, V. Ivanov, A. Blok [Poetry of the Word]. 1922.
Vospominaniia o Bloke [Reminiscences of A.A. Blok]. 1922–23.

Odna iz obiteley tsarstva tenei [In the Kingdom of the Shades]. 1924; as *In the Kingdom of Shadows*, translated by Catherine Spitzer, 2001.

Veter s Kavkaza [A Wind from the Caucasus]. 1928.

Ritm kak dialektika i "Mednyi vsadnik" [Rhythm as Dialectic and "The Bronze Horseman"]. 1929.

Na rubezhe dvukh stoletii [On the Brink of Two Centuries]. 1930.

Nachalo veka [The Turn of the Century]. 1933.

Masterstvo Gogolia [The Art of Gogol']. 1934.

Mezhdu dvukh revoliutsii [Between Two Revolutions]. 1934.

*

Critical Studies:: *The Frenzied Poets: Andrey Bely and the Russian Symbolists* by Oleg Maslennikov, 1952; *Andrey Bely* by Konstantin Mochulsky, 1955, reprinted as *Andrei Bely: His Life and Works*, translated by N. Szalavitz, 1977; *Andrey Bely*, 1972, and *Andrey Bely: A Critical Study of the Novels*, 1983, both by J.D. Elsworth; *The Apocalyptic Symbolism of Andrej Belyj* by Samuel D. Cioran, 1973; *Andrej Belyj: The "Symphonies"* by Anton Kovač, 1976; *The Poetic World of Andrey Bely*, by Boris Christa, 1977, and *Andrey Bely: Centenary Papers* edited by Christa, 1980; *Andrey Bely: A Critical Review* edited by Gerald Janeček, 1978; *Andrei Bely's Short Prose* by Ronald E. Peterson, 1980; *Word and Music in the Novels of Andrey Bely* by Ada Steinberg, 1982; *The Dream of Rebirth: A Study of Andrej Belyj's Novel "Peterburg"* by Magnus Ljunggren, 1982; *Andrei Bely: The Major Symbolist Fiction* by Vladimir E. Alexandrov, 1985; "From Fact to Fiction: The Role of the Red Domino in Belyi's *Peterburg*" by Milicz Banjanin, in *Russian Language Journal*, 40(135), 1986; *Andrey Bely: Spirit of Symbolism* edited by John E. Malmstad, 1987; *Body of Words: A Reading of Bely's "Kotik Letaev"* by M. Molnar, 1987; "The Grotesque Style of Belyi's *Moscow* Novels" by Olga Muller Cook, in *Slavic and East European Journal*, 32(3), 1988; "Andrej Belyi's *Dramatic Smphony*" by Willem G. Weststeijn, in *Avant-Garde: Interdisciplinary and International Review*, edited by Weststeijn and Jan van der Eng, 1991; *Bely, Joyce, and Döblin: Peripatetics in the City Novel* by Peter I. Barta, 1996; *The Reluctant Modernist: Andrei Belyi and the Development of Russian Fiction, 1902–1914* by Roger Keys, 1996.

* * *

Andrei Belyi, Russia's greatest modernist writer and a leading poet of that most remarkable period of Russian intellectual history which is called the Silver Age, was also a theorist of symbolism, a pioneer in the structural method of literary analysis, and, according to Briusov and later Pasternak, "the most interesting man in Russia." Before he became A. Belyi (in 1901), he considered himself a philosopher, a follower of the mystical philosopher Solovev, a scientist, and a composer, regarding himself as "simply a person who is searching."

In his search to find new forms of art, he wanted to fuse art with music and religion, "to escape into a primitive phase of culture, into rhythm and gesture. . ." ("About Myself as a Writer"). He maintained that life reveals itself only through creative activity which is "unanalysible, integral, and omnipotent." It is only expressible in symbolic images which envelop the idea. In the process of cognitive symbolization the symbol becomes reality, it can run ahead, depicting the future. He claimed that he had foreseen in his novels people and historical events, such as Rasputin in *Serebrianii golub'* (*The Silver Dove*), the downfall of tsarist Petersburg in *Peterburg* (*Petersburg*), and the fascist conspiracy in his projected novel *Germany*. Symbolism for Belyi was a way of thinking, writing, and living. The Belyi-Briusov-Petrovskaia triangle, and Belyi's dramatic affair with Blok's wife, conformed to the Symbolist doctrine that life and art should be unitary. The principal hero of his novels is a philosophizing eccentric, a madman-artist "whose only art is the creation of himself." Even the choice of the colour white (belyi) for his pseudonym was to be significant. White is a recurrent symbol in his poetry: it stands for the snowstorm, that vast elemental force, and for life itself. Sounds and colours always had for Belyi a mystical significance. As Belyi himself tells us, the subjects of his first four books "were drawn from musical leitmotifs, and I called them not stories or novels but *Symphonies*."

Belyi believed that, in moving towards music, a work of art becomes more profound. All his prose has distinct rhythmical qualities. The story *Kreshchenyi kitaets* (*The Christened Chinaman*), for example, was composed from the sounds of Schumann's *Kreisleriana*. The regular beat, the pause for breath are supposed to express a deep secret rhythm of the spirit. In poetry, too, phonetic structure is often more important than meaning. Words with similar consonants clutch at one another, cling to each other, echoing his favourite images of wind and storm. He deliberately obliterated all discourse from his poetry. There are hardly any developments of thought; instead Belyi repeats certain images pointing to a central theme. His poetry is, however, inferior to his prose. He saw rhythm as a "principle which unites poetry with prose." He called his last novel, *Maski* [Masks], a "lyrical epic poem." He often thought of himself more as a theoretician than as a poet. He devoted many years (from 1902 to 1910, and again from 1918 to 1921) to the development of the theory of symbolism. He gave many public lectures, wrote hundreds of essays, which were collected in the most complex book, *Simvolizm* [Symbolism]; he also conducted seminars and research work in the field of prosody. Only in 1924 did he return to literature completely, and he then began to fall into obscurity.

Like Blok, he saw the October Revolution as the birth of a new cosmical world. But Russia, risen anew, failed to appreciate him. In 1921, after Blok's death, he left Russia for Berlin only to find out that "the Russian émigré is as alien to me as the Bolsheviks." The two people he wanted to be with most, Asia Turgeneva and Rudolf Steiner, didn't need him. Bitterly disenchanted, exhausted and sick, he came back to Moscow: "I returned to my grave . . . all journals, all publishing houses are closed to me." After Trotskii's merciless attack, stating that Belyi's novels "poison your very existence," he appealed to Stalin (1931), and compromised with his conscience by becoming a Marxist. In Soviet Russia he remained a controversial writer, too modernist for the literary officials, too incomprehensible for the reading public. In the West his works have always been praised "without being understood or read," as the translators of *Petersburg* put it. Although Nabokov included *Petersburg* among the four "greatest masterpieces of 20th-century prose," Belyi never achieved such enormous popularity as Joyce, Kafka, and Proust. Like them he did his best to destroy the simplicity of forms, but it was precisely his linguistic experiments that cut him off from the foreign reader.

—Valentina Polukhina

See the essay on *Petersburg*.

BEMBO, Pietro

Born: Venice, Venetian Republic, 20 May 1470. Lived in Florence, where his father was ambassador, 1478–79. **Education:** Educated by the humanists Giovanni Alessandro Urticio and Giovanni Aurelio Augurello; studied Greek at the school of Costantino Lascaris, Messina, c. 1491–93. **Family:** Lived with Morosina (died 1535) in the 1520s, one daughter and two sons. **Career:** Accompanied his father on his ambassadorial mission in Rome, 1487–88; lived in Bergamo, where his father was podesta [governor], 1489–91, and subsequently returned to Venice; collaborated with the publisher Aldus Manutius: published his first work, *De Aetna*, at Manutius' press, 1496; lived in Ferrara, where his father was Vicedomino [co-ruler], 1497–99; studied philosophy under Niccolò Leoniceno; returned to Venice, 1499, and attempted to enter politics, with little success; lived at the court of Duke and Duchess of Urbino, 1506–12; lived in Rome, 1512–21; papal secretary to Leo X, 1513–21; settled in Padua, 1522; took up an ecclesiastical career, by virtue of his membership of the Order of Jerusalem; became historiographer and librarian of the Republic of Venice, 1530; elected to College of Cardinals, 1539, and moved to Rome; Bishop of Gubbio, 1541–44; lived in Rome, 1544–47. **Died:** 18 January 1547.

PUBLICATIONS

Collections

Opere, edited by A.F. Seghezzi. 4 vols., 1729.
Prose e rime, edited by Carlo Dionisotti. 1960,
Opere in volgare, edited by Mario Marti. 1961.

Verse

Rime. 1530; revised and enlarged editions, 1535, 1548.
Sonetti inediti, edited by Rinaldo Sperati. 1899.

Other

De Aetna (dialogue). 1496; as *On Etna*, translated by Betty Radice, in *De Aetna/On Etna* (bilingual edition), 1969.
Gli Asolani (treatise). 1505; revised edition, 1530; as *Gli Asolani*, translated by Rudolf Gottfried, 1954.
De imitatione Libellus. 1514 (unauthorized edition); 1530 (authorized edition).
Le prose della volgar lingua (treatise). 1525; revised edition, 1538; edited by Mario Marti, 1955, and by Carlo Dionisotti, 1955.
De Virgilii Culice et Terentii Fabulis. 1530.
De Guido Ubaldo Feretrio deque Elisabetha Gonzaga Urbini Ducibus. 1530.
Imitatione libri tres. 1541.
Carmina quinque illustrium poetarum. 1548; as *Carminum libellus*, 1552.
Lettere. 2 vols., 1548–50.
Rerum venetarum historiae libri XII. 1551; as *Delia historia vinitiana*, 1552.
Epistulae familiares (letters). 3 vols: 1552; as *Lettere*, 4 vols., 1562; edited by Ernesto Travi, 2 vols., 1987–90.
Lettere giovanili. 1554.
Nuove lettere famigliari (letters to his nephew G.M. Bembo). 1564.

Carteggio d'amore, with Maria Savorgnan (letters), edited by Carlo Dionisotti. 1950.
The Prettiest Love Letters in the World: Letters Between Lucrezia Borgia and Pietro Bembo, translated by Hugh Shankland. 1987.
Editor, *Le cose volgari*, by Petrarch. 1501.
Editor, *Commedia*, by Dante. 1502.
Editor, *Opera*, by Virgil. 1535.

*

Critical Studies:: *Un decennio della vita di M. Pietro Bembo (1521–1531)*, 1885, and *Un medaglione del Rinascimento: Cola Bruno messinese e le sue relazioni con Pietro Bembo*, 1901, both by Vittorio Cian; *La gioventù di M.P. Bembo e il suo dialogo Gli Asolani* by M. Tamburini, 1914; *Pietro Bembo e le sorti della lingua nazionale nel Veneto* by N. Schileo, 1923; *Pietro Bembo* by M. Santoro, 1937; *Il Bembo critico e il principio d'imitazione* by G. Santangelo, 1950; *La vita avventurosa di Pietro Bembo, umanista-poeta-cortigiano* by G. Meneghetti, 1961; *Il petrarchismo del Bembo e di altri poeti del '500* by Giorgio Santangelo, 1967; "Pietro Bembo's *Gli Asolani* of 1505" by C.H. Clough, in *Modern Language Notes*, 84(1), 1969; "Imitatio: Theory and Practice—The Example of Bembo the Poet" by Dante Della Terza, in *Yearbook of Italian Studies*, 1, 1971; *Pietro Bembo ed il suo epistolgario* by Ernesto Travi, 1972; "Bembo's Maneuvers from Virtue to Virtuosity in Gli Asolani" by Susan Delaney, in *Italian Quarterly*, 27(106), 1986; "Pietro Bembo and the Vat. Lat. 3226" by John N. Grant, in *Humanistica Lovaniensa*, 37, 1988; "Bembo and the Dialogic Path of Love" by Olga Zorzi Pugliese, in *Italiana 1988* edited by Albert N. Mancini and others, 1990; *Marsilio Ficino, Pietro Bembo, Baldassare Castiglione: Philosophical, Aesthetic, and Political Approaches in Renaissance Platonism* by Christine Raffini, 1998.

* * *

Pietro Bembo is remembered chiefly as the foremost pioneering theoretician of the Italian language and the architect of its use as a vehicle for serious literature fit to stand beside the Latin of humanistic culture, based on the example of the great medieval writers: Dante, Petrarch, and Boccaccio. In particular for poetry, Bembo proposed imitation of the model of Petrarch, and in *Gli Asolani*, a discussion of the issues of love between three men and three women, set in Asolo at the court of Caterina Cornaro, Queen of Cyprus, he established Petrarch as the model for Italian love poetry, just as in his *Prose della volgar lingua* he was to establish Florentine as the vernacular language, and rules for the correct use of the Italian language in prose that have been widely influential since.

A Venetian patrician, expert in the courtier arts, Bembo had travelled widely, including to the court of Urbino that had produced Castiglione's *Il libro del cortegiano* (*The Book of the Courtier*)—in which he appears as a fictional protagonist. He rose to eminent positions, firstly as papal secretary, and later as cardinal. Bembo was among the first Renaissance figures to study Greek; he wrote fluently in Latin, and acquired a unique position in the Italian Renaissance as an arbiter of literary taste. The now famous exchange of letters between Bembo and Giovan Francesco (nephew of the famous Pico) della Mirandola in 1512, in which the latter upheld the independence of style of the individual writer, became a classic text on the principle of literary imitation in Latin proposing Cicero as a model for prose and Virgil for poetry. Thus was reached an ideal of classical literary imitation, which would be elaborated for the Italian language using the models of Petrarch for poetry and Boccaccio for prose in Bembo's *Le prose della volgar lingua*. The Italian language would henceforth acquire the dignity and reverence previously accorded only to the classics.

In *Gli Asolani*, Bembo discusses the relative merits of erotic and platonic love, describing the different kinds of love whose parameters are clearly Petrarchan, although there is no explicit reference to Petrarch: a schematization of the love of Petrarch's Laura, with her counterpart (a less literary and more sensual ideal), which is contrasted, in the work's third book, in the discussion of earthly and platonic love, with the conclusion that platonic love is the more elevated spiritual kind and brings the lover closer to God. The exposition of platonic love in the third book of *Gli Asolani* has been called "love in a cold climate," but it looks forward to the concluding section of Castiglione's *The Book of the Courtier* where, quite deliberately, the defence of Platonic love is voiced by the character of Pietro Bembo himself.

Bembo's own lyric poetry is the first chapter in the long history of Petrarchism. The poems were published first in a collection in 1530 as *Rime* (although many were well known to contemporaries long before then), and they put into practice the theories established in *Gli Asolani*, The slavish imitation of Petrarch's *Canzoniere* is apparent everywhere, and even whole lines are quoted from the poetry of the master, as in the celebrated example of "Solingo augello, se piangendo vai," where critics have identified quotations from five different Petrarchan poems. The whole is refined, elevated, literary—an intellectual elaboration of the imitation principle—but without the passion or individuality of a basis in real life or love, in the eyes of both modern commentators and contemporary satirists and parodists such as Berni and Aretino. None the less, in spite of his detractors, Bembo's position as a figure of literary transition in the tradition of the love lyric was to be decisive.

Le prose della volgar lingua is Bembo's monumental contribution to the "questione della lingua" debate in the Italian Renaissance. It imagines a debate in Venice in 1502 between such celebrated contemporary authorities on the matter of the appropriate language for literature as Giuliano de'Medici, Federigo Fregoso, Ercole Strozzi, and Carlo Bembo (brother of the author, and so his spokesman), who vigorously advance the theory of the supremacy of Florentine as the only language for literature, on the models of Petrarch and Boccaccio. Bembo's standpoint is that of the maintenance of literary and artistic validity—not factors to do with the spoken language—in his strict adherence to the Ciceronian principle of imitation of one model. So, the questions of everyday usage, accessibility to speakers, and a widening of the circle of readers are scarcely parts of this thesis. Bembo is concerned above all with formal elegance and literary precedent, convinced that the fullest intellectual expression of a language is in the work of its writers. Writers will be writing for posterity as much as for contemporaries. The novelty for readers of his works in the early 16th century would have been that Italian—in the examples of its great literary masters from the past—was now to take its place alongside Latin and Greek as one of the languages for great literature.

Among Bembo's minor works (apart from the recently discovered letters to Maria Savorgnan, datable to Bembo's youth in 1500–01) only his letters, written while he was Pope Leo X's secretary, and his history of Venice are worthy of mention here. The first establishing his literary credentials as a humanist (Latin) writer, and the second the recognition of his cultural and literary pre-eminence in his own time

by his native Republic of Venice. A symbol and incarnation of all his efforts in a long career is his own translation of the history from Latin into Italian.

—Christopher Cairns

BEN JELLOUN, Tahar

Born: Fez, Morocco, 21 December 1944. **Education:** Attended primary school in Fez; French high school, Tangier, 1958–63; studied philosophy at Université Mohammed V, Rabat, 1963–71; Ph.D. in psychiatric social work, Université de Paris, 1975. **Military Service:** Served in Moroccan Army; spent 18 months in a disciplinary camp, 1966–1968. **Family:** Married Aicha in 1986; four children. **Career:** Teacher of philosophy in Tetouan and Casblanca, Morroco, 1967–71; emigrated to Paris, France, 1971; psychotherapist, 1972–75; contributor to many journals, particularly the Moroccan *Soufflés* and the French *Le Monde*, *Le Monde Diplomatique*, *Le Nouvel Observateur*, and *Les Lettres Nouvelles*, from 1971; hosted a weekly program for the Moroccan radio Médi I, from 1983; wrote for the Italian newspaper *La Repubblica*, 1999; appointed UN Ambassadeur de bonne volonté for the struggle against racism. **Awards:** Prix de l'Amitié Franco-Arabe, 1976; Prix de l'Association des Bibliothecaires de France et de Radio Montecarlo, 1978; Chevalier for Arts and Letters, 1983; Prix Goncourt for literature, 1987; Prix des Hemispheres for literature, 1991; Prix Maghreb, 1994; Chevalier de la Legion d'Honneur, 1998.

PUBLICATIONS

Collections

Poésie complète, 1966–1995. 1995.

Verse

Hommes sous linceul de silence. 1970.
Cicatrices du soleil. 1972.
Le discours du chameau. 1974.
Les amandiers sont morts de leurs blessures. 1976.
A l'insu du souvenir. 1980.
Sahara. 1987.
La remontée des cendres; suivi de Non identifees. 1991.

Fiction

Harrouda. 1973.
La reclusion solitaire. 1976; as *Solitaire*, translated by Nick Hindley, 1988.
Moha le fou, Moha le sage. 1978.
La Priére de l'absent. 1981.
Muha al-ma'twa, Muha al-hakîm. 1982.
L'ecrivain public: Recit. 1983.

L'enfant de sable. 1985; as *The Sand Child*, translated by Alan Sheridan, 1987.

La nuit sacrée. 1987; as *The Sacred Night*, translated by Alan Sheridan, 1989.

Jour de silence a Tanger. 1990; as *Silent Day in Tangier*, translated by David Lobdell, 1991.

Les yeux baissés. 1991; as *With Downcast Eyes*, translated by Joachim Neugroschel, 1993.

L'ange aveugle (short stories). 1992; as *State of Absence*, translated by James Kirkup, 1994.

L'homme rompu. 1994; as *Corruption*, translated by Carol Volk, 1997.

Le premier amour est toujours le dernier (short stories). 1995.

Le raisins de la galère. 1996.

La nuit de l'erreur. 1997.

L'auberge des pauvres. 1999.

Labyrinthe des sentiments. 1999.

Plays

Chronique d'une solitude. 1976.

Entretien avec Monsieur Said Hammadi, ouvrier Algerien. 1982.

La fiancé de l'eau. 1984.

Other

La plus haute des solitudes: Misere sexuelle d'emigrees nord-africains. 1977.

Haut Atlas: L'exil de Piérres. 1982.

Hospitalité française: Racisme et immigration maghrebine. 1984; as *French Hospitality: Racism and North African Immigrants*, translated by Barbara Bray, 1999.

Marseille, comme un matin d'insomnie. 1986.

Giacometti (essays). 1991.

Éloge de l'amitié: la soudure fraternelle. 1994.

Medinas. 1998; translated as *Medinas: Morocco's Hidden Cities*, 1998.

Le racisme expliqué a ma fille. 1999; as *Racism Explained to My Daughter*, translated by Carol Volk, 1999.

Cette aveuglante absence de lumiere. 2001; as *This Blinding Absence of Light*, translated by Linda Coverdale, 2002.

Les Italiens. 2002; translated as *The Italians*, 2002.

L'islam expliqué aux enfants. 2002.

Translator, *Le Pain nu: Recit autobiographique*, by Mohamed Choukri. 1980.

*

Critical Studies: *L'espace scriptural de Tahar Ben Jelloun* by Majid el-Houssi, 1983; ''Masculinity and Virility in Tahar Ben Jelloun's Work'' by Ouzgane Lahoucine, in *Contagion*, 1997; *Islam and Postcolonial Narrative* by John Erickson, 1998; *Tahar Ben Jelloun, l'ecrivain des villes de Fes* by Nadia Kamal-Trense, 1998; *Tahar Ben Jelloun* by Bernard Aresu, 1998; ''Female Impersonation and Male Desire in Tahar Ben Jelloun's *L'enfant de sable*'' by Laurel Taylor, in *Women in French*, 1999; *Étude sur Tahar Ben Jelloun. L'enfant de sable, La nuit sacrée* by Laurence Kohn-Pireux, 2000.

* * *

Tahar Ben Jelloun is one of the North Africa's most successful post-colonial writers. While still a university student, he began writing for the journal *Soufflés* [Breaths], but in 1971 completed his first poems, published in the collection *Hommes Sous Linceul de Silence* [Men under the Shroud of Silence]. Since 1977 Ben Jelloun has published regularly, but it was not until the publication, in 1985, of the novel *L'Enfant de Sable* (*The Sand Child*) that he became well known around the world. The final seal of his celebrity was the Prix Goncourt, received for his work *La Nuit Sacrée* (*The Sacred Night*) in 1987. Since then his works have been systematically translated into the most important Western languages, and he alternates between writing and participating in conferences related to matters of the Arab world.

Ben Jelloun's first book translated into English, *The Sand Child*, catapulted him into the literary spotlight and revealed the major themes of his work: gender identity in a male-dominated society, masking, storytelling and surrealism. The originality of Ben Jelloun's works resides in his ability to represent, in a remarkable synthesis, all the aspects of Moroccan tradition and culture with everyday life and the urgent problems of society. As a result, he produces a writing that disturbs the audience, since it stages taboo subjects and gives voice to characters normally debarred from speaking, such as prostitutes, immigrants, the demented, transsexuals, and other outcasts. These people, forced to silence or indifference, speak a forbidden language, related to the body, sensuality, and carnality. Their words usually provoke the sensibility of conformist readers, all the more so as these themes are frequently combined with the pitfalls of a chaotic and unfriendly writing, plagued by discontinuity and hallucination, which makes the narration impossible. This is true specially for the first novels, in particular *Harrouda* and *Moha le fou, Moha le sage* [Moha the Mad, Moha the Wise], whose erotic violence and exposure of the female body, together with the difficulties of the narrative, scandalize the reader and complicate the grasp of the plot. Nevertheless, with *La Prière de l'Absent* [The Absent's Prayer] and *L'Enfant de Sable*, Ben Jelloun's writing finds a more reassuring tone approaching the attitude of the traditional novel, at least at a first glance.

Although a native of Morocco and closely linked to Moroccan culture and hence to Arabic language, Ben Jelloun chose to write in French. When he started to write, he immediately found it natural to do so in French. It would be oversimplifying, however, to say that Arabic language has no part in his writing. In fact, bilingualism plays an active part in his life as well as in his works as a characterizing theme. He often plays with Arabic and French words, and this use of both languages adds to the complexity and sophistication of his writings.

Ben Jelloun's work represents a break with North Africa's literary tradition of the 1950–70s. The Moroccan audience, for instance, expected from the novelist a complete and committed awareness of the age, and Ben Jelloun's personages exist only in an *imaginary* world; they are creations of fantasy produced by everyday life's hallucinations and governed by the mess of memory and the intemperance of imagination. Therefore, not only does he write about Moroccan situations that may be seen as nonsensical or uncivilized, but he openly criticizes them. This has resulted in praise by certain strata of society, for example feminist groups, but disapproval from many critics, who protest that Ben Jelloun defends and appeals to

Westerners through stereotyping and a skewed perception of semi-traditional North African life.

It has been said by critics that Tahar Ben Jelloun is basically and primarily a poet; therefore his writing style resembles that of a poet. His novels are full of poetic images and lyrical language. Dream-like states, hallucinations, and lyrical visions give his work a magical and intoxicated atmosphere. His use of fictitious narrators, different points of view of the same story, and statements of unreliable characters add to a mystical quality as well. The creative space for doubt and wonder give Ben Jelloun's plots a surrealist feel.

—Alessandro Cancian

BENN, Gottfried

Born: Mansfeld, Germany, 2 May 1886. **Education:** Educated at the Gymnasium, Frankfurt, 1896–1903; studied philosophy and theology, University of Marburg, 1903–04; studied medicine, University of Berlin, 1904–05; Kaiser Wilhelm Academy, 1905–12, Ph.D. 1912. **Military Service:** Served in the army, discharged because of health problems 1912; served in the army medical corps, 1914–18, and 1935–45: awarded Iron Cross, second class, 1914. **Family:** Married 1) Edith Brosin in 1914 (died 1922), one son (from Brosin's previous marriage) and one daughter; 2) Herta von Wedemeyer in 1938 (committed suicide 1945); 3) Ilse Kaul in 1946. **Career:** Assistant, Pathological Institute Westend Hospital, 1912–13; ship's physician, 1913; after 1918, specialist in skin disease and sexually transmitted infection, Berlin; embraced National Socialism, 1932–34, renounced National Socialist Party, 1934; acting chairman, literary section of the Prussian Academy of Art, 1933; after World War II, forbidden to publish anything he had written since 1937; private medical practice, West Berlin, from 1945. **Awards:** Büchner prize, 1951; Order of Merit, first class, Federal Republic of Germany, 1952. **Member:** Prussian Academy of Art, 1932. **Died:** 7 July 1956.

PUBLICATIONS

Collections

Gesammelte Werke, edited by Dieter Wellershoff. 4 vols., 1958–61.
Primäre Tage: Gedichte und Fragmente aus dem Nachlass, edited by Dieter Wellershoff. 1958; as *Primal Vision: Selected Writings*, edited by E.B. Ashton, 1960.
Medizinische Schriften, edited by Werner Rübe. 1965.
Späte Gedichte: Fragmente, Destillationen, Aprèslude. 1965.
Poems, translated by Michael Lebeck. 1967.
Selected Poems, edited by Friedrich Wilhelm Wodtke. 1970.
Sämtliche Erzählungen. 1970.
Gesammelte Werke in der Fassung der Erstdrucke, edited by B. Hillebrand. 1982–.
Sämtliche Werke, edited by Gerhard Schuster. 4 vols., 1986–89.
Prose, Essays, Poems, edited by Volkmar Sandor. 1987.
Poems 1937–1947, translated by Simona Dradhici. 1991.

Verse

Morgue und andere Gedichte. 1912.
Söhne. 1913.
Fleisch. 1917.
Schutt. 1924.
Betäubung. 1925.
Spaltung. 1925.
Die Dänin. 1925.
Gesammelte Gedichte. 1927.
Ausgewählte Gedichte: 1911–1936. 1936.
Zweiundzwanzig Gedichte: 1936–1943. 1943.
Statische Gedichte. 1948.
Trunkene Flut: Ausgewählte Gedichte. 1949.
Fragmente. 1951.
Destillationen. 1953.
Aprèslude. 1955.
Gesammelte Gedichte 1912–1956. 1956.
Lyrik: Auswahl letzter Hand. 1956.
Sämtliche Gedichte. 1998.

Plays

Ithaka. 1919.
Etappe. 1919.
Der Vermessungsdirigent. 1919.
Das Unaufhörliche (oratorio), music by Paul Hindemith (produced 1931). 1931.

Radio Plays: *Die Stimme hinter dem Vorhang*, 1952.

Fiction

Gehirne. 1916.
Diesterweg. 1918.
Die gesammelten Schriften. 1922.

Other

Das moderne Ich. 1920.
Gesammelte Prosa. 1928.
Fazit der Perspektiven. 1930.
Nach dem Nihilismus (essays). 1932.
Der neue Staat und die Intellektuellen (essays). 1933.
Kunst und Macht (essays). 1934.
Ausdruckswelt: Essays und Aphorismen. 1949.
Drei alte Männer. 1949.
Goethe und die Naturwissenschaften. 1949.
Der Ptolemäer. 1949.
Doppelleben: Zwei Selbstdarstellungen (autobiography). 1950.
Frühe Prosa und Reden. 1950.
Essays. 1951.
Probleme der Lyrik (speech). 1951.
Frühe Lyrik und Dramen. 1952.
Monologische Kunst: Ein Briefwechsel zwischen Alexander Lernet-Holenia und Gottfried Benn. 1953.
Altern als Problem für Künstler. 1954.
Provoziertes Leben: Eine Auswahl aus den Prosaschriften. 1955.
Reden. 1955.

Soll die Dichtung das Leben bessern?, with Reinhold Schneider. 1956.
Über mich selbst: 1886–1956. 1956.
Dr. Rönne: Frühe Prosa, edited by Ernst Neff. 1957.
Ausgewählte Briefe. 1957.
Briefe an Carl Werckshagen. 1958.
Roman des Phänotyp: Landsberger Fragment, 1944. 1961.
Das gezeichnete Ich: Briefe aus den Jahren 1900–1956. 1962.
Weinhaus Wolf und andere Prosa. 1967.
Briefe an F.W. Oelze, edited by Harald Steinhagen and Jürgen Schröder. 3 vols., 1977–80.
Briefwechsel mit Paul Hindemith, edited by Ann Clark Fehn. 1978.
Gottfried Benn, Max Rychner: Briefwechsel 1930–1956, edited by Gerhard Schuster. 1986.
Briefe an Tilly Wedekind 1939–1955. 1986.
Lieber Bennito: Briefe an Gottfried Benn, 1946–1951. 1995.
Hernach: Gottfried Benns Briefe an Ursula Ziebarth. 2001.
Editor, *Lyrik des expressionistischen Jahrzehnts.* 1955.

*

Critical Studies: *Gottfried Benn, Phänotyp dieser Stunde: Eine Studie über den Problemgehalt seines Werkes* by Dieter Wellershoff, 1958; *Gottfried Benn's Critique of Substance* by Marion L. Adams, 1969; *Die Statischen Gedichte von Gottfried Benn* by Harald Steinhagen, 1969; *Gottfried Benn: The Unreconstructed Expressionist* by J.M Ritchie, 1972; *Gottfried Benn: The Artist and Politics 1910–1934* by Reinhard Alter, 1976; *Change and Permanence: Gottfried Benn's Text for Paul Hindemith's Oratorio Das Unaufhörliche* by Ann Clark Fehn, 1977; *Consistency of Phenotype: A Study of Gottfried Benn's Views on Lyric Poetry* by Angelika Manyoni, 1983; *Gottfried Benn, Johannes R. Becher* by Jürgen Haupt, 1994; *Gottfried Benn: Essay und Dokumentation* by Karl Schwedhelm, 1995; *Gottfried Benn, Rainald Goetz: Medium Literatur zwischen Pathologie und Poetologie* by Thomas Doktor and Carla Spies, 1997.

* * *

Gottfried Benn was one of the most important German poets of the 20th century. His early work—notably the poems of *Morgue* and the innovative prose works of the years 1915–21 (the so-called "önne stories")—forms a significant but not always typical part of the German Expressionist movement. The poems of *Morgue* take up themes and topics not unknown in European poetry since Baudelaire, but approach them with a sense of the grotesque which is quite removed from all sentimentality, and with a metonymic technique which strongly alienates and shocks the reader. After this collection, a landmark in German literature, Benn's development in poetry was towards a Dionysian, ecstatic voice and—after a deep crisis in his life and work in 1921—subsequently towards a more and more absolutist cult of formal art.

During the 1920s, when Benn was working as a doctor in Berlin, the city to which he remained loyal throughout his life, his cult of art was based on a growing rejection of civilization and reason and on the withdrawal of the poetic into a hermetic world of dream, trance, and hallucination. His essays of this period—on history, technology, alternative medicine, and the psychopathology of the artist—have a provocative and critical tone that at the time caused Benn to be

considered a radical critic of bourgeois society. Increasingly, however, public disputes with representatives of the political left, who were unwilling to accept the party-political independence of his aesthetic position, caused Benn to identify with the right. In 1933 he was one of the most prominent (and certainly one of the most surprising) writers to remain in Germany after the fascist takeover. He identified with Hitler's Germany not just in acquiescence but through active support for the state: a support that led to the celebrated controversy with Klaus Mann, who had appealed to Benn to recognize the barbarity of the National Socialist state (Benn's reply was the infamous speech "To the Literary Emigrés: A Reply," 1933). Benn went so far as to express naive yet disquieting support for aspects of the new state's eugenic measures ("Züchtung 1" [Breeding I], 1933) and finally completely compromised his own cherished principles of the self-referential nature of formal poetry (on whose distance from reality and social life he had insisted), as he identified aesthetic form with the brutal order of National Socialist Germany. Of Stefan George's poetry he wrote perhaps the most extraordinary sentence to be found in the unappetizing debris of cultural fascism: in one of George's most sensitive autumnal poems Benn claims to identify the spirit of the stormtroopers, for, he writes, discipline moves "in George's art and in the march-step of the brown batallions as *one* imperative."

Disillusionment set in after the Röhm putsch in 1934, and Benn took refuge in the German army—in an insensitive phrase he referred to his move as "the aristocratic form of emigration"—and continued to publish until 1938, when (as part of the general hostility of the state to artistic modernism) his works were banned. The lyrical products of these years are collected in *Statische Gedichte* [Static Poems], which, after initial problems with allied censorship, appeared in 1948. In the following year the volume *Der Ptolemäer* [The Ptolemean] appeared. It contains the prose works that he had written in 1944, most notably the remarkable *Roman des Phänotyp* [Novel of the Phenotype], in which the pursuit of a world of pure expression and form—what Benn calls the *Ausdruckswelt*—leads to prose of a rare and formal innovation and intensity. Benn referred to these works as "absolute prose." The controversial autobiography *Doppelleben* [Double Life]—the title refers to the double life of the artist in society—made clear that Benn's involvement with fascism was a topic for neither personal analysis nor regret.

The poems of the 1950s, by common critical consent, seldom attain the quality of *Statische Gedichte*. The speech *Probleme der Lyrik* [Problems of Lyric Poetry] became one of the most influential poetological works of the 1950s in West Germany. In this speech Benn tried to bring developments in modern poetry to the attention of a post-war German public whom—it has been argued—the Third Reich had cut off from international developments. Benn's judgements, like the language and themes of his own poetry at the time, were highly influential in the succeeding generation. The rehabilitation of Expressionism in West Germany (following its abrupt fall from grace in the 1930s) owes much to Benn's essays and anthologies in the years immediately before his death.

Voices critical of Benn had not been silent in the 1950s, but his influence waned sharply with the student revolt of the 1960s. The increasing interest in the socio-political function of literature and the subsequent (but by no means co-extensive) interest in the poetry of Bertolt Brecht contributed further to this decline. It was felt by young poets that aspects of Benn's language and poetic technique had exhausted themselves and that new models were called for. Benn's work came to be strongly identified with the restorative nature of the

Adenauer years. The subsequent eclipse of Marxist positions and the establishment of post-modernism cleared a way for Benn's re-emergence. It is to be feared that present opinion is open more to the tired, sophisticated resignation of the later Benn than to the magnificent modernist experiments of the early poetry and prose.

—Hugh Ridley

See the essay on "Palau."

BEOLCO, Angelo

See RUZZANTE

BERGERAC, Cyrano de

See CYRANO DE BERGERAC

BERNANOS, Georges

Born: Paris, France, 20 February, 1888. **Education:** Educated at Jesuit school, Paris, 1897–1900; Notre-Dame-des-Champs, Paris, 1901–03; Collège Saint-Célestin, Bourges, 1903–04; Collège Sainte-Marie, Aire-sur-la-Lys, baccalauréat, 1905 and 1906; studied law and literature, University of Paris, 1906–09. **Military Service:** 1909–10, served in the French army, 1914–19. **Family:** Married Jehanne Pauline Marie Talbert d'Arc in 1917; three sons and three daughters. **Career:** Travelling salesman for an insurance company, 1922–26; editor, *L'Avant-garde de Normandie*, 1913–14; columnist, *Le Figaro*, 1930–32; evicted from family home due to financial difficulties; moved to Majorca, Spain, 1934–37; returned to France, 1937; travelled to Buenos Aires, via Rio de Janeiro, en route to Paraguay, in an attempt to establish a French colony, stayed in Paraguay for five days only and returned to Rio de Janeiro. Settled in Brazil, involved in the resistance movement, 1938–44; returned to France, 1945; contributor to numerous journals including *Combat, La Bataille,* and *Le Figaro*; travelled to North Africa, Switzerland, and Belgium giving lectures. **Awards:** prix Fémina, 1929; Grand prize for fiction, Académie française, 1936. **Died:** 5 July 1948.

PUBLICATIONS

Collections

Dialogue d'ombres (collected stories). 1955.
Oeuvres complètes, edited by Maurice Bardèche. 12 vols., 1955–65.
Oeuvres romanesques, edited by Michel Estève. 1961.
Essais et écrits de combat, edited by Yves Bridel, Jacques Charbot, and Joseph Jart. 1971.

Fiction

Sous le Soleil de Satan. 1926; edited by William Bush, 1982; as *The Star of Satan*, translated by Veronica Lucas, 1927; also translated

by Pamela Morris, 1940; as *Under the Sun of Satan*, translated by Harry L. Binsee, 1949.
L'Imposture. 1927; as *The Imposter*, translated by J.C. Whitehouse, 1999.
Dialogue d'ombres (stories). 1928.
La Joie. 1929; revised edition, edited by Albert Béguin, 1954; as *Joy*, translated by Louise Varèse, 1946.
Un crime. 1935; as *The Crime*, translated by Anne Green, 1936, as *A Crime*, translated by Green, 1946.
Journal d'un curé de campagne. 1936; edited by Eithne M. O'Sharkey, 1969; as *The Diary of a Country Priest*, translated by Pamela Morris, 1937.
Nouvelle histoire de Mouchette. 1937; as *Mouchette*, translated by J.C. Whitehouse, 1966.
Monsieur Ouine. 1943; revised edition, edited by Albert Béguin, 1955; translated and introduced by William S. Bush, 2000; as *The Open Mind*, translated by Geoffrey Dunlop, 1945.
Un mauvais rêve, edited by Albert Béguin. 1951; as *Night Is Darkest*, translated by Walter J. Strachan, 1953.
The Heroic Face of Innocence: Three Stories by Georges Bernanos, 1999.

Plays

Dialogue des Carmélites (produced 1949). 1949; as *The Fearless Heart*, translated by Michael Legat, 1952; as *The Carmelites*, translated by Gerard Hopkins, 1961.

Other

Saint Dominique. 1927.
Noël à la maison de France. 1928.
La Grande Peur des bien-pensants. 1931.
Jeanne, relapse et sainte. 1934; as *Sanctity Will Out: An Essay on St. Joan*, translated by R. Batchelor, 1947.
Les Grands Cimetières sous la lune. 1938; as *A Diary of My Times*, translated by Pamela Morris, 1938.
Scandale de la vérité. 1939.
Nous autres, Français. 1939.
Lettres aux Anglais. 1942; as *A Plea for Liberty*, translated by Harry Lorin Binsse, 1944; also translated by Binsse and Ruth Bethell, 1970.
Écrits de combat. 1943–44.
Le Chemin de la Croix-des-Ames (articles). 4 vols., 1943–45; 1 vol, 1948: revised edition, 1987.
La France contre les robots. 1944; edited by Albert Béguin, 1955; also edited by Jean Loup Bernanos, 1970; as *Tradition of Freedom*, translated by Helen Beau Clark, 1950.
Réflexions sur le cas de conscience français. 1945.
Oeuvres. 6 vols., 1947.
Les Enfants humiliés: journal 1939–1940, edited by Albert Béguin, 1949; as *The Tradition of Freedom*, 1950.
La Liberté pour quoi faire?, edited by Albert Béguin, 1953; as *Last Essays*, translated by Joan and Barry Ulanov, 1955; as *The Last Essays of Georges Bernanos*, translated by Green, 1968.
Bernanos par lui-même, edited by Albert Béguin. 1954.
Le Crépuscule des vieux (articles), edited by Albert Béguin. 1956.
Français, si vous saviez, 1945–1948 (articles). 1961.
Le Lendemain c'est vous!, edited by Jean-Loup Bernanos. 1969.
Correspondance inédite, edited by Albert Béguin and Jean Murray. 2 vols., 1971.

La Vocation spirituelle de la France, edited by Jean-Loup Bernanos. 1975.

Les Prédestinés (essays), edited by Jean-Loup Bernanos. 1983.

Lettres retrouvées 1904–1948, edited by Jean-Loup Bernanos. 1983.

Georges Bernanos à la merci des passants (selection), edited by Jean-Loup Bernanos. 1986.

Bernanos (autobiography), edited by Jean-Loup Bernanos. 1988.

*

Critical Studies: *The Double Image: Mutations of Christian Mythology in the Work of Four French Catholic Writers* by Rayner Heppenstall, 1947; *The Poetic Imagination of Georges Bernanos* by Gerda Blumenthal, 1956; *Bernanos: His Political Thought and Prophecy* by Thomas Molnar, 1960; *Georges Bernanos*, 1965, and *Georges Bernanos: Un triple itinéraire*, 1981, both by Michel Estève; *Bernanos: An Introduction* by Peter Hebblethwaite, 1965; *Georges Bernanos* by Max Milner, 1967; *Bernanos* by Roger Pons, 1967; *Georges Bernanos* by William Bush, 1969; *Georges Bernanos: Journal d'un curé de campagne* by John Flower, 1970; *Georges Bernanos: A Study of the Man and the Writer* by Robert Speaight, 1973; *Bernanos et la politique: La Société et la droite françaises de 1900 à 1950* by Serge Albouy, 1980; *Georges Bernanos: A Study of Christian Commitment* by John E. Cooke, 1981; *La France dans l'histoire selon Bernanos* by Alan R. Clark, 1983; *Bernanos et l'angoisse* by Pierre Gille, 1984; *Bernanos aujourd'hui* by Jean-Loup Bernanos and Luc Balbont, 1987; *Temps et récit dans l'oeuvre romanesque de Georges Bernanos* by Elisabeth Lagadec-Sadoulet, 1988; *Bernanos et le monde moderne* (essays) edited by Monique Gosselin and Max Milner, 1989; *From Heaven to Hell: Imagery of Earth, Air, Water and Fire in the Novels of Georges Bernanos* by Daniel R. Morris, 1989; *Les Dialogues dans l'oeuvre de Bernanos* by André Not, 1990; *Bernanos: An Ecclesial Existence* by Hans Urs von Balthasar, translated by Erasmo Leiva-Merikakas, 1996; *Bernanos: Journal d'un curé de campagne* by Malcolm Scott, 1997.

*   *   *

Today the fame of Georges Bernanos rests largely on three works that have been successfully translated for the stage and/or the screen. *Dialogue des Carmélites* (*The Fearless Heart*) was turned into an opera in 1957 by Francis Poulenc. *Journal d'un curé de campagne* (*The Diary of a Country Priest*), first adapted by Robert Bresson in a characteristically austere style, attracted a new generation of Bernanos enthusiasts when it was revived in the 1980s as a stage monologue starring Thierry Fortineau. Finally *Sous le Soleil de Satan* (*The Star of Satan*), made into a film starring Gérard Depardieu and Sandrine Bonnaire by Maurice Pialat, fuelled controversies at the Cannes Film Festival in 1987. However, for his contemporaries Bernanos was as much of a polemicist as he was a novelist. But breadth and variety of inspiration were never his trademark: both his essays and his fiction deal with a small number of themes: on a mundane level, the mediocrity or even corruption of secular and ecclesiastical authorities; on a metaphysical level, the inner tragedy brought about by pride, self-hatred, despair, or lack of faith.

Born in Paris in 1988, Bernanos owed his happiest and most vivid memories to his holidays in the north of France where hunting became one of his favourite pastimes at an early age (which would explain why firearms feature in most of his novels). A pupil of the Jesuits, he was soon noticed for his independent, passionate personality. The pantheon he selected for himself, composed of Barber d'Aurevilly, Chateaubriand, Balzac, Maurras, Barrès, and Leon Daudet among others, helped shape the course of his religious and political development. Just before World War I he was offered the editorship of a provincial monarchist weekly. The masterpiece of his later years, *The Fearless Heart*, presents a vision of the French Revolution predicated on his monarchist convictions. After the war, however, he had to give up journalism for a more lucrative job with an insurance company. He was nearly 40 when he published his first novel, *The Star of Satan*, to considerable critical acclaim. Bernanos had the idea of *The Star of Satan* as early as 1918, and the novel, published eventually in 1926, owes its coherence to certain thematic concerns rather than to its discontinuous structure. Donissan, who gives his name to the third part of the book, "The saint of Lumbres," is the first in the long series of priests who people Bernanos's fiction. After his encounter with the young murderess and suicide victim Germaine (nicknamed Mouchette), Donissan's spiritual crisis, which had culminated in a violent inner struggle with Satan, resolves itself. The novel follows Donissan's troubled spiritual itinerary. It is Donissan's fate to be first beset by doubts about his calling, and then to have to fight the temptation of desire at every step of the way.

Bernanos's decision to support himself and his family entirely through his writing from then on shows that he had come to trust in his creative gift. Yet, with six children born between 1918 and 1933, he was permanently under severe material pressure, a fact which obviously affected his career, though money was already a pervasive theme in his early stories. Thus, pressed for money, he abandoned his ambitious plan for a novel which was to be called *Les Ténèbres* (*Darkness*) in favour of an, in his eyes, unsatisfactory diptych, *L'Imposture* (*The Imposture*), ready for publication in book form at the end of 1927, and *La Joie* (*Joy*), published in 1929. In 1933 a motorbike accident crippled him for life. Ever more financially desperate, he then took two important steps: the first was to try and earn some easy money by writing thrillers, the second was to move to Majorca where the cost of living was lower than in France. History caught up with him in Spain. Moved by the Spanish Civil War, which he witnessed *de facto* at closer range than most European intellectuals, he felt called upon to give up fiction for committed writings. Admittedly, this change in focus probably coincided with a major crisis that revealed to him that his inspiration was running out. Such at least can be assumed from the most poignant passages about the exhausted novelist Ganse in *Un mauvais rêve* (*Night Is Darkest*). From 1938 to 1945 Bernanos lived in Brazil, where he carried on his work as a polemicist while trying his hand at farming. After the war he returned to France, but found it impossible to settle back into his own country after so many years abroad. His last residence was in Tunisia, but he died in Neuilly in 1948.

The Diary of a Country Priest is an important document because of the serious discussion it contains of Christian values in an indifferent society. But once again it is the outstanding portrayal of the priest that has grabbed the attention of generations of readers and spectators. This priest is a Christ-like figure but retains throughout the book his credibility as a human being. In *The Diary* Bernanos explores another type of saintliness—the country priest, unlike Donissan, attains sainthood through his humility and naive self-sacrifice.

Equally unique is Bernanos's skill at suggesting the power of evil. In *Un crime* (*The Crime*), the Simenon-inspired detective novel he always unjustly despised, he gives an hallucinatingly ambiguous portrayal of a young sapphic murderess who for a few days impersonates the priest she has killed before taking her own life. The choice of a lesbian dressed as a man of God for his heroine allows him to weave a brilliant web of images suggesting the Fallen Angel. Another study of a possessed soul is that of the priest and historian Cénabre who does not leave the Church even though he suddenly realizes that he has lost his faith. Cénabre is one of Bernanos's most interesting characters because of the writer's ability to make us empathize with Cénabre's excruciating terror in front of the void opened in his intellectual life by the loss of his faith. Bernanos is at his most oneiric when probing such dark areas of the mind and of the soul, a tendency still accentuated in his uncompleted novel *Monsieur Ouine* (*The Open Mind*), which accomplishes much more than a satire of the sterile introspective writer epitomized in his view by André Gide. At his best, Bernanos is indeed closest to Dostoevskii.

—Pascale Voilley

BERNHARD, Thomas

Born: Heerlen, near Maastricht, The Netherlands, 10 February 1931. Lived in Austria from 1932. **Education:** Educated at Salzburg Gymnasium, 1943–47, studied singing, directing, and theatrical technique, 1952–55, and at the Salzburg Mozarteum, 1955–57. **Career:** Commercial apprenticeship, Viennese Academy of Music and Drama, Salzburg, 1947–51; contracted tuberculosis and spent two years in convalescence, 1951–52; journalist for the socialist *Demokratisches Volksblatt*, from 1952, and contributor to the newspaper *Die Furche*, 1953–55; intermittent travel to Italy and Yugoslavia, 1953–57, to London, 1960, and to Poland, 1962–63; settled on a farm in Ohlsdorf an Herzversagen, Upper Austria, 1965. **Awards:** Bremen prize, 1965: Austrian State prize, 1967; Wildgans prize, 1968; Büchner prize, 1970; Grillparzer prize, 1971; Séguier prize, 1974; Premio prato, 1982; Premio Mondello, 1983; Prix Médicis, 1988. **Died:** 12 February 1989.

PUBLICATIONS

Collection

Gesammelte Gedichte, edited by Volker Bohn. 1991.

Fiction

Frost. 1963.
Amras. 1964.
Verstörung. 1967; as *Gargoyles*, translated by Richard and Clara Winston, 1970.
Prosa. 1967.
Ungenach (stories). 1968.
Watten: Ein Nachlass. 1969.
Ereignisse (stories). 1969.
An der Baumgrenze. 1969.

Das Kalkwerk. 1970; as *The Lime Works*, translated by Sophie Wilkins, 1973.
Gehen. 1971.
Midland in Stilfs: Drei Erzählungen. 1971.
Der Kulterer. 1974.
Korrektur. 1975; as *Correction*, translated by Sophie Wilkins, 1979.
Der Wetterfleck. 1976.
Der Stimmenimitator. 1978; as *The Voice Impersonator*, translated by Craig Kinosian, 1995; translated by Kenneth J. Northcott, 1997.
Ja. 1978; as *Yes*, translated by Ewald Osers, 1991.
Die Erzählungen, edited by Ulrich Greiner. 1979.
Die Billigesser. 1980; as *The Cheap-Eaters*, translated by Ewald Osers, 1990.
Beton. 1982; as *Concrete*, translated by David McLintock, 1984.
Der Untergeher. 1983; as *The Loser*, translated by Jack Dawson, 1991.
Holzfällen: Eine Erregung. 1984; as *Woodcutters*, translated by David McLintock, 1987; as *Cutting Timber: An Imitation*, translated by Ewald Osers, 1988.
Alte Meister: Komödie. 1985; as *Old Masters*, translated by Ewald Osers, 1989.
Auslöschung: Ein Zerfall. 1986; as *Extinction: A Novel*, translated by David McLintock, 1995.
In der Höhe: Rettungsversuch. 1989; as *On the Mountain: Rescue Attempt, Nonsense*, translated by Sophie Wilkins, 1991.

Plays

Die Rosen der Einöde: Fünf Sätze für Ballet, Stimmen und Orchester (opera libretti; includes *Die Rose; Der Kartenspieler; Unter den Pflaumenbäumen; Der Kalbskopf; Phantasie*). 1959.
Köpfe (libretto: produced 1960). 1960.
Ein Fest für Boris (produced 1970). 1970; as *A Party for Boris*, translated by Peter Jansen and Kenneth Northcott, in *Histrionics: Three Plays*, 1990.
Der Berg, in *Literatur und Kritik 5*. 1970.
Der Ignorant und der Wahnsinnige (produced 1972). 1972.
Die Jagdgesellschaft (produced 1974). 1974.
Die Macht der Gewohnheit (produced 1974). 1974; as *The Force of Habit* (produced 1976), translated by Neville and Stephen Plaice, 1976.
Die Salzburger Stücke (includes *Der Ignorant und der Wahnsinnige* and *Die Macht der Gewohnheit*). 1974.
Der Präsident (produced 1975). 1975; as *The President*, translated by Gitta Honegger, with *Eve of Retirement*, 1982.
Die Berühmten (produced 1976). 1976.
Minetti: Ein Porträt des Künsters als alter Mann (produced 1976). 1977.
Immanuel Kant (produced 1978). 1978.
Der Weltverbesserer (produced 1980). 1979.
Vor dem Ruhestand (produced 1980). 1979; as *Eve of Retirement*, translated by Gitta Honegger, with *The President*, 1982.
Über allen Gipfeln ist Ruh: Ein deutscher Dichertag um 1980. 1981.
Am Ziel (produced 1981). 1981.
Der Schein trügt (produced 1984). 1983; as *Appearances Are Deceiving*, translated by Gitta Honegger, 1983.
Die Stücke 1969–1981. 1983.
Der Theatermacher (produced 1986). 1984; as *Histrionics*, translated by Peter Jansen and Kenneth Northcott, in *Histrionics: Three Plays*, 1990.

Ritter, Dene, Voss (produced 1986). 1984; as *Ritter, Dene, Voss*,
translated by Peter Jansen and Kenneth Northcott, in *Histrionics:
Three Plays*, 1990.
Einfach kompliziert (produced 1986). 1986.
Elisabeth II (produced 1989). 1987.
Heldenplatz (produced 1988). 1988.
Der deutsche Mittagstisch: Dramolette. 1988.
Stücke. 4 vols., 1988.
*Claus Peymann kauft sich eine Hose und geht mit mir essen: Drei
Dramolette*, 1990.
Histrionics: Three Plays (includes *A Party for Boris*; *Histrionics*;
Ritter, Dene, Voss), translated by Peter Jansen and Kenneth
Northcott. 1990.

Screenplays: *Der Italiener*, 1971.

Verse

Auf der Erde und in der Hölle. 1957.
Unter dem Eisen des Mondes. 1958.
In hora mortis. 1958.
Psalm. 1960.
Die Irren—Die Häftlinge. 1962.
Ave Vergil. 1981.

Other

Die Ursache: Eine Andeutung. 1975.
Der Keller: Eine Entziehung. 1976.
Der Atem: Eine Entscheidung. 1978.
Die Kälte: Eine Isolation. 1981.
Ein Kind. 1982.
Wittgensteins Neffe: Eine Freundschaft. 1982; as *Wittgenstein's
Nephew: A Friendship*, translated by Eward Osers, 1986.
Gathering Evidence: A Memoir (includes *Die Ursache*; *Der Keller*;
Der Atem; *Die Kälte*; *Ein Kind*), translated by David McLintock.
1987.

*

Bibliography: *Bernhard Werkgeschichte* by Jens Dittmar, 1981.

Critical Studies: *Über Thomas Bernhard* edited by Anneliese Botond,
1970; *Thomas Bernhard* edited by Heinz Ludwig Arnold, 1974;
Thomas Bernhard by Herbert Gamper, 1977; *Thomas Bernhard* by
Bernard Sorg, 1977; "The Plays of Thomas Bernhard: A Report" by
Alfred Barthoder, in *Modern Austrian Literature*, (11), 1978;
"Bernhard's Austria: Neurosis, Symbol, or Expedient?" by A.P.
Dierick, in *Modern Austrian Literature*, (12), 1979; *New German
Dramatists* by Denis Calandra, 1983; "The Works of Thomas Bernhard:
Austrian Literature?" in *Modern Austrian Literature*, (17), 1984, and
"Life (and Death) after Life: The Portrayal of Old Age in the
Works of Thomas Bernhard" in *University of Dayton Review*, (20),
1990, both by Gerald A. Fetz; *Leiden an der "Natur": Thomas
Bernhards metaphysische Weltdeutung im Spiegel der Philosophie
Schopenhauers* by Gerald Jurdzinski, 1984; *Sprache, Handlung,
Wirklichkeit im deutschen Gegenwartsdrama: Studien zu Thomas
Berhard, Botho Strauss und Bobo Kirchoff* by Siegfried Steinmann,
1985; "Theatertheater/Theaterspiele: The Plays of Thomas Bernhard"
by Nicholas Eisner, in *Modern Drama*, (30), 1987; "Thomas Bernhard
Issue" of *Modern Austrian Literature*, (20), 1988; *Thomas Bernhard
and his Grandfather Johannes Freumbichler: Our Grandfathers Are
Our Teachers* by Caroline Markolin, translated by Petra Hartweg,
1993; *The Nihilism of Thomas Bernhard: The Portrayal of Existential
and Social Problems in his Prose Works* by Charles W. Martin, 1995;
*The Imperative of Narration: Beckett, Bernhard, Schopenhauer,
Lacan* by Catharina Wulf, 1997; *The Rhetoric of National Dissent in
Thomas Bernhard, Peter Handke, and Elfriede Jelinek* by Matthias
Konzett, 2000; *Thomas Bernhard: The Making of an Austrian* by
Gitta Honegger, 2001; *The Novels of Thomas Bernhard: Form and Its
Function* by J.J. Long, 2001.

*   *   *

Praised for his radical exposure of a disintegrating world and for
his calculating and uncompromising prose style, Thomas Bernhard
developed in his writing a singlemindedly pessimistic view of life, in
which cruelty, disease, and injustice dominate the world. The
pointlessness and bleakness of human existence pervade his vast
output, which ranges through poetry, plays, novels, and autobiographical works. With its intricate black humour and satirical portraits of the Austrian culture, society, and authorities, Bernhard's
literary *oeuvre* has often evoked comparison with Kafka's labyrinthine irony, Beckett's theatre of the absurd, and Artaud's theatre
of cruelty.

The element of melancholy and despair permeated his writing
from the outset. Three early volumes of poetry deal with suffering and
depression, *Auf der Erde und in der Hölle* [On Earth and in Hell], *In
hora mortis* [In the Hour of Death], and *Unter dem Eisen des Mondes*
[Under the Iron of the Moon]. The imagery of death and mourning in
these early poems reveals what Bernhard described as the "uncertainty of the dim Gods." "Death is my theme because life is my
theme," said Bernhard, and the early novel *Frost* pursues this idea
through the narration of the report of a medical student about a
doomed painter, while *Amras* intensified this theme. *Verstörung*
(*Gargoyles*) continued the macabre tone, with a doctor visiting a
succession of grotesque figures and deformed consciousnesses: a
diabetic industrialist in an incestuous relationship with his half-sister;
three brothers who delight in strangling exotic birds; and a crippled
musical prodigy whose sister keeps him locked in a cage. These
stories of illness, brutality, and malice are characteristic of the
preoccupations of Bernhard's fiction. Often dealing with the mentally
ill or physically disabled, Bernhard asserts that all life is motivated by
madness and disease. In *Das Kalkwerk* (*The Lime Works*), the story
begins with Konrad having just blown off his wife's head, after
imprisoning himself and her in a disused lime works so that he may
experiment with sounds, in preparation for his masterwork, "A Sense
of Hearing." The story is narrated by a life-insurance salesman, and
tells of the events leading up to this dramatic opening. Again, in *Ein
Fest für Boris* (*A Party for Boris*), legless guests attend a party hosted
by a wealthy woman who is herself legless. Indeed, physical disability, mental disturbance, and obsessively cruel behaviour are not
considered as extraordinary characteristics in humans, but exemplary
of the overall pattern of things. People's activities are merely pathetic
distractions from this basic and fundamental truth.

The five volumes of Bernhard's autobiography, *Die Ursache* [The
Cause], *Der Keller* [The Cellar], *Der Atem* [The Breath], *Die Kälte*
[The Cold], and *Ein Kind* [A Child], recount a disturbed and unhappy
childhood: unsettled by illegitimate birth, the oppressive regimes of
Nazi and Catholic boarding schools, a debilitating illness which

developed into tuberculosis, and years of poverty as a student. Attempting to exorcise the misery of his past, he explodes the myth of Salzburg as a centre of cultural value in familiar terms in *Der Keller*: "My home city is in reality a deadly disease." He vents his criticism of Austrian society and its cultural community further in *Holzfällen* (*Cutting Timber* or *Woodcutters*).

Individual freedom and development are often curtailed by circumstances beyond one's control. Family relationships are frequently the locus of social imprisonment and repression, wherein a master-slave dialectic operates (as for example in *A Party for Boris* and *Am Zeil*). Elsewhere, subjects find themselves engaged in artistic projects which are fated to fail—Konrad's study of hearing in *The Lime Works*, or Rudolf's work on Mendelssohn in *Beton* (*Concrete*). Alternatively, the exigencies of creative practice placed upon artists transform them into performing automatons indistinguishable from circus creatures—as in the plays *Der Ignorant und der Wahnsinnige* [The Ignoramus and the Madman] and *Die Macht der Gewohnheit* (*The Force of Habit*).

It is noted frequently how Bernhard's prose, utilizing a variety of unusual techniques, embodies a musical structure, with its counter-point and fugal patterns, its leitmotif and harmony. The repetition and variation evident in the overall formal structure of the novels are complemented by an intricate, interlaced structure at the level of the sentence. His circular sentences and syntactical experimentation often set up the framework of traditional fictional expectations, only to undermine it. Describing the novel *Korrektur* (*Correction*), which recounts the self-corrective and self-refining actions which prompt Roithamer's suicide, George Steiner has described Bernhard's style as a "recursive and tidal motion," and commented on the "clipped understatement" and "the bone-bleached economy" of the language. A characteristic sense of life appears in *Correction*. "Peace is not life, Roithamer wrote, perfect peace is death, as Pascal said, wrote Roithamer, I shouldn't waste my time on truisms already demonstrated by history." Bernhard deliberately models some of his subjects on real people, as when in this novel the character Roithamer is a reflective allusion to Ludwig Wittgenstein; while Paul Wittgenstein appears in *Wittgensteins Neffe* (*Wittgenstein's Nephew*), the pianist Glenn Gould in *Der Untergeher* (*The Loser*), the philosopher in *Immanuel Kant*, and the actor in *Minetti*.

Bernhard's plays tend to be long monologues with a scarcity of action and satirical of human foibles, especially intellectual and artistic pretensions, as in *Der Weltverbesserer*, *Über allen Gipfeln ist Ruh*, and *Der Theatermacher* (*Histrionics*). With dark and forbidding subjects like the Third Reich in *Vor dem Ruhestand* (*Eve of Retirement*) and his assertion that anti-semitism is rife in Austria in *Heldenplatz* or the more general political satire in *Der Präsident* (*The President*), his plays are usually made palatable by a lighter, ironic streak.

Nothing in Bernhard's world is left sacred, including his own status as a writer, which he constantly calls into question. He considers, like Nietzsche, that truths are illusions, only just not recognized as such. Bernhard's despair over the impersonality, the dreariness, of a manic world devoid of God, and his representations of lonely individuals trying to cast aside their isolation through the temporary use of language, are nevertheless offset by his unerring dedication and commitment to a quest for truth.

—Tim Woods

See the essay on *The Lime Works*.

BETTI, Ugo

Born: Camerino, Italy, 4 February 1892. **Education:** Educated at Parma University, law degree 1914. **Family:** Married Andreina Frosini in 1930. **Career:** Artillery officer during World War I: captured by the Germans after the Italian defeat at Caporetto, 1917: prisoner-of-war October 1917–December 1918; magistrate, 1919–23, then judge, 1923–26, in Parma; judge in Rome, 1930–43; contributor to *Oggi*, from 1933; retired to Camerino, 1943, later officially cleared of charges of supporting Mussolini; librarian, Ministry of Justice, 1944; spent last years as legal adviser for the Coordinamento Spettacolo, a national association for writers and publishers. **Awards:** Mondadori Academy prize, 1932; Italian Institute of Drama prize, 1949. **Died:** 9 June 1953.

PUBLICATIONS

Collections

Teatro. 1955.
Teatro postumo. 1955.
Teatro completo. 1957.
Scritti inediti, edited by Antonio di Pietro. 1964.
Teatro completo. 1971.

Plays

La padrona (produced 1926). 1929.
La donna sullo scudo, with Osvaldo Gibertini (produced 1927). 1957.
La casa sull'acqua (produced 1929). 1935.
L'isola meravigliosa (produced 1929). In *Teatro*, 1955.
Un albergo sul porto (produced 1933). In *Teatro*, 1955.
Frana allo scalo nord (produced 1936). 1939; as *Landslide*, translated by G.H. McWilliam, in *Three Plays on Justice*, 1964.
Una bella domenica di settembre (produced 1937). In *Teatro*, 1955.
I nostri sogni (produced 1937). In *Teatro*, 1955.
Il cacciatore d'anitre (produced 1940). In *Teatro*, 1955.
Il paese delle vacanze (produced 1942). 1942; as *Summertime*, translated by Henry Reed, in *Three Plays*, 1956.
Notte in casa del ricco (produced 1942). In *Teatro*, 1955.
Il diluvio (produced 1943). In *Teatro*, 1955.
Il vento notturno (produced 1945). In *Teatro*, 1955.
Ispezione (produced 1947). In *Teatro*, 1955; as *The Inquiry*, translated by D. Gullette and Gino Rizzo, in *Ugo Betti: Three Plays*, 1966.
Marito e moglie (produced 1947). In *Teatro*, 1955.
Favola di Natale (produced 1948). In *Teatro*, 1955.
Corruzione al palazzo di giustizia (produced 1949). In *Teatro*, 1955; as *Corruption in the Palace of Justice*, translated by Henry Reed, in *The New Theatre of Europe 1*, edited by Robert Corrigan, 1962.
Lotta fino all'alba (produced 1949). In *Teatro*, 1955; as *Struggle Till Dawn*, translated by G.H. McWilliam, in *Three Plays on Justice*, 1964.
Irene innocente (produced 1950). In *Teatro*, 1955.
Spiritismo nell'antica casa (produced 1950). In *Teatro*, 1955.
Delitto all'isola delle capre (produced 1950). In *Teatro*, 1955; as *Goat Island*, translated by Henry Reed, 1960; as *Crime on Goat Island*, translated by D. Gullette and Gino Rizzo, in *Ugo Betti: Three Plays*, 1966.

La Regina e gli insorti (produced 1951). In *Teatro*, 1955; as *The Queen and the Rebels*, translated by Henry Reed, in *Three Plays*, 1956.

Il giocatore (produced 1951). In *Teatro*, 1955; as *The Gambler*, translated by B. Kennedy, in *Ugo Betti: Three Plays*, 1966.

L'aiuola bruciata (produced 1953). 1953; as *The Burnt Flower-Bed*, translated by Henry Reed, in *Three Plays*, 1956.

La fuggitiva (produced 1953). 1953; as *The Fugitive*, translated by G.H. McWilliam, in *Three Plays on Justice*, 1964.

Acque turbate; o, Il fratello protegge e ama (produced 1962). In *Teatro postumo*, 1955.

Three Plays (includes *Summertime; The Queen and the Rebels*; *The Burnt Flower-Bed*), translated by Henry Reed. 1956.

Three Plays on Justice (includes *Landslide*; *Struggle Till Dawn*; *The Fugitive*), translated by G.H. McWilliam. 1964.

I tre del pra' di sopra (screenplay). In *Scritti inediti*, 1964.

Ugo Betti: Three Plays (includes *The Inquiry*; *Crime on Goat Island*; *The Gambler*), translated by D. Gullette, B. Kennedy, and Gino Rizzo, edited by Rizzo. 1966.

Fiction

Caino (stories). 1928.
Le case (stories). 1933.
Una strana serata (stories). 1948.
La piera alta, from his screenplay *I tre del pra' di sopra*. 1948.
Raccolta di novelle, edited by Lia Fava. 1963.
Novelle (stories), edited by Mario Ortolani. 1968.

Verse

Il re pensieroso. 1922.
Canzonette—La morte. 1932.
Uomo e donna. 1937.
Poesie (includes poems written 1938–53). 1957.
Il filo verde, poesie, edited by L. Fontanella. 1993.

Other

Considerazioni sulla forza maggiore come limite di responsabilità del vettore ferroviario (essay). 1920.
Religione e teatro. 1957; as "Religion and Theatre," translated by Gino Rizzo, in *Tulane Drama Review*, 8, 1964.
Translator, *Le nozze di Teti e di Peleo*, from poems by Catullus. 1910.

*

Critical Studies: *La poesia di Ugo Betti* by E. de Michelis, 1937; *Il teatro di Ugo Betti* by E. Barbetti, 1943; *Ugo Betti* by N.D. Aloisio, 1952; *Ugo Betti* by A. Fiocco, 1954; *La fortuna del Teatro di Ugo Betti*, 1959, and *Ugo Betti*, 1960, both by F. Cologni; "Interpreting Betti" by G.H. McWilliam, in *Tulane Drama Review*, 5, 1960; *Ugo Betti* by A. Alessio, 1963; "Regression-Progression in Ugo Betti's Drama" by G. Rizzo, in *Tulane Drama Review*, 8(1), 1963; *L'opera di Ugo Betti* by Antonio di Pietro, 2 vols., 1966–68; "Ugo Betti: The Theater of Shame" by Harold Watts, in *Modern Drama*, 12, 1969; "The Purgatorial Theatre of Ugo Betti" by Robert Corrigan, in his *The Theatre in Search of a Fix*, 1973; *Il teatro di Ugo Betti* by Gildo Moro, 1973; *Impegno e astrazione nell'opera di Ugo Betti* by F. Musarra, 1974; "Ugo Betti's Last Plays" by Antonio Illiano, in *Perspectives on Contemporary Literature*, 1(1), 1975; *Coscienza e*

responsabilità nell'opera di Ugo Betti: Da La padrona a Corruzione al palazzo di giustizia by Gianni Spera, 1977; *Atti del congresso internazionale Betti drammaturgo* edited by F. Doglio and W. Raspolini, 1984; *Il teatro di Ugo Betti* by Giorgio Fontanelli, 1985; *Ugo Betti: An Introduction* by Emanuele Licastro, 1985; *La drammatica di Ugo Betti. Tematiche e archetipi* by Gaetana Marrone, 1988; "Tragedy in a Postmodern Vein: Ugo Betti, Our Contemporary?" by Lloyd A. Arnett, in *Modern Drama*, 33, 1990.

*   *   *

Of all the Italian dramatists, Ugo Betti is undoubtedly one of the best known and yet still little understood. Such critics as Pandolfi, Quasimodo, and Momigliano have addressed his thematic texts in a variety of ways, but have failed to grasp the core of Betti's artistic world, its "vibrant poetic truth" as philosopher Gabriel Marcel has called it. After World War I, during the years of disillusionment and despair which brought to power Benito Mussolini, Betti, a socialist, emerged with poems, short stories, and plays that debated modern man's metaphysical predicament and moral anguish. Betti's work is often compared to that of his illustrious contemporary Luigi Pirandello. Like the Sicilian playwright, the basic terms of Betti's existentialist discourse are alienation and authenticity, but their conclusions ostensibly differ. With modern notions of absurdity and nihilism, Pirandello dissects man's soul and traditional values. A passionate reader of Tolstoi and Dostoevskii, Betti revitalizes formal techniques for the projection of haunting images of death and loneliness. He is concerned with the immediate realities of the human experience and refuses to abide on nothingness, whereas Pirandello's appeal is toward the appropriation of the absurd in order to discover man's ambivalent nature. Anyone who attempts to acquire a comprehensive view of Betti discovers that, beyond the familiar paradigms of guilt, justice, and redemption, his is a disconcertingly complex road to follow.

Chronologically, any fundamental approach to Betti ought to begin with *La padrona* [The Mistress], which became an instant success in 1926. Simple in plot and naturalistic in style, *La padrona* is remembered mostly for its "Preface," an ideal introduction to Betti's theatre. From the beginning, the playwright promotes a plane of existence that is ethical. He explores the power of determining one's choice, the freedom of will that displaced Adam's progeny into a liminal stage of suffering. To Betti, "we are all poor, restless creatures, who try to understand the incongruity between our actual existence and the potential nature given to us." Guilt is a *felix culpa* motif. Angelo says in *Delitto all'isola delle capre* (*Crime on Goat Island*): "Our salvation is in sin; it's only our wretched pride that doesn't want to accept it." The ontological basis of Betti's tragic vision rests upon the myth of the Fall, which supports the heroic dimension of life, an idea of disorder which initiates the character's revolt and search for self-knowledge.

Betti's theatre evolves from realism into myth. The earlier plays evoke the dark settings of French naturalism. For example, in *Un albergo sul porto* [An Inn on the Harbour], the emblems of estrangement are foreshadowed by sailors, unscrupulous merchants, and prostitutes: in *Il cacciatore d'anitre* [The Duck Hunter], the symbolic inquiry into the unconscious is personified by the diabolic Michial, a wealthy merchant, and by Marco, an idealistic young man who uses logos and intuition to comprehend the most obscure part of himself, and chooses death over psychological chaos. The archetype of the unconscious is fully explored in *La fuggitiva* (*The Fugitive*), a posthumous play. The fugitive of the title is Nina, a neurotic character in whom Betti portrays the dialectic of the ascent from the abyss (a demonic parody of the Lost Eden) to the top of the mountain—the sacred space that defines microcosm and macrocosm. For Betti, man's test starts at the bottom: ''What I would like to do, in my writings, is to place certain characters and certain feelings, naked and alone, almost at the bottom of a big ladder. And to watch if there is in them, without any help, the capacity and the need to climb.'' This premise is implied in the dramas of Eros. *Crime on Goat Island, La padrona*, and *Acque turbate* [Troubled Waters] examine a theology of sin embodied in devouring female figures; they represent an epitome of desire and transgression, and yet are instrumental in any aspiration to a superior level of being. In *Crime on Goat Island*, Agata debates the causality of good and evil before letting Angelo die in the well; in *Acque turbate*, Alda's incestuous love for her brother, revealed by anamnesis, promotes cosmic awareness. Betti's plays on justice implement this investigation into man's existential stance by representing the legal responsibilities of guilt through an inquiry that is both judicial and metaphysical. To Betti, we are all part of ''a machine that moves us.'' Consequently, a crime triggers reactions that invalidate any individual punishment and call for collective responsibility. In *Ispezione* (*The Inquiry*), *Frana allo scalo nord* (*Landslide*), and *Corruzione al palazzo di giustizia* (*Corruption in the Palace of Justice*), Betti's Kafkaesque inspectors search for individual guilt, but they ultimately formulate a broader definition that transforms the verdict into a crisis of conscience. In existentialist terms, guilt is an essential liminal situation.

Betti's minor works are also worthy of consideration—poems, short stories, screenplays, essays, and a novel—most of which are an orchestration of his dramatic themes. Excluding a translation of Catullus' *Epithalamion*, Betti's first literary endeavour was a collection of poems, *Il re pensieroso* [The Pensive King], written in German prison camps between 1917 and 1918. This overture—like the subsequent *Canzonette—La morte* [Little Songs—Death] and *Uomo e donna* [Man and Woman]—seems designed to serve as a meditation on human suffering. The adult's cosmic terror, often symbolized by the myth of the child, remains a vital motif in the short story collections, *Caino, Le case* [Houses], *Una strana serata* [A Strange Evening], and the novel *La piera alta* [The High Stone], all of which are an elaboration on loneliness and authenticity. In the dramatic ballet *L'isola meravigliosa* [The Marvellous Island], the solitary King Nadir and his elusive quest for happiness symbolize the alienation of 20th-century guilt-ridden man. During the 1930s, Betti's escapist mood was translated into fables and farcical comedies. *Il diluvio* [The Flood], *Una bella domenica di settembre* [A Beautiful September Sunday], *Il paese delle vacanze (Summertime), I nostri sogni* [Our Dreams], and *Favola di Natale* [Christmas Story] engage in a critique of bourgeois values. Through the analysis of mediocre characters, obsessed by the urge to hide their defeats and weaknesses, Betti exposes the inauthenticity of conventional living.

Betti was not a formalist. In emphasizing his thought, as well as his theatrical achievements, we must remember, however, that Betti considered himself primarily a poet whose interest was ethical, and whose ultimate goal was artistic. Betti sought to restore to mankind a meaningful contact with transcendence. As in *Il giocatore* (*The Gambler*), should the protagonist dare to pass the threshold, there is the promise of an unprecedented encounter with the mystery of man himself. Ennio's leap of faith will be rewarded: ''He is a bad gambler who cannot risk all at the last moment.'' Compelled at every step to realize himself freely, but without the support of any established certainties, modern man must risk it all. Betti's theatre affirms faith not as a theological speculation but as a norm, bound to the moral life of the individual in society.

—Gaetana Marrone

BIBBIENA, Bernardo Dovizi da

See DOVIZI DA BIBBIENA, Bernardo

BILDERDIJK, Willem

Born: Amsterdam, The Netherlands, 7 September 1756. **Education:** Studied law at Leiden, 1780–82. **Family:** Married 1) Catharina Rebecca Woesthoven in 1785 (marriage not dissolved), one daughter; 2) Katharina Wilhelmina Schweikhardt. **Career:** Lawyer in The Hague; because of his loyalty to the House of Orange he was forced to leave the Netherlands after French troops proclaimed it a republic in 1795; lived in exile in London, then in Germany; returned to the Netherlands in 1806; King Louis Napoleon's court poet and private tutor in Dutch; nominated member of Royal Dutch Institute, 1808; sheltered from financial difficulties by the king; promised university post in 1813 by Regent William I but blocked by other academics. **Died:** 18 December 1831.

PUBLICATIONS

Collections

Geschiedenis des Vaderlands [History of the Fatherland], edited by H.W. Tydeman. 13 vols., 1832–53.
Brieven [Letters], edited by W. Meeschert. 5 vols., 1836.
Dichtwerken [Poetical Works], edited by I. da Costa. 16 vols., 1856–59.

Verse

Prijsvaerzen [Prize Verses]. 2 vols., 1776–77.
Op het afsterven van den dichter Lucas Pater [On the Death of the Poet Lucas Pater]. 1781.
De Leydsche Weezen aan de burgery. 1781.
Myn verlustiging [My Delight]. 1781.
Ellius. 1788.
Vertoogen van Salomo [Sayings of Solomon]. 1788.
De alleenheersching [Sole Rule]. 1793.
Treurzang van Ibn Doreid [Lament of Ibn Doreid]. 1795.
Urzijn en Valentijn [Urzijn and Valentijn]. 1795.
Mengelpoezy [Miscellaneous Verse]. 1799.
Raad van een Hollander aan Engeland [Advice from a Dutchman to England]. 1799.
Losse stukken in verzen [Loose Pieces in Verse]. 1803.
Mengelingen [Miscellaneous]. 1804.

Vaderlandsche oranjezucht [Patriotic Longings for the House of Orange]. 1805.
Ode aan Napoleon [Ode to Napoleon]. 1806.
Nieuwe mengelingen [New Miscellany]. 1806.
Aan den Koning [To the King]. 1807.
De ziekte der geleerden [The Disease of the Learned]. 1807.
Najaarsbladen [Autumn Leaves]. 1808.
Odilde. 1808.
Vreugdezang [Song of Joy]. 1808.
Konings komst tot den throon [Accession of the King]. 1809.
Pestel. 1809.
Verspreide gedichten [Scattered Poems]. 1809.
Wapenkreet [Call to Arms]. 1809.
Hulde aan Zijne Koninklijke en Keizerlijke Majesteit [Homage to His Royal and Imperial Majesty]. 1810.
De geestenwereld [The Spirit World]. 1811.
Winterbloemen [Winter Flowers]. 1811.
De echt. 1812.
Geologie. 1813.
Krijgsdans [War Dance]. 1813.
Affodillen [Asphodels]. 1814.
Nieuwe uitspruitsels [New Shoots]. 1817.
Wit en rood [White and Red]. 2 vols., 1818.
De ondergang der eerste waereld [The Ruin of the First World] (unfinished). 1820; edited by J. Bosch, 1959.
Zedelijke gispingen [Moral Strictures]. 1820.
Taal en dichtkundige verscheidenheden [Linguistic and Poetical Varieties]. 4 vols., 1820–22.
De muis en kikvorschkrijg [The Battle of Mice and Frogs], from Homer. 1821.
Sprokkelingen [Gleanings]. 1821.
Ter uitvaart van Nicolaas Schotsman [On the Passing of Nicholas Scotsman]. 1822.
Krekelzangen [Cricket Songs]. 3 vols., 1822–23.
De derde october [The Third of October]. 1823.
Aan de Roomsch-Katholieken dezer dagen [To Present-Day Catholics]. 1823.
Spreuken [Sayings]. 1823.
Rotsgalmen [Rock Echoes]. 2 vols., 1824.
Navonkeling [Afterglow]. 1826.
Oprakeling [Raking Up]. 1826.
Afscheid aan Leyden [Farewell to Leiden]. 1827.
Nieuwe oprakeling [New Raking Up]. 1827.
De voet in 't graf [A Foot in the Grave]. 1827.
Avondschemering [Twilight]. 1828.
Naklank [Echo]. 1828.
Vermaking [Amusement]. 1828.
Nieuwe vermaking [New Amusement]. 1829.
Schemerschijn [Twilight]. 1829.
Proeve eener navolging van Ovidius' gedaanterverwisselingen [Result of an Adaptation of Ovid's Metamorphoses]. 1829.
Nasprokkeling [Late Gleaning]. 1830.
Rondedans [Round Dance]. 1832.
Nederland hersteld [The Netherlands Reinstated]. 1836.

Plays

Floris de Vijfde [Floris V]. 1808.
Treurspelen [Tragedies], with K.W. Bilderdijk. 3 vols., 1808–09.

Fiction

Kort verhaal van eene aanmerkelijke luchtreis (story). 1813; as *A Remarkable Aerial Voyage and Discovery of a New Planet*, translated by Paul Vincent, 1986.

Other

Brief van den navolger van Sofokles' Edipus [Letter from the Adaptor of Sophocles' Oedipus]. 1780.
Redevoering over de voortreffelijkheid der schilderkunst [Discourse on the Excellence of Poetry]. 1794.
Verhandeling over de geslachten der naamwoorden [Treatise on the Gender of Nouns]. 1805.
De kunst der poezy [The Art of Poetry]. 1808.
Het treurspel [Tragedy]. 1808.
Van het letterschrift. 1820.
Geslachtslijst der Nederduitsche naamwoorden [List of Gender of Low-German Nouns]. 1821.
Korte ontwikkeling der gronden van het natuurrecht [Short Essay on the Fundamentals of Natural Law]. 1821.
Verhandelingen de zede en rechtsleer betreffende [Discourse on Morality and Law], 1821.
De bezwaren tegen den geest der eeuw van Mr I. da Costa toegelicht [Objections to the Spirit of the Age Elucidated by Mr I. da Costa]. 1823.
Bijdragen tot de toneelpoezy [Contributions to Dramatic Poetry]. 1823.
Nieuwe taal- en dichtkundige verscheidenheden [New Linguistic and Poetical Varieties] (collected works on philology). 4 vols., 1824–25.
Nederlandsche spraakleer [Dutch Grammar]. 1826.
Korte aanmerkingen op Huydecopers Proeve van taal en dichtkunde [Brief Remarks on Huydecoper's Essay on Language and Poetry]. 1827.
Grondregelen der perspectief of doorzichtkunde [Ground Rules of Perspective]. 1828.
Uitzicht op mijn dood [Prospect of My Death]. 1829.
Beginschels der woordvorsching [Principles of Linguistic Research]. 1831.
Translator, *Edipus, Koning van Thebe*, by Sophocles. 1780.
Translator, *De Dood Van Edipus*, by Sophocles. 1789.
Translator, *Het Buitenleven*, by J. Delille. 1803.
Translator, *Fingal, in zes gezangen*, by "Ossian" [James Macpherson]. 1805.
Translator, *Lofzangen*, by Callimachus. 1808.
Translator, *De Mensch*, by Pope. 1808.
Translator, *Hekeldichten*, by Persius. 1820.
Translator, *Cinna*, by Corneille. 1824.
Translator, *De Cycloop*, by Euripides. 1828.
Translator, *Redevoeringen*, by St. John Chrysostom. 1832.
Translator, *Kerkredenen*, by Merle d'Aubigné. 1833.
Translator, *Het Bewijs en gezag der Christelijke openbaring*, by T. Chalmers. 1833.

*

Critical Studies: *De mensch en de dichter Willem Bilderdijk* by I. da Costa, 1859; *Bilderdijk, zijn leven en zijn werken* by R.A. Kollewijn, 1891; *Bilderdijk als denker en dichter* by H. Bavinck, 1906; *Gedenkboek voor Mr. W. Bilderdijk* by R.A. Kollewijn, 1906; *Willem Bilderdijk als dichter* by A. Heyting, 2 vols., 1931–40; *Een Eeuw strijd om*

Bilderdijk by P. Geyl, 1958; *Folia Bilderdijkiana* edited by M. van Hattum and others, 1985; *Bilderdijk en het Jodendom: Bilderdijks waardering van het joodse denken in confrontatie met zijn tijd* by L. Engelfriet, 1995; *Hogere sferen: de ideeënwereld van Willem Bilderdijk (1756–1831)* by Joris van Eijnatten, 1998; *Wie leert 't krekeltjen zijn lied?: de poëtische oorspronkelijkheid van Willem Bilderdijk: negen beschouwingen over gedichten van Bilderdijk* by Piet Gerbrandy and Marinus van Hattum, 2000.

* * *

Willem Bilderdijk is without a doubt the most prolific Dutch writer but probably the least read, both by his countrymen and by the world at large. Virtually none of his huge output has been translated into English. His large output was caused mainly by the fact that he had to live off his pen, but also because he found writing easy. Bilderdijk was probably one of the last Dutch writers to be seen as a major figure on the cultural, social, and political scene of his time, but his influence scarcely survived his death. Although his many works had been brought out by different publishers, when one of them tried to launch a collected edition a few years after Bilderdijk's death, the project had to be abandoned for lack of interest.

Bilderdijk made his most lasting mark as one of the leading figures of what Dutch historians have called the "Réveil," or national awakening, under the leadership of the still largely autocratic first king of the Netherlands, William I. Bilderdijk's anti-republican, ultra-patriotic, and exceedingly conservative ideas proliferate in his lectures on the history of the Netherlands which he gave in his own living room in Leyden (at no point in his life did he become linked to any Dutch university) to a select group of people who were to become the leaders of the new Dutch state after 1815. Not only did Bilderdijk write an *oeuvre* of almost unbelievable volume, he did so in different languages and on a variety of topics. He wrote about law in Latin and in Dutch, about philology and literature in French and in Dutch, about botany in French, and about philosophy, theology, and history in Dutch. Three years before his death he published a theoretical book on perspective.

Bilderdijk probably learned to write with such ease in the *dichtgenootschappen* (poetry clubs) that existed throughout the Netherlands until the French occupation and beyond. His father belonged to one, and that is probably where the young Bilderdijk acquired what was then known as "Parnassian language," the polished, ornamental, somewhat obscure, sonorous, and mostly bombastic diction, replete with classical and mythological references, which he used both in his verse and in his prose. He supplemented it however, with strict metrical schemes in his verse, the only part of his *oeuvre* ever to be republished in anything resembling a collected edition.

The diction that greatly facilitated Bilderdijk's enormous production also proved an insurmountable barrier between his work and those who tried to read it in later generations. One has the feeling of a machine running on, endlessly and effortlessly, and only very few readers ever catch a glimpse of the sensitive, honest, sometimes even witty ghost imprisoned within it. Bilderdijk wrote in all the genres expected of a true man of letters at the time: prose, mainly polemical, political, and scientific, with his greatest output in verse. His tragedies were inspired by Dutch history and more exotic tales; an epic, *De ondergang der eerste waereld* [The Ruin of the First World], published unfinished during his lifetime, became his most popular work, and is perhaps the best example of his stature in the Dutch world of letters during his lifetime. Perhaps the truest measure of the reversal

of fate Bilderdijk has suffered since his death is the fact that his only complete work that is readily available in Dutch bookstores today is *Kort verhaal van eene aanmerkelijke luchtreis* (*A Remarkable Aerial Voyage and Discovery of a New Planet*), published in 1813, the first work of science fiction to be written in Dutch. Science fiction was the only genre in which Bilderdijk was an innovator in Dutch literature, albeit not consciously so. He probably believed that he was continuing 18th-century travel writing, but with other means: after the discovery of Australia, strange lands had to be looked for, and found, on other planets.

In his other works Bilderdijk never progressed beyond the "Parnassian speech" he found so easy. What is still published on Bilderdijk today is published in the form of articles on certain manageable aspects of his work, not on the work as a whole. Those few literary historians tempted to tackle Bilderdijk find his translations easier and more rewarding to read than his original work. Bilderdijk translated Ossian, Delille, and Alexander Pope, but also Sophocles, Persius, and Ovid. His Ossian translation was highly influential in the development of Dutch pre-Romanticism. One gets the impression that only in his translations does his work become less self-referential. Here Bilderdijk was relieved to be the craftsman and nothing more. In his other writings, whatever the subject, the reader is extremely likely to meet Bilderdijk. Many of the tragedies and the narrative poems contain thinly veiled autobiographical passages, and Bilderdijk unashamedly pushes his own views in his more "scientific" writings as well. His literary craftsmanship allowed him to cut a wide path for himself through the contemporary world of letters, so wide that none attempted to follow. Similarly, his unselfconscious egocentrism served as a protective armour. He was in his world but not really of it, like the sickly child not expected to take too great a part in everyday life.

In many ways Bilderdijk occupies a position in Dutch literature and culture not unlike that of Goethe in German literature and culture. Goethe, however, was a genius, whereas Bilderdijk was, in the words of the Dutch historians Annie and Jan Romein, a "genius crippled," a prophet with a club foot.

—André Lefevere

BJØRNSON, Bjørnstjerne (Martinius)

Born: Kvikne, Norway (then united with Sweden), 8 December 1832. **Education:** Educated at Molde grammar school, 1844–49; Christiania University, Christiania (now Oslo), 1852–54. **Family:** Married the actress Karoline Reimers in 1858. **Career:** Contributed articles to newspapers while at university; theatre reviewer, *Morgenbladet*, 1854–56; editor and contributor, *Illustreret Folkeblad*, from 1856; director (succeeding Ibsen, *q.v.*), Det Norske Theater [Norwegian Theatre], Bergen, 1857–59; editor, *Bergensposten*, Bergen; returned to Christiania to edit the newspaper *Aftenbladet*, 1859, but subsequently had to resign because of his political views; founder, Norwegian Cultural Society; lived in Rome, 1860–62; director, Christiania Theatre, 1865–67; editor, *Norsk Folkeblad*, 1866–71; returned to Rome, 1873; became increasingly involved in political and social debate in the late 1870s; travelled and lectured in the United States, 1880–81; lived in Paris, 1882–87; promoter of world peace and minority rights during the 1890s. **Awards:** Nobel prize for literature, 1903. **Died:** 26 April 1910.

PUBLICATIONS

Collections

Works, edited and translated by Rasmus B. Anderson. 6 vols., 1882.
Novels, edited by Edmund Gosse. 13 vols., 1895–1909.
Samlede værker, edited Carl Nærup. 11 vols., 1900–02.
Samlede digter-verker, edited by Francis Bull. 9 vols., 1919–20.
Samlede digte, edited by Francis Bull. 2 vols., 1926.
Samlede verker. 5 vols., 1960.

Plays

Mellem slagene (produced 1857). 1857; translated as *Between the Battles*, in *The Nobel Prize Treasury*, 1948.
Halte-Hulda [Limping Hulda] (produced 1858). 1858.
Kong Sverre [King Sverre] (produced 1861). 1861.
Sigurd Slembe (produced 1863). 1862; as *Sigurd Slembe*, translated by William Morton Payne, 1888.
Maria Stuart i Skotland (produced 1864). 1864; as *Mary Stuart in Scotland*, translated by August Sahlberg, 1912; as *Mary, Queen of Scots*, translated by Sahlberg, 1912.
De nygifte (produced 1865). 1865; as *The Newly-Married Couple*, translated by Sivert and Elizabeth Hjerleid, 1870; also translated by R. Farquharson Sharp, in *Three Comedies*, 1912; as *The Newly Married*, translated by John Volk, 1885; as *A Lesson in Marriage*, translated by Grace Isabel Colbron, 1910.
Sigurd Jorsalfar [Sigurd the Crusader]. 1872; in *Kongebrødrene*, edited by Francis Bull, 1932.
Redaktøren (produced 1875). 1874; as *The Editor*, translated by R. Farquharson Sharp, in *Three Dramas*, 1914.
En fallit (produced 1875). 1874; as *The Bankrupt*, translated by R. Farquharson Sharp, in *Three Dramas*, 1914.
Kongen (produced 1902). 1877; as *The King*, translated by R. Farquharson Sharp, in *Three Dramas*, 1914.
Det ny system (produced 1878). 1879; as *The New System*, translated by Edwin Brörkman, in *Plays 1*, 1913.
Leonarda (produced 1879). 1879; as *Leonarda*, translated by Daniel L. Hanson, in *The Drama*, 3, 1911; also translated by R. Farquharson Sharp, in *Three Comedies*, 1912.
En hanske (produced 1883). 1883; as *A Gauntlet*, translated by H.L. Brækstad, 1880; also translated by Osman Edwards, 1894; R. Farquharson Sharp, in *Three Comedies*, 1912; as *The Gauntlet*, translated by Edwin Björkman, in *Plays 1*, 1913.
Over ævne I (produced 1886). 1883; as *Pastor Sang*, translated by William Wilson, 1893; as *Beyond Our Power*, translated by Edwin Björkman, in *Plays 1*, 1913; as *Beyond Human Power*, translated by Lee M. Hollander, in *Chief Contemporary Dramatists*, edited by T.H. Dickinson, 1915.
Geografi og kjærlighed (produced 1885). 1885; as *Love and Geography*, translated by Edwin Björkman, in *Plays 2*, 1914.
Over ævne II (produced 1895). 1895; as *Beyond Human Might*, translated by Edwin Björkman, in *Plays 2*, 1914.
Lyset (libretto). 1895.
Paul Lunge og Tora Parsberg (produced 1901). 1898; as *Paul Lange and Tora Parsberg*, translated by H.L. Brækstad, 1899.
Laboremus (produced 1901). 1901; translated as *Laboremus*, 1901; also translated by Edwin Björkman, in *Plays 2*, 1914.
På Storhove [At Storhove] (produced 1902). 1902.
Daglannet [Dag's Farm] (produced 1905). 1904.

Når den ny vin blomstrer (produced 1909). 1909; as *When the New Wine Blooms*, translated by Lee M. Hollander, 1911.
Three Comedies (includes *The Newly-Married Couple; Leonarda; A Gauntlet*), translated by R. Farquharson Sharp. 1912.
Plays (vol. 1 includes *The Gauntlet; Beyond Our Power; The New System*; vol. 2 includes *Love and Geography; Beyond Human Might; Laboremus*), translated by Edwin Björkman. 2 vols., 1913–14.
Three Dramas (includes *The Bankrupt; The Editor; The King*), translated by R. Farquharson Sharp. 1914.
Kongebrødrene (includes *Sigurd Jorsalfar* and *Kong Eystejn*), edited by Francis Bull, 1932.

Fiction

Synnøve Solbakken. 1857; as *Trust and Trial*, translated by Mary Howitt, 1858; as *Love and Life in Norway*, translated by Augusta Bethell and Augusta Plesner, 1870; as *Betrothal*, translated in *Half Hours with Foreign Novelists*, 1880; as *Synnove Solbakken*, translated by Julie Sutter, 1881; also translated by Rasmus B. Anderson, 1881; part translated as *Sunny Hill*, 1932.
Arne. 1858; translated as *Arne*, 1861; also translated by Augusta Plesner and S. Rugeley-Powers, 1866; Rasmus B. Anderson, 1881; Walter Low, with *The Fisher Lassie*, 1890.
En glad gut. 1859; as *Ovind*, translated by Sivert and Elizabeth Hjerleid, 1869; as *The Happy Boy*, translated by Helen R.A. Gade, 1870; as *A Happy Boy*, translated by Rasmus B. Anderson, 1881; also translated by W. Archer, 1896; translated as *The Happy Lad*, in *"The Happy Lad" and Other Tales*, 1882.
Smaastykker [Sketches]. 1860.
Fiskerjenten. 1868; as *The Fisher-Maiden*, translated by M.E. Niles, 1869; as *The Fishing Girl*, translated by Augusta Plesner and Frederika Richardson, 1870; as *The Fisher Girl*, translated by Sivert and Elizabeth Hjerleid, 1871; as *The Fisher Maiden*, translated by Rasmus B. Anderson, 1882; as *The Fisher Lassie*, translated by Walter Low, with *Arne*, 1890; translated as *The Fisher Lass*, 1896.
Fortællinger [Tales]. 2 vols., 1872.
Brudeslåtten. 1872; as *The Bridal March*, in *Life by the Fells and Fjords*, translated by Augusta Plesner and S. Rugeley-Powers, 1879; also translated by Rasmus B. Anderson, in *"The Bridal March" and Other Stories*, 1882; J. Evan Williams, 1893.
Magnhild. 1877; as *Magnhild*, translated by Rasmus B. Anderson, 1883.
Life by the Fells and Fjords. 1879.
Kaptejn Mansana. 1879; as *Captain Mansana*, in *"Captain Mansana" and Other Stories*, translated by Rasmus B. Anderson, 1882; also translated by Marian Ford, 1883.
Frygten for flertallet. 1881.
"The Bridal March" and Other Stories, translated by Rasmus B. Anderson. 1882.
"Captain Mansana" and Other Stories, translated by Rasmus B. Anderson. 1882.
Det flager i byen og på havnen. 1884; as *The Heritage of the Kurts*, translated by Cecil Fairfax, 1890.
Støv. 1887.
På guds veje. 1889; as *In God's Way*, translated by Elizabeth Carmichael, 1890.
Nye fortællinger [New Tales]. 3 vols., 1893–94.
Mary. 1906; as *Mary*, translated by Mary Morison, 1909.

Verse

Digte og sange [Poems and Songs]. 1870.
Arnljot Gelline. 1870; as *Arnljot Gelline*, translated by William Morton Payne, 1917.
Poems and Songs (collection), translated by Arthur Hubbell Palmer. 1915.

Other

Mine brev til Petersburgskija Vjedomosti m.m. (letters). 1898.
Udvalgte artikler og taler (articles and speeches). 4 vols., 1902–04.
Aulestad-breve til Bergliot Ibsen, edited by Bergliot Ibsen. 1911.
Gro-tid: Breve fra årene 1857–1870, edited by Halvdan Koht. 2 vols., 1912.
Udvalgte artikler og taler (articles and speeches), edited by Christen Collin and H. Eitrem. 2 vols., 1912–13.
Brytnings-år: Breve fra årene 1871–1878, edited by Halvdan Koht. 2 vols., 1921.
Breve til Alexander L. Kielland, edited by Francis Bull. 1930.
Kamp-liv: Breve fra årene 1879–1884, edited by Halvdan Koht. 2 vols., 1932.
Bjørnstjerne Bjørnsons og Christen Collins brevveksling, 1889–1909, edited by Dagny Bjørnson Sautreau. 1937.
Brevveksling med danske 1875–1910, edited by Øyvind Anker, Francis Bull, and Torben Nielsen. 3 vols., 1953.
Din venn far, edited by Dagny Bjørnson Sautreau. 1956.
Breve til Karoline 1858–1907, edited by Dagny Bjørnson Sautreau. 1957.
Brevveksling med svenske 1858–1909, edited by Øyvind Anker, Francis Bull, and Örjan Lindberger. 3 vols., 1960–61.
Brevveksling med danske 1854–1874, edited by Øyvind Anker, Francis Bull, and Torben Nielsen. 3 vols., 1970–74.
Selvstændighedens Æresfølelse: artikler og taler i utvalg 1879–1905, edited by Knut Johansen. 1974.
Land of the Free: Bjørnson's American Letters, 1880–1881, edited and translated by Eva Lund Haugen and Einar Haugen. 1978.
"Og nu vil jeg tale ut"—"men nu vil jeg også tale ud," brevvekslingen mellom Bjørnstjerne Bjørnson og Amalie Skram 1878–1904, edited by Øyvind Anker and Edvard Beyer. 1982.
Briefwechsel mit Deutschen, edited by Aldo Keel. 1986.
God morgen, Rosalinde! brev til Rosalinde Thomsen, Bjørnstjerne Bjørnson, edited by Bodil Nævdal. 1990.

*

Bibliography: *Bjørnson-bibliografi* by Arthur Thuesen, 5 vols., 1948–57.

Critical Studies: *Critical Studies of Ibsen and Bjørnson* by Georg Brandes, 1899; *Bjørnstjerne Bjørnson: Hans barndom og ungdom* [Bjørnstjerne Bjørnson: His Childhood and Youth] by Christen Collen, 1907, revised edition, 2 vols., 1923; *Bjørnstjerne Bjarnson 1832–1910* by William Morton Payne, 1910; *The Norwegian-American Reaction to Ibsen and Bjørnson, 1850–1900* by Arthur Paulson, 1937; *Bjørnstjerne Bjørnson: A Study in Norwegian Nationalism* by Harold Larson, 1944; *Bjørnstjerne Bjørnson, the Man and His Work* by Øyvind Anker, 1955; "Bjørnson and Tragedy," in *Scandinavica*, 1(1), 1962, and "Björnson," in his *Modern Norwegian Literature, 1860–1918*, 1966, both by Brian Downs; "Bjørnson Research: A

Survey" by Harald Noreng, in *Scandinavica*, 4(1), 1965: "Bjørnson's 'Trond' and Popular Tradition," in *Scandinavian Studies*, 41(1), 1969, *Bjørnson's Bondefortellinger and Norwegian Folk Literature*, 1970, and "The Self in Isolation: A New Reading of Bjørnson's *Arne*," in *Scandinavian Studies*, 45(4), 1973, all by Henning K. Sehmsdorf; "The Multifarious Bjørnson" by Øystein Rottem, in *Scandinavica*, 24(1), 1985; *Bjørnstjerne Bjørnson: kunstneren og samfunnsmennesket 1832–1880* by Per Amdam, 1993; *Hvor gjerne vilde jeg have været i deres sted: Bjørnstjerne Bjørnson, de intellektuelle og Dreyfus-saken* by Bernt Hagtvet, 1998.

*   *   *

Bjørnstjerne Bjørnson, along with Henrik Ibsen and August Strindberg, focused the attention of the world upon Scandinavian theatre during the late 19th century. Each of these authors began his career by drawing upon the stories and myths of the Nordic tradition. Bjørnson, a Norwegian, was a prolific and distinguished writer in a number of fields, leaving 21 plays, eight novels, many short stories and poems, several epic-lyric works, critical articles, and nearly 20 volumes of letters. The variety of his literary interest was clear early in his career. In 1857 he published *Svnnøve Solbakken*, the first of the Norwegian peasant tales that gained him renown throughout Scandinavia, as well as his first play, *Mellem slagene (Between the Battles)*, a one-act work set in the 12th century. The following year saw the play *Halte-Hulda* [Limping Hulda] and the story *Arne*. The eponymous Synnøve and Arne, placed in poetically rendered northern landscapes, can be taken as two aspects of the Norwegian peasant, the one rough and swaggering, the other gifted with fancy and imagination, both seen (in a somewhat less sympathetic treatment) in Ibsen's more famous *Peer Gynt*. *Kong Sverre* [King Sverre] continued to work the popular vein of Romantic interest in national history and folklore, and was staged by Ibsen at the nationalist Norwegian Theatre in Christiania (now Oslo). The first of several epic poems on Nordic themes, "Bergliot," appeared the following year.

The play that first gained Bjørnson a major following was the brilliant historical trilogy *Sigurd Slembe*, much admired by Ibsen, and echoed to some extent in Ibsen's great success in historical drama, *Kongs-Emnerne (The Pretenders)*. This was followed by *Maria Stuart i Skotland (Mary Stuart in Scotland)* in 1864. Having achieved success in national historical dramas, Bjørnson, like Ibsen, but over a decade earlier, then turned to a realistic study of contemporary domestic life. His popular problem play, *De nygifte (The Newly-Married Couple)*, looks backward to Augier and Dumas *fils* and forward to Ibsen's *Et dukkehjem (A Doll's House)*. Indeed, Ibsen's play may be seen in part as a corrective to Bjørnson's, which focuses upon the adjustment of the husband to married life: a husband who, in Bjørnson's own phrase, is treated "like a doll." Ibsen, once embarked upon his studies of contemporary life, continued to work that vein consistently for a series of brilliant dramas, but Bjørnson, after *The Newly-Married Couple*, returned to the themes and subjects of his earlier years, producing some of his most popular works, beginning with the short story *Fiskerjenten (The Fisher Maiden)* in 1868. Two years later appeared both the short but tremendously influential and popular collection of lyric and patriotic verse *Digte og sange* [Poems and Songs] and the lengthy poem *Arnljot Gelline*, with an epic imagination and lyric beauty as powerful as anything in this artist's extensive canon. Another Romantic historical work, *Sigurd Jorsalfar* [Sigurd the Crusader], was completed in 1872.

In 1875, encouraged perhaps by Georg Brandes's call in 1871 for a Nordic literature engaged with the problems of the present, Bjørnson returned to the territory opened by *The Newly-Married Couple* with two new problem dramas: *Redaktøren* (*The Editor*), showing how an unscrupulous journalist destroys the reputation of a leading citizen, and *En fallit* (*The Bankrupt*), his best-known work internationally and Norway's first drama on a financial theme. The latter is a naturalistic study of a wealthy family achieving a happier, if more modest, domestic life after the loss of its ill-gotten riches. Despite its rather dry and untheatrical discussions, *Kongen* (*The King*), which questioned the significance of royalty in a democratic era, aroused strong protest from those who considered it an attack not only on the monarchy, but on the Church and other traditional institutions. *Det ny system* (*The New System*) responded, like Ibsen's later *En folkefiende* (*An Enemy of the People*), to such attacks with an allegory depicting the social martyrdom of a protagonist who dares to express an unpopular truth. Bjørnson's Kampe, however, is a closer relative to Holberg's Erasmus Montanus than to Ibsen's Dr. Stockmann, giving up at last to the superior social force of his opponents.

Bjørnson's two "women's" plays, *Leonarda* and *En hanske* (*A Gauntlet*), continued to bring their author under attack as unsocial and immoral, since the first sympathetically portrays the efforts of a divorced woman to make her way in society and the second attacks a social system that has different laws of morality for men and for women. Both plays, however, were overshadowed at the time and subsequently by the much more radical and more richly textured contemporary social dramas of Ibsen, beginning with *A Doll's House* in 1879.

Like many European authors of his generation, Bjørnson experienced the tension between traditional religious beliefs and the new scientism represented by such authors as Hippolyte Taine, J. Ernest Renan, and Charles Darwin. This tension forms the basis for what has often been considered his greatest play, *Over ævne I* (*Beyond Human Power*), depicting the agony of the Nordic Pastor Sang, whose miraculous powers of healing cannot save his dying and unbelieving wife. The faith and power of God are shown at last beyond human control or comprehension, even by so inspired a figure as Sang. In a much weaker sequel, *Over ævne II* (*Beyond Human Might*), Sang's two sons carry on his quest, seeking salvation on the social level through the new religion of revolution. This dynamic is also proven to be beyond their control, and the ever pragmatic Bjørnson seems to advocate a kind of Fabian gradualism to the solving of human problems.

The suicide of a former friend, in whose political downfall Bjørnson may have played a role, inspired the scathing *Paul Lange og Tora Parsberg* (*Paul Lange and Tora Parsberg*), which returns to the condemnation of political intolerance previously dealt with in *The Editor*. Of Bjørnson's final plays, including *Laboremus, På Storhove* [At Storhove], and *Daglannet* [Dag's Farm], only the last, *Når den ny vin blomstrer* (*When the New Wine Blooms*), a gently ironic study of a somewhat eccentric family disturbed by the stresses of the new feminism, achieved a continuing success.

—Marvin Carlson

See the essay on "peasant tales."

BLIXEN, Karen

See DINESEN, Isak

BLOK, Aleksandr (Alexandrovich)

Born: St. Petersburg, Russia, 28 November 1880. **Education:** Educated at Vvedenskii School, St. Petersburg, 1891–99; studied law, 1899–1901, and philology, 1901–06, University of St. Petersburg. **Family:** Married Liubov Dmitrievna Mendeleeva in 1903, **Career:** Professional writer from 1906; served behind the lines in 1916; later had government jobs: verbatim reporter, Extraordinary Investigating Commission, 1917–18; on various cultural committees after 1918: in theatrical department of People's Commissariat for Education (and chairman of Repertory Section), 1918–19, and involved with Gor'kii's publishing house Vsemirnaia Literatura [World Literature], 1918–21; adviser, Union of Practitioners of Literature as an Art, 1919; chairman of Directorate of Bolshoi Theatre, 1919–21. **Died:** 7 August 1921.

PUBLICATIONS

Collections

Sobranie stikhotvorenii [Collected Poetry]. 3 vols., 1911–12.
Sobranie sochinenii [Collected Works]. 7 vols. (of 9 planned), 1922–23; edited by Vladimir N. Orlov and others, 8 vols., 1960–63 (includes diaries and letters), in 6 vols., 1971 (includes notebooks).
Selected Poems, edited by James B. Woodward. 1968.
Selected Poems, edited by Avril Pyman. 1972.
Selected Poems, translated by Jon Stallworthy and Peter France. 1974.
Collected Poems, translated by Sidney Guthrie-Smith. 1975.
Teatr, edited by P.P. Gromova. 1981.
Selected Poems, translated by Alex Miller. 1981.

Verse

Stikhi o prekrasnoi dame [Verses on a Most Beautiful Lady]. 1905.
Nechaiannaya radost' [Unexpected Joy]. *1907.*
Snezhnaia maska [The Snow Mask]. 1907.
Zemlia v snegu [The Earth in Snow]. 1908.
Nochnye chasy [The Night Watches]. 1911.
Skazki: Stikhi dlia detei [Fairy Tales: Poems for Children]. 1913.
Kruglyi god: Stikhotvoreniia dlia detei [All the Year Round: Poetry for Children]. 1913.
Stikhi o Rossii [Poems about Russia]. 1915.
Solov'inyi sad [The Nightingale Garden]. 1918.
Dvenadtsat', with *Skify.* 1918; *Dvenadtsat'* (bilingual edition), edited by Avril Pyman, 1989; as *The Twelve,* translated by C.E. Bechhofer, 1920; also translated by B. Deutsch and Avrahm Yarmolinsky, 1931; Robin Fulton, 1968; as *The Twelve and the Scythians,* translated by Jack Lindsay, 1982.
Iamby: Sovremennye stikhi (1907–1914) [Iambs: Contemporary Poems]. 1919.
Za gran'iu proshlykh dnei [Beyond the Bounds of Days Gone By]. 1920.
Sedoe utro [The Grey Morning], 1920.
Stikhotvoreniia [Poetry]. 1921.
The Twelve and Other Poems. translated by Peter France and Jon Stallworthy. 1970.
Stikhotvoreniia i poemy. 1998.

Plays

Balaganchik (produced 1906). In *Liricheskie dramy*, 1908; as *The Puppet Show*, translated by M. Kriger and Gleb Struve, in *Slavonic Review*, 28 (71), 1949–50.

Korol' na ploshchadi [The King in the Square]. 1907.

O lyubvi, poezii i gosudarstvennoi sluzhbe; as *Love, Poetry and the Civil Service*, translated by F. O'Dempsey, 1953. 1907.

Pesnia sud'by [The Song of Fate]. 1907; revised edition, 1919.

Liricheskie dramy [Lyrical Dramas]. 1908.

Neznakomka [The Stranger] (produced 1914). In *Liricheskie dramy*, 1908.

Primater' [The Ancestress], from a play by Grillparzer (produced 1908).

Roza i krest (produced 1921). 1913; translated as *The Rose and the Cross*, in *The Russian Symbolist Theatre*, edited and translated by Michael Green. 1986.

Ramzes [Ramses]. 1921(?).

Other

Molnii iskusstva [Lightning Flashes of Art] (travel sketches; unfinished). 1909–20(?).

Sobranie stikhotvorenii i teatr [Collected Poetry and Plays]. 4 vols., 1916.

Rossiia i intelligentsiia (1907–1918) [Russia and the Intelligentsia] (essays). 1918; revised edition, 1919; translated in part in *The Spirit of Music*, 1943.

Katilina. 1919.

Otrocheskie stikhi; Avtobiografiia [Adolescent Poems; Autobiography]. 1922.

The Spirit of Music, translated by I. Freiman. 1943.

An Anthology of Essays and Memoirs, edited by Lucy E. Vogel. 1982.

Editor, *Poslednye dni imperatorskoi vlasti* [The Last Days of the Imperial Regime]. 1921.

*

Bibliography: *Blok* by N. Ashukin, 1923; in *O Bloke* by E. Blium and V. Goltsev, 1929; by E. Kolpakova and others, in *Vilniusskii gosudarstvennyi pedagogicheskii Institut 6*, 1959; by Avril Pyman, in *Blokovskii Sbornik 1*, 1964, and in *Selected Poems*, 1972; by P.E. Pomirchiy, in *Blokovskii Sbornik 2*, 1972.

Critical Studies: *Blok, Prophet of Revolution* by C.H. Kisch, 1960; *Aleksandr Blok: Between Image and Idea* by F.D. Reeve, 1962; *Alexander Blok: A Study in Rhythm and Metre* by Robin Kemball, 1965; *Aleksandr Blok: The Journey to Italy* (includes translations) by Lucy Vogel, 1973; *The Poet and the Revolution: Aleksandr Blok's "The Twelve"* by Sergei Hackel (includes translation), 1975; *Listening to the Wind: An Introduction to Alexander Blok* by James Forsyth, 1977; *The Life of Aleksandr Blok* by Avril Pyman, 2 vols., 1979–80; *Hamayun: The Life of Aleksandr Blok* by Vladimir N. Orlov, translated by Olga Shartse, 1981; *Alexander Blok as Man and Poet* by Kornei Chukovsky, translated and edited by Diana Burgin and Katherine O'Connor, 1982; *Aleksandr Blok* by Konstantin Mochulsky, 1983; *Aleksandr Blok's Ital'yanskie stikhi: Confrontation and Disillusionment* by Gerald Pirog, 1983; *Aleksandr Blok Centennial Conference* edited by Walter N. Vickery, 1984; "The Structure and Theme of Blok's Cycle *Jamby*" by James B. Woodward, in *Seando-Slavica*, 31, 1985; *Aleksandr Blok and the Dynamics of the Lyric Cycle* by David A. Sloane, 1987; *Between Time and Eternity: Nine Essays* by P. Kirschner, 1992; *Aspects of Dramatic Communication: Action, Non-action, Interaction* by J. Stelleman, 1992; *Alesandr Blok: A Life* by Nina Berberova, translated by Robyn Marsack, 1996.

*   *   *

Aleksandr Blok is Russia's last great Romantic poet and one of her most charismatic personalities. Blok's legend began when he discovered his great theme of the Eternal Feminine—this myth-making Symbolists' ideal, which they saw as the link between the earthly and the divine. His first book of poems, *Stikhi o prekrasnoi dame* [Verses on a Most Beautiful Lady], comprised 800 "romantic hymns to one woman," his future wife Liubov Mendeleeva. These, the most immaterial, rarified lyrics in Russian literature, are "poems of praise," "heavenly songs" to idealistic Beauty. Blok believed that the world was created according to absolute Beauty. The ecstatic vision of the Beautiful Lady appeared in Blok's poetry in various incarnations representing the spirit of harmony. It became the Symbolists' symbol of symbols and "passions" game. B. Eikhenbaum called Blok a "dictator of feelings," saying that Blok always lived in the "aura of those emotions which he himself aroused." Blok, indeed, "went from cult to cult" (Mandel'shtam), from the Beautiful Lady and "The Unknown Lady" through "The Snow Mask" and "Carmen" to Russia and the Revolution. He tried to find "the truth" through intensely lived emotional experiences, and his poetry mirrored his inner life which was essentially dualistic. "I am afraid of my two-faced soul," he confessed, "and carefully bury its demonic and fierce visage in shining armour." He was torn between his apocalyptical predictions and hope for future harmony, between the music of the spheres and the tumult-rhythms of the coming social upheavals.

Russia, as the theme of his life, also troubled him with her two faces—beautiful and hungry, great and drunken. The dissonance between vision and reality constitutes Blok's tragedy: "The love and hate I have within me—no one could endure." He found irony as the best weapon to deal with discontent and despair. He ridiculed mysticism in his dramatic trilogy *Balaganchik* (*The Puppet Show*), *Korol' na ploshchadi* [The King in the Square], and *Neznakomka* [The Stranger]. Blok shed his mysticism by 1906 but wanted to stay in touch with the infinite, having the capacity to hear the music of the "world's orchestra."

Music was the "essence of the world" for Blok. He built his metaphysical system on the conception of the "spirit of music": "There are . . . two times, two dimensions," he wrote in his essay "The Downfall of Humanism," "one historical, chronological, the other immeasurable and musical." Unlike Belyi, Blok was never a theorist or a thinker. He possessed enormous sensitivity and an impeccable ear, but not a great intellect. Blok's strictly poetic achievement has usually been exaggerated. As Mandel'shtam said: "In literary matters Blok was an enlightened conservative. He was exceedingly cautious with everything concerning style, metrics or imagery: not one overt break with the past." Harmony between the ear and the eye led him to use symbols of an auditory nature, elemental sounds, the wild howl of violins, the tune of the wind, the harps and strings of a blizzard. He incorporated the lilting rhythms of gypsy songs, their uneven beat and abrupt alternations of fire and melancholy. Many of his best lyrics are a curious transposition of gypsy tunes into the moods, forms, and vocabularies of modern symbolism. The predominance of the musical over the discursive and the logical was a feature of his poetry as much as of his character.

Blok dreamt all his life about creating a musical poem that would reflect this antimusical world. He realized his dream in the poem *Dvenadtsat'* (*The Twelve*), which he wrote in two days. Here chaos and music almost fuse. The imagery of snow-storms formed the background of the birth of the new world. Twelve Red soldiers, spreading terror and death, become 12 apostles with Christ as their invisible leader. In the Revolution Blok saw a new manifestation of "the Spirit of Music." But it was too loud for Blok's hypersensitive ear: soon after *The Twelve* and *Skify* (*The Scythians*), 1918, he ceased to "hear." "I have not heard any new sounds for a long time; they have all vanished for me and probably for all of us . . . it would be blasphemous and deceitful to try deliberately to call them back into our soundless space," he told Chukovsky, and he ceased writing poetry. Not all Blok's friends shared his belief that the time had come for the intellectuals to sacrifice themselves under the wheels of the "troika." Hostility toward Blok was inevitable. He was told to his face that "he had outlived his time and was inwardly dead"—a fact with which, Pasternak told us, he calmly agreed. Russia's last poet-nobleman with Decembrist blood in his veins was out of time. It was unfortunate for Blok that greater poets followed him so quickly. For them, however, Blok, as a man and a poet, became a symbol, a "monument of the beginning of the century" and the "tragic tenor of the epoch" (Akhmatova).

—Valentina Polukhina

See the essay on *The Twelve*.

BOBROWSKI, Johannes

Born: Tilsit, East Prussia (now Sovetsk, CIS) 9 April 1917. **Education:** Educated at high school in Königsberg (now Kaliningrad); studied art history, University of Berlin, 1937–41. **Military Service:** Served in the army 1939–45; prisoner of war in Russia, captured 1945, released 1949. **Family:** Married Johanna Buddrus in 1943; four children. **Career:** Editor, Lucie Groszer, children's book publishers, Berlin, 1950–59, and with Union Verlag, East Berlin, 1959. **Awards:** Gruppe 47 prize, 1962; Alma König prize, 1962; Heinrich Mann prize 1965; Veillon prize (Switzerland), 1965; Weiskopf prize, 1967 (posthumously). **Died:** 2 September 1965.

PUBLICATIONS

Collections

Gesammelte Werke, edited by Eberhard Haufe. 3 vols., 1987.
Shadow Lands: Selected Poems (includes the collections *Shadow Land* and *From the Rivers* and other poems), translated by Ruth and Matthew Mead. 1984.

Verse

Sarmatische Zeit. 1961.
Schattenland Ströme. 1962.
Wetterzeichen. 1966.
Shadow Land, translated by Ruth and Matthew Mead. 1966.
Im Windgesträuch, edited by Eberhard Haufe. 1970.

Selected Poems: Johannes Bobrowski, Horst Bienek, translated by Ruth and Matthew Mead. 1971.
Gedichte 1952–1965. 1974.
From the Rivers, translated by Ruth and Matthew Mead. 1975.
Literarisches Klima: Ganz neue Xenien, doppelte Ausführung. 1978.
Yesterday I Was Leaving, translated by Rich Ives. 1986.
The White Mirror: Poems, translated by Muska Nagel, 1993.

Fiction

Levins Mühle. 1964; as *Levin's Mill,* translated by Janet Cropper, 1970.
Böhlendorff und andere: Erzählungen. 1965.
Mäusefest und andere Erzählungen. 1965.
Litauische Claviere. 1966.
Der Mahner: Erzählungen und andere Prosa. 1968.
Erzählungen. 1969.
Drei Erzählungen. 1970.
I Taste Bitterness (stories), translated by Marc Linder. 1970.
Die Erzählungen. 1979.
Böhlendorff: A Short Story and Seven Poems, translated by Francis Golffing. 1989.
Darkness and a Little Light, translated by Leila Vennewitz, 1994.

Other

Nachbarschaft: Neun Gedichte; Drei Erzählungen; Zwei Interviews; Zwei Grabreden; Zwei Schallplatten; Lebensdaten. 1967.
Editor, *Die schönsten Sagen des klassichen Altertums,* by Gustav Schwab. 1954.
Editor, *Die Sagen von Troja und von der Irrfahrt und Heimkehr des Odysseus,* by Gustav Schwab. 1955.
Editor, *Der märkische Eulenspiegel,* by Hans Clauert. 1956.
Editor, *Leben Fibels,* by Jean Paul. 1963.
Editor, *Wer mich und Ilse sieht im Grase: Deutsche Poeten des 18. Jahrhunderts über die Liebe und das Frauenzimmer*. 1964.
Translator, with Günther Deicke, *Initialen der Leidenschaft,* by Boris Pasternak. 1969.

*

Bibliography: *Das Werk von Johannes Bobrowski* by Curt Grützmacher, 1974; bibliography by Adolf Sckerl, in *Schattenfabel von den Versuchungen. Johannes Bobrowski. Zur 20. Wiederkehr seines Todestages*, 1985.

Critical Studies: *West-Östliches in der Lyrik Johannes Bobrowski* by Sigrid Höfert, 1966; *Johannes Bobrowski: Selbstzeugnisse und Beiträge über sein Werk*, 1967, expanded edition, 1982; *Bobrowski und andere. Die Chronik des Peter Jokostra*, 1967; *Johannes Bobrowski. Leben und Werk*, 1967, and *Beschreibung eines Zimmers. 15 Kapitel über Johannes Bobrowski*, 1971, both by Gerhard Wolf; *Johannes Bobrowski. Versuch einer Interpretation* by Rudolf Bohren, 1968; *Johannes Bobrowski* by Brian Keith-Smith, 1970; *Beschwörung und Reflexion. Bobrowskis sarmatische Gedichte* by Wolfram Mauser, 1970; *Johannes Bobrowksi. Prosa. Interpretationen* by Mechthild and Wilhelm Dehn, 1972; *Johannes Bobrowski. Chronik, Einführung, Bibliographie* by Bernhard Gajek and Eberhard Haufe, 1977; *Facetten. Untersuchungen zum Werk Johannes Bobrowskis* by Alfred Behrmann, 1977; *Erinnerung Johannes Bobrowski* by Christoph Meckel, 1978;

Ahornallee 26; oder, Epitaph für Johannes Bobrowski edited by Gerhard Rostin, 1978: *Johannes Bobrowski. Studien und Interpretationen* by Bernd Leistner, 1981; *Johannes Bobrowskis Lyrik und die Tradition* by Fritz Minde, 1981; *Die aufgehobene Zeit. Zeitstruktur und Zeitelemente in der Lyrik Johannes Bobrowksis* by Werner Schulz, 1983; *Schattenfabel von den Versuchungen. Johannes Bobrowski. Zur 20. Wiederkehr seines Todestages,* 1985; *Understanding Johannes Bobrowski* by David Scrase, 1995; *Between Sarmatia and Socialism: The Life and Works of Johannes Bobrowski* by John P. Wieczorek, 1999.

*   *   *

Johannes Bobrowski, who died from peritonitis in 1965 at the age of 45, was one of the most humane German writers of the 20th century, and the concept of "humanitas" to bind communities together informs his works. This implies a willingness to learn from past mistakes and an openness to the needs of others. His declared central theme of atonement for German crimes against Eastern neighbours implies an awareness both of hidden, half-forgotten forces in the landscape and of a variety of ethnic characteristics among the villages and small towns along the river Memel. His combination of locally-based prejudices and events—the novel *Levins Mühle* (*Levin's Mill*) and a sophisticated application of culture from the classical world (the sapphic form of "Ode to Thomas Chatterton"), 18th-century writers and musicians (the story "Epitaph for Pinnau" and his unpublished anthology "Lieder von Heinrich Albert") produced a highly personal style. Essential was the relationship of the individual to his environment and to language (the poem "Dead Language"). This led him to search for the lifestyle and history of his ancestors (as can be seen from documents in his posthumous papers), and also to speak out against the inhumanity of his time, especially the Nazi period (the poem "eport"). The border atmosphere and village life as a world theatre in miniature form the background to his landscape poetry (the poems "Das Holzhaus über der Wilna," "Village," and "The Sarmatian Plain," also the stories "Lipmann's Leib" [Lipmann's Body] and "In Pursuance of City Planning Considerations"). Equally important to him were the river landscapes (the poems "In the Stream," "By the River," "The Don") that he presents as coordinates of both time and place. School in Königsberg—the town of Hamann and Kant—opened up to him a rich literary and musical heritage, and he developed a taste for Baroque music, for Bach, Buxtehude, and Mozart. He also learnt to appreciate the form and discipline of classical Greek and Latin writers. War service, especially in the army invading Poland, made him realize how fragile common humanity can be. This influenced much of his early, sometimes unpublished poetry and some of his short prose texts (the poems on Russia and texts such as "Mouse Banquet" and "The Dancer Malige").

The link between his poetry and prose, which was written mainly during the last few years of his life, lies in the use of signs, on which Minde and Behrmann among others have written. Yet he was constantly aware of the foreshortening, deadening, and dehumanizing potentials of language—hence the search in his second novel *Litauische Claviere* for an operatic form where reconciliation of political views and fusion of modes of expression might be fully explored. His works, set in a frontier land of German and Lithuanian districts (e.g. the novels *Levin's Mill* and *Litauische Claviere*) include examples of a level of consciousness between dream and wide-awake reality (the

poem "Eichendorff" and the short story "Das Käiuzchen" [The Little Owl]) where memories bring an awakening to a further dimension of reality. Through an unexpected event the everyday is revealed as only one level of experience (the poem "Elder Blossom").

Literature can function as a breaker of time barriers and create a sense of mythic existence as in the poem "Die Günderrode" [Gunderrode]. A *Weg nach innen* (way inwards) à la Novalis is based on the magic power of the word, yet Bobrowski used myth not to expand into the elemental, endless, or universal as with the Romantics, but to refer with his metaphors to a more intense understanding on the local human level. His works were thus a deliberate quest for cultural, historical, and natural roots. The use of open form bringing heterogenous elements together in an apparently often unresolved manner was designed to shock the reader, assist him sometimes to laugh, and help him to comprehend more fully the nature of the reasons behind his existence (the poem "Village Music" and the short story "De homine publico tractatus"). In both prose and poetry he paid strict attention to metric as opposed to strophic or linear structure as basic building blocks, thus emphasizing his sense of control, of *Bebauung* over his material.

The more "naïve" evocation of the past in his poems of the 1950s—"Der litauische Brunnen" [The Lithuanian Well], "Der Singschwan" [Singing Swan], "Die alte Heerstrasse" [The Old Army Road]—contained a definite epic quality. This gave way to a tone of lament for the loss of a previous world, and the poetic images began to assume the qualities of a cipher ("Always to Be Named," "Nänie"), He became a master of finding objective correlatives and set them with great verbal economy and rich variety of poetic device. Most of his poems are short, but they are full of nuances and hidden allusions. His prose works also developed from evocation and direct assimilation of the past towards emphatic statements of a new sense of community service ("Contemplation of a Picture"). Basic to poems and prose is often a structure that includes a negative warning that registers the past, followed by a call for closer involvement with nature, and finally an act of naming or finding the fitting poetic language to resuscitate a lost dimension of human awareness.

By including the perspective of a narrator, Bobrowski often ensured that sentimentality is cut out and the reader becomes aware of a directed form of detailed portrayal highlighting the co-existence of different worlds (especially in the longest of his short prose works "Böhlendorff"). A form of score with variants and counterpoint emerged in his prose works, just as with a work for an organ, an instrument that Bobrowski particularly cherished.

Since his early death Bobrowski has become known throughout the world because he developed a poetic language with a mastery of imagery, rhythm, and musicality. He understood the everyday world and political theories to be sterile and non-creative—the interplay of history and landscape seemed to him healthier and closer to the secret wishes of man in general. He combined a serious-minded, peace-loving message with an almost therapeutically ironic distancing from all human foibles. It is not surprising that half of his posthumous papers consist of letters from friends from many countries, for he sought above everything dialogue between all human beings (the poem "The Word Man"). The freshness of his works depends on his success in keeping them free from nostalgia and sentimentality, his rare mastery of technical detail, knowledge of several historical atmospheres, a light touch, and an eye for positive humanity.

—Brian Keith-Smith

BOCCACCIO, Giovanni

Born: Florence or Certaldo between June and July in 1313. **Education:** Apprentice in his father's banking business, Naples, 1327–31; studied canon law, 1331–36. **Career:** Worked in banking in Naples until 1341; returned to Florence in 1341 and was there during the Black Death, 1348; met Petrarch, *q.v.*, in 1350 and thereafter devoted himself to humanistic scholarship; took minor clerical orders, 1357; active in Florentine public life, and went on several diplomatic missions in the 1350s and 1360s; lectured on Dante, *q.v.*, in Florence, 1373–74. **Died:** 21 December 1375.

PUBLICATIONS

Collections

Opere latine minori, edited by A.F. Massèra. 1928.
Opere, edited by Vittore Branca and others. 12 vols., 1964.
Opere minori in volgare, edited by Mario Marti. 4 vols., 1969–72.
Opere, edited by Cesare Segre. 1980.
Poetry through Typography, compiled by Hermann Zapf, 1993.

Fiction

Elegia di Madonna Fiammetta, edited by Cesare Segre, 1966, and by Mario Marti, in *Opere minori,* 3, 1971; as *Amorous Fiammetta,* translated by Bartholomew Young, 1587, reprinted 1926; as *The Elegy of Lady Fiammetta,* edited and translated by Mariangela Causa-Steindler and Thomas Hauch, 1990.
Decameron, edited by Vittore Branca. 1976; as *The Decameron,* translated anonymously, 1620; numerous subsequent translations including by John Payne, 1866 (revised edition by Charles Singleton, 1984); Richard Aldington, 1930; Frances Winwar, 1930; G.H. McWilliam, 1972; Mark Musa and Peter E. Bondanella, 1977; J.M. Rigg, 1978.
Il filocolo, edited by Antonio Enzo Quaglio. 1967; translated in part as *Thirteen Questions of Love,* edited by Harry Carter, 1974.
Boccaccio's First Fiction, edited and translated by Anthony K. Cassel and Victoria Kirkham. 1991.

Plays

L'ameto, edited by Antonio Enzo Quaglio, in *Opere,* 2. 1964; as *L'ameto,* translated by Judith Powers Serafini-Sauli. 1985.

Verse

Il filostrato, edited by Vittore Branca, in *Opere,* 2. 1964; as *The Filostrato,* translated by N.E. Griffin and A.B. Myrick, 1929; as *Il Filostrato: The Story of the Love of Troilo,* translated by Hubertis Cummings, 1934.
Rime, edited by Vittore Branca. 1958.
Il ninfale fiesolano, edited by Armando Balduino. 1974; as *The Nymph of Fiesole,* translated by Daniel J. Donno, 1960; as *Nymphs of Fiesole,* translated by Joseph Tusiani, 1971.
La caccia di Diana, edited by Vittore Branca, in *Opere,* 1. 1964.
Il Teseida, edited by Alberto Limentani, in *Opere,* 2. 1964; as *The Book of Theseus,* translated by Bernadette Marie McCoy, 1974.

L'amorosa visione, edited by Vittore Branca, in *Opere,* 3. 1964; translated by Robert Hollander, Timothy Hampton, and Margherita Frankel, 1986.
Eclogues, translated by Janet Levarie Smarr. 1987.

Other

Le lettere, edited by Francesco Corazzini. 1877.
Trattatello in laude di Dante, edited by Pier Giorgio Ricci. 1974; translated in *The Early Lives of Dante,* 1904; as *The Life of Dante,* translated by Vincenzo Zin Bollettino, 1990.
Il commento alto Divina Commedia e altri scritti intorno a Dante, edited by Domenico Guerri. 4 vols., 1918–26.
De genealogia deorum gentilium [The Genealogies of the Gentile Gods], edited by Vincenzo Romano. 1951; section as *Boccaccio on Poetry,* translated by Charles Osgood, 1930; as *Boccaccio: In Defense of Poetry,* edited by Jeremiah Reedy, 1978.
De claris mulieribus, edited by Vittorio Zaccaria. 1967; as *Concerning Famous Women,* translated by Guido A, Guarino. 1963; as *Famous Women,* edited and translated by Virginia Brown, 2001.
De casibus virorum illustrium, abridged as*The Fates of Illustrious Men,* translated by Louis Hall. 1965.
Il corbaccio, edited by Tauno Nurmela. 1968; as *The Corbaccio,* edited and translated by Anthony K. Cassell, 1975.

*

Bibliography: *Linee di una storia della critica al Decameron. Con bibliografia boccaccesca completemente e aggiornata* by Vittore Branca, 1939; *Boccacciana: Bibliografia delle edizioni e degli scritti critici 1939–1974* by Enzo Esposito, 1976; *Giovanni Boccaccio: An Annotated Bibliography* by Joseph P. Consoli, 1992; *Boccaccio in English: A Bibliography of Editions, Adaptations, and Criticism* by F.S. Stych, 1995.

Critical Studies: *Boccaccio: A Biographical Study* by E. Hutton, 1910; *The Life of Giovanni Boccaccio* by Thomas C. Chubb, 1930; *The Tranquil Heart: Portrait of Giovanni Boccaccio* by Catherine Carswell, 1937; *Boccaccio* by Francis MacManus, 1947; *Boccaccio in England from Chaucer to Tennyson* by Herbert G. Wright, 1957; *Nature and Love in the Middle Ages: An Essay on the Cultural Context of the Decameron* by Aldo D. Scaglione, 1963; *An Anatomy of Boccaccio's Style,* 1968, and *Order from Chaos: Social and Aesthetic Harmonies in Boccaccio's Decameron,* 1982, both by Marga Cottino-Jones; *The Writer as Liar: Narrative Technique in the "Decameron"* by Guido Almansi, 1975; *Nature and Reason in the Decameron* by Robert Hastings, 1975; *Critical Perspectives on the Decameron* edited by Robert S. Dombrowski, 1976; *Boccaccio: The Man and His Works* by Vittore Branca, translated by Richard Monges, 1976, and *Boccaccio medievale e nuovi studi sul Decameron* by Branca, 1986; *Boccaccio's Two Venuses,* 1977, and *Boccaccio's Last Fiction: Il Corbaccio,* 1989, both by Robert Hollander; *Studies on Petrarch and Boccaccio* by Ernest H. Wilkins, 1978; *An Allegory of Form: Literary Self-Consciousness in the Decameron* by Millicent Joy Marcus, 1979; *Boccaccio* by Thomas G. Bergin, 1981; *Five Frames for the Decameron: Communication and Social Systems in the Cornice* by Joy Hambuechen Potter, 1982; *Giovanni Boccaccio* by Judith Powers Serafini-Sauli, 1982; *Religion and the Clergy in Boccaccio's Decameron* by Cormac O'Cuilleanáin, 1984; *Chaucer and the Early Writings of Boccaccio* by David Wallace, 1985; *Boccaccio and Fiammetta: The Narrator as Lover* by Janet Levarie

Smarr, 1986; *The World at Play in Boccaccio's Decameron* by Giuseppe Mazzotta, 1986; *Before the Knight's Tale: Imitation of Classical Epic in Boccaccio's Teseida* by David Anderson, 1988; *The Shades of Aeneas: The Imitation of Vergil and the History of Paganism in Boccaccio's Filostrato, Filocolo and Teseida* by James H. MacGregor, 1991; *Ambiguity and Illusion in Boccaccio's Filocolo* by Steven Grossvogel, 1992; *The Sign of Reason in Boccaccio's Fiction* by Victoria Kirkham, 1993; *Boccaccio's and Chaucer's Cressida* by Laura D. Kellogg, 1995; *Boccaccio's Des cleres et nobles femmes: Systems of Signification in an Illuminated Manuscript* by Brigitte Buettner, 1996; *Chaucer, Boccaccio, and the Debate of Love: A Comparative Study of the Decameron and the Canterbury Tales* by N.S. Thompson, 1996; *Adventures in Speech: Rhetoric and Narration in Boccaccio's Decameron* by Pier Massimo Forni, 1996; *Boccaccio's Dante and the Shaping Force of Satire* by Robert Hollander, 1997; *Visualizing Boccaccio: Studies on Illustrations of The Decameron, from Giotto to Pasolini* by Jill M. Ricketts, 1997; *The Ethics of Nature in the Middle Ages: On Boccaccio's Poetaphysics* by Gregory B. Stone, 1998; *The Decameron and the Canterbury Tales: New Essays on an Old Question*, edited by Leonard Michael Koff and Brenda Deen Schildgen, 2000; *Fabulous Vernacular: Boccaccio's Filocolo and the Art of Medieval Fiction* by Victoria Kirkham, 2001.

* * *

Boccaccio's literary production is characterized by an unusual versatility; his work, both in prose and verse, contains a variety of genres, many of which were pioneer ventures, destined to exercise a powerful influence on succeeding generations. His essay in the field of narrative in verse was *La caccia di Diana* [Diana's Hunt], an allegory of love, designed, it would seem, to memorialize the glamorous ladies of the Neapolitan court. It is a very "Dantean" composition, written in *terza rima* and with numerous echoes of *Commedia* (*The Divine Comedy*); it is a trifle but a well-constructed trifle. Of the same period is *Il filocolo* (*Thirteen Questions of Love*), a prose romance of Byzantine stamp composed, the author tells us, in honour of his "Fiammetta," the Neapolitan siren who charmed and betrayed him. Called by some critics "the first prose romance in European literature," *Thirteen Questions of Love* is long and digressive; although the central characters are of royal blood, the peripatetic plot anticipates the picaresque. For all its rhetoric and prolixity the narrative is well told and the characters in the main believable. This cumbrous initiative was followed by *Il filostrato* (*The Filostrato*), telling in *ottava rima* of the ill-starred love of the Trojan prince Troiolo for the faithless Criseida. It is a skilfully planned composition, set forth with economy, and successful in its depiction of characters; the romantic prince is artfully paired with the worldly Pandaro, his friend and counsellor. *Il Teseida* (*The Book of Theseus*), which followed a few years later, is, in spite of its Greek title and background, essentially a medieval work; the "epic" is actually a love story. All of these early productions reflect the feudal tastes of the Neapolitan court.

A change of inspiration becomes evident in the works written after Boccaccio's return to Tuscany in 1341. *L'ameto* is a moralizing allegory, combining prose and verse (as had Dante's *La vita nuova*) yet the use of "frame" to serve as a background for moralizing tales (paradoxically erotic in tone) points to *The Decameron*. In *L'amorosa visione* [Vision of Love] (a somewhat confused allegory) the presence of Dante is even more patent. *Elegia di Madonna Fiammetta* (*The Elegy of Lady Fiammetta*), which follows, is by contrast, original and strikingly "modern"—one might say timeless. The abandoned Fiammetta, who tells in her own words (in prose) of her misplaced obsession for a false lover, though somewhat prolix, wins our sympathy. In one sense the *Fiammetta* is a reversion, for the background is Naples. Truly Tuscan, on the other hand, is the charming idyll *Il ninfale fiesolano* (*The Nymph of Fiesoe*). With winning simplicity in *ottava rima* of unpretentious construction, the story is told of a simple shepherd and his beloved "nymph of Diana" who is in effect a simple *contadina*.

The Decameron, Boccaccio's masterpiece, marks a new departure in the author's trajectory. We deal no more with Trojan princes or even woodland nymphs—we have left Naples for good, and allegory has no part in the author's intention (though it must be conceded that in the flight of the narrators of the "frame" from the plague-stricken city one can argue some implications regarding the relation of art to its subject matter). The essential feature of *The Decameron* is realism; the world of the tales is the world of here and now. The demographic range is wide: it includes not only lords and princes but merchants, bankers, doctors, scholars, peasants, priests, monks—and a surprising number of women. A token of the feminist thrust of the work may be seen in the fact that seven of the ten "frame characters" or narrators are women. All of the actors in this extensive comedy are presented deftly, with sympathetic tolerance for their motivation and participant relish in their adventures, vicissitudes, and resourceful stratagems. If the work is without didactic intent—"Boccaccio doesn't want to teach us anything," the Italian critic Umberto Bosco has justly observed—yet the nature of its substance carries its own implications. *The Decameron* is democratic, feminist, and *au fond* optimistic. No doubt heaven is our destination but life can be joyous too, given a certain amount of wit and adaptability. Only in the last day does a kind of medievalism creep in, as the author sets before us a series of *exempla*, signifying sundry abstract virtues. Yet the narratives told even on that day are set forth with skill and verve and without undue lingering on their moralizing purpose; Griselda, for example, may seem an absurdly morbid creature (as in fact she does to some of the frame characters), but her story is told with a *brio* that compels the reader's attention. As entertaining today as when it was written, Boccaccio's great work both reflects and inspires a new appreciation of the human pilgrimage.

Save for *Il corbaccio*, a violent misogynistic satire, *The Decameron* is the last work of a creative nature to issue from Boccaccio's pen—and the last work in the vernacular as well. Moved by the example of Petrarch, he put aside fiction and turned to exercises in erudition, notably the massive compilation of the *De genealogia deorum gentilium* [The Genealogies of the Gentile Gods], an encyclopedia that would serve scholars for generations to come, and the catalogue of rivers, lakes, and mountains, both composed in Latin, as were his *Eclogues* (*Buccolicum Carmen*), patently in imitation of his revered master. After *The Decameron*, too, a certain inner spiritual change is apparent in the hitherto worldly Boccaccio; he took holy orders, and although the instinct for storytelling was still strong—witness *La vita di Dante* (*The Life of Dante*) and *De claris mulieribus* (*Concerning Famous Women*)—it was clearly affected by his new outlook on life. A letter suggests even a repudiation of *The Decameron*. His last work, and one of importance to Dantists, was his exposition of *The Divine Comedy*, a series of lectures given in Florence.

Many of Boccaccio's creative works are seminal: *The Book of Theseus* foreshadows the Renaissance epic, *The Filostrato* has left a trail of progeny ranging from Chaucer through Shakespeare to many contemporary writers. *The Nymph of Fiesole* has 15th-century echoes. And *The Decameron* has had many imitators. Boccaccio's contribution to the literature of the Western world is of impressive and all but unique dimensions.

—Thomas G. Bergin

See the essay on "The Ninth Tale of the Fifth Day of *The Decameron*."

BOETHIUS

Born: Anicius Manlius Severinus Boethius, probably in Rome, c. AD 480. **Family:** Married to Rusticiana; two sons. **Career:** Consul under the Ostrogothic King Theodoric, 510; head of government and court services (*magister officiorum*), 520; accused of treason, practising magic, and sacrilege: sentence ratified by the Senate, and he was imprisoned near Pavia, 522. Also a Hellenist: translator (with commentary) of works of Aristotle, Plato, and Porphyry. **Died:** (executed) in AD 524.

PUBLICATIONS

Collections

[Works], edited by J.P. Migne, in *Patrologia Latina.*, vols. 63–64. 2 vols., 1847.
The Theological Tractates and The Consolation of Philosophy [Loeb Edition], translated by S.J. Tester, H.F. Stewart, and E.K. Rand. 1918, revised edition, 1973.

Works

De arithmetica, De musica, edited by G. Friedlein. 1867.
De consolatione philosophiae (prose and verse), edited by Rudolph Peiper. 1871; also edited by A. Fortescue and G.D. Smith, 1925, G. Weinburger, 1934, and Ludwig Bieler, 1957; as *The Consolation of Philosophy*, translated by "I.T.," 1609, revised by H.F. Stewart [Loeb Edition], with *Tractates*, 1918; also translated by Richard Green, 1963; V.E. Watts, 1969; R.W. Sharpies, 1992; P.G. Walsh, 1999; commentaries by H. Scheible, 1972, J. Gruber, 1978, and J.J. O'Donnell, 1984; as *John Bracegirdle's Psychopharmacon: A Translation of Boethius' De consolatione philosophiae*, 1999.
De divisione, edited by Paulus Maria de Loe. 1913; as *Anicii Manlii Severini Boethii De divisione liber*, translated by John Magee, 1998.
De institutione musica, as *Fundamentals of Music*, translated by Calvin H. Bower. 1989.
De syllogismo hypothetico, edited by Luca Obertello. 1969.
De topicis differentiis, translated by Eleanore Stump. 1978.

In Ciceronis topica, edited by J.C. Orelli and G. Baiterus, in *Ciceronis opera*, vol. 5, pt 1. 1833; translated by Eleanore Stump, 1988.
In Isagogen, edited by Samuel Brandt. 1906.
In Perihermeneias, edited by Carl Meiser. 1880.
Tractates, edited and translated by E. Rapisarda. 1960; as *Tractates* [Loeb Edition], translated by H.F. Stewart and E.K. Rand, with *The Consolation of Philosophy*, 1918.
[Commentaries on *De interpretatione* by Aristotle], edited by Carl Meiser. 2 vols., 1877–80.
[Commentaries on Porphyry], edited by G. Schepss and Samuel Brandt. 1906; translated by E.W. Warren, 1975.
Translator, *Categoriae, De interpretatione, Analytica priora, Topica, Elenchi sophistici*, by Aristotle, edited by Lorenzo Minio-Paluello, in *Aristoteles Latinus*. 1961–.

*

Critical Studies: *The Tradition of Boethius: A Study of His Importance in Mediaeval Culture* by Howard R. Patch, 1935; *Boethius: Some Aspects of His Times and Works* by Helen M. Barrett, 1940; *Poetic Diction in the Old English Meters of Boethius* by Allan A. Metcalf, 1973; *Boethian Fictions: Narratives in the Medieval French* by Richard A. Dwyer, 1976; *Boethius and the Liberal Arts: A Collection of Essays* edited by Michael Masi, 1981; *Boethius: His Life, Thought, and Influence* edited by Margaret Gibson, 1981; *Boethius: The Consolations of Music, Logic, Theology, and Philosophy* by Henry Chadwick, 1981; *The Tradition of the Topics in the Middle Ages: The Commentaries on Aristotle's and Boethius' Topics* by Niels Jørgen Green-Pedersen, 1984; *Boethius and Dialogue: Literary Method in The Consolation of Philosophy* by Seth Lerer, 1985; *The Fate of Fortune in the Early Middle Ages: The Boethian Tradition* by Jerold C. Frakes, 1988; *Boethius on Signification and Mind* by John C. Magee, 1989; *The Poetry of Boethius* by Gerard O'Daly, 1991; *The Consolation of Boethius: An Analytical Inquiry into His Intellectual Processes and Goals* by Stephen Varvis, 1991; *Chaucer's "Boece" and the Medieval Tradition of Boethius*, edited by A.J. Minnis, 1993; *Clarembald of Arras as a Boethian Commentator* by John R. Fortin, 1995; *Boethius in the Middle Ages: Latin and Vernacular Traditions of the Consolatio philosophiae*, edited by Maarten J.F.M. Hoenen and Lodi Nauta, 1997.

*   *   *

As a member of the Roman senatorial class, which still kept its identity in the barbarian Italy of c. AD 500, Boethius expected to hold political and ceremonial office: he was consul and (fatally) *magister officiorum*, the dispenser of patronage at Theodoric's court in Ravenna. But most of his time was his own. He lived in his town house and his country estates immersed in his books, and also entertaining his friends: see Sidonius Apollinaris' letters and poems on the life of "senatorial ease" in Roman Gaul in the later 5th century. It was for these friends and protegés of his own family and class that Boethius wrote his literary and scholarly works. He was no schoolmaster, no compiler of encyclopedias, dependent on an unknown popular audience.

Boethius' interest in language and the structure of argument is seen in his many studies of logic and rhetoric. He translated some key texts from the Greek, and much of his analysis derived from Greek writers and teachers in the universities of Athens and Alexandria. These translations gave readers who knew only Latin access to mainstream philosophical discussion. In the same way Boethius' highly technical writing on mathematics and musical theory made Greek thought available to a Roman audience. That is the context for his ''papers''—they are too brief to be called books—on Christian doctrine: Boethius' careful definitions have a solid basis in Greek philosophy.

His masterpiece, *De consolatione philosophiae* (*The Consolation of Philosophy*), is his most readable and literary work. He had been informed on by his enemies and faced almost certain death. Could he face it? He argues through issue after conflicting issue, still the practised logician: but now he himself is a term in the problem. Why me? Why do the wicked prosper? Doesn't God care? Can God care? His partner in the argument is the Lady Philosophy, who is the traditional literary, mathematical, and philosophical learning to which he has devoted most of his life. Later readers thought of her as the Wisdom of the Old Testament: ''Wisdom hath builded her house, she hath hewn out her seven pillars.'' But Boethius is not so easily brought into line. His argument with himself in *The Consolation of Philosophy* reaches the point of an omniscient God, who is fully in control of the universe. Because it is an argument—rather than, for example, a vision or a confession—it *can* go no further. *The Consolation of Philosophy* stops short of the Christianity in which Boethius, judging by his theological papers (above), was an informed believer.

Boethius was executed in 524. His books seem to have lain undisturbed until about the time of Charlemagne (c. 800), when Alcuin and succeeding medieval scholars with little or no Greek read and transcribed and discussed this treasury of material on argument and on mathematics. Above all they welcomed *The Consolation*, in which the great questions of justice, chance, and freedom were analysed by the man who, in a changed intellectual climate, was now regarded as ''Boethius, the Christian philosopher.''

—Margaret Gibson

See the essay on *The Consolation of Philosophy*.

BOILEAU (-DESPRÉAUX), Nicolas

Born: Paris, France, 1 November 1636. **Education:** Educated at Collège d'Harcourt, Paris, 1643–48; Collège de Beauvais, Paris, 1648–52; studied law, University of Paris, 1652–56; admitted to the bar 1656. **Career:** Writer from 1657: slowly achieved a reputation; friend of Molière, Racine, La Fontaine; favoured by the court from 1674; historiographer to Louis XIV (with Racine), 1677. **Member:** Académie française, 1684. **Died:** 13 March 1711.

PUBLICATIONS

Collections

Works, translated by Nicholas Rowe. 3 vols., 1711–13.
Oeuvres complètes, edited by Charles-H. Boudhors. 7 vols., 1932–43.
Oeuvres complètes, edited by Françoise Escal. 1966.

Verse

Satires (12). 1666–1711; edited by A. Adam, 1941: translated as *Satires*, 1904.
Épîtres (12). 1670–98; edited by A. Cahen, 1937.
Oeuvres diverses. 1674; enlarged edition, 1683.
L'Art poétique, in *Oeuvres diverses*. 1674; edited by V. Delaporte, 3 vols., 1888; as *The Art of Poetry*, translated by William Soames (in verse), 1683; revised edition by John Dryden, 1710.
Le Lutrin. 1674–83; translated by Nicholas Rowe, 1708.

Other

L'Arrêt burlesque. 1671.
Réflexions sur Longin. 1694; as *On Longinus*, edited by John Ozell. 1972.
Selected Criticism, translated by Ernest Dilworth. 1965.
Lettres d'une amitié: Correspondance 1687–1698, edited by Pierre-Eugène Leroy, 2001.
Translator, *Traité du sublime*, by Longinus, in *Oeuvres diverses*. 1674.

*

Critical Studies: *Boileau and the Classical Critics in England* by Alexander F.B. Clark, 1925; *Racine and the ''Art Poétique'' of Boileau* by Sister M. Haley, 1938; *Boileau and Longinus* by Jules Brody, 1958; *Pour le commentaire linguistique de l'Art poétique* by John Orr, 1963; *Boileau* by Julian Eugene White, Jr., 1969; *Boileau and the Nature of Neo-Classicism* by Gordon Pocock, 1980; *Du sublime: (De Boileau à Schiller: Suivi de la traduction de Über das Erhabene de Friedrich Schiller)* by Pierre Hartmann, 1997; *Reading Boileau: An Integrative Study of the Early Satires* by Robert T. Corum, Jr., 1998.

* * *

Although Nicolas Boileau's fame has rested as much on his reputation as high-priest of French classicism as on his poetry, it is doubtful whether he added much to the critical ideas of his day, or significantly influenced his contemporaries.

His literary personality is complex. His iconoclasm comes out strongly in his early satires, and remains in his later work, even when he was in favour at court. His early series of *Satires* (I–IX) is concerned with literary and social themes. In his social satires (I, III, IV, V, VI, and VIII), he often paints with representational detail, but his comic exuberance lifts them well beyond realism. In the literary satires, he is less a critic of specific authors than a creator of startling images of poetry at war with dunces. The best of his satires (especially VII and IX) are dramatic in method. They bring together with kaleidoscopic brilliance wit, word-play, eloquence, and straight-speaking, leading the reader to heightened awareness of his responses which transcends the often banal content. The first series of *Epistles* (I–IX) is frequently plainer and more didactic, but even those addressed to Louis XIV (the *Discourse to the King, Epistles I, IV*, and *VIII*) mix humour with seriousness. *Epistles VII* and *IX*, on literary themes, express poignantly Boileau's sense of the high role of poetry, and its vulnerability in the face of ignorance and barbarism.

His verse *L'Art poétique* (*The Art of Poetry*) is on the surface an assertion of the Classical demand for rationalism and craftsmanship, with summaries of the neo-Aristotelian rules for different kinds of poem. More fundamentally, however, it demonstrates again Boileau's use of verbal dexterity (it is full of puns) to dramatize the effect of good and bad poetry on the reader. The mock-heroic *Le Lutrin* [The Lectern] is in lighter vein, but dazzles by its mixture of comedy with genuine grandeur.

His later works show a slackening of verve. The best are the long *Satire X* [On Women] in which some of the portraits recapture his earlier mordant vigour, and *Epistles X* and *XI*, in which he skilfully represents himself as a man of honest but endearing simplicity. The last works, much concerned with theological disputes, are clumsily written and hectoring in tone.

Boileau's lyrics have little merit. His ambitious *Ode on the Capture of Namur* fails to accommodate in lyric form his mixture of grandiloquence and satire. Of his prose, the early *L'Arrêt burlesque* [Mock Edict] is the liveliest, with its exuberant satire on official hostility to new ideas. His translation of Longinus with his *Remarks* and *Reflections* on it and his 1701 preface to his works, gave him the opportunity to reassert the moral and aesthetic dignity of poetry, against what he saw as the triviality and decadence of his contemporaries. Of his work as historiographer to Louis XIV (a post he shared with Racine) only a few occasional pieces remain. His surviving letters, mainly from his old age, display his passionate and quirky temperament.

—Gordon Pocock

See the essay on *The Art of Poetry*.

BÖLL, Heinrich (Theodor)

Born: Cologne, Germany, 21 December 1917. **Education:** Educated at Gymnasium, Cologne; University of Cologne. **Military:** Served in the German army, 1939–45; prisoner of war, 1945. **Family:** Married Annemarie Cech in 1942; three sons. **Career:** Joiner in his father's shop, then apprentice in the book trade before the war; full-time writer from 1947; co-editor, *Labyrinth*, 1960–61, and *L*, from 1976; president, PEN International, 1971–74. **Awards:** Bundesverband der Deutschen Industrie grant; Gruppe 47 prize, 1951; Rene Schickele prize, 1952; Tribune de Paris prize, 1953; Prix du Meilleur Roman Étranger, 1955; Heydt prize, 1958; Bavarian Academy of Fine Arts award, 1958; Nordrhein-Westfalen prize, 1959; Veillon prize, 1960; Cologne prize, 1961; Elba prize, 1965; Büchner prize, 1967; Nobel prize for literature, 1972; Scottish Arts Council fellowship, 1973. Honorary degrees: D.Sc.: Aston University, Birmingham, 1973; O.Tech.: Brunel University, Uxbridge, Middlesex, 1973; Litt.D.: Trinity College, Dublin, 1973. **Died:** 16 July 1985.

PUBLICATIONS

Fiction

Der Zug war pünktlich. 1949; as *The Train Was on Time*, translated by Richard Graves, 1956; also translated by Leila Vennewitz, 1973.

Wanderer, kommst du nach Spa.... 1950; as *Traveller, If You Come to Spa*, translated by Mervyn Savill, 1956.

Die schwarzen Schafe. 1951.

Wo warst du, Adam? 1951; as *Adam, Where Art Thou?*, translated by Mervyn Savill, 1955; as *And Where Were You Adam?*, translated by Leila Vennewitz, 1973.

Nicht nur zur Weihnachtszeit. 1952.

Und sagte kein einziges Wort. 1953; as *Acquainted with the Night*, translated by Richard Graves, 1954; as *And Never Said a Word*, translated by Leila Vennewitz, 1978.

Haus ohne Hüter. 1954; as *Tomorrow and Yesterday*, translated by Mervyn Savill, 1957; as *The Unguarded House*, translated by Savill, 1957.

Das Brot der frühen Jahre. 1955; as *The Bread of Our Early Years*, translated by Mervyn Savill, 1957; as *The Bread of Those Early Years*, translated by Leila Vennewitz, 1976.

So ward Abend und Morgen. 1955.

Unberechenbare Gäste: Heitere Erzählungen. 1956.

Im Tal der donnernden Hufe. 1957.

Doktor Murkes gesammelte Schweigen und andere Satiren. 1958.

Der Mann mit den Messern. 1958.

Die Waage der Baleks und andere Erzählungen. 1958.

Der Bahnhof von Zimpren. 1959.

Billard um halb zehn. 1959; as *Billiards at Half-Past Nine*, translated by Patrick Bowles, 1961.

Als der Krieg ausbrach, Als der Krieg zu Ende war. 1962; as *Absent Without Leave* (2 novellas), translated by Leila Vennewitz, 1965.

Ansichten eines Clowns. 1963; as *The Clown*, translated by Leila Vennewitz, 1965.

Entfernung von der Truppe. 1964.

Ende einer Dienstfahrt. 1966; as *The End of a Mission*, translated by Leila Vennewitz, 1967; as *End of a Mission*, translated by Leila Vennewitz, 1994.

Eighteen Stories, translated by Leila Vennewitz. 1966.

Absent Without Leave and Other Stories, translated by Leila Vennewitz. 1967.

Geschichten aus zwölf Jahren. 1969.

Children Are Civilians Too (stories), translated by Leila Vennewitz. 1970.

Gruppenbild mit Dame. 1971; as *Group Portrait with Lady*, translated by Leila Vennewitz, 1973.

Der Mann mit den Messern: Erzählungen (selection). 1972.

Die verlorene Ehre der Katharina Blum. 1974; as *The Lost Honor of Katharina Blum*, translated by Leila Vennewitz, 1975.

Berichte zur Gesinnungslage der Nation. 1975.

Fürsorgliche Belagerung. 1979; as *The Safety Net*, translated by Leila Vennewitz, 1982.

Du fährst zu oft nach Heidelberg und andere Erzählungen. 1979.

Gesammelte Erzählungen. 2 vols., 1981.

Das Vermächtnis. 1982; as *A Soldier's Legacy*, translated by Leila Vennewitz, 1985.

Die Verwundung und andere frühe Erzählungen. 1983; as *The Casualty*, translated by Leila Vennewitz, 1986.

Der Angriff: Erzählungen 1947–1949. 1983.

Veränderungen in Staeck: Erzählungen 1962–1980. 1984.

Mein trauriges Gesicht: Erzählungen. 1984.

Frauen vor Flusslandschaft: Roman in Dialogen und Selbstgesprächen. 1985; as *Women in a River Landscape: A Novel in Dialogues and Soliloquies*, translated by David McLintock, 1988.

Stories, translated by Leila Vennewitz. 1986.

Der Engel schwieg. 1992; as *The Silent Angel*, translated by Breon Mitchell, 1994.

The Mad Dog: Stories, translated by Breon Mitchell, 1997.

Plays

Die Brücke von Berczaba (broadcast 1952). In *Zauberei auf dem Sender und andere Hörspiele*, 1962.

Der Heilige und der Räuber (broadcast 1953). In *Hörspielbuch des Nordwestdeutschen und Süddeutschen Rundfunks*, 4, 1953; as *Mönch und Räuber*, in *Erzählungen, Hörspiele, Aufsätze*, 1961.

Ein Tag wie sonst (broadcast 1953). 1980.

Zum Tee bei Dr. Borsig (broadcast 1955). In *Erzählungen, Hörspiele, Aufsätze*, 1961.

Eine Stunde Aufenthalt (broadcast 1957). In *Erzählungen, Hörspiele, Aufsätze*, 1961.

Die Spurlosen (broadcast 1957). 1957.

Bilanz (broadcast 1957). With *Klopfzeichen*, 1961.

Klopfzeichen (broadcast 1960). With *Bilanz*, 1961.

Ein Schluck Erde (produced 1961). 1962.

Zum Tee bei Dr. Borsig (includes *Mönch und Räuber; Eine Stunde Aufenthalt; Bilanz; Die Spurlosen; Klopfzeichen; Sprechanlage; Konzert für vier Stimmen*). 1964.

Hausfriedensbruch (broadcast 1969). 1969.

Aussatz (produced 1970). With *Hausfriedensbruch*, 1969.

Radio Plays:: *Die Brücke von Berczaba*, 1952; *Ein Tag wie sonst*, 1953; *Der Heilige und der Räuber*, 1953; *Zum Tee bei Dr. Borsig*, 1955; *Anita und das Existenzminimum*, 1955, revised version, as *Ich habe nichts gegen Tiere*, 1958; *Die Spurlosen*, 1957; *Bilanz*, 1957; *Eine Stunde Aufenthalt*, 1957; *Die Stunde der Wahrheit*, 1958; *Klopfzeichen*, 1960; *Hausfriedensbruch*, 1969.

Verse

Gedichte. 1972.

Other

Irisches Tagebuch. 1957; as *Irish Journal*, translated by Leila Vennewitz, 1967.

Im Ruhrgebiet, photographs by Karl Hargesheimer. 1958.

Unter Krahnenbäumen, photographs by Karl Hargesheimer. 1958.

Menschen am Rhein, photographs by Karl Hargesheimer. 1960.

Brief an einen jungen Katholiken. 1961.

Erzählungen, Hörspiele, Aufsätze. 1961.

Assisi. 1962.

Hierzulande. 1963.

Frankfurter Vorlesungen. 1966.

Aufsätze, Kritiken, Reden. 1967.

Leben im Zustand des Frevels. 1969.

Neue politische und literarische Schriften. 1973.

Politische Meditationen zu Glück und Vergeblichkeit, with Dorothee Sölle. 1973.

Der Lorbeer ist immer noch bitter: Literarische Schriften. 1974.

Drei Tage in März, with Christian Linder. 1975.

Der Fall Staeck; oder, Wie politisch darf die Kunst sein?, with others. 1975.

Briefe zur Verteidigung der Republik, with Freimut Duve and Klaus Staeck. 1977.

Einmischung erwünscht: Schriften zur Zeit. 1977.

Missing Persons and Other Essays, translated by Leila Vennewitz. 1977.

Querschnitte: Aus Interviews, Aufsätzen, und Reden, edited by Viktor Böll and Renate Matthaei. 1977.

Werke, edited by Bernd Balzer. 10 vols., 1977–78.

Gefahren von falschen Brüdern: Politische Schriften. 1980. *Warum haben wir aufeinander geschossen?*, with Lew Kopelew. 1981.

Rendezvous mit Margaret. Liebesgeschichten. 1981.

Was soll aus dem Jungen bloss werden?; oder, Irgendwas mit Büchern. 1981; as *What's to Become of the Boy?; or, Something to Do with Books* (memoir), translated by Leila Vennewitz, 1984.

Der Autor ist immer noch versteckt. 1981.

Vermintes Gelände: Essayistische Schriften 1977–1981. 1982.

Antikommunismus in Ost und West. 1982.

Ich hau dem Mädche nix jedonn, ich hart et bloss ens kräje. Texte, Bilder, Dokumente zur Verteilung des Ehrenbürgerrechts der Stadt Köln, 29 April 1983. 1983.

Ein- und Zusprüche: Schriften, Reden und Prosa 1981–83. 1984.

Weil die Stadt so fremd geworden ist. 1985.

Bild-Bonn-Boenish. 1985.

Die Fähigkeit zu trauern: Schriften und Reden 1983–1985. 1986.

Denken mit Heinrich Böll. 1986.

Rom auf den ersten Blick. Landschaften, Städte, Reisen. 1987.

Editor, with Erich Kock, *Unfertig ist der Mensch*. 1967.

Editor, with Freimut Duve and Klaus Staeck, *Verantwortlich für Polen?*. 1982.

Translator, with Annemarie Böll:

Kein Name bei den Leuten [No Name in the Street], by Kay Cicellis. 1953.

Ein unordentlicher Mensch, by Adriaan Morriën. 1955.

Tod einer Stadt [Death of a Town], by Kay Cicellis. 1956.

Weihnachtsabend in San Cristobal [The Saintmaker's Christmas Eve], by Paul Horgan. 1956.

Zur Ruhe kam der Baum des Menschen nie [The Tree of Man], by Patrick White. 1957.

Der Teufel in der Wüste [The Devil in the Desert], by Paul Horgan. 1958.

Die Geisel [The Hostage], by Brendan Behan. 1958.

Der Mann von morgen früh [The Quare Fellow], by Brendan Behan. 1958.

Ein wahrer Held [The Playboy of the Western World], by J.M. Synge. 1960.

Die Boote fahren nicht mehr aus [The Islandman], by Tomás O'Crohan. 1960.

Eine Rose zur Weihnachtszeit [One Red Rose for Christmas], by Paul Horgan. 1960.

Der Gehilfe [The Assistant], by Bernard Malamud. 1960.

Kurz vor dem Krieg gegen die Eskimos, by J.D. Salinger. 1961.

Das Zauberfass [The Magic Barrel], by Bernard Malamud. 1962.

Der Fänger im Roggen [The Catcher in the Rye], by J.D. Salinger. 1962.

Ein Gutshaus in Irland [The Big House], by Brendan Behan, in *Stücke*. 1962.

Franny und Zooey, by J.D. Salinger. 1963.

Die Insel der Pferde [The Island of Horses], by Eilís Dillon. 1964.

Hebt den Dachbalken hoch, Zimmerleute; Seymour wird vorgestellt [Raise High the Roof Beam, Carpenters; Seymour: An Introduction], by J.D. Salinger. 1965.

Caesar und Cleopatra, by G.B. Shaw. 1965.

Der Spanner [The Scarperer], by Brendan Behan. 1966.

Die Insel des grossen John [The Coriander], by Eilís Dillon. 1966.

Das harte Leben [The Hard Life], by Flann O'Brien. 1966.

Neun Erzählungen [Nine Stories], by J.D. Salinger. 1966.

Die schwarzen Füchse [A Family of Foxes], by Eilís Dillon. 1967.

Die Irrfahrt der Santa Maria [The Cruise of the Santa Maria], by Eilís Dillon. 1968.

Die Springflut [The Sea Wall], by Eilís Dillon. 1969.

Seehunde SOS [The Seals], by Eilís Dillon. 1970.

Erwachen in Mississippi [Coming of Age in Mississippi], by Anne Moody. 1970.

Candida, Der Kaiser von Amerika, Mensch und Übermensch [Candida, The King of America, Man and Superman], by G.B. Shaw. 1970.

Handbuch des Revolutionärs, by G.B. Shaw. 1972.

*

Bibliography: *Heinrich Böll: Eine Bibliographie seiner Werke* by Werner Martin, 1975; *Der Schriftsteller Böll: Ein biographisch-bibliographischer Abriss* edited by Werner Lenging, 5th edition, 1977; *Heinrich Böll in America 1954–1970* by Ray Lewis White, 1979; *Heinrich Böll Auswahlbibliographie zur Primär- und Sekundärliteratur* edited by Gerhard Redemacher, 1989.

Critical Studies: *Böll, Teller of Tales: A Study of His Works and Characters* by Wilhelm Johannes Schwartz, 1969; *A Student's Guide to Böll* by Enid Macpherson, 1972; *Böll: Withdrawal and Re-Emergence*, 1973, and *Heinrich Böll: A German for His Time*, 1986, both by J.H. Reid; *The Major Works of Böll: A Critical Commentary* by Erhard Friedrichsmeyer, 1974; *The Writer and Society: Studies in the Fiction of Günter Grass and Heinrich Böll* by Charlotte W. Ghurye, 1976; *The Imagery in Böll's Novels* by Thor Prodaniuk, 1979; *Heinrich Böll* by Robert C. Conard, 1981; *Heinrich Böll* by Klaus Schröter, 1982; *Heinrich Böll and the Challenge of Literature* by Michael Butler, 1988; *Heinrich Böll: Forty Years of Criticism* by Reinhard K. Zachau, 1994; *The Narrative Fiction of Heinrich Böll: Social Conscience and Literary Achievement*, edited by Michael Butler, 1995; *On the Rationality of Poetry: Heinrich Böll's Aesthetic Thinking* by Frank Finlay, 1996.

* * *

More consistently than any of his contemporaries Heinrich Böll documented the development of the Federal Republic from its inception. In doing so he achieved the remarkable feat of becoming a best-selling author who was under constant attack from the popular press. His works are invariably provocative and the subject of critical disagreement in both academic and non-academic circles. Abroad he had a solid reputation as "the good German" who unambiguously condemned fascism and the less appealing features of the land of the Economic Miracle. Sales of his books in Eastern Europe are still considerable and in the former Soviet Union he is one of the best-known Western writers.

Implicit in all his works is the theme of the individual under threat from impersonal forces of all kinds. In *Wo warst du, Adam?* (*And Where Were You Adam?*) and *Ende einer Dienstfahrt* (*The End of a*

Mission) it is the war machine; in *Und sagte kein einziges Wort* (*And Never Said a Word*) and *Ansichten eines Clowns* (*The Clown*) it is the Roman Catholic church; in *Gruppenbild mit Dame* (*Group Portrait with Lady*) it is big business; in *Die verlorene Ehre der Katharina Blum* (*The Lost Honor of Katharina Blum*) and *Fürsorgliche Belagerung* (*The Safety Net*) it is the unholy empire of press and industry working hand in hand with the police. His standpoint is that of left-wing humanism tinged with a strong element of non-conformist, anti-clerical Catholicism. He was publicly involved in all the important issues of his day. Böll's particular literary strength lies in satire, the medium most suited to his conception of a literature which must in content be socially committed and in technique "exaggerate" ("Second Wuppertal Speech," 1960), test the limits to artistic freedom by "going too far" ("The Freedom of Art," 1966); it also relates to his notable sense of humour allied to his eye for the significant, absurd detail. His most memorable writings include those on the broadcaster who collects "silences," the family which celebrates Christmas all the year round, and the man who is employed to defeat the packaging industry by *unpacking* goods for the customer.

Böll was essentially a writer of prose fiction—his few excursions into other genres were unsuccessful. He experimented in a moderate way with narrative techniques. In the 1950s his favourite form was the short story, that genre peculiarly suited to existentialist statement. His novels of these years are marked by a preoccupation with the phenomenon of time and make extensive play with fluctuating narrative perspectives. *Billard um halb zehn* (*Billiards at Half-Past Nine*) comes closest to the *nouveau roman* of the day. In the more politically charged atmosphere of the 1960s and later, his writing became deliberately more casual and direct, although the ironic play with the convention of a first-person biographer-narrator in *Group Portrait with Lady* betrays a continued concern for questions of form. It is interesting therefore that *The Safety Net* reverts to the peculiar narrative economy of the earlier works with its condensation of narrated time and its use of multiple limited points of view.

—J.H. Reid

See the essays on *Group Portrait with Lady* and *The Lost Honor of Katharina Blum*.

BORGES, Jorge Luis

Born: Buenos Aires, Argentina, 24 August 1899. **Education:** Educated at Collège de Genève, Switzerland; Cambridge University. **Family:** Married 1) Elsa Millan in 1967 (separated 1970); 2) María Kodama in 1986. **Career:** Lived in Europe with his family, 1914–21; co-founding editor, *Proa*, 1924–26, and *Sur*, 1931; also associated with *Prisma*; literary adviser, Emecé Editores, Buenos Aires; columnist *El Hogár* weekly, Buenos Aires, 1936–39; municipal librarian, Buenos Aires, (fired from his post by the Péron regime) 1939–46; poultry inspector, 1946–54; went blind, 1955; director, National Library (after Péron's deposition), 1955–73; professor of English literature, University of Buenos Aires, 1955–70; Norton professor of poetry, Harvard University, Cambridge, Massachusetts; visiting lecturer, University of Oklahoma, Norman, 1969. President, Argentine Writers Society, 1950–53. **Awards:** Buenos Aires Municipal prize, 1928; Argentine Writers Society prize, 1945; National prize for literature, 1957; Prix Formentor, 1961; Ingram Merrill award, 1966; Bienal Foundation Inter-American prize, 1970; Jerusalem prize, 1971; Alfonso Reyes prize, 1973; Cervantes prize, 1979; Yoliztli prize, 1981. Honorary Degrees: D.Litt.: University of Cuyo, Argentina, 1956; Oxford University, 1971; Columbia University, New York, 1971; University of Michigan, East Lansing, 1972; University of Chile, 1976; University of Cincinnati, 1976; Ph.D.: University of Jerusalem, 1971. Honorary fellow, Modern Language Association (United States), 1961. Order of Merit (Italy), 1968; Order of Merit (German Federal Republic), 1979. Honorary KBE (Knight Commander, Order of the British Empire). Légion d'honneur. **Member:** Argentine National Academy; Uruguayan Academy of Letters. **Died:** 14 June 1986.

PUBLICATIONS

Collections

Collected Fictions, translated by Andrew Hurley, 1998.
Selected Non-fictions, edited by Eliot Weinberger, translated by Esther Allen, Suzanne Jill Levine, and Eliot Weinberger, 1999.
Everything and Nothing, translated by Donald A. Yates, 1999.

Fiction

Historia universal de la infamia. 1935; as *A Universal History of Infamy*, translated by Norman Thomas di Giovanni, 1971.
El jardín de senderos que se bifurcan. 1942.
Seis problemas para don Isidro Parido, with Adolfo Bioy Casares (as H. Bustos Domecq). 1942; as *Six Problems for Don Isidro Parodi*, translated by Norman Thomas di Giovanni, 1981.
Ficciones (1935–1944). 1944; enlarged edition, 1956; as *Ficciones*, edited and translated by Anthony Kerrigan, 1962; edited and translated by Gordon Brotherston and Peter Hulme, 1999; as *Fictions*, translated by Kerrigan, 1965.
Dos fantasías memorables, with Adolfo Bioy Casares. 1946.
Un modelo para la muerte, with Adolfo Bioy Casares (as B. Suárez Lynch). 1946.
El Aleph. 1949; as *The Aleph and Other Stories 1933–1969*, edited and translated by Norman Thomas di Giovanni, 1970.
La muerte y la brújula. 1951.
La hermana de Eloísa, with Luisa Mercedes Levinson. 1955.
Crónicas de Bustos Domecq, with Adolfo Bioy Casares. 1967; as *Chronicles of Bustos Domecq*, translated by Norman Thomas di Giovanni, 1976.
El informe de Brodie. 1970; as *Dr. Brodie's Report*, translated by Norman Thomas di Giovanni, 1972.
El congreso. 1970; as *The Congress*, translated by Norman Thomas di Giovanni, 1974.
El libro de arena. 1975; as *The Book of Sand*, translated by Norman Thomas di Giovanni (includes *The Gold of the Tigers*), 1977.

Verse

Fervor de Buenos Aires. 1923.
Luna de enfrente. 1925.
Cuaderno San Martín. 1929.
Poemas 1922–1943. 1943.
Poemas 1923–1958. 1958.

El hacedor (includes prose). 1960; as *Dreamtigers*, translated by Mildred Boyer and Harold Morland, 1964.
Obra poética. 6 vols., 1964–78.
Para las seis cuerdas. 1965; revised edition, 1970.
Nueva antología personal. 1968.
Elogio de la sombra. 1969; as *In Praise of Darkness*, translated by Norman Thomas di Giovanni (bilingual edition), 1974.
El otro, el mismo. 1969.
El oro de los tigres. 1972.
Selected Poems 1923–1967, edited by Norman Thomas di Giovanni. 1972.
La rosa profunda. 1975.
La moneda de hierro. 1976.
Historia de la noche. 1976.
The Gold of the Tigers: Selected Later Poems, translated by Alastair Reid, in *The Book of Sand*, 1977.
Adrogué (includes prose). 1977.
La cifra. 1981.
Antología poética, 1923–1977. 1981.

Screenplays: *Los orilleros; El paraíso de los creyentes*, with Adolfo Bioy Casares. 1955.

Other

Inquisiciones (essays). 1925.
El tamaño de mi esperanza (essays). 1926.
El idioma de los Argentinos (essays). 1928; enlarged edition, as *El lenguaje de Buenos Aires*, with José Edmundo Clemente, 1963.
Evaristo Carriego (essays). 1930; as *Evaristo Carriego: A Book about Old-Time Buenos Aires*, translated by Norman Thomas di Giovanni, 1983.
Discusión. 1932.
Las Kennigar. 1933.
Historia de la eternidad. 1936; enlarged edition, 1953.
Nueva refutación del tiempo. 1947.
Aspectos de la literatura gauchesca. 1950.
Antiguas literaturas germánicas, with Delia Ingenieros. 1951.
Otras inquisiciones 1937–1952. 1952; as *Other Inquisitions 1937–1952*, translated by Ruth L.C. Simms, 1964.
El "Martín Fierro", with Margarita Guerrero. 1953.
Obras completas, edited by José Edmundo Clemente. 9 vols., 1953–60.
Leopoldo Lugones, with Betina Edelberg. 1955.
Manual de zoología fantástica, with Margarita Guerrero. 1957; revised edition, as *El libro de los seres imaginarios*, 1967; as *The Imaginary Zoo*, translated by Tim Reynolds, 1969; revised edition, as *The Book of Imaginary Beings*, translated by Norman Thomas de Giovanni, 1969.
Antología personal. 1961; as *A Personal Anthology*, edited and translated by Anthony Kerrigan, 1967.
Labyrinths: Selected Stories and Other Writings, edited and translated by Donald A. Yates and James E. Irby, 1962; enlarged edition, 1964.
The Spanish Language in South America: A Literary Problem; El Gaucho Martín Fierro (lectures). 1964.
Introducción a la literatura inglesa, with María Esther Vázquez. 1965; as *An Introduction to English Literature*, edited and translated by L. Clark Keating and Robert O. Evans, 1974.

Literaturas germánicas medievales, with María Esther Vázquez. 1966.

Introducción a la literatura norteamericana, with Esther Zemborain de Torres. 1967; as *An Introduction to American Literature*, translated by L. Clark Keating and Robert O. Evans, 1973.

Nueva antología personal. 1968.

Conversations with Borges, by Richard Burgin. 1968.

Borges on Writing, edited by Norman Thomas di Giovanni, Daniel Halpern, and Frank MacShane. 1973.

Obras completas, edited by Carlos V. Frías. 1974.

Tongues of Fallen Angels: Conversations with Borges, edited by Selden Roman, 1974.

Prólogos. 1975.

Qué es el budismo?, with Alicia Jurado. 1976.

Libros de sueños. 1976.

Borges oral (lectures). 1979.

Siete noches (essays). 1980; as *Seven Nights*, translated by Eliot Weinberger, 1984.

Prosa completa. 2 vols., 1980.

Borges, A Reader: Selections from the Writings, edited by Emir Rodríguez Monegal and Alastair Reid. 1981.

Nueve ensayos dantescos. 1982.

Borges at Eighty: Conversations, edited by Willis Barnstone. 1982.

Atlas, with María Kodama. 1985; as *Atlas*, translated by Anthony Kerrigan, 1985.

Conversaciones, with Alicia Moreau de Justo. 1985.

Borges en dialogo, with Osvaldo Ferrari. 1985.

Los conjurados. 1985.

Conversaciones, with Roberto Alifano. 1986.

Conversaciones, with Francisco Tokos. 1986.

Textos Cautivos: Ensayos y reseñas en El Hogar (1936–1939), edited by Enrique Socerio-Gari and Emir Rodríguez Monegal. 1987.

Paginas escogidas, edited by Roberto Fernandez Retamar. 1988.

Biblioteca personal: Prólogos. 1988.

Ultimas conversaciones con Borges, with Roberto Alifano. 1988.

The Secret Books: Writings by Jorge Luis Borges, with photographs by Sean Kernan, 1999.

The Craft of Verse, edited by Calin-Andrei Mihailescu, 2000.

The Library of Babel, translated by Andrew Hurley, 2000.

Editor, with Pedro Henriques Ureña, *Antología clásica de la literatura argentina.* 1937.

Editor, with Silvana Ocampo and Adolfo Bioy Casares, *Antología de la literatura fantástica.* 1940; as *The Book of Fantasy*, 1988.

Editor, with Silvana Ocampo and Adolfo Bioy Casares, *Antología poética argentina.* 1941.

Editor, with Adolfo Bioy Casares, *Los mejores cuentos policiales.* 2 vols., 1943–51.

Editor, with Silvina Bullrich Palenque, *El Campadrito: Su destino, sus barrios, su música.* 1945.

Editor, with Adolfo Bioy Casares, *Prosa y verso*, by Francisco de Quevedo. 1948.

Editor, with Adolfo Bioy Casares, *Cuentos breves y extraordinarios.* 1955; as *Extraordinary Tales*, edited and translated by Anthony Kerrigan, 1971.

Editor, with Adolfo Bioy Casares, *Libro del cielo y del infierno.* 1960.

Editor, *Paulino Lucero, Aniceto y gallo, Santos Vega*, by Hilario Ascasubi. 1960.

Editor, *Macedonia Fernández* (selection). 1961.

Editor, *Páginas de historia y de autobiografía*, by Edward Gibbon. 1961.

Editor, *Prosa y poesía*, by Almafuerte. 1962.

Editor, *Versos*, by Evaristo Carriego. 1963.

Editor, with Maria Komada, *Breve antología anglosajona.* 1978.

Editor, *Micromegas*, by Voltaire. 1979.

Editor, *Cuentistas y pintores argentinos.* 1985.

Editor and translator, with Adolfo Bioy Casares, *Poesía gauchesca.* 2 vols., 1955.

Translator, *La metamorfosis*, by Kafka. 1938.

Translator, *Bartleby*, by Herman Melville. 1944.

Translator, *De los héroes; Hombres representativos*, by Carlyle and Emerson. 1949.

*

Bibliography: *Borges: Bibliografía total 1923–1973* by Horacio Jorge Becco, 1973; *Jorge Luis Borges: An Annotated Primary and Secondary Bibliography* by David William Foster, 1984.

Critical Studies: *Borges, The Labyrinth Maker* by Ana María Barrenchea edited and translated by Robert Lima, 1965; *The Narrow Act: Borges's Art of Illusion* by Ronald J. Christ, 1969; *The Mythmaker: A Study of Motif and Symbol in the Short Stories of Borges* by Carter Wheelock, 1969; *Jorge Luis Borges*, 1971, and *Borges and the Kabbalah and Other Essays on His Fiction and Poetry*, 1988, both by Jaime Alazraki, and *Critical Essays on Jorge Luis Borges* edited by Alazraki, 1987; *Borges*, 1971, and *Borges Revisited*, 1991, both by Martin S. Stabb; *The Cardinal Points of Borges* edited by Lowell Dunham and Ivor Ivask, 1971; *Jorge Luis Borges* by John M. Cohen, 1973; *Prose for Borges* edited by Charles Newman and Mary Kinzie, 1974; *Borges: Ficciones* by Donald Leslie Shaw, 1976; *Paper Tigers: The Ideal Fictions of Borges* by John Sturrock, 1977; *Borges: Sources and Illumination* by Giovanna De Garayalde, 1978; *Jorge Luis Borges: A Literary Biography* by Emír Rodríguez Monegal, 1978; *Jorge Luis Borges* by George R. McMurray, 1980; *Borges and His Fiction: A Guide to His Mind and Art* by Gene H. Bell-Villada, 1981; *The German Response to Latin American Literature and the Reception of Jorge Luis Borges and Pablo Neruda* by Yolanda Julia Broyles, 1981; *The Aleph Weaver: Biblical, Kabbalistic and Judaic Elements in Borges* by Edna Aizenberg, 1984, and *Borges and His Successors: The Borges Impact on Literature and the Arts* edited by Aizenberg, 1990; *The Prose of Jorge Luis Borges: Existentialism and the Dynamics of Surprise*, 1984, and *The Meaning of Experience in the Prose of Jorge Luis Borges*, 1988, both by Ion Tudro Agheana; *Jorge Luis Borges: Life, Work and Criticism* by Donald Yates, 1985; *Jorge Luis Borges* edited by Harold Bloom, 1986; *The Literary Universe of Jorge Luis Borges: An Index to References and Allusions to Persons, Titles and Places in His Writings*, 1986, and *Out of Context: Historical Reference and the Representation of Reality in Borges*, 1993, both by Daniel Balderston; *The Poetry and Poetics of Jorge Luis Borges* by Paul Cheselka, 1987; *The Emperor's Kites: A Morphology of Borges's Tales* by Mary Lusky Friedman, 1987; *In Memory of Borges* edited by Norman Thomas Di Giovanni, 1988; *A Dictionary of Borges* by Evelyn Fishburn, 1990; *Jorge Luis Borges: A Study of the Short Fiction* by Naomi Lindstrom, 1990; *Orientalism in the Hispanic Literary Tradition: In Dialogue with Borges, Paz and Sarduy* by Julia A. Kushigian, 1991; *Borges and Artificial Intelligence: An Analysis in the Style of Pierre Menard* by Ema Lapidot,

1991; *The Contemporary Praxis of the Fantastic: Borges and Cortázar* by Julio Rodríguez-Luis, 1991; *Jorge Luis Borges: A Writer at the Edge* by Beatriz Sarlo, 1992; *Jorge Luis Borges and His Predecessors, or, Notes Towards a Materialist History of Linguistic Idealism* by Malcolm K. Read, 1993; *With Borges on an Ordinary Evening in Buenos Aires: A Memoir* by Willis Barnstone, 1993; *Signes of Borges* by Sylvia Molloy, translated and adapted by Oscar Montero, 1994; *The Borges Tradition*, edited with introduction by Norman Thomas di Giovanni, 1995; *The Man in the Mirror of the Book: A Life of Jorge Luis Borges* by James Woodall, 1996; *Ravishing Tradition: Cultural Forces and Literary History* by Daniel Cottom, 1996; *Nightglow: Borges' Poetics of Blindness* by Florence L. Yudin, 1997; *Borges and Europe Revisited*, edited by Evelyn Fishburn, 1998; *Borges and the Politics of Form* by Jose Eduardo Gonzalez, 1998; *Jorge Luis Borges: Thought and Knowledge in the XXth Century* by Alfonso de Toro, 1999; *Humor in Borges* by René de Costa, 2000.

* * *

Jorge Luis Borges was one of the most influential writers of the 20th century. His lasting contribution to world literature is to be found in his short stories. *Ficciones* (*Fictions*) and *El Aleph* (*The Aleph and Other Stories*) collect his classic tales, the ones that secured his place among the masters of world literature and became the cornerstone of the new Spanish-American narrative. It is in these two books, along with the essays of *Inquisiciones* [Inquisitions] and the texts (prose, poetry, fragments) of *El hacedor* (*Dreamtigers*) that the synthesis of his literary art can be found. In later books of short stories, such as *El informe de Brodie* (*Dr. Brodie's Report*), he turned to simplicity, to straightforward storytelling. *El libro de arena* (*The Book of Sand*), however, his last collection of short stories, returned to the creative lines developed earlier. The recurrent aesthetic and philosophical concerns of his writing (time, the identity of the self, human destiny, eternity, infinite multiplicity, the double, the mirages of reality) remained predominant themes, but the rigorous verbal precision of his celebrated stories becomes a freer, simpler, and more direct prose.

His narrative develops within a tradition that has been called fantastic literature. Borges himself highlights the four basic procedures of fantastic fiction: the work of art within the work of art, the contamination of reality by dream, travels through time, and the use of the double. These procedures, along with his favourite devices and symbols (the labyrinth, mirrors, symmetry, plurality and multiplicity, infinite bifurcations, the cyclical nature of reality), contribute to reveal the essential unreality of all human constructions. His stories focus on man's relation with the world and convey a deep and disquieting uneasiness. Borges's fictions are a lengthy interrogation (philosophical, theological, metaphysical) without a possible answer, a terrifying questioning of the problematic and illusory nature of reality, of the existence itself of the universe. The anguish caused by the implacable destiny of humanity haunted by the passing of time and by the dissolution of the image of the self is a basic motif of all his writing.

Borges founded an imaginary universe based on intellectual premises (idealism is a guiding principle of his fiction), and discovered in literature a coherent order in contrast with the chaos of the world, but his fictions always ended up by being a terrifying duplication of our chaotic universe. Incapable of comprehending reality, he wrote self-reflective, involuted, ironic, or *ludic* stories, that become continuous dialogues with nothingness, where reality and dream are indistinguishable.

Borges's technical control, the evocative and allusive strength of his prose, the verbal rigour, the subtle conceptual irony, the lucid exercise of intelligence, and the power to create a world of his own, distinguishable from any other, are lasting contributions of his prose. He proposed that literature be, above all, literature, and that fiction accept, in the words of Rodríguez Monegal, "deliberately and explicitly its character of fiction, of verbal artifice."

Borges's writing can be seen, in short, as an elaborate way to justify life through art. His inexhaustible imagination justified, aesthetically, his reason for being. Borges found in the creative act and in the invention of ideal worlds a provisory salvation. He created his own reality in order to erase the inscrutable chaos of the world. "Unreality is the condition of art," he wrote in "The Secret Miracle," and in "Examination of the Work of Herbert Quain" he affirmed that "of the many joys that literature can provide, the highest is invention." Borges's scepticism with regard to the elusive and inexplicable universe becomes elaborately constructed fictions, games that mirror life but undermine all facile assumptions.

—Hugo J. Verani

See the essay on "Death and the Compass."

BOROWSKI, Tadeusz

Born: Zhitomir, Ukraine (Soviet Union), 12 November 1922. **Education:** Primary and secondary in Soviet Union and Poland 1928–32, 1933–40; Polish philology, underground University of Warsaw 1941–43. **Family:** Married Maria Rundo. **Career:** Father sent to a labor camp, 1926; mother to Siberia, 1930; Borowski left in the care of his aunt; Repatriated to Poland 1932. Underground cultural activity in German-occupied Warsaw 1939–43; arrested by the Nazis April 1943; spent over two months in the notorious Pawiak Prison, was then sent to Auschwitz, where his fiancée had also been taken; transferred to a camp near Stuttgart (Natzweiler-Dautmergen), August 1944, and subsequently to Dachau-Allach; liberated by the American Seventh Army on 1 May 1945, stayed in the West until 1946, and worked for the Red Cross; returned to Poland; until 1948 worked as a bibliography researcher at the University of Warsaw, contributed to several periodicals, edited the Gazette of the Congress of Intellectuals for Peace in Wroclaw 1948; joined the Communist Party 1948; Cultural officer in the Polish Press Bureau in East Berlin 1949–50, worked also for the Polish Secret Police; Member of the Executive of the Union of Polish Writers 1950. **Died:** 1 July 1951, committed suicide in Warsaw by opening the valves of a gas oven.

PUBLICATIONS

Collections

Utwory zebrane. 5 vols, 1954.
Utwory wybrane. 1991.

This Way for the Gas, Ladies and Gentlemen and Other Stories, edited and translated by Barbara Vedder, with an introduction by Jan Kott. 1967; reprinted 1976 and several other times.

Fiction

Byliśmy w Oświęcimiu, with Nel Siedlecki and K. Olszewski. 1946 (contains four Auschwitz stories by Borowski, and several other stories written collaboratively).
Pewien żolnierz. Opowieści szkolne. 1947.
Kamienny świat. Opowiadanie w dwudziestu obrazach. 1948.
Pożegnanie z Marią. Opowiadania. 1948, 1987.
Opowiadania z książek i gazet. 1949.

Poetry

Gdziekolwiek ziemia . . . Cykl poetycki (self-published). 1942.
Arkusz poetycki. 1944.
Imiona nurtu (poems). 1945.
Poszukiwania. Tracing (with K. Olszewski). 1945.
Poezje wybrane. 1971.
Poezje. 1972.

Other

Do młodych agitatorów pokoju. 1951.
Mała kronika wielkich spraw. 1951.

*

Critical Studies: "Beta, the Disappointed Lover," in *The Captive Mind* by Czesław Miłosz, 1953; "A Discovery of Tragedy (The Incomplete Account of T.B.)" by Andrzej Wirth, in *Polish Review*, 1967; *Zwyczajna apokalipsa* by Andrzej Werner, 1971, 1981; "Reise an die Grenzen einer Moral: Tadeusz Borowskis Auseinandersetzung mit Auschwitz als einen Modell des faschistischen Systems," in *Zeitschrift fur Slawistik*, 1971; *Sugestie interpretacyjne* by Andrzej Tauber-Ziółkowski, 1972; *Ucieczka z kamiennego świata* by Tadeusz Drewnowski, 1977; *Wielka choroba* by Jan Walc, 1992.

* * *

Tadeusz Borowski's significance as a writer rests primarily on his Auschwitz stories, which are perhaps the most incisive literary treatment of life and death in the Auschwitz camp. But he was also a poet as well as a writer of critical and political prose. The latter, full of ideological cant and simplistic argument, is a stark contrast to most of his short stories and poems, as by this time Borowski treated literature as a weapon in anti-imperialist and class struggle. The apprehension that in writing these pieces he had destroyed himself as a writer probably contributed to Borowski's decision to commit suicide.

His poetry, traditional in form, but written with considerable expressive power comprises: a cycle of poems written before his arrest, *Gdziekolwiek ziemia* [*Wherever the Earth. . .*] which is apocalyptic in theme and contains some powerful passages; poems written in Auschwitz and the other camps (three of which are included in Hilda Schiff's anthology *Holocaust Poetry*, 1995); and poems written after his liberation, which are on the whole less accomplished, and at times shockingly brutal. However, there are among them some remarkable lyrics.

Borowski's short stories fall into two groups—the Auschwitz stories proper and those dealing with his experiences immediately after the liberation, and stories unrelated to these experiences, which are of limited interest only. The first group forms a thematic cycle: the depiction of the behavior and fate of people in Auschwitz is followed by the depiction of the behavior of the survivors and their liberators. It is most of these stories that make up the English volume *This Way for the Gas, Ladies and Gentlemen*.

In a review of Zofia Kossak-Szczucka's account of her experiences in Auschwitz, *Z otchłani*, (*From the Abyss*, 1946) Borowski wondered angrily why the author failed to describe how she had managed to survive. And he asserted that no book by an inmate of German concentration camps had credibility unless the author described openly his or her own behavior. In Borowski's case the narrator, Vorarbeiter Tadek is clearly identifiable with the author. Another significant aspect of the stories concerns their genre. Borowski's stories are not reminiscences or a factual account. Yet what motivated Borowski in writing them was the moral obligation to bear witness and to tell the truth. They are thus best described as fictionalized documentary narrative. The crucial question is: how strong is the fictional element? The 1946 edition contains brief introductory comments appended to some of the pieces (which the later editions and the English translations omit). One of the comments reads: "The events here described have been placed within the span of one day. People have no surnames, but the first names remain unchanged, except for the name of one woman. Only Becker had a different name. The real Becker worked on the Kommando, but he did not come from Poznań." This suggests, and is borne out by comparing Borowski's stories with other accounts, that fictionalization affects not the types of happenings and behavior, but the plotting of incidents and the treatment of characters, who are not necessarily identical in all respects with real people in the camp. The character that is in part a deliberate construct is the narrator, who is presented as behaving worse than did his prototype, the author. In fact, the narrator is presented in the cycle in two different ways: as a character, and as the author of letters to his fiancée. This long story in letters, which with poignant irony makes Auschwitz almost sound like home, "U nas, w Auschwitzu" (translated as "Auschwitz, Our Home") is a reconstruction of letters Borowski actually wrote to his fiancée in Birkenau, and it shows a very different person from that of the self-serving and unscrupulous Vorarbeiter Tadek. We thus have a double perspective on Auschwitz, one that is chillingly objective (some have said nihilistic), and another one in which a poet and a man in love writes about his experiences, reflections and feelings to another person in the same camp. It is in this story that moral values, which are at best indirect in the other stories, are fully articulated.

What contributes further to the effectiveness of the stories is Borowski's style, which uses dialogue extensively, is spare and sharply realistic in description, and lets the narrated incidents themselves convey the horror, the suffering and the monstrosity of what human beings are capable of doing to their fellow men. Finally, there is Borowski's choice of scenes and incidents, many of which evoke the most powerful emotions of pity mixed with moral outrage.

Borowski's Auschwitz stories focus not on the efficient, professionalized barbarism of the camp authorities, but rather emphasize the fact that without the complicity of the victims, the camp could not have achieved its purposes, the chief one of which was the extermination of the Jews and Gypsies in the gas chambers. And the horrifying character of Auschwitz is perhaps best conveyed by his explicit argument, that what made the death of hundreds of thousands possible was not only the desire to survive at all costs and without regard to other human beings, but that it was also hope:

It is that very hope that makes people go without a murmur to the gas chambers, keeps them from risking a revolt, paralyses them into numb inactivity. It is hope that breaks down family ties, makes mothers renounce their children, or wives sell their bodies for bread, or husbands kill. It is hope that compels man to hold on to one more day of life, because that day may be the day of liberation . . . Never before in the history of mankind has hope been stronger than man, but never also has it done so much harm as it has in this war, in this concentration camp. We were never taught how to give up hope, and that is why today we perish in gas chambers.

It was the hope of surviving the Auschwitz hell that made the victims almost as humanly inhuman as were those who ran the camp. That is the supreme irony of Borowski's unique collection of stories.

Borowski's Auchwitz stories will remain, like Kafka's ''Penal Colony,'' Conrad's *Heart of Darkness*, and Céline's *Journey to the End of the Night*, a classic of the horror that human beings are capable of creating for themselves, except that in his stories the degree of the imagined unimaginable is unfortunately minimal.

—Bogdan Czaykowski

BRANT, Sebastian

Born: Strasbourg, Germany, 1457. **Education:** Educated privately; studied law, Basle University, 1475–77, baccalauréat, 1477. **Family:** Married Elisabeth Burg in 1485. **Career:** Licentiate in Canon law, 1484; doctor of Roman and Canon law, 1492, dean of the faculty of law, 1496, Basle University; editor for numerous publishing houses in Basle; set up as legal adviser to city council, Strasbourg, 1501; summoned to Innsbruck by Emperor Maximilian as a consultant, 1502 and 1509; town clerk, 1503, and municipal secretary, 1504, Strasbourg. **Died:** 10 May 1521.

PUBLICATIONS

Verse

Rosarium ex floribus vitae passionisque domini nostri Jesu Christi consertum. 1492.

Das Narrenschiff. 1494; edited by Friedrich Zarncke, 1854; reprinted 1964, also edited by H.A. Junghans (modern German translation and commentary), 1966, and by Manfred Lemmer, 1968; as *The Ship of Fools of the World*, translated from the Latin version by J. Locher and adapted by Alexander Barclay, 1509, reprinted 1874 and 1970; as *The Great Ship of Fools of the World*, translated by Henry Watson, 1517; as *The Ship of Fools*, translated by Edwin H. Zeydel, 1944, reprinted 1966; also translated by William Gillis, 1971.

Carmina in Laudem B. Mariae Virginis multorumque sanctorum. 1494.

Varia carmina. 1498.

Other (selection)

Von der wunderbaren geburd des kinds bey wurmbs. 1495.

Von der wunderlichen zamefügung der öbersten Planeten. 1504.

Von dem anfang und Wesen der statt Jerusalem. 1518.

In Laudem divi Maximiliani Caesaris invict. 1520.

Kleine Texte, edited by Thomas Wilhelmi. 1998.

Editor, *De civitate Dei* by Saint Augustine. 1489.

Editor, *De moribus et facetijs mense Thesmophagia*, by Reinerus. 1490.

Editor, *Opera Sancti Ambrosii.* 1492.

Editor, *De conceptu et triplici Mariae Virginis gloriosissimae candore.* 1494.

Editor, *Vita beati Brunonis.* 1495.

Editor, *Concordantiae maiores Bibli.* 1496.

Editor, *Theologica emphasis*, by Jacob Locher. 1496.

Editor, *Passio St. Meynrhadi martyris et heremite.* 1496.

Editor, *Librorum Francisci Petrarchae Annotatio.* 1496.

Editor, *Joannis Reuchlin Phorcensis Scenica Progymnasmata.* 1498.

Editor, *Aesopus appologi sive Mythologi cum quibusdam carminum et fabularum.* 1501.

Editor, *De philosophico consolatu sive de consolatione philosophie*, by Boethius. 1501.

Editor, *Hortulus animae.* 1501.

Editor, *Der heilgen leben nüw mit vil Heilgen, und clarz der Passion und die Grossen fest, das lessen, mit figuren zierlich und nutzlich den menschen.* 1502.

Editor, *Opera*, by Virgil. 1502.

Editor, *De laudibus crucis*, by Hrabanus. 1503.

Editor, *Bescheidenheit*, by Freidank. 1508.

Editor, with Jacob Locher, *Layen Spiegel*, by Ulrich Tengler. 1509.

Editor, *In mortem Johannis Keiserspergii.* 1510.

Editor, *Der richterlich Clagspiegel.* 1516.

Editor, *Von der Artzney beyder Glück, der guten und widerwertigen.* 1532.

Translator, *Phagifacetus seu de moribus et facetiis mensae.* 1490.

Translator, *Liber faceti.* 1496.

Translator, *Liber moreti.* 1496.

Translator, *Disticha Catonis.* 1498.

*

Bibliography: *Sebastian Brant Bibliographie* by Thomas Wilhelmi, 1990; *Sebastian-Brant-Bibliographie. Forschungsliteratur von 1800 bis 1985* by Joachim Knape and Dieter Wuttke, 1990.

Critical Studies: *The English Versions of the Ship of Fools* by A. Pompen, 1925; *Sebastian Brant: Studies in Religious Aspects of His Life and Works with Special Reference to the Varia Carmina* by Mary A. Rajewski, 1944; *Studien zu Sebastian Brants Narrenschiff* by Ulrich Gaier, 1966; *Sebastian Brant, Das Narrenschiff* by Barbara Könneker, 1966; *Sebastian Brant* by Edwin H. Zeydel, 1967; *Das Narrenschiff* by Klaus Manger, 1983; *Dichtung, Recht und*

Freiheit. Studien zu Leben und Werk Sebastian Brants 1457–1521 by Joachim Knape, 1992; *Sebastian Brant's The Ship of Fools in Critical Perspective, 1800–1991* by John Van Cleve, 1993; *Das Mittelniederdeutsche Narrenschiff (Lübeck 1497) und Seine Hochdeutschen Vorlagen* by Friederike Voss, 1994; *Ein Interpretierendes Wörterbuch der Nominalabstrakta im Narrenschiff Sebastian Brants von Abenteuer bis Zwietracht* by Dietmar Benkartek, 1996; *Sebastian Brant als Politischer Publizist: Zwei Flugblatt-Satiren aus den Folgejahren des Sogenannten Reformreichstags von 1495* by Vera Sack, 1997.

* * *

After graduating from the University of Basle in 1477 Sebastian Brandt studied and subsequently taught and practised law there, receiving his doctorate in 1489. From 1486–96 he also lectured on poetics. During this period he wrote occasional verse, some of it published as broadsides illustrated with woodcuts, on such topics as floods on the Rhine in 1480, an eclipse in 1485, or a hailstorm in 1487. A collection of his religious verse appeared in 1494, followed in 1498 by his *Varia carmina* [Diverse Lyric Poems], containing many panegyrics on Maximilian I and poems on various historical and contemporary personalities. Most of this early verse was in Latin and pedantic in style, but he soon started experimenting with translation into German, publishing versions of medieval didactic works: *Thesmophagia, Disticha Catonis, Facetus,* and *Moretus* in 1490. His interest in such writings points forward to the work for which he is chiefly remembered today, *Das Narrenschiff* (*The Ship of Fools*).

The Ship of Fools was an instant success. The first edition (Basle 1494) was followed in the same year by unauthorized reprints from Nuremberg, Reutlingen, and Augsburg, as well as by a Strasbourg edition with interpolations. New editions and adaptations continued to appear right down to 1625. The learned abbot Johannes Trithemius declared *The Ship of Fools* to be a "Divine Satire," the equal of Dante's *Commedia* (*Divine Comedy*), and the Strasbourg humanist Jacob Wimpheling likewise compared Brant to Dante and Petrarch and considered that even Homer could not have produced a poem to match it; he proposed to introduce *The Ship of Fools* as a school textbook. The renowned Strasbourg preacher Johann Geiler von Kaisersberg delivered more than a hundred sermons based on it in Strasbourg Minster in 1498, as though it were a canonical book of the church. Its success was not confined to southern Germany. Low German versions were published at Lübeck in 1497 and Rostock in 1519. The year 1497 also saw the publication of a Latin translation, made by Jacob Locher and supervised by Brant, and printed at Basle under the title *Stultifera navis*. Through this translation the book came to the attention not only of a humanist public but of an international readership too; indeed it was the only work of German literature to achieve international acclaim before Goethe's *The Sufferings of Young Werther* (1774). The Latin text was soon translated into French, English (by Alexander Barclay and Henry Watson), and Dutch, these versions becoming popular in their turn. The work had a major role in establishing "folly literature" as a genre which was cultivated by writers like Thomas Murner, Hans Sachs, and Johann Fischart and would remain popular down to the 17th century. To the modern reader, the book's extraordinary success is something of a mystery. Even specialists in the field have been baffled. Thus Zarncke,

who edited the work in 1854, felt that it was only "the intellectual impoverishment" of Brant's age which could explain the success of this "compilation" which bore the marks of "laboured industry and countless sleepless nights!"

One reason for its success is the appeal of the figure of the fool, though Brant cannot be credited with creating it—it has both medieval and classical antecedents, and of course the distinction between fools and wise men is as old as the Bible. Brant parades before us 112 fools, each of them standing for a different kind of breach of moral or social convention. In its way, the book is an illuminating document on the intellectual and moral history of the period. Brant is a stern moralist, conservative in his religious convictions, who does not share the humanists' sneaking belief in the innate goodness of man. For him it is foolish to sacrifice eternal salvation for passing pleasures. The "follies" that he castigates—whether blasphemy, adultery, or slavery to fashion, gluttony, sloth, or gossiping in church, bibliomania, failing to follow doctor's orders, or selling forged relics—seem to him to be equally reprehensible. The fool is not seen as a social outcast but rather as a person who fails to heed a warning about the folly of his ways, Brant's criticism being aimed at people who, despite warnings, persist in their sinful folly. The satire is rarely relieved with flashes of humour.

Each chapter can be read independently of the whole. Some scholars have believed that the individual chapters may originally have been published as separate poems. While this cannot be substantiated, it is certainly the case that approximately two-thirds of the chapters, especially in the first half of the work, were designed to fill neatly a two-page opening of the book, with the left-hand page having a three-line motto and a woodcut; the main text, usually 34 lines of rhyming couplets, then fills the rest of the page and the whole of the recto. The later chapters vary considerably in length. Another indication of Brant's changing approach to the work is that the allegory of the ship voyaging with a full complement of fools is treated in a sustained manner only in the second half of the work and in the prologue (which was probably written last). The concept of the ship of fools is not Brant's invention; the most likely source, albeit perhaps indirect, was a sermon, apparently preached in Strasbourg in the 1460s or 1470s, in which the anonymous preacher describes a ship laden with 21 fools who are invited by Christ to board his own St. Ursula's ship. What Brant did invent is the pun on German *Narr* "fool" when he says that the starting point of the voyage is Narbonne and the destination is the land of Narragonia.

The Ship of Fools can be said to have "grown" rather than to have been planned. In another sense, too, the work is a compilation. Brant is always at pains to buttress his arguments by citing recognized authorities, principally the Bible (notably Proverbs and Ecclesiastes), then canon law, the Church Fathers, and ancient writers (particularly Plutarch, Xenophon, Homer, Ovid, Juvenal, and Seneca). Gaier (1966) has also revealed the classical rhetorical structures underpinning the chapters, so that we are again able to understand more readily some of the subtleties appreciated by Brant's contemporaries.

But one feature that appeals to us as much as it did to them is the woodcuts which are an indispensable, integral part of the work. Brant himself says that he wanted to ensure that even fools unable to read might recognize themselves in the pictures. The woodcuts, which are remarkable for their vitality, are clearly the work of several artists; some have been attributed to the young Albrecht Dürer. Though Brant claims in the preface (line 25) to have designed the pictures, this doubtless means no more than that he suggested motifs and collaborated closely with the artists.

—John L. Flood

See the essay on *The Ship of Fools*.

BRASILLACH, Robert

Born: Perpignan, France, 31 March 1909. **Education:** Educated at Lycée Louis-le-Grand, Paris, 1925–28; École Normale Supérieure, Paris. **Military:** Served in the French army during World War II, taken prisoner, released 1941. **Career:** Associated with the fascist press during the 1930s; literary critic, *L'Action française*, 1929; contributor, *Le Coq Catalan*, Perpignan, *L'Intransigeant*, and *Candide*, both Paris, during 1930s; staff writer, *La Revue Universelle*, 1930s; member of the editorial board, with Marcel Aymé, *q.v.*, and Jean Anouilh, *q.v.*, *Je Suis Partout*, 1936–44 (resigned). Gave himself up to the Resistance, imprisoned and tried. **Died:** (executed) 6 February 1945.

PUBLICATIONS

Collection

Oeuvres complètes, edited by Maurice Bardèche. 12 vols., 1963–66.

Fiction

Le Voleur d'étincelles. 1932.
L'Enfant de la nuit. 1934.
Le Marchand d'oiseaux. 1936.
Comme le temps passe. 1937; as *Youth Goes Over*, translated by Warre Bradley Wells, 1938.
Les Sept Couleurs. 1939; with preface by Anne Brassié, 1995.
La Conquérante. 1943.
Six heures à perdre. 1953.
Los Captifs (unfinished), 1974.

Plays

Bérénice. 1954; as *La Reine de Césarée* (produced 1957). 1957.
Domrémy. 1961.

Verse

Poèmes. 1944.
Poèmes de Fresnes. 1949.

Other

Présence de Virgile. 1931.
Portraits. 1935.

L'Histoire du cinéma, with Maurice Bardèche. 1935; as *History of the Film*, translated by Iris Barry, 1938; as *History of Motion Pictures*, translated by Barry, 1970.
Animateurs de théâtre. 1936.
Léon Degrelle et l'avenir de Rex. 1936.
Les Cadets de l'Alcazar, with Henri Massis. 1936; as *The Cadets of the Alcazar*, translated anonymously, 1937.
Le Siège de l'Alcazar, with Henri Massis. 1936.
Pierre Corneille. 1938.
Histoire de la guerre d'Espagne, with Maurice Bardèche. 1939.
Notre avant-guerre. 1941; as *Une génération dans l'orage*, 1941.
Le Procès de Jeanne d'Arc. 1941.
Les Quatre Jeudis. 1944.
Chénier. 1947.
Morceaux choisis, edited by Marie Madeleine Martin. 1949.
Lettres écrites en prison (correspondence). 1952.
Journal d'un homme occupé. 1955.
Lettre à un soldat de la classe 60, suivie de textes écrits en prison. 1960.
Poètes oubliés. 1961.
Ecrit à Fresnes (correspondence). 1967.
Vingt lettres de Robert Brasillach. 1970.
Editor and translator, *Anthologie de la poésie grecque*. 1950.

*

Critical Studies: *Robert Brasillach* (in French) by Bernard George, 1968; *The Fascist Ego: A Political Biography of Robert Brasillach* by William Rayburn Tucker, 1975; *The Mystique of Fascism: Ideological and Artistic Function in the Works of Brasillach* by Peter Tame, 1980; *Robert Brasillach; ou, Encore un instant de bonheur* by Anne Brassié 1987; *Brasillach; ou, La célébration du mépris* by Jacqueline Baldran and Claude Bochurberg, 1988; *Robert Brasillach maître de l'évasion* by Marie-Lute Parton Monferron, 1988; *Brasillach: L'Illusion fasciste* by Pascal Louvrier, 1989; *Littérature et fascisme: les romans de Robert Brasillach* by Luc Rasson. 1991; *The Collaborator: The Trial and Execution of Robert Brasillach* by Alice Kaplan, 2000.

* * *

Robert Brasillach's short life had to it many aspects of that of a 19th-century Romantic struck with a severe case of the *mal du siècle*. That boredom, or *ennui*, which was essentially a rejection of traditional bourgeois values, had no real political dimension to it, but its 20th-century counterpart, fascism, had a strong attraction for young men like Brasillach. Somewhat anarchistic by nature (but not without a great deal of ambition), he left the provinces as a boy to attend the Lycée Louis-le-Grand in Paris at the age of 16. From there he passed the difficult competitive entrance examination for the École Normale Supérieure, yet he seems to have frittered away his time there, spending all too much energy as an extreme right activist in rebellion against the status quo.

He began his career as a right-wing journalist in 1931, working on the literary staff of the *L'Action française*, Maurras's royalist newspaper. He embarked on a parallel career as a critic and novelist at the same time. Having excelled in his studies of Greek and Latin, his first book, *Présence de Virgile*, established one of the underpinnings of his life's work: his admiration for classicism and Mediterranean culture.

His later admiration for Mussolini would be partly attributable to this, as were later books on Corneille and the *Anthologie de la poésie grecque*, which he prepared in prison shortly before his death in 1945.

Brasillach continued to spread himself very thin throughout this decade, using his vast energies to study and elucidate widely divergent fields. Thus, in collaboration with his brother-in-law Maurice Bardèche, he published the *Histoire du cinéma* (*History of the Film*) and the *Histoire de la guerre d'Espagne* [History of the Spanish War]. From 1937 to 1943 he was a key member of the right wing and later collaborationist daily newspaper *Je Suis Partout* [I Am Everywhere], which in its heyday boasted a circulation of 300,000. Brasillach had an enormous audience before he resigned from the paper in 1943 because it had gone too far in its pro-German commitment. In the European civil war of the day, Brasillach was surely a "national" who bitterly opposed the Allied "cosmopolitans," but at the same time he refused to allow his identity as a Frenchman to be lost in the alliance with Germany. After the Liberation of Paris, he deliberately did not listen to the advice of friends who counselled emigration to Switzerland. Instead, he chose to face up to what he seems to have known would be his fate. He was arrested in September 1944; his trial in January of the following year was delayed while the authorities looked for a judge who would be willing to decree the death sentence for the crime of having an unpopular opinion. When that judge was found, the trial was conducted quickly and Brasillach was predictably sentenced to death, like so many other victims of the *épuration* (purge). Despite a petition signed by many intellectuals of both Left and Right, including a direct appeal to General de Gaulle by François Mauriac (who had so often been on the receiving end of Brasillach's barbs during the war), he was executed on 6 February 1945. In the last half century he has taken on the status of a martyr among French nationalists, who liken him to Joan of Arc in his honesty and courage in standing up to the English-led cosmopolitan coalition of the 1940s.

Interest in recent years has turned to Brasillach the novelist. The blacklisting of his work by intellectuals was far more effective than the one used on Céline, for example, and it remained in effect well into the 1970s. If Brasillach is to be truly rehabilitated, as his admirers seek to do, he must be shown to have been more than a mere journalist, albeit a courageous one. His first novel, *Le Voleur d'étincelles*, appeared in 1932. The hero, Lazare, like Brasillach, is about 23 years old. In his desire to escape from the dreaded landscape of bourgeois conformity, he discovers a mythological world of dreams. Brasillach's classical background and his own personal debt to the author of *Le Grand Meaulnes* (*The Wanderer*) are evident influences here. This theme of escape was continued in the next novel, *L'Enfant de la nuit* [Child of the Night], but with an important modification. Brasillach, still young and looking for something to say, links the notion of escape to that of discovery. Thus his young hero, Robert, breaks out from his rather self-centred bourgeois universe to discover the everyday world of ordinary Parisians. Literary populism was in the air and the novel of social concern was thriving. In addition, a film like René Clair's *Sous les toits de Paris* [Beneath the Roofs of Paris], which brought out whatever poetic elements were to be found in working class existence of the day, had been an enormous success. Brasillach's novel tries to exploit, but unconvincingly, this formula. *Le Marchand d'oiseaux* [The Bird Seller] continues in the same vein. *Comme le temps passe* (*Youth Goes Over*) utilizes once again Robert, the narrator of *L'Enfant de la nuit*, but here his escape takes place not so much in space as in time—back to the days before World War I. Like many people who could see a new war coming, Brasillach seemed to be trying to stop the passage of time in this novel, as if to somehow stave off World War I. Some critics have seen this as his best fictional effort, but it has the same self-referential and somewhat decadent limitation as the earlier ones. Brasillach's hero never really overcomes his obsession with himself.

Les Sept Couleurs [The Seven Colours] signalled a new and welcome departure. It is a political novel whose action is set in the late 1930s. It was widely read and commented upon at the time, and nominated for the Goncourt prize. The seven colours of the title represent as many different fictional techniques, which are used in the various sections of the novel. Brasillach exhibits impressive control over each form while depicting the lure of escape for his young hero, Patrice, who discovers fascism in Italy and who attends the Nazi Party Congress in Nuremburg in 1938. This is Brasillach's major literary achievement, although to date it has not been studied seriously. It combines in potent form his interest in ancient Mediterranean culture (rekindled in Italian fascism) with the desire to escape into a world of dreams (as represented in the disciplined and anti-bourgeois *mise en scène* at Nuremburg). Patrice's fantasy is skilfully played off against the lucidity of his friend and classmate Catherine, who is able to accept bourgeois reality. This lucidity sets the work apart from the earlier novels as well as from *La Conquérante* [The Conquering Woman], an escapist work set in Morocco at the turn of the century, and *Six heures à perdre*, a pseudo-detective novel written in the spring of 1944 before Brasillach's arrest and execution.

Brasillach has emerged from literary and civil purgatory in the last several years and a large amount of research is now being done, mostly biographical. An objective assessment of the quality of his aesthetic achievement as a novelist has not yet begun, but this will be a critical stage in the process of rehabilitation if he is to be remembered as more than a mere journalist. In the meantime, the arbitrary and unjust death sentence that was imposed upon him for political reasons will continue to exert a powerful attraction for many.

—David O'Connell

BRECHT, Bertolt

Born: Eugen Berthold Friedrich Brecht in Augsburg, Germany, 10 February 1898. **Education:** Educated at elementary school, 1904–08, and Gymnasium, Augsburg, 1908–17; University of Munich, 1917–18, 1919. **Military Service:** Served as medical orderly during World War I. **Family:** Married 1) Marianne Zoff in 1922 (divorced 1927), one daughter; 2) the actress Helene Weigel in 1929, one son and one daughter; also had one son by Paula Banholzer. **Career:** Drama critic, *Der Volkswille*, Augsburg, 1919–21; dramaturg, Munich Kammerspiele, 1923–24; in Berlin, 1924–33; dramaturg, Deutsches Theater; following Hitler's assumption of power, left Germany, 1933; based in Denmark, 1933–39; stripped of German citizenship, 1935; editor, with Lion Feuchtwanger and Willi Bredel, *Das Wort*, 1936–39; moved to Sweden, 1939; fled Sweden, 1941, arrived in the United States via Moscow and Vladivostock; based in California, 1941–47, called before the House Un-American Activities Committee, 1947; flew to Europe immediately after testifying; based in Switzerland, 1947–49; became Austrian citizen, 1950; moved to East Berlin after 1949: artistic adviser, Berliner Ensemble (directed by his wife), 1949–56. **Awards:** Kleist prize, 1922; Stalin Peace prize, 1954. **Died:** 14 August 1956.

PUBLICATIONS

Collections

Gesammelte Werke (Stücke, Gedichte, Prosa, and *Schriften)*. 20 vols., 1967; supplemented with: *Texte für Filme*, 2 vols., 1969; *Arbeitsjournal*, 2 vols., 1974; *Gedichte aus dem Nachlass*, 2 vols., 1982.

Collected Plays, edited by John Willett and Ralph Manheim. 1970–; the United Kingdom and United States versions of this collection have a slightly different arrangement; some translations reprinted as *Plays*.

Poems 1913–1956, edited and translated by John Willett and Ralph Manheim. 3 vols., 1976; revised edition, 1979.

Collected Short Stories: 1921–1946, edited by John Willett and Ralph Manheim, translated by Yvonne Kapp, Hugh Rorrison, and Anthony Tatlow. 1983.

Werke: Grosse kommentierte Berliner und Frankfurter Ausgabe, edited by Werner Hecht and others. 1989–.

Plays

Baal (produced 1922; revised version 1926). 1922; revised version, in *Stücke*, 1, 1955; edited by Dieter Schmidt, 1968; as *Baal*, translated by Eric Bentley, in *Baal; A Man's A Man; The Elephant Calf*, 1964; also translated by Peter Tegel, in *Collected Plays*, 1970.

Trommeln in der Nacht (produced 1922). 1922; as *Drums in the Night*, translated by Frank Jones, in *Jungle of Cities and Other Plays*, 1966; also translated by John Willett, in *Collected Plays*, 1, 1970.

Im Dickicht der Städte (as *Im Dickicht*, produced 1923; revised version 1927). 1927; edited by Gisela E. Bahr, 1968; as *In the Jungle of Cities*, translated by Gerhard Nellhaus, 1957; as *Jungle of Cities*, translated by Anselm Hollo, in *Jungle of Cities and Other Plays*, 1966.

Pastor Ephraim Magnus, with Arnolt Bronnen, from the work by Hans Henry John (produced 1923).

Leben Eduards des Zweiten von England, with Lion Feuchtwanger, from the play by Christopher Marlowe (produced 1924). 1924; edited by Reinhold Grimm, 1968; as *Edward II*, translated by Eric Bentley, 1966; as *The Life of Edward II of England*, translated by Jean Benedetti, in *Collected Plays*, 1, 1970.

Die Kleinbürgerhochzeit (as *Die Hochzeit*, produced 1926). 1966; as *A Respectable Wedding*, translated by Jean Benedetti, in *Collected Plays*, 1, 1970.

Mann ist Mann, with others (produced 1926). 1927; as *Man Equals Man*, translated by Eric Bentley, in *Seven Plays*, 1961, also translated by Gerhard Nellhaus, in *Collected Plays*, 2, 1979; as *A Man's a Man*, also translated by Bentley, in *Baal; A Man's a Man; The Elephant Calf*, 1964.

Das Elefantenkalb. With *Mann ist Mann*, 1927; as *The Elephant Calf*, translated by Eric Bentley, in *Baal; A Man's A Man; The Elephant Calf*, 1964; also translated by Gerhard Nellhaus, in *Collected Plays*, 2, 1979.

Kalkutta 4 Mai, with Lion Feuchtwanger, from a play by Feuchtwanger, in *Drei Angelsächsische Stücke*. 1927; translated as *Warren Hastings*, in *Two Anglo-Saxon Plays*, 1928.

Die Dreigroschenoper, music by Kurt Weill, from the play *The Beggar's Opera* by John Gay (produced 1928). 1929; as *The Threepenny Opera*, translated by Desmond I. Vesey and Eric Bentley, in *From the Modern Repertoire*, edited by Bentley, 1958; also translated by Hugh McDiarmid, 1973; Ralph Manheim and John Willett, in *Collected Plays*, 2, 1979.

Happy End, with Elisabeth Hauptmann, music by Kurt Weill (produced 1929). *Happy End*, translated and adapted by Michael Feingold, 1982.

Lindberghflug, music by Kurt Weill and Paul Hindemith (produced 1929). 1929; retitled *Der Ozeanflug*.

Aufstieg und Fall der Stadt Mahagonny, music by Kurt Weill (produced 1930). 1929; as *The Rise and Fall of the City of Mahagonny*, translated by W.H. Auden and Chester Kallman, 1976.

Das Badener Lehrstück vom Einverständnis, music by Paul Hindemith (produced 1929). In *Versuche*, 2, 1930; as *The Didactic Play of Baden-Baden on Consent*, in *Tulane Drama Review*, May 1960.

Der Jasager/Der Neinsager, music by Kurt Weill (produced 1930). In *Versuche*, 4, 1931; edited by Peter Szondi, 1966; as *He Who Said Yes; He Who Said No*, translated by Wolfgang Sauerlander, in *The Measures Taken and Other Lehrstücke*, 1977.

Die Massnahme, music by Hanns Eisler (produced 1930). In *Versuche*, 4, 1931; edited by Reiner Steinweg, 1972; as *The Measures Taken*, translated by Eric Bentley, in *The Modern Theatre*, 6, edited by Bentley, 1960; in *The Jewish Wife and Other Short Plays*, 1965; also translated by Carl R. Müller, in *The Measures Taken and Other Lehrstücke*, 1977.

Versuche, 1–7, 9–15. 14 vols., 1930–57.

Die heilige Johanna der Schlachthöfe (broadcast 1932; produced 1959). In *Versuche*, 5, 1932; edited by Gisela E. Bahr, 1971; as *Saint Joan of the Stockyards*, translated by Frank Jones, in *From the Modern Repertoire*, series 3, edited by Eric Bentley, 1956; also translated by Ralph Manheim, in *Collected Plays*, 3, 1991.

Die Mutter, music by Hanns Eisler, from the novel by Gor'kii (produced 1932). In *Versuche*, 7, 1932; edited by W. Hecht, 1969; as *The Mother*, translated by Lee Baxandall, 1965; also translated by Steve Gooch, 1978.

Die Sieben Todsünden der Kleinbürger, music by Kurt Weill (produced 1933). 1959; as *The Seven Deadly Sins of the Petty Bourgeoisie*, in *Plays*, 1979.

Die Rundköpfe und die Spitzköpfe, music by Hanns Eisler (produced 1936). In *Gesammelte Werke*, 2, 1938; as *Roundheads and Peakheads*, translated by N. Goold-Verschoyle, in *Jungle of Cities and Other Plays*, 1966.

Die Gewehre der Frau Carrar (produced 1937). 1938; as *The Guns of Carrar*, 1971; as *Señora Carrar's Rifles*, in *Collected Plays*, 4, 1983.

Furcht und Elend des Dritten Reiches (produced as *99%*, 1938). 1945; as *The Private Life of the Master Race*, translated by Eric Bentley, 1944; as *Fear and Misery in the Third Reich*, in *Collected Plays*, 4, 1983.

Die Ausnahme und die Regel, music by Paul Dessau (produced 1938). In *Gesammelte Werke*, 2, 1938; as *The Exception and the Rule*, translated by Eric Bentley, in *The Jewish Wife and Other Short Plays*, 1965; also translated by Ralph Manheim, 1977.

Die Horatier und die Kuriatier, music by Kurt Schwän (produced 1958). In *Gesammelte Werke*, 2, 1938; as *The Horatians and the Curiatians*, in *Accent*, 1947.

Das Verhör des Lukullus (broadcast 1940; revised version, music by Paul Dessau, produced 1951). 1951; as *The Trial of Lucullus*, translated by H.R. Hays, 1943; as *Lucullus*, in *Plays*, 1, 1960.

Mutter Courage und ihre Kinder (produced 1941). 1949; In *Versuche*, 9, 1949; revised edition, 1950; edited by W. Hecht, 1964; as

Mother Courage and Her Children, translated by H.R. Hays, 1941; also translated by Eric Bentley, in *Seven Plays*, 1961, and *Collected Plays*, 2, 1962; John Willett, in *Collected Plays*, 5, 1980; translated by David Hare, 1995.

Der gute Mensch von Sezuan (produced 1943). In *Versuche*, 12, 1953; revised edition, 1958; edited by W. Hecht, 1968; as *The Good Woman of Setzuan*, translated by Eric Bentley, in *Parables for the Theatre*, 1948; as *The Good Person of Szechwan*, translated by John Willett, in *Plays*, 2, 1962; as *The Good Person of Sichuan*, translated by Michael Hofmann, 1989.

Galileo (produced 1943; revised version, with Charles Laughton, produced 1947; revised version, as *Leben des Galilei*, produced 1955). 1955; edited by W. Hecht, 1963; as *Galileo*, translated by Brecht and Charles Laughton, in *From the Modern Repertoire*, series 2, edited by Eric Bentley, 1953; as *The Life of Galileo*, translated by Desmond I. Vesey, 1960; also translated by John Willett, in *Collected Plays*, 5, 1980.

Der kaukasische Kreidekreis (produced 1948). In *Sinn und Form— Sonderheft*, 1949; as *The Caucasian Chalk Circle*, translated by Eric Bentley, in *Parables for the Theatre*, 1948; also translated by James and Tania Stern, with W.H. Auden, in *Collected Plays*, 7, 1960.

Herr Puntila und sein Knecht Matti (produced 1948). In *Versuche*, 10, 1950; as *Mr. Puntila and His Man Matti*, translated by John Willett, in *Collected Plays*, 6, 1977.

Die Antigone des Sophokles, from Hölderlin's translation of Sophocles' play (produced 1948). 1955; translated as *Antigone*, 1989.

Der Hofmeister, from the play by J.M.R. Lenz (produced 1950). In *Versuche*, 11, 1951; as *The Tutor*, in *Collected Plays*, 9, 1973 (United States edition only); also translated and adapted by Pip Broughton, 1988.

Herrnburger Bericht, music by Paul Dessau (produced 1951). 1951.

Der Prozess der Jeanne d'Arc zu Rouen 1431, from his radio play (produced 1952). In *Stücke*, 12, 1959; as *The Trial of Joan of Arc*, in *Collected Plays*, 9, 1973 (United States edition only).

Don Juan, from the play by Molière (produced 1953). In *Stücke*, 12, 1959: as *Don Juan*, in *Collected Plays*, 9, 1973 (United States edition only).

Die Gesichte der Simone Machard, with Lion Feuchtwanger (produced 1957). In *Sinn und Form*, 5–6, 1956: as *The Visions of Simone Machard*, translated by Hugh and Ellen Rank, in *Collected Plays*, 7, 1976.

Die Tage der Kommune, music by Hanns Eisler (produced 1956). In *Versuche*, 15, and *Stücke*, 10, both 1957; as *The Days of the Commune*, in *Dunster Drama Review*, 1971; also translated by Clive Barker and Arno Reinfrank, 1978.

Pauken und Trompeten, with Elisabeth Hauptmann and Benno Besson, music by Rudolf Wagner-Regeny, from a play by George Farquhar (produced 1956). In *Stücke*, 12, 1959; as *Trumpets and Drums*, in *Collected Plays*, 9, 1973 (United States edition only).

Der aufhaltsame Aufstieg des Arturo Ui (produced 1958). In *Stücke*, 9, 1957; as *The Resistible Rise of Arturo Ui*, translated by Ralph Manheim, in *Collected Plays*, 6, 1976.

Schweik im zweiten Weltkrieg, music by Hanns Eisler (produced 1957). In *Stücke*, 10, 1957; edited by Herbert Knust, 1974; as *Schweik in the Second World War*, translated by William Rowlinson, in *Collected Plays*, 7, 1976.

Coriolan, from the play by Shakespeare (produced 1962). In *Stücke*, 11, 1959; as *Coriolanus*, in *Collected Plays*, 9, 1973 (United States edition only).

Seven Plays (includes *Jungle of Cities; Man Equals Man; St. Joan of the Stockyards; Mother Courage and Her Children; Galileo; The Good Woman of Setzuan; The Caucasian Chalk Circle*), edited and translated by Eric Bentley. 1961.

Der Bettler; oder, Der tote Hund. In *Stücke*, 13, 1966; as *The Beggar; or, the Dead Dog*, translated by Michael Hamburger, in *Collected Plays*, 1, 1970.

Er treibt den Teufel aus. In *Stücke*, 13, 1966; as *Driving Out a Devil*, translated by Richard Greenburger, in *Collected Plays*, 1, 1970.

Lux in Tenebris. In *Stücke*, 13, 1966; as *Lux in Tenebris*, translated by Eva Geisel and Ernest Borneman, in *Collected Plays*, 1, 1970.

Der Fischzug. In *Stücke*, 13, 1966; as *The Catch*, translated by John Willett, in *Collected Plays*, 1, 1970.

Jungle of Cities and Other Plays (includes *Jungle of Cities; Drums in the Night; Roundheads and Peakheads*), translated by Anselm Hollo and others. 1966.

Turandot; oder, Der Kongress der Weisswäscher, music by Harms Eisler (produced 1969). In *Gesammelte Werke*, 1967.

Der Brotladen (produced 1967). 1969.

Kühle Wampe: Protokoll des Films und Materialien, edited by W. Gersch and W. Hecht. 1969.

Screenplays: *Kühle Wampe*, with others, 1932; *Hangmen Also Die*, with John Wexley and Fritz Lang, 1943.

Radio Plays: *Macbeth*, from the play by Shakespeare, 1927; *Hamlet*, from the play by Shakespeare, 1931; *Die heilige Johanna der Schlachthöfe*, 1932.

Fiction

Der Dreigroschenroman. 1934; as *A Penny for the Poor*, translated by Desmond I. Vesey and Christopher Isherwood, 1937; as *Threepenny Novel*, translated by Vesey and Isherwood, 1956.

Kalendergeschichten. 1948; as *Tales from the Calendar*, translated by Yvonne Kapp and Michael Hamburger, 1961.

Die Geschäfte des Herrn Julius Cäsar. 1957.

Stories of Mr. Keuner, translated by Martin Chalmers, 2001.

Verse

Taschenpostille. 1926.

Hauspostille. 1927; as *Manual of Piety*, translated by Eric Bentley, 1966.

Lieder Gedichte Chöre, with Hanns Eisler. 1934.

Svendborger Gedichte. 1939.

Selected Poems. 1947.

Die Erziehung der Hirse. 1951.

Hundert Gedichte. 1951.

Gedichte, edited by S. Streller. 1955.

Gedichte und Lieder, edited by P. Suhrkamp. 1956.

Selected Poems, translated by H.R. Hays. 1959.

Poems on the Theatre, translated by John Berger and Anna Bostock. 1961.

Gedichte aus dem Nachlass, edited by Herta Ramthun. 2 vols., 1982.

Poems and Songs from the Plays, translated by John Willett. 1990.

Other

Gesammelte Werke. 2 vols., 1938.
Theaterarbeit, with others. 1952.
Gesammelte Werke. 40 vols., 1953–.
Kriegsfibel. 1955; as *War Primer*, translated by John Willett, 1998.
Schriften zum Theater. 1957; as *Brecht on Theater*, edited and translated by John Willett, 1964.
Flüchtlingsgespräche. 1961.
Dialoge aus dem Messingkauf. 1964; as *The Messingkauf Dialogues*, translated by John Willett, 1965.
Arbeitsjournal, edited by Werner Hecht. 2 vols., 1973; as *Journals, 1934–1955*, edited by John Willett, translated by Hugh Rorrison, 1993.
Autobiographische Aufzeichnungen 1920–1954, Tagebücher 1920–22, edited by Herta Ramthun. 1975; *Tagebücher* as *Diaries 1920–22*, translated by John Willett, 1979.
Briefe, edited by Günter Gläser. 2 vols., 1981.
Über die bildenden Künste, edited by Jost Hermand. 1983.
Letters 1913–1956, edited by John Willett, translated by Ralph Manheim. 1990.
Bertolt Brecht: Bad Time for Poetry: Was It? Is It?: 150 Poems and Songs, edited and introduced by John Willett, 1995.
Brecht on Film and Radio, translated and edited by Marc Silberman, 2000.
Translator, with Margarete Steffin, *Die Kindheit*, by Martin Andersen-Nexö. 1945.

*

Bibliography: in *Sinn und Form*, 1957; *Brecht-Bibliographie* by Gerhard Seidel, 1975–.

Critical Studies: *Die dramatischen Versuche Bertolt Brechts 1918–1933*, 1955, and *Drama und Geschichte. Bertolt Brechts "Leben des Galilei" und andere Stücke*, 1965, both by Ernst Schumacher; *Brecht: A Choice of Evils: A Critical Study of the Man, His Work, and His Opinions* by Martin Esslin, 1959, 4th revised edition, 1984; *The Theatre of Bertolt Brecht*, 1959, revised edition, 1977, and *Brecht in Context: Comparative Approaches*, 1984, both by John Willett; *Brecht: A Collection of Critical Essays* edited by Peter Demetz, 1962; *Bertolt Brecht: The Despair and the Polemic* by C.R. Lyons, 1968; *Bertolt Brecht: His Life, His Art, and His Times* by Frederic Ewen, 1970; *The Essential Brecht*, 1972, and *Bertolt Brecht: Chaos, According to Plan*, 1987, both by John Fuegi; *Understanding Brecht* by Walter Benjamin, 1973; *Essays on Brecht: Theater and Politics* edited by Siegfried Mews and Herbert Knust, 1974; *Brecht Chronicle*, 1975, and *Brecht: A Biography*, translated by John Nowell, 1979, both by Klaus Völker; *The Dialectic and the Early Brecht: An Interpretative Study of "Trommeln in der Nacht"* by David Bathrick, 1975; *Bertolt Brecht's Adaptations for the Berliner Ensemble* by Arrigo Subiotto, 1975; *Brecht the Dramatist* by Ronald Gray, 1976; *Der Hofmeister: A Critical Analysis of Bertolt Brecht's Adaptation of Lenz's Drama* by Laurence P.A. Kitching, 1976; *The Mask of Evil: Brecht's Response to the Poetry, Theatre and Thought of China and Japan* by Anthony Tatlow, 1977; *Brecht: A Study* by Michael Morley, 1977; *Towards Utopia: A Study of Brecht* by Keith Dickson, 1978; *Bertolt Brecht and Post-War French Drama* by Victoria Williams Hill, 1978; *Bertolt Brecht* by Karl H. Schoeps, 1978; *Bertolt Brecht's Great Plays* by Alfred D. White, 1978; *Brecht's Misgivings* by Roy Pascal, 1978; *Approaching "Mother Courage," or, Who's Afraid of Bertolt Brecht?*

by Christopher Michael Sperberg, 1979; *Brecht as Thinker: Studies in Literary Marxism and Existentialism* by Ralph J. Ley, 1979; *Bertolt Brecht in America* by James K. Lyon, 1980; *Bertolt Brecht: Political Theory and Literary Practice* edited by Betty N. Weber and Hubert Heinen, 1980; *The Morality of Doubt: Brecht and the German Dramatic Tradition* by Edward McInnes, 1980; *Brecht* by Jan Needle, 1981; *Brecht's America* by Patty Lee Parmalee, 1981; *The Brecht Commentaries 1943–1980*, 1981, and *The Brecht Memoir*, 1985, both by Eric Bentley; *Brecht in Perspective* edited by Graham Bartram and Anthony Waine, 1982; *Characterisation of Women in the Plays of Bertolt Brecht* by Bernard Fenn, 1982; *Brecht's Early Plays*, 1982, and *Bertolt Brecht*, 1987, both by Ronald Speirs; *Brecht in Exile* by Bruce Cook, 1983; *Brecht: A Biography*, 1983, and *Bertolt Brecht: The Plays*, 1984, both by Ronald Hayman; *Brecht's Poetry: A Critical Study* by Peter Whitaker, 1985; *Lukács and Brecht* by David Pike, 1985; *Exception and Rules: Brecht, Planchon and "The Good Person of Szechwan"* by Pia Kleber, 1987, and *Re-interpreting Brecht: His Influence on Contemporary Drama and Film*, edited by Kleber and Colin Visser, 1990; *Bertolt Brecht: Dialectics, Poetry and Politics* by Peter Brooker, 1988; *Critical Essays on Bertolt Brecht* edited by Siegfried Mews, 1989; *Brecht and the West German Theatre: The Practice and Politics of Interpretation* by John Rouse, 1989; *The Poetry of Brecht* by Philip J. Thomson, 1989; *Postmodern Brecht: A Re-presentation* by Elizabeth Wright, 1989; *Brecht and the Theory of the Media* by Roswitha Müller, 1990; *Leitmotif and Drama: Wagner, Brecht and the Limits of "Epic" Theatre* by H.M. Brown, 1991; *Received Truths: Bertolt Brecht and the Problem of Gestus and Musical Meaning* by Kenneth Fowler, 1991; *The Young Brecht* by Hanns Otto Münsterer, translated by Tom Kuhn and Karen Leeder, 1992; *Citation and Modernity: Derrida, Joyce, and Brecht* by Claudette Sartiliot, 1993; *After Brecht: British Epic Theater* by Janelle Reinelt, 1994; *Brecht and Company: Sex, Politics, and the Making of the Modern Drama*, 1994; *The Cambridge Companion to Brecht*, edited by Peter Thomson and Glendyr Sacks, 1994; *Brecht and France* by Chetana Nagavajara, 1994; *Brecht's Reception in Brazil* by Lorena B. Ellis, 1995; *Elisabeth Hauptmann: Brecht's Silent Collaborator* by Paula Hanssen, 1995; *Brecht: Leben des Galilei* by John J. White, 1996; *Performing Brecht: Forty Years of British Performances* by Margaret Eddershaw, 1996; *Brecht: Mother Courage and Her Children* by Peter Thomson, with conclusion by Viv Gardner, 1997; *Proletarian Performance in Weimar Berlin: Agitprop, Chorus, and Brecht* by Richard Bodek, 1997; *A Bertolt Brecht Reference Companion*, edited by Siegfried Mews, 1997; *Brecht and Method* by Fredric Jameson, 1998; *Bentley on Brecht* by Eric Bentley, 1999; *Space and Time in Epic Theater: The Brechtian Legacy* by Sarah Bryant-Bertrail, 2000; *Brecht Sourcebook*, edited by Carol Martin and Henry Bial, 2000; *Shakespeare, Brecht, and the Intercultural Sign* by Antony Tatlow, 2001.

* * *

Bertolt Brecht is the single most innovative and influential force in 20th-century theatre. He wrote some three dozen plays, and these, together with his theories and productions, prose and verse, are all of a unity, generated by and contributing to a coherent and rational philosophy of man and society. This philosophy is essentially political in the widest sense, defining theatre as the depiction in artistic terms of the interaction of individuals in social situations, affecting each other's lives. Brecht was not satisfied with illusory depiction—the mimetic reproduction of the world, he was a realist who aimed at illuminating his audience's perception of society. He sought to articulate the underlying, objective "truth" of a situation, to explain how "what is" comes about. Such a view rested on the conviction that all human actions are explicable in terms of the workings of society, that "the fate of a man is determined by other men."

For most of his life Brecht was a Marxist. He endeavoured to assimilate into drama the investigative methods and findings of the "new" sciences of sociological, political, and economic analysis, and tried to evolve for the theatre a strategy of writing, acting, and production that would render it adequate to its role in the contemporary world. This he called "epic" theatre because of its fundamental rejection of the primacy of illusion and emotion, and its emphasis on the "narrative," reflective stance of the historian.

In his early plays after World War I Brecht showed a predilection for the rejects of society, victims of the grinding capitalism of the bourgeois world. The "beaten hero," as Walter Benjamin called him, reflected the imbalance of overwhelming economic forces and individual powerlessness. *Baal* showed an asocial hero in an asocial world; *Im Dickicht der Städte* (*Jungle of Cities*) provided a model of the isolated individual's struggle for survival in a capitalist structure; and the dismantling and reassembly of the hero in *Mann ist Mann* (*Man Equals Man*) thematized the manipulation of human beings by exploitative powers. During the period of his systematic study of Marxism after 1926 Brecht evolved from a rebellious to a disciplined supporter of the working-class struggle. The idiosyncratic "learning plays" like *Die Massnahme* (*The Measures Taken*) and *Die Ausnahme und die Regel* (*The Exception and the Rule*) are milestones in Brecht's developing conception of the function of theatre in a social context, offering openly didactic Marxist studies in models of (political) action. Even the apparently innocuous entertainment of *Die Dreigroschenoper* (*The Threepenny Opera*)—audiences have long been captivated by Kurt Weill's catchy tunes—masked a virulent attack on the bandit morality of bourgeois capitalism.

On the accession to power of the Nazi regime in 1933 Brecht immediately went into exile. This caesura paradoxically signalled the start of his most productive period, an astounding output of major plays, theoretical essays, prose writing, and a stream of poetry from 1933 to 1945. It is symptomatic of Brecht's single-mindedness, perseverance, and vision that at this time, driven as he was from one country to another and almost entirely deprived of a German-speaking public—Denmark, Finland, and the United States were his major staging-posts—he created a handful of plays that were to establish his truly international reputation: *Mutter Courage und ihre Kinder* (*Mother Courage and Her Children*), *Galileo* (*The Life of Galileo*), *Der gute Mensch von Sezuan* (*The Good Person of Szechwan*), *Herr Puntila und sein Knecht Matti* (*Mr. Puntila and His Man Matti*), *Der kaukasische Kreidekreis* (*The Caucasian Chalk Circle*). To some extent these plays compromise with the traditional Aristotelian drama from which Brecht had earlier dissociated himself so vehemently. They rely partly for their effect—and certainly for their popularity—on full-bodied characters caught in the classical dilemmas of dramatic heroes. Yet Brecht does ascribe the emotionally absorbing contradictions of human behaviour to the dialectics of society and its distorting, brutalizing effects on human personality.

The Nazis provided Brecht with a precise and concrete target in place of the formless, anonymous capitalism of Marxist theory and rhetoric, for he saw the actual fascist regime in Germany as a manifestation of "the most naked, shameless, oppressive and deceitful form of capitalism." His literary attacks on this virulent menace range from the sober documented realism of *Furcht und Elend des Dritten Reiches* (*The Private Life of the Master Race*), culled from newspaper items and information leaking from inside Germany, to the gangster satire of *Der aufhaltsame Aufstieg des Arturo Ui* (*The Resistible Rise of Arturo Ui*), and a range of vitriolic, elegiac, admonishing, hopeful poems.

After World War II Brecht eventually made his way back to Europe, settling in East Berlin in 1949. Here he was afforded every facility as the most prized cultural figure in the German Democratic Republic; supported by generous subsidies, he founded the world-renowned Berliner Ensemble with his wife, the actress Helene Weigel. Under Brecht's direction this theatre company established a wide-ranging repertoire, including Brecht's own plays as well as his free adaptations of many classics, such as Shakespeare's *Coriolanus* and Molière's *Don Juan*. Brecht also had the freedom and complete control of theatrical resources to try out, alter, and refine his ideas on epic writing, acting, and production. It was largely in these years until his death in 1956 that Brecht's dramatic style and theories were disseminated throughout the world to establish him as the focal point of 20th-century theatre.

The most important element in Brecht's theories was the celebrated "alienation effect" (*Verfremdungseffekt*), a term he used to describe the technique of "distancing" the audience from the play. The purpose of this was to enable the spectator to retain a detached, dispassionate, critical view of the events being enacted on stage, and not to be totally absorbed emotionally with a consequent loss of rational judgement. Brecht demanded that an alienating depiction should be "one that allows the object to be recognized but at the same time makes it appear unfamiliar"; it requires "a technique of taking the human social incidents to be portrayed and labelling them as something striking, something that calls for explanation, and is not to be taken for granted, not just natural. The object of this 'effect' is to allow the spectator to criticize constructively from a social point of view." Alienation, Brecht found, could be induced in many ways. Hence his free borrowing and parodying of other writers, his liberal use of music and songs (along with all the other "sister arts" of theatre), his exploitation of full lighting, placards, masks, "montage" and cinematic techniques—all to break the "atmosphere" of the stage and prevent the mystification of the spectator. By these means Brecht tried to reflect in the dialogue, structure, and production of individual scenes and whole plays the inconsistencies, ironical illogicalities, and dialectical contradictions of history and of individuals. His purpose was to foster insight into the workings of society and open the way to progress by emancipating man's thinking from the rigidities of tradition.

—Arrigo V. Subiotto

See the essays on *Baal*, *The Caucasian Chalk Circle*, *The Good Person of Szechwan*, *The Life of Galileo*, *Mother Courage and Her Children*, and *The Threepenny Opera*.

BREDERO, Gerbrand Adriaensz

Born: Amsterdam, The Netherlands, in 1585. **Career:** Studied painting with Francesco Badens: only one painting survives. Associated with the Amsterdam Rederijkerskamer (Rhetoricians' Club, established by Burgundians in 15th century for staging of plays and pageants) and d'Eglantier; broke to join the Nederduytsche Academie; ensign in Schutterij (local militia). Lived in Amsterdam all his life; friend of Pieter Hooft, *q.v.*, and Hugo Grotius. **Died:** 23 August 1618.

PUBLICATIONS

Collections

Alle de spelen [Complete Plays], edited by P. van Waesberge. 1622.
Werken [Works], edited by J. ten Brink, H.E. Moltzer, G. Kalff, and others. 3 vols., 1890.
Werken [Works], edited by J.A.N. Knuttel. 3 vols., 1918–29.
Verspreid werk [Extended Work], edited by G.A. Stuiveling and B.C. Damsteegt. 1986.

Plays

Treur-spel van Rodd'rick ende Alphonsus [Tragedy of Roderick and Alphonse] (produced 1611). 1616.
Griane (produced 1612). 1616.
Klucht van de koe [Farce of the Cow] (produced 1612). 1619, reprinted 1971.
Klucht van den molenaer [Farce of the Miller] (produced 1613). 1618, reprinted 1971.
Het Moortje [The Little Moor], adaptation of *Eunuchus* by Terence (produced 1615). 1617.
Lucelle. 1616.
De Spaanschen Brabander Ierolimo. 1618; as *The Spanish Brabanter*, translated by H. Dixon Brumble, 1982.
De stomme ridder [The Mute Knight] (produced 1618). 1619.
De Klucht van Symen sonder soeticheyt [The Farce of Simon Without Sweetness]. 1619, reprinted 1971.
Klucht van den hoochduytschen quacksalver [Farce of the German Quack], from Terence. 1619.
Van een huys-man en een barbier [Of a Householder and a Barber]. 1622.
Claes Cloet met een roumantel [Claes Cloet in Penitential Garb]. 1622.
Angeniet, completed by Jan Starter (produced 1628). 1623.
Schijn-heylich [Hypocrite]. 1624.

Verse

Apollo of Ghesangh der Musen [Apollo or Song of the Muses]. 1615.
Geestigh Liedt-Boecxken [Spiritual Verse Book]. 1616; corrected posthumous edition, 1621.
Boertigh, amoreus, en aendachtig groot Lied-Boek [Comic, Amorous, and Religious Verse Book]. 1622, reprinted 1974; two poems and two songs translated by Paul Vincent, in *Dutch Crossing*, 25 and 27, 1985.

*

Bibliography: *G.A. Bredero: Eene bibliographie* by J.H.W. Unger, 1884.

Critical Studies: *Bredero* by J.A.N. Knuttel, 1949; *De Waardering van Gerbr. Adr. Bredero* by J.P. Naeff, 1960; *Memoriaal van Bredero* and *Rondom Bredero, een viertal verkenningen*, both by Garmt

Stuiveling, 1970; *'t Kan verkeren, Leven en werk van Gerbrandt Bredero* by H. Cartens, 1972; *Bredero* edited by M.A. Schenkeveld van der Dussen and others, 1985.

*   *   *

Like his contemporaries Pieter Hooft and Joost van den Vondel, Gerbrand Adriaensz Bredero belongs to the generation of Dutch writers that made the transition between the Middle Ages and the Renaissance. He learned to write in the medieval genres and traditions established and propagated by the Rederijkerskamers (Rhetoricians' Club), but celebrated his greatest successes with works that adhered more closely to the emerging Renaissance poetics.

Bredero's first works for the stage were *kluchten*, or farces, often realistic and sometimes more than a trifle scatological, in the medieval tradition that confronted the audience with its failings in order to cure it of them. Bredero succeeded admirably in the former, as he was to prove again in his farces *Klucht van de koe* [Farce of the Cow], *Klucht van den molenaer* [Farce of the Miller], and *Klucht van den hoochduytschen quacksalver* [Farce of the German Quack]. Like his contemporaries, he wrote for a double audience. The farces and, generally speaking, the works more attributable to the Middle Ages, were aimed at the less educated, whereas the Renaissance comedies were addressed to the educated but written in a way that appealed to every spectator and reader. Of all the Dutch writers of the "Golden 17th Century," Bredero had perhaps the closest personal experience of this dichotomy. Unlike his contemporaries, he did not receive a classical education, although he knew French. As a result, even though he could read the Classics in translation, he did not—with the exception of *Het Moortje* [The Little Moor], a transposition to Amsterdam of Terence's *Eunuchus*—write any of his works on a Classical theme, as other writers of his time did as a matter of course.

Bredero's tragicomedies and poems may be said to occupy a middle position between medieval and Renaissance poetics. The tragicomedies continue the Dutch medieval tradition of the *abele spelen* by dramatizing epic/novelistic sources, while the title of Bredero's final collection of poems very obviously reflects the traditional division of poetry (humorous, amorous, and religious) established by the Rhetoricians. This mid-way position may well have made Bredero's poems popular with the readers of his day; they were given the highest accolade readers could bestow on them at the time—three pirated editions (of which not a single copy survives, suggesting that they were literally "read to pieces") appeared before Bredero himself prepared a more or less authorized fourth one, published posthumously.

Romantic critics, in particular, have tried to reveal Bredero, the man behind the poet, but to little avail. The myth of the *poète maudit*, driven to drink because he could not marry any of the better-educated women he wooed, and who repented on his death bed, has been shattered by the discovery that the very poem often quoted as "proof" of the man's heartfelt repentance was, in fact, a translation of a French original made by the poet interested in a fellow poet's work. Today Bredero the poet is generally considered a consummate craftsman, trying his hand at various genres, not only with a view to emulating them in the Renaissance tradition, but also with a sound instinct for what would go down well with the audiences of his time.

He first established himself as a writer for the theatre which, in his time, led a somewhat precarious existence in Amsterdam under the stern gaze of orthodox Calvinist preachers. While continuing to produce farces, he began to write tragicomedies, modelled not on

Aristotle, but rather on contemporary English and Spanish drama. This "modern" theatre was much more popular than the "classical" comedies and tragedies written for the élite. Bredero found the material for his tragicomedies in the immensely popular Spanish romances of chivalry published, in his time, as frequently in Antwerp (the richest city in the Spanish Empire, a day's journey south of Amsterdam) as in Madrid, and translated into Dutch. They are constructed around the age-old "boy meets, loses, weds girl" sequence. Bredero's own hand can be seen in the transposition of the material to the Netherlands, in particular Amsterdam, the city whose speech he incorporated into many of his works, giving it literary respectability at a time when his contemporaries tried to write a less regionally marked Dutch, more closely modelled on Greek and Latin.

Bredero's most celebrated play is the comedy *De Spaanschen Brabander Ierolimo* (*The Spanish Brabanter*). Its protagonist, Ierolimo, is one of the many immigrants from what is now Flanders, in the north of Belgium, who flocked to Amsterdam after the Spanish armies reconquered Antwerp. These immigrants, usually much richer and better educated than the Amsterdammers themselves, were to no small extent responsible for the phenomenal growth of their adopted city. They also caused enormous resentment, thematized in the play by the exchanges between the would-be rich and educated, foppish and Hispanicized Ierolimo, and his down-to-earth Amsterdam servant Robbeknol, who confirms the native Amsterdammers in the audience in their self-esteem. Even though Bredero used as his source *Lazarillo de Tormes*, recently published in Antwerp, Ierolimo and Robbeknol are to some extent reminiscent of Don Quixote and Sancho Panza. The archetypal nature of both the characters and their situation has allowed them to transcend the context of 17th-century Amsterdam.

Because of the "uncouth" nature of his material, Bredero was held in low esteem by subsequent writers and critics who propagated the ideals of French neo-classicism. By casting him in the role of a *poète maudit*, Romantic critics managed to credit him with a certain acceptability. In recent years, Bredero has regained his popularity—his works are taught in literature courses and, more importantly, staged in theatres. These historical metamorphoses seem fitting for a writer who signed most of his works with the motto "Things change."

—André Lefevere

BRENTANO, Clemens (Maria Wenzeslaus)

Born: Ehrenbreitstein, Germany, 9 September 1778. Grandson of the writer Sophie von La Roche and brother of the writer Bettina von Arnim, *q.v.* Spent his youth in Frankfurt and Koblenz. **Education:** Educated at the University of Bonn, 1794; Halle University, 1794; studied medicine at the University of Jena, 1798–1800. **Family:** Married 1) Sophie Mereau in 1803 (died in childbirth 1806); three children (all deceased in infancy); 2) Auguste Busmann in 1807 (dissolved 1810, divorced 1812). **Career:** Met Achim von Arnim in Göttingen, 1801 and travelled the Rhine with him, 1802; associated with the Heidelberg group of Romantics; founding editor, with von Arnim, of the journal *Zeitung für Einsiedler*, 1808; lived in Bohemia, 1811–13 and Vienna, 1813–14. Amanuensis for the nun Anna Katharina Emmerich, 1817–24. **Died:** 28 July 1842.

PUBLICATIONS

Collections

Die Märchen, edited by Guido Görres. 2 vols., 1847.
Gesammelte Schriften, edited by Christian Brentano. 9 vols., 1851–55.
Ausgewählte Schriften, edited by J. Diel. 2 vols., 1873.
Die Märchen von Clemens Brentano, edited by Hans E. Giehrl. 1955.
Gedichte, Erzählungen, Briefe, edited by Hans Magnus Enzensberger. 1958.
Werke, edited by Friedhelm Kemp. 4 vols., 1963–68.
Gedichte, edited by Wolfgang Frühwald. 1968.
Werke, edited by Max Preitz. 3 vols., 1974.
Sämtliche Werke und Briefe, edited by Jürgen Behrens, Wolfgang Frühwald, and Detlev Lüders. 6 vols., 1975–85.
The Legend of Rosepetal, translated by Anthea Bell. 1985.
Gedichte und Erzählungen, edited by Hans-Georg Werner. 1986.
Romantic Fairy Tales, translated and edited by Carol Tully. 2000.

Plays

Satiren und poetisehe Spiele. Gustav Wasa. 1800.
Die lustigen Musikanten (opera libretto), music by E.T.A. Hoffmann (produced 1805). 1803.
Ponce de Leon. 1804; as *Valeria: oder, Vaterlist* (produced 1804), 1901.
Die Gründung Prags. 1815.
Viktoria und ihre Geschwister mit fliegenden Fahnen und brennender Lunte. 1817.
Aloys und Imelde, edited by Agnes Harnack. 1912.

Fiction

Godwi; oder, Das steinerne Bild der Mutter. 1801.
Entweder wunderbare Geschichte von Bogs dem Uhrmacher, wie er zwar alas menschliche Leben längst verlassen, nun aber doch, nach vielen musikalischen Leiden zu Wasser und zu Lande, in die bürgerliche Schützengesellschaft aufgenommen zu werden Hoffnung hat; oder, die über die Ufer der badischen Wochenschrift als Beilage ausgetretene Konzert-Anzeige, with Joseph von Görres. 1807.
Geschichte vom braven Kasperl und dem schönen Annerl. 1817; published separately, 1838; as *Honor; or, The Story of Brave Caspar and the Fair Annerl*, translated by T.W. Appell, 1847; as *The Story of Just Caspar and Fair Annie*, translated by Helene Scher, in *Four Romantic Tales*, 1975.
Die drei Nüsse. 1834.
Gockel, Hinkel, und Gackeleia (stories). 1838; as *The Wondrous Tale of Cocky, Clucky, and Cackle*, translated by C.W. Heckethorn, 1889; as *The Tale of Gockel, Hinkel and Gacketiah*, translated by Doris Orgel, 1961.
Die mehreren Wehmüller und ungarischen Nationalgesichter. 1843.
Fairy Tales from Brentano, translated by Kate Freiligrath Kroeker. 1885.
New Fairy Tales from Brentano, translated by Kate Freiligrath Kroeker. 1888.
Das Märchen von dem Baron von Hüpfenstich (stories). 1918.
Die Schachtel mit der Friedenspuppe, edited by Josef Körner. 1922.
Chronika eines fahrenden Schülers (stories). 1923.

Verse

Legende von der heiligen Marina. 1841.
Romanzen vom Rosenkranz. 1852.
Gedichte. 1854.

Other

Universitati Litterariae Kantate auf den 15 October 1810. 1810.
Der Philister vor, in und nach der Geschichte. 1811.
Rheinübergang; Kriegsrundgesang. 1814.
Das Lied vom Korporal. 1815.
Das Mosel-Eisgangs-Lied von einer wunderbar erhaltenen Familie und einem traurig untergegangenen Magdlein in dem Dorf Lay bei Koblenz. 1830.
Die Barmherzigen Schwestern in Bezug auf Armen-und Krankenpflege; Nebst einem Bericht über das Bürgerhospital in Koblenz und erläuternden Beilagen. 1831.
Das bittere Leiden unseres Herrn Jesu Christi. Nach den Betrachtungen der gottseligen Klosterfrau Anna Katharina Emmerich. 1833; as *The Passion of Our Lord Jesus Christ According to the Revelations of Anna Catharina Emmerich,* 1914.
Rothkehlchens, Liebseelchens, Ermordung und Begräbnis. 1843.
Der unglückliche Franzose, oder der deutschen Freiheit Himmelfahrt, ein Schattenspiel mit Bildern, edited by Christian Brentano. 1850.
Leben der heil. Jungfrau Maria. Nach den Betrachtungen der gottseligen Anna Katharina Emmerich. 1852; as *Das Marienleben nach Betrachtungen der Anna Katherina Emmerich,* edited by Claire Brauflacht, 1952; as *The Life of the Blessed Virgin Mary from the Visions of Anne Catherine Emmerich,* translated by Michael Palairet, 1954.
Das Leben unseres Herrn und Heilandes Jesu Christi, edited by Karl E. Schmöger. 3 vols., 1858–60; as *The Life of Our Lord and Saviour Jesus Christ, combined with the Bitter Passion of the Life of Mary from the Revelations of Anne Catherine Emmerich as Recorded in the Journals of Clemens Brentano,* 1954.
Lied von eines Studenten Ankunft in Heidelberg. 1882.
Briefe an Johann Georg. 1888.
Briefwechsel zwischen Clemens Brentano und Sophie Mereau, edited by Heinz Amelung. 1908.
Clemens Brentano and Edward von Steinle, edited by Alexander von Bernus and Alfons M. von Steinel. 1909.
Clemens Brentano und Minna Reichenbach. Ungedruckte Briefe des Dichters, edited by W. Limburger. 1921.
Rheinmärchen: für die romantische Gemeinde neu bearbeitet, edited by Vereger Werneck. 1926.
Satiren und Parodien, edited by Andreas Müller. 1935.
Das unsterbliche Leben. Unbekannte Briefe von Clemens Brentano, edited by Wilhelm Schellberg and Friedrich Fuchs. 1939.
Clemens und Bettina: Geschwisterbriefe, edited by Ina Seidel. 1948.
Briefe, edited by Friedrich Seebass. 2 vols., 1951.
Briefwechsel mit Heinrich Remigius Sauerländer, edited by Anton Krättli. 1962.
Briefe an Emile Linder, edited by Wolfgang Frühwald. 1969.
Clemens Brentano (correspondence), edited by Werner Vordtriede and Gabriele Bartenschläger. 1970.
Clemens Brentano, Philipp Otto Runge: Briefwechsel, edited by Konrad Feilchenfeldt. 1974.
Visionen und Leben: Anna Katharina Emmerich aufgezeichnet, edited by Anton Brieger. 1974.

Lebe der Liebe und liebe das Leben: der Briefwechsel von Clemens Brentano und Sophie Mereau. 1981.
Freundschaftsbriefe: Achim von Arnim und Clemens Brentano: vollständige und kritische Edition von Hartwig Schultz. 1998.
Editor, with Sophie Brentano, *Spanische und italienische Novellen.* 2 vols., 1804–06.
Editor, with Ludwig Achim von Arnim, *Des Knaben Wunderhorn: Alte deutsche Lieder.* 3 vols., 1806–08; translated in part by Margarete Münsterberg as "The Boy's Magic Horn," in *The German Classics of the Nineteenth and Twentieth Centuries,* edited by Kuno Francke and W.G. Howard, vol. 5, 1913.
Editor, *Der Goldfaden: Eine Schöne alte Geschichte,* by Jörg Wickram. 1809.
Editor, *Trutz Nachtigall, ein geistlich poetisches Lustwäldlein,* by Friedrich Spee. 1817.
Editor, *Goldnes Tugendbuch,* by Friedrich Spee. 2 vols., 1829.

*

Bibliography: *Clemens Brentano: Ein Lebensbild nach gedruckten und ungedruckten Quellen* by Johannes B. Diel and Wilhelm Kreiten, 2 vols., 1877–78.

Critical Studies: *Romantic Orpheus: Profiles of Clemens Brentano,* 1974, and *Clemens Brentano,* 1981, both by John F. Fetzer; "Anxiety of the Spirit: Brentano and Arnim" by Eric A. Blackall, in *The Novels of the German Romantics,* 1983; *Negative Spring: Crisis Imagery in the Works of Brentano, Lenau, Rilke, and T.S. Eliot* by David B. Dickens, 1989; *Poetic Wreaths: Art, Death and Narration in the Märchen of Clemens Brentano* by Lawrence O. Frye, 1989; *Schwarzer Schmetterling: zwanzig Kapitel aus dem Leben des romantischen Dichters Clemens Brentano* by Hartwig Schultz, 2000.

* * *

Clemens Brentano's work is both intensely personal and extensively reflective. The contemporary satire in early works such as *Gustav Wasa* and *Entweder wunderbare Geschichte von Bogs dem Uhrmacher* [Bogs, The Watchmaker] made them effective only within the age they depicted. In spite of their linguistic virtuosity they are now considered merely as literary-historical documents.

If the same fate has been shared by Brentano's first novel *Godwi,* it is due mainly to the overly complex plot and the often slight characterization, both typical failings of the 18th-century novel. There is much in this work that demonstrates the influence of the Romantic school. The construction of the narrative in the form of letters, with each character presenting their own view of events, is reminiscent of Ludwig Tieck's *William Lovell* and reflects a modern, Romantic awareness of reality as a purely subjective category. The epistolary framework breaks down in the second part of the work, and in discussions between the main character and the fictional author on the writing of the novel the fiction reflects on itself as fiction: an illustration of Friedrich Schlegel's theory of "poetry of poetry." *Godwi* also confirms to Schlegel's concept of the novel as a mixed form, incorporating prose, lyric, and drama: a principle which was to characterize all Brentano's work.

Brentano's receptiveness to outside influence explains the importance he placed on joint literary ventures. He worked with Achim von Arnim on the collection of folktales *Des Knaben Wunderhorn* (*The Boy's Magic Horn*) and with Joseph yon Görres on "Bogs, The

Watchmaker.'' His *Romanzen vom Rosenkranz* [Romances of the Rosary] was conceived in conjunction with illustrations by the artist Philipp Otto Runge, and Brentano's interest in the project faded after Runge's death. More significantly, Brentano's own work is ''contaminated'' by outside influences. Rather than merely copying or quoting, this procedure involves the reworking of sources into a new and personal construct. In the editing of *The Boy's Magic Horn* this entailed both contributors adapting their sources and even inserting examples of their own work, while in the publication of the poetry of Brentano's wife Sophie Mereau and later of Luise Hensel, and finally in the recording of the visions of the ecstatic nun Anna Katharina Emmerick, Brentano interwove his own ideas inextricably with those of his subject.

Subjective adaptation also informs Brentano's creative writing. Much is inspired by old material, but all is imbued with the poet's own personality and style. Wherever Brentano turns to sources he blends report with interpretation, fact with opinion. This results in a complex mix of history and mythology in its widest sense in the prose fragment ''Poor Raymond,'' the drama *Die Gründung Prags* [The Foundation of Prague], the revised version of the fairytale *Gockel, Hinkel and Gackeliah*, and the ambitious cycle of poetry *Romanzen vom Rosenkranz*, which was to unite Biblical themes (the flight into Egypt; original sin and redemption) with legend (Tannhäuser), history (the arrival of the gypsies in Europe; the Crusades), and mythology (the origin of the Rosary).

Brentano's Italian fairytales are based on Giovanni Battista Basile's *Il Pentamerone* (*The Pentamerone*), but Brentano devises his own tales, which become tales for their own sake, told and enjoyed for the linguistic exuberance of the plays on words, sounds, and meanings, and the verbal leitmotifs which culminate in the endless variations of the egg theme in ''Gockel and Hinkel.'' His Rhine fairy-tales are inspired by the traditional folktales of this area, but again Brentano allows his fertile imagination full rein, and these stories, with their digressive, oral style, are a further testimony to his talent as a storyteller and to his linguistic inventiveness. Brentano's true virtuosity in these tales, however, lies in his amalgamation of simplicity and subtlety in both structure and content. These are sophisticated revisions of children's stories, which do not lose the freshness and vigour of the original.

Brentano's poetry likewise combines old and new, spontaneity and self-awareness. In ''The Song of the Spinning-Woman'' and ''On the Rhine'' the simple language and tone of the folksong is enriched by subtle imagery and intricate construction. In the poem ''Spring Song'' Brentano takes a medieval love lyric as the basis for a complex personal statement. His sensitivity to language is evident in the exploitation of sound, rhythm, and rhyme, for example, in ''Nightingale'' or in Radlauf's song in ''The Story of Miller Radlauf.''

It is perhaps in his poetry that Brentano expresses his most personal feelings. Erotic and religious sentiments are repeatedly interlinked, for example, in ''Love's Despair at Love'' and ''The Evening Breezes Blow,'' reflecting his unceasing attempt to reconcile these two kinds of love and achieve sanctuary from isolation. The poem ''A Servant's Spring Cry from the Depths'' is the anguished cry of a sinner for redemption.

Brentano's work on *The Boy's Magic Horn* and the folktale orientation of his own poetic creations indicate his profound interest in the common people and his genuine belief in the aesthetic stature of their art. ''The Rose,'' ''The Minstrel,'' and ''The Chronicle of the Travelling Scholar'' turn to the idealized simplicity of the middle ages to depict young and innocent men in harmony with God and

nature. The naïvety is, however, studied. These works express the longing for innocence by the sinner, for simplicity by the sophisticate. In such works the self-conscious author adopts the mask of spontaneity, aware that this is a game. In the poem ''On the Rhine'' the mask is of a fisherman, dreaming of his dead lover. In the final stanza the third-person narrative voice reveals itself as a first-person lyrical self, expressing personal experience in the guise of objective report. In the poem ''Lore Lay'' the same device is employed in triplicate.

It is in this sense that art becomes understood as artificiality in Brentano's work, reflected, for example, in the melancholy Johannes feels when comparing his mother's song to that of the nightingale (representing nature and naturalness) in the poem ''The Song of the Spinning-Woman,'' in ''The Chronicle of the Travelling Scholar,'' and in the despair of the siren in the poem ''Lore Lay,'' whose evil magic is poetry itself. The poet's alienation and his tragic yearning for lost innocence and harmony are articulated in the poems ''Echoes of Beethoven's Music'' and ''When the Crippled Weaver Dreams'' which, like *Godwi*, exemplify modern aesthetic self-reflection.

In the novella *Geschichte vom braven Kasperl und dem schönen Annerl* (*The Story of Just Caspar and Fair Annie*), the contrast of naïve and self-aware is presented through the confrontation of a poet, torn by religious and poetic selfdoubt, with an old woman, a genuine folk figure secure in her beliefs, who weaves her personal experience quite unconsciously into an artistic tale. The poet as scribe to the natural folkpoet was the role Brentano wished for himself, but he never succeeded in eliminating subjectivity and self-consciousness from his work.

—Sheila J. Dickson

See the essay on *The Story of Just Caspar and Fair Annie*.

BRETON, André (Robert)

Born: Tinchebray, France, 19 February 1896. **Education:** Educated at Collége Chaptal, Paris, 1906–12; Faculté de Médecine, Paris, 1913–15. **Military Service:** Served as medical assistant in army psychiatric centres, 1915–19, and medical director of Ecole de Pilotage, Poitiers, 1939–40. **Family:** Married 1) Simone Kahn in 1921 (divorced); 2) Jacqueline Lamba in 1934 (divorced), one daughter; 3) Elisa Bindhoff in 1945. **Career:** Co-founding editor, with Louis Aragon *q.v.* and Philippe Soupault, *Littérature*, 1919–24; founded Bureau of Surrealist Research, 1924; editor, *La Révolution Surréaliste*, 1925–29, *Le Surréalisme au Service de la Révolution*, 1930–33, and *Minotaure*, 1933–39; joined the Communist Party, 1927; broadcaster, Voice of America, 1942–45; editor, *VVV*, 1942–44; director, Galerie à l'Étoile Scellée, 1952–54; editor, *Le Surréalisme Même*, 1956–57. Organized exhibitions of Surrealist art from 1936. **Died:** 28 September 1966.

PUBLICATIONS

Collection

Oeuvres complètes [Pléiade Edition], edited by Marguerite Bonnet. 1988–.

Verse

Mont de piété. 1919.

Les Champs magnétiques, with Philippe Soupault. 1920; as *The Magnetic Fields*, translated by David Gascoyne, 1985.

Clair de terre. 1923; as *Earthlight*, translated by Bill Zavatsky and Zack Rogow, 1993.

Ralentir travaux, with René Char and Paul Éluard. 1930.

L'Union libre. 1931.

Le Revolver à cheveux blancs. 1932.

L'Air de l'eau. 1934.

Le Château étoilé. 1937.

Fata morgana. 1941; as *Fata Morgana*, translated by Clark Mills, 1969.

Les États-Généraux. 1943.

Pleine marge. 1943.

Young Cherry Trees Secured Against Hares, translated by Edouard Roditi. 1946.

Ode à Charles Fourier. 1947; as *Ode to Charles Fourier*, translated by Kenneth White, 1969.

Martinique charmeuse de serpents. 1948.

Poèmes. 1948.

Au regard des divinités. 1949.

Constellations. 1959.

Le là. 1961.

Selected Poems, translated by Kenneth White. 1969.

Poems (bilingual edition), translated by Jean-Pierre Cauvin and Mary Ann Caws. 1982.

Earthlight, translated by Bill Zavatsky and Zack Rogow. 1993.

Other

Manifeste du surréalisme; Poisson soluble. 1924, enlarged edition, 1929.

Les Pus perdus (essays). 1924; as *The Lost Steps*, translated by Mark Polizzotti, 1996.

Légitime défense. 1926.

Introduction au discours sur le peu de réalité. 1927.

Le Surréalisme et la peinture. 1928, enlarged edition, 1965; as *Surrealism and Painting*, translated by Simon Watson Taylor, 1972.

Nadja. 1928, revised edition, 1963; as *Nadja*, translated by Richard Howard, 1960.

Second manifeste du surréalisme. 1930.

L'Immaculée Conception, with Paul Éluard. 1930.

Misère de la poésie: "L'Affaire Aragon" devant l'opinion publique. 1932.

Les Vases communicants. 1932; as *Communicating Vessels*, translated by Mary Ann Caws and Geoffrey T. Harris, 1990.

Point du jour (essays). 1934, revised editions, 1970, 1992; as *Break of Day*, translated by Mark Polizzotti and Mary Ann Caws, 1999.

Qu'est-ce que le surrélisme? 1934; as *What Is Surrealism?*, translated by David Gascoyne, 1936.

Position politique du surréalisme. 1935.

Notes sur la poésie, with Paul Éluard. 1936.

L'Amour fou. 1937; as *Mad Love*, translated by Mary Ann Caws, 1987.

Arcane 17. 1944, enlarged edition, 1947; as *Arcanum 17: With Apertures Grafted to the End*, translated by Zack Rogow, 1994.

Situation du surréalisme entre les deux guerres. 1945.

Yves Tanguy (bilingual edition). 1946.

Les Manifestes du surréalisme. 1947, revised editions, 1955, 1962; complete edition, 1972; as *Manifestations of Surrealism*, translated by Richard Seaver and Helen R. Lane, 1969.

La Lampe duns l'horloge. 1948.

Flagrant délit: Rimbaud devant la conjuration de l'imposture et du truquage. 1949.

Entretiens 1913–1952. 1952, revised edition, 1973.

La Clé des champs (essays). 1953; as *Free Rein*, translated by Michel Parmentier and Jacqueline d'Amboise, 1995.

Toyen, with Jindrich Heisler and Benjamin Péret. 1953.

Adieu ne plaise. 1954.

Farouche à quatre feuilles, with others. 1954.

L'Art magique, with Gérard Legrand. 1957.

Pierre Moliner: Un film de Raymond Borde. 1964.

Perspective cavaliére (essays), edited by Marguerite Bonnet. 1970.

Conversations: The Autobiography of Surrealism with André Parinaud, 1993.

The Automatic Message: The Magnetic Fields: The Immaculate Conception with Paul Éluard and Philippe Soupault, translated by David Gascoyne, Antony Melville and Jon Graham, 1997.

Editor, *Trajectoire du rêve.* 1938.

Editor, with Paul Éluard, *Dictionnaire abrégé du surréalisme.* 1938.

Editor, *Anthologie de l'humour noir.* 1940(?), enlarged edition, 1950; as *Anthology of Black Humor*, translated by Mark Polizzotti, 1997.

*

Bibliography: *André Breton: A Bibliography* by Michael Sheringham, 1972; *André Breton: A Bibliography (1972–1989)* by Elza Adamowicz, 1992.

Critical Studies: *Surrealism and the Literary Imagination: A Study of Breton and Bachelard*, 1966, *The Poetry of Dada and Surrealism*, 1970, and *Breton*, 1971, all by Mary Ann Caws; *Breton, Arbiter of Surrealism* by Clifford Browder, 1967; *André Breton, Magus of Surrealism* by Anna E. Balakian, 1971, and *André Breton Today* edited by Balakian and Rudolf E. Kuenzli, 1989; *André Breton and the Basic Concepts of Surrealism* by Michael Carrouges, translated by Maura Prendergast, 1974; *Breton and the First Principles of Surrealism* by Franklin Rosemont, 1978; *Breton: "Nadja"* by Roger Cardinal, 1986; *André Breton: Sketch for an Early Portrait* by J.H. Matthews, 1986; *André Breton the Poet* by Keith Aspley, 1989; *Revolution of the Mind: The Life of André Breton* by Mark Polizzoti, 1995; *Issues of Otherness and Identity in the Works of Izquierdo, Kahlo, Artaud, and Breton* by Gina McDaniel Tarver, 1996; *André Breton* by Mary Ann Caws, 1996; *Literary Polemics: Bataille, Sartre, Valéry, Breton* by Suzanne Guerlac, 1997.

*   *   *

Founder of the Surrealist movement, André Breton was one of the 20th century's great writers; his highly poetic prose, even more than his poems, bears witness to a magnetic power of language as the equivalent of thought.

Believing that we can remake the world by our imagination as it is activated by and through our words, Breton was able to persuade, by those words, a whole generation of thinkers and artists to pay attention to their inner gifts and intuitions as they could be seen not only to respond to the world outside but even to discover in that world "an answer to a question we were not conscious of having." By what he called the law of objective chance, it comes about that the inner and the outer experiences mingle in an ongoing constant communion he compared to the scientific experiment of *Les Vases communicants* (*Communicating Vessels*). Like the mingling of day and night, life and death, up and down, the two contraries are held in balance and provide the dynamism of the activated images which make over, for us, what we live by, ''the unacceptable human condition.''

Surrealism is, then, by the vision of Breton, turned towards a positive future possibility; surrealist sight insists—with the Zen master Basho—that, instead of, for example, removing the wings from a dragonfly and calling it a red pepper, we add wings to the pepper to have it become that dragonfly. The attitude is characteristic of the entire movement, whose comportment Breton repeatedly defined as ''lyric.''

In his own works, Breton stressed the overwhelming power and frightening effect of love *L'Amour fou* (*Mad Love*) as it participates in the irrational mystery of complete surprise. Walking amid the garbage peelings on the streets of the marketplace at midnight, wondering whether it is not too late to turn back, the narrator and the poet are one with the observer of that love itself, always to be kept as marvellous, safe from the ''null and void moments'' that go to make up an ordinary life.

Nadja, Breton's quite unordinary heroine, herself mad, is no more adapted to ''real'' life than were the alchemists, with whom Breton feels such a bond—they aimed at transmuting our own base metal into our highest or golden selves. The impulse towards the arcane (*Arcane 17*) in no way rules out an openness to the simple everyday things; nor does madness invalidate the love of the marvellous, that child-like expectation of the next moment, this *disponibilité* or openness to chance that infuses surrealist writing and thinking at its best.

Nor was Breton separated from dailiness: against the worst of it, he insisted that art had to maintain its own urgency, ''for the problem is no longer, as it used to be, whether a canvas can hold its own in a wheat field, but whether it can stand up against the daily paper, open or closed, which is a jungle.'' Art has to hold good against famine, against reality, and against what people have done and thought.

Surrealism, as Breton conceived it, was directed against habit and against the predictable: the famous experiments in automatic writing, made to unleash the dams of imagination as the Surrealist manifestos point out, provocatively, worked towards this end, as did the images in the poems, upsetting to ''normal'' ways of seeing. But always the style and the vision of Breton went far past the limits of any experiment, and worked together to—as he put it—''prevent the paths of desire from being overgrown.''

In a time of despair and uncaring, Breton may be read as resolutely turned towards what he perceived as just, with an ardour we know as genuine, and with a poetic temperament that is all too rare.

—Mary Ann Caws

See the essays on ''Free Union,'' *Mad Love*, and *Ode to Charles Fourier*.

BROCH, Hermann

Born: Vienna, Austria, 1 November 1886. **Education:** Educated privately, 1892–96; Imperial and Royal State Secondary School, Vienna, 1897–1904; Technical College for Textile Manufacture, Vienna, 1904–06; Spinning and Weaving College, Mülhausen, 1906–07. **Military Service:** Administrator for Austrian Red Cross during World War I. **Family:** Married 1) Franziska von Rothermann in 1909 (divorced 1923), one son; 2) AnneMarie Meier-Gräfe in 1949. **Career:** Managed family's factory in Teesdorf, 1907–27; reviewer, *Moderne Welt*, Vienna, 1919; studied mathematics, philosophy, and pyschology, Vienna University, 1926–30; then writer; arrested by the Nazis and detained briefly, 1938; moved to London, 1938; then settled in the United States; involved in refugee work, from 1940; became American citizen, 1944; fellow, Saybrook College, Yale University, New Haven, Connecticut, 1949. **Awards:** Guggenheim fellowship, 1941. **Member:** American Academy, 1942. **Died:** 30 May 1951.

PUBLICATIONS

Collections

Gesammelte Werke, edited by Felix Stössinger and others. 10 vols., 1953–61.
Kommentierte Werkausgabe, edited by Paul Michael Lützeler. 13 vols., 1976–86.

Fiction

Die Schlafwandler: Ein Romantrilogie. 1952; as *The Sleepwalkers: A Trilogy*, translated by Edwin and Willa Muir, 1932.
   Pasenow; oder, Die Romantik—1888. 1931; as *The Romantic*, translated by Willa Muir and Edwin Muir, 2000.
   Esch; oder, Die Anarchie—1903. 1931.
   Hugenau; oder, Die Sachlichkeit—1918. 1932.
Die unbekannte Grösse. 1933; as *The Unknown Quantity*, translated by Edwin and Willa Muir, 1935.
Der Tod des Vergil. 1945; as *The Death of Virgil*, translated by Jean Starr Untermeyer, 1945.
Die Schuldlosen. 1950; as *The Guiltless*, translated by Ralph Manheim, 1974.
Der Versucher, edited by Felix Stössinger. In *Gesammelte Werke*, 4. 1953.
Der Bergroman, edited by Frank Kress and Hans Albert Maier. 4 vols., 1969.
Barbara und andere Novellen, edited by Paul Michael Lützeler. 1973.
Die Verzauberung, edited by Paul Michael Lützeler, 1976; as *The Spell*, translated by H.F. Broch de Rothermann. 1987.

Plays

Die Entsühnung (produced 1934).
Aus der Luft gegriffen; oder, die Geschäfte des Baron Laborde (produced 1981).

Other

Zur Universitätsreform, edited by Götz Wienold. 1969.
Gedanken zur Politik, edited by Dieter Hildebrand. 1970.
Briefwechsel 1930–1951, with Daniel Brody, edited by Bertold Hack and Marietta Kleiss. 1971.
Völkerbund-Resolution, edited by Paul Michael Lützeler. 1973.

Hofmannsthal und seine Zeit: Eine Studie. 1974; as *Hugo von Hofmannsthal and His Time: The European Imagination 1860–1920*, edited and translated by Michael P. Steinberg, 1984.

Menschenrecht und Demokratie: Politische Schriften, edited by Paul Michael Lützeler. 1978.

Briefe über Deutschland, 1945–1949: Die Korrespondenz mit Volkmar von Zühlsdorff, edited by Paul Michael Lützeler. 1986.

*

Critical Studies: *Broch* by Theodore Ziolkowski, 1964; *The Sleep-walkers: Elucidations of Broch's Trilogy* by Dorrit C. Cohn, 1966; *The Novels of Hermann Broch* by Malcolm R. Simpson, 1977; *Hermann Broch* by Ernestine Schlant, 1978; *Hermann Broch: Eine Biographie* by Paul Michael Lützeler, 1985, translated by Janice Furness, 1987; *Sprache und Metaphorik in Hermann Broch's Roman Der Tod des Vergil* by Barbara Lube, 1986; *Sympathy for the Abyss: A Study in the Novel of German Modernism: Kafka, Broch, Musil, and Thomas Mann* by Stephen D. Dowden, 1986, and *Broch: Literature, Philosophy, Politics* edited by Dowden, 1988; *Hermann Broch* by Rudolf Koester, 1987; *Culture and Catastrophe: German and Jewish Confrontations with National Socialism and Other Crises* by Steven E. Aschheim, 1996; *The Problem of Autonomy in the Works of Hermann Broch* by Robert Halsall, 2000.

* * *

At the age of 42, Hermann Broch gave up a distinguished career in industry to devote himself to writing. His first major work, the trilogy *Die Schlafwandler* (*The Sleepwalkers*), is set in Germany between 1880 and 1918. It depicts a society in crisis: the old social and political order is breaking up, traditional ethical and religious tenets are being challenged. People, left without moral guidance, seem like sleep-walkers, only dimly aware of their course of action.

The first novel of the trilogy, *Pasenow; oder, Die Romantik—1888* [The Romantic], portrays the symptoms of decline among the aristocracy; in the second part, *Esch; oder, Die Anarchie—1903* [The Anarchist], a bookkeeper, failing in his search for justice, turns against society. The last novel, *Hugenau; oder, Die Sachlichkeit—1918* [The Realist], set during the revolution of 1918, shows how the total disregard for moral values leads to betrayal and murder.

In the course of writing, Broch began to experiment with new modes of narration. His essay "James Joyce und die Gegenwart" ["James Joyce and the Present"] (1936) is a tribute to Joyce and to the modern novel in general. It also reveals much about Broch's own thoughts about art. He rejects the purely aesthetic point of view as "Kitsch," arguing that as science promotes man's material well-being, art should set standards for his ethical conduct. The main theme of Broch's works is a plea for a re-evaluation of moral values without which he thought the political and social decay of modern society could not be prevented.

Besides being a prolific essayist, Broch wrote plays and poems which, however, do not seem to measure up to his accomplishments as a novelist.

In the light of Broch's earlier dedication to modern narrative techniques, his next major work, *Der Bergroman* (which went through three versions), marked a surprise return to the traditional form of the novel. The narrator is an old country doctor who witnesses with horror and some fascination how a charlatan is able to gain, at least for a short time, control over the minds of his villagers.

Der Tod des Vergil (*The Death of Virgil*), considered by many critics to be Broch's greatest achievement, depicts in the form of inner monologue Virgil's visions and dreams during the last 18 hours before his death.

Broch's last work, the short story cycle *Die Schuldlosen* (*The Guiltless*), is essentially a reworking of earlier published material. *The Death of Virgil*, therefore, remains, as Broch had wished it to be, his true farewell as a writer.

—Helena Szépe

See the essays on *The Death of Virgil* and *The Sleepwalkers*.

BRODSKII, Iosif (Aleksandrovich)

Also known as Joseph Brodsky. **Born:** Leningrad, Union of Soviet Socialist Republics, 24 May 1940; emigrated to the United States in 1972, naturalized 1977. **Education:** Educated at schools in Leningrad to age 15. **Family:** Married; one son and one daughter. **Career:** Convicted as a "social parasite" in 1964 and served 20 months of a five-year sentence of hard labour in the far north; later exiled by the Soviet government; poet-in-residence and special lecturer, University of Michigan, Ann Arbor, 1972–73, 1974–80; has taught at Queen's College, City University of New York, Columbia University, New York, New York University, Smith College, Northampton, Massa-chusetts, Amherst College, Massachusetts, and Hampshire College. Andrew W. Mellon Professor of literature, Mount Holyoke College, South Hadley, Massachusetts, 1990–96. **Awards:** Guggenheim fel-lowship; MacArthur fellowship; Mondello prize (Italy), 1979; National Book Critics' Circle award, 1987; Nobel prize for literature, 1987; Légion d'honneur (France), 1991. D.Litt.: Yale University, New Haven, Connecticut, 1978; Oxford University, 1991. United States Poet Laureate, 1991–92. **Member:** American Academy of Arts and Letters: resigned in 1987 to protest against Evgenii Evtushenko, *q.v.*, being made an honorary member; corresponding member, Bavarian Academy of Sciences. **Died:** Of heart failure, 28 January 1996, in Brooklyn Heights, New York.

PUBLICATIONS

Verse

Stikhotvoreniia i poemy [Poems and Narrative Verse]. 1965.

Elegy to John Donne and Other Poems, edited and translated by Nicholas Bethell. 1967.

Ostanovka v pustyne [A Halt in the Wilderness]. 1970; corrected edition, 1988.

Selected Poems, translated by George L. Kline. 1973.

Debut, translated by Carl R. Proffer. 1973.

The Funeral of Bobo, translated by Richard Wilbur. 1974.

Three Slavic Poets, with Tymoteusz Karpowicz and Djordje Nikolic, edited by John Rezek. 1975.

Konets prekrasnoi epokhi: Stikhotvoreniia 1964–1971 [The End of the Belle Epoque: Poetry]. 1977.

Chast' rechi: Stikhotvoreniia 1972–1976 [A Part of Speech: Poetry]. 1977.

V Anglii [In England]. 1977.

A Part of Speech, translated by Anthony Hecht and others. 1980.

Verses on the Winter Campaign 1980, translated by Alan Meyers. 1981.

Rimskie elegii [Roman Elegies]. 1982.

Novye stasy k Avguste: Stikhi k M.B. 1962–1982 [New Stanzas to Augusta: Poems to M.B.]. 1983.

Uraniia [Urania]. 1987.

To Urania: Selected Poems 1965–1985, translated by Brodskii and others. 1988.

Primechaniia paporotnika [A Fern's Commentary]. 1990.

Osennii krik iastreba [The Hawk's Cry in Autumn]. 1990.

Stikhotvoreniia [Poetry]. 1990.

Chast' rechi: Izbrannye stikhi 1962–1989 [A Part of Speech: Selected Poems]. 1990.

Nazidanie [Edification]. 1990.

Pis'ma rimskomu drugu [Letters to a Roman Friend]. 1991.

Kholmy: bol'shie stikhotvoreniia i poemy [Hills: Poetry and Narrative Verse]. 1991.

Rozhdestvenskie stikhi [Christmas Poems]. 1992.

Forma vremeni [The Form of Time] (vol. 2 includes essays and plays). 2 vols., 1992.

Kappadokia: stikhi [Cappadocia: Poems]. 1993.

Izbrannoe [Selected Poems]. 1993.

Izbrannye stikhotvoreniia [Selected Poetry]. 1994.

Persian Arrow, with etchings by Edik Steinberg, 1994.

So Forth: Poems, 1996.

Collected Poems in English, edited by Ann Kjellberg, 2000.

Plays

Mramor. 1984; as *Marbles: A Play in Three Acts*, translated by Alan Myers, 1989.

Demokratiia!/Démocratie!, translated by Véronique Schiltz (bilingual edition in Russian and French). 1990; translated as *Democracy*, 1990.

Other

Less than One: Selected Essays (in English). 1986.

The Nobel Lecture. 1988.

Razmerom podlinnika [In the Metre of the Original] (essays; includes essays by others about Brodskii's work). 1990.

Ballada o malen'kom buksire: detskie stikhi [Ballad about a Small Tugboat: Children's Poems]. 1991.

Bog sokhraniaet vse: stikhi i perevody [God Preserves All: Poems and Translations]. 1992.

Watermark. 1992.

Vspominaia Akhmatovu [Remembering Akhmatova] (interview), with Solomon Volkov. 1992.

Sochineniia [Works]. 4 vols., 1992–95.

On Grief and Reason: Essays, 1995

Conversations with Joseph Brodsky: A Poet's Journey Through the Twentieth Century by Solomon Volkov, translated by Marian Schwartz, 1998.

Portrait of the Poet: 1978–1996: Joseph Brodsky by Marianna Volkova, 1998.

Editor, with Carl R. Proffer, *Modern Russian Poets on Poetry: Blok, Mandelstam, Pasternak, Mayakovsky, Gumilev, Tsvetaeva*. 1982.

Editor, *An Age Ago: A Selection of Nineteenth-Century Russian Poetry*. 1988.

*

Bibliography: by George L. Kline, in *Ten Bibliographies of Twentieth Century Russian Literature*, 1977; in *Joseph Brodsky: A Poet for Our Time* by Valentina Polukhina, 1989.

Critical Studies: "A Struggle against Suffocation" by Czeslaw Miłosz, in *New York Review of Books*, 14 August 1980; *Joseph Brodsky: A Poet for Our Time*, 1989, and *Brodsky Through the Eyes of His Contemporaries*, 1992, both by Valentina Polukhina, and *Joseph Brodsky's Poetics and Aesthetics* edited by Polukhina and Lev Loseff, 1990; *Joseph Brodsky and the Creation of Exile* by David M. Bethea, 1994; *The Poet as Traveler* by Alice J. Speh, 1996; *Joseph Brodsky and the Baroque* by David MacFadyen, 1998; *Joseph Brodsky: The Art of the Poem*, edited by Lev Loseff and Valentina Polukhina, 1999; *Styles of Ruin: Joseph Brodsky and the Postmodernist Elegy* by David Rigsbee, 1999; *Joseph Brodsky and the Soviet Muse* by David MacFadyen, 2000.

* * *

Iosif Brodskii seems to be condemned to success not only by his enormous talent and his desire "to go always for a greater thought," but also by the attention of the state. On the latter, Anna Akhmatova commented: "What a biography they're fashioning for our red-haired friend! It's as if he'd hired them to do it on purpose." On the basis of the former she declared him a genius after he read his "Bol'shaia elegiia. Dzhonu Donnu" ("Great Elegy to John Donne") to her in 1963 and endorsed him as the heir of Mandel'shtam. It looks as if he justified her judgement by becoming, in 1987, the youngest ever poet to receive the Nobel prize for literature. His unique position in Russian literature is underlined by the fact that as a poet, essayist, and playwright he is widely known and read in the English-speaking world: in May 1991 he was appointed as Poet Laureate of the United States. His complex cultural inheritance includes the Latin and English Metaphysical poets, Derzhavin and Tsvetaeva, Frost and Auden. He also learned a great deal from classical music.

Right from the start he struck a searingly tragic note in his poetry that set him apart from the work of his contemporaries. His first collection of poetry, *Stikhotvoreniia i poemy* [Poetry and Narrative Verse], was published in the United States while he was still in his northern exile. It reveals him as a lyrical and melancholic ironist brimming with understatement. It was followed by his second book, *Ostanovka v pustyne* [A Halt in the Wilderness]. The vulgarity of the human heart is his greatest enemy and a target for his art: "I'm trying to see how inhuman you can become and still remain a human being." His superiority lies, however, not so much in the subject matter as in its treatment. His main concern has always been to write better. He experiments with various poetic genres—descriptive poems, odes, elegies, and sonnets—by introducing new and provocative elements in their structure, prosody, and syntax. It is on the level of syntax, of this "circulatory system of poetry" (Mandel'shtam) which can so easily be struck by sclerosis, that Brodskii's innovations are especially significant. He used ellipses, short nominative phrases alternating with cumbersome periods, which occupy an entire stanza. In his extensive use of enjambment, which allows the renovation of Russian rhymes, he took after Tsvetaeva, another metaphysical maximalist. If he did not aim to surpass her, he moved in that direction: like Tsvetaeva he was a poet of ultimate truth, and as with Tsvetaeva all his devices display the unity of ethics and aesthetics, craftsmanship and humility. Unlike her, he was always restrained both in his grief and in his joy. His was the style of coolness, of irony with an air of reserve.

With the physical journey away from his native city, Brodskii began his anti-lyrical journey. In the poetry he published after he was forced into exile, the stylistic vector was clearly directed towards abstraction, rationalism, and even greater tonal neutrality. To use Coleridge's expression, Brodskii did not operate under the "despotism of the eye," but under that of reason. What made his poetry so semantically saturated was his intense thought. Trying to re-examine traditional conceptions of good and evil, he forced his poetry to discuss the "accursed" questions in the context of the post-Christian situation. In changing his angle of vision, intensifying his focus, Brodskii carried on from where Dostoevskii, Berdiaev, and Shestov left off. Like these predecessors, he was not afraid to admit aloud: "Here is one more/combination of numbers/that hasn't opened the door." Brodskii did for Russian poetry what Dostoevskii did for Russian prose: he stripped it of naïvety and innocence.

The greatest compensation for all the losses of 1972 was the meeting with W.H. Auden. Their meeting is commemorated in the poem "York" in the cycle of poems dedicated to England (in his collection *Uraniia* [Urania]). Here Brodskii clearly orientated himself towards the Auden text, in which landscape is used for meditating on death, love, and poetry. The elegy's deliberate prosaic quality was supported by excess of enjambments that were motivated by one of the themes of the elegy, the theme of death. He learned from Auden the poetic qualities he admired most: intellectual wit, unpredictability of plot, dry tone, and the sense of perspective. He was captivated by English poetry from youth, and this lasting love affair brought something qualitatively new to Russian poetry: he adjusted some aspects of Russian prosody, introduced an unusually restrained tone to his poems, and to a quite incredible extent widened the harmonic range in Russian poetic tradition.

For the English reader Brodskii's greatness was made clear by his prose more than by his poetry. His collection of essays, *Less than One*, won the United States National Book Critics' award for criticism in 1987. It is the best introduction to Brodskii's poetry because most of his essays have "borrowed the clothes of poetry itself" or, to use Brodskii's own words, they are "nothing but continuation of poetry by other means." This book includes his historical and culturological musings, homages to his favourite poets (Cavafy, Montale, Auden, Walcott, Akhmatova, Mandel'shtam, Tsvetaeva) and writers (Dostoevskii, Platonov, Nadezhda Mandel'shtam), and a personal memoir. Broad in scope, they stress the unity of European culture.

Critics are more ambiguous about Brodskii the playwright. His first play, *Mramor* (*Marbles*), was a philosophical dialogue between two prisoners in a luxury cell in Rome which is part ancient and part futuristic. This ironic journey to antiquity is a variation on some of Brodskii's main themes: empire, time, and the fate of culture in the post-Christian civilization. Here Brodskii also deals with the "after end" theme which he touched upon in many of his poems—after the end of love, after the end of life in Russia, after the end of Christianity. Furthermore, the play echoed his two masterpieces: a long poem

dialogue, "Gorbunov i Gorchakov" (1965–68), a reflection on his own experience in the Soviet prison, and *Rimskie elegii* [Roman Elegies], a brilliant succession of snapshots of the city in August where one "runs the risk of being turned to stone" (George Nivat). Brodskii's second play, *Demokratiia!* (*Democracy*), is a humorous musing on the collapse of communism in the Soviet Union. In both plays, with a certain dose of puns, paradox, and irony, Brodskii doesn't quite succeed in creating effective stage characters.

But, whatever Brodskii writes, his readers are aware of his relentless thinking on the grand scale. Finding himself outside his own culture, Brodskii continued to serve it by introducing to Russian culture an entirely different sensibility. Trying to get rid of its sentimentality, Brodskii encountered all kinds of fierce resistance and criticism. At the same time his universality earned him comparison with Pushkin himself. No Russian poet could ask for more.

—Valentina Polukhina

See the essay on *A Part of Speech*.

BRODSKY, Joseph

See BRODSKII, Iosif

BROSSARD, Nicole

Born: Montreal, Quebec, 27 November 1943. **Education:** Attended Collège Marguerite-Bourgeoys, 1955–60; Université de Montreal, B.A. 1965, Licence en lettres, 1968, Scolarité de maitrise en lettres, 1972; Université du Quebec à Montreal, Baccalaureate specialisé en pedagogie, 1971. **Family:** Married Roger Soublière, 1966 (divorced); one daughter. **Career:** Poet and novelist. Worked as a secretary, 1961–63; began publishing poetry and cofounded influential literary journal *La Barre du Jour*, 1965; organized jazz and poetry shows at the Pavilion de la jeunesse at Montreal's Expo 67, 1967; taught high school, Regina Mundi School, Ville Saint-Laurent, 1969–70 and 1971–72; codirected the film *Some American Feminists*, 1976; cofounded feminist journal *Les Têtes de pioche*, 1976–79; codirector *La Nouvelle Barre du Jour*, 1977–79; codirector of *Collections réelles*, 1979–81; founded and directed publishing house L'Integrale, 1982; visiting professor at Queen's University, Kingston, Ontario, 1982, 1984; short term fellow, Princeton University, New Jersey, 1991; organized and participated in numerous conferences, colloquiums, and festivals. Lives in Quebec, Canada. **Awards:** Governor General's award for *Mecanique jonglease*, 1975; Governor General's award for *Double Impression*,1984; Le Grand Prix de Poesie de la Foundation Les Forges, 1989; Le prix Athanase-David, 1991; Prix du Quebec, 1991; The Harbourfront Festival Prize, 1991. Honorary doctorate: l'Université de Sherbrooke, 1997.

PUBLICATIONS

Collections

Le Centre blanc: poèmes 1965–75. 1978.
Double Impression: Poemes et textes 1967–1984. 1985.

Verse

Aube a la saison. 1965.
Mordre en sa chair. 1966.
L'Echo bouge beau. 1968.
Suite logique. 1970.
Le Centre blanc. 1970.
Mecanique jongleuse. 1973; as *Daydream Mechanics*, translated by Larry Shouldice, 1980.
Mecanique jongleuse; Masculin grammaticale. 1974.
La Partie pour le tout. 1975.
D'Arcs de cycle la derive. 1979.
Amantes, Quinze. 1980; as *Lovhers*, translated by Barbara Godard, 1986.
L'Aviva. 1985.
Mauve, with Daphne Marlatt. 1985.
Domaine d'ecriture. 1985.
Character/Jeu de lettres, with Daphne Marlatt. 1986.
Sous la langue/Under the Tongue, translation by Susanne de Lotbimier-Harwood. 1987.
A tout regard, with Daphne Marlatt. 1989.
Installations: avec et sans pronoms. 1989; as *Installations*, translated by Erin Mouré and Robert Mejtels, 2000.
Langues obscures. 1992.
Typhon dru. 1990.
La Nuit Verte du Parc Labyrinthe. 1992; as *Green Night of Labyrinth Park*, translated by Lou Nelson and Marina Fe, 1992.
Vertige de l'avant scène. 1997.
Raddle Moon 17. 1998.
Musée de l'os et de l'eau. 1999.
Au présent des veines. 1999.
Installations. 2000.

Fiction

Un Livre. 1970; as *A Book*, translated by Larry Shouldice, 1976.
Sold-out: Etreinte/illustration. 1973; as *Turn of a Pang*, translated by Patricia Claxton, 1976.
French Kiss: Etreinte/exploration. 1974; as *French Kiss; or, A Pang's Progress*, translated by Patricia Claxton, 1986.
Picture Theory. 1982; translated by Barbara Godard, 1991.
Le Desert mauve. 1987; as *Mauve Desert*, translated by Susanne De Lotbiniere-Harwood, 1990.
Baroque d'aube: roman. 1995; as *Baroque at Dawn*, translated by Patricia Claxton, 1997.
Elle serait la première phrase de mon prochain roman. 1998; as *She Would Be the First Sentence of My Next Novel*, translated by Susanne de Lotbinière-Harwood, 1998.

Essays

L'Amer ou, Le Chapitre effrite: Fiction theorique. 1977; revised, 1988; as *These Our Mothers; or, The Disintegrating Chapter*, translated by Barbara Godard, 1983.
Le Sens apparent. 1980; as *Surfaces of Meaning*, translated by Fiona Strachan, 1989.
La Lettre aerienne. 1985; as *The Aerial Letter*, translated by Marlene Wilderman, 1988.

Plays

Narrateur et personnages. First aired by Radio Canada, 1971.
L'Ecrivain (produced 1976). In *La Nef des sorcieres*, 1976; as *The Writer*, translated by Linda Gaborian, in *A Clash of Symbols*, 1979.
Une Impression de fiction dans le retroviseur (produced 1978).
Journal intimes; ou, Voila donc un manuscrit (produced, 1983). 1984.
La Falaise (produced 1985).

Other

Contributor, *Emergence d'une culture au feminin*. 1987.
Editor, *The Story so Far: Les Strategies du reel* (anthology). 1979.
Editor with Lisette Girouard, *Anthologie de la poesie des femmes au Quebec*. 1991.

*

Critical Studies: "La Passion De La Beauté: Entretien avec Nicole Brossard," by Cépald Gaudet, in *Lettres québécoisse*, no. 57, Spring 1990; *Discoveries of the Other: Alterity in the Work of Leonard Cohen, Hubert Aquin, Michael Ondaatje, and Nicole Brossard* by Winfried Siemerling, 1994; "From Lesbos to Montreal: Nicole Brossard's Urban Fictions" by Lynne Huffer, in *Yale French Studies*, no. 90, 1996; "Region/Body: In? Of? And? Or? (Alter/native) Separatism in the Politics of Nicole Brossard" by Kimberly Verwaayen, in *Essays on Canadian Writing*, no. 61, Spring 1997; *Liminal Visions of Nicole Brossard* by Alice Parker, 1998; "Nothing Sacred: Nicole Brossard's *Baroque at Dawn* at the Limits of Lesbian Feminist Discourses of Sexuality" by Lianne Moyes, in *Essays on Canadian Writing*, no. 70, Spring 2000; *Narrative in the Feminine: Daphne Marlatt and Nicole Brossard*, by Susan Knutson, 2000; "Delirium and Desire in Nicole Brossard's *Le Desert Mauve/Mauve Desert*" by Susan Holbrook, in *Differences*, 12, no. 2, Summer 2001.

*   *   *

One of Quebec's foremost writers, Nicole Brossard is an innovative lesbian-feminist poet and novelist who began publishing her writing during the early days of the modern feminist movement. Early in the women's liberation movement of the late 1960s and 1970s, feminists began to question the masculine assumptions they felt were present in everyday language. As a poet who grew up in a French-speaking province of a largely English-speaking nation, Brossard had become fascinated with language and the way language shapes perception and experience. These interests meshed well with developing feminist philosophy, and Brossard's experiments with language made her a very influential feminist writer.

In *La Lettre aerienne* (*The Aerial Letter*), Brossard writes, "I think the wild love between two women is so totally inconceivable that to talk or write that in all its dimension, one almost has to rethink the world, to understand what it is that happens to us. And we can rethink the world only through words." A major element of early feminist thought was the idea that most language had been developed under patriarchy, or the rule of men. A new feminist literature would require more than simply replacing the hero with a heroine. Expressing the lives and experiences of women would require a new language, and that language would be developed by women themselves. Much of Brossard's work has been devoted to developing a language that expresses the experience and inner landscape of women and lesbians.

Brossard is also considered an important post-modernist writer. As such, she combines classical elements of the past with technologies of the present to present a complex point of view that encompasses both past and present. Her multi-layered writing style has been called baroque after a seventeenth century fashion of elaborate ornamentation, but it also includes elements from such twenty-first century fields as internet communication, holography, quantum physics, and atomic weaponry. In her 1998 work *Elle serait la premiere phrase de mon prochain roman* (*She Would Be the First Sentence of My Next Novel*), Brossard describes herself:

> I'm a woman of the present fascinated by the history that enters into the composition of the words with which each generation bears witness to its anguish, invents its hope, modifies the collective tale. I am interested in what confines each generation inside themes, metaphors, theoretical and stylistic attitudes. I imagine the passion of the language that is allowed to escape from this. The turbulence that cracks open history.

Though Brossard writes poetry, novels, plays and essays, she is most consistently a poet, deeply interested in and motivated by language and words. She approaches every genre with a poet's consciousness, giving great attention to the play, motion, and juxtaposition of words. Her writing is always dense and layered with meaning, challenging the reader to explore the limitations and possibilities of language. As a Quebecoise, she essentially grew up in a country within a country, surrounded by French, English, and Joual, the working class Quebecois dialect that is almost a hybrid of French and English. Therefore the notion of translation became an integral part of Brossard's work, denoting not only translation from one language to another but also translation of one person's experience to another and the translation of experience and thought to the written page. Much of her writing is devoted to the exploration of what is lost and what is gained through translation.

Brossard is also deeply interested in the creative process. The complexity of translation shows up clearly in her novels and her books of essays exploring the many facets of the artist's experience. Her 1987 novel, *Le Desert Mauve* (*Mauve Desert*), is at its core an examination of the writer's creative process. A novel within a novel, *Mauve Desert* begins with a short novel written by fifteen-year-old Melanie, who lives in the southwestern United States. Melanie writes of her love of driving at high speed over the highways of her desert home and her obsession with a woman who died as a result of the atomic bomb tests there. Her novel is found by an older woman writer, who in turn becomes obsessed with expanding and re-imagining Melanie's vision. She then translates the young woman's novel, not into another language, but into another vision, titled *Mauve, l'horizon*.

Mauve Desert is, like much of Brossard's work, a blend of poetry, fiction, and theory. In other works as well, she approaches the idea of the artist's attempt to communicate experience. *Baroque d'aube* (*Baroque at Dawn*) also describes this creation process. Using vibrant imagery and wordplay, Brossard tells the story of three women, a writer, a photographer and an oceanographer, who combine energies to create a symbolic representation of the sea. *She Would Be the First Sentence of My Next Novel* is an autobiographical, confessional essay about being a novelist and how a novelist sees the world and translates that vision to the page.

Though Brossard is a demanding writer who challenges the reader to leave behind old forms and assumptions, her complexity is never somber or dreary. In *Picture Theory* she leaves behind the traditional (and, in her view, patriarchal) linear narrative and uses an unconventional experimental narrative form that some critics have called "holographic hyperfiction." She manipulates language playfully and erotically to convey feelings as well as ideas, as in: "Responding to certain signs, with complete fluidity, our bodies interlaced m'urged to fuse in astonishment or fascination."

Brossard's work, with its focus on the constant creation of new language to describe and communicate new experience, continues to fascinate and inspire readers into a new millenium. Reading Brossard is not a passive experience, for she demands a questioning, flexible reader, who will conspire with her in the creative process. Perhaps the best example of this is media artist Adriene Jenek, who read *Le Desert Mauve* and became so inspired by it, that, in 1992, she created an appropriate companion work, an interactive CD-ROM titled *Mauve Desert*.

—Tina Gianoulis

BRUNO, Giordano

Born: Filippo Bruno, in Nola, Kingdom of Naples, in January or February 1548. **Education:** Studied theology, 1572–75; taught and studied (degree in theology), University of Toulouse, 1579–81. **Career:** Admitted as a novice to the Dominican monastery of San Domenico Maggiore, 1565, assumed the monastic name Giordano; lived in various priories in the Kingdom of Naples, 1565–76; left Naples after charges of heresy were levelled against him by the Inquisition, 1576, and spent 15 years travelling in Europe: travelled through the northern Italian states, Savoy and Lyon, 1577–79, before arriving in Geneva, where he was briefly a follower of Calvinism; reached Paris, 1581, found favour with Henri III, who awarded him a lectureship, and first published his writings, 1582; accompanied French ambassador to England, lectured briefly at Oxford University, and lived in London, 1583–85, published prolifically and frequented the court of Elizabeth I (and was associated with Sir Philip Sidney and Robert Dudley); returned to Paris, 1586; moved to Marburg, 1586; lectured at the University of Wittenberg, 1586–88, and converted to Lutheranism; visited Prague, 1589, and Helmstädt; lectured in Frankfurt, 1590–91; returned to Venice, 1591, and lived in the household of Giovanni Mocenigo; denounced to the Inquisition by Mocenigo, 1592: on trial in Venice, 1593, and in Rome, 1593–1600, found guilty of heresy. **Died:** (burned at the stake) 17 February 1600.

PUBLICATIONS

Collections

Opere italiane. 2 vols., 1830; edited by P. de Lagarde, 2 vols., 1888; edited by Giovanni Gentile and Vincenzo Spampanato, 3 vols., 1925–1927.

Opera latine conscripta publicis sumptis edita, edited by F. Fiorentino, Felice Tocco, and G. Vitelli. 3 vols., 1879–91; reprinted 1962.

Le opere latine esposte e confrontate con le italiane, edited by Felice Tocco. 1889.

Scritti scelti, edited by Luigi Firpo. 1950.

Opere, edited by A. Guzzo and Romano Amerio. 1953.

Opera Latine, edited by Carlo Monti. 1980.

Prose

De umbris idearum (includes *Ars memoriae*). 1582.

Cantus Circaeus. 1582.

De compendiosa architectura et complemento artis Lullii. 1582.

Ars reminiscendi; Explicatio triginta sigillorum; Sigillus sigillorum. 1583.

La cena delle ceneri. 1584; edited by Giovanni Aquilecchia, 1955; as *The Ash Wednesday Supper*, translated by Stanley L. Jaki, 1965; also translated by E.A. Gosselin and L.S. Lerner, 1977.

De la Causa, Principio et Uno. 1584; edited by A. Guzzo, 1933, and by Giovanni Aquilecchia, 1973; as *Concerning the Cause, Principle and One*, translated by D.W. Singer, in *The Infinite in Giordano Bruno*, by Sidney T. Greenberg, 1950; as *Five Dialogues by Giordano Bruno: Cause, Principle and Unity*, translated by Jack Lindsay, 1962; second dialogue translated by I. and K. Royce, in *Rand's Modern Classical Philosophies*, 1908; as *Cause, Principle, and Unity*, translated and edited by Robert de Lucca, 1998.

De l'Infinito Universo et Mondi. 1584; as *On the Infinite Universe and Worlds*, translated by D.W. Singer, in *Giordano Bruno: His Life and Thought*, 1950.

Lo spaccio de la bestia trionfante. 1584; as *The Expulsion of the Triumphant Beast*, translated by W. Morehead, 1713; also translated by Arthur D. Imerti, 1964.

La cabala del cavallo pegaseo. 1584.

L'asino cillenico del Nolano. 1584.

De gli eroici furori. 1585; as *The Heroic Enthusiasts*, translated (first part only) by L. Williams, 2 vols., 1887–89; as *The Heroic Frenzies*, translated by Paul E. Memmo, 1964.

Dialogi duo de Fabricii Mordentis Salernitani. 1586.

Idiota triumphans; De somnii interpretatione; Dialogi duo de Fabricii Mordentis Salernitani. 1586.

Centum et viginti articuli de natura et mundo adversus peripateticos. 1586.

De lampade combinatoria Lulliana. 1587; translated in part by J. Lewis McIntyre, in *Giordano Bruno*, 1903.

De progressu et lampade venatoria logicorum. 1587.

De specierum scrutinio et lampade combinatoria Raymondi Lullii Doctoris. 1588.

Camoeracensis acrotismus. 1588.

Articuli centum et sexaginta adversus huius tempestatis mathematicos atque philosophos. 1588.

Summa terminorum metaphysicorum ad capessendum logicae et philosophiae studium. 1595; edited by Eugenio Canone, 1979.

In tristitia hilaris, in hilaritate tristis, edited by E. Troilo. 1922.

Documenti della vita di Giordano Bruno, edited by Vincenzo Spampanato. 1933.

Due dialoghi sconosciuti e due dialoghi noti: Idiota triumphans; De somnii interpretatione; Mordentius; De Mordentii Circino, edited by Giovanni Aquilecchia. 1957.

Dialoghi italiani: Dialoghi metafisici e Dialoghi morali, edited by Giovanni Aquilecchia and Giovanni Gentile. 1958.

Praelectiones geometricae e ars deformationum: Testi inediti, edited by Giovanni Aquilecchia. 1964.

Verse

De monade, numero et figura libea consequens quinque de minimo magno. Menura. 1591.

De innumerabilibus, immenso et infigurabilii seu de universo et mundis. 1591.

De triplici minimo et mensura ad trium speculativarum scientiarum et multarum activarum artium principia. 1591.

De imaginum, signorum, et idearum compositione. 1591; as *On the Composition of Images, Signs and Ideas*, translated by Dick Higgins, 1991.

Plays

Il Candelaio. 1582; edited by Vincenzo Spampanato, 1923, and by G. Barbieri Squarotti, 1964; as *The Candle Bearer*, translated by J.R. Hale, in *The Genius of the Italian Theater*, edited by Eric Bentley, 1964; as *Candlebearer*, translated with notes by Gino Moliterno, 2000.

*

Bibliography: *Bibliografia delle opere di Giordano Bruno e degli scritti a esso attinenti* by Virgilio Salvestrini, 1926; revised edition, as *Bibliografia di Giordano Bruno (1582–1950)*, by Luigi Firpo, 1958.

Critical Studies: *Life of Giordano Bruno* by J. Frith, 1887; *Giordano Bruno* by J. Lewis McIntyre, 1903; *La filosofia di Giordano Bruno* by E. Troilo, 1907; *Giordano Bruno, His Life, Thought and Martyrdom* by W. Boulting, 1914; *Giordano Bruno e il pensiero del Rinascimento* by Giovanni Gentile, 1920, revised edition, 1925; *Vita di Giordano Bruno con documenti editi ed inediti* by Vincenzo Spampanato, 1921; *Giordano Bruno* by L. Olschki, 1927; *Il pensiero di Giordano Bruno nel suo svolgimento* by A. Corsano, 1940; *II processo di Giordano Bruno* by Luigi Firpo, 1949; *The Infinite in Giordano Bruno* by Sidney T. Greenberg, 1950; *Giordano Bruno: His Life and Thought* by D.W. Singer, 1950; *The Renaissance Philosophy of Giordano Bruno* by I.L. Horowitz, 1952; *La filosofia di Giordano Bruno* by N. Badolini, 1955; *From the Closed World to the Infinite Universe* by A. Koyré, 1957; *The Individual and the Cosmos in Renaissance Philosophy* by E. Cassirer, 1963; *Eight Philosophers of the Italian Renaissance* by O. Kristeller, 1964; *Giordano Bruno and the Hermetic Tradition*, 1964, *The Art of Memory*, 1966, and *Lull and Bruno*, 1982, all by Frances A. Yates; *Giordano Bruno* by E. Garin, 1966; *The Infinite Worlds of Giordano Bruno* by A. Mann Paterson, 1970; *Giordano Bruno* by Giovanni Aquilecchia, 1971; *La ruota del tempo: interpretazione di Giordano Bruno*, 1986, and *Giordano Bruno* (includes critical bibliography) both by M. Ciliberto, 1990; *The Renaissance Drama of Knowledge: Giordano Bruno in England* by Hilary Gatti, 1989; *Giordano Bruno and the Embassy Affair* by John Bossy, 1991; *Giordano Bruno and the Philosophy of the Ass* by Nuccio Ordine, translated by Henryk Baranski and Arielle Saiber, 1996; *Giordano Bruno and the Kabbalah: Prophets, Magicians, and Rabbis* by Karen Silvia De León-Jones, 1997; *The Last Confession* by Morris West, 2000.

* * *

The number of Giordano Bruno's writings exceeds 60 works, the majority written in Latin. These include works concerning philosophy, astronomy, mathematics, mnemonics (which was not "a mere set of mechanical rules for aiding memory, but was freighted with a very large content of mysticism and magic," as Gosselin and Lerner point out in the introduction to *The Ash Wednesday Supper*, 1977), and the various controversies in which Bruno was engaged. Bruno was asked on several occasions to give lectures on a variety of subjects; he became famous especially for his interest in mnemonics and the works of the 14th-century Catalan monk Ramón Lull.

By the time he left Naples, Bruno had embraced the system of belief called hermetic Neoplatonism or Hermeticism. In the Renaissance the prestige of this system was fostered by the belief that it was based on the writings of Hermes Trismegistus, an Egyptian sage who foretold the advent of Christianity, and whose wisdom had inspired Plato and the Platonists. Bruno held the belief that the Hermetic religion (with its magical component) was the only true religion, and felt a need to return to the beliefs of the Egyptians. He also believed in metempsychosis (the transmigration of souls at the time of death) and that the living earth moved around the divine sun; this latter belief brought him to embrace Copernicus' ideas and to formulate his most notable theories on the infinite universe and the multiplicity of worlds. Bruno's religion cannot be separated from his philosophy, and while he was conciliatory towards religious practices, he was intolerant of pedants and those who would not, or could not, accept occult truths: hence his anti-Aristotelianism. A brief survey of his major works will illustrate the broad spectrum of Bruno's ideas.

The *De umbris idearum* [The Shadows of Ideas], with the *Ars memoriae* [The Art of Memory,] in appendix, was published in Paris during Bruno's first visit to that city. These two works consolidated his fame as an expert in mnemonics, and earned him the privilege of entering the group of *lecteurs royaux* (royal lecturers) whose attitudes, in contrast with their Sorbonne counterparts, were anti-Aristotelian. In the first part of the *De umbris*, Bruno re-elaborates material dealing with Lull and mnemonics with a didactic purpose: he intends proving, from a platonic point of view, the correspondence between the physical and the ideal world. The Neoplatonists relied on the directness of intuition concerning high matters since man is incapable of achieving the essence of truth; hence our ideas are only shadows of truth and, in mnemonics, are shadows (signs) of these shadows. The second and third parts of the *De umbris* are a mnemotechnic manual purporting to instruct the reader, as Bruno does in the *Ars memoriae*, by drawing upon elements from the astrological and Hermetic traditions. The art of memory in its incantational perception—since the nature of memory is occult, the recall of ideas may be regarded as a magical exercise—forms the basis for the *Cantus Circaeus* [The Incantation of Circe]. By far the most successful and enjoyable publication of Bruno's first visit to Paris is *Il Candelaio* (*The Candle Bearer*), a play in five acts with 18 characters, written in popular Italian, but with many plebeian expressions derived from Neapolitan dialect. The play mainly satirizes three aspects of human behaviour and belief in Bonifacio's love, Bartolomeo's alchemy, and Manfurio's pedantry.

In 1583, while a guest of the French ambassador in London, Michel de Casteineau, Bruno lectured at Oxford on the Copernican theory of the movement of the earth, thus anticipating by one year what he says in *La cena delle ceneri* (*The Ash Wednesday Supper*). It is in the five dialogues making up this work that Bruno recaptures the ill-fated evening of 14 February 1584, when he walked out of a dinner party at Sir Fulke Greville's house because of the intolerance shown by two Oxonian doctors towards his explanation of heliocentric theories. From Copernicus, Bruno moves on to other theories of astronomy (plurality of worlds in an infinite universe), language (repudiation of Latin and adoption of vulgar Italian in scientific treatises), and politics (support for Robert Dudley's puritanical faction). Besides its philosophical and theological content (God is defined along the lines of the Hermetic tradition as an infinite sphere, the centre of which is everywhere and the circumference of which is nowhere), *The Ash Wednesday Supper* lashes out at the English society of the times and, particularly, at the pedantry of the Oxonian doctors who had prevented Bruno, the year before, from completing his course of lectures on the grounds that he had been plagiarizing Marsilio Ficino's *De vita Coelitus Comparanda*. Bruno's publication of *De la Causa, Principio et Uno* (*Cause, Principle and Unity*) was intended to fend off the criticism aroused by his previous work. Bruno failed to do this, but produced a most brilliant and original treatise on metaphysics, dealing with the concepts of "causa" and "principio" which, according to his physical theory, are to be considered the equivalents of "forma" [form] and "materia" [matter]: together they form an inextricable unity ["l'uno"]. In elaborating this theory, Bruno rejects the traditional dualism inherent in Aristotelian physics, and moves instead towards a monistic conception of the world. These ideas are also reaffirmed in the *De l'Infinito Universo et Mondi* (*On the Infinite Universe and Worlds*).

The first dialogue of *Lo spaccio de la bestia trionfante* (*The Expulsion of the Triumphant Beast*) is a satire on contemporary superstitions and vices, embodied in the "triumphant beast," which, Bruno implies, have distorted man's reason in all ages and cultures. In *The Expulsion* Bruno reaffirms that the search for truth is the very foundation of the ethical system, and he equates truth with Divinity itself. Bruno leans heavily upon the Pythagorean belief in metempsychosis, a teaching considered heretical by the Catholic Church since it does not uphold the ultimate return of the soul to its resurrected body. The relationship between the individual and universal soul is taken up in the *Cabala*. In *De gli eroici furori* (*The Heroic Frenzies*), dedicated to Sir Philip Sidney, Bruno establishes the premise that intellectual love is superior to physical love, and declares that the soul, in its pursuit of truth, progressively strives for an intellectual understanding of the Being, Truth itself. Couched in Ficinian terminology the ten dialogues also become testimony to Bruno's criticism of Aristotelian poetics and imitation of Petrarch in the 16th century.

The remainder of Bruno's works that were published in his lifetime are all in Latin, and are, to a large extent, a re-elaboration of the theories expounded in the Italian dialogues. Worthy of mention however, are the three verse dialogues published in Frankfurt in 1591. In the *De minimo* [Concerning the Least], the argument is concerned with three units: God (the unit of units), the soul (the eternal minimum) and the atom (the physical minimum). *De monade* is filled chiefly with mystical, philosophical and geometrical constructions, founded upon the theory of mathematical *minima* invested with metaphysical significance: one is the perfect number, the source of infinite series. The *De immenso* [Concerning the Immeasurable] amplifies Bruno's philosophy of the infinite universe and the innumerable worlds, which Bruno had derived from Lucretius, "animating it with the universal animation of the magical philosophy and using it in the Hermetic manner, to reflect in the *mens* the universe in this immensely extended form and so to absorb the infinite divinity'' (Frances A. Yates, *Giordano Bruno and the Hermetic Tradition*).

Bruno's originality and legacy appear to be ambiguous: on the one hand he transformed the art of memory from a fairly rational technique into a magical and religious instrument for reaching towards the divine, and, he thought, obtaining divine powers. Even the concepts of an infinite universe, of planetary life derived from the sun, and of the cosmic insights (which anticipate the findings of Galileo, Kepler, and Newton) are connected to his attempts to picture the intangible, the unknown, the arcane: this approach is in line with the Hermetic aim of becoming one with the universe through imaginative effort (as Yates explains). On the other hand, Bruno, in his endeavour to establish truth, defied the ecclesiastical authorities, most blatantly when he embraced the Copernican theories of heliocentricity; on account of this, Bruno is regarded as a precursor of modern scientific thought. At his trial Bruno made several attempts to demonstrate that his views were not incompatible with the Catholic conception of God and creation. He first retracted some of the contentious theological points on which he was to be found guilty, but, at the end, he refused to do so because he did not know any longer (after eight years' imprisonment) what he was expected to retract. It is his final stance at the trial (well documented in Luigi Firpo's *Il processo di Giordano Bruno*) and his horrific death that have made him a symbol of freedom and humanistic activism, while his emphasis on the magical and the occult dimmed his image as scientific investigator. The fact remains, however, that Bruno stands as one of the most thought-provoking and complex figures in the history of western thought.

—Bruno Ferraro

BÜCHNER, Georg

Born: Goddelau, Duchy of Hesse Darmstadt, Germany, 17 October 1813. **Education:** Educated at Carl Weitershausen's school, 1822–25; Gymnasium, Darmstadt, 1825–31; studied medicine at University of Strasbourg, 1831–33, and University of Giessen, 1833–34; studied biology: arned membership of the Strasbourg Société d'Histoire Naturelle and a doctorate from University of Zurich, 1836. **Career:** Politically active as a student in Darmstadt, founded the society, Gesellschaft der Menschenrechte, 1834, and wrote the political pamphlet *Der hessische Landbote*, 1834; fled Germany to escape impending arrest for sedition, 1835, and sought refuge in Strasbourg. Lecturer in comparative anatomy, University of Zurich, 1836–37. **Died:** 19 February 1837.

PUBLICATIONS

Collections

Nachgelassene Schriften, edited by Ludwig Büchner. 1850.
Sämtliche Werke, edited by K. Franzos. 1879.
Gesammelte Werke und Briefe, edited by Fritz Bergemann. 1922.
Complete Plays and Prose, translated by Carl Richard Mueller. 1963.
Sämtliche Werke und Briefe, edited by Werner R. Lehmann. 2 vols., 1967–71.

Plays, translated by Victor Price. 1971; also translated by Michael Hamburger, 1972.
Complete Works and Letters, edited by Walter Hinderer, translated by Henry J. Schmidt. 1986.
Complete Plays, edited by Michael Patterson, translated by John MacKendrick. 1987.
Werke und Briefe, edited by Karl Pörnbacher. 1988.
Complete Plays, Lenz and Other Writings, edited and translated by John Reddick. 1993.
Dantons Tod and Woyzeck, edited with introduction and notes by Margaret Jacobs, 1996.

Plays

Dantons Tod (produced 1902). 1835 (incomplete version); complete version in *Nachgelassene Schriften*, 1850; as *Danton's Death*, translated by Stephen Spender and Goronwy Rees, 1939; also translated by T.H. Lustig, in *Classical German Drama*, edited by Lustig, 1963; James Maxwell, 1968; Victor Price, 1971; Jane Fry and Howard Brenton, 1982; John MacKendrick, 1987.
Leonce und Lena (produced 1895). In *Mosaik, Novellen, und Skizzen*, edited by K. Gutzkow, 1842; as *Leonce and Lena*, translated by Eric Bentley, in *From the Modern Repertoire*, 3, 1956; also translated by Victor Price, 1971.
Woyzeck (produced 1913). As *Wozzeck*, in *Sämtliche Werke*, 1879; as *Woyzeck*, translated by Theodore Hoffmann, in *The Modern Theatre*, 1, edited by Eric Bentley, 1955; also translated by Carl Richard Mueller, in *Complete Plays and Prose*, 1963; Henry J. Schmidt, 1969; Victor Price, 1971; Michael Hamburger, 1972; John MacKendrick, 1979.

Fiction

Lenz. In *Telegraph für Deutschland*, January 1839; as *Lenz*, translated by Carl Richard Mueller, in *Complete Plays and Prose*, 1963; also translated by Michael Hamburger, in *Three German Classics*, edited by Ronald Taylor, 1966; F.J. Lamport, in *The Penguin Book of Short Stories*, 1974; John MacKendrick, in *Complete Plays*, 1987.

Other

Der hessische Landbote, with Pastor Weidig (pamphlet). 1834 (privately printed); as *The Hessian Courier*, translated by John MacKendrick, in *Complete Plays*, 1987; as *The Hessian Messenger*, translated by Henry J. Schmidt, in *Complete Works and Letters*, 1987.

*

Bibliography: *Das Büchner Schrifttum bis 1965* by Werner Schlick, 1968; ''Kommentierte Bibliographie zu Büchner'' by Gerhard P. Knapp, in *Text und Kritik Sonderband Büchner*, 1979; revised edition, 1984; *Georg Büchner* by Marianne Beese, 1983.

Critical Studies: *Georg Büchner* by Arthur Knight, 1951; *Georg Büchner* by Herbert Lindenberger, 1964; *Satire, Caricature, and Perspectivism in the Works of Büchner* by Henry J. Schmidt, 1970; *Georg Büchner* by Ronald Hauser, 1974; *The Drama of Revolt: A Critical Study of Georg Büchner* by Maurice B. Benn, 1976; *Georg*

Büchner and the Birth of Modern Drama by David G. Richards, 1977; *Georg Büchner* by William C. Reeve, 1979; *Georg Büchner* by Julian Hilton, 1982; *Georg Büchner's "Dantons Tod": A Reappraisal* by Dorothy James, 1982; *Lenz and Büchner: Studies in Dramatic Form* by John Guthrie, 1984; *Love, Lust, and Rebellion: New Approaches to Georg Büchner* by Reinhold Grimm, 1985; *Büchner in Britain: A Passport to Georg Büchner* edited by Brian Keith-Smith and Ken Mills, 1987; *Georg Büchner's Woyzeck* by Michael Ewans, 1989; *George Büchner: Tradition and Innovation: Fourteen Essays*, 1990; *Büchner, Woyzeck* by Edward McInnes, 1991; *Georg Büchner: The Shattered Whole* by John Reddick, 1994; *Büchner and Madness: Schizophrenia in Georg Büchner's Lenz and Woyzeck* by James Crighton, 1998; *Georg Büchner's Woyzeck: A History of Its Criticism* by David G. Richards, 2001.

* * *

Georg Büchner died in 1837 at the age of 23 with only one play, *Dantons Tod* (*Danton's Death*), in print and that in a bowdlerized version. His *Woyzeck* was not performed until the centenary of his birth. Yet he is now acknowledged to be a crucial link in the chain of innovative German drama which stretches from J.M.R. Lenz through Büchner, Frank Wedekind, the Expressionists, and Bertolt Brecht to the present day. In a wider context he is recognized as a seminal figure in the history of modern drama.

At Giessen University Büchner was a republican activist and co-editor of *Der hessische Landbote* (*The Hessian Courier*), an inflammatory pamphlet exposing the exploitative taxation which kept the aristocracy in Hesse in luxury. This led to a warrant being issued for his arrest, and he had to flee the country and complete his studies in Strasbourg. It was while he was in hiding on the way that he wrote *Danton's Death*, which broke with the idealist drama of Schiller and tried to present history "as it really happened." He revealed the bloody and bawdy side of revolution, showing the clash between Robespierre's ideological asceticism ("Virtue is the strength . . . terror the weapon of the Republic") and Danton's liberal hedonism as a mere phase in the inexorable, inscrutable cycle of history. It is a powerful but bleak piece of writing, in which the masses feature mainly as rabble, and it is so poised that left and right wing interpreters have struggled in vain for half a century to make it their own. *Leonce und Lena* (*Leonce and Lena*) is an ironic, satirical variant of the romantic comedy, set among the blasé and inane aristocrats of the lands of Pipi and Popo.

Büchner left his most important work, *Woyzeck*, unfinished, with only vague indications of possible endings. It is a study of social victimization. The passive, plebeian hero, Woyzeck, is a common soldier who acts as barber to his Captain and as dietetic guinea-pig to a demented physician in order to support his mistress and child. She succumbs haplessly to the crude blandishments of the virile drummajor, and Woyzeck, hounded by imaginary voices, stabs her to death. The fragment, of which there are several drafts, ends with Woyzeck wading into a pond to recover the murder weapon he has thrown away, but the play would not have ended there. Büchner based it on the controversial case of a murderer who was executed in Leipzig in 1824 after two years of medical examinations to determine whether he was responsible for his actions, and here, as in *Danton's Death*, historically authentic speeches are woven seamlessly into the dialogue. Büchner presents a *crime passionnel* in which degradation, debility, sexuality, love, and Christian conscience weave an intricate,

compelling pattern which, one is tempted to say, positively benefits from being incomplete. Its 24–29 brief scenes (depending on the edition), which add up to a longish one-act play, are the model for the *montages* of short scenes that are characteristic of Expressionism and epic theatre. Like Danton and Robespierre, Woyzeck is a puppet with an inscrutable controller. Inside themselves, Büchner's more positive characters see an abyss. Büchner was a humane pessimist to whom human life seemed locked in the grip of events. He has the unblinking vision of the moderns, and he provides his suffering characters, no matter what their station, with a voice that is natural and authentic, and at the same time universal and poetic.

—Hugh Rorrison

See the essays on *Danton's Death* and *Woyzeck*.

BULGAKOV, Mikhail (Afanas'evich)

Born: Kiev, Ukraine, 3 May 1891. **Education:** Educated at First Kiev High School, 1900–09; Medical Faculty, Kiev University, 1909–16, doctor's degree 1916. **Military Service:** Served as doctor in frontline and district hospitals, 1916–18. **Family:** Married 1) Tatiana Nikolaevna Lappa in 1913; 2) Liubov' Evgenievna Belozerskaia in 1924; 3) Elena Sergeevna Shilovskaia in 1932. **Career:** Doctor in Kiev, 1918–19, but abandoned medicine in 1920; organized a "sub-department of the arts," Vladikavkaz, 1920–21; in Moscow from 1921: journalist for various groups and papers; associated with the Moscow Art Theatre from 1925: assistant producer, 1930–36; librettist and consultant, Bolshoi Theatre, Moscow, 1936–40. Much of his writing was published posthumously. **Died:** 10 March 1940.

PUBLICATIONS

Collections

P'esy [Plays]. 1962.
Dramy i komedii [Dramas and Comedies]. 1965.
Izbrannaia proza [Selected Prose]. 1966.
The Early Plays, edited by Ellendea Proffer, translated by Ellendea and Carl R. Proffer. 1972.
Sobranie sochinenii [Collected Works], edited by Ellendea Proffer. 1982–90.
Romany [Novels]. 1988.
P'esy 1920-kh godov [Plays of the 1920s]. 1989.
Sobranie sochinenii v piati tomakh [Collected Works]. 5 vols., 1989–91.
Izbrannye proizvedeniia [Selected Works]. 1990.

Fiction

Zapiski na manzhetakh [Notes on the Cuff]. 1923.
Diavoliada: Rasskazy. 1925; as *Diaboliad and Other Stories,* edited by Ellendea and Carl R. Proffer, translated by Carl R. Proffer, 1972.
Rasskazy [Stories]. 1926.

Dni Turbinykh (Belaia gvardiia). 2 vols., 1927–29; as *The White Guard,* translated by Michael Glenny, 1971.

Rokovye iaitsa [The Fatal Eggs] (stories). 1928.

Zapiski iunogo vracha. 1963; enlarged edition as *A Country Doctor's Notebook,* translated by Michael Glenny, 1975.

Zapiski pokoinika (Teatralnyi roman), in *Izbrannaia proza.* 1966; as *Black Snow: A Theatrical Novel,* translated by Michael Glenny, 1967.

Master i Margarita. 1965–66; uncut version, 1969; complete version, 1973; as *The Master and Margarita,* translated by Mirra Ginsburg, 1967; uncut version, translated by Michael Glenny, 1967; translated by Diana Burgin and Katherine Tiernan O'Connor, 1995.

Sobach'e serdtse. 1969; as *The Heart of a Dog,* translated by Michael Glenny, 1968; also translated by Mirra Ginsburg, 1990.

Notes on the Cuff and Other Stories, edited by Ellendea Proffer, translated by Alison Rice. 1992.

Plays

Dni Turbinykh, from his novel (produced 1926). With *Poslednie dni (Pushkin),* 1955; as *The Days of the Turbins,* in *Six Soviet Plays,* translated by Eugene Lyons, 1935; also in *The Early Plays,* edited by Ellendea Proffer, 1972; as *The White Guard,* translated by Michael Glenny, 1979.

Zoikina kvartira (produced 1926). Edited by Ellendea Proffer, 1971; as *Zoya's Apartment,* in *The Early Plays,* edited by Proffer, 1972; as *Madame Zoya,* translated by Michael Glenny, in *Six Plays,* 1991.

Bagrovyi ostrov (produced 1928). In *P'esy,* 1971; as *The Crimson Island,* in *The Early Plays,* edited by Ellendea Proffer, 1972.

Mertvye dushi [Dead Souls], from the novel by Gogol' (produced 1932). With *Ivan Vasil'evich,* 1964.

Kabala sviatosh (as *Mol'er,* produced 1936). In *P'esy,* 1962; as *A Cabal of Hypocrites,* in *The Early Plays,* edited by Ellendea Proffer, 1972; as *Molière,* translated by Michael Glenny, in *Six Plays,* 1991.

Skupoi [The Miser], from the play by Molière, in *Polnoe sobranie sochinenii,* 4, by Molière. 1939.

Don Kikhot [Don Quixote], from the novel by Cervantes (produced 1940). In *P'esy,* 1962.

Poslednie dni (Pushkin) (produced 1943). With *Dni Turbinykh,* 1955; as *The Last Days (Pushkin),* in *Russian Literature Triquarterly,* 15, 1976; also translated by William Powell and Michael Earley, in *Six Plays,* 1991.

Rashel', edited by Margarita Aliger, music by R.M. Glière (broadcast 1943; produced 1947). Edited by A. Colin Wright, in *Novyi zhurnal,* 108, September 1972; Bulgakov's original text, 1988.

Beg (produced 1957). In *P'esy,* 1962; as *Flight,* translated by Mirra Ginsburg, 1969, and with *Bliss,* 1985, also translated by Michael Glenny, in *Six Plays,* 1991; as *On the Run,* translated by Avril Pyman, 1972.

Ivan Vasil'evich (produced 1966). With *Mertvye dushi,* 1964; as *Ivan Vasilievich,* in *Modern International Drama,* 7(2), 1974; as *Beg = Flight,* edited with introduction and notes by J.A.E. Curtis, 1997.

Poloumnyi Zhurden, from *Le Bourgeois Gentilhomme* by Molière (produced 1972). In *Dramy i komedii,* 1965.

Blazhenstvo (Son inzhenera Reina v 4-kh deistviakh), in *Zvezda vostoka,* 7. 1966; as *Bliss,* translated by Mirra Ginsburg, with *Flight,* 1985.

P'esy: Adam i Eva; Bagrovyi ostrov; Zoikina kvartira. 1971.

Adam i Eva, in *P'esy.* 1971; as *Adam and Eve,* in *Russian Literature Triquarterly,* 1, Fall 1971; also translated by Michael Glenny, in *Six Plays,* 1991.

Minin i Pozharskii, music by Boris Asafiev, edited by A. Colin Wright, in *Russian Literature Triquarterly,* 15. 1976.

Voina i mir [War and Peace], from the novel by Tolstoi, edited by A. Colin Wright, in *Canadian-American Slavic Studies,* 15, Summer–Fall. 1981.

Batum. 1988.

Chernoye more [The Black Sea]. 1988.

Petr Veliky [Peter the Great]. 1988.

Six Plays (includes *The White Guard; Madame Zoya; Flight; Molière; Adam and Eve; The Last Days),* edited by Lesley Milne, translated by Michael Glenny, William Powell, and Michael Earley. 1991.

Other

Zhizn' gospodina de Mol'era. 1962; as *The Life of Monsieur de Molière,* translated by Mirra Ginsburg, 1970.

Rannjaja neizdannaja proza [Early Unpublished Prose] (German edition). 1976.

Rannjaja nesobrannaja proza [Early Uncollected Prose] (German edition). 1978.

Rannjaja neizvestnaja proza [Early Unknown Prose] (German edition). 1981.

Pod piatoi. Moi dnevnik (early diary entries). 1990.

Manuscripts Don't Burn: A Life in Letters and Diaries, edited by J.A.E. Curtis. 1991.

*

Bibliography: *An International Bibliography of Works by and about Bulgakov* by Ellendea Proffer, 1976; *A Bibliography of Works by and about Mikhail Bulgakov* by Nadine Natov, in *Canadian-American Slavic Studies,* XV, 1981; *Mikhail Bulgakov in English: A Bibliography 1891–1991* by Garth M. Terry, 1991.

Critical Studies: *Bulgakov's "The Master and Margarita": The Text as a Cipher* by Elena N. Mahlow, 1975; *The Master and Margarita: A Comedy of Victory,* 1977, and *Mikhail Bulgakov: A Critical Biography,* 1990, both by Lesley Milne; *Mikhail Bulgakov: Life and Interpretations* by A. Colin Wright, 1978; *My Life with Mikhail Bulgakov* by L.E. Belozerskaia-Bulgakova, 1983; *Bulgakov: Life and Work* by Ellendea Proffer, 1984; *A Mind in Ferment: Mikhail Bulgakov's Prose* by Kalpana Sahni, 1984; *Mikhail Bulgakov* by Nadine Natov, 1985; *Mikhail Butgakov v Khudozhestvennom teatre* by Anatolii Smel'ianskii, 1986; *Between Two Worlds: A Critical Introduction to the Master and Margarita* by Andrew Barratt, 1987; *Bulgakov's Last Decade: The Writer as Hero* by J.A.E. Curtis, 1987; *Vospominaniia o Mikhaile Bulgakove,* 1988; *Zhizn' i smert' Mikhaila Bulgakova* by Anatolii Shvartz, 1988; *Zhizneopisanie Mikhaila Bulgakova* by M. Chudakova, 1988; Mikhail Bulgakov issue, *Soviet Literature,* 7(484), 1988; *Pis'ma. Zhizneopisanie v dokumentakh* edited by V.I. Losev and V.V. Petelin, 1989; *Biografiia M.A. Bulgakova. Pis'ma. Zhizneopisanie v dokumentakh* by P.S. Popov, 1989; *The Apocalyptic Vision of Mikhail Bulgakov's The Master and Margarita* by Edwin Mellen, 1991; *The Writer's Divided Self in Bulgakov's The Master and Margarita* by Riitta H. Pittman, 1991; *Is Comrade Bulgakov Dead?: Mikhail Bulgakov at the Moscow Art Theatre* by

Anatoly Smeliansky, translated by Arch Tait, 1993; *Bulgakov: The Novelist Playwright*, edited by Lesley Milne, 1995; *Bulgakov's Apocalyptic Critique of Literature* by Derek J. Hunns, 1996; *The Master and Margarita: A Critical Companion*, edited by Laura D. Weeks, 1996.

*   *   *

Mikhail Bulgakov is today one of the best-loved writers in the former Soviet Union, seen by many as reflecting the absurdities of that society under Stalinism and—although he died in 1940—of a later period as well. Although he was generally acclaimed following the publication of his masterpiece *Master i Margarita (The Master and Margarita)* in 1965–66, official attitudes towards him remained tolerant rather than acclamatory (with many works remaining unpublished) until the advent of *glasnost'* in the late 1980s. The first Soviet edition of his *Sobranie sochinenii* [Collected Works] was published just in time for the centenary of his birth in 1991, and his plays are now widely performed throughout Russia and other former republics of the Union of Soviet Socialist Republics, as well as in Eastern Europe.

Bulgakov began his career as a doctor, and his experiences in a country hospital during World War I became the basis for a number of humorous stories which may be seen as self-satire (later collected under the title *Zapiski iunogo vracha* [*A Country Doctor's Notebook*]). After leaving his native Kiev in 1919 for Vladikavkaz in the Caucasus—the result of being forcibly mobilized into various different armies during the Civil War and then attempting to find his younger brother—he abandoned medicine for literature, becoming "literary manager" for a "sub-department of the arts" and writing five plays (which have not survived) for the local population. Returning to Moscow in 1921, he supported himself and his wife by journalism, writing feuilletons which, although of minor literary value, provide an interesting and amusing picture of Russian life in the 1920s. He also published a number of satirical stories, of which *Sobach'e serdtse (The Heart of a Dog)* is best known. With its bitter criticism of Communist society, this story long remained unprintable—and indeed unmentionable—in the Soviet Union, but, with *glasnost'*, not only has it been widely published but dramatizations of it have been performed in most major cities (Bulgakov himself had intended to adapt it for the stage in 1926). Bulgakov's first major work was his novel, *Belaia gvardiia (The White Guard)*, based on his own experiences in Kiev during the Civil War. After its publication in 1925—although only in part, since the journal in which it appeared was closed down—Bulgakov was invited to rewrite it as a play for the Moscow Art Theatre. Its performance in 1926 as *Dni Turbinykh (The Days of the Turbins)* was a major theatrical event in that, despite the necessary changes to make it more politically acceptable, it was a sensitive portrayal of the problems of a "white" family during the upheavals that followed the revolution. (It has now been performed in an earlier version, without the politically motivated changes.) Withdrawn in 1929, along with two further plays *Zoikina kvartira (Madame Zoya)*, a surrealistic tragi-farce, and *Bagrovyi ostrov (The Crimson Island)*, an allegory on the revolution and a satire on censorship, *The Days of the Turbins* was restaged in 1932 with Stalin's approval. Indeed, in the later, oppressive post-war years of Stalinism, when Bulgakov's name could not even be mentioned publicly, he would be remembered, if at all, only as the author of this play. Another play *Beg (Flight)*, with its psychological study of a white general in the Civil War, was banned while still at the rehearsal stage.

In 1930, after an unsuccessful appeal to Stalin to be allowed to leave the country, Bulgakov was found employment with the Moscow Art Theatre, which led ultimately to his (uncompleted) satire *Teatralnyi roman (Black Snow: A Theatrical Novel)* including a humorous portrait of Stanislavskii in his later years. Bulgakov's stage version of Gogol's *Mertvye dushi (Dead Souls)* enjoyed a modest success, as did too, posthumously, an adaptation of Cervante's *Don Quixote* and a play about Pushkin, *Poslednie dni (The Last Days)*. The failure of his major play *Mol'er (Molière)*, in which he treated the French dramatist as a fallible human being instead of the "great man" Stanislavskii demanded, led to his resignation from the Art Theatre in 1936, when he became a librettist for the Bolshoi. Further works include an imaginative biography, *Zhizn' gospodina de Mol'era (The Life of Monsieur de Molière)*; a pacifist and anti-Communist play, *Adam i Eva (Adam and Eve)*; two comedies, *Blazhenstvo (Bliss)* and *Ivan Vasil'evich*; an adaptation of Tolstoi's *Voina i mir (War and Peace)*; various film scenarios and opera librettos; and a play based on the young Stalin, *Batum*, none of which appeared during Bulgakov's lifetime.

Aware that he was suffering from nephrosclerosis and had little time remaining to him, Bulgakov devoted his last years to a major effort to complete *The Master and Margarita*, dictating the final changes to his wife (his third, on whom the figure of Margarita was based) on his deathbed after he had become blind. His principal claim to fame in the West rests on this novel, arguably one of the major works of world literature of the 20th century. Published 25 years after his death, it combines an account of the devil's visit to Moscow in the 1930s with an unorthodox interpretation of Christ before Pilate in ancient Jerusalem: this presented through a "novel" written by the book's hero. As well as being fantasy, satire, comedy, mystery, and romance, it is a work of considerable philosophical depth, drawing equally on biblical and apocryphal sources and on the Faust tradition. Its basic postulates are that "Jesus existed," that "manuscripts don't burn"—a belief in the enduring nature of art—and that "everything will turn out right. That's what the world is built on": an extraordinary metaphysical optimism for a man whose life was characterized by recurring disappointment.

—A. Colin Wright

See the essays on *The Master and the Margarita* and *The White Guard*.

BUNIN, Ivan Alekseevich

Born: Voronezh, Russia, 10 October 1870. **Education:** Educated at the Gymnasium, Elets, 1881–85, and then at home in Ozerki; University of Moscow. **Family:** Married 1) Anna Nikolaevna Tsakni in 1898 (separated 1900), one son; 2) Vera Muromtseva, with whom he had lived since 1907, in 1921. **Career:** Editorial assistant, *Orlovskii vestnik* [Orel Courier], 1889–91; secretary, department of statistics, Poltava district administration, 1892–94; opened bookstore, 1894, and distributed publications of Tolstoi's, *q.v.*, publishing house, Posrednik: arrested for selling books without a license, but escaped prison sentence; entered literary circles in St. Petersburg and Moscow, 1895: in early years associated with the Symbolist publishing house Skorpion, and, after 1901, with Gor'kii's, *q.v.*, Znanie publishing house until 1909; travelled to Switzerland and Germany, 1900,

Constantinople (now Istanbul), 1903, Egypt, Ceylon (now Sri Lanka), and Singapore, 1911, and three times to Capri, visiting Gor'kii, 1911–14; lived in Moscow, Kiev, and Odessa during Revolutionary turmoil, 1918–20; moved to Constantinople, 1920, and eventually arrived in Paris, 1923, via Serbia and Bulgaria: settled in Grasse, southern France. Elected to the Russian Academy of Sciences, 1909. **Awards:** Pushkin prize, 1903, 1909; Nobel prize for literature, 1933. **Died:** 8 November 1953.

PUBLICATIONS

Collections

Sobranie sochinenii [Collected Works]. 5 vols., 1956.
Sobranie sochinenii [Collected Works]. 9 vols., 1965–67.
Sochineniia [Works]. 3 vols., 1982–84.
Sobranie sochinenii [Collected Works], edited by A.K. Baboreko. 6 vols., 1987.
Sobranie sochinenii [Collected Works]. 4 vols., 1988.

Fiction

Derevnia. 1910; as *The Village*, translated by Isabel F. Hapgood, 1923.
Sukhodol [Dry Valley]. 1911.
Grammatika liubvi. 1915; as *The Grammar of Love*, translated by John Cournos, 1977.
Gospodin iz San-Frantsisko. 1915; as *The Gentleman from San Francisco and Other Stories*, translated by Bernard Guilbert Guerney, 1934.
Fifteen Tales, translated by Bernard Guilbert Guerney. 1924.
Zhizn' Arsen'eva [The Life of Arsen'ev]. 1933; complete edition, 1952; translated in part as *The Well of Days*, by Gleb Struve and Hamish Miles, 1934.
The Dreams of Chang and Other Stories, translated by Gleb Struve and Hamish Miles. 1935.
The Elaghin Affair and Other Stories, translated by Bernard Guilbert Guerney. 1935.
Temnye allei [Dark Avenues] (stories). 1943.
Dark Avenues and Other Stories, translated by Richard Hare. 1949.
Vesnoi, v Iudee [Spring, in Judea]. 1953.
Petlistye ushi i drugie rasskazy [Loop Ears and Other Stories]. 1954.
Rasskazy [Stories]. 1955.
Lika. 1958.
Shadowed Paths, translated by Olga Shartse. 1958.
Povesti. Rasskazy. Vospominaniia [Short Stories. Stories. Reminiscences]. 1961.
Rasskazy [Stories]. 1962.
Rasskazy [Stories]. 1971.
Povesti. Rasskazy [Short Stories]. 1973.
Sueta suet [The Fuss of Vanities]. 1973.
Povesti i rasskazy [Short Stories]. 1977.
Poslednee svidanie [The Last Meeting]. 1978.
Stories and Poems, translated by Olga Shartse and Irina Zheleznova. 1979.
Rasskazy [Stories]. 1980.
Chasha zhizni [The Cup of Life]. 1983.
In a Far Distant Land: Selected Stories, translated by Robert Bowie. 1983.

Long Ago: Fourteen Stories, translated by David Richards and Sophie Lund. 1984.
Kholodnaia vesna [Cold Spring]. 1986.
Poeziia i proza [Poetry and Prose]. 1986.
Light Breathing and Other Stories, translated by Olga Shartse. 1988.
Velga (for children), translated by Guy Daniels. 1989.
Wolves and Other Love Stories, translated by Mark C. Scott. 1989.
Povesti i rasskazy [Short Stories and Stories]. 1990.

Verse

Stikhotvoreniia [Poetry]. 1956.
Listopad [Autumn]. 1982.
Stikhotvoreniia. Rasskazy [Poetry. Stories]. 1986.

Other

Sobranie sochinenii [Collected Works]. 1934–35.
Osvobozhdenie Tolstogo [The Emancipation of Tolstoi] (biography). 1937.
O Chekhove [About Chekhov] (unfinished manuscript). 1955.
Okaiannye dni: k dvadtsatiletiiu so dnia smerti I.A. Bunina [The Last Days: Twenty Years after the Death of I.A. Bunin]. 1973.
Buninskii sbornik [Bunin's Notebook]. 1974.
Pis'ma Buninykh k khudozhnitse T. Loginovoi-Murav'evoi (1936–1961) [Letters from the Bunins to the Artist T. Loginova-Murav'eva]. 1982.
Ivan Bunin i literaturnyi protsess nachala XX veka [Ivan Bunin and the Literary Process at the Beginning of the 20th Century]. 1985.
Stikhotvoreniia i perevody [Poetry and Translations]. 1985.
I sled moi v mire est' . . . = j'ai laissé une trace dans ce monde. . . [I Have Left My Mark on the World]. 1989.
Lish' slovu zhizn' dana. . . [Life is Given Only to the Word. . .]. 1990. [Life is Given Only to the Word. . .]. 1990.
Ivan Bunin (collections). 1991.
Solnechnii udar [Sunstroke]. 1992.
Russian Requiem 1885–1920: A Portrait from Letters, Diaries and Fiction, edited by Thomas Gaiton Marullo. 1993.
Catalogue of the I.A. Bunin, V.N. Bunina, L.F. Zurov and E.M. Lopatina Collections by Anthony J. Heywood, 2000.
Translator, *Pesn' o Gaivate*, by G.V. Longfellow. 1941.
Translator, *Zolotoi disk* (poems). 1975.

*

Critical Studies: "The Art of Ivan Bunin" by Gleb Struve, in *Slavonic and East European Review*, 11, 1932–33; "The Art of Ivan Bunin" by Renato Poggioli, in *The Phoenix and the Spider*, 1957; *The Works of Ivan Bunin* by Serge Kryzytski, 1971; *Ivan Bunin: A Study of His Fiction* by James B. Woodward, 1980; *Ivan Bunin* by Julian W. Connolly, 1982; *The Narratology of the Autobiography: An Analysis of the Literary Devices Employed in Ivan Bunin's "The Life of Arsenev"* by Alexander F. Zweers, 1997; *If You See the Buddha: Studies in the Fiction of Ivan Bunin* by Thomas Gaiton Marullo, 1998.

* * *

Ivan Bunin was the last major Russian writer to emerge from the ranks of the landed gentry and the first Russian writer to win the Nobel prize for literature. His most notable early successes were achieved as a poet and translator of poetry, and he continued to write poetry throughout his career. His reputation rests chiefly, however, on his two short novels *Derevnia* (*The Village*) and *Sukhodol* ("Dry Valley"), the autobiographical novel *Zhizn' Arsen'eva* [The Life of Arsen'ev], and, above all, his collections of short stories. All his work reflects the loyalty to the 19th-century realistic tradition which he advocated passionately in the literary polemics of the pre-revolutionary years. But the mark of the "Silver Age" is nevertheless visible in his outlook as a writer, in the poetic qualities of his prose and meticulous attention to matters of style and craftsmanship, and in the general character of an art that eschews ideas and attaches greater importance to tone than to incident.

One of the most frequently noted features of Bunin's art is the impression of coldness that it conveys, and his fastidiousness as a stylist is commonly adduced in this connection as a contributory factor. The explanation lies mainly, however, in the conception of life that informs almost all his work and in its implications for the status of the individual in his fiction. It is a view of man's life as governed by irrational forces that perpetually defy and subvert all his efforts to control it. In his early stories, such as "Antonovskie iabloki" ("Antonov Apples") and "Epitafiia" ("The Epitaph"), these forces are social. Reflecting the experience of his own family, they evoke lyrically and nostalgically the passing of the traditional rural way of life in which the landed gentry and peasantry, in Bunin's somewhat idealistic portrayal, lived in harmony with each other and in contented communion with nature. But in the transition from these stories to *The Village* and *Sukhodol* nostalgia and sorrow give way not only to anger and embitterment, but also to a broader philosophical understanding, according to which this process of social change is seen as the expression of an impersonal law of nature, of the natural law of decay to which societies, he had come to believe, like individuals, are unalterably subject and which begins ineluctably to operate as soon as the communion with nature is broken. In the two short novels, as in the stories "Veselyi dvor" ("A Happy Farmhouse"), 1911, "Ermil" (1912), and "Vesennii vecher" ("An Evening in Spring"), 1914, the behaviour and attitudes of individual landowners and peasants are examined as reflections of the moral and psychological effects of this law which Bunin interprets as inducing a kind of mental paralysis, a compulsion to maim and destroy, and a crippling insensitivity to the irrational aspects of life. By 1914, drawing on the experience of his travels in Europe and his journeys to Turkey and the Middle East described in "Ten' ptitsy" [The Shadow of the Bird] (1907–11), he was already intent on demonstrating the universal implications of this judgement. Hence "Brat'ia" ("The Brothers") and his most famous tale, *Gospodin iz San-Frantsisko* (*The Gentleman from San Francisco*), in which the same symptoms of moral decay, attributed to essentially the same basic cause, are explored in the portraits of an English traveller in Ceylon and an American capitalist on a voyage to Europe.

The most striking feature of all these works is the switch of emphasis from character to setting that results from the impersonality of Bunin's thought. Here action results not from rational decisions or free moral choices but from psychological conditions represented as reflecting the relation of the characters to the world about them. Thus the murder committed by the brutal Sokolovich in "Petlistye ushi" ("Loop Ears"), in which Bunin directly challenges Dostoevskii's faith in conscience and free will, is implicitly explained by nature's exclusion, by the transposition of the action to the dehumanizing urban setting of Petrograd. The result in each case is that descriptions of the setting acquire an unusual prominence. Often describing the structure and style of these works in musical terms, Bunin regarded them as performing an essentially musical function, as evoking a sense of the "rhythms" of life that determine the conduct of men and societies. He conceived of motivation as deriving less from events than from "harmonies" or "discords" between these "rhythms" and the human psyche.

The philosophical impersonality that gave birth to this distinctive kind of short story explains the profound interest, documented in "The Brothers" and later in "Noch" ("Night") and *Osvobozhdenie Tolstogo* [The Emancipation of Tolstoy] (1937), that Bunin had in Buddhism and the Buddhist conception of personality. It also determined his treatment of the theme that developed ultimately into the principal expression of his view of life—the theme of love. The most notable pre-revolutionary stories devoted to this theme are "Ignat," "Pri doroge" ("By the Road"), "Legkoe dykhanie" ("Light Breathing"), and "Syn" ("The Son"), and after his emigration to France it became almost his only theme, inspiring such well known works as "Mitina liubov" ("Mitia's Love"), "Delo Korneta Elagina" ("The Elaghin Affair"), *Solnechnii udar* ("Sunstroke"), and the stories that comprise his final volume *Temnye allei* [Dark Avenues]. As depicted by Bunin, love is always a pre-eminently sensual experience, a blinding flash of light that briefly illuminates the ultimate realities of life: the impotence of human reason, the impermanence of everything on earth, and man's inescapable thraldom to remorseless impersonal forces. With few exceptions, therefore, the love stories are tragic tales, the characters of which are torn by passion from the normal routines of their lives and repeatedly impelled, like automata, to embark on self-destructive courses of action. Here love is almost invariably experienced in the shadow of death. Yet the tragic conclusions of these tales are to be taken as expressing a judgement less on love than on life. For, as "Sunstroke" and the stories of *Temnye allei* make abundantly clear, love was also for Bunin the source of the greatest happiness that life affords man, offering an intensity of experience that transforms all preconceived notions of life and its meaning. Like *Zhizn' Arsen'eva*, the love stories convey the supreme value attached to sensory experience by a writer who thanked God for every moment that he spent on earth, yet was able to conceive of Him only as the creator of the laws of nature. For this reason Bunin continued to wrestle to the end with the mystery of man's ephemeral existence, for the representation of which he developed his highly personal and expressive medium.

—James B. Woodward

See the essay on *The Gentleman from San Francisco*.

BUZZATI, Dino

Born: Dino Buzzati-Traverso in San Pellegrino, near Belluno, Italy, 16 October 1906. **Education:** Educated at the Ginnasio Parini, Milan, 1916–24; University of Milan, 1924–26, 1927–28, degree in law 1928. **Military Service:** Served 1926–27: 2nd lieutenant. **Family:** Married Almerina Antoniazzi in 1966. **Career:** Correspondent, *Il Corriere della Sera*, Milan, 1928–72, which first published much of his writing; contributor, *Il Popolo di Lombardia*, from 1931; war correspondent for various newspapers, 1940–43; reporter in Tokyo, 1963, Jerusalem, New York, Washington, DC, and Bombay, 1964, Prague and New York, 1965. Also a painter (first exhibition, 1958, and subsequent exhibitions in Milan and Paris, 1966, Rome, 1971,

Milan 1972) and occasional director of plays, operas, and ballets. **Awards:** Gargano prize, 1951; Naples prize, 1954; Strega prize, 1958; Paese Sera prize, 1969; Mario Massai prize (for journalism), 1970. **Died:** 28 January 1972.

PUBLICATIONS

Collection

Teatro, edited by Guido Davico Bonino. 1980; selections as *Un caso clinico e altre commedie in un atto*, 1985.
Opere Scelte, edited by Giulio Carnazzi, 1998.
Il Borghese Stregato e Altri Racconti, with introduction by Carmen Covito, 1994.

Fiction

Barnabò delle montagne. 1933.
Il segreto del Bosco Vecchio. 1935.
Il deserto dei Tartari. 1940; as *The Tartar Steppe*, translated by Stuart C. Hood, 1952.
I sette messaggeri (stories). 1942.
La famosa invasione degli orsi in Sicilia (for children), illustrations by Buzzati. 1945; as *The Bears' Famous Invasion of Sicily*, translated by Frances Lobb, 1947.
Paura alla Scala (stories). 1949.
Il crollo della Baliverna (stories). 1954.
Esperimento di magia. 1958.
Sessanta racconti (includes *I sette messaggeri; Paura alla Scala; Il crollo della Baliverna*). 1958.
Il grande ritratto. 1960; as *Larger Than Life*, translated by Henry Reed, 1962.
Egregio signore, siamo spiacenti di. . . (stories). 1960.
Un amore. 1963; as *A Love Affair*, translated by Joseph Green, 1964.
Il colombre e altri cinquanta racconti (stories). 1966.
Catastrophe: The Strange Stories of Dino Buzzati, translated by Judith Landry and Cynthia Jolly. 1966; as *Catastrophe and Other Stories*, translated by Landry and Jolly, 1982.
La boutique del mistero. 1968.
Poema a fumetti. 1969.
Le notti difficili (stories). 1971.
Romanzi e racconti, edited by Giuliano Gramigna. 1975.
180 racconti, edited by Carlo Della Corte. 1982.
Restless Nights: Selected Stories, translated by Lawrence Venuti. 1984.

Verse

Il capitano Pic e altre poesie. 1965.
Due poemetti. 1967.
Poesie. 1982.

Plays

Piccola passeggiata (produced 1942). 1942.
La rivolta dei poveri (produced 1946). In *Teatro*, 1980.
Un caso clinico, from his story "Sette piani" (produced 1953). 1953.
Ferrovia soprelevata, music by Luciano Chailly (produced 1955). 1960.

Drammatica fine di un noto musicista (produced 1955). In *Teatro*, 1980.
Sola in casa (produced 1958). In *Teatro*, 1980.
Una ragazza arrivò (radio play; broadcast 1959). 1958.
Le finestre (produced 1959). In *Teatro*, 1980.
L'orologio (produced 1959). In *Teatro*, 1980.
Procedura penale, music by Luciano Chailly (produced 1959). 1959.
Il mantello (produced 1960). In *Teatro*, 1980; revised version, music by Luciano Chailly (produced 1960), 1960.
Un verme al ministero (produced 1960). In *Teatro*, 1980.
I suggeritori (produced 1960). In *Teatro*, 1980.
L'uomo che andrà in America (produced 1962). 1968.
La colonna infame (produced 1962). In *Teatro*, 1980.
Battono alla porta, music by Riccardo Malipiero (television opera; broadcast 1962; produced 1963). 1963.
Era proibito (produced 1962). 1963.
La fine del borghese (produced 1966). 1968.

Radio Plays: *Una ragazza arrivò*, 1959.

Television Writing: *Battono alla porta*, music by Riccardo Malipiero, 1962.

Other

Il capitano delle pipe, with Eppe Ramazzotti. 1945.
In quel preciso momento (miscellany). 1950; enlarged edition, 1955.
Miracoli di Val Morel (sketches). 1971.
Cronache terrestri (essays), edited by Domenico Porzio. 1972.
Il pianeta Buzzati (biographical documents, photographs), edited by Almerina Buzzati. 1974.
I misteri d'Italia. 1978.
Dino Buzzati al Giro d'Italia. 1981; as *The Giro d'Italia: Coppi Versus Bartali at the 1949 Tour of Italy*, introduced by John Wilcockson, 1999.
Cronache nere (essays), edited by Oreste Del Buono. 1984.
Il reggimento parte all'alba. 1985.
Lettere a Brambilla, edited by Luciano Simonelli. 1987.
Le montagne di vetro (stories and articles). 1989.

*

Critical Studies: *Dino Buzzati* by Fausto Gianfranceschi, 1967; *Il racconto fantastico da Tarchetti a Buzzati* by Neuro Bonifazi, 1971; *Dino Buzzati: Un autoritratto* by Yves Panafieu, 1971; *Invito alla lettura di Dino Buzzati*, by Antonia Arslan Veronese, 1974; *Come leggere Il deserto dei Tartari* by Marcello Carlino, 1976; "Spatial Structures in the Narrative of Dino Buzzati" by Elaine D. Cancalon, in *Forum Italicum*, 11(36–46), 1977; *Dino Buzzati* by Ilaria Crotti, 1977; *Anormalità e angoscia nella narrativa di Dino Buzzati* by Mario B. Mignone, 1981; *Guida all lettura di Dino Buzzati* by Claudio Toscani, 1987; *Dino Buzzati* by Giovanna Ioli, 1988; *Il coraggio della fantasia. Studi e ricerche intorno a Dino Buzzati* by Nella Giannetto, 1989; *Dino Buzzati tra fantastico e realistico* by Antonia Arslan, 1993; *Tre voci sospete: Buzzati, Piovene, Parise* by Ilaria Crotti, 1994; *Il sudario delle caligini: Significati e fortune dell'opera buzzatiana* by Nella Giannetto, 1996; *Dino Buzzati e il segreto della montagna* by Luigi De Anna, 1997; *Buzzati: Il limite dell'ombra* by Giorgio Cavallini, 1997; *Dino Buzzati: Le laboratoire secret* by Michel Suffran, 1998.

* * *

The critical fortunes of Dino Buzzati have fluctuated with the times. In the 1950s and 1960s he was extremely highly regarded as a writer, but after his death in 1972 his international popularity declined in the face of more fashionable Italian writers, such as Italo Calvino, Umberto Eco, and Primo Levi. Nevertheless, as the less ephemeral aspects of his output are being reassessed he is once again recognized as a major writer, both within and outside Italy.

A journalist for most of his life on Italy's leading daily newspaper, *Il Corriere della Sera*, Buzzati was convinced in theory, and proved in practice, that the best journalism could also be good literature. His first novel, *Barnabò delle montagne* [Barnabò of the Mountains], concerns a young woodsman who waits years for revenge, but when he finally has his enemy in his sights he refuses to shoot him. The two themes of waiting and abnegation, as well as a passion for mountain landscapes, recur in all Buzzati's works. His second novel, *Il segreto del Bosco Vecchio* [The Secret of the Old Wood], is, in its woodland setting, reminiscent of Tolkien; but it was his third and most ambitious novel that established the authentic Buzzati style.

Buzzati wrote *Il deserto dei Tartari* (*The Tartar Steppe*) in the first year of World War II, typing it in the mornings after he finished night shift at the *Corriere*. Perhaps these circumstances account for some of the pessimistic *ennui* of the novel, but there was also a considerable streak of innate melancholy in Buzzati himself. The novel's hero, Giovanni Drogo, sets out for military duty in a fortress that guards the steppe across which the Tartars may invade at any moment. Drogo spends the whole of his life there, waiting for the attack which only materializes when he is too old and too ill to fight. At the end, Drogo's true moment of glory arrives when he learns to face his own death, in an anonymous hotel room, with a stoicism that would have befitted the battlefield. The novel, later translated into French by Camus, was a resounding success. Its Kafkaesque pessimism suited the dark days of its composition; but there are many memorable passages which still appeal. Particularly powerful are his exploration of the passing of time, his visual descriptions of the mountains and the desert, his attention to sonorous detail in describing military routine, and his celebration of the mediocre existence of an everyman.

After this work, Buzzati was to write only two more novels, and both were flawed affairs, inspired by external contingencies rather than by an inner compulsion to write: *Il grande ritratto* (*Larger Than Life*) was submitted anonymously to a competition run by the magazine *Oggi*, while *Un amore* (*A Love Affair*) was written only after the death of Buzzati's mother, with whom he had lived until he was 55, and after he himself had fallen seriously in love for the first time.

In the meantime, Buzzati had found his true vein as a writer of short stories. His first collection, *I sette messaggeri* [The Seven Messengers] was enlarged to become *Sessanta racconti* [Sixty Stories], which included the best of his output to date, and which won him Italy's major literary prize, the Strega prize, in 1958. This latter volume includes some of the masterpieces in the genre. "Il mantello" ("The Cloak"), for example, which is like *The Tartar Steppe*, in miniature, has a haunting opening passage reminiscent of Poe at his best; it contains dialogue full of pathos in the exchanges between a mother and her son who, unknown to her, has died in battle but has been allowed to visit her; and it concludes with an evocative finale, as the black figure waiting outside the garden gate accompanies the son to his final destination. "Qualcosa era successo" ("Something Had Happened") is in the same dark vein: the passengers in the north-bound express realize some unknown disaster must have occurred in the north, since from the window they can see the inhabitants fleeing southwards in cars and trains. As they arrive in the deserted northern station a woman's scream concludes the tale in a verbal equivalent of Edvard Munch's famous painting "The Scream." There are also sunnier stories in the collection. "Il disco si posò" ("The Saucer Landed"), for instance, opens with a village priest noticing a flying saucer landing on the church roof and two Martians coming out to investigate its cross. When Don Pietro launches into the story from the Bible in order to convert them, he learns, to his chagrin, that the Tree of Good and Evil is still blooming on Mars, since the ancestors of these superior intelligences obeyed God's command. Yet, underneath this more humorous style, Buzzati remains melancholic about the imperfection of humanity. He published other volumes of short stories, including *Egregio signore, siamo spacienti di. . .* [We Are Sorry To. . .], *Il colombre*, the title story being about a mythical sea monster, and *Le notti difficili* [Difficult Nights]. However, none of them has attained the impressive consistency of *Sessanta racconti*.

Buzzati's abilities as a visual artist not only inform some of the stories and adorn most of his own book covers, but also led to his publication of picture books, including a children's book, *La famosa invasione degli orsi in Sicilia* (*The Bears' Famous Invasion of Sicily*), a book about curious ex-votos in Northern Italy, and *Miracoli di Val Morel* [Miracles of Val Morel], as well as a reworking of the Orpheus myth, in which Orpheus is a rock singer in 1960s Milan.

The themes of Buzzati's work are co-terminous with some of the key themes of 20th-century literature: man's solitude, the ineluctability of time and destiny, and the frisson of pleasure and terror inspired by landscapes of mountains, deserts, and cities. Though many critics have written of Kafka's influence, Buzzati evolved, in his best short stories and in his major novel, a compelling and distinctive style with which to elaborate these motifs.

—Martin L. McLaughlin

BYKAW, Vasil (Vladimirovich)

Born: Chernovshchina, Vitebsk region, Belorussia, Soviet Union (now independent as Belarus), 19 June 1924. **Education:** Educated at art academy, Vitebsk. **Military Service:** Served in the army during World War II: officer; remained in the army for ten more years. **Career:** Journalist for newspaper in Grodno; deputy of the Supreme Soviet of Belorussia. Lives in Minsk. **Awards:** Belorussian Republic Yakub Kolas prize; State prize, 1974; Lenin prize, 1986. **Member:** Bureau of the secretariat of the Writers Union of the Union of Soviet Socialist Republics, 1986.

PUBLICATIONS

Fiction

U toy dzien' [That Day]. 1949.
U pershym bai [In the First Battle]. 1949.
Abaznik [The Transport Driver] (story). 1956.
Žhurawliny kryk [The Cry of the Crane] (stories). 1956.
Zdrada [Treachery]. 1961.

Tretstsya raketa (stories). 1962; as *The Third Flare*, translated by Robert Daglish, 1966.

Al'piyskaya balada. 1964; as *Alpine Ballad*, translated by George Hanna, 1966.

Mertvym ne balits' [The Dead Feel No Pain]. 1965.

Praklyataya vyshynya [The Accursed Hill]. 1968.

Kruhlyansky most [The Bridge at Kruhlyany]. 1969.

Sotnikaw. 1970; as *The Ordeal*, translated by Gordon Clough, 1972; as *Sotnikov*, translated by Brian Bean, in *Soviet War Stories*, 1990.

Abelisk [The Obelisk] (story). 1971.

Dažhyts' da svitannya (story). 1973; as *His Battalion and Live until Dawn*, translated by Jennifer and Robert Woodhouse, 1981.

Vowčhaya zhraya (story). 1974; translated as ''The Wolf Pack,'' in *Soviet Literature*, 5, 1975; as *A Pack of Wolves*, 1981.

Paystsi i ne viarnutstsa [To Go and Not Return]. 1978.

Znak byady. 1982; as *Sign of Misfortune*, translated by Alan Myers, 1990.

Kar'er [The Pit]. 1987.

V tumane [In the Mist]. 1987.

Ablava [The Swoop]. 1989.

Plays

Rashenne [The Decision]. 1972.
Aposhni shants [The Last Chance]. 1974.

Other

Reč' na s'ezde Soiza pisatelei Belorussii [Speech to the Union of Belarusian Writers], in *Grani*, 61. 1966.

*

Critical Studies: *Vasil Bykaw: Narys tvorchastsi* by Vasil Buran, 1976; ''Vasil' Bykov and the Soviet Byelorussian Novel,'' in *The Languages and Literatures of the Non-Russian Peoples of the Soviet Union*, 1977, ''War and Peace in the Prose of Vasil Bykau,'' in *Die Welt der Slaven*, 8(1), 1983, and ''Recovery of the Past and Struggle for the Future: Vasil' Bykaw's Recent War Fiction,'' in *World War II and the Soviet People*, edited by John and Carol Garrard, 1993, all by Arnold B. McMillin; *Vasil' Bykov: Ocherk tvorchestva*, 1979, and *Vasil Bykov* (in English; includes interviews with Bykaw), 1987, both by L. Lazarev; ''The Growth of Crystal: Vasil' Bykov, Characters and Circumstances'' by Igor' Shtokman, in *Soviet Studies in Literature*, 15(2), 1979; *Vasil' Bykov: Ocherk tvorchestva* by I. Dedkov, 1980; *Vasil' Bykov: Povesti o voine* by A. Shagalov, 1989; ''The Art of Vasil' Bykov'' by Deming Brown, in *Zapisy Belaruskaha Instytuta Navuki i Mastatstva*, 20, 1992; *Belarusian Literature in the 1950s and 1960s: Release and Renewal* by Arnold McMillin, 1999.

* * *

Vasil Bykaw, an outstanding figure in present-day Belarusian prose, has chosen to write almost exclusively about World War II, raising the genre of war literature from one beset by cliché and hollow heroics to a level of sophistication marked by unvarnished realistic description of small-scale events, and a psychological truthfulness matched by few, if any, of his contemporaries. The consistent and unflinching moral focus of Bykaw's prose fiction brought him great popularity in the post-Stalin era, and, particularly in the last years of the Soviet Union, he has played a major role in the struggle for

Belarus's true independence. He has more than once been described by his fellow-countrymen as ''the conscience of the Belarusian people.''

Bykaw's writing came to prominence in the atmosphere of comparative freedom associated with the Thaw. Only 17 when the war broke out, he characteristically makes very young men the central figures in his stories and novellas, seeing events, actions and moral decisions through their eyes, and often contrasting them with the demagogy, self-seeking, bullying, and, at times, treachery and cowardice of their superiors, whose actions in the fight against a cruel enemy can sometimes be hardly less ruthless. Bykaw depicts the war on a human rather than epic scale, using tight spatial and temporal contexts, often at moments of life-and-death crisis for a small group of soldiers or partisans. Stark moral choices are to the fore, and it is Bykaw's highlighting of uncomfortable questions, often with a strong contemporary resonance that, with his avoidance of cant and stereotyping, helps to account for his works' great popularity and also for the fierce attacks he sustained from Communist critics in the 1960s and 1980s.

The narrow compass of Bykaw's works is often extended by means of memory, flashback, and dreams. Alluding to such features of Stalinism as sudden arrests and collectivization, Bykaw shows how their consequences affected the conduct of Soviet citizens during the war. For example, an episode in *Zdrada* [Treachery] tells the story of how a popular Komsomol secretary had been declared an ''enemy of the people'' in the 1930s before reappearing as a regular frontline soldier; in a later work, *Znak byady* (*Sign of Misfortune*), the behaviour of some Nazi collaborators is implicitly traced back to the bitter injustices suffered by their parents during the enforced collectivization of agriculture a decade earlier.

Often, too, Bykaw relates his war fiction to the present day, underlining the lessons of Stalinist immorality for Belarus and, indeed, the whole Soviet Union in the 1960s and 1970s. In his most expansive, autobiographical, and controversial novel, *Mertvym ne balits'* [The Dead Feel No Pain], a work long banned by the authorities, cruel and immoral Stalinist attitudes are graphically shown as being no less strong in Belarus of the 1960s than in the war; in *Abelisk* [The Obelisk] wartime injustices are hard to put right, even in the conditions of peace, and at the end of the novella Bykaw, never a dogmatist, seems to leave the ultimate decision to the reader: ''And now let the reader decide. Let him sort it out. Each according to his outlook on the world, his view of the war, of heroism, of his obligation to conscience and to history . . . .'' The linking of past and present is continued in Bykaw's latest works, such as *Kar'er* [The Pit].

Bykaw's thematic consistency has led to hostile critics accusing him of repetition, but there is a world of difference between his first major novella, *Žhurawliny kryk* [The Cry of the Crane], the outstanding story, *Kruhlyansky most* [The Bridge at Kruhlyany], the novel *Mertvym ne balits'*, his gripping first partisan novella, *Sotnikaw* (*The Ordeal*), and *Sign of Misfortune*. Not only does the last centre on old people rather than young heroes, it is set not in an area of conflict but in a run-down and deserted farm which has been taken over by the Germans and is being plagued by their henchmen. Again moral choices are prominent, but Bykaw shows a sensitive understanding of the various shades of grey, at the same time creating two memorable and contrasting peasant characters, and throwing much light on the misery of their lot in Soviet peacetime as well as war.

The moral imperative found throughout Bykaw's writing does not in any way impair his works' literary quality. His prose is always muscular and often lapidary, capable of vivid description and concise characterization, with sparing but effective imagery. The crises around which nearly all his works revolve make them both exciting and thought-provoking to read, both at a universal level and for a specifically Soviet readership, all too well aware that Khruschchev's denunciation of Stalin in 1956 did not mean abolition of Stalinist attitudes.

Translated into many languages (usually from Russian versions, no longer subjected to political bowdlerization in the process),

Bykaw's works have set new moral and artistic standards for Soviet and Belarusian literature. Topicality and universality combine in what is amongst the most powerful war prose in any language.

—Arnold McMillin

See the essay on *The Ordeal*.

C

CAESAR, (Gaius) Julius

Born: Rome in 100 or 102 BC. **Family:** Married 1) Cornelia in 83 BC (died); 2) Pompeia in 67 BC (divorced 62 BC); 3) Calpurnia in 59 BC. **Career:** Exiled in Asia because of opposition to Sulla, 82–78 BC; fought his first military campaign in Asia, 81 BC; on return to Rome entered politics and may have assisted in Catiline's conspiracy against Cicero, *q.v.*, and other senators; after a successful military campaign and governorship in Spain (61 BC), returned to Rome in 60 BC and formed a triumvirate with Pompey and Lucinius Crassus; consul, 59 and 56 BC; won support by his conquest of the province of Gaul, of which he was made governor, 58–50 BC; invaded Britain in 55 and 54 BC, subduing part of the country; crossed the river Rubicon without the authorization of the Senate, in effect declaring war on Pompey, his rival for power, but was victorious in the three months of civil war that followed; appointed dictator for one year; after Pompey's death, appointed for another year, and consul for five years; subdued Egypt and placed Cleopatra on the throne; made consul for ten years, and, in February 44 BC, dictator for life. **Died:** (assassinated) 15 March 44 BC.

PUBLICATIONS

Collections

[Commentaries], edited by Bernard Hübler. 3 vols., 1893–97; also edited by Alfred Klotz, 3 vols., 1920–27, and by Klotz, Otto Seel, and Winifried Trillitzsch, 1961–; as *War Commentaries*, edited and translated by John Warrington, 1953; as *The Commentaries*, translated by William Duncan, 1753; also translated by Somerset de Chair, 1951; as *The Gallic War and Other Writings*, translated by Moses Hadas, 1957; as *War Commentaries of Caesar*, translated by Rex Warner, 1960.

Works

De bello civili, edited by Charles E. Moberly, 1872; also edited by F. Kraner and F. Hofmann, revised by H. Meusel, 1906; Books I and II edited and translated by J.M. Carter, 1991; Book III edited and translated by J.M. Carter, 1993; as *Civil War with Pompeius*, translated by F.P. Long, 1906; as *The Civil Wars* [Loeb Edition], translated by A.G. Peskett, 1914; as *The Civil War*, translated by Jane F. Mitchell (now Gardner), 1967; as *The Civil War: With the Anonymous Alexandrian, African, and Spanish Wars*, translated with introduction by J.M. Carter, 1997.

De bello Gallico, edited by Charles E. Moberly. 2 vols., 1871; also edited by John Brown, 7 vols., 1900–03, T. Rice Holmes, 1914, and E.C. Kennedy, 1959–; as *Commentaries on the Gallic War*, translated by F.P. Long, 1906; also translated by T. Rice Holmes, 1908; as *The Gallic War*, translated by H.J. Edwards, 1917; as *The*

Conquest of Gaul, translated by S.A. Handford, 1951; also translated by Anne and Peter Wiseman, 1980; as *The Gallic Wars*, translated by John Warrington, 1954; as *Seven Commentaries on the Gallic War*, translated by Carolyn Hammond, 1996.

*

Critical Studies: *Julius Caesar* by Alfred Duggan, 1955; *Caesar as Man of Letters* by Franz E. Adcock, 1956; *Julius Caesar* by Michael Grant, 1969; *Caesar and Roman Politics 60–50 BC* by James S. Clare, 1971; *Caesar and Contemporary Roman Society* by Erik Wistrand, 1979; *End of the Ancient Republic: Essays on Julius Caesar* by Jan H. Blits, 1983; *Julius Caesar and His Public Image* by Zwi Yaetz, 1983; *Julius Caesar, the Pursuit of Power* by Ernle Bradford, 1984; *Fortune's Favorites* by Colleen McCullough, 1993; *Cicero's Caesarian Speeches: A Stylistic Commentary*, edited by Harold C. Gotoff, 1993; *Caesar* by Allan Massie, 1993; *Caesar* by Christian Meier, translated by David McLintock, 1995; *Caesar Against the Celts* by Ramon L. Jiménez, 1996; *Caesar's Women* by Colleen McCullough, 1996; *The Comet of 44 B.C. and Caesar's Funeral Games* by John T. Ramsey and A. Lewis Licht, 1997; *Julius Caesar as Artful Reporter: The War Commentaries as Political Instruments*, edited by Kathryn Welch and Anton Powell, 1998; *Caesar Against Rome: The Great Roman Civil War* by Ramon L. Jiménez, 2000; *Tense and Aspect in Caesar's Narrative* by Fredrik Oldsjö, 2001.

* * *

"In eloquence and in military skill Julius Caesar equalled or even surpassed the most famous." This was the judgement of Suetonius, a biographer not given to excessive praise, and what is particularly noteworthy is that Caesar is praised as much for his excellence in the arts of language as for his prowess as a soldier. This tireless man of action, one of history's most accomplished captains, a politician whose burning ambition was matched by his consummate skill, and a lover whose passions have beguiled the imaginations of later generations, was also an orator whose reputation in Rome in the first century BC was second only to Cicero's and a writer whose excellence won the admiration of all around him.

Such was Caesar's personality that it might be supposed his was an untutored talent. However, nothing could be further from the truth. In his early years he received a basic training in oratory from the freed slave Antonius Gnipho and put his newly acquired skills to use when, in a speech which he is reported to have delivered in a somewhat high pitched voice with great fluency and vehement gestures, he accused the provincial governor Dolabella of extortion. He did not secure a conviction but he succeeded in his primary aim of drawing attention to himself. Shortly afterwards, on his way to the island of Rhodes, Caesar was taken prisoner by pirates, released on ransom, and then returned to punish his captors with condign severity. That characteristic and colourful episode becomes even more interesting when it is recalled that his motive for this journey was, in fact, the desire to study under Apollonius Molon, one of the great teachers of rhetoric of the time. Whether or not the politically clever speech attacking Catiline,

177

which is cited by Sallust, is in fact an accurate reproduction of the words Caesar actually spoke, we certainly have further evidence here of his importance as an orator. Cicero himself draws particular attention in his *Brutus* to the purity of Caesar's Latin style.

Caesar's speeches are, however, no more the most important part of his literary output than is a work he wrote on philological concerns, though that too shows his concern for language. What really counts, of course, are the seven books of his *De bello Gallico* (*The Gallic War*) and the three of his *De bellum civile* (*The Civil War*). As an account of major events related by the principal actor in the unfolding drama, this is a work without parallel in ancient historical writing. The literary aspect, however, is hardly less remarkable. *The Gallic War* and *The Civil War* are categorized technically as "commentaries." They are not what the Greeks and Romans of the days would have classed as "histories." What commentaries were supposed to provide was only a bald, factual narrative of events. This was thought to be only the bare bones of history, considered a high literary form, replete with graphic battle scenes, for instance, and stirring speeches allegedly delivered to the troops by eloquent generals at suitable moments in the campaign. Nowadays we set the highest premium on the truthfulness of any historical narrative, but for antiquity some embellishment of fact was deemed legitimate in turning commentaries into the distinctly superior literary form of history.

Although Caesar purported to be writing only commentaries, it seems likely that he saw in their plain style an ideal way of presenting himself favourably to the public as an energetic man of deeds. "Gaul is all divided into three parts," the famous opening of *The Gallic War*, reveals something of his manner, especially when it is recalled that the sequence of Latin words permitted Caesar to place the word "three" emphatically after the noun "parts." It was notorious that Gaul was a vast, inchoate mish-mash of warring tribes, but the business-like commander Caesar cut the problem down to size. He likewise rejected the contemporary fashion of seeking to impress both by complexity in syntax and by inexhaustible variety in vocabulary, opting for something far more straightforward. His contemporaries, with their expertise in rhetoric, recognized that Caesar was, in fact, turning away from the so-called Asiatic style and using instead the Attic. Whether Caesar consciously adopted it may perhaps be debated, but that his choice was educated is undeniable. Successive generations have lauded Caesar's language as the reflection of a soldier's mind. The point that has not always been properly understood is that Caesar composed his commentaries precisely in order to create that impression.

The Gallic War, with its accounts of vast conquests north of the Alps and including, at the end of Book IV and the beginning of Book V, fascinating information about the Romans' first two raids on Britain, and *The Civil War*, describing the complex operations after 50 BC, were most likely written year by year after campaigning stopped. They succeeded admirably in ensuring that heed is paid above all to Caesar's role in events and to an interpretation that is most flattering to himself. What is more, it was recognized from the outset that there was in fact no way in which some man of letters could improve these particular commentaries by giving them literary polish and transforming them into history. Typically enough, Caesar had triumphed in yet another field of human endeavour.

—Christopher Smith

CALDERÓN DE LA BARCA, Pedro

Born: Madrid, Spain, 17 January 1600. **Education:** Educated at the Jesuit Colegio Imperial; studied canon law at the University of Alcalá, 1614–15, and University of Salamanca, 1615–c. 1621, no degree. **Career:** Entered the household of the Constable of Castille, Don Bernardino Fernández de Velasco, 1621; began writing plays for the court from 1623; entered order of St. James, 1637; served in the campaign against the Catalans, 1640–42; served in the household of the Duke of Alba from 1645; became a priest in 1651, but continued to write plays as court dramatist for Philip IV; chaplain of the Chapel of Reyes Nuevos, Toledo, from 1653, but lived in Madrid after 1657: Honorary Chaplain to the King, 1663. **Died:** 25 May 1681.

PUBLICATIONS

Collections

Obras, edited by Joseph Calderón. 5 vols., 1636–77.
Autos sacramentales. 1677.
Obras, edited by J. de Vera Tassis. 9 vols., 1682–91.
Poesias, edited by Adolfo de Castro Cádiz. 1845.
Dramas of Calderón: Tragic, Comic and Legendary (includes *Love after Death; The Scarf and the Flower; The Physician of His Own Honour; The Constant Prince; The Purgatory of St. Patrick*), translated by Denis F. McCarthy. 2 vols., 1853.
Six Dramas of Calderón (includes *The Mayor of Zalamea; Beware of Smooth Water; Gil Perez the Gallician; Keep Your Own Secret; The Painter of His Own Dishonour; Three Judgements at a Blow*), translated by Edward Fitzgerald. 1853; revised and enlarged edition as *Eight Dramas* (including additionally the adaptations *Such Stuff as Dreams Are Made Of* and *The Mighty Magician*), 1906.
Mysteries of Corpus Christi (includes *The Divine Philothea; Belshazzar's Feast; The Poison and the Antidote*), translated by Denis F. McCarthy. 1867.
Three Dramas of Calderón (includes *The Devotion of the Cross; The Sorceries of Sin; Love Is the Greatest Enchantment*), translated by Denis F. McCarthy. 1870.
Calderón's Dramas, translated by Denis F. McCarthy. 1873.
Obras escogidas. 1940.
Obra lírica, edited by M. de Montoliu. 1943.
Obras completas, edited by Luis Astrana Marín and Ángel Valbuena Briones. 3 vols., 1956–59:
    Dramas, edited by Luis Astrana Marín. 1959.
    Comedias, edited by Ángel Valbuena Briones. 1956.
    Autos sacramentales, edited by Ángel Valbuena Prat. 1959.
Four Plays (includes *Secret Vengeance for Secret Insult; The Devotion of the Cross; The Mayor of Zalamea; The Phantom Lady*), translated by Edwin Honig. 1961.
Tragedias, edited by Francisco Ruiz Ramón. 3 vols., 1967–69.
Four Comedies (includes *From Bad to Worse; The Secret Spoken Aloud; The Worst Is Not Always Spoken; The Advantages and Disadvantages of a Name*), translated by Kenneth Muir. 1980.
Three Comedies (includes *A House with Two Doors Is Difficult to Guard; Mornings of April and May; No Trifling with Love*), translated by Kenneth Muir and Ann L. Mackenzie. 1985.
Teatro cómico breve, edited by María Luisa Lobato. 1989.

Plays 1 (*The Surgeon of Honour; Three Judgements in One; Life Is a Dream*), translated by Gwynne Edwards. 1990.

Plays (selection: modern editions or plays translated into English)

A María el corazón, edited by Giacomo Vaifro Sabatelli (with *La hidalga del valle*). 1962.

A secreto agravio, secreta venganza, edited by Edward Nagy. 1966; in *Tragedias*, 2, 1968; as *Secret Vengeance for Secret Insult*, translated by Edwin Honig, in *Four Plays*, 1961.

El alcalde de Zalamea, edited by Peter N. Dunn. 1966; also edited by Alberto Porqueras Mayo, 1977; as *The Mayor of Zalamea*, translated by Edward Fitzgerald, in *Six Dramas*, 1853, and *Eight Dramas*, 1906; also translated by William E. Colford, 1959; Edwin Honig, in *Four Plays*, 1961; Walter Starkie, in *Eight Spanish Plays of the Golden Age*, 1964; adapted by Adrian Mitchell, 1981.

Amar después de la muerte, as *Love after Death*, translated by Denis F. McCarthy, in *Dramas of Calderón*. 1853; also translated by Roy Campbell, in *Classic Theatre*, 3, edited by Eric Bentley, 1960.

Amar y ser amado; divina Filotea, as *The Divine Philothea*, translated by Denis F. McCarthy, in *Mysteries of Corpus Christi*. 1867.

La aurora en Copacabana, edited by Antonio Pages Larraya. 1956.

La banda y la flor, as *The Scarf and the Flower*, translated by Denis F. McCarthy, in *Dramas of Calderón*. 1853.

Los cabellos de Absalón, edited by Helmy F. Giacoman. 1968, also edited by Evangelina Rodríguez Cuadros, 1989.

Cada uno para sí, edited by José M. Ruano de la Haza. 1982.

Casa con dos puertas mala es de guardar, edited by G.T. Northrup, in *Three Plays*. 1926; as *A House with Two Doors Is Difficult to Guard*, translated by Kenneth Muir and Ann L. Mackenzie, in *Three Comedies*, 1985.

El castillo de Lindabridis, edited by Victoria B. Torres. 1987.

Celos aun del aire matan, edited by J. Subirá. 1933; as *Even Baseless Jealousy Can Kill*, translated by M. Stroud, 1981.

La cena de Baltazar, in *Tragedias*, 3. 1969; as *Belshazzar's Feast*, translated by Denis F. McCarthy, in *Mysteries of Corpus Christi*, 1867.

La cisma de Inglaterra, as *The Schism in England*, edited and translated by Ann L. Mackenzie and Kenneth Muir. 1990.

La dama duende, edited by José Luis Alonso. 1966; as *The Phantom Lady*, translated by Edwin Honig, in *Four Plays*, 1961.

La desdicha de la voz, edited by Gwynne Edwards. 1970.

La devoción de la Cruz, edited by Sidney F. Wexler. 1966; in *Tragedias*, 3, 1969; as *The Devotion of the Cross*, translated by Denis F. McCarthy, in *Three Dramas of Calderón*, 1870; also translated by Edwin Honig, in *Four Plays*, 1961.

Dicha y desdicha del nombre, as *The Advantages and Disadvantages of a Name*, translated by Kenneth Muir, in *Four Comedies*. 1980.

La divina Filotea, edited by José Carlos de Torres Martínez, in *Segismundo 3*. 1967.

El divino Jasón, edited by Ignacio Arellano and Ángel L. Cilveti. 1992.

Eco y Narciso, edited by Charles V. Aubrun. 1961.

En esta vida todo es verdad y todo mentira, edited by D.W. Cruickshank. 1971.

Los encantos de la culpa, as *The Sorceries of Sin*, translated by Denis F. McCarthy, in *Three Dramas of Calderón*. 1870.

La estatua de Prometeo, edited by Charles V. Aubrun. 1961; also edited by Margaret Rich Greer, 1986.

Fieras afemina amor, edited by Edward M. Wilson. 1984.

El golfo de las sirenas, edited by Sandra L. Nielson. 1989.

El gran duque de Gandía, edited by Václav Cerný. 1963.

El gran teatro del mundo, edited by Eugenio Frutos Cortés. 1958; also edited by Domingo Ynduráin, 1973; as *The Great Theatre of the World and Genius of Calderón*, translated by Richard C. Trench, 1856; as *The Great World Theatre*, translated by Francis E. Sipman, 1955; as *The Great Stage of the World*, translated by George W. Brandt, 1976.

Guárdate del agua mansa, edited by Ignacio Arellano and Víctor García Ruiz. 1989; as *Beware of Smooth Water*, translated by Edward Fitzgerald, in *Six Dramas*, 1853, and *Eight Dramas*, 1906.

Gustos y disgustos son no más que imaginación, edited by Claudio Y. Silva. 1974.

La hidalga del valle, edited by Giacomo Vaifro Sabatelli (with *A María el corazón*). 1962.

La hija del aire, edited by Gwynne Edwards. 1970; also edited by Francisco Ruiz Ramón, 1987.

Luis Pérez el gallego, as *Gil Perez the Gallician*, translated by Edward Fitzgerald, in *Six Dramas*, 1853, and *Eight Dramas*, 1906.

El mágico prodigioso, edited by Alexander A. Parker and Malveena McKendrick. 1972; as *The Wonderworking Magician*, translated by Denis F. McCarthy, in *Calderón's Dramas*, 1873; also translated by Bruce W. Wardropper, 1982; as *The Mighty Magician*, translated by Edward Fitzgerald, in *Eight Dramas*, 1906; as *The Prodigious Magician*, translated by Wardropper, 1982.

Mañanas de abril y mayo, as *Mornings of April and May*, translated by Kenneth Muir and Ann L. Mackenzie, in *Three Comedies*. 1985.

El mayor encanto amor, as *Love Is the Greatest Enchantment*, translated by Denis F. McCarthy, in *Three Dramas of Calderón*. 1870.

El mayor monstruo los celos, edited by Everett W. Hess. 1965; in *Tragedias*, 1, 1967.

El médico de su honra, edited by C.A. Jones. 1961; in *Tragedias*, 2, 1968; also edited by D. W. Cruickshank, 1981; as *The Physician of His Own Honour*, translated by Denis F. McCarthy, in *Dramas of Calderón*, 1853; as *The Surgeon of His Honour*, translated by Roy Campbell, 1960; as *The Surgeon of Honour*, translated by Gwynne Edwards, in *Plays 1*, 1990; as *The Physician of His Honour*, translated by Dian Fox with Donald Hindley, 1997.

Mejor está que estaba, as *Fortune Mends*, in *The Theatrical Recorder*, 2. 1806.

Nadie fíe su secreto, as *Keep Your Own Secret*, translated by Edward Fitzgerald, in *Six Dramas*. 1853, and *Eight Dramas*, 1906.

No hay burlas con el amor, edited by I. Arellano. 1981; as *No Trifling with Love*, translated by Kenneth Muir and Ann L. Mackenzie, in *Three Comedies*, 1985.

No hay cosa como callar, edited by Ángel Valbuena Briones, in *Comedias de capa y espada*, 2. 1954.

No hay más fortuna que Dios, edited by Alexander A. Parker. 1949.

No hay que creer ni en la verdad, edited by Václav Cerný. 1968.

No siempre lo peor es cierto, edited by Luis G. Villaverde and Lucile Fariñas. 1977; as *The Worst Is Not Always Certain*, translated by Kenneth Muir, in *Four Comedies*, 1980.

Peor está que estaba, as *From Bad to Worse*, translated by Kenneth Muir, in *Four Comedies*. 1980.

El pintor de su deshonra, edited by Manuel Ruiz Lagos. 1969; as *The Painter of His Own Dishonour*, translated by Edward Fitzgerald, in *Six Dramas*, 1853, and *Eight Dramas*, 1906; as *The Painter of His Dishonour*, edited and translated by A.K.G. Paterson, 1991.

El pleito matrimonial del cuerpo y el alma, edited by Manfred Engelbert. 1969.

El postrer duelo de España, edited by Guy Rossetti. 1977.

El príncipe constante, edited by Alexander A. Parker. 1975; as *The Constant Prince*, translated by Denis F. McCarthy, in *Dramas of Calderón*, 1853.

Tu prójimo como a ti, edited by Mary Lorene Thomas. 1989.

El purgatorio de san Patricio, as *The Purgatory of St. Patrick*, translated by Denis F. McCarthy, in *Dramas of Calderón*. 1853.

El secreto a voces, edited by José M. de Osma. 1938; as *The Secret Spoken Aloud*, translated by Kenneth Muir, in *Four Comedies*, 1980.

El sitio de Bredá, edited by Johanna R. Schrek. 1957.

Las tres justicias en una, as *Three Judgements at a Blow*, translated by Edward Fitzgerald, in *Six Dramas*. 1853, and *Eight Dramas*, 1906; as *Three Judgements in One*, translated by Gwynne Edwards, in *Plays 1*, 1990.

El veneno y la triaca, translated in part as *The Poison and the Antidote* by Denis F. McCarthy, in *Mysteries of Corpus Christi*. 1867.

El verdadero dios Pan, edited by José M. de Osma. 1949.

La vida es sueño, edited by Augusta Cortina. 1955; also edited by A.E. Sloman, 1961, Everett W. Hesse, 1978, José María García Martín, 1983, J.M. Ruano de la Haza, 1992, and by Ann L. Mackenzie, 1992; as *Such Stuff as Dreams Are Made Of*, translated by Edward Fitzgerald, in *Eight Dramas*, 1906; several subsequent translations as *Life Is a Dream*, including by William E. Colford, 1958, Roy Campbell, in *The Classic Theatre 3*, edited by Eric Bentley, 1960, Kathleen Raine and R.M. Nadal, 1968, and by Gwynne Edwards, in *Plays 1*, 1990.

Verse

Psalle et sile, edited by Leopoldo Trenor. 1936.

Other

Obras menores, edited by A. Pérez Gómez. 1969.

*

Bibliography: *A Chronology of the Plays of Calderón de la Barca* by H.W. Bilborn, 1928; *Bibliografía temática de estudios sabre el teatro español antiguo* by Warren T. McCready, 1966; *Calderón de la Barca Studies 1951–69* by Jack H. Parker and Arthur M. Fox, 1971.

Critical Studies: *The Allegorical and Metaphorical Language in the Autos Sacramentales of Calderón* by Frances de Sales MacGarry, 1937; *The Allegorical Drama of Calderón*, 1943, and *The Mind and Art of Calderón: Essays on the "Comedies,"* 1988, both by Alexander A. Parker; *The Dramatic Craftsmanship of Calderón: His Use of Earlier Plays* by Albert E. Sloman, 1958; *Pedro Calderón de la Barca: A Biography* by Harry, Lund, 1964; *Critical Essays on the Theatre of Calderón* edited by Bruce W. Wardropper, 1965; *A Literary History of Spain: The Golden Age: Drama* by Edward M. Wilson and Duncan Moir, 1971; *Calderón and the Seizures of Honor* by Edwin Honig, 1972; *The Textual Criticism of Calderón's Comedias* by E.M. Wilson and D.W. Cruikshank, 1973; *Calderón de la Barca: Imagery, Rhetoric, and Drama* by John V. Bryans, 1977; *The Prison and the Labyrinth: Studies in Calderonian Tragedy* by Gwynne Edwards, 1978; *On Calderón* by James E. Maraniss, 1978; *Calderón's Characters: An Existential Point of View* by Barbara Louise Mujica, 1980; *Critical Perspectives on Calderón de la Barca* edited by Frederick A. De Armas and others, 1981, and *The Return of Astrea: An Astral-Imperial Myth in Calderón* by De Armas, 1986; *The Characters, Plots and Settings of Calderón's Comedias* by W. Richard Tyler and Sergio D. Elizondo, 1981; *Calderón de la Barca at the Tercentenary: Comparative Views* edited by P. Sydney Cravens, 1982: *Reason and the Passions in the "Comedias" of Calderón* by David Jonathan Hildner, 1982; *Calderón: The Secular Plays* by Robert Ter Horst, 1982; *Approaches to the Theater of Calderón* edited by Michael McGaha, 1982; *The Development of Imagery in Calderón's Comedias* by William R. Blue, 1983; *Calderón in the German Lands and the Low Countries: His Reception and Influence 1654–1780* by Henry W. Sullivan, 1983; *The Limits of Illusion: A Critical Study of Calderón* by Anthony J. Cascardi, 1984; *Calderón and the Baroque Tradition* edited by Kurt Levy, Jesús Ava, and Gethin Hughes, 1985; *Kings in Calderón: A Study in Characterization and Political Theory* by Dian Fox, 1986; *Myth and Mythology in the Theater of Pedro Calderón de la Barca* by Thomas Austin O'Connor, 1988; *The Mind and Art of Calderón: Essays on the Comedias* by Alexander A. Parker, 1989; *On the Boards and in the Press: Calderón's "Las tres justicias en una"* by Isaac Benazbu, 1991; *The Play of Power: Mythological Court Dramas of Calderón de la Barca* by Margaret Rich Greer, 1991; *Calderón: The Imagery of Tragedy* by Charlene E. Suscavage, 1991; *The Prince in the Tower: Perceptions of "La Vida es Sueño,"* edited by Frederick A. de Armas, 1993; *Allegories of Kingship: Calderón and the Anti-Machiavellian Tradition* by Stephen Rupp, 1996; *The Calderonian Stage: Body and Soul*, edited by Manuel Delgado Morales, 1997; *Calderón del la Barca: "La Vida es Sueño"* by Paul Lewis-Smith, 1998; *Metaphors of Conversion in Seventeenth-century Spanish Drama* by Leslie Levin, 1999.

*   *   *

Don Pedro Calderón de la Barca, one of the two greatest dramatists of the Spanish Golden Age, was extremely prolific, and his work was of many different kinds. Although he was not ordained until he was over 50, his plays are frequently religious in spirit, and many of them are directly doctrinal. In particular he wrote more than 70 one-act allegorical dramas which Shelley, although an atheist, called "incomparable autos." They resemble, but are greatly superior to, English Morality plays; and, like the Mystery cycles, they were performed on wagons in the open air. The best known of the *autos*, outside Spain, is *El gran teatro del mundo* (*The Great Stage of the World*) in which representative human beings are put into the world to perform their allotted parts on the stage of life. Calderón sometimes rewrote his secular plays as allegories: there is, for example, an *auto* of *La vida es sueño* (*Life Is a Dream*) and another based on *El mayor encanto amor* (*Love Is the Greatest Enchantment*), dramatizing the story of Ulysses and Circe.

Several of Calderón's full-length plays, written for performance in the public theatres of Madrid, have religious themes. It is arguable that *El mágico prodigioso* (*The Wonderworking Magician*) is the finest religious play in any language; and *El príncipe constante* (*The Constant Prince*), in which the phantom of the martyred prince leads the Portuguese army to victory, and *La devoción de la Cruz* (*The Devotion of the Cross*), which ends in the miraculous resurrection and repentance of a scoundrel, are among Calderón's most admired plays. When he wrote about Henry VIII in *La cisma de Inglaterra* (*The Schism in England*), he concentrated, in a way Shakespeare did not, on the religious issue. His most famous play, *Life Is a Dream*, is directly didactic, demonstrating that the pursuit of fame or wealth is foolish, that we ought to overcome our passions, and set our hearts on eternal things. Segismundo, returned to prison, is made to believe that he has only dreamed that he was a prince with absolute power; but when he is released again he decides to behave morally instead of selfishly.

Several of Calderón's important plays are marriage tragedies, demonstrating the disastrous effects of the code of honour under which husbands were expected to kill their wives on the mere suspicion of infidelity. In two of these plays the wives are innocent and in a third the imprudent wife has been compelled to marry a man she does not love. In *El médico de su honra* (*The Surgeon of Honour*) a husband has his wife bled to death; in *A secreto agravio, secreta venganza* (*Secret Vengeance for Secret Insult*) another deluded husband murders both his wife and her lover; and in *El pintor de su deshonra* (*The Painter of His Own Dishonour*) Juan Roca kills the innocent wife whom he still loves. Calderón contrasts the honour code with Christian ethics, most obviously in the first of these plays, but the husbands are regarded as mistaken rather than evil: one is provided by the King with another wife, another, tortured with remorse, is allowed to go free, and the third seeks to die in battle. Othello, who commits suicide when he discovers that Desdemona was innocent, provides an illuminating contrast. A modern reader has to make an effort of imagination to put himself in the place of the original audience; but it is important to note that the cruelty of the code is criticized by a number of sympathetic characters, even by those who conform to it in practice.

One of the most popular of Calderón's dramas, *El alcalde de Zalamea* (*The Mayor of Zalamea*), contrasts two conceptions of honour: that of the aristocratic rapist who prefers to die rather than marry the woman he has wronged, and that of her father, the Mayor, who believes that his own honour can be redeemed by the marriage of the rapist to his daughter or, failing that, by his execution. The King, who arrives opportunely, commends the justice of the execution, although the man should properly have been given a court-martial.

Calderón also wrote a large number of love comedies—cloak and sword plays, as they are often called. These have ingenious plots, witty dialogue, charming poetry, comic jealousy, sword fights, confusion over identity, humorous servants, and romantic lovemaking. The heroes, fashionable gallants, are, as Goethe complained, often indistinguishable; but the heroines, whether unjustly suspected of unchastity or gay flouters of convention, are expertly characterized. In a male-dominated society, with rigid notions of female propriety, they can obtain the husbands of their choice only by refusing to conform. One of the two heroines of *Mañanas de abril y mayo* (*Mornings of April and May*) finally persuades her jealous lover to trust her, and not to insist on a proof of her innocence; the other one exposes, and refuses to marry, a conceited philanderer. Marcela, in *Casa con dos puertas malas es de guardar* (*A House with Two Doors Is Difficult to Guard*), secures a husband by meeting her brother's guest clandestinely; Angela in *La dama duende* (*The Phantom Lady*) uses a concealed door to obtain access to a guest's room; and the lovers in *El secreto a voces* (*The Secret Spoken Aloud*) communicate with each other in public by use of an ingenious code.

These comedies often have an element of satire, as of the affected Beatriz in *No hay burlas con el amor* (*No Trifling with Love*). Other plays in this genre raise more serious issues: *Dicha y desdicha del nombre* (*The Advantages and Disadvantages of a Name*) contains an attempted murder and an attempted rape; and *No hay cosa como callar* begins with a rape and ends, years later, with the marriage of the rapist to his victim.

In his later years Calderón wrote mainly for the Court theatres, and here he made use of elaborate scenery, spectacle, and music. The plays were often on classical and mythological subjects, and usually didactic.

There were adaptations of some of Calderón's plays in France and England during the second half of the 17th century; but if one compares, for example, Wycherley's *Love in a Wood* with *Mornings of April and May*, Calderón's plots are submerged in several others; the tone is vulgarized: the rake is rewarded with a bride; and undistinguished prose is substituted for the delicate verse of the original.

—Kenneth Muir

See the essays on *The Great Stage of the World* and *Life Is a Dream*.

CALLIMACHUS

Born: Cyrene, North Africa (now Libya), c. 310–305 BC; active during first half of 3rd century BC and until at least 246 BC. **Career:** Said to have been a schoolteacher in the Alexandrian suburb of Eleusis before working at the royal library and museum at Alexandria; once believed to have been librarian, but apparently never held that post, though he was responsible for compiling the main bio-bibliographical reference catalogue (*Pinaces*) from which is derived much of the information we have today about ancient Greek writers and their works. Traditionally supposed to have quarrelled with Apollonius of Rhodes, *q.v.*, but evidence for this is poor, though he does seem to have been involved in numerous literary enmities. The scholars Eratosthenes and Aristophanes of Byzantium were among his pupils. **Died:** c. 240 BC.

PUBLICATIONS

Collections

[Works], edited by R. Pfeiffer. 2 vols., 1949–53; supplemented by P. Parsons and H. Lloyd-Jones, in *Supplementum Hellenisticum (Texte und Kommentare 11)*, 1983; translated by A.W. and G.R. Mari [Loeb Edition], 1921, and C.A. Trypanis [Loeb Edition], 1958; selection translated by Robert A. Furness, 1931.

Verse

Hymn to Zeus, edited by G.R. McLennan (with commentary). 1977.
Hymn to Apollo, edited by F. Williams (with commentary). 1978.
Hymn to Delos, edited by W.H. Mineur (with commentary). 1984.
Hymn to Demeter, edited by N. Hopkinson (with commentary). 1984.
The Fifth Hymn, edited by A.W. Bulloch. 1985.

Hymns, Epigrams, Select Fragments, translated by Stanley Lombardo
   and Diane Rayor. 1988.
Hecale, edited by A.S. Hollis (with commentary). 1990.
The Poems of Callimachus, translated by Frank Nisetich, 2001.

*

Critical Studies: *The Discovery of the Mind* by Bruno Snell, 1953;
*History of Classical Scholarship from the Beginnings to the End of the
Hellenistic Age* by R. Pfeiffer, 1968; *Callimachus' Iambi* by D.L.
Clayman, 1980; *Callimachus* by John Ferguson, 1980; *Cambridge
History of Classical Literature I: Greek Literature* edited by P.E.
Easterling and B.M.W. Knox, 1984; *The Well-Read Muse: Present
and Past in Callimachus and the Hellenistic Poets* by Peter Bing,
1988; *Callimachus: Hecale* by A.S. Hollis, 1990; *The Song of
the Swan: Lucretius and the Influence of Callimachus* by Harold
Donohue, 1993; *Callimachus and his Critics* by Alan Cameron, 1995;
Callimachus' Book of Iambi by Arnd Kerkhecker, 1999.

* * *

Callimachus was the most brilliant intellectual and poet of his
time, and, although an extremely controversial figure, had a more
radical influence on the course of Greek (and Roman) poetry than
almost any other writer except Homer. He wrote prolifically, but few
of his works now survive (or they are known only in fragmentary
form), and we have to gauge Callimachus' importance from his effect
on other writers. Yet his vivacious, penetrating, and rather quixotic
intelligence shows through in almost every line that we have. He was
said to have written more than 800 works altogether, and was one of
the few writers who was equally scholar and poet, in both activity
and achievement.

His research involved compilation and classification of data rather
than speculative thinking; he wrote scarcely anything of a philosophical or historical nature, and although some of his works have titles
such as *On Birds*, or *On Winds*, these were surveys rather than
scientific enquiries based on independent observation. However, his
work was of fundamental importance in another way: he lived at a
point in history when modern scholarship was just beginning to
evolve, and in a place where the resources to conduct that scholarship
were being assembled for the first time; the principles of philosophical and scientific enquiry were laid down in Athens by Plato and
Aristotle and their pupils, but the idea of a body of *knowledge*, and its
collection and transmission, came to maturity in 3rd-century BC
Alexandria. Callimachus played a key part in the evolution of the
principles and standards of true, energetic scholarship, and was one of
its most important practitioners; many of the great intellectuals of the
next generation were his pupils. His most important work, the
Pinaces, the reference catalogue to the library, consisted of 120
books, and was the first of its kind and exemplary: it classified the
works of all Greek writers of any importance and attempted to provide
all the basic information that a reader might need (biography, contents, authenticity, etc.). In effect the *Pinaces* was the first encyclopedia in Western culture.

As a poet Callimachus was equally vigorous and idiosyncratic. He
thought that he diagnosed muddle and mediocrity in the mainstream
of contemporary Greek poetry, and set a premium in his own work on
originality and refreshment of the language. Late in his career
Callimachus produced a collection of his own poetry, and wrote a
preface for it, in verse, expounding the critical principles that had

guided him as a writer ("The Prologue" to the *Aetia*). He claimed to
have avoided the trite, uninspired, hackneyed, "high" manner which
was popular at the time and to have been uncompromisingly unorthodox and original, even if that took him "along a narrower path."
Concision and clarity were of the utmost importance in his work; he
was fascinated by language and words, and set out, almost ideologically, to transform the linguistic material of poetry. Like any Greek
poet he was thoroughly imbued with Homer, but was too great a
writer to think that Homer needed to be overthrown: he advocated
passionately the creation of a "fine," spare, even elegant style, with
none of the inflation of unthinking traditionality. Poetry had to be
wrought, and writing was the result of work. Despite being a court
poet, dependent on, and gratefully acknowledging, the support of
royal patronage, he was a nonconformist, an experimenter, at times an
iconoclast, and seems always to have been controversial and involved
in fierce argument and criticism. He had a perpetual sense of the odd
or bizarre. Thus it was the mundane dimensions of what were
supposed to be the ideal realms that intrigued him: what are the
practicalities of being a hero, and what are the day-to-day effects
when man encounters god? His gods are often children and his men
involved in pursuing their own odd rituals, and although he represents
religious passion with sympathetic insight, he suggests that the only
real meaning comes from the limited warmth of human friendship,
not from the spiritual or the sublime.

His most important work was the *Aetia* [Origins or Causes], an
eccentrically learned work in 4,000–6,000 lines, which mixed strange
and wonderful stories into an episodic, almost picaresque narrative of
religious rituals and practices: the length was epic, but the style and
concerns crankily different, with off-beat accounts, bizarre humour,
unpredictable climaxes, and intricate but razor-sharp language. Narrative poetry was never the same again. The *Hecale* was an inverted
epic, nominally "about" Theseus' defeat of the bull of Marathon, but
mostly comprising an account of his stay overnight, during a rain-
storm, in the hut of a solitary peasant woman. His 13 *Iambi* were
mostly social satire, with some personal invective, directed at the
foibles of human ambition. None of these works survives in full, but
we do possess the complete text of six "hymns." All are complex but
fine texts, superficially dealing with the myths and rituals connected
with some of the principal Olympian deities, with some recognition of
the semi-divine power of his royal patrons; but their overall effect is to
convey, behind a brilliant, edgy, and often entertaining manner, that
traditional religion is puzzling and disturbing. All is not, in fact, right
with the world. Callimachus also wrote epigrams which are taut, wry,
witty, and pungent, and among the very best in the long history of
the genre.

Callimachus changed the course of Greek poetry: writers who saw
themselves as "mainstream" thereafter were deeply influenced by
both his style and outlook, and for poets rebelling against their own
traditions he was the archetypal avant-garde nonconformist.

—A.W. Bulloch

See the essays on *Aetia* and *Hecale*.

CALVINO, Italo

Born: Santiago de las Vegas, Cuba, 15 October 1923. Family moved
to San Remo, Italy, 1925. **Education:** Educated at Ginnasio-liceo

Cassini, San Remo; University of Turin, 1941–47; Royal University, Florence, 1943. **Family:** Married Esther Judith Singer ("Chichita") in 1964, one daughter. **Career:** Conscripted into the Young Fascists, 1940: left, sought refuge in the Alps with his brother, and joined the Communist Resistance, 1943–45. Contributor, *La Nostra Lotta, Il Garibaldino, Voce Della Democrazia,* and other periodicals, from 1945; first contributed to *L'Unità,* 1945; member of the editorial staff, Einaudi, publishers, Turin, 1948–84; contributor, *Contemporaneo* and *Città Aperta,* from 1954; co-editor, with Elio Vittorini, *Il Menabò,* Milan, 1959–67; travelled to the Union of Soviet Socialist Republics, 1952, and the United States, 1959–60; settled in Paris, 1967, while continuing to work for Einaudi; contributor, *La Repubblica,* from 1979; moved to Rome, 1980; member, editorial board, Garzanti, publishers, 1984. **Awards:** *L'Unità* prize, 1945; Viareggio prize, 1957; Bagutta prize, 1959; Veillon prize, 1963; Feltrinelli prize, 1972; Austrian State prize for European literature, 1976; Nice Festival prize, 1982. **Member:** Honorary member, American Academy, 1975. **Died:** 19 September 1985.

PUBLICATIONS

Collections

Romanzi e racconti, edited by Claudio Milanini, Mario Barenghi, and Bruno Falcetto. 1991–.

Fiction

Il sentiero dei nidi di ragno. 1947; as *The Path to the Nest of Spiders,* translated by Archibald Colquhoun, 1956.
Ultimo viene il corvo. 1949; as *Adam, One Afternoon, and Other Stories,* translated by Archibald Colquhoun and Peggy Wright, 1957.
I nostri antenati. 1960; as *Our Ancestors,* translated by Archibald Colquhoun, 1980.
    Il visconte dimezzato. 1952; as *The Cloven Viscount,* translated by Archibald Colquhoun, with *The Non-Existent Knight,* 1962.
    Il barone rampante. 1957; edited by J.M. Woodhouse, 1988; as *The Baron in the Trees,* translated by Archibald Colquhoun, 1959.
    Il cavaliere inesistente. 1959; as *The Non-Existent Knight,* translated by Archibald Colquhoun, with *The Cloven Viscount,* 1962.
L'entrata in guerra (trilogy of stories). 1954.
I racconti (stories). 1958.
Marcovaldo; ovvero, Le stagioni in città, illustrations by Sergio Tofano. 1963; as *Marcovaldo; or, The Seasons in the City,* translated by William Weaver, 1983.
La giornata d'uno scrutatore. 1963.
La nuvola di smog e La formica argentina. 1965; *La nuvola di smog* as *Smog,* in *Difficult Loves; Smog; A Plunge Into Real Estate,* 1983.
Le cosmicomiche (stories). 1965; enlarged edition, as *Cosmicomiche, vecchie e nuove,* 1984; as *Cosmicomics,* translated by William Weaver, 1969.
Ti con zero (stories). 1967; as *T Zero,* translated by William Weaver, 1969; as *Time and the Hunter,* translated by Weaver, 1969.
La memoria del mondo e altre storie cosmicomiche. 1968.
Gli amori difficili. 1970; as *Difficult Loves,* in *Difficult Loves; Smog; A Plunge Into Real Estate,* 1983.

The Watcher and Other Stories, translated by William Weaver and Archibald Colquhoun. 1971.
Le città invisibili. 1972; as *Invisible Cities,* translated by William Weaver, 1974.
Il castello dei destini incrociati. 1973; as *The Castle of Crossed Destinies,* translated by William Weaver, 1976.
Il gigante orripilante. 1975.
Se una notte d'inverno un viaggiatore. 1979; as *If on a Winter's Night a Traveller,* translated by William Weaver, 1981.
Palomar. 1983; as *Mr. Palomar,* translated by William Weaver, 1985.
Difficult Loves; Smog; A Plunge Into Real Estate, translated by William Weaver, Archibald Colquhoun, and Peggy Wright. 1983.
Sotto il sole giaguaro (unfinished). 1986; as *Under the Jaguar Sun,* translated by William Weaver, 1988.
Prima che tu dica "Pronto." 1993; as *Numbers in the Dark: And Other Stories,* translated by Tim Parks, 1995.

Plays

La panchina (libretto), music by Sergio Liberovici (produced 1956).
La vera storia (libretto), music by Luciano Berio (produced 1982).
Un re in ascolto (libretto), music by Luciano Berio (produced 1984).

Other

Italo Calvino racconta l'Orlando furioso di Ludovico Ariosto, edited by Carlo Minoia. 1970.
Una pietra sopra: Discorsi di letteratura e società (essays). 1980; as *The Uses of Literature,* translated by Patrick Creagh, 1986; as *The Literature Machine,* translated by Creagh, 1987.
Collezione di sabbia: Emblemi bizzarri e inquietanti del nostro passato e del nostro futuro gli oggetti raccontano il mondo. 1984.
Lezioni americane: Sei proposte per il prossimo millennio (texts for Charles Eliot Norton lectures). 1988; as *Six Memos for the Next Millenium,* translated by Patrick Creagh, 1988.
Sulla fiaba, edited by Mario Lavagetto. 1988.
La strada di San Giovanni. 1990; as *The Road to San Giovanni,* translated by Tim Parks, 1993.
Perchè leggere i classici (essays). 1992.
Editor, *Fiabe italiane: Raccolte della tradizione popolare durante gli ultimi cento anni e trascritte in lingua dai vari dialetti.* 1956, re-edited by Ersilia Zamponi, 3 vols., 1986–89; selections as *Italian Fables,* translated by Louis Brigante, 1959; as *Italian Folk Tales,* translated by Sylvia Mulcahey, 1975; as *Italian Folktales* (complete), translated by George Martin, 1980.
Editor, *Poesie edite e inedite,* by Cesare Pavese. 1962.
Editor, *Lettere 1945–1950,* by Cesare Pavese. 1966.
Editor, with Lorenzo Mondo, *Lettere 1924–1950,* by Cesare Pavese. 1966.
Editor, *Vittorini: Progettazione e letteratura.* 1968.
Editor, *Teoria dei quattro movimenti: Il nuovo mondo amoroso e altri scritti,* by Charles Fourier. 1971.
Editor, *Porfira,* by Silvina Ocampo. 1973.
Editor, *Il Principe Granchio e altre fiabe italiane.* 1974.
Editor, *Le più belle pagine,* by Tommaso Landolfi. 1982.
Editor, *Racconti fantastici dell'Ottocento.* 2 vols., 1983.
Translator, *I fiori blu,* by Raymond Queneau. 1967.
Translator, *La canzone di polistirene,* by Raymond Queneau. 1985.

*

Critical Studies: *Italo Calvino* by Germana Pescio Bottino, 1967; *Italo Calvino: A Reappraisal and an Appreciation of the Trilogy* by J.R. Woodhouse, 1968; *Invito alla lettura di Calvino* by Giuseppe Bonura, 1972, revised edition, 1987; *Italo Calvino* by Contardo Calligaris, 1973, augmented by G.P. Bernasconi, 1985; *I segni nuovi di Italo Calvino* by Francesca Bernardini Napoletano, 1977; *Italo Calvino: Writer and Critic* by Jo Ann Cannon, 1981; *With Pleated Eye and Garnet Wing: Symmetries of Italo Calvino* by I.T. Olken, 1984; Calvino issue of *Review of Contemporary Fiction*, 6(2), 1986; *Italo Calvino: Metamorphoses of Fantasy* by Albert Howard Carter III, 1987; *Italo Calvino: Tra realtà e favola* by Giovanna Finocchiaro Chimirri, 1987; *Italo Calvino: Introduzione e guida allo studio dell'opera calviniana: Storia e antologia della critica* by Giorgio Baroni, 1988; *Introduzione a Calvino* by Cristina Benussi, 1989; *Le capre di Bikini: Calvino giornalista e Saggista 1945–1985* by Gian Carlo Ferretti, 1989; *Calvino Revisited* edited by Franco Ricci, 1989; *L'Utopia discontinua. Saggio su Italo Calvino* by Claudio Milanini, 1990; *Calvino and the Age of Neorealism: Fables of Estrangement* by Lucia Re, 1990; *Difficult Games: A Reading of I racconti* by Franci Ricci, 1990; *Italo Calvino: a San Remo* by Piero Ferrua, 1991; *Calvino's Fictions: Cogito and Cosmos* by Kathryn Hume, 1992; *Understanding Italo Calvino* by Beno Weiss, 1993; *Italo Calvino: Eros and Language* by Tommasina Gabriele, 1994; *Humility's Deceit: Calvino Reading Ariosto Reading Calvino* by Wiley Feinstein, 1995; *Italo Calvino* by Martin McLaughlin, 1998; *Italo Calvino: A Journey Towards Postmodernism* by Constance Markey, 1999; *Under the Radiant Sun and Crescent Moon: Italo Calvino's Storytelling* by Angela M. Jeannet, 2000.

* * *

Italo Calvino was perhaps the greatest, and certainly the most versatile, Italian novelist in the second half of the 20th century. This versatility is apparent not only in the sophisticated content of his prolific output, but also in the complex structuring devices and the range of styles he deployed in his many fictions.

He began as a "neorealist", one of the post-World War II generation of Italians who sought to depict, in a new, explicit style influenced by American novelists, the new realism of Italy which had been ignored in the 20 years of Fascist rule. His first novel, *Il sentiero dei nidi di ragno* (*The Path to the Nest of Spiders*), examined the partisan movement not in hagiographic terms, but as seen through the naive eye of an engaging urchin, Pin. This technique allowed Calvino to mix a serious message with irony, and blend realism with elements borrowed from fairy-tales and Robert Louis Stevenson's *Treasure Island*.

At the beginning of the 1950s, disillusioned with trying to deliver a serious socialist message in tales that could no longer narrate the heroics of the Resistance, Calvino turned to writing the kind of story he himself would have liked to read. *I nostri antenati* (*Our Ancestors*) is a trilogy which, in its three separate parts, owes much, respectively, to the fairy-tale, the adventure story, and the chivalric romance. In *Il visconte dimezzato* (*The Cloven Viscount*), a viscount is torn in two by a cannonball, and the two halves, the Good Half and the Bad Half, return to torment his kingdom with both excessive goodness and excessive cruelty. *Il barone rampante* (*The Baron in the Trees*) also has an allegorical dimension, but is a fuller story; indeed it is the longest novel Calvino ever wrote. It recounts the life of a rebel aristocrat who rejects the outmoded values of his eccentric family to embrace the ideals of the French Enlightenment and Revolution. Although the cause (refusing to eat a plate of snails) and nature (climbing into the trees and staying there) of his rebellion seem trivial, the book argues a profound view about the place of the intellectual in society during times of ideological upheaval. *Il cavaliere inesistente* (*The Non-Existent Knight*) narrates a young knight's search for identity between the extremes offered by Agilulf, who is a perfect being devoid of body but inhabiting a suit of armour, and Gurdulù, who is all body and no intellect. Yet the novel is also about narratology, most of the characters opening with the thoughts of Suor Teodora, who is the narrator and who speculates about the limits of realism and other authorial problems. The final volte-face, in which the nun Teodora is revealed to be the female warrior Bradamante, typifies Calvino's anxieties in this period about his own role as contemplative intellectual, as opposed to active political partisan.

The rest of Calvino's output up to 1963 was in the form of short stories or novellas, either in a fantasy vein, as in the humorous cycle of Marcovaldo stories, or in ironic attempts at realism, as in *Gli amori difficili* (*Difficult Loves*), "La speculazione edilizia" (*A Plunge into Real Estate*), and *La nuvola di smog* (*Smog*). The year 1963 was a turning point in the author's career, neatly encapsulated by the publication of *La giornata d'uno scrutatore* [The Watcher], the last "full-length" novel he published (though even it is under 100 pages long) and of *Marcovaldo*, the first work of Calvino's new "serial" manner, based on a sequence of modular units combined to form a single, composite macrotext. In a prophetic passage in *La giornata d'uno scrutatore* the protagonist rejects novels about people and turns instead to scientific works.

Le cosmicomiche (*Cosmicomics*) inaugurated fully this new anti-novelistic and "scientific" period. The stories which comprise the volume are each introduced by an epigraph from a scientific text (about the Big Bang, the appearance of the first mammals, etc.), which is then illustrated in a comical manner by the protagonist with the unpronounceable name, Qfwfq. Calvino here is consciously challenging some of the assumptions of realism—about human protagonists, with human lifespans and recognizable names. *Ti con zero* (*Time and the Hunter*) contains more Qfwfq tales, but also includes others that showed Calvino's new interest in deductive logic and mathematical constraints on narrative, as practised then by Calvino's friends Queneau and other members of the "Ouvroir de littérature potentielle." Further experiments with combinatorial narrative technique followed: in *Il castello dei destini incrociati* (*The Castle of Crossed Destinies*), in which storytelling is carried out by means of tarot cards, since the knights in the enchanted castle have all been struck dumb; and in *Le città invisibili* (*Invisible Cities*), in which Marco Polo describes to the Great Khan, in 55 sections of poetic prose, the cities of his empire. These last two books, broadly based on works by Ariosto and Marco Polo, testify to Calvino's interest in rewriting texts. This fascination is also evident in his masterpiece, *Se una notte d'inverno un viaggiatore* (*If on a Winter's Night a Traveller*), which in structure is a reworking of *The Thousand and One Nights*. This "hypernovel" consists of a frame of 12 chapters, in which "you," the reader (a male subject) and a female reader try to read Calvino's *If on a Winter's Night*, but instead are given an apocryphal first chapter from ten different novels. This approach allows Calvino to parade his virtuosity in reproducing widely differing styles of contemporary fiction, and at the same time to play off the events in the frame-story against the episodes read by the readers. The whole book is informed by Calvino's narrative verve, as well as his sense of humour and his interest in contemporary literary theory.

The final work published in his lifetime, *Palomar* (*Mr. Palomar*), represents a complete change of style, since it consists of the meditations of Mr. Palomar, an elderly man living in 1980s Italy, but it is divided into 27 sections, each of which is subdivided into three units. The protagonist takes his name from the huge astronomical telescope in California, thus linking Calvino's twin fascinations— observation and scientific exploration of the universe. *Sotto il sole giaguaro* (*Under the Jaguar Sun*), published posthumously, continues Calvino's predilection for narrative patternings. An unfinished work, it was to have consisted of five stories about the five senses; but in the end only those concerning smell, taste, and hearing were written.

A provocative essayist as well as occasional librettist, Calvino holds an important place in world literature because of his constant awareness of the limits of realism and the written word in general, and his brilliant and humorous attempts to expand those limits, to innovate constantly, and to inscribe history, science, and philosophy within literature.

—Martin L. McLaughlin

See the essay on *If on a Winter's Night a Traveller*.

CAMÕES, Luís (Vaz) de

Born: Portugal, possibly in 1525. **Education:** May have attended the University of Coimbra. **Career:** Served as a soldier in North Africa, and may have lost an eye, perhaps in combat; went to India as a soldier, 1553; stayed for a year or two in East Africa, and possibly went to Macao and Goa; returned to Lisbon, 1569; received a small pension from the king. **Died:** 1580.

PUBLICATIONS

Collections

Obras completas, edited by Hernâni Cidade. 5 vols., 1946–47.
Obra completa, edited by Antônio Salgado, Jr. 1963.

Verse

Os Lusíadas. 1572; edited by Frank Pierce, 1973; as *The Lusiads*, translated by Richard Fanshawe, 1655; also translated by Leonard Bacon, 1950; William C. Atkinson, 1952; Landeg White, 1997.
Rhythmas. 1595, as *The Lyricks,* translated by Richard Burton, 2 vols., 1884.
Lírica completa, edited by Maria de Lurdes Saraiva. 3 vols., 1980–81.

Plays

Auto dos Enfatriões, from a play by Plautus, in *Autos e comedias portuguesas.* 1587.
Auto de Filodemo, in *Autos e comedias portuguesas.* 1587.
El Rei-Seleuco, in *Rimas.* 1645.

*

Critical Studies: *The Lusiads*, in *From Virgil to Milton* by C.M. Bowra, 1945; *Forms of Nationhood: The Elizabethan Writing of England* by Richard Helgerson, 1992; *Epic and Empire: Politics and Epic Form from Virgil to Milton* by David Quint, 1993; *The Presence of Camoes: Influences on the Literature of England, America, and Southern Africa* by George Monteiro, 1996; *The Poetics of Empire in the Indies: Prophesy and Imitation in La Araucana and Os Lusíadas* by James Nicolopulos, 2000.

*   *   *

Luís de Camões's most important work is his epic poem, *Os Lusíadas* (*The Lusiads*), which deals with Vasco da Gama's successful attempt to discover a sea route to India. Camões's poem owes a great deal to classical epic, and especially to Virgil's *Aeneid*. Gama is not, however, the protagonist of Camões's poem, as Aeneas is of Virgil's. For much of the poem he is not an actor at all but a narrator, and the story he tells is not just that of his own voyage, like the account of his adventures that Aeneas gives Dido, but embraces the whole history of Portugal from its legendary beginnings right down to Camões's own day.

The Lusiads offers abundant evidence of Camões's mastery of the sublime style that he inherited from Virgil. Like Virgil, Camões is fond of complex sentences, full of subordinate clauses, but, again like Virgil, his predilection for elaborate patterns of subordination does not keep him from being a superb storyteller. On the contrary, it can be said, as C.S. Lewis said of Milton, that he "avoids discontinuity by avoidance of what grammarians call the simple sentence" and that he "compensates for the complexity of his syntax by the simplicity of the broad imaginative effects beneath it and the perfect rightness of their sequence."

The Lusiads is not merely a faithful imitation of an admired model. Perhaps the most striking feature of the poem is the way it combines repeated reminders that it belongs to the noblest of the established literary kinds, the epic, with daring innovations. Camões repeatedly acknowledges Homer and Virgil as his models, but he insists just as firmly on the differences that separate his work from theirs. The most important difference is that the story he tells is true. Many passages of the poem follow closely the accounts given by the great Portuguese historians of Asia who were Camões's contemporaries, most notably João de Barros. Camões repeatedly asserts that the real achievements of the Portuguese rival can even outdo the fictional ones attributed to Odysseus and Aeneas. It is because he has a greater subject than the ancient epic poets that his poem may hope to surpass theirs. Camões stresses not only the truthfulness of his account but also its exemplary character. He believes, like Dryden, that "the design of [the heroic poem] is to form the mind to heroic virtue by example." Camões's conception of heroic virtue is, however, one that many modern readers find hard to accept; *The Lusiads* can serve as a magnificent example of Wallace Stevens's assertion that "poetry is a cemetery of nobilities." Another obstacle for many modern readers is Camões's readiness to evoke the hand of God to explain the course of historical events, a readiness he shares with many 16th-century historians.

Much of the poem is, of course, invention, not historical reporting. Sixteenth-century poets saw the marvellous as an indispensable element in poetry, and Camões supplies it in his mythological framestory which pits Venus against Bacchus, one aiding Gama and the other opposing him. For many readers the most memorable episodes in the poem are those that spring from Camões's imagination, often sparked, of course, by his memories of classical poetry: the giant Adamastor, for example, a personification of the Cape of Good Hope, who represents the hostile forces of nature that the Portuguese must confront on their voyages of discovery, on the Isle of Love, where Venus and her nymphs offer Gama and his men an erotic romp on their return voyage to Portugal.

The Lusiads is an extremely personal poem. Just how personal is difficult to appreciate without some familiarity with Camões's lyrics, which elaborate many of the motifs touched on in the epic, most notably a note of melancholy which has much in common with the Virgilian *lacrimae return*. The lyrics are not autobiographical poetry; they do not deal directly with the experiences of the poet's life but rather with their emotional effect on him. For this reason, and because so little is known with certainty about Camões's life, they have often served as points of departure for arbitrary and incompatible biographical interpretations. Like *The Lusiads*, Camões's lyrics offer an astonishing fusion of tradition and innovation. He is a master of both the principal currents that flow into 16th-century Portuguese poetry, one deriving from the 15th-century *cancioneiros* (songbooks, though the poems in them were not always intended to be sung) and the other from the love-poetry of Petrarch and his 16th-century Spanish followers, notably Garcilaso de la Vega. Camões sometimes combines elements of both traditions in a single poem, just as he sometimes combines traditional materials with an intensely individual development presumably drawn from his own lived experience. An outstanding example is the long poem "Sôbolos rios," which begins as a paraphrase of Psalm 137 ("By the waters of Babylon. . . ") and turns into a moving meditation on the poet's own life, expressed with incomparable grace in an inimitably personal style that nevertheless is firmly rooted in the tradition of the songbooks.

Camões's three plays turn away from the classical comedies and tragedies of Francisco de Sá de Miranda and António Ferreira and return to the tradition established by Gil Vicente, though with important differences, most notably Camões's choice, in two of the three, of subjects drawn from classical antiquity. The apparent amorality of Camões's theatre also sets it apart from that of Vicente. The prose passages in the *Auto de Filodemo*, like Camões's letters, show a mastery of language comparable to that of his lyrics or of *The Lusiads*, though both style and subject matter are entirely different. In the plays and letters we often encounter a playful and mocking Camões quite unlike the despairing lover of some of the lyrics or the inspired bard of *The Lusiads*.

—Thomas R. Hart

See the essay on *The Lusiads*.

CAMPANELLA, Tommaso

Born: Giovan Domenico Campanella in Stilo, Calabria, Spanish Viceroyalty of Naples, 5 September 1568. **Education:** Studied law in Naples. **Career:** Entered Dominican Order, 1582, took the monastic name Tommaso, and studied logic, physics, and Aristotelian metaphysics at the Convent of San Giorgio Morgeto, 1583–85; lived in Nicastro, 1586–87, Cosenza, 1588, Altomonte, 1588–89; returned to Naples, 1589, and moved into the palazzo of Mario del Tufo, 1590;

his views and writings brought him into increasing conflict with the Order, from 1592; travelled throughout Italy, 1592–93; first arrest by the Inquisition, 1594: imprisoned and tortured, 1595–96, and forbidden to publish; rearrested, 1597, on accusations of heresy, released and returned to Calabria, settled in Stilo, 1598; forced to flee to Franciscan monastery in Stignano, 1599, subsequently captured and imprisoned in Naples for involvement with (and possible organization of) an abortive anti-Spanish rebellion; sentenced by the Holy Office in Rome to life imprisonment for heresy, 1602, remained in confinement in the castles of Uovo, Sant'Elmo, and Nuovo, 1602–26, where he continued writing; released in May, 1626, but rearrested in June and taken to Rome; allowed by the Inquisition to live under house arrest, and settled in the Dominican Convent of Santa Maria sopra Minerva; pardoned completely by Pope Urban VIII, 1629, and his name and works deleted from the Inquisition's Index; named a Master of Theology by the Dominican Order, 1629; lived under papal patronage, 1629–34; fled to Paris, via Marseilles, because of the repercussions of a pupil's involvement in an anti-Spanish plot, 1634; received a pension from Louis XIII, 1635, and spent final years publishing many of his works. **Died:** 21 May 1639.

PUBLICATIONS

Collections

Opere, edited by Alessandro d'Ancona. 2 vols., 1854.
Tutte le opere, edited by Luigi Firpo. 1954.
Opera Latina Francofurti Impressa Annis 1617–1630, edited by Luigi Firpo. 1975.
Opere letterarie, edited by Lina Bolzoni. 1977.

Works

Philosophia sensibus demonstrata. 1591; as *La filosofia che i sensi ci additano*, edited by Luigi De Franco, 1974.
Prodromus philosophia instaurandae (*Compendium de return natura*). 1617.
De belgio sub hispani potestatem redigendo. 1617.
Monarchia di Spagna. In German, as *Von der spanischen Monarchie*, 1620; as *De monarchia hispanica*, 1640; as *Monarchia di Spagna*, 1854; as *A Discourse Touching the Spanish Monarchy*, translated by Edmund Chilmead, 1654; as *Tommaso Campanella . . . His Advice to the King of Spain*, 1659.
De sensu return et magia, edited by Tobias Adami. 1620; as *Del senso delle cose e della magia*, edited by Antonio Bruers, 1925.
Apologia pro Galileo. 1620; edited by R. Carebba, 1911, also edited by Salvatore Femiano, 1971; as *Apologia di Galileo*, edited by Luigi Firpo, 1969; as *The Defense of Galileo*, translated by Grant McColley, 1937; as *A Defense of Galileo, the Mathematician of Florence: Which Is an Inquiry as to Whether the Philosophical View Advocated by Galileo is in Agreement with, or Is Opposed to, the Sacred Scriptures*, translated by Richard J. Blackwell, 1994.
Civitatis solis. In *Realis philosophae epilogisticae partes quatuor*, 1623; single edition, 1643; in Italian, as *La città del sole*, 1840; edited by Edmondo Solmi, 1904, also edited by Norberto Bobbio (Italian and Latin), 1941, Adriano Seroni, 1977, F. Bartoletta, 1985, and by G. Berrettoni, 1991; as *The City of the Sun*, translated by Thomas W. Halliday, in *Ideal Commonwealths*, edited by

Henry Morley, 1885, revised edition, 1901; reprinted in *Ideal Empires and Republics*, 1901, *Famous New Deals of History*, 1935, and *Famous Utopias of the Renaissance*, 1948; also translated by William J. Gilstrap, in *The Quest for Utopias*, edited by Glenn Negley and J. Max Patrick, 1952; Daniel J. Donno (bilingual edition), 1981; R. Millner and A.M Elliott, 1981.

Realis philosophae epilogisticae partes quatuor. 1623; revised and enlarged edition, as *Disputationum in quatuor partes suae philosophiae realis*, 4 vols., 1637.

Astrologicorum. 7 vols., 1629; 8 vols., 1630.

Atheismus triumphatus. 1631.

Monarchia messiae (political treatise). 1633; edited by Luigi Firpo, 1960.

Medicinalium iuxta propria principia. 7 vols., 1635.

Philosophiae rationalis. 5 vols., 1638.

Universalis philosophiae, seu metaphysicarum rerum iuxta propria dogmata partes tres. 18 vols., 1638; as *Metafisica*, edited by Giovanni Di Napoli, 3 vols., 1967.

De libris propriis et de recta ratione studendi syntagma. 1642; edited by Vincenzo Spampanato, 1927.

Discorsi politici ai principi d'Italia, edited by Pietro Garzilli. 1848; also edited by Luigi Firpo, 1945.

Opere scelte, edited by Alessandro d'Ancona. 2 vols., 1854.

Theologicorum, edited by Romano Amerio. 1936–88; of the 30 books in Campanella's manuscript, the following have been edited:
Teologia (Book I). 1936; as *Dio e la predestinazione*, 2 vols., 1949–51.
La prima e la seconda resurrezione (Books XXVII–XXVIII). 1955.
Magia e grazia (Book XIV). 1957.
De sancta monotriade (Book II). 1958.
Cristologia (Book XVIII). 2 vols., 1958.
Della grazia gratificante (Book XIII). 1959.
Il peccato originale (Book XVI). 1960.
De homine (Book IV, part II), 1961.
Vita Christi (Book XXI). 1962.
Cosmologia (Book III). 1964.
I sacri segni (Book XXIV). 5 vols., 1965–68.
De Antichristo (Book XXVI). 1965.
De dictis Christi (Book XXIII). 1969.
E scatalogia (Books XXIX–XXX). 1969.
Le creature sovrannaturali (Book V). 1970.
Della beatitudine (Book VII). 1971.
Origine temporale di Cristo (Book XIX). 1972.
Le profezie di Cristo (Book XXV). 1973.
De remediis malorum (Book XVII). 1975.
Delle virtú e dei vizi in particolare (Book X). 1976; as *De virtutibus et vitiis Speciatum*, 1984.
De virtutibus supernaturalibus quibus ad beatitudinem homo regitur (Books XI–XII). 1988.

Epilogo magno, edited by Carmelo Ottaviano. 1939.

Aforismi politici, edited by Luigi Firpo. 1941.

Poetica, edited by Luigi Firpo. 1944.

Antiveneti, edited by Luigi Firpo. 1945.

Opuscoli inediti, edited by Luigi Firpo. 1951.

Articuli prophetales, edited by Germana Ernst. 1977.

Parole universali della dottrina politica, edited by Giuseppe Campanella. 1980.

Mathematica, edited by Armando Brissoni. 1989.

Verse

Scelta d'alcune poesie filosofiche. 1622; edited by Vincenzo Paladino, 1977, enlarged edition, 1983; as *Poesie filosofiche*, edited by Giovanni Gaspare Orelli, 1834, and by Marziano Guglielminetti, 1982; as *Le poesie*, edited by Giovanni Papini, 2 vols., 1913, by Giovanni Gentile, 1915, and by Mario Vinciguerra, 1938; parts translated by J.A. Symonds, in *The Sonnets of Michael Angelo Buonarroti and Tommaso Campanella*, 1878; as *Sonnets*, translated by John Addington Symonds, 1999.

Ecloga Christianissimus regi et reginae in portentosam delphini. 1639.

Other

Lettere, edited by Vincenzo Spampanato. 1927.

*

Bibliography: *Bibliografia degli scritti di Tommaso Campanella* by Luigi Firpo, 1940; *Tommaso Campanella in America: A Critical Bibliography and a Profile*, 1954, and *A Supplement to the Critical Bibliography*, 1957, by Francesco Grillo.

Critical Studies: *Campanella* by Léon Blanchet, 1920; *Tommaso Campanella*, by C. Dentice D'Accadia, 1921; *Tommaso Campanella and His Poetry* by Edmund Gardner, 1923; *Tommaso Campanella, metafisico* by Maria M. Rossi, 1923; *La filosofia politica di Tommaso Campanella* by Paolo Treves, 1930; *Campanella* by Nino Valeri, 1931; *Studi campanelliani* by Romano Amerio, 1934; *Famous Utopias* edited by Charles Andrews, 1937; *Tommaso Campanella* by Aldo Testa, 1941; *Studi campanelliani* by R. De Mattei, 1943; *Tommaso Campanella* by A. Corsano, 1944, revised edition, 1961; *Ricerche campanelliane* by Luigi Firpo, 1947; *Tommaso Campanella filosofo della restaurazione cattolica* by G. Di Napoli, 1947; *Tommaso Campanella* by Alfio and Antonietta Nicotra, 1948; *Tommaso Campanella: La crisi della coscienza in sè* by A. Maria Jacobelli Isoldi, 1953; *Tommaso Campanella* by Nicola Badaloni, 1965; *Lo spiritualismo di Tommaso Campanella* by Salvatore Femiano, 2 vols., 1965; *Renaissance Philosophers: The Italian Philosophers* edited by Arturo B. Fallico and Herman Schapiro, 1967; *Il sistema teologico di Tommaso Campanella* by R. Amerio, 1972; *L'eresia cattolica e riformatrice di T. Campanella e il Concilio Vaticano II* by F. Grillo, 1975; "Tommaso Campanella's *La città del sole*: Topography and Astrology" by Ilona Klein, in *Italiana 1987* edited by Albert N. Mancini and others, 1989; "Tommaso Campanella and the End of the Renaissance," in *Journal of Medieval and Renaissance Studies*, 20 (2), 1990, and "Tommaso Campanella and Jean de Launoy: The Controversy over Aristotle and His Reception in the West," in *Renaissance Quarterly*, 43 (3), 1990, both by John M. Headley; *Tommaso Campanella and the Transformation of the World* by John M. Headley, 1997.

* * *

Born in Calabria amid the harsh realities of Southern Italy and of an illiterate family sunk in the most extreme poverty, Campanella was educated in the only way possible for the poor—by taking priestly vows as a Dominican monk. He lived a life of incredible hardship, torture, persecution, and rejection by his contemporaries. However, upheld by an insatiable thirst for knowledge, an irrepressible intellectual curiosity, and a highly developed memory, he rose above the most extreme misfortune and the cruelty of the Inquisition to compose works on every subject imaginable—from philosophy to science and literature (over 100 works)—publicly championed Galileo at both his trials, yet he received only abuse in return, and lived in exile in Paris, at last recognized by educated society as a phenomenal intellectual, and able to oversee publication of many of his works. In a sense, the last Italian "Renaissance" man and a champion of the inexhaustibility of human knowledge, Campanella also preserved enough faith in human destiny to compose his own utopia (in the wake of Plato's *Republic* and More's *Utopia*), *La città del sole* (*The City of the Sun*), and composed moving poems and letters to contemporaries.

After initially devouring the knowledge available in his first monastery library, his first attempt to broaden his knowledge by moving to another monastery was harshly suppressed by his superiors, obliging him to flee to Northern Italy. By the age of 27 he had already been forced to adjure heresy by the Roman Inquisition, and by 1598 was obliged by the church to return to Calabria, where he became involved in an idealistic attempt to found an independent utopian state in the mountains, one governed by egalitarian principles and freed from the yoke of foreign domination. The harsh repression by the vice-regal government, with its mass arrests and executions, brought a swift end to this conspiracy, and Campanella, an acknowledged ringleader, was dragged in chains to Rome, only escaping execution by his resistance to torture and by feigning madness, to languish in prison almost forgotten, for 27 years.

Nevertheless, the creation of an enduring work of the literary imagination from first-hand experience of utopian idealism gave posterity *The City of the Sun*, the only work by Campanella to survive the test of time. In it, he described an utopian civilization located on a remote island in the Indian Ocean, founded on egalitarian principles and the rule of reason, where the Christian religion has not arrived to favour the life to come over earthly happiness, and where greed and corruption are not society's prime movers. Nature becomes the universal law, and a communistic sharing of property and duties characterizes this society, while children are brought up not by families, but by society, generated by principles of selection that smack (perhaps uncomfortably) of far more modern times. The city is laid out according to principles of the greatest benefit to all, while eating, sleeping, and working are all controlled by rigid rules, as are the clothes worn by the citizens—reminiscent to us of the uniforms of the science fiction imagination. Work is for all—of both sexes—and absolute equality between men and women extends even to military service.

The only hierarchy permitted is that of merit—an archetypal meritocracy—but defined in the terms of Campanella's time as the search for knowledge of all things: he who can understand more of nature's knowledge has the whip-hand in guiding those who know less, in working together for the common good. Thus we have a portrait of a society of happiness and peaceful concord, where private ambitions and clan affinities have been abandoned and family affection and concern for the future have been swept aside in favour of zealous dedication to the common good, leaving time for the cultivation of genial pursuits and learning.

It is clear that this utopian vision is the fruit of wide reading and not only of Campanella's experience of the failed Calabrian insurrection (and we have mentioned Plato and More in this connection). But there is also an autobiographical element stemming from Campanella's memories of his native Calabria—of the discipline of the monastic regime with its rigid rules, of the hardships of poverty, ignorance, and superstition that characterized Southern Italy. These were elevated here by one of the region's most distinguished sons—against impossible odds and through incredible hardships—to the dignity of great literature, almost constituting a cry for a better society, founded on saner principles and guided by the light of reason, that resounds down the centuries to the present, where, however dated and naïve it is in certain respects, it nonetheless seems to have an enduring vitality.

—Christopher Cairns

CAMUS, Albert

Born: Mondovi, Algeria, 7 November 1913. **Education:** Educated at the University of Algiers, graduated 1936. **Family:** Married 1) Simone Hié in 1934 (divorced); 2) Francine Faure in 1940 (died 1979), twin son and daughter. **Career:** Worked as meteorologist, shipbroker's clerk, automobile parts salesman, clerk in the automobile registry division of the prefecture, actor and amateur theatre producer, Algiers, 1935–39; staff member, *Alger-Républicain*, 1938–39, and editor, *Soir-Républicain*, 1939–40, both Algiers; sub-editor for layout, *Paris-Soir*, 1940; teacher, Oran, Algeria, 1940–42; convalescent in central France, 1942–43; joined Resistance in Lyon region, 1943; journalist, Paris, 1943–45; reader, and editor of Espoir series, Gallimard, publishers, Paris, 1943–60; co-founding editor, *Combat*, 1945–47. **Awards:** Critics prize (France), 1947; Nobel prize for literature, 1957. **Member:** Communist Party, 1935–39. **Died:** 4 January 1960.

PUBLICATIONS

Collections

Complete Fiction, translated by Stuart Gilbert and Justin O'Brien. 1960.
Théâtre, récits, nouvelles; Essais, edited by Roger Quilliot. 2 vols., 1962–65.
Collected Plays, translated by Stuart Gilbert and Justin O'Brien. 1965.
Oeuvres complètes. 5 vols., 1983.

Fiction

L'Étranger, 1942; as *The Stranger*, translated by Stuart Gilbert, 1946; as *The Outsider*, translated by Gilbert, 1946; also translated by K. Griffith, 1982; Joseph Laredo, 1984.
La Peste. 1947; as *The Plague*, translated by Stuart Gilbert, 1948.
La Chute. 1956; as *The Fall*, translated by Justin O'Brien, 1957.
L'Exil et le royaume (stories). 1957; as *Exile and the Kingdom*, translated by Justin O'Brien, 1958.
La Mort heureuse. 1971; as *A Happy Death*, translated by Richard Howard, 1972.
Le Premier Homme (unfinished). 1994; as *The First Man*, translated by David Hapgood, 1995.

Plays

Le Malentendu (produced 1944). With *Caligula*, 1944; as *Cross Purpose*, translated by Stuart Gilbert, with *Caligula*, 1948.

Caligula (produced 1945). With *Le Malentendu*, 1944; 1941 version (produced 1983), 1984; as *Caligula*, translated by Stuart Gilbert, with *Cross Purpose*, 1948.

L'État de siège (produced 1948). 1948; as *State of Siege*, translated by Stuart Gilbert, in *Caligula and Three Other Plays*, 1958.

Les Justes (produced 1949). 1950; as *The Just Assassins*, translated by Stuart Gilbert, in *Caligula and Three Other Plays*, 1958; as *The Just*, translated by Henry Jones, 1965.

La Dévotion à la croix, from the play by Calderón (produced 1953). 1953.

Les Esprits, from a work by Pierre de Larivey (produced 1953). 1953.

Un cas intéressant, from a work by Dino Buzzati (produced 1955). 1955.

Requiem pour une nonne, from the novel by William Faulkner (produced 1956). 1956.

Le Chevalier d'Olmedo, from the play by Lope de Vega (produced 1957). 1957.

Caligula and Three Other Plays (incudes *Cross Purpose; State of Seige; The Just Assassins*), translated by Stuart Gilbert. 1958.

Les Possédés, from the novel by Dostoevskii (produced 1959). 1959; as *The Possessed*, translated by Justin O'Brien, 1960.

Other

L'Envers et l'endroit. 1937.

Noces. 1939.

Le Mythe de Sisyphe. 1942; as *The Myth of Sisyphus and Other Essays*, translated by Justin O'Brien, 1955.

Lettres à un ami allemand. 1945.

L'Existence. 1945.

Le Minotaure; ou, La Halte d'Oran. 1950.

Actuelles [1]–3: Chroniques 1944–1948, Chroniques 1948–1953, Chronique algérienne 1939–1958. 3 vols., 1950–58.

L'Homme révolté. 1951; as *The Rebel: An Essay on Man in Revolt*, translated by Anthony Bower, 1953.

L'Été. 1954.

Réflexions sur la guillotine, in *Réflexions sur la peine capitale*, with Arthur Koestler. 1957; as *Reflections on the Guillotine*, translated by Richard Howard, 1960.

Discours de Suède. 1958; as *Speech of Acceptance upon the Award of the Nobel Prize for Literature*, translated by Justin O'Brien, 1958.

Resistance, Rebellion, and Death (selection), translated by Justin O'Brien. 1960.

Méditation sur le théâtre et la vie. 1961.

Carnets: Mai 1935–fevrier 1942. 1962; as *Carnets 1935–1942*, translated by Philip Thody, 1963; as *Notebooks 1935–1942*, 1963.

Lettre à Bernanos. 1963.

Carnets: Janvier 1942–mars 1951. 1964; as *Notebooks 1942–1951*, edited and translated by Justin O'Brien, 1965.

Lyrical and Critical (essays), edited and translated by Philip Thody. 1967.

Le Combat d'Albert Camus, edited by Norman Stokle. 1970.

Selected Essays and Notebooks, edited and translated by Philip Thody. 1970.

Le Premier Camus. 1973; as *Youthful Writings*, translated by Ellen Conroy Kennedy, 1977.

Journaux de voyage, edited by Roger Quilliot. 1978; as *American Journals*, translated by Hugh Levick, 1987.

Fragments d'un combat 1938–1940: Alger-Républicain, Le Soir-Républicain, edited by Jacqueline Lévi-Valensi and André Abbou. 1978.

Correspondance 1932–1960, with Jean Grenier, edited by Marguerite Dobrenn. 1981.

Selected Political Writings, edited by Jonathan King. 1981.

Oeuvre fermée, oeuvre ouverte, edited by Raymond Gay-Croisier and Jacqueline Lévi-Valensi. 1985.

Carnets: Mars 1951–Décembre 1959. 1989.

Translator, *La Dernière Fleur*, by James Thurber. 1952.

*

Bibliography: *Camus: A Bibliography* by Robert F. Roeming, 1968; and subsequent editions by R. Gay-Crosier, in *A Critical Bibliography of French Literature*, 6, 1980; *Camus in English: An Annotated Bibliography of Albert Camus's Contributions to English and American Periodicals and Newspapers* by Peter C. Hoy, 2nd edition, 1971.

Critical Studies: *Albert Camus: A Study of His Work*, 1957, *Albert Camus, 1913–1960: A Biographical Study*, 1961, and *Albert Camus*, 1989, all by Philip Thody, 1961; *Camus* by Germaine Brée, 1959, revised edition, 1972, and *Camus: A Collection of Critical Essays* edited by Brée, 1962; *Albert Camus: The Artist in the Arena* by Emmett Parker, 1965; *Camus* by Phillip H. Rhein, 1969, revised edition, 1989; *Albert Camus* by Conor Cruise O'Brien, 1970; *The Theatre of Albert Camus* by Edward Freeman, 1971; *Camus: The Invincible Summer* by Albert Maquet, 1972; *The Unique Creation of Albert Camus* by Donald Lazere, 1973; *Witness of Decline: Albert Camus: Moralist of the Absurd* by Lev Braun, 1974; *Albert Camus: A Biography* by Herbert R. Lottman, 1979; *The Descent of the Doves: Camus's Journey to the Spirit* by Alfred Cordes, 1980; *Camus's Imperial Vision* by Anthony Rizzuto, 1981; *The Narcissistic Text: A Reading of Camus's Fiction* by Brian T. Fitch, 1982; *Camus: A Critical Study of His Life and Work*, 1982, and *Camus: The Stranger*, 1988, both by Patrick McCarthy; *Exiles and Strangers: A Reading of Camus's Exile and the Kingdom* by Elaine Showalter, Jr., 1984; *Exile and Kingdom: A Political Rereading of Albert Camus* by Susan Tarrow, 1985; *The Ethical Pragmatism of Albert Camus: Two Studies in the History of Ideas* by Dean Vasil, 1985; *Beyond Absurdity: The Philosophy of Albert Camus* by Robert C. Trundle, 1987; *Camus: A Critical Examination* by David Sprintzen, 1988; *Albert Camus and Indian Thought* by Sharad Chaedra, 1989; *Understanding Albert Camus* by David R. Ellison, 1990; *Camus's L'Étranger: Fifty Years On* edited by Adele King, 1992; *Albert Camus: Le Premier Homme, La Peste* by Edward J. Hughes, 1995; *Looking for Heroes in Postwar France: Albert Camus, Max Jacob, Simone Weil* by Neal Oxenhandler, 1996; *Camus: The Challenge of Dostoevsky* by Ray Davison, 1997; *Albert Camus: A Life* by Oliver Todd, translated by Benjamin Ivry, 1997; *The Burden of Responsibility: Blum, Camus, Aron, and the French Twentieth Century* by Tony Judt, 1998; *Camus: Love and Sexuality* by Anthony Rizzuto, 1998; *Camus: Portrait of a Moralist* by Stephen Eric Bronner, 1999; *Camus: La Peste* by James S. Williams, 2000; *On Camus* by Richard Kamber, 2001.

*   *   *

Although French critics on the Right and the Left have proclaimed Albert Camus *passé* for every imaginable reason, he has remained the bestselling author of France's largest and most prestigious literary publisher, Gallimard. In 1971, eleven years after his death at the age of 46, the publication of an early novel that Camus had had the good sense to abandon stimulated sales that pushed the French edition of *La Mort heureuse* (*A Happy Death*) to the top of the bestseller list within a few weeks. This is but one belated aspect of the paradox of Camus's career and reputation as a writer. When he was selected in 1957 to receive the Nobel prize for literature, he was, at 44, the youngest literary laureate but one, Rudyard Kipling having received the prize at 42. He himself stated publicly at the time that he would have voted for Malraux.

Camus is exceptional among French writers, the majority of whom have come from comfortable middle-class origins even in recent times. He was reared in Algiers by his mother, an illiterate charwoman. His first writings published in Paris catapulted him to a literary celebrity for which he was ill prepared. The climate of the immediate post-war period, combined with his position as a popular editorial writer for the Resistance newspaper *Combat*, rapidly created an aura about Camus that he had not sought and that was to cause him considerable difficulty a decade later.

In the first important review of *L'Étranger* (*The Outsider* or *The Stranger*), Jean-Paul Sartre was struck by the contemporaneity of this objective, apparently dispassionate, non-novel. An essay on the notion of the Absurd, entitled *Le Mythe de Sisyphe* (*The Myth of Sisyphus*), has been taken by many readers since Sartre to be the theory of which *The Outsider* is the illustration. Camus's Absurd is a description of a state more familiar to some English-speaking readers as a variety of contemporary thought posited on the death of God. It owes a great deal to such thinkers as Pascal, Kierkegaard, Dostoevskii, and Nietzsche. Camus was at pains to point out that there were, in his view, few points of contact between the Absurd and Sartrean existentialism, a distinction that readers, critics, and historians have tended to honour in the breach. The third piece in this cycle is *Caligula*, which remains the most important and the most popular of his plays.

Camus's view of his own career involved cycles of trilogies. The cycle of the Absurd antedates his experience of the war in the Resistance. It was essentially complete by 1941, and in 1942 he began work on the cycle of Revolt which owed a great deal more to the war than did its predecessor. Once again the trilogy included a novel, *La Peste* (*The Plague*), an essay, *L'Homme révolté* (*The Rebel*), and a play, *Les Justes* (*The Just Assassins*). *The Rebel* was attacked in *Les Temps Modernes*, a pro-communist magazine edited by Sartre. The subsequent polemic caused Camus to break with Sartre and to become disgusted with left-wing intellectuals. Several works written after this experience testify to a deepened awareness of human motivation, resulting in a more complex and satisfying style. The most substantial of these is *La Chute* (*The Fall*). During the 1950s Camus turned progressively to the theatre for both solace and stimulation. At the time of his death he was preparing a third cycle, to be called Nemesis, and had begun a novel entitled *Le Premier Homme* (*The First Man*), which was published in 1994. He left interesting *Carnets* (*Notebooks*), in three volumes, and an important collection of journalistic writings, *Actuelles*.

—A. James Arnold

See the essays on *The Fall*, *The Outsider*, and *The Plague*.

CANETTI, Elias

Born: Ruse (Ruschuk), Bulgaria, 25 July 1905. **Education:** Educated at schools in England, Austria, Switzerland, and Germany; University of Vienna, Ph.D. in chemistry, 1929. **Family:** Married 1) Venetia Taubner-Calderón in 1934 (died 1963); 2) Hera Buschor in 1971 (died 1988), one daughter. **Career:** Full-time writer; resident of England from 1939. **Awards:** Foreign Book prize (France), 1949; Vienna prize, 1966; Critics prize (Germany), 1967; Great Austrian State prize, 1967; Büchner prize, 1972; Nelly Sachs prize, 1975; Franz Nabl prize (Graz), 1975; Keller prize, 1977; Order of Merit (Bonn), 1979; Europa Prato prize (Italy), 1980; Order of Merit (Germany), 1980(?); Hebbel prize, 1980; Nobel prize for literature, 1981; Kafka prize, 1981; Great Service Cross (Germany), 1983. D.Litt.: University of Manchester. Honorary Ph.D.: University of Munich. **Died:** 14 August 1994.

PUBLICATIONS

Fiction

Die Blendung. 1936; as *Auto-da-Fé,* translated by C.V. Wedgwood, 1946; as *The Tower of Babel,* translated by Wedgwood, 1947.

Plays

Hochzeit (produced 1965). 1932; as *The Wedding,* 1986.
Komödie der Eitelkeit (produced 1965). 1950; as *Comedy of Vanity,* translated by Gitta Honegger, with *Life-Terms,* 1982.
Die Befristeten (produced 1967). In *Dramen,* 1964; as *Life-Terms,* translated by Gitta Honegger, with *Comedy of Vanity,* 1982; as *The Numbered,* translated by Carol Stewart, 1984.
Dramen (includes *Hochzeit; Komödie der Eitelkeit; Die Befristeten*). 1964.
Comedy of Vanity and Life-Terms, translated by Gitta Honegger. 1982.

Other

Fritz Wotruba. 1955.
Masse und Macht. 1960; as *Crowds and Power,* translated by Carol Stewart, 1962.
Welt im Kopf (selection), edited by Erich Fried. 1962.
Aufzeichnungen 1942–1948. 1965.
Die Stimmen von Marrakesch: Aufzeichnungen nach einer Reise. 1967; as *The Voices of Marrakesh,* translated by J.A. Underwood, 1978.
Der andere Prozess: Kafkas Briefe an Felice. 1969; as *Kafka's Other Trial: The Letters to Felice,* translated by Christopher Middleton, 1974.
Alle vergeudete Verehrung: Aufzeichnungen 1949–1960. 1970.
Die gespaltene Zukunft: Aufsätze und Gespräche. 1972.
Macht und Überleben: Drei Essays. 1972.
Die Provinz des Menschen: Aufzeichnungen 1942–1972. 1973; as *The Human Province,* translated by Joachim Neugroschel, 1978.
Der Ohrenzeuge: 50 Charaktere. 1974; as *Earwitness: Fifty Characters,* translated by Joachim Neugroschel, 1979.

Das Gewissen der Worte: Essays. 1975; as *The Conscience of Words*, translated by Joachim Neugroschel, 1979.
Der Überlebende. 1975.
Der Beruf des Dichters. 1976.
Die gerettete Zunge: Geschichte einer Jugend. 1977; as *The Tongue Set Free: Remembrance of a European Childhood*, translated by Joachim Neugroschel, 1979.
Die Fackel im Ohr: Lebensgeschichte 1921–1931. 1980; as *The Torch in My Ear,* translated by Joachim Neugroschel, 1982.
Das Augenspiel: Lebensgeschichte 1931–1937. 1985; as *The Play of the Eyes*, translated by Ralph Manheim, 1986.
Das Geheimherz der Uhr: Aufzeichnungen 1973–1985. 1987; as *The Secret Heart of the Clock: Notes, Aphorisms, Fragments 1973–1985*, translated by Joel Agee, 1989.
Notes from Hampstead: The Writer's Notes, 1954–1971, translated by John Hargraves, 1998.
Translator, *Leidweg der Liebe*, by Upton Sinclair. 1930.
Translator, *Das Geld schreibt: Eine Studie über die amerikanische Literatur*, by Upton Sinclair. 1930.
Translator, *Alkohol*, by Upton Sinclair. 1932.

*

Critical Studies: *Canetti: Stationen zum Werk* by Alfons-M. Bischoff, 1973; *Kopf und Welt: Canettis Roman "Die Blendung"* by D.G.J. Roberts, 1975; *Canetti* by Dagmar Barnouw, 1979; *Essays in Honor of Elias Canetti*, translated by Michael Hulse, 1987; *Elias Canetti* by Thomas H. Falk, 1993; *Blind Reflections: Gender in Elias Canetti's Die Blendung* by Kristie A. Foell, 1994; *Canetti and Nietzsche: Theories of Humor in Die Blendung* by Harriet Murphy, 1997; *Metaphor as Thought in Elias Canetti's Mass und Macht* by David Scott, 1999; *The End of Modernism: Elias Canetti's Auto-da-fé* by William Collins Donahue, 2001; *Anthropology as Memory: Elias Canetti's and Franz Baermann Steiner's Responses to the Shoah* by Michael Mack, 2001.

*   *   *

Elias Canetti has never been widely known in Britain, although he lived in England from 1939. From 1981, when he won the Nobel prize for literature, the contemporary relevance of his work once again attracted attention. A reticent man, Canetti dedicated his life to the study of a single theme: the behaviour of the individual within the mass and the power struggle associated with this conflict.

His best known works are the novel, *Die Blendung* (*Auto-da-Fé*), and a study of the behaviour of the mass, *Masse und Macht* (*Crowds and Power*). His autobiographies of more recent years, *Die gerettete Zunge* (*The Tongue Set Free*), *Die Fackel im Ohr* (*The Torch in My Ear*), and *Das Augenspiel* (*The Play of the Eyes*) have underlined the origins of and inspiration for his lifetime's work. His dramas and essays, too, reflect a preoccupation with hallucination, political pressure, linguistic ambiguity, and the destructive power of the masses.

The events of most outstanding significance for Canetti in the formation of his interest in crowd psychology and the hypnotic power of the masses were the awaited arrival of a comet in Ruse, the sinking of the Titanic, the fire at the Law Courts in Vienna in 1927, and an experience in Vienna's Alserstrasse in the winter of 1924–25. These powerful emotional experiences are linked in Canetti's mind and work by images of great energy, of blood, of a rushing sound, and of fire. Fire is frequently seen as a magnetic driving force and is associated with the uncontrolled rhythm of the masses. These symbols recur in Canetti's work. Sight and blindness, insight and illusion are related themes. In *Auto-da-Fé* the central character, Kien, who becomes increasingly deluded by his world of books, eventually perishes in a fire with them. Canetti is always at pains to point out the contrasts and similarities between a character's external appearance, his environment, and his use of language. Each character, e.g., the man of books, the collector, the spend-thrift, has "fixed ideas" which stand out because reality is portrayed as fragmented, communication as very partial. Canetti distanced himself from the suggestiveness of his characters, and yet he had clearly been closely involved with the experience of each of them. Attempts at communication between these different kinds of people are often portrayed as grotesque, leading only to an intensification of individual isolation.

Despite themes which are characteristic of a period of social and political upheaval, Canetti's style is serene, controlled, and lucid, almost part of another era and tradition. His work reflects self-assurance and composure. Its stylistic poise and balance based on an authoritative use of language, rich in imagery, set him apart from many younger contemporary writers.

Nevertheless, his subject matter is complex and his vision powerful—a confidence in one's own destiny, a respect for the experience of others, and a resistance to illusion, manipulation, and death.

—Barbara Saunders

See the essay on *Auto-da-Fé*.

ČAPEK, Karel

Born: Malé Svatoňovice, Bohemia (now in the Czech Republic), 9 January 1890; brother of the writer Josef Čapek. **Education:** Educated at Charles University, Prague, 1909–15, Ph.D. in philosophy 1915; universities of Paris and Berlin, 1909–10. **Family:** Married the actress Olga Scheinpflugová in 1935. **Career:** Journalist, *Lidové noviny*; co-founder, with Josef Čapek, František-Langer, and with Edmond Konrad, of the avant-garde circle "The Pragmatists"; stage director and dramaturg, Vinohrady Theatre, Prague, 1921–23. **Died:** 25 December 1938.

PUBLICATIONS

Collections

Spisy bratří [Collected Works]. 51 vols., 1928–47.
Spisy [Works]. 1981.
Toward the Radical Center: A Karel Čapek Reader, edited by Peter Kussi. 1990.

Fiction

Zářivé hlubiny a jiné prózy [The Luminous Depths and Other Prose Works], with Josef Čapek. 1916.
Boží muka [Stations of the Cross]. 1917.
Krakonošova zahrada [The Garden of Krakonos], with Josef Čapek. 1918.

Trapné povídky. 1921; as *Money and Other Stories*, translated by Francis P. Marchant, Dora Round, F.P. Casey, and O. Vočadlo, 1929.

Továrna na absolutno. 1922; as *The Absolute at Large*, translated by M. and R. Weatherall, 1927.

Krakatit. 1924; as *Krakatit*, translated by Lawrence Hyde, 1925; as *An Atomic Fantasy*, translated by Hyde, 1948.

Povídky z jedné kapsy [Tales from One Pocket], *Povídky z druhé kapsy* [Tales from the Other Pocket]. 2 vols., 1929; in part as *Tales from Two Pockets*, translated by Paul Selver, 1932; also translated by Norma Comrada, 1994.

Apokryfy; Kniha apokryfů. 2 vols., 1932–45; as *Apocryphal Stories*, translated by Dora Round, 1949; as *Apocryphal Tales: With a Selection of Fables and Would-be Tales*, translated by Norma Comrada, 1997.

Devatero pohádek a ještě jedna od Josefa Čapek jako přívažek. 1932; as *Fairy Tales with One Extra as a Makeweight*, translated by M. and R. Weatherall, 1933.

Hordubal. 1933; as *Hordubal*, translated by M. and R. Weatherall, 1934.

Povětroň. 1934; as *Meteor*, translated by M. and R. Weatherall, 1935.

Obyčejný život. 1934; as *An Ordinary Life*, translated by M. and R. Weatherall, 1936.

Válka s mloky. 1936; as *War with the Newts*, translated by M. and R. Weatherall, 1937; also translated by Ewald Osers, 1985.

První parta. 1937; as *The First Rescue Party*, translated by M. and R. Weatherall, 1939.

Život a dílo skladatele Foltýna. 1939; as *The Cheat*, translated by M. and R. Weatherall, 1941.

Nine Fairy Tales and One More, translated by Dagmar Hermann. 1990.

Plays

Lásky hra osudná [The Fateful Game of Love], with Josef Čapek (produced 1922). 1910.

R.U.R. (produced 1920). 1920; as *R.U.R.* (*Rossum's Universal Robots*), translated by Paul Selver, 1923.

Loupežník (produced 1921). 1920; as *The Robber*, translated by Rudolph C. Bednar, 1931.

Ze života hmyzu, with Josef Čapek (produced 1922). 1921; as *And So Ad Infinitum (The Life of the Insect): An Entomological Review*, translated by Paul Selver, 1923; as *The Insect Play*, translated by Selver, 1923; as *The World We Live In (The Insect Comedy)*, adapted by Owen Davis, 1933.

Věc Makropulos (produced 1922). 1922; as *The Macropoulos Secret*, translated by Paul Selver, 1927.

Adam Stvořitel, with Josef Čapek (produced 1927). 1927; as *Adam the Creator*, translated by Dora Round, 1929.

Bílá nemoc (produced 1937). 1937; as *Power and Glory*, translated by Paul Selver and Ralph Neale, 1938.

Matka (produced 1938). 1938; as *The Mother*, translated by Paul Selver, 1939.

Other

Pragmatismus; čili, Filosofie praktického života [Pragmatism; or, a Philosophy of Practical Life]. 1918.

Kritika slov [A Critique of Words]. 1920.

Italské listy. 1923; as *Letters from Italy*, translated by Francis P. Marchant, 1929.

Anglické listy. 1924; as *Letters from England*, translated by Paul Selver, 1925.

O nejbližších věcech. 1925; as *Intimate Things*, translated by Dora Round, 1935.

Jak vzniká divadelní hra a průvodce po zákulisí. 1925; as *How a Play Is Produced*, translated by P. Beaumont Wadsworth, 1928.

Skandální aféra Josefa Holouška [The Scandalous Affair of Josef Holoušek]. 1927.

Hovory s T.G. Masarykem. 3 vols., 1928–35; as *President Masaryk Tells His Story*, 1934, and *Masaryk on Thought and Life*, 1938, both translated by M. and R. Weatherall; as *Talks with T.G. Masaryk*, translated by Michael Henry Heim, 1995.

Zahradníkův rok. 1929; as *The Gardener's Year*, translated by M. and R. Weatherall, 1931.

Výlet do Španěl. 1930; as *Letters from Spain*, translated by Paul Selver, 1932.

Minda; čili, Ochova psu. 1930; translated as *Minda; or, On Breeding Dogs*, 1940.

Obrázky z Holandska. 1932; as *Letters from Holland*, translated by Paul Selver, 1933.

O věcech obecných; čili, Zoon politikos [Ordinary Things; or, Zoon Politikon]. 1932.

Dášeňka čili Život štěněte. 1933; as *Dashenka; or, the Life of a Puppy*, translated by M. and R. Weatherall, 1940.

Legenda o člověku zahradníkovi [Legend of a Gardening Man]. 1935.

Cesta na sever. 1936; as *Travels in the North*, translated by M. and R. Weatherall, 1939.

Jak se co dělá. 1938; as *How They Do It*, translated by M. and R. Weatherall, 1945.

Kalendář [Calendar]. 1940.

O lidech [About People]. 1940.

Vzrušené tance [Wild Dances]. 1946.

Bajky a podpovídky [Fables and Would-Be Tales]. 1946.

Sedm rozhlásku [Seven Notes for the Wireless]. 1946.

Ratolest a vavřín [The Sprig and the Laurel]. 1947.

In Praise of Newspapers and Other Essays on the Margin of Literature, translated by M. and R. Weatherall. 1951.

Obrázky z domova [Letters from Home]. 1953.

Sloupkový ambit [The Pillared Cloister]. 1957.

Poznámky o tvorbě [Comments on Creation]. 1959.

Na břehu dnů [On the Boundaries of Days]. 1966.

Divadelníkem proti své vuli [A Drama Expert Against My Will]. 1968.

V zajetí slov [In the Bondage of Words]. 1969.

Ctení o T.G. Masarykovi [Readings about T.G. Masaryk]. 1969.

Místo pro Janathana! [Make Way for Jonathan]. 1970.

Listy Olze 1920–38 [Letters to Olga]. 1971.

Drobty pod stolem doby [Crumbs under the Table of the Age]. 1975.

Listy Anielce [Letter to Anielce]. 1978.

Neuskutečněný dialog [Selected Essays], edited by Gustav Földi. 1978.

Dopisy ze zásuvky [Letters Out of a Drawer] (letters to Vera Hruzová), edited by Jiří Opelik. 1980.

Cesty k přátelství [Selected Correspondence]. 1987.

Od člověka k člověku [From Person to Person]. 1988.

Filmová libreta [Film Libretto]. 1989.

*

Bibliography: *Bibliografie Karla Čapka: soupis jeho díla*, 1990; *Karel Čapek, bibliografie díla a literatury o životě a díle, publikace v Československu a v Sovětském svazu* by Margita Křepinská, 4 vols., 1991.

Critical Studies: *Karel Čapek* by William E. Harkins, 1962; *Karel Čapek: An Essay* by Alexander Matuška, 1964; *Karel Čapek* (in German) by Eckehard Thiele, 1988; *The Narratives of Čapek and Cexov: A Typological Comparison of the Authors' World Views* by Peter Z. Schubert, 1997; *Karel Čapek: In Pursuit of Truth, Tolerance, and Trust* by Bohuslava R. Bradbrook, 1998.

* * *

Karel Čapek sprang into world fame with his play *R.U.R.* about the production and commercial exploitation of semi-human automata. It gave the English language a new word—"robot." He and his brother Josef followed this up with *Ze Života hmyzu* (*The Insect Play*), where the jungle law of the insect world was portrayed as a reflection of the amorality of human society. Later plays included *Věc Makropulos* (*The Macropoulos Secret*; best known today in Janáček's operatic version) about a woman who was the victim of an experiment to prolong life, in which Čapek, unlike Shaw, reached the comforting conclusion that our existing life span is about right.

Although Čapek was a gifted playwright, his best work did not lie in the theatre. The world publicity he received for his plays with their sensational themes obscured the merit of his more philosophical works like his "Trilogy"—*Hordubal, Povětroň* (*Meteor*), and *Obyčejný život* (*An Ordinary Life*)—his series of short stories *Povídky z jedné kapsy* and *Povídky z druhé kapsy* (*Tales from Two Pockets*), and his *feuilletons,*. which were admirably suited to his particular genius. His delightful travel books, some of which he illustrated himself, achieved popularity in the countries he was describing.

In his "Trilogy" Čapek expresses his relativist view of life by showing that human personality comprises many disparate elements, some completely hidden and others only rarely coming to the surface. The Ukrainian peasant Hordubal is murdered by his wife and her paramour, but at the trial it is clear that the facts and motives are impossible for outsiders to determine. In *Meteor* three people make conflicting but plausible conjectures about the past history of an unknown airman who has been brought into a hospital unconscious, while in *An Ordinary Life* a man discovers, in retrospect, that he has had not one personality but several. Čapek adopts the same approach in his last, unfinished novel, *Život a dílo skladatele Foltýna* (*The Cheat*).

In his brilliant "Pocket" tales Čapek shows himself to be a master of short-story writing, following the example of G.K. Chesterton, just as his "utopian" plays and novels show the influence of H.G. Wells,

Less successful was his satirical fantasy *Továrna na absolutno* (*The Absolute at Large*), which tells how the discovery of the power of electrons and their application in a factory lead to overproduction and unemployment (including not "butter mountains" but all other "mountains" from tacks to rolls of paper) and release "fall-out" in the form of widespread religious hysteria; *Krakatit*, a half-mystical and strongly erotic story of the struggle of foreign powers to obtain the secret of an atomic bomb; and *První parta* (*The First Rescue Party*), a social realist novel about working-class heroism during an accident in a coal mine. His novel *Válka s mloky* (*War with the Newts*)—an extension of the theme in *R.U.R.*—was particularly topical at the time as it reflected the alarm felt at the power of the Nazi system and the threat of Hitler's aggression.

Čapek's writings are the product of his highly original imagination and deep philosophical thought. They are strongly influenced by his preoccupation with epistemology. His novels and plays are full of thought-provoking ideas and intriguing situations but lack fully rounded characters. He has continued to maintain his hold over the Czech reading public in spite of (or perhaps because of) his close identification with the officially rejected Masaryk Republic, but his work is today less well-known abroad, perhaps because many of the problems he dealt with so imaginatively have been overtaken or are seen today in a more modern light. The failure of existing English translations to match his highly individual literary style has proved an additional handicap to full appreciation of his talents. He had great faith in the West, and the Munich "betrayal" robbed him of his will to live. "It's not so bad. They haven't sold us out, only given us away" (*Bajky* [*Fables*]).

—Cecil Parrott

See the essays on *The Insect Play* and *R.U.R.*

CARDENAL, Ernesto

Born: Granada, Nicaragua, 20 January 1925. Family moved to León, 1930. **Education:** Educated at the Colegio Centro América, Granada; National Autonomous University, Mexico City, 1944–48, degree 1948; Columbia University, New York, 1948–49. **Career:** Travelled through France, Italy, Spain, and Switzerland, 1949; co-founder, Hilo Azul publishers, 1951; member, National Union for Popular Action, and contributor of political articles to *La Prensa*, 1950s; Trappist novice, Gethsemani, Kentucky, 1957–59; member of Benedictine monastery of Santa María de la Resurrección, Cuernavaca, Mexico, 1959–65, and a seminary in Colombia, 1961; ordained Roman Catholic priest, 1965; founder and leader, religious community "Nuestra Señora de Solentiname," Solentiname Archipelago, Nicaragua, during the 1960s and 1970s; visited Cuba to serve on poetry jury, 1970; chaplain, anti-government Sandinista Front, and subsequently appointed Minister of Culture in the Sandinista government in 1979. Lives in Managua. **Awards:** Managua Centenary prize, 1952; Christopher Book award, 1972; La Paz prize grant, 1980.

PUBLICATIONS

Verse

La ciudad deshabitada. 1946.
Proclama del conquistador. 1947.
Gethsemani, Ky. 1960.
La hora 0. 1960.
Epigramas: Poemas. 1961.

Oración por Marilyn Monroe, y otros poemas. 1965; as *Marilyn Monroe and Other Poems*, edited and translated by Robert Pring-Mill, 1975.

El estrecho dudoso. 1966; as *The Doubtful Strait*, translated by John Lyons, 1995.

Antología. 1967.

Poemas. 1967.

Salmos. 1967; as *Psalms of Struggle and Liberation*, translated by Emile G. McAnany, 1971; as *Psalms*, translated by Thomas Blackburn, 1981.

Mayapán. 1968.

Poemas reunidos 1949–1969. 1969.

Homenaje a los indios americanos. 1969; as *Homage to the American Indians*, translated by Carlos and Monique Altschul, 1973.

La hora 0 y otros poemas. 1971; as *Zero Hour and Other Documentary Poems*, edited by Donald D. Walsh, translated by Paul W. Borgeson, Jr. and Jonathan Cohen, 1980.

Antología, edited by Pablo Antonio Cuadro. 1971.

Poemas. 1971.

Antología. 1972.

Canto nacional. 1973.

Oráculo sobre Managua. 1973.

Poesía escogida. 1975.

Apocalypse and Other Poems, edited and translated by Robert Pring-Mill and Donald D. Walsh. 1977.

Antología. 1978.

Canto a un país que nace. 1978.

Poesía de uso: Antología, 1949–1978. 1979.

Poesía. 1979.

Nueva antología poética. 1979.

Tocar el cielo. 1981.

Waslala, translated by Fidel López-Criado and R.A. Kerr. 1983.

Antología: Ernesto Cardenal. 1983.

Poesia de la nueva Nicaragua. 1983.

Vuelos de victoria. 1984; as *Flights of Victory: Songs of Celebration of the Nicaraguan Revolution*, translated by Marc Zimmerman (bilingual edition), 1985.

Quetzalcóatl. 1985.

With Walker in Nicaragua and Other Early Poems, 1949–1954, translated by Jonathan Cohen. 1985.

From Nicaragua with Love: Poems, 1976–1986, translated by Jonathan Cohen. 1987.

Cántico cósmico. 1989; as *The Music of the Spheres* (bilingual edition), translated by Dinah Livingstone, 1990; as *Cosmic Canticle*, translated by John Lyons, 1993.

Los ovnis de oro: Poemas indios. 1991; as *Golden UFOs: The Indian Poems*, edited by Russell O. Salmon, translated by Carlos and Monique Altschul. 1992.

Other

Vida en el amor. 1970; as *To Live Is to Love*, translated by Kurt Reinhardt, 1972; as *Vida en el amor/Love*, translated by Dinah Livingstone, 1974; as *Abide in Love*, translated by Dinah Livingstone, 1995.

En Cuba. 1972; as *In Cuba*, translated by Donald D. Walsh, 1974.

Cristianismo y revolución, with Fidel Castro. 1974.

Cardenal en Valencia (interviews). 1974.

El Evangelio en Solentiname. 1975; as *The Gospel in Solentiname*, translated by Donald D. Walsh, 1976; as *Love in Practice: The Gospel in Solentiname*, 1977; selections as *Evangelio, pueblo, y arte*, 1983; selections as *The Gospel in Art by the Peasants of Solentiname*, edited by Philip and Sally Sharper, 1984.

La santidad de la revolución. 1976.

La paz mundial y la revolución de Nicaragua. 1981.

Nostalgia del futuro: Pintura y buena noticia en Solentiname. 1982.

La democratización de la cultura. 1982.

Nicaragua: La guerra de liberación—der Befreiungskrieg, with Richard Cross. 1982(?).

Nuevo cieto y tierra nueva. 1985.

Del Monasterio al Mundo: Correspondencia entre Ernesto Cardenal y Thomas Merton (1959–1968), edited by Santiago Daydí-Tolson. N.d.

Editor, with José Coronel Urtecho, *Antología de la poesia norteamericana.* 1963.

Editor, with Jorge Montoya Toro, *Literatura indígena americana: Antologia.* 1964.

Editor, *Poesía nicaragüense.* 1973.

Editor, *Poesía nueva de Nicaragua.* 1974.

Editor, *Poesía cubana de la revolución.* 1976.

Editor, *Antología de poesía primitiva.* 1979.

Editor, *Poemas de un joven*, by Joaquín Pasos. 1983.

Editor, *Antologia: Azarias H. Pallais.* 1986.

Translator, *Catulo-Marcial en versión de Ernesto Cardenal.* 1978.

Translator, *Ezra Pound: Antología*, with José Coronel Urtecho. 1979.

Translator, *Tu paz es mi paz*, by Ursula Schulz. 1982.

*

Bibliography: *An Annotated Bibliography of and about Ernesto Cardenal* by Janet Lynne Smith, 1979.

Critical Studies: *Poetas de América en España: Cardenal, político* by M.R. Barnatán, 1973; *Emblems of a Season of Fury* by T. Merton, 1973; *Homenaje a Ernesto Cardenal*, edited by P.R. Gutierrez, 1975; "Daniel Boone, Moses and the Indians: Ernesto Cardenal's Evolution from Alienation to Social Commitment", in *Chasqui*, 11(1), 1981, and "The Image of the United States in the Poetry of René Depestre and Ernesto Cardenal," in *Revista/Review Interamericana*, 11(2), 1981, both by Henry Cohen; "A Search for Utopia on Earth: Toward an Understanding of the Literary Production of Ernesto Cardenal" by C. Schaefer, in *Crítica Hispánica*, 4(2), 1982; *Ernesto Cardenal en Sotentiname* by H. Tones, 1982; "The Evolution of Ernesto Cardenal's Prophetic Poetry," in *Latin American Literary Review*, 12(23), 1983, "Cardenal's Poetic Style: Cinematic Parallels," in *Revista Canadiense de Estudios Hispanicos*, 11(1), 1986, and "Cardenal's Exteriorismo: The Ideology Underlying the Esthetic," in *Mid Hudson Languages Studies*, 10, 1987, all by Jorge H. Valdés; "Prophecy of Liberation: The Poetry of Ernesto Cardenal" by Edward Elias, in *Poetic Prophecy in Western Literature* edited by Jan Wojcik and Raymond-Jean Frontain, 1984; *La poesía de Ernesto Cardenal: Cristianismo y revolución* by E. Urdanivia Bertarelli, 1984; "Poetry in the Central American Revolution: Ernesto Cardenal and Roque Dalton" by John Beverley, in *Literature and Contemporary Revolutionary Culture*, 1, 1984–85; "Peace, Poetry and Popular

Culture: Ernesto Cardenal and the Nicaraguan Revolution" by Claudia Scharfer-Rodríguez, in *Latin American Literary Review*, 13(26), 1985; "Tradition and Originality in the *Denunciator y Salmos* of Ernesto Cardenal" by G.B. Barrow, in *Chispa*, 1987; "Political Poetry and the Example of Ernesto Cardenal" by Reginald Gibbons, in *Critical Inquiry*, 13(3), 1987; "Ernesto Cardenal and North American Literature: Intertextuality and Reality and the Formulation of an Ethical Identity," in *Inti*, 31, 1990, and "Ernesto Cardenal's *El estrecho dudoso*: Reading/Re-Writing History," in *Revista Canadiense de Estudios Hispánicos*, 15(1), 1990, both by Steven F. White; *La Poesía Cósmica de Ernesto Cardenal* by Ma. Angeles Pastor Alonso, 1998; *Poets of Contemporary Latin America: History and the Inner Life* by William Rowe, 2000.

* * *

In reading Ernesto Cardenal's poetry one must separate the charismatic personality of the ex-Sandinista Minister of Culture, and once Trappist priest, from the actual poems. Cardenal's crucial position in the Nicaraguan hierarchy, and his public image, have lead to him being heavily criticized in Mario Vargas Llosa's novel about a failed revolutionary in Peru, *Historia de Mayta* (*The Real Life of Alejandro Mayta*), and positively celebrated in Julio Cortázar's short story "Apocalypse in Solentiname."

When Cardenal began publishing his poems in the 1940s it was under two crucial influences, one literary, the other political. Literary surrealism had an enormous liberating impact on Latin American poetry, for it seemed to combine personal freedom of expression with a revolutionary context. Cardenal first published poems in the magazine *Letras de México* in 1946 in free verse, and he has acknowledged his debt to the "mad" Nicaraguan poet Alfonso Cortës. However, the ferocious political situation under the successive dictatorships of the Somozas made Cardenal reconsider the ambition of a merely personal liberation in a written text. From this questioning emerged one of the constants of Cardenal's developing poetics. The position of the poet's "ego" is made secondary to the need to write a poem that urges action. By taking the *effect* of the poem on the reader as central to the poem's area of action, the poet relegates the more Romantic notion of the poem as the sincere expression of his own inner world.

Cardenal discovered the means to carry out his new perception of the role of the poet in an illiterate country like Nicaragua through reading Ezra Pound while studying at Columbia University in New York. He began translating Pound, William Carlos Williams, and others, aware that most of the Latin American poets of his generation were still, like Rubén Darío before him, looking towards French culture, and especially French surrealism, for their examples. To Cardenal, Pound's *Cantos*, with their incorporation of quotations, with the collage technique of confronting documentary texts with Chinese poems, and with their ambitious attempt to go beyond the limitations of an individual's private world, suggested a new sound to poetry. Cardenal called this technique "exteriorismo" (exteriorism), the term denoting an attitude that pays more attention to the outer world than to the inner one. It must be emphasized that Cardenal sounded strange and new to most of his contemporaries because he had turned to another literary tradition. Over time Cardenal published his translations in *Antología de la poesía norteamericana* [Anthology of North American Poetry], and *Ezra Pound: Antología*.

The briefly mentioned political context to Cardenal's poetry further drives the ego-obsessed Romantic out of the poems. In 1961, in Mexico, Cardenal published his *Epigramas*, based, through Pound, on his reading of Latin and Greek poets. Cardenal develops a counterpointing technique of opposing the past (Caesar and others) with the present (Somoza), and by pretending to write love poems avoids direct political denunciation. His little poem "Imitation of Propertius" ends, "And she prefers me, poor, to all Somoza's millions." Through Pound, Cardenal also learnt that a poem must be clear and understood immediately. The epigrams remain fresh and provocative.

For protest poetry to work on its audience it must be direct, immediately comprehensible, and, in Latin America, readable aloud. The Chilean poet Pablo Neruda had led the way in the early 1950s with his realization that a poem must be read aloud to spread beyond the confines of the printed word and the few who can afford to buy books. Surrealism, with its twisted dark metaphors, its forays into the unconscious, would not do. All Cardenal's post-1960s poetry is narrative. It avoids the condensation of meaning in metaphors and uses the syntax of prose.

In some ways Cardenal, by expanding what can be included in a lyrical poem, has become the unofficial historian of Nicaragua, then Central America, and finally for the whole Latin American sub-continent. In *La hora 0* ("Zero Hour") there are poems with specific references to local Nicaraguan revolutionaries like Adolfo Báez Bone or Sandino; Cardenal names places, dictators, characters from the past and the present that have no universal poetic appeal as such, but who represent his version of evil. It is this moral vision that allows Cardenal to blend his Christian messianism (he was ordained as a priest in 1965) with his reading of Karl Marx. *Salmos* (*Psalms of Struggle and Liberation*) combines a rewriting of the Biblical psalms with a critique of Somoza. This political-religious vein continues through the poems of *Oración por Marilyn Monroe, y otros poemas* (*Marilyn Monroe and Other Poems*) where, in the title poem, Cardenal mentions Monroe's last unanswered phone call and ends "Lord answer that phone." The title of that poem shows how Cardenal has moved beyond Pound to the pop culture of 1960s America; but he gives Warhol's icon a moral value. His criticism of the United States' consumer culture flows from this stance.

In the collections *El estrecho dudoso* (*The Doubtful Strait*) and *Homenaje a los indios americanos* (*Homage to the American Indians*) Cardenal expands his poems by recreating the history of the conquest of Central America and catalogues the pre-Columbian Indian heritage, basing his work on archival studies, and incorporating voices and historical documents into the poems so that a reader actually learns about the forgotten past. A good example is "Economy of Tahuantinsuyu," where Cardenal contrasts capitalist North American uses of money with pre-Columbian ones, where political truth and religious truth "were but the one truth for the people." The poem that best conveys Cardenal's radical moral vision is his lament on the death of his mentor, the Trappist poet Thomas Merton (whose poems Cardenal has translated into Spanish), which ends, "We only love and only are on dying/The final deed the gift of all one's being/okay." On reading this poem in conjunction with the notes he was allowed to write during his stay at the Trappist monastery (see his *Gethsemani, Ky*) few would doubt Cardenal's deserved position as a much-admired poet.

Cardenal has written *Vida en el amor* (*To Live Is to Love*), a book on love, which is close in form to a sermon, *En Cuba* (*In Cuba*) on his crucial stay in Cuba, *El Evangelio en Solentiname* (*The Gospel in Solentiname*) on his religious beliefs, as well as poems celebrating the Sandinista victory of 1979, *Vuelos de victoria* (*Flights of Victory*). His poem *Cántico cósmico* (*Cosmic Canticle*) is a celebration of the energy of the cosmos, based on his reading of science and cosmology in pursuit of an interest that derives from his earlier reading of the theologian Teilhard de Chardin. However, in this later poetry the fertile juxtaposition of his moral stance with his readings of Pound and his opposition to Somoza has given way to a lax prose syntax that carries few poetic surprises.

—Jason Wilson

CARDUCCI, Giosuè (Alessandro Giuseppe)

Also known as Giosue Carducci. **Born:** Valdicastello, near Pisa, territory of Tuscany, 27 July 1835. Lived in Maremma, 1838–49. **Education:** Educated at home; studied the humanities, rhetoric, and philosophy in Florence, from 1849; Scuola Normale, Pisa, 1853–56, degree in philology and philosophy 1856. **Family:** Married Elvira Menicucci in 1859, two sons and three daughters; had affair with Carolina Cristofori Piva ("Lina") in the 1870s. **Career:** Co-founder, Amici Pedanti society; teacher of rhetoric, Ginnasio di San Miniato al Tedesco, 1856–57; returned to live with his family in Florence, 1857; private tutor, and edited and wrote prefaces to the Diamante series of classics produced by Barbèra, publishers, Florence, from 1858; professor of Greek, then Italian and Latin, Liceo Forteguerri, Pistoia, 1860; professor of Italian, University of Bologna, 1861–1904 (retired). Elected as republican deputy to parliament, 1876; later a monarchist candidate, but failed to get elected; named a senator, 1890. **Awards:** Nobel prize for literature, 1906. **Died:** 16 February 1907.

PUBLICATIONS

Collections

Opere. 20 vols., 1889–1909.
Edizione nazionale delle opere. 30 vols., 1935–42; supplemented with *Lettere* (21 vols.), 1938–60, and *Aggiunte* (1 vol.), 1968.
Poesie, edited by Albano Sorbelli. 1950.
Poesie scelte, edited by P. Treves. 1968.
Poesie scelte, edited by Luigi Baldacci. 1974.
Poesie e prose scelte, edited by Aulo Greco. 1974.
Poesie, edited by Giorgio Barberi Squarotti. 1978.
Poesie, edited by Guido Davico Bonino. 1980.

Verse

Rime. 1857; as *Juvenilia* (definitive edition), 1880.
Leviia gravia. 1868; definitive edition, 1881.

Poesie: Decennalia, Levia Gravia, Juvenilia. 1871; revisededition, 1875.
Primavere elleniche. 1872.
Nuove poesie. 1873.
Odi barbare. 3 vols., 1877–89; in 2 vols., 1893; edited by M. Valgimigli, 1959, and Gianni A. Papini, 1988; parts translated in *Poems*, 1907, and by J.E. Watson as *To the Sources of the Clitumnus*, 1912; as *The Barbarian Odes*, translated by William Fletcher Smith, 1939, revised (bilingual edition), 1950.
Il canto dell'amore. 1878.
Satana e polemiche sataniche. 1879.
Giambi ed Epodi. 1882; edited by E. Palmieri, 1959.
Ça ira. 1883.
Rime nuove. 1887; edited by P.P. Trompeo and G.B. Salinari, 1961; parts translated in *Poems*, 1907; as *Rime nuove*, translated by Laura Fullerton Gilbert, 1916; as *The New Lyrics*, translated by William Fletcher Smith, 1942.
Poems, translated by Frank Sewall. 1892.
La chiesa di Polenta. 1897.
Rime e ritmi. 1899; edited by M. Valgimigli and G.B. Salinari, 1964; parts translated in *Poems*, 1907; as *The Lyrics and Rhythms*, translated by William Fletcher Smith, 1942.
Poesie, edited by Carducci. 1901.
Poems of Italy, translated by M.W. Arms. 1906.
Poems (selections), translated by Maud Holland. 1907.
Carducci: A Selection of His Poems, translated by G.L. Bickersteth. 1913.
A Selection from the Poems, translated by Emily A. Tribe. 1921.
From the Poems of Giosuè Carducci, translated by Romilda Rendel. 1929.
Political and Satirical Verse, translated by William Fletcher Smith. 1942.
24 Sonnets, translated by Arthur Burkhard (bilingual edition). 1947.
Selected Verse, translated by David H. Higgins, 1994.

Other

Studi letterari. 1874.
Delle poesie latine edite ed inedite di L. Ariosto. 1875; as *La gioventù di L. Ariosto e le sue poesie latine*, 1881.
Ai parentali di Giovanni Boccaccio in Certaldo. 1876.
Bozzetti critici e discorsi letterari. 1876.
Confessioni e battaglie. 3 vols., 1882–84.
Eterno femminino regale: Dalle mie memorie. 1882.
Conversazioni critiche. 1884.
Petrarca e Boccaccio. 1884.
Il libro delle prefazioni. 1888.
L'opera di Dante: Discorso. 1888; as *Dante's Work*, translated by Gina Dogliotti, 1923.
Lo studio bolognese: Discorso. 1888.
La libertà perpetua di San Marino. 1894.
Degli spiriti e delle forme nella poesia di Giacomo Leopardi: Considerazioni. 1898.
Discorsi letterari e storici. 1899.
Da un carteggio inedito (letters to Countess Silvia Pasolini-Zanelli). 1907.
Antologia carducciana: Poesie e prose, edited by Guido Mazzoni and Giuseppe Picciola. 1908; several subsequent editions.

Lettere, edited by Alberto Dallolio and Guido Mazzoni. 2 vols., 1911–13.

Pagine di storia letteraria (selection), edited by G. Lipparini. 1913.

Pagine autobiografiche, edited by G. Lipparini. 1914.

Prose scelte, edited by L. Bianchi and P. Nediani. 1935.

Lettere (supplement to *Opere*). 21 vols., 1938–60.

Il Carducci (selection), edited by F. Selmi. 1965.

Prose e poesie, edited by G. Getto and Guido Davico Bonino. 1965.

Poesie e prose scelte, edited by M. Fubini and R. Ceserani. 1968.

Lettere scelte, edited by G. Ponte and F. De Nicola. 1985.

Prose critiche, edited by Giovanni Falaschi. 1987.

Editor, *Satire e poesie minori*, by V. Alfieri. 1858.

Editor, *La secchia rapita e l'Oceano*, by A. Tassoni. 1858.

Editor, *Poesie minori*, by G. Parini. 1858.

Editor, *Poesie liriche*, by V. Monti. 1858.

Editor, *Del Principe e delle lettere con altre prose*, by V. Alfieri. 1859.

Editor, *Poesie di Lorenzo de'Medici*. 1859.

Editor, *Poesie di G. Giusti*. 1859.

Editor, *Satire odi e lettere di S. Rosa*. 1860.

Editor, *Poesie di Gabriele Rossetti*. 1861.

Editor, *Rime di M. Cino da Pistoia e d'altri del Secolo XIV*. 1862.

Editor, *Canti e poemi di V. Monti*. 1862.

Editor, *Le Stanze l'Orfeo e le Rime di Messer A. Ambrogini Poliziano*. 1863.

Editor, *Di T. Lucrezio Caro Della natura delle cose Libri VI volgarizzati da A. Marchetti*. 1864.

Editor, *Tragedie drammi e cantate di V. Monti*. 1865.

Editor, *Rime di Matteo e di Dino Frescobaldi*. 1866.

Editor, *Poeti erotici del Sec. XVIII*. 1868.

Editor, *Versioni poetiche di V. Monti*. 1869.

Editor, *Lirica del Sec. XVII*. 1871.

Editor, *Cantilene e ballate, strambotti e madrigali nei secoli XIII e XIV*. 1871.

Editor, *Satire, rime e lettere scelte*, by B. Menzini. 1874.

Editor, *Rime di F. Petrarca sopra argomenti storici morali e diversi*. 1876.

Editor, *Strambotti e rispetti dei secoli XIV, XV e XVI*. 1877.

Editor, *Lettere*, by F.D. Guerrazzi. 2 vols., 1880–82.

Editor, *La poesia barbara nei secoli XV e XVI*. 1881.

Editor, *G. Garibaldi: Versi e prose*. 1882.

Editor, with U. Brilli, *Letture italiane*. 1883.

Editor, *Lettere disperse e inedite di Pietro Metastasio*. 1883.

Editor, *Scelte poesie di V. Monti, con le varie lezioni*. 1885.

Editor, *Cacce in rima dei secoli XIV, XV*. 1896.

Editor, *Letture del Risorgimento italiano*. 2 vols., 1896–97.

Editor, with S. Ferrari, *Le rime di Francesco Petrarca di su gli originali*. 1899.

Editor, with others, *Raccolta degli storici italiani dal 500 al 1500 ordinata da L.A. Muratori*. 1900.

Editor, *Scritti politici*, by A. Mario. 1901.

Editor, *Scritti letterari e artistici*, by A. Mario. 1901.

Editor, *Primavera e fiore della lirica italiana*. 1903.

Editor, *Carlo Goldoni: Sonetti*. 1903.

Editor, *Giuseppe Monti: Epodo. . . : Documenti storici*. 1904.

Illustrator, *Della Scelta di curiosità letterarie inedite o rare illustrazione*. 1863.

*

Bibliography: *A Bibliography of Critical Material (1859–1940) on Giosue Carducci* by William Fletcher Smith, 1942.

Critical Studies: *Giosuè Carducci* (in English) by Orlo Williams, 1914; *L'uomo Carducci* by G. Papini, 1918; *Giosuè Carducci: Studio intorno alla critica e alla lirica carducciana* by E. Palmieri, 1926; *Giosuè Carducci: L'uomo e il poeta* by G. Petronio, 1930; *L'opera critica di Giosuè Carducci* by D. Mattalia, 1934; *I giorni e le opere di Giosuè Carducci* by Giulio Natali, 1935, reprinted as *Giosuè Carducci*, 1950; *Giosuè Carducci: Studio critico* by Benedetto Croce, 1937; *Carducci: His Critics and Translators in England and America 1881–1932* by S.E. Scalia, 1937; *La prosa di Giosuè Carducci* by A. Cerea, 1957; *Carducci senza retorica* by L. Russo, 1957; *Giosuè Carducci: L'uomo, il poeta, il critico e il prosatore* by N. Busetto, 1958; *Il grande Carducci* by F. Giannessi, 1958; *La poesie e la prosa di Giosuè Carducci* by Francesco Flora, 1959; *Discorsi nel cinquantenario della morte di Giosuè Carducci* by various authors, 1959; *Il poeta della Terza Italia: Vita di Giosuè Carducci* by M. Biagini, 1961; *Carducci nelle lettere* by R. Bruscagli, 1973; *Carducci* (survey of criticism) by Giorgio Santangelo, 1973; *Per una lettura storica di Carducci* by F. Mattesini, 1975; *Carducci poeta barbaro* by Franco Robecchi, 1981; "The Mixed Blessings of Tradition: An Examination of Carducci's 'Idillio maremmano'" by Remo Catani, in *The Italian Lyric Tradition*, 1993; *Carducciana* by Renato Serra, 1996; *Carducci di Carducci* by Umberto Panozzo, 2000.

* * *

Giosuè Carducci's critical fortune has swung sharply from inordinate veneration to out-and-out rejection. With the passing of the historical and political circumstances of a united Italy, which had assured the fame of Carducci's patriotic compositions, he came to be regarded as rhetorical, outdated, and of doubtful creative ability. This view has, however, been moderately redressed in recent decades through a quiet appreciation of more intimate aspects of his writings.

His reputation owes much to a vast output of critical, occasional, and epistolary prose, but his contribution to creative literature is his verse. The collections, as definitively established by Carducci himself, are the result of a meticulous lifelong process of reordering and reworking. These give the mistaken impression that, after youthful experimentation, a period in which his work had a socio-political orientation was succeeded by a calmer phase, imbued with classical myth, whereas the two aspects in fact co-existed throughout his productive life. The reordering process responds to the desire for a classical ideal of harmony and represents the attempt to transcend a dialectic that sees the poetry of commitment vying with that of aesthetic purity.

The imitative early poems of *Rime* (*Juvenilia*) draw heavily on the classical tradition, but often herald the mature Carducci, both in their robust tone and in the combination of personal sadness (memories of his brother Dante's tragic suicide) and patriotic feeling (support of the house of Savoy in its quest to unify Italy). A similar amalgam can be found in *Levia gravia*, where Carducci finds something of his own voice in the forceful expression of socio-political sentiment and a new-found republicanism, and in the introduction of elegiac and idyllic notes. Important, too, in the evolution of his style, is the controversial "Inno a Satana" ("Hymn to Satan") of 1863 where, in a vigorous outburst of anti-clerical materialism, he exalts the forces of science, progress, and freedom of thought. His satire and political invective culminate in *Giambi ed Epodi* [Iambs and Epodes], which are classical in form, as the title indicates, but are concerned with contemporary issues and, in part, influenced by Hugo. It can be argued that here Carducci gives vent to his indignation and anti-papal feeling in too strident a voice; yet the collection has been admired by Natalino Sapegno who sees it as the most vital part of the poet's opus.

Carducci's creative peak, however, is generally perceived in the poems of *Rime nuove* (*The New Lyrics*) and parts of *Odi barbare* (*The Barbarian Odes*). While maintaining a thematic mixture, these collections introduce a restrained intimacy, the hallmark of his maturity, in the intense poems of longing, suffering, nostalgia and melancholy, as well as in the more imaginative of the historico-literary compositions. The expression of these feelings is not dissipated in sentimental effusion but translated into rapid movements and sharp visions that have found the approval of even the harshest critics.

Although some poems in *The New Lyrics* are inspired by history (like the ''Ça ira'' cycle on the French Revolution), the majority are personal, recalling Carducci's childhood in the Maremma—''Davanti a San Guido'' (''In Front of San Guido'')—and the death of his son Dante—''Pianto antico'' (''Ancient Lament'')—or animated by his love for Lina Piva. Many depict the simple attractions of rustic life—''Il bove'' (''The Ox'') or ''Idillio maremmano'' (''Maremman Idyll''). The collection also amply illustrates Carducci's mastery of the sonnet form.

The Barbarian Odes reproduce the rhythm of quantitative classical metre through the ''barbarian'' use of the tonic accents of modern Italian. Although this erudite experiment, with its origins in the Renaissance, had little following and now seems idiosyncratic, it was a bold and partially successful attempt to renew Italian verse. But too many odes seem outmoded in their rhetorical exaltation of the values of ancient Rome—''Alle fonti del Clitumno'' (''At the Source of the Clitumnus'')—in their scholastic idealization of epic and dramatic literature—''Presso l'urna di P.B. Shelley'' (''Near P.B. Shelley's Urn'')—or in their pedantic examination of the workings of historical Nemesis—''Per la morte di Napoleone Eugenio'' (''On the Death of Napoleon Eugene''). Yet the collection is largely redeemed, and the potential of Carducci's innovations revealed, in a few simple odes that present the ancient world as an ideal source of solace, as in ''Fantasia'' (''Fantasy''), or which express a universal feeling of melancholy and transience that communicates the *ennui* of the modern psyche, as in ''Alla stazione in una mattina d'autunno'' (''At the Station on an Autumn Morning'') and ''Nevicata'' (''Snowfall'').

The later poems collected in *Rime e ritmi* (*The Lyrics and Rhythms*) show a tired Carducci flagging in inspiration, producing commemorative verses that accentuate his academic shortcomings, and they are only occasionally relieved by more felicitous, impressionistic moments.

Although it is often claimed that Carducci's classicism and rhetorical nationalism, which dominated the second half of the 19th century, exerted a regressive influence on Italian culture, isolating it from avantgarde Europe, a total repudiation of Benedetto Croce's fundamental approbation would be extreme. It has nevertheless been argued convincingly that Carducci marks the end of an era, and that the moral basis of his poetry separates him from Giovanni Pascoli and Gabriele D'Annunzio with whom he is traditionally linked. Conversely, one should not disregard the merits of his rigorously traditional aesthetics in the crisis and confusion of post-unification culture. His classicism is polemical: it militates against the excesses of

both the late Romantics and the bohemian Scapigliati, and strives for a return to ancient naturalism in the name of lay values and scientific progress. What is more, his poetry was enriched by an assimilation of writers such as Hugo, Heine, and Shelley; and recent critical examination of unpretentious moments of everyday realism and inner feeling has brought out a modern affinity: Carducci emerges, at least in part, not as the national poet of yester-year, but as an elegiac poet of wider appeal, who, while remaining undaunted in his classicism, reveals a Romantic need for the illusion of beauty in the ephemerality of the past.

—Remo Catani

CARLET DE CHAMBLAIN DE MARIVAUX, Pierre

See MARIVAUX

CARPENTIER (Y VALMONT), Alejo

Born: Havana, Cuba, 26 December 1904. **Education:** Educated at the University of Havana. **Family:** Married Andrea Esteban. **Career:** Journalist, Havana, 1921–24; editor, *Carteles* magazine, Havana, 1924–28; director, Foniric Studios, Paris, 1928–39; writer and producer, CMZ radio station, Havana, 1939–41; professor of history of music, Conservatorio Nacional, Havana, 1941–43; lived in Haiti, Europe, the United States, and South America, 1943–59; director, Cuban Publishing House, Havana, 1960–67; cultural attaché, Cuban Embassy, Paris, from 1967. Columnist, *El Nacional*, Caracas; editor, *Imam*, Paris. **Died:** 24 April 1980.

PUBLICATIONS

Collections

Obras completas. 9 vols., 1983–86.

Fiction

¡Écue-yamba-Ó! 1933.

Viaje a la semilla (story). 1944.

El reino de este mundo. 1949; as *The Kingdom of This World*, translated by Harriet de Onís, 1957.

Los pasos perdidos. 1953; as *The Lost Steps*, translated by Harriet de Onís, 1956.

El acoso. 1956; as *The Chase*, translated by Alfred MacAdam, 1989.

Guerra del tiempo: Tres relatos y una novela: El Camino de Santiago, Viaje a la semilla, Semejante a la noche, y El acoso. 1958; as *War of Time* (includes *The Highroad of Saint James*; *Right of Sanctuary*; *Journey Back to the Source*; *Like the Night*; *The Chosen*), translated by Frances Partridge, 1970.

El siglo de las luces. 1962; as *Explosion in a Cathedral*, translated by John Sturrock, 1963.

El derecho de asilo, Dibujos de Marcel Berges (stories). 1972.

Los convidados de plata. 1972.

Concierto barroco. 1974; as *Baroque Concerto,* translated by Asa Zatz, 1991.

El recurso del método. 1974; as *Reasons of State,* translated by Frances Partridge, 1976.

Cuentos (stories). 1976.

La consagración de la primavera. 1978.

El arpa y la sombra. 1979; as *The Harp and the Shadow,* translated by Thomas and Carol Christensen, 1990.

Plays

Yamba-Ó, music by M.F. Gaillard (produced 1928).

La passion noire, music by M.F. Gaillard (produced 1932).

Verse

Dos poemas afrocubanos, music by A. García Caturla. 1929.

Poèmes des Antilles, music by M.F. Gaillard. 1929.

Other

La música en Cuba. 1946; as *Music in Cuba,* translated by Alan West-Durán, 2001.

Tientos y diferencias: Ensayos. 1964.

Literatura y consciencia política en América Latina. 1969.

La ciudad de las columnas (on Havana architecture), photographs by Paolo Gasparini. 1970.

Letra y solfa (articles), edited by Alexis Márquez Rodríguez. 1975.

Crónicas (articles). 1975.

Críticas de arte: 1922–39. 1975.

Razón de ser (lectures). 1976.

Bajo el Signo de la Cibeles: Crónicas sobre España y los españoles, 1925–1937, edited by Julio Rodríguez Puértolas. 1979.

El adjectivo y sus arrugas. 1980.

Ese músico que llevo dentro (selection), edited by Zolla Gómez. 1980.

La novela latinoamericana en vísperas de un nuevo siglo y otros ensayos. 1981.

Ensayos (essays). 1984.

Entrevistas, edited by Virgilio López Lemus. 1985.

Conferencias, edited by Virgilio López Lemus. 1987.

*

Bibliography: *Carpentier: 45 años de trabajo intelectual,* 1966; *Bibliografía de Alejo Carpentier* by Araceli García-Garranza, 1984.

Critical Studies: *Three Authors of Alienation: Bombal, Onetti, Carpentier* by M. Ian Adams, 1975; *Major Cuban Novelists: Innovation and Tradition* by Raymond D. Souza, 1976; *Alejo Carpentier: The Pilgrim at Home* by Roberto González Echevarría, 1977, revised edition, 1990; *Alejo Carpentier and His Early Works* by Frank Janney, 1981; *Carpentier: Los pasos perdidos* (in English) by Verity Smith, 1983; *Alchemy of a Hero: A Comparative Study of the Works of Alejo Carpentier and Mario Vargas Llosa* by Bob M. Tusa, 1983; *Alejo Carpentier* by Donald L. Shaw, 1985; *Myth and History in Caribbean Fiction: Alejo Carpentier, Wilson Harris and Édouard Glissant* by Barbara J. Webb, 1992; *Carpentier's Proustian Fiction: The Influence of Marcel Proust on Alejo Carpentier* by Sally Harvey, 1994; *Postmodern Tales of Slavery in the Americas: From Alejo Carpentier to Charles Johnson* by Timothy J. Cox, 2001.

* * *

Musicologist, journalist, critic, leader in the Afro-Cuban and vanguardia movements in Cuba in the 1920s, associate of the surrealists in Paris in the 1930s, Alejo Carpentier gave to 20th-century Latin American letters an important critical concept and a distinctive vision of American identity through history. In the prologue to *El reino de este mundo* (*The Kingdom of This World*), Carpentier proposed that there exists ''lo real maravilloso americano'' (''marvellous American reality''). A conflation of the vocabulary of surrealism (''marvellous'') and the primitivism of the Afro-Cuban movement, the term has, along with ''magic realism,'' been used to justify and to describe the element of the fantastic so prominent in much Latin American writing of the 20th century. (Among the authors significantly influenced by Carpentier's precept and practice is the Colombian Gabriel García Márquez.) Almost as soon as he had elaborated the concept, however, Carpentier turned in his own work from the marvellous as the impossible and folkloric to the marvellous as the real, perceived by a modern, alienated eye, struck by the incongruity and irreality of what it really sees.

His early works include the first history of Cuban music, a scenario for an Afro-Cuban ballet, poems on Afro-Cuban themes, and a novel, *¡Écue-yamba-Ó!* (*God Be Praised*), which follows a contemporary rural black into the city and through the rites of the santería and ñañigo cults. His second novel was a product of his middle age, and in it he began to redefine the essentially American less as the primitive than as a paradoxical synthesis of times, peoples, cultures, and styles, simultaneously primitive and sophisticated, European, African, and Indian. While his fictions remained conventional in structure, over time he elaborated an allusive, witty, ornately encrusted style, heterogeneous and baroque, itself both original and a synthesis.

Set in Haiti during the period of the French Revolution, *The Kingdom of This World* juxtaposes the effete high culture of Europeans with the primitive powers of their black slaves. Such folkloric impossibilities as taking animal shapes parallel cyclic political metamorphoses in which a black revolution re-enacts and intensifies the white oppression violently thrown off and is in its turn violently replaced by the oppressive rule of mulattoes. In *Los pasos perdidos* (*The Lost Steps*) a modern protagonist is on a search for primitive musical instruments from inauthentic, synthetic Paris through a Latin American city in the grip of a civil war that appears to be a quarrel ''between the Guelphs and the Ghibellines'' to the upper reaches of the Orinoco, a journey still further back in time, to ''the roots of life.'' In part a parable of Carpentier's own efforts to discover the essential America, the project of modern man's finding himself by losing himself in the primitive is doomed: the journey cannot be made twice.

Thereafter, Carpentier embraced his distinctive vision of Latin America as a place and a history split between its American realities and its European origins and consciousness. A volume of short stories, obsessed with origins, returns, and time, four novels and a fragment, all of the first order, complete an *oeuvre* distinguished by a paradoxical habit of seeing things twice, as past and as present, a multiplication of illusions with artifice as the nature of man, fallen into history, committed to ''Adam's task of naming things.'' *El siglo de las luces* (*Explosion in a Cathedral*) returned to the Caribbean to chart once again the betrayals of the French Revolution, but this time from the perspective of the creole bourgeoisie. *El recurso del método* (*Reasons of State*) set an exemplary dictator amid real and fictive personages in Paris in 1913, and followed him back and forth across the Atlantic, never fully at home on either side, until his death in homesick Parisian exile, sometime in the 1940s, with a brief epilogue dated 1972. *Concierto barroco* (*Baroque Concerto*) reached an apotheosis of heterogeneous synthesis as a Mexican and his black servant give Vivaldi a topic for an opera, *Motezuma*, and as the trumpet in Handel's *Messiah* becomes the trumpet of Louis Armstrong, a glorious concert of incongruities in which all is transformed, but nothing is lost. It is a final, fitting paradox that Carpentier, still writing at the age of 76, should have died while at work on a novel celebrating a triumph of the Cuban revolution—in Paris.

—Regina Janes

See the essays on *The Kingdom of this World* and *The Lost Steps*.

CASSOLA, Carlo

Born: Rome, Italy, 17 March 1917. **Education:** Educated at the University of Rome, 1935–39, degree in law 1939. **Military Service:** In Spoleto, 1937. **Family:** Married Giuseppina Rabage, one daughter. **Career:** Journalist after World War II; lived in Grosseto, Tuscany, from 1950, where he was a teacher of history and philosophy; contributor, *Il Contemporaneo, Il Mondo, Nuovi Argomenti,* and other publications. **Awards:** Prato prize, 1955; Salento prize, 1958; Marzotto prize, 1959; Strega prize, 1960; Naples prize, 1970; Bancarella prize, 1976; Bagutta prize, 1978. **Died:** 29 January 1987.

PUBLICATIONS

Fiction

Alla periferia (stories). 1942.
La visita (stories). 1942; enlarged edition (includes *Alla periferia*), 1962.
Fausto e Anna. 1952; revised edition, 1958; as *Fausto and Anna,* translated by Isabel Quigly, 1960.
I vecchi compagni. 1953.
Il taglio del bosco (stories). 1954; edited by Tom O'Neill, 1970; as *The Cutting of the Woods,* translated by Raymond Rosenthal, in *Six Modern Italian Novellas,* edited by William Arrowsmith, 1964.
La casa di via Valadier. 1956.
Un matrimonio del dopoguerra. 1957.
Il soldato. i958.
La ragazza di Bube. 1960; as *Bebo's Girl,* translated by Marguerite Waldman, 1962.
Un cuore arido. 1961; as *An Arid Heart,* translated by William Weaver, 1964.
Il cacciatore. 1964.
Tempi memorabili. 1966.
Storia di Ada (includes *La maestra*). 1967.
Il soldato e Rosa Gagliardi. 1967.
Ferrovia locale. 1968.
Una relazione. 1969.
Paura e tristezza. 1970; as *Fear and Sadness,* translated by Peter N. Petroni, in *Portland Review,* Fall-Winter 1981.

Monte Mario. 1973; as *Portrait of Helena,* translated by Sebastian Roberts, 1975.
Gisella. 1974.
Troppo tardi. 1975.
L'antagonista. 1976.
La disavventura. 1977.
L'uomo e il cane. 1977.
Un uomo solo. 1978.
Il superstite. 1978.
Il paradiso degli animali. 1979.
La morale del branco. 1980.
Vita d'artista. 1980.
Ferragosto di morte. 1980.
Il ribelle. 1980.
L'amore tanto per fare. 1981.
La zampa d'oca. 1981.
Gli anni passano. 1982.
Colloquio con le ombre. 1982.
Mio padre. 1983.

Other

Viaggio in Cina. 1956.
I minatori della Maremma, with Luciano Biancardi. 1956.
Poesia e romanzo, with Mario Luzi. 1973.
Fogli di diario. 1974.
Ultima frontiera. 1976.
Il gigante cieco. 1976.
Conversazione su una cultura compromessa, edited by Antonio Cardella. 1977.
La lezione della storia. 1978.
Letteratura e disarmo: Intervista e testi, edited by Domenico Tarizzo. 1978.
Il mondo senza nessuno. 1980.
Il romanzo moderno. 1981.
Cassola racconta (interview), edited by Pietro Poiana. 1981.
La rivoluzione disarmista. 1983.

*

Critical Studies: *Letteratura e ideologia: Bassani, Cassola, Pasolini* by Gian Carlo Ferretti, 1964; *Carlo Cassola* by Rodolfo Macchioni Jodi, 1967, revised edition, 1975; *Carlo Cassola* by Renato Bertacchini, 1977; *Invito all lettura di Cassola* by G. Manacorda, 1981; *Existence as Theme in Carlo Cassola's Fiction* by Peter N. Pedroni, 1985; *Il realismo esistenziale di Carlo Cassola* by Vittorio Spinazzola, 1993.

*   *   *

Although born in Rome in 1917, Carlo Cassola chose Tuscany and the Maremma as the background against which he placed much of his early work, including the autobiographical novel *Fausto e Anna* (*Fausto and Anna*), based on his experiences as a partisan in 1944. This choice of a topographical setting that is neither city nor countryside but a twilight zone between the two—it is significant that one of his early works was in fact called *Alla periferia* [On the Outskirts]—provided Cassola with the possibility of exploiting to the full his predilection for an understated, almost colourless style of writing such as that used by Joyce in *Dubliners*, a book that Cassola admitted influenced him profoundly. More significantly, however, the peripheral setting of much of Cassola's early—and best—work underlines his attitude to life and the transformation of life into art. In other words it gives him the possibility of expressing his fascination with a life lived on the margins of society, a life that does not have any precise or easily defined characteristics or outlines. Hence Cassola's adoption, at the beginning of his career, of the word *sublimare* to describe his poetics, which he saw as the translation of the subconscious emotions of the artist into a language that was divested of all overt ideological, ethical, or psychological attributes. This early understated style adopted by Cassola reached its highest point artistically in the short novel *Il taglio del bosco* (*The Cutting of the Woods*), written shortly after the death of his wife.

In the novels published after *The Cutting of the Woods*, and in particular in *Fausto and Anna, I vecchi compagni* [The Old Companions], *La casa di via Valadier* [The House in the Via Valadier], and *Un matrimonio del dopoguerra* [A Post-War Marriage], there emerges a rather polemical tone, as the author seeks to investigate the disappointed hopes and aspirations of the partisans. His often ambiguous attitude to the achievements of the Resistance movement as expressed through the dialogue and through the protagonists' attitudes characterizes this second phase of Cassola's writing, and has been criticized by the Italian Left, including such writers as Pier Paolo Pasolini and Giorgio Bassani: when, for instance, the prizewinning *La ragazza di Bube* (*Bebo's Girl*) was published in 1960.

From 1961 onwards, with the publication of *Un cuore arido* (*An Arid Heart*), Cassola may be said to have returned, more or less, to his early style in which the rhythm of the narration seems to coincide with the rhythm of life itself—the humble, usually uneventful life of unsophisticated characters who nevertheless impart dignity to that life by virtue of their calm and stoical acceptance of the odds against them, mostly of an economic kind. It must be added, however, that it is only in such works as *Ferrovia locale* [Local Railway] that Cassola manages to recapture the high artistic tone of his best work. For the most part, unfortunately, in this last phase, the reader is made increasingly uneasy by a sense of aridity in the lives of Cassola's protagonists—a sense of lost opportunities and in the last analysis, of an inability to live life in any full or meaningful human sense of the term.

—Gabrielle Barfoot

CASTELLANOS, Rosario

Born: Mexico City, Mexico, 25 May 1925. Grew up in Comitán; family moved to Mexico City, 1941, after losing its estate in land reforms. **Education:** Educated at the National Autonomous University, Mexico City, 1944–50, M.A. in philosophy 1950; University of Madrid, 1950–51. **Family:** Married Ricardo Guerra in 1958 (divorced); one son. **Career:** Visited Spain, France, Austria, Italy, the Netherlands, and Germany, 1951; director, Chiapas cultural programmes, 1951–53, and staff member, Institute of Arts and Sciences, both in Tuxtla Gutiérrez; director, El Teatro Guiñol (puppet theatre) for the National Indigenist Institute, San Cristóbal, 1956–59, and toured Chiapas, 1956–58; journalist for various Mexico City newspapers and periodicals, from 1960; press and information director, 1960–66, and professor of comparative literature, 1967–71, National

Autonomous University, Mexico City, 1960–66; visiting professor of Latin American literature at the United States universities of Wisconsin, Indiana, and Colorado, all 1967; Mexican ambassador to Israel, Tel Aviv, and lecturer in Mexican literature, Hebrew University, Jerusalem, 1971–74. **Awards:** Mexican Critics' award, 1957; Chiapas prize, 1958; Xavier Villaurrutia prize, 1961; Woman of the Year award, Mexico, 1967. **Died:** 7 August 1974.

PUBLICATIONS

Collections

A Rosario Castellanos Reader, edited and translated by Maureen Ahern, with others. 1988.
Obras, edited by Eduardo Mejía. 1989.
Another Way To Be: Selected Works (poetry, essays, stories), edited and translated by Myralyn F. Allgood. 1990.

Fiction

Balún Canán. 1957; as *The Nine Guardians,* translated by Irene Nicholson, 1959.
Ciudad Real: Cuentos (stories). 1960; as *The City of Kings*, edited by Yvette E. Miller, translated by Gloria Chacon de Arjona and Robert S. Rudder, 1993.
Oficio de tinieblas. 1962; fragment as *Office of Tenebrae*, translated by Anne and Christopher Fremantle, in *Latin American Literature Today,* 1977.
Los convidados de agosto (stories). 1964.
Álbum de familia (stories). 1971.

Verse

Trayectoria del polvo. 1948.
Apuntes para una declaración de fe. 1948.
De la vigilia estéril. 1950.
Dos poemas. 1950.
Presentación al templo: Poemas (Madrid, 1951), with *El rescate del mundo.* 1952.
Poemas 1953–1955. 1957.
Al pie de la letra. 1959.
Salomé y Judith: Poemas dramáticos. 1959.
Lívida luz. 1960.
Materia memorable (verse and essays). 1969.
Poesía no eres tú: Obra poética 1948–1971. 1972.
Looking at the Mona Lisa, translated by Maureen Ahern. 1981.
Bella dama sin piedad y otros poemas. 1984.
Meditación en el umbral: Antologiá poética, edited by Julian Palley. 1985; as *Meditation on the Threshold* (bilingual edition), translated by Palley, 1988.
Selected Poems (bilingual edition), edited by Cecilia Vicuñ and Magda Bogin, translated by Bogin. 1988.

Plays

Tablero de damas: Pieza en un acto. In *América: Revista Antológica*, 68, 1952.
El eterno femenino. 1975; as *Just Like a Woman*, translated by V.M. Bouvier, 1984; as *The Eternal Feminine*, in *A Rosario Castellanos Reader*, 1988.

Other

Sobre cultura femenina (essays). 1950.
La novela mexicana contemporánea y su valor testimonial. 1965.
Rostros de México, photographs by Bernice Kolko. 1966.
Juicios sumarios: Ensayos. 1966; revised edition, as *Juicios sumarios: Ensayos sobre literatura,* 2 vols., 1984.
Mujer que sabe latín (criticism). 1973.
El uso de la palabra (essays), edited by J.E. Pacheco. 1974.
El mar y sus pescaditos (criticism). 1975.

*

Bibliography: 'Rosario Castellanos (1925–1974) by Maureen Aherne, in *Spanish American Women Writers,* edited by Diane E. Marting, 1990; ''Rosario Castellanos'' in *Mexican Literature: A Bibliography of Secondary Sources* by William David Foster, 1992 (2nd edition).

Critical Studies: *Rosario Castellanos: Biografía y novelística* by Rhoda Dybvig, 1965; *La obra poética de Rosario Castellanos* by Víctor N. Baptiste, 1972; *Rosario Castellanos* by Beatriz Reyes Nevares, 1976; ''Images of Women in Castellanos' Prose'' by Phyllis Rodríguez-Peralta, in *Latin American Literary Review,* 6, 1977; ''Women and Feminism in the Works of Rosario Castellanos'' by Beth Miller, in *Feminist Criticism: Essays on Theory, Poetry, and Prose,* edited by Cheryl L. Brown and Karen Olson, 1978; *El universo poético de Rosario Castellanos* by Germaine Calderón, 1979; *Homenaje a Rosario Castellanos* edited by Maureen Ahern and Mary Seale Vásquez, 1980; ''Point of View in Selected Poems by Rosario Castellanos'' by Esther W. Nelson, in *Revista/Review Interamericana,* 12(1), 1982; ''Women in the Work of Rosario Castellanos'' by Claire Tron de Bouchony, in *Cultures,* 8(3), 1982; ''Rosario Castellanos and the Structures of Power'' by Helene M. Anderson, in *Contemporary Women Authors of Latin America: Introductory Essays,* 1983; *Rosario* by Oscar Bonifaz Caballero, 1984, as *Remembering Rosario: A Personal Glimpse into the Life and Works,* translated by Myralyn F. Allgood, 1990; ''*Balún-Canán*: A Model Demonstration of Discourse as Power,'' in *Revista de Estudios Hispánicos,* 19(3), 1985, and ''Onomastics and Thematics in *Balún-Canán,*'' in *Literary Onomastic Studies,* 13, 1986, both by Sandra Messinger Cypress; ''The Function of Interiorization in *Oficio de tinieblas*'' by Frank R. Dorward, in *Neophilologus,* 69, 1985; *The Double Strand: Five Contemporary Mexican Poets* by Frank N. Dauster, 1987; ''Toward the Ransom of Eve: Myth and History in the Poetry of Rosario Castellanos'' by N. Mandlove, in *Retrospect: Essays on Latin American Literature* edited by E.S. and T.J. Rogers, 1987; *Lives on the Line: The Testimony of Contemporary Latin American Authors* edited by Doris Meyer, 1988; *Women's Voice* by Naomi Lindstrom, 1989; ''Rosario Castellanos: Demythification through Laughter'' by Nina M. Scott, in *Humor,* 2(1), 1989; ''Confronting Myths of Oppression: The Short Stories of Castellanos'' by Chloe Funival, in *Knives and Angels* edited by Susan Bassnett, 1990; *Prospero's Daughter: The Prose of Rosario Castellanos* by Joanna O'Connell, 1995; *Testamento de Hécuba: Mujeres e Indígenas en la Obra de Rosario Castellanos* by María Luisa Gil Iriarte, 1999.

* * *

In ''If Not Poetry, Then What?'' Rosario Castellanos identifies three points she considers cardinal in her writing: ''humour, solemn meditation, and contact with my carnal and historical roots.'' Her complete works give evidence that she kept these points in mind. Her historical and carnal roots are most evident in ''El hombre del destino'' (''Man of Destiny''), an essay about Lázaro Cárdenas (post-revolutionary Mexican president), and in ''Tres nudos en la red'' (''Three Knots in the Net'') and *Balún Canán* (*The Nine Guardians*), works that chronicle fictionally her family's adjustment to the loss of their properties when Cárdenas's administration implemented agrarian reform. In fact, most of her writing is intimately bound to her biography, reflecting from her personal perspective events and conditions around her. A preferred mode of approach to ''solemn meditation'' in her writing is through a domestic vignette which then yields to thoughtful reflection. Humour in her writing takes the form of irony.

In Castellanos's works, significant thematic unity exists across genres. Themes in her essays (weekly newspaper columns written for several Mexico City newspapers) such as social inequality, injustice, and feminist thought, along with a sense of personal isolation and an almost obsessive concern with death, are echoed in her novels, short stories, theatre, and, especially, poetry.

Her early fiction portrays the lives of contemporary native peoples in her home state of Chiapas, defining the people's existence in terms of their history and mythology and the relation to, and contrast with, the history and mythology of Creole society. Castellanos's natives are neither Romanticism's ''noble savages'' nor the positive pole of the Manichean opposition (good native victim/evil Creole oppressor) of the Indigenist movement. Her native characters seem authentic because they emerge from her first-hand observation of, and personal contact with, the Tzotzil-Tzeltal of Chiapas. Her recognition of the unequal status of natives in relation to Creoles is evident in ''La suerte de Teodoro Méndez Acubal'' (''The Luck of Teodoro Méndez Acubal''). Inequality of status and the tragedy to which it often leads are explored in her essays such as ''Discriminación en Estados Unidos y en Chiapas'' (''Discrimination in the United States and in Chiapas''), her novels (*The Nine Guardians* and *Oficio de tinieblas*— a fragment of which has been translated as *Office of Tenebrae*), and many of her short stories.

Oficio de tinieblas provides a bridge between her advocacy of the native and her focus on women from a feminist perspective, The protagonist is deemed inferior by both natives and Creoles because she is a woman, a native, and barren. However, by mastering the healing arts, she becomes a leader in her community and catalyses actions that lead to an native boy's expiatory crucifixion. Castellanos's concern for the natives oppressed by Chiapas's feudal society yields to probing examinations of the subordinate status of all women in that society. The questions of the subjugation of women—who are expected to be ''under a man's hand,'' ''be it her father's, her brother's, her husband's, or her priest's''—and of masculine honour, which depends upon the behaviour of women, are given fictional form in many of her short stories, notably ''El viudo Roman'' (''The Widower Román''), ''El advenimiento del águila'' (''The Eagle''), and ''Las amistades efímeras'' (''Fleeting Friendships''). An evolution from Rosario's concepts of woman's inherent intellectual inferiority expressed in *Sobre cultura femenina* [On Feminine Culture], to feminist conviction is easily discernible. She labours to raise the consciousness of her contemporaries, pointing out inequalities between the sexes in Mexico, yet insisting (as in ''Self-Sacrifice Is a Mad Virtue'') that Mexican women have no right to complain about their subordinate status because they remain subjugated by choice in their failure to avail themselves of ''what the constitution gives them: the category of human being.''

Castellanos's theatrical works include two long dramatic poems and a play. *El eterno femenino* (*The Eternal Feminine*), despite its ironic humour, is a serious work, which deserves to be regarded as the pinnacle of her feminist writings. Using a double stage, Castellanos criticizes the reality of contemporary Mexican women as they play the roles dictated by the present-day myths of innocent bride, self-sacrificing wife, fulfilled mother, emancipated woman, mistress, and prostitute, while simultaneously recreating more authentic portraits of historical women long ago rendered into myths in Mexico: Eve, Sor Juana Inés de la Cruz, the Empress Carlotta, Malinche (Cortés's native mistress/translator), and so on.

Women's alienation and their oppression in contemporary urban life is the thread that runs through the short stories of *Los convidados de agosto* [The Guests of August] and *Álbum de familia* [Family Album]. The best known of these is "Lección de cocina" ("Cookery Lesson") a story that alternates the preparation of a meat recipe with acerbic comments on the life of a new bride.

A consummate poet, Castellanos once acknowledged that she "came to poetry after discovering that other roads were not viable for survival"; that for her, "the words of poetry constituted the only way to achieve permanence in this world." Still, in "An Attempt at Self-Criticism," she admits that it was not until 1950 that she "was beginning to discover [her] individuality and validity which, in poetry, has to express the moods of the soul." But discover it she did: her poems have unequivocally a woman's poetic voice. She speaks directly and intimately to her women readers about their isolation and the constraints that have limited their lives. By defamiliarizing the feminine context, she makes it, and its inequalities, visible, and leads her readers in the search for another way of being female, as she says in "Meditación en el umbral" ("Meditation on the Brink"), one "que no se llame Safo/ni Mesalina ni María Egipciaca/ni Magdalena ni Clemencia Isaura" ("that's not named Sappho/or Messalina or Mary of Egypt/or Magdalene or Clémence Isaure").

Both in her early works expressing concern for the Indian's unjust existence in Chiapas and in her later writings about woman's inequitable situation in the world, Castellanos acknowledged "the other" and attempted to span the space of alienation with her poetic words.

—Oralia Preble-Niemi

CASTIGLIONE, Baldassarre

Also known as Baldesar Castiglione. **Born:** Casatico, territory of Mantua, 6 December 1478. **Education:** Studied Latin and Greek at the school of Giorgio Merula and Demetrio Calcondila, Milan, early 1490s. **Family:** Married Ippolita Torelli in 1516 (died 1520); one son and two daughters. **Career:** Attended the Court of Ludovico Sforza ("il Moro") in Milan, c. 1494–99; returned to Mantua, 1499, and entered service of the French-sponsored Francesco Gonzaga, ruler of Mantua, as diplomat and military commissioner: participated in the Battle of Garigliano against the Spanish-controlled Vice-royalty of Naples, 1503; entered the service of Guidobaldo di Montefeltro, Duke of Urbino, and his wife Elisabetta, 1504: commanded 50 men-at-arms to recapture lost territory for Urbino, 1504; travelled to England to receive the Order of the Garter from Henry VII, 1506; ambassador in Milan, 1507; on death of Guidobaldo, 1508, continued service with his successor, Francesco Maria, nephew of Pope Julius II; participated with papal forces in the Romagna campaign against Venice,

1509, the siege of Mirandola, 1511, and the reconquest of Romagna and Emilia after the Battle of Ravenna, 1512; wrote the prologue for *La calandria* by Dovizi da Bibbiena, *q.v.*, 1513; ambassador in Rome on the death of Julius II and election of Leo X, 1513; received the castle of Novilara for his diplomatic and literary services, 1513, but settled in Rome as ambassador, 1514–16; followed Francesco Maria into exile in Mantua after the conquest of Urbino by papal forces, 1516; re-established stable relations between Rome and Mantua, 1519; resettled in Rome, 1520, and remained in the service of Rome and Mantua, 1520–24; neutral broker between Milan, France, and Spain to decide the fate of Lombardy, 1524; nuncio for Pope Clement VII at the Court of Emperor Charles V, Madrid, 1525–29. **Died:** 1529.

PUBLICATIONS

Collections

Opere volgari e latine, edited by G.A. and G. Volpi. 1733.
Opere di Baldassarre Castiglione e Giovanni Della Casa, edited by G. Prezzolini. 1937.
Il libro del cortegiano con una scelta delle opere minori, edited by Bruno Maier. 1955; second edition, 1964; third, supplemented edition, 1981.
Opere di Baldassarre Castiglione, Giovanni della Casa, Benvenuto Cellini, edited by Carlo Cordié. 1960.

Prose

Il libro del cortegiano. 1528; edited by Vittorio Cian, 1894, revised editions, 1910, 1929, and 1947, also edited by G. Preti, 1960, Ettore Bonora, 1972, Salvator Battaglia, 1988, and Carlo Cordié, 1991; as *The Book of the Courtier*, translated by Sir Thomas Hoby, 1561, reprinted 1974; also translated by Robert Samber, 1724; Leonard Eckstein, 1901; Charles Singleton, 1959; George Bull, 1967.

Plays

Il tirsi, with Cesare Gonzaga (produced 1506). 1553; edited by F. Torraca, in *Teatro italiano dei seccoli XII–XV*, 1885.

Other

L'epistola ad regem Henricum de Guidubaldo Urbini duce. 1513.
Lettere (includes the Latin poetry and vernacular works). 2 vols., 1769–71.
Lettere inedite o rari, edited by G. Gorini. 1969.
Tutte le opere: Lettere, edited by Guido La Rocca. 1978.

*

Bibliography: "Studi sul Castiglione" by G.G. Ferrero, in *Rivista di Sintesi Letterari*, II, 1935.

Critical Studies: *Baldassarre Castiglione, the Perfect Courtier: His Life and Letters* by Julia Cartwright, 2 vols., 1908; *Baldassarre Castiglione* by G. Bongiovanni, 1929; *Baldassarre Castiglione: Il cortegiano, il letterato, il politico* by A. Vicinelli, 1931; *La lingua di*

Baldassarre Castiglione, 1942, and *Un illustre nunzio pontificio del Rinascimento: Baldassarre Castiglione*, 1951, both by Vittorio Cian; *Baldassarre Castiglione: La sua personalità; la sua prosa* by Mario Rossi, 1946; *Il Cortegiano nella trattatistica del Rinascimento* by G. Toffanin, 1962; *La seconda redazione del Cortegiano di Baldassarre Castiglione* edited by Ghino Ghinassi, 1968; *Courtly Performances: Masking and Festivity in Castiglione's Book of the Courtier* by Wayne A. Rebhorn, 1978; *La misura e la grazia sul Libro del cortegiano* by Antonio Gagliardi, 1989; *The Economy of Human Relations: Castiglione's Libro del Cortegiano* by Joseph D. Falvo, 1992; *The Fortunes of the Courtier: The European Reception of Castiglione's Cortegiano* by Peter Burke, 1996; *Marsilio Ficino, Pietro Bembo, Baldassare Castiglione: Philosophical, Aesthetic, and Political Approaches in Renaissance Platonism* by Christine Raffini, 1998; *Donne, Castiglione, and the Poetry of Courtliness* by Peter DeSa Wiggins, 2000; *The Absence of Grace: Sprezzatura and Suspicion in Two Renaissance Courtesy Books* by Harry Berger Jr., 2000.

* * *

Combining a noble upbringing with a humanistic education, Baldassare Castiglione's life—as a soldier, diplomat, courtier, and papal legate—never gave him the freedom to develop a literary career in the generation of Bembo, Ariosto, and Machiavelli, and gave rise to his *Il libro del cortegiano* (*The Book of the Courtier*) for which he is best remembered, as well as an eclogue, *Il tirsi*, and Latin and Italian verses. He is also remembered for a production at Urbino in 1513 of Bibbiena's comedy, *La Calandria* (*The Follies of Calandro*), for which it was long held that he had written a prologue.

The genesis of *The Book of the Courtier* took place at, and the work was modelled on, the court of Urbino under Francesco Gonzaga, where Castiglione resided between 1504 and 1513, though it is really more of a nostalgic memoir of the rule of Frederico da Montefeltro some years before. This exposition of the qualities of the ideal courtier, the archetype and model for many treatises on behaviour and books of manners that were to follow, was circulated among scholars for suggestions, debate, and corrections from the time of its inception in 1507–08 until publication in 1528, and translated the Ciceronian idea of the perfect orator (*De Oratore*) into the Renaissance concept of a manual and formula for the perfectibility of the gentleman (and lady) at court. Others had written treatises for the perfect cardinal (Cortese) and the perfect prince (Machiavelli). Yet the realism of Machiavelli's *Il principe* (*The Prince*) contrasted starkly with the idealism of Castiglione's *The Book of the Courtier*: like the theoretical writings on language by Bembo, the latter was a refined and cultivated literary ideal, based as much on cultural antecedents and tradition as on observed experience at the court of Urbino. Castiglione's treatise provided a model for the educated and cultivated gentleman at court (the basic social structure for the power base and government of many European states, and most, though not all, of the Italian states in the Renaissance period) and projected into the arena of politics and government the idea of the polymath, an educated ideal of the multi-talented humanist, an ideal that has had a measurable impact on subsequent educational systems. All this was articulated as the ideal in spite of the traditional clash of interests between the form of the principality as an absolutist state and the freedom of an artist's creativity, enshrined in the complaints of writers from Ariosto to Tasso (and projected by the iconoclasm or anti-classicism of satirists like Aretino), which began in Castiglione's own generation and

continued long after him. By 1525, Castiglione's refined ideal courtier had its antidote in the satire of the papal court in Aretino's courtesan (*La cortigiana*), since, as noted, the book had been widely read long before its official publication.

The Book of the Courtier identifies the qualities a successful courtier should possess, from the martial arts to artistic flair in poetry and music, from *sprezzatura* (an effortless gracefulness in accomplishments that eschews the boastful and arrogant) to a finely developed aesthetic sense. Already we have the formula for a gentleman which was to be widely influential. But the gentleman must have his mate, and the *donna di palazzo* is given similar arts and graces (and similar artfulness and gracefulness) in the work, and a notable equality with man that is in tune with the prominence of women (as warriors, as poetesses, as governors) in the society of Ariosto and Castiglione. On the appropriate language for discourse (as opposed to writing) Castiglione is more pragmatic than Bembo is in *Le prose della volgar lingua*, since usage is admitted as arbiter, though in the conclusion to *The Book of the Courtier* the supremacy of the Platonic ideals of Ficino is given to Bembo to expound. In broadest outline then, *The Book of the Courtier* is a discussion between Castiglione's authoritative contemporaries, and roughly approximates to the three ages of man: youth, maturity, and old age. The first part, from Ludoviso di Canossa and Federico Fregoso, represents the earthly and humanistic courtier; the second, from Ottaviano Fregoso, projects the ideal courtier as wise counsellor to the prince; whereas the third proposes the sublimation of love into the metaphysical Neoplatonic philosophy of Ficino, through the mouth of Pietro Bembo.

Politically, of course, *The Book of the Courtier* had to favour the form of a principality, for this is its explicit frame of reference; but the work does not blind itself to other possibilities, and contemporary "mixed" forms of government (from Machiavelli in the most recent exposition) find their way in with election of councils of nobles and the people, even if, with the image of Duke Federico da Montefeltro in the background as memory and inspiration, the figure of the prince is benignly paternalistic, caring, civilizing, and morally upright—at some remove, therefore, from the opportunism and pragmatism of the Machiavellian idea. As a window on the world of the Italian Renaissance—whether escapist fantasy fossilized in an already outdated cultural ideal, or a manual for courtly deportment and a survival package in an age of rapidly changing values—*The Book of the Courtier* has had an enduring influence on educational and political thinking ever since it was written, and seems resolutely contemporary in several of its themes—in man's sense of cultural identity and the function of the arts in his make-up and personal ambitions, in the notion of *mens sana in corpore sano*, and, not least, in the long debate between service (servility) and freedom in politics.

—Christopher Cairns

CATULLUS

Born: Gaius Valerius Catullus, c. 84 BC; father a citizen of Verona. **Career:** Lived in Rome, and probably had a villa near Tivoli; also owned property at Sirmio (now Sirmione); friend of Cicero and other important men; accompanied C. Memmius Gemellus on visit to Bithynia, Asia Minor, 57–56 BC. **Died:** c. 54 BC.

PUBLICATIONS

* * *

Verse

[Verse], edited by R.A.B. Mynors. 1958, revised edition, 1972; also edited by Henry Bardon, 2nd edition, 1973, D.F.S. Thomson, 1978; edited and translated by G.P. Goold, 1983; translated by Frederick A. Wright, 1926; also translated by Jack Lindsay, 1929; Horace Gregory, 1956; Frank Copley, 1957; R.A. Swanson, 1959; C.H. Sisson, 1966; Peter Whigham, 1966; Reney Myers and Robert J. Ormsby, 1972; James Michie, 1972; Frederic Raphael and Kenneth McLeish, 1978; Charles Martin, 1979; Guy Lee, 1990; commentaries by Robinson Ellis, 1876; Elmer T. Merrill, 1893, reprinted 1951; C.J. Fordyce (in part), 1961; Kenneth Quinn, 1970, revised edition, 1973; and J. Ferguson, 1985; as *Catullus: Poems 61–68*, edited and translated by John Godwin, 1995; as *Catullus: The Shorter Poems*, edited and translated by John Godwin, 1999.

*

Bibliography: *A Bibliography to Catullus* by Hermann Harrauer, 1979; *Gaius Valerius Catullus: A Systematic Bibliography* by James P. Holoka, 1985.

Critical Studies: *Catullus and His Influence* by Karl P. Harrington, 1923; *Catullus in English Poetry* by E.S. Duckett, 1925; *Catullus and Horace: Two Poets in Their Environment* by Frank Tenney, 1928; *Catullus and the Traditions of Ancient Poetry* by A.L. Wheeler, 1934; *Catullus and the Traditions of Ancient Poetry* by E.A. Havelock, 1939, revised edition, 1967; *Catullus in Strange and Distant Britain* by J.A.S. McPeek, 1939; *The Catullan Revolution*, 1959, revised edition, 1969, and *Catullus: An Interpretation*, 1973, both by Kenneth Quinn, and *Approaches to Catullus* edited by Quinn, 1972; *Enarratio Catulliana* by C. Witke, 1968; *Style and Tradition in Catullus* by David O. Ross, Jr., 1969; *Catullan Questions*, 1969, and *Catullus and His World*, 1985, both by T.P. Wiseman; *Studies in Catullan Verse* by Julia W. Loomis, 1972; *Interpreting Catullus* by G.P. Goold, 1974; *Catullus' Indictment of Rome: The Meaning of Catullus 64* by David Konstan, 1977; *Catullan Self-Revelation* by E. Adler, 1981; *Catullus' "Passer": The Arrangement of the Book of Polymetric Poems* by M.B. Skinner, 1981; *Sexuality in Catullus* by Brian Arkins, 1982; *Three Classical Poets: Sappho, Catullus, and Juvenal* by Richard Jenkyns, 1982; *Catullus 68: An Interpretation* by John Sarkissian, 1983; *Catullus: A Reader's Guide to the Poems* by Stuart P. Small, 1983; *Catullus* by John Ferguson, 1988; *The Student's Catullus* by David H. Garrison, 1989; *The Abhorrence of Love: Studies in Rituals and Mystic Aspects in Catullus' Poem of Attis* by Britt-Mari Näsström, 1989; *Roman Catullus and the Modification of the Alexandrian Sensibility* by J.K. Newman, 1990; *Catullus* by Charles Martin, 1992; *Catullus and His Renaissance Readers* by Julia Haig Gaisser, 1993; *"When the Lamp Is Shattered": Desire and Narrative in Catullus* by Micaela Janan, 1994; *Martial's Catullus: The Reception of an Epigrammatic Rival* by Bruce W. Swann, 1994; *Catullan Provocations: Lyric Poetry and the Drama of Position* by William Fitzgerald, 1995; *The Child and the Hero: Coming of Age in Catullus and Vergil* by Mark Petrini, 1997; *The Catullan Revolution* by Kenneth Quinn, 1999; *Catullus in English*, edited by Julia Haig Gaisser, 2001; *Cicero, Catullus, and the Language of Social Performance* by Brian A. Krostenko, 2001.

* * *

Catullus' poems are traditionally divided into three distinct groups: the short polymetric poems (1–60), the long poems (61–68), and the epigrams (69–116). Whether this arrangement, and that of the poems within each group, were Catullus' own work is much disputed; some, for example, believe that he intended 65–116 as a group, since they are all written in elegiacs. At present, the weight of scholarly opinion favours the view that at least the majority of the polymetrics were arranged in their present order by the poet, though some interference by a later editor is generally accepted to be evident.

Two types of poem, by virtue of their frequency, dominate the polymetrics and epigrams. First, there are roughly three dozen poems of invective (e.g., 28–29, 39, 69, 71, 94), which very often employ obscene language (incest is a recurrent theme) and of which several are directed at a single target (thus 74, 88–91, 116 against one Gellius). Second, and most famously, there are between two dozen and 30 poems which relate to Catullus' love affair with Lesbia (the exact number is uncertain because she is named explicitly in only 13). This woman ("Lesbia" is a pseudonym) is usually identified with Clodia, the wife of Q. Metellus Celer who was consul in 60 BC and died the following year.

These two main types of poem are interspersed with a refreshing variety of others: e.g., poems on homecoming (4, 9, 31, 46), homosexual love (e.g., 15, 48, 81, 99), his dead brother (101) the death of a friend's wife (96), and literature (e.g., 35, 50, 95); there are mock hymns (36, 44) and a real hymn (34); and there is *vers de société* (e.g., 10, 12–13, 25, 55, 84, 103), sometimes of a risqué nature (e.g., 6, 32, 56, 110). As for the group of long poems, there are two on weddings (61–62); one (63) on the fanatical cult of the goddess Cybele, depicting the self-castration of her devotee Attis; an epyllion (miniature epic) on the marriage of Peleus and Thetis (64); a translation into Latin of Callimachus' "Lock of Berenice" (66), together with its epistolary introduction in verse (65); a dialogue with a door (67); another verse letter, on the death of his brother (68A); and an elegy which combines the themes of his brother's death and his love for Lesbia with a complicated series of mythological illustrations (68B) (these last two are written as a single poem in the MSS and are still so regarded by many scholars). Of these long poems, 63 is one of the most remarkable poems in Latin on account of its theme; 64 is the only epyllion which survives from the literature of the late republic and early empire; and 68B is the forerunner of the poetry, of Propertius, Tibullus, and Ovid. On these grounds alone, Catullus' work would be significant; but his principal achievement lies elsewhere.

Such long poems as 64, 68, and 68B are characterized above all by the *doctrina* (learning, scholarship) which was dear to the other *novi poetae* (new poets) of Catullus' generation and which was inspired by the work of the Greek librarian-poet Callimachus (ft. 250 BC). Until fairly recently it was often thought that there were, so to speak, "two Catulluses": the scholar-poet of the long poems, whose obscure and allusive verse was very much an acquired taste; and the simple poet of the polymetrics and epigrams, whose direct and passionate language had impressed centuries of readers. Yet this myth has been exploded by more recent scholarship, which has shown that learning, allusiveness, and technical refinement are not restricted to the long poems but permeate much of the other poetry too. Indeed it is precisely in the area where *doctrina* interacts with the portrayal of emotion that Catullus holds most fascination for the reader who knows Latin and Greek and is prepared to put his knowledge to good use. For it is by no means easy to fully appreciate the poetry written by Callimachus and his followers, and many of Catullus' polymetrics and epigrams require considerable effort for their understanding. Six examples, which appear to reflect his love affair from its beginning to its end, will make this clear.

Poem 51 is an expression of Catullus' love for Lesbia, yet the poem is a translation and adaptation of a famous poem by Sappho (31); and the fact that Catullus has troubled to clarify the meaning of his exemplar suggests that he expected his readers, including Lesbia, to be aware of the problems raised by Sappho's poem and to notice his own view of their solution. Poems 7 and 70 both have a "twin" (5 and 72 respectively), which suggests that all four poems reflect episodes in the poet's affair and are thus heavily biographical; yet 7 is full of learned allusion to the life and works of Callimachus, quite apart from treating us to a virtuoso display of oral imagery, while 70 is actually an adaptation of an epigram by Callimachus (25), which Catullus has completely transformed. Poem 85 is a two-line epigram of deceptive simplicity; yet its first three words (*Odi et amo*, "I hate and love") recall a theme which echoes back to the beginnings of Greek personal poetry, and the remainder of the couplet is a superb example of the arrangement and suggestiveness of apparently simple words. Poems 8 and 11 reflect the end of the affair, with all its bitterness; yet the former seems inspired by a soliloquy from the comic playwright Menander's *Samia (The Girl from Samos),* and in the latter Catullus finds time to demonstrate his knowledge of the vernacular name for Egypt, of the original name for the Nile, and of the etymology of the word "Alps" (we must remember that Callimachus' most famous work was entitled *Origins* and that another work dealt with the foundations of islands and cities and their changes of name).

To the modern reader, these and countless other instances of *doctrina* may seem strange; but it is vital to appreciate that they in no way detract from, but rather enhance, the conviction with which Catullus expresses himself. He achieved that fusion of form and emotion which many believe to be the quintessence of poetry and which has made his work everlastingly memorable.

—A.J. Woodman

See the essays on "poem 85" and "three poems: 2, 63, and 76."

CAVAFY, C(onstantine) P(etrou)

Born: Alexandria, Egypt, 29 April 1863. Lived in England as a child, 1872–79, and in Constantinople, 1882–85; otherwise lived in Alexandria. **Education:** Educated at Hermis Lyceum, 1879. **Career:** Worked at Egyptian Stock Exchange, 1888; clerk, Irrigation Service, Ministry of Public Works, 1892–1922. Issued one private pamphlet of his verse in 1904, and thereafter compiled notebooks of verse for distributing to friends. **Died:** 29 April 1933.

PUBLICATIONS

Collections

Poiemata, edited by Alexander Singopoulos. 1935.
Poems, translated by John Mavrogordato. 1951.
Complete Poems, translated by Rae Dalven. 1961; enlarged edition, 1976.

Collected Poems, edited by G.P. Savidis, translated by Edmund Keeley and Philip Sherrard. 1975.
The Greek Poems, translated by Memas Kolaitis. 2 vols., 1989.
Before Time Could Change Them: The Complete Poems of Constantine P. Cavafy, translated by Theoharis Constantine Theoharis. 2001.
The Essential Cavafy, translated by Edmund Keeley and Philip Sherrard. 1995.

Verse

Fourteen Poems, translated by Nikos Stangos and Stephen Spender. 1966.
Anecdota poiemata 1882–1923 [Unpublished Poems], edited by G.P. Savidis. 1968.
Passions and Ancient Days: Twenty One New Poems, translated by Edmund Keeley and G.P. Savidis. 1972.
Ta Apokirigmena: Poiemata kai Metafrasis [The Rejected Works: Poems and Translation]. 1983.

Other

Peza [Prose], edited by G. Papoutsakis. 1963.
Anecdota Peza [Unpublished Prose], edited by M. Peridis. 1963.
Epistoles ston Mario Valano [Letters to Mario Valano], edited by E.N. Moschou. 1979.

*

Critical Studies: *Constantine Cavafy,* 1964, and *Three Generations of Greek Writers: Introductions to Cavafy, Kazantzakis, Ritsos,* 1983, both by Peter Bien; *Cavafy: A Critical Biography* by Robert Liddell, 1974; *Cavafy's Alexandria: Study of a Myth in Progress* by Edmund Keeley, 1976; "A Concise Introduction to Cavafy" by Marguerite Yourcenar, in *Shenandoah,* 32(1), 1980; "Cavafy Issue" of *Journal of the Hellenic Diaspora,* 10, 1983; *The Mind and Art of C.P. Cavafy: Essays on His Life and Work* by Denise Harvey, 1983; *The Poetics of Cavafy: Textuality, Eroticism, History* by Gregory Jusdanis, 1987; *C.P. Cavafy* by Christopher Robinson, 1988.

* * *

Solemnly asked his opinion of his own work, C.P. Cavafy towards the end of his life is said to have replied, "Cavafy in my opinion is an ultra-modern poet, a poet of future generations." History has proved him right, but the tone of the reply also reveals an important ingredient of the unique poetic voice that is Cavafy's: a gentle mockery of all pretension, even that of the poet interviewed about his own work, and a light-hearted concealment of his true self at the very moment when he appears about to lay his cards on the table. "Cavafy," he says, not "I," as if "Cavafy" were someone different.

Cavafy's poetry is distinguished by many subtle forms of irony, and also by an intriguing self-effacement in poems that purport to tell of personal experience and feeling. The subject matter of his poems is equally unusual. Approximately half of what that he published in his lifetime (consisting of 154 fairly short poems) and a similar proportion of those published posthumously, are devoted to subjects taken from Greek history, chiefly between 340 BC and AD 1453, while the remainder deal more or less explicitly with homosexual encounters against a backdrop of contemporary Alexandria. Cavafy's uniqueness has posed a problem for critics, for whom he continues to exercise a profound fascination. To many his erotic poetry is a disreputable appendage to more "sublime" poetry dedicated to the Greek past, but Cavafy's uncompromisingly "historical" treatment of that past has also disconcerted many. And those critics who have not chosen to ignore the erotic poems have been hard put to identify the source of powerful emotion, felt by many readers, in response to poems from which all reference to love is lacking, and the sordidness and triviality of the sexual encounters evoked are freely confessed.

The common denominator between Cavafy's two principal preoccupations, the distant Greek past and contemporary homosexual experiences, is time, which plays a major role in both types of poem. Often it appears that the true subject of the erotic poems is not the experience described so much as its loss to the passage of time. Time takes away and alienates all real experience, but through art the poet can sometimes regain it in the creation of a poem, though what is regained is both more and less than the original. More, because, as the poet frankly says in several of these poems, he is free to touch up reality in the imaginative act of writing; less, because, no matter how "perfect" an experience can become thus imaginatively recreated, it is only imaginary, the real thing remaining lost to the past. This sense of "lost to the past" is central, too, to Cavafy's historical poems, in which he juxtaposes vivid pictures of flesh-and-blood, fallible human beings with a chillingly historical sense of how remote they are, and how futile are these people's preoccupations now.

In their treatment of time, *all* Cavafy's poems can be said to belong to his third type, into which he once said his work could be divided, namely "philosophical" poetry.

—Roderick Beaton

See the essay on "Waiting for the Barbarians."

CAVALCANTI, Guido

Born: Florence, c. 1255; member of a Guelph merchant family. **Family:** Engaged to Bice, a member of the Ghibelline family, in 1267. **Career:** Guelph guarantor for a peace settlement, 1280; member of the general council of the commune, 1284 and 1290; an ardent supporter of the white Guelph faction, he was banished on 24 June 1300 by order of the council on which Dante, *q.v.*, served as a prior (from June to August) and confined to Sarzana. Contracted malaria and was recalled to Florence in August but died soon after. Friend of Dante, whose *La vita nuova* was dedicated to him but who no longer spoke of him after his death. **Died:** Buried 29 August 1300.

PUBLICATIONS

Collections

The Poetry, edited and translated by Lowry Nelson, Jr. 1986.
The Complete Poems, translated by Marc Cirigliano (bilingual edition). 1992.
Thirty-three Sonnets of Guido Cavalcanti, translated by Ezra Pound. 1991.

Verse

Rime, edited by Guido Favati. 1957; edited by Marcello Ciccuto, 1978; also edited by Letterio Cassata, 1993; translated by Dante Gabriel Rossetti, in *The Early Italian Poets,* 1861, revised edition, as *Dante and His Circle,* 1874; as *The Sonnets and Ballate,* translated by Ezra Pound, 1912.

*

Critical Studies: *Guido Cavalcanti's Theory of Love: The "Canzone d'Amore" and Other Related Problems* by J.E. Shaw, 1949; "Cavalcanti" by Ezra Pound, in *Literary Essays,* 1954; *Medieval Latin and the Rise of the European Love Lyric* by Peter Dronke, 2 vols., 1968; "Pound and Cavalcanti" by G. Singh, in *Essays in Honour of J.H. Whitfield,* 1975.

* * *

Guido Cavalcanti's merit as a lyricist has never been overshadowed by the genius of his close friend Dante. A *dolce stil nuovo* poet, he imposed on the conventions of that school his own particular individuality and moulded them to suit his own taste and poetic exigency. Ezra Pound, the creator of modern poetry, singled him out as an inspiration in his own poetry, and as an embodiment of something authentically modern. He put Cavalcanti in the same category as Sappho and Theocritus—poets who have sung, "not all the modes of life, but some of them, unsurpassedly; those who in their chosen or fated field have bowed to no one." What characterizes Cavalcanti's lyricism as such is the dramatic intensity of his passions as well as the stark individuality of diction in which it is couched, together with the conceptual richness and subtlety of his content. If, as Pound said, "no psychologist of emotions is more keen in his understanding, more precise in his expression" than Cavalcanti, it is because he conveys the feelings, intuitions, and convictions of a highly gifted mind and because of his use of a singularly concrete and poetically charged language with no trace of conventionality.

Cavalcanti's concept of love—and love is the leitmotif of the *dolce stil nuovo* school of poetry—is significantly different from that of a contemporary like Guido Guinizzelli, in that it is conceived more in earthly and sensuous terms than in mystical and transcendental ones, and the language Cavalcanti uses to characterize it is direct and graphic rather than symbolic or abstract. And this in spite of the fact that he brought to bear on his treatment of love all his philosophic learning and intellectual curiosity, a large share of it derived from Averroès, so that his similes, metaphors, and descriptions, even though they might at times appear to be arid and prosaic, always embody a definite concept or meaning as well as a fineness of perception. Apropos of this, Pound's evaluative comparison between Cavalcanti and Petrarch, or between Cavalcanti and Dante, is worth quoting. After noting how Cavalcanti "thought in accurate terms" and how his phrases "correspond to definite sensations undergone," Pound goes on to argue that "the 'figure,' the strong metaphoric or 'picturesque' expression in him is there to convey or to interpret a definite meaning. In Petrarch, on the other hand, it is ornament, the prettiest ornament he could find, but not an irreplaceable ornament, or one that he couldn't have used just about as well somewhere else." Pound's comparison between Cavalcanti and Dante is equally illuminating—Dante "qui était diablement dans les idées reçues," Cavalcanti more independent and unconventional; Dante willing "to take on any sort of holy and orthodox furniture," Cavalcanti "eclectic," swallowing "none of his authors whole," and lastly, "Dante himself never wrote more poignantly, or with greater intensity than Cavalcanti . . . a spirit more imperious, more passionate, less likely to give ear to sophistries; his literary relation to Dante is not unlike Marlowe's to Shakespeare" (though, Pound adds, "such comparisons are always unsafe").

—G. Singh

CELA (TRULOCK), Camilo José

Born: Iria Flavia, La Coruña, Galicia, Spain, 11 May 1916. **Education:** Educated at the University of Madrid, 1933–36, 1939–43. **Military Service:** Served in General Franco's forces during the Spanish Civil War, 1936–39: corporal. **Family:** Married 1) Maria del Rosario Conde Picavea in 1944 (divorced 1990), one son; 2) Marina Castaño in 1991. **Career:** Freelance writer in Madrid until 1954, then in Palma de Mallorca; travelled to Chile, 1952, and Venezuela, 1953; founder, *Papeles de Son Armadans*, 1956–79; travelled to Italy, France, and the United States, 1990. **Awards:** Critics prize, 1956; National literature prize, 1984; Prince of Asturias prize for literature, 1987; Nobel prize for literature, 1989; Santiago de Compostela gold medal, 1990. Honorary doctorates: Syracuse University, USA, 1965; University of Santiago (Chile), 1974 (refused); University of Birmingham (England), 1976; John F. Kennedy University, Buenos Aires, 1978; Interamericana University, Puerto Rico, 1980; University of Palma, Mallorca, 1980; Hebrew University, Jerusalem, 1986; University of Miami, University of Tel Aviv, University of San Marcos, Peru, Dowling College, New York, Millersville University, Pennsylvania, and University of Murcia, all 1990; Universidad Complutense, Madrid, and La Trobe University, Australia, 1991. Honorary professor, University of Santo Domingo, 1990. **Member:** Spanish Royal Academy, since 1957. Created Royal Senator, 1977. **Died:** 17 January 2002.

PUBLICATIONS

Fiction

La familia de Pascual Duarte. 1942; edited by Jorge Urrutia, 1977, and by Harold L. Boudreau and John W. Kronik, 1989; as *Pascual Duarte's Family*, translated by John Marks, 1946; as *The Family of Pascual Duarte*, translated by Anthony Kerrigan, 1964.
Pabellón de reposo. 1943; as *Rest Home*, translated by Herma Briffault, 1961.
Nuevas andanzas y desventuras de Lazarillo de Tormes. 1944.
Esas nubes que pasan. . . 1945.
El bonito crimen del carabinero y otras invenciones. 1947.
El gallego y su cuadrilla y otros apuntes carpetovetónicos. 1949; enlarged edition (includes "En el lomo de la cubierta dice"), 1951.
La colmena. 1951; edited by Jorge Urrutia, 1988; as *The Hive*, translated by J.M. Cohen, 1953.
Santa Balbina 37, gas en cada piso. 1952.
Timoteo, el incomprendido. 1952.
Café de artistas. 1953.

Mrs. Caldwell habla con su hijo. 1953; as *Mrs. Caldwell Speaks to Her Son*, translated by J.S. Bernstein, 1968.
Baraja de invenciones. 1953.
Historias de Venezuela: La catira. 1955.
El molino de viento y otras novelas cortas. 1956.
Nuevo retablo de Don Cristobita: Invenciones, figuraciones y alucinaciones. 1957.
Cajón de sastre. 1957.
Historias de España: Los ciegos, Los tontos. 1958.
Los viejos amigos. 2 vols., 1960–61.
Gavilla de fábulas sin amor. 1962.
Tobogán de hambrientos. 1962.
Once cuentos de fútbol. 1963.
Las compañías convenientes y otros fingimientos y cegueras. 1963.
El solitario; Los sueños de Quesada. 1963.
Garito de hospicianos o Guirigay de imposturas y bambollas. 1963.
Cuentos 1941–1953; Nuevo retablo de Don Cristobita. 1964.
Apuntes carpetovetónicos: Novelas cortas 1949–56. 1965.
A la pata de palo: Historias de España; La familia del héroe; El ciudadano Iscariote Reclús; Viaje a USA. 4 vols., 1965–67; selection as *El tacatá oxidado: Florilegio de carpetovetonismos, y otras lindezas*, 1973.
Nuevas escenas matritenses. 7 vols., 1965–66; as *Fotografías al minuto*, 1972.
San Camilo, 1936: Vísperas, festividad y octava de San Camilo del año 1936 en Madrid. 1969; as *San Camilo, 1936: The Eve, Feast and Octave of St. Camillus of the Year 1936 in Madrid*, translated by J.H.R. Holt, 1992.
Café de artistas y otros cuentos. 1969.
Timoteo et incomprendido y otros papeles ibéricos. 1970.
Obras selectas. 1971.
Oficio de tinieblas 5 o Novela de tesis escrita para ser cantada por un coro de enfermos. 1973.
Cuentos para leer despues del baño. 1974.
Prosa, edited by Jacinto-Luis Guerña. 1974.
Café de artistas y otros papeles volanderos. 1978.
El espejo y otros cuentos. 1981.
Mazurca para dos muertos. 1983; as *Mazurka for Two Dead Men*, translated by Patricia Haugaard, 1993.
Cristo versus Arizona. 1988.
Las orejas del niño Raúl (for children). 1989.
Cachondeos, escareos y otros meneos. 1991.
O Camaleón solteiro. 1991.

Plays

Maria Sabina, music by Balada (produced 1970). 1967.
Homenaje al Bosco I: El carro de heno o El inventor de la guillotina. 1969.

Verse

Poemas de una adolescencia cruel. 1945; as *Pisando la dudosa luz del día*, 1945.
Cancionero de la Alcarria. 1987.

Other

Mesa revuelta. 1945; enlarged edition (includes *Ensueños y figuraciones*), 1957.
San Juan de la Cruz (as Matilde Verdú). 1948.

Las botas de siete leguas: Viaje a la Alcarria. 1948; as Journey to the Alcarria, translated by Frances M. Lopez Morillas, 1964.

Ávila. 1952; revised edition, 1968.

Del Miño al Bidasoa: Notas de un vagabundaje. 1952.

Ensueños y figuraciones. 1954.

Vagabundo por Castilla. 1955.

Mis páginas preferidas (selection). 1956.

Judíos, moros y cristianos: Notas de un vagabundaje por Ávila, Segovia y sus tierras. 1956.

La rueda de los ocios. 1957.

La obra literaria del pintor Solana. 1957.

Recuerdo de don Pío Baroja. 1958.

La cucaña: Memorias. 1959.

Primer viaje andaluz: Notas de un vagabundaje por Jaén, Córdoba, Sevilla, Huelva y sus tierras. 1959.

Cuaderno del Guadarrama. 1959.

Cuatro figuras del '98: Unamuno, Valle-Inclán, Baroja, Azorín y otros retratos y ensayos españoles. 1961.

Obra completa. 17 vols., 1962–86.

Toreo de salón. 1963.

Izas, rabizas y colipoterras. 1964.

Páginas de geografía errabunda. 1965.

Viaje al Pirineo de Lérida: Notas de un paseo a pie por el Pallars Sobira, el Valle de Aran y el Condado de Ribagorza. 1965.

Viajes por España. 3 vols., 1965–68.

Madrid. 1966.

El solitario, illustrated by Rafael Zabaleta. 1966.

Calidoscopio callejero, marítimo y campestre de Camilo José Cela para el reino y ultramar. 1966.

Xam, with Cesáreo Rodríguez Aguilera, 1966.

Viaje a USA. 1967.

Diccionario secreto. 2 vols., 1968–71.

Al servicio de algo. 1969.

La bandada de palomas (for children). 1969.

Barcelona, illustrated by Federico Lloveras. 1970.

La Mancha en el corazón y en los ojos. 1971.

La bola del mundo: Escenas cotidianas. 1972.

Fotografías al minuto. 1972.

A vueltas con España. 1973.

Cristina Mallo (monograph). 1973.

Balada del vagabundo sin suerte y otros papeles volanderos. 1973.

Diccionario manual castellá-catalá, catalá-castellá. 1974.

Danza de las gigantas amorosas. 1975.

Rol de cornudos. 1976.

Crónica del cipote de Archidona. 1977.

La rosa. 1979.

Los sueños vanos, los ángeles curiosos. 1980.

Lectura de Quijote. 4 vols., 1981.

Vuelta de hoja. 1981.

Los vasos comunicantes. 1981.

Album de taller (art commentary). 1981.

Enciclopedia de erotismo. 4 vols., 1982–86; revised edition, as Diccionario del erotismo, 2 vols., 1988.

El juego de los tres madroños. 1983.

Madrid, color y siluta. 1985.

Nuevo viaje a la Alcarria. 1986.

El asno de Buridán (articles). 1986.

Of Genes, Gods, and Tyrants: The Biological Causation of Reality. 1987.

Conversaciones españolas. 1987.

Los caprichos de Francisco de Goya y Lucientes. 1989.

Vocación de repartidor. 1989.

Toda ta vida a una carta, 1989.

Obras completas. 37 vols., 1989–90.

Cela, lo que dijo en TVE. 1989.

Galicia. 1990.

Blanquito, peón de Brega. 1991.

Páginas escogidas (anthology). 1991.

Desde et palomar de Hita. 1991.

Torerías: El gallego y su cuadrilla; Madrid toreo de salón. 1991.

El camaleón. 1992.

El huevo del juicio. 1993.

Memorias, entendimientos y voluntades. 1993.

Editor, Homenaje y recuerdo a Gregorio Marañon (1887–1960). 1961.

Translator, La Celestina, by Fernando de Rojas. 1979.

Translator, La resistible ascensión de Arturo Ui, by Bertolt Brecht. 1986.

*

Critical Studies: El sistema estético de Camilo José Cela by Olga Prjevalinsky, 1960; Camilo José Cela: Acercamiento a un escritor by Alonso Zamora Vicente, 1962; The Novels and Travels of Camilo José Cela, 1963, and "Camilo José Cela's Quest for a Tragic Sense of Life," in Romance Quarterly, 17, 1970, both by Robert Kirsner; "Social Criticism, Existentialism and Tremendismo in Camilo José Cela's La familia de Pascual Duarte," in Romance Quarterly, 13 (supplement), 1967, and Forms of the Novel in the Work of Camilo José Cela, 1967, both by David William Foster; El léxico de Camilo José Cela by Sara Suárez Solís, 1969; Camilo José Cela by D.W. McPheeters, 1969; Cela by Mariano Tudela, 1970; La novelística de Camilo José Cela, 1971, and "The Politics of Obscenity in San Camilo, 1936," in Anales de la Novela de Posguerra, 1, 1976, both by Paul Ilie; Cela issue of Contemporary Fiction, 4(3), 1984; Cela: Masculino singular: Biografía by Francisco García Marquina, 1991; La familia de Pascual Duarte by Alan Hoyle, 1994; La Familia de Pascual Duarte und El Túnel: Correspondences and Divergencies in the Exercise of Craft by Cedric Busette, 1994; Novel Into Film: The Case of La familia de Pascual Duarte and Los Santos Inocentes by Patricia J. Santoro, 1996; Understanding Camilo José Cela by Lucile C. Charlebois, 1998; Camilo José Cela Revisited: The Later Novels by Janet Pérez, 2000.

*   *   *

Camilo José Cela's first novel, La familia de Pascual Duarte (Pascual Duarte's Family), is a strange hybrid, reading in parts like a picaresque novel (though managing, unlike the later Nuevas andanzas y desventuras de Lazarillo de Tormes [Further Adventures of Lazarillo de Tormes], to keep away from pastiche), and in parts like a Lorca "rural tragedy." These sources of inspiration reveal the combined ideological intentions that underlie the book: nationalism, vitalism, and aestheticism. The nationalism is most evident in the choice of the picaresque as a model, while it is in the passages inspired by "rural tragedy" that can best be seen the vitalistic philosophy that pervades the whole story and provides its main message: Pascual is a primitive man who has not learned to interpose between his actions and the mysterious natural forces that rule them—as they rule all other men's—the distorting screen of civilization. In return, however, Pascual keeps in close contact with those same forces and, unlike the rest of us, is able to understand them intuitively, which is the only way in which they *can* be understood. Pascual is a nationalistic Spanish version of a Nietzschean hero, and the novel, rather then the isolated exception it is usually made out to be, is arguably the best example of the Spanish brand of fascist literature that flourished briefly during the very early Franco years.

The aestheticist dimension of *Pascual Duarte's Family* is developed more fully in some of Cela's early stories and in his second novel, *Pabellón de reposo* (*Rest Home*), in which the flimsy story line is entirely subservient to the elegant narrative orchestration and the poetic prose. This purely aestheticist strain remains a constant, if secondary, aspect of Cela's work, re-emerging in occasional short stories, in the never completed pseudo-memoirs "La cucaña" [The Greasepole] and, in tediously extreme form, in *Mrs. Caldwell habla con su hijo* (*Mrs. Caldwell Speaks to Her Son*). But, above all, aestheticism is inseparable from the other two essential dimensions of Cela's literature, and the full measure of it is given precisely by the marriage of the crudeness of the subject matter to the lyricism of the prose, as illustrated by his best short stories, like "Marelo Brito," "La naranja es una fruta de invierno" [Oranges Are Winter Fruit], or the significantly entitled "El bonito crimen del carabinero" [The Carabinero's Lovely Murder]. With *Viaje a la Alcarria* (*Journey to the Alcarria*), Cela's nationalism too gets partly shunted off into a special genre, though description is not Cela's forte and his travelogues tend to become a series of vignettes of (largely imaginary) encounters with odd characters. Yet nationalism is also an essential component of Cela's work as a whole, embedded in the stories themselves: the sickening brutality of their world is to be seen as a vital national Spanish characteristic, not to be decried, but to be upheld as such.

Cela's best work is undoubtedly *La colmena* (*The Hive*), which, however, is neither the technically sophisticated nor the social-realist novel it is often made out to be. It was, in the Spain of its day, innovative, but it is most emphatically not objectivist: its supposedly life-like randomness is largely an illusion. It does reflect very accurately the reality of 1940s Spain, not so much on the surface, where it leans often to the atypical, but at a deeper level, conveying the essential truth about that society—its sharp division between winners and losers, and the uninhibited exploitation and constant humiliation of the latter by the former. This it does, however, almost entirely by accident, for Cela believed that Spanish society was like that not because of its recent history, but because any human society must always be like that. The specific circumstances of Franco's Spain simply fitted his social and Darwinistic preconceptions. Still, *The Hive* remains an accurate portrayal of post-war Spain, and is also the best expression of Cela's artistic powers. It manages to keep a balance between being moving and being outrageously funny, and to retain its coherence in spite of its very fragmented structure, and, though many of its characters are on the fringes of normality or even beyond it, it gives, somehow, an overall impression of social realism. Here also, Cela's distinctive style reaches its perfection. The style is very simple, based almost entirely on one single technique, the delaying of the conclusion of his sentences by a series of triple repetitions at every syntactical level. It works, however, to great effect, thanks above all to Cela's extremely rich lexical resources.

After *The Hive*, Cela's work declined sharply. His travelogues became collections of improbable anecdotes involving freakish characters and having little to do with any actual place, and his stories degenerated into hackneyed portraits of misfits with ludicrous names and ludicrous lives, generously spiced for titillation with vulgarity and gratuitous violence. In fact, Cela simply parodied himself endlessly, in a descent into the pits of shallow commercialism which reached its bottom with *Enciclopedia del erotismo* [Encyclopedia of Eroticism]. He eventually tried his hand again at some real writing with *San Camilo, 1936,* a version of *The Hive* translated to the days of the outbreak of the Spanish Civil War. Unfortunately, the vision had not changed. At the very time when their collective destiny is being decided, the characters of *San Camilo* are all shown scurrying about purposelessly, obsessed only with the urge to satisfy their most basic needs. This is demonstrably false: there is abundant evidence that, at that fateful moment, many Spaniards were only too conscious of what was happening to them and were determined to shape history one way or another. But the worst thing about *San Camilo* is that Cela, having neglected his artistic powers for so long, failed to recapture them. The precarious but real balance between outrageous humour, lyricism, and social observation that he had achieved in *The Hive* eluded him this time, and his characters were too much the hacked versions of *Los viejos amigos* [Old Friends] and *Tobogán de hambrientos* [Tramps Down the Chute] rather than their original selves.

—J.F. Marfany

See the essay on *Pascual Duarte's Family.*

CELAN, Paul

Born: Paul Antschel in Czernowitz, Bukovina, Romania, 23 November 1920. **Education:** Educated at the Czernowitz Gymnasium; École de Médecine, Tours, France, 1938–39; University of Czernowitz, 1939–41; studied for a Licence-ès-Lettres in Paris, 1950. **Family:** Married Gisèle Lestrange in 1952. **Career:** In a forced labour camp during World War II; emigrated to Vienna, 1947; settled in Paris in 1948: language teacher and translator. **Awards:** Bremen literary prize, 1958; Büchner prize, 1960; Nordrhein-Westfalen prize, 1964. **Died:** (suicide) 20 April 1970.

PUBLICATIONS

Collections

Gedichte. 2 vols., 1975.
Gesammelte Werke, edited by Beda Allemann and S. Reichert. 5 vols., 1983; volume 3 as *Collected Prose*, translated by Rosemarie Waldrop, 1986.
Gedichte 1938–1944. 1985.

Verse

Der Sand aus den Urnen. 1948.
Mohn und Gedächtnis. 1952.
Von Schwelle zu Schwelle. 1955.
Sprachgitter. 1959.
Die Niemandsrose. 1963.

Atemwende. 1967; as *Breathturn*, translated and introduced by Pierre Joris, 1995.

Totnauberg. 1968.

Fadensonnen. 1968; as *Threadsuns*, translated and introduced by Pierre Joris, 2000.

Lichtzwang. 1970.

Speech-Grille and Selected Poems, translated by Joachim Neugroschel. 1971.

Schneepart. 1971.

Selected Poems, translated by Michael Hamburger and Christopher Middleton. 1972.

Nineteen Poems, translated by Michael Hamburger. 1972.

Zeitgehoft: Späte Gedichte aus dem Nachlass. 1976.

Poems (bilingual edition), translated by Michael Hamburger. 1980.

65 Poems, translated by Brian Lynch and Peter Jankowsky. 1985.

Thirty-Two Poems, translated by Michael Hamburger. 1985.

Last Poems (bilingual edition), translated by Katharine Washburn and Margaret Guillemin. 1986.

Other

Edgar Jené und der Traum vom Traume. 1948.

Der Meridian. 1961.

Übertragungen aus dem Russischen. 1986.

Paul Celan, Nelly Sachs: Correspondence by Paul Celan, translated by Christopher Clark. 1995.

Translator (into Romanian), *Taranii*, by Chekhov. 1946.

Translator (into Romanian), *Un eroual timpalu*, by Mikhail Lermontov. 1946.

Translator (into Romanian), *Chestinnea Rusa*, by Konstantin Simonov. 1947.

Translator, *Lehre vom Zerfall*, by E.M. Cioran. 1953.

Translator, *Die Zwölf*, by Aleksandr Blok. 1958.

Translator, *Das trunkene Schiff*, by Arthur Rimbaud. 1958.

Translator, *Gedichte*, by Osip Mandel'shtam. 1959.

Translator, *Die junge Parze*, by Paul Valéry. 1960.

Translator, *Gedichte*, by Sergei Esenin. 1961.

Translator, *Im Bereich einer Nacht*, by Jean Cayrol. 1961.

Translator, *Maigret und die schrecklichen Kinder; Hier irrt Maigret*, by Georges Simenon. 1963.

Translator, *Dichtungen*, by Henri Michaux. 1966.

Translator, *Einundzwanzig Sonette*, by Shakespeare. 1967.

Translator, *Gedichte*, by Jules Supervielle. 1968.

Translator, *Vakante Glut: Gedichte*, by André du Bouchet. 1968.

Translator, *Das verheissene Land*, by Giuseppe Ungaretti. 1968.

*

Critical Studies: *Zur Lyrik Celans* by P.H. Neumann, 1968; *Über Celan* edited by Dietlind Meinecke, 1970, revised edition, 1973; *Celan* by Jerry Glenn, 1973; *Celans Poetik* by Gerhard Buhr, 1976; ''Celan Issue'' of *Text + Kritik* (53–54), edited by H.L. Arnold, 1977; *Paul Celan* by Holger A. Pausch, 1987; ''Celan Issue'' of *Acts: A Journal of New Writing*, (8–9), 1989; *Paul Celan: Holograms of Darkness* by Amy Colin, 1990; *Paul Celan: A Biography of His Youth* by Israel Chalfen, translated by Maximilian Bleyleben, 1991; *Word Traces: Readings of Paul Celan* edited by Floretas Aris, 1994; *Holocaust Visions: Surrealism and Existentialism in the Poetry of Paul Celan* by Clarise Samuels, 1994; *Word Traces: Readings of Paul Celan*, edited by Aris Fioretos, 1994; *Language Mysticism: The Negative Way of Language in Eliot, Beckett, and Celan* by Shira Wolosky, 1995; *Paul Celan: Poet, Survivor, Jew* by John Felstiner, 1995; *Gadamer on Celan: ''Who am I and who are you?'' and Other Essays* by Hans-Georg Gadamer, translated by Richard Heinemann and Bruce Krajewski, 1997; *The Early Poetry of Paul Celan: In the Beginning was the Word* by Adrian Del Caro, 1997; *Economy of the Unlost: (Reading Simonides of Keos with Paul Celan)* by Anne Carson, 1999; *Ethics and Dialogue: In the Works of Levinas, Bakhtin, Mandelshtam, and Celan* by Michael Eskin, 2000; *Remnants of Song: Trauma and the Experience of Modernity in Charles Baudelaire and Paul Celan* by Ulrich Baer, 2000; *Five Portraits: Modernity and the Imagination in Twentieth-century German Writing* by Michael André Bernstein, 2000.

*   *   *

Paul Celan is arguably the most important poet who wrote in German in the period after 1945. His poetry met with early and widespread recognition, although critics have always found difficulty in reconciling its manifestly superior stature—it has an immediate and haunting appeal—with its considerable resistance to interpretation.

Celan's complex poetic idiom is rooted in the Jewish-Hasidic mystical tradition of his ancestors, and also in the heritage of European symbolism. The uncompromisingly reflexive nature of his language—as elusive as it is allusive—has, however, less in common with the hermeticism of Mallarmé's art, than with the extreme tendency towards internalization that characterized the work of Hölderlin, Trakl, and Rilke.

Celan's poetry is a profoundly serious response to the darkest period of modern history, and a statement, too, of its own invalidity in such an age of crisis. One cannot afford to overlook the significance of Celan's position as a Jew writing in German after the Holocaust; the poet's parents were among the millions who are mourned in countless of his poems. The most famous of these—''Todesfuge'' (''Death Fugue'')—in *Mohn und Gedächtnis* [Poppy and Memory]—superbly illustrates his ability to fuse the historically specific with the universal; to term his poetry political is indeed to underestimate its power and relevance, for, above all, the fate of the Jew in the Diaspora is for Celan a metaphor for the existential condition of humanity as a whole.

Acutely aware of the chasm dividing individual perception from the generalities of speech, which can convey but a ''darkling splinterecho'' of a distorted, fragmented reality, Celan's poetic voice withdraws into extreme semantic privacy. The metaphor of the ''Sprachgitter'' (*Speech-Grille*)—the title of one poem and the collection in which it stands—is applicable to his poetry as a whole. Representing language as a complex framework which obstructs man's relation to reality, it is also a metaphor for the net of words and associations with which we attempt to capture that reality. Such paradox is central to Celan's art. As the bars of the grille delimit and connect empty spaces, so Celan used language to circumscribe the silent interstices between words. He was constantly preoccupied with the poem's precarious, marginal existence ''on the verge of falling silent.'' However, his poetry remains essentially dialogic (between man and woman, man and God, life and death—the situation is rarely fully defined), and this communicative quality constitutes a dimension of hope.

Celan's work does not allow for easy division into ''phases'': from the flowing rhythms and surrealistic imagery of *Mohn und Gedächtnis* it developed steadily towards increasing concentration

211

and fragmentation, while continuing to draw and elaborate on a wide range of recurring metaphors and highly expressive neologisms, and making intricate use of repetition, allusion, antithesis, and paradox. The same features mark Celan's prose poem "Gespräch im Gebirg" [Conversation in the Mountains] (in *Neue Rundschau*, 71[2], 1960), which directly complements his theoretical discussion of his art in *Der Meridian* [Meridian].

—Andrea C. Cervi

See the essay on "Death Fugue."

CÉLINE, Louis-Ferdinand

Born: Louis-Ferdinand Destouches in Courbevoie, France, 27 May 1894. Adopted the pseudonym Céline. **Education:** Educated at a school in Paris; Diepholz Volksschule in Germany, 1908; a school in Rochester, Kent, 1909; Rennes Medical School, 1919–24, qualified as doctor 1924. **Military Service:** Served in the French cavalry, 1912–15: sergeant; military medal; worked in French passport office, London, 1915; worked as ship's doctor, 1939–40. **Family:** Married 1) Suzanne Nebout in 1915 (marriage never registered); 2) Edith Follet in 1919 (divorced 1926), one daughter; 3) Lucette Almanzoe in 1943. **Career:** Worked as a clerk in a silk shop, an errand boy in Paris and Nice, and for a goldsmith while studying for his baccalauréat; Trader for a French forestry company, West Africa, 1917; practising doctor: in Rennes, then with League of Nations, 1925–28; in Clichy, 1928–38; in Bezons 1940–44, Germany, 1944–45, and Denmark, 1945; imprisoned in Denmark, 1945–47; returned to France in 1950: found guilty of collaboration with Germany during World War II, and sentenced to one year in prison: pardoned in 1951; then lived in Meudon, near Paris. **Awards:** Prix Renaudot, 1933. **Died:** 1 July 1961.

PUBLICATIONS

Collections

Oeuvres complètes, edited by Henri Godard. 2 vols., 1962–74.
Oeuvres, edited by Jean Ducourneau. 5 vols., 1966–69.
Oeuvres, edited by Frédéric Vitoux. 1981–.

Fiction

Voyage au bout de la nuit. 1932; revised edition, 1952; as *Journey to the End of the Night*, translated by John H.P. Marks, 1934, revised edition, 1983; also translated by Ralph Manheim, 1988.
Mort à crédit. 1936; as *Death on the Installment Plan*, translated by John H.P. Marks, 1938; also translated by Ralph Manheim, 1966; as *Death on Credit*, translated by Manheim, 1989.
Guignol's Band. 1944; translated as *Guignol's Band*, translated by Bernard Frechtman and Jack T. Nile, 1954.
Féerie pour une autre fois. 1952; edited by Henri Godard, 1985.
Normance, 1954.
D'un château à l'autre. 1957; as *Castle to Castle*, translated by Ralph Manheim, 1968; also translated by Ralph Manheim, 1997.
Nord. 1960; as *North*, translated by Ralph Manheim, 1972.

Le Pont de Londres. 1964; as *London Bridge: Guignol's Band II*, translated by Dominic Di Bernardi, 1995.
Rigodon. 1969; as *Rigodon*, translated by Ralph Manheim, 1974.
Maudits soupirs pour une autre fois, edited by Henri Godard. 1986.
Cannon Fodder, translated by K. De Coninck and B. Childish. 1988.

Plays

L'Eglise. 1933.
Ballets, sans musique, sans personne, sans rien (includes *La Naissance d'une fée* and *Voyou Paul, Pauvre Virginie*). 1959; as *Ballets without Music, without Dancers, without Anything*, translated by Thomas and Carol Christensen, 1999.
Progrès. 1978.

Other

La Quinine en therapeutique. 1925.
Mea Culpa, suivi de La Vie et l'oeuvre de Semmelweis. 1936; as *Mea Culpa and the Life and Work of Semmelweis*, translated by Robert A. Parker, 1937.
Bagatelles pour un massacre. 1937.
L'École des cadavres. 1938.
Les Beaux Draps. 1941.
A l'agité du bocal. 1948.
Foudres et flèches. 1948.
Casse-pipe: suivi du Carnet du Cuirassier Detouches. 1949.
Scandale aux abysses. 1950.
Entretiens avec le Professor Y. 1955; as *Conversations with Professor Y* (bilingual edition), translated by Stanford Luce, 1986.
Céline et l'actualité littéraire 1932–1957 and *1957–1961*, edited by Jean-Pierre Dauphin and Henri Godard. 2 vols., 1976.
Cahiers. 1976–.
Semmelweis et autres écrits médicaux, edited by Jean-Pierre Dauphin and Henri Godard. 1977.
Lettres et premier écrits d'Afrique (1916–1917), edited by Jean-Pierre Dauphin. 1978.
Lettres à des amies, edited by Colin W. Nettelbeck. 1979.
Lettres à Albert Paraz, 1947–1957, edited by Jean-Paul Louis, 1980.
Chansons, edited by Frédéric Monnier. 1981.
Lettres à son avocat: 118 lettres inédites à maître Albert Naud, edited by Frédéric Monnier. 1984.
Lettres à Tixier: 44 lettres inédites à maître Tixier-Vignancourt, edited by Frédéric Monnier. 1985.
Lettres à Joseph Garcin (1929–1938), edited by Pierre Lainé. 1987.
Lettres à N.R.F: 1931–1961, edited by Pascal Fouché. 1991.
Lettres à Marie Bell Céline, edited by Jean Paul Louis. 1991.
Céline et les éditions Denoël 1932–48: Correspondances et documents, edited by Pierre-Edmond Robert. 1991.

*

Bibliography: *Essai de bibliographie des études en langue française consacrées à Louis-Ferdinand Céline*, 1977; *A Half-Century of Céline: An Annotated Bibliography, 1932–1982* by Stanford Luce, 1983.

Critical Studies: *The Crippled Giant: A Literary Relationship with Louis-Ferdinand Céline* by Milton Hindus, 1950, revised edition, 1986; *Céline* by David Hayman, 1965; *Céline and His Vision*, 1967, and *Voyeur Voyant: A Portrait of L.-F. Céline*, 1971, both by Erika

Ostrovsky; *Céline: The Novel as Delirium* by Allen Thiher, 1972; *Céline, Man of Hate* by Bettina L. Knapp, 1974; *Céline* by Patrick McCarthy, 1975; *Louis-Ferdinand Céline* by David O'Connell, 1976; *Louis-Ferdinand Céline* by Merlin Thomas, 1979; *Understanding Céline* by James Flynn and C.K. Mertz, 1984; *Céline and His Critics* edited by Stanford Luce, 1986; *Céline's Imaginative Space* by Jane Carson, 1987; *The Golden Age of Louis-Ferdinand Céline* by Nicholas Hewitt, 1987; *Language and Narration in Céline's Writings: The Challenge of Disorder* by Ian Noble, 1987; *Enfin Céline vint: A Contextualist Reading of Journey to the End of the Night and Death on the Installment Plan* by Wayne Burns, 1988; *Louis-Ferdinand Céline: Journey to the End of the Night* by John Sturrock, 1990; *Louis-Ferdinand Céline: The I of the Storm* by Charles Krance, 1992; *Understanding Céline* by Philip Solomon, 1992; *Céline and the Politics of Difference*, edited by Rosemarie Scullion, Philip H. Solomon, and Thomas C. Spear, 1995; *The Life of Céline: A Critical Biography* by Nicholas Hewitt, 1999; *Céline, Gadda, Beckett: Experimental Writings of the 1930s* by Norma Bouchard, 2000.

*   *   *

Louis-Ferdinand Céline emerged as a great writer in 1932 with his first novel, *Voyage au bout de la nuit* (*Journey to the End of the Night*). Although the early pages, which depict the carnage of World War I and hallucinatory journeys to Africa and America, are more brilliant and were responsible for the book's immediate success, the second half of the book may be of greater significance. The doctor-hero, Bardamu, undertakes a quest to understand and absorb the suffering of modern life, which allows Céline to demonstrate not merely the collapse of traditional values but the inadequacy of traditional fiction with its reliance on plot, rounded characters, and familiar language.

So in *Mort à crédit* (*Death on Credit*) he dismembers his sentences and introduces a tide of Parisian slang that is meant more as a lyrical than as a realistic device. This novel reverses the conventional view of childhood in order to depict the pain the child undergoes as he awakens to his surroundings, and the broken rhythms, the slang, and the obscenity permit Céline to render the child's world with great immediacy.

Obsessed with his own nightmares and convinced that another world war was imminent, Céline then wrote his pamphlets *Bagatelles pour un massacre* [Bagatelles for a Massacre] and *L'École des cadavres* [School for Corpses]. Although their message is appalling, they are an integral part of his work and cannot be ignored. The solution to Hitler's threat is, Céline maintains, appeasement and the author of all the world's evil is the Jew. Whereas evil in Céline's novels is not so easily explained away, for it is inherent in the human condition, here it is personified in the figure of the Jew. During the Occupation Céline remained in France and continued to publish and, while in no sense a leading collaborator, he certainly helped the cause of anti-Semitism.

For this reason his work was banned at the Liberation, was afterwards long neglected and has only in the last several decades been widely read. His later novels are generally considered to be less good than the early ones, but one of them, *Féerie pour une autre fois* [Fairy-Tale for Another Time], is a fascinating work that is an investigation both of World War II and of artistic creation itself. Céline attempts to incorporate into the novel other arts like painting and film while giving pride of place to the ballet. Art is depicted as

making and unmaking the universe, and its demonic, destructive quality is emphasized, although the role of the ballet-dancer is to restore harmony. In this novel Céline created a multiple work of art that is not governed by a single point of view and invites many different readings.

The only one of his later novels to be appreciated in his lifetime was *D'un château a l'autre* (*Castle to Castle*), a satire of the collaborators and a good example of Céline's black humour. In general Céline was the voice of the 1930s and 1940s who sought to express with a novel intensity the violence of his age. But he was also a consummate artist whose experiments with the language and structure of novels have influenced contemporary writers, both French and foreign.

—Patrick McCarthy

See the essay on *Journey to the End of the Night*.

CENDRARS, Blaise

Born: Frédéric Sauser Hall in La Chaux-de-Fonds, Switzerland, 1 September 1887. Naturalized French citizen, 1916. **Education:** Educated at International School, Naples; Basle Gymnasium; L'École de commerce, Neuchâtel, 1903–04; studied medicine and philosophy, University of Berne, 1908–09. **Military Service:** Served with the French Foreign Legion during World War I; injured in Navarin, right arm amputated, 1916: Order of the Army, Croix de Guerre, and Médaille Militaire, all 1915. **Family:** Married 1) Fela Poznanska in 1914 (divorced), one daughter and two sons; 2) Raymone Duchâteau in 1949. **Career:** Assistant to the film director, Abel Gance, Rome, 1918–20. Worked at a variety of jobs including juggling, prospecting, journalism; producer and director of films in France, Italy, and Hollywood; travelled extensively throughout Africa and South America. Editor, *Les Hommes Nouveaux* and *Paris-Soir;* reporter for several provincial newspapers, including *Le Jour* and *Paris-Soir,* 1934–40. Associated with the early Cubist movement. **Awards:** Grand prix littéraire de la ville de Paris, 1961. **Died:** 21 January 1961.

PUBLICATIONS

Collections

Oeuvres completes [Denoël Edition]. 8 vols., 1960–65.
Selected Writings, edited by Walter Albert, translated by Albert, John Dos Passos, and Scott Bates. 1962.
Poésies complètes 1912–1924. 1967.
Oeuvres complètes. 16 vols., 1968–71.
Selected Poems, translated by Peter Hoida, 1979.

Fiction

La Fin du monde. 1919.
L'Anthologie nègre (folklore). 1921; as *The African Saga,* translated by Margery Bianco, 1927.
La Perle fiévreuse. 1921–22.

L'Or, la merveilleuse histoire du Général Johann August Sutter. 1925; as *Sutter's Gold,* translated by Henry Longan Stuart, 1926; as *Gold: The Marvellous History of General John Augustus Sutter,* translated by Nina Rootes, 1982.

Moravagine. 1926; revised edition, 1956; as *Moravagine,* translated by Alan Brown, 1968.

L'Eubage: Aux antipodes de l'unité 1926; as *At the Antipodes of Unity,* 1922.

Petits contes nègres pour les enfants des Blancs. 1928; as *Little Black Stories for Little White Children,* translated by Margery Bianco, 1929.

Le Plan de l'aiguille. 1929; as *Antarctic Fugue,* translated anonymously, 1948; as *Dan Yack,* translated by Nina Rootes, 1987.

Les Confessions de Dan Yack. 1929; as *Confessions of Dan Yack,* translated by Nina Rootes, 1990.

Rhum, ou l'aventure de Jean Galmot. 1930.

Comment les Blancs sont d'anciens Noirs (stories). 1930.

Carolina (story). 1931.

Vol à voile. 1932.

Histoires vraies (stories). 1937.

La Vie dangereuse (stories). 1938.

D'Oultremer à Indigo (stories). 1940.

Emmène-moi au bout du monde!. . . 1956; as *To the End of the World,* translated by Alan Brown, 1967.

Verse

Les Pâques. 1912; as *Les Pâques à New York,* 1918; as *Easter in New York,* translated by Scott Bates, 1918.

La Prose du Transsibérien et de la petite Jehanne de France. 1913; as *The Trans-Siberian,* translated by John Dos Passos, in *Panama; or, the Adventures of My Seven Uncles,* 1931.

Séquences. 1913.

La Guerre au Luxembourg. 1916.

Le Panama; ou, les Aventures de mes sept oncles. 1918; as *Panama: or the Adventures of My Seven Uncles,* translated by John Dos Passos, 1931.

Dix-neuf poèmes élastiques. 1919; edited by Jean-Pierre Goldenstein, 1986.

Sonnets dénaturés. 1923.

Feuilles de route I: Le Formose. 1924; with parts I and II, in *Poésies complètes,* 1944; in *Complete Postcards from the Americas,* translated by Monique Chefdor, 1976.

Kodak. 1924; as *Kodak,* translated by Ron Padgett, 1976; in *Complete Postcards from the Americas,* translated by Monique Chefdor, 1976.

Poésies complètes. 1944; as *Complete Poems,* translated by Ron Padgett, 1992.

Du monde entier au coeur du monde (complete poems). 1957.

Amours. 1961.

Shadow, translated by Marcia Brown, 1996.

Plays

Danse macabre de l'amour. 1912.

La Création du monde (ballet, with Darius Milhaud and Fernand Léger; produced 1923). 1931.

Films sans images (radio plays). 1959.

Screenplays: *La Roue,* 1922; *La Fin du monde,* 1931.

Other

Le Cahier noir, le cahier rouge (lectures). 1906.

Novogorod, la légende de l'or gris et du silence. 1909.

Le Dernier des masques: Rémy de Gourmont. 1910.

Moganni Nameh. 1912.

Profond aujourd'hui. 1917; as *Profound Today,* translated by Harold Loeb, 1922.

J'ai tué. 1918; as *I Have Killed,* translated by Harold Ward, 1919.

Peintres. 1919.

L'A B C du cinéma. 1926.

L'Éloge de la vie dangereuse. 1926.

La Métaphysique du café. 1927.

Une nuit dans la forêt. 1929; as *Night in the Forest,* translated by Margaret Ewing, 1985.

Aujourd'hui. 1931.

Cassandra. 1933.

Panorama de la pègre (articles). 3 vols., 1935.

Hollywood, la Mecque du cinéma. 1936; as *Hollywood: Mecca of the Movies,* translated by Garrett White, 1995.

Chez l'armée anglaise (articles). 1940.

L'Homme foudroyé (autobiography). 1945; as *The Astonished Man,* translated by Nina Rootes, 1970.

La Main coupée (autobiography). 1946; as *Lice,* translated by Nina Rootes, 1973.

Bourlinguer (autobiography). 1948; as *Planus,* translated by Nina Rootes, 1972.

La Banlieue de Paris (on Robert Doisneau's photographs). 1949.

Le Lotissement du ciel, photographs by Robert Doisneau. 1949.

Blaise Cendrars vous parle (interviews with Michel Manoll). 1952.

Le Brésil—Des hommes sont venus, photographs by Jean Manzon. 1952.

Noël aux quatre coins du monde (radio broadcasts). 1953; as *Christmas at the Four Corners of the Earth,* translated by Bertrand Mathieu, 1994.

Trop c'est trop (articles and stories). 1957.

A l'aventure (selection). 1958.

Films sans images: Sarajevo, Gilles de Rais, Le Divin Arétin (radio broadcasts). 1959.

Dites-nous, Monsieur Blaise Cendrars, edited by Hughes Richard. 1969.

Inédits secrets (journals, correspondence, plays), edited by Miriam Cendrars. 1969.

Paris ma ville. 1987.

John Paul Jones; ou, L'Ambition. 1989.

J'écris. Écrivez-moi: Correspondance Blaise Cendrars—Jacques-Henry Lévesque: 1924–1959, edited by Monique Chefdor. 1991.

Modernities and Other Writings (essays), edited by Monique Chefdor, translated by Esther Allen. 1992.

Correspondance, 1934–1979: 45 Ans d'Amitié, introduction by Frédéric-Jacques Temple, 1995.

Translator, *Hors la loi!,* by Alphonso J. Jennings. 1936.

Translator, *Forêt vierge,* by Ferreira de Castro. 1938.

*

Bibliography: *Bibliographie générale de l'oeuvre de Blaise Cendrars* by Hughes Richard, 1965.

Critical Studies: *Blaise Cendrars* by Henry Miller, 1951; *Blaise Cendrars* by Jean Buhler, 1960; *Situation de Blaise Cendrars* by

Jean-Claude Lovey, 1965; *Blaise Cendrars; ou, La Passion de l'écriture* by Yvette Bozon-Scalzitti, 1977; *Cendrars aujourd'hui; présence d'un romancier* edited by Michel Décaudin, 1977; *Au coeur du texte: essai sur Blaise Cendrars* by John Carlo Flückiger, 1977; *Blaise Cendrars: Bilans nègres* by Martin Steins, 1977; *Blaise Cendrars: Discovery and Re-Creation* by Jay Bochner, 1978; *Blaise Cendrars* by Monique Chefdor, 1980; *Blaise Cendrars* by Miriam Cendrars, 1984; *Le Premier Siècle de Cendrars 1887–1987*, 1987, and *Cendrars et l'Homme Foudroyé*, 1989, both edited by Claude LeRoy; *Genèse et dossier d'une polémique: "La Prose du Transsibérien et de la petite Jehanne de France"* by Antoine Sidoti, 1987; *Le Texte cendrarsien* edited by Jacqueline Bernard, 1988; *Blaise Cendrars* by Anne-Marie Jaton, 1991; *La Main de Cendrars*, preface by Miriam Cendrars, 1996; *Blaise Cendrars: Le Désir du Roman, 1920–1930* by Michéle Touret, 1999.

* * *

A fast-moving, exciting novel whose graphic events come gradually to take on a mythic character, *L'Or (Sutter's Gold)* is a work that reflects in fiction many of the factors making up Blaise Cendrars's complex personality, including a tendency to mingle fact and fantasy in an inextricable web. General John Augustus Sutter, based on a historical figure, is Swiss, like Cendrars, and around his life story the novelist weaves a tale of travel, violence, and adventure. This man, "bankrupt, vagabond, thief and swindler," as he is uncompromisingly described, sets out from his village, makes his way through France to Le Havre, whence, on a square-rigged paddle-steamer, he crosses the Atlantic to New York where in 1834 "all the shipwrecked souls from the Old World disembark." Before long Sutter is making his way west, farming in Missouri and then moving eventually on to California where he acquires land and becomes master of a vast domain. All might seem set fair. In 1848, however, gold is discovered on his land, and in the rough and tumble of the gold rush, Sutter finds, not prosperity, but personal ruination. At the end we see the figure of a pathetic old man in his second childhood. Told in short chapters and laconic prose, *Sutter's Gold* captures all the excitement of an epic life that rises from the depths only to fall again, and the novel, which has been translated into many languages, remains Cendrars's most popular work.

Before writing it, Cendrars had had an exciting life which included journeys from his native Switzerland to Russia and to the United States. His period of service in the French Foreign Legion ended with the amputation of his right arm after he had been wounded in the Battle of the Marne in September 1915. Though his education had been cut short, he had, from his childhood on, always been a voracious reader, especially of the French Romantic authors, and he had soon also begun to find expression of his restless and enquiring spirit in the more advanced forms of literature and the other arts. He wrote experimental poetry, and he became particularly involved in the emergence of Cubism. The cinema was another medium that seemed to him to have great potential, and a collection of his film reviews was published in his *L'A B C du cinéma* in 1926. Another interest was jazz, at a time when its lively rhythms and vivid instrumental colour struck European ears as the sort of music that had genuine elemental vigour. A product of this interest was Cendrars's collaboration with Darius Milhaud, one of the group of French avant-garde composers known as "Les Six," on the jazz ballet *La Création du monde*. It was first performed by the Ballets Suédois in Paris in 1923, with its "African" idiom inevitably provoking something of an

outcry. Work of this sort appealed, however, only to a relatively restricted coterie, and Cendrars owes his wider reputation to his prose works.

Sutter's Gold was published in 1925, and *Moravagine*, of which excerpts had been printed half a decade earlier, followed the year after. In it is reflected the Surrealists' passionate curiosity about the nature of insanity. This topic is explored through the investigations carried out by a young psychiatrist on Moravagine, a particularly fascinating patient. Moravagine is an old man who turns out to be the heir to the Hungarian throne. Having been brought up in isolation, he has become excessively inward-looking and consequently developed a morbid sensitivity. Doctor and patient flee from the Swiss sanatorium. Moravagine subsequently becomes a serial killer of women before getting involved in terrorist activity in Moscow at the time of the 1905 uprising then escaping to the New World. *Les Confessions de Dan Yack* (*Confessions of Dan Yack*) also has adventurous journeying as one of its major structures, this time by a playboy from St. Petersburg who goes to the Antarctic, but the second volume of the two in which it was originally published is an exploration of the hero's relationship with his wife who had died some time earlier.

Rhum, l'aventure de Jean Galmot [Rum, Jean Galmot's Adventure] owes something to the style and to the inspiration of *Sutter's Gold*. It is based on a real-life event that Cendrars was invited to report on for the Paris newspaper, *Vu*—the trial of the murderer of Jean Galmot, a *député* for Guiana in the French National Assembly whose rise and fall in exotic surroundings had been as spectacular as that of Sutter.

Cendrars continued to write throughout his life, producing film criticism and a book on Hollywood as well as novels and verse. In the first year of World War II he was attached as a war correspondent to the British Headquarters in France, publishing a collection of his newspaper articles in *Chez l'armée anglaise* [With the British Army] in 1940. Cendrars also wrote a number of autobiographical books, the exact veracity of which has been increasingly questioned by critics who are now more inclined to see them either as exercises in mystification or as quasi-fictional works.

—Christopher Smith

CERNUDA (Y BIDÓN), Luis

Born: Seville, Spain, 21 September 1902. **Education:** Educated at school in Seville, 1914–18; University of Seville, 1919–25, degree in law 1925. **Military Service:** Served in 1923. **Career:** Lecturer in Spanish literature, Ècole Normale, Toulouse, 1928–29; worked in bookshop, Madrid, 1929; contributor to *Heraldo de Madrid*, 1933–34; worked for the government Misiones Pedagógicas, 1934; secretary to Spanish ambassador in Paris, 1936; returned to Madrid, 1936, and wrote for several newspapers; Spanish assistant, Cranleigh School, Surrey, England, and gave pro-Republican lectures, 1938; reader in Spanish, Glasgow University, 1939–43, Cambridge University, 1943–45; lecturer, Instituto Español, London, 1945; professor of Spanish, Mount Holyoke College, Massachusetts, 1947–52; moved to Mexico, 1952; professor of Spanish, Autonomous University of Mexico, Mexico City, 1954–60; visiting professor, University of California, Los Angeles, and San Francisco State College, 1960–62. **Died:** 5 November 1963.

PUBLICATIONS

Collections

Poesía, edited by A.E. Kins and D. Morris. 1971.
Poesía completa, edited by Derek Harris and Luis Maristany. 1974; revised edition, 1977.
Prosa completa, edited by Derek Harris and Luis Maristany. 1975.
Obra Completa, 1993.

Verse

Perfil del aire. 1927.
La invitación a la poesía. 1933.
Donde habite el olvido. 1934.
El joven marino. 1936.
La realidad y el deseo. 1936; revised editions, 1940, 1958, 1964; edited by Miguel Flys, 1982.
Ocnos (prose poems). 1942; revised and enlarged editions, 1949, 1963; edited by D. Musacchio, 1977.
Las nubes. 1943; edited by Luis Antonio de Villena, with *Desolación de la quimera*, 1984.
Como quien espera el alba. 1947.
Poemas para un cuerpo. 1957.
Díptico español (1960–1961). 1961.
Desolación de la quimera. 1962; edited by Luis Antonio de Villena, with *Las nubes*, 1984.
Antología poética, edited by P.L. Ávila. 1966; also edited by César López, 1996.
Antología poética, edited by Rafael Santos Torroella. 1970.
Eglogà, edited by Gregorio Prieto. 1970.
Perfil del aire; Con otras obras olvidadas e inéditas, edited by Derek Harris. 1971.
The Poetry of Luis Cernuda, edited by Anthony Edkins and Derek Harris. 1971.
Invitación a la poesía de Luis Cernuda, edited by Carlos Peregrin Otero. 1975.
Antología poética, edited by Philip W. Silver. 1975.
Selected Poems, translated by Reginald Gibbons. 1977.
El exilio en la poesía de Luis Cernuda (selection), edited by Douglas Barnette. 1984.
Sonetos clásicos sevillanos. 1986.
The Young Sailor and Other Poems, translated by Rick Lipinski. 1987.
Luis Cernuda para niños. 1992.
Un río, un amor; Los placeres prohibidos, edited by Derek Harris, 1999.

Fiction

Tres narraciones. 1948.

Other

Variaciones sobre tema mexicano. 1952.
Estudios sobre poesía española contemporánea. 1957.
El pensamiento poético en la lírica inglesa (siglo XIX). 1958.
Poesía y literatura. 2 vols., 1960–64; in one volume, 1971.
Crítica, ensayos y evocaciones, edited by Luis Maristany. 1970.
Cartas a Eugenio de Andrade, edited by Ángel Crespo. 1979.
Epistolario inédito. 1981.

La familia interrumpida; Juegos de memoria y olvido por Octavio Paz. 1988.
Translator, *Poemas*, by Friedrich Hölderlin. 1942; revised edition, 1974.
Translator, *Troilo y Cresida*, by Shakespeare. 1953.

*

Critical Studies: *Cuadrivio* (on Darío, López Velarde, Pessoa, Cernuda) by Octavio Paz, 1965; *Et in Arcadia Ego: A Study of the Poetry of Luis Cernuda*, 1966, and *De la mano de Cernuda*, 1989, both by Philip W. Silver; *Other Voices: A Study of the Late Poetry of Luis Cernuda* by J. Alexander Coleman, 1969; *A Generation of Spanish Poets 1920–1936* by Cyril Brian Morris, 1969; *El periodo sevillano de Luis Cernuda*, 1971, and *El surrealismo en la poesía de Luis Cernuda*, 1976, both by J.E. Capote Benot; *La poesía de Luis Cernuda: Estudio cuantitativo del léxico de La realidad y el deseo* by J.A. Bellón Cazabán, 1973; *Luis Cernuda: A Study of the Poetry* by Derek Harris, 1973, and *Luis Cernuda* (in Spanish) edited by Harris, 1977; *La poética de Luis Cernuda* by Agustín Delgado, 1975; *Luis Cernuda y su obra poética*, 1975, and *Luis Cernuda y la generación del 27*, 1983, both by C. Real Ramos; *El espacio y las máscaras: Introducción a la lectura de Luis Cernuda* by Jenaro Talens, 1975; *Luis Cernuda* edited by Gil de Biedma and others, 1977; *Luis Cernuda* (in English) by Salvador Jiménez-Fajardo, 1978, and *The Word as Mirror: Critical Essays on the Poetry of Luis Cernuda* edited by Jiménez-Fajardo, 1989; *Arte, amor y otras soledades en Luis Cernuda* by Carlos Ruiz Silva, 1979; *Españoles en la Gran Bretaña: Luis Cernuda: El hombre y sus temas* by Rafael Martínez Nadal, 1983; *Cernuda y el poema en prosa*, 1984, and *La prosa narrativa de Luis Cernuda*, both by James Valender, 1984; *En torno a la poesía de Luis Cernuda* by Richard K. Curry, 1985; *Luis Cernuda: Escritura cuerpo y deseo* by Manuel Ulacia, 1986; *Luis Cernuda and the Modern English Poets* by Brian Hughes, 1988; *Los finales poemáticos en la obra de Luis Cernuda* by Hilda Pato, 1988; *The Poetry of Luis Cernuda: Order in a World of Chaos* by Neil C. McKinlay, 1999; *Art, Gender, and Sexuality: New Readings of Cernuda's Later Poetry* by Philip Martin-Clark, 2000.

* * *

Luis Cernuda was a member of that brilliant group of Spanish poets known as the Generation of 1927, which included such major poets as Federico García Lorca, Jorge Guillén, Pedro Salinas, Gerardo Diego, and Rafael Alberti. Not until the decade of the 1960s did Cernuda achieve his just recognition as one of the most original and profound poets of 20th-century Spain. With exemplary versatility, depth, and poetic skill he explored a number of poetic techniques from the romantic to the surrealistic. Thematically, Cernuda's is a poetry of continuous tension, grounded in his desperate attempt to escape the conflicts between reality and desire, appearances and truth. He sought to escape an alienating and hostile world in the dream of some transcendent existence which would unify self and world. *La realidad y el deseo* [Reality and Desire] became the title of his collected work, and has continued to influence the generations of Spanish poets that followed him.

The first book of poetry by Cernuda was entitled *Perfil del aire* [Profile of the Air]. In an impressionistic and melancholy work, the young poet seeks to fuse his personal experience and the surrounding environment. Recreating the memories of his childhood, he retreats to a hidden garden symbolic of Paradise and escapes the threatening world of objective reality. This first collection is reminiscent of the impressionistic techniques of Juan Ramón Jiménez and the refined Romantic verse of Gustavo Adolfo Bécquer, and the classical forms and elegance recall the poetry of Jorge Guillén. The theme of the artist isolated in a lost Paradise continues in "Égloga, elegía, oda" [Eclogue, Elegy, Ode], with its extended verse and classical form.

Cernuda himself later repudiated what he felt to be the artificiality and imitative beauty of these early volumes, and with "Un río, un amor" [A River, a Love] embraced the techniques of surrealism, which offered a new freedom in its use of free association to explore the subconscious. This collection initiates the perception of the vital conflict between reality and desire, an opposition which evolves into the dominant force in the poetry of Cernuda. The persona of the poems is hurled into a fractured and alien world of tearless sorrow, pits of snakes, thorns, and ashes—pain upon pain. The poem "As the Wind" portrays the weary speaker abandoned, as the reality of love becomes the threat of death:

> As the wind throughout the night
> Love in torment or lonely body,
> Knocks in rain against the glass,
> Abandons corners, sobbing.

> (translated by Anthony Edkins)

"Los placeres prohibidos" [Forbidden Pleasures] continues the theme of rejection and, in a number of poems, the surrealistic technique. The defence of erotic desire as a part of the self implies an increasingly apparent ethical concern on the part of the poet. As the eroticism of the verse intensifies, so does the indictment of a blind and repressive society paralysed in the false dichotomy of good versus evil. Surrealism not only liberated Cernuda's poetics; it also encouraged a more intellectualized response to his feelings. Because the poet finds the knowledge of self in memory, a bond is created between image and memory.

Donde habite el olvido [Where Oblivion Dwells], whose title is taken from Bécquer, moves from surrealism to the dark images of romanticism and its idea of an Edenic private world created by the dual attraction of love and death. While the verse is calmer and more measured, the reader encounters a cold scepticism and disillusionment as Cernuda reflects on the adolescent years. The private dream has become a spiritual wasteland, and desire becomes suffering. With this collection, Cernuda enters a more meditative phase. Seeking knowledge of himself by confronting reality, he discovers solitude and alienation as the truth of the human condition. If love can lead only to destruction and pain, then the only exit leads to oblivion and insensibility:

> Where oblivion dwells
> In vast gardens without a dawn;
> Where I shall only be
> The memory of a stone. . .

> (translated by Anthony Edkins)

Acute consciousness of the vocation of the poet is apparent in the poems of "Invocaciones" which Cernuda began in 1935 and which were later included in *La realidad y el deseo*. While it is somewhat more hopeful than the verse of *Donde habite el olvido*, the themes of evasion, isolation, and solitude dominate the work.

The title of Cernuda's masterpiece, *La realidad y el deseo*, is an encapsulation of his experience, poetry, and philosophy of life. The work ultimately was to include 11 separate editions under the same title. From its inception, the verse of Cernuda merged an erotic awareness with the essence of poetry. The struggle to acknowledge his homosexuality and to identify its relationship with his poetry was arduous and painful. In the later poetry this becomes the defence of his own identity and an attempt to unify self and world. Yet, as Derek Harris observes in *Luis Cernuda: A Study of the Poetry* (1973), this vital existential question of Cernuda's homosexuality creates a metaphor for the alienation of the human condition, for "he was not a homosexual poet, but a homosexual *and* a poet."

The tone of the elegiac form of *Las nubes* [The Clouds] is distant and aloof. This verse represents the mature poetry of Cernuda, with the appearance of autodialogue and monologue. Poems like "Elegía española" [Spanish Elegy] and "A un poeta muerto" [To a Poet Dead]—dedicated to the assassinated poet Federico García Lorca— lament the destruction of the values, vitality, and spirit of Mother Spain by her sons. Spain as a social and political entity is a new theme, although Cernuda does not address the horrible reality of the Civil War directly. In one of the most acclaimed of the poems, "La adoración de los Magos" [The Adoration of the Magi], the Wise Men find the God for whom they are sent, but cannot recognize him. "They sought a new god, and some say they found him/I rarely saw men. I have never seen any gods." Man is estranged from any idea of God or gods. Some of Cernuda's finest poetry appears in this collection, which reveals a compelling artistry in the complexity of its images, metaphors, and symbols.

In another work of this period *Como quien espera el alba* [Like Someone Waiting for the Dawn], Cernuda continues to seek both engagement with the world and the discovery of his identity in the essence of his poetry. Such poems as "La familia" [The Family] and "Las ruinas" [The Ruins] give voice to his alienation and defiance. "Noche del hombre y su demonio" [A Man's Night with His Demons] finds the poet alone in tormented dialectic with the demonic, as the demon tempts him with the idea of social acceptance and attacks the illusion that there is immortality in art. The commitment of the poet to the meaning and authenticity of his verse holds firm as the poem ends in sad resignation. Death itself is viewed as offering dimensions and a sense to life, as well as providing energy to create and even to love. In the mature verse, Cernuda finds beauty, however transitory, superior to reality, and several of the poems are devoted to the creation of pure lyric.

The next two collections of exile poetry, "Vivir sin estar viviendo" [Living Without Being Alive] and "Con las horas contadas" [With Time Running Out], became part of the 1958 edition of *La realidad y el deseo*. The perception of time as fleeting and escaping becomes more intense, as the preoccupation with self-analysis is reflected in only slightly disguised self-portraits. There is a new acceptance of alienation and suffering as real and inseparable from the eminent calling of the poet. In "Sombra de mí" [Shadow of Myself] the poet suffers, weeps, and desires, but possesses ". . . the shadow/of love which exists in me/While my time is still not run out."

The final work of Cernuda, *Desolación de la quimera* [The Disconsolate Chimera], takes its title from *The Four Quartets* by T.S. Eliot, whom Cernuda greatly admired. It is clearly intended as a final testament of his poetic creed, and his attitudes regarding Spain, art, and beauty—in sum, his life philosophy. A good number of the verses reveal a dark cynicism and anger regarding what he denounces as a spiteful misunderstanding of his personality and work. It is a work of incredible honesty, however, without apology or false humility. Cernuda fuses art and the self, and, in the process of recreating and restructuring reality, art creates its own vision and ultimate reality. With complex imagery and multiple metaphors, Cernuda offers changing and increasing planes of meaning which evoke the universal from personal experience in such celebrated poems as "Luis de Baviera escucha *Lohengrin*" [Ludwig of Bavaria listens to *Lohengrin*].

Cernuda's poetry is the chronicle of a proud and sensitive man's search for individual truth. He sought to flee an alienating and hostile world in a dream of Paradise inspired by his Andalusian youth. The dream of unity somewhere between reality and desire was never fully realized; the existential pain of the confrontation between the poet's experience and his personal desires endured. Finally, he learned to accept the tension of an imperfect reality in the understanding that the poetic and vital struggle itself was the instrument of self-realization. His work reflects a singular dimension of passion, integrity, and ethical dignity in the pursuit of truth and beauty.

—Jerry Phillips Winfield

CERVANTES (SAAVEDRA), Miguel de

Born: Alcalá de Henares, Spain, October 1547. Grew up in Córdoba, Cabra, and Seville. **Education:** Attended the Estudio de la Villa, Madrid, 1567–68, and studied under the Erasmian humanist, López de Hoyos. **Family:** Married Catalina de Salazar y Palacios in 1584; had one daughter by Ana Franca de Rojas. **Career:** Went to Rome in 1569, possibly after a brawl in Madrid; chamberlain to Cardinal Giulio Acquaviva, 1570; enlisted as soldier by 1571; fought with the Spanish fleet at the battle of Lepanto, 1571, sustaining an injury; later, expeditions to Corfu and Navarino, 1572, and to Tunis, 1573, then in garrisons at Palermo, Sardinia, and Naples; was captured by pirates and imprisoned by Turks in Algiers, 1575–80: ransomed, 1580; went on diplomatic mission to Oran, North Africa, 1581; returned to Spain, tax inspector and purchasing agent (excommunicated briefly in 1587 for financial zeal); suffered bankruptcy and two short prison terms (1597 and 1602) for financial irregularities; application for administrative post in America denied; lived mainly in Seville, 1596–1600, and Madrid after c. 1606. **Died:** 23 April 1616.

PUBLICATIONS

Collections

Obras, edited by B.C. Aribau and Francisco Ynduráin. 2 vols., 1846.
Obras completas, edited by J.E. Hartzenbusch and C. Rosell. 1863.
Complete Works, edited by James Fitzmaurice-Kelly. 1901–03.
Obras completas, edited by R. Schevill and A. Benilla y San Martín. 16 vols., 1914–41.
The Portable Cervantes, edited and translated by Samuel Putnam. 1947.
Obras completas, edited by Ángel Valbuena Prat. 10th edition, 1956.
Obras completas, edited by Germán de Argumosa. 2 vols., 1964–65.

Fiction

La Galatea. 1585; edited by Juan Bautista Avalle-Arce, 1987; as *La Galatea*, translated by Gordon W.J. Gyll, 1867.
El ingenioso hidalgo Don Quijote de la Mancha. 2 vols., 1605–15; edited by Francisco Rodríguez Marín, 8 vols., 1911, and by Vicente Gaos, 3 vols., 1987; as *The History of Don Quixote of the Mancha*, translated by Thomas Shelton, 1612; numerous subsequent translations including by Tobias Smollett, 1755, Charles Jarvis, 1883, Samuel Putnam, 1949, J.M. Cohen, 1950, Walter Starkie, 1957, and P.A. Motteux, 1991, Burton Raffel, 1995.
Novelas ejemplares. 1613: edited by F. Rodríguez Marín, 2 vols., 1969, also edited by Juan Bautista Avalle-Arce, 3 vols., 1987; as *Exemplary Novels*, translated in part by James Mabbe, 1640; B.W. Ife and others, 4 vols., 1992; as *Six Exemplary Novels*, translated by Harriet de Onís, 1961; as *Exemplary Stories*, translated by C.A. Jones, 1972, translated by Lesley Lipson, 1998.
Los trabajos de Persiles y Sigismunda. 1617; as *The Travels of Persiles and Sigismunda*, translated by "M.L.," 1619; also translated by Louisa Dorothea Stanley, 1854; as *The Trials of Persiles and Sigismunda*, translated by Celia Richmond Weller and Clark A. Colahan, 1989.
A Dialogue Between Scipio and Bergansa; The Comical History of Rincon and Corlado (in English). 1767.
The Captive's Tale, translated with introduction by Donald P. McCrory, 1994.

Plays

Ocho comedias y ocho entremeses nuevos. 1615; as *Eight Interludes*, translated and edited by Dawn L. Smith, 1996.
La Numancia, El trato de Argel (with *Viage del Parnaso*). 1784; as *El cerco de Numancia*, edited by Robert Marrast, 1984; as *Numantia; The Commerce of Algiers*, translated by Gordon W.J. Gyll, 1870.
Entremeses, edited by Miguel Herrero García. 1945; also edited by Alonso Zamora Vicente, 1979, and by Nicholas Spadaccini, 1985; as *The Interludes*, translated by S. Griswold Morley, 1948, also translated by Edwin Honig, 1964; as *Interludes/Entremeses*, translated by Randall W. Listerman, 1991.
El viejo celosos and El Celoso extremeño, edited by Paul Lewis-Smith, 2001.

Verse

Viaje del Parnaso. 1614; edited by Miguel Herrero García, 1983; as *Journey to Parnassus*, translated by J.Y. Gibson, 1883.
Viaje del Parnaso y poesías varias, edited by Elias L. Rivers. 1991.

*

Bibliography: *Cervantes: A Bibliography* by R.L. Grismer, 1946; *An Analytical and Bibliographical Guide to Criticism on Don Quixote (1790–1893)* by Dana B. Drake and Dominick L. Finello, 1987.

Critical Studies: *Cervantes* by Aubrey F.G. Bell, 1947; *Cervantes in Arcadia* by J.B Trend, 1954; *Don Quixote's Profession* by Mark Van Doren, 1958; *Don Quixote: An Introductory Essay in Psychology* by Salvador de Madariaga, 1961; *Cervantes's Theory of the Novel* by Edward C. Riley, 1962; *Cervantes and the Art of Fiction* by George D. Trotter, 1965; *Cervantes: A Collection of Critical Essays* edited by

L. Nelson, Jr., 1969; *Cervantes: His Life, His Times, His Works* edited by Arnaldo Mondadori, 1970; *Cervantes, The Man and the Genius* by Francisco Navarro y Ledesma, 1973; *Cervantes* by Manuel Durán, 1974; *The Golden Dial: Temporal Configuration in Don Quixote*, 1975, and *A Critical Introduction to Don Quixote*, 1988, both by L.A. Murillo; *Cervantes: A Biography* by William Byron, 1978; *The Romantic Approach to "Don Quixote": A Critical History of the Romantic Tradition in "Quixote" Criticism*, 1978, and *Miguel de Cervantes: Don Quixote*, 1990 both by Anthony Close; *The Individuated Self: Cervantes and the Emergence of the Individual*, 1979, *The Substance of Cervantes*, 1985, and *In the Margins of Cervantes*, 1988, all by John G. Weiger; *Don Quixote in World Literature* by Dana B. Drake, 1980; *Cervantes* by Melveena McKendrick, 1980; *The Unifying Concept: Approaches to the Structure of Cervantes's Comedias* by Edward H. Friedman, 1981; *Cervantes: Pioneer and Plagiarist* by E.T. Aylward, 1982; *Cervantes and the Humanist Vision: A Study of Four Exemplary Novels*, 1982, and *Cervantes and the Mystery of Lawlessness: A Study of El casamiento engañoso y El coloquio de los perros*, 1984, both by Alban K. Forcione; *Don Quixote and the Shelton Translation: A Stylistic Analysis* by Sandra Forbes Gerhard, 1982; *Skeptisism in Cervantes* by Maureen Ihrie, 1982; *The Chivalric World of Don Quixote: Style, Structure and Narrative Technique* by Howard Mancing, 1982: *Madness and Lust: A Psychoanalytical Approach to Don Quixote* by Carroll B. Johnson, 1983; *Beyond Fiction: The Recovery of the Feminine in the Novels of Cervantes* by Ruth El Saffar, 1984; *The Half-Way House of Fiction: Don Quixote and Arthurian Romance* by Edwin Williamson, 1984; *Cervantes* by P.E. Russell, 1985; *Don Quixote* by E.C. Riley, 1986; *Cervantes: Modern Critical Views* edited by Harold Bloom, 1987; *Don Quixote: An Anatomy of Subversive Discourse* by James A. Parr, 1988; *Cervantes the Writer and Painter of Don Quixote* by Helena Percas de Ponseti, 1988; *The Novel According to Cervantes* by Stephen Gilman, 1989; *Cervantes and Ariosto* by Thomas R. Hart, 1989; *Cervantes* by Jean Canavaggio, translated by J.R. Jones, 1990; *The Solitary Journey: Cervantes' Voyage to Parnassus* by Ellen D. Lokos, 1991; *Cervantes and the Burlesque Sonnet* by Adrienne Laskier Martin, 1991; *Allegories of Love: Cervantes's Persiles and Sigismunda* by Diana de Armas Wilson, 1991, and *Quixotic Desire: Psychoanalytic Perspectives on Cervantes*, edited by de Armas Wilson and Ruth Anthony El Soffar, 1993; *Through the Shattering Glass: Cervantes and the Self-Made World* by Nicholas Spadaccini and Jenaro Talens, 1992; *Pastoral Themes and Forms in Cervantes's Fiction* by Dominic Finello, 1994; *Cervantes and the Modernists: The Question of Influence*, edited by Edwin Williamson, 1994; *Refiguring Authority: Reading, Writing, and Rewriting in Cervantes* by E. Michael Gerli, 1995; *Eros and Empire: Politics and Christianity in Don Quixote* by Henry Higuera, 1995; *Grotesque Purgatory: A Study of Cervantes's Don Quixote, Part II* by Henry W. Sullivan, 1996; *Cervantes: Essays on Social and Literary Polemics* by Dominick Finello, 1998; *Don Quixote in England: The Aesthetics of Laughter* by Ronald Paulson, 1998; *Don Quijote Dictionary*, compiled by Tom Lathrop, 1999; *Critical Images: The Canonization of Don Quixote Through Illustrated Editions of the Eighteenth Century* by Rachel Schmidt, 1999; *Cervantes and His Postmodern Constituencies*, edited by Anne J. Cruz and Carroll B. Johnson, 1999; *Meditations on Quixote* by José Ortega y Gasset, translated by Evelyn Rugg and Diego Martín, 2000; *Cervantes and the Comic Mind of His Age* by Anthony Close, 2000; *Adventures in Paradox: Don Quixote and the Western Tradition* by Charles D. Presberg, 2001; *Cervantes' Los trabajos de Persiles y Sigismunda: A Study of Genre* by Maria Alberta Sacchetti, 2001.

* * *

Biographers and critics of Miguel de Cervantes have been no less fascinated by his remarkable life and personality than by the quality of his literary work. Few of our great geniuses have been more stringently treated by luck or fortune, and fewer still have borne life's ill will with greater magnanimity and creative resignation. Cervantes suffered, precisely in the period which for most men offers the opportunity to build a foundation for their future lives, the most arduous fate that might befall a Spaniard of his times: five years of imprisonment and slavery under the Moors in Algeria, from the age of 28 to 33. His heroism as a soldier in the battle of Lepanto and other encounters with the Turks had been rewarded with highly laudatory letters of recommendation. On the basis of these commendations, his captors set a correspondingly high price for his ransom.

When this was finally achieved, and he returned to Spain, he found that his exploits were not to be rewarded with favouritism in the court. He was a valiant but minor hero of battles now forgotten. The wounded veteran, now well into the fourth decade of his life, decided to pursue a literary career and very consciously modelled his early works on currently popular genres. The pastoral novel was enjoying vogue, and his first novel, *La Galatea*, was cast in that mode. Few read the work today, but it was certainly among the best of the Spanish mannerist style and represented fertile possibilities to this new author, who prided himself on his elegant prose style, his gift for dialogue and plot, and his ability as a poet. *La Galatea* was an ample showcase for these talents, and to the end of his life the author promised a continuation of the novel, but it was never written.

Cervantes proved to be an untalented literary businessman. He was never able to make his living by the pen, although most of his works had moderate success for the period, and translations and pirated editions, while they brought him no income, established his name quite firmly in the literary world. He was forced to seek his livelihood with commissions as a tax collector and purchasing agent for the Spanish government. Through bad management or actual misappropriation, he was twice imprisoned—a popular conjecture is that he wrote the early chapters of *El ingenioso hidalgo Don Quijote de la Mancha* (*Don Quixote*) in the infamous dungeons of Seville—and he was briefly excommunicated for expropriating grain from Church stores.

While pursuing such minor bureaucratic and commercial occupations, Cervantes seems never to have stopped writing—poetry, plays, short comedies, some works of prose. Much of his early work is lost, but it is doubtful that it would have added much of value to the Cervantine corpus we have. The writer did not prize very highly the forgotten plays and poetry to which he refers in passing, and he had little success even with those works that were produced. Better dramatic writers than he—especially Lope de Vega—had "run off with the monarchy of the theatre," and his poetry, he admitted ruefully, was never of the highest quality.

Cervantes's talent lay above all in narration, in the novel, a genre which was just achieving solidity and definition at the beginning of the 17th century. He claims in the prologue to his *Novelas ejemplares* (*Exemplary Novels*) that he is the first to "novelize" in Castilian, a boast that is only partly true. The novella was well established in Italy and had been introduced to Spain at least half a century earlier in the form of very short narrative pieces taken from a variety of sources, and Mateo Alemán, his contemporary, had intercalated *novelas* in his picaresque work *Guzmán de Alfarache* (1599). But it is true that

Cervantes brought wholly new dimensions to the form in terms of giving each of the 12 tales autonomy and a much broader development of plot and character.

Don Quixote, which began as a parody of the popular books of chivalry, was his superb creation. The immense body of critical examination and eulogy stresses his perspectivism, his ability to create character, contrast, and believable dialogue; his comprehensive knowledge of his own time and of the currents of the age, and the tone of optimistic good humour and moral clarity that characterizes his treatment of the society of his time. *Don Quixote* is referred to frequently as the first modern novel, and very rightly so. It is the first extensive work of narrative fiction conceived on a grand scale which engages the reader with basic human questions of integrity, folly, social honesty, moralistic delusion, idealism, practical interest, basic concepts of justice, and the strengths and weaknesses of our best resolve. It is certainly the first work of western literature to offer the reader a world view and, as well as telling him an involved and entertaining story, it invites him to think about life and experience in very broad terms.

The first part of *Don Quixote* (1605) had very wide success, but Cervantes had sold his rights to the book for a ridiculously small sum of money. He had begun the promised second part of the novel when a plagiarist published a spurious continuation (1614), probably based on an incomplete manuscript which Cervantes had allowed to circulate in the literary court of Madrid. The real identity of the plagiarist is still unknown, but the apocryphal work, not entirely without merit, is decidedly inferior to the first part of *Don Quixote* or to Cervantes's own continuation (1615). The authentic second part abandons much of the parodic quality with which the novel had begun, to enquire more deeply into the nature of human consciousness, faith in ourselves and beyond ourselves, and the moral perspectives by which we live. Most critics have seen more conceptual depth in the second part, but it is the first which continues to be more widely read and which forms the basis for our English adaptation of the word "quixotic."

Cervantes was a writer totally, perhaps obsessively, committed to his craft, and it is with the urgency of impending death that he completed his last novel, *Los trabajos de Persiles y Sigismunda* (*The Trials of Persiles and Sigismunda*), a rambling account of adventures, separations, reunions, and recognitions, a form rare in Spanish Golden Age literature: the Byzantine novel. He had long planned the work, and had extravagant hopes for its success. Aware that his time was mercilessly short, Cervantes was forced to write the last chapters hurriedly. Perhaps the last strokes of his pen were the lines of the dedicatory prologue to the Count of Lemos, which quotes an ancient poem that begins, "puesto ya el pie en el estribo"—"with one foot already placed in death's stirrup." This last book was not a success either in popular or critical terms, although many later Cervantists have sought to find value in the work.

Cervantes must be read and re-read in his masterpieces, not sought in his minor works, where so many flaws are overwhelmingly evident to the most ingenuous and tolerant eye. These great works are half a dozen of the *Exemplary Novels* and, above all in western literature of the 17th century, the two parts of *Don Quixote*, where the incredible mind of Cervantes lays bare the human soul in all of its possibilities for good, for hope, and for imaginative moral creation.

—James Russell Stamm

See the essay on *Don Quixote*.

CHAMISSO, Adelbert von

Born: Louis Charles Adelaide de Chamisso de Boncourt in Champagne region, France, 3 January 1781. Emigrated with his parents to Prussia to escape the French Revolution in 1790. **Education:** Educated at Berlin University, studied medicine, 1812–13. **Military Service:** Commissioned as ensign in the Prussian army, 1798, lieutenant, 1801, engaged in active service in Hameln 1806; discharged 1808. **Family:** Married Antonie Piaste in 1819 (died 1837); several children. **Career:** Lived in the Hague, Düsseldorf, Würzburg, and Bayreuth, settled in Berlin from 1796; attendant to Queen Friederike Luise, 1796; co-founding member of the liberal literary club Nordsternbund [North Star Alliance], 1803; travelled throughout France and Switzerland, 1806–12; naturalist on Otto von Kotzebue's expedition to the South Seas and to the Northern Pacific, 1815–18; curator, Berlin Museum Botanical Gardens, Berlin 1819; co-editor, with Gustav Schwab, *Deutscher Musenalmanach*, Berlin, 1833–38. **Awards:** Hononary doctorate: University of Berlin, 1819. **Member:** Berlin Academy of Sciences, 1835. **Died:** 21 August 1838.

PUBLICATIONS

Collections

Poetische Werke. 1868.
Aus Chamissos Frühzeit: Ungedruckte Briefe nebst Studien, edited by Ludwig Geiger. 1905.
Sümtliche Werke, edited by Ludwig Geiger. 4 vols., 1907.
Werke, edited by Hermann Tardel. 8 vols., 1907–08.
Werke, edited by Peter Wersig. 1967.
Sämtliche Werke, edited by Jost Perfahl. 2 vols., 1975.

Fiction

Peter Schlemihls wundersame Geschichte, edited by Friedrich de la Motte Fouqué. 1814; revised edition 1827; as "Zauberposse," 1817; as *Peter Schlemihl*, translated by John Bowring, 1823; also translated by Leopold von Löwenstein-Wertheim, 1957; as *The Wonderful History of Peter Schlemihl*, translated by William Howitt, 1843; also translated by Frederic Henry Hedge, 1899, Theodore Bolton, 1923, and Peter Rudland, 1954; as *The Shadowless Man; or, the Wonderful History of Peter Schlemihl*, 1845; as *Peter Schlemiel: The Man Who Sold His Shadow*, translated by Peter Wortsman, 1993.
Erzählungen. 1947.

Verse

Gedichte. 1831.
Zwei Gedichte (ein altes und ein neues): Zum Besten der alten Waschfrau. 1838.
Frauen-Liebe und Leben: Ein Lieder-Cyklus. 1879; as *Women's Love and Life: A Cycle of Song*, translated by Frank V. Macdonald, 1881.
The Castle of Boncourt and Other Poems, translated by Alfred Baskerville, in *German Classics of the Nineteenth and Twentieth Centuries*, vol. 5, 1913.

Plays

Faust. 1803; in *Musenalmanach auf das Jahr 1804*, edited by
Chamisso and Karl August Varnhagen von Ense, 1804; as *Faust:
A Dramatic Sketch*, translated by Henry Phillips, Jr., 1881.
Die Wunderkur (produced 1825).
Der Wunder-Doktor, from a play by Molière. 1828.
Fortunati Glückseckel und Wunschhütlein, edited by E.F. Kossmann.
1895.

Other

*De animalibus quibusdam e classe Vermium Linnaeana in
circumnavigatione terræ auspicate comite N. Romannzoff, duce
Ottone de Kotzebue annis 1815. ad 1818.* 1819.
*Bemerkungen und Ansichten auf einer Entdeckungs-Reise,
unternommen in den Jahren 1815–1818...*, in *Entdeckungsreise
in die Südsee und nach der Berrings-Strasse zur Erforschung
einer nordöstlichen Durchfahrt unternommen in den Jahren
1815–1818*, by Otto von Kotzebue, vol. 3, 1821; as *Remarks and
Opinions of the Naturalist of the Expedition*, translated by H.E.
Lloyd, in *A Voyage of Discovery into the South Sea and Beering's
Straits, for the Purpose of Exploring a North-east Passage,
Undertaken under the Command of the Lieutenant in the Russian
Imperial Navy, Otto von Kotzebue*, 1821.
Cetaceorum maris Kamtschatici imagines, ab Aleutis e ligno fictas.
1825.
*Übersicht der nutzbarsten und der schädlichsten Gewächse, welche
wild oder angebaut in Norddeutschland vorkommen: Nebst
Ansichten von der Pflanzenkunde und dem Pflanzenreiche.* 1827.
*Plantae Ecklonianæ Gentianearum et rosacearum novearum
descriptiones fusiorea.* 1833.
Werke. 6 vols., 1836–39; vols. 5–6 edited by Julius Eduard Hitzig.
*Reise um die Welt mit der Romanzoffischen Entdeckungs Expedition
in den Jahren 1815–1818.* 1836; as *A Voyage Around the World
with the Romanzov Exploring Expedition in the Years 1815–1818
in the Brig Rurik*, edited and translated by Henry Katz, 1986;
translated in part by Robert Fortuine as *The Alaska Diary of
Adelbert von Chamisso Naturalist on the Kotzebue Voyage
1815–1818*, 1986.
*Über die Hawaiische Sprache: Versuch einer Grammatik der Sprache
der Sanwich-Inseln.* 1837.
Leben und Briefe, edited by Julius Eduard Hitzig. 1839; revised
edition, 1842.
*Adelbert von Chamisso und Helmina von Chézy: Bruchstücke ihres
Briefwechsels*, edited by Julius Petersen and Helmuth Rogge.
1923.
Editor, with Karl August Varnhagen von Ense, *Musenalmanach auf
das Jahr 1804* [*1805, 1806*]. 3 vols., 1804–06.
Editor, with Gustav Schwab, *Deutscher Musenalmanach für das Jahr
1833* [*1834, 1835, 1836, 1837, 1838*]. 6 vols, 1833–38.
Editor, with Franz Gaudy, *Deutscher Musenalmanach für das Jahr
1839.* 1839.
Editor and translator, with Franz Gaudy, *Bérangers Lieder*, by Pierre
Jean de Béranger. 1838.

*

Bibliography: *Bibliotheca Schlemihliana: Ein Verzeichnis der
Ausgaben und Übersetzungen des Peter Schlemihl* by Philipp Rath,
1919; *Chamisso als Naturforscher: Eine Bibliographie* by Günther
Schmid, 1942.

Critical Studies: *Chamisso: A Sketch of His Life and Work* by Karl
August Lentzner, 1893; *A Poet Among Explorers: Chamisso in the
South Seas* by Niklaus R. Schweizer, 1973; *Adelbert von Chamisso vu
de France, 1905–1840: Genèse et réception d'une image* by René-
Marc Pille, 1993; *Die Poesie des Fremden: Neue Einblicke in
Adelbert von Chamissos "Peter Schlemihls wundersame Geschichte"*
by Alexandra Hildebrandt, 1998.

* * *

Forced into exile from France by the Revolution, Adelbert von
Chamisso learned German in his teenage years, and fell under the
spell of German Romanticism when he settled in Berlin in the early
years of the 19th century. His verse reflects in various ways the
burden of his cosmopolitan inheritance. Poems set in France include
the "Das Schloss Boncourt" [Boncourt Castle], in which Chamisso
accepts the ruin of his ancestral home and blesses the farmer who now
tills the soil where the family residence once stood; its calm, conciliatory tone is in marked contrast to the impassioned idealism of earlier
Romantics. Many of his poems retell legends that had recently been
collected and anthologized by the Grimm brothers; in these "German
sagas," Chamisso seems more intent on evoking situations with
precision than on creating a nostalgic atmosphere. The emphasis is
often on the pragmatic need to deal honestly and tolerantly with one's
subordinates. Thus the giant's daughter in "Das Riesenspielzeug"
[The Giant's Plaything] is rebuked by her father for treating the
farmer she comes across as a mere toy; here the poet reinterprets the
ancient saga in order to comment on some of the factors that brought
down the aristocracy in France. In "Die Weiber von Winsperg" [The
Wives of Winsperg], Emperor Conrad's advisers try in vain to make
their master retract his generous promise to the women of Winsperg,
and the poem ends with a dark hint that future rulers may turn out to be
less honourable in dealing with their subjects. Sympathy with the
poor and sick is vividly documented in many other works, such as
"Die alte Waschfrau" [The Old Washerwoman] and "Der Invalid im
Irrenhaus" [The Invalid Soldier in the Madhouse].

It was partly Chamisso's lightness of touch that made him more
popular with the reading public of his time than many of his more
literary contemporaries. A wry sense of humour comes through in
many sketches of odd individuals and curious scenes from modern
life. His poem "Das Dampfross" [The Steam Horse] is one of the
earliest to deal with the potential of the railway. But he was especially
interested in psychology, as is evidenced by his sensitive exploration
of feminine aspirations in the cycle *Frauen-Liebe und Leben* (*Women's
Love and Life*). His most harrowing investigation of the inner recesses
of the human mind is found in the narrative poem "Salas y Gomez."
Comparable in some ways to Coleridge's "Rime of the Ancient
Mariner," it relates the experiences, visions, and hallucinations of a
shipwrecked sailor who survives in complete solitude for nearly a
century on a small island in the Pacific. This poem is again no ideal
Romantic vision, but is firmly based on experiences which Chamisso
gained on his journey around the world and constitutes a far from
idyllic counterblast to the myth of Robinson Crusoe.

Chamisso's most celebrated prose narrative is the story *Peter
Schlemihls wundersame Geschichte* (*Peter Schlemihl*), an account of

a man who is persuaded to sell his shadow to a diabolical stranger. In some ways reminiscent of the *Faust* tradition, this story has been read both as an allegory of the artist as a social outcast and as an autobiographical statement by the deracinated poet. Eventually, the hero finds solace in travel and in the contemplation of Nature. Like Schlemihl, but unlike many Romantics whose tormented fantasies expressed frustrated longings for freedom, Chamisso was able to live out a vision of himself as a restless wanderer during his voyage around the world between 1815 and 1818. He showed a particular interest in the negative consequences of European colonization and was fascinated by the uncontacted tribes of the remote Marshall Islands. This journey provided Chamisso with unique insights into the biology, botany, and culture of the Pacific, many of which are recorded in the autobiographical *Reise um die Welt* (*A Voyage Around the World*). Back in Germany, he became increasingly active as a botanist, collecting and classifying more than 2,500 plant species, and eventually obtaining a research post in the Berlin botanical gardens.

Chamisso stands at the threshold between the dreamy world of Romanticism and the empirically determined attitudes that were to gain ground during the 19th century. All poetry, he once remarked, should be based on events that can be retold in the manner of a short story, and his own neatly constructed and clearly focused poems have little in common with the often formless outpourings of his predecessors. He was undoubtedly a victim of prejudice in a society where Germans saw him as French while the French treated him as a German. Protestants and Catholics, democrats and aristocrats viewed him with misgivings, but he survived the petty antagonisms of his contemporaries and gave his name to the Chamisso prize, which is reserved for distinguished non-German authors writing in German.

—Osman Durrani

See the essay on *Peter Schlemihl*.

CHAMOISEAU, Patrick

Born: Fort-de-France, Martinique, 3 December 1953. **Education:** Attended school in Fort-de-France; Attended university in Paris, where he studied sociology and law. **Career:** Trained as an educator, returned to Martinique after completing his studies in Paris, and worked as a journalist and political activist before acheiving success as a writer. **Awards:** Prix Kléber Haedens for *Chronique des sept misères*, 1986; Prix de l'île Maurice for *Chronique des sept misères*, 1986; Grand Prix de la littérature de jeunesse for *Au temps de l'antan*, 1988; Prix Goncourt for *Texaco*, 1992; Grand Prix Carbet de la Caraïbe for *Antan d'enfance*, 1993.

PUBLICATIONS

Fiction

Manman Dio contre la Fée Carabosse. 1981.

Chronique des sept misères. 1986; as *Chronicle of the Seven Sorrows*, by Linda Coverdale, 1999.
Au temps de l'antan. 1988; as *Creole Folktales* [also known as *Strange Words*] translated by Linda Coverdale, 1997.
Solibo Magnifique. 1988; as *Solibo Magnificent*, translated by Rose-Myriam Réjouis and Val Vinokurov, 1998.
Une enfance créole I: Antan d'enfance. 1990; as *Childhood*, translated by Carol Volk, 1999.
Texaco. 1992; as *Texaco*, translated by Linda Coverdale, 1998.
Une enfance créole II: Chemin d'école. 1994; as *School Days*, translated by Linda Coverdale, 1998.
L'esclave vieil homme et le molosse. 1997.
Elmire des sept bonheurs. 1998; as *Seven Dreams of Elmira*, translated by Mark Polzzotti, 1999.
Emerveilles. 1998.
Biblique des dernier gestes. 2001.

Other

Delgres: les Antilles sous Bonaparte. 1981.
Éloge de la créolité. 1989; with Jean Bernabé and Raphaël Confiant; as *In Praise of Creoleness*, translated by M.B. Taleb-Khyar, 1993.
Lettres Créoles, with Raphaël Confiant. 1991.
Martinique. 1991.
Écrire la parole de nuit: la nouvelle littérature antillaise. 1994.
Guyane, traces-mémoires du bagne. 1994.
Écrire en pays dominé. 1997.
Cases des îles Pays-mêlés. 2000.
Métiers créoles: tracées de melancolie. 2001.
Livret des villes du deuxième monde. 2002.

*

Critical Studies: *Decolonizing the Text: Glissantian Readings in Caribbean and African Literatures* by Debra L. Anderson, 1995; *French and West Indian* by Richard D. Burton and Fred Reno, 1995; *Afro Creole: Power, Opposition and Play in the Caribbean* by Richard D. Burton, 1997; *Islands and Exiles: The Creole Identities of Post/colonial Literature* by Chris Bongie, 1998; *Vers un concept de littérature nationale martiniquaise* by Luciano C. Picanco, 2000; *La créolité: espace de création* by Delphine Perret, 2001.

*   *   *

Patrick Chamoiseau's work is most closely identified with the *créolité* movement that had its origins in his native island of Martinique. Proclaimed in the 1989 manifesto *Éloge de la créolité* (*In Praise of Creoleness*), which Chamoiseau co-authored with fellow Martinicans Jean Barnabé and Raphaël Confiant, *créolité* proclaimed the existence and specificity of Caribbean cultures, languages, and experience, and affirmed the need for a literature that both embraced and embodied this specificity. Highly influenced by the writings of Edouard Glissant, *créolité* in general and Chamoiseau's work, in particular, are predicated on the assumption that while Western, and particularly French, culture have contributed to the evolution of

Caribbean/Martinican culture, the two are now distinct and quite often at odds. Moreover, Chamoiseau's texts, in particular, call, sometimes quite openly, for the separation of Martinique from France in order to preserve such specificity.

In many ways, *In Praise of Creoleness* functions as a guide to the rest of Chamoiseau's project. His novels, for example, take up the call by the manifesto to attempt to produce a literature that is truly Creole, that incorporates Creole oral forms, the specific oral history of Martinique, while at the same time reflecting the diverse influences that have formed Martinican culture. To that end, for example, Chamoiseau carefully inscribes the oral storyteller in all of his texts, as well as his own presence as writer, in an effort to consciously point to his own work as a hybrid form that embodies both the written and the oral.

Moreover, there is, in all of Chamoiseau's literary texts, a historical consciousness at work, that seeks quite consciously to create in literature the myths and histories of origin that Martinique lacks, but which are requisite to the formation of any national consciousness. Nowhere is this more apparent than in his third novel, *Texaco*, for which he won the prestigious Prix Goncourt. Texaco is the story of Marie-Sophie Laborieux, the founding mother of the township of Texaco, located on the outskirts of Fort-de-France. It is also, however, a sort of creation myth, or what Chamoiseau has elsewhere called a *myth fondateur* (founding myth) of Martinique itself. This myth is carefully woven through the oral narrative of Marie-Sophie's own life, and that of her father Esternome, whose combined experiences approximate the entire history of Martinique from slavery to departmentalization.

Beyond its mythical function, *Texaco* also embodies all of the other central aspects of Chamoiseau's literary work, such as the interweaving of Creole speech into the narrative, a play with written and oral forms, an exploration of the role of the oral and of storytelling in Martinican culture, a presentation of the various aspects of Martinican society, and an insistence on the need for Martinique to separate itself from the French mainland. All of these aspects can be found, in one form or another, in all of Chamoiseau's novels, including those that are formally autobiographical, such as *Antan d'enfance* (*Childhood*) and *Chemin d'école* (*School Days*).

Chamoiseau's simultaneous affirmation of the specificity of Martinique and of the need for political separation can also be found, sometimes implicitly, sometimes explicitly, in his works of nonfiction. In *Écrire en pays dominé*, for example, there is a fairly clear call for political and cultural separation that is evident even in the title. In *Martinique*, however, a sort of tour guide/introduction to the island that Chamoiseau wrote in 1991, such over political positioning is replaced by a more subtle insistence on Martinique as a *pays* (country) with a unique history, language, and culture.

It must be noted that although Chamoiseau is widely acclaimed, widely translated, and widely read in both French and English, his work is not without controversy. Edouard Glissant, for example, whom Chamoiseau claims as a sort of literary father, has, on occasion, openly distanced himself from the *créolité* movement, criticizing it for essentializing Martinican identity, and thereby replicating the closed logic of Western thought that Glissant himself rejects. Moreover, some literary scholars in both France and the United States have accused Chamoiseau of exoticizing his native Martinique and of creating a stereotyped, commercialized literary product that caters to

that very French culture he criticizes in his work. Despite such critiques, however, Chamoiseau's literary reputation continues to grow, and to those who have read him widely, it is clear that he wrestles with these issues quite openly in his writing, and that he remains true to the project he has set himself, however controversial that project might be.

—Dayna Oscherwitz

CHAR, René (-Émile)

Born: L'Isle-sur-Sorgue, Vaucluse, France, 14 June 1907. **Education:** Educated at Lycée d'Avignon, baccalauréat; École-de-Commerce, Marseilles, 1925. **Military Service:** Served in the French artillery, Nîmes, 1927–28, and Alsace, 1939–40; served during the Resistance in France and North Africa: Médaille de la Résistance; Croix de Guerre. **Family:** Married 1) Georgette Goldstein in 1933 (divorced 1949); 2) Marie-Claude de Saint-Seine in 1987. **Career:** Moved to Paris in 1929 and met Aragon, Éluard, and Breton: associated with the Surrealists during the second period of the movement, 1930–34. Contributor to *Le Surréalisme au service de la Révolution*, 1930. **Awards:** Critics prize (France), 1966. Chevalier, Légion d'honneur. **Member:** Bavarian Academy; honorary member, Modern Language Association (United States). **Died:** 19 February 1988.

PUBLICATIONS

Collection

Selected Poems, edited and translated by Mary Ann Caws and Tina Jolas. 1992.

Verse

Les Cloches sur le coeur, illustrated by Louis Serrière-Renoux. 1928.
Arsenal. 1929; as *De la main à la main*, 1930.
Artine. 1930; enlarged edition, as *Artine et autres poèmes*, 1967.
Ralentir travaux, with André Breton and Paul Éluard. 1930; revised edition, 1989.
Le Tombeau des secrets. 1930.
L'Action de la justice est éteinte. 1931.
Le Marteau sans maître, etchings by Miró. 1934; revised edition with *Moulin premier*, 1945.
Dépendance de l'adieu. 1936.
Placard pour un chemin des écoliers. 1937.
Dehors la nuit est gouvernée. 1938.
Seuls demeurent. 1945.
Premières alluvions. 1946.
Le Poème pulvérisé, illustrated by Braque. 1947.
Fureur et mystère. 1948; revised edition, 1962.
Fête des arbres et du chasseur. 1948.

Les Matinaux. 1950; revised edition, 1964; as *The Dawn Breakers*, edited and translated by Michael Worton, 1990.

Art bref, suivi de Premières alluvions. 1950.

Amitié cachetée. 1951.

La Lettre I du dictionnaire. 1951.

Pourquoi le ciel se voûte-t-il?. 1951.

Quatre fascinants: La Minutieuse. 1951.

D'une sérénité crispée. 1951.

Poèmes. 1951.

La Paroi et la prairie. 1952.

Le Rempart de brindilles. 1952.

Homo poeticus. 1953.

Lettera amorosa. 1953.

Choix de poèmes. 1953.

A la santé du serpent. 1954.

Le Deuil des Nevons. 1954.

Poèmes des deux années 1953–1954, illustrated by Giacometti. 1955.

Chanson des étages. 1955.

La Bibliothèque est en feu, etchings by Braque. 1956.

Les Compagnons duns le jardin. 1956.

Hypnos Waking: Poems and Prose, edited by Jackson Mathews, translated by Mathews, William Carlos Williams, and others. 1956.

Jeanne qu'on brûla verte. 1956.

Pour nous, Rimbaud. 1956.

En trente-trois morceaux. 1956.

L'Abominable Homme des neiges. 1957.

La Bibliothèque est en feu et autres poèmes. 1957.

L'Une et l'autre. 1957.

Épitaphe. 1957.

De moment en moment, engravings by Miró. 1957.

Poèmes et prose choisis. 1957.

Le Poète au sortir des demeures. 1957.

Rengain d'Odin le Roc. 1957.

Élizabeth, petite fille. 1958.

Cinq poésies en hommage à Georges Braque. 1958.

L'Escalier de Flore, illustrated by Braque. 1958.

La Faux relevée. 1959.

Nous avons (prose poem), illustrated by Miró. 1959.

L'Allégresse. 1960.

Anthologie. 1960; revised edition as *Anthologie 1934–1969*, 1970.

Les Dentelles de Montmirail. 1960.

Deux poèmes, with Paul Éluard. 1960.

Éros suspendu. 1960.

Pourquoi la journée vole. 1960.

Le Rebanque. 1960.

L'Inclémence lointaine (selection). 1961.

L'Issue. 1961.

La Montée de la nuit. 1961.

La Parole en archipel. 1962.

Deux poèmes. 1963.

Impressions anciennes. 1964.

Commune présence (anthology). 1964; revised edition, 1978.

L'An 1964. 1964.

L'Âge cassant. 1965.

La Provence, point Oméga. 1965.

Retour amont, illustrated by Giacometti. 1966.

Le Terme épars. 1966.

Les Transparents. 1967.

Dans la pluie giboyeuse. 1968.

Le Chien de coeur. 1969; as *The Dog of Hearts*, translated by Paul Mann, 1973.

Dent prompte, illustrated by Max Ernst. 1969.

L'Effroi la joie. 1971.

Le Nu perdu. 1971.

La Nuit talismanique. 1972; revised edition, 1983.

Le Monde de l'art n'est pas le monde du pardon. 1974.

Contre une maison sèche. 1975.

Aromates chasseurs. 1975.

Faire du chemin avec. . . 1976.

Poems, edited and translated by Mary Ann Caws and Jonathan Griffin. 1976.

Chants de la Balandrame 1975–1977. 1977.

Tous partis!. 1978.

Fenêtres dormantes et porte sur le toit. 1979.

D'Ailleurs. 1981.

Joyeuse. 1981.

La Condamnée. 1982.

Loin de nos cendres. 1982.

Los Voisinages de Van Gogh. 1985.

Le Gisant mis en lumière. 1987.

Éloge d'une soupçonnée. 1988.

Plays

La Conjuration (ballet). 1947.

Claire. 1949.

Le Soleil des eaux. 1951.

Trois coups sous les arbres: Théâtre saisonnier (includes *Sur les hauteurs, L'Abominable Homme des neiges*; *Claire*; *Le Soleil des eaux*; *L'Homme qui marchait dans un rayon de soleil*; *La Conjuration*). 1967.

Other

Moulin premier. 1936.

Feuillets d'Hypnos (war journal). 1946; as *Leaves of Hypnos*, translated by Cid Corman, 1973.

Arrière-histoire de "Poème pulvérisé." 1953.

Recherche de la base et du sommet; Pauvreté et privilège (essays). 1955; revised edition, 1965.

Arthur Rimbaud. 1957.

Le Dernier Couac. 1958.

Sur la poésie. 1958.

Aux riverains de la Sorgue. 1959.

Flux de l'aimant. 1964.

La Postérité du soleil, with Camus. 1965.

L'Endurance de la pensée, with Martin Heidegger. 1968.

L'Egalité des jours heureux. 1970.

Boyan sculpteur. 1971.

Picasso sous les vents étésiens. 1973.

Le Monde de l'art n'est pas le monde du pardon. 1974.

Sur la poésie 1936–1974. 1974.

Oeuvres complètes. 1983.

Correspondance 1935–1970, edited by Jeannine Baude. 1993.

Translator, *Le Bleu de l'aile*, by Tiggie Ghika. 1948.

Translator (into English), *Le Réveil et les orchidées*, by Théodore Roethke. In *Preuves*, 1959.

Translator, with Tina Jolas, *La Planche de vivre: Poésies.* 1981.

*

Bibliography: *Bibliographie des oeuvres de Char de 1928 à 1963* by Pierre André Benoit, 1964.

Critical Studies: *René Char* by Pierre Guerre, 1961; René Char issue of *L'Arc*, 1963; *The Poetry and Poetics of René Char* by Virginia La Charité, 1968; René Char issue of *Liberté*, 1968; René Char issue of *L'Herne*, 1971; *The Presence of René Char*, 1976, and *Char*, 1977, both by Mary Ann Caws; *Worlds Apart: Structural Parallels in the Poetry of Paul Valéry, Saint-John Perse, Benjamin Péret, and René Char* by Elizabeth Jackson, 1976; René Char issue of *World Literature Today*, 1977; *Char: The Myth and the Poem* by James R. Lawler, 1978; *Orien Resurgent. René Char: Poet of Presence* by Mechthild Cranston, 1979; *Lightning: The Poetry of Char* by Nancy Kline Piore, 1981; René Char issue of *Sud*, 1984; *La Poésie de René Char* by Jean-Claude Mathieu, 2 vols., 1984–85; *René Char* (includes bibliography) by Christine Dupouy, 1987; René Char issue of *Europe*, 1988; *René Char: Traces* by Philippe Castellin, 1989; *René Char: faire du chemin avec* by Marie-Claude Billet, 1990; *René Char: Lea Dernières Années* by Michael Bishop, 1990; *René Char* by Eric Marty, 1990; *Lectures de René Char* edited by Paul Smith and Tineke Kingma, 1990; *René Char et ses poèmes* by Paul Veyne, 1991; *Figuring Things: Char, Ponge, and Poetry in the Twentieth Century* edited by Charles D. Minahen, 1994.

* * *

If being is indeed a storehouse of insurgent impulse, as the title of one of René Char's earliest works, *Arsenal*, would seem to imply, the poet's ceaseless task is to stir, channel, and articulate such impulse as unflinching and passionate response to the surrounding world and to one's condition in it. Char's is, from the beginning, a metaphysical vision of "man massacred and yet victorious," of defeat breeding new aspiration, of suffering mysteriously shaping unexpected affirmation. So Char remains the protector of being's "infinite faces," of being at once exultant and weak, ferocious and muted, emphatic and evasive, and the poem, set against the abundant forces of nature, becomes the very birthplace of an ungleaned and myriad truth by which, once again, we may begin to know ourselves and, consequently, gather strength.

The Surrealist movement provided Char with initial models of expression and disclosure, but it was his experience of war, accompanied by a purposeful self-distancing from Surrealism, that determined the more evaluative and succinct nature of his writing. From a self willed event, the poet is forced to turn to the immediate import of external event. From the teeming images upheld in *Le Marteau sans maître* [The Hammer Without a Master] that bespeak a linguistic unfettering of the unconscious, he progresses, through *Dehors la nuit est gouvernée* [Outside the Night Is Governed], to a broader, more universal summoning that embraces the real as a source not only of present oppression and limitation, but also of undying breadth and possibility. "We oppose consciousness of the event to the gratuitous," he declares in his wartime journal included in *Fureur et mystère* [Fury and Mystery], a stunning volume containing some of Char's most powerful and poignant writings. Playful outpouring yields to urgent response; oneiric indulgence is indeed obliterated by the impact of many brutish and unpardonable acts. The expansive majesty of the poem is replaced by dense aphorisms, clustered shards

of reflection that express, in the very face of death and destruction, the enduring desire for a dignified and resistant whole. Through brevity, the poet avoids useless obsession. Through and with his other, wedded at the same time to an earthy locality of place in his native Provence, he comes to a true knowledge of his condition as man and his function as poet.

It is his tremendous regard for the other that allows Char a writing ever practised and diversified beyond the narrow constraints of self. While such figures as Heraclitus and Georges de La Tour, Nietzsche and Heidegger, remain central to his development as a poet and thinker, many are those who touch him and spawn in his work an arterial complexity of connection shunning all boundaries. "Moving, horrible, exquisite earth and heterogeneous human condition seize upon each other and qualify each other mutually," he declares. The poem is the attempted sum of these (inter)relations mingling being and nature, for though the latter, divided within, also prove infinitely warring in their differences without, they remain wondrously bound together as an inexhaustible whole. Thus Char draws, from a language at once shared and intensely private, the revelation of a unity fraught with contradiction, but a unity nevertheless—endlessly emergent, furiously willed. Enlightened by the will of others, dependent in many ways on past and present models of ardent literary and artistic endeavour, he shapes his writing as a coercive act that seeks, not least through violence, ever increased measures of inclusion. So, onwards, from *Les Matinaux* (*The Dawn Breakers*) through, for example, *Le Nu perdu* [The Lost Nude] and *Aromates chasseurs* [Hunting Aromatics] to *Les Voisinages de Van Gogh* [The Vicinities of Van Gogh] and *Éloge d'une soupçonnée* [Praise for a Suspected One], Char imperatively restakes and redefines the shifting ground of our existence, as others have previously viewed it and as many to come, through furious toil, will continue to transform and secure it.

There can be no end to such an effort, no final (re)solution, for living, as Char teaches us, is a constant becoming. From the prehistoric visions of the Lascaux paintings to the fierce fragility of Vincent Van Gogh, from the timeless myth of Orion resurgent to the particular predicament of those caught in war, a vast array of references bear witness to a shared condition that escapes single definition but lies ever-changing around and within us, demanding constant reacquaintance. Thus Char's work encourages less familiarization than pursuit; it does not flatter immediate comprehension but, rather, a searching poised on the threshold of things dawning and passing; it rejects mastery in the hope of ample and passionate exchange. The hunter, a recurrent figure in this poetry, does not seek a mere victim in the hunted but a joining that will fuel new desire. His embrace of the other, as apparent to Char in a Lascaux painting, is also the accepted dissolution of an old self. Each meeting is never one of simple possession but enacts simultaneous degrees of communion and erosion, of tolerance and severance, of triumph and Less. Indeed, from and beyond such an active and indisputable erotic grappling, new appetite and vigour are born.

Chaos and dislocation, though ineradicable, are countered for Char by the promise of an eternal remaking that is ever the gift of being and nature, of being with nature, and it is the exploration of this gift that he obstinately and durably charts for us. His poetry thus remains an opening for desire and hope, its message never simple since it pleads not only for what we have lost and forgotten but for what, through combined and renewed effort, we must yet come to welcome, celebrate, and magnanimously release.

—Michael Brophy

CHATEAUBRIAND, (François-René August), Vicomte de

Born: Saint-Malo, France, 4 September 1768. **Education:** Educated at schools in Saint-Malo and Dol, 1777–81; Collège de Rennes, 1781–83; Collège de Dinan, 1783–84. **Family:** Married Céleste Buisson de la Vigne in 1792. **Career:** Entered the army, 1786; visited America, 1791; served in the Prussian army briefly, 1792; taught French in Beccles and Bungay, Suffolk, 1792–1800; returned to France and joined state service: secretary to Embassy in Rome, 1803; appointed Chargé d'Affaires to Swiss canton of Valais, 1804, but resigned, 1804; appointed Minister of Interior of Government in exile, 1815, and Ambassador to Sweden (not taken up); honorary Minister of State, 1815–16; made Peer of France, 1815, and President of Electoral College of Orleans, 1815; envoy extraordinary to Berlin, 1821; ambassador to London, 1822; attended Congress of Verona, 1822; minister of Foreign Affairs, 1823; ambassador to Rome, 1828. Editor, *Le Mercure*, 1800s. Many women friends, especially Mme Récamier. **Member:** Academie française, 1815. **Died:** 4 July 1848.

PUBLICATIONS

Collections

Oeuvres complètes. 31 vols., 1826–31, and later revised editions.
Oeuvres romanesques et voyages, edited by Maurice Regard. 2 vols., 1969.

Fiction

Atala; ou, Les Amours de deux sauvages dans le désert. 1801; edited by J.M. Gautier, 1973; as *Atala*, translated anonymously, 1825; also translated by James Spence Harry, 1867; Irving Putter, 1952; Walter J. Cobb, 1962; Rayner Heppenstall, 1965.
René; ou, Les Effets des passions. 1802; edited by Armand Weil, 1947, also edited by J.M. Gautier, 1970; as *René: A Tale*, translated anonymously, 1813; also translated by Irving Putter, 1952; Rayner Heppenstall, 1965.
Les Martyrs; ou, Le Triomphe de la religion chrétienne. 1809; original version edited by B. d'Andlau, 1951; as *The Martyrs*, translated by W. Joseph Walter, 1812, revised translation by O.W. Wight, 1859; *The Two Martyrs*, translated by Walter, 1819.
Les Aventures du dernier Abencérage, in *Oeuvres complètes.* 1826; as *Aben-Hamet, the Last of the Abencérages*, translated, 1826; as *The Adventures of the Last of the Abencérages*, translated by H.W. Carter, 1870; as *The Last Abencerage*, translated by Edith M. Nuttall, 1922.
Les Natchez. 1827; edited by G. Chinard, 1932; as *The Natchez*, translated anonymously, 1827.

Other

Essai historique, politique, et moral sur les révolutions anciennes et modernes. 1797; edited by Maurice Regard, 1978.
Le Génie du christianisme; ou, Beautés de la religion chrétienne. 5 vols., 1802; edited by Maurice Regard, 1978; as *The Genius of Christianity*, translated by Charles I. White, 1802; also translated by Rev. E. O'Donnell, 1854; as *The Beauties of Christianity*, 3 vols., translated by Frederic Shoberl, 1813.
Itinéraire de Paris à Jérusalem et de Jérusalem à Paris. 3 vols., 1811; as *Travels in Greece, Palestine, Egypt, and Barbary*, translated by Frederic Shoberl, 2 vols., 1812.
De Buonaparte et des Bourbons. 1814.
Réflexions politiques. 1814; as *Political Reflections*, translated anonymously, 1814.
Mélanges de politique. 2 vols., 1816.
De la monarchie selon la charte. 1816; as *The Monarchy According to the Charter*, translated anonymously, 1816.
Mémoires, lettres, et pièces authentiques touchant la vie et la mort du duc de Berry. 1820.
Maison de France; ou, Recueil de pièces relatives à la légitimité et à la famille royale. 2 vols., 1825.
Voyage en Amerique, Voyage en Italie. 2 vols., 1827; as *Travels in America and Italy*, translated anonymously, 2 vols., 1828.
Mélanges et poésies. 1828.
Études ou discours historiques sur la chute de l'empire romain, la naissance et les progrès du christianisme, et l'invasion des barbares. 4 vols., 1831.
Mémoires sur la captivité de Mme la duchesse de Berry. 1833.
La Vie de Rancé. 1844; edited by Fernand Letessier, 1955.
Les Mémoires d'outre-tombe. 12 vols., 1849–50; edited by Maurice Levaillant and Georges Moulinier, 2 vols., 1951; as *Memoirs*, translated anonymously, 3 vols., 1848; complete version, 1902; selections edited and translated by Robert Baldick, 1961.
Souvenirs d'enfance et de jeunesse. 1874.
Correspondance générale, edited by Louis Thomas. 5 vols., 1912–24.
Le Roman de l'occitanienne et de Chateaubriand (letters). 1925.
Lettres à la comtesse de Castellane. 1927.
Lettres à Mme. Récamier pendant son ambassade à Rome, edited by Emmanuel Beau de Loménie. 1929.
Lettres à Mine Récamier, edited by Maurice Levaillant. 1951.
Mémoires de ma vie: Manuscrit de 1826, edited by J.M. Gautier. 1976.
Correspondance générale, edited by Pierre Riberette. 1977–.
Translator, *Le Paradis perdu*, by Milton. 2 vols., 1836.

*

Bibliography: *Bibliographie de la critique sur François-René de Chateaubriand: 1801–1986* by Pierre H. and Ann Dubé, 1988.

Critical Studies: Société Chateaubriand *Bulletin*, 1930–; *Chateaubriand, Poet, Statesman, and Lover* by André Maurois, 1938; *Chateaubriand: A Biography* by Joan Evans, 1939; *Chateaubriand* by Friedrich Sieburg, translated by Violet M. Macdonald, 1961; *Chateaubriand* by Richard Switzer, 1971; *Chateaubriand: A Biography* by George D. Painter, vol. 1, 1977; *Chateaubriand: Composition, Imagination, and Poetry* by Charles A. Porter, 1978; *Back to the Garden: Chateaubriand, Senancour and Constant* by Michael J. Call, 1988; *Chateaubriand, Atala and René* by Colin Smethurst, 1995; *One Hundred Years of Melancholy* by Naomi Schor, 1996; *Les vanités de Chateaubriand* by Agnès Verlet, 2001.

* * *

Chateaubriand's dozen and a half major works and copious tracts, discourses, and parliamentary opinions appeared during that most political half century beginning with the Revolution and ending with the fall of the July Monarchy. His most original narratives portray the emotions and yearnings of the Romantic self amid historical European landscapes or against the background of the North American wilderness. In his vigorous and wide-ranging polemical writings he argues the Christian and royalist cause with sarcasm and an idealistic vision. His major literary distinction has been as a stylist.

Not all Chateaubriand's narrative writings are frankly autobiographical. The figure of the brooding, proud, aristocratic European in the post-Revolutionary world, partially discernable in the Native American, Chactas of *Atala* and *Les Natchez* (*The Natchez*), appears more clearly as the protagonist of Chateaubriand's best-known story, *René*, confession of a self-exiled Frenchman in the American forest in the early 18th century. The life of the 17th-century Trappist serves in the late *La Vie de Rancé* as the locus of curious digressions about both Chateaubriand and 17th-century France. *Itinéraire de Paris à Jérusalem et de Jérusalem à Paris* (*Travels in Greece, Palestine, Egypt, and Barbary*) is Chateaubriand's first autobiographical book. His most important work, composed and often refashioned over 30 years into the 1840s, is his autobiography, *Les Mémoires d'outre-tombe* (*Memoirs*).

Much of the charm of Chateaubriand's narratives comes from evocative descriptions and the metaphors and complex rhythms of his prose. His descriptions of America in the "Indian" works, and of his childhood Brittany, Rome, the Near East in the autobiographical writings, present a nearly seamless web of memories of earlier travel accounts, his own personal observation, and, no doubt, brilliant invention: scholars will continue to differ over how much of the America he described he ever actually saw. His descriptive prose, characterized by visual detail and suggestive, often exotic names, is arranged in rhythmically ordered sentences and chapters. His polemical writings scan more like oratory; there too nouns and figures of speech focus the meaning. The Château de Chambord, with all its chimneys, is personified in the *La Vie de Rancé* as "une femme dont le vent aurait soufflé en l'air la chevelure" ("a woman with wind-blown hair"); in 1815 in Louis XVIII's antechamber he sees a "vision infernale": Talleyrand supported by Fouché, "le vice appuyé sur le bras du crime" ("vice leaning on the arm of crime").

The force of his narratives stems from their subtle analysis of the difficulties of modern life: how to be both an aristocrat and a leader in the new democratic world, appreciate the beauties of religion in the age of science, live true to one's own sensibilities without shirking one's duties toward others. Unfortunately the autobiography—though not the autobiographical fictions—is weakened by Chateaubriand's determination to hide almost everything intimate, including his many passionate liaisons. The strength of the polemical writings lies in their juxtaposition of noble themes—fidelity, honor, national pride—with a quick, savage denunciation of posturing and opportunism.

Abundance characterizes his rhetoric; his writing displays ease and vigour in invention, high colour, passion and sentiment. Admiration, anger, scorn, enthusiasm animate sometimes flowing, sometimes cadenced and elaborate prose. The criticism though often harsh is never mean, the praise though sentimental is grand, and the ever-present portrait of the self is pompous, often insincere, indiscreetly long—and lucid, probing, subtle, and finally very moving.

—Charles A. Porter

See the essays on *Memoirs* and *René*.

CHEKHOV, Anton (Pavlovich)

Born: Taganrog, Russia, 17 January 1860. **Education:** Educated at a school for Greek boys, Taganrog, 1867–68; Taganrog grammar school, 1868–79; Moscow University Medical School, 1879–84, graduated as doctor, 1884. **Family:** Married the actress Olga Knipper in 1901. **Career:** Practising doctor in Moscow, 1884–92, Melikhovo, 1892–99, and in Yalta after 1899. Freelance writer while still in medical school, especially for humorous magazines, and later for serious ones; travelled to Sakhalin Island, 1890; suffered severe haemorrhage of the lungs, 1897. **Awards:** Pushkin prize, 1888. **Member:** Imperial Academy of Sciences, 1900 (resigned 1902). **Died:** 2 July 1904.

PUBLICATIONS

Collections

Plays, translated by Marian Fell. 1912.
Plays, translated by Julius West. 1916.
The Cherry Orchard and Other Plays, translated by Constance Garnett. 1923.
Plays, translated by Constance Garnett. 1929; retitled *Nine Plays*, 1946.
Polnoe sobranie sochinenii i pisem [Complete Works and Letters], edited by S.D. Balukhatyi and others. 20 vols., 1944–51; new edition in 30 vols., 1974–83.
The Brute and Other Farces, translated by Eric Bentley and Theodore Hoffman. 1958.
Plays, translated by Elisaveta Fen. 1959.
Six Plays, translated by Robert Corrigan. 1962.
The Oxford Chekhov, edited and translated by Ronald Hingley. 9 vols., 1964–80; excerpts as *Seven Stories*, 1974; *Eleven Stories*, 1975; *Five Major Plays*, 1977; *The Russian Master and Other Stories*, 1984; *Ward Number Six and Other Stories*, 1988; *A Woman's Kingdom and Other Stories*, 1989, *The Princess and Other Stories*, 1990; *The Steppe and Other Stories*, 1991.
The Major Plays, translated by Ann Dunnigan. 1964.
Ten Early Plays, translated by Alex Szogyi. 1965.
Four Plays, translated by David Magarshack. 1969.
Plays, edited and translated by Eugene K. Bristow. 1977.
The Early Stories 1883–1888, edited and translated by Patrick Miles and Harvey Pitcher. 1982.
Plays, translated by Michael Frayn. 1988.
The Sneeze: Plays and Stories, translated by Michael Frayn. 1989.
Chekhov: The Major Plays, translated by Jean-Claude van Itallie. 1994.
Chekhov's Major Plays: Ivanov, The Seagull, Uncle Vanya, and The Three Sisters, translated by Karl Kramer and Margaret Booker. 1996.

Plays

O vrede tabaka, in *Peterburgskaia gazeta* [Petersburg Gazette]. 1886; several revisions: final version in *Sobranie sochinenii*, 1903; as *On the Harmfulness of Tobacco*, translated by Constance Garnett, in *Plays*, 1935; as *The Harmfulness of Tobacco*, translated by Eric Bentley and Theodore Hoffman, in *The Brute and Other Farces*, 1958; as *Smoking Is Bad for You*, translated by Ronald Hingley, in

The Oxford Chekhov, 1968; as *On the Injurious Effects of Tobacco*, translated by Eugene K. Bristow, in *Plays*, 1977.

Ivanov (produced 1887; revised version, produced 1889). In *P'esy*, 1897; as *Ivanov*, translated by Marian Fell, in *Plays*, 1912; numerous subsequent translations including by Elisaveta Fen, in *Three Plays*, 1951; Robert Corrigan, in *Six Plays of Chekhov*, 1962; Alex Szogyi, in *Ten Early Plays*, 1965; David Magarshack, 1966; Ariadne Nicolaeff, 1966; Ronald Hingley, in *The Oxford Chekhov*, 1967; as *Ivanov: A Play in Four Acts* by David Hare, 1997.

Lebedinaia pesnia (produced 1888). In *P'esy*, 1897; as *Swan Song*, translated by Marian Fell, in *Plays*, 1912; also translated by Theodore Hoffman, in *The Brute and Other Farces*, 1958; Ronald Hingley, in *The Oxford Chekhov*, 1968; Alex Szogyi, in *Ten Early Plays*, 1965.

Medved' (produced 1888). In *Novoe vremia* [New Time], 1888; as *The Bear*, translated by Julius West, in *Plays*, 1916; also translated by Constance Garnett, in *The Cherry Orchard and Other Plays*, 1923; Elisaveta Fen, in *Plays*, 1959; Ronald Hingley, in *The Oxford Chekhov*, 1968; as *The Boor*, 1915; as *The Brute*, translated by Theodore Hoffman, in *The Brute and Other Farces*, 1958.

Leshii (produced 1889). 1890; as *The Wood Demon*, in *Calender of Modern Letters*, 2, 1925–26; also translated by Robert Corrigan, in *Six Plays of Chekhov*, 1962; Ronald Hingley, in *The Oxford Chekhov*, 1964; Alex Szogyi, in *Ten Early Plays*, 1965.

Predlozhenie (produced 1889). 1889; as *A Marriage Proposal*, 1914; also translated by Theodore Hoffman, in *The Brute and Other Farces*, 1958; as *The Proposal*, translated by Julius West, in *Plays*, 1916; also translated by Constance Garnett, in *The Cherry Orchard and Other Plays*, 1923; Elisaveta Fen, in *Plays*, 1959; Ronald Hingley, in *The Oxford Chekhov*, 1968; Alex Szogyi, in *Ten Early Plays*, 1965.

Tragik ponevole (produced 1889). 1890; as *A Tragedian in Spite of Himself*, translated by Julius West, in *Plays*, 1916; as *The Reluctant Tragedian*, translated by Alex Szogyi, in *Ten Early Plays*, 1965; as *A Tragic Role*, translated by Ronald Hingley, in *The Oxford Chekhov*, 1968.

Svad'ba (produced 1900). 1889; as *The Wedding*, translated by Julius West, in *Plays*, 1916; also translated by Constance Garnett, in *Plays*, 1929; Ronald Hingley, in *The Oxford Chekhov*, 1968; Alex Szogyi, in *Ten Early Plays*, 1965; as *A Wedding*, translated by Theodore Hoffman, in *The Brute and Other Farces*, 1958.

Iubilei (produced 1900). 1892; as *The Anniversary*, translated by Julius West, in *Plays*, 1916; also translated by Constance Garnett, in *Plays*, 1929; Ronald Hingley, in *The Oxford Chekhov*, 1968; Alex Szogyi, in *Ten Early Plays*, 1965; as *A Jubilee*, translated by Elisaveta Fen, in *The Seagull and Other Plays*, 1953; as *The Celebration*, translated by Theodore Hoffman, in *The Brute and Other Farces*, 1958.

Chaika (produced 1896). In *P'esy*, 1897; revised version (produced 1898), 1901; as *The Sea Gull*, translated by Marian Fell, in *Plays*, 1912; numerous subsequent translations including by Constance Garnett, in *The Cherry Orchard and Other Plays*, 1923; Stark Young, 1939; Robert Corrigan, in *Six Plays of Chekhov*, 1962; Fred Eisemann, 1965; David Magarshack, in *Four Plays*, 1969; Lawrence Senelick, 1977; Milton Ehre, in *Chekhov for the Stage*, 1992; as *The Seagull*, translated by Elisaveta Fen, in *Plays*, 1959;

also translated by Ronald Hingley, in *The Oxford Chekhov*, 1967; Eugene K. Bristow, in *Plays*, 1977; John-Claude von Italie, 1977; David French, 1978; Tania Alexander and Charles Sturridge, 1986; Michael Frayn, 1986; Pam Gems 1994; Tom Stoppard, 1997.

Diadia Vania (produced 1897). In *P'esy*, 1897; as *Uncle Vanya*, translated by Marian Fell, in *Plays*, 1912; numerous subsequent translations including by Jennie Covan, 1922; Constance Garnett, in *The Cherry Orchard and Other Plays*, 1923; Rose Caylor, 1930; Elisaveta Fen, in *The Seagull and Other Plays*, 1953; Stark Young, 1956; David Magarshack, in *The Storm and Other Russian Plays*, 1960; Robert Corrigan, in *Six Plays of Chekhov*, 1962; Ronald Hingley, in *The Oxford Chekhov*, 1964; Eugene K. Bristow, in *Plays*, 1977; Michael Frayn, 1987; Milton Ehre, in *Chekhov for the Stage*, 1992; as *August: An Adaptation of Chekhov's Uncle Vanya* by Julian Mitchell, 1994; as *Uncle Vanya: A Version of the Play by Anton Chekhov* by Brian Friel, 1998.

Tri sestry (produced 1901). 1901; as *The Three Sisters*, translated by Julius West, in *Plays*, 1916; numerous subsequent translations including by Robert Corrigan, in *Six Plays of Chekhov*, 1962; David Magarshack, in *Four Plays*, 1969; Eugene K. Bristow, in *Plays*, 1977; Milton Ehre, in *Chekhov for the Stage*, 1992; as *Three Sisters*, translated by Constance Garnett, in *Plays*, 1929; Elisaveta Fen, in *Three Plays*, 1951; Ronald Hingley, in *The Oxford Chekhov*, 1964; Randall Jarrell, 1969; Michael Frayn, 1983; Stephen Mulrine, 1994.

Vishnevyi sad (produced 1904). 1904; as *The Cherry Orchard*, translated by M. Mandell, 1908; numerous subsequent translations including by Julius West, in *Plays*, 1916; Constance Garnett, 1923; Jenny Covan, 1923; C.C. Daniels, and G.R. Noyes, in *Masterpieces of the Russian Drama*, edited by Noyes, 1933; Hubert Butler, 1934; S.S. Kotelianskii, 1940; Stark Young, 1947; Elisaveta Fen, in *Three Plays*, 1951; Ronald Hingley, in *The Oxford Chekhov*, 1964; Tyrone Guthrie and Leonis Kipnis, 1965; David Magarshack, in *Four Plays*, 1969; Eugene K. Bristow, in *Plays*, 1977; Laurence Senelick, 1977; Michael Frayn, 1978; Jean-Claude von Italie, 1979; Milton Ehre, in *Chekhov for the Stage*, 1992; adapted by Robert Brustein, translated by George Calderon, 1996; version by Pam Gems, translated by Tania Alexander, 1996; as *The Cherry Orchard: A Comedy*, version by Peter Gill, translated by Ted Braun, 1995.

Neizdannaia p'esa, edited by N.F. Belchikov. 1923; as *That Worthless Fellow Platonov*, 1930; as *Don Juan (in the Russian Manner)*, translated by Basil Ashmore, 1952; as *Platonov*, translated by David Magarshack, 1964, translated by Ronald Hingley, in *The Oxford Chekhov*, 1967; as *Wild Honey*, translated by Michael Frayn, 1984; also translated by Susan Coyne and Laszlo Marton, 2001.

Tatiana Repina, in *Polnoe sobranie sochinenii i pisem*. 1944–51; as *Tatyana Repin*, translated by S.S. Kotelianskii, in *Literary and Theatrical Reminiscences*, 1927; also translated by Ronald Hingley, in *The Oxford Chekhov*, 1968.

Na bolshoi doroge, in *Polnoe sobranie sochinenii i pisem*. 1944–51; as *On the Highway*, in *Drama*, 22, 1916; as *On the High Road*, translated by Julius West, in *Plays*, 1916; also translated by Constance Garnett, in *Plays*, 1929; Ronald Hingley, in *The Oxford Chekhov*, 1968; Alex Szogyi, in *Ten Early Plays*, 1965.

Fiction

Pestrye rasskazy [Motley Tales]. 1886; revised edition, 1891; in *Motley Tales and a Play*, translated by Constance Garnett and Vlada Chernomordik, 1998.

Vsumerkakh [In the Twilight]. 1887.

Nevinnye rechi [Innocent Tales]. 1887.

Rasskazy [Tales]. 1889.

Khmurye liudi [Gloomy People]. 1890.

Duel [The Duel]. 1892.

Palata No. 6 [Ward No. 6]. 1893.

Tales, translated by Constance Garnett. 13 vols., 1916–22.

The Unknown Chekhov: Stories and Other Writings Hitherto Untranslated, edited by Avrahm Yarmolinsky. 1954.

Early Stories, translated by Nora Gottlieb. 1960.

The Image of Chekhov (selected stories), translated by Robert Payne. 1963.

The Lady with Lapdog and Other Stories, translated by David Magarshack. 1964.

Chuckle with Chekhov: A Selection of Comic Stories, translated by Harvey Pitcher. 1975.

The Kiss and Other Stories, translated by Ronald Wilks. 1982.

The Duel and Other Stories, translated by Ronald Wilks. 1984.

The Party and Other Stories, translated by Ronald Wilks. 1985.

The Black Monk and Other Stories, translated by Alan Sutton. 1985.

The Fiancée and Other Stories, translated by Ronald Wilks. 1986.

Longer Stories from the Last Decade, translated by Constance Garnett. 1994.

Kashtanka, adapted by Ronald Meyer. 1995.

Intrigues: Nine Stories, translated by Peter Constantine. 1997.

The Undiscovered Chekhov: Thirty-eight New Stories, translated by Peter Constantine, 1998.

Other

Ostrov Sakhalin [Sakhalin Island]. 1895; as *The Island: A Journey to Sakhalin*, translated by Luba and Michael Terpak, 1967; as *A Journey to Sakhalin*, translated by Brian Reeve, 1993.

Sobranie sochinenii [Collected Works]. 11 vols., 1899–1906.

Pis'ma [Letters]. 1909; *Sobranie pis'ma*, 1910; *Pis'ma*, 1912–16, and later editions.

Zapisnye knizhki. 1914; as *The Note-Books*, translated by S.S. Kotelianskii and Leonard Woolf, 1921.

Letters to Olga Knipper. 1925.

Literary and Theatrical Reminiscences, edited by S.S. Kotelianskii. 1927.

Personal Papers. 1948.

Selected Letters, edited by Lillian Hellman. 1955.

Anton Chekhov's Life and Thought: Selected Letters and Commentary, edited by Simon Karlinsky, translated by Michael Henry Heim. 1973.

A Life in Letters, edited and translated by Gordon McVay. 1994.

Dear Writer—Dear Actress—: The Love Letters of Olga Knipper and Anton Chekhov, translated and edited by Jean Benedetti, 1996.

*

Bibliography: *Chekhov in English: A List of Works by and about Him* edited by Anna Heifetz and Avrahm Yarmolinsky, 1949; *The Chekhov Centennial: Chekhov in English: A Selective List of Works by and about Him 1949–60* by Rissa Yachnin, 1960; *Anton Chekhov: A Reference Guide to Literature* by K.A. Lantz, 1985; *Chekhov Bibliography: Works in English by and about Anton Chekhov*, 1985, and *Chekhov Criticism: 1880 Through 1986*, 1989, both by Charles W. Meister; *Anton Chekhov Rediscovered: A Collection of New Studies with a Comprehensive Bibliography* edited by Savely Senderovich and Munir Sendich, 1987.

Critical Studies: *Anton Chehov: A Critical Study* by William Gerhardie, 1923, revised edition, 1972; *Chekhov: A Biographical and Critical Study*, 1950, revised edition, 1966, and *A New Life of Anton Chekhov*, 1976, both by Ronald Hingley; *Chekhov: A Life*, 1953, *Chekhov the Dramatist*, 1960, and *The Real Chekhov: An Introduction to Chekhov's Last Plays*, 1972, all by David Magarshack; *Anton Chekhov* by Walter Horace Bruford, 1957; *Tchekov, the Man* by Beatrice Saunders, 1960; *Chekhov: A Biography* by Ernest J. Simmons, 1962; *The Breaking String: The Plays of Anton Chekhov* by Maurice Valency, 1966; *Chekhov and His Prose* by Thomas Winner, 1966; *Chekhov: A Collection of Critical Essays* edited by Robert Louis Jackson, 1967; *Anton Chekhov* by J.B. Priestley, 1970; *Chekhov in Performance: A Commentary on the Major Plays* by J.L. Styan, 1971; *The Chekhov Play: A New Interpretation* by Harvey Pitcher, 1973; *Chekhov: The Evolution of His Art* by Donald Rayfield, 1975; *Chekhov: A Study of the Major Stories and Plays* by Beverly Hahn, 1977; *On the Theory of Descriptive Poetics: Anton Chekhov as Storyteller and Playwright* by Jan van der Eng, 1978; *Chekhov as Viewed by His Russian Literary Contemporaries* by Henry Urbanski, 1979; *Chekhov: A Structuralist Study* by John Tulloch, 1980; *Chekhov's Great Plays: A Critical Anthology* edited by Jean P. Barricelli, 1981; *Chekhov: The Critical Heritage* edited by Victor Emeljanow, 1981; *Anton Chekhov* by Irina Kirk, 1981; *Chekhov and the Vaudeville: A Study of Chekhov's One-Act Plays*, 1982, and *Chekhov in Performance in Russia and Soviet Russia*, 1984, both by Vera Gottlieb; *Chekhov's Art: A Stylistic Analysis* by Peter M. Bitsilli, 1983; *Chekhov's Poetics* by Aleksandr Pavlovich Chudakov, 1983; *Chekhov: A Study of the Four Major Plays* by Richard Peace, 1983; *Chekhov: New Perspectives* edited by René and Nonna D. Wellek, 1984; *A Chekhov Companion* edited by Toby W. Clyman, 1985; *Anton Chekhov* by Laurence Senelick, 1985; *Chekhov* (biography) by Henri Troyat, translated by Michael Henry Heim, 1986; *File on Chekhov* by Nick Worrall, 1986; *Chekhov and Women: Women in the Life and Work of Chekhov* by Carolina de Maegd-Soëp, 1987; *Chekhov on the British Stage, 1909–1987: An Essay in Cultural Exchange* by Patrick Miles, 1987; *Chekhov: The Silent Voice of Freedom* by Valentine Tschebotarioff Bill, 1987; *Chekhov: A Spirit Set Free* by V.S. Pritchett, 1988; *Critical Essays on Anton Chekhov* edited by Thomas A. Eekman, 1989; *Chekhov on the British Stage* edited by Patrick Miles, 1993; *The Cherry Orchard: Catastrophe and Comedy* by Donald Rayfield, 1994; *Time and Temporal Structure in Chekhov* by C.J.G. Turner, 1994; *Chekhov's Plays: An Opening into Eternity* by Richard Gilman, 1995; *Chekhov* by Edward Sanders, 1995; *Chekhov's Uncle Vanya and The Wood Demon* by Donald Rayfield, 1995; *Chekhov's Three Sisters* by Gordon McVay, 1995; *Chekhov and Russian Religious Culture: The Poetics of the Marian Paradigm* by Julie W. de Sherbinin, 1997; *Anton Chekhov: A Life* by Donald Rayfield, 1997; *Chekhov Then and Now: The Reception of Chekhov in World Culture*, edited by J. Douglas Clayton, 1997; *A Systems Approach to Literature: Mythopoetics of Chekhov's Four Major Plays* by Vera Zubarev, 1997; *Chekhov, The Hidden Ground: A Biography* by Philip Callow, 1998; *Understanding Chekhov: A Critical Study of Chekhov's Prose and Drama* by Donald Rayfield,

1999; *Stella Adler on Ibsen, Strindberg, and Chekhov* by Stella Adler, 1999; *Performing Chekhov* by David Allen, 2000.

* * *

The leading exponent of the short story and the drama in modern Russian literature, which is otherwise dominated by poetry and the novel, Anton Chekhov began to write for money while he was a medical student. The majority of his early comic stories are characterized by the muddles and confusions of life. They portray overweening Russian respect for authority and hilarious conflicts between the sexes and the generations, in which the expected "triggers" of social occasions, chance meetings, love entanglements and relatives, children and animals rarely fail to appear. Nevertheless, the best of these stories already illustrate the serious aspects of Chekhov's vision. "The Death of a Clerk" is a reworking of Gogolian menace. "Daughter of Albion," "The Upheaval," and "Spat khochetsia" ("Sleepy") all explore the relationship between master and servant. None of these is actually funny: the first two reveal the humiliation of servants, while the third is an early demonstration of Chekhov's ability to conjure horror out of commonplace situations, as the exhausted girl servant unemotionally smothers her masters' crying baby. Chekhov's medical training, to be evident later in the illnesses that afflict many of his characters, influences his study of adolescence, "Volodia," with its themes of corruption, sexuality, and suicide. In stories such as "The Huntsman," "Happiness," and "The Steppe," Chekhov showed his ability to describe the natural settings and atmosphere of rural Russia, featuring within them episodic moments of communication between man and his world or between men themselves against a background of silence, emptiness, and timelessness.

Later, the comic element in Chekhov ceases to be the framework of an attitude to life and becomes instead the sometimes relieving, always revealing observation, a perception of the continuity of life and of man's remarkable ability to endure it. In the stories of 1888–96 the still young Chekhov captures the loss of momentum in middle age ("A Dreary Story"). The grim *Palata No. 6* (*Ward No. 6*) and "The Black Monk" study psychological alienation, while other stories explore sexual relations. A wife's abuse of a weak, loving husband in "The Butterfly" is counterbalanced by the wife's triumph over her husband in "The Order of St. Anne." In "The Artist's Story" romance itself is shown to be imbued with misunderstanding, potential disaster, and the loss of opportunity. The most positive story of this period is undoubtedly "The Student," in which myth and beauty inspire a moment of communication against the background of an atmospherically evoked rural evening and the passage of centuries.

In Chekhov's last years stories of loneliness and isolation reveal fear of life ("A Hard Case"), the sadness of missed opportunities for happiness ("Concerning Love"), and estrangement ("The Bishop"). Chekhov also exposes the suffocating power of bourgeois self-satisfaction, materialism, and philistinism that is contained in the one Russian word *poshlost'*: this is what overcomes the vitality of Startsev in "Ionych" and what permeates the life of Olga Semenovna in "The Darling." In "A Case History" the gentry shelter helplessly from the world of peasant-workers and alien factories, while "The Peasants" and "In the Hollow" take us to the primitive world of the peasant and the kulak. Here materialism and greed emerge as violent weapons by which the strong abuse the weak. One of Chekhov's last stories is perhaps his best creation, "Dama s sobachkoi" ("The Lady with a Dog"): for once, a story of mature love, of genuine communication

and self-sacrifice, in which the characters respect each other enough to face their uncertain future consciously and courageously.

Chekhov's "vaudevilles," his comic one-act plays—such as *Medved'* (*The Bear*) and *Predlozhenie* (*A Marriage Proposal*)—are mainly dramatized encounters, in which human feelings and follies undermine the solemnity of social occasions and rituals. Here, as in the major plays, dialogue and the revelation of character and atmosphere predominate over event. The major plays themselves, the foundation of Chekhov's reputation in the West, give dramatic form to the themes of the later stories. The way in which history overtakes the gentry is illustrated in Chekhov's bewildered central characters as they confront their own failure, the success of others, and the new strangeness of the world beyond their estates. Characters "in mourning for their lives" immerse themselves in nostalgia, petty rivalries, games, and hopeless dreaming or planning, while the forces of *poshlost'* and social change threaten their way of life and their future. The pathos and bathos of the unloved pervade *Chaika* (*The Seagull*), while *Diadia Vania* (*Uncle Vanya*) traces the erosion of hopes and dreams by age and failure. The despair of provincial life is all too evident in *Tri sestry* (*The Three Sisters*), but this play also shows how the characters' own self-indulgences and self-delusions frustrate their yearning for "Moscow." Finally, in *Vishnevyi sad* (*The Cherry Orchard*), the axes are being sharpened not just for trees, but for the softer material of a self-obsessed gentry that has lost the will to resist.

Chekhov does not abandon plot altogether, but he creates a startling division between the extreme events of his plays, whether on or off stage (suicide, duel, attempted murder, fire, and death), and the spelling-out through stage direction, dialogue, and sub-text of the ironies of man's hopes and fears. The atmosphere created by the charcaters' inertia, the sounds of their surroundings, and their own silences resonates at one moment with amusement, affectation, and confusion and at the next with bitterness, recrimination, and loss. Chekhov's integration of these resonances into frameworks of "everyday life" was a major dramatic innovation, one which was not accomplished without difficulty or with complete success. The balance between laughter and tears is sometimes too precarious in these plays, the relationship between exposition and natural discourse too artificial. Nevertheless, they are dramatic masterpieces, which have had the most significant influence on 20th-century Western drama.

Throughout, Chekhov preserved his humanity and his practical activity. Continuing to practise frequently as a doctor, he made a remarkable journey in 1890 across Siberia to visit the penal colony on Sakhalin Island, later producing an extensive account of conditions there, and in 1892 he helped in famine relief (as did Tolstoi). Although he was not devoid of the prejudices and shortcomings of his age, the simplicity, modesty, and gentle but firm truthfulness of Chekhov's vision mark him out among modern Russian writers.

—Christopher R. Pike

See the essays on *The Cherry Orchard*, "The Lady with a Dog," *The Seagull*, *The Three Sisters*, and *Uncle Vanya*.

CHIKAMATSU Monzaemon

Born: Suigimori Jirokichi (adult name Nobumori) into a samurai family, in Echizen Province (now in Fukui district), Japan, in 1653.

Family moved to Kyoto, c. 1667. **Family:** Married (wife died 1734); two sons. **Career:** In the service of the nobleman Ichijo Zenkakuekan until c. 1671–72; began writing plays, at first for Uji Kadayū [Kagano-jō] and other chanters of the *jōruri* (puppet) theatre; wrote for the chanter Takemoto Gidayū's theatre, Takemoto-za, Osaka, from 1686; also wrote kabuki plays, from 1684; house writer for Sakata Tōjūrō I's theatre, Miyako-za, Kyoto, 1695–1703; following Tōjūrō's retirement, c. 1703, resumed collaboration with Gidayū in Osaka; wrote solely for the puppet theatre, chiefly in the genres of the domestic drama (*sewamono*) and historical play (*jidaimono*), after c. 1705; moved back to Osaka, and became staff writer for the Takemoto-za, 1706. **Died:** 1725.

PUBLICATIONS

Collections

[Works], edited by Takam Tatsuyuki and Kuroki Kanzo. 10 vols., 1924.

[Works], edited by Kitano Hogi. 16 vols., 1925.

Masterpieces of Chikamatsu (includes *The Courier for Hades*; *The Love Suicide at Amijima*; *The Adventures of the Hakata Damsel*; *The Tethered Steed*; *Fair Ladies at a Game of Poem-Cards*; *The Almanac of Love*), translated by Asatoro Miyamori. 1926.

Chikamatsu zenshū [Complete Works], edited by Fujii Otoo. 12 vols., 1927.

Major Plays of Chikamatsu (includes *The Love Suicides at Sonezaki*; *The Drum of the Waves of Horikawa*; *Yosaku from Tamba*; *The Love Suicides in the Women's Temple*; *The Courier for Hell*; *The Battles of Coxinga*; *Gonza the Lancer*; *The Uprooted Pine*; *The Girl from Hakata*; *The Love Suicides at Amijima*; *The Woman-Killer and the Hell of Oil*), translated by Donald Keene. 1961.

Plays (selected *jōruri* plays)

Yotsugi Soga [The Soga Heir] (produced 1683).

Shusse Kagekiyo [Kagekiyo Victorious] (produced 1686).

Semimaru (produced 1686). As *Semimaru*, in *The Legend of Semimaru*, translated by S. Matisoff, 1978.

Sonezaki shinjū (produced 1703). As *The Love Suicides at Sonezaki*, translated by Donald Keene, in *Major Plays of Chikamatsu*, 1961.

Yomei tenno shokunin kagami (produced 1705).

Horikawa Nami no tsuzami (produced 1706). As *The Drum of the Waves of Horikawa*, translated by Donald Keene, in *Major Plays of Chikamatsu*, 1961.

Shinjū nimai ezōshi [Love Suicide and the Double-Folded Picture Books] (produced 1706).

Shinjū kasaneizutsu [Love Suicide at the Sunken Well] (produced 1707).

Tamba Yosaku (produced 1708). As *Yosaku from Tamba*, translated by Donald Keene, in *Major Plays of Chikamatsu*, 1961.

Shinjū mannenso (produced 1708). As *The Love Suicides in the Women's Temple*, translated by Donald Keene, in *Major Plays of Chikamatsu*, 1961.

Keisei hangoko (produced 1708).

Imamiya shinjū [Love Suicide at Imamiya] (produced 1711).

Meido no Hikyaku (produced 1711). As *The Courier for Hades*, translated by Asatoro Miyamori, in *Masterpieces of Chikamatsu*,

1926; as *The Courier for Hell*, translated by Donald Keene, in *Major Plays of Chikamatsu*, 1961.

Yugiri awa no naruto (produced 1712). Part translated as *Love Letter from the Licensed Quarter*, in *Kabuki*, by James R. Brandon, 1975.

Kokusenyā Kassen (produced 1715). As *The Battles of Coxinga*, edited and translated by Donald Keene, 1951, and in *Major Plays of Chikamatsu*, 1961.

Ikudama shinjū [Love Suicide at Ikudama] (produced 1715).

Yari no Gonza (produced 1717). As *Gonza the Lancer*, translated by Donald Keene, in *Major Plays of Chikamatsu*, 1961.

Nebiki no kadomatsu (produced 1718). As *The Uprooted Pine*, translated by Donald Keene, in *Major Plays of Chikamatsu*, 1961.

Soga kaikeizan (produced 1718). As *The Soga Revenge*, translated by Frank A. Lombard, in *Outline History of the Japanese Drama*, 1928.

Heike Nyogo no shima (produced 1719). Part translated by Samuel L. Leiter, in *The Art of Kabuki: Famous Plays in Performance*, 1979.

Hakata kojorō namimakura (produced 1719). As *The Adventures of the Hakata Damsel*, translated by Asatoro Miyamori, in *Masterpieces of Chikamatsu*, 1926; as *The Girl from Hakata*, translated by Donald Keene, in *Major Plays of Chikamatsu*, 1961.

Shinjū ten no Amijima (produced 1721). As *The Love Suicide at Amijima*, translated by Asatoro Miyamori, in *Masterpieces of Chikamatsu*, 1926; as *The Love Suicides at Amijima*, translated by Donald Keene, in *Major Plays of Chikamatsu*, 1961.

Onnagoroshi abura jigoku (produced 1721). As *The Woman Killer and the Hell of Oil*, translated by Donald Keene, in *Major Plays of Chikamatsu*, 1961.

Kwan-hasshu tsunagi, as *The Tethered Steed*, translated by Asatoro Miyamori, in *Masterpieces of Chikamatsu*. 1926.

Kaoyo utragaruta, as *Fair Ladies at a Game of Poem-Cards*, translated by Asatoro Miyamori, in *Masterpieces of Chikamatsu*. 1926; as *Fair Ladies at a Game of Poem Cards: A Verse Play* by Peter Oswald, 1996.

Koi hakkée hashiragoyomi, as *The Almanac of Love*, translated by Asatoro Miyamori, in *Masterpieces of Chikamatsu*. 1926.

*

Critical Studies: *Studien zu Chikamatsu Monzaemon* by Detlef Schauwacker, 1975; *World Within Walls* by Donald Keene, 1976; *Circles of Fantasy: Convention in the Plays of Chikamatsu* by Andrew C. Gerstle, 1986; *Hero as Murderer in the Plays of Chikamatsu: An Inaugural Lecture Delivered on 9 March 1994* by C.A. Gerstle, 1994.

* * *

Chikamatsu, sometimes referred to as the "Japanese Shakespeare," is widely considered Japan's most notable dramatist. Born in 1653, he became a major writer of the end of the 17th century and beginning of the 18th, producing plays for the puppet theatre (*ningyo jōruri*) and, in the middle period of his career, for the kabuki stage.

In Chikamatsu's day, the puppet theatre consisted of relatively simple puppets, operated from beneath the stage, with music provided by a *shamisen* player, and the dialogue, scenic evocations, and commentary delivered by a chanter. The plots drew largely on traditional forms and subject matter, including semi-historical stories of war and scenes of allegorical journeys (*michiyuki* scenes), but, as with any great dramatist, Chikamatsu is notable for his distinctive use of, and modifications to, existing conventions. Thus, the first play to which Chikamatsu's name is attached, *Yotsugi Soga* [The Soga Heir], based its plot on a traditional revenge tale concerning the Soga brothers, but introduces two courtesans who imbue the play with a level of pathos through their discussions of the pitfalls of love with the mother of the dead Soga brothers. Though this play is often considered crude and clumsy in many respects, already evident in it is the increased sophistication of emotional content brought about through the use of the mistress/courtesan figure—a figure that was to become characteristic of Chikamatsu. In his next important play, *Shusse Kagekiyo* [Kagekiyo Victorious], the mistress of Kagekiyo is, according to one critic, "a believable woman with the contradictions and complexities that distinguish human beings from puppets," and possesses a "genuine tragic intensity."

Shusse Kagekiyo was written for the famous chanter Takemoto Gidayū, with whom Chikamatsu was collaborating from 1686. But (and perhaps logically, considering his increasing "humanization" of character-types) Chikamatsu turned increasingly towards the kabuki theatre of live actors, and wrote almost exclusively for the kabuki stage from 1693 to 1703, becoming a contracted writer for the actor Sakata Tōjūrō I in Kyoto. He probably wrote about 30 kabuki plays, but those that have survived (rarely in complete form) are not regarded as highly as the puppet plays by most commentators. Above all, and perhaps to Chikamatsu's disappointment, kabuki theatre was one in which the actor was preeminent, and the writer's scripts, often produced in collaboration, were more bases for histrionic improvisation than structured, literary products.

Whether because of artistic limitations of the kabuki stage, the retirement of Tōjūrō, the resurgence in popularity of Gidayū's puppet theatre, or other reasons (an open biographical question which has intrigued scholars and theatre historians), Chikamatsu returned to writing puppet plays in the early 1790s, and wrote almost wholly in this form after 1795. It is from this period that those works generally considered his masterpieces derive. The later puppet plays fall into two categories—the *sewamono* form (domestic tragedies, also described as "dramas of contemporary life") and the *jidaimono* form (historical plays).

In the *sewamono* category are the "love suicide" plays, notably *Sonezaki Shinjū* (The Love Suicides at Sonezaki) and *Shinjū Ten no Amijima* (The Love Suicides at Amijima). The former of these drew on actual reports of the suicide of a pair of lovers, a shop assistant and a prostitute, and formed the basis for this entire genre of puppet plays. Chikamatsu wrote more than 11 "love suicide" plays, whose plots were usually based on the efforts of the male lover to buy his beloved from the brothel where she has been sent by her father, with the tragic element often involving the destitution brought about thereby. The characters' heroism does not derive from any innate "superhuman" qualities or attributes, but emerges through their struggles, sacrifices, and the depth of their love—elements brought out particularly in the *michiyuki* scenes. Chikamatsu was able to make extensive use of irony, tragic pathos, and social and economic realism to produce an extremely popular dramatic concoction—indeed one so popular that the plays increased the rate of such suicides in real life, causing consternation for the authorities and new legislation criminalizing such suicide attempts.

Most of the plays of the *jidaimono* category, the historical plays, have faded into relative obscurity, although Chikamatsu composed around 50 of them, and they were given higher priority in the theatre

of his time. Nevertheless, the category does contain the play sometimes cited as his greatest achievement—*Kokusenyā Kassen* (The Battles of Coxinga). It was certainly his greatest popular success, achieving an extraordinary run of around 17 months. Its treatment of history is highly fantastic—it presents the story of the almost single-handed rescue of the Ming dynasty in China from the Tartar tyranny by a half-Chinese, half-Japanese fisherman—and its contrasts are stark in tone, including broad humour, heroic and sensational feats, vivid exploitation of the audience's unfamiliarity with a foreign setting, and, by virtue of the hero's semi-Japanese lineage, patriotic appeal. Such a play as *The Battles of Coxinga* is a world away from the concerns of the *sewamono* works, and it is the latter which tend to be the better known today, particularly in the West.

—Noel Stanley

CHRÉTIEN DE TROYES

Career: Almost nothing is known of his life; because of dedications of his works, it is commonly assumed that he knew or served Countess Marie de Champagne at her court in Troyes and Philip of Alsace, Count of Flanders; works were probably written in the 1170s and 1180s.

PUBLICATIONS

Collections

Sämtliche Werke, edited by Wendelin Foerster. 4 vols., 1884–99; reprinted 1965.

Arthurian Romances (includes translations of *Erec and Énide; Cligès; Yvain; Lancelot*), edited by D.D.R. Owen, translated by W.W. Comfort. 1914; reprinted 1975.

Arthurian Romances (includes translations of *Erec and Énide; Cligès; Lancelot; Yvain; Perceval*), translated by D.D.R. Owen. 1987.

The Complete Romances, translated by Donald Staines. 1990.

Arthurian Romances (includes translations of *Eric and Énide; Cligès; The Knight of the Cart* [*Lancelot*]; *The Knight with the Lion* [*Yvain*]; *The Story of the Grail* [*Perceval*]), translated by William W. Kilber and Carleton W. Carroll. 1991.

Verse

Philomena, edited by C. de Boer. 1909.

Erec et Énide, edited by Mario Roques. 1952: as *Erec and Enid*, edited and translated by Carleton W. Carroll, 1987; also translated by Dorothy Gilbert, 1992; as *Erec and Enide*, translated by Ruth Harwood Cline, 2000.

Cligès, edited by Alexandre Micha, 1957; also edited by Claude Luttrell and Stewart Gregory, 1993.

Yvain (*Le Chevalier au Lion*), edited by Mario Roques. 1960; also edited by T.B.W. Reid, 1967; as *Yvain*, translated by Robert W. Ackerman and Frederick W. Locke, 1957; also translated by Ruth Harwood Cline, 1975; edited and translated by William W. Kibler, 1985; Burton Raffel, 1987.

Lancelot (*Le Chevalier de la charrette*), edited by Mario Roques. 1958; as *Lancelot; or, The Knight of the Cart*, edited and translated by William W. Kibler, 1981; also translated by Deborah Webster Rogers, 1984; Ruth Harwood Cline, 1990; as *Lancelot: The Knight of the Cart*, translated by Burton Raffel, 1997.

Le Conte du Graal (*Perceval*), edited by William Roach. 1959; also edited by Félix Lecoy, 2 vols., 1972–75; as *Perceval: The Story of the Grail*, translated by Nigel Bryant, 1982; also translated by Ruth Harwood Cline, 1985; translated by William W. Kibler, edited by Rupert T. Pickens, 1990; as *The Story of the Grail*, translated by Robert White Linker, 1952.

*

Bibliography: *Chrétien de Troyes: An Analytic Bibliography* by Douglas Kelly, 1976.

Critical Studies: *Arthurian Tradition and Chrétien de Troyes* by Roger Sherman Loomis, 1949: *Romance in the Making: Chrétien de Troyes and the Earliest French Romance*, 1954, and *Chrétien de Troyes: Inventor of the Modern Novel*, 1957, both by Foster E. Guyer; *The Portrait in Twelfth-Century French Literature: An Example of the Stylistic Originality of Chrétien de Troyes* by Alice M. Colby, 1965; *Aesthetic Distance in Chrétien de Troyes: Irony and Comedy in Cligès and Perceval* by Peter Haidu, 1968; *Chrétien de Troyes* by Urban T. Holmes, 1970; *Chrétien Studies* by Z.P. Zaddy, 1972; *The Allegory of Adventure: Reading Chrétien's Erec and Yvain* by Tom Artin, 1974; *The Creation of the First Arthurian Romance: A Quest* by Claude A. Luttrell, 1974; *Chrétien's Jewish Grail: A New Investigation of the Imagery and Significance of Chrétien de Troyes's Grail Episode Based Upon Medieval Hebraic Sources* by Eugene J. Weinraub, 1976; *Structure and Sacring: The Systematic Kingdom in Chrétien's Erec et Énide*, 1978, and *The Arthurian Romances of Chrétien de Troyes: Once and Future Fictions*, 1991, both by Donald Maddox; *The Craft of Chrétien de Troyes: An Essay on Narrative Art* by Norris J. Lacy, 1980, and *The Legacy of Chrétien de Troyes* edited by Lacy, Douglas Kelly, and Keith Busby, 2 vols., 1987–88; *Chrétien de Troyes: A Study of the Arthurian Romances* by Leslie T. Topsfield, 1981; *Chrétien de Troyes: The Man and His Work* by Jean Frappier, translated by Raymond J. Cormier, 1982; *The Dream of Chivalry: A Study of Chrétien de Troyes's Yvain and Hartmann von Aue's Iwein* by Ojars Kratins, 1982; *Love and Marriage in Chrétien de Troyes* by Peter S. Noble, 1982, and *Chrétien de Troyes and the Troubadours* edited by Noble and Linda M. Paterson, 1984; *Chrétien de Troyes* by Lucie Polak, 1982; *The Sower and His Seed: Essays on Chrétien de Troyes* edited by Rupert T. Pickens, 1983; *The Portrayal of the Heroine in Chrétien de Troyes's Erec et Énide; Gottfried von Strassburg's Tristan and Flamenca* by Nancy C. Zak, 1983: *Chrétien de Troyes: Erec et Énide* by Glynn S. Burgess, 1984; *The Romances of Chrétien de Troyes: A Symposium* edited by Douglas Kelly, 1985; *Chrétien de Troyes: Yvain (Le Chevalier au Lion)* by Tony Hunt, 1986; *From Topic to Tale: Logic and Narrativity in the Middle Ages* by Eugene Vance, 1987; *Chrétien de Troyes: Perceval (Le conte du Graal)* by Keith Busby, 1993; *Chrétien de Troyes and the German Middle Ages: Papers from an International Symposium*, edited with introduction by Martin H. Jones and Roy Wisbey, 1993; *Sealed in Parchment: Rereadings of Knighthood in the Illuminated Manuscripts of Chrétien de Troyes* by Sandra Hindman, 1994; *Chrétien de Troyes Revisited* by Karl D. Uitti with Michelle A. Freeman, 1995; *The Unholy Grail: A Social Reading of Chrétien de Troyes's Conte du Graal* by Brigitte Cazelles, 1996; *The Romances of Chrétien de Troyes* by Joseph J. Duggan, 2001.

* * *

Chrétien de Troyes brought the nascent romance form to one of its highest points and gave Arthurian characters and situations their courtly cast. Some of his early works—adaptations of Ovid and a version of the Tristan story—have not survived; others are of doubtful attribution or of marginal interest (the *Philomena*, the *Guillaume d'Angleterre*, and two short lyrical poems); on the other hand, his five major romances have earned him great critical acclaim. A product of the revival of interest in the classics, notably Ovid, and of the vogue of Celtic tales and of courtly love, these compositions written in octosyllabic rhymed couplets are among the most sophisticated literary creations of the 12th-century Renaissance. Chrétien was encouraged and probably supported for a while by Countess Marie of Champagne, daughter of King Louis VII of France and Eleanor of Aquitaine.

Erec et Énide (*Erec and Énide*) is the first full-blown account of King Arthur and the knights of the Round Table. After Erec weds the fair Énide, he becomes so enamoured of her that he loses interest in chivalry. Prodded into taking up arms again by his bride's hasty words, the hero forces her to accompany him on a series of perilous adventures in the course of which he proves his valour and Énide her loyalty and devotion to him.

Cligès (written c. 1176) appears to have been modelled in part on Thomas's *Tristan* whose heroine Chrétien criticized. Unlike Isolt, Fenice refuses to become involved with two lovers simultaneously. With the aid of magic potions, she prevents her husband from consummating their marriage, then, after feigning death, flees with Cligès to an idyllic hideaway. When the husband succumbs, the lovers are finally free to marry. In this romance, Chrétien developed the soliloquy as a means of analysing love's torments.

There is some evidence that Chrétien worked alternately on his next two romances in the late 1170s. *Lancelot* (*Le Chevalier de la charrette*) (*Lancelot; or, The Knight of the Cart*) is perhaps the author's best-known story. Held hostage by the evil Meleagant, Queen Guinevere is rescued by her secret lover Lancelot who must first overcome several obstacles and, above all, suffer the humiliation of mounting a cart driven by a dwarf. Guinevere is a haughty and demanding mistress who makes her lover give in to all her caprices; Lancelot is a model of chivalry and courtesy for whom love-service has many of the characteristics of religious devotion and even mysticism.

Yvain (*Le Chevalier au Lion*) (*Yvain; or, The Knight of the Lion*) recounts the adventures of a hero who weds the widow of a man he has slain. Though passionately in love with his bride, Yvain becomes so preoccupied with tourneying that she is soon out of his mind. The two are eventually reconciled after Yvain expiates his fault.

Le Conte du Graal (*Perceval*) (*Perceval: The Story of the Grail*), of 1181 or later, is about a naive young man who, after receiving training in chivalry and courtesy at King Arthur's court, happens upon a mysterious castle whose host is the Fisher King. There he witnesses a curious procession that includes a bleeding lance and a grail. Perceval fails to inquire about the significance of these objects and must then face the consequences. Medieval continuators gave a Christian interpretation to this story and some scholars believe

Chrétien intended to provide this kind of explanation. However, the poem was left unfinished and constitutes one of the most fascinating literary conundrums of all time.

—Gerard J. Brault

See the essays on *Erec and Énide* and *Lancelot*.

CHRISTINE DE PIZAN (OR PISAN)

Born: Venice, Italy, c. 1365. Moved to Paris at an early age. **Family:** Father was medical adviser and astrologer to Charles V. Married Étienne de Castel in 1380 (died 1390); two sons (one died in infancy) and one daughter. **Career:** Started writing career shortly after the death of her husband; attracted the attention of members of the French Royal Court and became society poet; worked as a copyist in the book trade; fled to a Dominican Abbey in Poissy to escape the civil war. **Died:** c. 1430.

PUBLICATIONS

Collections

Oeuvres poétiques, edited by Maurice Roy. 3 vols., 1886–96; reprinted 1965.
Ballades, Rondeaux and Virelais, edited by Kenneth Varty. 1965.
The Writings of Christine de Pizan, edited by Charity Cannon Willard, 1994.
The Selected Writings of Christine de Pizan: New Translations, Criticism, translated by Renate Blumenfeld-Kosinski and Kevin Brownlee, 1997.

Works

L'Avision-Christine, edited by Sister Mary Louise Towner. 1932.
Les Cent Ballades d'amant et de dame, edited by Jacqueline Cerquiglini. 1982.
Le Débat sur le Roman de la Rose, edited by Eric Hicks. 1977.
Le Ditié de Jehanne d'Arc, edited and translated by Angus J. Kennedy and Kenneth Varty. 1977.
L'Epistre de la prison de vie humaine, edited by Angus J. Kennedy. 1984.
L'Epitre d'Othéa, as *The Epistle of Othea to Hector*, edited by George F. Warner, 1904; also edited by James D. Gordon and translated by Anthony Babington, 1942; as *The Epistle of Othéa*, edited by C.F. Bühler and translated by Stephen Scrope, 1970.
Le Livre de la cité des dames, edited by M.C. Curnow. 2 vols., 1975; as *The Book of the City of Ladies*, translated by Earl J. Richards, 1982; also translated by Thérèse Moreau and Eric Hicks, 1986.
Le Livre de la mutacion de Fortune, edited by Suzanne Solente. 4 vols., 1959–66.
Le Livre de la paix, edited by Charity Cannon Willard. 1958.
Le Livre des faits et bonnes meurs du sage roy Charles V, edited by Suzanne Solente. 2 vols, 1936–40.
Le Livre des faits d'armes et de la chevalerie, as *The Book of Feats of Arms and of Chivalry*, translated by William Caxton, 1498, reprinted and edited by A.T.P. Byles, 1932; revised edition, 1937;

as *The Book of Deeds of Arms and of Chivalry*, translated by Sumner Willard, 1999.
Le Livre des trois vertus; ou, le Trésor de la citié des dames, edited by Eric Hicks. 1989; as *Le Livre des III vertus a l'enseignement des dames*, edited by Charity Cannon Willard, 1989; as *The Treasures of the City of Ladies; or, The Book of the Three Virtues*, translated by Sarah Lawson, 1985; *A Medieval Woman's Mirror of Honor*, translated by Willard, 1989.
Le Livre du chemin de long estude, edited by Robert Püschell. 1881; revised edition, 1887, reprinted 1974.
Le Livre du corps de policie, edited by Robert H. Lucas. 1967; edited and translated by Kate Langdon Forhan, 1994.
L'Oroyson nostre dame: Prayer to Our Lady (bilingual edition), translated by Jean Misrahi and Margaret Marks. 1953.
Les Sept Psaumes allégorisés, edited by Ruth Ringland Rains. 1965.
The Book of the Duke of True Lovers, translated by Alice Kemp-Welch. 1966.
The Epistle of the Prison of Human Life with An Epistle to the Queen of France and Lament of the Evils of the Civil War, edited by Josette A. Wisman. 1984.
Poems of Cupid, God of Love (includes *Epistre au dieu d'amours* and *Le Dit de la rose*), edited and translated by Thelma S. Fenster and Mary Carpenter Erler. 1990.

*

Bibliography: *Christine de Pisan: A Bibliography of Writings by Her and About Her*, 1982, and *Christine de Pisan: A Bibliography*, 2nd edition, 1989, both by Edith Yenal; *Christine de Pisan: A Bibliographical Guide* by Angus J. Kennedy, 1984.

Critical Studies: *Christine de Pizan: Ballades, Rondeaux and Virelais*, 1965, and *Epistre de la prison de vie humaine*, 1984, both by Angus J. Kennedy; *The Order of the Rose: The Life and Ideas of Christine de Pizan* by Enid McLeod, 1976; *Ideals for Women in the Works of Christine de Pizan* edited by Diane Bornstein, 1981; *Christine de Pisan* by Régine Pernond, 1982; *Christine de Pizan: Her Life and Works* by Charity Cannon Willard, 1984; *Politics, Gender and Genre: The Political Thought of Christine de Pizan* edited by Margaret Brabant, 1992; *Reinterpreting Christine de Pizan* edited by Earl Jeffrey Richards, 1992; *The City of Scholars: New Approaches to Christine de Pizan*, edited by Margarete Zimmermann and Dina De Rentiis, 1994; *Le livre du duc des vrais amans*, a critical edition by Thelma S. Fenster, 1995; *The Love Debate Poems of Christine de Pizan* by Barbara K. Altmann, 1998; *Christine de Pizan and Medieval French Lyric*, edited by Earl Jeffrey Richards, 1998; *Christine de Pizan and the Categories of Difference*, edited by Marilynn Desmond, 1998.

* * *

Christine de Pizan, the early 14th-century writer, composed a voluminous body of works. Writing both poetry and prose, she produced autobiographical texts, love lyrics, religious works, and treatises on education, warfare, peacemaking, and proper behaviour, as well as polemics on the "woman question." She was also the official biographer of Charles V of France.

Christine began her literary career from necessity, after her husband died leaving her virtually impoverished with three small children and considerable debts. Since she earned her living solely by her pen, she is often referred to as the first professional writer. Her first endeavours were poems lamenting her husband's death and depicting her grief. She wrote about 20 such ballads. Soon she began to produce more traditional love lyrics and to experiment with both themes and lyrical forms.

Two of her longer poems, *Epistre au dieu d'amours* [Epistle to the God of Love], written in 1399, and *Le Dit de la rose* [The Story of the Rose], written in 1402, were composed as part of Christine's challenge to Jean de Meung's slanderous depiction of women in the second half of the *Roman de la rose* (*The Romance of the Rose*). Christine was in fact the main correspondent in the Quarrel of the Rose in which she and others such as Jean de Gerson, chancellor of the University of Paris, attacked the immorality and misogyny of Jean de Meung's poem.

The *Epistre au dieu d'amours* presents ladies from all social classes who complain to Cupid about those who slander them, Ovid and Jean de Meung in particular. It concludes with the banishment of all defamers of women from the court. In *Le Dit de la rose* she founds the Order of the Rose which rewards those knights who defend the honour of woman. The Quarrel of the Rose extended Christine's fame throughout Europe.

With the exception of two poems treating common courtly love themes, "Le Dit de deux amans" [The Story of Two Lovers] and "Le Livre des trois jugements" [Story of the Three Judgements], dedicated to the Seneschal de Hainaut, the only other major poem not connected to Christine's personal life is *Le Ditié de Jehanne D'Arc* [Joan of Arc's Story]. Christine had been in retirement at Poissy and had not written for years, when she heard about Joan of Arc and wrote this poem celebrating Joan as the saviour of France. For Christine, she was proof of the value of women and of their worth in God. The poem was the only work written in Joan of Arc's honour during her lifetime.

Among the personal or autobiographical poems, we find a poem written for Christine de Pizan's son, Jean de Castel. This work, "Enseignements et proverbes moraux" [Moral Proverbs], became very popular in England. "Le Livre du dit de Poissy" describes an elaborate party given for guests at the convent where her daughter lived. *Le Livre de la Mutacion de Fortune* [Mutation of Fortune] composed between 1400 and 1403, is the longest of her works in verse. It includes an allegorical sea voyage in which Christine depicts her transformation from wife to writer. She is adrift and helpless; Fortune takes pity upon her and by touching her renders her stronger in every sense. Her wedding band falls symbolically from her finger, for, as Christine tells us, she has become a man (lines 1,359–61). She is no longer a wife, but a person alone. The second part contains a description of Fortune's castle. In the *Le Livre du chemin de long estude* [The Long Study], Christine, in a dream vision, visits the Court of Reason and then returns to earth with the knowledge necessary to correct the Earth's faults by founding a world empire.

Christine's prose works explore the same topics as her poems. There are a number of letters that she wrote as part of her polemic against Jean de Meung. She addresses the subject of world reform in *L'Avision-Christine* and the problem of strife and the necessity for peace in *Le Livre du corps de policie* [Book of the Body Politic], written 1406–07 and based on John of Salisbury's *Policraticus*, and in *Le Livre de la paix* [Book of Peace], 1412–14, which was actually a book of instruction written for the dauphin. Her interest in politics, society, and history is also evidenced in her manual on military ethics, *Le Livre des faits d'armes et de chevalerie* (*The Book of Feats of Arms and of Chivalry*) and in her commissioned work on the reign of Charles V, *Le Livre des faits et bonnes meurs du sage roy Charles V* [Deeds and Manners of Charles V], which was intended as a manual

of good government for the dauphin. In addition, Christine wrote two religious works: *Les Sept Psaumes allégorisés* [Seven Allegorical Psalms] with a prose meditation for Charles le Noble, and the consolation, *L'Epistre de la prison de vie humaine* [Prison of Human Life], dedicated to Mary of Berry, who had lost so many of her family in the civil strife.

Her two major prose works, *Le Livre de la cité des dames* (*The Book of the City of Ladies*) and *Le Livre des trois vertus; ou, le Trésor de la citié des dames* (*The Treasures of the City of Ladies; or, The Book of the Three Virtues*), develop further the subject of greatest concern to her, the rehabilitation of the image of women. In these two works, we find a detailed presentation of her basic beliefs and her own view of woman's place in society. In the *City of Ladies*, using once again an allegorical setting and a subtle method of attack, she refutes the many accusations against women. Drawing examples from various sources, Christine compiles a gallery of heroic, intelligent, virtuous women. Using an allegory of three ladies sent by God to help her build in the City, she enhances her work with divine approval and strengthens her refutation of the then popular belief that women were less holy, less valuable. This motif of Christine as an intermediary between the misguided world and the elements of right-thinking, justice, and holiness appears in several of her works (*L'Avision-Christine, Le Livre du chemin de long estude*).

Having established the value and talents of women, she continued her work on women by writing a manual of proper conduct in the companion text, *The Treasures of the City of Ladies*. In spite of her own unorthodox life as a professional writer and her decision to remain a widow, Christine saw woman's role as primarily that of a wife. Some feminists have tended to shy away from her because of this aspect of her work; however, given the world in which she was living, her stand against the accepted devaluation of women, supported by the Church as well as the majority of male intellectuals was a bold move. To have believed that women's situation could have been totally transformed would have been impractical, even foolish. Moreover, Christine had enjoyed a happy marriage. Her goal was to gain respect for women in their established role in society, not to revolutionize her world. Nevertheless, for her period, Christine was a strong advocate of women and deserves to be considered one of the first feminists. During her time, she was recognized as both an accomplished lyric poet and a respected authority on the status of women.

—Shawncey J. Webb

See the essay on *The Book of the City of Ladies*.

CICERO

Born: Marcus Tullius Cicero in Arpinum (now Arpino), central Italy, 3 January 106 BC. **Education:** Educated in Rome, and studied rhetoric and oratory in Athens and Rhodes, 79–77 BC. **Military Service:** Served in the army of Pompeius Strabo, 89 BC. **Family:** Married 1) Terentia in 80 BC (divorced 47 BC), one daughter and one son; 2) Publilia (divorced 45 BC). **Career:** Lawyer: first appearance in courts, 81 BC; usually appeared for the defence, but his prosecution of Verres (70 BC) is his most famous case. Financial administrator (*quaestor*), western Sicily, 75 BC; judicial officer (*praetor*), 66 BC; consul, 63 BC:

exposed Catiline's conspiracy to carry out uprisings in Italy and arson in Rome; declared an exile by Clodius in 58 BC, and lived in Thessalonica and Illyricum, but recalled with help of Pompey, 57 BC; reluctantly allied himself with triumvirate of Pompey, Caesar, and Crassus, 56 BC, and retired from public life until 51 BC; elected augur of the college of diviners, 53 BC; governor of Cilicia, Asia Minor, 51–50 BC; allied with Pompey in civil war, 49–48 BC: after Pompey's defeat Cicero's safety was guaranteed by Caesar; after Caesar's assassination, 44 BC, supported general amnesty (delivered 14 Philippic orations against Antony, 44–43 BC); the triumvirate of Octavian, Antony, and Lepidus put Cicero on the execution list, 43 BC, and he was captured and killed. **Died:** 7 December 43 BC.

PUBLICATIONS

Collections

[Works], edited by C.F.W. Mueller. 1884–1917; also edited by K. Simbeck and others, 1923–; translated by various hands [Loeb Edition], 28 vols., 1912–58.
[Letters], edited by R.Y. Tyrrell and L.C. Purser. 7 vols., 1899–1918; selections as *Letters*, translated by L.P. Wilkinson, 1949; *Selected Letters*, translated by D.R. Shackleton Bailey, 1980.
[Poems], edited by W.W. Ewbank. 1933; translated by A.E. Douglas, 1985.
Selected Works, translated by Michael Grant. 1960.
Selected Political Speeches, translated by Michael Grant. 1969, revised edition, 1973.

Works

Academica, edited by J.S. Reid. 1885.
De amicitia, with *De senectute* and *De divinatione*, translated by William Armistead Falcolner. 1922.
Brutus, edited by H. Malcovati. 1963; also edited by A.E. Douglas, 1966; translated by H.M. Poteat, 1950.
The Caesarian Orations, translated by G.J. Acheson. 1965.
De divinatione, edited by Arthur S. Pease. 4 vols., 1920–23; as *De divinatione*, with *De senectute* and *De amicitia*, translated by William Arthur Falcolner, 1922; as *On Divination*, translated by H.M. Poteat, 1950.
De domo sua, edited by R.G. Nisbet. 1939.
Epistulae ad Atticum: Letters to Atticus, edited by W.S. Watt. 2 vols., 1961–65; edited and translated by D.R. Shackleton Bailey, 7 vols., 1965–70.
Epistulae ad familiares [Letters to His Friends], edited by D.R. Shackleton Bailey. 2 vols., 1977; also edited by W.S. Watt, 1982; translated by D.R. Shackleton Bailey, 1978.
Epistulae ad Quintum frateum et M. Brutum, edited by D.R. Shackleton Bailey. 1980; also edited by W.S. Watt, 1958; translated by D.R. Shackleton Bailey, 1978.
De finibus, edited by J.N. Madrid. 3rd edition, 1876; Books I–II edited by J.S. Reid, 1925.
In Pisonem, edited by R.G. Nisbet. 1961.
In Vatinium, edited by L.F. Pocock. 1926.
Kerrines II, translated by T.N. Mitchell. 1986.
Laelius, edited by Frank Stock, revised edition. 1930; as *On Friendship*, translated by Frank Copley, 1967; also translated by J.G.F. Powell, 1990.
Murder Trials (selected orations), translated by Michael Grant. 1975.

De natura deorum, edited by A.S. Pease. 2 vols., 1955–58; as *On the Nature of the Gods*, translated by H.M. Poteat, 1950; also translated by H.C.P. McGregor, 1972.
Nine Orations and the Dream of Scipio, translated by Smith P. Bovie. 1967.
De officiis, edited by P. Fedeli. 1965; as *On Duties*, translated by H.M. Poteat, 1950; also translated by John Higginbotham, 1967; Harry G. Edinger, 1974; M.T. Griffin and E.M. Atkins, 1991.
On Fate, edited and translated by R.W. Sharples. 1992.
On the Good Life (selections), translated by Michael Grant. 1971.
De oratore, edited by A.S. Wilkins. 1892.
Philippics I–II, edited by J.D. Denniston. 1939; also edited by D.R. Shackleton Bailey, 1986.
Pro M. Caelio, edited by R.G. Austin. 1960.
De republica, as *On the Commonwealth*, translated by G.H. Sabine and S.B. Smith. 1929; selections as *Res Publica*, translated by W.K. Lacey and Harry G. Edinger, 1974.
De senectute, edited by Leonard Huxley, revised edition. 1923; also edited by J.G.F. Powell, 1988; translated (from the French) as *De senectute*, 1481; with *De amicitia* and *De divinatione*, translated by William Armistead Falconer, 1922; as *Cato Major, or His Discourse of Old-Age*, translated by James Logan, 1744; as *On Old Age*, translated by Frank Copley, 1967.
Somnium Scipionis, as *The Dream of Scipio*, with *Nine Orations*, translated by Smith P. Bovie. 1967; also translated by Percy Bullock, 1983; J.G.F. Powell, 1990.
Tusculanae disputationes, edited by Thomas W. Dougan and Robert M. Henry. 2 vols., 1905; as *Tusculan Disputations* [Loeb Edition], translated by J.E. King, 1927; 2 and 5 translated by A.E. Douglas, 1990.

*

Critical Studies: *Cicero and the Roman Republic* by Frank R. Crowell, 1948; *The Humanism of Cicero* by H.A.K. Hunt, 1954; *Cicero on the Art of Growing Old* by H.W. Couch, 1959; *Cicero* by T.A. Dorey, 1965; *Cicero on Old Age* by E.M. Blaiklock, 1966; *Cicero the Statesman* by Richard E. Smith, 1966; *Cicero* by D.R. Shackleton Bailey, 1971; *Cicero: A Political Biography* by David Stockton, 1971; *Cicero and the State Religion* by R.J. Goar, 1972; *Cicero and Rome* by David Taylor, 1973; *Cicero: A Portrait* by Elizabeth Rawson, 1975; *Cicero and the End of the Roman Republic* edited by W.K. Lacey, 1978; *Cicero's Elegant Style: An Analysis of the "Pro Archia"* by Harold C. Gotoff, 1979; *Cicero: The Ascending Years*, 1979, and *Cicero the Senior Statesman*, 1991, both by Thomas N. Mitchell; *The Style and the Composition of Cicero's Speech "Pro Q. Rescio Comoedo": Origin and Function* by Jerzy Axer, 1980; *Cicero's Philippics and their Demosthenic Model: The Rhetoric of Crisis* by Cecil W. Wooten, 1983; *Trials of Character: The Eloquence of Ciceronian Ethos* by James M. May, 1988; *Cicero's Social and Political Thought* by Neal Wood, 1988; *The Philosophical Books of Cicero* by Paul MacKendrick, 1989; *Cicero the Politician* by Christian Habicht, 1990; *Cicero and the Roman Republic* by Manfred Fuhrmann, 1992; *Representations: Images of the World in Ciceronian Oratory* by Ann Vasaly, 1993; *Form as Argument in Cicero's Speeches: A Study of Dilemma* by Christopher P. Craig, 1993; *Cicero's Caesarian Speeches: A Stylistic Commentary*, edited by Harold C. Gotoff, 1993; *The Letters of January to April 43 BC*, translated with commentary by M.M. Willcock, 1995; *Onomasticon to Cicero's Letters* by D.R. Shackleton Bailey, 1995; *Cicero the*

Philosopher: Twelve Papers, edited with introduction by J.G.F. Powell, 1995; *The Speeches of Cicero: Context, Law, Rhetoric* by Paul MacKendrick, 1995; *Cicero's Cilician Letters*, translated with notes by Susan Treggiari, 1996; *Cicero's Accretive Style: Rhetorical Strategies in the Exordia of the Judicial Speeches* by Stephen M. Cerutti, 1996; *Cicero's Correspondence: A Literary Study* by G.O. Hutchinson, 1997; *Master Tully: Cicero in Tudor England* by Howard Jones, 1998; *Crime and Community in Ciceronian Rome* by Andrew M. Riggsby, 1999; *Cicero's Republic*, edited by J.G.F. Powell and J.A. North, 2001; *Cicero, Catullus, and the Language of Social Performance* by Brian A. Krostenko, 2001.

* * *

Cicero was one of the most prolific and versatile of Latin authors, but his literary reputation has varied more than most. In antiquity he was generally accepted as the prince of Roman orators, though sometimes with reservations. In the Middle Ages, when his speeches and letters were almost forgotten, the less technical of his philosophical works became vastly popular and influential. Petrarch was his devout admirer, and among the humanists of the Renaissance his Latin style was a fetish. The 18th century found him congenial, the 19th less so.

In the 20th the most valuable part of Cicero's literary legacy seems to be the part he never intended to leave: his private correspondence. It was published at intervals after his death, apparently with scarcely any editing. The first extant letter was written when Cicero was 38 and they continue in uneven flow down to within a few months of his death. Many were to his closest intimates, his brother and his lifelong friend, Pomponius Atticus. They take us behind the political and domestic scenes, and thanks to them the colourful history of the last two decades of the Roman Republic is more than a bare chronicle of events. The famous names—Pompey, Cato, Crassus, Julius Caesar—come to life, and Cicero's own complex personality gets ample exposure. Incidentally, they show him to be a master of vivid narrative and description in a colloquial style very different from that of his publications. Nothing in the remains of Greco-Roman literature takes us so close to an individual and a society.

The speeches, too, offer much of this kind of interest and some of them, like the letters, are an important source of information about the speaker and his times. Covering a period of nearly 40 years, almost the whole of Cicero's public career, they range from legalistic pleas on behalf of obscure clients to grand occasions when Cicero held forth to the Senate or the People in its assemblies on great political issues. To a modern eye the faults of his eloquence are often all too plain: inflation, false pathos, egotism, verbosity, and what Theodor Mommsen called a dreadful barrenness of thought. Even so, a receptive reader may let himself be swept along with the tide of impeccably constructed periods, especially if he can read the Latin aloud. And sometimes there is more, as in the rhetorical drive of the *Catilines*, the genuine pathos of the 14th Philippic, or the brilliant badinage in the defence of Murena. As for Cicero's prose style, even Mommsen admired it. It was his most creative achievement.

Cicero was not an original thinker, but like many educated Romans of his time he was much interested in Greek philosophy. Late in life he conceived the plan to present it, at least its more recent developments, in Latin form. The result was a rapidly produced series of metaphysical and moral treatises based on Greek sources. As literature, the gem of the collection is the little tract on old age (*De senectute*), perhaps Cicero's one unqualified artistic success. Another

attractive piece, on friendship, characteristically tells us nothing about the actualities of Roman *amicitia*, as Cicero knew them from his own experience. Even the works on rhetoric have this second-hand quality, except the *Brutus*, a survey of Roman orators which often reads like a catalogue but contains some highly interesting sketches of speakers whom Cicero had heard and personally known.

Cicero also wrote poetry, mostly in his youth. It had a considerable vogue, until Catullus and the "New Poets" brought their fresh inspiration. Posterity would have none of it, and enough survives to show that posterity was right. Even the advance in verse technique as compared with the remnants of earlier writing need not have been due to Cicero.

—D.R. Shackleton Bailey

See the essays on *In Defence of Marcus Caelius Rufus*, *On Old Age*, and *On the Commonwealth*.

CLAUDEL, Paul (Louis Charles Marie)

Born: Villeneuve-sur-Fère, France, 6 August 1868. **Education:** Educated at schools in Bar-le-Duc, 1870–75, Nogent-sur-Seine, 1876–79, and Wassy-sur-Blaise, 1879–81; Lycée Louis-le-Grand, Paris, 1882–85; law school, and École des Sciences Politiques. **Family:** Married Reine Sainte-Marie-Perrin in 1906; five children. **Career:** In the French diplomatic service from 1890: commercial department, Paris, 1890–92, New York, 1893, Boston, 1894, China, 1894–1909, Prague, 1909–11, Frankfurt, 1911–14, Berlin, 1914, Rome and Brazil during World War I; ambassador to Japan, 1921–25, to the United States, 1926–33, and to Belgium, 1933–35; retired 1935; served in the Ministry of Propaganda during World War II. **Member:** Académie française, 1946. **Died:** 23 February 1955.

PUBLICATIONS

Collections

Théâtre. 4 vols., 1911–12; revised edition, 2 vols., 1947–48.
Oeuvres complètes. 26 vols., 1950–67; supplement, 1990.
Théâtre, edited by Jacques Madaule and Jacques Petit. 2 vols., 1956; revised edition, 1965–67.
Oeuvres poétiques, edited by Stanislas Fumet. 1957.
Oeuvres en prose, edited by Jacques Petit and Charles Galperine. 1965.

Plays

Tête d'or. 1890; revised version (produced 1924), in *L'Arbre*, 1901; as *Tete-d'or*, translated by John S. Newberry, 1919.
La Ville. 1893; revised version (produced 1931), in *L'Arbre*, 1901; edited by Jacques Petit, 1967; as *The City*, translated by John S. Newberry, 1920.
L'Agamemnon, from the play by Aeschylus (produced 1963). 1896.
L'Échange (produced 1914). In *L'Arbre*, 1901; revised version (produced 1951), 1954; as *The Trade*, translated by Donald L. Holley and Jean-Pierre Krémer, 1995.

La Jeune Fille Violaine, in *L'Arbre*. 1901; revised version, as *L'Annonce faite à Marie* (produced 1912), 1912; revised version (produced 1948), 1948; as *The Tidings Brought to Mary*, translated by Louise Morgan Sill, 1916; also translated by Wallace Fowlie, in *Two Dramas*, 1960.

Le Repos du septième jour (produced 1928). In *L'Arbre*, 1901.

Partage de midi (produced 1921). 1906; revised version (produced 1948), 1914, 1949; as *Break of Noon*, translated by Wallace Fowlie, in *Two Dramas*, 1960; also translated by Jonathon Griffin, 1990.

L'Otage (produced 1913). 1911; edited by Jean-Pierre Kempf, 1977; as *The Hostage*, translated by Pierre Chavannes, 1917; also translated by John Heard, in *Three Plays*, 1945.

Protée, in *Deux poèmes d'été*. 1914; revised version (produced 1929), in *Deux farces lyriques*, 1927.

La Nuit de Noël 1914. 1915.

La Pain dur (produced in German, 1926; in French, 1949). 1918; edited by Jacques Petit, 1975, as *Crusts*, translated by John Heard, in *Three Plays*, 1945.

L'Ours et la lune (produced 1948). 1919.

Le Père humilié (produced in German 1928). 1920; as *The Humiliation of the Father*, translated by John Heard, in *Three Plays*, 1945.

Les Choéphores, music by Darius Milhaud, from the play by Aeschylus (produced 1935). 1920.

Les Euménides, music by Darius Milhaud, from the play by Aeschylus (produced 1949). 1920.

L'Homme et son désir, music by Darius Milhaud (ballet; produced 1921). In *Le Livre de Christophe Colomb*, 1929.

La Femme et son ombre (produced 1923). In *Le Livre de Christophe Colomb*, 1929.

Sous le rempart d'Athènes, music by Germaine Taillefer (produced 1929). 1928.

Le Soulier de satin. 1928–29; revised version (produced 1943), 1944; as *The Satin Slipper*, translated by John O'Connor, 1931.

Le Livre de Christophe Colomb, music by Darius Milhaud (produced 1930). 1929; as *The Book of Christopher Columbus*, translated anonymously, 1930.

Jeanne d'Arc au bûcher, music by Arthur Honegger (produced 1939). 1939.

La Sagesse; ou, La Parabole du Festin, music by Darius Milhaud (broadcast, 1945; produced 1949). 1939.

L'Histoire de Tobie et de Sara (produced 1947). 1947; as *Tobias and Sara*, translated by Adele Fiske, in *Port-Royal and Other Plays*, edited by Richard Hayes, 1962.

L'Endormie. 1947.

Three Plays, translated by John Heard. 1945.

Two Dramas, translated by Wallace Fowlie. 1960.

Radio Play:: *La Sagesse; ou, La Parabole du Festin*, 1945.

Verse

Vers d'exile. 1895.

Connaissance du temps. 1904.

Cinq grandes odes suivies d'un processional pour saluer le siècle nouveau. 1910; as *Five Great Odes*, translated by Edward Lucie Smith, 1967.

Cette heure qui est entre le printemps et l'été. 1913; as *La Cantate à trois voix*, 1931.

Corona benignitatis anni dei. 1915; as *Coronal*, translated by Sister Mary David, 1943.

Trois poèmes de guerre. 1915; as *Three Poems of the War*, translated by Edward J. O'Brien, 1919.

Autres poèmes durant la guerre. 1916.

Poèmes et paroles durant la guerre. 1916.

La Messe là-bas. 1919.

Poèmes de guerre. 1922.

Feuilles de saints. 1925.

Écoute, ma fille. 1934.

La Légende de Prakriti. 1934.

Poèmes et paroles durant la guerre de trente ans. 1945.

Visages radieux. 1946.

Paul Claudel répond les psaumes. 1948; as *Psaumes: Traductions 1918–1959*, edited by Renée Nantet and Jacques Petit, 1966.

Sainte Agnès et poèmes inédits. 1963.

A Hundred Movements for a Fan (haiku), translated by Andrew Harvey and Iain Watson. 1992

Other

Connaissance de l'est. 1900; enlarged edition, 1907; edited by Gilbert Gadoffre, 1973; as *The East I Know*, translated by Teresa Frances and William Rose Benét, 1914.

Art poétique. 1907; as *Poetic Art*, translated by Renée Spodheim, 1948.

Correspondance 1907–1914, with Jacques Rivière. 1926; as *Letters to a Doubter*, translated by Henry Longan Stuart, 1929.

Positions et propositions. 2 vols., 1928–34; vol. 1 as *Ways and Crossways*, translated by John O'Connor, 1933.

L'Oiseau noir dans le soleil levant. 1929.

Introduction à la peinture hollandaise. 1935.

Conversations dans le Loir-et-Cher. 1935.

Toi, qui es-tu? Tu quis es? 1936.

Figures et paraboles. 1936; edited by Andrée Hirschi, 1974.

Vitraux des cathédrales de France. 1937.

L'Aventure de Sophie. 1937.

Un poète regarde la croix. 1938; as *A Poet Before the Cross*, translated by Wallace Fowlie, 1958.

L'Épée et le miroir. 1939.

Contacts et circonstances. 1940.

La Rose et le rosaire. 1946.

L'Oeil écoute (essays). 1946; as *The Eye Listens*, translated by Elsie Pell, 1950.

Chine, photographs by Hélène Hoppenot. 1946.

Présence et prophétie. 1947.

Lord, Teach Us to Pray, translated by Ruth Bethell. 1947.

Sous le signe du dragon. 1948.

Paul Claudel interroge le Cantique des Cantiques. 1948.

Accompagnements. 1949.

Correspondance 1899–1926, with André Gide, edited by Robert Mallet. 1949; as *Correspondence*, translated by John Russell, 1952.

Emmaüs. 1950.

L'Évangile d'Isaïe. 1951.

Correspondance 1904–1938, with André Saurés. 1951.

Paul Claudel interroge l'Apocalypse. 1952.

Mémoires improvisés, edited by Jean Amrouche. 1954.

J'aime la Bible. 1955; as *The Essence of the Bible*, translated by Wade Baskin, 1957.

Correspondance 1918–1953, with Darius Milhaud, edited by Jacques Petit. 1961.

I Believe in God: A Commentary on the Apostles Creed, edited by Agnes du Sarment, translated by Helen Weaver. 1963.

Au milieu des vitraux de l'Apocalypse, edited by Pierre Claudel and Jacques Petit. 1966.

Mes idées sur le théâtre, edited by Jacques Petit and Jean-Pierre Kempf. 1966; as *Claudel on the Theatre*, translated by Christine Trollope, 1972.

Journal, edited by Jacques Petit and François Varillon. 2 vols., 1968–69.

Correspondance 1908–1914, with Louis Massignon, edited by Michel Malicet. 1973.

Correspondance, with Jean-Louis Barrault, edited by Michel Lioure. 1974.

Chroniques du Journal de Clichy, with François Mauriac (includes Claudel-Fontaine correspondence), edited by François Norlot and Jean Touzot. 1978.

La Vague et le rocher: Paul Claudel, François Mauriac correspondance 1911–1954, edited by Michel Malicet and Marie-Chantal Praicheux, 1989.

Lettre à son fils Henri et sa famille, edited by Marianne and Michel Malicet. 1990.

Henri Pourrat-Paul Claudel: Correspondance, edited by Michel Lioure. 1990.

Translator, *Poèmes*, by Coventry Patmore. 1912.

*

Bibliography: *Bibliographie des oeuvres de Claudel* by Jacques Petit, 1973; *Claudel and the English-Speaking World: A Critical Bibliography*, 1973.

Critical Studies: *The Double Image: Mutations of Christian Mythology in the Work of Four French Catholic Writers* by Rayner Heppenstall, 1947; *The Theme of Beatrice in the Plays of Claudel* by Ernest Beaumont, 1954; *The Poetic Drama of Claudel* by Joseph Chiari, 1954; *Paul Claudel* by Wallace Fowlie, 1957; *Paul Claudel: The Man and the Mystic* by Louis Chaigne, 1961; *Claudel and Aeschylus* by William H. Matheson, 1965; *The Inner Stage: An Essay on the Conflict of Vocations in the Early Works of Claudel* by Richard Berchan, 1966; *Claudel et l'univers chinois* by Gilbert Gadoffre, 1968; *Claudel: A Reappraisal* by Richard M. Griffiths, 1968; *Paul Claudel* by Harold A. Waters, 1970; *Claudel and Saint-John Perse* by Ruth N. Horry, 1971; *Claudel's Immortal Heroes: A Choice of Deaths* by Harold Watson, 1971; *The Prince and the Genie: A Study of Rimbaud's Influence on Claudel* by John A. MacCombie, 1972; *Paul Claudel's Le Soulier de satin: A Stylistic, Structuralist, and Psychoanalytic Interpretation* by Joan S. Freilich, 1973; *Two Against Time: A Study of the Very Present Worlds of Claudel and Charles Péguy* by Joy Nachod Humes, 1978; *In/stability: The Shape and Space of Claudel's Art* by Lynne L. Gelber, 1980; *Paul Claudel* by Bettina L. Knapp, 1982; *Paul Claudel: Biographie* by Marie-Josèphe Guers, 1987; *Claudel: Beauty and Grace* by Angelo Caranfa, 1989; *Mis-reading the Creative Impulse: The Poetic Subject in Rimbaud and Claudel, Restaged* by Adrianna M. Paliyenko, 1997; *The Instruction of Philosophy and Psychoanalysis by Tragedy: Jacques Lacan and Gabriel Marcel Read Paul Claudel* by Ann Bugliani, 1999.

* * *

Despite the high praise of Charles Du Bos, who called him the greatest genius of the west, and despite the judgment of Jacques Madaule, who compared him to Dante, Paul Claudel's place in literature and in Catholic thought is still vigorously disputed. At the time of his death, in his mid-eighties, he appeared as belligerent as ever, having maintained to the end not only his full powers as a writer but also his violent temper and his animosities. His detractors are still legion and his admirers come from many varying quarters differing widely in their religious, political, and aesthetic beliefs.

During his last year at the Lycée Louis-le-Grand, he read Baudelaire and Verlaine, but the first major revelation to Claudel of both a literary and spiritual order was to be Rimbaud. He has described in a passage justly celebrated and justly disputed the profound effect which the reading of the *Illuminations* had on him. He first came upon some of the prose poems in the July issue of *La Vogue* of 1886. To him it meant release from what he called the hideous world of Taine, Renan, and other Molochs of the 19th century. ''J'avais la révélation du surnaturel,'' he wrote to Jacques Rivière.

After a spiritual experience at Christmas 1886, in Notre Dame, Claudel began to study the Bible, the history of the Church and its liturgy, and discovered that what he had once valued as poetry was indissolubly associated with religion. He attended Mallarmé's Tuesday evening gatherings and learned from the master of symbolism to look at the universe as if it were a text to be deciphered. To Rimbaud's doctrine on the power of poetic language and to Mallarmé's doctrine on the symbolism of the universe Claudel added the gigantic synthesis of Aquinas and the religious interpretation of metaphorical language.

Taken as a whole, Claudel's work is praise to God and praise to His creation. It does not reflect the exaltation of a mystic but is rather the expression of the natural joy of a man who has found an order in the universe and believes in a certain relationship between this world and the next. In whatever he wrote—poems, letters, plays, essays, Biblical exegesis—he steadfastly explored the central drama of the human soul engaged in its adventure with eternity. His dramas are not a combination of the comic and the tragic; they are works of one piece and one texture—simultaneously dramatic speech and poetry.

The French literary mind has been predominantly analytical in each century. Claudel's mind was more inclined toward the creation of a synthesis. His fundamental preoccupations are more metaphysical than is usual in French writers who tend to psychological and moralistic preoccupations. Moreover, the seeming bluntness of his style, its vehemence, its violence, separates his work from the central tradition of the French literary style. Claudel believed that at our birth we enter into a secret pact with all beings and all objects. The poet's mission is that of pointing out our relationship with all the realities of the world.

—Wallace Fowlie

See the essay on *The Satin Slipper*.

CLAUDIAN

Born: Claudius Claudianus in Alexandria, Egypt, c. AD 370. **Family:** Married in c. AD 404. **Career:** Went to Rome before 395, then lived in Milan for five years, from c. AD 395; became a successful court poet under the western emperor Honorius. He was a favourite of and spokesman for General Stilicho, defender of the Roman empire against the Goths and the Vandals. **Died:** Rome c. AD 404.

PUBLICATIONS

Collections

[Works], edited by Ludwig Jeep. 2 vols., 1876–79; also edited by
Theodor Birt, in *Monumenta Germaniae historica*, vol. 10, 1892,
Julius Koch, 1893, and J.B. Hall, 1985; edited and translated
(prose) by Maurice Platnauer [Loeb Edition], 2 vols., 1922;
translated by A, Hawkins, 2 vols., 1817.

Works

De raptu Proserpine, edited by Ludwig Jeep. 1874; also edited by J.B.
Hall, 1969; edited and translated by Claire Gruzelier (with com-
mentary), 1993; as *The Rape of Proserpine*, translated by Leonard
Digges, 1628, reprinted 1959; also translated by Jabez Hughes,
1714; Jacob G. Strutt, 1814; Henry E.J. Howard, 1854; Martin
Pope, 1934.
Eidyllia, as *The Phoenix of Claudian*, translated by Arthur Smith(?).
1714.
Epigrammata, as *De Sene Veronensi*, translated by Andrew Symon.
1708.
Epithalamium for the Marriage of Honorius, translated by H. Isbell,
in *The Last Poets of Imperial Rome*. 1971.
In Eutropium, edited by P. Fargues. 1933.
In Rufinum, edited by Harry L. Levy. 1935; translated as *Rufinus; or,
the Favourite*, 1712; as *Elegant History of Rufinus*, translated by
Jabez Hughes, in *Miscellanies in Verse and Prose*, 1737; com-
mentary by Harry L. Levy, 1971.
Panegyric on the Third Consulate of Honorius, translated by William
Warburton. 1724.
Panegyric on the Fourth Consulate of Honorius, edited and translated
by William Barr. 1981.
Panegyricus de sexto consulatu Honorii Augusti, edited and trans-
lated by Michael Dewar, 1996.

*

Critical Studies: *Claudian as an Historical Authority* by James
Crees, 1906; *The Influence of Ovid on Claudian* by Annette Hawkins
Eaton, 1943; *Secular Latin Poetry* by F.J.E. Raby, 1957; *The Use of
Images by Claudius Ctaudianus* by Peder G. Christiansen, 1969;
Claudian, Poet of Declining Empire and Morals by Oswald A.W.
Dilke, 1969; *Claudian: Poetry and Propaganda at the Court of
Honorius* by Alan D.E. Cameron, 1970; *Prolegomena to Claudian* by
J.B. Hall, 1986; *A Concordance to Claudianus* edited by Peder G.
Christiansen, 1988; *Claudian's In Eutropium, or, How, When, and
Why to Slander a Eunuch* by Jacqueline Long, 1996.

*   *   *

Claudian most deserves fame for resuscitating the secular traditions of Latin hexameter poetry. Roman historical and mythological
epic, having thrived during the era of Virgil and Ovid, lapsed after that
of Silius Italicus and Valerius Flaccus at the close of the 1st century
AD. Claudian was not the first poet of the 4th century to revive these
forms, but he was the most popular and influential.

Claudian was not born into Latin traditions, but in the Greek-
speaking Egyptian metropolis of Alexandria. Like others of the same
background, he became an itinerant hired poet (see Alan Cameron,
"Wandering Poets: a Literary Movement in Byzantine Egypt" in
Historia, 14, 1965); but Claudian, uniquely, travelled West. He first
published in Rome on the New Year of 395, panegyrizing two young
nobles of the ancient capital who had been named consuls for that
year. To have a panegyric in verse revolutionized western fashion.
Claudian also ingeniously turned the traditional structure to focus
neither on the consuls themselves nor on the emperor who appointed
them, but on their famous and recently deceased father Probus. He not
only earned his commission for the immediate occasion, but also bid
for patronage among Roman aristocrats who honoured Probus' memory.

The imperial court at Milan took up the bait. Claudian next
celebrated the third consulate of the Western emperor Honorius in
396. Not only did he praise Honorius and forecast favourably for the
year, as the occasion required, but he also introduced a hero behind
the throne. Between the resplendent scene of Honorius' triumphal
arrival at the Western court and the concluding prayers for worldwide triumphs of the Roman empire under Honorius' joint rule with
his brother Arcadius, he inserted a scene in which Honorius' and
Arcadius' father Theodosius entrusts the care of both sons to his son-
in-law, the general Stilicho. This historically dubious claim, superfluous to the panegyric structure, launched a theme which Claudian
continued to pursue in political poems for the next eight years:
exaltation of Stilicho as the true preserver of Roman values and glory.
Alan Cameron has argued that Claudian did not simply admire
Stilicho but was actually commissioned to portray him flatteringly
before Western aristocrats (*Claudian: Poetry and Propaganda at the
Court of Honorius*). Cameron's interpretation has been accepted
widely if not universally (see the reviews of Diegmar Dopp, *Anzeiger
für die Altertumswissenschaft*, 28, 1975, and Christian Gnilka, *Gno-
mon*, 49, 1977); but certainly Stilicho did receive favourable press
from Claudian, and manuscript evidence suggests that Stilicho sponsored collection and republication of Claudian's poems after he died
(see J.B. Hall, *Prolegomena to Claudian*). Claudian's long tenure as
court poet also guaranteed his works illustrious audiences.

The political relevance of many of Claudian's poems and his own
social prominence, however, only made his work conspicuous. His
artistry secured them long-lived popularity, just as it had secured his
prominence. His major poems divide between three books of an
unfinished mythological epic, *De raptu Proserpine* (*The Rape of
Proserpine*), and historical or political poems; they include panegyrics of
Honorius and other Western consuls including Stilicho; invectives
against ministers of Arcadius who were hostile to Stilicho; poems
celebrating Honorius' marriage to Stilicho's daughter, and epics that
display Stilicho's triumphant generalship. All are dominated structurally by visual tableaux, reported speeches, and expostulations in the
poet's own voice; this emphasis exceeds the norms of classical epic
but resembles contemporary Greek epic and encomiastic poetry.

Claudian stirred emotions with full rhetorical verve. He drew out
his central themes, finding ever newer points of view. His invective
against the eunuch Eutropius, for example, calls attention to his
emasculation in more than 60 separate passages. They range from
explicit references, to meditations on effeminacy, to extended portraits casting Eutropius in the female roles of an abandoned heroine
(burlesqued), a decaying bawd, and a bibulous old nursemaid. Modern critics sometimes deplore the endlessness of Claudian's fluency,
but contemporary audiences clearly delighted in the panoplies of
ideas and images that it spread. Michael Roberts has illuminated a late
antique aesthetic preference for brilliance in poetic descriptions and
construction as well as in visual arts (*The Jewelled Style: Poetry and*

Poetics in Late Antiquity, 1989). The triumphal processions of Honorius in the panegyrics for his third, fourth, and sixth consulates provide lush examples with gleaming robes, glittering armour, and dragon-banners that rustle and hiss in the wind like real snakes.

The majority of Claudian's minor poems, elegant and fashionable epigrams, describe marvels of both nature and art. In "The Gothic War," a flash of light from Stilicho's white hair first tells the anxious Romans that they will soon be rescued, and shows how excitingly such details can figure in epic narrative. Curiously, this latter item almost alone in Claudian's poetry reveals what anyone looked like. Eutropius' ghastly decrepitude, insect-ridden scalp and flapping wrinkles, which contrasted with his gorgeous consular robes, demonstrate Claudian's use of description not for its own sake, but for its emotional impact. His dense allusions to earlier Roman poets display a poetic consciousness of the past that would also have stirred the emotions of listeners equally imbued with poetical traditions. They reinforce Claudian's explicit emphasis on Roman themes in his political poems and operate no less in the mythological *The Rape of Proserpine* (Gualandri, 1969, and Moroni, 1982).

Claudian's poems perfectly fulfilled the sensibilities of his age. They consequently reinforced them and set a trend for subsequent Latin epic. He can be particularly credited with reviving the epic form in Latin; in his political poems he fused it so successfully with encomium as to have invented a new genre, which later generations of poets perpetuated (Heinz Hofmann, "Überlegungen zu einer Theorie der nichtchristlichen Epik der lateinischen Spätantike," *Philotogus*, 132, 1988). His political poems are thus seminal as well as vivid aesthetic documents, and, incidentally, major historical sources.

—Jacqueline Long

See the essay on *The Rape of Proserpine*.

CLAUS, Hugo

Born: Bruges, Belgium, 5 April 1929. **Education:** Primary education at various boarding schools; abandoned school before completing secondary education. **Military service:** 1949. **Family:** Married 1) Elly Overzier 1955, one son; relationship with Kitty Courbois and subsequently with Sylvia Kristel, who bore him a son; 2) Veerle de Wit, 1993. **Career:** Left home in 1946 to begin life as an independent artist and writer; lived in Paris, 1950–53, and Rome, 1953–55, and participated in the COBRA movement of avant-garde painters; moved to Ghent, 1955–66, and Nukerke, 1966–70, to build a career as a novelist, poet, playwright, painter, film and stage director, and author of film scenarios and opera libretti; incurred a four-month prison sentence (suspended) in 1968 for staging one of his plays featuring three nude men; moved to Amsterdam, 1970, back to Paris and then back to Ghent in 1978. Lives in Antwerp. **Awards:** *In Belgium:* Triennial prize for drama, 1955, 1967, 1973 and 1979; Triennial State prize for poetry, 1971; Triennial State prize for fiction, 1984; Triennial Culture prize of the Flemish Community, 1999. *Dutch-Flemish awards:* Constantijn Huygens prize, 1979; prize of Dutch Letters, 1986; prize of the Society of Dutch Letters, 1995. *International awards:* Prix Lugné-Poe (France), 1955; Ford Foundation grant (United States), 1959; Grand Prix de l'Humour Noir (France), 1989; Prix International Pier Paolo Pasolini (Italy), 1997; Aristeion prize (European Union), 1998; Premio Nonino (Italy), 2000; Preis für Europäische Poesie (City of Münster, Germany), 2001.

PUBLICATIONS

Collections

Gedichten. 1965, 1979.
Acht toneelstukken. 1966.
Gedichten 1969–1978. 1979.
Gedichten 1948–1993. 1994.
Toneel I–IV. 1988–93.
Toneel. 1999.
Verhalen. 1999.
Een andere keer: de andere verhalen. 1999.
Selected Poems 1953–1973, edited by Theo Hermans, translated by Theo Hermans, Paul Brown and Peter Nijmeijer. 1986.
Four Works for the Theatre by Hugo Claus, edited by David Willinger, translated by David Willinger, Lucas Truyts and Luc Deneulin. 1990.

Fiction

De Metsiers. 1950; as *The Duck Hunt*, translated by George Libaire, 1955; as *Sister of Earth*, translated by George Libaire. 1966.
De hondsdagen. 1952.
Natuurgetrouw. 1954.
De koele minnaar. 1956.
De zwarte keizer. 1958.
Het mes. 1961.
De verwondering. 1962.
Omtrent Deedee. 1963.
Natuurgetrouwer. 1969.
Schaamte. 1972.
Het jaar van de kreeft. 1972.
Jessica!. 1977.
Het verlangen. 1978; as *Desire*, translated by Stacey Knecht. 1997.
De verzoeking. 1981; as *The Temptation*, translated by David Willinger and Luc Deneulin, 1984, 1990.
Het verdriet van België. 1983; as *The Sorrow of Belgium*, translated by Arnold Pomerans, 1990.
De mensen hiernaast. 1985.
Een zachte vernieling. 1988.
Gilles en de nacht. 1989.
De zwaardvis. 1989; as *The Swordfish*, translated by Ruth Levitt, 1996.
Belladonna. 1994.
De geruchten. 1996.
Onvoltooid verleden. 1998.
Het laatste bed. 1998.
Een slaapwandeling. 2000.

Plays

Een bruid in de morgen. 1955.
Het lied van de moordenaar. 1957.
Suiker. 1958.
Mama, kijk, zonder handen!. 1959.
De dans van de reiger. 1962.

Vrijdag. 1969; as *Friday*, translated by Christopher Logue and the author, 1972; by David Willinger and Lucas Truyts, 1986, 1990.

Tand om tand. 1970.

Het leven en de werken van Leopold II. 1970; as *The Life and Works of Leopold II*, translated by David Willinger and Lucas Truyts, in *An Anthology of Contemporary Belgian Plays*, 1984.

Interieur. 1971.

Pas de deux. 1973.

Thuis. 1975; as *Back Home*, translated by David Willinger and Lucas Truyts, in *An Anthology of Contemporary Belgian Plays*, 1984.

Het huis van Labdakos. 1977.

Jessica!. 1977.

De verzoeking. 1981.

Het haar van de hond. 1982; as *The Hair of the Dog*, translated by David Willinger and Lucas Truyts, 1988, 1990.

Serenade. 1984; as *Serenade*, translated by David Willinger and Lucas Truyts, 1985, 1990.

Gilles!. 1988.

Het schommelpaard. 1988.

Onder de torens. 1993.

De eieren van de kaaiman. 1996.

De verlossing. 1996.

Visite. 1996.

Winteravond. 1996; as *Winter Evening*, translated by Paul Charters, Katheryn Ronnau Bradbeer and Paul Vincent, in *Modern Poetry in Translation* (n.s.) 12, 1998.

De komedianten. 1997.

Poetry

Kleine reeks. 1947.

Registreren. 1948.

Zonder vorm van process. 1950.

Tancredo infrasonic. 1952.

Een huis dat tussen nacht en morgen staat. 1953.

Paal en perk. 1955.

De Oostakkerse gedichten. 1955.

Een geverfde ruiter. 1961.

Het teken van de hamster. 1963; as *The Sign of the Hamster*, translated by Paul Claes, Christine D'haen, Theo Hermans and Yann Lovelock, 1986.

Heer Everzwijn. 1970.

Van horen zeggen. 1970.

Dag, jij. 1971.

Figuratief. 1973.

De wangebeden. 1978.

Claustrum. 1980.

Almanak. 1982.

Alibi. 1985.

Sonnetten. 1988.

De sporen. 1993.

Wreed geluk. 1999.

De groeten. 2002.

*

Bibliography: *Studie- en Documentatiecentrum Hugo Claus*. [Online] http://pcger46.uia.ac.be/homepage.htm. Accessed June 2002.

Critical Studies: *Het geclausuleerde beest* by Theo Goovaert, 1962; *Hugo Claus, traditie en experiment* by Jean Weisgerber, 1970; *Over Claus' tonee* by Jacques de Decker, 1971; *Hugo Claus of Oedipus in het paradijs* by Georges Wildemeersch, 1973; *Claus Quadrifrons* by Paul Claes, 1978; *Over De Verwondering van Hugo Claus* by Joris Duytschaever, 1979; *Over De hondsdagen van Hugo Claus* by G.F.H. Raat, 1980; *De pen gaat waar het hart niet kan* edited by Gerd de Ley, 1980; *De mot zit in de mythe* by Paul Claes, 1984; *Claus-reading* by Paul Claes, 1984; *Hugo Claus* by Freddy de Vree, 1984; *Hugo Claus* by Bert Kooijman, 1984; *Over Hugo Claus via bestaande modellen*, edited by H. Dütting, 1984; *Onbewoonbare huizen zijn de woorden* by Dirk de Geest, 1989; *Het spiegelpaleis van Hugo Claus* edited by Daan Cartens and Freddy de Vree, 1991; *Dodelijke dikke wolken* by Rudi van der Paardt and Freddy Decreus, 1992; *Het paard begeerte* by Johan Thielemans, 1994; *Claus geheimschrift* by Dina and Jean Weisgerber, 1995; *Het teken van de ram. Jaarboek van de Claus-studie*, yearbook from 1995; *Hugo Claus—wat bekommert zich de leeuw om de vlooien in zijn vacht?* edited by Georges Wildemeersch, 1999; 'Claus the Chameleon' by Paul Claes in *The Low Countries* 1, 1993–94.

*   *   *

Hugo Claus' literary output, which runs to around 150 titles to date, is daunting for its complexity and diversity as well as for its size. At once the *enfant terrible* of contemporary Dutch-language writing and its most prized and celebrated author, his work ranges across genres and styles. He varies literary modes and linguistic registers with astonishing ease and alternates between elemental passion and political satire, unabashed naturalism and allusive erudition, Oedipal imagery and grotesque humour. A restless experimental streak runs through his entire oeuvre. His original output is supplemented with a large number of translations and adaptations, especially for the stage—including work by Shakespeare, Cyril Tourneur, Ben Jonson, Christopher Marlowe, Dylan Thomas, Noel Coward, Georg Büchner, Federico García Lorca, Seneca, Sophocles, Euripides, Aristophanes and others. He has also rewritten his own prose for the stage and vice versa.

An uncompromising, anarchic zest for life informs much of Claus' work, but he is not a writer given to pursuing a single theme or form. Indeed the other side of the insistence on the libidinal is Claus' expert use of allusion and wordplay, often deployed together in dense intertextual webs. His most important work of fiction, the epic novel *Het verdriet van België* (*The Sorrow of Belgium*), may be read autobiographically as an account of his own development as a writer. Set in the years before, during, and just after World War II, the book tells the story of a young Flemish boy who observes the chaotic world around him with wilful incomprehension and ironic detachment. Fragmented and kaleidoscopic, tender and carnivalesque, the novel presents a portrait of the artist as a recalcitrant young man but also offers biting social criticism and an engaging period evocation. In the end, however, the protagonist's decision to go his own stubbornly independent way is existential rather than political.

Although Claus' work is much too varied to allow the application of a single label to characterize it, it is, on the whole, more concerned with a violent distaste for the constraints imposed by social conventions, family ties, church and state than with any positive ideals. In that sense its hankering after freedom is overshadowed by a pervasive, illusionless pessimism. The dark, brooding secrets of the past which cloud personal and social relationships in many of his novels, stories, and plays appear both as Oedipal drives and as the signs of political and moral corruption. The only redeeming force is a strongly physical, blind love that does not ask questions but takes the here and now for what it is worth.

In all the genres that he practises Claus pushes his portrayal of human nature beyond the limits of conventional realism. As a result, some characters are larger than life and assume mythical proportions, while others turn into grimacing caricatures, primitive brutes or tormented victims. Like Francis Bacon's—and indeed his own— paintings, Claus' literary works intrigue and shock because they intensify the human condition to the point where its raw nerves are rendered visible through the distortion.

—Theo Hermans

COCTEAU, Jean (Maurice Eugène Clément)

Born: Maisons-Laffitte, France, 5 July 1889. **Education:** Educated at the Lycée Condorcet, Paris, and privately. **Career:** Entered Parisian literary and theatrical circles, giving readings and attending functions; cofounder, *Shéhérazade* magazine, 1909; collaborated with Diaghilev's Ballets Russes as librettist, designer and painter, from c. 1911; joined the Red Cross, 1914; co-editor, *le Mot*, 1914–15; contributor, *Paris-Midi*, 1919; travelled around the world, under commission to write articles for *Paris-Soir*, 1936–37; travelled to the United States, 1949. President, Jazz Academy; Honorary President, Cannes Film Festival. **Awards:** Louions-Delluc prize, 1946; Avant-garde Film Grand prize, 1950. D.Litt.: Oxford University, 1956. Commander, Légion d'honneur, 1961. **Member:** Académie française, 1955; Royal Academy of Belgium; honorary member, American Academy and German Academy. **Died:** 11 October 1963.

PUBLICATIONS

Plays

Les Mariés de la Tour Eiffel (produced 1921). 1924; as *The Eiffel Tower Wedding Party*, translated by Dudley Fitts, in *The Infernal Machine and Other Plays*, 1963; as *The Wedding on the Eiffel Tower*, translated by Michael Benedikt, in *Modern French Plays*, edited by Benedikt and George Wellwarth, 1965.
Antigone (produced 1922; revised version, music by Arthur Honegger, produced 1927). 1927; as *Antigone*, translated by Carl Wildman, in *Five Plays*, 1961.
Roméo et Juliette, from the play by Shakespeare (produced 1924). 1926.
Orphée (produced 1926). 1927: as *Orpheus*, translated by Carl Wildman, 1933; also translated by John Savacool, in *The Infernal Machine and Other Plays*, 1963; Carol Martin-Sperry, 1972.
Le Pauvre Matelot, music by Darius Milhaud (produced 1927). 1927.
Oedipus Rex, music by Stravinsky (produced 1927). 1949.
Oedipe-Roi (produced 1937). 1928.
La Voix humaine (produced 1930). 1930; as *The Human Voice*, translated by Carl Wildman, 1951.

La Machine infernale (produced 1934). 1934; as *The Infernal Machine*, translated by Carl Wildman, 1936, revised version, in *International Modern Plays*, edited by Anthony Bent, 1950; also translated by Albert Bermel, in *The Infernal Machine and Other Plays*, 1963.
Les Chevaliers de la table ronde (produced 1937). 1937; as *The Knights of the Round Table*, translated by W.H. Auden, in *The Infernal Machine and Other Plays*, 1963.
Les Parents terribles (produced 1938). 1938; edited by R.K. Totton, 1972; translated by Jeremy Sans, 1994; as *Intimate Relations*, translated by Charles Franck, in *Five Plays*, 1962.
Les Monstres sacrés (produced 1940). 1940; as *The Holy Terrors*, translated by E.O. Marsh, in *Five Plays*, 1962.
La Machine à écrire (produced 1941). 1941; as *The Typewriter*, translated by Ronald Duncan, 1947.
Renaud et Armide (produced 1943). 1943.
L'Aigle à deux têtes (produced 1946). 1946; as *The Eagle Has Two Heads,* translated by Ronald Duncan, 1948; as *The Eagle with Two Heads,* translated by Carl Wildman, 1961.
Ruy Blas (screenplay). 1947.
Le Sang d'un poète (screenplay). 1948; as *The Blood of a Poet,* translated by Lily Pons, 1949; also translated by Carol Martin-Sperry, in *Two Screenplays*, 1968.
Un tramway nommé désir, from the play by Tennessee Williams (produced 1949). 1949.
Théâtre de poche (includes scenarios, sketches, and radio works). 1949.
Orphée (screenplay). 1951; as *Orpheé*, in *Three Screenplays*, 1972.
Bacchus (produced 1951). 1952; as *Bacchus,* translated by Mary Hoeck, in *The Infernal Machine and Other Plays*, 1963.
La Belle et la bête (screenplay). 1958; as *La Belle et la bête*, translated by Carol Martin-Sperry, in *Three Screenplays*, 1972.
Cher menteur, from the play by Jerome Kilty (produced 1960). 1960.
Le Testament d'Orphée (screenplay). 1961; as *The Testament of Orpheus,* translated by Carol Martin-Sperry, in *Two Screenplays*, 1968.
L'Impromptu du Palais-Royal (produced 1962). 1962.
L'Éternel Retour (screenplay), as *L'éternel retour,* translated by Carol Martin Sperry, in *Three Screenplays.* 1972.

Screenplays: *Le Sang d'un poète,* 1930; *La Comédie du bonheur,* 1940; *Le Baron fantôme,* with Serge de Poligny, 1943; *L'Éternel Retour,* 1943; *Les Dames du Bois du Boulogne,* with Robert Bresson, 1945; *La Belle et la bête,* 1946; *Ruy Blas,* 1947; *L'Aigle à deux têtes,* 1948; *Les Parents terribles,* 1948; *Noces de sable,* 1949; *Les Enfants terribles,* 1950; *Orphée,* 1950; *La Villa Santo-Sospiro,* 1952; *La Corona Negra,* 1952; *Le Testament d'Orphée,* 1960; *La Princesse de Clèves,* 1961; *Thomas l'imposteur,* 1965.

Ballet scenarios: *Le Dieu bleu,* 1912; *Parade,* 1917; *Le Boeuf sur le toit,* 1920; *Le Train bleu,* 1924; *Le Jeune Homme et la mort,* 1946; *La Dame à la licorne,* 1953; *Le Poète et sa muse,* 1959.

Fiction

Le Potomak. 1919; revised edition, 1934.
Le Grand Écart. 1923; as *The Grand Écart*, translated by Lewis Galantière, 1925; as *The Miscreant*, translated by Dorothy Williams, 1958.

Thomas l'imposteur. 1923; as *Thomas the Imposter,* translated by Lewis Galantière, 1925; as *The Imposter,* translated by Dorothy Williams, 1957.

Le Livre blanc. 1928; as *The White Paper,* 1957; as *The White Book,* translated by Margaret Crosland, 1989.

Les Enfants terribles. 1929; as *Enfants Terribles,* translated by Samuel Putnam, 1930; as *Children of the Game,* translated by Rosamond Lehmann, 1955; as *The Holy Terrors,* translated by Lehmann, 1957.

Le Fantôme de Marseille. 1936.

Le Fin du Potomak. 1940.

Deux travestis. 1947.

Verse

La Lampe d'Aladin. 1909.

Le Prince frivole. 1910.

La Danse de Sophocle. 1912.

Le Cap de Bonne-espérance. 1919.

Ode à Picasso. 1919.

Discours du grand sommeil. 1920.

Escales, with André Lhote. 1920.

Poésies 1917–20. 1920.

Vocabulaire. 1922.

Plain-chant. 1923.

La Rose de François. 1923.

Poésie 1916–23. 1924.

Cri écrit. 1925.

Prière mutilée. 1925.

L'Ange Heurtebise. 1926.

Opéra: Oeuvres poétiques 1925–27. 1927.

Morceaux choisis. 1932.

Mythologie. 1934.

Allégories. 1941.

Les Poèmes allemands. 1944.

Léone. 1945; translated as *Leoun,* 1960.

La Crucifixion. 1946.

Poèmes. 1948.

Le Chiffre. 1952.

Appogiatures. 1953.

Dentelle d'éternité. 1953.

Clair-obscur. 1954.

Poèmes 1916–1955. 1956.

Gondole des morts. 1959.

Cérémonial espagnol du phénix; La Partie d'échecs. 1961.

Le Requiem. 1961.

Faire-part. 1969.

Tempest of Stars: Selected Poems (bilingual edition), translated by Jeremy Reed. 1992.

Other

Le Coq et l'arlequin: Notes autour de la musique. 1918; as *Cock and Harlequin,* translated by Rollo H. Myers, 1921.

Dans le ciel de la patrie. 1918.

Carte blanche. 1920.

La Noce massacrée. 1921.

Le Secret professionnel. 1922; *Professional Secrets: An Autobiography,* edited by Robert Phelps, translated by Richard Howard, 1970.

Dessins. 1923.

Picasso. 1923.

Ferat. 1924.

Le Mystère de l'oiseleur. 1925.

Lettre à Jacques Maritain. 1926.

Le Rappel à l'ordre (essays). 1926; as *A Call to Order,* translated by Rollo H. Myers, 1926.

Maison de santé: dessins. 1926.

Le Mystère laïc. 1928.

Une entrevue sur la critique avec Maurice Rouzaud. 1929.

25 Dessins d'un dormeur. 1929.

Essai de critique indirecte. 1932; as *An Essay in Indirect Criticism,* translated by Olga Rudge, 1936.

Opium. 1932; as *Opium: Diary of an Addict,* translated by Ernest Boyd, 1932: also translated by Margaret Crosland and Sinclair Rood, 1957.

Portraits-souvenir 1900–1914. 1935; as *Paris Album 1900–1914,* translated by Margaret Crosland, 1956; as *Souvenir Portraits: Paris in the Belle Epoch,* translated by Jesse Browner, 1991.

60 Dessins pour "Les Enfants terribles." 1935.

Mon Premier Voyage: Tour du monde en 80 jours. 1936; as *Round the World Again in Eighty Days,* translated by Stuart Gilbert, 1937; as *My Journey Round the World,* translated by Walter J. Strachan, 1958.

Énigme. 1939.

Dessins en marge du texte des "Chevaliers de la table ronde." 1941.

Le Greco. 1943.

Serge Lifar à l'opéra. 1944.

Portrait de Mounet-Sully. 1945.

La Belle et la bête: Journal d'un film. 1946; as *The Diary of a Film,* translated by Ronald Duncan, 1950.

Poésie critique. 1946.

Oeuvres complètes. 11 vols., 1946–51.

La Difficulté d'être. 1947; as *The Difficulty of Being,* translated by Elizabeth Sprigge, 1966.

Le Foyer des artistes. 1947.

Art and Faith: Letters Between Jacques Maritain and Jean Cocteau, translated by John Coleman. 1948.

Drôle de ménage. 1948.

Reines de France. 1948.

Lettre aux américains. 1949.

Maalesh: Journal d'une tournée de théâtre. 1949; as *Maalesh: A Theatrical Tour in the Middle-East,* translated by Mary C. Hoeck, 1956.

Dufy. 1949.

Orson Welles, with André Bazin. 1950.

Modigliani, 1950.

Jean Marais. 1951.

Entretiens autour du cinématographe, edited by André Fraigneau. 1951; revised edition, edited by André Bernard and Claude Gauteur, 1973; as *Cocteau on Film,* translated by Vera Traill, 1954; as *The Art of Cinema,* translated by Robin Buss, 1992.

Gide vivant, with Julien Green. 1952.

La Nappe du Catalan. 1952.

Journal d'un inconnu. 1953; as *The Hand of a Stranger,* translated by Alec Brown, 1956; as *Diary of an Unknown,* translated by Jesse Browner, 1988.

Aux confins de la Chine. 1955.

Lettre sur la poésie. 1955.

Le Dragon des mets. 1955.

Journals, edited and translated by Wallace Fowlie. 1956.

Adieu à Mistinguett. 1956.

L'Art est un sport. 1956.

Impression: Arts de la rue. 1956.

Cocteau chez les sirènes, edited by Jean Dauven. 1956.

Témoignage. 1956.

Entretiens sur la musée de Dresde, with Louis Aragon. 1957; as *Conversations in the Dresden Gallery,* 1983.

Erik Satie. 1957.

La Chapelle Saint-Pierre, Villefranche-sur-Mer. 1957.

La Corrida du premier mai. 1957.

Comme un miel noir (in French and English). 1958.

Paraprosodies, précédées de 7 dialogues. 1958.

La Salle des mariages, Hôtel de Ville de Menton. 1958.

La Canne blanche. 1959.

Poésie critique: Monologues. 1960.

Notes sur ''Le Testament d'Orphée.'' 1960.

Le Cordon ombilical: Souvenirs. 1962.

Hommage. 1962.

Anna de Noailles oui et non. 1963.

Adieux d'Antonio Ordonez. 1963.

La Mésangère. 1963.

Entretien avec Roger Stéphane. 1964.

Entretien avec André Fraigneau. 1965.

Pégase. 1965.

My Contemporaries, edited and translated by Margaret Crosland. 1967.

Entre Radiguet et Picasso. 1967.

Lettres à André Gide, edited by Jean-Jacques Kihm. 1970.

Cocteau's World (selections), edited and translated by Margaret Crosland. 1972.

Cocteau, poète graphique, edited by Pierre Chanel. 1975.

Lettres à Milorad, edited by Milorad. 1975.

Le Passé défini (journals), edited by Pierre Chanel. 2 vols., 1986; as *Past Tense: The Cocteau Diaries,* translated by Richard Howard, 2 vols., 1987–90.

Lettres à Jean Marais. 1987.

Journal 1942–1945, edited by Jean Touzot. 1989.

Correspondance, 1911–1931, with Anna de Noailles, edited by Claude Mignot-Ogliastri. 1989.

Lettres à sa mère 1: 1898–1918, edited by Pierre Caizergues. 1989.

Correspondance, with Lucien Clerque. 1989.

Correspondance, with Guillaume Apollinaire, edited by Pierre Caizergues and Michel Décaudin. 1991.

The Passionate Penis: Drawings, with introduction by Margaret Crosland. 1993.

A Day With Picasso: Twenty-four Photographs by Jean Cocteau by Billy Klüver

Editor, *Almanach du théâtre et du cinéma.* 1949.

Editor, *Choix de lettres de Max Jacob à Jean Cocteau 1919–1944.* 1949.

Editor, *Amadeo Modigliani: Quinze dessins.* 1960.

*

Critical Studies: *Cocteau* by Margaret Crosland, 1956; *Scandal and Parade: The Theatre of Jean Cocteau* by Neal Oxenhandler, 1957; *Jean Cocteau: The History of a Poet's Age* by Wallace Fowlie, 1966; *Cocteau: The Man and the Mirror* by Elizabeth Sprigge and Jean-Jacques Kihm, 1968; *An Impersonation of Angels: A Biography of Jean Cocteau* by Frederick Brown, 1968; *Cocteau: A Biography* by Francis Steegmuller, 1970; *Jean Cocteau* by Bettina L. Knapp, 1970, revised edition, 1989; *Jean Cocteau and André Gide: An Abrasive Friendship* by Arthur King Peters, 1973; *Jean Cocteau* by William Fifield, 1974; *Jean Cocteau and His Films of Orphic Identity* by Arthur B. Evans, 1977; *The Esthetic of Cocteau* by Lydia Crowson, 1978; *Jean Cocteau and the French Scene* edited by Arthur Peters, 1984; *The Dance Theatre of Jean Cocteau* by Frank W.D. Ries, 1985; *Les Enfants terribles* by Robin Buss, 1986; *Jean Cocteau and the Dance* by Erik Aschengreen, 1986; *Jean Cocteau and His World* by Arthur K. Peter, 1987; *Reviewing Orpheus: Essays on the Cinema and Art of Jean Cocteau,* edited by Cornelia A. Tsakiridou, 1997; *Jean Cocteau* by Patrick Mauriès, 1998.

* * *

Precociously Jean Cocteau published his first volume of verse at the age of 19. A small public flattered him and applauded the facile brilliance of the poems. Between 1917 and 1919, with three very different works, Cocteau became a public figure. *Parade,* of 1917, a ballet performed in Rome, was an early experiment with the theatre. *Le Coq et l'arlequin* (*Cock and Harlequin*), a manifesto against the disciples of Debussy and Wagner, revealed his interest in aesthetics and his powers as a critic. *Le Cap de Bonne-espérance* [The Cape of Good Hope], a volume of war poems, placed him in the ranks of the best young poets. Poetry was the mark of all three works, and the principle which was thereafter to direct Cocteau's varied activities.

His sentence is swift and seemingly lucid, but the content is mysterious and enigmatical. Cocteau's style became a manner of expressing complicated matters with discerning simplicity. The poems of *Vocabulaire* contained the key words of his poetic experience, symbols and characters projected out of his imagination that were to form in time his mythology—episodes, myths, and characters charged with the duty of narrating the poet's drama. Kidnappers, sailors, angels, and cyclists appear and disappear as if searching for their poet.

The play *Orphée* (*Orpheus*), performed in Paris in 1926 by Georges and Ludmilla Pitoëff, was his first work to reach a fairly wide public. In *Orpheus,* the poet appears to be the combined characters of Orpheus and Angel Heurtebise. The action of the play is both familiar and esoteric; in it Orpheus is both poet and hierophant, both husband and priest.

Les Enfants terribles (*The Holy Terrors*) was written in three weeks and published in 1929. This book has now become a classic, both as a novel belonging to the central tradition of the short French novel, and as a document of historical-psychological significance in the study it offers of the type of adolescent referred to in the title. The intertwined destinies of brother and sister, Paul and Elisabeth, with the dark forbidding figure of Dargelos behind them, provide an unusual picture of adolescence in its actions and speech and games.

The theme of Cocteau's first film, *Le Sang d'un poète* (*The Blood of a Poet*), was an idea close to the romantics a century earlier, in which the poet writes with his own blood. Much later, in the film *Orphée* Cocteau developed this lesson of the poet and borrowed from

The Blood of a Poet and his play *Orpheus*. These films are two esoteric poems for the screen.

In his plays, as in *La Machine infernale* (*The Infernal Machine*), on the Oedipus theme, Cocteau presented experimentations on the stage with the enthusiasm of a dramatist enamoured of the theatre and of the idea of a spectacle. Between the death of Apollinaire in 1918 and his own death in 1963, Cocteau occupied an active position in all the domains of French art.

—Wallace Fowlie

See the essays on *The Holy Terrors* and *The Infernal Machine*.

COLETTE, (Sidonie-Gabrielle)

Born: Saint-Saveur en Puisaye, France, 28 January 1873. **Education:** Educated at local school to age 16. **Family:** Married 1) the writer Henry Gauthier-Villars ("Willy") in 1893 (divorced 1910); 2) Henry de Jouvenal in 1912 (divorced 1925), one daughter; 3) Maurice Goudeket in 1935. **Career:** Actress and revue performer, 1906–27; columnist, 1910–19, and literary editor, 1919–24, *Le Matin*; drama critic, *La Revue de Paris*, 1929, *Le Journal*, 1934–39, *L'Éclair*, and *Le Petit Parisien*; operated a beauty clinic, Paris, 1932–33. **Awards:** Chevalier, 1920, officer, 1928, commander, 1936, and grand officer, 1953, Légion d'honneur; City of Paris Grande Médaille, 1953. **Member:** Belgian Royal Academy, 1936; member, 1945, and president, 1949, Académie Goncourt; honorary member, American Academy, 1953. **Died:** 3 August 1954.

PUBLICATIONS

Collections

Works. 17 vols., 1951–64.
Oeuvres complètes. 16 vols., 1973.
Collected Stories, edited by Robert Phelps. 1983.
Oeuvres, edited by Claude Pichois. 1984–.

Fiction

Claudine à l'école, with Willy. 1900; as *Claudine at School*, translated by Janet Flanner, 1930; also translated by H. Mirande, 1930; Antonia White, 1956.
Claudine à Paris, with Willy. 1901; as *Claudine in Paris*, 1931; as *Young Lady of Paris*, translated by James Whitall, 1931; also translated by Antonia White, 1958.
Claudine amoureuse, with Willy. 1902; as *Claudine en ménage*, 1902; as *The Indulgent Husband*, translated by Frederick A. Blossom, 1935; as *Claudine Married*, translated by Antonia White, 1960.
Claudine s'en va, with Willy. 1903; as *The Innocent Wife*, translated by Frederick A. Blossom, 1934; as *Claudine and Annie*, translated by Antonia White, 1962.
Minne; Les Égarements de Minne. 2 vols., 1903–05; revised version, as *L'Ingénue libertine*, 1909; as *The Gentle Libertine*, translated by Rosemary Carr Benét, 1931; as *The Innocent Libertine*, translated by Antonia White, 1968.

La Retraite sentimentale. 1907; as *Retreat from Love*, translated by Margaret Crosland, 1974.
Les Vrilles de la vigne. 1908.
La Vagabonde. 1911; as *The Vagrant*, 1912; as *Renée la vagabonde*, translated by Charlotte Remfry-Kidd, 1931; as *The Vagabond*, translated by Enid McLeod, 1954.
L'Entrave. 1913; as *Recaptured*, translated by Viola Gerard Garvin, 1931; as *The Shackle*, translated by Antonia White, 1963.
Les Enfants dans les ruines. 1917.
Dans la foule. 1918.
Mitsou; ou, Comment l'esprit vient aux filles. 1919; as *Mitsou; or, How Girls Grow Wise*, translated by Jane Terry, 1930.
La Chambre éclairée. 1920.
Chéri. 1920; as *Chéri*, translated by Janet Flanner, 1929; also translated by Roger Senhouse, 1974.
Le Blé en herbe. 1923; as *The Ripening Corn*, translated by Phyllis Mégroz, 1921; as *The Ripening*, translated by Ida Zeitlin, 1932; as *The Ripening Seed*, translated by Roger Senhouse, 1956.
La Femme cachée. 1924; as *The Other Woman*, translated by Margaret Crosland, 1971.
Quatre saisons. 1925.
La Fin de Chéri. 1926; as *The Last of Chéri*, translated anonymously, 1932; also translated by Viola Gerard Garvin, 1933; Roger Senhouse, 1951.
La Naissance du jour. 1928; as *A Lesson in Love*, translated by Rosemary Carr Benét, 1932; as *Morning Glory*, 1932; as *The Break of Day*, translated by Enid McLeod, 1961.
La Seconde. 1929; as *The Other One*, translated by Elizabeth Tait and Roger Senhouse, 1931; as *Fanny and Jane*, translated by Viola Gerard Garvin, 1931.
Paradises terrestres. 1932.
La Chatte. 1933; as *The Cat*, translated by Morris Bentinck, 1936, also translated by Antonia White, 1955; as *Saha the Cat*, 1936.
Duo. 1934; as *Duo*, translated by Frederick A. Blossom, 1935; also translated by Margaret Crosland, with *The Toutounier*, 1974; as *The Married Lover*, translated by Marjorie Laurie, 1935.
Bella-Vista. 1937.
Le Toutounier. 1939; as *The Toutounier*, translated by Margaret Crosland, with *Duo*, 1974.
Chambre d'hôtel. 1940; in *Julie de Carneilhan and Chance Acquaintances*, translated by Patrick Leigh Fermor, 1952.
Julie de Carneilhan. 1941; as *Julie de Carneilhan*, in *Julie de Carneilhan and Chance Acquaintances* translated by Patrick Leigh Fermor, 1952.
Le Képi. 1943.
Gigi et autres nouvelles. 1944; as *Gigi*, translated by Roger Senhouse, 1952.
Stories, translated by Antonia White. 1958; as *The Tender Shoot and Other Stories*, 1959.

Plays

En camerades (produced 1909). In *Oeuvres complètes*, 15, 1950.
Claudine, music by Rodolphe Berger, from the novel by Colette (produced 1910). 1910.
Chéri, with Léopold Marchand, from the novel by Colette (produced 1921). 1922; translated as *Cheri*, 1959.
La Vagabonde, with Léopold Marchand, from the novel by Colette (produced 1923), 1923.

L'Enfant et les sortilèges, music by Maurice Ravel (produced 1925). 1925; as *The Boy and the Magic*, translated by Christopher Fry, 1964.

La Décapitée (ballet scenario), in *Mes Cahiers*. 1941.

Gigi, with Anita Loos, from the story by Colette (produced 1951). 1952; in French, 1954.

Jeune filles en uniform, Lac aux dames, Divine (screenplays), in *Au Cinéma*. 1975.

Screenplays: *La Vagabonde*, 1917, remake, 1931; *La Femme cachée*, 1919; *Jeunes filles en uniform* (French dialogue for German film *Mädchen in Uniform*), 1932; *Lac aux dames*, 1934; *Divine*, 1935.

Other

Dialogues de bêtes. 1904; enlarged edition, as *Sept dialogues de bêtes*, 1905; as *Douze dialogues de bêtes*, 1930; as *Barks and Purrs*, translated by Marie Kelly, 1913; as *Creatures Great and Small*, translated by Enid McLeod, 1951.

L'Envers du music-hall. 1913; as *Music-Hall Sidelights*, translated by Anne-Marie Callimachi, 1957.

Prrou, Poucette, et quelques autres. 1913; revised edition, as *La Paix chez les bêtes*, 1916; as *Cats, Dogs, and I*, translated by Alexandre Gagarine, 1924; also translated by Enid McLeod, in *Creatures Great and Small*, 1951.

Les Heures longues 1914–1917. 1917.

La Maison de Claudine. 1922; as *The Mother of Claudine*, translated by Charles King, 1937; as *My Mother's House*, translated by Enid McLeod and Una Vicenzo Troubridge, with *Sido*, 1953.

Le Voyage égoïste. 1922; translated in part by David Le Vay as *Journey for Myself: Selfish Memoirs*, 1971.

Rêverie du nouvel an. 1923.

Aventures quotidiennes. 1924; translated by David Le Vay, in *Journey for Myself: Selfish Memoirs*, 1971.

Renée Vivien. 1928.

Sido. 1929; as *Sido*, translated by Enid McLeod, with *My Mother's House*, 1953.

Histoires pour Bel-Gazou. 1930.

La Treille Muscate. 1932.

Prisons et paradis. 1932; translated in part by David Le Vay, in *Places*, 1970.

Ces plaisirs. 1932; as *Le Pur et l'impur*, 1941; as *The Pure and the Impure*, translated by Edith Dally, 1933, and by Herma Briffault, 1968; as *These Pleasures*, translated anonymously, 1934.

La Jumelle noire (theatre criticism). 4 vols., 1934–38.

Mes apprentissages. 1936; as *My Apprenticeships*, translated by Helen Beauclerk, 1957.

Chats. 1936.

Splendeur des papillons. 1937.

Mes cahiers. 1941.

Journal à rebours. 1941; as *Looking Backwards*, translated by David Le Vay 1975.

De ma fenêtre. 1942; enlarged edition, as *Paris de ma fenêtre*, 1944; translated by David Le Vay, in *Looking Backwards*, 1975.

De la patte à l'aile. 1943.

Flore et Pomone. 1943; as *Flowers and Fruit*, edited by Robert Phelps, translated by Matthew Ward, 1986.

Nudités. 1943.

Broderie ancienne. 1944.

Trois . . . six . . . neuf. 1944.

Belles Saisons. 1945; as *Belles Saisons: A Colette Scrapbook*, edited by Robert Phelps, 1978.

Une amitié inattendue (correspondence with Francis Jammes), edited by Robert Mallet. 1945.

L'Étoile vesper. 1946; as *The Evening Star: Recollections*, translated by David Le Vay, 1973.

Pour un herbier. 1948; as *For a Flower Album*, translated by Roger Senhouse, 1959.

Oeuvres complètes. 15 vols., 1948–50.

Trait pour trait. 1949.

Journal intermittent. 1949.

Le Fanal bleu. 1949; as *The Blue Lantern*, translated by Roger Senhouse, 1963.

La Fleur de l'âge. 1949.

En pays connu. 1949.

Chats de Colette. 1949.

Paysages et portraits. 1958.

Lettres â Hélène Picard, edited by Claude Pichois. 1958.

Lettres à Marguerite Moréno, edited by Claude Pichois. 1959.

Lettres de la vagabonde, edited by Claude Pichois and Roberte Forbin. 1961.

Lettres au petit corsaire, edited by Claude Pichois and Roberte Forbin. 1963.

Earthly Paradise: An Autobiography Drawn from Her Lifetime of Writing, edited by Robert Phelps, translated by Helen Beauclerk and others. 1966.

Places (miscellany; in English), translated by David Le Vay, 1970.

Contes de mille et un matins. 1970; as *The Thousand and One Mornings*, translated by Margaret Crosland and David Le Vay. 1973.

Journey for Myself: Selfish Memoirs (selection), translated by David Le Vay. 1971.

Lettres à ses pairs, edited by Claude Pichois and Roberte Forbin. 1973.

Au cinéma, edited by Alain and Odette Virmaux. 1975.

Letters from Colette, edited and translated by Robert Phelps. 1980.

*

Bibliography: *Colette: An Annotated Primary and Secondary Bibliography*, compiled and annotated by Donna M. Norell, 1993.

Critical Studies: *Madame Colette: A Provincial in Paris*, 1952, and *Colette: The Difficulty of Loving*, 1973, both by Margaret Crosland; *Colette* by Elaine Marks, 1960; *Colette* by Margaret Davies, 1961; *Colette* by Robert D. Cottrell, 1974; *Colette: A Taste for Life* by Yvonne Mitchell, 1975; *Colette: Free and Fettered* by Michèle Sarde, translated by Richard Miller, 1980; *Colette: The Woman, The Writer* edited by Erica M. Eisinger and Mari McCarty, 1981; *Colette* by Joan Hinde Stewart, 1983; *Colette* by Joanna Richardson, 1983; *Colette: A Passion for Life* by Genevieve Dormann, translated by David Macey, 1985; *Colette* by Allan Massie, 1986; *Colette* by Nicola Ward Jouve, 1987; *Colette: A Life* by Herbert Lottman, 1991; *Colette* by Diana Holmes, 1991; *Colette and the Fantom Subject of Autobiography* by Jerry Aline Flieger, 1992; *Colette: A Study of the Short Fiction* by Dana Strand, 1995; *Creating Colette* by Claude Francis and Fernande Gontier, 1998; *Secrets of the Flesh: A Life of Colette* by Judith Thurman, 1999; *Colette, Beauvoir, and Duras: Age and Women Writers* by Bethany Ladimer, 1999.

*   *   *

Colette began her literary career under the tutelage of a man, her husband Willy; her first novels were written in collaboration with him and were published under his name. But the partnership was not a happy one, and after their divorce she branched out on her own. She wrote many more books, and survived into the second half of the 20th century, but she is essentially a *fin de siècle* writer who captures with great finesse and depth of perception the particular world which we call the *belle époque*: middle-class society in France (especially Paris) before 1914. She is particularly adept at exploring human relationships, such as the tragic love of a young man for a woman of 50 in *Chéri* and *La Fin de Chéri* (*The Last of Chéri*), or a husband's destructive jealousy of his wife in *Duo*, but she also writes with great sensitivity about children—in, for instance, *Claudine à l'école* (*Claudine at School*), her first book—and about nature, especially animals. This is not to imply, however, that she is a sentimental writer, quite the reverse: there is a toughness and a sharpness in her analysis of her characters' moods and whims which is firmly in the great French tradition of psychological precision inaugurated by Madame de Lafayette and continued by Constant and Stendhal. At her best she sustains comparison with these illustrious forebears in her unclouded perception of the ravages of love.

But her books, fine as some of them are, constitute only a part of her legacy. Like George Sand nearly a century earlier she worked hard as a professional woman of letters, and even, after her divorce from Willy, plunged for a time into the gruelling life of a professional actress and performer. This was a brave and original thing to do then, but it is characteristic of the lack of pretentiousness and of the nononsense attitude manifested in her fiction. Since she had to earn her own living after the break with Willy, she put her talents to good use. Unsentimental in her attitudes as in her art, she accepted that if she was to be free and independent she had to raise income by her own unaided efforts. Like Simone de Beauvoir, who is perhaps more of an intellectual though not necessarily more intelligent, she may in the last analysis be a minor writer only, but there is no doubt that she is a great woman, a figure of whom women of today can be proud. In spite of knowing great personal unhappiness in her younger days, she lived to become one of most famous and honoured writers of her generation, and this, in a male-dominated society, is no small achievement.

—John Fletcher

See the essay on *Chéri*.

COLONNA, Vittoria

Born: Colonna Castle, Marino (near Rome), Papal States, 25 February 1492. **Family:** Married Ferrante Francesco D'Avalos, Marquis of Pescara, in 1509 (died in battle, 1525). **Career:** Lived in the convents of Santa Caterina, Viterbo, and San Silvestro, Rome, after her husband's death (although she did not become a nun), and began to write poetry; became a leading literary figure to whom many significant humanist writers dedicated their works: had notable friendships with Pietro Bembo, *q.v.*, Baldassarre Castiglione, *q.v.*, and, particularly, Michelangelo (who painted her, and to whom she dedicated poetry). **Died:** 1547.

PUBLICATIONS

Collection

Rime e lettere, edited by E. Saltini. 1860.

Verse

Rime. 1538; revised edition, 1539; edited by Pietro Ercole Visconti, 1840, and by Alan Bullock, 1982; selections translated by Alethea J. Lawley, in *Vittoria Colonna,* 1888, anonymously, in *The "In Memoriam" of Italy: A Century of Sonnets from the Poems of Vittoria Colonna,* 1894, and by Joseph Tusiani, in *Italian Poets of the Renaissance,* 1971.

Other

Lettere inedite, edited by Giuseppe Piccioni. 1875.
Carteggio (correspondence), edited by Ermanno Ferrero and Giuseppe Müller. 1889; annotated by Domenico Tordi, 1892.

*

Critical Studies: *Vittoria Colonna: Her Life and Poems* by Maria Roscoe, 1868; *Vittoria Colonna* by Alethea J. Lawley, 1888; *The Romance of Woman's Influence* by Alice Corkran, 1906; *Vittoria Colonna and Some Account of Her Friends and Her Times* by Maud F. Jerrold, 1906: *La vita e l'opera di Vittoria Colonna* by A.A. Bernardy, 1927; *Vittoria Colonna* by Thomas Pawsey, 1953; "A Hitherto Unexplored Manuscript of One Hundred Poems by Vittoria Colonna in the Biblioteca Nazionale Centrale" by Alan Bullock, in *Italian Studies,* 21, 1966; *Un cénacle humaniste de la Renaissance autour de Vittoria Colonna châtelaine d'Ischia* by Suzanne Therault, 1968; "Vittoria Colonna" by Roland Bainton, in *Women of the Reformation in Germany and Italy,* 1971; "Vittoria Colonna's Friendship with the English Cardinal Reginald Pole" by Diane Dyer, in *Riscontri,* 7(1–2), 1985; "Neoplatonism in Vittoria Colonna's Poetry: From the Secular to the Divine" by Dennis J. McAuliffe, in *Ficino and Renaissance Neoplatonism* edited by Olga Zorzi Pugliese, 1986; "Vittoria Colonna: Child, Woman and Poet" by Joseph Gibaldi, in *Women Writers of the Renaissance and Reformation* edited by Katharina M. Wilson, 1987.

*   *   *

Renaissance Italy produced an extraordinary number of talented women writers, most of whom remain forgotten. Despite the advances in feminist scholarship that have brought the work of many earlier women writers back into focus, the Italian poets of the 15th and 16th centuries remain, for the most part, in obscurity. Vittoria Colonna is probably the best known of these poets, and was described by Buckhardt as the "most famous woman in Italy." Born into a noble family and married young, she was widowed at the age of 35 and never remarried. She moved to the Convent of San Silvestro in Rome, though did not actually join a religious order, using it as a base from which to travel extensively throughout Italy. She enjoyed close friendships with a number of leading contemporary intellectuals and artists, including Pietro Bembo, the cardinal-poet who encouraged her to write her own poetry, Castiglione, and Michelangelo. Her friendship with Michelangelo, in particular, led to an exchange of poems and letters that continued until her death in 1547, when Michelangelo wrote a series of moving poems about his loss, describing her as his "sun of suns," the woman whose strength in life lifted him closer to God.

Though Colonna was a Beatrice figure to Michelangelo, her own poetry was not written for any single person. Unlike Gaspara Stampa or Veronica Franco, two other important women poets of her day, her poetry does not deal with the delights of physical passion or with disappointment and unrequited love. Her love poems, written after her husband's death on the battlefield, are full of sadness, and although she uses the conventions of the Petrarchan tradition, her imagery is particularly powerful, and she writes of the illuminating force of her memories with great energy and power. Curiously, however, her first known poem, written when her husband was still alive, is completely different in tone. Her "Epistle to Ferrante Francesco d'Avalos, Her Husband, After the Battle of Ravenna" (written 1512) is an angry poem protesting about his preference for war over staying at home with his young wife:

> You live happily and have no cares:
> thinking only of your new won fame,
> you care not if I go hungry for your love;
> but I, with anger and sadness in my face,
> lie in your bed, abandoned and alone.

Reluctant to publish her poems, Colonna finally allowed a collection to appear in 1538, and it is clear that she saw poetry as an essentially private activity, even after the poems had come out and she had begun to be acclaimed as a major poet. (Some 20 editions appeared in the 16th century). Her "love poems" were written in the years immediately after her husband's death, and she then began to write what came to be called her "spiritual poems." Her long poem, 'Poi ch'il mio sol, d'eterni raggi cinto' ("The Triumph of Christ's Cross") praises the glories of divine love over worldly passions:

> Blessed is she who scorned worldly fruit,
> root and all, for now from her Lord
> she receives other, everlasting sweetness.

Divine love for Colonna is not a source of anguish or torment, it is a fount of perfection, a healing, consoling beauty. She appeals to Christ to tear off the veils, to unfasten the chains that have bound her in darkness. The imagery of her "spiritual poems" depicts a gentle Christ, bringing nourishment and consolation, a figure of healing, redemption, and liberation. Significantly, she writes movingly of Mary, whose suffering as Christ's mother provides a model for women, and of Mary Magdalene. In a sonnet on Mary Magdalene, "La bella donna, a cui dolente preme" [The Beautiful Woman Oppressed by Sorrows], she depicts Mary's loneliness and desperation at being abandoned by man and God, and contrasts that anguish with the security offered by the vision of the risen Christ in the garden:

> And those strong men, privileged
> by grace, huddled together in fear;
> the true Light seemed to them merely a shadow.
>
> So that, if truth is not overwhelmed by falsehood
> we must grant to women all the prize
> of having more loving and more constant hearts.

In Colonna's exquisitely crafted Petrarchan sonnets, through her Neoplatonic idealism, there is a clear portrait of a world of binary oppositions, a world in which women are forced to submit passively to whatever society decreed, while men go out into that world to try and change it through their actions. Yet, while she recognizes the inevitability of this pattern of behaviour, Colonna also protests against the injustice of it. From her early poem angrily chiding her military husband for leaving her at home uncared-for, to her later poetry extolling the joys that illuminate the heart of Mary Magdalene, she seems to be consistently demanding to be heard and speaking out for other women in similar positions. Her poetry is full of references to other women's pain; "Mentre la nave mia, lungi dal porto," one of her longer "love poems," compares her own suffering and wifely resignation to that of women from classical mythology—to Penelope and Laodmia, Ariadne and Medea, or Portia, wife of Brutus, the noblest Roman of them all—while "Poi ch'l mio sol, d'eterni raggi cinto" depicts the Virgin Mary and Mary Magdalene as examples of supreme womanhood.

Colonna's language has a clarity and precision that testify to her great poetic talent. In an age of many superbly gifted poets (and even more derivative, second-rate ones) her voice comes through powerfully and directly. She deserves to be more widely read and translated, because her poetry speaks to women (and men) of all times.

—Susan Bassnett

CORNEILLE, Pierre

Born: Rouen, France, June 1606; elder brother of the writer Thomas Corneille. **Education:** Educated in Jesuit college, Rouen, 1615–22; studied law, 1622–24, licensed lawyer, 1624. **Family:** Married Marie de Lampérière in 1641; seven children. **Career:** Member of the Rouen *Parlement,* 1629–50: held offices as King's advocate in water and forests court and in Rouen port Admiralty court. Lived in Paris after 1662. Elected to the Académie française, 1647. **Died:** 1 October 1684.

PUBLICATIONS

Collections

Oeuvres, edited by Charles Marty-Leaveaux. 12 vols., 1862–68.
Oeuvres completes, edited by A. Stegman. 1963.
Oeuvres complètes, edited by Georges Couton. 3 vols., 1980–87.
Théâtre complet, edited by Alain Niderst. 1984–.
Le Cid; Cinna; Polyeuct: Three Plays, translated by Noel Clark. 1993.
Three Masterpieces: The Liar, The Illusion, Le Cid, translated and adapted by Ranjit Bolt. 2000.

Plays

Mélite; ou, Les Fausses Lettres (produced 1629–30). 1633; translated as *Melite*, 1776.

Clitandre; ou, L'Innocence délivrée (produced 1630–31). 1632.

La Veuve; ou, Le Traître trahi (produced 1631–32). 1634.

La Galerie du Palais; ou, L'Amie rivale (produced 1632–33). 1637; edited by Milorad R. Margitic, 1981.

La Suivante (produced c. 1633–34). 1637; edited by Milorad R. Margitic, 1978.

La Place Royale; ou, L'Amoureux extravagant (produced c. 1633–34). 1637.

Médée (produced c. 1634–35). 1639; edited by André de Leyssac, 1978.

La Comédie des Tuileries, with others (produced 1635). 1638.

L'Illusion comique (produced 1635–36). 1639; as *The Theatrical Illusion,* with *The Cid* and *Cinna,* 1975; as *The Illusion,* with *The Liar,* 1989; as *The Comedy of Illusion,* translated with introduction by Lynette R. Muir, 2000.

Le Cid (produced 1637). 1637; revised version, 1682; translated as *The Cid,* 1637; several subsequent translations.

L'Aveugle de Smyrne, with Rotrou and others (produced 1637). 1638.

Horace (produced 1640). 1641; translated as *Horatius,* 1656; as *Horace,* in *The Chief Plays of Corneille,* 1952; translated by Albert Bernell, 1962; also translated by Alan Brownjohn, 1996.

Cinna; ou, La Clémence d'Auguste (produced 1642). 1643; as *Cinna's Conspiracy,* 1713; also translated as *Cinna.*

Polyeucte, Martyr (produced 1642–43). 1643; translated as *Polyeuctes,* 1655; as *Polyeucte,* in *The Chief Plays of Corneille,* 1952; as *Polyeuctus,* with *The Liar* and *Nicomedes,* 1980.

La Mort de Pompée (produced 1643–44). 1644; as *Pompey the Great,* 1664; as *La Mort de Pompée,* translated by Lacey Lockert, in *Moot Plays of Corneille,* 1959.

Le Menteur (produced 1643–44). 1644; as *The Mistaken Beauty; or, The Liar,* 1685; as *The Lying Lover,* 1717; as *The Liar,* with *Polyeuctus* and *Nicolmenedes,* 1980.

Oeuvres (plays). 1644; and later editions.

La Suite du Menteur (produced 1644–45). 1645.

Rodogune, Princesse des Parthes (produced 1644–45). 1645; translated as *Rodogune,* 1765.

Théodore, vierge et martyre (produced 1645–46). 1646 or 1647.

Héraclius, Empereur d'Orient (produced 1646–47). 1647; as *Heraclius, Emperor of the East,* 1664.

Andromède (produced 1650). 1650.

Don Sanche d'Aragon (produced 1649–50). 1650; as *The Conflict,* in *Plays and Poems,* 1798; as *Don Sanche d'Aragon,* translated by Lacey Lockert, in *Moot Plays of Corneille,* 1959.

Nicomède (produced 1651). 1651; translated as *Nicomede,* 1671.

Pertharite, Roi des Lombards (produced 1651–52). 1653.

Oedipe (produced 1659). 1659.

La Conquête de la toison d'or (produced 1660). 1661.

Sertorius (produced 1662). 1662; as *Sertorius,* translated by Lacey Lockert, in *Moot Play's of Corneille,* 1959.

Sophonisbe (produced 1663). 1663.

Othon (produced 1664). 1665; as *Othon,* translated by Lacey Lockert, in *Moot Plays of Corneille,* 1959.

Agésilas (produced 1666). 1666.

Attila, Roi des Huns (produced 1667). 1667; as *Attila,* translated by Lacey Lockert, in *Moot Plays of Corneille,* 1959.

Tite et Bérénice (produced 1670). 1671.

Psyché, with Molière and Quinault, music by Lully (produced 1671). 1671.

Pulchérie (produced 1672). 1673.

Suréna, Général des Parthes (produced 1674). 1675; translated as *Surenas,* 1969.

Other

Oeuvres diverses. 1738.

Writings on the Theatre, edited by H.T. Barnwell. 1965.

Translator, *L'Imitation de Jésus-Christ,* by Thomas à Kempis. 1651–56.

Translator, *Louanges de la Sainte Vierge,* by St. Bonaventure. 1665.

Translator, *L'Office de la Sainte Vierge,* by St. Bonaventure. 1670.

*

Critical Studies: *The Classical Moment: Studies of Corneille, Molière, and Racine* by Martin Turnell, 1947; *Corneille: His Heroes and Their Worlds* by Robert J. Nelson, 1963, and *Corneille and Racine: Parallels and Contrasts* edited by Nelson, 1966; *Corneille* by P.J. Yarrow, 1963; *The Cornelian Hero* by Albert West, 1963: *The Criticism of Cornelian Tragedy* by Herbert Fogel, 1967; *Corneille* by Claude K. Abraham, 1972; *Corneille and Racine: Problems of Tragic Form* by Gordon Pocock, 1973; *Corneille: Horace* by R.C. Knight, 1981; *The Tragic Drama of Corneille and Racine: An Old Parallel Revisited* by H.T. Barnwell, 1982; *The Comedies of Corneille* by G.J. Mallinson, 1984; *The Liar and the Lieutenant in the Plays of Pierre Corneille* by I.D. McFarlane, 1984; *Corneille, Classicism and the Ruses of Symmetry* by Mitchell Greenberg, 1986; *If There Are No More Heroes, There Are Heroines: A Feminist Critique of Corneille's Heroines 1637–1644* by Josephine A. Schmidt, 1987; *Le Cid: Corneille* by W.D. Howarth, 1988; *The Poetic Style of Corneille's Tragedies: An Aesthetic Interpretation* by Sharon Harwood Gordon, 1989; *Dissonant Harmonies: Drama and Ideology in Five Neglected Plays of Pierre Corneille* by Susan Read Baker, 1990; *Corneillian Theater: The Metadramatic Dimension* by M.J. Muratore, 1990; *Corneille's Tragedies: The Role of the Unexpected* by R.C. Knight, 1991; *Pierre Corneille: The Poetics and Political Drama under Louis XII* by David Clarke, 1992; *In the Grip of Minos: Confessional Discourse in Dante, Corneille, and Racine* by Matthew Senior, 1994; *La Gloire: The Roman Empire of Corneille and Racine* by Louis Auchincloss, 1996; *The Tragedy of Origins: Pierre Corneille and Historical Perspective* by John D. Lyons, 1996; *Corneille: Cinna* by C.J. Gossip, 1998; *Pierre Corneille Revisted* by Claire L. Carlin, 1998.

* * *

Pierre Corneille is the earliest of the great French Classical playwrights. "Cornelian" has become an adjective to describe qualities of grandeur, heroism, and the subordination of passion to duty which are apparent in many of his plays.

His production was in fact very various. He showed a constant desire to astound—by extreme gestures and situations, by complication, surprise, verbal display, variety. As a poet, his great gift is for emphatic and weighty eloquence, admirably suited to his "Cornelian" moments. But his range is wide—tenderness, lyricism, irony, with a talent (not only in his comedies) for realistic dialogue and repartee. His changes of tone and delight in verbal ingenuity have often led to complaints of bathos and bad taste, but can be seen as indications of his breadth and daring. He shows a fascination with human behaviour in bizarre and confused situations, and especially with the complexity of moral decisions, sometimes reflecting contemporary events and controversies. This fascination is most memorably focused on the hero's struggle to fulfil the demands of his "gloire" (literally "honour" or "reputation," but in Corneille's best work a subtle concept involving self-realization at a high moral level). There is also a sense of the complexity of life in a more obvious way. Even in his loftiest plays there is an awareness of the self-seeking, even comical, elements which accompany and oppose or corrupt the heroic impulse. In many of his works, this shades into irony and a disabused realism.

Corneille's early plays are mainly comedies on the intrigues of young lovers. They are best read in the original versions, before Corneille toned them down. Free in form, with a mixture of realism and fantasy, they show a Baroque concern with illusion and the falsity of appearances, especially in the play-within-a-play-within-a-play of *L'Illusion comique (The Theatrical Illusion)*. Despite their often frank realism and comedy, deeper themes emerge: real or assumed madness and real grief at a supposed death (*Mélite*); misery caused by a young man's rejection of love in order to preserve his freedom (*La Place Royale*); the bitterness of a woman at her social status (*La Suivante*). *Clitandre*, though labelled a tragedy, is a romantic comedy. *Médée* signals Corneille's approach to tragedy. It sets the selfish triviality of Jason and the Court against the lonely figure of Medea, who asserts her identity by a terrible revenge.

Le Cid (The Cid) shows the crisis in the hero's life when he has to kill the father of his beloved Chimène in order to fulfil his heroic destiny, and she, to match his integrity, has to seek his death. Although Corneille blurs the ending, the poignancy and dramatic boldness of the situations, together with the lyricism and energy of the verse, make this his most accessible play. *Horace,* the first play within the strict unities (though Corneille, as often, has difficulty in unifying his action), shows the hero isolating himself in his destiny, which leads him both to save his country and to murder his sister. Corneille resolves the crisis ambiguously, showing the hero both glorious and flawed. *Cinna* is perhaps his most unified achievement. In a shifting drama of love and political intrigue, it focuses on the effort of the Emperor Augustus to transcend his past and convert by forgiveness those who have conspired against him. *Polyeucte (Polyeuctus)* deals with a clash between Christianity and Paganism in the Roman Empire, and shows how the heroic Polyeucte, in seeking martyrdom, brings to Christianity not only his passionate wife but also his cynical father-in-law. Powerful in structure, characterization, and verse, it is often regarded as his masterpiece though some have found the ending unconvincing.

Corneille's later plays only achieve this level intermittently. Until the failure of *Pertharite,* he produced a series of very varied plays—tragedies, plays with music and spectacular effects, and *comédies héroïques* (plays with noble characters, but less serious than tragedies). The best are the comedy *Le Menteur (The Liar)* and the tragedy *Nicomède (Nicomede)*, a play of complex ironies showing the hero triumphing (largely through the efforts of others) over the hostility of Rome and the intrigues of his stepmother, who dominates his realistic and weak father. *Rodogune* and *Héraclius (Heraclius)*, both tragedies, are more typical, in their schematic characterization, exciting plots, and melodramatic verve.

The plays after Corneille's return to the theatre in 1659 are uneven, but in some ways his most interesting. The heroic mode of his masterpieces and the melodrama of his middle plays give way to a subtle blend of political and psychological intrigue, with flashes of both grandeur and comedy. The finest are *Sertorius,* dramatizing the clash of personal and political ambitions in the civil wars of the Roman Republic, and *Suréna (Surenas)*, his last play. *Surenas,* with its atmosphere of ambiguity and menace, has an emotional and tragic resonance rare in Corneille.

As well as various prefatory pieces, Corneille wrote the substantial critical *Discourses* and critiques (*Examens*) of individual plays prefixed to each volume of his 1660 *Works.* Although not very illuminating on individual plays, they show his difficulties with the contemporary critical concern for verisimilitude and moral utility in poetry. He stresses pleasure as the aim of drama, and historical truth as an aid to credibility.

Apart from some lively personal pieces, his non-dramatic poetry is of little interest.

—Gordon Pocock

See the essays on *The Cid* and *The Theatrical Illusion.*

CORREIA DA ROCHA, Adolfo

See TORGA, Miguel

CORTÁZAR, Julio

Born: Brussels, Belgium, 26 August 1914. Family returned to Argentina, 1918. **Education:** Educated at the Escuela Normal de Profesores Mariano Acosta (teachers college), Buenos Aires, degree as primary-level teacher, 1932, degree as secondary-level teacher, 1935; University of Buenos Aires, 1936–37. **Family:** Married Aurora Bernárdez in 1953 (separated); lived with Carol Dunlop in later years. **Career:** Taught in secondary schools in Bolívar, Chivilcoy, and Mendoza, 1937–44; professor of French literature, University of Cuyo, Mendoza, 1944–45, and imprisoned briefly for involvement in anti-Peronist demonstrations at the university, 1945; manager, Cámara Argentina del Libro [Publishing Association of Argentina], 1946–48; passed examinations in law and languages, and worked as translator, Buenos Aires, 1948–51; travelled to Paris on a scholarship, 1951, and settled there; writer and freelance translator for UNESCO, from 1952; visited Cuba, 1961, Argentina, Peru, Ecuador, and Chile, all 1973, Nicaragua and (after the lifting of a seven-year ban on his entry into the country) Argentina, 1983; visiting lecturer, University of Oklahoma, Norman, 1975, and Gildersleeve lecturer, Barnard College, New York, 1980; acquired French citizenship (in addition to existing Argentinian citizenship), 1981. **Awards:** Médicis prize (France), 1974; Great Golden Eagle (Nice), 1976; Rubén Darío Order of Cultural Independence (Nicaragua), 1983. **Member:** Second Russell Tribunal for investigation of human rights abuses in Latin America, 1975. **Died:** 12 February 1984.

PUBLICATIONS

Fiction

Bestiario (stories). 1951; title story as "Bestiary," translated by J.M. Cohen, in *Latin American Writing Today,* edited by Cohen, 1967;

as *Bestiary: Selected Stories*, translated by Alberto Manguel, Paul Blackburn, Gregory and Clementine Rabassa, and Suzanne Jill Levine, 1998.

Final del juego (stories), 1956; enlarged edition, 1964.

Las armas secretas (stories). 1959.

Los premios. 1960; as *The Winners*, translated by Elaine Kerrigan, 1965.

Historias de cronopios y de famas (stories). 1962; as *Cronopios and Famas*, translated by Paul Blackburn, 1969.

Rayuela. 1963; edited by Julio Ortega and Saúl Yurkievich, 1991; as *Hopscotch*, translated by Gregory Rabassa, 1966.

Cuentos, edited by Anton Arrufat. 1964.

Todos los fuegos el fuego (stories). 1966; as *All Fires the Fire and Other Stories*, translated by Suzanne Jill Levine, 1973.

End of the Game and Other Stories, translated by Paul Blackburn. 1967; as *Blow-Up and Other Stories*, translated by Blackburn, 1968.

El perseguidor y otros cuentos. 1967; edited by Alberto Couste, 1979.

62: Modelo para armar. 1968; as *62: A Model Kit*, translated by Gregory Rabassa, 1972.

Ceremonias (includes *Final del juego* and *Las armas secretas*). 1968.

Casa tomada. 1969.

Relatos (selection). 1970.

La isla a mediodia y otros relatos. 1971.

Libro de Manuel. 1973; as *A Manual for Manuel*, translated by Gregory Rabassa, 1978.

Octaedro (stories). 1974; parts translated in *A Change of Light and Other Stories*, 1980.

Los relatos. 3 vols., 1976.

Alguien que anda por ahí y otros relatos. 1977; parts translated in *A Change of Light and Other Stories*, 1980.

Un tal Lucas. 1979; as *A Certain Lucas*, translated by Gregory Rabassa, 1984.

A Change of Light and Other Stories, translated by Gregory Rabassa. 1980.

Queremos tanto a Glenda. 1981; as *We Love Glenda So Much and Other Tales*, translated by Gregory Rabassa, 1983.

Deshoras (stories). 1983; as *Unreasonable Hours*, translated by Alberto Manguel, 1995.

El examen. 1986.

Divertimento. 1986.

Siete Cuentos by Julio Cortazar, edited with introduction by Peter Beardsell. 1994.

Verse

Presencia (as Julio Denis). 1938.

Pameos y meopas. 1971.

Poemas, meopas y prosemas. 1984.

Salvo el crepúsculo. 1984; as *Save Twilight: Selected Poems of Julio Cortázar*, translated by Stephen Kessler, 1997.

Plays

Los reyes. 1949.

Nada a Pehuajó, y Adiós, Robinson. 1984.

Other

Fantomas contra los vampiros internacionales. 1965.

La vuelta al día en ochenta mundos (essays). 1967; as *Around the Day in Eighty Worlds*, translated by Thomas Christensen, 1986.

Buenos Aires, Buenos Aires, photographs by Alicia d'Amico and Sara Facio (includes English translation). 1968.

Último round. 1969.

La literatura en la revolución y revolución en la literatura, with Oscar Collazos and Mario Vargas Llosa. 1970.

Viaje alrededor de una mesa. 1970.

Prosa del observatorio, photographs by Cortázar, with Antonio Galvez. 1972.

La casilla de los Morelli y otros textos (miscellany), edited by Julio Ortega. 1973.

Antología, edited by Nicolás Bratosevich. 1975.

Silvalandia (on the paintings of Julio Silva). 1975.

Estrictamente no profesional: Humanario (on the photographs of Aticia D'Amico and Sara Facio). 1976.

Territorios (miscellany). 1978.

Conversaciones con Cortázar, with Ernesto González Bermejo. 1978; as *Revelaciones de un cronopio: Conversaciones con Cortázar*, 1986.

Monsieur Lautrec, with Hermenegildo Sabat. 1980.

Un elogio del tres (on the paintings of Luis Tomasello). 1980.

París: Ritmos de una ciudad, photographs by Alecio de Andrade. 1981; as *Paris: The Essence of an Image*, translated by Gregory Rabassa, 1981.

Los autonautas de la cosmopista; o, Un viaje atemporal París—Marsella, with Carol Dunlop. 1983.

Cuaderno de bitácora de Rayuela, with Ana María Barrenechea. 1983.

El edad presente es de lucha/The Present Age Is One of Struggle, with Sergio Ramírez Mercado. 1983.

Nicaragua, tan violentamente dulce. 1983; as *Nicaraguan Sketches*, translated by K. Weaver, 1989.

Negro el diez (on the lithographs of Luis Tomasello). 1983.

Argentina: Años de alambradas culturales, edited by Saúl Yurkievich. 1984.

Alto el Perú (on the photographs of Manja Offerhaus). 1984.

La fascinación de las palabras: Conversaciones con Julio Cortázar, with Omar Prego. 1985.

Cortázar: Iconografía, edited by Alba C. de Rojo and Felipe Garrido. 1985.

Policrítica en la hora de los chacales. 1987.

Voicing, with others, edited by Don Wellman, translated by Cola Franzen and others. 1989.

Cartas a una pelirroja, edited by Evelyn Picon Garfield. 1990.

Translator, *Robinson Crusoe*, by Daniel Defoe. 1945.

Translator, *El hombre que sabía demasiado*, by G.K. Chesterton. 1946.

Translator, *Nacimiento de la Odisea*, by Jean Giono. 1946.

Translator, *La poesía pura* by Henri Brémond. 1947

Translator, *El inmoralista*, by André Gide. 1947.

Translator, *Filosofía de la risa y el llanto*, by Alfred Stern. 1950.

Translator, *Mujercitas*, by Louisa May Alcott. 1951.

Translator, *Tom Brown en la escuela*, by Thomas Hughes. 1951.

Translator, *La filosofía existencial de Jean-Paul Sartre,* by Alfred Stern. 1951.

Translator, *La víbora,* by Marcel Aymé. 1952.

Translator, *La vida de los otros,* by Ladislas Dormandi. 1952.

Translator, *Así sea; o, La suerte está echada,* by André Gide. 1953.

Translator, *Vida y cartas de John Keats,* by Lord Houghton. 1955.

Translator, *Memorias de Adriano,* by Marguerite Yourcenar. 1955.

Translator, *Obras en prosa,* by Edgar Allan Poe. 1956.

Translator, *Cuentos,* by Edgar Allan Poe. 1963.

Translator, *Eureka,* by Edgar Allan Poe. 1972.

Translator, *Ensayos y críticos,* by Edgar Allan Poe. 1973.

Translator, *Memorias de una enana,* by Walter de la Mare. N.d.

*

Bibliography: "Bibliografía de y sobre Julio Cortázar" by Marta Paley de Francescato, in *Revista Iberoamericana de Literatura,* 59(84–85), 1973; *Julio Cortázar: His Works and His Critics: A Bibliography* by Sara de Mundo Lo, 1985.

Critical Studies: *Moyano, Benedetto, Cortázar* by Eugenio Castelli, 1968; *Cortázar: Una antropología poética* by Néstor García Canclini, 1968; *Cinco miradas sobre Cortázar* edited by Ana María Simo, 1968; *Julio Cortázar y el hombre nuevo* by Graciela de Sola, 1968; *La vuelta a Cortázar en nueve ensayos,* various authors, 1968; *Sobre Cortázar* by José Amícola, 1969; *Julio Cortázar: El escritor y sus máscaras* by Mercedes Rein, 1969; *Julio Cortázar: Visión de conjunto* by Roberto Escamilla Molina, 1970; *De Sarmiento a Cortázar* by David Viñas, 1970; *El individuo y el otro: Crítica a los cuentos de Julio Cortázar* by Alfred J. MacAdam, 1971; *Cortázar: La novela moderna* by Lida Aronne Amestoy, 1972; *Julio Cortázar; o, La crítica de la razón pragmática* by Juan Carlos Curutchet, 1972; *Homenaje a Julio Cortázar* edited by Helmy F. Giacoman, 1972; *Seven Voices* by Rita Guibert, 1973; *Julio Cortázar: Una búsqueda mítica* by Saúl Sosnowski, 1973; *Julio Cortázar ante su sociedad* by Joaquín Roy, 1974; *¿Es Julio Cortázar un surrealista?,* 1975, *Julia Cortázar* (in English), 1975, and *Cortázar por Cortázar,* 1978, all by Evelyn Picon Garfield; *Estudios sobre los cuentos de Julio Cortázar* edited by David Lagmanovich, 1975; *Currents in the Contemporary Argentine Novel: Arlt, Mallea, Sábato and Cortázar* by William David Foster, 1975; Cortázar issue of *Books Abroad,* 50(3), 1976; *Julio Cortázar: Rayuela* by Robert Brady, 1976; *The Final Island: The Fiction of Cortázar* (includes bibliography) edited by Ivar Ivask and Jaime Alazraki, 1978, and *En busca del unicornio: Los cuentos de Julio Cortázar* by Alazraki, 1983; *The Novels of Cortázar* by Steven Boldy, 1980; *Keats, Poe, and the Shaping of Cortázar's Mythopoesis* by Ana Hernández del Castillo, 1981; *Julio Cortázar* edited by Pedro Lastra, 1981; Cortázar issue of *Casa de las Américas,* 25(145–146), 1984; *Julio Cortázar: Life, Work, and Criticism* by E.D. Carter, Jr., 1986; *Lo lúdico y lo fantástico: Coloquio,* edited by Keith Cohen, 2 vols., 1986; *Los ochenta mundos de Cortázar: Ensayos* edited by Fernando Burgos, 1987; *Otro Round: Ensayos sobre la obra de Julio Cortázar* edited by E. Dale Carter, 1988; *The Politics of Style in the Fiction of Balzac, Beckett, and Cortázar* by M.R. Axelrod, 1991; *Julio Cortázar: A Study of the Short Fiction* by Ilan Stavans, 1996; *Julio Cortázar: New Readings,* edited by Carlos J. Alonso, 1998; *Critical Essays on Julio Cortázar,* edited by Jaime Alazraki, 1999; *Questions of the Liminal in the Fiction of Julio Cortázar* by Dominic Moran, 2000; *Understanding Julio Cortázar* by Peter Standish, 2001.

* * *

Julio Cortázar is one of the most widely recognized Spanish American writers outside the Spanish-speaking world, due particularly to the critical acclaim of *Rayuela* (*Hopscotch*), a novel where the most experimental narrative innovations find an original form, and to the filming by Michelangelo Antonioni of one of his best short stories, "Blow-Up."

Cortázar's narrative is unclassifiable. His fiction breaks away from the habitual categories of narrative and all conventional forms, and blurs the uncertain boundaries between reality and the fantastic. The realistic and social milieu of his stories (be it Buenos Aires or Paris) is continuously compromised by elements of the absurd, the mythic, and the oneiric, by surrealist undercurrents where artistic freedom and imaginative possibilities disturb all routine representations of reality. Cortázar searches for an opening toward the other side of reality, toward—in his own words—"a more secret and less communicable order."

Cortázar's experimentation with the techniques of narrative can best be exemplified with *Hopscotch,* his masterpiece. The novel is written in loose fragments—the collage is the basic associative procedure—sequences of a totality that the reader is forced to recompose. The search for harmony and authenticity is the guiding motif of the novel; the search for the "key," "the other side," "the centre," "the heaven of the hopscotch," "the love-passport," "the wishful kibbutz," illustrate Cortázar's attempts to apprehend an absolute order, a "sacred space" or mandala (a mystical labyrinth used by the Buddhists as a spiritual exercise), where integration and ultimate harmony can be attained. This ontological search for unity is one of the distinctive aspects of Cortázar's narrative. In his fiction it is common to find a character embarked on the search for a secret order, pursuing something undefinable to bring him inner harmony. Some characters intuitively explore the mysteries of the self (Johnny Carter, the jazz musician of "The Pursuer"), others chase truth and self-knowledge—Medrano in *Los premios* (*The Winners*)—but most attempt failed intellectual projections into a world of their dreams: Oliveira in *Hopscotch,* Juan in *62: Modelo para armar* (*62: A Model Kit*), Andrés in *Libro de Manuel* (*A Manual for Manuel*). Fascinated by the unreachable absolute, all of Cortázar's major characters seek to jump into authenticity, rebel against a civilization governed by reason.

Hopscotch is a questioning of the art of storytelling, as well as a questioning of reality and all rational knowledge, an attempt to break away from all routine narrative formulas. The disintegration of the traditional novel begins with "The Table of Instructions," where Cortázar suggests at least two ways of reading the novel and the reader is invited to select between expendable and unexpendable chapters. The complex point of view, movable chapters, montage, *dédoublement,* dissociation of personality, simultaneity of creation and theoretical reflection within the novel, and, above all, the destruction of inherited language and syntax, the search for a new syntax to reunite unreconcilable languages, are the predominant features of Cortázar's writing. The constant questioning of the capability of language to represent reality can best be seen by quoting the opening paragraph of "Blow-Up":

It'll never be known how this has to be told, in the first person or in the second, using the first person plural or continually inventing modes that will serve for nothing. If one might say: I will see the moon rose, or: we hurt me at the back of my eyes, and especially: you the blond woman was the clouds that race before my your his our yours their faces. What the hell.

These two aspects of Cortázar's narrative—innovation of language and form, and the metaphysical search—reveal his talent as a storyteller of universal appeal.

—Hugo J. Verani

COUPERUS, Louis Marie Anne

Born: The Hague, The Netherlands, 10 June 1863. Spent part of his youth on Java. **Education:** Failed his school exams, 1886. **Family:** Married his niece Elizabeth Baud in 1891. **Career:** After 1891 spent most of his life in the south of France and in Italy; travelled to Indonesia, 1899. Worked for the magazine *Nederlandsch Spectator;* also wrote for The Hague newspaper *Het Vaderland.* **Died:** 16 July 1923.

PUBLICATIONS

Collections

Verzamelde werken [Collected Works]. 12 vols., 1952–57.
Nagelaten werk. 1976.

Fiction

Eline Vere. 1889; as *Eline Vere,* translated by J.T. Grein, 1892.
Noodlot. 1890; as *Footsteps of Fate,* translated by Clara Bell, 1891.
Extase. 1892; as *Ecstasy,* translated by Alexander Teixeira de Mattos and John Gray, 1892.
Eene illuzie [An Illusion]. 1892.
Majesteit. 1893; as *Majesty,* translated by Alexander Teixeira de Mattos and Ernest Dowson, 1894.
Wereldvrede [World Peace]. 1895, reprinted 1991.
Willeswinde [Wind of Will]. 1895.
Hooge troeven [High Stakes]. 1896.
Metamorfoze. 1897.
Psyche. 1897; as *Psyche,* translated by B.S. Berrington, 1908.
Fidessa. 1899.
Langs lijnen van geleidelijkheid. 1900; as *The Law Inevitable,* translated by Alexander Teixeira de Mattos, 1921.
De stille kracht. 1900; as *The Hidden Force,* translated by Alexander Teixeira de Mattos, 1922, revised and edited by E.M. Beekman, 1985.
Babel. 1901; as *Babel,* translated by A.A. Betham, n.d.
De boeken der kleine zielen. 4 vols., 1901–04; as *The Book of the Small Souls,* translated by Alexander Teixeira de Mattos, 4 vols., 1914–18.
Over lichtende drempels. 1902.
Van oude menschen, de dingen die voorbijgaan. 2 vols., 1902; as *Old People and the Things That Pass,* translated by Alexander Teixeira de Mattos, 1918.
God en goden [God and Gods]. 1903.
Dionyzos. 1904.
De berg van licht [The Mountain of Light]. 3 vols., 1905–06.
Aan den weg der vreugde [Along the Road of Joy]. 1908.

Van en over mijzelf en anderen [Of and About Myself and Others]. 4 vols., 1910–17.
Korte arabesken (stories). 1911; selection as *Eighteen Tales,* translated by J. Kooistra, 1924.
Antiek toerisme. 1911; as *The Tour,* translated by Alexander Teixeira de Mattos, 1920.
Antieke verhalen [Antique Stories]. 1911.
Herakles. 2 vols., 1913.
Van en over alles en iedereen [Of and About Everything and Everyone]. 5 vols., 1915.
De ongelukkige [The Unfortunate One]. 1915.
De komedianten. 1917; as *The Comedians, a Story of Ancient Rome,* translated by J. Menzies-Wilson, 1926.
De ode. 1918.
Legende, mythe en fantazie. 1918.
De verliefde ezel [The Enamoured Ass]. 1918.
Xerxes of de hoogmoed. 1919; as *Arrogance, the Conquests of Xerxes,* translated by Frederick H. Martens, 1930.
Lucrezia. 1920.
Iskander. 1920.
Het zwevend schaakbord [The Hovering Chessboard]. 1922.
Het snoer der ontferming en Japansche legenden [The String of Mercy and Japanese Legends]. 1924.
Via appia. 1972.
De zwaluwen neer gestreken [The Alighted Swallows]. 1974.
Endymion. 1976.

Verse

Een Lent van vaerzen [A Lent of Verses]. 1884.
Orchideën. 1886; selection in *Flowers from a Foreign Garden,* translated by A.L. Snell, 1902.

Other

Schimmen van schoonheid [Phantoms of Beauty] (sketches). 1912.
Uit blanke steden onder blauwe lucht [From White Cities under Blue Skies] (sketches and impressions). 2 vols., 1912–13.
Brieven van een nutteloozen toeschouwer [Letters of a Useless Spectator] (anti-war polemic). 1918.
Met L. Couperus in Afrika (journalism). 1921.
Oostwaarts. 1924; as *Eastward,* translated by J. Menzies-Wilson and C.C. Crispin, 1924.
Nippon. 1925; as *Nippon,* translated by J. de la Vallette, 1926.
Kindersouvenirs [Childhood Memories]. 1978.
Epigrammen. 1982.
Translator, *Verzoeking van den Heiligen Antonius,* by Flaubert. 1896, reprinted 1992.

*

Critical Studies: *Leven en werken van Louis Couperus* by Henri van Booven, 1933; *Verhaal en lezer* by W. Block, 1960; *Couperus in de kritiek* by M. Galle, 1963; *Louis Couperus: Een verkenning* by H.W. van Tricht, 1965; *Beschouwingen over het werk van Louis Couperus* by K.J. Popma, 1968; *De antieke wereld van Louis Couperus* by T. Bogaerts, 1969; *Couperus, grieken en barbaren* by E. Visser, 1969; *De man met de orchidee. Het levensverhaal van Louis Couperus* by Albert Vogel, 1973, 2nd revised edition, 1980; *Een zuil in de mist. Van en over Louis Couperus* by F.L. Bastet, 1980; *Eenheid in* *verscheidenheid: over de werkwijze van Louis Couperus* by H.T.N. van Vliet, 1996.

* * *

A novelist of international stature, Louis Couperus belonged to two late 19th-century literary traditions of naturalist and decadent prose. He was born in The Hague in 1863 into a formal, conventional, and aristocratic milieu where colonial administration was one of the traditional professions. Consequently, the family of the young Couperus spent six years in the Dutch colony of Indonesia, returning to the Netherlands in 1877.

As an aspiring literary figure, he did not immediately find his natural form. In 1884 he published a none-too-successful collection of poems, *Een Lent van vaerzen* [A Lent of Verses], and in 1886 a second collection, *Orchidëen* [Orchids]. The tepid reaction to these poetry collections encouraged him to concentrate on prose. Nevertheless, in the eyes of many critics, his persistent love for poetic, "beautiful" language and extended ornate description was to mar a number of his novels.

However, when *Eline Vere,* his first novel, appeared in 1889, Couperus was an immediate success. In 1888, when the novel was serialized in the newspaper *Het Vaderland,* it coincided with the appearance of two other naturalist novels: *Een liefde* by Lodewijk van Deyssel and *Juffrouw Lina* by Marcellus Emants. Dutch naturalism differed from the scientific-minded French naturalism in several respects. The works tend to focus on middle-class milieux, and the main characters are anti-heroes, frequently over-sensitive, over-civilized men and women reacting against the smug calm of the surrounding prosaic, bourgeois society. There is frequently an investigation of taboo subjects like homosexuality or self-gratification. The text aims at objective representation of the characters, and combines colloquial dialogue with *woordkunst* ("artistic writing"), highly descriptive, evocative passages full of adjectives and neologisms.

In the novel Eline Vere, a victim of her class and her gender, can find no escape for her pent-up energy. Too finely tuned for her own good and consequently misunderstood, she takes an overdose as the result of an unhappy love affair. Unlike other Dutch naturalists, Couperus stressed the laws of deterministic inheritance: Eline Vere has inherited her character from her father, while her cousin Vincent suffers from a similar clash between his personality and his environment.

In a logical step, Couperus's next novel was entitled *Noodlot* (*Footsteps of Fate*), associating family hereditary factors with a fate the three main characters cannot escape. Meijers suggests that *Footsteps of Fate* and the next novel *Extase* (*Ecstasy*) partially attempt to work through Couperus's homosexuality by transferring it onto a sublimated desire for heterosexual love.

Couperus's generally recognized masterpiece is a novel written during a year-long return to the Dutch East Indies, and once again deals with the disintegration of character and the notion of fate. In *De stille kracht* (*The Hidden Force*), the senior colonial administrator Van Oudijck is undermined by his wife's infidelities, which weakens his resistance to the pervasive atmosphere of Indonesian magic, "goena goena." The rational Dutch colonials one by one become completely submerged in the alien culture they are trying to control and suppress. As Dutch pianos and furniture disintegrate because of the heat, humidity, and termites, their mental and physical health is drained by the atmosphere. In fact there is a suggestion that it is their own moral corruption that allows the silent forces of magic to take hold of their minds.

Back in the bourgeois atmosphere of The Hague, the four novels that make up *De boeken der kleine zielen* (*The Book of the Small Souls*) present another Dutch family slowly falling apart under outside strain, with the addition of typically *fin-de-siècle* mystical elements.

Van oude menschen, de dingen die voorbijgaan (*Old People and the Things That Pass*) is sometimes likened to a psychological detective novel, as the reader slowly learns how the old people, a 94-year-old man and a 97-year-old woman, murdered the woman's husband 60 years earlier, with the guilty knowledge of the family doctor. In what is generally regarded as one of his best novels, Couperus slowly peels away this family secret that is affecting the younger generations.

Less well-liked are the novels where Couperus shows a clearer connection with European decadent writers like Baudelaire, de Maupassant, and Wilde. A number of long novels are situated in antiquity or Eastern history, like *De berg van licht* [The Mountain of Light], about the Roman child-emperor Heliogabalus, *Herakles* [Hercules], and *Xerxes*. Above all, *Iskander* depicts Alexander the Great's conquest of the Persian empire, with prolonged evocations of the exotic Persian court. These novels are frequently faulted by critics for an overindulgence in long descriptions of luxurious, decadent palaces, sounds, smells, and wines. Frequently, a certain shying away from the homoerotic subtext is also partly the cause for the unpopularity of these novels. However, while these novels are hard-going at times, their opulence and excess can be regarded more positively. By means of their very textual excesses Couperus was in fact able to evoke the exotic, alien quality of long-gone cultures and lifestyles, thus along with his other works, contributing to his highly original and enduring position in Dutch literature.

—Sabine Vanacker

CRAVEIRINHA, José

Born: Lourenco Marques (now Maputo), 28 May 1922. **Education:** Attended primary school only, thereafter an autodidact. **Family:** Married Maria de Lurdes (died in 1979). **Career:** Began to write very early and established himself as a journalist in local media publications such as *O Brado Africano, Notícias da Beira, Tribuna, O Tempo,* and *O Notícias,* where for many years he wrote a weekly piece; after Mozambique gained its independence, Craveirinha became the first President of the Associaçao dos Escritores Moçambicanos (AEMO; Mozambican Writers' Guild), a position he held between 1982 and 1987; also the President of the Associaçao Moçambicana da Língua Portuguesa (AMOLP; Mozambican Association of the Portuguese Language), and Vice-President of Maputo's chapter of the Fundo Bibliográfico da Língua Portuguesa (Bibliographic Fund for the Portuguese Language); librarian of the Faculty of Economy at Mondlane University in Maputo; continues to live in Maputo, a place frequently referred to in his writing. **Awards:** Lourenço Marques Prix, 1959; Reinaldo Ferreira prize, 1961; National poetry prize, Italy, 1975; gold medal of the commune of Concesio, Italy, 1975; Lotus prize, awarded by the Afro-Asiatic Writers' Association, 1983; Prémio Camões, 1990, the most prestigious literary prize for work in the Portuguese language.

PUBLICATIONS

Verse

Chigubo. 1964.
Xigubo. 1980; reprinted in 1995.
Karingana ua karingana. 1974; reprinted in 1982 and 1995.
Cela 1. 1980.
Maria. 1988; reprinted in 1998.
Babalaze das hienas. 1997.
Haminas. 1997.

*

Critical Studies: *Sobre a Poesia de José Craveirinha* by Rui Baltazar, 1988; *Echoes of the Sunbird: An Anthology of Contemporary African Poetry* by Donald Burness, 1993; *The Postcolonial Literature of Lusophone Africa* by Patrick Chabal et al, 1996; *Vozes Mocambicanas: Literatura and Nacionalidade*, 1994; "The Edge of Discourse: Bodies and Rhythms in the Poetry of Craveirinha" by M. L. de Cortez, in *Portuguese Studies*, 9, 1993; *Voices of an Empire* by Russell Hamilton, 1975; *A Poética de José Craveirinha* by Ana Mafalda Leite, 1991; *A construçao da imagem de Moçambicanidade em José Craveirinha, Mia Couto e Ungulani ba ka Khosa* by Gilberto Matusse, 1998; *Literatura Moçambicana: A história e as escritas* by Fátima Mendonça, 1988; *Do alheio ao próprio: a poesia em Moçambique* by Manoel Souza e Silva, 1996.

* * *

Now over 80 years old, José Craveirinha is the foremost Mozambican poet and one of the most innovative African poets working in the Portuguese language. A quiet and unassuming man, his work in contrast is characterised by a vibrant and subversive political edge. Although he writes in a simple and common language, there is little in his work that is not cleverly crafted to get the most out of language's inherent potential for ambiguity and wilful misconstruction. His diction veers between the poetic and the bombastic, the sophisticated and the vulgar. He often incorporates a tone of mimicry in his writing that is intrinsic to a colonial view of the native as *potentially* civilisable, which signifies a profoundly self-conscious challenge to colonial inscription. Indeed, in his subversive use of irony, but one often of a quasi-idiotic nature, resides much of his writing's anti-colonialist message. Craveirinha *chooses* to play the role of "the dumb black bastard," the *mamparra* in the discourses of Portuguese colonial domination. In what is a common characteristic of his work, in poems such as "Aforismo" [Aphorism] and "Poemeto" [Little Poem] for instance, Craveirinha deploys to great effect the role of rumour in the destabilization of colonial structures of control. Ironically, there is in his wily and resourceful native persona, which is capable of a challenge to the system as outspoken as is found in "Quero ser tambor" [I Want to Be a Drum] and "Grito Negro" [African Cry], an uncanny vulnerability that speaks of that "poisoning of the blood" that Derek Walcott underlines in "A Far Cry to Africa" ("I who am poisoned with the blood of both, / where shall I turn, divided to the vein?"). But unlike Walcott, who was born and raised in the Caribbean, Craveirinha's poetry has added meaning since he has both African and European roots.

Craveirinha is of mixed race, born of Portuguese and Ronga parents, and his work is dominated by an engagement with racial

issues and creolised cultural identities. His poetic oeuvre draws simultaneously on African and European influences, and in this way it exists in the space that Walcott identifies as one of tortured angst and infinite creative plenitude. In poems such as "Miserere em Lhanguene" [Miserere In Lhanguene], "A Morte de Camoes" [Camoens' Death], and "O Bule e o Blue" [The Teapot and the Blues], Craveirinha underlines this uniquely delicate double-bind. In "O Bule e o Blue," the alliteration allowed for in Portuguese evokes at once a local and a diasporic mood; the musical reference to Afro-American identity is a clear identification with the pan-African tendencies of so much writing of the African diaspora.

Identity is thus one of the central themes in Craveirinha's writing. It is something he returns to time and again and often articulates through a focus on the body, specifically the black body. In poems such as "Grito Negro," "Quero Ser Tambor," and "Africa," among others, there is a direct connection between the black body—an African body—and an African identity. Clearly anchored on the *Négritude* models imagined by Césafre and Senghor, this appeal to an identity that is at once personal, racial, and cultural is central to Craveirinha's work. In "Hino à minha terra" [Hymn to my Country], and "Sangue de Minha Mae" [Blood of my Mother], Craveirinha explores the poet's own personal being in existential terms but, crucially, in the context of the racialised hierarchies of Portuguese Africa.

Thus even in the poems found in *Maria*, a collection named after his wife and a declaration of his undying love for her, Craveirinha brings together the discourse of the intimate self and that of a public intellectual. The poet is alone following the death of his wife, but his poetry articulates a care for someone with whom he had looked forward to living with in the newly independent Mozambique. When the speaker of his poem addresses his wife's experience during his imprisonment, having been ostracised by her so-called friends, his own suffering at the hands of the Portuguese political police from 1965–69 is framed by a concern for another. Much as the poet often will speak of his writing as innocuous and incidental, few of his poems are about anything other than the politics of self in a colonial society. In his verse he speaks of and to a dispossessed but proud people who refuse to submit to the brutality their colonial oppressor. He speaks, in sum, of *Moçambicanidade*, a way of being in the world that is both inextricable from a Portuguese sensibility and lived in defiance of it.

In the post-independence climate, and despite a pressing need re-assert one's political credentials, Craveirinha has continued to refrain from adopting an overtly political style. As a person of mixed ethnicity, he knows that he is often considered to be as much of an alien in the post-independence society based on rigid racial structures as he was in colonised society, since his racial duality does not always fall within the hegemonic demands of the new nation's search for a common point of reference. He continues to write in the simple, elegant, casually ironic tone he had made his trademark. In turn joyous and morbid, genial and sarcastic, his is a stance that has always gained its subversive power from a refusal to be easily classifiable. However, in *O Babalaze das Hienas* [Babalaze of the Hyenas, 1997], a collection of his new poetry, a new direction seems to be emerging. His verse dealing with the ongoing Mozambican civil war now suggests a more self-conscious repositioning within Mozambique's political and cultural paradigms. In poems such as "Carreira de Gaza" [Gaza's Shooting Range], "Outra Beleza" [Another Beauty], or in "Eles foram lá" [They Went There], "Barbearia" [Barber Shop], and "A Boca" [The Mouth], Craveirinha's old detachment has given rise to a new tone, one of anger and bitterness that demonstrates the disillusionment of a postcolonial intellectual who is capable of using the power of language to bring about real political change. His legendary verbal dexterity, which critics like Gerald Moser, Patrick Chabal, Ana Mafalda Leite, and others have identified as the crucial sign of his unique poetic voice, has now been replaced by a clumsiness of expression in which a brutal irony does as much to shock as it does to confirm the utter hopelessness of the political situation in the new Mozambique. The shifting persona, once playful and wilful in works such as *Xigubo, Karingana ua Karingana,* and even *Cela 1* [Cell 1], now bears witness to what seems like a never-ending postcolonial war, pointing accusingly at the cavernous face of death, at the limbs hanging from trees, or at the heads impaled on stakes. The mimicry of much of the earlier poems, which were considered to be subversive, resourceful, and challenging, has been replaced by a fatalistic attitude exemplified by works such as *Machimbombo queimado* [Burned-bus Barbecued Human Bits]. In this new phase of Craveirinha's work, physical mutilation stands as a metonym for the futile role of poetry in the new nation. In "A Boca," Craveirinha speaks of one of the more horrific practices in which RENAMO, one of the two political groups fighting for control of Mozambique, is said to have engaged: the slicing of the lips of their victims who would then often be left to die. Ultimately, Craveirinha remains, now as during the colonial period, a voice narrating the history of the Mozambican nation.

—Tony Simoes da Silva

CRUZ, Sor Juana Inés de la

See JUANA INÉS DE LA CRUZ

CYRANO DE BERGERAC, Savinien

Born: Paris, France, 1619. **Education:** Educated at Collège de Beauvais, Paris, 1632–37; Collège de Lisieux, Paris, 1641. **Military Service:** Enlisted with M. de Carbon de Casteljoux's Company of Guards; soldier and duellist; retired from military career, wounded, 1640. **Career:** Renowned for his grotesque appearance and long nose and as the subject of Edmond Rostand's play. **Died:** July 1655.

PUBLICATIONS

Collections

Les Oeuvres libertines de Cyrano de Bergerac parisien, edited by Frédéric Lachèvre. 2 vols., 1921.
Oeuvres, edited by Georges Ribermont-Dessaignes. 1957.
Oeuvres complètes, edited by Jacques Prévot. 1977.
Oeuvres complètes, edited by Madeleine Alcover, 2000.

Fiction

Voyage dans la lune (part one), edited by Le Bret. 1657; *L'Histoire des états et empires du soleil* (part two; unfinished), 1662; complete version as *L'Autre Monde; ou, Les États et empires de la lune,* 1920; edited by H. Weber, 1959; also edited by Jacques

Prévot, 1977; Madeleine Alcover, 1977; as *Voyages to the Moon and the Sun,* translated by Richard Aldington, 1923; as *Other Worlds: The Comical History of the States and the Empires of the Moon and the Sun,* translated by Geoffrey Strachan, 1965.

Plays

La Mort d'Agrippine. 1654.
Le Pédant joué. 1654.

Other

Lettres. 1654; as *Satyrical Characters and Handsome Descriptions in Letters,* translated anonymously, 1658, reprinted 1914.

*

Critical Studies: *Cyrano de Bergerac* by G. Mongrédien, 1964; *Cyrano de Bergerac and the Universe of the Imagination* by Edward W. Lanius, 1967; *La Pensée philosophique et scientifique de Cyrano de Bergerac,* 1970, and *Cyrano relu et corrigé: Lettres, Estats du soleil, Fragment de physique,* 1990, both by Madeleine Alcover; *Cyrano de Bergerac and the Polemics of Modernity* by E. Harth, 1970; *Cyrano de Bergerac romancier,* 1977, and *Cyrano de Bergerac: Poète et dramaturge,* 1978, both by Jacques Prévot; *Cyrano de Bergerac, L'Autre Monde* by Haydn Mason, 1984; *Cyrano de Bergerac: L'Esprit de révolte* by Willy de Spens, 1989.

*   *   *

The name Savinien Cyrano de Bergerac seems, with its "de," to suggest aristocratic rank, while "Bergerac" might point to Gascon origins which would be some warrant for military swagger and a tendency towards boastful vanity. The sober truth is that Cyrano's origins were Parisian and bourgeois. Born in 1619, he was in fact the son of a successful lawyer, practising at the *parlement de Paris,* whose program for social aggrandizement took the orthodox form of purchasing a modest estate not far from the capital. Even though the property at Bergerac was to be sold after a few years, Cyrano had no scruples about flaunting its name for the rest of his life. He received, most probably at the Collège de Beauvais in Paris, an education that was largely classical in orientation, and then, inspired perhaps in part by a desire to enhance his social status, he joined Carbon de Casteljoux's Company of Guards. Its members were all supposed to be of noble birth and to come from Gascony, so there must have been either some flexibility or some hiding of the truth when it came to Cyrano's entry. What he may have lacked in hereditary qualifications, however, he made up for by his conduct. He participated in many duels, fighting, it is said, not as a principal but as a "second," for at the time it was customary for them to join in to defend their friend's honour and not just stand by and ensure fair play. He was also wounded twice, at the siege of Mouzon in 1639 and the siege of Arras a year later. With his health undermined, he decided to return to civilian life.

The basis of the often repeated story that Cyrano then went back to college, and possibly even became a junior teacher at the Collège de Lisieux in Paris, is dubious, as is that for the statement that he was taught by the Epicurean philosopher Pierre Gassendi (1592–1655). What is clear, however, is that Cyrano had a wild life and became associated with a number of notorious free thinkers, among them Tristan l'Hermite. It was not long before he began to write, but without the regular support of a patron he had difficulty making a living, and after his father's death he soon squandered his inheritance. He was seriously injured by a falling beam in 1654 and died, reconciled to the Catholic church, a year later. Contemporary portraits show that he indeed had a very prominent, remarkably shaped nose.

Like many other writers in France in the 17th century, Cyrano tried his hand at a number of genres, and it could well be that at least some of his writing was influenced by a desire to win the favour of a patron. This is particularly true of his contributions to political controversy at the time of the Fronde rebellions, unless we accept the more implausible hypothesis that his attitudes towards Cardinal Mazarin's policies underwent a rapid and radical change. Cyrano's *Lettres* are not letters in the everyday sense, but rather what the humanists called ''themes,'' that is to say, exercises in the literary development of a variety of topics. In 1645 Cyrano tried his hand at comedy. *Le Pédant joué*, in prose, makes fun of Jean Grangier, principal of the Collège de Beauvais when Cyrano was there. Though not without merit, the play was apparently never performed, and it is best known in literary history because Molière, never over-fussy

about borrowing other people's good ideas, turned to it for a key scene in *Les Fourberies de Scapin* (*The Rogueries of Scapin*) a quarter of a century later. *La Mort d'Agrippine* [Agrippina's Death] is a classical verse tragedy about a conspiracy against Tiberius; it was published in 1654, after causing a sensation when performed in Paris at the Hôtel de Bourgogne because of the outrageous sentiments it expressed.

Cyrano's most famous works are, however, his two fantastic satires, *Voyage dans la lune* and *L'Histoire des états et empires du soleil* (translated together as *Voyages to the Moon and the Sun*). With their blend of apparently realistic detail and free speculation about controversial issues, these stand in the tradition of Renaissance utopian writing, as exemplified by Thomas More, Tommaso Campanella, and Francis Godwin, whose *Man in the Moon* was published posthumously in England in 1638 and translated into French within a decade. Cyrano's astronomical romances show eclectic erudition, general irreverence, and great verve in burlesque.

—Christopher Smith

See the essay on *Voyages to the Moon and the Sun*.

D

D'ANNUNZIO, Gabriele

Born: Pescara, Italy, 12 March 1863. **Education:** Educated at a secondary school, Prato, 1874–81; University of Rome, 1881. **Military Service:** Served in the Italian infantry, navy, and air force during World War I: injury led to loss of sight in one eye. **Family:** Married Duchess Maria Hardouin di Gallese in 1883, three children; had romance with the actress Eleonora Duse, 1894–1904. **Career:** Staff member, *Tribuna,* Rome, in the 1880s; elected to Chamber of Deputies, 1897–1900 (defeated 1900); lived in Tuscany, 1899–1910; forced by debts to live in France, 1910–15; after the Treaty of Versailles, seized Fiume with other patriots and held the city, 1919–20; supported the Fascists: granted a title by Mussolini; spent last years at his home, the Vittoriale, on Lake Garda. **Died:** 1 March 1938.

PUBLICATIONS

Collections

Tutte le opere, edited by Egidio Bianchetti. 10 vols., 1939–50.
Poesie; Teatro; Prose, edited by Mario Praz. 1966.
Poesie, edited by Federico Roncoroni. 1978.
Carteggio D'Annunzio—Ojetti (1894–1937), edited by Cosimo Ceccuti. 1979.
Prose, edited by Federico Roncoroni. 1983.

Verse

Primo vere. 1879; revised edition, 1880.
Canto novo. 1882.
Intermezzo di rime. 1883.
San Pantaleone. 1886.
Isaotta Guttadàuro ed altre poesie. 1886; revised edition, as *L'Isottèo, La Chimera,* 1890.
Elegie romane 1887–1891. 1892.
Odi navali. 1893.
L'allegoria dell' autunno. 1895.
La canzone di Garibaldi. 1901.
Laudi del cielo, del mare, della terra, e degli eroi: Anno 1903—Maia; Anno 1904—Elettra, Alcyone; Libro IV—Merope, 3 vols., 1903–12; *Alcyone* as *Halcyon,* translated by J.G. Nichols, 1988.
L'orazione e la canzone in morte di Giosuè Carducci. 1907.
Canto novo. 1907.
Le città del silenzio. 1926.
Versi d'amore e di gloria, edited by Annamaria Andreoli and Niva Lorenzini. 2 vols., 1982–84.

Plays

Sogno d'un mattino di primavera (produced 1897). 1897; as *The Dream of a Spring Morning,* translated by Anna Colby Schenck, 1911.

La città morta (as *La Ville morte,* produced 1898). 1898; as *The Dead City,* translated by Arthur Symons, 1900; also translated by Gaetano Mantellani, 1902.
La Gioconda (produced 1899). 1898; as *Gioconda,* translated by Arthur Symons, 1902.
Sogno di un tramonto d'autunno (produced 1905). 1898; as *The Dream of an Autumn Sunset,* translated by Anna Colby Schenck, 1903.
La gloria (produced 1899). 1899.
Francesca da Rimini (produced 1901). 1901; revised version, music by Riccardo Zandonai (produced 1914), 1914; as *Francesca da Rimini,* translated by Arthur Symons, 1902.
La figlia di Iorio (produced 1904). 1904; revised version, music by Alberto Franchetti (produced 1906), 1906; as *The Daughter of Jorio,* translated by C. Porter, and others. 1907.
La fiaccola sotto il moggio (produced 1905). 1905.
Più che l'amore (produced 1906). 1907.
La nave (produced 1908). 1908; as *La Nave,* translated and adapted by R.H. Elkin, 1919.
Fedra (produced 1909). 1909.
Le Martyre de Saint Sébastien, music by Debussy (produced 1911). 1911.
Il ferro (produced as *Le Chèvrefeuille,* 1913; revised version, as *Il ferro,* produced 1914). 1914; as *The Honeysuckle,* translated by Cecile Sartoris and G. Enthoven, 1911.
La Pisanelle (produced 1913). In *Tutte le opere,* 1935.
La Parisina, music by Mascagni (produced 1913). 1913.
Cabiria. 1914.

Screenplays: *La crociata degli innocenti,* 1911.

Fiction

Terra vergine (stories). 1882.
Il libro delle vergine. 1884.
Il piacere. 1889; as *The Child of Pleasure,* translated by Georgina Harding, 1898.
L'innocente. 1892; as *The Intruder,* translated by Arthur Hornblow, 1898; as *The Victim,* translated by Georgina Harding, 1899, reprinted 1991.
Giovanni Episcopo. 1892; as *Episcopo and Company,* translated by Myrta Leonora Jones, 1896.
Il trionfo della morte, 1894; as *The Triumph of Death,* translated by Georgina Harding, 1896.
Le vergini delle rocce. 1896; as *The Maidens of the Rocks,* translated by Annette Halliday-Antona and Giuseppe Antona, 1898; as *The Virgins of the Rocks,* translated by A. Hughes, 1899.
Il fuoco. 1900; as *The Flame of Life,* translated by K. Vivaria, 1900; as *The Flame,* translated by Dora Knowlton Ranous, 1906; also translated by Susan Bassnett, 1991.
Le novelle della Pescara. 1902; as *Tales of My Native Town* (12 of 18 tales), translated by Gaetano Mantellini, 1920.
Forse che si, forse che no. 1910.
La leda senza cigno. 1916.

Other

Notturno (autobiographical prose). 1921.

Tutte le opere, edited by Angelo Sodini. 49 vols., 1927–36.

Carteggio D'Annunzio—Duse: Superstiti missive: Lettere, cartoline, telegrammi, dediche 1898–1923, edited by Piero Nardi. 1975.

Lettere a una donna. 1975.

Lettere inedite. In *Quaderni del Vittoriale,* July-August, 1980.

Scritti politici, edited by Paolo Alatri. 1980.

Nocturne and Five Tales of Love and Death, translated by R. Rosenthal. 1991.

*

Bibliography: *D'Annunzio Abroad: A Bibliographical Essay* by Joseph G. Fucilla and Joseph M. Carrière, 2 vols., 1935–37; *Bibliografia critica di Gabriele D'Annunzio* by Mario Vecchioni, 1970; *Bibliografia della critica dannunziana nei periodici italiani dal 1880 al 1938* by Anna Baldazzi, 1977; ''Bibliografia dannunziana,'' in issues of *Quaderni vittoriale.*

Critical Studies: *D'Annunzio* by Tom Antongini, 1938; *Age Cannot Wither: The Story of Duse and D'Annunzio* by Bertita L. de Harding, 1947; *Wings of Fire: A Biography of Gabriele D'Annunzio and Eleonora Duse* by Frances Winwar, 1957; *D'Annunzio: The Poet as Superman* by Anthony Rhodes, 1959; *D'Annunzio in France: A Study in Cultural Relations* by Giovanni Gullace, 1966; *D'Annunzio* by Philippe Julian, 1973; *The First Duce: D'Annunzio at Fiume* by Michael A. Ledeen, 1977; *Gabriele D'Annunzio* by Charles Klopp, 1988; *Gabriele D'Annunzio: The Dark Flame* by Paolo Valesio, 1992; *D'Annunzio and the Great War* by Alfredo Bonadeo, 1995; *Gabriele D'Annunzio: Defiant Archangel* by John Woodhouse, 1997.

*   *   *

The grounds for regarding Gabriele D'Annunzio as a major 20th-century Italian poet are aptly summed up by Eugenio Montale: ''D'Annunzio experimented or touched upon all the linguistic and prosodic possibilities of our time . . . Not to have learned anything from him would be a very bad sign.'' Yet Montale as well as Giuseppe Ungaretti and Umberto Saba reacted against him, just as D'Annunzio himself had reacted against the poetic tradition represented by Giosuè Carducci and Giovanni Pascoli. D'Annunzio's metrical and linguistic innovations altered expression and reflected a new sensibility. He was a prolific writer (in French and in Italian): his first book of poems, *Primo vere,* came out in 1879 and his last, *Teneo te, Africa* (in *Tutte le opere*), in 1936. In between he published several important books of lyrics; *Alcyone* (*Halcyon*)—the third of four books (*Maia, Elettra,* and *Merope* are the others) in the cycle of poems called *Laudi del cielo, del mare, della terra, e degli eroi* [Praises of the Skies, the Sea, the Earth, and the Heroes]—is an impressive synthesis of his naturalistic creed and rhythmic mastery and control, and is deservedly regarded as his most inspired and most successful book of lyrics.

The characteristic qualities of D'Annunzio's best work are exuberant naturalism, plastic and pictorial talent, rhythmic, metric, and imagistic skill, mastery over landscape, in depicting which D'Annunzio achieves a creative fusion between ''physicality'' and ''sensuousness'' and between profound inwardness and spirituality.

But such qualities in D'Annunzio's work went hand in hand with certain defects and weaknesses, such as a self-indulgent dilettantism

in dealing with things that are not rooted in his life and experience; a kind of amoral impressionistic exhibitionism unredeemed by the vitality and concreteness of a fully realized experience; and a rhetorical, musical, and aesthetic artifice which aims at and at times achieves a kind of perfection which is essentially hollow and therefore unconvincing.

D'Annunzio also wrote novels and plays. Of the former those most indicative of his powers as a decadent aesthete are *Il piacere* (*The Child of Pleasure*), *Le vergini delle rocce* (*The Virgins of the Rocks*), *Il fuoco* (*The Flame*), and *Forse che sì forse che no* [Maybe Yes, Maybe No]; and of the latter *La città morta* (*The Dead City*), *La Gioconda, Francesca da Rimini,* and the best-known of all, *La figlia di Iorio* (*The Daughter of Jorio*), are the most characteristic. Both in the plays and the novels one underlying theme is the Nietzschean myth of the superman; another is the cult of sensuality.

—G. Singh

See the essays on *The Flame, Francesca da Rimini,* and ''Rain in the Pine Forest.''

DANTE Alighieri

See ALIGHIERI, Dante

DARÍO, Rubén

Born: Félix Rubén García Sarmiento in Metapa, Nicaragua, 18 January, 1867. **Education:** Educated at various schools; then a Jesuit school, 1878–80; Instituto de Occidente, Léon, 1881. **Family:** Married 1) Rafaela Contreras in 1890 (died 1892), one son; 2) Rosario Emelina Murillo in 1893, one son; also one daughter and two sons by Francisca Sánchez. **Career:** Journalist from age 14: worked on papers in Nicaragua, Valparaíso, Santiago and Buenos Aires; then correspondent for Latin American papers in various parts of Latin America as well as in Paris and Madrid; also served Guatemala in various diplomatic and representative functions; consul of Cambodia to Argentina, 1893–94; suffered from alcoholic depression, 1895. **Died:** 6 February 1916.

PUBLICATIONS

Collections

Obras completas. 22 vols., 1917–20.

Obras completas, edited by Alberto Ghiraldo and Andrés González-Blanco. 21 vols., 1923–29.

Obras completas, edited by Sanmiguel Raimúndez and Emilio Gascó Contell. 5 vols., 1950–55.

Poesías completas, edited by Alfonso Méndez Plancarte. 1952; revised edition, edited by Antonio Oliver Belmás, 2 vols., 1967.

Selected Poems, translated by Lysander Kemp. 1965.

Poesía, edited by Ernesto Mejía Sánchez. 1977.

Poesías inéditas, edited by Ricardo Llopesa. 1988.

Selected Poems of Rubén Darío: A Bilingual Anthology, translated, edited with introduction by Alberto Acereda and Will Derusha. 2001.

Verse

Epístolas y poemas. 1885.
Abrojos. 1887.
Las rosas andinas: Rimas y contra-rimas, with Rubén Rubí 1888.
Azul. 1888; revised edition, 1890; also edited by Andrew P. Debicki and Michael J. Doudoroff, 1985.
Rimas, 1889.
Prosas profanas y otros poemas. 1896; revised edition, 1901; as *Prosas Profanas and Other Poems,* translated by Charles B. McMichael. 1922.
Cantos de vida y esperanza, Los cisnes, y otros poemas. 1905.
El canto errante. 1907.
Poema del otoño y otros poemas. 1910.
Canto a la Argentina y otros poemas. 1914.
Obra poética. 4 vols., 1914–16.
Eleven Poems, translated by Thomas Walsh and Salomón de la Selva. 1916.
Sol del domingo: Poesías inéditas. 1917.

Fiction

Emelina, with Eduardo Poirier. 1887.
Edelmira, edited by Francisco Contreras. 1926(?).
Cuentos fantásticos, edited by José Olivio Jiménez. 1979.
Cuentos, edited by José Emilio Balladares. 1986.

Other

La canción del oro; La isla del oro; El oro de Mallorca. 1886.
A. de Gilbert. 1890.
Los raros. 1893.
Castelar, 1899.
Peregrinaciones. 1901.
España contemporánea. 1901.
La caravana pasa. 1902.
Tierras solares. 1904.
Opiniones. 1906.
Parisiana. 1907.
El viaje a Nicaragua. 1909.
Blanco. 1911.
Letras. 1911.
Todo al vuelo. 1912.
Autobiografía. 1912.
La casa de las ideas. 1916.
La vida de Rubén Darío, escrita por el mismo. 1916.
El mundo de los sueños: Prosas póstumas. 1917; edited by Angel Rama, 1973.
Impresiones y sensaciones, edited by Alberto Ghiraldo. 1925.
Escritos inéditos, edited by E.K. Mapes. 1938.
Cartas: Epistolario inedito, edited by Dictino Álvarez Hernández. 1963.
Escritos dispersos, edited by Pedro Luis Barcia. 2 vols., 1968–73.
Páginas desconocidas, edited by Roberta Ibáñez. 1970.
La isla del oro/El oro de Mallorca, edited by Luis Maristany. 1978.
Textos socio-políticos, edited by Jorge Eduardo Arellano and Francisco Valle, 1980.

*

Bibliography: *A Bibliography of Darío* by Henry Grattan Doyle, 1935; *Rubén Darío: A Selective Classified and Annotated Bibliography* by Hensley C. Woodbridge, 1975; *Bibliografía de Rubén Darío* by Jorge Eduardo Arellano, 1981.

Critical Studies: *Poet-Errant: A Biography of Darío* by Charles D. Watland, 1965; *Cuadrivio* (on Darío, López Velarde, Pessoa, Cernuda) by Octavio Paz, 1965; *Critical Approaches to Rubén Darío* by Keith Ellis, 1974; *Rubén Darío and the Pythagorean Tradition* by Raymond Skyrme, 1975; *Rubén Darío and the Romantic Search for Unity: The Modernist Recourse to Esoteric Tradition* by Cathy Logan Jrade, 1983; *Light and Longing: Silva and Darío: Modernism and Religious Heterodoxy* by Sonya A. Ingwersen, 1986; *Los espacios poéticos de Rubén Darío* by José María Martínez Domingo, 1995; *Poesía Mallorquina de Rubén Darío* by Carlos Menese, 1997; *Beyond the Glitter: The Language of Gems in Modernista Writers Rubén Darío, Ramón del Valle-Inclán, and José Asunción Silva* by Rosemary C. LoDato, 1999.

* * *

Throughout the Spanish-speaking literary world Rubén Darío is known as the great innovator, the poet who transformed the prosody of that language. At the turn of the century he emerged as the leader of the movement known as ''Modernismo,'' and as the first American writer seriously to influence the literary conventions of metropolitan Spain.

His first important collection, *Azul* [Blue], shows an obvious allegiance to 19th-century French poetry, from Hugo through the Parnassians to the symbolists and Verlaine, otherwise evident in the sketches collected in *Los raros [The Rare Ones]*; in fact the coda of *Azul,* ''Échos,'' is actually written in French. The core of the book is a ''lyrical year,'' in which the four seasons are experienced in terms less appropriate to the poet's native Nicaragua than to a Europe whose culture dazzled Darío from the start of his career. None the less there are characteristic American notes in the sonnets to Caupolicán, the Mapuche hero of Chile, and to the poet Salvador Díaz Mirón, a fellow modernist whom Darío had known in Mexico and whose ''unfettered'' verses are said to resound like a herd of American buffalo.

Usually thought of as his most decadent and precious collection, *Prosas profanas* [Profane Prose] is by any account his least American in terms of overt theme and subject matter, despite, that is, his famous invocation of Palenque and Utatlán, Montezuma and the Inca, in the introduction. For example, the past evoked in the section ''ecreaciones arqueológicas'' definitely belongs to the classic Mediterranean, also the backdrop for the extensive ''Coloquio de los centauros,'' with its Pythagoreanism. Elsewhere in this collection Darío turns to the Cid and medieval Spain, much as Ezra Pound (triumphant in London not long after Darío was in Madrid) turned to medieval England. Indeed, this parallel helps us to focus on what is a new cosmopolitanism in the poetry of Darío and the Spanish language in general. Associated repeatedly with Buenos Aires, where Darío began the collection, this cosmopolitanism is most fully expressed in the poem ''Divagación,'' a spiralling journey through cultures and time.

From a technical point of view, *Prosas profanas* announces spectacular innovations in prosody, notably in the syncopation of the alexandrine, which continue to be used to great effect in Darío's three subsequent collections *Cantos de vida y esperanza* [Songs of Love and Hope] *El canto errante* [Wandering Song], and *Poema del otoño*

[Poem of Autumn], though less so in the somewhat stentorian *Canto a la Argentina,* the last collection published in his lifetime. (In his nomadic career, he left a good deal of work uncollected.) Typical of the more sombre agility of his later period are the Nocturnes in *Cantos de vida,* notably the arresting alexandrine that opens the second: "Los que auscultasteis el corazón de la noche." The alexandrine is also the verse form chosen by Darío in *El canto errante* for his "Epístola a Madame Lugones," she being the wife of another fellow modernist, the Argentinian Leopoldo Lugones. Remarkable for its colloquialism, its shifts of mood and tone, as well as its technical virtuosity, this poem has received brilliant elucidation in "El caracol y la sirena," Octavio Paz's indispensable vindication of Darío as the father not just of modernist but of modern poetry in Spanish.

—Gordon Brotherston

See the essay on "Mía."

DAZAI Osamu

Born: Tsushima Shuji in Kanagi, Japan, 19 June 1909. **Education:** Educated in Kanagi grade school; middle school in Aomori City; higher school in Hirosaki, 1927–30; Tokyo Imperial University, from 1930. **Family:** Married 1) Oyama Hatsuyo in 1931; 2) Ishihara Michiko in 1939. **Career:** Journalist and writer: illness, alcohol, and drugs led to several suicide attempts. **Awards:** Kitamura Tōkoku award, 1939. **Died:** 13 June 1948.

PUBLICATIONS

Collections

Zenshū [Works]. 12 vols., 1955–57; revised editions, 1967–68, 1979.

Fiction

Bannen [The Declining Years]. 1936.
Doke No hana [The Flower of Buffoonery]. 1937.
Dasu gemaine [Das Gemeine]. 1940.
Hashire Merosu [Run Melos]. 1940.
Shin Hamuretto [The New Hamlet]. 1941.
Kojiki gakusei [Beggar-Student]. 1941.
Kakekomi uttae [The Indictment]. 1941.
Seigi to bisho [Justice and Smile]. 1942.
Udaijin Sanetomo [Lord Sanetomo]. 1943.
Tsugaru. 1944; as *Return to Tsugaru: Travels of a Purple Tramp,* translated by James Westerhoven, 1985.
Shinshaku shokoku banashi [A Retelling of the Tales from the Province]. 1945.
Otogi zoshi [A Collection of Fairy-Tales]. 1945.
Pandora no hako [Pandora's Box]. 1946.
Shayō. 1947; as *The Declining Sun,* translated by Takehide Kikuchi, 1950; as *The Setting Sun,* translated Donald Keene, 1956.
Biyon no tsuma [Villon's Wife]. 1947.
Ningen shikkaku. 1948; as *No Longer Human,* translated by Donald Keene, 1953.
Selected Stories and Sketches, translated by James O'Brien. 1982.

Crackling Mountain and Other Stories, translated by James O'Brien. 1989.
Self Portraits (stories), translated by Ralph F. McCarthy. 1991.
Blue Bamboo: Tales of Fantasy and Romance, translated by Ralph F. McCarthy. 1993.

Other

Human Lost (diary; in Japanese). 1937.
Fugaku Hyakkei [One Hundred Views of Mt. Fuji]. 1940.
Tokyo Hakkei [Eight Views of Tokyo]. 1941.

*

Critical Studies: *Landscapes and Portraits* by Donald Keene, 1971; *Accomplices of Silence: The Modern Japanese Novel* by Masao Miyoshi, 1974; *Dazai Osamu* by James A. O'Brien, 1975; *Modern Japanese Writers and the Nature of Literature* by Makoto Ueda, 1976; "Art Is Me": Dazai Osamu's Narrative Voice as a Permeable Self,' in *Harvard Journal of Asiatic Studies,* 41, 1981, and *The Saga of Dazai Osamu: A Critical Study with Translations,* 1985, both by Phyllis I. Lyons; *Suicidal Narrative in Modern Japan: The Case of Dazai Osamu,* by Alan Wolfe, 1990; *Studies in the Cosmic Spirit in Modern Japanese Fiction* by Joel R. Cohn, 1998.

* * *

Dazai Osamu is regarded as one of the greatest stylists of modern Japanese literature, though his own life may be considered his masterpiece. Virtually all of his works were reflections of that life. For Dazai, fiction was ultimately a lie, and in his often nostalgic quest for sincerity he strove to strip bare the authorial self and let it speak directly to the reader. In this respect, Dazai can be associated with the autobiographical strain in modern Japanese fiction, the *watakushi-shosetsu* or "I-novel." The practitioners of this form felt that reality could only be portrayed through the unmediated perspective of the author, presented as the first-person narrator in the text. This mode coincided with traditional tendencies to view literature as a mode of self-expression and to hold a somewhat skeptical attitude towards "objective" reality.

Dazai consciously conceived of his life as art, as the subject matter of his writings. Dazai the man became "Dazai" the text, and his works represented various readings of that text. The Dazai persona was that of the sensitive but cynical dissolute, the sloppy drunk who arouses more pity than disgust. It was characterized by an all-too-human weakness that was designed to elicit compassion, the highest virtue. Born to a wealthy landholding family, Dazai developed a rebellious streak that he briefly tried to channel into political activism, but it seems that he could not even believe in communism. Distrusting virtually all social institutions, he lived a scandalous life. Hypocrisy, arrogance, and pretension are denounced everywhere in his works, while simplicity, sincerity, and honesty are praised. In Dazai's literary world, consciousness is the curse that keeps one from living a true life. While idealizing simple people who live day-to-day in an unselfconscious manner, Dazai found himself irresistibly drawn to despair and death.

Many of Dazai's writings are in the "I-novel" vein. Such works as *Tokyo Hakkei* [Eight Views of Tokyo], *Fugaku Hyakkei* [One Hundred Views of Mt. Fuji], and *Tsugaru (Return to Tsugaru)* are first-person narratives by the archetypal "Dazai" character. In *Shin Hamuretto* [The New Hamlet], *Otogi Zoshi* [A Collection of Fairy-Tales], and similar works, old literary works are retold in a uniquely Dazaiesque manner, irreverent yet profoundly human. Dazai's most accomplished works of fiction—the short story *Biyon no tsuma* [Villon's Wife] and the novels *Shayō (The Setting Sun)* and *Ningen Shikkaku (No Longer Human)*—appeared shortly after the end of World War II. Taken together, the works present a deep and multi-faceted composite image of the "Dazai" persona. *The Setting Sun*, Dazai's most famous work, has been praised for its portrayal of the desolation and hope of post-war Japan. Yet although one of the central characters, Kazuko, appears to have made an existentialist decision at the end, even her resolve is cloaked in ambiguity.

If Dazai's *oeuvre* suffers from its narrowly drawn subject, it nevertheless contains some of the most beautiful prose in 20th-century Japanese literature. Because of his basic love of humanity, Dazai possessed an extraordinary sensitivity to the rhythm and flow of speech, revealed in a limpid, entertaining, and often humorous literary style that makes his works a joy to read, and must account for some of the popularity he maintains among Japanese readers to this day.

—Matthew Mizenko

DE FILIPPO, Eduardo

Born: Naples, Italy, 24 May 1900. Illegitimate son of playwright and actor-manager Eduardo Scarpetta. **Education:** Educated at Istituto Chierchia, Naples, 1911. **Military Service:** Served in the Italian army, 1920–22. **Family:** Married 1) the actress Dorothy Pennington in 1928 (marriage annulled in San Marino, 1952, recognized in Italy, 1956); 2) Thea Prandi in 1956 (separated 1959; died 1961), one son and one daughter before marriage; 3) Isabella Quarantotti in 1977. **Career:** Child actor with family troupe: debut, 1904; actor with Vincenzo Scarpetta's company, 1914–20, Francesco Corbindi's troupe, 1922, Peppino Villani's troupe, 1928, and the Riviste Molinari company, 1930–31; co-founder, with his brother Peppino and sister Titina, Il Teatro Umoristico, 1929, and toured with it until Peppino's departure in 1945; co-founder, with Titina, Il Teatro di Eduardo, 1945–54; director and owner, Teatro San Ferdinando, Naples, from 1954; toured Austria, Belgium, Hungary, Poland, and Russia, 1962. Also film actor, and director of films and operas. **Awards:** Institute of Italian Drama prize, 1951, 1968; Simoni prize, 1969; Feltrinelli prize, 1972; Pirandello prize, 1975. D.Litt.: University of Birmingham, England, 1977; University of Rome, 1980. Named Senator for Life of the Italian Republic, 1981. **Died:** 31 October 1984.

PUBLICATIONS

Collections

Three Plays (includes *The Local Authority; Grand Magic; The Best House in Naples—Filumena Marturano*), translated by Carlo Ardito. 1976.
Four Plays, with introduction by Carlo Ardito. 1992.
Eduardo de Filippo: Four Plays, translated by Maria Tucci. 2001.

Plays

Sik-Sik, L'artefice magico (produced 1929). 1932; as *Sik-Sik, The Masterful Magician*, translated by Robert G. Bender, in *Italian Quarterly*, 11, 1967.
Natale in casa Cupiello (produced 1931; revised version produced 1942). In *Cantata dei giorni pari*, 1959.
Farmacia di turno (produced 1931). In *Cantata dei giorni pari*, 1959.
Ogni anno punto e da capo (produced 1931). 1971.
Quei figuri di trent'anni fa (produced 1932). In *Cantata dei giorni pari*, 1959.
Chi è cchiù felice 'e me!. . . (produced 1932). In *Cantata dei giorni pari*, 1959.
Gennariniello (produced 1932). In *Cantata dei giorni pari*, 1959.
Ditegli sempre di sì (produced 1932). In *Cantata dei giorni pari*, 1959.
I morti non fanno paura (as *Requie all'anima soia*, produced 1932; revised version, as *I morti non fanno paura*, produced 1952). In *Cantata dei giorni dispari 2*, 1958.
L'ultimo bottone (produced 1932).
Cuoco della mala cucina, with Maria Scarpetta (produced 1932).
Uomo e galantuomo (produced 1933). In *Cantata dei giorni pari*, 1959.
Parlate al portiere, with Maria Scarpetta (produced 1933).
Scorzetta di limone, from a play by Gino Rocca (produced 1933).
Il dono di Natale (produced 1934). In *Cantata dei giorni pari*, 1959.
Tre mesi dopo (produced 1934).
Sintetici a qualunque costo (produced 1934).
Il berretto a sonagli, from a play by Pirandello (produced 1936).
Quinto piano, ti saluto! (produced 1936). In *Cantata dei giorni pari*, 1959.
L'abito nuovo, from a story by Pirandello (produced 1937). In *Cantata dei giorni pari*, 1959.
Uno coi capelli bianchi (produced 1938). In *Cantata dei giorni pari*, 1959.
Si salvi chi può, from a work by Gino Rocca (produced 1940).
Non ti pago! (produced 1940). 1943.
La parte di Amleto (produced 1940). In *Cantata dei giorni pari*, 1959.
In licenza, from a work by Eduardo Scarpetta (produced 1941).
La fortuna con l'effe maiuscola, with Armando Curcio and R. De Angelis (produced 1942).
Io, l'erede (produced 1942). In *Cantata dei giorni pari*, 1959.
Il diluvio, from the play by Ugo Betti (produced 1943).
Napoli milionaria! (produced 1945). 1946; as *Eduardo de Filippo's Napoli milionaria*, translated and adapted by Tori Haring-Smith, 1996.
Occhiali neri (produced 1945). In *Cantata dei giorni dispari 2*, 1958.
Questi fantasmi! (produced 1946). In *Cantata dei giorni dispari 1*, 1951; as *Oh, These Ghosts*, translated by Marguerite Carra and Louise H. Warner, in *Tulane Drama Review*, 8, 1963.
Filumena Marturano (produced 1946). In *Cantata dei giorni dipari 1*, 1951; as *The Best House in Naples*, translated by Carlo Ardito, in *Three Plays*, 1976; as *Filumena*, translated by Keith Waterhouse and Willis Hall, 1978; also translated by Timberlake Wertenbaker, 1998.
Pericolosamente (produced 1947). In *Cantata dei giorni pari*, 1959.
Le bugie con le gambe lunghe (produced 1948). In *Cantata dei giorni dispari 1*, 1951.
Le voci di dentro (produced 1948). In *Cantata dei giorni dispari 1*, 1951; as *Inner Voices*, translated by N.F. Simpson, 1983.

La grande magia (produced 1949). In *Cantata dei giorni dispari 1*, 1951; as *Grand Magic*, translated by Carlo Ardito, in *Three Plays*, 1976.

La paura numero uno (produced 1950). In *Cantata dei giorni dispari 2*, 1958.

Cantata dei giorni dispari. 3 vols., 1951–66; revised edition, 1971.

Amicizia (produced 1952). In *Cantata dei giorni dispari 2*, 1958.

Miseria e nobiltà from a play by Eduardo Scarpetta (produced 1953).

Bene mio e core mio (produced 1955). 1956.

Mia famiglia (produced 1955). 1955.

Il medico dei pazzi, from a work by Eduardo Scarpetta (produced 1957).

De Pretore Vincenzo (produced 1957). 1957.

Tre cazune fortunate, from a play by Eduardo Scarpetta (produced 1958).

Sabato, domenica e lunedì (produced 1959). 1960; as *Saturday, Sunday, Monday*, translated by Keith Waterhouse and Willis Hall, 1974.

Cantata dei giorni pari. 1959.

Il sindaco del Rione Sanità (produced 1960). 1961; as *The Local Authority*, translated by Carlo Ardito, in *Three Plays*, 1976.

Il figlio di Pulcinella (produced 1962). In *Cantata dei giorni dispari 3*, 1966.

Peppino Girella, with Isabella Quaratotti (televised 1963). 1964.

Farse e commedie. 2 vols., 1964.

Dolore sotto chiave (produced 1964). With *L'arte della commedia*, 1965.

L'arte della commedia (produced 1965). With *Dolore sotto chiave*, 1965.

Tommaso D'Amalfi. In *Cantata dei giorni dispari 3*, 1966.

Il cilindro (produced 1966). In *Cantata dei giorni dispari 3*, 1966.

Il contratto (produced 1967). 1967.

Cani e gatti, from a work by Eduardo Scarpetta (produced 1970).

Il monumento (produced 1970). 1971.

'Na santarella, from a work by Eduardo Scarpetta (produced 1972).

I capolavori. 2 vols., 1973.

Gli esami non finiscono mai (produced 1973). 1973.

Lu curaggio de nu pumpiere napulitano, from a work by Eduardo Scarpetta (produced 1974).

L'erede di Shylock, from the play by Shakespeare. 1984.

La Tempesta, from the play by Shakespeare. 1984.

Nativity Scene: A Play, translated by Anthony Molino and Paul Feinberg, 1997.

Screenplays: "Adelina" episode, with Isabella Quarantotti, of *Ieri, oggi e domani (Yesterday, Today and Tomorrow)*, 1963; *Matrimonio all'italiana (Marriage Italian Style)*, 1964; *Spara forte, più forte . . . non capisco (Shoot Loud, Louder . . . I Don't Understand)*, with Suso Cecchi D'Amico, 1966.

Television Plays: *Peppino Girella*, with Isabella Quarantotti, 1963; *Li nepute de lu sinecco*, 1975; *'O Tuono 'e marzo*, 1975; and adaptations of about 20 of his own plays.

Verse

Il paese di Pulcinetta. 1951.
'O canisto. 1971.
Le poesie. 1975.

Other

Editor, *Manzù: Album inedito*. 1977.
Teatro, edited by Nicola Di Blasi and Paola Quarenghi. 2000.
Tre adattamenti teatrali. 1999.

*

Critical Studies: *In Search of Theatre* by Eric Bentley, 1953; *L'esperienza comica di Eduardo De Filippo* by Laura Pizer, 1972; *Eduardo* by Federico Frascani, 1974; *Il teatro di Eduardo*, 1975, and *Eduardo De Filippo*, 1978, by Fiorenza Di Franco; *Eduardo nel mondo* edited by Isabella De Filippo, 1978, and *Eduardo De Filippo: Vita e opere 1900–1984* edited by De Filippo and Sergio Martin, 1986; *Eduardo De Filippo: Poeta comico del tragico quotidiano* by Carla Filosa, 1978; *Eduardo De Filippo: Introduzione e guida alia studio dell' opera eduardiana, storia e antologia della critica* by Giovanni Antonucci, 1980; *Eduardo segreto* by Federico Frascani, 1982; *De Filippo* (in English) by Mario Mignone, 1984; *Eduardo drammaturgo* by Anna Barsotti, 1988; *The Theatre of Eduardo De Filippo: An Introductory Study* by Marco Ciolli, 1993; *Vita di Eduardo* by Maurizio Giammusso, 1993.

* * *

Eduardo De Filippo's entire life was spent in the theatre. At the age of four he first appeared on stage; at 14 he joined the company in which his father, Eduardo Scarpetta, the prominent Neapolitan actor, director, and author, was a member. De Filippo was born into a thespian family but he was also educated in the still lively, century-old tradition of the Neapolitan theatre, the popular and dialectal heir to the *commedia dell'arte*. He became an author, actor, and later director and manager of his own company. It is not surprising that even in his least inspired works one cannot fail to notice his consummate stage craftsmanship.

His plays are either a continuous crescendo or a combination of crescendo and diminuendo. An example of the latter is *La paura numero uno* [Fear Number One]: Matteo, fearing World War II, tries to postpone indefinitely his daughter's wedding; Luisa, the other protagonist and the fiancé's mother, who has lost her husband in World War I and one son in World War II, does not want her only remaining son to risk the danger of war, and walls him up in a room. Matteo first appears comical, then ridiculous, then morally acceptable; Luisa is first seemingly mad, then pathetic, then irreproachable.

Filumena Marturano, on the other hand, is an example of the plays of crescendo. By the end of each of its three acts we are surprised: in Act I, characters and audience discover that the main character is the mother of three grown sons; in Act II, one of the three proves to be that of Domenico, her lover; in Act III, the lovers reveal to each other their inner feelings. These revelations disclose, to odd effect, the real meaning of what went on before: some of the comic elements become serious, and the serious, comic: the sentimental becomes real, while the insane becomes normal.

Although De Filippo was a product of Neapolitan popular theatre in his craft and often in his language, the theatricality of that tradition did not compromise his originality. The farce of Eduardo Scarpetta and the grotesquerie of Raffaele Viviani, another famous Neapolitan playwright, become, in De Filippo, humorous, bittersweet, or pathetic. In the first poem of his collection *Il paese di Pulcinella* [Pulcinella's Land], the question "Is it a laughing matter when I portray comical situations arising from everyday life?'' is answered with ''I don't think so.'' Of course, we may still laugh, but we must also perceive that his comedy carries a streak of melancholy.

The locus of De Filippo's drama is Naples, and its subject the Neapolitan in his daily struggle for physical, social, or emotional survival. The solidity of De Filippo's plots and the characterization of his Neapolitan personae generate irresistible laughter, but also reveal man's existential finitude: a hint of the tragic is evoked. These dramas pitch the individual against society, which is generally represented by the family. In fact, some of De Filippo's most famous and successful plays, such as *Napoli milionaria!*, *Filumena Marturano*, and *Sabato, domenica e lunedì* (*Saturday, Sunday, Monday*), present in tones of bittersweet realism conflicts among family members with different desires, morals, or beliefs. However, it is when De Filippo shatters the realistic mould that his plays achieve their greatest originality.

In his first major play, and one of his own favourites, *Natale in casa Cupiello* [Christmas at the Cupiellos], the protagonist, Luca, detaches himself completely from the reality surrounding him by clinging stubbornly to his ideals, his world of illusions. A human being unable to see the obvious may evoke in the audience a smile of compassion and pity. But the audience is also made aware that Luca is unconsciously rejecting the obvious in order to preserve his ego, in order to prevent existence from drowning essence. Our smile of compassion becomes self-conscious, for we all share in Luca's hopeless effort. To pity is added a tinge of terror.

While Luca defends his illusions with the myth of universal brotherhood, symbolized by his construction of the Nativity scene, and remains within realistic coordinates, the protagonists of two of the most important of De Filippo's plays break through the frame of realism and enter the world of fantasy and the surreal.

In *Questi fantasmi!* (*Oh, These Ghosts*), Pasquale convinces himself that there are ghosts: he manufactures them instead of accepting the fact that his wife has a lover. He abandons the reality of pain by living in a world of fantasy. In *La grande magia* (*Grand Magic*), Calogero, who does not want to admit that his wife has run away with her lover, believes what he is told by Otto, a magician: that his wife is being kept in a small box. By opening it, says Otto, he can make her reappear, but only if he has faith in her. Calogero refuses to open the box; he does not want to face the reality of his adulterous wife. Four years later Maria comes back, but Calogero refuses to accept her because she appeared the moment before he was about to open the box; he concludes that the woman before him is not Maria. He will keep the box closed forever so that he can always believe his wife has been faithful.

De Filippo's two kinds of ''reality''—fact and fantasy—do not imply a kind of Pirandellian relativism or an ontological questioning of the real. But his characters, like some of Pirandello's, do use fantasy to avoid being thrown into the abyss of despair or emptiness. Their defences against the abyss are what makes De Filippo's comedies serious.

—Emanuele Licastro

See the essay on *Filumena Marturano*.

DE QUEIRÓS, José Maria de Eça

See EÇA DE QUEIRÓS, José Maria de

DE QUEIROZ, Rachel

See QUEIROZ, Rachel de

DELEDDA, Grazia

Born: Nuoro, Sardinia, Italy, 27 September 1871. **Education:** Educated to age 11. **Family:** Married Palmiro Modesani in 1900; two sons. **Career:** Regular contributor to the periodicals *L'Ultima Moda* and *Il Paradiso dei Bambini*, from 1888, and *Rivista di Letteratura popolare*, 1893–95; moved to Cagliari, 1899; settled in Rome, 1900. **Awards:** Nobel prize for literature, 1926. **Died:** 15 August 1936.

PUBLICATIONS

Collections

Romanzi e novelle, edited by Emilio Cecchi. 5 vols., 1941–61.
Opere scelte, edited by Euralio De Michelis. 2 vols., 1964.

Fiction

Sangue sarde (for children). 1888.
Nell'azzurro. 1890.
Amore regale (stories). 1891.
Fior di Sardegna. 1892.
Amori fatali; La leggenda nera; Il ritratto (stories). 1892.
Racconti sardi. 1894.
Anime oneste. 1895.
La via del male. 1896.
L'ospite (stories). 1897.
Il tesoro. 1897.
Le tentazioni (stories). 1899.
Giaffah (stories; for children). 1899.
Il vecchio della montagna. 1900; edited by Joseph G. Fucilla, 1932.
La regina delle tenebre (stories). 1902.
Dopo il divorzio. 1902; as *Naufraghi in porto*, 1920; as *After the Divorce*, translated by Maria Hornor Landsdale, 1905; also translated by Susan Ashe, 1985.
Elias Portolu. 1903; translated by Martha King, 1992.
Cenere. 1904; as *Ashes*, translated by Helen Hester Colvill, 1908.
Nostalgie. 1905; as *Nostalgia*, translated by Helen Hester Colvill, 1905.
I giuochi della vita (stories). 1905.
L'edera. 1906.
L'ombra del passato. In *Nuova antologia*, 13, 1907.
Amori moderni (stories). 1907.
Il nonno. 1909; as *Cattive compagnie*, 1921.
Il nostro padrone. 1910.
Sino al confine. 1910.
Nel deserto. 1911.
Chiaroscuro (stories). 1912; as *Chiaroscuro and Other Stories*, translated with introduction by Martha King, 1994.
Colombi e sparvieri. 1912.

Canne al vento. 1913; as *Reeds in the Wind*, translated by Martha King, 1999.
Le colpe altrui. 1914.
Il fanciullo nascosto (stories). 1915.
Marianna Sirca. 1915; edited by Maro Beath Jones and Armando T. Bissiri, 1940.
L'incendio nell'oliveto. 1918.
Il ritorno del figlio; La bambina rubata. 1919.
La madre. 1920; as *The Woman and the Priest*, translated by Mary G. Steegman, 1923; as *The Mother*, translated by Steegman, 1928.
Il segreto dell'uomo solitario. 1921.
Il Dio dei viventi. 1921.
Il flauto del bosco (stories). 1923.
La danza della collana. With *A sinistra*, 1924.
La fuga in Egitto. 1925.
Il sigillo d'amore (stories). 1926.
Annalena Bilsini. 1927.
Il vecchio e i fanciulli. 1928.
Il dono di Natale (stories). 1930.
La casa del poeta (stories). 1930.
Il paese del vento. 1932.
La vigna sul mare (stories). 1932.
Sole d'estate (stories). 1933.
L'argine. 1934.
La chiesa della solitudine. 1936; as *The Church of Solitude*, translated by E. Ann Matter, 2002.
Cosima, edited by Antonio Baldini. 1937; translated by Martha King, 1991.
Il cedro del Libano. 1939.
Romanzi e novelle, edited by Natalino Sapegno. 1972.
La Feste del Cristo, e altre novelle, edited by L. Nicastro. 1972.
Romanzi Sardi, edited by Vittorio Spinazzola. 1981.

Verse

Paesaggi sardi. 1897.

Plays

Odio vince. With *Il vecchio della montagna*, 1912.
L'edera (produced 1909), from her novel, with Camillo Antona Traversi. 1912.
La grazia (libretto), with C. Guastella and V. Michetti, music by Vincenzo Michetti (produced 1923). 1922.
A sinistra. With *La danza della collana*, 1924.

Screenplays: *Cenere*, 1916.

Other

Tradizioni popolari di Nuoro in Sardegna. 1894.
Versi e prose giovanili, edited by Antonio Scano. 1938.
Lettera di Grazia Deledda a Marino Moretti (1913–1923). 1959.
Editor, *Le più belle pagine di Silvio Pellico*. 1923.
Translator, *Eugenia Grandet*, by Balzac. 1930.

*

Bibliography: *Bibliografia deleddiana* by Remo Branca, 1938.

Critical Studies: *Grazia Deledda* by Mercedes Mundula, 1929; *Grazia Deledda* by Francesco Bruno, 1935; *L'opera di Grazia Deledda* by Luigi Falchi, 1937; *Grazia Deledda e il Decadentismo* by Euralio De Michelis, 1938; *L'arte di Grazia Deledda* by Licia Roncarati, 1949; *Grazia Deledda* by E. Buono, 1951; *Deledda* by Giancarlo Buzzi, 1952; *Vocazione narrativa di Grazia Deledda* by Floro Di Zeno, 1967; *Grazia Deledda* by Antonio Piromalli, 1968; *Deledda* by Maria Tettamanzi, 1969; *Il segreto di Grazia Deledda* by Remo Branca, 1971; *Grazia Deledda: Ricordi e testimonianze* by Lina Sacchetti, 1971; *Grazia Deledda* by Antonio Tobia, 1971; *Grazia Deledda* by Nicola Valle, 1971; *Atti del convegno nazionale di studi deleddiani*, 1974; *A Self-Made Woman* by Carolyn Balducci, 1975; *Deledda* by Mario Miccinesi, 1975; *Invito alla lettura di Grazia Deledda* by Olga Lombardi, 1979; *Grazia Deledda: Ethnic Novelist* (includes bibliographies) by Mario Aste, 1990; *Women in Modern Italian Literature: Four Studies* by Bruce Merry, 1990.

*   *   *

Grazia Deledda, Italian novelist and short story writer, was born in Sardinia and always remained a passionately committed Sardinian. She was awarded the Nobel prize for literature in 1926. Her journey to Stockholm to receive it was the only occasion in her life when she travelled abroad. A prolific writer, she started writing early in life, and at the age of 17 published her first novel, *Sangue sardo* [Sardinian Blood]. In 1896 she published *La via del male* [The Path of Evil], which was reviewed by the Sicilian novelist Luigi Capuana, in a review that made her well-known in the world of Italian letters. Among the writers she studied in her childhood and early youth, she was most influenced by De Amicis, Hugo, Dumas *père*, and Paul Bourget. After her marriage, Deledda moved to Rome where she lived for the rest of her life.

Although Deledda wrote more than 30 novels and about 15 collections of short stories, it is difficult to pinpoint any particular novel as her masterpiece. Among the more famous and successful are *Elias Portolu, Cenere* (*Ashes*), *Colombi e sparvieri* [Pigeons and Sparrows], *Canne al vento* [*Reeds in the Wind*], *L'incendio nell'oliveto* [The Fire in the Olive-Grove], and *La madre* (*The Mother*). Among her later novels, the more important are *Il segreto dell'uomo solitario* [The Secret of a Lonely Man], *Il Dio dei viventi* [The God of the Living], *Il paese del vento* [The Country of the Wind], and her last novel, which is largely autobiographical, *Cosima*.

Both the novels she wrote while still living in Sardinia, and those produced after she had moved to Rome, have a strongly ethnic and regional vein running through them. Sardinia, its history and geography, its folklore and landscape, its people, customs, and superstitions, its religion and morality, are not only vividly described and passionately celebrated in Deledda's writings, but also constitute the very fabric of her narrative art. Her characters, with their passions and sentiments, fears and feelings of guilt, their primitive as well as romantic impulses, are portrayed convincingly. In this respect, as well as in her adoption of the technique and ethos of "verism" in her writings, Deledda may be compared to Giovanni Verga. But the kind of self-discipline found in Verga, which accounts for his more austere, compact and, on the whole, more accomplished kind of narrative art and realism, is not to be found in Deledda, even in her most mature novels. Little wonder, therefore, that Verga made a point of detaching himself from Deledda, considering his own view of life and truth to be more bitter and tragic than that of Deledda.

It is only in her later and more mature novels that Deledda manages to drop description for its own sake and do away with mechanical repetition of theme, character, and landscape. To some extent this development was brought about by her contact with the French and Russian naturalists as well as with Tolstoi, Dostoevskii, and Thomas Hardy. However, neither her naturalism or "verism," nor her contact with such foreign writers, went far enough to free her from both her instinctive tendency to idealize or lyricize her subject matter and from her own self-absorption, which accounts for the essentially autobiographical nature of her art. Thus, her native land, with its savage and primitive landscape, and her own emotionally rich childhood and memories may be regarded as the main protagonists of her work, so that such characters as servants and landlords, or priests and bandits, seem to be secondary. And it is in the context of such a landscape and such protagonists that Deledda manages to depict, like Verga and Hardy, but not with the same degree of moral depth and stoic richness, the workings of the human fate, the nature of the Montalian "evil of living," the drama and turmoil of human passions.

But while Deledda was deeply involved in portraying the life and passions of the land and the people of Sardinia, her involvement was more emotional than moral or psychological in nature. She could not detach herself from her subject matter, because she lacked what D.H. Lawrence called the psychological technique. But then this is both her weakness *and* her strength; it is her strength in the sense that what she did achieve (which prompted Lawrence, in his introduction to the translation of *La madre*, to locate some parallels between Deledda and Emily Brontë) would not have been possible had she been able to contemplate objectively that with which she was so emotionally involved.

—Gabrielle Barfoot

DEMOSTHENES

Born: Athens, c. 384 BC. **Education:** Studied rhetoric and law, overcoming speech impediments. **Career:** Speech writer and teacher, then practised constitutional law; also active in politics from age 30, rousing the Athenians to resist the growing threat from Philip II of Macedon; formed an anti-Macedonian party, 346–340 BC, and an alliance with Thebes, 339 BC, and made his great speeches against Philip: *Olynthiacae* in 349 BC; *Philippicae* in 352, 344, and 341 BC; was present when the Greeks were defeated at the battle of Chaeronea in 338 BC. Accused of theft, 324 BC, condemned, fined, and exiled; recalled after the death of Alexander in 323 BC to direct the Greek rebellion against Macedon; sentenced to death by Demades, a supporter of the Macedonian rule; fled to the island of Calaureia, where he took poison. **Died:** 322 BC.

PUBLICATIONS

Collections

[Works], edited by F. Blass. 4th revised edition, 3 vols., 1885–89; translated by J.H. and C. Vince, A.T. Murray, N.W. and N.J. de Witt [Loeb Edition], 7 vols., 1926–49.
Orations, edited by S.H. Butcher. 3 vols., 1938; as *All the Orations of Demosthenes*, translated by Thomas Leland, 3 vols., 1770; also

translated by Charles R. Kennedy, 5 vols., 1852–63; as *Public Orations*, translated by A.W. Pickard-Cambridge, 1912; selection as *Olynthiacs, Philippics, Minor Public Speeches* (bilingual edition), translated by J.H. Vince, 1930; as *On the False Embassy (Oration 19)*, translated and edited by Douglas M. MacDowell, 2000.

Works

Adversus Leptinem, translated by F.E.A. Trayes. 1893; translated as *The Oration Against the Law of Leptines*, 1879; also translated by J. Harold Boardman, 1892.
De corona, edited by Arthur Holmes. 1871; also edited by George and William Simcox, 1871, Martin L. D'Ooge, 1875, B. Drake, revised by Thomas Gwatkin, 1880, William W. Goodwin, 1901, Milton W. Humphreys, 1913, and Evelyn Abbott and P.E. Matheson, 2 vols., 1926; as *The Crown*, translated by William Brandt, 1870; also translated by Robert Collier, 1875; Francis P. Simpson, 1882; Charles R. Kennedy, 1888; Henry, Lord Brougham, 1893; T. Jeffrey, 1896; Otho Lloyd Holland, 1926; A.N.W. Saunders, in *Demosthenes and Aeschines*, 1975; as *The Oration of Demosthenes upon the Crown*, translated by Charles Rann Kennedy, 1988; as *On the Crown (De Corona)*, translated with introduction and commentary by S. Usher, 1993.
De falsa legatione, edited by Richard Shilleto. 9th edition, 1901; translated by A.N.W. Saunders, in *Demosthenes and Aeschines*, 1975.
In Androtionem, translated as *Androtion*. 1888.
In Midiam, as *Against Meidias*, edited by John R. King. 1901; also edited by William W. Goodwin, 1906, S.H. Butcher, 1907, J.H. Vince [Loeb Edition], 1935, Ioannes Sykutris, 1937, and Jean Humbert, 1959; translated by J.H. Vince (bilingual edition), 1930; also translated by Douglas M. MacDowell, 1990.
Olynthiacae, edited by T.R. Glover. 1897; also edited by H. Sharpley, 1900, J.M. Macgregor, 1915, and E.I. McQueen (with commentary), 1986; as *The Olynthiacs*, translated by E.L. Hawkins, 1905.
Philippicae, edited by Gilbert A. Davies. 1907; translated by *The Philippic Orations*, 1885.
Selected Private Speeches (with commentary.), edited by C. Carey and R.A. Reid. 1985.

*

Critical Studies: *Demosthenes and the Last Days of Greek Freedom* by A.W. Pickard-Cambridge, 1914; *Demosthenes: The Original and Growth of His Policy* by Werner W. Jaeger, translated by Edward S. Robinson, 1938; *Demosthenes' On the Crown: A Critical Case Study* by George Kennedy, 1967; *The General Demosthenes and His Use of Military Surprise* by Joseph Roisman, 1993; *Demosthenes and His Time: A Study in Defeat* by Raphael Sealey, 1993; *Demosthenes: Statesman and Orator*, edited by Ian Worthington, 2000.

* * *

The legacy of the great orator Demosthenes, as handed down to us in the manuscripts, consists of 61 speeches, 56 *exordia*, or opening paragraphs of speeches, and six letters. The speeches, which naturally form the centrepiece of his *oeuvre*, are distributed among the three major forms of ancient oratory. The first 17 are deliberative, composed as contributions to debate in the Assembly, the sovereign body of democratic Athens. Two of the remainder, the *Funeral Speech* and the *Erotic Essay*, are epideictic display pieces. The rest, forming by far the largest portion, are forensic pieces, written to impress jurors in the law courts. The fact that not all the works handed down to us in the corpus Demosthenicum are by Demosthenes himself was recognized already in antiquity. Some are the works of contemporaries, like Apollodorus, for instance, to whom several, including the famous 59th speech, *Against Neaera*, are ascribed. They were probably collected with the great orator's works by accident. Others, especially some of the letters, are probably exercises composed in the rhetorical schools of the Hellenistic and Roman periods, although one or two may be deliberate forgeries, designed for the ancient trade in rare and obscure works by famous figures of the classical golden age. In acknowledgement of these false attributions, several works in the corpus are generally and universally ascribed to a pseudo-Demosthenes, although the authenticity of some others continues to attract controversy.

Demosthenes was a *rhetor*, which means in Greek simply "speaker," an unassuming label that designates an unofficial role, which was the closest the Athenians came to "politician" or "statesman." Demosthenes wrote speeches for himself and his friends, and at the beginning of his career he was a *logographos*, a professional speech-writer, who would listen to the facts of his client's case and then write a speech for him to deliver, since the Athenian system tried to preserve an equal and amateur democracy by insisting that each man should conduct his own prosecution or defence. Accordingly, this profession was rather looked down upon by the Athenians and Demosthenes probably abandoned it as soon as he could, to concentrate on his own political and forensic battles, which carried their own considerable financial rewards both of a legitimate and an illegitimate kind. However, the particular skill of the *logographos*, the creation of convincing characterizations (*ethopoeia*), was important for the development of Demosthenes' oratorical skills. There were three sets of characterizations to be worked on: that of the speaker, that of his audience, and that of the other participants in the narrative, including the opposing side. Obviously, the depiction of one's enemies, and of any other figures in the narrative of events (*katastasis*), had to be convincing enough to make the speaker's own version of what happened plausible, as well as painting his opponents as darkly as possible. In his speech "Against Conon," the hubristic nature of the defendant and his associates is carefully constructed by the use of vivid accounts of brawls and boorish behaviour, including one scene in which Conon is described flapping his arms and crowing like a game-cock that has just won a fight. The second layer of characterization, concerning the way the audience could be depicted, was rather more awkward. This kind of *ethopoeia* was especially important in the deliberative speeches, when the Athenians were being urged into a certain mode of action. They had to be cajoled without feeling insulted and alienated by the speaker: frightened into action, but not terrified into inertia by too strong a sense of their own inadequacies. This kind of construction of "the Athenians" could be effected with rather subtle means, by getting past the audience controversial statements disguised as *opiniones communes*, making quiet assumptions about the class of the spectators and thereby attempting to co-opt them into a ready-made set of values, or by rather more brutal tactics: heavy-handed contrasts between the sharp and decisive monarch Philip and the shiftless, feckless, and fickle populace of the democratic city, or comparisons between the decadent and lazy citizens of the present and their energetic, more moral, and more successful ancestors of the 5th century.

The final type of *ethopoeia* was perhaps the trickiest of all, the characterization of the speaker himself. Demosthenes perhaps never quite reached the heights attained by the acknowledged master of this technique, the *logographos* Lysias, in the very early 4th century, but one or two speeches show that he could pull it off if he tried. The clearest example is perhaps the speech "Against Callicles," in which the master of Greek prose style writes words for the mouth of someone purporting to be a simple farmer, defending himself against claims for flood damage, but the general principle that "ars est celare artem" would apply even to the major public speeches in which Demosthenes was speaking his own words in the position of a great statesman. Too much awareness by the audience of the speaker's skills as an orator would detract from the honesty of his case and distract attention from the policies he was championing. A great speaker had to seduce without the slightest hint or suspicion that he was a seducer. Demosthenes' original solution to this paradox in his public speeches is to describe a dialogue with himself, so that he seems to be exposing his own thought-patterns in the form of an agonizing struggle, inviting the audience to sympathize and empathize directly.

This problem of disguising cleverness brings us to the question of Demosthenes' own art, his style, the foundation of his reputation as "the orator," and the reason why his works were preserved as models for students of rhetoric. Since antiquity, readers have observed two closely related characteristics in particular: the rich variety of effects he could command, and his *bia* or forcefulness. While his predecessors cultivated a highly finished, intellectual conciseness, the texture of Demosthenes' speeches is terribly uneven. Long periods, carefully constructed with a precisely chosen vocabulary, can suddenly give way to extreme abruptness. Lofty abstractions are succeeded by concrete metaphors and metonymies. High-falutin' poetic language yields to colloquialisms and oaths. Narrative passages are suddenly brought to life with direct speech. The overall effect is of spontaneity, of a carefully composed piece of prose disrupted by true feeling and uncontrollable passions, usually but not always of violent anger.

This at any rate is the Demosthenes who survives in the manuscripts, and whose reputation as the great master of Greek prose is disputed only by Plato. It could be, however, that what the orator himself considered his greatest achievement has been lost to us, for the story was told among later generations that when he was asked what the three most important elements of rhetoric were, he replied, "Delivery, delivery and delivery."

—James N. Davidson

See the essay on *On the Crown*.

DEPESTRE, René

Born: Jacmel, Haiti, 29 August 1926. **Education:** High School in Port-au-Prince, Haiti; attended Insititut d'Etudes Politiques de Paris and Sorbonne University. Received a degree in History and Art from Musée de l'Homme, Paris. **Career:** Lived and studied in France,

1946–58; lived and a taught in Cuba, where he published extensively and translated Spanish American poetry into French, 1958–78; returned to Paris, where he worked for Unesco, 1978. **Awards:** Bourse Goncourt de la nouvelle prize, for *Alléluia pour une femme-jardin*, 1982; John Simon Guggenheim Memorial Foundation award, 1995; Grand Prix de Poésie de l'Académie Française, 1998.

PUBLICATIONS

Collections

Anthologie personnelle. 1993.

Poetry

Étincelles [Sparks]. 1945.
Gerbe du sang. 1946.
Végétations de clartés [Vegetations of Splendor]. 1951.
Traduit du grand large, poeme de ma patrie enchanee. 1952.
Minerai Noir. 1957.
Journal d'un animal marine. 1964.
Un arc-en-ciel pour l'occident chretien. 1967; as *A Rainbow for the Christian West*, translated by Joan Dayan, 1977.
Cantate d'octobre. 1968.
Poète à Cuba. 1976.
En état de poésie. 1980.
Au matin de la négritude. 1990.

Fiction

Le Mât Cocagne, 1979, as *The Festival of the Greasy Pole*, translated by Carrol F. Coates, 1990.
Alléluia pour une femme-jardin. 1981.
Hadriana dans tous mes rêves. 1988.
Éros dans un train chinois. 1990.

Essays

Bonjour et Adieu à la negritude. 1980.

*

Critical Studies: *René Depestre* by Claude Couffon, 1986; ''France Reads Haiti: René Depestre's *Hadriana dans tous mes rêves*'' by Joan Dayan, in *Yale French Studies*, vol. 83, 1993; *Shaping and Reshaping the Caribbean: The Work of Aimé Césaire and René Depestre* by Martin Munro, 2000.

*   *   *

René Depestre published his first book of poetry, Étincelles [Sparks] very young, at the age of 19. He actively engaged in political activities and founded and directed the journal ''La Ruche,'' the official publication of the Haitian revolutionary youth. In 1945 he met the French poet André Breton, a figure that deeply influenced him. In January 1946, after ''La Ruche'' was prohibited, a revolutionary movement overthrew and sent to exile President Elie Lescot. But the

new regime didn't satisfy his political expectations and Depestre went to exile in France. He spent twelve years in France taking courses at Sorbonne University and other institutions of higher education in Paris and obtained a degree in History and Arts at Musée de l'Homme. Depestre returned to Haiti in 1958, but displeased with the dictatorship of ''Papa Doc'' Duvalier, he abandoned his country again to settle in Cuba, where he lived for the next twenty years. In Cuba he published *Un arc-en-ciel pour l'occident chrétien (A Rainbow For the Christian West)*, an extensive poem where he depicts the dramatic position of black people in the context of modern white capitalism. This book puts him close to the Négritude movement that was founded by the Martinican poet Aimé Césaire with whom Depestre had a political and literary relationship. Césaire wrote the prologue for his book *Vegetations de clartés [Vegetations of Splendor]*.

During his stay in Cuba Depestre taught at University of La Habana and also at University of West Indies at Mona, Jamaica. He translated Cuban poets into French such as Nicolás Guillén, Heberto Padilla and Roberto Fernández Retamar; and was a founder of the Casa de las Americas publishing house. He also published frequently in the literary magazine of the same name. In 1978 he left Cuba and returned to Paris, where he worked for Unesco until his retirement in 1988.

Rene Depestre's poetry expresses a profound desire for representing the richness of the Haitian and the Caribbean world and makes reference not exclusively to his natal country but to the global condition of the Afro-Caribbean people. His first poems talk of a pure and innocent world but they soon become an expression of his political views, a medium by which he denounces the mechanisms of capitalist exploitation. His body of *engagé* works, with books like *Végétations de clartés* and *Traduit du grand large* [Translated from the High Seas] not only address Haiti's social and political problems, but also the plight of oppressed black people in Africa, the Caribbean and in other parts of the world. All his work is influenced by the problem of cultural identity linked to ethnicity and the historical experience of slavery. His esthetical and political contributions made his work comparable to other Afro-Caribbean poets related to the Négritude movement.

Nevertheless, his essay *Bonjour et Adieu à la négritude* [Hello and Goodbye to Négritude] marks a turning point from certain ideas of racial identity present in the Négritude movement. In this book Depestre asks himself whether the self-assurance reached by the black man through his historical quest is enough to abandon the prejudices and racial hatreds that weighed upon him. After a critical balance of the values and deficiencies of Negritude, he proclaims the necessity of a ''panhuman'' identity that would allow the Caribbean man to project himself beyond the barrier of the color of his skin.

Both in his poems and in his prose, the latter developed during the mature phase of his literary production, there exists a strong presence of popular culture, in particular of the African-Haiti religion, the ''voodoo.'' The presence of the inexplicable in his work has been compared with the Latin American magic realism. In his novels he also treats political issues such as the dictatorship in Haiti as in *The Festival of the Greasy Pole*, published in 1979. This book is not so much a novel as a political fable that explains the crushing conditions of his country during the Duvalier regime. As a political exile for most of his life, Depestre must have harbored deep despair for the fate of his country, forever wrapped in oppression, poverty, and ecological degradation. His literature is full of erotic references (*Hadriana dans tout mes rêves* [Hadrianna In All My Dreams]). His poetry has appeared in many French and Spanish anthologies and collections and has been translated into French, English, Spanish, and Russian.

—Alvaro Fernández Bravo

DESTOUCHES, Louis-Ferdinand

See CÉLINE, Louis-Ferdinand

DIDEROT, Denis

Born: Langres, France, 5 October 1713. **Education:** Educated at Jesuit school in Langres, 1723–28, became an abbé in 1726; in Paris from 1728: University of Paris, master of arts 1732; studied theology at the university and read law for a short time, 1732–35. **Family:** Married Antoinette Champion in 1743; two daughters and two sons. **Career:** Tutor, and freelance writer and translator from 1734; imprisoned briefly in 1749 for *Lettre sur les aveugles*; commissioned by the publisher Le Breton to edit the *Encyclopédie*, which appeared from 1751 to 1772: also a major contributor; writer for F.M. Grimm's private periodical *Correspondance Littéraire* from 1759; patronized by Catherine the Great from 1765, and visited Russia, 1773–74. **Member:** Prussian Royal Academy, 1751; Foreign Member, Russian Academy of Sciences, 1773. **Died:** 31 July 1784.

PUBLICATIONS

Collections

Oeuvres. 15 vols., 1798.
Oeuvres complètes, edited by Jean Assézat and Maurice Tourneux. 20 vols., 1875–77, reprinted 1966.
Oeuvres, edited by A. Billy. 1951.
Oeuvres philosophiques, edited by Paul Vernière. 1956.
Oeuvres esthétiques, edited by Paul Vernière. 1959.
Oeuvres romanesques, edited by Henri Bénac. 1962.
Oeuvres politiques, edited by Paul Vernière. 1963.
Oeuvres complètes [Chronological Edition], edited by Roger Lewinter. 15 vols., 1969–73.
Oeuvres complètes, edited by H. Dieckmann, Jean Varloot, and Jacques Proust. 1975–.
Oeuvres complètes, edited by Arthur M. Wilson and others. 1975–.
Oeuvres romanesques, edited by Lucette Perol. 1981.
The Irresistible Diderot (selections), edited by John Hope Mason. 1982.

Fiction

Les Bijoux indiscrets. 1748; as *The Indiscreet Toys*, 2 vols., 1749.
Contes moraux et nouvelles idylles, with Salomon Gessner, edited by J.-H. Meister. 1773.

Jacques le fataliste et son maître. 1796; edited by Simone Lecointre and Jean Le Galliot, 1976; as *Jacques the Fataliste*, edited by Martin Hall and translated by M. Henry, 1986; as *James the Fatalist and His Master*, translated anonymously, 3 vols., 1797; as *Jacques the Fatalist*, translated by J. Robert Loy, 1962; as *Jacques the Fatalist and His Master*, translated with introduction by David Coward, 1999.
La Religieuse. 1796; edited by Robert Mauzi, 1972; as *The Nun*, translated by Brett Smith, 1797; also translated by Marianne Sinclair, 1966; and Leonard Tancock, 1972; as *Memoirs of a Nun*, translated by Francis Birreil, 1928.
Le Neveu de Rameau. 1821; edited by Jean Fabre, 1950; as *Rameau's Nephew*, translated by Sylvia M. Hill, 1897; also translated by Mrs. Wilfrid Jackson, 1926; Jacques Barzun and Ralph H. Bowen, 1956; and Leonard Tancock, 1966.
Récits, edited by Ph. Van Tieghem. 1959.

Plays

Le Père de famille (produced 1759). 1758; as *The Father*, translated 1770; as *The Family Picture*, translated 1781.
Le Fils naturel; ou, Les Épreuves de la vertu (produced 1771). 1757; as *Dorval; or, The Test of Virtue*, translated anonymously, 1767.
Est-il bon est-il méchant? (produced 1913). 1784; as *Wicked Philanthropy*, translated by Gabriel John Brogyanyi, 1986.
Le Joueur, from the play *The Gamester* by Edward Moore. 1819.
Comédie Française (previously unpublished plays). 1984.

Other

Essai sur le merité et la vertu. 1745.
Pensées philosophiques. 1746; as *Philosophical Thoughts*, translated by Margaret Jourdain, in *Early Philosophical Works*, 1916.
Mémoires sur différents sujets de mathématiques. 1748.
Lettre sur les aveugles. 1749; as *An Essay on Blindness*, translated 1750; as *A Letter Upon the Blind*, translated by S.C. Howe, 1857.
Lettre sur les sourds et muets. 1751; edited by Paul Hugo Meyer, 1965; as *Letter on the Deaf and Dumb*, translated by Margaret Jourdain, in *Early Philosophical Works*, 1916.
Pensées sur l'interprétation de la nature. 1753.
Leçons de clavecin et principes d'harmonie. 1771.
Oeuvres philosophiques. 6 vols., 1772.
Select Essays from the Encyclopedy, translated anonymously. 1772.
Essai sur Sénèque. 1778; revised edition, as *Essai sur les règnes de Claude et de Néron*, 1782.
Supplément au voyage de Bougainville. In *Opuscules Philosophiques et Littéraires*, edited by S.J. Bourlet de Vauxcelles, 1786; published separately in 1796; also edited by Herbert Dieckmann, 1955.
Essai sur la peinture. 1795; edited by Gita May, 1984.
Correspondance Littéraire 1753–90. 1813.
Mémoires, correspondances, et ouvrages inédits. 4 vols., 1830–31.
The Paradox of Acting, translated by Walter H. Pollock. 1883.
Mémoires pour Cathérine II. In *Diderot et Catherine*, edited by Maurice Tourneux, 1899; also edited by Paul Vernière, 1966.
Diderot's Thoughts on Art and Style, With Some of His Shorter Essays, translated by Beatrix L. Tollemache. 1904.
Early Philosophical Works, edited and translated by Margaret Jourdain. 1916, reprinted 1973.
Observations sur la Nakaz. 1920.
Dialogues, translated by Francis Birrell. 1927.

Lettres à Sophie Volland, edited by André Babelon. 3 vols., 1938; as *Letters to Sophie Volland*, translated by Peter France, 1972.

Diderot, Interpreter of Nature: Selected Writings, edited by Jonathan Kemp and translated by Kemp and Jean Stewart. 1937.

Correspondance, edited by Georges Roth. 16 vols., 1955–70.

Salons, edited by Jean Séznec and Jean Adhémar. 4 vols., 1957–67.

Le Rêve de d'Alembert, edited by Jean Varloot. 1962; as *D'Alembert's Dream*, translated by Leonard Tancock, 1966.

Rameau's Nephew and Other Works, edited by R.H. Bowen. 1964.

Éléments de physiologie, edited by Jean Mayer. 1964.

Encyclopedia: Selections, edited and translated by Nelly S. Hoyt and Thomas Cassirer. 1965; another selection edited by Stephen Gendzier, 1967.

Selected Writings, edited by Lester G. Crocker, translated by Derek Coltman. 1966.

Voyage en Hollande. 1982.

Écrits sur la musique, edited by Béatrice Durand-Sendrail. 1987.

Selected Philosophical Writings, edited by John Lough. 1987.

Voyages à Bourbonne, à Langres, et autres récits, edited by Anne-Marie Chouillet. 1989.

Political Writings, edited by R. Wokler and J.H. Mason. 1992.

Architecture in the Encyclopédie of Diderot and d'Alembert: The Letterpress Articles and Selected Engravings by Terence M. Russell. 1993.

Diderot on Art, edited and translated by John Goodman. 1995.

The Architectural Plates from the "Encyclopédie," edited by Denis Diderot. 1995.

Editor, and contributor, *Encyclopédie; ou, Dictionnaire raisonné des sciences, des arts, et des métiers, par une société de gens de lettres*. 17 vols., 1751–65; as *Pictorial Encyclopaedia of Trades and Industry*, 2 vols., 1959; *Recueil de planches*, 11 vols., 1762–72.

Translator, *Histoire de Grèce*, by Temple Stanyan. 3 vols., 1743.

Translator, *Principes de la philosophie morale*, by Shaftesbury. 1745; revised edition, as *Philosophie morale réduite à ses principes*, 1751.

Translator, with Marc-Antoine Eidous and François-Vincent Toussaint, *Dictionnaire universel de médecine*, by Robert James. 6 vols., 1746–48.

Translator, *Les Oeuvres de Shaftesbury*. 3 vols., 1769.

*

Bibliography: *Bibliographie de Diderot* by Frederick A. Spear, 1980.

Critical Studies: *Diderot Studies*, 1949–; *Diderot's Determined Fatalist: A Critical Appreciation of Jacques le Fataliste* by J. Robert Loy, 1950; *Two Diderot Studies: Ethics and Esthetics*, 1952, *The Embattled Philosopher: A Biography of Denis Diderot*, 1954, revised edition, 1966, and *Diderot's Chaotic Order*, 1974, all by Lester G. Crocker; *Diderot, The Testing Years 1713–1739*, 1957, and *Diderot*, 1972, both by Arthur M. Wilson; *Essays on the Encyclopédie of Diderot and d'Alembert* by John Lough, 1968; *Diderot the Satirist: Le Neveu de Rameau and Related Works* by Donal O'Gorman, 1971; *Inventory of Diderot's Encyclopédie*, 6 vols., 1971, and vol. 7, *Inventory of the Plates, With a Study of the Contributors to the Encyclopédie*, 1984, both by Richard N. Schwab and Walter E. Rex; *Vacant Mirror: A Study of Diderot* by Thomas M. Kavanagh, 1973; *Diderot and the Eighteenth-Century French Press* by Gary B. Rodgers, 1973; *Diderot's Politics* by Anthony Strugnell, 1973; *Diderot: The Virtue of a Philosopher* by Carol Blum, 1974; *Diderot's Essai sur*

Seneque by William Thomas Conroy, 1975; *Diderot's Great Scroll: Narrative Art in Jacques le Fataliste*, 1975, and *Socratic Satire: An Essay on Diderot and Le Neveu de Rameau*, 1987, both by Stephen Werner; *Diderot and the Art of Dialogue* by Carol Sherman, 1976; *Diderot's "femme savante"* by Lawrence Louis Bongie, 1977; *Diderot* by Otis Fellows, 1977; revised edition, 1989; *Diderot and Goethe: A Study in Science and Humanism* by Gerhard M. Vasco, 1978; *The Business of Enlightenment: A Publishing History of the Encyclopédie, 1775–1800* by Robert Darnton, 1979; *Cataract: A Study in Diderot* by Jeffrey Mehlman, 1979; *Le Neveu de Rameau and The Praise of Folly: Literary Cognates* by Apostolos P. Kouidis, 1981; *Diderot: La Religieuse* by Vivienne Mylne, 1981; *Diderot and the Jews* by Leon Schwartz, 1981; *Diderot: Reason and Resonance* by E. de Fontenay, 1982; *Diderot and the Space-Time Continuum: His Philosophy, Aesthetics and Politics* by Merle L. Perkins, 1982; *Diderot's Imagery* by Eric M. Steel, 1982; *Order and Chance: The Pattern of Diderot's Thought*, 1983, and *Diderot: Jacques le Fataliste*, 1985, both by Geoffrey Bremner; *Diderot* by Peter France, 1983; *The Irresistible Diderot* by John Hope Mason, 1983; *Sex and Enlightenment: Women in Richardson and Diderot* by Rita Goldberg, 1984; *Diderot: Digression and Dispersion* edited by J. Undank and H. Josephs, 1984; *Diderot, Jacques le Fataliste* by Geoffrey Bremner, 1985; *Diderot and the Family: A Conflict of Nature and Law* by William F. Edmiston, 1985; *Diderot: Le Neveu de Rameau* by John Falvey, 1985; *Diderot, Dialogue and Debate* by D.J. Adams, 1986; *Framed Narratives: Diderot's Genealogy of the Beholder* by Jay Caplan, 1986; *Diderot: Thresholds of Representation* by James Creech, 1986; *Diderot and a Poetics of Science* by Suzanne L. Pucci, 1986; *Denis Diderot* by Tamara Dlugach, 1988; *The Encyclopedists as Individuals: A Biographical Dictionary of the Authors of the Encyclopédie* by Frank A. and Serena L. Kafker, 1988; *Diderot's Vie de Seneque: A Swan Song Revised* by Douglas Bonneville, 1989; *Innovation and Renewal: A Study of the Theatrical Works of Diderot* by Derek F. Connon, 1989; *Diderot: Supplément au Voyage de Bougainville* by Peter Jimack, 1989; *Diderot's Dream* by Wilda C. Anderson, 1990; *Satirizing the Satirist: Critical Dynamics in Swift, Diderot and Jean Paul* by Stephanie B. Hammer, 1990; *Success in Circuit Lies: Diderot's Communicational Practice* by Rosalind de la Carrera, 1991; *Diderot: A Critical Biography* by P.N. Furbank, 1992; *The Discourse of Enlightenment in Eighteenth-century France: Diderot and the Art of Philosophizing* by Daniel Brewer, 1993; *Art Criticism as Narrative: Diderot's Salon de 1767* by Julie Wegner Arnold, 1995; *Mass Enlightenment: Critical Studies in Rousseau and Diderot* by Julia Simon, 1995; *Diderot's Counterpoints: The Dynamics of Contrariety in His Major Works* by Walter E. Rex, 1998; *Voicing Desire: Family and Sexuality in Diderot's Narrative* by J.E. Fowler, 2000; *Diderot and the Body* by Angelica Goodden, 2001; *Sublime Disorder: Physical Monstrosity in Diderot's Universe* by Andrew Curran, 2001.

* * *

Denis Diderot is best remembered as the general editor of the *Encyclopédie* (*Encyclopedia*) and as one of its main contributors. The project absorbed most of his energies from 1750 to 1772. Conceived initially as a translation of the Chambers *Cyclopaedia*, the *Encyclopedia* developed into an overview of world knowledge and was intended to illustrate its inherent harmony and order. In Diderot's hands the work became an organ of radical and anti-reactionary propaganda; hence publication was from time to time impeded by the French authorities. Technology figures largely in the text and in the accompanying plates, and the work also contains numerous articles on ethical, philosophical, and aesthetic topics. Though produced in a society still dominated by the Roman Catholic Church, the *Encyclopedia* reflects its editor's hostility to religious authority, and, while many of the contributors were priests, Diderot contrived to incorporate heterodox or "dangerous" views in seemingly minor articles to which the reader is directed by cross-references given in the more prominent, orthodox ones. The *Encyclopedia* encapsulates the spirit of the French Enlightenment and is its most noteworthy product.

From early adherence to a deism derived from the English deists (principally Shaftesbury), Diderot moved to an openly atheistic viewpoint in the *Lettre sur les aveugles* (*An Essay on Blindness*) of 1749, which earned him a brief spell in the Vincennes prison. In his novel *La Religieuse* (*The Nun*), which was not in general circulation in his lifetime, Diderot uses a protagonist forced to take the veil against her will in order to explore the pernicious effects on nuns of life in the convent, separated as it is from normal society. A film based on the novel, directed by Jacques Rivette, was banned in France in 1966 and released in the UK in the following year. Among his other novels, the best known is the picaresque *Jacques le fataliste et son maître* (*Jacques the Fatalist*), partially inspired by Laurence Sterne's *Tristram Shandy*. As well as being a rather ambivalent examination of philosophical determinism, this novel is notable for the strikingly modern way in which Diderot engages the active participation of the reader in the unfolding of the episodes, through authorial harangues, questions, puzzles, alternative versions, and ascribed reactions. Both *Jacques the Fatalist* and *The Nun* are perfectly accessible to the modern reader.

Diderot was a polymath very familiar with the scientific trends of his day. He was especially fascinated by discoveries in the biological sciences of the 1740s and 1750s onwards and, in works which include *Pensées sur l'interprétation de la nature* [On the Interpretation of Nature], the *Dialogue between D'Alembert and Diderot, Le Rêve de d'Alembert* (*D'Alembert's Dream*) and the *Éléments de physiologie* [Elements of Physiology], developed theories of the cellular structure of matter and of animal adaptation which prefigured the work of Lamarck and Darwin.

While intellectually a philosophical materialist and a determinist, believing that individual character was principally the product of heredity, Diderot thought man was generally susceptible to modification by environmental influences. He ascribed most of the evil he saw around him to the baleful influence of European (especially French) society, but his attempts, in works like his *Supplément au voyage de Bougainville* [Supplement to Bougainville's Voyage], to develop a moral code based on "natural" principles were doomed to failure by the impossibility of formulating a definition of nature which could underpin social morality.

Like a number of his contemporaries, he clung in his published works to the belief that only the virtuous man can know true happiness and that even apparently prospering evil-doers suffer in their conscience. However, *Le Neveu de Rameau* (*Rameau's Nephew*), a polythematic dialogue which he began in 1761 and polished over the next 20 years without ever attempting to publish it, casts doubts on this view. In the belief that the theatre could serve to further ethical progress—and that both the writer and the state could exploit it in this way—he wrote three very detailed treatises on dramatic art, which Lessing admired, and three original plays (discounting adaptations) which fail to match the dynamism of the theoretical works.

In his *Salons*, written for readers unable actually to see the pictures described, he proves himself a judicious and sensitive art critic and was the first to interest himself in the technical processes ancillary to painting.

—John Dunkley

See the essays on *Jacques the Fatalist* and *The Test of Virtue*.

DINESEN, Isak

Born: Karen Christentze Dinesen in Rungsted, Denmark, 17 April 1885. **Education:** Educated privately; studied art at Academy of Art, Copenhagen, 1902–06, in Paris, 1910, and in Rome. **Family:** Married Baron Bror von Blixen-Finecke in 1914 (divorced 1921). **Career:** Managed a coffee plantation near Nairobi, Kenya, with her husband, 1913–21, and alone, 1921–31; lived in Rungsted after 1931; co-founder, with Ole Wivel, Bjørn Poulson, and Thorkild Bjørnvig, of the literary journal *Heretica*. **Awards:** Holberg medal, 1949; Ingenio e Arti medal, 1950; Nathansen Memorial Fund award, 1951; Golden Laurels, 1952; Hans Christian Andersen prize, 1955; Danish Critics prize, 1957. **Member:** Founding Member, Danish Academy, 1960; Honorary Member, American Academy 1957; Corresponding Member, Bavarian Academy of Fine Arts. **Died:** 7 September 1962.

PUBLICATIONS

Collection

Mindeudgave. 7 vols., 1964.

Fiction

Seven Gothic Tales. 1934; as *Syv fantastiske fortællinger*, translated by Dinesen, 1935.
Winter's Tales. 1942; as *Vinter eventyr*, translated by Dinesen, 1942.
Gengældelsens veje (as Pierre Andrézel), translated into Danish by Clara Svendsen. 1944; as *The Angelic Avengers*, 1946.
Babette's Feast, in *Ladies' Home Journal*. 1950; in book form, in *Anecdotes of Destiny*, 1958; as *Babettes gæstebud*, translated by Jørgen Claudi, 1952.
Kardinalens tredie historie [The Cardinal's Third Tale]. 1952.
Last Tales. 1957; as *Sidste fortællinger*, translated by Dinesen, 1957.
Anecdotes of Destiny (stories). 1958; as *Babette's Feast and Other Anecdotes of Destiny*, 1988; as *Skæbne-anekdoter*, translated by Dinesen, 1958.
Ehrengard. 1963; as *Ehrengard*, translated into Danish by Clara Svendsen, 1963.
Efterladte fortællinger (stories), edited by Frans Lasson. 1975; as *Carnival: Entertainments and Posthumous Tales*, translated by P.M. Mitchell, W.D. Paden, and others, 1977.

Plays

Sandhedens hævn: En marionetkomedie (produced 1936). 1960; as *The Revenge of Truth: A Marionette Comedy*, in *"Isak Dinesen" and Karen Blixen*, by Donald Hannah, 1971.

Other

Out of Africa. 1937; as *Den afrikanske farm*, translated by Dinesen, 1937.

Om restkrivning: politiken 23–24 marts 1938 [About Spelling: Politiken 23–24 March 1938]. 1949.

Farah [Name]. 1950.

Daguerrotypier (radio talks). 1951; in *Daguerrotypes and Other Essays*, translated by P.M. Mitchell and W.D. Paden, 1979.

Omkring den nye lov om dyreforsøg [The New Law on Vivisection]. 1952.

En baaetale med 14 aars forsinkelse [A Bonfire Speech 14 Years Later]. 1953.

Skygger paa græsset. 1960; translated as *Shadows on the Glass*, 1960.

On Mottoes of My Life. 1960.

Osceola, edited by Clara Svendsen. 1962.

Essays. 1965.

Karen Blixens tegninger: med to essays of Karen Blixen, edited by Frans Lasson. 1969.

Breve fra Afrika 1914–31, edited by Frans Lasson. 2 vols., 1978; as *Letters from Africa 1914–1931*, translated by Anne Born, 1981.

Daguerrotypes and Other Essays, translated by P.M. Mitchell and W.D. Paden. 1979.

Samlede essays. 1985.

On Modern Marriage and Other Observations, translated by Anne Born. 1986.

*

Bibliography: *Dinesen: A Bibliography* by Liselotte Henriksen, 1977; supplement in *Blixeniana 1979*, 1979; *Karen Blixen/Isak Dinesen: A Select Bibliography* by Aage Jørgensen, 1985.

Critical Studies: *Isak Dinesen* by Louise Bogan, in *Selected Criticism*, 1955; *The World of Isak Dinesen* by Eric O. Johannesson, 1961; *Isak Dinesen: A Memorial* edited by Clara Svendsen, 1964, *The Life and Destiny of Isak Dinesen* by Svendsen and Frans Lasson, 1970, and *Karen Blixen: Isak Dinesen: A Chronology* by Lasson, 1985; *The Gayety of Vision: A Study of Isak Dinesen's Art* by Robert Langbaum, 1965; *Titania: the Biography of Dinesen* by Parmenia Migel, 1967; *Isak Dinesen, 1885–1962* by Hannah Arendt, in *Men in Park Times*, 1968; *"Isak Dinesen" and Karen Blixen: The Mask and the Reality* by Donald Hannah, 1971; *Isak Dinesen's Aesthetics* by Thomas Reid Whissen, 1973; *My Sister, Isak Dinesen* by Thomas Dinesen, translated by Joan Tate, 1975; *Dinesen: The Life of a Storyteller* by Judith Thurman, 1982, as *Isak Dinesen: The Life of Karen Blixen*, 1982; *The Pact: My Friendship with Isak Dinesen* by Thorkild Bjørnvig, 1984; *Diana's Revenge: Two Lines In Isak Dinesen's Authorship* by Marianne Juhl, 1985; *Out of Denmark* edited by Bodil Wamberg, 1985; *The Witch and the Goddess in the Stories of Isak Dinesen: A Feminist Reading* by Sarah Stambaugh, 1988; *Isak Dinesen and the Engendering of Narrative* by Susan Hardy Aiken, 1990; *Isak Dinesen: The Life and Imagination of a Seducer* by Olga Anastasia Pelensky, 1991; *Isak Dinesen: Critical Views*, edited by Olga Anastasia Pelensky, 1993; *Isak Dinesen and Narrativity: Reassessments for the 1990s*, edited by Gurli A. Woods, 1994; *Out of Isak Dinesen in Africa: The Untold Story* by Linda Donelson, 1995; *Difficult Women, Artful Lives: Olive Schreiner and Isak Dinesen, In and Out of Africa* by Susan R. Horton, 1995; *By Europe, Out of Africa: White Women Writers on Farms and Their African Invention* by Simon Lewis, 1996; *Understanding Isak Dinesen* by Susan C. Brantly, 2001.

*   *   *

Isak Dinesen liked to disclaim the complex erudition of her tales and to speak of herself as a "storyteller," a Scheherazade, whose mission was simply to "entertain" people. Entertain them she did, with leisurely and urbane philosophical discourse, painterly descriptions of nature, a wry and refined eroticism, and in narratives as intricate and polished as Chinese boxes that took her years of reworking to perfect. But the lightness of her tone and the preciousness of her surfaces have tended to obscure her scope of vision, which is that of a major and highly original writer.

In Denmark, Dinesen was accused of decadence and an indifference to social issues. These were charges deserved, perhaps, by Baroness Karen Blixen, who cultivated a sybilline persona and liked to *épater les bourgeois*, not to mention *les socialistes*. But Dinesen, the storyteller, was a passionate and rather pure-hearted immoralist, rather than a decadent, The erotic daredevils and demonic heroes of Romantic literature had given her the first glimpse of emotional freedom, and she perceived the attempt to spare oneself repression, at whatever price, as heroic and ennobling. This was the lion hunt, the great gesture, the daring fantasy, the mortal sin. In Marxist terms, her heroes may be decadents; in Freudian terms they may be perverts of one sort or another; but in Dinesen's terms they are *dreamers—* planted in the soil of life like a coffee tree with a bent taproot. "That tree will never thrive," she wrote, "nor bear fruit, but will flower more richly than the others."

Dinesen did, of course, "neglect social issues." Her choice of form—the tale, rather than the novel or the short story—was a way of taking sides with the past against her contemporaries, although she was also never without a keen sense of irony about her own absurd position, in modern Denmark, as the defender of a way of life that had vanished, to general applause. She set her tales a hundred years in the past, defining her period as "the last great phase of aristocratic culture," and aware that it was also the first great phase of bourgeois culture, when wealth was shifting from the land to the cities and to currency; when the feudal world, with all its certainties and inequities, the one inseparable from the other, was dissolving. By taking such a distance, she was able to gain clarity and a certain imaginative freedom. She was also better able to describe the tension between her own aristocratic idealism and the materialism that had triumphed over it. And she was able to understand the nature of a certain kind of Fall: the loss that occurs to a culture or to a child when values that have once been absolute become relative.

Dinesen's work does, despite its great literary sophistication, have a common ground with the old tales, which she defined as Nemesis: "the thread in the course of events that is determined by the psychic assumptions of a person." By psychic assumptions, she meant the scenarios that we absorb from our family and our culture, the patterns we unconsciously repeat. Like the old storytellers, but also like Mann, Joyce, or Yeats, Dinesen is interested in the points at which the individual and the typical, psychology and culture, intersect as *myth*, and she works with myth in an innovative modern way. The climax of a Dinesen tale comes at the moment that the hero and the reader recognize how the forces that have been shaping the events of the story have also shaped their perception of it: history from without, desire from within.

Dinesen stands at the end of a long cultural process, looking back ironically upon it. She sums up the Romantic tradition as she carries it forward. Perhaps her vision could only belong to a writer who took up her pen at the age of 46, when she had lost everything of importance to her, except the thing with the greatest value of all: experience itself.

—Judith Thurman

DING LING

Courtesy name: Jiang Bingzhi. **Pseudonyms:** Bin Zhi, Cong Xuan. **Born:** Jiangwei in Lingli county, Hunan province, China, 12 October, 1904. **Education:** Primary and junior high school in Taoyuan and Changsha; Common Girls' High School in Shanghai, 1921; Shanghai University, 1923. *Family:* Lived with poet Hu Yepin, 1924–31; one son; lived with Feng Da, 1931–35; one daughter; married Chen Ming, 1942. **Career:** Became member of the League of Leftwing Writers, 1930; joined the Communist Party at the beginning of 1933; arrested by the Nanking Nationalist Government on 4 May 1933; after she was released in 1937 went to Yan'an; established a women's league called Women's National Salvation Association in northwest China; participated in land reform work, 1946; became Vice-President of the Chinese Writers Association, 1950; accused of being a rightist during the Anti-Rightist Movement, 1957; her books were banned, 1957–78; was sent to Heilongjiang province to work manual labour, 1958; imprisoned for five years during the Cultural Revolution, 1970; exiled to Shaanxi, 1975–78; returned to Beijing, 1978; officially rehabilitated, 1979; visited the United States in 1981, Canada and France in 1983, and Australia in 1985; vice president of the Chinese Writers Association; member of Chinese People's Political Consultative Conference. **Awards:** Soviet Union's Stalin second prize for Literature, 1951. **Died:** Beijing, 4 March 1986.

PUBLICATIONS

Collections

Zai hei'an zhong [In the Darkness]. 1928.
Zisha riji [Diary of a Suicide]. 1928.
Yige nuren [A Woman]. 1928.
Shujia zhong [During the Summer Holidays]. 1928.
Awei guniang [The Girl Awei]. 1928.
Shui [Water]. 1930.
Yehui [Night Meeting]. 1930.
Zai yiyuan zhong [In the Hospital]. 1941.
Ding Ling wenji [Works of Ding Ling], Hunan Renmin Chubanshe. 6 vols. 1982.
Ding Ling xuanji [Selected Works of Ding Ling], Sichuan Renmin Chubanshe. 3 vols. 1984.

Fiction

Meng Ke. 1927.
Shafei nüshi riji. February 1928, *Xiaoshuo yuebao* (short story magazine); as *Miss Sophie's Diary*, translated by Gary Bjorge, 1981.
Weihu. 1930.
Muqin. 1930; as *Mother*, translated by Tani Barlow, 1989.
1930 Chun Shanghai. 1930; as *Shanghai, Spring, 1930*, translated by Tani Barlow, 1989.

Zai yiyuan zhong. 1941; as *In the Hospital*, translated by Gary Bjorge, 1981.
Wo zai Xia cun de shihou. 1941; as *When I Was in Xia Village*, translated by Gary Bjorge, 1981.
Taiyang zhao zai sanggan he shang. Guanghua shudian. September 1948; as *The Sun Shines Over Sanggan River*, translated by Gladys Yang and Yang Xianyi, Panda Books, 1984.
Du Wanxiang. 1978; as *Du Wanxiang*, translated by Tani Barlow, 1989.

Other

San ba jie yougan [Thoughts on March 8th], in *Jiefang ribao* [Liberation Daily]. 9 March 1942.
Co-editor, *Hong he Hei* [Red and Black] Literary Supplement to *Zhongyang ribao*. 1928.
Co-editor, *Renjian* monthly. 1928.
Editor, Literary Supplement of *Jiefang Ribao* [Liberation Daily]. 1936–42.
Editor, *Renmin wenxue* [People Literature]. 1950–53.
Editor, *Wenyi Bao* [Literary Gazette]. 1950–52.

*

Critical Studies: *Ding Ling, Her life and Her Work* by Jun-Mei Chang, 1978; *Ding Ling's Fiction: Ideology and Narrative in Modern Chinese Literature* by Yi-tsi Mei Feuerwerkwer, 1982; *Essays in Modern Chinese Literature and Literary Criticism* by Wolfgang Kubin, 1982; "Feminism and Literary Techique in Ting Ling's Early Short Stories," by Tani Barlow, in *Women Writers of the 20th Century China*, 1982; "Gender and Identity in Ding Ling's 'Mother'" by Tani Barlow, in *MCL 2, 2*, 1986; "Shanghai Spring 1930: Engendering the Revolutionary Body" in *Chinese Modernism: The Heroic and the Quotidian*, by Tang Xiaobing, 2000.

*   *   *

Although she was born in a conservative family, Ding Ling spent her childhood with her progressive mother, whose teachings and examples greatly influenced her education. In the early 1920s she moved to Beijing, attracted by the new ideas spread by the promoters of the May 4th 1919 Movement. In Beijing she met many famous writers and intellectuals of this period; she became a close friend of Hunan writer Shen Congwen and the poet Hu Yepin, who soon became her lover. Right from the beginning of her career she showed a remarkable personality, a strong mind of her own, which led her first to pursue the issues of women's emancipation and freedom of marriage. Later she became aware of the need for a profound political change in China and became actively involved in social and political issues. She became a well known writer in the late 1920s, and her reputation on the literary scene did not decline for almost sixty years despite the numerous punishments and purges she, and many other Chinese intellectuals of that time, were subjected to.

Her first novel, *Shafei nüshi riji* (*Miss Sophie's Diary*), is a daring document on the condition of twentieth-century "modern" Chinese women, torn between semi-feudal taboos and ambition of freedom, romantic sentimentalism and materialistic cynicism. Ding Ling names the main character Sophie after the Russian revolutionary heroine Sofia Perovskaja; nevertheless the young and passionate Sophie, who was confined to bed by tuberculosis, resembles a Madame Bovary, who feels sexual tensions and conflicting feelings towards two different men depicted as well-intentioned but weak and vacuous. The novel ends with Sophie's decision to reject their love, and her move to the South where nobody knows her to live in solitude. Publication of *Miss Sophie's Diary* aroused strong reactions among conservatives who criticized it for its uninhibited content. It was an absolute novelty for the Chinese audience of this time—never before had a young woman writer openly explored her feelings and given voice to her tormented interior life.

The works published after she joined the Leftwing Writers Association, such as *1930 Chun Shanghai* (*Shanghai Spring*) and *Yehui* [Night Meeting] focus more on social issues and describe the life of ordinary people. *Night* is a very short and poetic story which draws an impressive sketch of the life of a local cadre, depicting one particular night he spent in solitude enveloped by thoughts of divorce, love, work and future. *Zai yiyuan zhong* (*In the Hospital*) tells the story of Lu Ping, an obstetrician transferred to a new hospital, where she soon realizes the incompetence of the hospital administration composed of old, conservative cadres and their indifference towards the problems of patients and doctors. The heroine attempts to correct medical abuses but is censured undeservedly. The story disturbed the Party authorities who convened meetings to criticize it.

Ding Ling was openly criticized in the literary page of the Party organ *Liberation Daily* only after the publication of *San ba jie yougan* [Thoughts on March 8]. In the story, the author condemned the condition and fate of women living in the liberated area of Yan'an, their disillusionment and bitterness due to the inequality and discrimination they were subjected to, instead of enjoying equal rights. *Wo zai Xia run de shihou* (*When I was in Xia Village*) tells the story of a young girl, Zhenzhen who is raped by Japanese soldiers during a raid, and decides to become a prostitute to the Japanese retinue in order to gather secret information for the Liberation Army. On returning home to recover from a venereal disease, she receives a hostile welcome from the villagers, then she decides to leave for Yan'an to start a new life.

Taiyang zhao zai sanggan he shang (*The Sun Shines Over Sanggan River*), written during the land reform, describes the difficulties of the mobilization and organizational work in the countryside, focusing also on the complexity of social and human relations. The novel was widely acclaimed and won the Stalin Literature prize. It was the first Chinese novel to receive such an honour.

During the Hundred Flower Campaign, Ding Ling was accused of carrying out political activities subversive to the regime. She was labelled as rightist and sent into exile.

Du Wanxiang, written in the 1960s but published only in 1979, portrays the harsh life of Du Wanxiang, a poor peasant girl married at the aged of thirteen. Du Wanxiang embodies all the qualities of a traditional woman, she is hardworking courageous, honest and reliable, but also has the strong independent character of modern Chinese women as depicted in other stories by Ding Ling.

—Rosa Lombardi

DJEBAR, Assia

Born: Fatima-Zohra Imalayen in Cherchell, Algeria, 4 August 1936. **Education:** Attended Lycee Fenelon, Paris, 1954; studied at the École Normale Superieure de Sevres, France, 1955–56; studied history, University of Algiers, 1958. **Family:** Married 1) Walid Garn (divorced); 2) Malek Alloula. **Career:** Author and filmmaker; teacher in Rabat, 1955–62; assistant professor of history, University of Algiers, 1962 to late 1980s; director of the Center for French and Francophone Studies at Louisiana State University, Baton Rouge, 1990s. **Awards:** Venice Biennale Critics prize, 1979; Prix Maurice Maeterlink, 1995; Neustadt prize for Contributions to World Literature, 1996; Yourcenar prize, 1997; International prize of Palmi, Italy, 1998; International Peace prize, German Book Trade Association, 2000; Commandeur des Arts et des Lettres, Paris, 2001. Honorary doctorates, University of Vienna, 1995, and University of Concordia, Montreal, 2000.

PUBLICATIONS

Fiction

La Soif: Roman. 1957; as *The Mischief*, translated by Frances Frenaye, 1958.
Les Impatients. 1958.
Les Enfants du nouveau monde: Roman. 1962.
Les Alouettes naïves: Roman. 1967.
Femmes d'Alger dans leur appartement: Nouvelles (short stories). 1980; as *Women of Algiers in Their Apartment*, translated by Marjolijin de Jager, 1992.
L'Amour, la fantasia: Roman. 1985; as *Fantasia: An Algerian Cavalcade*, translated by Dorothy S. Blair, 1993.
Ombre Sultane: Roman. 1987; as *A Sister to Scheherazade*, translated by Dorothy S. Blair, 1988.
Loin de Médine: Filles d'Ismaël: Roman. 1991; as *Far from Medina*, 1994.
Vaste est la prison: Roman. 1994; as *So Vast the Prison: A Novel*, translated by Betsy Wing, 1999.
Le Blanc de l'Algérie: Recit. 1996; as *Algerian White: A Narrative*, translated by David Kelley and Marjolijn de Jager, 2000.
Oran, Langue Morte (short stories). 1997.
Les Nuits de Strasbourg: Roman. 1997.

Poems

Poemes pour l'Algerie heureuse. 1969.

Plays

Rouge l'aube, with Walid Garn. 1969.

Other

Women of Islam, translated by Jean MacGibbon. 1961.
La Nouba des femmes du Mont Chenoua (film). 1979.
La Zerda ou les chants de l'oubli (film). 1982.
Ces voix qui m'assiègent:—en marge de ma francophonie (essays). 1999.
Preface, *Chronique d'un été Algérien: Ici et la-bas.* 1993.

*

Critical Studies: ''Introduction'' by Dorothy S. Blair, in *Fantasia, An Algerian Cavalcade* by Assia Djebar, 1989; *Journeys Through the French African Novel* by Mildred Mortimer, 1990; *Transfigurations* *of the Maghreb: Feminism, Decolonization and Literatures* by Winifred Woodhull, 1993; "Unmasking Women: The Female Persona in Algerian Fiction" by Farida Bu-Haidar, in *African Francophone Writing*, edited by Laila ibnlfassi and Nicki Hitchott, 1996; *Assia Djebar: Ecrire, Transgresser, Resister* by Jeanne Marie Clerc, 1997; *L'écrivain francophone à la croisée des langues: entretiens* by Lise Gauvin, 1997; "Women's Writings between Two Algerian Wars" by Benjamin Stora, in *Research in African Literature*, vol. 30, no. 3, Fall 1999; "Translating the Untranslated: Djebar's Le blanc de l'Algérie" by John Erickson, in *Research in African Literature*, vol. 30, no. 3, Fall 1999; "Women's Prison: Literally and Figuratively" by Michelle Reale, in *Al-Jadid*, no. 37, Fall 2001; *Recasting Postcolonialism: Women Writing between Worlds* by Anne Donadey, 2001; *Trances, Dances, and Vociferations: Agency and Resistance in African Women's Narratives* by Nada Elia, 2001.

* * *

Assia Djebar is an Algerian novelist, playwright, documentary film director and producer, and poet. It is in fiction, however, that her contribution has been the most substantive and valuable. She writes in French and her plans to write in Arabic have never materialized. She has been the dominant woman writer in Maghribi literature for almost half a century, achieving both national and international fame and recognition.

Djebar finished her school education in a French lycee in Algeria, where she was considered an excellent student, but pursued her higher education in Paris, receiving a bachelors degree in history and geography. She spent most of the years of the war of independence, from 1955 to 1962, outside her country, teaching in Rabat. Following Algeria's independence in 1962, she took a position as assistant professor of history at the University of Algiers. With the deteriorating political situation in Algeria in the late 1980s she chose to reside in France. She was later appointed distinguished professor and Director of the Center for French and Francophone Studies at Louisiana State University.

It is possible to divide Djebar's literary trajectory into three phases, beginning with a formative period inaugurated by a youthful novel *La Soif* (*The Mischief*), generally considered an immature work as it ignored the fight for independence taking place on the Algerian soil. Soon however, she adopted a more responsible position and turned her attention to Algerian women's involvement in the war of independence, as distant observers in *Les Impatients* [The Impatients] and as participants in *Les Enfants du nouveau monde* [The Children of the New World]. It is her novel *Les Alouettes naives* [The Innocent Larks], however, that reveals a deep understanding of the political challenges awaiting an independent Algeria.

The second phase in her literary career was marked by a new approach to the writing of fiction in which she used her background as historian. She intermingles history and autobiography, moving between the distant past of her country's tragic colonial history and her childhood memories, and focusing on the way the colonial rule shaped the present, both hers and that of the Algerian women. Through her own life as a colonized Algerian, looking in at the "colons" from the outside, Djebar portrays the experience of a large section of the Algerian population, especially that of a certain class with access to French education. The historian and the novelist are at work in most novels of this phase, particularly in *L'Amour, la fantasia* (*Fantasia: An Algerian Cavalcade*), where she succeeds in recreating the tragic atmosphere of the early years of the French conquest.

Djebar planned a quartet to paint the panorama of the conquest, and three of the series have been published so far, *Fantasia: An Algerian Cavalcade*, *Ombre Sultane* (*A Sister to Scheherazade*), and *Vaste est la prison* (*So Vast The Prison*). In her focus on her country's colonial history, Djebar imbued her works with symbols of Arabic culture and relied on the structure of the well known classic *Arabian Nights* in *A Sister to Scheherazade*.

Soon however, in a third phase, the novelist's attention was absorbed by the tragic events of the early 1990s which resulted in the loss of many of her friends and colleagues, prompting her to address the situation in *Le Blanc de l'Algérie* (*Algerian White: A Narrative*) and interrupt the writing of another novel, *Les Nuits de Strasbourg* [The Nights of Strasbourg]. In *Le Blanc d'Algérie*, Djebar tries to comprehend the bewildering bloody events of the 1990s, while mourning and lamenting the assassination of her three friends, Mahfoud Boucebci, M'Hamed Boukhobza, and Abdelkader Alloula. The book portrays the feeling of disarray provoked by their brutal deaths as well as that of other named and anonymous victims. It brings back the sad memory of other writers who passed away.

There is throughout Djebar's writings a linear progression displaying Algerian women's search for their rights in a society where men do not seem to move at the speed of their emancipated women. This discovery is made at a price, as can be observed in *So Vast the Prison*, where women's expectations go beyond society's perimeters. Reflecting the author's personality, most female characters drawn by Djebar convey a dichotomy between modernity and traditions. Djebar considers this unbalanced development within the life of the married couple, where intimacy leads to greater openness but also to tragic consequences in the absence of mutual acceptance of women's liberation. This concentration on Algerian women's world, their poetic expression and their vision of themselves, distinguishes Djebar's writings. She gives it an audible dimension in her films, *La Zerda et les Chants de l'oubli* (1982) and *La Nouba des femmes du Mont Chenoua*, which received the international critics award at the Venice Biennale in 1979. There is also in those films the liberating effect of the use of the author's native languages, Arabic and Berber, in contrast to her reliance on French in the written texts, which keeps the author in the shadow of the colonial past.

Djebar has achieved world fame and was recognized by the international literary community, which awarded her the Neustadt International prize for literature in 1996, and the International Peace prize of the German Book Trade Association in 2000.

—Aida Bamia

See the essay on *Fantasia: An Algerian Cavalcade*.

DÖBLIN, Alfred

Born: Stettin, Germany, 10 August 1878. **Education:** Educated at the Gymnasium, Stettin, 1888, 1891–1900; studied medicine at Berlin University, 1900–04; Freiburg University, 1904–05, medical degree 1905. **Military Service:** Served as a medical officer in the German army during World War I. **Family:** Married Erna Reiss in 1912; two sons. **Career:** Worked in a psychiatric hospital, Regensburg; general practitioner, Berlin, 1911–14; member, Schutzverband deutscher Schriftsteller [Association of German Writers], 1920, and president, 1924; theatre reviewer, *Prager Tageblatt*, 1921–24; visited Poland, 1924; member of the discussion group, Group 1925, with Bertolt Brecht; fled to France to escape the Nazi regime, 1933: became French citizen, 1936, emigrated to the United States, 1940; script writer, Metro Goldwyn Mayer, 1940–41; converted to Roman Catholicism, 1941; returned to Germany, 1945; education officer, Baden-Baden, 1945; editor, *Das Goldene Tor*, 1946–51; co-founder, 1949 and vice-president of literature section, 1949–51, Academy for Science and Literature, Mainz; moved to Paris, 1951; entered sanatorium at Freiburg in Breisgau, 1956. **Awards:** Fontane prize, 1916. **Member:** Prussian Academy of the Arts, 1928. **Died:** 26 June 1957.

PUBLICATIONS

Collections

Ausgewählte Werke, edited by Walter Muschg, Heinz Graber, and Anthony W. Riley. 23 vols., 1960–85.
Die Zeitlupe: Kleine Prosa, edited by Walter Muschg. 1962.
Die Vertreibung der Gespenster, edited by Manfred Beyer. 1968.
Gesammelte Erzählungen. 1971.
Schriften zur Politik und Gesellschaft 1896–1951, edited by Heinz Graber. 1972.
Ein Kerl muss eine Meinung haben, edited by Manfred Beyer. 1976.

Fiction

Die Ermordung einer Butterblume und andere Erzählungen (stories). 1913.
Das Stiftsfräulein und der Tod. 1913.
Die drei Sprünge des Wang-lun. 1915; as *The Three Leaps of Wang Lun: A Chinese Novel*, translated with introduction by C.D. Godwin, 1991.
Die Lobensteiner reisen nach Böhmen (stories). 1917.
Wadzeks Kampf mit der Dampfturbine. 1918.
Der schwarze Vorhang: Roman von den Worten und Zufällen. 1919.
Wallenstein. 1920.
Blaubart und Miss Ilsebill. 1923.
Berge, Meere und Giganten. 1924; revised edition as *Giganten*, 1932.
Die beiden Freundinnen und ihr Giftmord. 1925.
Feldzeugmeister Cratz. Der Kaplan. Zwei Erzählungen. 1926.
Berlin Alexanderplatz. Die Geschichte vom Franz Biberkopf. 1929; as *Alexanderplatz, Berlin: The Story of Franz Biberkopf*, translated by Eugene Jolas, 1931; as *Berlin Alexanderplatz: The Story of Franz Biberkopf*, 1978.
Babylonische Wandrung; oder, Hochmut kommt vor dem Fall. 1934.
Pardon wird nicht gegeben. 1935; as *Men Without Mercy*, translated by Trevor and Phyllis Blewitt, 1937.
Das Land ohne Tod. 1937–38; as *Amazonas*, edited by Walter Muschg, 1963.
Die Fahrt ins Land ohne Tod. 1937.
Der blaue Tiger. 1938.
Der neue Urwald. 1948.
November 1918: Eine deutsche Revolution. 1949; selections from volumes 1 and 2 as *A People Betrayed*, translated by John E. Woods, 1983.
> *Bürger und Soldaten 1918*. 1939; revised edition as *Verratenes Volk*, 1948.
> *Heimkehr der Fronttruppen*. 1949.

Karl und Rosa. 1950; as *Karl and Rosa*, translated by John E. Woods, 1983.
Der Oberst und der Dichter; oder, Das menschliche Herz. 1946.
Heitere Magie, zwei Erzählungen. 1948.
Sinn und Form. 1954.
Hamlet; oder, die lange Nacht nimmt ein Ende. 1956.
Jagende Rösser, Der schwarze Vorhang, und andere frühe Erzählwerke (stories). 1981.

Plays

Lydia and Mäxchen: Tiefe Verbeugung in Einem Akt (produced 1905). 1906.
Lusitania (produced 1926). 1920.
Die Gefährten (includes *Lydia und Mäxchen; Lusitania; Das verwerfliche Schwein*). 1920.
Die Nonnen von Kemnade (produced 1923). 1923.
Die Ehe (produced 1931). 1931.

Verse

Manas: Epische Dichtung. 1927

Other

Gespräche mit Kalypso: Über die Gedächtnisstörungen bei der koraskoffschen Psychose Liebe und die Musik (essays). 1906.
Der deutsche Maskenball (essays). 1921.
Staat und Schriftsteller. 1921.
Feldzeugmeister Cratz, Der Kaplan. 1926.
Reise in Polen. 1926; as *Journey to Poland*, translated by Joachim Neugroschel, 1991.
Das Ich über der Natur. 1927.
Im Buch—Zu Haus—Auf der Strasse, with Oskar Loerke. 1928.
Der Bau des epischen Werkes. 1929.
Der Überfall. 1929.
Wissen und Verändern! Offene Briefe an einen jungen Menschen. 1931.
Jüdische Erneuerung. 1933.
Unser Dasein (essays). 1933.
Flucht und Sammlung des Judenvolkes: Aufsätze und Erzählungen. 1935.
Der historische Roman. 1936.
Die deutsche Literatur: Ein Dialog zwischen Politik und Kunst. 1938.
Nocturno. 1944.
Sieger und Besiegte: Eine wahre Geschichte. 1946.
Nürnberger Lehrprozess. 1946.
Der unsterbliche Mensch: Ein Religionsgespräch. 1946; with *Der Kampf mit dem Engel: Religionsgerpräch*, 1980.
Die literarische Situation. 1947.
Auswahl aus dem erzählenden Werk. 1948.
Heitere Magie: Zwei Erzählungen. 1948.
Unsere Sorge—der Mensch. 1948.
Schicksalsreise: Bericht und Bekenntnis. 1949; as *Destiny's Journey*, edited by Edgar Pässler, translated by Edna McCown, 1992.
Die Dichtung, ihre Natur und ihre Rolle. 1950.
Die Zeitlupe: Kleine Prosa (essays). 1962.
Briefe, edited by Walter Muschg. 1970.
Doktor Döblin (autobiography), edited by Heinz Graber. 1970.

Ein Kerl muss eine Meinung haben: Berichte und Kritiken 1921–1924. 1974.

Griffe ins Leben: Theater-Feuilletons, edited by Manfred Beyer. 1978.

Autobiographische Schriften und letzte Aufzeichnungen, edited by Edgar Pässler. 1980.

Editor, *The Living Thoughts of Confucius.* 1940.

Editor, *Die Revolution der Lyrik,* by Arno Holz. 1951.

Editor, *Minotaurus.* 1953.

*

Bibliography: *Bibliographie Alfred Döblin* by Louis Huguet, 1972.

Critical Studies: *Dimensions of the Modern Novel: German Texts and European Contexts* by Theodore Ziolkowski, 1969; *The Humorous and Grotesque Elements in Döblin's Berlin Alexanderplatz* by Henrietta S. Schoonover, 1977; *Alfred Döblin* by Matthias Prangel, 1987; *The Berlin Novels of Alfred Döblin: Wadzek's Battle with the Steam Turbine, Men Without Mercy and November 1918* by David B. Dollenmayer, 1988; *A Chinese Story from a Berlin Practice: Alfred Döblin's Narrative Technique in Die drei Sprünge des Wang-lun* by John Henry Collins, 1990; *Bely Joyce, and Döblin: Peripatetics in the City Novel* by Peter I. Barta, 1996; *Alfred Döblin* by Armin Arnold, 1996.

* * *

One of the most versatile and enigmatic figures in the field of 20th-century German letters, Alfred Döblin was, like Kafka, born into the social environment of deracinated eastern European Jewry. The poverty endured in his youth and the fascination exerted by the cultural ferment of the city that became his home left their mark on the novel which is commonly viewed as his supreme achievement: *Berlin Alexanderplatz,* the great "urban novel" of 1929. What is often overlooked is the fact that Döblin, as well as leading an active life as a medical practitioner, was the author of literary manifestos, didactic dramas, historical and utopian novels, philosophic essays, and even an Indian verse epic, and was a major formative influence on Brecht, whose theory of epic theatre he helped to shape. No subject was too remote or too obscure. After much painstaking research, he located his first major novel, *Die drei Sprünge des Wang-lun* (*The Three Leaps of Wang-lun*) in 18th-century China. It chronicles the fortunes of a little-known religious group, who wage a campaign of passive resistance against the Imperial authorities and are brutally annihilated. Other major novels of his early years were set in the 17th century (*Wallenstein*), and in a remote, technology-dominated future (*Berge, Meere und Giganten* [Mountains, Seas, and Giants]).

It is not so much the range or the exoticism of his subjects that elicits surprise as the means by which he evokes them. On one level, Döblin strives to be ultra-realistic, using historical sources to create an overpoweringly vivid background. "I was in love with the facts and documents, and wanted to incorporate them without alteration," he says of his work on the Thirty Years War. The direct portrayal of events is enhanced by the extensive use of a specialist vocabulary with which he assumes the reader to be familiar. But besides the documentary layer in Döblin's work, other methods are employed to produce expressive effects: these include interior monologues, cinematic editing techniques, and scenes of lyrical and at times nightmarish intensity. Several such devices seem calculated to make the reader aware of the "fictionality" of the text. Like James Joyce, with whom he is often compared, Döblin was involved in extending the range of narrative perspectives within the novel, and regularly experimented with methods which subsequently came to be recognized as features of post-modernism.

Berlin Alexanderplatz is not only the story of a humble furniture-removal-man with a personality that encompasses the extremes of criminality and sainthood, but also the definitive chronicle of a modern metropolis and a probing interrogation of the values of its secularized inhabitants. The career of Franz Biberkopf is examined over a period of 18 months, during which he abandons his initial quest for "respectability" and becomes increasingly involved in the activities of a gang of thieves and swindlers, loses an arm in a car-chase, and sustains a final blow when his girlfriend, Mieze, is murdered by fellow crook, Reinhold. But, as always in Döblin, the medium is no less important than the events. Innovatory techniques abound: soft-focusing is often used, and material from various walks of life is mounted onto the narrative as in the collages of Expressionist and Dadaist painters. Language is pushed to new extremes: documentary source-material, news items, statistics, popular songs, hymns, and biblical references intertwine to create an at times clinically realistic, at times symbolic canvas, at the heart of which is an impassioned plea for our sympathetic understanding of a disoriented, marginal man, and through him, of his entire generation.

In much of his work, Döblin shows himself to be keenly aware of injustice and hypocrisy in society. His passion for detail, his medical experience, and his familiarity with the low life of inter-war Berlin made him deeply suspicious of officialdom and superficial notions of respectability. Incompetent and mendacious bureaucracy, corruption in high places, and the gross materialism of the well-to-do recur as themes in the novels, whatever their setting. His central characters tend to be from undistinguished backgrounds, ordinary men buffeted about by an ill-functioning system. In the 1920s, Döblin published political commentaries in a variety of formats. From 1927 onwards, he claimed to have become more interested in the individual than in the collective. Several works deal directly with revolutionary and fascist tendencies in Germany, notably *November 1918* and *Pardon wird nicht gegeben* (*Men Without Mercy*). His exile is vividly recalled in the autobiographical *Schicksalsreise* (*Destiny's Journey*). Unlike Brecht and Thomas Mann, Döblin was unable to find his feet in America and returned after the war to Germany, where he had been all but forgotten. There was little interest in his kaleidoscopic, experimental style, and his later manuscripts were ignored by the major commercial publishing houses of West Germany. After his death in 1957, an unreliable, fragmentary, and expensive collected edition began to appear. Public interest was re-awakened in part by the efforts of East German critics and publishers, who were keen to stress his social commitment. A complete edition of Döblin's works was at last forthcoming, and his reputation has been further enhanced by the attentions of the film director Rainer Werner Fassbinder, whose last major work was a monumental 15-hour version of *Berlin Alexanderplatz.*

—Osman Durrani

See the essay on *Berlin Alexanderplatz.*

DODERER, Heimito von

Born: Weidlingau, Austria, 5 September 1896. **Education:** Educated at the Landstrasser Gymnasium, graduated 1914; University of Vienna, 1921–25, Ph.D. in history, 1925. **Military Service:** Served as a reserve officer, Austrian dragoon regiment, 1915, prisoner of war in Siberia, 1916, repatriated 1920; conscripted to the German Air Force, 1940; examiner of potential Luftwaffe officers, Vienna, 1943; prisoner of war in Norway, 1945, released 1946. **Family:** Married 1) Gusti Hasterlik in 1930 (divorced 1934); 2) Maria Thoma in 1952. **Career:** Converted to Roman Catholicism, 1940; publisher's reader, Vienna, 1946; banned from publishing works until 1950. **Awards:** Confederation of German Industry, Novelist's prize, 1954; Austrian State grand award, 1954; Prikheim medal of Nuremberg, 1958; Raabe prize, 1966; Ring of Honour of the City of Vienna, 1966. **Member:** Nazi Party, 1933–38; Institute for Research in Austrian History, 1950. **Died:** 23 December 1966.

PUBLICATIONS

Collections

Frühe Prosa, edited by Hans Flesch-Brunningen. 1968.
Die Erzählungen, edited by Wendelin Schmidt-Dengler. 2 vols., 1973–76.
Commentarii: Tagebücher aus dem Nachlass, edited by Wendelin Schmidt-Dengler. 2 vols., 1976–86.
Das Doderer-Buch: Eine Auswahl aus dem Werk Heimito von Doderers, edited by Karl Heinz Kramberg. 1976.

Fiction

Die Bresche: Ein Vorgang in vierundzwanzig Stunden. 1924.
Das Geheimnis des Reichs. 1930; as *The Secret of the Empire: A Novel of the Russian Civil War*, translated with foreword and afterword by John S. Barrett, 1998.
Ein Mord, den jeder begeht. 1938; as *Every Man a Murderer*, translated by Richard and Clara Winston, 1964.
Ein Umweg. 1940.
Die erleuchteten Fenster; oder, die Menschwerdung des Amtsrates Julius Zihal. 1950; as *The Lighted Windows; or, The Humanization of the Bureaucrat Julius Zihal*, translated with afterword by John S. Barrett, 2000.
Die Strudlhofstiege; oder, Melzer und die Tiefe der Jahre. 1951.
Das letzte Abenteuer. 1953.
Die Dämonen. 1956; as *The Demons*, translated by Richard and Clara Winston, 1961.
Die Posaunen von Jericho: Neues Divertimento. 1958; as "The Trumpets of Jericho," translated by Vincent Kling, in *Chicago Review*, 26(2), 1974.
Die Peinigung der Lederbeutelchen (stories). 1959.
Die Merowinger; oder, die totale Familie. 1962.
Roman No. 7
    Die Wasserfälle von Slunj. 1963; as *The Waterfalls of Slunj*, translated by Eithne Wilkins and Ernst Kaiser, 1966.
    Der Grenzwald (fragment). 1967.
Unter schwarzen Sternen (stories). 1966.
Meine neunzehn Lebensläufe und neun andere Geschichten. 1966.

Die Wiederkehr der Drachen: Aufsätze, Traktate, Reden, edited by Wendelin Schmidt-Dengler. 1972.

Verse

Gassen und Landschaft. 1923.
Ein Weg im Dunklen: Gedichte und epigrammatische Verse. 1957.

Other

Der Fall Gütersloh: Ein Schicksal und seine Deutung. 1930.
Von der Unschuld des Indirekten. 1947.
Grundlagen und Funktion des Romans. 1959; as "Principles and Functions of the Novel," in *30th International Congress of the P.E.N. Clubs*, 1959.
Wege und Unwege, edited by Herbert Eisenreich. 1960.
Die Ortung des Kritikers. 1960.
Albert Paris Gütersloh: Autor und Werk, with others. 1962.
Tangenten. Tagebuch eines Schriftstellers 1940–1950 (correspondence). 1964.
Mit der Sprache leben, with Herbert Meier and Josef Mühlberger. 1965.
Repertorium: Ein Begreifbuch von höheren und niederen Lebens-Sachen, edited by Dietrich Weber. 1969.
Briefwechsel 1928–1962, with Albert Paris Gütersloh, edited by Reinhold Treml. 1986.
Editor, *Gewaltig staunt der Mensch*, by Albert Paris Gütersloh. 1963.

*

Critical Studies: *From Prophecy to Exorcism: The Premises of Modern German Literature* by Michael Hamburger, 1965; "Heimito von Doderer's Demons and the Modern Kakanian Novel by Engelbert Pfeiffer," in *The Contemporary Novel in German* edited by Robert H. Heitner, 1967; "A Commentary on Heimito von Doderer" by Dietrich Weber, translated by Brian L. Harris, in *Dimension*, (1), 1968; *Heimito von Doderer* by Michael Bachem, 1981; *Twentieth-Century Odyssey: A Study of Heimito von Doderer's Die Dämonen* by Elizabeth C. Hesson, 1982; *Doderer and the Politics of Marriage: Personal and Social History in Die Dämonen* by Bruce Irvin Turner, 1982; *Begegnung mit Heimito von Doderer* edited by Michael Horowitz, 1983; *Heimito von Doderer* by Dietrich Weber, 1987; "Heimito von Doderer and National Socialism" by Andrew W. Barker, in *German Life and Letters*, 41(2), 1988; *The Writer's Place: Heimito von Doderer and the Alsergrund District of Vienna* by Engelbert Pfeiffer, translated by Vincent Kling, 2001.

*   *   *

Friedrich Torberg contended that Heimito von Doderer would have enjoyed the reputation of being the most Austrian of Austrian authors. Few authors' works are so intimately linked with locations and milieux as his. Vienna's third district, the site of his former school between the "diplomats' quarter" and the *Prater* as well as the *Alsergrund*, are his preferred settings, for example *Die Wasserfälle von Slunj* (*The Waterfalls of Slunj*) and *Die Strudlhofstiege* [The Strudlhof Steps]. Doderer describes not only streets, but also houses in such detail that they are easily identifiable. His actual protagonist is Vienna as the former capital of the Austro-Hungarian empire and the multicultural metropolis which he loved: his family's aristocratic and bourgeois circles and his own bohemian environment. In his portrayal of urban life, Doderer displays his familiarity with various social groups: the coffee house culture, ladies of leisure, civil servants, state officials, and workers. He is no stranger to the Viennese underworld and their transactions in the canal and sewer systems. The monumental novels, *Die Strudlhofstiege* and *Die Dämonen* (*The Demons*), like *romans à clef*, frequently refer to historical persons and events.

Doderer's depiction of the anxiety of the Austrian bourgeoisie is unmatched, because he shared their general lack of interest in democracy and resented the newly-formed republic despite the fact that in the 1920s Vienna was a model of social progress. His perspective is that of an upper-class man and a World War I officer of a dragoon elite unit, who was not even stripped of his privileges in a Siberian prison camp. As a prisoner of war he wrote, studied, and encountered the work of the novelist Albert Paris Gütersloh, his "venerated master" and friend, whose concept of the total novel shaped his own theories. This Russian experience, his captivity and escape, defined to a large extent his view of reality. For example, in *The Demons* a hands-on fight delivers Imre Gyurkicz, a character caught up in military reveries, from the twilight-zone of alienation. Dying as a fighter, he realizes his human potential. Other protagonists, like the socially awkward René Stangeler, a reflection of Doderer as a young man, and his fiancée Grete Siebenschein, mirror Doderer's exacting courtship and unsuccessful marriage to Gusti Hasterlik, the daughter of a Jewish surgeon, from whom Doderer was divorced in 1938 when the Hasterliks went into exile.

Doderer's literary cosmos evolved organically. The protagonists from earlier texts are followed up in later ones, aging and changing with time. Doderer writes in a "realistic" and a "grotesque" mode. The former is assigned to the inner world of the civilized Sektionsrat Geyrenhoff, an image of the mature Doderer, the latter to the "horrible" Dr. Döblinger, alias Kajetan von Schlaggenberg, reminiscent of the middle-age author in his Nazi phase—the name Döblinger alludes to Doderer's residence in the suburb of Döbling between 1928 and 1936. This compartmentalization of texts suggests a Jekyll-and-Hyde disposition, which Doderer ascribes to the world, coining the concept of a "dual reality." The "Döblinger" texts introduce the readers to extreme, sadistic relationships, taking them on excursions into psychological aberrations and perversions, for example *Die Posaunen von Jericho* ("The Trumpets of Jericho") and *Die Merowinger; oder, die totale Familie* [The Merovingians, or the Total Family]. The "Geyrenhoff" texts present society from a rational and benevolent point of view—Geyrenhoff is the chronicler of *The Demons*, a detached insightful spectator. In larger works the rational and the bizarre spheres overlap. The result is an extreme narrative tension. In the short story "Eine Person aus Porzellan" [A Porcelain Person] one character combines both aspects: a young women who hides her vampire-like nature under a perfect facade. In *The Demons* the digressions about late medieval witch hunts written in archaic German—an offshoot of Doderer's historical studies—reveal the dual reality in terms of culture. The poetry in *Gassen und Landschaft* [Alleys and Landscape] represents yet another literary sensibility, that of a perceptive observer of nature and urban atmospheres.

Doderer's inability to cope with diversity goes hand in hand with a passionate rejection of "ideology" and a yearning for authenticity. While his work abounds with idiosyncratic characters intended to produce the effect of universality, it is precisely this narrow focus on the unique and private which undermines the author's intent. It fosters the notion that nothing in this hermetic cosmos happens by accident: all characters interconnect in causally related plots, by lineage, or

through mutual acquaintances. The desire, if not for uniformity, at least for a group spirit—the protagonists in *The Demons* call their intimate circle "Our People"—reveals an all-pervasive suspicion, particularly of Socialist politics, which is bolstered by Doderer's portrayal of the proletarian masses as rabble as well as his revisionist assessment of the 1927 riots. His texts propose that it takes personal initiative rather than political involvement to overcome the crippling bewilderment supposedly caused by too much indoctrination. Any passionate activity commensurate with one's character may lead to fulfilling one's destiny. While Doderer's concept of character echoes German idealism, it also has a fascist ring to it. His acute awareness of otherness based on gender and ethnicity corresponds with the views held by his psychology professor Hermann Swoboda who, like himself, advocated the principles of one of the most virulent proponents of anti-semitism and misogyny, Otto Weininger.

In Doderer's post-war publications, the inflammatory pronouncements, the prejudice against groups and individuals, but most of all the anti-semitism, are toned down—the later was most prevalent in his projects of the 1930s, following the estrangement from his wife. He had actually planned the first, lost version of *The Demons* as a celebration of anti-semitism. However, some of these tendencies survived, explaining Doderer's attraction to National Socialism. The novel *Ein Mord, den jeder begeht* (*Every Man a Murderer*), written during his Nazi phase, refutes the concept of individual responsibility as a young man realizes his involvement in his sister-in-law's murder. *Die erleuchteten Fenster; oder, die Menschwerdung des Amtsrates Julius Zihal* (*The Lighted Windows; or, The Humanization of the Bureaucrat Julius Zihal*) submits that objective structures support any kind of activity: Zihal changes from a devoted, punctual civil servant to an equally serious voyeur. Only love can deliver him from his obsession. Despite their admirable stylistic qualities, the same problematic tendencies persist in Doderer's postwar novels. Purporting to present a critical literary survey of the inter-war years, they do not discuss the events following the burning of the Palace of Justice in 1927. The protagonists of *The Demons* disband and go into exile, including Mary K., a Jewish woman who has found her true self in a relationship with a working-class man, who, in turn, became a "better" person through his intellectual pursuits. Even after 1945, marriage and assimilation to the gentile middle-classes represent Doderer's ultimate vision of hope to offset the collapse of the civilized world as he perceived it.

—Dagmar C.G. Lorenz

See the essay on *Die Strudlhofstiege*.

DOSTOEVSKII, Fedor (Mikhailovich)

Also known as Fyodor Dostoevsky. **Born:** Moscow, Russia, 30 October 1821. **Education:** Educated at home to age 12; Chermak's School, Moscow; Army Chief Engineering Academy, St. Petersburg, 1838–43: commissioned as ensign, 1839, as 2nd lieutenant, 1842, graduated 1843 as War Ministry draftsman; resigned 1844. **Family:** Married 1) Maria Dmitrievna Isaeva in 1857 (died 1864), one stepson; 2) Anna Grigorievna Snitkina in 1867, two daughters and two sons. **Career:** Writer; political involvement caused his arrest,

1849: sentenced to death, but sentence commuted at the last moment to penal servitude, in Omsk, Siberia, 1850–54; exiled as soldier at Semipalatinsk, 1854: corporal, 1855, ensign, 1856, resigned as 2nd lieutenant for health reasons, and exile ended, 1859; editor, *Vremia* [Time], 1861–63; took over *Epokha* [Epoch] on his brother's death, 1864–65; in Western Europe, 1867–71; editor, *Grazhdanin* [Citizen], 1873–74. **Died:** 28 January 1881.

PUBLICATIONS

Collections

Novels, translated by Constance Garnett. 12 vols., 1912–20.
Polnoe sobranie khudozhestvennykh proizvedenii [Complete Works]. 3 vols., 1933.
Sobranie sochinenii [Collected Works], edited by Leonid Grossman. 10 vols., 1956–58.
Polnoe sobranie sochinenii [Complete Works], edited by G.M. Fridlender and others. 30 vols., 1972–90.
Sochineniia [Works]. 2 vols., 1987–.
Sobranie sochinenii [Collected Works]. 15 vols., 1988.
Izbrannye sochineniia [Selected Works], edited by N.I. Iakushin. 1990.
White Nights; A Gentle Creature; The Dream of a Ridiculous Man, translated by Alan Myers. 1995.

Fiction

Bednye liudi. 1846; as *Poor Folk*, 1887; also translated by L. Milman, 1894; C.J. Hogarth, with *The Gambler*, 1916; Constance Garnett, in *Novels*, 1917; L. Nazrozov, 1956; Robert Dessaix, 1982; David McDuff, 1988.
Dvoinik. 1846; as *The Double*, translated by Constance Garnett, in *Novels*, 1917; also translated by Jessie Coulson, 1972; as *The Double: A Poem of St. Petersburg*, translated by George Bird, 1956; as *The Double: Two Versions*, translated by Evelyn Harden, 1985.
Belye nochi. 1848; as *White Nights*, translated by Constance Garnett, in *Novels*, 1918; also translated by Olga Shartse, 1958.
Netochka Nezvanova. 1849; as *Netochka Nezvanova*, translated by Constance Garnett, in *Novels*, 1920; also translated by Ann Dunnigan, 1970; Jane Kentish, 1985.
Selo Stepanchikogo i ego obitateli [The Village Stepanchikogo and Its Inhabitants]. 1859; as *The Village of Stepanchikovo and Its Inhabitants: From the Notes of an Unknown*, translated with introduction by Ignat Avsey, 1995.
Zapiski iz podpol'ia. 1864; edited by A.D.P. Briggs, 1994; as *Letters from the Underworld*, translated by C.J. Hogarth, 1913; as *Notes from the Underground*, translated by Jessie Coulson, 1972; as *Notes from Underground*, translated by Constance Garnett, in *Novels*, 1918; also translated by Mirra Ginsburg, 1974; Michael R. Katz, 1989; Jane Kentish, with *The Gambler*, 1991; Richard Pevear and Larissa Volokhonsky, 1992.
Igrok. 1866; as *The Gambler*, translated by F. Whishaw, with *The Friend of the Family*, 1887; also translated by C.J. Hogarth, with *Poor Folk*, 1916; Jessie Coulson, 1966; Victor Terras, with *Diary*, by Polina Suslova, 1973; Jane Kentish, with *Notes from the Underground*, 1991.
Prestuplenie i nakazanie. 1867; as *Crime and Punishment*, translated by Frederick Whishaw, 1886; also translated by Constance Garnett,

1881; David Magarshack, 1951; Jessie Coulson, 1953 (this translation edited by George Gibian, 1989; with an introduction by Richard Peace, 1995); Sidney Monas, 1968; J. Katzer, 1985; David McDuff, 1991; Richard Pevear and Larissa Volokhonsky, 1993.
Idiot. 1869; as *The Idiot*, translated by Frederick Whishaw, 1887; also translated by Constance Garnett, in *Novels*, 1913; E. Martin, 1914; David Magarshack, 1954; Henry and Olga Carlisle, 1969; J. Katzer, 1978; Alan Myers, 1992; Richard Pevear and Larissa Volokhonsky, 1993.
Vechnyi muzh. 1870; as *The Permanent Husband*, translated by Frederick Whishaw, with *Uncle's Dream*, 1888; as *The Eternal Husband*, translated by Constance Garnett, in *Novels*, 1917.
Besy. 1872; as *The Possessed*, translated by Constance Garnett, in *Novels*, 1913; as *The Devils*, translated by David Magarshack, 1953; as *Devils*, translated by Michael R. Katz, 1992; as *Demons: A Novel in Three Parts*, translated by Richard Pevear and Larissa Volokhonsky, 1994.
Podrostok. 1875; as *A Raw Youth*, translated by Constance Garnett, in *Novels*, 1916.
Brat'ia Karamazovy. 1880; as *The Brothers Karamazov*, translated by Constance Garnett, in *Novels*, 1912; also translated by A. Kropotkin, 1953; David Magarshack, 1958; Andrew R. MacAndrew, 1970; Julius Katzer, 1980; W.J. Leatherbarrow, 1990; Richard Pevear and Larissa Volokhonsky, 1990; David McDuff, 1993.
Injury and Insult, translated by Frederick Whishaw. 1886; as *The Insulted and Injured*, translated by Constance Garnett, in *Novels*, 1915; also translated by Olga Shartse, 1977; as *The Insulted and Humiliated*, 1956.
The Friend of the Family and The Gambler, translated by Frederick Whishaw. 1887.
Uncle's Dream, translated by Frederick Whishaw, with *The Permanent Husband*. 1888; also translated by Constance Garnett, in *Novels*, 1919; as *My Uncle's Dream*, translated by Ivy Litvinova, 1956.
Letters from the Underworld and Other Stories, translated by C.J. Hogarth. 1913.
A Gentle Spirit, translated by Constance Garnett, in *Novels*. 1917; as *A Gentle Creature and Other Stories*, translated by David Magarshack, 1950.
Best Short Stories, translated by David Magarshack, 1954.
Winter Notes on Summer Impressions, translated by R. Renfield. 1954; as *Summer Impressions*, translated by Kyril FitzLyon, 1954; translated by David Patterson, 1997.
The Gambler; Bobok; A Nasty Story, translated by Jessie Coulson. 1966.
Notes from the Underground; The Double, translated by Jessie Coulson. 1972.
Poor Folk and Other Stories, translated by David McDuff. 1988.
Uncle's Dream and Other Stories, translated by David McDuff. 1989.
An Accidental Family, edited and translated by Richard Freeborn. 1994.

Other

Zapiski iz mertvogo doma. 1861–62; as *Buried Alive; or, Ten Years of Penal Servitude in Siberia*, translated by M. Von Thilo, 1881; as *Prison Life in Siberia*, translated by H. Edwards, 1881; as *The*

House of the Dead, 1911; also translated by Constance Garnett, in
Novels, 1915; David McDuff, 1985; as *Memoirs from the House of
the Dead*, translated by Jessie Coulson, 1955; as *Notes from a
Dead House*, translated by L. Nazrozov and J. Guralsky, 1958.

Dnevnik pisatelia. 1876–81; as *The Diary of a Writer*, translated by
Boris Leo Brasol, 2 vols., 1949; as *A Writer's Diary 1873–1876*,
translated by Brasol, 2 vols., 1949; also translated by Kenneth
Lantz, 1993.

*Letters of Fyodor Michailovitch Dostoevsky to His Family and
Friends*, translated by E. Mayne. 1914.

Pages from the Journal of an Author, translated by S.S. Kotelianskii
and J.M. Murry. 1916.

Letters and Reminiscences, translated by S.S. Kotelianskii and J.M.
Murry. 1923.

Pis'ma k zhene, edited by V.F. Pereverzev. 1926; as *Letters to His
Wife*, translated by E. Hill and D. Mudie, 1930.

New Dostoevsky Letters, translated by S.S. Kotelianskii. 1929.

Zapisnye tetradi [Notebooks]. 4 vols., 1935.

The Grand Inquisitor, translated by S.S. Kotelianskii. 1935; also
translated by Constance Garnett, 1948.

Pis'ma [Letters]. 4 vols., 1959.

Occasional Writings, edited and translated by David Magarshack.
1961.

The Notebooks for The Idiot [*Crime and Punishment, The Possessed,
A Raw Youth, The Brothers Karamazov*], edited by Edward
Wasiolek, translated by Wasiolek, Victor Terras, and Katharine
Strelsky. 5 vols., 1967–71.

Neizdannyi Dostoevskii. Zapisnye knizhki i tetradi 1860–1881. 1971;
as *The Unpublished Dostoevsky: Diaries and Notebooks, 1860–81*,
edited by Carl R. Proffer, 3 vols., 1973–76.

Self Portrait, edited by Jessie Coulson. 1976.

Selected Letters, edited by Joseph Frank and David I. Goldstein,
translated by Andrew R. MacAndrew. 1987.

Complete Letters (Vol. 1, 1832–59; Vol. 2, 1860–67; Vol. 3, (1868–71);
Vol. 4 (1872–77); Vol. 5, 1878–81), edited and translated by
David Lowe and Ronald Meyer. 1988–91.

Vozvrashchenie cheloveka [The Return of Man], edited by M.M.
Stakhanova. 1989.

*

Bibliography: *Dostoevskii, Bibliografiia proizvedenii Dostoevskogo
i literatury o nem 1917–65* edited by A.A. Belkin, A.S. Dolinin, and
V.V. Kozhinov, 1968; "Dostoevsky Studies in Great Britain: A
Bibliographical Survey" by Garth M. Terry in *New Essays on
Dostoevsky* edited by Malcolm V. Jones and Garth M. Terry, 1983;
Fedor Dostoevsky: A Reference Guide by W.J. Leatherbarrow, 1990;
*The Dostoevsky Archive: Firsthand Accounts of the Novelist from
Contemporarie's Memoirs and Rare Periodicals, Most Translated
for the First Time, With a Detailed Lifetime Chronology and Anno-
tated Bibliography*, compiled by Peter Sekirin, 1997.

Critical Studies: *Fyodor Dostoevsky: A Study* by Aimee Dostoevskii,
1922; *Dostoevsky: The Man and His Work* by Julius Meier Graefe,
1928; *The Mighty Three: Pushkin, Gogol, Dostoevsky* by Boris
Leo Brasol, 1934; *Dostoevsky in Russian Literary Criticism 1846–1954*,
1957, *Dostoevskii's Image in Russia Today*, 1975, and *Dostoevskii
in Russian and World Theatre*, 1977, all by Vladimir Seduro;
Dostoevsky: His Life and Art by Avrahm Yarmolinsky, 1957;

Dostoevsky by David Magarshack, 1961; *The Undiscovered
Dostoevsky*, 1962, and *Dostoevsky: His Life and Work*, 1978, both by
Ronald Hingley; *Dostoevsky: A Collection of Critical Essays* edited
by Rene Wellek, 1962; *Notes on Dostoevsky's "Crime and Punish-
ment,"* 1963, and *Notes on Dostoevsky's "Notes from the Underground,"* 1970, both by James L. Roberts, and *Notes on Dostoevsky's
"Brothers Karamazov"* by Roberts and Gary Carey, 1967; *Dostoevsky:
The Major Fiction* by Edward Wasiolek, 1964; *Dostoevsky's Quest
for Form*, 1966, *The Art of Dostoevsky*, 1981, and *Dostoevsky's
Underground Man in Russian Literature*, 1982, all by Robert Louis
Jackson; *Dostoevsky and Romantic Realism* by Donald Fangler,
1967; *Dostoevsky: His Life and Work* by Konstantin Mochulskii,
1967; *Dostoevsky: An Examination of the Major Novels* by Richard
Peace, 1971; *Political Apocalypse: A Study of Dostoevsky's Grand
Inquisitor* by Ellis Sandoz, 1971; *The Religion of Dostoevsky* by A.
Boyce Gibson, 1973; *Dostoevsky and the Age of Intensity* by Alex de
Jong, 1975; *Starets Zosima in the Brothers Karamazov: A Study in the
Mimesis of Virtue* by Sven Linnér, 1975; *Dostoevsky: The Novel of
Discord*, 1976, and *Dostoevsky after Bakhtin: Readings in Dostoevsky's
Fantastic Realism*, 1990, both by Malcolm V. Jones, 1976, and *New
Essays on Dostoevsky* edited by Jones and Garth M. Terry, 1983;
Dostoevsky: The Literary Artist by Erik Krag, 1976; *Dostoevsky: The
Seeds of Revolt 1821–1849*, 1977, *The Years of Ordeal 1850–1859*,
1984, and *The Stir of Liberation 1860–1865*, 1987, all by Joseph
Frank; *Dostoevsky and the Novel* by Michael Holquist, 1977; *A
"Handbook" to the Russian Text of Crime and Punishment* by Edgar
H. Lehrmann, 1977; *Atheism and the Rejection of God: Contempo-
rary Philosophy and the Brothers Karamazov* by Stewart Sutherland,
1977; *Dostoevsky and Christ: A Study of Dostoevsky's Rebellion
Against Belinsky* by Ivan Dolenc, 1978; *Ideology and Imagination:
The Image of Society in Dostoevsky* by Geoffrey C. Kabat, 1978;
Dostoevsky and the Psychologists by Maria Kravchenko, 1978;
Crime and Punishment: Murder as Philosophic Experiment by A.D.
Nuttall, 1978; *Crime and Punishment: The Techniques of the Omnis-
cient Author* by Gary Rosenshield, 1978; *Unconscious Structure in
The Idiot: A Study in Literature and Psychoanalysis* by Elizabeth
Dalton, 1979; *Narrative Principles in Dostoevskij's Besy: A Struc-
tural Analysis* by Slobodanka B. Vladiv, 1979; *Tolstoy or Dostoevsky:
An Essay in Contrast* by George Steiner, 1980; *F.M. Dostoevsky
(1821–1881): A Centenary Collection* edited by Leo Burnett, 1981;
Fedor Dostoevsky, 1981, and *Fyodor Dostoevsky; "The Brothers
Karamazov,"* 1992, both by W.J. Leatherbarrow; *Dostoevsky and
The Idiot: Author, Narrator and Reader* by Robin Feuer Miller, 1981;
*A Karamazov Companion: Commentary on the Genesis, Language
and Style of Dostoevsky's Novel* by Victor Terras, 1981; *The Under-
ground Man and Raskolnikov: A Comparative Study* by Preben
Villadsen, 1981; *Dostoevsky* by Gerald Abraham, 1982; *Fyodor
Dostoevsky* by John Arthur Thomas Lloyd, 1982; *Dostoevsky* by
Stanislaw Mackiewicz, 1982; *Dostoevsky* by Dimitri Merejkowski,
1982; *Character Names in Dostoevsky's Fiction* by Charles Passage,
1982; *Dostoevsky* by John Cowper Powys, 1982; *Dostoevsky* by C.M.
Woodhouse, 1982; *Dostoevsky* by L.A. Zander, 1982; *New Essays on
Dostoevsky*, 1983; *A Dostoevsky Dictionary* by Richard Chapple,
1983; *Dostoevsky* by John Jones, 1983; *The Idiot: Dostoevsky's
Fantastic Prince: A Phenomenological Approach* by Dennis Patrick
Slattery, 1983; *Problems of Dostoevsky's Poetics* by Mikhail M.
Bakhtin, translated by Caryl Emerson, 1984; *Tyrant and Victim in
Dostoevsky* by Gary Cox, 1984; *Dostoevsky and His New Testament*,
1984, and *Dostoevsky: A Writer's Life*, 1988, both by Geir Kjetsaa;

The Experience of Time in Crime and Punishment by Leslie A. Johnson, 1985; *Varieties of Poetic Utterance: Quotation in The Brothers Karamazov* by Nina Perlina, 1985; *Dostoevsky and the Healing Art: An Essay in Literary and Medical History* by James L. Rice, 1985; *Dostoevsky: The Myths of Duality* by Roger B. Anderson, 1986; *Dostoevsky and the Human Condition after a Century* edited by Alexej Ugrinsky, Frank S. Lambasa, and Valija K. Ozolins, 1986; *Dostoyevsky's Critique of the West: The Quest for the Earthly Paradise* by Bruce K. Ward, 1986; *Humor in the Novels of F.M. Dostoevsky* by R.L. Busch, 1987; *The Aesthetics of Dostoevsky* by Nadezhda Kashina, 1987; *Summer in Baden-Baden: From the Life of Dostoyevsky* by Leonid Tsypkin, 1987; *Fyodor Dostoevsky* by Peter Conradi, 1988; *Poverty and Power in the Early Works of Dostoevskij* by S.K. Somerwil-Ayrton, 1988; *Furnace of Doubt: Dostoevsky and The Brothers Karamazov* by Arthur Trace, 1988; *The Genesis of the Brothers Karamazov: The Aesthetics, Ideology and Psychology of Making a Text* by Robert Belknap, 1989; *Dostoevsky: The Author as Psychoanalyst* by Louis Breger, 1989; *Dostoevsky and the Process of Literary Creation* by Jacques Catteau, 1989; *Literary Portraits in the Novels of F.M. Dostoevskij* by Edmund Heier, 1989; *Dostoevsky: Dreamer and Prophet* by Judith Gunn, 1990; *The Political and Social Thought of F.M. Dostoevsky* by Stephen Carter, 1991; *The Brothers Karamazov and the Poetics of Memory* by Diana Oenning Thompson, 1991; *Fedor Dostoevsky* by Alloa Amoia, 1993; *Dostoevsky's Notes from Underground* by Richard Peace, 1993; *Dostoevsky and the Twentieth Century: The Ljubljana Papers*, edited by Malcolm V. Jones, 1993; *Dostoevsky and the Woman Question: Rereadings at the End of a Century* by Nina Pelikan Straus, 1994; *Dostoevsky: The Miraculous Years* by Joseph Frank, 1995; *Dostoevskii and Britain*, edited by W.J. Leatherbarrow, 1995; *The Annihilation of Inertia: Dostoevsky and Metaphysics* by Liza Knapp, 1996; *Dostoevsky's Crime and Punishment: An Aesthetic Interpretation* by Henry Buchanan, 1996; *The Perverted Ideal in Dostoevsky's "The Devils"* by Nancy K. Anderson, 1997; *Dostoevsky and Soloviev: The Art of Integral Vision* by Marina Kostalevsky, 1997; *Resurrection From the Underground: Feodor Dostoevsky* by René Girard, translated and edited by James G. Williams, 1997; *Reading Dostoevsky* by Victor Terras, 1998; *Dostoevsky's The Idiot: A Critical Companion*, edited by Liza Knapp, 1998; *Dostoevsky and English Modernism, 1900–1930* by Peter Kaye, 1999; *Dimensions of Laughter in Crime and Punishment* by John (János) Spiegel, 2000; *Dostoevsky and the Christian Tradition*, edited by George Pattison and Diane Oenning Thompson, 2001; *Retelling Dostoyevsky: Literary Responses and Other Observations* by Gary Adelman, 2001.

* * *

The darkness of Fedor Dostoevskii's life—a murdered father, epilepsy, near-execution and exile, debt, compulsive gambling, estrangement from friends, and a tormented sexuality—reflects the rapidly overheating Russian society of the later 19th century. So does his literature. His early work, including *Bednye liudi* (*Poor Folk*), *Dvoinik* (*The Double*), and *Belye nochi* (*White Nights*), surfaces in a post-Gogolian "civic realism," with a compassion for the little man, but this feature is quickly overshadowed by his characteristic and seminal perceptions of the paranoia, deception, emptiness, and illusion of modern urban life. In the score of years following his penal servitude and exile for "socialist" activities (1849–59) Dostoevskii produced a series of works of lasting significance for 20th-century

literature. The Underground Man (central character of *Zapiski iz podpol'ia*, translated as *Notes from the Underground*) is a determining forerunner to most of the later heroes: a frustrated modern man, adrift in a moral void. Estranged from the roots of land, tradition, and faith, he attempts to establish, if only negatively, his own identity and dignity against the palliatives and platitudes of authority on the one hand and the serious, but dangerous appeal of "rationalism" on the other. Rationalism, in Dostoevskii's view, came to embrace utilitarianism, materialism, socialism, and the temporal power of Roman Catholicism. Throughout his work Dostoevskii seeks to counteract rationalism by appeal to the intuitive Christian faith which he sees embodied, however imperfectly, in the beliefs of the Russian people.

The conflicting interplay between the rationalist analysis of existence and the natural response to life is pursued in stronger terms in the characters and plots of the major novels. In *Prestuplenie i nakazanie* (*Crime and Punishment*) Raskol'nikov's espousal of a "rational" superman morality results only in the squalid murder of a pawnbroker, followed by Raskol'nikov's own self-torment which eventually leads him to an unconvincing "salvation." In *Idiot* (*The Idiot*) Prince Myshkin's passive beauty and his all too perceptive innocence stimulate, rather than reconcile, the perverse impulses of his society. In *Besy* (*The Possessed* or *The Devils*), a Messianic, anti-revolutionary novel, Stavrogin's unique strength and individuality is sapped to suicide by disillusionment with ideologies, causes, and beliefs. Finally, in *Brat'ia Karamazovy* (*The Brothers Karamazov*) the Karamazov family, beset by jealousy, pride, and hatred, disintegrates into parricide, a crisis that tests the extremes of Christianity and atheism. It is only in this last novel that Dostoevskii's attempt to give a positive depiction of active Christian love (in the persons of Father Zosima and Alesha Karamazov) is artistically successful, although even here it often fails to match the power of Ivan Karamazov's reasoned objections to "God's world."

Dostoevskii's heroes are strong but divided personalities, engaged in intimate and frequently mortal debate with themselves, their "doubles," and the reader over the moral basis of their actions. His murder-centred plots are a visionary, fantastic, and mythically structured re-working of the sensational and extremist life observed in his journalism. The polarized themes of reason and unreason, faith and unbelief, moral freedom and moral slavery, frame the tension of modern man, a tension which finds a precarious resolution in the vision of Christ, Dostoevskii's moral-aesthetic ideal. His journal chronicle *Dnevnik pisatelia* (*The Diary of a Writer*) portrays these issues in the form of justification of tradition, discussion of psychology and education, and nationalistic, reactionary vaunting of the Russian destiny over a corrupt Europe.

The essence of Dostoevskii's work is dialogue. Vladimir Nabokov, a noted critic of Dostoevskii's otherwise largely undisputed reputation, describes him as a writer who "seems to have been chosen by the destiny of Russian letters to become Russia's greatest playwright," but who "took the wrong turning and wrote novels" (*Lectures on Russian Literature*, 1982). Those novels are constantly destabilized by narrators, chroniclers, and a host of narrating characters who run amok through authorial corridors. Mikhail Bakhtin's identification of this dialogic structure as "polyphony" (in his *Problems of Dostoevsky's Poetics*) has been revolutionary to the understanding of Dostoevskii and highly influential in the development of modern structuralism. Dostoevskii creates from his settings of fateful threshold and crowded room, grubby town and fantastic city the fragmented universe inherited by the 20th-century novel. Nothing in Dostoevskii's work is single, whole, or certain, but his imperfective vision looks forward with a desperate hope for perfection.

—Christopher R. Pike

See the essays on *The Brothers Karamazov*, *Crime and Punishment*, *The Devils*, *The Idiot*, and *Notes from the Underground*.

DOUWES DEKKER, Edouard

See MULTATULI

DOVIZI DA BIBBINA, Bernardo

Born: Bernardo Dovizi, in Bibbiena, Casentino, Florentine Republic, 4 August 1470. **Career:** Entered the service of the Medicis at an early age: Florentine ambassador to Pope Alexander VI in Rome, 1492, and to King Alfonso II of Aragon and Naples, 1494; followed Pietro de'Medici into exile following his expulsion from Florence by the French, 1494, and, after Pietro's death in 1503, served his brother, Cardinal Giovanni de'Medici, as secretary; plenipotentiary for the Pope at the Congress of Mantua, 1512; on Giovanni's election as Pope Leo X in 1513, became papal treasurer and Cardinal of Santa Maria, Portico; thereafter pursued papal diplomatic and religious interests: enabled papal alliance with Austria, Switzerland, Venice, and Milan, 1515, acted as legate to the papal armies besieging Urbino, 1516, and travelled to France, 1518–19, to raise support for a new crusade against the Turks; obtained the bishop's palace in Costanza, 1518, but gave it to his friend Pietro Bembo, *q.v.* **Died:** 9 November 1520.

PUBLICATIONS

Plays

La Calandria (produced 1513). 1521; as *La Calandria*, 1786; edited by N. Borsellino, in *Commedie del Cinquecento 1*, 1967, also edited by P. Fossati, 1967, and by Giorgio Padoan, 1970; as *The Follies of Calandro*, translated by Oliver Evans, in *The Genius of the Italian Theater*, edited by Eric Bentley, 1964.

Other

Epistolario, edited by G.L. Moncallero. 2 vols., 1955–64.

*

Critical Studies: *Il cardinale Bibbiena* by A. Santelli, 1931; *Commedie fiorentine del Cinquecento: Mandragola; Clizia; Calandria* by Luigi Russo, 1939; *Il cardinale Bernardo Dovizi da Bibbiena, umanista e diplomatico (1470–1520)* by Giuseppe L. Mocallero, 1953; *The Birth of Modern Comedy in Renaissance Italy* by Douglas Radcliff-Umstead, 1969; "Women and the Management of Dramaturgy in *La Calandria*" by Laurie Detenbeck, in *Women in Italian Culture* edited by Ada Testaferri, 1989; "Drama and the Court in *La Calandria*" by Jack D'Amico, in *Theatre Journal*, 43(1), 1991.

*   *   *

In the Rome of the Medici popes, and at the court of Urbino that had produced Castiglione's *Il libro del cortegiano* (*The Book of the Courtier*), Bernardo Dovizi da Bibbiena had been a papal courtier from an early age, and later a politician, ambassador, and ultimately cardinal. Literature was a pastime for him and (other than some letters to contemporaries) the comedy *La Calandria* (*The Follies of Calandro*) is all that survives of his works. He assisted Giovanni de' Medici to become Pope Leo X in 1513, and there was speculation that Dovizi da Bibbiena may have been poisoned as his powerful position suggested that he might have been involved in an intrigue to succeed to the papacy. His influence and prestige are indicated by the number of references to him in *The Book of the Courtier*; Castiglione was also responsible for the celebrated production of *The Follies of Calandro* at Urbino in 1513 (and it is to Castiglione that the second prologue to the play has been attributed). This was the earliest production of an Italian play of which we have a full account. The comedy was published first in Siena in 1521, but was consistently staged (at least eight productions are recorded before 1550). An entertaining courtier and consummate literary craftsman, Dovizi da Bibbiena is characterized above all by humour and intelligence.

Dovizi da Bibbiena's masterpiece was first staged at the court of Urbino in the throne room of the ducal palace, with a set by Girolamo Genga. It was directed and staged-managed by Castiglione, whose letter about the staging provides a unique insight into the production. The principle of courtly patronage, in deference to the Duke of Urbino, was represented in hanging tapestries of stories from the history of Troy, reflecting the Duke's recent reconquest of the city, in an inscription in large letters which figured in the design, and in the proscenium arch, which has been compared with the twin towers and façade of the ducal palace itself, making an analogy between the playing space, the power of the Duke, and the Duke's "ideal" city-state. The surviving documentation identifies the playing space, seats for spectators, entries and exits, and the location of musicians.

In 1514, *The Follies of Calandro* was staged in Rome, in a production organized by Dovizi da Bibbiena himself with a set designed by the celebrated designer Peruzzi. A sketch survives that may have been for this production, showing the Urbino ducal palace façade translated into "Roman" terms, with twin temples based on the Pantheon replacing the two towers. This production has been seen as seminal for the entire subsequent history of the perspective set because of the link with Peruzzi (whose model "tragic" and "comic" set designs were to become standard points of reference), and since reference was made specifically to the Urbino staging for the Roman production.

In 1532 Mantua saw a production of the comedy. The unique documentation charts the progress of a dispute between the celebrated artist Giulio Romano, who designed the set, and the "director," Ippolito Calandra, over the question of whether the set should contain "flat" painted houses or representations of architecture in relief. But the most spectacular production of all was staged in Lyon in 1548, by the community of Florentines resident in the city, organized and funded by the Cardinal Ippolito d'Este, Archbishop of Lyon. Mounted in the great hall of the Archbishop's palace, the play was performed before a set depicting Florence, with recognizable monuments reproduced and the hall embellished with 12 giant statues of Florentine warriors and artists in a Parnassus celebrating the glories of Florence for resident expatriates. The performance was attended by the King of France, Henry II, and the *intermezzi* between the acts (of which full descriptive documentation survives) set a pattern in the courtier/patronage relationship, between the play and its illustrious patron, which was to be influential, and looks forward to the celebrated production of Bargagli's *Pellegrina* in Florence in 1589. Allegorical figures representing the ages of Iron, Bronze, Silver, and Gold dispute for the favours of the King, and are unrelated to the text of the comedy itself.

Uniquely therefore, the history of the staging of Dovizi da Bibbiena's *The Follies of Calandro* documents the importance of this comedy among the earliest in the ''vulgar'' tongue, sets the tone for dramatic representation of the stories from Boccaccio's *The Decameron* (its source), and establishes the relationship between comedy in performance, the city-state as playing space (in the reproduction of reality in the perspective set), the patronage network, and the intermingling of political and practical life with creativity in all the arts (painting, architecture, sculpture, writing, comedy, acting, and so on). And the multi-faceted façade of this concept of theatre echoes the careers of two of the most successful courtiers in the Renaissance: Dovizi da Bibbiena, the play's author, and Castiglione, its first director.

—Christopher Cairns

DROSTE-HÜLSHOFF, Annette von

Born: Anna Elisabeth Franziska Adolfine Wilhelmina Luisa Maria in Schloss Hülshoff near Münster, Westphalia, Germany, 10 January 1797. **Education:** Educated by private tutors. **Career:** Moved with her mother and sister to Rüschhaus following the death of her father in 1826; collaborated with the writer Levin Schücking from 1840 who encouraged her poetic activity; lived in Meersburg from 1846. Suffered from ill health throughout her life. **Died:** 24 May 1848.

PUBLICATIONS

Collections

Gesammelte Schriften, edited by Levin Schücking. 3 vols., 1878–79.
Sämtliche Werke, edited by Karl Schulte Kemminghausen. 4 vols., 1925–30.
Poems, edited by Margaret Atkinson. 1968.
Historisch-kritische Ausgabe: Werke, Briefwechsel, edited by Winfried Woesler. 14 vols., 1978–85.
Werke, edited by Clemens Heselhaus. 1984.

Verse

Walther. 1818.
Gedichte. 1838.
Das malerische und romantische Westfalen. 1839.
Gedichte. 1844.

Das geistliche Jahr. Nebst einem Anhang Religiöser Gedichte, edited by C.B. Schülter and Wilhelm Junkmann. 1851.
Letzte Gaben, edited by Levin Schücking. 1860.
Lebensgang, edited by Marie Silling. 1917.
Balladen. 1922.

Fiction

Die Judenbuche. 1851; as *The Jew's Beech*, translated by Lionel and Doris Thomas, 1958; as *The Jew's Beech Tree*, translated by Michael Bullock, in *Three Eerie Tales from 19th Century German*, 1975.
Ledwina (fragment). 1923.

Plays

Perdu; oder, Dichter, Verleger und Blaustrümpfe. 1840.

Other

Bilder aus Westfalen. 1845.
Briefe, edited by C. Schlueter. 1877.
Die Briefe von Annette von Droste-Hülshoff und Levin Schücking, edited by Theo Schücking. 1893.
Die Briefe der Dichterin Annette von Droste-Hülshoff, edited by Hermann Cardauns. 1909.
Dreiundzwanzig neue Droste-Briefe, edited by Manfred Schneider. 1923.
Briefe, edited by Karl Schulte Kemminghausen. 2 vols., 1944.
Lieder und Gesänge, edited by Karl Gustav Fellerer. 1954.

*

Bibliography: *Droste-Hülshoff Bibliographie* by Eduard Arens and Karl Schulte Kemminghausen, 1932.

Critical Studies: *Annette von Droste-Hülshoff* by Margaret Mare, 1965; *Annette von Droste-Hülshoff in Selbstzeugnissen und Bilddokumenten* by Peter Berglar, 1967; *Annette von Droste-Hülshoff. Werk und Leben* by Clemens Heselhaus, 1971; *Sinnbildsprache. Zur Bildstruktur des Geistlichen Jahres der Annette von Droste-Hülshoff* by Stephan Berning, 1975; *Annette von Droste-Hülshoff* by Ronald Schneider, 1977; *Annette von Droste-Hülshoff: A Woman of Letters in a Period of Transition*, 1981, and *Annette von Droste-Hülshoff: A Biography*, 1984, both by Mary Morgan; *Annette von Droste-Hülshoff: Die Judenbuche* by Klaus Moritz, 1981; *Annette von Droste-Hülshoff: A German Poet Between Romanticism and Realism* by John Guthrie, 1989; *Annette von Droste-Hülshoff: Die Judenbuche* by Heinz Rölleke, 1989; *Ambivalence Transcended: A Study of the Writings of Annette von Droste-Hülshoff* by Gertrude Bauer Pickar, 1997.

* * *

Annette von Droste-Hülshoff belonged to the group *Junges Deutschland* and is considered a writer of classical stature, certainly as one of Germany's greatest women poets.

Her interest in poetry was early stimulated by a one-time friend of August Bürger, a certain A. Spickmann. In 1814 she began a two-act romantic verse tragedy entitled *Berta*, a drama fragment of 2,000 lines which foreshadows her later mastery of writing. *Berta* deals with intrigue and with criticism of the ambitious nobility, and it contains a conspiracy against the prince, an evil Italian servant, diplomatic wedding negotiations, and a pair of true lovers separated by the exigencies of rank as well as by intrigue. Its author was wise to realize early on that the work was not a success and that drama was not her strength.

Another early work, the epic poem *Walther*, was completed in 1818, and is considered a most ambitious finished product. The poem mingles medieval cruelty and knightly idealism with modern sensibility. It contains lines of exceptional promise, as well as some narrative skill and the ability to sustain and round off her theme. The problem of man's deliberate waywardness and estrangement from God through a cherished "idol" is raised but not thoroughly worked out. In this poem, Droste-Hülshoff imitates Walther von der Vogelweide's *Kreuzlied* in an attempt to draw on genuine medieval sources as well as on nature. *Walther*, however, remained unsuccessful.

In 1824 Droste-Hülshoff began a novel *Ledwina*, which remained unfinished although some 50 pages were published posthumously. It is a fragment of her early prose work, having been begun about the year 1819. It was to remain a fragment, although she worked on it over the next five years of her life. There are elements in the prose passages which seem to belong expressly to a highly "romantic" phase of Droste-Hülshoff's life. Some critics believe that these "romantic" elements in her early work reveal, as well as Droste-Hülshoff's acquaintance with the literature of the time or at least with its mood, her own lifelong tendency to dwell on decay and death and the transience of all things. One reason for her decision not to finish *Ledwina* is to be found in her half-humorous remarks in a letter to her friend Spickmann on 8 February 1819 (*Die Briefe von Annette von Droste-Hülshoff*, vol. 1) that consumptive heroines were becoming rather too common, featuring in all the second-rate, sentimental literature.

Towards the end of 1820 Droste-Hülshoff began to write a cycle of devotional poems for her grandmother, reflecting the ecclesiastical calendar: *Das geistliche Jahr* [The Spiritual Year], published posthumously in 1851. It is a cycle of 72 poems which are of a confessional character and reflect not only piety but also a conscientious struggle with doubt. There is a song devoted to each Sunday of the year, and one for every church holiday. Although Droste-Hülshoff was a devout Catholic, there are few specific references to the Catholic church in her poems. *Das geistliche Jahr* gives the impression that Droste-Hülshoff was seeking a God who could not be found and that she had to go on seeking until death (in fact, she continued to revise the manuscript until a few months before her death).

In *Das geistliche Jahr* Droste-Hülshoff drew from such varied sources as books of scientific knowledge, like those her father had been interested in collecting for his library, containing facts about phenomena such as the "Phosphorpflanze," and from accounts of oriental travel, as well as the Bible, mystical literature and baroque verse, books of popular hymns, and classical and romantic verses. Her other poems, too, were indebted to such books. However, direct experience also plays a major role in shaping the poems.

Three epic poems, "Das Hospiz auf dem grossen St. Bernhard" [The Hospice on the St. Bernhard], "Des Arztes Vermächtnis" [The Doctor's Legacy], and "Die Schlacht am Loener Bruch" [The Battle at Loener Bog], were all published in her first collection of poems. "Das Hospiz" is apparently modelled on Sir Walter Scott's *Lady of the Lake* since Droste-Hülshoff was an enthusiastic devoteé of Scott's

work. These verses rarely express lyric sweetness or romantic sentiment; indeed, they are often repellent in their acerbic realism. But her love for the red soil of her native Westphalia, its forests, and its moors, is perhaps deeper than that of any other German poet for the homeland; and for nature's most hidden secrets she has an almost preternatural clearness of vision. Her technical mastery and self-abnegating restraint are classical in the pre-Romantic sense of the word, but her language is full of colour. In the above-mentioned epic poems, Droste-Hülshoff shows herself to be a woman of great earnestness, realistic observation, and deep psychological insight.

Her friend and literary adviser, the critic Levin Schücking, inspired her to work on her most famous works: the novella, *Die Judenbuche* (*The Jew's Beech Tree*), and the poems "Der Knabe im Moor" [The Young Boy in the Bog] and "Mondesaufgang" [The Rising Moon]. These three works are realistic and detailed descriptions contributing to an atmosphere of horror and gloom previously absent in her works.

The Jew's Beech Tree is a tragic tale of ignorance, crime, and social prejudice in which the sins of the fathers are visited upon the sons. The story was inspired by an actual murder in Westphalia. An old town drunk, Mergel, neglected and debauched, is found dead one day near an old beech tree. His son, Friedrich, disreputable and unsocial, murders a Jewish merchant to whom he owes money and places him beside the same beech tree where his own father died of drunkenness, then flees. All the Jews in the area come with a mysterious inscription in Hebrew and place it on the tree. After many years Friedrich returns; no one recognizes him, but the remembrance of his own act of murder leaves him no peace and he is found hanged on the beech tree. In this work, Droste-Hülshoff introduces new and modern elements: social injustice, environmental influence, the role of the conscience, and the psychology of crime.

After the publication of *The Jew's Beech Tree*, on which her reputation as a writer for a long time depended, Droste-Hülshoff began on the "Spiritus Familiaris des Rosstäuschers" [The Familiar Spirit of the Horse-Dealer]. In this work, her last ballad, Droste-Hülshoff shows a deep and genuine faith; in the old folklorist tradition, it tells of a man who accepts help from the devil and imperils his soul. It is a cross between a ballad and an epic poem and is considered one of her most mature works.

Bilder aus Westfalen [Pictures of Westphalia] appeared at first anonymously. These sketches of Westphalia describe the differing mental and physical types found in the districts of Sauerland, Paderborn, and Munsterland. They are shrewd and bold, so much so that they could not appear under her own name, but they were written with the same empathy as *The Jew's Beech Tree*, which was written as a result of Droste-Hülshoff's studies for *Bilder aus Westfalen*. These later writings show the remarkable nuances of wit and irony which balance, but never obscure, the humanity of her mature style. Until comparatively recently the aspect of Droste-Hülshoff's work most stressed by the literary historian was the amazing exactness and the visual and auditory quality of her descriptions. Other elements in her poems which contribute even more to her greatness were thus overlooked. What lends fascination to her thoughts are the symbols and images in which they are often clothed.

—Brigitte Edith Zapp Archibald

See the essay on *The Jew's Beech Tree*.

DU BELLAY, Joachim

Born: at the Château de la Turmelière, Liré, France, probably in 1522. **Education:** Studied law at the University of Poitiers, c. 1545. **Career:** Took minor clerical orders; writer by 1547: at Collège de Coqueret, Paris, with Ronsard and other writers; lived in Rome in the service of his relation, cardinal Jean Du Bellay, 1553–57. **Died:** 1 January 1560.

PUBLICATIONS

Collections

Oeuvres françaises, edited by Guillaume Aubert and Jean Morel. 1568.

Oeuvres poétiques, edited by Henri Chamard. 6 vols., 1907–31; revised by Yvonne Bellenger, 1982–85.

Collected Translations by C.H. Sisson. 1996.

Verse

L'Olive. 1549; enlarged edition, 1550.

Antérotique. 1549.

Vers lyriques. 1549.

Recueil de poésie. 1549; enlarged edition, 1553.

Oeuvres. 1552.

Hymnes. 2 vols., 1555–56.

Premier livre des antiquités de Rome. 1558; as *Ruins of Rome*, translated by Edmund Spenser, in *Complaints*, 1591.

Les Regrets et autres oeuvres poétiques. 1558; as *The Regrets*, translated by C.H. Sisson, 1984.

Divers jeux rustiques. 1558.

Poemata (in Latin). 1558.

Discours sur le sacre du treschrétien roi François I. 1558.

Ample discours au roi. 1567.

Xenia. 1569.

The Visions of Bellay [*Songe*], translated Edmund Spenser, in *Theatre for Worldlings*, edited by Jan Van Der Noot, 1569, reprinted 1939; revised in *Complaints*, 1591.

Poems, edited by Harold Walter Lawton, 1961.

Du Bellay (selected poems), edited by Marie-Hélène Richard. 1973.

La Monomachie de David et de Goliath (and other poems), edited by E. Caldarini. 1981.

L'Olive: An Anthology, edited by Thomas Thomson. 1986.

A Critical Edition of the Circumstantial Verse of Joachim Du Bellay, edited by David Julian Hartley. 2000.

Other

La Défence et illustration de la langue française. 1549; as *The Defence and Glorification of the French Language*, translated by Elizabeth Smulders, 1935; as *The Defence and Illustration of the French Language*, translated by Gladys M. Turquet, 1939.

Lettres, edited by Pierre de Nolhac. 1883.

*

Bibliography: *Du Bellay: A Bibliography* by Margaret B. Wells, 1974.

Critical Studies: *The Platonism of Du Bellay* by R.V. Merrill, 1925; *Histoire de la Pléiade* by Henri Chamard, 4 vols., 1939–40; *Du Bellay in Rome* by Gladys Dickinson, 1960; *Les Sources italiennes de la "Deffense et illustration de la langue françoise" de Joachim du Bellay* by Pierre Villey, 1970; *Du Bellay* by Louis C. Keating, 1971; *Spenser, Ronsard, and Du Bellay: A Renaissance Comparison* by Alfred W. Satterthwaite, 1972; *The Chaste Muse: A Study of Du Bellay's Poetry* by Dorothy Gabe Coleman, 1980; *Trials of Desire: Renaissance Defenses of Poetry* by Margaret W. Ferguson, 1983; *Du Bellay: Poems* by Kathleen M. Hall and Margaret Wells, 1985; *The Ordered Text: The Sonnet Sequences of Du Bellay* by Richard A. Katz, 1985; *Three French Short-Verse Satirists: Marot, Magny and Du Bellay* by William F. Panici, 1990; *The Poet's Odyssey: Joachim Du Bellay and the "Antiquitez de Rome"* by George Hugo Tucker, 1990; *Patriotism in the Work of Joachim Du Bellay: A Study of the Relationship Between the Poet and France* by David Hartley, 1993; *Ronsard and Du Bellay Versus Bèze: Allusiveness in Renaissance Literary Texts* by Malcolm C. Smith, 1995.

* * *

It was perhaps inevitable that Joachim Du Bellay should be overshadowed both in and after his lifetime by his friend and contemporary, Ronsard. Yet the fact remains that he is the author of some of the finest and best-known sonnets in the French language. These are for the most part to be found among the 191 sonnets of the *Les Regrets et autres oeuvres poétiques* (*The Regrets*) which, a mixture of elegy and satire, owe their inspiration to his progressive disenchantment with his life as a minor diplomat in Rome. Other, less famous, sonnets in the same collection are delightfully sharp sketches of Roman life in the 1550s and in particular of the intrigues of the papal court.

However, it was not just this personal frustration which triggered off Du Bellay's disillusionment. He seems to have been by temperament a melancholy man and as early as 1549 had written a "Chant du désespéré." Compared to Ronsard he was something of a lightweight intellectually, but he can appear more sensitive, and certainly more vulnerable. He seems indeed to have been a sick man (or at the very least a chronic hypochondriac) much of his life, which fact makes it all the more surprising that he should adopt the aggressive posture of a young man in a hurry in his first major publication, *La Défence et illustration de la langue française* (*The Defense and Illustration of the French Language*) published in 1549. This short work quickly established itself as the manifesto of the "Brigade" which had gathered around Ronsard, but later developments cast doubt on the extent to which Du Bellay himself subscribed to the views he expounded. In fact, parts of this "defence" of the French language were cribbed from an Italian treatise by Sperone Speroni (1542). Du Bellay seems concerned above all with demolishing the achievements of his predecessors among the French poets, whom he compares unfavourably with the Greek and Roman masters and with the Italians such as Petrarch. He soon outgrew his theories: his *L'Olive* is a Petrarchist *canzoniere* but within a few years Du Bellay claimed that he had forgotten the art of "petrarchizing," and one of the main strands of his work—the admonition against writing in Latin—is similarly forgotten in the mid-1550s when he set about composing his *Poemata*. In *The Regrets* he even renounces the *imitatio* which was supposed to raise the level of French poetry by a close imitation of Greek and Roman models. Du Bellay claims in this collection that he will write only what his "passion" dictates, thereby suggesting that he will restrict himself to his own personal misfortunes, without reference to illustrious examples or personal glory. Such disclaimers are perhaps more apparent than real. Certainly, in the 32 sonnets in the *Premier livre des antiquités de Rome* (*Ruins of Rome*) he sought to universalize his sense of bewilderment at the change of fortune of this once great city, victim of its own hubris.

But it is above all to *The Regrets* that the non-specialist poetry lover will wish to return again and again. In this sequence of sonnets Du Bellay emerges as one of the great poets of nostalgia, for a far-away country and for the illusions of youth; a poet, too, of solitude, who peoples his poems, mysteriously, with absences, and who turns his back both on the ambitions of his youth and on the meagre consolation of immortality through verse.

—Michael Freeman

See the essay on "Heureux qui, comme Ulysse, a fait un beau voyage."

DU FU

Also known as Tu Fu. **Pseudonym:** Pen name: Du Gonglou [Su of the East Slope]. **Born:** Xiangyang, Gong county, Henan province, China, in 712. Brought up by an aunt after his mother's death. **Education:** Received traditional Confucian education. **Family:** Married, with children. **Career:** Celebrated locally as a poet by age 15; traveller by 731; failed imperial examinations, 735, but finally obtained minor official posts, 751 and 757; thereafter often in poverty and unable to support his family; received patronage from an old friend in Chengdu, 760–65; travelled again in last years, contracting fatal illness while sailing up the Xiang River. His work received little attention until 1039, when an edition of 1,405 poems and 29 prose pieces was compiled. **Died:** 770.

PUBLICATIONS

Works

Qian qianyi [Works]. 1667 (includes 1,457 poems and 32 prose pieces); as *Dushi xiangzhu*, 1713 ("standard" text); as *Jiuja jizhu Dushi* (after 1181 compilation), 1796–1812; modern editions as: *Sibu beiyao*, 6 vols., 1936; *A Concordance to the Poetry of Tu Fu* (text and concordance), 3 vols., 1940, reprinted 1967; *Du shi quianzhu*, 1974; *Du shi xiangzhu*, 5 vols., 1979; selections: in *Gems of Chinese Literature*, translated by H.A. Giles, 1923; *The Autobiography of a Chinese Poet*, 1929, and *The Travels of a Chinese Poet*, 1936, both translated by Florence Ayscough; in *The White Pony*, translated by R. Payne, 1947; in *One Hundred Poems from the Chinese* (includes 35 poems by Du Fu), translated by Kenneth Rexroth, 1956; *Selected Poems*, edited by Feng Chih, translated by Rewi Alley, 1962; *A Little Primer of Tu Fu* (bilingual edition), edited and translated by David Hawkes, 1967; *Li Po and Tu Fu: Selected Poetry*, edited and translated by Arthur Cooper, 1973; *Selected Poems*, translated by David Hinton, 1989; *Three Chinese Poets: Translations of Poems by Wang Wei, Li Bai, and Du Fu*, translated by Vikram Seth, 1992; *Ruan Ji's Island and Tu*

Fu's In the Cities by Graham Hartill, 1993; *Endless River: Li Po and Tu Fu: A Friendship in Poetry*, edited by Sam Hamill, 1993; *Li-Tu: Ch'iu-p'u Verses & Scattered Sentiments: Poetic Cycles*, translation by Bradford S. Miller, 1997.

*

Critical Studies: *Tu Fu: China's Greatest Poet* (includes translations) by Wei Lien Hung, 1952; "Tu Fu, Lover of His People" by C. Feng, in *Chinese Literature*, 1955; *A Little Primer of Tu Fu* by D. Hawkes, 1967; *Tu Fu* by A.R. Davis, 1971; *The Great Age of Chinese Poetry: The High Tang* by Stephen Owen, 1980; *Du Fu's Laments from the South* by David R. McCraw, 1992; *Reconsidering Tu Fu: Literary Greatness and Cultural Context* by Eva Shan Chou, 1995.

*   *   *

Honoured as a the "Sage of Poetry," Du Fu is considered one of the greatest poets not only of the Tang dynasty but also in the history of Chinese literature, and his verse has been widely translated.

He travelled across the country for more than ten years when he was young. But judging from his extant poems, he did not write much during this happy period. He is best remembered for his later works. He thought of himself as a poet who had read "tens of thousands of books" and "could write poems like magic." So when he went to the city of Luoyang to sit for an imperial examination, he had full confidence in his success. However, he unexpectedly failed the exam, and thereafter began to travel extensively again.

Du Fu lived in an age when the feudal rulers became decadent and corrupt, during the demise of the Tang dynasty after it had enjoyed prosperity for more than a hundred years. Through various means he tried to get an official position, but without success. He was given only low-status positions, and for only brief periods. He returned to his itinerant life in later years, and lived in poverty till his death. The harshness of his life is reflected in one poem about his homecoming after an absence of ten years: "I heard loud wailing, entering the house; And found my youngest son had died of hunger." The misery of his life and his bitter experiences gave him a chance to see with his own eyes the chaos, poverty, and tragedy of the war-weary nation. His poems, which are filled with social themes mirroring this period of Chinese history, are thus often called "poetic history."

Du Fu was, on the whole, a realist poet. His poems explicitly express his concern for the common people and lament their sufferings, while implicitly satirizing the extravagant and licentious life of the Emperor and his concubines. His poem "A Ballad of Beautiful Women" exposes the decadence in the palace and the cruelty of the imperial prime minister. In his often-quoted lines "Meat and wine behind the doors of the powerful rich are becoming stinking, while in the streets corpses of the miserable people frozen to death are lying" he makes a striking contrast between the extravagant rich and the suffering poor.

Corruption and war were the root cause of the misery he described. The cruel and corrupt officials robbed the people, leaving them destitute—a situation compounded by the successive wars. In one poem he describes the desperate state of a typical village: "No one has been able to attend to farming. And since we're still in the midst of battles, All our children have gone to the eastern front." Many of his poems reflect the grief of lovers separated by war, and, above all, the desolate scene all over the war-torn country. Poems like "The Song of Chariots," "Farewell of the Newlyweds," and "Husband on an Expedition," epitomize the bitter and tragic situation during the war: "Grass smells of the lying corpses, The vast plains are flooded with blood." In "Farewell of an Old Man," the narrator pours out his grievances: "My sons and grandsons lost in war, What's the use of staying home to save my skin?" Another poem, "Recruiting Officer of Shihao," presents a heartbreaking picture of an old woman whose "three sons have have left for garrison duty at Ye." She receives a letter from one of them breaking the news that the other two have recently died in battle: "Now there's no other man in the house, Only a grandson at his mother's breast. The child's mother has not gone away; She has only a tattered skirt to wear." In other words, there is no one left for the officer to recruit except the feeble old woman herself. In numerous poems Du Fu expresses the hope that war will soon come to an end and that the people will be allowed to live in peace. He used his poems to show his sympathy with ordinary people, comment on state affairs, and reproach the wrong-doings of the rulers.

Du Fu was more than a political poet, however. His verse covers a wide range of subjects and includes various forms including pastoral, narrative and lyric poetry, folk songs and ballads (*yuefu*). His "Autumn Thoughts," "A Spring Night—Rejoicing in the Rain," and a number of other poems portray the beauty of nature. His genius for diction, excellent mastery of rhythm and rhyme, and astonishing skill at creating images, gave such beauty to his poetry and won him so much renown that no poet in the history of Chinese literature has attracted so many followers and influenced so much later poetry.

—Binghong Lu

DU GARD, Roger Martin

See MARTIN DU GARD, Roger

DU GONGLOU

See DU FU

DUMAS *FILS*, Alexandre

Born: Paris, France, 28 July 1824, the illegitimate son of the writer Alexandre Dumas *père, q.v.* **Education:** Educated at the Pension Goubaux and the Collège Bourbon. **Family:** Married 1) Nadejda Knorring (neé Naryschkine) in 1864 (died 1895), two daughters, one before marriage; 2) Henriette Régnier de la Brière in 1895. **Career:** Lived with father in Saint-Germain-en-Laye, 1843–51; travelled with father to Spain and Algeria, 1846–47; wrote for the Théâtre du Gymnase, and later in career, for the Comédie-Française. Elected to the Académie française, 1875. **Died:** 28 November 1895.

PUBLICATIONS

Collection

Théâtre complet. 10 vols., 1923.

Fiction

Aventures de quatre femmes et d'un perroquet. 6 vols., 1846–47.
La Dame aux camélias. 2 vols., 1848; as *The Lady with the Camelias*, translated anonymously, 1856; as *The Camelia-Lady*, translated anonymously, 1857; as *The Lady of the Camellias*, translated by William Walton, 1897; as *Camille*, translated by Henrietta Metcalf, 1931; also translated by Edmund Gosse, 1952; David Coward, 1986.
Césarine. 1848.
Le Docteur Servans. 2 vols., 1848–49.
Le Roman d'une femme. 4 vols., 1849.
Antoine. 2 vols., 1849.
La Vie à vingt ans. 2 vols., 1850; as *Paris Life at Twenty*, translated anonymously, 1863; as *The American Girl in Paris*, translated by Llewellyn Williams, 1891.
Tristan le roux. 3 vols., 1850; as *The Beggar of Nimes*, 1988.
Trois hommes forts. 4 vols., 1850.
Diane de Lys et Grangette. 3 vols., 1850.
Le Régent Mustel. 2 vols., 1852 (originally published as *Les Revenants* as an offprint from *Le Pays*, 1852); as *The Resuscitated*, translated by G. de Croij, 1877.
Contes et nouvelles. 1853.
La Dame aux perles. 4 vols., 1853; as *The Lady with the Pearl Necklace*, translated by M. Maury, 1901.
Sophie Printems. 2 vols., 1854.
Un Cas de rupture. 1854.
L'Affaire Clemenceau. 1866; as *The Clemenceau Case*, translated anonymously, n.d; as *Wife Murderer*, translated by H.L. Williams, 1866; as *Belle*, translated anonymously, 1888.

Plays

Atala, music by P. Varney. 1848.
La Dame aux camélias (produced 1852). 1852; edited by Roger J.B. Clark, 1972; as *La Dame aux camélias*, translated by Frederick A. Schwab, 1880; as *The Lady of the Camelias*, translated by Edith Reynolds and Nigel Playfair, 1930, in *Camille*, edited by S.S. Stanton, 1958; as *Camille*, translated by Henriette Metcalf, 1931; also translated by Edmund Gosse, 1937; Barbara Bray, 1975.
Diane de Lys (produced 1853). 1853.
Éva, with A. Montjoye and R. Deslandes (produced 1854). 1854.
Le Bijou de la reine (produced 1855). In *Théâtre complet.* 1868.
Le Demi-monde (produced 1855). 1855: as *The Demi-Monde: A Satire on Society*, translated by E.G. Squier, 1858; as *The Outer Edge of Society*, translated by Allison Smith and Robert Bell Michell, 1921.
Comment la trouves-tu?, with others (produced 1857). 1857.
La Question d'argent (produced 1857). 1857; as *The Money Question*, translated by B.W. Cragin and others, in *Poet Lore*, 26, 1915.
Le Fils naturel (produced 1858). 1858; as *Le fils naturel*, translated by T.L. Oxley, 1879.
Un Mariage dans un chapeau, with Auguste Vivier (produced 1859). 1859.
Un Père prodigue (produced 1859). 1859.

L'Ami des femmes (produced 1864). 1864; as *The Friend of Women*, translated anonymously, n.d.

Le Supplice d'une femme, with Émile de Girardin (produced 1865). 1865.

Héloïse Paranquet, with Anne-Adrien-Armand Durantin (produced 1866). 1866.

Les Idées de Madame Aubray (produced 1867). 1867.

Le Filleul de Pompignac, with A. de Jolin and N. Fournier (produced 1869). 1869.

Une visite de noces (produced 1871). 1872.

La Princesse Georges (produced 1871). 1872; translated as *La Princesse Georges*, 1881.

La Femme de Claude (produced 1873). 1873; as *Claude's Wife*, translated anonymously, n.d.

Monsieur Alphonse (produced 1873). 1874; as *M. Alphonse*, translated anonymously, 1886.

Les Danicheff, with Pyotr Korvin-Krukovsky (produced 1876). 1879.

La Comtesse Romani, with Gustave-Eugène Fould (produced 1876). 1878.

L'Étrangère (produced 1876). 1877; as *The Foreigner*, translated anonymously, 1881; as *L'Étrangère*, translated by Frederick A. Schwab, 1888.

La Princesse de Bagdad (produced 1881). 1881; as *The Princess of Bagdad*, translated anonymously, 1881.

Théâtre complet. 7 vols., 1882–93.

Denise (produced 1885). 1885; as *Denise*, translated anonymously, 1888.

Francillon (produced 1887). 1887.

Théâtres des autres (includes collaborative works). 2 vols., 1894.

Verse

Péchés de jeunesse. 1847.

Other

Histoire de la loterie. 1851.

Histoire du "Supplice d'une femme." 1865.

Les Madeleines repenties. 1869.

Nouvelle lettre de Junius à son ami A.D. 1871.

La Révolution plébéienne: Lettres à Junius. 1871.

Une lettre sur les choses du jour. 1871.

Nouvelle lettre sur les choses du jour. 1871.

L'Homme-Femme. 1872; as *Man-Woman*, edited and translated by George Vandenhoff, 1873.

Entr'actes. 3 vols., 1878–79.

Les Femmes qui tuent et les femmes qui votent. 1880.

La Question du divorce. 1880.

Lettre à M. Naquet. 1882.

La Recherche de la paternité. 1883.

Nouveaux Entr'actes. 1890.

*

Critical Studies: *Les Idées sociales dans le théâtre de Dumas* by C.M. Noël, 1912; *Dumas, Father and Son* by Francis Gribble, 1930; *Le Théâtre de Dumas fils et la société contemporaine* by O. Cheorgiu, 1931; *The Theatre of Alexandre Dumas fils* by F.A. Taylor, 1937; *The Prodigal Father: Dumas Père et Fils and "The Lady of the Camellias"* by Edith Saunders, 1951; *Three Musketeers: A Study of the Dumas Family* by André Maurois, translated, 1957; *Alexandre Dumas*

fils by A. Lebois, 1969; *La fleur du mal: La véritable histoire de la Dame aux camélias* by Micheline Boudet, 1993; *Dumas: Père et fils* by Yves-Marie Lucot, 1997; *A Critical Edition of La route de Thèbes*, edited with introduction by H.D. Lewis, 1998.

* * *

Like his father, Alexandre Dumas *fils* was a prolific author of both novels and plays, though his major success was on the stage. After an early volume of poetry, *Péchés de jeunesse* [Sins of Youth], Dumas *fils* turned to the novel, writing 14 between 1846 and 1854. Although the best of these, *La Dame aux camélias* (*Camille*), *Diane de Lys*, and *La Dame aux perles* (*The Lady with the Pearl Necklace*), showed promise, the work that truly established his literary career was his stage adaptation of *Camille*. This presented a social situation new to the French stage, with characters speaking a language which, if flowery and rhetorical to modern ears, was far closer to everyday speech than mid-19th-century audiences were accustomed to hearing on stage. With its sympathetic portrayal of the doomed courtesan who finds love too late to escape the fatal result of her dissipated life, *Camille*, after an initial battle with censorship, achieved an enormous success.

Dumas *fils*'s second stage adaptation, *Diane de Lys*, is a distinctly grimmer study of a neglected wife who pursues an affair with a young artist whom her husband finally kills. Although Dumas was attempting to preach a moral lesson here, the contribution of the husband to his own problems was so clear that he gained little sympathy. Much clearer morally was the more original and more successful *Le Demimonde* (*The Outer Edge of Society*), an unsentimental study of a world on the fringes of polite society, eager at any price to achieve the respectability society could offer. Suzanne d'Ange dreams of a proper marriage that will confirm her respectability, but Olivier de Jain, a protector of polite society from such contamination, frustrates her ambitions. De Jain is the first of Dumas *fils*'s *raisonneurs*, a key figure in the new "thesis play," which illustrates some contemporary social or moral question, with the *raisonneur* serving as spokesman for the author.

The Outer Edge of Society differs from most thesis plays in that the social point of view it expresses is essentially the same as the members of society who would attend this play. Later thesis plays, from Dumas's own to those of Ibsen and Shaw, regularly challenged widely held social and moral beliefs and practice. Dumas turned in this direction with *La Question d'argent* (*The Money Question*), which challenged certain ideas prevalent in Dumas's society concerning the acquisition of wealth, and *Le Fils naturel*, which challenged social attitudes toward illegitimate children, with the added titillation of the author's own birth being illegitimate. *Un Père prodigue* [A Prodigal Father] clearly serves as a companion piece to *Le Fils naturel* and if the traits of Dumas *fils* are rather difficult to trace in the melodramatically idealized Jacques, those of Dumas *père* seem clearly in evidence in the larger-than-life prodigal father, presented, for all his faults, with obvious affection.

L'Ami des femmes (*The Friend of Women*) utilized Dumas *fils*'s new interest in psychology. His *raisonneur*, de Ryons, "the woman's friend," has made a study of the female mind and thus is able to anticipate and to thwart Jane de Simerose's temptation toward adultery. More novels appeared after 1854, but only one, *L'Affaire*

Clemenceau (*The Clemenceau Case*), had a real success. It claimed to be the prison journal of a husband who has murdered his unfaithful wife after a last night of love.

Les Idées de Madame Aubray [Madame Aubray's Ideas] was one of Dumas's most unconventional works, not only because he turned at last to a strong central female character, but also because of its religious theme. Mme. Aubray is a zealous Christian torn between her beliefs and her desire to save her son from a marriage to a "fallen woman." Less openly religious but similarly admirable is Séverine, the heroine of *La Princesse Georges*, who redeems her unfaithful husband by forgiving him. During the late 1860s Dumas began to create long prefaces in the later manner of Shaw, carrying out his project for a "useful theatre" by promulgating his ideas on love, marriage, divorce, abortion, and a whole range of social and moral concerns. The 1870 Franco-Prussian War also inspired a series of important public letters from him, as had the uprisings of 1848, letters expressing a fear of democratic government leading to anarchy.

La Femme de Claude (*Claude's Wife*) attempted a symbolic statement on the war and its causes, but the realistic context and melodramatic characters confused the public. Claude, a noble, patriotic Frenchman, marries a foreign wife who betrays his love and steals military secrets. Claude, discovering her perfidy, kills her. A much lighter note was struck this same year by *Monsieur Alphonse*, another study of a fallen woman, this one repentant and forgiven by a magnanimous husband. Monsieur Alphonse, the manipulative seducer, is one of Dumas's most successful characters.

L'Etrangère (*The Foreigner*), Dumas *fils*'s first play written for the Comédie-Française, depicts an unhappy arranged marriage, and although in this story the villainous husband is conveniently killed in a duel, Dumas felt clearly that society should provide a more thoughtful solution. The result was his famous pamphlet *La Question du divorce*, followed by a statement championing women's rights, *Les Femmes qui tuent et les femmes qui votent* [Women who Kill and Women who Vote], and one on illegitimacy, *La Recherche de la paternité* [A Study on Paternity]. Although each of these aroused great controversy, all were instrumental in inspiring important new social legislation in France.

Dumas *fils*'s political statements encouraged a negative public reaction to *La Princesse de Bagdad* (*The Princess of Bagdad*), but it is one of his weaker plays, another study of a spoiled, headstrong wife and a forgiving husband. His last two plays were more substantial and more successful. *Denise* presents a moving and convincing picture of a young woman who gives up her present happiness by confessing a sexual sin in her past in order to protect another young woman from marrying her seducer. *Francillon* shows a wife, tired of her husband's amorous intrigues, who boasts to him (falsely) of carrying out an affair of her own, thus curing him.

With the exception of *Camille*, none of Dumas *fils*'s theatre survives today, and even *Camille* is often regarded as little more than sentimental melodrama. In his own time, however, Dumas *fils* was regarded as a bold portrayer of contemporary life with a powerful and often effective commitment to social concerns. The modern "problem play" of Ibsen, Shaw, and their followers would scarcely have been possible without his example.

—Marvin Carlson

See the essay on *Camille*.

DUMAS *PÈRE*, Alexandre (Davy de la Pailleterie)

Born: Villers-Cotterêts, France, 24 July 1802. **Education:** Educated at local school. **Family:** Married Ida Ferrier in 1840 (separated 1844; died 1861); had a son, the writer Alexandre Dumas *fils*, *q.v.*, by Catharine Labay, a daughter by Mélanie Serre, a son by Anna Bauër, and a daughter by Émilie Cordier. **Career:** Articled at age 14 to a solicitor in Villers-Cotterêts, and one in Crépy, until 1822; employed in the secretariat of the Duc d'Orléans, 1822–29, and entered literary circle of Charles Nodier: librarian, Palais Royal, 1829; successful playright, then historical novelist (often revising and polishing works written first by someone else); co-founder, Théâtre Historique, Paris, 1847–50; editor (and copious contributor), *La Liberté*, 1848; founding editor, *La France nouvelle*, 1848, and *Le Mois*, 1848–50; declared bankrupt and moved to Brussels, 1852, returned to Paris in 1853; founding editor, *Le Mousquetaire*, 1853–57, and the weekly *Le Monte-Cristo*, 1857–60; aided Garibaldi's invasion of Sicily, 1860–61; director of excavations and museums, Naples, 1860–61; editor *Journal de Jeudi*, 1860, and *L'indipendente*, Naples, 1860–64; returned to France, 1864; revived *Le Mousquetaire*, 1866–67; editor, *Le D'Artagnan*, 1868, and *Théâtre Journal*, 1868–69. **Awards:** Chevalier, Légion d'honneur, 1837; Order of Isabella the Catholic (Belgium); Cross of Gustavus Vasa (Sweden); Order of St. John of Jerusalem. **Died:** 5 December 1870.

PUBLICATIONS

Collections

Oeuvres complètes. 286 vols., 1848–1900.
Théâtre complet. 15 vols., 1863–74.
Oeuvres complètes. 301 vols., 1885–88.
The Romances. 60 vols., 1893–97; 10 vols., 1896.
The Novels, translated by Alfred Allinson. 56 vols., 1903–11.

Fiction

Nouvelles contemporaines. 1826.
Souvenirs d'Antony. 1835; as *The Recollections of Antony*, translated by Jeremy Griswold, 1849; as *The Reminiscences of Antony*, 1905.
Guelfes et Gibelins. 1836; as *Guelphs and Ghibellines*, 1905.
Isabelle de Bavière. 1836; as *Isabel of Bavaria*, translated by William Barrow, 1846.
La Main droite du Sire de Giac. 1838; as *The King's Favourite*, 1906.
Le Capitaine Paul, with Adrien Dauzats. 2 vols., 1838; as *Captain Paul*, translated by Thomas Williams, 1846; as *Paul Jones*, translated by William Berger, 1839; as *Paul Jones, the Son of the Sea*, translated 1849; as *Paul Jones: A Nautical Romance*, translated by Henry Llewellyn Williams, 1889; as *Paul Jones, the Bold Privateer*, n.d.
La Salle d'armes (includes *Pauline*; *Pascal Bruno*; *Murat*). 1838; parts translated under the following titles: *Pascal Bruno*, edited by Theodore Hook, 1837; *Pauline: A Tale of Normandy*, translated by "A Lady of Virginia," 1842; *The Sicilian Bandit*, 1859; *Pauline, Pascal Bruno, and Bontekoe*, translated by Alfred Allinson, 1904.

Acté. 1839; as *Acté*, translated by Henry William Herbert, 1847; also translated by Alfred Allinson, 1904.

Les Crimes célèbres, with others. 1839–40; as *Celebrated Crimes*, translated 1843; also translated by I.G. Burnham, 8 vols., 1887; as *The Celebrated Crimes of History*, 8 vols., 1895; parts published as *The Crimes of the Borgias and Others*, 1907; *The Crimes of Urbain Grandier and Others*, 1907; *The Crimes of Ali Pacha and Others*, 1908; *The Crimes of the Marquise de Brinvilliers and Others*, 1908.

La Comtesse de Salisbury. 1839; as *The Countess of Salisbury*, 1851.

Monseigneur Gaston Phoebus. 1839.

Mémoires d'un maître d'armes. 1840; as *The Fencing-Master*, translated by G. Griswold, 1850.

Aventures de John Davys. 1840.

Maître Adam le Calabrais. 1840.

Othon l'archer. 1840; as *Otho the Archer*, 1860.

Praxéde. 1841.

La Chasse au Chastre. 1841; as *The Bird of Fate*, 1906.

Aventures de Lyderic. 1842; as *Lyderic, Count of Flanders*, 1903; as *Adventures of Lyderic*, 1981.

Jehanne la Pucelle. 1842; as *Joan the Heroic Maiden*, 1847.

Albine. 1843; as *Le Château d'Eppstein*, 1844; as *The Spectre Mother*, 1864; as *The Castle of Eppstein*, translated by Alfred Allinson, 1904.

Le Chevalier d'Harmental, with Auguste Maquet. 1843; as *The Chevalier d'Harmental*, translated by P.F Christin and Eugene Lies, 1846; as *The Chateau d'Harmental*, 1856; as *The Orange Plume*, translated by Henry L. Williams, Jr., 1860; as *The Conspirators*, 1910.

La Comtesse de Saint-Géran; as *The Countess of Saint-Géran*, 1843.

Georges. 1843; as *George*, translated by G.J. Knox, 1846; also translated by Samuel Spring, 1847; as *Georges*, translated by Alfred Allinson, 1904.

Ascanio, with Paul Meurice. 1843–44; as *Ascanio*, translated by Eugene Lies and Eugene Plunkett, 1846; as *Francis I*, 1849.

Le Comte de Monte-Cristo, with Auguste Maquet. 1844–45; edited by David Coward (in English), 1990; as *The Count of Monte Cristo*, 1846; also translated by Henry Llewellyn Williams, 1892; William Thiese, 1892; Steven Grant, 1990; as *The Chateau d'If: A Romance*, translated by Emma Hardy, 1846.

Amaury, with Paul Meurice. 1844; as *Amaury*, translated by "E.P.," 1844; also translated by Alfred Allinson, 1904.

Une âime à naître [*Histoire d'une âme*]. 1844.

Cécile. 1844; as *La Robe de noces*, 1844; as *Cecile*, translated by Eugene Plunkett, 1847; also translated by Alfred Allinson, 1904; as *The Wedding Dress*, translated by Fayette Robinson, 1851.

Fernande. 1844; as *Fernande*, 1904; also translated by A. Craig Bell, 1988.

Une fille du régent, with Auguste Maquet. 1844; as *The Regent's Daughter*, translated by Charles H. Town, 1845.

Les Frères corses. 1844; as *The Corsican Brothers*, translated by Henry William Herbert, 1845; also translated by Gerardus Van Dam, 1883; Alfred Allison, 1904.

Les Trois Mousquetaires, with Auguste Maquet. 1844; edited by David Coward (in English), 1991; as *The Three Guardsmen*, translated by Park Benjamin, 1846; as *The Three Musketeers*, translated by William Barrow, 1846; also translated by William Robson, 1860; Henry Llewellyn Williams, 1892; A. Curtis Bond, 1894; Alfred Allinson, 1903; Philip Schuyler Allen, 1923; J. Walker McSpadden, 1926; Jacques Le Clercq, 1950; Isabel Ely Lord, 1952; Lord Sudley, 1952; Marcus Clapham and Clive Reynard, 1992.

Gabriel Lambert. 1844; translated as *The Galley Slave*, 1849; as *Gabriel Lambert*, 1904.

Invraisemblance [*Histoire d'un mort*]. 1844.

Sylvandire, with Auguste Maquet. 1844; as *Sylvandire*, translated by Thomas Williams, 1847, as *The Disputed Inheritance*, translated by Williams, 1847; as *The Young Chevalier*, 1850; as *Beau Tancrede*, 1861.

La Guerre des femmes, with Auguste Maquet. 1845–46; as *Nanon*, 1847; as *The War of Women*, translated by Samuel Spring, 1850.

La Reine Margot, with Auguste Maquet. 1845; as *Margaret de Navarre*, 1845; as *Marguerite de Valois*, 1846; also translated by S. Fowler Wright, 1947; as *Queen Margot*, translated 1885.

Vingt ans après, with Auguste Maquet. 1845; edited by David Coward (in English), 1993; as *Cardinal Mazarin; or, Twenty Years After*, n.d.; as *Twenty Years After*, translated by "E.P.," 1846; also translated by William Barrow, 1846; Henry Llewellyn Williams, 1899; Alfred Allinson, 1904; as *Cromwell and Mazarin*, 1847.

Le Chevalier de Maison-Rouge, with Auguste Maquet. 1845; translated as *Marie Antoinette*, 1846; as *Genevieve*, translated by Henry William Herbert, 1846; as *Chateau-Rouge*, 1859; as *The Knight of Redcastle*, translated by Henry Llewellyn Williams, 1893; as *The Chevalier de Maison-Rouge*, 1877.

La Dame de Monsoreau, with Auguste Maquet. 1846; as *Diana of Meridor*, 1846; as *Chicot the Jester*, 1857; as *La Dame de Monsoreau*, 1889; also translated by J. Walker McSpadden, 1926; as *Diane*, 1901.

Mémoires d'un médecin: Joseph Balsamo, with August Maquet. 1846–48; parts translated under the following titles: *Memoirs of a Physician*, 1847; *Andrée de Taverney; or, The Downfall of French Monarchy*, translated by Henry L. Williams, Jr., 2 vols., 1862; *The Chevalier*, 1864; *Balsamo; or, Memoirs of a Physician*, 1878; *Joseph Balsamo*, 1878; *The Mesmerist's Victim*, translated by Henry Llewellyn Williams, 1893.

Le Bâtard de Mauléon, with Auguste Maquet. 1846; as *The Bastard of Mauleon*, 1849; as *The Knight of Mauléon*, 1850; as *The Half Brothers*, 1858; as *The Iron Hand, or, The Knight of Mauleon*, 1858; as *Agénor de Mauléon*, 1897.

Les Quarante-cinq, with Auguste Maquet. 1848; as *The Forty-Five Guardsmen*, 1847; also translated by J. Walker McSpadden, 1926; as *The Forty-Five*, 1889.

Le Vicomte de Bragelonne; ou, Dix ans plus tard, with Auguste Maquet. 1848–50; edited by John Kennett (in English), 1970, and by David Coward (in English), 1991; as *The Vicomte de Bragelonne*, translated by Thomas Williams, 1848, as *Bragelonne, the Son of Athos; or, Ten Years Later*, translated by Williams, 1848, as *The Iron Mask*, 1850; as *Louise La Vallière*, 1851; also translated by Alfred Allinson, 1904; as *The Man in the Iron Mask*, translated by Henry Llewellyn Williams, 1889, this translation also published as *The Vicomte de Bragelonne*, 1892, and *Louise de la Vallière*, 1892; as *Louise de la Vallière*, translated by J. Walker McSpadden, 1901; as *The Man in the Iron Mask*, revised and updated by Jacqueline Rogers, 1998.

Les mille et un fantômes. 1848–51; as *Tales of the Supernatural* [*Strange Adventures, Terror*], 1907–09.

Le Collier de la Reine, with Auguste Maquet. 1849; as *The Queen's Necklace*, translated by Thomas Williams, 1850; also translated by Henry Llewellyn Williams, 1892.

Ange Pitou, with Auguste Maquet. 1849; as *Taking the Bastille*, n.d.; as *Six Years Later*, translated by Thomas Williams, 1851; as *The Royal Life-Guard*, translated by Henry Llewellyn Williams, 1893; as *Ange Pitou*, 1907.

Les Mariages du père Olifus, with Paul Bocage. 1849; as *The Man with Five Wives*, 1850.

Le Trou de l'enfer. 1850–51; as *The Mouth of Hell*, 1906.

La Tulipe noire. 1850; as *Rosa; or, The Black Tulip*, translated by Franz Demmler, 1854, and edited by David Coward, 1993; as *The Black Tulip*, translated by A.J. O'Connor, 1902; also translated by Mary D. Frost, 1902; S.J. Adair Fitz-Gerald, 1951.

La Colombe. 1851; as *The Dove*, 1906.

Dieu dispose. 1851–52; as *God's Will Be Done*, 1909.

La Comtesse de Charny. 1852–55; as *The Countess de Charny*, translated 1853; as *La Comtesse de Charny*, 1890; as *The Countess of Charny*, translated by Henry Llewellyn Williams, 1892.

Un Gil-Blas en Californie. 1852; as *A Gil Blas in California*, 1933.

Isaac Laquedem. 1852–53.

Conscience l'innocent. 1852; as *The Conscript*, 1855; as *Conscience*, translated by Alfred Allinson, 1902.

Olympe de Clèves. 1852; as *Olympia of Cleves; or, The Loves of a King*, 1887; as *Olympe de Clèves*, 1893; as *Madame de Mailly*, 1896.

Emmanuel Philibert. 1852–54; as *Le Page du duc de Savoie*, 1855; as *Emmanuel-Philibert*, 1854; as *The Page of the Duke of Savoy*, 1861.

Le Pasteur d'Ashbourne. 1853.

El Saltéador. 1854; as *The Brigand*, translated with *Blanche de Beaulieu*, 1897; with *The Horoscope*, 1897.

Ingénue. 1854; as *Ingénue; or, The First Days of Blood*, translated by Julie de Marguerittes, 1855.

Les Mohicans de Paris; Salvator le Commissionnaire, with Paul Bocage. 1854–59; as *The Mohicans of Paris*, 1859; also translated by R.S. Garnett, 1926; *The Horrors of Paris*, 1875; parts translated by Mary Neal Sherwood under the following titles: *Salvator*, 1882, *Conrad de Valgeneuse*, 1900, *Rose-de-noël*, 1900, *The Chief of Police*, 1900, *Monsieur Sarranti*, 1900, and *Princess Régina*, 1900.

Catherine Blum. 1854; as *The Foresters*, 1854; as *Catherine Blum*, 1861.

Les Compagnons de Jéhu. 1857; as *Roland of Montreval*, 1860; as *The Company of Jehu*, translated by Katharine Prescott Wormeley, 1894; as *The Companions of Jehu*, 1894; as *The Aide-de-Camp of Napoleon*, 1897.

Charles le téméraire. 2 vols., 1857; as *Charles the Bold*, 1860.

Le Meneur de loups. 1857; as *The Wolf-Leader*, translated by Alfred Allinson, 1904.

Black. 1858; as *Black*, 1895.

Le Capitaine Richard. 1858; as *The Twin Captains*, 1861; as *The Young Captain*, 1870; as *The Twin Lieutentants*, 1877.

Herminie. 1858.

L'Horoscope. 1858; as *The Horoscope*, with *The Brigand*, 1897; also translated by Mary Stuart Smith, 1900.

Les Louves de Machecoul. 1859; as *The Castle of Souday*, translated by Henry L. Williams, Jr., 1862, this translation also published as *Royalist Daughters*, 1862; as *The Last Vendee; or, The She-Wolves of Machecoul*, 1894; as *The She-Wolves of Machecoul*, with *The Corsican Brothers*, 1894.

Ammalet Beg. 1859; as *Sultanetta*, translated in *Tales of the Caucasus*, 1895.

L'Histoire d'un cabanon et d'un chalet. 1859; as *Monsieur Coumbes*, 1860; as *Le Fils de Forçat*, 1864; as *The Convict's Son*, 1905.

La Princesse Flora. 1859.

Jane. 1859; as *Jane*, with *Crop-Ear Jacquot*, 1903.

Le Chasseur de Sauvagine. 1859; as *The Wild Duck Shooter*, 1906.

Le Médecin de Java. 1859(?); as *L'Île de feu*, 1870; as *Doctor Basilius*, translated 1860.

Madame de Chamblay, 1859.

Une aventure d'amour. 1860.

Le Père la Ruine, with de Cherville. 1860; as *Père la Ruine*, translated by Alfred Allinson, 1905.

La Maison de glace, 1860; as *The Russian Gipsy*, 1860.

Jacquot sans oreilles. 1860; as *Crop-Ear Jacquot*, with *Jane*, 1903; also translated by Alfred Allinson, in *Crop-Eared Jacquot and Other Stories*, 1905.

Les Drames galants, La Marquise d'Escoman. 1860.

Une nuit à Florence. 1861.

La San-Felice [*Emma Lyonna*]. 1864–65; as *Love and Liberty*, 1869; as *The Lovely Lady Hamilton*, 1903; as *Love and Liberty; or, Nelson at Naples*, translated by R.S. Garnett, 1917; as *The Neapolitan Lovers*, translated by Garnett, 1917.

La Pêche aux filets. 1864.

Le Comte de Moret. 1866; as *The Count of Moret*, translated by Henry L. Williams, Jr., 1868.

La Terreur prussienne. 1867; as *The Prussian Terror*, translated by R.S. Garnett, 1915.

Les Blancs et les bleus. 1867–68; as *The Polish Spy*, 1869; as *The First Republic*, 1894; as *The Whites and the Blues*, 1894.

Les Hommes de fer. 1867.

L'Huitième Croisade. 1868; as *The Eighth Crusade*, 1890.

Parisiens et provinciaux, with de Cherville. 1868; as *Parisians and Provincials*, translated and edited by A. Craig Bell, 1995.

Création et rédemption: Le Docteur mystérieux, La Fille du marquis. 1872.

Le Comte de Beuzeval; as The Count of Beuzeval, 1889.

Short Stories (in English). 1927.

Plays

La Chasse et l'amour, with Adolphe de Leuven and Pierre-Joseph Rousseau (produced 1825).

La Noce et l'enterrement, with E.H. Lassagne (produced 1826).

Henri III et sa cour (produced 1829). 1829.

Christine (produced 1830). 1830.

Antony (produced 1831). 1831; edited by Maurice Baudin (in English), 1929; as *Antony*, translated by Frederick A. Schwab, 1880.

Napoléon Bonaparte (produced 1831). 1831.

Charles VII chez ses grands vassaux (produced 1831). 1831; as *Charles VII at the Homes of His Great Vassals*, translated by D.T. Bonett, 1992.

Richard Darlington, with Dinaux (produced 1831). 1832.

La Tour de Nesle, from play by Frédéric Gaillardet (produced 1832). 1832; as *The Tower of Nesle*, translated by George Almar, 1850(?); also translated by Henry Llewellyn Williams, 1904; Adam L. Gowans, 1906; Edwin Stanton De Poncet, 1934.

Térésa, with Anicet Bourgeois (produced 1832). 1832.

Perinet Leclerc; ou, Paris en 1418 (produced 1832). 1832.

Le Fils de l'émigré, with Anicet Bourgeois (produced 1832).

Le Mari de la veuve, with Anicet Bourgeois and Eugène Durieu (produced 1832). 1832.

Angèle, with Anicet Bourgeois (produced 1833). 1834.

La Vénitienne, with Anicet Bourgeois (produced 1834). 1834.

Catherine Howard (produced 1834). 1834; as *Catherine Howard*, 1859; translated and adapted by William E. Suter, 1870(?).

La Tour de Babel, with others (produced 1834). 1834.

Cromwell et Charles Ier, with Cordellier Delanoue (produced 1835). 1835.

Don Juan de Marana (produced 1836). 1836.

Kean; ou, Désordre et génie, with Théaulon (produced 1836). 1836; as *Edmund Kean; or, The Genius and the Libertine*, 1847.

Le Marquis de Brunoy, with others (produced 1836). 1836.

Caligula (produced 1837). 1838.

Piquillo, with Gérard de Nerval, music by Hippolyte Monpou (produced 1837). 1837.

Paul Jones (produced 1838). 1838.

Le Bourgeois de Gand; ou, Le Secrétaire du Duc d'Albe, with Hippolyte Romand (produced 1838). 1838.

Mademoiselle de Belle-Isle (produced 1839). 1839; as *Mademoiselle de Belle-Isle* (bilingual edition), 1855; also translated by F.A. Kemble, in *Plays*, 1863; as *The Lady of Belle Isle*, translated by J.M. Gully, 1872; as *Gabrielle de Belle Isle*, 1880; as *The Great Lover*, 1979.

Bathilde, with Auguste Maquet (produced 1839). 1839.

L'Alchimiste, with Gérard de Nerval (produced 1839). 1839; as *The Alchemist*, translated by Henry Bertram Lister, 1940.

Léo Burckart, with Gérard de Nerval (produced 1839). 1839.

Jarvis l'honnête homme, with Charles Lafont (produced 1840). 1840.

Un mariage sous Louis XV (produced 1841). 1841; as A *Marriage of Convenience*, translated and adapted by Sydney Grundy, 1897.

Jeannil le Breton; ou, Le Gérant responsable, with Eugène Bourgeois (produced 1841). 1842.

Le Séducteur et le mari, with Charles Lafont (produced 1842). 1842.

Halifax, with Adolphe d'Ennery (produced 1842). 1842.

Lorenzino (produced 1842). 1842.

Les Demoiselles de Saint-Cyr (produced 1843). 1843; as *The Ladies of Saint-Cyr*, 1870.

Le Laird de Dumbicky, with Adolphe de Leuven and Léon Lhérie (produced 1843). 1844.

Louise Bernard, with Adolphe de Leuven and Léon Lhérie (produced 1843). 1843.

L'Ecole de princes (produced 1843). 1843.

Le Mariage au tambour (produced 1843). 1843.

Le Garde-Forestier, with Adolphe de Leuven and Léon Lhérie (produced 1845). 1845.

Un conte de fées, with Adolphe de Leuven and Léon Lhérie (produced 1845). 1845.

Sylvandire, with Adolphe de Leuven and Léon Lhérie, from the novel by Dumas and Maquet (produced 1845). 1845.

Les Mousquetaires, with Auguste Maquet, from the novel *Vingt ans après* by Dumas and Maquet (produced 1845). 1845.

Une fille du régent, from the novel by Dumas and Maquet (produced 1846). 1846.

Échec et mat, with Octave Feuillet and Paul Bocage (produced 1846). 1846.

Intrigue et amour, from a play by Schiller (produced 1847). In *Théâtre complet*, 1864.

Hamlet, with Paul Meurice, from the play by Shakespeare (produced 1847). 1848.

La Reine Margot, with Auguste Maquet, from the novel by Dumas and Maquet (produced 1847) 1847.

Le Chevalier de Maison-Rouge, with Auguste Maquet, from the novel by Dumas and Maquet (produced 1847). 1847; as *The Chevalier de Maison-Rouge*, 1859.

Catalina, with Auguste Maquet (produced 1848). 1848.

Monte-Cristo, parts 1–2, with Auguste Maquet, from the novel *Le Comte de Monte-Cristo* by Dumas and Maquet (produced 1848). 2 vols., 1848; translated 1850.

Le Cachemire vert, with Eugène Nus (produced 1849). 1850.

Le Comte Hermann (produced 1849). 1849.

La Jeunesse des mousquetaires, with Auguste Maquet, from the novel *Les Trois Mousquetaires* by Dumas and Maquet (produced 1849). 1849; as *The Three Musketeers*, 1855; as *The Musketeers*, 1898.

Le Chevalier d'Harmental, with Auguste Maquet, from the novel by Dumas and Maquet (produced 1849). 1849.

La Guerre des femmes, with Auguste Maquet, from the novel by Dumas and Maquet (produced 1849). 1849.

Le Connétable de Bourbon; ou, L'Italie au seizième siècle, with Eugène Grangé and Xavier de Montépin (produced 1849). 1849.

Le Testament de César, with Jules Lacroix (produced 1849). 1849.

Pauline, with Eugène Grangé and Xavier de Montépin (produced 1850). 1850; as *Pauline*, translated and adapted 1855.

Les Frères corses, with Eugène Grangé and Xavier de Montépin, from the novel (produced 1850).

Trois Entr'actes pour l'amour médecin (produced 1850). 1850.

La Chasse au Chastre, from his own novel (produced 1850). 1850.

Les Chevalier du Lansquenet, with Eugène Grangé and Xavier de Montépin (produced 1850). 1850.

Urbain Grandier, with Auguste Maquet (produced 1850). 1850.

Le Vingt-quatre février (produced 1850). 1850.

La Barrière de Clichy (produced 1851). 1851.

Le Vampire, with Auguste Maquet (produced 1851). 1851.

Le Comte de Morcerf; Villefort, with Auguste Maquet, from the novel *Le Comte de Monte-Cristo* by Dumas and Maquet (produced 1851). 2 vols., 1851.

La Conscience (produced 1854). 1851.

La Jeunesse de Louis XIV (produced 1854). 1854; as *Young King Louis*, 1979.

Le Marbrier, with Paul Bocage (produced 1854). 1854.

Romulus (produced 1854). 1854; as *Romulus*, 1969.

L'Orestie (produced 1856). 1856.

La Tour Saint-Jacques, with Xavier de Montépin (produced 1856). 1856.

Le Verrou de la reine (produced 1856). In *Théâtre complet*, 1865.

Samson, music by E. Duprez (produced 1857). Parts published, 1856.

L'Invitation à la valse, with P. Bocage (produced 1857). 1857; as *Childhood's Dreams*, 1881.

La Bacchante (Thais), with Adolphe de Leuven and A. de Beauplan, music by Eugène Gautier (produced 1858).

L'Honneur est satisfait (produced 1858). 1858.

Les Forestiers, from his novel *Catherine Blum* (produced 1858). In *Théâtre complet*, 13, 1865.

L'Envers d'une conspiration (produced 1860). 1860.

Le Roman d'Elvire, with Adolphe de Leuven, music by Ambroise Thomas (produced 1860). 1860.

Le Gentilhomme de la montagne, from his novel *El Saltéador* (produced 1860). 1860.

La Dame de Monsoreau, with Auguste Maquet, from the novel by Dumas and Maquet (produced 1860). 1860.

Le Prisonnier de la Bastille: Fin des Mousquetaires, with Auguste Maquet, from the novel *Le Vicomte de Bragelonne* by Dumas and Maquet (produced 1861). 1861.

La Veillée Allemande, with Bernard Lopez (produced 1863).

Les Mohicans de Paris, from the novel by Dumas and Bocage (produced 1864). 1864.

Gabriel Lambert, with Amédée de Jallais, from the novel by Dumas (produced 1866; as *Gabriel le Faussaire*, produced 1868). 1866.

Madame de Chamblay, from his own novel (produced 1868). 1869.

Les Blancs et les bleus, from his own novel (produced 1869). 1874.

Ivanhoë; Fiesque de Lavagna. 1974.

Other

La Vendée et Madame. 1833; as *The Duchess of Berri in La Vendée*, 1833.

Gaule et France. 1833.

Impressions de voyage: En Suisse. 5 vols., 1833–37; as *Glacier Land*, translated by Mrs. W.R. Kilds, 1852; as *Swiss Travel*, edited by C.H. Parry, 1890; as *Adventures in Switzerland*, 1960.

Impressions de voyage: France. 1835–37; as *Pictures of Travel in the South of France*, 1852; as *Sketches in France*, 1860(?).

Quinze Jours à Sinaï, with Adrien Dauzats. 2 vols., 1839, also published as *Voyage au Orient*, and *Le Sinaï*; as *Impressions of Travel, in Egypt and Arabia Petraea*, translated by ''A Lady of New York,'' 1839; as *Travelling Sketches in Egypt and Sinai*, translated by ''A Biblical Student,'' 1839.

Napoléon. 1840; as *Napoleon*, translated by John B. Larner, 1894.

Le Capitaine Pamphile (for children). 1840; edited by A.R. Florian, 1912; as *The Adventures of Captain Pamphile*, translated by James Herald, 1845(?); also translated by Alfred Allinson, 1905; as *Captain Pamphile*, 1850.

Les Stuarts. 2 vols., 1840.

Excursions sur les bords du Rhin. 3 vols., 1841.

Une année à Florence. 2 vols., 1841.

Midi de la France. 3 vols., 1841.

Le Speronare. 4 vols., 1842; as *The Speronara*, translated by Katharine Prescott Wormeley, with *Journeys with Dumas*, 1902.

Souvenirs de voyage en Italie. 1841–42; comprises *Une année à Florence* and *Le Speronare*.

Le Capitaine Aréna. 2 vols., 1842; as *Captain Marion*, translated by F.W. Reed, 1949.

Le Corricolo. 4 vols., 1843; part translated as *Sketches of Naples*, by A. Roland, 1845.

La Villa Palmieri. 2 vols., 1843.

Filles, lorettes, et courtisanes. 1843.

Louis XIV et son siécle. 2 vols., 1844–45.

Histoire d'un casse-noisette (for children). 2 vols., 1845; as *The Story of a Nutcracker*, 1846; as *The History of a Nutcracker*, 1872; as *Princess Pirlipatine and the Nutcracker*, translated and continued by O. Eliphaz Keat, 1920; as *The Nutcracker of Nuremberg*, translated by Grace Gingras, 1930.

La Bouillie de la Comtesse Berthe (for children). 1845; edited by Cornell Price, 1889; as *The Honey-Stew of the Countess Bertha*, translated by Mrs. Cooke Taylor, 1846; as *Good Lady Bertha's Honey Broth*, 1846; as *The Countess Bertha's Honey-Feast*, translated by Harry A. Spurr, in *Fairy Tales*, 1904; as *The Honey Feast*, 1980.

Italiens et Flamands. 1845.

Les Médicis. 2 vols., 1845.

De Paris à Cadix. 5 vols., 1848; as *Adventures in Spain*, 1959.

Le Véloce; ou, Tanger, Alger, et Tunis. 4 vols., 1848–51; as *Adventures in Algeria*, 1959; as *Tangier to Tunis*, translated by A.E. Murch, 1959; as *Tales of Algeria; or, Life Among the Arabs*, translated by Richard Meade Bache, 1868.

Louis XV et sa cour. 4 vols., 1849.

La Régence. 2 vols., 1849.

Montevideo; ou, Une nouvelle Troie. 1850.

Histoire de Louis XVI et la révolution. 3 vols., 1850–51.

Mémoires de Talma. 3 vols., 1850.

Le Drame de '93. 7 vols., 1851–52.

Les Drames de la mer. 2 vols., 1852.

Histoire de Louis-Philippe. 1852; as *The Last King; or, The New France*, 1915.

Mes Mémoires. 22 vols., 1852–54; annotated edition, 5 vols., 1954–68; selections as *Memoirs*, translated by A.F. Davidson, 5 vols., 1891; as *My Memoirs*, translated by E.M. Waller, 6 vols., 1907–09.

Une vie d'artiste. 2 vols., 1854; as *A Life's Ambition*, translated by R.S. Garnett, with *My Odyssey*, 1924.

La Jeunesse de Pierrot (for children). 1854; as *When Pierrot Was Young*, translated by Douglas Munro, 1975.

La Dernière Année de Marie Dorval. 1855.

Isabel Constant. 2 vols., 1855.

Les Grands Hommes en robe de chambre: Henri IV, Louis XIII, et Richelieu; César. 12 vols., 1856–57.

L'Homme aux contes (for children). 1857.

Le Lièvre de mon grand-père (for children), with de Cherville. 1857; as *The Phantom White Hare and Other Tales*, translated by Douglas Munro, 1989.

Marianna. 1859.

Les Baleiniers, with Félix Meynard. 3 vols., 1860.

Le Caucase; depuis Prométhée jusqu'à Chamyll. 7 vols. in 3, 1859, also published as *Impressions de Voyage: Le Caucase*, 1865; as *Adventures in Caucasia*, translated by A.E. Murch, 1962.

L'Art et les artistes contemporains au salon de 1859. 1859.

Contes pour les grands et les petits enfants (for children). 2 vols., 1859.

Causeries. 2 vols., 1860.

La Route de Varennes. 1860; as *Flight to Varennes*, translated by A. Craig Bell, 1962.

Les Garibaldiens: Révolution de Sicile et du Naples. 1861; as *The Garibaldians in Sicily*, 1861; complete version, as *On Board the ''Emma'': Adventures with Garibaldi's ''Thousand'' in Sicily*, edited by R.S. Garnett, 1929.

Bric-à-brac. 2 vols., 1861.

Les Morts vont vites. 2 vols., 1861.

Le Pape devant les évangiles. 1861.

I Borboni di Napoli. 10 vols., 1862–64.

Impressions de voyage: En Russie, 4 vols. 1865, also published as *De Paris à Astrakan*, 1858(?); as *Voyage en Russie*, edited by Jacques Suffel, 1960; excerpts as *Celebrated Crimes of the Russian Court*, 1905; as *Adventures in Czarist Russia*, 1960; also translated by A.E. Murch, 1976.

Bouts-rimés. 1865.

Étude sur ''Hamlet'' et sur William Shakespeare. 1867.

Histoire de mes bêtes. 1868; as *My Pets*, translated by Alfred Allinson, 1909; as *Adventures with My Pets*, 1960.

Souvenirs dramatiques. 2 vols., 1868.

Le Grand Dictionnaire de cuisine. 1873; as *Dictionary of Cuisine*, translated 1958; selection as *Dumas on Food: Selections From "Le Grand Dictionnaire de Cuisine,"* translated by Alan and Jane Davidson, 1978.

Propos d'art et de cuisine. 1877.

Fairy Tales, edited and translated by Harry A. Spurr. 1904.

The Dumas Fairy Tale Book, edited by Harry A. Spurr. 1924.

Lettres d'Alexandre Dumas à Mélanie Waldor, edited by Claude Schopp. 1982.

Sur Gérard de Nerval: Nouveaux mémoires. 1990.

Editor, *Un pays inconnu.* 1845.

Editor, *Pierre précieuse*, by Saphir. 1854.

Editor, *L'Arabie heureuse.* 1855.

Editor, *Le Journal de Madame Giovanni.* 4 vols., 1856; as *The Journal of Madame Giovanni,* translated by Marguerite E. Wilbur, 1944.

Editor, *Pélerinage de Hadji-abd-el-Hamid-Bey (à la Mecque).* 6 vols., 1856–57.

Editor, *Les Baleiniers*, by Felix Maynard. 1861; as *The Whalers*, translated by F.W. Reed, 1937.

Translator, *Mémoires de Garibaldi.* 2 vols., 1860; revised edition, 5 vols., 1860–61; 3 vols., 1861; as *Garibaldi: An Autobiography*, 1860; revised edition, as *The Memoirs of Garibaldi*, translated by R.S. Garnett, 1931.

*

Bibliography: *A Bibliography of Alexandre Dumas Père* by F.W. Reed, 1933; *Dumas père: Works Published in French. Works Translated into English* by Douglas Munro, 2 vols., 1978–81; *Alexandre Dumas père: A Secondary Bibliography of French and English Sources to 1983: With Appendices* by Douglas Munro, 1985.

Critical Studies: *The Life and Writings of Alexandre Dumas* by H.A. Spurr, 1929; *Alexandre Dumas père* by Richard S. Stowe, 1976; *The King of Romance: A Portrait of Alexandre Dumas* by F.W.J. Hemmings, 1979; *Alexandre Dumas* by Michael Ross, 1981; *"Missing" Works of Alexandre Dumas Père* by Douglas Munro, 1983; *Notes on Dumas' "Count of Monte Cristo"* by Arnie Jacobson, 1985; *Alexandre Dumas: Genius of Life* by Claude Schopp, translated by A.J. Koch, 1988; *Humeurs et humour d'Alexandre Dumas* by Claude Sylvain, 1993; *Alexandre Dumas: Le Vicomte de Bragelonne (The Man in the Iron Mask): A Critical Study* by A. Craig Bell, 1995.

* * *

Victor Hugo said: "No popularity of this century has surpassed that of Alexandre Dumas. The name of Alexandre Dumas is more than French . . . it is universal. Alexandre Dumas seduces, fascinates, interests, amuses, teaches." Dumas was too large in scope, too dynamic, too overpowering to be judged merely by the 40 years in which he dominated every field of writing in France.

Victorien Sardou called Dumas the greatest theatrical craftsman of the century. From 1829 until 1868 he had at least one play on the boards each year, often two or three, and in 1849, five. He inaugurated the Romantic movement with his play *Henri III et sa cour* [Henry III and His Court] in 1829. His *Antony*, in 1831, was the first modern Romantic play, and imitations are in the hundreds. An 1833 trip to

Switzerland started Dumas on another type of writing—travel impressions, but a new kind of travelogue that was as interesting as a novel.

In 1844, his novel *Les Trois Mousquetaires* (*The Three Musketeers*) was the literary sensation of the century. Within ten years he had covered most of the history of France in his novels, and also turned out other gems such as *Le Comte de Monte-Cristo* (*The Count of Monte Cristo*), *La Tulipe noire* (*The Black Tulip*), and *Les Frères corses* (*The Corsican Brothers*). He also wrote purely historical works such as *Gaule et France, Louis XIV et son siècle, Napoléon* (*Napoleon*), and many others, probably the least boring history books ever written.

Dumas had collaborators on many of his novels, but their work consisted of research and planning; Dumas rewrote everything in his own hand. Critics have been amazed at his enormous output, but this was a man who could entertain a group of people for hours with facts and anecdotes drawn from the deep well of his memory; this was a man who could write 14 hours a day with scarcely a single erasure or reference. Whatever he heard or read remained in his fertile brain—history, mythology, swordsmanship, geography, names, dates. At a gathering, he was describing the battle of Waterloo in great detail when he was interrupted by a pompous general who said: "But it wasn't like that; I was there!" "I'm sorry, general," replied Dumas, "but you were not paying attention to what was going on." Dumas often had an entire novel or play in his head before he ever put it on paper. One of his finest plays, *Mademoiselle de Belle-Isle* (*The Lady of Belle Isle*), which had 500 performances, was recited for the committee of the Comédie-Française, and was accepted by acclamation before one word of it had ever been written.

Dumas has had his detractors, mostly writers who were jealous of his great popularity. He was often slighted in histories of French literature. His son, Alexandre Dumas *fils*, became a playwright, and for a decade or more almost eclipsed his father. But time works in favour of Dumas *père*. Except for *Camille*, his son's plays are virtually forgotten, even in France, but the father's works are being reprinted constantly, and more than 300 films have been made from his novels, his plays, and his life.

Dumas *père* was a master storyteller. His style, as Robert Louis Stevenson said, "is light as a whipped trifle, strong as silk." Dumas will survive. Two hundred years from now, you can be sure that at any given moment, someone, in some far-off place, will be reading *The Three Musketeers* or *The Count Of Monte Cristo* in one of the dozens of languages into which Dumas has been translated.

—Barnett Shaw

See the essay on *The Three Musketeers*.

DURANTI, Francesca

Born: Maria Francesca Rossi in Genova, Italy, 2 January 1935. **Education:** Law degree, University of Pisa, 1960. **Family:** Married 1) Enrico Magnani, 1956 (divorced), one son; 2) Massimo Duranti, early 1970s (divorced), one daughter. **Career:** Writer since early 1970s; worked as a translator and editor, 1980–84. Lives in Milan, Italy. **Member:** PEN. **Awards:** Premio Martinafranca, 1984, Premocitta Di Milano, 1984, Bagutta prize for best Italian novel of the year 1985, all for *La casa sul lago della luna*; Premio Basilicate, 1988, Premio Hemingway, 1988, Premio Campiello, 1989, all for *Effetti personali*.

PUBLICATIONS

Fiction

La Bambina. 1976.
Piazza mia bella piazza. 1978.
La casa sul lago della luna. 1984; as *The House on Moon Lake*, translated by Stephen Sartarelli, 1986.
Lieto fine. 1987; as *Happy Ending*, translated by Annapaola Cancogni, 1991.
Effetti Personali. 1988, as *Personal Effects*, translated by Stephen Sartarelli, 1993.
Ultima stesura. 1991.
Progetto Burlamacchi. 1994.
Sogni mancini. 1996; as *Left-Handed Dreams*, translated by the author, 2000.
Il commune senso delle proporzioni: piccolo thriller da viaggio. 2000.

Other

Translator, *Lunedi o martedi: tutti i racconti*, by Virginia Woolf. 1980.

*

Critical Studies: "Writing in a Changing World: An Interview With Francesca Duranti" by Sharon Wood, in *The Italianist*, vol. 12, 1992; "Francesca Duranti: Reflections and Inventions" by S.W. Vinall, in *The New Italian Novel*, edited by Zygmunt G. Baranski and Lino Pertile, 1993; "Writing an Identity: The Case of Francesca Duranti" by Rita Wilson, in *Studi d'Italianistica nell'Africa Australe*, vol. 9, No. 2, 1996; "Bio-fictive Conversations and the Uncentred Woman in Francesca Duranti's Novels" by Janice Kozma, in *The Italianist*, vol. 16; "Francesca Duranti and Metafiction" by Shirley Smith, in *Quaderni d'Italianistica*, vol. 18, No.1, Spring 1997; "The Language of Tolerance: Dialogism and Orality in Francesca Duranti's *Sogni Mancini*" by Marina Spunta, in *MLN*, vol. 115, No. 1, January 2000.

* * *

Francesca Duranti's life spans from the Nazi occupation of Italy during World War II to the post-modern computer age of the twenty-first century. Her novels of identity and experience have made her one of Italy's most popular and important modern novelists. Duranti's work has been translated into English, Spanish, Portuguese, Dutch, Finnish, Swedish, and Hebrew among other languages, proving that her explorations of modern society speak to readers of many different cultures. While her work always has a strong autobiographical base, Duranti reaches out from that base to delve into such age-old artistic themes as the source of identity and the complex relationship of fiction and reality.

Raised in an upper-class family, Duranti frequently uses her novels to examine the unsatisfying lives of the rich and the struggle of bourgeois intellectuals to make a place for themselves in society and

in their own lives. Her first novel, acclaimed by Italian readers, was a largely autobiographical tale of childhood titled *La Bambina* [The Child]. The novel tells the story of the earliest years of Francesca Rossi (Duranti's own maiden name) as she begins her life during the last years of World War I. Duranti makes creative use of language to approximate the way a child's thoughts might develop as she learns to understand the new, fascinating, and often terrifying world in which she finds herself.

Just as *La Bambina* explores the developing identity of a child, Duranti's later novels also focus on the continuing development of identity. As her protagonists become adults, their identities become many-layered as their experiences increase and their philosophical self-examination deepens. In fact, most of her novels are explorations of the trappings of identity and what happens to the self when those trappings are stripped away.

In *Piazza, mia bella piazza* [My Town Square, My Beautiful Square], Duranti's second novel, the protagonist is Paola, a young married woman. The book tells the story of Paola's struggle to take herself seriously as a writer. To do this, she must leave her husband, who is threatened by his wife's consuming work and strong sense of independence. Pulling herself free from the ties of marriage shakes Paola's very sense of self and she feels that, "to be without a man to care for her seemed like having lost her papers in a foreign and hostile country." She not only has to rebuild a life on her own, but also reconstruct an identity separate from her role as a wife. Though *Piazza* is clearly a forerunner to Duranti's later, more developed, works, she herself considers it an inferior novel and has refused to allow it to be reprinted.

With *La casa sul lago della luna* (*The House on Moon Lake*), Duranti received her first major popular and critical success. The award-winning novel was on Italian bestseller lists for weeks and was translated into seventeen languages. In *The House on Moon Lake*, Duranti continues to examine the quest for identity in the face of loss and failure. However, it is here she begins to reveal herself as a true postmodern writer, also fascinated by the relationship of reality to art and creation to fact.

The House on Moon Lake is actually a novel within a novel, and its format accentuates Duranti's interest in the multi-layered personality and the multi-leveled experience. The protagonist, Fabrizio (a name quite close to Francesca), is the depressed, embittered product of a wealthy family that has lost its position and money. He works in a plodding, hopeless way as a translator, a sort of transmitter for other people's experiences. In the course of his work, he stumbles upon an unknown Austrian writer and becomes the first to translate the author's novel, *Das Haus am Mondsee*, or *The House on Moon Lake*.

Fabrizio's success with his Italian translation of the novel leads him to write a biography of the little-known Austrian novelist. When he cannot find information about the end of the writer's life, he invents a life for him, complete with a dynamic romance. Readers not only accept the fictitious biography, but they begin to participate in the creation of the false reality, contacting Fabrizio to say that they knew the Austrian novelist's beautiful love, Maria. The novel ends with Fabrizio moving to Moon Lake to live out his life with a ghostly, mysterious woman who claims to be the fictional Maria's granddaughter. Having risked everything to make an identity, "a name for himself," Fabrizio is trapped in the end, living out someone else's identity.

The House on Moon Lake represents a change in style and tone from Duranti's earlier works. With a sure wit and generous humor, Duranti began to craft literary thrillers, psychological detective novels where the mystery is internal. The task of the detective/ protagonist is to uncover the roots of identity and experience and how they affect each other. In some novels, like *Progetto Burlamacchi* [The Burlamacchi Project], experience and self are explored in the context of Italian culture, society, and politics. In others, like *Effetti personali (Personal Effects)*, the context is more deeply personal, as a young woman rediscovers her identity after the desertion of her husband leaves her feeling empty. She succeeds, completing the journey started in *Piazza, mia bella piazza.*

Sogni mancini (Left-Handed Dreams) joins both the construction of the self and the search for cultural identity. The heroine of the novel, Martina, is a single Italian woman living and working as a college professor in New York. She experiences the dissolution of her childhood world with the death of her mother, and the loss of cultural assumptions living so far from the world where she grew up. At the same time, she is obsessed with a machine that helps her to remember and analyze her dreams. Her dreams convince her that she was born left-handed and forced to learn to use her right hand. This discovery shakes her on the deepest level, for who would she be if she had grown up as her left-handed self?

This is the crux of the mystery to Duranti, then. What is the self, and what would that self be if the outward things that shaped it had been different? In *Personal Effects,* she writes, ''I no longer knew where to start from in order to say I.'' This is Duranti's chief goal, and what makes her such an important writer for the ever-changing, fast-paced twenty-first century: to constantly shift the perspective of the reader in order to demonstrate just what a complex thing it is to know where to start from to say I.

—Tina Gianoulis

DURAS, Marguerite

Born: Marguerite Donnadieu in Gia Dinh, near Saigon, French Indochina (now Vietnam), 4 April 1914. **Education:** Educated at Lycée de Saigon, baccalauréat 1931; the Sorbonne, Paris, 1933–34, degree in law and political science, 1935. **Family:** Married Robert Antelme in 1939 (divorced 1946); had one son by Dionys Mascolo. **Career:** Moved to France, 1932. Secretary, Ministry of Colonies, Paris, 1935–41; freelance writer, after 1943; journalist, *Observateur*; also film writer and director. **Awards:** Cocteau prize, 1954/55; Cannes Film Festival Palme d'Or, with Gérard Jarot, 1962; Ibsen prize, 1970; Cannes Film Festival special prize, 1975; Académie française grand prize for theatre, 1983; Goncourt prize, 1984; Ritz Paris Hemingway prize, 1986. **Member:** French Communist Party, 1940s, expelled 1950. **Died:** 3 March 1996.

PUBLICATIONS

Fiction

Les Impudents. 1943.
La Vie tranquille. 1944.
Un Barrage contre le Pacifique. 1950; as *The Sea Wall*, translated by Herma Briffault, 1952; as *A Sea of Troubles*, translated by Antonia

White, 1953; as *A Dam Against an Ocean*, translated by Sofka Skipworth, 1966.
Le Marin de Gibraltar. 1952; as *The Sailor from Gibraltar*, translated by Barbara Bray, 1966.
Les Petits Chevaux de Tarquinia. 1953; as *The Little Horses of Tarquinia*, translated by Peter DuBerg, 1960.
Des journées entières dans les arbres (stories). 1954; as *Whole Days in the Trees and Other Stories*, translated by Anita Barrows, 1983.
Le Square. 1955; as *The Square*, translated by Sonia Pitt-Rivers and Irina Morduch, 1959, also in *Four Novels*, 1965, and in *Three Novels*, 1977.
Moderato cantabile. 1958; as *Moderato Cantabile*, translated by Richard Seaver, 1960, also in *Four Novels*, 1965.
Dix heures et demi du soir en été. 1960; as *Ten-Thirty on a Summer Night*, translated by Anne Borchardt, 1962, also in *Four Novels*, 1965, and in *Three Novels*, 1977.
L'Après-midi de Monsieur Andesmas. 1962; as *The Afternoon of Monsieur Andesmas*, translated by Anne Borchardt, with *The Rivers and Forests*, 1964, also in *Four Novels*, 1965; published separately, 1968.
Le Ravissement de Lol V. Stein. 1964; as *The Ravishing of Lol V. Stein*, translated by Richard Seaver, 1966; as *The Rapture of Lol V. Stein*, translated by Eileen Ellenbogen, 1967.
Four Novels (includes *The Square; Moderato Cantabile; Ten-Thirty on a Summer Night; The Afternoon of Monsieur Andesmas*), translated by Sonia Pitt-Rivers, Irina Morduch, Richard Seaver, and Anne Borchardt. 1965.
Le Vice-Consul. 1966; as *The Vice-Consul*, translated by Eileen Ellenbogen, 1968.
L'Amante anglaise. 1967; as *L'Amante Anglaise*, translated by Barbara Bray, 1968.
Détruire, dit-elle. 1969; as *Destroy, She Said*, translated by Barabara Bray, 1970; as *Destroy. . .* , translated by Bray, 1970.
Abahn Sabana David. 1970.
L'Amour. 1971.
Ah! Ernesto, with Bernard Bonhomme. 1971.
La Maladie de la mort. 1983; as *The Malady of Death*, translated by Barbara Bray, 1986.
L'Amant. 1984; as *The Lover*, translated by Barbara Bray, 1985.
Les Yeux bleus cheveux noirs. 1986; as *Blue Eyes, Black Hair*, translated by Barbara Bray, 1989.
Emily L. 1987; as *Emily L.*, translated by Barbara Bray, 1989.
La Pluie d'été. 1990; as *Summer Rain*, translated by Barbara Bray, 1992.
La Vie tranquille (selection). 1990.
L'Amant de la Chine du Nord. 1991; as *The North China Lover*, translated by Leigh Hafrey, 1992.
Yann Andrea Steiner. 1993; as *Yann Andrea Steiner*, translated by Barbara Bray, 1994.
Two by Duras, translated by Alberto Manguel. 1993.

Plays and Texts for Voices

Le Square, with Claude Martin, from her own novel (produced 1957; revised version produced 1965). In *Théâtre 1*, 1965; as *The Square*, translated by Barbara Bray and Sonia Orwell, in *Three Plays*, 1967.
Hiroshima mon amour (screenplay). 1960; as *Hiroshima mon amour*, translated by Richard Seaver, 1961, also with *Une aussi longue absence*, 1966.

Les Viaducs de la Seine-et-oise (produced 1960). 1960; as *The Viaducts of the Seine-et-oise*, translated by Barbara Bray, in *Three Plays*, 1967.

Une aussi longue absence (screenplay), with Gérard Jarlot. 1961; as *Une Aussi Longue Absence*, translated by Barbara Wright, with *Hiroshima Mon Amour*, 1966.

Les Papiers d'Aspern, with Robert Antelme, from the play *The Aspern Papers* by Michael Redgrave based on the story by Henry James (produced 1961). 1970.

Miracle en Alabama, with Gérard Jarlot, from a play by William Gibson (produced 1961). With *L'Homme qui se taisait*, by Pierre Gaillot, 1962.

La Bête dans la jungle, with James Lord, from a story by Henry James (produced 1962).

Théâtre I (includes *Les Eaux et fôrets; Le Square; La Musica*). 1965.

Les Eaux et fôrets (produced 1965). In *Théâtre I*, 1965; as *The Rivers and Forests*, translated by Barbara Bray, with *The Afternoon of Monsieur Andesmas*, 1964.

La Musica (produced 1965). In *Théâtre I*, 1965; as *La Musica*, translated by Barbara Bray, in *Suzanna Andler, La Musica and L'Amante Anglaise*, 1975, also in *Four Plays*, 1992.

Des journées entières dans les arbres (produced 1965). In *Théâtre II*, 1968; as *Days in the Trees*, translated by Sonia Oswell and Barbara Bray, 1966.

Three Plays (includes *Days in the Trees; The Square; The Viaducts of Seine-et-Oise*). 1967.

Théâtre II (includes *Susanna Andler; Yes, peut-être; Le Shaga; Des journées entières dans les arbres; Un Homme est venu me voir*). 1968.

Le Shaga (produced 1968). In *Théâtre II*, 1968.

Susanna Andler (produced 1969). In *Théâtre II*, 1968; as *Suzanna Andler*, translated by Barbara Bray in, *Suzanna Andler, La Musica and L'Amante Anglaise*, 1975.

L'Amante anglaise, from her own novel (produced 1969). 1968; as *A Place without Doors*, translated by Barbara Bray, in *Suzanna Andler, La Musica and L'Amante anglaise*, 1975.

Yes, peut-être (produced 1968). In *Théâtre II*, 1968.

La Danse de mort, d'après August Strindberg (produced 1970). In *Théâtre III*, 1984.

Nathalie Granger; La Femme du Gange (screenplays). 1973.

India Song (in English, produced 1993). 1973; as *India Song*, translated by Barbara Bray, 1976; with *Eden Cinema* (bilingual edition), 1988, also in *Four Plays*, 1992.

Home (in French), from the play by David Storey. 1973.

Suzanna Andler, La Musica and L'Amante Anglaise. 1975.

L'Éden Cinéma (produced 1977). 1977; as *Eden Cinema*, translated by Barbara Bray, with *India Song* (bilingual edition), 1988; translated by Bray, in *Four Plays*, 1992.

Le Camion (screenplay). 1977.

Le Navire Night, Césarée, Les Mains négatives, Aurélia Steiner (screenplays). 1979.

Véra Baxter; ou, Les Plages de l'Atlantique (screenplay). 1980; translated as *Vera Baxter; or, the Atlantic Beaches*, in *Drama Contemporary: France*, edited by Philippa Wehle, 1988.

L'Homme assis dans le couloir. 1980; as *The Seated Man in the Passage*, translated by Mary Lydon, in *Contemporary Literature 24*, 1983.

Agatha (screenplay). 1981.

L'Homme Atlantique (screenplay). 1982.

Savannah Bay (produced 1984). 1982; revised edition, 1983; as *Savannah Bay*, translated by Barbara Bray, in *Four Plays*, 1992.

Théâtre III (includes *La Bête dans la jungle, d'après Henry James*, with James Lord; *Les Papiers d'Aspern, d'après Henry James*, with Robert Antelme; *La Danse de mort, d'après August Strindberg*). 1984.

La Musica deuxième (produced 1985). 1985.

Four Plays (includes *La Musica; India Song; Eden Cinema; Savannah Bay*), translated by Barbara Bray. 1992.

Screenplays: *Hiroshima mon amour*, 1960; *Moderato cantabile*, with Gérard Jarlot and Peter Brook, 1960; *Une aussi longue absence* (The Long Absence), with Gérard Jarlot, 1961; *10.30 P.M. Summer*, with Jules Dassin, 1966; *La Musica*, 1966; *Les Rideaux blancs*, 1966; *Détruire, dit-elle (Destroy, She Said)*, 1969; *Jaune le soleil*, 1971; *Nathalie Granger*, 1972; *La ragazza di Passaggio/La Femme du Gange*, 1973; *Ce que savait Morgan*, with others, 1974; *India Song*, 1975; *Des journées entières dans les arbres*, 1976; *Son nom de Venises dans Calcutta désert*, 1976; *Baxter-Véra Baxter*, 1976; *Le Camion*, 1977; *Le Navire Night*, 1978; *Césarée; Les Mains négatives; Aurélia Steiner; L'Homme assis dans le couloir*, 1980; *Agatha et les lectures illimitées*, 1981; *L'Homme Atlantique*, 1981; *Dialogue de Rome*, 1982; *Les Enfants*, 1985.

Television Play: *Sans merveille*, with Gérard Jarlot, 1964.

Other

Les Parleuses (interviews), with Xavière Gauthier. 1974; as *Woman to Woman*, translated by Katherine Jensen, 1987.

Étude sur l'oeuvre littéraire, théâtrale, et cinématographique de Marguerite Duras, with Jacques Lacan and Maurice Blanchot. 1975.

Territoires du féminin, with Marcelle Marini. 1977.

Les Lieux de Marguerite Duras (interview), with Michelle Porte. 1978.

L'Été 80. 1980.

Les Yeux ouverts. In *Cahiers du Cinema* (special Duras issue), 312–313, June 1980.

Outside: Papiers d'un jour. 1981; revised edition, 1984; as *Outside: Selected Writings*, translated by Arthur Goldhammer, 1986.

Marguerite Duras à Montréal (interviews and lectures), edited by Suzanne Lamy and André Roy. 1981.

La Douleur. 1985; as *La Douleur*, translated by Barbara Bray, 1986; as *The War*, translated by Bray, 1986.

La Pute de la côte normande. 1986.

La Vie matérielle: Marguerite Duras parle à Jérôme Beaujour. 1987; as *Practicalities: Marguerite Duras Speaks to Jérôme Beaujour*, translated by Barbara Bray, 1990.

Les Yeux verts. 1987; as *Green Eyes*, translated by Carol Barko, 1990.

Marguerite Duras (interview). 1987.

Écrire (autobiography). 1993; as *Writing*, translated by Mark Polizzotti, 1998.

Yves Saint Laurent and Fashion Photography, with an essay by Marguerite Duras. 1998.

Translator, *La Mouette*, by Anton Chekhov. 1985.

*

Critical Studies: *Marguerite Duras* by Alfred Cismaru, 1971; *Marguerite Duras* by François Barat and Joel Farges, 1975; *Marguerite*

Duras: Moderato cantabile by David Coward, 1981; *Alienation and Absence in the Novels of Marguerite Duras* by Carol J. Murphy, 1982; *Marguerite Duras* by Mieheline Tison-Braun, 1985; *Marguerite Duras* by Jean Pierrot, 1986; "Space Invasions: Voice-Overs in Works by Samuel Beckett and Marguerite Duras" by Mary K. Martin, in *The Theatrical Space* edited by James Redmond, 1987; *Marguerite Duras: Writing on the Body* by Sharon Willis, 1987; *Remains to Be Seen: Essays on Marguerite Duras* edited by Sanford Ames, 1988; *L'Autre Scène: Le Théâtre de Marguerite Duras* by Liliane Papin, 1988; *Marguerite Duras* edited by Ilma Rakusa, 1988; *The Other Woman: Feminity in the Work of Marguerite Duras* by Trista Selous, 1988; "Women Writing Across Purpose: The Theater of Marguerite Duras and Nathalie Sarraute" by Janice B. Gross, in *Modern Drama*, 32, 1989; *Marguerite Duras: Fascinating Vision and Narrative Cure* by Deborah N. Glassman, 1991; *Forgetting and Marguerite Duras* by Carol Hofmann, 1991; *Écriture feminine et violence: Une étude de Marguerite Duras* by Janine Ricouart, 1991; *Du rythme au sens: Une lecture de "L'Amour" de Marguerite Duras* by Claire Cerasi, 1992; *Welcome Unreason: A Study of "Madness" in the Novels of Marguerite Duras* by Raynelle Udris, 1992; *Women and Discourse in the Fiction of Marguerite Duras: Love, Legends, Language* by Susan D. Cohen, 1993; *Marguerite Duras: Apocalyptic Desires* by Leslie Hill, 1993; *Le Ravissement de Lol V. Stein and L'Amant* by Renate Gunther, 1994; *Marguerite Duras Revisited* by Marilyn R. Schuster, 1993; *Beyond the Book: Marguerite Duras: Infans* by Mechthild Cranston, 1996; *The Erotics of Passage: Pleasure, Politics, and Form in the Later Work of Marguerite Duras* by James S. Williams, 1997; *Marguerite Duras: A Bio-bibliography* by Robert Harvey and Hélène Volat, 1997; *Art and Politics in Duras' India Cycle* by Lucy Stone McNeece, 1997; *Critical Essays on Marguerite Duras*, edited by Bettina L. Knapp, 1998; *Marguerite Duras: A Life* by Laure Adler, translated by Anne-Marie Glasheen, 2000; *Revisioning Duras: Film, Race, Sex*, edited by James S. Williams, 2000; *Duras, Writing, and the Ethical: Making the Broken Whole* by Martin Crowley, 2000; *Postcolonial Duras: Cultural Memory in Postwar France* by Jane Bradley Winston, 2001.

*   *   *

Marguerite Duras's early narratives present young women struggling with their own identity within the traditional aesthetic of third-person (*Les Impudents* [The Shameless]) and first-person (Françou in *La Vie tranquille* [The Quiet Life]) narrative perspectives. In both novels women are trying to put their lives together by struggling for independence from their families. Men appear to offer redemptive possibilities through marriage and fatherhood. However, promises are broken, and the men are not there when the women need them. This conflict between men and women who are tied by family or impossible love affairs recurs throughout Duras's work and engenders pain and suffering in the women's and sometimes the men's lives.

Le Square (*The Square*) shows the mature stage of Duras's narrative style. An encounter and a separation between a man and a woman in a public square are examined through their dialogue. Duras's allusive style, that reveals compassion towards the characters, according to Frank Towne, is henceforward characteristic of her fiction, plays, and films. Many of her narrators are obsessed with drinking as a means of forgetting their problems. The zigzag narrative style, as Carol Murphy describes Duras's mature writing, is evocative of characters who wander aimlessly through life, attracted to other

erotically, passionately, and violently while trying to piece together their own past and present.

Duras's filmmaking career began at about the same time as her adoption of the zigzag style. The plots and techniques of her motion pictures, her plays, and her novels are intertwined. Her script for Alain Resnais's *Hiroshima mon amour* contains many references to the intersecting influences of forgetting and remembering in the narrative process. The meeting of the Orient and the Occident, in this case a French actress and a Japanese businessman, is paradigmatic of her work. *Un Barrage contre le Pacifique* (*A Sea of Troubles*), *Le Vice-Consul* (*The Vice-Consul*), *India Song*, *L'Amant* (*The Lover*), *Emily L.*, and *L'Amant de la Chine du Nord* (*The North China Lover*) explore the impossible meeting and unavoidable separation not only of men and women but also of other profoundly different orientations, such as the young and old (*L'Après-midi de Monsieur Andesmas* [The Afternoon of Monsieur Andesmas]), mothers and daughters, husbands and wives (*La Douleur* [The War]), brothers and sisters (*Agatha*), as well as those between a prostitute and a homosexual in *Les Yeux bleus cheveux noirs* (*Blue Eyes, Black Hair*) and between races (*The Lover*; *The North China Lover*).

Mutilation and fragmentation are connected activities of the memory and narration in the numerous stories about women as lovers and as mothers. The film techniques of *découpage* and frame-sequencing promote this sense of disconnectedness among characters in the stories. Insecure mothers continue their cycle of insecurity by threatening their daughters (Françou) with prearranged marriages (Maud in *Les Impudents*), and abandonment (the beggar woman in *The Vice-Consul*), resulting in unwanted pregnancies (Maud), wandering (Anne in *Moderato cantabile*) and general schizophrenia (Lol in *Le Ravissement de Lol V. Stein* [The Ravishing of Lol V. Stein]). Duras's women become invigorated by rejection to desire what they do not have. The story of Lol V. Stein, a saga known as the India Cycle, still continues in Duras's work as if to signify that the violence done in women's lives cannot be encompassed and closed.

The slow repeating cycle of women's insecurity begins with abandonment (Lol V. Stein) and leads to crimes such as murder (the husband in the café in *Moderato cantabile*), self-immolation (Claire's murder of her twin self, Marie-Thérèse, in *L'Amante anglaise*, and incest (Joseph and Suzanne in *A Sea of Troubles*). Alissa's prophetic word "destroy" in *Détruire, dit-elle* (*Destroy, She Said*), becomes the rallying cry for women who want to be in control of their lives. While the sea threatens the livelihood of the family in *A Sea of Troubles* and devours both brother and sister in *Agatha*, it is the sea-like rhythm of Duras's narratives, oscillating between silence and disconnected words, forgetting and remembering, that yearns for the impossible desire and produces an incantation to the tension between those who are powerful and those who are denied. This incantation is often lost in the haze of music (Indiana's Song in *The Vice-Consul*; Diabelli's sonata in *Moderato cantabile*).

These themes could be Freudian or Lacanian, but most of all they represent women in the trauma of searching for their identities and trying to constitute their stories from their past and towards their imaginary future. The strategic use of silence gives the readers and/or spectators a space in which to put together lives that are fragmented and typically destroyed by past experiences. Duras herself refuses an intellectual or essentialist reading of her work that allows a feminist or any other community-orientated meaning. Instead, the prototypical character of Anne (Anna in *Le Marin de Gibraltar* [The Sailor from Gibraltar]; Anne-Marie Stretter in *The Vice-Consul*, *Lol V. Stein* and

India Song; Anne Desbaresdes in *Moderato cantabile*) wanders, as if in mourning, object of a desire that is constantly frustrated and misdirected. Anne's own desire returns in attempts to retell her story, many times embedded with lies and half-truths. One can never "get it right." The pleasure is in the piecing together of a dizzying, hazy state of imagination.

—Roland A. Champagne

DÜRRENMATT, Friedrich

Born: Konolfingen, near Berne, Switzerland, 5 January 1921. **Education:** Educated at Grosshöchstetten school; Freies Gymnasium and Humboldtianum, Bern; University of Zurich, one term; University of Bern, 1941–45. **Family:** Married 1) Lotti Geissler in 1946 (died 1983), one son and two daughters; 2) Charlotte Kerr in 1984. **Career:** Drama critic, *Die Weltwoche*, Zurich, 1951–53; co-director, Basle Theatres, 1968–69; co-owner, *Zürcher Sonntags-Journal*, 1969–71; writer-in-residence, University of Southern California, Los Angeles, 1981; travelled to the USSR, 1964 and 1967, Israel, 1974, Greece and South America, 1983–84, and to Egypt, 1985, and the United States. Also television director. **Awards:** City of Berne prize, 1954, 1979; Radio Play prize (Berlin), 1957; Italia prize, for radio play, 1958; Schiller prize (Mannheim), 1959; New York Drama Critics Circle award, 1959; Schiller prize (Switzerland), 1960; Grillparzer prize, 1968; Kanton Berne prize, 1969; Welsh Arts Council International Writers prize, 1976; Buber-Rosenzweig medal, 1977; Zuckmayer medal, 1984; Austrian State prize, 1984; Bavarian literature prize, 1985; Büchner prize, 1986; Schiller prize (Stuttgart), 1986; Ernst Robert Curtis prize, for essays, 1989. Honorary doctorate: Temple University, Philadelphia, 1969; Hebrew University, Jerusalem, 1977; University of Nice, 1977; University of Neuchâtel, 1981; University of Zurich, 1983. Honorary Fellow, Modern Language Association (United States). **Died:** 14 December 1990.

PUBLICATIONS

Plays

Es steht geschrieben (produced 1947). 1947; revised version, as *Die Wiedertäufer* (produced 1967), 1969.
Der Blinde (produced 1948). 1960; revised edition, 1965.
Romulus der Grosse (produced 1949). 1956; revised version (produced 1957), 1958; translated as *Romulus*, 1962; as *Romulus the Great*, translated by Gerhard Nellhaus, in *Four Plays*, 1964.
Die Ehe des Herrn Mississippi (produced 1952). 1952; revised version, 1957; film version, 1961; as *The Marriage of Mr. Mississippi*, translated by Michael Bullock, in *Four Plays*, 1964.
Ein Engel kommt nach Babylon (produced 1953). 1954; revised version (produced 1957), 1958; as *An Angel Comes to Babylon*, translated by Wiliam McElwee, in *Four Plays*, 1964.
Der Besuch der alten Dame (produced 1956). 1956; film version, 1963; as *The Visit*, translated by Maurice Valency, 1958; also translated by Patrick Bowles, 1962.

Nächtliches Gespräch mit einem verachteten Menschen (radio play). 1957; as *Conversation at Night with a Despised Character*, n.d.
Komödien I–III. 3 vols., 1957–70.
Das Unternehmen der Wega (radio play). 1958.
Frank V, music by Paul Burkhard (produced 1959). 1960.
Der Prozess um des Esels Schatten (radio play). 1959.
Stranitzky und der Nationalheld (radio play). 1959.
Abendstunde im Spätherbst (radio play; also produced on stage 1959). 1959; as *Episode on an Autumn Evening*, translated by Myron B. Gubitz, 1959; as *Incident at Twilight*, in *Postwar German Theatre*, edited by Michael Benedikt and George E. Wellwarth, 1968,
Der Doppelgänger (radio play). 1960.
Herkules und der Stall des Augias (radio play; also produced on stage 1963). 1960; translated as *Hercules and the Augean Stables*, n.d.
Die Panne, from his own novel (radio play: also televised 1957; produced on stage 1979). 1961; revised version, 1979.
Gesammelte Hörspiele (includes *Abendstunde im Spätherbst*; *Der Doppelgänger*; *Herkules und der Stall des Augias*; *Nächtliches Gespräch mit einem verachteten Menschen*; *Die Panne*; *Der Prozess um des Esels Schatten*; *Stranitzky und der Nationalheld*; *Das Unternehem der Wega*). 1961.
Die Physiker (produced 1962). 1962; television version, 1963; as *The Physicists*, adapted by Maurice Valency, 1958; translated by James Kirkup, 1963.
Four Plays 1957–62 (includes *Romulus the Great*; *The Marriage of Mr. Mississippi*; *An Angel Comes to Babylon*; *The Physicists*), translated by Gerhard Nellhaus and others. 1964.
Der Meteor (produced 1966). 1966; as *The Meteor*, translated by James Kirkup, 1973.
König Johann, from the play by Shakespeare (produced 1968). 1968.
Play Strindberg: Totentanz nach August Strindberg (produced 1969). 1969; as *Play Strindberg: The Dance of Death*, translated by James Kirkup, 1972.
Titus Andronicus, from the play by Shakespeare (produced 1970). 1970.
Porträt eines Planeten (produced 1970; revised version, produced 1971). 1970.
Urfaust, from the play by Goethe (produced 1970). 1980.
Woyzeck, from the play by Büchner (produced 1972). 1980.
Der Mitmacher (produced 1973). 1973; enlarged edition, *Der Mitmacher-Ein Komplex* (includes notes, essays, narratives), 1976.
Die Frist (produced 1977). 1977.
Achterloo (produced 1983). 1984.
Achterloo IV (produced 1988).

Screenplays: *Es geschah am hellichten Tag* (*It Happened in Broad Daylight*), 1960; *Die Ehe des Herrn Mississippi*, 1961; *Der Besuch der alten Dame*, 1963.

Radio Plays: *Der Prozess um des Esels Schatten*, 1951; *Stranitzky und der Nationalheld*, 1952; *Nächtliches Gespräch mit einem verachteten Mensch*, 1952; *Herkules und der Stall des Augias*, 1954; *Das Unternehmen der Wega*, 1954; *Die Panne*, 1956; *Abendstunde im Spätherbst*, 1958; *Der Doppelgänger*, 1961.

Fiction

Pilatus. 1949.
Der Nihilist. 1950; reprinted as *Die Falle*.

Der Richter und sein Henker. 1952: as *The Judge and His Hangman*, translated by Cyrus Brooks, 1954.

Die Stadt: Prose 1–4. 1952.

Das Bild des Sisyphos. 1952.

Der Verdacht. 1953; as *The Quarry*, translated by Eva H. Morreale, 1961.

Grieche sucht Griechin. 1955; as *Once a Greek...*, translated by Richard and Clara Winston, 1965.

Das Versprechen: Requiem auf den Kriminalroman. 1958; as *The Pledge*, translated by Richard and Clara Winston, 1959.

Die Panne: Eine noch mögliche Geschichte. 1960; as *Traps*, translated by Richard and Clara Winston, 1960; as *A Dangerous Game*, translated by Richard and Clara Winston, 1960.

Der Sturz. 1971.

The Judge and His Hangman; The Quarry: Two Hans Barlach Mysteries, translated by George Stade. 1983.

Minotaurus: Eine Ballade, illustrated by Düirrenmatt. 1985.

Dürrenmatt: His Five Novels (includes *The Judge and His Hangman; The Quarry; Once a Greek; A Dangerous Game; The Pledge*). 1985.

Justiz. 1985; as *The Execution of Justice*, translated by John E. Woods, 1989.

Der Auftrag; oder, Vom Beobachten des Beobachters der Beobachter. 1986; as *The Assignment; or, On Observing of the Observer of the Observers*, translated by Joel Agee, 1988.

Durcheinanderthal. 1989.

Other

Theaterprobleme. 1955; as *Problems on the Theatre*, translated by Gerhard Nellhaus, in *Four Plays*, 1964, and with *The Marriage of Mr. Mississippi*, 1966.

Friedrich Schiller: Rede (address). 1960.

Der Rest ist Dank (addresses), with Werner Weber. 1961.

Die Heimat im Plakat: Ein Buch für Schweizer Kinder (drawings). 1963.

Theater-Schriften und Reden, edited by Elisabeth Brock-Sulzer. 2 vols., 1966–72; translated in part as *Writings on Theatre and Drama*, edited by H.M. Waidson, 1976.

Monstervortrag über Gerechtigkeit und Recht. 1968.

Sätze aus Amerika. 1970.

Zusammenhäinge: Essay über Israel. 1976.

Gespräch mit Heinz Ludwig Arnold. 1976.

Frankfurter Rede. 1977.

Lesebuch. 1978.

Bilder und Zeichnungen, edited by Christian Strich. 1978.

Albert Einstein: Ein Vortrag. 1979.

Werkausgabe. 30 vols., 1980–86.

Stoffe 1–3: Winterkrieg in Tibet, Mondfinsternis, Der Rebell. 1981.

Plays and Essays, edited by Volkmar Sander. 1982.

Denken mit Düirrenmatt, edited by Daniel Keel. 1982.

Die Welt als Labyrinth, 1982.

Rollenspiele: Protokoll einer fiktiven Inszenierung und "Achterloo III" (includes text of play *Achterloo III*). 1986.

Versuche. 1988.

Midas; oder, Die Schwarze Leinwand. 1991.

Kants Hoffnung. 1991.

Gedankenfuge. 1992.

*

Bibliography: *Friedrich Dürrenmatt Bibliografie* by Johanes Hansel, 1968; *Friedrich Dürrenmatt* by Gerhard B. Knapp, 1980.

Critical Studies: *Friedrich Dürrenmatt* by Murray B. Peppard, 1969; *Friedrich Dürrenmatt* by Armin Arnold, 1972; *To Heaven and Back: The New Morality in the Plays of Friedrich Dürrenmatt* by Kurt J. Fickert, 1972; *Friedrich Dürrenmatt* by H.L. Arnold, 2 vols., 1976–77; *Dürrenmatt: A Study in Plays, Prose, and Theory* by Timo Tiusanen, 1977; *Dürrenmatt: A Study of His Plays* by Urs Jenny, 1978; *Friedrich Dürrenmatt: A Collection of Critical Essays* edited by Bodo Fritzen and H.F. Taylor, 1979; *The Theatre of Dürrenmatt: A Study in the Possibility of Freedom*, 1980, and *Dürrenmatt: Reinterpretation in Retrospect*, 1990, both by Kenneth S. Whitton; *Play Dürrenmatt* edited by Moshe Lazar, 1983; *Dürrenmatt* by H. Goertz, 1987; *Friedrich Dürrenmatt: Moralist und Komödiant* by Lutz Tantow, 1992; *Understanding Friedrich Dürrenmatt* by Roger A. Crockett, 1998; *Tradition und Verfremdung: Friedrich Dürrenmatt und der klassische Detektivroman* by Stefan Riedlinger, 2000.

* * *

Born in Switzerland in 1921, Friedrich Dürrenmatt occupied a major place among writers in German since the *succès de scandale* of his first play, *Es steht geschrieben* [It Is Written], in Zurich in 1947.

His witty, provocative, grotesque caricatures of his fellow human beings seemed to mirror the chaotic post-World War II conditions and ensured his plays and prose works a permanent place on the bestseller lists. Dürrenmatt wrote of the human condition, of the shifting moral values in government and politics, of the loosening of familial and societal bonds, and of the despair of "the little man," suffering at the hands of well-organized, tyrannical bureaucracies. His shafted barbs of humour were directed at the "bringing-down," a true *reductio ad absurdum*, of the pompous and the entrepreneurial, the over-rich and the over-powerful.

His vehicle was "die Komödie," not the lighthearted, frothy social comedy of the western world, of Molière and Noël Coward, but that savage, grotesque, satirical comedy deriving ultimately from the satires of Aristophanes, and often presented in the farcical form of the medieval "commedia dell'arte." Dürrenmatt's reputation rests on his two great international stage successes, *Der Besuch der alten Dame* (*The Visit*) and *Die Physiker* (*The Physicists*), presented throughout the world, and on his short novels, e.g., *Der Richter und sein Henker* (*The Judge and His Hangman*) and *Die Panne* (*A Dangerous Game*), which have been studied in schools and universities worldwide.

The Visit deserves its phenomenal success because of the brilliant simplicity of what Dürrenmatt calls the "Einfall," that "germ-idea" which lies behind and illuminates a play—here philosophically effective and scenically and dramatically masterly: an aged grotesque, Claire Zachanassian, once driven out of her little village because she had been made pregnant by the village shopkeeper, Alfred Ill, returns to seek revenge. Now the richest woman in the world, she will give the ailing village "eine Milliarde" (a billion) if one of them will kill Alfred. The hypocrisy of the villagers as they declare their firm resolve to stand by Alfred (now in the running for mayor) and at the same time crowd into his shop to buy goods on credit in anticipation of the flood of gold, has been taken to be a symbolical attack on the then prevailing western capitalist values—but Dürrenmatt has never flailed exclusively one side. In *The Physicists*, Möbius, the brilliant scientist who has fled into an asylum to bury with him his potentially dangerous, revolutionary discovery, finds that his two "fellow-patients" are in fact American and Soviet agents bent on extracting his secrets.

Dürrenmatt attacked both sides of the Iron Curtain again in two biting prose works, *Der Sturz,* [The Fall], a story about "a" Polit-buro, and *Sätze aus Amerika* [Sentences from America], written after a visit to the United States to receive a doctorate which showed that his target was cruel bureaucratization and the denial of freedom to *all* sorts and conditions of men.

After his gradual withdrawal from the stage, Dürrenmatt busied himself with political and philosophical treatises—he was one of the few Europeans to support Israel in the Yom Kippur war—and with his grotesque paintings. Dürrenmatt's withdrawal from the public gaze turned out to be more than temporary; he turned instead to another "pulpit" (as Lessing did), the reflective, philosophical essay, in which he developed the theme of the helpless, hapless Minotaur condemned in his mirror-lined loneliness, representing symbolically the fate of those condemned to be misunderstood while they struggle against the folly and the inhumanity of man to man. When Dürrenmatt died in 1990, he left a rich legacy of witty yet deeply philosophical works whose importance has yet to be fully recognized in the world of letters. The Nachlass bequeathed to the Swiss National Archive in Berne may help scholars to interpret this legacy for the world.

—Kenneth S. Whitton

See the essays on *The Physicists* and *The Visit.*

E

EÇA DE QUEIRÓS, José Maria de

Born: Póvoa de Varzim, Portugal, 25 November 1845. **Education:** Educated at Colégio da Lapa, Oporto, 1855–60; Faculty of Law, Coimbra, 1861–66. **Family:** Married Emília de Castro Pamplona (Resende) in 1886; one daughter and one son. **Career:** Advocate in Lisbon, 1867–70; visited Egypt, and attended the inauguration of the Suez Canal, 1869; appointed administrator of the Council of Leiria, 1870; passed diplomatic service examinations, 1870; Portuguese consul in Havana, Cuba (then part of the Spanish Antilles), 1872–74; travelled through Canada, the United States, and Central America, 1873; consul to Great Britain, in Newcastle-upon-Tyne, 1874–78, and Bristol, 1878–88; consul in Paris, 1888–1900. Contributor, *Gazeta na Portugal*, from 1866, and *Gazeta de Notícias*, Rio de Janeiro, from 1878; editor, *Revista de Portugal*, 1889; also contributed to *Diário de Notícias, Revista Ocidental, A Actualidade, Diário de Portugal, O Atlântico, Revue Univérselle Internationale* (Paris), *Réporter, Revista Moderna* (Paris). **Died:** 16 August 1900.

PUBLICATIONS

Collections

Obras. 1986.
Obras completas [Resomnia Edition]. 20 vols., 1988.

Fiction

O crime do Padre Amaro. 1875; revised edition, 1880; as *The Sin of Father Amaro*, translated by Ned Flanagan, 1962.
O primo Basílio. 1878; revised editions, 1878, 1887; as *The Dragon's Teeth*, translated by Mary J. Serrano, 1889; as *Cousin Bazilio*, translated by Roy Campbell, 1953.
O mandarim. 1880; edited by Helena Cidade Moura, 1969; as *The Mandarin*, in *The Mandarin and Other Stories*, 1965.
O mistério da Estrada de Sintra. 1884.
A relíquia. 1887; as *The Relic*, translated by Aubrey F. Bell, 1954; also translated by Margaret Jull Costa, 1994.
Os Maias. 1888; as *The Maias*, translated by Patricia McGowan Pinheiro and Ann Stevens, 1965.
A ilustre casa de Ramires. 1900; as *The Illustrious House of Ramires*, translated by Ann Stevens, 1968.
A cidade e as serras. 1901; as *The City and the Mountains*, translated by Roy Campbell, 1955.
Contos. 1902; edited by Luiz Fagundes Duarte and Joaquim Mendes, 1989.
Prosas bárbaras. 1903.
The Sweet Miracle, translated by E. Prestage. 1905; also translated by A. de Alberti, 1913; Henry Gaffney, 1928.
Our Lady of the Pillar, translated by E. Prestage. 1906.
Perfection, translated by Charles Marriott. 1923.
Alves & ca. 1925; as *Alves & Co.*, translated by Robert M. Fedorchek, 1988.

O conde de Abranhos; A Catastrophe, edited by José Maria de Eça de Queirós the Younger. 1925.
A capital. 1925; as *To the Capital*, translated by John Vetch, 1995.
The Mandarin and Other Stories, translated by Richard Franko Goldman. 1965.
A tragédia da Rua das Flores. 1980.
The Yellow Sofa and Three Portraits, translated by John Vetch, Richard Franko Goldman, and Luís Marques. 1993.

Plays

Filidor, from a play by José Bouchardy (produced 1866).

Other

As farpas (articles), with Ramalho Ortigão. 42 vols., 1871–83; edited by David Corazzi, 13 vols., 1887–90.
Antero de Quental—In Memoriam, with others. 1896.
A correspondência de Fradique Mendes: memorias e notas. 1900.
Dicionário de Milagres . . . outros escriptos dispersos. 1900.
Prosas bárbaras (articles), edited by Jaime Batalha Reis. 1903.
Cartas de Inglaterra. 1905; as *Letters from England*, translated by Ann Stevens, 1970; as *Eça's English Letters*, translated by Alison Aiken and Ann Stevens, 2000.
Ecos de Paris. 1905.
Cartas familiares e bilhetes de Paris (1893–1896). 1907.
Notas contemporâneas. 1909.
Últimas páginas: S. Cristávão, S. to Onofre, S. Frei Gil. 1912.
Correspondência. 1925.
O Egipto: notas de viagem. 1926.
Cartas inéditas de Fradique Mendes e mais páginas esquecidas. 1929.
Novas cartas inéditas de Eça de Queiroz a Ramalho Ortigão. 1940.
Crónicas de Londres. 1944.
Cartas. 1945.
Eça de Queiroz entre os seus. 1949.
Cartas de Eça de Queiroz aos seus editores Genelioux e Lugan (1887–1894). 1961.
Páginas esquecidas, edited by Alberto Machado da Rosa. 5 vols., 1965–66.
Eça de Queiroz e Jaime Batalha Reis: Cartas e Recordações do Seu Convívio. 1966.
Folhas soltas (travel writing). 1966.
Páginas de journalismo. 2 vols., 1980.
Correspondência. 2 vols., 1983.
Cartas inéditas. 1987.
Love Letters Written by Anna Conover and Mollie Bidwell to José Maria Eça de Queiroz in *Cartas de amor de Anna Conover e Mollie Bidwell para José Maria Eça de Queiroz, Cônsul de Portugal em Havana (1873–1874)*, introduction by Alice Lomath Ferreira. 1998.
Editor, with José Sarmento and Henrique Marques, *O almanaque enciclopédico para 1896* [*1897*]. 2 vols., 1896–97.
Translator, *As minas de Salomão*, by Henry Rider Haggard. 1891.

*

Bibliography: *Lengua y estilo de Eça de Queiroz: Bibliografía queriociana sistemática e anotada* by Ernesto Guerra da Cal, 6 vols., 1975–84.

Critical Studies: *Eça, Fialho, Aquilino* by C. da Costa, 1923; *Estudos críticos* by Castelo Branco Chaves, 1932; *História literária de Eça de Queiroz* by Álvaro Lins, 1939, revised edition, 1964; *Eça de Queiroz* by Antônio Cabral, 1936; *Eça de Queiroz* by Clovis Ramalhette, 1939; *O realismo de Eça de Queiroz e a sua expressão artística* by Manuel de Paiva Boléo, 1941; *Eça de Queiroz: o homem e o artista* by João Gaspar Simões, 1945; *Eça de Queiroz: uma estética da ironia* by Mário Sacramento, 1945; *Eça de Queiroz: In Memoriam* edited by Eloy de Amaral and Cardoso Martha, 1947; *As ideias de Eça de Queiroz* by António José Saraiva, 1947; *Crític social de Eça de Queiroz* by Djacar Menezes, 1950, revised edition, 1962; *Lengua y estilo de Eça de Queiroz* by Ernesto Guerra, 1954; "amalho Ortigão and the Generation of 1870" by Walter J. Schnerr, in *Hispania*, 44, 1961; *Eça e Wilde* by A. Casemiro da Silva, 1962; *Eça, discípulo de Machado?* by Alberto Machado de Rosa, 1963; "Eça de Queiroz as a Literary Critic" by Peter Demetz, in *Comparative Literature*, 19, 1967; *Ensaios queirosianos* by António Coimbra Martins, 1967; "*Alves e Ca.* as Comedy" by Timothy Brown, Jr., in *Kentucky Romance Quarterly*, 16, 1969; *Eça de Queiroz e a questão social* by Jaime Cortesão, 1970; *Eça, político*, 1970, *Eça de Queiroz e o seu tempo*, 1972, and *Eça de Queiroz e a Geração de 70*, 1980, all by João Medina; *Eça de Queiroz e o século XIX* by Vianna Moog, 1977 (6th edition); "Presentation of Protagonist in *Alves & Ca.*", in *Kentucky Romance Quarterly*, 25, 1978, and "The Opera Motif in Eça's Lisbon Novels," in *Luso-Brazilian Review*, 16, 1979, both by Robert M. Fedorchek; *Introdução a leitura d'Os Maias* by Carlos Reis, 1978(?); *Eça de Queiroz and European Realism* by Alexander Coleman, 1980; *A vida de Eça de Queiroz* by Luís Viana Filho, 1983; *Imagens do Portugal queirosiano* by A. Campos Matos, 1987; *Dicionário de Eça de Queiroz* edited by A. Campos Matos, 1988; *Os vencidos da vida* by the Circulo Eça de Queiroz, 1989; *A construção da narrativa queirosiana* by Carlos Reis and Maria do Rosário Milheiro, 1989; *O leitor e a verdade oculta: ensaio sobre Os Maias* by Alan Freeland, 1990; *Eça e Os Maias: actas do 1° Encontro Internacional de Queirosianes, 1988*, 1990.

* * *

José Maria de Eça de Queirós, beyond dispute the greatest Portuguese novelist of the 19th century, has long deserved wider recognition among the major European novelists of the last century. It is as a novelist that he is best known in Portugal and beyond, yet the major novels only amount to half a dozen or so works while the rest of his very considerable literary output consists of hundreds of journalistic articles on a whole range of topics, as well as novels, short stories, tales of fantasy and imagination, essays, travel notes, a translation of *King Solomon's Mines* and numerous collections of letters to family and friends.

Eça de Queirós's earliest writings, *Prosas bárbaras* [Barbaric Tales], dating from as early as 1866 and 1867, reveal the contemporary prevailing taste for romanticism, imported from France and Germany; their pervading atmosphere of fantasy, Satanism, grotesqueness and mystery is enhanced by the rhythmic, lyrical and evocative style. Already Eça de Queirós's concern with the expressive potential of language is evident.

A few years later, in 1871, in a revolutionary public lecture, *The New Literature*, given in Lisbon, Eça de Queirós severely criticized and rejected the traditional Portuguese Romantic manner of writing as being conventional, sentimental, escapist, limited in interest, and lacking in purpose and originality, and expounded realism/naturalism after the French manner as the only way forward for literature. He declared that literature should teach and correct, that society should be depicted just as it was so that the evils of society could be condemned. This enthusiastic embracing of realism and the accompanying critical attitude to traditional practices and values gave rise to a series of *Farpas* [Barbs] in which Eça de Queirós condemned the state of torpor and stagnation he saw in society, literature and politics, and to his first major novel, *O crime do Padre Amaro* (*The Sin of Father Amaro*). This was a landmark, the first Portuguese work of realist fiction and Eça de Queirós's strongest reaction against romanticism. The novel provided the perfect opportunity for Eça de Queirós to put his theories into practice and the hypocrisy and immorality of provincial society and in particular, the greed and lust of the clergy, are scrutinized and depicted without reserve. In his second realist work, *O primo Basílio* (*Cousin Bazilio*), "the most doctrinal work printed in Portugal to date," the decadence, indolence, and false values of the Lisbon bourgeoisie are attacked. *Os Maias* (*The Maias*), Eça de Queirós's longest and most ambitious work, generally considered to be his masterpiece, tells the story of the decline of an ill-fated aristocratic family. In this Portuguese equivalent of Galdós's *Fortunata and Jacinta* Eça de Queirós paints a vast canvas of Lisbon high society, with gatherings of intellectuals, cosmopolitan types, fashionable women, intrigues, contemporary customs, excursions in and around Lisbon and many detailed descriptions of interiors and gardens, as part of his mission to depict contemporary Portugal with all its flaws.

With *O mandarim* (*The Mandarin*), which appeared less than ten years after Eça de Queirós had rebelled against tradition to uphold the cause of realism, he broke away from the realist novel in favour of a tale of invention, not observation, a world of fantasy, mystery, and exoticism, which was much more in harmony with his natural preferences. Similarly with *A relíquia* (*The Relic*) some years later Eça de Queirós is no longer the critical observer but revels in the role of storyteller. Fantasy combines with realism to create a tale of adventure, whose aim was to entertain rather than simply instruct and censure, though the greed and duplicity of the anti-hero, Teodorico, received their just deserts. Here we see Eça de Queirós's humour at its best, no longer the caustic irony of his realist period but a more playful brand, sometimes a rather macabre juxtaposition of comic and tragic, a bathetic cutting down to size of pompous behaviour or an impressive event, or imparting a lighter, frivolous touch to a sad, even tragic scene.

Eça de Queirós spent many years away from Portugal, returning only for occasional short vacations and the last 12 years of his life were spent in Paris. Years before this would have given him great pleasure and satisfaction, but ironically France, the French way of life, literature, culture, and attitudes had lost its charm for him while his former critical appraisal of Portugal and most things Portuguese had mellowed. This latter nostalgic mood is echoed in his two final novels, *A ilustre casa de Ramires* (*The Illustrious House of Ramires*) and *A cidade e as serras* (*The City and the Mountains*). The setting for *The Illustrious House*, which could be described as a historical novel dealing with contemporary life and the glories of the past, is not Lisbon or a seedy provincial town but a remote rural area. In the final novel Eça de Queirós presents his version of the popular contemporary theme of urban civilization versus the simple country life. Humour abounds in the descriptions of the hero's Parisian mansion with its wealth of gadgetry and the latest aids to easy living. The enforced return of the protagonist to his estate in northern Portugal provides the opportunity to contrast the wholesome pastoral existence in which he eventually finds happiness and fulfilment with the evils of super-civilization, epitomized by his former life in Paris.

Eça de Queirós's journalistic works and his letters, particularly those of his invented character, Fradique Mendes, who wrote on all manner of subjects (as Eça de Queirós himself says, "from the immortality of the soul to the price of coal"!), provide a fascinating insight into Eça de Queirós's personal thoughts—his nostalgia for his country, his opinion on politics, literature, culture, and controversial contemporary issues. In addition, in these writings Eça de Queirós expresses his views of many of his fictional works and his perpetual dissatisfaction with his writing, plagued by his apparent inability to provide a great work or create a new and vital style.

As well as boldly rejecting what he regarded as the fetters of traditional Portuguese literary norms in order to embrace the cause of realism/naturalism, thereby changing the course of development of the novel, Eça de Queirós rebelled against the heavy rhetorical, bombastic literary manner to create a very personal style that he strove to perfect throughout his literary career. From the lyrical, sonorous prose of *Prosas bárbaras*, overladen with adjectives, Eça de Queirós's style became more disciplined, versatile, flexible, and expressive. He always sought the precise word or combination of words to express the desired effect, and Eça de Queirós's capacity to create a humorous or ironic impression by means of verbal dexterity is without par. He combined words in novel, unexpected ways, made ironic use of paradox and hyperbole and is the master of the transferred epithet. His letters reveal that this gift for innovation and flexibility, whose influence is still felt today, was not simply a literary device to be used in novels but an essential part of his persona.

Although he has been described as the Zola of Portugal, naturalism in Eça de Queirós's case was, as he himself admitted, always more theoretical than practical. Naturalism played its part in his literary evolution by disciplining his imagination and leading him to base his novels on the critical observation of society, but he was essentially too much an artist and man of imagination to maintain the realist/naturalist stance with conviction and his socio-critical works are best described as *semi*-realist depictions of society, a mix of comedy and tragedy. No other Portuguese novelist has painted such a gallery of colourful, acutely observed portraits, accompanied by such mordant wit or playful humour.

Throughout his literary evolution his writings reveal a fusion of styles and genres which, together with his very personal use of humour and irony, his concern for words and their effect, his fondness for storytelling, his fascination with the exotic and fantastic, his underlying tolerance towards his characters, make his work defy easy definition. Eça de Queirós frequently attempted to define the Portuguese character, often contrasting his countrymen with the French, as in his preface to *The Mandarin* where he describes the Portuguese as man of imagination not reason, always preferring a beautiful phrase to a precise idea, and Eça de Queirós himself, in spite of the strong French influence on his early career and his admiration for French novelists, particularly Flaubert, could never escape his own essential Portugueseness.

—Shirley Clarke

ECO, Umberto

Born: Alessandria, Italy, 5 January 1932. **Education:** Received his doctoral degree at University of Turin. **Military Service:** Served in the Italian Army, 1958–59. **Family:** Married Renate Ramge, one son and one daughter. **Career:** Cultural editor for RAI, Italian Radio-Television, 1954–59; as a journalist, has written frequently in newspapers and magazines; taught at universities of Turin, Milan and Florence; Honorary President of the International Association for Semiotic Studies (IASS/AIS); Visiting Professor at Yale (1977 and 1980–81), Columbia (1984), Harvard (1992–93), and Paris (1992–93); appointed professor of Semiotics at University of Bologna, 1971, where he still teaches. **Awards:** Strega prize, 1981; Viareggio prize, 1981; Anghiari prize, 1981; Medicis prize, 1982; McLuhan Teleglobe prize, 1985. Received the Legion d'Honneur in France, 1993; Doctor Honoris Causa of 25 universities around the world, among them Brown, 1988; Paris Sorbonne Nouvelle, 1989; Tel Aviv, 1994; Buenos Aires, 1994; Athens, 1994; and Berlin Free University, 1998.

PUBLICATIONS

Collections

Diario minimo. 1963; as *Misreadings*, translated by William Weaver, 1993.
Il costume di casa. 1973.
Dalla periferia dell'Impero. 1977.
Il secondo diario minimo. 1992; as *How to Travel with a Salmon and Other Essays*, translated by William Weaver, 1994.
Sette anni di desiderio. 1983; as *Travels in Hyperreality: Essays*, translated by William Weaver, 1990.

Essays

Il problema estetico in San Tommaso. 1956; as *The Aesthetics of Thomas Aquinas* by Hugh Bredin, 1988.
Sviluppo dell'estetico medievale. 1959; as *Art and Beauty in the Middle Ages*, translated by Hugh Bredin, 1985.
Opera aperta: forma e indeterminazione nelle poetiche contemporanee. 1962, revised edition 1972; as *The Open Work*, translated by Anna Cancogni, 1989.
Apocalipticci e integrati. 1964, revised edition 1977; as *Apocalypse Postponed*, edited by Robert Lumley, 1994.
Il Caso Bond: el origini, la natura, gli effetti del fenomeno 007, with Oreste del Buono. 1965; as *The Bond Affair*, translated by R.A. Downie, 1966.
La poetishce di Joyce: dall "summa" al "Finnegans Wake". 1966; as *The Aesthetics of Chaosmos: The Middle Ages of James Joyce*, translated by Ellen Esrock, 1989.
La definizione dell'arte. 1968.
La strutura assente. 1968.
Le forme del contenuto. 1971.
Il segno. 1973.
Il costume di casa. 1973.
Beato di Liébana. 1973.
Semiotica della leteratura in URSS. 1974.
Trattato di semiotica generale. 1975; as *A Theory of Semiotics*, 1976.
Il superuomo di massa. 1976.
Come si fa una tesi di laurea. 1977.

Lector in fabula: la coperazioni interpretativa nei testi narrativi. 1979; partly translated as *The Role of the Reader: Explorations in the Semiotics of Texts*, 1981 (this book contains essays from other works).

Sette anni di desiderio. 1983.

Postille al nome della rosa. 1983; as *Postcript to The Name of the Rose*, translated by William Weaber, 1984.

Semiotica e filosofia del linguaggio. 1984; as *Semiotics and the Philosophy of Language*, 1984.

Sugli specchi e altri saggi. 1985.

Lo strano caso della Hanau 1609. 1989.

Limiti dell'interpretazione. 1990; translated as *The Limits of Interpretation*, 1990.

Stelle e stellette. 1991.

Vocali. 1991.

Sguardi venuti da lontano. 1991.

La ricerca della lingua perfetta nella cultura europea. 1993; as *The Search for the Perfect Language*, translated by James Fentress, 1997.

Povero Pinocchio: giochi linguistici di studenti del corso di comunicazione. 1997.

Six Walks in the Fictional Woods. 1994.

In cosa crede chi non crede?, with Carlo Maria Martini. 1996; as *Belief or Nonbelief?: A Confrontation*, translated by Minna Proctor, 2000.

Kant e l'ornitorrinco. 1997; as *Kant and the Platypus: Essays on Language and Cognition*, translated by Alastair McEwen, 1997.

Cinque scritti morali. 1997; as *Five Moral Pieces*, translated by Alastair McEwen, 2001.

Serendipities. Language and Lunacy. 1998.

Tra menzogna e ironia. 1998.

La bustina di Minerva. 2000.

Experiences in translation. 2000.

Fiction

Il nome della rosa. 1980; as *The Name of the Rose*, translated by William Weaber, 1983.

Il pendolo di Foucault. 1988; as *Foucault's Pendulum*, translated by William Weaber, 1989.

L'isola del giorno prima. 1994; as *The Island of the Day Before*, translated by William Weaber, 1995.

Baudolino. 2000; as *Baudolino*, translated by William Weaber, 2002.

Other

Tre cosmonauti (children's book). 1975; as *The Three Astronauts*, translated by Eugenio Carmi, 1989.

*

Bibliography: *Il "caso" Eco* by Margherita Ganeri, 1991.

Critical Studies: *Umberto Eco and the Open Text: Semiotics, Fiction, Popular Culture* by Peter Bondanella, 1997; *Reading Eco. An Anthology*, edited by Rocco Capozzi, 1997; *Umberto Eco's Alternative. The Politics of Culture and the Ambiguities of Interpretation*, edited by N. Bouchard and V. Pravadelli, 1998; *Umberto Eco: Philosophy, Semiotics and the Work of Fiction* by Caesar Michael, 1999; *Naming the Rose: Eco, Medieval Signs and Modern Theory* by Theresa Coletti, 1988; *Out of Chaos. Semiotics. A Festschrift in Honor of Umberto Eco*, edited by E. Tanner, et al, 1991; *Swinging Foucault's Pendulum* by Carl Rubino, 1992; *Umberto Eco's Alternative: The Politics of Culture and the Ambiguities of Interpretation*, edited by Norma Bouchard and Veronica Pravadelli, 1998; *Literary Philosophers?: Borges, Calvino, Eco*, edited by Jorge J.E. Gracia, Carolyn Korsmeyer, and Rudolphe Gasché, 2002.

* * *

Umberto Eco is a leading figure of contemporary Italian culture. He was born in Alessandria, in the Piedmonte Province of Italy, 60 miles south of Milan, to a large family of thirteen children. As a child he watched the shoot-outs between Fascists and Partisans during World War II. Urged by his father to become a lawyer, he entered the University of Turin, but abandoned his studies of law, and against his father's wishes, he took up medieval philosophy and literature.

He has an extensive oeuvre in the fields of Aesthetic, the Middle Ages, Literary Criticism, Semiotics, Cultural Analysis, and fiction for adults and children. Eco also has a journalistic production as a columnist for newspapers and magazines. His articles cover a wide range of topics, from football to airplane food, and many of them have been collected in books. Since 1960, when he began collaborating to the press, he has written for two separate audiences—academic specialists on one hand, and general readers on the other. He graduated in Philosophy in 1954 from the University of Turin at the age of 24, with a thesis on the aesthetics of Thomas Aquinas, and began his research as a Medievalist. His first publications pursued the focus he developed as a student, as in his first book, an extension of his thesis, *Il problema estetico in San Tommasso* (*The Aesthetics of Thomas Aquinas*). But soon his interest combined a strong erudition on the Middle Ages with a concern for the new discipline of semiotics.

In 1962 he published *Opera aperta* (*The Open Work*), his first major work in the field of semiotics. His academic career was very successful for the next two decades through his activity as a professor and author of books on semiotics and theory of signs. Two important books established his position in the field: *Trattato si semiotica generale* (*A Theory of Semiotics*) and *Semiotica e Filosofia del linguaggio* (*Semiotics and the Philosophy of Language*). Both works study a theory of codes and of sign production discussing key concepts developed in the writings of Charles Sanders Peirce. The first one marks the shift from medieval aesthetics into a more general interest in cultural values and literature as a whole. In the second book he argues that a sign is not only something that stands for something else, but must also be interpreted.

But Eco's most important contribution to the study of culture probably lies in the role he attributed to the reader. While taking many of the fundamentals of the structuralist theory of Ferdinand de Saussure, Claude Levy-Strauss, and Roman Jakobson, he drastically differs from them. In *The Open Work* and *Lector in Fabula* (*The Role of the Reader*) he criticized the view that meaning is the production of a structure, and saw that the reader uses two main concepts in the process of interpretative cooperation: the reader inserts in the text the "possible worlds" and the "frames," situations or sequences of action, in order to complete its meaning. The addressee of the work of art, therefore, becomes an active element in bringing that work to provisional completion. In a recent statement on reading and interpretation, Eco has stressed that the "anything goes" version of postmodern criticism is not what is implied in the notion of an open work. Rather, every literary work can be said to propose a "model reader" corresponding to the real possibilities set by the text. For Eco, to propose that an infinite number of readings is possible for any text is a wholly empty gesture. On the contrary, every work of art implies an "encyclopedia of the reader" that implies a specific amount of knowledge necessary to understand that work of art.

By the late 1970s he had established a solid reputation as a semiotician, but no one expected the radical shift his career would take when he published his first novel *Il nome della rosa* (*The Name of the Rose*) in 1980, of which more than 26 million copies have been sold. The book launched his career as a writer of fiction, that today includes four novels and two books of fiction for children. In his novels, Eco makes reference to many of the topics he has written in his academic production, such as problems of literary interpretation, reader's competence, Medieval culture, and classic philosophy. His books of criticism and fiction have been translated to more than twenty languages. He continues teaching and contributing weekly to Italian magazines and newspapers.

—Alvaro Fernández Bravo

See the essay on *The Name of the Rose*.

EDUARDO

See DE FILIPPO, Eduardo

EICH, Günter

Born: Lebus/Oder, Mecklenburg, Germany, 1 February 1907. **Education:** Educated at Leipzig Gymnasium, graduated 1925; studied Chinese and Law, University of Berlin, 1925–27; Leipzig University, 1927–29; the Sorbonne, Paris, 1929–30. **Military Service:** Served during World War II; prisoner of war, 1945, released 1946. **Family:** Married the writer Ilse Aichinger (second marriage) in 1953; one son and one daughter. **Career:** Full-time writer from 1946. **Awards:** Gruppe 47 prize, 1950; Bavarian Academy of Fine Arts literature prize, 1952; Büchner prize, 1959; Schiller prize, 1968. **Died:** 20 December 1972.

PUBLICATIONS

Collections

Gesammelte Werke, edited by Ilse Aichinger and others. 4 vols., 1973.
Gedichte, edited by Ilse Aichinger. 1973.

Tage mit Hähern: Ausgewählte Gedichte, edited by Klaus Schumann. 1975.
Pigeons and Moles: Selected Writings, translated by Michael Hamburger. 1990.

Verse

Gedichte. 1930.
Abgelegene Gehöfte. 1948.
Untergrundbahn. 1949.
Botschaften des Regens. 1955.
Ausgewählte Gedichte, edited by Walter Höllerer. 1960.
Zu den Akten. 1964.
Anlässe und Steingärten. 1966.
Nach Seumes Papieren. 1972.
Valuable Nail: Selected Poems, translated by Stuart Friebert, David Walker, and David Young. 1981.

Plays

Die Glücksritter. 1933.
Träume (radio plays; includes *Geh nicht nach El Kuwehd; Der Tiger Jussuf; Subeth; Träume*). 1953.
Stimmen: Sieben Hörspiele (radio plays; includes *Die Andere und ich; Allah hat hundert Namen; Das Jahr Lazertis; Die Mädchen aus Viterbo; Zinngeschrei; Festianus Märtyrer; Die Brandung vor Setúbal*). 1958.
Die Brandung vor Setúbal, Das Jahr Lazertis: Zwei Hörspiele (radio plays), edited by Robert Browning. 1963; as *Journeys: Two Radio Plays, The Rolling Sea at Setúbal, The Year Lacertis*, translated by Michael Hamburger, 1968.
In Anderern Sprachen: Vier Hörspiele (radio plays; includes *Meine sieben jungen Freunde; Die Stunde des Huflattichs; Blick auf Venedig; Man bittet zu läuten*). 1964.
Unter Wasser; Böhmische Schneider: Marionettenspiele. 1964.
Fünfzehn Hörspiele (radio plays). 1966.

Radio Plays: *Das festliche Jahr*, with Martin Raschke, 1936; *Zinngeschrei*, 1955; *Die Brandung vor Setúbal*, 1957; *Allah hat hundert Namen*, 1957; *Die Mädchen aus Viterbo*, 1960; *Festianus Märtyrer*, 1966.

Fiction

Katharina. 1936.
Kulka, Hilpert, Elefanten. 1968.
Maulwürfe. 1968.
Ein Tibeter in meinem Büro. 1970.

Other

Ein Lesebuch, edited by Susanne Müller-Hanpft. 1972.
Semmelformen, drawings by Sven Knebel. 1972.
Translator, *Lyrik des Ostens: China* (verse), edited by Wilhelm Gundert, A. Schimmel and Walther Schubring. 1958.
Translator, *Aus dem Chinesischen* (verse). 1973.

*

Critical Studies: *Günter Eich* by Egbert Krispyn, 1971; *Günter Eich* edited by Bernd Jentzsch, 1973; *Committed Aestheticism: The Poetic Theory and Practice of Günter Eich* by Larry L. Ricardson,

1983; *Career at the Cost of Compromise: Günter Eich's Life and Work in the Years 1933–1945* by Glenn R. Cuomo, 1989; *Der eigenen Fehlbarkeit begegnet: Günter Eichs Realitäten 1933–1945* by Axel Vieregg, 1993; *Günter Eich und der Rundfunk: Essay und Dokumentation* by Hans-Ulrich Wagner, 1999; *Günter Eich 1907–1972: Nach dem Ende der Biographie*, edited by Peter Walther, 2000.

* * *

Günter Eich was among those writers who helped provide a sense of continuity in German literature from the early 1930s through to the post-World War II period. In the pre-war years he gradually gained public recognition; however, unlike many writers, he remained in Germany after Hitler came to power and served his country during the war.

Eich's first collection of verse, *Gedichte* [Poems], published in 1930, warrants his description of himself as a late expressionist and nature poet, and reflects his association with the literary group at Dresden centred on the journal *Die Kolonne*. Such poems as "Die Flusse entlang" [Along the Rivers] and "Der Anfang kühlerer Tage" [The Start of Cold Weather] illustrate this mood and approach at the time. The 1930s also marked the beginning of a lifelong involvement on Eich's part with the radio play. Schwitzke has noted several plays and their broadcasts between 1932 and—interestingly in the historical context—the late 1930s.

In an American prisoner-of-war camp in 1945 Eich resumed his interest in poetry and soon after embarked upon literary collaboration with Hans Werner Richter. He contributed to numerous journals and became a founding member of the newly established Gruppe 47 and the first recipient of its prize in 1950 (it was only the first of several literary recognitions awarded to Eich over the years). By that time Eich had established himself as a leading post-war writer in West Germany.

In 1948 his first post-war collection of verse, *Abgelegene Gehöhfte* [Isolated Farms] was published. Eich's occupation with the theme of remoteness, be it of time or place, is already suggested in the title poem or in "Wiepersdorf, die Arminschen Gräber" and "Wie grau es auch regnet." In Eich's evocation of bygone times there is evidence of the melancholic tone which becomes an increasingly characteristic feature of his verse. These poems in fact are still a reminder of the *Kolonne* period, but the volume also contains a number that starkly relate to his war experiences. "Inventur" [Stocktaking], one of the best-known of all early post-war poems, catalogues matter-of-factly and with the sparsest language the few yet precious belongings of the prisoner-of-war; it is rightly regarded as typically illustrating the so-called *Kahlschlag* technique. The rhyming juxtaposition of "Hölderlin/Urin" in "Latrine," may have caused offense to some readers' susceptibilities at the time, but Eich's concern was always to challenge. Lines from his radio play *Träume* [Dreams] effectively serve as a motto for his work: "no, don't sleep, while those who order the world are busy!/Be mistrustful of their power. . .!/. . ./Do that which is not useful, sing the songs that are not expected from your mouth!/Be irritating, be sand, not oil, in the world machine!"

Träume [Dreams] was but one of the barrage of radio plays from Eich's pen and some 40 plays are credited to him in the span of a quarter of a century after the war. The development of the radio play as a literary genre in the 1950s is synonymous with Eich's own work in the field. The medium encouraged anti-naturalist techniques, with the use of acoustic devices, and these Eich exploited to the full. In this context the titles of his first collections of radio plays are pertinent: *Träume* (it was to prove highly popular, with over 50,000 copies sold) and *Stimmen* [Voices]. The individual pieces show the ready transposition of dream and reality. In *Der Tiger Jussuf*, for instance, the soul of a lion enters different people, while in *Die Andere und ich* [The Other Woman and I] Ellend Harland, a rich American woman, experiences the miserable existence of an Italian fisherman's wife. Catarina in *Die Brandung von Setúbal* (*The Rolling Sea at Setúbal*) is similarly placed in a transformational situation, as Eich juggles with the theme of time and the two worlds of life and death. The presence of a strong comic-absurd, satiric, even grotesque dimension here as elsewhere in his work serves to heighten the underlying seriousness of Eich's intent. One may seek to play out the game of fulfilling logic through dreams, but as Goldschmidt reminds us in *Die Mädchen aus Viterbo* [The Girls from Viterbo], there comes a point when the time for dreaming is over. For three years during World War II the old Jew and his granddaughter have fearfully awaited the knock on the door that portends death. To combat their fears they indulge themselves with the story of schoolgirls lost with their teacher in the catacombs of Rome. The interplay, perhaps rather the counterbalancing, of make-believe and reality allows Eich once more to present a marginal situation. Only when the knock does come is the moment reached of recognizing life for what it is, including the notion that God too is a component in the established order of evil, lies, and illusion. It is a viewpoint that Eich formulates both in his radio plays and in his verse. Anarchy or the perceived sense of ordered life is the challenge Eich poses himself and us. *Man bittet zu läuten* [Please Ring the Bell], Eich's penultimate radio play, is arguably his most powerful expression of indictment, but equally is seen as marking a departure from the conventional understanding of the *hörspiel* (radio play) towards the *sprechstück* (spoken drama).

By the time Eich's third post-war and most popular volume of verse, *Botschaften des Regens* [Messages of the Rain], was published in 1955 (the second *Untergrundbahn* [Subway] had appeared in 1949), the melancholic tone had become more marked and the language more sparse. The simple routine and details of everyday life is not completely absent (for example in "Weg zum Bahnhof" [The Way to the Station]), but an actual journey can become also the journey of the mind ("D-Zug-München-Frankfurt" [The Munich to Frankfurt Express]). A locality can conjure up memories, but also evoke darker responses: "Der Beginn der Einsamkeit, Das Schilf der Verzweiflung/der trigonometrische Punkt/Abnessung im Nichts" [The beginning of solitude, the need of despair/of the trigonometric point/measurement in the void] ("Der grosse Lübbe-See"). The emphasis still lies on the theme of transience, as the first poem of the collection, "Ende eines-Sommers" [End of a Summer], immediately establishes. The initial positive note in the poem gives way before the awareness of the inevitability of the process of death. Equally, the title poem spells out the gloomy portents carried by the rain—portents of despair, privation, and guilt.

Zu den Akten did not appear until almost a decade later, in 1964. By then Eich had travelled extensively through North America, but more significantly to the Orient, and his apparent growing preference for the latter's way of life is reflected not only in the poem "Fussnote zu Rom" [Footnote to Rome], but also in the very title of the subsequent collection *Anlässe und Steingärten* [Reasons and

Rockeries]. Objects themselves become the sources of existential experience, as in the case of the stones placed artificially in the sand in those places of meditation, the Japanese stone gardens. In "Zum Berspiel" Eich becomes engaged with the difficulty experienced in translating meaning and truth by a word ("ein wort in ein Wort übersetzen") inferring the need rather for "transposition." For Eich, it becomes a matter of seeking a symbol instead of a metaphor. With the passing years, his distrust of life increases and his goals correspondingly appear to lessen. Occasionally, the old aggressive note surfaces ("Seminar für Hinterbliebene" [School for Survivors], "Geometrischer Ort" [Geometrical Point], "Optik" [Optics]), even a trace of bitter humour and self mockery can be detected ("Zuversicht" [Optimism]), to become subsumed in the more prevailing mood of a resigned acceptance of ultimate silence. Thematically, the late poems centre on departure and death.

Eich would expound occasionally on the nature of poetry, but essentially he never saw himself as a theoretician. A poem such as "Kunsttheorien" would confirm that view, as would a series of short prose pieces undertaken by Eich towards the end of the 1960s. Under the title *Maulwürfe* [Moles] (1968; a second collection, *Ein Tibeter in meinem Büro* [A Tibetan in My Office] was published in 1970), they are fundamentally short paragraph-like passages that illustrate Eich's apparent unwillingness to make a direct statement. They constitute a deliberate jumbling of aphorisms, clichés, and touches of lyricism that produce an odd mixture of sense and nonsense. The anarchic factor still proclaims itself: "If I were a negative writer, I'd rather be a negative carpenter, long live anarchy!" ("Späne" [Woodshavings]). Basically, the passages reflect the view that nothing is self-evident in life or in literature.

Despite his limited verse output, Eich proved a significant influence on the development of the German lyric after World War II, while the progress of the radio play during that same period (and particularly in the 1950s) is indelibly linked with Eich's own creative performance in that field.

—Ian Hilton

EICHENDORFF, Joseph (Karl Benedikt, Freiherr) von

Born: Lubowitz, Silesia, Germany, 10 March 1788. **Education:** Educated at Katholisches Gymnasium, Breslau, 1801–04; Halle University, 1805–06; Heidelberg University, 1807–08; continued to study law in Vienna, 1810–12. **Military Service:** Served in the volunteer forces during the War of Liberation, 1813–14 and 1815; commissioned 1813. **Family:** Married Aloysia (Luise) von Larisch in 1815 (died 1855); two sons and three daughters. **Career:** Undertook a walking tour through the Harz mountains, 1805; travelled to Paris and Vienna, 1808; returned to Lubowitz to manage father's estate, 1809; lived in Berlin, 1809–10; dispatch clerk, War Ministry, Berlin, 1815; trainee civil servant, 1816–19, and assessor, 1819–21, Prussian Royal Government; government councillor, Danzig, 1821, Ministry of Education and Cultural Affairs, Berlin, 1823, 1831–44, and Königsberg, 1824. **Died:** 26 November 1857.

PUBLICATIONS

Collections

Sämtliche Werke. 6 vols., 2nd edition, 1864.
Vermischte Schriften. 5 vols., 1866–67.
Werke, edited by Richard Dietze. 2 vols., 1891.
Werke, edited by Ludwig Krähe. 2 vols., 1908.
Sämtliche Werke, edited by Wilhelm Kosch and August Sauer; continued by Hermann Kunisch and Helmut Koopmann. 9 vols., 1908–50; 2nd edition, 1962–.
Gedichte, Erzählungen, Biographisches, edited by Max Wehrli. 1945.
[Selected Poems], edited by Gerhard Prager. 1946.
Neue Gesamtausgabe der Werke und Schriften, edited by Gerhart Baumann and Siegfried Grosse. 4 vols., 1957–58.
Werke, edited by Ansgar Hillach and Klaus Dieter Krabiel. 5 vols., 1970–88.
Werke, edited by Wolfgang Frühwald, Brigitte Schillbach and Hartwig Schultz. 6 vols., 1985–.

Fiction

Ahnung und Gegenwart. 1815.
Aus dem Leben eines Taugenichts und Das Marmorbild. Zwei Novellen nebst einem Anhange von Liedern und Romanzen. 1826; reprinted 1981; as *Memoirs of a Good-for-Nothing*, translated by Charles Godfrey Leland, 1866, also translated by Bayard Quincy Morgan, 1955; Ronald Taylor, 1966; as *The Happy-Go-Lucky*, translated by A.L. Wister, 1906; as *The Life of a Good-for-Nothing*, translated by Michael Glenny, 1966; *Das Marmorbild* as "The Marble Statue," translated by F.E. Pierce, in *Fiction and Fantasy of German Romance*, edited by Pierce and C.F. Schreiber, 1927.
Viel Lärmen um Nichts, in *Der Gesellschafter*, edited by F.W. Gubitz. 1832.
Dichter und ihre Gesellen. 1834.
Das Schloss Dürande. 1837.
Die Entführung. 1839.
Die Glücksritter. 1841.
Libertas und ihr Freier. 1864.
Eine Meerfahrt. 1864.
Auch ich war in Arkadien. 1866.
Novellen. 1927.
Erzählungen. 1946.
Erzählungen, edited by Werner Bergengruen. 1955.
Das Wiedersehen, edited by Hermann Kunisch. 1966.

Verse

Gedichte. 1837; revised edition, 1843.
Neue Gedichte. 1847.
Julian. 1853.
Robert und Guiscard. 1855.
Lucius. 1857.
Gedichte aus dem Nachlasse, edited by Heinrich Meisner. 1888.
Joseph und Wilhelm von Eichendorffs Jugendgedichte, edited by Raimund Pissin. 1906.
Eichendorffs Jugendgedichte aus seiner Schulzeit, edited by Hilda Schulhof. 1915; reprinted 1974.
Gedichte, edited by A. Schaeffer. 1919.

The Happy Wanderer and Other Poems, translated by Marjorie Rossy. 1925.

Gedichte. Ahnung und Gegenwart, edited by Werner Bergengruen. 1955.

Plays

Krieg den Philistern!. 1824.

Meierbeths Glack und Ende, in *Der Gesellschafter*, edited by F.W. Gubitz. 1827.

Ezelin von Romano. 1828.

Der letzte Held von Marienburg. 1830.

Die Freier. 1833.

Das Incognito: Ein Puppenspiel. Mit Fragmenten und Entwürfen anderer Dichtungen nach den Handschriften, edited by Konrad Weichberger. 1901; also edited by Gerhard Kluge, with *Das Loch; oder, das wiedergefundene Paradies: Ein Schattenspiel*, by Ludwig Achim von Arnim, 1968.

Other

Die Wiederherstellung des Schlosses der deutschen Ordensritter zu Marienburg. 1844.

Zur Geschichte der neueren romantischen Poesie in Deutschland. 1846.

Über die ethische und religiöse Bedeutung der neueren romantischen Poesie in Deutschland. 1847.

Die geistliche Poesie in Deutschland. 1847.

Der deutsche Roman des achtzehnten Jahrhunderts in seinem Verhältnis zum Christenthum. 1851.

Zur Geschichte des Dramas. 1854.

Geschichte der poetischen Literatur Deutschlands. 2 vols., 1857.

Aus dem Nachlass. Briefe und Dichtungen, edited by Wilhelm Kosch. 1906.

Fahrten und Wanderungen 1802–1814 der Freiherren Joseph und Wilhelm Eichendorff, edited by Alfons Nowack. 1907.

Lubowitzer Tagebuchblätter, edited by Alfons Nowack. 1907.

Liederbuch, illustrated by Josua Leander Gampp. 1922.

Schlesische Tagebücher (diaries), edited by Alfred Riemen. 1988.

Editor, *Gedichte,* by Lebrecht Dreves. 1849.

Translator, *Der Graf Lucanor*, by Juan Manuel. 1840.

Translator, *Geistliche Schauspiele* by Pedro Calderón de la Barca. 2 vols., 1846–53.

Translator, *Fünf Zwischenspiele*, by Miguel de Cervantes, edited by A. Potthoff. 1924.

*

Critical Studies: *Der Dichter des Taugenichts: Eichendorffs Welt und Leben, geschildert von ihm selbst und von Zeitgenossen* edited by Paul Stöcklein and Inge Feuchtmayer, 1957, and *Eichendorff heute* edited by Stöcklein, 1960; ''Zum Gedächtnis Eichendorffs'' by Theodor W. Adorno, in *Akzente*, (5), 1958; *Eichendorff: Aus dem Leben eines Taugenichts* by G.T. Hughes, 1961; *Versuche über Eichendorff* by Oskar Seidlin, 1965, 2nd edition, 1978; ''The Metaphor of Death in Eichendorff,'' in *Oxford German Studies*, (4), 1969, and ''Eichendorff und Shakespeare,'' in *German Romantics in Context: Selected Essays*, 1992, both by Elisabeth Stopp; *Eichendorff: The Spiritual Geometer* by Lawrence Radner, 1970;

Eichendorff-Kommentar by Ansgar Hillach and Klaus-Dieter Krabiel, 2 vols., 1971–72; *Joseph von Eichendorff* by Egon Schwarz, 1972; *Spatiotemporal Consciousness in English and German Romanticism. A Comparative Study of Novalis, Blake, Wordsworth, and Eichendorff* by Amala M. Hanke, 1981; *Eichendorff und die Spätromantik* edited by Hans-Georg Pott, 1985; *Hieroglyphenschrift. Untersuchungen zu Eichendorffs Erzählungen* by Klaus Köhnke, 1986; *Lyric Descent in the German Romantic Tradition* by Brigitte Peucker, 1986; *Joseph von Eichendorff* by Wolfgang Frühwald and Franz Heiduk, 1988; *Ansichten zu Eichendorff. Beiträge der Forschung 1985 bis 1988* edited by Alfred Riemen, 1988; Eichendorff Issue of *German Life and Letters*, 42(3), 1989; *Hindeutung auf das Höhere: A Structural Study of the Novels of Joseph von Eichendorff* by Judith Purver, 1989; *Lebendige Allegorie. Studien zu Eichendorffs Leben und Werk* by Robert Mühlher, 1990; *Eichendorff's Scholarly Reputation: A Survey* by Robert O. Goebel, 1994; *Classical Rhetoric and the German Poet 1620 to the Present: A Study of Opitz, Bürger and Eichendorff* by Anna Carrdus, 1996; *Schumann's Eichendorff Liederkreis and the Genre of the Romantic Cycle* by David Ferris, 2000; *Italy in the German Literary Imagination: Goethe's Italian Journey and Its Reception by Eichendorff, Platen, and Heine* by Gretchen L. Hachmeister, 2002.

*   *   *

Joseph von Eichendorff's fame as the quintessential German Romantic writer rests primarily on a narrow segment of his total output: a selection of his lyric poetry and two or three stories, the most celebrated of which is *Aus dem Leben eines Taugenichts* (*Memoirs of a Good-for-Nothing*). Since very little of his work, apart from this tale and a few poems, has been translated into English, he is best known in the English-speaking world through the musical settings of his lyrics by such composers as Mendelssohn, Schumann (especially ''Dichterliebe,'' Opus 39, 1840), Brahms, Hugo Wolf, Hans Pfitzner (the cantata ''Von deutscher Seele'' [Of the German Soul], Opus 28, 1921), and Richard Strauss. His poems have been set to music more frequently than those of almost any other German writer; thus his importance in the context of the German *Lied* and its development is considerable. His work also influenced more 19th-century German poets than that of any other writer except Goethe, and has been assimilated, imitated, parodied, praised, and quoted to a remarkable degree by a wide variety of authors, from Theodor Storm and Theodor Fontane to Thomas Mann, Hermann Hesse, and Günter Grass.

The full range of Eichendorff's literary and other writings is, however, still relatively little known. He wrote over 500 lyric poems, nine stories, five plays, three epic poems, two novels, and a number of narrative, dramatic, and autobiographical fragments. His diaries (1798 to 1815) reveal many of the decisive influences on his formative years, including the Romantic thinkers and writers Joseph Görres, Friedrich Schlegel, Henrik Steffens, Achim von Arnim, Clemens Brentano, and the Grimm brothers, whose example probably inspired him to begin, in 1808–09, a collection of Upper Silesian fairytales. In his later years, he again followed the Romantic example, both by translating from Spanish a number of ballads, as well as dramas by Calderón and Cervantes, and a 14th-century prose text, *El Conde Lucanor* [Count Lucanor] by Don Juan Manual, and by composing several essays and treatises on literature, the last and most comprehensive of which, *Geschichte der poetischen Literatur Deutschlands* [History of the Poetic Literature of Germany], appeared in 1857, the year of his death. In the same year, he began a biography of St. Hedwig, the patron saint of Silesia. In connection with his career in the Prussian Civil Service, Eichendorff also produced a number of historical and political writings, including pieces on secularization, constitutional questions, and press censorship, and on the two great symbolic Prussian architectural undertakings of the time, the completion of Cologne Cathedral and the restoration of the Marienburg castle near Danzig, with both of which he was, personally as well as professionally, closely involved. His correspondence, while less extensive than that of some of his contemporaries, provides valuable insights into his life, work, and thought, and into the unsettled times in which he lived.

The chaotic period of the Napoleonic Wars forms the background to Eichendorff's first novel, *Ahnung und Gegenwart* [Divination and the Present], written 1810–12 in Vienna, but not published until 1815. Eichendorff's intention in this work was to provide a "complete picture . . . of that strange time of expectation, longing and grief, heavy with foreboding of the storm to come" which had preceded the Wars of Liberation in the German lands. Though by no means devoid of realistic detail, the novel is not a mimetic portrayal of the period, but rather an attempt to create, in the spirit of the theory and practice of the novel among the German Romantics, a structural and symbolic counterpart both to the confusion of the times, as it appeared to Eichendorff, and to the underlying order of the universe, guaranteed for him by his Catholic faith and his trust in an ultimate divine purpose shaping the world as a whole and the individual human life within it. Characteristically, the lyrical prose of the novel is interspersed with a large number of poems, among which are some of Eichendorff's best known, such as "Das zerbrochene Ringlein" ["The Broken Ring"], "Abschied" ["Farewell"], and "Waldgespräch" ["Conversation in the Forest"].

Apart from *Memoirs of a Good-for-Nothing*, two of Eichendorff's shorter narrative works, *Das Marmorbild* ("The Marble Statue") and *Das Schloss Dürande* [Dürande Castle] deserve special mention. The first is based on a traditional European story concerning the betrothal of a young man to a statue of Venus, a theme which preoccupied Eichendorff throughout his life and which he here uses to reveal the psychological roots and destructive potential of the erotic drive, as well as the lure of an unbridled poetic imagination, both of which he saw as manifestations of the demonic forces of subjectivism which could only be controlled by Christianity. He saw the same forces at work in the French Revolution, which provides the subject matter of *Das Schloss Dürande*. Yet while he regards the Revolution as an unmitigated disaster, he is also sharply critical of the behaviour of the nobility which led up to it.

The first edition of Eichendorff's collected poems appeared in 1837. Characteristic of his lyric vocabulary is the recurrence of a limited number of archetypal words and images, particularly nouns (often in the plural) referring to basic features of the landscape, such as mountains, forests, valleys, and rivers, verbs conveying movement and sense impressions, and unspecific but emotionally charged adjectives. These combine to give his verse an incantatory quality and an instantly recognizable tone, adapted from the folk-song tradition as transmitted through Arnim and Brentano's collection *Des Knaben Wunderhorn* (*The Boy's Magic Horn*). Eichendorff's conscious use of elements of popular tradition has often been misinterpreted as naive; in fact, it is subtle and ambivalent, stirring unconscious depths in the reader and evoking, through a densely woven net of symbols, a transcendent sphere beyond the physical world. He is also a fine prose stylist and spirited polemicist, using satire and irony to attack, in a manner somewhat reminiscent of his ideological opponent, Heine, both Romantic excesses and unromantic philistinism.

—Judith Purver

See the essay on *Memoirs of a Good-for-Nothing*.

ELIADE, Mircea

Born: Bucharest, Romania 9 March 1907. **Education:** Spiru Haret Lyceum, Bucharest, 1917–25; studied philosophy, University of Bucharest, 1925–28, doctorate in philosophy, 1933; studied Indian philosophy, Calcutta, 1929–31. **Military Service:** Artillery regiment, 1932. **Family:** Married 1) Nina Mareş, 1934 (died 1944); 2) Christinel Cotrescu, 1950. **Career:** Lecturer, University of Bucharest, 1933–39; cultural attaché, Romanian legation, London, 1940–41; cultural counselor, Romanian legation, Lisbon, Spain, 1941–45; lecturer, École Pratique des Hautes Études, Paris, 1946–48; lecturer, Sorbonne, Paris, 1948–56; fellow, Bollingen Foundation, 1951–55; visiting professor, 1956–57, and professor, 1957–86, of the history of religions, University of Chicago. **Awards:** Numerous honorary doctorates, including Yale, 1966, Oberlin, 1972, and the Sorbonne, 1976. **Member:** American Academy of Arts and Sciences, 1966; Royal Academy of Belgium, 1975; corresponding member, Austrian Academy of Sciences, 1973. **Died:** Chicago, Illinois, 22 April 1986.

PUBLICATIONS

Fiction

Isabel şi apele diavolului. 1930.
Maitreyi. 1933; as *Bengal Nights*, 1993, translated by Catherine Spencer.
Întoarcerea din rai. 1934.
Lumina ce se stinge. 1934.
Huliganii. 2 vols. 1935.
Domnişoara Christina. 1936.
Şarpele. 1937.
Nunta în cer. 1939.
Secretul doctorului Honigberger and *Nopţi la Serampore.* 1940; as *Two Tales of the Occult*, translated by W. A. Coates, 1970.
Pe strada Mântuleasa. 1968.
La tigănci şi alte povestiri. 1969.
Noaptea de Sânziene. 2 vols, 1971; as *The Forbidden Forest*, translated by M. L. Ricketts and M. P. Stevenson, 1978.
Tales of the Sacred and Supernatural. 1981.
Mystic Stories: The Sacred and the Profane, translated by Ana Cartianu. 1992.

Nonfiction

India. 1934.
Alchimia Asiatică. 1935.
Yoga: Essai sur les origines de la mystique indienne. 1936.
Cosmologie şi alchimie babiloniană. 1937.
Metallurgy, Magic, and Alchemy. 1938.
Mitul reîntegrării. 1942.
Comentarii la legenda Meşterului Manole. 1943.

Traité d'histoire des religions. 1949; as *Patterns in Comparative Religion*, translated by R. Sheed, 1958.

Le Mythe de l'éternel retour. 1949; as *The Myth of the Eternal Return*, translated by W. R. Trask, 1954.

Le Chamanisme et les techniques archaïques de l'extase. 1951; as *Shamanism. Archaic Techniques of Extasy*, translated by W. R. Trask, 1964.

Images et symboles. Essai sur le symbolisme magico-religieux. 1952; as *Images and Symbols*, translated by P. Mairet, 1961.

Le Yoga: Immortalité et liberté. 1954; as *Yoga: Immortality and Freedom*, translated by W. R. Trask, 1958.

Forgerons et alchimistes. 1956; as *The Forge and the Crucible*, translated by S. Corrin, 1962.

Das Heilige und das Profane. 1957; translated from the French manuscript by E. Grassi; as *The Sacred and the Profane: The Nature of Religion*, translated by W. R. Trask, 1959.

Mythes, rêves et mystères. 1957; as *Myths, Dreams, and Mysteries*, translated by P. Mairet, 1960.

Naissances mystiques: Essai sur quelques types d'initiation. 1959; as *Birth and Rebirth: The Religious Meaning of Initiation in Human Culture*, translated by W. R. Trask, 1958.

Méphistophélès et l'Androgyne. 1962; as *Mephistopheles and the Androgyne*, translated by J. M. Cohen, 1965.

Patanjali et le Yoga. 1962; as *Patanjali and Yoga*, translated by C. L. Markmann, 1969.

Aspects du mythe. 1963; as *Myth and Reality*, translated by W. R. Trask, 1963.

The Quest: History and Meaning in Religion. 1969.

De Zalmoxis à Gengis Khan. 1970; as *Zalmoxis: The Vanishing God*, translated by W. R. Trask, 1972.

Australian Religions: An Introduction. 1973.

Occultism, Witchcraft, and Cultural Fashions: Essays in Comparative Religions. 1976.

Histoire des croyances et des idées religieuses. 3 vols. 1976–83; as *A History of Religious Ideas*, 3 vols., translated by W. R. Trask, A. Hiltebeitel, and D. Apostolos-Cappadona, 1978–85.

The Eliade Guide to World Religions, with Ioan P. Couliano and Hillary S. Wiesner. 1991.

Biblioteca Maharajului. 1991.

Erotica mistică în Bengal. 1994.

Misterele şi inițierea orientală: Scrieri din tinerețe. (1926), 1998.

Essays

Soliloquii. 1932.

Oceanografie. 1934.

Fragmentarium. 1939.

Insula lui Euthanasius. 1943.

Symbolism, the Sacred, and the Arts, edited by Diane Apostolos-Cappadona. 1985.

Other

Şantier. 1935.

Amintiri. I (1907–28). 1966.

Fragments d'un journal. 1973; as *No Souvenirs: Journal, 1957–1969*, translated by F. H. Johnson, Jr., 1977.

L'Épreuve du labyrinthe: Entretiens avec Claude-Henri Rocquet. 1978; as *Ordeal by Labyrinth: Conversations with Claude-Henri Rocquet*, translated by D. Coltman, 1982.

Autobiography, translated by Mac Linscott Ricketts, 2 vols., 1981–88.

Journal I (1949–1955), *II* (1957–1969), *III* (1970–1978), *IV* (1979–1985). 1989–90.

L'histoire des religions a-t-elle un sens?: correspondance, 1926–1959, edited by Natale Spineto. 1994.

Editor, *Zalmoxis.* 1938–42.

Editor, *From Pimitives to Zen: A Thematic Sourcebook of the History of Religions.* 1967.

Editor in Chief, *Encyclopedia of Religion.* 16 vols, 1987

*

Bibliography: *Mircea Eliade: An Annotated Bibliography* by Douglas Allen and Dennis Doeing, 1980.

Critical Studies: *Religion on Trial: Mircea Eliade and His Critics* by Guilford Dudley III, 1977; *Mircea Eliade*, in *Cahiers de l'Herne*, no. 33, edited by Constantine Tacou, 1978; *Hermeneutica lui Mircea Eliade* by Adrian Marino, 1980; *Waiting for the Dawn: Mircea Eliade in Perspective*, edited by David Carrasco and Jane Swanberg, 1985, 1991; *Mircea Eliade: The Romanian Roots, 1907–1945* by Mac Linscott Ricketts, 2 vols., 1988; *The Theology and Philosophy of Eliade: A Search for the Centre* by Carl Olson, 1992; *Mircea Eliade's Vision for a New Humanism* by David Cave, 1993; *Mircea Eliade, spirit al amplitudinii* by Eugen Simion, 1995; *Reconstructing Eliade: Making Sense of Religion* by Bryan S. Rennie, 1996; *Changing Religious Worlds: The Meaning and End of Mircea Eliade*, edited by Bryan Rennie, 2000; *Dosarul Eliade*, 5 vols., by Mircea Handoca, 1998–2001.

* * *

Mircea Eliade pursued two careers throughout his life, that of the scholar and that of the creative writer. He first achieved fame in his native Romania as a novelist in the decade before the outbreak of World War II. It was a time when he was deepening his knowledge of Indian religions and myths and publishing the first of a remarkable series of works on these subjects. After he left Romania he gained an international reputation as an exegete of religions and myths, initially in France, from 1945 to 1956, and then in the United States, from 1956 to 1986. He ranged widely in his chosen field from the occult beliefs of the ancient Dacians to the mythologies of India and the supernatural in Australian aboriginal religions. His work was pioneering, and he contributed enormously to the advancement of the humanistic sciences. Scholarship now came first, and fiction was a secondary preoccupation, though he wrote several of his prose masterpieces during these later years.

Eliade himself perceived no barrier between science and fiction. For him, the one illuminated the other. His main concern was to grasp the human spirit and to chart the human destiny, tasks, he was convinced, that could best be accomplished if culture were taken as a whole and not separated into compartments. Not surprisingly, then, certain themes are common to both his scholarly research and his literary creativity. His studies of Indian civilization in India between

1929 and 1931 exerted an enormous enduring influence on him as a scholar, a teacher, and a novelist. He was struck especially by the contrast between India, a civilization that had preserved a mysterious link to the world of myth and the spirit, and the West, a civilization in thrall to rationalism and technology. Thus *Maitreyi* (*Bengal Nights*) is both a love story between a European man and an Indian woman and a philosophical novel on the impermeability of civilizations, while *Noaptea de Sânziene* (*The Forbidden Forest*), his other masterpiece of fiction, combines the real and the fantastic and draws on his investigations of myth and his skill at delineating character.

In contrast to his scholarly works, Eliade's fiction is little known outside Romania. But in Romania, ever since the appearance of his first important novels in the early 1930s, his literary work has aroused lively criticism and discussion. His admirers and even some of his detractors recognize his innovations of theme and character as powerful stimulants in the development of the Romanian novel. He took the Romanian novel out of its traditional modes, endowing it with another kind of conflict. His heroes were no longer the young men from the countryside who struggled to adapt to urban life or or the small town intellectuals who were overwhelmed by the inertia of provincial life. Rather, they thought differently about the world, and they perceived their own destiny differently from that of their fathers as traditional values crumbled and nothing filled the void.

Eliade was intent on "renewing" the Romanian novel by introducing new subject matter and "authentic" characters. He championed the novel of ideas and strong characters who experienced ideas and had their own view of the world and a consciousness of their place in it. He changed the emphasis in the novel from the sentimental drama to the drama of cognition. Perhaps this is why he gave young men, rather than old men and women, a privileged place in his novels; he thought them better able to endure the curse of existence. As for form, he was conservative. Although he was reading Gide, Huxley, Joyce, and others who were experimenting with form, he insisted that the novel preserve traditional structures. He thought that the "novel should be a novel," that the author should let his characters be themselves and refrain from analyzing them or even commenting upon them.

Eliade's novels fall into several stylistic categories. The first consisted of his "Indian" novels, notably *Bengal Nights*, which gained recognition for him in Romania as a significant writer. Based on his own experiences in Calcutta, *Bengal Nights* recounts his love for a charming and puzzling young Indian woman. But love is also a mode of cognition; through it he discovers the Indian spirit and experiences a revelation of his own soul. In *Huliganii* [The Hooligans] he tried a formula new to Romanian literature—the existentialist revolt. He thus moved from the autobiographical novel to the novel of observation and the creation of character types. It is realistic, as he turns to Romanian society and the younger generation, frenetic, confused, and certain that it was descending into tragedy. In this novel of ideas Eliade has captured the spirit of a society that is slowly disintegrating, where the hooligans test various philosophies of existence but are united in their abandonment of the moral values their parents defended. The solutions he proposed—revolt, a philosophy of despair, the experience of the tragic—were unusual for readers of the time.

Eliade was a master of the fantastic tale, and *Domnişoara Christina* [Miss Christina] was the first modern fantastic novel in Romanian

literature. It tells of a woman, dead at a young age, who returns as a ghost in the dreams of persons staying at her sister's house through her will, not theirs. Eliade, drawing upon Romanian folklore, is intrigued by the ways in which the fantastic manifests itself in normal people and how they cope with the chaos it causes.

The Forbidden Forest, which Eliade composed between 1949 and 1954 and which many critics regard as his masterpiece, combines in one vast fresco the major themes of his fiction. It is a novel of manners, a political novel, and an erotic novel that portrays Romanian society in the fateful years between 1936 and 1948. But it is, above all, an intellectual novel and a mystic novel. It is about young men who are desperate to escape from history and time and who seek to live in some other dimension and in accordance with other rules.

In his fiction no less than in his explorations of religions and myths, Eliade was moved by the urge to pose fundamental questions about existence. Novels served him as tools to sound the inner life of man in search of the eternal.

—Keith Hitchins

ÉLUARD, Paul

Born: Eugène-Émile-Paul Grindel in Paris, France, 14 December 1895. **Education:** Educated at École communale, Aulnay-sous-Bois, 1901–09; École primaire supérieure Colbert, Paris, 1909. **Military Service:** Served in the French army during World War I and World War II. **Family:** Married 1) Hélène Dimitrovnie (Gala) Diakonova in 1917 (separated 1930), one daughter; 2) Maria Benz in 1934 (died 1946); 3) Dominique Lemor in 1951. **Career:** Confined in a sanatorium in Davos, 1912–14; leading member of the Surrealist movement between 1919 and 1938; co-founder *La Révolution surréaliste*, 1924; joined Association of Revolutionary Writers and Artists, Paris, 1931; worked for the Resistance, from 1942; founder, with Louis Parrot, *L'Éternelle Revue*, 1944; travelled to Czechoslovakia, Italy, Yugoslavia, Greece, and Poland after World War II. **Member:** Communist Party, 1927–33, and from 1938. **Died:** 18 November 1952.

PUBLICATIONS

Collections

Poésies choisies, edited by Claude Roy. 1959.
Anthologie Éluard, edited by Clive Scott. 1968.
Oeuvres complètes, edited by Marcelle Dumas and Lucien Scheler. 2 vols., 1968.
Poèmes choisis, edited by Pierre Gamarra and Rouben Melik. 1982.
Oeuvres poétiques complètes, edited by Hubert Juin. 6 vols., 1986.
Selected Poems, translated by Gilbert Bowen. 1987.
Ombres et soleil: Shadows and Sun: Selected Writings of 1913–1952, translated by Lloyd Alexander and Cicely Buckley. 1995.
The Automatic Message; The Magnetic Fields; The Immaculate Conception by André Breton, Paul Éluard and Philippe Soupault, translated by David Gascoyne, Antony Melville and Jon Graham. 1997.

Verse

Premiers poèmes. 1913.
Le Devoir et l'inquiétude. 1917.
Poèmes pour la paix. 1918.
Les Animaux et leurs hommes. Les Hommes et leurs animaux. 1920.
Répétitions. 1922.
Les Malheurs des immortels, with Max Ernst. 1922.
Mourir de ne pas mourir. 1924.
152 proverbes mis au goût du jour, with Benjamin Péret. 1925.
Capitale de la douleur. 1926.
Les Dessous d'une vie ou la pyramide humaine. 1926.
L'Amour la poésie. 1929.
A toute épreuve. 1930.
La Vie immédiate. 1932.
La Rose publique. 1934.
Facile. 1935.
Nuits partagées. 1935.
Les Yeux fertiles. 1936.
Thorns of Thunder: Selected Poems, edited by George Reavey, translated by Samuel Beckett and others. 1936.
Les Mains libres, illustrated by Man Ray. 1937.
Cours naturel. 1938.
Chanson complète. 1939.
Donner à voir (includes prose). 1939.
Le Livre ouvert I (1938–1940). 1940.
Choix de poèmes, edited by A. Bosquet. 1941; revised edition, 1946.
Sur les pentes inférieures. 1941.
Le Livre ouvert II (1939–1941). 1942.
Poésie et vérité. 1942; as *Poetry and Truth*, translated by Roland Penrose and E.L.T. Mesens, 1944.
Poésie involontaire, poésie intentionnelle (selection). 1942.
Les Sept poèmes d'amour en guerre. 1943.
Dignes de vivre. 1944.
Le Lit, la table. 1944.
Au rendez-vous allemand. 1944; revised edition, 1946.
Pour vivre ici. 1944.
Doubles d'ombre, illustrated by Éluard. 1945.
Lingères légères. 1945.
Une longue réflexion amoureuse. 1945.
Poésie ininterrompue I. 1946.
Le Dur Désir de durer. 1946; as *Le Dur Désir de durer*, translated by Stephen Spender and Frances Cornford, 1950.
Corps mémorable. 1947.
Le Temps déborde. 1947.
Choix de poèmes, edited by Louis Parrot. 1948.
Poèmes politiques. 1948.
Voir: Poèmes, peintures, dessins. 1948.
Le Bestiare. 1949.
Une leçon de morale. 1949.
Pouvoir tout dire. 1951.
Le Phénix. 1951.
Les Sentiers et les routes de la poésie. 1952.
Poésie ininterrompue II. 1953.
Deux poèmes, with René Char. 1960.
Derniers poèmes d'amour. 1966; as *Last Love Poems of Paul Éluard* (bilingual edition), translated by Marilyn Kallet, 1980.
Max Ernst: Peintures pour Paul Éluard. 1969.
Poésies 1913–1926. 1970.

Uninterrupted Poetry: Selected Writings, translated by Lloyd Alexander. 1975.
Poèmes de jeunesse, edited by Lucien Scheler and Clavreuil. 1978.
L'Enfant qui ne voulait pas grandir. 1980.

Other

Les Nécessités de la vie et les conséquences des rêves. 1921.
L'Immaculée Conception, with André Breton. 1930.
Appliquée. 1937.
A Pablo Picasso. 1944.
A L'Intérieur de la vue. 1948.
Selected Writings, translated by Lloyd Alexander. 1951.
Lettres de jeunesse, edited by Robert D. Valette. 1962.
Anthologie des écrits sur l'art. 3 vols., 1952–54; 1 vol., 1972.
Le Poète et son ombre: Textes inédits. 1963; revised edition, 1989.
Lettres à Joë Bousquet, edited by Lucien Scheler. 1973.
Lettres à Gala: (1924–1948), edited by Pierre Dreyfus. 1984.
Seconde nature. 1990.
Dictionnaire abrégé du surréalisme, with André Breton. 1991.
Translator, *Oeuvres choisies*, by Christo Botev, 1966.

*

Critical Studies: *Le Je universal chez Paul Éluard* by P. Emmanuel, 1938; *Paul Éluard* by Louis Perche, 1963; *Le Poète et son ombre*, 1963, and *Éluard: Livre d'identité*, 1967, revised edition, 1968, both by Robert D. Valette; *Paul Éluard: L'Amour, la révolte, le rêve*, 1965, and *Paul Éluard: Biographie pour une approche*, 1965, both by Luc Decaunes; *La Poésie de Paul Éluard et le thème de la pureté* by Ursula Jucker-Wehrli, 1965; *Éluard par lui-même*, 1968, and *La Poétique du désir*, 1974, both by Raymond Jean; *Album Éluard* by Roger J. Ségalat, 1968; *The Poetry of Dada and Surrealism: Aragon, Breton, Tzara, Éluard and Desnos* by Mary Ann Caws, 1970; *Le Vocabulaire politique de Paul Éluard* by Marie-Renée Guyard, 1974; *Paul Éluard* by Robert Nugent, 1974; *"Nuits partagées" and The Prose Poem in Éluard* by Eric Hill Wayne, 1976; *Éluard; ou, le pouvoir du mot* by Jean-Yves Debreuille, 1977; *Les Mots la vie* by C. Guedj, 1980; *Éluard; ou, le rayonnement de l'être* by Daniel Bergez, 1982; *La Poésie de Paul Éluard: La rupture et le partage 1913–1936* by Nicole Boulestreau, 1985; *Paul Éluard; ou, Le Frère voyant* by Jean-Charles Gateau, 1988.

* * *

Paul Éluard was a prolific if uneven poet. Between 1916 and 1952 he composed verse and prose poems of astonishing lyrical power and verbal invention. His reputation as a major 20th-century lyric poet rests chiefly on his surrealist love poetry (1924–38) and his Resistance poems (1940–44). He also produced Dadaist poems, surrealist experimental collaborations (with Breton on the *Dictionnaire abrégé du surréalisme* [Abridged Dictionary of Surrealism] and on *L'Immaculée Conception* [The Immaculate Conception]—a linguistic exploration of madness using automatic writing techniques, poetic translations (of García Lorca, Botev), critical writings on poetry, demagogical communist verse, political pamphlets, anthologies of poetry and of writings on art, and scripts for a series of radio broadcasts. The broad trajectory of his work reflects an increasing commitment to militant communism, although many critics feel that his later work does not rise above sentimentality or dogma.

In Éluard's poetry a language of an amoral sensory world is pitched against that of moral statement. Fighting alongside fellow Surrealists in a crusade against artificially maintained rational categories, Éluard believed that the moral and sensory domains are inseparable. For Éluard there is an immediacy of perception by the self of the world. Moreover, all the world's objects cooperate in the act of perception by mutually foregrounding each other. Éluard called this idea "transparence." This transparency is observed in many of the poems in *Capitale de la douleur* [Capital of Pain]: "The space between things has the shape of my words/ . . . The space has the shape of my looks" (from "Ne plus partager"); "Tes yeux sont livrés à ce qu'ils voient/Vus par ce qu'ils regardent" [Your eyes are delivered to what they see/Seen by what they observe] (from "Nusch"). Transparency is ensured by the figure of Woman that for Éluard is a principle of Being ("resemblance").

This myth of seeing is predominant in many of Éluard's poems presenting the world altered by the radical perception of lovers. However, the proliferation of perspectives and matter created and sustained by Éluard's vertiginous visual imagery points up a disturbance at the heart of looking. The purity of vision paradoxically requires impurity in the form of dissolved identity. A poem such as "L'Amoureuse" celebrates the marvellous, yet shows it to be a burden. The full presence of the external world both delights and oppresses: "Elle est debout sur mes paupières" (she is standing on my eyelids). The event of looking takes place inside the eye, as experience accrues in an endless set of transparencies. The unsettling nature of this sensory plenitude is in evidence in poems such as "Le plus jeune" and in many of the poems in "La vie immédiate" and *La Rose publique* [The Public Rose].

The highly volatile universe of images in the Éluardian sensory world is matched by the equally destabilizing moral diction in the poems. This is as true of Éluard's first serious political poem "La Victoire de Guernica," as in these opening lines from "Premièrement": "La terre est bleue comme une orange/Jamais une erreur les mots ne mentent pas" [The earth is blue like an orange/Never an error words do not lie]. The dizzying, and irritating, effect of these lines resides in the way in which both domains collide. The programmatic symmetry here moralizes the sensory, just as the moral is made sensory; the reader witnesses simultaneous substitution and interpenetration.

Such strategies are to be found in *Poésie ininterrompue I* [Uninterrupted Poetry I], a long poem that demonstrates the full range of Éluard's poetic language. This extraordinary work, which is at the same time an autobiographical *apologia* and a poem of the Liberation, grafts surrealist techniques (used long after his objective break with Breton and the Surrealists in 1938) onto a vision of communist utopia. The peculiar rhetoric of this poem presents the paradise experienced by the reader as the next and inevitable evolutionary step for humankind. As elsewhere in Éluard's work, but here concentrated and refined, the "linguistic democracy" of Éluard's syntax reflects his anti-hierarchical views, creating a poetic Marxism in which all classes are dissolved. Paratactic enumeration and sententious aphorism, which Éluard had exploited in earlier poems, gather momentum through hallucinatory verbal incantation. In *Poésie ininterrompe I*, with its wearisome and elating intertwining of programmatic exhortations and surrealist imagery, Éluard achieved a new kind of poem.

If the themes of Éluard's love poetry are perennial—purity, passion, the lovers' look, the world made marvellous by the state of romance, the loneliness experienced in the absence of love—he nevertheless proves to be an unconventional poet, in two essential ways. Firstly, an analysis of his poetic language reveals a specific and idiosyncratic revitalizing of stock, contemporary, diction. A microhistory of the period is detectable in the incestuous surrealist magazines and, during the war, in the echoes and loans of key words in the many Resistance journals to which Éluard subscribed and contributed. Secondly, Éluard promulgated in his poems the belief that love, like poetry itself, was a revolutionary act capable of transforming both perception and societal life. In so doing, the amorous couple is placed at the service of humanity, as an example and a building block for an abundant world.

Although Éluard wrote some execrable verse ("Joseph Staline" for example) at a time (1950) when the French Communist Party was nurturing its cultural mascots, his overall project was not to incorporate Marxist ideas into poems, but to set down his sympathies for victims of social injustice and of the stultification of perception in bourgeois life. To this end, Éluard created a hybrid poetry of moral didacticism and pure lyricism. Not since Hugo has there been such an intriguing conflation of private imagination and public pronouncement in French poetry.

—Rolf Venner

See the essay on "You the only one."

ELYTIS, Odysseus

Born: Odysseus Alepoudelis in Heraklion, Crete, 2 November 1911. **Education:** Studied law at the University of Athens, 1930–33, no degree; studied literature at the Sorbonne, Paris, 1948–52. **Military Service:** Served in the First Army Corps, in Albania, 1940–41: Lieutenant. **Career:** Programme director, National Broadcasting Institution, 1945–47, 1953–54; art and literary critic, *Kathimerini* newspaper, 1946–48, adviser to Art Theatre, 1955–56, and Greek National Theatre, 1965–68. President of the Governing Board, Greek Ballet, 1956–58, and Greek Broadcasting and Television, 1974; member of the Administrative Board, Greek National Theatre, 1974–76. **Member:** Order of the Phoenix, 1965; Grand Commander, Order of Honour, 1979; Commandeur de l'Ordre des Arts et des Lettres (France), 1984; Commandeur, Légion d'honneur (France), 1989. **Awards:** National prize for poetry, 1960; Nobel prize for literature, 1979; Royal Society of Literature Benson medal (UK), 1981. D.Litt.: University of Salonica, 1976; the Sorbonne, 1980; University of London, 1981. **Died:** 18 March 1996.

PUBLICATIONS

Collections

The Collected Poems of Odysseus Elytis, translated by Jeffrey Carson and Nikos Sarris. 1997.

Eros, Eros, Eros: Selected and Last Poems, translated by Olga Broumas. 1998.

Verse

Prosanatolismi [Orientations]. 1936.

O Ilios o Protos, mazi me tis Parallayes pano se mian Ahtida [Sun the First Together with Variations on a Sunbeam]. 1943.

Asma Iroiko ke Penthimo yia ton Hameno Anthipolohago tis Alvanias [Heroic and Elegiac Song for the Lost Second Lieutenant of the Albanian Campaign]. 1945.

I Kalosini stis Likopories [Kindness in the Wolfpasses]. 1946.

To Axion Esti. 1959; as *The Axion Esti*, translated by Edmund Keeley and G.P. Savidis, 1974.

Exi ke Mia Tipsis yia ton Ourano [Six and One Regrets for the Sky]. 1960.

To Fotodendro ke i Dekati Tetarti Omorfia [The Light Tree and the Fourteenth Beauty]. 1971.

O Ilios o Iliatoras [The Sovereign Sun]. 1971.

Thanatos ke Anastasis tou Konstantinou Paleologou [Death and Resurrection of Constantine Palaiologos]. 1971.

To Monogramma [The Monogram]. 1972.

To Ro tou Erota [The Ro of Eros] (songs). 1972.

Clear Days: Poems by Palamas and Elytis, in Versions by Nikos Tselepides, edited by Kenneth O. Hanson. 1972.

Villa Natacha. 1973.

O Fillomantis [The Leaf Diviner]. 1973.

Ta Eterothali [The Stepchildren]. 1974.

The Sovereign Sun: Selected Poems, translated by Kimon Friar. 1974.

Maria Nefeli. 1978; as *Maria Nefeli,* translated by Athan Anagnostopoulos, 1981.

Selected Poems, edited and translated by Edmund Keeley and Philip Sherrard. 1981.

Tria Poemata me Simea Evkerias [Three Poems under a Flag of Convenience]. 1982.

Hemerologio henos atheatou Apriliou [Diary of an Unseen April]. 1984.

O Mikros Naftilos. 1985; as *The Little Mariner,* translated by Olga Broumas, 1988.

What I Love: Selected Poems of Odysseas Elytis, translated by Olga Broumas. 1986.

Krinagoras. 1987.

Ta Elegia tis Oxopetras [The Elegies of Oxopetras]. 1991.

Other

O Zografos Theofilos [The Painter Theophilos]. 1973.

Anoichta Hartia [Open Book]. 1974; as *Open Papers,* translated by Olga Broumas and T. Begley, 1995.

He Mageia tou Papadiamanti [The Magic of Papadiamantis]. 1976.

Anafora ston Andrea Embiriko [Report to Andreas Embirikos]. 1980.

To Domatio me tis Ikones [The Room of Images]. 1986.

Ta Dimosia ke ta Idiotika [Public and Private Matters]. 1990.

I Idiotiki Odos [Private Way]. 1990.

En Lefko [In White]. 1992.

Translator, *Defteri Graphi* [Second Writing] (poems of Lorca, Rimbaud, Éluard, Maiakovskii, and others). 1976.

Translator, *Ioannis, I Apokalipsi* [St. John, Apocalypse]. 1985.

Translator, *Sappho—Anasinthesi ke Apodosi* [Sappho—Synthesis and Rendering]. 1985.

*

Critical Studies: Elytis issue of *Books Abroad*, Autumn 1975; *Odysseus Elytis: Anthologies of Light*, edited by Ivar Ivask, 1981; "Maria Nefeli and the Changeful Sameness of Elytis: Variations on a Theme" by Andonis Decavalles, and "Elytis and the Greek Tradition" by Edmund Keeley, both in *Charioteer*, 1982–83; "Odysseus Elytis and the Discovery of Greece" by Philip Sherrard, in *Journal of Modern Greek Studies*, 1(2), 1983; "Eliot and Elytis: Poet of Time, Poet of Space" by Karl Malkoff, in *Comparative Literature*, 36(3), 1984; "Odysseus Elytis in the 1980s" by Andonis Decavalles, in *World Literature Today*, 62(1), 1988.

*   *   *

Ever since Odysseus Elytis first appeared on the Greek literary scene in 1935, critical attention has focused on the new world his poetry created: a world of sun and sea, the Aegean landscape, love, and communion with nature. Yet the world of Elytis, consistently developed since the poet's earliest collection, *Prosanatolismi* [Orientations], would seem to be rather more complex than some critics have allowed. His subsequent work indicates that this world is correlative to his view of poetry as an alternative to reality. Within this world, as Elytis has said with reference to a fellow poet, Andreas Embirikos, actual problems may not be solved, but something more radical occurs: the logic that created these problems is abolished.

One of the methods Elytis has employed for the creation of his world is surrealism. Together with Embirikos, Nikos Engonopoulos, and Nikos Gatsos, he introduced surrealism into Greek literary life in the 1930s and 1940s. Having experimented with surrealism before publishing anything, Elytis finally rejected certain surrealist techniques, such as automatic writing, but adopted some aspects of its philosophy, viewing surrealism as a quest for spiritual health and a reaction against the rationalism prevalent in Western thought. Another method he used is the establishing of connections between the natural elements of his poetic world and attitudes to life; as he says in *O Mikros Naftilos (The Little Mariner)*, the exploration of the hidden relationships between meanings leads to poetry which, like one's view of the sky, depends on one's vantage point.

The "Greekness" of Elytis's poetic landscape has frequently been the subject of critical commentary. If, however, at the beginning of his poetic career, this landscape was a celebration of love, in *To Axion Esti (The Axion Esti)* it also becomes a place where the joy and pain of existence and creation combine with the historical adventures of the Greek nation, where good fights against evil, universal values are established, and death is defeated. This world, created by and simultaneously with poetry, is proclaimed in the end to be eternal, while the poet states that "WORTHY is the price paid." The tragic aspects of this sunlit world are also confronted in *Exi ke Mia Tipsis yia ton Ourano* [Six and One Regrets for the Sky]. There, the poet affirms "the lawfulness of the Unhoped-For," and at the same time states: "Well then, he whom I sought *I am*"—an achievement that Elytis has elsewhere characterized as the most difficult thing in the world, defining the process of becoming what one is as poetry.

When the components of Elytis's world have acquired these new dimensions, some of which are explored through the dialogue of a girl called Maria Nefeli [Maria Cloud] and her interlocutor who seems to represent the poet, in *Maria Nefeli,* they manage to incorporate death too. Aspects of death are explored in *Hemerologio henos atheatou Apriliou* [Diary of an Unseen April] and in *Ta Elegia tis Oxopetras* [The Elegies of Oxopetras]. Through its polymorphous connections with sun, sea, gardens, and love, death is proclaimed in the latter collections to be the blue, endless sea and the unsetting sun, while in the former ones, the poet contemplates the "Unknown" and declares that he has worked there for years and that his fingers were scorched just as he was about to see Paradise opening. Thus, death is not presented as the reverse of love, since antitheses in the world of Elytis are often resolved into a synthesis; as the poet said about himself in *Prosanatolismi*, from the other side he is the same.

This sameness persists in the "other side" of Elytis's main poetic work, that is, in his songs and essays. His songs were published in 1972 under the general title *To Ro tou Erota* [The Ro of Eros] and many of them were set to music, as also was a large part of *The Axion Esti*, by Mikis Theodorakis. Apart from the subject matter, one of the obvious resemblances between these songs and Elytis's poems is found in the insistence on magic numbers: most of these songs are grouped in sevens or multiples of seven, a number which occurs both in titles of collections (*Exi ke Mia Tipsis yia ton Ourano*, *To Fotodendro ke i Dekati Tetarti Omorfia* [The Light Tree and the Fourteenth Beauty]) and in the structure of his collections and compositions. His preoccupation with numbers is probably related to his preoccupation with the metrical forms of his poems. Although his verse usually falls under the general heading of "free verse," Elytis has himself commented on the strict metrical and formal rules he imposes on his verse. Most of his essays have been collected in a book entitled *Anoichta Hartia* (*Open Papers*), where he gives a chronicle of his literary generation (the "Generation of the 1930s"), describes their explorations and poetics, and deals with surrealism and dreams, painters, and poets. One of his other, separately published, essays takes the form of *Anafora ston Andrea Embiriko* [Report to Andreas Embirikos], combining memories of his friend and fellow poet with an account of surrealist poetics. The integral position which Elytis's translations occupy in his work is apparent from the titles he gives them: *Defteri Graphi* [Second Writing] for translations of Lorca, Rimbaud, Éluard, Maiakovskii, and others; *Sappho—Anasinthesi ke Apodosi* [Sappho—Synthesis and Rendering] for his arrangement and translation of the Sapphic fragments.

The creation of the poetic world, adjacent to the real one, both dependent on and independent from it, makes the poet's role a dangerous one, quite different from the image of the "carefree Elytis" projected by critics of his early work. In *To Fotodendro ke i Dekati Tetarti Omorfia* the poet defines his position as painful but unshakeable ("still standing firm with burnt fingers") in a world of his own creation.

—Elli Philokyprou

ENDŌ Shūsaku (Paul)

Born: Tokyo, Japan, 27 March 1923. **Education:** Educated at Keio University, Tokyo, B.A. in French literature 1949; University of Lyons, 1950–53. **Family:** Married Junko Okada in 1955; one son. **Career:** Contracted tuberculosis in 1959. Former editor of the literary journal *Mita Bungaku*; chair, Bungeika Kyōkai (Literary Artists' Association); manager, Kiza amateur theatrical troupe. President, Japanese PEN. **Awards:** Akutagawa prize, 1955; Tanizaki prize, 1967; Grupo de Oficial da Ordem do Infante dom Henrique (Portugal), 1968; Sancti Silvestri (award by Pope Paul VI), 1970; Noma

prize, 1980; Mainichi cultural prize; Dag Hammarskjold prize. Honorary doctorate: Georgetown University, Washington, DC; University of California, Santa Clara. **Member:** Nihon Geijutsuin (Japanese Arts Academy), 1981. **Died:** 29 September 1996.

PUBLICATIONS

Collections

Five by Endo: Stories, translated by Van C. Gessel. 2000.

Fiction

Aden made [Till Aden], in *Mita bungaku*. November 1954.
Shiroi hito [White Man]. 1955.
Kiiroi hito [Yellow Man]. 1955.
Aoi chiisana budō [Green Little Grapes], in *Bungakukau*. January-June 1956.
Umi to dokuyaku. 1957; as *The Sea and Poison*, translated by Michael Gallagher, 1972.
Kazan. 1959; as *Volcano*, translated by Richard Schucherl, 1978.
Obakasan, in *Asahi shinbun*. April-August 1959; as *Wonderful Fool*, translated by Francis Mathy, 1974.
Otoko to kyūkanchō [Three Men and a Starling], in *Bungakukai*. January 1963.
Watashi no mono. 1963; translated as "Mine," in *Japan Christian Quarterly*, 40(4), 1974.
Watashi ga suteta onna. 1964; as *The Girl I Left Behind*, translated by Mark Williams, 1994.
Aika [Elegies] (stories). 1965.
Ryūgaku, in *Gunzō*. March 1965; as *Foreign Studies*, translated by Mark Williams, 1989.
Chinmoku. 1966; as *Silence*, translated by William Johnston, 1969.
Taihen daa! [Good Grief!]. 1969.
Shikai no hotori [By the Dead Sea]. 1973.
Iesu no shogai. 1973; as *A Life of Jesus*, translated by Richard Schucherl, 1978.
Yumoa shōsetsu shū [Collection of Humorous Stories]. 1973.
Waga seishun ni kui ari [Regrets for Our Youth]. 1974.
Kuchibue o fuku toki. 1974; as *When I Whistle*, translated by Van C. Gessel, 1979.
Sekai kikō [Travels Around the World]. 1975.
Hechimakun [Master Snake-Gourd]. 1975.
Kitsunegata tanukigata [In the Shape of a Fox, in the Shape of a Badger]. 1976.
Gūtara mandanshū [Lazybones]. 1978.
Marie Antoinette. 1979.
Jūichi no iro garasu [11 Pieces of Stained Glass] (stories). 1979.
Samurai. 1980; as *The Samurai*, translated by Van C. Gessel, 1982.
Onna no isshō [A Woman's Life]. 1982.
Akuryō no gogo [Afternoon of the Evil Spirit]. 1983.
Stained Glass Elegies: Stories (includes stories from *Aika* and *Jūichi no iro garasu*), translated by Van C. Gessel. 1984.
Sukyandaru. 1986; as *Scandal*, translated by Van C. Gessel, 1988.
Hangyaku [Rebellion]. 2 vols., 1989.
The Final Martyrs: Stories, translated by Van C. Gessel. 1993.
Fukai kawa. 1993; as *Deep River*, translated by Van C. Gessel. 1994.

Plays

Ōgon no kuni (produced 1966). 1969; as *The Golden Country*, translated by Francis Mathy, 1970.
Bara no yakata [A House Surrounded by Roses]. 1969.

Other

Furansu no daigakusei [Students in France, 1951–52]. 1953.
Seisho no naka no joseitachi [Women in the Bible]. 1968.
Korian vs Manbō, with Kita Morio. 1974.
Bungaku Zenshū [Collected Literary Works]. 11 vols., 1975.
Ukiaru kotoba [Floating Words]. 1976.
Ai no akebono [Dawn of Love], with Miura Shumon. 1976.
Nihonjin wa kirisuto kyō o shinjirareru ka [Can Japanese People Believe in Christianity?]. 1977.
Kirisuto no tanjō [The Birth of Christ]. 1978.
Ningen no naka no X [X Inside Human Beings]. 1978.
Rakuten taishō [Great Victory of Optimism]. 1978.
Kare no ikikata [His Way of Life]. 1978.
Jū to jūjika (biography of Pedro Cassini). 1979.
Shinran, with Masutani Fumio. 1979.
Sakka no nikki [Writer's Diary]. 1980.
Chichioya [Father]. 1980.
Kekkonron [On Marriage]. 1980.
Endō Shūsaku ni yoru Endō Shūsaku [Endo Shusaku According to Himself]. 1980.
Meiga Iesu junrei [Pilgrimage to Famous Pictures of Jesus]. 1981.
Ai to jinsei o meguru danso [Faults in Love and Life]. 1981.
Ōkoku e no michi [The Way to the Kingdom]. 1981.
Fuyu no yasashisa [The Gentleness of Winter]. 1982.
Watakushi ni totte kami to wa [My View of God]. 1983.
Kokoro [Heart]. 1984.
Ikiru gakkō [School of Life]. 1984.
Watakushi no aishita shōsetsu [A Novel I Have Loved]. 1985.
Rakudai bōzu no rirekisho [Resumé of a Failed Priest]. 1989.
Kawaru mono to kawaranu mono: hanadokei [Things That Change and Things That Do Not Change: Flower-Clocks]. 1990.

*

Critical Studies: "Shusaku Endo: The Second Period" by Francis Mathy, in *Japan Christian Quarterly*, 40, 1974; "Tradition and Contemporary Consciousness: Ibuse, Endo, Kaiko, Abe" by J. Thomas Rimer, in his *Modern Japanese Fiction and Its Traditions*, 1978; "Mr. Shusaku Endo Talks about His Life and Works as a Catholic Writer" (interview), in *Chesterton Review*, 12(4), 1986; "The Roots of Guilt and Responsibility in Shusaku Endo's *The Sea and Poison*" by Hans-Peter Breuer, in *Literature and Medicine*, 7, 1988; "Rediscovering Japan's Christian Tradition: Text-Immanent Hermeneutics in Two Short Stories by Shusaku Endo" by Rolf J. Goebel, in *Studies in Language and Culture*, 14(63), 1988; "Graham Greene: *The Power and the Glory*: A Comparative Essay with *Silence* by Shusaku Endo" by Kazuie Hamada, in *Collected Essays by the Members of the Faculty* (*Kyoritsu Women's Junior College*), 31, February 1988; "Christianity in the Intellectual Climate of Modern Japan" by Shunichi Takayanagi, in *Chesterton Review*, 14(3), 1988; "Salvation

of the Weak: Endo Shusaku," in *The Sting of Life: Four Contemporary Japanese Novelists*, 1989, and "The Voice of the Doppelgänger," in *Japan Quarterly*, 38(2), 1991, both by Van C. Gessel; *The Image of Christ in the Fiction of Endō Shūsaku* by Leith Morton, 1994; *Endō Shūsaku: A Literature of Reconciliation* by Mark B. Williams, 1999.

* * *

Ever since his emergence on the literary scene, Endō Shūsaku has consistently sought resolution of the conflict he has perceived between, on the one hand, his "adopted" religion, Christianity, and, on the other, his chosen profession as author. Derived in part from his study of several French Catholic novelists, and informing his entire *oeuvre*, is the desire for a reconciliation between his perceived duty, as Christian, to seek within man the potential for salvation and the necessity, accruing to him as author, to remain totally honest to his observations of human nature. In the case of Endō, a Japanese national, moreover, the tension was further exacerbated by the need to operate within a cultural and spiritual framework that provides less encouragement for the development of literary themes dealing with the spiritual drama of the relationship between God and man, leading him to conclude: "As a Christian, Japanese and an author, I am constantly concerned with the relationship and conflict created by these three tensions . . . Unfortunately, these three tensions continue to appear as contradictory in my mind."

The result, in the case of Endō, is an author whose self-professed desire "to find God on the streets of Shinjuku and Shibuya, districts which seem so far removed from Him" has been constantly tempered by a realization that he was "not writing in order to proselytize," and that, if he were, his "works would certainly suffer as literature." Thereafter, the more he has found himself drawn to privilege his obligations as literary artist, the more he has come to recognize the need to create "living human beings," a task that requires, not merely external observation, but also scrutiny of the internal psychology of his creations, a faithful depiction of their inner being, however unattractive. The result is a body of works that increasingly mirrors Endō's conviction that "to describe man's inner self, we must probe to the third dimension [within the unconscious] . . . to the territory of demons. One cannot describe man's inner being completely unless one closes in on this demonic part."

The paradox is readily apparent: in focusing on a realm in which "our desire for Good conflicts with our penchant for Evil, where our appreciation of Beauty conflicts with our attachment to the Ugly," Endō was drawn increasingly to focus on the weakness of human nature, in the belief that only thus could he portray, behind the sin depicted, "the glimmer of light . . . the light of God's grace"—the potential for salvation which he saw as underlying the entire human drama. The consequent vision of the unconscious as both the fount of all sin and the "place where God works and has His being" is reflected in the Endō text by an increasing focus on the "monstrous duality of man," this assuming the literary guise of a gradual fusion of two qualities, initially established as in opposition. In several texts, like *Chinmoku* (*Silence*) and *The Samurai*, the central dichotomy thus established is that between East and West, with the distance between the two, initially depicted as unfathomable (as evidenced by the Western missionaries appearing unable to penetrate the "mudswamp" of Japan), steadily eroded during the course of the novels as a result of the author's increasing focus, not on external distinctions, but on internal similarities that allow for meaningful communication across various national, religious, and cultural divides. Thus, at the outset of

Silence, Rodrigues, the Portuguese missionary, is portrayed as entirely confident of his own inner resources. Confronted by the choice, imposed upon him by the Japanese shogunate authorities, between on the one hand adherence to his faith and the consequent death of the Japanese converts being tortured before his eyes, and, on the other, renunciation of all that his life to date had stood for, Rodrigues ultimately succumbs and tramples on the crucifix that had been placed before him in an outward act of apostasy. Internally, however, there is evidence, supported in the text by the erosion of the apparently irreconcilable distinction between the "strong" martyr and the "weak" apostate, of the protagonist's augmented love of God at the end of the novel, the narrator acknowledging Rodrigues's decision, following shortly after his act of public apostasy, to hear the confession of the Japanese man who had betrayed him to the authorities: "He may have been betraying [his fellow priests], but he was not betraying 'that man, [Christ].' He loved Him now in a totally different way. 'Everything in my life to date was necessary in order to know that love. I am still the last priest in this land.'"

A similar process can be seen at work in *The Samurai*, a novel in which the distance between the "Western" missionary, Velasco, and the lower-ranking samurai, symbol of "Eastern" values, is initially portrayed as unfathomable. As the novel progresses, however, so Endō's narrator succeeds in breaking down the various obstacles to reconciliation, this being acknowledged at the personal level by Velasco in his eventual recognition: "It was as if a firm bond of solidarity had formed between the envoys and myself."

In these, and other examples of oppositions subjected to similar fusion in Endō's novels, the emphasis is on a steady growth in self-awareness and, as the Endō protagonist becomes more and more aware of some previously unconscious aspect of his being, so he appears increasingly well equipped to participate in this process of reconciliation. Seen in this light, Endō's 1986 novel, *Sukyandaru* (*Scandal*), a text heralded by several critics as an abrupt abandonment of earlier Endō motifs, comes to appear rather as a progression, a work that addresses more directly than ever before the inherent human duality. During the course of the novel, the protagonist, Suguro, grows steadily in his conviction that the "impostor" he initially dismisses as a chance look-alike is none other than his own double—that "he could no longer conceal that part of himself, no longer deny its existence"—the pervading impression being of an author confident in the assessment of human nature he offered at the time: "Man is a splendid and beautiful being, and, at the same time, man is a terrible being as we recognized in Auschwitz—God knows well this monstrous dual quality of man."

—Mark Williams

See the essay on *Silence*.

ENNIUS, Quintus

Born: Rudiae, Calabria, southern Italy, 239 BC. Probably of Greek extraction. **Career:** Served in the Roman army in Sardinia, where in 204 BC he met Cato the Elder, who took him to Rome; in 189 BC went on the Aetolian campaign with consul M. Fulvius Nobilior, through whose son he acquired Roman citizenship, 184 BC. Became a friend of Scipio Africanus the Elder. **Died:** 169 BC.

PUBLICATIONS

Collections

[Works], edited by I. Vahlen. 1854, 2nd edition, 1903.
Fragments, edited and translated by Eric H. Warmington, in *Remains of Old Latin* [Loeb Edition], vol. 1, 1935; as *The Tragedies of Ennius*, edited by H.D. Jocelyn, 1967.

Works

Annales, as *The Annals*, edited and translated by E.M. Steuart. 1925; also translated by Otto Skutsch, 1953; with introduction by Enrico Flores, 2000.

*

Critical Studies: *Die Formenlehre des Ennius* by R. Frobenius, 1907; *Ennius und Vergilius* by E. Norden, 1915; *Ennius und Homer* by H. von Kameke, 1927; *Studia Enniana* (in English) by Otto Skutsch, 1968.

*   *   *

Quintus Ennius, the acknowledged father of Latin epic poetry, was an innovative poet who made striking advances in several literary genres. A Messapian from Rudiae, he came in 204 BC to Rome, aged 35, where he worked as a teacher, poet, and playwright. Ennius boasted of possessing three hearts, *tria corda*, meaning the Oscan, Greek, and Latin languages. His literary achievement owed much to his familiarity with the entire Greek heritage, from Homer to the Hellenistic writers.

The work which established Ennius' reputation for posterity was his epic poem, the *Annales* (*The Annals*), whose title recalled that of the Pontifical Annals, although it bore little resemblance to those arid records. Ennius' poem covered the whole range of Roman history from the sack of Troy to at least 179 BC. It contained 15 (later extended to 18) books, each of between 1,000 and 1,700 lines (compared with an average of just over 800 for those of Virgil's *Aeneid*). Only about 600 lines survive, but these suffice to indicate the general pattern of the work, which was arranged in groups, each consisting of three books. Of these I–III dealt with Aeneas' flight from Troy and the Roman kings; IV–VI with Rome's Italian wars down to the time of Pyrrhus; VII–IX with the Punic Wars; X–XII with the wars against Philip V of Macedonia and Nabis of Sparta; and XIII–XVI with the Syrian War. Books XVI–XVIII recounted "more recent wars" (after 187 BC), but the content of this triad is obscure.

There were Hellenistic precedents for historical epic, but a poem which took the whole history of a single people as its theme was unique. Ennius' work soon became a classic, to be studied at school, and it influenced writers in all fields down to the first century BC. Its wide appeal rested on its patriotic theme, as it dealt largely with wars, and its stress on traditional Roman qualities, reflecting the ideals of an aristocratic society, in particular *virtus* (manliness), enlisted in the service of Rome. *The Annals* were intended to replace Naevius' poem on the First Punic War as the national epic of Rome, and Ennius' success was achieved partly by his rich and highly original narrative style, marked by bold effects of alliteration and assonance; partly by his use of the Greek hexameter (in place of Naevius' ungainly Saturnians); and partly by the varied contents of his verse, which incorporated biographical details, polemic, and a scattering of philosophical and learned comments.

Ennius conjures up a variety of moods, now light, now solemn, by his vivid style, which used, for example, archaisms such as "induperator" for "imperator" (general), or weighty spondaic lines at critical moments: "olli respondit rex Albai Longai" (to him replied the king of Alba Longa). Some aspects of his style, it is true, struck later generations as primitive; to Ovid his native genius (*ingenium*) was undeniable, but he lacked literary subtlety (*ars*). Occasionally he pushed his effects to the point of bathos, as in the alliterative lines "At tuba terribili sonitu taratantara dixit" (But the trumpet with frightening sound said "taratantara") or "O Tite, tute, Tati, tibi tanta, tyranne, tulisti" (such terrible evils, Titus Tatius, broughtest thou, tyrant, on thyself). Ennius' hexameter was still rough, with its tolerance of elided "s" before a consonant, non-elision of "m" before a vowel, and laxity regarding the caesura. However, among the surviving lines are several famous for their lapidary dignity, like the famous comment on Fabius, the opponent of Hannibal: "Unus homo nobis cunctando restituit rem" (one man by procrastinating gave us back our state). Ennius kept the "Olympic machinery" of Homer and in a famous prologue to Book I, invoking the Muses, recounted a dream in which Homer appeared to him to announce his reincarnation in the Latin poet. It is unclear how far this was symbolic and how far to be taken seriously, for Ennius wrote at a time when Pythagorean ideas of reincarnation were prevalent in Rome.

The Annals were written only in Ennius' later years, but he composed tragedies throughout his life. Some 24 titles and about 400 lines survive. Except for two works, *Sabine Women* and *Ambracia*, based on Roman themes, Ennius followed the stories of Greek mythology. Up to a dozen titles are based on Euripides, his *Eumenides* on Aeschylus and *Achilles* on a work by Euripides' contemporary, Aristarchus. Ennius' tragedies, however, were far from being literal translations. Cicero remarks that Ennius gives us the sense (*vis*) rather than the word (*verba*) of his models. Moreover, he occasionally combined two Greek plays to make one: thus his *Medea* draws on both the *Medea* and the *Aegeus* of Euripides. More importantly, however, Ennius adapted his originals to suit a Roman audience, compressing or expanding, modifying the presentation, and introducing powerful bombastic and emotional language. The chorus had a smaller role and frequent arias, *cantica*, contributed a melodramatic tone, which in some ways foreshadowed Seneca.

Besides epic and tragedy, Ennius was prolific in other fields. He wrote some comedies. His four books of *Satires* combined moralizing and homespun philosophizing in a variety of metres and in a way that points ahead to Lucilius and Horace. And there were other works, now lost: the *Euhemerus*, a translation of that author's *Sacred Relation*, the *Hedyphagetica*, probably a parody of epic dealing with food, *Scipio* praising Africanus, and *Sota*, a translation of scurrilous verses by Sotades. Ennius also composed epigrams, including his own alliterative epitaph (in elegiac metre):

nemo me lacrimis decoret nec funera fletu
faxit. cur? volito vivus per ora virum

(Let no one honour me with tears nor weep
at my funeral. Why? Because I live, flitting from mouth
to mouth)

Ennius dominated Roman poetry down to Virgil's time; but the *Aeneid* ousted *The Annals* from its position as the great Roman epic.

There was a reaction against Ennius in Nero's time, but a revival under Hadrian, who preferred him to Virgil.

—Frank W. Walbank

EÖTVÖS, Baron József

Born: Buda, Hungary (then in the Austrian Empire), 3 September 1813. **Education:** Educated at home, then at schools in Buda until 1824; University of Pest, from 1826. **Family:** Married Ágnes Rosty in 1842. **Career:** Attended parliament in Pozsony, 1832; served as deputy clerk of Fehér County; travelled in Switzerland, England, France, and Germany, 1836–37; appointed Minister of Religion and Public Education in Hungary, 1848: resigned and left the country several months later; returned to Buda, 1851; reappointed Minister of Religion and Public Education, 1867–71. **Member:** Hungarian Academy, 1835. **Died:** 2 February 1871.

PUBLICATIONS

Collections

Összes munkái [Complete Works], edited by Mór Ráth. 13 vols., 1886–93.
Összes munkái [Complete Works], edited by Géza Voinovich. 20 vols., 1901–03.

Fiction

A karthausi [The Carthusian], in *Budapesti Árvizkönyv*. January 1839–July 1841; in book form, 2 vols., 1842.
A falu jegyzője. 3 vols., 1845; as *The Village Notary*, translated (from German) by Otto Wenckstern, 3 vols., 1850.
Magyarország 1514-ben [Hungary in 1514]. 1847.
A nővérek [The Sisters]. 1857.
Elbeszélések [Short Stories]. 1859.

Verse

Költeményei [Poems]. 1868.

Plays

A házasulók [Getting Married]. 1833.
Bosszú [Revenge]. 1834.

Other

A kritikus apotheosisa [The Apotheosis of the Critic]. 1831.
Vélemény a fogházjavítás ügyében [An Opinion on Prison Reform]. 1838.
Die Emanzipation der Juden [The Emancipation of the Jews]. 1840.
Kelet népe és a Pesti Hirlap [People of the East and Pesti Hirlap]. 1841.
Emlékbeszéd Kőrösi Csoma Sándor felett [Memorial Speech on Sándor Kőrösi Csoma]. 1842.
Reform [Reform]. 1846.

A XIX. század uralkodó eszméinek befolyása az álladalomra [The Dominant Ideas of the 19th Century and Their Influence on the State]. 2 vols., 1851–54; translated by D. Mervyn Jones, 1996.

Die Garantien der Macht und Einheit Oesterreichs [Guarantees for the Power and Unity of Austria]. 1859.

Die Sonderstellung Ungarns vom Standpunkte der Einigheit Deutschlands [The Exceptional Position of Hungary from the Perspective of German Unity]. 1859.

Emlékbeszéd gróf Széchenyi István felett [Memorial Speech on Count István Széchenyi]. 1860.

Felelet báró Kemény Gábor néhány szavára [Reply to a Few Remarks by Gábor Kemény]. 1860.

Gondolatok [Thoughts]. 1864.

A nemzetiségi kérdés [The Nationality Problem]. 1865.

Translator, *Angelo*, by Victor Hugo. 1836.

*

Bibliography: *Hungarian Authors: A Bibliographical Handbook* by Albert Tezla, 1970; *A magyar irodalomtörténet bibliográfiája, 1772–1849* by György Kókay, 1975.

Critical Studies: *Báró Eötvös József, mint regényíró* [Baron József Eötvös as a Novelist] by Jenő Péterfy, 1901; "József Eötvös" by D. Mervyn Jones, in *Five Hungarian Writers*, 1966; *Eötvös József* by István Sőtér, 2nd enlarged edition, 1967; *Baron József Eötvös* by Béla Várdy, 1969; *Joseph Eötvös and the Modernization of Hungary* by Paul Bödy, 1972.

* * *

Baron József Eötvös's works include verse, drama, novels, short stories, and political studies, but his literary reputation rests mainly on his four novels. He believed firmly that all writing must have a serious purpose, but should also give pleasure, though this was never to be its main aim. He was a determined reformer of the Hungarian social and political system, and he viewed literature as a means of conveying his message.

An extended visit to Western Europe in 1836–37 had a profound effect on his thought: he then saw how the revolution of July 1830 in France had failed to usher in a new and better era and how the ideals of the 1789 French Revolution had faded. His reflections, spurred by a chance encounter at the Grande Chartreuse, inspired his first novel, *A karthausi* [The Carthusian]. It takes the form of a memoir containing the confessions of a selfish young French count; overcome with self-disgust after two unhappy love affairs, he withdraws from the world to seek peace among the Carthusians. He gives his confessions to a friend, who records his death, noting that he had not found the solace he sought. The novel is intensely introspective and emotional, and contains lengthy reflective passages. While there are some splendid descriptive and dramatic episodes, many of the characters seem overdrawn and reliance upon coincidences betrays the inexperienced novelist. Yet his message is clear: it is a warning against selfishness and the corruption of high ideals, and is as applicable to Hungary as to France.

Eötvös's second and best-known novel, *A falu jegyzője* (*The Village Notary*), appeared in 1845 when political reform was under active discussion. It is a full-blooded attack on the Hungarian county-system, which the author viewed as corrupt and hostile to reform. He depicts a fictitious county, exposing all its shortcomings and the social evils generated by them. It embraces all classes from the aristocracy to the outlaw, and the resulting unflattering picture led early critics to declare that it was more like a reformist leading article than a novel. Yet the scene is not entirely bleak; hope for the future rests with the young nobility, whose reforming zeal contrasts sharply with the arid conservatism of their elders. Here Eötvös's style is appropriate to his contemporary theme; it is incisive, dramatic and satirical, laced with sardonic humour. He weaves skilfully the varied episodes into a convincing whole, and only occasionally holds up the action to reflect on a particular concern such as prison reform. In this novel he best achieved his aim of combining entertaining fiction with a political message, and the result was widely acclaimed, notably in Britain.

If *The Village Notary* portrayed contemporary reality, Eötvös's third novel, *Magyarország 1514-ben* [Hungary in 1514], explored the origins of the social system then prevailing. In 1514 an abortive crusade against the Turks turned into full-scale peasant revolt. The rebellion was crushed and the leaders savagely punished—at the very time when the legal rights of the various classes were being codified. So the punitive legislation of 1514 relating to non-nobles passed into laws which remained in force till 1848. Eötvös's novel places history in the foreground, as his copious footnotes attest.

The action proceeds in a series of personal conflicts, without any central heroic figure; this is deliberate, since it allows Eötvös to express his doubts about revolution as a means to improve the lot of mankind and his misgivings about such ideals as liberty and equality, themes which occupied him in his later works. Justice, according to Eötvös, cannot be achieved by violence. The novel, again on a vast scale, maintains an uneasy balance between history and fiction; it seeks to interpret history, not to use it as a background. Thus while the historical characters are vividly portrayed, their fictional counterparts are somewhat drab, indicating an unresolved conflict between the historian and the novelist, to whom the message was more important than the medium.

The message came too late. Eötvös left Hungary before revolution erupted in 1848. In exile till 1850, he expounded his political views in *A XIX. század uralkodó eszméinek befolyása az álladalomra* [The Dominant Ideas of the 19th Century and Their Influence on the State], a magisterial survey demonstrating how the ideals inherited from the French Revolution—liberty, equality, and nationality to replace fraternity—might well prove incompatible in mankind's endeavours to progress, and offering his own solution to the problem. Published in two volumes in 1851 and 1854, in both German and Hungarian, it received wider recognition abroad than in Hungary.

On his return to Hungary in 1851, Eötvös resumed his literary pursuits. A number of skillfully written short stories set in rural Hungary were followed by his novel *A nővérek* [The Sisters] in 1857. Here new problems are faced, including the decay of the Hungarian gentry, a theme pursued by many later writers. Eötvös introduces the superfluous aristocrat, whose life is characterized by uneventfulness, boredom, and illusion. It is a psychological novel, remarkable for its insight into feminine psychology. Alongside the main theme, the author stresses the importance of children's education, a subject that he was to pursue vigorously after 1867 as Minister of Religion and Public Education. Once again he suits his style to his theme: it is muted and colourless, prompting critics to deplore the lack of his previous vitality, even in a comparatively brief work.

Such strictures ignore his unrivalled skill, at a time when the novel was an undefined genre, of altering both form and style to suit his theme; no other writer attempted such variety, from the memoir to realistic description, history, and psychology, to proclaim his views. Eötvös served his age not only as statesman and political thinker, but also as thought-provoking novelist.

—G.F. Cushing

See the essay on *The Village Notary*.

ERASMUS, Desiderius

Born: Rotterdam, The Netherlands (then under Spanish rule), probably 27/28 October 1467. **Education:** Educated at a school in Gouda, ages 4–9; at Deventer, 1478–93; a seminary at 's Hertogenbosch. **Career:** Entered monastery of Canons Regular of S. Augustine, Steyn, 1487: ordained priest, 1492; released from monastic confinement, and entered secretarial service of Bishop of Cambrai, 1493–95; studied at College of Montaigue, Paris, 1495–99, 1500–01; became Doctor of Divinity, University of Turin, 1506. Lived or travelled in England, 1499, 1505–06, 1509–14 (lectured on Greek in Cambridge), 1515, 1516, 1517; lived in Italy, 1506–09: lived in Louvain, 1517–21; general editor of John Froben's press, Basle, 1521–29; lived in Freiburg, 1529–35, and in Basle again, 1535–36: declined offer of becoming a Cardinal. **Died:** 12 July 1536.

PUBLICATIONS

Collections

Opera omnia, edited by Jean Leclerc. 10 vols., 1703–06.
The Essential Erasmus, edited by John P. Dolan. 1964.
Essential Works, edited by W.T.H. Jackson. 1965.
Opera omnia. 1969– (9 vols. to 1983).
Collected Works. 1974– (72 vols. to 1992).
The Erasmus Reader, edited by Erika Rummel. 1990.

Works

Adagia. 1500, and later augmented editions; as *Proverbs or Adages*, translated by Richard Taverner, 1539; translated anonymously, 1622; as *Adages*, translated by Margaret Mann Phillips, in *The Adages: A Study*, 1964; also translated by R.A.B. Mynors, in *Collected Works*, 1982.
Enchiridion militis Christiani. 1503; as *The Manual of the Christian Knight*, translated by William Tyndale, 1533, reprinted 1905; also translated by Anne M. O'Donnell, 1981; as *The Christian Manual*, translated by John Spier, 1752; as *The Handbook of the Militant Christian*, translated by John P. Dolan, 1962; as *The Enchiridion*, translated by Raymond Himelick, 1963.
Encomium moriae. 1511; revised edition, 1514; edited and translated by Hoyt H. Hudson, 1941; as *The Praise of Folly*, translated by

Thomas Chaloner, 1549; also translated by John Wilson, 1668, reprinted 1961; White Kennett, 1683; James Copner, 1878; Leonard F. Dean, 1946; A.H.T. Levi and Betty Radice, 1971; Clarence H. Miller, 1979.
De ratione studii. 1512; revised edition, 1514; edited by Jean-Claude Margolin, in *Opera omnia*, 1971; translated as *On the Aim and Method of Education*, edited by W.H. Woodward, 1904; as *A Method of Study*, translated by Brian McGregor, in *Collected Works*, 1978.
De copia. 1512; revised edition, 1514; as *On Copia of Words and Ideas*, translated by Donald B. King and H. David Rix, 1963; as *On Copia*, translated by Betty I. Knott, in *Collected Works*, 1978.
Institutio principis Christiani. 1516; as *The Education of a Christian Prince*, translated by Lester K. Born, 1936; also translated by Neil M. Cheshire and Michael J. Heath, 1997.
Julius Exclusus. 1517; as *The Dialogue Between Julius the Second Genius and Saint Peter*, translated anonymously, 1534; translated as *The Pope Shut Out of Heaven Gates*, 1673; also translated by J.A. Froude, in *Life and Letters of Erasmus*, 1894, reprint edited by Edwin Johnson, 1916.
Colloquia familiaria. 1518, and later augmented editions; edited by L.-E. Halkin, F. Bierlaire, and R. Hoven, in *Opera omnia*, 1972; as *The Colloquies*, translated by H.M. London, 1671; also translated by Roger L'Estrange, in *Twenty Select Colloquies*, 1680, revised edition, 1923; Nathan Bailey, 1725, reprinted 1905; Craig R. Thompson, 1965; in part as *Ten Colloquies*, translated by Craig R. Thompson, 1957.
De libero arbitro. 1524; edited by J. Walter, 1910; as *Discourse on the Freedom of the Will*, edited and translated by Ernest F. Winter, 1961.
Dialogus Ciceronianus. 1528; edited by Pierre Mesnard, in *Opera omnia*, 1971; as *Ciceronianus; or, A Dialogue on the Best Style of Speaking*, edited and translated by Izora Scott, 1900.
Apophthegmes, translated by Nicholas Udall. 1542, reprinted 1877.
The Complaint of Peace, translated by Thomas Paynell. 1559; revised edition, 1946.
Life and Letters of Erasmus, translated by J.A. Froude. 1894, reprinted 1916.
Opus epistolarum, edited by P.S. Allen and others. 12 vols. (in Latin and English), 1906–58; as *The Epistles*, edited and translated by Francis M. Nichols, 3 vols., 1901–18; as *Correspondence*, translated by R.A.B. Mynors and D.F.S. Thomson, annotated by Wallace K. Ferguson, James K. McConica, and Peter G. Bietenholz, in *Collected Works*, 1974.
Opuscula, edited by W.K. Ferguson. 1933.
The Poems, edited by Cornelis Reedijk. 1956.
Erasmus and Cambridge: The Cambridge Letters, edited by H.C. Porter, translated by D.F.S. Thomson. 1963.
Christian Humanism and the Reformation: Selected Writings, edited by John C. Olin. 1965.
Erasmus and Fisher: Their Correspondence 1511–1524, edited by Jean Rouschausse. 1968.
Erasmus and His Age: Selected Letters, edited by Hans J. Hillerbrand. 1970.
De conscribendis epistolis, as *On the Writing of Letters*, edited and translated by Charles Fantazzi, in *Collected Works*. 1985.
De pueris ... instituendis declamatio, as *A Declamation on the Subject of Early Liberal Education for Children*, edited and translated by Beert C. Vorstraete, in *Collected Works*. 1985.

De recta latini graecique sermonis pronuntiatione, as *The Right Way of Speaking Latin and Greek*, edited and translated by Maurice Pope, in *Collected Works*. 1985.

The Praise of Folly, and Other Writings. 1990.

Paraphrase on The Acts of the Apostles, edited by John J. Bateman, translated and annotated by Robert D. Sider, 1995.

Erasmus on Women, edited by Erika Rummel, 1996.

Expositions of the Psalms, edited by Dominic Baker-Smith, translated and annotated by Michael J. Heath, 1997.

Editor and translator (into Latin), *Novum instrumentum* [New Testament]. 1516; revised edition, 1527.

Translator (into Latin), with Thomas More, *Lucian*. 1506.

Translator (into Latin), *Hecuba, Iphigenia in Aulide*, by Euripides. 1506.

Also edited works by Ambrose, Aristotle, Augustine, Basil, Cato, Chrysostom, Cicero, Cyprian, Hilary, Irenaeus, Jerome, Lactantius, Origen, Plutarch, Pseudo-Arnobius, Seneca, and others; commentary on the Bible.

*

Bibliography: *Renaissance Translations of Erasmus: A Bibliography to 1700* by E.J. Devereux, 1983.

Critical Studies: *Erasmus and the Northern Renaissance*, 1949, and *The Adages of Erasmus: A Study*, 1964, both by Margaret Mann Phillips; *Thomas More and Erasmus* by Ernest E. Reynolds, 1965; *Erasmus and Luther* by Rosemary D. Jones, 1968; *Erasmus of Christendom* by Roland H. Bainton, 1969; *Twentieth Century Interpretations of The Praise of Folly* edited by Kathleen Williams, 1969; *Erasmus of Rotterdam*, 1971, and *Essays on the Work of Erasmus*, 1978, both edited by Richard L. DeMolen, and *The Spirituality of Erasmus of Rotterdam* by DeMolen, 1987; *Erasmus: The Growth of a Mind* by James D. Tracy, 1972; *The Tragedy of Erasmus* by Harry S. May, 1975; *Desiderius Erasmus* by J. Kelley Sowards, 1975; *Erasmus on Language and Method in Theology*, 1977, *Christening Pagan Mysteries: Erasmus in Pursuit of Wisdom*, 1981, and *Rhetoric and Reform: Erasmus' Civil Dispute with Luther*, 1983, all by Marjorie O'Rourke Boyle; *Phoenix of His Age: Interpretations of Erasmus, c. 1550–1750*, 1979, and *Man on His Own: Interpretations of Erasmus c. 1750–1920*, 1992, both by Bruce Mansfield; *Six Essays on Erasmus, and a Translation of Erasmus' Letter to Carondelet, 1523* by John C. Olin, 1979, and *A Biography of Erasmus*, edited by Olin, 1988; *Erasmus: The Right to Heresy* by Stephan Zweig, 1979; *Erasmus: Ecstasy and The Praise of Folly* by M.A. Screech, 1980; *Le Neveu de Rameau and The Praise of Folly: Literary Cognates* by Apostolos P. Kouidos, 1981; *Erasmus and His Times* edited by G.S. Facer, 1982; *The Praise of Folly: Structure and Irony* by Zoja Pavlovskis, 1983; *Erasmus and the Jews* by Shimon Markish, 1986; *Erasmus Grandescens: The Growth of a Humanist's Mind and Spirituality*, 1988, and *Erasmus of Europe: The Making of a Humanist*, 1990, both by Richard J. Schoeck; *Erasmus and His Catholic Critics* by Erika Rummel, 1989; *Humanist Play and Belief: The Seriocomic Art of Desiderius Erasmus* by Walter M. Gordon, 1990; *Erasmus: His Life, Works and Influence* by Cornelius Augustijn, translated by J.C. Grayson, 1991; *Erasmus* by James McConica, 1991; *Erasmus, Colet and More: The Early Tudor Humanists and Their Books* by J.B.

Trapp, 1991; *Erasmus, Lee and the Correction of the Volgate: The Shaking of the Foundations* by Robert Coogan, 1992; *Erasmus: A Critical Biography* by Leon E. Halkin, translated by John Tonkin, 1992; *Erasmus, Man of Letters: The Construction of Charisma in Print* by Lisa Jardine, 1993; *Rhetoric and Theology: The Hermeneutic of Erasmus* by Manfred Hoffmann, 1994; *Erasmus the Reformer* by A.G. Dickens and Whitney R.D. Jones, 1994; *Erasmus, Utopia, and the Jesuits: Essays on the Outreach of Humanism* by John C. Olin, 1994; *Erasmianism: Idea and Reality*, edited by M.E.H.N. Mout, H. Smolinsky and J. Trapman, 1997; *Conversing with God: Prayer in Erasmus' Pastoral Writings* by Hilmar M. Pabel, 1997; *Silenos: Erasmus in Elizabethan Literature*, edited by Claudia Corti, 1998; *Erasmus, the Anabaptists, and the Great Commission* by Abraham Friesen, 1998; *Erasmus and the Middle Ages: The Historical Consciousness of a Christian Humanist* by István Pieter Bejczy, 2001.

*   *   *

Desiderius Erasmus of Rotterdam was the most famous man of letters of early 16th-century Europe, a figure who dominated the intellectual world of his time as clearly as Petrarch, Voltaire, or Goethe did theirs. He was acclaimed "the prince of humanists." He was the leading biblical scholar of his time, and the editor of the first modern critical text of the Greek New Testament. He was an advocate of educational reform and an author of textbooks and educational tracts. He was a passionate advocate of peace. Additionally, and perhaps most important of all, he was one of the most tireless advocates of religious reform in the age of the Reformation. The titles of his books run into the hundreds, but his most famous works were his satirical books, especially the *Encomium moriae* (*The Praise of Folly*) and the *Colloquia familiaria* (*The Colloquies*).

The Praise of Folly, Erasmus' single best-known book, is a complex, multi-layered satire of the outworn classical form of the oration of praise, a parody of such worthy abstractions as Dame Philosophy or The Seven Liberal Arts—in this case the goddess Folly. Folly, arising before the court of mankind, intends to praise herself, since no one else will praise her. She proves with impeccable logic that all important actions and accomplishments are owing to her influence. She claims as hers all manner and conditions of men, from kings and nobles and wealthy merchants to calamity-ridden and tormented teachers of grammar, even husbands and wives, parents and children. But Folly also claims theologians with their pride of learning and endless hair-splitting definitions; monks with their empty formalism and self-serving piety; and the powerful, cynical rulers of the church, including the popes, the vicars of Christ so unlike him in every way. Then Folly claims that true Christians are the greatest of fools, that no people behave more foolishly, giving away their goods, overlooking wrongs and injuries, forgiving their enemies. And finally, Folly argues, Christ himself became something like a fool to cure the folly of mankind by the foolishness of the cross.

The serious religious-reforming purpose of *The Praise of Folly* is equally clearly expressed in Erasmus' other major satiric work, *The Colloquies*. This was probably the most frequently printed of Erasmus' books in his lifetime. It began as a series of brief and simple Latin conversational exercises for students which proved to be so popular that Erasmus prepared expanded editions through the 1520s and early 1530s, adding many new colloquies. Most are little satiric dialogues directed at the targets of his reforming efforts—corrupt monks and ignorant priests; the excesses of the veneration of saints and relics and pilgrimages; the senseless preference for the formalities of religion to the neglect of its spirit; and his hatred of war. Several of the colloquies—*Charon, Naufragium* (*The Shipwreck*), *Peregrinatio Religionis ergo* (*The Pilgrimage for Religion's Sake*), *Abbatis et eruditae* (*The Abbot and the Learned Lady*), *Exorcismus, sive spectrum* (*Exorcism or the Spectre*)—can be compared with the best satiric writing of the 16th century.

—J. Kelley Sowards

See the essays on *The Colloquies* and *The Praise of Folly*.

ESENIN, Sergei Aleksandrovich

Also known as Sergey Yesenin. **Born:** Konstantinovo, Riazan' Province, Russia, 3 October 1895. **Education:** Educated at the Konstantinovo primary school, 1904–09; church school, Spas-Klepiki, 1909–12; Shaniavskii University, 1913. **Military Service:** Military service, 1916; deserted, 1917. **Family:** Married 1) Anna Romanova Izriadnova in 1914 (divorced), one son; 2) Zinaida Nikolaevna Raikh in 1917 (separated 1918, divorced 1921), one daughter and one son; 3) the dancer Isadora Duncan in 1922 (divorced 1924); 4) Sof'ia Tolstaia in 1925 (separated); also had a son in 1925. **Career:** Made poetic debut in Petrograd, 1915; settled in Moscow, 1918; member of the Imaginist poetic movement, 1919; travelled to Turkestan and Tashkent, 1921; travelled through Belgium, Germany, France, Italy, and the United States, with Isadora Duncan, 1922–23; returned to Russia, 1923; suffered from declining mental health from c. 1922, with spells in sanatoriums, 1924–25; travelled in the Caucasus, 1924–25. **Died:** (suicide) 28 December 1925.

PUBLICATIONS

Collections

Sobranie stikhotvorenii [Collected Poetry]. 4 vols., 1926–27.
Sobranie sochinenii [Collected Works], 5 vols., 1961–62, 1966–68.
Sobranie sochinenii [Collected Works], edited by Iu.L. Prokushev. 3 vols., 1970.
Sochineniia [Works], edited by P.S. Vykhodtsev. 1975.
Sobranie sochinenii [Collected Works], edited by V.G. Bazanov. 6 vols., 1977–80.
Sochineniia, 1910–1925 [Works, 1910–1925], edited by V.G. Bazanov. 1980.
Izbrannye sochineniia [Selected Works], edited by Aleksei Kozlovskii. 1983.
Sochineniia [Works], edited by Aleksei Kozlovskii. 1988.
Sobranie sochinenii [Collected Works], edited by Iu.L. Prokushev. 2 vols., 1990.
Stikhotvoreniia; Poemy: Izbrannoe [Poetry; Narrative Verse; Selections], edited by D.A. Ovinnikov. 1992.
I Do Not Regret: Selected Poems, edited by Uolter Mei. 1997.

The Collected Poems of Yesenin, translated by Gregory Brengauz. 2000.

Verse

Radunitsa. 1916.
Preobrazhenie [Transfiguration]. 1918.
Sel'skii chasoslov [A Village Prayerbook]. 1918.
Inoniia. 1918.
Goluben' [Azure]. 1920.
Treriadnitsa. 1920.
Ispoved' khuligana [Confessions of a Hooligan]. 1920.
Pugachov. 1922.
Stikhi skandalisa [Scandalous Poems]. 1923.
Tovarishch; Inoniia [Comrade; Inoniia]. 1923.
Moskva kabatskaia [Moscow of the Taverns]. 1924.
Stikhi [Poems]. 1924.
Rus' sovetskaia [Soviet Russia]. 1925.
Berezovyi sitets [The Birch-Tree Cotton Print]. 1925.
Persidskie motivy [Persian Motifs]. 1925.
Stikhotvoreniia [Poetry]. 1940.
Stikhotvoreniia. Poemy [Poetry. Narrative Verse]. 1956.
Stikhotvoreniia i poemy [Poetry and Narrative Verse]. 1957.
Zarianka. 1964.
Slovesnykh rek kipenie i shorokh [The Boiling and Rustle of the River of Words]. 1965.
Otchee slovo [The Father's Word]. 1968.
Sinii mai. Lirika [Dark Blue May. Lyric Poems]. 1973.
Confessions of a Hooligan: Fifty Poems, translated by Geoffrey Thurley. 1973.
Anna Snegina. 1974.
Riabinovyi koster: Stikhotvoreniia [The Rowan-Tree Bonfire: Poetry]. 1975.
Plesk golubogo livnia [The Splash of the Blue Downpour]. 1975.
Zlatoi posev [Golden Crops], edited by S. Koshechkin. 1976.
Neskazannoe, sinee, nezhnoe [Unspeakable, Dark Blue, Tender]. 1978.
Belykh iablon' dym [White Smoke of the Apple-Trees] 1978.
Selected Poems, translated by Jessie Davies. 1979.
Volnuias' serdtsem i stikhom. . . [Agitated in My Heart and Verse]. 1981.
Izbrannye stikhotvoreniia i poemy/Selected Poetry (bilingual edition), translated by Peter Tempest. 1982.
"Ia bolee vsego vesnu liubliu. . . " [I More than Anything Love Spring]. 1984.
Snezhnye vetry [Snowy Winds]. 1985.
Serdtsu snitsia mai: Stikhi o liubvi [A Heart Dreaming of May: Love Poems]. 1985.
Sin', upavshaia v reku [Blue Colour, Falling into the River]. 1985.
Stikhotvoreniia i proza [Poetry and Prose]. 1985.
Cheremukha [Bird-Cherry]. 1985.
Poemy i stikhotvoreniia [Narrative Verse and Poetry]. 1986.
Zakruzhilas' listva zolotaia [The Twisted Gold Foliage]. 1988.
Strana negodiaev [A Country of Scoundrels]. 1991.

*

Critical Studies: *Esenin: A Life* by Gordon McVay, 1976; *Sergey Esenin* by Constantin V. Ponomareff, 1978; *Sergei Yesenin: The*

Man, the Verse, the Age by Yuri Prokushev, 1979; *Sergei Esenin: Poet of the Crossroads* by Lynn Visson, 1980; *Esenin: A Biography in Memoirs, Letters, and Documents* edited and translated by Jessie Davies, 1982; *Poetika Esenina* by A.N. Zakharov, 1995.

* * *

Sergei Esenin led a short and turbulent life, which quickly passed into legend and myth. From his meteoric literary debut in Petrograd in 1915 until his suicide in a Leningrad hotel in 1925, Esenin assumed in rapid succession a number of literary "masks"—pastoral angel (1915–16), peasant prophet (1917–18), last poet of the village, tender hooligan (1919–21), tavern rake (1922–23), ex-hooligan (late 1923), would-be bard of the new Soviet Russia (mid-1924 until March 1925), and, finally, elegiac foreteller of his own imminent death (1925).

Although Esenin's poetry is highly autobiographical and even "confessional," the connection between the private man and his poetic persona is not entirely straightforward. By single-mindedly dedicating himself to the writing of poetry and the achievement of fame, Esenin blurred the boundaries between his "mask" and his "real face," sacrificing the possibility of ordinary human happiness.

A peasant from Riazan' province, Esenin enjoyed conspicuous success in the pre-revolutionary literary salons of Petrograd. His first volume of poetry, *Radunitsa*, reflected the decorative, traditional aspects of village life. Rus', his ancient Russian motherland, was already the beloved heroine of his verse, a motherland which may be sad and impoverished, yet is also calm and imbued with a simple peasant religiousness. Jesus and the saints wandered as lowly pilgrims in the forests and along the paths of rural Rus', and the poet knelt in prayer before the temple of Nature.

Esenin's life was drastically affected by the February and October Revolutions of 1917. He welcomed these upheavals enthusiastically but vaguely in a series of longish "Scythian" poems, couched in abstruse religious and animal symbolism. These poems, which alternate between optimism and anxiety, prayerfulness and blasphemy, maintain a lofty cosmic tone far removed from the grim reality of earth-born Bolshevism.

By 1919, Esenin appeared a promising peasant poet, whose natural gifts displayed the influence of folk poetry, Kliuev, and Blok. Thenceforth, however, pursuing national fame, he sought creative independence within Moscow's anarchic literary bohemia. The last six years of Esenin's life witnessed the blossoming of his poetic talent and the disintegration of his inner peace.

As a founding member of the enterprisingly avant-garde "Imaginist" group, Esenin achieved instant notoriety by emphasizing the unresolved dissonances in his personality and plight. Voicing his deep-rooted romantic attachment to old-fashioned, non-industrialized Rus', he lamented the imminent encroachment of the "iron guest" (urban industrialization) in "Ia poslednii poet derevni" [I'm the Last Poet of the Village] (1920), and cursed the "vile guest" (the train which defeats the living horse) in "Sorokoust" (1920). In *Ispoved' khuligana* [The Confessions of a Hooligan], his lyrical hero is coarse and tender, desperate and kind; full of provocative vulgarity, and yet also "gently sick with childhood recollections."

After his marriage to Isadora Duncan in 1922, and an ill-starred 15-month tour of western Europe and the United States, Esenin composed the controversial cycle *Moskva kabatskaia* [Moscow of the Taverns]. The setting is the tavern, the inhabitants are prostitutes and bandits, syphilitic accordionists, down-and-outs seeking to drown their misery in alcohol and dreams. Written in a universally understandable, non-Imaginistic language, these poems immediately appealed to thousands of Russians who saw in them a reflection of their own anguish.

The poetry of Esenin's last two years, after his return to Russia in 1923, combines a new-found "Pushkinian" simplicity of style with a mood of ever-deepening tragic isolation. In the cycle "Liubov' khuligana" [A Hooligan's Love], his lyrical hero sought to break with hooliganism, passing into autumnal resignation. A profoundly elegiac mood permeates the outstanding lyrics of 1924, "My teper' ukhodim ponemnogu" [We Are Now Gradually Departing] and "Otgovorila roshcha zolotaia" [The Golden Grove Has Ceased to Speak].

Esenin had never been openly counter-revolutionary and, after his disillusioning travels in the west, he strove at times to compose pro-Soviet verse, praising Lenin and endeavouring to accept the changed face of Russia. Such attempts often proved poetically lifeless, however, with many critics doubting his sincerity and aptness for such topics.

Towards the end of 1925 Esenin's poetry entered its most tragic phase. Isolated, alcoholic, vulnerable, and despairing, he created a sequence of short poems set in a winter landscape. Instead of autumnal fading, his mood was now echoed by wintry iciness, evoking memories of lost youth and lost happiness. On 12–13 November 1925 he wrote down the only extant version of his poem "Chernyi chelovek" [The Black Man], revealing his desperate struggle against alcoholic hallucinations and a tormented conscience. On 27 December Esenin wrote his last poem, "Do svidan'ia, drug moi, do svidan'ia" [Goodbye, My Friend, Goodbye], in his own blood, and the next day he was found hanging in a Leningrad hotel room.

As a literary phenomenon, Esenin has been compared with Robert Burns and Arthur Rimbaud, with Dylan Thomas and, above all, François Villon; yet such is his complexity that he has also been characterized as the "Don Quixote of the village and the birch-tree" (V. Shershenevich, in *Trud*, Klintsy, 19 January 1926), and even likened to St. Francis of Assisi. He has been called a poet of death, and a poet of eternal youth.

Despite a prolonged period of disfavour during the Stalin years, Esenin remains the most popular and most widely read Russian poet of the 20th century. He is exceptionally "Russian," a temperamental peasant embodying tragic pathos and the forlorn dream of a rural idyll. Scholars in the West (mainly non-Russian urban intellectuals) often disparage the simplicity, emotionality and melodiousness of Esenin's verse, preferring the sophisticated subtlety of Pasternak, Mandel'shtam, Akhmatova, and Tsvetaeva. It is perhaps time to challenge this elitist judgement. A Russian critic perceptively observed during Esenin's lifetime (Andrei Shipov [Ivan Rozanov], in *Narodnyi uchitel'*, 2, 1925):

> In certain respects Esenin should without doubt seem inferior to some of his contemporaries: he lacks the sweep and crude strength of Maiakovskii, the cultural saturation of Mandel'shtam, or the dazzling lyrical intensity of Boris Pasternak, but he has a quality which is perhaps the most valuable of all for a lyric poet—the ability to reach the reader's heart and even—a thing to which we are now especially unaccustomed—the ability at times to move and touch us . . . Mandel'shtam and Pasternak are too intellectual as poets, in the last resort they are

poets for the few ... Esenin, on the other hand, can be understood by everyone from the lowly to the grand . . . .

—Gordon McVay

ESTERHÁZY, (Count) Péter

Pseudonym: Lili Csokonai. **Born:** Budapest, Hungary, 1 April 1950. **Education:** Studied mathematics at Eötvös Loránd University, Budapest, 1969–74. **Military Service:** Served in the army. **Family:** Married Gitti Reen in 1973; four children. **Career:** Began publishing in literary journals in the 1970s; works as an independent writer. Lives in Budapest, Hungary. **Awards:** Research fellow, Andrew W. Mellon Foundation; Kossuth prize (Hungary), 1996; Berliner Wissenschaftkolleg, 1996–97; Osterreichischen Staatspreis for European Literature, Vienna, 1999; Hungarian Literary award, 2001; Capo Circeo, Rome, 2001; Herder prize, Vienna, 2002. **Member:** Society of Digital Immortals (Hungary).

PUBLICATIONS

Collections

Bevezetés a szépirodalomba (novels). 1986.
A kitömött hattyú (essays). 1988.

Fiction

Fancsikó és Pinta. 1976.
Pápai vizeken ne kalozkodj. 1977.
Termelési regény. 1979.
Függő. 1981.
Ki szavatol a lady biztonságáért?. 1982.
Ágnes. 1982.
Fuharosok. 1983; as *The Transporters*, translated by Ferenc Takacs, in *A Hungarian Quartet.* 1991.
Kis magyar pornográfia. 1983; as *A Little Hungarian Pornography*, translated by Judith Sollosy, 1995.
A szív segédigéi. 1985; as *Helping Verbs of the Heart*, translated by Michael Henry Heim, 1991.
Tizenhét hattyúk. 1986.
Hrabal könyve. 1990; as *The Book of Hrabal*, translated by Judith Sollosy, 1993.
Hahn-Hahn grofno pillantása. 1991; as *The Glance of Countess Hahn-Hahn (Down the Danube)*, translated by Richard Aczel, 1994.
Búcsúszimfónia. 1994.
Egó nő. 1995; as *She Loves Me*, translated by Judith Sollosy, 1997.
Harmonia Caelestis. 2000.

Other

"Investigating the Bath Tub" in *Index on Censorship.* 1988.
"On Laziness" translated by Zsuzsanna Ozváth and Martha Satz, in *Partisan Review.* 1989.
"God's Hat" translated by Michael Henry Heim, in *Partisan Review.* 1990.
"Want to See Golden Budapest?" in *Cross Currents.* 1990.

"The Problem Facing the Writer Today" translated by Judith Sollosy, in *Partisan Review.* 1996.

*

Critical Studies: "Mekhanizm literatury: Pushkin i Esterkhazi" by E. Boitar, translated by Nadezhda Nikulina, in *Studia Slavica Academiae Scientiarum Hungaricae*, vol. 28, nos. 1–4, 1982; "Peter Esterhazy" by Ferenc Takacs, in *The Hungarian P.E.N./Le P.E.N. Hongrois*, vol. 26, 1985; "Torment and Sacrifice" by Miklos Gyorffy, in *New Hungarian Quarterly*, vol. 26, no. 97, 1985; "(Selbstzensur) und (Textverderben): Konflikte und Losungen in den neuesten Schriften von Peter Esterhazy" by Tiborc Fazekas, in *Festschrift fur Istvan Futaky*, edited by Wolfgang Veenker and Tibor Kesztyus, 1986; "Irasok" by Gyorgy Poszler, in *Kortars: Irodalmi Es Kritikai Folyoirat*, vol. 32, no. 7, 1988; "Delicate Balance: Coherence and Mutual Knowledge in a Short Story" by Istvan Siklaki, in *Poetics*, vol. 17, nos. 4–5, 1988; "Textualitat und Dialogizitat: Versuch der Wesensbestimmung der 'Postmoderne' bei P. Esterhazy" by Laszlo Onodi, in *Neohelicon*, vol. 16, no. 1, 1989; "The Concealed Eye/The Elusive 'I': An Update on Peter Esterhazy" by Marianna D. Birnbaum, in *Cross Currents*, vol. 11, 1992; "Peter Nadas, Peter Esterhazy und die deutsche Literatur im Zeitalter der Moderne und Postmoderne" by Arpad Bernath, in *Neohelicon*, vol. 20, no. 1, 1993; "Peter Esterhazys 'Hilfsverben des Herzens' und Peter Handkes 'Wunschloses Ungluck': Ein komparatistischer Versuch" by Maria Kajtar, in *Die Zeit und die Schrift: Osterreichische Literatur nach 1945*, edited by Karlheinz Auckenthaler, 1993; "Postmodernism in Hungary: The Example of Peter Esterhazy against the Background of Analysing John Barth's Later Fiction" by Judit Friedrich, in *Anachronist*, 1996; "Introducing Péter Esterházy" in *Hungarian Rhapsodies* by Richard Teleky, 1997; "Gender Benders: Naughtiness in the post-Communist World" by John Updike, in *The New Yorker*, 25 May 1998; "Der religiose Horizont in den Romanen Peter Esterhazys" by Istvan Dobos, translated by Christina Kunze, in *Epoche-Text-Modalitat: Diskurs der Moderne in der ungarischen Literaturwissenschaft*, edited by Erno Kulcsar-Szabo and Mihaly Szegedy-Maszak, 1999; "Configurations of Postcoloniality and National Identity: In-between Peripherality and Narratives of Change" by Steven Totosy de Zepetnek, in *The Comparatist*, vol. 23, 1999.

* * *

Péter Esterházy is one of the most popular and successful writers in Hungary. Born a count, Esterházy is the scion of one of the oldest noble Hungarian families. His relatives were patrons of Haydn and Liszt, while the Duke Pál Esterházy (who died in 1713) is remembered for his sacred cantatas, collected as *Harmonia Caelestis*. Recently, Péter Esterházy has himself used the title of his ancestor's musical collection for a long narrative history of his family. *Harmonia Caelestis*, published in 2000, has been a bestseller in Hungary and in German translation as well.

Although Esterházy has had great critical and commercial success in his native Hungary and is well-known throughout Europe, Anglophone critics' response to Esterházy's works has been mixed. Only six of his novels have been translated into English, due perhaps in equal parts to the difficulty of Hungarian and of Esterházy's writing. Although he calls them "novels," Esterházy does not write novels in the 19th century sense. He eschews linear plots and sustained character development, preferring instead shifting, discontinuous scenes and anonymous narrators. In addition, until 1989 Hungary was part of the USSR, and that cultural and political reality forms the background (and occasionally the foreground) of Esterházy's works. *Termelési regény* [Production Novel], a satire of socialist production, and *Ki szavatol a lady biztonságáért?* [Who Does Guarantee the Lady's Security?], which is about transvestites, are in part a reaction against the Socialist Realism imposed by the Soviets. As a result, very little in Esterházy's writing could be termed realism, socialist or not.

In his defiance of the conventions of the traditional novel, Esterházy's works tend to be short (*Termelési regény* is about 50 pages) and combine various genres (historical drama, romance, psychological realism, verse, and travelogue) in an eclectic rhapsody. Yet the word "postmodern," often applied to his novels, misses the point. Esterházy has said that Hungary never experienced modernism; therefore, his works may be termed "pre-modern," while true Hungarian modernism remains in the future. That being said, however, Esterházy's novels nonetheless share elements of postmodernism, including fractured narratives and relentless intertextuality. The author quotes from sources as diverse as contemporary journalism, American blues standards, German philosophy, and his favorite authors. In *Kis magyar pornográfia* (*A Little Hungarian Pornography*), Esterházy warns the reader, "if you find an especially clever sentence in the book, the chances are better than even that it is a quote. If it is clever but you don't know what it means, it is from Wittgenstein." The narrator further explains that introducing a "foreign text (body)" creates "tension" between the various voices and points of view. Historical figures may also become characters to engage in impossible and anachronistic conversations; in *Hrabal könyve* (*The Book of Hrabal*), Charlie Parker teaches God (who has some attributes very similar to Esterházy's) to play the saxophone.

In *A szív segédigéi* (*Helping Verbs of the Heart*), the narrator mourns the death of his mother. To underscore the universal nature of grief, Esterházy refers to the family members not by names, but by their relationship to the narrator: Mother, Father, Sister, Brother. The book consists of two parts: the first is the son's narrative, while in the second half the mother discusses her life and her family. One critic interpreted the novel's final sentence, "Some day I'll write about all this in more detail," as the author's admission of failing to convey the profundity of his subject; others contend that Esterházy has already told all he could possibly say about death, leaving only the inexpressible for the readers to imagine for themselves.

European history is another topic for Esterházy's invention. His particular relationship to history goes against the conventions of dialectical Marxism: Esterházy's history is largely plotless and non-chronological—even *anti*-chronological. The incompleteness of the historical record prevents a deeper understanding of those events and their interrelatedness. Esterházy recognizes this overvaluation of the importance and sanctity of fact, and presents events in his narratives outside their chronology and stripped of most of their specifying—and thus limiting—facts and dates. Anna, the heroine of *The Book of Hrabal*, realizes history's deceptiveness when she confesses that she never really knew her mother. Her mother's generation, born before World War II and the Communist takeover, had witnessed terrible destruction. When Anna was still a teenager, her mother criticized her boldness; only years later does Anna begin to understand her mother's quiet will to survive. Boldness is not necessarily courage, and timidity is not necessarily cowardice. With this in mind, Anna redeems Bohumil Hrabal, the great Czech writer castigated for his allegiance

to the Soviet Party's 1975 congress. History is thus shown to obscure as much as it reveals.

By the same token, for readers who pick up *Hahn-Hahn grofno pillantása* (*The Glance of the Countess Hahn-Hahn*) expecting a history lesson on East Central Europe or the political significance of the Danube, the author's coyness with dates and facts can be frustrating. Yet what Esterházy tries to achieve with his reordering of events is history as it is experienced subjectively. Even the map in the front of the book flouts convention; cities and rivers are marked, but although the names of countries appear on the map, their political boundaries are conspicuously absent. In other words, though geographic variations exist and people have come to identify with their regions, political borders are neither natural nor inevitable. Questioning the assumptions of unchallenged ethnic or national identity, the narrator asks, "What does it mean to be Austrian?" His narrator records changes in his state of mind as he travels from the source of the Danube in the Black Forest to its mouth at the Black Sea. In Ulm, Germany, he feels one way, in Vienna, Austria, another; in his native Hungary, he thinks of himself differently, whereas in Romania the narrator modifies his behavior completely. Esterházy would likely agree with Sander Gilman's statement that identity is not *who* you are, but *where* you are.

In *Egó nõ* (*She Loves Me*), Esterházy challenges ideas of romance and character development. The book consists of 97 chapters, some no more than a few sentences in length. Each chapter begins with some variant of "There's this woman, she loves me," or "she hates me," although not all of the love objects are women. Esterházy explores the variety of relationships covered by the umbrella term "love," a love that is sometimes indistinguishable from hate, and hatred that is occasionally indistinguishable from love. Ultimately the novel is not about the object of love, but love itself.

Péter Esterházy continues to be prominent in Hungarian society. One of Esterházy's novels is the basis for the 1996 Hungarian film by Andras Solyom, *Erzekek Iskolaja* (*School of Sensitivity*). In 2001 Esterházy supported France's involvement in the fate of Roma refugees and he has been commended for his promotion of interethnic relations in Europe.

—Natalie Smith

EURIPIDES

Born: 480 or 485 BC. **Family:** Married to Melito; three sons. **Career:** Held a local priesthood at Phlya; not prominent politically, but did go on an embassy to Syracuse; also went to the court of Archelaus in Macedon, c. 408 BC; first competed in the City Dionysia in 455 BC: won four prizes during his lifetime, and one posthumously; of the 92 plays he is said to have written, 80 titles are known, and 19 are extant. **Died:** Before February/March 406 BC.

PUBLICATIONS

Collections

[Plays], edited by Gilbert Murray. 3 vols., 1902–13; also edited by James Diggle, 3 vols., 1982–94; as *The Tragedies*, translated by

Robert Potter. 2 vols., 1781–83; as *The Nineteen Tragedies*, translated by Michael Woodhull, 4 vols., 1782; also translated by T.A. Buckley, 2 vols., 1850; W.B. Donne, 1872; Arthur S. Way, 3 vols., 1894–98, revised edition [Loeb Edition], 4 vols., 1912; Percy Bysshe Shelley and others, 2 vols., 1906; Moses Hadas and J.M. McLean, 1936; edited by David Grene and Richmond Lattimore, various translators, in *Complete Greek Tragedies*, 5 vols., 1955–59; translated (prose) by Edward P. Coleridge, 2 vols., 1891; as *Euripides*, edited and translated by David Kovacs, 1994; as *After the Trojan War: Women of Troy, Hecuba, Helen: Three Plays*, translated and introduced by Kenneth McLeish, 1995; as *Alcestis and Other Plays*, translated by John Davie, 1996; as *Plays: Three*, introduced by J. Michael Walton and Kenneth McLeish, 1997; as *Plays: Four*, introduced by J. Michael Walton and Kenneth McLeish, 1997; as *Plays: Five*, introduced by J. Michael Walton and Kenneth McLeish, 1997; as *Plays: Six*, introduced by J. Michael Walton, Frederic Raphael and Kenneth McLeish, 1997; as *Medea; Hippolytus; Electra; Helen*, translated with notes by James Morwood, 1997; as *Euripides*, edited by David R. Slavitt and Palmer Bovie, 1998; as *Electra and Other Plays*, translated by John Davie, 1998; as *Iphigenia Among the Taurians; Bacchae; Iphigenia at Aulis; Rhesus*, translated by James Morwood, 1999; as *Women on the Edge: Four Plays*, translated and edited by Ruby Blondell, 1999; as *Hecuba; The Trojan Women; Andromache*, translated by James Morwood, 2000; as *Orestes and Other Plays*, translated by Robin Waterfield, 2001.

Plays

Alcestis (produced 438 BC). Edited by W.S. Hadley, 1896; also edited by E.H. Blakeney, 1899, revised edition, 1933, Amy Marjorie Dale, 1954, revised edition, 1978, and Antonio Garzya, 1980; edited and translated (with commentary) by Desmond J. Conacher, 1988; as *Alcestis*, translated by Robert Browning, 1871; also translated by H. Kynaston, 1906; Gilbert Murray, 1915; Richard Aldington, 1930; Dudley Fitts and Robert Fitzgerald, 1933; D.W. Lucas, 1951; Philip Vellacott, in *Three Plays*, 1953, revised edition, 1974; Richmond Lattimore, in *Complete Greek Tragedies*, 1955; Alistair Elliot, 1965; C.R. Beye, 1973; William Arrowsmith, 1974; Ted Hughes, 1999.

Medea (produced 431 BC). Edited by A.W. Verrall, 1881; also edited by Clinton E.S. Headlam, 1897, Denys L. Page, 1938, and Alan F. Elliott, 1969; as *Medea*, translated by Gilbert Murray, 1910; also translated by John Jay Chapman, in *Two Greek Plays*, 1928; Countee Cullen, 1935; R.C. Trevelyan, 1939; Rex Warner, 1944, in *Complete Greek Tragedies*, 1955, and in *Three Great Plays*, 1958; Frederick Prokosch, in *Greek Plays in Modern Translation*, 1947; D.W. Lucas, 1950; Moses Hadas and John McLean, in *Ten Plays*, 1960; Philip Vellacott, in *Medea and Other Plays*, 1963; Peter D. Arnott, in *Three Greek Plays*, 1964; Michael Townsend, 1966; Kenneth McLeish, 1970; Jeremy Brooks, in *Plays One*, 1988; D. Egan, 1991; Nicholas Rudall, 2000.

Heracleidae (produced c. 430–28 BC). Edited by Antonio Garzya, 1972; also edited by John Wilkins, 1993; as *Children of Heracles*, translated by Ralph Gladstone, in *Complete Greek Tragedies*, 1955; also translated by Philip Vellacott, in *Orestes and Other Plays*, 1972; Henry Taylor and Robert A. Brooks, 1981; John Wilkins, 1993.

Hippolytus (produced 428 BC). Edited by J.P. Mahaffy and J.B. Bury, 1881; also edited by W.S. Hadley, 1889, W.S. Barrett, 1964, and John Ferguson, 1984; as *Hippolytus*, translated by Gilbert Murray, 1900; also translated by David Grene, in *Three Greek Tragedies*, 1942, and in *Complete Greek Tragedies*, 1955; Rex Warner, 1949, and in *Three Great Plays*, 1958; Philip Vellacott, in *Three Plays*, 1953, revised edition, 1974; E.P. Coleridge, in *Three Great Greek Plays*, 1960; Donald Sutherland, in *Hippolytus in Drama and Myth*, 1960; Kenneth Cavander, 1962; Robert Bragg, 1974; Gilbert and Sarah Lawall, 1986; Michael R. Halleran, 1995.

Andromache (produced c. 426–25 BC). Edited by Philip Theodore Stevens, 1971; also edited by Antonio Garzya, 1978; as *Andromache*, translated by Hugh Meredith, in *Four Dramas*, 1937; also translated by L.R. Lind, 1957; John Frederick Nims, in *Complete Greek Tragedies*, 1958; Philip Vellacott, in *Orestes and Other Plays*, 1972; Michael Lloyd, 1994; Susan Stewart and Wesley D. Smith, 2001.

Hecuba (produced c. 424 BC). Edited by Michael Tierney, 1946; also edited by Stephen G. Daitz, 1973, and C. Collard, 1991; as *Hecuba*, translated by Hugh Meredith, in *Four Dramas*, 1937; also translated by William Arrowsmith, in *Complete Greek Tragedies*, 1958; Peter D. Arnott, 1969; Janet Lembke and Kenneth J. Reckford, 1991; as *Hecabe*, translated by Philip Vellacott, in *Medea and Other Plays*, 1963; as *Eupriides Hekabe: Freely Translated from the Greek* by Robert Emmet Meagher, 1995.

Supplices (produced c. 423–22 BC). Edited by Christopher Collard, 2 vols., 1975; as *The Suppliants*, translated by L.R. Lind, 1957; as *The Suppliant Women*, translated by Frank Jones, in *Complete Greek Tragedies*, 1958; also translated by Philip Vellacott, in *Orestes and Other Plays*, 1972; as *Suppliant Women*, translated by Rosanna Warren and Stephen Scully, 1995.

Electra (produced c. 422–16 BC). Edited by C.H. Keene, 1893; also edited by J.D. Denniston, 1939; edited and translated by Arthur S. Way, 1919: Martin J. Cropp, 1988; as *Electra*, translated by Gilbert Murray, 1905; also translated by Moses Hadas, 1950; D.W. Lucas, 1951; Emily Townsend Vermeule, in *Complete Greek Tragedies*, 1959; Philip Vellacott, in *Medea and Other Plays*, 1963; David Thompson, 1964; Janet Lembke and Kenneth J. Reckford, 1994.

Ion (produced c. 421–13 BC). Edited by A.S. Owen, 1939; also edited by Werner Biehl, 1979, and K.H. Lee, 1992; as *Ion*, translated by Ronald Frederick Willetts, in *Complete Greek Tragedies*, 1958; also translated by HD, 1937; D.W. Lucas, 1950; Philip Vellacott, in *The Bacchae and Other Plays*, 1954; A.P. Burnett, 1970; David Lan, 1994; Peter Burian, 1996.

Heracles (produced c. 417–15 BC). Edited by Godfrey W. Bond, 1981; as *Heracles*, translated by Robert Browning, in *Aristophanes' Apology*, 1875; also translated by Hugh Meredith, in *Four Dramas*, 1937; William Arrowsmith, in *Complete Greek Tragedies*, 1956; Philip Vellacott, in *Medea and Other Plays*, 1963; Michael R. Halleran, 1988; Shirley A. Barlow, 1996; Tom Sleigh, 2001; as *The Madness of Heracles*, translated by Peter D. Arnott, 1969.

Troades (produced 415 BC). Edited by F.A. Paley, 1881; also edited by Robert Yelverton Tyrrell, 1882, revised edition, 1897, Werner Biehl, 1970, and K.H. Lee, 1976; as *The Trojan Women*, translated by Gilbert Murray, 1905; also translated by Edith Hamilton, in *Three Greek Plays*, 1937; Richmond Lattimore, in *Greek Plays in Modern Translation*, 1944, and in *Complete Greek Tragedies*, 1958; Nell Curry, 1946; Shirley A. Barlow, 1986; as *The Women of Troy*, translated by Philip Vellacott, in *The Bacchae and Other Plays*, 1954; also translated by Don Taylor, in *The War Plays*, 1990; translated by Brendan Kennelly, 1993; Nicholas Rudall, 1999.

Iphigeneia Taurica (produced c. 414–13 BC). Edited by E.B. England, 1926; also edited by C.B. Watts, 1930, Maurice Platnauer, 1938, and David Sansone, 1981; as *Iphigenia in Tauris*, translated by Gilbert Murray, 1910; also translated by Witter Bynner, 1915, and in *Complete Greek Tragedies*, 1956; Philip Vellacott, in *Three Plays*, 1953, revised edition, 1974; Richmond Lattimore, 1974; as *Iphigeneia in Taurica* [Loeb Edition], translated by Arthur S. Way, 1912; as *Iphigenia Among the Taurians*, translated by Nicholas Rudall, 1997; M.J. Cropp, 2000.

Helena (produced 412 BC). Edited by A.Y. Campbell, 1950; also edited by Amy Marjorie Dale, 1967, and Richard Kannicht, 1969; as *Helen*, translated by J.T. Sheppard, 1925; also translated by Rex Warner, 1951, and in *Three Great Plays*, 1958; Philip Vellacott, in *The Bacchae and Other Plays*, 1954; Richmond Lattimore, in *Complete Greek Tragedies*, 1956; Neil Curry, 1981; James Michie and Colin Leach, 1981; R.E. Meagher, 1986; Don Taylor, in *The War Plays*, 1990.

Phoenissae (produced c. 412–08 BC). Edited by Donald J. Mastronarde (with commentary), 1994; as *The Phoenician Women*, translated by Elizabeth Wychoff, in *Complete Greek Tragedies*, 1959; also translated by Philip Vellacott, in *Orestes and Other Plays*, 1972; Peter Burian and Brian Swann, 1981; Elizabeth M. Craik, 1988; David Thompson, in *Plays One*, 1988.

Orestes (produced 408 BC). Edited by C.W. Willink, 1986; edited and translated by M.L. West, 1987; as *Orestes*, translated by Hugh Meredith, in *Four Dramas*, 1937; also translated by William Arrowsmith, in *Complete Greek Tragedies*, 1958; Philip Vellacott, in *Orestes and Other Plays*, 1972; John Peck and Frank Nisetich, 1995.

Bacchae (produced c. 405 BC). Edited by J.E. Sandys, 1880; also edited by E.R. Dodds, 1960, and E. Christian Kopff, 1982; as *The Bacchae*, translated by Henry Hart Milman, 1865; also translated by Margaret Kinmont Tennant, 1926; D.W. Lucas, 1930; Philip Vellacott, in *The Bacchae and Other Plays*, 1954; Henry Birkhead, 1957; William Arrowsmith, in *Complete Greek Tragedies*, 1959; G.S. Kirk, 1970; Neil Curry, 1981; M. Cacoyannis, 1983; J. Michael Walton, in *Plays One*, 1988; John Buller, 1992; Robert Emmet Meagher, 1995; Richard Seaford, 1996; Nicholas Rudall, 1996; Paul Woodruff, 1998; Herbert Golder, 2001; Reginald Gibbons, 2001.

Iphigeneia Aulidensis, completed by another writer (produced c. 405 BC). Edited by E.S. Headlam, 1939; as *Iphigenia in Aulis*, translated by F.M. Stawell, 1929; Charles R. Walker, in *Complete Greek Tragedies*, 1958; Philip Vellacott, in *Orestes and Other Plays*, 1972; Kenneth Cavander, 1973; W.S. Merwin and George E. Dimock, Jr., 1978; as *Iphigenia at Aulis*, translated by Don Taylor, in *The War Plays*, 1990; Nicholas Rudall, 1997.

Cyclops, edited by Jacqueline Duchemin. 1945; also edited by R.G. Ussher, 1978, and Richard Seaford, 1984; as *Cyclops*, translated by J.T. Sheppard, 1923; also translated by William Arrowsmith, in *Complete Greek Tragedies*, 1956; Roger Lancelyn Green, in *Two Satyr Plays*, 1957; Peter D. Arnott, in *Three Greek Plays*, 1964; Heather McHugh, 2001.

Hypsipyle (fragmentary play), edited by G.W. Bond. 1963; also edited by W.E.H. Cockle, 1987.

Phaethon (fragmentary play), edited by James Diggle. 1970.

Rhesus (probably not by Euripides), edited by James Diggle, in *Fabulae*, vol. 3. 1994; as *Rhesus*, translated by Richmond Lattimore, in *Complete Greek Tragedies*, 1958; also translated by Richard Emil Braun, 1973.

Four Dramas (includes *Andromache; Hecuba; Heracles; Orestes*), translated by Hugh Meredith. 1937.

Three Plays (includes *Hippolytus; Iphigeneia in Taurica; Alcestis*), translated by Philip Vellacott. 1953; revised edition, 1974.

The Bacchae and Other Plays (includes *Ion; The Women of Troy; Helen*), translated by Philip Vellacott. 1954.

Three Great Plays (includes *Helen; Hippolytus; Medea*), translated by Rex Warner. 1958.

Ten Plays, translated by Moses Hadas and John McLean. 1960.

Medea and Other Plays (includes *Medea; Hecabe; Electra; Heracles*), translated by Philip Vellacott. 1963.

Orestes and Other Plays (includes *The Children of Heracles; Andromache; The Suppliant Women; The Phoenician Women; Orestes; Iphigenia in Aulis*), translated by Philip Vellacott. 1972.

Plays One (includes *Medea; The Phoenician Women; Bacchae*), translated by Jeremy Brooks, David Thompson, and J. Michael Walton. 1988.

The War Plays: Iphigenia at Aulis; The Women of Troy; Helen, translated by Don Taylor. 1990.

Plays Two (includes *Hecuba; The Women of Troy; Iphigenia at Aulis; Cyclops*), translated by Don Taylor, Peter D. Arnott, and J. Michael Walton. 1991.

*

Critical Studies: *Chronology of the Extant Plays of Euripides* by Grace Harriet Macurdy, 1911; *Euripides and His Age* by Gilbert Murray, 1913, revised edition, 1946; *Euripides and His Influence* by F.L. Lucas, 1924; *The Drama of Euripides* by G.M.A. Grube, 1941; *Essays on Euripidean Drama* by Gilbert Norwood, 1954; *The Political Plays of Euripides*, 1955, revised edition, 1963, and *An Inquiry into the Transmission of the Plays of Euripides*, 1966, both by Gunther Zuntz; *Euripides* by W.N. Bates, 1961; *Notes on Euripides' Medea and Electra* by Robert J. Milch, 1965; *Euripides and the Judgement of Paris* by T.C.W. Stinton, 1965; *Euripidean Drama: Myth, Theme, and Structure* by Desmond J. Conacher, 1967; *The Tragedies of Euripides* by T.B.L. Webster, 1967; *Euripides: A Collection of Critical Essays* edited by Erich Segal, 1968; *The Imagery of Euripides: A Study in the Dramatic Use of Pictorial Language* by Shirley A. Barlow, 1970; *Catastrophe Survived: Euripides' Plays of Mixed Reversal* by Anne P. Burnett, 1971; *The New Oxyrhynchus Papyrus: Hypothesis of Euripides' "Alexandros"* by R.A. Coles, 1974; *Euripides and the Full Circle of Myth* by Cedric H. Whitman, 1974; *Ironic Drama: A Study of Euripides: Method and Meaning* by Philip Vellacott, 1975; *Colloquial Expressions in Euripides* by P.T. Stevens, 1976; *"God, or not God, or Between the Two?" Euripides' Helen* by George E. Dimock, 1977; *Existentialism and Euripides: Sickness, Tragedy and Divinity in The Medea, The Hippolytus and The Bacchae* by William Sale, 1977; *On the Concept of Slavery in Euripides* by Katerina Syodinou, 1977; *Terms for Happiness in Euripides* by Marianne McDonald, 1978; *The Violence of Pity in Euripides' Medea* by Pietro Pucci, 1980; *The Trojan Trilogy of Euripides* by Ruth Scodel, 1980; *Euripides* by Christopher Collard, 1981; *Studies on the Text of Euripides: Supplices, Electra, Heracles, Troades, Iphigenia in Tauris, Ion*, 1981, *The Textual Tradition of*

Euripides' Orestes, 1990, and *Euripides: Collected Essays*, 1994, all by James Diggle; *The Textual Tradition of Euripides' Phoinissai* by Donald J. Mastronarde, 1982; *Dionysiac Poetics and Euripides' Bacchae* by Charles Segal, 1982; *Euripides' Bacchae: The Play and Its Audience* by Hans Oranje, 1984; *New Directions in Euripidean Criticism: A Collection of Essays* edited by Peter Burian, 1985; *Ritual Irony: Poetry and Sacrifice in Euripides* by Helene P. Foley, 1985; *Stagecraft in Euripides* by Michael R. Halleran, 1985; *Euripides' Medea and Electra: A Companion to the Penguin Translation of Philip Vellacott* by John Ferguson, 1987; *The Heroic Muse: Studies in the Hippolytus and the Hecuba of Euripides* by David Kovacs, 1987; *Euripides and the Tragic Tradition* by Ann Norris Michelini, 1987; *Aspects of Human Sacrifice in the Tragedies of Euripides* by E.A.M.E. O'Connor-Visser, 1987; *Two Lost Plays of Euripides* by Dana F. Sutton, 1987; *The God of Ecstasy: Sex-Roles and the Madness of Dionysos* by Arthur Evans, 1988; *Time Holds the Mirror: A Study of Knowledge in Euripides' Hippolytus* by C.A.E. Luschnig, 1988; *A New Creed: Fundamental Religious Beliefs in the Athenian Polis and Euripidean Drama* by Harvey Yunis, 1988; *Euripides' Medea: The Incarnation of Disorder* by Emily A. McDermott, 1989; *The Noose of Words: Readings of Desire, Violence and Language in Euripides' Hippolytus* by Barbara E. Goff, 1990; *Euripides, Women and Sexuality* by Anton Powell, 1990; *Euripides and the Instruction of the Athenians* by Justina Gregory, 1991; *Ambiguity and Self-Deception: The Apollo and Artemis Plays of Euripides* by Karelisa V. Hartigan, 1991; *Narrative in Drama: The Art of the Euripidean Messenger-Speech* by I.J.F. de Jong, 1991; *The Agon in Euripides* by Michael Lloyd, 1992; *Anxiety Veiled: Euripides and the Traffic in Women* by Nancy Sorkin Rabinowitz, 1994; *Euripidean Polemic: The Trojan Women and the Function of Tragedy* by N.T. Croally, 1994; *Euripidea: Collected Essays* by James Diggle, 1994; *Euripidea* by David Kovacs, 1994; *Wild Justice: A Study of Euripides' Hecuba* by Judith Mossman, 1995; *The City of Dionysos: A Study of Euripides' Bakchai* by Vladis Leinieks, 1996; *Tragedy's End: Closure and Innovation in Euripidean Drama* by Francis M. Dunn, 1996; *Theseus, Tragedy, and the Athenian Empire* by Sophie Mills, 1997; *Euripides and Alcestis: Speculations, Simulations, and Stories of Love in the Athenian Culture* by Kiki Gounaridou, 1998; *Euripides and the Sophists: Some Dramatic Treatments of Philosophical Ideas* by Desmond J. Conacher, 1998; *Eurykleia and Her Successors: Female Figures of Authority in Greek Poetics* by Helen Pournara Karydas, 1998; *Intimate Commerce: Exchange, Gender, and Subjectivity in Greek Tragedy* by Victoria Wohl, 1998; *Nothing Is As it Seems: The Tragedy of the Implicit in Euripides' Hippolytus* by Hanna M. Roisman, 1999; *The Andromache and Euripidean Tragedy* by William Allen, 2000; *Euripides' Use of Psychological Terminology* by Shirley Darcus Sullivan, 2000.

* * *

Euripides was the youngest of the famous tragedians of 5th-century Athens; he is regarded by some as responsible for a breakdown in the lofty spirit of Greek tragedy from which it never recovered; by others as introducing a new and enduring humanism, a sense of the pathos of the human condition, which expressed more powerfully than that of his predecessors the tragic realities of life.

To some degree, perhaps, the impression of contrast which the Euripidean corpus of plays provides with that of Aeschylus and Sophocles may be due to the fact that we possess a greater number of his plays (18 or 19 as compared with seven of each of the other two) and so a wider variety of Euripidean themes. However, this explanation of "the difference" is, at best, a very partial one, for all of Euripides' plays betray, to a greater or lesser degree, a distinctly new tragic style and approach to traditional myth.

These "new directions" of Euripidean tragedy are in part traceable to two major influences, those of the sophistic movement and of the Peloponnesian War, both of which appear to have affected Euripides more than they did his elder contemporary Sophocles. The sophists (the first professional teachers in Greece) imbued Euripides with their rationalistic way of looking at traditional beliefs and values and strongly influenced his dramatic style by the rhetorical emphasis of their teaching. In a very different way, Euripides' tragic outlook was also affected by certain dire events of the Peloponnesian War and their effects on Athenian morale and policy.

As implied above, Euripides was something of an iconoclast, a "reducer" of the ancient mythological tradition on which the plot material of Greek tragedy was, by convention, based. Thus he tended to reinterpret and reformulate the tales of arbitrary, often vengeful anthropomorphic gods and of heroes from a remote and glorious past in ways which related them more closely to recognizable human experience. In a few plays, such as *Hippolytus* and *Bacchae* (which I shall call "the mythological tragedies") these anthropomorphic gods still play a major role, but even here, though they are presented physically as dramatically real personages in the tragedies, they clearly symbolize mysterious forces governing the emotional and irrational areas of human experience. Thus, in *Hippolytus*, Aphrodite, goddess of sexual passion, declares that she will take vengeance on the hero for his refusal to do her honour. However, the actual action of the play (once the intentions of the goddess have been expressed in the Prologue) is worked out in essentially human terms: the catastrophe comes about from the conflict between the woman-hating Hippolytus and his stepmother Phaedra, the unwilling victim of guilty love for him. Here the poet makes it clear that it is the excess of Hippolytus' scorn for sex and his failure to understand the power of sexual passion that leads to his destruction. So, too, in *Bacchae* King Pentheus, the puritanical rationalist, suffers for suppressing in his state the mystical ecstasy and emotional release brought by the communal singing, drinking, and dancing of Dionysian worship.

In other, quite different plays of Euripides, such as *Medea* and *Electra*, the catastrophe occurs as a result of the destructive power of hate and vengeance within the soul of the individual tragic figure. Here the mythological dimension is notably less marked, since no divine figure is needed to represent the actively destructive power now embodied in the tragic personality itself. *Medea* is perhaps the most powerful example of this kind of Euripidean tragedy, which presents in psychologically "realistic" terms the destructive power of passion. Medea, who loves her children, slays them in order to be avenged on her faithless husband Jason. "My passion is stronger than my reason!" she exclaims at the climax of her struggle between mother-love and vengeful fury: a very Euripidean expression of what this poet felt to be one of the mainsprings of human tragedies. Other plays which I would describe (despite certain supernatural overtones) as psychologically "realistic" human tragedies are *Electra* and *Hecuba* (in which the same power of vengeful hatred, in very different circumstances, corrupts and destroys noble tragic figures) and (apart from its melodramatic finale) *Orestes*, which studies the effects of guilt and social rejection on the condemned matricide Orestes.

"Tragedies of War and of Politics [in the broadest sense]" might be selected as the label (with all the inadequacies which such labelling entails) for a third group of Euripidean tragedies. Here the issues are almost exclusively human and social, and the tragic situations arise, not from any divine vengeance (however "symbolically" understood) or from individual human passions, but from man's more impersonal inhumanity to his fellow men. In *Supplices* (*The Suppliant Women*) and *Heracleidae* (*Children of Heracles*), "just wars" are fought by legendary Athenian kings on behalf of just such victims of human cruelty, but in each case the plays end with an ironic undermining of the noble purpose of the war or else of the just pretensions of the suppliants themselves. In *Troades* (*The Trojan Women*) and *Hecuba* (which belongs as well in this group as in the preceding one), we witness the destructive results of war's cruelties on the helpless survivors of the defeated: in the one case, collectively, on the women and children of the slain Trojan heroes, in the other, individually, on the tragic (and initially noble) figure of the Trojan Queen. Again the setting is in the mythological past, but the themes are universal and, *mutatis mutandis*, apply in some respects all too tellingly to certain historical circumstances and events of Euripides' own day.

Another group of Euripidean plays, very different from the sombre "war plays," comprises such plays as *Ion, Helena* (*Helen*), and *Iphigeneia Taurica* (*Iphigenia in Tauris*), which have been variously described by modern critics as "tragicomedy," "romantic tragedy," and (here some would include *Orestes*) "melodrama." Of these, *Helen* is, perhaps, at the furthest remove from traditional Greek tragedy. Euripides bases this play on a variant version of the Trojan War myth according to which Helen spent the Trojan War secretly hidden away in Egypt while the goddess Hera caused a wraith of Helen to be substituted (and mistaken) for the real Helen of Troy. The plot includes a highly comic "recognition scene" (in which shipwrecked Menelaus, returning from Troy with the wraith, has great difficulty in recognizing his "real," and somewhat indignant, wife) and an ingenious and exciting "escape" sequence, in which Helen and Menelaus outwit the wicked Egyptian King and escape over the seas to Sparta with the King's ship and generous provisions of arms and supplies. In this and similar plays the poet seems to be taking traditional myth rather less seriously than in the more properly "tragic" plays and to adopt a satirical tone (not always absent even in the most "serious" tragedies) concerning the more improbable and anthropomorphic treatments of the gods. However, even in these less tragic plays, there are sometimes serious overtones: the Trojan War, the Chorus reminds us in *Helen*, was fought for a wraith: perhaps all wars, including the war currently ruining the poet's own beloved city, could be avoided if men allowed words and reasoning (*logoi*) instead of bloody strife (*eris*) to settle their differences.

This brief account inevitably fails to do justice to the great variety in the Euripidean treatment of human experience and human folly. If the reader has been left with the wrong impression that, in questioning traditional mythology, Euripides rejects the supernatural element in that experience, he should read *Bacchae*, one of the last, and surely the most terrifying, of Euripides' extant tragedies. Here he will discover, with King Pentheus, what sort of fate awaits those scorning the timeless and universal powers ("even stronger than a god, if that were possible," as we are reminded of Aphrodite in *Hippolytus*) which Euripides recognized as dominating certain crucial areas in the life of man.

—Desmond J. Conacher

See the essays on *Electra, Hippolytus, Ion, Medea, Orestes,* and *The Trojan Women.*

EVTUSHENKO, Evgenii (Alexandrovich)

Also known as Yevgeny Yevtushenko. **Born:** Stantsiia Zima, Irkutsk region, Siberia, 18 July 1933. **Education:** Educated at the Gor'kii Institute, Moscow, early 1950s. **Family:** Married 1) Bella Akhmadulina in 1954 (divorced); 2) Galina Semenova; 3) Jan Butler in 1978; 4) Maria Novika in 1986; five sons. **Career:** Went on geological expeditions with father to Kazakhstan, 1948, and the Altai, 1950. Member, Congress of People's Deputies of USSR, since 1989; vice president, Russian PEN, since 1990. Lives in Moscow. **Member:** Honorary member, American Academy of Arts and Sciences, 1987. **Awards:** USSR Committee for Defence of Peace award, 1965; Order of Red Banner of Labour (twice); State prize, 1984.

PUBLICATIONS

Collection

The Collected Poems 1952–1990, edited by Albert C. Todd, various translators. 1991.

Verse

Razvedchiki griadushchevo [The Prospectors of the Future]. 1952.
Tretii sneg [Third Snow]. 1955.
Shosse entuziastov [Highway of the Enthusiasts]. 1956.
Stantsiia Zima, in *Oktiabr',* 10. 1956; as *Winter Station,* translated by Oliver J. Frederiksen, 1964.
Obeshchanie [Promise]. 1957.
Dye liubimykh [Two Loves], in *Grani,* 38. 1958.
Luk i lira [The Bow and the Lyre]. 1959.
Stikhi raznykh let [Poems of Several Years]. 1959.
Iabloko [The Apple]. 1960.
Red Cats. 1961.
Vzmakh ruki [A Wave of the Hand]. 1962.
Selected Poems, translated by Peter Levi and Robin Milner-Gulland. 1962.
Nezhnost': novye stikhi [Tenderness: New Poems]. 1962.
Posle Stalina [After Stalin]. 1962.
The Heirs of Stalin, in *Current Digest of the Soviet Press,* 14(40). 1962; as *Nasledniki Stalina,* 1963.
Selected Poems. 1962.
Selected Poetry. 1963.
Khochu ia stat' nemnozhko staromodnym [I Want to Become a Bit Old-Fashioned], in *Novyi mir,* 7. 1964.
The Poetry of Yevgeny Yevtushenko, edited and translated by George Reavey. 1964; revised edition, 1981; as *Early Poems,* 1989.
Bratskaia GES. 1965; as *The Bratsk Station,* in *New Works: The Bratsk Station,* 1966.
Khotiat li russkie voiny? [Do They Want Russian Wars?]. 1965.
So mnoiu vot chto proiskhodit: izbrannaia lirika [Here's What Happens to Me: Selected Lyrics]. 1966.
Kater sviazi [Torpedo Boat Signalling]. 1966.
Kachka [Swing-Boat]. 1966.
New Works: The Bratsk Station, translated by Tina Tupikina-Glaessner, Geoffrey Dutton, and Igor Mezhakoff Koviakin. 1966; as *The Bratsk Station and Other New Poems,* 1967.

Yevtushenko Poems (bilingual edition), translated by Herbert Marshall. 1966.

Poems, translated by Herbert Marshall. 1966.

Poems Chosen by the Author, translated by Peter Levi and Robin Milner-Gulland. 1966.

The City of Yes and the City of No and Other Poems. 1966.

Stikhi [Poems]. 1967.

New Poems. 1968.

Tramvai poezii [Tram of Poetry]. 1968.

Tiaga val'dshnepov [Roding Woodcock]. 1968.

Idut belye snegi [The White Snows Are Falling]. 1969.

Flowers and Bullets, and Freedom to Kill. 1970.

Ia sibirskoi porody [I'm of Siberian Stock]. 1971.

Stolen Apples, translated by James Dickey. 1971.

Kazanskii universitet. 1971; as *Kazan University and Other New Poems*, translated by Eleanor Jacks and Geoffrey Dutton, 1973.

Doroga nomer odin [Highway Number One]. 1972.

Poiushchaia damba [The Singing Dam]. 1972.

Poet v Rossii—bol'she, chem poet [A Poet in Russia Is More than a Poet]. 1973.

Intimnaia lirika [Intimate Lyrics]. 1973.

Ottsovskii slukh [Father's Hearing]. 1975.

Izbrannye proizvedeniia [Selected Works]. 1975.

Proseka [The Track]. 1976.

Spasibo [Thank You]. 1976.

From Desire to Desire. 1976; as *Love Poems*, 1977.

V polnyi rost: novaia kniga stikhov i poem [At Full Growth: New Book of Poetry and Verse]. 1977.

Zaklinanie [A Spell]. 1977.

Utrennii narod: novaia kniga stikhov [The Morning Crowds: New Book of Poetry]. 1978.

Prisiaga prostoru: stikhi [An Oath to Space: Poems]. 1978.

A Choice of Poems by Evgeny Evtushenko. 1978.

Kompromiss Kompromissovich [Compromise Kompromissovich]. 1978.

The Face Behind the Face, translated by Arthur Boyars and Simon Franklin. 1979.

Ivan the Terrible and Ivan the Fool, translated by Daniel Weissbort. 1979.

Tiazhelee zemli [Heavier than Earth]. 1979.

Kogda muzhchine sorok let [When a Man Is 40]. 1979.

Doroga, ukhodiashchaia vdal' [The Road, Leading Far]. 1979.

Svarka vzryvom: stikhotvoreniia i poemy [Explosion Welding: Poetry and Narrative Verse]. 1980.

Tret'ia pamiat' [Third Memory]. 1980.

Poslushaite menia [Listen to Me]. 1980.

Tochka opory [Fulcrum] (includes *Pirl-kharbor* [Pearl Harbour]). 1981.

Ia sibiriak [I'm a Siberian]. 1981.

Dye pary lyzh [A Pair of Skis]. 1982.

Belye snegi [White Snows]. 1982.

A Dove in Santiago (novella in verse), translated by D.M. Thomas. 1982.

Mama i neitronaiia bomba i drugie poemy [Mother and Neutron Bomb and Other Poems]. 1983.

Otkuda rodom ia [Where I Come From]. 1983.

Sobranie sochinenii [Collected Works]. 3 vols., 1983–84.

Dva goroda [Two Towns]. 1985.

More [Sea]. 1985.

Pochti naposledok: novaia kniga. 1985; as *Almost at the End*, translated by Antonina W. Bouis and Albert C. Todd, 1987.

Poltravinochki [Half a Blade of Grass]. 1986.

Stikhi [Poems]. 1986.

Zavtrashnii veter [Tomorrow's Wind]. 1987.

Stikhotvoreniia [Poetry]. 1987.

Sud [The Trial], in *Novyi mir*, 11. 1987.

Stikhotvoreniia i poemy 1951–1986 [Poetry and Narrative Verse]. 3 vols., 1987.

Posledniaia popytka: stikhotvoreniia iz starykh i novykh tetradei [Last Attempt: Poetry from Old and New Books]. 1988.

Pochti v poslednii mig [Almost at the Last Moment]. 1988.

Nezhnost' [Tenderness]. 1988.

Poemy o mire [Verses on Peace]. 1989.

Stikhi [Poems]. 1989.

Grazhdane, poslushaite menia. . . [Citizens, Listen to Me. . .]. 1989.

Liubimaia, spi. . . [Loved One, Sleep . . .]. 1989.

Pomozhem svobode! [We Will Help Freedom!], in *Znamia*, 4. 1990.

Ne umirai prezhde smerti [Don't Die Before Death], in *Ogonek*, 10. 1992; as *Don't Die Before You're Dead*, translated by Antonina W. Bouis, 1995.

Pre-morning: A New Book of Poetry in English and Russian. 1995.

The Best of the Best: A New Book of Poetry in English and Russian. 1999.

Fiction

Chetvertaia meshchanskaia [Four Vulgar Women], in *Iunost'*, 2. 1959.

Iagodnye mesta. 1982; as *Wild Berries*, translated by Antonina W. Bouis, 1984.

Ardabiola. 1984.

Izbrannaia proza. 1998.

Plays

Bratskaia GES (produced 1968). 1967.

Under the Skin of the Statue of Liberty (produced 1972).

Screenplays: Screenplays: *Kindergarten*, 1984; *Detskii sad Moscow*, 1989.

Other

Avtobiografiia. 1963; as *A Precocious Autobiography*, translated by Andrew R. MacAndrew, 1963.

Yevtushenko's Reader: The Spirit of Elbe, A Precocious Autobiography, Poems. 1966.

Izbrannye proizedeniia [Selected Works]. 2 vols., 1975.

Talent est' chudo nesluchainoe [Talent Is a Miracle Coming Not by Chance]. 1980.

Invisible Threads. 1981.

Voina—eto antikultura [War Is Anti-Culture]. 1983.

Divided Twins = Razdel ennye blizne t sy: Alaska and Siberia, photographs by Evtushenko and Boyd Norton. 1988.

Politika privilegiia vsekh [Everybody's Privilege]. 1990.

Propast'—v dva pryzhka? [The Precipice—in Two Leaps?]. 1990.

Fatal Half Measures: The Culture of Democracy in the Soviet Union,
   with Antonina W. Bouis. 1991.
Translator, *Mlechnyi put'*, by D. Ulzytuev. 1961.
Translator, *Seti zvezd*, by T. Chiladze. 1961.
Translator, *Na koleni ne padat'!*, by G. Dzhagarov. 1961.
Translator, *Tiazhelee zemli: stikhi o Gruzii, poety Gruzii*. 1979.

*

Critical Studies: "Herbert and Yevtushenko: On Whose Side Is
History?" by George Gömöri, in *Mosaic*, 3(1), 1969: "The Politics of
Poetry: The Sad Case of Yevgeny Yevtushenko" by Robert Con-
quest, in *New York Times Magazine*, 30 September, 1973; "An
Interview with Evgeniy Evtushenko" by Gordon McVay, in *Journal
of Russian Studies*, 1977; "Women in Evtushenko's Poetry" by
Vickie A. Rebenko, in *Russian Review*, 36, 1977: "Yevtushenko as a
Critic" by Vladimir Ognev, in *Soviet Studies in Literature*, 18(3),
1981; "Yevgeni Yevtushenko's Solo: On His 50th Birthday" by
Yevgeni Sidorov, in *Soviet Literature*, 7(424), 1983; "Two Opinions
about Evgenii Evtushenko's Narrative Poem: "Man and the Neutron
Bomb": And What If This Is Prose? And What If It Is Not?" by
Adol'f Urban and Gennadii Krasnikov, in *Soviet Studies in Litera-
ture*, 20(1), 1983–84; "The Poetry of Yevgeny Yevtushenko in the
1970's" by Irma Mercedes Kaszuba, in *USF Language Quarterly*,
25(1–2), 1986; "Evtušenko's *Jagodnye mesta*: The Poet as Prose
Writer" by Richard N. Porter, in *Russian Language Journal*, 40(135),
1986; "'Queuing for Hope': About Yevgeni Yevtushenko's Poem
'Fuku!'" by Pavel Ulyashov, in *Soviet Literature*, 9(462), 1986;
"Yevtushenko's *Stantsiya Zima*: A Reassessment" by Michael
Pursglove, in *New Zealand Slavonic Journal*, 2, 1988.

*   *   *

In the 1950s and 1960s Evgenii Evtushenko became the poet and
spokesman for the younger post-Stalinist generation of Russian
writers. He was responsible for reviving the brash, slangy, and direct
poetic language of the revolutionary poets like Maiakovskii and
Esenin, and reintroducing the personal and love lyrics so frowned
upon by the authorities. The open demands he made on the international scene for greater artistic freedom, and for a literature based on
aesthetic criteria rather than ideological standards, were partially
responsible for the gradual easing of control over writers in the USSR.

Evtushenko's writing has always been rooted in the autobiographical. His poetry is topical and journalistic, as in *Stantsiia Zima*
(*Winter Station*), a celebration of his birthplace, a small provincial
town situated on the famous Trans-Siberian railway, in the Irkutsk
region. This poem records a visit in the summer of 1953 to Zima,
describing the relatives and other people he encounters there, and his
endeavours to come to terms with his anxieties and the public moral
problems raised by Stalin's death and the revelations that followed.
Similarly, in "Svad'by" ("Weddings"), 1955, he records the atmosphere of the terrible years he spent as a child evacuee from Moscow at
Zima Station during the war. Not only did Zima Station provide a
source for country characters and scenery, but Evtushenko also began
to be influenced by Siberian folklore and folk song, an impact which
was to shape many of his later poems.

Evtushenko's poetic career began in earnest when he was given
the chance to study at the Gor'kii Literary Institute in Moscow, the
official training school for many of the Soviet writers after the war.
He published widely in established journals in the 1950s, and his early

books, *Tretii sneg* [Third Snow], *Shosse entuziastov* [Highway of the
Enthusiasts], and *Obeshchanie* [Promise], made him famous and
controversial with their outspokenness and flamboyance. *Luk i lira*
[The Bow and the Lyre] followed, a volume that was the result of a
stay in Georgia and contains many translations of Georgian poetry,
and then the final volume of this series, *Stikhi raznykh let* [Poems of
Several Years]. His poetry demonstrated a distinctive lyrical note in
his treatment of nature, love, and various patriotic beliefs, celebrating
the original ideals of the Revolution and condemning their corruption
at the hands of the bureaucrats. It is compared frequently with the
poetry of Maiakovskii with whom Evtushenko shares a dislike of
hypocrisy and decadence, and a forthright, declamatory style.

Evtushenko began to write more boldly and to touch upon issues
that had until then been kept under wraps. Such concerns included
admitting the terrible mistakes of the Stalinist purges of the 1930s and
1940s and insisting that the truth be told. Such poems naturally caused
a great deal of displeasure in certain circles: "It will go hard with me
at times,/and they will say: 'He'd better hold his tongue!'." This
sharp political edge to the poetry went hand in hand with the youth's
general desire to reassess the direction of the revolution. Poetry for
Evtushenko was not merely negative and critical; rather, it was a form
of aesthetic affirmation and ideal statement. In "Rakety i telegi"
("Rockets and Carts"), 1960, he declared the need for rocket-like
art against the persistence of dull, plodding, "cart-like" novels
and operas. This stance, adopted by Evtushenko and others like
Voznesenskii, was hugely popular and caused a large increase in book
sales and attendances at poetry readings. In a poetry that desires "art
to be/as diverse as myself," Evtushenko sought to write a more
dynamic verse that challenged the orthodoxy of Soviet Realism with
the emergence of a new subjective element. As he declared in
"Svezhesti" ("Freshness") (1960), "Freshness!/Freshness!/We
want freshness!"

Evtushenko's work and activities in the early 1960s were often
stimulated by his wide travels, including visits to England, France,
Catalonia, Ghana, Liberia, Togo, and Bulgaria, and in April 1961 to
the United States. These years saw the publication of one of his most
notable collections, *Vzmakh ruki* [A Wave of the Hand], which
contains many of his poems written as a result of his worldwide
travels; and *Nezhnost'* [Tenderness], which includes more of his
travel poems and impressions of foreign cultures and societies,
particularly the last section with its poems on Cuba, which he had
visited in 1962. Nevertheless, his political poems continued, with
immense popularity: the controversial "Babii Iar" (1961), a poem
that mourns the Nazi massacre of Ukrainian Jews but which also
attacks the vestiges of Soviet anti-semitism; *Nasledniki Stalina* (*The
Heirs of Stalin*), published originally in *Pravda*, satirizes Stalin's
politics and his followers; "Kar'era" ("A Career"), which deals
with Galileo's fight for truth against the authority of the church; and
"Iumor" ("Humour"), in which the power of laughter emerges
triumphant over despotic power. However, the publication in Paris of
his *Avtobiografiia* (*A Precocious Autobiography*), with its vivid
sequence of scenes from his life and his idiosyncratic interpretation of
Soviet history without submission to the Soviet censors, incurred
official disfavour and privileges were withdrawn.

Favour was restored with the publication in 1965 of an ambitious
cycle of poems entitled *Bratskaia GES* (*The Bratsk Station*), in which
he juxtaposes the symbol of a Siberian power plant generating light in
Russia with Siberia's symbolic status as a prison throughout Russian
history. The poems sought to reconnect modern Russia with its past,
and were later adapted and performed as a play. More recently, he has

turned increasingly to prose and the theatre. His play *Under the Skin of the Statue of Liberty*, composed of selections from his earlier poems about the United States that attack its violence but celebrate the idealism of its youth, was performed in Moscow to great acclaim. This was followed by a novel, *Iagodnge mesta* (*Wild Berries*), and the novella *Ardabiola*.

Evtushenko has always demonstrated commitment in his writing and although appearing to be slapdash in style he nevertheless shifts adroitly from intimate to public themes. He has been influential principally as a consolidator of certain revived traditions, while his ringing militancy, stylistic versatility, and challenging self-assertiveness in poetry have encouraged his contemporaries to emulate him.

—Tim Woods

F

FERDOWSI, Abu'l Qāsim

Born: Persia (now Iran), c. 932–36. Came from a landowning family near Tus, Khorāsān. **Family:** Had one daughter. **Career:** According to tradition, began writing his epic poem the *Shāh-nāma* at about the age of 35, dedicating it to the Ghaznavid Sultan Mahmud, whose failure to reward it generously led Ferdowsi to write a satire about him and then return to his birthplace. **Died:** c. 1020.

PUBLICATIONS

Verse

Shāh-nāma, edited by Djalal Khaleghi-Motlagh. 6 vols., 1988– (3 vols. to 1992); as *Shahnama*, translated by Arthur George Warner and Edmond Warner, 9 vols., 1905–25; abridged versions translated by J. Atkinson, 1814, Alexander Rogers, 1907, and as *The Epic of the Kings, Shah-Nama, the National Epic of Persia*, translated by Reuben Levy, 1967; part as *The Poems of Ferdosi*, translated by J. Champion, 1785; part as *The Tragedy of Sohrab and Rostam: From the Persian National Epic of Shahname*, translated by Jerome W. Clinton, 1987; part as *The Legend of Seyavash*, translated by Dick Davis, 1992.
Fathers and Sons, translated by Dick Davis. 2000.
The Lion and the Throne, translated by Dick Davis. 1998.

*

Critical Studies: in *Early Persian Poetry* by W. Jackson, 1920; *Ferdowsi: A Critical Biography* by A. Shapur Shahbazi, 1991; *Epic and Sedition: the Case of Ferdowsi's Shahnameh* by Dick Davis, 1992; *Poet and Hero in the Persian Book of Kings* by Olga H. Davidson, 1994; *Comparative Literature and Classical Persian Poetics: Seven Essays* by Olga H. Davidson, 2000.

* * *

Abu'l Qāsim Ferdowsi was born between 932 and 936 and the date of his death is placed in either 1020 or 1021. He lived in Khorāsān, in the environs of Tus near present-day Mashhad and was apparently a small farmer of the *dehqan* class, a squirarchy that in early Islamic times may have represented a stratum of landlords reduced in status following the Arab conquest in the 7th century. He is justly regarded as one of the world's greatest poets for his composition of Iran's national epic, the *Shāh-nāma* (*Shahnama* or *The Epic of theKings*). It is an epic which has the distinction of encompassing the whole history of ancient Iran from about the 9th century BC to the 7th century AD—legendary as well as factual, and in so far as there is a subtle layer of the facts of human experience in mythology, basically factual enough to have universal appeal. It is, not surprisingly, one of the world's longest poems, of some 50,000 rhyming couplets in the same martially inspiring *mutaqarib* metre throughout; it is chanted to furnish the rhythm for athletes exercising in Iranian *zurkanehs*, "Houses of Strength," the traditional gymnasiums.

The chronological scheme of the work provides unity as it moves from monarch to monarch, although scope is given to the *gestes* of Herculean heroes who at times overshadow less competent kings, as is especially evident in the feats and courage of Rustam. He is known to readers of English literature through Matthew Arnold's *Sohrab and Rustum*, published in 1853, after Arnold had seen Sainte-Beuve's *Causerie du Lundi* of February 1850, which reviewed Jules Mohl's French translation of *Le Livre des Rois*, begun in 1838; Arnold was already aware of the story, of a father's slaying the son he did not recognize, from Sir John Malcolm's reference to it in his *History of Persia*, published in 1815. Various other English versions of the *Shahnama* exist, but the translation of the whole by Arthur George Warner and Edmond Warner, is recommended.

Ferdowsi's sources may be summarized as a recension of ancient Iranian history by an Abu Mansur; tales retained in folk memory; and, more than probably (he explicitly speaks of reports from a venerable *mobed*, a Zoroastrian priest, and his mythical kings are named in the *Avesta*) sources related to Iran's pre-Islamic religion and scriptures. His lofty purpose, in a work to which it seems he devoted nearly 30 years of his life, was apparently to remind Iran of past glories, not least in the continuing conflict between the sedentary, cultivating people of its north-eastern province and pastoralist invaders from the Central Asian Steppes. A dominant theme is war between Iran and Turan: the latter has been read as the land of the Turks beyond the River Oxus. In taking up the unfinished few verses of a predecessor, Daqiqi, who was murdered sometime between 976 and 981, Ferdowsi might have started his epic as a paean befitting the regime then still in power, that of the Iranian Samanids, sympathetic to memorials of Iran's pre-Islamic eras. The paean became more of a nostalgic lament when these rulers were ousted at the end of the 10th century, to be replaced in Iran by the House of their former Turkish military commanders, called the Ghaznavids.

Pessimism and an element of dignified resignation to the blows of fate tinge the overall melancholy strain of an epic concerned, not least in the poet's asides, with life's mutabilities and man's inability to control them. It is tempting to attribute the story of initial rejection of the work at the hands of the ruler whose patronage Ferdowsi sought on its completion, the Ghaznavid Sultan Mahmūd, who ruled from 998 to 1030, to the latter's seeing it as an innuendo against the Turks, but it would be pure speculation. A 12th-century writer, Nizami the Prosodist, attributed the rigorously orthodox Sultan's underpayment of the poet to Ferdowsi's alleged inclination for Muslim heresies with echoes of older Iranian beliefs. Fable has it that, on perceiving encouragement of military bravery in one of Ferdowsi's verses, the great warlord repented. Returning from conquest in India he sent Ferdowsi recompense in a caravan of indigo, but as the caravan entered one gate of Ferdowsi's hometown, the poet's bier was being carried to the grave out of another. Ferdowsi's only child, his daughter, refused the gift, which was devoted to providing a resthouse for travellers.

In his *Chahar Maqala* (*Four Discourses*) Nizami the Prosodist gives an illuminating, if partly fabulous, account of Ferdowsi, noteworthy for his remark that Ferdowsi's verse had a "sweet fluency to resemble running water." It must be added that, in spite of its length, the poem never sinks to mediocrity and contains memorable depictions of nature and colours, those of banners before and the dust and blood during battles, for example, which later Persian miniaturists revelled in presenting in illustrations to some of the great manuscripts of the *Shahnama* that have reached our museums and libraries despite tumults of the time in the lands where they were produced. The text has suffered through time, copyists having often been ignorant of dialect usages of Ferdowsi's day in Khorāsān, but at last, after a fine effort by Soviet scholars, a more reliable text than even theirs is now appearing, edited by Djalal Khaleghi-Motlagh and based, for as much as the manuscript covers, on the very ancient text discovered in Florence in 1977.

—Peter Avery

FEYDEAU, Georges (Léon-Jules-Marie)

Born: Paris, France, 8 December 1862, son of the writer Ernest-Aimé Feydeau. **Education:** Educated at boarding school, 1871–79. **Military Service:** 1883–84; **Family:** Married Marianne Duran in 1889 (divorced 1914); one son, Jacques, and other children. **Career:** Lawyer's clerk, 1879; began writing and reciting monologues in the early 1880s; established career with the long run of *Champignol malgré lui*, from 1892; lived at the Hôtel Terminus, Paris, 1909–19; suffered declining mental health, due to syphilis, after 1916; committed by his family to a sanatorium in Rueil-Malmaison, 1919. **Died:** 5 June 1921.

PUBLICATIONS

Collections

Théâtre complet. 9 vols., 1948–56.
Théâtre complet. 4 vols., 1988–89.

Plays

La Petite Révoltée (monologue). 1880.
Le Mouchoir (monologue). 1881.
Par la fenêtre (produced 1881). 1887; as *Wooed and Viewed*, translated by Norman Shapiro, in *Four Farces*, 1970; in *Feydeau, First to Last*, 1982.
Un Coup de tête (monologue). 1882.
J'ai mal au dents (monologue). 1882.
Un monsieur qui n'aime pas les monologues (monologue). 1882.
Trop vieux! (monologue). 1882.
Notre futur (produced 1894). 1882; as *Ladies' Man*, translated by Norman Shapiro, in *Feydeau, First to Last*, 1982.
Le Diapason. 1883.
Le Potache. 1883.
Aux antipodes (monologue). 1883.
Patte-en-l'air (monologue). 1883.
Le Petit Ménage (monologue). 1883.
Amour et piano (produced 1883). 1887; as *Romance in a Flat*, translated by Norman Shapiro, in *Feydeau, First to Last*, 1982; as *The Music Lovers*, translated by Reggie Oliver, 1992.

Gibier de potence (produced 1884). 1885; as *Fit to Be Tried; or, Stepbrothers in Crime*, translated by Norman Shapiro, in *Feydeau, First to Last*, 1982.
Les Célèbres (monologue). 1884.
Le Volontaire (monologue). 1884.
Le Billet de mille (monologue). 1885.
Le Colis (monologue). 1885.
L'Homme économe (monologue). 1885.
Les Réformes (monologue). 1885.
L'Homme intègre (monologue). 1886.
Fiancés en herbe (produced 1886). 1886; as *Budding Lovers*, translated by Barnett Shaw, 1969.
Tailleur pour dames (produced 1886). 1888; as *A Gown for His Mistress*, translated by Barnett Shaw, 1969; as *Fitting for Ladies*, translated by Peter Meyer, in *Three Farces*, 1974; as *Love By the Bolt*, translated by J. Paul Marcoux, in *Three Farces*, 1976.
Les Enfants (monologue). 1887.
La Lycéenne, music by G. Serpette (produced 1887). 1887.
Le Fiancés de Loche, with Maurice Desvallières. 1888.
Le Chat en poche (produced 1888).
Un bain de ménage (produced 1888). 1889.
L'Affaire Édouard, with Maurice Desvallières (produced 1889). 1889.
Monsieur Nounou, with Maurice Desvallières (produced 1890).
C'est une femme du monde!, with Maurice Desvallières (produced 1890). 1890; as *Mixed Doubles*, translated by Norman Shapiro, 1982.
Tout à Brown-Séquart! (monologue). 1890.
Le Mariage de Barillon, with Maurice Desvallières (produced 1890). 1890; as *On the Marry-Go-Wrong*, translated by Norman Shapiro, in *Four Farces*, 1970; as *All My Husband*, translated by J. Paul Marcoux, in *Three Farces*, 1976.
Madame Sganarelle (produced 1891).
Monsieur Chasse (produced 1892). 1896; as *13, Rue de L'Amour*, translated by Mawby Green and Ed Feilbert, 1972; as *The Happy Hunter*, translated by Barnett Shaw, 1973; as *A-Hunting We Will Go*, translated by Ray Barron, 1976.
Champignol malgré lui, with Maurice Desvaillières (produced 1892). 1925; as *A Close Shave*, translated by Peter Meyer, in *Three Farces*, 1974.
Le Système Ribadier (produced 1892). 1925.
Un fil à la patte (produced 1894). 1899; as *Cat Among the Pigeons*, translated by John Mortimer, 1970; as *Not by Bed Alone*, translated by Norman Shapiro, in *Four Farces*, 1970; as *Get Out of My Hair!*, translated by Frederick Davies, 1973.
L'Hôtel du Libre-Échange, with Maurice Desvaillières (produced 1894). 1928; as *Hotel Paradiso*, translated by Peter Glenville, 1956; as *A Little Hotel on the Side*, translated by John Mortimer, in *Three Boulevard Farces*, 1985; as *Paradise Hotel*, translated by Nicholas Rudall, 1990.
Le Ruban, with Maurice Desvaillières (produced 1894). In *Théâtre complet*, 1948–56.
Le Dindon (produced 1896). In *Théâtre complet*, 1948–56; as *There is One in Every Marriage*, translated by Suzanne Grossmann and Paxton Whitehead, 1970; as *Sauce for the Goose*, translated by Peter Meyer, in *Three Farces*, 1974; as *The French Have a Word for It*, translated by Barnett Shaw, 1983; as *An Absolute Turkey*, translated by Nicki Frei and Peter Hall, 1994.

Les Pavés de l'ours (produced 1896). In *Théâtre complet*, 1948–56; as *The Boor Hug*, translated by Norman Shapiro, in *Feydeau, First to Last*, 1982.

Séance de nuit (produced 1897). In *Théâtre complet*, 1948–56.

Dormez, je le veux! (produced 1897). In *Théâtre complet*, 1948–56; as *Caught with His Trance Down*, translated by Norman Shapiro, in *Feydeau, First to Last*, 1982.

La Bulle d'amour, music by F. Thomé (ballet scenario; produced 1898).

Le Juré (monologue). 1898.

Un monsieur qui est condamné à mort (monologue). 1899.

La Dame de chez Maxim (produced 1899). 1914; as *The Lady from Maxim's*, translated by Gene Feist, 1971; also translated by John Mortimer, 1977.

La Duchesse des Folies-Bergères (produced 1902). In *Théâtre complet*, 1948–56.

Le Billet de Joséphine, with J. Méry and A. Kaiser (produced 1902).

La Main passe (produced 1904). 1907; as *Chemin de Fer*, translated by Suzanne Grossmann and Paxton Whitehead, 1968.

L'Âge d'or, with Maurice Desvallières, music by L. Varney (produced 1905). In *Théâtre complet*, 1948–56.

Le Bourgeon. 1907.

La Puce à l'oreille (produced 1907). 1909; as *A Flea in Her Ear*, translated by John Mortimer, 1968; also translated by Barnett Shaw, 1975; Frank Galati, from a literal translation by Abbott Chrisman, 1989; Graham Anderson, 1993.

Feu la mère de Madame (produced 1908). 1923; as *Better Late*, translated by Peter Mayer, 1976; as *Night Errant*, translated by Michael Pilch, 1990.

Occupe-toi d'Amélie (produced 1908). 1911; as *Keep an Eye on Amélie*, translated by Brainerd Duffield, in *Let's Get A Divorce and Other Plays*, edited by Eric Bentley, 1958; also translated by Robert Cogo-Fawett and Braham Murray, 1991; as *Look After Lulu*, translated and adapted by Noël Coward, 1959; as *That's My Girl*, translated by J. Paul Marcoux, in *Three Farces*, 1976.

Le Circuit, with Francis Croisset (produced 1909). In *Théâtre complet*, 1948–56.

On purge bébé (produced 1910). 1910; as *Going to Pot*, translated by Norman Shapiro, in *Four Farces*, 1970; as *The Purging*, translated by Peter Barnes, 1977.

Mais n'te promène donc pas toute nue! (produced 1911). 1912; as *Put Some Clothes on Clarisse!*, translated by Reggie Oliver. 1990.

Léonie est en avance; ou, Le Mal joli (produced 1911). 1920.

Cent millions qui tombent (produced 1911).

On va faire la cocotte (produced 1913). In *Théâtre complet*, 1948–56.

Je ne trompe pas mon mari, with René Peter (produced 1914). 1921.

Complainte du pauvr' propriétaire. 1915.

Hortense a dit: "Je m'en fous!" (produced 1916). In *Théâtre complet*, 1948–56; as *Tooth and Consequences; or, Hortense Said: "No Skin off My Ass!"*, translated by Norman Shapiro, 1978; also translated by Shapiro, in *Feydeau, First to Last*, 1982.

Four Farces (includes *Wooed and Viewed; On the Marry-Go-Wrong; Not By Bed Alone; Going to Pot*), translated by Norman Shapiro. 1970.

Three Farces (includes *Fitting for Ladies; A Close Shave; Sauce for the Goose*), translated by Peter Meyer. 1974.

Three Farces (includes *Love By the Bolt; All My Husband; That's My Girl*), translated by J. Paul Marcoux. 1976.

Feydeau, First to Last: Eight One-Act Comedies, translated by Norman Shapiro. 1982.

Three Boulevard Farces (includes *The Lady from Maxim's; A Flea in Her Ear; A Little Hotel on the Side*), translated by John Mortimer. 1985.

The Pregnant Pause; or, Love's Labor Lost, translated by Norman Shapiro. 1987.

Five by Feydeau, translated by J. Paul Marcoux. 1994.

From Marriage to Divorce, translated by Peter Meyer. 1998.

*

Bibliography: *Théâtre complet 1*, 1988.

Critical Studies: "Suffering and Punishment in the Theatre of Georges Feydeau" by Norman R. Shapiro, in *Tulane Drama Review*, 5(1), 1960; *Georges Feydeau* (in English) by Jacques Lorcey, 1972; *Georges Feydeau: Textes de Feydeau, points de vue critique, témoignages, chronologie, bibliographie, illustrations* by Arlette Shenkan, 1972; *Georges Feydeau* (in English), 1975, and *Eugène Labiche and Georges Feydeau*, 1982, both by Leonard C. Pronko; *Le Théâtre de Georges Feydeau* by Henry Gidel, 1979; *Georges Feydeau and the Aesthetics of Farce* by Stuart E. Baker, 1981; *Georges Feydeau* (in English) by Manuel A. Esteban, 1983; "Feydeau 1862–1921: Dossier" by Henry Gidel, in *Comédie-Française* 139–140, 1985; *Georges Feydeau* by Henry Gidel, 1991.

*   *   *

Georges Feydeau's lengthy and successful dramatic career falls into four fairly distinct periods. During the first, from 1881 to 1886, he developed his skills by producing a series of dramatic monologues and short skits called *saynètes* which provided amusing entertainment in the fashionable drawing rooms of the period. Although necessarily possessing little of the manic activity and complex imbroglios of the brilliant later works, these early essays still offer certain features and themes that form the basis of later and more elaborate works—misunderstood or deceitful spouses, amorous intrigues, absurdly logical complications arising from outré premises, titillating misunderstandings, eccentric characters in bizarre situations. Such features mark *Amour et piano* (*The Music Lovers*), the one-act play that was Feydeau's first work produced in Paris.

Tailleur pour dames (*Love By the Bolt*) inaugurated a new phase in Feydeau's career; it was his first three-act comedy and his first major success. Already he had achieved considerable skill in weaving together a number of complex plots and subplots and an almost continuous web of misunderstandings and deceptions. The basic intrigue of the play is typically built on a romantic intrigue—Dr. Moulineaux's attempted seduction of Suzanne—but in standard Feydeau fashion, Moulineaux's wife, Suzanne's husband, and a variety of others are drawn one after another into an escalating round of mistaken identity, misdirection, and inopportune encounters. The plays immediately following *Love By the Bolt*, several, such as *L'Affaire Édouard* [The Edouard Affair], written in collaboration with Maurice Desvallières, were distinctly less successful, and in 1890 Feydeau took a two-year voluntary "exile" from the stage to polish his craft. According to his later collaborator René Peter, he gave particular attention to three contemporary authors who had gained considerable success in vaudeville and farce—Henri Meilhac for his dialogue, Eugène Labiche for his keen observation of contemporary characters and society, and Alfred Hennequin for his skill at dramatic construction.

Whatever his activities during this retreat, he returned with enormous energy and success, producing seven major plays, alone or in collaboration, during the next four years. These include some of his most famous and most elaborate imbroglios of marital intrigue, *Monsieur Chasse* (*A-Hunting We Will Go*), again with Desvallières, *Le Système Ribadier* [The Ribadier System] with Alfred Hennique's son Maurice, *Champignol malgré lui* (*A Close Shave*), *L'Hôtel du Libre-Échange* (*Paradise Hotel*), with Desvallières, *Un fil à la patte* (*Cat Among the Pigeons*), and *Le Dindon* (*The French Have a Word for It*). Although the actual or attempted amorous escapades of a bourgeois husband provide a departure point for almost all of these works, some, such as *A-Hunting We Will Go*, give major attention to the domestic situation and to the wife, often not above a bit of romancing herself but stoutly opposed to any such activity on the part of her partner, while others, such as *Cat Among the Pigeons*, pay more attention to the coquette who arouses the husband's interest, and to her quest for material success. Such character configurations recur again and again in Feydeau, so that *La Puce à l'oreille* (*A Flea in Her Ear*) may be classified as a "wife" play, and *Occupe-toi d'Amélie* (*Keep an Eye on Amélie*) a "coquette" play.

During the mid-1890s Feydeau attempted to depart from the rather mechanical farce to attempt a comedy of character in *Le Ruban* [The Ribbon] with Desvallières, written for the Odéon, France's second national theatre. Dr. Paginet, a scientific researcher whose passion to be awarded a prestigious national decoration recalls the obsessive drives of characters in the Molière tradition, was well received, but producers and public seemed to prefer the less thoughtful comic structures of Feydeau's successes in the boulevard theatres, and he returned to that approach with new one-act pieces and another of his comic masterpieces *La Dame de chez Maxim* (*The Lady from Maxim's*), his longest and most complex work. When the happily married Dr. Petypon wakes up one morning, on the floor of his bedroom, after an evening at Maxim's, and with a strange dancer from the Moulin Rouge in his bed, we are plunged at once into a racy and outrageous world of bizarre events and unexpected turns that never allows a moment of relaxation until the final masterful tying off of every loose end.

After such a success, a certain falling-off was perhaps inevitable, and although the public strongly supported *La Duchesse des Folies-Bergères* [The Duchess of the Folies-Bergère], critics suggested that Feydeau's themes and technique were beginning to show signs of wear. It may have been such criticism that encouraged Feydeau during his final period to divide his attention fairly equally between new examples of his most successful formulas and more "serious" comedies of character and personal relationships rather more in the style of his earlier *Le Ruban*. The most serious of the later works, indeed it is rather closer to drama than comedy, is *Le Bourgeon* [The Bud], dealing with a young seminarian's struggle with carnality. Immediately after this, however, came *A Flea in Her Ear* and *Keep an Eye on Amélie*, two of Feydeau's most elaborate and most successful farces.

In his final one-act and full-length plays, beginning with *Feu la mère de Madame* (*Night Errant*) and continuing through *Hortense a dit: "Je m'en fous!"* (*Tooth and Consequences*), Feydeau concentrated on confusions and conflicts within married life. The serious tonality that characterized much of his later work is found in all of these plays, but shot through with inventive comic elements. Although such plays as *Mais n'te promène donc pas toute nue!* (*Put Some Clothes on Clarisse!*) have lost nothing of the humour that marks all of Feydeau's best work, this humour no longer draws significantly upon such farce material as disguises, elaborate deceptions, or unexpected and unlikely encounters, but upon the irritants of everyday married life. The befuddled husbands and outrageous wives of these plays are developed with an intensity that at times almost suggests Strindberg in the mode of farce. The increasing grimness of the husband-wife relationship in these final works is suggested by Feydeau's plan to gather them in a collection to be called "From Marriage to Divorce."

—Marvin Carlson

See the essay on *A Flea in Her Ear*.

FILIPPO, Eduardo de

See DE FILIPPO, Eduardo

FLAUBERT, Gustave

Born: Rouen, France, 12 December 1821. **Education:** Educated at Collège Royal, 1831–39 (expelled); baccalauréat, 1840; studied law at École de Droit, Paris, 1841–45. **Career:** Suffered a seizure in 1844 which left him in poor health; after 1845 lived with his family at Croisset, near Rouen, where he stayed for the rest of his life; spent winters in Paris after 1856; visited Egypt and the Near East, 1849–51; publication of *Madame Bovary*, 1857, led to unsuccessful prosecution for indecency; returned to North Africa, 1858. State pension, 1879. **Award:** Chevalier, Légion d'honneur, 1866. **Died:** 8 May 1880.

PUBLICATIONS

Collections

Oeuvres complètes (includes correspondence). 35 vols., 1926–54.
Oeuvres, edited by Albert Thibaudet and René Dumesnil. 2 vols., 1946–48.
Complete Works. 10 vols., 1926.
Oeuvres complètes, edited by Bernard Masson. 1964.
Oeuvres complètes, edited by M. Bardèche. 16 vols., 1971–75.

Fiction

Madame Bovary. 1857; as *Madame Bovary*, translated by Eleanor Marx-Aveling, 1886; numerous subsequent translations including by Gerard Hopkins, 1949; Alan Russell, 1950; J.L. May, 1953; Francis Steegmuller, 1957, reprinted 1993; Lowell Bair, 1959; Mildred Marmur, 1964; Paul de Man, 1965; Geoffrey Wall, 1992.
Salammbô. 1862; edited by P. Moreau, 1970; as *Salammbô*, translated by J.S. Chartres, 1886; numerous subsequent translations including by E. Powys Mathers, 1950; A.J. Krailsheimer, 1977.
L'Éducation sentimentale. 1869; edited by C. Gothot-Mersch, 1985; as *Sentimental Education*, translated by D.F. Hannigan, 1896;

numerous subsequent translations including by A. Goldsmith, 1941; Robert Baldick, 1964; Douglas Parmée, 1989.

La Tentation de Saint Antoine. 1874; edited by C. Gothot-Mersch, 1983; as *The Temptation of Saint Anthony*, translated by D.F. Hannigan, 1895; numerous subsequent translations including by Lafcadio Hearn, 1932; Kitty Mrosovsky, 1980.

Trois Contes (includes *Un coeur simple; La Légende de Saint Julien l'hospitalier; Hérodias*). 1877; edited by S. de Sasy, 1973; as *Three Tales*, translated by George Burnham Ives, 1903; also translated by Mervyn Savill, 1950; Robert Baldick, 1961; A.J. Krailsheimer, 1991.

Bouvard et Pécuchet. 1881; edited by Alberto Cento, 1964, and by C. Gothot-Mersch, 1979; as *Bouvard and Pécuchet*, translated by D.F. Hannigan, 1896; also translated by A.J. Krailsheimer, 1976; reprinted in part as *Dictionnaire des idées reçues*, edited by Lea Caminiti, 1966; as *A Dictionary of Platitudes*, edited and translated by E.J. Fluck, 1954; as *The Dictionary of Accepted Ideas*, translated by Jacques Barzun, 1954; also translated by Robert Baldick, 1976.

La première Éducation sentimentale. 1963; as *The First Sentimental Education*, 1972.

Plays

Le Candidat (produced 1874). 1874.
Le Château des coeurs, with Louis Bouilhet and Charles d'Osmoy (produced 1874). In *Oeuvres complètes*, 1910.

Other

Par les champs et par les grèves. 1886.
Mémoires d'un fou. 1901.
Souvenirs, notes, et pensées intimes, edited by L. Chevally-Sabatier. 1965, and by J.P. Germain, 1987; as *Intimate Notebook 1840–1841*, edited by Francis Steegmuller, 1967.
November, edited by Francis Steegmuller. 1966.
Flaubert in Egypt: A Sensibility on Tour, edited by Francis Steegmuller. 1972.
Correspondance, edited by Jean Bruneau. 3 vols., 1973–91.
Letters, edited and translated by Francis Steegmuller. 2 vols., 1980–82.
Correspondance, with George Sand, edited by Alphonse Jacobs. 1981; as *Flaubert-Sand: The Correspondence*, translated by Francis Steegmuller and Barbara Bray, 1993.
Flaubert and Turgenev: A Friendship in Letters: The Complete Correspondence, edited and translated by Barbara Beaumont, 1985.
Carnets de travail, edited by Pierre-Marc de Biasi. 1988.
Early Writings, translated by Robert Griffin. 1991.
Correspondance, with Guy de Maupassant, edited by Yvan Leclerc. 1994.
Editor, *Dernières chansons*, by Louis Bouilhet. 1872.

*

Bibliography: *Bibliographie de Flaubert* by D.L. Demorest and R. Dumesnil, 1947; *Bibliographie des études sur Gustave Flaubert*, edited by D.J. Colwell, 1988–90.

Critical Studies: *Flaubert and Madame Bovary* by Francis Steegmuller, 1947; *Flaubert and the Art of Realism* by Anthony Thorlby, 1956; *On Reading Flaubert* by Margaret G. Tillett, 1961;

Flaubert: Madame Bovary by Alison Fairlie, 1962; *Flaubert: A Collection of Critical Essays* edited by Raymond D. Giraud, 1964; *The Novels of Flaubert: A Study of Themes and Techniques* by Victor Brombert, 1966, revised edition, 1968; *Madame Bovary and the Critics* edited by Benjamin F. Bart, 1966, *Flaubert*, 1967, and *The Legendary Sources of Flaubert's Saint Julien*, 1977, both by Bart; *Flaubert* by Stratton Buck, 1966; *The Sentimental Adventure* by Peter Cortland, 1967; *Flaubert* by Enid Starkie, 2 vols., 1967–71; *Three Novels by Flaubert: A Study of Techniques* by R.J. Sherrington, 1970; *The Discovery of Illusion: Flaubert's Early Works, 1835–37*, 1971, and *Madame Bovary: The End of Romance*, 1989, both by Eric L. Gans; *The Greatness of Flaubert* by Maurice Nadeau, 1972; *Flaubert: The Uses of Uncertainty* by Jonathan Culler, 1974, revised edition, 1985; *Flaubert: The Problem of Aesthetic Discontinuity* by Marie J. Diamond, 1975; *Sartre and Flaubert* by Hazel E. Barnes, 1981; *The Family Idiot: Gustave Flaubert 1821–1857* by Jean-Paul Sartre, translated by Carol Cosman, 5 vols., 1981–93; *Saint/Oedipus: Psychocritical Approaches to Flaubert's Art* by William J. Berg, 1982; *Flaubert and the Historical Novel: Salammbô Reassessed* by Anne Green, 1982; *Madame Bovary on Trial* by Dominick La Capra, 1982; *Towards the Real Flaubert: A Study of Madame Bovary* by Margaret Lowe, 1984; *Flaubert and Postmodernism* by Naomi Schor and Henry F. Majewski, 1984; *Madame Bovary: A Psychoanalytical Reading* by Ion K. Collas, 1985; *Flaubert's Characters: The Language of Illusion* by Diana Knight, 1985; *Flaubert and the Gift of Speech: Dialogue and Drama in Four Modern Novels*, 1986, and *The Madame Bovary Blues: The Pursuit of Illusion in Nineteenth Century French Fiction*, 1987, both by Stirling Haig; *Critical Essays on Gustave Flaubert* by Laurence Porter, 1986; *The Perpetual Orgy: Flaubert and Madame Bovary* by Mario Vargas Llosa, translated by Helen Lane, 1986; *Gustave Flaubert's Madame Bovary* edited by Harold Bloom, 1988; *Rape of the Lock: Flaubert's Mythic Realism* by Robert Griffin, 1988; *The Free Indirect Mode: Flaubert and the Poetics of Irony* by Yaheed R. Ramazani, 1988; *The Hidden Life at Its Source: A Study of Flaubert's L'Éducation sentimentale* by D.A. Williams, 1988; *Madame Bovary* by Alastair B. Duncan, 1989; *Madame Bovary* by Rosemary Lloyd, 1989; *Flaubert: A Biography* by Herbert Lottman, 1989; *Gustave Flaubert* by David Roe, 1989; *Flaubert Remembers: Memory and the Creative Experience* by William VanderWalk, 1990; *Flaubert's Straight and Suspect Saints: The Unity of Trois Contes* by Aimée Israel-Pelletier, 1991; *Gustave Flaubert: Madame Bovary* by Stephen Heath, 1992; *Sentimental Education: The Complexity of Disenchantment* by William Paulson, 1992; *The Script of Decadence: Essays on the Fictions of Flaubert and the Poetics of Romanticism* by Eugenio Donato, 1993; *Realism and Narrative Modality: The Hero and Heroine in Eliot, Tolstoy and Flaubert* by Jill Felicity Durey, 1993; *When Flaubert Lies: Chronology, Mythology and History* by Claire Addison, 1996; *Gustave Flaubert* by William J. Berg and Laurey K. Martin, 1997; *Processes of Literary Creation: Flaubert and Proust* by Marion Schmid, 1998; *Searching for Emma: Gustave Flaubert and Madame Bovary* by Dacia Maraini, 1998; *Flaubert: Writing the Masculine* by Mary Orr, 2000; *Flaubert and the Pictorial Arts: From Image to Text* by Adrianne Tooke, 2000; *Flaubert: A Life* by Geoffrey Wall, 2001; *A Gustave Flaubert Encyclopedia*, edited by Laurence M. Porter, 2001.

* * *

Gustave Flaubert's best and best-known novel, *Madame Bovary*, marked a turning point in the history of the European novel. For the first time, an ordinary, middle to lower-middle-class woman occupied the central place in a detailed study of how dull everyday life could be in a small town, and the romantic myth that true love could be found in successfully consummated adultery was convincingly presented as a total illusion. In the wider history of fiction, Emma Bovary resembles Cervantes's *Don Quixote* (1615) in that she is a person who tries to live her life in terms of ideas derived from books but fails, and she also, perhaps more significantly, represents the first version of the ''miserable married woman'' who recurs in Tolstoi's *Anna Karenina* (1875–77), in the Irene of John Galsworthy's *Forsyte Saga* (1906–29), in Mauriac's *Thérèse Desqueyroux* (1927), and even—though here the problem finds a satisfactory solution—in D.H. Lawrence's *Lady Chatterley's Lover* (1928). Like her fictional successors, Emma is married to a worthy but dull man, and the fact that she is, for all her self-centredness and folly, by far the most enterprising and interesting character in the novel does enable *Madame Bovary* to be interpreted nowadays as a not entirely unsympathetic account of the problems to which feminism seeks to find a solution.

As his other novels, especially *L'Éducation sentimentale* (*Sentimental Education*), show, and as his voluminous *Correspondance* confirms, Flaubert was an unremitting pessimist who did not believe that human beings either could achieve happiness or deserved to do so. For him, the only activity deserving any consideration was the construction of perfect works of art, and it was to this that he devoted the whole of his life. He rewrote incessantly, spending sometimes a week on one paragraph, and it took him five years to complete *Madame Bovary*. It is consequently slightly surprising that the heroine of what is otherwise rightly regarded as a masterpiece of realism should have eyes that are blue on one page but black on another, and the modern French critics who profess to admire Flaubert do so because of his mastery of form. His other novels, especially the exotic *Salammbô* and *La Tentation de Saint Antoine* (*The Temptation of Saint Anthony*), have a less immediate appeal to the modern reader, though the various versions through which the latter book passed between 1848 and 1874 make it the work on which Flaubert spent most time. Flaubert's attitude of caustic superiority to the modern world joined with an obsession with stupidity to produce *Bouvard et Pécuchet* (*Bouvard and Pécuchet*), although he died before it was completed, as well as the shorter and more amusing *Dictionnaire des idées reçues* (*The Dictionary of Accepted Ideas*). Although he was himself of impeccably middle-class origins, and adopted a very middle-class lifestyle, he contributed greatly to the growth of the now universal custom in France whereby imaginative writers have only contempt for the members of the middle class who buy and read their books.

His literary influence showed itself in the 19th century principally in the development of the realist movement with Zola and Maupassant, and in the 20th in the self-styled ''nouveaux romanciers'' of the 1950s. Thus Robbe-Grillet saw in Flaubert a writer with a comparable interest to his own in the minute description of inanimate physical objects, and tended to pay less attention to the concern for pitiless psychological analysis which led to Flaubert being shown, in his lifetime, in a cartoon depicting him as a surgeon in a bloodstained apron holding up the dissected heart of the unhappy Emma Bovary.

There is general unanimity among critics of all tendencies to admire the long short stories in *Trois Contes* (*Three Tales*) as undisputed masterpieces. ''Un coeur simple'' (''A Simple Heart''),

an account of how a servant woman devotes herself entirely to the welfare of others, is indeed a masterpiece. It is certainly the work in which Flaubert shows something of the sympathy for his own creations which traditionally characterizes the novelist, and in which the hatred of normal humanity which so often informs his work gives way to a more charitable vision of our limitations. Those who consider singleness of purpose in the pursuit of aesthetic perfection will admire the hermit-like existence which Flaubert imposed upon himself, and detach themselves from Jean-Paul Sartre's view that Flaubert, like the other 19th-century French writers who retired to their ''ivory tower,'' is to be held responsible for the massacres which followed the Commune of 1871 because they did not write a single line to protest against them. Those who admire the vigour and even the vulgarity of a Dickens or a Balzac, or who share the sympathy with ordinary life which so often shows itself in Tolstoi, will speculate more on the paradox of how a man who disliked human beings so much managed to write novels at all. The subtitle of *Madame Bovary* is ''Moeurs de Province'' (''Customs of the Provinces''), and this draws attention to the character of the local pharmacist Homais, the embodiment of all that Flaubert most disliked in the optimism and enthusiasm for scientific progress which were so marked a feature of mid-19th-century France.

—Philip Thody

See the essays on *Madame Bovary*, *Sentimental Education*, and ''A Simple Heart.''

FONTAINE, Jean de la

See LA FONTAINE, Jean de

FONTANE, Theodor

Born: Henri Théodore Fontane in Neuruppin, Germany, 30 December 1819. **Education:** Educated at Gymnasium, Neuruppin, 1832–33; Gewerbeschule K.F. Klödens, Berlin, 1833–36. **Military Service:** 1844. **Family:** Married Emilie Rouanet-Kummer in 1850, three sons and one daughter. **Career:** Apprenticed to an apothecary, Berlin, 1836–40, and worked in Burg, Leipzig, Dresden, and Berlin, 1841–49; then freelance writer; worked for Prussian government press bureau, 1851–55; London correspondent for Berlin papers, 1855–59; editor for London affairs, *Kreuzzeitung*, 1860–70; theatre critic, *Vossische Zeitung*, 1870–89; secretary Berlin Academy of Arts, 1876 (resigned, 1876). **Awards:** Schiller prize (Prussia), 1891. **Died:** 20 September 1898.

PUBLICATIONS

Collections

Sämtliche Werke, edited by Edgar Gross and others. 30 vols., 1959–75.

Werke, Schriften, und Briefe, edited by Walter Keitel and Helmuth Nürnberger. 1962–.

Romane und Erzählungen, edited by Peter Goldammer and others. 8 vols., 1969.

Fiction

Vor dem Sturm. 1878; as *Before the Storm*, translated by R.J. Hollingdale, 1985.

Grete Minde. 1880.

Ellernklipp. 1881.

L'Adultera. 1882; as *A Woman Taken in Adultery*, translated by Gabriele Annan, with *The Poggenpuhl Family*, 1979.

Schach von Wuthenow. 1883; as *A Man of Honor*, translated by E.M. Valk, 1975.

Graf Petöfy. 1884.

Unterm Birnbaum. 1885.

Cecile. 1887; translated by Stanley Radcliffe, 1992.

Irrungen, Wirrungen. 1888; as *Trials and Tribulations*, 1917; as *A Suitable Match*, translated by Sandra Morris, 1968; as *Entanglements: An Everyday Berlin Story*, translated by Derek Bowman, 1986.

Quitt. 1890.

Stine. 1890; translated as *Stine*, 1977.

Unwiederbringlich. 1891; as *Beyond Recall*, translated by Douglas Parmée, 1964.

Frau Jenny Treibel. 1892; as *Jenny Treibel*, translated by Ulf Zimmermann, 1976.

Effi Briest. 1895; translated by Douglas Parmée, 1967; also translated by Hugh Rorrison and Helen Chambers, 1995.

Die Poggenpuhls. 1896; as *The Poggenpuhl Family*, translated by Gabriele Annan, with *A Woman Taken in Adultery*, 1979.

Der Stechlin. 1899; as *The Stechlin*, translated with introduction and notes by William L. Zwiebel, 1995.

Mathilde Möhring. 1906; revised version, 1969.

Short Novels and Other Writings (includes *A Man of Honor*; *Jenny Treibel*; *The Eighteenth of March*), edited by Peter Demetz. 1982.

Delusions, Confusions; and The Poggenpuhl Family, edited by Peter Demetz. 1989.

Verse

Von der schönen Rosamunde. 1850.

Männer und Helden. 1850.

Gedichte. 2 vols., 1851–75.

Balladen. 1861.

Die schönsten Gedichte und Balladen. 1982.

Bilder und Balladen, edited by Werner Feudell. 1984.

Other

Ein Sommer in London. 1854.

Bilderbuch Aus England. 1860; as *Journeys to England in Victoria's Early Days 1844–1859*, translated by Dorothy Harrison, 1939.

Jenseit des Tweed. 1860; as *Across the Tweed*, translated by Brian Battershaw, 1965; as *Beyond the Tweed: A Tour of Scotland in 1858*, translated by Brian Battershaw, 1998.

Wanderungen dutch die Mark Brandenburg. 4 vols., 1862–82.

Kriegsgefangen. 1871.

Aus den Tagen der Okkupation. 1872.

Der Krieg gegen Frankreich, 1870–1871. 2 vols., 1873–76.

Christian Friedrich Scherenberg und der literarische Berlin von 1840 bis 1860. 1885.

Fünf Schlösser. 1889.

Meine Kinderjahre (memoirs). 1894.

Von Zwanzig bis Dreissig (memoirs). 1898.

Aus dem Nachlass, edited by Joseph Ettlinger. 1908.

Briefwechsel, with Wilhelm Wolfsohn, edited by Wilhelm Walters. 1910.

Briefe, edited by Kurt Schreinert and Charlotte Jolles. 4 vols., 1968–71.

Briefwechsel, with Paul Heyse, edited by Gotthard Erler. 1972.

Briefe, edited by Gotthard Erler. 2 vols., 1980.

Briefwechsel, with Theodor Storm, edited by Jacob Steiner. 1981.

Ein Leben in Briefen, edited by Otto Drude, 1981.

Autobiographische Schriften, edited by Gotthard Erler, Peter Goldammer, and Joachim Krueger. 3 vols., 1982.

Briefe an den Verleger Rudolf von Decker. 1988.

Shakespeare in the London Theatre 1855–58, translated with introduction and notes by Russell Jackson, 1999.

*

Critical Studies: *Formen des Realismus* by Peter Demetz, 1964; *The Gentle Critic: Theodor Fontane and German Politics 1848–98* by Joachim Remak, 1964; *Theodor Fontane: An Introduction to the Novels and Novellen* by H.C. Sasse, 1968; *Theodor Fontane: An Introduction to the Man and His Work* by A.R. Robinson, 1976; *The Preparation of the Future: Techniques of Anticipation in the Novels of Theodor Fontane and Thomas Mann* by Gertrude Michielsen, 1978; *Some Aspects of Balladesque Art and Their Relevance for the Novels of Fontane* by R. Geoffrey Lackey, 1979; *Supernatural and Irrational Elements in the Works of Fontane* by Helen Elizabeth Chambers, 1980; *The Berlin Novels of Theodor Fontane* by Henry Garland, 1980; *Theodor Fontane: The Major Novels* by Alan F. Bance, 1982; *The German "Gesellschaftsroman" at the Turn of the Century: A Comparison of the Works of Theodor Fontane and Eduard von Keyserling* by Richard A. Koc, 1982; *Novel Associations: Theodor Fontane and George Eliot within the Context of Nineteenth-Century Realism* by Gabriele A. Wittig Davis, 1983; *Meyer or Fontane? German Literature after the Franco-Prussian War 1870–71* by John Osborne, 1983; *Anekdoten aus allen fünf Weltteilen: The Anecdote in Fontane's Fiction and Autobiography* by Andrea MhicFhionnbhairr, 1985; *Social Integration and Narrative Structure: Patterns of Realism in Auerbach, Freytag, Fontane, and Raabe* by Nancy A. Kaiser, 1986; *Effi Briest* by Stanley Radcliffe, 1986; *The Changing Image of Theodor Fontane* by Helen Chambers, 1997; *New Approaches to Theodor Fontane: Cultural Codes in Flux*, edited by Marion Doebeling, 2000.

* * *

It was as a writer of ballads that Theodor Fontane first made his way in the literary world, and it was on the ballad, and on his historical researches, *Wanderungen durch die Mark Brandenburg*, that Fontane's reputation rested for most of his own lifetime. He emerged as a novelist only in his late fifties, with the historical novel *Vor dem*

Sturm (*Before the Storm*), on the mood of Prussia on the eve of the Wars of Liberation against Napoleon.

Fontane is typically concerned here to present large-scale events through the details of everyday life, and this predilection for the actual conditions of life (albeit within a limited social range) is somewhat un-German. In fact, Fontane and Heinrich Heine were perhaps the only two 19th-century writers of rank to grapple closely with the political reality of their country. The author himself thought his wealth of topical references would render him unreadable in the next century (yet Ernst Jünger was sustained by the love story *Irrungen, Wirrungen* (*A Suitable Match*) in the trenches of World War I).

Everything Fontane writes is in a sense political, and yet everything is conveyed through the intimate medium of a private fate. Thus his novella on the decadent state of Prussian society in the era of its defeat at Napoleon's hands in 1806 reveals the nature of the times through the character of an individual, the Prussian officer Schach von Wuthenow (after whom the story is named), a vacillating conformist. Fontane's highly developed handling of conversation is the most praised quality of his art, and it especially offers him scope for revealing the link between private existence and the public totality of an epoch. His preference for reticence and discretion as a narrator has allowed him to be read as an apologist for the accommodations required of the individual in society. But he is at heart a romantic, who knows, however, that individuals only exist within the given of their society and cannot transcend it. Yet it is *through* these individuals that Fontane must convey his sense of an alternative world, and he does so often through female characters who possess a mysterious natural attraction, and whose potential the world stifles or leaves unrealized. The most poetic expression of this confrontation of nature and society is the figure of Effi Briest in Fontane's best-known novel; and yet this book more than any other makes clear that society is known and understood only through individuals who are products of their society and cannot stand outside it. His last novel, *Der Stechlin*, is a serene and yet politically astute analysis of the tension between reified "facts"—the facts of self-interest and power politics which became a dominant fetish in Wilhelm II's materialistic Second Reich—and the possibility of change. Fontane's life-long attraction to England, prominent in *Der Stechlin*, was precisely to do with the contrast between English political culture and Prussia's difficulty in evolving social structures commensurate with the dynamic forces of its modernization.

—Alan F. Bance

See the essays on *Before the Storm* and *Effi Briest*.

FONVIZIN, Denis (Ivanovich)

Born: Moscow, Russia, 3 April 1745. **Education:** Educated at Moscow University Gymnasium, 1755–60; Moscow University, 1760–62. **Family:** Married Ekaterina Khlopova in 1774. **Career:** After university, moved to St. Petersburg and entered the civil service: secretary to Ivan Elagin in the Foreign Ministry, 1763–69; secretary to the statesman Count Nikita Ivanovich Panin, from 1769;

received an estate, 1773; travelled to France and Germany, 1777–78; achieved dramatic success with the St. Petersburg production of *The Minor*; retired from public life, 1783, following the death of Panin and after incurring the displeasure of Catherine the Great; a founding member of the Russian Academy, 1783; his works banned temporarily in the early 1780s; travelled to Germany and Italy, 1784–85; suffered stroke, 1785; planned to launch a periodical, *Starodum* [Old Thought], which never appeared because of censorship; travelled to Austria for health reasons, 1786–87. **Died:** 1 December 1792.

PUBLICATIONS

Collections

Polnoe sobranie sochinenii [Complete Works]. 4 vols., 1830.
Pervoe polnoe sobranie sochinenii [First Complete Works]. 1888.
Izbrannye sochineniia i pis'ma [Selected Works and Letters]. 1946.
Izbrannoe [Selection], edited by B. Derkach. 1957.
Sobranie sochinenii [Collected Works], edited by G.P. Makogonenko. 2 vols., 1959.
Sochineniia [Works], edited by A.I. Vredinskii. 1983.
Izbrannoe: Stikhotvoreniia; Komedii; Satiricheskie proza publitsistika; Avtobiograficheskaia proza; Pis'ma [Selection: Poetry; Comedies; Satirical Prose and Publications; Autobiographical Prose; Letters], edited by Iu.V. Stennik. 1983.
Sochineniia [Works], edited by N.N. Akopova. 1987.
Izbrannye sochineniia [Selected Works], with A.S. Griboedov and A.N. Ostrovskii, edited by V.N. Turbin. 1989.

Plays

Korion [Korion], from a play by Jean-Baptiste Gresset (produced 1764).
Brigadir (produced 1780). In *Polnoe sobranie sochinenii*, 1830; single edition, 1950; as *The Brigadier*, translated by Harold B. Segel, in *The Literature of Eighteenth-Century Russia*, 2, edited by Segel, 1968; also translated by Marvin Kantor, in *The Dramatic Works*, 1974.
Nedorosl' (produced 1782). 1937; as *The Young Hopeful*, translated by George Z. Patrick and G.R. Noyes, in *Masterpieces of the Russian Drama*, edited by Noyes, 1933; as *The Minor*, translated by Frank D. Reeve, in *Anthology of Russian Plays*, 1, edited by Reeve, 1961; also translated by Marvin Kantor, in *The Dramatic Works*, 1974; as *The Infant*, in *Four Russian Plays*, translated by Joshua Cooper, 1972, reprinted as *The Government Inspector and Other Plays*, 1990.
Vybor guvernera (produced 1790). As *The Choice of a Tutor*, in *Five Russian Plays with One from the Ukraine*, edited and translated by C.E.B. Roberts, 1916; as *The Selection of a Tutor*, translated by Marvin Kantor, in *The Dramatic Works*, 1974.
Alzir; ili, Amerikantsii [Alzire; or, The Americans], from a play by Voltaire, in *Pervoe polnoe sobranie sochinenii*. 1888.
Komedii (includes *Vseobshchaia pridvornaia grammatika*). 1950.
The Dramatic Works (includes *The Minor; The Brigadier; The Selection of a Tutor;* and the fragment *A Good Mentor*), translated by Marvin Kantor. 1974.

Other

Zhizn' grafa N.I. Panin [The Life of Count N.I. Panin]. 1784 (in French); 1796 (in Russian).

Brigadir; Nedorosl'; Satiricheskaia proza; Pis'ma iz Peterburga [The Brigadier; The Minor; Satirical Prose; Letters from Petersburg]. 1987.

Lettres de France (1777–1778), translated into French with commentary by Henri Grosse, Jacques Proust, and Piotr Zaborov, 1995.

Translator, *Basni nravouchitel' ne siz'' iasneniami*, from Holberg's fables. 1761; enlarged edition, 1765.

Translator, *Geroiskaia dobrodetel'; ili, zhizn' Sife* [Heroic Virtue], by Jean Terrasson. 4 vols., 1762–68.

Translator, *Liubov' Karity i Polidora* [The Love of Carita and Polidore], by Jean-Jacques Berthélémy. 1763.

Translator, *Torguiushchee dvorianstvo* [The Commercial Nobility], by Gabriel-François Coyer. 1766.

Translator, *Sidnii i Sillii* [Sidney and Silly], by François-Thomas Baculard d'Arnaud, 1769.

Translator, *Joseph*, by Paul-Jérémie Bitaube. 1769.

Translator, *Rassuzhdenie o natsional'nom liubochestie* [An Essay on National Patriotism], by Johann Zimmermann. 1785.

*

Critical Studies: *Russian Comedy 1765–1823* by D. Walsh, 1966; *Denis Fonvizine* by Alexis Strychek, 1976; *Denis Fonvizin* by Charles A. Moser, 1979; *Russian Drama from Its Beginnings to the Age of Pushkin* by Simon Karlinsky, 1985.

* * *

The Russian theatre before Denis Fonvizin, after its official inception during the reign of Tsar Alexei in 1672, progressed by fits and starts. Very little of lasting value was produced and the period is of little more than historical interest. The mid-18th century, did, however, witness some notable developments and a few original plays were written, the best of them by Aleksandr Sumarokov. The style was highly imitative and followed the conventions of French neo-classicism. During the reign of Catherine the Great marked progress was made, not entirely unconnected with her own interest in writing plays, and the theatre was given encouragement, state support, and financial assistance. The two best plays of the period are undoubtedly Fonvizin's *Brigadir* (*The Brigadier*) and *Nedorosl'* (*The Minor*).

Fonvizin was a well-educated, cultured, and widely-travelled man but his work as a dramatist was not central to his career. His interest in drama derived from his leisure-time activity of translating from French and German—his version of Holberg's *Fables* (1761) led to a lasting interest in his plays, a few of which he attempted to translate. Fonvizin's first attempt at dramatic composition was a version in Russian of Gresset's *Sidney* (1764), to which he gave the un-Russian title of *Korion*. Although it is a good example of travesty that was extremely popular at the time and it was rendered in competent verse, it is best regarded only as an immature experiment. These early experiences did, however, stand Fonvizin in good stead, for the two plays for which he is remembered are unquestionably the best in Russian before Griboedov's *Gore ot uma* (*Woe from Wit*), composed in the early 1820s. They are both written in prose and follow the rules of neo-classical dramatic form. They are comedies of manners and social satires with a marked didactic element.

When *The Brigadier* first appeared it was an immediate success. Its plot revolves around a young couple who hope to marry and whose respective parents meet in order to become better acquainted and to decide whether their offspring are suitable for each other. The comedy springs from the efforts of each of the two fathers to form a liaison with the other's wife, while simultaneously the young man courts his prospective mother-in-law, thus becoming a rival to his own father. Ultimately such disgraceful behaviour gets its just reward: the parents are ridiculed, the young man is unsuccessful, and the daughter's eyes are opened to the ways of the world before she finds true love with someone else. Consequently the sanctity of the family is upheld and love based on sincere feelings and mutual respect encouraged. Fonvizin, however, keeps his most biting satire for the then pervasive Gallomania, endemic at court but imitated, although not understood, by society at large. Fonvizin was by no means opposed to the French or their ways, but wished his fellow-countrymen to be selective, balanced, and rational in what they accepted, thus developing some sense of their own worth. The play is amusing in both its action and its dialogue, the latter being the most natural-sounding yet heard on the Russian stage. For the first time in Russia a play had been written that was recognizably Russian in subject matter, characterization, and feel, even though many of the human foibles satirized are universal.

Although less well constructed and more obviously didactic and closer to the conventions of neo-classicism than *The Brigadier*, *The Minor* was the better-known in its day and the one for which he is now chiefly remembered. It features a pair of conventional lovers who have to suffer the machinations of the young girl's guardian to marry her off, first to her brother, and then when it transpires that her ward is the heiress to a considerable fortune, to her son, the minor of the title. Everything is sorted out finally, the lovers are free to marry and the guardian punished, although not so much for her dealings with her family as for maltreating her serfs. The plot is rather conventional and uninvolving. The central focus of the satire is squarely on the brutal, uneducated, unthinking, and selfish provincial landowners of the minor gentry and their equally uninspiring entourage of servants, relations, and ignorant tutors. The negative characters, with hardly a redeeming feature among them, are wonderfully comic creations and are in sharp contrast to the positive, moralizing, and tediously didactic representatives of the good and true, the wealthy, honest, and educated. The language of the former is lively, natural, and colloquial while that of the latter is formal and stilted. Fonvizin is proposing virtuous behaviour in human relations and the legitimate claims of social justice, both of which can be guaranteed by a proper education, while the state must do all it can to promote the necessary conditions. Even Catherine is reported to have approved of the play, although there were some suggestions that Fonvizin had drawn very near to the limits of the permissible.

Vybor guvernera (*The Selection of a Tutor*), although continuing the theme of the importance of education to the country's well-being, is rather more political than social. Politics, Fonvizin affirms, has to concern itself with questions of the freedom and the equality of citizens, the former being the more crucial. There will always be differences between various social classes and consequently inequality is inevitable, but civil liberties are to be ensured wherever possible. It is not Russia's institutions, including serfdom, which are at fault in themselves, rather the shortcomings of those who manage them. In all of his plays Fonvizin shows himself to be a man of his times, but a humane and considerate one who believed that Russia needed change but that she had enough intrinsic worth not simply to imitate others.

—A.V. Knowles

See the essay on *The Minor*.

FOUQUÉ, Caroline (Auguste) de la Motte

Born: Caroline von Briest, in Nennhausen, Germany, 7 October 1775(?). **Family:** Married 1) Friedrich Ehrenreich Adolph Ludwig von Rochow in 1789; two sons and one illegitimate daughter (marriage dissolved 1799; died [suicide] 1799); 2) the writer Friedrich de la Motte Fouqué, *q.v.*, in 1803. **Died:** 21 July 1831.

PUBLICATIONS

Fiction

Drei Märchen. 1806.
Rodrich. 1806–07.
Die Frau des Falkensteins. 1810.
Kleine Erzählungen von der Verfasserin des Rodrich, der Frau des Falkensteins und der Briefe über weibliche Bildung. 1811.
Die Magie der Natur: Eine Revolutionsgeschichte. 1812; edited with introduction by Gerhart Hoffmeister, 1989.
Der Spanier und der Freiwillige in Paris. Eine Geschichte aus dem heiligen Kriege. 1814.
Feodora. 1814.
Edmunds Wege und Irrwege. Ein Roman aus der nächsten Vergangenheit. 1815.
Das Heldenmädchen aus der Vendée. 1816.
Neue Erzählungen. 1817. Includes ''Die Verwünschung''; as ''The Curse: A Tale'', translated by N. Stenhouse, 1825.
Die früheste Geschichte der Welt: Ein Geschenk für Kinder. 1818.
Frauenliebe. 1818.
Blumenstrauss gewunden aus den neusten Romanen und Erzählungen, with Friedrich de la Motte Fouqué. 1818.
Fragmente aus dem Leben der heutigen Welt. 1820.
Ida. 1820.
Lodoiska und ihre Tochter. 1820.
Kleine Romane und Erzählungen. 1820.
Heinrich und Marie. 1821.
Die blinde Führerin. 1821.
Vergangenheit und Gegenwart. 1822.
Die Herzogin von Montmorency. 1822.
Die Vertriebenen: Eine Novelle aus der Zeit der Königin Elisabeth von England. 1823; as *The Outcasts: A Romance*, translated by George Soane, 1824.
Neueste gesammelte Erzählungen. 1824.
Die beiden Freunde. 1824.
Bodo von Hohenried. 1825.
Aurelio. 1825.

Valerie, Die Sinnesänderung, und Der Weihnachtsbaum (stories). 1827.
Resignation. 1829.
Memoiren einer Ungenannten. 1831.
Der Schreibtisch; oder, Alte und neue Zeit. 1833.
The Physician of Marseilles, The Revolutionists: Four Tales from the German. 1845.

Other

Briefe über Zweck und Richtung weiblicher Bildung. 1811.
Briefe über die griechische Mythologie für Frauen. 1812.
Ruf an die deutschen Frauen. 1812.
Über deutsche Geselligkeit, in Antwort auf das Urtheil der Frau von Staël. 1814.
Briefe über Berlin im Winter 1821. 1822.
Reiseerinnerungen, with Friedrich de la Motte Fouqué. 1823.
Die Frauen in der grossen Welt: Bildungsbuch beim Eintritt in das gesellige Leben. 1826.
Geschichte der Moden, vom Jahre 1785 bis 1829, als Beitrag zur Geschichte der Zeit. 1830.
Editor, with others, *Für müssige Stunden: Vierteljahrsschrift.* 7 vols., 1816–21; reprinted 1971.

*

Critical Studies: *Märchen-Dichtung der Romantiker* by Richard Benz, 1926; *Caroline de la Motte Fouqué* by Vera Prill, 1933; *The Romantic Realist: Caroline de la Motte Fouqué* by Jean T. Wilde, 1955.

* * *

Caroline de la Motte Fouqué was a writer of some significance in the literary, cultural, and social history of Germany. For a number of years she and her husband, Friedrich, were the country's most successful literary couple, and her works were praised by major writers such as Goethe and Kleist. Yet she has been even more neglected than her husband, and the few references to her in critical literature tend to be derogatory.

Her career spans the quarter century from the defeat of Prussia by Napoleon in 1806 to her death eight months before that of Goethe. During this period of political and social upheaval she published more than 100 works, including 20 novels, over 60 stories, a number of poems and reviews, and some 20 non-fiction pieces of didactic, social, and cultural import aimed primarily at women. Besides pursuing her own career she collaborated in her husband's editorial ventures and co-authored with him two volumes of *Reiseerinnerungen* [Travel Reminiscences].

The range and quantity of Fouqué's output testify not only to the diversity of her interests and her facility in writing, but also to her need to earn money, which became acute when her husband's popularity waned after 1815. Although acquainted with most of the important writers of the day and admitted to the highest court circles in Prussia, she was under financial pressures, as reflected in the concessions to popular taste, the prolixity, and the uneven quality of much of her work. Deeply conservative in outlook, with a strong belief in monarchy, aristocracy, religion, family honour, and the military ethos, she yet experienced, like many women of her time, marital breakdown and the birth of an illegitimate child. She was, too, an educated professional writer in a society which discouraged the serious pursuit of art or scholarship by women. These contradictions, characteristic of an age of transition, are mirrored in her writing through the strategies that she adopts in order to cope with them and to make her work acceptable to the reading public, and through the tension between Romantic and realistic features in her style.

Several of her earliest works, two anonymous poems and the collection *Drei Märchen* [Three Fairy Tales], show the influence of Romantic models, particularly Novalis and Tieck. However, her first novel, *Rodrich*, already displays the mixture of Romanticism and realism which characterizes her later work. It includes Romantic motifs such as verse interpolations, visions, dreams, symbolism, and a mystery concerning the hero's birth and ancestry, as well as realistic descriptions, social criticism, and discussions between characters on various topics. It probably influenced E.T.A. Hoffmann's novel *Die Elixiere des Teufels* (*The Devil's Elixirs*, 1815–16).

Fouqué's second novel, *Die Frau des Falkensteins* [The Lady of Castle Falkenstein], is a tale of passion and renunciation with autobiographical overtones, and a number of the characters are based on Fouqué's acquaintances. It has many of the trappings of the Gothic novel—an old castle, a family curse, an ancestral ghost, a mysterious portrait, dreams, premonitions, and forebodings—which appear repeatedly in her work, but it also emphasizes the importance of self-restraint, convention, and useful, settled activity. These concerns suggest the influence of Goethe but also show Fouqué seeking fictional solutions to problems of her own. Several of her other novels and stories, such as *Feodora, Frauenliebe* [A Woman's Love], *Ida, Lodoiska und ihre Tochter* [Lodoiska and Her Daughter], and "Arnold und Marie" (1811), which, exceptionally for Fouqué, is set wholly in a non-aristocratic milieu, likewise deal with marriage and relationships between the sexes.

Fouqué's conviction that traditional forms must be preserved is expressed in "Das Frälein vom Thurme" [The Girl in the Tower] (1811), a cautionary tale about the dangers of marrying below one's station, and *Die Magie der Natur* [The Magic of Nature], which is set against the background of the French Revolution and carries an antirevolutionary message as well as a warning not to meddle in the mysteries of the universe. This novel may have been influenced by Goethe's *Elective Affinities*; he certainly read and approved of it. Its concern with the dangers of unfettered scientific enquiry is characteristic of its time (compare Mary Shelley's *Frankenstein*, 1818). *Das Heldenmädchen aus der Vendée* [The Heroic Girl of the Vendée Nobility], one of Fouqué's best historical novels, is again set in revolutionary France. Based on the memoirs of the Marquise de la Rochejaquelein (1814), it concerns the Vendean Wars of 1793–96, and interweaves fact and fiction, events in the Vendée and in Paris, to create a vivid picture of opposing forces during a controversial episode of French history. Fouqué's idealization of the Vendeans stands in striking contrast to their denigration in official French historiography.

English history of the Elizabethan era provides the background to *Die Vertriebenen* (*The Outcasts*), which was influenced by Sir Walter Scott. Here, as in *Das Heldenmädchen* and *Die Herzogin von Montmorency* [The Duchess of Montmorency], which recounts the Massacre of St. Bartholomew, Fouqué shows a particular flair for character drawing and vivid description, especially of crowd scenes. Other strengths of her writing are her depiction of nature and gift for detail, often of a domestic or everyday kind.

Her capacity for observation is also evident in her nonfiction works, in which she comments on and seeks to influence the society of her time. While conforming to contemporary prejudice in warning women against scholarly and artistic virtuosity, she pursues her own ambitions as writer and guide on women's education, etiquette, mythology, history, social events, and cultural phenomena. Whereas her earlier pieces are strongly patriotic, her later work is marked by increasing disillusionment. Yet her *Geschichte der Moden, vom Jahre 1785 bis 1829, als Beitrag zur Geschichte der Zeit* [History of Fashion, from 1785 to 1829, as a Contribution to the History of the Age] shows originality in its insight that changes in fashions reflect intellectual and social changes, and suggests unfulfilled potential that, in an age less restrictive of women, might have come to more complete fruition.

—Judith Purver

FOUQUÉ, Friedrich (Heinrich Karl, Baron) de la Motte

Born: Brandenburg, Germany, 12 February 1777. **Education:** Educated privately by A.L. Hülsen, 1788–94. **Military Service:** Served with the Weimar Dragoons, 1794, took part in the Rhine campaign, invalided out, 1795; Prussian cavalry officer, 1812–13: Major. **Family:** Married 1) Marianne von Schubaert in 1798; 2) the writer Caroline von Briest, *q.v.*, in 1803 (died 1831); 3) Albertine Tode in 1833, two sons. **Career:** Visited Weimar, 1802 and met Goethe and Schiller; encouraged to proceed with career as a writer by Friedrich and August Wilhelm Schlegel, *q.v.*; lived in Nennhausen after 1803. Editor, *Taschenbuch*, 1809; *Die Jahreszeiten*, 1811–14; *Die Musen*, 1812–14; *Das Frauentaschenbuch*, 1815–21; *Für müssige Stunden*, 1816–20; *Berlinische Blätter für deutsche Frauen*, 1829–30; gave private lectures in history and poetry, Halle, 1840; co-editor, *Zeitung für den deutschen Adel*, Berlin, 1840–42. **Died:** 23 January 1843.

PUBLICATIONS

Collections

Works. 6 vols., 1845–46.
Geistliche Gedichte, edited by Albertine de la Motte Fouqué. 1846.
Werke, edited by Walther Ziesemer. 3 vols., 1908.
Werke, edited by C.G. von Maassen. 2 vols., 1922.

Fiction

Alwin. 1807.
Das Galgenmännlein. 1810; as "The Bottle-Imp," in *Popular Tales and Romances of the Northern Nations*, 1, 1823; as "The Vial-Genie and Mad Farthing," translated by Thomas Tracy, in *Miniature Romances from the German*, 1841.
Der Todesbund. 1811.
Undine. 1811; as *Undine*, translated by George Soane, 1818; also translated by Thomas Tracy, 1839; C.L. Lyttleton, 1845; Fanny Elizabeth Bunnett, 1867; Edmund Gosse, 1896; Abby L. Alger, 1897; George P. Upton, 1908; Paul Turner, 1960.

Sintram und seine Gefährten. 1811; as *Sintram and His Companions*, translated by Julius C. Hare, 1820; also translated by J. Burns, 1848; A.M. Richards, 1900; A.C. Farquharson, 1908.

Der Zauberring. 1812; as *The Magic Ring; or, Ingratitude Punished*, 1812; as *The Magic Ring: A Knightly Romance*, translated by Alexander Platt, 1846.

Die beiden Hauptleute. 1812; as *The Two Captains*, 1846; in *Undine and Other Tales*, translated by Fanny Elizabeth Bunnett, 1867.

Erzählungen. 1812.

Aslaugas Ritter und Alpha und Jucunde. 1813; ''Aslaugas Ritter'' translated as ''Aslauga's Knight,'' in *German Romance: Specimens of Its Chief Authors*, by Thomas Carlyle, 1827.

Neue Erzählungen. 1814.

Kleine Romane und Erzählungen. 6 vols., 1814–19.

Die Fahrten Thiodolfs des Isländers. 1815; as *Thiodolf, the Icelander*, 1845.

Sängerliebe: Eine provenzalische Sage in drei Büchern. 1816; as *Minstrel-Love*, translated by George Soane, 1821.

Reidmar und Diona. 1816.

Kindermärchen, with Karl Wilhelm Contessa and E.T.A. Hoffmann. 1817.

Die wunderbaren Begebenheiten des Grafen Alethes von Lindenstein. 1817.

Blumenstrauss: Gewunden aus den neusten Romanen und Erzählungen (stories), with Caroline de la Motte Fouqué. 1818.

Altsächsischer Bildersaal (stories). 1818–20.

Der Verfolgte. 1821.

Ritter Elidouc: Eine altbretannische Sage. 1822; as *Sir Elidoc: An Old Breton Legend*, 1849.

Wilde Liebe. 1823; as *Wild Love and Other Tales*, 1844.

Der Refugié; oder, Heimath und Fremde. 1824.

Sophie Ariele. 1825.

Die Saga von dem Gunlaugur, genannt Drachenzunge und Rafn dem Skalden: Eine Islandskunde des elften Jahrhunderts. 1826.

Erdmann und Fiammetta. 1826.

Mandragora. 1827.

Fata Morgana. 1836.

Der Geheimrath (stories). 1838.

Ausgewählte Werke. Ausgabe letzter Hand. 12 vols., 1841.

Abfall und Busse; oder, Die Seelenspiegel. 1844.

Joseph und seine Geige: Kaiser Karls V. Angriff auf Algier (stories). 1845.

Der Parcival, edited by Tilman Spreckelsen. 1997.

Plays

Dramatische Spiele, edited by A.W. Schlegel. 1804.

Zwei Schauspiele. 1805.

Die Zwerge. 1805.

Historie vom edlen Ritter Glamy und einer schönen Herzogin aus Bretagne. 1806.

Der Held des Nordens (includes *Sigurd der Schlangentödter; Sigurds Rache; Aslauga*). 1810.

Eginhard und Emma. 1811.

Vaterländische Schauspiele. 1811.

Alboin der Langobardenkönig. 1813.

Dramatische Dichtungen für Deutsche. 1813.

Die Pilgerfahrt, edited by Franz Horn. 1816.

Arien und Gesänge der Zauber-Oper gennant: Undine, music by E.T.A. Hoffmann. 1816.

Liebesrache. 1817.

Die zwei Brüder. 1817.

Heldenspiel. 1818.

Herrmann. 1818.

Hieronymous von Stauf. 1819.

Der Leibeigene. 1820.

Don Carlos, Infant von Spanien. 1823.

Der Sängerkrieg auf der Wartburg. 1828.

Mortiz Gottlieb Saphir und Berlin, with Willibald Alexis. 1828.

Der Jarl der Orkney-Inseln. 1829.

Der Pappenheimer Kürassier: Scenen aus der Zeit des dreissigjährigen Krieges. 1842.

Violiante. 1845.

Verse

Romanzen vom Thale Ronceval. 1805.

Gedichte vor und während dem Kriege 1813. 1813.

Corona: Ein Rittergedicht in drei Büchern. 1814.

Jahrbüchlein Deutscher Gedichte auf 1815, with others. 1815.

Tassilo: Vorspiel, music by E.T.A. Hoffmann. 1815.

Karls des Grossen Geburt und Jugendjahre: Ein Ritterlied, edited by Franz Horn. 1816.

Gedichte. 5 vols., 1816–27.

Jäger und Jägerlieder. 1818.

Romantische Dichtungen, with others. 1818.

Bertrand du Guesclin. 1821.

Feierlieder eines Preussen im Herbste 1823. 1823.

Geistliche Lieder: Erstes Bändchen. Missions-Lieder. 1823.

Erhörung: Sechs Psalme. 1827.

Christlicher Leiderschatz zur Erbauung von Jung und Alt, edited by Albertine de la Motte Fouqué. 1862.

Other

Gespräch zweier Preussischen. Edelleute über dem Odel. 1808.

Uber den sogenannten falschen Waldemar. 1811.

An Christian Grafen zu Stolberg (letter). 1815.

Auch ein Wort über die neueste Zeit: Nebst einigen Beilagen (essay). 1815.

Abendunterhaltungen zu gemüthlicher Erheiterung des Geistes, with others. 1817.

Der Mord Augusts von Kotzebue: Freundes Ruf an Deutschlands Jugend. 1819.

Etwas über den deutschen Adel, über Rittersinn und Militärehre in Briefen (essays), with Friedrich Perthes. 1819.

Gefühle, Bilder und Ansichten: Sammlung kleiner prosaischer Schriften. 1819.

Wahrheit und Lüge (essays). 1820.

Betrachtungen über Türken, Griechen und Türkenkrieg (essays). 1822.

Reise Erinnerungen, with Caroline de la Motte Fouqué. 1823.

Die Fahrt in die neue Welt with *Das Grab der Mutter*, by Alexis dem Wanderer. 1824.

Lebensbeschreibung des königlich preussischen Generals der Infanterie Heinrich August Baron de la Motte Fouqué: Verfasst von Seinem Enkel (biography). 1824.

Geschichte der Jungfrau von Orleans, nach authentischen Urkundern und dem französischen Werke des Herrn Le Brun de Charmettes. 2 vols., 1826.

Ernst Friedrich Wilhelm Philipp von Rüchel, Königlich Preussischer General Infanterie (biography). 1828.

Der Mensch des Südens und der Mensch des Nordens: Sendschreiben in Bezug auf das gleichnamige Werk des Herrn von Bonstettin an den Freiherrn Alexander von Humboldt. 1829.

Jakob Böhme (biography). 1831.

Sendschreiben an den Verfasser der Betrachtungen über die neuesten Begebenheiten in Deutschland (essay). 1831.

Von der Liebes-Lehre (essay). 1837.

Goethe und einer seiner Bewunderer: Ein Stück Lebensgeschichte (essay). 1840.

Lebengeschichte (autobiography). 1840.

Preussische Trauersprüche und Huldigungsgrüsse für das Jahr 1840. 1840.

Ausgewählte Werke: Ausgabe letzer Hand. 12 vols., 1841–73.

Denkschrift über Friedrich Wilhelm III, König von Preussen: Eine biographische Mittheilung. 1842.

Novellen-Mappe, with others. 1843.

Briefe an Friedrich Baron de la Motte Fouqué von Chamisso, Cherzy, Collin, u.a., edited by Albertine de la Motte Fouqué. 1848.

Stories by Musäus and Fouqué, translated by Thomas Carlyle, 1991.

Editor, with Wilhelm Neumann, *Die Musen: Eine norddeutsche Zeitschrift.* 3 vols., 1812–14.

Editor, *Peter Schlemihl's wundersame Geschichte*, by Adelbert von Chamisso. 1814.

Editor, *Thomas Aniella*, by August Fresenius. 3 vols., 1817.

Editor, *Hinterlassene Schriften: Erster Band*, by August Fresenius. 1818.

Editor, with Friedrich Laun, *Aus der Geisterwelt: Geschichten, Sagen und Dichtungen.* 2 vols., 1818.

Editor, with L. von Alvensleben, *Zeitung für den deutschen Adel.* 3 vols., 1840–42.

Translator, *Numancia*, by Cervantes. 1810.

Translator, *Lalla Rukh; oder, Die mongolische Prinzessin*, by Thomas Moore. 1822.

Translator, *Pique-Dame: Berichte aus dem Irrenhause, in Briefen. Nach dem Schwedischen.* 1825.

Translator, with others, *Der fünfte May: Ode auf Napoleons Tod*, by Alessandro Manzoni. 1828.

Translator, *Drei Erzählungen: Aus dem Dänischen*, by Bernhard Severin Ingemann. 1837.

Translator, *Bilderbuch ohne Bilder: Aus dem Dänischen.* 1842.

*

Critical Studies: *"Sich in die Poesie zu flüchten, wie in unantastbare Eilande der Seeligen": Analysen zu ausgewählten Romanen von Friedrich Baron de La Motte Fouqué* by Katja Diegmann-Hornig, 1999; *Das dramatische Werk Friedrich de la Motte Fouqué: Ein Beitrag zur Geschichte des romantischen Dramas* by Claudia Stockinger, 2000.

* * *

Friedrich Baron de la Motte Fouqué was one of the most prolific and widely-read writers of his time, as well as being one of the first members of the German Romantic movement to be translated into English. He experimented with a wide variety of literary forms, including verse dramas, novels, stories, fairytales, and lyric poetry, and he was also influential as an editor of literary periodicals, encouraging a number of younger writers. Today, however, with the exception of *Undine*, the tale of the water nymph who gains a human soul, his work has fallen into almost total popular and critical neglect and in most surveys of the period is either overlooked completely or else dismissed as trivial. Although such a fall from grace was to a large extent prefigured towards the end of his own life, conjecture as to the reasons for it have not always been well-informed, and a critical reevaluation of his work is long overdue.

One of the most striking features of Fouqué's dramatic and narrative *oeuvre* is his use of various mythological sources. These he manipulates to form a pseudo-medieval fairytale world, which serves as a physical and symbolic setting for the exploits of his heroic protagonists. This can be seen as early as 1810 in his dramatic trilogy *Der Held des Nordens* [The Hero of the North]. Fouqué draws not only on Germanic legend, but also, for example, on Norse mythology and the writings of the 16th-century physician and alchemist Paracelsus, as well as adding inventions of his own. The result is an apparently chaotic and deliberately artificial network of real and supernatural elements, covering a geographical area from Scandinavia in the north to Normandy in the west and Italy and Spain in the south. Central to this network are the motifs of the forest and the valley, which symbolize chaos and confusion and which typically provide the scene for the crucial testing of the hero in his physical and spiritual quest. The titular hero of the story *Sintram und seine Gefährten* (*Sintram and His Companions*), to take one example, must undertake a solitary horseback ride through the Valley of Death before he can achieve the ultimate status of the true Christian knight.

Fouqué's heroes in fact present something of a problem to the modern reader. They seem idealized, one-dimensional figures, most of them almost indistinguishable from each other, and Joseph von Eichendorff was not the only contemporary of Fouqué to claim that they represented a somewhat naive projection of the author's own self-image. What is interesting, however, about Fouqué's heroes is that nearly all of them are characterized by a dichotomy between the terrestrial and the spiritual, as represented in the figures of the knight and the poet. The novels in particular tend accordingly to follow a pattern of alternation between narrative sections, in which the protagonist's heroic deeds and supernatural encounters are described, and more lyrical passages, often featuring interpolated verse, in which the hero, in repose, discovers a wider, more spiritual perspective for his exploits. The ideal of Christian knighthood to which Fouqué's heroes aspire is presented as a conflict, which can only be resolved if the hero succeeds in overcoming the series of barriers which strew his path.

The charges most frequently levelled at Fouqué are that his reliance on mythological and supernatural elements represents a form of literary escapism, a retreat from social and political realities at a time when Europe was struggling to come to terms with the upheavals of the Napoleonic Wars, and that his persistence with allegedly trivial forms, such as the *Ritterroman* (the novel with the knight as hero) led to staleness and repetition. What such judgements largely ignore is the artificiality with which the mythological/supernatural network is constructed and the degree of manipulation with which Fouqué exploits popular forms, especially in his prose fiction. The narrative framework of much of Fouqué's best work is consciously stylized, and the reader is quite deliberately distanced from events by a fragmentary form of narration and an often quite dazzling array of perspectives: in the novel *Alwin*, for example, events from the hero's past are presented in the form of an overheard dream narrative; in *Sintram* the crucial links between the various episodes are withheld from the reader by means of a complicated framework of inner narratives and tableaux; and the narrators of most of the novels are not only omniscient but also highly visible figures, whose rare but crucial interjections exist on a temporal plane clearly separate from the plots.

The distance created between reader and text by such devices is the key to an understanding of Fouqué's work and its purpose. The chaos which reigns in the forest and the valley does not in fact reflect a retreat from reality: rather it acts as a mirror of the social and political unrest prevailing in early 19th-century Europe, and Fouqué's narrator steps back from such confusion not as a means of escape, but in an attempt to make sense of it from a clearer perspective. Fouqué is in fact revealed as a highly moral and didactic writer, and his appeal to a wide public deserves to be seen in this context. His basic response to the political upheaval of the Napoleonic Wars was an appeal to national pride and a firm conviction that Christianity alone could restore unity to Europe. Nowhere is this belief more clearly illustrated than in the final tableau of the novel *Der Zauberring* (*The Magic Ring*), where the heathen symbol of the ring itself is shattered and replaced by an idealized picture of family unity and Christian harmony. The ideal of Christian knighthood at the centre of Fouqué's philosophy may hark back to a bygone era, the *goldene Zeit* (golden age) beloved of so many German Romantics, but for Fouqué it had a definite contemporary relevance.

Friedrich Baron de la Motte Fouqué deserves to be remembered as more than merely a trivial figure in the German Romantic movement, who happened to achieve mass popularity through his vast output of work. Closer examination reveals not only a master of narrative, but also an author with a serious didactic purpose, much more responsive to the spirit of his times than is generally supposed.

—Howard Atkinson

FOURNIER, Henri Alban

See ALAIN-FOURNIER

FRANCE, Anatole

Born: Jacques-Anatole-François Thibault in Paris, France, 16 April 1844. **Education:** Educated at the Collège Stanislas. **Family:** Married 1) Marie-Valérie Guérin de Sauville in 1877 (divorced 1893), one daughter; 2) Emma Laprevotte in 1920. **Career:** Assistant at his father's bookshop, Librairie de France, Paris, 1860s; editorial assistant, Bachelin-Deflorenne, publishers, Paris, mid-1860s; schoolteacher, Ivry-sur-Seine, 1869; reader and editor, Lemerre, publishers, 1869–75; librarian, Senate library, Paris, 1876–90; regular contributor to *Le Globe* and *L'Univers illustré*; literary editor, *Le Temps*, 1888; associated with Mme. Armand de Caillavet. **Awards:** Académie française

award, 1881; Nobel prize for literature, 1921. Chevalier, Légion d'honneur, 1884. Honorary degree: University of Athens, 1919. **Member:** Académie française, 1897. **Died:** 12 October 1924.

PUBLICATIONS

Collections

Complete Works, edited by Frederic Chapman. 21 vols., 1908–28.
Oeuvres complètes, edited by Léon Carias and Gérard Le Prat. 26 vols., 1925–37.
Oeuvres complètes. 1968–70.
Works. 40 vols., 1975.
Oeuvres, edited by Marie-Claire Bancquart. 2 vols., 1984–87.

Fiction

Jocaste et le chat maigre. 1879; as *Jocasta and the Famished Cat*, translated by Agnes Farley, 1912.
Le Stratagème. 1880.
Le Crime de Sylvestre Bonnard, membre de l'Institut. 1881; revised edition, 1902; edited by R.L. Graeme Ritchie, 1927; as *The Crime of Sylvestre Bonnard, Member of the Institute*, translated by Lafcadio Hearn, 1890; also translated by Arabella Ward, 1897.
Les Désirs de Jean Servien. 1882; as *The Aspirations of Jean Servien*, translated by Alfred Allinson, 1912.
Abeille: Contes (stories). 1883; as *Honey-Bee*, translated by Mrs John Lane, 1911; as *Bee: The Princess of the Dwarves*, translated by Peter Wright, 1912.
Le Livre de mon ami. 1885; edited by J. Heywood Thomas, 1942; as *My Friend's Book*, translated by J. Lewis May, 1913; also translated by Rosalie Feltenstein, 1950.
Nos Enfants: Scènes de la ville et des champs (stories). 1887; in 2 vols., 1900; as *Child Life in Town and Country*, translated by Alfred Allinson, with *The Merrie Tales of Jacques Tournebroche*, 1910; as *Girls and Boys: Scenes from the Country and the Town*, 2 vols., 1913, and as *Our Children: Scenes from the Country and the Town*, 2 vols., 1917, both translated by Allinson; as *In All France: Children in Town and Country*, translated by A.G. Wippern, 1930.
Balthasar (stories, includes *Abeille*). 1889; as *Balthasar*, translated by Mrs. John Lane, 1909.
Thaïs. 1890; revised edition, 1928; as *Thaïs; or, The Vengeance of Venus*, translated by Ernest DeLancey Pierson, 1892; as *Thaïs*, translated by A.D. Hall, 1891; also translated by Ernest Tristan, 1902; as *Thaïs or The Monk's Temptation*, translated by Robert B. Douglas, 1909; also translated by Basia Gulati, 1976.
L'Étui de nacre (stories). 1892; as *Tales from a Mother-of-Pearl Casket*, translated by Henri Pène du Bois, 1896; as *Mother of Pearl*, translated by Frederic Chapman, 1908.
La Rôtisserie de la Reine Pédauque. 1893; as *The Queen Pedauque*, translated by Joseph A.V. Stritzko, 1910; as *At the Sign of the Reine Pédauque*, translated by Mrs Wilfrid Jackson, 1912; as *At the Sign of the Queen Pédauque*, 1933; as *The Romance of the Queen Pedauque*, translated by Jackson, 1950.
Le Lys rouge. 1894; as *The Red Lily*, translated by Winifred Stevens, 1908.
Le Puits de sainte Claire. 1895, as *The Well of Saint Claire*, translated by Alfred Allinson, 1909.
Histoire contemporaine. 4 vols., 1897–1901.

L'Orme du mail. 1897; as *The Elm-Tree on the Mall: A Chronicle of Our Own Times*, translated by M.P. Willcocks, 1910.

Le Mannequin d'osier. 1897; as *The Wicker-Work Woman: A Chronicle of Our Own Times*, translated by M.P. Willcocks, 1910.

L'Anneau d'améthyste. 1899; as *The Amethyst Ring*, translated by B. Drillien, 1919.

Monsieur Bergeret à Paris. 1901; as *Monsieur Bergeret in Paris*, translated by B. Drillien, 1921.

La Leçon bien apprise. 1898.

Pierre Nozière. 1899; as *Pierre Nozière*, translated by J. Lewis May, 1916.

Clio. 1900; as *Clio*, translated by Winifred Stephens, 1922.

L'Affaire Crainquebille. 1901; revised edition as *Crainquebille, Putois, Riquet, et plusieurs autres récits profitables*, 1904; as *Crainquebille, Putois, Riquet, and Other Profitable Tales*, translated by Winifred Stephens, 1915; as *Crainquebille*, translated by Jacques Le Clerq, 1949.

Histoire de Dona Maria d'Avala et de Don Fabricio, duc d'Andria. 1902.

Mémoires d' un volontaire (selection). 1902.

Histoire Comique. 1903; as *A Mummer's Tale*, translated by Charles E. Roche, 1921.

Sur la pierre blanche. 1903; as *The White Stone*, translated by Charles E. Roche, 1910.

Les Contes de Jacques Tournebroche. 1908; as *The Merry Tales of Jacques Tournebroche*, translated by Alfred Allinson, 1910.

L'Île des pingouins. 1908; as *Penguin Island*, translated by A.W. Evans, 1909; also translated by Belle Notkin Burke, 1968.

Les Sept Femmes de la Barbe-Bleue et autres contes merveilleux. 1909; as *The Seven Wives of Bluebeard and Other Marvellous Tales*, translated by D.B. Stewart, 1920.

Les Dieux ont soif. 1912; as *The Gods Are Athirst*, translated by Alfred Allinson, 1913; also translated by Mrs. Wilfrid Jackson, 1925; Alec Brown, 1951; Linda Frey, Marsh Frey, and Roman Zylawy, 1978; as *The Gods Will Have Blood*, translated by Frederick Davies, 1979.

Les Anges. 1913; revised edition as *La Révolte des anges*, 1914; as *The Revolt of the Angels*, translated by Mrs. Wilfrid Jackson, 1914.

Amycus et Célestin. 1916.

Le Petit Pierre. 1918; edited by Isabelle H. Clarke, 1925; as *Little Pierre*, translated by J. Lewis May, 1920.

Marguerite. 1920; as *Marguerite*, translated by J. Lewis May, 1921; with *Alfred de Vigny* and *The Path of Glory*, 1927.

Le Comte Morin, député. 1921; as *Count Morin, Deputy*, translated by J. Lewis May, 1921; with *Alfred de Vigny* and *The Path of Glory*, 1927.

La Vie en fleur. 1922; as *The Bloom of Life*, translated by J. Lewis May, 1923.

Contes, edited by C.J.M. Adie and P.C.H. de Satgé. 1923.

Little Sea Dogs (selection), translated by Alfred Allinson and J. Lewis May. 1925.

Les Autels de la peur. 1926.

Golden Tales, translated anonymously. 1926.

Le Jongleur de Notre-Dame and Other Stories, translated by Margaret Weale. 1948.

Verse

Les Poèmes dorés. 1873.

Les Noces corinthiennes. 1876; as *The Bride of Corinth and Other Poems and Plays*, translated by Wilfrid and Emilie Jackson, 1920.

Poésies. 1896.

Les Poèmes du souvenir. 1910.

Plays

Au Petit bonheur (produced 1898). 1898.

Le Lys rouge, with Gaston de Caillavet, from his own novel (produced 1899). In *Oeuvres complètes*, 1970.

Les Noces corinthiennes (produced 1902). 1876.

Crainquebille, from his own story (produced 1903). 1913; as *Crainquebille*, translated by Barrett H. Clark, 1915; also translated by Jacques Le Clerq, 1949.

Le Mannequin d'osier, from his own novel (produced 1904). 1928.

La Comédie de celui qui épousa une femme muette (produced 1912). 1913; as *The Man Who Married a Dumb Wife*, translated by Curtis Hidden Page, 1915.

Other

Alfred de Vigny. 1868; revised edition, 1923.

Le Livre du bibliophile. 1874.

Les Poèmes de Jules Breton. 1875.

La Vie littéraire. 4 vols., 1888–92; as *On Life and Letters*, translated by A.W. Evans, D.B. Stewart, and Bernard Miall, 4 vols., 1911–14.

L'Elvire de Lamartine: Notes sur M. et Mme. Charles. 1893.

Les Opinions de M. Jérôme Coignard. 1893; as *The Opinions of Jérôme Coignard*, translated by Mrs. Wilfrid Jackson, 1913.

La Société historique d'Auteuil et de Passy. 1894.

Le Jardin d'Épicure. 1895; as *The Garden of Epicurus*, translated by Alfred Allinson, 1908.

La Liberté par l'étude. 1902.

Madame de Luzy. 1902.

Opinions sociales. 2 vols., 1902.

L'Église et la république. 1904.

Vers les temps meilleurs. 3 vols., 1906; as *Vers les temps meilleurs: Trente ans de vie sociale*, edited by Claude Aveline and Henriette Psichar, 3 vols., 1949–67; as *The Unrisen Dawn: Speeches and Addresses*, 1928.

Vie de Jeanne d'Arc. 2 vols., 1908; as *The Life of Joan of Arc*, translated by Winifred Stephens, 1909.

Le Génie latin (criticism). 1909; revised edition, 1917; as *The Latin Genius*, translated by Wilfrid Jackson, 1924.

Aux étudiants (lecture). 1910.

La Comédie de celui qui épousa une femme muette. 1912.

Sur la voie glorieuse. 1916; as *The Path of Glory*, translated by Alfred Allinson, 1916.

Ce que disent nos morts. 1916.

La Vie en fleur. 1922.

Epigrams of Love, Life and Laughter, edited and translated by Sylvestre Dorian. 1924.

Dernières pages inédites. 1925.

Promenades félibréennes. 1925.

Under the Rose (essays), translated by J. Lewis May. 1926.

Prefaces, Introductions, and Other Uncollected Papers, translated by
  J. Lewis May. 1927.
Les Dieux asiatiques aux premiers siècles de l'ère chrétienne. 1928.
Rabelais, translated by Ernest Boyd. 1929.
*Le Secret du "Lys rouge": Anatole France et Madame de Caillavet:
  lettres intimes (1888–1889)*, edited by Jacques Suffel. 1984.
Editor, *Oeuvres de Jean Racine*. 5 vols., 1874–75.
Editor, *Lucile de Chateaubriand*. 1889.
Editor, *Les Poèmes du souvenir*. 1910.

*

Critical Studies: *Anatole France: The Degeneration of a Great
Artist* by Barry Cerf, 1927; *Anatole France Abroad* by Jean J.
Brousson, translated by John Pollock, 1928; *Anatole France and His
Time: The Ironic Temper* by Haakon Chevalier, 1932; *Anatole
France: A Life Without Illusions 1844–1924* by Jacob Axelrad, 1944;
Anatole France and the Greek World by Loring B. Walton, 1950;
Seven Against the Night by Paul Eldridge, 1960; *Anatole France
polémiste*, 1962, and *Anatole France: Un sceptique passionné*, 1984,
both by Marie-Claire Bancquart; *Anatole France: The Politics of
Skepticism* by Carter Jefferson, 1965; *Anatole France* by David
Tylden-Wright, 1967: *Anatole France* by Reino Virtanen, 1968; *The
Art of Anatole France* by Duskan Bresky, 1969; *Anatole France: The
Short Stories* by Murray Sachs, 1974; *The Saint and the Skep-
tics* by William Searle, 1976; "Techniques of Irony in Anatole
France: Essays on 'Les Sept femmes de la Barbe-Bleue'" by Diane
Wolfe Levy in *North Carolina Studies in the Romance Languages
and Literatures*, 201, 1978; *Anatole France inconnu* by Edith
Tendron, 1995.

*   *   *

Urbane, erudite and eminently civilized, Anatole France was
generally considered at the turn of this century to be the foremost
contemporary French novelist and man of letters. To an extent seldom
found in the career of any other writer, he also represented the literary
and philosophical values of a previous age.

His first full-length novel, *Le Crime de Sylvestre Bonnard* (*The
Crime of Sylvestre Bonnard*) is an early example of fiction in diary
form. Its hero, an elderly and artless scholar, kind-hearted and
sceptical in outlook, abducts the orphaned granddaughter of the
woman he had once loved from the drudgery of a menial job at her old
boardingschool; he sells his beloved books to provide her with a
dowry. The same theme of self-sacrifice, more convincingly presented in exotic lands and remote historical times, is central to both
the short story "Balthasar" and the novel *Thaïs*. The former tells how
Balthazar, one of the Magi, overcomes lust in order to follow the star
of Bethlehem, whilst one of the other kings overcomes cruelty and the
third masters his pride. *Thaïs*, set in 4th-century Egypt, is perhaps the
most skilful of all of France's narrations. Its eponymous heroine is an
Alexandrian courtesan converted to Christianity by the hermit
Paphnuce, her former lover. The theme of renunciation is twofold;
Paphnuce's in the first instance, though Thaïs's self-abnegation is
more complete. More importantly, however, France seems to suggest
that the life to which Paphnuce tries to win Thaïs back is not the work

of the devil: it is a life of love and vitality which, whether God-
inspired or not, is the diametrical opposite of asceticism.

The collection *L'Étui de nacre* (*Mother of Pearl*) contains two
important stories, "Le Procurateur de Judée" and "Le Jongleur de
Notre-Dame." In the first of these Pontius Pilate recalls his time as
ruler of Judaea. His friend Lamia happens to mention one Jesus of
Nazareth, "a young wonder-worker from Galilee" who was crucified
for some crime or other, Pilate cannot remember him! In the second
the juggler Barnabé is converted to the monastic life. He is about to be
expelled from the monastery chapel where he has been secretly
performing a juggling act as his particular tribute to Our Lady when
she descends the altar steps, pronouncing the sixth beatitude: "Blessed
are the pure in heart."

In "Balthasar," *Thaïs*, "Le Procurateur de Judée," and "Le
Jongleur de Notre-Dame" the influence of Flaubert's *Tentation de
saint Antoine* (*The Temptation of Saint Anthony*) and *Trois Contes*
(*Three Tales*) upon France is unmistakable, France chooses themes of
the Nativity, Pontius Pilate and the monastic life, treating self-
abnegation with that enigmatic detachment shown by Flaubert in "Un
coeur simple" ("A Simple Heart"). But the historical relativism of
"Le Procurateur de Judée," stupendous as it is at the narrative level,
smacks a little of artifice.

La Rôtisserie de la Reine Pédauque (*The Queen Pedauque*)
reveals France's fascination with the 18th century. Jérôme Coignard,
a priest with a *philosophe*'s outlook, is deeply respectful of religion
despite his voluptuousness and moral laxity. Tournebrouche, the
narrative voice in this novel, is the landlord's son at the inn regularly
visited by Coignard; he becomes the Abbé's loyal pupil, even to the
extent of helping him and a raffish nobleman in an abduction which
results in Coignard's murder. With his unusual sceptical irony France
mocks belief in the occult. Through the medium of *Les Opinions de
M. Jérôme Coignard* (*The Opinions of Jérôme Coignard*), a compilation of the Abbé's thoughts produced by Tournebrouche, France also
expresses sharp criticism of contemporary society.

In the *Histoire contemporaine* series, the hero, Lucien Bergeret, is
a further embodiment of the scholar, sceptic, epicurean humanist, and
keen but detached observer of daily life which France himself was. At
the heart of his four-volume cycle is the Dreyfus affair; also evident is
the author's growing anti-clericalism. In the third volume, *L'Anneau
d'améthyste* (*The Amethyst Ring*), ecclesiastical rivalries are prominent; also portrayed are the intrigues of a provincial town. Differing
greatly from Balzac, France treats the latter theme with gentle
good humour.

The eponymous hero of the short novel *L'Affaire Crainquebille*
(*Crainquebille*) is an elderly street trader imprisoned after conviction
on a false charge of shouting abuse at the police. Unable to make a
living after his release from jail, he decides he would be better off
behind bars again and so, on seeing another policeman, he actually
does shout abuse. But he is simply moved on. Nothing illustrates
better the even-handedness of France's outlook than *Crainquebille*,
which recognizes that there is kindliness, and hence durability, in
existing institutions.

Nevertheless, in consequence of the Dreyfus affair, France be-
came increasingly committed to social change from 1900 onwards.
Further scope for incisive satire was afforded by *L'Île des pingouins*
(*Penguin Island*, which again dealt with the Dreyfus affair), *Les
Dieux ont soif* (*The Gods Are Athirst*), and *Les Anges* (*The Revolt of*

the Angels). In the second of these France returns to the 18th century, providing a broad picture of varying Revolutionary attitudes. None of these novels, however, shows much belief in that cornerstone of 18th-century thinking, the inevitability—or even the likelihood—of social progress.

The many review notices which make up *La Vie littéraire* (*On Life and Letters*) reveal a subjective critic whose role models in this genre were Taine and Sainte-Beuve: he admired their immense erudition. But although Taine prized objectivity above all things, France's philosophical relativism would not allow him to believe in the absoluteness of any judgement. For the same reason he rejected Zola's view that Naturalism was the summation of literary art.

France has too often been denigrated for the episodic nature of his plots and for his lack of imaginative power. Though he was the author of one ill-researched work—*Vie de Jeanne d'Arc* (*The Life of Joan of Arc*), extreme in its anticlericalism—his writings are remarkable for their depth of understanding and for their linguistic and philosophical clarity reminiscent of Voltaire. His qualities of euphony, wit, well-balanced scepticism, and the whimsical fantasy and discursiveness seen at their best in *The Queen Pedauque* were sustained at a level of near-perfection throughout his literary life.

—Donald Adamson

See the essay on *The Gods Are Athirst*.

FREYRE, Gilberto (de Melo)

Born: Recife, Pernambuco, Brazil, 15 March 1900. **Education:** Educated at American Colégio Gilreath, Recife, to 1917; Baylor University, Waco, Texas, 1918–21, BA 1921; Columbia University, New York, 1921–22, MA in anthropology 1922. **Family:** Married Maria Magdalena Guedes Pereira in 1941; one daughter and one son. **Career:** Travelled in Europe, 1922–23, and returned to Brazil, 1923; co-organizer, Regionalist Artistic Movement's Congress, Recife, 1926; private secretary to the Governor of Pernambuco, Recife, 1927–30; editor, *A Província*, Recife, 1928–30; assistant professor of sociology, Escola Normal, Recife, 1928; went into exile to Portugal, 1930; travelled to Africa, 1930; visiting professor, Stanford University, California, 1931; professor of sociology, Faculty of Law, Recife, 1935, and appointed to the chair of sociology and social anthropology, Federal University, 1935; visiting professor, Columbia University, New York, 1938; representative for Pernambuco, National Assembly, 1946, and in the House of Deputies, 1947–50; Brazilian Ambassador to the United Nations General Assembly, 1949; visiting professor, Indiana University, Bloomington, United States, 1966. Founder, Joaquim Nabuco Institute, Recife, 1949. **Awards:** Felippe d'Oliveira award, 1934; Anisfield-Wolf award, 1957; Machado de Assis prize, 1963; Aspen award, 1967; La Madonnina International literary prize (Italy), 1969; José Vasconcelos gold medal (Mexico), 1974; Moinho Santista prize, 1974. Honorary doctorates: Columbia University, 1954; University of Coimbra, 1962; University of Paris, 1965; University of Sussex, Falmer, 1965; University of Münster, 1965. KBE (Knight Commander, Order of the British Empire), 1971;

Commander, Légion d'honneur, 1986. **Member:** American Philosophical Association (United States); Council for the Philosophy of Law and Sociology, Paris; São Paulo Academy of Letters, 1961; Brazilian Academy of Letters, 1962; Royal Anthropological Institute; American Academy of Arts and Sciences. **Died:** 18 July 1987.

PUBLICATIONS

Fiction

Dona Sinhá e o filho padre. 1964; as *Mother and Son*, translated by Barbara Shelby, 1967.
O outro amor do Dr. Paulo. 1977.

Verse

Bahia de todos os santos e todos os pecados. 1926.
Talvez poesia. 1962.
Gilberto poeta: algumas confissões. 1980.
Poesia reunida. 1980.

Other

Casa-grande & Senzala. 1933; revised edition, 2 vols., 1943; as *The Masters and the Slaves: A Study in the Development of Brazilian Civilization*, translated by Samuel Putnam, 1946; revised edition, 1964.
Guia prático, histórico, e sentimental de cidade do Recife. 1934; revised edition, 1968.
Artigos de jornal. 1935.
Sobrados e mucambos. 1936; revised edition, 1961; as *The Mansions and the Shanties: The Making of Modern Brazil*, translated by Harriet de Onís, 1963.
Mucambos de Nordeste. 1937.
Nordeste. 1937; revised edition, 1961.
Olinda: 2° guia prático, histórico, e sentimental de cidade Brasileira. 1939; revised edition, 1968.
Açúcar. 1939; enlarged edition, 1969.
Um engenheiro francês no Brasil. 1940; revised edition, 2 vols., 1960.
O mundo que o Português criou. 1940.
Região e tradição. 1941.
Uma cultura ameaçada. 1942.
Ingleses. 1942.
Problemas brasileiros de antropologia. 1943; revised edition, 1954.
Na Bahia em 1943. 1944.
Perfil de Euclides e outros perfís. 1944.
Sociologia. 2 vols., 1945; revised edition, 1962.
Brazil: An Introduction (written in English). 1945; revised edition, as *New World in the Tropics: The Culture of Modern Brazil*, 1959.
Ingleses no Brasil. 1948.
Quase política. 1950; revised edition, 1966.
Aventura e rotina. 1953.
Um brasileiro em terras portuguêsas. 1953.
Assombrações do Recife velho. 1955.
Manifesto regionalista 1926. 1955.
Sugestões para uma nova política no Brasil: a Rurbana. 1956.
Integração portuguesa nos trópicos. 1958; as *Portuguese Integration in the Tropics*, translated anonymously, 1961.
A propósito de frades. 1959.
A propósito de Morão, Rosa, e Pimenta. 1959.

Ordem e progresso. 2 vols., 1959; as *Order and Progress: Brazil from Monarchy to Republic*, edited and translated by Rod W. Horton, 1970.

Obras reunidas. 12 vols, 1959–66.

Brasis, Brasil, e Brasília. 1960; revised edition, 1968.

O Luso e o trópico. 1961; as *The Portuguese and the Tropics*, translated by Helen M. d'O. Matthew and F. de Mello Moser, 1961.

Vida, forma, e côr. 1962.

Homen, cultura, e trópico. 1962.

O escravo nos anúncios de jornais brasileiros do século XIX. 1963; revised and enlarged edition, 1979.

Retalhos de jornais velhos. 1964.

The Racial Factor in Contemporary Politics. 1966.

O Recife, sim! Recife, não!. 1967.

Sociologia da medicina. 1967.

Como e porque sou e não sou sociólogo. 1968.

Contribução para uma sociologia de biografia. 2 vols., 1968.

Oliveira Lima, Don Quixote gordo. 1968.

A casa brasileira. 1971.

Nós e a Europa germânica. 1971.

Seleta para jovens de Gilberto Freyre. 1971; as *The Gilberto Freyre Reader*, translated by Barbara Shelby, 1974.

A condição humana e outros temas, edited by Maria Elisa Dias Collier. 1972.

Além do apenas moderno. 1973.

A presença do açúcar na formação brasileira. 1975.

Tempo morto e outros tempos: trechos du um diário de adolescência e primeira mocidade 1915–1930. 1975.

O brasileiro entre os outros hispanos. 1975.

Alhos & bugalhos. 1978.

Cartas de próprio punho sobre pessoas e coisas do Brasil e do estrangeiro, edited by Sylvio Rabello. 1978.

Prefácios desgarrados, edited by Edson Nery da Fonseca. 2 vols., 1978.

Heróis e vilões no romance brasileiro, edited by Edson Nery da Fonseca. 1979.

Livro de Nordeste, with others. 1979.

Oh de casa!. 1979.

Tempo de aprendiz (articles 1918–26), edited by José Antônio Gonsalves de Mello. 1979.

Arte, ciencia, e trópico. 1980.

Pessoas, coisas e animals: ensaios. 1981.

Insurgências e ressurgências atuais: cruzamentos de sins e nãos num mundo em transição. 1983.

Médicos, doentes e contextos sociais. 1983.

Editor, *Coleção documentos brasileiros.* 161 vols., 1936–73.

Editor, *Desenvolvimento brasileiro & tropico.* 1985.

Translator, *Vida social no Brasil nos meados do século XIX*, by Waldemar Valente. 1977.

*

Bibliography: *Brazilian Literature: A Research Guide* by David William Foster and Walter Rela, 1990.

Critical Studies: *Gilberto Freyre* by Diogo de Melo Menezes, 1944; *Gilberto Freyre: sua ciencia, sua filosofia, sua arte* by various authors, 1962; "Gilberto Freyre and José Honório Rodrigues: Old and New Horizons for Brazil" by Richard A. Mazzara, in *Hispania*, May 1964; "Gilberto Freyre as a Literary Figure: An Introductory Study" by Dorothy S. Loos, in *Revista Hispánica Moderna*, 34, 1968; *Gilberto Freyre: Uma biografia intelectual* by Vamireh Chacon, 1993; *Guerra e paz: Casa-Grande & Senzala e a obra de Gilberto Freyre nos anos 30* by Ricardo Benzaquen de Araùjo, 1994; *A obra em tempos vários: Livro comemorativo dos 95 anos de nascimento de Gilberto Freyre*, organized and presented by Fátima Quintas, 1999; *Gilberto Freyre: Entre tradição & ruptura* by Gustavo Henrique Tuna, 2000; *Gilberto Freyre e a invenção do Brasil* by Roberto Cavalcanti de Albuquerque, 2000; *Gilberto Freyre* by Maria Inês de França Roland, 2000.

*   *   *

Gilberto Freyre is the single most influential Brazilian intellectual of the 20th century. His extraordinary reputation is based largely upon his social history of colonial Brazil, *Casa-grande & Senzala* (*The Masters and the Slaves*), which Freyre wrote to accomplish three separate and sometimes contradictory goals: to deny the validity of 19th-century "scientific" racism, still almost universally accepted among the Brazilian elite, by endeavouring "to discriminate between the effects of purely genetic relationships and those resulting from social influences, the cultural heritage and the milieu"; to insist that Brazil was a multiracial nation, and that no Brazilian could claim to have escaped the genetic and cultural influence of the nation's Amerindian and African populations; and to assert that his own ancestors, the plantation aristocrats and slave owners of the Northeast, had created a remarkably humane social system which encouraged both cultural fusion and sexual miscegenation between blacks and whites.

A few Brazilian intellectuals had presented some of the same ideas earlier, but their works had been ignored. Freyre succeeded because his education abroad enabled him to buttress his claims with dozens of references to North American and European theorists almost unknown in Brazil; their prestige, as foreigners, finally put to rest the ghosts of Gobineau, Haeckel, and Le Bon. Secondly, Freyre exemplified his theories with masses of detailed information about every aspect of plantation life. Moreover, because he was convinced that sex was the primary vehicle of both physical and cultural change in Brazilian society, Freyre included a great deal of very racy anecdotal material, which helped to popularize his works and his ideas. All of these theories and details were presented superbly in complex and powerful prose.

The Masters and the Slaves and Freyre's many subsequent works—including some rather mediocre verse and two semi-autobiographical novels—have sometimes been utilized in ways he did not envision: to defend the continued existence of Portuguese colonialism in Africa, for example, or to insist that contemporary Brazil is a harmonious racial paradise entirely free of any sort of prejudice. It is also clear that Freyre sometimes contradicted himself, and that some of his judgements are the products of privilege and naivety—as in his belief that Africans were perfectly adapted for hard labour in the tropics because they, unlike Europeans, were able to sweat all over their bodies. One of Freyre's fundamental ideas, that slavery was generally far more humane in Brazil than elsewhere in the Americas, has been vigorously attacked by a number of Brazilian and foreign scholars.

None the less, there is no doubt that the popularization of Freyre's works has transformed the ways in which educated Brazilians think about their nation and about themselves—freeing them from a self-destructive conviction of racial and cultural inferiority and bringing about a psychological and intellectual liberation which has profoundly influenced contemporary Brazil.

—David T. Haberly

FRISCH, Max (Rudolf)

Born: Zurich, Switzerland, 15 May 1911. **Education:** Educated at the Kantonale Realgymnasium, Zurich, 1924–30; University of Zurich, 1930–33; Zurich Technische Hochschule (Institute of Technology), 1936–41, diploma in architecture 1941. **Military Service:** Served in the Swiss army, 1939–45. **Family:** Married 1) Gertrud Anna Constance von Meyenburg in 1942 (divorced 1959), two daughters and one son; 2) Marianne Oellers in 1968. **Career:** Freelance journalist from 1933; architect in Zurich, 1942–54; then full-time writer; visited Germany, France, and Italy, in 1946, Poland and Czechoslovakia in 1948, Spain in 1950; spent a year in the United States and Mexico, 1951–52; based in Rome, 1960–65. **Awards:** Raabe prize, 1954; Schleussner Schüller prize, for radio play, 1955; Büchner prize, 1958; Zurich prize, 1958; Veillon prize, 1958; Nordrhein-Westfalen prize, 1962; Jerusalem prize, 1965; Schiller prize (Baden-Württemberg), 1965; Schiller prize (Switzerland), 1974; German Book Trade Freedom prize, 1976; Commonwealth award, 1985; Neustadt International prize, 1986; Heine prize (Düsseldorf), 1989. Honorary doctorate: University of Marburg, 1962; Bard College, Annandale-on-Hudson, New York, 1980; City University of New York, 1982; University of Birmingham, West Midlands, 1985; University of Berlin, 1987. **Member:** Honorary Member, American Academy, 1974. **Died:** 4 April 1991.

PUBLICATIONS

Plays

Nun singen sie wieder: Versuch eines Requiems (produced 1945). 1946; as *Now They Sing Again*, translated by David Lommen, in *Contemporary German Theatre*, edited by Michael Roloff, 1972.
Santa Cruz (produced 1946). 1947.
Die chinesische Mauer (produced 1946). 1947; revised version, 1955; as *The Chinese Wall*, translated by James L. Rosenberg, 1961; as *The Great Wall of China*, translated by Michael Bullock, in *Four Plays*, 1969.
Als der Krieg zu Ende war (produced 1948). 1949; as *When the War Was Over*, translated by James L. Rosenberg, in *Three Plays*, 1967.
Graf Öderland (produced 1951). 1951; as *Count Oederland*, translated by Michael Bullock, in *Three Plays*, 1962.
Don Juan; oder, Die Liebe zur Geometrie (produced 1953). 1953; translated as *Don Juan; or, the Love of Geometry*, by James L. Rosenberg, in *Three Plays*, 1967; also translated by Michael Bullock, in *Four Plays*, 1969.
Rip van Winkle, from the story by Washington Irving (broadcast 1953). 1969.
Biedermann und die Brandstifter (broadcast 1953; produced 1958). 1958; as *The Fire Raisers*, translated by Michael Bullock, in *Three Plays*, 1962, revised edition, 1985; as *The Firebugs*, translated by Mordecai Gorelik, 1963.

Die grosse Wut des Philipp Hotz (produced 1958). 1958; as *The Great Rage of Philipp Hotz*, translated by James L. Rosenberg, in *Three Plays*, 1967; as *Philipp Hotz's Fury*, translated by Michael Bullock, in *Four Plays*, 1969.
Andorra (produced 1961). 1962; translated as *Andorra*, by Michael Bullock, in *Three Plays*, 1962; also translated by Geoffrey Skelton, 1964.
Stücke. 2 vols., 1962; enlarged edition, 1972.
Three Plays (includes *The Fire Raisers*; *Count Oederland*; *Andorra*), translated by Michael Bullock, 1962.
Zurich Transit (televised 1966). 1966.
Biografie (produced 1968). 1967; as *Biography: A Game*, translated by Michael Bullock, in *Four Plays*, 1969.
Three Plays (includes *Don Juan; or, the Love of Geometry*; *The Great Rage of Philipp Hotz*; *When the War Was Over*), translated by James L. Rosenberg. 1967.
Four Plays (includes *The Great Wall of China*; *Don Juan*; *or, the Love of Geometry*; *Philipp Hotz's Fury*; *Biography: A Game*), translated by Michael Bullock. 1969.
Triptychon: Drei szenische Bilder (produced 1979). 1978; revised edition, 1980; as *Triptych: Three Scenic Panels*, translated by Geoffrey Skelton, 1981.

Radio Plays: *Rip van Winkle*, 1953; *Biedermann und die Brandstifter*, 1953.

Television Plays: *Zurich Transit*, 1966.

Fiction

Jürg Reinhart: Eine sommerliche Schicksalsfahrt. 1934.
Antwort aus der Stille: Eine Erzählung aus den Bergen. 1937.
J'adore ce qui me brûte; oder, Die Schwierigen. 1943.
Bin; oder, Die Reise nach Peking. 1945.
Marion und die Marionotten: Ein Fragment. 1946.
Stiller. 1954; as *I'm Not Stiller*, translated by Michael Bullock, 1958.
Homo Faber. 1957; as *Homo Faber*, translated by Michael Bullock, 1959.
Mein Name sei Gantenbein. 1964; as *A Wilderness of Mirrors*, translated by Michael Bullock, 1965; as *Gantenbein*, 1982.
Wilhelm Tell für die Schule. 1971.
Montauk. 1975; as *Montauk*, translated by Geoffrey Skelton, 1976.
Der Mensch erscheint im Holozän. 1979; as *Man in the Holocene*, translated by Geoffrey Skelton, 1980.
Blaubart. 1982; as *Bluebeard*, translated by Geoffrey Skelton, 1983.

Other

Blätter aus dem Brotsack (diary). 1940.
Tagebuch mit Marion (diary). 1947; revised edition, as *Tagebuch 1946–1949*, 1950; as *Sketchbook 1946–1949*, translated by Geoffrey Skelton, 1977.
Achtung: Die Schweiz. 1955.
Die neue Stadt: Beiträge zur Diskussion. 1956.
Ausgewählte Prosa. 1961.
Öffentlichkeit als Partner. 1967.
Tagebuch 1966–1971. 1972; as *Sketchbook 1966–1971*, translated by Geoffrey Skelton, 1974.
Dienstbüchlein (memoir). 1974.
Stich-Worte (selection), edited by Uwe Johnson. 1975.

Gesammelte Werke, edited by Hans Mayer and Walter Schmitz. 12
    vols., 1976; same texts also published in 6 vols., 1976, with
    supplementary volume, 1987.
Kritik, Thesen, Analysen. 1977.
Erzählende Prosa 1939–1979. 1980.
Forderungen des Tages: Porträts, Skizzen, Reden, 1943–82, edited
    by Walter Schmitz. 1983.
Gesammelte Werke [Jubiläums Edition]. 7 vols., 1986.
Schweiz ohne Armee? Ein Palaver. 1989.
Schweiz als Heimat? Versuche über 50 Jahre, edited by Walter
    Obschlager. 1990.
Jetzt ist Sehenzeit: Briefe, Notate, Dokumente, 1943–1963. 1998.
Der Briefwechsel: Max Frisch, Uwe Johnson, 1964–1983, edited by
    Eberhard Fahlke. 1999.
Correspondence: Selections, edited by Carl Zuckmayer. 2000.

*

Critical Studies: *Max Frisch* by Ulrich Weisstein, 1967; *The Novels
of Max Frisch*, 1976, and *The Plays of Max Frisch*, 1985, both by
Michael Butler; *The Dramatic Works of Max Frisch* by Gertrud Bauer
Pickar, 1977; *Max Frisch: His Work and Its Swiss Background* by
Malcolm Pender, 1979; *Gombrowicz and Frisch: Aspects of the
Literary Diary* by Alex Kurczaba, 1980; *Perspectives on Max Frisch*
edited by Gerhard F. Probst and Jay F. Bodine, 1982; *Frisch: Andorra*
by Michael Butler, 1985; *Understanding Max Frisch* by Wulf Koepke,
1990; *Life as a Man: Contemporary Male-Female Relationships in
the Novels of Max Frisch* by Claus Reschke, 1990; *Frisch und
Dürrenmatt* by Hans Mayer, 1992; *Max Frisch Rollen-Spiele* by
Ulrich Ramer, 1993; *Mythos der Weiblichkeit im Werke Max Frischs*
by Liette Bohler, 1998; *Dass der Mensch allein nicht das Ganze ist!:
Versuche menschlicher Zweisamkeit im Werk Max Frischs* by Iris
Block, 1998; *Typologie des modernen Menschen im Schaffen von
Max Frisch* by Antoni Hodak, 1999.

* * *

Max Frisch has attained wide popularity both as a novelist and
dramatist. His central theme from his very earliest works is the
individual's longing to discover and realize his "true" self, but the
works themselves encompass a rich variety of emphases, moods, and
styles. The early novels such as *Jürg Reinhart* derive from the
German Bildungsroman tradition (novel of development), but in the
immediate post-war years Frisch began to experiment much more
with genre and form. *Bin; oder, Die Reise nach Peking*, for example,
is a whimsical, dream-like reflection on unfulfilled longing, while a
drama such as *Nun singen sie wieder* (*Now They Sing Again*) uses
harsh, almost surrealistic pictures to capture the conflict of self-
centredness and humanitarian feeling in war. Some dramas like *Santa
Cruz* or *Graf Öderland* (*Count Oederland*) are quasi-mythical presentations of the problem of marrying personal dream to social reality,
but though Brechtian in structure they ultimately lack Brecht's
intellectual clarity. Nevertheless, it is in this period that Frisch's
major *leitmotif* emerges, the concept of "image-making"—the imposition of arbitrary, labels, social, racial, psychological, upon our fellows.

In the late 1950s and 1960s Frisch began to produce the works
upon which his international reputation is really founded: *Biedermann
und die Brandstifter* (*The Fire Raisers*) and *Andorra*, for example,
have become stage classics. The former is a satirical attack upon

middle-class concern for the "right image," and not just in the usual
sense of keeping up appearances. Frisch shows his central characters'
exploitation of others on the one hand and attempts to retain a belief in
their own "decency" on the other. With sharp comic insight the play
illustrates the hypocritical bourgeois desire to exercise power and yet
still bask in a shared sense of common humanity, ranging from the
status-conscious superficiality of "hospitality" rituals and the emptiness of "polite" discourse to the profound and dangerous gullibility
that results from inability to confront self-contradiction. At this level
the play has multiple political associations—variously interpreted
over the years as referring to the threat of fascism or communism—
since it reveals how such social hypocrisy invites destruction without
unmasking its own falsity. Despite such serious overtones, however,
the text remains playful throughout, trapping the audience through
laughter into self-recognition. In the more immediately serious *Andorra*
Frisch probes the destructive effects of the image we create of others
as well as of ourselves—through fear, self-interest, convenience. The
mistaken assumption that the central figure is Jewish is used to reveal
both the selfish origins and the insidious growth of prejudice, and its
disastrous physical and spiritual effects on the victim. Though not
intended as a comment on the Holocaust—it is as much about
"otherness" as anti-semitism—this has often been the context in
which the play has been read, and thus misjudged. Its true power
derives from the very ordinariness of its figures and initial events, and
from the recognition—as in *The Fire Raisers*—that unthinking "normality," the petty weakness of everyday life, can lead to terrible
consequences. Both plays have a tellingly spare, episodic structure
again reminiscent of Brechtian distancing devices, but especially in
the case of *Andorra* there is also highly emotive visual symbolism
demanding something closer to the emotional involvement of traditional tragedy, yet without cathartic release. Indeed, it is the—
sometimes comic, sometimes tragic—inevitability of human weakness, rather than a Brechtian view of alterable social structures, that
shape the pointed stage effects in both texts.

Inventive formal structure is also the hallmark of *Stiller* (*I'm Not
Stiller*), perhaps Frisch's finest work. This novel combines sheer
entertainment in the constant mystery surrounding the main figure's
identity, with a probing investigation into Swiss national self-images
and into the deeper, personal meaning of "identity." Frisch quite
logically abandons omniscient narration and allows Stiller to reflect
his own complex self, a battleground between the images others
would impose, those implied by modern media or inherent in language itself, and those fashioned by the self even in moments of
apparent existential insight. The novel's wonderful intricacy and
"unfinished" narrative structure force the reader to confront his own
desire for completion, to reassess his own modes of judgment. And
the same is true of Frisch's subsequent novels. *Homo Faber* is an
attack upon the complacent belief that technology "explains" the
world. The engineer Walter Faber's neat image of a calculable,
controllable reality is shattered—at first by random, chance events,
but increasingly by previously excluded factors such as age, emotion,
and the incursion of his own unacknowledged past. His tortuous
account of tragic events, for which he cannot evade personal responsibility, embodies the breakdown of his simplistic reading of the world,
though the textual complexity with its Oedipal fate motifs is more
contrived than in *I'm Not Stiller*.

Frisch's last major novel *Mein Name sei Gantenbein* (*A Wilderness of Mirrors*) again explores the essential complexity of individual
personality, but in a delightfully comic interplay of multiple
"experimental" identities.

Frisch's concern with modern issues also extended to the political: in his diaries and various essays he confronts Swiss myths and attitudes directly. In his later works, however, he turned increasingly to the more individual concerns such as loneliness and ageing, though again with great variety, from sophisticated comedy in the drama *Biografie* (*Biography*), through painful confession in the diary-like *Montauk* to sombre reflection or scurrilous wit in the short tales *Der Mensch erscheint im Holozän* (*Man in the Holocene*) and *Blaubart* (*Bluebeard*). What is perhaps most characteristic of this late phase of his writing is a profounder scepticism than ever before about the possibility of escaping either from externally imposed images or from those created by age, gender, or selfish desire.

—Mary E. Stewart

See the essays on *Andorra*, *The Fire Raisers*, and *I'm Not Stiller*.

FROISSART, Jean

Born: Valenciennes, Hainault c. 1337. **Education:** Educated in Valenciennes. **Career:** Travelled to England in 1361; obtained protection of Queen Philippa. Accompanied the Black Prince to Bordeaux in 1366, and the Duke of Clarence to Milan, 1368. Returned to Valenciennes in 1369, following the death of Queen Philippa. Took religious orders and became priest of Lestines, c. 1370; secretary to Wenceslas of Luxembourg, 1381–83. Travelled in Flanders and France and revisited England 1394–95. **Died:** Date of death is unknown.

PUBLICATIONS

Collections

Oeuvres, edited by Kervyn de Lettenhove. 28 vols., 1867–1870.
Poésies, edited by A. Scheler. 3 vols., 1870–72.
The Chronicles of Jean Froissart in Lord Berners' Translation, edited by Gillian and William Anderson. 1963.
Ballades et rondeaux, edited by R.S. Baudouin. 1978.
Jean Froissart: An Anthology of Narrative and Lyric Poetry, edited and translated by Kristen M. Figg with R. Barton Palmer. 2001.

Verse

Chroniques. 1350s–c. 1400; edited by S. Luce, G. Raymond, A. Mirot and L. Mirot, 13 vols., 1869–1957; also edited and abridged by G.C. Macauley, 1895; W.P. Ker, 1901–03; C.E. Mills and H.B. Mills, 1929; Georges T. Diller, 1972 and 1991; M. de Medeiros, 1988; as *The Chronicles of England, France and Spain*, translated by Johan Bourchier, 2 vols., 1523–25; also translated by Thomas Johnes, 2 vols., 1848; John H. Joliffe, 1967; Geoffrey Brereton, 1968.
Trois récits de Froissart, edited by Marguerite Ninet. 1902.
Honour and Arms (selection), edited by Mary Macleod. 1910.
Histoires de Froissart, edited by H. Longnon. 1931.
Voyage en Béarn, edited by A.H. Diverres. 1953.
L'Espinette amoureuse, edited by Anthime Fourrier. 1963.
La Prison amoureuse, edited by Anthime Fourrier. 1974; as *The Prison of Love*, translated and edited by Laurence De Looze, 1994.
Le Joli buisson de jonece, edited by Anthime Fourrier. 1975.

The Lyric Poems of Jean Froissart, edited by Rob Roy McGregor, Jr. 1975.
"Dits" et "Débats," edited by Anthime Fourrier. 1979.
Dit du florin, edited by Anthime Fourrier. 1979.
Le Paradis d'amour, L'Orloge amoureus, edited by P.F. Dembowski. 1986.

Fiction

Méliador, edited by A. Longnon. 1895–99.

Other

Ci sensient un trettie de morelité à s'appelle le temple donneur. 1845.

*

Critical Studies: *Froissart: Chronicler and Poet* by F.S. Shears, 1930; "The Geography of Britain in Froissart's *Méliador*" by A.H. Diverres in *Medieval Miscellany Presented to E. Vinaver* edited by F. Whitehead, A.H. Diverres, and F.E. Sutcliffe, 1965; "Historians Reconsidered: Froissart" by C.T. Allmand in *History Today*, 16, 1966; *I, John Froissart* by Grant Uden, 1968; "The Concept of Advancement in the Fourteenth Century in the Chroniques of Jean Froissart" by K. McRobbie in *The Canadian Journal of History*, 6, 1971; *Le Vocabulaire psychologique dans les Chroniques de Froissart* by Jacqueline Picoche, 2 vols., 1976–84; *Froissart: Historian* edited by J.J.N. Palmer, 1981; *Jean Froissart and His "Méliador": Context, Craft and Sense* by Peter F. Dembowski, 1983; "Froissart, Chronicler of Chivalry" by K. Fowler in *History Today*, 36, 1986; "Froissart's *Chroniques*: Knightly Adventures and Warrior Forays" by G.T. Diller in *Fifteenth-Century Studies*, 12, 1987; *Jean Froissart and the Fabric of History: Truth, Myth and Fiction in the Chroniques* by Peter F. Ainsworth, 1990; *The Short Lyric Poems of Jean Froissart: Fixed Forms and the Expression of the Courtly Ideal* by Kristen Mossler Figg, 1994; *Pseudo-autobiography in the Fourteenth Century: Juan Ruiz, Guillaume de Machaut, Jean Froissart, and Geoffrey Chaucer* by Laurence de Looze, 1997; *Froissart Across the Genres*, edited by Donald Maddox and Sara Sturm-Maddox, 1998; *The Evolution of Arthurian Romance: The Verse Tradition from Chrétien to Froissart* by Beate Schmolke-Hasselmann, translated by Margaret and Roger Middleton, 1998.

* * *

Jean Froissart is recognized as being one of the most important and prolific authors writing in late medieval French. His passionate interest in aristocratic chivalry lent his work a truly international dimension: indeed, he can be viewed as a proto-European whose French was at that time the language of chivalry *par excellence*. Appointed at an early stage of his career to the household of Queen Philippa of England, he moved in august circles (his patrons included Gui de Châtillon, Wenceslas of Brabant and Albrecht of Bavaria). Although his earliest sympathies were fired by all he had learned of the impressive military triumphs of Edward III and the Black Prince, Froissart also had connections with the French and Scottish courts, and travelled extensively through England, Wales, Scotland, the Low Countries, France, and Italy. Affection for his patrons did not preclude avoidance of partiality (as he understood it). Where his work betrays bias, this is essentially chivalrous rather than "national." His avowed aim as a conscious artist was to write of arms and love, a task he fulfilled with panache, both in his verse and in his prose.

Froissart saw himself primarily as a poet: the two extant manuscripts contain his *ballades, virelais,* and *rondeaux* together with his *pastourelles* and longer narrative poems, show evidence of considerable versatility and wit, and of a constant preoccupation with the aesthetic arrangement of these works within their particular manuscripts. Heavily influenced by the diction and forms of *Le Roman de la rose* (*The Romance of the Rose*), Froissart also found inspiration for themes or situations in the works of his near-contemporary Guillaume de Machaut. A further important influence was the early 14th-century *Ovide moralisé* (from Ovid's *Metamorphoses*), though Froissart was not afraid to out-ovid Ovid: some of the "Ovidian" tales in his poems are pure inventions. The longer narrative *dits* owe much to the allegorical diction of Jean de Meung. Their occasional sententiousness is relieved by a lightness of touch encountered, for instance, in passages where Froissart writes obliquely about his craft as writer, via a first-person narrator whose complexities have been analysed recently (Bennett, 1991). These often engaging poems (*L'Espinette amoureuse* [Love's Hawthorn], *Le Joli buisson de jonece* [The Gallant Bush of Youth], or the *L'Orloge amoureus* [Love's Timepiece/The Clockwork of Gallantry]) display an appealingly wry irony directed towards the poet-narrator, through whose adventures Froissart explores the delights and vicissitudes of love and of literary creation. Jacqueline Cerquiglini has highlighted the metaphorical valency of the images Froissart uses to delineate the activities of poetic creation and "finishing": garlands, crowns, wreaths, and boxes. The *Poésies* also include shorter, semi-autobiographical pieces such as the "Débat du Cheval et du Levrier" in which the poet's horse and the greyhound, returning with their master from a Scottish journey, argue about who has the harsher lot in life; or the *Dit du florin*, which allows us to hear the irreverent observations of Froissart's last remaining florin concerning the fate of his erstwhile fellows in the hands of a spendthrift poet-chronicler possessed of an inordinate appetite for wine and parchment. The lighthearted prosopopoeia of these works affords the author a further opportunity to be ironic about his own preoccupations and obsessions, and to do so without a trace of pomposity.

Less accessible to modern readers is Froissart's self-consciously archaic Arthurian romance *Méliador*. Thirty-thousand lines of verse (by this time unusual for romance) relate a quest—for the hand of Hermondine, daughter of the king of Scotland. Peter Dembowski's monograph (1983) has established interesting parallels between the chivalry celebrated in *Méliador*, where knightly achievement is graded on an "Olympic" model ("gold, silver and bronze medallist. . .") and that delineated by the French knight Geoffrey de Charny in his *Demandes* and *Livre Charny*. The romance is also graced by a somnambulist named Camel de Camois, as by some highly-coloured Irish episodes and a journey to the Other World undertaken by the enigmatic Sagremor, episodes which one can compare with analogues in Froissart's greatest work *Chroniques* (*The Chronicles*).

Still widely read, *The Chronicles* were written to preserve the memory of what their author viewed as the Golden Age of Chivalry—and therefore to offer exemplary and inspirational material for young men aspiring to knighthood, however modest their background. Comprising four books, they cover the years 1325–99 in a prose deservedly famous for its graceful rhythms and stylistic vividness. Book I (first prose redaction c. 1355–78; Amiens MS: 1377–80; both possibly revised in part *post* 1392; final redaction, Rome MS: 1399–c. 1405) probably began as a rhymed history, but Froissart was prompted

by the prose *Chronicle* of Jean le Bel (composed 1352–61) to eschew verse for history-writing: Froissart's first prose redaction virtually reproduces le Bel's work (an affirmation of probity rather than "plagiarism"), but the later books testify to the chronicler's developing confidence. Book II (1379–85) offers a vivid, sometimes shrewd account of political and socio-economic affairs in the troubled Low Countries, together with what many British readers will quickly recognize as the chronicler's lively account of the Peasants' Revolt of 1381. Modern historians have rightly drawn attention to the pitfalls of this kind of narrative history, which rarely uses sources as we understand them. Yet *The Chronicles* are not devoid of critical perspective or judgement, despite their markedly aristocratic viewpoint. In any case, it is profitable to read them as commemorative, moral chronicles, while recognizing in them (particularly in Books III and IV) an increasing disparity between the writer's avowed aims and the result—reflected in a correspondingly greater tonal and formal variety. Book III (1390–91, revised *post* 1392) places the chronicler centerstage, as protagonist—offering us an enthralling narrative (travelogue, diary, memoir, chronicle. . .) which is essentially "about" being a writer, while Book IV (1392–c. 1400) contains episodes that stand on their own as virtual novellas. Of most interest to the modern reader, finally, are the different editorial recensions of Book I: for here we engage with the hesitations, doubts, and revisions of the author.

—Peter F. Ainsworth

FUENTES, Carlos

Born: Panama City, Panama, 11 November 1928. Lived in the United States (1934–40), Chile, and Argentina; moved to Mexico at age 16. **Education:** Educated at schools in New York, Mexico, and Chile; Colegio Frances Morelos, Mexico City, 1946–48, LL.B. 1948; graduate work in law at the National Autonomous University, Mexico City, 1950, and Institut des Hautes Études Internationales, Geneva, 1950–52. **Family:** Married 1) Rita Macedo in 1959 (divorced 1966), one daughter; 2) Sylvia Lemus in 1973, one son and one daughter. **Career:** Member, then secretary, Mexican delegation, International Labor Organization, Geneva, 1950–52; assistant chief of press section, Ministry of Foreign Affairs, Mexico City, 1954; press secretary, United Nations Information Center, Mexico City, 1954; co-founder and editor, *Revista Mexicana de Literatura*, 1954–58; secretary, then assistant director of Cultural Department, National Autonomous University, Mexico City, 1955–56; head of department of cultural relations, Ministry of Foreign Affairs, 1957–59; editor, *El Espectador*, 1959–61, *Siempre* and *Política* from 1960; lived in Europe during much of the 1960s; Mexican Ambassador to France, 1974–77. Fellow, Woodrow Wilson Center, Smithsonian Institute, Washington, DC, 1974; Virginia Gildersleeve visiting professor, Barnard College, New York, 1977; Norman Maccoll lecturer, 1977, and Simón Bolívar professor of Latin American studies, 1986–87, University of Cambridge; Henry L. Tinker lecturer, Columbia University, New York, 1978; professor of English, University of Pennsylvania, Philadelphia, 1978–83; fellow of humanities, Princeton University, New Jersey; professor of comparative literature, 1984–86, and Robert F. Kennedy professor of Latin American studies, since 1987, Harvard University, Cambridge, Massachusetts. President, Modern Humanities Research Association, since 1989. Lives in Mexico City and

London. **Awards:** Mexican Writers Center fellowship, 1956; Seix-Barral Biblioteca Breve prize, 1967; Xavier Villaurrutia prize, 1975; Rómulo Gallegos prize (Venezuela), 1977; Alfonso Reyes prize, 1979; Mexican National prize for literature, 1984; Cervantes prize, 1987; Rubén Darío prize, 1988; Instituto Italo-Latino Americano prize, 1988; New York City National Arts Club Medal of Honor, 1988; Order of Cultural Independence (Nicaragua), 1988; IUA prize, 1989; Prince of Asturias prize (Spain), 1994. D.Litt.: Wesleyan University, Middletown, Connecticut, 1982; University of Cambridge, 1987; D.Univ.: University of Essex, Colchester, England, 1987; LL.D.: Harvard University; other honorary doctorates: Columbia College, Chicago State University, Washington University (St. Louis). **Member:** El Colegio Nacional, since 1974; American Academy and Institute of Arts and Letters, 1986.

PUBLICATIONS

Collections

The Writings of Carlos Fuentes, edited by Raymond L. Williams, 1996.

Fiction

Los días enmascarados (stories). 1954.
La región más transparente. 1958; as *Where the Air Is Clear,* translated by Sam Hileman, 1960.
Las buenas conciencias. 1959; as *The Good Conscience,* translated by Sam Hileman, 1961.
La muerte de Artemio Cruz. 1962; as *The Death of Artemio Cruz,* translated by Sam Hileman, 1964; also translated by Alfred MacAdam, 1991.
Aura. 1962; as *Aura,* translated by Lysander Kemp, 1965.
Cantar de ciegos (stories). 1964.
Zona sagrada. 1967; as *Holy Places,* translated by Suzanne Jill Levine, in *Triple Cross,* 1972.
Cambio de piel. 1967; as *A Change of Skin,* translated by Sam Hileman, 1968.
Cumpleaños. 1969.
Chac Mool y otros cuentos. 1973.
Terra Nostra. 1975; as *Terra Nostra,* translated by Margaret Sayers Peden, 1976.
La cabeza de la hidra. 1978; as *The Hydra Head,* translated by Margaret Sayers Peden, 1978.
Una familia lejana. 1980; as *Distant Relations,* translated by Margaret Sayers Peden, 1982.
Agua quemada. 1981; as *Burnt Water,* translated by Margaret Sayers Peden, 1981; as *Agua quemada: Cuarteto narrativo,* edited with introduction and notes by Steven Boldy, 1995.
El gringo viejo. 1985; as *The Old Gringo,* translated by Margaret Sayers Peden, 1985.
Cristóbal nonato. 1987; as *Christopher Unborn,* translated by Fuentes and Alfred MacAdam, 1989.
Constancia, y otras novelas para vírgenes. 1989; as *Constancia and Other Stories for Virgins,* translated by Thomas Christensen, 1990.
La campaña. 1990; as *The Campaign,* translated by Alfred MacAdam, 1991.
The Orange Tree (stories). 1994.

Diana, o, La cazadora solitaria. 1994; as *Diana, the Goddess Who Hunts Alone,* translated by Alfred Mac Adam, 1995.
La frontera de cristal: Una novela en nueve cuentos. 1995; as *The Crystal Frontier: A Novel in Nine Stories,* translated by Alfred Mac Adam, 1997.
Años con Laura Díaz. 1999; as *The Years with Laura Díaz,* translated by Alfred Mac Adam, 2000.
Instinto de Inez. 2001.

Plays

Todos los gatos son pardos. 1970; revised edition, as *Ceremonias del alba,* 1991.
El tuerto es rey (produced in French, 1970). 1970.
Las reinos originarios (includes *Todos los gatos son pardos* and *El tuerto es rey*). 1971.
Orquídeas a la luz de la luna (produced in English, 1982). 1982; as *Orchids in the Moonlight,* translated by Fuentes, in *Drama Contemporary: Latin America,* edited by George W. Woodyard and Marion Peter Holt, 1986.

Screenplays: *Pedro Páramo,* 1966; *Tiempo de morir,* 1966; *Los caifanes,* 1967.

Television series: *The Buried Mirror* (on Christopher Columbus), 1991.

Verse

Poemas de amor: cuentos del alma. 1971.

Other

The Argument of Latin America: Words for North Americans. 1963.
Paris: La revolución de Mayo. 1968.
La nueva novela hispanoamericana. 1969.
El mundo de José Luis Cuevas. 1969.
Casa con dos puertas. 1970.
Tiempo mexicano. 1971.
Cuerpos y ofrendas. 1972.
Cervantes; o, La crítica de la lectura (Hackett memorial lectures). 1976; as *Don Quixote; or, The Critique of Reading,* translated anonymously, 1976.
Latin American Literature Today: A Symposium, with others, edited by Rose S. Minc. 1980.
High Noon in Latin America. 1983.
Juan Soriano y su obra, with Teresa del Conde. 1984.
On Human Rights: A Speech. 1984.
Latin America: At War with the Past. 1985.
Palacio Nacional, with Guillermo Tovar y de Teresa. 1986.
Gabriel García Márquez and the Invention of America (lecture). 1987.
Myself with Others: Selected Essays. 1988.
Valiente mundo nuevo (essays). 1990.
The Buried Mirror: Reflections on Spain and the New World. 1992.
Return to Mexico: Journeys behind the Mask. 1992.
Henri Cartier-Bresson: Mexican Notebooks, 1934–1964, translated by Michelle Beaver. 1995.
The Diary of Frida Kahlo: An Intimate Self-portrait, with introduction by Carlos Fuentes. 1995.
A New Time for Mexico. 1996.
El Espejo Enterrado. 2001.
Editor, *Los signos en rotación y otros ensayos,* by Octavio Paz. 1971.

*

Bibliography: "Carlos Fuentes: A Bibliography" by Sandra L. Dunn, in *Review of Contemporary Fiction*, 8, 1988; "Carlos Fuentes," in *Mexican Literature: A Bibliography of Secondary Sources* by David William Foster, 1992.

Critical Studies: *Carlos Fuentes y Las buenas conciencias* by Agustín Velarde, 1962; *Carlos Fuentes y la realidad de México* by Fidel Ortega Martínez, 1969; *The Mexican Novel Comes of Age* by Walter M. Langford, 1971; *Carlos Fuentes* by Daniel de Guzman, 1972; *Nostalgia del futuro en la obra de Carlos Fuentes* by Liliana Befumo Boschi and Elisa Cabrera, 1973; *Cambio de piel; or, The Myth of Literature* by Michael González, 1974; *La magia y las brujas en la obra de Carlos Fuentes* by Gloria Durán, 1976, translated as *The Archetypes of Carlos Fuentes: From Witch to Androgyne*, 1980; *Simposio Carlos Fuentes: Actas* (University of South Carolina), 1978; *Cinco novelas claves de la literatura hispanoamericana* by Antonio Sacoto, 1979; *Los disfraces: La obra mestiza de Carlos Fuentes* by G. Garcí Gutiérrez, 1981; *Carlos Fuentes: A Critical View* edited by Robert Brody and Charles Rossman, 1982; *Yáñez, Rulfo y Fuentes: El tema de la muerte en tres novelas mexicanas* by K.M. Taggart, 1982; *Carlos Fuentes* by Wendy B. Faris, 1983; *La narrativa de Carlos Fuentes* by Aida Elsa Ramírez Mattei, 1983; *El cuento mexicano contemporáneo: Rulfo, Arreola y Fuentes* by Bertie Acker, 1984; *Lo fantástico en los relatos de Carlos Fuentes* by G. Feijoo, 1985; *The Lost Rib: Female Characters in the Spanish-American Novel* by Sharon Magnarelli, 1985; *Carlos Fuentes: Life, Work, and Criticism* by Alfonso González, 1987; *El mito en la obra narrativa de Carlos Fuentes* by Francisco J. Ordiz, 1987; *La obra de Carlos Fuentes: Una visión múltiple* by Ann Maria Hernández de López, 1988; *Fabulación de la fe: Carlos Fuentes* by Fernando García Núñez, 1989; *Realidad y ficción en Terra nostra de Carlos Fuentes* by Ingrid Simson, 1989; *A Marxist Reading of Fuentes, Vargas Llosa and Puig* by Victor Manuel Durán, 1993; *Author, Text, and Reader in the Novels of Carlos Fuentes* by Kristine Ibsen, 1993; *The Postmodern Fuentes* by Chalene Helmuth, 1997; *Carlos Fuentes, Mexico and Modernity* by Maarten van Delden, 1998.

* * *

Carlos Fuentes for some years now has been one of the most imposing figures in Latin America. His fame extends beyond literary achievements, and certainly beyond his mother country Mexico (actually he was born in Panama where his father, who was in the diplomatic service, was stationed at the time). He belongs to the Latin American generation of great writers who are known as the authors of "the Boom." Along with Fuentes, other such luminaries as Gabriel García Márquez and Octavio Paz (both Nobel prize winners) have made the world aware of the great accomplishments of Latin American literature. In 1987 Fuentes was awarded Spain's most prestigious literary prize, "el premio Cervantes." He has received numerous other important prizes from many countries, including the Venezuelan Rómulo Gallegos national prize, equivalent to the Cervantes prize in Spain.

Fuentes has a rich and varied professional life. He is equally at home when speaking French, English, or Spanish, and in the subject areas of literature, history, politics, or journalism. He has been visiting professor in the United States at some of the most distinguished universities, and has received honorary degrees from many more. In matters of diplomatic positions, he has attained the highest cultural post available to any artist in a Latin American country, as his nation's Ambassador to France. In England and France he has been involved with the intellectual pursuits of the intelligentsia. Moreover, he has been quite active in meetings and conferences in underdeveloped countries. His passion, of course, has been his dedication to understanding, and expressing in literary form the essence of Mexican civilization, and by extension the substance of Latin American life and thought. His quest is inexorably linked to capturing the spiritual structure of those countries, Spain and the United States in particular, whose values are interwoven by patrimony as in the case of Spain, or by propinquity and political dominance as in the case of the United States, with the destiny of Latin America.

Fuentes distinguished himself as a writer of note with *La muerte de Artemio Cruz* (*The Death of Artemio Cruz*), later becoming a truly international figure as a man of letters. *The Death of Artemio Cruz*, which depicts the dying days of a former general of the Mexican Revolution, re-creates the history of Mexico from 1910, when the Revolution broke out. As the old moribund patriot of the struggle for freedom chronicles the idealistic quest for liberty and for an equitable distribution of land, he wonders, as did Don Quixote towards the end of his life, what, if anything, was accomplished. At the same time that Artemio Cruz reflects on the uselessness of the past, he comments on his surviving heirs to whom the impending death of an old man is essentially nothing but an annoying event that interferes with their immediate pursuit of personal happiness. Unbeknownst to the young, the dying patriot is able to listen in on the conversations around him. Yet there is no bitterness; *The Death of Artemio Cruz* smiles ironically on humanity. Disillusionment is conceived as but an inexorable experience of living. Idealism is as necessary as disenchantment is inevitable.

The 1985 novel *El gringo viejo* (*The Old Gringo*), which was subsequently made into a film starring Jane Fonda and Gregory Peck, projected the continuity of personal tyranny in Mexico. Revolutions and more revolutions fail to quench the thirst for power among the brave Mexican *machos*. Idealism, fuelled by adulation, makes despots or political bosses (*caciques*) of them all. Here we have the microcosm of the apparent neverending growth of *caciques* throughout Latin America. Principles and ideals give way to personal hegemony, and all members of society in one way or another participate in creating a form of government that befits the abiding faith that one man can inspire. The old gringo is a naive, innocent observer who cannot fully grasp the prevailing form of life in a Latin American country. Even when the gringo means well, he is basically lost in another culture.

Fuentes's writings are indeed varied and numerous. However, *The Buried Mirror: Reflections on Spain and the New World* stands out as a most ambitious project. It is a kind of celebration of what has become the polemical quincentenary observance of Christopher Columbus's arrival in the New World. *The Buried Mirror* is akin to a self-examining quest for truth and reality. In the highest humanistic tradition, with a sense of compassion for human imperfection, Fuentes feelingly re-creates history for all participants, victors and vanquished alike. Perhaps they are all mere victims of their own passions. In the long run, the distinction between them is blurred. New World countries as well as Spain have experienced—and survived—all sorts of leaders and seemingly untenable situations. While not "history" in the traditional sense, Fuentes's account affords us a living experience of the essence of the Hispanic and Hispanic American way of life.

—Robert Kirsner

G

GAO Xingjian

Born: Ganzhou, Jiangxi province, China, 4 January 1940; naturalized French citizen, 1997. **Education:** Early education at home due to poor health; attended Number Ten Middle School, Nanjing, 1951–57; majored in French at the Beijing Foreign Languages Institute, graduating in 1962. **Career:** Assigned to work as a translator of French, Foreign Languages Press, Beijing, 1962–79; during the Cultural Revolution worked for five years as a peasant, 1970–75; traveled to France as interpreter for a delegation of writers from the Chinese Writers' Association, 1979; re-assigned to work as a writer for the People's Arts Theatre, Beijing, and traveled to France and Italy as a member of the Chinese Writers' Association, 1980; came under attack for promoting the modernist literature of decadent Western capitalism with the publication of his *Xiandai xiaoshuo jiqiao chu tan* [Preliminary Discussion on the Art of Modern Fiction], 1982; his play *Chezhan* (*The Bus Stop*) was banned after a few performances, and publication of his writings were banned during the stamp out spiritual pollution campaign of that year, 1983; his play *Yeren* (*Wild Man*) was staged, 1985; in the same year traveled on a D.A.A.D fellowship to Germany and from there twice visited Paris; his play *Bi'an* (*The Other Shore*) was banned while being rehearsed, 1986; in 1987 invited to Germany by the Morat Institut für Kunst und Kunstwissenschaft, and from Germany relocated permanently to Paris where his prolific creative output successfully expanded in the three areas of drama, fiction and art. **Awards:** Chevalier d'Ordre des Arts et des Lettres, 1992; Nobel prize for literature, 2000; Premio Letterario Feronia, 2000; Chevalier de l'Ordre de la Légion d'honneur, 2000; American Academy of Achievement Golden Plate award, 2002.

PUBLICATIONS

Collections

Gao Xingjian xiju ji. 1985.
Gei wo laoye mai yugan. 1988.
Gao Xingjian xiju liuzhong. 7 vols., 1995.
Meiyou zhuyi. 1996.
The Other Shore: Plays by Gao Xingjian. 1999.
Gao Xingjian xiju ji. 10 vols., 2001.
Wenxue de liyou. 2001.
Gao Xingjian. 1999.

Plays

Juedui xinhao (produced 1982). 1982; as *Alarm Signal*, translated by Shiao-Ling S. Yu, in *Chinese Drama after the Cultural Revolution, 1979–1989*, edited by Shiao-Ling S. Yu, 1996.
Chezhan (produced 1983). 1983; as *The Bus Stop*, translated by Shiao-Ling S. Yu, in *Chinese Drama after the Cultural Revolution, 1979–1989*, edited by Shiao-Ling S. Yu, 1996; also as *Bus Stop*, translated by Kimberley Besio, in "Bus Stop: A Lyrical

Comedy on Life in One Act," *Theatre and Society: An Anthology of Contemporary Chinese Drama* edited by Haiping Yan, 1998.
Duo yu (produced 1987). 1984.
Yeren (produced 1985). 1985; as *Wild Man*, translated by Bruno Roubicek, in "Wild Man: A Contemporary Chinese Spoken Drama" 1990.
Bi'an (produced 1990). 1986; as *The Other Side*, translated by Jo Riley, in "The Other Side: A Contemporary Drama Without Acts," in *An Oxford Anthology of Contemporary Chinese Drama* edited by Martha P. Y. Cheung and Jane C. C. Lai, 1997; also as *The Other Shore* translated by Gilbert C. F. Fong, in *The Other Shore: Plays by Gao Xingjian*, 1999.
Sheng sheng man bianzhou (produced 1989). 1990.
Taowang (produced 1992). 1990; as *Fugitives*, translated by Gregory B. Lee, in *Chinese Writing and Exile*, edited by Gregory B. Lee, 1993; as *La Fuite* [*Fleeing*], translated by Michele Guyot, Editions Lansman, 1992.
Sheng si jie (produced 1993). 1991, and also as *Au bord de la vie* in 1993; as *Between Life and Death*, translated by Gilbert C. F. Fong, in *The Other Shore: Plays by Gao Xingjian*, 1999.
Duihua yu fanjie (produced 1992). 1993; as *Dialogue and Rebuttal*, translated by Gilbert C. F. Fong, in *The Other Shore: Plays by Gao Xingjian*, 1999.
Shanhaijing zhuan. 1993.
Le Somnambule (produced 1999). As *Yeyoushen* in 1995; as *Nocturnal Wanderer*, translated by Gilbert C. F. Fong, in *The Other Shore: Plays by Gao Xingjian*, 1999.
Zhoumo sichongzou. 1996; also as *Quatre quatuors pour un week-end*, 1998; as *Weekend Quartet*, translated by Gilbert Fong, in *The Other Shore: Plays by Gao Xingjian*, 1999.
Mingcheng (produced 1988). 1995.
Bayue xue (produced 2002). 2001.

Novels

Lingshan. 1990; as *Soul Mountain*, translated by Mabel Lee, 2000.
Yige ren de shengjing. 1999; as *One Man's Bible*, translated by Mabel Lee, 2002.

Selected Essays

"Xiandai jiqiao yu minzu jingshen." 1981; as "Contemporary Technique and National Character in Fiction," translated by Mau-sang Ng, *Renditions*, 19 & 20, 1983.
"Geren de shengyin." 1993; as "The Voice of the Individual," translated by Lena Aspfors and Torbjörn Lodén, *The Stockholm Journal of East Asian Studies*, 6, 1995.
"Meiyou zhuyi." 1993; as "Without Isms," translated by Winnie Lau, Deborah Sauviat, and Martin Williams, *The Journal of the Oriental Society of Australia*, 27 & 28, 1995–96.
"Wenxue de liyou," Nobel Lecture. 2000; as "The Case for Literature" translated by Mabel Lee, 2001.
"Wenxue de jianzheng: dui zhenshi de zuiqiu," Nobel Centenary Lecture. 2001; as "Literature as Testimony: the Search for Truth" translated by Mabel Lee, 2002.

Other

Xiandai xiaoshuo jiqiao chutan (non-fiction). 1981.
Dui yizhong xiandai xiju de zuiqiu (non-fiction). 1988.
Ink Paintings by Gao Xingjian. 1995.
Gout de l'encre (art). 1996.
Au plus près du réel: Dialogues sur l'écriture (1994–1997), co-authoed with Denis Bourgeois. 1997.
L'Encre et la lumiere (art). 1998.
Une Autre esthétique (art). 2000; also as *Ling yizhong meixue*, 2001; and *Return to Painting*, 2002.

*

Critical Studies: "Personal Freedom in Twentieth Century China: Reclaiming the Self in Yang Lian's *Yi* and Gao Xingjian's *Lingshan*," in *History, Literature and Society: Essays in Honour of S. N. Mukherjee*, edited by Mabel Lee and Michael Wilding, 1997, "Walking Out of Other People's Prisons: Liu Zaifu and Gao Xingjian on Chinese Literature in the 1990s," in *Asian & African Studies*, vol. 5, no. 1, 1996, "Without Politics: Gao Xingjian on Literary Creation," in *The Stockholm Journal of East Asian Studies*, vol. 6, 1995, all by Mabel Lee; "Searching for Alternative Aesthetics in the Chinese Theatre: The Odyssey of Huang Zuolin and Gao Xingjian" by Quah Sy Ren, in *Asian Culture*, vol. 24, 2000; *Towards a Modern Zen Theatre: Gao Xingjian and Chinese Theatre Experimentalism* by Henry Y. H. Zhao, 2000; *Lun Gao Xingjian zhuangtai* by Liu Zaifu, 2000; *Soul of Chaos: Critical perspectives on Gao Xingjian* edited by Kwok-Kan Tam, 2001; "Gao Xingjian: The Playwright As an Intellectual" by Quah Sy Ren, in *Nantah Journal of Chinese Language and Culture*, vol. 5.1, 2002; *Gao Xingjian: An Alternative Transcultural Response to Chinese Theatre* by Quah Sy Ren, 2003.

* * *

Proclaimed Nobel laureate for literature in 2000, Gao Xingjian was the first writer to be awarded the prize for a body of writings in the Chinese language. His win caused a controversy as experts who had read at most only one or two of his early works, if any, came forward to criticize the award. The controversy was fanned by political or personal motives and clearly had nothing to do with Gao's achievements in literature. Gao had become a French citizen in 1997, his plays were being performed internationally, and a substantial part of his major works had also been published in French, Swedish, and English translation.

Gao Xingjian rose to prominence in the Chinese literary world immediately following the end of the Cultural Revolution (1966–76). At the height of the Cultural Revolution he had burnt twenty years of unpublished manuscripts (plays, essays, poems, short stories and a novella) rather than face the consequence of having them discovered. The first of his many short stories and essays on European writers began to appear in literary publications in 1980. When, in 1982, several veteran writers applauded his *Xiandai xiaoshuo jiqiao chutan* [*Preliminary Discussion on the Art of Modern Fiction*], the book was banned for promoting the "decadent modernism" of Western literature. In the same year, staged at the People's Art Theatre to packed houses, his play *Juedui xinhao* (*Alarm Signal*) caused great excitement in the literary world, but, in the following year, when his play *Chezhan* (*The Bus Stop*) was staged, again to packed houses, it

created a sensation. *Bus Stop* portrays a group of people waiting for a bus that never comes and of the passage of years in futile waiting; its ambiguity and Absurdist approach represented a clear departure from the official guidelines for literature, and it was closed by the authorities after a few performances. Gao was targeted for criticism during the campaign to stamp out "spiritual pollution" and a ban placed on the publication of his writings. The ban lasted for over a year, after which he continued to publish short stories, plays, as well as his translations of Jacques Prévert's *Paroles*, in 1984, and Eugène Ionesco's *La Cantatrice chauve*, in 1985. His play *Yeren* (*Wild Man*) was staged in 1985, but in the following year *Bi'an* (*The Other Shore*) was banned while it was being rehearsed.

In late 1987 he traveled to Germany as a guest of the Morat Institut für Kunst und Kunstwissenschaft and, while there, applied for a French visa. Gao was acutely aware of a physiological need to write, but, in China, even when he exercised self-censorship, his works were criticized. By the end of the 1987 he had relocated to Paris and began to support himself by selling his Chinese ink paintings. He soon found publishers in Taipei and Hong Kong for his prolific writings and, to begin with, though translations in French and Swedish, new stages for his play productions.

Following the brutal military crackdown on student protesters in Beijing on 4 June, 1989, Gao Xingjian was commissioned to write a play "about China" by an American theatre company. When his play *Taowang* [*Fleeing*] was submitted in English translation, he was asked to make revisions. He paid for the translation and withdrew the manuscript. *Fleeing* was published in early 1990 and premiered in Stockholm in Swedish. In "Guanyu *Taowang*" [About *Fleeing*], Gao states that the Chinese Communist Party could not get him to change what he had written, and an American theatre company certainly would not. He was aware that the play had displeased members of the Chinese democracy movement because it was critical of the naivete of the student movement, and did not portray the students as heroes. However, he had written the play not to denounce only this particular massacre and had stated in the stage instructions: "This is not a socialist-realist play." While as an individual he had denounced the military crackdown in the French and Italian media, he was adamantly opposed to "tying literature to the war chariot of a particular camp." As a writer he saw literary truth as his only criterion, truth as he perceived it and not truth as dictated by others, no matter how noble the cause. In his subsequent writings he coined the terms "cold literature" and "no -isms" to define the sort of literature to which he was committed.

—Mabel Lee

GARCÍA LORCA, Federico

Born: Fuente Vaqueros, near Granada, Spain, 5 June 1898. **Education:** Educated at Colegio del Sagrado Corazón de Jesús, Granada; also studied piano at Granada conservatory; University of Granada, 1914–19; travelled in Spain, 1915–17; Residencia de Estudiantes, Madrid, 1919–29; Columbia University, New York, 1929–30. **Career:** Editor of artistic review, *El Gallo*, 1928; travelled to Paris, London, New York, and Havana (Cuba), 1929–30; founder and director of itinerant government-sponsored student theatre group, La Barraca, in the 1930s (grant withdrawn 1935); visited Buenos Aires

(Argentina) in 1933. Arrested and shot by Franco supporters immediately following the outbreak of the Spanish Civil War. **Died:** (executed) 18/19 August 1936.

PUBLICATIONS

Collections

Obras completas, edited by Guillermo de Torre. 7 vols., 1938–42.

Obras completas, edited by Arturo del Hoyo. 1954; revised editions, 2 vols., 1973; 3 vols., 1986; edited and translated by J.L. Gili, 1960.

Collected Plays (includes the texts of *Three Tragedies*, 1947, and *Five Plays*, 1963), translated by James Graham-Luján and Richard L. O'Connell. 1976.

Obras, edited by Miguel García-Posada. 6 vols., 1980.

Plays, translated by Gwynne Edwards and Peter Luke. 3 vols., 1987–91.

Collected Poems, edited by Christopher Maurer. 1991.

Four Major Plays, translated by John Edmunds. 1997.

A Season in Granada: Uncollected Poems & Prose, edited and translated by Christopher Maurer. 1998.

In Search of Duende, translated by Christopher Maurer and Norman di Giovanni. 1998.

Lorca/Blackburn: Poems of Federico García Lorca, edited and translated by Paul Blackburn, 2000.

Plays

El maleficio de la mariposa (produced 1920). In *Obras completas*, 1954; as *The Butterfly's Evil Spell*, translated by James Graham-Luján and Richard L. O'Connell, in *Five Plays*, 1963.

Mariana Pineda (produced 1927). 1928; as *Mariana Pineda*, translated by James Graham-Luján, in *Tulane Drama Review*, 7(2), 1962; also translated by Robert G. Havard, 1987; Gwynne Edwards, with *The Public* and *Play Without a Title*, 1991.

Quimera. In *El Gallo*, May 1928; in book form, in *Teatro breve*, 1954.

El paseo de Buster Keaton (produced 1986). In *El Gallo*, May 1928; in book form, in *Teatro breve*, 1954; as *Buster Keaton's Promenade*, translated by Tim Reynolds, in *Accent*, 17(3), 1957.

La doncella, el marinero y el estudiante (produced 1986). In *El Gallo*, May 1928; in book form, in *Teatro breve*, 1954.

La zapatera prodigiosa (produced 1930; revised version produced 1933). In *Obras completas*, 1938; edited by J. and F. Street, 1962; as *The Shoemaker's Prodigious Wife*, translated by James Graham-Luján and Richard L. O'Connell, in *From Lorca's Theatre*, 1941, and in *Five Plays*, 1963; as *The Shoemaker's Wonderful Wife*, translated by Gwynne Edwards, in *Plays 2*, 1990.

El amor de Don Perlimplín con Belisa en su jardín (produced 1933). In *Obras completas*, 1938; as *The Love of Don Perlimplín*, translated by James Graham-Luján and Richard L. O'Connell, in *From Lorca's Theatre*, 1941, and in *Five Plays*, 1963; as *The Love of Don Perlimplín for Belisa in the Garden*, translated by David Johnston, 1990.

Bodas de sangre (produced 1933). 1935; edited by H. Ramsden, 1980; as *Blood Wedding*, translated by Gilbert Murray, 1939; also translated by James Graham-Luján and Richard L. O'Connell, in *Three Tragedies*, 1947; Sue Bradbury, in *Three Tragedies*, 1977;

Michael Dewell and Carmen Zapata, in *The Rural Trilogy*, 1987; Gwynne Edwards, in *Three Plays*, 1988; David Johnston, 1989; Brendan Kennelly, 1996; Ted Hughes, 1996.

La dama boba, from a play by Lope de Vega (produced 1934).

Yerma (produced 1934). 1937; as *Yerma*, in *From Lorca's Theatre*, translated by James Graham-Luján and Richard L. O'Connell, 1941, and in *Three Tragedies*, 1947; also translated by Sue Bradbury, in *Three Tragedies*, 1977; Ian MacPherson and Jacqueline Minett, 1987; Michael Dewell and Carmen Zapata, in *The Rural Trilogy*, 1987; Peter Luke, in *Three Plays*, 1988; David Johnston, 1990; edited with introduction and notes by Robin Warner, 1995.

Doña Rosita la soltera (produced 1935). In *Obras completas*, 1938; as *Doña Rosita the Spinster*, translated by James Graham-Luján and Richard L. O'Connell, in *From Lorca's Theatre*, 1941, and in *Five Plays*, 1963; translated by Gwynne Edwards and Peter Luke, in *Three Plays*, 1988.

El "retablillo" de Don Cristóbal (produced 1935). In *Obras completas*, 1938; as *The Tragicomedy of Don Cristóbal and Doña Rosita*, translated by Will I. Oliver, in *New World Writing*, 8, 1955; as *The Puppet Play of Don Cristóbal*, translated by Gwynne Edwards, in *Plays*, 2, 1990.

Los títeres de Cachiporra (produced 1937). 1949; as *The Billy-Club Puppets*, translated by James Graham-Luján and Richard L. O'Connell, in *Five Plays*, 1963.

Así que pasen cinco años (produced in English 1945; produced in Spanish 1978). In *Obras completas*, 1938; as *If Five Years Pass*, translated by James Graham-Luján and Richard L. O'Connell, in *From Lorca's Theatre*, 1941; as *When Five Years Pass*, translated by Gwynne Edwards, in *Plays*, 2, 1990; as *Once Five Years Pass*, translated by W.B. Logan and A.G. Orrios, in *Once Five Years Pass, and Other Dramatic Works*, 1990.

From Lorca's Theatre: Five Plays (includes *If Five Years Pass; Yerma; The Love of Don Perlimplín; Doña Rosita the Spinster; The Shoemaker's Prodigious Wife*), translated by James Graham-Luján and Richard L. O'Connell. 1941.

La casa de Bernarda Alba (produced 1945). 1945; edited by H. Ramsden, 1984; as *The House of Bernarda Alba*, translated by James Graham-Luján and Richard L. O'Connell, in *Three Tragedies*, 1947; also translated by Sue Bradbury, in *Three Tragedies*, 1977; Michael Dewell and Carmen Zapata, in *The Rural Trilogy*, 1987.

Three Tragedies (includes *Blood Wedding; The House of Bernarda Alba; Yerma*), edited and translated by James Graham-Luján and Richard L. O'Connell. 1947.

Playlets (includes *Buster Keaton's Promenade; Chimera; The Virgin, the Sailor and the Student*), translated by Tim Reynolds, in *Accent*, 17(3), 1957.

Five Plays: Comedies and Tragedies (includes *The Butterfly's Evil Spell; The Billy-Club Puppets; The Shoemaker's Prodigious Wife; The Love of Don Perlimplín; Doña Rosita the Spinster*), translated by James Graham-Luján and Richard L. O'Connell. 1963.

El público (produced in English 1972; produced in Spanish 1986). With *Comedia sin título*, 1978; as *The Public*, translated by Carlos Bauer, 1983; also translated by Gwynne Edwards, 1991.

Three Tragedies (includes *Blood Wedding; Yerma; Bernarda Alba*), translated by Sue Bradbury. 1977.

El público y Comedia sin título: Dos obras teatrales póstumas, edited by Rafael Martínez Nadal. 1978; as *The Public, and Play Without a Title: Two Posthumous Plays*, translated by Carlos Bauer, 1983; as *The Public and Play Without a Title*, translated by Gwynne Edwards, with *Mariana Pineda*, 1991.

Comedia sin título (produced 1989). With *El público*, 1978; as *Play Without a Title*, translated by Carlos Bauer, 1983; also translated by Gwynne Edwards, 1991.

The Rural Trilogy (includes *Blood Wedding; Yerma; The House of Bernarda Alba*), translated by Michael Dewell and Carmen Zapata. 1987; as *Three Plays*, 1992.

Three Plays (includes *Blood Wedding; Doña Rosita the Spinster; Yerma*), translated by Gwynne Edwards and Peter Luke. 1988; as *Plays 1*, 1991.

Once Five Years Pass, and Other Dramatic Works, translated by W.B. Logan and A.G. Orrios. 1990.

Screenplays: *Trip to the Moon*, translated by Bernice C. Duncan, in *New Directions*, 18, 1964.

Verse

Libro de poemas. 1921; reprinted 1974.

Canciones. 1927; as *Canciones*, edited by Daniel Eisenberg, translated by Philip Cummings, 1976.

Primer romancero gitano. 1928; edited by H. Ramsden, 1988, and by Derek Harris, 1991; as *Gypsy Ballads*, translated by Rolfe Humphries, 1953; also translated by Michael Hartnett, 1973; Carl W. Cobb, 1983; Robert G. Havard, 1990.

Poema del cante jondo. 1931; as *Poem of the Deep Song*, translated by Christopher Bauer, 1987.

Oda a Walt Whitman. 1933.

Llanto por la muerte de Ignacio Sánchez Mejías. 1935.

Primeras canciones. 1936.

Seis poemas galegos. 1936.

Lament for the Death of a Bullfighter and Other Poems, translated by A.L. Lloyd. 1937.

Poems, translated by Stephen Spender and J.L. Gili. 1939.

Diván del Tamarit. 1940; as *Divan*, translated by Edwin Honig, in *Divan and Other Writings*, 1974.

Poeta en Nueva York. 1940; edited by Christopher Maurer, translated by Greg Simon and Steven White, 1989; as *Poet in New York*, translated by Rolfe Humphries, 1940; also translated by Ben Belitt, 1955.

Selected Poems, translated by Lloyd Mallan. 1941.

Selected Poems, translated by J.L. Gili and Stephen Spender. 1947.

Poemas sueltos. 1954.

Cantares populares. 1954.

Selected Poems, translated by Francisco García Lorca and Donald M. Allen. 1955.

Selected Poems, translated by J.L. Gili (prose). 1960.

Lorca and Jiménez, translated by Robert Bly. 1973.

Divan and Other Writings, translated by Edwin Honig. 1974.

Canciones y poemas para niños. As *The Cricket Sings: Poems and Songs for Children*, translated by Will Kirkland, 1980.

Suites (selected poetry), edited by André Belamich. 1983; translated by Jerome Rothenberg, 2001.

Canciones y primeras canciones, edited by Piero Menarini. 1986.

Diván del Tamarit; Seis poemas galegos; Llanto por Ignacio Sánchez Mejías; Poemas sueltos, edited by Andrew A. Anderson. 1988.

Ode to Walt Whitman and Other Poems, translated by Carlos Bauer. 1988.

The Towers of Cordova: Selected Poems, translated by Merryn Williams. 1990.

Songs and Ballads, translated by R. Skelton. 1992.

Other

Impresiones y paisajes. 1918; as *Impressions and Landscapes*, translated by L.H. Klibbe, 1987.

Homenaje al Poeta Federico García Lorca (selection and commentary), edited by Antonio Machado and Emilio Prados. 1937.

Cartas a sus amigos, edited by S. Gasch. 1950.

Cartas; postales; poemas y dibujos, edited by A. Gallego Morell. 1968.

Granada, Paraíso Cerrado y otras páginas granadinas, edited by Enrique Martínez López. 1971.

Autográfos, edited by Rafael Martínez Nadal. 1975–76.

Deep Song and Other Prose, edited by Christopher Maurer. 1980.

Selected Letters, edited and translated by David Gershator. 1983.

Oda y burla de Sesostris y Sardanápalo, edited by Miguel García-Posada. 1985.

Diván del Tamarit y otros textos, edited by Aída O'Ward and Carlos Arredondo. 1988.

Four Puppet Plays, Play Without a Title, the Divan Poems, and Other Prose Poems and Dramatic Pieces, translated by Edwin Honig. 1990.

Poeta en Nueva York y otras hojas y poemas: Manuscritos neoyorquinos, edited by Mario Fernández. 1990.

Barbarous Nights: Legends and Plays, translated by C.S. Laucanno. 1991.

The Unknown Lorca: Dialogues, Dramatic Projects, Unfinished Plays and a Filmscript, edited and translated by John London. 1996.

A Life of Lorca: Drawings, Photographs, Words, compiled and edited by Andrew Dempsey, 1997.

Editor, *El Gallo: Revista de Granada*, in 1928.

*

Bibliography: *García Lorca: A Selectively Annotated Bibliography of Criticism*, 1980, and *García Lorca: An Annotated Primary Bibliography*, 1982, both edited by Francesca Colecchia; *Federico García Lorca: A Bibliography* by Everett E. Larson, 1987.

Critical Studies: *Federico García Lorca* by Edwin Honig, 1944; *Lorca: The Poet and His People* by Arturo Barea, 1945; *Federico García Lorca* by John A. Crow, 1945; *Lorca: An Appreciation of His Poetry* by Roy Campbell, 1952; *Lorca and the Spanish Poetic Tradition* by J.B. Trend, 1955; *Lorca: A Collection of Critical Essays* edited by Manuel Durán, 1962 and *Lorca's Legacy* edited by Durán and Francesca Colecchia, 1991; *The Theatre of García Lorca* by Robert Lima, 1963; *The Victorious Expression: A Study of Four Contemporary Spanish Poets: Miguel de Unamuno, Antonio Machado, Juan Ramón Jiménez, Federico García Lorca* by Howard T. Young, 1964; *García Lorca* by Rafael Alberti, 1966; *Federico García Lorca* by Carl W. Cobb, 1967; *Federico García Lorca* by Rolf Michaelis, 1969; *The Symbolic World of García Lorca*, 1972, and *Psyche and Symbol in the Theatre of Federico García Lorca*, 1974, both by

Rupert Allen; *The Death of Lorca*, 1973, revised edition, as *The Assassination of Federico García Lorca*, 1979, and *Federico García Lorca: A Life*, 1989, both by Ian Gibson; *Lorca's The Public* by Rafael Martínez Nadal, 1974; *A Concordance to the Plays and Poems of Federico García Lorca*, 1975; *La Barraca and the Spanish National Theatre* by Suzanne W. Byrd, 1975; *The Comic Spirit of Federico García Lorca* by Virginia Higginbotham, 1976; *García Lorca, Playwright and Poet* by Mildred Adams, 1977; *Lorca's Poet in New York: The Fall Into Consciousness* by Betty Jean Craige, 1977; *Federico García Lorca and Sean O'Casey: Powerful Voices in the Wilderness* by Katie Brittain Adams Davis, 1978; *García Lorca: Poeta en Nueva York* by Derek Harris, 1978; *Federico García Lorca: The Poetry of Limits* by David K. Loughran, 1978; *García Lorca's Poema del Cante Jondo* by Norman C. Miller, 1978; *The Tragic Myth: Lorca and Cante Jondo* by Edward F. Stanton, 1978; *Lorca: The Theatre Beneath the Sands*, 1980, and *Dramatists in Perspective: Spanish Theatre in the Twentieth Century*, 1985, both by Gwynne Edwards; *Lorca's New York Poetry: Social Injustice, Dark Love, Lost Faith* by Richard Predmore, 1980; *García Lorca: Bodas de Sangre*, 1981, and *García Lorca: La Casa de Bernarda Alba*, 1990, both by Cyril Brian Morris, and *"Cuando yo me Muera. . . ": Essays in Memory of Federico García Lorca*, 1988 edited by Morris; *Lorca's Impresiones y Paisajes: The Young Artist* by Laurence Hadfield Klibbe, 1983; *Federico García Lorca* by Reed Anderson, 1984; *Federico García Lorca* by Felicia Hardison Londres, 1984; *Lorca: The Gay Imagination* by Paul Binding, 1985; *Federico García Lorca: Life, Work and Criticism* by C. Grant McCurdy, 1986; *In the Green Morning: Memories of Federico* by Francisco García Lorca, translated by Christopher Maurer, 1986; *Lorca, the Drawings: Their Relation to the Poet's Life and Work* by Helen Oppenheimer, 1986; *Lorca's Romancero Gitano: Eighteen Commentaries* by H. Ramsden, 1988; *Leeds Papers on Lorca and on Civil War Verse* edited by Margaret A. Rees, 1988; *Lorca's Late Poetry: A Critical Study*, 1990, and *García Lorca: La Zapatera Prodigiosa*, 1991, both by Andrew A. Anderson; *Line of Light and Shadow: The Drawings of Federico García Lorca* by Mario Hernandez, 1991; *File on Lorca* edited by Andy Piasecki, 1991; *Lorca: Poet and Playwright—Essays in Honour of J.M. Aguirre* edited by Robert G. Havard, 1992; *Souls in Anguish: Religion and Spirituality in Lorca's Theatre* by Ronald Cueto, 1994; *Lorca's Drawings and Poems: Forming the Eye of the Beholder* by Cecelia J. Cavanaugh, 1995; *Understanding Federico García Lorca* by Candelas Newton, 1995; *Audience and Authority in the Modernist Theater of Federico García Lorca* by C. Christopher Soufas, 1996; *Son of Andalusia: The Lyrical Landscapes of Federico García Lorca* by C. Brian Morris, 1997; *Federico García Lorca* by Jonathan Buckley, 1998; *Lorca: A Dream of Life* by Leslie Stainton, 1998; *The Theatre of García Lorca: Text, Performance, Psychoanalysis* by Paul Julian Smith, 1998; *The Trickster-function in the Theatre of García Lorca* by Sarah Wright, 2000; *Lorca, Buñuel, Dalí: Art and Theory*, edited by Manuel Delgado Morales and Alice J. Proust, 2001.

* * *

Federico García Lorca has come to be one of the most widely read and admired authors who have written in Spanish in the 20th century. His execution by fascists at the outbreak of the Spanish Civil War abruptly brought his name into world focus, but since then his work as a poet and playwright has endured the test of political notoriety and has continued to prosper on the strength of its intrinsic worth.

Leonardo, the protagonist of *Bodas de sangre* (*Blood Wedding*), one of Lorca's most famous plays, defends adulterous love in these terms: "The fault is not mine / The fault belongs to the earth." A case could readily be made to substantiate the point of view that all of Lorca's protagonists, including the poet-narrator himself, struggle in the grip of telluric passions. Smugglers, gypsies, suppressed women, and ultimately the poet have but one goal: to exult, by means of startling metaphors fashioned against the backdrop of Andalusia, their pain and grief at the indifference of society and the silence of death. In a celebrated lecture, Lorca pointed to the Andalusian *duende* (goblin) as the embodiment of dark and dangerous feelings. In Lorca's canon, the greatest crime is to stifle the expression of these emotions and the greatest fear is the total tranquillity of death.

By emphasizing the demonic inspiration of his verse, Lorca placed himself in the tradition of those who believe in the Platonic seizure, or in Housman's shivers down the spine. A master of details of form, he nevertheless insisted that the totality of the poem was something over which he had no control. "If it is true" he once said, "that I am a poet through the grace of God (or the devil), I have also got where I am by virtue of work and technical skill, without having the slightest notion of what a poem is."

Constantly requested to read his poetry aloud (which he did with great effect), Lorca had all the appearances of a latter-day bard. His strong sense of the oral tradition led him at times to display indifference toward the printed word. Many poems circulated among friends, or survived in the intimacy of small public readings before they became fixed between the covers of books.

Childhood memories of playing in meadows with crumpled purple mountains in the distance, such is Lorca's own characterization of his first book of verse *Libro de poemas* [Book of Poems]. Graceful combinations of humour, irony, and whimsy bestow a tone notably lacking in most of his subsequent poetry. A strong sense of mystery and magic pervade this Andalusian pastoral.

In *Poema del cante jondo* (*Poem of the Deep Song*), Lorca sought to capture in verse the impact of the heady, monotonous, and pathetic chant that had been introduced into Spain from oriental sources. He personifies the *cante*, turns it into a baleful, dark-haired woman, attributes cosmic powers to it (the shout of the singer causes olive groves to tremble and even silence quivers), and finally makes it an expression of elemental grief. By now, the characteristics of Lorca's modernism have become clear: using an acute sense of local culture (Andalusia), he will express in bold metaphorical terms the loneliness, grief, and frustration of the human predicament.

The *Primer romancero gitano* (*Gypsy Ballads*) raises the plight of the persecuted gypsies of Spain to the level of poetry by inventing a mythology for them. In doing so, Lorca went back beyond the Greek and Roman myths and intuited a primitive mythology in which there is a close relationship between man and cosmic reality. The moon opens the book by stealing away a gypsy boy, and under her influence, the fortunes of the gypsies wax and wane. The wind attempts to rape a gypsy girl, and all of nature reacts in sympathy to her plight. By skilfully employing the eight-syllable line and the strong dramatic dialogue form of the old Spanish *romance* (ballad), Lorca demonstrates once again his ability to meld traditional elements into his modern outlook. The bedazzling, sometimes disturbing metaphors of this popular book have still not worn thin.

Seeking to step aside from the success accorded him in Madrid, Lorca went to New York in the summer of 1929. His sensitivities, developed in an agrarian and conservative European region, were overwhelmed by the vast concreteness of New York, its technological power, and the festering racial prejudice. *Poeta en Nueva York* (*Poet in New York*), making use of a modified form of surrealism, is a description of the collapse of his personal world and the painful process of picking up the pieces again. In terms of its denunciation of modern civilization, it is often compared to T.S. Eliot's *The Waste Land*. Lorca's outraged feeling of social justice and his sympathy for the underdog come through loud and clear. The section on Harlem, with its forecast of violence between blacks and whites, has turned out to be remarkably prescient. The death of a bullfighter friend inspired *Llanto por la muerte de Ignacio Sánchez Mejías* (*Lament for the Death of a Bullfighter*), considered by many critics to be one of the most impressive of modern elegies.

Aside from the playfulness and sense of humour sporadically present in the early verse, the register of Lorca's poetic voice is intense, dark, and sombre. Passionate descriptions rather than philosophical reflections mark his work. Once again, his regional background plays a role, for the *andaluz*, he once remarked, is either asleep in the dust or shouting at the stars.

Lorca's plays have been performed around the world. *Blood Wedding, Yerma*, and *La casa de Bernarda Alba* (*The House of Bernarda Alba*), dealing with sexual frustration, are his best known works for the theatre, but there is a strong interest in an experimental play, *El público* (*The Public*) (finished in 1930 but not produced in Spain until 1987) that, well before Genet, deals with homosexuality on the stage. In the so-called rural trilogy, the violent punishment of adultery, the tortures of sterility imposed by environment as well as nature, and the oppressiveness of a matriarchal family are handled powerfully. The first two make extensive use of poetry and have earned Lorca a reputation among modern dramatists for his ability to incorporate lyrics in his plays.

—Howard T. Young

See the essays on *Blood Wedding, The House of Bernarda Alba*, and *Yerma*.

GARCÍA MÁRQUEZ, Gabriel

Born: Aracataca, Colombia, 6 March 1928. **Education:** Educated at the Jesuit Colegio San José, Barranquilla, 1940–42; Jesuit Colegio Nacional, Zipaquirá, to 1946; studied law and journalism at the National University of Colombia, Bogotá, 1947–48: studies interrupted by civil strife, and continued at University of Cartagena, 1948–49. **Family:** Married Mercedes Barcha in 1958; two sons. **Career:** Contributor of stories to *El Espectador*, 1947–52; journalist, *El Universal*, Cartegena, 1948–50; correspondent, *El Heraldo*, Barranquilla, 1950–54; journalist, 1954–55, and Paris correspondent, 1955, *El Espectador*: paper closed by government, 1955; lived in Europe, 1955–57; travelled through Eastern Europe, 1957; journalist in Caracas, 1958–59; joined Prensa Latina (Cuban press agency),

1959: opened its office in Bogotá, then worked in Havana, 1959, and New York until his resignation in 1961; lived in Mexico, 1961–67, working as journalist (editor, *Sucesos* and *La Familia*), advertising agent, and scriptwriter; lived in Spain, 1967–75; founder, left-wing *Alternativa*, Bogotá, 1974; returned to Mexico, 1975, and to Colombia in 1981; founder, *El Otro*, Bogotá, 1963; member, Panamanian delegation for the United States-Panama treaty, Washington, DC, 1978; member, UNESCO commission on Third World Communications Problems, 1979; founder, 1979, and president, from 1979, Fundación Habeas; director, Foundation for New Latin American Cinema, Havana, 1986–88. Lives in Colombia. **Awards:** Colombian Association of Writers and Artists award, 1954; National Short Story Competition prize, 1955; Esso literary prize, 1961; Chianchiano prize (Italy), 1968; Foreign Book prize (France), 1970; Rómulo Gallegos prize (Venezuela), 1972; Neustadt international prize, 1972; Nobel prize for literature, 1982; Los Angeles *Times* prize, 1988. Honorary doctorate: Columbia University, New York, 1971. Légion d'honneur, 1981. **Member:** American Academy.

PUBLICATIONS

Fiction

La hojarasca. 1955; as *Leaf Storm*, in *Leaf Storm and Other Stories*, translated by Gregory Rabassa, 1972.

El coronel no tiene quien le escriba. 1957; as *No One Writes to the Colonel*, translated by J.S. Bernstein, in *No One Writes to the Colonel and Other Stories*, 1968.

La mala hora. 1962; as *In Evil Hour*, translated by Gregory Rabassa, 1979.

Los funerales de la Mamá Grande (stories). 1962; as *Big Mama's Funeral*, translated by J.S. Bernstein, in *No One Writes to the Colonel and Other Stories*, 1968.

Isabel viendo llover en Macondo. 1967.

Cien años de soledad. 1967; as *One Hundred Years of Solitude*, translated by Gregory Rabassa, 1970.

Relato de un náufrago. 1970; as *The Story of a Shipwrecked Sailor*, translated by Randolph Hogan, 1989.

Leaf Storm and Other Stories, translated by Gregory Rabassa. 1972.

La increíble y triste historia de la cándida Eréndira y de su abuela desalmada: Siete cuentos. 1972; as *Innocent Erendira and Other Stories*, translated by Gregory Rabassa, 1978.

El negro que hizo esperar a los ángeles. 1972.

Ojos de perro azul: Nueve cuentos desconocidos. 1972.

Cuatro cuentos. 1974.

Todos los cuentos 1947–1972. 1975; as *Collected Stories*, translated by Gregory Rabassa, 1984, revised edition, 1991.

El otoño del patriarca. 1975; as *The Autumn of the Patriarch*, translated by Gregory Rabassa, 1976.

El último viaje del buque fantasma. 1976.

Crónica de una muerte anunciada. 1981; as *Chronicle of a Death Foretold*, translated by Gregory Rabassa, 1982.

El amor en los tiempos del cólera. 1985; as *Love in the Time of Cholera*, translated by Edith Grossman, 1988.

El general en su laberinto. 1989; as *The General in His Labyrinth*, translated by Edith Grossman, 1990.

Collected Novellas, translated by Gregory Rabassa and J.S. Bernstein. 1990.

Three Novellas (includes *Leaf Storm; No One Writes to the Colonel; Chronicle of a Death Foretold*), translated by Gregory Rabassa and J.S. Bernstein. 1991.

Doce cuentos peregrinos. 1992; as *Strange Pilgrims: Twelve Stories*, translated by Edith Grossman, 1993.

Del amor y otros demonios. 1994; as *Of Love and Other Demons*, translated by Edith Grossman, 1995.

Plays

Viva Sandino. 1982; as *El asalto: u; operativo con que el FSLN se lanzó al mundo*, 1983.

El rastro de tu sangre en la nieve; El verano de la Señora Forbes (screenplays). 1982.

Diatribe of Love Against a Seated Man (produced 1988).

Screenplays: *El secuestro*, 1982; *María de mi corazón*, with J.H. Hermosillo, 1983; *Eréndira*, from his own novella, 1983.

Other

La novela en América Latina: diálogo, with Mario Vargas Llosa. 1968.

Cuando era feliz e indocumentado. 1973.

De viaje por los países socialistas: 90 días en la Cortina de hierro. 1978.

Crónicas y reportajes. 1978.

Periodismo militante. 1978.

La batalla de Nicaragua, with Gregorio Selser and Daniel Waksman Schinca. 1979.

García Márquez habla de García Márquez. 1979.

Obra periodística, (includes vol. 1: *Textos costeños*; vols. 2–3: *Entre cachacos*; vol. 4: *De Europa y América (1955–1960)*), edited by Jacques Gilard. 4 vols, 1981–83.

El olor de la guayaba, with Plinio Apuleyo Mendoza. 1982; as *The Fragrance of Guava*, translated by Ann Wright, 1983.

La soledad de América Latina; Brindis por la poesía. 1983.

Persecución y muerte de minorías, with Guillermo Nolasco-Juárez. 1984.

La aventura de Miguel Littín, clandestino en Chile: Un reportaje. 1986; as *Clandestine in Chile: The Adventures of Miguel Littín*, translated by Asa Zatz, 1987.

El cataclismo de Damocles/The Doom of Damocles (bilingual edition). 1986.

Dialogo sobre la novela latinoamericana, with Mario Vargas Llosa. 1988.

Noticia de un secuestro. 1996; as *News of a Kidnapping*, translated by Edith Grossman. 1997.

*

Bibliography: *Gabriel García Márquez: An Annotated Bibliography 1947–1979* by Margaret Eustella Fau, 1980; *A Bibliographical Guide to Gabriel García Márquez 1979–1985* by Margaret Eustella Fau and Nelly Sfeir de González, 1986.

Critical Studies: *García Márquez; o, El olvidado arte de contar* by R. Gullon, 1970; *Sobre García Márquez* edited by P.S. Martínez, 1971; *García Márquez: Historia de un deicidio* by Mario Vargas Llosa, 1971; *Homenaje a Gabriel García Márquez* edited by Helmy F. Giacoman, 1972; *Cien años de soledad: Una interpretación* by J. Ludmer, 1972; *Gabriel García Márquez*, 1977, and *Gabriel García Márquez: Life, Work, and Criticism*, 1987, both by George R. McMurray; *Gabriel García Márquez: El escritor y la crítica* by P.G. Earle, 1981; *Melquiades, Alchemy and Narrative Theory: The Quest for Gold in Cien años de soledad* by C.S. Halka, 1981; *Gabriel García Márquez: Revolutions in Wonderland*, 1981, and *One Hundred Years of Solitude: Modes of Reading*, 1991, both by Regina Janes; *The Evolution of Myth in García Márquez from La hojarasca to Cien años de soledad* by Robert Lewis Sims, 1981; *La soledad de Gabriel García Márquez: Una conversación infinita* by M. Braso Fernandez, 1982; *García Márquez: La soledad y la gloria: Su vida y su obra* by O. Collazos, 1983; *Gabriel García Márquez: El coronel no tiene quien le escriba* (in English) by J.B.H. Box, 1984; *Essays on Gabriel García Márquez* edited by K. Oyarzum and W.W. Megenny, 1984; *Gabriel García Márquez* by Raymond L. Williams, 1984; *En el punto de mira: Gabriel García Márquez* edited by A.M. López, 1985; *Interpretaciones a la obra de García Márquez* (anthology), 1986; *Critical Perspectives on Gabriel García Márquez* edited by B.A. Shaw and N. Vera-Godwin, 1986; *Gabriel García Márquez and Latin America* edited by Alok Bhalla, 1987; *Gabriel García Márquez and the Invention of America* by Carlos Fuentes, 1987; *Gabriel García Márquez: New Readings* edited by Bernard McGuirk and Richard Cardwell, 1987; *Critical Essays on Gabriel García Márquez* edited by George R. McMurray, 1987; *Gabriel García Márquez, Writer of Colombia* by Stephen Minta, 1987; *Guía para la lectura de Cien años de soledad* by M.E. Montaner Ferrer, 1987; *García Márquez: Edificación de un arte nacional y popular* by E. Rama, 1987; *Gabriel García Márquez and the Powers of Fiction* edited by Julio Ortega and C. Elliott, 1988; *Gabriel García Márquez* edited by Harold Bloom, 1989; *Understanding Gabriel García Márquez* by Kathleen McNerney, 1989; *Como leer a García Márquez: Una interpretacion sociologica* by J.L. Mendez, 1989; *Gabriel García Márquez: The Man and His Work* by Gene H. Bell-Villada, 1990; *Gabriel García Márquez: One Hundred Years of Solitude* by Michael Wood, 1990; *Gabriel García Márquez: A Study of the Short Fiction* by Harley D. Oberhelman, 1991; *Gabriel García Márquez: Solitude and Solidarity* by Michael Bell, 1993; *Home as Creation: The Influence of Early Childhood Experience in the Literary Creation of Gabriel García Márquez, Agustín Yáxez, and Juan Rulfo* by Wilma E. Detjens, 1993; *Painting Literature: Dostoevsky, Kafka, Pirandello, and Gabriel García Márquez, in Living Color* by Constance A. Pedoto, 1993; *Circularity and Visions of the New World in William Faulkner, Gabriel García Márquez and Osman Lins* by Rosa Sims, 1993; *García Márquez: Crónica de una muerte anunciada* by Stephen M. Hart, 1994; *Intertextuality in García Márquez* by Arnold M. Penuel, 1994; *Rescuing History: Faulkner, García Márquez, and Morrison as Postcolonial Writers of the Americas* by Barbara J. Wilcots, 1995; *García Márquez*, edited and introduced by Robin Fiddian, 1995; *Gabriel Garcí Márquez: A Critical Companion* by Ruben Pelayo, 2001.

*   *   *

Novelist, storyteller, polemical journalist, recipient of the Nobel prize for literature, the Colombian Gabriel García Márquez has been among the most influential of 20th-century Latin American writers. Appearing at the crest of ''the Boom'' in Latin American literature in the 1960s, his novel, *Cien años de soledad* (*One Hundred Years of Solitude*), made ''magic realism'' a common critical term, and the novel still generates imitators from Chile to London, Bombay to Massachusetts. Definitively postmodern in its self-referentiality, its foregrounding of the act of writing, and its temporal warps, the book is also firmly grounded in the Colombian-Venezuelan regionalist tradition, a wider Latin American tradition of fantastic literature, and in the typically American project of national self-definition in the face of an imperial past and present cultural diversity.

Simultaneously an account of a nation, a town, a family, a house, and a book, the novel tells an episodic and realistic story of development and decline, remarkable for the sheer quantity of storytelling it accommodates. Instead of a single plot line taking a few characters through hundreds of pages, a seemingly inexhaustible invention produces story after story through some six generations. Always precisely individuated, episodes and characters parallel and contrast with each other, creating constantly shifting, intricate patterns within a lucid, accessible narrative. If the novel's fecundity violates expectations, so do its events.

Brought back are episodes conventionally excluded by the rationalist criteria which, developing in the 17th and 18th centuries along with the novel, had separated the novel from the romance. The effect is to interrogate the reader's sense of possibility, to put into question what constitutes reality. Creating a town, Macondo, where it seems almost anything can happen, García Márquez's new epic narrator reintegrates events for long ruled out as too bizarre because they do not happen at all (virgins rising into the heavens holding onto the family sheets, or men returning from the dead), because they are no longer believed to happen (priests who levitate or magicians who return from the dead), or because although they may happen, they fail to fit into dominant rationalist categories (Aristotle's possible improbabilities, such as a rain of dead birds or a plague of butterflies).

Effecting a radical defamiliarization, García Márquez also makes appear wonderful events or objects that modernity takes for granted and that no longer seem strange (the original sense of ''magic realism'' in art criticism), such as the television or a block of ice. Nor are the inventions ever entirely arbitrary: the most immediately accessible ones create patterns of cultural history, economic development, or political conflict, which are usually satirical, but occasionally pathetic or sentimental. Many create powerful symbols, readily transferrable to other contexts, such as a plague of insomnia inducing forgetfulness of words and their referents. Creating an alternative to the conventions of social or psychological realism and modernist fragmentation, the novel represents a world on the cultural margin without condescending to it as primitive, mythologizing it as nobly mysterious, or pitying it as deprived. As fiction, it is clearly a much livelier, more stimulating, more historically and politically conscious work than most of the American and European fiction of its period.

From his earliest short stories, García Márquez has manifested his impatience with ''meat-and-potatoes'' realism. The earliest fictions evoke dreams, doubles, and ghosts, altered states of consciousness, ''real'' hallucinations, in stories that omit, or barely allude to, their most crucial concern. Under the helpfully foreign influence of Faulkner and Hemingway, he turned to more realistic representations and subjects, to social history and politics: the history of a family and

town in the Faulknerian monologues of *La hojarasca* (*Leaf Storm*), or of a town and *La violencia* (the major Colombian political conflict of the mid-20th century) in the intercut episodic structure of *La mala hora* (*In Evil Hour*), and in the spare short stories of *Los funerales de la Mamá Grande* (*Big Mama's Funeral*). In some of the stories of that volume, and in the short novel *El coronel no tiene quien le escriba* (*No One Writes to the Colonel*), García Márquez discovered the power of humour and ironic juxtaposition to both relieve and intensify the oppressive political atmosphere he communicates. Through *One Hundred Years of Solitude*, *El otoño del patriarca* (*The Autumn of the Patriarch*), *La increíble y triste historia de la cándida Eréndira. . .* (*Innocent Erendira*), and some short stories, García Márquez deployed the fantastic or impossible element often taken to characterize his fiction, and then abandoned it.

This abandonment is characteristic of García Márquez. In addition to the inventiveness and originality of his fictional fabling, he is a master craftsman, intent on locating unique shapes or structures for each fiction. While certain stylistic features remain constant (and have become perhaps too habitual for the writer himself: the winds of disillusion waft too frequently), he works very hard *not* to give his readers what many of them may want: a hundred *One Hundred Years of Solitude*s. Each work develops a distinct structural principle. *One Hundred Years of Solitude* depends on the making of a book through the destruction of the town, family, and house that are the subjects of the book; *The Autumn of the Patriarch* on the swirl of voices and constant resurrections that constitute the power of dictators and their eternal, invasive presence; *Crónica de una muerte anunciada* (*Chronicle of a Death Foretold*) on the predictive shape of classical Greek tragedy; *El amor en los tiempos del cólera* (*Love in the Time of Cholera*) on an impossible openness established by the refusal to close off the fiction; *El general en su laberinto* (*The General in His Labyrinth*) on a journey to an ending that attempts to start again but cannot. As Phil West has observed, myths always provide a second chance; history never does. Suggesting an ambiguous relationship with history and fiction, García Márquez's fictions characteristically provide second chances in the body of the fiction, but deny them at the end, as the fiction moves into the reader's history.

Often humorous, at times bitterly ironic or grotesque, occasionally tinged with pathos, García Márquez's work possesses a rare power of invention. Deficient in the psychological and linguistic density characteristic of some modern writers, García Márquez at his best achieves continuous surprise in the elaboration of a rococo, tessellated prose surface that makes the reader aware of the simultaneous insistence and insufficiency of interpretation.

—Regina Janes

See the essays on *Love in the Time of Cholera* and *One Hundred Years of Solitude*.

GAUTIER, (Pierre-Jules) Théophile

Born: Tarbes, France, 30 August 1811. **Education:** Educated at Lycée Louis-le-Grand and Lyée Charlemagne, both Paris; studied art in Paris. **Family:** One son, by Eugénie Fort, and two daughters, by Ernesta Grisi. **Career:** Member of the circle of French Romantic writers including Gérard de Nerval, *q.v.*, and Pétrus Borel; journalist, 1831–36; contributed to *Chronique de Paris*, from 1835; art and drama critic, *La Presse*, 1836–55 and *Le Moniteur universel*, from 1845; also contributed to *Revue de Paris, Le Figaro, Ariel, Le Cabinet de lecture*, and *La France littéraire*; travelled to Spain to advise on art collecting, 1840. **Died:** 23 October 1872.

PUBLICATIONS

Collections

Poésies complètes. 1845; edited by René Jasinski. 3 vols., 1858; 2 vols., 1932; revised edition, 1970.
Oeuvres. 2 vols., 1890.
Oeuvres. 1893.
Oeuvres érotiques. 1953.
Nouvelles, edited by Claudine Lacoste. 1979.
Récits fantastiques, edited by Jean-Jacques Eideldinger. 1981.

Fiction

Les Jeunes-France: Romans goguenards. 1833.
Mademoiselle de Maupin. 2 vols., 1835; revised edition, 1845; edited by Adolphe Boschot, 1966; as *Mademoiselle de Maupin*, translated anonymously, 1836; as *A Romance of the Impossible*, translated by Paul Hookham, 1912; also translated by Burton Rascoe, 1922; R. and E. Powys Mathers, 1938; Paul Seiver, 1948; Joanna Richardson, 1981.
L'Eldorado. 1837.
Nouvelles. 1845; as *Stories*, translated by Lafcadio Hearn, 1908.
Militona. 1847.
Les Roués innocents. 1847.
Les Deux Étoiles. 2 vols., 1848.
La Peau de tigre. 3 vols., 1852.
Un trio de romans (includes *Militona; Jean et Jeannette; Arria Marcella*). 1852.
Avatar. 1856.
La Croix de Berny. 1857.
Jettatura. 1857; edited by V.J.T. Spiers, 1891.
Le Roman de la momie. 1858; as *The Romance of a Mummy*, translated by M. Young, 1886; as *The Mummy's Romance*, translated by G.F. Monkshood, 1908.
Le Capitaine Fracasse. 2 vols., 1863; edited by G.F. Monkshood, 1910; as *Captain Fracasse*, translated by E.M. Beam, 1898.
Romans et contes. 1863.
La Belle-Jenny. 1866; as *Partie carrée*, 1889.
Spirite. 1866; edited by Reginald and Douglas Menville, 1890, Adolphe Boschot, 1961, and by Marc Eigeldinger, 1970; translated by Patrick Jenkins, 1995.
Mademoiselle Daphné. 1881; revised edition, 1984.
One of Cleopatra's Nights and Other Fantastic Romances, translated by Lafcadio Hearn. 1886.
Une Nuit de Cléopâtre. 1894.
Le Pavillon sur l'eau, edited by W.G. Hartog. 1902.
The Romances. 10 vols., 1903.

The Beautiful Vampire—La Morte Amoureuse, translated by Paul Hookham. 1926.
Triple Mirror, translated by Mervyn Savill. 1951.
The Bridge of Asses, translated by Albert Meltzer. 1953.
Skin-Deep, translated by Mervyn Savill. 1955.
Short Stories, translated by George Burnham Ives. 1970.
My Fantoms, translated by David Farris. 1976.
Three Supernatural Tales, edited by Robert Navon, translated by George Burnham Ives. 1989.

Verse

Poésies. 1830; edited and translated by Harry Cockerham, 1985.
Albertus; ou, L'Âme et le péché. 1832.
La Comédie de la mort. 1838.
Poésies complètes. 1845.
España. 1845; edited by René Jasinski, 1929.
Émaux et Camées. 1852; 3rd edition (includes "L'Art"), 1858.
Premières poésies 1830–1845. 1870.
Obscenia: Lettre à la Présidente. Poésies érotiques. 1907.
Gentle Enchanter, translated by Brian Hill. 1960.

Plays

Une larme du diable. 1839.
Giselle (ballet scenario; produced 1841). 1841; as *Giselle; or, The Wilis*, translated by Violette Verdy, 1970.
La Péri (ballet scenario; produced 1843). 1843.
Un voyage en Espagne. 1843.
La Juive de Constantine. 1846.
Le Selam. 1850.
Pâquerette (ballet scenario; produced 1851). 1851.
Gemma (ballet scenario; produced 1854). 1854.
Théâtre de poche. 1855.
Sakountala (ballet scenario; produced 1858). 1858.
Théâtre (includes *Une larme du diable; Le Tricorne enchanté; La Fausse Conversion; Le Pierrot posthume; L'Amour souffle où il veut; Giselle; La Péri; Gemma; Sakountala*). 1872.

Other

Tra los montes. 2 vols., 1843; as *Voyage en Espagne*, 1843; as *The Romantic in Spain*, translated by Catherine A. Phillips, 1926.
Les Grotesques. 2 vols., 1844.
Les Beautés de l'opéra, with Jules Janin and Philarète Chasles. 1845.
Zigzags. 1845.
Les Fêtes de Madrid. 1847.
Salon de 1847. 1847.
Lettre à la Présidente. 1850.
Oeuvres humoristiques. 1851.
Caprices et zigzags. 1852.
Italia. 1852.
Celle-ci et celle-là. 1853.
Constantinople. 1853; as *Constantinople of Today*, translated by Robert Howe Gould, 1854.
Les Beaux-Arts en Europe. 2 vols., 1855–56.
L'Art moderne. 1856.
De la mode. 1858.

Histoire de l'art dramatique en France depuis vingt-cinq ans. 6 vols., 1858–59; translated in part as *The Romantic Ballet*, by Cyril W. Beaumont, 1932.

Honoré de Balzac. 1858; revised edition, 1859.

Les Peintres vivants. 1858.

Abécédaire du Salon de 1861. 1861.

Les Dieux et les demi-dieux de la peinture, with A. Houssaye and P. de Saint-Victor. 1864.

Loin de Paris. 1865.

Quand on voyage. 1865.

Voyage en Russie. 2 vols., 1865; as *Russia, by Théophile Gautier and Other French Travellers of Note*, translated by Florence MacIntyre, 1970.

Les Progrès de la poésie française depuis 1830. 1868.

Ménagerie intime. 1869; as *A Domestic Menagerie*, translated by Mrs. W. Chance, 1899.

La Nature chez elle. 1870.

Tableaux de siège, Paris, 1870–1871. 1871.

Henri Regnault. 1872.

Histoire du romantisme. 1872.

Portraits contemporains, 1874.

Portraits et souvenirs littéraires. 1875.

Voyage en Italie. 1876; as *Journeys in Italy*, translated by D.B. Vermilye, 1903.

L'Orient (essays). 2 vols., 1877.

Fusains et eaux-fortes. 1880.

Guide de l'amateur au musée du Louvre. 1882.

Souvenirs de théâtre, d'art et de critique. 1883.

Omphale: histoire rococo. 1896.

La Musique (reviews). 1911.

Les Plus Belles Lettres de Théophile Gautier, edited by Pierre Descaves. 1962.

Correspondance générale, edited by Claudine Lacoste-Veysseyre. 1985.

Gautier on Dance (reviews), edited and translated by Ivor Guest. 1986.

*

Critical Studies: *Théophile Gautier, souvenirs intimes* by Ernest Feydeau, 1874; *Histoire des oeuvres de Théophile Gautier* by Charles Spoelberch de Lovenjoul, 1887; *The Dramatic Criticism of Théophile Gautier* by Helen Patch, 1922; *The Creative Imagination of Théophile Gautier* by Louise Dillingham, 1927; *Gautier and the Romantics* by John Palache, 1927; *Théophile Gautier: His Life and Times* by Joanna Richardson, 1958; *Les Ballets de Théophile Gautier* by Edwin Binney, 1965; *Ideal and Reality in the Fictional Narratives of Théophile Gautier* by Albert B. Smith, 1969; *The Art Criticism of Théophile Gautier* by Michael Clifford Spencer, 1969; *Théophile Gautier, auteur dramatique* by C. Book-Seninger, 1972; *Théophile Gautier* by Serge Fauchereau, 1972; *Théophile Gautier* (in English) by Richard B. Grant, 1975; *Théophile Gautier* by Philip E. Tennant, 1975; Gautier issue of *Europe*, May 1979; *Études et recherches sur Théophile Gautier, prosateur* by Jean Richer, 1981; *Théophile Gautier: A Romantic Critic of the Visual Arts* by Robert Snell, 1982; *Le Regard de Narcisse: Romans et nouvelles de Théophile Gautier* by Marie-Claude Schapira, 1984; *La Critique d'art de Théophile Gautier* by Claudine Lacoste-Vesseyre, 1985; *Rève de Pierre: La Quète de la femme chez Théophile Gautier* by Natalie David-Weill, 1989; *Three Nineteenth-century French Writer/Artists and the Maghreb: The*

Literary and Artistic Depictions of North Africa by Théophile Gautier, Eugène Fromentin, and Pierre Loti by Elwood Hartman, 1994.

*   *   *

Poet, writer of novellas and short stories, novelist, critic, journalist, and author of inimitably vivid travel books, Théophile Gautier stands out among French writers of his generation.

Being, as he himself told the Goncourt brothers, a "man for whom the visible world exists," he became an art student at the age of 19. He soon realized, however, that he was lacking in technical perfection and turned to literature, bringing to his new medium not only a painterly love of form and colour but also an imagination deeply imbued with impressions of the visual arts. His career as an art student had brought him into contact with the young Romantic fraternity of painters and writers and he was later to write a history of the Romantic movement, not published until after his death.

Seldom highly creative but always a flawless craftsman, Gautier supplied a much needed corrective to the Romantics' diffuse style. In his preface to *Premières poésies* [First Poems] he displayed an indifference towards politics, society, and even nature, that was uncharacteristic of the French Romantic movement. A work closer to that movement, in theme if not in technique, is the lengthy narrative poem *Albertus*, jaunty in style and showing obvious traces of Byronic influence, which describes how a young painter falls into a sorceress's hands. Gautier continued his flight from Romanticism in *Les Jeunes-France*, mocking both himself and his youthful fellow artists for their callow extravagances of thought, dress, and behaviour.

Turning aside from Romanticism, Gautier reverted to the theme already foreshadowed in his preface to *Albertus*, advocating the doctrine of "art for art's sake" in the celebrated—indeed almost notorious—preface to *Mademoiselle de Maupin* (*A Romance of the Impossible*). Here he pours scorn upon the hypocrisies of contemporary society, rejects conventional notions of morality, and emphasizes the cult of beauty. In the novel itself the eponymous heroine, dressed as a man, engages in numerous exploits and is loved by a woman but also by d'Albert, whose mistress she finally becomes. *A Romance of the Impossible* implicitly condemns the formless sentimentalizing which, in Gautier's judgment, was the unworthy ideal of so many of his contemporaries.

Giving further expression to his Romantic leanings, *La Comédie de la mort* [Comedy of Death] treats the theme of *memento mori* which had perhaps been suggested to Gautier by his growing interest in Spanish engraving and painting. His critical work *Les Grotesques* extolled the personal and literary merits of French poets of the earlier part of the 17th century such as Théophile de Viau, Saint-Amant, and Scarron, who, not only in their writings but also in their individualism, seemed to him to foreshadow the Romantic outlook.

Gautier's travels in Greece confirmed his conviction that the literary artist should seek only Classical purity of form, without the need to impart any moral lesson. In *Émaux et Camées* [Enamels and Cameos] he emerged as the leading proponent, and practitioner, of "art for art's sake" and thus as the inspiration of the Parnassian school. Composed (with the notable exception of "L'Art") in octosyllabic quatrains and with many *rimes riches*, rhyming in the manner of the English or German ballad, these short poems avoid the 12-syllable alexandrine favoured by the (French) Romantics. They teem with images of plastic beauty, burning with a hard gem-like quality that perfectly conveys their underlying theme that life is short whereas art is eternal. But "Symphonie en blanc majeur," "Affinités secrètes,'' ''Clair de lune sentimental,'' and other poems in *Émaux et Camées* foreshadow symbolism in their tonal sensitivity, synaesthesia (or use of artistic transposition), and latent-fluidity of form.

Gautier was also the author of *Le Roman de la momie* (*The Romance of a Mummy*), in which he admirably juxtaposes ancient Egypt and the contemporary world, and of *Le Capitaine Fracasse* (*Captain Fracasse*), the last, in terms of year of publication, of the great French works in the Romantic tradition of the historical novel. *Captain Fracasse* is a lengthy and picaresque rehandling of Scarron's 17th-century *Le Roman comique* (*The Comic Romance*). A young nobleman, Sigognac, forsakes his ancestral home on falling in love with an actress. He accompanies her and the group of strolling players to which she belongs on their travels throughout France, experiencing many prodigious adventures along the way.

In *La Presse*, mainly during the years 1836–40, and in *Le Moniteur universel*, from 1845, Gautier published more than 2,000 *feuilletons* on painting, ballet, and literature. Of his feuilletons about the Salons and visits to art collections those recording his admiration of Rubens, Goya, and Delacroix are outstanding; several volumes of art criticism, largely based on these feuilletons, also came from his pen. In his day he was an unrivalled ballet critic. He was also the author of numerous comedies and ballets, and the joint author of *Giselle*. His literary criticism is notable for its studies of Lamartine, Baudelaire, and Balzac (whose short story ''The Unknown Masterpiece'' he may even have helped to write). In *Tra los monies* (*The Romantic in Spain*) he proved himself to be a fine writer of travel sketches; in the former book the visual inspiration is especially evident.

More clearly than any other French writer, Gautier represents the transition from Romanticism to Parnassianism. Balzac, Flaubert, Sainte-Beuve, Baudelaire, Banville, the Goncourt brothers, and other literary contemporaries held him in high esteem. His work is often derivative, however. His verse, in particular, lacks an emotional and intellectual content commensurate with its perfection of form. His output was enormous, *Émaux et Camées, Spirite* (a short novel of the supernatural), novellas such as *Militona, Avatar, Arria Marcella,* and *Jettatura* are among his finest achievements. Maupassant appears to have been influenced by the subject matter of these shorter fictions.

—Donald Adamson

See the essay on ''Art.''

GENET, Jean

Born: Paris, France, 19 December 1910 (illegitimate); took his mother's surname. Abandoned by his parents, and reared by foster parents in Le Morvan. **Career:** Sent to reformatory, Mettray, 1926–29, for petty crimes; enlisted in the Foreign Legion, served in Morocco 1932–33, but deserted in 1936 and again in 1939; lived the life of a criminal in several countries until 1942; began writing during term in Fresnes Prison; met Jean Cocteau, *q.v.*, in the early 1940s; began publishing his works in the mid-1940s; met Jean-Paul Sartre, *q.v.*, and Simone de Beauvoir, *q.v.*, in 1944; sentenced to life imprisonment for recurrent theft, 1948, until friends and supporters secured a presidential pardon in 1949; writing all but ceased after 1966; subsequently supporter of various radical causes, including the Black Panthers in the United States, Palestinian liberation groups, and the Baader-Meinhof group in Germany. **Died:** 15 April 1986.

PUBLICATIONS

Collections

The Selected Writings of Jean Genet, edited with introduction by Edmund White, 1993.

Fiction

Notre Dame des Fleurs. 1944; revised version, in *Oeuvres complètes*, 2, 1951; as *Our Lady of the Flowers*, translated by Bernard Frechtman, 1949; as *Gutter in the Sky*, translated by Frechtman, 1955.

Miracle de la rose. 1946; revised version, in *Oeuvres complètes*, 2, 1951; as *Miracle of the Rose*, translated by Bernard Frechtman, 1965.

Pompes funèbres. 1947; revised version, in *Oeuvres complètes*, 3, 1953; as *Funeral Rites*, translated by Bernard Frechtman, 1969.

Querelle de Brest. 1947; revised version, in *Oeuvres complètes*, 3, 1953; as *Querelle of Brest*, translated by Gregory Streatham, 1966.

Plays

Les Bonnes (produced 1947; revised version, produced 1954). 1948; revised versions 1954, 1958; as *The Maids*, translated by Bernard Frechtman, with *Deathwatch*, 1954.

'Adame Miroir (ballet scenario), music by Darius Milhaud. 1948.

Haute surveillance (produced 1949). 1949; revised versions, 1965, and in *Oeuvres complètes*, 4, 1968; as *Deathwatch*, with *The Maids*, translated by Bernard Frechtman, 1954.

Le Balcon (produced 1957). 1956; revised versions, 1960, 1962; edited by David Walker, 1982; as *The Balcony*, translated by Bernard Frechtman, 1958; revised translation, 1966; also translated by Barbara Wright and Terry Hands, 1991.

Les Nègres (produced 1959). 1958; as *The Blacks*, translated by Bernard Frechtman, 1960.

Les Paravents (produced 1961). 1961; revised version, 1976; as *The Screens*, translated by Bernard Frechtman, 1962.

Splendid's, translated by Neil Bartlett. 1995.

Screenplays: *Un chant d'amour*, 1950; *Goubbiah*, 1955; *Mademoiselle*, 1966.

Verse

Chants secrets. 1947.

La Galère. 1947.

Poèmes. 1948; revised edition, 1966.

Poems. 1980.

Treasures of the Night: Collected Poems, translated by Steven Finch. 1981.

Other

Journal du voleur. 1949; as *The Thief's Journal*, translated by Bernard Frechtman, 1954.

L'Enfant criminel, 'Adame Miroir. 1949.

Oeuvres complètes. 4 vols., 1951–68.

Lettres à Roger Blin. 1966; as *Letters to Roger Blin: Reflections on the Theatre*, translated by Richard Seaver, 1969.
May Day Speech. 1970.
Reflections on the Theatre and Other Writings. 1972.
Lettres à Olga et Marc Barbezat. 1988.
Fragments et autres textes. 1990.
L'Ennemi déclaré: Textes et entretiens, edited by Albert Dichy. 1991.
Editor, with R. Gallet, *Poètes anglais contemporains: Geoffrey Hill, Philip Larkin, Kathleen Raine, R.S. Thomas, K. White*. 1982.

*

Bibliography: *Jean Genet: A Checklist of His Works in French, English and German* by Richard N. Coe, in *Australian Journal of French Studies*, VI, 1969; *Jean Genet and His Critics: An Annotated Bibliography 1943–1980* by Richard C. and Suzanne A. Webb, 1982.

Critical Studies: *Saint Genet, Comédien et martyr* by Jean-Paul Sartre, 1952; *The Imagination of Jean Genet* by Joseph H. McMahon, 1963; *Jean Genet* by Tom F. Driver, 1966; *The Vision of Jean Genet* by Richard N. Coe, 1968, and *The Theatre of Jean Genet: A Casebook* edited by Coe, 1970; *Jean Genet* by Bettina L. Knapp, 1968, revised edition, 1989; *Jean Genet: A Study of His Novels and Plays* by Philip Thody, 1968; *Profane Play, Ritual, and Jean Genet: A Study of His Drama* by Lewis T. Cetta, 1974; *Jean Genet in Tangier* by Mohamed Choukri, 1974; *A Genetic Approach to Structures in the Work of Jean Genet* by Camille Naish, 1978; *Genet: A Collection of Critical Essays* edited by Peter Brooks and Joseph Halpern, 1979; *Genet's Ritual Play* [*Les Bonnes*] by Sylvie Debevec Henning, 1981; *Jean Genet* by Jeannette L. Savona, 1983: *No Man's Stage: A Semiotic Study of Jean Genet's Major Plays* by Una Chaudhuri, 1986; *Jean Genet and the Semiotics of Performance* by Laura Oswald, 1989; *Jean Genet: A Biography of Deceit, 1910–1951* by Harry E. Stewart and Rob Roy McGregor, 1989; *Genet, Les Nègres* by J.P. Little, 1990; *The Cinema of Jean Genet: Un chant d'amour* by Jane Giles, 1991; *The Rites of Passage of Jean Genet: The Art and Aesthetics of Risk Taking* by Gene A. Plunka, 1992; *File on Genet* by Richard Webb, 1992; *Genet* by Edmund White, 1993; *Artaud, Genet, Shange: The Absence of the Theatre of Cruelty* by Sean Carney, 1994; *Flowers for Jean Genet* by Josef Winkler, translated by Michael Roloff, 1997; *Flowers and Revolution: A Collection of Writings on Jean Genet*, edited by Barbara Read with Ian Birchall, 1997; *The Body Abject: Self and Text in Jean Genet and Samuel Beckett* by David Houston Jones, 2000.

*   *   *

When Jean-Paul Sartre published his long study, *Saint Genet, Comédien et martyr* (*Saint Genet, Actor and Martyr*) in 1952, many readers came to Jean Genet through Sartre's evaluation and sympathy. The book proposed that Genet be classified among the greatest French writers of the century. At every step of the way, Genet had known what he was doing. Hence Sartre's term to designate him *comédien* or actor. Genet never failed to acknowledge the condition imposed upon him by society when he was young; hence the second term in the title of *martyr*.

One day the parallels will be studied that exist between Rimbaud's revolt against his condition in the world, and Genet's submission to his fate. A world only half-seen by Rimbaud in episodes of *Une saison en enfer* (*A Season in Hell*) is raucously dramatized in Genet's first novel *Notre Dame des Fleurs* (*Our Lady of the Flowers*). Extravagant in every sense, this late adolescent world of Montmartre, engendered by the early adolescent world in the prisons of Mettray and Fontevrault, is the *légende dorée* of Genet, in which existence is a cult, a ceremony of evil where the male is female. Death in violence obsesses the minds of the tough heroes of Genet (*les durs*: Bulkaen, Pilorge, Harcamone), and martyrdom obsesses the minds of the effeminate (Divine and Notre-Dame). The guillotine is the symbol of the male and of his greatest glory.

The central drama in his books is always the struggle between the man in authority and the man to whom he is attracted. The psychological varieties of this struggle are many. Each of the novels and each of the plays is a different world in which the same drama unfolds. *Querelle de Brest* is the ship: naval officers and sailors. *Pompes funèbres* (*Funeral Rites*) is the Occupation: Nazi officers and young Frenchmen of the capital. *Our Lady of the Flowers* is Montmartre, with its world of male prostitutes and pimps. *Miracle de la rose* (*Miracle of the Rose*) is the prison, with the notorious convicts and slaves.

The play *Haute surveillance* (*Deathwatch*) is also the prison cell with the intricate hierarchy of criminals where those standing under the death sentence exert the greatest power and prestige over those with lesser sentences. *Les Bonnes* (*The Maids*) is the household, where in the absence of the mistress one of the maids plays her part. *Les Nègres* (*The Blacks*) is the world of colonialism: the conflict between whites and blacks. It is much more than a satire on colonialism. The oppression from which the blacks suffer is so hostile, so incomprehensible, as to be easily the oppression of mankind. The hostility which Genet persistently celebrates throughout all his work, in his opulent language, is the strangely distorted love joining the saint and the criminal, the guard and the prisoner, the policeman and the thief, the master and the slave, the white and the black.

—Wallace Fowlie

See the essays on *The Balcony* and *The Maids*.

GEZELLE, Guido

Born: Bruges, Austrian Netherlands (now Belgium), 1 May 1803.
Education: Educated at a seminary in Roeselare, 1846–49. **Career:** Became priest in 1854; appointed to teaching post at his old school, where his unorthodox pedagogical methods caused his dismissal; co-director, English College, Bruges, 1860–61; teacher of philosophy, Seminarium Anglo-Belgicum, 1861–65; journalist for anti-liberal magazine *'t Jaer 30*, 1864–70, and *'t Jaer 70*, 1870–72; founder and journalist for the illustrated weekly *Rond den Heerd* [Round the Hearth], 1865–71; parish priest of St. Walburgis, 1865–72; moved to Kortrijk, where he worked as chaplain; continued ecclesiastical and journalistic work for *De Vrijheid* and *Gazette van Kortrijk*; recalled to Bruges in 1899, and granted position of rector of the English Convent. **Died:** 27 November 1899.

PUBLICATIONS

Collections

Dichtwerken [Poetical Works]. 10 vols., 1903–05, revised edition, 14 vols., 1913.
Jubileumuitgave [Jubilee Edition]. 18 vols., 1930–39.
Werken [Works], edited by Frank Baur. 4 vols., 1949–50.
Briefwisseling [Correspondence], edited by R.F. Lissens. 1970.
Verzameld dichtwerk [Collected Poetry], edited by K. de Busschere. 1980–92.
Evening and the Rose: 30 Poems, translated by Paul Claes and Christine D'Haen, 1989.

Verse

Boodschap van de vogels en andere opgezette dieren [Message from the Birds and Other Stuffed Animals]. 1856.
Vlaemsche dichtoefeningen [Flemish Poetry Exercises]. 1858.
Kerkhofblommen [Graveyard Flowers]. 1858.
XXXIII Kleengedichtjes [Thirty-Three Little Poems]. 1860.
Gedichten, gezangen en gebeden [Poems, Songs, and Prayers]. 1862, reprinted 1976.
Liederen, eerdichten et reliqua [Songs, Poems of Praise, and Relics]. 1880.
Driemaal XXXIII Kleengedichtjes [Thrice Thirty-Three Little Poems]. 1881.
Tijdkrans [Garland of Time]. 1893.
Rijmsnoer [Rhyme String]. 1897.
Laatste verzen [Last Poems]. 1901.
[Selection], translated by M. Swepstone. 1937.
[15 Poems], translated by C. and F. Stillman, in *Lyrica Belgica I*. 1960.
Poems, translated by Christine d'Haen. 1971.
[12 Poems], translated by A. van Eyken, in *Dutch Crossing*, 35. 1988.

Other

Uitstap in de Warande [Excursion in the Warande]. 1882.
De ring om 't kerkelijk jaar [Ring Around the Church Year]. 1908.
Brieven van, aan, over Gezelle (letters; some in English). 2 vols., 1937–39.
De Briefwisseling tussen G. Gezelle en Ernest Rembry 1872–1899, edited by C. Verstraeten. 1987.
Translator, *Hiawatha*, by Longfellow. 1886.

*

Critical Studies: *Woordkunst van Guido Gezelle* by J. Craynet, 1904; *Het leven van Guido Gezelle* by A. Walgrave, 1924; *Guido Gezelle* by Henriette Roland Hoist, 1931; *Guido Gezelle* by A. Visser, 1949; *Guido Gezelle en de andere* by H. Bruning, 1954; *Guido Gezelle* by A. van Duinkerken, 1958; *Van het leven naar het boek* by J.J.M. Westenbroek, 1967; *Guido Gezelle katholiek vrijmetselaar* by R. Reniers, 1973; *De taalkunst van Guido Gezelle* by Albert Westerlinck, 1980; *Guido Gezelle: Flemish Priest and Poet* by Hermine J. van Nuis, 1986; *De wonde in 't hert* by Christine d'Haen, 1988; *Mijnheer Gezelle* by Michel van der Plas, 1991; *Gezelle, de dichter: Studies* by Jan J.M. Westenbroek, 1995; *Gezelle: Humorist* by Johan van Iseghem, 1999.

*   *   *

Guido Gezelle is the Dutch poet who singlehandedly took the Dutch language to a summit of beauty and complexity hitherto undreamt of. There are at least five Gezelles. Perhaps the least interesting for literary purposes is Gezelle the journalist. Since he was a priest who could obviously write well, Gezelle was forced by his bishop to invest much time and energy in political journalism, both to expound the policies of the Catholic People's Party and to attack and chastise its opponents. In that capacity he made a number of enemies, and the stress connected with his journalistic work brought him to the brink of a nervous breakdown.

Gezelle the linguist or, as he would have preferred to think of himself, the philologist, was interested in the Dutch language in general, and in his own West Flemish dialect in particular. He cultivated the latter for two reasons. The use of this dialect enhanced his poetry, especially in the later phase, as it was more effortlessly melodious than standard Dutch. It was also, he felt (and many agreed), a "Catholic" Dutch, as opposed to the "Calvinist" variant that had come to dominate Holland.

The third Gezelle is the educator, whether as teacher in the classroom or as editor (who also often filled whole issues with the fruit of his labour) of weekly magazines designed to teach and to entertain the faithful, particularly those whose education had progressed little beyond acquiring the basic skill of reading itself.

The fourth Gezelle is the priest-poet, responsible for a sizeable part of the poetry that has come down to us. As a priest, Gezelle felt both close to and responsible for the people entrusted to his care and would often write small poems, *kleengedichtjes*, to commemorate important events in their lives.

The fifth Gezelle, the most interesting, wrote experimental poetry before the term was even conceived of, and *poésie pure* long before Brémond. For many it is he who represents the "real" Gezelle. His poetry is constructed around several main themes. Many poems reflect his highly-strung religious idealism. Some are marred by didacticism, while others achieve a level of mystical lyricism rarely equalled in world literature. Other poems represent the reverse of his idealism: a feeling of inadequacy, sinfulness, and despair that is also to be found in the so-called "terrible sonnets" of Gerard Manley Hopkins, the poet to whom Gezelle is most often compared. Gezelle, however, wrote few sonnets; he preferred experimenting with sound, rhythm, and metre.

Another principal theme is that of friendship. A number of close friends stayed loyal to Gezelle all his life, and he commemorated his affection for them in a number of poems, the best known of which is probably "Dien avond en die rooze" [That Evening and That Rose].

Throughout his life Gezelle fought for the recognition of Dutch as an official language by the Belgian state, and against the dominant position of French, which was used almost exclusively by the civil service and in the courts, even though the majority of people in Flanders, the northern half of the country, were hardly able to understand it, let alone communicate in it. Some of Gezelle's "Flemish" poems are evocations of the glorious past in a somewhat romantic vein. Others, the more interesting, range from parody to an almost incantatory celebration of the sheer range of the language itself.

The last, but certainly not least, main theme is that of nature, which to Gezelle represented the "visible words" of God, according to the old mystical belief that God spoke to man in words destined for his ears, and written down in the Bible, but also in words destined for his eyes, and present in nature all around him. On the basis of this attitude, any and every celebration of nature, even of the smallest insects, is also a celebration of God himself, and all poetic meditations on nature automatically become religious utterances of prayer. Since Gezelle was a keen observer of all that went on around him, not only (as a philologist) of the language his people spoke, but also (as a poet) of the nature they lived in, or sometimes had to struggle against, he produced many poems that are prayers, or prayers that are poems.

The final 15 years of Gezelle's life saw his consecration as the national poet of the Flemish people. He was awarded many honours, including a state funeral. The ultimate paradox of his life as a poet is, perhaps, that he will always remain the prisoner of his own excellence. The very virtuosity, inventiveness, and exuberant revelling in the power of the Dutch language that establishes so many of his greatest poems as truly of world stature also militates against their being translatable effectively. For this reason he has not been translated frequently or successfully into any of the more widely spoken languages.

—André Lefevere

GHĀLIB, (Mīrzā Muḥammad) Asadullāh Khān

Born: Agra, Uttar Pradesh, India, in 1797. Father killed when he was five; guardian uncle died when he was nine. **Education:** Self-educated: well-versed in classical subjects, Arabic, and developed interests in philosophy, Sufism, and astrology. **Family:** Married nobleman's daughter in 1810. **Career:** Began writing poetry in Urdu from the age of ten, but after 1847 wrote mostly in Persian. On uncle's death, his estate was confiscated: subsequently devoted much time attempting to regain control of his share; lived for most of his life in Delhi, apart from two years (1827–29) in Calcutta; attended the court of the Mughal rulers, from 1847; commissioned to write official history of the Mughal dynasty, in Persian, 1850; appointed official poetry teacher, 1854; witnessed the Indian Mutiny 1857–58, and recorded his experiences in letters and journals. **Died:** 1869.

PUBLICATIONS

Verse

Dī vā-i Ghālib [Ghālib's Works]. 1841; 5th edition, 1863; modern editions: (Nizami edition) 1915, 1958, 1965, 1969, 1989; selections translated in collections listed below, and in *The Falcon and the Hunted Bird* (anthology of different poets), 1950; *The Golden Tradition: An Anthology of Urdu Love Poetry* (80 poems, with critical study), translated by Ahmed Ali, 1973; *An Anthology of Classical Urdu Love Lyrics*, translated by David J. Mathews and Christopher Shackle, 1972; *Classical Urdu Poetry 2*, translated by M.A.R. Barker and Shah Abdus Salam, 1977.
[MS Amroha Verses], edited by Nisar Ahmad Farooqi. 1857.
Nuskha-i-Hāmidīa, edited by Abdur Rahman Bijnori. 1921.
Intikhāb i Ghālib (selection), edited by Imtiyāz Ali 'Arshī. 1942.
Dīvān-i Ourdu (Urdu verses). 1954.

Shish jihat-i Ghālib (Persian verse), edited by Chaudhuri Nabi Ahmad Bajwa. 1962.
Selected Verses, translated by Sufia Sadullah. 1965.
Selected Poems, translated by Ahmed Ali. 1969.
Ghālib Urdu kalamka intikhab (selection), edited by Mukatabah Jam'ah. 1969.
Mata'-i Ghālib: Intikhab-i ghazaliyat-i farsi (Persian selection). 1969.
Twenty Five Verses, translated by C.M. Nain. 1970.
Ghazals of Ghalib, edited and translated by Aijaz Ahmad, adapted by various poets. 1971.
Ham Kalām, Fārsī rubā'iyāt-i Ghālib kā tarjamah, ṣ Akbārabādī. 1986.
Galib: The Man and His Couplets, translated by Umesh Joshi. 1998.

Other

Khatut-i-Ghālib (letters), edited by Ghulam Rasul Mehr. 3rd edition, 1969.
Ghālib aur fann-i tanqīd [murattib] Akhlāq Ḥsain Ārif (correspondence). 1977.
Urdu Letters, translated and annotated by Daub Rahbar. 1987.
Panj ahang men makatib-i Ghālib (Persian letters). 1989.
Dastanbuy: A Diary of the Indian Revolt of 1857. N.d.
Ghalib: 1797–1869, translated and edited by Ralph Russell and Khurshidul Islam. 1994.
Quest for New Horizons. 1996.

*

Critical Studies: *The Aligarh Urdu Magazine: Ghālib Number* edited by Mukhtar Uddin Ahmad Arzu, 1949; *Studies in Urdu Literature* by Fazl Mahmud Asiri, 1952; *Interpretations of Ghālib* by J.L. Kaul, 1957; *Ghālib, The Man and His Verse* by P.L. Lakhanpal, 1960; *Ghālib: Two Essays* by Ahmed Ali and Alessandro Bausani, 1969, and *The Problem of Style and Technique in Ghālib*, 1969, and *The Golden Tradition*, 1973, reprinted 1991, both by Ali; *Ghālib* by M. Mujeeb, 1969; *Ghālib: Life and Letters* by Ralph Russell and Khurshidul Islam, 1969; *Mirza Ghālib: The Poet of Poets* by S. Saran, 1976; *A Dance of Sparks: Imagery of Fire in Ghālib's Poetry* by Annemarie Schimmel, 1979; *Ghālib: The Man, the Times* by Pavan K. Varmer, 1989; *Yadgar-e-Ghālib: A Biography of Ghālib* by Maulana Altaf Hussain Hali, translated by K.H. Qadiri, 1990; *Ghālib* by Anis Nagore, 1990; *Ghalib: The Poet and His Age*, edited by Ralph Russell, 1997.

* * *

Asadullāh Khān Ghālib died having lost both his sense of hearing and all interest in a life which, in any case, had not treated him kindly. Unappreciated during his lifetime, he stands in great esteem today, and his reputation has spread far and wide during the last two decades through translations into English and appraisals in other languages. He is a highly individualistic, sophisticated, and difficult poet, whose mind was far in advance of his age, and whose poetry retains its sophisticated and difficult nature today.

The 19th century was an age in India of upheaval, uncertainty, religious controversy, revolt, decay, and disorder, but also one of hope as a new order was emerging, in Ghālib's own words, like "Dispersed light in the mirror, a speck of dust / Caught in the sunlight in the window." Psychologically it was a difficult period of warring loyalties, with instinct demanding attachment to national feeling, but with expediency suggesting alignment with an alien power that had almost complete control over India. Attitudes underwent a change. Some patriotic souls revolted against the dominance of the West, like Momin who reflected Ghālib's own sentiments "O Doomsday, come, rend up the world, / Shake it up and down, about . . . ."

These currents produced sentiments and attitudes that are difficult to analyse. Ghālib's developed sensibility accepted a variety of thought as valid experience. His peculiar mind unified experiences so that the sifting of their elements becomes a hopeless task, the more so as Ghālib had a comprehension of his age similar to that of Baudelaire, while the changing pattern of the age was still incomplete and unrecognized by his contemporaries. As a result he was considered incomprehensible and obscure, so that one commentator said in exasperation, "What he writes he alone / Or God can understand." But Ghālib was a poet of passion with a philosophical conception of life and the universe, like the Metaphysical poets of England, and he carried his search for the truth to a more metaphysical plane. Endowed with a visionary imagination, his mind fused perception and thought so that he could see creation and the creator involved together in the situation:

Life's leisure is a mirror of the hundred hues
Of self-adoration;
And night and day the great dismay
Of the onlooker of the scene.

Here, conventional belief is upturned. Life is engrossed with its multifarious forms, and the Maker, bound by His own laws, then turns into a helpless beholder of the scene he has created:

Intelligence unconcerned
Is caught in the great despair
Of encirclement, and man's
Image remains imprisoned
In the mirror of the world.

Ghālib's poetry reflects the movement of thought, and his passion creates an imagery that is both picturesque and startling in its suddenness. His poetic experience was more conscious than intuitive, presenting an object after the idea of it, as in "The heat engendered by thought is indescribable; / I had just thought of despair when the desert went up in flames."

This quality of his thought is so breathtaking that he remained beyond the reach of the average critic of his era. Yet his intensive mind needed a new diction and grammar to express itself: "Where is, O Lord, the other foot of Hope? / I found the desert of contingent existence a mere footprint." From this to the opening poem of his *Dīvān*, "Of whose gay tracery is the picture a complainant?," is only a continuation of the great leap forward, where the style is highly elliptical and the meaning seemingly incomprehensible, as words and images are strung together pell-mell, as in Gerard Manley Hopkins (a contemporary of Ghālib). Ghālib's elliptical style is indeed as startling in Urdu as Hopkins's is in English:

No, it was not these.
The jading and jar of the cart,
Time's tasking, it is fathers that asking for ease
Of the sodden-with-its-sorrowing heart,
Nor danger, electrical horror; then further it finds
The appealing of the passion is tender in prayer apart.
. . .

The elliptical fourth line is less complicated and breathtaking, however, than:

The joy-of-creation-of-image-producing-
Coquetry-of-expressing-
The-intense-desire-of-being-killed.
In the furnace-of-fire is the hoof
Of the prey from the beloved's scimitar.

The first three lines here are a series of ellipses, constituting a single emotive state. This is wit, conceit, hyperbole, all in one. Ghālib created metaphors out of the conditions of his mind and feeling. It is a complex, composite picture of overlapping and interlinked states in the devotional opening poem, where words and grammar, image and idea, fact and fiction, intellect and emotion, all play their part singly and collectively, transcending the realm of words to form an imagery of abstractions; if John Donne could find a parallel between a pair of lovers and a pair of compasses, Ghālib could find ecstasy in the way to the altar of sacrifice itself: "With what joy in front of the executioner I walk / That from my shadow the head is two steps ahead of the feet . . . ."

This was an idiom his contemporaries and the generations that followed could not understand, so that between 1892 and 1972 at least 54 keys to his *she'rs* (unit of two lines) were published. It was not until the 1960s that Ghālib could find his rightful place in the ranks of the world's great poets.

—Ahmed Ali

GIDE, André (Paul-Guillaume)

Born: Paris, France, 22 November 1869. **Education:** Educated at École Alsacienne, Paris, 1878–80; Lycée in Montpellier, 1881; boarder at M. Henri Bauer, 1883–85; and at M. Jacob Keller, 1886–87; École Alsacienne, 1887; École Henri IV: baccalauréat, 1890. **Family:** Married Madeleine Rondeaux in 1895 (died 1938); had one daughter by Elisabeth van Bysselberghe. **Career:** Mayor of a Normandy commune, 1896; juror in Rouen, 1912; special envoy of Colonial Ministry on trip to Africa, 1925–26. Helped found *Nouvelle Revue française*, 1909. **Awards:** Nobel prize for literature, 1947. Ph.D.: Oxford University. **Member:** Honorary Member, American Academy, 1950. **Died:** 19 February 1951.

PUBLICATIONS

Collection

Romans, récits, et soties; Oeuvres lyriques, edited by Yvonne Davet and Jean-Jacques Thierry. 1958.

Fiction

Les Cahiers d'André Walter. 1891; translated in part as *The White Notebook*, by Wade Baskin, 1965; complete translation as *The Notebooks of André Walter*, 1968.

La Tentative amoureuse. 1893; as *The Lovers' Attempt*, translated by Dorothy Bussy, in *The Return of the Prodigal*, 1953.

Le Voyage d'Urien. 1893; as *Urien's Voyage*, translated by Wade Baskin, 1964.

Paludes. 1895; as *Marshlands*, translated by George D. Painter, with *Prometheus Misbound*, 1953.

Les Nourritures terrestres. 1897; as *Fruits of the Earth*, translated by Dorothy Bussy, 1949.

Le Prométhée mal enchaîné. 1899; as *Prometheus Illbound*, translated by Lilian Rothermere, 1919; as *Prometheus Misbound*, translated by George D. Painter, with *Marshlands*, 1953.

L'Immoraliste. 1902; as *The Immoralist*, translated by Dorothy Bussy, 1930; translated by Stanley Appelbaum, 1996; also translated by David Watson, 2001.

Le Retour de l'enfant prodigue. 1907; as *The Return of the Prodigal*, translated by Dorothy Bussy, 1953.

La Porte étroite. 1909; as *Strait Is the Gate*, translated by Dorothy Bussy, 1924.

Isabelle. 1911; as *Isabelle*, translated by Dorothy Bussy, in *Two Symphonies*, 1931.

Les Caves du Vatican. 1914; as *The Vatican Cellars*, translated by Dorothy Bussy, 1914; as *The Vatican Swindle*, translated by Bussy, 1925; as *Lafcadio's Adventures*, 1927.

La Symphonie pastorale. 1919; as *The Pastoral Symphony*, translated by Dorothy Bussy, in *Two Symphonies*, 1931.

Les Faux-monnayeurs. 1926; as *The Counterfeiters*, translated by Dorothy Bussy, 1927; as *The Coiners*, translated by Bussy, 1950.

L'École des femmes. 1929; as *The School for Wives*, translated by Dorothy Bussy, 1929.

Two Symphonies (includes *Isabelle* and *The Pastoral Symphony*), translated by Dorothy Bussy. 1931.

Deux récits. 1938.

Thésée. 1946, as *Theseus*, translated by John Russell, 1948.

Plays

Philoctète (produced 1919). 1899; as *Philoctetes*, translated by Jackson Mathews, in *My Theater*, 1952; also translated by Dorothy Bussy, in *The Return of the Prodigal*, 1953.

Le Roi Candaule (produced 1901). 1901; as *King Candaules*, translated by Jackson Mathews, in *My Theater*, 1952.

Saül (produced 1922). 1903; as *Saul*, translated by Jackson Mathews, in *My Theater*, 1952; also translated by Dorothy Bussy, in *The Return of the Prodigal*, 1953.

Le Retour de l'enfant prodigue (produced 1928), 1909.

Bethsabé. 1912; as *Bathsheba*, translated by Jackson Mathews, in *My Theater*, 1951; also translated by Dorothy Bussy, in *The Return of the Prodigal*, 1953.

Antoine et Cléopatre, from the play by Shakespeare (produced 1920). In *Théâtre complet*, 1947.

Amal; ou, La Lettre du roi, from the play by Tagore (produced 1928). 1922.

Robert: Supplément à L'École des femmes (produced 1946). 1930; as *Robert; ou, L'Intérêt général*, 1949.

Oedipe (produced 1931). 1931; as *Oedipus*, translated by John Russell, in *Two Legends*, 1950.

Les Caves du Vatican, from his own novel (produced 1933). In *Théâtre complet*, 1948.

Perséphone (libretto), music by Igor Stravinsky (produced 1934). 1934; edited by Patrick Pollard, 1977; as *Persephone*, translated by Jackson Mathews, in *My Theater*, 1952.

Geneviève. 1936.

Le Treizième Arbre (produced 1939). In *Théâtre*, 1942; as *The Thirteenth Tree*, translated and adapted by Diane Moore, 1987.

Théâtre. 1942; as *My Theater*, translated by Jackson Mathews, 1952.

Hamlet, from the play by Shakespeare (produced 1946). In *Théâtre complet*, 1949.

Le Procès, with Jean-Louis Barrault, from the novel by Kafka (produced 1947). 1947; as *The Trial*, translated by Jacqueline and Frank Sundstrom, 1950.

Théâtre complet. 8 vols., 1947–49.

Verse

Les Poésies d'André Walter. 1892.

Other

Le Traité du Narcisse. 1892; as *Narcissus*, translated by Dorothy Bussy, in *The Return of the Prodigal*, 1953.

Réflexions sur quelques points de littérature et de morale. 1897.

Feuilles de route 1895–1896. 1899.

Philoctète, suivi de Le Traité du Narcisse, La Tentative amoureuse, El Hadj. 1899; all translated by Dorothy Bussy, in *The Return of the Prodigal*, 1953.

De l'influence en littérature. 1900.

Lettres à Angèle (1898–1899). 1900.

Les Limites de l'art. 1901.

De l'importance du public. 1903.

Prétextes. 1903; enlarged edition, 1913; translated in *Pretexts: Reflections on Literature and Morality*, edited by Justin O'Brien. 1959.

Amyntas. 1906; as *Amyntas*, translated by Villiers David, 1958; also translated by Richard Howard, 1988.

Dostoïevsky d'après sa correspondance. 1908.

Oscar Wilde. 1910; as *Oscar Wilde*, translated by Bernard Frechtman, 1951.

Charles-Louis Philippe. 1911.

C.R.D.N. 1911; enlarged edition as *Corydon* (privately printed), 1920; 2nd edition, 1925; as *Corydon*, translated by Hugh Gibb, 1950; also translated by Richard Howard, 1983.

Nouveaux prétextes. 1911; translated in *Pretexts: Reflections on Literature and Morality*, edited by Justin O'Brien, 1959.

Souvenirs de la cour d'assises. 1914; as *Recollections of the Assize Court*, translated by Philip A. Wilkins, 1941.

Si le grain ne meurt. 2 vols., 1920–21; as *If It Die. . .* , translated by Dorothy Bussy, 1935.

Numquid et tu . . . ? 1922; translated in *Journal*, 1952.

Dostoïevsky. 1923; as *Dostoevsky*, translated by Arnold Bennett, 1925.

Incidences. 1924.

Caractères. 1925.

Le Journal des faux-monnayeurs. 1926; as *Journal of The Counterfeiters*, translated by Justin O'Brien, 1951; as *Logbook of The Coiners*, 1952.

Dindiki. 1927.

Émile Verhaeren. 1927.

Joseph Conrad. 1927.

Voyage au Congo. 1927; translated by Dorothy Bussy, in *Travels in the Congo.* 1929.

Le Retour du Tchad, suivi du Voyage au Congo, Carnets de route. 1928; translated by Dorothy Bussy, in *Travels in the Congo*, 1929.

Travels in the Congo, translated by Dorothy Bussy. 1929.

Essai sur Montaigne. 1929; as *Montaigne: An Essay in Two Parts*, translated by Stephen H. Guest and Trevor E. Blewitt, 1929.

Un esprit non prévenu. 1929.

Lettres. 1930.

L'Affaire Redureau, suivie de Faits divers. 1930.

Le Sequestré de Poitiers. 1930.

Jacques Rivière. 1931.

Divers. 1931.

Oeuvres complètes, edited by Louis Martin-Chauffier. 15 vols., 1932–39; *Index*, 1954.

Les Nouvelles Nourritures. 1935; translated in *Fruits of the Earth*, 1949.

Retour de l'URSS. 1936; as *Return from the USSR*, translated by Dorothy Bussy, 1937; as *Back from the USSR*, 1937.

Retouches à mon Retour de l'URSS. 1937; as *Afterthoughts: A Sequel to Back from the USSR*, translated by Dorothy Bussy, 1938.

Journal 1889–1939. 1939; *1939–1942*, 1946; *1942–1949*, 1950; as *Journals 1889–1949*, edited and translated by Justin O'Brien, 4 vols., 1947–1951.

Découvrons Henri Michaux. 1941.

Attendu que. 1943.

Interviews imaginaires. 1943; as *Imaginary Interviews*, translated by Malcolm Cowley, 1944.

Jeunesse. 1945.

Lettres à Christian Beck. 1946.

Souvenirs littéraires el problèmes actuels. 1946.

Et nunc manet in te. 1947; as *The Secret Drama of My Life*, translated by Keen Wallis, 1951; as *Madeleine*, translated by Justin O'Brien, 1952.

Paul Valéry. 1947.

Poétique. 1947.

Correspondance 1893–1938, with Francis Jammes, edited by Robert Mallet. 1948.

Notes sur Chopin. 1948; as *Notes on Chopin*, translated by Bernard Frechtman, 1949.

Préfaces. 1948.

Rencontres. 1948.

Correspondance 1899–1926, with Paul Claudel, edited by Robert Mallet. 1949; as *The Correspondence 1899–1926*, translated by John Russell, 1952.

Feuillets d'automne. 1949; as *Autumn Leaves*, translated by Elsie Pell, 1950.

Lettres, with Charles du Bos. 1950.

Littérature engagée, edited by Yvonne Davet. 1950.

Égypte 1939. 1951.

Ainsi soit-il; ou, Les Jeux sont faits. 1952; as *So Be It; or, The Chips Are Down*, translated by Justin O'Brien, 1960.

Correspondance 1909–1926, with Rainer Maria Rilke, edited by Renée Lang. 1952.

Lettres à un sculpteur (Simone Marye). 1952.

The Return of the Prodigal (includes *Narcissus; The Lovers' Attempt; El Hadj; Philoctetes; Bathsheba; Saul*), translated by Dorothy Bussy, 1953.

Correspondance 1890–1942, with Paul Valéry, edited by Robert Mallet. 1955; as *Self-Portraits: The Gide Valéry Letters 1890–1942* (abridged edition), edited by Robert Mallet, translated by June Guicharnaud. 1966.

Lettres au Docteur Willy Schuermans (1920–1928). 1955.

Correspondance inédite, with Rilke and Verhaeren, edited by C. Bronne. 1955.

Correspondance, with Marcel Jouhandeau. 1958.

Correspondance 1905–1912, with Charles Péguy, edited by Alfred Saffrey. 1958.

Correspondance 1904–1928, with Edmund Gosse, edited by Linette F. Brugmans. 1960.

Correspondance 1908–1920, with André Suarès, edited by Sidney D. Braun. 1963.

Correspondance 1911–1931, with Arnold Bennett, edited by Linette F. Brugmans. 1964.

Correspondance 1909–1951, with André Rouveyre, edited by Claude Martin. 1967.

Correspondance 1913–1951, with Roger Martin du Gard, edited by Jean Delay. 2 vols., 1968.

Lettres, with Jean Cocteau, edited by Jean-Jacques Kihm. 1970.

Correspondance 1912–1950, with François Mauriac, edited by Jacqueline Morton. 1971.

Le Récit de Michel, edited by Claude Martin. 1972.

Correspondance, with Charles Brunard. 1974.

Correspondance 1891–1938, with Albert Mockel, edited by Gustave Vanwelkenhuyzen. 1975.

Correspondance, with Jules Romains, edited by Claude Martin. 1976; supplement, 1979.

Correspondance 1897–1944, with Henri Ghéon, edited by Jean Tipy. 2 vols., 1976.

Correspondance 1892–1939, with Jacques-Émile Blanche, edited by Georges-Paul Collet. 1979.

Correspondance, with Justin O'Brien, edited by Jacqueline Morton. 1979.

Correspondance, with Dorothy Bussy, edited by Jean Lambert. 3 vols., 1979–82; as *Selected Letters*, edited and translated by Richard Tedeschi, 1983.

Correspondance 1907–1950, with François-Paul Alibert, edited by Claude Martin. 1982.

Correspondance 1929–1940, with Jean Giono, edited by Roland Bourneuf and Jacques Cotnam. 1983.

Correspondance 1934–1950, with Jef Last, edited by C.J. Greshoff. 1985.

La Correspondance générale de André Gide, edited by Claude Martin. 1985.

Correspondance, with Harry Kessler, edited by Claude Foucart. 1985.

Correspondance 1927–1950, with Thea Sternheim, edited by Claude Foucart. 1986.

Correspondance 1891–1931, with Francis Viélé-Griffin, edited by Henri de Paysac. 1986.

Correspondance 1902–1928, with Anna de Noailles, edited by Claude Mignot-Ogliastri. 1986.

Correspondance, with Jacques Copeau, edited by Jean Claude. 2 vols., 1987–88.

Correspondance avec sa mère 1880–1895, edited by Claude Martin. 1988.

Correspondance 1903–1938, with Valery Larbaud, edited by Françoise Lioure. 1989.

Correspondance, with André Ruyters, edited by Claude Martin and Victor Martin-Schmets. 2 vols, 1990.

Correspondance 1901–1950, with Jean Schlumberger, edited by Pascal Mercier and Peter Fawcett. 1994.

Editor, *The Living Thoughts of Montaigne*. 1939.

Editor, *Anthologie de la poésie française*. 1949.

Translator, *Typhon*, by Joseph Conrad. 1918.

Translator, with J. Schiffrin, *Nouvelles; Récits*, by Aleksandr Pushkin. 2 vols., 1929–35.

Translator, *Arden of Faversham*, in *Le Théâtre élizabethain*. 1933.

Translator, *Prométhée*, by Goethe. 1951.

*

Bibliography: *Bibliographie des écrits de Gide* by Arnold Naville, 1949, supplement, 1953; *An Annotated Bibliography of Criticism on André Gide 1973–1988* by Catharine Savage Brosman, 1990.

Critical Studies: *Gide*, 1951, and *Gide: A Critical Biography*, 1968, both by George D. Painter; *Gide* by Enid Starkie, 1953; *The Theatre of André Gide* by J.C. McLaren, 1953; *Gide and the Hound of Heaven* by H. March, 1953; *Portrait of Gide* by Justin O'Brien, 1953; *Gide* by Albert Guerard, 1963, revised edition, 1969; *Gide: His Life and Work* by Wallace Fowlie, 1965; *Gide: The Evolution of an Aesthetic* by Vinio Rossi, 1967; *Gide and the Greek Myth* by Helen Watson-Williams, 1967; *André Gide* by Thomas Cordle, 1969; *André Gide: The Theism of an Atheist* by H.J. Nersoyan, 1969; *André Gide and the Roman d'aventure* by Kevin O'Neill, 1969; *Gide: A Study of His Creative Writings* by G.W, Ireland, 1970; *Gide: A Collection of Critical Essays* edited by David Littlejohn, 1970; *Gide's Art of the Fugue: A Thematic Study of Les Faux-monnayeurs* by Karin Nordenhaug Gihdas, 1974; *Gide and the Art of Autobiography: A Study of Si le grain ne meurt* by C.D.E. Tolton, 1975; *A Student's Guide to Gide* by Christopher Bettinson, 1977; *Gide: Les Faux-monnayeurs* by Michael J. Tilby, 1981; *André Gide and the Codes of Homotextuality* by Emily S. Apter, 1987; *Gide* by David H. Walker, 1990; *André Gide: Homosexual Moralist* by Patrick Pollard, 1991; *Gide: Les caves du Vatican* by Peter Broome, 1995; *Gide's Bent: Sexuality, Politics, Writing* by Michael Lucey, 1995; *Void and Voice: Questioning Narrative and Conventions in André Gide's Major First-person Narratives* by Charles O'Keefe, 1996; *Conrad and Gide: Translation, Transference and Intertextuality* by Russell West, 1996; *André and Oscar: Gide, Wilde and the Gay Art of Living* by Jonathan Fryer, 1997; *André Gide: A Life in the Present* by Alan Sheridan, 1998; *André Gide: Pederasty and Pedagogy* by Naomi Segal, 1998; *André Gide's Politics: Rebellion and Ambivalence*, edited by Tom Conner, 2000.

*   *   *

By the end of his life, André Gide had received the official sign of consecration, the recognition of his century, that he was one of its major writers. The Nobel prize for literature, awarded to him in 1947, indicated that his work had attained a degree of accepted universality. The miracle was that Gide had become a "classical" writer by the time of his death while remaining a "dangerous" writer. This man who invented for his age the term "restlessness" (*inquiétude*) ended his life in apparent calm and resignation. A tone of affirmation, a marked denial of God, and a belief in the void of death provided a different portrait of Gide that has been added to the long series of self-portraits his books had already fashioned.

Gide's vast literary output is, in a sense, a written confession, initiated by a need to communicate what he felt to be true about himself. He knew that he possessed nothing of the anguish of a Pascal. That trait he left to Mauriac, and accepted for himself the characteristics of a Montaigne—of a wavering and diverse mind, as Montaigne had described himself: *esprit ondoyant et divers*. He remained at all times the writer who profited from every kind of experience, important or trivial.

Marc Allégret's film *Avec André Gide* opens with a few solemn pictures of the funeral at Cuverville and Gide's own reading of the opening pages of his autobiography *Si le grain ne meurt* (*If It Die. . .*). There are pictures showing the two contrasting family origins of Gide: Normandy and Languedoc, the north and the south, the Catholic and the Protestant background. The landscape pictures of Algeria and Tunisia provide a documentation for many of his works, from the earliest, such as *Les Nourritures terrestres* (*Fruits of the Earth*) to his *Journal* in 1941–42. Among the most curious episodes are the trip to the Congo, the walk with Valéry, the home of his daughter Catherine in Brignoles, the speech made in Moscow in the presence of Stalin, the visit with Roger Martin du Gard in Bellème.

A genius is a person who considers passionately what other people do not see. In the tradition of French letters, Montaigne was pre-eminently this type of genius, seizing every occasion of pleasure, every meeting, for the subject matter of his writing. The art of both the 16th-century essayist and the 20th-century moralist is based upon an indefatigable curiosity and a relentless critical spirit. Gide's enthusiasm for whatever came within his vision was usually followed by an admirable detachment from it. Once the conquest was made, he refused to be subjugated by it, to be dominated by his conquest. The image of the Minotaur's labyrinth, elaborated in his last important book, *Thésée* (*Theseus*), represents any body of doctrine that might constrict or imprison the thinking powers of a man. The problem for Theseus, as it was for Gide, was that of surpassing his adventures. The one moral error to be avoided at all cost was immobility, fixation. The meaning of Gide's celebrated word *disponibilité* seems to be the power of remaining dissatisfied, capable of change and growth.

From his avid curiosity about everything, whether it was the coloration of a leaf or the first book of a new author, his ideas were engendered. In the manifold forms of attentiveness with which his life seems to have been spent, there were no traces of misanthropy, of pessimism, of class prejudice, or of fatuous satisfaction with self. From a nature that accepted all contradictions—a will to freedom as well as a sense of destiny, good as well as evil—Gide's mind grew into one of the most critical of our age, a mind of infinite subtlety and unexpected boldness.

Gide began writing about 1890, at a time of great peacefulness in Europe, and continued to write during the next 60 years. He remained a constant and fervent witness to every ominous development in Europe and the world, from the period in which a religion of science and a rational vision of the universe dominated Europe to the mid-century of deep unrest.

There is little doubt that Gide hoped to compose a new gospel. With his favourite themes of adolescence, revolt, escape, the gratuitous act, he was able to upset the convictions of his readers, particularly his youthful readers, without creating in them feelings of terror or dismay. He tried to write in all the genres because he was unwilling to restrict himself to any one form and because each book, once it was well under way, became irksome to him; he would finish it off quickly in order to move on to a newer work. He had planned, for example, several further chapters for *Les Faux-monnayeurs* (*The Counterfeiters* or *The Coiners*), but when he wrote the sentence, "Je suis bien curieux de connaître Caloub" ("I am very curious to know Caloub"), it appeared to him such an admirable final sentence that he felt freed from continuing farther.

Whenever Christianity appeared to him in the form of a system, of a body of principles, he refused to accept it. His was an attitude of detachment and adventure, which permitted him the practice of what has been so often called his "sincerity." Problems of ethics worried Gide far more than religion. He was more concerned with justice than salvation. His knowledge of the Bible and his love for the Gospels always gave hope to his Catholic friends (Claudel, Jammes, DuBos, Ghéon, Copeau) that he would finally submit.

What appears as conformity to the world's law was seriously castigated in *Fruits of the Earth* and in *L'Immoraliste* (*The Immoralist*). And yet the very difficulty involved in living within a new freedom provided the moral problem of most of his subsequent books, such as *Les Caves du Vatican* (*The Vatican Swindle*), *The Counterfeiters*, *Theseus*. For the expression of human freedom, for its power and its peril, Gide created massive formulas that have returned, only slightly modified, in the writings of Sartre, Camus, and René Char. His long life was one of self-examination, of courage in liberating himself in such experiences as his African visits, communism, Catholicism. Gide developed one need—that of doubting everything—and one obligation—that of never doubting himself.

—Wallace Fowlie

See the essays on *The Counterfeiters* and *The Immoralist*.

GINZBURG, Natalia

Born: Natalia Levi in Palermo, Sicily, 14 July 1916. Family moved to Turin, 1919. **Education:** Educated at home and at schools in Turin to 1935; entered University of Turin, 1935, left before graduating. **Family:** Married 1) Leone Ginzburg in 1938 (died in captivity, 1944), three children; 2) Gabriele Baldini in 1950 (died 1969). **Career:** Exiled to Pizzoli, in the Abruzzo region, 1940–43; returned to Rome after the fall of Mussolini's fascist government, 1943; went into hiding in Rome, then Florence, 1944, but returned to Rome after the Allied Liberation; worked for Einaudi publishers, Rome and Turin, 1944–49; settled in Rome, 1952; lived in London, where her second husband headed the Italian Cultural Institute, 1959–61; returned to Rome, 1961; elected to parliament as independent left-wing deputy, 1983. **Awards:** Tempo prize, 1947; Veillon prize, 1952; Viareggio prize, 1957; Chianciano prize, 1961; Strega prize, 1963; Marzotto prize, for play, 1965; Bargutta prize, 1983. **Died:** 8 October 1991.

PUBLICATIONS

Collections

Place to Live: Selected Essays of Natalia Ginzburg, translated and edited by Lynne Sharon Schwartz. 2002.

Fiction

I bambini (as Natalia Levi). 1934.
Giulietta (as Natalia Levi). 1934.
Un'assenza (as Natalia Levi). 1934.
Casa al mare (as Alessandra Tornimparte). 1937.
La strada che va in città (as Alessandra Tornimparte). 1942; revised edition, 1945; as *The Road to the City*, translated by Francis Frenaye, in *The Road to the City: Two Novelettes*, 1949.
Passaggio di tedeschi a Erra. 1945.
É stato così. 1947; as *The Dry Heart*, translated by Francis Frenaye, in *The Road to the City: Two Novelettes*, 1949.
The Road to the City: Two Novelettes, translated by Francis Frenaye. 1949.
Tutti i nostri ieri. 1952; as *Dead Yesterdays*, translated by Angus Davidson, 1956; as *A Light for Fools*, translated by Davidson, 1956; as *All Our Yesterdays*, translated by Davidson, 1985.
Valentino (includes *La madre* and *Sagittario*). 1957; *La madre*, as *The Mother*, translated by Isabel Quigly, 1965; two stories as *Valentino and Sagittarius: Two Novellas*, translated by Avril Bardoni, 1987.
Le voci della sera. 1961; edited by S. Pacifici, 1971, and by Alan Bullock, 1982; as *Voices in the Evening*, translated by D.M. Low, 1963.
Lessico famigliare. 1963; as *Family Sayings*, translated by D.M. Low, 1967; revised translation, 1984; as *Things We Used to Say*, translated with introduction by Judith Woolf, 1997.
Mio marito. 1964.
Il maresciallo. 1965.
Caro Michele. 1973; as *No Way*, translated by Sheila Cudahy, 1974; as *Dear Michael*, translated by Cudahy, 1975.
Lessico famigliare No. 2: La luna pallidassi. 1975.
Lessico famigliare No. 2: Il cocchio d'oro. 1975.
Borghesia. 1977; as *Borghesia*, translated by Beryl Stockman, 1988.
Famiglia (includes *Borghesia*). 1977; as *Family*, translated by Beryl Stockman, 1988.
La famiglia Manzoni. 1983; as *The Manzoni Family*, translated by Marie Evans, 1987.

La città e la casa. 1984; as *The City and the House*, translated by Dick Davis, 1986.
Four Novellas (includes *Valentino; Sagittarius; Family; Borghesia*), translated by Avril Bardoni and Beryl Stockman. 1990.

Plays

Ti ho sposato per allegria (produced 1966). 1965.
L'inserzione (produced 1968). In *Ti ho sposato per allegria e altre commedie*, 1968; as *The Advertisement*, translated by Henry Reed, 1969.
Ti ho sposato per allegria e altre commedie (includes *L'inserzione; Fragola e panna; La segretaria*). 1968.
Paese di mare e altre commedie (includes *Dialogo; La porta sbagliata; La parrucca*). 1973.
La poltrona. In *Opere raccolte e ordinate dall'autore*, vol. 2, 1987.
L'intervista. 1989.
Teatro (includes *L'intervista; La poltrona; Dialogo; Paese di mare; La porta sbagliata; La parrucca*). 1990.
Il cormorano. 1991.

Other

Le piccole virtù (essays). 1962, as *The Little Virtues*, translated by Dick Davis, 1985.
Mai devi domandarmi (essays). 1970; as *Never Must You Ask Me*, translated by Isabel Quigly, 1973.
Vita immaginaria (essays). 1974.
Opere, edited by Cesare Garboli. 2 vols., 1986–87.
Serena Cruz; o, La vera giustizia. 1990.
Editor, *La carta del cielo* (stories), by Mario Soldati. 1980.
Editor, with Giovanna Delfini, *Diari 1927–1961*, by Antonio Delfini. 1982.
Translator, *Alla ricerca del tempo perduto: La strada di Swann*, by Marcel Proust. 1953.
Translator, *La signora Bovary*, by Gustave Flaubert. 1983.

*

Critical Studies: "Natalia Ginzburg: The Fabric of Voices" by Donald Heiney, in *The Iowa Review*, 1(4), 1970; *Invito alla lettura di Natalia Ginzburg* by Elena Clementelli, 1972, revised edition, 1986; "The Narrative Strategy of Natalia Ginzburg" by Clotilde S. Bowe, in *Modern Language Review*, 68(4), 1973; "Natalia Ginzburg" by Luciana Marchionne Picchione, in *Il castoro*, 137, 1978; "Forms and Figures in the Novels of Natalia Ginzburg" by R.D. Piclardi, in *World Literature Today*, 53(4), 1979; "Some Thoughts on Internal and External Monologue in the Writings of Natalia Ginzburg," in *Moving in Measure: Essays in Honour of Brian Moloney* edited by Judith Bryce and Doug Thompson, 1989, and *Natalia Ginzburg: Human Relationships in a Changing World*, 1991, both by Alan Bullock; "A Lexicon for Both Sexes: Natalia Ginzburg and the Family Saga" by Corinna Del Greco Lobner, in *Contemporary Women Writers in Italy*, edited by Santo L. Aricò, 1990; *Natalia Ginzburg: A Voice of the Twentieth Century*, edited by Angela M. Jeannet and Giuliana Sanguinetti Katz, 2000; *Material Desire: Natalia Ginzburg's Bonded and Separating Daughters* by Teresa Picarazzi, 2002.

* * *

Described by Ian Thomson in his review of her last novel as "the most interesting of Italian female writers" (*Sunday Times*, 10 October 1986) Natalia Ginzburg remained throughout her life a controversial author, evoking deeply contrasting reactions from both the critical establishment and the general public. Responsive and sympathetic to the problems of both sexes, and highly sensitive to the rhythms of family life, she has analysed problems inherent in emotional relationships which transcend their immediate context to become universally recognizable, exposing the ambiguous feelings that motivate actions, and which frequently ensure that individuals are at greatest risk from those closest to them emotionally. Conscious that the traditional concept of male superiority is a myth based on women's continued acceptance of subordinate roles she was also aware that men are ultimately equally vulnerable human beings, and are thus deserving of sympathy—a view that has inevitably alienated both male chauvinists and militant feminists. Essentially a pessimistic writer, she also possesses a sharp sense of humour, pinpointing the absurdity of much human activity, in which comic and tragic elements are frequently intermingled, and has thereby offended those unable to accept that something as supposedly frivolous as humour can have a place in creative writing. In addition her straightforward and sparse narrative style, far removed from the ornate traditions of Italian literary composition, has led in some quarters to disapproval.

Ginzburg's main theme is the isolation of the individual, usually female, in an environment in which, surrounded by well-intentioned friends or relatives, there is paradoxically no real communication, and thus no possibility of genuine fulfilment. Oblivious to the generation gap and its implications, parents are unaware that their adult children have become individuals whose needs may be radically different from their own, and are thus incapable of providing emotional support when it is most needed. Thus although female roles in postwar society are increasingly released from traditional domestic passivity and ignorance, the older generation continues to educate its offspring in the same way, ensuring that daughters who choose to work for their living are incapable of coping with the pressures of the urban rat race or the problems of sexual emancipation. Meanwhile marriage, traditionally seen by women as a goal rather than a new beginning, is frequently a source of deep disillusion as they discover that sexual intimacy cannot compensate for radical differences in temperament and is no substitute for the meeting of minds.

Though principally focusing in her early work on the plight of women Ginzburg was always concerned to expose victimization irrespective of gender, as is clear from her first work of fiction deemed worthy of publication, *Un'assenza* [An Absence], whose protagonist is a wealthy young man lacking any emotional drive, trapped in a loveless marriage of convenience, and with no interests to fill up his empty days—someone who has unthinkingly embraced appropriate stereotypes only to find them insufficient for his needs. If Ginzburg's output over the next 30 years may appear uncompromisingly feminist, dealing largely with unhappy wives afflicted with uncomprehending husbands in *Casa al mare* [The House by the Seaside] and *Mio marito* [My Husband], or young women neglected or oppressed by their families, in *La strada che va in città* (*The Road to the City*) and *Valentino*, unable to develop successful relationships, as in *Le voci della sera* (*Voices in the Evening*), or to cope adequately with their maternal duties, as in *La madre* (*The Mother*) and *É stato così* (*The Dry Heart*), she also saw fit to continue extending her sympathy to males, as is clear from her portrait of Ippolito in *Tutti i nostri ieri* (*All Our Yesterdays*). In this work, a sensitive youth deprived of parental guidance who is unable to withstand the implications of the German advance in World War II and thus commits suicide is contrasted with the figure of Cenzo Rena, a hard-headed businessman and anti-fascist who resolves a family crisis by marrying Ippolito's sister, pregnant by her feckless teenage lover, and defends the impoverished peasants of his southern village against the terrors of German occupation—a rare example in Ginzburg's work of masculine strength and positive awareness. These themes are developed further in her autobiographical novel *Lessico famigliare* (*Family Sayings*), a loose collage of events from her earliest childhood to her second marriage, in which her father, a benevolent despot, and her mother, totally immersed in domesticity, are revealed as lovable but supremely ineffectual parents, with no interest in Natalia's creative talent and unable to understand or communicate with their sons, who none the less achieve success in their chosen careers.

Ginzburg's plays, dating from the mid-1960s, continue to reflect awareness of the complexity of human relationships, and include both the familiar figure of the naive female, oppressed and exploited in an alien environment—Giuliana in *Ti ho sposato per allegria* [I Married You For Fun], Teresa in *L'inserzione* (*The Advertisement*)—and the difficulties experienced by men unable to discharge adequately traditional roles such as that of vengeful husband (Paolo in *Fragola e panna* [The Strawberry Ice]), publisher (Edoardo in *La segretaria* [The Secretary]), or academic (Stefano in *La porta sbagliata* [The Wrong Door]). Now older, and thus more susceptible to the many disturbing changes in moral attitudes in post-1968 Europe, she then turned her attention to the problems of an older generation, a theme already touched on in the character of the unnamed mother in *Sagittario* (*Sagittarius*) and now more fully developed in *Caro Michele* (*Dear Michael*), where she combines an intense realization of the grim implications of social breakdown with an awareness that blanket rejections of contemporary reality by the elderly amount to mere short-sightedness and a reassuring belief that parents who make an effort to come to terms with the new world can still perhaps establish a meaningful rapport with their adult children.

This theme, here only tentatively suggested, is fully realized in her last novel, *La città e la casa* (*The City and the House*), where Giuseppe, who has long been estranged from his son, gradually re-establishes contact through a protracted correspondence between Princeton, New Jersey, where he has retired, and Rome, where his son still lives. In both cases, however, the bond so carefully established between the disaffected generations is shattered by the unexpected assassination of the son, confirming Ginzburg's essential pessimism. This pessimism was already reiterated in her two previous novels *Borghesia* and *Famiglia* (*Family*), in which rootless members of the younger generation are unable to use their newfound freedom to achieve happiness, while their elders likewise suffer both directly and indirectly from their inability to cope with the relaxation of traditional norms.

Ginzburg's last two full-length creative works, the short plays *La poltrona* [The Armchair] and *L'intervista* [The Interview], both focus on inadequate males deserving of sympathy, while also showing how they can adversely affect the lives of their female partners—a return

to her original interest in emotional relationships in which both sexes are now given equal attention. In the short fragment *Il cormorano* [The Cormorant] these feelings are extended to cover the threat to animal and plant life in the Gulf War, while her many essays on a wide variety of subjects provide a more direct expression of her views than in her fiction, reaching their climax in a lengthy polemic on the laws concerning adoption, *Serena Cruz; o, La vera giustizia* [Serena Cruz; or, True Justice], typical of her activity as a left-wing parliamentarian in her final years.

—Alan Bullock

See the essay on *Voices in the Evening*.

GIONO, Jean

Born: Manosque, Provence, France, 30 March 1895. **Education:** Educated at École Saint-Charles, 1900–02; Collège Municipal de Manosque, 1902–11. **Military Service:** Served in the Alpine Infantry, 1915–19. **Family:** Married Élise Maurin in 1920; two daughters. **Career:** Bank clerk, Comptoir National d'Escompte de Paris, Manosque, 1911–14 and 1918–28; full-time writer from 1928; founded his own film company, 1958. Founder member, the Contadour movement, to promote collectivism and pacifism, 1935; imprisoned briefly at Saint Nicolas, Marseille, for refusal to join in the war effort, 1939, and at Saint-Vincent-les-Forts, 1944, for collaboration. **Awards:** Brentano prize, 1929; Northcliffe prize, 1930; Corrard prize, 1931; Monaco prize for literature, 1953. Chevalier, Légion d'honneur. Elected to the Académie Goncourt, 1954. **Died:** 9 October 1970.

PUBLICATIONS

Collections

Oeuvres Romanesques complètes, edited by Robert Ricatte. 6 vols., 1971–83
Oeuvres cinématographiques, edited by Jacques Mény. 1980.
Récits et essais, edited by Pierre Citron. 1989.
Romans et essais 1928–1941, edited by Henri Godard. 1992.

Fiction

Présentation de Pan. 1930.
    Colline. 1929; as *Hill of Destiny*, translated by Jacques Le Clercq, 1929.
    Un de Baumugnes. 1929; as *Lovers Are Never Losers*, translated by Jacques Le Clercq, 1931.
    Regain. 1930; revised edition, edited by Dominique Baudouin, 1967; as *Harvest*, translated by Henri Fluchère and Geoffrey Myers, 1939, 1999.
La Naissance de l'Odyssée. 1930.
Le Grand troupeau. 1931; as *To the Slaughterhouse*, translated by Norman Glass, 1969.
Eglogues. 1931.

Jean le bleu. 1932; edited by Marian Giles Jones, 1968; as *Blue Boy*, translated by Katherine Allen Clarke, 1946.

Solitude de la pitié (stories). 1932.

Le Serpent d'étoiles. 1933.

Le Chant du monde. 1934; as *The Song of the World*, translated by Henri Fluchère and Geoffrey Myers, 1937.

Que ma joie demeure. 1935; as *Joy of Man's Desiring*, translated by Katherine Allen Clarke, 1940.

Batailles dans la montagne. 1937.

L'Eau vive. 1943.

Noé. 1947.

Un roi sans divertissement. 1947.

Les Âmes fortes. 1949.

Mort d'un personnage. 1949.

Les Grands Chemins. 1951.

Le Hussard sur le toit. 1951; as *The Hussar on the Roof*, translated by Jonathan Griffin, 1953; as *The Horseman on the Roof*, translated by Griffin, 1954.

Le Moulin de Pologne. 1952; as *The Malediction*, translated by Peter de Mendelssohn, 1955.

L'Ecossais. 1955.

Le Bonheur fou. 1957; as *The Straw Man*, translated by Phyllis Johnson, 1959.

Angélo. 1958; as *Angelo*, translated by Alma E. Murch, 1960.

Chroniques romanesques (includes *Un roi sans divertissement; Les Grands Chemins*). 1962.

Deux Cavaliers de l'orage. 1965; as *Two Riders of the Storm*, translated by Alan Brown, 1967.

Ennemonde et autres caractères. 1968; as *Ennemonde and Other Characters*, translated by David Le Vay, 1970.

Une histoire d'amour. 1969.

L'Iris de Suse. 1970.

Les Récits de la demi-brigade (stories). 1972.

Le Déserteur et autres récits (stories). 1973.

Faust au village (stories). 1977.

L'Homme qui plantait des arbres. 1980; as *The Man Who Planted Trees*, translated by Frédéric Back, 1985; translated by Barbara Bray, 1995.

Dragoon; suivi de Olympe (unfinished, in two versions). 1982.

Verse

Accompagnés de la flûte. 1924.

Premières proses et premiers poèmes. 1938–39, *Fragments d'un déluge, Fragments d'un paradis.* 1948.

Plays

Le Lanceur de graines (produced 1932). In *Théâtre*, 1943.

Le Bout de la route (produced 1941). In *Théâtre*, 1943.

La Femme du boulanger (produced 1944). In *Théâtre*, 1943.

Théâtre (includes *Le Bout de la route; Le Lanceur de graines; La Femme du boulanger; Esquisse d'une mort d'Hélène*). 1943.

Le Voyage en calèche (produced 1947). 1946.

Hortense; ou, L'Eau vive, with Alain Allioux (screenplay). 1958.

Théâtre II: Domitien, suivi de Joseph à Dotham. 1959.

Crésus (screenplay). 1961.

Le Cheval fou. 1974.

Screenplays: *L'Eau vive*, with Alain Allioux, 1958; *Crésus,* 1960; *Un roi sans divertissement*, 1963.

Other

Manosque des plateaux. 1930.

Solitude de la pitié. 1932.

Le Serpent d'étoiles. 1933.

Les Vraies Richesses (essays). 1936.

Rondeur des jours. 1936.

Refus d'obéissance. 1937.

Le Poids du ciel. 1938.

Vivre Libre I: Lettre aux paysans sur la pauvreté et la paix. 1938.

Etrée du printemps. 1938.

Mort du blé. 1938.

Vivre Libre II: Précisions. 1939.

Provence (travel guide). 1939.

Pour saluer Melville, with *Moby Dick.* 1941.

Triomphe de la vie (essays). 1941.

Pages immortelles de Virgile. 1947.

La Chasse au bonheur. 1953.

Recherches de la pureté. 1953.

Voyage en Italie. 1953; as *An Italian Journey*, translated by John Cumming, 1998.

Arcadie, Arcadie!. 1953.

Notes sur l'affaire Dominici. 1955; as *The Dominici Affair*, translated by Peter de Mendelssohn, 1956.

Giono par lui-même, edited by Claudine Chonez. 1956.

Bernard Buffet. 1956.

Lundi. 1956.

Lucien Jacques. 1956.

Sur les oliviers morts. 1958.

Oppède le vieux. 1959.

Rome, with others. 1959.

Camargue. 1960.

Le Grand Théâtre. 1961.

Images de Provence. 1961.

Tableau de la littérature française. 1962.

Le Désastre de Pavie, 24 février 1525. 1963; as *The Battle of Pavia 24 February 1525*, translated by Alma E. Murch, 1965.

Animalités. 1965.

Selections, edited by Maxwell A. Smith. 1965.

Le Déserteur. 1966.

Le Génie du sud, edited by Claude Annick Jacquet. 1967.

Provence perdue. 1967.

Terre d'or. 1967.

La Mission. 1971.

Les Terrasses de l'île d'Elbe (articles). 1976.

Écrits pacifistes. 1978.

Voilà le pays magique, edited by Marcel Arlaud. 1980.

Correspondance, edited by Pierre Citron. 2 vols., 1981.

Coeurs, passions, caractères. 1982.

Correspondance, with André Gide, edited by Roland Bourneuf and Jacques Cotnam. 1983.

Les Territoires heureux. 1984.

Les Trois Arbres de Palzem (articles). 1984.

Giono à Manosque (selection). 1986.

Entretiens avec Jean Amrouche et Taos Amrouche, edited by Henri Godard. 1990.

Yves Brayer, with Yves Dentan. 1990.

Correspondance 1928–1969, with Jean Guéhenno, edited by Pierre Citron. 1991.

Translator, with Lucien Jacques and Joan Smith, *Moby Dick*, by Herman Melville. 1941.

Translator, with Catherine d'Ivernois, *L'Expédition d'Humphry Clinker*, by Tobias Smollett. 1955.

*

Critical Studies: *Jean Giono et les religions de la terre* by Christian Michelfelder, 1938; *Jean Giono* by Jacques Pugnet, 1955; *Jean Giono et les techniques du roman* (includes bibliography) by Pierre Robert, 1961; *Giono* by Pierre de Boisdeffre, 1965; *Jean Giono* by Maxwell A. Smith, 1966; *The Private World of Jean Giono* by Walter D. Redfern, 1967; *Giono, Master of Fictional Modes* by Norma L. Goodrich, 1973; *Jean Giono*, 3 vols., 1974–81, *Pour une poétique de la parole chez Giono*, 1978, and *Jean Giono, imaginaire et écriture*, 1985, all edited by Alan J. Clayton; *Les Critiques de notre temps et Giono* edited by Roland Bourneuf, 1977; *Giono et l'art du récit* edited by Yves-Alain Favre, 1978; *Jean Giono et le cinéma* by Jacques Mény, 1978; *La Provence de Giono* by Jacques Chabot, 1980; *Jean Giono* by Jean Carrière, 1985; *Giono et la mer* by Michèle Belghmi, 1987; *Dialectique de la fleur: Angélique matrice de l'oeuvre gionienne* by Laurent Fourcaut, 1989; *L'Imagionnare: Essay* by Jacques Chabot, 1990; *Giono* (in English) by Pierre Citron, 1990; *Jean Giono: Le hussard sur le toit* by Walter Redfern, 1997.

*   *   *

Jean Giono was born in the small medieval town of Manosque in Upper Provence and lived there for the rest of his life, his birthplace providing the inspiration for much of his writing. He had already published several poems in a regional magazine, when, in 1929, his first novel *Colline* (*Hill of Destiny*) appeared. This was serialized in a review edited by Paul Valéry, and greeted with critical acclaim by André Gide. It was to be the first of a trilogy, dedicated to the spirit of Pan, and recounting peasant life in the isolated hills of Les Bastides, the unforgettable haunt of his childhood. His evocation of this landscape is filled with its own quasi-religious spirit, beneficent when the peasants live in harmony with it, but menacing when the harmony is broken by thoughtless or wanton action. The presence of Pan is felt in the water of the village spring, on whose flow the peasants are totally dependent, and it is this spirit which punishes with drought and fire their inability to live together in peace. In the second part of the trilogy, *Un de Baumugnes* (*Lovers Are Never Losers*), Pan appears as the inventor of the flute, through whose music happiness is restored to a young peasant woman after her betrayal by a smooth, cynical town dweller. *Regain* (*Harvest*) celebrates Pan as the renewing life force, bringing back civilization and fertility to a tiny community that had seemed doomed to wither away. Although the presence of the spirit of Pan only loosely joins the three novels, they have in common a lyrical celebration of the elemental forces of nature, and a deliberate simplicity of language that can both surprise and move the reader.

Giono's reputation was by now firmly established, and he continued to publish regularly until his death in 1970. More than anything, his versatility has ensured him a devoted readership, for although his output can be divided into a number of broad categories, it is never repetitive and his style evolved to suit his thematic material.

The Pan novels were followed by two semi-autobiographical novels. In *Le Grand troupeau* (*To the Slaughterhouse*) Giono explores the senseless waste of war through the demoralization of the old men left to tend the herds and land while the young men are dragged off to pointless suffering at the front. This bitter evocation of war is replaced by affectionate memories of childhood and family in *Jean le bleu* (*Blue Boy*).

In *Le Chant du monde* (*The Song of the World*), *Que ma joie demeure* (*Joy of Man's Desiring*), and *Batailles dans la montagne* [Battles on the Mountain], Pan is replaced by Dionysus, who personifies the seasonal renewal of life and gives supernatural powers to his followers. Although still belonging to the "regionalist" tradition, these works represent a move away from the realistic presentation of the countryside towards a symbolic expression of the issues that were currently preoccupying the author. The power of love, the goodness of life, man's relationship with society and with nature are central themes, and although the poetry remains, it is often submerged by Giono's "message." It was only a small step from these three novels to the polemical writing of the late 1930s and early 1940s. With war imminent, he argues in *Refus d'obéissance* [Refusal to Obey] and *Vivre Libre I: Lettre aux paysans sur la pauvreté et la paix* [Letter to the Peasants on Poverty and Peace] that if the peasants were to stop providing the towns and battle zones with food, then war would grind to a halt. In *Les Vraies Richesses* [True Riches], *Le Poids du ciel* [The Weight of the Sky], and *Triomphe de la vie* [Triumph of Life] he sees contemporary society threatened by increasing mechanization and urban life, and urges a return to the natural order of the world together with a renunciation of materialistic values.

When war was declared in 1939, Giono remained faithful to his pacifist principles. Refusing to obey his mobilization orders, he was imprisoned from September to November of 1939. His release was secured through the indignant intervention of Gide, the Queen Mother of Belgium, and the student body of Yale University. On his return to Manosque, he wrote *Pour saluer Melville* [Regards to Melville] to complement his translation of *Moby Dick*. These were accompanied by *Fragments d'un paradis* [Fragments of a Paradise], *Triomphe de la vie* and *Le Voyage en calèche* [Journey by Barouche]. The latter work was banned by the German censor, an ironic event in view of Giono's second imprisonment when France was liberated in 1944. He was accused of collaboration with the enemy for not speaking out against the Germans, and for having one of his books serialized in a collaborationist paper.

Although these accusations were blatantly spurious, this second experience of prison hurt Giono deeply, and his post-World War II writings are marked by a shift away from the poetic celebration of peasant life to a series of novels with an historical background, drawing on the traditions of Stendhal and Balzac. *Chroniques* [Chronicles] consists of several novels published between 1947 and 1958, whose central hero, Angélo, is clearly based upon Giono's paternal grandfather, the Italian Carbonaro. The best known of the series is *Le Hussard sur le toit* (*The Hussar on the Roof*), which narrates Angélo's adventures as he crosses a plague-infested Provence to rejoin the *Risorgimento* in Italy.

Although Giono's work has always appealed to intellectuals, his books reached an even wider audience through his screen adaptations and original film scenarios. In all, some 16 films have been adapted from his works, the most celebrated of which is *La Femme du boulanger* [The Baker's Wife], made with Raimu in 1938. In addition he was the author of eight plays.

Giono's reputation has, if anything, increased in the years since his death. He was recognized initially as a great poet in prose and a regional novelist, but his main appeal lies in his handling of such themes as the struggle for survival against elemental forces, the strength of love and hatred, the destructive power of jealousy, and above all the creative power of friendship.

—Jane McAdoo

See the essay on *The Hussar on the Roof*.

GIRAUDOUX, Jean (Hippolyte)

Born: Bellac, France, 29 October 1882. **Education:** Educated at a school in Pellevoisin; lycée, Chateauroux, 1893–1900; Lycée Lakanal, Paris, 1900–02; École Normale Supérieure, Paris, 1903–05. **Military Service:** 1902–03; served in World War I; wounded twice; High Commissioner for Information, 1939–40. **Family:** Married Suzanne Boland in 1918; one son. **Career:** Travelled in Europe, 1905–07; secretary and editor of *Le Matin*; in French diplomatic service, 1910; worked in the Press Office, Ministry of Foreign Affairs, 1910–14; mission to Russia and the East, 1911; military instructor in Portugal, 1916; in United States, 1917, thereafter liaison officer with the United States army in Paris; head of "Service des oeuvres françaises à l'étranger" [Foreign Cultural Service], 1920–24; secretary to Embassy in Berlin, 1924; chief government press officer, 1924; in Turkey, 1926; with the inspectorate of consulates, 1934; director general of Information Services, 1939; retired to live with his brother in Cusset, 1940. **Awards:** Légion d'honneur. **Died:** 31 January 1944.

PUBLICATIONS

Collections

Théâtre complet. 16 vols., 1945–53.
Oeuvre romanesque; Oeuvres littéraires diverses. 3 vols., 1955–58.
Théâtre complet. 1971.
Théâtre complet, edited by Jacques Body and others. 1982.
Oeuvres romanesques complètes, edited by Jacques Body, Brett Dawson, and others. 1990.

Plays

Siegfried (produced 1928). 1928; edited by Gerald V. Banks, 1975; as *Siegfried,* translated by Philip Carr, 1930; also translated by Phyllis La Farge and Peter H. Judd, in *Three Plays*, 1964.
Amphitryon 38 (produced 1929). 1929; as *Amphitryon 38,* translated and adapted by S.N. Behrman, 1938; also translated by Phyllis La Farge and Peter H. Judd, in *Three Plays*, 1964; and Roger Gellert, in *Plays 2*, 1967.
Judith (produced 1931). 1931; as *Judith,* translated by J.K. Savacool, in *From the Modern Theatre,* vol. 3, edited by Eric Bentley, 1955; also translated by Christopher Fry, in *Plays 1*, 1963.

Intermezzo (produced 1933). 1933; edited by Colette Weil, 1975; as *The Enchanted,* translated by Maurice Valency, 1950, and in *Four Plays*, 1958; as *Intermezzo,* translated by Roger Gellert, in *Plays 2*, 1967.
Tessa, from the play *The Constant Nymph* by Margaret Kennedy and Basil Dean (produced 1934). 1934.
La Fin de Siegfried. 1934.
Supplément au voyage de Cook (produced 1935). 1937; as *The Virtuous Island,* adapted by Maurice Valency, 1956.
La Guerre de Troie n'aura pas lieu (produced 1935). 1935; as *Tiger at the Gates,* translated by Christopher Fry, 1955, and in *Plays 1*, 1963, also published as *The Trojan War Will Not Take Place*, 1983.
Électre (produced 1937). 1937; as *Electra,* translated by Winifred Smith, 1952; also translated by Winifred Smith, in *From the Modern Repertoire,* edited by Eric Bentley, 1952, and in *The Modern Theatre 1,* edited by Bentley, 1955; Phyllis La Farge and Peter H. Judd, in *Three Plays*, 1964.
L'Impromptu du Paris (produced 1937). 1937.
Cantique des cantiques (produced 1938). 1939.
Ondine (produced 1939). 1939; as *Ondine,* translated by Maurice Valency, 1954, and in *Four Plays*, 1958; translated by Roger Gellert, in *Plays 2*, 1967.
L'Apollon de Bellac (as *L'Apollon de Marsac,* produced 1942). 1946; as *The Apollo of Bellac,* adapted by Maurice Valency, 1954, and in *Four Plays*, 1958.
Sodome et Gomorrhe (produced 1943). 1943; as *Sodom and Gomorrha,* translated by Herma Briffault, in *The Makers of the Modern Theatre,* edited by Barry Ulanov, 1961.
La Folle de Chaillot (produced 1945). 1945; as *The Madwoman of Chaillot,* adapted by Maurice Valency, 1947, and in *Four Plays*, 1958.
Pour Lucrèce (produced 1953). 1953; as *Duel of Angels,* translated by Christopher Fry, 1958; also translated by Christopher Fry, in *Plays 1*, 1963.
Les Gracques, edited by R.M. Albérès and Jean-Pierre Giraudoux. 1958.
Four Plays (includes *The Madwoman of Chaillot; The Apollo of Bellac; The Enchanted; Ondine*), adapted by Maurice Valency. 1958.
Plays 1 (includes *Judith; Tiger at the Gates; Duel of Angels*), translated by Christopher Fry. 1963.
Three Plays (includes *Siegfried; Amphytrion 38; Electra*), translated by Phyllis La Farge and Peter H. Judd. 1964.
Plays 2 (includes *Amphytrion 38; Intermezzo; Ondine*), translated by Roger Gellert. 1967.

Screenplays: *La Duchesse de Langeais,* 1942; *Les Anges du péché,* with R.-L. Bruckberger and Robert Bresson, 1943 (published as *Le Film de Béthanie: Texte du "Les Anges du péché"*, 1944).

Fiction

Provinciales. 1909.
L'École des indifférents. 1911.
Simon le pathétique. 1918.
Elpénor. 1919; as *Elpénor,* translated by Richard Howard and Bernard Bruce, 1958.
Adorable Clio. 1920.
Suzanne et le Pacifique. 1921; as *Suzanne and the Pacific,* translated by Ben Ray Redman, 1923.

Siegfried et le Limousin. 1922; as *My Friend from Limousin*, translated by Louis M. Wilcox, 1923.
Juliette au pays des hommes. 1924.
Le Cerf, with *Premier rêve signé.* 1926.
Bella. 1926; as *Bella*, translated by J.F. Scanlan, 1927.
Églantine. 1927.
Les Aventures de Jérôme Bardini. 1930.
La France sentimentale. 1932.
Combat avec l'ange. 1934.
Choix des élues. 1939.
Les Contes d'un matin. 1952.
La Menteuse. 1958; as *Lying Woman*, translated by Richard Howard, 1969.

Other

Retour d'Alsace, août 1914. 1916.
Lectures pour une ombre. 1917.
Adieu à la guerre. 1919.
Amica America. 1919.
Visite chez le prince. 1924.
Le Sport. 1928.
Racine. 1930; as *Racine*, translated by P. Mansell Jones, 1938.
Fugues sur Siegfried. 1930.
Fontrages au Niagara. 1932.
De pleins pouvoirs à sans pouvoirs. 1935.
Les Cinq Tentations de La Fontaine. 1938.
Le Futur Armistice. 1939.
Pleins pouvoirs. 1939.
Apropos de la rentrée des classes. 1939.
Littérature. 1941.
Écrits dans l'ombre. 1944.
Armistice à Bordeaux. 1945.
Sans pouvoirs. 1946.
Pour une politique urbaine. 1947.
La Française et la France. 1951.
Visitations. 1952.
Portugal, suivi de Combat avec l'image. 1958.
Or dans la nuit: Chroniques et préfaces littéraires 1910–1943. 1969.
Cornets des Dardanelles, edited by Jacques Body. 1969.
Souvenir de deux existences. 1975.
Messages du continental: Allocutions radiodiffusées du Commissaire général à l'Information (1939–1940) (speeches). 1987.
Lettres à Lilita: 1910–1928, edited by Mauricette Berne. 1989.

*

Bibliography: *Bibliographie de l'oeuvre de Giraudoux 1899–1982*, by Brett Dawson, 1982.

Critical Studies: *Jean Giraudoux: The Making of a Dramatist* by Donald Inskip, 1958; *Jean Giraudoux: His Life and Works* by Laurence LeSage, 1959; *Jean Giraudoux: The Theatre of Victory and Defeat* by Agnes G. Raymond, 1966; *Giraudoux: Three Faces of Destiny* by Robert Cohen, 1968; *Jean Giraudoux: The Writer and His Work* by Georges Lemaître, 1971; *Giraudoux: La Guerre de Troie n'aura pas lieu* by Roy A. Lewis, 1971; *Precious Irony: The Theatre of Giraudoux* by Paul A. Mankin, 1971; *Giraudoux* by Chris Marker, 1978; *Jean Giraudoux* by John H. Reilly, 1978; *Jean Giraudoux and Oriental Thought: A Study of Affinities* by Arthur C. Buck, 1984; *Jean Giraudoux: The Legend and the Secret* by Jacques Body, translated by James Norwood, 1991; *Heroine as Social Redeemer in the Plays of Jean Giraudoux* by Victoria B. Korzeniowska, 2001.

*   *   *

Jean Giraudoux's theatre dominated the French stage in the period between the two World Wars. When he first began writing plays in the late 1920s, his stylistic inventiveness, his witty sense of the incongruity of life, and his search for purity made Giraudoux's work unique and individual. Since then, his fame has spread worldwide and there have been numerous translations and productions of his dramatic works in English and in other languages.

What makes this even more extraordinary is that the dramatist did not begin writing for the stage until he was 46 years old. Before that time, he had achieved some renown, although on a minor scale, as a novelist. Such works as *Suzanne et le Pacifique* (*Suzanne and the Pacific*) and *Juliette au pays des hommes* [Juliette in the Land of Men] gave him a reputation as a writer of complex and subtle novels that reached only a very small public. Indeed, it is only in recent years that his fiction has begun to receive greater recognition.

The presentation of his first play, *Siegfried*, catapulted Giraudoux from the ranks of the minor novelists to the forefront of the French theatre movement. This startling success with both audiences and critics was to last throughout his lifetime and beyond, as some of his later works were not performed until after his death, including one of his most popular, *La Folle de Chaillot* (*The Madwoman of Chaillot*). At first glance, the fanciful creativity and the unusual turn of mind of the writer would seem ill-suited to the more restrictive demands of the stage. Several factors, however, played a role in his achievement. Certainly, Louis Jouvet, the actor-director who formed a close collaboration with Giraudoux and who directed most of his plays, was one of the principal reasons that the dramatist established himself so easily. Another important element was evidently Giraudoux's major theme—man's search for a purity and an ideal beyond the imperfections of reality—a theme that touched a sensitive nerve with the theatre-going public of the 1930s. It found its expression in whimsical comedies like *Amphitryon 38* and *Intermezzo* in which the central characters flirt with the attractiveness of the unknown, only to accept a compromise with the appeal of everyday reality. And the theme also appears in a more concrete form in *La Guerre de Troie n'aura pas lieu* (*Tiger at the Gates*) in which the characters debate the issue of peace and war. In the final analysis, however, it can be argued that the real reason for Giraudoux's appeal was his style—his elegant, civilized, witty account of life in its diverse aspects. The writer's special use of metaphors and symbols, his ironic view of reality, and his sense of the spontaneous and the unexpected were basically responsible for the singular universe that enchanted and delighted his public.

Giraudoux is no longer the major force in French drama that he once was. The contemporary theatre has taken a number of new directions in recent years, passing from the theatre of the absurd of Eugène Ionesco or Samuel Beckett to a theatre in which the director assumes the prominent role, the writer and his words becoming only one part of the whole. Giraudoux's plays, based upon dialogue and discussion, hold language in high esteem. As a result, he could seem less current today. Nevertheless, his imaginative views of man and man's role in the universe and his creative use of language are likely to endure and he should remain one of the major French playwrights of the 20th century.

—John H. Reilly

See the essays on *The Madwoman of Chaillot* and *Tiger at the Gates*.

GIRONELLA (POUS), José María

Born: Darnius, near Gerona, Spain, 31 December 1917. **Education:** Educated at a seminary, Gerona, 1928–30. **Family:** Married Magda Castañer in 1946. **Career:** Worked as labourer and factory hand, early 1930s; bank clerk, Gerona, 1935–36; on the outbreak of the Spanish Civil War, 1936, volunteered for the Nationalist forces, and served with mountain patrols in Huesca, Pyrenees; journalist in Gerona, 1940; correspondent for Italian *Informazione*, Rome, 1942; left Spain covertly, 1947, and lived in France, Italy, Austria, and Sweden, 1947–52; suffered nervous breakdown in Paris, 1951, and travelled between clinics in Vienna and Helsinki, 1951–53; travelled to New York, Cuba (during its revolution), and Mexico, 1959–60, the Far East (twice), 1962–64, Israel, 1975, and Egypt, Iran, and Kuwait, 1979. **Awards:** Nadal prize, 1946; Planeta prize, 1971. **Died:** 1991.

PUBLICATIONS

Fiction

Un hombre. 1947; as *Where the Soil Was Shallow*, translated by Anthony Kerrigan, 1957.
La marea. 1949.
Los cipreses creen en Dios. 1953; as *The Cypresses Believe in God*, translated by Harriet de Onís, 1956.
Muerte y juicio de Giovanni Papini: Cuento fantástico. 1959.
Un millón de muertos. 1961; as *One Million Dead*, translated by Joan Maclean, 1963; as *The Million Dead*, translated by Maclean, 1963.
Mujer, levántate y anda. 1962.
Ha estallado la paz. 1966; as *Peace after War*, translated by Joan Maclean, 1969.
Los hombres lloran solos. 1971.
Condenados a vivir. 2 vols., 1971.
Cita en el cementerio. 1983.
La duda inquietante (novella). 1986.
Se hace camino al andar. 1997.
El apocalipsis. 2001.

Verse

Ha llegado el invierno y tú no estás aquí. 1945.

Other

El novelista ante el mundo. 1954.
Los fantasmas de mi cerebro. 1959; as *Phantoms and Fugitives: Journeys to the Improbable*, translated by Terry Broch Fontsere, 1964.

Todos somos fugitivos (stories and essays). 1961, and in *Phantoms and Fugitives; Journeys to the Improbable*, 1964.
On China and Cuba, translated by John F. Byrne. 1963.
Personas, ideas, mares (travel writing). 1963.
El Japón y su duende (travel writing). 1964.
China, lágrima innumerable (history). 1965.
Gritos del mar (essays). 1967.
Conversaciones con Don Juan de Borbón. 1968.
La sociedad actual en el mundo asiático: Experiencia de un viaje. 1968.
100 españoles y Dios (essays). 1969.
Gritos de la tierra (essays). 1970.
En Asia se muere bajo las estrellas (travel writing). 1971.
El Mediterráneo es un hombre disfrazado de mar (travel writing). 1974.
El escándalo de Tierra Santa (travel writing). 1977.
Carta a mi padre muerto (autobiographical writings). 1978.
100 españoles y Franco (essays). 1979.
Mundo tierno, mundo cruel. 1981.
El escándalo del Islam (travel writing). 1982.
A la sombra de Chopin. 1990.
Yo, Mahoma. 1992.
Jerusalén de los evangelios. 1992.
Carta a mi madra muerta (autobiographical writings). 1992.
Nuevos 100 españoles y Dios. 1994.
El corazón alberga muchas sombras. 1995.

*

Critical Studies: "José María Gironella, Spanish Novelist" by William J. Grupp, in *Kentucky Foreign Language Quarterly*, 4(3), 1957; "Arturo Barea and J.M. Gironella: Two Interpreters of the Spanish Civil War" by J.J. Devlin, in *Hispania*, 41, 1958; "Revolutionary Novels of Gironella and Pasternak" by Edmund S. Urbanski, in *Hispania*, 43, 1960; *Crítica y glosa de Un millón de muertos* by L.E. Calvo Sotelo, 1961; "Gironella and Hemingway: Novelists of the Spanish Civil War" by R.L. Sheehan, in *Studies in Honor of Samuel Montefiore Waxman*, 1969; *José María Gironella* (in English) by Ronald Schwartz, 1972; *Perspectivas humorísticas en la trilogía de Gironella* by J. David Suárez-Torres, 1972; "Gironella's Chronicles Revisited: A Panorama on Fratricide" by John E. Dial, in *Papers on Language and Literature*, 10(1), 1974; "Fictive History in Gironella" by Peter Ilie, in *Journal of Spanish Studies*, 2, 1974; *José María Gironella* by J.A. Salso, 1982; *The Novel of the Spanish Civil War (1936–1939)* by Gareth Thomas, 1990.

* * *

The outstanding literary creations of José María Gironella deal with the Spanish Civil War, 1936–39. The predominant theme of his best received novels, *Los cipreses creen en Dios* (*The Cypresses Believe in God*) and *Un millón de muertos* (*One Million Dead*), focuses on the suffering and disintegration of family life. Gironella, a traditionalist in all respects, intones the lament of a society which has forsaken its sense of order. Vengeful survival becomes a way of life. In his portrayal of war-torn Spain, the author attempts, really tries very hard, to be objective. However, he cannot divest himself of his strong commitment to his orthodox religious background, and consequently to the conservative political position. Unquestionably, his devotion to his personal principles has a marked influence on his characters; although seemingly they confront their tragic circumstances as individuals, in truth they carry with them symbolic identities. That is to say, in the last analysis, they are "types" rather than singular characters. Yet, even as generic projections of an agonizing existence, they achieve a significant measure of artistic reality. Through the description of their lives, the reader is able to identify with the day-to-day struggle for subsistence amid the ravages of a war which tears families asunder, as fanaticism grows in intensity on all sides of the political spectrum.

The warring hostilities depicted in *The Cypresses Believe in God* violently expand in *One Million Dead* which, as the title suggests, dwells on the terrible loss of life. (Even though "one million" is an exaggeration, the number of dead did run into the hundreds of thousands.) Historical events are interwoven with fictional accounts quite skilfully; on the surface, both novels would appear to be a reliable recording of dramatic incidents through the personal vicissitudes of the Alvear family, which microcosmically serves as the axis for the national catastrophe. Essentially, the tragedy of Spain is reflected in the misfortunes that befall one family. To be sure, it is a family that predominantly leans toward the cause of Franco.

The third volume of Gironella's trilogy on the Civil War, *Ha estallado la paz* (*Peace after War*), hardly deserves the same recognition. The first two, voluminous indeed, will give Gironella a respectable place in the annals of Spanish literature. While not achieving, by any means, the stature of a weaver of fictionalized history like Pérez Galdós in the 19th century, Gironella has succeeded in establishing himself as the literary historian of the Spanish Civil War. Other novelists have centred their attention on the consequences of the consanguineous conflict, but Gironella has been the only outstanding writer who has addressed the question in the form of novels.

Gironella's other writings comprise many themes: religion, death, politics, and a variety of subjects that refer to human problems as they affect daily existence. However, they are by and large essay-type expressions of the author's concern for life and death. In themselves they would not constitute a testimony to a writer who is worthy of being considered as the novelistic chronicler of the three most harrowing years that Spaniards have ever known. Without a doubt, for those who would want to view the drama of a Spain embarked on self-destruction, *The Cypresses Believe in God* and *One Million Dead* are indispensable reading.

—Robert Kirsner

GLISSANT, Edouard

Born: Bezaudin (Sainte-Marie), Martinique, 21 September 1928.
Education: Attended primary school in Lamentin, Martinique; lycée Schoelcher (studied under Aimé Césaire, along with fellow student Frantz Fanon), Fort-de-France, Martinique 1939–1945; Studied at the Sorbonne (received a Licence in Philosophy), Paris, 1946–1953.
Career: Worked and studied in Paris where he was politically active in the Société Africaine de Culture [African Society for Culture] and the Front Antillo-Guynais pour l'Indépendence [Antillo-Guyanais Front for Independance] (which he co-founded), 1953–60; placed under surveillance and banned from leaving France as a result of his political activities, 1959–60; professor of philosophy at the Lycée des Jeunes Filles [High School for Young Girls], Fort-de-France, 1965; founded and taught at the Institut Martiniquais d'Études [Martinican

Institute of Studies], Fort-de-France, 1967–70; founder and editor of the Caribbean studies journal *Acoma*, 1971–74; returned to Paris to become editor of the UNESCO *Courrier*, 1980; moved to the United States to become Distinguished Professor at Louisiana State University, Baton Rouge, 1988; moved to New York to become distinguished Professor of French at the City University of New York, 1997. **Awards:** Prix Renaudot for *La Lézarde*, 1958; Prix Charles Veillon for *Le quatrième siècle*, 1964; Puterbaugh award for literature, 1989; honorary doctorate: York University of Toronto, 1989.

PUBLICATIONS

Collections

Poèmes. 1963.
Poèmes complets. 1994.

Fiction

La Lézarde. 1958; as *The Ripening*, translated by J. Michael Dash, 1985.
Le quatrième siècle. 1964.
Malemort. 1975.
La case du commandeur. 1981.
Mahagony. 1987.
Tout-monde. 1993.
Sartorius: le roman des Batoutos. 1999.

Poetry

Un champ d'îles. 1953.
La terre inquiète. 1954.
Les Indes: poème de l'une et l'autre terre. 1956; as *The Indies*, translated by Dominique O'Neill, 1992.
Le sel noir. 1960; as *Black Salt*, translated by Betsy Wing, 1999.
Le sang rivé. 1961.
L'Intention poétique. 1969.
Boises: histoire naturelle d'une aridité. 1979.
Pays rêvé, pays réel. 1985.
Fastes. 1992

Other

Soleil de la conscience. 1956.
Monsieur Toussaint (play). 1978; as *Monsieur Toussaint*, translated by Joseph G. Foster and Barbara A. Franklin, 1981.
Le Discours antillais. 1981; as *Caribbean Discourse: Selected Essays*, translated by J. Michael Dash, 1989.
Poétique de la relation. 1990; as *Poetics of Relation*, translated by Betsy Wing, 1997.
Discours de Glendon. 1990.
Introduction à une poétique du divers. 1995.
Faulkner, Mississippi. 1996; as *Faulkner, Mississippi*, translated by Barbara Lewis and Thomas C. Spear, 1999.
Traité du tout-monde. 1997.

*

Bibliography: *Bibliographie annotée d'Edouard Glissant* by Alain Baudot, 1993.

Critical Studies: *Edouard Glissant* by Daniel Radford, 1982; *Conquérants de la nuit nue: Edouard Glissant et l'Histoire antillaise* by Bernadette Cailler, 1988; *Myth and History in Caribbean Fiction: Aléjo Carpentier, Wilson Harris, and Edouard Glissant*, 1992; *Decolonizing the Text: Glissantian Readings in Caribbean and African Literatures* by Debra L. Anderson, 1995; *Edouard Glissant* by J. Michael Dash, 1995; *Edouard Glissant and Postcolonial Theory: Strategies of Language and Resistance* by Celia Britton, 1999.

* * *

Although his creative works far outnumber his theoretical texts, Edouard Glissant has received the most critical attention for the latter, and in particular *Le Discours antillais* (*Caribbean Discourse*) and *Poétique de la relation* (*Poetics of Relation*). Glissant's most important theoretical contribution is his conception of Caribbean identity in general and Martinican identity in particular. Specifically, Glissant suggests in his theoretical works that Caribbean identity, which has typically been read in terms of an absence—an absence of traditional history, of clear origins, of a distinct language, for example—is in fact a new form of identity freed from the violence and domination of typically Western forms. Moreover, Glissant sees Caribbean identity, which he terms *antillanité*, as a model for a new world order. Precisely because Caribbean identity was born of rupture, of transplantation, of intermixing, it is, according to Glissant, ideally suited for a world in which migration, diversity, and multiculturalism have created a reality in which stable origins, nations, histories, languages are not possible.

Antillanité for Glissant refers to Caribbean (Martinican) identity as it exists. Whereas, he gives the name *relation* to the model for global identity and interaction based on antillanité. According to Glissant, a world characterized by relation is one in which interpersonal and political interaction results not in the domination or suppression of one group by another, but rather in the mutual interaction and transformation of peoples and cultures. Glissant sees relation as a direct contrast to traditional, Western conceptions of identity, which he reads as being rooted in fixed, stable categories such as race, nation, and religion. According to Glissant, the need for stability and rootedness leads to a fear of others that in turn leads to violent domination (such as colonization) and war. He presents relation as an alternative—one that accepts the reality of a constantly destabilized and unpredictable world, which he calls *le chaos monde*, or "the chaos world." However, he sees chaos not as negative, but rather as the act of embracing the world in its true, ever-changing state.

In his creative works, Glissant both explores and illustrates the ideas of antillanité, relation, and chaos as they are later articulated in his theoretical texts. His poetry, which marks the beginning of his creative endeavor, demonstrates, even at his creative beginning, his preoccupation with capturing the hybridity and paradox of Caribbean experience. His poems are experiments in form and language, which attempt to bridge the gap between the Caribbean present and its past. These poems are filled with images of the sea, the land, and with historical references to slavery, to Departmentalization and even to Christopher Columbus. What they have in common is their attempt to capture Martinican experience through language.

Glissant's novels, like his poems, are also generically somewhat hybrid and are also preoccupied with capturing Caribbean and particularly Martinican reality. The two most widely studied of his novels, *La Lézarde* (*The Ripening*) and *La case du commandeur*, are in many ways narrative attempts to articulate and interpret the confused reality of contemporary Martinique. Both novels are characterized by Glissant's hybrid writing style, which merges elements of poetry and prose, and which reflects his conceptions of Martinican space and time through the rejection of linear narrative. In both novels, as in the majority of Glissant's *oeuvre*, the plot is secondary to the exploration of the nature of Martinique and of Martinican identity.

The Ripening centers on a political plot during the 1945 elections in Martinique. However, it may be argued that the Lézarde River, which winds throughout the narrative, connecting characters to one another, event to event, past to present, is actually the center of the text. In fact, the river, in the text, comes to function as Glissant's narrative embodiment of Martinican experience, precisely because of its ability to transcend time and space, and to connect diverse people, events, and realities.

La case du commandeur continues the exploration of the essence of Martinique, through the story of madwoman Marie Celat, or Mycéa, who escapes from a mental hospital and ends up in the cabin of an overseer. Mycéa, like the river in *The Ripening*, becomes the focal point of the text, although it can not be clearly said that her story is the novel's center. Rather, as in the earlier novel, Mycéa becomes a conduit or focal point through which the forces of time and nature, and the actions and events of others pass and become interconnected. Like the river of *The Ripening*, she becomes the representation of what Glissant is able to capture of Martinique, rather than a character in the traditional sense.

In its quest to simultaneously affirm and narrate a Caribbean/Martinican essence Glissant's work functions as the bridge between two generations of Martinican writers. Glissant is clearly influenced by Aimé Césaire and the *négritude* movement, which is often seen as the moment of awakening of Caribbean literary identity. However, Glissant differs from Césaire in that he does not seek to return to some fundamental African origin. Instead, he insists on the specificity of Caribbean experience, precisely in its rupture from all origins. In that respect, he can be seen as the intellectual predecessor of the contemporary generation of Martinican writers, the *créolists*, who embrace the hybridity of Martinican language and identity, and who claim the rupture and negotiation as a new origin of a new (world) identity.

—Dayna Oscherwitz

GOETHE, Johann Wolfgang von

Born: Frankfurt, Germany, 28 August 1749. **Education:** Studied law at Leipzig University, 1765–68, and drawing with Adam Oeser; after a period of illness, resumed his studies in Strasbourg, 1770–71, licentiate in law 1771. **Family:** Lived with Christiane Vulpius from 1788; married her in 1806 (died 1816); one son. **Career:** Practised law in Frankfurt, 1771–72, and Wetzlar, 1772; contributor, *Frankfurter Gelehrte Anzeigen*, 1772–73; at invitation of Duke Karl August, joined the small court of Weimar in 1775: member of the council, 1776, president, war commission, 1779, director of roads and services, 1779, ennobled 1782, took over much of the financial affairs of the court; after a visit to Italy, 1786–88, released from day-to-day government business: general supervisor for arts and sciences, 1788, and director of the court theatres, 1791–1817. Editor of a variety of yearbooks and magazines, including, with Schiller, *Xenien*, 1796–97; with J.H. Meyer, *Die Propyläen*, 1798–1800; *Kunst und Altertum*,

1816–32; and *Zur Naturwissenschaft,* 1817–24. Chancellor of the University of Jena. **Died:** 22 March 1832.

PUBLICATIONS

Collections

Schriften. 8 vols., 1787–90; later editions, as *Werke,* 13 vols., 1806–10, etc.; 69 vols., 1826–42.
Complete Works [Bohn Standard Library]. 14 vols., 1848–90.
Werke [Sophie or Weimar Edition]. 134 vols., 1887–1919.
Sämtliche Werke [Jubiläum Edition], edited by Eduard von der Hellen. 40 vols., 1902–07.
Werke [Hamburg Edition], edited by Erich Trunz and others. 14 vols., 1948–69; subsequent revisions, last reprinted 1981.
Gedenkausgabe der Werke, Briefe, und Gespräche, edited by Ernst Beutler. 27 vols., 1948–71.
Collected Works, edited by Christopher Middleton and others, translated by Michael Hamburger and others. 12 vols., 1983–88.
Sämtliche Werke [Munich Edition], edited by Karl Richter and others. 1986–.
Goethe: The Collected Works, edited by Thomas P. Saine and Jeffrey L. Sammons. 1994.
Fairy Tales, Short Stories, and Poems by Johann von Goethe, edited and translated by J.W. Thomas. 1998.
Selected Poems, translated by John Whalley. 1998.
Selected Poems, edited with introduction by T.J. Reed. 1999.
Selected Works: Including the Sorrows of Young Werther, Elective Affinities, Italian Journey, Faust, introduced by Nicholas Boyle. 1999.

Fiction

Die Leiden des jungen Werthers. 1774; revised edition, 1787; as *The Sorrows of Werter,* translated by Richard Graves or Daniel Malthus, 1780; numerous subsequent translations including as *The Sufferings of Young Werther,* translated by Michael Hulse, 1989.
Wilhelm Meisters Lehrjahre [and *Wanderjahre*]. 1795–1821; as *Wilhelm Meister's Apprenticeship* [and *Travels*], translated by Thomas Carlyle, 1824–27, revised editions 1842, 1865; several subsequent translations including by H.M. Waidson, 1977–79.
Die Wahlverwandtschaften. 1809; as *Elective Affinities,* in *Works;* as *Kindred by Choice,* translated by H.M. Waidson, 1960; as *Elective Affinities,* translated by Elizabeth Mayer and Louise Brogan, 1963; also translated by R.J. Hollingdale, 1971; John Winkelman, 1987.
Novelle. 1826.

Plays

Götz von Berlichingen mit tier eisernen Hand (produced 1774). 1773; as *Goetz of Berlichingen with the Iron Hand,* translated by Walter Scott, 1799; as *Ironhand,* translated by John Arden, 1965; as *Götz von Berlichingen,* translated by Charles E. Passage, in *Plays,* 1980.
Clavigo (produced 1774). 1774; as *Clavidgo,* translated by Charles Leftley, 1798.
Götter, Helden, und Wieland. 1774.
Erwin und Elmire, music by Jean André (produced 1775). 1775; revised version, in verse, in *Schriften,* 5, 1788.

Stella. 1776; revised version (produced 1806), in *Werke,* 6, 1816; translated as *Stella,* 1798.
Claudine von Villa Bella (produced 1777). 1776; revised version (produced 1789), in *Schriften,* 5, 1788.
Die Geschwister (produced 1776). In *Schriften,* 1, 1787.
Die Mitschuldigen (produced 1777). In *Schriften,* 2, 1787; as *Fellow Culprits,* translated by Charles E. Passage, in *Plays,* 1980.
Lila, music by Sigmund von Seckendorff (produced 1777). In *Schriften,* 1790.
Das Jahrmarktsfest zu Plundersweilern (produced 1778). In *Schriften,* 6, 1790.
Der Triumph der Empfindsamkeit (produced 1778). In *Schriften,* 4, 1787; revised version, as *Proserpina,* music by Karl Eberwein (produced 1915), in *Werke,* 1808.
Die Laune des Verliebten (produced 1779). In *Werke,* 4, 1806; as *The Lover's Whim,* translated by Charles E. Passage, in *Plays,* 1980.
Iphigenie (produced 1779; revised version, in verse, as *Iphigenie auf Tauris,* produced 1802). In *Schriften,* 3, 1787; as *Iphigenia in Tauris,* translated by William Taylor, 1793; several subsequent translations including by Charles E. Passage, in *Plays,* 1980.
Die Vögel, from the play by Aristophanes (produced 1780). 1787.
Jery und Bätely, music by Sigmund von Seckendorff (produced 1780). 1790.
Die Fischerin, music by Corona Schröter (produced 1782). 1782.
Egmont (produced 1784). 1788; translated as *Egmont,* 1848; also translated by Michael Hamburger, in *The Classic Theatre,* edited by Eric Bentley, 1959; F.J. Lamport, in *Five German Tragedies,* 1969; Charles E. Passage, in *Plays,* 1980.
Torquato Tasso (produced 1807). In *Schriften,* 6, 1790; as *Torquato Tasso,* translated by C. des Voeux, 1827; also translated by A. Swanwick, in *Dramatic Works,* 1846; John Prudhoe, 1979; Charles E. Passage, in *Plays,* 1980; Alan Brownjohn, 1985; as *Tasso (Torquato Tasso),* translated by Robert David MacDonald, 1994.
Scherz, List und Rache (opera libretto; produced 1790). In *Schriften,* 7, 1790.
Der Gross-Cophta (produced 1791). 1792.
Der Bürgergeneral (produced 1793). 1793.
Mahomet, from the play by Voltaire (produced 1799). 1802.
Paläophron und Neoterpe (produced 1800; revised version, produced 1803). In *Werke,* 1808.
Tancred, from the play by Voltaire (produced 1801). 1802.
Die natürliche Tochter (produced 1803). 1804.
Faust, Part One (produced 1819). In *Werke,* 8, 1808; translated as *Faustus,* 1821; numerous subsequent translations.
Pandora. 1810.
Romeo und Juliet, from the play by Shakespeare (produced 1812).
Des Epimenides Erwachen (produced 1815). 1815.
Faust, Part Two (produced 1854). In *Werke: Ausgabe letzter Hand,* 41, 1832 (first complete publication); numerous translations with Part One as *Faust* including by Philip Wayne, 2 vols., 1949–59.
Plays (includes *Götz von Berlichingen; Fellow Culprits; The Lover's Whim: Iphigenia in Tauris; Egmont; Torquato Tasso; Faust*), translated by Charles E. Passage. 1980.
Plays: Egmont, Iphigenia in Tauris, Torquato Tasso, edited by Frank Ryder. 1992.

Verse

Neue Lieder mit Melodien, music by Bernhard Breitkopf. 1770.
Gedichte, in *Schriften,* 8, 1789; and subsequent editions.

Römische Elegien. 1789; as *Roman Elegies,* translated by David Luke, 1977; as *Roman Elegies and Other Poems,* translated and edited by Michael Hamburger, 1996.

Reineke Fuchs. 1794; as *Reynard the Fox,* translated by Thomas Arnold, 1855; as *Reineke Fox,* translated by A. Rogers, 1888.

Hermann und Dorothea. 1798; as *Herman and Dorothea,* translated by Thomas Holcroft, 1801; several subsequent translations.

West-östlicher Divan. 1819; as *West-Easterly Divan,* translated by J. Weiss, 1876; as *West-Eastern Divan,* translated by Alexander Rogers, 1890; also translated by E. Dowden, 1914.

Selected Verse (bilingual edition), edited by David Luke. 1964.

Selected Poems (bilingual edition), edited by Christopher Middleton, translated by Michael Hamburger. 1983.

Erotic Poems, translated by David Luke. 1997.

Other

Beiträge zur Optik. 1790.

Versuch, die Metamorphose der Pflanzen zu erklären. 1790; as *Goethe's Botany,* translated by Agnes Arber, 1946.

Winckelmann und sein Jahrhundert. 1805.

Zur Farbenlehre. 1810; as *Goethe's Theory of Colours,* translated by C.L. Eastlake, 1840.

Aus meinem Leben: Dichtung und Wahrheit. 4 vols., 1811–33; as *Memoirs of Goethe: Written by Himself,* 1824; as *The Autobiography of Goethe,* translated by John Oxenford, 1848; as *From My Life,* translated by Robert Heitner, in *Collected Works,* 4, 1987.

Italienische Reise. 1816–17; as *Travels in Italy,* translated by Alexander James Morrison, 1849; as *Italian Journey,* translated by W.H. Auden and Elizabeth Mayer, 1962; edited by Thomas P. Saine and Jeffrey L. Sammons, translated by Robert R. Heitner, 1989; as *The Flight to Italy: Diary and Selected Letters,* edited and translated with introduction by T.J. Reed, 1999.

Tag- und Jahreshefte, in *Werke 31–32.* 1830; as *Annals,* translated by Charles Nisbet, 1901.

Gespräche mit Goethe, by Johann Peter Eckermann. 1836; edited by Fritz Bergemann, 1955; as *Conversations with Goethe,* translated by S.M. Fuller, 1839.

Correspondence with Goethe, by Carlyle. 1887.

Die Schriften zur Naturwissenschaft. 1947.

Amtliche Schriften, edited by Willy Flach and Helma Dahl. 3 vols., 1950–72.

Briefe, edited by K.R. Mandelkow and B. Morawe. 6 vols., 1962–69.

Gespräche, edited by W.F. and F. von Biedermann, revised by Wolfgang Herwig. 3 vols., 1965–72.

Goethe on Art, edited and translated by John Gage. 1980.

Schriften zur Biologie, edited by Konrad Dietzfelbinger. 1982.

Briefe aus Italien 1786 bis 1788 (selected letters), edited by Eugen Thurnher. 1985.

Early Letters of Goethe, with introduction by Christoph E. Schweitzer. 1993.

Published Essays: 1940–1952, edited with introduction by Ellis Sandoz. 2000.

*

Bibliography: *Goethe-Bibliographie* by Hans Pyritz, Heinz Nicolai, and Gerhard Burckhardt, 1954; supplement, 1968; *Goethe-Bibliographie* by Helmut G. Hermann, 1991.

Critical Studies: *A Study of Goethe,* 1947, and *Goethe's Faust, Six Essays,* 1953, both by Barker Fairley; *Goethe: The Story of a Man* by Ludwig Lewisohn, 1949; *The Testament of Werther in Poetry and Drama,* 1949, and *Goethe's Faust: A Literary Analysis,* 1958, both by Stuart P. Atkins; *Goethe's Major Plays* by Ronald Peacock, 1959; *Goethe, Poet and Thinker* by E. Wilkinson and L.A. Willoughby, 1962; *Goethe: A Critical Introduction* by Henry C. Hatfield, 1963; *Goethe: His Life and Times* by Richard Friedenthal, 1965; *The Drama of Goethe,* 1966, *The Beautiful Soul: A Study of Eighteenth-Century Idealism as Exemplified by Rousseau's La Nouvelle Héloïse and Goethe's Die Leiden des jungen Werthers,* 1981, and *The Misinterpreting of Goethe's Gretchen Tragedy,* 1992, all by R.D. Miller; *Goethe's Faust: Its Genesis and Purport* by Eudo C. Mason, 1967; *A Student's Guide to Goethe* by F.J. Lamport, 1971; *Goethe's Faust: A Critical Reading,* 1972, and *Johann Wolfgang Goethe,* 1974, both by Liselotte Dieckmann; *"Wine That Maketh Glad": The Interplay of Reality and Symbol in Goethe's Life and Work* by L.A. Willoughby, 1975; *Goethe and the Novel* by Eric A. Blackall, 1976; *Goethe's Faust: Seven Essays* by Alan Cottrell, 1976; *Faust and the Bible: A Study of Goethe's Use of Scriptural Allusions and Christian Religious Motifs in Faust I and II* by Osman Durrani, 1977; *Goethe: Portrait of the Artist* by Ilse Graham, 1977; *Goethe and the Weimar Theatre* by Marvin Carlson, 1978; *Invitation to Goethe's Faust* by Harry G. Haile, 1978; *The Form of Faust: The Work of Art and its Intrinsic Structures* by Harold Jantz, 1978; *Studies in Goethe's Lyric Cycles* by Meredith Lee, 1978; *Time Structure in Drama: Goethe's Sturm und Drang Plays* by Walter K. Stewart, 1978; *Goethe's Search for the Muse: Translation and Creativity* by David B. Richards, 1979; *The Classical Centre: Goethe and Weimar 1775–1832,* 1980, *Goethe,* 1984, and *Nobody's Master: Goethe and the Authority of the Writer,* 1990, all by T.J. Reed; *Goethe's Faust: The Making of Part I,* 1981, and *Goethe's Other Faust: The Drama, Part Two,* 1993, both by John Gearey; *Goethe's Narrative Fiction* edited by William J. Lillyman, 1983; *Spirited Women Heroes: Major Female Characters in the Dramas of Goethe, Schiller and Kleist* by Julie D. Prandi, 1983; *Figures of Identity: Goethe's Novels and the Enigmatic Self* by Clark S. Muenzer, 1984; *Goethe's Theory of Poetry: Faust and the Regeneration of Language* by Benjamin Bennett, 1986; *Goethe's Faust: The German Tragedy* by Jane K. Brown, 1986 and *Interpreting Goethe's Faust Today,* edited by Brown and others, 1994; *Goethe's Faust: Part One,* 1987, and *Goethe: The Poet of the Age—The Poetry of Desire,* 1991, both by Nicholas Boyle; *Our Faust? Roots and Ramifications of a German Myth* edited by Reinhold Grimm and Jost Hermand, 1987; *Images of Identity: Goethe and the Problem of Self-Conception in the Nineteenth Century* by Benjamin C. Sax, 1987; *Goethe: The Sorrows of Young Werther* by Martin Swales, 1987; *The Eternity of Being: On the Experience of Time in Goethe's Faust* by Deirdre Vincent, 1987; *Echoes of Lucian in Goethe's Faust* by Ida H. Washington, 1987; *Goethe's Faust* by John R. Williams, 1987; *Apollo in the Wilderness: An Analysis of Critical Reception of Goethe in America, 1806–1840* by Maxine Grefe, 1988; *The Paradoxical Quest: A Study of Faustian Vicissitudes* by Alfred Hoelzel, 1988; *Goethe in Italy, 1786–1986: A Bicentennial Symposium* edited by Gerhardt Hoffmeister, 1988; *Faust through Four Centuries: Retrospect and Analysis* edited by Sidney Johnson, 1989; *Goethe's Römische Elegien: The Lover and the Poet* by Eva Dessau Bernhardt, 1990; *Goethe's Faust: Notes for a Jungian Commentary* by Edward F.

Edinger, 1990; *The Critical Idyll: Traditional Values and the French Revolution in Goethe's Hermann und Dorothea* by Peter Morgan, 1990; *Idioms of Uncertainty: Goethe and the Essay* by Peter J. Burgard, 1993; *The Life of Goethe: A Critical Biography* by John R. Williams, 1998; *Goethe* by Irmgard Wagner, 1999; *Goethe and Schubert: The Unseen Bond* by Kenneth S. Whitton, 1999.

*   *   *

Johann Wolfgang von Goethe is the dominant figure in the history of modern German literature, whose works established, in all the principal genres, models or norms which have dominated succeeding generations (whether they have sought to follow or emulate, or to rebel against them). His creative life is customarily divided into three principal periods. The first embraces his youth and early manhood and coincides with (or, indeed, determines) the rise and fall of the *Sturm und Drang* movement in German literature. The second comprises his maturity and middle age, from the Italian journey of 1786 through the years of his collaboration with Schiller and their joint attempt to establish a "classical" German literature; the third, the last quarter-century of his life, after Schiller's death, in which he appears as an increasingly solitary figure. Goethe himself spoke of the Italian journey as a "rebirth," of the death of Schiller as "the loss of half of myself." In each of these phases Goethe made contributions of the highest rank and importance to German lyric and dramatic poetry and prose fiction.

Goethe's literary beginnings were more or less conventional, but in 1770 his own characteristic individuality was liberated by his meeting with the critic Herder. Herder introduced him to new ideas of spontaneous creation and inspiration and of national character in literature, to the beauties of folksong and of other "unsophisticated" forms free of the rules and precepts of continental neo-classicism, such as the plays of Shakespeare. Before he was 25, Goethe had effectively created models for the whole European Romantic movement: with the exuberant outpourings of his lyrical poetry on the themes of nature, love, individuality, genius, and creativity; with the sprawling, shapeless, but powerful pseudo-Shakespearian historical drama *Götz von Berlichingen mit tier eisernen Hand* (*Goetz of Berlichingen with the Iron Hand*) and the as yet unfinished and unpublished *Faust*; not least with the tragic, "confessional" epistolary novel *Die Leiden des jungen Werthers* (*The Sufferings of Young Werther*), which established his European reputation at a stroke—somewhat to his subsequent chagrin. But it was to the reputation thus earned that he owed his appointment to the court of the young Duke Karl August of Weimar, with whom he soon established a close relationship.

Before long, court life began to impose its restraints on the hitherto unfettered genius, and the idealistic spiritual drama *Iphigenie auf Tauris* (*Iphigenia in Tauris*) exhibits a highly "classical" formal balance and discipline appropriate to its content and message, even in its original prose version (only after the journey to Italy was it recast in polished blank verse). In the lyric poetry written in the aftermath of the Italian journey Goethe carries this formal "classicism" to the extent of writing almost exclusively in the ancient Greek and Latin metres, hexameter and elegiac distich. This poetry is also concerned with balance and harmony, with a wholeness of all aspects of human life, of art and nature, of intellect, emotion, and sensuality. In respect

of the last-named, however, it marks the overcoming of courtly restraint: the *Römische Elegien* (*Roman Elegies*) celebrate a ripe sense of sexual fulfilment quite different from the youthful "romantic" passion of the earlier poetry. But that the Romantic spirit was still alive in the classical Goethe is demonstrated above all by the poetic drama *Torquato Tasso*, which introduces into European literature that quintessentially Romantic figure, the lonely artist tragically at odds with society.

A fragment of *Faust* was published in 1790, but it was during the period of his collaboration with Schiller that Goethe was able to create an overall design for the work—now conceived not as the tragedy of a heaven-storming genius, but as a celebration of universal human striving. The first of its two parts was completed in 1805, the year of Schiller's death. The novel *Wilhelm Meisters Lehrjahre* (*Wilhelm Meister's Apprenticeship*) was another recasting of an earlier project. Originally concerned with Wilhelm's "theatrical mission," typical of the attempts of earlier generations of German writers to create a national dramatic literature, it is now extended to embrace the much wider theme of his "apprenticeship" to life, of his development and growth into a complete human being, into some sort of modern equivalent (with all the necessary limitation that that implies) of the *kalokagathos* of classical antiquity. The novel is the prototype of the Bildungsroman, which has represented the apogee of the novel form to many German writers, from the Romantics, Goethe's immediate successors, to Thomas Mann, Hesse, and even Grass in the 20th century.

Despite or indeed because of their self-consciously "classical" and exemplary character, many of the works of Goethe's middle period have often been felt to lack the vigour and immediacy of his earlier writing: many readers have found in their balance and restraint a certain blandness or evasiveness. In the works of his old age these very qualities are, paradoxically, intensified into a uniquely personal obliquity and ironical allusiveness, particularly in the second part of *Faust* and in the novels *Wilhelm Meisters Wanderjahre* (*Wilhelm Meister's Travels*)—the sequel to the *Apprenticeship*—and *Die Wahlverwandtschaften* (*Elective Affinities*). But much of his late lyrical poetry is of a mysterious, luminous simplicity, and there is direct expression of powerful emotion in the love-poems of the *West-östlicher Divan* (*West-Eastern Divan*) and in the "Marienbad Elegy."

The chief ever-present theme of all Goethe's work is nature, with its all-pervading harmonies, its universal laws of metamorphosis, of evolution, of permanence in change, of death and rebirth. Man, both as an individual and in his social and political life, is seen essentially as part of this natural order. Goethe devoted much effort to scientific work. His anti-Newtonian theory of light and colours has found little favour, but his work in geology and biology, in comparative anatomy, and in plant and animal morphology still commands respect. He was profoundly drawn to evolutionary theories of geological and of human development—which made him politically a conservative, an enemy of the French Revolution and of all arbitrary violence. Despite the many upheavals he witnessed in his long life, he remained essentially an optimist: despite the tragedy that has accompanied his strivings, his Faust is ultimately—untraditionally and un-Romantically—redeemed.

—F.J. Lamport

See the essays on *Elective Affinities, Faust, Goetz of Berlichingen with the Iron Hand, The Sufferings of Young Werther, Torquato Tasso,* and *Wilhelm Meister's Apprenticeship.*

GOGOL' (IANOVSKY), Nikolai (Vasilevieh)

Born: Sorochintsy, Poltava, Ukraine, 19 March 1809. **Education:** Educated at Poltava boarding school 1819–21, and Nezhin high school, 1821–28. **Career:** Civil servant in St. Petersburg, 1829–31; history teacher, Patriotic Institute, St. Petersburg, and private tutor, 1831–34; assistant lecturer in history, University of St. Petersburg, 1834–35; visited Germany, Switzerland, and France, 1836; in Rome, 1837–39; travelled in western Europe and Russia, 1839–48; began association with the spiritual leader, Father Konstantinovskii, 1847; visited the Holy Land, 1848; resettled in Russia, 1849. **Died:** 21 February 1852.

PUBLICATIONS

Collections

Collected Works (includes *Dead Souls; The Overcoat and Other Stories; Evenings on a Farm near Dikanka; The Government Inspector and Other Stories*), translated by Constance Garnett. 6 vols., 1922–27.
Polnoe sobranie sochinenii [Complete Works]. 14 vols., 1937–52.
Sobranie sochinenii [Collected Works], edited by S.A. Mashinskii. 7 vols., 1966–67.
The Collected Tales and Plays (translations), edited by Leonard J. Kent. 1969.
The Theater of Nikolay Gogol: Plays and Selected Writings (includes *Marriage; The Government Inspector; The Gamblers*; extracts from Gogol's notes, letters, and essays), edited by Milton Ehre, translated by Ehre and Fruma Gottschalk. 1980.
Sobranie sochinenii [Collected Works], edited by V.R. Shcherbina. 8 vols., 1984.
The Complete Tales, edited by Leonard J. Kent. 2 vols., 1985.
Gogol: Plays and Selected Writings, edited with introduction and notes by Milton Ehre, translated by Milton Ehre and Fruma Gottschalk, 1994.

Fiction

Vechera na khutore bliz Dikan'ki (stories). 2 vols., 1831–32; as *Evenings in Little Russia*, translated by E.W. Underwood and W.H. Cline, 1903; as *Evenings on a Farm near Dikanka*, translated by Constance Garnett, in *Collected Works*, 1926; as *Evenings near the Village of Dikanka*, translated by Ovid Gorchakov, 1960; translated and edited by Christopher English, 1994.
Mirgorod (stories). 1835; as *Mirgorod, Being a Continuation of Evenings in a Village near Dikanka*, translated by Constance Garnett, 1928; as *Mirgorod*, translated by David Magarshack, 1962.
Arabeski (stories). 1835; as *Arabesques*, translated by Alexander Tulloch, 1982.
Mertvye dushi. 1842; as *Home Life in Russia*, 1854; as *Tchitchikoff's Journeys or Dead Souls*, translated by Isabel F. Hapgood, 2 vols., 1886; as *Dead Souls*, translated by S. Graham, 2nd edition, 1915; also translated by C.J. Hogarth, 1916; George Reavey, 1936; Andrew R. MacAndrew, 1961; David Magarshack, 1961; Helen

Michailoff, 1964; as *Chichikov's Journeys; or, Home-Life in Old Russia*, translated by Bernard G. Guerney, 1942; translated by Bernard Guilbert Guerney, 1996; translated by Richard Pevear and Larissa Volokhonsky, 1996.
Cossack Tales (includes "The Night of Christmas Eve"; "Taras Bulba"), translated by G. Tolstoi. 1861.
St. John's Eve and Other Stories from Evenings at the Farm and St. Petersburg Stories (includes "St. John's Eve"; "Old-Fashioned Farmers"; "The Tale of How Ivan Ivanovich Quarrelled with Ivan Nikiforovich"; "The Portrait"; "The Cloak"), translated by Isabel F. Hapgood. 1886.
Taras Bulba, St. John's Eve and Other Stories (includes "Taras Bulba"; "St. John's Eve"; "The Cloak"; "The Quarrel of the Two Ivans"; "The Mysterious Portrait"; "The Calash"), translated anonymously. 1887.
Russian Romances (includes "Taras Bulba"; "St. John's Eve"; "Akakiy Akakievitch's New Cloak"; "How the Two Ivans Quarrelled"; "The Mysterious Portrait"; "The King of the Gnomes"; "The Calash"), translated anonymously. 1899.
The Mantle and Other Stories (includes "The Mantle"; "The Nose"; "Memoirs of a Madman"; "A May Night"; "The Viy"), translated by Claud Field. 1915.
Taras Bulba and Other Tales, translated by John Cournos. 1917.
Tales, translated by Constance Garnett. 1926.
Diary of a Madman, translated by D. Mirsky. 1929; also translated by Beatrice Scott, with *Nevsky Prospekt*, 1945; Andrew R. MacAndrew, in *Diary of a Madman and Other Stories*, 1962; Ronald Wilks, in *Diary of a Madman and Other Stories*, 1972; as *A Madman's Diary*, in *The Humor of Russia*, edited by Ethel Lilian Voynich, 1895; as *Memoirs of a Madman*, in *Gems of the World's Best Classics*, edited by Llewellyn Jones and C.C. Gaul, 1927; translated by Constance Garnett, 1998.
Tales from Gogol (includes "Sorochinsky Fair"; "The Coach"; "Christmas Eve"; "Nevsky Prospekt"; "How the Ivans Quarrelled"; "The Nose"), translated by Rosa Portnova. 1945.
Tales of Good and Evil (includes "The Terrible Vengeance"; "The Portrait"; "Nevsky Avenue"; "Taras Bulba"; "The Overcoat"), translated by David Magarshack. 1949; new edition, 1957 (includes additionally "Ivan Fyodorovich Shponka and His Aunt" and "The Nose," but omits "Taras Bulba").
Taras Bulba and Other Tales, translated by Nikolay Andreyev. 1962.
Taras Bulba; The Lost Letters; The Terrible Vengeance, translated by Andrew R. MacAndrew. 1962.
Diary of a Madman and Other Stories (includes "Diary of a Madman"; "The Nose"; "The Carriage"; "The Overcoat"; "Taras Bulba"), translated by Andrew R. MacAndrew. 1962.
Shinel', edited by J. Forsyth. 1965; as *The Cloak*, in *Short Story Classics*, vol. 1, edited by W. Patten, 1907; in *Best Russian Short Stories*, edited by Thomas Seltzer, 1917; in *Russian Short Stories*, edited by Harry Christian Schweikert, 1919; translated by Isabel F. Hapgood, in *Great Russian Short Stories*, edited by Stephen Graham, 1929; as *The Overcoat*, translated by Constance Garnett, in *The Overcoat and Other Stories*, 1923; also translated by David Magarshack, 1956; Andrew R. MacAndrew, in *Diary of a Madman and Other Stories*, 1962; Ronald Wilks, in *Diary of a Madman and Other Stories*, 1972; adapted by Tom Lanter and Frank S. Torok, 1975; as *The Greatcoat*, translated by Bernard G. Guerney, 1943; Z. Shoenberg and J. Domb, 1944.
Diary of a Madman and Other Stories (includes "Diary of a Madman"; "The Nose"; "The Overcoat"; "How Ivan Ivanovich

Quarrelled with Ivan Nikiforovich''; ''Ivan Fyodorovich and His Aunt Shponka''), translated by Ronald Wilks. 1972.

Plays

Utro delovogo cheloveka (produced 1871). 1836; as *An Official's Morning*, translated by Constance Garnett, in *The Government Inspector and Other Plays*, 1926.

Revizor (produced 1836). 1836; revised versions, 1841, and in *Sochineniia*, 1842; edited by D. Bondar, 1945; as *The Inspector*, translated by T. Hart-Davies, 1892; as *Revizor: A Comedy*, translated by M. Mandell, 1910; as *The Inspector-General*, translated by A.A. Sykes, 1892; T. Seltzer, 1916; J. Anderson, 1931; J. Dolman and B. Rothberg, 1937; Andrew R. MacAndrew, 1976; as *The Government Inspector*, translated by Constance Garnett, in *The Government Inspector and Other Plays*, 1926, and in *Works*, 1927; also translated by D.J. Campbell, 1947; W.L. Goodman and Henry S. Taylor, 1962; Edward O. Marsh and Jeremy Brooks, 1968; Milton Ehre and Fruma Gottschalk, in *The Theater of Nikolay Gogol*, 1980; adapted by Guy Williams, 1980; also adapted by Adrian Mitchell, 1985; translated by John Laurence Seymour and George Rapall Noyes, 1995; adapted by John Byrne, translated by Alex Wilbraham, 1997.

Zhenit'ba (produced 1842). 1841; translated as *Zhenitba*, in *The Humor of Russia*, edited by Ethel Lilian Voynich, 1895; as *Marriage*, translated by Alexander Bakshy and Elizabeth Pennell, 1923; also translated by A. Berkman, with *The Gamblers*, 1927; Bella Costello, 1969; Milton Ehre and Fruma Gottschalk, in *The Theater of Nikolay Gogol*, 1980; as *The Marriage*, translated by Constance Garnett, in *The Government Inspector and Other Plays*, 1926, and in *Works*, 1927.

Tiazhba (produced 1844). In *Sochineniia*, 1842; as *A Lawsuit*, translated by Constance Garnett, in *The Government Inspector and Other Plays*, 1926; also translated by B. Pares, 1926.

Teatralnyi razyezd posle predstavleniia novoi komedii, in *Sochineniia*. 1842; as *After the Play*, translated by David Magarshack, 1959; in part as *Leaving the Theatre after a Performance of a New Comedy*, translated by Milton Ehre and Fruma Gottschalk, in *The Theater of Nikolay Gogol*, 1980, and in *Hanz Kuechelgarten, Leaving the Theatre and Other Works*, edited and translated by Ronald Meyer, 1990.

Igroki (produced 1843). In *Sochineniia*, 1842; as *The Gamblers*, translated by Constance Garnett, in *The Government Inspector and Other Plays*, 1926; numerous subsequent translations including by G. Wallerstein and B. Pares, 1926, A. Berkman, with *Marriage*, 1927, and Eric Bentley, 1957.

Otryvok (produced 1860). In *Sochineniia*, 1842; as *A Fragment*, translated by Constance Garnett, in *The Government Inspector and Other Plays*, 1926.

Lakeiskaia (produced 1863). In *Sochineniia*, 1842; as *The Servants' Hall*, translated by Constance Garnett, in *The Government Inspector and Other Plays*, 1926.

The Government Inspector and Other Plays (includes *Marriage; The Gamblers; Dramatic Sketches and Fragments: An Official's Morning, A Lawsuit, The Servants' Hall, A Fragment*), translated by Constance Garnett. 1926.

Other

Sochineniia [Works]. 4 vols., 1842.

Vybrannye mesta iz perepiski s druz'iami. 1847; as *Selected Passages from Correspondence with Friends*, translated by Jesse Zeldin, 1969.

Razmyshleniia o bozhestvennoi liturgii; as *Meditations on the Divine Liturgy*, translated by L. Alexieff. 1913; as *The Divine Liturgy of the Eastern Orthodox Church*, translated by Rosemary Edmonds, 1960.

Letters of Nikolai Gogol (translations), edited by Carl R. Proffer, translated by Proffer and Vera Krivoshein. 1967.

Nikolai Gogol: A Selection, translated by Christopher English. 1980.

Hanz Kuechelgarten, Leaving the Theater and Other Works, edited and translated by Ronald Meyer. 1990.

Avtorskaia ispoved' [An Author's Confession]. 1990.

V poiskakh zhivoi dushi [In the Raid of a Living Soul]. 1990.

*

Bibliography: *Gogol: A Bibliography* by Philip E. Frantz, 1989.

Critical Studies: *Gogol* by Janko Lavrin, 1926; *The Mighty Three: Pushkin, Gogol, Dostoevsky* by Boris Leo Brasol, 1934; *Nikolai Gogol* by Vladimir Nabokov, 1944; *Gogol: A Life* by David Magarshack, 1957; *Gogol as a Short Story Writer: A Study of His Technique of Composition* by F.C. Driessen, 1965; *Gogol: His Life and Works* by Vsevolod Setchkarev, 1965; *The Simile and Gogol's Dead Souls* by Carl. R. Proffer, 1967; *Gogol* by Victor Ehrlich, 1969; *Gogol: A Life* by Hugh McLean, 1969; *Reading the Russian Text of the Memoirs of a Madman of N.V. Gogol* by D.R. Hitchcock, 1974; *Gogol from the Twentieth Century: Eleven Essays* edited by Robert A. Maguire, 1974, revised edition, 1976; *Gogol: The Biography of a Divided Soul* by Henri Troyat, 1974; *The Sexual Labyrinth of Nikolai Gogol* by Simon Karlinsky, 1976; *Through Gogol's Looking Glass: Reverse Vision, False Focus, and Precarious Logic* by William W. Rowe, 1976; *Gogol's Dead Souls*, 1978, and *The Symbolic Art of Gogol: Essays on His Short Fiction*, 1982, both by James B. Woodward; *The Creation of Nikolai Gogol* by Donald Fanger, 1979; *Are There Any Digressions in Pushkin's Evgenij Onegin and Gogol's Dead Souls?: A Review of the Critical Literature with Commentary* by László Dienes, 1981; *Gogol* by V.V. Gippius, 1981; *The Enigma of Gogol: An Examination of the Writings of N.V. Gogol and Their Place in the Russian Literary Tradition* by Richard Peace, 1981; *Out from under Gogol's Overcoat: A Psychoanalytic Study* by Daniel Rancour-Laferrière, 1982; *Gogol's Overcoat: An Anthology of Critical Essays* edited by Elizabeth Trahan, 1982; *Nikolai Gogol and Ivan Turgenev* by Nick Worrall, 1982; *Gogol and the Natural School* by Victor V. Vinogradov, 1987; ''*Such Things Happen in the World*'': *Deixis in Three Short Stories by N.V. Gogol* by P.M. Waszink, 1988; *Nikolai Gogol: Text and Context* edited by Jane Grayson and Faith Wigzell, 1989; *Essays on Gogol: Logos and the Russian Word* edited by Susanne Fusso and Priscilla Meyer, 1992, and *Designing Dead Souls: An Anatomy of Disorder in Gogol* by Fusso, 1993; *Nikolai Gogol and the Baroque Heritage* by Gavriel Shapiro, 1993; *The Pragmatics of Insignificance: Chekhov, Zoshchenko, Gogol* by Cathy Popkin, 1993; *Exploring Gogol* by Robert A. Maguire, 1994; *Gogol's The Government Inspector* by Michael Beresford, 1997; *The Anguish of Mykola Hohol a.k.a. Nikolai Gogol* by George Luckyj, 1998; *Russian Devils and Diabolic Conditionality in Nikolai Gogol's Evening on a Farm Near Dikanka* by Christopher Putney, 1999; *Frames of the Imagination: Gogol's Arabesques and the Romantic Question of Genre* by Melissa Frazier, 2000.

* * *

The contribution of Nikolai Gogol' to the remarkable renaissance of Russian literature in the 19th century is exceeded only by that of Pushkin. With his three volumes of stories and his novel *Mertvye dushi* (*Dead Souls*) he not only ensured that the prose genres would predominate until the advent of Symbolism; he also effected with his subject-matter, themes, and character-types and his highly complex style the enormous expansion of the range of Russian literature and the Russian literary language, without which the major works of his successors, particularly Dostoevskii, could hardly have been written. In addition, his fiction and plays laid the foundations of Russian satire, and his central concern with the themes of guilt and redemption and with the contradictions and fragmentation of society marked the transition from a disinterested art to a committed one, to the conception of art as service and a spur to action, which has given modern Russian literature its characteristic sense of engagement.

But although Gogol's influence on the development of the modern Russian literary tradition was far-reaching, his works represent a unique body of writing that differs from that tradition in numerous fundamental respects. Herein lies the first of the many paradoxes which confront the reader. Thus neither of the two most conspicuous elements of that tradition, realism and penetrating psychological analysis, can be readily ascribed to Gogol's own art, in which the boundaries between the real, the supernatural, and the grotesque are always likely to dissolve, and the inner man is usually seen only through the props of his portrait. Similarly his elaborate style, in which extremes converge and a sentence or simile can encompass a paragraph or page, remained an inimitable testimony to the uniqueness of his genius.

The transition from his first two volumes of stories, *Vechera na khutore bliz Dikan'ki* (*Evenings on a Farm near Dikanka*) and *Mirgorod* (*Mirgorod, Being a Continuation of Evenings in a Village near Dikanka*), to his uncompleted novel conveys the impression of a complex evolution. In seven of the eight tales of *Evenings on a Farm near Dikanka* he drew extensively on his intimate knowledge of the Ukrainian folklore tradition, responding both to the contemporary vogue for exotic regionalism and to the taste for Gothic horror stories whetted by such German Romantic writers as Hoffmann and Tieck. The result is a bizarre mixture of the mundane and the supernatural, the comic and the horrific, which immediately established contrast as the central feature of Gogol's art. But the most striking contrast of all is created by the volume's penultimate story "Ivan Fedorovich Shpon'ka and His Aunt" in which the scene is switched abruptly to the Russian provinces of the 1820s and detailed characterization replaces tortuous plots. The story presents the first intriguing foretaste of the manner and preoccupations of the later works.

In the four works which comprise the volume *Mirgorod* the Ukrainian setting is retained, and the particular forms of contrast here serve significantly to clarify the underlying theme of Gogol's Ukrainian tales. The four works are essentially parodies of four literary genres—the idyll ("Old-Fashioned Farmers"), the heroic epic ("Taras Bulba"), the folktale ("The Viy"), and the comic tale ("The Tale of How Ivan Ivanovich Quarrelled with Ivan Nikiforovich")—which in combination express a powerful lament on the social and moral decline of Gogol's native land. In each case the reader's expectations are abruptly confounded by the intrusion of unfamiliar elements that evoke a pervasive sense of degeneration, aberration, and debilitating betrayal. Love yields to habit, heroism to inertia, and the appetites and senses replace honour and duty as the ultimate arbiters of human conduct. Greeted with wide acclaim, the four works are the first major embodiments of the theme to which Gogol's art was thereafter to be devoted—the theme of moral decline, of the emasculation and perversion of the human spirit.

On moving to St. Petersburg Gogol' soon found congenial material for the further development of this theme in the dehumanizing world of the capital's bureaucracy in which he spent a few wretched months. The most celebrated of his so-called "Petersburg Tales"— "Shinel" ("The Overcoat") and "Zapiski Sumasshedshego" ("Diary of a Madman")—were the fruits of this experience. Here again a disconcerting effect is produced by the coexistence of contrasting elements—in this case compassion for the depersonalized "little man" and detached, ironic scorn both for his abject surrender of his human dignity and for his belated, grotesque attempts to restore it. At the same time these and other stories in Gogol's third volume— "Nevskii prospekt" ("The Nevsky Prospect"), "Portret" ("The Portrait"), and especially "Nos" ("The Nose")—make abundantly clear the umbilical connection between his deceptive, nightmarish St. Petersburg and the folktale world of his Ukrainian tales. Again comedy and horror, the real and the fantastic are inseparably fused, and the devil and the witch retain their prominent roles, now clothed anew in the elegant attire of dignitaries, generals, and imperious ladies.

It was in the play *Revizor* (*The Government Inspector*) and the novel *Dead Souls*, however, that the contrasting elements of Gogol's art combined to produce two of the masterpieces of world literature. Selecting the vacuous Khlestakov and the acquisitive Chichikov as his itinerant heroes and employing in both works the simple plot device of confronting them with the senior citizens of the provincial towns in which they briefly alight, he was able to bring his unique gifts as humorist and satirist and his mature art of portraiture to bear on the task which he had now come to believe he was called on to perform: to expose the limitless extent of human folly and corruption and to infect his readers with his personal craving for moral rebirth. But the appearance of Part One of the projected three-part novel in 1842 marked the death of Gogol' the artist. Only fragments of Part Two have survived, together with his collection of essays *Vybrannye mesta iz perepiski s druz'iami* (*Selected Passages from Correspondence with Friends*), to illuminate the agonies that he experienced in exchanging his role as a castigator of evil for that of a guilt-ridden instrument of divine revelation. The struggle continued for ten long years before his body succumbed to the fate of his art.

—James B. Woodward

See the essays on *Dead Souls*, "Diary of a Madman," and *The Government Inspector*.

GOLDONI, Carlo

Born: Venice, Italy, 25 February 1707. **Education:** Educated in Venice; at a Jesuit school in Perugia; with Domenicans in Rimini; studied law at Papal College in Pavia, 1723–25. **Family:** Married Nicoletta Conio in 1736. **Career:** Assistant to his physician father in Chioggia, 1721–23, and in other towns; clerk in criminal court,

Chioggia, 1728–29, and Feltre, 1729–30; passed law examinations in Padua in 1731, and called to the Venetian bar, 1732; wrote plays for amateur companies as early as 1729–30, and for Giuseppe Imer's company, 1734–44, beginning with bare scenarios and gradually working towards completely written scripts; director of the opera house Teatro San Giovanni Crisostomo in Venice; lawyer in Pisa, 1744–47; house dramatist for Girolamo Medebach's acting company, 1748–53, and writer with the Teatro San Luca, 1753–62, both in Venice (in Rome, 1757–58); with the Comédie-Italienne, Paris, 1762–64; Italian tutor to the daughter of Louis XV, Princess Adelaide, 1764–65, and to royal children, 1768–80, in Versailles; in Paris after 1780. Wrote plays in both Italian and Venetian dialect, and some plays in French; also wrote libretti for cantatas and operas. **Died:** 6 February 1793.

PUBLICATIONS

Collections

Opere teatrali (first complete edition). 44 vols., 1788–95.
Raccolta completa di tutte le commedie in prosa ed in verso del signor Carlo Goldoni. 15 vols., 1794–98.
Opere complete, edited by Giuseppe Ortolani, E. Maddalena, and C. Musatti. 40 vols., 1907–60.
Tutte le opere (includes letters), edited by Giuseppe Ortolani. 14 vols., 1935–56.
Opere, edited by Fitippo Zampieri. 1954.
Teatro (selected plays), edited by Marzia Pieri. 3 vols., 1991.
The Comic Theatre of Carlo Goldoni, translated and introduced by L. Paris Saiko. 2000.

Plays

Belisario (produced 1734). 1798.
Rosmonda (produced 1734). 1793.
Don Giovanni Tenorio; o, Sia il dissoluto (produced 1736). 1754.
Rinaldo di Montalbano (produced 1736). 1774.
Enrico, Re di Sicilia (produced 1736). 1740.
Momolo cortesan, o, L'uomo di mondo (produced 1738). 1757.
Il prodigo (also known as *Momolo sulla Brenta;* produced 1739). 1757.
La bancarotta (produced 1740).
La donna di garbo (produced 1743). 1747; edited by Gastone Geron, 1984.
Il figlio d'Arlecchino perduto e ritrovato (produced c. 1745).
Il servitore di due padroni (produced 1745). 1753; edited by Eugenio Levi, 1957; as *Arlecchino servitore di due padroni,* edited by Luigi Lunari, Giorgio Strehler, and Carlo Pedretti, 1979; as *The Servant of Two Masters,* translated by Edward J. Dent, 1928; also translated by Tom Cone, 1980; Eric Bentley, in *Servant of Two Masters and Other Italian Classics,* 1986; translated and adapted by Shelley Berc and Andrei Belgrader, 1992; translated by Christina Sibul, adapted by Constance Congdon, 2000.
I due gemelli veneziani (produced 1748). 1750; edited by Guido Davico Bonino, 1975; as *The Venetian Twins,* translated by Frederick H. Davies, in *Four Comedies,* 1968; translated by Ranjit Bolt in *The Venetian Twins; Mirandolina: Two Plays,* 1993.
L'uomo prudente (produced 1748). 1750.

La vedova scaltra (produced 1748). 1750; edited by Avancinio Avancini, 1935, and by Gastone Geron, 1984; as *The Artful Widow,* translated by Frederick H. Davies, in *Four Comedies,* 1968.
Tonin Bella Grazie; o, Il frappatore (produced 1748). 1757.
La buona moglie (produced 1749). 1751.
Il cavaliere e la dama; o, I cicisbei (produced 1749). 1751; edited by Nicola Mangini, 1964.
La putta onorata (produced 1749). 1751; edited by Gastone Geron, 1984.
Il poeta fanatico (produced 1750).
Il padre di famiglia (produced c. 1750). 1751; as *The Father of a Family,* 1757.
Il teatro comico (produced 1750). 1751; edited by Gerolamo Bottoni, 1926, and by Guido Davico Bonino, 1983; as *The Comic Theatre,* translated by John W. Miller, 1969.
La famiglia dell'Antiquario (produced 1750). 1752; edited by Pietro Azzarone, 1961, by Guido Davico Bonino, 1983, and by Nicola Mangini and Nella Pavese, 1988.
L'avvocato veneziano (produced 1750). 1752.
Le feminine puntigliose (produced 1750). 1753.
La bottega del caffè (produced 1750). 1753; edited by Gianni Di Stefano, 1967, and by Carlo Pedretti, 1984; as *The Coffee House,* translated by Henry B. Fuller, 1925; translated by Robert Cornthwaite, 1995; also translated by Jeremy Parzen, 1998.
Il bugiardo (produced 1750). 1753; edited by Pietro Azzarone, 1967; with *La donna di garbo,* 1980; as *The Liar,* translated by Grace Lovat Fraser, 1922; also translated and adapted by Frederick H. Davies, 1963.
L'adulatore (produced 1750). 1753.
La Pamela, from the novel by Richardson (produced 1750). 1753; edited by Carmine Montella, 1968; translated as *Pamela,* 1756.
Il cavalier di buon gusto (produced 1750). 1753.
Il giuocatore (produced 1750). 1754.
Il vero amico (produced 1750). 1753.
L'erede fortunata (produced 1750). 1752.
Commedie. 1750–55, 1753–57, 1757–63, 1761–78.
La finta ammalata (produced 1751). 1753.
La dama prudente (produced 1751). 1753.
L'incognita perseguitata dal bravo impertinente (produced 1751). 1754.
L'avventuriere onorato (produced 1751). 1753.
La donna volubile (produced 1751). 1755.
I pettegolezzi delle donne (produced 1751). 1753; edited by Antonio Marenduzzo, 1942.
Il Moliere (produced 1751).
L'amante militare (produced 1751). 1755.
La castalda (produced 1751). 1753.
Il tu tare (produced 1752). 1753.
La moglie saggia (produced 1752). 1753.
Il feudatario (produced 1752). 1753.
La figlia obbediente (produced 1752). 1754; as *The Good Girl,* translated by M. Tracy, in *Four Comedies,* 1922.
La serva amorosa (produced 1752). 1753.
Le donne gelose (produced 1752). 1753; edited by Gastone Geron, 1988; as *The Good-Humoured Ladies,* translated by Richard Aldington, 1922.
I puntigli domestici (produced 1752). 1754.
I mercatanti (produced 1752). 1754.

Le donne curiose (produced 1753). 1753; edited by Ettore Allodoli, 1960, and by Gastone Geron, 1988.

La locandiera (produced 1753). 1753; edited by Gian Piero Brunetta, 1967; as *La locandiera (The Mistress of the Inn)*, translated by Merle Pierson, 1912; as *Mistress of the Inn*, translated by Helen Lohman, 1926, and by Anthony Intreglia, 1964; as *Mine Hostess*, in *Four Comedies*, 1922; also translated by Clifford Bax, in *Three Comedies*, 1961; as *Mirandolina*, translated by Frederick H. Davies, in *Four Comedies*, 1968; translated by Ranjit Bolt in *The Venetian Twins; Mirandolina: Two Plays*, 1993.

Il contrattempo; o, Il chiaccherione imprudente (produced 1753). 1754.

La donna vendicativa (produced 1753). 1754.

Il geloso avaro (produced 1753). 1757.

La donna di testa debole (produced 1753). 1757.

La sposa persiana (produced 1753). 1757.

L'impostore (produced 1754). 1754.

La cameriera brillante (produced 1754). 1757.

Il filosofo inglese (produced 1754). 1757.

Il vecchio bizzarro (produced 1754). 1757.

Il festino (produced 1754). 1757.

La peruviana (produced 1754). 1757.

La madre amorosa (produced 1754). 1757.

Terenzio (produced 1754). 1758.

I malcontenti (produced 1755). 1755.

Torquato Tasso (produced 1755). 1757.

Le massere (produced 1755). 1758.

Il cavaliere giocondo (produced 1755). 1758.

Le donne di casa soa (produced 1755). 1758; edited by Gastone Geron, 1988.

Ircana in Julfa (produced 1755). 1758.

La buona famiglia (produced 1755). 1758; edited by Polisseno Fegejo, 1942.

La villeggiatura (produced 1755). 1758; edited by Manlio Dazzi, 1954; as *Carlo Goldoni's Villeggiatura: A Trilogy Condensed*, translated by Robert Cornthwaite, 1994.

Il campiello (produced 1756). 1758; edited by Luigi Lunari, 1975, and by Guido Davico Bonino, 1986; as *Il Campiello*, translated by Susanna Graham-Jones and Bill Bryden, 1976.

Il raggiratore (produced 1756). 1758.

Il medico olandese (produced 1756). 1760.

Ircana in Ispahan (produced 1756). 1760.

La dalmatina (produced 1756). 1763.

La donna stravagante (produced 1756). 1760.

L'avaro (produced 1756). 1762; edited by Antonio Marenduzzo, 1946.

Il buon compatriotto (produced 1756). 1790.

La donna sola (produced 1757).

L'amante di se medesimo (produced 1757). 1760.

La vedova spiritosa (verse version produced 1757; prose version 1758). Prose version published 1759; verse version 1761.

Il padre per amore (produced 1757). 1763.

Un curioso accidente (produced 1757). 1768; as *A Curious Mishap*, translated by Helen Zimmern, in *Comedies*, 1892; also translated by Charles Lloyd, in *Three Comedies*, 1907; translated and adapted by Richard D.T. Hollister, 1924.

Il cavaliere di spirito (produced 1757). 1764.

L'impresario delle Smirne (produced 1757). 1774; as *The Impresario from Smyrna*, translated by Clifford Bax, in *Four Comedies*, 1922.

La bella selvaggia (produced 1758). 1761.

Il ricco insidiato (produced 1758). 1761.

La donna di governo (produced 1758). 1761.

La sposa sagace (produced 1758). 1761.

Lo spirito di contraddizione (produced 1758). 1761.

Le morbinose (produced 1758). 1761.

La donna bizzarra (produced 1758). 1760.

L'apatista; o, Sia l'indifferente (produced 1758). 1760.

Pamela maritata (produced 1759). 1761.

Gl'innamorati (produced 1759). 1761; edited by Andrea Sangiuolo, 1965, and by Guido Davico Bonino, 1986.

La scuola di ballo (produced 1759). 1792.

Artemisia (produced 1759). 1793.

La buona madre (produced 1759). 1764.

Le donne di buonumore (produced 1759). 1789.

La donna capricciosa. 1760.

I rusteghi (produced 1760). 1761; edited by Guido Davico Bonino, 1970; as *The Boors*, translated by I.M. Rawson, in *Three Comedies*, 1961.

La guerra (produced 1760). 1764; edited by Franco Fido, with *Il quartiere fortunato*, 1988.

Eneo nel Lazi (produced 1760). 1793.

Zoroaster (produced 1760), 1793.

La donna forte. 1761.

Le smanie della villeggiatura (produced 1761). 1768; edited by E. Maddalena, 1963, by Gastone Garon, 1984, and by Nicola Mangini and Nella Pavese, 1988.

Le avventure della villeggiatura (produced 1761). 1768; edited by Giorgio Strehler, Luigi Lunari, and Carlo Pedretti, 1982, by Gastone Geron, 1984, and by Nicola Mangini and Nella Pavese, 1988.

Il ritorno dalla villeggiatura (produced 1761). 1768; edited by Giorgio Strehler, Luigi Lunari, and Carlo Pedretti, 1982.

La casa nova (produced 1761). 1768; edited by Antonia Veronese Arslan, 1969; as *The Superior Residence*, translated by Frederick H. Davies, in *Four Comedies*, 1968.

Sior Todero Brontolon (produced 1761). 1774.

La scozzese (produced 1761). 1774.

La bella Giorgiana (produced 1761). 1792.

Le baruffe chiozzote (produced 1762). 1774; edited by Carlo Pedretti, 1978; as *The Squabbles of Chioggia*, translated by Charles W. Lemmi, in *The Drama*, 15, 1914; as *It Happened in Venice*, translated and adapted by Frederick H. Davies, 1965.

Una della ultime sere di carnevale (produced 1762). 1777.

L'osteria della posta (produced 1762). Edited by Antonio Marenduzzo, 1935; as *The Post-Inn*, translated by W.H.H. Chambers, in *The Drama 5*, edited by A. Bates, 1902.

L'amor paterno; o, La serva riconoscente (produced 1763).

Il matrimonio per concorso (produced 1763). 1778.

Il ventaglio (produced 1763). 1789; edited by Luigi Squarzina, 1979, and by Carlo Pedretti, 1980; as *The Fan*, translated by Helen Zimmern, in *Comedies*, 1892; also translated by Charles Lloyd, in *Three Comedies*, 1907; Kenneth McKenzie, 1911; E. and H. Farjeon, in *Four Comedies*, 1922, and in *Three Comedies*, 1961; Henry B. Fuller, 1925; translated and adapted by Frederick H. Davies, 1968.

Il ritratto d'Arlecchino (produced 1764). 1777.

Chi la fa l'aspetta (produced 1765). 1789.

Le Bourru bienfaisant (produced 1771). Edited by Gerolamo Bottoni; as *The Times*, 1780; as *The Beneficent Bear*, translated by Helen Zimmern, in *Comedies*, 1892; also translated by Charles Lloyd, in *Three Comedies*, 1907; Barrett H. Clark, 1915; as *Il burboro benefico*, translated 1964.

Il filosofo di campagna; as The Wedding Ring. 1773.

L'Avare fastueux (produced 1776). 1789; as *The Spendthrift Miser*, translated by Helen Zimmern, in *Comedies*, 1892.

L'amore artigiano, music by Florian Gassman, translated as *L'amore artigiano.* 1778.

I metempsicosi, 1793.

Gli amori di Alessandro Magno. 1793.

The Comedies (includes *The Beneficent Bear; A Curious Mishap; The Fan; The Spendthrift Miser*), edited and translated by Helen Zimmern. 1892.

Three Comedies (includes *The Fan; An Odd Misunderstanding; The Beneficent Bear*), translated by Charles Lloyd. 1907.

Four Comedies (includes *Mine Hostess; The Impresario from Smyrna; The Good Girl; The Fan*), translated by Clifford Bax, M. Tracy, and H. and E. Farjeon. 1922.

Three Comedies (includes *Mine Hostess; The Boors; The Fan*), translated by Clifford Bax, I.M. Rawson, and H. and E. Farjeon. 1961.

Four Comedies (includes *The Venetian Twins; The Artful Widow; Mirandolina; The Superior Residence*), translated by Frederick H. Davies. 1968.

Commedie, edited by Kurt Ringger. 1972.

Il quartiere fortunato, with *La guerra*, edited by Franco Fido. 1988.

Other

Mémoires, pour servir à l'histoire de sa vie, et à celle de son théâtre. 3 vols., 1787; as *Memoirs*, translated by John Black, 2 vols., 1814.

On Play-Writing, edited by F.C.L. van Steenderen. 1919.

Il teatro comico; Memorie italiane, edited by Guido Davico Bonino. 1983.

*

Bibliography: *Saggio di una bibliografia delle opere intorno a Carlo Goldoni (1793–1907)* by A. Della Torre, 1908; *Bibliografia goldoniana 1908–1957*, 1961, and *Bibliografia goldoniana 1958–1967*, 1961, both by Nicola Mangini, supplemented in the journal *Studi goldoniani*, 1968–79.

Critical Studies: *Goldoni: A Biography* by H.C. Chatfield-Taylor, 1913; *Goldoni and the Venice of His Time* by Joseph Spencer Kennard, 1920; *Carlo Goldoni, Librettist: The Early, Years* by P.E. Weiss, 1970; *Goldoni* by Heinz Riedt, 1974; *A Servant of Many Masters: The Life and Times of Carlo Goldoni* by Timothy Holme, 1976; *Language and Dialect in Ruzzante and Goldoni* by Linda L. Carroll, 1981; *Goldoni as Librettist: Theatrical Reform and the drammi giocosi per musica* by Ted Emery, 1991; *Goldoni and the Musical Theatre*, edited by Domenico Pietropaolo, 1995; *Carlo Goldoni and Eighteenth-century Theatre*, edited by Joseph Farrell, 1997.

* * *

Carlo Goldoni's career as a dramatist can be plotted easily in terms of his relationship to the historical development of drama in Italy, and, in fact, he is usually presented in such terms. In the first half of the 18th century, Italian comedy was essentially that of the *commedia dell'arte* (as opposed to the erudite comedy based on classical models). The plays were not written out, but a scenario was prepared around which the players improvised. All the characters were conventional, and in Venice four of the players still wore the *commedia dell'arte* masks: a miserly old man (Pantalone); a pretentious old man called the Doctor, usually learned and absurd; and two "zany" servants, one lively and simple (Arlecchino), one clever and roguish (Brighella). The masks themselves instantly revealed to the audience the players' characters; other characters—various servants, banal lovers—might be the basis of the simple plot, but the masked characters were the leading players. The "creative" element of each play was centred on the ingenuity of the stage business and the verbal dexterity of the permanent company members. Many of these practices are shown in Goldoni's play *Il teatro comico* (*The Comic Theatre*).

Goldoni, a youthful enthusiast for the theatre, slid into this theatrical world almost by accident, if his *Memoirs* are to be believed. After an early involvement with a touring company, he became a lawyer, married, and set up a law practice in Pisa. A play he had earlier written out in complete form became a success in Venice, and he was approached by the "Pantalone" character of the Medebach company to write some more plays for them. Goldoni agreed, but insisted on a written text, gradually ensuring that natural speech replaced the exaggerated and obscene dialogue used formerly, and, most revolutionary of all, he insisted that the masks be abandoned. The success of one of his first plays, *I due gemelli veneziani* (*The Venetian Twins*), lay in having a leading actor play both twin brothers—one a clever romantic hero, the other a simple country boy—so that the mask would have become a liability rather than an aid.

His "new" plays proved so successful that he was gradually able to bring about these changes in the next 15 years of playwriting in Venice. His interest in these "reforms" is clear only from the prefaces he wrote for editions of his plays: he never formalized his ideas in theoretical works.

That his plays did not represent a complete break with the past is obvious from the way in which many of his leading characters are based on the conventional *commedia dell'arte* characters: Pantalone usually reappears in the guise of a hard-up nobleman, always on he look-out for a free meal or a present—for instance, the Count in both *La locandiera* (*The Mistress of the Inn*) and *Il ventaglio* (*The Fan*); the Doctor is also often placed among the aristocracy, as a pretentious or "literary" man; comic servants are still well-employed, since the plots spring from mistaken identity or trivial misunderstandings—but such a character as Fabrizio, the servant of Mirandolina in *The Mistress of the Inn*, is complex, with doubts concerning his position and a past that acts on his character; and other servants or working-class characters are often full of individuality as well as zest.

The most interesting transformation in his characterizations—those in his romantic heroines—leads to the other major point to be made about Goldoni: his amiability and good nature, based on a perception of the world that is missing from *commedia dell'arte*. The timid conventional heroine has become a sensible and intelligent young woman, if not well educated, at least aware of her own dignity and worth, and not averse to fighting for her right to choose her own mate. Many of the plays have such a woman: usually she is concerned in overturning the prejudices of the male relative who is in charge of arranging her marriage (often to a fool or fortune-hunter). The most advanced example of this character type is Mirandolina, who has no guardian to protect (or dictate) to her, and whose heart is set on marriage with her servant and childhood friend, Fabrizio. Before her hopes are realized, however, she has to fend off the advances of the men who have fallen for her obvious charm and prospects (she runs an inn), and even to prove to herself that she is in charge of her own fate by wilfully making a misogynist staying at the inn fall in love with her. This plot would sound tragic if it were not so funny—no one is harmed by the intrigue; in fact, all the male characters learn something about themselves from the experience.

This interest in the naturalness of love and marriage, and in the natural relations of people in a social group, also led Goldoni often to centre his plays on a milieu—a shop or an inn, a small village, or a square in a city—where no single character emerges as an obvious hero or heroine, and where the good will and acceptance of the outcome seem to be the end in view; there is usually a liberated spokesman for the group—often a woman. Examples of this sort of play are *Il campiello*, *I rusteghi* (*The Boors*), *Le baruffe chiozzote* (*The Squabbles of Chioggia*), and *The Fan*. *La casa nova* (*The Superior Residence*), though involving only two families in an apartment house in Venice, and with a smaller cast, also promotes good nature, lack of pretensions, and the value of simple love.

Goldoni's plays are not deep, and his *Memoirs* reflect this lack of theoretical or intellectual interest, but his characters, like those of Marivaux, are human and often complex, and his plots are arranged to bring out this complexity rather than to submerge it in a conventional framework.

—George Walsh

See the essays on *The Comic Theatre* and *The Mistress of the Inn*.

GOLL, Ivan

Born: Isaac Lang in Saint Dié, Alsace, Germany, 29 March 1891. Moved to Switzerland in 1915 after the outbreak of hostilities. **Education:** Educated at Metz; studied jurisprudence at the University of Strasbourg, 1912–14; University of Lausanne, 1915–18. **Family:** Married Claire Studer. **Career:** Founder, Rhein Verlag, publishers, Zurich; lived in Paris, 1919–39, associated with Picasso, Chagall, Breton and Éluard; moved to New York, 1939; founding editor, *Hémisphères*, New York, 1943–46; diagnosed as suffering from leukaemia, 1944; returned to Paris, 1947. **Died:** 27 February 1950.

PUBLICATIONS

Collections

Dichtung, Lyrik, Prosa, Dramen, edited by Claire Goll. 1960. *Oeuvres*, edited by Claire Goll and François Xavier Jaujard. 2 vols., 1968–70.

Selected Poems, edited by Paul Zweig, translated by Zweig, Robert Bly, George Hitchcock, and Galway Kinnell. 1968.
Gedichte 1924–1950, edited by Horst Bienek. 1976.

Verse

Der Panamakanal. 1912.
Films. 1914.
Élégies Internationales. 1915.
Dithyramben. 1918.
Der Torso. 1918.
Der neue Orpheus. 1918; as *Le Nouvel Orpheé*, translated by Goll, 1923.
Die Unterwelt. 1919.
Astral. 1920.
Paris brennt. 1920.
Der Eiffelturm: Gesammelte Dichtung. 1924.
Poèmes d'amour, with Claire Goll. 1925; as *Love Poems*, 1947.
Poèmes de jalousie, with Claire Goll. 1926.
Poèmes de la vie et de la mort, with Claire Goll. 1927.
Die siebente Rose. 1928.
Deux Chansons de la Seine. N.d.
Chansons malaises. 1934; as *Songs of a Malay Girl*, translated by Clark Mills, 1942; as *Malaiische Liebeslieder* (bilingual edition), translated by Goll, 1967.
Métro de la mort. 1936.
La Chanson de Jean sans Terre. 1936; revised edition, 1957; edited by Francis J. Carmody, 1962; as *John sans Terre: Landless John*, translated by Lionel Abel, William Carlos Williams, and others, 1944.
Le mythe de la roche percée. 1945; as ''The Myth of the Pierced Rock,'' translated by Louise Bogan, in *Four Poems of the Occult*, edited by Francis J. Carmody, 1962.
Atom Elegy. 1946.
Fruit from Saturn. 1946.
Élégiè d'Ihpétonga suivie de Masques de cendre. 1949; as *Elegy of Ihpetonga and Masks of Ashes*, translated by Babette Deutsch, Louise Bogan, and Claire Goll, 1954.
Le Char triomphal de l'antimoine. 1949.
Les géorgiques parisiennes. 1951.
Dix Mille Aubes, with Claire Goll. 1951.
Les Cerdes magiques. 1951; as ''The Magic Circles,'' translated by Claire Goll and Eric Sellin, in *Four Poems of the Occult*, edited by Francis J. Carmody, 1962.
Traumkraut, edited by Claire Goll. 1951.
Zehntausend Morgenröten, with Claire Goll. 1954.
Abendgesang (Neila); letzte Gedichte, edited by Claire Goll. 1954.
Multiple femme, edited by Claire Goll. 1956; as *Multiple Woman*, translated by Francis J. Carmody, in *Four Poems of the Occult*, edited by Carmody, 1962.
Der Mythus vom durchbrochenen Felsen. 1956.
Neue Blümlein des heiligen Franziskus, with Claire Goll. 1957.
Duo d'Amour: Poèmes d'amour 1920–1950, with Claire Goll. 1959.
Four Poems of the Occult, edited by Francis J. Carmody. 1962.
L'Antirose, with Claire Goll. 1965; as *Die Antirose*, 1967.
Gedichte, edited by René A. Strasser. 1968.
Élégie de Lackawanna. 1973; as *Lackawanna Elegy* (bilingual edition), translated by Galway Kinnell, 1970.

Fiction

Le Microbe de l'or. 1927.
Die Eurokokke. 1927.
Der Goldbazillus. 1927.
Der Mitropäer. 1928.
À bas l'Europe. 1928.
Agnus Dei. 1929.
Sodome et Berlin. 1929.
Lucifer vieillissant. 1934.
Nouvelles Petites Fleurs de Saint François d'Assise, with Claire Goll. 1958.

Plays

Die Unsterblichen: zwei Possen (includes *Der Unsterbliche* and *Der Ungestorbene*). 1920; as *The Immortal One*, translated by Walter H. and Jacqueline Sokel, in *An Anthology of German Expressionist Drama*, edited by Walter H. Sokel, 1963.
Die Chapliniade. 1920.
Melusine (produced 1956). 1922.
Mathusalem; oder, Der ewige Bürger (produced 1927). 1922; translated by Arthur S. Wensinger and Clinton J. Atkinson, in *Plays for a New Theatre*, 1966; also translated by J.M. Ritchie, in *Seven Expressionist Plays*, 1968.
Assurance contre le suicide (produced 1926). 1923.
Der neue Orpheus, music by Kurt Weill (produced 1928). 1923.
Der Stall des Agias. 1924.
Royal Palace (opera libretto), music by Kurt Weill. 1926.
Théâtre. Mathusalem. Les Immortels. 1963.

Other

Requiem pour les morts de L'Europe. 1916.
Requiem für die Gefallenen von Europa. 1917.
Die drei guten Geister Frankreichs (essays). 1919.
Oberrealismus, Vorwort zu Methusalem. 1922.
Germaine Berton. 1925.
Pascin (essays). 1929.
Iwan Goll, Claire Goll: Briefe. 1966.
Selected Correspondence, edited by Barbara Glauert. 1978.
Editor, with Claire Goll, *Dos Herz Frankreichs, eine Anthologie französischer Freiheitslyrik.* 1920.
Editor and translator, *Das Lächeln. Voltaire: Ein Buch in Diese Zeit.* 1921.
Editor and translator, *Les Cinq Continents: Anthologie de poésie contemporaine.* 1922.
Translator, with Gustav Laudauer, *Der Wundarzt: Briefe Aufzeichnungen und Gedichte aus dem amerikanischen Sezessionskreig*, by Walt Whitman. 1919.
Translator, *Der Schimmer im abgrund: Ein Manifest an alle Denkenden*, by Henri Barbusse. 1920.
Translator, *Die Goldsucher von Wien: Ein Bergebenheit unter Schriebern*, by Pierre Hamp. 1922.
Translator, *Der Aussätzige und die Heilige*, by François Mauriac. 1928.
Translator, *Schwarz und Weiss, die Wahrheit über Afrika*, by Albert Londres. 1929.
Translator, *César*, by Mirko Jelusich. 1937.
Translator, *Le Chant de Bernadette*, by Franz Werfel, 1942.

*

Critical Studies:: *The Poetry of Ivan Goll* by F.J. Carmody, 1956; *Ivan Goll: Quatre études par Jules Romains, Marcel Brion, Francis Carmody, Richard Exner*, 1956; *Yvan Goll: An Iconographical Study of His Poetry* by Vivien Perkins, 1970; *Interpretations of Ivan Goll's Late Poetry* by Vera B. Profit, 1977; *Ivan Goll: The Development of His Poetic Themes and Their Imagery* by Margaret A. Parmée, 1981; *Yvan Goll and Bilingual Poetry* by James Phillips, 1984; *Yvan Goll—Claire Goll: Texts and Contexts*, edited by Eric Robertson and Robert Vilain, 1997.

* * *

Ivan Goll is remembered today chiefly for his cycles of poems, though he expresses himself in many different forms: essays, plays, novels, and the *avant-garde* film. His writing was in many ways an attempt to come to terms with his peculiarly uneasy position in Europe in the first half of the 20th century. He described himself as being "by fate a Jew, by chance a Frenchman, by virtue of a piece of paper a German." It has been felt by some that his poetry belongs more firmly to German literary history than to that of France, yet he found it impossible to align himself wholeheartedly with any one aspect of this tripartite division and, like his Alsatian compatriot, Hans Arp, expressed himself with equal felicity in French and German. (Later, during his American exile, he also wrote poems in English.)

Goll's first published poem of note was *Der Panamakanal* [The Panama Canal] of 1912, a work that reveals clearly his affinities with the new movement of Expressionism. The poem, which seems at first to be a Romantic lament for a natural world destroyed by civilization, ends on a positive note, evoking universal love and the brotherhood of mankind. This is in keeping with the spirit of his requiem for the dead of Europe in World War I and indicates his commitment to the branch of Expressionism more dedicated to building the future than revelling in the decline of a passing world. However, a later version of "Der Panamakanal" in 1918 ends with the belief that man's lot does not, after all, improve, and points forward to the pessimistic tone of much of the later poetry.

In his essays, such as *Die drei guten Geister Frankreichs* [The Three Good Spirits of France], Goll attempted to foster a better understanding between the peoples of France and Germany, but he himself was attracted more to France by the greater liveliness of the artistic scene. Here his Expressionist style began to develop towards Surrealism, manifested first in drama and film scenarios, such as *Die Chapliniade* [The Chaplinade] and *Mathusalem* (*Methusalem*). These works blend fantasy, reality, and the absurd in a way that recalls the work of German Expressionist dramatists, continuing and extending their desire to arouse audience response by means of shock effects. They are evidence of the autobiographical nature of much of Goll's writing, but also of his tendency to appear in the guise of a persona rather than in the first person. By this means he endows his figures with more general validity; the problems he explores are in some senses peculiarly his own, yet the character of Charlot in *Die Chapliniade* is an evocative portrayal of a well-known clown image, whose melancholy is concealed by his fixed smile.

The cyclical poem that Goll regarded as his major work, *La Chanson de Jean sans Terre* (*Landless John*), is the most significant example of such autobiographical writing. If one imagines the character of John replaced by "I," claims Jules Romains in *Yvan Goll*

(1956), one will notice a surprising change of colour and persuasive force. The central figure, who wanders the earth through 69 poems, belongs everywhere and nowhere. He seeks love and identity and yet the absence of these things also bestows a form of freedom. His searching and his problems are not ended by the end of the cycle. The final verse of the poem gives Goll's own definition of John:

> Landless John walks the roads leading nowhere
> He walks to escape his shadow which binds him to the soil
> He wants to possess nothing on this earth. Will he
> —By singing—get free of his shadow, his other I?

(translated by Galway Kinnell)

It would be a mistake to regard *Landless John* as simply a version of the Wandering Jew. The work follows on from the novels of the 1920s, such as *À bas l'Europe* [Down with Europe], which are concerned with the economic and moral decline of the age. John too inhabits the modern, materialistic world and Goll describes him as a contemporary individual, battling against internal and external forces.

The uncertainty of love is a theme of poems written both before and after *Landless John*. Goll composed the cycle *Poèmes d'amour* (*Love Poems*) together with his wife Claire, also a poet of note, who translated much of his work. They reflect in a pure and limpid style the poets' love, their need of each other, but also jealousy, fear of betrayal, and a clash of temperaments. Love also runs as a constant thread through the last work, *Traumkraut* [Grasses of Dreams]. On his deathbed the poet reverted to the language of his earliest writings and was able to say that only now had he truly learned to master his craft. It was for this reason that he asked Claire Goll, as she tells us in her preface, to destroy all his previous work. As the title implies, the poems are concerned with nature, but often nature seen in a surreal context: the images spring from spiritual rather than physical experience.

Because of the change of style (but more especially of language) that took place in Goll's writing when he settled in France, he is often regarded in Germany first and foremost as an Expressionist and in France as a Surrealist. Yet his plays and poems show clearly the way in which his Surrealism grew out of his Expressionism. He made a conscious break with the latter in 1921, aware that it was nearing its end, but the break was a gradual one and there are many echoes of the earlier movement in his later work. The many distinguished artists who have illustrated his work are also representative of both groups; they include Hans Arp, Salvador Dali, George Grosz, Fernand Léger and above all Marc Chagall. Like them, Goll was in the mainstream of the artistic movements of his time.

—Margaret K. Rogister

GOMBROWICZ, Witold

Born: Maloszyce, Poland, 4 August 1904. **Education:** Educated privately; St. Stanislas Kostka (Catholic high school), 1916–22; Warsaw University, 1922–26, law degree 1926; Institut des Hautes Études Internationales, Paris, 1926–27. **Family:** Married Marie-Rita Labrosse in 1968. **Career:** Part-time law clerk, Warsaw, 1928–34; reviewer for several Warsaw newspapers, 1935; travelled to Argentina and cut off from Poland because of war, 1939; reviewer (under pseudonym) for newspapers in Buenos Aires from 1940; secretary for the Polish Bank, Buenos Aires, 1947–55; left Argentina, 1963; Ford Foundation fellow, Berlin, 1963–64; lived in Vence, France, 1964–69. **Awards:** Kultura prize (Paris), 1961; International literary prize, 1967. **Died:** 25 July 1969.

PUBLICATIONS

Collection

Dzieła zebrane [Collected Works]. 11 vols., 1969–77.

Fiction

Pamiętnik z okresu dojrzewania [Memoirs from Adolescence]. 1933.
Ferdydurke. 1937; as *Ferdydurke*, translated by Eric Mosbacher, 1961; also translated by Danuta Borchardt, 2000.
Trans-Atlantyk, with *Ślub*. 1953; as *Trans-Atlantyk*, translated by Carolyn French and Nina Karsov, 1994.
Bakakaj (selections). 1957.
Pornografia. 1960; as *Pornografia*, translated by Alastair Hamilton, 1966.
Kosmos. 1965; as *Cosmos*, translated by Eric Mosbacher, 1966.
Opętani. 1973; as *Possessed; or, The Secret of Myslotch*, translated (from French) by J.A. Underwood, 1980.
Zdarzenia na brygu Banbury. 1982.

Plays

Iwona, Księżniczka Burgunda (produced 1957). In *Skamander*, 1935; as *Princess Ivona*, translated by Krystyna Griffith-Jones and Catherine Robins, 1969.
Ślub (produced 1964). With *Trans-Atlantyk*, 1953; as *The Marriage*, translated by Louis Iribarne, 1970.
Operetka (produced 1969). 1966; as *Operetta*, translated by Louis Iribarne, 1971.
Historia [History] (unfinished). 1975.

Other

Dziennik 1953–1956. 3 vols., 1957–66; as *Diary*, edited by Jan Kott, translated by Lillian Vallee, 3 vols., 1988–93.
Entretiens avec Gombrowicz, edited by Dominique de Roux. 1968; as *A Kind of Testament*, translated by Alastair Hamilton, 1973.
Wspomnienia polskie [Polish Reminiscences]. 1977.
Listy 1950–1969 [Letters], with Jerzy Giedroyc, edited by Andrzej Kowalczyk. 1993.
Correspondance, with Jean Dubuffet. 1995.
Philosophy in Six Lessons and a Quarter, edited with preface by Simona Draghici. 1999.

*

Critical Studies: *Gombrowicz* (in French) by Constantin Jeleński and Dominique de Roux, 1971; *Gombrowicz: Bourreau-martyr* by Jacques Volle, 1972; *Gombrowicz* (in French) by Rosine Georgin, 1977; *Gombrowicz* by Ewa M. Thompson, 1979; *Gombrowicz and Frisch: Aspects of the Literary Diary* by Alex Kurczaba, 1980; *Gombrowicz, vingt ans après* edited by Manuel Carcassone and others, 1989; *Gombrowicz's Grimaces: Modernism, Gender, Nationality*, edited by Ewa Plonowska Ziarek, 1998; *Lines of Desire: Reading Gombrowicz's Fiction with Lacan* by Hanjo Berressem, 1998.

* * *

Witold Gombrowicz is one of the most original Polish writers of the 20th century. His first book *Pamiętnik z okresu dojrzewania* [Memoirs from Adolescence], a collection of grotesque short stories, already established his obsessive themes which he was to pursue in later years. These can be described as a desire for sexual domination and/or submission, and the manipulation (sexual and intellectual) of others. In *Ferdydurke*, his most striking novel, all these themes are woven into the plot which follows the adventures of Joey, a 30-year-old man forced back into the immaturity of adolescence by a determined schoolteacher. *Ferdydurke* is a parody of traditional Polish and fashionable Western values which are displayed and then effectively discredited in three different domains of life: at school, in the "progressive" household of an engineer, and in the old-fashioned manor-house. The conclusion of this very entertaining novel is that however much we may try to break out of the prison of Form, there is no escape from play-acting.

In 1939 Gombrowicz visited Argentina and after the outbreak of World War II decided to stay there, so it was this country that became the backdrop to his next novel *Trans-Atlantyk*. It depicts a conflict between the old and new generation of Polish emigrés in Argentina, the author acting as a narrator/chronicler of a fairly trivial quarrel which he tells with the panache of Polish memoirs from the Baroque period. What Gombrowicz really questions in this novel is the relevance of the Polish national myth. He continues to investigate this and other controversial issues in the three volumes of his *Dziennik* (*Diary*) which has been called an "autobiographical novel" as well as a running commentary on the philosophical, cultural, and political problems of the day. Gombrowicz's *Diary* exhibits the same sharp wit and far-reaching scepticism to traditional values as his novels, but it also lays bare the author's obsessions, complexes, and narcissistic tendencies. These reappear in a less striking form in the novels *Pornografia* and *Kosmos* (*Cosmos*), which are both essays on the possibilities and limits of psychological manipulation—of the young by the old, and of the normal by the obsessed.

Gombrowicz was also a playwright; indeed, his first international successes were due to the production of his plays in Paris and in Germany in the 1960s. There are altogether four plays by Gombrowicz, one of which, the amusing but perhaps too ambitious *Historia* [History], was left unfinished. The earliest play, *Iwona, Księżniczka Burgunda* (*Princess Ivona*), is a "tragifarce." It takes place in a mythical kingdom where the young heir to the throne plans but eventually fails to marry the singularly ugly and unpleasant girl whom he chose in a moment of malicious whim. Ivona acts as a catalyst of suppressed guilt for everyone, so in the end she has to be eliminated in the name of state interests. There are, pseudo-Shakespearean undertones in the excellent *Ślub* (*The Marriage*), which, on one level, is the story of human beings shaping each other through words, gestures, and acts of homage or defiance, while on another level it is the tragedy of overstrained human will. The sacralization of certain symbols can force society into their temporary acceptance, but not even the most charismatic figure can "give himself" a wedding which would restore the lost innocence of a fallen bride. *Operetka* (*Operetta*) is a bizarre tragi-comedy which through the parody of this "idiotic art form" manages to convey a philosophical message. Although its starting-point is the striving of an overformalized society towards "nakedness" (i.e. freedom), anarchy and totalitarianism are alternative "forms" also to be experienced. While Gombrowicz's savage parody of the past hundred years of European history, brings

the play very close to the theatre of the absurd, it nevertheless ends on an optimistic note, hailing "nudity eternally youthful" and "youth eternally nude," that expresses faith in the mysterious self-regenerating forces of mankind.

—George Gömöri

See the essay on *Ferdydurke*.

GONCHAROV, Ivan (Aleksandrovich)

Born: Simbirsk, Russia, 18 June 1812. **Education:** Educated at local boarding school, 1820–22; Moscow Commercial School, 1822–31; University of Moscow, 1831–34. **Military Service:** Civil servant in St. Petersburg from 1834: secretary to Admiral Pitiatin on trip to Far East, 1852–55; **Career:** Official censor, St. Petersburg, 1856–60, and member of the committee of review of Russian censorship groups, 1863–67; retired from civil service as Actual Councillor of State, 1867. **Died:** 27 September 1891.

PUBLICATIONS

Collections

Povesti i ocherki [Stories and Essays], edited by B.M. Engelgardt. 1937.
Sobranie sochinenii [Collected Works], edited by A.P. Rybasov. 8 vols., 1952–55.
Sobranie sochinenii [Collected Works], edited by S.I. Mashinskii. 8 vols., 1977–80.
Izbrannye sochineniia [Selected Works], edited by G.I. Belen'kii. 1990.

Fiction

Obyknovennaia istoriia. 1848; as *A Common Story*, translated by Constance Garnett, 1894; as *The Same Old Story*, translated by Ivy Litvinova, 1956; as *An Ordinary Story*, with *Viktor Rovoz*, edited and translated by Marjorie L. Hoover, 1993.
Oblomov. 1859; as *Oblomov*, translated by C.J. Hogarth, 1915; also translated by Natalie Duddington, 1929; David Magarshack, 1954; Ann Dunnigan, 1963.
Obryv. 1870; as *The Precipice*, translated by M. Bryant, 1915; translated by Laury Magnus and Boris Jakim, 1993.

Other

Russkie v Iaponii v kontse 1853 i v nachale 1854 godov [Russians in Japan in the End of 1853 and the Beginning of 1854]. 1855; revised edition, as *Fregat Pallada*, 1858; edited by D.V. Oznobishin, 1986; as *The Frigate Pallas: Notes on a Journey*, translated by N.W. Wilson, 1965.
Literaturno-kriticheskie stat'i i pis'ma [Literary Critical Articles and Letters], edited by A.P. Rybasova. 1938.
I.A. Goncharov-kritik (selection), edited by V.I. Korobov. 1981.
Ocherki. Stat'i. Pis'ma. Vospominaniia sovremennikov [Essays. Articles. Letters. Reminiscences of Contemporaries]. 1986.

*

Bibliography:: *Bibliografiia Goncharova 1832–1964* by A.D. Alekseev, 1968; *Ivan Goncharov: A Bibliography* edited by Garth M. Terry, 1986.

Critical Studies:: *Goncharov* by Janko Lavrin, 1954; *Goncharov* by Alexandra and Sverre Lyngstad, 1971; *Oblomov and His Creator: The Life and Art of Ivan Goncharov* by Milton Ehre, 1973; *Goncharov: His Life and His Works* by V. Setchkarev, 1974; *Oblomov: A Critical Examination of Goncharov's Novels* by Richard Peace, 1991; *The Autobiographical Novel of Co-consciousness: Goncharov, Woolf, and Joyce* by Gayla Diment, 1994; *Goncharov's Oblomov: A Critical Companion*, edited by Gayla Diment, 1998.

* * *

Oblomov, Ivan Goncharov's best known novel, so dwarfs his other fiction that, in the West, at least, he tends to be known for this work alone. This is regrettable because, for all its uniqueness, it is still arguable that *Oblomov* achieves its fullest resonance against the background of its predecessor, *Obyknovennaia istoriia* (*A Common Story*), and its successor, *Obryv* (*The Precipice*).

All three novels are concerned with the confrontation between the rising pragmatism of the mid-19th century and the comparatively established norms of Romantic idealism. *A Common Story* explores the relationship between Aleksandr Aduev, a young idealist dreaming of love and literary success and his uncle who has become reconciled to the uninspiring realities of the world. Somewhat too schematically, perhaps, Goncharov plots the course of Aduev's disenchantment to its issue: assimilation to the uncle's viewpoint. In *The Precipice* the ineffective Raiskii, another idealist, vies with a nihilist for the heroine's hand. Although the nihilist manages to seduce her, both he and Raiskii are ultimately rejected in favour of Tushin, a solid, commonsensical neighbour of the heroine.

The triumph of the pragmatic outlook is also an essential feature of *Oblomov*. Stolz, the half-German friend of the eponymous hero, attempts to awaken the latter from his torpid inactivity, urging him to use his talents in the real world before it is too late. Encouraged by the practical Stolz and by the heroine, Olga, with whom he has an affair, Oblomov makes some progress in extricating himself from the mire before succumbing once more to the temptations of inertia. Oblomov dies of a stroke and Stolz marries the heroine. Oblomov's slothful attachment to his bed, his almost symbiotic relationship with his aged servant Zakhar and his addiction to comfort are generally seen as satirized characteristics of the declining Russian landed gentry of the mid-19th century. Stolz embodies the entrepreneurial class that will oust the aristocracy unless it adapts.

However, the status of *Oblomov* as a world classic derives from the fact that Oblomov, like Hamlet (whose indecisiveness he shares) transcends his *chronotopos* to personify a universal human predicament. Oblomov is the passive romantic who instinctively resists every incursion from the real world of disturbing activity. This passivity is represented in the novel as something akin to sleep, and, like sleep, is solaced by dreaming.

''Oblomov's Dream,'' a pivotal section of the novel, was published separately in 1849. It offers an idyllic vision of the hero's rural childhood that has so fatefully shaped his later life. The dream is not just a representation of the past but an abiding subconscious reality that continues to exert a stultifying influence on Oblomov's will. Such is its fatally soothing power that, after his brief awakening by

Olga and Stolz, Oblomov is unable to resist his landlady's adult reconstruction of the old childhood comforts.

The use of dream, both for subliminal analysis and as a means of representing contradictions inherent in the romantic outlook, makes *Oblomov* a profoundly psychological novel. It is Goncharov's achievement to have successfully grafted psychological portrayal on to the Gogolian stock of external characterization. To this extent *Oblomov* may be held to anticipate the great novels of Tolstoi and Dostoevskii and must be assigned a crucial role in the development of the Russian novel.

—Robert Reid

See the essay on *Oblomov*.

GONCOURT, Edmond (-Louis-Antoine Huot) de, and Jules (-Alfred) de

Edmond de Goncourt: **Born:** Nancy, France, 26 May 1822. **Education:** Educated at Pension Goubaux; Lycée Henri IV; Collège Bourbon; studied law, 1841. **Career:** Worked for the city finance department. Travelled through France and Algeria with his brother, sketching and noting impressions in their now famous diary, 1848–49; travelled to Switzerland, Belgium, and Normandy, 1850; contributed to the literary daily, *Paris*, and to *Revue de Paris*, 1852–53; travelled to Italy, 1855–56, and 1867; important collector and connoisseur of Japanese art. Bequeathed money to found the Académie Goncourt that awards the annual literary prize. **Died:** 16 July 1896. *Jules de Goncourt:* **Born:** Paris, France, 17 December 1830. **Education:** Educated at Lycée Condorcet and Collège Bourbon, Paris. **Career:** Travelled through France and Algeria with his brother, sketching and writing their now famous diary, 1848–49; travelled to Switzerland, Belgium and Normandy, 1850; contracted syphilis, 1850; contributed to the literary daily, *Paris*, and to *Revue de Paris*, 1852–53; co-founder, with his brother and their cousin, Pierre-Charles de Villedeuil, *L'Éclair*, 1850s; travelled to Italy, 1855–56, and 1867. **Died:** 20 June 1870.

PUBLICATIONS BY EDMOND AND JULES DE GONCOURT

Collections

Théâtre. 1879.
Bibliothèque des Goncourt. 1897.
Collection des Goncourt. 1897.

Fiction

En 18. . . 1851.
La Lorette. 1853.
Les Hommes de lettres. 1860; as *Charles Demailly*, 1896.
Soeur Philomène. 1861; as *Sister Philomene*, translated by Laura Ensor, 1890; also translated by Madeline Jay, 1989.
Germinie Lacerteux. 1865; as *Germinie Lacerteux*, translated anonymously, 1887; also translated by John Chestershire, 1897; Leonard Tancock, 1984; as *Germinie*, translated by Jonathan Griffith, 1955.

Renée Mauperin. 1864; as *Renée Mauperin*, translated by Alys Hallard, 1902; also translated by James Fitzmaurice-Kelly, 1904.
Manette Salomon. 1867.
Madame Gervaisais. 1869.
Quelques créatures de ce temps (stories). 1876.
Première amoureuse (stories). 1896.

Plays

La Nuit de la Saint-Sylvestre. 1852.
Henriette Maréchal (produced 1865). 1866.
La Patrie en danger. 1873.

Other

Salon de 1852 (criticism). 1852.
Mystères des théâtres, 1852. 1853.
Oeuvres complètes. 21 vols., 1854.
La Révolution dans les moeurs. 1854.
Histoire de la société française pendant la Révolution. 1854.
Histoire de la société française pendant le Directoire. 1855.
La Peinture à l'exposition de 1855. 1855.
Une voiture de masques. 1856; revised edition, 1990.
Les Actrices. 1856.
Sophie Arnould, d'après sa correspondance et ses mémoires inédits. 1857.
Portraits intimes du dix-huitième siècle. 2 vols., 1857–58.
Histoire de Marie-Antoinette. 1858; revised edition, 1859; revised, with letters, 1863; revised editions, 2 vols., 1873–74, 2 vols., 1880–82, 3 vols., 1881–82.
Les Saint-Aubin. 1859.
L'Art du dix-huitième siècle. 11 vols., 1859–75; complete edition, 1875; as *French 18th-Century Painters*, edited and translated by Robin Ironside, 1948.
Les Hommes de lettres. 1860.
Les Maîtresses de Louis XV. 2 vols., 1860; as *The Confidantes of a King*, translated by Ernest Dowson, 1907.
La Femme au dix-huitième siècle. 1862; as *The Woman of the 18th-Century*, translated by Jacques Le Clerq and Ralph Roeder, 1927.
Idées et sensations. 1866.
Les Vignettistes. 1868.
Deuxième mille. 1886.
Gavarni, l'homme et l'oeuvre. 1873.
La Du Barry. 1878; revised edition, 1880; as *Madame du Barry*, translated anonymously, 1914.
Madame de Pompadour. 1878; revised editions 1881, and 1888.
Journal des Goncourt: Mémoires de la vie littéraire. 9 vols., 1887–96; 9 vols., 1935–36; 22 vols., 1956–59; edited by Robert Ricatte, 4 vols., 1956: as *The Journal of the Goncourts* (selection), translated by Julius West, 1908; as *Goncourt Journals 1851–70*, edited and translated by Lewis Galantière, 1937; as *Pages from the Goncourt Journal* (selection), translated by Robert Baldick, 1962; as *Paris Under Siege, 1870–71*, edited and translated by George J. Becker, 1969.
Armande, illustrated by Marold, 1892; as *Armande*, translated by Alfred E. Haserick, 1894.
Pages retrouvées. 1886.
Edmond and Jules de Goncourt (correspondence and journal), edited and translated by M.A. Belloc and M. Shedlock. 2 vols., 1894.
L'Italie d'hier: Notes de voyages 1855–56. 1894.
Selections, edited by Arnold Cameron. 1898.

Paris and the Arts 1851–96, edited and translated by George J. Becker and Edith Philips. 1971
Lettres de jeunesse inédites, edited by Alain Nicolas. 1981.

PUBLICATIONS BY EDMOND GONCOURT

Fiction

La Fille Élisa. 1877; as *Elisa: The Story of a Prostitute*, translated by Margaret Crosland, 1959; as *Woman of Paris*, translated by Cedric Harrald, 1959.
Les Frères Zemganno. 1879; as *The Zemganno Brothers*, translated anonymously, 1886; also translated by Leonard Clark and Iris Allam, 1957.
La Faustin. 1882; as *La Faustin: A Life Study*, translated by John Stirling, 1882; as *La Faustin*, translated by G.F. Monkshood and Ernest Tristan, 1906.
Chérie. 1884.

Other

L'Amour au dix-huitième siècle. 1875; as *Love in the 18th Century*, 1905.
La Duchesse de Châteauroux et ses soeurs. 1879; revised edition, 1892.
La Maison d'un artiste. 2 vols., 1881; definitive edition, 2 vols., 1931.
Madame Saint-Huberty. 1882; definitive edition, 1925.
Lettres de Jules de Goncourt. 1885.
Préfaces et manifestes littéraires. 1888.
Mademoiselle Clairon. 1890.
L'Art japonais du XVIIIe siècle. 2 vols., 1891–96.
Outamaro, le peintre des maisons vertes. 1891.
A bas le progrès!. 1893.
Le Guimard. 1893.
L'Italie d'hier. 1894.
Hokousaï. 1896.
Lettres. 1930.
Edmond de Goncourt et Henri Céard: correspondance inédite 1876–1896. 1965.
Gustave Flaubert-les Goncourt: Correspondance, edited and prefaced by Pierre-Jean Dufief. 1998.
Correspondance, with Alphonse Daudet, edited by Pierre Dufief with Anne-Simone Dufief. 1996.

*

Critical Studies:: *Création romanesque chez les Goncourt* by Robert Ricatte, 1953; *The Goncourt Brothers* by André Billy, translated by M. Shaw, 1960; *The Goncourts* by Robert Baldick, 1960; *Réalisme et impressionnisme dans l'oeuvre des frères Goncourt* by Enzo Caramaschi, 1971; *The Goncourt Brothers* by Richard B. Grant, 1972; *Les frères Goncourt: Art et écriture*, edited by Jean-Louis Cabanès, 1997.

* * *

Edmond and Jules de Goncourt form one of the most remarkable literary partnerships that has ever existed. Jules had the greater literary talent, but died in early middle age of syphilis. His brother continued to write after his death, but generally with less mastery and success than the joint works.

En 18. . . , the first of their novels, is a slight work, recounting its hero's disappointments in love. *Les Hommes de lettres*, later entitled *Charles Demailly*, is both a story of marital discord culminating in the husband's madness and also a *roman à clef* vehemently denouncing unprincipled literary journalism. *Soeur Philomène* (*Sister Philomene*), a far less episodic novel, is notable for its bleak evocation of a hospital environment. *Renée Mauperin,* describing the shallow conventional life of a wealthy middle-class family, is marred by legal and historical inaccuracies which deny it any claim to narrow "realism" in the sense in which that term is applied to Balzac's work. Renée, seeking to prevent her brother's marriage, involves him in a duel in which he is killed; grief-stricken, she falls into a lengthy decline (admirably described by the Goncourts) and dies. *Germinie Lacerteux,* modelled on the hidden life of the brothers' own maid, resembles *Sister Philomene* and *Renée Mauperin* in that it concerns degradation and death; it tells of the heroine's two secret love-affairs, the second more squalid that the first, and both unsuspected by her employer. *Manette Salomon,* a novel of artistic life, contrasts four types of artist and explores the (generally destructive) influence exerted by women upon artists' lives. *Madame Gervaisais,* a study in religious mania, shows the destructive influence of Catholicism upon the lives of the heroine and her young son. Each of these works, so different in their ambience and subject-matter, was considered by the Goncourt brothers to be a venture into a new field of human experience; each was a challenge. Each was carefully documented, as when the two brothers spent six weeks in Rome gathering material for *Madame Gervaisais.* Whether actively seeking out such researched material or else modelling Germinie on the secret life of their maid, they looked upon the subject matter of their novels as "history which might have taken place." But this documentary aspect of their work was as far as their "naturalism" went.

Their method of writing was unusual even by the standards of literary partnerships. So closely attuned were their ways of viewing and writing about the world that it is impossible to make precise attributions of particular passages; Edmond went so far as to write of their "twin mind." Jules, however, had a better ear for dialogue, where Edmond's gifts lay more in the direction of scene-setting and background detail. Nevertheless, each chapter of each novel was separately drafted out by both novelists, who (living under the same roof and working in adjacent rooms) would then meet to compare and conflate their two versions: thus, one novel was made out of the best elements of each. But both wrote to a storyline that had been mapped out initially in fine detail by the two brothers working in concert.

Like Musset, Edmond and Jules de Goncourt were men of essentially artistic temperament: artistic in their leanings towards the visual arts, in which they took a keen interest. They even evolved a literary style peculiarly adapted to their purposes. This was the *écriture artiste,* full of neologisms and the specialized vocabularies of medicine, art criticism, and other disciplines; its contorted syntax was meant to convey all the complexities and obscurities of contemporary life. Unjustly maligned by many critics, this *écriture artiste* was a sort of literary mannerism in which all too often the manner of saying a thing seemed to predominate over the thing said. The very tortuousness of the Goncourts' writing, febrile, hypersensitive, and so hard to translate, suggests inner torments: they claimed that the whole of their writing was based upon neurosis. Yet the sheer technical virtuosity of that writing must surely be deemed a literary quality in itself, and they strove to avoid preciosity at all times.

The brothers' interest in the visual arts also found expression in the sharp focus of individual scenes. While the prevalence of dialogue suggests their desire to emulate the theatre, they foreshadow cinematic techniques in the way in which they move into the very centre and heart of the action as each brief chapter opens. These chapters are sometimes so visually concentrated as to resemble tableaux. In their rapid juxtaposition of colourful details the Goncourt brothers achieve a sort of impressionism, though Gautier's influence upon them is also evident—not only in their literary practice but also (to a lesser extent) in their theory of the fine arts.

The *Journal des Goncourt* (*Goncourt Journals*), kept by the two brothers from 1851 until Jules's death and afterwards by Edmond alone, is a store of information about such writers as Flaubert, Gautier, Zola, Daudet, Hugo, and Turgenev and about marginal historical figures such as Princess Mathilde Bonaparte. The very reverse of a confessional diary, it is crammed with anecdotes and has the deft touch of the gossip column, of which it is a main forerunner. A vivid impression is given of Paris at the time of the Franco-Prussian War and the Commune. That part of the *Journal* for which Edmond was solely responsible (from March 1870 until July 1896) outshines even the joint diary; however, the four novels written by him alone—even *La Fille Élisa* (*Woman of Paris*) and *Les Fréres Zemganno* (*The Zemganno Brothers*)—are but pale reflections of the brilliance of the joint novels.

Together with Zola, the Goncourt brothers are generally considered to be the founders of the French school of Naturalism. Earlier than Zola, they described sordid—sometimes pathological—subject matter, but always in brilliant painterly terms. They did much to pioneer novels of working-class life. They took great care to see, seek, verify, and investigate the facts, by which they generally meant the physical settings. The term "naturalist" was not, however, a distinction they ever claimed for themselves. In Zola's own words, "the analysis of things artistic, plastic, and neurotic" was the heart of their achievement.

—Donald Adamson

GÓNGORA (Y ARGOTE), Luis de

Born: Córdoba, Spain, 11 July 1561. **Education:** Educated at Jesuit school in Córdoba; University of Salamanca, 1576–80, no degree. **Career:** Took minor orders at university, and deacon's orders, 1586: prebendary of Córdoba Cathedral, 1586–1617: undertook various business trips for the Cathedral; ordained priest, 1617, and royal chaplain in Madrid, 1617–25. **Died:** 23 May 1627.

PUBLICATIONS

Collections

Obras en verso del Homero español, edited by Juan López de Vicuña. 1627; also edited by Dàmaso Alonso, 1963.
Todas las obras, edited by Gonzalo de Hozes y Córdoba. 1633.
Obras completas, edited by Juan and Isabel Millé y Giménez. 1972.
Luis de Góngora: Selected Shorter Poems, translated by Michael Smith. 1995
Obras completas, edited with prologue by Antonio Carreira. 2000.

Verse

Soledades, edited by Dámaso Alonso. 1927, revised edition, 1956; also edited by Alfonso Gallejo and María Teresa Pajares, with *Fábula de Polifemo y Galatea,* 1985; as *The Solitudes,* translated by Edward M. Wilson, 1931; translated by Gilbert F. Cunningham, 1968; also translated by Philip Polack, 1997.

Fâbula de Polifemo y Galatea, as *Góngora y el "Potifemo,"* edited by Dámaso Alonso. 1960, revised edition, 2 vols., 1961; also edited by Alfonso Gallejo and María Teresa Pajares, with *Las Soledades,* 1985; as *Polyphemus and Galatea,* translated by Gilbert F. Cunningham, 1977; as *The Fable of Polyphemus and Galatea,* translated by Miroslav John Hanak, 1988.

Romance de "Angélica y Medoro," edited by Dámaso Alonso. 1962.

Sonetos completos, edited by Biruté Ciplijauskaité. 1969.

Romances (selection), edited by José María de Cossno. 1980.

Las firmezas de Isabela, edited by Robert Jammes. 1984.

Fábula de Píramo y Tisbe, edited by David Garrison. 1985.

Cuadernos de varias poesías, manuscrito patentino, edited by Lorenzo Rubio González. 1985.

*

Critical Studies: *The Metaphors of Góngora* by E.J. Gates, 1933; *Góngora* by D.W. and V.R. Foster, 1973; *Góngora: Polyphemus and Galatea: A Study in the Interpretation of a Baroque Poem* (includes text and translation by Gilbert F. Cunningham) by Alexander A. Parker, 1977; *The Poet and the Natural World in the Age of Góngora* by M.J. Woods, 1978; *Aspects of Góngora's "Soledades"* by John R. Beverley, 1980; *The Sonnets of Luis de Góngora* by R.P. Calcraft, 1980; *Góngora's Poetic Textual Tradition: An Analysis of Selected Variants, Versions, and Imitations of His Shorter Poems* by Diane Chaffee-Sorace, 1988; *Poetry as Play: "Gongorismo" and the "Comedia"* by Maria Cristina Quintero, 1991; *Silva gongorina* by Andrés Sánchez Robayna, 1993; *Combinatorias hispánicas* by José Lezama Lima, 1993; *Gracián Meets Góngora* by M.J. Woods, 1995; *The Transforming Text: A Study of Luis de Góngora's Soledades* by R. John McCaw, 2000.

* * *

Luis de Góngora was a remarkable poet who made a significant contribution in a variety of poetic fields, expanding the range of poetry by his conception of the ballad as a more sophisticated, artistically balanced form than was traditional, by his promotion of the burlesque as a valid artistic form, and, in the case of his most famous major poem, *Soledades* (*The Solitudes*), by creating a work that not only did not fit into any recognized genre, but also had a dazzling stylistic novelty.

Having already acquired a reputation as a writer of fine sonnets and ballads from the publication of a number of his poems in a general anthology in 1605, Góngora in his native Andalusia dreamed of making a career for himself at the court in Madrid. Hence in 1614 copies of his *Solitudes* and his *Polifemo y Galatea* (*Polyphemus and Galatea*), major poems he had recently completed, were being circulated at court and caused a major literary controversy which centred upon the original and exceptionally difficult style in which they were written. There was a spate of letters, pamphlets, and poems attacking and defending Góngora. Although he never achieved the patronage he sought, he attracted many imitators, and detailed explanatory commentaries of his works were published later in the century.

The features of Góngora's style attracting comment were his use of neologisms (so-called *cultismos*), his liberties with syntax, particularly word order, and frequency and complexity of his metaphors. But it is misleading to portray Góngora's novelty as merely stylistic, a question of mode of expression rather than of what was being said. Thematically, the major poems give a novel prominence to the world of nature. With his *Polyphemus and Galatea,* which retells the story found in Ovid's *Metamorphoses* of the giant Polyphemus' love for Galatea and his enraged killing of her lover, Acis, despite the importance that Góngora gives the rural Sicilian setting we still have basically a narrative poem. But in his *Solitudes,* of which there are two of an originally planned four, the second being unfinished, we have basically a descriptive poem, which is in itself a novelty. Góngora shows the hospitality offered by a rustic community to a shipwrecked young courtier, presenting their way of life and the environment in which they live in an enthusiastic way. When we consider Góngora's use of metaphor as a means of presenting this positive vision, again it is clear that we are dealing with a mode of thought, not merely one of speech. It is through metaphor that he draws attention to surprising patterns and relationships in the world, inviting us to wonder at them. Hence, when he calls the sea "a Libya of waves," he invites us to consider the parallels between desert and sea, their common vastness and inhospitability, dunes mirroring waves, and at the same time surprises us by describing the extremely wet in terms of the extremely dry. Through such explorations of relationships Góngora reveals himself as a major exponent of wit.

—M.J. Woods

GORAN, Abdulla

Born: Abdulla Sulayman in Halabja, Ottoman Empire (now Iraq), September 1904; son of a minor official in the Ottoman administration. **Education:** Attended elementary school in Halabja, and medrese in Kirkuk, 1919–21; State Pedagogical Institute, Kirkuk, 1921. **Career:** School teacher, Sulaimniya, 1925–37; Iraqi Ministry of Communications, late 1930s; worked at a radio station in Jaffa, Palestine, 1942–45; editor of the weekly cultural journal *Jin,* early 1950s; founder, Committee for the Defense of Peace, Iraq, 1951. **Died:** Sulaimainya, Iraq, 18 November 1962.

PUBLICATIONS

Collections

Dîwanî Goran, edited by Muhammadi Mela Karim. 1980.

Verse

Behesht u yadgar. 1950.

Firmêsk u huner. 1950.

Sirâsht u derûn. 1968.

Lawuk u peyman. 1969.

Plays

Guli Hiwênawi. 1950.
Bûkêki nakam. 1950.

Other

Translator, *Helbijarde.* 1953.

*

Critical Studies: *Shi'ir u edebieti kurdi,* vol. 2, by Rafik Hilmi, 1956; *Müasir kürd shairi: Abdulla Goranyn poezijasy* by Hüseyn Alyshanov, 1969.

* * *

Abdulla Goran is generally recognized as the leading Kurdish poet of the twentieth century. He combined the heritage of indigenous classical and folk creativity with the intentions and techniques of modern lyricism to endow Kurdish poetry with new means of expression and a diverse subject matter. The form and content of his poetry evolved continuously as his acquaintance with Kurdish society broadened. His early poems were suffused with the romantic spirit and themes characteristic of traditional and much contemporary Kurdish verse, but as his sympathy for the hard life of the ordinary Kurd grew and his social conscience became fully awakened, he increasingly drew inspiration from the joys and sorrows of everyday life. In so doing, he became one of the founders of Kurdish realism.

The main task he set for himself was to reveal all the poetic capabilities of the Kurdish language. He thus brought new vigor and freshness to Kurdish poetry by introducing the prose poem and blank verse and by adopting a syllabic rhythm close to the rhythms of folk poetry. In "Awati duri" [Distant Longing], for example, he abandoned the traditional *aruz* in favor of a prosody that allowed him to vary the number of syllables in a line and to introduce new rhymes. He also experimented with form. He was particularly fond of verse dramas, which suited his lyrical temperament. Whether his mood was romantic or realist, he wrote in a remarkably pure, flowing language, and many of his poems, because of their simple, easy rhythms, were set to music. His early poetry of the 1920s and 1930s, was romantic, and his favorite themes were nature and love. Two longer poems, "Gesht Is Hewraman" [Journey to Hewraman] and "Gesht le Keredag" [Journey to Keredag], both of which appeared in the volume *Behesht u yadgar* [Paradise and Remembrance], attest to his skill at painting native landscapes and describing the customs and rituals of daily life. The focus of his love poetry is woman, portrayed as the source of all that is beautiful and good. But even his most idyllic poetry revealed traces of the later, dominant realism; he curbed the hyperbole of classical Kurdish verse and sought to move the reader by genuineness and depth of feeling. In his "romantic period" he was also animated by strong ethnic sentiments. In "Demi raperine" [The Voice Awakens] he expressed his ardent love of country (Kurdistan) and his yearning for its liberation, and in "Derwêsh Ebdulla" [Dervish Abdulla] he urged the famous Kurdish balladeer to assuage his melancholy by singing pure Kurdish melodies.

Goran's dramas in verse, a new genre in Kurdish literature, were decidedly realistic, despite their preoccupation with romantic love. They gave him freedom to express his growing civic sense by allowing him to confront contemporary social issues more directly than was possible in traditional genres. Perhaps the most popular of these dramas was "Guli hinênawi" [The Bloody Rose], the story of tragic love in an unjust world, which became a modern Kurdish classic. An equally powerful piece, "Bûkêki nakam" [An Unhappy Bride], emphasizes social themes as two lovers from different classes try to overcome deeply rooted family prejudices.

Goran pursued other literary interests alongside poetry. He was an accomplished prose writer and composed numerous short stories and sketches, especially on social themes. An avid student of languages, he translated into Kurdish poems from Persian, Arabic, Turkish, and English and a volume of short stories, *Helbijarde* [Selections], by French and English authors. He was also a skilled essayist and polemicist, as his commitment to social justice for the downtrodden suggests. But he could be passionate also about literary matters and was in the forefront of the effort to create a single Kurdish literary language, a tool he thought essential if writers were to express the true essence of the Kurdish genius and way of life. Convinced that the two main dialects—Kûrmanjî, used in Turkey, Syria, Iran, and northwest Iraq, and Sorânî, the literary language of the Kurds of Iraq, which he himself used—were gradually coming together, he railed against extremists who would interfere with the process by removing Arabic and Persian elements and replace them with "dead" words and "false" neologisms.

Through his innovative use of language and meter, his commitment to new themes, and his harmonious blending of form and subject, Goran created a watershed in the development of modern Kurdish poetry. The generation that followed him no longer composed in accordance with the classical canon, but eagerly assimilated the experiences of ordinary life and boldly experimented with new modes of expression.

—Keith Hitchins

GOR'KII, Maksim

Also known as Maxim Gorky. **Born:** Alexei Maksimovich Peshkov, in Nizhnyi Novgorod, Russia, 16 March 1868. **Education:** Educated in parish school, Nizhnyi Novgorod; Kumavino elementary school, 1877–78. **Family:** Married Ekaterina Pavlovna Volzhina in 1896 (separated); one son and one daughter. **Career:** Apprenticed to a shoemaker at age 11; then draughtsman's clerk and cook's boy on a Volga steamer; from 1888, associated with revolutionary politics: first arrest, 1889; travelled on foot through much of Russia; began publishing in prominent journals by the mid-1890s; member of publishing co-operative Knowledge, and literary editor, *Zhizn'* [Life], St. Petersburg, from 1899; worked for the publishing house Znanie, 1900, and was subsequently its leading editor; exiled to Arzamas, central Russia, for involvement with a covert printing press, 1901; joined the Bolshevik Party, 1905; travelled to the United States, 1906; lived in Capri, 1906–13; set up revolutionary propaganda school, 1909; returned to Russia after general amnesty, 1913: founding editor, *Letopis'* [Chronicles] magazine, 1915–17, and newspaper *Novaia Zhizn'* [New Life], 1917–18; established publishing house Vsemirnaia Literatura [World Literature]; involved in Petrograd Workers and Soldiers Soviet; left Russia in 1921: editor, *Dialogue,* Berlin, 1923–25, and in Sorrento during most of 1924–32; editor, *Literary Apprenticeship* magazine, 1930; returned to Russia permanently in 1933: helped set up the Biblioteka Poeta [Poet's Library] publishing project; travelled widely throughout USSR, took a leading role at the All-Union Congress of Soviet Writers, 1934, and was associated with the implementation of Socialist Realism as the artistic orthodoxy. **Awards:** Order of Lenin, 1932. Gor'kii Literary Institute established in his honour. **Died:** 18 June 1936.

PUBLICATIONS

Collections

Selected Works, translated by Margaret Wettlin and others. 2 vols., 1948.
Polnoe sobranie sochinenii: Khudozhestvennaia literatura [Complete Collected Works]. 25 vols., 1968–76.
Collected Works. 10 vols., 1978–83.
Sobranie sochinenii [Collected Works], edited by N.N. Zhegalov. 16 vols., 1979.
Sobranie sochinenii [Collected Works], edited by S.A. Nebol'shim. 8 vols., 1987.
Sobranie sochinenii [Collected Works], edited by A.I. Ovcharenko, 12 vols., 1987.
Collected Short Stories, edited by Avrahm Yarmolinsky and Moura Budberg. 1988.

Plays

Meshchane (produced 1902). 1902; as *The Smug Citizens,* translated by Edwin Hopkins, 1906; as *The Courageous One,* translated by M. Goldina and H. Choat, 1958; as *The Petty Bourgeois,* in *Collected Works 4,* 1979.
Na dne (produced 1902). 1903; as *A Night's Lodging,* translated by Edwin Hopkins, in *Poet Lore,* 16, 1905; as *The Lower Depths,* translated by L. Irving, 1912; also translated by Alexander Bakshy with Paul S. Nathan, in *Seven Plays,* 1945, Moura Budberg, 1959, Margaret Wettlin, in *Five Plays,* 1959, David Magarshack, in *The Storm and Other Russian Plays,* 1960, Andrew R. MacAndrew, in *Twentieth Century Russian Drama,* 1963, and Kitty H. Blair and Jeremy Brooks, 1973; as *Submerged,* translated by Edwin Hopkins, 1914; as *At the Bottom,* translated by W. Laurence, 1930; as *Down and Out,* translated by G.R. Noyes and Alexander Kaun, in *Masterpieces of the Russian Drama,* edited by Noyes, 1933; as *Lower Depths,* edited with introduction, notes and vocabulary by Kurt Klein and Ira Goetz, 1993; translated by Jennie Covan, 1999.
Dachniki (produced 1904). 1904; as *Summerfolk,* translated by A. Delano, in *Poet Lore,* 16, 1905; translated by Kitty H. Blair and Jeremy Brooks, in *Five Plays,* 1988; also translated by Nicholas Saunders and Frank Dwyer, 1995.
Varvary. 1905; as *Barbarians,* translated by Alexander Bakshy with Paul S. Nathan, in *Seven Plays,* 1945; also translated by Kitty H. Blair and Jeremy Brooks, in *Five Plays,* 1988; as *Philistines,* translated by Dusty Hughes, 1986.
Deti solntsa. 1905; as *Children of the Sun,* translated by John Wolfe, 1906; also translated by Kitty H. Blair and Jeremy Brooks, in *Five Plays,* 1988.
Vragi (produced 1907). 1906; as *Enemies,* translated by Alexander Bakshy with Paul S. Nathan, in *Seven Plays,* 1945; also translated by Kitty H. Blair and Jeremy Brooks, 1972.
Poslednie [The Last Ones] (produced 1908). 1908.

Vassa Zheleznova (produced 1911). 1910; revised version, 1935; as *Vassa Zheleznova,* translated by Alexander Bakshy with Paul S. Nathan, in *Seven Plays,* 1945.
Vstrecha [The Meeting] (produced 1910). 1910.
Chudaki. 1910; as *Queer People,* translated by Alexander Bakshy with Paul S. Nathan, in *Seven Plays,* 1945.
Zykovy. 1913; as *The Zykovs,* translated by Alexander Bakshy with Paul S. Nathan, in *Seven Plays,* 1945.
Starik (produced 1919). 1918; as *The Judge,* translated by M. Zakhrevsky and B.H. Clark, 1924; as *The Old Man,* translated by Margaret Wettlin, 1956.
Somov i drugie [Somov and Others]. 1931.
Egor Bulychov i drugie (produced 1932). 1932; as *Yegor Bulichoff and Others,* translated by W.L. Gibson-Cowan, in *The Last Plays,* 1937; as *Yegor Bulychov and the Others,* translated by Alexander Bakshy with Paul S. Nathan, in *Seven Plays,* 1945.
Dostigaev i drugie (produced 1934). 1933; as *Dostigaeff and the Others,* translated by W.L. Gibson-Cowan, in *The Last Plays,* 1937.
The Last Plays (includes *Yegor Bulichoff and Others; Dostigaeff and the Others*), translated by W.L. Gibson-Cowan, 1937.
Seven Plays (includes *Barbarians; Enemies; Vassa Zheleznova; The Lower Depths; Queer People; The Zykovs; Yegor Bulychov and Others*), translated by Alexander Bakshy with Paul S. Nathan. 1945.
Five Plays (includes *The Petty Bourgeois; Philistines; The Lower Depths; Summerfolk; Enemies*), translated by Margaret Wettlin. 1956.
The Lower Depths and Other Plays, translated by Alexander Bakshy and Paul S. Nathan. 1959.
Five Plays (includes *The Lower Depths; Summerfolk; Children of the Sun; Barbarians; Enemies*), translated by Kitty H. Blair and Jeremy Brooks. 1988.

Fiction

Ocherki i rasskazy (stories). 3 vols., 1898–99; in part as *Tales,* translated by R. Bain, 1902.
Foma Gordeev. 1899; as *Foma Gordeyev,* translated by Herman Bernstein, 1901; also translated by Margaret Wettlin, 1956; as *The Man Who Was Afraid,* translated by Bernstein, 1905; as *Foma,* 1945.
Troe. 1900; as *Three of Them,* translated by Alexandra Linden, 1902; as *Three Men,* translated by Charles Horne, 1902; also translated by A. Frumkin, 1919; as *The Three,* translated by Margaret Wettlin, 1958.
Orloff and His Wife: Tales of the Barefoot Brigade, translated by Isabel F. Hapgood. 1901.
The Orloff Couple, and Malva, translated by Emily Jankowleff and Dora B. Montefiore. 1901.
Tales, translated by R. Bain. 1902.
The Outcasts and Other Stories, translated by Dora B. Montefiore, Emily Jankowleff, and V. Volkhovsky. 1902.
Chelkash and Other Stories, translated by Emily Jankowleff and Dora B. Montefiore. 1902.
Twenty-Six Men and a Girl and Other Stories, translated by Dora B. Montefiore and Emily Jankowleff. 1902.
Twenty-Six and One and Other Stories, translated by I. Strannik. 1902.
Tales, translated by C. Alexandroff. 1903.

Mat'. 1906; as *Mother,* 1907; revised translation, by Isidor Schneider, 1947; as *Comrades,* 1907.

Zhizn' nenuzhnogo cheloveka. 1907–08; as *The Spy: The Story of a Superfluous Man,* translated by Thomas Seltzer, 1908; as *The Life of a Useless Man,* translated by Moura Budberg, 1971.

Ispoved'. 1908; as *A Confession,* translated by Frederick Harvey, 1910; as *The Confession,* translated by Rose Strunsky, n.d.

Gorodok Okurov [Okurov City]. 1909.

Leto [Summer]. 1909.

Zhizn' Matveia Kozhemiakina. 1910–11; as *The Life of Matvei Kozhemyakin,* translated by Margaret Wettlin, 1960.

Tales, translated by R. Nisbet Bain. 1912.

Tales of Two Countries. 1914.

Twenty-Six Men and a Girl and Other Stories, translated by S. Michel. 1915.

Stories of the Steppe, translated by H. Schnittkind and I. Goldberg. 1918.

Creatures That Once Were Men (stories), translated by J.M. Shirazi. 1918.

Delo Artamonovykh. 1925; as *Decadence,* translated by Veronica Dewey, 1927; as *The Artamonov Business,* translated by A. Brown, 1948; as *The Artamonovs,* translated by H. Altschuler, 1952.

The Story of a Novel and Other Stories, translated by M. Zakrevsky. 1925.

Zhizn' Klima Samgina [The Life of Klim Samgin] (unfinished). 1925–36; as *The Bystander, The Magnet, Other Fires,* and *The Spectre,* translated by Bernard Guilbert Bakshy, 4 vols., 1931–38.

Best Short Stories, edited and translated by Avrahm Yarmolinsky and Moura Budberg. 1939; as *A Book of Short Stories,* 1939.

Song of the Stormy Petrel and Other Short Stories, translated by M. Trommer. 1942.

Unrequited Love and Other Stories, translated by Moura Budberg. 1949.

Selected Short Stories 1892–1901, translated by Margaret Wettlin. 1954.

A Sky-Blue Life and Other Stories, translated by George Reavey. 1964.

Verse

Pesnia o Sokole. 1895; as *The Song of the Falcon,* translated by ''M.G.,'' 1896.

Chelovek. 1903; translated as *Man,* 1905.

Devushka i smert' [The Little Gift and Death]. 1917.

Other

A.P. Chekhov. 1905; as *Anton Tchekhov: Fragments of Recollections,* translated by S.S. Kotelianskii and Leonard Woolf, 1921.

Detstvo V liudiakh Moi universitety. 1913–22; as *My Childhood in the World [My Apprenticeship] My University Days [My Universities],* 1915–23; as *Autobiography,* translated by Isidor Schneider, 1949; as *My Apprenticeship, My Childhood, My Universities,* translated by Ronald Wilks, 3 vols., 1966–79; *My Childhood* also translated by Gertrude M. Foakes, 1915, and as *Childhood,* by Margaret Wettlin, 1950, revised by Jessie Coulson, 1961.

Vospominaniia o Tolstom. 1919; as *Reminiscences of Tolstoi,* translated by S.S. Kotelianskii and Leonard Woolf, 1920.

Revoliutsiia i kul'tura [Revolution and Culture]. 1920.

O russkom krestianstve. 1922; translated as *On the Russian Peasantry,* 1976.

Zametki iz dnevnika. 1924; translated as *Fragments from My Diary,* 1924; also translated by Moura Budberg, 1972, revised edition, 1975.

V.I. Lenin. 1924; as *V.I. Lenin,* translated by C.W. Parker-Arkhangelskaya, 1931; as *Days with Lenin,* 1932.

O literature. 1933; revised edition, 1935, 1955; as *On Literature: Selected Articles,* translated by Julius Katzer and Ivy Litvinova, 1960.

On Guard for the Soviet Union. 1933.

Reminiscences of Tolstoy, Chekhov and Andreyev, translated by Katherine Mansfield, S.S. Kotelianskii, Virginia Woolf, and Leonard Woolf. 1934.

Culture and the People. 1940.

Creative Labour and Culture. 1945.

Literature and Life: A Selection from the Writings, edited and translated by Edith Bone. 1946.

History of the Civil War, translated by J. Fineberg. 1946.

Articles and Pamphlets. 1950.

Letters of Maxim Gor'kij to V.F. Xodasevič, 1922–1925, edited and translated by Hugh McLean, in *Harvard Slavonic Studies,* I. 1953.

F.I. Chaliapin. 2 vols., 1957–58; as *Chaliapin: An Autobiography,* edited and translated by Nina Froud and James Hanley, 1967.

Letters of Gorky and Andreev 1899–1912, edited by Peter Yershov, translated by Lydia Weston. 1958.

Letters, translated by P. Cockerell. 1966.

Nesvoyevremennye mysli. 1971; as *Untimely Thoughts,* edited and translated by Herman Ermolaev, 1968; as *Untimely Thoughts: Essays on Revolution, Culture and the Bolsheviks, 1917–1918,* translated with notes by Herman Ermolaev, 1995.

The City of the Yellow Devil: Pamphlets, Articles and Letters about America. 1972.

Rasskazy i povesti 1892–1917 (selection). 1976.

Perepiska M Gor'kogo (selected correspondence). 2 vols., 1986.

Gorky and His Contemporaries (letters), edited by Galina Belaya, translated by Cynthia Carlile. 1989.

Selected Letters, edited by Andrew Barratt and Barry P. Scherr. 1997.

Editor, *Belomor. An Account of the Construction of the New Canal Between the White Sea and the Baltic Sea.* 1935.

*

Bibliography: *Maxim Gorky in English: A Bibliography, 1868–1986* by Garth M. Terry, 1986; *Maxim Gorky: A Reference Guide* by Edith Clowes, 1987.

Critical Studies: *Maxim Gorky and His Russia* by Alexander Kaun, 1931; *The Young Maxim Gorky 1868–1902* by Filia Holtzman, 1948; *Maxim Gorky: Romantic Realist and Conservative Revolutionary* by Richard Hare, 1962; *Stormy Petrel: The Life and Work of Maxim Gorky* by Dan Levin, 1965; *Gorky: His Literary Development and Influence on Soviet Intellectual Life* by I. Weil, 1966; *Maxim Gorky, The Writer: An Interpretation* by F.M. Borras, 1967; *The Bridge and the Abyss: The Troubled Friendship of Maxim Gorky and V.I. Lenin* by Bertram D. Wolfe, 1967; *Maxim Gorky* by Gerhard E. Habermann, 1971; *Three Russians Consider America: America in the Works of Maksim Gor'kij, Aleksandr Blok, and Vladimir Mayakovskij* by Charles Rougle, 1976; *Maxim Gorky and the Literary Quests of the*

Twentieth Century by A.I. Ovcharenko, 1985; *Maxim Gorky Fifty, Years On: Gorky and His Time* edited by Nicholas Luker, 1987; *Maxim Gorky* by Barry P. Scherr, 1988; *Gorky and His Contemporaries: Memoirs and Letters* edited by Galina Belaya, 1989; *Gorky* by Henri Troyat, translated by Lowell Bair, 1989; *File on Gorky*, compiled by Cynthia Marsh, 1993; *The Early Fiction of Maksim Gorky: Six Essays in Interpretation* by Andrew Barratt, 1993; *Vicissitudes of Genre in the Russian Novel* by Russell Scott Valentino, 2001.

* * *

For many years Maksim Gor'kii was revered in the Soviet Union as the founder of Socialist Realism, the father of Soviet literature, and one of the greatest 20th-century writers. Critical opinion of him in the West was always more mixed, and since the collapse of the Soviet Union attitudes towards him in Russia have also evolved. The city of his birth and one of Moscow's largest streets, both once named in his honour, have reverted to their former designations. Even though his sometime differences with Bolshevik leaders rather than his statements on behalf of the Communist Party now receive more attention, he remains a writer for whom it is difficult to separate the literary and the non-literary achievements.

Before the revolution he was active both politically, as a supporter of revolutionary causes, and, among his fellow writers, as a leader of the so-called "critical realists" and the organizer of various publishing enterprises. After the revolution his political connections enabled him to protect, aid, and encourage an entire generation of writers, at the same time that he was again instrumental in establishing major publication projects, some of which continue to the present day.

As a writer Gor'kii introduced or at least popularized many topics that had largely been ignored by 19th-century Russian writers. He drew upon his own experiences to depict the vagrants and social outcasts who were the main characters in many of his early stories, while his upbringing provided the material for graphic descriptions of Russia's merchant class and its emergent capitalists, many of whom, especially in the provinces, retained the superstitions and habits instilled by peasant backgrounds. His particular talent lay in his descriptive skills. He created unforgettable portraits of his main characters and also brought out vividly the most mundane details of their everyday lives. That ability, along with the exotic quality of his subject matter, was sufficient to ensure the near-instant fame that he achieved. On the other hand, his fiction was occasionally marred by faults that he never completely overcame: a political tendentiousness that sometimes led to exaggeration and overly broad generalizations, the appearance of florid passages and lack of simplicity in his style, and difficulty in creating narratives with sufficient drama and cohesiveness to serve as vehicles for the characters he created.

This last feature of his writing perhaps explains why he achieved mixed success with his novels and plays but had more consistent results with his short stories and, particularly, his autobiographical writings and memoirs. In early stories such as "Chelkash" (1894) and "Konovalov" (1896) the single vagrant figure predominates and is sufficient to hold the reader's interest throughout. Further, since Gor'kii's vagrants turn out to originate from widely divergent classes, they possess sufficient variety so that the stories as a group do not become repetitive. Also notable among his stories is "Dvadsta' shest' i odna" ("Twenty-Six Men and a Girl"), in which Gor'kii offers a concise and powerful treatment of a theme that was to be important for much of his subsequent work: the need for many people, especially those who have virtually nothing, to create illusions to sustain themselves, and the ease with which those illusions may be destroyed. The novels too are most notable for their central figures, as well as for the social milieu that Gor'kii depicts with his customary skill and knowledge. In this genre, though, Gor'kii's problems with narrative are particularly telling. Typical are *Foma Gordeev*, in which the title character rejects the merchant-class society into which he is born, and *Mat'* (*Mother*), which passionately describes the birth of a revolutionary consciousness in the mother of an imprisoned worker and which is regarded by Soviet critics as a model work for what became known as Socialist Realism. In both instances the introduction of fascinating characters dominates the first third or so of the work, but the action then becomes diffuse until the concluding pages.

Gor'kii's last novels could all be classsifed as chronicles, in which the recording of social and political events comes to take precedence over dramatic narrative. If the title character in *Zhizn' Matveia Kozhemiakina* (*The Life of Matvei Kozhemyakin*) at least remains in the centre of the action, then in *Delo Artamonovykh* (*The Artamonov Business*) the focus is more on how generational changes are reflected in the rise and fall of a family dynasty during the years leading up to the Bolshevik Revolution. Gor'kii's final novel, *Zhizn' Klima Samgina* [The Life of Klim Samgin], remained unfinished at his death; it consists of four large volumes, each of which has a separate title in the English translation. Here he again reverts to tracing the life of a single individual, but Gor'kii's real interest lies elsewhere: epic in scope and filled with historical figures and events, the novel represents an attempt to portray intellectual and political developments in Russian life during the 40 years that culminated in the overthrow of the old regime in 1917.

Remarkably, Gor'kii created his best play with only his second effort as a dramatist, *Na dne* (*The Lower Depths*). The play lacks any single predominant figure, but its collection of cast-offs, who seem to be refugees from several of his early stories, offers originality and dramatic interaction that more than compensate for the lack of a strong plot. In other plays of this type the static quality of Gor'kii's writing tends to undercut his efforts, though he still succeeds in those plays that are dominated by a strong figure, such as *Egor Bulychov i drugie* (*Yegor Bulichoff and Others*). In more recent years Gor'kii's plays have enjoyed renewed interest in both England and North America, with stagings of both these works as well as *Dachniki* (*Summerfolk*) and *Vragi* (*Enemies*). However, Gor'kii's best writing occurred when he was writing directly about himself or about those whom he knew intimately. At such moments he was able to give full vent to his descriptive abilities at the same time that the necessity to invent a plot was removed. The brilliant portrayal of his grandparents in his *Detstvo* (*My Childhood*) and the skilful capturing of the complexities and contradictions exhibited by a great writer in his memoir devoted to Tolstoi are typical of the qualities that make Gor'kii's autobiography and various reminiscences his major contributions to world literature.

—Barry P. Scherr

See the essays on *The Lower Depths* and "Twenty-Six Men and a Girl."

GORKY, Maxim

See GOR'KII, Maksim

GOTTFRIED VON STRASSBURG

Career: Active in Alsace, possibly at the episcopal court in Strasbourg, in the years around 1200.

PUBLICATIONS

Verse

Tristan, edited by Friedrich Ranke. 1930, also edited by Rüdiger Krohn, 1981; as *Tristan und Isolde*, edited by Reinhold Bechstein, revised by P.F. Ganz, 1978, also edited by Hermann Kurtz and Wolfgang Mohr, 1979; as *Tristan and Isolde*, translated by Edwin H. Zeydel, 1948; as *Tristan*, translated by A.T. Hatto, 1960; a shortened version, as *The Story of Tristan and Iseult*, translated by Jessie L. Weston, 1899.

*

Bibliography: *Bibliographie zu Gottfried von Strassburg*, 1971, and *Bibliographie zu Gottfried von Strassburg, II, Berichtszeitraum 1971–1983*, 1986, both by Hans H. Steinhoff.

Critical Studies: *Gottfried von Strassburg* by Michael S. Bates, 1971; *The Anatomy of Love: The "Tristan" of Gottfried* by W.T.H. Jackson, 1971; *A History of Tristan Scholarship* by Rosemary Picozzi, 1971; *The Tristan of Gottfried von Strassburg: An Ironic Perspective* by Ruth Goldsmith Kunzer, 1973; *The Poetics of Conversion: Number Symbolism and Alchemy in Gottfried's "Tristan"* by Susan L. Clark and Julian N. Wasserman, 1977; *Medieval Humanism in Gottfried's Tristan und Isolde* by C. Stephen Jaeger, 1977; *Gottfried's Tristan: Journey Through the Realm of Eros* by Hugo Bekker, 1987; *Gottfried von Strassburg and the Medieval Tristan Legend: Papers from an Anglo-American Symposium* edited by Adrian Stevens and Roy Wisbey, 1990; *Tristan in the Underworld: A Study of Gottfried von Strassburg's "Tristan" Together with the "Tristran" of Thomas* by Nell Thomas, 1991; *Complete Concordance to Gottfried von Strassburg's Tristan* by Clifton D. Hall, 1992; *History, Fiction, Verisimilitude: Studies in the Poetics of Gottfried's Tristan* by Mark Chinca, 1993; *Gottfried von Strassburg: Tristan* by Mark Chinca, 1997.

* * *

In the flourishing of courtly literature in Germany around 1200 Gottfried von Strassburg must be counted among the most profound narrative poets, and certainly the most enigmatic. Of his life nothing is known but his name and designation; he did work in Alsace, but his social position, whether aristocratic or bourgeois, cannot be determined, although the latter seems most likely; nor any patron identified. Manifestly he enjoyed a clerical education, but his attitude

towards the chivalric culture of aristocracy and in manners of religion remains elusive. His courtly romance *Tristan*, the supreme poetic account of the ill-fated lovers Tristan and Isolde at the court of Marke, king of Cornwall, remains incomplete, and breaks off (probably because of Gottfried's death) at v. 19 548. Running through this romance are complex strands of reflection and commentary on matters literary, social, ethical, and religious which render difficult any unitary interpretation according to customary categories.

Tristan, a romance in rhymed couplets, shows Gottfried's sovereign command of Latin poetics and vernacular narrative techniques, within the traditions of clerical historical writing. The stylistic richness of the work's verbal figures matches the dialectic artistry with which the story unfolds its model of a love-force which transforms human existence, and the poem gives a masterful presentation of the social and aesthetic functions of courtly ceremony.

Contemporary literary references indicate that Gottfried's romance was composed between 1200 and 1220. It is recorded in a strong, early tradition from the 13th century, with 11 manuscripts complete (to the break-off point) and 16 fragments. Later poets, Ulrich von Türheim and Heinrich von Freiberg wrote continuations, praising Gottfried warmly.

The Tristan story has its origins in the Celtic realism of the heroic age in Britain in the fourth to sixth centuries, but the relation of Celtic myth to medieval romance is elusive. No extant insular text gives definite information about the early shaping of the legend, and its literary origins are to be found rather in the early continental texts of Brittany and France. Gottfried presents in general the adventure sequences familiar in diverse European Tristan texts since the late 12th century, including a German version by Eilhart von Oberge (usually dated 1170–75). He claims to follow specifically the account of Thomas of Brittany, whose extant text, dated between 1155 and 1190, while fragmentary, in essence complements the unfinished German work in a most valuable way: its significance in the interpretation of Gottfried's poem is debated. Gottfried himself insists on the authenticity of his source as guarantee of the moral truth and validity of his work in contrast to that of disreputable minstrels. Such professional polemic underlies, too, his important literary review of contemporary German courtly poets, including Hartmann von Aue and Heinrich von Veldeke, Wolfram von Eschenbach (whom he does not name) and Walther von der Vogelweide.

Tristan is born the orphan son of Riwalin and Blanchefleur, his story a variant of the widespread theme of the Fair Unknown; the tragic love of Tristan's parents anticipates the entanglements of his own love for Isolde, who is his queen and the wife of his uncle, when the two, joined by mischance through a love potion, feel driven to abuse the bonds of court, society, and religion in order to nurture their illicit love. After episodes of mounting hazard and bold deception Tristan finally succumbs to the contradictions of his plight and flees the court, vainly seeking solace for his psychological torment in the company of another Isolde.

In contrast to the protagonist of Arthurian romance, Tristan does not develop through experience towards maturity. From the outset he displays his consummate skill in every sphere of chivalric life and culture; frequently he assumes the role of *spilman* (entertainer), and deceptions play a major role in the narrative. Tristan's artistic accomplishments serve in a sense to indicate his status as outsider in the courtly world, for he avails himself constantly of a certain

independence from norms that pertain to those who are fully integrated into society. Hand in hand with this aesthetic orientation is his
indifference to martial values (despite, of course, his mastery of arms
and strategy). Often the events reflect material familiar from medieval fabliaux, comic tales which reward cunning and delight in the
bawdy and irreverent, The many episodes are linked in a tectonic
pattern of analogies and contrasts which reflect the mystical, paradoxical power of the love that dominates the romance.

Indeed, high ideals are Gottfried's constant concern in this narrative which deals with the conflict between the individual and society.
In numerous reflective passages the poet probes chivalric aristocratic
society, its military ethos, its values, and its use of religion (in, for
example, a blatant piece of trickery which serves as critique of trial by
ordeal). In episodes which focus upon the vacillating insensitivity of
Marke, the all-too-human centre of social authority in this fictional
world, he explores the implications for feudal society of unregulated
love. Through the use of allégory (in the introduction and the Cave of
Lovers, where in a cathedral-like natural setting the couple finds a
paradisal bliss outside of society which is short-lived) he postulates a
mystical community of *edele herzen* (noble hearts) who embody the
power of this fateful love. Gottfried addresses himself to this elite
audience of ''noble hearts'' who alone are culturally and ethically
capable of apprehending the nature of the love which is depicted in the
romance as an overwhelming, paradoxical force. This passionate
love, absolute and compulsive, is in flagrant conflict with the normal
standards of law, religion, and ethics. Through its dialectic of *liebe
unde leit* (the joy and suffering of love), this love force raises the
exceptional individual to an autonomy beyond the social constraints
which encompass human beings in medieval courtly society, but it
leads finally to self-loss and death. The poet's attitude to this love is
imparted in subtle allusion and demands discerning critical analysis:
the love of Tristan and Isolde may briefly defy society in their
moments of aesthetic and erotic fulfilment, which give listeners to
their tale great solace, but the lovers must in the end experience bitter
deprivation. Gottfried's romance is perhaps the most radical exploration of the potential of the individual in medieval literature.

—Lewis Jillings

GOTTHELF, Jeremias

Born: Albert Bitzius in Murten, Switzerland, 4 October 1797. **Education:** Studied theology at Berne Academy, 1814–20; Göttingen
University, for one year. **Family:** Married Henriette Elisabeth Zeender
in 1833. **Career:** Ordained in 1820; curate, Utzenstorf, 1820, and
1822–24; Herzongenbuchsee, 1824–29, transferred to Berne, 1829–31;
pastor, Lützelflüh, Emmental, 1832; school commissioner and founder
of educational institute for poor boys, 1835–45. Suffered from heart
disease, apoplexy, and dropsy in the 1850s. **Died:** 22 October 1854.

PUBLICATIONS

Collections

Gesammelte Schriften. 24 vols., 1856–58.
Ausgewahlte Erzählungen, edited by Adolf Bartels. 4 vols., 1907.

Sämtliche Werke, edited by Rudolph Hunziker and Hans Bloesch. 24
vols., 1911–59.
Werke, edited by Walter Muschg. 20 vols., 1948–53.
Werke, edited by Henri Poschmann. 1971.
Schwänke und Witze, edited by Eduard Strübin. 1986.

Fiction

Der Bauernspiegel; oder, Lebensgeschichte des Jeremias Gotthelf.
1837; as *The Mirror of Peasants*, translated by Mary Augusta
Ward, in *Macmillans Magazine*, 1883.
Wie fünf Mädchen im Branntwein jämmerlich umkamen. 1838.
Leiden und Freuden eines Schuhneisters. 1839; as *The Joys and
Griefs of a National Schoolmaster*, translated by Mary Augusta
Ward, in *Macmillans Magazine*, 1883; as *The Joys and Sorrows of
a Schoolmaster*, 1864.
Dursli, der Brannteweinsäufer; oder, der Heilige Weihnachtsabend.
1839.
Wie Uli der Knecht glücklich wird. 1841; as *Uli der Knecht*, 1846; as
Ulric the Farm-Servant, translated by Julia Firth, 1866.
Ein Sylvester-Traum (stories). 1842.
Bilder und Sagen aus der Schweiz (stories). 6 vols., 1842–46.
Anne Bäbi Jowäger. 1843–44.
Geld und Geist; oder, die Versöhnung. 1843; as *Wealth and Welfare*,
1866; as *Soul and Money*, translated by Julia Guarterick Vere,
1872.
Eines Schweizers Wort an den Schweizerischen Schützenverein.
1844.
Wie Christen eine Frau gewinnt. 1845.
Der Gelstag; oder, Die Wirthschaft nach tier neuen Mode. 1846.
Der Knabe des Tell. 1846.
Jakobs, des Handwerksgesellen, Wanderungen durch die Schweiz. 2
vols., 1846–48.
Käthi die Grossmutter. 1847; as *The Story of an Alpine Valley; or,
Katie the Grandmother*, translated by L.G. Smith, 1896.
Hans Joggeli der Erbvetter. 1848.
Uli der Pächter. 1849.
*Doctor Dorbach, der Wühler und die Bürglenherren in der heiligen
Weihnachtsnacht Anno 1847.* 1849.
Die Käserei in der Vehfreude. 1850.
Erzählungen und Bilder aus dem Volksleben der Schweiz. 1850–55.
Hans Jakob und Heiri; oder, die beiden Seidenweber. 1851.
Die Erbbase; oder, Freunde in der Not gehen hundert auf en Lot.
1851.
Zeitgeist und Berner Geist. 1852.
Der Patrizierspiegel. 1853.
Erlebnisse eines Schuldenbauers. 1854.
Das Erdbeeri Mareili. 1858.
Elsi, die seltsame Magd. 1858.
Die Schwarze Spinne. 1917; as *The Black Spider*, translated by Mary
Hottinger, in *Nineteenth Century German Tales*, 1958; also trans-
lated by H.M. Waidson, 1958.
Der Schwarze Spinne und andere Erzählungen (stories). 1970.

Other

Bericht über Gemeinde Utzenstorf. 1824.
Benz am Weihnachtdonnstag. 1825.
Zum Bollodingeer Schulstreit. 1829.
Aufruf der Bürgerschaft von Bern an die Landschaft. 1830.

Bericht über die Schulen von Latzelflüh und das Erziehungsdepartment. 1832.

Bettagspredigt für die eidgenössischen Regenten, welche weder in den Kirchen noch in den Herzen den eidgenössischen Bettag mit den eidgenössischen Christen feiern. 1839.

Die Armennoth. 1840.

Verfasser ins Hoehdeutsche übertragne Ausgabe. 1846.

Durchgesehene über mit einem Schlusskapitel vermehrte Aufl. 1851.

Jeremias Gotthelf und Karl Rudolf Hegenbach; ihr Briefwechsel aus den Jahren 1841 bis 1853, edited by Ferdinand Vetter. 1910.

Uzwil. 1923.

Langensalza. 1923.

Familienbriefe Jeremias Gotthelf, edited by Hedwig Wäber. 1929.

Donauwörth. 1931.

*

Bibliography: *Jeremias Gotthelf, 1797–1854* by Bee Juker and Giseal Martorelli, 1983.

Critical Studies: *The Rural Novel: Jeremias Gotthelf, Thomas Hardy and C.R. Ramuz* by Michael H. Parkinson, 1984; *Narrative Strategies in the Novels of Jeremias Gotthelf* by Robert Godwin-Jones, 1986; *Three Swiss Realists: Gotthelf, Keller, and Meyer* by Robert Godwin-Jones and Margaret T. Peischl, 1988.

* * *

Jeremias Gotthelf was considered by Gottfried Keller an epic genius, and has come to be recognized as a great epic writer not only in German-speaking countries but worldwide. Ernst Alker, the German literary critic, even goes so far as to classify Gotthelf with Cervantes, Tolstoi, Dickens, and Homer. Alker considers Gotthelf more than a great novelist, seeing him as a man who created a new world in his poetical works. In his realism, Gotthelf is furthermore the forerunner of German naturalism as found in the latter half of the 19th century.

Gotthelf, who is often referred to as the classical writer of *Dorfgeschichten* and *Heimatkunst* or regional literature, actually belongs to the school of German realism. A Swiss Protestant pastor, he portrayed a narrow segment of his native Switzerland: the peasants of the Bernese hinterland, among whom he spent his entire life. Like his more famous contemporaries, Gotthelf attempted to portray real human beings with all their shortcomings and deficiencies. Gotthelf took his figures, as Dickens did, from definite walks of life, and specifically from the region he knew best, the Swiss *Bernbiet* (Bern region) with its farming population. He often wrote the dialogue in his novels in local dialect. Like Dickens too, Gotthelf had a weakness for moralizing; this is not surprising, since Gotthelf was greatly influenced by the teachings of his countryman, Johann Heinrich Pestalozzi, the Swiss educationist.

Education is one of the main themes in Gotthelf's first novel, *Der Bauernspiegel; oder, Lebensgeschichte des Jeremias Gotthelf* (*The Mirror of Peasants*). This novel was written in the form of a fictional autobiography and shows the development of a young orphan from farmers' helper to freelance writer. In this work, Gotthelf attacks social prejudice, drawing on his own experience of paupers' establishments, and shows, through the character of the boy Jeremias, how poverty leads to crime. Jeremias is eventually saved from final degradation as a mercenary in a foreign army; yet on his return home, a changed man, he cannot find employment. It was Gotthelf's aim to open people's eyes to reality and to make the peasants in the canton of Berne aware of the social inequities within their parish. Gotthelf points the finger for these inequities and injustices not at a backward government but at man himself. Because of his indifference, his selfishness, his covetousness, and his lack of true Christian charity, man is his own enemy. The first part of the novel is vivid and forceful; the second part loses some of its *élan* and becomes somewhat theoretical.

The main impulse of Gotthelf's second work, *Leiden und Freuden eines Schulmeisters* (*The Joys and Sorrows of a Schoolmaster*) shows the resentment of Peter Kiser, a man who refused to be a mere puppet as a member of a local school board. Like *The Mirror of Peasants*, it is written in the first person; it describes, transcending time and place, the pandemonium of a provincial school system.

Following these two early works, Gotthelf depicted the sunny side of peasant life in his novel *Uli der Knecht* (*Ulric the Farm-Servant*). It is a narrative in which Gotthelf shifts from first to third person narration, and becomes more objective and less didactic in his writing. Indeed, in this *Entwicklungsroman* (novel of character development), Gotthelf avoids all pedagogic tendencies and departs from the form of his first two novels. *Ulric the Farm-Servant* remains one of his most popular works, with its vivid characters and realistic detail, and eulogy of life on the land, the blessings of work, the triumph of the will, and purification through suffering. Here as elsewhere, Gotthelf is particularly successful in probing the depths of his female characters. He depicts village attitudes to marriage and pregnancy, drunkenness and duel fighting.

Uli der Pächter [Uli the Tenant], not a sequel to *Ulric the Farm-Servant*, is one of those stories in which Gotthelf could not refrain from sermonizing. Here Gotthelf revived the good old farmers' customs, and poured venom on those of his countrymen who aped foreign fashions or gave up their ancient religion, Neither did he spare the intellectuals, whether teachers, physicians, or even parsons, and his criticism was blunt. Gotthelf always bore in mind that his village readers would never accept evasive words.

Christian humility and moderation appear as dominant concerns in the novel *Hans Joggeli der Erbvetter* [Hans Joggeli the Inheritor]. In this work, Gotthelf steers a middle course between asceticism and worldliness. Again, as in so many of his novels, he reveals his fascination with man and especially with man's striving spiritual potential.

The most discussed and perhaps the greatest of Gotthelf's works is the novella *Die Schwarze Spinne* (*The Black Spider*). It presents a colourful picture of rural life, a banquet reminiscent of a Homeric idyll. But this humorous description of the present is soon interrupted by an eruption from the solemn past, as an old farmer tells the story of his family, which has achieved prosperity by fighting the black spider. This spider was the progeny of a woman who called upon the devil for help, and defaulted on her promise to repay him by sending him a soul. The vengeful spider had thereupon killed everyone and everything in its way until the pious farmer caught it and imprisoned it in a hole in a beam. If any generation became too arrogant, the spider would, once again, find its way to freedom. Thus, in mythical manner and without direct sermonizing, Gotthelf points to piety as the basis of the village's present prosperity. Inevitably the author's own vocation as a pastor and his Christian world-view led to allegorical interpretations of the story based on Catholic doctrine denying the full beatific vision to the unbaptized. Rationalist interpreters saw in the black spider an unenlightened stage in the progressive development of man. The influence of psychoanalysis led later critics to see the black spider as a female mother-symbol. Probably none of these allegorical or one-sided interpretations does justice to Gotthelf's poetic achievement. In broader terms, one can claim that in this work, Gotthelf depicts the world in a perilous situation. Humanity is constantly threatened. It is by no means established that evil is punished and good rewarded. So-called earthly justice is the work of fallible human hands. The devil can seize power in this world and the innocent are victimized along with the guilty. It seems to be a mystery of divine justice that only the sacrifice of the innocent has expiatory power. Gotthelf gains depth and perspective for his picture of well-to-do farmers by bringing in past crises and temptations. *The Black Spider* is short, but substantial and full of meaning. An entire nation is presented in its dependence on the heavenly powers, in a masterly story that has few equals.

Das Erdbeeri Mareili [Strawberry Mary] and *Elsi, die seltsame Magd* [Elsie, the Strange Farm Servant], are other masterpieces from Gotthelf's pen. Both are rooted in history and present the Swiss environment realistically. Gotthelf's work as a whole is proof of his love for the tiller of the soil and of his understanding of Swiss national particularities. Although he was inclined, at times, to sentimentalize rural life, the immediacy with which he describes it stands out in an age of emerging realism.

Over a span of 18 years, Gotthelf wrote more than 12 long novels and over 50 separate works; in the last years of his life he was swamped with requests for novels, short stories, and anecdotes for all manner of publications. In later life he also became increasingly concerned with politics, often to the detriment of the broad, flowing style of his novels. Gotthelf restricted himself to narrative fiction: he produced no rhymed poems or ballads and he scarcely considered writing a drama, though he was acquainted with the works of Schiller and Shakespeare. The stories of his maturity, particularly the shorter ones, show great skill in construction; their language is lively and full of vivid images, a blend of dialect forms and standard constructions, reflecting his desire to fuse the elevated world of the Bible with the real world of the canton of Berne and to make the many Bernese dialects serve the purposes of art.

—Brigitte Edith Zapp Archibald

GRABBE, Christian Dietrich

Born: Detmold, Westphalia, 11 December 1801. **Education:** Educated at Gymnasium, Detmold; studied law at Leipzig University, 1820–22; and also in Berlin. **Family:** Married Luise Clostermeier (separated). **Career:** Attempted, unsuccessfully, to become an actor, 1823; established a legal practice in Detmold, 1824; military legal officer, 1826–34, resigning under pressure because of his dissolute lifestyle; quarrelled with Heinrich Heine, Ludwig Tieck, and Karl Immermann, losing their friendship and support; lived in Düsseldorf, 1835; contracted a spinal illness, and returned to Detmold. **Died:** 12 September 1836.

PUBLICATIONS

Collections

Werke und Briefe, edited by Alfred Bergmann. 6 vols., 1960–73.
Werke, edited by Roy C. Cowen. 3 vols., 1975–77.

Plays

Herzog Theodor von Gothland (produced 1892). In *Dramatische Dichtungen*, 1827.
Scherz, Satire, Ironie und tiefere Bedeutung (produced 1876). In *Dramatische Dichtungen*, 1827; translated as *Comedy, Satire, Irony and Deeper Meaning*, 1955.
Marius und Sulla (produced 1936). In *Dramatische Dichtungen*, 1827.
Nannette und Maria (produced 1914). In *Dramatische Dichtungen*, 1827.
Dramatische Dichtungen. 2 vols., 1827.
Don Juan und Faust (produced 1829). 1829; translated 1963.
Die Hohenstaufen I: Kaiser Friedrich Barbarossa (produced 1875). 1829
Die Hohenstaufen II: Kaiser Heinrich der Sechste (produced 1875). 1830.
Napoleon; oder, Die hundert Tage (produced in a shortened version, 1869; complete version produced 1895). 1831.
Aschenbrödel (produced 1937). 1835.
Kosciuszko (incomplete; produced 1940). 1835.
Hannibal (produced 1918). 1835.
Die Hermannsschlacht (produced 1934). 1838

*

Bibliography: *Grabbe Bibliographie*, by Alfred Bergmann, 1973.

Critical Studies: *Grabbes Leben und Charakter* by Karl Ziegler, 1885, reprinted 1981; *Christian Dietrich Grabbe* by R. von Gottschall, 1901; *Christian Dietrich Grabbe: Sein Leben und seine Werke* by O. Nieten, 1908, reprinted 1978; *Die Glaubwürdigkeit der Zeugnisse für den Lebensgang und Charakter Christian Dietrich Grabbes*, 1933, and *Christian Dietrich Grabbe: Chronik seines Lebens*, 1954, both by Alfred Bergmann; *Grabbes Werke in der zeitgenössischen Kritik*, 6 vols., 1958–66, and *Grabbe in Berichten seiner Zeitgenossen*, 1968, both edited by Alfred Bergmann; *Grabbe: Glanz und Elend eines Dichters* by F. Böttger, 1963; *Idea and Reality in the Dramas of Christian Dietrich Grabbe* by A.W. Hornsey, 1966; *Christian Dietrich Grabbe* by W. Steffens, 1966, revised edition, 1972; *The Dramas of Christian Dietrich Grabbe* by R.A. Nicholls, 1969; *Grabbes Dramenformen* by W. Hegele, 1970; *Christian Dietrich Grabbe* by R.C. Cowen, 1972; *Deutung und Dokumentation: Studien zum Geschichtsdrama Christian Dietrich Grabbes*, 1973, and *Brecht und Grabbe: Rezeption eines dramatischen Erbes*, 1979, both by Hans-Werner Nieschmidt; *Destruktion und utopische Gemeinschaft. Zur Thematik und Dramaturgie des Heroischen im Werk Christian Dietrich Grabbes* by Manfred Schneider, 1973; *Grabbe-Studien* by Alfred Bergmann, 1977; *Byron und Grabbe: Ein geistesgeschichtlicher Vergleich* by Ulrich Wesche, 1978; *Grabbe und sein Verhältnis zur Tradition* by David Horton, 1980; *Geschichte und Gesellschaft in den Dramen Christian Dietrich Grabbes* by Detlev Kopp, 1982; *Christian Dietrich Grabbe: Leben, Werk, Wirkung* by Lothar Ehrlich, 1983; *Literaturrezeption und historische Krisenerfahrung: Die Rezeption der Dramen Christian Dietrich Grabbes 1827–1945* by M. Vogt, 1983; *Grabbe im Dritten Reich. Zum nationalsozialistischen Grabbe-Kult*, 1986, and *Christian Dietrich Grabbe: Ein Symposium*, 1987, both edited by W. Broer and W. Kopp; *Die Logik yon Zerstörung und Grössenphantasie in den Dramen Christian Dietrich Grabbes* by Antonio Cortesi, 1986; *Christian Dietrich Grabbe: Leben und Werk* by Lothar Ehrlich, 1986;

Grabbes Gegenentwürfe: Neue Deutungen seiner Dramen edited by W. Freund, 1986; *Christian Dietrich Grabbe* by Ladislaus Löb, 1996; *Christian Dietrich Grabbe: Dramatiker ungelöster Widersprüche* by Ron C. Cowen, 1998; *Lachen der Verzweiflung: Grabbe, ein Leben* by Jörg Aufenanger, 2001.

* * *

"What is to become of a person whose first memory is taking an old murderer for a walk in the open air?," Christian Dietrich Grabbe asked Karl Immermann in a reminiscence about his childhood. While the question, as usual with Grabbe, contained an overstatement of the truth, the answer is that he became one of Germany's major dramatists. He was described by Sigmund Freud as "an original and rather peculiar poet," by Heine as "a drunken Shakespeare," and by Immermann as both "a wild, ruined nature" and "an outstanding talent." Although the image of a flawed genius, which dogged Grabbe in his lifetime, still persists, the irregularities of his plays are now more often regarded as an integral part of their originality.

The only child of the local jailer, Grabbe felt oppressed and alienated in his provincial home town of Detmold where, as he wrote to Ludwig Tieck, "an educated person is looked upon as an inferior kind of fattened ox" (letter of 29 August 1823). Physically sickly and emotionally unstable, swinging between sullen shyness and aggressive self-assertion, arrogantly demanding recognition but unwilling to please or to conform, uncouth in company, erratic in his post as army legal officer, entangled in a destructive marriage, and precipitating an early death by excessive drinking, he appeared as the archetype of the dissolute bohemian artist. While it is not clear how far his "bizarreness" was natural or assumed in order to shock, the "Grabbe legend" soon became confused with, and has often overshadowed, his work.

After his death Grabbe was forgotten owing to the classical orientation of literary fashion until later in the 19th century when both nationalists and naturalists rediscovered him as a kindred spirit. In the 20th century, expressionists welcomed him as a fellow-outcast from bourgeois society, dadaists and surrealists acclaimed him as another rebel against rationality, the Nazis celebrated him as a champion of "blood and soil," and Brecht placed him alongside J.M.R. Lenz and Georg Büchner in the "non-Aristotelian" strain leading from the Elizabethans to his own Marxist epic theatre. On the German stage he was first adopted in the 1870s, revived in the early 1920s and late 1930s, and finally included in the standard repertory—chiefly with *Scherz, Satire, Ironie und tiefere Bedeutung* (*Comedy, Satire, Irony and Deeper Meaning*) and *Napoleon; oder, Die hundert Tage* [Napoleon, or, The Hundred Days]—in the 1950s, although he is still largely unknown in other countries.

In philosophical terms Grabbe is generally seen—together with Byron, Lamartine, Leopardi, and Heine—as the product of a period in which idealism was superseded by materialism, with young writers facing a spiritual void in a mood of post-romantic scepticism and melancholy. His early plays—particularly *Herzog Theodor von Gothland* and *Comedy, Satire, Irony and Deeper Meaning*, a gothic melodrama and a black comedy—reveal the despair of "intellect spent and emotion shattered" (letter to George Ferdinand Kettembeil, 4 May 1827). A similar disillusionment awakens superhuman desires in *Don Juan und Faust* (*Don Juan and Faust*)—his only play to be performed while he was alive—which "glorifies the tragic fall of the sensualist and the metaphysician" alike (letter to Christian von

Meien, 6 January 1829). Nihilism also underlies his later plays—notably *Napoleon* and *Hannibal*—which blend the longing for powerful heroes with a sense of futility in view of the baseness of human nature and the impermanence of all things. Current affairs were of little interest to him. Thus he abandoned a trendily patriotic *Hohenstaufen* cycle after two instalments on the Emperors Barbarossa and Heinrich VI, while his last play, *Die Hermannsschlacht* [Arminius's Battle], was inspired by his "best childhood memories" (letter to Louise Grabbe, 8 January 1835) of its setting in the Teutoburg Forest near Detmold, rather than by the chauvinism traditionally associated with the topic. Nevertheless, his pessimism and cynicism can be interpreted as an oblique response to the uncongenial socio-political conditions of the "Restauration" era.

By common consent Grabbe's prime achievement consists in his innovations in historical drama. Unlike the historical plays of Schiller and his followers, which were classical in style and idealistic in message, his are prosaic in language, episodic in structure, and realistic in outlook. They portray history as determined not by ideas or individuals but by mass movements and the contingencies of time, place, and circumstance. Foreshadowed in *Marius und Sulla*, further developed in *Die Hohenstaufen*, and culminating in *Napoleon* and *Hannibal*, his re-creation of the broad flow of history itself has been much admired. He was hardly exaggerating when—referring to *Napoleon* but with his historical drama as a whole in mind—he claimed to have brought about "a dramatic-epic-revolution" (letter to Kettembeil, 25 February 1831).

Grabbe's "revolution" in historical drama involved a revolutionary handling of drama as such. Dismissed in the past as signs of ineptitude, capriciousness, or a pathological psyche, his approaches now seem eminently modern. Teeming with incongruities and distortions, deliberately avoiding harmony or beauty, his disjoined actions, ambiguous characters, and dissonant dialogues not only express the conflicts he experienced in his own age but anticipate the "open" form and "absurd" content favoured by dramatists today.

Commenting on *Napoleon*, Grabbe once declared: "I haven't taken any trouble over its shape as a drama. The present stage doesn't deserve it" (letter to Kettembeil, 2 October 1830). On another occasion, however, he noted: "Drama is not bound to the stage . . . the proper theatre is—the imagination of the reader" (letter to Wolfgang Menzel, 15 January 1831). We cannot tell whether Grabbe's refusal to compromise with the stage resulted from his anger over the theatrical conventions of his day or from more general doubts about theatrical production as a vehicle for poetic utterances. If the latter is true, then the paradox of a born dramatist who does not believe in theatre could be the key to both the successes and the failures of this maverick in the evolution of German drama.

—Ladislaus Löb

GRASS, Günter (Wilhelm)

Born: Danzig, Germany (now Gdansk, Poland), 16 October 1927. **Education:** Educated at Volksschule and Gymnasium, Danzig; trained as stone mason and sculptor; attended Academy of Art, Düsseldorf, 1948–52, and State Academy of Fine Arts, Berlin, 1953–55. **Military Service:** Served in World War II: prisoner of war, Marienbad,

Czechoslovakia, 1945–46. **Family:** Married 1) Anna Margareta Schwarz in 1954, three sons and one daughter; 2) Ute Grunert in 1979. **Career:** Worked as farm labourer, miner, apprentice stonecutter, jazz musician; speech writer for Willy Brandt when Mayor of West Berlin; writer-in-residence, Columbia University, New York, 1966; also artist and illustrator; co-editor, *L*, since 1976, and Verlages L'80, publishing house, since 1980. Member, Gruppe 47. Lives in Berlin, Germany. **Awards:** Süddeutscher Rundfunk Lyrikpreis, 1955; Gruppe 47 prize, 1958; Berlin Critics prize, 1960; City of Bremen prize, 1960 (withdrawn); Foreign Book prize (France), 1962; Büchner prize, 1965; Fontane prize, 1968; Theodor Heuss prize, 1969; Mondello prize (Palermo), 1977; Carl von Ossietsky medal, 1977; International literature prize, 1978; Alexander Majkowski medal, 1978; Vienna literature prize, 1980; Feltrinelli prize, 1982; Leonhard Frank ring, 1988. Honorary doctorate: Kenyon College, Gambier, Ohio, 1965; Harvard University, Cambridge, Massachusetts, 1976; Adam Mieckiewicz University, Poznan; Nobel prize for literature, 1999. **Member:** Member, 1963, and president, 1983–86 (resigned), Academy of Art, Berlin; American Academy of Arts and Sciences.

PUBLICATIONS

Fiction

Danziger Trilogie. 1980; as *The Danzig Trilogy*, translated by Ralph Manheim, 1987.
Die Blechtrommel. 1959; as *The Tin Drum*, translated by Ralph Manheim, 1962.
Katz und Maus. 1961; as *Cat and Mouse*, translated by Ralph Manheim, 1963; as *Cat and Mouse and Other Writings*, edited by A. Leslie Willson, 1994.
Hundejahre. 1963; as *Dog Years*, translated by Ralph Manheim, 1965.
Geschichten (as Artur Knoff). 1968. *Örtlich betäubt*. 1969; as *Local Anaesthetic*, translated by Ralph Manheim, 1969.
Aus dem Tagebuch einer Schnecke. 1972; as *From the Diary of a Snail*, translated by Ralph Manheim, 1973.
Der Butt. 1977; as *The Flounder*, translated by Ralph Manheim, 1978.
Das Treffen in Telgte. 1979; as *The Meeting at Telgte*, translated by Ralph Manheim, 1981.
Kopfgeburten; oder, Die Deutschen sterben aus. 1980; as *Headbirths; or, The Germans Are Dying Out*, translated by Ralph Manheim, 1982.
Die Rättin. 1986; as *The Rat*, translated by Ralph Manheim, 1988.
Unkenrufe. 1992; as *The Call of the Toad*, translated by Ralph Manheim, 1992.
Ein weites Feld: Roman. 1995.
Auf einem anderen Blatt: Zeichnungen. 1999.

Plays

Hochwasser (produced 1957). 1963; as *Flood*, translated by Ralph Manheim, in *Four Plays*, 1967.
Onkel, Onkel (produced 1958). 1965; as *Onkel, Onkel*, translated by Ralph Manheim, in *Four Plays*, 1967. *Noch zehn Minuten his Buffalo* (produced 1959). In *Theaterspiele*, 1970; as *Only Ten Minutes to Buffalo*, translated by Ralph Manheim, in *Four Plays*, 1967.
Beritten hin und zurück (produced 1959).

Die bösen Köche (produced 1961). In *Theaterspiele*, 1970; as *The Wicked Cooks*, translated by A. Leslie Willson, in *Four Plays*, 1967.
Goldmäuschen (produced 1964).
Die Plebejer proben den Aufstand (produced 1966). 1966; as *The Plebeians Rehearse the Uprising*, translated by Ralph Manheim, 1966.
Four Plays (includes *Flood; Onkeh Onkel; Only Ten Minutes to Buffalo; The Wicked Cooks*). 1967.
Davor (produced 1969). In *Theaterspiele*, 1970; as *Max*, translated by A. Leslie Willson and Ralph Manheim, 1972.
Theaterspiele (includes *Noch zehn Minuten bis Buffalo; Hochwasser; Onkel, Onkel; Die Plebejer proben den Aufstand; Davor*). 1970.
Die Blechtrommel als Film (screenplay), with Volker Schlöndorff. 1979.

Screenplays: *Katz und Maus*, 1967; *Die Blechtrommel*, with Volker Schlöndorff, 1979.

Ballet Scenarios: *Fünf Köche*, 1957; *Stoffreste*, 1959; *Die Vogelscheuchen*, 1970.

Radio Plays: *Zweiunddreissig Zähne*, 1959; *Noch zehn Minuten bis Buffalo*, 1962; *Eine öffentliche Diskussion*, 1963; *Die Plebejer proben den Aufstand*, 1966; *Hochwasser*, 1977.

Verse

Die Vorzüge der Windhühner. 1956.
Gleisdreieck. 1960.
Selected Poems, translated by Michael Hamburger and Christopher Middleton. 1966; as Poems *of Günter Grass*, 1969.
März. 1966.
Ausgefragt. 1967; as *New Poems*, translated by Michael Hamburger, 1968.
Danach. 1968.
Die Schweinekopfsülze. 1969.
Gesammelte Gedichte. 1971.
Mariazuehren/Hommageàmarie/Inmarypraise. 1973; as *Inmarypraise*, translated by Christopher Middleton, 1974.
Liebe geprüft. 1974.
Mit Sophie in die Pilze gegangen. 1976; revised edition, 1987.
In the Egg and Other Poems (bilingual edition), translated by Michael Hamburger and Christopher Middleton. 1977.
Als vom Butt nur die Gräte geblieben war. 1977.
Kinderlied: Verse and Etchings. 1982.
Nachruf auf einen Handschuh: Sieben Radierungen und ein Gedicht. 1982.
Ach, Butt, dein Märchen geht böse aus. 1983.
Gedichte. 1985.
Die Rättin: 3 Radierungen und 1 Gedicht. 1985.
Die Gedichte 1955–1986. 1988.
Tiersehutz. 1990.
Novemberland: 13 Sonnette. 1993.

Other

O Susanna: Ein Jazzbilderbuch: Blues, Balladen, Spirituals, Jazz, with H. Geldmacher and H. Wilson. 1959.
Die Ballerina. 1963.
Dich singe ich Demokratie (pamphlets). 5 vols., 1965.
Der Fall Axel C. Springer am Beispiel Arnold Zweig. 1967.

Briefe über die Grenze; Versuch eines Ost-West-Dialogs, with Pavel Kohout. 1968.

Über meinen Lehrer Döblin und andere Vorträge. 1968.

Ausgewählte Texte, Abbildungen, Faksimiles, Bio-Bibliographie, edited by Theodor Wieser. 1968; as *Porträt und Poesie*, 1968.

Über das Selbstverständliche: Reden, Aufsätze, Offene Briefe, Kommentare. 1968; revised and enlarged edition as *Über das Selbstverständliche: Politische Schriften*, 1969; translated in part by Ralph Manheim, as *Speak Out! Speeches, Open Letters, Commentaries*, 1969.

Die Schweinekopfsülze. 1969.

Originalgraphik. 1970.

Dokumente zur potitischen Wirkung, edited by Heinz Ludwig Arnold and Franz Josef Görtz. 1971.

Der Schriftsteller als Bürger—eine Siebenjahresbilanz. 1973.

Der Bürger und seine Stimme. 1974.

Denkzettel: Potitische Reden und Aufsätze 1965–76. 1978.

Aufsätze zur Literatur. 1980.

Werkverzeichnis der Radierungen (exhibition catalogue). 1980.

Bin ich nun Schreiber; oder, Zeichner? (exhibition catalogue). 1982.

Vatertag (lithographs). 1982.

Zeichnen und Schreiben: das bildnerisehe Werk des Schriftstellers Günter Grass:

Zeichnungen und Texte 1954–1977. 1982; as *Drawings and Words 1954–1977*, translated by Michael Hamburger and Walter Arndt, 1983.

Radierungen und Texte 1972–1982. 1984; as *Etchings and Words 1972–1982*, translated by Michael Hamburger and others, 1985.

Günter Grass: Lithographien: 19. Juni bis 24. Juli 1983 (exhibition catalogue). 1983.

Die Vernichtung der Menschheit hat begonnen. 1983.

Widerstand lernen: Politische Gegenreden 1980–1983. 1984.

Geschenkte Freiheit: Rede zum 8. Mai 1945. 1985.

On Writing and Politics, 1967–1983 (selection), translated by Ralph Manheim. 1985.

Erfolgreiche Musterreden für den Bürgermeister. 1986.

In Kupfer, auf Stein. 1986.

Werkausgabe, edited by Volker Neuhaus. 10 vols., 1987.

Radierungen, Lithographien, Zeichnungen, Plastiken, Gedichte (exhibition catalogue). 1987.

Es war einmal ein Land: Lyrik und Prosa, Schlagzeug und Perkussion, with Günter "Baby" Sommer. 1987.

Zunge Zeigen (travel). 1988; as *Show Your Tongue*, translated by John E. Woods, 1989.

Skizzenbuch. 1989.

Meine grüne Wiese: Kurzprosa. 1989.

Wenn wir von Europa sprechen: ein Dialog, with Françoise Giroud. 1989.

Alptraum und Hoffnung: zwei Reden vor dem Club of Rome, with T. Aitmatow. 1989.

Deutscher Lastenausgleich: wider das dumpfe Einheitsgebot: Reden und Gespräche. 1990; as *Two States—One Nation? The Case Against Reunification*, translated by Krishna Winston and A.S. Wensinger, 1990.

Totes Holz: Ein Nachruf. 1990.

Ausstellung Güinter Grass, Kahlschlag in unseren Köpfen (1990–1991 Berlin) (exhibition catalogue). 1990.

Deutschland, einig Vaterland? Ein Streitgespräch, with Rudolph Augstein. 1990.

Erfolgreiche Mustergrussworte und Musterbriefe für Bürgermeister und Kommunalpolitiker. 1990.

Droht der deutsche Einheitsstaat?. 1990.

Ein Schnäppchen namens DDR: Letzte Reden vorm Glockengeläut. 1990.

Schreiben nach Auschwitz: Frankfurter Poetik-Vorlesung. 1990.

Gegen die verstreichende Zeit: Reden, Aufsäitze und Gesprache 1989–1991. 1991.

Vier Jahrzehnte: Ein Werkstattbericht, edited by G. Fritze Margull. 1991.

Editor, with Elisabeth Borchers and Klaus Roehler, *Luchterhands Loseblatt Lyrik: eine Auswahl.* 2 vols., 1983.

*

Bibliography: *Günter Grass: A Bibliography 1955–1975* by Patrick O'Neill, 1976; *Günter Grass in America: The Early Years* edited by Ray Lewis White, 1981; in *Erstausgaben deutscher Dichtung*, 1992.

Critical Studies: *Günter Grass: A Critical Essay* by Norris W. Yates, 1967; *Günter Grass* by W. Gordon Cunliffe, 1969; *Grass* by Kurt Lothar Tank, 1969; *A Grass Symposium* edited by A. Leslie Willson, 1971; *Günter Grass* by Irène Leonard, 1974; *A Mythic Journey: Günter Grass's Tin Drum* by Edward Diller, 1974; *Günter Grass* by Keith Miles, 1975; *The "Danzig Trilogy" of Günter Grass* by John Reddick, 1975; *The Writer and Society: Studies in the Fiction of Günter Grass and Heinrich Böll* by Charlotte W. Ghurye, 1976; *Günter Grass: The Writer in a Pluralist Society* by Michael Hollington, 1980; *Adventures of a Flounder: Critical Essays on Günter Grass' "Der Butt"* edited by Gertrude Bauer Pickar, 1982; *The Narrative Works of Günter Grass: A Critical Interpretation*, 1982, and *Grass: Die Blechtrommel*, 1985, both by Noel L. Thomas; *The Fisherman and His Wife: Günter Grass's "The Flounder" in Critical Perspective* edited by Siegfried Mews, 1983; *Günter Grass* by Ronald Hayman, 1985; *Günter Grass* by Richard H. Lawson, 1985; *Grass and Grimmelshausen: Günter Grass's "Das Treffen in Telgte" and Rezeptionstheorie* by Susan C. Anderson, 1986; *Critical Essays on Günter Grass* edited by Patrick O'Neill, 1987; *Understanding Günter Grass* by Alan Frank Keele, 1988; *Günter Grass's "Der Butt": Sexual Politics and the Male Myth of History* edited by Philip Brady, Timothy McFarland, and John J. White, 1990; *Günter Grass's Use of Baroque Literature* by Alexander Weber, 1995; *Distorted Reflections: The Public and Private Uses of the Author in the Work of Uwe Johnson, Günter Grass and Martin Walser, 1965–1975* by Stuart Tabener, 1998; *Günter Grass Revisited* by Patrick O'Neill, 1999; *The Life and Work of Günter Grass: Literature, History, Politics* by Julian Preece, 2001.

* * *

Günter Grass has shown in his novels that he is one of the most acute observers and critics of West Germany. After beginning in the 1950s with short prose pieces, poems, and plays in the then dominant "absurd" style, he made a dramatic impact on the literary scene with *Die Blechtrommel* (*The Tin Drum*), *Katz und Maus* (*Cat and Mouse*), and *Hundejahre* (*Dog Years*). These were later named the *Danziger Trilogie* (*The Danzig Trilogy*) after Grass's native city which, detached and distant like Joyce's Dublin, became the prism through which he conveyed his vision of the world about him. In Danzig, with its mixed German and Polish population, World War II began. The city was a paradigmatic setting for the gradual growth of Nazism amid the banality of the petty bourgeoisie, and symbolized the lost homelands from which millions of Germans would be forever exiled after 1945. In this picaresque trilogy Grass, with great zest and wide-ranging scope, imaginatively investigated both recent German history—the monstrous crimes of the Nazis, the acquiescence and cowardice of the ordinary citizen, and contemporary post-war reality—the suppression of guilt, economic reconstruction and the return to affluence and complacency, the loss of moral values. Inevitably Grass became identified with the new generation of critical realists, which included Heinrich Böll and Martin Walser, who implacably satirized the faults and errors of their fellow-countrymen and untiringly reminded them of the guilty involvement in Nazi Germany they were eager to forget.

Grass's sense of social justice and his contentious nature took him into the political arena where he threw his authority and weight behind the Social Democratic Party in the general elections of the 1960s. His personal friend Willy Brandt became Chancellor in 1969 and Grass's fiery, hard-hitting campaign speeches, open letters, and commentaries were variously published in *Über das Selbstverständliche* (*Speak Out!*) and *Der Bürger und seine Stimme* [The Citizen and His Voice]. The creative work accompanying this intense activity was also coloured by Grass's political commitment; the play *Davor* (*Max*) and the novel *Örtlich betäubt* (*Local Anaesthetic*) thematize the dominant preoccupations of intellectual and public life, namely the war in Vietnam and radical student protest in German universities. Though imbued with socialist ideas Grass stopped short of violence and destruction, advocating reform rather than revolution, practical measures for eradicating injustice rather than ideological posturings.

The anti-ideological scepticism of Grass's political stance is articulated in the novel *Aus dem Tagebuch einer Schnecke* (*From the Diary of a Snail*), which charts the author's reflections on his active participation in the election campaign of 1969 as well as telling the fictional story of the teacher Ott, "nicknamed Doubt," who resisted the Nazis and clandestinely helped the persecuted Jews to the best of his ability. During the mid-1970s Grass seemed to be out of tune with the more extreme progressive forces in Germany and his literary talents appeared to lie dormant and inactive. In fact this proved to be the period of gestation of another epic masterpiece. *Der Butt* (*The Flounder*) incorporates so many autobiographical details that the blurring of the distinction between author and narrator already initiated in *From the Diary of a Snail* is here completed. *The Flounder* is a complementary piece to *The Danzig Trilogy*; where the latter focuses on the enormities of contemporary events, *The Flounder* embraces in its narrative structure the whole sweep of German social and political history. The perennial human endeavour to ascribe progress and meaning to historical process as well as the more topical question of feminism and the secular domination of women by men are central themes given expression by Grass.

In the "fictional" work, *Kopfgeburten; oder, Die Deutschen sterben aus* (*Headbirths; or, The Germans Are Dying Out*), Grass displayed his political persona once more, thematizing the massive and urgent problems facing the industrialized nations: energy crisis, the threat of nuclear war, a declining birth-rate, the Third World. Yet, despite all his concern as a citizen with the struggles of the real world, Grass's faith in the significance of literature and the aesthetic dimension still shines through; he maintains that even in the most catastrophic destruction of civilization "a hand holding a pen would reach up out of the rubble."

Political concerns of national and global proportions have continued as fictional and polemical themes in Grass's subsequent work.

Die Rättin (*The Rat*) envisaged a dystopian world following a nuclear catastrophe where the human race, in its self-destructive hubris, has appropriately been superseded by pullulating rodents. His most recent novel, *Unkenrufe* (*The Call of the Toad*), also revels in near-cloacal and lugubriously funereal imagery, returning to Grass's beloved Danzig to re-enact the historically fraught and bitter relations between Germany and Poland. Grass encapsulated his nostalgia in the love-affair of an older couple (Alexander, the German, and his Polish mistress, Alexandra) who found a Cemetery Society to enable the German dead to at least rest in graves in the city from where they had been driven. But the story ends in tragedy.

Grass spent some time in Calcutta during 1986 and 1987, and expressed in *Zunge Zeigen* (*Show Your Tongue*) his deep horror and shame at the chaotic world of filth, violence, and death he encountered there. The inexorable process of merging the two Germanies that got under way in 1989 provoked violent opposition from Grass, who protested vehemently in *Deutscher Lastenausgleich: wider das dumpfe Einheitsgebot* (*Two States—One Nation?*) and *Ein Schnäppchen namens DDR* [The GDR, a Real Snip] at the juggernaut of reunification, its nationalistic repercussions and the cynically arrogant takeover of Eastern Länder by the Federal Republic. Going against the tide of public opinion Grass prophesied that nothing but ill would result from the euphoria and complacency of an inflated Germany situated at the heart of a Europe in flux.

—Arrigo V. Subiotto

See the essay on *The Tin Drum*.

GRIBOEDOV, Aleksandr (Sergeevich)

Also known as Alexander Griboyedov. **Born:** Moscow, Russia, 15 January 1795. **Education:** Educated at the University of Moscow, 1806–08, graduated in law; education interrupted by Napoleon's invasion of Russia, 1812. **Military Service:** Joined the Moscow hussars (General Kologryvov's reserve), 1812, but saw no military action; discharged, 1816. **Family:** Married daughter of the poet Prince Aleksandr Chavchavadze in 1828. **Career:** Joined Ministry of Foreign Affairs in St. Petersburg, 1816: diplomatic secretary to Russian legation in Persia, 1818, and to General A.P. Ermolov, 1821–23, both in Tiflis; diplomat in Tehran, 1819–21; returned to Georgia, 1825; arrested and imprisoned for four months on suspicion of involvement in the Decembrist uprising, 1825; returned to Caucasus after release, 1826; prepared the text of the Treaty of Turkmenchai, concluding the Russo-Persian war, 1826; Russian Minister to Persia, 1828. **Died:** Killed during the storming of the Russian embassy, Tehran, by a mob of insurgents, 11 February 1829.

PUBLICATIONS

Collections

Polnoe sobranie sochinenii [Collected Works]. 1911–17.
Sochineniia v stikhakh [Works], edited by I.N. Medvedeva. 1967.
Izbrannoe [Selections], edited by S.A. Fomicheva. 1978.

Plays

Molodye suprugi [The Young Married Couple], from a play by
  Creuzé de Lesser (produced 1815). 1815.
Student [Student], with Pavel A. Katenin (produced 1904). 1817.
Svoia sem'ia; ili, Zamuzhniaia nevesta [All in the Family; or, The
  Married Fiancée], with Aleksandr Shakovskoi and Nikolai
  Khmel'nitskii (produced 1818).
Pritvornaia nevernost' [False Infidelity], with A.A. Gendre, from a
  play by Nicolas Barthe (produced 1818). 1818.
Proba intermedy [Test of an Interlude] (produced 1819). In *Polnoe
  sobranie sochinenii*, 1911–17.
Kto brat, kto sestra; ili, Obman za obmanom [Who's the Brother,
  Who's the Sister; or, Deception for Deception], with Prince Peter
  Viazemskii and others (libretto; produced 1824).
Gore ot uma [Woes of Wit] (produced 1825; complete version
  produced 1831). 1825 (partial version); 1833 (censored version);
  1861 (uncensored version); edited by D.P. Costello, 1951; trans-
  lated as *Intelligence Comes to Grief*, in *Anthology of Russian
  Literature*, 2, edited by Leo Wiener, 1902; as *The Misfortune of
  Being Clever*, translated by S.W. Pring, 1914; as *The Mischief of
  Being Clever*, translated by Bernard Pares, 1925; as *Wit Works
  Woe*, in *Masterpieces of Russian Drama*, 1, edited by G.R. Noyes,
  1933; as *Chatsky*, translated by Joshua Cooper, in *Four Russian
  Plays*, 1972, reprinted as *The Government Inspector and Other
  Plays*, 1990; as *Woes of Wit: A Comedy in Four Acts*, translated by
  Alan Shaw, 1992; as *Distress from Cleverness: A Four-Act
  Comedy in Verse*, translated by Beatrice Yusem, 1993.

*

Critical Studies: "The Murder of Griboedov" by D.P. Costello, in
Oxford Slavonic Papers, 1958; *Griboedov et la vie littéraire de son
temps* by Jean Bonamour, 1965; *The Murder of Griboedov: New
Materials* by Evelyn J. Harden, 1979; *Diplomacy and Murder in
Tehran: Alexander Griboyedov and Imperial Russia's Mission to the
Shah of Persia* by Laurence Kelly, 2002.

*   *   *

Aleksandr Griboedov's first dramatic production was a one-act
comedy in alexandrines, *Molodye suprugi* [The Young Married
Couple], adapted from Creuzé de Lesser's *Le Secret du ménage*, and
produced in September 1815. A second play was *Student*, a three-act
comedy in prose, written in 1817 in conjunction with Pavel A.
Katenin, which satirized and parodied such older writers as Nikolai Karamzin (1766–1824), Vasilii Zhukovskii (1783–1852), and
Konstantin Batiushkov (1787–1855). A third comedy, first produced
in January 1818, *Svoia sem'ia; ili, Zamuzhniaia nevesta* [All in the
Family; or, The Married Fiancée], was written in collaboration with
the two most celebrated comic writers of his day, Aleksandr Shakovskoi
and Nikolai Khmel'nitskii. It is, however, for his masterpiece *Gore ot
uma* (*Woes of Wit*), a classically structured four-act comedy in free
iambic verse, that Griboedov has won one of the most illustrious
places in all Russian literature.

Woes of Wit is a *tour de force* of supple versification, brilliantly
aphoristic repartee, and abundant topical allusion that also affords an
unrivalled portrait of Moscow high society in about 1820. The verse
form of the play, free iambs with arbitrary rhyme patterning, recalls
strongly the form of the Russian fable, which in turn reflected the

influence of Lafontaine. Adopted for a few plays in the early 19th
century, free iambs were rarely used after *Woes of Wit*. In Griboedov's
play they ranged from one to 13 syllables with nearly half the
lines alexandrines.

Woes of Wit's repartee, in part reminiscent of Molière, depends
both on sparkling colloquial language and virtuosic timing. After first
hearing the play, Pushkin remarked that "half the lines are bound to
become proverbs," and it has indeed become the most quoted literary
work in the Russian language. For contemporaries an additional
quality was provided by the pithy topical references in which this
comedy abounds, ranging from the Russian order of battle in 1813 to
serf theatres, Carbonarism, freemasonry, and new educational ideas.
In this respect *Woes of Wit* recalls the allusory and referential nature
of Pushkin's almost contemporaneous novel in verse, *Eugene Onegin*. It
was the topical allusions, with their generally liberal tenor, which
meant the play could not be published in full until 1861, the year
serfdom was abolished, although a censored version was first published in 1833. In the meantime some 40,000 manuscript copies are
said to have circulated throughout Russia.

The Moscow aristocratic society in *Woes of Wit* is depicted as
hospitable, relaxed, venial, superficially cultured, and, above all,
politically conservative in the years preceding the Decembrist Uprising. Into it comes the alienated but undoubtedly heroic central
protagonist Chatskii, "straight from the boat into a ball," and it is the
inevitable clash between on the one hand the clever, eloquent,
tactless, and intolerant hero, who once loved the daughter of the
house, and on the other the sleepily unprepared Muscovite society
that lends the play its tension. Chatskii's qualities, positive and
negative alike, have proved to be universal, and he has easily outlived
contemporary literary heroes like Lermontov's Pechorin or, indeed,
Onegin. His bewildered beloved Sofiia and her genial but nervous and
cautious father Famusov (Mr. Rumours), her ambitious lickspittle
suitor Molchalin (Mr. Silent), and arch-gossip and intriguer Repetilov
(Mr. Reptilian Repeater), and the mindless soldier Skalozub (Mr.
Teeth-barer) are all very convincingly characterized, while Sofiia's
maid Liza is the only character to begin to match Chatskii's quick
aphoristic wit.

Modern audiences, for whom the ubiquitous topical references are
bound to be at least partially obscure, find the play's most enduring
qualities to be the wittily portrayed clash of cultures between impetuous liberal youth and somnolent conservative society, but above all
the use of richly colloquial syntax and vocabulary in conjunction with
verse of the highest sophistication. Such qualities ensure that
Griboedov's masterpiece will last as long as the Russian language itself.

—Arnold McMillin

See the essay on *Woes of Wit*.

GRILLET, Alain Robbe

See ROBBE-GRILLET, Alain

GRILLPARZER, Franz

Born: Vienna, Austria, 15 January 1791. **Education:** Educated at
Anna-Gymnasium, Vienna, 1800–07; studied law at University of

Vienna, 1807–11. **Family:** Engaged for 50 years to Katharina Fröhlich. **Career:** Tutor in law studies to nephew of Graf von Seilern, 1812; unpaid assistant in court library, 1813; civil servant from 1814: appointed Theaterdichter, 1818; travelled to Italy, 1819, and to Germany, 1826, director of court archives, 1832: retired 1856, as Hofrat; created a member of the Herrenhaus (upper house of the Austrian parliament), 1861. **Award:** Honorary Doctorate: University of Leipzig, 1859. **Member:** Founder-member, Austrian Academy of Sciences, 1847. **Died:** 21 January 1872.

PUBLICATIONS

Collections

Sämtliche Werke, edited by August Sauer and Reinhold Backmann. 42 vols., 1909–48.
Sämtliche Werke, edited by Peter Frank and Karl Pörnbacher. 4 vols., 1960–65.
Werke, edited by Helmut Bachmaier. 1986–.

Plays

Die Ahnfrau (produced 1817). 1817; as *The Ancestress*, translated by Herman L. Spahr, 1938.
Sappho (produced 1818). 1819; as *Sappho*, translated by J. Bramsen, 1820; also translated by E.B. Lee, 1846; Lucy C. Cumming, 1855; E. Frothingham, 1876; Arthur Burkhard, 1953.
Das Goldene Vlies (trilogy; produced 1821). 1822; as *Medea*, translated by F.W. Thurstan and S.A. Wittmann, 1879, also translated by Arthur Burkhard, 1941; as *The Golden Fleece*, translated by Burkhard, 1942; as *The Guest-Friend* and *The Argonauts*, translated by Burkhard, 2 vols., 1942.
König Ottokars Glück und Ende (produced 1825). 1825; as *Ottokar*, translated by Thomas Carlyle, 1840; as *King Ottokar, His Rise and Fall*, translated by G. Pollack, 1907; also translated by Arthur Burkhard, 1932; Henry H. Stevens, 1938.
Ein treuer Diener seines Herrn (produced 1828). 1830; as *A Faithful Servant of His Master*, translated by Arthur Burkhard, 1941.
Des Meeres und der Liebe Wellen (produced 1831). 1839; edited by E.E. Pabst, 1967; edited by Mark Ward, 1981; as *Hero and Leander*, translated by Henry H. Stevens, 1938, also translated by Arthur Burkhard, 1962; as *The Waves of Sea and Love*, translated by Samuel Solomon, in *Plays on Classic Themes*, 1969.
Melusina, music by Konradin Kreutzer (produced 1833). 1833.
Der Traum ein Leben (produced 1834). 1840; edited by W.E. Yuill, 1955; as *A Dream Is Life*, translated by Henry H. Stevens, 1947.
Weh dem, der lügt (produced 1838). 1840; as *Thou Shalt Not Lie*, translated by Henry H. Stevens, 1939.
Esther (produced 1868). In *Gesamtausgabe*, 1872; as *Esther*, translated by Arthur Burkhard, with *The Jewess of Toledo*, 1953.
Ein Bruderzwist in Habsburg (produced 1872). In *Gesamtausgabe*, 1872; edited by Bruce Thompson, 1982; as *Family Strife in Hapsburg*, translated by Arthur Burkhard, 1940.
Die Jüdin von Toledo (produced 1872). In *Gesamtausgabe*, 1872; as *The Jewess of Toledo*, translated by Arthur Burkhard, with *Esther*, 1953.
Libussa (produced 1874). In *Gesamtausgabe*, 1872; as *Libussa*, translated by Henry H. Stevens, 1941.

Fiction

Das Kloster bei Sendomir. In *Aglaja*, 1828; in *Sämtliche Werke*, 1930.
Der arme Spielmann. In *Iris*, 1847; in *Sämtliche Werke*, 1930; as *The Poor Musician*, translated by A. Remy, 1914; as *The Poor Fiddler*, translated by Alexander and Elizabeth Henderson, 1969.

Verse

Tristia ex Ponto. In *Vesta*, 1827.
Gedichte, edited by P. von Matt. 1970.

Other

Selbstbiographie. 1872.
Gespräche und Charakteristiken seiner Persönlichkeit durch die Zeitgenossen, edited by August Sauer. 6 vols., 1904–16; supplementary volume, edited by Reinhold Backmann, 1941.
Tagebücher und Reiseberichte, edited by Klaus Geissler. 1981.

*

Critical Studies: *Grillparzer, Lessing, and Goethe in the Perspective of European Literature* by Fred. O. Nolte, 1938; *Grillparzer: A Critical Biography* (vol. 1 only) by Douglas Yates, 1946; *The Inspiration Motif in the Works of Franz Grillparzer* by Gisela Stein, 1955; *The Plays of Grillparzer* by George A. Wells, 1969; *Grillparzer: A Critical Introduction* by W.E. Yates, 1972; *A Sense of Irony: An Examination of the Tragedies of Franz Grillparzer*, 1976, and *Franz Grillparzer*, 1981, both by Bruce Thompson, and *Essays on Grillparzer* edited by Thompson and Mark Ward, 1978; *Grillparzer's Aesthetic Theory* by William Norman Boyd Mullan, 1979; *The World as Theatre in the Works of Franz Grillparzer* by Sybil Hitchman, 1979; *Grillparzer's Der arme Spielmann: New Directions in Criticism* edited by Clifford Albrecht Bernd, 1988; *An Introduction to the Major Works of Franz Grillparzer* by Ian F. Roe, 1991; *Analysis of Franz Grillparzer's Dramas: Fate, Guilt, and Tragedy* by Eva Wagner, 1992; *The Federfuchser/Penpusher from Lessing to Grillparzer: A Study Focused on Grillparzer's Ein Bruderzwist in Habsburg* by William C. Reeve, 1995; *Franz Grillparzer: A Century of Criticism*, 1995; *Grillparzer's Libussa: The Tragedy of Separation* by William C. Reeve, 1999.

* * *

Nothing ever went right for Franz Grillparzer, a fact he viewed with grim satisfaction. He was the archetypal Viennese grumbler, and a wealth of anecdote testifies to his melancholy and his crusty hypochondria. At 81, still beset by a conflict between literature and marriage, he died in the arms of his "eternal betrothed" Katharina Fröhlich, to whom he had been engaged for 50 years.

Grillparzer's writing is rooted in the rich cultural heritage of the multi-lingual Hapsburg Empire. As a child he marvelled at the musical fantasies and magical transformations of Viennese popular comedy in which the spectacular visual effects of the baroque survived in a naive form. His comedy *Weh dem, der lügt* (*Thou Shalt Not Lie*), in which a cook's boy rescues a Frankish bishop's nephew from the heathen Germans, barely, but humorously, managing not to perjure himself in the process, uses the fun and wealth of incident of popular comedy to make a moral point. *Der Traum ein Leben* (*A Dream Is Life*) translates the hero into a dream to live out his ambitions then brings him back to renounce the life of action because of the inevitable guilt it involves.

Grillparzer was, however, drawn to the more austere world of German classicism, and even visited Goethe in Weimar, with disastrous results for his always parlous self-confidence. He set three plays in the ancient world. *Sappho*, in which the heroine forsakes poetry for a young lover and commits suicide when he abandons her, and *Des Meeres und der Liebe Wellen* (*The Waves of Sea and Love*), in which a novice priestess forsakes religion, only to have her lover drown in the Hellespont when the high priest extinguishes the lamp she has lit to guide him, are lyrical, tragic verse dramas of the conflict between the spirit and the flesh. In *Das Goldene Vlies* (*The Golden Fleece*) there is a foretaste of Strindberg's sexual psychology in the clash of the exotic alien Medea with her husband Jason in his sophisticated Greek homeland, but the tame sagacity of Grillparzer's conclusion underlines the gap between Biedermeier Vienna and the tragic ferocity of Greece.

Grillparzer's finest achievements were his historical dramas in verse. He was a rationalist and a liberal whom the nationalism of the mid-century turned into a conservative. *König Ottokars Glück und Ende* (*King Ottokar, His Rise and Fall*) celebrates the first Hapsburg Holy Roman Emperor, Rudolf I. *Ein treuer Diener seines Herrn* (*A Faithful Servant of His Master*), on the theme of loyalty, is set in Hungary. *Libussa* dramatizes the legendary founding of Prague in Bohemia. The best of these Austrian dramas is *Ein Bruderzwist in Habsburg* (*Family Strife in Hapsburg*) which unites Grillparzer's main themes in the drama of the self-abnegating, intellectual Emperor Rudolf II who struggles in vain to prevent the Reformation from splitting his empire. It was a plea for a supranational concept, and took on a new meaning when the empire was broken up in 1918. *King Ottokar*, with Ottokar von Horneck's hymn to Austria, is staged at the Burgtheater in Vienna on days of public celebration. But the Austrian national dramatist's complex language has defied translation and even in Germany his plays have never shown the power to move and entertain.

—Hugh Rorrison

See the essay on *Family Strife in Hapsburg*.

GRIMM, Jacob and Wilhelm

Jacob (Ludwig Karl) Grimm: **Born:** Hanau, Germany, 4 January 1785. **Education:** Educated at Kassel Lyceum, 1798–1802; University of Marburg, studied law, 1802–05. **Career:** Researcher for Friedrich Karl von Savigny in Paris, 1805; civil servant, secretariat of the War Office, Kassel, 1806; librarian for King Jérôme Bonaparte's private library, Wilhelmshöhe, 1808–14, co-editor with Wilhelm Grimm, *Altdeutsche Wälder*, 1813–16; legation secretary for the Hessian delegation at the Congress of Vienna, 1814–15; librarian, Kassel, 1816; chair, archaeology and librarianship, University of Göttingen, Hanover, 1830–37, dismissed from the university for political reasons by Ernst August in 1837; lived in Kassel, 1837–41; president, Conferences of Germanists, Frankfurt am Main, 1846, Lubeck, 1847; elected to the Frankfurt parliament, 1848. **Awards:** Order of Merit, 1842. Honorary doctorate: University of Marburg, 1819; Berlin University, 1828; Berslau University, 1829. **Member:** Academy of Science, Berlin, 1841. **Died:** 20 September 1863.

Wilhelm (Karl) Grimm: **Born:** Hanau, Germany, 24 February 1786. **Education:** Educated at Kassel Lyceum, 1798–1803; University of Marburg, 1803–06; law degree, 1806. **Family:** Married Henriette Dorothea Wild in 1825; one daughter and three sons. **Career:** Co-editor with Jacob Grimm, *Altdeutsche Wälder*, 1813–16; assistant librarian, electoral library, Kassel, 1814–29; professor, University of Göttingen, 1830, dismissed from the university for political reasons by Ernst August in 1837; lived in Kassel, 1837–41. **Member:** Academy of Science, Berlin, 1841. **Awards:** Honorary doctorate, Marburg University, 1819. **Died:** 16 December 1859.

PUBLICATIONS

Collections

Complete Works. 62 vols., 1974–.
Die älteste Märchensammlung der Brüder Grimm, edited by Heinz Rölleke. 1975.
Grimm's Tales for Young and Old: The Complete Stories, translated by Ralph Manheim. 1977.
The Complete Fairy Tales of the Brothers Grimm, edited and translated by Jack Zipes. 2 vols., 1987.

Fiction

Kinder- und Hausmärchen. 2 vols, 1812–15; revised editions, 3 vols., 1819–22 (includes *Anmerkungen zu den einzelnen Märchen*), 1837, 1840, 1843, 1850, 1857; edited by Friedrich Panzer, 1975, and by Heinz Rölleke, 1982; numerous subsequent translations including as *German Popular Stories*, translated by Edgar Taylor, 2 vols., 1823–26; revised edition as *Gammer Grethel; or, German Fairy Tales and Popular Stories*, 1839; as *Home Stories*, translated by Matilda Louisa Davis, 1855; *Grimm's Popular Stories*, 1868; as *Grimm's Fairy Tales*, translated by H.H.B. Paull, 1872; also translated by L.L. Weedon, 1898, Edgar Lucas, 1900, Beatrice Marshall, 1900, N.J. Davidson, 1906, Ernest Beeson, 1916, and Peter Carter, 1982; as *Grimm's Goblins*, 1876; as *The Complete Grimm's Fairy Tales*, translated by Margaret Hunt, 1944, reprinted 1975; as *Grimm Tales* by Tim Supple, 1996; as *Grimm's Grimmest*, edited by Marisa Bulzone and Stefan Matzig, 1997.
Deutsche Sagen. 1816–18; as *The German Legends of the Brothers Grimm*, edited and translated by Donald Ward, 1981.

Other

Deutsches Wörterbuch, with others. 32 vols., 1854–1961.
Freundesbriefe von Wilhelm und Jacob Grimm: Mit Anmerkungen, edited by Alexander Reifferscheid. 1878.
Briefwechsel des Freiherrn K.H.G. von Meusebach mit Jacob und Wilhelm Grimm. 1880.
Briefwechsel zwischen Jacob und Wilhelm Grimm aus der Jegendzeit, edited by Herman Grimm and Gustav Hinrichs. 1881; revised edition, edited by Wilhelm Schoof, 1963.
Briefwechsel der Gebrüder Grimm mit nordischen Gelehrten, edited by Ernst Schmidt. 1885.
Briefwechsel zwischen Jacob und Wilhelm Grimm, Dahlmann und Gervinus, edited by Eduard Ippel. 2 vols., 1885–86.
Briefe der Brüder Jacob und Wilhelm Grimm an Georg Friedrich Benecke aus den Jahren 1808–1829, edited by Wilhelm Müller. 1889.

Briefwechsel F. Lückes mit dell Brüdern Jacob und Wilhelm Grimm. 1891.

Briefe der Brüder Grimm an Paul Wigand, edited by Edmund Stengel. 1910.

Briefwechsel Johann Kaspar Bluntschlis mit Jacob Grimm. 1915.

Briefe der Brüder Grimm, edited by Albert Leitzmann and Hans Gürtler. 1923.

Briefwechsel der Brüder Jacob und Wilhelm Grimm mit Karl Lachmann, edited by Albert Leitzmann. 2 vols., 1927.

Briefwechsel zwischen Jacob Grimm und Karl Goedeke, edited by Johannes Bolte. 1927.

Briefe der Brüder Grimm an Savigny, edited by Wilhelm Schoof. 1953.

Unbekannte Briefe der Brüder Grimm, edited by Wilhelm Schoof. 1960.

John Mitchell Kemble and Jacob Grimm: A Correspondence 1832–1852. 1971.

Briefwechsel der Bruder Grimm mit Hans Georg von Hammerstein, edited by Carola Gottzmann. 1985.

Editors, *Die beiden ältesten deutschen Gedichte aus dem achten Jahrhundert: Das Lied von Hildebrand und Hadubrand und das Weissenbrunner Gebet.* 1812.

Editors, *Lieder der alien Edda.* 1815.

Editors, *Der arme Heinrich*, by Hartmann von Aue. 1815.

Editors and translators, *Irische Elfenmärchen*, by Thomas Croften Croker. 1826.

PUBLICATIONS BY JACOB GRIMM

Collections

Reden und Aufsätze, edited by Wilhelm Schoof. 1966.
Selbstbiographie: Ausgewählte Schriften, Reden und Abhandlungen. 1984.

Fiction

Irmenstrasse und Irmensäule: Eine mythologische Abhandlung. 1815.
Deutsche Mythologie. 3 vols., 1835–37; as *Teutonic Mythology*, translated by James Stevens Stallybrass, 4 vols., 1883–88.
Frau Aventiure klopft an Beneckes Thür. 1842.
Der Fundevogel: Ein Märlein. 1845.

Other

Über den altdeutschen Meistergesang. 1811.
Deutsche Grammatik. 4 vols., 1819–37.
Zur Recension der deutschen Grammatik. 1826.
Deutsche Rechtsalterthümer. 1828.
Hymnorum veteris ecclesiae XXVI interpretatio Theodisca nunc primum edita. 1830.
Bericht . . . an die Hannoversche Regierung. 1833.
Reinhart Fuchs. 1834.
Über meine Entlassung (pamphlet). 1838.
Sendschreiben an Karl Lachmann über Reinhart Fuchs. 1840.
Über zwei entdeckte Gedichte aus der Zeit des deutschen Heidenthums. 1842.
Grammatik der Hochdeutschen Sprache unserer Zeit. 1843.
Deutsche Grenzalterthümer. 1844.
Über Diphthonge nach weggefallnen Consonanten. 1845.

Über Iornandes und die Geten: Eine in der Akademie der Wissenschaften am 5. März 1846 von Jacob Grimm gehaltene Vorlesung (lecture). 1846.
Geschichte der deutschen Sprache. 2 vols., 1848.
Über Marcellus Burdingalensis. 1849.
Das Wort des Besitzes: Eine linguistische Abhandlung. 1850.
Rede auf Lachmann, gehalten in der öffentlichen Sitzung der Akademie der Wissenschaften am 3. Juli 1851 (lecture). 1851.
Über den Liebesgott: Gelesen in der Akademie am 6. Januar 1851 (lecture). 1851.
Über den Ursprung der Sprache. 1851.
Über Frauennamen aus Blumen. 1852.
Über die Namen des Donners. 1855.
Über die Marcellischen Formeln, with Adolf Pictet. 1855.
Über den Personenwechsel in der Rede. 1856.
Über einige Fälle der Attraction. 1858.
Von Vertretung männlicher durch weibliche Namensformen. 1858.
Über Schule, Universität, Academie. 1859.
Über das Verbrennen der Leichen: Eine in der Academie der Wissenschaften am 29 November 1849. . . (lecture). 1859.
Rede auf Schiller, gehalten in der feierlichen Sitzung der König. 1859.
Rede auf Wilhelm Grimm und Rede über das Alter, edited by Herman Grimm. 1863.
Kleinere Schriften, edited by Karl Victor Müllenhoff and Eduard Ippel. 8 vols., 1864–90.
Briefwechsel zwischen Jacob Grimm und Friedrich David Graeter aus den Jahren 1810–1813, edited by Hermann Fischer. 1877.
Briefe an Hendrik Willem Tydeman: Mit einem Anhange und Anmerkungen, edited by Alexander Reifferscheid. 1883.
Briefwechsel von Jacob Grimm und Hoffmann von Fallersleben mit Henrik van Wyn: Nebst anderen Briefen zur deutschen Literatur, edited by Karl Theodor Gaedertz. 1888.
Kopitars Briefwechsel mit Jakob Grimm, edited by Max Vasmer. 1938.
Editor, *Silva de romances viejos.* 1815.
Editor, *Zur Recension der deutschen Grammatik.* 1826.
Editor, *Taciti Germania edidit et qua as res Germanorum pertinere videntur e reliquo Tacitino oere excerpsit.* 1835.
Editor, with Andreas Schmeller, *Lateinische Gedichte des X. und XI. Jahrhunderts.* 1838.
Editor, *Andreas und Elene.* 1840.
Editor, *Gedichte des Mittelalters aus König Freidrich I., dem Staufer, und aus seiner, sowie der nächstfolgenden Zeit.* 1844.
Translator, *Kleine serbische Grammatik*, by Vuk Stefanovic Karadzic. 1824.

PUBLICATIONS BY WILHELM GRIMM

Other

Über deutsche Runen. 1821.
Grâve Ruodolf: Ein Altdeutsches Gedicht. 1828.
Zur Literatur der Runen. 1828.
Bruchstücke aus einem Gedichte von Assundin. 1829.
Die deutsche Heldensage. 1829.
De Hildebrando antiquissimi carminis teutonici fragmentum. 1830.
Die Sage vom Ursprung der Christusbilder. 1843.

Exhortatio ad plebem christianam Glossae Cassellanae: Über die Bedeutung der deutschen Fingernamen. 1848.

Über Freidank: Zwei Nachträge. 1850.

Altdeutsche Gespräche: Nachtrag. 1851.

Zur Geschichte des Reims. 1852.

Nachtrag zu den Casseler glossen. 1855.

Thierfabeln bei den Meistersängern. 1855.

Die Sage von Polyphem. 1857.

Kleinere Schriften, edited by Gustav Hinrichs. 4 vols., 1881–87.

Unsere Sprachlaute als Stimmbildner. 1897.

Editor, *Vrídankes Bescheidenheit.* 1834.

Editor, *Der Rosengarten.* 1836.

Editor, *Ruolandes Liet.* 1838.

Editor, *Wernher vom Niederrhein.* 1839.

Editor, *Goldene Schmiede*, by Konrad von Würzburg. 1840.

Editor, *Silvester*, by Konrad von Würzburg. 1841.

Editor, *Athis und Prophilias: Mit Nachtrag.* 2 vols., 1846–52.

Editor, *Altdeutsche Gespräche: Mit Nachtrag.* 2 vols., 1851.

Editor, with Bettina von Arnim and Karl August Varnhagen von Ense, *Sämmtliche Werke*, by Ludwig Achim von Arnim. 22 vols., 1853–56; revised edition, 21 vols., 1857; reprinted 1982.

Editor, *Bruchstücke aus einem unbekannten Gedicht vom Rosengarten.* 1860.

Editor and translator, *Drei altschottische Lieder.* 1813.

Translator, *Altdänische Heldenlieder, Balladen und Märchen.* 1811.

Translator, *Irische Land-und Seenmärchen*, by Thomas Crofton Croker, edited by Werner Moritz and Charlotte Oberfeld. 1986.

*

Bibliography: "Bibliographie der Briefe von und an Wilhelm und Jacob Grimm: Mit einer Einführung", by Ludwig Denecke, in *Aurora* (43), 1983.

Critical Studies: *Jacob Grimm: Aus seinem Leben*, 1961, and *Die Brüder Grimm in Berlin*, 1964, both by Wilhelm Schoof; *Der junge Jacob Grimm 1805–1819* by Gunhild Ginschel, 1967; *The Brothers Grimm* by Ruth Michaelis-Jena, 1970; *Jacob Grimm und sein Bruder Wilhelm* by Ludwig Denecke, 1971, and *Die Brüder Grimm in Bildern ihrer Zeit*, 1980, by Ludwig Denecke and Karl Schulte Kemminhausen; *Paths Through the Forest: A Biography of the Brothers Grimm* by Murray B. Peppard, 1971; *Jacob Grimm's Conception of German Studies* by Peter F. Ganz, 1973; *Brüder Grimm* by Hermann Gerstner, 1973; *The Uses of Enchantment: The Meaning and Importance of Fairy Tales* by Bruno Bettelheim, 1977; *The German Legends of the Brothers Grimm* edited and translated by Donald Ward, 1981; *One Fairy Story Too Many: The Brothers Grimm and Their Tales* by John M. Ellis, 1983; *Die Brüder Grimm: Leben, Werke, Zeit* by Gabriele Seitz, 1984; *Wilhelm Grimms Nibelungenkolleg* edited by Else Ebel, 1985; *Die Brüder Grimm in ihrer amtlichen und politischen Tätigkeit* edited by Hans-Bernd Harder and Eckehard Kaufmann, 1985; *Die Brüder Grimm: Dokumente ihres Lebens und Wirkens* edited by Dieter Hennig and Bernhard Lauer, 1985; *Die Märchen der Brüder Grimm* by Heinz Rölleke, 1985; *Die Märchenbrüder: Jacob und Wilhelm Grimm—ihr Leben und Wirken* by Jürgen Weishaupt, 1985; *Grimms' Bad Girls and Bold Boys: The Moral and Social Vision of the Tales* by Ruth B. Bottigheimer, 1987; *The Hard Facts of the Grimms' Fairy Tales* by Maria M. Tatar, 1987; *The Brothers Grimm and the Folktale* edited by James M. McGlathery, 1988; *The Brothers Grimm: From Enchanted Forests to the Modern World* by Jack Zipes, 1988; *The Grimm Brothers and the Germanic Past: International Bicentenary Symposium on the Brothers Grimm*, 1990; *The Brothers Grimm and Their Critics: Folktales and the Quest for Meaning* by Christa Kamenetsky, 1992; *The Reception of Grimms' Fairy Tales: Responses, Reactions, Revisions*, edited by Donald Haase, 1993; *Grimm's Fairy Tales: A History of Criticism on a Popular Classic* by James M. McGlathery, 1994; *The Sin-complex: A Critical Study of English Versions of the Grimms' Kinder-und Hausmärchen in the Nineteenth Century* by Martin Sutton, 1996; *The Owl, the Raven and the Dove: The Religious Meaning of the Grimms' Magic Fairy Tales* by G. Ronald Murphy, 2000.

*   *   *

The Brothers Grimm, Jacob and Wilhelm, are universally known for their *Tales* (or *Fairy Tales*), the single most often translated and republished book in German. Inseparable in life as in legend, the Grimm brothers also co-founded three 19th-century academic disciplines: European historical linguistics, or philology; folklore studies; and German *Germanistik*—the study of the history of German culture, language, and literature. Finally the *German Dictionary* became their gigantic epitaph. It was initially planned as a small book for household use; "snowed under" with words, as he put it, Jacob had reached the letter F and, it is always said, the word *Frucht* (fruit), when he died. The Berlin Academy of Sciences did not complete the dictionary, which contains some 400,000 entries, until 1960.

Kinder- und Hausmärchen (*Fairy Tales*) was their first book—the shortened edition of 1825, illustrated by their brother Ludwig Emil, established it as a popular classic—and it is the only one of their major works, published jointly or singly, which does not have the word *Deutsch* (normally meaning "Germanic") in the title. This may be regarded as a concession to the fact that most of the tales, and the motifs, too, are by no means German or indeed Germanic, but are international. Many are certainly ancient; but a high proportion are equally certainly of medieval origin. The Grimms took as much from older written sources as from oral ones. And at least some of their key "oral" informants were women of their own acquaintance, well-to-do, well-educated, and in a number of cases bilingual and notedly talented, rather than belonging to the illiterate, unindividuated peasantry invoked by their prefaces.

If the Grimms failed to make these facts clear (and some of them are still controversial, as is the assessment of Wilhelm's role as editor and writer), it is because their wider project was specifically a revival of Germanic culture, animated by a Romantic faith in a myth of history. This myth posited both an original state of linguistic and cultural unity (eventually located in the speakers of an "Indo-Germanic" original tongue from which, they thought, all other languages derived); and also a manifest destiny, not only of Germans but of the whole world, to return to that monolingual condition. This theory appears to imply that the rest of the world will return to its origins under German tutelage. Be that as it may, their life's work was no matter of neutral scholarship. The *Tales* and the less popularly successful *Deutsche Sagen* (*German Legends*), were compilations of those "threads" of folk tradition which "finally link it directly to ancient times" (Wilhelm Grimm, preface to the *Tales*). These ancient times were then revived in ever more detail in the monumental editions of Old German texts, the compilations and exhaustive collations of material on the history of Germanic tribal religion and law, and the historical studies in grammar, vocabulary, and phonetics. Dedicating his *Geschichte der deutschen Sprache* [History of the

Germanic Language] (1848)—a collection of diverse studies in ancient culture and religion, grammar and philology—to the patriotic historian Gervinus, Jacob Grimm called his work "thoroughly political" in the context of "our fatherland [which is] divided contrary to nature (*unser widernatürlich geteiltes Vaterland*)."

This was the same year as the European revolutions and of the first, short-lived German National Assembly in Frankfurt-am-Main, at which Jacob served as a deputy. Eleven years earlier, both brothers had been among seven professors dismissed from Göttingen after protesting against the King of Hanover's suspension of the constitution. The brothers' work embodied the nationalist aspirations of the Romantic generation. It proved unfortunately exploitable by later generations of aggressive nationalists. But the Grimms had no party politics: they were patriots and liberal constitutionalists, in the era of the Napoleonic Wars followed by the restoration of territorial principalities in the space left vacant by the end of the Holy Roman Empire. Their generation speculated eagerly about past and future German unity, freedom, and greatness. The brothers' inspiration came from several sources. Since the 1770s, J.G. Herder had called for collections of folk (oral) traditions to be made, and the Grimms adopted his postulate that *Völker* (peoples/nations) were unconsciously unified collectives linked by language, custom, and history, which were now on the way to becoming conscious of their unity. The *Volk* had once spontaneously, without individual effort, brought forth poetry on a grand scale, poetry which now survived in precious fragments in early writing and in oral tradition. It was the task of present writers to (re)create cultural unity. Thus the Romantics of the 1790s had called for a "new mythology" (A.W. Schlegel) and set about constructing it out of the traces of past mythologies. This programme determined the Grimms' lifelong work. Their collection of tales also followed in the immediate wake of their friends Achim von Armin and Clemens Brentano's collection of songtexts, *Des Knaben Wunderhorn* (*The Boy's Magic Horn*, 3 vols., 1806–8). There too—notoriously today—the "discovery" and "invention" of "national tradition" are inseparable.

Romantic historians, as A.W. Schlegel had put it, are "prophets facing backwards." The Grimms were far from wanting merely to document the past, though they did much to develop historical methodology; they hoped to spur present and future creativity and to teach Germans to seek unity. They were peculiarly fitted by their personal background to become spokesmen for their generation (and in the *Tales*, spokesmen for later generations of mainly middle-class readers, parents and children, too). They coped with the traumatic early loss of their father by assuming joint responsibility for the family, which entailed unremitting labour in order to maintain their respectability. The energy animating their researches is that of the desire to retrieve their lost father, as much as the "lost" or "denatured" fatherland. The ethic promoted by the *Tales*—resourceful individualism tempered by a very strong sense of amicable, fraternal generosity—is that of a family determined, against the odds, to maintain if not enhance its social standing, as much as it is that of a quite narrowly middle-class nationalist movement struggling to make good a history of cultural division and decadence.

In *Deutsche Grammatik* [Germanic Grammar], Jacob—a more assiduous philologist and historian, though a much less gifted storyteller than Wilhelm—built on the work of the Danish philologist, Rasmus Rank, in order to formulate what has become known as "Grimm's Law" of sound shifts in the transition from Indo-European to Germanic (2000 to 1000 BC). The poet Heinrich Heine wrote that this book is "a Gothic cathedral in which all the Germanic peoples

raise their voices, like giant choirs, each in their dialect." The metaphor aptly described the Grimms' utopian vision: their work orchestrated masses of disparate material in an edifice erected to the glory of the German language. Their achievements are monumental; they remain legendary, and their work's complex, central significance for "German identity" continues to be highly controversial, as do the many and varied mythical, psychoanalytical, formalist, structuralist, functionalist, social historical, and pedagogical interpretations of their *Tales*.

—Tom Cheeseman

See the essay on "Hansel and Gretel."

GRIMMELSHAUSEN, Hans Jakob Christoffel von

Published under pseudonym: authorship not established until the 19th century. **Born:** Gelnhausen, near Frankfurt am Main, Germany, in 1622. **Education:** Educated at Lutheran Latin School, Gelnhausen, 1627. **Family:** Married Katharina Henninger in 1649. **Career:** Family fled to Hanau, 1634, after Gelnhausen was plundered in the Thirty Years War; served in the Kaiser's army after 1637: garrison soldier in Offenburg, 1639, clerk, 1645, then secretary, 1648, in regimental office; steward for the von Schauenburg family in Gaisbach bei Oberkirch, 1649; innkeeper in Gaisbach, 1658; steward for Dr. Küeller, 1662; innkeeper, 1665; mayor of Renchen, 1667; temporary soldier, 1675. **Died:** 17 August 1676.

PUBLICATIONS

Collections

[Collected Works], edited by H. Kurz. 4 vols., 1863–64.
Gesammelte Werke, edited by Rolf Tarot. 1966–.

Works

Der Abenteuerliche Simplicissimus Teutsch und Continuatio, edited by Rolf Tarot. 1967; as *The Adventurous Simplicissimus*, translated by A.T.S. Goodrich, 1912; as *Simplicissimus the Vagabond*, 1924; as *The Adventures of a Simpleton*, translated by Walter Wallich, 1962; as *Simplicius Simplicissimus*, translated by Monte Adair, 1986; as *The Adventures of Simplicius Simplicissimus*, translated by George Schulz-Behrend, 1993; as *Simplicissimus*, translated by Mike Mitchell, 1999.
Dietwalts und Amelindens anmutige Lieb- und Leidsbeschreibung, edited by Rolf Tarot. 1967.
Trutz Simplex; oder, . . . Lebensbeschreibung der Erzbetrügerin und Landstörzerin Courasche, edited by Wolfgang Bender. 1967; as *Mother Courage*, translated by Walter Wallich, 1965; as *The Life of Courage: The Notorious Thief, Whore, and Vagabond*, translated by Mike Mitchell, 2001.
Des durchleuchtigen Prinzen Proximi . . . und Lympidae Liebs-Geschicht-Erzählung, edited by Franz Günter Sieveke. 1967.
Des vortrefflich keuschen Josephs in Ägypten Lebensbeschreibung samt des Musai Lebenslauf, edited by Wolfgang Bender. 1968.

Simplicianischer Zweiköpfiger Ratio Status, edited by Rolf Tarot. 1968.

Der seltsame Springinsfeld, edited by Franz Günter Sieveke. 1969; as *The Singular Life Story of Heedless Hopalong*, translated by Robert L. Hiller and John C. Osborne, 1981.

Satyrischer Pilgram, edited by Wolfgang Bender. 1970.

Das wunderbarliche Vogelnest, edited by Rolf Tarot. 1970.

Die verkehrte Welt, edited by Franz Günter Sieveke. 1973.

Kleinere Schriften (*Beernhäuter, Gauckeltasche, Stolze Melcher, Bart-Krieg, Galgen-Männlin*, etc.), edited by Rolf Tarot. 1973.

Ratstübel Plutonis, edited by Wolfgang Bender. 1975.

Teutscher Michel und Ewigwährender Kalender, edited by Rolf Tarot. 1976.

*

Bibliography: *Grimmelshausen-Bibliographie 1666–1972* by Italo Michele Battafarano, 1975.

Critical Studies: *Grimmelshausen* by Kenneth C. Hayens, 1932; *Grimmelshausen* by Kenneth Negus, 1974; *Grimmelshausen in Selbstzeugnissen und Bilddokumenten* by Curt Hohoff, 1978; *The Nature of Realism in Grimmelshausen's Simplicissimus Cycle of Novels* by R.P.T. Aylett, 1982; *Grimmelshausen the Storyteller: A Study of the "Simplician" Novels* by Alan Menhennet, 1997.

* * *

Reading Hans Jakob Christoffel von Grimmelshausen we feel ourselves to be in the immediate company of a narrator; stories are told—to fictional listeners and to us—and much of the material rings like first-hand truth. But the narrative voices have to be listened to critically; they are continually ironized and relativized by other perspectives offered in the text. The text itself supplies its own commentary—from the perspective of the narrator's old age, for example—or we ourselves, among the listeners, are encouraged to comment.

Grimmelshausen is a great realist. He worked in a genre, the picaresque, marvellously suited to his times, his purposes, and his gifts. The picaresque novel, imported from Spain in the service of the Counter-Reformation by Aegidus Albertinus, is realistic and anti-heroic. In Spain it flourished during the Moorish Wars, and the Thirty Years War makes up all of Grimmelshausen's world. The picaro is a delinquent, and he lives in delinquent times. In times of licensed immorality he lives his immoral life.

War is depicted truthfully by Grimmelshausen, as pointless and horrible. He repeatedly mocks the lying heroic tradition. War is the licence, under arbitrary creeds and slogans, to commit atrocities. War is seen from the true, the lowest point of view: from among the dead, for example, as the scavengers come round. We learn most, to our greatest horror, quite incidentally. What happens to an officer's mistress when he tires of her? She is given to the stable boys: a detail, Grimmelshausen implies, too ordinary to dwell on. War is continually rendered strange; it has to be, or we should not see it for what it is, so accustomed have we become.

Grimmelshausen works to the important Baroque principle of "mögliche Realität" ("possible reality"). More happens to his heroes than really could; he accumulates around them an implausible number of truthful incidents. For realism is not an end in itself; it serves an urgent moral and religious purpose. Man must be shown as he is, as he really lives, in order that he may change. All human life is

precarious and war only accentuates that fact; and in war man behaves according to his nature, which is greedy, cruel, and selfish. Much of Baroque literature rests on a simple antithesis: the World or God. To be in the world is to be apart from God. The ordinary state of the world, for Grimmelshausen, is war. What the child last sees of the world as he enters the forest is his family home pillaged and its inhabitants raped or tortured; and what he first sees when he leaves the forest is again torture. That is the world.

Simplicissimus passes, without plausible inner motivation, through the predetermined stages of a religious and ethical career. He begins life in brute ignorance; in the forest with the hermit (his true father) he acquires *sancta simplicitas*; leaving the forest he is for a time a holy fool (Christianity in such a world appearing necessarily foolish); then, as court fool, he becomes a knowing social critic. Next, for most of the book, he lives not as a critic of the world but as its exemplar, as a worldling. Finally, with only nominal motivation, he leaves the world to resume his innocent hermit's state. He undergoes an exemplary disillusioning, an *Enttäuschung*.

Grimmelshausen's books are still, as he intended them, amusing and instructive. They are enjoyable and affirmative in their exuberance of language and invention; and salutary in their truthful exposure of man living badly.

—David Constantine

GRYPHIUS, Andreas

Born: Glogau, Silesia, 22 October 1616. **Education:** Educated at schools in Glogau, 1631, Goerlitz and Fraustadt, 1632–34. **Family:** Married Rosina Deutschländer in 1647. **Career:** Private tutor to Georg von Schönborn's children, Danzig, 1634–36; travelled to Holland, studied and lectured at the University of Leyden, 1638–42; went on Grand Tour, 1644–47, lived in Paris and Strasbourg, visited Florence, Rome, Ferrara, and Venice. Secretary to the estates, Glogau, 1650. **Died:** 16 July 1664.

PUBLICATIONS

Collections

Dramatische Dichtung, edited by Julius Tittmann. 4 vols., 1870.

Lustspiele, Trauerspiele, Lyrische Gedichte, edited by Hermann Palm. 3 vols., 1878–84.

Gedichte, edited by Johannes Pfeiffer. 1948.

Werke, edited by Marian Szyrocki. 1963.

Gesamtausgabe der deutschprachigen Werke, edited by Marian Szyrocki and Hugh Powell. 8 vols., 1963–72.

Ergänzungsband. 4 vols., 1983–87.

Werke. 1985.

Plays

Ermordete Majestät; oder, Carolus Stuardus, König von Gross Britannien (produced 1650). 1657; as *Murdered Majesty; or, Charles Stuart*, edited by Hugh Powell, 1955.

Leo Armenius (produced 1651). 1650.

Gibeoniter; oder, die sieben Bruder, from the play by Joost van den Vondel (produced 1652). 1698.

Majuma. 1653.

Catharina von Georgien (produced 1655). 1657.

Beständige Mutter; oder, Die Heilige Felicitas (produced 1657). 1657.

Cardenio und Celinde; oder, Unglücklich Verliebte (produced 1661). 1657; edited by Hugh Powell, 1961.

Absurda Comica; oder, Herr Peter Squentz. 1658; edited by Sydney H. Moore, 1908; also edited by Hugh Powell, 1957.

Freuden und Trauer-Spiele, auch oden und Sonnette sampt Herr Peter Squentz. 1658.

Der grossmüthige Rechtsgelehrte; oder, Der Sterbende Ämilius Paulus Papinianus (produced 1660). 1659.

Verlibtes Gespenst and *Die geliebte Dornrose.* 1661.

Horribilicribrifax; oder, Wählende Liebhaber (produced 1674). 1663.

Verse

Sonnete. 1637.

Sonn-und Feiertags Sonnete. 1639.

Sonnete. 1643.

Oden. 1643.

Epigrammatica. 1643.

Olivetum. 1646.

Teutsche Reim-Gedichte. 1650.

Kirchhofsgedanken, Oden. 1657.

Andreae Gryphii Deutscher Gedichte. 1657.

Epigrammata; oder, Bey Schrifften. 1663.

Other

Fewrige Freystadt. 1673.

Dissertationes funebres; oder, Leich-Abdankungen, bey unter schiedlichen hoch-und ansehnlichen Leich-Begängnüssen gehalten. Auch nebenst seinem letzten Ehren-Gedächtnuss und Lebens-Lauft. 1683.

Translator, *Die Seugamme, oder Untreues Hausgesinde*, by Girolamo Razzi. 1663.

Translator, *Der Schwärmende Schaffer*, by Thomas Corneille. 1663.

*

Bibliography: *Auswahlbibliographie zu Andreas Gryphius* by K.H. Habersetzer in *Text + Kritik*, 1980.

Critical Studies: *Die Lyrik des Andreas Gryphius* by Victor Manheimer, 1904; *Die Bildlichkeit in der Dichtung des Andreas Gryphius* by Gerhard Fricke, 1933; *Der junge Gryphius*, 1959, and *Andreas Gryphius: Leben und Werk*, 1964, both by Marian Szyrocki; *Andreas Gryphius: Leo Armenius* by Herman J. Tisch, 1968; *The Sonnets of Andreas Gryphius: Use of the Poetic Word in the Seventeenth Century* by Marvin S. Schindler, 1971; *Andreas Gryphius: Poet between Epochs* by Hugo Becker, 1973; *The Constructive Art of Andreas Gryphius's Historical Tragedies* by Janifer Gerd, 1986; *Andreas Gryphius* by Eberhard Mannack, 1986; *Andreas Gryphius: A Modern Perspective* by Blake Lee Spahr, 1993; *Reading Andreas Gryphius: Critical Trends 1664–1993* by Erika A. Metzger and Michael M. Metzger, 1994; *Form und Funktion des Komischen in den Komödien von Andreas Gryphius* by Daniela Toscan, 2000.

*　*　*

Andreas Gryphius exerted considerable influence as a dramatist, but his carefully crafted sonnets, odes, epigrams, and religious songs also helped to stabilize and invigorate the German literary language of the Baroque age. Underpinned by neo-classical scholarship and the religious and spiritual anguish of the Thirty Years War, his works eclectically refashioned a wide range of native and non-native forms with remarkable consistency. Six years at Leiden and travels in England, France, and Italy made him aware of the need to raise German drama to a higher level, although his primarily allegorical mode precluded the psychological depth of his European counterparts. His tragedies and poetry are suffused with an intense personal conviction, typical of the 17th century, that God is the sole source of constancy in a world of inconstancy and illusion. Stressing the vanity and transience of earthly endeavour, his antithetically structured plots and dialogues reflect the stark polarity and duality of existence: good struggles with evil, constancy with inconstancy, illusion with reality, and eternity with the fleeting moment, while life itself is a perpetual battle in which the individual, like a rudderless ship in a storm, is tossed helplessly toward the rocks of destruction.

Gryphius rarely blurred the prevailing socially based distinctions between comedy and tragedy. In accordance with Opitz's advocacy of the unities and stylistic decorum, the major tragedies, *Leo Armenius, Catharina von Georgien* [Catharine of Georgia], *Ermordete Majestät; oder, Carolus Stuardus* (*Murdered Majesty; or, Charles Stuart*), and *Paulus Papinianus*, dignify historical material and affairs of state with predominantly alexandrine verse and the more elevated poetic forms. Gryphius often lent linguistic dynamism to the declamatory, rhetorical, and circumscriptive "high style," but neo-classical concepts of form sat somewhat uneasily with his Baroque profusion and subordination of art to the Christian message. Catharina, the Christian Queen of Georgia, for example, is put to death by her enamoured captor, the Persian Sheikh Abas, for refusing to marry him. After her death the pagan Abas is metaphorically consumed by the flames of hell experienced in his guilt-ridden imagination. Despite a certain political topicality, these events of 1624 are "spiritualized," rather than dramatized. Moral edification toward Christian stoicism was more important than the psychological coherence of the basically allegorical plot and exemplary characters. In these "martyr tragedies" the protagonist is the divinely-ordained head of state who offers stability, yet whose crown is also an emblem of the Wheel of Fortune and the Crown of Thorns. Any attempt to remove them is portrayed as a villainous transgression of the divine order. The villain is the driving force of the plot, whereas the hero or heroine is trapped in a passive role of suffering victim, which allows ample opportunity for rhetorical, bombastic lament on the vicissitudes of human existence. Earthly attachments like human love may appear fleetingly, but only as past vices which the hero has firmly overcome: there is little to deflect the "martyr" from welcoming death as a desirable release. As Walter Benjamin (*The Origin of German Tragic Drama*) and others have suggested, Aristotle's fear and pity are separately allocated to villain and hero(ine), so that a bloody physical catastrophe, often recounted in gruesome detail, replaces a truly tragic denouement.

Gryphius gradually reduced the narrative element in his tragedies and increased the presentation of important events on stage, but he also relied on the visual spectacle of operatic tradition: impressive stage sets, pomp and ceremony, and lavish costumes counteracted the frequent stasis of a slow-moving plot. Linked to this is his use of visions, dreams, and ghosts, any of which may appear at crucial points as a means of warning reprobates about eternal retribution. The most spectacular such device occurs in *Cardenio und Celinde*, where the lustful Cardenio believes he sees his former lover, Olympia, but she reveals herself as a skeleton exhorting him to repent or be damned. This "conversion therapy" is reinforced shortly afterwards when he sees a corpse emerge from and re-enter its grave! Such supernatural elements are often dogmatically interpreted by a Chorus or "eyen" of allegorical figures who proclaim the *vanitas mundi*.

Cardenio und Celinde, however, breaks down some of the traditional barriers between tragedy and comedy. The characters, claims Gryphius in his preface, are "almost too lowly for a tragedy," for they belong to the low aristocracy, not far from the bourgeoisie. The action concentrates not on affairs of state, but on purely personal problems in normal human relationships. The language is marginally closer to that of everyday speech, although it still remains elevated enough to lend dignity to the subject matter. A double, interlinked plot illustrates the two kinds of earthly love, one rational and sanctioned by God in marriage, the other sensual and irrational. A hint of almost Shakespearean comic relief occurs in IV.ii, when two servants are momentarily pushed to the centre stage. It is difficult, however, to see the action as tragic, because all the characters are reconciled, overcome their earthly lusts, and live piously ever after.

The comedies, which satirize the lower social orders and use prose to reflect the "mundanity" of the action, appear more realistic in their earthy language, naive characters, and freer plots, yet they too employ type characters and are directed towards edification. The comedy of Gryphius which has best stood the test of time is *Absurda Comica; oder, Herr Peter Squentz* [Absurd Comedy; or, Mr. Peter Squentz], which was probably written between 1647 and 1650, and first appeared in 1657 or 1658. The artisans' comical performance of Ovid's tale of Piramus and Thisbe is well-known to English audiences from Shakespeare's *A Midsummer Night's Dream*. Although Shakespeare's version was performed by wandering English actors in Europe during the 17th century, Gryphius is more likely to have known Dutch and German versions. In his preface, Gryphius says that his *Peter Squentz* was to be performed alongside one of his tragedies. This was probably *Cardenio und Celinde*, with which it shares thematic affinities, especially with regard to human love and notions of illusion. In contrast to Shakespeare, who satirizes all social levels, Gryphius uses the aristans' performance, which is the main body of his play, to attack the outdated notions of popular bourgeois culture from the viewpoint of courtly, high culture. The different social classes appear on stage, but the device of a play within a play, with the courtiers and educated court officials patronizingly mocking the artisans' performance, reinforces social and cultural distinctions. The main butt of the literary (and implicitly social) satire is Hans Sachs, the great 16th-century popular dramatist, whose work is mercilessly condemned. Despite its harsh satirical tone, however, the play provides delightful linguistic and visual humour of some sophistication and vivacity.

Horribilicribrifax takes up the type of the braggart soldier returning from the war, but the hero is often submerged in rapid scene changes, a multiplicity of characters, and shifting dramatic focus. The main themes, the nature of human love and the necessity to distinguish between illusions and reality, are also explored in the double-play *Verlibtes Gespenst/Die geliebte Dornrose* [The Amorous Ghost/ Beloved Domrose], where once again the different social classes are kept separate, but their love affairs are skilfully paralleled.

—E.A. McCobb

GUILLAUME DE MACHAUT

Born: Rheims (?) c. 1300. **Education:** May have been educated at Rheims, where he spent much of his later life. **Career:** Entered the service of John of Luxemburg, King of Bohemia around 1323, and remained his secretary until the king's death in 1346, subsequently attached to the houses of Charles, King of Navarre, John, Duke of Berry, and the princes of France; held chaplaincy at Verdun, 1330, Arras, 1332, and Rheims, 1333. Prolific composer: the most important figure of the French Ars Nova. Spent much of his later years producing works in manuscript for his royal patrons. **Died:** 13 April 1377.

PUBLICATIONS

Collections

Les Oeuvres, edited by Prosper Tarbe. 1849.
Oeuvres, edited by Ernest Hoepffner. 3 vols., 1908–21.
Poésies lyriques, edited by Vladimir Chichmaref. 2 vols., 1909; 1 vol., 1973.

Verse

Le Confort d'ami, edited and translated by R. Barton Palmer. 1992.
Le Dit de la harpe, edited by K. Young. 1943.
15 poésies inédites, edited by Bernard Monod. 1903.
The Fountain of Love and Two Other Love Vision Poems, edited and translated by R. Burton Palmer. 1993.
Le Jugement du roy de Behaigne; and Remede de fortune, edited by James L. Wimsatt and William W. Kibler. 1988.
The Judgement of the King of Bavaria, edited and translated by R. Barton Palmer, 1984.
Le Jugement du roy de Navarre, as *The Judgement of the King of Navarre*, edited and translated by R. Barton Palmer. 1988.
Le Livre du Voir dit, edited by P. Paris. 1875, reprinted 1969, and by P. Imbs, 1988.
La Louange des dames, edited by Nigel Wilkins. 1972.
Prise d'Alexandrie, edited by L. de Mas Latrie. 1877; as *Guillaume de Machaut: The Capture of Alexandria*, translated by Janet Shirley, 2001.
Quelques poèmes de Guillaume de Machaut. In *"Dits" et "débats"* by Jean Froissart, edited by Anthime Fourrier, 1979.
Recueil de Galantries, edited by A. Vitale Brovarone. 1980.
The Tale of the Alerion, edited and translated by Minnette Gaudet and Constance B. Hieatt. 1994.

Other

Guillaume de Machaut: Musikalische Werke, edited by Friedrich Ludwig. 4 vols., 1926–54.

*

Bibliography: *Guillaume de Machaut: An Analytic Bibliography* by Kevin Brownlee, 1990.

Critical Studies: *Guillaume de Machaut: Musicien et poète rémois* by André Douce, 1948; *Guillaume de Machaut* by Siegmund Levarie,

1954; *Guillaume de Machaut, 1300–1377: La Vie et l'oeuvre musicale* by Armand Machabey, 2 vols., 1955; *Le Poète et le Prince: L'Évolution du lyrisme courtois de Guillaume de Machaut à Charles d'Orléans* by Daniel Poiron, 1965; *The Marguerite Poetry of Guillaume de Machaut* edited by James Wimsatt, 1970; *Guillaume de Machaut* by Gilbert Reaney, 1971; *A Poet at the Fountain: Essays on the Narrative Verse of Guillaume de Machaut* by William Calin, 1974; *Poetic Identity in Guillaume de Machaut* by Kevin Brownlee, 1984; *Guillaume de Machaut et l'écriture au XIVe siècle: "Un engin si soutil"* by Jacqueline Cerquiglini, 1985; *Machaut's Mass: An Introduction* by Daniel Leech-Wilkinson, 1990; *Le Voir-dit de Guillaume de Machaut, étude littéraire* by Paul Imbs, 1991; *The Grammar of 14th Century Melody: Tonal Organization and Compositional Process in the Chansons of Guillaume de Machaut and the ars subtilior* by Yolanda Plumley, 1996; *Pseudo-autobiography in the Fourteenth Century: Juan Ruiz, Guillaume de Machaut, Jean Froissart, and Geoffrey Chaucer* by Laurence de Looze, 1997; *Logos as Number and Proportion in Amiens Cathedral and in the Kyrie of the Messe de Nostre Dame by Guillaume de Machaut* by Dominique Pascale Bardet, 1999.

*   *   *

After the death of Guillaume de Machaut in 1377, the poet Eustache Deschamps wrote a moving *déploration* (put to music by Andrieu) in which he lamented the death of the man who was universally considered to be the greatest poet and musician of his age. All those who care about music and poetry are invited to mourn the passing of a figure who, in the words of William Calin, "as a musician and as a poet, is one of the great international masters of the 14th century." And yet, after his death, Guillaume de Machaut's reputation went into something of a decline, and it is only in the last 30 years or so that he has come to be recognized as an outstanding author. For the genres that he perfected—and to a certain degree invented—such as the *dit*, the *motet*, the *virelai*, and the polyphonic *ballade* and *rondeau*, were soon to go out of fashion, to be replaced by genres borrowed from classical antiquity. Born in 1300, he was the dominant figure both in lyric poetry and in music in 14th-century France. His output was enormous and wide-ranging. Although a canon of the church (he spent his later years in Rheims, in his native Champagne), he wrote much verse that was profane and gently erotic in tone, as well as sacred music. He was also very much a court poet, depending on wealthy patrons for his livelihood and forced to write works to their taste as much as to his own. Nonetheless, a distinctive authorial voice comes through in his work, especially in his *dits*, a genre which he effectively made his own.

Guillaume de Machaut wrote ten long *dits* and four shorter ones. Among the long ones, the most famous are perhaps the *Le Livre du Voir dit*, the *Remede de fortune*, *Le Jugement du roy de Behaigne* [The Judgement of the King of Behaigne], and *Le Jugement du roy de Navarre* (*The Judgement of the King of Navarre*). Despite their apparent diversity, these narrative *dits* share a common pattern. The narrator, usually preoccupied with love, embarks on a quest that will be both a physical journey and an imaginative adventure of experience and learning. He will return a happier and wiser man. The trappings of the quest are recognizably courtly, with gardens of love, fine castles, and of course beautiful women. But these works are much more complex than this structure and subject-matter would appear to allow. As Calin has pointed out, all the *dits* (a very flexible genre) are "poems of consolation." Guillaume de Machaut uses these long narrative poems to provide the reader with a very clear idea of his world-view. The progression of the protagonist from being an inexperienced outsider to being welcomed in his maturity to the civilized play world of courtly society is typical. On the way, however, the author gives his views of a series of topics that range from etiquette to morality and even flights of philosophical fancy. The (inevitable) unwillingness of the courtly ladies in these poems to appear anything other than unattainable also allows the author to indulge in pseudoautobiographical musings on the vagaries of love. He invests these poetic fictions with a realistic veneer that lends them an air of authenticity, so much so that critics have sometimes seen his *Le Livre du Voir dit* as the real-life confessions of an old poet infatuated with a young woman. Whether or not Peronne did exist in the way she is described in Guillaume de Machaut's poem is perhaps immaterial; what matters more is the realistic depiction of the pangs of love.

Guillaume de Machaut is best known today for his music. Although he is associated in most people's minds with the *Ars nova*, he was not in fact especially radical in his musical and poetical tastes and ambitions. In a career lasting 40 years he naturally tried his hand at different styles and forms, and there is an impressive variety of theme, message, and tone in his work. He is remembered as the composer of the first complete polyphonic setting of the "Ordinary of the Mass." His output of sacred music is huge, but he is most accessible today as the composer of poems of profane love. The *ballade* (both monophonic and polyphonic) was his favourite form, but he also wrote memorable *virelais* such as the haunting "Quant je suis mis au retour" ["When I return"] and works of outstanding complexity. As David Munrow remarked, Guillaume de Machaut's genius "lies in the way he combined a mastery of all the musical techniques of his age with a gift of melody and expressiveness. He was as good at writing a simple tune as he was at writing an elaborate isorhythmic motet and he approached the business of composition with the freedom of genius." The same critic claimed that Guillaume de Machaut's motets were "one of the high points of medieval art." With such technical expertise, such a range of forms and expressions, it is little wonder that Guillaume de Machaut was admired by contemporaries and praised so memorably in words and music by those who survived him.

—Michael Freeman

GUILLÉN, Jorge

Born: Valladolid, Spain, 18 January 1893. **Education:** Educated at the Instituto de Valladolid, 1903–09; Maison Perreyve, Fribourg, Switzerland, 1909–11; University of Madrid, Faculty of Philosophy and Letters, 1911–13; University of Granada, 1913, degree 1913; University of Madrid, Ph.D. 1924. **Family:** Married 1) Germain Cahen in 1921 (died 1947), one daughter and one son; 2) Irene Mochi-Sismondi in 1961. **Career:** Contributor to *El Norte de Castilla*, from 1918; lecturer or professor of Spanish, the Sorbonne, Paris, 1917–23, University of Murcia, 1926–29, Oxford University, 1929–31, and University of Seville, 1931–38; jailed briefly in Pamplona by Nationalist forces, on suspicion of spying, 1936; went into exile, 1938; taught at Middlebury College, Vermont, 1938–39, and McGill University, Montreal, 1939–40; professor of Spanish, Wellesley College,

Massachusetts, 1940–57: retired as emeritus professor; Charles Eliot Norton lecturer, Harvard University, Cambridge, Massachusetts, 1957, 1958. Also taught at Yale University, New Haven, Connecticut, 1947, Colegio de Mexico, 1950, University of California, Berkeley, 1951, Ohio State University, Columbus, 1952–53, University of the Andes, Bogota, 1961, University of Puerto Rico, Rio Piedras, 1962, 1964, University of Pittsburgh, 1966, and University of California, San Diego, 1968. Returned to Spain, 1978, and settled in Malaga. **Awards:** Guggenheim fellowship, 1954; American Academy award of merit, 1955; City of Florence poetry prize, 1957; Etna-Taormina prize (Italy), 1959; International Grand prize for poetry (Belgium), 1961; San Luca prize (Florence), 1964; Bennett prize (*Hudson Review*), 1975; Cervantes prize, 1976; Feltrinelli prize (Italy), 1977; Alfonso Reyes prize (Mexico), 1977; Yoliztli prize (Mexico), 1982. **Died:** 6 February 1984.

PUBLICATIONS

Verse

Cántico. 1928; enlarged edition, 1936, edited by José Manuel Blecua, 1970; further enlarged edition, as *Cántico, fe de vida*, 1945; complete edition, as *Cántico, fe de vida*, 1950; as *Cántico: A Selection*, translated by Norman Thomas di Giovanni and others, 1965; also translated by Donald McCrory, 1998.
Tercer cántico. 1944.
El encanto de las sirenas. 1953.
Luzbel desconcertado. 1956.
Del amanecer y el despertar. 1956.
Clamor. 3 vols., 1957–63:
   Maremágnum. 1957.
   Que van a dar en la mar. 1960.
   A la altura de las circunstancias. 1963.
Lugar de Lázaro. 1957.
Viviendo, y otros poemas. 1958.
Historia natural: Breve antología con versos inéditos. 1960.
Poemas de Castilla. 1960.
Poesias. 1960.
Versos, edited by Miguel Pizarro. 1961.
Anita. 1961.
Flores. 1961.
Las tentaciones de Antonio. 1962.
Según las horas. 1962.
Tréboles. 1964.
Suite italienne. 1964; enlarged edition, 1968.
Selección de poemas. 1965; enlarged edition, 1970.
El trasnochador. 1967.
Homenaje: Reunión de vidas. 1967.
Affirmation: A Bilingual Anthology, edited and translated by Julian Palley. 1968.
Aire nuestro (includes *Cántico; Clamor; Homenaje*). 1968; enlarged edition (includes *Y otros poemas* and *Final*), 5 vols., 1977–81.
Obra poética: Antología, edited by José Manuel Blecua. 1970.
Guirnalda civil. 1970.
Obra poética. 1970.
Al margen. 1972.
Y otros poemas. 1973.
Convivencia. 1975.
Plaza major: Antología civil. 1977.
Final. 1981.

Poemas malagueños (selection), edited by Antonio Gómez Yebra. 1983.
Jorge Guillén para niños, edited by Antonio Gómez Yebra. 1984.
Sonetos completos, edited by Antonio Gómez Yebra. 1988.
Horses in the Air and Other Poems, translated by Cola Franzen, 1999.

Plays

El huerto de Melibea (dramatic poem) (produced 1955). 1954.

Other

Federico en persona: Semblanza y epistolario (on García Lorca). 1959.
El argumento de la obra (Cántico) (essays), edited by V. Scheiwiller. 1961; also edited by José Manuel Blecua, 1970.
Language and Poetry: Some Poets of Spain (Charles Eliot Norton lectures). 1961; Spanish edition, as *Lenguaje y poesía*, 1962.
En torno a Gabriel Miró: Breve epistolario. 1970.
La poética de Bécquer. 1973.
Mientras el aire es nuestro, edited by Philip W. Silver. 1978.
Guillén on Guillén: The Poetry and the Poet (readings and commentary), translated by Reginald Gibbons and Anthony L. Geist. 1979.
Paseo marítimo. 1990.
Correspondencia (1923–1951), with Pedro Salinas, edited by Andrés Soria Olmedo. 1992.
Translator, *El cementerio marino*, by Paul Valéry. 1930.

*

Critical Studies: *The Poetry of Jorge Guillén* by Frances Avery Pleak, 1942; *La poesía de Jorge Guillén* edited by R. Gullón and José Manuel Blecua, 1949; *Jorge Guillén* by J.B. Trend, 1952; *La realidad y Jorge Guillén* by J. Muela González, 1962; *A. Machado; P. Salinas; J. Guillén* by P. Darmangeat, 1969; *A Generation of Spanish Poets 1920–1936* by Cyril Brian Morris, 1969; *Luminous Reality: The Poetry of Guillén* edited by Ivar Ivask and Juan Marichal, 1969; *Poesía de Guillén* by Andrew P. Debicki, 1973; *El cántico americano de Jorge Guillén* by J. Ruiz de Conde, 1973; *Cántico de Guillén y Aire nuestro* by Joaquín Casalduero, 1974; *Jorge Guillén* by Joaquín Caro Romero, 1974; *The Vibrant Silence of Jorge Guillén's Aire nuestro* by Florence L. Yudin, 1974; *Jorge Guillén* edited by B. Ciplijauskaité, 1975; *La obra poética de Jorge Guillén* (includes bibliography) by Oreste Macrí, 1976; *Homenaje a Jorge Guillén* by the Wellesley College Department of Spanish, 1978; *Jorge Guillén* by S. Carretero and C. Meneses, 1981; *Jorge Guillén: Sus raíces: Recuerdos al paso* by J. Guerrero Martín, 1982; *Jorge Guillén* (in English) by G. Grant MacCurdy, 1982; *The Structured World of Jorge Guillén: A Study of Cántico and Clamor* (includes translations) by Elizabeth Matthews, 1985; *Jorge Guillén: Cántico* by Robert Havard, 1986; *Guillén at McGill: Essays for a Centenary Celebration*, edited by K.M. Sibbald, 1996.

* * *

It is a cliché to say that a poet creates order out of chaos, but it is one supremely applicable to Jorge Guillén. Guillén always found a sense of order, whether it was among the proliferation of literary movements following World War I, from the experience of living most of his life in an exile both physical and linguistic, or in a recoil from the atrocities and horrors of war. This passion for order can be seen in the careful control of structure, in the reworking of many of his early poems, and in the unhurried perfection that finds its most peaceful expression in his recurrent opening and closing image of a dawn always followed by nightfall. This search for order has led his work to be compared to Baudelaire's *Les Fleurs du mal* (*The Flowers of Evil*) and Whitman's *Leaves of Grass*.

A poet who has won awards in the United States and in Europe, Guillén belongs to the Generation of 1927, so-called after their tricentenary celebration of the death of the eclectic Golden-Age poet, Luis de Góngora. Theirs was a short-lived generation: after the Civil War most went into exile, some were in prison, and García Lorca had been killed. However, in that short time the quality of their work led critics to proclaim a new golden age of Spanish poetry, and their work managed a successful fusion of influences, from the Spanish Golden Age to literary trends from France, in particular those of "pure poetry" and surrealism. Guillén himself was particularly impressed by Jorge Manrique and Paul Valéry.

As a university lecturer he published important critical essays and translations of poetry as well as his own work, of which the main parts were combined in the 1968 volume *Aire nuestro* [Our Air]. This edition is made up of the three collections, *Cántico* [Song], *Clamor* [Clamour], and *Homenaje* [Homage], each superficially quite different in range and theme. *Cántico*, with its focus on harmony, revels in life in a way the more sombre poems of *Clamor* would seem to deny. *Clamor* provides a shadowy mirror image of *Cántico*. It reflects the ferocity of life rather than its potential harmony, tracing the destruction and suffering caused by war and death, while *Homenaje* is a wide-ranging eulogy to the poetry of all ages, from Genesis to Guillén himself, offering an impressive mixture of translation and originality. This collection was supplemented by "Y otros poemas" [And Other Poems], the modest title at once a gesture of self-effacement and a hint to the more central significance of the earlier work, and *Final*.

Cántico evolved from its first publication in 1928 to a definitive version in 1950. It is the most widely known of his works and owes much to the influence of Paul Valéry whom Guillén grew to know well during his stay in France. Subtitled *Fe de vida* (the name of a document proving a person is still alive), it is an affirmation of the beauty and coherence of life, a search for a perfection of form involving precision, interaction, and fusion. The importance placed on the present tense in the search for purity of expression is equalled by that placed upon fusion and interaction, as humanity and nature work in a symbiotic relationship. This is a search for a paradise on this earth, the perfection of which is portrayed in images of solid geometric forms that have often led Guillén's work to be considered in relation to cubism. Faith and love are constants in this search for an illumination attainable only through the experience and creation of a solid harmony and the potential of poetic form to resolve contradiction.

Clamor complements *Cántico* with the same rigour and control; their main difference lies in the attention given to the themes of exile, grief, and war. *Clamor* is about transcending the oppositions of order versus chaos, life versus death, and love versus hate, which threaten to disrupt our faith in life. That Guillén saw *Clamor* as the dramatization of an age can be seen in its subtitle *Tiempo de historia*. Where *Cántico* was an ecstatic song to life, *Clamor* is a dialogue between a man and his time, but this does not detract from the poet's faith in life, and if *Clamor* contains tones of disgust at the world of human creation it

does not lose the exclamatory tone of pleasure that punctuated *Cántico*, nor the intensely tactile and sensual evocation of the poet's immediate surroundings.

Homenaje continues to explore this affirmation of life and poetry. Guillén has always expressed a commitment to humanity; but here there is a progression that allows the voices of other poets to blend in with this own. His wish to overcome division and chaos has meant an attempt to bridge the gap between individual and collective perception, which is nowhere more clear that in this work. *Homenaje* is a gesture of thanks, an invitation to a gathering where we find Calderón, Bécquer, Machado, Pascal, Mallarmé, and Tolstoi, among others, joined in a postmodern celebration of the death of the author and the rebirth of intertextuality.

Guillén's work, then, traces a familiar journey from harmony to discord, and beyond. For Guillén, life is an adventure and poetry an attempt to resolve its confusion. His is a vital, optimistic, and illuminating poetry, a love poetry in its most universal sense of self-abandonment to life itself. His work is therefore, in this ecology-conscious and first decade of the 21st century, no less contemporary now than it was on its initial publication.

—Jo Evans

GUILLÉN (BATISTA), Nicolás (Cristóbal)

Born: Camagüey, Cuba, 10 July 1902. **Education:** Educated at the Instituto de Segunda Enseñanza, Camagüey, to 1920; studied law at the University of Havana, 1920 and 1921–22: abandoned studies. **Career:** Worked for *El Nacional* as printer and typesetter while taking evening classes, 1918–19; contributor, *Camagüey Gráfico*, 1919, *Orto*, 1920 and 1927, *Las Dos Repúblicas*, 1920, and *Alma Mater*, 1922; co-founder and editor, *Lis*, 1923; editor, *El Camagüeyano*, 1923; typist, Ministry of the Interior, Havana, 1926; contributor, *Diario de la Marina*, from 1928, editor, *Información* and *El Loco*, from 1934; worked in the Havana Ministry of Culture, 1935–36; editor, *Mediodía*, 1936–38; travelled to Spain and attended pro-Republican conferences, 1937; joined National Committee of the Cuban Communist Party, 1938, and worked on its journal *Hoy*, 1938–50 (closed by the authorities) and from its revival in 1959; unsuccessful mayoral candidate, Camagüey, 1940; travelled to Haiti, 1942, and throughout Latin America on lecture and recital tour, 1945–48; co-editor, *Gaceta del Caribe*, 1944; travelled widely throughout Europe, USSR, and China, attending conferences and cultural events, 1948–52; contributor, *La Última Hora*, 1952; detained twice for activities against the Batista regime, 1952; left Cuba for Chile, 1953, and, though based in Paris, 1955–58, continued travelling widely during the 1950s; lived in Buenos Aires, 1958–59; returned to Cuba after the Castro Revolution, 1959, and thereafter combined career as writer with attendances at numerous international conferences, lectures, and cultural events, often in other countries of the socialist bloc, and often in an official capacity as Cuban ambassador at large or president of the Cuban Union of Writers and Artists (UNEAC) (appointed 1961); member, Central Committee of the Communist Party of Cuba, from 1975; had leg amputated, June 1989. Professor of Merit, University of Camagüey, 1981. **Awards:** International Lenin Peace prize, 1954; Jesús Suárez Gayol prize, 1972;

Union of Journalists' Félix Elmuza prize, 1972; Viareggio prize (Italy), 1972; Jamaican Institute Musgrave medal, 1974; Ricardo Miró National Poetry prize (Panama), 1979; Julius Fucik medal for journalism, 1981; Maurice Bishop prize, 1989. Honorary doctorates: University of Havana, 1974; University of the West Indies, 1975; University of Bordeaux (France), 1978. Cirilo and Metodio medal (Bulgaria), 1972; Red Band of Achievement (USSR), 1972; Order of Merit (Poland), 1974; Distinguished Son of the Cuban Popular Assembly, 1981; Cuban Order of José Marti, 1981. **Died:** 16 July 1989.

PUBLICATIONS

Verse

Motivos de son. 1930.
Sóngoro cosongo: Poemas mulatos. 1931.
West Indies Limited: Poemas. 1934.
España: Poema en cuatro angustias y una esperanza. 1937.
Cantos para soldados y sones para turistas. 1937.
El son entero; Suma poética 1929–1946. 1947.
Elegía a Jacques Roumain en el cielo de Haiti. 1948.
Cuba Libre: Poems, translated by Langston Hughes and Ben Frederic Carruthers. 1948.
Versos negros (selection), edited by José Luis Varela. 1950.
Elegía a Jesús Menéndez. 1951.
Elegía cubana. 1952.
La paloma de vuelo popular: Elegías. 1958.
Buenos días, Fidel. 1959.
Sus mejores poemas. 1959.
Los mejores versos. 1961.
Balada. 1962.
Poesías. 1962.
Poemas de amor. 1964.
Tengo. 1964; as *Tengo*, translated by Richard J. Carr, 1974.
Antología mayor: El son entero y otros poemas (selection). 1964; enlarged edition, 1969.
Che comandante. 1967.
El gran zoo. 1967; as "The Great Zoo," in *¡Patria o muerte!: The Great Zoo and Other Poems*, 1973.
Cuatro canciones para el Che. 1969.
Antologiía clave. 1971.
El diario que a diario. 1972; corrected edition, 1979; as *The Daily Daily*, translated by Vera Kutzinski, 1989.
La rueda dentada. 1972.
Man-Making Words: Selected Poems, translated by Robert Márquez and David Arthur McMurray. 1972.
Obra poética, edited by Ángel Augier. 2 vols., 1972–73; enlarged and corrected edition, 1979; revised edition, 1985.
¡Patria o muerte!: The Great Zoo and Other Poems (bilingual edition), edited and translated by Robert Márquez. 1973.
El corazón con que vivo. 1975.
Poemas manuables. 1975.
Suma poética, edited by Luis Iñigo. 1976.
Por el mar de las Antillas anda un barco de papel. 1977.
Música de cámara. 1979.
Coplas de Juan Descalzo. 1979.
El libro de las décimas (selection), edited by Nancy Morejón. 1980.
Sol de domingo. 1982.
New Love Poetry; In Some Springtime Place; Elegy, translated and edited with commentary by Keith Ellis. 1994.

Plays

Poema con niños (produced 1943). In *Sóngoro cosongo y otros poemas*, 1942.
Soyán, music by Jorge Berroa (produced 1980).

Other

Prosa de prisa; Crónicas. 1962; revised and enlarged edition, as *Prosa de prisa 1929–1972*, edited by Ángel Augier, 3 vols., 1975–76.
Páginas vueltas; Memorias. 1982.

*

Bibliography: *Bibliografía de Nicolás Guillén* by Mará Luisa Antuña and Josefina García Carranza, 1975, supplemented in *Revista de la Biblioteca Nacional José Martí*, 3rd series, 19(3), 1977; "Nicolás Guillén" in *Cuban Literature: A Research Guide* by David William Foster, 1985; "Nicolás Guillén" in *Dictionary of Twentieth Century Cuban Literature* by Julio A. Martínez, 1990.

Critical Studies: *Nicolás Guillén: Notas para un estudio biográfico-crótico*, 2 vols., 1965, *La revolución cubana en la poesía de Nicolás Guillén*, 1979, and *Nicolás Guillén: Estudio biográfico-crítico*, 1984, all by Ángel Augier; *La poesía afro-cubana de Nicolás Guillén* by Ezequiel Martínez Estrada, 1966, revised edition, as *La poesía de Nicolás Guillén*, 1977; *La poesía de Nicolás Guillén* by Adriana Tous, 1971; *Recopilación de textos sobre Nicolás Guillén* edited by Nancy Morejón, 1974, and *Nación y mestizaje en Nicolás Guillén* by Morejón, 1982; *La poesía de Nicolás Guillén* by Jorge M. Ruscalleda Bercedóniz, 1975; *El sentimiento de la negritud en la poesía de Nicolás Guillén* by Armando González-Pérez, 1976; *Hazaña y triunfo americanos de Nicolás Guillén* by Juan Marinello, 1976; *The Poetry of Nicolás Guillén: An Introduction* by Dennis Sardinha, 1976; *Harlem, Haiti, and Havana: A Comparative Critical Study of Langston Hughes, Jacques Roumain, and Nicolas Guillén* by Martha K. Cobb, 1979; *Black Writers in Latin America* by Richard Jackson, 1979; *Self and Society in the Poetry of Nicolás Guillén* by Lorna V. Williams, 1982; *Against the American Grain: Myth and History in William Carlos Williams, Jay Wright, and Nicolás Guillén*, 1987, and Guillén issue of *Callaloo 31*, 10(2), 1987, both by Vera M. Kutzinski; *Nicolás Guillén: Popular Poet of the Caribbean* by Ian Isidore Smart, 1990; *Nicolás Guillén: Growth of a Revolutionary Consciousness* by J.A. George Irish, 1990; *Decoding the Word: Nicolás Guillén as Maker and Debunker of Myth* by Clement A. White, 1993.

* * *

Nicolás Guillén forsook his youthful imitation of Rubén Darío and the modernist aesthetic to focus a revolutionary's eye on social and political matters and on formal innovation. His message of protest, he once said, was sometimes "dissimulated by the rhythm, the picturesque elements," characteristic of his early poetry. Until recently, critics considered his works only in the light of these elements, his unveiling of Cuba's black heritage, or of his communist ideology. Critics classified his poetry, as "black" and related it to the "Afro-Caribbean" movement or the "negritude" of black francophone Caribbean poets. This classification was made on the basis of his evocative imagery of African nature, his musicality reminiscent of African ritual-dance rhythms, and his reproduction of Cuban black speech (recently acknowledged as the popular speech of Cubans of all races). Contrary to "Afro-Caribbean" and "negritude" poetry that tends to exacerbate divisions among the races, Guillén's work aims to consolidate.

The subtitle of *Sóngoro cosongo: Poemas mulatos* [Songoro Cosongo: Mulatto Poems] expresses such an integrative intent. In the prologue to the first edition, Guillén indicated that he wanted his poetry to reflect the ethnic composition of Cuba. He also claimed that Cuban society, by excluding "blackness" from its writings, disavowing its African roots, and perceiving itself as "white," had failed to create an authentic Cuban national literature. To rectify this lack, Guillén created a consciously "mestizo" (of racially mixed ancestry) poetry which used the Spanish language to express Cuba's African essence. In *Motivos de son* [*Son* Motifs], *Sóngoro consongo, West Indies Limited*, and to some extent in later collections, Guillén used his revolutionary poetic form based on the *son*, a popular Cuban musical form with roots in Spanish, African, and Arawak traditional forms. Guillén's *son*-poem uses the eight-syllable lines of the Spanish "romance" (ballad) and an "estribillo" (chorus), similar to the antiphonal chants of African and/or Arawak ritual traditions. In addition, Guillén revolutionized Cuban poetry by using expressions long perceived as "jitanjáforas" (onomatopoeic neologisms) that subsequently have been identified as words in various African languages. These sounds (such as "sóngoro consongo") provide rhythmic auditory effects evocative of Africa and, through their encrypted meaning, of its culture.

Guillén also proposed to legitimize blacks and mulattos as images in Cuban literature and to assert their beauty and positive value. In "Negro bembón" ("Thick-Lipped Cullud Boy"), for example, the reader's perception is refocused to recognize the beauty of those generally disdained thick lips. The black/white dichotomy (evil/good in white societies) is debunked in "¿Qué color?" ("What Color?"), a poem commemorating the assassination of Martin Luther King. The negative value judgement implicit in the image of the black-skinned pastor who, nevertheless, had "such a white soul" is repudiated and replaced with awe before his "powerful black soul."

Guillén also rebelled against Cuban society's hypocritical modesty—hypocritical because by the 1950s Cuba had become the brothel and playground of America's affluent and gangster classes. Instead, Guillén's poetry evokes voluptuous images of dark women that are unabashedly sensuous.

This period of Afro-Cuban synthesis in Guillén's work was followed by one of revolutionary political preoccupation. His solidarity with the Republican cause during the Spanish Civil War is evident in *España: Poema en cuatro angustias y una esperanza* [Spain: Poem in Four Anguishes and One Hope]. The grievances of the oppressed classes in Cuba are depicted in the poems of *Cantos para soldados y sones para turistas* [Songs for Soldiers and Sones for Tourists] and *El son entero* [The Whole Son]. His protest against the Spanish slayer's lash disfiguring his black grandfather's back in "Balada de los dos abuelos" ("Ballad of the Two Grandfathers") is as intense as that in "Mau-maus" for the failure to indict the slain Englishman because he "pierced the lung of Africa / with an Empire-dagger of / alphabetizing steel . . . / of syphilis, gunpowder, / *money, business, yes*." Published after the Cuban Revolution, the collection *Tengo*, extols the more egalitarian society that struggle created.

Guillén's revolutionary poetic form reaches its zenith in *El gran zoo* (*The Great Zoo*) and *El diario que a diario* (*The Daily Daily*). The former, a neo-bestiary, portrays the denizens of the zoo not as animals, but as inanimate objects, character types, or institutions that caustically satirize capitalist society. Form in *The Great Zoo* ranges from haiku-like brevity to polymetric free verse. *The Daily Daily* is a collection of newspaper items recounting Cuba's history since colonial times. Some are authentic journalistic items, others are creations of the author; some are in recognizably poetic forms, others are classified advertisements, display advertisements, social items, or municipal announcements. His early humour reappears in this volume with a demythologizing effect. The bullfight—the mythic paradigm of Spanish masculinity—collapses in "Bulls," in which bullfighters do everything from taking "a great leap over a bull," to "stick[ing] a new kind of banderilla into another from the top of a stool," to making "fun of the animal's ferocity by dancing 'La Cucaracha' on a table." The sharp criticism of the capitalist establishment contained in this book crowns a career dedicated to exposing the flaws and abuses of the moneyed classes.

Guillén revolutionized Cuban literature by making it mirror Cuba's mixed racial heritage, in his new form, the *son*-poem, and by using "jitanjáforas" and ritual-like rhythm. With renewed language and formal innovations, he denounced oppression, and, through satire, demythologized the "reality" imposed by the dominant classes.

—Oralia Preble-Niemi

GUIMARÃES ROSA, João

Born: Cordisburgo, Minas Gerais, Brazil, 27 June 1908. **Education:** Educated at the Colégio Arnaldo, Belo Horizonte; Medical School of Minas Gerais, Belo Horizonte, 1925–30, degree 1930. **Family:** Married 1) Lygia Cabral Pena in 1930, two daughters; 2) Aracy Moebius de Carvalho in 1938. **Career:** Public servant, Statistical Service, Minas Gerais, 1929–31; doctor in private practice, Itaguara, Minas Gerais, 1931–32; volunteered as military medical officer, Belo Horizonte, 1932; medical officer, Ninth Infantry Battalion, Barbacena, Minas Gerais, 1934; passed civil service examinations and joined Ministry of Foreign Affairs, 1934; vice-consul, Hamburg, Germany, 1938–42: briefly interned in Baden Baden, following Brazil's entry into World War II, 1942; secretary, Brazilian Embassy in Bogotá, Colombia, 1942–44; director, Ministry of State's Documentation Service, 1944–46; secretary, Brazilian Delegation to Paris Peace Conference, 1946; secretary-general, Brazilian Delegation to Ninth Pan-American Conference, Bogotá, 1948; principal secretary, Brazilian Embassy, Paris, 1949–51; cabinet head, Ministry of Foreign Affairs, Rio de Janeiro, 1951–53; budget director, Ministry of State, Rio de Janeiro, 1953–58; head of Frontier Demarcation Service, 1962–67. Vice-president, First Latin American Writers Conference, Mexico City, 1965. **Awards:** Brazilian Academy of Letters poetry prize, 1936; Carmen Dolores Barbosa prize, 1957; Paula Brito prize, 1957; Brazilian Academy Machado de Assis prize, 1961. **Member:** Brazilian Academy of Letters, 1963. **Died:** 19 November 1967.

PUBLICATIONS

Fiction

Sagarana (stories). 1946; revised edition, 1951; as *Sagarana: A Cycle of Stories*, translated by Harriet de Onís, 1966.

Corpo de baile: sete novelas (includes *Manuelzão e Miguilim; No Urubùquaquá, no pinhém; Noites do Sertão*). 2 vols., 1956; 3 vols., 1964–66.

Grande Sertão: Veredas. 1956; as *The Devil to Pay in the Backlands*, translated by James L. Taylor and Harriet de Onís, 1963.

Primeiras estórias. 1962; as *The Third Bank of the River and Other Stories*, translated by Barbara Shelby, 1968.

Os sete pecados capitais (novellas), with others. 1964.

Campo geral (stories). 1964.

Tutaméia: terceiras estórias. 1967.

Estas estórias. 1969.

Contos (stories), edited by Heitor Megale and Marilena Matsuola. 1978.

Other

Ave, palavra (prose and verse). 1970.

Correspondência com o traductor italiano [Edorado Bizzarri]. 1972.

Seleta (anthology), edited by Paulo Rónai, 1973.

Sagarana emotiva: cartas de Guimarães Rosa a Paulo Danteas. 1975.

Rosiana: uma coletánea de conceitos, máximas e brocardos, edited by Paulo Rónai. 1983.

*

Bibliography: *Bibliografia de e sobre Guimarães Rosa* by Plínio Doyle, 1968; *Brazilian Literature: A Research Guide* by David William Foster and Walter Rela, 1990.

Critical Studies: *Trilhas no Grande Sertão* by M. Calvalcânti Proença, 1958; *Guimarães Rosa* edited by Heriqueta Lisboa and others, 1966; *João Guimarães Rosa: travessia literária*, 1968, and "João Guimarães Rosa," in *Studies in Short Fiction*, 8(1), 1971, both by Mary L. Daniel; *Em memória de João Guimarães Rosa* by various authors, 1968; *Guimarães Rosa* by Adonias Filho and others, 1969; *Guimarães Rosa* by Francisco Assis Brasil, 1969; *Guimarães Rosa* by Guilhermino César and others, 1969; *Guimarães Rosa em três dimensões* by Pedro Xosto, Augusto de Campos, and Harolde de Campos, 1970; *O mundo movente de Guimarães Rosa* by José Carlos Garbuglio, 1972; *Structural Perspectivism in Guimarães Rosa* by W. Martins, 1973; *Guimarães Rosa: dois estudos* by Nelly Novaes Coelho and Ivana Versiani, 1975; *O insólito em Guimarães Rosa e Borges* by Lenira Marques Covizzi, 1978; *A Construção do Romance em Guimarães Rosa* by Wendel Santos, 1978; *O diálogo no Grande Sertão: Veredas* by Paulo de Tarso Santos, 1978; *João Guimarães Rosa* (in English) by Jon S. Vincent, 1978; *The Process of Revitalization of the Language and Narrative Structure in the Fiction of João Guimarães Rosa and Julio Cortázar*, 1980, and *The Synthesis Novel in Latin America: A Study of Grande Sertão: Veredas*, 1991, both by Eduardo de Faria Coutinho; *Guimarães Rosa: signo e sentimento* by Suzi Frankl Sperber, 1982; *Guimarães Rosa* edited by Eduardo de Faria Coutinho, 1983; *A cultura popular em Grande Sertão: Veredas* by Leonardo Arroyo, 1984; *O discurso oral em Grande Sertão: Veredas* by Teresinha Souto Ward, 1984; *Logos and the Word: The Novel of Language and Linguistic Motivation in Grande Sertão: Veredas and Três tristes tigres* by Stephanie Merrim, 1988; *Guimarães Rosa: O alquimista do coração* by José Maria Martins, 1994; *O roteiro de Deus: Dois estudos sobre Guimarães Rosa* by Heloísa Vilhena de Araújo, 1996; *Viagem ao sertão brasileiro: Leitura geo-socio-antropológica de Ariano Suassuna, Euclides da Cunha,* *Guimarães Rosa* by Vernaide Wanderley and Eugénia Menezes, 1997; *O mito de Fausto em Grande sertão: Veredas* by Fani Schiffer Durães, 1999; *Guimarães Rosa* by Walnice Nogueira Galvão, 2000; *Guimarães Rosa: Magma e gênese da obra* by Maria Célia Leonel, 2000; *Palavra e tempo: Ensaios sobre Dante, Carroll e Guimarães Rosa* by Heloísa Vilhena de Araújo, 2001.

*   *   *

When João Guimarães Rosa died on 19 November 1967 at the age of 59, he had published only five works of prose fiction; however, these five volumes had earned him a seat in the Brazilian Academy of Letters and undisputed recognition as the greatest writer of prose fiction to emerge in Brazil since 1945.

He was born in Cordisburgo in the state of Minas Gerais in 1908. He studied medicine but practised it for only four years—first in the backlands of the Brazilian *sertão* and later in the army—before joining the Brazilian diplomatic service in which he would serve for the remainder of his life. His childhood and his time spent as a country doctor provided the raw material with which he fashioned an extraordinary fictional world—an amalgam of fantasy, folklore, and myth, yet invariably resting upon a bedrock of harsh reality in which the life of the inhabitants of the vast wilderness, or *sertão*, of northern Minas Gerais and southern Bahia comes vividly and exuberantly to life. The way of life of the farmers, traders, ranchers, cowboys, and bandits of the *sertão* is closely observed and painstakingly described. To call these fictions regionalist would be to misunderstand totally the scope and richness of a fictional world that attains a mythic grandeur and universal significance. This attainment of the universal through the particular is well illustrated by the title of Guimarães Rosa's first book, a collection of novellas entitled *Sagarana*. Sagarana is a neologism combining the Germanic "saga" with a Tupi Indian word, "rana," meaning "in the manner of." Naturalistic and magical by turns, sometimes simultaneously, these novellas tell of a world in which animals talk and think like human beings, a young man insults a warlock and is punished with temporary blindness during which he learns much about himself, and a murderous bully wins redemption after a lifetime of tribulation and wandering. *Sagarana* was followed ten years later by a second volume of novellas entitled *Corpo de baile* [Corps de Ballet] and the vast novel, *Grande Sertão: Veredas* (*The Devil to Pay in the Backlands*) which appeared in the same year. A literal translation of the latter would be something like "Great Backlands: Paths." The novel is as enigmatic and elusive as its title. It consists of an autobiography told by an ageing rancher to an unseen interlocutor. Riobaldo relates the story of his career as a *jagunço*, or bandit of the *sertão*, of his love for his mysterious, hermaphrodite comrade-in-arms, Diadorim, and of his existential anguish over the possibility that he may have sold his soul to the devil. Riobaldo tells his story in the hope that his listener may be able to pronounce on the mystery and thus release him from his torment. It is a story of love, hate, revenge, and betrayal, a tale of epic proportions in which bandit armies quarter the *sertão* in search of their enemy, and in Riobaldo's case, so that his destiny may be charted and realized.

It also reveals Guimarães Rosa as a profound student of medieval and Renaissance European literature. Like the world of the medieval epic and romance, Guimarães Rosa's fictional world tells of the constant struggle between good and evil, and contains large doses of tragedy and ecstasy as well as an underlying current of poetic justice. It is epic as well as mythic, because its protagonist's trajectory is clearly, on one hand, a rite of passage, and on the other, a chivalric quest during which deeds are done in the name of an absent lady, Otacília, and in order to fulfil the chivalric enterprise: the defeat of the traitor in the midst, bandit leader Hermógenes, so as to avenge the death of the betrayed—supreme commander Juca Ramiro. The *sertão* becomes a vast natural theatre or cosmic space in which the *jagunços* act out this drama and become at one with their environment. Neither the individual nor the space in which they move has primacy. In its scope and ambition, *The Devil to Pay in the Backlands* has been compared to *The Divine Comedy, Don Quixote, Hamlet, Faust, Moby Dick*, and *Ulysses*. In its themes, the work is certainly Faustian, but linguistically-speaking, the comparison with Joyce's *Ulysses* is the most useful one; for the language in which the novel and the novellas that preceded it are expressed is baroque and intensely poetic. Guimarães Rosa employs alliteration, assonance, onomatopoeia, and verse rhythms. His vocabulary is enormous, and as in the case of Joyce, there is a constant recourse to neologisms of which there can be as many as a dozen on a single page. The language is poetic not only in its evocations of the Brazilian *sertão*, but also in the fundamental sense that it offers incessant renewal of a Portuguese enriched by a lexis borrowed from numerous languages. Guimarães Rosa also has a taste for metaphor. His fourth book, *Primeiras estórias (The Third*

Book of the River and Other Stories), is a set of short stories in one of which a family man, for no apparent reason, says goodbye to his family, paddles in a canoe to the centre of a wide river, and remains there until his son, years later, offers to take his place. The English title of this story, chosen as the title story for the volume when it was translated and published in 1968, reads "The Third Bank of the River," a notion bespeaking mysticism and utter dislocation.

Guimarães Rosa's remaining books are *Tutaméia* [Trifle], another set of even briefer stories, the posthumous short stories of *Estas estórias* [These Tales], and the miscellany, *Ave, palavra* [Hail, Word]. His prose fiction is little known in Europe. This is due to the fact that translating him into any other language has proved a daunting task and because, in any case, he wrote in Portuguese. This last fact has meant that, unlike the great Spanish-American writers of the Latin American "Boom," he has yet to be "discovered" by the English-speaking world. The day this happens, the Old World will encounter, with astonishment, a rural, Brazilian post-modernist whose total achievement constitutes the great watershed of Brazilian literature, a literary phenomenon commensurate with that of Joyce in English letters.

—R.J. Oakley

H

HADEWIJCH

Career: Lived c. 1250, possibly near Antwerp, The Netherlands (now Belgium). Facts of her life uncertain; possibly from an aristocratic background; spiritual leanings show affinities with the Beguines as well as with the mysticism of Hugh of St. Victor, William of St. Thierry, and St. Bernard (of Clairvaux). Her fame spread as far as Germany (where she was known as Adelwîp).

PUBLICATIONS

Collections

Werken [Works], edited by F.J. Heremans. 3 vols., 1875–1905.
The Complete Works, translated by Mother Colomba Hart. 1981.
Poetry of Hadewijch, translated and introduction by Marieke J.E.H.T. van Baest. 1998.

Verse

Strophische gedichten [Strophic Poems], edited by J. van Mierlo. 1942.
Mengeldichten [Poems], edited by J. van Mierlo. 1952.
Strofische gedichten [Strophic Poems], edited by E. Rombants and N. de Paepe. 1961.

Other

Visioenen [Visions], edited by J. van Mierlo. 2 vols., 1924–25.
Brieven [Letters], edited by J. van Mierlo. 2 vols., 1947.
Brieven [Letters], translated (into modern Dutch) by M. Ortmanns-Cornet. 1986.

*

Critical Studies: *Hadewijch* by M.H. van der Zeyde, 1934; *Hadewijch d'Anvers* by J.B. Porion, 1954; *Hadewijch en Heer Hendrik van Breda* by P.C. Boeren, 1962; *Medieval Netherlands Religious Literature* by T. Weevers, translated by E. Colledge, 1965; *Some Aspects of Hadewijch's Poetic Form* by T.M. Guest, 1975; *The Measure of Mystic Thought: A Study of Hadewijch's Mengeldichten* by S. Murk-Jansen, 1991; *Geschichte der abendländischen Mystik: Frauenmystik und Franziskanische Mystik der Frühzeit* by Kurt Ruh, 1993; *Hadewijch and Her Sisters: Other Ways of Loving and Knowing* by John Giles Milhaven, 1993; *Meister Eckhart and the Beguine Mystics: Hadewijch of Brabant, Mechthild of Magdeburg, and Marguerite Porete*, edited by Bernard McGinn, 1994; *Begeerte in het werk van Hadewijch* by Rob Faesen, 2000.

* * *

The 13th-century Christian mystic Hadewijch wrote in Middle Dutch and her work, some of the finest literature in the Dutch language, is preserved in five closely related manuscripts, the earliest of which dates from the late 14th century. Three of these contain the substantial part of the corpus and the other two only smaller selections. The works attributed to Hadewijch consist of 31 letters, 14 visions, the "List of the Perfect Ones," 45 stanzaic poems, and 16 epistolary poems. The manuscripts also contain two other collections of poems, the smaller of which consists of four poems which may have been written later than Hadewijch. The other collection of lyric poems is almost certainly contemporary to her and should perhaps also be attributed to her.

The currently accepted date for Hadewijch's literary activity is c. 1240–50. This deduction is based on scraps of evidence gleaned from one of her works, the "List of the Perfect Ones," which occurs at the end of her visions. In it she refers to two facts that can be dated: the death at the hands of the Inquisitor "Meester Robbaert" of a Beguine, and the presence of hermits on the walls of Jerusalem. The Beguine has been tentatively identified as a certain Aelais whom Robert le Bougre had put to death in 1236, in which case the List would not have been drawn up before that date. Jerusalem finally fell to the Khorezmians on 23 August 1244 and there would not have been any Christian hermits on its walls after that time. Allowing for a certain time lapse before the news reached the author of the List, it seems unlikely that she would have drawn it up much after 1250. There is of course no way of knowing at what point in her career Hadewijch composed the List but, in view of some references in the Visions which precede it, it seems reasonable to assume that she did so in the second half of her career.

We know little about Hadewijch's life, her circumstances, or her origins. A note on the flyleaf of one of the manuscripts refers to her as "de Antverpia," but no independent evidence has been found linking her to Antwerp or any other city. Attempts have been made to guess at the possible course of her life from evidence within her works. However, such evidence is extremely sparse and ambiguous. Recently Kurt Ruh has re-opened the debate on Hadewijch's social status by putting forward powerful circumstantial arguments in favour of her being a member of the aristocracy.

Arguably Hadewijch's most remarkable literary achievement are the 45 stanzaic poems, written in the style and using the conventions of the courtly love poetry of the period. Many have the *Natureingang* and complicated rhyme-schemes so typical of much troubadour and *trouvère* love lyrics. However, Hadewijch uses the conventional themes not to lament the trials of the faithful knight in the service of a demanding and fickle lady, but to lament her own suffering in the service of God. The extended metaphor, combining themes of feudal service and secular love, works particularly well as Hadewijch uses the feminine noun *minne* (love) to refer to God, which naturally takes feminine adjectives and pronouns, while she refers to herself using the masculine noun *sen*, meaning reason or mental awareness.

Hadewijch appears to have written for a group of like-minded laywomen. She may have had at some point a position of leadership among them, but her letters certainly suggest that there were also times when she was distant from those whom she exhorted to good works and growth in love. In view of the growing antagonism to such activity in the second half of the 13th century, the fact that she was able to exhort and teach with no apparent expectation or consciousness of ecclesiastical criticism supports the date of her literary activity as being in the earlier part of the century. However personal some of the expressions in her work appear to be, it is likely that everything she wrote was intended to be read out loud, or in the case of the poetry sung, to an audience. Her teaching is rooted in her own experience, as is her theology, and she uses her sufferings and doubts as object lessons to her audience.

The texts attributed to Hadewijch are significant evidence for the development in the 13th century of what could be described as "vernacular theology," namely a mode of theological writing that is neither that of the theology of the monasteries, with its source in experience and contemplation, nor that of the scholastics, which has its source in reason. Vernacular theology is rooted in the experience of living in the world rather than withdrawing from it, and tends to be expressed in a language rich in images that seek to connect the reality of that experience, including the problem of suffering, with the transcendent reality of the soul's relationship to God. Themes similar to those found in Hadewijch's work are to be found in numerous texts from this period as well as in the works of later mystics such as Eckhart and Marguerite Porete.

—S.M. Murk-Jansen

HAFIZ

Born: Shams al-Din Muhammad [or Shamsu'd-Din Muhammad] Hafiz in Shiraz, Persia (now Iran), in 1325/26. **Education:** Studied Islamic literature and mastered Arabic (the name Hafiz indicates one who has memorized the *Koran*). **Career:** Patronized by Shah Abu Ishaq-i Inju, 1341–53, by Shah Shuja, 1358–68/69, and Muzaffarid Shah Mansur in late 1380s; lectured on theology, and wrote commentaries on religious classics. Little is known of his private life. **Died:** 1389/90.

PUBLICATIONS

Collections

Fifty Poems of Hafiz, translated and annotated by Arthur J. Arberry. 1993.
The Poems of Hafez, translated by Reza Saberi. 1995.
The Hafez Poems of Gertrude Bell: With the Original Persian on the Facing Page, introduced by E. Denison Ross. 1995.

Verse

Divan, edited by J. von Hammer. 2 vols., 1812–13; also edited by Hermann Brockhaus, 3 vols., 1854–63, Vincenz von Rosenzweig-Schwannau, 3 vols., 1858–64, and Mohammed Qazvini and Qasem Ghani. 1941; as *Diwan-i-Hafiz*, translated by H. Wilberforce-Clarke (prose), 3 vols., 1891, reprinted 1974; as *The Poems*, translated by John Payne (verse), 3 vols., 1901; selections in translation include: [Selections], edited by Algernon S. Bicknell, translated by Hermann Bicknell, 1875; *Versions from Hafiz* by Walter Leaf, 1898; *Poems from the Divan* by G. Bell, 2nd edition, 1928; *Hafiz in Quatrains* by C.K. Street, 1946; *Fifty Poems* by A.J. Arberry, 1947; *Thirty Poems* by Peter Avery and John Heath-Stubbs, 1952; *Poetical Horoscope or Odes* by A. Aryanpur, 1965; *Odes of Hafiz: Poetical Horoscope* by Abbas Aryanpur Kashani,

1984; *Tongue of the Hidden: Poems from the Divan* by P. Smith, 1990; *The Green Sea of Heaven: Fifty Ghazals from the Díwán of Háfiz*, translated by T. Gray, Jr., 1995; *In Search of Hafiz: 109 Poems from the Diwan of Hafiz*, translated by A.J. Alston, 1996.

*

Bibliography: *Towards a Hafiz Bibliography* by Henri Broms, 1969.

Critical Studies: *A Literary History of Persia* by Edward G. Browne, 1928; *Classical Persian Literature* by A.J. Arberry, 1958; *History of Iranian Literature* by Jan Rypka, edited by Karl Jahn, 1968; *Hafez* by G.M. Wickens, in *Encyclopedia of Islam*, revised edition, 1971; *Unity in the Ghazals of Hafez* by Michael C. Hillmann, 1976; *The Spiritual Wisdom of Haféz: Teachings of the Philosopher of Love* by Haleh Pourafzal and Roger Montgomery, 1998.

* * *

Even in his lifetime, the fame of Hafiz had extended beyond his homeland—eastward to India and westward to other portions of the Islamic realm. In the first centuries after his death, it was still Islam's taste for Persian poetry that nourished his reputation; but in the last two or three centuries, when the East and the West have impacted upon each other, Hafiz has become truly a world poet, read in many languages, both Eastern and Western.

Not all readers will agree with Ralph Waldo Emerson (who read him in German translation) that Hafiz ranks with Shakespeare as the type of the true poet; or with John Payne (who translated him into English verse) that he is, along with Shakespeare and Dante, one of the three greatest poets of the world; but there is a consensus that he is "the Prince of Persian poets" and the fullest flowering of the lyric gift in a nation famed for its poetry. Regarding the substance of his poetic thought, however, there is again considerable difference of opinion.

His compatriots and fellow Muslims have for the most part accepted his native reputation as *Lisān-al-ghaib* [The Tongue of the Hidden]: that is, as a mystical poet of the Sufi school, whose allusions to love, wine, roses, and revelry signify spiritual concepts. A few Westerners, too, have accepted this view—including the philosopher Hegel—but the majority of his European and American readers have had different opinions. Sir William Jones, who in the late 18th century introduced Hafiz to the West, regarded him as "the Persian Anacreon." Goethe, whose *West-östlicher Divan* was composed in emulation of the *Divan* of Hafiz, was disposed to stress the poet's joy in love and life, as suited the taste of the Romantic age. Emerson, who learned from Hafiz to take deeper poetic drafts than his Puritan heritage allowed, believed the poet's wine stood for intellectual liberation rather than for the divine afflatus on the one hand or [Thomas] "Moore's best Port" on the other. The English Victorians, reflecting their own anxieties over faith and doubt, heard in Hafiz the voice of weeping and loud lament; and the *fin de siècle* hedonists and sceptics saw in him a latter-day Omar Khayyam. In this century, A.J. Arberry, has described him as a philosophical nihilist propounding the gospel of Unreason.

Unfortunately, the *ghazal* form in which Hafiz wrote (and which, in the opinion of G.M. Wickens, he took "so far beyond the work of his predecessors that he practically cut off all succession") does not lend itself to easy translation. It has variously been likened to the ode and the sonnet, and, by Arberry, to the late sonatas of Beethoven. The "wonderful inconsecutiveness" of the Persian *ghazal* (in Emerson's phrase) has led Arberry, Wickens, and Michael Hillmann to seek in the form a kind of organic unity that is quite unlike the linear and dramatic continuity characteristic of Western poetry. Some hint of the suggestive ambiguity of Hafiz, and of his mellifluous music, might be gleaned from the following couplet:

Hameh kass tāleb-i-yārand, che hushyār che mast
Hameh jā khāneh-i-ishq ast, che masjid che kunasht.

(Everyone is desirous of the Friend, what is sober what is drunk?
Every place is the house of love, what is temple what is mosque?)

—John D. Yohannan

HAGIWARA Sakutarō

Born: Maebashi, Gunma Prefecture, Japan, 1 November 1886.
Education: Prefectural Normal School elementary school, 1893–1897; higher level elementary school, 1897–1900; Prefectural Middle School, 1900–1906; failed entrance exam to Osaka Higher Medical School and entered Higher School as an English literature major in Kumamoto, Kyushu, 1907–1908; failed first year of study, entered High School in Okayama as a German literature and law major, 1908; failed his first year, 1909; entered and then dropped out of Keio College Preparatory School, 1910; contracted typhus and dropped out of Okayama high school, 1910; began studying the mandolin in Tokyo and entered then dropped out of the Keio College Preparatory School, 1911; studied guitar and Italian in Tokyo, 1912. **Family:** Married 1) Ueda Ineko in 1919 (divorced 1929), two daughters; 2) Otani Mitsuko in 1938 (separated 1940). **Career:** Editor of *tanka* column in the local newspaper, *Jōshū Shinpō*, 1913; mandolin concert performances around Maebashi, 1914; lecturer in modern poetry at Meiji University, 1933–1942; gave talks at Bunka Gakuin, 1933; appointed to editorial board of the literary journal *Shiki*, 1936; became member of the editorial board of *Shin Nippon*, 1938. **Awards:** Eighth prizes, Bungakkai journal [Literary World], awarded for essays of poetry criticism in the journal, 1936; Kitamura Tōkoku prize for *Kikyōsha* [Homecoming], 1940. **Member:** With Murō Saisei and Yamamura Bochō, established the Ningyo shisha [Mermaid Poetry Society], 1914; established the Gondola Western Music Club (later the Jōmō Mandolin club) in Maebashi, 1915; appointed to selection committee for Bungei Hanron poetry prize, 1936; joined Nihon Roman-ha [Japanese Romantic School], 1936; joined Shin Nihon Bunka no Kai [New Japan Cultural Society], 1937; joined Tokyo Amateur Magicians Club, 1937; member of Nakahara Chūya poetry prize committee, 1938. **Died:** 11 May 1942 of pneumonia; buried in family plot outside Maebashi.

PUBLICATIONS

Collections

Hagiwara Sakutarō zenshū. 1943.
Hagiwara Sakutarō zenshū, edited by Murō Saisei and others. 1959–1962.
Hagiwara Sakutarō zenshū. 1975–1978.

Face at the Bottom of the World and Other Poems, translated by Graeme Wilson. 1969.
Rats' Nests: The Collected Poetry of Hagiwara Sakutarō, translated by Robert Epp. 1993.

Verse

Tsuki ni hoeru. 1917; as *Howling at the Moon*, translated by Hiroaki Satō, 1978.
Atarashiki Yokujō. 1922.
Aoneko [Blue Cat]. 1923; revised as *Teihon Aoneko*, 1936; as *Howling at the Moon and Blue Cat*, translated by Hiroaki Satō, forthcoming.
Chō o Yumemu. 1923.
Junjō Shōkyokushū. 1925.
Hyōtō [The Iceland]. 1934.
Shukumei (prose poems). 1939.

Other

Shiron to Kansō. 1928.
Shi no Genri. 1928; as *Principles of Poetry*, translated by Chester Wang and Isamu P. Fukuchi, 1998.
Kyomō no Seigi. 1929.
Zetsubō no Tōsō. 1935.
"Nekomachi" (short story). 1935.
Kyōshū no Shijin Yosa Buson (critical study on poet Yosa Buson). 1936.
Rōka to Shitsubō. 1936.
Shijin no Shimei. 1937.
Mu kara no Kōsō. 1937.
Nihon e no Kaiki (essay). 1938.
Kikyōsha. 1940.
Minato ni te. 1940.
Adai. 1940.
Hagiwara Sakutarō Shashin Sakuhin: Nostalgia, photographs by Hagiwara Sakutarō, essays by Hagiwara Yoko and Hagiwara Sakumi. 1994.
Editor, *Ren'ai Meikashū.* 1931.
Editor, *Gendai Shishū.* 1940.
Editor, *Shōwa Shishō.* 1940.

*

Critical Studies: "Introduction" in *An Anthology of Modern Japanese Poetry* edited and translated by Ichiro Kōno and Rikutaro Fukuda, 1959; "Hagiwara Sakutarō" in *Dawn to the West: Japanese Literature in the Modern Era: Poetry, Drama, Criticism* by Donald Keene, 1984; "Introduction" in *Face at the Bottom of the World and Other Poems* by Graeme Wilson, 1969; "Introduction" in *Howling at the Moon* by Hiroaki Satō, 1978; *The Language of Symbolism in Yeats and Hagiwara* by Reiko Tsukimura, 1968; "Hagiwara Sakutarō" in *Modern Japanese Poets and the Nature of Literature* by Makoto Ueda, 1983; "Introduction" in *Rats' Nests: The Collected Poetry of Hagiwara Sakutarō* by Robert Epps, 1993.

*   *   *

Hagiwara Sakutarō is one of the key figures in modern Japanese poetry. He was among the first to abandon the traditional forms of Japanese poetry (*waka*) and to free his verse from the constraints of traditional metric rhythms (in particular the 5–7–5–7–7 syllabic pattern characteristic of *tanka*, the most popular form of Japanese poetry since ancient times). Much of his poetry was also marked by a pioneering use of colloquial language as a medium for lyrical poetic expression. Hagiwara's success with these new forms paved the way for a whole generation of Japanese poets and played a large part in establishing the foundations of modern Japanese verse. His three major collections *Tsuki ni hoeru* (*Howling at the Moon*), *Aoneko* (*Blue Cat*), and *Hyōtō* [The Iceland] had a huge impact on the development of poetry in Japan, and although Hagiwara was not alone in moving away from traditional forms of versification, he was perhaps the first to incorporate successfully many of the revolutionary new ideas entering Japan from the West at this time. He was hailed both for the innovative style and for the deeply personal imagery of his poems, many of which are marked by highly lyrical modes of expression.

Hagiwara's first published poems were a series of *tanka* that were submitted to major Tokyo magazines while he was still in school. Often ill as a child, and so absorbed in poetry that he often neglected his schoolwork and missed classes, he did not graduate from middle school until he was 20, and never graduated from high school at all. As the eldest son of a successful doctor, he could afford to explore his many artistic interests at leisure. In addition to his poetry, Hagiwara was also an accomplished musician and photographer.

In 1913, Hagiwara moved back home to Maebashi and had a Western-style study built in the garden, where he would relax by strumming on his mandolin or reading European literature while sipping on black tea. In addition to his interest in contemporary European movements, Hagiwara also had read a good deal of classical Japanese poetry in school and was familiar with the work of modern poets such as Yosano Akiko. His interest in European poetic movements (primarily Romanticism and French Symbolism) was no doubt encouraged by the publication of Ueda Bin's *Kaichōon* [The Sound of the Tide], a collection of European Symbolist poetry translated into somewhat free forms of traditional Japanese prosody. Hagiwara was clearly influenced by the poetry of Baudelaire and the French Symbolists but he also borrowed heavily from the conventional images of Japanese poetry. Together, elements from these two widely disparate traditions provided the landscape for a world of pessimism and despair.

His first collection, *Howling at the Moon*, was recognized as a major breakthrough in poetic technique. In it he turned away from the classical diction of his early poetry and made wide use of colloquial language for the first time, imbuing his verse with a rhythm and sensibility quite different from anything seen in Japan before. Classical motifs were still important elements of Hagiwara's poetics, but they were no longer a part of an abstract, idealized view of a benign and beautiful natural world. Reassuringly familiar tropes such as cherry blossoms, bamboo shoots, and the harvest moon were now incorporated into a world typified by striking new images of rotting shellfish, clanking steam trains, and the overwhelming stench of chrysanthemums. Two poems that dealt with love, "Airen" ("Love") and "Koi wo koi suru Hito" ("A Man Who Loves Love"), were banned by the censors, judged to be "injurious to public morals."

His second collection, *Blue Cat* (later revised and published as *Teihon Aoneko*), was quite different both in tone and atmosphere. The psychological background of alienation and decay that had marked *Howling at the Moon* remained prominent, but now Hagiwara seemed to place greater emphasis on lyrical expressions of sadness and loneliness. In *Aoneko*, meaning "Blue Cat," the "blue" of the title is suggestive of the melancholy and longing that Hagiwara associated with life in modern society. For Hagiwara, an important part of poetry's appeal was its ability to provide a world of escape. All around him, the world was changing at an unprecedented pace; artists and scientists were able to travel abroad in large numbers for the first time, and older traditions were being rejected in favor of new ideas from Europe. Much of Hagiwara's work is marked by the contradictory desire typical of the times; like many of his contemporaries, Hagiwara was torn between his enthusiasm for the new and a desire to hold on to the spirit of his past.

Hagiwara's dilemma finds perhaps its clearest expression in his last major collection, *Hyōtō*, in which Hagiwara returned to a more classical style. Many of the poems seem to deal more directly with Hagiwara's personal life than had generally been the case in earlier collections, and the autobiographical notes that Hagiwara added to several of them served to ground them firmly in the prosaic circumstances of the poet's life. Critics are divided in their view of *Hyōtō*. Some have criticized these later poems for a vision of life that can seem narrow and somewhat limited in comparison to the wild imagination and creativity of *Howling at the Moon* and *Blue Cat*. These critics have often seen Hagiwara's return to a classical style as an admission of his "failure" to break new ground. Others, however, have preferred this later poetry, in which Hagiwara finally "graduated" from the escapist fantasy world of his early work. Despite the classical language, the choppy rhythms, and the scattered neologisms, Hagiwara's last poems represent an honest attempt to look at reality and the world the poet inhabited.

Hagiwara continued to write essays, aphorisms, and prose poems after *Hyōtō*, but hardly any more poetry in verse. In later life, he admitted that this last collection had been a "shameful retreat." Hagiwara was pessimistic in his appraisal of his own writing and achievements. For the rest of his life, he regretted what he regarded as his failure to discover a truly new poetic language, and often expressed a hope that others would succeed where he had failed. Posterity has been kinder to Hagiwara than he was to himself, however, and today his position as the "father of modern Japanese poetry" seems unassailable.

—Emi Shimokawa

HAMSUN, Knut

Born: Knut Pedersen in Lom, Norway, 4 August 1859. **Family:** Married 1) Bergliot Goepfert in 1898 (divorced 1909), one daughter; 2) Marie Andersen in 1909, two sons and two daughters. **Career:** Apprenticed to a shoemaker in Bodö; then a road worker and wanderer for 10 years; lived in the United States, 1882–84, 1886–88: streetcar conductor in Chicago, farmhand in North Dakota, and secretary, and lecturer in Minneapolis; lived for several years in Paris, early 1890s; travelled in Finland, Russia, and Denmark during the 1890s and 1900s; writer after 1890, and after 1911 farmer in Hamarøy, later near Grimstad; openly supported Quisling's pro-German party during World War II: indicted, fined, and briefly confined to a mental institution after the war, **Awards:** Nobel prize for literature, 1920. **Died:** 19 February 1952.

Collection

Samlede Verker. 15 vols., 1954–56.

Fiction

Den gaadefulde [The Mysterious One]. 1877.
Bjørger. 1878.
Sult. 1890; as *Hunger*, translated by George Egerton, 1899; translated by Robert Bly, 1967; also translated by Sverre Lyngstad, 1998.
Mysterier. 1892; as *Mysteries*, translated by Arthur G. Chater, 1927; also translated by Gerry Bothmer, 1971.
Ny jord. 1893; as *Shallow Soil*, translated by Carl Christian Hyllested, 1914.
Redaktør Lynge [Editor Lynge]. 1893.
Pan. 1894; as *Pan*, translated by W.W. Worster, 1920; also translated by James W. McFarlane, 1955.
Siesta. 1897.
Victoria. 1898; as *Victoria*, translated by Arthur G. Chater, 1923; as *Victoria: A Love Story* translated by Oliver Stallybrass, 1969.
Kratskrog [Brushwood]. 1903.
Sværmere. 1904; as *Mothwise*, translated by W.W. Worster, 1921, as *Dreamers*, 1921; also translated by Tom Geddes, 1995.
Stridende liv [Struggling Life]. 1905.
Under Høststjærnen. 1906; as *Autumn*, translated by W.W. Worster, in *Wanderers*, 1922; as *Under the Autumn Star*, translated by Oliver and Gunnvor Stallybrass, in *The Wanderer*, 1975.
Benoni. 1908; as *Benoni*, translated by Arthur G. Chater, 1925.
Rosa. 1908; as *Rosa*, translated by Arthur G. Chater, 1925.
En vandrer spiller med sordin. 1909; as *With Muted Strings*, translated by W.W. Worster, in *Wanderers*, 1922; as *A Wanderer Plays on Mute Strings*, translated by Worster, 1922; as *On Muted Strings*, translated by Oliver and Gunnvor Stallybrass, in *The Wanderer*, 1975.
Den siste glæde. 1912; as *Look Back on Happiness*, translated by Paula Wiking, 1940; as *The Last Joy*, translated by Sverre Lynstad, 2002.
Børn av tiden. 1913; as *Children of the Age*, translated by J.S. Scott, 1924.
Segelfoss by. 1915; as *Segelfoss Town*, translated by J.S. Scott, 1925.
Markens grøde. 1917; as *The Growth of the Soil*, translated by W.W. Worster, 1920.
Konerne ved Vandposten. 1920; as *The Women at the Pump*, translated by Arthur G. Chater, 1928; also translated by Oliver and Gunnvor Stallybrass, 1978.
Wanderers (includes *Autumn; With Muted Strings*), translated by W.W. Worster. 1922.
Siste kapitel. 1923; as *Chapter the Last*, translated by Arthur G. Chater, 1929.
Landstrykere. 1927; as *Vagabonds*, translated by Eugene Gay-Tifft, 1930; as *Wayfarers*, translated by James W. McFarlane, 1980.
August. 1930; as *August*, translated by Eugene Gay-Tifft, 1931.
Men livet lever. 1933; as *The Road Leads On*, translated by Eugene Gay-Tifft, 1934.
Ringen sluttet. 1936; as *The Ring Is Closed*, translated by Eugene Gay-Tifft, 1937.
Paa gjengrodde Stier. 1949; as *On Overgrown Paths*, translated by Carl L. Anderson, 1968; also translated by Sverre Lyngstad, 1999.

The Wanderer (includes *Under the Autumn Stars; On Muted Strings*), translated by Oliver and Gunnvor Stallybrass. 1975.
Night Roamers and Other Stories, translated by Tiina Nunnally. 1992.

Plays

Ved rigets port [At the Gates of the Kingdom] (produced 1896). 1895.
Livets Spil [The Game of Life] (produced 1896). 1896.
Aftenrøde [Evening Glow] (produced 1898). 1898.
Munken Vendt [Friar Vendt] (produced 1926). 1902.
Dronning Tamara [Queen Tamara] (produced 1903). 1903.
Livet i void (produced 1910). 1910; as *In the Grip of Life*, translated by Graham and Tristan Rawson, 1924.

Verse

Det vilde kor [The Wild Chorus]. 1904.
Dikte. 1921.

Other

Lars Oftedal (articles). 1889.
Fra det moderne Amerikas aandsliv. 1889; as *The Cultural Life of Modern America*, edited and translated by Barbara Gordon Morgridge, 1969.
I Æventyrland [In the Land of Fairy Tales]. 1903.
Sproget i fare [Language in Danger]. 1918.
Samlede Verker [Collected Works]. 12 vols., 1918; revised edition, 17 vols., 1936.
Artikler 1899–1928, edited by Francis Bull. 1939.
Knut Hamsun som hun var [Letters 1879–1949], edited by Tore Hamsun. 1956,
Paa Turné tre foredrag om Litteratur [On Tour]. 1960.
On the Prairie: A Sketch of the Red River Valley, translated by John Christianson. 1961.
Brev til Marie [Letters to Marie 1908–38], edited by Tore Hamsun. 1970.
Over havet: artikler, reisebrev, edited by Lars Frode Larsen. 1990.
Selected Letters [vol. 1] 1879–1898, edited by Harald Naess and James W. McFarlane. 1990.

*

Bibliography: *Hamsun: En bibliografi* by Arvid Østby, 1972.

Critical Studies: *Hamsun* by Hanna Astrup Larsen, 1922; *Six Scandinavian Novelists: Lie, Jacobsen, Heidenstam, Selma Lagerlöf, Hamsun, Sigrid Undset* by Alrik Gustafson, 1940; *Hamsun* (in Norwegian) by Tore Hamsun, 1959; *Konflikt og visjon* by Rolf Nyboe Nettum, 1970; ''Critical Attitudes to Hamsun 1890–1969'' by Ronald Popperwell, in *Scandinavica*, 9, 1970; ''Knut Hamsun's *Pan*: Myth and Symbol'' by Henning Sehmsdorf, in *Edda*, 1974; *Knut Hamsun som modernist* by Peter Kierkegaard, 1975; *The Hero in Scandinavian Literature* edited by John M. Weinstock and Robert T. Rovinsky, 1975; ''Knut Hamsun's Anti-Semitism'' by Allen Simpson, in *Edda*, 1977; *Knut Hamsun* by Harald Naess, 1984; *Enigma: The*

Life of Knut Hamsun by Robert Ferguson, 1987; *The Roots of Modernist Narrative: Knut Hamsun's Novels Hunger, Mysteries, and Pan* by Martin Humpal, 1999.

* * *

Knut Hamsun burst upon Norwegian literature in 1890 with a series of lectures attacking the realist writers, including Ibsen; he appealed instead for a new kind of writing, which he called "psychological literature." His first novel, *Sult* (*Hunger*), published in the same year, embodies his theories. It is the story of a mind—a lively, fantastic, creative mind which ever and again rises irrepressibly above the vicissitudes of a mundane bodily existence. "The unconscious life of the soul" is the centre of focus; the starving artist pacing the streets of Christiania is not an occasion for an attack on social injustice but a creator of a vibrant inner world.

Inspired, often unstable visionaries are the heroes of Hamsun's other early novels *Mysterier* (*Mysteries*), *Pan*, and *Victoria*. With these novels Hamsun became the first Modernist writer in Scandinavia, reflecting the turbulent inner conflict of modern man; Nietzsche and Dostoevskii were among his antecedents. The interplay of instinct and impulse, the celebration of spontaneity over sober reflection and nature over civilization give his heroes a quixotic air of inconsistency which made his contemporaries dismiss them as "erratic." His prose style is equally innovative, and has proved inimitable—though many have since tried to imitate it. There is a lyrical intensity in his phrasing which makes whole chapters of *Pan* and *Victoria* read like prose poems; the rhythms are incantatory, the mood ecstatic. The novels are hymns to love—but it is a self-destructive, impossible love which bars the way to its own fulfilment and mocks at its own despair.

Hamsun's heroes grew older as he himself grew old; and the exuberance of youth gave way to a more disillusioned world-weariness. Social issues, which he had previously dismissed, also preoccupied him increasingly. In *Børn av tiden* (*Children of the Age*) and *Segelfoss by* (*Segelfoss Town*) he attacked the decadence of modern capitalist society and the emergent workers' movements. *Markens grøde* (*The Growth of the Soil*) celebrated instead his ideal, the noble peasant who rejects the softness of city ways and chooses the harsh, unremitting struggle of the pioneering farming life.

Nostalgia for a lost patriarchal era and dislike of modern industrial society were among the factors which led Hamsun towards the end of his long life to support Hitler, a fateful choice for which his countrymen have still not forgiven him. However, the best of his writing is not marred by his political blindness. In his final trilogy, *Landstrykere* (*Wayfarers*), *August*, and *Men rivet lever* (*The Road Leads On*), the vitality of his inventiveness and the suppleness of his style are undiminished. August, the central character, is Hamsun's last great adventurer and orchestrator of humanity's dreams—though his stock is running low, and the chill winds of old age and bankruptcy are felt with increasing keenness. But like his creator, he is dogged to the end, and the rich gallery of characters around him is depicted with discerning clarity and a fine sense of life's ironies.

—Janet Garton

See the essay on *Hunger*.

HARTMANN VON AUE

Born: Swabia, Germany, 1160. **Education:** Educated in a monastery. **Career:** Minister in the service of a lord. Took part in a crusade, 1189–90 or 1197. **Died:** Between 1210 and 1220.

PUBLICATIONS

Collections

Selections from Hartmann von Aue, translated by Margaret F. Richey. 1962.
Das Hartmann-Liederbuch, edited by Richard Kienast. 1963.
Werke, edited by E. Schwarz. 2 vols., 1967.
Die Lieder Hartmanns von Aue, edited by Ekkehard Blattmann. 1968.
The Narrative Works of Hartmann von Aue, translated by R.W. Fisher. 1983.
Arthurian Romances, Tales, and Lyric Poetry: The Complete Works of Hartmann von Aue, translated with commentary by Frank Tobin, Kim Vivian, Richard H. Lawson. 2001.

Verse

Der arme Heinrich, edited by Johann Gustav Büsching. 1810; also edited by Jacob and Wilhelm Grimm, 1815; Karl Simrok, 1830; W. Wackernagel, 1835; Franz Kocian, 1878; H. Raul, 1882; J.G. Robertson, 1895; E. Gierach, 1911; C.H. Bell, 1931; F. Maurer, 1958; Helmut de Boor, 1967, revised edition by H. Henne, 1987; translated by R.W. Fisher, in *The Narrative Works of Hartmann von Aue*, 1983.
Das Büchlein, edited by Petrus W. Tax. 1979.
Erec, edited by Moriz Haupt. 1839, revised edition, 1871; also edited by O. von Heinemann, 1898; Albert Litzmann, 1939, revised edition, 1972; as *Erec*, translated by J.W. Thomas, 1979; also translated by R.W. Fisher, in *The Narrative Works of Hartmann von Aue*, 1983; Michael Resler, 1987; Thomas L. Keller, 1987.
Gregorius, edited by Karl Lachmann. 1838; also edited by Hermann Paul, 1873; F. Neumann, 1958; as *Gregorius: A Medieval Oedipus Legend*, translated by Edwin H. Zeydel, 1955; as *Gregorius: The Good Sinner*, translated by Sheema Zeben Buehne, 1966; as *Gregorius*, translated by R.W. Fisher, in *The Narrative Works of Hartmann von Aue*, 1983.
Gedichte, edited by Fedor Bech. 1867.
Iwein, edited by G.F. Benecke and K. Lachmann. 1827; also edited by A. Pernhoffer, 1857; as *Iwein*, translated by J.W. Thomas, 1979; also translated by R.W. Fisher, in *The Narrative Works of Hartmann von Aue*, 1983; Patrick M. McConeghy, 1984.
Die Klage, edited by Herta Zutt. 1968.
Das Klagenbüchlein: Hartmann von Aue und das zweite Büchlein, edited by Ludwig Wolff. 1972; edited and translated by Thomas L. Keller, 1986.

*

Bibliography: *Bibliographie zu Hartmann von Aue* by Elfriede Neubuhr, 1977; revised edition, 1987.

Critical Studies: "An Interpretation of Hartmann's *Iwein*" by H. Sacker, in *Germanic Review*, (36), 1961; "Heinrich's Metanoia:

Intention and Practice in *Der Arme Heinrich*'' by T. Buck, in *Modern Language Review*, (60), 1965; *Hartmann von Aue and His Lyric Poetry* by Leslie Seiffert, 1968; ''Christian Allegory in Hartmann's *Iwein*'' by J. Clifton-Everest, in *Germanic Review*, (48), 1973; *Hartmann von Aue* edited by Hugo Kuhn and Christoph Cormeau, 1973; *Gregorius and Der arme Heinrich: Hartmann's Dualistic and Gradualistic Views of Reality* by Frank J. Tobin, 1973; *Symbolism in Hartmann's Iwein* by R.E. Lewis, 1975; *Hartmann von Aue* by P. Wapnewski, 1976; ''The Fortune in Hartmann's *Erec*'' by F. Pickering, in *German Life and Letters*, (30), 1976–77; ''The ex lege Rite of Passage in Hartmann's *Iwein*'' by T.L. Markey, in *Colloquia Germanica* (II), 1978; ''The Maiden in Hartmann's *Armen Heinrich*: Enrite Redux?'' by W.C. McDonald, in *Deutsche Vierteljahrsschrift*, (53), 1979; ''Hartmann's Gregorius and the Paradox of Sin'' by R. Fisher, in *Seminar*, (17), 1981; *Hartmann von Aue: Changing Perspectives* edited by Timothy McFarland and Silvia Ranawake, 1988; *Hartmann von Aue: Landscapes of the Mind* by Susan L. Clark, 1989; *Chivalry in Twelfth-Century Germany: The Works of Hartmann von Aue* by W.H. Jackson, 1994; *The Pilgrimage Motif in the Works of the Medieval German Author Hartmann von Aue* by Mary Vandegrift Mills, 1996; *Adventures in Interpretation: The Works of Hartman von Aue and Their Critical Reception* by Will Hasty, 1996; *Bodies of Pain: Suffering in the Works of Hartmann von Aue* by Scott E. Pincikowski, 2002.

*   *   *

According to contemporaries, Hartmann von Aue set the standard for the great generation of German poets flourishing around 1200. Hartmann identifies himself as a *''dienstman''* (*ministerialis*) *''von Ouwe.''* On linguistic grounds we know that he came from Swabia (south-western Germany), a member of the unfree class of *ministeriales* who, through service as functionaries of the high aristocracy, won noble status for themselves in the course of the 12th century; in his depiction of an ideal knighthood, noble status is legitimated by service to society. He emphasizes his Latin clerical education, unusual for a layman. It is not possible to identify Hartmann's family—or even his patrons—with any reliability; he may have belonged to the sphere of the Dukes of Zähringen. His literary activity can with confidence be said to extend from about 1180 to around 1205, and he seems to have participated in the Crusade in either 1189–90 or 1197–98; testimony of other poets indicates that he died before 1220.

Hartmann's *oeuvre* comprises a youthful disputation on love, *Die Klage* [The Lover's Lament]; a substantial corpus of love lyrics whose chronology cannot reliably be determined; and four narrative works: two courtly romances, *Erec* and *Iwein*, and between them two religious legends, *Gregorius* and *Der arme Heinrich* [Poor Sir Henry]. This sequence for his compositions, posited early on stylistic grounds, has long been accepted.

Hartmann's two Arthurian romances, *Erec* and *Iwein*, were based upon two romances by the French poet Chrétien de Troyes, who inaugurated the genre of Arthurian romance. These works present critically an ideal by which the problematical nature of knightly ways can be explored. Common to Arthurian texts on the model of Chrétien is a tectonic structure in which the hero, accepted into chivalric society, incurs guilt through some specific fault, is repudiated by the community, and must in a second sequence of exploits make good this fault in order to achieve a new, higher integration into aristocratic society. In a system of thematic harmonics which embody the statement of the narrative, the events and persons of these adventures reflect through repetition, parallel, and contrast the nature of the deficiency which is to be remedied.

In spite of its significance as the first German Arthurian romance, *Erec*, composed soon after 1180, is preserved whole in only a single, large manuscript (the Ambraser MS, a compendium of chivalric poetry) from the early 16th century, and even then its opening is lost; the test has 10,135 verses. Significant divergences from Chrétien show that Hartmann also knew other versions of the story. *Erec* treats marital sexuality, chivalric violence, and their proper regulation as socially beneficial functions. The compulsive Erec and his devoted wife Enite succumb to the erotic delights of marriage and accordingly neglect their public duty as king and queen; once apprised of his disgrace, Erec imposes absolute silence upon his wife during his quest for rehabilitation, but after repeatedly being saved only through her warnings is forced to acknowledge their marital interdependence. Similarly, he learns to exercise his martial prowess in works of rescue and liberation rather than as an end in itself, and finally through social responsibility merits his crown. Enite, growing in maturity and perception before her husband, can be deemed an equal protagonist. Hartmann points up more strongly than his French source the religious dimension of this idealized chivalry.

Iwein, completed by about 1205, is 8,165 verses in length and adhered much more closely to its French source. It is widely recorded, being preserved in 32 manuscripts (some fragmentary). The foreground theme reflects that of *Erec*, for the protagonist has here to curb his eagerness for chivalric exploits in order to regain the favour of his wife, whom he has neglected. The essential theme here too, however, is the social function which alone legitimates chivalric feats of arms, for after total breakdown and loss of self, Iwein overcomes his frivolous desire for *âventiure*—the term means both ''a chivalric encounter'' and ''a story about chivalric encounters''—and directs his knightly endeavours to deeds of rescue and the defence of what is just. The plot requires feats of diplomatic persuasion in order to motivate the reconciliations between Iwein and his lady. With its myth and fairytale elements the narrative has less inherent linear focus than *Erec*. Irony embedded in the work serves to convey the author's critical play with the values of conventional knighthood and the assumptions of chivalric romance.

In narrative structure Hartmann's religious legends resemble the romances: the protagonist in all his worldly glory is suddenly struck down because he has failed to live according to God's ordinance, presuming his fortune to be his by right. *Gregorius*, 4,007 verses in length and composed either in 1188 or in the 1190s, is recorded in 11 manuscripts. Based on a version of the contemporary French *Life of Pope Gregory*, it portrays the son of a sibling relationship who, after renouncing a monastic life for the world of chivalry, unknowingly commits incest with his mother. After 17 years of harsh penance he is called to the papal throne, and mother and son devote themselves to God's service in Rome. This work is probably related to a legend type recorded by the Persian Firdousi (10th century) rather than the Oedipus myth, and it focuses more on the need for penance than on the incurring of guilt. *Der arme Heinrich*, 1,520 verses long and composed probably around 1195, survives in six manuscripts; it depicts an ideal, courtly knight who, visited with leprosy, fails still to acknowledge God's sovereignty and is prepared even to countenance the willing sacrifice of a pure young virgin for the sake of his cure. Relenting finally as the surgeon prepares the sacrifice, Henry recognizes God's will and accepts his life as penance for the sin of worldliness. The peasant girl, his counterpart in delusion, denied immediate salvation by means of her sacrifice, must accept that life on earth is meant to be lived. God rewards their acceptance of his will by curing Henry, who marries the girl below his rank and lives in marriage and penance isolated from courtly society.

With their lucid expression and crafted composition, Hartmann's works illustrate vividly the interaction between clerical learning and the aspirations of the lay aristocracy in a period of dynamic social evolution. Their manuscript transmission suggests that they were perceived to be in distinct categories rather than the work of a single personality; none the less they ranked from the outset as classical models in their genres. *Gregorius* was translated into Latin as early as 1210, and *Iwein* served from the 13th century as the basis for cycles of frescoes in Rodeneck in the Tyrol and Schmalkalden in Thuringia. Hartmann's legends have been reworked in the past century by Thomas Mann and Gerhart Hauptmann.

—Lewis Jillings

HAŠEK, Jaroslav

Born: Prague, Bohemia (now Czech Republic), 30 April 1883. **Education:** Educated at St. Stephen's School, 1891–93; Imperial and Royal Junior Gymnasium, 1893–97, expelled; Czechoslavonic Commercial Academy, 1899–1902. **Family:** Married Jarmila Mayerová in 1910 (separated 1912), one son; bigamous marriage with Shura Lvova in 1920. **Career:** Worked for a chemist in late 1890s; wrote stories and sketches for several humorous and political magazines from 1901; also wrote and performed cabaret sketches; clerk, Insurance Bank of Slavie, 1902–03; jailed for anarchist rioting, 1907; editor, *Svět zvírat* [Animal World], 1909–10; assistant editor, *Czech Word*, 1911; conscripted into the Austrian army, 1915; captured by the Russians: allowed to work for Czech forces in Russia, and staff member, *Cechoslovan*, Kiev, 1916–18; after a propaganda battle, 1917–18, left Czech group and entered political department of the Siberian Army: editor, *Our Path* (later *Red Arrow*), 1919, *Red Europe*, 1919, and other propaganda journals in Russia and Siberia; sent to Czechoslovakia to do propaganda work, 1920; lived in Lipnice from 1921. **Died:** 3 January 1923.

PUBLICATIONS

Collection

Spisy [Works]. 16 vols., 1955–68.

Fiction

Dobrý voják Švejk a jiné podivné historky [The Good Soldier Svejk and Other Strange Stories]. 1912.
Trampoty pana Tenkráta [The Tribulations of Mr. That-Time]. 1912.
Průvodčí cizincu a jiné satiry [The Tourists' Guide and Other Satires from Home]. 1913.
Mùj obchod se psy a jiné humoresky [My Trade with Dogs and Other Humoresques]. 1915.

Dobrý voják Švejk v zajetí [The Good Soldier Svejk in Captivity]. 1917.
[Two Dozen Stories]. 1920.
Pepíček Nový a jiné povídky [Pepíček Nový and Other Stories]. 1921.
Osudy dobrého vojáka Švejka za světové války. 4 vols., 1921–23; as *The Good Soldier Schweik*, translated by Paul Selver, 1930; complete version, as *The Good Soldier Švejk and His Fortunes in the World War*, translated by Cecil Parrott, 1973; as *The Fateful Adventures of the Good Soldier Svejk During the World War*, translated by Zenny K. Sadlon, 2000.
Tři muži se žralokem a jiné poučné historky [Three Men and a Shark and Other Instructive Stories]. 1921.
Mírová Konference ajiné humoresky [The Peace Conference and Other Humoresques]. 1922.
Idylky z pekla (stories), edited by Evžen Paloncy. 1974.
The Red Commissar, Including Further Adventures of the Good Soldier Svejk and Other Stories, translated by Cecil Parrott, 1981.
Povídky (stories). 2 vols., 1988.
The Bachura Scandal and Other Stories and Sketches, translated by Alan Menhennet. 1991.

Other

Lidský profil Jaroslava Haška: korespondence a dokumenty (selected letters 1920–22), edited by Radko Pytlík. 1979.
Tajemství mého pobytu v Rusku (selected essays), edited by Zdeněk Horění. 1985.

*

Bibliography: *Bibliografie Jaroslava Haška* by Boris Mědílek, 1983.

Critical Studies: *Hašek, the Creator of Schweik* by Emanuel Frynta, 1965; *The Bad Bohemian: The Life of Jaroslav Hašek*, 1978, and *Jaroslav Hašek: A Study of Svejk and the Short Stories*, 1982, both by Cecil Parrott; *Jaroslav Hašek and the Good Soldier Schweik* by Radko Pytlík, translated by David Short, 1983.

* * *

Jaroslav Hašek wrote his one and only novel, *Osudy dobrého vojáka Švejka za světové války* (*The Good Soldier Švejk and His Fortunes in the World War*), in 1921 and 1922, at the very end of his adventurous and chequered life, and left it unfinished at his death. It has been translated into countless languages and is now far better known in the world than any other Czech book—a development which he could never have foreseen. At first the Czech literary "establishment" dismissed the book as unliterary, and it was only when it was translated into German in 1926 and presented by Erwin Piscator in dramatized form at the famous Theater am Nollendorfplatz in Berlin in 1928 that it achieved European fame.

When it was published in final form in 1923, it anticipated by several years the wave of popular war books which appeared at the end of the decade, like *All Quiet on the Western Front* (*Im Westen nichts Neues*) by Erich Maria Remarque and others. But whereas the authors of such books mostly dwelt on the horror and suffering of war and their disillusionment with it, Hašek, to quote the perceptive judgement of a contemporary Czech writer, Ivan Olbracht, "stood above it" and "just laughed at it." Olbracht went on to say that he had read several war novels and even written one himself, but none of them showed up World War I "in all its infamy, idiocy and inhumanity" so vividly as Hašek's.

Hašek found the material for his novel during the one year he spent in the Austrian army on the way to the Eastern Front. Most of its leading characters are modelled on the officers, NCOs, and men of the regiment he served in. He had already invented the character of "The Good Soldier" in 1911, when he wrote five short stories about him, but in his final novel Švejk had become a much rounder and more enigmatic figure. Was he an idiot or only pretending to be one? In consequence of this ambiguity Švejk was caught up in the political struggles between Left and Right in the young republic. The Left wanted to see him as a revolutionary, while the Right condemned him as a dodger and a threat to national morale. While most other readers of the book would laugh aloud at Švejk's misadventures, Czechoslovakia's leading critic, F.X. Šalda, saw their tragic side. For all its comedy, he wrote, it was a desperately sad book, because in it the individual was fighting against a giant power, against the war.

Hašek himself would have been greatly surprised to know that his book had given rise to such discussions, because he just dictated it as it came into his head—sometimes in the middle of a pub bar—with nothing but a map to go on. He filled the pages of his book with a vast array of fascinating types, whom he involved more often than not in ludicrous situations. He had a Dickensian gift for describing character, although unlike Dickens he did not dwell on their appearance but rather on their actions and manner of speech. He was particularly successful in reproducing the conversations of ordinary men and the anecdotes they tell. And he described in a masterly fashion the scrapes they got into and the idiotic ideas they had, saying under his breath, "Lord, what fools these mortals be." The book is as much a condemnation of the Austrian Army as it is of the war. Its generals are shown either as inept fuddy-duddies or potential hangmen. (Hašek was of course free for the first time to say exactly what he thought of the monarchy, as it no longer existed.)

In writing his novel Hašek drew on his long experience in contributing short stories and feuilletons to the Czech press, which are said to have amounted to over 1,200. He wrote them for Prague dailies before the war, for the Czech Legion's newspaper in Kiev during it, and Soviet journals in Siberia after it was over. He wrote easily, but carelessly. He once described a feuilleton as "something which can be read in the morning at breakfast, when a man is still yawning, and in the afternoon, when after lunch he lies agreeably stretched out on a soft sofa, a kind of writing in which one can skip half a column without missing it." His short stories prove his inexhaustible ingenuity in inventing comic situations, but as the newspapers he contributed to seldom allowed him more than a little over a thousand words they almost all suffer from compression and sometimes end with the point only half made. His best stories are the Bugulma tales, which he published in Prague on his return from Russia after the war, and which recount his experiences as deputy-commandant of a little town beyond the Volga. Although in these he ridicules Soviet petty officials, he is more indulgent to them than he is to Austrians or indeed to his own people.

In the years before the war Hašek acquired something of a reputation as a popular entertainer, when he helped to create a mock political party and posed as its candidate in the national elections. People flocked to hear his improvised speeches, in which he mercilessly pilloried the activities of the Czech political parties. When the elections were over he sat down and wrote up the "annals" of his

"party" and ascribed to its members various imaginary exploits, but much of what he wrote was too personal and defamatory to be published at the time and only found its way into print as late as 1963.

None of Hašek's flamboyant posturings as electioneering agent, speaker at Anarchist rallies, or cabaret entertainer earned him much respect, and his lampoons and tomfoolery alienated many who might otherwise have helped him. By the time war broke out Prague had become rather too hot for him, and he no doubt joined up with a certain feeling of relief. But it can be said of him that he added another dimension to conventional humorous writing by acting and actually living his stories. All his experiences, whether lived or written, bore fruit later, when he drew on them for his one great novel.

—Cecil Parrott

See the essay on *The Good Soldier Švejk and His Fortunes in the World War.*

HAUPTMANN, Gerhart (Johann Robert)

Born: Ober-Salzbrunn, Silesia, 15 November 1862. **Education:** Educated at a school in Breslau, from 1874; studied sculpture at Royal College of Art, Breslau, 1880–82; also studied at University of Jena, 1882–83. **Family:** Married 1) Marie Thienemann in 1885 (divorced 1904; died 1915), three sons; 2) Margarete Marschalk in 1905, one son. **Career:** Sculptor in Rome, 1883–84; also worked as actor in Berlin, before becoming a full-time writer; co-founder of the literary group *Durch.* **Awards:** Grillparzer prize, 1896, 1899, 1905; Goethebünde Schiller prize, 1905; Nobel prize for literature, 1912: Goethe prize (Frankfurt), 1932. Honorary degrees: Oxford University, 1905; University of Leipzig, 1909; University of Prague, 1921; Columbia University, New York, 1932. Ordre pour le Mérite, 1922. **Died:** 8 June 1946.

PUBLICATIONS

Collections

Dramatic Works, edited by Ludwig Lewisohn, translated by Lewisohn and others. 9 vols., 1912–29.
Sämtliche Werke, edited by Hans-Egon Hass. 11 vols., 1962–74.
Plays, edited by Reinhold Grimm and Caroline Molina y Vedia, 1994.

Plays

Vor Sonnenaufgang (produced 1889). 1889; as *Before Dawn,* translated by Leonard Bloomfield, 1909; also translated by Richard Newnham, in *Three German Plays,* 1963; as *Before Daybreak,* translated by Peter Bauland, 1978; as *Before Sunrise,* translated by James Joyce, edited by Jill Perkins, 1978.
Das Friedenfest (produced 1890). 1890; as *The Coming of Peace,* translated by Janet Achurch and C.E. Wheeler, 1900; as *The Reconciliation,* in *Dramatic Works,* 1914.
Einsame Menschen (produced 1891). 1891; as *Lonely Lives,* translated by Mary Morrison, 1898.

Die Weber (produced 1893). 1892; as *The Weavers*, translated by Mary Morrison, 1899; also translated by T.H. Lustig, in *Five Plays*, 1961; Frank Marcus, 1980.

Kollege Crampton (produced 1892). 1892; as *Colleague Crampton*, translated by Roy Temple House and Ludwig Lewisohn, in *Dramatic Works*, 1914.

Der Biberpelz (produced 1893). 1893; as *The Beaver Coat*, translated by Ludwig Lewisohn, 1912; also translated by T.H. Lustig, in *Five Plays*, 1961.

Hanneles Himmelfahrt (produced 1893). 1893; as *Hannele*, translated by William Archer, 1894; also translated by Charles Henry Meltzer, 1908; T.H. Lustig, in *Five Plays*, 1961.

Florian Geyer (produced 1896). 1896; as *Florian Geyer*, translated by Bayard Quincy Morgan, in *Dramatic Works*, 1929.

Die versunkene Glocke (produced 1896). 1896; as *The Sunken Bell*, translated by Mary Harned, 1898; also translated by Charles Henry Meltzer, 1899.

Fuhrmann Henschel (produced 1898). 1898; as *Drayman Henschel*, translated by Marion A. Redlich, in *Dramatic Works*, 1913; also translated by T.H. Lustig, in *Five Plays*, 1961.

Schluck und Jau (produced 1900). 1900; as *Schluck and Jau*, translated by Ludwig Lewisohn, in *Dramatic Works*, 1919.

Michael Kramer (produced 1900). 1900; as *Michael Kramer*, translated by Ludwig Lewisohn, in *Dramatic Works*, 1914.

Der rote Hahn (produced 1901). 1901; as *The Conflagration*, translated by Ludwig Lewisohn, in *Dramatic Works*, 1913.

Der arme Heinrich (produced 1902). 1902; as *Henry of Auë*, translated by Ludwig Lewisohn, in *Dramatic Works*, 1914.

Rose Bernd (produced 1903). 1903; as *Rose Bernd*, translated by Ludwig Lewisohn, in *Dramatic Works*, 1913; also translated by T.H. Lustig, in *Five Plays*, 1961.

Elga (produced 1905). 1905; as *Elga*, translated by Mary Harned, in *Dramatic Works*, 1919.

Und Pippa tanzt! (produced 1906). 1906; translated as *And Pippa Dances*, 1907.

Die Jungfrau vom Bischofsberg (produced 1907). 1907; as *Maidens of the Mount*, translated by Ludwig Lewisohn, in *Dramatic Works*, 1919.

Kaiser Karls Geisel (produced 1908). 1908; as *Charlemagne's Hostage*, translated by Ludwig Lewisohn, in *Dramatic Works*, 1919.

Griselda (produced 1909). 1909; as *Griselda*, translated by Alice Kauser, in *Dramatic Works*, 1919.

Die Ratten (produced 1911). 1911; as *The Rats*, translated by Ludwig Lewisohn, in *Dramatic Works*, 1913.

Gabriel Schillings Flucht (produced 1912). 1912; as *Gabriel Schilling's Flight*, translated by Ludwig Lewisohn, in *Dramatic Works*, 1919.

Festspiel in deutschen Reimen (produced 1913). 1913; as *Commemoration Masque*, translated by Bayard Quincy Morgan, in *Dramatic Works*, 1919.

Der Bogen des Odysseus (produced 1914). 1914; as *The Bow of Ulysses*, translated by Bayard Quincy Morgan, in *Dramatic Works*, 1919.

Winterballade (produced 1917). 1917; as *A Winter Ballad*, translated by Edwin and Willa Muir, in *Dramatic Works*, 1925.

Der weisse Heiland (produced 1920). 1920; as *The White Savior*, translated by Edwin and Willa Muir, in *Dramatic Works*, 1925.

Indipohdi (produced 1920). 1920; as *Indipohdi*, translated by Edwin and Willa Muir, in *Dramatic Works*, 1925.

Peter Bauer (produced 1921). 1921.

Veland. 1925; as *Veland*, translated by Edwin Muir, in *Dramatic Works*, 1929.

Dorothea Angermann (produced 1926). 1926.

Spuk; oder, Die schwarze Maske und Hexenritt (produced 1929). 1929.

Vor Sonnenuntergang (produced 1932). 1932.

Die goldene Harfe (produced 1933). 1933.

Hamlet in Wittenberg (produced 1935). 1935.

Ulrich von Lichtenstein (produced 1939). 1939.

Die Tochter der Kathedrale (produced 1939). 1939.

Atridentetralogie: Iphigenie in Aulis; Agamemnons Tod; Elektra; Iphigenie in Delphi (produced 1940–44). 4 vols., 1941–48.

Magnus Garbe (produced 1942). 1942.

Die Finsternisse. 1947.

Herbert Engelmann, completed by Carl Zuckmayer (produced 1952). 1952.

Five Plays, translated by T.H. Lustig. 1961.

Fiction

Fasching. 1887.

Bahnwärter Thiel. 1888.

Der Apostel. 1890.

Der Narr in Christo, Emanuel Quint. 1910; as *The Fool in Christ, Emanuel Quint*, translated by Thomas Seltzer, 1911.

Atlantis. 1912; as *Atlantis*, translated by Adele and Thomas Seltzer, 1913.

Lohengrin. 1913.

Parsival. 1914; as *Parsifal*, translated by Oakley Williams, 1915.

Der Ketzer von Soana. 1918; as *The Heretic of Soana*, translated by Bayard Quincy Morgan, 1923.

Phantom. 1922; as *Phantom*, translated by Bayard Quincy Morgan, 1923.

Die Insel der grossen Mutter. 1924; as *The Island of the Great Mother*, translated by Edwin and Willa Muir, 1925.

Wanda. 1928.

Buch der Leidenschaft. 1930.

Die Hochzeit auf Buchenhorst. 1931.

Das Meerwunder. 1934.

Im Wirbel der Berufung. 1936.

Der Schuss im Park. 1939.

Das Märchen. 1941.

Mignon. 1944.

Lineman Thiel and Other Tales, translated by Stanley Radcliffe, 1989.

Verse

Promethidenlos. 1885.

Das bunte Buch. 1888.

Anna. 1921.

Die blaue Blume. 1924.

Till Eulenspiegel. 1928.

Ährenlese. 1939.

Der grosse Traum. 1942.

Neue Gedichte. 1946.

Other

Griechischer Frühling. 1908.
Ausblicke. 1922.
Gesammelte Werke. 12 vols., 1922.
Um Volk und Geist. 1932.
Gespräche, edited by Josef Chapiro. 1932.
Das Abenteuer meiner Jugend. 2 vols., 1937.
Italienische Reise 1897: Tagebuchaufzeichnungen, edited by Martin Machatzke. 1976.
Diarium 1917 bis 1933, edited by Martin Machatzke. 1980.
Notiz-Kalender 1889 bis 1891, edited by Martin Machatzke. 1982.
Gerhart Hauptmann—Ludwig von Hofmann: Briefwechsel 1894–1944, edited by Herta Hesse-Frielinghaus. 1983.
Otto Brahm, Gerhart Hauptmann: Briefwechsel 1889–1912, edited by Peter Sprengel. 1985.
Tagebuch 1892 bis 1894, edited by Martin Machatzke. 1985.
Tagebücher 1897 bis 1905, edited by Martin Machatzke. 1987.
Ein Leben für Gerhart Hauptmann: Aufsätze aus den Jahren 1929–1990, edited by Walter A. Reichart. 1991.
Gespräche und Interviews mit Gerhart Hauptmann (1894–1946), edited by H.D. Tschörtner, 1994.

*

Bibliography: *Gerhart-Hauptmann-Bibliographie* by Walter Requardt, 3 vols., 1931; *Gerhart-Hauptmann-Bibliographie* by Walter A. Reichart, 1969; *Gerhart-Hauptmann-Bibliographie* by Heinz D. Tschörtner, 1971; *Internationale Bibliographie zum Werk Gerhart Hauptmanns* by Sigfried Hoefert, 2 vols., 1986–89.

Critical Studies: *The Death Problem in the Life and Works of Hauptmann* by Frederick A. Klemm, 1939; *Gerhart Hauptmann* by Hugh F. Garten, 1954; *Gerhart Hauptmann: His Life and Work* by C.F.W. Behl, 1956; *Gerhart Hauptmann: The Prose Plays* by Margaret Sinden, 1957; *Witness of Deceit: Gerhart Hauptmann as a Critic of Society* by Leroy R. Shaw, 1958; *Hauptmann: Centenary Lectures* edited by K.G. Knight and F. Norman, 1964; *Gerhart Hauptmann in Russia, 1889–1917: Reception and Impact* by Albert A. Kipa, 1974; *From Lessing to Hauptmann: Studies in German Drama* by Ladislaus Löb, 1974; *Gerhart Hauptmann and Utopia*, 1976, and *Gerhart Hauptmann: Religious Syncretism and Eastern Religions*, 1984, both by Philip Mellen; *The Image of the Primitive Giant in the Works of Gerhart Hauptmann* by Carolyn Thomas Dussère, 1979; *The German Naturalists and Gerhart Hauptmann: Reception and Influence* by Alan Marshall, 1982; *Hauptmann, Wedekind and Schnitzler* by Peter Skrine, 19891; *Understanding Gerhart Hauptmann* by Warren R. Maurer, 1992.

* * *

Gerhart Hauptmann's reputation as the leading representative of German naturalism has tended to obscure the fact that he enjoyed a period of literary creativity which lasted for more than 60 years. Apart from Goethe, few German writers have succeeded in bequeathing a life's work of such astonishing variety, richness, and breadth. From naturalism to neo-romanticism to 20th-century mysticism and neo-classicism, there are few literary movements between 1880 and 1940 which failed to influence Hauptmann or indeed to be influenced by him.

Hauptmann's plays, ranging from the crude but powerful *Vor Sonnenaufgang* (*Before Dawn*), 1889, to the deeply pessimistic recasting of antique sources in the *Atridentetralogie* [Atriden tetralogy], 1940–44, are remarkable for the easy assurance with which the author displays his mastery of diverse registers, themes, styles, and genres. The raucous naturalism of his earliest work was tempered in 1891 by the performance in Berlin of *Einsame Menschen* (*Lonely Lives*), a poignant middle-class tragedy which, in its probing analysis of the roles ascribed by society to women, has lost none of its topicality. Realism re-emerged in *Die Weber* (*The Weavers*), a moving account of the ill-fated uprising of the Silesian weavers in 1844, in the comedies *Der Biberpelz* (*The Beaver Coat*) and *Der rote Hahn* (*The Conflagration*), and in the tightly knit dialect tragedy *Fuhrmann Henschel* (*Drayman Henschel*). Even in this early period Hauptmann was not willing to accept the dictates of naturalism in any doctrinaire sense, for in *Hanneles Himmelfahrt* (*Hannele*) the techniques of realism are employed as a means of making visual the delirious dreams and mental states of a dying child. Hannele's hallucinations, which express the reality of her wretched childhood and at once represent a flight from it, symbolize Hauptmann's own deepening interest in the workings of the imagination and its relationship to the human capacity to apprehend reality in mythical and poetic ways. This development is carried much further in the dramatic fairytale *Die versunkene Glocke* (*The Sunken Bell*), and in a more realistic framework it is evident in the father/son conflict portrayed in the artist tragedy *Michael Kramer*. The subtlest and most magical expression of this thematic material is the drama *Und Pippa tanzt!* (*And Pippa Dances*), a work which owes much to Hauptmann's intensive study of the myths and legends of his native Silesia.

Hauptmann's works of prose fiction reflect in both theme and style the main trends discernible in his development as a dramatist. And similarly, the earlier naturalistic stories such as *Fasching* and *Bahnwärter Thiel* have had a greater impact than the mythological and symbolic works of the later period: *Der Narr in Christo, Emanuel Quint* (*The Fool in Christ, Emanuel Quint*), *Der Ketzer von Soana* (*The Heretic of Soana*), and *Die Insel der grossen Mutter* (*The Island of the Great Mother*). Narratives such as *Bahnwärter Thiel* reveal even more clearly than the naturalistic plays, however, that Hauptmann was transcending naturalism in those very works which explored its themes and its expressive possibilities. The story certainly abounds in fashionable literary touches: the low social position of Thiel, the second-by-second description of trains appearing on the horizon and disappearing in the distance, the realistic "close-up" of a spade turning over the soil, and so on. At the same time, the narrative penetrates beyond realism to suggest the existence of realities and levels of perception which can be grasped only through symbol and myth. The train which kills Thiel's son and destroys Thiel is depicted on one level with all the photographic detail and meticulous accuracy which one expects to find in late 19th-century fiction; on a different level, the train's headlights transform the falling rain into droplets of blood and the train comes to symbolize the unpredictable and chaotic forces of destruction which, in Hauptmann's fictional world, are never very far from surface reality, however rational and well ordered it might appear.

—A.P. Foulkes

See the essay on *The Weavers*.

HAVEL, Václav

Born: Prague, Czechoslovakia (now Czech Republic), 5 October 1936. **Education:** Completed compulsory schooling, 1951; difficulty in obtaining higher education because of his "bourgeois" background; attended evening courses while working as apprentice at Prague's Technical High School 1951–55; after several applications for admission to humanities departments at Charles University were refused he studied economics at Technical High School 1955–57; refused entry to the Academy of Arts in Prague 1959–60. **Military Service:** 1957–59. **Family:** Married Olga Šplíchalová in 1964. **Career:** During the political thaw in the 1960s, after working as stage hand, assistant to the director and dramaturge at various Prague theaters, became resident playwright at Prague's Theater on the Balustrade where several of his plays were performed; on editorial staff of monthly *Tvář*; chairman of Czechoslovak Writers' Association, April 1968; all was cut short by the Soviet-led invasion of Czechoslovakia in August 1968; numerous activities as a "dissident" include letters, reports, editorial works published in *samizdat* and abroad in numerous translations, involvement in the Charter 77 movement and its famous "Declaration" of 1 January 1977, and serving several prison sentences, one of which was four and a half years; since the demise of Communism in 1990 became President of Czechoslovakia, and in 1992, after the separation of Slovakia, President of the Czech Republic. He was reelected in 1996. **Awards:** Numerous honorary doctorates; most important awards: Obie prize (United States), 1968, 1970; Austrian prize for European Literature, 1968; Erasmus prize (Netherlands), 1986; German Booksellers' prize, 1989; International prize of Charles the Great (Germany), 1991; Sonning prize for contribution to European Civilization (Denmark), 1991; Onassis prize for Man and Mankind (Greece), 1993; Indira Gandhi prize (India), 1994; Philadelphia Liberty medal (United States), 1994; Future of Hope medal (Hiroshima), 1995; Fulbright prize (United States), 1997; Honourary doctorate of Oxford University, 1998; Open Society prize (Hungary), 1999.

PUBLICATIONS

Collections

Spisy [Works]. 7 vols., 1999.
Open Letters: Selected Writings 1965–1990 (selected essays), translated by Paul Wilson et al.; selected and edited by Paul Wilson.

Plays

Rodinný večer. 1960.
Zahradní slavnost (produced in Prague 1963). 1963; as *The Garden Party*, translated by Vera Blackwell, 1969; also in *Selected Plays 1963–1983*, 1992; and in *The Garden Party and Other Plays*, 1993.
Vyrozumění (produced in Prague 1965). 1966; as *The Memorandum*, translated by Vera Blackwell, 1967, 1980; also in *Selected Plays 1963–1983*.
Anděl strážný (radio play). 1968.
Motýl na anténě. 1968.

Ztížena možnost soustředění (produced in Prague 1968). 1968; as *The Increased Difficulty of Concentration*, translated by Vera Blackwell, 1972, 1976; also in *Selected Plays 1963–1983*.
Spiklenci. 1971.
Audience (first appeared in *samizdat* 1975). 1975; as *Audience*, translated by Vera Blackwell, 1978; also translated by George Theiner as *Conversation*, 1976; by Jan Novak as *Audience*, 1985; in *The Vaněk Plays: Four Authors One Character*, 1987; also the *Three Vaněk Plays*, 1990; and in *Selected Plays 1963–1983*.
Unveiling (first appeared in *samizdat* 1975). 1975; as translated by Jan Novak, 1985; also as *Private View* in *Sorry. . .* , translated by Vera Blackwell, 1978; as *Unveiling* in *The Vaněk Plays: Four Authors One Character*, 1987; also in *Three Vaněk Plays*; and in *Selected Plays 1963–1983*.
Žebrácká opera (first appeared in *samizdat* 1974). 1972; as *The Beggar's Opera*, translated by Paul Wilson, 2001.
Horský hotel (first appeared in *samizdat* 1978). 1976.
Protest (first appeared in *samizdat* 1978). 1978; as *Protest*, translated by Vera Blackwell, 1985; in *DramaContemporary: Czechoslovakia*, 1985; also in *Three Vaněk Plays*; and in *Selected Plays 1963–1983*.
Chyba (first appeared in *samizdat* 1983). As *The Mistake*, translated by George Theiner, 1984; in *Index on Censorship*, 1984.
Largo Desolato (first appeared in *samizdat* 1984). 1984; as *Largo desolato*, English version by Tom Stoppard, 1987.
Pokoušení (first appeared in *samizdat* 1985). 1985; as *Temptation*, translated by George Theiner, 1986, in *Index on Censorship* 1986; also by Marie Winn, 1989.
Asanace (first appeared in *samizdat* 1987). 1987; as *Redevelopment or Slum Clearance*, adapted by James Saunders from a literal translation by Marie Winn, 1990.
Zítra to spustíme!. 1988. As *Tomorrow!*, translated by Barbara Day, in *Czech Plays*, 1994.

SELECTED ESSAYS

"Na téma opozice." 1968; as "On the Theme of Opposition."
"Dopis Gustávu Husákovi." 1975; as "Letter to Dr. Gustav Husák, General Secretary of the Czechoslovak Communist Party."
"Moc bezmocných." 1978; as "The Power of the Powerless."
"Politika a svědomí." 1984; as "Politics and Conscience."
"Šest poznámek o kultuře." 1984; as "Six Asides about Culture."
"Anatomie jedné zdrženlivosti." 1985; as "Anatomy of Reticence."
"Slovo o slovu." 1989; as "A Word About Words."

Speeches

Projev na konferenci Svazy československých spisovatelů (speech at a conference of the Union of Czechoslovak writers). 1965; as "On Evasive Thinking."
The Art of the Impossible: Politics as Morality in Practice, Speeches and Writings 1990–1996. 1997; translated by Paul Wilson and others.

Other Texts

Dopisy Olze (červen 1979–září 1982) (first appeared in *samizdat*). 1983; as *Letters to Olga: June 1979–September 1982*, translated by Paul Wilson, 1988.

Dálkový výslech 1985–1986 (a book-length interview conducted by Karel Hvížd'ala). As *Disturbing the Peace*, translated by Paul Wilson, 1990.

Letní přemítání. 1991; as *Summer Meditations*, translated by Paul Wilson, 1992

*

Critical Studies: *Czech Drama Since World War II* by Paul Trensky, 1978; *The Silenced Theatre: Czech Playwrights Without a Stage* by Marketa Goetz-Stankiewicz, 1979; *The Reluctant President: a Political Life of Václav Havel* by Michael Simmons, 1991; *Václav Havel* by Eda Kriseová, 1993; *Questions of Identity: Czech and Slovak Ideas of Nationality and Personality* by Robert Pynsent, 1994; *Václav Havel: a Political Tragedy in Six Acts* by John Keane, 1999; *Critical Essays on Václav Havel* ed. by Marketa Goetz-Stankiewicz and Phyllis Carey, 1999.

* * *

Václav Havel's work can be viewed under three aspects: there is the dramatist whose plays are known in many translations, the ''dissident'' writer of eloquent essays, and the author of numerous speeches delivered across the world as president of his country after 1990. It seems ironic that Havel's stature as playwright has been overshadowed by his prose for two reasons: between the Soviet-led occupation of Czechoslovakia in 1968 and the demise of Communism in 1989 Havel's powerful essays illuminating the machinery of the Communist system had a strong impact in the West; since 1990 his eloquent presidential speeches have captured the attention of people in all walks of life.

However, although at present receding into the background because of what could be called the sensational extremes of his life, Havel's plays are bound to reemerge in their full importance for our culture. They show the complex relationship of human beings and the system under which they live and are part of; they explore the progressive mechanization of people in our technology-oriented age; and, perhaps most importantly, they put language itself on display and let us watch how language conceals as much as it reveals, how the word can become a tool of enlightenment or obfuscation. Although this may not sound like the stuff that good theater is made of, Havel's plays are highly theatrical, consistently amusing, yet challenging in their many-layered exploration of what it means to be a human being in today's world.

In the background of Havel's plays there always hovers a moral issue but is never pressed explicitly. It concerns, for example, the way ''politically correct'' language can absurdly lead to success (*Zahradní slavnost* [*The Garden Party*]), the talent to rationalize one's decisions even if they are dubious (*Protest*), the temptation to play ''dependable guy'' to two opposing sides (*Pokoušení* [*Temptation*]), the possible collaboration between guardians and opponents of the law (*Žebrárká opera* [*The Beggar's Opera*]), the nature of bureaucratic constellations (*Vyrozumění* [*The Memorandum*], *Asanace* [*Slum Clearance*], and others). The importance of Havel's dramatic exploration of language—reified and encased in frozen concepts that manipulate the characters' consciousness—cannot be overstated. Although these plays were written under the pressure of a coercive regime, they illuminate issues of topical importance in today's world in a depth that is likely to become increasingly apparent.

Havel's prose writings during the 1970s and 1980 taken abroad via various channels while their author was denied a voice in his own country, made a strong impact on international readership. Their titles speak for themselves: they deal with questions of conscience, conformity, power, culture, and again language as a molder of thought. Refreshingly free of jargon, they are candid and, under the circumstances, bold reflections on human beings and their lives under political pressure.

Since 1990 President Havel has given numerous speeches (invariably written by himself) all over the world. Again, intellectual openness, a sharp eye for the pitfalls of politics, pervasive tolerance, a strong sense of ethical values, and constant stress on human responsibility distinguish these speeches from what we have come to regard as the essential stuff of politics. The horizon of the speeches widens with time, and Havel explores the philosophical, scientific and cultural roots of various civilizations, all merging into the vast question of human identity. His is a significant voice for our times.

—Marketa Goetz-Stankiewicz

HEBBEL, (Christian) Friedrich

Born: Wesselburen, Holstein, Denmark (now Germany), 18 March 1813. **Education:** Educated in a dame's school, 1817–19; primary school, Wesselburen, 1819–25; in Hamburg a group of benefactors supported him in his studies, and helped send him to the University of Heidelberg, 1836; studied in Munich, 1836; returned to Hamburg, 1839; doctorate, University of Erlangen, 1844. **Family:** Married Christine Enghaus in 1846, two children; also had two sons (both died in infancy) by Elise Lensing. **Career:** Servant and clerk for local official, 1827–35; freelance writer in Munich, 1836–39, Hamburg, 1839–43; travel allowance from Christian VIII, King of Denmark, allowed him to live in Paris, 1843–44, and Rome, 1844–45; lived in Vienna from 1845; honorary court librarian, Weimar, 1863. **Awards:** Schiller prize, 1863. **Died:** 13 December 1863.

PUBLICATIONS

Collections

Sämtliche Werke, edited by Richard Maria Werner. 27 vols., 1904–22.
Werke, edited by Gerhard Fricke, Werner Keller, and Karl Pörnbacher. 5 vols., 1963–67.

Plays

Judith (produced 1840). 1840; as *Judith*, translated by Carl van Doren, 1914.
Genoveva (produced 1849). 1843.
Maria Magdalena (produced 1846). 1844; as *Maria Magdalena*, translated by Barker Fairley, in *Three Plays*, 1914; also translated by Carl Richard Mueller, 1962; Sarah Somekh, 1990.
Der Diamant (produced 1852). 1847.
Julia (produced 1903). 1848.

Herodes und Mariamne (produced 1849). 1850; as *Herod and Mariamne*, translated by L.H. Allen, in *Three Plays*, 1914.
Der Rubin (produced 1849). 1851.
Michel Angelo (produced 1861). 1851.
Ein Trauerspiel in Sizilien (produced 1907). 1851.
Agnes Bernauer (produced 1852). 1852; as *Agnes Bernauer*, translated by L. Pattee, in *Poet Lore*, 1909.
Gyges und sein Ring (produced 1889). 1856; as *Gyges and His Ring*, translated by L.H. Allen, in *Three Plays*, 1914.
Die Nibelungen (produced 1861). 2 vols., 1862; as *The Nibelungs*, translated by H. Goldberger, 1921.
Demetrius, from a play by Schiller (produced 1869). 1864.
Ein Steinwurf. 1883.
Three Plays (includes *Maria Magdalena; Herod and Mariamne; Gyges and His Ring*), translated by L.H. Allen and Barker Fairley, 1914.

Fiction

Schnock: Ein niederländisches Gemälde. 1850.
Erzählungen und Novellen. 1855.

Verse

Gedichte. 1842.
Neue Gedichte. 1848.
Gedichte. 1857.
Mutter und Kind. 1859.

Other

Mein Wort über das Drama! 1843; as "My View on the Drama," translated by Moody Campbell, 1922.
Über den Stil des Dramas. 1857.
Tagebücher, edited by F. Bamberg. 2 vols., 1885–87.
Neue Hebbel-Briefe, edited by Anni Meetz. 1963.
Der einsame Weg (diaries), edited by Klaus Geissler. 1966.
Briefe, edited by U. Henry Gerlach. 2 vols., 1975–78.

*

Bibliography: *Hebbel-Bibliographie 1910–1970* by Ulrich H. Gerlach, 1973; supplements: *1970–1980*, in *Hebbel-Jahrbuch*, 1983; *1981–1984*, in *Hebbel-Jahrbuch*, 1986.

Critical Studies: *Friedrich Hebbel as a Dramatic Artist* by G. Brychan Rees, 1930; *Hebbel: A Study of His Life and Work* by Edna Purdie, 1932; *Motivation in the Drama of Hebbel* by William F. Oechler, 1948; *Friedrich Hebbel's Conception of Movement in the Absolute and History*, 1952, and *Friedrich Hebbel*, 1968, both by Sten G. Flygt; *Hebbel as a Critic of His Own Works* by Ulrich H. Gerlach, 1972; *Hebbel's Prose Tragedies* by Mary Garland, 1973; *From Lessing to Hauptmann: Studies in German Drama* by Ladislaus Löb, 1974; *The Reception of Friedrich Hebbel in Germany in the Era of National Socialism* by William John Niven, 1984; *Studien zu Hebbels Tagebüchern* by Günter Häntzschel, Hg., 1994; *Hebbel, Mensch und Dichter im Werk: Sittlicher Revolutionär zur Zeitenwende*, edited by Ida Koller-Andorf and Gerda Benesch-Tschanett, 2000.

* * *

Poised between the fading beliefs of philosophical idealism and the positivism that came to replace them in the mid-19th century, Friedrich Hebbel sought for compromises between the literary approaches of German classicism and the new realism in European literature. While he also wrote stories, poems, and comedies, he is chiefly remembered today for a number of tragedies, based mostly on history or legend and inclining towards the "closed" dramatic form.

As a "poetic realist" who held that art should be both a record of empirical observation and a symbol of timeless truth, he defined drama as "the art of mixing the general and the specific so that the law all living things obey never appears naked and is never completely missed" ("Schiller und Körner"). It has been argued that his chief weakness derives from the fact that, despite his acutely realistic awareness of psychological and social determination within a framework of historical change, he resorts to metaphysical notions and orthodox techniques in an attempt to regain idealistic certainties and to elicit meaning from an existence which he feels to be meaningless. As Brecht put it: "Wherever German playwrights started thinking, like Hebbel and before him Schiller, they started contriving."

Suffering considerable poverty and humiliation before he achieved fame in his fifth and last decade, and inflicting pain on others—particularly on Elise Lensing, a seamstress who supported him for ten years and bore him two sons before he abandoned her to marry the celebrated actress Christine Enghaus—Hebbel was not an attractive personality. Dour and uncompromising, depressive and touchy, yet ruthless and domineering, bristling with the awkwardness of the self-taught and self-made, devoid of humour and beset by brooding pessimism, he maintained that "all life is a struggle of the individual against the universe" (Diaries, September 1840). Individuals, he explains in his treatise *Mein Wort über das Drama!* ("My View on the Drama"), are obliged by their very nature to incur the guilt—existential rather than moral—of self-assertion, for which they must be destroyed: the destruction occurs through strife with other individuals, although it serves the universal order which itself changes in the process. At times he finds solace in the assumption of the dialectical progress of the universe, but his main emphasis rests on human misery, and he suspects that even the divinity is subject to incongruity and impermanence. These views, which owe something to the unacknowledged influence of Hegel and Schelling, are at the centre of his world-picture and his theory of tragedy.

In all of Hebbel's major plays the clash of overbearing heroes and victimized heroines reflects both his personal experiences and his Kantian maxim, "To use a human being as a means to an end: the worst sin" (Diaries, May? 1839). However, although his greatest artistic asset is his understanding of the sado-masochistic battle of the sexes, which anticipates Ibsen and Strindberg, he often weakens the impact of his acute insights into emotional quandaries by imposing his transcendental theories on them. In *Judith*, the idea that the heroine, by killing her adversary Holofernes, will help replace universal idol-worship with monotheism forms an uneasy union with the intriguing exploration of a woman's confusion of her sense of divine mission and her personal revenge on a brutal lover. In *Herodes und Mariamne* (*Herod and Mariamne*) the advent of Christianity to supplant Judaeo-Roman despotism seems an inconsequential afterthought to the fascinating picture of possessiveness and resentment, devotion, hostility, and mutually incompatible desire in marriage, which destroy the heroine and leave the hero in lonely desolation. In *Gyges und sein Ring* (*Gyges and His Ring*) the king's pathological urge to exhibit the beauty of the Queen and her equally pathological modesty merge uncomfortably with the figurative reconciliation of tradition and reformation under their successor to the throne.

There are, however, two instances where Hebbel avoids abstruse speculation. In *Agnes Bernauer*, a historical tragedy set in the 15th century—in which a barber's daughter marries the son of a ruler, who has her assassinated to prevent a war of succession—his conservative proposition that the citizen must always be sacrificed to the state represents one of his rare political statements and may raise liberal objections, but his handling of the confrontation of love and politics links concrete human reality with abstract thought in a dramatically convincing manner. In *Maria Magdalena* any abstract thought that may be present is even more effectively transformed into tangible drama. Set in Hebbel's own time, this play—as he argues in his renowned preface—represents a significant innovation in the development of German domestic tragedy since Lessing and Schiller, by deriving the decisive conflict no longer from the opposition of the bourgeoisie and the aristocracy but from the prejudices of the petty bourgeoisie itself. The tragedy of the provincial joiner's daughter—who, on becoming pregnant, is driven to suicide by the desertion of her mercenary seducer and the threats of her bitterly puritanical father—combines the claustrophobically compelling portrayal of characters and circumstances with merciless social criticism to produce not only Hebbel's masterpiece, which Ibsen for one greatly admired, but one of the outstanding works of European realism as a whole.

At the level of dramatic structure, Hebbel's preference for classical methods is liable to prove inconsistent with his modern intuitions. At the level of language, he is most successful when writing contemporary prose, whereas his blank verse is prone to clumsiness, bombast, and anti-climax. At their worst, his plays are hysterical in atmosphere, extravagant in characterization, artificial in situation, and tortuous in argument. At their best, however, they powerfully convey the perplexities of an uncommon mind in an age of transition. Just as his personal egotism was the reverse side of his commitment to his calling, his art with all its harsh idiosyncrasies represents a remarkable document of the struggle of creativity against physical, mental, and social odds.

—Ladislaus Löb

See the essay on *Maria Magdalena*.

HEINE, Heinrich

Born: Harry Heine in Düsseldorf, Germany, probably 13 December 1797; baptized as protestant, Christian Johann Heinrieh Heine, 1825. **Education:** Educated in a dame's school for 2 years; Hebrew school; Catholic schools, 1804–14; business school, 1814–15; studied law at universities of Bonn, 1819–20, Göttingen, 1820–21, Berlin, 1821–24, Göttingen, 1824–25, doctor of law 1825. **Family:** Married Crescence Eugénie Mirat in 1841. **Career:** Apprenticed to a banking house and to a grocery dealer, Frankfurt, 1815; worked in his uncle Salomon's bank, Hamburg, 1816, and was set up in a cloth business, 1818–19; writer in Lüneberg and Hamburg, 1825–27; co-editor, *Neue Allgemeine Politische Annalen*, Munich, 1827–28; Italy, 1828; Hamburg and Berlin, 1829–31; in Paris from 1831: correspondent for Augsburg

Allgemeine Zeitung; ill after 1845, and bed-ridden after 1848. **Died:** 17 February 1856.

PUBLICATIONS

Collections

Sämtliche Werke, edited by Ernst Elster. 7 vols., 1887–90.
Works, translated by Charles Geoffrey Leland and others. 16 vols., 1905.
Sämtliche Schriften, edited by Klaus Briegleb and others. 7 vols., 1968–76.
Säkularausgabe: Werke, Briefwechsel, Lebenszeugnisse. 1970–.
Historisch-kritische Gesamtausgabe der Werke, edited by Manfred Windfuhr. 1973–.
Selected Works, translated by Helen M. Mustard and Max Knight. 1973.
Complete Poems, edited and translated by Hal Draper. 1982.
Selected Prose, edited and translated by Ritchie Robertson. 1993.
Songs of Love & Grief: A Bilingual Anthology in the Verse Forms of the Originals, translated by Walter W. Arndt, 1995.

Verse

Gedichte. 1822.
Tragödien nebst einem lyrischen Intermezzo (includes the plays *Almansor* and *William Ratcliff*). 1823.
Buch der Lieder. 1827; revised edition, 1844; as *Book of Songs*, translated by J.E. Wallis, 1856; also translated by Charles Godfrey Leland, 1864; Stratheir, 1882; Theodore Martin and E.A. Bowring, 1884; John Todhunter, 1907; R. Levy, 1909; Robert R. Garran, 1924.
Neue Gedichte. 1844; revised edition, 1851; as *New Poems*, 1910.
Deutschland: Ein Wintermärchen. 1844; as *Germany: A Winter's Tale*, translated by H. Salinger, 1944; as *Deutschland: A Winter's Tale*, translated by T.J. Reed, 1986; as *Deutschland, Deutschland: An Unsentimental Journey*, translated by Reed, 1987.
Atta Troll: Ein Sommernachtstraum. 1847; as *Atta Troll: A Midsummer Night's Dream*, translated by Thomas Selby Egan, in *Atta Troll and Other Poems*, 1876; also translated by Herman Scheffauer, 1913.
Romanzero. 1851; translated as *Romancero*, 1905.
Paradox and Poet: The Poems, translated by Louis Untermeyer. 1937.
The Lazarus Poems (bilingual edition), translated by Alistair Elliott. 1979.
Jewish Stories and Hebrew Melodies, translated by Charles Godfrey Leland, Frederic Ewen, and Hal Draper. 1987.

Other

Reisebilder (includes *Die Harzreise; Die Heimkehr; Die Nordsee; Ideen: Das Buch Le Grand; Reise von München nach Genua; Die Bäden von Lucca; Die Stadt Lucca, Englische Fragmente*). 4 vols., 1826–31; as *Pictures of Travel*, translated by Charles Godfrey Leland, 1855; also translated by Russell Davis Gilmann, 1907; as *Travel Pictures*, translated by F. Storr, 1887; as *The Italian Travel Sketches*, translated by Elizabeth A. Sharp, 1892; as *The Harz Journey*, translated by Charles G. Leland, 1995.
Französische Zustände. 1833; as *French Affairs*, 1889.

Zur Geschichte der neueren schönen Literatur in Deutschland. 1833; as *Die Romantische Schule,* 1836; as *The Romantic School,* translated by S.L. Fleishman, 1882.

Der Salon. 4 vols., 1834–40.

Shakespeares Mädchen und Frauen. 1839; as *Heine on Shakespeare,* translated by Ida Benecke, 1895.

Ludwig Börne: Eine Denkschrift. 1840; as *Ludwig Börne: Portrait of a Revolutionist,* translated by T.S. Egan, 1881.

Der Doktor Faust (ballet scenario). 1851; as *Doctor Faust: A Dance Poem,* translated by Basil Ashmore, 1952.

Vermischte Schriften (includes *Geständnisse, Lutezia*). 3 vols., 1854.

Memoiren und neugesammelte Gedichte, Prosa, und Briefe, edited by Eduard Engel. 1884; as *Memoirs,* translated by T.W. Evans, 1884; also translated by G. Cannon, 1910.

Works of Prose, edited by Hermann Kesten, translated by E.B. Ashton. 1943.

Poetry and Prose, edited by Frederic Ewen, translated by Ewen, Louis Untermeyer, and others. 1948.

Briefe, edited by Friedrich Hirth. 6 vols., 1950–51.

The Sword and the Flame (selected prose), edited by Alfred Werner. 1960.

Begegnungen mit Heine: Berichte der Zeitgenossen, edited by Michael Werner. 2 vols., 1973.

Poetry and Prose, edited by Jost Hermand and Robert C. Holub. 1982.

The Romantic School and Other Essays, edited by Jost Hermand and Robert C. Holub. 1985.

Heinrich Heine und die Musik: publizistische Arbeiten und poetische Reflexionen (selections), edited by Gerhard Müller. 1987.

*

Bibliography: *Heine in England and America: A Bibliographical Check-List* by Armin Arnold, 1959; *Heine-Bibliographie* by Gottfried Wilhelm and Eberhard Galley, 2 vols., 1960; supplement by Siegfried Seifert, 1968, and by Siegfried Seifert and Albina A. Volgina, 1986; *Heinrich Heine: A Selected Critical Bibliography of the Secondary Literature, 1956–1980* by Jeffrey L. Sammons, 1982; *Heine in der Musik: Bibliographie der Heine-Vertonungen* by Günter Metzner, 1989–.

Critical Studies: *Heinrich Heine: Paradox and the Poet, the Life* by Louis Untermeyer, 1937; *Judaic Lore in Heine* by Israel Tabak, 1948; *Heinrich Heine: An Interpretation* by Barker Fairley, 1954; *The English Legend of Heinrich Heine* by Sol Liptzin, 1954; *Heinrich Heine: A Biography* by Elizabeth M. Butler, 1956; *Heine: Two Studies of His Thought and Feeling,* 1956, and *The Early Love Poetry of Heinrich Heine: An Enquiry into Poetic Inspiration,* 1962, both by William Rose; *Heinrich Heine: The Artist in Revolt* by Max Brod, 1957; *Heine: Buch der Lieder,* 1960, *Heine, The Tragic Satirist: A Study of the Later Poetry 1827–1856,* 1962, *Heine's Shakespeare: A Study in Contexts,* 1970, *Heine's Jewish Comedy: A Study of His Portraits of Jews and Judaism,* 1983, *Coal-Smoke and Englishmen: A Study of Verbal Caricature in the Writings of Heinrich Heine,* 1984, and *Frankenstein's Island: England and the English in the Writings of Heinrich Heine,* 1986, all by S.S. Prawer; *Heine* by Laura Hofrichter, 1963; *The Exile of Gods: Interpretation of a Theme, a Theory and a Technique in the Work of Heinrich Heine* by A.I. Sandor, 1967; *Heinrich Heine, The Elusive Poet,* 1969, and *Heinrich Heine: A Modern Biography,* 1979, both by Jeffrey L. Sammons; *Heine: Poetry and Politics* by Nigel Reeves, 1974; *Heinrich Heine's Reisebilder: The Tendency of the Text and the Identity of the Age* by Edward A. Zlotkowski, 1980; *Heine's Reception of German Grecophilia* by Robert C. Holub, 1981; *Heinrich Heine* by Hanna Spencer, 1982; *Valiant Heart: A Biography of Heinrich Heine* by Philip Kossoff, 1983; *Exiles and Ironists: Essays on the Kinship of Heine and Laforgue* by Ursula Franklin, 1988; *Heine* by Ritchie Robertson, 1988; *Heine: Poetry in Context: A Study of Buch der Lieder* by Michael Perraudin, 1989; *Paintings on the Move: Heinrich Heine and the Visual Arts* edited by Susanne Zantop, 1989; *Heinrich Heine and the Occident: Multiple Identities, Multiple Receptions* edited by Peter Uwe Hohendahl and Sander L. Gilman, 1992; *The Jewish Reception of Heinrich Heine* edited by Mark H. Gelber, 1992; *The Poet Dying: Heinrich Heine's Last Years in Paris* by Ernst Pawel, 1995; *Virtuosity of the Nineteenth Century: Performing Music and Language in Heine, Liszt, and Baudelaire* by Susan Bernstein, 1998; *By the Rivers of Babylon: Heinrich Heine's Late Songs and Reflections* by Roger F. Cook, 1998; *Heinrich Heine's Contested Identities: Politics, Religion, and Nationalism in Nineteenth-Century Germany,* edited by Jost Hermand and Robert C. Holub, 1999; *The Poet as Provocateur: Heinrich Heine and His Critics* by George F. Peters, 2000.

* * *

Heinrich Heine is the most widely read or, perhaps one should say, *heard,* poet to have written in the German language. His poetry has been carried around the world, in his own phrase, ''on wings of song,'' in more than eight thousand musical settings. It can be difficult to apprehend the poetry accurately through all that music, which in some cases re-romanticizes and resentimentalizes it. For Heine had an exceptionally tense relationship to poetry, including his own. Through much of his career he was a more reactive than strikingly original poet. While he had a great lyrical gift, genuinely fuelled by an experience of unrequited love that became virtually archetypal for him, he doubted the relevance of poetry and its traditional materials in his politically and socially stressed post-Romantic environment. Thus, from within, he undermined the tradition with his bitterly accusatory tone directed toward the beloved, with abrasive irony and jarring stylistic dissonances, with ingenious dexterity and a visible manipulation of poetic devices that exposes them as fictions, ultimately with studied salaciousness and fiercely aggressive political verse. Not until *Romanzero* in 1851 did he find a genuinely original, mid-19th-century style, a bleak, ironically serious verse composed in the suffering of his ''mattress-grave.'' With all his misgivings, however, he regarded the poetic vocation as one of high dignity and by mid-life he had doubtless achieved his ambition to succeed Goethe as the major living poet in the German language.

With his prose *Reisebilder* (*Pictures of Travel*) beginning in the mid-1820s he developed greater originality of form. With sparkling wit, they weld together essay and fiction, imaginative autobiographical reminiscence and acute contemporary observation, high and low comedy and sardonic social criticism. Though he pretends to easy-going free association, as though setting down the first thing that came into his head, they are, like all of his writing, meticulously formulated and ordered. The comedy and wit, as always with Heine, have a seriously committed purpose. For he lived in gloomily repressive times and was determined to take up arms against the reactionary political order of the neo-feudal Metternichian system, under whose heavy-handed censorship he suffered unremittingly. He came to subsume political and cultural phenomena under a dichotomy of "spiritualism" versus "sensualism" or, in his later vocabulary, "Nazarenism" versus "Hellenism." What he perceived in the repressive order was a denial of gratification and plenitude, a reservation of aristocratic luxuries and erotic liberty to the privileged few, while the mass of people were kept in superstitious ignorance, compensated for their deprivation by promises of mythical joys in the other world. Since he regarded religion and especially Christianity as part of this conspiracy, he attacked religious institutions and Christian doctrine with an explicitness unparalleled in his generation.

Heine's at first voluntary, then involuntary exile in France beginning in 1831 was initially motivated by his interest in the Saint-Simonian movement, which for a time he thought congruent with his own vision of emancipation and sensualism. He reported on France in two series of newspaper articles in 1830–32 and 1840–43, published in book form as *Französische Zustände* (*French Affairs*), 1833 and *Lutezia*, 1854. He covers not only political and public events but also music, theatre, art, and the common life of the people. It was a report on the painting exhibition of 1831 that gave the title to a four-volume collection of essays, fiction, and poetry, *Der Salon*. At the same time he endeavoured to explain Germany to France in terms of a secret revolutionary doctrine of sensualism, in a book directed against Madame de Staël and bearing her title *De l'Allemagne*, it appeared in two parts in German, as *Zur Geschichte der Religion und Philosophie in Deutschland* [On the History of Religion and Philosophy in Germany] in *Salon II*, 1834, and *Die Romantische Schute* (*The Romantic School*), 1836. Heine's views, despite all their vigour and forthrightness, were complex and sometimes gave an impression of capriciousness because of his contradictory commitments. He insisted that he was a democrat, but the commanding figure of his heroic imagination was the conqueror Napoleon, and he sometimes claimed to be a monarchist; he championed the proletariat against the dominant order and yet feared a barbarian destruction of cultural and civilized values; and he turned against his liberal and radical contemporaries because he suspected them of nationalism, which he always strongly opposed, and of puritanical spiritualism. Thus in 1840 he greatly damaged his reputation with an ill-considered book directed against the deceased spokesman of the German dissidents, Ludwig Börne, and then exhibited the opposing vectors of his outlook in two contrasting mock-epic poems, *Atta Troll: Ein Sommernachtstraum* (*Atta Troll: A Midsummer Night's Dream*), which spoofs the radical poets of his time, and *Deutschland: Ein Wintermärchen* (*Germany: A Winter's Tale*), a tough satire on German conditions. The latter, considered the greatest of German political poems, was written during his months of friendship with the young Karl Marx and is the chief product of his most radical phase. With the collapse of his health into painful paralysis, he became more thoughtful and discouraged, and also underwent a religious reversal, though not abandoning his habits of irony, independence, and impudence. He occupied himself with his memoirs, a segment of which appeared as *Geständnisse* (*Confessions*) in 1854; the remainder was suppressed by his relatives, with whom he had had a violent public feud over his uncle's inheritance, and was not published until 28 years after his death.

Few writers of literature have had such an embattled reputation as Heine; he has been scorned by nationalists, conservatives, and anti-semites, and for a long time his reputation was stronger outside Germany. During the current era of his rehabilitation it is sometimes forgotten how much he was himself responsible for the hostility of his public and posterity; he scoffed at their cherished values and his career was often marked by ethical carelessness. But he lucidly drew into himself and exposed with ultimate sincerity the critical dilemmas of his time, and he stands as not only one of the wittiest but also one of the most penetrating writers in European letters.

—Jeffrey L. Sammons

See the essay on "The Homecoming."

HEINESEN, William

Born: Tórshavn, Faroe Islands (Danish Territory), 15 January 1900. **Education:** Educated at Copenhagen School of Commerce, 1916–19. **Family:** Married Elisa Johansen in 1932; three sons. **Career:** Journalist in Ringsted and Copenhagen, 1919–32, then settled in Tórshavn. Also musician and artist: chair, Faroese Museum of Fine Art, 1969. **Awards:** Nathansen prize, 1956; Holberg medal, 1960; Danish-Faroese Cultural Fund prize, 1962; Nordic Council prize, 1965; Scandinavian literary prize, 1965; Aarestrup medal, 1968. **Member:** Danish Academy, 1961. **Died:** 12 March 1991.

PUBLICATIONS

Fiction

Stjernerne vaagner [The Stars Awaken]. 1930.
Blæsende gry [Windswept Dawn]. 1934; revised edition, 1962.
Noatun. 1938; as *Niels Peter*, translated by Jan Noble, 1939.
Den sorte gryde. 1949; as *The Black Cauldron*, translated by W. Glyn Jones, 1992.
De fortabte spillemænd. 1950; as *The Lost Musicians*, translated by Erik J. Friis, 1971.
Moder syvstjerne. 1952; as *The Kingdom of the Earth*, translated by Hedin Brønner, 1974.
Det fortryllede lys [The Enchanted Light]. 1957.
Gamaliels besættelse [Gamaliel's Bewitchment]. 1960.
Det gode Håb. 1964; as *The Good Hope*, translated by John F. West, 1981.
Kur mod onde ånder [Cure Against Evil Spirits]. 1967.
Don Juan fra Tranhuset [Don Juan from the Blubber Works]. 1970.
Fortællinger fra Thorshavn [Stories from Tórshavn], edited by Erik Vagn Jensen. 1973.
Tårnet ved verdens ende. 1976; as *The Tower at the Edge of the World*, translated by Maja Jackson, 1981; also translated by Anne Born, 1982.
Her skal danses: Seks fortællinger [Let the Dance Go On: Six Stories]. 1980.
The Winged Darkness and Other Stories, translated by Hedin Brønner. 1983.
Laterna magica, nye erindringsnoveller. 1985; as *Laterna Magica*, translated by Tiina Nunnally, 1987.
Godaften måne, godaften min ven [Good Evening Moon, Good Evening My Friend]. 1989.

Verse

Arktiske elegier [Arctic Elegies]. 1921.
Høbjergning ved havet [Haymaking by the Sea]. 1924.
Sange mod vaardybet [Songs at the Spring Deep]. 1927.
Den dunkle sol [The Dark Sun]. 1936.
Digte i udvalg [Selected Poems], edited by Regin Dahl and Ole
    Wivel. 1955.
Hymne og harmsang [Hymn and Song of Indignation]. 1961.
Panorama med regnbue [Panorama with Rainbow]. 1972.
Arctis: Selected Poems, 1921–1972, translated by Anne Born. 1980.
Vinter-drøm: Digte i udvalg 1920–30 [Winter Dream: Selected
    Poems 1920–30]. 1983.
Samlede digte [Collected Poems]. 1985.

Plays

Ranafelli, in *Varthin*. 1929.

Other

Tann deiliga Havn [Fair Tórshavn], with John Davidsen. 1953.
Det dyrebare liv [Precious Life] (biography of J.F. Jacobsen). 1958.
*Færøerne, de magiske øer/Førayar, Gandaoyggjarnar/The Faroe
    Islands, The Magic Islands*, photographs by Gérard Franceschi.
    1971.
Editor, *Nýføroyskur skaldskapur*. 1930.
Editor, with H.A. Djurhuus, *Livet på Færøerne i billeder og tekst*.
    1950.

*

Bibliography: *William Heinesen—en bibliografi* by Mia Thorkenholdt
and Lars Øhlenschläger, 1984.

Critical Studies: ''*Noatun* and the Collective Novel,'' in *Scandina-vian Studies*, 42(3), 1969, ''William Heinesen and the Myth of Conflict,'' in *Scandinavica*, 9, 1970, *William Heinesen*, 1974, ''*Tårnet ved verdens ende*: A Restatement and an Extension,'' in *Scandina-vian Studies*, 50(1), 1978, ''Towards Totality: The Poetry of William Heinesen,'' in *World Literature Today*, 62(1), 1988, and ''Cultural Perspectives in the Late Work of William Heinesen,'' in *Grenzerfahrung—Grenzüberschreitung: Studien zu den Literaturen Skandinaviens und Deutschlands*, edited by Leonie Marx and Herbert Knust, 1989, all by W. Glyn Jones; *Three Faroese Novelists: An Appreciation of Jorgen-Frantz Jacobsen, William Heinesen and Hein Brú*, 1973, and ''William Heinesen: Faroese Voice—Danish Pen,'' in *American-Scandinavian Review*, 61(2), 1973, both by Hedin Brønner; *Godheds ubændige vælde: En lille bog om William Heinesen, Færøernes store danske digter* by Ejgil Søholm, 2000.

* * *

William Heinesen was one of the outstanding poets and novelists of Scandinavia in the 20th century, distinguished for the breadth of his imagination and for his linguistic and stylistic brilliance. After moving from his native Tórshavn to Copenhagen, he published exclusively lyric poetry in the 1920s, echoing the neo-Romantic and Symbolist poetry of the turn of the century, but clearly influenced by

Johannes V. Jensen, a writer who remained a major source of inspiration to him throughout his life. Originally elegiac and expressive of an awareness of the passage of time and the constant presence of death, the poems gradually develop a more optimistic and dynamic approach, though still bearing the traces of religious speculation caused by the death of the poet's brother in 1927. The 1930s saw a change, and Heinesen progressed to poems expressing political awareness, often painting satirical portraits of a society dominated by materialism and money. The later poems are often strikingly modernist in idiom, a mixture of the satirical and the more reflective youthful poetry.

Heinesen is, however, chiefly famed for his prose. His novel *Blæsende gry* [Windswept Dawn] was influenced by the Danish collective novel, but showed a greater interest in the individual personality than was usual in this genre. It was formless but powerful, and was completely recast for a second edition in 1962, in which the emphasis is moved from religious considerations to social questions. *Noatun* (*Niels Peter*) continued the collective genre, but towards the end of the 1940s Heinesen started on his major works, *Den sorte gryde* (*The Black Cauldron*), *De fortabte spillemænd* (*The Lost Musicians*), *Moder syvstjerne* (*The Kingdom of the Earth*), and *Det gode Håb* (*The Good Hope*). Here he moves from a more or less sober account into the realm of fantasy and imagination, reflecting on man's place in the universe, the confrontation of life and death forces, the role of woman as the vehicle of life, the mystery of the human psyche. *The Good Hope*, Heinesen's only historical novel, is an allegory of a fascist dictatorship as well as a penetrating study of human personality; full of conscious anachronisms and written in a language that smacks of the 17th century without any attempt to be authentic, it is considered by many to be Heinesen's masterpiece.

After this novel, which took 40 years to complete, Heinesen concentrated on the short story, in which he further explored the themes of his earlier years, though with increasing concentration on the mystery of human nature. His portraits of children are warm and sensitive, often humorous; in particular, he is fond of portraying puberty, revealing the incipient erotic instincts in children unaware of what is happening to them. In the volume of short stories *Her skal danses* [Let the Dance Go On], he adds to these themes a moving story centred on the cultic significance of the Faroese chain dance, a profound homage to life, with violent death as its background.

It is a matter of regret to many Faroese that Heinesen chose to write in Danish, thereby becoming as much identified with Danish literature as with Faroese. His works are nevertheless intensely Faroese, and uniquely he presents the Faroe Islands as a microcosm in such a way that they are immediately intelligible to the outsider with no previous knowledge of them whatever.

—W. Glyn Jones

HERLIANY, Dorothea Rosa

Born: Magelang, Central Java, 20 October 1963. **Education:** Elementary school and junior high school in Magelang; senior high school at the Stella Duce High School, Yogyakarta; graduated from the Faculty of Indonesian Language and Literature, Sanata Dharma Teachers College (now University), Yogyakarta, Central Java, 1987.

Family: Married, 1991, two daughters. **Career:** After graduation, worked for several years as a teacher and part-time journalist before becoming a freelance writer; currently resides in a small village near Magelang, Central Java, where she is a Director of IndonesiaTera, a publishing firm, which she established in 1998. IndonesiaTera also works in the areas of social and cultural research, and the development of information networks relating to culture, education and social awareness.

PUBLICATIONS

Verse

Nyanyian Gaduh. 1987.
Matahari yang Mengalir. 1990.
Kepompong Sunyi. 1993.
Nikah Ilalang. 1995.
Mimpi Gugur Daun Zaitun. 1999.
Kill the Radio: Sebuah Radio, Kumatikan. 2001; bilingual, with
    English translations and introduction by Harry Aveling.
Para Pembunuh Waktu, Sajak-sajak 1985–2000. 2002.

Fiction

Blencong. 1995.
Karikatur dan Sepotong Cinta. 1996.
Perempuan yang Menunggu. 2000.

* * *

In 1974, the Indonesian government launched a program for women which was designed to promote "community well being." The Family Welfare Guidance scheme proposed five principles for women's lives. Each woman was encouraged to (1) support her husband's career and duties; (2) bear children; (3) care for and raise the children; (4) be a good housekeeper; and (5) be a guardian of the community.

These conventional female roles of wife, mother, and moral exemplar, are the staple of most poetry written by Indonesian men about Indonesian women. At times, the woman on whom the poem focuses is simply described as "you," without a name, a distinct personality or any clear purpose. At other times, she is the subject of the male gaze; his words describe, direct, and—in a sense—even serve to create her. Sometimes masculine power is clearly expressed in this poetry without reservation. The extremely popular poem "Isteri" ("Wife," 1980), by Darmanto Yatman (1942–), using the persona of a simple farmer, describes a wife as necessary "to look after us / To sweep the yard / Cook in the kitchen / Wash at the well"; as well as to care for our children "the way we care for our hens, our ducks, the goat and the corn." The poem concludes: "Honor your wife / as you honor Dewi Sri, / goddess of the rice, / the source of your life. / Eat her, / for so it is written, / and you will be changed / forever."

The amount of contemporary poetry written in the Indonesian language by women is far less than that written by men. But on the whole, their work also supports these assumptions about the nature of women. Poets such as Selasih (1909–), Hamidah (1915–53), Walujati (1924–), S. Rukiah (1927–), Siti Nuraini (1931–), Isma Sawitri (1940–) and Poppy Hutagalung (1941–), deal with the joys and pains of love and marriage, the delights of motherhood, and the problems of diminishing physical beauty. Until the 1979 anthology *Seserpih Pinang Sepucuk Sirih* (*A Taste of Betel and Lime*, edited by Toeti Heraty), poetry by women has also tended to be under-represented in collections of Indonesian literature.

There are, however, a few women writers who have refused to accept these narrow prescriptions. One such is Toeti Heraty (1933–) herself. An academic and scholar, with graduate degrees from the Netherlands and Indonesia, a dominant image in her heavily ironic work is that of the mask, behind which people hide their true personality and feelings. In her work, Heraty seeks a man who will treat her as an equal, face her honestly and openly, instead of pretending to be "*manusia jantan, semacam dewa,*" a male, almost a god, who demands absolute control over his partner ("Pria," "Man," 1970). She has also regrets the almost deliberately self-destructive lack of intimacy between women. The poem "Wanita" ("Woman," 1967), laments: "how much affection throughout your life / is never expressed, is never enough, / because you don't care, can't be bothered / you bear your unhealed sorrow, / without ever realising it, without ever realising it." The cost of writing without dissimulation or ornamentation is, she admits in "Post scriptum" ("Postscript," 1995), almost impossible. "To do so," she confesses, "I would have to reveal myself / and hide / tell lies / and the truth."

Another non-conventional woman poet is the much younger Dorothea Rosa Herliany, a teacher who now manages a small press in Magelang, Central Java. Herliany began writing in 1985 and has now established herself one of the most important poets writing in Indonesia.

Her poetry shares little of Toeti Heraty's concern for self-concealment or hesitant reticence. "When I married you," the poem "Buku Harian Perkawinan" ["Wedding Diary," 2000] begins, "I never promised to be faithful." In fact, she continues, "you agreed to be my slave." The poem sees the marriage as a field of battle, on which the female narrator must surely triumph, conquering him and satisfying both their sexual hungers, hers first, then his through her active intervention. The sense that sexual intercourse is a field of struggle, of both pain and satisfaction, occurs in many of her other poems, sometimes even with a final gesture of castration towards the man who causes woman such suffering. "Nikah Pisau" ("Married to a Knife," 1992) ends with the graphic assertion: "I stab you in the heart and / tear off your prick / in my pain."

What makes Herliany's poetry so threatening is her simple inversion of the usual conventions of Indonesian society. It is the women who are aggressive and sexually predatory, it is the men who are passive victims and unable to protect themselves. These strategies are further reinforced by her use of dark images that she relates to the human body in various ways. Valleys and ravines, maggots, illness and decay, death and corruption, all feature strongly in much of her mature work.

Herliany also explores the realm of love outside marriage. Within the repressive attitudes of Indonesian society, however, the result of such adventures is guilt rather than personal liberation. "Surat Cinta" ("Love Letter") sets out confidently: "I decided on a pretty act of betrayal / when I left to satisfy a simple desire." It ends in frustration and anger: "awareness showed me too / how fierce disappointment can be." Significantly, in a number of poems addressed to various women, Herliany does find a comfort to which Heraty can only gesture in the poem "Woman."

Dorothea Rosa Herliany's willingness to explore all dimensions of human experience, through her emotions rather than through her intellect, gives her writing a graphic, often shocking quality, with which few other Indonesian writers can compare. As a still comparatively young writer, with an enormous potential yet to be developed, this poetry demands our ongoing attention.

—Harry Aveling

HERNÁNDEZ, José

Born: Pueyrredón (now part of San Martín), Argentina, 10 November 1834. **Education:** Educated to elementary level at the school of Don Pedro Sánchez, Barracas, 1841–45, **Family:** Married Carolina González del Solar in 1863; four daughters and one son. **Career:** Worked with his father, in Camarones and Laguna de los Padres, 1846–52; supported the Federalists against the Unitarians (joined the Federal Reform Party, 1855), and fought at the battles of Rincón de San Gregorio (1853) and El Tala (1854), then travelled to Paraña, capital of the Confederation of Argentina, to escape persecution in Buenos Aires; store assistant and judicial scribe, Paraná, 1856–58; stenographer for the Confederation Senate, 1859; appointed Second Official to the Confederation's government, 1859; fought at the battle of Cepeda, 1859; private secretary to President Juan Esteban Pedernera, 1860; received promotion to Captain, and fought at the battle of Pavón, 1861; secretary, Convention of Nogoyá, 1864; state attorney and secretary of the legislature, Corrientes, 1867–68; editor, *El Eco de Corrientes*, 1867–68; joined the resistance movement of Evaristo López Jordán, 1868: ministerial secretary under López, La Paz, 1868; co-founder, Club de los Libres, 1869; fought under Ricardo López Jordán against President Sarmiento at the battle of Ñaembé, 1871; lived in Buenos Aires, 1872–73; followed Jordán into exile into Montevideo, Uruguay (then part of Brazil), 1873–75; settled in Belgrano, following amnesty from the new President Avellaneda, 1875; deputy for the provincial legislature, 1879–80; vice-president, Chamber of Deputies, 1880; provincial senator, 1881–86; co-founder, national insurance company "La Previsora," 1884; board-member, Banco Hipotecario, from 1884. Also political journalist, including: contributor, *La Reforma Pacífica*, from 1856, and *El Argentino*, from 1863; editor, *El Nacional Argentino*, 1860, and *El Argentino*, 1863; founding editor, *Río de la Plata*, 1869–70, and *La Patria*, Montevideo, 1873–75. **Died:** 21 October 1886.

PUBLICATIONS

Verse

El gaucho Martín Fierro; La vuelta de Martín Fierro. 2 vols., 1872–79; edited by Eleuterio F. Tiscornia, 1925 (corrected by Santiago M. Lugones, 1926), Ramón Estrella Gutiérrez, 1953, José Edmundo Clemente, 1953, Augusto Raúl Cortázar, 1961, Jorge Becco, 1962, Walter Rela, 1963, Pilo Mayo, 1970, Luis Sáinz de Medrono, 1979, and Gisela Frechou and Mónica García, 1984; as *The Gaucho Martín Fierro*, translated and adapted by Walter Owen, 1935; also translated by Catherine E. Ward (bilingual edition), annotated by Frank G. Carrino and Alberto J. Carlos, 1967; as *Martín Fierro: The Argentine Gaucho Epic*, translated by Henry Alfred Holmes, 1948.
Los otros poemas. 1968.

Other

Rasgos biográficos del general Ángel V. Peñazola. 1863.
Vida del Chacho: rasgos biográficos del general Angel Vicente Peñaloza. 1863 (in magazine); 1947 (as book).
Instrucción del estanciero (cattle rancher's guide). 1882.
Las Malvinas (writings about Falkland Islands). 1982.

*

Bibliography: *Itinerario bibliográfico y hemerográfico del Martín Fierro* by José Carlos Maubé 1943; *José Hernández: Martín Fierro y su crítica* by Augusto Raúl Cortázar, 1960.

Critical Studies: *Martín Fierro: An Epic of the Argentine* by Henry Alfred Holmes, 1923; *La lengua de Martín Fierro* by Eluterio Tiscornia, 1930; *El poeta creador: Cómo hizo Hernández La vuelta de Martín Fierro* by Carlos Alberto Leumann, 1945; *Los motivos del Martín Fierro en la vida de José Hernández* by Pedro de Paoli, 1947; *El mito gaucho: Martín Fierro y el hombre argentino* by Carlos Astrada, 1948; *Muerte y transfigurarcíon de Martín Fierro* by Ezequiel Martínez Estrada, 1948, revised edition, 2 vols., 1958; *Martín Fierro* by Enrique Bianchi, 1952; *Prosas del Martín Fierro* by Antonio Pagés Larraya, 1952; *El Martín Fierro* by Jorge Luis Borges and Margarita Guerrero, 1953; *José Hernández: Periodista, político y poeta*, 1959, and *La vuelta de José Hernández*, 1973, both by Fermín Chávez; *La elaboración literaria del Martín Fierro*, 1960, and *Con el Martín Fierro*, 1968, both by Ángel Héctor Azeves; *Martín Fierro y La justicia social* by Eduardo B. Astesano, 1963; *El nombre, el pago y la frontera de Martin Fierro* by R. Darío Capdevila, 1967; *Arte y sentido del Martín Fierro* by John B. Hughes, 1970; *Valoración de Martín Fierro* by Héctor Adolfo Cordero, 1971; *José Hernández* by Noé Jitrik, 1971; *Genio y figura de José Hernández* by Roque Raúl Aragón, 1972; *Ida y vuelta de José Hernández* by Andrés Carretero, 1972; *Contenido histórico-social del Martín Fierro* by Néstor A. Fayo, 1972; *José Hernández* by Hialmar E. Gammalsson, 1972; *Tiempo y vida de José Hernández* by Horacio Zorraquín Becú, 1972; *Hernández: Poesiá y política* by Rodolfo Borello, 1973; *De las aguas profundas en el Martín Fierro* by Bernardo Cana-Feijóo, 1973; *La creación del Martín Fierro* by Emilio Carilla, 1973; *Hernandismo y martin-fierrismo* by Elías Giménez Vega and Julio González, 1975; *Prehistoria del Martín Fierro* by Olga Fernández Latour de Botas, 1977; *José Hernández y sus mundos* by Tulio Halperín Donghi, 1985; *José Hernández: Sus ideas políticas* by Enrique de Gandía, 1985; *Martín Fierro: Cien años de crítica* edited by José Isaacson, 1986; *Cuatro Versiones del Martín Fierro* by Alba Omil, 1994; *Las Vidas de José Hernández* by Beatriz Celina Doallo, 1995; *Concordancias del poema Martín Fierro* by Angela B. Dellepiane, 1995; *Tres arquetipos argentinos: Sarmiento, Hernández, Lugones* by César Rosales, 1999; *Las voces secretas del Martin Fierro* by Víctor Zenobi, 2000.

* * *

José Hernández was the last of a series of 19th-century Argentinian writers of gauchesque poetry: they were educated men who imitated in their works the idiom and naive style of the songs of the pampas cowboys. (The best known of the others are Bartolomé Hidalgo, Hilario de Ascasubi and Estanislao del Campo.) This genre tended to treat the gaucho as a figure of fun; Hernández, however, exalted the gaucho's virtues of courage, endurance, and honour, while also denouncing the abuses to which contemporary society subjected such men.

In travel literature, and in anthropological and sociological writing, the gauchos had frequently been described as ill-educated, workshy, violent, nomadic, and antisocial, and in the quarrel between Unitarians (Centralists) and Federalists which divided Argentinians for most of the 19th century, they were depicted by Unitarian writers as an obstacle to democracy and progress because of their support for the *caudillos*, men who had led their own armies in the Independence wars and became *de facto* political leaders in the power-vacuum left by the departure of the Spanish. In Domingo Sarmiento's *Life in the Argentine Republic in the Days of the Tyrants* not merely the cowboy, but cattle-ranching itself, is seen as barbaric.

Hernández's book, *Vida del Chacho* [The Life of El Chacho] is a polemical and uplifting portrait of the Federalist General Peñaloza, who had been killed by the Unitarians. Much of Hernández's writing took the form of political journalism. In 1869 he founded a newspaper, in which he published fierce attacks on several aspects of Sarmiento's government's policy, particularly the use of vagrancy laws to conscript gauchos forcibly into service in the wars against the natives.

Hernández's best-known work is his long narrative poem published in two parts, *El gaucho Martín Fierro* [The Gaucho Martín Fierro], 1872, entitled in some later editions *La ida de Martín Fierro* [Martín Fierro's Departure] and *La vuelta de Martín Fierro* [The Return of Martín Fierro], 1879. There are many humorous moments, but the prevailing tone of the first part of the poem is one of bitter moral indignation, and the contemporary audience would have recognized it immediately as a polemical work directed against the government of the day, although there are aspects of the poem that contradict or modify this political intention: for example, Martín Fierro often uses concepts such as "fate" or "luck" in commenting on his predicament.

In contrast to the humanitarian sentiments experienced in relation to the gaucho, the 20th-century reader may be struck by the expression of racist feelings in the poem. Martín Fierro, at one point, addresses racial insults to a black man. Fierro admits that he is drunk and feels like picking a fight, but in the course of the duel the black man offends against the gaucho fighting code by being the first to take out a knife, thereby restoring Martín Fierro's position as the man of honour. Italian and English immigrants are also portrayed unfavourably in the poem: Hernández thus expresses his opposition to Sarmiento's policy of encouraging European immigration as a means of reducing Argentina's dependence on the cattle industry and the cowboys. The portrayal of the native pampas Indians is more complex: Hernández's main aim, in the first part of the poem, is to criticize the conduct of the Indian wars. To this end, he depicts the natives as fierce warriors and excellent horsemen, that is, as formidable opponents who should have been countered with well-fed and well-equipped troops. He has no particular interest in depicting the natives negatively in any other respect, and in fact Fierro and his friend Cruz state confidently, at the end of this part of the poem, that the life they propose with the natives will be preferable to life under Sarmiento.

The first part of the poem proved immensely popular with both the educated audience and the gauchos it depicted. Two years after its publication, political circumstances changed in Argentina. President Avellaneda ushered in an era of national reconciliation and Hernández was elected to the Senate. *The Gaucho Martín Fierro* strikes a mellower note than the first part of the poem. Many critics, such as

Noé Jitrik, consider the second part inferior to the first: it is more consciously literary, seeking to tie up the loose ends of the story, yet the structure is more diffuse, for the sequel narrates not only the subsequent adventures of Fierro and Cruz (until the latter's death), but also those of Fierro's two sons, whom he re-encounters, and that of Cruz's son, Picardía. All are shown to have suffered misfortune, but the powerful moral anger of the first part seems to have been dissipated. The mood of national reconciliation is expressed in the final episode, in which Martín Fierro is confronted by the brother of the black man he had killed in part one. Instead of the expected duel with knives, they are persuaded to settle their differences by means of a *payada* or improvised singing contest. Martín Fierro wins, and the black man leaves, though still threatening that he may one day return and exact vengeance.

The mood of reconciliation does not extend to the natives. Hernández seems eager in this second part of the poem to establish the native peoples as the ethnic and religious enemy, depicting them as barbarous, cruel, and unfeeling, a vision that is at odds with the majority of the anthropological evidence. Ángel Héctor Azeves suggests in *La elaboración literaria del Martín Fierro* that Hernández drew on information supplied by an uncle who had published a study of the native peoples written from a military rather than an anthropological viewpoint.

The poem has been described by Santiago Lugones and others as the national epic of Argentina. While the term is perhaps not appropriate in its strict rhetorical sense, it may be considered apt in that the poem exalts the gauchos, who were instrumental in winning independence from Spain, and who made a vital contribution to the main economic activity of the nation—cattle-raising. Today the poem is familiar to all Argentinians.

—A. McDermott

See the essay on *The Gaucho Martín Fierro*.

HERODOTUS

Born: c. 490–84 BC. Possibly related to the ruling family of Halicarnassus, Asia Minor. **Career:** Moved to Samos during civil strife, c. 460 BC; travelled and lectured in Greece, including Athens, and settled in the Athenian colony of Thurii in south Italy (founded 444–43 BC); also travelled in south Italy, Egypt, the Near East and Babylon, Scythia and the Black Sea, and the north Aegean. **Died:** Probably before 420 BC.

PUBLICATIONS

Works

[History], edited by Carl Hude. 2 vols., 1927; also edited by P.E. Legrand, 11 vols., 1932–54; as *The History*, translated by George Rawlinson, 4 vols., 1858–60, this translation edited by A.W. Lawrence, 1935, and abridged by W.G. Forrest, 1966; also translated by A.D. Godley [Loeb Edition], 4 vols., 1920–24; Enoch Powell, 1949; Aubrey de Selincourt, 1954; H. Carter, 1962; David

Grene, 1987; translated in part by Walter Blanco and Jennifer Tolbert Roberts, 1992; as *The Histories*, translated by Robin Waterfield, 1998.

Selections, edited by Amy L. Barbour. 1985.

*

Critical Studies: *Commentary on Herodotus* by W.W. How and Joseph Wells, 2 vols., 1912, revised edition, 1928; *The World of Herodotus* by Aubrey de Selincourt, 1962; *Form and Thought in Herodotus* by H.R. Immerwahr, 1966; *Herodotus: An Interpretative Essay* by C.W. Fornara, 1971; *Herodotus, Father of History* by J.L. Myres, 1971; *The Histories of Herodotus: An Analysis of the Formal Structure* by H. Wood, 1972; *The Interrelation of Speech and Action in the Histories of Herodotus* by Paavo Hohti, 1976; *Herodotus and Greek History* by John Hart, 1982; *Past and Process in Herodotus and Thucydides* by Virginia J. Hunter, 1982; *Aspectual Usage of the Dynamic Infinitives in Herodotus* by Peter Stork, 1982; *Herodotean Narrative and Discourse* by Mabel Lang, 1984; *Herodotus: Persian Wars—A Companion to the Penguin Translation of Histories V–IX* edited by Stephen Usher, 1988; *Herodotus and His "Sources": Citation, Invention and Narrative Art* by Detlev Fehling, 1989; *Herodotus*, 1989, and *Give and Take in Herodotus*, 1991, both by John Gould; *Herodotus, Explorer of the Past* by J.A.S. Evans, 1991; *Heroes in Herodotus: The Interaction of Myth and History* by Elizabeth Vandiver, 1991; *Herodotus, The Histories: New Translation, Selection, Backgrounds, Commentaries* edited by Walter Blanco and Jennifer Tolbert Roberts, 1992; *The Malice of Herodotus* by Plutarch, translated by A.J. Bowen, 1992; *The Historical Method of Herodotus* by Donald Lateiner, 1992; *The Liar School of Herodotos* by W. Kendrick Pritchett, 1993; *The Relationship Between Herodotus' History and Primary History* by Sara Mandell and David Noel Freedman, 1993; *Word Order in Ancient Greek: A Pragmatic Account of Word Order Variation in Herodotus* by Helma Dik, 1995; *Discourses on the First Book of Herodotus* by James A. Arieti, 1995; *The Significant and the Insignificant: Five Studies in Herodotus' View of History* by J.E. van der Veen, 1996; *Herodotus and the Origins of the Political Community: Arion's Leap* by Norma Thompson, 1996; *The Tragedy in History: Herodotus and Deuteronomistic History* by Flemming A.J. Nielsen, 1997; *Herodotus* by James Romm, 1998; *Slaves, Warfare, and Ideology in the Greek Historians* by Peter Hunt, 1998; *Herodotean Inquiries* by Seth Benardete, 1999; *Herodotus in Context: Ethnography, Science and the Art of Persuasion* by Rosalind Thomas, 2000; *Divinity and History: The Religion of Herodotus* by Thomas Harrison, 2000; *The Historian's Craft in the Age of Herodotus*, edited by Nino Luraghi, 2001; *Telling Wonders: Ethnographic and Political Discourse in the Work of Herodotus* by Rosaria Vignolo Munson, 2001.

* * *

Herodotus is traditionally styled "Father of History," and rightly so—he invented it. There were before him a few local chronicles and geographical studies, which have entirely perished; no one had essayed a great and significant theme, nor assembled masses of material from diverse sources and organized them into a coherent whole. As there is no reason to think that those lost works were of any great literary merit, Herodotus is also entitled to be regarded as a pioneer of artistic prose composition.

Yet there is nothing primitive or unsophisticated about Herodotus. He aims to record for posterity the great deeds of men, and his chosen vehicle is the conflict between the Greeks and the Persians that reached its climax with Xerxes' defeat by the Greeks in 480–79 BC. His handling of that tremendous theme shows a remarkable sense of planning and design: the first half of the work is devoted to the rise of Persia to her greatest extent; the second, by a smoothly negotiated transition, to her wars against the Greeks. The story unfolds in no crude annalistic way: instead it proceeds by a mixture of narrative and digression. The digressions are sometimes little more than footnotes; equally often they are substantial chapters, carefully designed to explain the background to the main narrative, while spacing out its climactic points. Some of these are miniature narratives themselves; others are extended essays in ethnology or sociology, such as the full-length study of Egypt (Book II).

Herodotus understands the broad tides of history, making it clear that Persia's aggression was motivated by imperialist expansion; he is equally good on the grand strategy of the combatants in 480–79 BC—such non-narrative issues being conveyed through direct speech put into the mouths of his characters. He is noticeably weaker on detailed military tactics, however, and tends to personalize the causes of lesser events. He does not gloss over the failings of the Greeks at war—their occasional loss of nerve, the inter-allied bickerings; war itself he hates, despite the glorious exploits associated with it.

Accepting the Homeric picture of man's relationship with the gods, he emphasizes the role of oracles in Greek life, and often quotes oracular texts, many authentic, some spurious. His "theological" passages, such as the story of Xerxes' cabinet meeting (VII), teach the lesson that man cannot escape his destiny, and that the gods are envious of excessive prosperity in mortals. This pessimistic view informs his whole work, which is tinged with sadness and pity for human suffering; yet this is lightened by passages of irresistible sparkle and humour—Aristagoras' appeal to Sparta (V), "Hippocleides doesn't care" (VI), and dozens of others. His Greek is unmannered and effortless, resembling an educated man's friendly conversation.

Herodotus was a man of broad sympathies. His travels furnished him with a wide variety of oral sources, and enabled him to appreciate the "barbarian" point of view; but he was equally at home with the Athenian nobility, some of whose family history he records. His interests include poetry (he quotes from Pindar, Simonides, and many others), the visual arts, and medicine. But above all, he is concerned with humanity, and, like Homer, describes man's behaviour as he finds it: heroism, generosity, foresight, loyalty, vindictiveness, xenophobia, cowardice, treachery, corruption, paranoia, sacrilege—all these, and more, are exemplified many times over in his pages. But what sets Herodotus apart from most other ancient historians is his conviction that history is more than war, politics, and diplomacy. Today, students of social and cultural history can regard Herodotus as their truest ancestor.

—John Hart

HESIOD

Career: Lived c. 700 BC. According to the poet himself, he lived in Ascra in Boeotia (central Greece), and tended sheep on Mount

Helicon; won a tripod at the funeral games of Amphidamas in Chalcis; the story of his meeting and contest with Homer was probably a fictional account. **Died:** Said to have died in Locri or Orchomenus.

PUBLICATIONS

Collections

[Works], edited by Friedrich Solmsen, R. Merkelbach, and M.L. West. 1970; revised edition, 1983; translated by J. Mair, 1908; also translated by Hugh G. Evelyn-White [Loeb Edition; prose], 1936; also translated by Richmond Lattimore, 1959; Dorothea Wender, 1973; Apostolos N. Athanassakis, 1983; R.M. Frazer, 1983; selection as *The Essential Hesiod*, translated by C.J. Rowe, 1978; as *Works and Days; and Theogony*, translated by Stanley Lombardo, 1993; as *Hesiod's Works and Days*, translation with commentary by David W. Tandy and Walter C. Neale, 1996; also translated by David Grene, 1998.

Verse

Theogonia, edited by M.L. West (with commentary). 1966; edited and translated by Richard Caldwell, 1988; as *Theogony*, translated by Norman O. Brown (prose), 1953; also translated by M.L. West, with *Works and Days*, 1988.
Opera et dies, edited by M.L. West (with commentary). 1978; as *Works and Days*, translated by M.L. West, with *Theogony*, 1988.

*

Critical Studies: *Hesiod and Aeschylus* by Friedrich Solmsen, 1949; *The World of Hesiod: A Study of the Greek Middle Ages c. 900–700 BC* by A.R. Burn, 1966; *Hesiod and the Near East* by Peter Walcot, 1966; *The Language of Hesiod in Its Traditional Context* by G.P. Edwards, 1971; *The Winged Word: A Study in the Technique of Ancient Greek Oral Composition as Seen Principally Through Hesiod's "Works and Days"* by B. Peabody, 1975; *Hesiod and the Language of Poetry* by Pietro Pucci, 1976; *Hesiod and Parmenides* by M.E. Pelikaan-Engel, 1977; *The Hesiodic Catalogue of Women: Its Nature, Structure, and Origins* by M.L. West, 1985; *The Architecture of Hesiodic Poetry* by Richard Hamilton, 1988; *Hesiod* by Robert Lamberton, 1988; *Heat and Lust: Hesiod's Midsummer Festival Scene Revisited* by J.C.B. Petropoulos, 1994; *Greek Myths and Mesopotamia: Parallels and Influence in the Homeric Hymns and Hesiod* by Charles Penglase, 1994; *Hesiod and Aeschylus* by Friedrich Solmsen, 1995; *God and the Land: The Metaphysics of Farming in Hesiod and Vergil* by Stephanie A. Nelson, 1998; *Homer and Hesiod: Myth and Philosophy* by Richard Gotshalk, 2000.

*   *   *

Antiquity attributed a number of poems to Hesiod: besides *Theogonia* (*Theogony*) and *Opera et dies* (*Works and Days*), the only ones which are both nearly intact and probably genuine, there is a fragmentary *Catalogue of Women* (or *Eoiai*), a spurious *Shield of Herakles*, and some others of which we know little more than the titles.

The *Theogony* begins with a prayer-song celebrating the Muses, recounting their encounter with the poet on the foothills of Helicon, and invoking their power to fill him with true song. They start with a cosmogony. Chaos, the primal chasm, came first into being, then Earth, the Underworld, and Eros, sexual desire, the primal energy from which further creation flowed. Once he has established that primordial being is a unity, and material if also divine, the poet interests himself mainly in the emergence of the various gods, and the generations of their rulers. First in power were nature gods, Earth and Heaven; then came Cronus and the Titans, who ruled by force and violence; these were replaced by Zeus and the Olympians, the present regime, characterized by intelligence as well as power, and a deathless being which transcends nature. The shift in power from Earth and Sky is accomplished by a savage fulfilment of the Freudian Oedipal wish: the boy Cronus, at the instigation of his mother Earth, castrates his father Heaven and takes his throne. The triumph of Zeus over Cronus is different, a triumph of practical intelligence. Cronus is deceived by his mother Earth into swallowing a stone when he intended to devour his son Zeus. Zeus had the sense to free the spirits of lightning and thunder, who armed him with weapons to crush Cronus and the Titans, weapons he still uses. Mental agility will keep Zeus in power: warned that his first wife Metis (Intelligence) is to give birth to Athena, her father's equal in strength and wisdom, and a son destined to rule, Zeus swallows Metis and procures her power for himself: Athena is born from his head, and the son is never conceived.

A myth is needed to illustrate the quality of intelligence that rules the world, and Hesiod adapts *Prometheus*. The hero first tricks Zeus into granting humans the better share of sacrifices. Zeus does not undo, but rather compensates, by withholding fire from mortals. Prometheus steals the fire; again Zeus compensates, fashioning the first woman, regarded by Hesiod as a mixed blessing at best. Divine retribution is creative rather than destructive, a balancing which achieves a kind of justice.

If the cosmos began as a unity, it is a unity no longer: the transcendent has seemingly emerged from primal matter and become Olympian. But Olympus is not born, any more than it was present at the beginning: its becoming is as mysterious as its supernatural being. Though beyond nature, it is somehow above us; occasionally called Heaven, it is in fact a place beyond the sky. At the other pole lies Tartarus, the Underworld, where the defeated Titans dwell, along with Night, Sleep, and Death. Above Tartarus is a chasm, perhaps identical with primordial Chaos; then comes the natural world and the monsters "beyond the sea," such as the Gorgons, Echidna, and the defunct Medusa.

The *Theogony*'s suggestion of a close connection among Zeus, Earth, and Justice is developed into an elaborate theodicy in the *Works and Days*. The premises are, not unexpectedly, questionable; but the argument is highly rational. Zeus is a just god, who rewards the good and punishes the wicked. The good, in this Iron age of ours, are those who honour the goddess good Strife, competition; the wicked are worshippers of bad Strife—battle, disputation, and theft legal and illegal. Strife (Eris) is thus the energy of human purposes, just as Sexual Desire (Eros) is the energy of the *Theogony*. We all desire wealth, but it must be acquired justly, through good strife, or else the gods will destroy us, our offspring, our cities. And this means that we must work. It was not always thus: as the myths of Prometheus-Pandora and of the Decadence from the Golden Age reveal, Zeus has punished human arrogance by hiding our livelihood. But the life of hard work is not a mere avoidance of evil, rather a fulfilment of justice, an honourable response to the act of a just Zeus. Hesiod's paradigm for work is the life of the farmer, who struggles to be in harmony with Zeus, Heaven and Earth, divinities of Olympus and of Nature. This life is depicted in the imperative mood: "Now plough, now sow, now reap," a device which combines description with prudential—and moral—imperative. The poem ends with a superstitious Catalogue of Good and Bad Days for doing things, which many scholars have adjudged spurious. But the bulk of the poem is a well thought-out and logical vindication of a life of honourable competition in harmony with nature and a just God.

The style of Hesiod is the oral-epic style of Homer. Whether Hesiod utilized writing is not known, but he probably shaped and reshaped his poems for many years. Their final form is somewhat, but probably not radically, different from what we read. Catalogue poetry such as the *Theogony*, didactic verse such as the *Works and Days*, will have its wearisome moments for modern readers. But—to name only a sample—the opening portions of both poems, and the description of Zeus' battle with the Titans and of the Underworld in the *Theogony*, are exceedingly powerful reflections of apocalyptic inspiration.

—William Merritt Sale

HESSE, Hermann

Born: Calw, Württemberg, Germany, 2 July 1877. **Education:** Educated at Basle Mission; Rector Otto Bauer's latin school, Göppingen, 1890–91; Protestant Seminary, Maulbronn, 1891–92; Cannstatt Gymnasium, 1892–93. **Military Service:** Volunteer, as editor of books and magazines for prisoners of war in Switzerland during World War I. **Family:** Married 1) Marie Bernoulli in 1904 (divorced 1923), three sons; 2) Ruth Wenger in 1924 (divorced 1927); 3) Ninon Auslander Boldin in 1931. **Career:** Clock factory apprentice, Calw, 1894–95; apprentice, 1895–98, then assistant, 1898–99, Heckenhauer bookshop, Tübingen; worked for bookdealers in Basle, 1899–1903; freelance writer from 1903; editor, *März*, 1907–15; co-editor, *Vivos Voco*, 1919–20; also editor of publishers' book series in 1910s and 1920s; regular contributor to *Corona* and *Bonniers Litterära Magasin* in 1930s. Lived in Gaienhofen, Germany, 1904–12, near Berne, Switzerland, 1912–19, and Montagnola, Switzerland, 1919–62. **Awards:** Bauernfeldpreis (Vienna), 1904; Fontane prize (refused), 1919; Keller prize, 1936; Nobel prize for literature, 1946; Goethe prize, 1946; Raabe prize, 1950; German Book Trade Peace prize, 1955. Honorary doctorate: University of Berne, 1947. **Died:** 9 August 1962.

PUBLICATIONS

Collection

Werkausgabe, edited by Volker Michels. 12 vols., 1970; supplement, 2 vols., 1972.

Fiction

Peter Camenzind. 1904; as *Peter Camenzind*, translated by W.J. Strachan, 1961; also translated by Michael Roloff, 1969.

Unterm Rad. 1906; as *The Prodigy*, translated by W.J. Strachan, 1957; as *Beneath the Wheel*, translated by Michael Roloff, 1968.

Diesseits: Erzählungen. 1907; revised edition, 1930.

Nachbarn: Erzählungen. 1908.

Gertrud. 1910; as *Gertrude and I*, translated by Adèle Lewisohn, 1915; as *Gertrude*, translated by Hilda Rosner, 1955.

Umwege: Erzählungen. 1912.

Anton Schievelbeyns ohn-freywillige Reise nacher Ost-Indien. 1914.

Der Hausierer. 1914.

Rosshalde. 1914; as *Rosshalde*, translated by Ralph Manheim, 1970.

Knulp: Drei Geschichten aus dem Leben Knulps. 1915; as *Knulp: Three Tales from the Life of Knulp*, translated by Ralph Manheim, 1971.

Am Weg. 1915.

Schön ist die Jugend: Zwei Erzählungen. 1916.

Hans Dierlamms Lehrzeit. 1916.

Alte Geschichten: Zwei Erzählungen. 1918.

Zwei Märchen. 1919; revised edition, 1946, 1955; as *Strange News from Another Star and Other Tales*, translated by Denver Lindley, 1972.

Demian: Geschichte einer Jugend. 1919; as *Demian*, translated by N.H. Priday, 1923; translated by W.J. Strachan, 1958; also translated by Stanley Appelbaum, 2002.

Im Pressel'schen Gartenhaus. 1920.

Klingsors letzter Sommer: Erzählungen. 1920; as *Klingsor's Last Summer*, translated by Richard and Clara Winston, 1970.

Siddhartha: Eine indische Dichtung. 1922; as *Siddhartha*, translated by Hilda Rosner, 1951; as *Siddhartha: An Indian Tale*, translated by Joachim Neugroschel, 1999; translated by Stanley Appelbaum, 1999; also translated by Sherab Chödzin Kohn, 2000.

Psychologia balnearia; oder, Glossen eines Badener Kurgastes. 1924; as *Kurgast*, 1925.

Die Verlogung: Erzählungen. 1924.

Der Steppenwolf. 1927; as *Steppenwolf*, translated by Basil Creighton, 1929; revised edition by Joseph Mileck, 1963.

Narziss und Goldmund. 1930; as *Death and the Lover*, translated by Geoffrey Dunlop, 1932; as *Goldmund*, 1959; as *Narcissus and Goldmund*, translated by Ursule Molinaro, 1968, also translated by Leila Vennewitz, 1993.

Die Morgenlandfahrt. 1932; as *The Journey to the East*, translated by Hilda Rosner, 1956.

Kleine Welt: Erzählungen. 1933.

Fabulierbuch: Erzählungen. 1935.

Das Glasperlenspiel. 1943; as *Magister Ludi*, translated by Mervyn Savill, 1949; as *The Glass Bead Game*, translated by Richard and Clara Winston, 1969.

Der Pfirsichbaum und andere Erzählungen. 1945.

Traumfährte: Neue Erzählungen und Märchen. 1945.

Berthold: Ein Romanfragment. 1945.

Glück (collection). 1952.

Zwei jugendliche Erzählungen. 1957.

Freunde: Erzählungen. 1957.

Geheimnisse: Letzte Erzählungen. 1964.

Erwin. 1965.

Aus Kinderzeiten und andere Erzählungen. 1968.

Stories of Five Decades, edited by Theodore Ziolkowski, translated by Ralph Manheim. 1972.

Die Erzählungen. 2 vols., 1973.

Six Novels, with Other Stories and Essays. 1980.

Pictor's Metamorphoses and Other Fantasies, edited by Theodor Ziolowski, translated by Rika Lesser, 1982.

The Fairy Tales of Hermann Hesse, translated with introduction by Jack Zipes, 1995.

Verse

Romantische Lieder. 1899.

Hinterlassene Schriften und Gedichte von Hermann Lauscher. 1901; revised edition as *Hermann Lauscher*, 1907.

Gedichte. 1902.

Unterwegs. 1911.

Musik des Einsamen: Neue Gedichte. 1915.

Gedichte des Malers. 1920.

Ausgewählte Gedichte. 1921.

Trost der Nacht: Neue Gedichte. 1929.

Vom Baum des Lebens: Ausgewählte Gedichte. 1934.

Das Haus der Träume. 1936.

Stunden im Garten: Eine Idylle. 1936.

Neue Gedichte. 1937.

Die Gedichte. 1942.

Der Blütenzweig: Eine Auswahl aus den Gedichten. 1945.

Bericht an die Freunde: Letzte Gedichte. 1961.

Die späten Gedichte. 1963.

Poems, translated by James Wright. 1970.

Hours in the Garden and Other Poems, translated by Rika Lesser. 1979.

Other

Eine Stunde hinter Mitternacht. 1899.

Boccaccio. 1904.

Franz von Assisi. 1904.

Aus Indien: Aufzeichnungen von einer indische Reise. 1913.

Zum Sieg. 1915.

Brief ins Feld. 1916.

Zarathustras Wiederkehr: Ein Wort an die deutsche Jugend. 1919.

Kleiner Garten: Erlebnisse und Dichtungen. 1919.

Wanderung: Aufzeichnungen. 1920; as *Wandering: Notes and Sketches*, translated by James Wright, 1972.

Blick ins Chaos: Drei Aufsätze. 1920; as *In Sight of Chaos*, translated by Stephen Hudson, 1923.

Elf Aquarelle aus dem Tessin. 1921.

Sinclairs Notizbuch. 1923.

Erinnerung an Lektüre. 1925.

Bilderbuch: Schilderungen. 1926.

Die schwere Weg. 1927.

Die Nürnberger Reise. 1927.

Betrachtungen. 1928.

Krisis: Ein Stück Tagebuch. 1928: as *Crisis: Pages from a Diary*, translated by Ralph Manheim, 1975.

Eine Bibliothek der Weltliteratur. 1929; revised edition, 1957.

Zum Gedächtnis unseres Vaters, with Adele Hesse. 1930.

Gedenkblätter. 1937.

Aus der Kindheit der heiligen Franz von Assisi. 1938.

Der Novalis: Aus den Papieren eines Altmodischen. 1940.

Kleine Betrachtungen: Sechs Aufsätze. 1941.

Dank an Goethe. 1946.

Der Europäer. 1946.

Krieg und Frieden: Betrachtungen zu Krieg und Politik seit dem Jahr 1914. 1946; revised edition, 1949; as *If the War Goes On. . . : Reflections on War and Politics*, translated by Ralph Manheim, 1971.

Stufen der Menschwerdung. 1947.

Frühe Prosa. 1948.

Berg und See: Zwei Landschaftsstudien. 1948.

Gerbersau. 2 vols., 1949.

Aus vielen Jahren. 1949.

Späte Prosa. 1951.

Briefe. 1951; revised edition, 1959, 1964.

Eine Handvoll Briefe. 1951.

Gesammelte Dichtungen. 6 vols., 1952; enlarged edition as *Gesammelte Schriften*, 7 vols., 1957.

Über das Alter. 1954.

Briefe, with Romain Rolland. 1954.

Aquarelle aus dem Tessin. 1955.

Beschwörungen: Späte Prosa, neue Folge. 1955.

Abendwolken: Zwei Aufsätze. 1956.

Aus einem Tagebuch des Jahres 1920. 1960.

Aerzte: Ein paar Erinnerungen. 1963.

Prosa aus dem Nachlass, edited by Ninon Hesse. 1965.

Neue deutscher Bücher. 1965.

Kindheit und Jugend vor Neunzehnhundert, edited by Ninon Hesse. 1966.

Briefwechsel, with Thomas Mann, edited by Anni Carlsson. 1968; revised edition, 1975; also edited by Hans Wysling, 1984; as *The Hesse/Mann Letters: The Correspondence of Hermann Hesse and Thomas Mann, 1910–1955*, translated by Ralph Manheim, 1975.

Briefwechsel 1945–1959, with Peter Suhrkamp, edited by Siegfried Unseld. 1969.

Politische Betrachtungen. 1970.

Eine Literaturgeschichte in Rezensionen und Aufsätzen, edited by Volker Michels. 1970.

Beschreibung einer Landschaft. 1971.

Lektüre für Minuten, edited by Volker Michels. 1971; as *Reflections*, translated by Ralph Manheim, 1974.

Meine Glaube, edited by Siegfried Unseld. 1971; as *My Belief: Essays on Life and Art*, edited by Theodore Ziolkowski, translated by Denver Lindley and Ralph Manheim, 1974.

Zwei Autorenporträts in Briefen 1897 bis 1900: Hesse—Helene Voigt-Diederichs. 1971.

Eigensinn: Autobiographische Schriften, edited by Siegfried Unseld. 1972; as *Autobiographical Writings*, edited by Theodore Ziolkowski, translated by Denver Lindley, 1972.

Briefwechsel aus der Nähe, with Karl Kerenyi, edited by Magda Kerenyi. 1972.

Gesammelte Briefe, edited by Ursula and Volker Michels. 4 vols., 1972–86.

Die Kunst des Müssiggangs: Kurze Prosa aus dem Nachlass, edited by Volker Michels. 1973.

Hermann Hesse, R.J. Humm: Briefwechsel, edited by Ursula and Volker Michels. 1977.

Politik des Gewissens: die politische Schriften 1914–1932, edited by Volker Michels. 2 vols., 1977.

Die Welt im Buch, edited by Volker Michels. 1977.

Briefwechsel mit Heinrich Wiegand, 1924–1934, edited by Klaus Pezold. 1978.

Hermann Hesse/Hans Sturzenegger: Briefwechsel, edited by Kurt Bächtold. 1984.

Bodensee: Betrachungen, Erzählungen, Gedichte, edited by Volker Michels. 1986.

Soul of the Age: The Selected Letters, 1891–1962, edited by Theodore Ziolkowski. 1991.

Editor, with others, *Der Lindenbaum, deutsche Volkslieder.* 1910.

Editor, *Der Zauberbrunnen.* 1913.

Editor, *Der Wandsbecker Bote*, by Matthias Claudias. 1916.

Editor, *Alemannenbuch.* 1919.

Editor, with Walter Stich, *Ein Schwabenbuch für die deutschen Kriegsgefangenen.* 1919.

Editor, *Ein Luzerner Junker vor hundert Jahren*, by Xaver Schnyder von Wartensee. 1920.

Editor, *Dichtungen*, by Solomon Gessner. 1922.

Editor, *Mordprozesse.* 1922.

Editor, *Novellino.* 1922.

Editor, with Karl Isenberg, *Novalis: Dokumente seines Lebens und Sterbens.* 1925.

Editor, with Karl Isenburg, *Hölderlin: Dokumente seines Lebens.* 1925.

Editor, *Geschichten aus dem Mittelalter.* 1925.

Editor, *Sesam: Orientalische Erzählungen.* 1925.

*

Bibliography:: *Hermann-Hesse-Bibliographie* by M. Pfeifer, 1973; *Hermann Hesse: Biography and Bibliography* by Joseph Mileck, 2 vols., 1977.

Critical Studies:: *Faith from the Abyss: Hermann Hesse's Way from Romanticism to Modernity* by Ernst Rose, 1965; *The Novels of Hermann Hesse*, 1965, and *Hesse*, 1966, both by Theodore Ziolkowski, and *Hesse: A Collection of Critical Essays* edited by Ziolkowski, 1973; *Hermann Hesse: His Mind and Art* by Mark Boulby, 1967; *Hermann Hesse* by G.W Field, 1970; *Hesse: An Illustrated Biography* by Bernhard Zeller, 1971; *Hermann Hesse* by Edwin F. Casebeer, 1972; *Hesse's Futuristic Idealism* by Roger C. Norton, 1973; *Hermann Hesse, The Man Who Sought and Found Himself* by Walter Sorrell, 1974; *Hesse: A Pictorial Biography* by Volker Michels, translated by Theodore and Yetta Ziolkowski, 1975; *Hermann Hesse: A Collection of Criticism* edited by Judith Lieberman, 1977; *Hermann Hesse: Life and Art* by Joseph Mileck, 1978; *Hermann Hesse's Fictions of the Self: Autobiography and the Confessional Imagination* by Eugene L. Stelzig, 1978; *Hermann Hesse's Quest: The Evolution of the Dichter Figure in His Work* by Kurt J. Fickert, 1978; *Hermann Hesse: Pilgrim of Crisis: A Biography* by Ralph Freedman, 1979; *Hermann Hesse's Das Glasperlenspiel: A Concealed Defense of the Mother World* by Edmund Ray, 1983; *Hermann Hesse: Politische und wirkungsgechichtliche Aspekte* edited by Sigrid Bauschinger and Albert Reh, 1986; *The Hero's Quest for the Self: An Archetypal Approach to Hesse's Demian and Other Novels* by David G. Richards, 1987; *The Ideal of Heimat in the Works of Hermann Hesse* by Andreas Kiryakakis, 1988; *A Poet or Nothing At All: The Tübingen and Basel Years of Hermann Hesse* by Richard C. Helt, 1996; *Exploring the Divided Self: Hermann Hesse's Steppenwolf and Its Critics* by David G. Richards, 1996; *Understanding Hermann Hesse: The Man, His Myth, His Metaphor* by Lewis W. Tusken, 1998.

* * *

Hermann Hesse's work has its roots in many areas of culture, especially German romanticism, Eastern religious thought, Nietzschean philosophy, and Jungian psychoanalytic theory. It has always appealed particularly to the young because of its recurrent stress—already perhaps implied in these sources—on breaking barriers, on the individual's need to emancipate itself from all ties and follow its own star. His first major work was the novel *Demian*, which attained widespread popularity as one of the earliest texts to deal sympathetically with adolescence. Here Hesse strikingly—if perhaps over-eclectically—combines new interpretations of Old Testament and gnostic symbolism with Jungian motifs to trace the moral and spiritual emancipation of his typical hero: the man who learns how to put comforting bourgeois security behind him, to accept fully the unconventional, even amoral, complexity of his soul and thus gain control of his own destiny. A heady optimism attaches to his ''rebirth,'' expressed through images redolent both of a Jungian journey into the Collective Unconscious and a Nietzschean Will to Power. However, this elated confidence becomes tempered over the years in Hesse's subsequent works.

This is already the case in *Siddhartha*, another stylized but gentler picture of the search for self. The text has the simplified form of an Eastern myth, and the new idiom indicates a new depth of understanding: the goal of self-overcoming may be attainable but the search is lifelong, and culminates not in redirected activity but rather in changed vision, in the hard-won capacity to embrace all oppositions intellectually and emotionally, to cease thinking ''exclusively.'' The most remarkable aspect of this novel is its beautifully sustained imagery and simplicity of style. It is here that Hesse first shows himself a master of the German language: it flows with wonderful euphony, and elsewhere—as in *Klingsors letzter Sommer* (*Klingsor's Last Summer*)—can attain a splendidly rich sensuousness.

Hesse's next major work, *Der Steppenwolf* (*Steppenwolf*), is perhaps his best-known novel and one that bears clear autobiographical reference to its author's at times tortured middle years. Far removed from the archetypal serenity of *Siddhartha*, it is a remarkable, graphic portrayal of unresolved personal problems. Hesse captures the agonizing simultaneity of violent oppositions in one and the same personality, for whom life becomes a battle between the longing for simple security and the painful awareness of inner division and self-hatred. Where in earlier works the less ''acceptable'' aspects of personality are portrayed fairly conventionally as sensuality or Nietzschean will-power, here the depths of degradation are plumbed with ruthless honesty, from aggressive sexuality to bestial destructiveness. The same honesty extends to the social setting; through Harry Haller's alienation we see something of the disturbing mix of jingoism, complacency, and self-gratification of the inter-war years. Yet despite Haller's agony, there are intimations of how this deep sense of dislocation, both internal and external, might be overcome by sublime acceptance, for which the ''Immortals''—great artists such as Goethe and Mozart—stand as models. Haller must learn like them to turn life itself into art; if he can abandon not only conventional moral disapprobation but all rational categorization and embrace discreteness, he might rewrite the whole concept of identity, learning to see personality no longer as circumscribed unity but as infinite, capable of embracing all experience as part of the potential self. This theme has interesting aesthetic consequences in the text, which no longer seeks to tell a sequentially developing, finite story, but rather to create a sense of simultaneity and openness via a structure reminiscent of a musical theme and variations, or of a series of interrelated mirrors—an explicit leitmotif in the text. Above all Hesse succeeds in blurring the distinction between internal and external action, dream and actuality. The whole text is both multivalent and "unfinished"; it has echoes—more subtly handled than in *Demian*—of romanticism, Freudian and Jungian analysis, Zen Buddhism, which undercut but never destroy the level of social realism and thus create a fluid view of personality as multidimensional. So too does the fact that no one part of the text has an objective narrative source, and thus the reader also is detached from inherited models of character definition and textual interpretation. The linguistic problems involved in attempting to present simultaneity in epic form are returned to explicitly in *Kurgast*.

Surprisingly, Hesse's next novel *Narziss und Goldmund* (*Narcissus and Goldmund*) lacks all such complexity and manifests a return to much more basic narrative skills. Set in medieval times, it tells a broadly allegorical tale about the inescapable responsibility of individual self-discovery. Two friends, one a sensuous artist and the other an ascetic intellectual, gradually both learn that the road to defining one's own personal truth is long; as in earlier texts, Hesse shows that friends may act as valuable mentors but can never release the individual from the journey towards selfhood that encompasses both pain and joy. While charming in its narrative simplicity, it lacks conviction at a deeper level, especially when compared with Hesse's great work *Das Glasperlenspiel* (*The Glass Bead Game*). Set in a post-20th-century future, this summation of all his inspiration from Goethe to the Orient projects the theme of personal multiplicity onto a cultural plane, and explores the grandiose possibility of harmonizing all knowledge, as an antidote to what Hesse sees as the dangerous cultural and spiritual narrowness of our century. Yet the text offers no final answers and raises many profound questions about the relationship between intellect and practical activity, harmony and extremism, culture and barbarism, stasis and progress. Like his central figure Josef Knecht, Hesse remained self-questioning until the end.

In addition to these major works Hesse produced many short stories, autobiographical sketches, and essays of great delicacy and perceptive insight both into himself and his age. His poetry, while lacking the originality of his prose, still has the power to charm by its romantic sensitivity to nature and inwardness of imagery. Some of it has indeed been set to music, notably by Richard Strauss (*Four Last Songs*).

—Mary E. Stewart

See the essays on *The Glass Bead Game*, *Siddhartha*, and *Steppenwolf*.

HOCHWÄLDER, Fritz

Born: Vienna, Austria, 28 May 1911. **Education:** Educated at Reform-Realgymnasium, Vienna, and in evening classes at the Volkshochshule. **Family:** Married 1) Ursula Büchi in 1951 (divorced 1957); 2) Susanne Schreiner in 1960, one daughter. **Career:** Apprentice upholsterer in Vienna; moved to Switzerland in 1938 to escape the Nazi regime; lived in refugee camps in Switzerland, 1938–42; freelance writer in Zurich, from 1945. **Awards:** Vienna prize, 1955, and Ehrenring, 1972; Grillparzer prize, 1956; Wildgans prize, 1963; Austrian State prize, 1966; Austrian Ehrenkreuz für Kunst und Wissenschaft, 1971. Named Professor by Austrian government, 1963. **Died:** 20 October 1986.

PUBLICATIONS

Plays

Jehr (produced 1933).
Liebe in Florenz; oder, Die unziemliche Neugier (produced 1936).
Das heilige Experiment (produced 1943). 1947; as *The Strong Are Lonely*, translated by Eva Le Galienen, 1954; as *The Holy Experiment* (televised 1985); also translated by Todd C. Hanlin and Heidi Hutchinson in *Holy Experiment and Other Plays*, 1998.
Der Flüchtling, from a work by Georg Kaiser (produced 1945). 1954.
Hotel du commerce (produced 1946). 1954.
Meier Helmbrecht (produced 1947). 1956.
Der öffentliche Ankläger (produced 1948). 1954; as *The Public Prosecutor*, translated by Kitty Black, 1958; and in *The Public Prosecutor and Other Plays*, 1980.
Der Unschuldige (produced 1958). Privately printed, 1949; 1958.
Virginia (produced 1951).
Donadieu (produced 1953). 1953.
Die Herberge (produced 1957). 1956; as *The Inn* (produced 1962).
Donnerstag (produced 1959). In *Dramen*, 1, 1959.
Dramen. 2 vols., 1959–64.
Esther. 1960.
1003 (produced 1964). In *Dramen*, 2, 1964.
Der Himbeerpflücker (televised 1965; produced 1965). 1965; as *The Raspberry Picker*, translated by Michael Bullock, in *The Public Prosecutor and Other Plays*, 1980.
Der Befehl (televised 1967; produced 1968). 1967; as *The Order*, in *Modern International Drama*, 3(2), 1970.
Dramen. 1968.
Dramen. 4 vols., 1975–85.
Lazaretti; oder, Der Säbeltiger (produced 1975). 1975; as *Lazaretti; or, the Saber-Toothed Tiger*, translated by James Schmittin, in *The Public Prosecutor and Other Plays*, 1980.
The Public Prosecutor and Other Plays (includes *The Raspberry Picker; The Public Prosecutor; The Strong Are Lonely; Lazaretti; or, the Saber-Toothed Tiger*), edited by Martin Esslin. 1980.
Die Prinzessin von Chimay. 1982.
Der verschwundene Mond. 1985.
Die Burgschaft. 1985.

Radio Plays: *Der Reigen*, from the play by Arthur Schnitzler; *Weinsberger Ostern 1525*, 1939.

Television Plays: *Der Himbeerpflücker*, 1965; *Der Befehl*, 1967.

Other

Im Wechsel der Zeit: Autobiographische Skizzen und Essays. 1980.

*

Bibliography: Fritz Hochwälder Bibliography' by James Schmitt, in *Modern Austrian Literature*, 11(1), 1978.

Critical Studies: *The Theater of Protest and Paradox: Developments in the Avant-Garde Drama* edited by George E. Wellwarth, 1964; "Tradition and Experiment in the Work of Fritz Hochwälder" by Anthony J. Harper, in *New German Studies*, 5, 1977; "The Theatre of Fritz Hochwälder: Its Background and Development" by James Schmitt, in *Modern Austrian Literature*, 11(1), 1978; *Der Dramatiker*

Hochwälder by Wilhelm Bortenschlager, 1979; "Fritz Hochwälder's Range of Theme and Form" by Donald G. Daviau, in *Austrian Literature*, 18(2), 1985; "The Classical Theater-of-Illusion Modernized: The Conflicting Messages of the Moral Imperative in Fritz Hochwälder's Drama *Das heilige Experiment*" by Edward R. McDonald, in *Maske und Kothurn*, 31, 1985.

* * *

In the years following World War II Fritz Hochwälder's plays were at the forefront of German-speaking and indeed European drama, challenging the audience to come to terms with the recent past.

Hochwälder saw himself as part of the vigorous tradition of Viennese folk theatre, revitalized in the 1930s by Ödön von Horváth. When the angry young men of the Austrian theatre announced in the 1960s that "Grandpa's theatre is dead," Hochwälder's reply was characteristically tart: no one had ever fallen asleep in any of *his* plays! Throughout his career his works relied on the characteristic devices of the *Volksstück*, stock characters, unexpected twists to the story line, cases of mistaken identity, and a nice turn to the dialogue with moments of unexpected comedy to lighten the mood.

Above all, however, Hochwälder was a moralist and the light touch of his pen never disguised the fact that he was dealing with serious issues. It would be surprising were this not so. A Jew forced into exile and living through the Europe of the Third Reich could not but be affected. Behind the costume drama lies a grim political and moral reality. The fact that his plays move, over the years, from historical pieces (*Das heilige Experiment* [The Strong Are Lonely], *Der öffentliche Ankläger* [The Public Prosecutor], to allegory (*Donnerstag, 1003, Die Herberge* [The Inn]), to works dealing with the second half of the 20th century (*Der Himbeerpflücker* [The Raspberry Picker], *Der Befehl* [The Order]), reflects the innate Austrianism in his soul. The Austrian tradition shies away from immediacy, preferring to depict the present from the safer, apparently objective context of history and costume drama; the first National Socialist to appear explicitly as such in Hochwälder's work does not walk on stage until the mid 1960s, by when, of course, Nazi uniforms have begun to become historical pieces in their own right.

Behind the surface Hochwälder probes deep into the psyche of his protagonists and emerges with a picture of hell. Hochwälder's hell is knowledge of the inner self, gained at the cost of considerable personal pain. There is much of *Oedipus Rex* in Hochwälder's work. A characteristic example is the mild-mannered Dutch police inspector in *The Order*, given the task of hunting down the perpetrator of a brutal war crime and child murder by a military policeman in occupied Holland. As he penetrates the past, the inspector unravels his own repressed subconscious until he is forced to realize that he is the brutal war monster he is seeking.

Power versus justice, the demands of the ideal set against the limitations of reality: these are the axes of Hochwälder's plays. Jesuit black in Latin America, although an apparent world away from the Gestapo black of Europe, is used by Hochwälder to show the danger of unquestioning acceptance of a cause (however noble). Read as a study of the evil of individual reliance on external support and the seductive appeal of "Order," *The Strong Are Lonely* regains much of the relevance many would today deny the work. The shadow of the Gestapo is equally apparent behind the Terror of revolutionary France in *The Public Prosecutor*. The public prosecutor's relentless commitment to the Thermidor government is used by his opponents to engineer his self-destruction.

Hochwälder does not make his public prosecutor a monster; he shows him as a man with feelings who would like to be humane but who has fallen victim to the machine he serves. The true tragedy in both plays is that of the individual lost in the morass of a system where individualism has no place. Hochwälder's virtual disappearance from the theatrical scene in recent years does him scant justice. It is difficult to believe that the European stage can afford to ignore *The Strong Are Lonely* and *The Public Prosecutor*. He himself felt he would be remembered for these two and, and, surprisingly, *The Inn*, an allegory on the theme of justice which offers this profoundly pessimistic thought: "Only one thing protects us from our neighbours—and that is order. There is no such thing as justice, we have to make do with order."

Towards the end of his career Hochwälder ran out of creative steam. Both *Lazaretti* and *Die Prinzessin von Chimay* [The Princess of Chimay] lack the bite of his earlier works. The *Prinzessin* is a tired attempt to take forward the threads of *The Public Prosecutor*, and *Lazaretti* has been described as an old man's play for old men.

Hochwälder's more allegorical plays continue the theme of security and individual responsibility. In *Donnerstag*, a modern mystery play, an architect, Niklaus Pomfrit, sells his soul to Belial Incorporated in order to gain understanding of the meaning of the world; in *1003* (with clear echoes from *Don Giovanni*) he has become invincible and invulnerable: "He's like the man in the fairytale: his heart has frozen solid."

What is attainable in allegory is impossible in reality, and the plays in a contemporary setting explore the legacy of the National Socialist security that has been so cruelly dashed from its adherents' grasp. *The Raspberry Picker*, a mischievously malicious farce, neatly pillories the capacity for self-deception and collective amnesia of a group of former Nazis in post-war Austria. Hochwälder milks the device of mistaken identity to good effect as his characters erroneously identify a petty criminal as a former SS official come back to claim his share of war-loot. The discrepancy between the pathetic figure the criminal cuts on stage and the grandiose past he is supposed to embody is not lost on the audience who are in possession of both sides of the story and can draw their own conclusions.

Much of what Hochwälder wrote has a particularly Austrian timbre and loses much in translation. Best approached with an awareness of the social and political context in which he wrote, his dramatic work, like that of Friedrich Schiller before him, uses the theatre as a moral institution to expose and challenge the great and petty tyrannies of life that could otherwise not be brought to book.

—Alan Best

HØEG, Peter

Also known as Peter Hoeg. **Born:** Copenhagen, Denmark, 17 May 1957. **Education:** Graduated from Frederiksberg Gymnasium, 1976; studied literary theory, University of Copenhagen, M.A. 1984. **Family:** Married Kenyan dancer Akinyi, late 1980s; two daughters. **Career:** Full-time writer, since the late 1980s; in the late 1970s and early 1980s he alternately worked as a crewman on yachts, danced with the Royal Danish Ballet, fenced professionally, and acted in the theater in Paris and Sweden; taught acting in a high school in Odense and at the University of Odense in Denmark, 1984; started the Lolwe

Foundation to aid poor mothers and children in developing nations, 1996. Lives in Denmark. **Awards:** De Gyldne Laurbar (Golden Laurel) award for Danish literature, 1994.

PUBLICATIONS

Fiction

Forestilling om det tyvende århundrede. 1988; as *The History of Danish Dreams*, translated by Barbara Haveland, 1995.
Fortallinger om natten. 1990; as *Tales of the Night*, translated by Barbara Haveland, 1997.
Frøken Smillas fornemmelse for sne. 1992; as *Smilla's Sense of Snow*, translated by Tiina Nunnally, 1993; as *Miss Smilla's Feeling for Snow*, translated by F. David, 1993.
De måske egnede. 1993; as *Borderliners*, translated by Barbara Haveland, 1994.
Kvinden og aben. 1996; as *The Woman and the Ape*, translated by Barbara Haveland, 1996.

Other

Preface, *Point of View*, photographs by Henrik Saxgren. 1998.

*

Bibliography: Entry in *Danske digtere i det 20. århundrede* by Per Stounbjerg, 3 vols., 2000–2002.

Critical Studies: "Strangers in Paradise" by Nader Mousavizadeh, in *New Republic*, no. 212, 1993; "Fleeing Literary Limelight for Calm Obscurity" (interview) by Sarah Lyall, in *New York Times*, 6 October 1993; "Peter Høeg and the Critical Apes" by Lars Henrik Aagaard, translated by W. Glyn Jones, in *Danish Literary Magazine*, no. 10, 1996; "Smilla's Sense of Success: Peter Hoeg Believes that *The Woman And The Ape* Represents a Breakthrough, Yet He Tempers His Enthusiasm" (interview) by Dan Cryer, in *Newsday*, 3 December 1996; "A House of Mourning: *Frøken Smillas fornemmelse for sne*" by Mary Kay Norseng and "Peter Høeg and the Sense of Writing" by Hans Henrik Møller, in *Scandinavian Studies*, no. 69, 1997; "Film Must Speak to the Heart: A Conversation Between Peter Høeg and Bille August" by Jes Stein Pedersen, in *Smilla's Sense of Snow: The Making of a Film by Bille August, Adapted from the Novel by Peter Høeg* by Karin Trolle, 1997; "Smilla's Sense of Gender Identity" by Rachel Schaffer, in *Clues: A Journal of Detection*, no. 19, 1998.

*   *   *

A writer with an unmistakable disdain for literary celebrity, Peter Høeg is an enigmatic figure whose life and works, with one major exception, have remained somewhat obscure. The aura surrounding his international best-seller *Smilla's Sense of Snow* has largely overshadowed his other four books, none of which enjoyed the same degree of near-unanimous critical praise or commercial success. Although he was hailed as a rising literary star when he published *Smilla's Sense of Snow* at the age of 34—at which point he had already published the novel *Forestilling om det tyvende århundrede* (*The History of Danish Dreams*) and the collection of stories

Fortallinger om natten (*Tales of the Night*)—Høeg has not published a novel since 1996, when his *Kvinden og aben* (*The Woman and the Ape*) was released to mixed reviews. As a result, his status within world literature is still rather ambiguous, although he remains very popular in his native Denmark.

Smilla's Sense of Snow established Høeg's reputation, but in doing so also set expectations about his style and subject matter that have perhaps unjustly skewed the response to his other works, all of which have since been translated into English. *Smilla's Sense of Snow* was billed by many reviewers as a mystery novel, and the plot that revolves around its heroine, an Inuit/Danish woman named Smilla Qaavigaaq Jaspersen who studies glaciers for a living, certainly contains many of the conventions of this genre. However, in examining the seemingly accidental death of a young neighbor who has fallen from a snowy roof, Smilla finds herself entangled in a far-reaching conspiracy that allows Høeg to do much more than simply spin out a thrilling detective tale. Smilla's mixed heritage provides Høeg with the opportunity to comment critically on the historical maltreatment of the Inuit natives of Greenland by the Danes. Furthermore, the novel contains a subplot about a wondrous meteorite that may be alive, through which Høeg engages in an examination of the ethics of contemporary science and scientists.

The theme of a marginalized group's struggles and elements of fantasy literature or "magical realism" that are found in *Smilla's Sense of Snow* are more representative of Høeg's overall body of work than the conventions of the mystery genre, which he adapted for this particular novel and has not returned to since, albeit to the chagrin of many readers. Høeg's novels, like his personal life, demonstrate sympathy for those whose relation to the dominant forces of "civilization" is either grudging, unwilling, or doomed. His characters wrestle with the consequences of cultural oppression in a wide variety of forms—from the implications of Smilla's mixed ethnicity to the abuses heaped upon students at an ostensibly progressive boarding school for troubled youths in Høeg's third novel, *De måske egnede* (*Borderliners*).

This concept is perhaps most fully developed in *Kvinden og aben*, for which Høeg drew extensively upon his experiences in visiting his wife's native country of Kenya, which the couple has repeatedly done for months at a time. Although the novel itself only addresses African culture obliquely, the inclusive worldview that Høeg came into contact with during his travels there is expressed in the bond he depicts between Madelene, an upper-class Danish woman living in London, and Erasmus, an ape who is the subject of study—and potential exploitation—by Madelene's husband Adam, a blindly ambitious animal behaviorist. Høeg initially presents their relationship in a relatively realistic manner, showing how Madelene's sympathy for Erasmus in light of her husband's unethical treatment of the extraordinarily intelligent ape leads her to reevaluate her life, which is filled with trifles and alcoholic numbness. The tone and style changes dramatically in the middle of the novel, however, when Erasmus and Madelene escape together from the stifling environment of the house/laboratory where they both have been confined. While on the run, they become lovers and Madelene develops Erasmus's language skills, teaching him to speak fluently in both Danish and English.

Many critics objected to what they claimed was a heavy-handed animal rights message in the book (an intention Høeg denied repeatedly in the few interviews he gave to promote the book), and others accused Høeg of essentially restating the message of past works of science fiction such as the *Planet of the Apes* series—that humans and apes are more similar than humans might wish to accept. However, neither of these criticisms places the novel within the scope of the author's other books. The dual heroes of *Kvinden og aben* closely resemble Høeg's collection of sympathetically depicted ''misfits,'' from Mads, the narrator of complex and often disturbing stories that span the 20th century in *The History of Danish Dreams*, through Smilla and Peter, the troubled yet unmistakably admirable adolescent who narrates *Borderliners*.

Høeg's seeming inability to please his most outspoken critics seems to stem from his unwillingness to accommodate the expectations of those who want him to write either conventional genre fictions or highbrow philosophical novels. Høeg is equally comfortable (and interested in) writing about the complexities of theories concerning the nature of time—a subject that shows up in most of his books—as he is making allusions to popular culture, from thrillers in the vein of John LeCarre to B-movie science fiction like *King Kong*. Although this combination won him millions of readers in *Smilla's Sense of Snow*, it has not resulted in similarly broad acclaim for his subsequent efforts.

Opinions regarding Høeg's intensely private personal life demonstrate a similar misunderstanding. The fact that he and his family live willingly without such modern amenities as a television, a telephone, or a car has been interpreted by many of his commentators as evidence of his withdrawal from contemporary life. Høeg's practice of personally delivering his manuscripts—which he writes out in longhand—to his publisher on bicycle has become an almost inseparable part of this legend of supposed reclusion. He has frequently denied this interpretation, though, countering that his simple lifestyle is an indispensable part of his writing process because it frees him from distraction and allows him to focus his broad-ranging imagination. His willingness to engage with the world for the purpose of improving it is shown clearly by his establishment of the Lolwe Foundation, to which he donated all his profits from worldwide sales of *The Woman and the Ape*. This organization is dedicated to improving conditions in least developed nations through such projects as funding refugee camps for exiled Tibetans in Nepal or supporting independent businesswomen in Tanzania.

Høeg still has ample time to cement his place in world literature, but the combination of his deliberate pace of publication and his social and literary non-conformity complicates assessment of his contributions at the present time.

—Derek Maus

HOFFMANN, E(rnst) T(heodor) A(madeus)

Born: Ernst Theodor Wilhelm Hoffmann in Königsberg, Germany, 24 January 1776. **Education:** Educated at Burgschule, Königsberg, 1782–92; studied law at University of Königsberg, 1792–95. **Family:** Married Maria Thekla Michalina Rorer-Trzynska in 1802; one daughter. **Career:** In legal civil service: posts in Glogau, 1796–98, Berlin, 1798–1800, Posen, 1800–02, Plozk, 1802–04, Warsaw, 1804–08, and, after Napoleon's defeat, Berlin, 1814–22. Also a composer: Kappellmeister, 1808–09, house composer and designer, 1810–12, Bamberg Theatre, and conductor for Sekonda Company, Leipzig and Dresden, 1813–14; composer of operas, and editor of musical works by Beethoven, Mozart, Gluck, and others, 1809–21. **Died:** 25 June 1822.

PUBLICATIONS

Collections

Werke, edited by Georg Ellinger. 15 vols., 1912; 2nd edition, 1927.
Sämtliche Werke, edited by Walter Müller-Seidel and others. 5 vols., 1960–65.
Gesammelte Werke, edited by Rudolf Mingau and Hans-Joachim Kruse. 1976–.
Sämtliche Werke, edited by Wulf Segebrecht, Hartmut Steinecke, and others. 1985–.

Fiction

Fantasiestücke in Callots Manier. 4 vols., 1814–15; as *Fantasy Pieces in Callot's Manner: Pages From the Diary of a Traveling Romantic*, translated by Joseph M. Hayse, 1996.
Die Elixiere des Teufels. 1815–16; as *The Devil's Elixir*, translated by R. Gillies, 1824; as *The Devil's Elixirs*, translated by Ronald Taylor, 1963.
Nachtstücke. 2 vols., 1817.
Seltsame Leiden eines Theater-Direktors. 1819.
Klein Zaches genannt Zinnober. 1819.
Die Serapions-Brüder: Gesammelte Erzälungen und Märchen. 4 vols., 1819–21; as *The Serapion Brethren*, translated by Alexander Ewing, 1886–92.
Lebens-Ansichten des Katers Murr. 1820–22.
Prinzessin Brambilla. 1821.
Meister Floh. 1822; as *Master Flea*, translated by G. Sloane, in *Specimens of German Romance*, vol. 2, 1826.
Die letzten Erzählungen. 2 vols., 1825.
Tales, edited by Christopher Lazare. 1959.
The Tales of Hoffmann, translated by Michael Bullock. 1963.
Tales, translated by James Kirkup. 1966.
The Best Tales of Hoffmann, edited by E.F. Bleiler. 1967.
Tales, edited by Victor Lange. 1982.
Tales of Hoffmann, edited and translated by R.J. Hollingdale. 1982.
Golden Pot, and Other Tales, translated and edited by Ritchie Robertson. 1992.
Life and Opinions of the Tomcat Murr: Together With a Fragmentary Biography of Kapellmeister Johannes Kreisler on Random Sheets of Waste Paper, translated by Anthea Bell. 1999.

Plays

Die Maske, edited by Friedrich Schnapp. 1923.

Verse

Poetische Werke, edited by Gerhard Seidel. 6 vols., 1958.

Other

Die Vision auf dem Schlachtfelde bei Dresden. 1814.
Briefwechsel, edited by Hans von Müller and Friedrich Schnapp. 3 vols., 1967–69.
Selected Writings, edited and translated by Leonard J. Kent and Elizabeth C. Knight. 2 vols., 1969.
Tagebücher, edited by Friedrich Schnapp. 1971.
Juristische Arbeiten, edited by Friedrich Schnapp. 1973.

Selected Letters of E.T.A. Hoffmann, edited and translated by Johanna C. Sahlin. 1977.

*

Bibliography: *E.T.A. Hoffmann: Bibliographic* by Gerhard Salomon, 1963; *E.T.A. Hoffmann Bibliographic* by Curt Grützmacher, 1981.

Critical Studies: *Hoffmann, Author of the Tales* by Harvey Hewett-Thayer, 1948; *Hoffmann* by Ronald Taylor, 1963; *E.T.A. Hoffmann's Other World: The Romantic Author and His "New Mythology"* by Kenneth Negus, 1965; *Music: The Medium of the Metaphysical in Hoffmann* by Pauline Watts, 1972; *The Shattered Self: E.T.A. Hoffmann's Tragic Vision* by Horst S. Daemmrich, 1973; *E.T.A. Hoffmann and Music* by R. Murray Schafer, 1975; *Hoffmann and the Rhetoric of Terror* by Elizabeth Wright, 1978; *Spellbound: Studies on Mesmerism and Literature* by Maria M. Tatar, 1978; *Baudelaire et Hoffmann* by Rosemary Lloyd, 1979; *Mysticism and Sexuality: E.T.A. Hoffmann* by James M. McGlathery, 2 vols., 1981–85; *Hoffmann's Musical Writings: Kreisleriana, The Poet and Composer, Musical Criticism* by David Charlton, 1989; *Authorship as Alchemy: Subversive Writing in Pushkin, Scott, Hoffmann* by David Glenn Kropf, 1994; *E.T.A. Hoffmann* by James M. McGlathery, 1997.

* * *

E.T.A. Hoffmann is one of the few authors belonging to German romanticism who has attained international status. As an exponent of "black romanticism," as it is called in Europe, he was hailed by Baudelaire and scorned by Sir Walter Scott for his preoccupation with the grotesque and the bizarre. He managed to combine this trait with, on the one hand, the most astringent satire, criticizing the injustices of his day in *Meister Floh* (*Master Flea*), and on the other hand, with a modern concern regarding a writer's identity in *Lebens-Ansichten des Katers Murr* [The Life and Opinions of Tomcat Murr].

He made the best possible use of the literary conventions of his day, such as the popular Gothic novel, the epistolary novel, and the short story or novella. He was a diarist and a keen letter writer; like most of his fellow-romanticists he constantly reflected on what he did and on how and why he did it. Interspersed with his fictional writings he developed a theory of representation which accounts for the artist's fascination and concern with subjective phenomena, what he called his "inner world," and he argued that the persuasiveness of the artist's vision depended on his ability to project this world accurately into the external. But it also depended on a reader, playfully addressed by the narrator as "dear reader," and placed within the fictional world of the novel, an example of Romantic irony whereby the artist asserted his supremacy. This reader was expected to suspend disbelief and to open himself up to the experience offered by the novels and stories.

Hoffmann's modernity rests in the powerful description of this inner world, later systematically examined by Freud's new science of the mind, a science not like the physical sciences but like the human ones, depending on interpretation of subjective phenomena. One of Freud's key essays, "The Uncanny," uses one of Hoffmann's stories, "Der Sandmann" ("The Sand-Man"), in order to capture a certain kind of aesthetic experience. Hoffmann was himself interested in parapsychological phenomena of all kinds, being well acquainted with the work of Anton Mesmer, who played a key role in the history of medicine and psychoanalysis. Hoffmann wrote a number of stories

about strange characters, hypnotized and possessed by powerful and threatening figures.

A major theme in Hoffmann's work is that of the divided self, now almost a cliché of Hoffmann scholarship. Whereas in Goethe's *Faust* this can be seen as a benign split, in Hoffmann's work it is usually catastrophic, a prime instance being *Die Elixiere des Teufels* (*The Devil's Elixirs*), though it sometimes resolves itself ironically, as in "Der goldene Topf" ("The Golden Pot"), or satirically, as in *Prinzessin Brambilla* [Princess Brambilla]. The split is between the hero's desire to belong to the world of art and music, and his desire to partake of the pleasures and security of the life of an average citizen. These dual desires manifest themselves in a simultaneous love for two different women, an idealized figure, usually connected with the world of art and music, and a domestic figure who promises the joys of marriage. This precarious stance also parallels the situation in Hoffmann's life, where he simultaneously maintained a satisfactory marriage and an unconsummated but passionate love for an erstwhile music pupil, from the days when he earned his living by giving music lessons. He was similarly divided in his profession, earning his living in one sphere and following his bent in another, the career of civil servant later replacing that of music teacher.

Those who do not recognize him as an author may be acquainted with him as the inspiration behind Offenbach's opera *The Tales of Hoffmann* and Delibes's ballet *Coppélia*.

—Elizabeth Wright

See the essay on *The Devil's Elixirs*.

HOFMANNSTHAL, Hugo (Laurenz August Hofmann, Edler) von

Born: Vienna, Austria, 1 February 1874. **Education:** Educated at Akademisches Gymnasium, Vienna, 1884–92; studied law, 1892–94; and romantic philology: dissertation on Pléiade poets, 1897, and habilitation work on Victor Hugo, 1900–01, University of Vienna. **Military Service:** Served with 6th Dragoon Regiment in Göding, 1894–95. **Family:** Married Gertrud Schlesinger in 1901; one daughter and two sons. **Career:** Full-time writer, from 1901; collaborated with Richard Strauss on operas, from 1909; editor, Österreichische Bibliothek, 1915–17; co-founder, with Max Reinhardt, Salzburg Festival, 1919. **Died:** 15 July 1929.

Publications

Collections

Gesammelte Werke in Einzelausgaben, edited by Herbert Steiner. 15 vols., 1945–59.
Selected Writings: Prose, Poems and Verse Plays, Plays and Libretti, edited by Mary Hottinger, Tania and James Stern, and Michael Hamburger. 3 vols., 1952–64.
Sämtliche Werke, edited by Heinz Otto Burger and others. 1975–.

Plays

Gestern (produced 1928). 1896.

Der Tor und der Tod (produced 1898). 1900; as *Death and the Fool*, translated by Elisabeth Walker, 1914; also translated by Michael Hamburger, in *Selected Writings*, 2, 1961; Alfred Schwarz, in *Three Plays*, 1966.

Die Frau im Fenster (as *Madonna Dianora*, produced 1898). In *Theater in Versen*, 1899; as *Madonna Dionara*, translated by Harriet Betty Boas, 1916.

Theater in Versen. 1899.

Der Abenteurer und die Sängerin (produced 1899). In *Theater in Versen*, 1899; revised version, 1909.

Die Hochzeit der Sobeide (as *Sobeide, Abenteurer*, produced 1899). In *Theater in Versen*, 1899; as *The Marriage of Sobeide*, translated by Bayard Quincy Morgan, in *German Classics of the Nineteenth and Twentieth Centuries*, edited by Kuno Francke and William G. Howard, 20, 1916; as *The Marriage of Zobeide*, translated by Christopher Middleton, in *Selected Writings*, 2, 1961.

Das Bergwerk zu Falun, from a story by E.T.A. Hoffmann (produced 1899). 1933; as *The Mine at Falun*, translated by Michael Hamburger, in *Selected Writings*, 2, 1961.

Der Kaiser und die Hexe (produced 1926). In *Die Insel*, 1900; as *The Emperor and the Witch*, translated by Christopher Middleton, in *Selected Writings*, 2, 1961.

Der Tod der Tizian. 1901; as *The Death of Titian*, translated by John Heard, 1920.

Elektra (produced 1903). 1904; revised version, music by Strauss (produced 1909), 1908; as *Electra*, translated by Arthur Symons, 1908; also translated by Alfred Schwarz, in *Selected Writings*, 3, 1964, and in *Three Plays*, 1966.

Das kleine Welttheater; oder, Die Glücklichen (produced 1929). 1903; as *The Little Theatre of the World*, translated by Walter R. Eberlein, 1945; also translated by Michael Hamburger, in *Selected Writings*, 2, 1961.

Das gerettete Venedig, from the play *Venice Preserved* by Otway (produced 1905). 1905.

Ödipus und die Sphinx (produced 1905). 1906.

Kleine Dramen. 2 vols., 1906–07.

Der weisse Fächer (produced 1927). 1907.

Vorspiele. 1908.

Die Begegnung mit Carlo. 1909.

Alkestis, from the play by Euripides, music by Egon Wellesz (produced 1916). 1909.

Lucidor. 1910.

Christinas Heimreise (produced 1910). 1910; as *Christina's Journey Home*, translated by Roy Temple House, 1916.

König Ödipus, from the play by Sophocles (produced 1910). 1910.

Die Heirat wider Willen, from a play by Molière. 1910.

Amor und Psyche. 1911.

Das fremde Mädchen. 1911.

Der Rosenkavalier, music by Strauss (produced 1911). 1911; edited by Willi Schuh, 1971; as *The Rose-Bearer*, translated by Alfred Kalisch, 1912; as *The Cavalier of the Rose*, translated by Christopher Holme, in *Selected Writings*, 3, 1964.

Jedermann: Das Spiel vom Sterben des reichen Mannes (produced 1911). 1911; as *The Play of Everyman*, translated by G. Sterling, 1917; as *The Salzburg Everyman*, translated by M.E. Tafler, 1930.

Ariadne auf Naxos, music by Strauss (produced 1912). 1912; revised version (produced 1916), 1916; as *Ariadne on Naxos*, translated by Alfred Kalisch, 1912.

Josephs Legende (ballet scenario), with Harry Graf Kessler, music by Strauss (produced 1914). 1914.

Die Frau ohne Schatten, music by Strauss (produced 1919). 1916; as *The Woman without a Shadow*, 1927; translated by Jean Hollander, 1993.

Die grüine Flöte (ballet scenario), music by Mozart (produced 1916). 1925.

Die Lästigen, from a play by Molière (produced 1916). In *Marsyas*, 1917.

Der Bürger als Edelmann, from a play by Molière, music by Strauss (produced 1918). 1918.

Dame Kobold, from a play by Calderón (produced 1920). 1920.

Der Schwierige (produced 1921). 1921; as *The Difficult Man*, translated by Willa Muir, in *Selected Writings*, 3, 1964.

Florindo und die Unbekannte (produced 1921). 1923.

Das Salzburger grosse Welttheater, from a play by Calderón (produced 1922). 1922; as *The Salzburg Great Theatre of the World*, translated by Vernon Watkins, in *Selected Writings*, 3, 1964.

Prima Ballerina (ballet scenario). 1923(?).

Der Unbestechliche (produced 1923). With *Der Schwierige*, 1958.

Die Ruinen von Athen (produced 1924). 1925.

Der Turm, from a play by Calderón. 1925; revised version (produced 1928), 1927; as *The Tower*, translated by Michael Hamburger, in *Selected Writings*, 3, 1964; also translated by Alfred Schwarz, in *Three Plays*, 1966.

Die ägyptische Helena, music by Strauss (produced 1928). 1928; as *Helen in Egypt*, translated by Alfred Kalisch, 1928.

Semiramis: Die beiden Götter. 1933.

Arabella, music by Strauss (produced 1933). 1933; as *Arabella*, translated by John Gutman, 1955; also translated by Nora Wydenbruck and Christopher Middleton, in *Selected Writings*, 3, 1964.

Dramatische Entwürfe aus dem Nachlass, edited by Heinrich Zimmer. 1936.

Danae; oder, Die Vernunftheirat. 1952.

Three Plays (includes *Death and the Fool; Electra; The Tower*), translated by Alfred Schwarz. 1966.

Fiction

Prinz Eugen der edle Ritter. 1905.

Das Märchen der 672. Nacht und andere Erzählungen (includes "Ein Brief" [The Chandos Letter]). 1905.

Die Frau ohne Schatten. 1919.

Andreas; oder, Die Vereinigten. 1932; as *Andreas; or, The United*, translated by Marie D. Hottinger, 1936.

Four Stories, edited by Margaret Jacobs. 1968.

Verse

Ausgewählte Gedichte. 1903.

Die gesammelten Gedichte. 1907.

Die Gedichte und kleinen Dramen. 1911.

Lyrical Poems, translated by Charles Wharton Stork. 1918.

Gedichte. 1922.

Nachlese der Gedichte. 1934.

Other

Stüdie über die Entwicklung des Dichters Victor Hugo. 1901; as *Victor Hugo*, 1904; as *Versuch über Victor Hugo*, 1925.

Unterhaltungen über literarische Gegenstände. 1904.

Die prosaischen Schriften gesammelt. 2 vols., 1907; vol. 3, 1917.

Hesperus: Ein Jahrbuch, with Rudolf Borchardt and Rudolf Alexander Schröder. 1909.
Grete Wiesenthal in Amor und Psyche und das fremde Mädchen. 1911.
Die Wege und die Begegnungen. 1913.
Rodauner Nachträge. 3 vols., 1918.
Reden und Aufsätze. 1921.
Buch der Freunde. 1922; edited by Ernst Zinn, 1965.
Gesammelte Werke. 6 vols., 1924; revised edition, 3 vols., 1934.
Augenblicke in Griechenland. 1924.
Früheste Prosastücke. 1926.
Grillparzers politisches Vermächtnis. 1926.
Loris: Die Prosa des jungen Hoffmansthals. 1930.
Die Berührung der Sphären. 1931.
Briefe. 2 vols., 1935–37.
Briefwechsel, with Anton Wildgans, edited by Joseph A. von Bradish. 1935.
Briefwechsel, with Stefan George, edited by Robert Boehringer. 1938; revised edition, 1953.
Briefwechsel, with Richard Strauss, edited by Franz and Alice Strauss. 1952; revised edition, edited by Willi Schuh, 1954; as *Correspondence*, translated by Hans Hammelmann and Ewald Osers, 1961.
Briefe der Freundschaft, with Eberhard von Bodenhausen, edited by Dora von Bodenhausen. 1953.
Briefwechsel, with Rudolf Borchardt, edited by Marie Luise Borchardt and Herbert Steiner. 1954.
Briefwechsel, with Carl J. Burckhardt, edited by Burckhardt. 1956.
Sylvia in "Stern", edited by Martin Stern. 1959.
Briefwechsel, with Arthur Schnitzler, edited by Theresa Nickl and Heinrich Schnitzler. 1964.
Briefwechsel, with Helene von Nostitz, edited by Oswalt von Nostitz. 1965.
Briefwechsel, with Edgar Karl von Bebenburg, edited by Mary E. Gilbert. 1966.
Briefwechsel, with Leopold von Andrian. 1968.
Briefwechsel, with Willy Haas. 1968.
Briefwechsel, with Harry Graf Kessler. 1968.
Briefwechsel, with Josef Redlich. 1971.
Briefwechsel, with Richard Beer-Hofmann. 1972.
Briefwechsel, with Max Rychner, Samuel and Hedwig Fischer, Oscar Bie, and Moritz Heimann, edited by Claudia Mertz-Rychner and others. 1973.
Briefwechsel, with Ottonie Gräfin Degenfeld, edited by Marie Therese Miller-Degenfeld. 1974.
Briefwechsel 1899–1925, with Rainer Mafia Rilke, edited by Rudolf Hirsch and Ingeborg Schnack. 1978.
Briefwechsel, with Max Mell, edited by Margret Dietrich and Heinz Kindermann. 1982.
Briefwechsel, with Ria Schmujlow-Claasen. 1982.
Briefwechsel, with Paul Zifferer, edited by Hilde Burger. 1983.
The Poet and the Countess: Hugo von Hofmannsthal's Correspondence with Countess Ottonie Degenfeld, edited by Marie-Therese Miller-Degenfeld, translated by W. Eric Barcel. 2000.
Editor, *Deutsche Erzähler.* 4 vols., 1912.

*

Bibliography: *Hofmannsthal: Bibliographie des Schrifttums 1892–1963*, 1966, and *Hugo von Hofmannsthal: Bibliographie: Werke, Briefe, Gespräche, Übersetzungen, Vertonungen*, 1972, both by Horst Weber; *Hugo von Hofmannsthal Bibliographie 1964–1976* by H.A. and U. Koch, 1976; ''Hofmannsthal Bibliographie'' by C. Köttelwesch, in *Hofmannsthal Blätter* from 1979.

Critical Studies: *Hugo von Hofmannsthal* by Hans Hammelmann, 1957; *Hofmannsthal's Festival Dramas* by B. Coughlin, 1964; *Hofmannsthal's Novel "Andreas"* by David Miles, 1972; *Hugo von Hofmannsthal: Three Essays* by Michael Hamburger, 1972; *Hofmannsthal and the French Symbolist Tradition* by Steven P. Sondrup, 1976; *Hugo von Hofmannsthal* by Lowell A. Bangerter, 1977; *The Banal Object: Theme and Thematics in Proust, Rilke, Hofmannsthal, and Sartre* by Naomi Segal, 1981; *Hugo von Hofmannsthal: Commemorative Essays* edited by W.E. Yuill and Patricia Howe, 1981; *Hugo von Hofmannsthal and His Time: The European Imagination, 1860–1920* by Hermann Broch, 1984; *Hofmannsthal and Symbolism: Art and Life in the Work of a Modern Poet* by Thomas A. Kovach, 1985; *Animal Symbolism in Hofmannsthal's Works* by Helen Frink, 1987; *Hugo yon Hofmannsthal: The Theatres of Consciousness* by Benjamin Bennett, 1988; *Narrative Transgression and the Foregrounding of Language in Selected Prose Works of Poe, Valdéry and Hofmannsthal* by Leroy T. Day, 1988; *Selten Augenblicke: Interpretations of Poems by Hugo von Hofmannsthal* by Margit Resch, 1989; *The Challenge of Belatedness: Goethe, Kleist, Hofmannsthal* by Jean Wilson, 1991; *Schnitzler, Hofmannsthal and the Austrian Theatre* by W.E. Yates, 1992; *Hugo Von Hofmannsthal* by Mathias Mayer, 1993; *Hugo Von Hofmannsthal: Poets and The Language of Life* by Adrian Del Caro, 1993; *The Poetry of Hugo Von Hofmannsthal and French Symbolism* by Robert Vilain, 2000.

* * *

Hugo von Hofmannsthal is chiefly remembered as the successful librettist who partnered with Richard Strauss. Their operas, including the famous *Der Rosenkavalier* (*The Cavalier of the Rose*), are lively and powerful, rich in register and motif.

Hofmannsthal's fame, however, neither begins nor ends with Strauss. He had enjoyed some 15 years of precocious celebrity before their collaboration began. His schoolboy lyrics established his reputation as one of the foremost young poets in Vienna. Even his earliest works, among them *Gestern* [Yesterday], *Der Tor und der Tod* (*Death and the Fool*), and *Die Hochzeit der Sobeide* (*The Marriage of Zobeide*), reveal his remarkable insight into some of the questions most crucial to man: the passing of time, the problem of death, the dangers of excessive aestheticism, the role of women in society. His range, even in the 1890s, is vast.

The turn of the century brought a change of style. There were several reasons for this change. One, metaphysical reason prompting him to abandon his lyrical mode, is expressed in the fictitious Chandos Letter. A more immediate reason can be found in his desire to stage his dramas more successfully. They made good reading, but as theatre they were indicted by critics as ''lukewarm'' and ''boring.'' Hofmannsthal began to write with a specific theatre in mind, that of Max Reinhardt in Berlin. He made increasing use of stage technology in order to enhance the sensuous impact of his works. Lighting, music, the rhythms of movement are all incorporated into the text, as the stage directions of the powerfully visual *Elektra* (*Electra*) demonstrate.

Further factors influencing Hofmannsthal's change of style include the literary trend of "anti-erotic" writers such as Wilde, Strindberg, and Wedekind, and also the writings of Freud. Their influence shows most overtly in the so-called "Greek" plays, *Electra* and *Ödipus und die Sphinx* [Oedipus and the Sphinx], where Hofmannsthal probes the depths of sexual antagonism, repression, and perversion—a radical departure from his Sophoclean model. Greek myth is here used to underline the most primitive aspects of human behaviour. Hofmannsthal was to return to the symbolic world of myth in his operas *Ariadne auf Naxos* (*Ariadne on Naxos*) and *Die ägyptische Helena* (*Helen in Egypt*), explaining in his late essay on the latter work that mythological opera was the only form in which the "atmosphere of the present" could be expressed adequately.

Hofmannsthal had already explored other possible modes of expression. Moving away from the "armchair playlets" of the 1890s, and the Greek plays of 1903 and 1905, he wrote his *Jedermann* (*The Play of Everyman*), and *Das Satzburger grosse Welttheater* (*The Salzburg Great Theatre of the World*), expressing fundamental human truths in the universalizing form of the medieval mystery play. Social satires, such as *Der Schwierige* (*The Difficult Man*), again treat universal themes, but this time in the context of modern Austria. Yet another mode is the magical setting of *Die Frau ohne Schatten* (*The Woman without a Shadow*), and of *Der Turm* (*The Tower*) which, with its oblique references to politics and its background of language scepticism, constitutes one of Hofmannsthal's most difficult plays.

The range and density of Hofmannsthal's poems and plays, essays and correspondence, account for the continuing interest in these works today.

—Sally McMullen (Croft)

See the essays on *Andreas*, *The Difficult Man*, and *The Tower*.

HOLBERG, Ludvig

Born: Bergen, Norway (then part of the Kingdom of Norway and Denmark), 3 December 1684. **Education:** Studied at school and university in Bergen; University of Copenhagen, 1702–04; travelled in the Netherlands and Germany, 1704–06; travelled in England, and studied in Oxford and London, 1706–08. **Career:** Tutor in Germany, 1708–09; at Borch's College, Copenhagen, 1709–14; appointed unpaid associate professor at University of Copenhagen, 1714, but spent the time of the appointment travelling in the Low Countries, Paris, and Rome, 1714–16; professor of metaphysics, 1717, professor of Latin, 1720, member of the University Council, 1720, professor of history and geography, 1730, and University bursar (*quaestor*), 1737–51, University of Copenhagen; wrote for Montaigu's troupe at the newly organized Danish Theatre, the Lille Grønnegade Theatre, Copenhagen, from 1722 until its closure in 1728; ceased writing plays during the reign of Christian VI, 1730–46, who banned all theatrical activity in Denmark and Norway; unofficial adviser and writer for the Kongelige Teater [Theatre Royal], Copenhagen, established shortly after the succession of Frederik V, in 1748. Made a baron, 1747. **Died:** 28 January 1754.

PUBLICATIONS

Collections

Udvalgte skrifter, edited by Knud Lyne Rahbek. 21 vols., 1804–14.
Samlede skrifter, edited by Carl S. Petersen. 18 vols., 1913–63.
Samtlige komedier i tre bind, edited by F.J. Billeskov Jansen. 3 vols., 1984.
No; Jeppe of the Hill; The Scatterbrain, translated by Michael Meyer. 1999.

Plays (selection)

Den politiske kandestøber (produced 1722). 1723; as *The Blue-Apron Statesman*, translated by T. Weber, 1885; as *The Political Tinker*, translated by Oscar James Campbell, Jr. and Frederick Schenck, in *Comedies*, 1914.
Den vægelsindede (produced 1722). 1724; as *The Weathercock*, translated by Henry Alexander, in *Four Plays*, 1946.
Jeppe på bjerget; eller, Den forvandlede bonde (produced 1722). 1723; as *Jepp on the Hill*, translated by Waldemar C. Westergaard and Martin B. Ruud, 1906; as *Jeppe of the Hill*, translated by Oscar James Campbell, Jr. and Frederick Schenck, in *Comedies*, 1914; also translated by M. Jagendorf, 1953; as *Barney Brae: A Comedy Set in Northern Ireland*, translated and adapted by G.V.C. Young, 1980.
Mester Gert Westphaler; eller, Den meget talende barbeer (produced 1722). 1723; as *The Loquacious Barber*, translated by W.H.H. Chambers, 1903; translated as *Mester Gert Westphaler; or, The Very Loquacious Barber*, in *The Drama 17*, edited by A. Bates, 1903–04; as *The Talkative Barber*, translated by Henry Alexander, in *Seven One-Act Plays*, 1950.
Jean de France; eller, Hans Fritz (produced 1722). 1731; translated (from the German) as *Jean de France; or, Hans Fritz*, 1922.
Nye-Aars prologos [New Year's Prologue] (produced 1723).
Erasmus Montanus (produced 1748). 1723; as *Erasmus Montanus*, translated by T. Weber, 1885; also translated by Oscar James Campbell, Jr. and Frederick Schenck in *Comedies*, 1914; also translated in *The Chief Modern Dramatists*, edited by B. Mathews, 1916.
Den ellefte Juni [The Eleventh of June] (produced 1723). 1724.
Barselstuen [Room of the Child's Birth] (produced 1723). 1731.
Komedier. 3 vols., 1723–25.
Det arabiske pulver (produced 1724). 1724; as *The Arabian Powder*, translated by Henry Alexander, in *Seven One-Act Plays*, 1950; also translated by Reginald Spink, in *Three Comedies*, 1957.
Julestuen (produced 1724). 1724; as *The Christmas Party*, translated by Henry Alexander, in *Seven One-Act Plays*, 1950.
Mascarade (produced 1724). 1724; as *Masquerade*, translated by Henry Alexander, in *Four Plays*, 1946.
Ulysses von Ithacia; eller, En tysk comoedie [Ulysses of Ithaca; or, A German Comedy] (produced 1724). 1725.
Diderich Menschenschreck (produced 1724). 1731; as *Captain Bombastes Thunderton*, translated by H.W.L. Hime, in *Three Comedies*, 1912; as *Diderich the Terrible*, translated by Henry Alexander, in *Seven One-Act Plays*, 1950.
Henrik og Pernille (produced 1724). 1731; as *Henry and Pernilla*, translated by H.W.L. Hime, in *Three Comedies*, 1912.
Melampe [Melampe] (produced 1724). 1725.

Kilderejsen (produced 1724). 1725; as *The Healing Spring*, translated by Reginald Spink, in *Three Comedies*, 1957.

Jacob von Tyboe; eller, Den stortalende soldat [Jacob von Tyboe; or, The Braggart Soldier]. 1725.

Uden hoved og hale [Without Head or Tail]. 1725.

Den stundeløse (produced 1726). 1731; as *Scatterbrains*, translated by H.W.L. Hime, in *Three Comedies*, 1912; as *The Fussy Man*, translated by Henry Alexander, in *Four Plays*, 1946.

Den pantsatte bondedreng (produced 1726). 1731; as *The Peasant in Pawn*, translated by Henry Alexander, in *Seven One-Act Plays*, 1950; as *The Transformed Peasant*, translated by Reginald Spink, in *Three Comedies*, 1957.

Den danske comoedies liigbegiængelse [The Danish Drama's Funeral] (produced 1727). 1746.

Hexerie; eller, Blind allarm [Witchcraft; or, False Alarm] (produced 1750). 1731.

Det lykkelige skibbrud [The Fortuitous Shipwreck] (produced 1754). 1731.

De usynlige (produced 1747). 1731; as *The Masked Ladies*, translated by Henry Alexander, in *Four Plays*, 1946.

Pernilles korte frøikenstand [Pernille's Short Ladyship] (produced 1747). 1731.

Den honnete Ambition [Social Aspiration] (produced 1747). 1731.

Don Ranudo de Colibrados; eller, Fattigdom og hoffærdighed [Don Ranudo de Colibrados; or, Poverty and Pride]. 1745.

Sganarels reyse til det Philosophiske Land (produced c. 1751–53). 1751; as *Sganarel's Journey to the Land of the Philosophers*, translated by Henry Alexander, in *Seven One-Act Plays*, 1950.

Plutus (produced 1751). 1753.

Abracadabra; eller, Huus-spøgelse [Abracadabra; or, The House-Ghost] (produced 1752).

Den forvandlede brudgom (produced 1882). 1753; as *The Changed Bridegroom*, translated by Henry Alexander, in *Seven One-Act Plays*, 1950.

Republigven; eller, Det gemene Bedste [The Republic; or, The General Good] (produced 1754). 1754.

Philosophus udi egen Inbildung (produced 1754). 1754.

Three Comedies (includes *Henry and Pernilla*; *Captain Bombastes Thunderton*; *Scatterbrains*), translated by H.W.L. Hime. 1912.

Comedies (includes *Erasmus Montanus*; *Jeppe of the Hill*; *The Political Tinker*), translated by Oscar James Campbell, Jr. and Frederick Schenck. 1914.

Four Plays (includes *The Fussy Man*; *The Masked Ladies*; *The Weathercock*; *Masquerade*), translated by Henry Alexander. 1946.

Seven One-Act Plays (includes *The Talkative Barber*; *The Arabian Powder*; *The Christmas Party*; *Diderich the Terrible*; *The Peasant in Pawn*; *Sganarel's Journey to the Land of the Philosophers*; *The Changed Bridegroom*), translated by Henry Alexander. 1950.

Three Comedies (includes *The Transformed Peasant*; *The Arabian Powder*; *The Healing Spring*), translated by Reginald Spink. 1957.

Fiction

Nicolai Klimii iter subterraneum (in Latin). 1741; as *A Journey to the World Under-Ground*, translated 1742, as *The Journey of Niels Klim to the World Underground*, edited by James McNelis, Jr., 1960; as *Niels Klim's Journey under the Ground*, translated by John Gierlow, 1845.

Verse

Peder Paars. 2 vols., 1719–20; in part as *Peter Paars*, translated and adapted by Bergliot Stromsoe, 1862, complete version, translated by Stromsoe, 1962.

Opuscula latina. 2 vols., 1737–43.

Mindre poetiske skrifter. 1746.

Other

Introduction til de formemste Europæiske Rigers Historier. 1711; revised edition, 1728.

Introduction til natur og folke-retten [Introduction to Natural Law]. 1715; revised edition, 1734.

Epistola ad virum perillustrem [Letter to a Person of Renown]. 1728; in part as *Virtues and Faults of Some European Nations*, translated by J. Christian Bay, 1958.

Dannemarks og Norges beskrivelse. 1729; in part as *The History of Norway*, translated by A.A. Feldborg, 1817.

Den danske Skue-Plads. 5 vols., 1731–54.

Dannemarks riges historie [History of the Kingdom of Denmark]. 1732–35.

Synopsis historiae universalis. 1733; as *An Introduction to Universal History*, translated by Gregory Sharpe, 1755.

Bergens beskrivelse [Description of Bergen]. 1737.

Almindelig kirkehistorie [General Church History]. 1738.

Heltehistorier [Achievements of Great Men]. 1739.

Jødisk historie [History of the Jews]. 2 vols., 1742.

Moralske tanker. 1744; edited by F.J. Billeskov Jansen, 1943; as *Moral Reflections and Epistles*, edited and translated by P.M. Mitchell, 1991.

Heltindehistorier [Comparative History of Famous Women]. 1745.

Epistler. 2 vols., 1748–54; edited by F.J. Billeskov Jansen, 8 vols., 1944–54; in part as *Selected Essays*, edited and translated by P.M. Mitchell, 1955, and with *Moral Reflections*, 1991.

Moralske fabler [Moral Fables]. 1751.

Remarques sur quelques positions qui se trouvent dans l'esprit des lois (written in French). 1753.

Memoirs: An Eighteenth-Century Danish Contribution to International Understanding (translation based on various sections of works). 1827; edited by Stewart E. Fraser, 1970.

Memoirer, edited by F.J. Billeskov Jansen. 1943.

Essays, edited by Kjell Heggelund. 1977.

Den radikale Holberg, edited by Thomas Bredsdorff. 1984.

Holberg og Juristerne: en antologi, edited by Klaus Neiiendam and Ditlev Tamm. 1984.

Moral Reflections and Epistles, edited and translated by P.M. Mitchell. 1991.

Translator, *Herodiani historie*. 1746.

*

Bibliography: *Bibliografi over Holbergs skrifter*, 3 vols., 1933–35; *Holberg-Ordbog*, 1981–.

Critical Studies: *The Comedies of Holberg* by Oscar James Campbell, Jr., 1914; *Holberg* by F.J. Billeskov Jansen, 1974; *A Guide to the Writings of Ludwig Holberg and to His Manor-House Tersløsegaard* by F.J. Billeskov Jansen, 1979; *Ludwig Holberg's Comedies: A Biographical Essay* by Gerald S. Argetsinger, 1983; *Ludvig Holberg: The Playwright and His Age Up to 1730*, translated by Jean and Tom Lundskær-Nielsen, 1993; *Ludvig Holberg—a European Writer: A Study in Influence and Reception*, edited by Sven Hakon Rossel, 1994.

* * *

When Holberg wrote his first comedies in 1722, there was effectively no tradition of playwriting in Scandinavia to which he could turn for inspiration. He was at the time a much-travelled scholar, recently appointed to the Chair of Metaphysics at the University of Copenhagen. He felt a deep sympathy with the rationalist, conservative ethos of French neo-classicism, and it was accordingly to the work of Molière that he looked for dramatic inspiration. Between 1722 and 1723, he wrote some 15 comedies, all of which, in the best neo-classical tradition, brilliantly satirize socially deviant behaviour in a way that is both entertaining and yet unmistakably didactic. Holberg uses the weapons of ridicule and irony to highlight the folly of characters such as the feckless peasant in *Jeppe på bjerget* (*Jeppe of the Hill*), the know-all amateur politician in *Den politiske kandestøber* (*The Political Tinker*), and the pretentious undergraduate from peasant stock in *Erasmus Montanus*. Like Molière, Holberg felt an obvious sympathy for his unfortunate victims, never losing sight of the transparently human qualities of even his most outrageous fools. This gives his plays, underneath the satiric thrust, a feeling of warmth, at times almost endearment.

Holberg was a precise observer of human behaviour, and his plays faithfully reflect the unsophisticated earthiness of peasant and middle-class culture in 18th-century Denmark. Despite the classical framework, his plays are manifestly Danish in spirit and texture (which may explain why so few have been performed in English). This is as true of the boasting warrior plays modelled on Plautus, such as *Diderich Menschenschreck* (*Diderich the Terrible*) or *Jacob von Tyboe*, as it is of plays like *Den stundesløse* (*The Fussy Man*) or *Den vægelsindede* (*The Weathercock*), modelled on *Le Malade imaginaire* by Molière.

Holberg had begun his literary career with a mock epic poem in 1720 called *Peder Paars* (*Peter Paars*). Based on the *Aeneid*, it follows the mock heroic journey of Peder Paars between two Danish provincial towns, Kalundborg and Aarhus. His comedies were written in 1722 at the invitation of a French actor called Montaigu who was given a licence to set up the first public theatre in Copenhagen with Danish actors. After the theatre went bankrupt in 1727, Holberg concentrated on his academic duties, publishing a number of important historical works. In 1741, he published a long satirical novel in the style of Swift called *Nicolai Klimii iter subterraneum* (*Niels Klim's Journey under the Ground*) and, in 1744, published a collection of essays called *Moralske tanker* (*Moral Reflections and Epistles*), similar in tone to those of Addison in *The Spectator*.

When a new theatre was established in Copenhagen in 1748, with the official title of the Theatre Royal, Holberg wrote a set of six new comedies to celebrate the occasion. However, these late plays lack the charm and appeal of his early work. His satiric, neo-classical approach to comedy was out of tune with an age that was increasingly embracing the liberal, sentimental values of English and French writers. By now a baron and a conservative pillar of the establishment, Holberg, in 1748, found himself writing for a culture that no longer existed. However, his fame as the founding father of Danish comedy was beyond question. Today, his plays still occupy an important and much-loved place in the repertoire of the Theatre Royal in Copenhagen.

—David Thomas

HÖLDERLIN, (Johann Christian) Friedrich

Born: Lauffen, Germany, 20 March 1770. **Education:** Educated at Latin school, Nürtingen, 1776–84; theological seminary, Denkendorff, 1784–86, and Maulbronn, 1786–88; Tübingen Seminary, 1788–93, master of philosophy, 1790. **Career:** Tutor to son of Charlotte von Kalb, in Waltershausen, 1793–94, and in Weimar, 1794–95; lived in Jena, 1795; tutor to son of Herr Gontard, Frankfurt, 1795–98; tutor in house of Herr Gonzenbach, Hauptweil, Switzerland, 1801, and of a German official in Bordeaux, 1801–02; librarian, Homburg, 1804–06. Mentally ill after 1805: confined first in clinic in Tübingen, 1806–07, and privately after 1807. **Died:** 7 June 1843.

PUBLICATIONS

Collections

Sämtliche Werke, edited by Friedrich Beissner and Adolf Beck. 8 vols., 1943–85.
Sämtliche Werke und Briefe, edited by Günter Mieth. 4 vols., 1970.
Sämtliche Werke, edited by Dietrich E. Sattler. 1975–.

Verse

Gedichte, edited by Gustav Schwab and Ludwig Uhland. 1826.
Selected Poems, translated by J.B. Leishman. 1944.
[Selection], translated by Michael Hamburger. 1943; revised edition, 1952; revised edition as *Selected Verse*, 1961.
Alcaic Poems (bilingual edition), translated by Elizabeth Henderson. 1962.
Poems and Fragments (bilingual edition), edited and translated by Michael Hamburger. 1966; revised edition, 1980.
Selected Poems (with *Selected Poems* by Mörike), translated by Christopher Middleton. 1972.
Hymns and Fragments (bilingual edition), translated by Richard Sieburth. 1984.
Selected Verse, edited and translated by Michael Hamburger. 1986.
Selected Poems, translated by David Constantine. 1990.

Fiction

Hyperion; oder, Der Eremit in Griechenland. 2 vols., 1797–99; as *Hyperion; or, the Hermit in Greece*, translated by Willard R. Trask, 1965.
Hyperion and Selected Poems, edited by Eric L. Santer. 1990.

Other

Ausgewählte Briefe, edited by Wilhelm Böhm. 1910.
Briefe, edited by Erich Lichtenstein. 1922.
Gesammelte Briefe, edited by Ernst Bertram. 1935.
Briefe, edited by Friedrich Seeba. 1944.
Briefe zur Erziehung, edited by K. Lothar Wolf. 1950.
Einundzwanzig Briefe, edited by Bertold Hack. 1966.
Essays and Letters of Theory, edited and translated by Thomas Pfau. 1988.
Hölderlin's Sophocles: Oedipus and Antigone, translated by David Constantine, 2001.
Translator, *Die Trauerspiele des Sophokles*. 2 vols., 1804–06.

*

Bibliography: *Internationale Hölderlin-Bibliographie* edited by Maria Kohler, 1985.

Critical Studies: *Hölderlin* by Ronald Peacock, 1938; *Hölderlin* by Agnes Stansfield, 1944; *Hölderlin* by L.S. Salzberger, 1952; *A Study of Hölderlin* by R.D. Miller, 1958; *Hölderlins Elegie "Brot und Wein": Die Entwicklung des hymnischen Stils in der elegischen Dichtung* by Jochen Schmidt, 1968; *Hölderlin's Hyperion: A Critical Reading* by Walter Silz, 1969; *The Young Hölderlin* by Roy C. Shelton, 1973; *Hölderlin and Greek Literature* by Robin Burnett Harrison, 1975; *Hölderlin and Goethe* by Eudo C. Mason, 1975; *Hölderlin's Major Poetry: The Dialectics of Unity*, 1975, and *Friedrich Hölderlin*, 1984, both by Richard Unger; *Hölderlin and the Left: The Search for a Dialectic of Art and Life* by Helen Fehervary, 1977; *The Significance of Locality in the Poetry of Hölderlin*, 1979, and *Hölderlin*, 1988, both by David Constantine; *Hölderlin's Hyperion* by Howard Gaskill, 1984; *Text, Geschichte und Subjektivität in Hölderlins Dichtung—"Unessbarer Schrift gleich"* by Rainer Nägele, 1985; *Narrative Vigilance and the Poetic Imagination* by Eric L. Santer, 1986; *Hölderlin's Silence* by Thomas Eldon Ryan, 1988; *Friedrich Hölderlin: The Theory and Practice of Religious Poetry: Studies in the Elegies* by Martin F.A. Simon, 1988; *The Problem of Christ in the Work of Friedrich Hölderlin* by Mark Ogden, 1991; *Hölderlin: The Poetics of Being* by Adrian Del Caro, 1991; *A Foretaste of Heaven: Friedrich Hölderlin in the Context of Württemberg Pietism* by Priscilla A. Hayden-Roy, 1994; *The Poet as Thinker: Hölderlin in France* by Geert Lernout, 1994; *Hölderlin's Hymn "The Ister"* by Martin Heidegger, translated by William McNeill and Julia Davis, 1996; *Leaves of Mourning: Hölderlin's Late Work, With an Essay on Keats and Melancholy* by Anselm Haverkamp, translated by Vernon Chadwick, 1996; *The Course of Remembrance and Other Essays on Hölderlin* by Dieter Henrich, edited by Eckart Förster, 1997; *Hölderlin and the Dynamics of Translation* by Charlie Louth, 1998; *The Solid Letter: Readings of Friedrich Hölderlin*, edited by Aris Fioretos, 1999; *The Recalcitrant Art: Diotima's Letters of Hölderlin and Related Missives*, edited and translated by Douglas F. Kenney and Sabine Menner-Bettscheid, 2000; *Narrating Community After Kant: Schiller, Goethe, and Hölderlin* by Karin Schutjer, 2001.

* * *

Poetry—"this most innocent of occupations"—was Friedrich Hölderlin's vocation, and he had from the start the highest ambitions in it. His models as a young man were Pindar, Klopstock, and, closer to home, Schiller—whom he adulated, to his own detriment. He shared with his companions at school and in the seminary (several of them highly gifted) a passion for liberty excited by events in France, and a belief that poetry might, in its manner, serve the revolutionary cause. The regime in Württemberg, especially as it touched the students in Tübingen, was oppressive, and poetry served as a medium of revolt. The language of Hölderlin's early poems is often very violent; they depict the beleaguering of the Good, in whatever definition, by the forces of Wrong—of injustice, tyranny, philistinism, etc. In the Tübingen Hymns these oppositions are expressed in abstract terms, and the poetry suffers accordingly.

Hölderlin was educated for the Church but avoided entry into it by taking the customary house-tutor jobs. In the second of these, in Frankfurt, he met and fell in love with Susette Gontard. Through her he found his own true poetic voice; Frankfurt, in a late fragment, he called "the navel of the earth." His first poems for her, whom he addressed as Diotima, are marvellously expressive of love and joy; thereafter, as social circumstances oppressed the lovers, he turned to lament and the determined celebration of the Good he was losing. The loss of Susette confirmed him in his elegiac character.

Hölderlin had been working on the novel *Hyperion* before he met Susette (she had read fragments of it in Schiller's *Thalia*), but meeting her he continued it as their book. "Forgive me that Diotima dies," he wrote. Hyperion, the modern Greek fighting for the recovery of the Hellenic Ideal in the abortive rising of 1770, sees his ideals founder in the bitterest fashion; his attempt to realize them costs him Diotima too. There is almost a will to failure in the book; as though the hero pushes the foreboding that he will fail to its ultimate proof, and salvages his ideals out of a wretched reality into the spirit.

Forced to leave the Gontard household Hölderlin held out in nearby Homburg for as long as he could. There he schooled himself for his greatest poetry. He translated Pindar literally, to learn what his own German language might do; he reflected on the nature and practice of poetry, especially the crucial question of how form might express the spirit without imprisoning or travestying it. Further, he worked at the drama *Empedokles*; but having written extensive notes and attempted three versions, he abandoned the work. Attractive though the idea was and although much of the poetry, especially that of the second version, has an exciting vitality, in essence the conception itself was undramatic and could not have been executed satisfactorily.

The world of Hölderlin's mature poetry, of the great hymns and elegies, is conceived in very concrete terms: it can be mapped, it has two poles—Greece and Hesperia—and numerous renowned features—rivers, mountains, islands, and cities. It incorporates a simple idea (deriving from Herder but also from contemporary Pietist beliefs): that the Spirit of Civilization, having flourished in the East and most splendidly in Periclean Athens, will alight and flourish now north of the Alps, in Germany. The Revolutionary Wars, and the momentousness attaching to the turn of the century, inclined the determinedly optimistic Hölderlin to believe in such a renaissance. In his cosmology we inhabit an Age of Night—initiated by Christ, the last of the Greek gods. We are benighted and await the new daylight; the poet's task is to encourage us not to despair. This benighted age is characterized by restlessness and wandering; an ideal homeland (Hölderlin's childhood Swabia) is a focus of longing. These are not so much ideas or beliefs as poetic images of immense persuasive power; they express certain readily identifiable conditions: alienation, loss, nostalgia. The theme of Hölderlin's poetry is, *in nuce*: love in absence—how to survive and continue to hold to ideals in times of their manifest absence.

It will not do, when reading Hölderlin, simply to abstract the above adumbrated scheme. That is paraphrase. Instead we have to attend to the rhythms of his poetry, which are very subtle. Contradictions (inclination to despair, insistence on hope, longing for the past, assertion of a better future) are expressed less in statement than in rhythm, in the running of the verse itself against the exact constraints of form. His handling of hexameters and the elegiac couplet is infinitely finer than Goethe's or Schiller's. There is a movement of tones in Hölderlin's verse, there are oscillations of feeling, shifts, transitions through discord and harmony. In a sense, the poems do not end; their constituent emotions have been so finely rendered that we feel them to be still in play. There is no neat conclusion, as of a logical argument. There could not be. The spirit resists such finality. In this manner, in what he himself called a "loving conflict," Hölderlin's poetry serves the cause of perpetual renewal, of revolt against oppression, deadness, and despair of whatever kind.

After the time in Bordeaux, after the death of Susette Gontard, Hölderlin's poetic world expanded and disintegrated. It is much to be regretted that his mind, because of illness, could not compose the terrific richness of his last creative years. There are moments of vision unlike any others in his poetry, of an intense sensuousness and particularity.

During his years in the tower, half his life, Hölderlin wrote, very often to order, rhyming stanzas on the view through his window of the Neckar and the fields and hills beyond; or, less successfully, on abstract topics. These last poems are very moving, sometimes in their own flat simplicity (*tension* being a hallmark of the mature poetry) but often, alas, only as documents.

Nobody nowadays would be likely, as earlier generations did, to disregard anything Hölderlin wrote on the grounds of his presumed insanity. In his life and in all his work he is a poet for our times. He confronts us with benightedness, and demonstrates the spirit's will to survive.

—David Constantine

See the essay on "Bread and Wine."

HOLUB, Miroslav

Born: Plzeň, Czechoslovakia (now the Czech Republic), 13 September 1923. **Education:** Completed secondary school, 1942; while Czech universities remained closed under Nazi occupation, worked as a labourer at a warehouse and at a railway station, 1942–45; studied at Charles University, 1945–53, received an M.D., 1953. **Family:** Married 1) Věra Koktová, 1948 (divorced,1952); 2) Marta Svikruhová, 1963 (divorced, 1971); 3) Jitka Langrová, 1971, three children. **Career:** Worked as a pathologist in a Prague hospital, 1953, was employed at the Institute of Biology (later Microbiology) at the Czechoslovak Academy of Sciences 1954–70; fired in 1970 for political reasons; executive editor of *Vesmír (The Universe)* 1951–65, after making a degrading public statement of self-criticism he was given employment at the Institute for Clinical and Experimental Medicine in Prague, 1970; he was re-admitted to the Institute of Microbiology, 1995. From 1970–82 he was a banned author in Czechoslovakia, until mid 1980s he could only publish his literary and journalistic work with difficulty. **Awards:** Honorary Doctorate, Oberlin University, 1985. **Died:** 14 July 1998.

PUBLICATIONS

Collections

Selected Poems, translated by Ian Milner and George Theiner. 1967.
Notes of a Clay Pigeon, translated by Ian and Jarmila Milner. 1977.
Poems Before and After, translated by Ian and Jarmila Milner, Ewald Osers and George Theiner. 1990.
Intensive Care: New and Selected Poems. 1997.
The Rampage, translated by Miroslav Holub, David Young, Dana Hábová and Rebekah Bloyd. 1997.

Verse

Denní služba [Day Duty]. 1958.
Achilles a želva [Achilles and the Tortoise]. 1960.
Slabikář [School Reader]. 1961.
Jdi a otevři dveře [Go and Open the Door]. 1962.
Kam teče krev [Where Blood Flows]. 1963.
Tak zvané srdce [The So-Called Heart]. 1963.
Ačkoli. 1969; as *Although*, translated by Ian and Jarmila Milner, 1971.
Beton [Concrete]. 1970.
Události [Events]. 1971.
Sagitální řez. 1988; as as *Sagittal Section: Poems, New and Selected*, translated by Stuart Friebert and Dana Hábová, 1980.
Naopak. 1982; as *On the Contrary and Other Poems*, translated by Ewald Osers, 1984.
Interferon čili O divadle. 1986; as *Interferon or On Theater*, translated by David Young and Dana Hábová, 1982.
Syndrom mizející plíce. 1990, as *Vanishing Lung Syndrome*, translated by David Young and Dana Hábová, 1990.
Ono se letělo: Suita z rodného města. 1994; as *Supposed to Fly. A Sequence from Pilsen, Czechoslovakia*, translated by Ewald Osers, 1996.
Narození Sisyfovo. Básně 1989–1997 [The Birth of Sisyphos. Poems 1989–1997]. 1998.

Other

Zcela nesoustavná zoologie [Quite Unsystematic Zoology], with Květoslav Přibyl. 1963.
Anděl na kolečkách: Poloreportáž z USA [An Angel on Wheels: Half a Report from the USA]. 1963, extended 1964.
Tři kroky po zemi: Příběhy a myšlenky kolem vědy [Three Steps on the Ground: Stories and Ideas about Science]. 1965.
Žít v New Yorku [To Live in New York]. 1969.
Struktura imunitního systému [The Structure of the Immunity System]. 1979.
K principu rolničky. 1987; as *The Jingle Bell Principle*, translated by James Naughton, 1992.
Immunology of Nude Mice. 1989.
Maxwellův démon čili O tvořivosti [Maxwelás Demon or On Creativity]. 1988.
Nepatrně ne [Imperceptibly, No]. 1989.
The Dimension of the Present Moment and Other Essays, edited by David Young. 1990.
Skrytá zášť věků [The Hidden Hatred of the Ages]. 1990.
O příčinách porušení a zkázy těl lidských. 1992; as *Shedding Life: Disease, Politics and Other Human Conditions*, translated by David Young, Rebekhah Bloyd and others, 1997.
Aladinova lampa [Alladiñs Lamp]. 1996.

*

Bibliography: *MUDr. Miroslav Holub, CSc. Publikované práce 1956–1983 (MUDr. Miroslav Holub, CSc. Published Work 1956–1983),* edited by A. Nováková, 1983.

Critical Studies: "Syntagmatic Structure in the Free Verse of Miroslav Holub" by Herbert Eagle, in *Rackham Literary Studies*, vol. 3, 1972; "The Fully Exposed Poem" by Seamus Heaney, in *Parnassus*, vol. 11, Spring-Summer, 1983; "Miroslav Holub" by Dennis ÓDriscoll, in *Poetry Review*, vol. 75, October, 1985; "Three Contemporary Slavic Poets: A View from the Other Side" by Rueul Wilson, in *New Querterly Cave*, vol. 1, no. 4, 1976; "Miroslav Holub" by Jan Čulík and Jiří Holý, in *Dictionary of Literary Biography*, vol. 232, 2001.

*   *   *

Miroslav Holub was a poet and a scientist, a medical doctor and an internationally respected immunologist. His poetry is unique because it combines a literary tradition with the analytical incisivenes of a scientific mind. Holub began writing poetry at the end of World War II under the influence of the Czech interwar poetic avant garde. Surrealist motives—used within the strictly cerebral structures of his poems—remained a characteristic feature of his poetry throughout his literary career. He was also influenced by the civilist poetry of Jacques Prévert.

After the communist takeover in 1948, when all published literature in Czechoslovakia was forced to conform to strict propagandist norms, Holub did not publish any of his work. It was not until the second half of the 1950s that he became a member of a literary circle centered around the journal *Květen* [*May*], which rejected the rhetoric of official pro-communist literature and in response to its bathos chose to be deliberately anti-ideological. The writers centered around *Květen* used a casual writing style, and were interested in the life of ordinary people, in what they called the "poetry of the everyday." Holub avoided lyricism and wrote irregular, free verse. His poetry used themes from his work as a scientist: researchers were for Holub unassuming individuals who by solving problems and making discoveries brought about progress. Holub's poems are effective because they are extremely logical and semantically precise: sometimes they feel like riddles, often they are based on paradoxes. They contain humor. They translate well into other languages because their structure is based on the confrontation of ideas, not on linguistic experimentation.

Even Holub's early poetry could be construed as implicit comment on the frustrations of life under the communism—as well as on the bleakness of the human condition in general. But in the early 1960s, Holub was still quite optimistic. He felt one must always ask questions, try to "go and open the door": "even if there's only / the darkness ticking / even if there's only the hollow wind / even if nothing is there. / At least there'll be / a draft." Poems like these had a subversive, political charge within the besieged society of communist Czechoslovakia, and Holub's writing became a significant part of the movement of Czech intellectuals to liberalise the communist system through questioning, outspoken, liberal and democratic art. In the 1960s, like many of his colleagues, Holub still seemed to believe in human progress.

The 1968 Warsaw Pact invasion of Czechoslovakia ended the liberalising reforms and threw the country into a harsh neo-Stalinist mode for twenty years. The mood of Holub's poetry darkened. Life was difficult for Holub in the 1970s and 1980s: like many of his colleagues, he was banned as a writer and could not publish his work until 1982, in spite of the fact that he made a degrading public statement in order to win favor with the communist authorities as early as 1973. The publication of this statement alienated Holub from many of his former literary friends who had by this time become persecuted political dissidents. Holub tried to remain out of trouble with the communist authorities, but the secret police harassed him nevertheless. While he was ostracised in his own country, internationally, his literary and scientific work fame grew. His poetry came to be translated into more than thirty languages and in the last years of his life Holub was frequently invited to attend public readings of his poetry in many countries.

In the 1980s and 1990s, Holub mostly commented in essays on the current technological civilisation and on the place of poetry in today's world. His poetry continued in the line of development, started in the late 1960s: in spite of all effort, life now seemed absurd, ambiguous, unintelligible, and undecipherable.

After the fall of communism in Czechoslovakia in 1989, Holub never regained the standing that he had enjoyed along with his liberal colleagues in the 1960s in his native country. Czechoslovakia had quickly succumbed to low-brow commercial entertainment and the arts no longer played such a significant role as they did in the 1960s. Many Prague intellectuals could not forgive Holub that he never came out openly against communism in the 1970s and 1980s. Holub's rational and matter-of-fact literary style felt alien and "non-poetic" to many Czech critics.

—Jan Čulík

HOMER

Career: Nothing is known of his life: possibly lived 8th century BC; generally thought to have come from Ionia in Asia Minor, specifically Chios or Smyrna; ancient tradition that he was blind may be true.

PUBLICATIONS

Collection

Opera, edited by D.B. Munro and Thomas W. Allen. 5 vols., 1912–20.

Verse

Iliad, edited by Walter Leaf. 2 vols., 1900–02, reprinted 1960; also edited by D.B. Munro and Thomas W. Allen, 1920, A.J. Church, 1965, and M.M. Willcock, Books I–XII, 1978, Books XIII–XXIV, 1983; Book XXIV edited by C.W. MacLeod, 1982; as *The Iliad*, translated by George Chapman, 1611; also translated by Thomas Hobbes, 1676; John Ozell, W. Broome, and W. Oldisworth (from the French), 5 vols., 1712; Alexander Pope, 6 vols., 1715–20; William Cowper, 2 vols., 1802, reprinted 1992; P. Williams, 1806; James Mortice, 1809; William Sotheby, 2 vols., 1831; William Munford, 2 vols., 1846; T.S. Brandreth, 2 vols., 1846; F.W. Newman, 1856; I.C. Wright, 2 vols., 1861–65; Lord Derby, 2 vols., 1864; T.S. Norgate, 1864; J. Henry Dart, 1865; Edwin M. Simcox, 1865; P.S. Worsley and John Conington, 2 vols., 1865–68;

John F.W. Herschel, 1866; J.I. Cochrane, 1867; Charles Merivale, 2 vols., 1869; W.C. Bryant, 2 vols., 1870; W.G. Caldcleugh, 2 vols., 1870; J.G. Cordery, 2 vols., 1871; John Benson Rose, 1874; W. Lucas Collins, 1876; C.B. Cayley, 1877; A.S. Way, 1885; John Purves, 1891; Samuel Butler, 1898; E.A. Tibbetts, 1907; E.H. Blakeney, 1909; A.G. Lewis, 1911; A.F. Murison, 1933; William Marris, 1934; W.B. Smith and W. Miller, 1944; A.H. Chase and W.G. Perry, Jr., 1950; Richmond Lattimore, 1951; Robert Fitzgerald, 1974; J.P. Kurton, 1977; E. Rees, 1977; D.B. Hull, 1983; Martin Hammond, 1987; Robert Fagles, 1990; Michael Reck, 1990; as *The Anger of Achilles*, translated by Robert Graves, 1959; translations into prose: by James MacPherson, 2 vols., 1773; Theodore Alois Buckley, 1851; Andrew Lang, Walter Leaf, and Ernest Myers, 1882; A.T. Murray [Loeb Edition], 2 vols., 1924–25; Robinson Smith, 1937; W.H.D. Rouse, 1938; E.V. Rieu, 1950; commentaries: Books I–VI by M.M. Willcock, 1970, Books I–IV and Books V–VIII by G.S. Kirk, 1985 and 1990, Books IX–XII by J.B. Hainsworth, 1993, Books XIII–XVI by Richard Janko, 1991, Books XVII–XX by Mark W. Edwards, 1991, Books XXI–XXIV by Nicholas Richardson, 1993; Book Nine, edited by Jasper Griffin, 1995; Books VIII and IX, edited with translation by Christopher H. Wilson, 1996; translated by Stanley Lombardo, 1997; as *Illiad Book One*, translated by Simon Pulleyn, 2000.

Odyssey, edited by J.J. Owen. 1845; also edited by Thomas W. Allen, 1906, and W.B. Stanford, 2 vols., 1947–48, revised edition, 1965; as *The Odyssey*, translated by George Chapman, 1615; also translated by Thomas Hobbes, 1675; Alexander Pope, 1725; William Cowper, 1792; Theodore Alois Buckley, 1851; P.S. Worsley, 2 vols., 1861–62; T.S. Norgate, 1863; George Musgrave, 2 vols., 1865; L. Bigge-Wither, 1869; G.W. Edginton, 1869; W.C. Bryant, 1871; Mordaunt Barnard, 2 vols., 1876; W. Walter Merry, and James Riddell, 2 vols., 1878; G.A. Schomberg, 2 vols., 1879–82; A.S. Way, 1880; William Morris, 2 vols., 1887; J.G. Cordery, 1897; Samuel Butler, 1900; J.W. Mackail, 3 vols., 1903–10; H.B. Cotterill, 1911; Francis Caulfeild, 1921; William Marris, 1925; S.O. Andrew, 1948; Robert Fitzgerald, 1961; Richmond Lattimore, 1965; Albert Cook, 1973; E, Rees, 1977; Walter Shewring, 1980; P.V. Jones, 1991; translated into prose by S.H. Bryant and A. Lang, 1879; translations into prose: by G.H. Palmer (Books I–XII), 1884; A.T. Murray [Loeb Edition], 2 vols., 1919; Robert H. Hiller, 1927; T.E. Lawrence, 1932; W.H.D. Rouse, 1937; E.V. Rieu, 1945; commentaries: on vol. 1 by A. Heubeck, Stephanie West, and J.B. Hainsworth, 1985, col. 2 by A. Heubeck and Arie Hoekstra, 1988; Books VI–VIII, edited by A.F. Garvie, 1994; translated by Martin Hammond, 2000; translated by R.L. Eickhoff, 2001.

The Homeric Hymns, translated by Thomas W. Allen, W.R. Holliday, and E.E. Sikes. 1904; also translated by C. Boer, 1972; Apostolos N. Athanassakis, 1976.

*

Bibliography: *A Bibliography of Homeric Scholarship 1930–1970* by D.W. Packard, 1973; ''Homer and Oral Tradition'' by Mark W. Edwards, in *Oral Tradition*, 1/2, 1986; ''Homeric Studies 1978–83'' by J.P. Holoka, in *Classical World*, 1990.

Critical Studies: *Homer and the Epic*, 1893, and *The World of Homer*, 1910, both by Andrew Lang; *External Evidence for Interpolation in Homer* by G.M. Bolling, 1925; *The Unity of Homer* by J.A. Scott, 1925; *The Composition of Homer's Odyssey* by W.J. Woodhouse,

1930; *The Idea of God in Homer* by E. Ehnmark, 1935; *The Poetry of Homer* by S.E. Bassett, 1938; *The Iliad; or, The Poem of Force* by S. Weil, translated by M. McCarthy, 1945; *Homer in English Criticism: The Historical Approach in the Eighteenth Century* edited by D.M. Foerster, 1947; *Homer and the Monuments* by H.L. Lorimer, 1950; *The Poet of the Iliad* by H.T. Wade-Gery, 1952; *The World of Odysseus* by M.I. Finley, 1954; *The Homeric Gods* by W.F. Otto, translated by M. Hadas, 1954; *The Homeric Odyssey*, 1955, *History and the Homeric Iliad*, 1959, and *Folktales in the Odyssey*, 1972, all by Denys L. Page; *Homer and His Critics* by J.L. Myres, 1958; *From Mycenae to Homer* by T.B.L. Webster, 1958; *Homer and the Homeric Tradition* by Cedric H. Whitman, 1958; *The Singer of Tales* by A.B. Lord, 1960; *A Complete Concordance to the Odyssey of Homer* by H. Dunbar, edited by B. Marzullo, 2nd edition, 1962; *The Songs of Homer*, 1962 (as *Homer and the Epic*, 1965), *The Language and Background of Homer*, 1965, and *Homer and the Oral Tradition*, 1976, all by G.S. Kirk; *A Complete Concordance to the Iliad of Homer* by G.L. Prendergast, edited by B. Marzullo, 2nd edition, 1962; *A Companion to Homer* edited by A.J.B. Wace and Frank H. Stubbings, 1962; *Homer: A Collection of Critical Essays* edited by George Steiner and Robert Fagles, 1963; *Essays on the Odyssey: Selected Modern Criticism* edited by Charles H. Taylor, 1963; *Prolegomena to Homer* by F.A. Wolf, edited by R. Peppmüller, 1963; *Typical Battle Scenes in the Iliad* by Bernard Fenik, 1965, *Homer: Tradition and Invention*, edited by Fenik, 1978, and *Homer and the Nibelungenlied*, by Fenik, 1986; *Homeric Modifications of Formulaic Prototypes* by A. Hoekstra, 1965; *Notes on Homer's Odyssey* by Robert J. Milch, 1966; *The Art of the Odyssey* by Howard W. Clark, 1967; *The Iliad, the Odyssey and the Epic Tradition* by C.R. Beye, 1968; *The Flexibility of the Homeric Formula*, 1968, and *Homer*, 1969, both by J.B. Hainsworth; *Homer's Odyssey: A Critical Handbook* edited by C.E. Nelson, 1969; *People and Themes in Homer's Odyssey*, 1970, and *Homer's Iliad: Its Composition and the Motif of Supplication*, 1984, both by Agathe Thornton; *The Making of Homeric Verse: The Collected Papers of Milman Parry* edited by Adam Parry, 1971; *The Theme of the Mutilation of the Corpse in the Iliad* by Charles Segal, 1971; *Homer* by C.M. Bowra, 1972; *The Conference Sequence: Patterned Narrative and Narrative Inconsistency in the Odyssey* by William F. Hansen, 1972; *Studies in the Language of Homer* by G.P. Shipp, 2nd edition, 1972; *Spontaneity and Tradition: A Study of the Oral Art of Homer* by M.N. Nagler, 1974; *The Homeric Hymn to Demeter* by N.J. Richardson, 1974; *Archery at the Dark of the Moon: Poetic Problems in Homer's Odyssey* by Norman Austin, 1975; *Nature and Culture in the Iliad: The Tragedy of Hector* by James Michael Redfield, 1975; *The Meaning of Homeric EYCHOMAI Through Its Formulas* by Leonard Charles Muellner, 1976; *The Disguised Guest: Rank, Role and Identity in the Odyssey* by Douglas J. Stewart, 1976; *An Essay on the Original Genius of Homer* by R. Wood, 1976; *Similes in the Homeric Poems* by Carroll Moulton, 1977; *Composition by Theme in the Odyssey*, 1977, and *Homer and the Origin of the Greek Alphabet*, 1991, both by Barry Powell; *The Homeric Epics* by C.A. Trypanis, 1977; *Nature and Background of Major Concepts of Divine Power in Homer*, 1977, and *Form and Content in Homer*, 1982, both by Odysseus Tsagarakis; *Homer's Iliad: The Shield of Memory* by Kenneth John Atchity, 1978; *Studies in Characterization in the Iliad* by Leslie Collins, 1978; *Homer's Odyssey* by John H. Finley, J.r, 1978; *The Greek Concept of Justice: From Its Shadow in Homer to Its Substance in Plato* by Eric A. Havelock, 1978; *The Last Scenes of the Odyssey* by Dorothea Wender, 1978; *Essays on the Iliad: Selected Modern Criticism* edited by J. Wright, 1978; *The Best of the Achaeans* by G. Nagy, 1979; *An Introduction to Homer* by W.A. Camps, 1980; *Homer on Life and Death*, 1980, and *Homer: Odyssey*, 1987, both by Jasper Griffin; *The Homeric Question and the Oral-Formulaic Theory* by Minna Skafte Jensen, 1980; *Achilles, Patroklos and the Meaning of Philos* by Dale S. Sinos, 1980; *Homer's Readers: A Historical Introduction to the Iliad and the Odyssey* by Howard W. Clarke, 1981; *Homer, Hesiod and the Hymns: Diachronic Development in Epic Diction* by Richard Janko, 1982; *Childlike Achilles: Ontogeny and Philogeny in the Iliad* by W.T. MacCary, 1982; *Improvisation, Typology, Culture, and "the New Orthodoxy": How Oral Is Homer?* by D.G. Miller, 1982; *The Epithets in Homer: A Study in Poetic Values*, 1982, and *Homer*, 1985, both by Paolo Vivante; *The Wrath of Athena: Gods and Men in the Odyssey* by Jenny Strauss Clay, 1983; *Approaches to Homer* edited by Carl A. Rubeno and Cynthia W. Shelmerdine, 1983; *Twentieth-Century Interpretations of the Odyssey: A Collection of Critical Essays*, 1983; *The Mortal Hero* by S. Schein, 1984; *Traditional Themes and the Homeric Hymns* by Cora Angier Sowra, 1984; *Achilles in the Odyssey* by Anthony T. Edwards, 1985; *Prolegomena to Homer* translated by A. Grafton, G.W. Most, and J.E.G. Zetzel, 1985; *Notes on Homer's Iliad* edited by Robin Sowerby, 1985, and *Homer, the Odyssey: Notes* by Sowerby, 1986; *Homer the Theologian* by Robert Lamberton, 1986, and *Homer's Ancient Readers: The Hermeneutics of Greek's Earliest Epic Exegeses* edited by Lamberton and John Jo Keaney, 1992; *Notes on Homer's Iliad* by Elaine Strongskill, 1986; *Homer* by Martin Thorpe, 1986; *Homer: Beyond Oral Poetry: Recent Trends in Homeric Interpretation* by J.M. Bremner, I.J.F. De Jong, and J. Kalff, 1987; *Homer: Poet of the Iliad* by Mark W. Edwards, 1987; *Disguise and Recognition in the Odyssey* by Sheila Murnaghan, 1987; *Odysseus Polutropos: Intertextual Readings in the Odyssey and the Iliad* by Pietro Pucci, 1987; *Naming Achilles* by David Shire, 1987; *Homer: Iliad* by M.S. Silk, 1987; *Linguistics and Formulas in Homer: Scalarity and the Description of the Particle Per* by E.J. Bakker, 1988; *Notes on Homer's Odyssey* edited by A. Norman Jeffares and Suheil Badi Bushrui, 1988; *The Ironies of War: An Introduction to Homer's Iliad* by Ian C. Johnston, 1988; *Homer's Odyssey: A Companion to the English Translation of Richmond Lattimore* by Peter Jones, 1988; *War Music: An Account of Books 16–19 of Homer's Iliad* by Christopher Logue, 1988; *Epos: Word, Narrative and the Iliad* by Michael Lynn-George, 1988; *Homer, 1987: Colloquium Proceedings* edited by John Pinsent and H.V. Hurt, 1988; *The Unity of the Odyssey* by George E. Dimock, 1989; *Pindar and Homer* by Frank Nisetich, 1989; *Psychological Activity in Homer: A Study of Phren* by Shirley D. Sullivan, 1989; *Traditional Oral Epic* by John Foley, 1990; *Measure and Music* by Caroline Higbie, 1990; *The Language of Heroes: Speech and Performance in the Iliad* by Richard P. Martin, 1990; *Man in the Middle Voice: Name and Narration in the Odyssey* by John Peradotto, 1990; *Homer and the Sacred City* by S. Scully, 1990; *Homer* edited by Harold Bloom, 1991; *The Gods in Epic* by D.C. Feeney, 1991; *Penelope's Renown* by M. A. Katz, 1991; *Homer: Readings and Images* by Chris Emlyn-Jones, Loina Hardwick, and John Purkis, 1992; *Regarding Penelope* by N. Felson-Rubin, 1992; *Homer: The Poetry of the Past* by Andrew Ford, 1992; *Classical Epic: Homer and Virgil* by Richard Jenkyns, 1992; *Homeric Misdirection: False Predictions in the Iliad* by James V. Morrison, 1992; *Homeric Soundings: The Shaping of the Iliad* by Oliver Taplin, 1992; *The Stranger's Welcome: Oral Theory and the Aesthetics of the Homeric Hospitality Scene* by Steve Reece, 1992; "Homer and the *Roland*" by William M. Sale, in *Oral Tradition*, 8.1 and 8.2, 1993; *The Shield of Homer:*

Narrative Structure in the Iliad by Keith Stanley, 1993; *The Poetics of Supplication: Homer's Iliad and Odyssey* by Kevin Crotty, 1994; *Singers, Heroes, and Gods in the Odyssey* by Charles Segal, 1994; *Reciprocity and Ritual: Homer and Tragedy in the Developing City-State* by Richard Seaford, 1994; *Homer*, edited by Katherine Callen King, 1994; *Greek Myths and Mesopotamia: Parallels and Influence in the Homeric Hymns and Hesiod* and Charles Penglase, 1994; *The Heart of Achilles: Characterizations of Personal Ethics in the Iliad* by Graham Zanker, 1994; *The Interpretation of Order: A Study in the Poetics of Homeric Repetition* by Ahuvia Kahane, 1994; *The Distaff Side: Representing the Female in Homer's Odyssey*, edited by Beth Cohen, 1995; *Siren Songs: Gender, Audiences, and Narrators in the Odyssey* by Lillian Eileen Doherty, 1995; *The Odyssey in Athens: Myths of Cultural Origins* by Erwin F. Cook, 1995; *Turning: From Persuasion to Philosophy: A Reading of Homer's Iliad* by Michael Naas, 1995; *Homer, His Art and His World* by Joachim Latacz, translated by James P. Holoka, 1996; *Homer* by R.B. Rutherford, 1996; *Essay on the Life and Poetry of Homer* by Plutarch, edited by J.J. Keaney and Robert Lamberton, 1996; *Talking Trojan: Speech and Community in the Iliad* by Hilary Mackie, 1996; *Homeric Questions* by Gregory Nagy, 1996; *The Odyssey Re-formed* by Frederick Ahl and Hanna M. Roisman, 1996; *Reading the Odyssey: Selective Interpretive Essays*, edited with an introduction by Seth L. Schein, 1996; *Out of Line: Homeric Composition Beyond the Hexameter* by Matthew Clark, 1997; *Plot and Point of View in the Iliad* by Robert J. Rabel, 1997; *Poetry in Speech: Orality and Homeric Discourse* by Egbert J. Bakker, 1997; *Readings on Homer*, edited by Don Nardo, 1998; *Homer*, edited by Ian McAuslan and Peter Walcot, 1998; *The Swineherd and the Bow: Representations of Class in the Odyssey* by William G. Thalmann, 1998; *The Song of the Sirens: Essays on Homer* by Pietro Pucci, 1998; *Homer: Critical Assessments*, edited by Irene J.F. de Jong, 1999; *Flesh and Spirit in the Songs of Homer: A Study of Words and Myths* by Michael Clarke, 1999; *Homer's Secret Iliad: The Epic of the Night Skies Decoded* by Florence Wood and Kenneth Wood, 1999; *Homer's Traditional Art* by John Miles Foley, 1999; *Nine Essays on Homer*, edited by Miriam Carlisle and Olga Levaniouk, 1999; *The Odyssey: Structure, Narration, and Meaning* by Bruce Louden, 1999; *Homer's Iliad: A Commentary on the Translation of Richmond Lattimore* by Norman Postlethwaite, 2000; *Homer Beside Himself: Para-narratives in the Iliad* by Maureen Alden, 2000; *Sense and Nonsense in Homer: A Consideration of the Inconsistencies and Incoherencies in the Texts of the Iliad and Odyssey* by John Wilson, 2000; *The Pity of Achilles: Oral Style and the Unity of the Iliad* by Jinyo Kim, 2000; *Homer* by Jasper Griffin, 2001; *The Tradition of the Trojan War in Homer and the Epic Cycle* by Jonathan S. Burgess, 2001; *Studies in the Text and Transmission of the Iliad* by Martin L. West, 2001; *The Raft of Odysseus: The Ethnographic Imagination of Homer's Odyssey* by Carol Dougherty, 2001.

* * *

The Iliad and *The Odyssey* come at the end of a 500-year-long tradition of oral epic, and parts of them—phrases, lines, perhaps even passages—must have been composed at the beginning of this tradition, when the city of Troy fell to the Achaean armies commanded by King Agamemnon of Mycenae. The oral epic style is a formulaic style, and most of the verses contain formulae: half-lines consisting of a noun plus an adjective, adverb, verb, or another noun, repeated exactly throughout the poem; whole lines stating a recurring fact, such as the coming of dawn; and a few passages of several lines describing, e.g. the preparation and eating of a meal. The formulae exist in order to ensure that the improvising oral poet can keep his metre from breaking down.

Such poetry and its audiences are not offended by repetitions that serve metrical needs, nor by epithets that are otiose or even slightly inappropriate: Achilles is ''swift-footed,'' whether running, standing, or seated. Repetition weakens the adjective, not so as to render it meaningless, but to make it seem part of the name. Repeated adjectives never, or very rarely, mean the wrong thing, but they need hardly be the *mot juste*.

The oral-formulaic style did not evolve in order that poems of the length of *The Iliad* be composed, and the Homeric compositions are extraordinary achievements even as craftworks. It is quite possible, even probable, that they were composed with the aid of writing: perhaps they were dictated, perhaps the poet learned how to write. That they were preserved orally is of course possible, but in that case what we read undoubtedly suffered distortion during oral transmission. Since most Homeric critics prefer to talk about a text assumed to go back to the 7th or 8th centuries BC, criticism cannot safely rest its analyses on one or two passages; or if it does, it must recognize that it is analysing a text that may well not be Homer's. Granted this caveat, it is safe to look on each poem as a unity, not an editorial amalgamation of previously existing long passages. Whether one poet composed both poems cannot be decided.

The theme of *The Iliad* is the Wrath of Achilles, directed first at Agamemnon, who robbed Achilles of his battleprize Briseis, and then at Hector, who killed Achilles' beloved companion Patroclus. The young Achilles had dedicated himself to the heroic code, the most attractive concept of values in his Achaean society. To be a hero is to be publicly recognized for one's valour on the battlefield, in combat fought no further from the enemy than a spear's throw. Such recognition is symbolized by the battleprize, awarded by the troops or by Agamemnon after a city is sacked. To take away one's prize is to shatter one's honour, and Achilles is quite justified in withdrawing from battle. Agamemnon, his cause seriously threatened by Achilles' absence, sends an embassy offering vast recompense. Achilles, still in the grip of his wrath, has by now come to question the value of heroism: life and love seem more important, and the pleas of Odysseus—representing Agamemnon—and of Achilles' old teacher Phoenix, are turned aside. Ajax's brilliant appeal to Achilles' love for his comrades has better luck. Achilles agrees with him intellectually, though he is still too angry to rejoin the battle. But he does allow his companion Patroclus to lead his troops back to fight; when Hector kills Patroclus, Achilles conceives a blind hatred for Hector which is not satisfied even by Hector's death. Priam comes seeking his son's body, offering the ransom appropriate to the heroic code, and more importantly basing his appeal on the love between father and son. To this common human value Achilles responds, and the Wrath comes to an end.

Achilles' movement from heroism to love is interlaced with the poet's exploration of other perceptions of value and of the conflicts such differing perceptions create. Agamemnon, at least initially, believes himself justified by his superior power: his ability to field the most troops. Odysseus is the professional soldier who most honours success: never to return from war empty-handed. The Achaeans and their codes are essentially military; the Trojans are more diverse. We never forget that their city was once at peace, and prosperous. One of

the king's sons, Paris, is a skilled bowman in battle, but has no interest in war; he values beauty, and is not only the consort of Helen, but was the architect of his own palace. The shipbuilder Phereclus, no great warrior, is none the less eminent enough to merit a pedigree. The individual Achaean nations are under the absolute command of their kings, while Troy is loosely governed by a council of elders dominated, but hardly dictated to, by Priam's family. Corresponding to such institutional looseness is a moral pluralism: unlike his brother Paris, Hector values heroism, while their father Priam is broadly tolerant, kindly, and sympathetic. Troy's acceptance of diversity is the reason for its destruction: it does not force Paris to return the stolen Helen, nor Hector to re-enter his city and shun the duel with Achilles. Achaean society will always put the military goal first, while the Trojans will sacrifice national security to preserve individual freedom of choice. This is Troy's tragedy, played against Achilles' finding value in love, at the price of losing his friend and becoming forever alienated spiritually from his own society. Homer's vision is pessimistic, but affirmative: human life has more ill than good, but it has value, in heroism and in love.

The Odyssey moves in very different worlds. Odysseus, returning from the Trojan War, is thrust into a fairyland world inhabited by the one-eyed giant Cyclops, the witch Circe, the seductive Sirens, the inexorable Scylla and Charybdis. Reluctant, fascinated, curious, self-indulgent, Odysseus pits himself against the temptations and dangers of this world with considerable personal success, but with the loss of his entire army. His various adventures usually have a ready symbolic interpretation: the Sirens represent the danger of losing one's soul to the power of great art; Scylla and Charybdis, the need to choose to surrender a part to save the whole; Calypso, the surrender of one's humanity to a world without death or domestic responsibility. Odysseus visits the underworld and hears from Achilles how any kind of life is preferable to non-existence. Despite this gloomy prospect, and despite the lure of the beauty of Calypso and her island, Odysseus chooses to be a mortal, a human being, and to go home.

Before this picture of the temptations of sensuality, adventure, and escape from the human lot, Homer places a ''Telemachy'' revealing how desperately Odysseus is needed at home in Ithaca. His wife Penelope, not knowing if her husband is alive, is besieged by suitors: though anxious to remain faithful, she cannot afford to reject a second marriage out of hand. Her son Telemachus is beginning to grow up in this hostile world: he acts creditably enough, but clearly requires a father's help. Odysseus' household—in Greek, his *oikos*, the fundamental unit of Ithacan society—is being consumed by the suitors, and pleas to fellow citizens receive no effective response. The last half of the poem describes Odysseus' return to Ithaca, where he reclaims his household and restores order. Husband and wife reunite in their wedding bed; and it appears at this moment that the destiny of humanity, male and female, is essentially domestic, and that ultimate fulfilment lies in establishing and maintaining the *oikos*.

Yet the poem's vision is larger than this. Odysseus must one day journey to an inland place and there dedicate his oar to Poseidon, thus placating the hostile god of the sea. The life of Odysseus, as of Penelope, is defined by two movements: one is a struggle to attain domestic stability; the other is the fascination offered by the adventures and challenges along the way.

—William Merritt Sale

See the essays on *The Iliad* and *The Odyssey*.

HOOFT, Pieter Corneliszoon

Born: Amsterdam, Dutch Republic (now The Netherlands), 15 March 1581. **Education:** Educated at the Amsterdam Latin School; studied law at Leiden, 1605–07. **Family:** Married 1) Christina van Erp in 1610 (died 1624); 2) Leonora Hellemans in 1627. **Career:** Travelled in Europe, then settled in the Netherlands; Justice of Muiden, from 1609; after 1627 his official residence became the leading literary circle of his time, the Muiderkring. **Awards:** Granted title "Knight of St. Michael" for his biography of Henry IV, 1639. **Member:** d'Eglantier; joined Samuel Coster's Nederduytsche Academie. **Died:** 21 May 1647.

PUBLICATIONS

Collections

Alle de werken [Complete Works]. 4 vols., 1703–04.
Historieën [Histories], edited by W. Hecker. 5 vols., 1843–46.
Brieven [Letters], edited by J. van Vloten. 4 vols., 1855–57.
Volledige uitgave der gedichten [Complete Edition of the Poems], edited by P. Leendertz. 2 vols., 1871–75; revised by F.A. Stoet, 2 vols., 1899–1900.
Lyriek [Lyrics], edited by C.A. Zaalberg. 1963.
Alle de gedrukte werken [All the Printed Works], edited by W. Hellinga and P. Tuynman. 9 vols., 1971.

Plays

Geeraerdt van Velsen. 1613; as *The Tragedy of Gerard van Velsen*, translated by Theo Hermans and Paul Vincent, in *Dutch Crossing*, 45, 1991.
Achilles en Polyxena. 1614.
Theseus en Ariadne. 1614, reprinted 1988.
Granida, from *Pastor fido* by Guarini. 1615, reprinted 1958.
Warenar [A True Fool], from *Aulularia* by Plautus. 1617.
Schijnheyligh [Hypocrite], from *L'ipocrito* by Aretino. 1617.
Baeto oft oorsprong der Hollanderen [Baeto or the Origins of the Dutch]. 1626.

Verse

Emblemata amatoria. 1611.
Brief van Menelaus aan Helena [Letter from Menelaus to Helena]. 1615.
Bruiloftzang [Wedding Song]. 1623.
Klaghte der Princesse van Oranjen over 't oorloogh voor s'Hartogenbosch [Lament of the Princess of Orange Concerning the War in Den Bosch]. 1629.
Gedichten [Poems], edited by J. van der Burgh. 1636.
Erotische gedichten [Erotic Poems], edited by C.C. van Sloten. 1956.
Sonnetten, edited by P. Tuynman. 1971.

Other

Henrick de Grote [Henry the Great]. 1626.
Waernemingen op de Hollandsche tael [Observations on Dutch Language]. 1638.
Neederlandsche histoorien [History of the Netherlands]. 20 vols., 1642; 7 vols. completed by his son, 1654.

Rampzaeligheden der verheffinge van den Huize Medicis [Disasters of the Rise of the House of Medici]. 1638, revised 1649.
Reden van de waerdicheit der poesie, edited by J. van Krimpen and A.A.M. Stols. 1925, reprinted 1971; as *An Oration Concerning the Excellence of Poetry*, translated by Lesley Gilbert, in *Dutch Crossing*, 47, 1992.

*

Critical Studies: *Het vers van Hooft* by G. Kazemier, 1932; *Hooft en Tacitus* by J.D.M. Cornelissen, 1938; *Bijdrage tot de kennis van de invloeden op Hooft*, 1946, and *Ethiek en moral bij P.C. Hooft*, 1967, both by F. Veenstra; *P.C. Hooft* by H.W. van Tricht, 1951; *Hooft en dia* by W.A.P. Smit, 1968; *Dramatische struktuur in tweevoud* by E.K. Grootes, 1973; *Bijdragen tot de P.C. Hooft filologie* by P. Tuynman, 1973; *Uyt liefde geschreven: Studies over Hooft*, 1981; *Hooft als historienschrijver* by S. Groeneveld, 1981.

*   *   *

Pieter Corneliszoon Hooft was born into a rich merchant's family and took full advantage of the privileges of such a background: he received a good classical education, and he helped administer his country. He devoted himself to writing early in life, and the poetics he espoused were those of the Renaissance rather than of the Rhetoricians of "d'Eglantier," the Amsterdam chapter of Rhetoricians where he first learned his trade. He was later to break with them altogether, and to become instrumental in the founding of the first Amsterdam theatre dedicated to the new Aristotelian drama.

Like many Dutch painters of his time, Hooft discovered the Renaissance in Italy and helped introduce it to the Netherlands on his return to his native country and city. The influence of Italian models on his poetry and his pastoral play *Granida* is as obvious as is the influence of Tacitus on his historiographical writings. In the first half of his literary career Hooft concentrated on writing for the stage, although he also wrote poetry, but rather as an expression of his amorous pursuits than of his main intellectual and philosophical interests. Hooft wrote the first Renaissance play in Dutch, *Achilles en Polyxena*, based on the Homer continuations by Dictus Cretensis and Dares Phrygius. He came into his own as a playwright with *Granida*, inspired by Italian examples. Hooft used the play, written in a genre that was extremely popular in his time, to test his views on the conflict between *liefde*, by which he understood what his medieval predecessors would have referred to as "high love," and *min*, which he used to mean eroticism. A happy ending is achieved, wholly in keeping with the conventions of the genre, when love and eroticism are combined in the harmony of lasting relationships. The same tension between love and eroticism pervades much of Hooft's more personal poetry, mainly the earlier work, although it is never quite absent from later productions. This private Hooft coexisted with the public Hooft, not just in discharging administrative duties, but also in poetry. Like many of his contemporaries, Hooft produced many "public" poems to celebrate victories, dedicate buildings, or praise public figures or the city of Amsterdam itself.

The poetry also reveals another side to Hooft: the conscientious craftsman who tried to emulate Petrarch and his school. The many sonnets he wrote are probably not meant to be read at a personal level, but as "masterpieces" in the original sense of the word, a piece to show that the apprentice had "mastered" his trade and could therefore set up as a master himself. Hooft was a master who used a diction more refined and a metre more subtle than any of his predecessors. He was, however, a slightly different kind of master in his official residence, the Muiderslot, where he lived during the summer. After his second marriage in 1627, he played host there to many writers and creative spirits who gathered at the castle for evenings of discussion, not just of literature, but also of matters of more philosophical and political import.

Hooft ventured into comedy with *Warenar* [A True Fool], an adaptation of Plautus' *Aulularia* (*The Pot of Gold*), in which he also displayed his knowledge and mastery of the Amsterdam dialect. He had always been interested in the different variants of Dutch spoken around him and in the evolution of the language, and even tried to standardize its spelling, to little avail. *Warenar* also illustrated that Hooft knew how to write successfully for a less educated audience, thereby beating at their own game the Rhetoricians, who claimed to be writing for a general rather than an elite audience. Hooft could and did write for a general audience not only as a playwright, but also as a poet. His *Emblemata amatoria*, which represents his contribution to the then thriving genre of "emblem literature," became very popular during his lifetime and remained so for at least a century after his death.

In both his later tragedies and his prose, Hooft explored the problem of power, probably the central problem of his life, not primarily because he exercised some kind of limited power himself, but because his life coincided almost exactly with the lengthy but unexpectedly victorious war of independence waged by the emerging Dutch Republic against Spain, then the most important power in Europe.

Geeraerdt van Velsen (*The Tragedy of Gerard van Velsen*) provides a rationale for revolt against an unjust ruler. Once the Count of Holland, Floris V, no longer behaves as he should, his subjects are entitled to rise against him and depose him, just as the Netherlands rose against Philip II of Spain and deposed him as its ruler. *Baeto oft oorsprong der Hollanderen* [Baeto or the Origins of the Dutch], based not so much on Dutch history as on the emerging national mythology all new states create to legitimize their existence, is Hooft's portrayal of the just ruler who would rather forsake his throne than plunge his country into civil war. Hooft also depicted the just ruler in prose in his biography of the French king Henry IV (*Henrick de Grote*), considered an example to all kings by many intellectuals in Europe of the time. Hooft wrote his biography of Henry IV to sharpen his skills for the major task ahead: the history of the Dutch war of independence against Spain. This project, undertaken in the spirit of Tacitus for whom, as for Hooft, history was a literary genre that could be used to inform and instruct, was to occupy Hooft for the last part of his life. The published version, *Neederlandsche histoorien* [History of the Netherlands] runs to 20 books of stately prose, interspersed with pithy sayings on the Tacitian model. It contains Hooft's final and most incisive analyses of power, loyalty, tyranny, and revolt.

—André Lefevere

HORACE

Born: Quintus Horatius Flaccus in Venusia (now Venosa), Apulia, Italy, 8 December 65 BC. **Education:** Educated in Rome and Athens, c. 46 BC. **Career:** Joined Brutus' army in Athens, 44 BC, and probably accompanied him to Asia Minor, then fought at the battle of Philippi, 42 BC; returned to Italy, 41 BC, to find his father's land had been confiscated; became treasury clerk, c. 39 BC; friend of Virgil, *q.v.*, who introduced him to Maecenas: became part of his circle of writers; given a farm in the Sabine country by Augustus. **Died:** 27 November 8 BC.

PUBLICATIONS

Collections

[Works], edited by Otto Keller and Alfred Holder. 2 vols., 1899; also edited by Edward C. Wickham, revised by Heathcote William Garrod, 1912, Adolph Kiessling, revised by Richard Heinze, 3 vols., 1930, Friedrich Klinger, 1959, S. Borszák, 1984, and D.R. Shackleton Bailey, 1985; translated by John Conington, 2 vols., 1863–69; also translated by Theodore Martin, 1881; C.E. Bennett, 1914; H.R. Fairclough, 1926; Lord Dunsany and Michael Oakley, 1961; Charles E. Passage, 1983.

The Essential Horace, translated by Burton Raffel. 1983.

"Ecce Homo Amore!": The Love Poems of Horace, edited and translated by Louis Francis. 1993.

Horace in English, edited by D.S. Carne-Ross and Kenneth Haynes. 1996.

The Complete Odes and Epodes, translated with introduction and notes by David West. 1997.

The Complete Odes and Satires of Horace, translated with introduction and notes by Sidney Alexander. 1999.

Verse

Ad Pyrrham (Ode I.5), several hundred translations, mostly into English, edited by R. Storrs. 1959.

Ars poetica, edited and translated by A.F. Watt. 1905; also edited by C.O. Brink, 1971; as *Ars poetica*, translated by H.R. Fairclough [Loeb Edition], 1926; also translated by R.C. Trevelyan, 1940; Burton Raffel, 1974; Niall Rudd, 1989; as *The Poetic Art*, translated and adapted by C.H. Sisson, 1975.

Epistles, edited by A.S. Wilkins (with commentary). 1892; also edited by O.A.W. Dilke, 1954, revised edition, 1961; Book II edited by Niall Rudd, 1989; edited and translated by Francis Platstowe and Frank P. Shipham, 1893; edited and translated by Howard H. Erskine-Hill, 1964; translated by Philip Francis, 1906; also translated by H.R. Fairclough [Loeb Edition], 1926; R.C. Trevelyan, 1940; Smith P. Bovie, 1959; Colin MacLeod, 1986; Book I translated by O.A.W. Dilke, 1966; Book II translated by C.O. Brink, 1982; commentary by E.P. Morris, 1909–11; Book I, edited by Roland Mayer, 1994.

Epodes, edited by Henry Darnley Naylor. 1978; also edited by D.H. Garrison, 1991; translated by Joseph P. Clancy, 1960; translated by John Penman, 1980; W.G. Shepherd, 1983; translated with introduction by David Mulroy, 1994; edited by David Mankin, 1995.

Odes, edited by F. Plessis. 1924; also edited by Henry Darnley Naylor, 1978, Arthur Sherbo, 1979, Kenneth Quinn, 1980, and D.H. Garrison, 1991; Books I–II edited by R.G.M. Nisbet and M. Hubbard, 2 vols., 1970–78; Book III edited and translated by Gordon Williams, 1969; translated by Christopher Smart, 1767; also translated by J.B. Leishman, in *Translating Horace*, 1956; Joseph P. Clancy, 1960; Helen Rowe Henze, 1961; James Michie, 1964; W.G. Shepherd, 1983; commentaries by P. Shorey and G.J.

Laing, 2nd edition, 1910; as *Horace Odes II: Vatis amici*, translated by David West, 1998; as *Odes and Carmen Saeculare*, translated by Guy Lee, 1998.

Satires, edited by A. Palmer (with commentary). 1883; edited and translated by Howard H. Erskine-Hill, 1964; translated by H.R. Fairclough [Loeb Edition], 1926; also translated by Smith P. Bovie, 1959; Niall Rudd, 1973, revised edition, 1979; commentaries by E.P. Morris, 1909–11; as *Satires I*, translated by P. Michael Brown, 1993.

*

Critical Studies: *Studies in Horace* by A.W. Verrall, 1884; *Horace and the Elegiac Poets* by W.Y. Sellar, 1892; *Horace and His Age* by J.F. D'Alton, 1917; *Horace and His Influence* by G. Showerman, 1922; *Horace: A New Interpretation* by Archibald Young Campbell, 1924; *Horace and His Lyric Poetry* by L.P. Wilkinson, 1945, revised edition, 1968; *Horace* by E. Fraenkel, 1957; *The Structure of Horace's Odes* by Neville E. Collinge, 1961; *The Odes of Horace: A Critical Study* by Steele Commager, 1962; *Horace on Poetry* by C.O. Brink, 1963; *Horace* by J. Perret, 1964; *The Satires of Horace* by Niall Rudd, 1966; *Reading Horace* by David A. West, 1967; *The Epodes of Horace* by R.W. Carrubba, 1969; *Word, Sound, and Image in the Odes of Horace* by M.O. Lee, 1969; *Studies in Horace's First Book of Epistles* by M.J. McGann, 1969; *Horace* by Kenneth J. Reckford, 1969; *A Commentary on Horace, Odes Book 1* by R.G.M. Nisbet, 1970; *Horace* by Gordon Williams, 1972; *Horace* edited by C.D.N. Costa, 1973; *Horace and Callimachean Aesthetics* by J.V. Cody, 1976; *Horace in His Odes* by James A. Harrison, 1981; *Profile of Horace* by D.R. Shackleton Bailey, 1982; *The Golden Plectrum: Sexual Symbolism in Horace's Odes* by Richard Minadeo, 1982; *Horace: A Study in Structure* by Helena Dettmer, 1983; *Horace's Roman Odes: A Critical Examination* by Charles Witke, 1983; *The Poetry of Friendship: Horace, Epistles I*, 1986, and *The Poetry of Criticism*, 1990, both by Ross S. Kilpatrick; *Artifices of Eternity: Horace's Fourth Book of Odes* by Michael C.J. Putnam, 1986; *Unity and Design in Horace's Odes* by Matthew S. Santirocco, 1986; *Horace's Lyric Poetry* by Peter Connor, 1987; *Horace* by David Armstrong, 1989; *Horace* by Marjorie Newman, 1990; *Polyhymnia: The Rhetoric of Horatian Lyric Discourse* by G. Davis, 1991; *Horace* by Holly Keller, 1991; *The Walking Muse: Horace and the Theory of Satire* by Kirk Freudenburg, 1993; *Horace Made New: Horatian Influences on British Writing from the Renaissance to the Twentieth Century* edited by Charles Martindale and David Hopkins, 1993; *Horace 2000: A Celebration: Essays for the Bimillennium*, edited by Niall Rudd, 1993; *Horace and the Dialectic of Freedom: Readings in "Epistles I"* by W.R. Johnson, 1994; *Time and the Erotic in Horace's Odes* by Ronnie Ancona, 1994; *Horace's Epistles, Wieland and the Reader: A Three-way Relationship* by Jane Veronica Curran, 1995; *Homage to Horace: A Bimillenary Celebration*, edited by S.J. Harrison, 1995; *Philodemus and Poetry: Poetic Theory and Practice in Lucretius, Philodemus, and Horace*, edited by Dirk Obbink, 1995; *Horace: Behind the Public Poetry* by R.O.A.M. Lyne, 1995; *Horace's Narrative Odes* by Michèle Lowrie, 1997; *Horace: A Life* by Peter Levi, 1997; *Horace and the Rhetoric of Authority* by Ellen Oliensis, 1998; *Horace: Poetics and Politics* by V.G. Kiernan, 1999; *Horace's Carmen saeculare: Ritual Magic and the Poet's Art* by Michael C.J. Putnam, 2000; *Horace: Image, Identity, and Audience* by Randall L.B. McNeill, 2001; *Horace and the Gift Economy of Patronage* by Phebe Lowell Bowditch, 2001.

* * *

Horace's achievement is to have mastered two completely different types of poetry, each of which is remarkable for its originality and each of which has endeared itself to generations of readers.

The first type is his hexameter poetry. In 36/35 BC Horace produced *Satires 1*, a collection of ten poems written in the manner of Lucilius (a Roman landowner and littérateur of the late 2nd century BC) and described by Horace himself as *sermones* (conversation pieces). Lucilius had been famous for his invective and biting wit; but though Horace subjects certain individuals to intermittent mockery throughout his collection, and though the first three satires deal with such moral questions as discontent and adultery, the book as a whole is hardly satirical at all in our sense of the word. Among the matters described or discussed are literary criticism (4, 10), a journey from Rome to Brundisium (5), and the poet's own life and his relationship with his patron Maecenas (6). Several representative features are combined brilliantly in satire 9, in which Horace describes how, on a walk through Rome, he was pursued by a stranger claiming to be a poet and hoping for an introduction to Maecenas. The satire, which begins with an allusion to Lucilius, is almost wholly taken up with dialogue, in which the pest's importunity is matched by Horace's politeness, the latter's irony by the former's insensitivity. Since both protagonists are poets, the satire resembles the traditional form of the literary *agon* (contest); yet the pest unwittingly presents his own work in terms which, as the reader well knows, Horace (and Maecenas) can only regard with contempt. Further wit is displayed by means of epic motifs and military imagery, which are used throughout to suggest that the combatants are a pair of Homeric heroes; yet this language is entirely belied by the appalling behaviour of the pest, by whom Horace is nevertheless characteristically worsted until the very last moment, when he is rescued by the surprise intervention of a third party. The rescue itself is expressed in language which is again borrowed from Lucilius. The whole poem exhibits a confident combination of humour and humanity, and in the dialogue form the resources of metre and language are exploited to the full. Yet underneath the wit Horace has a serious message for his readers about admission to Maecenas' circle and hence, by implication, to the entourage of Octavian (the future emperor Augustus) himself.

A second book of *Satires*, containing eight poems, followed in 30 BC, and ten years later, 20 more hexameter poems which are known as *Epistles 1*. Finally, there are three very long letters, the first two of which are collectively known as *Epistles 2*: to Augustus, to Florus, and to the Pisones (the *Ars poetica*, or *The Poetic Art*). Although the *Satires* and *Epistles* are conventionally distinguished by their titles, and though the latter display some epistolographical features which are naturally absent from the former, there is little otherwise to distinguish the two sets of poems. Since the verse letter had no significant analogue in Greek, and satire no analogue at all, Horace in these works produced a body of poetry which for its principal inspiration owes virtually nothing to the world of Greece. In this his poetry differs fundamentally both from that of other Roman poets, almost all of whom wrote in rivalry of Greek genres, and from the rest of the poetry which he wrote himself.

At the same time as he was engaged with *Satires 1*, Horace was also writing iambic poetry in the manner of the early Greek iambist Archilochus. Iambics were traditionally associated with invective and disillusionment, and Horace's *Epodes* (as the 17 poems, which appeared around 30 BC, are known) include examples of this type (e.g. 2, 4, 8, 10, 12); but there is a wider range of subjects too, e.g. civil war

(7, 16), the battle of Actium (1, 9), life (13), and love (11, 14, 15). Thus the *Epodes* have affinities not only with the satires but also with Horace's second major achievement, the three books of *Odes* which appeared in 23 BC. These 88 poems, all written in lyric metres, cover an enormous variety of subject matter: famous examples are, in Book I: 4 (spring), 5 (the flirtatious Pyrrha, this being one of the most translated poems in Latin), 9 (Mt. Soracte), and 37 (Cleopatra); in Book II: 3 and 14 (death); and in Book III: 1 (ambition), 29 (life), and 30 (the immortality of the *Odes*). These three books represent Horace's attempt at producing a substantial collection of Latin lyric poetry, which would be a cultural adornment of Augustan Rome and which would rival the lyrics written by the Greek monodists Sappho and Alcaeus. Characteristic in many ways is II.7, in which Horace welcomes back to Italy a friend with whom he served on the republican side at the battle of Philippi many years before. Metaphor is used with striking originality to contrast the old soldiers' periods of enforced idleness with their bursts of frenzied activity, their comradely carousing with their defeat on the field of battle. Whereas his friend was sucked away by the tides of war, Horace had a fortunate escape. Ever conscious of the imminence of death, Horace presents his escape in epic terms; but there is no hint of self-congratulation, for he has already described his own part in the battle ignominiously, symbolized by his abandoned shield. This last is a motif found in several archaic Greek poets, including Alcaeus; Horace thus aligns his experience with theirs and underscores his poetic relationship with them. Now that his friend has returned to Italy, tellingly evoked by its sky and native gods, Horace conveys his delight by the detailed preparations he is making for their renewed carousing; and though the poet seems proud to have fought alongside Brutus, the reader is subtly reminded that his friend's return, and Horace's own prosperity, are due to the clemency and beneficence of the victor. This ode, in its linguistic brilliance, its feeling for friends and home, its blending of pride and understatement and of literature and life, illustrates much that is outstanding in Horace's lyric work.

There can be no question that Horace's achievement in the *Odes* was triumphantly successful. Official recognition of that success came when he was commissioned by the emperor to write the *Carmen saeculare* [Secular Hymn] for the important Secular Games of 17 BC. The emperor also requested poems celebrating the military exploits of his stepsons; these poems duly appear (4, 14) in Book IV of the *Odes*, which came out separately around 13 BC.

In metre and form the *Odes* could hardly be more different from the *Satires* and *Epistles*; yet all are recognizably written by the same poet, all have certain features in common, and all evince a concern for the same subjects. Horace is one of the few great classical writers whom readers easily convince themselves that they know intimately; yet his remarkable habit of partly revealing and partly concealing his personality means that, while throughout his different types of poetry the common link is provided by the poet himself, one person's Horace is never the next person's, and the "real Horace" is a source of endless fascination. Horace similarly tantalizes us in his manner of expression. Common features of his hexameter and lyric works are the wit and subtlety of their argumentation; yet his unrivalled facility with words means that apparently key sentences can look both forwards and backwards in such a way that his effortless transitions provide constant delight to the reader who, after much labour, thinks he has worked them out. Similarly ambivalent are Horace's favourite topics. He can combine support for the emperor's efforts at moral rearmament with hedonistic recommendations to drink and make love before the summons of death. He can profess to prefer light poetry to

grand and at the same time produce the noblest of political poems. Horace's work has that capacity for constantly surprising the reader which we associate with great art; yet nothing could be more familiar than the many famous lines which he wrote and which are among the most memorable statements ever uttered about the human condition.

—A.J. Woodman

See the essays on *The Poetic Art*, "Odes Book I, Poem 5," and "Odes Book IV, Poem 7."

HORVÁTH, Ödön (Josef) von

Born: Fiume (now Rijeka), Austro-Hungarian Empire, 9 December 1901. **Education:** Educated at Episcopal School, Budapest, 1909–13; Wilhelmsgymnasium and Realschule, Munich, 1913–16; school in Pressburg, 1916; Realgymnasium, Vienna, 1916–19; University of Munich, 1919–22. **Family:** Married Maria Elsner in 1933 (divorced 1934). **Career:** Involved in politics from an early age; writer from 1922; contributor to various newspapers and journals; settled in Berlin, 1926; freelance writer, from 1929; increasingly attacked by the Nazis, from 1931; dialogue writer for the German film industry, 1934; left Germany to retain Hungarian citizenship, 1933; returned briefly to Berlin in early 1933; moved to Austria until the German annexation, then emigrated to Zurich, 1934. **Awards:** Kleist prize, 1931. **Died:** 7 June 1938.

PUBLICATIONS

Collections

Stücke, edited by Traugott Krischke. 1961.
Gesammelte Werke, edited by Traugott Krischke, Walter Huder, and Dieter Hildebrandt. 4 vols., 1970; also edition in 8 vols., 1972.
Gesammelte Werke, edited by Traugott Krischke. 4 vols., 1988.
Plays One: "Sladek," A Sexual Congress, translated by Penny Black. 2000.
Plays Two. 2000.

Plays

Das Buch der Tänze (libretto; produced 1922). 1922.
Revolte auf Côte 3018 (produced 1927). 1927; as *Die Bergbahn* (produced 1929), 1928.
Zur schönen Aussicht (produced 1969). 1927.
Sladek; oder, die schwarze Armee (produced 1972). 1928; revised version, as *Sladek, der schwarze Reichswehrmann* (produced 1929), 1929.
Rund um den Kongress (produced 1959). 1929.
Italienische Nacht (produced 1931). 1930; edited by Ian Huish, 1986.
Geschichten aus dem Wienerwald (produced 1931). 1931; edited by Hugh Rank, 1980; as *Tales from the Vienna Woods*, translated by Christopher Hampton, 1977.
Kasimir und Karoline (produced 1932). 1932; edited by Traugott Krischke, 1973; as *Kasimir and Karoline*, translated by Violet B. Ketes, in *Four Plays*, 1986.
Glaube, Liebe, Hoffnung (as *Liebe, Pflicht und Hoffnung*, produced 1936). 1932; edited by Traugott Krischke, 1973; also edited by Ian

Huish, 1986; as *Faith, Hope and Charity*, translated by Paul Foster and Richard Dixon, in *Four Plays*, 1986; also translated by Christopher Hampton, 1989.

Die Unbekannte aus der Seine (produced 1949). 1933.

Hin und Her (produced 1934). In *Gesammelte Werke*, 1970.

Mit dem Kopf durch die Wand (produced 1935). 1935.

Figaro lässt sich scheiden (produced 1937). 1959; as *Figaro Gets a Divorce*, translated by Roger Downey, in *Four Plays*, 1986; as *Figaro Gets Divorced*, translated by Ian Huish, in *Two Plays*, 1991.

Der jüngste Tag (produced 1937). 1955; edited by Ian Huish, 1985; as *Judgement Day*, translated by Martin and Renate Esslin, in *Four Plays*, 1986.

Ein Dorf ohne Männer, from a novel by Koloman van Mikszáth (produced 1937). In *Gesammelte Werke*, 1970.

Himmelwärts (produced 1950). In *Gesammelte Werke*, 1970.

Don Juan kommt aus dem Krieg (produced 1952). In *Stücke*, 1961; as *Don Juan Comes Back from the War*, translated by Christopher Hampton, 1978.

Pompeji (produced 1959). In *Stücke*, 1961.

Four Plays (includes *Kasimir and Karoline*; *Faith, Hope and Charity*; *Figaro Gets a Divorce*; *Judgement Day*). 1986.

Two Plays (includes *Don Juan Comes Back from the War* and *Figaro Gets Divorced*), translated by Ian Huish and Christopher Hampton. 1991.

Fiction

Der ewige Spiesser. 1930.

Ein Kind unserer Zeit; *Jugend ohne Gott.* 2 vols., 1938; as *Zeitalter der Fische*, 1953; as *A Child of Our Time*, translated by R. Wills Thomas, 1938; as *The Age of the Fish*, 1939.

*

Critical Studies: *Materialien zu Horváth* edited by Traugott Krischke, 1970, and *Horváth: Ein Lesebuch* by Krischke, 1978; *Über Horváth* (includes bibliography) edited by Dieter Hildebrandt and Traugott Krischke, 1972; *Symposium on Horváth* published by Austrian Institute, London, 1977; *Horváth Studies: Close Readings of Six Plays* by Krishna Winston, 1977; *A Student's Guide to Horváth* by Ian Huish, 1980, and *Ödön von Horváth Fifty Years On* edited by Huish and Alan Bance, 1988; *Prostitution in the Works of Ödön von Horváth* by Belinda Horton Carstens, 1982; *The Reformation of Comedy: Genre Critique in the Comedies of Ödön von Horváth* by Christopher B. Balme, 1985; *Ödön von Horváth* by Kurt Bartsch, 2000.

*   *   *

Ödön von Horváth, the most representative dramatist of the Weimar Republic, saw himself as "a faithful chronicler" of his times. His uncompromising veracity and oppositional stance to the politics of nascent Nazism (who burnt his books) compelled him to emigrate in 1933 and left him without a stage to write for. His plays portray, as he once laconically observed, the "gigantic struggle between the individual and society, that eternal slaughter in which there is to be no peace" (Randbemerkung, marginal comment). While he saw contemporary political and social life in dramatic terms, he had a sharp eye for the tell-tale or typical detail. His dramatic

technique tended not towards the drastic, but to subtler stage effects: moments of critical illumination and finely moderated accents. His characters are conceived as representative "creatures of an ailing age," smug mediocraties in the main, trapped in the confines of a petty-bourgeois prejudice and conformity. His vision of humanity remained soberly critical and unheroic.

His plays are divided between the genres of comedy, dialect theatre, and period drama yet they anticipate the theatre of the absurd in their mixture of the comic, the tragic, and the gruesome. Though he adopted the naive, established conventions of Austrian popular theatre in a conscious attempt to revitalize that tradition, his plays are ironic-realistic portrayals of the contemporary historical scene, set in the years 1925–37 against a background of inflation, unemployment, political extremism, and the rise of fascism. The chosen social milieu is almost exclusively that of the lower-middle class in Vienna and Munich whose typical lifestyle, ideology, and speech habits are sharply set in focus.

The critical irony which pervades Horváth's plays stems largely from his subtle handling of dialogue. Horváth's language exploits the latent contradictions between overt and covert meanings, the intentional and unintentional in speech. Language betrays and exposes its inept user. The frequent points of conflict which arise within his dialogues are usually marked by the stage direction: "silence." These momentary pauses which punctuate speech have the effect of a searching concentration on language and consciousness, yet always with reference to the unspoken. The use of unreflective speech, the pretentious jargon and clichés of the semi-educated, as the principal key both to individual psychology and to the consciousness of a class, is a dramatic device which Horváth developed and perfected. His attempted "synthesis between irony and realism," in his own words, produces a form of theatre which combines life-like representation with critical distancing. Though a kind of "alienation," in theatrical terms, is achieved by subversive and ironic use of dialect and stereotyped language, what distinguishes Horváth from Brecht is the avoidance of dialectical debate and of didacticism.

In Horváth not action but the word is the principal carrier of drama, and he insisted on a stylized manner of performance. Dialogue is used with a fine sense of its force, ambiguities, and psychological implications. "Demaskierung des Bewusstseins" (the unmasking of consciousness) is Horváth's phrase for his technique of allowing characters involuntarily to reveal their inner natures, intentions, and thoughts, through the words they use. The conflict between appearance and reality, pretence and truth is thus dramatically enacted. The social dimension is at the same time manifested, since the conventions of language used by the classes portrayed are equally subject to critical scrutiny. The menacing political reality behind an apparently harmless facade is best exemplified in *Geschichten aus dem Wienerwald* (*Tales from the Vienna Woods*), which presents a suspect image of "the old honest true golden Viennese heart" compounded of sentimentalism, kitsch, and brutality. This richly diverse mirror of the times shows the playwright at the pinnacle of his achievement. A number of other plays (*Glaube, Liebe, Hoffnung* [Faith, Hope, and Charity]; *Kasimir und Karoline*; *Die Unbekannte aus der Seine* [The Unknown Girl from the Seine]; *Hin und Her* [Back and Forth]) portray the cold indifference of a bureaucratized society which exploits and ultimately destroys the individual. Yet tragic intensity is always held in check by a dramatist who chooses to explore the darker side of existence within the sordidness, pettiness, and banalities of life. His influence on the leading playwrights of the post-war years (Handke, Kroetz, Bauer, Turrini) has been fundamental.

Deprived of a stage for his plays, the exiled Horváth latterly turned to prose and wrote three short novels (*Der ewige Spiesser, Ein Kind unserer Zeit* [A Child of Our Time], *Jugend ohne Gott*). These depict the stark realities of the day in a sparse, economic style derivative of "Neue Sachlichkeit" (the New Objectivity). Thomas Mann judged *Jugend ohne Gott*, a compelling study of the cold amorality of the Hitler Youth movement, to be one of the most important novels of that generation.

—Alexander Stillmark

See the essay on *Tales from the Vienna Woods*.

HUANG Chunming

Also known as Hwang Chun-ming, Hwang Ch'un-ming, Huang Ch'un-ming. **Pseudonym:** Qiu Wenqi. **Born:** Luodong township, Yilan county, 13 February 1935; oldest of five children; mother died when he was eight years old; had a strained relationship with his stepmother; ran away from home. **Education:** Had a reputation as a rambunctious student; after studying at Taipei Normal and Tainan Normal Colleges, eventually graduated from Pingdong Normal College, the southernmost in Taiwan, in 1958. **Military Service:** Served in R.O.C. military from 1961 to 1963. **Family:** Married Lin Meizhu, 1 June 1966, two sons. **Career:** Employed in a wide variety of occupations, including grammar school teacher, 1958–61, broadcaster for China Broadcasting Radio Network, 1963–65, in sales at Adidas, 1978–84, and several advertising firms, among other sundry positions; produced several documentary films; wrote television and film scripts, and children's literature and plays, many of which he directed to the stage. Produced many collage and multi-media art works. Lives in Taipei, Taiwan. **Awards:** Taiwan Literature prize (for *The Man and the Dagger*), 1967; Wu Sanlian prize for Literature, 1980; National Endowment for Culture and Art (Taiwan) Literary prize, 1998; China Times Literary prize (for *Set Free*), 2000.

PUBLICATIONS

Collections

Erzide Da Wan'ou. 1969.
Shayuenala, Zaijian. 1974.
Luo. 1974.
Xiao Guafu. 1975.
Collected Fiction of Huang Chunming. 3 vols. 1985.
Dengdai Yiduohuade mingzi. 1989.
Huang Chunming's Children's Stories. 5 vols. 1993.
Fangsheng. 1999.

Fiction

"Qingdaofude haizi." 1956.
"Chengzai luoche." 1962.
"Kanhaide rizi." 1967; as "A Flower in the Rainy Night," translated by Earl Weiman, 1967.
"Nisi yizhi laomao." 1967; as "The Drowning of an Old Cat," translated by Howard Goldblatt, 1980 and 2001.

"Qingfangongde gushi." 1967; as "The Story of Grandfather Ch'ing Fan," translated by Stephen Field, 1981.
"Ahban yu jingcha." 1968; as "Ah-Ban and the Cop," translated by Howard Goldblatt, 1981.
"Erzide da wan'ou." 1968; as "His Son's Big Doll," translated by Howard Goldblatt, 1980 and 2001.
"Xian." 1968; as "Ringworms," translated by Howard Goldblatt, 1980 and 2001.
"Yu." 1968; as "The Fish," translated by Howard Goldblatt, 1980 and 2001.
"Luo." 1969; as "The Gong," translated by Howard Goldblatt, 1980 and 2001.
"Liangge youqijiang." 1971; as "The Two Signpainters," translated by Howard Goldblatt, 1980 and 2001.
"Pingguode ziwei." 1972; as "The Taste of Apples," translated by Howard Goldblatt, 2001.
"Shayuenala, zaijian." 1973; as "Sayonara, Goodbye," translated by Howard Goldblatt, 1980 and 2001.
"Xiaoqide na yi ding maozi." 1974; as "Xiaoqi's Hat," translated by Howard Goldblatt, 2001.
"Xiao guafu." 1975; as "Young Widow," translated by Rosemary Haddon, 1996.
"Wo ai mali." 1977; as "I Love Mary," translated by Howard Goldblatt, 1983.
"Da bing." 1983; as "A Big Cake," translated by Shu-fang Lai, 1998.
"Fangsheng." 1987; as "Set Free," translated by Howard Goldblatt, 2001.
"Shoupiao kou." 1999; as "The Ticket Booth," translated by Carlos Tee, 2000.

Essays

"Wangshi zhineng huiwei." 1974; as "We Can't Bring Back the Past," translated by David Pollard, 2000.
"Dengdai yiduo huade mingzi." 1987; as "Waiting for the Name of a Flower," translated by David Pollard, 2000.
"Yongjiao du dili." 1999; as "Using One's Own Two Feet to Study Geography," translated by Jonathan Barnard, 2000.

*

Critical Studies: "The Rural Stories of Hwang Chun-ming" by Howard Goldblatt, 1980; "Images of Suffering in Taiwan Fiction" by Cyril Birch, 1980; "Echoes of the May Fourth movement in Taiwan Hsiang-t'u Fiction" by Joseph S. M. Lau, 1983; *Huang Chunming qianzhuan*, by Liu Chuncheng, 1987; *Modern Chinese Literature and the Nativist Resistance*, by Yvonne Chang, 1991; "Taiwanese Nativism and the Colonial/Post-Colonial Discourse" by Rosemary Haddon, 1996.

* * *

The 1960s in Taiwan was a period of great flourishing in the realm of literature, and the young Huang Chunming was a central figure in it. Though largely understood as an era involving first a Modernist movement that stressed literary technique over anti-Communist ideology followed by a "Nativist resistance" comprised mainly of "native" Taiwanese who reacted against the less politically-engaged and more urban-focused Modernists, in fact Huang and most of his fellow Nativists actually began writing and publishing only slightly later than the Modernists. Moreover, though more locally concerned and rurally focused, his stories exhibit considerable polish and attention to the craft of fiction. Huang, still an active and prolific writer, will be remembered as a teller of the simple person's tale, offering endearing portraits that seek insight into the consciousness of those whom mainstream society tends to view as silent objects of our perception rather than as perceiving subjects themselves. These characters include, for example, prostitutes, menial office assistants, gong drummers (the equivalent of the town crier), men saddling sandwich board advertisements, sign painters fresh from the country-side, pre-adolescent apprentices, elderly rural folk, and others of the impoverished, downtrodden class. In spite of this fascination with the marginal, his depictions are never bathetic. He brings these characters to life with an "insider's" touch, balancing humor and empathy, adding Taiwanese local language and folk mannerisms to the dia-logue, establishing himself as one of the genuine working class writers of modern Chinese literature.

After writing some juvenilia in the late 1950s, Huang gained the attention of Lin Haiyin, literary editor of the influential *United Daily News*, who began publishing his works in 1962. A few years later, he began submitting to a new coterie journal known as *Literary Quarterly*, edited by Yao Yiwei and Yu Tiancong, that promoted several native Taiwanese writers such as Chen Yingzhen, Wang Zhenhe, Wang Tuo, and Yang Qingchu. One of Huang's early "classics," "Kanhaide rizi" [Sea Gazing Days] (translated as "A Flower in the Rainy Night"), was first published in *Literary Quarterly*. The story features a prostitute named Baimei who is seeking a new path for her life. The avenue through which deliverance from prostitution is afforded to her is pregnancy and the birth of a son, thereby indicating an ambivalent attitude toward patriarchal society. The richly woven plot of this work established Huang's reputation as a gifted story-teller, one who could lead the reader deeply into the lives of his characters with little strain, employing an innate talent seldom matched in contemporary literature. Though the story can legiti-mately be read as an exposé on the social abuse of women trapped in the underclass, its artistry is never overshadowed by critique.

Baimei returns to her native village to give birth to her child and becomes a sort of auspicious omen, improving the lot of her family and neighbors as they struggle with physical challenges, land rights, and the price their crops will garner at the market. Other stories written near the same time that underscore the special relationship of the people with the land include "Yu" ("The Fish"), which depicts a young boy pedaling home on furlough as a carpenter's apprentice to present a fresh fish to his grandfather, only to have it lost in an accident along the way. The grandfather eventually beats the boy, not for failing to deliver but for the scene all the stress has caused, and the reader is left to ponder how the exploitation of innocents in the countryside has led to the perversion of their once natural and positive relationships. A story that probes the psyche of the marginal, telling it from their perspective, is "Erzide da wan'ou" ("His Son's Big Doll"). The drama of this work hinges on the extent to which one becomes an inseparable part of the labor that enslaves yet ensures one's continued existence. For his job, the protagonist Kunshu must shoulder a sandwich board advertisement and walk in the heat all day, his face caked with grease paint. The mask becomes the man by the end of the story, as his anticipated "liberation" from the makeup used in his job is removed to reveal his own face; however, his son does not

recognize the "true" him and begins to cry in fear and rejection. This story and others were made into films that began the careers of illustrious Taiwan directors such as Hou Xiaoxian and Yang Dechang.

While there always has been some degree of social commentary in Huang's fiction, this quality becomes more pronounced in his works of the 1970s after a series of diplomatic humiliations for Taiwan at the hands of the United States and Japan. Stories such as "Shayuenala, zaijian" ("Sayonara, Goodbye"), in which the protagonist is forced into being a pimp for a Japanese sex tour, "Wo ai mali" ("I Love Mary"), in which a Taiwanese office executive inherits the dog of his former American boss, which then proceeds to dominate his life and ruin his marriage, and, in particular, "Xiao guafu" ("Young Widow"), in which a prostitute bar is established for U.S. soldiers on leave from the Vietnam conflict, all exemplify this turn toward political satire. Yet even in "Young Widow," Huang cannot resist etching each character with a sympathetic brush stroke, as the G.I.s' lives are shown in loneliness and despair, mere emissaries of destruction in the geopolitical chess game of the Cold War.

Besides Huang's political acerbity during this stage and his affectionately wrought characterization of subsistence level country folk in the earlier period, there also exists an impish aspect to his style. Huang is given to embellishing otherwise grave situations with a degree of levity. "Luo" ("The Gong"), for example, is a richly textured narrative of a laid off gong drummer called Kam Kim-ah, a buffoonish fellow who has lost his calling and now must eke out a living with fellow ne'er-do-wells. His antics include "summoning" a corpse to help a casket maker's business and being falsely implicated in the pregnancy of a woman of limited mental faculties. In the end, however, Kam is rendered with comedic tenderness as he squanders his one last chance to regain his former job. A vestige of a bygone era, Kam Kim-ah embodies the common peoples' dilemma in the face of modernity.

The impish dimension is even more discernible in his essays. While best known for his fiction, Huang has authored several beloved works of prose that relate humorous anecdotes of idyllic life. Many of them, like "Waiting for the Name of a Flower," are lighthearted yet somewhat crude occasional pieces with a disarming earthiness that abjures high culture and effete sensibility. Also well known as a writer of children's literature, Huang has invested much time in the nurturing of the younger generation.

More recently, Huang has returned to some of the gentler tones of his youthful stories and to the bucolic setting as well. These stories nevertheless retain an element of critique. "Fangsheng" ("Set Free"), for example, tells a parallel story: first, of how the elderly Zhang Awei saves an egret from the contamination of a nearby factory conjuring in turn the memory of an egret his son Wentong once raised as a boy; second, of Wentong's imprisonment for striking someone presum-ably on the payroll of the polluting factories. In an adroit interlacing, Huang unites the two strands when the healing egret is set free while Wentong clandestinely observes from a distance, himself just re-leased from prison. The story is one of effortless beauty and poign-ancy, the work of a master storyteller whose underlying message never disrupts the flow of the narrative nor undermines the reader's ability to gain an affection for the characters. It is precisely this ability to forge together the various tendencies—formal skill with an en-gaged spirit, sympathetic portrayal with an impish humor—that has assured Huang a place in the annals of fine literature.

—Christopher Lupke

HUGO, Victor (Marie)

Born: Besançon, France, 26 February 1802. **Education:** Educated at Cordier and Decotte's school, Paris, 1814–18. **Family:** Married Adéle Foucher in 1822 (died 1868); three sons and two daughters; lived with Juliette Drouet from 1868 (she had been his mistress from 1833; died 1883). **Career:** Editor, with his two brothers, *Le Conservateur littéraire*, 1819–21; involved in politics: founded newspaper *L'Événement* (later *L'Événement du Peuple*), 1848; elected to assembly, 1849, but exiled in 1851, first in Brussels, then in Jersey and Guernsey to 1870, and intermittently after that; visited France, 1870–71; deputy at Bordeaux Assembly, 1871; defeated in 1872 election because of his tolerance of Communards; elected to Senate, 1876. **Awards:** Chevalier, Légion d'honneur, 1825; ennobled as Vicomte Hugo, 1845. **Member:** Académie française, 1841. **Died:** 22 May 1885.

PUBLICATIONS

Collections

Works, translated by Frederick L. Slous and Camilla Crosland. 5 vols., 1887.
Dramas, translated by Frederick L. Slous and Camilla Crosland. 1887.
Works, translated by Alfred Barbou. 30 vols., 1892.
Dramas, translated by I.G. Burnham. 10 vols., 1895–96.
Works, edited by Henry Llewellyn Williams. 20 vols., 1907.
Romans, edited by Henri Guillemin. 3 vols., 1963.
Théâtre complet, edited by Roland Purnal. 2 vols., 1963–64.
Oeuvres poétiques, edited by Pierre Albouy. 3 vols., 1964–74.
Oeuvres complètes, edited by Jean Massin. 18 vols., 1967–70.
Poésies, edited by Bernard Leuilliot. 3 vols., 1972.

Fiction

Han d'Islande. 1823; as *Hans of Iceland*, translated anonymously, 1825; also translated by A. Langdon Alger, 1891; John Chesterfield, 1894; Huntington Smith, 1896; as *Hans of Iceland; or, The Demon of the North*, translated by J.T. Hudson, 1843; as *The Demon Dwarf*, 1847; as *The Outlaw of Iceland*, translated by Gilbert Campbell, 1885.
Bug-Jargal. 1826; as *The Slave King*, translated anonymously, 1833; as *Bug-Jargal*, translated anonymously, 1844; also translated by "Eugenia de B," 1894; Arabella Ward, 1896; as *The Noble Rival*, 1845; as *Jargal*, translated by Charles E. Wilbour, 1866; as *Told Under Canvas*, translated by Gilbert Campbell, 1886.
Le Dernier Jour d'un condamné. 1829; as *The Last Day of a Condemned Man*, translated by P. Hesketh Fleetwood, 1840; also translated by Arabella Ward, 1896; and Metcalfe Wood, 1931; as *Under Sentence of Death; or, A Criminal's Last Hours*, translated by Gilbert Campbell, 1886; as *The Last Day of a Condemned*, translated by G.W.M. Reynolds, 1840; also translated by "Eugenia de B," 1894; and Lascelles Wraxall, 1909; as *The Last Day of a Condemned Man*, edited and translated by Geoff Woollen, in *The Last Day of a Condemned Man and Other Prison Writings*, 1992.
Notre-Dame de Paris. 1831; edited by Jacques Seebacher and Yves Gohin, 1975; as *Notre Dame de Paris*, translated by A. Langdon

Alger, 1832(?); also translated by Isabel F. Hapgood, 1888; Jessie Haynes, 1902; M. Dupres, 1949; as *The Hunchback of Notre-Dame*, translated by Frederic Shoberl, 1833; also translated by Henry Llewellyn Williams, 1862; Lowell Bair, 1982; as *La Esmeralda*, 1844; as *Notre Dame of Paris*, translated by J. Carroll Beckwith, 1892; also translated by John Sturrock, 1978; translated by Walter J. Cobb, 2001; translated by Catherine Liu, 2002.
Claude Gueux. 1834; as *Claude Gueux*, translated by Gilbert Campbell, 1886; also translated by "Eugenia de B," 1894; Arabella Ward, 1896; edited and translated by Geoff Woollen, in *The Last Day of a Condemned Man and Other Prison Writings*, 1992.
Les Misérables. 1862: edited by Marcus Clapham and Clive Reynard, 1992; as *Les Misérables*, translated by Charles E. Wilbour, 1862; also translated by Lascelles Wraxall, 1862; Isabel F. Hapgood, 1887; William Walton and others, 1892–93; Norman Denny, 1976.
Les Travailleurs de la mer. 1866; edited by Jacques Seebacher and Yves Gohin, 1975; as *The Toilers of the Sea*, translated by W. Moy Thomas, 1860; also translated by Isabel F. Hapgood, 1888; Mary W. Artois, 1892; as *The Workers of the Sea*, translated by Gilbert Campbell, 1887.
L'Homme qui rit. 1869; as *The Man Who Laughs*, translated by William Young, 1869; also translated by Isabel F. Hapgood, 1888; as *By Order of the King*, translated by Mrs. A.C. Steele, 3 vols., 1870; also translated by Hapgood, 1888; as *The Laughing Man*, 1887; also translated by Bellina Phillips, 1894.
Quatre-Vingt-Treize. 1874; as *Ninety-Three*, translated by Frank Lee Benedict and J. Hain Friswell, 1874; Gilbert Campbell, 1886; Aline Delano, 1888; Helen B. Dole, 1888; Jules Gray, 1894; Lowell Bair, 1962; as *'93*, translated by E.B. d'Espinville Picot, 1874.
The Last Day of a Condemned Man and Other Prison Writings (includes *Claude Gueux; My Visit to the Concierge; The Condemned Cells at La Roquette*), edited and translated by Geoff Woollen. 1992.
Conversations with Eternity: The Forgotten Masterpiece of Victor Hugo, translated by John Chambers. 1998.

Plays

Amy Robsart, from *Kenilworth* by Scott (produced 1827); as *Amy Robsart*, translated by I.G. Burnham, 1896; also translated with *Angelo* and *The Twin Brothers*, 1901; and by Ethel T. and Evelyn Blair, 1933.
Cromwell (produced 1956). 1827; edited by Annie Ubersfeld, 1968; as *Oliver Cromwell* (vols. 1–2), translated by I.G. Burnham, 1896.
Marion Delorme (produced 1831). 1829; as *The King's Edict*, translated and adapted by B. Fairclough, 1872; as *Marion de Lorme*, translated by I.G. Burnham, 1895; as *Red Robe and Grey Robe; or, Richelieu Defied*, translated by Henry Llewellyn Williams, 1901.
Hernani (produced 1830). 1830; as *Hernani*, translated by Lord Gower, 1830; also translated by Camilla Crosland, 1887; I.G. Burnham, 1895; R. Farquharson Sharp, 1898.
Le Roi s'amuse (produced 1832). 1832; as *The King's Fool*, translated by H.T. Haley, 1842; as *Le Roi s'amuse*, translated by Frederick L. Slous, 1843; also translated by I.G. Burnham, 1895; as *The King's Diversion*, translated by Frederick L. Slous and Camilla Crosland,

1887; as *His Kingly Pleasure*, translated by Edward John Harding, 1902; as *The King Enjoys Himself*, translated by T.M.R. von Keler, 1925; as *The Prince's Play* by Tony Harrison, 1996.

Lucrèce Borgia (produced 1833). 1833; as *Lucretia Borgia*, translated by W.T. Haley, 1842; as *Lucrezia Borgia*, translated and adapted by W. Young, 1847; also translated by I.G. Burnham, 1896.

Marie Tudor (produced 1833). 1833; as *Mary Tudor*, translated by I.G. Burnham, 1896.

Angelo, Tyran de Padoue (produced 1835). 1835; as *Angelo*, translated and adapted by Charles Reade, 1851; also translated by Ernest O. Coe, 1880; translated with *Amy Robsart* and *The Twin Brothers*, 1901; as *Angelo; or, The Tyrant of Padua*, 1855; as *Angelo and the Actress of Padua*, translated by G.H. Davidson, 1855; as *Angelo; or, The Actress of Padua*, translated by G. A'Beckett, 1857; as *Angelo, Tyrant of Padua*, translated by I.G. Burnham, 1896; also translated by Charles Alfred Byrne (bilingual edition), 1905.

La Esméralda, music by Louise Bertin, from *Notre-Dame de Paris* by Hugo (produced 1836). 1836; as *Esmeralda*, translated by I.G. Burnham, 1895.

Ruy Blas (produced 1838). 1838; edited by Annie Ubersfeld, 2 vols., 1971–72; as *Ruy Blas*, translated and adapted by Charles Webb, 1860; also translated by Camilla Crosland, 1887; I.G. Burnham, 1895; Brian Hooker, 1931; adapted by Charles Fechter, 1870.

Les Burgraves (produced 1843). 1843; as *The Burgraves*, translated by I.G. Burnham, 1896.

Torquemada. 1882; edited by John J. Jance, 1989; as *Torquemada*, translated by I.G. Burnham, 1896.

Théâtre en liberté (short plays). 1886.

La Grand'mère (produced 1898). In *Théâtre en liberté*, 1886.

Mangeront-ils? (produced 1907). In *Théâtre en liberté*, 1886.

Théâtre de jeunesse. 1934.

Mille francs de récompense (produced 1961). In *Théâtre de jeunesse*, 1934.

Les Jumeaux. In *Théâtre complet*, 1964; as *The Twins*, translated by I.G. Burnham, 1896; as *The Twin Brothers*, with *Angelo* and *Amy Robsart*, 1901.

Verse

Odes et poésies diverses. 1822.

Nouvelles odes. 1824.

Odes et ballades. 1826; edited by Pierre Albouy, 1980.

Les Orientales. 1829; edited by Pierre Albouy, 1981.

Les Feuilles d'automne. 1831; edited by Pierre Albouy, 1981.

Les Chants du crépuscule. 1835; as *Songs of Twilight*, translated by George W.M. Reynolds, 1836.

Les Voix intérieures. 1837.

Les Rayons et les ombres. 1840.

Le Rhin. 1842; as *The Rhine*, translated by D.M. Aird, 1843; as *Excursions Along the Banks of the Rhine*, 1843; as *Sketches and Legends of the Rhine*, 1845; as *The Story of the Bold Pécopin*, translated by Eleanor and Augustine Birrell, 1902.

Les Châtiments. 1853; edited by P.J. Yarrow, 1975; and René Journet, 1977.

Les Contemplations. 1856; edited by Pierre Albouy, 1973.

La Légende des siècles. 3 vols., 1859–83; edited by André Dumas, 1974; as *The Legend of the Centuries*, translated by George S. Burleigh, 1867.

Les Chansons des rues et des bois. 1865.

L'Année terrible. 1872.

L'Art d'être grand-père. 1877.

Le Pape. 1878.

La Pitié suprême. 1879.

Religions et religion. 1880.

L'Âne. 1880; edited by Pierre Albouy, 1966.

Les Quatre vents de l'esprit. 1881.

The Literary Life and Poetical Works, edited by Henry Llewellyn Williams. 1883.

Translations from the Poems, translated by Henry Carrington. 1885.

La Fin de Satan. 1886.

Poems. 1888.

Toute la lyre. 2 vols., 1888–93.

Dieu. 1891; edited by René Journet and Guy Robert, 3 vols., 1969.

Poems, translated by George Young. 1901.

Selected Poems, edited by Alfred T. Baker. 1929.

The Distance, The Shadows: Selected Poems, translated by Harry Guest. 1981.

Selected Poems of Victor Hugo: A Bilingual Edition, translated by E. H. and A. M. Blackmore. 2001.

Other

Littérature et philosophie mêlées. 1834; edited by Anthony R.W. James, 1976.

Lettres sur le Rhin. 1846.

Congrès de la paix (International Peace Congress address). 1849; as *The United States of Europe*, 1914.

Napoléon le Petit. 1852; as *Napoleon the Little*, 1852; also translated by George Burnham Ives, 1909; as *The Destroyer of the Second Republic*, translated by "A Clergyman," 1870.

John Brown, translated as *Letter on John Brown*, in *Echoes of Harper's Ferry*, edited by James Redpath. 1860; also translated by Lionel Strachey, 1902.

Dessins de Hugo (art criticism). 1862; edited by J. Sergent, 1955.

L'Archipel de la Manche. 1863; as *The Channel Islands*, translated by Isabel Hapgood, in *The Toilers of the Sea*, 1961; also translated by John W. Watson (bilingual edition), 1985.

Hugo raconté par un témoin de sa vie. 1863.

William Shakespeare. 1864; as *William Shakespeare*, translated by A. Baillot, 1864; also translated by Meville B. Anderson, 1886.

Actes et paroles. 3 vols., 1875–76.

Histoire d'un crime; Déposition d'un témoin. 2 vols., 1877–78; as *History of a Crime; Testimony of an Eyewitness*, translated by T.H. Joyce and Arthur Locker, 4 vols., 1877–78; Gilbert Campbell, 1888; Huntington Smith, 1888.

Le Discours pour Voltaire. 1878; as *Oration on Voltaire*, translated by James Parton, 1883.

Works. 8 vols., 1883, revised as 12 vols., 1887.

Selections, Chiefly Lyrical, edited by Henry Llewellyn Williams. 1883.

Choses vues. 2 vols., 1887–1900; edited by Hubert Juin, 4 vols., 1972; translated in part as *Things Seen*, 2 vols., 1887; revised edition, edited by David Kimber, 1964.

Alpes et Pyrénées. 1890; as *The Alps and Pyrenees*, translated by John Manson, 1898.

Selected Poems and Tragedies, translated by Gilbert Campbell and others. 1890.

France et Belgique. 1892; edited by Claude Gély, 1974.

Letters to His Wife and Others, translated by Nathan H. Dole. 1895.

Les Années funestes. 1896.

Letters, translated by F. Clarke. 1896.

Letters to His Family, to Sainte-Beuve and Others, edited by Paul Meurice. 1896.

Correspondance [1815–82]. 2 vols., 1896–98.

Letters from Exile and After the Fall of the Empire, edited by Paul Meurice. 1898.

Mémoires. 1899; as *Memoirs*, translated by John W. Harding, 1899.

Post-scriptum de ma vie. 1901; edited by Henri Guillemin, 1961; as *Hugo's Intellectual Autobiography*, translated by Lorenzo O'ourke, 1907.

Love Letters 1820–22, translated by Elizabeth W. Latimer. 1901.

Dernière gerbe. 1902.

Correspondance, with Paul Meurice. 1909.

Correspondance, with Michelet. 1924.

Océan, tas de Pierres. 1942.

Correspondance [1814–85]. 4 vols., 1947–52.

Pierres: Vers et prose, edited by Henri Guillemin. 1951.

Carnets intimes, edited by Henri Guillemin. 1953.

Journal 1830–1848, edited by Henri Guillemin. 1954.

Hugo dessinateur, edited by Roger Cornaille and Georges Herscher. 1963.

Lettres à Juliette Drouet 1833–1883, edited by Jean Gaudon. 1964.

Correspondance, with Pierre-Jules Hetzel, edited by Sheila Gaudon. 1979–.

*

Bibliography: *Victor Hugo's Drama: An Annotated Bibliography 1900–1980* by Ruth Lestha Doyle, 1981.

Critical Studies: *The Career of Hugo*, 1945, and *The Perilous Quest: Image, Myth, and Prophecy in the Narratives of Hugo*, 1968, both by Elliott M. Grant; *Hugo*, 1956, and *Hugo and His World*, 1966, both by André Maurois; *Notes on Hugo's "Les Misérables"* by George Klin and Amy Marsland, 1968; *A Stage for Poets: Studies in the Theatre of Hugo and Musset* by Charles Affron, 1971; *Hugo* by John Porter Houston, 1974, revised edition, 1989; *Victor Hugo: A Biography* by Samuel Edwards, 1975; *The Medievalism of Victor Hugo* by Patricia A. Ward, 1975; *Victor Hugo* by Joanna Richardson, 1976; *"Les Contemplations" of Hugo: An Allegory of the Creative Process* by Suzanne Nash, 1977; *Victor Hugo: Philosophy and Poetry* by Henri Peyre, 1980; *Hugo, Hernani and Ruy Blas* by Keith Wren, 1982; *Victor Hugo and the Visionary Novel* by Victor Brombert, 1984; *Hugo: "Les Contemplations"* by Peter Cogman, 1984; *Victor Hugo* by Gregory Stevens Cox, 1985; *The Power of Rhetoric: Hugo's Metaphor and poetics* by Wendy Nicholas Greenberg, 1985; *Victor Hugo in Jersey* by Phil Stevens, 1985; *The Early Novels of Victor Hugo* by Kathryn M. Grossman, 1986; *"Les Contemplations" of Victor Hugo: The Ash Wednesday Liturgy* by John A. Frey, 1988; *Figuring Transcendence in "Les Misérables": Hugo's Romantic Sublime* by Kathryn M. Grossman, 1994; *Victor Hugo: "Notre-Dame de Paris"* by Rachel Killick, 1994; *To Kill a Text: The Dialogic Fiction of Hugo, Dickens, and Zola* by Ilinca Zarifopol-Johnston, 1995; *Les Misérables: Conversion, Revolution, Redemption* by Kathryn M. Grossman, 1996; *Victor Hugo: A Companion to His Poetry* by J.C. Ireson, 1997; *Victor Hugo* by Graham Robb, 1997; *Victor Hugo and*

the Romantic Drama by Albert W. Halsall, 1998; *A Victor Hugo Encyclopedia* by John Andrew Frey, 1999; *Victor Hugo* by Laurence M. Porter, 1999.

*   *   *

When Gide was asked to name France's greatest poet, his reply was "Victor Hugo, hélas!," a response expressing Hugo's undeniable stature and a concomitant embarrassment on the part of a mature Frenchman in acknowledging such a fact. Hugo spanned the 19th century, and dealt in his works with all the major issues central to individuals, society, literature, politics and religion through this period of violent and frequent change. Along with the published novels, plays, poems, and essays go more volumes of fragments, ideas, images, word-associations, rhymes, all scribbled on whatever piece of paper was at hand. His output is monumental, indeed he himself referred to it as a single edifice in which individual works were merely stones. Given such a proliferation it is perhaps natural that among the marks of genius there should also be much that is trite, oversimplified, and self-indulgent.

The main explanation for this apparent paradox is that Hugo was a great primitive, who approached his subjects with intensity, simplicity, and an unshakeable confidence in the validity of his own vision. All his writings were informed by the belief that creation was a composite of forces of good and evil and this dualism provides both the structural security of his works, which deal invariably with conflicting opposites, and the richness of an imagery whose prism translates everything into a battle between light and darkness. His attempts thus to categorize and render accessible the mysterious absolutes that are the dynamics of existence take account also of another omnipresent sensation, that of vertigo. It is the feeling, absorbed during childhood and adolescence from the traumas of Imperial and Restoration society and shared by an entire generation, that the fragile hold on faith, reason, or any human construct may dissolve and leave only "le gouffre." It is not a distortion to describe the fundamental Hugolian experience as a play of day and night on the edge of an abyss.

His philosophy, intuited early and evolved and refined through the middle years, placed man at the centre of an axis stretching between God and earth. Once again the condition is that of antithesis which seeks synthesis. Matter is evil, its very weight and substance separating it from spirit, and therefore God. Original sin is literally a fall and only by a progressively greater awareness of and recourse to things of the spirit may the prison of matter be breached and the soul released up to its source. More than any other writer Hugo was aware of his Messianic role in such a context. With sometimes disarming and sometimes infuriating conceit he places himself above his fellow-mortals to act as a visionary, a gifted intermediary between God and his creatures. Writing was the manipulation of material things to reveal spiritual truths, an interface between concrete and abstract, and Hugo recognized the importance of the fact that "In the beginning was the word . . . ." Words to him were simultaneously "things" and "mysterious wanderers of the soul," the black and literal object on the page was the envelope of a spreading transcendent truth, and thus the ingredients and processes of artistic creativity mirrored those of Creation itself.

He began writing his poetry in a climate of dissatisfaction. Although his earliest works expressed conventional attitudes to Church and King and execrated Napoleon, the recognition that the *ancien régime* was stifling progress quickly began to break the moulds of poetry as well as those of belief. A collection of poems like *Les Orientales* demonstrates the true Romantic revolution of lyric poetry. The forms are new, the rhythms daring and mysterious, the subject-matter exotic, and Hugo's contemporaries acknowledged the fact that their literary generation had found its leader. He himself claimed later in life to have "dislocated" the alexandrine, liberated French versification, and revolutionized poetic vocabulary, a boast entirely validated by the collections of the 1820s and 1830s. The works are those of a man totally involved in the moods and movements of his times. Enforced exile, however, removed him from the literary barricades and allowed time for reflection, or more properly contemplation. In the Channel Islands, his own exile, the death of his daughter, his "crimes" and his sexuality are examined and, through the alchemy of the poetic process, transformed into a strong, single affirmation of divine purpose. *Les Contemplations* is a masterpiece, containing poems brilliant in themselves and yet also important as components within the deliberate architecture of an overall poetic narrative. The conviction at which he arrives in the making of this work provides the basis for the great epic collections of his middle and later years, the gigantic stories of myth, creation, history which continue his exploration of verse, image, and language through poetic registers more varied than those of any of the poets who had preceded him.

His pre-eminence extended to the world of the theatre. The preface to his play *Cromwell* became the manifesto of the French Romantics, not because its ideas were particularly new, but because the power of Hugo's rhetoric gave it coherence and force. Its main original contribution to the debate between Classical and Romantic adherents was the theory of the grotesque. This proposed not, as is sometimes mistakenly suggested, that emphasis should fall only on the ugly and misshapen, but that art should mix extremes of the beautiful and the grotesque in order to convey a more complete picture of the world than that which had been proposed by the Classical imitators with their ideals of beauty. His own plays adopted the morality of popular melodrama, and criticism of them has always been directed at their "unreality" and the fact that he created only stereotypes. Hugo himself, however, never claimed verisimilitude, and if the plays are experienced as dramatic poems, then character, like symbol and image, is seen to be a constituent part of an artistic whole which conveys its meanings through the totality of its impact rather than from the activities of some of its parts; when Hernani confronts Don Salluste it is not merely a young man facing an old one, it is the whole tangle of Ancien Régime, the Restoration's desire to perpetuate it and the frustrating and inexpressible need of the new generation to be liberated from both.

It is easy also to offer facile criticisms of his novels. Indeed the earliest are in themselves Gothic parodies, the hero of one making meals of human flesh washed down with seawater drunk from his son's skull. His linguistic facility, however, and the vast imagination of the visionary produced the great evocation of medieval Paris clutched around the cathedral in *Notre-Dame de Paris* (*The Hunchback of Notre-Dame*), the socio-political tapestry of *Les Misérables* which contains enough themes and sub-plots to fill several novels, and the mysticism of *Les Travailleurs de la mer* (*The Toilers of the Sea*) in which the central character defeats wind and waves, and Hugo reminds the reader that reality consists of more than just conscious imaginings. The prose is as sonorous as the poetry and in all the works the great unifying tendency of the visionary is the controlling factor.

Hugo's work is monolithic. In it the Romantics, the Symbolists, and even the Surrealists found examples of their own desired effects.

It is inhabited by monsters, Gods, and men, sprawling, digressing, and yet simultaneously rendering accessible the moods and movements of the human spirit in its own time and beyond.

—W.J.S. Kirton

See the essays on *The Hunchback of Notre-Dame* and *Les Misérables*.

HÜLSHOFF, Annette von Droste

See DROSTE-HÜLSHOFF, Annette von

HUYGENS, Constantijn

Born: The Hague, Dutch Republic (now The Netherlands), 4 September 1596. **Education:** Studied law at Leiden. **Family:** Married his niece Susanna van Baerle in 1627 (died 1637); five children, including the scientist Christiaan Huygens. **Career:** Travelled to Venice in 1619, and several times to England, once as secretary to a diplomatic mission, 1618, and again as secretary at the embassy, 1620; knighted by James I, 1622; secretary to successive Stadtholders, Frederik Henry, William II and III, from 1625. Associated with Descartes, Daniel Heinsius, Francis Bacon, Ben Jonson, and Pierre Corneille, *q.v.*. Designed his own country house at Hofwijk. **Died:** 28 March 1687.

PUBLICATIONS

Collections

De gedichten [The Poems], edited by J.A. Worp. 9 vols., 1892–99.
De briefwisseling [Correspondence], edited by J.A. Worp. 6 vols., 1911–17.
A Selection of the Poems of Sir Constantijn Huygens (1596–1687): A Parallel Text, translated with introduction and appendices by Peter Davidson and Adriaan van der Weel, 1996.

Verse

Misogamos. 1620.
Batave Tempe dat is 't voorhout van 's Gravenhage [Batavian Temple, That Is the Voorhout in The Hague]. 1621, reprinted 1973.
Costetick mal [Costly Folly]. 1622, reprinted 1973.
De uytlandighe herder [The Exiled Shepherd]. 1622.
Zedeprinten [Characters]. 1623–24.
Dorpen en stedestemmen [Voices of Villages and Towns]. 1624; edited by C.W. de Kruyter, 1981.
Otia of ledighe uren [Idleness or Empty Hours]. 1625.
Momenta desultoria. 1644.
Eufrasia. Ooghentroost [Solace for the Sightless]. 1647, reprinted 1984.
Vitaulium. Hofwijck. Hofstede vanden Heere van Zuylichem onder Voorburgh [Hofwijck, Seat of Lord of Zuylichem]. 1653.
Korenbloemen [Cornflowers]. 1658.
Dagh-werck [Daily Work]. 1658; edited by F.L. Zwaan, 1973.

Triomfdichten ter eeren de doorluchte Huizen van Nassauw, Oranje en Anhalt [Triumphal Poem in Honour of the Illustrious Houses of Nassau, Orange, and Anhalt]. 1660.
De nieuwe zee-straet van 's Gravenhage op Scheveningen [The New Sea Promenade from The Hague to Scheveningen]. 1667.
Cluyswerck [Work in Seclusion]. 1681.
Dichten op de knie, 500 sneldichten [Rhyming on the Knee, 500 Quick Rhymes], edited by G.W. and W.G. Hellinga. 1956.
Dromen met open ogen [Dreaming with Eyes Open] (selection), edited by M.A. Schenkeveld van der Dussen, L. Strengholt, and P.E.L. Verkuyl. 1984.
Sneldichten [Quick Rhymes], edited by H. Blijlevens, M. van Drunen, and P. Lavrijssen. 1988.

Plays

Trijntje Cornelis. 1653; edited by H.M. Hermkens, 1987.

Other

Ghebruyck of onghebruyck van 't orgel [Use and Misuse of the Organ]. 1641, reprinted 1974.
Heilighe daghen [Holy Days]. 1645, reprinted 1974; translated by Koos Daley, 2001.
De vita propria (autobiography, in Latin). 1678; as *Mijn Jeugd* [My Youth], translated (into Dutch) by C.L. Heesakkers, 1987.
Dagboek van Constantijn Huygens [Diary]. 1885.
Lettres du Seigneur de Zuylichem à Pierre Corneille. 1890.
Journaal van zijne reis naar Venetië in 1620 (Travel Journal). 1894.
Correspondence of Descartes and Huygens, 1635–47 (in French), edited by Leon Roth. 1926.

*

Critical Studies: *"Some Thankfulness to Constantine": A Study of English Influence upon the Early Work of Constantine Huygens* by Rosalie Littel Colie, 1956; *Constantine Huygens and Britain* by A.G.H. Bachrach, 1962; *Driemaal Huygens*, 1966 and *De grootmeester van woord- en snarenspel. Het leven van Constantijn Huygens*, 1980, both by J. Smit; *Constantijn Huygens' Oogentroost: Een interpretatieve studie* by C.W. de Kruyter, 1971; *Dromen is denken: Constantijn Huygens over dromen en denken en dichten* by L. Strengholt, 1977; *Constantijn Huygens, mengeling* by A. van Strien, 1990.

* * *

Cast in the Renaissance mould of the *uomo universale*, Constantijn Huygens, like his contemporary, Jacob Cats, was a Calvinist moralist. Unlike Cats, however, his bearing was aristocratic and his literary work erudite, even obscure. In his autobiographical poem *Dagh-werck* [Daily Work], written between 1627 and 1638, he even added a note that true poetry should require elucidation, and he made his point by giving prose summaries of each stanza, concerning his daily life and his views on religion and poetry. It is significant that he described his poems as "cornflowers" along the path of his life, suggesting that they are all autobiographical and provide a welcome creative redress from his onerous business career.

His first long poem is an ode of 105 eight-line stanzas in the humanist tradition, *Batave Tempe dat is 't voorhout van 's Gravenhage* [Batavian Temple, That Is the Voorhout in The Hague]. The Voorhout was (and still is) a fine tree-lined avenue in the centre of a town greatly loved by the poet, and he expatiates on its virtues by applying the theories of rhetoric appropriate to his theme. So we find a variety of styles and genres: lyrical, georgic, satirical, farcical, and emblematic. Yet there is a highly personal feeling in his sometimes humorous, sometimes bitter irony or parody, and an entirely individual use of circumlocution, condensation, and metaphor.

His moral indignation comes fully to light, however, in the mordant sarcasm of his next poem, *Costelick mal* [Costly Folly]. In some 500 lines of alexandrines, Huygens ridicules what, according to his strict biblical morality, is absurd and culpable in the fashionable society of his day. As such it provides a valuable historical record of society at that time, and because it conforms to the Horatian ideal of *utile dulci*, it was a work (dedicated to Cats) for which Huygens retained an affection.

In both poems there are mannerisms that recall the style of Marino in Italy and the metaphysical poets in England, yet there is no evidence of a direct influence of the Marinists on Huygens. Though in his love poetry, as we shall see, there is a Petrarchan influence, in *Costelick mal* there is evidence, in his attitudes to women, of anti-Petrarchanism. So, steeped in the learning and theories of his age as he was, Huygens brings an individualism to his work that remains its hallmark.

If *Costelick mal* was an outward-looking commentary, however personal, on social behaviour, *De uytlandighe herder* [The Exiled Shepherd] is entirely introspective, and seems to have been written in a fit of depression. It is a pastoral with a difference; the first-person narrator, the shepherd, conducts an interior monologue between his emotional and rational selves.

Huygens's familiarity with English poetry, and not just John Donne's, is evident from his *Zedeprinten* [Characters]. Character sketches were a literary genre known in the Netherlands through Daniel Heinsius's translations of Theophrastus of Eresus, but *Zedeprinten* reproduces some of the characters of the English poets who were popular at that time, as well as a number of original moralistic satires on Dutch "types," with the sophisticated wit that is Huygens's alone.

Dorpen en stedestemmen [Voices of Villages and Towns] devotes ten-line verses to each of 18 towns and six villages, and these, along with the character sketches and *Costelick mal*, add a further contemporary, if subjective, picture of 17th-century Dutch life. The personal and local sketches were reprinted in a collection published in 1625 with the title *Otia of ledighe uren* [Idleness or Empty Hours]. It is true that Huygens wrote rapidly, and often filled the time spent on his many journeys by writing. But the disdainful tone of this title merely echoes a Renaissance convention of false modesty, and does not belie his earlier insistence that poetry is a serious, cultivated art.

Dagh-werck [Daily Work] covers the years of Huygens's marriage to his beautiful and wealthy niece, Susanna van Baerle. There is every reason to assume utter sincerity in his Petrarchan protestations of love for his *sterre* (star), the shining light in his firmament, whose premature death in 1637 evoked his finest sonnet "On the Death of *Sterre*."

Ooghentroost [Solace for the Sightless] was written for a friend who had lost the sight of one eye. Typically, its moral tone extols the virtue of those who though physically blind are spiritually whole, while attacking those who are spiritually blind: the arrogant, the prodigal, the malicious, and the ostentatious. The conclusion sums up the underlying faith throughout Huygens's poetry, that sighted or blind, only the virtuous will see God.

There are two autobiographical sequels to *Ooghentroost: Hofwijck* and *Cluyswerck* [Work in Seclusion]. Hofwijck was the country house that Huygens had built on the river Vliet as a refuge from his busy court life and as an antidote to his bereavement. This long, georgic poem represents an important contribution to the popular Stoical, bucolic literature of the Renaissance. The planning of country estates was considered consistent with the divine intention that man should restore the order of the garden of paradise from the wilderness, in which a Stoical balance should be observed, for ''too orderly would be too formal, too wild would be all too coarse.'' To Huygens, creation is God's revelation:

> From all things trivial, even things that miss our gaze
> To distil creation's purpose, sing the Maker's praise.

Where he speaks of God's two books, he is referring to the Bible and nature.

> This book, this Book of Books
> Has as much to teach us, as many instructive nooks,
> As there are leaves on Hofwijck's trees and plants.

In 1653 Huygens wrote his only play, *Trijntje Cornelis*, named after the protagonist, a young Dutch skipper's wife who is seduced by two Flemish street lads and ends up in men's clothes on a manure heap. She has her revenge when the following day she, unrecognized, lures them onto her ship where they are roundly thrashed and put ashore. An accomplished linguist with a good ear, Huygens clearly relished writing in the two dialects of the Netherlands and Antwerp, and spicing the humour with bawdy obscenities, which were by no means only the prerogative of fairground dramatists in the 17th century.

In his mid-eighties, Huygens wrote the last of his autobiographical trilogy, *Cluyswerck* [Work in Seclusion]. Though still William III's secretary, Huygens's retirement from full employment, with his freedom to enjoy his library, his music, and visits from friends, is celebrated here in some 600 alexandrines of scarcely diminished vitality and perception. Up to the last he also continued jotting down his *Sneldichten* [Quick Rhymes], which are simply frivolous nonsense rhymes, succeeding best where Huygens's wit comes out in contemporary-seeming wordplay.

—Peter King

HUYSMANS, Joris-Karl

Born: Charles-Marie-Georges in Paris, France, 5 February 1848. **Education:** Educated at Lycée Saint-Louis, Paris, 1862–65; baccalauréat, after private tuition, 1866; law student, Paris, 1866. **Military Service:** 1870. **Career:** Civil servant, French Ministry of the Interior, 1866–76; internal security and crime prevention officer, Sûreté Générale, 1876–98; throughout career contributed reviews and stories to various French and Belgian publications, including *Revue Mensuelle, La République de lettres,* and *L'Art universel.* Associated with Zola and the Naturalist movement, became interested in Black Magic, retreated to Trappist monastery at Igny in 1892, returned to the Catholic faith; retired to a monastry at Ligugé. **Awards:** Chevalier, Légion d'honneur, 1893. **Died:** 12 May 1907.

PUBLICATIONS

Collection

Oeuvres complètes, edited by Lucien Descaves. 18 vols., 1928–40.

Fiction

Marthe, histoire d'une fille. 1876; as *Marthe,* translated by Samuel Putnam, in *Down Stream and Other Works,* 1927; as *Martha, the Story of a Woman,* translated by Robert Baldick, 1948; as *Marthe,* translated by Baldick, 1958.
Sac-au-dos. 1877; in *Les Soirées de Médan,* 1880; as *Sac-au-dos,* translated by L.G. Meyer, 1907.
Les Soeurs Vatard. 1879; as *The Vatard Sisters,* translated by James Babcock, 1983.
En ménage. 1881; as *Living Together,* translated by J. Sandisford-Pelle, 1969.
À vau-l'eau. 1882; in *Croquis parisiens,* 1905; as *Downstream,* translated by Robert Baldick, 1952.
À Rebours. 1884; as *Against the Grain,* translated by John Howard, 1922; as *Against Nature,* translated by Robert Baldick, 1959; translated by Margaret Mauldon, 1998.
En Rade. 1887; as *Becalmed,* translated by Terry Hale, 1992.
Un dilemme. 1887.
Là-bas. 1891; as *Down There,* translated by Keene Wallis, 1928.
En route. 1895; as *En Route,* translated by C. Kegan Paul, 1896.
La Cathédrale. 1898; as *La Cathédrale-Chartres,* edited by Helen Trudgian, 1936; as *The Cathedral,* translated by Clara Bell, 1898.
L'Oblat. 1903; as *The Oblate,* translated by Eduard Perceval, 1924.

Other

Le Drageoir à épices (prose poems). 1874; as *Le Drageoir aux épices,* 1874; as *A Dish of Spices,* translated by Samuel Putnam, in *Down Stream and Other Works,* 1927.
Pierrot sceptique, with Léon Hennique. 1881.
L'Art moderne. 1883; selections translated by Samuel Putnam, in *Down Stream and Other Works,* 1927.
Croquis parisiens. 1885; as *Parisien Sketches,* translated by Richard Griffiths, 1962.
Certains (articles). 1889; selections translated by Samuel Putnam in *Down Stream and Other Works,* 1927.
La Bièvre. 1890; with *Les Gobelins* and *Saint-Séverin,* 1901; as *The Bièvre River,* translated by Darius Halpern and Ellen Moerman, 1986.
Les Vieux Quartiers de Paris. 1890.
L'Oeuvre érotique de Félicien Rops. 1897.
Pages catholiques. 1899.
La Magie en Poitou: Gilles Rais. 1899.
Sainte Lydwine de Schiedam. 1901; as *Saint Lydwine of Schiedam,* translated by Agnes Hastings, 1923.
De tout. 1902.
Esquisse biographique sur Don Bosco. 1902.
Trois primitifs. 1904; as *Grunewald,* translated by Robert Baldick, 1958.
Le Quartier Notre-Dame. 1905.

Les Foules de Lourdes. 1906; as *The Crowds of Lourdes*, translated by W.H. Mitchell, 1925.

Trois églises et trois primitifs. 1908.

Prières et pensées chrétiennes de J.K. Huysmans. 1910.

Pages choisies, edited by Lucien Descaves. 1916.

Down Stream and Other Works, translated by Samuel Putnam. 1927.

En marge (essays), edited by Lucien Descaves. 1927.

Correspondance, with Madame Cécile Bruyère, edited by R. Rancoeur. 1950.

Lettres inédites à Emile Zola, edited by Pierre Lambert. 1953.

Lettres inédites à Edmond de Goncourt, edited by Pierre Lambert and Pierre Cogny. 1956.

Lettres inédites à Camille Lemonnier, edited by G. Vanwelkenhuyzen. 1957.

Le Retraite de M. Bougran. 1964.

Là-haut; ou, Notre-Dame de la Salette, edited by Pierre Cogny, Artine Artinian, and Pierre Lambert. 1965.

Lettres inédites à Jules Destrée, edited by G. Vanwelkenhuyzen. 1967.

Une étape de la vie de J.-K. Huysmans: Lettres inédites de J.-K. Huysmans à l'abbé Ferret, edited by Elisabeth Bourget-Besnier. 1973.

Lettres inédites à Arij Prins, edited by L. Gillet. 1977.

Bloy, Villiers, Huysmans: lettres, edited by D. Habrekorn. 1980.

Lettres à Théodore Hannon (1876–1886), edited by Pierre Cogny and Christian Berg. 1985.

The Road from Decadence: From Brothel to Cloister: The Selected Letters of J.-K. Huysmans, edited and translated by Barbara Beaumont. 1988.

*

Bibliography: *J.-K. Huysmans in England and America: A Bibliographical Study* by George A. Cevasco, 1960.

Critical Studies: *The First Decadent* by James Laver, 1954; *The Life of J.-K. Huysmans* by Robert Baldick, 1955; *Huysmans* by Henry R.T. Brandreth, 1963; *The Reactionary Revolution: The Catholic Revival in French Literature 1870–1914* by Richard Griffiths, 1966; *Joris Karl Huysmans* by George R. Ridge, 1968; *The Genius of the Future* by Anita Brookner, 1971; *The Violent Mystique: Thematics of Retribution and Expiation in Balzac, Barbey d'Aurevilly, Bloy and Huysmans* by Joyce O. Lowrie, 1974; "*A vau-l'eau*—A Naturalist Sotie" by C.G. Shenton, in *Modern Language Review*, 72, 1977; *Reality and Illusion in the Novels of J.-K. Huysmans* by Ruth B. Antosh, 1986; "J.-K. Huysmans: Novelist, Poet, and Art Critic" by Annette Kahn, in *Studies in the Fine Arts*, 19, 1987; *J.-K. Huysmans and the Fin de Siècle Novel* by Christopher Lloyd, 1990; *The Image of Huysmans* by Brian R. Banks, 1992; *Huysmans* by Jean Borie, 1992; *Beyond the Paradox of the Nostalgic Modernist Temporality in the Works of J. K. Huysmans* by Elisabeth M. Donato, 2001.

*   *   *

Joris-Karl Huysmans was among those writers marked by a series of startling events in France beginning in 1848 and lasting into the early 20th century. Born in February 1848, reputedly at the very moment when the Parliament declared the inception of the Second Republic, he witnessed the subsequent changes in government—from a republic to the reinstitution of the Empire under Napoleon III in 1852—as well as the establishment of the Third Republic after the Commune of Paris was defeated, and ultimately the political and economic preparations for World War I. In addition to this intense political activity, social, economic, and intellectual developments were also little short of revolutionary: the urbanization of France, accompanying its evolving democratization, resulted in a literal and figurative change of landscape and the new ideas of socialism had their impact on politics as Positivism, Realism, and Naturalism had theirs on literature. Writers like Huysmans could either participate in this ferment by supporting or criticizing these new concepts and their social or literary results, or they could in various ways withdraw from the life of these innovations.

Huysmans in his career did both. At first, a partisan of Naturalism and admirer of Zola, Huysmans abandoned Zola's form of Naturalism in *À Rebours* (*Against Nature*) and turned towards a spiritual Naturalism. Des Esseintes, the hero of the novel, is the prototype of the decadent hero whose only solution for an unacceptable environment is to isolate himself completely from it and seek an alternative in artifice and ultimately religion. Published in May 1884, *Against Nature* is a novel of *fin-de-siècle* aestheticism, considered to be the masterpiece of this genre in French literature of the late 19th century.

Des Esseintes recalls the Baudelairian character who suffers from the disease of the century: boredom. Huysmans's hero cannot tolerate contemporary society and decides to escape it, adopting Baudelaire's motto, "Anywhere out of the world." Plot and action are practically nonexistent in the novel. Curiously, however, one of the principal motifs is travel; travel, though, that takes place in the mind of Des Esseintes, who frees himself from his surroundings by means of imaginary journeys. For example, he decides to travel to England, a country in vogue at the time and the centre of dandyism. It is also the home of Charles Dickens, whose works had stimulated Des Esseintes's conception of London's grey skies and the general mood of England. To prepare for his trip, Des Esseintes consults a guidebook in a bookshop. Inspired by his reading, his imagination takes him to London and its museums, but his wandering is interrupted by the presence of the bookseller. To continue his imaginary trip, he escapes to the "Bodega" to recreate in his mind the land of clergymen and of Dickens by drinking glasses of port. Des Esseintes's imaginary voyage in place of the real one does not disappoint him: it allows him to get away from reality. His reading of the guidebook enables him to make his trip to England in accordance with his wishes; a real trip would have eventually brought disillusion in the form of a train ride home. He has succeeded in escaping from the daily routine and killing his boredom at least for a few hours.

At the beginning of the novel Des Esseintes had sold his family's manor house and had left Paris and his tumultuous life there to seek refuge in his ideal house at Fontenay-aux-Roses, where he is waited on by his two faithful servants. Having left no forwarding address, he is completely isolated from the world. His only company consists of religious objects, posters, aquariums, and books. He has created an entirely artificial milieu, imitating theatre sets decorated in flamboyant colours. On occasion he drapes his dining room in black and has a funeral meal served accompanied by dirges. On other occasions the atmosphere of a cloister dominates the whole house, imposing an air of sanctity and silence. For Des Esseintes, artifice is the distinctive sign of man's genius. Consequently he is uninterested in, and repulsed by, the human condition. His indifference extends as well to all that is associated with progress and the modern. Instead he shuts himself up in his study to cultivate his admiration for the painter Gustave Moreau, whose two paintings of Salome Des Esseintes owns. Depicted in the novel as a double to Des Esseintes, Moreau had been able to escape reality even though he lived in Paris.

Finally, Des Esseintes realizes that his artificial refuge at Fontenay-aux-Roses will not help him escape from the nihilism into which he has sunk. He becomes physically and mentally lethargic. The country doctor warns him of the danger of a life lead in such strange and luxurious conditions and advises him to return to Paris if he wishes to recover his health and mental stability. ''In two days I shall be in Paris,'' Des Esseintes replies. ''All is finished.'' He gives himself up to God in the hope of finding a solution to his dilemma, and prays: ''Lord, take pity on a Christian who is in doubt, on the unbeliever who would like to believe.'' Thus finishes *Against Nature*.

The autobiographical aspect of the book (Des Esseintes is the alter ego of Huysmans) is evident. Like his hero's life, Huysmans's was notable for its gradual progress towards a state of spirituality. Like Des Esseintes, Huysmans withdrew from the world, but he actually retired to a Trappist monastery at Notre-Dame d'Igny, causing something of a scandal in late 19th-century anti-clerical France. Ironically, although Huysmans, like Des Esseintes, detested modern civilization, he wrote in *Against Nature* a novel that exhibits many of the features of French Modernism, particularly its surrealistic tone and its impressionistic style.

—Nicole Mosher

HYDER, Qurratulain

Also known as Aini Apa. **Born:** Aligarh, India, 1927. **Education:** Primary school in Aligarh, 1937; attended high school in Aligarh, 1938–1943; Master's degree in English language and literature, University of Lucknow, Uttar Pradesh. **Career:** Became involved in journalism as a teenager through her mother, an editor of a children's magazine; began to write for several Urdu magazines at age 20; worked as a broadcaster; served as a visiting lecturer at the universities of California, Chicago, Wisconsin, and Arizona. Lives in Uttar Pradesh, India. **Awards:** Sahitya Academy award for literature, 1969; Soviet Land Nehru award, 1969; Ghalib award for literature, 1985; Governmental Padma Shri for Urdu literature, 1989; Jnanpith award for the novel *Aakhir-i shab ki hamsafar* (*Fireflies in the Mist*), 1989.

PUBLICATIONS

Collections

A Woman's Life or Tea Gardens of Sylhet. 1979.
Muntakhab Kahaniyan. 1991.
The Street Singers of Lucknow and Other Stories. 1996.
Sheeshay kay ghar. 1998.
A Season of Betrayals. 1999.

Novels and Novelettes

Aag ka darya. 1959; as *The River of Fire*, translated by the author, 1999.
Chaa'i ki baagh. 1965.

Patjar ki awaz. 1965; as *The Sound of Falling Leaves*, translated by the author, 1997.
Shitaa haran. 1968.
Pat jhar ki avaz. 1970.
Dilrubaa. 1976.
Aakhir-i shab ki hamsafar. 1979; as *Fireflies in the Mist*, translated by the author, 1994.
Pikchar gailri. 1983.
Gardish-i rang-i chaman. 1991.
Chaandn-i Begam. 1990.
Jugnu'o ki dunyaa. 1990.
Eka larak ki zindagi. 1996.
A Season of Betrayals. 1999.

Other

Kar-i jahan daraaz hay. 1990.
Koh-i Damavand. 2000.
Translator, *The Nautch Girl: A Novel*, by Hasan Shah. 1790; as *The Dancing Girl*, 1993.

*

Critical Studies: *Feminine Sense and Sensibility: A Comparative Study of Six Modern Women Short Story Fiction Writers in Hindi and Urdu: Rashid Jahan, Ismet Chugtai, Qurratal-ain-Hyder, Mannu Bhandari, Usha Priyamavada, Vijay Chauhan* by S. M. Poulos, 1975; *Muslim Self-Identity in Qurratulain Hyder's ''Aag ka darya''* by L. A. Fleming, in *Studies in Urdu Ghazal and Prose Fiction* edited by M. U. Memon, 1979; *Qurratul'ain Haidar kaafan* by M. Abd al-Mughanni, 1985; *Qurratul'ain Haidar* by A. Tufail, 1991; *Qurratul'ain Haidar, ek mutala'a* edited by K. Irtiza', 1992; *First Urdu Novel*, in *Annual Urdu Studies* by M. Asaduddin, 2001; *Reclaiming the Past*, in *Annual Urdu Studies* by C. Byer, 2001. *Qurratulain Hyder's Art of Fiction* by M. Asaduddin, in *Manushi*, 2002.

*   *   *

Qurratulain Hyder, widely recognized as the most important writer of Urdu fiction, is one of the most celebrated Indian contemporary writers. She began writing in Urdu, the language of the Muslim people of the Subcontinent, as an act of self-consciousness, and began writing novels at a time when fiction was not yet widely used as a form of expression in the poetry-oriented world of Urdu literature. She brought new life to the genre and purged it of its conventions with energy, romance, and realism, instilling a new sense of thought and imagination henceforth unknown in the field.

Aag ka darya (*The River of Fire*), the most celebrated of Hyder's novels was published in 1959 and ''transcreated'' in English by the author in 1988. It is a landmark work that explores the wide sweep of historical time. Its narration, conceptually divided into four distinct plots, passes through a period that encompasses 2400 years of Indian history, moving from the 4th century BC to the post-Independence period both of India and Pakistan, lingering to look at the many crucial turning points of the subcontinental history. Hyder, in her voluminous masterpiece, shows an unusual ability to encompass, even in brief passages, the great historical narratives of the most important cultural phenomena of her land: Bhuddism, Hinduism, the coming of Islam, the age of the Mughal empire, the British occupation, the 1857 War of Independence, the two World Wars, and the consequences of the Partition in the Hindu as well as in the Muslim milieu. It was years after the novel was first published before its magical realism and other formal devices reshaped the novel genre in the regional literatures of India. The common human experiences of art and love are the means by which the author, in the mirror of the characters' souls, enables the reader to participate in 24 centuries of imagined history.

At a time when Urdu literature was dominated by the Progressive writers movement and used to voice leftist opinion, Hyder—scandalously for some—wrote not about the paradigmatic peasant and plough, but about her own privileged literate surroundings and the destruction of its composite culture. However, Hyder's work could also be used for political expression; her personal background and education, together with creative experimentation, led her to express in fictional form her own commitment to social change. With *A Season of Betrayals*, originally published in 1960, Hyder began the trend of feminist literature in India, which sought to rewrite the patriarchal *Weltanschauung* and challenged the set order. Her energetic characters—though caught in a parochial society—have the strength to face their struggles. The themes of identity and self play a central role almost in all Hyder's work: the necessity of recovering one's primary or youthful self is usually present as a clashing paradigm, illustrating the difficulties a person will have in realizing and accepting his past, especially after life has fashioned him into what seems like a completely different person.

On the same hand, *Aakhir-i shab ki hamsafar* (*Fireflies in the Mist*) constitutes an attempt to link the subcontinental experience to that of the international, postcolonial cultural renewal. Despite the fact that it also explores the themes of time and history, Hyder uses a relativistic approach toward the more modern themes of the social and cultural uprooting by the powerful Western influence, analyzing in detail the impact of British rule over the Hindu, Muslim, and Christian traditional identities and how it deeply unsettled the lives of so many people. In Hyder's view, one's early, primary self is not entrapping, disgraceful, or something to be shunned as a source of contradiction, but an entity which every person must come to terms with and accept.

Although the period of intellectual revolution that characterized much of her career is now past, Qurratulain Hyder remains a fascinating alchemy of scholarship and sudden compassion, and—although in comparison with some other Indian literatures as Bangla, Malayalam, or Marathi, Urdu has not produced enough writers of promise who could have contributed to the development of a novel tradition—one may assert that she is to be considered the real founder of modern Urdu prose.

—Alessandro Cancian

I

IBN AL-ARABI, Muhyi al-Din

Also known as Ibn Arabi. **Pseudonym:** al-Shaykh al-Akbar (Greatest Teacher). **Born:** Murcia, Spain, 17th of Ramadan, 560 Hijri/27 July AD 1165. **Education:** Educated at home in Qur'an and religious sciences; studied Qur'an and hadith in Seville, c. AD 1182. **Family:** From a wealthy family; two or three wives, two surviving sons. **Career:** About age twenty took up the mystical path; trained in Sufism under a number of Andalusian and Maghrebi teachers; moved to the central Islamic lands, AD 1201; taught and wrote in Cairo, Mecca, Medina, Jerusalem, Mosul, Konya, Baghdad, Malatya, Aleppo, and Damascus. **Died:** Damascus, 22 Rab' II, 638 Hijri/8 November AD 1240.

PUBLICATIONS

Mystic Writings

Al-Futuhat al-Makkiyya. 4 vols. 1911; incomplete critical edition, 14 vols., 1972–; sections published in *Les Illuminations de la Mecque: Textes Choisis [The Meccan Illuminations: Selected Texts]*, translated by M. Chodkiewicz, W. Chittick, Ch. Chodkiewicz, D. Gril, and J. Morris, 1989.

Fusus al-Hikam. 1946; as *Ibn al-Arabi: The Bezels of Wisdom*, translated by R.W.J. Austin, 1981.

Rasa'il Ibn al-Arabi (which contains *Istilahat al-Sufiyya, Hilyat al-Abdal, Al-Tajalliyat, Al-Alif, Risalat al-Shaykh ila al-Imam al-Razi, Al-Wasaya, Masa'il, Al-Anwar, Ayyam al-Sha'n, Al-Azal*). 1948; *Al-Anwar* as *Journey to the Lord of Power*, translated by R. Harris, 1981.

Tarjuman al-Ashwaq. 1911; translated and edited by R.A. Nicholson; also sections in *Stations of Desire*, translated by M. Sells, 2000.

Insha al-Dawa'ir, in *Kleinere Schriften des Ibn al-Arabi*. 1919; as *La Production des Cercles*, translated by P. Fenton and M. Gloton, 1996.

Kitab Anqa Maghrib fi khatm al-awliya wa shams al-Maghrib. 1954.

*

Bibliography: *Histoire et classification de l'oeuvre d'Ibn Arabi* by Osman Yahia, 1964; *Fihrist al-Mu'allafat* in "The Works of Ibn Arabi" by A. Affifi, in *Revue de la faculté de lettres de l'Université d'Alexandrie*, no. 8, 1954.

Critical Studies: *The Mystical Philosophy of Muhy al-Din Ibn al-Arabi* by A. Affifi, 1964; *Creative Imagination in the Sufism of Ibn Arabi* by H. Corbin, 1969; *Sufism and Taoism* by T. Izutsu, 1983; *The Sufi Path of Knowledge: Ibn Arabi's Metaphysics of Imagination* by W. Chittick, 1989; *Ibn Arabi wa Mawlid Lugha Jadida (Ibn Arabi and the Birth of New Language)* by S. Hakim, 1991; *Seal of the Saints: Prophethood and Sainthood in the Doctrine of Ibn Arabi* by M. Chodkiewicz, 1993; *An Ocean Without Shore; Ibn Arabi, the Book and the Law* by M. Chodkiewicz, 1993; *Quest for the Red Sulphur: The Life of Ibn Arabi* by Claude Addas, 1993; *The Self-disclosure of God: Principles of Ibn Arabi's Cosmology* by W. Chittick, 1998; *Ibn Arabi and the Later Islamic Tradition* by A. Knysh, 1999.

*   *   *

The thirteenth century mystical philosopher Muhyi al-Din Ibn al-Arabi was a truly prolific writer. Osman Yahia has listed up to 700 separate works attributed to him, 400 of which have survived. It is not an exaggeration to say that the works of Ibn al-Arabi marked the high point in Islamic mystical writing. Any survey of the history of Sufi writing must distinguish between a pre and a post-Ibn al-Arabi landscape. His works have been studied throughout the Islamic world, from Morocco to Indonesia.

Ibn al-Arabi's writings range from short devotional and didactic pieces for aspirants on the Sufi path, to the imposing *Al-Futuhat al-Makkiyya* [Mekkan Openings], containing 560 chapters, which has been printed without notes or references in an edition of over 2500 pages in small type. A critical edition of this work begun by O. Yahia will take up more than twenty volumes. Ibn al-Arabi also composed a significant work of mystical poetry, the *Tarjuman al-Ashwaq* [Interpreter of Desires]. Most of his writings however, remain in manuscript form awaiting proper editing and publication.

Central to his approach is a sophisticated hermeneutical style based on the Qur'anic revelation. This revelation is logo-centric; that is, God's message to humanity takes the form of the divine (Arabic) Word. Ibn al-Arabi's approach holds to this understanding, yet it opens up vast new insights into this Word by avoiding dogmatic and hence stifling interpretation. The issue here is not simply a distinction between a literalist and an interpretive reading. Ibn al-Arabi makes it clear that all readings bring with them preconceptions, and that they are all presumptuous when they claim to represent any "true" meaning with regard to revelation. After all, humanity's efforts can only ever be incomplete and imperfect in relation to God and his Word. With this insight in mind, Ibn al-Arabi takes up his own approach. He does put the various Islamic "sciences" to work in his writings. He uses grammar, law, hadith and often neo-Platonism as tools, but his touchstone is mystical inspiration. For him this is neither infallible nor can it fully encompass God's Word, but it is less of a human construct than the other approaches and for him (and other mystics) it is certainly more direct and convincing. In the end of course he is also interpreting the Word, but in basing his hermeneutic on spiritual principles, religious experience, and divine inspiration, he is uncovering realities as valid and as sound as those reached by any other method. Significantly, his hermeneutic starting point is open to change, since divine inspiration cannot be predicted, codified, or systematized. Mystical insight as an interpretive basis can thus never be a "school" or a set philosophy laying claim to a totalizing truth. This makes for a dynamic infinite hermeneutic, one that responds (in its own fallible and incomplete human way) to the incomprehensible infinite that is God. At one point he succinctly states, "I only speak of what I taste."

Ibn al-Arabi is best known for his development of a concept that became known in short as the "oneness of being." Although he himself did not coin the phrase, it came to represent his position on the nature of existence. In a number of works, he argued that the only real existence is that properly of God; and all of creation simply shares temporarily in that existence. This is not to say that Ibn al-Arabi was a pantheist (holding that creation is simply part of God). He insisted on a qualified but significant independence of creation from its creator. Ibn al-Arabi also made an impact through his developments on the idea of "walaya" or sainthood. The concept had been discussed from at least the tenth century, but Ibn al-Arabi took it to new heights. In particular he wrote in detail on the final or "seal" of saints, his function, and his identity. At stake here were ideas such as the continuation of divine guidance, the relation of sainthood to prophethood, and certain apocalyptic elements. Ibn al-Arabi was also known for his cosmological ideas. Probably the most innovative were his elaborations on the "imaginal world." Although not without simpler precedents in Islamic thought, for Ibn al-Arabi it is the realm in which imagined entities (including intentions, words, spiritual insights) take form. This imagination may be human or it may be God's.

The writings of Ibn al-Arabi from the 13th century to the present day have not been without their critics. *Fusus al-Hikam (The Bezels of Wisdom)*, for example, with its rehabilitation of Pharaoh and its apparent criticism of the prophet Noah, has been a convenient target. Conservative figures, in particular Ibn Taymiyya (d. 1328) and al-Sakhawi (d. 1496), objected to ideas such as the "oneness of being" (smacking of pantheism), Ibn al-Arabi's priority of God's mercy over his wrath (the non-eternity of God's punishment), and his doctrine of sainthood (which might compromise the function of the prophet Muhammad). These criticisms have never halted the circulation of Ibn al-Arabi's writings, but they have certainly kept them out of the hands of the general public. Even in the modern period Ibn al-Arabi must be handled with care: the publication of his *Al-Futuhat al-Makkiyya* was temporarily halted in the 1970s by the Egyptian government. Nevertheless, generations of Muslims (in particular intellectuals open to the mystical side of their religion, and many students of Islamic philosophy more generally) have read his works. The impact of these books (among both Sunnis and Shi'is) has been felt in the Arabic, Persianate, Turkic, and Asian regions of the Islamic world. The Western world has also recently begun to explore the Greatest Teacher.

—Richard J.A. McGregor

IBN AL-FÂRID, 'Umar

Born: Cairo, Egypt, 4 Dhû al-Qa'dah, 576 AH/March, 1181 AD **Education:** Raised to be a scholar of literature and religion by his father; studied the traditions of the prophet Muhammad (*hadîth*) with al-Qâsim ibn 'Alî Ibn 'Asâkir (d. 600 AH/1203 AD); studied Islamic mysticism, and Arabic literature; member of the Shâfi'î law school. **Family:** Married; at least two sons and a daughter. **Career:** As a young man, traveled and stayed in Mecca for about 15 years; returned to Cairo and taught poetry and the traditions of the prophet Muhammad at the al-Azhar mosque. **Died:** Cairo, Egypt, 2 Jumâdâ I, 632 AH/ January, 1235 AD

PUBLICATIONS

Collections

Dîwân Ibn al-Fârid, multiple editions including that edited by 'Abd al-Khâliq Mahmûd. 1984.

*

Critical Studies: *Studies in Islamic Mysticism* by R.A. Nicholson, 1921; *Ibn al-Fârid wa-al-hubb al-ilâhî* by Muhammad Mustafâ Hilmî, 1945; *The Mystical Poems of Ibn al-Fârid* by A.J. Arberry, 2 vols., 1952–56; *The Poem of the Way* by A.J. Arberry, 1952; *From Arab Poet to Muslim Saint: Ibn al-Fârid, His Verse, and His Shrine* by Th. Emil Homerin, 1994; *'Umar Ibn al-Fârid: Sufi Verse, Saintly Life by* Th. Emil Homerin, 2001.

* * *

'Umar Ibn al-Fârid is the most renowned mystical poet in Arabic. Born in Cairo, he grew up in the scholarly home of his father, a noted *fârid* in the religious courts, hence his title Ibn al-Fârid or "son of the women's advocate." As a youth, he memorized traditions of the prophet Muhammad (*hadîth*) and pursued studies in Islamic mysticism and Arabic literature. Ibn al-Fârid lived for a time in Mecca, but spent most of his life in Cairo where he taught the traditions of the prophet Muhammad and Arabic poetry until his death in 632 AH/1235 CE

A master of the Arabic poetic tradition, Ibn al-Fârid composed verse in a number of genres including the quatrain, love poetry (*ghazal*), and the formal ode (*qasîdah*). Ibn al-Fârid's verse is very polished and highly lyrical, though mannered and occasionally didactic. Generally, he addresses themes involving love, longing, and union:

> Ancient is my tale of love for her;
> it has, she knows, no beginning, no end.
> There is none like me in passion for her,
> while her enchanting beauty has no equal.

Here, Ibn al-Fârid praises the beloved's unique beauty with words that echo the Qur'ân's frequent declarations that God "has no equal." This phrasing suggests the spiritual nature of the relationship, and Ibn al-Fârid's verse is filled with allusions to God, Muhammad, the Qur'ân, and, especially, to Islamic mystical doctrines and practice. Often, Ibn al-Fârid describes the lover's pain that is necessary to purify his heart of selfishness:

> So it happened that passion's fire filled him;
> he sees its burning but no relief.
> Thirsty, his ribs embrace a sorrow
> beyond the doctors' power,
> So he clinched his teeth as pain bit deep.

Yet, by suffering patiently, the lover learns true humility, which may then result in rapture and a state of union, as the lover passes away to reside with the beloved:

I rubbed my face in the dust for her to step on,
so she said: "Glad tidings for you; kiss my veil!"
But my soul would not have it, guarding me,
jealous to keep my longing pure.
So we passed the night together
as I controlled desire:
I saw kingship my kingdom and time my slave.

A distinguishing feature of Ibn al-Fârid's poems is the many places he cites within them. Significantly, most of the names refer to actual sites in Arabia found on the Cairo to Mecca pilgrimage route, a route Ibn al-Fârid probably knew from personal experience. With these detailed itineraries, Ibn al-Fârid links his physical residence in Cairo with his spiritual home in Mecca, Islam's sacred center. Moreover, the poet often refers to the beloved as the object of his prayers and pilgrimage, and he may recall hallowed memories of an earlier pilgrimage to Mecca. This, again, suggests the holy nature of both the poet's love and his beloved, and thus Ibn al-Fârid's poems may be read as love songs to God and His prophet Muhammad.

Furthermore, throughout his verse, Ibn al-Fârid expresses a mystical view of life in which creation mirrors its divine creator such that, when seen aright, all things shine with primordial light. This is perhaps best seen in two of his poems that have been especially cherished as classics of Islamic mystical literature, the al-Khamrîyah ("Wine Ode"), and the Nazm al-Sulûk ("Poem of the Sufi Way"). Beginning his al-Khamrîyah, the poet declares:

In memory of the beloved, we drank a wine.
We were drunk with it, before creation of the vine!

Clearly this timeless vintage is not that of the grape, and Ibn al-Fârid goes on to describe the miraculous healing properties of this heavenly ambrosia. Both in this verse and elsewhere in the al-Khamrîyah, he links this wine with dhikr ("memory") and the name of the Muslim mystical practice of recollection. Ibn al-Fârid elaborates on this and other aspects of Islamic mysticism in the 760 verses of his Nazm al-Sulûk, one of the longest poems ever composed in Arabic. This poem, in particular, revolves around the transformation of a mystic from a self-absorbed individual into an embodiment of the all-embracing Light of Muhammad, God's instrument of creation and revelation. Though at times complex and abstruse, this progressive mystical illumination must still rely on the simple power of love between God and His worshipper, an eternal love that underlies all of existence:

This is not some feeble guess:
beloveds and lovers appear to us from us
As we reveal ourselves in love and splendor.
So every hero in love am I,
And she the beloved of every hero,
all names of a disguise.

Ibn al-Fârid's poems were popular in his own day, and they have been read, studied, and imitated by Arab and Muslim poets for centuries. On occasion, he has been criticized by more conservative Muslims for his unitive vision of existence, using a female beloved to symbolize God, and for likening God's love to an intoxicating wine, a drink prohibited by the Qur'ân. For the vast majority of Muslims, however, Ibn al-Fârid's devotion to love and the beautiful and moving qualities of his verse have earned him the lasting title of "the sultan of lovers." In fact, Ibn al-Fârid's verse and later accounts of his life and

work have inspired many Muslims to venerate him as a saint and make pilgrimage to his grave, which is still a revered shrine in Egypt today.

—Th. Emil Homerin

IBN KHAFAJAH, Ibrahim ibn Abi al-Fath Abu Ishaq

Born: 450 AH/1058 AD on Shuqr Island on a river near Valencia in Andalusia (Spain). **Career:** Independently wealthy; primarily composed nature poetry; left off writing poetry in midlife, perhaps in the wake of the Spanish conquest of Valencia; brief travel to Morocco; praised the Almoravids, especially the ruler Yusuf ibn Tashfin, in Valencia, Granada, and Murcia. **Died:** 533 AH/1117 AD on Shuqr Island.

PUBLICATIONS

Collections

Diwan Ibn Khafajah (poetry). c. 533 AH/1117 CE; as The Diwan of Abu Ishaq ibn Ibrahim ibn Abu al Fath ibn Khafaja, translated by Arthur Wormhoudt, 1987.

*

Critical Studies: Ibn Khafajah by Muhammad Radwan, 1972; Hayat wa-athar al-sha'ir al-Andalusi Ibn Khafajah by Hamdan Hajaji, 1974; Ibn Khafajah al-Andalusi by Abd al-Rahman Jubayr, 1980; Ibn Khafajah: Sha'ir sharq al-Andalus: 450–533 H by Hasan Muhammad Nur al-Din, 1990; The Poetry of Ibn Khafajah: A Literary Analysis by Magda al-Nowaihi, 1993.

* * *

Ibrahim ibn Abi al-Fath Abu Ishaq Ibn Khafajah's privileged background enabled him to devote most of his creative energy to nature poetry, rather than the panegyric poetry that was the main source of income for many poets of his time. Although his nature poetry encompasses both the "Arabian" style, or depiction of bleak desert scenes in the tradition of the eastern Arab poets, and the "Andalusian" style, or depiction of pleasant garden scenes, it is the latter style that predominates in his work and for which he is best known. Ibn Khafajah's importance as a nature poet is emphasized in the classical anthologies and biographies. In addition, the references to him as "the gardener" and as "al-Sanawbari of the west"— linking him to the eastern Arab poet best known for his descriptive poetry—display the central role of nature poetry in his work. Ibn Khafajah's talent in portraying nature also appears in other genres such as his panegyrics and his elegies.

His Andalusian nature poetry can be viewed in the broader context of Andalusian Arabic poetry, in which the description of pleasant garden scenes was proportionally more important than in eastern Arabic poetry. This may be due in part to the lush gardens throughout the region, including the island of Shuqr where Ibn Khafajah was born and raised. His nephew Ibn Zuqqaq is considered his imitator, while his style in nature poetry is said to be emulated by subsequent generations of Andalusian Arab poets.

Ibn Khafajah refers to the major eastern poets al-Mutanabbi, Mihyar al-Daylami, and al-Sharif al-Radi as his inspiration, although this inspiration has more to do with rhetorical style and "Arabian" themes than the garden poetry for which Ibn Khafajah is best known. Ibn Khafajah's style is noteworthy for his seamless interweaving of different spheres of experience, such as the animate and the inanimate, the human and the non-human, and the cosmos and the natural environment on earth. The depiction of human beauty is made vivid through the use of natural imagery, while the depiction of nature comes alive through the use of human imagery with physical, intellectual, and emotive dimensions. Within the depiction of nature, the cosmos and the natural environment on earth reflect one another and interact with one another. These rhetorical features give Ibn Khafajah's poetry a magical quality. While mannerist elaboration of poetic expression was a common feature of Andalusian Arabic poetry, Ibn Khafajah's manipulation of this potential stands out for both classical and modern critics.

As a privileged owner of plantations, Ibn Khafajah was able to enjoy a playful and adventurous youth, referred to by classical biographers as *mujun*, which refers to sexual promiscuity, especially homosexual, drinking and partying, and carefree living in general. This lifestyle may be related to his focus on pleasant garden scenes, where much of this type of socializing took place. However, he apparently repented for these youthful adventures later in life, and this repentance is assumed to be the source of much of his wisdom poetry. The best known example of this wisdom poetry is his fatalistic description of himself as a traveler who hears a mountain lamenting the loss of all who pass by. As in his garden poetry, the rhetorical integration of the animate and the inanimate in this poem contributes to its emotive force.

Ibn Khafajah is also noted for his ode on the Spanish conquest of Valencia. Like many Andalusian poets, he composed poetry on yearning for Andalusia during his travels in North Africa. As the compiler of his own poetry later in life, Ibn Khafajah included an introduction to his compilation that has been valuable for his classical and modern critics.

—Jocelyn Sharlet

IBSEN, Henrik (Johan)

Born: Skien, Norway (then united with Sweden), 20 March 1828. **Education:** Educated at local schools, and a private school in Skien; attended the University of Christiania (now Oslo), 1850–51. **Family:** Married Suzannah Thoresen in 1858; one son; also had one son by Else Jonsdatter. **Career:** Pharmacist's assistant in Grimstad, 1844–50; drama critic, *Manden*, later *Andhrimner*, 1851; contributor to the radical newspaper *Arbejderforeningernes blad*, until it was shut down by the police, 1851; house dramatist, Det Norske Theater [Norwegian Theatre], Bergen, 1851–57; visited Copenhagen and Dresden, 1852; artistic director, Det Norske Theater, Christiania, 1857–62: theatre declared bankrupt, 1862; travelled in northern Norway on grant to collect folktales, 1862; consultant, Christiania Theater, 1863; awarded a small travelling scholarship by the state in 1864, and left for Italy,

where he lived until 1868; visited Egypt, 1869; lived in Dresden, 1868–75, Munich, 1875–78, Rome, 1878–85, Munich, 1885–91; returned to Norway and settled in Christiania, 1891–1906. Government pension, 1866. Doctor of Letters, Uppsala University, 1877. **Died:** 23 May 1906.

PUBLICATIONS

Collections

Samlede verker [Collected Works] (includes letters), edited by Francis Bull, Halvdan Koht, and Didrik Arup Seip. 21 vols., 1928–58.
Samlede verker [Collected Works]. 7 vols., 1978.
Prose Dramas (includes *The League of Youth*; *The Pillars of Society*; *A Doll's House*; *Ghosts*; *An Enemy of the People*; *The Wild Duck*; *Lady Inger of Östråt*; *The Vikings at Helgeland*; *The Pretenders*; *The Emperor and Galilean*; *Rosmersholm*; *The Lady from the Sea*; *Hedda Gabler*), edited by William Archer, translated by Archer, Frances E. Archer, Eleanor Marx-Aveling, Charles Archer, Catherine Ray. 5 vols., 1890.
Collected Works, edited by William Archer, translated by Archer, Edmund Gosse, Charles Archer, Frances E. Archer, Eleanor Marx-Aveling, Mary Morison, C.H. Herford, and A.G. Chater. 12 vols., 1906–12.
The Oxford Ibsen, edited by James W. McFarlane, translated by McFarlane and others. 8 vols., 1960–77.
The Complete Major Prose Plays, translated by Roll Fjelde. 1978.
Plays, translated by Michael Meyer. 6 vols., 1980–87.

Plays

Catalina (produced 1882). 1850; as *Cataline*, translated by Anders Orbeck, in *Early Plays*, 1921; as *Catiline*, translated by Graham Orton, in *The Oxford Ibsen*, 1, 1960.
Kjæmpehøjen (produced 1850). 1902; as *The Warrior's Barrow*, translated by Anders Orbeck, in *Early Plays*, 1921; as *The Burial Mound*, translated by James McFarlane, in *The Oxford Ibsen 1*, 1960.
Norma; eller, En politikers kjærlighed, in *Andhrimmer*. 1 and 8 June, 1851; as *Norma; or, A Politician's Love*, translated by James McFarlane, in *The Oxford Ibsen 1*, 1960.
Sankthansnatten (produced 1853). 1909; as *St. John's Night*, translated by James and Kathleen McFarlane, in *The Oxford Ibsen 1*, 1960.
Fru Inger til Østråt (produced 1855). 1857; revised edition, 1874; as *Lady Inger of Östråt*, translated by Charles Archer, in *Prose Dramas*, 1890; also translated by R. Farquharson-Sharp, with *Love's Comedy* and *The League of Youth*, 1915; as *Lady Inger*, translated by Graham Orton, in *The Oxford Ibsen 1*, 1960.
Gildet på Solhaug (produced 1856). 1856; as *The Feast at Solhaug*, translated by William Archer and Mary Morison, in *Collected Works*, 1906–12.
Olaf Liljekrans (produced 1857). 1898; as *Olaf Liljekrans*, translated by Anders Orbeck, in *Early Plays*, 1921.
Hærmændene på Helgeland (produced 1858). 1857; as *The Vikings at Helgeland*, translated by William Archer, in *Prose Dramas*, 1890; also translated by Sam Oakland, 1978; as *The Warriors at Helgeland*, translated by R. Farquharson-Sharp, with *Ghosts* and *An Enemy of the People*, 1911; translated by James McFarlane, in *The Oxford Ibsen 2*, 1962.

Kjærlighedens komedie (produced 1873). 1862; as *Love's Comedy*, translated by C.H. Herford, 1900; also translated by R. Farquharson-Sharp, with *Lady Inger of Ostraat* and *The League of Youth*, 1915; Jens Arup, 1962.

Kongs-Emnerne (produced 1864). 1863; as *The Pretenders*, translated by William Archer, in *Prose Dramas*, 1890; also translated by R. Farquharson-Sharp, with *The Pillars of Society* and *Rosmersholm*, 1913; William Archer, 1913.

Brand (produced in part, 1866; complete version, 1885). 1866; as *Brand*, translated by W. Wilson, 1891; also translated by C.H. Herford, 1894; F.E. Garrett, 1894; J.M. Olberman, 1912; Miles M. Dawson, 1916; Theodore Jorgenson, 1962; G.M. Gathorne-Hardy, 1966; Michael Meyer, 1967; Geoffrey Hill, 1978; R.D. MacDonald, 1991.

Peer Gynt (produced 1876). 1867; as *Peer Gynt*, translated by William and Charles Archer, 1892; also translated by R. Ellis-Roberts, 1912; R. Farquharson-Sharp, 1921; Gottfried Hult, 1933; Norman Ginsbury, 1945; Paul Green, 1951; Horace Maynard Finney, 1955; Rolf Fjelde, 1964; Christopher Fry and Johan Fillinger, 1970; Peter Watts, 1970; David Rudkin, 1983; James W. McFarlane, 1989; Anne Bamborough, adapted by Frank McGuiness, 1990; Kenneth McLeish, 1990.

De unges forbund (produced 1869). 1869; as *The League of Youth*, translated by William Archer, in *Prose Dramas*, 1890; R. Farquharson-Sharp, with *Love's Comedy* and *Lady Inger of Ostraat*, 1915; Peter Watts, with *A Doll's House* and *The Lady From the Sea*, 1965.

Kejser og Galilæer (produced in part 1896). 1873; as *The Emperor and the Galilean*, translated by Catherine Ray, 1876; also translated by Graham Orton, 1963.

Samfundets støtter (produced 1877). 1877; as *The Pillars of Society*, translated by William Archer, in *The Pillars of Society and Other Plays*, 1888; also translated by R. Farquharson-Sharp, with *The Pretenders* and *Rosmersholm*, 1913; Garrett H. Leverton, 1937; Norman Ginsbury, 1962; as *The Pillars of the Community*, translated by Una Ellis-Fermor, in *Three Plays*, 1950.

Et dukkehjem (produced 1879). 1879; as *Nora*, translated by T. Weber, 1880; also translated by Henrietta Frances Lord, 1882; as *A Doll's House*, translated by William Archer, 1889; also translated by Norman Ginsbury, 1904; R. Farquharson-Sharp, with *The Wild Duck* and *The Lady From the Sea*, 1910; Norman Ginsbury, 1950; Peter Watts, with *The League of Youth* and *The Lady From the Sea*, 1965; Roll Fjelde, in *Four Major Plays*, 1965; James W. McFarlane, in *Four Major Plays*, 1981; Frank McGuinness, from a literal translation by Charlotte Barslund, 1996; translated by Nicholas Rudall, 1999.

Gengangere (produced 1881). 1881; as *Ghosts*, translated by William Archer, in *The Pillars of Society and Other Plays*, 1888; also translated by Henrietta Frances Lord, 1890; R. Farquharson-Sharp, with *The Warriors at Helgeland* and *An Enemy of the People*, 1911; Norman Ginsbury, 1938; Bjorn Koefoed, 1950; Peter Watts, with *A Public Enemy* and *When We Dead Wake*, 1964; Michael Meyer, 1970; James W. McFarlane, in *Four Major Plays*, 1981; Christopher Hampton, 1983; Nicholas Rudall, 1990.

En folkefiende (produced 1883). 1882; as *An Enemy of Society*, translated by Eleanor Marx-Aveling, in *The Pillars of Society and Other Plays*, 1888; as *An Enemy of the People*, translated by R. Farquharson-Sharp, with *Ghosts* and *The Warriors at Helgeland*, 1911; Norman Ginsbury, 1939; Lars Nordenson, adapted by Arthur Miller, 1951; James W. McFarlane, with *The Wild Duck*

and *Rosmersholm*, 1960; Inger Lignell, adapted by Henry S. Taylor, 1960; Michael Meyer, 1970; as *A Public Enemy*, translated by Peter Watts, with *Ghosts* and *When We Dead Wake*, 1964; as *An Enemy of the People*, adapted by Max Faber, 1967; adapted by Christopher Hampton, 1997.

Vildanden (produced 1885). 1884; as *The Wild Duck*, translated by Frances E. Archer, in *Prose Dramas*, 1890; also translated by R. Farquharson-Sharp, with *A Doll's House* and *The Lady From the Sea*, 1910; William Archer, in *Four Plays*, 1941; Una Ellis-Fermor, in *Three Plays*, 1950; James W. McFarlane, with *Enemy of the People* and *Rosmersholm*, 1960; Rolf Fjelde, in *Four Major Plays*, 1965; Michael Meyer, 1970; Inga-Stina Ewbank and Peter Hall, with *John Gabriel Borkman*, 1975; Dounia Christiani, 1980; Christopher Hampton, 1980; adapted by Max Faber, 1958; adapted by Robert Brustein, 1997.

Rosmersholm (produced 1887). 1886; as *Rosmersholm*, translated by L.N. Parker, 1889; also translated by M. Carmichael, in *Prose Dramas*, 1890; R. Farquharson-Sharp, with *The Pretenders* and *The Pillars of Society*, 1913; Una Ellis-Fermor, in *The Master Builder and Other Plays*, 1958; James W. McFarlane, with *Enemy of the People* and *The Wild Duck*, 1960; Norman Ginsbury, 1961; Ann Jellicoe, 1961; Arvid Paulson, in *Last Plays*, 1962; D. Rudkin, with *When We Dead Awaken*, 1990; as *The House of Rosmer*, adapted by Brian J. Burton, 1959.

The Pillars of Society and Other Plays (includes *The Pillars of Society*; *Ghosts*; *An Enemy of Society*), edited by Havelock Ellis, translated by William Archer and Eleanor Marx-Aveling. 1888.

Fruen fra havet (produced 1889). 1888; as *The Lady from the Sea*, translated by Eleanor Marx-Aveling, 1890; also translated by Frances E. Archer, in *Prose Dramas*, 1890; Peter Watts, with *The League of Youth* and *A Doll's House*, 1965; James W. McFarlane, 1977.

Prose Dramas, edited by Edmund Gosse. 5 vols., 1890.

Hedda Gabler (produced 1891). 1890; as *Hedda Gabler*, translated by William Archer, in *Prose Dramas*, 1890; also translated by Edmund Gosse, 1891; Una Ellis-Fermor, in *Three Plays*, 1950; Eva Le Gallienne, 1953; Arvid Paulson, in *Last Plays*, 1962; Rolf Fjelde, in *Four Major Plays*, 1965; Michael Meyer, 1970; Christopher Hampton, 1972; Jens Arup, in *Four Major Plays*, 1981; Nicholas Rudall, 1992; adapted by John Osborne, 1972, and with Strindberg's *The Father*, 1989; adapted by Jon Robin Baitz, from a translation by Anne-Charlotte Hanes Harvey, 2000.

Bygmester Solness (produced 1893). 1892; as *The Master Builder*, translated by J.W. Arctander, 1893; also translated by Edmund Gosse and William Archer, 1893; Eva Le Gallienne, 1955; Una Ellis-Fermor, in *The Master Builder and Other Plays*, 1958; Arvid Paulson, in *Last Plays*, 1962; Rolf Fjelde, in *Four Major Plays*, 1965; Michael Meyer, 1968; James W. McFarlane, in *Four Major Plays*, 1981; also translated by Nicholas Rudall, 1994.

Lille Eyolf (produced 1895). 1894; as *Little Eyolf*, translated by William Archer, 1895; also translated by Henry L. Mencken, 1909; Una Ellis-Fermor, in *The Master Builder and Other Plays*, 1958; James W. McFarlane, 1977.

John Gabriel Borkman (produced 1897). 1896; as *John Gabriel Borkman*, translated by William Archer, 1897; also translated by Una Ellis-Fermor, in *The Master Builder and Other Plays*, 1958; Norman Ginsbury, 1960; Arvid Paulson, in *Last Plays*, 1962; Inga-Stina Ewbank and Peter Hall, with *The Wild Duck*, 1975; Nicholas Wright, from a translation by Charlotte Barslund, 1996.

Når vi døde vågner (produced 1900). 1899; edited by Robert Brustein, 1992; as *When We Dead Awaken*, translated by William Archer, 1900; also translated by Arvid Paulson, in *Last Plays*, 1962; James W. McFarlane, 1977; D. Rudkin, with *Rosmersholm*, 1990; as *When We Dead Wake*, translated by Peter Watts, with *Ghosts* and *A Public Enemy*, 1964.

Prose Dramas (includes *The League of Youth*; *The Pillars of Society*; *A Doll's House*; *Ghosts*; *An Enemy of the People*), revised edition, edited by William Archer, translated by Archer and Eleanor Marx-Aveling (reprinted from *The Pillars of Society and Other Plays*, 1888, and *Prose Dramas*, 5 vols., 1890). 5 vols., 1900–01.

A Doll's House; The Wild Duck; The Lady from the Sea, translated by R. Farquharson-Sharp and Eleanor Marx-Aveling. 1910.

The Warriors at Helgeland; Ghosts; An Enemy of the People, translated by R. Farquharson-Sharp. 1911.

The Pretenders; The Pillars of Society; Rosmersholm, translated by R. Farquharson-Sharp. 1913.

Prose Dramas (includes *Rosmersholm*; *A Doll's House*; *The Lady from the Sea*). 1913.

Lady Inger of Ostraat; Love's Comedy; The League of Youth, translated by R. Farquharson-Sharp. 1915.

Early Plays (includes *Cataline*; *The Warrior's Barrow*; *Olaf Liljekrans*), translated by Anders Orbeck. 1921.

Four Plays (includes *A Doll's House*; *Ghosts*; *The Wild Duck*; *The Master Builder*), translated by William Archer. 1941.

Three Plays (includes *Hedda Gabler*; *The Wild Duck*; *The Pillars of the Community*), translated by Una Ellis-Fermor. 1950; as *Hedda Gabler and Other Plays*, 1963.

Seven Famous Plays, edited by William Archer and others. 1950.

The Master Builder and Other Plays (includes *The Master Builder*; *Rosmersholm*; *Little Eyolf*; *John Gabriel Borkman*), translated by Una Ellis-Fermor. 1958.

An Enemy of the People; *Rosmersholm*; *The Wild Duck*, translated by James W. McFarlane. 1960.

Last Plays (includes *Rosmersholm*; *Hedda Gabler*; *The Master Builder*; *John Gabriel Borkman*; *When We Dead Awaken*), translated by Arvid Paulson. 1962.

Ghosts; A Public Enemy; When We Dead Wake, translated by Peter Watts. 1964.

The League of Youth; A Doll's House; The Lady from the Sea, translated by Peter Watts. 1965.

Four Major Plays (includes *A Doll's House*; *The Wild Duck*; *Hedda Gabler*; *The Master Builder*), translated by Rolf Fjelde. 1965.

Ghosts; An Enemy of the People; Wild Duck; Hedda Gabler, translated by Michael Meyer. 1970.

Four Major Plays (includes *A Doll's House*; *Ghosts*; *The Master Builder*; *Hedda Gabler*), translated by James W. McFarlane and Jens Arup. 1981.

Verse

Digte [Verse]. 1871; enlarged edition, 1875.

Lyrical Poems, translated by R.A. Streatfeild. 1902.

På vidderne, as *On the Heights*, translated by William Norman Guthrie. 1910.

Lyrics and Poems, translated by F.E. Garrett. 1912.

Terje Viken, translated by M. Michelet and G.R. Vowles. 1918.

Poems, translated by John Northam. 1986.

Poems, translated by Brian Sourbut. 1993.

Other

Samlede verker [Collected Works]. 10 vols., 1898–1902.

Correspondence, edited and translated by Mary Morison. 1905.

Episke Brand (fragment), edited by Karl Larsen. 1907.

Speeches and New Letters, edited by Lee M. Hollander, translated by Arne Kildal. 1911, reprinted 1982.

Letters and Speeches, edited by Evert Sprinchorn, translated by Sprinchorn and others. 1965.

Brevveksling med Christiania Theater 1878–1899 (letters), edited by Øyvind Anker. 1965.

Brev 1845–1905 (letters), edited by Øyvind Anker. 1979.

*

Bibliography: *Henrik Ibsen: A Bibliography of Criticism and Biography, with an Index to Characters* by Ina Ten Eyck Firkins, 1921; *Ibsen 1828–1928* by H. Pettersen, 1928; *Ibsen Årbok* [Ibsen Yearbook] (later *Contemporary Approaches to Ibsen*), 195–; *Ibsen Bibliography 1928–1957* by I. Telford, 1961.

Critical Studies: *Henrik Ibsen: A Critical Biography* by Henrik B. Jaeger, translated by W.M. Payne 1901; *Henrik Ibsen: Plays and Problems* by Otto Heller, 1912; *Henrik Ibsen: Poet, Mystic and Moralist* by Henry Rose, 1913; *The Quintessence of Ibsenism* by G.B. Shaw, revised edition, 1913; *Ibsen and His Creation* by Janko Lavrin, 1921; *Henrik Ibsen: A Critical Study* by Richard E. Roberts, 1922; *The Modern Ibsen* by H.J. Weigand, 1925; *Henrik Ibsen: An Introduction to His Life and Works* by Paul H. Grummann, 1928; *Ibsen and the Actress* by Elizabeth Robins, 1928; *Henrik Ibsen: A Study in Art and Personality* by Theodore Jorgenson, 1945; *Ibsen the Norwegian* by M.C. Bradbrook, 1946, revised edition, 1966; *Ibsen: The Intellectual Background*, 1946, and *A Study of Six Plays by Ibsen*, 1950, both by Brian W. Downs; *Ibsen's Dramatic Technique* by P.F.D. Tennant, 1948; *Ibsen's Dramatic Method*, 1952, and *Ibsen: A Critical Study*, 1973, both by John Northam; *Ibsen: The Man and the Dramatist* by F. Bull, 1954; *Ibsen and the Temper of Norwegian Literature*, 1960, and *Ibsen and Meaning: Studies, Essays and Prefaces 1953–87*, 1987, both by James McFarlane, and *Ibsen: A Critical Anthology*, 1970, and *The Cambridge Companion to Ibsen*, 1994, both edited by McFarlane; *Henrik Ibsen* by G. Wilson Knight, 1962; *The Drama of Ibsen and Strindberg* by F.L. Lucas, 1962; *Henrik Ibsen: A Collection of Critical Essays* edited by Rolf Fjelde, 1965; *Notes on Ibsen's "Doll's House" and "Hedda Gabler,"* 1965, and *Notes on Ibsen's "Ghosts," "Enemy of the People" and "The Wild Duck"*, 1965, both by Marianne Sturman; *Henrik Ibsen* (biography), 3 vols., 1967–71, condensed single vol., 1974, *Ibsen on File*, 1985, and *Ibsen*, 1990, all by Michael Meyer; *Mythic Patterns in Ibsen's Last Plays* by O.I. Holtan, 1970; *The Life of Ibsen* by H. Koht, 1971; *Ibsen: The Critical Heritage* edited by Michael Egan, 1972; *Cataline's Dream: An Essay on Ibsen's Plays* by J. Hurt, 1972; *Henrik Ibsen: The Divided Consciousness* by Charles R. Lyons, 1972, and *Critical Essays on Henrik Ibsen* edited by Lyons, 1987; *Women in the Plays of Henrik Ibsen* by Clela Allphin, 1975; *Ibsen's Feminine Mystique* by Vincent J. Balice, 1975; *The Ibsen Cycle: The Design of the Plays from "Pillars of Society" to "When We Dead Awaken,"* 1975, revised 1992, *To the Third Empire: Ibsen's Early Drama*, 1980, and *Text and Supertext in Ibsen's Drama*, 1989, all by Brian Johnston; *Ibsen* by Harold Clurman, 1977; *The Real Drama of Henrik Ibsen?* by Arne Duve, 1977; *Ibsen: A Dissenting View* by Ronald Gray, 1977; *Ibsen: The Man and His Work*, 1978, and *Henrik Ibsen*, 1980, both by

Edvard Beyer; *Ibsen the Romantic: Analogues of Paradise in the Later Plays* by Errol Durbach, 1978, and *Ibsen and the Theatre: Essays in Celebration of the 150th Anniversary of Henrik Ibsen's Birth* edited by Durbach, 1980; *Ibsen's Drama: Author to Audience* by E. Haugen, 1979; *A Doll's House: Notes* by Bruce King, 1980; *Henrik Ibsen's Aesthetic and Dramatic Art* by J.E. Tammany, 1980; *Patterns in Ibsen's Middle Plays* by Richard Hornby, 1981; *Notes on Ibsen's "Doll's House"* edited by A. Norman Jeffares and Suheil Badi Bushrui, 1981; *Ghosts: Notes* by Adele King, 1981; *Ibsen: The Open Vision* by John Chamberlain, 1982; *Ibsen Studies* by Peter J. Eikeland, 1982; *Ibsen: Four Essays* edited by Angel Flores, 1982; *Hedda Gabler: Notes* by Helena Forsås-Scott, 1983; *Henrik Ibsen* by David Thomas, 1983; *William Archer on Ibsen: The Major Essays 1889–19* by William Archer, edited by Thomas Postlethwait, 1984; *An Ibsen Companion: A Dictionary Guide to the Life, Works and Critical Reception of Henrik Ibsen* by G.B. Bryan, 1984; *Ibsen and Shaw* by Keith M. May, 1985; *Henrik Ibsen: Life, Work and Criticism* by Yvonne Shafer, 1985; *Ibsen and the English Stage* by Gretchen P. Ackerman, 1987; *China's Ibsen: From Ibsen to Ibsenism* by Elisabeth Eide, 1987; *Ibsen in America: A Century of Change* by Robert A. Schanke, 1988; *Peer Gynt and Ghosts* by Asbjørn Aarseth, 1989; *Ibsen's Lively Art: A Performance Study of the Major Plays* by Frederick J. and Lise-Lone Marker, 1989; *Time's Disinherited Children: Childhood, Regression and Sacrifice in the Plays of Henrik Ibsen* by Robin Young, 1989; *Ibsen's Heroines* by Lou Andreas-Salome, translated by S. Mandel, 1990; *Ibsen and the Great World* by Naomi Lebowitz, 1990; *Divine Madness and the Absurd Paradox: Ibsen's "Peer Gynt" and the Philosophy of Kierkegaard* by Bruce G. Shapiro, 1990; *Ibsen's Forsaken Merman: Folklore in the Late Plays* by Per Schelde Jacobsen and Barbara Fass Leavy, 1991; *Ibsen: A Doll's House* by Egil Törnqvist, 1995; *Ibsen and the Greeks: The Classical Greek Dimension in Selected Works of Henrik Ibsen as Mediated by German and Scandinavian Culture* by Norman Rhodes, 1995; *Henrik Ibsen: A New Biography* by Robert Ferguson, 1996; *Ibsen's Drama: Right Action and Tragic Joy* by Theoharis Constantine Theoharis, 1996; *Ibsen's Women* by Joan Templeton, 1997; *Ibsen and Early Modernist Theatre, 1890–1900* by Kirsten Shepherd-Barr, 1997; *Theatrical and Narrative Space: Studies in Ibsen, Strindberg and J.P. Jacobsen* by Erik Østerud, 1998; *On Ibsen* by James Joyce, edited by Dennis Phillips, 1999; *Stella Adler on Ibsen, Strindberg, and Chekhov* by Stella Adler, edited by Barry Paris, 1999; *Ibsen: The Dramaturgy of Fear* by Michael Goldman, 1999.

*   *   *

"Anyone who wants to understand me must know Norway," Henrik Ibsen once remarked. This most European of Norwegian dramatists, still played regularly to packed houses the world over, often to theater-goers ignorant of his nationality, insisted upon the importance of his national heritage. There was much about Norway which irritated and depressed him—to such an extent that he spent 27 of his most creative years (1864–91) abroad, in Italy and Germany—yet his plays, almost without exception, are set in the land he had rejected. Trolls and hobgoblins, Viking legends, brooding fjord landscapes and deep sunless valleys, snow and ice and extreme cold and light, hectic summer nights—these permeate the lives and form the personalities of the characters in his plays.

Yet even before he left Norway, Ibsen was well versed in the European theatrical tradition. After an inauspicious and poverty-stricken beginning, he was appointed theatre director in Bergen (1851–57), then Christiania (now Oslo, 1857–62). The European stage at this period was dominated by French salon comedies, the "well-made play" written by dramatists such as Eugène Scribe; and it was largely these which Ibsen directed.

Most of Ibsen's early works are historical dramas, often in verse, which combine tales of Norway's heroic, half-legendary past with the techniques of Scribean drama: a complicated intrigue, involving convoluted misunderstanding and mistaken identity, and a neat tying-off of ends in conclusion—as in, for example, *Fru Inger til Østråt* (*Lady Inger of Östråt*) and *Gildet på Solhaug* (*The Feast at Solhaug*). They are lofty in style, with a tendency to melodrama; it was not until Ibsen turned to depiction of contemporary society in colloquial modern prose that he found his natural medium.

Before that, however, he had written the two vast and sprawling verse dramas *Brand* and *Peer Gynt*. They were "reading dramas," not intended for the stage, and could not be staged realistically; they required not only an enormous cast but (for *Brand*) whole mountain ranges, storms, and avalanches, and (for *Peer Gynt*) a removal across several continents, a shipwreck, and a multitude of supernatural and monstrous creatures. It was not until Ibsen had achieved success with his prose dramas that they were accepted into theatre repertoires. Nowadays, however, they are among the most frequently performed of the plays.

At the centre of each play is a loner, a man ostracized by his fellow men. Brand is a fanatical priest who demands unquestioning submission to his stern Jehovah, and destroys his family and finally himself in his obsessive devotion to his call. Peer Gynt is his antithesis, a man who stands for nothing, taking the line of least resistance throughout his life; yet both die equally unsure that they have achieved anything.

This pattern of antitheses—exposing the deficiencies of one extreme standpoint in one play and then those of its polar opposite in another—was to repeat itself in many of Ibsen's later plays. Ibsen's protagonists feel driven to take a stand: the lofty claims of the ideal clash with the more sordid compromise of the real, the egotistical drive for success and fame with the gentler values of love and friendship.

It was with the "social" dramas of his next period, from *Samfundets støtter* (*The Pillars of Society*) to *Vildanden* (*The Wild Duck*), that Ibsen won an international reputation and established himself as a European dramatist. Initially the success was often one of scandal rather than acclaim; for Ibsen wrote about such subjects, and in such a way, that polite society was outraged. The slamming of the door at the end of *Et dukkehjem* (*A Doll's House*), which announces Nora's abandonment of husband and children, and her determination to find self-fulfilment on her own terms, aroused furious condemnation. *Gengangere* (*Ghosts*), with its frank treatment of debauchery, illegitimacy, and syphilis, was banned and reviled. "An open drain," the *Daily Telegraph* called it. Posterity, however, has discovered that it was neither lubricity nor frankness which was the truly revolutionary aspect of these plays; it was rather Ibsen's determination to challenge social convention and hypocrisy, which barred the way to individual self-realization.

Ibsen read few books, but he did read newspapers, and his reading is reflected not only in his involvement in contemporary debates but in the language and style of his plays. His actors were not required to strike heroic poses and indulge in elevated conceits, but to talk to each other in the contemporary language of everyday life. Acting traditions had to change before Ibsen's ideas could be realized.

From 1877 Ibsen's plays are entirely in prose, and the centre of interest narrows to a small group of people, frequently a family within the four walls of their home, a refuge which grows more and more like a prison as the conflict intensifies. The mainspring of the action is often the revelation of a guilty secret, a past misdeed which returns to haunt the present and disrupt the fragile security which has been erected over its concealment. The end is often death or despair (*Ghosts, The Wild Duck, Rosmersholm*); with the relentlessness of Greek tragedy, the characters are doomed by their own acts even as they struggle to escape. It is but rarely that they find the strength to take charge of their own fates, as in *Fruen fra havet* (*The Lady from the Sea*), where understanding and tolerance break the vicious spiral of mutual destructiveness.

Ibsen's late plays puzzled critics and audiences; they found them obscure and disturbing. In the 1890s he began to depart from the familiar realistic form and to move towards a more experimental, modernistic drama. Complex images or symbols dominate the play, like the tower in *Bygmester Solness* (*The Master Builder*) or the iron mountains in *John Gabriel Borkman*; strange, surreal characters appear; the protagonists are groping uncertainly for the meaning of life. In Ibsen's last play, *Når vi døde vågner* (*When We Dead Awaken*), the artist and his muse disappear into the apocalypse hand in hand.

Ibsen wrote not just in one dramatic form but in many. There are few European dramatists since his day who do not owe something to his tightly controlled form and his sense of theatre.

—Janet Garton

See the essays on *Brand, A Doll's House, Ghosts, Hedda Gabler, The Master Builder, Peer Gynt,* and *The Wild Duck.*

IBUSE Masuji

Born: Kamo, Hiroshima Prefecture, Japan, 15 February 1898. **Education:** Tutored and intellectually mentored by his maternal grandfather from early childhood through adolescence; attended a prestigious and strongly traditional high school in Fukuyama; studied French literature at Waseda University in Tokyo, 1917–22; briefly studied painting at the Japanese School of Arts in Tokyo, 1921–22. **Military Service:** Drafted into Imperial Army, 22 November 1941; served as war correspondent in Malaya until November 1942. *Family:* Married Setsuyo Akimoto, 1927. *Career:* Grew up as a member of a moderately wealthy land-owning family; associated himself during and immediately after his time at Waseda with literary figures such as Hōmei Iwano, Seiji Tanizaki, and Kōtarō Tanaka; later became a close literary mentor to the writer Osamu Dazai; worked professionally as a writer throughout his life, often through associations with "group journals" (*dōjin zasshi*) such as *Seiki, Bungei toshi,* and *Sakuhin. Awards:* Naoki prize for popular literature by a rising author, 1938; Yomiuri prize for fiction, 1949; Art Academy prize, 1955; Noma prize for literature, 1966; Order of Cultural Merit, 1966. **Died:** 10 July 1993.

PUBLICATIONS

Collections

Ibuse Masuji zenshū [Collected Works]. 14 vols., 1965–74.

Ibuse Masuji jisen zenshū [Author-Selected Collected Works]. 13 vols., 1985–86.

Short Stories

"Yūhei." 1923.

"Yofuke to ume no hana." 1925; as "Plum Blossom by Night," translated by John Bester, in *Lieutenant Lookeast and Other Stories,* 1971; and in *Salamander and Other Stories,* 1981.

"Koi." 1926; as "Carp," translated by John Bester, in *Lieutenant Lookeast and Other Stories,* 1971; and in *Salamander and Other Stories,* 1981.

"Sanshōuo." 1929; as "The Salamander," translated by Tadao Katayama, 1956; and also translated by Leon Zolbrod, 1964; as "Salamander," translated by Sadamichi Yokoo and Sanford Goldstein, 1966; and also translated by John Bester, in *Lieutenant Lookeast and Other Stories,* 1971; and in *Salamander and Other Stories,* 1981.

"Yane no ue no Sawan." 1929; as "Sawan on the Roof," translated by Yokuchi Miyamoto with Frederick Will, 1966; and also translated by John Bester, in *Lieutenant Lookeast and Other Stories,* 1971; and in *Salamander and Other Stories,* 1981; as "Sawan on the Rooftop," translated by Tadao Katayama, 1967.

"Kuchisuke no iru tanima." 1929; as "Kuchisuke's Valley," translated by John Whittier Treat, in *The Showa Anthology,* edited by Van C. Gessel and Tomone Matsumoto, 1985.

"Tange-shi-tei." 1931; as "At Mr. Tange's," translated by Sadamichi Yokoo and Sanford Goldstein, 1969; as "Life at Mr. Tange's," translated by John Bester, in *Lieutenant Lookeast and Other Stories,* 1971; and in *Salamander and Other Stories,* 1981.

"Shoga kottō no sainan." 1933.

"Aogashima taigaiki." 1934.

"Mujintō Chōhei." 1936.

"Chōhei no haka." 1936.

"Yama o mite rōjin no kataru." 1939.

"Tajinko-mura hoi." 1940.

"Oki Beppu-mura no Morikichi." 1941.

"Gojinka." 1943.

"Kane kuyō no hi." 1943.

"Aru shōjo no senji nikki." 1943.

"Honjitsu kyūshin." 1949; as "No Consulation Today," translated by Edward Seidenstecker, 1964.

"Kakitsubata." 1951; as "The Crazy Iris," translated by Ivan Morris, 1956, and reprinted in *The Crazy Iris and Other Stories of the Atomic Aftermath,* edited by Oe Kenzaburo, 1985.

Fiction

Sazanami gunki (novella). 1930–38; as *Waves: A War Diary,* translated by David Aylward and Anthony Liman, in *Waves: Two Short Novels,* 1986.

Kawa. 1932.

Shūkin ryokō. 1935–37.

Jon Manjirō hyōryūki (novella). 1937; as "John Manjiro, the Castaway: His Life and Adventures," translated by Hisakazu Kaneko, 1940; as "John Manjiro: A Castaway's Chronicle," translated by David Aylward and Anthony Liman in *Castaways: Two Short Novels,* 1987.

Tajinko mura (novella). 1937; as "Tajinko Village," translated by John Bester, in *Lieutenant Lookeast and Other Stories*, 1971; and in *Salamander and Other Stories*, 1981.

Hana no machi. 1943.

Wabisuke (novella). 1946; as *Isle-on-the-Billows*, translated by David Aylward and Anthony Liman, in *Waves: Two Short Novels*, 1986.

Hikkoshi-yatsure. 1947.

Kashima ari. 1948.

Yōhai taichō (novella). 1950; as "A Far-worshipping Commander," translated by Glenn Shaw, 1954, and as "The Far-worshipping Commander," in *The Shadow of Sunrise*, edited by Shoichi Sakei, 1966; as "Lieutenant Lookeast," translated by John Bester, in *Lieutenant Lookeast and Other Stories*, 1971, and in *Salamander and Other Stories*, 1981.

Karusan yashiki. 1953.

Hyōmin Usaburō. 1954–55.

Ekimae ryokan. 1956–57.

Chimpindō shujin. 1959.

Bushū Hachigata-jō. 1961–62.

Kuroi ame. 1966; as *Black Rain*, translated by John Bester, 1966, 1969.

Tomonotsu chakaiki. 1983–1985.

Other

Zuihitsu (essays). 1933.

Keirokushū (memoir). 1936.

Jōkyō chokugo (memoir). 1936.

Kame (memoir). 1939.

Yama ya nodo (essays and sketches). 1941.

Shonan nikki (war diary). 1942.

Nankō Taigaiki (war diary). 1943.

Kawatsuri (stories and essays on fishing). 1952.

Nanatsu no kaidō (travel essays). 1952–57.

Tsurishi; Tsuriba (essays on fishing). 1960.

Hanseiki (memoir). 1970.

Tsuribito (essays on fishing). 1970.

Waseda no mori (memoir). 1971.

Chōyōchū no koto (memoir). 1977–80.

Umi-agari (essays). 1980–81.

Ogikubo fudoki (memoir). 1981–82.

Dazai Osamu (biography), 1989.

Translator, *Robinson hyoryuki*, by Daniel Defoe. 1961.

Translator, *Doritoru-sensei monogatari zenshu* by Hugh Lofting. 12 vols., 1961–62.

*

Bibliography: "Ibuse Masuji sankō bunken nempyō" by Terayoko Takeo, in *Ibuse Masuji kenkyu*, edited by Isogai Hideo, 1984; "Ibuse Masuji sankō bunken mokuroku" by Okoshi Kishichi, 1985; "Ibuse Masuji" by Anthony V. Liman, in *Dictionary of Literary Biography* (vol. 180), 1997.

Critical Studies: "Black Rain" by Robert J. Lifton, in *Death in Life: Survivors of Hiroshima*, 1967; "After the Bomb" by Arthur G. Kimball, in *Crisis in Identity and Contemporary Japanese Novels*, 1973; "Tradition and Contemporary Consciousness: Ibuse, Endo, Kaiko, Abe" by J. Thomas Rimer, in *Modern Japanese Fictions and Its Traditions*, 1978; *Pools of Water, Pillars of Fire: The Literature of Ibuse Masuji* by John Whittier Treat, 1988; *A Critical Study of the Literary Style of Ibuse Masuji* by Anthony V. Liman, 1992; "Ibuse Masuji: Nature, Nostalgia, Memory" by John Whittier Treat, in *Writing Ground Zero: Japanese Literature and the Atomic Bomb*, 1995.

*   *   *

Although his reputation outside Japan is still based chiefly on *Kuroi ame* (*Black Rain*), his novel about the atomic bombing of Hiroshima in 1945, Ibuse Masuji is without a doubt one of the most prolific and important Japanese writers of the 20th century. Ibuse's career spanned more than six decades and his literary output included dozens of volumes of fiction, essays, memoirs, and poems written in a direct, evocative style that obscured many of the distinctions among these genres. Largely because he refused to ally himself too closely with any particular political or aesthetic movement, Ibuse's voice was prominent not only during the post-Hiroshima era of reconstruction and recovery, but also during the tumultuous 1920s and 30s, when Japanese society alternated between the conservatism of traditional values and the radicalism of foreign ideas such as Marxism. In retrospect, Ibuse stands next among Akutagawa, Kawabata, Mishima, Murakami, Oe, and Tanizaki as one of the luminaries of contemporary Japanese literary culture.

Having studied literature—especially French, English, and Russian literature—in the midst of many of Japan's most noteworthy scholars and writers during his years at Waseda University, Ibuse rapidly burst onto the literary scene in the 1920s with a series of short stories including "Koi" ("Carp") and "Sanshōuo" ("The Salamander"). These tales not only reflect elements of traditional Japanese culture with which Ibuse was intimately familiar from his youth, but also show the early development Ibuse's uniquely perceptive narrative voice. Encouraged in his literary pursuits by his mentor and patron Kotaro Tanaka, Ibuse rapidly established himself by the early 1930s as a successful author. More than any other writer of his generation, Ibuse intermingled conventional Japanese literary themes and styles such as the sentimental *watakushi shosetsu* ("I-novel") or naturalistic *shaseibun* ("nature-sketching" forms) with a distinctly modern perspective in creating works that maintain a clear link to cultural tradition and heritage without descending into chauvinism (as was often the case with writers such as Yukio Mishima).

Throughout his career as a writer, Ibuse took an interest in history. Influences on his work ranged from medieval Japanese epics, whose style he imitated in his first longer work of fiction *Sazanami gunki* (*Waves: A War Diary*), to his own experiences of being drafted during World War II as a correspondent for the Imperial Army. In essays like *Nankō Taigaiki* ["An Account of My Voyage South"] or in fiction like his novellas *Wabisuke* (*Isle-on-the-Billows*) and *Yōhai taichō* ("Lieutenant Lookeast"), Ibuse refuses to moralize openly about events he witnessed while observing the Malayan campaign that were often shocking and dismaying to him. Instead, he allows his keen eye for detail and his sensitivity to human suffering to convey his intentions. Some critics have accused Ibuse of being overly uncritical in refusing to criticize the Japanese tactics in Singapore, but Ibuse extended a similar lack of judgment to most of his subject matter.

Coupled with his abiding interest in literal or figurative *hyōryūki* (''castaways''), this objectivity toward historical reality laid the foundation for his masterpiece, *Black Rain*.

As the only one of Ibuse's novels to have been translated into English, *Black Rain* stands out regardless of its subject matter. However, given that the atomic bombing of Hiroshima and Nagasaki had such a radical effect on the psyche of Japan as a whole—as well as that of individual *hibakusha* (survivors; literally ''the burned'')—Ibuse's 1966 novel represented an important new perspective on the reality of atomic weapons at a time when the nuclear tensions of the Cuban Missile Crisis were still a relatively recent memory for the entire world.

As was the case with many of his prior works, Ibuse thoroughly researched the details of the novel. Ibuse himself had been thirty miles away in the village of Kamo during the bombing, but not near enough to have experienced it first-hand. *Black Rain* is based on a number of documentary sources, including eyewitness accounts of the bombing. Most important, though, was the journal of Shizuma Shigematsu, a survivor with whom Ibuse had regularly gone fishing in the immediate post-war years and whose story he would transform into that of his protagonist Shigematsu Shizuma. Ibuse indirectly depicts the events of 6 August 1945, setting his novel nearly five years after the bombing. Shigematsu, his wife Shigeko, and their niece Yasuko are still dealing with the lingering physical, psychological, and societal after-effects of the bombing, especially the ''black rain'' contaminated with radioactive dust-particles that fell in and around Hiroshima in the hours after the explosion.

Shigematsu has been excused from normal work because of his mild radiation sickness. However, since he is not visibly ill, he is embarrassed at being perceived to be shirking his rightful share of labor. He decides to begin raising carp to restock a local lake that has been devoid of fish since the bombing. Shigematsu is also trying to arrange a marriage for Yasuko, but a false rumor that she was in Hiroshima at the time of the bombing (and thus would likely both to become ill and be infertile) has frustrated his attempts. In responding to an inquiry from a potential suitor, Shigematsu copies out excerpts from his niece's diary to dispel this rumor, but quickly realizes that her reminiscences of being soaked by the ''black rain'' will make her unmarriageable. He omits this passage and includes excerpts from his own journal instead. The remainder of the novel is made up of these excerpts, as well as pieces from other documents—e.g., an essay describing what survivors ate in Hiroshima, and a doctor's memoirs of treating radiation sickness in the days after the bombing—that Ibuse adapted for his fictional purposes. The novel ends on an ambiguously hopeful note as Yasuko admits she has been suffering symptoms of radiation-induced illness and rapidly declines at the same time that Shigematsu's carp pond begins to thrive.

Despite some mild protests that Ibuse's somewhat distanced depiction of the bombing of Hiroshima lessened the horror of the event, critics almost immediately hailed *Black Rain*, and it garnered several of the most prestigious literary awards in Japan. Its reputation has hardly diminished with the passage of time—it has never been out of print in either Japanese or English and it was voted in 1987 as the most significant post-war Japanese novel in a poll of Japanese scholars. Although Ibuse's output after the publication of *Black Rain* was mainly confined to collections of essays and memoirs, his status within Japanese literature has continued to grow, as demonstrated by

the popularity of a thirteen-volume set of his works released in the mid-1980s. Ibuse was nominated for the Nobel prize several times in the late 1980s and 1990s and continues to be the subject of scholarship both in Japan and the West.

—Derek Maus

IDRIS, Yusuf

Born: al-Bayrum village, Sharqiyya province, Egypt, 19 May 1927. **Education:** Attended school in Faqus in Sharqiyya; Dameitta; al-Mansura in Daqahliyya; Zaqaziq in Sharqiyya; Qasr al-'Ayni medical school, Cairo, 1945–51. **Military Service:** Secretary of the University Executive committee for armed combat, 1951. **Family:** Married; three children. **Career:** Physician, 1952; medical inspector in the poor section of Darb al-Ahmar district, Cairo; head of the literary department at *Rosa al-Yusuf, al-Sha'b, al-Masry, al-Jumhuriyya* then *al-Ahram* newspaper, 1961–91. **Awards:** Hiwar International Literary prize (refused), 1965; Medal of the Republic, 1966. **Died:** 1 August 1991.

PUBLICATIONS

Collections

Al-'Askary al-aswad. 1962.
Al-Sayyida Viryinna. 1977.
In the Eye of the Beholder: Tales of Egyptian Life from the Writings of Yusuf Idris, edited by Roger Allen. 1978.
Rings of Burnished Brass, translated by Catherine Cobham. 1984.
Al-Qisas al-qisirah. 2 vols. 1990–91.
Three Egyptian Short Stories; translated with introduction by Saad El-Gabalawy. 1991.

Short Stories

Arkhas al-layali. 1954; as *The Cheapest Nights and Other Stories,* translated by Wadida Wassef, 1990.
Qissat Hubb in *Jumhuriyyat Farahaat.* 1956; as *City of Love and Ashes,* translated by R. Neil Hewison, 1999.
Alysa kadhalika [Isn't It So]. 1957.
Al-Batal [The Hero]. 1957.
Hadithat sharaf [Matters of Honor]. 1959.
Akhir al-dunya [The End of the World]. 1961.
Qa' al-madina [City Dregs]. 1964.
Lughat al-ay ay [The Language of Pain]. 1965.
Al-Naddaha [The Siren].1969; as *La Sirene, et autres nouvelles,* translated by Luc Barbulesco and Phillipe Cardinal, 1986.
Mashuq al-hams. 1969.
Laylat sayf. 1970.
Bayt min lahm [House of Flesh]. 1971.
Ana sultan qanun al-wujud [I Am Sultan, the Law of Being]. 1980.
Jumhuriyyat Farahat [Farahat's Republic]. 1981.
Uqtulha [Kill Her]. 1982.
Al-'Atab 'ala al-nazar [Sight Is to Blame]. 1987.
Abu al-rijal. 1988; as *A Leader of Men,* translated by Saad Elkhadem, 1988.

Plays

Malik il-qutn [Cotton's King]. 1963.
Al-Lahza al-hariga [Critical Moment]. 1958.
Al-Mahzala al-ardiyya [The Face of the World]. 1966.
Al-Bahlawan [The Clown]. 1963.
Al-Farafir [The Flip Flaps]. 1963–64.
Al-Mukhattatin [The Stripped Ones]. 1969.
Al-Jins al-thalith [The Third Sex]. 1971.
Al-Irada. 1985.

Novels

Al-Haram (produced 1965). 1959; as *Sinners*, translated by Kristin
  Peterson-Ishaq, 1984; as *Le Tabou*, translated into French by
  France M. Douvier, 1987.
Al-'Ayb (produced 1967). [The Shame] 1963.
Rijal wa thiran. [Men and Oxen] 1964.
Al-Bayda'. [The White Woman] 1970.
Iktishaf qara. 1972.
Bisaraha ghayr Mutlaqa. 1968.
Niyu Yurk. 1980.
Al-Ab al-gha'ib. 1987.

Essays

Kitab nahwa masrah 'arabi. 1974.
Mufakkirat doctor Yusuf Idris. 2 vols., 1977.
Bahth 'an al-Sadat. 1984.
Ahammiyyat an natathaqqaf ya nas. 1985.
Faqr al-fikr wa fikr al-faqr. 1985.
Intiba'at mustafizza. 1986.
Khulw al-bal. 1986.
'Azf munfarid. 1987.
Al-'Idz al-'arabi. 1989.
Islam bi-la difaf. 1989.
Madinat al-mala'ika. 1989.
Dhikrayat Yusuf Idris. 1991.
Yusuf Idris 'ala fawhat burkan. 1991.
Jabarti al-sittinat. N.d.

*

Critical Studies: *Broken Idols: The Death of Religion as Reflected in
Two Short Stories by Idris and Mahfouz* by Mona Mikhail, 1974; *Sex
and Society in Yusuf Idris: Qa' al-Madina* by Catherine Cobham,
1975; *The Search for the Authentic Self within Idris's City* by Mona
Mikhail, 1977; *Studies in the Short Fiction of Naguib Mahfouz and
Yusuf Idris* by Mona Mikhail, 1992; *Yusuf Idris: Changing Vision* by
Dalya Cohen-Mor, 1992; *Egyptian Drama and Social Change: A
Study of Thematic and Artistic Development in Yusuf Idris's Plays* by
Dorota Rudnicka-Kassem, 1993; *Critical Perspectives on Yusuf Idris*,
edited by Roger Allen, 1994; *Critical Perspectives on Yusuf Idris* by
Issa J. Boullata, 1995; *The Western Encounter in the Works of Yusuf
Idris* by Rasheed El-Eanny, 1997; *The Short Stories of Yusuf Idris: A
Modern Egyptian Author* by P. M. Kurpershoek, 1997.

* * *

Yusuf Idris, though trained as a physician, was considered the
greatest short story writer of the Arab world. He was the first Egyptian

realist writer to break down the divide between fiction and reality,
introducing new themes, atmospheres, and social groups into Arab
fiction and drama. With vivid images of human interaction, he
explored the psychology of the oppressed classes in both the village
and the city and created narratives of social and political significance.
He explored themes of love, politics, and changing social and moral
values through stories of sexual relationships. For Idris, sex highlighted the hypocrisy in society, either by reinforcing the human
comedy or by shifting events in the direction of tragedy. Idris'
foremost accomplishment was his incorporation of the spoken language in the different dialogues of his characters. This incorporation
of the spoken Arabic language heightened the sense of realism in
creating a more truthful picture of characters' lives, traditions, failings, and virtues as they struggled against the restrictions of class in
Egyptian society.

Idris's stylistic devices varied from realism and existentialism to
absurdity, all in reaction to the changing political conditions of Egypt.
This variation is demonstrated in the chronology of Idris's work. He
began as a social realist in the 1950s, and his Marxist views led him to
address contemporary problems and their impact upon Egyptian life.
His themes during this early period included Egypt's transition from a
feudal to a socialist society, the plight of the Egyptian lower classes,
and issues of child labor, overpopulation, and migrant workers. The
setting for most of Idris's early work was the Egyptian village or the
urban slum areas of Cairo. The characters were mostly peasants and
migrant villagers with whom many readers could identify. Idris's
collection *Arkhas al-layali* (*The Cheapest Night*) depicted popular
literature, *Al-Batal* (*The Hero*) portrayed patriotic sentiments of
fighting the British occupation, *Love Story* (*Qissat hubb*) and *Al-
Bayda'* [White Woman] weaved a narrative of Egyptians' defense of
their country's independence and with love stories. *Al-Haram* (*Sinners*) addressed moral issues such as the permeation of corruption in
the government and described the group psychology of two poor
social groups, the unprivileged seasonal migrant workers and
the villagers.

Idris examined social injustice and class struggle through the
sexual relationships of his characters, especially the sexual relationships between people of different classes which highlighted the wide
gap between public morality and private behavior. In the village,
sexual relations are sanctioned within the marriage framework. The
moral codes overlap and are at odds among classes. Predictably it is
the affluent who can afford secrecy and successfully avoided punishment, a privilege not afforded to the working class. Generally, the
glamour of the city suggests misfortunes. The poor, whose identities
and lives change drastically in the city, struggle with varying standards of behavior that create confusion. For example, poverty and
deprivation lead a police sergeant to fantasize and drive a servant
woman to theft, immorality, and prostitution in *Al-'Ayb* (*The Shame*)
and *Qa' al-madina* [City Dregs]. In *Al-Naddaha* [Sirens], the loss of
innocence is a metaphor for the search for identity and freedom.

But Idris's vision later became absurd and surreal with an emphasis on the conflict between the vulnerable individual and the hostile or
cruelly indifferent institution. His style became more economical, and
the narrative mode became more experimental in its use of time and
imagery, with the line between reality and dream often blurred. This
change in the style developed from the degenerating political environment, the absence of freedom, and a desire to reconcile science and
metaphysics. Abandoning his realist approach for this metaphysical
style, Idris created new works that generated various responses, from

support to rejection from his realist fans as well as those opposing the use of dialects in literature. His foremost absurdist work, *Al-Farafir* [The Flip Flaps], written during a time of great change and challenge in Egypt, caused a literary uproar for two weeks in 1964 before it was banned. The play marked him as the leader of the post-socialist rebellion. *Fliplap*, named after its protagonist, is a two-person dialogue between a master and a slave. The slave, Fliplap, imparts Idris's social, political, moral, and metaphysical ideas through allusions and symbols. Although the play is a political satire of the regime, its distinctiveness stems from the way it engages the audience to find alternative social and political positions that secure dignity, self-respect, liberty, and egalitarianism. Among the other themes discussed are marriage, birth, death, the structural hierarchy of society, and social injustice. In this play, Idris argues that the problem is originally cosmic.

The significance of *Al-Farafir* lies in Idris's experimental approach to breaking down the barriers between actors and audiences by adopting an indigenous form of popular drama, particularly the shadow plays, to modern theatre. Such settings, in Idris's opinion, heighten the collective experience in which actors and audiences engage in an interactive dialogue to reach a solution to problems. In his work *Towards an Egyptian Theatre*, Idris asserted the existence of theatrical roots in Egyptian folklore and called for the exploration of settings and themes different from the traditional ones in an effort to reach a wide audience. Critics, however, accredited his new form of theatre to the Western dramatic tradition of Brecht and Pirandello. Subsequently, Idris wrote a second political allegory *Al-Mukhattatun* [The Stripped Ones] that lashes out at the totalitarian, one-party State and discusses man's control over his destiny. His fantasy *Al-Jins al-thalith* [The Third Sex], on the other hand, did not receive much critical attention.

Idris's existentialist views are illustrated in his parabolic religious story ("A Table from the Sky" from the collection of *Hadithat sharaf* [Matters of Honor]), in which folklore and religious metaphors are weaved together to discuss the relationship between man and God and to suggest that the protagonist challenge those teachings. As in "The Language of Pain," living is, according to Idris, freeing oneself from the standard rules of society through experiencing pain. Idris assumed the role of a historian recording the social and political conditions during Naser's era in his work *Jabarti of the Sixties*, al-Jabarti being the great Egyptian historian of the 19th century.

Idris enriched literary life with numerous productions in drama, fiction, and critical studies and his work provides an incandescent mirror of the time through which he lived.

—Hanaa Kilany

IHARA Saikaku

Pseudonyms: Kakuei (until 1673), Saikaku, and Saihō (1688–1691). **Born:** Hirayama Tōgo, evidently the fifth son of a merchant household in a chōnin (townsman, merchant and artisan) quarter near Ōsaka castle, Ōsaka, Japan, 1642. **Education:** Probably went to a temple school. **Family:** Married a women who was nine years his junior and an amateur poet (died at the age of 25); three daughters, one of whom was blind. **Career:** Served as an apprentice to a *tabi* (two-toed boots,

and in this case probably of leather) maker in Uemachi (Ōsaka) at about nine or ten years old; began writing haikai at fifteen and was a teacher of haikai at twenty-one, under the penname Kakuei (eternal crane; used as his pen name until late 1673); he then adopted Saikaku (western crane), the name by which he is known, and Saihō (western phoenix; used 1688–91 when the use of the crane character was banned by the Tokugawa Shogunate); a successful merchant; shaved his head and began living a monk-like existence, perhaps affiliated with the Pure Land Sect, early 1675 (nearly all extant portraits are of him with a shaved head); lived in Yariyamachi just to the west of warrior residences surrounding Ōsaka castle, from about 1679 till late in life; part of the Danrin haikai group of Nishiyama Sōin, who Saikaku succeeded as group leader (an indication of the unorthodoxy of Saikaku and his group was that they were labeled by contemporaries "orandaryū," the Holland School); recited 23,500 verses in one day at Sumiyoshi Shrine, 1684. Saikaku would not be much read today if not for his turn toward prose in 1682. In the last years of his life he composed a number of works that are universally considered part of the Japanese canon; Saikaku's death verse, "ukiyo no tsuki / misugoshi ni keri / sue ninen," Peter Nosco clearly rendered, "The span of human life is destined to be fifty years, which is rather too long for a man such as I. Nevertheless, I was allowed to enjoy the sight of the moon of this world for two extra years." **Died:** 9 September 1693.

PUBLICATIONS

Fiction

Kōshoku Ichidai Otoko. 1682; as *Life of an Amorous Man*, translated by Kenji Hamada, 1964.

Kōshoku Gonin Onna. 1686; as *Five Women Who Loved Love*, translated by Wm. Theodore de Bary, 1956.

Kōshoku Ichidai Onna. 1686; as *Life of an Amorous Woman*, translated and edited by Ivan Morris, 1963.

Nanshoku Ōkagami. 1687; as *Great Mirror of Male Love*, translated with introduction by Paul Gordon, 1990.

Budō Denraiki [A Record of the Traditions of the Warrior's Way]. 1687.

Nippon Eitai Kura. 1688; as *The Eternal Storehouse of Japan*, *The Japanese Family Storehouse*, and *The Millionaire's Gospel Modernised*, translated by G. W. Sargent, 1959.

Buke Giri Monogatari. 1688; as *Tales of Samuari Honor*, translated by Caryl Ann Callahan, 1981.

Seken Mune Sanyō. 1692; as *This Scheming World*, translated by Masanori Takasuka and David C. Stubbs, 1965.

Saikaku Oridome. 1694; as *The Last Fragments of Saikaku's Cloth or Some Final Words of Advice*, translated by Peter Nosco, 1980.

*

Critical Studies: *In the Shade of Spring Leaves* by Robert Danly, 1981; *Kindai Izen* by Etō Jun, 1985; "Saikaku and Burlesque Fiction" by Howard Hibbett, in *HJAS*, vol. 20, 1957; *The Floating World in Japanese Fiction*, 1959; *World within Walls* by Donald Keene, 1976; "The Beginnings of the Modern Japanese Novel: Kanazōshi, 1600–1682" by Richard Lane, in *HJAS*, vol. 20, 1957; "Saikaku and the Modern Japanese Novel," in *Japan's Modern Century*, 1968; *Japanese Thought in the Tokugawa Period* by Tetsuo Najita, 1978;

Visions of Virtue in Tokugawa Japan, 1987; *Saikaku Shinkō* by Noma Kōshin, 1981; *Saikaku Kenkyū Josetsu* by Taniwaki Masachika, 1992; *Saikaku Shinron* by Teruoka Yasutaka, 1981.

* * *

Ihara Saikaku is one of a trio of esteemed writers of the Genroku cultural period (the others being Matsuo Bashō and Chikamatsu Monzaemon) who along with thinkers such as Ōgyū Sorai and Arai Hakuseki, contribute to making the Genroku cultural period among the richest in Japanese history. Tetsuo Najita views the Genroku as a period of idiosyncratic iconoclasts and Saikaku was one of the earliest in a long line. Clear evidence of this is the fact that Saikaku's most important haikai collections and poetic events were performed alone, when haikai was quintessentially a product of group composition. His 23,500 verses at Sumiyoshi Shrine in 1684 could only be tallied by scribes. Danrin poetics were dominated by humor, punning, parody, assonance, alliteration, and a quick tempo. Such compositional energy naturally led to narrative composition late in his life.

Saikaku's work is known in Japan today as a predecessor to the first novels, if not actually the first novels, either modern or realistic. Taking cues from Noma Kōshin and Teruoka Yasutaka, Keene and Lane discuss *Kōshoku Ichidai Otoko* (*Life of an Amorous Man*) as the culmination and transcendence of the *kana-zōshi* tradition (1600–1682). It is universally accepted as the start of the *ukiyo-zōshi* genre (1682–1783), which, at least in its beginnings, developed hand-in-hand with the *ukiyo-e*, floating world prints. It may also be observed that Saikaku's work, especially in its playfulness, must have exerted great influence on the writers of *gesaku* fiction and particularly the genres, *sharebon*, *kibyōshi*, and *kokkeibon*, which reveled in the punning and word play possibilities in the homophonic quality of Japanese. However, Saikaku's work was increasingly ignored until the "Saikaku revival" in the 1890s. Subsequently, Saikaku was co-opted in the Meiji period (1868–1912) as a pre-European influence novelist. The artificiality of this construction is attacked by Etō Jun, who is of the "merchant energy" school of Saikaku criticism, contending that the rediscovery of Saikaku was largely ideological. Lane contends that even while the Meiji period fascination with the European novel held sway, Saikaku's style attracted writers such as Ōzaki Kōyō (1867–1903), Kōda Rohan (1867–1947), Mori Ōgai (1862–1922), and Higuchi Ichiyō (1872–1896). There is some combination of style, erotic aestheticism, and subject matter which carries Saikaku's influence over into the late Edo and Meiji novel. However, the eroticism came under periods of censorship leaving style the main and sometimes only focus of literary studies of Saikaku's texts. Donald Keene's synopsis of the elements of Saikaku's style describes sentences frequently ending in nouns, grammatical particles, and subjects missing, plays on words, the elliptical omission of an implied conclusion, borrowings from classics, shifts from classical idiom to contemporary colloquial earthy descriptions, poetic phraseology, colloquial flavor, and an oral delivery. One could add the mixture of classical and colloquial styles, long sentences consisting of short phrases, and the predominance of imagery. Robert Danly writes in *In the Shade of Spring Leaves* that Saikaku's fiction consisted of "extended light-hearted sequences of episodes or separate stories, often short on plot and long on what smacks of free association, bound by a common theme and written in a highly elliptical style." Saikaku's narrative production includes a broad range of portraiture and subject matter.

Saikaku is most remembered for the *kōshokubon* (novels of sensuality) published between 1682 and 1687, and his portraits of merchant life published between 1688 and 1696. The most esteemed texts of the *kōshokubon* are *Life of the Amorous Man*, *Koshoku Gonin Onna* (*Five Women Who Loved Love*), and *Koshoku Ichidai Onna* (*Life of an Amorous Woman*). In *Amorous Man* the main character, Yonosuke, wanders Japan seeking the perfect courtesan. With *Five Women*, Saikaku's focus shifts to the themes of *giri* (duty) and *ninjō* (human emotion). The couples involved in all the short stories have to choose between love, such as marriages outside one's caste, and some form of filial duty to one's family or society, and all but one of these novellas ends in death. *The Life of an Amorous Woman* deals with the fortunes of a courtesan who writes her own confessional tale. This novel moves between celebration and lamentation within the framework of a parody of the confessional tale.

The second group of narratives is a miscellany of short stories mostly spanning 1685 to 1689 which often parody legends and satirize folk wisdom. These include *Nanshoku Ōkagami* (*Great Mirror of Male Love*), *Budō Denraiki* [A Record of the Traditions of the Warrior's Way], and *Buke Giri Monogatari* (*Tales of Samurai Codes of Honor*). All of these samurai stories while compassionate, leave one with the sense of the outmoded morality of the samurai class.

The final group of Saikaku narratives makes up a portrait of the merchant class. *Nippon Eitai Kura* (*The Eternal Storehouse of Japan*), *Seken Mune Sanyō* (*This Scheming World*), and Saikaku's Parting Gift are the collections of this group published before his death in 1693. In addition, *Saikaku Oridome* (*Some Final Words of Advice*) was published posthumously. These narratives are largely the source of the "realism" label in that they portray the details of the daily lives of the merchant class. This substantial narrative production earned Saikaku one of the highest positions in Japanese literary history.

Saikaku's oeuvre contains some treatment of virtually every sector of the society of his day. The close contact of his narratives especially with the plebeian history of his time has earned him the title of "realist," however, as a small number of critics have observed, objective description is not Saikaku's intent. Comparisons are often made to Boccaccio, Fielding, Rabelais, Balzac, Cervantes, and most often to Defoe—the combination of playfulness, descriptions of the rising bourgeoisie, depictions of lowlife, and emphasis on material life, go part way in explaining these comparisons. However, the centrality of parody, punning, hyperbole, and satirical observation puts Saikaku closer to Boccaccio, Rabelais, Cervantes, and the picaresque. Keene's states in *World within Walls* that beyond entertainment, Saikaku's intent "may have been to challenge the literature of the past." Nonetheless, to date only Teruoka and Johnson have centered studies on Saikaku's comedy.

—Jeffrey Johnson

ILLYÉS, Gyula

Born: Rácegrespuszta, Hungary, 2 November 1902. **Education:** Educated in Budapest, 1916–19; the Sorbonne, Paris, in the 1920s. **Family:** Married Flóra Kozmutza; one daughter. **Career:** Forced to leave Hungary in 1921 because of leftist activity; lived in Paris until 1926, then returned to Hungary; contributor from 1928 and editor, with Mihály Babits, 1937–41, *Nyugat* [West]; founding editor, *Magyar Csillag* [Hungarian Star], 1941–44; editor, *Válasz* [The Answer], 1946–48. Co-founder, 1939, and parliamentary representative from 1945, National Peasant Party. Vice-president, International PEN, from 1970. **Awards:** Baumgarten prize, four times in the 1930s; Kossuth prize, 1948, 1953, 1970; International grand prize for poetry, 1965. Commandeur, l'Ordre des Arts et des Lettres (France), 1974. **Died:** 14 April 1983.

PUBLICATIONS

Verse

Nehéz föld [Heavy Earth]. 1928.
Sarjúrendek [Swaths of Hay]. 1931.
Három öreg [Three Old Men]. 1932.
Hősökről beszélek [I Speak of Heroes]. 1933.
Ifjúiság [Youth]. 1934.
Szálló egek alatt [Under a Moving Sky]. 1935.
Rend a romokban [Order Upon Ruins]. 1937.
Külön világban [In a Separate World]. 1939.
Összegyűjtött versei [Collected Poems]. 1940.
Válogatott versek [Selected Verse]. 1943.
Egy év [One Year]. 1945.
Összes versei [Complete Poems]. 3 vols., 1947.
Szembenézve [Face to Face]. 1947.
Tizenkét nap Bulgáriában [12 Days in Bulgaria]. 1947.
Két kéz [Two Hands]. 1950.
Válogatott versei [Selected Verses]. 1952.
Kézfogások [Handclasps]. 1956.
Új versek [New Poems]. 1961.
Nem volt elég. . . [It Was Not Enough. . .]. 1962.
Nyitott ajtó [Open Door]. 1963.
Dőlt vitorla [With Tilted Sail]. 1965.
Poharaim [My Cups]. 1967.
A Tribute to Gyula Illyés, edited by Thomas Kabdebo and Paul Tabori, various translators. 1968.
Fekete-fehér [Black-White]. 1968.
Kháron ladikján [In Charon's Boat]. 1969; as *Charon's Ferry: Fifty Poems*, translated with introduction by Bruce Berlind, 2000.
Selected Poems, edited by Thomas Kabdebo and Paul Tabori. 1971.
Abbahagyott versek [Unfinished Poems]. 1971.
Haza a magasban: Összegyűjtött versek 1920–1945 [Homeland in the Heights: Collected Poems]. 1972.
Teremteni: Összegyűjtött versek 1946–1968 [To Create: Collected Poems]. 1972.
Minden lehet: Új versek [Everything Is Possible: New Poems]. 1973.
Különös testamentum [A Strange Testament]. 1977.
Szemelt szőlő, válogatott versek, edited by Miklós Béládi. 1980.
Közügy [Public Matter]. 1981.
Konok kikelet [Stubborn Springtime]. 1981.
Mert szemben ülsz velem. 1982.
Táviratok. 1982.
A semmi közelít [The Approach of Nothingness]. 1983.
Szemben a támadással. összegyűjtött versek 1969–1981. edited by Miklós Borsos. 1984.
Menet a ködben. 1986.
What You Have Almost Forgotten: Selected Poems, edited with introduction by William Jay Smith. 1999.

Plays

A tű foka [The Eye of the Needle]. 1944.
Lélekbúvár [The Psychiatrist]. 1948.
Tűz-víz [Fire-Water]. 1952; revised version. as *Fáklyaláng* [Torch-bearers]. 1953.
Ozorai példa [The Example of Ozora]. 1952.
Tűvé-tevők [Turning the House Upside Down]. 1953.
Dózsa György [George Dózsa]. 1954.
Malom a Séden [Mill on the Séd]. 1960.
Bolhabál [Flea Dance]. 1962.
Különc [The Eccentric]. 1963.
Kegyenc [The Minion], from a play by László Teleki. 1963.
Az éden elvesztése: Oratórium [The Loss of Eden: An Oratorio]. 1967.
Drámák [Plays]. 2 vols., 1969.
Tiszták [The Pure Ones]. 1969.
Testvérek [Brothers]. 1972.
Bál a pusztán; Bölcsek a fán [Ball at the Ranch; Wise Men on the Tree]. 1972.
Újabb drámák [More Recent Plays]. 1974.
Dániel az övéi közt [Daniel among His Own People]. 1976.
Sorsválasztók. 1982.
Czak az igazat. 1983.

Fiction

Puszták népe. 1936; as *People of the Puszta*, translated by G.F. Cushing. 1967.
Kora tavasz [Early Spring]. 1941.
Húnok Párizsban [Huns in Paris]. 1946.
Két férfi [Two Men]. 1950.

Other

Oroszország [Russia]. 1934.
Petőfi (biography). 1936; as *Petőfi*, edited by Joseph M. Értavy-Barráth, translated by Anton N. Nyerges, 1973.
Magyarok [Hungarians]. 1938.
Ki a magyar? [The Hungarian—Who Is He?]. 1939.
Lélek és kenyér [Soul and Bread], with Flora Kozmutza. 1939.
Csizma az asztalon [Boots on the Table]. 1941.
Mint a darvak [Like Cranes]. 1942.
Honfoglalók között [Among the New Masters]. 1945.
Franciaországi változások [Changes in France]. 1947.
Ebéd a kastélyban [Lunch in the Castle]. 1962.
Ingyen lakoma: Tanulmányok, vallomások [A Free Feast: Studies. Confessions]. 2 vols., 1964.
Munkái [Works]. 1969–.
Hajszálgyökerek [Capillary. Roots]. 1971.
Hét meg hét népmese (for children). 1975.
Matt the Gooseherd (for children), retold by Illyés, translated by Paul Tabori. 1976.
Itt élned kell [You Have to Live Here]. 1976.
Beatrice apródjai [The Pages of Beatrice]. 1978.
Szellem es erőszak. 1978.
Szulofolden. 1984.
A kolto felel (interviews), with Anna Foldes. 1986.
Naplójegyzetek [Entries in a Diary]. 5 vols., 1986–91.

Editor. *A francia irodalom kincsesháza* [The Treasure-House of French Literature]. 1942.

Editor. *Once upon a Time: Forty Hungarian Folk-Tales*, translated by Barna Balogh and Susan Kun. 1970.

*

Bibliography: *A magyar irodalomtörténet bibliográfiája, 1905–1945* by Ferenc Botka and Kálmán Vargha, vol. 1, 1982.

Critical Studies: *Az ismeretlen Illyés* [The Unknown Illyés] by László Gara. 1965; "The Seventy Years of Illyés" by Miklós Béládi, in *New Hungarian Quarterly 48*, 1972; *Illyés Gyula költői viláképe* by József Izsák, 1982; "Gyula Illyés: An Appraisal" by George Gömöri, in *World Literature Today*, Summer 1984.

* * *

Gyula Illyés was a poet first and foremost, although he created works of importance in practically all literary genres. Born into a poor family on a manorial estate in western Hungary, he remained loyal to the cause of the underprivileged throughout his life, though in old age he was regarded by many as the most forceful literary representative of the whole Hungarian nation. His early poetry was influenced by French surrealism and the constructivism of Lajos Kassák but soon after his return to Hungary from Paris in 1926 he found his own distinctive voice. While in his epic poems he followed the traditions of popular realism, his lyrical verse was characterized by a supple syntax, admirable intellectual vigour, and sharp psychological intro-spection. In some pre-war poems such as "The Wonder Castle" Illyés foretold the collapse of the anachronistic social system of Hungary based on entrenched class privilege; to World War II he reacted with the lyrical diary *Egy év* [One Year] and with the rousing condemnation of the poem "It Did Not Help." Among his post-war collections probably *Kézfogások* [Handclasps] and *Dőlt vitorla* [With Tilted Sail] were the most accomplished. Outside Hungary he will be best remembered for the powerful "Egy mondat a zsarnokságról" ("A Sentence for Tyrrany"), a long litany of unfreedom told through a succession of poetic metaphors including this stanza:

Where seek tyranny? Think again:
Everyone is a link in the chain;
Of tyranny's stench you are not free:
You yourself are tyranny.

(translated by Vernon Watkins)

A Socialist since his youth, Illyés was bitterly disappointed at the unsocialist manner in which most communist regimes in central east Europe suppressed and forcibly tried to assimilate their Hungarian national minorities. His solidarity with fellow-Hungarians outside the borders of Hungary was expressed in a number of poems as well as essays; for example he wrote an introduction to Kálmán Janics's book on the persecution of the Hungarian ethnic minority in Czechoslovakia after 1945. Illyés was a master of the essay and published several collections of essays before and after World War II, *Hajszálgyökerek* [Capillary Roots] being the most comprehensive. He also wrote two autobiographical novels as well as an objective though cautious travelogue about Soviet Russia (following his visit there in 1934), but

his most memorable prose works were probably *Puszták népe* (*People of the Puszta*), which first focused attention on the semi-Asiatic living conditions of the Hungarian agrarian proletariat, and the short biography of the 19th-century revolutionary poet, Sándor Petőfi. The genuine radicalism and uncompromising character of Petőfi exerted a great attraction on the less passionate but no less committed Illyés; like Petőfi he also believed that a politically active literature can promote the democratization of society.

Illyés the playwright was particularly fertile in the 1950s and 1960s when he wrote a cycle of historical plays tackling national issues. Both *Fáklyaláng* [Torchbearers] and *Ozorai példa* [The Example of Ozora] are about events of the War of Independence which followed the Hungarian revolution of 1848. Later the character of László Teleki, a far-sighted but tragic political figure of the Kossuth emigration, captured Illyés's imagination and he wrote *Különc* [The Eccentric] about him, while another play entitled *Kegyenc* [The Minion] is the adaptation of a play by Teleki on a Roman theme, showing that it is impossible to serve tyranny without being dehumanized in the process. Of Illyés's later plays probably *Tiszták* [The Pure Ones] is the most interesting with its tale of moral conflict among the Cathar believers just before the fall of Monségur. By and large, Illyés's comedies are less successful than his dramas, though even the best plays suffer from an overdose of noble rhetoric and from too much concentration on national issues.

Apart from Hungary where since 1956 his standing has been exceptionally high, Illyés was better known in France than anywhere else in Europe; many French poets translated his work, and he reciprocated by translating French poetry into Hungarian and editing in 1942 an excellent anthology *A francia irodalom kincsesháza* [The Treasure-House of French Literature].

—George Gömöri

See the essay on "A Sentence for Tyrrany."

IONESCO, Eugène

Born: Slatina, Romania, 26 November 1909 (13 November according to Orthodox calendar; some sources erroneously give 1912); grew up in France; returned to Romania to join father after parents' divorce, 1922. **Education:** Educated at the lycée Sfântul-Sava, Bucharest; learned Romanian; lycée, Craiova, baccalauréat, 1928; studied French literature at the University of Bucharest, 1928–33, *Capacitate* (teaching dipoma) 1934. **Family:** Married Rodica Burileanu in 1936; one daughter. **Career:** Taught French in Cernavodà and Bucharest 1936–38; moved to Paris, 1939; contributed to *Viata Româneasca* [Romanian Life], 1939, travelled to Paris, 1939; lived in Marseille during World War II; settled in Paris after its liberation, 1944; proofreader, Éditions Administratives, Paris, c. 1945, and subsequently full-time writer. Also an artist: exhibited artwork in Biarritz and the Galérie Mouf, Paris, 1970. **Awards:** Tours Festival prize, for film, 1959; Prix Italia, 1963; Society of Authors theatre prize (France), 1966; National Grand Prix for Theatre, 1969; Monaco Grand Prix, 1969; Austrian State prize for European literature, 1970; Jerusalem prize, 1973. Honorary doctorates: New York University, 1971, and the universities of Louvain, Warwick, Tel Aviv. Chevalier, Légion d'honneur, 1970. **Member:** Académie française, 1970. **Died:** 18 March 1994.

PUBLICATIONS

Collection

Théâtre complet, edited by Emmanuel Jacquart, 1991.

Plays

La Cantatrice chauve (produced 1950). In *Théâtre I*, 1954; as *The Bald Prima Donna*, translated by Donald Watson, in *Plays I*, 1958; as *The Bald Soprano*, translated by Donald M. Allen, in *Four Plays*, 1958.

La Leçon (produced 1951). In *Théâtre I*, 1954; as *The Lesson*, translated by Donald Watson, in *Plays I*, 1958; also translated by Donald M. Allen, in *Four Plays*, 1958; and with *Rhinoceros* and *The Chairs*, 1989.

Les Chaises (produced 1952). In *Théâtre I*, 1954; as *The Chairs*, translated by Donald Watson, in *Plays I*, 1958; also translated by Donald M. Allen, in *Four Plays*, 1958; and with *Rhinoceros* and *The Lesson*, 1989.

Sept petits sketches (includes *Les Grandes Chaleurs*; *Le connaissez-vous?*; *Le Rhume onirique*; *La Jeune Fille à marier*; *Le Maître*; *La Nièce-Épouse*; *Le Salon de l'automobile*) (produced 1953). *La Jeune Fille à marier* in *Théâtre II*, 1958, as *Maid to Marry*, translated by Donald Watson, in *Plays III*, 1960; *Le Maître* in *Théâtre II*, 1958, as *The Leader*, translated by Derek Prouse, in *Plays IV*, 1960; *La Nièce-Épouse* as *The Niece-Wife*, translated by Richard N. Coe, in *Ionesco: A Study of His Plays*, revised edition, 1971; *Le Salon de l'automobile* in *Théâtre IV*, 1966, as *The Motor Show*, translated by Donald Watson, in *Plays V*, 1963.

Victimes du devoir (produced 1953). In *Theatre I*, 1954; as *Victims of Duty*, translated by Donald Watson, in *Plays II*, 1958.

Théâtre I (includes *La Cantatrice chauve*; *La Leçon*; *Jacques; ou, La Soumission*; *Les Chaises*; *Victimes du devoir*; *Amédée, ou, Comment s'en débarrasser*). 1954.

Amédée; ou, Comment s'en débarrasser (produced 1954). In *Théâtre I*, 1954; as *Amédée; or, How to Get Rid of It*, translated by Donald Watson, in *Plays II*, 1958.

Jacques; ou, La Soumission (produced 1955). In *Théâtre I*, 1954; as *Jacques, or Obedience*, translated by Donald Watson, in *Plays I*, 1958; as *Jack; or, The Submission*, translated by Donald M. Allen, in *Four Plays*, 1958.

Le Nouveau Locataire (produced 1955). In *Théâtre II*, 1958; as *The New Tenant*, translated by Donald Watson, in *Plays II*, 1958.

Le Tableau (produced 1955). In *Théâtre III*, 1963; as *The Picture*, translated by Donald Watson, in *Plays VII*, 1968.

L'Impromptu de l'Alma; ou, Le Caméléon du berger (produced 1956). In *Théâtre II*, 1958; as *Improvisation; or, The Shepherd's Chameleon*, translated by Donald Watson, in *Plays III*, 1960.

L'Avenir est dans les oeufs; ou, Il faut de tout pour faire un monde (produced 1957). In *Théâtre II*, 1958; as *The Future Is in Eggs; or, It Takes All Sorts to Make a World*, translated by Donald Watson, in *Plays IV*, 1960.

Impromptu pour la Duchesse de Windsor (produced 1957).

Plays I (includes *The Chairs*; *The Bald Prima Donna*; *The Lesson*; *Jacques, or Obedience*), translated by Donald Watson. 1958.

Four Plays (includes *The Bald Soprano*; *The Lesson*; *Jack; or, The Submission*; *The Chairs*), translated by Donald M. Allen. 1958.

Théâtre II (includes *L'Impromptu de l'Alma, ou, Le Caméléon du berger*; *Tueur sans gages*; *Le Nouveau Locataire*; *L'Avenir est*

dans les oeufs, ou, Il faut de tout pour faire un monde; *Le Maître*; *La Jeune Fille à marier*). 1958.

Tueur sans gages (produced 1959). In *Théâtre II*, 1958; as *The Killer*, translated by Donald Watson, in *Plays III*, 1960.

Plays II (includes *Amedee, or, How to Get Rid of It*; *The New Tenant*; *Victims of Duty*) translated by Donald Watson. 1958.

Rhinocéros (produced 1959). In *Théâtre III*, 1963; as *Rhinoceros*, translated by Derek Prouse, in *Plays IV*, 1960.

Scène à quatre (produced 1959). In *Théâtre III*, 1963; as *Foursome*, translated by Donald Watson, in *Plays V*, 1963.

Apprendre à marcher (ballet scenario; produced 1960). In *Théâtre IV*, 1966; as *Learning to Walk*, translated by Donald Watson, in *Plays IX*, 1973.

Plays III (includes *The Killer*; *Improvisation, or, The Shepherd's Chameleon*; *Maid to Marry*), translated by Donald Watson. 1960.

Plays IV (includes *Rhinoceros*; *The Leader*; *The Future Is in Eggs, or, It Takes All Sorts to Make a World*), translated by Derek Prouse. 1960.

Rhinoceros; The Chairs; The Lesson, translated by Donald Watson. 1962.

Délire à deux (produced 1962). In *Théâtre III*, 1963; as *Frenzy for Two*, translated by Donald Watson, in *Plays VI*, 1965.

Le Roi se meurt (produced 1962). 1963; as *Exit the King*, translated by Donald Watson, in *Plays V*, 1963.

Le Piéton de l'air (produced 1962). In *Théâtre III*, 1963; as *A Stroll in the Air*, translated by Donald Watson, in *Plays VI*, 1965.

Théâtre III (includes *Rhinocéros*; *Le Piéton de l'air*; *Délire à deux*; *Le Tableau*; *Scène à quatre*; *Les Salutations*; *La Colère*). 1963.

Plays V (includes *Exit the King*; *The Motor Show*; *Foursome*), translated by Donald Watson. 1963.

Plays (includes *The Chairs*; *The Killer*; *Maid to Marry*), translated by Donald Watson. 1963.

Les Salutations (produced 1970). In *Théâtre III*, 1963; as *Salutations*, translated by Donald Watson, in *Plays VII*, 1968.

La Soif et la faim (produced 1964). In *Théâtre IV*, 1966; as *Hunger and Thirst*, translated by Donald Watson, in *Plays VII*, 1968.

La Lacune (produced 1965). In *Théâtre IV*, 1966.

Plays VI (includes *A Stroll in the Air*; *Frenzy for Two*), translated by Donald Watson. 1965.

Pour préparer un oeuf dur (produced 1966). In *Théâtre IV*, 1966.

Théâtre IV (includes *Le Roi se meurt*; *La Soif et la faim*; *La Lacune*; *Le Salon de l'automobile*; *L'Oeuf dur*; *Pour préparer un oeuf dur*; *Le Jeune Homme à marier*; *Apprendre à marcher*). 1966.

L'Oeuf dur, in *Théâtre IV*, 1966; as *The Hard-Boiled Egg*, translated by Donald Watson, in *Plays X*, 1976.

Leçons de français pour Américains (produced 1966). As *Exercices de conversation et de diction françaises pour étudiants américains*, in *Théâtre V*, 1974.

Plays VII (includes *Hunger and Thirst*; *The Picture*; *Anger*; *Salutations*), translated by Donald Watson. 1968.

Jeux de massacre (produced 1970). 1970; as *Here Comes a Chopper*, translated by Donald Watson, in *Plays VIII*, 1971; as *Killing Game*, translated by Helen Gary Bishop, 1974.

Plays VIII (includes *Here Comes a Chopper*; *The Oversight*; *The Foot of the Wall*), translated by Donald Watson. 1971.

The Duel (produced 1971). In *Plays XI*, translated by Clifford Williams, 1979.

Double Act (produced 1971). In *Plays XI*, translated by Clifford Williams, 1979.

Macbett (produced 1972). 1972; as *Macbett*, translated by Donald Watson, in *Plays IX*, 1973.

Plays IX (includes *Macbett*; *The Mire*; *Learning to Walk*), translated by Donald Watson. 1973.

Ce formidable bordel (produced 1973). 1973; as *A Hell of a Mess*, translated by Helen Gary Bishop, 1975; as *Oh What a Bloody Circus*, in *Plays X*, translated by Donald Watson, 1976.

La Vase. In *Théâtre V*, 1974.

Théâtre V (includes *Jeux de massacre*; *Macbett*; *La Vase*; *Exercices de conversation et de diction françaises pour étudiants américains*). 1974.

L'Homme aux valises (produced 1975). 1975; as *Man with Bags*, translated by Marie-France Ionesco and adapted by Israel Horowitz, 1977; as *The Man with the Luggage*, translated by Donald Watson, in *Plays XI*, 1979.

Plays X (includes *Oh What a Bloody Circus*; *The Hard-Boiled Egg*; with essay *Ionesco and His Early English Critics* by Donald Watson), translated by Donald Watson. 1976.

Plays XI (includes *The Man with the Luggage*; *The Duel*; *Double Act*; with essay *Why Do I Write?*), translated by Donald Watson and Clifford Williams. 1979.

Voyages chez les morts (as *Voyages among the Dead*, 1980; scenes produced, 1983). As *Théâtre VIII* (*Voyages chez les morts: Thèmes et variations*), 1981; as *Plays XII* (*Journeys Among the Dead*), translated by Barbara Wright, 1985.

Plays XII (includes *Journeys Among the Dead*), translated by Barbara Wright. 1985.

Screenplays: "La Colère" episode in *Les Sept Péchés capitaux*, 1962; *Monsieur Tête* (animated film), 1970 (published in *Théâtre V*, 1974).

Ballet Scenarios: For television, with Fleming Flindt: *La Leçon*, 1963; *Le Jeune Homme à marier*, 1965; *La Vase*, 1970; *Le Triomphe de la mort*, 1971.

Fiction

La Photo du Colonel. 1962; as *The Colonel's Photograph*, translated by Jean Stewart and John Russell, 1967.

Le Solitaire. 1973; as *The Hermit*, translated by Richard Seaver, 1974.

Other

Elegii pentru fiinti mici. 1931.

Nu. 1934; as *Non* (in French), translated by Marie-France Ionesco, 1986.

Notes et contre-notes. 1962; revised edition, 1966; as *Notes and Counter-Notes*, translated by Donald Watson, 1964.

Entretiens avec Claude Bonnefoy. 1966; as *Conversations with Ionesco*, edited by Claude Bonnefoy, translated by Jan Dawson, 1970.

Journal en miettes. 1967; as *Fragments of a Journal*, translated by Jean Stewart, 1968.

Présent passé passé présent. 1968; as *Present Past, Past Present*, translated by Helen Lane, 1971.

Contes pour enfants. 4 vols., 1969–75; as *Story no. 1*, translated by Calvin K. Towle, 1968; *Story no. 2*, translated by Calvin K. Towle, 1970; *Story no. 3*, translated by Ciba Vaughan, 1971; *Story no. 4*, translated by Ciba Vaughan, 1973.

Découvertes, illustrated by Ionesco. 1969.

Mise en train: Première année de français, with Michael Benamou. 1969.

Discours de réception à l'Académie française. . . 1971.

Entre la vie et la rêve: Entretiens avec Claude Bonnefoy. 1977.

Antidotes. 1977.

Un homme en question. 1979.

Le Noir et le blanc. 1980.

Hugoliade. 1982; as *Hugoliad; or, The Grotesque and Tragic Life of Victor Hugo*, 1987.

Pourquoi j'écris. 1986; as *Why Do I Write?*, translated by Donald Watson, in *Plays XI*, 1979.

La Quëfe intermittente (autobiography). 1987; as *The Intermittent Quest*, 1988.

*

Bibliography: *Ionesco: A Bibliography* by Griffith R. Hughes and Ruth Bury, 1974; *Bibliographie et index thématique des études sur Ionesco* by Wolfgang Leiner, 1980.

Critical Studies: *Ionesco: A Study of His Plays* by Richard N. Coe, 1961, revised edition, 1971; *The Theatre of the Absurd* by Martin Esslin 1961, revised edition 1980. *Four Playwrights and a Postscript: Brecht, Ionesco, Beckett, Genet* by David I. Grossvogel, 1962; *Avant-Garde: The Experimental Theatre in France* by Leonard C. Pronko, 1962; *Eugène Ionesco* by Leonard C. Pronko, 1965; *Eugène Ionesco: An Introduction to His Work* by Kenneth R. Dutton, 1967; *Ionesco and Genet* by Josephine Jacobsen and William Randolph Mueller, 1968; *Brecht and Ionesco: Commitment in Context* by J.H. Wulbern, 1971; *Eugène Ionesco* by Ronald Hayman, 1972, revised edition, 1976; *Ionesco* by Allan Lewis, 1972; *Ionesco: A Collection of Critical Essays* edited by Rosette C. Lamont, 1973, and *The Two Faces of Ionesco* edited by Lamont and M.J. Friedman, 1978; *Ionesco: Rhinocéros* by C.E.J. Dolamore, 1984; *Langage et corps, fantasmé duns le théâtre des années cinquante: Ionesco, Beckett, Adamov* by Marie-Claude Hubert, 1987. *Ionesco's Imperatives: The Politics of Culture* by Rosette C. Lamont, 1993; *Understanding Eugene Ionesco* by Nancy Lane, 1994; *Eugène Ionesco Revisited* by Deborah B. Gaensbauer, 1996.

* * *

Eugène Ionesco's one-act plays of the early 1950s, together with those of Beckett, revitalized post-war drama and introduced what came to be known as the "theatre of the absurd." *La Cantatrice chauve* (*The Bald Prima Donna*), *La Leçon* (*The Lesson*), and *Les Chaises* (*The Chairs*) present different images of man's incomprehensible existence, expressed not so much through plot and characterization, which are minimal, as through the disintegration of language into chaos, silence, and death. The style is akin to farce, the tone a disturbing mixture of comic and tragic, for comedy, in Ionesco's view, is "the intuition of the absurd, . . . more despairing than tragedy." *The Bald Prima Donna*, which has enjoyed a continuous run at La Huchette since 1957, had its source in the conversational banalities of a beginner's English textbook. Superficially, it parodies petty-bourgeois life and the clichés of everyday speech, but the author's purpose was to express the astonishing meaninglessness of life and, with it, "the tragedy of language," that is, not the problem of social communication, but our inability to penetrate the silence that surrounds us.

509

This metaphysical theme, which underlies the whole of Ionesco's work, is most clearly expressed in *The Chairs*. An old couple look back regretfully on their inconsequential lives, while expressing vague nostalgia for a lost "City of Light." Wishing to leave a "message" for posterity before they die, they have invited a large number of guests to their isolated home. As the guests, who are invisible, arrive, the couple fill the stage with a vast number of chairs. The proliferation of meaningless objects, which has become a hallmark of Ionesco's plays, here signifies spiritual absence, the essential void: there is no message. With *The Lesson*, a further dimension emerges: the abuse of man's power, which is developed in more specific terms in later plays. During the course of a private lesson, the teacher gradually dominates his young female pupil by the manipulation of language (meaningless words which proliferate like the chairs) and pseudo-learning (reminiscent of ideological brainwashing). Finally carried away with his own power and desire, he kills the girl with the mesmerically repeated word "cou-teau" (knife), in an act of violation containing both sexual and political overtones.

The longer, more ambitious plays, which subsequently predominate in Ionesco's output, frequently use the raw material of dreams and introduce us directly into the playwright's private obsessions: his sense of guilt; his spiritual frustration; his fear of death; his bewilderment at mankind's murderous nature. At the same time, his inventiveness and comic genius produce audacious dramatic images both grotesque and memorable, such as the huge expanding corpse of *Amédée; ou, Comment s'en débarrasser* (*Amédée; or, How to Get Rid of It*), or the transformation of people into monstrous pachyderms in *Rhinocéros* (*Rhinoceros*).

Rhinoceros, probably his most successful full-length play, evokes the rapid advance of fascism in the 1930s and, more generally, the threat of all conformist ideologies. The strength of the play lies not in its condemnation of ideology as such, but in its dramatization of the experience of the individual, Bérenger, who resists the tide of mass transformation. By preserving, intuitively rather than heroically, his human qualities—his inner world of fears, complexes, passion—he stands alone against the threatening herd in a final image of great dramatic power.

The denunciation of evil, especially that which is politically motivated, is a major theme of many of Ionesco's works, e.g. *Tueur sans gages* (*The Killer*), *Délire à deux* (*Frenzy for Two*), *Macbett, Ce formidable bordel* (*Oh What a Bloody Circus*). The tone is one of naive astonishment rather than righteous indignation; the caricature and humour of farce remain predominant. *Macbett*, a parody of Shakespeare by way of Jarry's *Ubu Roi*, is one of Ionesco's blackest and funniest plays, satirizing the tyrant's lust for power. *Oh What a Bloody Circus*, a dramatization of his only novel, *Le Solitaire* (*The Hermit*), and containing echoes of the political unrest in France in 1968, is a despairing inventory of all the horrors of the world and a cry of metaphysical anguish; with bitter irony, the play ends in hysterical laughter at the "huge joke" God has played on mankind.

Ionesco's obsessional fear of death forms the subject of *Le Roi se meurt* (*Exit the King*), in which King Bérenger must prepare himself to die "at the end of the play," and of *Jeux de massacre* (*Killing Game*), a series of 18 tableaux, inspired by Defoe's *Journal of the Plague Year*, and presenting the fundamental tenet of the absurd: "That's what life is: dying." Ionesco's own search for spiritual enlightenment found expression in the image of the quest in a number of dream-inspired plays, from the psychoanalytical *Victimes du devoir* (*Victims of Duty*) to the less successful autobiographical sagas, *L'Homme aux valises* (*Man with Bags*) and *Voyages chez les morts*

(*Journeys among the Dead*), which rework dreams and memories already published in diary form. In *La Soif et la faim* (*Hunger and Thirst*) the protagonist, having finally rejected human love, goes vainly in search of higher spiritual fulfilment, finally to be trapped in a Kafkaesque, monastery-like institution characterized by tyranny and indoctrination and signifying "purgatory or hell."

This generally bleak picture of human life, marked by guilt, violence and metaphysical alienation, is offset by Ionesco's original sense of comedy, his childlike delight in nonsense, contradiction and wordplay. There are also flights—sometimes literally, as in *Le Piéton de l'air* (*A Stroll in the Air*)—of poetic wonderment and the hope of salvation through love. But wonder invariably gives way to horror, love constantly fails, and the smile freezes on our lips as comedy reveals its tragic face. In the later autobiographical plays, humour is a rare ingredient and provokes sparse, uneasy laughter.

In his volume of autobiography, *La Quête intermittente* (*The Intermittent Quest*), Ionesco rejects literature in favour of painting and the spiritual quest, acknowledging the failure of language to give meaning to human existence. In his last play, *Journeys among the Dead*, words finally disintegrate, without producing the anarchic humour which such an effect produced in *The Bald Prima Donna*. Their incoherence expresses the protagonist's, and the author's, bewildered incomprehension of life.

—C.E.J. Dolamore

See the essays on *The Bald Prima Donna* and *Rhinoceros*.

ISHIGAKI Rin

Born: Akasaka, Tokyo, 21 February 1920. **Education:** Kindergarten, 1925; local elementary school, 1926–32; Akasaka Higher Elementary School, and reading of poetry collections and young women's magazines (*shōjo zasshi*) at local library and home, 1932–34. **Career:** Worked in Industrial Bank of Japan, 1934–75. Began and edited literary magazine for women *Dansō* [Dislocation], 1938–43. **Awards:** 19th H prize of Japanese Contemporary Poets Society, 1969; 12th Tamura Ayako award, 1972; 4th Earth prize, 1979. **Member:** Union-sponsored literary groups, first *Ginkakei* [The Milky Way] and then *Jikan* [Time], 1948–50; Rekitei poet's group, 1965–88.

PUBLICATIONS

Collections

Gendai Shijin Bunko 46 Ishigaki Rin Shishū. 1971.
Gendai no Shijin 5 Ishigaki Rin. 1983.
Ishigaki Rin Bunko. 4 vols., 1987–1990.
Sora wo katsuide. 1997.
Ishigaki Rin Shishū. 1998.

Poetry

Watakushi no mae ni aru nabe to okama to moeru hi to. 1959.
Hyōsatsu nado. 1968.
Ryakureki. 1979.
Yasashii Kotoba. 1984.

Essays

Yuumoa no Sakoku. 1973.
Honō ni te wo kazashite. 1980.
Yoru no Taiko. 1989.

Other

Katei no shi. 1980.
Shi no Fūkei. 1992.

*

Critical Studies: Chapters in *Jojō no zensen* [On the front lines of lyricism] by Kiyooka Takayuki, 1970; *Seikimatsu no bikō—Ayukawa Nobuo, sono ta* [The thin light of the fin de siecle—Ayukawa Nobuo and others] by Kitamura Tarō, 1988; *Gendai josei shijinron—jidai wo kakeru joseitachi* [Contemporary women poets: women ahead of their time] by Asō Naoko, 1991; "Ishigaki Rin: The Venus of Tokyo" by Janine Beichman, in *Across Time and Genre: Reading and Writing Japanese Women's Texts*, ed. Janice Brown and Sonya Arntzen, 2002.

* * *

Ishigaki Rin is one of the foremost contemporary women poets of Japan, and in spite of her age, appeals strongly to the younger generation. Imaginative and elliptical, her exuberant, deeply-felt poetry expresses both social and metaphysical concerns.

In the difficult postwar days of the Occupation (1945–1952), Ishigaki struggled to support single-handedly her parents and two younger brothers, one unemployed and the other disabled. The ambivalence this aroused was intense. In her first collection, *Watakushi no mae ni aru nabe to okama to moeru hi to* [Before Me the Pot, the Pan, and the Burning Flame], a number of poems depict the hell of home and family. In other poems, confined domestic spaces are forgotten in favor of open-ended visions. Some are natural scenes of the sea and other landscapes in Izu, the rural area where her parents were born. Others are transcendent, supernatural vistas that evoke the infinite horizon of the heart and a powerful drive to self-actualization.

Ishigaki's most recent collections, *Ryakureki* [My Life in Brief] and *Yasashii Kotoba* [Gentle Words], were written when she was in her fifties and sixties. In a number of poems from that period, the poet simultaneously contemplates her own end and the lost past. Nor does she forget those who lost their lives in war, an important theme in her work from the early postwar period. The distinction between past and present is obliterated; both are part of one eternity in which life and death are dissolved. Death, in fact, is not so much an end as a surrender to a new mode of existence. The focus on death and aging was new in these collections, but the sense of matter-of-fact, unsentimental intimacy with everything alive, whether animal, vegetable or mineral, was not. In the poems of *Hyōsatsu nado* [Nameplates etc.], her second collection, self and other interpenetrate, as if the wall between them were porous.

Ishigaki believes that poetry can only come out of one's own life, but at the same time, she does not think of it as simple autobiography, but more as a distillation. Of her first collection, she wrote that because she "did not want anything that was not wholly cooked," it took her nine years to "boil down," and even then, it and her second collection still had some "raw parts" left in them. She considers herself an "amateur" poet in the sense that she does not separate life and poetry: "How else," she asks, "could you write poetry except from your own life?"

"The Japanese language," she writes, "is my first and only real home." Words are living creatures to her, and she refers to them with the suffix *-tachi*, ordinarily used only for human beings. The care with which she uses words (she once walked around Tokyo for several hours trying to decide whether to use the particle *o* or *wa* after a certain noun) gives her poems a surface simplicity, for everything unnecessary is pared away. At the same time, there is an elliptical quality to her work, for she believes in the necessity of leaving a certain amount of "blank space." Her poems are also notable for their lack of literary allusion.

Ishigaki's appeal lies in the high-spirited combination of anger, wit, and tenderness that animates her poetry; her tone is at once pungent and lyrical, pugnacious and forgiving, earthly and transcendent. She is, above all, a poet in whom individualism and a sense of community are interwined in a particularly compelling way. The chronicle of contemporary Japanese poetry is still being written, but it seems more than possible that Ishigaki Rin will be remembered as one of the representative poets of 20th century Japan.

—Janine Beichman

J

JACOB, Max

Born: Quimper, France, 11 July 1876. **Education:** Educated at École Coloniale, 1894. **Career:** Moved to Paris; gave piano lessons and attended art courses; art critic, *Le Gaulois*, Paris, 1898, resigned; returned to Quimper and had a variety of jobs; returned to Paris, 1901; clerk and labourer, the department store, Entrepôt Voltaire; closely associated with Apollinaire, *q.v.*, and Picasso, who became his godfather in 1915, after Jacob's conversion to Roman Catholicism; settled at a Benedictine monastery, Saint-Benoît-sur-Loire, after 1921; returned to Paris, 1928–35, and associated with Cocteau, *q.v.* Spent most of his retirement in poverty. Arrested as a Jew by the Nazis, 1944. **Award:** Légion d'honneur, 1932. **Died:** (in Drancy Concentration Camp) 5 March 1944.

PUBLICATIONS

Collections

Hesitant Fire: Selected Prose, edited and translated by Moishe Black and Maria Green. 1991.
Théâtre. 1953.
Selected Poems of Max Jacob, edited and translated by William Kulik, 1999.

Verse

Saint Matorel, illustrated by Picasso. 1911; enlarged edition, 1936.
La Côte: Recueil de chants celtiques inédits. 1911; reprinted with 17 watercolours by Jacob, 1927.
Les Oeuvres burlesques et mystiques de Frère Matorel, mort au couvent de Barcelone, illustrated by André Derain. 1912.
Les Alliés sont en Arménie: Poème. 1916; revised edition, 1976.
Le Cornet à dés: Poèmes en prose. 1917; as *The Dice Cup: Selected Prose Poems*, edited by Michael Brownstein, translated by John Ashbery, and others, 1979; selections translated by Judith Morganroth Schneider, in *The Play of the Text*, 1981, and in *Double Life: Thirty Prose Poems*, translated by Michael Bullock, 1989.
La Défense de Tartuffe: Extases, remords, visions, prières, poèmes, et Méditations d'un juif converti, illustrated by Picasso and Jacob. 1919.
Le Voyage en autobus. 1920.
Le Laboratoire central. 1921.
Visions infernales: poèmes en prose. 1924.
Les Pénitents en maillots roses. 1925.
Fond de l'eau. 1927.
Le Sacrifice impérial. 1929.
Rivage. 1931.
Cinq poèmes, music by Francis Poulenc. 1932.

Le Chemin de croix infernal, illustrated by Jean-Mario Prassinos. 1935.
Ballades. 1938.
L'Homme de cristal. 1946; revised edition, 1967.
Derniers poèmes en vers et en prose. 1945; revised edition, 1961.
Les Poèmes de Morvan le Gaëlique. 1953.
Trois quatrains. 1953.
A poèmes rompus. 1960.
Double Life: Thirty Prose Poems, translated by Michael Bullock. 1989.

Fiction

L'Histoire du roi Kaboul Ier et du Marmiton Gauwain (for children). 1903; revised edition, 1971; as *Story of King Kabul the First and Gawain the Kitchen-Boy*, translated by Moishe Black and Maria Green, 1994.
Le Géant du soleil (for children). 1904.
Le Siège de Jérusalem: Drame céleste, illustrated by Picasso. 1914.
La Phanérogame. 1918.
Cinématoma. 1919.
Le Roi de Boétie: nouvelles. 1921; revised edition 1971.
Wenceslas, ancien cocher. 1921; revised edition, 1971.
Filibuth; ou, La Montre en or. 1922.
Le Cabinet noir. 1922; enlarged edition, 1928.
La Couronne de vulcain (stories), illustrated by Suzanne Roger. 1923.
Le Terrain bouchaballe. 2 vols., 1923; revised edition, 1964.
L'Homme de chair et l'homme reflet. 1924.
Le Nom: nouvelle. 1926.
Aguedal II. 1944.

Plays

Isabelle et Pantalon (opera libretto), music by Roland Manuel. 1922.
Fable sans moralité (ballet scenario), music by H. Bordes. 1931.
Le Bal masqué (ballet scenario), music by Francis Poulenc. 1932.

Other

Matorel en province. 1921; revised edition, 1936.
Ne coupez pas, mademoiselle; ou, Les Erreurs des PTT: plaquette de grand luxe, illustrated by Juan Gris. 1921.
Dos d'Arlequin, illustrated by Jacob. 1921.
Art poétique. 1922.
Le Chien de pique. 1928.
Visions des souffrances et de la mort de Jésus, fils de Dieu, illustrated by Jacob. 1928.
Tableau de la bourgeoisie, illustrated by Jacob. 1929.
Bourgeois de France et d'ailleurs (portraits). 1932.
Morceaux choisis, edited by Paul Petit. 1936.

Conseits à un jeune poète, conseils à un jeune étudiant. 1945; as *Advice to a Young Poet*, translated by John Adlard, 1976.

Méditations religieuses. 1945.

Lettres à Edmond Jabès. 1945.

Lettres inédites du poète à Guillaume Apollinaire. 1946.

En février 1942, Max Jacob écrivait. 1947.

Le Symbolisme de la face. 1948.

Choix de lettres de Max Jacob à Jean Cocteau (1919–1944). 1949.

Miroir d'astrologie, with Claude Valence. 1949.

Choix de lettres à Jean Cocteau, 1919–1944. 1950.

Lettres à un ami: correspondance 1922–1937, with Jean Grenier. 1951.

Drawings and Poems, edited and translated by Stanley J. Collier. 1951.

Lettres à Bernard Esdras-Gosse (1924–1944). 1953.

Correspondance, edited by François Garnier. 2 vols., 1953–55.

Lettres aux Salacrou (août 1923–janvier 1926). 1957.

Lettres à Marcel Béalu. 1959.

Quatre problèmes à résoudre. 1962.

Max Jacob and Les Feux de Paris (correspondence), edited by Neal Oxenhandler. 1964.

Lettres à T. Briant et C. Valence (1920–1941), edited by Stanley J. Collier. 1966.

Lettres 1920–41. 1966.

Lettres à Michel Levanti, suivies des poèmes de Michel Levanti, edited by Lawrence A. Joseph. 1975.

Lettres à René Villard, suivies du Cahier des Maximes, edited by Yannick Pelletier. 1978.

Lettres à Marcel Jouhandeau, edited by Anne Kimball. 1979.

Lettres à Liane de Pougy. 1980.

Lettres à René Rimbert, edited by Christine Andréucci and Maria Green. 1983.

Max Jacob et Quimper (selection). 1984.

Lettres mystiques 1934–1944 à Clotilde Bauguion. 1984.

Lettres à Michel Manoll, edited by Maria Green. 1985.

Méditations religieuses: Derniers cahiers 1942–1943. 1986.

Chroniques d'art 1898–1900, with Léon David, edited by Lawrence A. Joseph. 1987.

Lettres à Pierre Minet, edited by Anne Kimball. 1988.

Lettres à Nino Frank, edited by Anne Kimball. 1989.

Lettres à Florent Fels, edited by Maria Green. 1990.

Translator, with A. de Barreau, *Le Livre de l'ami et de l'aimé,* by Raymond Lulle. 1920.

*

Bibliography: *Bibliographie et documentation sur Max Jacob* by Maria Green, 1988.

Critical Studies: *Max Jacob, mystique et martyr* by Pierre Lagarde, 1944; *Max Jacob* by André Billy, 1946; *Jacob* by Maurice Sachs in his *Witches Sabbath,* 1964; *Max Jacob and the Poetics of Cubism* by Gerald Kamber, 1971; "Realism and Fantasy in the Work of Max Jacob: Some Verse Poems" by S.I. Lockerbie, in *Order and Adventure in Post-Romantic French Poetry* edited by E.M. Beaumont, J.M. Cocking and J. Cruickshank, 1973; "Max Jacob: The Poetics of *Le Cornet à dés*" by Renée Riese Hubert, in *About French Poetry from Dada to "Tel Quel"* edited by Mary Ann Caws, 1974; "Max Jacob's Bourgeois Voices" by Renée Riese Hubert in *Folio,* 9, 1976; *Poetry and Antipoetry: A Study of Selected Aspects of Max Jacob's Poetic Style* by Annette Thau, 1976; "Max Jacob" by Francis Poulenc in his *My Friends and Myself* translated by James Harding, 1978; *Clown at the Altar: The Religious Poetry of Max Jacob* by Judith M. Schneider, 1978; *Max Jacob* by Lina Lachgar, 1981; *The Play of the Text: Max Jacob's Le Cornet à dés* by S. Lévy, 1981; "Max Jacob: Style, Situation" by Theo Hermans, in *The Structure of Modernist Poetry,* 1982; *Looking for Heroes in Postwar France: Albert Camus, Max Jacob, Simone Weil* by Neal Oxenhandler, 1996.

* * *

Although Max Jacob's work is very rich and varied, it is his book of prose poems, *Le Cornet à dés* (*The Dice Cup*), which has attracted the most readers and the most critical attention. Published in 1917, the collection brought together texts Jacob had been writing since the early 1900s and represented its author's major contribution to the literary and artistic modernism exemplified by Apollinaire and Picasso. Commentators have even spoken retrospectively of "literary Cubism," although no such notion existed at the time. The poems of *The Dice Cup* tend to be short and couched in relatively simple language, but they offer twists and turns of narrative and juxtapositions of fragmentary realities that defy the habits of logic and representation. The title itself suggests a notion of chance, as though the poet randomly selected or juggled with words and elements of stories. yet at the same time it is also the image of something multi-faceted and whole, like the die, which is implied. The prose poem as a genre had already attained a certain artistic maturity in the work of Baudelaire and Rimbaud, spelling liberation from the traditional approach to poetry based on prosody and, to a certain extent, the mimesis of external reality or inner feelings. Yet Jacob went one step further. In his preface to *The Dice Cup* he rejects Baudelaire and Rimbaud as models: the former identified the prose poem too closely with the fable, while the latter's work constituted the triumph of "Romantic disorder" leading inevitably to "exasperation." Jacob emphasizes instead what he terms "style" and "situation." "Style" is not simply the writer's use of language, but his ability to marshal and compose the various elements of his work. The more successful a work, the more it will give the impression of being an autonomous, self-enclosed unity, however disparate its component parts might otherwise have seemed. "Situation" refers to the distance between the reader and the work: if Baudelaire believed the prose poem should "surprise" the reader, Jacob felt that it should transplant him from the reality he normally accepts and inhabits into the reality of the work.

Both "style" and "situation" implied the assembling of apparently dissimilar fragments or view-points into a synthetic unity somewhat reminiscent of the Cubist painting or "*papier collé.*" And yet the often absurd combinations thrown up by the prose poems looked forward to Surrealism. In a later preface Jacob indeed spoke of the "unconscious" as manifested in random associations of words and ideas or in dreams and hallucinations. Where he differed from the automatic writing of the Surrealists was in his insistence that the poem should be not an out-pouring but a construction. Contrasting his own work with that of Rimbaud, he stipulated that the prose poem must be a "jewel" and not a "jeweller's shop window." His achievement lies in part in this balance between the surrender of conscious control and the will to shape and construct. In his view the essence of lyricism lay in "unconsciousness, but an unconsciousness that is watched over" (*Conseils à un jeune poète* [*Advice to a Young Poet*]).

The impression given by *The Dice Cup* is that of a kaleidoscope. Each poem either offers a multiplicity of scenes or magnifies some fragment that adds to the heteroclite effect of the collection as a whole. Frequently, illogical connections or consequences are presented with such linguistic and narrative casualness as to appear natural, as in "Il n'y a pas de valet de chambre pour un grand homme" ("A Great Man Needs No Valet"):

> Meanwhile the lobster banquet was giving rise to entrances through the roof, to conversations with legs dangling from skylights and to frying pans catching on fire.

The miniature phantasmagorias often revel in their own factitiousness: "Chariot au bord de la mer" ("Charlie Chaplin at the Seashore") ends, "A lady is minding a child on a bank of loose stones. I jostle him and the scene disappears." The result is a celebration of the ludicrous. Almost anything may appear, but its contours will always be brought into sharp focus within the restricted space of the prose poem. However, the kaleidoscope effect and the playful nature of the reality produced by the texts is not simply the result of brusque changes of scene or tense. It is also inherent in language itself. Wordplay and puns are made the basis of startling comparisons and sequences. One poem proclaims in its title: "Fausses nouvelles! Fosses nouvelles!"—or "Grave News! New Graves!" in Michael Browstein's rendering. Another poem speculates on the possible confusion of *"patte"* ("paw," "mitt") and "pâte" ("paste" or "cream"). Nearly all the texts aim to exploit playfully and subversively the well-trodden paths of language in the form of platitudes or literary and para-literary genres. Some poems read like bewildering snatches from some serialized pot-boiler or detective novel (two pieces even have the eponymous hero of the contemporary crime serial, *Fantômas*, as their title). Others seem to be speeded up medieval visions, burlesque news articles, or repositories of undiscovered popular wisdom. Overall, tile products of Jacob's dice cup tend to parody and cannibalize existing literature and patterns of language in an inventive and liberating fashion that was to be vital for Surrealism and successive avant-garde groups even into the 1970s.

The same multiplicity of sources and guises covering the range of high and low literature and spanning history characterizes most of Jacob's other works. In verse he sought inspiration in the Breton folk ballad (*La Côte* and *Les Poèmes de Morvan le Gaëlique*) as well as in the traditions of religious mysticism. Yet even here the bizarre irony of *The Dice Cup* often reappears, undercutting any pretensions to directly serious statement, but leaving an oblique emotion all the more striking for its apparent self-deprecation. "Exhortation" from *La Défense de Tartuffe* [The Defense of Tartuffe] shows the poet unable to read a message from heaven because it is Hebrew and ends: "The angel is furious at finding me so stupid." He could achieve sustained seriousness, as in "eportage de juin 1940" ("eportage June 1940") in *Derniers poèmes en vers et en prose* [Last Poems in Verse and Prose] on the fall of France—a key event in his own tragic destiny. His novels are varied. *Le Cabinet noir*, for example, is a collection of letters by different characters, satirically parodying human types and their discourses, while *Le Terrain bouchaballe* [The Terrain of Bouchaballe] deals with small town corruption. In all his work Jacob's main drive was to absorb the multiplicity of the world into the self, while retaining a self-deprecating irony:

> We don't know very well those we love
> But I understand them fairly well
> Being all these people myself
> I who am however but a baboon.
> ("Do You Know Meister Eckhart?," *Derniers poèmes en vers et en prose*)

—J.R. Stubbs

JARRY, Alfred (Henri)

Born: Laval, France, 8 September 1873. **Education:** Educated at schools in Saint-Brieuc, 1879–88, and Rennes, 1888–91; Lycée Henri IV, Paris, 1891–93. **Military Service:** Brief military service, June–November 1895; discharged because of poor health. **Career:** Contributor, *L'Art littéraire* in the 1890s; co-founder, with Rémy de Gourmont, art review *L'Ymagier*, 1894, and co-director, 1894–95; founder and publisher, art journal *Perhinderion*, 1896 (closed after second issue); assistant to Lugné-Poe, director of the Théâtre de l'Oeuvre, 1896; columnist, *La Revue blanche*, 1900–03; suffering from malnutrition and the consequences of alcoholism, attempted recuperation at his sister's home in Laval, 1906. **Died:** 1 November 1907.

PUBLICATIONS

Collections

Oeuvres poétiques complètes, edited by Henri Parisot. 1945.
Oeuvres complètes, edited by René Massat. 8 vols., 1948.
Selected Works (includes *The Ubu Cycle; Writings on the Theatre; Poems; Essays and Speculations; Fiction Selections*), edited by Roger Shattuck and Simon Watson Taylor. 1965.
Oeuvres complètes, edited by Michel Arrivé. 2 vols., 1972–87.

Plays

César-Antéchrist. 1895; as *Caesar Antichrist*, translated by James H. Bierman, 1971.
Tout Ubu (includes *Ubu Roi; Ubu cocu; Ubu enchaîné; Almanach du père Ubu; Ubu sur la butte*), edited by Maurice Saillet. 1962; as *Ubu*, edited by Noël Arnaud and Henri Bordillon, 1980; selection as *The Ubu Plays* (includes *Ubu Rex; Ubu Enchained; Ubu Cuckolded*), edited by Simon Watson Taylor, translated by Watson Taylor and Cyril Connolly. 1968.
Ubu Roi (produced 1896). 1896; as *Ubu Roi*, translated by Barbara Wright, 1951; as *King Turd*, translated by B. Keith and G. Legman, 1953; as *King Ubu*, in *Modern French Theatre*, edited by Michael Benedikt and George E. Wellwarth, 1964; as *Ubu Rex*, in *The Ubu Plays*, 1968; also translated by David Copelin, 1973; as *Ubu the King*, translated by Maya Slater in *Three Pre-surrealist Plays*, 1997.
Ubu enchaîné (produced 1937). 1900; as *Ubu Enslaved*, translated by Simon Watson Taylor, 1953; as *Ubu Enchained*, in *The Ubu Plays*, 1968.

Ubu sur la butte (condensed marionette version of *Ubu roi*, with songs; produced 1901). 1906.

Ubu cocu (produced 1946). 1944; as *Ubu Cuckolded*, translated by Cyril Connolly, 1965, and in *The Ubu Plays*, 1968.

Par la taille (for marionettes). 1906.

Le Moutardier du page. 1907; as *La Papesse Jeanne*, edited by Marc Voline, 1981.

Pantagruel, with Eugène Demolder, music by Claude Terrasse. 1911.

Les Silènes, from a play by Christian Dietrich Grabbe, edited by Pascal Pia. 1926.

L'Objet aimé (produced 1937). 1953.

Fiction

Les Jours et les nuits. 1897; as *Days and Nights: Novel of a Deserter*, translated by Alexis Lykiard, with *The Other Alcestis*, 1989.

L'Amour en visites. 1898.

L'Amour absolu. 1899; edited by Noël Arnaud and Henri Bordillon, 1980.

Messaline. 1900; as *The Garden of Priapus*, translated by Louis Colman, 1932; as *Messalina*, translated by John Harman, 1985.

Le Surmâle. 1902; as *The Supermale*, translated by Barbara Wright, 1968.

Les Gestes et opinions du docteur Faustroll, Pataphysicien. 1911; edited by Noël Arnaud and Henri Bordillon, 1980.

La Dragonne, completed by Charlotte Jarry. 1943.

Verse

La Revanche de la nuit, edited by Maurice Saillet. 1949.

Other

Les Minutes de sable, mémorial (miscellany). 1894.

Spéculations. 1911.

Le Manoir enchanté et quatre autres oeuvres inédites, edited by Noël Arnaud. 1974.

Adventures in 'Pataphysics, translated by Paul Edwards and Antony Melville. 2001.

Other works have been issued in *Cahiers* and *Dossiers* of the Collège de Pataphysique, since 1950.

*

Bibliography: ''Alfred Jarry: Essai de bibliographie critique,'' in *Interférences*, 9, 1979.

Critical Studies: *The Banquet Years: The Arts in France 1885–1918* by Roger Shattuck, 1959, revised edition, 1968; *Jarry: D'Ubu roi au Docteur Faustroll* by Noël Arnaud, 1974; *Ubu roi: An Analytical Study* by Judith Cooper, 1974; *Alfred Jarry, dramaturge*, 1980, and *Les Cultures de Jarry*, 1988, both by Henri Béhar, and *Jarry et cie: Communications du Colloque international*, 1985, edited by Béhar and Brunella Eruli; *Jarry: Nihilism and the Theatre of the Absurd* by Maurice Marc LaBelle, 1980; *Alfred Jarry: A Critical and Biographical Study*, 1984, and *Jarry: Ubu roi*, 1987, both by Keith Beaumont; *Alfred Jarry: The Man with the Axe* by Nigel Lennon, 1984; *Alfred Jarry and Guillaume Apollinaire* by Claude Schumacher, 1984;

Gestes et opinions de Alfred Jarry, écrivain by Henri Bordillon, 1986; *Alfred Jarry* by Vincenzo Accame, 1993; *The Pataphysician's Library: An Exploration of Alfred Jarry's Livres Pairs* by Ben Fisher, 2000.

* * *

Alfred Jarry was born in Laval, a town some distance from the Brittany whose traditions of Celtic magic and intense Catholicism he claimed later to have inherited and to represent. He saw little of his father, whose business collapsed in 1879 and who was forced to return to his original employment as a commercial traveller. Together with his sister, Caroline-Marie, he was brought up almost exclusively by his mother. His strong attachment to her may explain his homosexuality, a feature of his life which links him to the tradition of Gide, Proust, and Genet as well as to the relationship between Verlaine and Rimbaud. In spite of the priapism celebrated in the novel *Le Surmâle* (*The Supermale*), published in *La Revue blanche* in 1902, it is doubtful whether he ever enjoyed a sexual relationship with a woman. His admiration for the author, Marguerite Eymery, the wife of his friend Alfred Vallette, was based on the feeling that she alone really understood him. This may have been true in a way, since she is the only person who records him speaking in a normal voice and not in the stilted, aggressive, staccato tones which he borrowed for his most famous creation, père Ubu.

Jarry felt at home intellectually in the literary Paris of the 1890s where the Symbolist movement, under the influence of Mallarmé, encouraged him in his dislike of the earlier climate of naturalism, with its view that literature ought to talk about real life, and in his adoption instead of the solipsistic attitude embodied in Schopenhauer's phrase ''The world is my representation.'' The production at the Théâtre de l'Oeuvre on 10 December 1896 of his ''dramatic comedy'' *Ubu Roi* (*Ubu Rex*), the work to which he owes his literary survival and continued fame, provoked a great controversy.

After the first word, *merdre* (the translation as ''Shit!'' does not quite have the ring of the French), nothing could be heard for 20 minutes. Jarry subsequently went to the trouble to select all the most hostile reviews, paste them on to sheets of blue and pink notepaper, and bind them in a file. This was not discovered after his death. The bill for 1,300 francs in production costs, which reduced the young director of the Théâtre de l'Oeuvre, Lugné-Poe, to despair, was like all the other debts that Jarry incurred and left behind him: unpaid. Lugné-Poe had to console himself by contemplation of the fact that his theatre is now remembered principally for the events of December 1896. On 28 January 1898, *Ubu Rex* was performed successfully by the marionettes of the Théâtre des Pantins. This was more than a further sign of the rejection of the naturalistic conventions of 19th-century drama which helps to make *Ubu Rex* a precursor of the absurdist plays of Beckett, Ionesco, and Genet. It reflected Jarry's not unreasonable view that 19th-century actors and actresses expected to be, and were, given far too much importance by playwrights and audiences.

Ubu Rex, with its starting point as a schoolboy farce inspired by the antics of the physics master, a M. Hébert, at the lycée in Rennes, is virtually the only play written by a Frenchman in the 19th century to be performed nowadays as anything other than a museum piece. It has been particularly successful with English-speaking audiences and made into an opera, as well as a ballet. It is, nevertheless, the only work by Jarry to be anything but the expression of a disordered personality and of a fundamentally very sad life. André Breton's remark, in the first *Manifeste du surréalisme* (*Surrealist Manifesto*) in 1924, that Jarry was ''a surrealist in absinth'' is true in so far as Jarry did drink an enormous amount. This was, however, also because he could not afford to buy food, and it is not true that he died of alcoholic poisoning. The probable cause of his death was tubercular meningitis, brought on by a pulmonary infection produced by inadequate food, cold, and damp. There are other aspects of Jarry's behaviour that make him a precursor of surrealism, and his predilection for firearms may have inspired Breton's other remark that the simplest surrealist act was to go down into the street with a revolver and fire at random into the crowd. On one occasion, in a crowded restaurant, Jarry fired a shot at the sculptor Manoco, exclaiming as he did so how beautiful his action was as literature. He claimed also to have shot a nightingale which was disturbing his sleep, and witnesses confirmed how he terrified his landlady by using the wall between their rooms for target practice. When she complained that the bullets might go through the wall and kill her children, he replied that he would, if it happened, help her to have others. The remark was taken up in Gide's 1926 novel *Les Faux-monnayeurs* (*The Counterfeiters*), who used his depiction of a group of unpleasant adolescent schoolboys.

Like Rimbaud, whom he resembles by his eccentricity of behaviour, as well as by the impression given by his later life of great talents squandered needlessly, Jarry was looked after at the end of his life by his sister. Like Isabelle Rimbaud, Caroline-Marie encouraged the belief that her brother had undergone a late conversion to Catholicism. The evidence is unconvincing in both cases and goes against the predominant atmosphere in the work of both writers. What did characterize Jarry's attitude in the early 1890s was the adoption, in common with many others from the *Mercure de France* and *Revue blanche* groups, of a set of views that were highly nationalistic and violently anti-semitic. The taste for random violence that marked Jarry's own behaviour is also a fiction of the *Collège de Pataphysique*, whose members still take pleasure in interrupting lectures and meetings of which they disapprove. Jarry was undoubtedly the founder of what he also claimed was the ''science'' of pataphysics, described variously as the science of imaginary solutions, the destruction of all forms of knowledge to make way for a new mysticism, and the ''synthesis of immediate knowledge'' said to characterize the imaginative world of the child. Jarry's critical writings also insist on the primacy of form in literature and denigrate the importance of content.

—Philip Thody

See the essay on *Ubu Rex*.

JENSEN, Johannes V.

Born: Farsø, Denmark, 20 January, 1873. **Education:** Attended Cathedral School, Viborg, Denmark, 1889–93; finished the first part of a medical degree, University of Copenhagen, 1893–98. **Military Service:** Completed Danish military service as infantryman, 1899–1900. **Family:** Married Else Marie Ulrik, 1904; three sons. **Career:** After leaving the university, devoted himself to a life of writing and traveling; traveled to the United States, 1896; became correspondent in Spain, 1898, and at the World's Fair in Paris, 1900; journey around the world via Suez Canal, Singapore (living among natives in what is now Malaysia for five weeks), Japan, and the United States, especially Chicago and New York, 1902–03; married and established a home in Copenhagen, 1904; further subsequent travels to the United States (1905, 1914, 1937, 1939), Norway (1907, 1910, 1938), many parts of Asia (1912), Berlin, Egypt and Palestine (1925), Canary Islands, Berlin, and Rome (1928), Czechoslovakia (1932), London (1935), and France (1948). **Awards:** Honorary doctorate, University of Lund, Norway, 1929; Nobel prize for literature, 1944. **Died:** 25 November, 1950.

PUBLICATIONS

Collections

Himmerlandshistorier. 2 vols., 1904, 1910.
Himmerlandshistorier, edited by Aage Marcus. 1973, 1995.
Skrifter. 8 vols., 1916.
Skrifter. 5 vols., 1925.
Den Lange Rejse. 2 vols., 1938.
Digte, 1901–41. 1943.
Myter, edited by Aage Marcus. 2 vols., 1946, 1960.
Nordisfk Foraar: Myter, edited by Niels Birger Wamberg. 1999.

Fiction

Danskere. 1896.
Einar Elkær. 1898.
Himmerlandsfolk. 1898.
Intermezzo. 3 vols., 1900–1901; as *The Fall of the King.*
Kongens Fald. 1901.
Madame d'Ora. 1904.
Nye Himmerlandshistorier. 1904.
Skovene. 1904.
Hjulet. 1905.
Eksotiske Noveller
Singaporenoveller. 1907
Den Lange Rejse. 6 vols., 1908–22; as *The Long Journey.*
Bræen. 1908.
Lille Ahasverus. 1909
Skibet. 1912
Olivia Marianne. 1915
Norne-Gæst. 1919.
Det tabte Land. 1919.
Christofer Columbus. 1921.
Cimbrernes Tog. 1922.
Himmerlandshistorier. Tredie Samling. 1910.
Jørgine. 1926.
Dr. Renault's Fristelser. 1935.
Gudrun. 1936.

Myths

Myter og Jagter. 1907.
Nye Myter. 1908.
Myter, ny Samling. 1910.
Myter, fjerde Samling. 1912.
Myter. 3 vols., 1924.
Ved Livets Bred. 1928.
Pisangen. 1932.
Kornmarken. 1932.
Sælernes Ø. 1934.

Poetry

Digte. 1906.
Aarstiderne. 1923.
Verdens Lys. 1926.
Den jydske Blæst. 1931.
Paaskebadet. 1937.

Essays

Den gotiske Renaissance. 1901.
Den ny Verden. 1907.
Nordisk Aand. 1911.
Rudyard Kipling. 1912.
Introduktion til vor Tidsalder. 1915.
Aarbog 1916. 1916.
Aarbog 1917. 1917.
Johannes Larsen og hans Billeder. 1920.
Æstetik og Udvikling. 1923.
Hamlet. 1924.
Evolution og Moral. 1925.
Aarets Højtider. 1925.
Thorvaldsens Portrætbuster. 1926.
Dyrenes Forvandling. 1927.
Aandens Stadier. 1928.
Retninger i Tiden. 1930.
Form og Sjæl. 1931.
Paa danske Veje. 1931.
Det Blivende. 1934.
Jydske Folkelivsmalere. 1937.
Thorvaldsen. Haandværkeren og Manden. 1938.
Nordvejen. 1939.
Fra Fristaterne. 1939.
Gutenberg. 1939.
Mindets Tavle. 1941.
Vor Oprindelse. 1941.
Om Sproget og Undervisningen. 1942.
Kvinden i Sagatiden. 1942.
Folkeslagene i Østen. 1943.
Afrika. Opdagelsesrejserne. 1949.
Swift og Oehlenschläger. 1950.
Tilblivelsen. 1951.

Other

Sangerinden. 1921.
Darduse. 1937.

*

Bibliography: *Johannes V. Jensen. En bibliografi* by Frits Johansen and Aage Marcus, 2 vols., 1933–51; *Litteratur om Johannes V. Jensen* by Aage Jørgensen, 1998.

Critical Studies: *Johannes V. Jensen* by Alf Henriques, 1938; *Johannes V. Jensen: Kurven i hans Udvikling* by Otto Gelsted, 1938; *Johannes V. Jensen. 1873—20. january—1943* edited by Felix Nørgaard and Aage Marcus, 1943; *Johannes V. Jensen* by Niels Birger Wamberg, 1961; *Johannes V. Jensen. Liv of forfatterskab* by Leif Nedergaard, 1968; *Om sammenhængen i Johannes V. Jensens Forfatterskab* by Aage Schiøttz-Christensen, 1969; *Studier i Johannes V. Jensens forfatterskab* by Harry Andersen, 1972; *Den unge Johannes V. Jensen* by Oluf Friis, 2 vols., 1974; *Den titaniske eros. Drifts- og karakterfortolkning i Johannes V. Jensens forfatterskab* by Henrik Wivel, 1982; *Johannes V. Jensen* by Sven Rossel, 1984; *Johannes V. Jensen og den hvide mans byrde: eksotisme og imperialisme* by Bent Haugaard, 1984; *Johannes V. Jensen* by Jørgen Elbek; *Kongens Fald: en analyse af Johannes V. Jensens roman* by Poul Bager; *Et Spring ind i et Billede: Johannes V. Jensens Mytedigtning* edited by Aage Jørgensen and Anders Thyrring Andersen, 2000.

*   *   *

Johannes V. Jensen was, in many ways, a modern mythmaker. Winner of the Nobel prize in literature in 1944, he was a prolific novelist, short story writer, essayist, journalist, travel writer, and poet, and a key figure and trend-setter in early 20th century Danish literature. Jensen's enormous body of work impresses us today with its mythic scope—its ability to invest characters and settings with a sense of timeless, universal importance—and its rootedness in powerful experiences in nature, whether on the windswept flatlands of Western Denmark or the sweltering Malaysian jungle.

Jensen's most famous novel, *Kongens Fald (The Fall of the King)*, recently named the "Danish novel of the century," has considerable stature in Danish cultural consciousness. Set in the early 16th century, it tells the story of King Christian II, the last ruler to govern all three Scandinavian countries, but by focusing primarily on the adventures, meditations, and personal growth of the King's assistant, the mercenary Mikkel Thøgersen. The novel has been praised for passages of great lyric beauty as well as for harsh realism, notably a stirring and brutal scene in which a horse is butchered. It is also admired for its historically comprehensive depiction of Denmark's loss of stature and power, and for the symbolic portrayal of our impermanence as humans.

Jensen's talents as a mythmaker appear most clearly in two large bodies of work. The first is his major epic, *Den Lange Rejse (The Long Journey)*, a cycle of six novels recounting the history of humankind from the pre-Ice Age era to Columbus' voyage across the Atlantic. This sweeping story, heavily influenced by Darwin's evolutionary theories, follows the progress of different tribes and communities in northern Europe as they struggle with extreme natural hardships and yearn to discover and settle new territories. Jensen's prose is intense in its naturalistic descriptions, and lofty in its depiction of fundamental human themes and symbols.

The second kind of mythmaking appeared over several decades in many collections of approximately 160 short stories and essays which he called *Myter* [Myths]. Some of these short pieces seem "mythic" in a traditional sense, but many others are journalistic sketches, biographical anecdotes, and travel essays that are realistic works of non-fiction. Whether these "myths" are surreal fables, descriptions of scenes in nature (such as Mount Fujiyama, or a field of waving rye), or specific experiences from Jensen's life, Jensen uses a heightened, poetic language to convey how these moments are charged with timeless significance. Collectively, they reinforce one of his key concerns, which is to depict how each person, event in nature, or moment of observation carries a universal meaning by being linked to other moments across time.

Jensen has had a tremendous influence on modern Danish writing, thanks to his many essays, his vividly realistic tales of his native Jutland in *Himmerlandshistorier* [Tales from Himmerland], and his poetry, which was written in both traditional verse and in an innovative prose style. Jensen believed in an active, pragmatic attitude to life, but his writing is also permeated with a mythic vision of the interconnectedness and timeless significance of our daily experience of the world.

—Erik Christensen

JEROME, St.

Born: Eusebius Sophronius Hieronymus in Stridon Dalmatia, c. AD 347. **Education:** Studied Greek and Roman rhetoric in Rome under Aelius Donatus. **Career:** Went to Trèves (Trier) to dedicate himself to Christian religion; settled to a life of asceticism in Aquilea, on the Adriatic coast of Italy, 370; then went east, studying Greek in Antioch, where he fell ill. Retired to the desert of Chalcis, southeast of Antioch, to learn Hebrew and live as a hermit, c. 375; ordained as priest in Antioch, 377; met Greek theologian Gregory of Nazianzus while travelling to Rome, 382; in Rome became secretary to Pope Damasus I, and revised old Latin texts of the Gospels. Left Rome to lead a pilgrimage to Palestine in 385; travelled to Egypt; settled in Bethlehem, 386: founded a religious house, 389, and worked on his *Vulgate*, the first Latin translation of the Bible from the original Hebrew, completed c. 405. **Died:** AD 420.

PUBLICATIONS

Collections

[Works; Paris Edition]. 11 vols., 1842–46; also in *Patrologia Graeca*, edited by Jacque Paul Migne, vols. 19–24, 1857; also edited by J. Hausleiter, I. Hilberg, and S. Reiter, in *Corpus Scriptorum Ecclesiasticorum Latinorum*, vols. 49, 54–56, 59, 1866–1913; in *Corpus Christianorum: Series Latiana*, vols. 72, 78, 1958–59.
The Principal Works, translated by W.H. Freemantle, in *A Select Library of Nicene and Post-Nicene Fathers*, series 2, vol. 6. 1893.

Works

De nominis Hebraicis [Book on Hebrew Names], edited by P. de Lagarde. 1870.
De viris illustribus [On Famous Men], edited by G. Herdingius. 1879; also edited by C.A. Bernouilli, 1895, and E.C. Richardson, 1896; as *Lives of Illustrious Men*, translated by E.C. Richardson, in *A Select Library of Nicene and Post-Nicene Fathers*, series 2, vol. 3, 1892; as *On Illustrious Men*, translated by Thomas P. Halton, 1999.
Epistolae, as *Letters*, translated by Charles Christopher Mierow. 1963; edited by James Duff, 1942, and Carl Favus, 1956; selection edited and translated by F.A. Wright, 1933; selection as *Satirical Letters*, translated by Paul Carroll, 1956.
Prologus Galeatus: The Middle English Bible; Prefatory Epistles of St. Jerome, edited by C. Lindberg. 1978.
Quaestiones Hebraicae in Genesim [Hebrew Questions], edited by P. de Lagarde. 1868; as *Saint Jerome's Hebrew Questions on Genesis*, translated with introduction and commentary by C.T.R. Hayward, 1995.
Vitae Patrum [Lives of the Saints], as *The . . . Lyff of the Old Auncyent Holy Faders Hermytes*, translated by William Caxton. 1495, reprinted 1977; as *The History of the Monks*, translated by E.A.W.

Budge, 1934; selections as *Lives of St. Paul the First Hermit, St. Hilarion and Malchus*, translated by Sister Marie Liguori Ewald, in *Fathers of the Church*, vol. 15, 1952.
Vulgate (first Latin translation of Old and New Testaments). 1452–55.
Homilies, translated by Sister Marie Liguori Ewald. 2 vols., 1964–66.
Dogmatic and Political Works, translated by John N. Hritzu, in *Fathers of the Church*, vol. 53. 1965.
Translation of Jerome's Chronicon with Historical Commentary by Malcolm Drew Donalson. 1996.

Other

Correspondence (394–419), between Jerome and Augustine of Hippo, translated with introduction and notes by Carolinne White. 1990.

*

Critical Studies: *St. Jerome* by A. Largent, 1900; *Life and Times as Revealed in the Writings of St. Jerome* by Mary J. Kelly, 1944; *St. Jerome* by Mary Beattie, 1945; *Hieronymus* by L. Huizinga, 1946; *St. Jerome and the Bible* by George Sanderlin, 1961; *St. Jerome as a Biblical Translator* by William H. Semple, 1965; *The Vulgate as a Translation* by Benjamin Kedar-Kipfstein, 1968; *Jerome: His Life, Writings and Controversies* by John N.D. Kelly, 1975; *New Jerome Biblical Commentary*, edited by Raymond E. Brown, 1989; *Vir Trilinguis: A Study in the Biblical Exegesis of Saint Jerome* by Dennis Brown, 1992; *Consoling Heliodorus: Commentary of Jerome "Letter 60"* by J.H.D. Scourfield, 1992; *Jerome, Greek Scholarship and the Hebrew Bible: A Study of the "Quaestiones Hebraicae in Genesim"* by Adam Kamesar, 1993.

* * *

St. Jerome is one of the two famous Fathers of the Latin Church from the 4th and 5th centuries, the other being St. Augustine. He is chiefly remembered for having translated the Old and New Testaments from the original Hebrew and Greek into Latin. This translation, later known as the *Vulgate*, has been the authoritative version of the Catholic Church since the 16th century. St. Jerome's translations and commentaries on the Sacred Scriptures are the most serious intellectual attempt at biblical exegesis produced in Latin from the early Christian Church, written at a time when the Roman Empire was crumbling under the onslaught of the Barbarian invasions.

After studying the Seven Liberal Arts in Rome, Jerome converted to Christianity at the age of 20. A famous dream recounts how Jerome turned away from the Classical pagan authors, notably Cicero, to a new centre of interest, the writings of the Christian revelation, which preoccupied him all the rest of his life. The first stage of his career took place in the East, at Constantinople. Having perfected his knowledge of Greek in AD 379–80, Jerome translated a series of *Homilies* written by the 3rd-century Greek theologian, Origen of Alexandria. He translated into Latin 14 homilies on the prophet Jeremiah, the same number on Ezekiel, and nine on Isaiah. Later he translated Origen's commentary on the *Song of Songs* (AD 382–84), and 39 of his homilies on St. Luke (AD 386–90). It is thanks to Jerome's translation that Western Europe became familiar with some of Origen's teaching and thought. Origen remained a decisive influence on Jerome, although he was later moved to criticize what he considered to be heretical elements in Origen's writings.

Imbued with a strong historical sense, Jerome was familiar with the works of both the Latin and Greek historians—Tacitus, Livy, Suetonius, Herodotus, and Xenophon. In AD 382 Jerome set about translating the *Chronicle* of Eusebius of Caesarea, originally written in Greek at the beginning of the 4th century. Eusebius had written a history of the world from Adam to the reign of Constantine. Jerome, wishing to give Christianity a solid historical context, translated Eusebius' history, bringing it up to his own time. Jerome's work had a major influence during the Middle Ages, and served as a model for later chronicles of Church history, especially for Isidore of Seville (AD 570–636) and the Venerable Bede (c. AD 673–735).

Back in Rome in AD 382, Jerome, under the direction of Pope Damasus I, was entrusted with making a new translation of the Bible. By the 4th century it had become necessary to revise the Old Latin version of the Bible, a text compiled from various anonymous authors from the 2nd and 3rd centuries, and itself a translation from the *Septuagint*, a translation for Greek-speaking Jews of the Old Testament, made between 301 BC and 150 BC. As well as these two texts, Jerome was able to consult the now lost *Hexaplar Text* of Origen, a six-column version of the Old Testament in Hebrew and Greek. Jerome's originality and genius exist in his methodological approach. He gained a thorough knowledge of spoken and written Hebrew and studied Syriac, Coptic, and Aramaic, all of which prepared him for the 15-year task he had set himself: to translate the Old Testament from the original Hebrew and the New Testament from its Greek versions, as well as checking with previous translations for inconsistencies and errors. The translation produced by Jerome is the fruit of a vast encyclopaedic knowledge and the work of an extremely erudite man. It earned him the title *Doctor Maximus in sacris Scripturis explanandis*, the "Greatest Teacher in setting forth the Sacred Scripture." In a decree of 1546, the Council of Trent declared the *Vulgate* (a term first used by Roger Bacon in the 13th century to describe Jerome's translation) the authorized version of the Bible for the Catholic Church.

In 385 Jerome finally left Rome and moved to Bethlehem, where he remained until his death. It is here that he wrote a large number of exegeses, biblical commentaries, on both the Old and New Testaments, in the 390s and at the beginning of the 5th century. Origen is remembered for favouring the allegorical meaning of Scripture, but Jerome defended the theoretical principle of investigating and establishing its literal sense. He did not neglect interpreting biblical symbols and metaphors, with the help of Jewish scholars.

Three closely related works from the 390s are Jerome's *Quaestiones Hebraicae in Genesim* (*Hebrew Questions on Genesis*), a series of notes he made on various passages of the Book of Genesis, stemming from the work of Josephus, Origen, Philo, Porphyry, and Eusebius. In his *De nominus Hebraicis* [Book on Hebrew Names] and *Onomasticon urbium ac locorum sanctae Scriptorae* [Book on Cities and Sites of Holy Scripture], Jerome sought to explain the meaning of proper names which could not be translated. With often fanciful and popular etymologies, sometimes devoid of scientific exactness, Jerome, working from the *Onomasticon* by Eusebius, produced the main source of material on Hebrew proper names, later used during the Middle Ages.

Jerome is also the author of seven controversial treatises, written at times in an acerbic tongue against contemporaries who defended heretical doctrine. These polemical works were begun in the late 370s and Jerome was still venting his temper when *Contra pelagianos* [Against the Pelagians] was published in AD 415. The previous titles were: *Altercatio luciferiani et orthodoxi* [Debate of a Luciferian and an Orthodox] (AD 378) in which Jerome was concerned with the validity of heretical baptism; *Adversus Helvidium* [Against Helvidius]

(AD 383) who doubted the virginity of the Blessed Virgin; *Liber contra Jovinianum* [Against Jovinian] (AD 393) who criticized celibacy and asceticism; *Contra Joannem Hierosolymitanum* [Against John of Jerusalem] (AD 397) and *Apologia adversus Rufinum* [Against Rufinus] (AD 401) who both defended certain "heresies" of Origen; and *Contra Vigilantium liber* [Against Vigilantius] (AD 406), a critic of the worship of saints and relics. Like St. Augustine, Jerome saw his role as vigilant supporter of an orthodox Christianity, but his polemics sometimes degenerated into personal attacks on men rather than on ideas. Finally, Jerome wrote a handbook on 135 Christian authors, *De viris illustribus* (*On Illustrious Men*) (AD 392), based on Suetonius' secular manual, as well as 117 *Letters*, which enjoyed an enormous popularity during the Middle Ages.

—David Coad

JIMÉNEZ (MANTECÓN), Juan Ramón

Born: Moguer, Spain, 23 December 1881. **Education:** Educated at a Jesuit school in Cádiz, 1891–96; University of Seville, 1896. **Family:** Married Zenobia Camprubí Aymar in 1916 (died 1956). **Career:** In sanatoriums, 1901–05, then a writer: settled in Madrid, 1912, but left Spain in 1936; travelled and taught in Puerto Rico, Cuba, North Carolina, and Florida, 1939–42, Washington, DC, 1942–51; faculty member, University of Puerto Rico, Río Piedras, 1951–58. **Awards:** Nobel prize for literature, 1956. **Died:** 29 May 1958.

PUBLICATIONS

Collections

Libros de poesía, edited by Agustín Caballero. 1957.
Primeros libros de poesía, edited by Francisco Garfias. 1960.
Antología general en prosa, edited by Angel Crespo and Pilar Gómez Bedate. 1981.
Lorca and Jiménez: Selected Poems, edited and translated by Robert Bly, 1997.

Verse

Almas de violeta. 1900.
Ninfeas. 1900.
Rimas. 1902.
Arias tristes. 1903.
Jardines lejanos. 1904.
Elegías. 3 vols., 1908–10.
Olvidanzas. 1909; edited by Francisco Garfias, 1968.
Baladas de primavera. 1910.
La soledad sonora. 1911.
Pastorales. 1911.
Poemas mágicos y dolientes. 1911.
Melancolía. 1912.
Laberinto. 1913.
Platero y yo: Elegía andaluza. 1914; complete edition, 1917; edited by Michael P. Predmore, 1980, Francisco López Estrada, 1986, and Richard Cardwell, 1988; as *Platero and I*, translated by

William and Mary Roberts, 1956; translated by Eloise Roach, 1958; Antonio T. De Nicolás, 1986; S. O-Carboneres, 1990; also translated by Myra Cohn Livingston and Joseph F. Domínguez, 1994.

Estío. 1916.

Sonetos espirituales. 1917; as *Spiritual Sonnets*, translated by Carl W. Cobb, 1996.

Diario de un poeta recién casado. 1917; revised editions, as *Diario de poeta y mar*, 1948, 1955.

Poesías escogidas. 1917.

Eternidades. 1918.

Piedra y cielo. 1919.

Segunda antología poética. 1922.

Poesía. 1923.

Belleza. 1923.

Canción. 1936.

Voces de mi copla. 1945.

La estación total. 1946.

Romances de Coral Gables. 1948.

Animal de fondo. 1949.

Fifty Spanish Poems, translated by J.B. Trend. 1950.

Tercera antología poética 1898–1953. 1957.

Three Hundred Poems 1903–1953, translated by Eloise Roach. 1962.

Dios deseado y deseante. 1964; as *God Desired and Desiring*, translated by Antonio T. De Nicolás, 1987.

Lorca and Jiménez, translated by Robert Bly. 1973.

Jiménez and Machado, translated by J.B. Trend and J.L. Gili. 1974.

Naked Music: Poems, translated by Dennis Maloney. 1976.

Leyenda, edited by A. Sánchez Romeralo. 1978.

The Flower Scenes (selection), translated by J.C.R. Green. 1982.

Realidad invisible: Libro inédito, edited by A. Sánchez Romeralo. 1984; as *Invisible Reality* (bilingual edition), translated by Antonio T. De Nicolás, 1987.

Time and Space: A Poetic Autobiography, translated by Antonio T. De Nicolás. 1988.

The Complete Perfectionist: A Poetics of Work, edited and translated by Christopher Maurer. 1997.

Other

Conferencias I: Política poética. 1936.

Ciego ante ciegos. 1938.

Españoles de tres mundos. 1942.

El zaratán. 1946.

Selected Writings, translated by H.R. Hays. 1957.

Olvidos de Granada. 1960.

Cuadernos, edited by Francisco Garfias. 1960.

La corriente infinita. 1961.

El trabajo gustoso. 1961.

Cartas, edited by Francisco Garfias. 1962.

Primeras prosas, edited by Francisco Garfias. 1962.

Estética y ética estética. 1967.

Libros de prosa. 1969–.

Stories of Life and Death, translated by Antonio T. De Nicolás. 1986.

Light and Shadows: Selected Poems and Prose, 1881–1958, translated by Dennis Maloney. 1987.

Ideología: 1897–1957: Metamórfosis IV, edited by Antonio Sánchez Romeralo. 1990.

Translator, with Z. Camprubí de Jiménez, *Jinetes hacia el mar*, by J.M. Synge. 1920.

*

Bibliography: *Bibliografía genered de Juan Ramón Jiménez* by Antonio Campoamor González, 1982.

Critical Studies: *The Victorious Expression: A Study of Four Contemporary Spanish Poets: Miguel de Unamuno, Antonio Machado, Juan Ramón Jiménez, Federico García Lorca*, 1964, and *The Line in the Margin: Juan Ramón Jiménez and His Readings in Blake, Shelley, and Yeats*, 1980, both by Howard T. Young; *The Religious Instinct in the Poetry of Jiménez* by Leo R. Cole, 1967; *Circles of Paradox: Time and Essence in the Poetry of Juan Ramón Jiménez* by Paul R. Olson, 1967; *Juan Ramón Jiménez* by Donald F. Fogelquist, 1976; *Jiménez: The Modernist Apprenticeship 1895–1900* by Richard A. Cardwell, 1977; *Word and Work in the Poetry of Juan Ramón Jiménez* by Mervyn Coke-Enguidanos, 1982; *Perfume and Poison: A Study of the Relationship Between José Bergamín and Juan Ramón Jimenez* by Nigel Dennis, 1985; *Self and Image in Juan Ramón Jiménez: Modern and Post-modern Readings* by John C. Wilcox, 1987; *Poesía Popular en la Obra de Juan Ramón Jiménez* by María Isabel López Martínez, 1992; *Encounters with Juan Ramón Jiménez* by William Kluback, 1995.

* * *

Although he could be looked upon as the juvenile filter of a highly sentimental form of *fin de siècle* decadence in his first two books (published in 1900), Juan Ramón Jiménez quickly grew more constrained and became a sensitive transmitter and adapter of Verlaine's style of symbolism, as well as a successor of Bécquer in such works as *Rimas* [Rhymes] and *Arias tristes* [Sad Airs]. This early lyrical stage led eventually to the triumph of the *Diario de un poeta recién casado* [Diary of a Newly-Married Poet]. Written as a result of its author's wedding in New York to Zenobia Camprubí Aymar, a Puerto Rican educated in America and Spain, the book exerted enormous influence on subsequent Hispanic poetry. It stands between the towers of Bécquer's *Rimas* (1871) and Lorca's *Primer romancero gitano* (*Gypsy Ballads*, 1928) as one of the indisputable landmarks of the modern Spanish lyric.

Leaving aside the prose descriptions of New York, Boston, and Philadelphia, the style of the *Diario* is lucid, stripped down to a minimum of adjectives and expressed in an unrhymed and brief free verse form. The imagists had introduced *verso libre* to the United States at about that time, and Jiménez reacted with a version he called *verso desnudo* (naked verse), a short stanza that had considerable impact on younger poets.

In the *Diario* the characteristic mature tone of Jiménez is set. Highly self-referential but less hermetic than Mallarmé, he began in this book a long series of poems that continue in *Eternidades* [Eternities] and *Belleza* [Beauty]. They record epiphanies that express the manifold aspects of a mind perceiving the indifferent beauty of the world. Pebbles and petals on the one hand and the sea and sidereal distances on the other were among the fragments of his surroundings that Jiménez sought to appraise, reconnoitre, and finally to possess.

However, for many readers, Jiménez is the author of only one book: *Platero y yo* (*Platero and I*). It is a pastoral prose poem that reveals many layers of meaning and nuance as the sombrely clad poet-narrator, with his Nazarene beard, rides the donkey Platero through the village of Moguer and out into the countryside. The book also contains astute observations on the poor and oppressed.

Jiménez returned to the United States at the outbreak of the Spanish Civil War in 1936. The flat open land of the Florida Everglades inspired the much admired "Espacio" [Space]. An audacious experiment with form, "Espacio" turns discourse into an examination of the possibilities of language. Contingency, the confluence of past and present, memory, spiritual versus carnal love, destiny, and mortality are its themes.

Animal de fondo [Enduring Animal] celebrates the encounter with a humanistic god. Like Blake, he discovered the divinity of the creative consciousness, which seemed to him a god within and without, desiring and desired. On this note of apodictic humanism, with "all the clouds ablaze," the best of Jiménez's work concludes.

Except for the uneven early books, his work, although repetitive and unduly extensive—30 books and a mass of unpublished material—sustains a remarkably high quality. He was a scrupulous self-critic and devoted much time to revising and rewriting large amounts of his poetry.

—Howard T. Young

See the essay on *Platero and I*.

JOHN OF THE CROSS, St.

Also known as San Juan de la Cruz. **Born:** Juan de Yepes y Ávarez in Fontiveros, Spain, 1542. **Education:** Studied at Jesuit college, Medina del Campo, 1559–63; took the habit as Fray Juan de Santo Matía; attended Carmelite College of San Andrés, University of Salamanca, 1564–68; ordained, 1567. **Career:** Boarded at an orphanage by his widowed mother; joined St. Teresa's reformed Discalced Order of Carmel in a priory at Duruelo, near Fontiveros, as San Juan de la Cruz, 1568–70, then at Mancera, 1570; rector of a new Carmelite college at University of Alcalá, 1571–72; confessor at convent in Avila, 1572–77; controversy over reformation of the Carmelite order caused him to be confined in conventual prison in Toledo, 1577–78, because of his reforming attitudes; escaped to a nearby convent; at El Calvario hermitage near convent at Beas de Segura, 1578–79; rector of new Carmelite college at Baeza, 1579–82; prior of Los Mártires, Granada, 1582–88; prior at Segovia, 1588–91; out of favour with head of Discalced Order, and made a simple friar at Priory of La Peñvela, 1591. Beatified, 1675; Canonized, 1726. **Died:** 14 December 1591.

PUBLICATIONS

Works

Complete Works, edited and translated by E. Allison Peers. 3 vols., 1934–35; poems also translated by Roy Campbell, 1951; John

Frederick Nims, 1959, revised edition, 1968; Kieran Kavanagh and Otilio Rodríguez, 1964, selection from this edition published as *A Song in the Night*, 1991; and Willis Barnstone, 1968; as *Poems of St. John of the Cross*, translated with introduction by Kathleen Jones, 1993; as *Poems of St. John of the Cross* , translated by Ken Krabbenhoft, 1999.

Vida y obras completas, edited by Crisógono de Jesús, Matías del Niño, and Lucinio Ruano. 1946; 6th edition, 1972.

Four Poems, translated by Yon Oria. 1984.

The Living Flame of Love, translated by J. Vernard. 1990; translated by E. Allison Peers, 1991; as *Living Flame of Love: Versions A and B*, translated with introduction by Jane Ackerman, 1995.

The Spiritual Canticle, translated by J. Vernard. 1991.

Prayers of Saint John of the Cross, compiled by Alphonse Ruiz. 1991.

Loving God Through the Darkness: Selected Writings of John of the Cross, selected, edited and introduced by Keith Beasley-Topliffe. 2000.

Ascent of Joy: Selected Spiritual Writings , selected, annotated and introduced by Marc Foley. 2002.

Dark Night of the Soul, translated and introduced by Mirabai Starr. 2002.

*

Bibliography: *Bibliografia di S. Juan de la Cruz* by Pier P. Ottonello, 1966.

Critical Studies: *St. John of the Cross and Other Lectures and Addresses*, 1946, and *Handbook to the Life and Times of Saint Teresa and Saint John of the Cross*, 1954, both by E. Allison Peers; *Medieval Mystical Tradition and Saint John of the Cross* by a Benedictine of Stanbrook Abbey, 1954; *San Juan de la Cruz, Saint John of the Cross* by Bernardo Gicovate, 1971; *St. John of the Cross: His Life and Poetry* by Gerald Brenan, 1973; *San Juan de la Cruz: Poems* by Margaret Wilson, 1975; *The Poet and the Mystic: A Study of the Cántico Espiritual of San Juan de la Cruz* by Colin P. Thompson, 1977; *St. John of the Cross: Alchemist of the Soul* by Antonio T. De Nicolás, 1989; *St. John of the Cross* by Bede Frost, 1991; *St. John of the Cross: Studies on His Life, Doctrine, and Times*, edited by Justin Panakal, 1991; *Knowledge and Symbolization in Saint John of the Cross* by Elizabeth Wilhelmsen, 1993; *The Contemporary Challenge of John the Cross: An Introduction to His Life and Teaching* by Leonard Doohan, 1995; *Canciones entre el alma y el esposo of Juan de la Cruz: A Hermeneutical Interpretation* by David Brian Perrin, 1996; *John of the Cross* by Wilfrid McGreal, 1996; *Words of Wisdom for Our World: The Precautions and Counsels of St. John of the Cross* by Susan Muto, 1996; *John of the Cross: Doctor of Light and Love* by Kieran Kavanaugh, 1999; *St. John of the Cross and the Bhagavad-Gita: Love, Union, and Renunciation* by Thomas Myladil, 2000; *Mysticism and Cognition: The Cognitive Development of John the Cross as Revealed in His Works* by Birgitta Mark, 2000.

* * *

The 22 poems of St. John of the Cross must certainly constitute one of the briefest opuses of any major poet, but, since the 1880s, they have exerted a significant influence on the course of European and American poetry. In his conviction that words provide, at best, only indirect access to experience and that meaning does not exist on a one-to-one basis but, instead, spills over from the play of rhetorical devices (see the 1584 prologue to "The Spiritual Canticle"), St. John anticipated the basic symbolist tenet of indirect expression as expounded by Mallarmé and Valéry (the latter acknowledged the importance to him of St. John). The highly polished lyrical quality of his lines in Spanish inspired Bécquer, whose work represents a transition from romanticism to symbolism, and found a worthy follower in the leading Spanish symbolist poet Juan Ramón Jiménez. St. John's presence may be discovered in "East Coker," the first of T.S. Eliot's *Four Quartets*, and the image "dark night of the soul" has gained much currency among modern writers.

The major theme of St. John's poetry is a description of the various stages of development that the soul undergoes in its efforts to become unified with God. In St. John's hands, this mystical undertaking achieves one of the highest levels of lyricism known to Western poetry. Delicate alliteration and simple diction endow the poems with pellucid beauty. St. John chose to recount the story of divine love by having recourse to the symbols and devices used to portray human love, and this accounts for the strong but refined sensuality that characterizes his work.

"The Dark Night," "The Spiritual Canticle," "The Living Flame of Love," and "Although by Night," to mention only some of the better-known poems, are nourished by three distinct sources: the pastoral tradition, exemplified in Spanish by Garcilaso de la Vega; the ballads (*romances*); and the Bible, above all "The Song of Songs." St. John drew heavily from Solomon's adaptation of Eastern nuptial songs to limn the marriage between the soul and God.

Part of the modern attraction of these poems is that they lend themselves so readily to multiple levels of meaning. "The Dark Night" is, at once, great amorous verse, a biographical description of escape from prison, and an allegory of mystical experience.

St. John left assiduously detailed comments on these poems. Those for "Ascent of Mount Carmel" and "Dark Night of the Soul" are incomplete; notes on the latter do not get beyond the first 11 lines. The glosses on "The Spiritual Canticle" and "The Living Flame of Love" are complete. Written within the hermeneutic tradition of the Counter-Reformation, these commentaries, except for scattered moments, display none of the consummate literary talent of the poetry. Such is the disparity that it is almost as if one were reading two different authors. *Sayings of Light and Love*, a collection of aphorisms, and, incidentally, the only autograph of his work extant, displays many pleasant paradoxes, but hardly surpasses any other such miscellany. Clearly, it was only as a lyrical poet that he excelled.

—Howard T. Young

JOHNSON, Uwe

Born: Kämmin, Pomerania (now in Poland), 20 July 1934. **Education:** Educated at school in Güstrow; University of Rostock, 1952–54; University of Leipzig, 1954–56, diploma in philosophy 1956. **Family:** Married Elisabeth Schmidt in 1962; one daughter. **Career:** Freelance writer; lived in Güstrow until 1959, in West Berlin, 1959–74, and in England from 1975; lecturer, Wayne State University, Detroit, and Harvard University, Cambridge, Massachusetts, 1961; editor of German writing, Harcourt Brace, publishers, New York, 1966–67. **Awards:** Berlin Academy Fontane prize, 1960; International Publishers prize, 1962; Villa Massino grant, 1962; Büchner prize, 1971; Raabe prize, 1975; Thomas Mann prize (Lübeck), 1978. **Died:** 15 March 1984.

PUBLICATIONS

Collections

Speculations about Jakob and Other Writings, edited by Alexander Stephan. 2000.

Fiction

Mutmassungen über Jakob. 1959; as *Speculations about Jakob*, translated by Ursule Molinaro, 1963; edited by Alexander Stephan, 2000.

Das dritte Buch über Achim. 1961; as *The Third Book about Achim*, translated by Ursule Molinaro, 1967.

Karsch und andere Prosa. 1964; translated in part as *An Absence*, by Richard and Clara Winston, 1969.

Zwei Ansichten. 1965; as *Two Views*, translated by Richard and Clara Winston, 1966.

Jahrestage: Aus dem Leben von Gesine Cresspahl. 1970–83; as *Anniversaries: From the Life of Gesine Cresspahl*, vols. 1–2 translated by Leila Vennewitz, 1975; vols. 2–4 translated by Vennewitz and Walter Arndt, 1987.

Von dem Fischer un syner Fru: Ein Märchen nach Philipp Otto Runge. 1976.

Skizze eines Verunglückten. 1982.

Ingrid Babendererde: Reifeprüfung 1953. 1985.

Versuch, einen Vater zu finden. Marthas Ferien. 1988.

Other

Eine Reise nach Klagenfurt. 1974.

Berliner Sachen: Aufsätze. 1975.

Begleitumstände: Frankfurter Vorlesungen. 1980.

Der 5. Kanal. 1987.

Ich überlege mir die Geschichte: Uwe Johnson im Gespräch, edited by Eberhard Fahlke. 1988.

Editor, *Me-ti: Buch der Wendungen*, by Bertolt Brecht. 1965.

Editor, with Hans Meyer, *Das Werk von Samuel Beckett—Berliner Colloquium*. 1975.

Editor, *Stich-Worte*, by Max Frisch. 1975.

Editor, *Verzweigungen*, by Margret Boveri. 1977.

Translator, *Israel Potter*, by Herman Melville. 1960.

Translator, *In diesem Land*, by John Knowles. 1963.

*

Bibliography: *Uwe Johnson: Bibliographie* by Nicolai Riedel, 2 vols., 1976; revised edition, 1981.

Critical Studies: *Uwe Johnson* by Mark Boulby, 1974; *Ich und Er: First and Third Person Self-Reference and Problems of Identity in Three Contemporary German-Language Novels* by Paul F. Botheroyd, 1976; *Beyond the Single Vision: Henry James, Michel Butor, Uwe Johnson* by Marianne Hirsch, 1981; *Uwe Johnson* edited by Rainer Gerlach and Matthias Richter, 1984; *Uwe Johnsons Jahrestage* edited by Michael Bengel, 1985; *Neither Left nor Right: The Politics of Individualism in Uwe Johnson's Work* by Kurt J. Fickert, 1987; *Difficulties of Saying "I": The Narrator as Protagonist in Uwe Johnson's Jahrestage and Christa Wolf's Kindheitsmuster* by Robert K. Shirer, 1988; *The Ethics of Narration: Uwe Johnson's Novels from Ingrid Babendererde to Jahrestage* by Colin Riordan, 1989; *Uwe Johnsons "Jahrestage." Erzählstruktur und politische Subjektivität* by Ulrich Fries, 1990; *Über Uwe Johnson* edited by Raimund Fellinger, 1992; *German History and German Identity: Uwe Johnson's Jahrestage* by D.G. Bond, 1993; *Dialogue With the Reader: The Narrative Stance in Uwe Johnson's Fiction* by Kurt Fickert, 1996; *Distorted Reflections: The Public and Private Uses of the Author in the Work of Uwe Johnson, Günter Grass and Martin Walser, 1965–1975* by Stuart Tabener, 1998; *Understanding Uwe Johnson* by Gary L. Baker, 1999.

* * *

Although less well known internationally than Heinrich Böll or Günter Grass, Uwe Johnson is unquestionably one of the towering figures of post-war German literature. Having grown up in the German Democratic Republic and moved to the West in 1959, he became the first German writer of stature to tackle the pre-eminent theme of post-war Germany: the division into separate States. In 1967, after three novels and a volume of short stories which drew on the divisions of Germany for wide-ranging analyses of historical, moral, and literary dilemmas, Johnson embarked on his epic novel *Jahrestage* (*Anniversaries*). Completed a year before the author's early death from heart disease in 1984, *Anniversaries* in its later stages was influenced by a debilitating personal crisis which dogged the last ten years of Johnson's life. A number of minor pieces written during the 1970s reflect both Johnson's life in England and his personal tribulations. Not until after his death did Johnson's first, originally unpublished novel appear.

Begun when Johnson was 19, rewritten four times and finished by the time he was 22, *Ingrid Babendererde*, published in 1985, is a novel of astonishing maturity. Rejected by publishers in the GDR as politically dangerous, and by a West German publisher as sympathetic to communism, the novel tells the story of the last few days in school of a class about to take school-leaving examinations in April 1953, shortly after Stalin's death and two months before the workers' uprising. The examination becomes political and moral rather than strictly educational, however, because the eponymous heroine comes into conflict with the authorities over the persecution by the State of a religious youth organization. Finally she is left with no choice but to leave for the West. While *Ingrid Babendererde*, as a school novel, does betray the youth of its author, it nevertheless displays the sensitivity to subtle moral and political dilemmas (presented in this case by life in an aspiring socialist, but actually totalitarian regime) which was to characterize much of Johnson's later work.

Mutmassungen über Jakob (*Speculations about Jakob*), written in the GDR but published in the Federal Republic in 1959, marked Johnson's emergence as a new literary talent. A young East German railway worker, Jakob Abs, is killed by a train after having been to the Federal Republic to visit his lover, Gesine Cresspahl, whom the secret police had hoped to recruit as an agent through Jakob. The novel concerns the efforts of the characters, including Gesine, the secret police captain Rohlfs, and Jonas, Jakob's friend, to reconstruct the last month of Jakob's life. This seems straightforward enough, but extensive use of flashback, unidentified interior monologue, and structural complexity reminiscent of William Faulkner give rise on first reading to a kind of foggy indistinctness which bewildered many early reviewers and critics. Close analysis shows, however, that the work's component parts can be reassembled in an easily comprehensible form. Despite the title, then, the reader is called upon not to speculate, but to observe with the utmost precision. The speculation in which the characters are forced to indulge, immersed as they are in an atmosphere of extreme mutual mistrust arising from the exigencies of the Cold War, reflects the reality of a divided Germany which was no more than partly penetrable by those caught up in its complexities.

Karsh, a Hamburg journalist, the hero of Johnson's second published novel, *Das dritte Buch über Achim* (*The Third Book about Achim*), similarly feels the effects of mutual inter-German mistrust upon his own person. In response to a telephone invitation from a former girlfriend, Karsch travels to the GDR. His former girlfriend is now closely involved with Joachim ("Achim") T., famous racing cyclist and folk-hero, and the subject of two biographies. Karsch is asked to produce a third book about Achim, which he works on but never finishes. The reasons for his failure form the main object of interest. The fallible workings of memory (and of literature), as well as the linguistic divergence between the two countries which engenders epistemological clashes, all contribute to the problems Karsch encounters. Ultimately, however, political pressures conflict with ethical dictates: unable to preserve his integrity as a writer and simultaneously connive at the State's self-interested remodelling of Achim's image, the journalist makes his decision to return empty-handed to the West, constrained by the moral imperatives which characterize so much of Johnson's work.

Johnson re-worked the Achim story in his collection of short prose *Karsch und andere Prosa* [Karsch and Other Prose], concentrating on the breakdown which Karsch suffered on his return to the West. The collection also contains a number of short stories prefiguring the later novel *Anniversaries*. *Zwei Ansichten* (*Two Views*), topped the West German bestseller lists with its topical tale of two lovers divided by the Berlin wall. This is no *Romeo and Juliet*, however, since the motives of both participants are complex and ambiguous. Although the young East German woman, Nurse D., does eventually reach West Berlin, there is no fairytale happy ending. The apparent simplicity of star-crossed lovers seeking happiness in each other's arms is superseded by the realization that the characters are in the grip of complex historical forces which they are unable to comprehend and powerless to control.

The effect which historical circumstances have on the lives of individuals forms a central concern in Johnson's greatest achievement, *Anniversaries*. The four-volume novel recounts a year in the life of Gesine Cresspahl (familiar from *Speculations about Jakob*), who lives and works as a single mother in New York with her 11-year-old daughter Marie (daughter of Jakob Abs). Each day of the year in question—20 August 1967 to 20 August 1968—is individually documented on two chronological levels. The first documents daily events in New York and the United States as perceived by Gesine through her reading of the *New York Times* and her personal experience. The second follows Gesine's efforts to retrace the story of her family and forebears in pre-war Germany, progressing through the war and the establishment of the GDR to the early 1960s when Gesine left for the United States. These two levels are connected using sophisticated narratological devices as anniversaries of events in the earlier story occur, though both can be read as stories in their own right. The novel encompasses a broad sweep of 20th-century history, concentrating particularly on the moral dilemmas faced by Gesine and her parents, dilemmas encapsulated in the "moral Switzerland" problem: "Where is the moral Switzerland that we can emigrate to?" asks Gesine in despair. While Gesine bitterly regrets her parents' failure to leave Nazi Germany when they had the opportunity, she finds herself bringing up her own daughter in a country riven by race-riots and embroiled in a hopeless, costly war. Gesine finds no solution, and her hopes of experiencing democratic, humane socialism are dashed as she plans a trip to Czechoslovakia on the day of the Soviet invasion, the final day of the *Anniversaries* year. Such a brief description cannot do justice to what is a richly interwoven, absorbing, and meticulously crafted text. *Anniversaries* stands out as one of the great German novels of the post-war era, indeed of the 20th century, encapsulating as it docs the origins and development of many of the problems which beset the world we know today.

—Colin Riordan

JUANA INÉS DE LA CRUZ, Sor

Born: Juana Inés Ramírez de Asbaje (or Asuaje) in San Miguel de Nepantla, Viceroyalty of New Spain (now Mexico), 12 November 1651 (some sources give 1648). **Education:** Largely self-educated. **Career:** Invited to attend the court of the Spanish Viceroy's wife, the Marquise de Mancera, in Mexico City, c. 1659, and subsequently wrote verses for official events; member of the Carmelite convent in Mexico City, 1667 (for three months); entered Jeronymite Convent of San Paula, Mexico City, 1669, and adopted the religious name Sor Juana Inés de la Cruz; abandoned writing, c. 1693, because of the increasing pressure from Church authorities after 1689. **Died:** 17 April 1695.

PUBLICATIONS

Collections

Obras escogidas, edited by Manuel Toussaint. 1928.
Obras completas, edited by Alfonso Mendez Plancarte and Alberto Salceda. 4 vols., 1951–57.
Poesía, teatro y prosa (selections), edited by Antonio Castro Leal. 1965.

Obras selectas, edited by Georgina Sabat de Rivers and Elias L. Rivers. 1976.
Obra selecta, edited by Lusi Sáinz de Medrano. 1987.
Answer: Including a Selection of Poems, translated by Electa Arenal and Amanda Powell. 1994.
Poems, Protest, and a Dream: Selected Writings, translated with notes by Margaret Sayers Peden. 1997.

Verse

Villancicos. 12 vols., 1676–91.
Poesías escogidas, edited by Antonio Elías de Molins. c. 1901.
Poesías completas, edited by Emilio Abreu Gómez. 1940.
Poesías (selection), edited by Elena Amat. 1941.
The Pathless Grove: Sonnets, translated by Pauline Cook. 1950.
El sueño, edited by Alfonso Méndez Plancarte. 1951; as *Primero sueño*, edited by Gerardo Moldenhauer and Juan Carlos Merlo, 1953; as *El sueño*, translated by John Campion, 1983; as *Sor Juana's Dream*, translated by Luis Harss, 1986.
Endechas, edited by Xavier Villaurrutia. 1952.
Sonetos y endechas, edited by Rosa Chacel. 1980.
Lírica, edited by Raquel Asún. 1983.
Poems: A Bilingual Anthology, edited and translated by Margaret Sayers Peden. 1985.
Sonnets of Sor Juana Ines de la Cruz in English Verse, translated by Carl W. Cobb. 2001.

Plays (individual 17th-century editions)

Auto sacramental de "El divino Narciso" (produced 1689). 1690; as *Divine Narcissus*, translated and annotated by Patricia A. Peters and Renée Domeier, 1998.
Los empeños de una casa (produced 1683). N.d; as *The House of Trials*, translated by David Pasto, 1996.
Amor es más laberinto. N.d.
Neptuno alegórico. N.d.
Three Secular Plays of Sor Juana Inés de la Cruz by Guillermo Schmidhuber in collaboration with Olga Marthat Peña Doria, translated by Shelby Thacker. 2000.

Other

Carta atenagórica. 1690.
Explicación sucinta del arco triunfal. . . N.d.
La respuesta a Sor Filotea de la Cruz. 1691; as *A Woman of Genius: The Intellectual Biography of Sor Juana Inés de la Cruz*, translated by Margaret Sayers Peden, 1982.
[Works]. 3 vols., 1691–1700.
   1. *Inundación castálida* (includes verse and the play *El neptuno alegórico*). 1689; as *Poemas*, 1690; edited by Georgina Sabat de Rivers, as *Inundación castálida*, 1982.
   2. *Segundo volumen de las obras* (includes "El sueño"; the autos *El cetro de José, El mártir del Sacramento, San Hermenegildo, El divino Narciso*; the comedies *Los empeños de una casa, Amor es más laberinto*; and *Crisis sobre un sermón: Carta atenagórica*). 1692.
   3. *Fama y obras póstumas* (includes *La respuesta a Sor Filotea*). 1700.

Carta atenagórica; Respuesta a Sor Filotea, edited by Emilio Abreu Gómez. 1934.

Poesía y teatro, edited by Matilde Muñoz. 1946.

Antología Sorjuanina, edited by Giuseppe Bellini. 1961.

Antología, edited by Elias L. Rivers. 1968.

Antología clave, edited by Hernán Loyola. 1971.

Selección, edited by L. Ortega Galindo. 1978.

A Sor Juana Anthology (bilingual edition), translated by Alan S. Trueblood. 1988.

Sor Juana's Love Poems; Poemas de amor: A Bilingual Edition, translated by Joan Larkin and Jaime Manrique. 1997.

*

Bibliography: *Bibliografía de Sor Juana Inés de la Cruz* by Dorothy Schons, 1927; *Sor Juana Inés de la Cruz: Bibliografía y biblioteca* by Emilio Abreu Gómez, 1934.

Critical Studies: "Some Obscure Points in the Life of Sor Juana Inés de la Cruz" by Dorothy Schons, in *Modern Philology*, 24, 1926; *La santificación de Sor Juana Inés de la Cruz* by Genaro Fernández MacGregor, 1932; *Vida de Sor Juana* by P. Diego Calleja, 1936; *La ruta de Sor Juana*, 1938, and *Semblanza de Sor Juana*, 1938, by Emilio Abreu Gómez; *Sor Juana Inés de la Cruz* by Clara Carilla, 1944; *Sor Juana Inés de la Cruz: Poetisa de corte y convento* by Elizabeth Wallace, 1944; *Juana de Asbaje* by Amado Nervo, 1946; *Cuatro documentos relativos a Sor Juana* by Lota Spell, 1947; "The Tenth Muse of America" by Alfonso Reyes in *The Position of America*, 1950; *Razón y pasión de Sor Juana* by Anita Arroyo, 1952; *Sor Juana Inés de la Cruz* by Patricia Cox, 1958; *Sor Juana Inés de la Cruz: Claro en la selva* by C.G. de Gullarte, 1958; *Baroque Times in Old Mexico* by Leonard Irving, 1959; "A Revision of the Philosophy of Sor Juana Inés de la Cruz," in *Hispania*, 43, 1960, "The Alleged Mysticism of Sor Juana Inés de la Cruz," in *Hispanic Review*, 28(3), 1960, "The *Primero sueño* of Sor Juana Inés de la Cruz: A Revision of the Criticism," in *Revista Iberoamericana de Literatura*, 15, 1965, and *Sor Juana Inés de la Cruz*, 1971, all by Gerard C. Flynn; *Sor Juana Inés de la Cruz: La décima musa de México* by Ludwig Pfandl, translated by Juan Antonio Ortega y Medina, 1963; *Genio y figura de Sor Juana Inés de la Cruz* by Ramón Xirau, 1967; *Autos sacramentales de Sor Juana Inés de la Cruz* by Sergio Fernández, 1970; "Human and Divine Love in the Poetry of Sor Juana Inés de la Cruz" by Arthur Terry, in *Studies in Spanish Literature of the Golden Age*, 1973; *Del encausto a la sangre: Sor Juana Inés de la Cruz* by Mirta Aguirre, 1975; *Lo americano en el teatro de Sor Juana Inés de la Cruz* by María E. Pérez, 1975; *Juana de Asbaje: Aproximación a la autobiografía de la Décima Musa* by Carlos E. Galeano Ospina, 1976; *El Sueño de Sor Juana Inés de la Cruz: Tradiciones literarias y originalidad* by Georgina Sabat de Rivers, 1977; "The Tenth Muse," in *Americas*, 30(2), 1978, and "Sor Juana Inés de la Cruz: Let Your Women Keep Silence in the Churches," in *Women's Studies in International Forum*, 5(8), 1985, both by Nina M. Scott; *Sor Juana Inés de la Cruz ante la historia* by Francisco de la Maza and Elías Trabulse, 1980, and *El hermetismo y Sor Juana Inés de la Cruz: Orígenes e interpretación* by Trabulse, 1980; *Virtue or Vice?: Sor Juana's Use of Thomistic Thought* by Constance M. Montross, 1981; "Sor Juana Inés de la Cruz Speaking the Mother Tongue," in *University of Dayton Review*, 16(2), 1983, and "The Convent as a Catalyst for Autonomy: Two Hispanic Nuns of the Seventeenth Century," in *Women in Hispanic Literature: Icons and Fallen Idols* edited by Beth Miller, 1983, and "This Life Within Me Won't Keep Still," in *Reinventing the Americas* edited by Bell Gale Chevigny and Gari Laguardia, 1986, all by Electra Arenal; "Hermetic Traditions in Sor Juana's *Primero sueño*" by Manuel Durán, in *University of Dayton Review*, 16(2), 1983; *Sor Juana Inés de la Cruz; o, Las trampas de la Fe* by Octavio Paz, 1982, as *Sor Juana; or, The Traps of Faith*, translated by Margaret Sayers Peden, 1988; *Plotting Women: Gender and Representation in Mexico* by Jean Franco, 1989; *Feminist Perspectives on Sor Juana Inés de la Cruz* edited by Stephanie Merrim, 1991; *Juana Inés de la Cruz and the Theology of Beauty* by George H. Tavard, 1991; *Sor Juana Inés de la Cruz: Religion, Art, and Feminism* by Pamela Kirk, 1998; *Early Modern Women's Writing and Sor Juana Inés de la Cruz* by Stephanie Merrim, 1999.

* * *

Sor Juana Inés de la Cruz has been hailed as the first great writer of Spanish America, and has been compared to Anne Bradstreet (1612–71), her New England contemporary whose poetry became one of the first literary landmarks of North America. That two such powerful writers in the New World of the 17th century should have been women has been the focus of feminist critical attention, especially since both wrote immensely personal poetry, and both questioned the subservient role of women generally accepted at the time.

Sor Juana was well-educated, and claims that her desire to study was a powerful motivating force from the age of barely three. She claimed to have pressed her mother to allow her to attend university in Mexico City dressed as a boy (women were not allowed to study at universities in the colonies). She became a nun in order to "live alone and avoid obligations that would disturb my freedom to study," even though she acknowledged that there would be aspects of convent life with which she might find it difficult to cope. She seems to have been a rebel all her life, refusing to accept easy solutions, writing, despite the misgivings of powerful members of the clergy, and searching for ways to express her radical views on the role of women in the world. Jean Franco has examined Sor Juana's attempts to move beyond gender, to escape from the limitations of a society structured along binary oppositions of male and female, in which the female was the subordinate partner. As a nun, she claimed to be outside sexual difference, and her poem *Primero sueño* (*Dream*), which she said was her only work written just for herself, is the metaphysical journey of a soul which, in dream, is set free from the constraints of gender categorization.

Most of her work (all of it, she claimed, in her autobiographical *La respuesta a Sor Filotea de la Cruz*, translated as *A Woman of Genius: The Intellectual Biography of Sor Juana Inés de la Cruz*), was written for specific purposes, at the request of a patron, or to celebrate a certain event. Her earliest poems were dedicated to the Viceroy's wife; a number of poems were written for religious or viceregal holidays; and she wrote ballads, songs, carols and poems on religious themes. Her play *Los empeños de una casa* (*The House of Trials*) was performed in 1683 for the Viceroys. Her later play, generally considered to be a masterpiece, *El divino Narciso* (*Divine Narcissus*) was written in 1688 and performed in Madrid the following year. At this time Sor Juana was at the height of her fame, but in 1690 the antagonism felt for her by some of the bishops reached crisis point. Sor Juana's interpretation of the Bible had a very definite slant: she consistently praised the virtues of heroic female figures, not only Mary and Mary Magdalene and the women of the New Testament, but powerfully symbolic women such as Esther, Rebecca, Deborah, and Judith. Her criticism of the Jesuit Father Vieyra's Maundy Thursday sermon, intended for private circulation only, was published without her consent by the Bishop of Puebla using the pseudonym of Sor Filotea under the title of *Carta atenagórica* [Letter Worthy of Athene]. The publication of this text caused a scandal, as did her reply that appeared three months later, *A Woman of Genius*. The effect of this crisis was a desperate one for Sor Juana: publicly humiliated and rebuked by the Church authorities, she was devastated by what she saw as an act of treachery by the Bishop of Puebla in publishing a private document. Although a new edition of her poems came out in 1689 (the *Inundación castálida*), and her religious *autos* were published in 1692 (see [Works], 3 vols., 1691–1700), she dismantled her library, and in 1694 again took her vows as a nun, to proclaim symbolically her decision to live under a new austerity. In 1695 she died during a plague epidemic.

The end of Sor Juana's writing career was poignant one. After a lifetime of struggle, during which she had asserted her voice with a power unique in the Americas—and in the Spanish-speaking world as a whole—she was finally silenced by the very forces of repressive authoritarianism against which she had fought. In *A Woman of Genius* she comments bitterly on how her desire to learn and to write "led me closer to the flames of persecution," declaring that never again would she speak out to defend herself. The dismantling of her personal library was a potent sign of her decision to choose silence in the face of overt hostility from her religious superiors.

The emotive details of Sor Juana's biography, and the fascination that the content of her works has for today's readers, has meant that less attention has been paid to the skills of her poetic technique. Influenced by Góngora and the Golden Age writers, Sor Juana can be described as a Baroque lyricist, whose use of rhyme, rhythm, and imagery distinguish her as a particularly gifted poet. Octavio Paz claims that Quevedo and Lope de Vega were ultimately greater writers, but that what makes Sor Juana's writing unique is the combination of passion and conscience, of dynamic energy and a questing soul. We might add to that the tragic conflict between a mind that wanted to explore the universe and tried to do so through the pen, and the body of a woman in a nun's habit, firmly and constrictingly located in the world of a 17th-century colonial convent.

—Susan Bassnett

JÜNGER, Ernst

Born: Heidelberg, Germany, 29 March 1895. **Education:** Educated at Lyceum II, 1901–05, Hanover Internaten, Hanover and Braunschweig, 1905–07; studied biology in Leipzig and Naples, 1923–26. **Military Service:** Joined the French Foreign Legion, 1913, brought back home by his father; volunteer with the German army during World War I, served on the Western Front, 1914–18; captain during World War II, discharged 1944. **Family:** Married 1) Gretha

von Jeinsen in 1925 (died 1960), two sons (one deceased); 2) Liselotte Lohrer in 1962. **Career:** Officer in the Reichswehr, 1919–23; contributor to radical right-wing journals including *Standarte, Arminius, Widerstand,* and *Der Vormarsch,* 1925–31; moved to Berlin, 1927; freelance writer from 1927; lived in Goslar, 1933–36; Überlingen, 1936–39; Kirchhorst, 1939–48; Revensburg, 1948–50; and Wilfingen, from 1950; banned from publishing his work in 1945; ban lifted, 1949; travelled extensively in the 1950s and 1960s; co-editor of the journal *Antaios,* 1959–71. **Awards:** Culture prize (Goslar), 1955; City of Bremen prize, 1955; literary prize of the Federal League of German Industry, 1960; Immermann prize (Düsseldorf), 1965; Humbolt Society gold medal, 1981, Goethe prize, 1982; Accademia Casentinese, Dante Alighieri International prize, 1987; Tevere Intern prize, 1987. Honorary Doctorate: University of Bilbao, Spain. Great Order of Merit, Federal Republic of Germany, 1959. **Died:** 17 February 1998 in Wilflingen, Germany.

Publications

Fiction

In Stahlgewittern: Aus dem Tagebuch eines Stosstruppführers. 1920; as *The Storm of Steel: From the Diary of a German Storm-Troop Officer on the Western Front,* translated by Basil Creighton, 1929.

Das Wäldchen 125: Eine Chronik aus den Grabenkämpfen 1918. 1925; as *Copse 125: A Chronicle from the Trench Warfare of 1918,* translated by Basil Creighton, 1930.

Afrikanische Spiele. 1936; as *African Diversions,* translated by Stuart Hood, 1954.

Auf den Marmorklippen. 1939; as *On the Marble Cliffs,* translated by Stuart Hood, 1947.

Heliopolis: Rückblick auf eine Stadt. 1949.

Besuch auf Godenholm (stories). 1952.

Gläserne Bienen. 1957; revised edition, 1960; as *The Glass Bees,* translated by Louise Bogan and Elizabeth Mayer, 1961.

Sturm. 1963.

Die Zwille. 1973.

Eumeswil. 1977; translated by Joachim Neugroschel, 1993.

Aladins Problem. 1983; as *Aladdin's Problems,* translated by Joachim Neugroschel, 1993.

Eine gefährliche Begegnung. 1985.

Other

Der Kampf als inneres Erlebnis. 1922.

Feuer und Blur: Ein kleiner Ausschnitt aus einer grossen Schlacht. 1925.

Das abenteuerliche Herz: Aufzeichnungen bei Tag und Nacht (essays). 1929.

Die totale Mobilmachung. 1931.

Hier spricht der Feind. 1931.

Der Arbeiter: Herrschaft und Gestalt. 1932.

Blätter und Steine (essays). 1934.

Geheimnisse der Sprache: Zwei Essays. 1934.

Lob der Vokale. 1937.

Gärten und Strassen: Aus den Tagebüchern von 1939 und 1940 (diaries). 2 vols., 1942.

Myrdun: Briefe aus Norwegen. 1943.

Der Friede: Ein Wort an die Jugend Europas, ein Wort an die Jugend der Welt. 1945; as *The Peace*, translated by Stuart Hood, 1948.

Atlantische Fahrt: Nur für Kriegsgefangene gedruckt (diaries). 1947.

Sprache und Körperbau. 1947; revised edition, 1949.

Ein Inselfrühling: Ein Tagebuch aus Rhodos. 1948.

Strahlungen (diary). 1949.

Über die Linie. 1950.

Das Haus der Briefe. 1951.

Am Kieselstrand. 1951.

Der Waldgang. 1951.

Drei Kiesel. 1952.

Der gordische Knoten. 1953.

Ernst Jünger: Eine Auswahl, edited by Arnim Mohler. 1953.

Das Sanduhrbuch. 1954.

Geburtstagsbrief: Zum 4. November 1955. 1955.

Die Herzmuschel. 1955.

Sonnentau: Pflanzenbilder. 1955.

Am Sarazenenturm (on Sardinia). 1955.

Die Schleife, Dokumente zum Weg. 1955.

Rivarol. 1956.

Serpentara. 1957.

San Pietro. 1957.

Jahre der Okkupation (diary). 1958.

Mantrana. 1958.

An der Zeitmauer. 1959.

Der Weltstaat: Organismus und Organisation. 1960.

Ein Vormittag in Antibes. 1960.

Sgraffiti (essays). 1960.

Werke. 10 vols., 1960–65.

Das spanische Mondhorn. 1962.

Fassungen. 1963.

An Friedrich Georg zum 65. Geburtstag. 1963.

Typus, Name, Gestalt. 1963.

Grenzgänge (essays). 1966.

Subtile Jagden (essays). 1967.

Im Granit (on Corsica). 1967.

Zwei Inseln: Formosa, Ceylon. 1968.

Federbälle. 1969.

Annäherungen: Drogen und Rausch. 1970.

Lettern und Ideogramme (on Japan). 1970.

Ad Hoc (essays). 1970.

Sinn und Bedeutung: Ein Figurenspiel (essays). 1971.

Zahlen und Götter. Philemon und Baucis: Zwei Essays. 1974.

Eine Begegnung: acht Abbildungen nach Zeichungen und Briefen von Ernst Jünger und Alfred Kubin. (correspondence). 1975.

Sämtlichte Werke. 18 vols., 1978–83.

Siebzig verweht (diary). 2 vols., 1980–81.

Flugträume (selections). 1983.

Autor und Autorschaft. 1984.

Die Schere. 1990.

Editor, *Aufmarsch des Nationalismus.* 1926.

Editor, *Die Unvergessenen.* 1928.

Editor, *Das Antlitz des Weltkrieges.* 1930.

Editor, *Krieg und Krieger.* 1930.

Editor, *Luftfahrt ist not!* 1930.

Editor, *Der feurige Weg*, by Franz Schauwecker. 1930.

Editor, *Der Kampf um das Reich.* 1931.

*

Bibliography: *Ernst Jünger: Eine Bibliographie* by Karl O. Paetel, 1953; *Bibliographie der Werke Ernst Jüngers* by Hans Peter des Coudres, 1970.

Critical Studies: *Ernst Jünger: A Writer of Our Time* by J.P. Stern, 1953; *Ernst Jünger* by Heinz Ludwig Arnold, 1966; *Ernst Jünger* by Wolfgang Kaempter, 1981; *Ernst Jünger and the Nature of Political Commitment* by Roger Woods, 1982; *Ernst Jünger: Leben und Werk in Bildern und Texten* edited by Heimo Schwilk, 1988; *Ernst Jünger* by Martin Meyer, 1990; *Ernst Jünger's Visions and Revisions on the European Right* by Marcus Paul Bullock, 1992; *The Details of Time: Conversations with Ernst Jünger* by Julien Hervier, translated by Joachim Neugroschel, 1995; *Ernst Jünger and Germany: Into the Abyss, 1914–1945* by Thomas Nevin, 1996; *A Dubious Past: Ernst Jünger and the Politics of Literature after Nazism* by Elliot Y. Neaman, 1999.

* * *

Ernst Jünger is not only German's longest-lived author, but also one of its most controversial literary figures. Considered to have been among the leading, most innovative, and most productive writers of the country's intellectual and political right in his earlier years, in mid-career he assumed the position of an iconoclast and an inhabitant of the proverbial ivory tower without, however, completely eschewing his earlier political and philosophical convictions. Distancing himself from the tenents and practices of National Socialism prior to and during the years of the Third Reich, he nonetheless did not espouse a very strong and open anti-Nazi stance, preferring the status of a not always clearly defined ''Inner Emigration'' to that of the Nazi opposition in exile. His later years are highlighted by extensive travels and keen stylistic and thematic experimentations in his literary endeavours.

An adventurer at heart who not merely fantasized about the outer limits of human existence in his fiction but actively sought to experience such situations and encounters throughout his life, Jünger combines the pursuits and experiences of the soldier/warrior with those of the investigator, researcher, and traveller in a fashion that betrays an intellectuality rooted in the Renaissance. Deeply steeped in the German classical intellectual tradition, yet also influenced by French moralism, his plots and themes deal not just with past and present settings and conditions, but imaginatively conjure up futuristic developments. His style can be said to have varied from ''heroic realism'' via surrealism to aberrant sado-masochism in his fiction. His extensive essayistic work, on the other hand, displays a stylistic lucidity which stands in sharp contrast to the enigmatic prose of Heidegger, a philosopher with whom Jünger engaged in a lively intellectual exchange of ideas for many years.

Jünger's work can be roughly divided into three segments, irrespective of the chronology involved. The perhaps most basic part of it, underlying the other two, is thematically guided by his war-time experiences from 1915 to 1918 and his post-war political convictions issuing therefrom and extending into World War II and beyond. It includes *In Stahlgewittern* (*The Storm of Steel*), *Das Wäldchen 125* (*Copse 125*), *Der Kampf als inneres Erlebnis* [Fighting as an Inner Experience], *Feuer und Blut* [Fire and Blood], *Die totale Mobilmachung* [Total Mobilization], Der Friede (*The Peace*), and *Der Weltstaat* [The

World State]. This segment reflects both the impact of World War I on his thinking and the reverberations of the experiences he gathered during and after World War II. The central core of his *oeuvre* consists of fiction. The principal works represented in this part are *Afrikanische Spiele* (*African Diversions*), *Auf den Marmorklippen* (*On the Marble Cliffs*), *Heliopolis*, *Gläserne Bienen* (*The Glass Bees*), *Eumeswil*, and *Eine gefährliche Begegnung* [A Dangerous Meeting]. Although these works also incorporate personal experience and philosophical constructs, they are primarily imaginative literature intent on both entertaining the reader and provoking his intellectual, if not visceral, reaction to themes of supreme interest to the author himself. The third part of his writings deals with nonpolitical observations, travel experiences, and investigations that occupy a middle ground between scientific enquiry and innermost reflections. Examples of this type of writing, though interspersed in and throughout his *oeuvre*, are principally *Das abenteuerliche Herz, Geheimnisse der Sprache, Sprache und Körperbau, Sgraffiti; Sonnentau: Pflanzenbilder*, and *Annäherungen: Drogen und Rausch.*

The Storm of Steel is not only the trend setter in Jünger's largest segment of writings with monographic leanings but also the work that established his national and international reputation. Written in diary form and covering his own war experiences from 1915 to 1918, the book gives an inside view of the plight and the glory of the soldier in modern warfare without, however, passing judgement on the moral dilemma it generates. Subsequent works—such as *Copse 125, Der Kampf als inneres Erlebnis,* and *Feuer und Blut*—deal with the same basic experiences and sentiments in a more systematic and deliberate manner. In *Der Kampf als inneres Erlebnis*, Jünger celebrates war as the expression of an elementary natural force. He puts this metaphysical sublimation of warfare on a more expansive philosophical and political basis in his treatise *Die totale Mobilmachung*. This work, in effect, advocates the total mobilization of society for total warfare. However, a complete reversal of attitude brought about the certainty of Germany's inevitable defeat in World War II is voiced in the treatise *Der Friede*. Jünger wrote this essay in secret at the height of Nazi power, and circulated it among friends for commentary. Field Marshal Envin Rommel, an avowed enemy of Hitler's military adventurism, saw it as an ethical basis for resistance to the Nazi regime. The two-part document not only envisages the achievement of a just and equitable peace, but also develops a political programme along philosophical lines that might serve as a guideline for both Europe and the world to avoid future conflicts. Nearly two decades later, Jünger wrote a sequel to *Der Friede*. He called it *Der Weltstaat: Organismus und Organisation*. In this work he envisages a world state that is no longer a source of external or internal conflict, as previous nation states had been, but a guarantor of a just, organic, and moral mode of human existence, freed from the coercive forces of organization.

Jünger's fiction is highlighted by two novels, *On the Marble Cliff* and *Heliopolis*. In contrast to his earlier narrative *African Diversions* which took many of its cues from his youthful excursion into Africa while attempting to join the Foreign Legion, *On the Marble Cliffs* is an abstract, surrealistic novel in a timeless setting that not only has futuristic and mythic features, but also reflects contemporary scenarios. Although the peaceful life of contemplation and pursuit of botanical and linguistic studies proves illusory to the anonymous narrator and his brother Otho in a belligerent human world bent on self-destruction, the brothers can escape annihilation and may be able to re-establish themselves at a distant shore. This novel with its thinly

veiled references to the political power struggles in Germany in the 1920s and 1930s has been hailed as an exemplary work of the "Inner Emigration," a loose movement of writers remaining in Germany during the Nazi era and criticizing the regime in symbolic and allegorical form. *Heliopolis*, by contrast, is a clearly futuristic novel in which man's possible future development is outlined in a highly politicized and philosophical fashion. The city-state Heliopolis is an imaginary place postdating the era of the second nihilism and that of the global workers' state. Yet it has not achieved internal peace. As in *On the Marble Cliffs*, dialectically opposed political forces, representing the opposite world views of technological perfection and human perfectibility, vie for political dominance. Although the novel's protagonist, Lucius de Geer, whose personal characteristics reflect Jünger's own, fails in his political undertakings on the side of humanist causes, he gains intellectually and spiritually. His celebration of free will and altruistic individualism and his rejection of collectivism and the heartless worship of power again betray Jünger's changed world-view in his maturing years. Later fiction, principally represented in *The Glass Bees* and *Eumeswil*, deals further with the ideas expounded in *Heliopolis*, albeit in more limited and less universal settings. Jünger's later novel, *Eine gefährliche Begegnung*, however, is a more traditional work that takes the reader back into the Paris of the late 19th century and the sensuality, intrigues, murderous plots, superficiality, and decadence of an epoch that in many ways reflects our own.

Jünger's reflective and pseudo-scientific writings, while basically also experiential, differ from his previously categorized works not only in content but also in style. They are stylistically more diverse than those dealing with his war-time experiences and their imprints in his intellectual and political psyche. What is most significant, however, is the fact that this body of writing is also endowed with a Goethean inclination toward the universal. The two most interesting works in this segment are *Das abenteuerliche Herz* [The Adventurous Heart] and *Annäherungen: Drogen und Rausch* [Approach: Drugs and Intoxication]. While *Das abenteuerliche Herz*, a collection of essays, was in its original version still very much influenced by his World War I experiences, Jünger's intention went from the very outset beyond the merely adventurous. His aim was both internal and external. Internally he meant to convey impressions of a more personal nature. Externally—and this became the overriding intent in the revised edition of the work—he aimed to discuss the whole gamut of the organic life of man, animal, and plant, a Goethean undertaking. In contrast to *Sgraffiti*, a volume of essays patterned after *Das abenteuerliche Herz* and an obvious sequel to this work, *Annäherungen: Drogen und Rausch* is a book about mind-altering drugs and their effect on the human psyche. Although Jünger experimented with drugs throughout his adult life, he was, unlike some of his literary predecessors in this area such as Thomas De Quincey, Charles Baudelaire, and Edgar Allan Poe, never an addict. The experimentation was another one of his attempts to penetrate the innermost core of his psyche.

This last discussed work in particular makes it clear that Jünger was basically a neo-Romantic at heart who was constantly journeying to and probing the higher as well as the innermost regions of both his consciousness and his intellect. This overwhelming urge on his part also helps to explain his argumentative, essayistic, observational, reflective, and speculative style, which defies easy labelling and categorization. His proto-fascist political leanings early in life have done much harm to his later reception. His contribution to literature and thought has consequently been vastly underrated, and his reputation as a major writer in 20th-century German, indeed world, literature appears to be in need of a revision.

—Carl Steiner

JUVENAL

Born: Decimus Junius Juvenalis, c. AD 50–65, or perhaps later. Possibly native of Aquinum. **Career:** Wrote his *Satires* under Trajan and Hadrian. May have been wealthy; does not mention a patron. Accounts of his army career and exile by Domitian have no foundation. Mentioned by Martial, and was acquainted with him, otherwise not well-known in his own lifetime. **Died:** after AD 130.

PUBLICATIONS

Works

[Satires], edited by A.E. Housman. 1931; also edited by W.V. Clausen (with satires by Persius), 1959, revised edition, 1992, J.D. Duff, 1970, and John Ferguson (with commentary), 1979; 1, 3, and 10 edited by Niall Rudd and Edward Courtney, 1977; edited and translated by G.G. Ramsey [Loeb Edition], 1918, revised edition, 1940; translated by John Dryden and others, 1735, reprinted 1979; also translated by T. Sheridan, 1739; Edward Owen, 2 vols., 1785; F. Hodgson, 1807; Charles Badham, 1814; James Sinclair, 1814; Lewis Evans, 1848; T.J. Arnold and R. Mongan, 1889; W. Gifford, 1906; Rolfe Humphries, 1958; Hubert Creekmore, 1963; Jerome Mazzaro, 1965; Peter Green, 1967; Charles Plumb, 1968; Steven Robinson, 1983; Niall Rudd, 1991; *13 Satires*, translated by J.E.B. Mayor, 1872–78; also translated by H.A. Strong and A. Leeper, 1882; Sidney G. Owen, 1903; commentary by J.E.B. Mayor (omits 2, 6, and 9), 2 vols., 1880–81, and J.D. Duff, 1898 (omits 2, 9, and selected passages).

*

Critical Studies: *The Grand Style in the Satires of Juvenal* by I.G. Smith, 1927; *Juvenal the Satirist*, 1954, and *The Anatomy of Satire*, 1962, both by Gilbert Highet; *Post-Augustan Poetry from Seneca to Juvenal* by Harold E. Butler, 1977; *Irony in Juvenal* by Alba Claudia Romano, 1979; *A Study of Juvenal's Tenth Satire* by E. Tengström, 1980; *Essays on Roman Satire* by William S. Anderson, 1982; *Three Classical Poets: Sappho, Catullus, and Juvenal* by Richard Jenkyns, 1982; *The Persona in Three Satires of Juvenal* by Martin M. Winkler, 1983; *Themes in Roman Satire* by Niall Rudd, 1986; *Juvenal and Boileau* by Robert C. Colton, 1987; *A Prosopography to the Poems of Juvenal* by John Ferguson, 1987; *The Imperial Muse: To Juvenal Through Ovid: Ramus Essays on Roman Literature of the Empire* edited by A.J. Boyle, 1988; *Beyond Anger: A Study of Juvenal's Third Book of Satires* by S.H. Braund, 1988; *The Satiric Voice: Program, Form and Meaning in Persius and Juvenal* by William Thomas Wehrle, 1992; *Figuring Out Roman Nobility: Juvenal's Eighth Satire* by John Henderson, 1997; *Satires of Rome: Threatening Poses from*

Lucilius to Juvenal by Kirk Freudenburg, 2001; *Juvenal in English*, edited by Martin M. Winkler, 2001.

*   *   *

Juvenal's entire *oeuvre* comprises 16 Satires in hexameters. They were published in five separate books during the reigns of the emperors Trajan and Hadrian.

In his first book (Satires 1–5) Juvenal adopts an indignant *persona*, following the convention of using a first-person mouthpiece expressing views not necessarily attributable to the poet himself. The angry man whose voice we hear in Book I was a type familiar to the Romans from philosophical works, for example, those of Seneca. As suits the angry man, the poems have the appearance of being a jumbled and excited outburst. Yet there is order behind the façade of disorder: Juvenal has arranged the poems in an alternating sequence featuring the patron-client relationship perverted by mercenary preoccupations (Satires 1, 3, and 5) and the corrupt nobility as a canker at the heart of Roman society (Satires 2 and 4). The satiric technique invites us to agree with the angry rantings *and* to ridicule the angry man for his narrow-minded, petty, and vicious obsessions. The high epic tone adopted ought to dignify the attack on society but the intrusion of mundane and crude words and ideas deflates the pretensions of the angry *persona*. The "angry" approach proved to be Juvenal's most important legacy to, and influence on, later European satire.

The angry stance is maintained in Book II (Satire 6), a huge attack of epic proportions and unparalleled length in Roman satire on women, couched as a dissuasion from marriage. The angry man reveals himself as utterly unreasonable (e.g., he cannot stand even a perfect woman!) and hence absurd.

Juvenal has now exhausted the "angry" approach and in his remaining three books he adopts an ironic and detached *persona*. In the three poems of Book III Juvenal applies this new approach to the main themes of Book I, patrons and clients (Satires 7 and 9) and the nobility (Satire 8). The poems of Books IV and V feature a wide variety of topics: men's prayers (Satire 10), a simple meal (Satire 11), true and false friendship (Satire 12); anger and vengeance (Satire 13), parents' bad examples to their children (Satire 14), the quality of humanness (Satire 15), the advantages of the soldier's life (Satire 16, incomplete). These poems are reminiscent of Horace's satire, sharing his interest in friendship and moderation and his double-edged ironic approach. At the same time, Juvenal's abandonment of the early angry *persona* emerges clearly from Satire 13 where anger is explicitly condemned.

Complementing the variety of the *Satires*, there are characteristic features present throughout Juvenal's work. The *Satires* constantly reflect the rhetorical nature of Roman education. Rhetoric is Juvenal's idiom which he exploits brilliantly to produce many memorable epigrammatic phrases. He is clearly steeped in Roman literature: the poems are packed with literary allusions, and throughout Juvenal shows his debt to his predecessors in the genre, Lucilius, Horace, and Persius. In every poem, Juvenal's powers of vivid visualization are evident. He prefers to depict vice in the concrete rather than the abstract, ranging from brief vignettes of crooks or perverts sumptuously dressed to extended descriptions, for example of a subhuman act of cannibalism.

Finally, Juvenal's essential satiric technique may perhaps be encapsulated in the word "surprise." Throughout his poems, Juvenal springs on his audience surprise after surprise, revealing his great fund of wit and humour. On a large scale, it is impossible to predict the direction or proportions of a poem: Juvenal often links two unconnected topics to create surprise. On a smaller scale, he often saves for the end of a section or sentence or line an unexpected word or idea: deflating, pompous, witty, funny, or absurd. Particularly powerful are pithy juxtapositions like ''princess whore'' and ''muleteer consul.'' All such surprises were highly effective in the original context of oral recitation. In short, Juvenal exemplifies Feinberg's definition of satire as ''the playfully critical distortion of the familiar.''

—S.H. Braund

See the essay on ''Satire 10.''

K

KABĪR

Born: Varanasi Benares, Uttar Pradesh, India, 1398 (some sources give c. 1440). **Family:** Probably brought up by Muslim foster parents in a poor weaver's family. **Career:** Probably a devotee of Rām, and a preacher; influenced by Hindu and Muslim ideas, and Sufi mysticism. Exiled from Benares by the Muslim emperor, Sikandar Lōdī. Wrote devotional (*bhakti*) poetry, mainly in a Hindi dialect. His major texts exist in three major regional variants (recensions): Eastern (the *Bījak*), Rajasthani (*Kābir-Granthāvalī*), and Punjabi with Hindi (contained in the *Adi Granth*). **Died:** 1448 (some sources give 1518).

PUBLICATIONS

Verse

Bījak [Account]. 1868; 1872 (with "Trijya" commentary); edited by Prem Chand, 1890; also edited by Bābā Puran Dās, 1905, Ahmed Shah, 1911, Vicardas Shastri, 1926, Hamsdas Shastri and Mahabir Prasad ("standard" edition), 1950, and Shukdev Singh (critical edition), 1972; as *Bijak Satguru Kabīr Sāhab Kā*, 1982; as *Bijaka* (Hindi text, English commentary), 1987; as *Bijak*, translated by Prem Chand, 1911; also translated by Ahmad Shah, 1917; Linda Hess and Shukdev Singh, 1983; as *Kabīr*, translated by S.H. Jhabvala, 1955.

The Adi Granth (including Kabīr's Punjabi/Hindi verse), translated by E. Trumpp. 1877.

Granthāvalī [Complete Works]. Edited by S.S. Das, 3 vols., 1928; also edited by P.N. Tiwari, 1961, M.P. Gupta, 1969, and Dr. Syamasundravadasa, 1976; as *Kabīr*, translated by Charlotte Vaudeville, 1974.

One Hundred Poems of Kabīr, translated by Rabindranath Tagore, with Evelyn Underhill. 1914.

Kabīr the Great Mystic (selection), translated by Isaac A. Exekiel. 1966.

Couplets from Kabir (bilingual edition), translated by G.N. Das. 1991.

Songs of Kabir from the Adi Granth, translated by Nirmal Dass. 1991.

Love Songs of Kabir (bilingual edition), translated by G.N. Das. 1992.

Mystical Poems of Kabir, translation and commentary by Swami Rama and Robert B. Regli. 1990.

Touch of Grace: Songs of Kabir, translated by Linda Hess and Shukdev Singh. 1994.

Kabir: In the Light of Kriyayoga, translated and edited by Jogesh Chandra Bhattacharya. 1997.

Selected Couplets from the Sakhi in Transversion: 400-odd Verses in Iambic Tetrameter Stanza Form/Kabir, translated by Mohan Singh Karki. 2001.

Other

The Sayings of Kabir, edited and translated by Lala Kannoo Mal. 1923.

Maxims of Kabir by G.N. Das. 1999.

The Thirsty Fish: Kabir bhajans, translated by Sushil Rao. 2000.

*

Critical Studies: *Kabir and the Kabir Panth* by George H. Westcott, 1907, reprinted 1974; *A History of Hindi Literature*, 1920, and *Kabir and His Followers*, 1931, both by Frank E. Keay; *Kabīr* (includes translations) by Charlotte Vaudeville, 1974; *Kabir, the Apostle of Hindu-Muslim Unity* (with bibliography) by M. Hedayetullah, 1977; *Kabir's Mythology: The Religious Perceptions, Doctrines and Practices of a Medieval Saint*, 1985; *A Weaver Named Kabir: Selected Verses with a Detailed Biographical and Historical Introduction* by Charlotte Vaudeville, 1993; *A New Look at Kabir* by Krishna P. Bahadur, 1997; *The Dialogues of Kabir* by B.K. Narayan and Rajeev Sawhney, 1998; *Lord Kabir* by Sharan Malhotra, 2000.

* * *

Kabīr is perhaps the most representative figure of the monotheistic movement that characterized 15th-century India. According to legend, he was the son of a widowed Brahmin woman who abandoned him. Although he seems to have been adopted by a Muslim weaver, he later became the greatest of the disciples of the Vaiṣṇava *bhakti* teacher Rāmaānanda.

Kabīr's fame led to many legends, but unfortunately we lack reliable information about his life. Whether he was a Muslim or not, the influence of the Islamic doctrine in his sayings is undeniable. He calls himself "the son of Allah and Rāma," and his poetry shows an influence of the Vedantic doctrine; but his rejection of most Hindu rituals and Muslim traditions caused the hatred of the most conservative sector of the Indian society, the Brahmanic caste, as well as that of the Muslims. He is said to have been persecuted by the Muslim Emperor Sikandar Lōdī, who exiled him from Benares. All these events earned him the reputation of a bold social reformer, and his impact on the masses of Northern India was profound. Further evidence of Kabīr's influence is found in the Kabīrpanthīs, the religious sect whose members claim to be the followers of Kabīr's teaching and preserve the poems and sayings attributed to him.

Although a large number of works have been attributed to Kabīr, there is no certainty about the authorship of many of them. Kabīr's humble origin and the decisive aversion for the written word that we see in his poems may be an indication of his illiteracy. Therefore, and although there is no conclusive evidence, we may assume that his poems were written by his disciples. Kabīr's verses are found in four compilations. The *Bījak* [Account] was the first of Kabīr's works to attract the attention of Western scholars. The members of the Kabīrpanth compiled this book after the death of Kabīr, and considered it the most important and most representative of his doctrine. The *Granth* [Book], compiled at the beginning of the 17th century, became the sacred book of the Sikh religion. A large number of poems traditionally attributed to Kabīr are also found in the *Pamcvānīs*, a collection of sayings of the "five saints." The five saints or "*dādū-panthīs*" are the followers of a Muslim cotton-cleaner, Dādū Dayāl, who seems to owe his inspiration to the teaching of Kabīr. Finally, the *Sarbangī* is the work of Rajjab, Dādū Dayāl's most distinguished disciple. It contains an important collection of Kabīr's verses, but unfortunately it has never been published.

Kabīr may have spoken the old Avadhi dialect of Hindi, but his poems are chiefly preserved in mixed dialect. They are characterized by an extraordinary vigour; yet they are often rough and unpolished. The absence of any kind of literary ornament in Kabīr's poetry proves his contempt for the sacred Brahmanic language. The metrical forms in his poems, *dohās* and *padas*, are popular in origin. The *dohās* were lyrical compositions in popular dialects, which the common people used to sing or quote; the *padas* were short, rhymed poems, originally folksongs adapted to religious purposes. In the *Granth* collection the lyrical compositions are called *saloku* (Sanskrit *śloka*, verse); elsewhere, they are called *sākhīs* (or witnesses): they are pithy utterances, "witnesses" of the ultimate truth. All the main compilations of Kabīr's poems contain a large number of these pithy utterances; but he also makes use of a variety of metres. Although his verses contain numerous allusions to the common realities of daily life, the use of the Tantric language and symbols often render his poetry obscure. This deliberate contrast, and the simultaneous use of Hindu and Muslim references and vocabulary, is the result of his bitter irony, a proof of his sarcastic irreverence to traditional formalism as well as to Islamic and Hindu beliefs.

Kabīr's poems convey the spiritual turmoil that pervaded Northern India in the 15th century. This turmoil began to take place two centuries before, both in the Deccan and in Northern India, and coincided with the permanent establishment of Muslim domination in the subcontinent. The 15th century is also the period in which the modern vernaculars of India were taking shape, so it is not strange to see that Kabīr's language and style has played such an important role in the development of Hindi. Kabīr's monotheism was part of the religious revival which found manifestation in the cult of popular divinities such as Rāma and Kṛṣṇa, and all these religious movements used the vernacular for their literature. Kabīr's poetry evidently denounces the rigidity of the Hindu social system. However, his debt to Hindu tradition is undeniable, not only in the numerous allusions to Brahma or to Rāma, but also in the importance attached to the guru or spiritual leader, and particularly to the relationship between the guru and his disciple. Moreover, despite his attacks on the bigotry of Muslims, he was obviously influenced by Islamic monotheism as well as by the eclectic mysticism of Sufis.

Kabīr reflects the efforts of a number of religious movements in Northern India to advocate tolerance and unity. But his role as a unifier of the two conflicting religions, Islam and Hinduism, makes him appear as a holy man who stands alone. On the one hand, Kabīr voiced the aspirations of the common people; on the other, he was considered a danger both by Hindus and by Muslims for the vehemence with which he attacks their beliefs. Kabīr is conscious of the contradictions that he incurred, and his poetry can be read as a means of justifying the confrontation with society and with himself. He, "the slave of the spirit of the quest," as he calls himself in one of the poems translated by Tagore, confesses that "the true path is rarely found," and this is perhaps the principal message that the poet has left to posterity.

—Ana M. Ranero

KADARE, Ismail

Also known as Ismaïl Kadaré. **Pseudonym:** Gent Arbana. **Born:** Gjirokastra, Albania, 28 January 1936; emigrated to Paris, October 1990. **Education:** Primary and secondary school education in Gjirokastra; studied at the University of Tirana, 1953–58; graduated as a teacher of Albanian language and literature, 1958; post-graduate studies in Moscow at the Gorky Institute for World Literature, 1958–60. **Family:** Married Helena Gushi (writer Elena Kadare), two daughters. **Career:** After a break in political relations between the Soviet Union and China (with which Stalinist Albania had taken sides) in 1961, Kadare was forced to interrupt his studies in Russia and return to Albania, where he embarked upon a career as a professional writer; trip to China, 1967; period of internal exile in late 1970s; return to Tirana, 1978. **Awards:** Académie des Sciences Morales et Politiques, France, 1996; Officier de la Légion d'Honneur, France.

PUBLICATIONS

Collections

Komplete veprash. 1980.
Vepra letrare 1–12. 1981.
Vepra 1–10. 1993–2001.
Oeuvres 1–10. 1993–2000.

Fiction

Gjenerali i ushtrisë së vdekur—roman. 1963, 1967; as *The General of the Dead Army*, translated from the French by Derek Coltman, 1971, 1983, 1986, 1991.
Dasma—roman. 1968.
Kështjella—roman. 1970; as *The Castle*, translated by Pavli Qesku, 1974.
Kronikë në gur—roman. 1971; as *Chronicle in Stone*, 1987.
Dimri i vetmisë së madhe—roman. 1973.
Nëntori i një kryeqyteti—roman. 1975.
Dimri i madh, botim i tretë—roman. 1977.
Emblema e dikurshme: tregime e novella. 1977.
Ura me tri harqe: triptik me një intermexo. 1978; as *The Three-arched Bridge*, translated from the Albanian by John Hodgson, 1997.
Gjakftohtësia—novela. 1980.
Kush e solli Doruntinën, published in the volume *Gjakftohtësia*. 1980; as *Doruntine: A Novel*, translated by Jon Rothschild, 1988.
Prilli i thyer, published in the volume *Gjakftohtësia*. 1980; as *Broken April*, 1990.
Koha e shkrimeve—tregime, novela, përshkrime. 1986.
Krushqit janë të ngrirë, published in the volume *Koha e shkrimeve*. 1986; as *The Wedding Procession Turned to Ice*, translated from the Albanian by Robert Elsie in *Kosovo: In the Heart of the Powder Keg*, edited by Robert Elsie, 1997.
Koncert në fund të dimrit—roman. 1988; as *The Concert*, translated by Barbara Bray from the French by Jusuf Vrioni, 1994, 1998.
Dosja H—roman. 1990; as *The File on H*, translated by David Bellos from the French version by Jusuf Vrioni, 1997.
Ftesë në studio. 1990.
Ëndërr mashtruese—tregime e novela. 1991.

Nga një dhjetor në tjetrin—kronikë, këmbim letrash, persiatje. 1991; as *Albanian Spring: The Anatomy of Tyranny*, 1994.

Përbindëshi. 1991.

Pesha e kryqit. 1991.

Piramida—roman. 1995; as *The Pyramid*, translated by David Bellos from the French version by Jusuf Vrioni, 1996.

Dialog me Alain Bosquet. 1996.

Nëpunësi i pallati i ëndrrave—versioni përfundimtar. 1996; as *The Palace of Dreams*, translated by Barbara Bray from the French version by Jusuf Vrioni, 1993.

Shkaba—roman. 1996.

Spiritus—roman me kaos, zbulesë dhe çmërs. 1996.

Tri këngë zie për Kosovën. 1998; as *Three Elegies for Kosovo*, translated from the Albanian by Peter Constantine, 2000.

Ikja e shtergut. 1999.

Qorrfermani. 1999.

Ra ky mort e u pamë: ditar për Kosovën, artikuj, letra. 1999.

Vjedhja e gjumit mbretëror—tregime. 1999.

Kohë barbare: nga Shqipëria në Kosovë—biseda. 2000.

Lulet e ftohta të Marsit—roman. 2000.

Qyteti pa reklama—roman. 2001.

Unaza në kthetra—sprova letrare, shkrime të ndryshme, intervista. 2001.

Poetry

Shekulli im—vjersha dhe poema. 1961.

Përse mendohen këto male—vjersha dhe poema. 1964.

Vjersha dhe poema. 1969.

Poèmes, 1957–1997 (French version by the author, Claude Durand, with Mira Meksi, Edmond Tupja, and Jusuf Vrioni). 1997.

*

Bibliography: *Kadare në gjuhët e botës* by Bashkim Kuçuku, 2001.

Critical Studies: "Subversion vs. Conformism: The Kadare phenomenon" by Arshi Pipa, in *Telos*, vol. 73, 1987; *Un rhapsode albanais: Ismail Kadaré* by Anne-Marie Mitchell, 1990; *Ismaïl Kadare: entretiens avec Eric Faye, en lisant en écrivant* and *Ismaïl Kadaré: Prométhée porte-feu* both by Eric Faye, 1991; *Mythologie am Werk: Kazantzakis, Andrif*, Kadare: eine vergleichende Untersuchung am besonderen Beispiel des Bauopfermotivs by Ardian Klosi, 1991; *Contemporary Albanian Literature* by Arshi Pipa, 1991; *Ismaïl Kadaré* by Fabien Terpan, 1992; *Présentation d'Ismail Kadaré* by Maurice Druon, 1993; *History of Albanian Literature* by Robert Elsie, 1995; *De Scanderbeg à Ismail Kadaré: propos d'histoire et de littérature albanaises* by Alexandre Zotos, 1997.

* * *

Ismail Kadare began his literary career with poetry but turned increasingly to prose, of which he soon became the undisputed master and by far the most popular writer of the whole of Albanian literature. Though he is not unadmired as a poet in Albania, his reputation and, in particular, his international reputation now rests entirely upon his prose.

Ismail Kadare's first major novel, and still one of his best known, was *Gjenerali i ushtrisë së vdekur* (*The General of the Dead Army*). It is the vision, or better nightmare, of an Italian general in the company of a laconic priest on a mission to Albania to recover the remains of his soldiers who had perished some twenty years earlier. After a revised Albanian edition in 1967, the French-language edition *Le général de l'armée morte*, laid the foundations for Kadare's renown abroad. The novel has been widely translated.

In the 1970s, Kadare turned increasingly to historical prose, a safer haven after the Cultural Revolution, and became an unrivalled master of the genre. The 244-page *Kështjella* (*The Castle*), a novel reminiscent of Dino Buzzati's *Il deserto dei Tatari* [The Tatar Steppe], 1940, takes us back to the 15th century, the age of the Albanian national hero Scanderbeg and, in carefully composed, minute detail, depicts the siege of a medieval Albanian fortress, symbolic of Albania itself, by the Turks during one of their numerous punitive expeditions to subdue the country. As in *The General of the Dead Army*, Albania is seen through the eyes of a foreigner, the Turkish pasha. Scanderbeg himself does not even appear in person. The allusion to political events of the 1960s as seen by many critics was not unintentional. In 1961, ties had been broken off with the mighty Soviet Union, and after the 1968 invasion of Czechoslovakia, the Albanian leaders felt the very real possibility that the Soviets might try to use military force to bring the country back into the fold.

In the period of relative calm between the end of the Cultural Revolution in 1969 and the Purge of the Liberals in 1973, Ismail Kadare published one of his most impressive works: *Kronikë në gur* (*Chronicle in Stone*). This novel in eighteen chapters and an epilogue is the chronicle of the beautiful city of Gjirokastra in southern Albania under occupation during World War II.

Dimri i madh (The Great Winter) is a literary digestion of the traumatic rupture of relations with the Soviet Union, a novel of monumental historical and political dimensions. The harsh winter of 1960–61 was indeed a momentous one in post-war Albanian history. It was that year which marked the break between Nikita Khrushchev and Enver Hoxha and saw the definitive withdrawal of Albania from the Soviet sphere. The principal character of the novel is Besnik Struga, a Tirana journalist, who finds himself assigned to the Albanian delegation as an interpreter and who departs for Moscow as the first snows of the great winter descend over Eastern Europe. There he takes part in negotiations, receptions and secret high-level talks, experiencing political intrigue and power politics first hand. Kadare's portrait of Enver Hoxha, as one might expect, is somewhat flattering and strengthened his position as the Party's "writer in residence." Kadare later alleged that it was *The Great Winter* that ensured his physical survival. Enver Hoxha appreciated the portrait made of him in *The Great Winter* and did not wish to jeopardize it. Kadare's liquidation would have been incompatible with the survival of the novel.

With *Ura me tri harqe* (*The Three-Arched Bridge*), Kadare returns to the mythical fountainhead of Albania's haunted history to bring to life one of the most awesome motifs of Balkan legendry, that of immurement. The legend of a human being walled in during the construction of a bridge or castle is widespread in Albanian oral literature (cf. *The Tale of Rozafat Castle*) and is based no doubt on a reality. The novel has been interpreted as an Albanian response to Bosnian Serb Nobel prize winner Ivo Andrić's *Na Drini ćuprija* (*Bridge on the Drina*). Kadare is at his best with Balkan themes.

Prilli i thyer (*Broken April*), published in the volume *Gjakftohtësia*, begins with a murder in the 1930s. Gjorg Berisha has accomplished what all his family and relatives insisted he must do: cleanse his honour by slaying his brother's murderer from the rival Kryeqyqe clan. There was no way out of the bloody rituals of vendetta, anchored in the ancient Code of Lekë Dukagjini. Whole families had been wiped out in the "taking of blood" and now he, too, was obliged to follow suit, only to set himself up as the next victim.

Nëpunësi i pallatit të ëndrrave (*The Palace of Dreams*) is considered one of Kadare's masterpieces. It is the world of Franz Kafka and of George Orwell's *1984* set in the sybaritic, if somewhat torpid atmosphere of the Ottoman Empire. Mark-Alemi, scion of a noted family of public servants, is appointed to work at the Tabir Saraj, the awesome government office responsible for the study of sleep and dreams. It is his duty to analyse and categorize the dreams and nightmares of the Sultan's subjects and interpret them in order to enable the authorities to stifle any incipient rebellion and prevent criminal acts. It is a surprisingly humorous novel, though perhaps not entirely so for those who have lived in a totalitarian state. The analogy for the Albanians was more than evident.

In contrast to his many shorter novels of the period, Kadare's *Koncert në fund të dimrit* (*The Concert*) returns to the epic proportions of *Dimri i madh* with which it has many parallels. This 700-page chronicle offers the reader here a monumental review of Albania's dramatic break with post-Maoist China in 1978.

In the novel *Dosja H* (*The File on H*), two fictive Irish-American scholars, Max Roth and Willy Norton, set off for the isolated mountains of pre-war northern Albania, tape recorder in hand, in search of the homeland of the epic. The two folklorists are intent on investigating the possibility of a direct link between Homeric verse and the heroic songs sung by the Albanian mountaineers on their one-stringed *lahutas*. *The File on H* is a delightful satire on two innocent foreigners endeavouring to fathom the Albanian soul and, in particular, on the foibles of Albanian life at which foreign visitors often marvel: the Balkan love of rumours and gossip, administrative incompetence, and a childish fear or suspicion on the part of the authorities of everything foreign. By placing his tale in the 1930s once again, Kadare was able to take a safe sideswipe at his country's isolationist proclivities and at the bungling interference of the security apparatus in all spheres of contemporary life.

The novel *Piramida* (*The Pyramid*), is an historical and political allegory that is set in ancient Egypt. The pyramid was, of course, the huge "Enver Hoxha Museum" erected on the main boulevard of Tirana. Like so many of the Albanian writer's works, this novel can only be understood properly if read as a political allegory. *The Pyramid* is the mind-boggling tale of the conception and construction of the Cheops pyramid in ancient Egypt, but also of absolute political power and indeed of human folly. The Egyptian masses set to work on an absurd construction in the desert, just as four and a half millennia after them, the Albanian people set to work on the building of literally hundreds of thousands of cement bunkers throughout the country to defend themselves against a supposedly imminent imperialist invasion, and on the construction of a marble mausoleum for their own pharaoh.

Ismail Kadare's talents both as a poet and as a prose writer have lost none of their innovative force over the last four decades. His courage in attacking literary mediocrity within the system brought a breath of fresh air to Albanian culture during the long years of the Stalinist dictatorship (1944–90). Kadare was privileged by the authorities, in particular once his works became known internationally. Indeed, he was able to pursue literary and personal objectives for which other writers would certainly have been sent into internal exile or to prison. But Kadare knew well that liberties in communist Albania could be withdrawn easily, by a stroke of the tyrant's quill,

and had to tread carefully at times. However, there is no doubt that he used his 'relative' freedom and his talent under the Stalinist dictatorship to launch many a subtle attack against the regime in the form of political allegories which occur throughout his works. Kadare was the most prominent representative of Albanian literature under the dictatorship of Enver Hoxha and, at the same time, its most talented adversary. His works were extremely influential throughout the 1970s and 1980s and, for many readers, he was the only ray of hope in the cold, grey prison that was communist Albania. Though some observers in Albania silently viewed him as a political opportunist and many Albanians in exile later criticized him vociferously for the compromises he made, it is Ismail Kadare more than anyone else who, from within the system, dealt the deathblow to the literature of Albanian socialist realism.

At the end of October 1990, a mere two months before the final collapse of the dictatorship, Kadare left Tirana and applied for political asylum in France. His departure enabled him, for the first time, to exercise his profession with complete freedom. His years of Parisian exile have been productive and have accorded him further success and recognition, both as a writer in Albanian and in French. He has published his collected works in ten thick volumes, each in an Albanian-language and a French-language edition, and has been honoured with membership in the prestigious Académie Française.

—Robert Elsie

KAFKA, Franz

Born: Prague, Austro-Hungarian Empire (now Czech Republic), 3 July 1883. **Education:** Educated at Staatsgymnasium, Prague, 1893–1902; studied jurisprudence at Karl Ferdinand University, Prague, 1901–06, qualified in law, 1907; unpaid work in law courts, 1906–07. **Family:** Engaged to Felice Bauer twice but never married. **Career:** Worked for Assicurazioni Generali insurance company, 1907–08; Workers Accident Insurance Institute, 1908–22: developed tuberculosis, 1917, confined to a sanatorium, 1920–21, retired because of ill health. **Died:** 3 June 1924.

PUBLICATIONS

Collections

Gesammelte Werke, edited by Max Brod and others. 11 vols., 1950–.
Sämtliche Erzählungen, edited by Paul Raabe. 1970.
Complete Stories, edited by Nahum N. Glatzer. 1971.
Shorter Works, edited and translated by Malcolm Pasley. 1973.
The Complete Novels, translated by Edwin and Willa Muir. 1983.
Schriften, Tagebücher, Briefe, edited by Nahum N. Glatzer and others. 1983–.
Collected Stories, edited by Gabriel Josipovici, translated by Edwin Muir. 1993.
The Metamorphosis and Other Stories, translated by Joachim Neugroschel. 1993.
Best Short Stories: Die schönsten Erzählungen: A Dual-language Book, edited and translated by Stanley Appelbaum. 1997.

Fiction

Betrachtung. 1913.

Der Heizer: ein Fragment. 1913.

Die Verwandlung. 1915; edited by Peter Hutchinson and Michael Minden, 1985; as *The Metamorphosis*, translated by A.L. Lloyd, 1937; also edited and translated by Stanley Corngold, 1972.

Das Urteil. 1916.

In der Strafkolonie. 1919; as *In the Penal Settlement: Tales and Short Prose Works*, translated by Ernst Kaiser and Eithne Wilkins, 1949.

Ein Landarzt. 1919; as *A Country Doctor*, translated by Kevin Blahut, 1997.

Ein Hungerkünstler (stories). 1924.

Der Prozess. 1925; edited by Malcolm Pasley, 1990; as *The Trial*, translated by Edwin and Willa Muir, 1937, revised edition, 1956; also translated by Douglas Scott and Chris Waller, 1977.

Das Schloss. 1926; as *The Castle*, translated by Edwin and Willa Muir, 1930; revised edition, 1953; translated with preface by Mark Harman, 1998.

Amerika. 1927; original version, as *Der Verschollene*, edited by Jost Schillemeit, 1983; as *America*, translated by Edwin and Willa Muir, 1938.

Beim Bau der chinesischen Mauer. 1931; as *The Great Wall of China, and Other Pieces*, translated by Edwin and Willa Muir, 1933.

Parables in German and English, translated by Edwin and Willa Muir. 1947.

The Penal Colony, Stories and Short Pieces, translated by Edwin and Willa Muir. 1948.

Wedding Preparations in the Country and Other Stories, translated by Ernst Kaiser and Eithne Wilkins. 1953.

Dearest Father: Stories and Other Writings, translated by Ernst Kaiser and Eithne Wilkins. 1954.

Metamorphosis and Other Stories, translated by Edwin and Willa Muir. 1961.

Parables and Paradoxes: Parabeln und Paradoxe (bilingual edition). 1961.

Description of a Struggle and Other Stories, translated by Willa Muir and others. 1979.

Stories 1904–1924, translated by J.A. Underwood. 1981.

The Transformation and Other Stories, edited and translated by Malcolm Pasley. 1992.

Selected Stories, translated by Edwin and Willa Muir. 1994.

Other

Tagebücher 1910–23. 1951; edited by Hans Gerd Koch, Michael Müller, and Malcolm Pasley, 1990; as *Diaries, 1919–1923*, edited by Max Brod, translated by Joseph Kresh, 1948; *Diaries, 1914–1923*, translated by Martin Greenberg, 1949.

Briefe an Milena, edited by Willy Haas. 1952; revised edition by Jürgen Born and Michael Müller, 1983; as *Letters to Milena*, translated by Tania and James Stern, 1953; also translated by Philip Boehm, 1990.

Briefe 1902–24, edited by Max Brod. 1958; as *Letters to Friends, Family and Editors*, translated by Richard and Clara Winston, 1977.

Briefe an Felice, edited by Erich Heller and Jürgen Born. 1967; as *Letters to Felice*, translated by James Stern and Elisabeth Duckworth, 1973.

Briefe an Ottla und die Familie, edited by Klaus Wagenbach and Hartmut Binder. 1974; as *Letters to Ottla and the Family*, translated by Richard and Clara Winston, 1982.

Max Brod, Franz Kafka: Ein Freundschaft. 2 vols., 1987–1989.

Briefe an die Eltern aus den Jahren 1922–1924, edited by Josef Čermăk and Martin Svatos. 1990.

*

Bibliography: *Franz Kafka: Eine Bibliographie* by Rudolph Hemmerle, 1958; *A Kafka Bibliography 1908–76* by Angel Flores, 1976; *Franz Kafkas Werke: Eine Bibliographie der Primärliteratur (1908–1980)* by Maria Luise Caputo-Mayr and Julius M. Herz, 1982; *Franz Kafka: Die Veröffentlichungen zu seinen Lebzeiten (1908–1924): Eine textkritische und kommentierte Bibliographie* by Ludwig Dietz, 1982.

Critical Studies: *The Kafka Problem*, 1946, and *The Kafka Debate: New Perspectives for Our Time*, 1977, both edited by Angel Flores; *Franz Kafka: A Biography* by Max Brod, 1947; *Kafka's Castle*, 1956, and *Franz Kafka*, 1973, both by Ronald Gray, and *Kafka: A Collection of Critical Essays* edited by Gray, 1962; *Franz Kafka: Parable and Paradox* by Heinz Politzer, 1962; *Franz Kafka* by Erich Heller, 1964; *Franz Kafka* by Walter H. Sokel, 1966; *The Reluctant Pessimist: A Study of Franz Kafka* by A.P. Foulkes, 1967; *The Process of Kafka's "Trial"* by Adrian Jaffe, 1967; *Franz Kafka: A Critical Study of His Writings* by Wilhelm Emrich, translated by Sheema Zeben Buehne, 1968; *The Terror of Art: Kafka and Modern Literature* by Martin Greenberg, 1968; *Dreams, Life, and Literature: A Study of Franz Kafka* by Curtis S. Hall and Richard E. Lind, 1970; *Kafka and the Yiddish Theater: Its Impact on His Work* by Evelyn Torton Beck, 1971; *Kafka and Prague*, by Johann Bauer, translated by P.S. Falla, 1971; *Conversations with Kafka* by Gustav Janouch, translated by Goronwy Rees, 2nd edition, 1971; *Kafka and Anarchism* by Mijal Levi, 1972; *Kafka: A Study* by Anthony Thorlby, 1972; *The Commentator's Despair: The Interpretation of Kafka's "Metamorphosis"*, 1973, and *Franz Kafka: The Necessity of Form*, 1988, both Stanley Corngold; *On Kafka's "Castle": A Study* by Richard Sheppard, 1973; *Moment of Torment: An Interpretation of Franz Kafka's Short Stories* by Ruth Tiefenbrun, 1973; *Kafka's Other Trial* by Elias Canetti, 1974; *Franz Kafka: A Collection of Criticism* edited by Leo Hamalian, 1974; *Franz Kafka: Literature as Corrective Punishment* by Franz Kuna, 1974, and *On Kafka: Semi-Centenary Perspectives* edited by Kuna, 1976; *Kafka's Narrative Theatre* by James Rolleston, 1974; *Kafka in Context* by John Hibberd, 1975; *Kafka's "Trial": The Case Against Josef K.* by Eric Marson, 1975; *Gesture as a Stylistic Device in Kleist's "Michael Kohlhaas" and Kafka's "Der Prozess"* by David E. Smith, 1976; *Franz Kafka* by Meno Spann, 1976; *A Complete Contextual Concordance to Franz Kafka's "Der Prozess"* by Walter H. Speidel, 1978; *Kafka's Doubles* by Kurt J. Flickert, 1979; *Franz Kafka: Geometrician of Metaphor* by Henry Sussman, 1979; *The Secret Raven: Conflict and Transformation in the Life of Franz Kafka* by Daryl Sharp, 1980; *The World of Franz Kafka* edited by J.P. Stern, 1980, and *Franz Kafka Symposium: Paths and Labyrinths* edited by Stern and J.J. White, 1985; *K: A Biography of Kafka* by Ronald Hayman, 1981; *Kafka: Geometrician of Metaphor* by Henry Sussman, 1981; *Kafka's Narrators: A Study of His Stories and Sketches* by Roy Pascal, 1982; *Franz Kafka of Prague* by Jiřéí Gruša, 1983; *The Nightmare of Reason: A Life of Franz Kafka* by Ernst Pawel, 1984; *Kafka: Judaism, Politics, and Literature* by Ritchie

Robertson, 1985; *Kafka's "Landarzt" Collection: Rhetoric and Interpretation* by Gregory B. Triffitt, 1985; *Franz Kafka*, 1986, *Frank Kafka's The Trial*, 1987, *Franz Kafka's The Castle*, 1988, and *Franz Kafka's The Metamorphosis*, 1988, all edited by Harold Bloom; *Sympathy for the Abyss: A Study in the Novel of German Modernism: Kafka, Broch, Musil and Thomas Mann* by Stephen D. Dowden, 1986; *The Loves of Franz Kafka* by Nahum N. Glatzer, 1986; *Franz Kafka's Use of Law in Fiction: A New Interpretation of In der Strafkolonie, Der Prozess and Das Schloss* by Lida Kirchberger, 1986; *Outside Humanity: A Study of Kafka's Fiction* by Ramón G. Mendoza, 1986; *As Lonely as Franz Kafka* by Marthe Robert, translated by Ralph Manheim, 1986; *Kafka's Contextuality*, 1986, and *Kafka and the Contemporary Critical Performance: Centenary Readings*, 1987, both edited by Alan Udoff; *Franz Kafka (1883–1983): His Craft and Thought* edited by Roman Struc and J.C. Yardley, 1986; *The Dove and the Mole: Kafka's Journey into Darkness and Creativity* edited by Ronald Gottesman and Moshe Lazar, 1987; *Kafka's Prussian Advocate: A Study of the Influence of Heinrich von Kleist on Franz Kafka* by John M. Grandin, 1987; *Constructive Destruction: Kafka's Aphorisms* by Richard T. Gray, 1987; *The Jewish Mystic in Kafka* by Jean Jofen, 1987; *On the Threshold of the New Kabbalah: Kafka's Later Tales* by Walter A. Strauss, 1988; *Reading Kafka: Prague, Politics and the fin de siècle* edited by Mark Anderson, 1989, and *Kafka's Clothes: Ornament and Aestheticism in the Habsburg fin de siècle* by Anderson, 1992; *Kafka's Rhetoric: The Passion of Reading* by Clayton Koelb, 1989; *A Hesitation before Birth: The Life of Franz Kafka* by Peter Mailloux, 1989; *After Kafka: The Influence of Kafka's Fiction* by Shimon Sandbank, 1989; *Kafka* by Pietro Citati, 1990; *Necessary Angels: Tradition and Modernity in Kafka, Benjamin and Scholem* by Robert Alter, 1991; *Kafka and Language: In the Stream of Thoughts and Life* by Gabriele von Natamer Cooper, 1991; *Someone Like K: Kafka's Novels* by Herbert Kraft, translated by R.J. Kavanagh, 1991; *The Landscape of Alienation: Ideological Subversion in Kafka, Céline and Onetti* by Jack Murray, 1991; *Kafka's Relatives: Their Lives and His Writing* by Anthony Northey, 1991; *A Life Study of Franz Kafka* by Ronald Gestwicki, 1992; *Franz Kafka: Representative Man* by Frederick Karl, 1993; *End of a Mission: Kafka's Search for Truth in His Last Stories* by Kurt Fickert, 1993; *Introducing Kafka* by David Zane Mairowitz and Robert Crumb, 1994; *Franz Kafka: A Writer's Life* by Joachim Unseld, translated by Paul F. Dvorak, 1994; *Kafka and Kabbalah* by Karl Erich Grözinger, translated by Susan Hecker Ray, 1994; *Everyone's Darling: Kafka and the Critics of His Fiction* by Franz R. Kempf, 1994; *The Intellectual Contexts of Kafka's Fictions: Philosophy, Law, Religion* by Arnold Heidsieck, 1994; *Kafka: The Metamorphosis, The Trial, and The Castle*, edited and introduced by William J. Dodd, 1995; *Franz Kafka: The Jewish Patient* by Sander L. Gilman, 1995; *Kafka's Castle and the Critical Imagination* by Stephen D. Dowden, 1995; *Meditations on Metamorphosis* by Steven Berkoff, 1995; *Franz Kafka and Prague* by Karol Kállay, 1996; *Kafka and China*, edited by Adrian Hsia, 1996; *Kafka: Gender, Class and Race in the Letters and Fictions* by Elizabeth Boa, 1996; *The Legacy of Kafka in Contemporary Austrian Literature*, edited by Frank Pilipp, 1997; *Constructing China: Kafka's Orientalist Discourse* by Rolf J. Goebel, 1997; *Franz Kafka* by Ronald Speirs and Beatrice Sandberg, 1997; *Franz Kafka and Prague* by Harald Salfellner, 1998; *Kafka and Pinter: Shadow-boxing: The Struggle between Father and Son* by Raymond Armstrong, 1999; *Prague Territories: National Conflict and Cultural Innovation in Franz Kafka's fin de siècle* by Scott Spector, 2000.

* * *

If one were to judge the worth of an author solely according to the amount of critical commentary which his works have generated, then there is no doubt that Franz Kafka has already earned his place beside Shakespeare, Goethe, and Cervantes. The primary attraction and challenge for the critic lie in the strange and enigmatic quality of the fiction, its disturbing capacity to invite and yet to resist interpretation, and at the same time the intuitive belief of many readers that they are being addressed by a writer who has managed to capture in words the very essence of 20th-century experience and angst. Kafka's stories, moreover, possess a degree of semantic openness which makes it possible to re-express many of his narrated scenes and images within the interpretative schemes which have come to dominate modern thought, be they derived from political systems, theological concerns, psychoanalysis, or philosophy. Nor is it difficult, once such an interpretation has been put forward, to "corroborate" it by referring to events in the author's life or indeed to more general cultural factors which helped shape early 20th-century views of the individual's relationship to society, to his own unconscious self, or to the Divine. And finally, the lack of specificity characteristic of Kafka's fiction can be resolved into conceptual systems derived from the author's non-fiction writings, for the critic has at his disposal a considerable collection of posthumously published letters, diaries, fragments, and conversations.

There is some evidence, when we consider Kafka's work in its chronological entirety, that the author was increasingly concerned to forestall the kind of criticism which might attempt to view his fictional creations as referring in a straightforward way to events, localities, or people outside the narratives. In the three novels this process is apparent in the progressive disappearance of all references to actual topographical entities as well as in the names of the three main protagonists, Karl Rossmann, Josef K., and K. Some of the later short stories, told through the first-person mental associations of shadowy animal narrators, carry this stylistic device to the point that the reader is deprived of almost any familiar landmark which might indicate a concealed meaning waiting to be discovered.

Kafka's earliest novel *Amerika* (*America*), first published in 1927, has attracted less critical attention than his later works, and is regarded by some as an only partially successful attempt to satirize the institutions of the New World by recounting them from the perspective of Karl Rossmann, a young European who has been packed off to America by his parents after he is seduced by a servant girl. The bizarre adventures which befall Karl certainly possess a Chaplin-like quality, and significantly they provide us with one of Kafka's few overt examples of social criticism, for the episodic narrative is a reversal of the Horatio Alger, poor-boy-makes-good myth; Karl, despite his unfailing optimism and his determination to succeed, is slowly destroyed by the very system of values in which he has faith. The novel is fragmentary and unfinished, and a final interpretation would have to speculate on the possible ending. Max Brod, Kafka's biographer and confidant, insisted that the novel was to end "on a note of reconciliation," but this is thrown into doubt by a diary entry

(30 September 1915) in which Kafka stated that the "innocent" Rossmann, just like the "guilty" K., was to meet his death.

Der Prozess and *Das Schloss*, translated respectively as *The Trial* and *The Castle*, are also fragmentary, and *The Castle*, like *America*, remained without an ending. The two later novels have in common a number of thematic similarities, and to a much greater extent than *America* they portray the singular and oppressive dreamlike sequences which have enriched many of the world's languages with the phrase "it's like something out of Kafka." Reflecting the two sides of Kafka's aphorism, according to which, "He who seeks, will not find; he who does not seek will be found," the two novels suggest the existence of aloof and inscrutable authorities which can reach out to destroy, as in *The Trial*, or which will withdraw into a state of total inaccessibility as in *The Castle*. In each case the authorities are represented by a lower hierarchy of pompous officials and libertine servants, and they have additionally given rise to a vast body of anecdotal and superstitious lore designed to divine their intentions in order that one may either cooperate with them or thwart their will. The diversity of opinion typical of Kafka interpretation is strikingly evident in the interpretations of these two novels. They have been seen as the vain struggle of the individual seeking to comprehend the faceless bureaucracies which govern him, as depictions of the alienated Jew in a hostile Christian world, as grotesque fictive transmutations of Kafka's obsession with his father's power, and as parables on humanity's eternal but fruitless striving for the Absolute. Before embracing any one of these interpretations, the reader might do well to heed the words of advice offered to Josef K. by the prison chaplain in *The Trial*: "You mustn't pay too much attention to opinions. The words are unchangeable, and the opinions are often just an expression of despair about that."

According to Max Brod, Kafka "thought in pictures and he spoke in pictures." This tendency to pictorialize inner thoughts and feelings, to lend visual form to the subjective and the abstract, is a feature which Kafka's writings share with dreams, and it can be seen as one of the guiding structural principles of the short stories and of the literary experimentation published in the volume *Wedding Preparations in the Country*. On the surface Kafka's short pieces treat a remarkable variety of themes and situations, including the father-son conflict in "The Judgement," the transformation of a commercial traveller into a monstrous insect in *Die Verwandlung* (*The Metamorphosis*), the horrifying method of execution described in *In der Strafkolonie* (*In the Penal Colony*), and the self-imposed death by starvation depicted in "A Hunger Artist." There are stories narrated both by and about animals, and pieces concerning themselves with circus riders, country doctors, mysterious hunters, Ulysses, and the Emperor of China. A unifying stylistic factor behind this thematic diversity is the fact that each story can be interpreted as the manifest portrayal of certain inner experiences and states of mind which recur constantly in Kafka's fiction. This does not mean of course that the stories should be regarded simply as variations to be reduced to the same theme, for each work contributes uniquely through its imagery and structure to the thematic aspect which it embodies. Nor should it be forgotten that the fiction, even though Kafka himself once described it as "the representation of my inner life," has been received as significant and compelling by countless readers who have related it to their own experience of the 20th century.

—A.P. Foulkes

See the essays on *The Castle*, *The Metamorphosis*, and *The Trial*.

KAISER, Georg

Born: Magdeburg, Germany, 25 November 1878. **Education:** Educated at the school of a Lutheran monastery, 1888–95. **Family:** Married Margarete Habenicht in 1908; two sons and one daughter; also had a daughter by Maria von Mühfeld in 1919. **Career:** Bookshop assistant in Magdeburg, 1895; apprentice with an import/export business, 1896–99; sailed to Buenos Aires, Argentina, worked with the local branch of the Berlin AEG [General Electric Company], 1899; contracted malaria, returned to Germany, 1901; in sanatorium, following a nervous breakdown, 1902; lost house through financial difficulties, moved to Munich, 1918; arrested on a charge of embezzlement, because of his selling of rented furniture, and imprisoned in Munich for six months, 1920–21; settled in Berlin after his release, 1921; became Germany's most widely performed dramatist, 1921–33; under the Nazi regime, his works banned from publication or production, from 1933, and his books burnt; continued writing in Berlin, 1934–37; learned of impending investigation by the Gestapo and fled to Switzerland via Amsterdam, 1938; lived in various parts of Switzerland, 1939–44. **Awards:** Elected to Prussian Academy of Arts, 1926, and the German Academy, 1930 (membership later withdrawn under Nazi pressure). Honorary president, Association for German Writers in Exile, 1945. **Died:** 4 June 1945.

PUBLICATIONS

Collections

Stücke, Erzählungen, Aufsätze, Gedichte, edited by Walther Huder. 1966.
Werke, edited by Walther Huder. 6 vols., 1971–72.

Plays

Die jüdische Witwe (produced 1921). 1911.
Claudius (produced 1918). In *Hyperion*, 1911.
Friedrich und Anna (produced 1918). In *Hyperion*, 1911.
König Hahnrei (produced 1931). 1913.
Der Fall des Schülers Vehgesack (produced 1915). 1914.
Rektor Kleist (produced 1918). 1914.
Grossbürger Möller (produced 1915). 1914; revised version, as *David und Goliath* (produced 1922). 1920; as *David and Goliath*, translated by B.J. Kenworthy, in *Plays 2*, 1981.
Die Bürger von Calais (produced 1917). 1914; as *The Burghers of Calais*, translated by J.M. Ritchie and Rex Last, in *Five Plays*, 1971.
Europa (produced 1920). 1915.
Der Zentaur (produced 1917). 1916.
Von Morgens bis mitternachts (produced 1917). 1916; as *From Morn to Midnight*, translated by Ashley Dukes, in *Poet Lore*, (21), 1920; also translated by Ulrich Weisstein, in *Plays for the Theatre: An Anthology of World Drama*, edited by O.G. and L. Brockett, 1967; as *From Morning to Midnight*, translated by J.M. Ritchie, in *Five Plays*, 1971.
Die Sorina; oder, Der Kindermord (produced 1917). 1917.
Die Versuchung (produced 1917). 1917.

Die Koralle (produced 1917). 1917; as *The Coral*, translated by Winifred Katzin, 1963; also translated by B.J. Kenworthy, in *Five Plays*, 1971.

Das Frauenopfer (produced 1918). 1918.

Juana (produced 1918). 1918.

Gas I (produced 1918). 1918; as *Gas I*, translated by Herman Scheffauer, 1957; also translated by B.J. Kenworthy, in *Five Plays*, 1971.

Der Brand im Opernhaus (produced 1918). 1919; as *Fire in the Opera House* translated by Winifred Katzin, in *Eight European Plays*, 1927.

Hölle Weg Erde (produced 1919). 1919.

Gas II (produced 1920). 1920; as *Gas II*, translated by Winifred Katzin, 1963; also translated by B.J. Kenworthy, in *Five Plays*, 1971.

Der gerettete Alkibiades (produced 1920). 1920; as *Alkibiades Saved*, translated by Bayard Quincy Morgan, in *An Anthology of German Expressionist Drama*, edited by Walter H. Sokel, 1963.

Der Protagonist (produced 1922). 1921; as *The Protagonist*, translated by H.F. Garten, in *Tulane Drama Review*, (5), 1960.

Noli me tangere. 1922.

Kanzlist Krehler (produced 1922). 1922.

Der Geist der Antike. 1923.

Gilles und Jeanne (produced 1923). 1923.

Die Flucht nach Venedig (produced 1923). 1923; as *The Flight to Venice*, translated by B.J. Kenworthy, in *Plays 2*, 1981.

Nebeneinander (produced 1923). 1923.

Kolportage (produced 1924). 1924.

Gats (produced 1925). 1925.

Der mutige Seefahrer (produced 1925). 1926.

Zweimal Oliver (produced 1926). 1926.

Papiermühle (produced 1926). 1927.

Der Zar lässt sich photographieren, music by Kurt Weill (produced 1928). 1927.

Der Präsident (produced 1928). 1927; as *The President*, translated by B.J. Kenworthy, in *Plays 2*, 1981.

Oktobertag (produced 1928). 1928; as *The Phantom Lover*, translated by Hermann Bernstein and Adolf E. Meyer, 1928; as *One Day in October*, translated by B.J. Kenworthy, in *Plays 2*, 1981.

Die Lederköpfe (produced 1928). 1928.

Hellseherei (produced 1929). 1929.

Zwei Krawatten (produced 1929). 1929.

Mississippi (produced 1930). 1930.

Der Silbersee (produced 1933). 1933.

Adrienne Ambrosat (produced 1935). 1948(?); translated as *Adrienne Ambrosat*, in *Continental Plays 2*, 1935.

Das Los des Ossian Balvesen (produced 1936). 1947(?).

Der Gärtner von Toulouse (produced 1945). 1938.

Der Schuss in die Öffentlichkeit (produced 1949). 1939.

Der Soldat Tanaka (produced 1940). 1940.

Rosamunde Floris (produced 1953). 1940.

Alain und Elise (produced 1954). 1940.

Die Spieldose (produced 1943). In *Stücke, Erzählungen, Aufsätze, Gedichte*, 1966.

Zweimal Amphitryon (produced 1944). In *Griechische Dramen*, 1948.

Das Floss der Medusa (produced 1945). 1963; as *The Raft of the Medusa*, translated by Ulrich Weisstein, in *First Stage*, 1, 1962; also translated by George Wellwarth, in *Postwar German Theater*,

edited by Michael Benedikt and George E. Wellwarth; H.F. Garten and Elizabeth Sprigge, in *Plays 2*, 1981.

Agnete (produced 1949). 1948(?).

Pygmalion (produced 1953). In *Griechische Dramen*, 1948.

Bellerophon (produced 1953). In *Griechische Dramen*, 1948.

Klawitter (produced 1949). 1949.

Napoleon in New Orleans (produced 1950). In *Stücke, Erzählungen, Aufsätze, Gedichte*, 1966.

Schellenkönig. In *Stücke, Erzählungen, Aufsätze, Gedichte*, 1966.

Das gordische Ei (unfinished). N.d.

Five Plays (includes *From Morn to Midnight; The Burghers of Calais; The Coral: Gas I; Gas II*), translated by B.J. Kenworthy, Rex Last, and J.M. Ritchie. 1971; as *Plays I*, 1985.

Plays 2, (includes *The Flight to Venice; One Day in October; The Raft of the Medusa; David and Goliath; The President*), translated by B.J. Kenworthy, H.F. Garten, and Elizabeth Sprigge. 1981.

Radio Plays: *Der englische Sender*, 1947.

Fiction

Es ist genug. 1932.

Villa Aurea. 1940.

Leutnant Welzeck (fragment). In *Stücke, Erzählungen, Aufsätze, Gedichte*, 1966.

Other

Vision und Figur. 1918.

Georg Kaiser in Sachen Georg Kaiser: Briefe 1916–1933, edited by Gesa M. Valk. 1989.

*

Bibliography: "Georg Kaiser (1878–1945): A Bio-Bibliographical Report" by Leroy W. Shaw, in *Texas Studies in Literature and Language*, (3), 1961.

Critical Studies: *Kaiser und seine Bühenwerke* by Willibald Omankowski, 1922; *Der Denkspieler, Georg Kaiser* by Bernhard Diebold, 1924; *Georg Kaisers Werk* by Max Freyhan, 1926; *Georg Kaiser* by Hugo Königsgarten, 1928; *Georg Kaiser und seine Stellung im Expressionismus* by Eric A. Fivian, 1946; *Georg Kaiser* by Brian J. Kenworthy, 1957; *Georg Kaiser: Die Perspektiven seines Werkes* by Wolfgang Paulsen, 1960; *Georg Kaiser* by Wilhelm Steffens, 1969; *Die Suche nach dem Menschen im Drama Georg Kaisers* by M. Kuxdorf, 1971; *Georg Kaiser und Bertolt Brecht* by Ernst Schürer, 1971; "Georg Kaiser Re-examined" by Hugo F. Garten, in *German and Dutch Literature*, edited by W.D. Robson-Scott, 1973; *Georg Kaisers Drama "Die Koralle": Persönliche Erfahrung und ästhetische Abstraktion* by Heinrich Breloer, 1977; *Georg Kaisers "Gas I": Textanalyse und Konzept einer szenischen Realisation* by Peter Schlapp, 1983; *German Expressionist Drama: Ernst Toller and Georg Kaiser* by Renate Benson, 1984, German edition, 1987; *The Reception of Georg Kaiser (1915–1945): Texts and Analysis* by Peter K. Tyson, 2 vols., 1984; *Théâtre expressionniste et le sacré: Georg Kaiser, Ernst Toller, Ernst Barlach* by Catherine Mazellier-Grünbeck, 1994; *Georg Kaiser and the Critics: A Profile of Expressionism's Leading Playwright* by Audrone B. Willeke, 1995.

* * *

Georg Kaiser, the greatest, most prolific, and certainly the most eccentric of the German Expressionist dramatists, was born in Magdeburg, the son of an insurance salesman, in 1878. Such was the diversity and profusion of his work (over a hundred dramas, as well as poetry and prose) that he was suspected by one critic of being a collective of writers toiling away under the company name of Kaiser.

Kaiser was convinced of the centrality and overwhelming significance of his mission as a writer, before which all else paled into insignificance. His central conviction found its clearest expression in his key essay *Vision und Figur* [Vision and Form] (1918), in which he states:

> The Vision is everything, because it is one. The forms which are bearers of this vision are manifold, laden by the fiery hand of the poet with the weighty burden of his message. In many ways does the poet fashion but one thing: the vision, which has existed since the dawn of time. And of what nature is this vision? There is only one: The renewal of man.

This quasi-religious idealism finds its most complete expression in Kaiser's difficult but rewarding masterpiece, *Die Bürger von Calais* (*The Burghers of Calais*), first performed with great success in 1917, when the tide of war was turning and audiences had become attuned to the strong pacifist element in the play's message. It borrows both from the historical account of the siege of Calais at the beginning of the Hundred Years War and from the New Testament. Duguesclin, commander of the French army, represents the forces of the old world, of the "chain of deeds" of violence which Eustache de Saint-Pierre, a leading Calais merchant, seeks to break with his concept of community effort towards an unselfish and peaceful society.

At first, Eustache endeavours to convert the whole community to his idealism, then he turns to the other volunteers for the self-sacrifice demanded by the besieging English forces (six citizens to be hanged as a penance for the town and to guarantee its safety), but ultimately only he achieves the ideal—through death.

Kaiser depicts the path to the ideal in terms of a sudden chance awakening or opportunity for escape from the trammels of the Old World. At that instant, the "New Man" is born, as at the death of the old and birth of the new in a Christian convert, and is utterly committed to the struggle toward the renewal of mankind.

Then the process of debate to persuade others to recognize and espouse that ideal begins in earnest. Such is the centrality of the dialectic in Kaiser's dramas that he describes writing a drama in terms of "thinking a thought to its end." In *The Burghers of Calais*, the debate takes place in a setting which deliberately parallels the Last Supper, and in which the aspiration toward self-sacrifice fights a losing battle against self-interest and fear of the unknown. At the end, Eustache commits suicide, and his old blind father paradoxically proclaims "I have seen the New Man! Last night was he born!"

Although that ideal—not untypically of German idealism through history—is far beyond mortal reach, Kaiser the activist stresses the key significance of the struggle to attain it. This awakening and commitment take place in a variety of contexts, from the purely personal, in a drama like *Oktobertag* (*One Day in October*), in which Catherine, made pregnant by a butcher's boy, persuades a certain lieutenant Marrien by an act of will that he is the father, literally demonstrating the power of mind over matter, to, at the other extreme, *Die Koralle* (*The Coral*) and the *Gas* plays, which explore the wider social scene in the conflict between the brute force of industry and human ideals. The workers would rather continue to manufacture gas, which in the last part of the trilogy becomes poison gas, than take a leap into uncertainty, demolish the factories, and return to a community lifestyle closer to the natural world. In his anti-industrial and anti-war stance, Kaiser anticipates many of the themes and preoccupations of the German Green movement, although his political preoccupations are too broad to be associated with any one political party.

The Coral also underlines Kaiser's fascination with the notion of the doppelgänger and the problems of personal identity, although it must be stressed that in his work Kaiser is concerned with the human psyche, rather than with human psychology.

The language and style of his works reflect the huge tensions which he is seeking to expose and cause to interact—paradox and the grotesque are never far from the centre stage, and the language itself oscillates between extreme concentration on isolated concrete nouns to rambling, expansive, and highly stylized speeches, in which the punctuation serves almost to orchestrate and define the style of delivery demanded of the actor.

In Kaiser's work there is to be found a great variety of different forms of drama, from the small domestic scale to the vast arena of Calais town hall or the six-day cycle races in Berlin; from traditional three-act dramatic form to the *Stationendrama* of the kind made most famous by Brecht, in which the action focuses not on plot but on theme, and is held together by one central figure.

Among all his writings, Kaiser's despairing but determined idealism is most vividly encapsulated in the closing moments of the grotesque comedy *Von Morgens bis mitternachts* (*From Morn to Midnight*), in which the bank clerk (a representative type rather than a psychologically delineated figure), who from being an automaton processing money in the bank is transformed by the touch of an exotic woman's hand into a parody of the New Man, steals a large sum from the bank, and goes off in pursuit of the ideal. Failing in a number of such endeavours, he finally comes to the Salvation Army Hall, where in a long speech he confesses the overwhelming significance of spirituality, proclaims that "money destroys true value . . . money is the most wretched swindle in the world," and casts his ill-gotten gains among the startled congregation.

After an astonished silence as the stolen banknotes fall through the air, the onlookers revert to type and grasp at the money, and even the Salvation Army girl who led the bank clerk there betrays him. At the end, he is spread-eagled, in a parody of the crucifixion, against the cross sewn into the curtain on the stage. Like Eustache, he has achieved his ideal; like Eustache he is alone; and like Eustache, he has left this world behind.

—Rex Last

See the essay on *The Gas Trilogy: The Coral* (*Die Koralle*), *, Gas I, Gas II*.

KĀLIDĀSA

Born: Date of birth unknown; flourished c. AD 400. **Career:** Poet and dramatist who wrote in Sanskrit and who may have been in the city of Ujjain, at the court of the North Indian ruler Chandragupta Vikramāditya or of his successor Kumāragupta, or both, for some years between about 388 and c. 455. Texts exist is several regional variants (recensions). **Died:** 5th century(?).

PUBLICATIONS

Collections

Shakuntala and Other Works, translated by Arthur Ryder. 1912; as *Shakuntala and Other Writings*, 1959.
Kālidāsa Lexicon (Sanskrit texts), edited by A. Scharpé. 5 vols., 1954–75.
Granthavali [Collected Works] (Hindi and Sanskrit). 1965.
Complete Works (Sanskrit), edited by V.P. Joshi. 1976.
Granthāvalī/Works (Sanskrit), edited by R.P. Dwivedī. 1976; 2nd edition, 1986.
The Loom of Time (includes *Ṛtusaṃhāram; Meghadūtam; Abhijnānaśākuntalam*), translated by Chandra Rajan. 1989.
Complete Works of Kalidasa, translated by Sudhanshu Chaturvedi. 2000.

Verse

Ṛtusaṃhāra, as *The Season: A Descriptive Poem*, edited by W. Jones. 1792; as *The Ritusamhara*, translated by M. Nandy, 1970; as *Ṛtusamhāram*, in *The Loom of Time*, 1989; as *The Seasons* (bilingual edition), translated by John T. Roberts, 1990.
Raghuvaṃśa, edited by G.N. Nandargikar (with Mallinātha's commentary). 1811 (reprinted 1982); also edited (with Latin translation) by F.A. Stenzler, 1832; as *The Story of Raghu's Line*, translated by P.D.L. Johnstone, 1902; as *The Dynasty of Raghu*, translated by Robert Antoine, 1972; as *Kalidasa's Raghuvamsham: An Account of the Family of Raghu*, edited by Lallanji Gopal, 1992.
Kumārasambhava, edited by F.A. Stenzler (songs 1–8, with Latin translation). 1838; critical edition, 1962; edited by M.S. Narayana Murti, in *Verzeichnis der orientalischen Handschriften in Deutschland*, supplement 20(1), 1980; as *The Birth of the War God*, translated by R.T.H. Griffith, 1877; as *The Origin of the Young God*, translated by Hank Heifetz, 1985.
Meghadūta, in *Meghaduta et Cringaratilaka*, edited by J. Gildemeister. 1841; edited by E. Hultzsch (with Vallabhadeva's commentary), 1911; also edited by S.K. De, 1957 (critical edition), and M.R. Kale (bilingual edition), 7th edition, 1967; as *Meghaduta; or, Cloud Messenger*, translated by H.H. Wilson, 1843; as *Meghaduta*, translated by G.H. Rooke, 1935; as *The Cloud Messenger*, translated by Franklin and Eleanor Edgerton, 1964; as *The Transport of Love*, translated by Leonard Nathan, 1976; as *Meghadūtam*, in *The Loom of Time*, 1989; edited by A.L. Sancheti and Dayanand Bhargava, 1998.

Plays

Abhijñāna Śakuntalā. 1761; edited by Richard Pischel (Bengali recension), 1922; edited by N.R. Acharya, with commentary by Rāghavabhaṭṭa (Devanagari recension), 1958 (12th edition); as *Shakuntala*, translated by William Jones, 1789; also translated by Arthur Ryder, in *Shakuntala and Other Works*, 1912; P. Lal, in *Great Sanskrit Plays*, 1957; as *Śakuntalā*, translated by M.

Monier-Williams, 1853: Michael Coulson, in *Three Sanskrit Plays*, 1981; as *Abhijnāśakuntalā*, translated by M.R. Kale, 1898; as *Sakuntala*, translated by J.G. Jennings, 1902; also translated by Murray Emeneau, 1962; as *Abhijna Shakuntala*, translated by Hemant Kanitkar, 1984; as *Sakuntala and the Ring of Recollection*, in *Theater of Memory: The Plays of Kālidāsa*, 1984; as *Abhijnānaśākuntalam*, in *The Loom of Time*, 1989; translated by V. Gowri Shanker, 1994; translated by P.C. Jain Daljeet, 1998; as *Recognition of Sakuntala: A Play in Seven Acts*, translated by W.J. Johnson, 2001; as *Sacontala, or, The Fatal Ring*, translated by William Jones, 2001.
Vikramorvaśīya, edited (with Latin translation) by R. Lenz. 1833; also edited by S.P. Pandit, 1889, H.D. Velankar, 1961; as *Vikramorvasiya* (bilingual edition), translated by M.R. Kale, 1889, and subsequent editions; also translated by Dhruva Sumana, 1912; as *Urvaśī Won By Valor*, in *Theater of Memory: The Plays of Kālidāsa*, 1984.
Mālavikāgnimitra, as *Malvika et Agnimitra*, edited by O.F. Tullberg. 1840; also edited by Friedrich Bollensen, 1879, C.S. Rama Sastri, 1929, N.R. Acharya, 1950, and K.A. Subramania, 1978; as *Malavikagnimitra*, edited and translated by D.S. Sane, G.H. Godbole, and H.S. Ursekar, 1950; also translated by C.H. Tawney, 1964 (3rd edition); as *Mālvikā and Agnimitra*, in *Theater of Memory: The Plays of Kālidāsa*, 1984.
Theater of Memory: The Plays of Kālidāsa, edited by Barbara Stoler Miller, translated by Edwin Gerow, David Gitomer, and Miller. 1984.

*

Bibliography: *Kalidasa Bibliography* by S.P. Narang, 1976.

Critical Studies: *The Sanskrit Drama: Its Origin, Development, Theory and Practice* by Arthur Berriedale Keith, 1924; *Kalidasa: His Period, Personality and Poetry* by K.S. Ramaswami, 1933; *Kalidasa: Poet of Nature* by Mary B. Harris, 1936 *India in Kalidasa* by B.S. Upadhyaya, 1947; *Kalidasa* by Walter Ruben, 1957; *The Classical Drama of India* by Henry Willis Wells, 1963; *Kalidasa: Date, Life, Works* by V.V. Mirashi, 1969; *A Critical Study of the Sources of Kalidasa* by B.R. Yadau, 1974; *The Imagery of Kalidasa* by V. Aggarwal, 1985; *Kalidasa as Dramatist* by P.C. Mandel, 1986; *The Literary Semantics of Kalidasa* by H.L. Shukla, 1987; *Kālidāsa* by K. Krishnamoorthy, 1994; *Juridical Studies in Kālidāsa* by Satya Pal Narang, 1996; *Sakuntala: Texts, Readings, Histories* by Romila Thapar, 1999; *Kālidāsa: The Man and the Mind* by P.N. Kawthekar, 1999.

*   *   *

Kālidāsa occupies a special place in world literature, a poet who has contributed outstanding examples of epic, lyric, and dramatic works. Later Indian poets, critics, and theorists have considered him the central reference point of the tradition, and for over 15 centuries his works have continued to attract devoted readers. Two lyric poems are ascribed to Kālidāsa (the first less certainly): *Ṛtusaṃhāra* (*The Seasons*) and *Meghadūta* (*The Cloud Messenger*). Both are poems of love and describe a natural universe transfigured by the lover's imagination and enthusiasm. *The Seasons* contains 140 stanzas, the first extended lyric poem in the literature. It is divided into six books corresponding to six parts of the year: Spring, Summer, the Rainy Season, Autumn, Early Winter, and Winter. In each, a newly married young man sees all of nature with the eyes of love: the sun, the sea, the rivers, trees and vines, birds and beasts, flowers and insects, all are seen as participating in the dance of love. The elaborateness and conviction of this sensual imagery set a new style in Sanskrit poetry, which had previously been more concerned with religious or patriotic themes. *The Cloud Messenger*, like *The Seasons*, is more a lyric meditation than a story. Here a lover is separated from his beloved and the same plants and flowers, rivers and lakes, birds and fish that inspired such ecstasies in *The Seasons* serve him as bitter reminders of his loss. He pours out his grief to a passing rain cloud and begs it to carry his love message to his beloved. The first book of the poem describes in loving and erotic detail the countryside over which the cloud passes on its journey. The second book, at the journey's end, describes the lover's pining wife and her reception of the comforting message borne to her by the cloud. Although the primary mood of the poem is lyric, it combines many elements; religious poetry is mixed with love poetry, elegiac and pastoral elements with the lyric.

Although Kālidāsa may be said to have originated the extended lyric poem, when he turned to the epic he had before him the great traditional works, the *Rāmāyana* and the *Mahābhārata*. Drawing upon these and other poetic sources, he created two major epics, *Kumārasambhava* (*The Birth of the War God*) and *Raghuvaṃśa* (*The Story of Raghu's Line*). The first poem contains 17 cantos, although most Sanskrit scholars consider only the first eight to be the work of Kālidāsa, and the rest a later addition, even though the war-god Kumāra is not in fact yet born in the first eight cantos. These eight, distinctly superior in poetic style and imagination, tell of the process by which the supreme god Śiva is drawn from a state of contemplation to enter into marriage with Pārvatī, a union that will produce a hero to destroy the evil demon Tāraka, who is troubling all the gods in the Hindu pantheon. Clearly, the subject allows Kālidāsa to explore again the poetry of love and nature, but also that of spiritual ecstasy, divine vision, and even the pain of death, in the famous elegy that is pronounced by Rati, the consort of Kāma and the god of love, who is destroyed by Śiva when he first attempts to interrupt the supreme deity's meditations. *The Story of Raghu's Line* concerns legendary kings rather than gods, and is not a single story but a sprawling collection of the deeds of great heroes. The careers of almost 30 dynastic rulers are traced, but the first three, Dilīpa, Raghu, and Aja, receive particularly detailed and loving attention.

Kālidāsa is probably best known in the West as a playwright. He is the author of three plays, one of which, *Śakuntalā*, is the most famous Sanskrit drama. His two other plays are *Mālavikāgnimitra* and *Vikramorvaśīya*. As might be expected from Kālidāsa's other works, all three plays deal with love, and all are examples of the *nātaka* type of Sanskrit drama, using history or legend with a king as a protagonist. *Mālavikāgnimitra* tells of the king's passion for a serving girl in the queen's retinue and how, through the manipulations of his clever jester and opportune political developments at the close of the play, his love succeeds. *Vikramorvaśīya* tells of a king who falls in love with a celestial nymph. Both undergo great suffering and torment but at the end Indra, Hindu god of the sky, intervenes to unite the lovers. Both of the plays provide a rich texture of poetry, music, and dance, but for Western tastes their rather arbitrary actions and thin characterizations are serious drawbacks.

Śakuntalā is much more satisfying on these points, though it, too, is set in a fairytale world of strange and unexpected events. King Duṣyanta, during a hunting expedition, meets Śakuntalā, the daughter of a nymph and a sage, and they fall in love. The king returns to his capital, leaving his new bride to follow him later. After his departure, Śakuntalā unwittingly offends a hermit who pronounces a curse on her: that her husband will forget her until he sees a ring he left with her as a token. Unhappily Śakuntalā, unaware of the curse, loses the ring in a river on her way to her husband and is rejected by him. She seeks refuge among the gods in heaven, where her son Bharata is born. Meanwhile, a fisherman discovers the ring inside a fish he has caught. He is suspected of having stolen it and brought before King Duṣyanta, whose memory of Śakuntalā is thus restored. Having provided us in the early section of the play with the expression of love's delights, Kālidāsa now turns to the sorrows of love lost.

Despite his anguish, the king wins an important battle for Indra, and, returning to his home from her heavenly realm, he stops at the hermitage of a sage, allowing Kālidāsa to laud the ascetic life in richly poetic terms. So peaceful is this site that the king observes a six-year-old boy playing happily with a lion cub. In a lengthy and moving recognition scene, Duṣyanta comes to realize that this is his own son, and Śakuntalā soon appears to complete his happiness. Their reunion is blessed by the sage, who explains the curse and prophesies future glory for Bharata. As in all his works, Kālidāsa creates a rich panorama of the effects of love, fulfilled and frustrated, and of the penetration of nature itself by the lovers' moods; but his canvas in this play is particularly rich and colourful, because of the complex gallery of dramatic characters and the sweep of the action, extending from earth to heaven. Goethe, one of the few authors whose range of poetic achievement resembles that of Kālidāsa, was one of the many Western admirers of *Śakuntalā*, commenting that it combined the flowers of youth and the fruits of age, delight and enchantment, heaven and earth, all in a single work.

—Marvin Carlson

See the essays on *The Cloud Messenger* and *Śakuntalā*.

KANZE ZEAMI MOTOKIYO
See ZEAMI

KAPLINSKI, Jaan

Born: Tartu, Estonia, 22 January 1941. **Education:** Attended primary and secondary school in Tartu, 1947–58; Tartu University, 1958–64. **Family:** Married 1) Küllike Kolk, one daughter; 2) Tiia Toomet in 1969; four sons and a daughter. **Career:** Freelance writer and translator since 1972; research assistant at botanical garden in Tallinn, 1974–80; worked for theatre *Ugala* in Viljandi, Estonia, 1980–82; lecturer at Tartu University, 1983–88; deputy of the Estonian Parliament (Riigikogu), 1992–95; member of the *Académie Universelle des Cultures*, since 1994; regular contributor to Estonian newspaper *Sõnumileht*, 1996–98; writer in residence at the Aberystwyth Arts Centre in Wales, 1997; guest professor, Tartu University, 2000–01. **Awards:** Juhan Liiv poetry prize, 1967; short list, Nobel prize in literature, 1996; Estonian Cultural Endowment prize, 1997; Baltic Assembly prize for literature, 1997.

PUBLICATIONS

Collections

The New Heaven and Earth of Jaan Kaplinski: Poems, selected and translated by Ants Eert. 1981.
Käoraamat: Luulet 1956–1980. 1986.
Kirjutatud: Valitud Luuletused. 2000.

Poetry

Jäljed allikal. 1965.
Kalad punuvad pesi. 1966.
Tolmust ja värvidest. 1967.
Valge joon Võrumaa kohale: 54 luuletust 1967–1968. 1972.
Ma vaatasin päikese aknasse: luulet. 1976.
Uute kivide kasvamine. 1977.
Raske on kergeks saada. 1982.
Tule tagasi helmemänd. 1984.
Õhtu toob tagasi kõik. 1985.
The Wandering Border, translated by Kaplinski with Sam Hamill and Riina Tamm. 1987.
Hinge tagasitulek: poeem. 1990.
I Am the Spring in Tartu and Other Poems Written in English, edited by Laurence P.A. Kitching. 1991.
Tükk elatud elu: tekste 1986–1989. 1991; as *Through the Forest*, translated by Hildi Hawkins, 1996.
Öölinnud, öömõtted, yölintuja, yöajatuksia: luuletusi 1995–1997. 1998.

Plays

Põgenik (produced 1976).
Neljakuningapäev (produced 1977).
Liblikas ja peegel (produced 1982).
Indiaaninägemused (produced 1995).

Children's Books

Kuhu need värvid jäävad, with Tiia Toomet. 1975.
Kes mida sööb, kes keda sööb. 1977.
Udujutt. 1977.
Jänes. 1980.
Jalgrataste talveuni. 1987.

Essays

Poliitika ja antipoliitika. 1992.
Teekond Ayia Triadasse. 1993.
Jää ja Titanic. 1995.
See ja teine. 1996.
Võimaluste võimalikkus. 1997.
Usk on uskumatus. 1998.
Kevad kahel rannikul ehk tundeline teekond Ameerikasse. 2000.
Kajakas võltsmunal. 2000.

Other

Kust tuli öö: proosat. 1990.
Mitu suve ja kevadet: luulet ja märkmeid. 1995.
Silm; Hektor. 2000.

*

Critical Studies: "Jaan Kaplinski. *Tolmust ja värvidest*" by Ivar Ivask, in *Books Abroad* [*World Literature Today*], no. 42, 1968; "For a New Heaven and a New Earth: Comments on the Poetry of Jaan Kaplinski" by Hellar Grabbi, in *Books Abroad* [*World Literature Today*], no. 47, 1973; "The Transcendence of Jaan Kaplinski's Poetry" by Jüri Talvet, in *Estonian Literary Magazine*, Spring 1998; "Escape Artists and Freedom's Children" by Thomas Salumets, in *Interlitteraria*, no. 3, 1998; "Crossing the Sea: Tomas Tranströmer and Jaan Kaplinski" by Ene-Reet Soovik, in *Interlitteraria*, no. 4, 1999.

*   *   *

Being both Estonian and Jewish-Polish ties Jaan Kaplinski to "two cultures that were not given a chance to develop fully, strangled and destroyed by the Western and Eastern imperialists. . . . As the Jews are mourning over the destruction of their temple . . . the Estonians, Finns, Saamis, Samoyeds, Maris and others can mourn over the destruction of their sacred groves, trees and lakes," he writes on his web page (http://jaan.kaplinski.com). From these "two fatal identities," a childhood in war-torn Estonia, and adolescence and adulthood in the grey depression of an occupied country there emerged a prolific author with an inspiring passion for nature and all things living.

Kaplinski is the author of numerous collections of poetry, plays, children's books, essays, and prose fiction. In 1968, at the age of 27, Kaplinski was awarded the prestigious Juhan Liiv poetry prize and people in the West began to take notice. Ivar Ivask wrote in *Books Abroad*: "With his second collection [*Tolmust ja Värvidest*], Jaan Kaplinski has clearly established himself as the most original and exciting young poet . . . writing in Soviet Estonia today. His interesting poetry would no doubt evoke a wide international echo if translated into one of the major Western languages." As the Iron Curtain began to lift with Soviet premier Gorbachev's perestroika in the 1980s, Kaplinski, a household name in his native Estonia since the mid-1960s, established himself on the international scene. In relatively quick succession, English translations appeared—*The Same Sea in Us All* (1985), *The Wandering Border* (1987), *I Am the Spring in Tartu* (1991)—as well as translations into thirteen other languages, among them Japanese, Icelandic, Dutch, Russian, Swedish, Czech and Spanish. In 1996 Kaplinski was short-listed for the Nobel prize in literature. Kaplinski, reluctant poet laureate of his small nordic country with its long colonial and ancient finno-ugric past, had arrived. Today, he is known well beyond the borders of his native Estonia.

The appeal of Kaplinski's poetry is apparent in his success at home and abroad, but the reasons for the attraction are difficult to describe. To write about Kaplinski's poetry is to engage with someone who works at the limits of what can be contained in words and conveyed through art. Moreover, while writing lightly on difficult matters, Kaplinski connects to greater, more complex, elusive, and often forgotten or otherwise endangered contexts. For Kaplinski, these greater contexts include the world of the Siberian shaman as guardian of folkloristic knowledge and mediator between animals, human beings, and nature, and between the living and the dead. He embraces the quest of Taoists, Buddhists, and other thinkers and religions open to paradox and mystical experiences. Seeking closeness to nature, his artistic imagination also extends into Native American culture and the vanishing pre-European, pre-Christian animistic past of his Estonian ancestors. If we are to move closer to one another poetry, in Kaplinski's view, is meant to remind us of something which we have forgotten or haven't noticed yet.

Sweeping across all sorts of boundaries, Kaplinski's poetry evokes many other aspects which go hand in hand with what could be called *interdependencies*. Among them are: seeing the individual as part of a continuously shifting, open-ended network of human beings who co-determine one-another, the primacy of change and the relational, the unintended consequences of planned action, resisting reification, the interconnectedness of past and present, and the social and natural world. Consequently, his poems emphasize ''the openness of things'' (*The Wandering Border*); being open to that which is outside the exclusively rational is central to his writing. As a result, for Kaplinski nouns are ''like ice and snow; in them is death and eternity, which is almost the same'' and he sometimes dreams ''of a language in which there are no nouns, only verbs,'' he writes in *Tükk elatud elu* (*Through the Forest*). Although Kaplinski ''ended up in literature,'' as he explained in *Through the Forest*, ''because it seems, perhaps, closest to [his] proper place,'' he does not think of it as a special place, a place somehow removed, on its own, or exotic. Such lines of separation are not real; they only appear to be. But when they are mistaken for reality, literature can point a way out of the confusion.

Kaplinski's relationship with words and literature is further complicated by his awareness of the limitations of language and art. Life, as Kaplinski's poetry evokes it—including his concern for all things living, the simple and small things we so easily overlook—''cannot be contained in words . . . cannot be explained or understood . . . can only be lived, and perhaps also protected,'' as he put it in *Through the Forest*. Poems are therefore best left unwritten, unless one ''cannot do otherwise,'' which is to say, unless poems help make us ''insiders of life again,'' they are not only superfluous but become part of the problem. To put it differently, as he did in an essay in *Võimaluste Võimalus*, we ''need writers just as we do physicians; we shouldn't think however, that this need for both could not disappear and that such a condition would be bad.'' Moreover, writing and living rarely go hand in hand. Instead, writing more often than not means having ''stepped away from life.'' What is implied here as the aim of literature—not the survival of art, but life itself—writers sometimes forget; Jaan Kaplinski rarely does.

—Thomas Salumets

KAWABATA Yasunari

Born: Osaka, Japan, 11 June 1899. **Education:** Educated at Ibaragi Middle School, 1915–17, and First Higher School 1917–20, Tokyo; Tokyo Imperial University, 1920–24, degree in Japanese literature 1924. **Family:** Married Hideko; one daughter. **Career:** Writer and journalist: helped found *Bungei Jidai* magazine, 1924, and Kamakura Bunko, publishers, Kamakura, later in Tokyo, 1945. Author-in-residence, University of Hawaii, Honolulu, 1969. President, Japanese PEN, 1959–69. **Awards:** Bungei Konwa Kai prize, 1937; Kikuchi Kan prize, 1944; Geijutsuin-shō prize, 1952; Japan Academy of Arts prize, 1952; Noma literary prize, 1954; Goethe medal (Frankfurt), 1959; Prix du Meilleur Livre Étranger, 1961; Nobel prize for literature, 1968. **Member:** Japan Academy of Arts, 1954. First Class Order of the Rising Sun, 1972. **Died:** (suicide) 16 April 1972.

PUBLICATIONS

Collection

Zenshū [Collected Works]. 19 vols., 1969–74.
Dancing Girl of Izu and Other Stories, translated by J. Martin Holman. 1998.

Fiction

Kanjo shushoku [Sentimental Decoration]. 1926.
Tenohira no shosetsu. 1926; as *Palm-of-the-Hand Stories*, translated by Lane Dunlop and J. Martin Helman, 1988.
Izu no odoriko. 1926; as *The Izu Dancer*, translated by Edward Seidensticker, in *The Izu Dancer and Others*, 1964.
Asakusa kurenaidan [The Red Gang of Asakusa]. 1930.
Jojōka [Lyrical Feelings]. 1934.
Kinjū. 1935; as *Of Birds and Beasts*, translated by Edward Seidensticker, in *House of the Sleeping Beauties and Other Stories*, 1969.
Hana no warutsu [The Flower Waltz]. 1936.
Yukiguni. 1937; revised, enlarged edition, 1948; as *Snow Country*, translated by Edward Seidensticker, 1957.
Aisuru hitotachi [Lovers]. 1941.
Utsukushii tabi [Beautiful Travel]. 1947.
Otome no minato [Sea-Port with a Girl]. 1948.
Shiroi mangetsu [White Full-Moon]. 1948.
Maihime [The Dancer]. 1951.
Meijin, in *Shincho*. 1951; revised, enlarged edition, in book form, 1954; shorter version as *The Master of Go*, translated by Edward Seidensticker, 1972.
Sembazuru. 1952; as *Thousand Cranes*, translated by Edward Seidensticker, 1959.
Hi mo tsuki mo [Days and Months]. 1953.
Suigetsu. 1953; as *The Moon on the Water*, translated by George Suitō, in *The Izu Dancer and Others*, 1964.
Yama no oto. 1954; as *The Sound of the Mountain*, translated by Edward Seidensticker, 1970.
Mizuumi. 1955; as *The Lake*, translated by Reiko Tsukimura, 1974.
Onna de aru koto [To Be a Woman]. 1956–58.
Nemureru bijō. 1961; as *House of the Sleeping Beauties*, translated by Edward Seidensticker, in *House of the Sleeping Beauties and Other Stories*, 1969.
The Izu Dancer and Others (includes *Izu Dancer; Reencounter; The Mole; The Moon on the Water*; bilingual edition), translated by Edward Seidensticker and others. 1964.
Kata-ude. 1965; as *One Arm*, translated by Edward Seidensticker, in *House of the Sleeping Beauties and Other Stories*, 1969.
Utsukushisa to kanashimi to. 1965; as *Beauty and Sadness*, translated by Howard S. Hibbett, 1975.
Sakuhin sen [Selected Works]. 1968.

House of the Sleeping Beauties and Other Stories, translated by Edward Seidensticker. 1969.
Tampopo [Dandelion]. 1972.
First Snow on Fuji, translated by Michael Emmerich. 1999.

Other

Bunsho [Prose Style]. 1942.
Zenshū [Collected Works]. 16 vols., 1948–54; revised edition, 12 vols., 1959–61.
Aishu [Sorrow] (stories and essays). 1949.
Asakusa monogatari [Asakusa Story]. 1950.
Shosetsu no kenkyū [Studies of the Novel]. 1953.
Tokyo no hito [The People of Tokyo]. 4 vols., 1955.
Who's Who among Japanese Writers, with Aono Suekichi. 1957.
Koto. 1962; as *The Old Capital*, translated by J. Martin Holman, 1987.
Senshū [Selected Works], edited by Yoshiyuki Junnosuke. 1968.
Utsukushii nihon no watakushi; Japan, The Beautiful, and Myself (Nobel prize lecture; bilingual edition), translated by Edward Seidensticker. 1969.
Shosetsu nyūmon [Introduction to the Novel]. 1970.

*

Critical Studies: *Accomplices of Silence: The Modern Japanese Novel* by Masao Miyoshi, 1974; *The Search for Authenticity in Modern Japanese Literature* by Hisaaki Yamanouchi, 1978; *The Moon in the Water: Understanding Tanizaki, Kawabata, and Mishima* by Gwenn Boardman Petersen, 1979; *Three Modern Novelists: Sōseki, Tanizaki, Kawabata* by Van C. Gessel, 1993; *Soundings in Time: The Fictive Art of Kawabata Yasunari* by Roy Starrs, 1998.

*   *   *

The first of two Japanese Nobel laureates in literature (Ōe Kenzaburo is the other), Kawabata Yasunari is perhaps better known than any other recent writer of his country. His standing at home, however, may not be quite so unchallenged: a large number of critics might mention more intellectual and ideological writers as truly representative of the modern Japanese tradition.

Kawabata's reputation rests on the subtly evocative images that continually startle the reader with clarity and brilliance. When successful—as in *Yukiguni* (*Snow Country*), *Yama no oto* (*The Sound of the Mountain*), or *Nemureru bijō* (*House of the Sleeping Beauties*)—the images serve to add dimensions to the straightforward narrative flow. They suspend the plot, deflect the causal expectation, and open up new spaces for meaning. The narrative vibrates with the fullness of sensory perception that reaches out toward what remains untold. When overcharged, however, the images tend to turn inert. In *Sembazuru* (*Thousand Cranes*) or *Utsukushisa to kanashimi to* (*Beauty and Sadness*), for instance, image after image lights up aimlessly, as if prettiness were the tale's sole objective. The result is an ostentatious display in the manner of airline posters. Kawabata is never completely free from such pitfalls.

Kawabata's dependence on visualization must be explained by the fact that he is essentially a short-story writer. By this it is not meant that he principally wrote short stories—though he in fact did write a great many—but that his "novels" were nearly always accumulated short stories. His longer works grew out of assembled modules, each managing to remain flexible and open-ended like individual verse-stanzas in a *renga* (linked poem). That is, his narrative is generated by spatialization and detemporalization of acts and events. Hence it is not causal but casual: it intersects time and offers the still moments pictorially. Neither psychological nor sociological, Kawabata's narrative is antithetical to novelistic representation and is likewise resistant to novelistic analysis. His characters are often unfulfilled swift sketches, and his plots are series of unconnected *tableaux vivants*. Both are embedded among the beauties of background. In the Kawabata territory, scenery is serious.

Although sensitive to popular demands, Kawabata had a streak of stubbornness that saved as well as damned him. During World War II, he was reluctant to play an active role in the militarist programmes, spending his time quietly reading the nation's classics. In the post-war years when most intellectuals switched their allegiance to Western humanism, Kawabata kept recalling Japan's traditional heritage. Later, when Mishima Yukio's self-destructive histrionics were increasingly antagonizing Japan's literary establishment, Kawabata steadfastly stood with the younger writer. His uncharacteristic involvement in municipal politics just before his own suicide, too, seems inseparable from his attachment to his nationalist friend.

It would be a mistake to latch on to Kawabata's art as the quintessence of the famed "Japanese lyricism." And yet one recalls even now how solacing and encouraging the sensitive images in his work were to the war-ravaged Japanese in those dark post-war years. Kawabata is thus remembered despite his refusal to propose any particular reflection or recommendation in his art.

—Masao Miyoshi

See the essay on *Snow Country*.

KAZANTZAKIS, Nikos

Born: Heraklion, Crete, 18 February 1883. **Education:** Educated at French School of Holy Cross, Naxos, 1897–99; Gymnasium, Heraklion, 1899–1902; University of Athens, 1902–06, degree in law; studied in Paris, Germany, and Italy, 1906–10. **Family:** Married 1) Galatea Alexiou in 1911 (divorced 1926); 2) Eleni Samios in 1945. **Career:** Writer and traveller; Director General of Ministry of Public Welfare, 1919–20; Cabinet Minister Without Portfolio, 1945; served in UNESCO's Department of Translations of the Classics, 1947–48. **Awards:** Lenin peace prize. **Died:** 26 October 1957.

PUBLICATIONS

Fiction

Ophis ke Krino. 1906; as *Serpent and Lily*, translated by Theodora Vasils, with *The Sickness of the Age*, 1980.
Toda Raba (written in French). 1933; as *Toda Raba*, translated by Amy Mims, 1964.
Vios ke Politia tou Alexi Zorba. 1946; as *Zorba the Greek*, translated by Carl Wildman, 1952.

O Kapetan Michalis. 1953; as *Freedom or Death*, translated by Jonathan Griffin, 1956; as *Freedom and Death*, translated by Griffin, 1956.

O Christos Xanastavronete. 1954; as *The Greek Passion*, translated by Jonathan Griffin, 1953; as *Christ Recrucified*, translated by Griffin, 1954.

O Telefteos Pirasmos. 1955; as *The Last Temptation*, translated by Peter Bien, 1960; as *The Last Temptation of Christ*, translated by Bien, 1960.

O Ftochoulis tou Theou. 1956; as *God's Pauper*, translated by Peter Bien, 1962; as *Saint Francis*, translated by Bien, 1962.

Le Jardin des rochers (written in French). 1959; as *The Rock Garden*, translated by Richard Howard (passages from *The Saviors of God* translated by Kimon Friar), 1963.

Aderfofades. 1963; as *The Fratricides*, translated by Athena Gianakas Dallas, 1964.

Sta Palatia tes Knossou. 1981; as *At the Palace of Knossos*, translated by Theodora and Themi Vasils, 1987.

Plays

Ximeroni [Day Is Breaking] (produced 1907). In *Nea Estia*, 1977.

O Protomastoras [The Master Builder] (produced as operatic version, music by Manolis Kalomiris, 1916). In *Panathinea*, 1910.

Nikoforos Fokas [Nicephoros Phokas] (produced 1984). 1927.

Christos [Christ]. 1928.

Melissa (produced in French, 1960; produced in Greek, 1962). In *Nea Estia*, 1939; in book form (author's own French translation), with *Thésée*, 1953; as *Melissa*, translated by Athena Gianakas Dallas, in *Three Plays*, 1969.

Ioulianos o Paravatis [Julian the Apostate] (produced in French, 1945; produced in Greek, 1959). 1945.

Kapodistrias [Capodistria] (produced 1946). 1946.

Sodhoma ke Ghomora (produced 1983). In *Nea Estia*, 1949; as *Sodom and Gomorrah*, translated by Kimon Friar, in *Two Plays*, 1982.

Konstantinos Paleologhos [Constantine Paleologos] (produced in operatic version, music by Manolis Kalomiris, 1962; produced as play 1965). In *Nea Estia*, 1953.

Kouros, from the radio play (produced in English, 1971; produced in Greek, 1977). In author's own French translation, as *Thésée*, with *Melissa*, 1953; in Greek, 1955; as *Kouros*, translated by Athena Gianakas Dallas, in *Three Plays*, 1969.

Prometheas [Prometheus]. In *Theatro*, vol. 1, 1955.

Theatro: Tragodies (includes *Prometheas; Kouros; Odhisseas; Melissa; Ioulianos; Nikoforos Fokas; Konstantinos Paleologhos; Kapodistrias; Christoforos Colomvos; Sodhoma ke Ghomora; Vudhas*). 3 vols., 1955–56.

Vudhas (produced 1978). In *Theatro*, vol. 3, 1956; as *The Buddha*, translated by Kimon Friar and Athena Dallis-Damis, 1983.

Christoforos Colomvos (produced 1975). In *Theatro*, vol. 3, 1956; as *Christopher Columbus*, translated by Athena Gianakas Dallas, in *Three Plays*, 1969.

Comodhia. In *Nea Estia*, 1958; as *Comedy*, translated by Kimon Friar, 1982.

O Othelos Xanayirizi [Othello Returns]. In *Nea Estia*, 1962.

Three Plays (includes *Melissa; Kouros; Christopher Columbus*), translated by Athena Gianakas Dallas. 1969.

Eos Pote [Until When]. In *Nea Estia*, 1977.

Fasgha [Swaddling Clothes]. In *Nea Estia*, 1977.

Two Plays (includes *Sodom and Gomorrah; Comedy*), translated by Kimon Friar. 1982.

Verse

Odhisseas. 1938; as *The Odyssey: A Modern Sequel*, translated by Kimon Friar, 1958.

Tertsines [Poems in Terza Rima]. 1960.

Symposium. 1971; as *Symposium*, translated by Theodora and Themi Vasils, 1973.

Other

O Friderikos Nitse [Friedrich Nietzsche]. 1909.

Salvatores Dei: Askitiki. 1927; revised edition, 1945; as *The Saviors of God: Spiritual Exercises*, translated by Kimon Friar, 1960.

Taxidevontas (travel writing). 1927.

Te eida set Rousia. 2 vols., 1928; later published as *Taxidevontas: Rousia*, 1956; translated as *Russia: A Chronicle of Three Journeys in the Aftermath of the Revolution*, 1989.

Historia tes Rosikes logotechnias [History of Russian Literature]. 2 vols., 1930.

Taxidevontas: Ispania. 1937; as *Spain*, translated by Amy Mims, 1963.

O Morias. 1937; as *Journey to the Morea*, translated by F.A. Reed, 1965; as *Travels in Greece*, translated by Reed, 1966.

Taxidevontas II: Iaponia, Kina. 1938; as *Japan, China*, translated by George Pappageotes, 1963; as *Travels in China and Japan*, translated by Pappageotes, 1964.

Taxidevontas III: Anglia. 1941; translated as *England: A Travel Journal*, 1965.

Epistoles pros te Galatia. 1958; as *The Suffering God: Selected Letters to Galatia and to Papastefanou*, translated by Philip Ramp and Katerina Anghelaki Rooke, 1979.

Anafora ston Greco. 1961; as *Report to Greco*, translated by Peter Bien, 1965.

Tetrakosia grammata tou Kazantzakis sto Prevelaki (letters). 1965.

Journeying: Travels in Italy, Egypt, Sinai, Jerusalem, and Cyprus, translated by Themi and Theodora Vasils. 1975.

Arrostia tou aionos, as *The Sickness of the Age*, translated by Theodora Vasils, with *Serpent and Lily*. 1980.

Megas Alexandros (for children), as *Alexander the Great*, translated by Theodora Vasils. 1982.

Translator, *The Divine Comedy* by Dante; *Faust* by Goethe; *Iliad* by Homer; several Platonic dialogues; *The Birth of Tragedy* and *Thus Spake Zarathustra* by Nietzsche; *The Prince* by Machiavelli; *Conversations with Goethe* by Eckermann; *Origin of Species* by Darwin; *On Laughter* by Bergson; and other works, including many books for children.

*

Bibliography: *Kazantzakis bibliografi* by G.K. Katsimpales, 1958; ''Kazantzakis in America: A Bibliography of Translations and Comment'' by Sandra A. Parker, in *Bulletin of Bibliography*, 25, 1968.

Critical Studies: *Kazantzakis and His Odyssey* by Pandelis Prevelakis, 1961; *Nikos Kazantzakis: A Biography Based on His Letters*, 1968, and *Kazantzakis*, 1970, both by Helen Kazantzakis; *Kazantzakis and* *the Linguistic Revolution in Greek Literature*, 1972, *Three Generations of Greek Writers: Introductions to Cavafy, Kazantzakis, Ritsos*, 1983, *Nikos Kazantzakis: Novelist*, 1989, and *Kazantzakis: Politics of the Spirit*, 1989, all by Peter Bien; *Kazantzakis: The Politics of Salvation* by James F. Lea, 1979; *The Cretan Glance: The World and Art of Nikos Kazantzakis* by Morton P. Levitt, 1980; *God's Struggler: Religion in the Writings of Nikos Kazantzakis*, edited by Darren J.N. Middleton and Peter Bien, 1996; *Kazantzakis and God* by Daniel A. Dombrowski, 1997.

*   *   *

Nikos Kazantzakis was an insatiable traveller, internally and externally. He visited many countries. He read a vast amount of books. He calls to mind Wordsworth's lines about Newton: "a mind for ever/voyaging through strange seas of thought, alone" (*Prelude* III, 62–3). No wonder he took as the hero of his epic a timeless, intellectual Odysseus. This ploy enabled him, in the course of 33,333 lines of great virtuosity, to explore again various answers to the human predicament which he had already considered in travel books, in the slim but significant *Salvatores Dei: Askitiki* (*The Saviors of God: Spiritual Exercises*), and in several plays of unrelieved seriousness. These answers include the philosophy of Nietzsche and Bergson, communism (which he had seen at first hand on visits to Russia in the 1920s), the idea of Christ (rather than any particular form of Christianity), Buddhism, anarchy, nihilism, and so on. In the end they are all found wanting.

Kazantzakis makes his Odysseus exclaim (II, 960): "Hail, my soul, whose homeland has always been the journey!". It is really the poet himself who is speaking. Kazantzakis's view of the world was too all-encompassing for him to be contained by any one literal homeland, even though his Cretan origins were tremendously important to him. Kazantzakis was forever moving on, from one country to another, from one creed to another. But, apart from the journey, there was one "homeland" to which he always remained loyal: "The demotic language is our homeland," he wrote in *Taxidevontas III: Anglia* (*England: A Travel Journal*). He loved natural, spoken Greek passionately. His *Odhisseas* (*The Odyssey*) is not only a hymn to the spirit of man, it is also a hymn to the Greek language.

If Kazantzakis had died in 1938, aged 55, he would probably be known only to a few researchers. The plays "smell of the ink-well," as the Greeks say. The travel books are charming, but slight. *The Odyssey* is too vast, rambling, and daunting. There the case would rest. But on the island of Aegina, during the German occupation, between 1941 and 1943, Kazantzakis wrote his novel *Vios ke Politia tou Alexi Zorba* [The Life and Times of Alexis Zorba], known in English as *Zorba the Greek*. In *Zorba* he exclaims: "if only I could do that, remain silent until the abstract idea reaches its highest point and becomes fable"—which is exactly what he did.

He managed, in his remaining 15 or so years, in five major novels—*O Kapetan Michalis* (*Freedom and Death*), *O Christos Xanastavronete* (*Christ Recrucified*), *O Telefteos Pirasmos* (*The Last Temptation*), *O Ftochoulis tou Theou* (*Saint Francis*), *Aderfofades* (*The Fratricides*)—and one autobiographical masterpiece, *Anafora ston Greco* (*Report to Greco*), to rework, as fables, all the themes that had preoccupied him for years with, for the first time, humanity and humour.

Among Kazantzakis's papers was found a note which said: "Major work—the *Odyssey*. Everything else—spin-offs." It might be more accurate to say that his real odyssey was his lifelong search for the meaning of existence, and that *all* his works, including the enormous epic, were spin-offs from that.

—Roger Green

See the essay on *The Last Temptation*.

KELLER, Gottfried

Born: Zurich, Switzerland, 19 July 1819. **Education:** Educated at Armenschule zum Brunnenturm; Landknabeninstitut, to age 13; Industrieschule, 1832–33; studied painting with Peter Steiger, 1834, and Rudolf Meyer, 1837; Munich Academy, 1840–42. **Career:** Gave up art for writing in Zurich, 1842: government grant to study at University of Heidelberg, 1848–50, and University of Berlin, 1850–55; cantonal secretary (Staatschreiber), 1861–76. **Awards:** Honorary doctorate: University of Zurich, 1869. Honorary Citizen, Zurich, 1878. **Member:** Order of Maximilian (Bavaria), 1876. **Died:** 15 July 1890.

PUBLICATIONS

Collections

Sämtliche Werke, edited by Jonas Fränkel and Carl Helbling. 24 vols., 1926–54.
Werke, edited by Clemens Heselhaus. 2 vols., 1982.

Fiction

Der grüne Heinrich. 1853–55; revised edition, 1880; as *Green Henry*, translated by A.M. Holt, 1960.
Die Leute von Seldwyla (includes *Frau Regel Amrain und ihr Jüngster; Kleider machen Leute; Pankraz, der Schmoller; Romeo und Julia auf dem Dorfe; Der Schmied seines Glückes*). 1856–74; as *The People of Seldwyla*, translated by Martin Wyness, 1911; also translated by M.D. Hottinger, with *Seven Legends*, 1929.
Sieben Legenden. 1872; edited by K. Reichert, 1965; as *Seven Legends*, translated by Martin Wyness, 1911; also translated by C.H. Handschin, 1911; M.D. Hottinger, with *The People of Seldwyla*, 1929.
Züricher Novellen (includes *Hadlaub; Der Landvogt von Greifensee*). 1877.
Das Sinngedicht. 1881.
Martin Salander. 1886; as *Martin Salander*, translated by Kenneth Halwas, 1963.
Clothes Maketh Man and Other Swiss Stories, translated by K. Freiligrath Kroeker. 1894.
Stories, edited by Frank G. Ryder. 1982.

Verse

Gedichte. 1846.
Neue Gedichte. 1852.
Gesammelte Gedichte. 1883.
Gedichte, edited by Albert Köster. 1922.

Other

Briefwechsel, with Theodor Storm, edited by Albert Köster. 1904.
Briefwechsel, with Paul Heyse, edited by Max Kalbeck. 1919.
Gottfried Keller in seinen Briefen, edited by Heinz Amelung. 1921.
Briefwechsel, with J.V. Widmann, edited by Max Widmann. 1922.
Briefe an Vieweg, edited by Jonas Fränkel. 1938.
Gesammelte Briefe, edited by Cart Helbling. 4 vols., 1950–54.
Briefwechsel, with Hermann Hettner, edited by Jürgen Jahn. 1964.
Aus Gottfried Kellers glücklicher Zeit: der Dichter im Briefwechsel mit Marie und Adolf Exner, edited by Irmgard Smidt. 1981.
Kellers Briefe, edited by Peter Goldammer. 1982.
Mein lieber Herr und bester Freund: Gottfried Keller im Briefwechsel mit Wilhelm Petersen, edited by Irmgard Smidt. 1984.
Briefwechsel, with Emil Kuh, edited by Irmgard Smidt and Erwin Streitfeld. 1988.

*

Bibliography: *Keller Bibliographie 1844–1934* by Charles C. Zippermann, 1935.

Critical Studies: *The Cyclical Method of Composition in Keller's "Sinngedicht"* by Priscilla M. Kramer, 1939; *Keller: Kleider machen Leute* by B.A. Rowley, 1960; *Keller: Life and Works* by J.M. Lindsay, 1968; *Light and Darkness in Keller's "Der grüne Heinrich"* by Lucie Karcic, 1976; *Gottfried Keller: Welterfahrung, Werkstruktur und Stil* by Kaspar T. Locher, 1985; *Gottfried Keller: Poet, Pedagogue and Humanist* by Richard R. Ruppel, 1988; *Readers and their Fictions in the Novels and Novellas of Gottfried Keller* by Gail K. Hart, 1989; *The Poetics of Scepticism: Gottfried Keller and Die Leute von Seldwyla* by Eric Swales, 1994; *Gottfried Keller and His Critics: A Case Study in Scholarly Criticism* by Richard R. Ruppel, 1998.

*　*　*

Gottfried Keller, together with Jeremias Gotthelf and Conrad Ferdinand Meyer, is today generally regarded as one of the three pillars of 19th-century Swiss-German literature. His poems are no longer widely read, and he is remembered chiefly for his novel *Der grüne Heinrich* (*Green Henry*), his four collections of short stories, and the correspondence he conducted with writers such as Theodor Storm and Paul Heyse. His reputation was slow to establish itself even in the German-speaking countries, and outside Germany his works have never attracted a readership which truly reflected Keller's standing as a master storyteller and an acute but humane observer of human passion and folly.

Green Henry, conceived as a novel of education (Bildungsroman) within a German tradition which stretches from the medieval *Parzival* to Thomas Mann's *Der Zauberberg* (*The Magic Mountain*) and beyond, depicts in sympathetic and at times painful detail the early life of Heinrich Lee, a young Swiss who is torn between the compulsion to be an artist and the demands of domestic and civic duty. Partly autobiographical, the novel portrays a number of scenes and situations familiar to Keller, ranging from the small Swiss village to student life in Munich. The descriptions of Heinrich's early childhood, his thoughts on religion, his encounters at school, above all his ability to project an inner poetic vision onto events and experiences, reveal strikingly Keller's powers of psychological observation and his capacity to bring out the symbolic and the significant in his treatment of everyday and indeed mundane occurrences.

The second version of the novel lacks the lyrical spontaneity and exuberance of the first; it is provided with a more conciliatory ending and is altogether more measured and distanced in tone and style. It no doubt reflects Keller's own mature view that to renounce art for the sake of duty was not of necessity a tragic choice.

Keller's ability to transcend the surface meaning of events and human actions, and to attribute to them a more universal significance, is even more clearly evident in his collections of stories and short novels, especially in *Die Leute von Seldwyla* (*The People of Seldwyla*) and the cycle of *Züricher Novellen* [Zurich Novellas]. The two groups of Seldwyla tales take as their fictional milieu a small town described by Keller as being "situated somewhere in Switzerland, surrounded by the same old city walls and towers as it was three hundred years ago." The narratives which revolve around this setting display a playful inventiveness and a sharp eye for incongruity and pretence. With humour and gentle irony they lay bare the realities underlying the seemingly placid exterior of peasant and bourgeois life in 19th-century Switzerland, and in doing so they illuminate and clarify the reader's understanding of the perennial conflicts deriving from personal and social relationships.

Literary history tends to assign Keller and his writings to the period of "poetic realism," a movement which some modern critics would disparage as a manifestation of political quiescence produced both for and by the German bourgeoisie. Such generalizations can on occasion be useful, but they would do scant justice to stories like "Romeo und Julia auf dem Dorfe" and "Der Landvogt von Greifensee" which, quite apart from their artistic perfection as narrative structures, touch upon the most basic contradictions which appear whenever individual conscience and consciousness seek to define themselves within systems of social values and traditional beliefs.

—A.P. Foulkes

KENKŌ

Also known as: Yoshida Kenkō; Kenkō hōshi; Urabe Kenkō. **Born:** Urabe Kaneyoshi, in Kyoto, or by one theory in Kamakura, in about 1283. **Education:** Received training appropriate to a low-ranking member of the aristocracy, including native and Chinese classics, poetry, court customs, and Shintō religious texts, in preparation for a hereditary career in shrine service; probably had brief training in scholastic Tendai Buddhism on Mt. Hiei at Yokawa; entrusted with transmissions of secret poetic knowledge by head of Nijō school of poetry. **Military Service:** Assistant Commander of the Left Military Guard (*sahyōe no suke*) at fifth rank before retiring from public life. **Career:** Steward (*keishi*) to Horikawa family, and through these connections became Sixth Rank Chamberlain (*rokui no kurōdo*) to the sovereign Go-Nijō (r.1301–1308); became a monk by 1313; lived as a recluse in Ono and Shūgakuin; traveled east to Kamakura in about 1306 and again perhaps in 1318; returned to live in capital of Kyoto during crisis in leadership of Nijō school of poetry; served as advisor on court customs to at least one military leader; no evidence that he lived at Mt. Yoshida, legends of which earned him the surname Yoshida centuries after his death. **Died:** Probably in Kyoto, no earlier than 1352.

PUBLICATIONS

Essays

Tsurezuregusa. Between 1308 and 1348?; as *Essays in Idleness*, translated by Donald Keene, 1967.

Verse

Kenkō hōshishû. c. 1346?; eight verses added in about 1349; parts translated in *Waiting for the Wind: Thirty-Six Poets of Japan's Late Medieval Age* by Steven D. Carter, 1989.
Minbukyōke hōhen waka. c. 1345–1350.

*

Critical Studies: "Japanese Aesthetics" by Donald Keene, *Philosophy East and West* vol. 19, no. 3, July 1969; "The Birth of the Essay: a Comparative Study of Michel de Montaigne and Yoshida Kenkō" by Naoko Fuwa Thornton, Ph.D. dissertation, Indiana University, 1973; *Formless in Form: Kenkō, Tsurezuregusa, and the Rhetoric of Japanese Fragmentary Prose* by Linda H. Chance, 1997.

*   *   *

A poet of renown in his own day, Kenkō made his mark on Japanese literary history with a work of prose. We have no knowledge of how or when he composed *Tsurezuregusa* (*Essays in Idleness*), and no evidence that his contemporaries knew of or read it. Yet this assemblage of miscellaneous jottings (an introduction and 243 segments, in modern editions) had an enormous impact on later generations, inspiring many readers to call it the most characteristically Japanese piece of literature.

The positive response to *Essays in Idleness* derives from both its form and content. It shares with other classics of Japanese literature a brevity and conciseness of expression. One section (number 192) reads in its entirety "It is best to pay reverence to the gods or the Buddhas on days when others do not, or at night." The aphoristic quality and plain language are common to Buddhist maxims. Other passages invoke the rhetoric and spirit of such female-authored fictions as *The Tale of Genji*. In them, Kenkō creates a romantic atmosphere as he sketches an elegant young man pushing his way through dew-drenched grass (section 44), or a lover pensively watching the moon (section 32). Each such episode finishes with a touch of resigned melancholy, noting, for example, that the young man's identity was a mystery, or that the protagonist has passed away.

Essays in Idleness' ground-note is the impermanence of life, and its renditions of the concept are some of the most famous in Japanese history. How would anything move us, he asks, if life were not fleeting? (section 7). We are most attached to that which is most easily lost, and most deceived about the swiftness with which time threatens to deprive us. From this he concludes that impermanence is not loss, but our highest positive value. Must we have our blossoms in abundance and the moon in a clear sky? Is it not more evocative to conjure spring in a room with the blinds drawn? he inquires (section 137). This emphasis is at the base of Japan's exemplary aesthetic

focus—seen in the arts from ink painting and gardening to ritual tea—on the understated, suggestive, and insufficient. That which is incomplete allows the observer to contribute to the process of its perfection. Rejecting attachment to successful love affairs, in one example, he writes: "To linger over the pain of meetings that ended without intimacy, lament a vow that came to nothing, spend the long night awake and alone, dwell on distant clouds beyond reach, yearn for the past spent in a dwelling overgrown with rushes—all this is within the pursuit of passion." Few can now comprehend what made Kenkō's fellow poets count him among the "Four Guardian Kings" of native verse (*waka no shitennō*). The lines of *Kenkō hōshishû* [Lay Priest Kenkō's Poetry Collection] follow medieval guidelines with scarcely a breath of originality, but his prose still sings to readers.

In addition to delicate, elliptical musings, Kenkō is a master of sharp-tongued pronouncements on the foolishness of humanity. He likens us to ants that scurry east and west, heedless of the futility of our labors (section 74); he warns that no one would be expected to waste time with trivial things were this known to be his or her last night on earth (section 108). Kenkō promotes attentiveness in all things. Each of the arts that a cultured individual might practice, calligraphy or horse-riding, poetry or tree-climbing, should be approached with mental discipline and dedication, as though it were a "Way" toward enlightenment. This pattern of thought had great currency in the 14th century, shaping religious and artistic practices equally. Aesthetic pursuits were the material embodiment of religious sentiment, in fact, an understanding that Kenkō often expresses. He exhorts us to attend to the matter of death, whether revealed in the flourishing of a cherry blossom or the deterioration of a grave, and to hasten on with our devotions.

The past had special attraction for Kenkō, who lamented the degeneracy of behavior the present. One of his professional interests was the transmission of court procedure and precedent. Comments in *Essays in Idleness* indicate that knowledge of the proper methods of tying pheasants to branches (section 66), caring for football fields (section 177), and attaching prisoners to a rack for whipping (section 204) was lost to his contemporaries, to his chagrin.

Kenkō provides some of the more endearing comic portrayals in the literature. A priest who went out for an evening of linked verse competition is attacked on the way home by a man-eating creature he had been warned of. When neighbors rescue him from the river, they learn the attacker was his own dog (section 89). An elderly nun continually mutters a magic word for her absent charge, in case he might be sneezing and in need of protection (section 47); a bishop fumes as people assign him ever more ridiculous nicknames (section 45).

Kenkō's ability to capture the telling moment was enhanced by his reading of *Makura no sōshi* [Pillow Book] of Sei Shōnagon, a work from the late 10th century. Sei is witty and opinionated; Kenkō borrows her technique of tersely enumerating the details that peg a bore or a bumpkin (section 78). Later critics put the two works together as exemplars of the same genre, which they called *zuihitsu*. This Chinese loanword, literally "following the brush," became acknowledged over the centuries as denoting the most amenable form of prose for Japanese sensibility. Capturing a flow of seemingly random thoughts in a work of reflection and restrained comment is still valued highly. Some would say its influence contaminates other genres, producing fiction that downplays plot and scholarly writing that eschews logic. There is a certain logic to the fragment, however, that writers such as Kenkō exploit to great effect. Fragments remind us of the contingency of existence; they force us to participate in a negotiation of meaning as we try to ferret out relationships among them.

Many, especially philosophers and educators, have searched for a single, consistent reading of *Essays in Idleness* nonetheless. At different points in its critical reception, Buddhist moralism, didactic Confucianism, lyricism, or gentlemanly advice have been called key. Critics often note the "contradictions" that surface at multiple points in the text. Whether there is a true contradiction between an injunction to avoid matrimony (section 190) and an observation that men without children have no human feeling (section 142) is open to debate. Yet the fact remains that whenever he seems to contradict himself via his variety of tones and topics, Kenkō incites readers to wonder what attitude he holds. This shifts attention away from the author, who remains at a distance even as he seems to provide strong opinions, while throwing the reader into the work of interpretation. In the process, the reader cannot help but notice that the great issues of life are not so settled after all, and that we must dedicate ourselves to determining how best to manage our short lives.

Some may fault *Tsurezuregusa* for lacking stylistic unity, but mainstream literary tradition accepts this as its primary virtue. From the late 16th century on, when it was first used as a tool for educating the young in the classical modes of Japanese literature, *Essays in Idleness* became an object of wide imitation. Some of those imitations were parodies that ranged from clever to vulgar, but others were serious works that absorbed its manner of moving from subject to subject without obvious transitions. Thus did a work that its author claimed (in a customary humble pose) he planned to tear up spread its imprint on the written heritage.

—Linda H. Chance

KHATIBI, Abdelkebir

Born: El Jadida, Morocco, 11 February 1938; son of Ahmed Belfassi, a theologian and a merchant who died when Khatibi was twelve, and grandson of a stucco craftsman from Fez. **Education:** Received primary education in his hometown, later attended school at the College Sidi Mohammed in Marrakesh, 1950–57; Lycee Lyautey in Casablanca, 1957–58; Sorbonne University, Paris, 1958–64, doctorate in Sociology in 1965. **Family:** Married; one son and one daughter. **Career:** Khatibi joined the faculty of Mohammed V University as a social scientist, Rabat, 1965; while working at the University he became extremely active, not only as a writer and teacher, but also as a significant voice in local politics; one of the founding members of the Union of University Teachers. Wrote his first literary work, *La mémoire tatouée*, which was published in Paris, 1971; wrote numerous fictional and autobiographical works as well as essays in art criticism, cultural inquiry, social science research and non-fiction reflection pieces; withdrew from teaching in order to devote himself to writing, 1979. Director, University Institute for Scientific Research, Rabat, 2002. **Awards:** Grand Prix de l'Académie Française, 1994; Chevalier (Fariss) de l'ordre du trône, 1996; Chevalier de l'Ordre Français des Arts et Lettres, 1997; Lauréat du Grand Prix Atlas, 1997; Grand Prix du Maroc, 1998.

PUBLICATIONS

Collected Essays

Le roman maghrébin. 1968; as *Der maghrebinische Roman*, German translation, 1971.
La blessure du nom proper. 1974.
Vomito blanco. 1974.
Maghreb pluriel. 1983.
Figures de l'étranger. 1987.
Par dessus l'épaule. 1988.
Penser le Maghreb. 1993.

Fiction

La mémoire tatouée. 1971; as *La memoria tatuada*, translated by Kadhim Jihad, 1986.
Le livre de sang. 1979; second edition, 1986; *Amour bilingue*, 1983; as *Love in Two Languages*, translated by Richard Howard, 1990; as *Amore bilingue*, Italian translation, 1992.
Un été à Stockholm. 1990; Arabic translation by Farid Zahi, 1992.
Triptyque de Rabat. 1993.

Poetry

Le lutteur de classe à la manière taoïste. 1979.
Dédicace a l'année qui vient. 1986.

Plays

Le prophète voile. 1979 (produced, Paris, 1973).

Selected essays in literary and cultural criticism

Roman maghrébin et culture nationale, in *Souffles 3*. 1966.
De la critique du langage a la lutte des classes, in *Le Monde*. 1971.
Le Maghreb comme horizon de pensée, in *Les temps modernes*. 1977.
La double critique, in *Liberation* 91. 1977.
De la bi-langue, in *Ecritures*. 1981.
De l'Aimance, in *Intersignes 6–7*. 1993.

Selected articles in sociology

Histoire et sociologie au Maroc. 1966.
Perception et fonction de l'enquête d'opinion. 1966.
Planification familiale et société marocaine. 1966.
Stratification sociale et développement. 1967.
Deux propositions sur le changement social et l'acculturation. 1968.
Bilan dela sociologie au Maroc. 1968.
Pouvoir et administrtion. 1970.
Ouvriers, bourgeois, fonctionnaires. 1970.
La manipulation des aspirations collectives, in *Aspirations et transformations sociales*. 1970.
Hiérarchies pré-coloniales. 1971.
Décolonisation de la sociologie au Maghreb. 1974.
Sociologie du monde arabe, as *Double Criticism in Contemporary North Africa*. 1984.
Mémoire d'une quête, as *Space-time-culture* in the proceedings of the international conference on urbanism in Islam, Tokyo. 1989.

Other

Anthologie de la littérature nord-africaine d'expression française,
     with A. Memmi et al. 1964.
Bibliographie de la littérature nord-africaine d'expresion française,
     with J. Dejeux, et al. 1965.
Ecrivains marocains, with M.T. Benjelloun et al. 1975.
L'art calligraphique arabe, with Mohammed Sijelmassi. 1976.
La peinture de Ahmed Charkaoui, with E.A. El Maleh, et al. 1976;
     second edition as *Ahmed Cherkaoui: La passion du signe*, 1996.
Le même livre, with Jacques Hassoun. 1985.
Du bilinguisme. 1985.
L'art contemporain au Maroc, with Mohamed Sijelmassi. 1989.
Du signe à l'image (le tapis marocain). 1995.
L'art calligraphique de l'islam. 1995; as *The Splendour of Islamic
     Calligraphy*, translated by James Hughes, 1995.

*

Bibliography: *L'Oeuvre de Abdelkebir Khatibi*, Marsam Publications, 1997.

Critical Studies: *Imaginaires de l'autre*, Paris, 1987; *Abdelkebir Khatibi*, Rabat, 1990; *Abdelkebir Khatibi*, Philadelphia, 1990; *Lectures de la pensée de Abdelkebir Khatibi*, 1990; "Itinéraires du politique dans le champ intellectuel marocain" by Abdellah Saaf, in *Politique et savoir*, 1991; "Abdelkebir Khatibi: Writing a Dynamic Identity" by Abdallah Mdarhri Alaoui, in *Research in African Literatures*, 1992; *A. Khatibi* by Marc Gontard, in *Le moi étrange*, 1993; "Decolonizing the Sign: Language and Identity in Abdelkebir Khatibi's *La Mémoire tatouée*" by L.S. McNeece, in *Yale French Studies*, 1993; *Abdelkebir Khatibi: l'écriture de la dualité* by Abdellah Memmes, 1994; "The Fiction of Translation: Abdelkebir Khatibi's *Love in Two Languages*" by Thomas O. Beebee, in *Sub-Stance*, 1994; *Les mots du monde* by Hassan Wahbi, 1995; *Lecture des récits de Abdelkebir Khatibi* by Rachida Saigh Bousta, 1996.

* * *

One of the leading Francophone writers of North Africa, Abdelkebir Khatibi occupies a unique position in the world of letters. A North African Arab steeped in Western culture, Khatibi represents the borderland condition of the postcolonial identity—a perpetually transitional condition of dislocation, providing a double vision, at once liberating and conflicting. Khatibi's writing defies categorization. His narratives, hardly definable as fiction, fall between the genres of poetry, essay, and autobiography; his essays, on the other hand, lyrical and elliptical, offer the reader no linear argument. Articulated in the French language, Khatibi's writing reveals Arabic structures of thought; it is thus a split language, a *bilangue* (a French word Khatibi uses: literally "bi-language"), containing an androgynous indeterminacy that frees it from the univocal, paraphrasable sense.

Bilingualism is one of Khatibi's key motifs. Perhaps his most important work, *Amour bilingue*, published in 1983 and translated into English by Richard Howard as *Love in Two Languages*, is both *about* the condition of bilingualism and *is itself* a passionate engagement with language that grows precisely out of this internal encounter of otherness—an encounter of self and other in the "two tongues" of the bilingual. According to Khatibi, bilingualism is a hybridity that does not assimilate but maintains difference; it is also a condition of language. Bilingualism, he maintains, is an inherent structural fact of

all languages. He emphasizes the split between spoken word and written text—diglossia—as an inherent quality of doubleness and desymmetry, creating endless linguistic possibilities. This dualism is again multiplied in the two languages of the bilingual—in Khatibi's case, French/Arabic. This linguistic duality tends to recur on various levels of self-expression, and shapes the nature of Khatibian thought in general.

But most significantly, for Khatibi, and particularly in *Love in Two Languages*, the language question is not one of choice or compromise—or even of reconciliation—between the two languages; rather, the task is one of furnishing the unthinkable space where both languages can inscribe their reality. Khatibi's vision—double, blurred, layered—redefines the language question for postcolonial culture and emerges in a play of discourse that finally accounts for the uniqueness of his style and the apparent opacity of his text.

The Khatibian reader is formed by the Khatibian text. The reader, too, like the writer, must allow language itself to lead. In an interview with Isabelle Larrivée in *L'Oeuvre de Abdelkebir Khatibi*, Khatibi explains that for him, reality is like a tapestry, and his (the writer's) task is simply to find a thread, to let himself be guided by the force of a moment. The author does not authorize language, but seeks to capture a tone and a rhythm, to embody life in the shape and sound of language: "to transplant from life into writing—this is my passion, my task." Khatibi speaks of being a guest in his own text. Khatibi's writing emerges from that interstitial space in an unexpected genre—elliptical and fragmented, the thought always seduced by the play of words and signs.

The seduction of the language continually leads the writer—and the good reader—in multiple directions. *Amour bilangue* becomes finally a space of the transcultural condition of the Francophone North African Arab. Within the framework of a love story, Khatibi's recit becomes a theoretical discourse, which itself verges on the lyrical and the poetic. The fiction itself becomes almost external, a "pre-text," as Rachida Saigh Bousta argues. Far from presenting a consumable object in the tradition of narrative fiction, she suggests that the Khatibian recit is primarily a literary embodiment of a theoretical reflection and a means of provoking the reader's diligence.

Readers have often complained about the recalcitrance of the Khatibian text, its resistance to interpretation, its elliptical nature, the dispersion of the storyline into various fragments of prose, its elusiveness. In response to a question posed during an interview concerning these difficulties that readers seem to encounter, Khatibi quoted Roland Barthes who had been reproached for the same reasons. When people ask you to be clear, Barthes had told Khatibi, it simply means that they are asking you to be like themselves. For Khatibi, a reader's experience of the difficulty of a text is a confession of that reader's difficult relation with the text. The reader must be engaged in the process of the text's emergence as language and not only a recipient of a message. For Khatibi, language is a process, a movement—both fluid and formative—rather than a vehicle to represent a referential reality.

Khatibi's relationship with language, his existence in several linguistic spaces at once, his painstaking chiseling (in words) of the postcolonial identity—all contribute to the interpenetration of different discourses and different genres in his narratives and essays. In *La mémoire tatouée* [The Tatooed Memory], Khatibi's first literary narrative and his most explicitly autobiographical work, the characteristic attempt to transcend established genres is already manifest.

The generic homogeneity of the narrative is deconstructed by the frequent intrusion of contrasting discourse—poetic and philosophical elements. Like all of Khatibi's texts, *La mémoire tattouée* is written in a continuous mirroring, from the inside out and from the outside in—representing the specular quality of the bilingual identity. In Khatibi's hand, the autobiographical novel is also an account of its theoretical genesis. In it, he dramatizes the genesis and affirmation of his cultural hybridity. The story is constantly being deferred by means of intruding utterances, creating a mosaic-like form of writing. Neither the beginning nor the end of the text is easily determined. The narrative proper is preceded by a prologue which, in turn, is preceded by a preface, written by the author himself, thus creating multiple beginnings. The end of the narrative rendered by the narrator is followed by a stylized parody of a ritualistic monologue, which is followed by a Socratic dialogue, which is followed by a "supplement." Each of these beginnings and endings is written in a clearly different register, contributing to the double-voicedness evident in the whole.

This method of intergenre writing has the important effect of destroying the convention of verisimilitude. Instead of pretending to recreate the temporal experience of a lived past, Khatibi presents us with reflections on the construction of identity in a context of multiple sign systems. The use of this technique—the grafting of various discourses in the narrative—common in the postmodern text, is one of the elements contributing to the opacity of the Khatibian text.

A second and more intriguing element that renders the Khatibian text recalcitrant is his use of images, signs, traces, marks, and letters to form his text. These reaffirm the inherent duality of the subject, for they are taken from Khatibi's Arabo-Islamic heritage and inscribed in the French language, thus remaining inside both signifying systems, yet belonging to neither. Signs, for the narrator in *La mémoire tatouée* for instance, are linked to the sacred; they radiate by association, and serve to bind the individual to his heritage.

Yet, asked about the thinkers who influenced him and to whom he feels indebted, Khatibi lists exclusively European thinkers: Sartre, Marx, Nietzsche, Kierkegaard, Derrida, Blanchot, and Foucault. And in spite of this very accurate perception of his intellectual formation, Khatibi remains a North African intellectual—a foreigner in his own culture, a host and a guest in the postcolonial text of the 21st century.

—Faiza Shereen

KHLEBNIKOV, Velimir

Born: Viktor Vladimirovich Khlebnikov in Malye Derbety, near Tundutovo, Astrakhan province, Russia, 28 October 1885. **Education:** Educated at Kazan' Third Gymnasium, 1898–1903; studied mathematics and natural sciences at University of Kazan', 1903–08; studied biology and Slavic languages, University of St. Petersburg, 1909–11. **Military Service:** Served in Tsarist army, 1916–17. **Career:** Associated with Futurist and other literary groups; wandering poet, travelled across Russia: arrested by Whites in Kharkov, then by Reds, 1919; worked in Caucasus propaganda bureau (Rosta) in Baku, 1920; lecturer in Revolutionary army headquarters in Persia, 1921; night watchman in Rosta office in Piatigorsk, 1921. **Died:** 28 June 1922.

PUBLICATIONS

Collections

Stikhi [Poems]. 1923.
Sobranie proizvedenii [Collected Works], edited by Yurii Tynianov and Nikolai Stepanov. 5 vols., 1928–33.
Neizdannye proizvedenii [Unpublished Works], edited by N. Khardziev and T. Grits. 1940.
Stikhotvoreniia i poemy [Poetry and Narrative Verse], edited by Nikolai Stepanov. 1960.
Sobranie sochinenii [Collected Works]. 4 vols., 1968–72.
Snake Train: Poetry and Prose, edited by Gary, Kern, translated by Kern, Richard Sheldon, Edward J. Brown, Neil Cornwell, and Lily Feiler. 1976.
The King of Time, edited by Charlotte Douglas, translated by Paul Schmidt. 1985.
Izbrannoe [Selection], edited by V. Smirnov. 1986.
Collected Works:
    1. *Letters and Theoretical Writings*, edited by Charlotte Douglas, translated by Paul Schmidt. 1987.
    2. *Prose, Plays and Supersagas*, edited by Ronald Vroon. 1989.

Works

Uchitel' i uchenik [Teacher and Pupil]. 1912.
Igra v adu [A Game in Hell]. 1912.
Riav! Perchatki 1908–1914 [Roar! The Gauntlets]. 1913.
Izbornik stikhov 1907–1914 [Selected Verse]. 1914.
Tvoreniia (1906–1908) [Creations]. 1914.
Bitvy 1915–1917: Novoe uchenie o voine [Battles: The New Teaching about War]. 1915.
Vremia mera mira [Time the Measure of the World]. 1916.
Truba marsian [The Martian Pipe]. 1916.
Oshibka smerti [Death's Mistake] (produced 1920). 1916.
Ladomir [Goodworld]. 1920.
Noch' v okope [A Night in the Trench]. 1921.
Vestnik [Herald]. 2 vols., 1922.
Zangezi. 1922.
Otryvok iz dosok sud'by [Fragment from the Boards of Destiny]. 3 vols., 1922–23.
Nastoiashchee [Genuine]. 1926.
Vsem: Nochnoi bal [For Everyone: The Night Ball]. 1927.
Zverinets [Menagerie]. 1930.
Voisko pesen [Military Song]. 1985.
Stikhotvoreniia. Poemy. Dramy. Proza [Poetry. Narrative Verse. Drama. Prose]. 1986.
Stikhotvoreniia [Poetry]. 1988.
Utes iz budushchego [The Rock of the Future]. 1988.
Proza [Prose]. 1990.
Stikhi, poemy [Poems, Narrative Verse]. 1991.

*

Critical Studies: *The Longer Poems of Khlebnikov*, 1961, and *Russian Futurism: A History*, 1968, both by Vladimir Markov; *Xlebnikov and Carnival: An Analysis of the Poem "Poet"* by Barbara

Lonnqvist, 1979; *Velimir Xlebnikov's Shorter Poems: A Key to the Coinages* by Ronald Vroon, 1983; *Velimir Chlebnikov and the Development of Poetical Language in Russian Symbolism and Futurism* by Willem G. Weststeijn, 1983.

* * *

When the Russian Futurists "slapped the face of public taste" it was largely with the gauntlet of Velimir Khlebnikov's work that they administered the blow. His experimentation with the Russian language and his ingenious neologisms helped to earn the Futurists the notoriety they were seeking. His work on the word was an embodiment of the Futurist aesthetic stance. He placed the word at the centre of attention, showed how it could develop according to an inner logic. A fossilized literary language came alive at his touch.

The Futurists proclaimed Khlebnikov "King of Russian Poetry." He could not, however, summon the regal presence or stentorian tones of such as Maiakovskii. Although the Futurists toured Russia, Khlebnikov did not take part. He seemed to have a pathological inability to perform in public. Yet, Russian Futurism without Khlebnikov would have been an empty shell.

Nevertheless, Khlebnikov's association with the Futurists was somewhat double-edged. Their tendency to publicize those of his works which reflected the movement's iconoclastic interests led to him acquiring a reputation as a poet of gibberish. This is a grave misjudgement. Despite his espousal of the "self-developed" word, Khlebnikov was a keen seeker after meaning. Even his transrational language (*zaum'*) was designed not to destroy meaning but to enhance it.

Khlebnikov's preoccupation with language should not be stressed unduly. His work reveals a considerable concern for the world as well as the word. Social and ideological motivations provided a major inspiration for his writing. Many works reflect militant pan-Slavist and revolutionary sentiments. He was opposed to Western influence and looked towards the folk art of the Russian and Slavic peoples. He also directed his gaze eastwards towards India, Persia, and Central Asia.

After the outbreak of World War I Khlebnikov directed his poetic militancy against war. This campaign soon intermingled with a general assault on the arbitrary nature of fate. He became increasingly preoccupied with numerological theories aimed at discovering the laws of time. By practical prophecy he wished to make man the master of his destiny, to make him capable of directing his passage through the centuries like a ship along the Volga. This utopian element finds expression in much of his work. However, running parallel to it is a vivid awareness of the conflict and disaster constantly threatening mankind. Convinced that events unfolded according to some determinable and rational schema, Khlebnikov proclaimed that "measure" had come to replace faith. Yet there is something irrational about his faith in "measure." His mathematical formulas can appear as incantational as his verse.

As well as his "experimental" works Khlebnikov was an author of long poems with an unusual epic sweep, of short lyric verse with surprising depth, of prose, and of drama. Above all he was a visionary, and it is this vision coupled with an acute sensitivity towards the world which makes some of his works among the best in Russian literature.

—Ray Cooke

See the essay on "Incantation by Laughter."

KIERKEGAARD, Søren

Pseudonyms: Victor Eremita, Johannes de Silentino, Constantin Constantinus, Virgilius Haufniensis, Johannes Climacus, Hilarius Bogbinder, Anti-Climacus, H.H. Moreover. **Born:** Søren Aabye Kierkegaard, in Copenhagen, Denmark, 5 May 1813. **Education:** Studied theology at the University of Copenhagen, graduating with distinction in 1840. **Family:** Engaged to Regine Olsen, 1840–41. **Career:** Entered the University of Copenhagen to study theology according to his father's wishes, and instead immersed himself in the study of literature, philosophy, and history, 1830; rejected Christianity and became estranged from father, 1830–36; resisted suicidal temptation, 1836; received a sizable inheritance when his father died, 1838; returned to Christianity after experience of "indescribable joy," 1838; defended his thesis, The Concept of Irony, decided against becoming a minister, 1841; published *Either/Or*, 1843; visited Berlin, Germany, 1846; attacked the publication *Corsair* and was lampooned by the publication; 1846; attacked the Danish State Church as an institution of secular humanism, 1848; increased his negative criticism of Danish State Church following death of family friend Bishop Mynster, 1854. **Died:** 4 November 1855, following a massive stroke suffered while passing out pamphlets on a Copenhagen street.

PUBLICATIONS

Collections

Papirer. 1909–48; as *Søren Kierkegaard's Journals and Papers*, 1967–78.
Samlede Vaerker. 1962–64.
Without Authority: Kierkegaard's Writings . 25 vols., edited and translated by Howard V. Hong and Edna H. Hong, with introduction and notes, 1997.

Philosophy

Om Begrebet Ironi med stadigt Hensyn til Socrates. 1841; as *On the Concept of Irony, with Special Reference to Socrates*, translated by Lee M. Capel, 1966; as *The Concept of Irony, with Continual Reference to Socrates: Together with Notes of Schelling's Berlin Lectures*, edited and translated by Howard V. Hong and Edna H. Hong, 1989.
Enten/Eller (as Victor Eremita). 1843; as *Either/Or: A Fragment of Life*, translated by David F. Swenson and Lillian Marvin Swenson, 1944; also translated by George L. Stengren, 1986; Howard V. Hong and Edna H. Hong, 1987; Alastair Hannay, 1992.
Frygt og Baeven (as Johannes de Silentino). 1843; as *Fear and Trembling: A Dialectical Lyric by Johannes de Silentino*, translated by Robert Payne, 1939; also translated by Walter Lowrie, 1941; Howard V. Hong and Edna H. Hong, 1983; Alastair Hannay, 1985.
Gjentaglesen: Et Forsog I den experimenterende Psychologi (as Constantin Constantinus). 1843; as *Repetition: An Essay in Experimental Psychology*, translated by Walter Lowrie, 1941.
Opbyggelige Taler. 1843–44; as *Edifying Discourses*, translated by David F. and Lillian Marvin Swenson, 1943–46.

Begrebet Angest (as Virgilius Haufniensis). 1844; as *The Concept of Anxiety*, translated with introduction and notes by Walter Lowrie, 1944.

Philosophiske Smuler (as Johannes Climacus). 1844; as *Philosophical Fragments; or, A Fragment of Philosophy*, translated by David F. Swenson, 1936; revised translation by Howard V. Hong, 1962.

Stadier paa Livets Vej (as Hilarius Bogbinder). 1845; as *Stages on Life's Way*, translated by Walter Lowrie, 1940; also translated by Howard V. Hong and Edna H. Hong, 1988.

Tre Taler ved taenkte Leiligheder. 1845; as *Thoughts on Crucial Situations in Human Life: Three Discourses on Imagined Occasions*, translated by David F. Swenson, 1941.

Afsluttende uvidenskabelig Efterskrift (as Johannes Climacus). 1846; as *Concluding Unscientific Postscript to the Philosophical Fragments*, translated by David F. Swenson and Walter Lowrie, 1941; also translated and edited by Howard V. Hong and Edna H. Hong, 1992.

En literair Anmeldelse. To Tidsaldre. 1846; as *Two Ages: The Age of Revolution and the Present Age, A Literary Review*, translated and edited by Howard V. Hong and Edna H. Hong, 1978.

Bogem om Adler. 1846–47; as *On Authority and Revelation: The Book on Adler*, translated with introduction by Walter Lowrie, 1955.

Kjerlighedens Gjerninger. 1847; as *Works of Love*, translated by David F. Swenson and Lillian Marvin Swenson, 1946.

Opbyggelige Taler I forskjellig Aand. 1847; as *Edifying Discourses in a Different Vein*, translated by David F. Swenson and Lillian Marvin Swenson, 1938.

Krisen og en Krise I en Skuespillerindes Liv. 1848; as *Crisis in the Life of an Actress* , in *Crisis in the Life of an Actress, and Other Essays on Drama by Søren Kierkegaard*, translated with introduction and notes by Stephen Crites, 1967; also translated by Howard V. Hong and Edna H. Hong, in *Christian Discourses: The Crisis and a Crisis in the Life of an Actress*, 1997.

Christelige Taler. 1848; as *Christian Discourses*, translated by Walter Lowrie, 1939; also translated by Howard V. Hong and Edna H. Hong, in *Christian Discourses: The Crisis and a Crisis in the Life of an Actress*, 1997.

Sygdommen til Doden (as Anti-Climacus). 1849; as *The Sickness unto Death*, translated by Walter Lowrie, 1941; also translated by Howard V. Hong and Edna H. Hong, 1980; Alastair Hannay, 1989.

Tre Taler ved Altergangen om Fredagen. 1849; as *Three Discourses at the Communion on Fridays*, translated by Walter Lowrie, 1939; also translated by Howard V. Hong and Edna H. Hong in *Kierkegaard's Writings: XVIII: Without Authority* , 1997.

Tvende ethisk-religieuse Smaa-Afhandlinger (as H.H. Moreover). 1849; as *Two Minor Ethico-Religious Treatises*, translated by Alexander Dru and Walter Lowrie, 1940.

Indovelse i Christendom (as Anti-Climacus). 1850; as *Training in Christianity*, translated by Walter Lowrie, 1941.

Om min Forfatter-Virksomhed. 1851; as *On My Work as an Author*, published in *The Point of View for My Work as an Author*, translated by Walter Lowrie, 1939; also translated by Howard V. Hong and Edna H. Hong, 1998.

Til Selprovelse. 1851; as *For Self-Examination*, translated by Walter Lowrie, 1940; also translated by Howard V. Hong and Edna H. Hong, 1990.

Hvad Christus dommer om official Christendom . 1855; as *Kierkegaard's Attack upon "Christendom," 1854–1855*, translated by Walter Lowrie, 1944.

*

Bibliography: *Søren Kierkegaard and His Critics: An International Bibliography of Criticism*, compiled by François H. Lapointe, 1980.

Critical Studies: *A History of Philosophy; Volume VII: Modern Philosophy from the Post-Kantian Idealists to Marx, Kierkegaard, and Nietzsche* by Frederick Copleston, S.J., 1965; *Socrates to Sartre: A History of Philosophy* by Samuel Enoch Stumpf, 1966; *Kierkegaard's Authorship: A Guide to the Writings of Kierkegaard* by George Bartholomow and George E. Arbaugh, 1968; *Philosophy & the Christian Faith* by Colin Brown, 1968; *Søren Kierkegaard* by Brita K. Stendahl, 1976; *A Kierkegaard Handbook* by Frederick Sontag, 1978; *Kierkegaard and Literature: Irony, Repetition, and Criticism* edited by Ronald Schleifer and Robert Markley, 1984; *Foundations of Kierkegaard's Vision of Community: Religion, Ethics, and Politics in Kierkegaard* edited by George B. Connell and C. Stephen Evans, 1992; *Kierkegaard for Beginners* by Donald D. Palmer, 1996.

*   *   *

Søren Kierkegaard is considered by many historians of philosophy as the progenitor of the existentialist school of thought. Existentialism, as named by French philosopher and novelist Jean-Paul Sartre—who considered Kierkegaard one of his major inspirations—emphasizes the individual and the personal, subjective choice to either exercise ultimate freedom or responsible restraint. Kierkegaard endured ridicule and had a reputation as a crackpot, especially in the years immediately preceding his death, in the then small, enclosed town of Copenhagen. About 70 years after his death, 20th-century philosophers and translators introduced Kierkegaard's works to a larger audience outside Denmark, causing him to be reassessed as one of the modern age's most prodigious and profound philosophical thinkers.

Many of Kierkegaard's writings were reactions against the predominant philosophy of the early 19th-century, primarily the writings of German metaphysical idealist Georg Wilhelm Friedrich Hegel. Hegel attempted to construct a dialectic that explained both the world and its divine governance according to human reason. Kierkegaard argued that Hegel's system relied too heavily on a belief in objective or universal truths and neglected to consider the choices made by individuals. Kierkegaard wrote that men and women exercise self-commitment in choosing one action or belief over another and, furthermore, that these acts of self-commitment are based upon the subjective determination of each individual rather than upon universally agreed-upon truths.

Central to Kierkegaard's system of belief is that individuals operate in one of three realms—the aesthetical, the ethical, or the religious. Aesthetical humans engage in a life of the senses and emotion. Rather than limit his definition of the aesthetic human to such hedonists as Don Juan, Kierkegaard included the Romantic poets who engaged in what he considered the worship of ultimate freedom, nature, and imagination. Kierkegaard believed that submission to an aesthetic life void of salvation led to a despair that could only be mediated by choosing to commit oneself to the ethical realm. The ethical human, represented by the Greek philosopher Socrates, believes that humans can overcome their individual foibles by acts of willpower guided by ethical ideals. For example, a hedonist may suppress his or her sexual impulses by choosing to adopt a life of marital fidelity, which Kierkegaard believed to be an ethical choice. This realm, however, is predicated on the assumption that humankind is capable of determining all differences between right and wrong without the acknowledgement of the existence of sin in terms of divine law. This determination can be achieved only through religious faith. To illustrate his point, Kierkegaard employed the Old Testament story of Abraham and Isaac. Abraham's choice to murder his son at the bequest of God, Kierkegaard said, was not an ethical choice, but a religious choice based upon Abraham's faith. Such a faith cannot be explained in terms of human reason and ethics, but only through an individual's relationship with God. The belief in such a God required what Kierkegaard called a "leap of faith," which is a conscious exercise of choice to accept the existence of God, and the willingness to trust in God's demands however contrary such demands are to human standards of morality.

—Bruce Walker

KIŠ, Danilo

Born: Subotica, Serbia, 22 February 1935. Jewish parents sent to Auschwitz in 1944; brought up by uncle in Cetinje, Yugoslavia. **Education:** Educated locally in Hungary to age 13, then high school in Cetinje; Belgrade University, degree in comparative literature 1958. **Career:** Editor, *Vidici*; lecturer in Serbo-Croat, Universities of Strasbourg, 1961–63, Bordeaux, 1973–76, and Lille, 1979–83; also translator from a number of languages; lived and worked in Paris, from 1979. **Awards:** NIN prize, 1973; Ivan Goran Kovacič prize, 1977; Grand Aigle d'Or (Nice), 1980; Ivo Andrić award, 1984; PEN Bruno Schulz prize 1989. **Died:** 15 October 1989.

PUBLICATIONS

Fiction

Mansarda; Psalam 44 [The Garret; Psalm 44]. 1962.
Bašta, pepeo. 1965; as *Garden, Ashes*, translated by William J. Hannaher, 1976.
Rani jadi [Early Sorrows] (stories). 1969; as *Early Sorrows: For Children and Senstive Readers*, translated by Michael Henry Heim, 1998.
Peščanik. 1972; as *Hourglass*, translated by Ralph Manheim, 1990.
Grobnica za Borisa Davidoviča (stories). 1976; as *A Tomb for Boris Davidovich*, translated by Duška Mikić-Mitchell, 1978.
Enciklopedija mrtvih. 1983; as *The Encyclopedia of the Dead*, translated by Michael Henry Heim, 1989.

Plays

Elektra (produced 1969).

Noć i magla [Night and Mist] (includes *Papagaj* [The Parrot]; *Drveni sanduk Tomasa Vulfa* [The Wooden Chest of Thomas Wolfe]; *Mehanički lavovi* [The Mechanical Lions]). 1983.

Other

Po-etika [Poetics]. 2 vols., 1972–74.
Caš anatomije [The Anatomy Lesson]. 1978.
Homo poeticus. 1983; as *Homo poeticus: Essays and Interviews*, edited with introduction by Susan Sontag, 1995.
Sabrana dela [Collected Works]. 10 vols., 1983.
Gorki talog iskustva (interviews), with Mirjana Miočinović. 1990.
Pesme i preperi, edited by Predrag Cudic. 1992.
Editor, with Mirjana Miočinović, *Sabrana dela* [Collected Works], by Lautréamont. 1964.
Translator of the poetry of Verlaine and Baudelaire.

*

Critical Studies: "Imaginary-Real Lives: On Danilo Kiš" by Norbert Czarny and Catherine Vincent, in *Cross Currents*, 3, 1984; "Danilo Kiš: From "Enchantment" to "Documentation"" by Branko Gorjup, in *Canadian Slavonic Papers*, 29(4), 1987; "Danilo Kiš: Encyclopedia of the Dead" by Predrag Matvejevic, in *Cross Currents*, 1988; "The Awakening of Sleepers in Danilo Kiš's *Encyclopedia of the Dead*" by Jelena S. Bankovic-Rosul, in *Serbian Studies*, Spring 1990; "Danilo Kiš, 1935–1989" by Gyorgy Spiro, in *New Hungarian Quarterly*, 31(119), 1990; "Silk, Scissors, Gardens, Ashes: The Autobiographical Writing of Irena Vrkljan and Danilo Kiš" by Celia Hawkesworth, in her *Literature and Politics in Eastern Europe*, 1992; *Proza Danila Kiśa* by Peter Pijanović, 1992.

* * *

Danilo Kiš occupied a pre-eminent position among contemporary Yugoslav writers on the strength of his carefully crafted fiction, but his other literary ventures—plays for radio and television, essays and translations from French, Hungarian, and Russian—have also been held in high esteem. His early novels, *Mansarda* [The Garret] and *Psalam 44* [Psalm 44], have clearly indicated two important features of Kiš as a fiction writer: his keen interest in the themes of human suffering and his lack of interest in the vestiges of traditional realistic narrative and classical psychological analysis.

Mansarda is basically a story of youthful love patterned on the myth of Orpheus and Eurydice, but what the novel captures best is the garret atmosphere of the hero's juvenile world of capricious daydreams, hallucinations, paradoxical reasoning, and cynicism from which he is "dethroned" and brought down to face the demanding banalities of everyday life. Many quotations and literary and mythological allusions give the novel a strong intellectual edge. The author's concern with the contrasting facets of existence and the playful dance of his language make this story of how innocence changes into experience one of the most original first novels published in Yugoslavia after World War II.

Psalam 44 is Kiš's attempt at the literature of the Holocaust. It is a stream-of-consciousness novel in which a young Jewish girl reveals her distressing history in the tense moments preceding her escape from the Birkenau concentration camp with her newborn baby and her French girlfriend. The account of her desperate efforts to survive after the escape is concluded with a qualified happy ending: the reunited family visit the camp six years afterwards in order to hand down to the child "the joy of those who, out of death and love, were able to create life." The most impressive feature of the novel is the dispassionate, almost lethargic calmness of the narrative, which recaptures in most grisly detail the abyss of human agony.

Kiš's next novel, *Bašta, pepeo* (*Garden, Ashes*), has a strong autobiographical element. The narrator-protagonist is the Jewish boy Andreas Sam, who grows up in the Danubian plains in the 1940s, before, during, and after the war. His memories concentrate on a small, tightly knit group of characters, but are dominated by the overpowering personality of his father, Eduard, a railway official who has compiled a gigantic Universal Timetable and who disappears during the Holocaust. The book is in large measure the search by a son for the father (a hypochondriac, lunatic dreamer, drunkard, and loner) he lost even before his death, in an attempt to establish distant and unnoticed connections which in his childhood he could not believe existed. A skilful interweaving of introspective poetic strands, striking intellectual displays, and reminiscences almost sensuously brought to life makes this book a particular kind of creative autobiography, clothed in a fine net of soft lyrical weave. Kiš followed it with a sequel, *Rani jadi* [Early Sorrows], a collection of short stories where the Sam family appears again portrayed in the same tone of melancholic lyricism and psychological subtlety.

Peščanik (*Hourglass*), where the same father-figure turns up under the initials E.S., is a novel which seemingly lacks all thematic and narrative coherence. It is composed of various texts referring to E.S., his motivations and actions, but the key to understanding these diverse writings (letters, documents, reports, and notes), which demand the reader's utmost concentration and patience, is given at the end of the book, in a letter written by E.S. to his sister. It casts a revealing light on Kiš's apparently chaotic narrative and discloses its moral seriousness in the history of a man who, in the inferno of history and amid the atmosphere of selfishness and indifference, tries to secure the survival of his family.

Grobnica za Borisa Davidoviča (*A Tomb for Boris Davidovich*), a collection of short stories concerned with the theme of suffering of the innocent, makes a new departure. All the stories except one, which takes place in southern France in 1330, describe the misfortunes of several characters (mostly Jewish) who perished in the Soviet labour camps or died in the USSR as the victims of forces of terror. The stories, based on authentic documents and case histories, are an original hybrid of fiction and "faction" and bear a general resemblance to Arthur Koestler's *Darkness at Noon*, "although surpassing it in both horrifying detail and narrative skill," as Joseph Brodskii said in his introduction to the English translation. Accused of plagiarism by some Yugoslav critics, Kiš refuted their allegations in the highly polemic *Čas anatomije* [The Anatomy Lesson], turning his defence into a virulent satire of his critics.

In his last volume of short stories, *Enciklopedija mrtvih* (*The Encyclopedia of the Dead*), Kiš widened his thematic range through his interest in ancient legends and metaphysical strata of existence. His paramount concern for human suffering caused by forces of history, however, preserved its centrality in all his writing.

—Dušan Puvačić

KLEIST, (Bernd) Heinrich (Wilhelm) von

Born: Frankfurt an der Oder, Brandenburg (now Germany), 18 October 1777. **Education:** Studied law, University of Frankfurt, 1799. **Military Service:** Entered the Prussian army in 1792; took part in the siege of Mainz, 1793, promoted to second lieutenant, 1979, resigned his commission, 1799. **Career:** Travelled throughout Germany, and to Paris and Switzerland, 1800–04; attempted to join the French army, 1803; civil servant, Königsberg, 1805–06; co-founder, with Adam Müller, and editor, *Phöbus*, Dresden, 1808–09; attempted unsuccessfully to publish the newspaper *Germania*, in Prague, 1809; editor, *Berliner Abendblätter*, 1810–11. Suffered many nervous breakdowns. **Died:** (suicide) 21 November 1811.

PUBLICATIONS

Collections

Hinterlassene Schriften, edited by Ludwig Tieck. 1821.
Gesammelte Schriften, edited by Ludwig Tieck. 3 vols., 1826.
Werke, edited by Erich Schmidt and others. 5 vols., 1904–05; revised edition, 7 vols., 1936–38.
Sämtliche Werke und Briefe, edited by Helmut Sembdner. 2 vols., 1961.
Three Plays, translated by Noel Clark. 1997.
Three Major Plays, translated by Carl R. Mueller. 2000.

Plays

Die Familie Schroffenstein (produced 1804). 1803; as *The Feud of the Schroffensteins*, translated by Mary J. and Lawrence M. Price, 1916.
Amphitryon (produced 1899). 1807; as *Amphitryon*, translated by Marion Sonnenfeld, 1962; also translated by Charles E. Passage, in *Amphitryon: Three Plays in New Verse Translations*, 1973; Martin Greenberg, in *Five Plays*, 1988; as *God's Gift: A Version of Amphitryon by Heinrich von Kleist* by John Banville, 2000.
Der zerbrochene Krug (produced 1808). 1811; as *The Broken Pitcher*, translated by Bayard Quincy Morgan, 1961; also translated by Jon Swan, in *Plays*, 1982; as *The Broken Jug*, translated by Lawrence P.R. Wilson, in *Four Continental Plays*, edited by John P. Allen, 1964; also translated by Roger Jones, 1977; Martin Greenberg, in *Five Plays*, 1988; translated and adapted by Blake Morrison as *The Cracked Pot: A Play*, 1996. Penthesilea (produced 1876). 1808; as *Penthesilea*, translated by Humphry Trevelyan, in *The Classic Theatre*, edited by Eric Bentley, 1959; also translated by Martin Greenberg, in *Five Plays*, 1988; as *Penthesilea: A Tragic Drama*, translated and introduced by Joel Agee, 1998.
Das Käthchen von Heilbronn (produced 1810). 1810; as *Kate of Heilbronn*, translated by Elijah B. Impey, in *Illustrations of German Poetry*, 1841; as *Käthchen of Heilbronn; or, the Test of Fire*, translated by Frederick E. Pierce, in *Fiction and Fantasy of German Literature*, 1927.
Prinz Friedrich von Homburg (produced 1821). In *Hinterlassene Schriften*, 1821; as *The Prince of Homburg*, translated by Charles E. Passage, 1956; also translated by James Kirkup, in *The Classic Theatre*, edited by Eric Bentley, 1959; as *Prince Frederick of*

Homburg, translated by Peggy Meyer Sherry, in *Plays*, 1982; also translated by Martin Greenberg, 1988.

Die Hermannsschlacht (produced 1839). In *Hinterlassene Schriften*, 1821.

Robert Guiskard (unfinished; produced 1901). In *Gesammelte Schriften*, 1826; as *A Fragment of the Tragedy of Robert Guiscard*, translated by Martin Greenberg, in *Five Plays*, 1988.

Plays (*The Broken Pitcher; Amphitryon; Penthesilea; Prince Frederick of Homburg*), edited by Walter Hinderer. 1982.

Five Plays (includes *Amphitryon; The Broken Jug; Penthesilea; Prince Frederick of Homburg; A Fragment of the Tragedy of Robert Guiscard*), translated by Martin Greenberg. 1988.

Fiction

Erzählungen. 2 vols., 1810–11.

The Marquise of O. and Other Stories, translated by Martin Greenberg. 1960; also translated by David Luke and Nigel Reeves, 1978.

Michael Kohlhaas, translated by J. Oxenford, 1844; also translated by F. Lloyd and W. Newton, 1875; F.H. King, 1919; James Kirkup, 1967; Harry Steinhauer, in *Twelve German Novellas*, 1977; David Luke and Nigel Reeves, in *The Marquiss of O. and Other Stories*, 1978.

Other

Briefe an seine Schwester Ulrike, edited by August Koberstein. 1860.

Briefe an seine Braut, edited by Karl Biedermann and others. 1884.

Über das Marionettentheater: Aufsätze und Anekdoten, edited by Helmut Sembdner. 1935; revised edition, 1980; as *On a Theatre of Marionettes*, translated by G. Wilford, 1989; as *On Puppetshows*, translated by David Paisley, 1991.

Lebensspuren: Dokumente und Berichte der Zeitgenossen, edited by Helmut Sembdner. 1964.

An Abyss Deep Enough: Letters of Heinrich von Kleist (includes essays), edited and translated by Philip B. Miller. 1982.

*

Bibliography: *Kleist-Bibliographie 1803–1862* by Helmut Sembdner, 1966.

Critical Studies: *Reason and Energy* by Michael Hamburger, 1957; *Kleist: Studies in His Work and Literary Character* by Walter Silz, 1961; *Heinrich von Kleist's Dramas* by E.L. Stahl, 1961; *Kleist's "Prinz Friedrich von Homburg": An Interpretation Through Word Patterns* by Mary Garland, 1968; *Kleist: A Study in Tragedy and Anxiety* by John Gearey, 1968; *Kleist's Prinz Friedrich von Homburg: A Critical Study*, 1970, and *Heinrich von Kleist*, 1979, both by J.M. Ellis; *From Lessing to Hauptmann: Studies in German Drama* by Ladislaus Löb, 1974; *The Major Works of Heinrich von Kleist* by R.E. Helbling, 1975; *Kleist and the Tragic Ideal: A Study of Penthesilea and its Relationship to Kleist's Personal and Literary Development, 1806–1808* by H.M. Brown, 1977; *The Stories of Kleist: A Critical Study* by Denys Dyer, 1977; *Heinrich von Kleist: Word into Flesh: A Poet's Quest for the Symbol* by Ilse Graham, 1977; *Von Kleist: From Hussar to Panzer Marshal* by Clyde R. Davis, 1979; *Heinrich von Kleist: Studies in the Character and Meaning of His Writings* by J.M. Ellis, 1979; *Kleist's Lost Year and the Quest for Robert Guiskard* by R.H. Samuel, 1981; *Kleist: A Biography* by Joachim Maass, translated by Ralph Manheim, 1983; *Desire's Sway: The Plays and Stories*

of Heinrich von Kleist by James M. McGlathery, 1983; *Spirited Women Heroes: Major Female Characters in the Dramas of Goethe, Schiller and Kleist* by Julie D. Prandi, 1983; *Prison and Idylls: Studies in Heinrich von Kleist's Fictional World* by Linda Dietrick, 1985; *Heirich von Kleist: A Critical Study* by Raymond Cooke, 1987; *The Manipulation of Reality in Works by Heinrich von Kleist* by Robert E. Glenny, 1987; *Kafka's Prussian Advocate: The Influence of Heinrich von Kleist on Franz Kafka* by John M. Grandin, 1987; *In Pursuit of Power: Heirich von Kleist's Machiavellian Protagonists*, 1987, *Kleist's Aristocratic Heritage and Das Käthchen von Heilbronn*, 1991, and *Kleist on Stage, 1804–1987*, 1993, all by William C. Reeve; *Laughter, Comedy and Aesthetics: Kleist's Der zerbrochene Krug* by Mark G. Ward, 1989; *Heinrich von Kleist: The Dramas and Stories* by Anthony Stephens, 1994; *The Poetics of Death: The Short Prose of Kleist and Balzac* by Beatrice Martina Guenther, 1996; *The Plays of Heinrich von Kleist: Ideals and Illusions* by Seán Allan, 1996; *The Retreat of Representation: The Concept of Darstellung in German Critical Discourse* by Martha B. Helfer, 1996; *Heinrich Von Kleist: The Ambiguity of Art and the Necessity of Form* by Hilda Meldrum Brown, 1998; *The School of Days: Heinrich von Kleist and the Traumas of Education* by Nancy Nobile, 1999.

*　　*　　*

Throughout his short life Heinrich von Kleist was bedevilled by contradictions and misfortunes. A Prussian aristocrat alienated from his class, brilliantly gifted yet deeply neurotic, he was torn between pedantry and passion, sensitivity and violence, furious ambition and a paralysing sense of failure. His obsessive striving for absolute certainties was confounded by doubts. His uncompromising search for fulfilment through love, friendship, nation, nature, or art foundered on external obstacles and on his own instability. Some moments of euphoria apart, his dominant mood was despair, leading to an early suicide. It is suitably ironic that, having been declared sick by Goethe and ignored for a century, he should have come to be regarded, not least by Kafka and Thomas Mann, as one of Germany's greatest writers. Kleist shared the subjectivism and spiritualism of the Romantics, but unlike them he incorporated, rather than suppressed, the recalcitrance of objective reality in his writing. Anticipating psychoanalysis, sceptical about communication, and rejecting traditional philosophical, moral, and social assumptions in his treatment of existential issues, he seems strikingly modern.

Kleist's central problem—documented in his correspondence and occasional essays—was that of knowledge. At first he sought happiness through both Enlightenment rationalism and Rousseauesque sensibility, but he was shattered when some ideas of Kant confirmed his suspicion that the intellect was "unable to decide whether what we call truth is truly the truth, or only appears so to us" (letter to Wilhelmine Zenge, 22 March 1801). He continued to commend "feeling," and he claimed—notably in *Über das Marionettentheater* (*On Puppetshows*)—that the pristine grace of an unthinking condition, which was upset by reflection, would be regained in a divine state of infinite awareness. Basically, however, he believed that emotion, in its inconstancy, was as unreliable as reason, and that the impossibility of making informed choices or recognizing any providential purpose rendered human freedom an illusion and fate synonymous with chance. His creative works explore these dilemmas from a variety of angles.

Kleist's first play, *Die Familie Schroffenstein* (*The Feud of the Schroffensteins*), is a Gothic melodrama in which the trust of the young lovers proves helpless against the accidents, errors, and enmities that destroy them. His next two plays mix hope and anxiety: in *Amphitryon*, an adaptation of Plautus and Molière, the tragicomedy of Jupiter impersonating the title hero to seduce his wife, alongside the farcical impersonation of the servant Sosias by Mercury, raises vexing questions about personal identity, the fallibility of perception, and the afflictions of love; in *Der zerbrochene Krug* (*The Broken Jug*), a rural comedy with overtones of Greek and Biblical myth, the truth emerges as the judge Adam convicts himself of his advances to the virtuous Eve, but her fiancé's distrustfulness almost causes disaster. Two subsequent plays, as Kleist noted, are complementary: in *Penthesilea*, a tragedy on Greek legend, the inefficacy of the intellect is compounded by the ambivalence of emotion as the Amazon queen, after many misunderstandings, slaughters the warrior Achilles in a paroxysm of love-hate and wills herself to death; in *Das Käthchen von Heilbronn* (*Käthchen of Heilbronn*), a medievalizing romance, the assurance of undivided devotion prevails as the heroine, supported by suprasensory promises, conquers the reluctant hero against all reasonable expectation. Kleist's vaguely historical last play, *Prinz Friedrich von Homburg* (*The Prince of Homburg*), is also his most celebrated. The hero, who disobeys orders but wins a battle and who after agonies of fear welcomes the death penalty but is rehabilitated, apparently achieves a "classical" reconciliation of subjective inclination and objective duty; but again misconceptions abound, destiny as embodied in the Elector remains arbitrary, the chauvinistic exaltation of the Prussian state rings hollow, and the happy ending which completes the hero's initial somnambulistic fantasy of love and glory is literally called "a dream."

Of Kleist's collected stories five are commonly regarded as the most important. In "The Earthquake in Chile" a young couple is lynched in a resurgence of religious hysteria after an interlude of idyllic peace following the collapse of the city. In "The Engagement in Santo Domingo" the hero, misinterpreting the heroine's attempt to save his life during a colonial uprising, kills her, and, on learning the truth, kills himself. In "The Marquise of O" the conundrum of the celibate but pregnant heroine is resolved by the confession of her eventual husband, who raped her while she was unconscious. In "The Duel" the champion's belief in his lady's innocence is vindicated when he recovers from the near-fatal wound he sustained in the trial by ordeal, while the villain, whose alibi rests on delusion, dies of a slight injury. In *Michael Kohlhaas*, Kleist's greatest story, a righteous horsedealer becomes a vindictive outlaw when he is denied a fair legal hearing, and triumphs, with supernatural aid, at the very moment of his execution, when his grievances are redressed and his enemies punished. Love, trust, and intuitive confidence thus thrive in some cases and perish in others. In all cases, however, deceptive appearances, intellectual fallacies, and emotional disturbances, allied with strange coincidences and baffling incongruities, reiterate Kleist's view of the irrationality and mystery of existence.

Kleist's style, which is highly original though not deliberately experimental, is marked by ambiguity, irony, and paradox. His characters, faced with surprising situations, locked in fierce conflicts or painful isolation, driven by forces they can neither understand nor control, represent extreme impulses rather than normal human behaviour. His superbly timed actions replace conventional linearity with cyclic recurrences, sudden reversals, abrupt contrasts, and complex symbolic variations on a relatively limited number of enigmatic themes. His restraint from authorial comment and analytical explanation, his shifting perspectives, his insistence on accurate detail in the midst of upheaval and confusion invest his subjective

concerns with a semblance of objectivity and provide solid realistic foundations for his visions. Rather than discussing his experience in conceptual terms, he conveys it directly through the structure of his language: blending fancy with matter-of-factness, dryness with lyricism, profuse rhetoric with explosive compression; revelling in bold metaphors, puns, equivocations, and relentless question-and-answer sequences; interrupting long hypotactical periods by encapsulated elucidations, qualifications, and objections before rushing headlong to their conclusion; and breaking down into speechless gestures, blushing and fainting, when words fail. It is this masterly use of dramatic, narrative, and linguistic devices that enables Kleist to impose aesthetic order on a chaotic world and to turn his torments into art.

—Ladislaus Löb

See the essay on *The Broken Jug*, *Michael Kohlhaas*, and *The Prince of Homburg*.

KLÍMA, Ivan

Born: Prague, Czech Republic, 14 September 1931. **Education:** Attended school in Prague; education interrupted when he spent three years in the concentration camp Terezín; high school in Prague, after 1945; studied Czech literature and philology at Charles University in Prague, graduating with a thesis on Karel Čapek, 1952–56. **Family:** Married Helena Malá (now the well-known psychotherapist Helena Klímová) in 1958; one daughter and one son. **Career:** Editor of *Květen*, a short-lived journal of young writers,1956–59; book editor for *Československý spisovatel*, 1959–63; joined the editorial staff of *Literární noviny*, the weekly journal of the Writers' Union, an outspoken prestigious publication (in 1968 renamed *Literární Listy*, then *Listy*), 1963; during the literary renaissance that peaked in the "Prague Spring" editor-in-chief (the journal was banned in 1969); Visiting Professor at The University of Michigan at Ann Arbor, 1969–70; decided to return to Czechoslovakia which, following the Soviet occupation in August 1968, was by then again under harsh Communist rule; no possibilities for carrying on his editorial work; held various jobs, e.g. as ambulance man, surveying assistant, messenger during the 1970s and 1980s; his writings were banned in Czechoslovakia but published abroad in several translations; involved in the initiation of the now renowned *samizdat* publication where most of his works appeared; continued writing against the greatest odds; after the demise of Communism in 1989 president of Czech PEN, 1990; his writings now published in translations into thirty languages; travels widely, lecturing and giving author's readings; from 1991 on contributor to literary journals and dailies (including Sweden and Germany).

Publications

Fiction

A Wonderful Day. 1960.
Hodina ticha. 1963.
Milenci na jednu noc. 1964.

Loď' jménem naděje. 1969; as *A Ship Named Hope* (includes two novels: *The Jury* and *A Ship Named Hope*); translated by Ewald Osers, 1970.

Markétčin zvěřinec (first appeared in *samizdat*). 1973.

Má veselá jitra (first appeared in *samizdat*). 1978; as *My Merry Mornings*, translated by George Theiner, 1985.

Moje první lásky (first appeared in *samizdat*). 1990; as *My First Loves*, translated by Ewald Osers, 1986.

Milostné léto. 1979; as *A Summer Affair*, 1979; revised edition translated by Ewald Osers, 1985.

Láska a smetí (first appeared in *samizdat*). 1986; as *Love and Garbage*, translated by Ewald Osers, 1990.

Soudce z Milosti (first appeared in *samizdat*). 1986; as *Judge on Trial*, translated by A.G. Brain [pseudonym for Alice and Gerald Turner], 1991.

Má zlatá řemesla. 1989; as *My Golden Trades*, translated by Paul Wilson, 1992.

Čekání na tmu, čekání na světlo (first appeared in *samizdat*). 1993; as *Waiting for the Dark, Waiting for the Light*, translated by Paul Wilson, 1994.

Milostné rozhovory [Lovers' Conversations]. 1995; some of these short texts appeared in the collection *Lovers for a Day.*

Poslední stupeň důvěrnosti. 1996; as *The Ultimate Intimacy*, translated by A.G. Brain, 1997.

Lovers for a Day [collected stories from the 1960s to the 1990s], translated by Gerald Turner. 1999.

Ani svatí ani andělé. 1999; as *No Saints or Angels*, translated by Gerald Turner, 2001.

Plays

Zámek. 1965.

Mistr. 1967.

Klára a dva páni (produced in Vancouver, B.C., 1985). 1968; as *Klara and Two Men*, translated by Peter Stenberg and Marketa Goetz-Stankiewicz in *Prism International*, XXI:4, summer 1983.

Cukrárna Myriam (produced as *Sweetshop Myriam* in New York, 1968). 1968.

Ženich pro Marcelu (produced as *Bridegroom for Marcela* in New York, 1969). 1968.

Porota (produced in Prague, 1969). 1969.

Pokoj pro dva a jiné hry (contains three plays; first appeared in *samizdat*). 1973.

Ministr a anděl (first appeared in *samizdat*). 1973.

Hromobití (first appeared in *samizdat*; produced in Vancouver, B.C. [in Czech], 1995). 1973.

Amerika, with Pavel Kohout [based on Franz Kafka's novel]. 1974.

Hry (contains four plays; first appeared in *samizdat*). 1974.

Hry (first appeared in *samizdat*; produced in Vancouver, B.C., 1981, in London, 1990). 1974; as *Games*, translated by Jan Drabek, in *Dramacontemporary Czechoslovakia*, 1985.

Franz a Felice (first appeared in *samizdat*). 1984; as *Franz and Felice*, translated by Jan Drabek, in *Cross Currents* 5, 1986.

Other

Karel Čapek (critical study). 1962.

The Spirit of Prague (essays written between 1974 and 1993) translated by Paul Wilson. 1994.

Kruh nepřátel českého jazyka (selected feuilletons). 1998.

Between Security and Insecurity (essays). 1999; translated by Gerry Turner.

*

Critical Studies: *Czech Theatre Since World War II* by Paul I. Trensky, 1978; *The Silenced Theatre: Czech Playwrights without a Stage* by Marketa Goetz-Stankiewicz, 1979; *Selfjustification through Writing* by Marlene A. Schiwy, M.A. thesis, University of British Columbia, 1983; ''Profile: Ivan Klíma'' by Igor Hájek, in *Index on Censorship*, vol. 12, no. 2, 1983; ''A Conversation in Prague'' by Philip Roth, *New York Review*, April 1990; ''Love and Garbage: Can Ivan Klíma Do Without an Adjective?'' by Marketa-Goetz-Stankiewicz, in *Czechoslovak and Central European Journal*, vol. 11, no. 2, Winter 1993.

* * *

When, in 1970, students and colleagues at the University of Michigan tried to talk Ivan Klíma into staying with his family in the United States, he explained the reason for his decision to return: in America all he could be—at best—was a professor, whereas in his home he could always remain a writer, even if he had to sweep the streets. It is ironic that this is just about what happened (see *Láska a smeti* [*Love and Garbage*]). But while going through a series of menial jobs, political harassment, banning of his works, loss of basic human rights, Ivan Klíma remained a writer. As such, he combines three qualities that are rarely found in the same person: he is a novelist and short story writer, a playwright (although this genre relates to his past) and a literary critic *cum* feuilletonist. What is called his ''career'' above, shows the complexity, indeed absurdity of his biography. For example, had he started writing a few years earlier, this writer, striving all through his life for understanding and tolerance between human beings and seeking to reveal ethical values, would have been censored or banned by two diametrically opposed political regimes—National Socialism and Communism. He shares this fate with another Prague writer whom he admires and whose work he adapted and discussed: Franz Kafka.

Broadly speaking, Klíma's work falls into three areas. There are (spanning his whole career): short stories that are veritable gems of finely drawn miniatures, dealing with the changeable reflections of human affection *Moje první lásky* (*My First Loves*); the comic/tragic incidents a banned writer experiences when he works at menial jobs and turns these often absurd experiences into gently ironic celebrations of human resilience *Má zlatá řemesla* (*My Golden Trades*); the shockingly funny or funnily shocking incidents of *Má veselá jitra* (*My Merry Mornings*); and the intimate encounters between man and woman, whose emotional fragility is illuminated by the sharp yet kindly lingering gaze of the author's eye *Milostné rozhovory* [Lovers' Conversations].

Then there are his novels: work on the mighty volume *Soudce z Milosti* (*Judge on Trial*) spanned two decades (the first version, under the title *There Stands a Gallows* appeared in *samizdat* in 1978, the final version almost twenty years later). Malcolm Bradbury wrote that ''it was likely to survive as the key version of the later 20th century Eastern European political novel.'' More austere and lacking the ironic humor that pervades Klíma's short stories and to a certain extent also his later novels, it moves, as all of the author's works do, on the borderline of ethical dilemmas: it is a trial of conscience of a man who seems to have done everything ''properly''; yet at the end, when the sum of his life is being tested, little of value remains. *Milostné léto* (*A Summer Affair*) explores a mature man's passion for an indifferent young woman, tracing a sort of finding and losing oneself; *Love and Garbage*, loosely based on Klíma's own experience, deals with a banned writer who becomes part of a street-sweeping crew and thus gains a view of society from below; merging political satire with a love story and the author's perennial meditations on the nature of guilt and innocence, compulsion and freedom of choice. The finely hued balance of moral condemnation and forgiving understanding also marks the succeeding two novels: In *Čekáni na tmu, čekáni na světlo* (*Waiting for the Dark, Waiting for the Light*), the first novel written after the Velvet Revolution, as a "free" writer, Klíma explores the timely topic of a man's many-layered moral confusion: the hero, a television cameraman who has carried on in the so-called "grey zone" by working, albeit uneasily, within the constraints of the Communist regime, finds himself unprepared for the challenging tasks demanded by the post-1990 era of new freedom and remains stuck in the mediocrity that used to be his safe haven and has now become his mental prison. The central figure of *Poslední stupeň důvěrnosti* (*The Ultimate Intimacy*) is another one of Klíma's ruminating and questioning figures, a Protestant pastor, whose life unravels before the reader's eyes, as the changes of the political scene intrude, and as he weighs love against eros, oppression against freedom, trust in God against trust in human beings.

As far as the third area of his work is concerned, Klíma moved away from the dramatic genre several decades ago. His one-act plays that could be called black comedies steeped in high-spirited irony, feed on the clash between the absurdities of the system and the partially resourceful, partially semi-tragic attempts of individuals to evade them. Klíma's innate ability to write good dialogue now enlivens his prose.

Of Klíma's numerous other writings, feuilletons, essays, commentaries, the two slim volumes *The Spirit of Prague* and *Between Security and Insecurity* ought to be mentioned. The former one charts five critical decades in the history of his country, yet remains a personal account of the author. The latter tackles problems that today concern us all: rationality and irrationality, apathy and aggressiveness, the mass media, the abdication of art, the nature of hope and the new problems that humanity faces. Invariably sharp-edged and critical, Klíma's voice is also deeply humane and wise.

—Marketa Goetz-Stankiewicz

KLOPSTOCK, Friedrich Gottlieb

Born: Quedlinburg, Saxony, Germany, 2 July 1724. **Education:** Educated in Quedlinburg, 1736–39 and Schulpforta, 1739–45; studied theology, University of Jena, 1745–46; University of Leipzig, 1746–48. **Family:** Married 1) Margareta (Meta) Moller in 1754 (died in childbirth 1758); 2) Johanna Elisabeth von Winthem in 1791. **Career:** Private tutor, Langensalza, Saxony, 1748–50; visited Zurich at the invitation of the influential Swiss literary figure Johann Jacob Bodmer, 1750; invited to Copenhagen in 1751; received life pension from Frederick V of Denmark at the behest of Count Bernstoff; left Denmark in 1770 and moved to Hamburg where he spent the rest of his life; awarded honorary citizenship of the French Republic, 1792. **Died:** 14 March 1803.

PUBLICATIONS

Collections

Werke. 12 vols., 1798–1817.
Odes of Klopstock from 1747 to 1780, translated by William Nind. 1848.
Oden, edited by F. Muncker and J. Pawel. 1889.
Ausgewählte Werke, edited by K.A. Schleiden. 1962.
Werke und Briefe [Hamburg Edition], edited by Horst Gronemeyer, Elisabeth Höpker-Herberg, Klaus Hurlebusch, and Rose-Maria Hurlebusch. 1974–.

Verse

Der Messias. 1751, enlarged editions, 1755, 1769, 1773, and 1780; translated in part as *The Messiah* by Mary and Joseph Collyer, 1763; also translated by Solomon Hallings, 1810; Mary Collyer and Mrs. Meeke, 1811; Thomas Raffles, 1814; G.H.C. Egestorff, 1821–22; Catharine Head, 1826.
Oden. 1750.
Ode an Gott. 1751.
Geistliche Lieder. 1758–69.
Die frühen Gräber. 1764.
Die Sommernacht. 1766.
Rothschilds Gräber. 1766.
Oden und Elegien: Vier und dreyssigmal gedrukt. 1771.
Kleine poetische und prosaische Werke, edited by Christian Friedrich Schubart. 1771.
Ode an den Kaiser. 1782.
Das Vaterunser, ein Psalm. 1790.
Poetische Werke. 1794–96.

Plays

Der Tod Adams. 1757; as *The Death of Adam*, translated by Robert Lloyd, 1763.
Salomo. 1764; as *Solomon*, translated by Robert Huish, 1809.
Hermanns Schlacht. 1769.
David. 1772.
Hermann und die Fürsten. 1784.
Hermanns Tod. 1787.

Other

Die Deutsche Gelehrtenrepublik. 1774.
Über die deutsche Rechtschreibung. 1778.
Über Sprache und Dichtkunst: Fragmente. 1779–80.
Grammatische Gespräche. 1794.
Memoirs of Frederick and Margaret Klopstock, translated by Elizabeth Smith. 1808.
Klopstock und seine Freunde: Briefwechsel der Familie Klopstock unter sich, und zwischen dieser Familie, Gleim, Schmidt, Fanny, Meta und andern Freunden, edited by Klamer Schmidt. 2 vols., 1810; as *Klopstock and His Friends: A Series of Family Letters, Written between the Years 1750 and 1803*, translated by Elizabeth Ogilvy, 1814.
Auswahl aus Klopstocks nachgelassenem Briefwechsel und übrigen Papieren: Ein Denkmal für seine Verehrer, edited by Christian August Heinrich Clodius. 2 vols., 1821.

Kurzer Briefwechsel zwischen Klopstock und Goethe im Jahre 1776. 1833.

Briefe an Herder. 1856.

Briefe von und an Klopstock: Ein Beitrag zur Literaturgeschichte seiner Zeit, edited by Johann Martin Lappenberg. 1867; reprinted 1970.

Briefwechsel zwischen Klopstock und den Grafen Christian und Friedrich Leopold zu Stolberg. Mit einem Anhang: Briefwechsel zwischen Klopstock und Herder, edited by Jürgen Behrens and Sabine Jodeleit. 1964.

Briefe 1738–1750, edited by Horst Gronemeyer. 1979.

Editor, *Hinterlassene Schriften,* by Meta Klopstock. 1759.

*

Bibliography: by Gerhard Burkhardt and Heinz Nicolai, in *Werke und Briefe,* 1975; *Die zeitgenössischen Drucke von Klopstocks Werken* by Christiane Boghardt, and others, 1981.

Critical Studies: "Klopstock's Occasional Poetry" by Terence K. Thayer, in *Lessing Yearbook,* (2), 1970; *Studien zu Klopstocks Poetik* by W. Grosse, 1977; "Klopstock's Poetic Innovations: The Emergence of German as a Prosodic Language" by Beth Bjorklund, in *Germanic Review,* 1981; "Klopstock's Temple Imagery," in *Lessing Yearbook,* (13), 1982, and "A Question of Influence: Goethe, Klopstock, and 'Wanderers Sturmlied,'" in *German Quarterly,* (55), 1982, both by Meredith Lee; *Philosophy, Letters, and the Fine Arts in Klopstock's Thought* by Kevin Hilliard, 1987; *Rhetoric, the Bible, and the Origins of Free Verse: The Early Hymns of Friedrich Gottlieb Klopstock* by Katrin M. Kohl, 1990; *Displacing Authority: Goethe's Poetic Reception of Klopstock* by Meredith Lee, 1999.

* * *

Der Messias (*The Messiah*) is the most ambitious large-scale epic poem on a religious subject in modern German literature. In 1748 the publication in a Bremen literary periodical of its first three cantos (there were to be 20 in all) was a landmark in the evolution of German literature. Discerning readers were quick to recognize that here, at last, was a new and distinctive voice. The young Friedrich Gottlieb Klopstock (he was 24 at the time) not only possessed a poetic vision of Miltonic proportions: he also had the command of language necessary to express that vision and communicate it to his readership. The poem was hailed as a work of genius.

When the first three cantos appeared, the creative literature of Germany had scarcely begun to fulfil the hopes and recommendations of the new school of literary theorists and critics who had been exploring the role of the imagination in artistic creation. In Zurich Johann Jakob Bodmer (1698–1783) and Johann Jakob Breitinger (1701–76) had formulated their pioneering conception of poetry in a joint treatise on the influence and use of the imagination (1727); this they had followed up with Bodmer's prose translation of Milton's *Paradise Lost* (1732), a work in which they saw that conception fully realized. It fell to the young North German poet to achieve a poetic masterpiece which rivalled Milton in scale and sublimity of theme and similarly appealed to both a critical readership and the general reader.

Klopstock had discovered Milton's work when he was a pupil at the famous school of Schulpforta at Bad Kösen near Halle in Saxony. He left school determined to create for Protestant Germany a work which would stand comparison with *Paradise Lost* itself. Milton's subject had been the Fall of Man: Klopstock responded by selecting Man's redemption through Christ's atonement. His epic poem focuses on the course of events from Christ's entry into Jerusalem on Palm Sunday to his completion of his redemptive mission and his ascension into heaven. But the relatively straightforward sequence of events retold by the evangelists is often little more than a framework for a spiritual, moral, and above all emotional experience of cosmic proportions. As a result, the dynamic forward impetus of epic poetry as exemplified by Homer and Virgil is replaced by a more discursive approach in which material of the poet's own invention swamps the simplicity of the Gospel narrative.

There is little realism of the Homeric kind in *The Messiah* and none of Virgil's nation-making mythical purpose. Instead Klopstock exploits his considerable descriptive and lyrical powers to construct a fantasy world which many of his original readers would have shunned had it not been more or less firmly anchored in orthodox Christian theology. Scarcely anything actually takes place before the reader's eyes: it is the reaction within the reader that counts. The epic's celebrated opening line ("Sing, immortal soul, the redemption of sinful mankind") sets the tone for what is to come. The soul, susceptible to a whole gamut of spiritual experiences, is the eyewitness of past events re-created by the poet: their quasi-symbolic and transcendent significance far outweighs their historical or narrative credibility. Time and again the modern reader is struck by anticipations of Blake in prophetic, visionary mood, though Klopstock is also sporadically capable of passages of graphic narrative such as Christ's harrowing ascent of Golgotha in Canto 8.

Underlying the whole extraordinary enterprise are two basic and complementary impulses. On the one hand the poet is intent on making his reader "feel" what hitherto he (and she) had been taught to ponder. On the other, he frequently appears to be displaying the power of language to evoke a poetic world that transcends the norms of reality by dissolving the normal dimensions of space and time. Thus the locations of much of the epic's storyline are vague in the extreme, whereas the mental and moral agonies and ecstasies of some of the many figures involved in it possess an extraordinary immediacy. As a result, the epic, though couched in a German equivalent of the Latin hexameter and characterized by highly stylized vocabulary and syntax appropriate to its sublime theme, contains many stretches which are closer to Samuel Richardson's epistolary novels and the intense self-scrutiny of their characters than to Milton's strongly visual yet intensely intellectual Biblical poem. It is no coincidence that *Clarissa* and *The Messiah* are contemporaneous and that both scored an enormous success with the predominantly middle-class mid-18th-century reading public.

In England the success of *The Messiah* was not as great as that of Richardson's novels in Germany, and it never achieved the popularity of *Der Tod Adams* (*The Death of Adam*), 1758, a religious work in somewhat similar vein by Klopstock's Swiss contemporary, Salomon Gessner. Nevertheless the prose translation of the first 10 cantos by Gessner's translator Mary Collyer and her husband Josiah Collyer ran to three editions during the 1760s.

Klopstock's contribution to the emergence of German classical literature in the mid-18th century was far-reaching; but his epic was too long. By the time he completed and published the last of its 20 cantos in 1773 it had swelled to almost 20,000 lines. Its novelty was past and its popularity was on the wane except among the large readership that continued to rank it second only to the Bible itself. However, long after its sprawling shapelessness and rapt intensity had been decried by a new generation, it continued to haunt the imagination. For instance the pure but ardent attachment between Cidli, the daughter of Jairus, and Semida, the son of the widow of Nain, both saved from death by miracles wrought by Christ (Canto 15), struck a responsive chord in readers eager for romance of an uplifting Christian kind such as could be safely read on a Sunday. The delicate sentimentality of such episodes provided a Protestant equivalent or echo of Tasso's *Gerusalemme liberata* (*Jerusalem Delivered*) which proved very acceptable well into the 19th century. In this respect Klopstock's greatest stroke of genius was the tormented figure of Abbadona, the remorseful devil. Originally one of the evil spirits who conspired against the Messiah, Abbadona's protracted remorse and ultimate pardon in heaven brought tears to many an eye in an age which regarded sentimentality differently from our own.

When in Goethe's epoch-making novel *Die Leiden des jungen Werthers* (*The Sufferings of Young Werther*) Lotte and Werther both utter the name "Klopstock" at the same moment, recognition is paid to the achievement of a writer whose masterpiece spans the years between Handel's oratorio *Messiah* (1742) and the climax of the *Sturm und Drang*.

—Peter Skrine

KOCHANOWSKI, Jan

Born: Sycyna, Poland, in 1530. **Education:** Educated at Cracow Academy, 1544–49; University of Królewiec, 1551–52; University of Padua, 1552–55. **Family:** Married Dorota Podłodowska in 1570; six daughters. **Career:** Courtier: secretary to King Zygmunt, 1560–68; retired to estate in Czarnolas, 1570. **Died:** 22 August 1584.

PUBLICATIONS

Collections

Dzieła wszystkie [Complete Works]. 4 vols., 1884–97.
Dzieła polskie [Polish Works], edited by Julian Krzyzanowski. 3 vols., 1960.
Dzieła wszystkie [Complete Works], edited by Maria Renata Mayenowa and others. 4 vols., 1982–91.

Verse

Zuzanna [Susanna]. 1562.
Szachy [A Game of Chess]. 1562(?); edited by Kazimierz Nitsch, 1923; also edited by Julian Krzyzanowski, 1966.
Zgoda [Concord]. 1564.
Satyr; albo, dziki mż [The Satyr; or, The Wild Man]. 1564; edited by Paulina Buchwald-Pelcowa, 1983.
Psałterz Dawidów [Psalms of David]. 1579, reprinted 1985.
Treny. 1583; edited by Wiktor Weintraub, 1943; also edited by Tadeusz Sinko, 1966, Julian Krzyzanowski, 1967, and Janusz Pelc, 1972; as *Laments*, translated by Dorothea Prall Radin, 1920; also translated by Seamus Heaney and Stanislaw Baranczak, 1995.
Lyricorum libellus. 1580.
Elegiarum libri IV, elusdem Foricoenia sive epigrammatum libellus [Four Books of Elegies and the Trifles]. 1584; as *Fraszki* [Trifles],

1612; edited by Antonina Jelicz, 1956; also edited by Aleksander Soszynski, 1980;
Pieśni [Songs]. 1586; edited by Tadeusz Sinko, 1948.
Elegie [Elegies], translated (from Latin) by K. Brodziński. 1829.
Poems, edited by G.R. Noyes, translated by Noyes, Dorothea Prall Radin, and others. 1928.

Plays

Odprawa posłów greckich (produced 1578). 1578; edited by Tadeusz Sinko, 1915; also edited by Tadeusz Ulewicz, 1962; as *The Dismissal of the Greek Envoys*, translated by G.R. Noyes and Ruth Earl Merrill (verse), 1918; also translated by Charles S. Kraszewski, 1994.

*

Bibliography: *Bibliografia dziel Jana Kochanowskiego: wiek XVI–XVII* by Kazimierz Piekarski, 1934.

Critical Studies: "The Medieval Dream Formula in Kochanowski's *Laments*" by Jerzy Peterkiewicz, in *Slavonic and East European Review*, 31(77), 1953; "Mythological Allusions in Kochanowski's *Laments*" by Ray J. Parrott, in *Polish Review*, 14(1), 1969; *Jan Kochanowski* by David J. Welsh, 1974; *Ian Kochanowski in Glasgow* edited by Donald Pirie, 1985; *The Polish Renaissance in Its European Context* edited by Samuel Fiszman, 1988.

* * *

Jan Kochanowski's reputation outside the Polish cultural sphere is small, and his significance in European terms is difficult to assess, though his works are of an ingenuity and sophistication that compete with the best among his international contemporaries.

His debut was as a cosmopolitan poet taking advantage of the medium of progressive humanist culture, Neo-Latin. The erudite and inventive Virgilian verse of his early work, widely circulated in manuscript after 1550, was published much later as the *Lyricorum libellus* in 1580. Well known among the small cultured élite of the Polish-Lithuanian Commonwealth's few courts, Kochanowski was patronized by both courtiers and clerics, eventually securing himself the position of Royal Secretary for most of the 1560s. It was in this milieu that he switched to his native idiom, in which he wrote first the vignettes of humorous verse in the anthology entitled *Fraszki* [Trifles], which satirize contemporary society and its mores.

Kochanowski soon advanced to a combination of the sophisticated style of Neo-Latin verse and its classical models and genres with Polish vocabulary and syntax in the *Pieśni* [Songs] (again, known widely, but published posthumously in 1586), closely modelled on Horace's *Odes*. In these highly polished "songs," he set the stylistic and thematic standards for almost two centuries. His subjects range from subtle (and not so subtle) panegyric dedicated to court patrons, through hymns on the beauty of Creation, to the erotic and melancholic, pastoral and religious. While some are artful paraphrases from Horace, most are entirely original, and stand as a testament of the achievements of the "Augustan" Golden Age under the sophisticated Zygmunt August (1548–72). The *Pieśni* are a fusing of two cultures (Roman and Sarmatian), two languages (Latin and Polish), and two poets (Horace the master, and Kochanowski the apprentice).

Towards 1570, however, for reasons that are unclear, Kochanowski had severed his dependence on court favour, and retired with his new wife to his estate at Czarnolas, evoked so lyrically in the "Pieśń świętojańska o Sobótce" (published with *Pieśni*). Despite irregular commissions from his earlier patrons, such as his experimental Euripidean tragedy in Polish, *Odprawa posłów greckich* (*The Dismissal of the Greek Envoys*), in this idyllic environment he concentrated on his true "vocation," a versified paraphrase of the Psalter in Polish. This huge work, the *Psałterz Dawidów* [Psalms of David], is another blending of biblical, classical Latin, and Polish vernacular ingredients. His version surpassed all others in originality, beauty, and popularity. On all levels it is the culmination of his life's work.

The last five years of the poet's life were overshadowed by the deaths of court friends, relatives, and in particular his own children. A record of the struggle between faith and despair following the death of his three-year-old daughter Orszula, entitled the *Treny* (*Laments*), was published in 1580. It contains a cycle of contemplative lyrics on the implications of Orszula's demise and his sense of loss. Once again there is the combination of contrasting elements—the classical and biblical, the philosophical and personal, the lyrical and dramatic, all focused by the factual event that inspired the cycle. Together they transform these laments from a conventional exercise into an extraordinarily honest psychological document, revealing much of the mentality of 16th-century man.

With the exception of some secondary political and panegyric verse, Kochanowski's sublime poetry is not the product of a provincial. Single-handedly he extended the Polish language's limits in all directions. The *Laments* are his last word, a personal legacy of the potential of Christian humanism, after which the poet abandoned his artificial lute for the rewards of David's faith.

—Donald Pirie

KOUROUMA, Ahmadou

Born: Togbala, French West Africa (now Ivory Coast), c. 1927.
Education: Attended École Technique Supérieure, Bamako (now Mali), 1947–49; Institut des Actuaires, Lyon, France, 1956–59.
Military Service: Enlisted in French army in present-day Mali; was sent to Abidjan (now Ivory Coast); service in Indochina, interpreter in Saigon, 1951–54. **Family:** Married; four children. **Career:** Returned to Ivory Coast, 1960; jailed, then exiled, 1963; actuary, Algeria, 1964–73; returned to Ivory Coast, exiled, 1974; Director General of the International Insurance Institute Yaoundé, Cameroon, then of the Compagnie Commune des Reassurances des Etats de l'Afrique Francophone, Lomé, Togo, 1974–93; retired 1994. Lives with family in France, travels frequently to Ivory Coast. **Awards:** Prix littéraire de la Francité, University of Montreal, Canada, 1967; Grand Prix Littéraire de l'Afrique Noire, Lifetime award, 1990; Prix Tropiques 1999, and Prix du Livre Inter 1999, Paris, France; Prix Renaudot 2000, Paris, France; Commandeur dans l'Ordre National de la Côte d'Ivoire, Abidjan, Ivory Coast, 2000.

PUBLICATIONS

Fiction

Les Soleils des independences. 1970; as *The Suns of Independence*, translated by Adrian Adams, 1981.

Monné: outrages et defies. 1990, as *Monnew*, translated by Nidra Poller, 1993.
Yacouba, chasseur africain [Yacuba, African Hunter] (juvenile). 1998.
En attendant le vote des bêtes sauvages. 1998; as *Waiting for the Vote of the Wild Beasts*, translated by Carrol Coates, 2001.
Une Journée avec le Griot [A Day with a Praise-singer] (juvenile). 1999.
Allah n'est pas obligé [Allah Is Not Obliged]. 2000.

Plays

Tougnantigui, ou le diseur de vérité [Tougnantigui, or the Speaker of Truth]. 1974.

*

Bibliography: "Ahmadou Kourouma: A Bibliography" by Carrol F. Coates, in *Callaloo*, vol. 23, no. 4, 2000.

Critical Studies: "End of the Line: Time in Kourouma's 'Les Soleils des Indépendances'" by H.R. Ireland, *Présence Francophone*, no. 23, 1981; *Comprendre 'Les Soleils des Indépendances' d'Ahmadou Kourouma* by Jean-Claude Nicolas, 1985; "La confrérie des chasseurs Malinké et Bambara" in *Mythes, rites et récits initiatiques* by Youssouf Cissé, 1994; "Independence Acquired—Hope or Disillusionment" by Mildred Mortimer, in *Research in African Literatures*, vol. 21, Summer 1990; "Bound to Textual Violence: Gabriel Okara and Ahmadou Kourouma" in *The African Palimpsest: Indigenization of Language in the West African Europhone Novel* by Chantal Zabus, 1991; *La Langue d'Ahmadou Kourouma, ou Le Français sous le soleil d'Afrique* by Makhily Gassama, 1995; *The Modernity of Witchcraft: Politics and the Occult in Postcolonial Africa* by Peter Geschiere, 1997; "Kourouma's 'Monné' as Aesthetics of Lying" by Karim Traoré, in *Callaloo*, vol. 23. no. 4, 2000; "Ahmadou Kourouma: Fiction Writer" by Carror F. Coates in, *Callaloo*, vol. 23, no. 4, 2000; "Entretien avec Ahmadou Kourouma" by Jean Ouedraogo, in *French Review*, no. 74, March 2001.

* * *

Ahmadou Kourouma's artistic talent and originality have attracted worldwide attention to his urgent message: corruption, dictatorship, and ethnic strife must end for Africans to be free and take their proper place in the world community. This, Kourouma believes, can happen only if Africans face the unvarnished truth of their history.

For Kourouma, truth must be spoken about the present as well as the past: an ancient past of contributions to human development, traditions, glories, and magic; a more recent past of victimization by slavery, colonialism, and cold war rivalries; and a present of disorientation, discord, and exploitation by power and money greedy post-independence African leaders. Yes, Kourouma says, Africa has been abused, but it must accept its own share of responsibility and move on. *La parole* [the word] will set Africa free. To this project he dedicates his writings, combining modern ideas with traditional images in a highly personal language he creates.

He began writing in mid-life. His first novel, *Les Soleils des independences* (*Suns of Independence*), reflects the values and knowledge he has acquired growing up in the tradition-steeped, educated Malinke hunter elite as well as his own disappointments under colonialism and post-colonialism, but is not autobiographical. Like all his fiction it is highly imaginative, though supported by thorough historical research.

The novel's protagonist is Fama, a fallen Malinke prince shaken first by colonialism, and then reduced to begging by the post-independence ruling tyrant. Fama's distress is compounded by family problems. His wives appear to be barren, notwithstanding recourse to Allah and magic alike. This condemns him to the worst fate of all, that of dying without progeny. Actually, Fama is the sterile one. He, the great prince, has lost all power. Unable to accept the truth, he makes a last desperate attempt to recapture his past by fleeing to his former Malinke lands, but is senselessly shot for illegally crossing a border that did not exist in his youth. Publisher after publisher, in both Africa and France, refused the politically explosive novel until after it had received a prize in Montreal.

Back in the Ivory Coast, Kourouma staged a play hoping that the spoken word would bring his message to a wider audience in the essentially non-reading country. In *Tougnantigui ou le diseur de vérité* [Tougnantigui, or the Speaker of Truth], two groups evoke a happy past when they were united. They are now disunited and unsure of their very identity. Foreigners have disrupted their society with alien concepts, but Africans have allowed this to happen. Kouroma indicates that accepting responsibility for the past and adopting an independent and more rational approach to problems will lead to better days. The success of the play in Abidjan in 1972 caused Kourouma to be exiled again.

Years of professional activity went by before Kourouma, the actuarian, wrote his second novel, entitled *Monné* (*Monnew*), a Malinke word signifying outrage, defiance, contempt, and humiliation. Here he shows myth and history as inseparable. He portrays Djigui, who has been ruling the African Kingdom of Soba for 100 years, losing control when confronted with the French conquest. Suffering is widespread in Soba, yet neither Djigui nor religious leaders are of any help and therefore they share responsibility for the disasters. All are subjected to the author's biting irony.

After another long hiatus, Kourouma wrote what is probably his most important work to date, *En attendant le vote des bêtes sauvages* (*Waiting for the Vote of the Wild Beasts*); an Orwellian satire of African dictatorships spawned and supported by foreign powers during the cold war with consequences which persist to this day. The novel is the story of Koyaga, the Malinke hunter with magic powers, narrated against the historical background of colonialism and post-colonialism. After World War II, Koyaga, a decorated veteran, overthrows the first president of the fictional independent Republic of the Gulf and rules it for 30 years thanks to his supernatural capabilities. Kourouma clearly indicates that while to understand Africa one must also understand its belief in magic, magic is useless: it has not prevented any of the ills which have befallen the population.

In the novel reality catches up with Koyaga when the sources of his powers, his mother and his main fetishist, both mysteriously disappear and he can no longer control the inhabitants of the Republic. The only solution left to him appears to be to persuade wild beasts to vote for him in the next election—a possibility made to seem almost realistic in that atmosphere of magic. The book, Kourouma explains, is a *donsonoma*, a traditional Malinke epic about a hunter's extraordinary deeds. Donsonoma are sung to purify the protagonist of the deeds, participants, and audience alike; but for them to work, the protagonist must listen and hear the truth presented. Koyaga does gather his hunters and praise-singers to truthfully celebrate his life. The irony and criticism of the praise-singers are stinging, but Koyaga is too vain to realize this. Purification does not occur.

Kourouma selected the Malinke format because he finds western narrative techniques ill suited to write about a continent where magic is a component of everyday life. Similarly he writes in a French which is close to Malinke. Ever since *The Suns of Independence* his fiction illustrates his concept that standard French cannot express African thought and experience adequately. His style is improvisational, as is the oral literature from which his writings derive. The narrator intervenes to address both characters and readers. Repetition, rhetorical questions, redundancy, Malinke words, images, proverbs, unusual sentence structures, and neologisms all reflect indigenous speech. Aphorisms convey African philosophy. He creates a language meant to strike a responsive chord in his fellow Africans, while also helping foreigners understand Africa better.

Consistent with Kourouma's goals is his recent novel, *Allah n'est pas obligé* [Allah Is Not Obliged], the story of children who soldier in the civil wars which continue to ravage West Africa. These child-soldiers have lost everything; they rob, maim, and kill at random, without really understanding their own actions. They play with machine guns, ruthlessly and naïvely at the same time. The picture is horrifyingly brutal, but Allah is not obliged to be just on the earth he created, hence the child protagonist, Brahima, has no such obligation either. The facts presented are historically correct; it is fiction only because everything is seen and told by a twelve-year-old as he perceives it. To relieve the horror the author lends him an ironic tone. Kourouma tells us that he wrote this book to keep a promise made to child soldiers he met in Ethiopia, who asked him to write about tribal wars. As all of Kourouma's fiction, this book is not merely good literature, but also a participatory act.

—L. Natalie Sandomirsky

KRASIŃSKI, Zygmunt

Born: Paris, France, 19 February 1812. Grew up on family estate in Opinogóra, Poland. **Education:** Educated at home, then in Warsaw until 1828; University of Warsaw until 1829; University of Geneva, c. 1830. **Military Service:** Short military service. **Family:** Married Countess Elżbieta Branicki in 1843. **Career:** Travelled to St. Petersburg with his father, where he met Tsar Nicholas I, 1832; returned to Poland, 1832, and in 1843–44. Seriously ill for much of his life; spent most of 1830s and 1840s in spas in France and Italy, rarely coming home. Published many works anonymously. **Died:** 23 February 1859.

PUBLICATIONS

Collections

Pisma [Works], edited by J. Czubek. 8 vols., 1912; also edited by L. Piwiński, 7 vols., 1931.
Dzieła literackie [Literary Works], edited by Paweł Hertz. 3 vols., 1973.

Plays

Nie-Boska Komedia (produced 1902). 1835; as *The Undivine Comedy*, translated by M.W. Cook, in *The Undivine Comedy and Other*

Poems, 1875; as The Un-Divine Comedy, translated by Harold B. Segel, in Polish Romantic Drama, 1977; as Undivine Comedy, translated by Charles S. Kraszewski, 1999.
Irydion (produced 1908). 1836; as Irydion, translated by Florence Noyes, 1927.

Fiction

Pan trzech pagórków [Lord of Three Hills]. 1828.
Grób rodziny Reichstalów [The Tomb of the Reichstal Family]. 1828.
Sen Elżbiey Pileckiej [Elizabeth Pilecka's Dream]. 1829.
Władysław Herman i dwór jego [Vladislav Herman and His Court]. 3 vols., 1830.
Agay-Han. 1834.

Verse

Modlitewnik [Prayer Book]. 1837.
Noc letnia [Summer Night]. 1841.
Pokusa [Temptation]. 1841.
Przedświt [Pre-Dawn]. 1843.
Psalmy przyszłości [Future Psalms]. 1845; enlarged edition, 1848.
Ostatni [The Last One]. 1847.
Dzień dzisiejszy [Today]. 1847.
Psalm żalu [Psalm of Regret]. 1848.
Psalm dobrej woli [Psalm of Goodwill]. 1848.
Niedokończony poemat [The Unfinished Poem]. 1860.
The Undivine Comedy and Other Poems (includes play), translated by M.W. Cook. 1875.

Other

Trzy myśli Henryka Ligenzy [Henry Ligenza's Three Thoughts].1840.
O stanowisku Polski z bożych i ludzkich względów [About Poland's Position from the Viewpoint of God and People]. 1841.
Lettres à Montalembert et . . . Lamartine. 1847.
Listy o poemacie Kajeta Koźmiana Stefan Czarniecki [Letters to S.C. Koźmian]. 1859.
Briefe. 1860.
Listy od roku 1835 do 1844 pisane do Edwarda Jaroszyńskiego [Letters to Edward Jaroszyński]. 1871.
Listy [Letters]. 3 vols., 1882–87.
Correspondance de Sigismond Krasinski et de Henry Reeve. 2 vols., 1902.
Listy [Letters], with Ary Scheffer. 1909.
Listy do Augusta Cieszkowskiego [Letters to August Cieszkowski]. 2 vols., 1912.
Listy do A. Potockiego [Letters to A. Potocki]. 1922.
Listy do Delfiny Potockiej [Letters to Delfina Potocka]. 3 vols., 1930–38.
Listy wybrane [Selected Letters]. 1937.
Listy do ojca [Letters to His Father]. 1963.
Listy do Jerzego Lubomirskiego [Letters to Jerzy Lubomirski]. 1965.
Listy do Adama Sołtana [Letters to Adam Sołtan]. 1970.
Listy do Konstantego Gaszyńskiego [Letters to Konstanty Gaszyński]. 1971.

*

Critical Studies: Zygmunt Krasiński by J. Kallenbach, 2 vols., 1904; The Anonymous Poet of Poland: A Life of Zygmunt Krasiński by Monica M. Gardner, 1919; Zygmunt Krasinski: Romantic Universalist: An International Tribute by W. Lednicki, 1964.

* * *

Zygmunt Krasiński came from a rich aristocratic family in Poland. His father, Wincenty, was a conservative general in the army of the Congress Kingdom and supported the Tsar and Poland's Russian rulers even during the November Uprising of 1830. Young Zygmunt was sent abroad to finish his higher studies, and it was in Geneva that he began writing plays that reflected the major philosophical and social questions of the age. While Krasiński first published his works anonymously (as the "Nameless Poet of Poland") to avoid embarrassment for his family, his entire mature life was characterized by a struggle between his conflicting loyalties—whether to side with his father or with the cause of national independence, the fatherland. Krasiński made his home abroad (mostly in Germany), wrote poetry, a vast number of letters, and two plays which—though unstaged in his lifetime—belong to the best achievements of Polish Romantic drama.

Although of the plays Irydion was conceived first, the final version of Nie-Boska Komedia (The Undivine Comedy) came to be published first in 1835 in Paris. The latter is a poetic drama in four "parts" (acts) which deals with one of the most crucial issues of the modern age beginning with the French Revolution—the struggle of the "haves" and the "have-nots," that of aristocracy with revolutionary democracy. The background to this historic conflict is provided by the career of Count Henryk. He is first shown to be a failure in private life for he is much more interested in poetry (symbolized by a demonic maiden) than in domestic happiness with his newly wedded wife. In fact, he leaves his wife and is almost killed by the Maiden who wants to lure him to a precipice. At the end of Act I, Henryk's wife dies with the wish that their son Orcio should become a poet—the wish is fulfilled, though Orcio remains incurably blind. The first two acts of the play are very sketchy, but they lead up to the powerful Act III, not unlike Juliusz Słowacki's play Kordian (1834). In one of the scenes of Act II Count Henryk declares: "Farewell, Mother Nature! I leave you, to become a man. I go to fight with my brethren." Abandoning all other myths of romanticism, Henryk tests the last one: that of progress in society.

The third act takes place some time in the undefined future when the rebellious masses have managed to take over most of the civilized world. Only the Castle of Holy Trinity holds out in a vain attempt to stem the tide. Here all the rich and mighty (aristocrats, bankers, bishops) assemble; down in the valley the vast coalition of the poor and their radical leaders set up their camp to lay siege to the castle. Henryk, at night and in disguise, visits the camp and is appalled by the wrath of the masses and their thirst for revenge. All the same, Krasiński observes and indicates certain latent conflicts between the simple participants of the struggle, their ideologues, and the military "technicians." Henryk's tour of the camp is followed by a return visit by Pankracy, the leader of the revolutionaries, to the castle; his confrontation with Count Henryk (who later is elected Commander-in-Chief by the beleaguered "aristocrats") produces some of the best scenes in the play. The values of both leaders are shown to be flawed; Henryk's concept of "honour" is hopelessly anachronistic, and Pankracy's promise of a radiant future is utopian and clearly unrealizable.

The Undivine Comedy nearly ends with the victory of the revolutionary mobs. Count Henryk prefers to commit suicide at the moment when they take the castle by storm. Nonetheless, the victorious Pankracy is suddenly smitten by a vision of Julian the Apostate: "Galileae vicisti!" ("You have won, O Christ!"). The message of this unexpected scene is fairly clear: no "godless" revolution can be truly victorious; the new age will not dawn until it finds a way to reconcile democracy with Christianity.

Staged for the first time in the 20th century, The Undivine Comedy has been steadily gaining topicality with the rise of (basically anti-Christian) mass totalitarian movements. Adam Mickiewicz, in the middle of the 19th century, regarded it as "the highest achievement of the Slavonic theatre"; Czesław Miłosz called it, more recently, "a truly pioneering work in its treatment of an unusual subject and in its visual elements." Although several English translations exist, the play has been, on the whole, ignored outside Poland, even by directors otherwise interested in the Polish theatre.

Krasiński's other play, Irydion, published in 1836, takes place in imperial Rome in the 3rd century AD. It is the story of a half-Greek, half-Germanic hero, Irydion ("the son of the rainbow"), who is bent on the destruction of corrupt, decadent Rome. To achieve this aim he is ready to sacrifice his sister Elsinoe to the lust of the Emperor Heliogabalus. His plot to subvert and then destroy Rome fails in the end because of the Christians' reluctance to take up arms against their rulers. Irydion was written as an indirect response to Mickiewicz's influential poem Konrad Wallenrod, a work which advocated revenge against the enemy by any means, including morally reprehensible methods. Krasiński's play is written in an "ornate arhythmical, utterly Romantic prose," as described by Miłosz, partly modelled on Chateaubriand, and while it enjoyed some popularity in the 19th century, it has not been resurrected on the stage in contemporary Poland.

—George Gömöri

KRLEŽA, Miroslav

Born: Zagreb, Croatia (then in the Austro-Hungarian Empire), 7 July 1893. **Education:** Educated at Lucoviceum military academy, Budapest. **Military Service:** Served in the Serbian Army, 1912: suspected of spying, expelled from Serbia and arrested by the Austrians; served in the Austrian Army during World War I. **Family:** Married Bela Kangrga. **Career:** Communist Party from 1918: expelled, 1939; rehabilitated by Tito, 1952; founded the periodicals Plamen [Flame], 1919, Književna republika [Literary Republic], 1923–27, Danas [Today], 1934, Pečat [Seal], 1939–40, and Republika, 1945–46; director, Lexicographic Institute, Zagreb, from 1952; editor, Pomorska enciklopedija, 1954–64, Enciklopedija Jugoslavije, 1955–71, and Enciklopedija Leksikografskog savoda, 1955–64. Deputy, Yugoslav National Assembly. President, Yugoslav Writers Union; vice-president, Yugoslav Academy of Science and Art. **Died:** 29 December 1981.

PUBLICATIONS

Collection

Sabrana djela [Collected Works]. 1980–.

Fiction

Tri kavalira gospoice Melanije [Three Suitors of Miss Melania]. 1920.
Magyar királyi honvéd novela [Short Story on the Royal Hungarian Homeguards]. 1921.
Hrvatski bog Mars [The Croatian God Mars]. 1922.
Novele. 1923.
Vražji otok [Devil's Island]. 1924.
Povratak Filipa Latinovicza. 1932; as The Return of Philip Latinovicz, translated by Zora Depolo, 1959.
Hiljadu i jedna smrt [A Thousand and One Deaths]. 1933.
Novele. 1937.
Na rubu pameti. 1938; as On the Edge of Reason, translated by Zora Depolo, 1976.
Banket u Blitvi [Banquet in Blitva]. 3 vols., 1938–64.
Tri domobrana [Three Homeguards]. 1950.
Zastave [Banners]. 4 vols., 1967.
The Cricket beneath the Waterfall and Other Stories, edited by Branco Lenski. 1972; as Cvrčak pod vodopadom, i druge novele, 1973.
Baraka pet be i druge novele (collection). 1976.

Verse

Pan. 1917.
Tri simfonije [Three Symphonies]. 1917.
Pjesme 1–3 [Poems]. 3 vols., 1918–19.
Lirika [Lyrics]. 1919.
Knjiga pjesama [A Book of Poems]. 1931.
Knjiga lirike [A Book of Lyrics]. 1932.
Simfonije [Symphonies]. 1933.
Balade Petrice Kerempuha [Ballads of Petrica Kerempuh]. 1936.
Pjesme u tmini [Poems in Darkness]. 1937.

Plays

Hrvatska rapsodija [Croatian Rhapsody]. 1918.
Golgota [Golgotha] (produced 1922). 1926.
Vučjak (produced 1922). 1923.
Michelangelo Buonarroti (produced 1925).
Adam i Eva [Adam and Eve] (produced 1925).
Gospoda Glembajevi [The Glembays] (produced 1929). 1928.
U agoniji (produced 1928; revised version produced 1959). 1931.
Leda (produced 1930).
Legende [Legends] (includes 6 plays). 1933.
U logoru [In the Camp] (produced 1937). With Vučjak, 1934.
Maskerata [Masquerade] (produced 1955).
Kraljevo [The Kermess] (produced 1955).
Kristofor Kolumbo (produced 1955).
Aretej; ili, Legenda o Svetoj Ancili [Aretheus; or, The Legend of St. Ancilla] (produced 1959). 1963.
Saloma [Salome] (produced 1963).
Put u raj [Journey to Paradise] (produced 1973). 1970.

Other

Izlet u Rusiju [Excursion to Russia]. 1926.
Eseji [Essays]. 1932.
Moj obračun s njima [My Squaring of Accounts]. 1932.
Podravski motivi [Motifs of Podravina]. 1933.
Evropa danas [Europe Today]. 1935.
Deset krvavih godina [Ten Years in Blood]. 1937.
Eppur si muove. 1938.
Knjiga proze [A Book of Prose]. 1938.
Dijalektički antibarbarus [A Dialectical Antibarbarian]. 1939.
Knjiga studija i putopisa [A Book of Studies and Travels]. 1939.
Goya. 1948.
O Marinu Držiću [On Marin Držić]. 1949.
Zlato i srebro Zadra. 1951; translated as *The Gold and Silver of Zadar*, 1972.
Djetinjstvo u Agramu godine 1902–1903 [Childhood in Agram]. 1952.
Kalendar jedne bitke 1942 [Almanac of a 1942 Battle]. 1953.
Kalendar jedne parlamentarne komedije [Almanac of a Parliamentary Comedy]. 1953.
O Erasmu Rotterdamskom [On Erasmus of Rotterdam]. 1953.
Sabrana djela [Collected Works]. 27 vols., 1953–72.
Davni dani [Long Bygone Days]. 1956.
Eseji [Essays]. 1958.
Eseji [Essays]. 6 vols., 1961–67.
Razgovori s Miroslavom Krležom [Conversations with Miroslav Krleža]. 1969.
99 varijacija lexicographica [99 Lexicographic Variations]. 1972.
Djetinjstvo 1902–1903 i drugi zapisi [Childhood and Other Pieces]. 1972.
Panorama pogleda, pojava i pojmova. 5 vols., 1975.
Dnevnik [Diary]. 5 vols., 1977.
Tito 1892–1937–1977, with Edvard Kardelj. 1977.
Eseji i članci (essays). 1979–.
Iz naše književne krčme. 1983.
Ratne teme. 1983.
Sa uredničkog stola. 1983.
Editor, with others, *Danas* [Today]. 2 vols., 1971.

*

Bibliography: *Bibliografia djela Miroslava Krleže* by T. Jakić, 1953; *Literatura o Miroslavu Krleži 1914–1963* by D. Kapetanić, 1967.

Critical Studies: *Studien zur Romantechnik Miroslav Krležas* by Sibylle Schneider, 1969; *La Vie et l'oeuvre de Miroslav Krleža* by Marijan Matković, 1977; *Miroslav Krleža und der deutsche Expressionismus* by Reinhard Lauer, 1984; *Die Gestalt des Künstlers bei Miroslav Krleža* by Andreas Leitner, 1986; *The Writer as Naysayer: Miroslav Krleža and the Aesthetic of Interwar Central Europe* by Ralph Bogert, 1990; *On the Edge of Reason*, translated by Zora Depolo, 1995; *Literature, History, and Postcolonial Cultural Identity in Africa and the Balkans: The Search for a Useable Past in Farah, Ngugi, Krleza, and Andric* by Dubravka Juraga, 1996.

* * *

Miroslav Krleža was the dominant figure in 20th-century Croatian literature. As the writer of novels, short stories, poems, essays, journals, travelogues, polemics, and memoirs, and as the editor of a series of leftist literary journals, he had a considerable influence on his contemporaries. His search for an enlightened humanism brought him to communism after the collapse of the Austro-Hungarian empire, but he was never an obedient Party member who marched uncritically, following the Party policy. His criticism of the Marxist dogmatism and of the notion of Socialist Realism in the arts as well as his outspoken demands ''for freedom of artistic expression, for the simultaneous existence of differing schools and styles, for liberty of choice and independence of moral and political convictions'' left their lasting mark on the cultural climate of post-World War II Yugoslavia.

Krleža began his literary career as a poet celebrating in pagan terms the triumph of life over the powers of darkness, mysticism, and death. However, World War I brought a dramatic change in his outlook. His war poems evoke in a series of striking expressionistic images the idea of the futility of life and the absurdity of death and have as their underlying theme one of Krleža's favourite notions, that of the supremacy of stupidity over reason in human life. The same theme, articulated as dehumanization caused by the horrors of the war, is central to his collection of short stories *Hrvatski bog Mars* [The Croatian God Mars], in which the useless squandering of lives of the Croats enlisted to fight for Austria in the war of 1914–18 is depicted in a dramatic and memorable narrative.

The poetry he continued to write in the 1920s and 1930s shows an increased social awareness and concerns itself primarily with the themes of social protest. The peak of his career as a poet was reached by the publication of his *Balade Petrice Kerempuha* [Ballads of Petrica Kerempuh], a collection of poems written in the dialect of north-western Croatia, used by the writers of the 17th and the 18th centuries. It is a unique satirical saga of Croatian history. Although overwhelmed with suffering, injustice, blood, and the symbol of gallows, the Croatian past is approached without any romantic illusions and rather treated in a bitter but mocking tone of Rabelaisian laughter.

In his youthful plays, published in a collection entitled *Legende* [Legends], Krleža used historical figures and themes as means of handling underlying themes of his time. His reputation as a dramatist was established with the piece *Golgota* [Golgotha], a socialist play set in a shipyard, and enhanced with two anti-war plays, *Vučjak* and *U logoru* [In the Camp]. The best known, and the best, of his plays make up his Glembay trilogy: *Gospoda Glembajevi* [The Glembays], *U agoniji* [In Agony], and *Leda* constitute an organic unity with the short stories of the same cycle. The plays and the short stories combine to portray the rise and decline of a rich Croatian family against the background of the agony of a dying civilization (the Austro-Hungarian empire). Ibsenesque in character and scope, these plays were written in the best vein of psychological realism.

Povratak Filipa Latinovicza (*The Return of Philip Latinovicz*) is the most popular of his four novels. It tells a story of an expatriate artist who, in a moment of personal and creative crisis, returns to his native Panonia to establish his paternity. But his pilgrimage turns into a quest for his own identity and a scathing portrayal of provincial decadence and his struggle to confront it. *Na rubu pameti* (*On the Edge of Reason*) is a novel of a model citizen who falls from society's grace after speaking his mind. Abandoned by both his family and his friends, persecuted and jailed, put into an asylum, he finishes as a lonely and desperate man listening in his hotel room to the discordant and meaningless sounds coming from the radio. Krleža's two other novels provide an imaginative and critical portrait of both Yugoslavia and Europe in the first decades of the 20th century, and make some major political, social, and psychological statements about the predicament of modern man. *Banket u Blitvi* [Banquet in Blitva] shows Krleža as a political satirist at his best. It is a political-allegorical novel with various references to those European countries (including his own) where, after World War I, people were deprived of their freedoms and democratic rights by military dictatorships. The vivid and dramatic story of a struggle between a dictator and a courageous political idealist is interspersed with typical Krleža polemics, soliloquies, and conversations with the intention of showing the amoral nature of politics in general. *Zastave* [Banners] spans the period between 1912 and 1922 in Croatian and Yugoslav history. The novel is built upon one of Krleža's recurring themes, that of the conflict between a father, a loyal and acquiescent servant of the Establishment, and his only son, the embittered, freedom-loving rebel. Their precarious relations are designed to bring out a psychological and ideological drama caused by the disillusionments of the two generations in the political upheavals of the early 20th century.

Alongside the best of Krleža's creative writing may be set the best of his non-fiction prose: the essays which reflect his vast reading and his moral and intellectual integrity; the two books of memoirs, *Djetinjstvo u Agramu godine 1902–1903* [Childhood in Agram] and *Davni dani* [Long Bygone Days]; the account of his visit to the USSR in 1925, *Izlet u Rusiju* [Excursion to Russia]; and, finally, his writings and annotations for the Yugoslav Encyclopedia, of which he was the *spiritus movens* and the editor-in-chief.

—Dušan Puvačić

KROSS, Jaan

Born: Tallinn, Estonia, 19 February 1920. **Education:** Attended Westholm high school, Tallinn, 1928–38; Tartu University, 1938–44. **Family:** Married 1) Helga Roos, 1954 (marriage ended, 1958); 2) Ellen Niit (née Hiob), 1958; two daughters. **Career:** Translator, 1943; arrested by German forces, 1944; lecturer at Tartu University, 1944–46; political prisoner, 1946–54; freelance writer and translator, since 1954; chair, Young Authors' Society, 1957–60; secretary, Estonian Writers' Union, 1976–81; member, Estonian Parliament (riigikogu), 1992–93. **Awards:** Eeva Joenpelto award, 1988; Amnesty International award, 1991; Herder prize, 1997. Honorary doctorate, Tartu University, 1989, and Helsinki University, 1990.

PUBLICATIONS

Collections

Voog ja kolmpii: Luuletusi 1938–1968. 1971.
Kogutud teosed [Works]. 1997.

Poetry

Söerikastaja. 1958.
Tuule-Juku: (Üle 16 a. vanustele keelatud). 1963.
Kivist viiulid. 1964.
Lauljad laevavööridel. 1966.
Hetk. 1968.
Vihm teeb toredaid asju. 1969.
Põhjatud silmapilgud. 1990.

Prose

Kolme katku vahel: Balthasar Russowi romaan. 1970–1977, 1980.
Neli monoloogi Püha Jüri asjus. 1970.
Michelsoni immatrikuleerimine: Tosin üksikkõnet trummi, väntoreli ja torupilliga tumma flöödi saatel. 1971.
Klio silma all. 1972.
Mardileib. 1973.
Kolmandad mäed. 1975.
Taevakivi. 1975; as *The Rock from the Sky*, 1983.
Keisri Hull. 1978; as *The Czar's Madman: A Novel*, translated by Anselm Hollo, 1993.
Kajalood. 1980.
Ülesõidukohad. 1981.
Rakvere romaan. 1982.
Professor Martensi ärasõit. 1984; as *Professor Martens' Departure*, translated by Anselm Hollo, 1994.
Vastutuulelaev: Bernhard Schmidti romaan. 1987.
Silmade avamise päev. 1988; as *The Conspiracy and Other Stories*, translated by Eric Dickens, 1995.
Wikmani poisid. 1988.
Väljakaevamised. 1990.
Tabamatus: Jüri Vilmsi romaan. 1993.
Järelehüüd. 1994.
Mesmeri ring: Romaniseeritud memuaarid nagu kõik memuaarid ja peaaegu iga romaan. 1995.
Paigallend: Ullo Paeranna romaan. 1998.
Tahtamaa. 2001.

Other

Muld ja marmor: Möödasõitnu meenutusi, with Ellen Niit. 1968.
Vahelugemised 1–6. 1968–95.

*

Bibliography: *Bibliograafia: Jaan Kross* by Vaime Kabur and Gerli Palk, 1997.

Critical Studies: *Der Verrückte des Zaren. Jaan Kross in Loccum*, edited by Olaf Schwencke, 1990; "The Antic Disposition of a Finno-Ugric Novelist" by Mardi Valgemäe, in *Journal of Baltic Studies*, vol. 24, no. 4, 1993; *Special Issue: Jaan Kross*, edited by Thomas Salumets, *Journal of Baltic Studies*, vol. 31, no. 3, 2000; "Jaan Kross: Negotiating Nation" by Thomas Salumets, in *Interlitteraria*, no. 5, 2000; *Die historischen Romane von Jaan Kross. Am Beispiel einer Untersuchung der deutschen und englischen Übersetzungen von Professor Martensi ärasõit* by Kerttu Wagner, 2001.

* * *

Shortly after Estonia was occupied by the Soviet Union, Jaan Kross was deported to Siberia, sharing the fate of tens of thousands of fellow Estonians and countless other victims of the widespread terror under Stalin's dictatorship. Following his release from a labor camp in 1954, Kross returned to Estonia's largest city, Tallinn. There he was able to work as a translator and writer. In the late 1950s and 1960s, during the period of relative liberalization in the Soviet Union, he published several collections of poems. Perhaps the most influential among them is *Söerikastaja* [The Coal Enricher]. None of his other publications, however, are as remarkable as his historical-autobiographical prose fiction. Among his twenty-one novels and collections of short stories are the trilogy *Kolme katku vahel* [Between Three Plagues], *Professor Martensi ärasõit* (*Professor Martens' Departure*), *Silmade avamise päev* (*The Conspiracy and Other Short Stories*), and *Paigallend* [Flying in Place]. His most successful novel internationally is *Keisri hull* (*The Czar's Madman*). It tells the story of a Baltic-German nobleman, Timotheus von Bock, who is asked by his friend, Czar Alexander I, to always speak the truth. He does. As a consequence of his outspokenness, he has to serve nine years in solitary confinement in one of the worst dungeons of the empire. Staying under close surveillance, he is allowed to return to his Estonian wife as long as he is deemed insane by the authorities. *The Czar's Madman* has been translated into English and more than twenty other languages.

With his prose fiction, Kross maps Estonia's past from the 16th century to the time shortly after Estonia regained its independence in 1991, the subject of his latest novel *Tahtamaa*. Although there often is a strong autobiographical element that characterizes his texts, they are not autobiographical novels. Instead, Kross writes about the often universal struggles of remarkable, but not so well known, characters in Estonian history. He tells stories about the entanglement of artists, scientists, physicians, aristocrats, academics, and others in a country ruled for centuries by Germans, Swedes, and Russians and, after a brief period of independence from 1918 to 1940, occupied by the Soviet Union. Kross asks questions about dissidence, conformism, truth, madness, betrayal, compromise, escape, and resistance. His latest novel, a bestseller in Estonia, is somewhat of an exception. It is set in contemporary, post-Communist Estonia and explores issues related to the transition to a free market economy, including the privatization boom that characterized much of independent Estonia in the 1990s.

Although Kross casts his novels in a wide and often very sophisticated, richly adorned, distinctly European cultural context, the stories turn on one single geographical pivot: his native Estonia. It is a profound and complex sense of loss, dignity and, at times, also guilt as well as a deep concern for the very survival of his people and their home and language that informs Kross' work. More than that, his novels and short stories are probably best understood as chapters of Estonian history. As such, in no small measure, they have shaped the idea of an independent Estonia, kept it alive during the better part of its almost fifty years of Communist colonization and cultural genocide, and served as a reminder of Estonia's identity as a nation.

Not surprisingly, the role of pain and suffering is of particular importance in this quest for nationhood and the struggle for survival as a people. However, as Maire Jaanus has pointed out, pain and suffering are not only a sign of lost freedom or masochistic delight; they are also a sign of survival. Thus, seemingly paradoxically, pain, where it turns into suffering, goes hand in hand with the kind of pleasure we experience when we are able to intervene, make a difference, contribute, be ourselves. This complex and often hidden dimension of the human condition in no small measure co-determines the consciousness of the Estonian people; Kross also explores this dimension in his writing, especially in his 1998 novel with the telling title *Paigallend*.

In addition to the psychological perspective, another perspective—the historical—also reveals the striking richness and significance of Kross' work. Whatever factual disputes there might be between historians and Jaan Kross, in his fiction, Estonia's history comes across as more real than the dominant discourse of professional historians, East and West, permitted for a long time. It is only recently that Estonian historiography, both in Estonia and elsewhere, has caught up with Kross and has become less driven by ideological concerns or the narrow, self-serving perspective that often informs the stories colonizers tell about the colonized. To be sure, at the core of Kross' narrative style is the voice of a native Estonian informant. After all, telling stories from the inside about struggles against dominant outsiders is among the distinguishing characteristics of Jaan Kross' autobiographical-historical fiction. But Kross' novels are not about ethnic singularity. Instead, they provide "thick," dynamic, and complex descriptions that bear witness to a cross-cultural Estonian identity shaped by a long history of colonization.

—Thomas Salumets

KUNCEWICZ, Maria

Also known as Maria Kuncewiczowa. **Born:** Maria Zofia Szczepańska in Samara, Russia, probably on 30 October 1895 (some sources quote 1897 or 1899); naturalized United States citizen, 1960. **Education:** Schooled internationally in languages, music, and French and Polish philology in Nancy, France, at the Jagiellonian University in Cracow and the University of Warsaw; considered a career as a concert singer following her studies at the conservatories in Warsaw and Paris. **Family:** Married Jerzy Kuncewicz, lawyer and writer, in 1921 (died 1984); one son. **Career:** Traveled before World War II (Europe, Middle East), debuted with stories, journalism, and translations in newly independent Poland, 1918; involved in the Polish PEN Club, from 1924, elected vice president, 1938; translated literary works from Russian, French, and English, wrote the first radio serial in Europe; by World War II widely recognized in Poland and abroad for her short stories and first novel, *Cudzoziemka* (*The Stranger*); fled to Romania, France, and England, 1939; engaged in émigré publications and radio broadcasts; wrote an appeal to the United Nations on behalf of post-war international refugees, 1949; one of the founders of the International Pen-Club Center for Writers in Exile, 1951, Honorary President, 1951–57; following their son, immigrated with husband to the United States, 1955; continued writing novels and autobiographical prose in Polish and English, taught at the University of Chicago, broadcast a radio serial with Radio Free Europe, edited anthologies and lectured on Polish literature; returned to Poland in 1958, resumed publishing in Polish journals and periodicals despite censorship, and resettled there in later years as an American citizen; communist government returned her family house "Kuncewiczówka" in Kazimierz nad Wisłą in the 1960s; re-joined the official Association of Polish Writers, 1962; continued travelling and paid regular visits to the United States; after husband's death in 1984 suffered from ill health; wrote until her death; her last will turned "Kuncewiczówka" into a cultural center. **Awards:** Krzyż Niepodległości, 1931; Literary award of the City of Warsaw, 1937; Złoty Krzyż Zasługi, 1938; American Council of Learned Societies award, 1963; Kosciuszko

Foundation medal for "Contributions to Polish and American Cultures," 1971; Polish National award, First Class, 1974; Krzyż Komandorski Orderu Odrodzenia Polski, declined in 1982, accepted 1987. **Died:** 15 July 1989 in Lublin.

PUBLICATIONS

Collections

Dzieła. Seria I–II. 1978–86.
Dzieła wybrane Marii i Jerzego Kuncewiczów. 8 vols, 1989–1997.

Prose

Tseu-Hi, władczyni bokserów. 1926.
Przymierze z dzieckiem. Powieść. 1927.
Twarz mężczyzny. Powieść. 1928.
Miłość Panieńska. Sztuka w 4 aktach. 1932.
Dwa Księżyce. 1933.
Dyliżans warszawski. 1935.
Cudzoziemka. 1936; as *The Stranger*, translated by B.W.A. Massey, 1944, 1945.
Dni powszednie państwa Kowalskich. Powieść radiowa. 1938; revised 1938, 1960; 1984.
Kowalscy się odnaleźli. Uzupełnienie powieści radiowej "Dni powszednie państwa Kowalskich." 1938.
Serce Kraju. 1938.
Przyjaciele ludzkości. 1939.
Miasto Heroda. Notatki palestyńskie. 1939.
W domu i w Polsce. 1939.
Zagranica. 1939.
Klucze. 1943; revised edition, 1948; as *The Keys: A Journey through Europe at War*, 1946.
Zmowa nieobecnych. Powieść. 1 vol., 1946; expanded, 2 vols., 1950; as *The Conspiracy of the Absent: A Novel*, translated by Maurice Michael and Harry Stevens, 1950.
Leśnik. Powieść. 1952; as *The Forester: A Novel*, translated by Stevens, 1954.
Odkrycie Patusanu. 1958.
Gaj oliwny. 1961; English version published as *The Olive Grove*, 1963.
Don Kichote i Niańki. 1965.
Tristan 1946. 1967; English version published as *Tristan: A Novel*, 1974.
Fantomy. 1971.
Natura. 1975.
Fantasia alla polacca. 1979.
Przezrocza. Notatki włoskie. 1985.
Listy do Jerzego. 1988.

Plays

Radio Plays: *Dni powszednie państwa Kowalskich. Powieść mowiona,* 1936–37; *Kowalscy się odnaleźli. Powieść mówiona,* 1937; *Dialog o zmierzchu. Powieść mówiona,* 1939; *Polskie żarna,* 1942; *Oblężenie i obrona Warszawy,* 1949; *Państwo Kowalscy na emigracji: Kowalscy w Anglii,* and *Kowalscy w Ameryce,* 1956.

Other

"Avec les réfugies," in *Paris aux yeux du monde*, edited by Boris Metzel. 1951.
Cudzoziemka (screenplay). 1986.
Editor, *The Modern Polish Mind: An Anthology.* 1962.
Editor, *Modern Polish Prose.* 1945.
Translator, *Gra* by Jack London. 1923.
Translator, *Podła kobieta* by Jack London. 1923.
Translator, *Arcybestia* by Jack London. 1926.
Translator, *Lato R. 1925* by Ilia Erenburg. 1927.
Translator, *Bella* by Jean Giraudoux. 1929.
Translator, *Pani Hjelde* by Sigrid Undset. 1931.
Translator, *Macierzyństwo* by Sigrid Undset. 1933.

*

Bibliography: *Maria Kuncewiczowa: Bibliografia* by Anna Palczak, 1989; *Maria Kuncewiczowa: monografia dokumentacyjna 1895–1989* by Alicja Szalagan, 1995; *Współcześni pisarze polscy i badacze literatury. Słownik bibliograficzny*, vol. 4, 1996.

Critical Studies: Introduction to *The Stranger* by Margaret Storm Jameson, 1945; *Kobiety piszą ... Sylwetki i szkice* by Stefania Podhorska-Okołów, 1938; "The Stranger: A Study and Note about Maria Kuncewicz" by Mary C. Smith, in *Polish Review*, 1969; "Cudzoziemka Marii Kunczewiczowej. Powstanie, dzieje, recepcja" by Alicja Szalagan, in *Pamiętnik Literacki*, vol. 3, 1986; *W stronę Kuncewiczowej. Studia i szkice*, edited by Włodzimierz Wójcik, 1988; "Ethnicity in Exile in Maria Kuncewicz's Writings" by Magdalena J. Zaborowska, in *Something of My Very Own to Say: American Women Writers of Polish Descent*, edited by Thomas S. Gladsky and Rita Holmes Gladsky, 1997; "In Alien Worlds: Transcending the Boundaries of Exile in the Works of Maria Kuncewicz" by Magdalena J. Zaborowska, in *How We Found America: Reading Gender through East European Immigrant Narratives*, 1995; "Writing the Virgin, Writing the Crone: Maria Kuncewicz's Embodiments of Faith," by Magdalena J. Zaborowska, in *Engendering Slavic Literatures*, edited by Sibelan Forrester and Pamela Chester, 1996; "W stronę utopii. Nad książkami Marii Kuncewiczowej" by Helena Zaworska, in *Odra*, 1987; *Maria Kuncewiczowa* by Helena Zaworska, 1973; *Maria Kuncewiczowa* by Stanisław Żak, 1971; *Kuncewiczowa* by Halina Ivanickova, translated by Krystyna Cękalska, 1974; *Roznowy z Maria Kuncewiczową*, edited by Helena Zaworska, 1983.

* * *

Maria Kuncewicz is one of the most engaging and important Polish writers of the 20th century. Her works span the genres of short story, novel, travel notebook, autobiography, reportage, radio serial, play, and essay. Upon her literary debut after World War I, she won acclaim from the most influential literary critics of the day with her stories focused on women's issues—motherhood, sexuality, puberty, marriage. But while later writing in exile, she expanded her thematic focus to authorship across cultures and languages, the impact of space and geographic location on identity, and the individual versus the state and international politics. Although she lived and wrote internationally, was nominated for the Nobel prize in literature in 1970s, and had her works translated into several languages, Kuncewicz has not gained wide recognition outside of Poland. One of the reasons for her relative obscurity is the continued hegemony of male writers from

Eastern Europe on the world's literary scene, which has been aided by the preferences of Western editors and critics. Another reason may be the unavailability of her work in English: there are no up-to-date translations of her works and the two novels she wrote in English have been out of print since 1970s.

Kuncewicz's writings display a keen sense of observation, attention to detail, and subtle depiction of mood and character; the narrative voice of her later, autobiographical notebooks *Fantomy* [Phantoms], *Natura* [Nature], *Przezrocza* [Slides] draws the reader in effortlessly by combining an intimate perspective on people and places in many countries with the distance and irony of a seasoned witness of history and human folly. Kuncewicz's writing can be deeply lyrical, daring, and experimental, as in the descriptions of music, desire, erotics, and nature in her early stories and her first novels, *Przymierze z dzieckiem* [Covenant with a Child], *Dwa Księżyce* [Two Moons], and *Cudzoziemka* (*The Stranger*). She is an astute reader of different aspects of identity—ethnicity, class, gender and sexuality—and thus able to paint a rich portrait of Poland between the wars and of some of its human types: bohemian artists, small-town Jews, petty bourgeoisie, anti-Semites, displaced persons (*Dwa Księżyce*, *Dyliżans warszawski* [Warsaw Stagecoach], *Miłość panieńska* [A Maiden's Love]). She excels at psychological sketches, especially of women (*Cudzoziemka, Tristan, Gaj oliwny* [The Olive Grove]), and belongs in the ranks of international feminist writers who boldly explored the complexities of women's psyche and physiology against the bourgeois mentality of the first half of the 20th century.

Well-traveled and then forced into exile by the war and the communist takeover of Poland, Kuncewicz is also a chronicler and a keen observer of contemporary events. The Keys, a war memoir, steers masterfully between profoundly personal and self-ironic, distanced observations of what seems to be the end of the world in Nazi invaded Poland, where the author's house is wiped out by an explosion, and under the bomb-filled sky of London, where she finds refuge. She is also the author of the first European radio serial, *Dni powszednie państwa Kowalskich*, which became famous and set the standard for the genre in Poland. It explored the lives of average, working class people and poor intelligentsia; it was later continued when Kuncewicz was living in England and the United States (*Państwo Kowalscy na emigracji: Kowalscy w Anglii, Kowalscy w Ameryce* [Mr. and Mrs. Kowalski in Exile: The Kowalskis in England, The Kowalskis in America]. However, enraged colleagues at Radio Free Europe cancelled the series and even destroyed some unaired episodes when Kuncewicz agreed, after the political "thaw" of 1956, to have her works published in Poland again. Following the end of Stalinism, changes in the Polish government and shifts in Moscow's foreign policy allowed for more cultural freedom, and Kuncewicz responded to the call of her family and readers to return home as a writer. Although she continued to be a "citizen of the world," which was easy with her American passport, her decision to be published in Poland made her unpopular among the "professional refugees," or those who thought it impossible to write under the constraints of the communist regime. It is not clear how much Kuncewicz had to compromise, although it is highly unlikely that she "collaborated" with the government in any way. Her works were subjected to censorship just as those by any other writer living in Poland; she chose to pay that price in order to return to her beloved house in Kazimierz and her mother tongue.

Kuncewicz's later writings—her autobiographical notebooks and her tribute to her late husband, *Listy do Jerzego* [Letters to George]— came perhaps ahead of their time, for the critical apparatus needed to assess her craft has been only very recently forged in the fields of interdisciplinary feminist and cultural studies. Her diverse oeuvre makes for a fascinating study, for it records and responds to the major events of the century—two world wars, the Cold War, the birth of Israel (*Miasto Heroda*), Soviet domination, and the 1960s in the United States. Her preoccupation with the creative process and political responsibility of writers, whom she saw as products/witnesses of their social and historical contexts, makes her worthy of sustained international attention.

—Magdalena J. Zaborowska

KUNDERA, Milan

Born: Brno, Czechoslovakia, 1 April 1929. **Education:** Graduated from a secondary school in Brno, 1948, began studying literature and aesthetics at the Arts Faculty of Charles University, Prague, 1948, after one year transferred to the Film Academy, Prague, where he studied film direction and scriptwriting, graduated in 1952. **Family:** Married Věra Hrabánková in 1967. **Career:** Taught world literature at the Film Academy, Prague, 1952–70; after the 1968 Warsaw Pact invasion of Czechoslovakia he became a banned writer and remained unemployed, 1970–75. Visiting professor at the University of Rennes, France, 1975, then he taught at the Ecoles des Hautes Etudes, Paris. **Awards:** Czechoslovak state prize, 1964, Czechoslovak Writers Union Prize, 1968, Prix Médicis, France, 1973, Premio letterario Mondello, Italy, 1978; American Commonwealth award, 1981, European literature prize, 1982, Doctor honoris causa of the University of Michigan, United States, 1983; Jerusalem prize, 1985; Critics' prize of the Academie Francaise, 1987; Austrian prize for European Literature, 1987; Knight of the Légion Étrangère, France, 1990; The Independent Newspaper prize for Foreign Literature, 1991; Jaroslav Seifert prize, Czech Republic, 1994, Herder prize, Austria 2000.

PUBLICATIONS

Fiction

Směšné lásky: tři melancholické anekdoty [Laughable Loves: Three Melancholy Anecdotes]. 1963.
Druhý sešit směšných lásek [Second volume of Laughable Loves]. 1965.
Třetí sešit směšných lásek [Third volume of Laughable Loves]. 1968.
Směšné lásky. 1970; definitive version published in French as *Risibles amours*, 1970; emigré Czech edition, 1981; as *Laughable Loves*, definitive English edition, translated by Suzanne Rappaport, 1987.
Žert. 1967; as *The Joke*, abridged English translation by David Hamblyn and Oliver Stallybrass, 1969; complete English translation by Michael Henry Heim, 1982; definitive English edition, 1992.
Život je jinde. As *La vie est ailleurs*, translated by François Kérel, 1973; as *Life is Elsewhere*, translated by Peter Kussi, 1974; emigré Czech edition, 1979; definitive English edition, 1986.
Valčík na rozloučenou. As *The Farewell Party*, translated by Peter Kussi, 1974; emigré Czech edition, 1979.
Kniha smíchu a zapomnění. As *Le livre du rire et de l'oubli*, translated by François Kérel, 1979; as *The Book of Laughter and Forgetting*,

translated by Michael Henry Heim, 1980; emigré Czech edition, 1981.

Nesnesitelná lehkost bytí. As *The Unbearable Lightness of Being,* translated by Michael Henry Heim, 1984; emigré Czech edition, 1985.

Nesmrtelnost. As *L'immortalité,* by Eva Bloch, 1990; as *Immortality,* translated by Peter Kussi, 1991; emigré Czech edition, 1993.

La Lenteur. 1995; as *Slowness,* translated by Linda Asher, 1996.

L'Identité: roman. 1997; as *Identity: A Novel,* translated by Linda Asher, 1998.

La ignorancia. Spanish translation from French by Beatriz de Moura, 2000; as *Ignorance,* translated from French by Linda Asher, 2002.

Verse

Člověk, zahrada šírá [Man, a Wide Garden]. 1953.

Poslední máj [The Last May]. 1955.

Monology [Monologues]. 1957; extended and rewritten, 1964; extended and rewritten 1965.

Plays

Majitelé klíčů [The Owners of the Keys]. 1962.

Jakub a jeho pán: pocta Denisi Diderotovi. As *Jacques et son maitre: Hommage à Denis Diderot en trois,* 1981; as *Jacques and His Master: An Homage to Diderot in Three Acts,* 1985.

Other

Umění románu: cesta Vladislava Vančury za velkou epikou [The Art of the Novel: Vladislav Vančura´s journey towards great epic writing]. 1960.

L'art du roman: essai. 1986; as *The Art of the Novel* by Linda Asher, 1988.

Les testaments trahis. 1993; as *Testaments Betrayed: An Essay in Nine Parts* by Linda Asher, 1995.

*

Bibliography: *Milan Kundera: An Annotated Bibliography* by Glen Brand, 1988.

Critical Studies: *Europäische Ideen,* vol. 20, 1976; *Liberté,* no. 121, 1979; *L'Infini,* no. 5, 1984; *Salmagundi,* no. 73, winter 1987; *The Review of Contemporary Fiction,* vol. 9, no. 2, summer 1989; *Proměny,* vol. 28, no. 1, 1991; *Milan Kundera and the Art of Fiction. Critical Essays,* edited by Aron Aji, 1992; *L'Infini,* no. 44, 1993; *Die Fallen der Welt. Der Romancier Milan Kundera* by Květoslav Chvatík, 1994; in Czech as *Svět románů Milana Kundery,* 1994; *Understanding Milan Kundera. Public Events, Private Affairs* by Fred Misurella, 1993; *Terminal Paradox: The Novels of Milan Kundera* by Maria Němcová-Banerjee, 1990; *Kundera ou La mémoire du désir* by Eva Le Grand, 1995, in English as *Kundera or The Memory of Desire,* 1999; ''Milan Kundera'' by Jan Čulík, in *Dictionary of Literary Biography,* vol. 232, 2001.

* * *

Milan Kundera is a major contemporary French/Czech writer who has succeeded in communicating the East European experience of life under totalitarian communism to a wide international public. Most recently, he has used his experience of life both in the East and in the West for commenting on contemporary Western civilization. Milan Kundera's knowledge of life in Czechoslovakia under Soviet rule has led him to important insights regarding the human condition of people living both in the East and in the West. Since Kundera moved to France in 1975, he has become an author of considerable international renown.

In Czechoslovakia after World War II, Kundera was a member of the young, idealist communist generation who were trying to bring about a ''paradise on Earth,'' a communist utopia. It was not until their middle age that they realised that the communist regime had abused their idealism and that they had brought their nation into subjugation. This realisation resulted in a feeling of guilt which Milan Kundera has been trying to exorcise by his literary work in which, especially after leaving for the West, he has been able, by contrasting the Western and the East European experience, to elucidate important aspects of contemporary human existence. Kundera's mature work serves as a warning: the author argues that human perception is flawed and that human beings fall prey to false interpretations of reality. The primary impulse for this cognitive scepticism is undoubtedly Kundera's traumatic experience of his younger years when he uncritically supported communist ideology.

While he lived in Czechoslovakia, Kundera was always in the forefront of indigenous public debate on cultural issues. In the 1950s, he published lyrical poetry which while conforming to the demands of official communist literary style of ''socialist realism'' highlighted the importance of individual personal experience. Later, Kundera came to abhor lyricism and sentimentality.

In his own words, he ''found himself'' as a writer when, in the mid-1960s, he wrote short stories, later gathered in *Laughable Loves.* These are miniature dramas of intimate human relationships. Most of these short stories are based on bittersweet anecdotes which deal with sexual relations of two or three characters. Kundera believes that looking at people through the prism of erotic relationships reveals much about human nature. Sex and love-making is an important instrument for Kundera which enables him to delve into the minds of his characters in all his mature works.

Many Czech critics regard Kundera's first novel, *Žert* (*The Joke*) as his finest achievement. Here Kundera develops for the first time his most important theme: the warning that it is impossible to understand and control reality. The novel is a story of a young communist student, Ludvík Jahn, who, out of frustration that he cannot get a female-fellow student into bed, sends her a postcard in which he mocks her political beliefs. The postcard is intercepted and Ludvík is punished by being expelled from university and sent to work in the mines. Throughout his later life, Ludvík bears a grudge against all his former fellow students who voted for his expulsion. He plans an intricate revenge. However, it is impossible to enter the same river twice and Ludvík´s plan misfires: although he prides himself on his intellectual capacity, his perception of reality is just as flawed as the perception of the ''emotional'' and ''lyrical'' women whom he despises. The structure of the novel is pluralist and polyphonic: the author compares and contrasts the testimonies of a number of different protagonists, thus forcing the reader to come to the conclusion that reality is unknowable. Most Western critics saw *The Joke* primarily as a criticism of Stalinist communism, yet Kundera rightly rejected such a simplistic interpretation.

Kundera further developed his writing style particularly in his novels *Kniha smíchu a zapomnění* (*The Book of Laughter and Forgetting*) and *Nesnesitelná lehkost bytí* (*The Unbearable Lightness of Being*), which made his name in the West in the 1980s. He argues that he has invented a new method of writing a novel. His major works written since the 1980s consist of a series of texts which are bound together by a number of salient themes rather than by the narrative itself. These themes are examined and analysed by means of variations, like in a musical composition.

In *The Book of Laughter and Forgetting*, a major theme when analysing people's insufficiences in perceiving reality, is forgetting. One of the main characters of the novel, Czech emigré Tamina, who leads a meaningless and isolated existence in France, is trying desperately and unsuccessfully to reconstruct her life in Czechoslovakia with her now dead husband. In *The Unbearable Lightness of Being*, a work which was hailed in the West as a masterpiece, Kundera's preoccupations with insufficiencies of perception, lyricism, privacy and misunderstanding are re-examined in a polyphonic structure with a more traditional narrative line. It is a story of two Czech emigrés, Tomáš and Tereza who return to communist Czechoslovakia on an impulse and suffer the consequences.

In his later works, Kundera deals with various frustrating features of human behaviour, and again returns to the themes of privacy, individuality, perception and herd behaviour. *Immortality*, ''a novel of debate,'' is—among other things—a strong criticism of contemporary, superficial, Western civilisation in which commercial media and advertising images rule supreme and reduce everything to manipulated, meaningless drivel. Kundera here stands in awe over the mystery and authenticity of life and protests with all his might against its trite, consumerist simplification.

—Jan Čulík

L

LA FONTAINE, Jean de

Born: Château-Thierry, France, 8 July 1621. **Family:** Married Marie Héricart in 1647 (separated 1658). **Career:** Succeeded his father as Maître des Eaux et Forêts of the Duchy of Château-Thierry; possibly licensed to practice as a lawyer; writer in Paris; patronized by Fouquet and others, especially Mme. de la Sablière. **Member:** Académie française, 1684. **Died:** 13 March 1695.

PUBLICATIONS

Collections

Oeuvres complètes, edited by H. de Regnier. 11 vols., 1883–92.
Oeuvres: Fables, contes, et nouvelles; Oeuvres diverses, edited by René Groos, Jacques Schiffrin, and Pierre Clarac. 2 vols., 1942–54.
The Complete Fables, translated by Norman B. Spector. 1988.
Oeuvres complètes, edited by Jean-Pierre Collinet. 1991–.
Selected Fables, translated by Christopher Wood. 1995.
Selected Fables: A Dual-language Book, edited and translated by Stanley Appelbaum. 1997.
Complete Tales in Verse, translated by Guido Waldman. 2000.
Love and Folly: Selected Fables and Tales of La Fontaine, translated by Marie Ponsot. 2002.

Verse

Élégie aux nymphes de Vaux. 1661.
Nouvelles en vers. 1665.
Contes et nouvelles en vers (4 parts). 4 vols., 1665–74; enlarged edition, 1686; edited by Jacqueline Zeugschmitt, 2 vols., 1972; as *Tales and Novels in Verse*, translated by Samuel Humphreys, 1735; as *La Fontaine's Bawdy: Of Libertines, Louts, and Lechers*, translations from the *Contes et nouvelles en vers* by Norman R. Shapiro, 1992.
Fables (12 parts). Vols. 1–6, 1668; vols. 7–11, 1678–79; vol. 12, 1693; translated as *Fables*, 1804; also translated by Edward Marsh, 1931; Marianne Moore, 1954; Reginald Jarman, 1962; Elizur Wright, 1975; James Michie, 1979; Francis Scarfe, 1985; Walter Thornbury, 1984; Liza Cornmager, 1985; Norman Shapiro, 1988.
Fables nouvelles et autres poésies. 1671; as *Fables and Other Poems*, translated by John Cairncross, 1982.
Poème du Quinquina et autres ouvrages en vers. 1682.

Fiction

Les Amours de Psyché et de Cupidon. 1669; as *The Loves of Cupid and Psyche*, translated by Joseph Lockman, 1744.

Plays

L'Eunuque, from the play by Terence. 1654.

Les Rieurs de Beau-Richard (ballet; produced 1659–60). In *Oeuvres*, 1827.
Astrée, music by Pascal Colasse (produced 1691). 1691.

Other

Voyage en Limousin. 1663.
Ouvrages de prose et de poésie, with Abbé François de Maucroix. 2 vols., 1685.
Oeuvres posthumes. 1696.

*

Critical Studies: *Young La Fontaine* by P. Wadsworth, 1952; *La Fontaine* by M. Sutherland, 1953; *La Fontaine: Fables* by Odette de Mourgues, 1960; *La Fontaine, Poet and Counterpoet* by Margaret O. Guiton, 1961; *The Style of La Fontaine's Fables* by Jean Dominique Biard, 1966; *The Esthetics of Negligence: La Fontaine's Contes* by John C. Lapp, 1971; *La Fontaine and His Friends: A Biography* by Agnes Ethel MacKay, 1972; *Fables in Frames: La Fontaine and Visual Culture in Nineteenth-Century France* by Kirsten H. Powell, 1997; *Reading Undercover: Audience and Authority in Jean de La Fontaine* by Anne L. Birberick, 1998; *The Fables of La Fontaine: Wisdom Brought Down to Earth* by Andrew Calder, 2001.

* * *

Jean de La Fontaine stands out as the one French writer of the 17th century to have written sympathetically about animals and the natural world, and the one poet in the classical period to have combined a deep respect for form with a readiness and ability to experiment in different types of versification. His two collections of *Fables* continue to make him probably the most frequently read and quoted of all French poets, and he is probably the only great French writer to be equally appreciated by children and by adults. His first book of *Fables* was written for the instruction of the Dauphin, the future Louis XIV, and offers a view of the world that contains a greater awareness of *Realpolitik* than of the nobler elements in the concept of Christian monarchy. Thus when, in "La Génisse, la chèvre, et la brebis en société avec le lion" ("The Heifer, the Goat, and the Sheep in company with the Lion"), the animals prepare to share out the spoils, the lion—the King of Beasts—takes the largest share on the indisputable grounds that he is called Lion and is the strongest. One of the best known fables, "Le Loup et l'Agneau" ("The Wolf and the Lamb") demonstrates the truth that might is right, and the qualities needed to succeed, or even to survive, in the social world depicted in La Fontaine's animal allegories are exactly those that Hobbes considered inseparable from the State of Nature. For it is indeed the war of all against all in which the cardinal virtues are force and fraud, and the human beings who make an appearance in this world tend to be on the same moral level as the animals who represent the various ranks in the extremely hierarchical society that La Fontaine knew. When a bird is wounded in a fight and lands in a field, a child casually throws a stone to kill it, thus illustrating the pre-Rousseauist view of children as "an age without pity." Only perhaps by adopting an attitude of suspicion, humility, and self-effacement can those at the bottom end of the social spectrum survive, and it is clear that La Fontaine had no vision of a society in which a king or any other kind of ruler might act or intervene to improve the lot of his subjects.

Most of the actual stories, of course, are traditional, coming down from Aesop and Phaedra, and the almost unremitting pessimism which is the quality that most strikes the modern reader may well have been more axiomatic and therefore less surprising for La Fontaine's contemporaries. This pessimism is also occasionally relieved by fables such as "Les Deux Amis" ("The Two Friends"), showing as it does an idealized vision of friendship, and is prevented from making a really deep emotional impact by the humour of versification and characterization that run through all the *Fables*. La Fontaine excels in matching verbal rhythms to the physical features of the animals he describes, writing about mice in short, neat, light, precise lines, and about bears and lions in more ponderous and self-important tones. You can see his animals moving as you read or listen to the *Fables*, and visualize the French countryside against which the action takes place.

In his lifetime, and by connoisseurs since the 17th century, La Fontaine was also known as the author of a number of *Contes et nouvelles en vers* (*Tales and Novels in Verse*), whose agreeably pagan inspiration gave way to a more orthodox Christian sensibility in the "ecueil de Poésies Chrétiennes" ("Collection of Christian Poetry") in 1671. It is traditional in France to refer to the author of the *Fables* as "le bon La Fontaine," a reference more to his genial disposition than to the view of humanity running through his work.

—Philip Thody

See the essay on *Fables*.

LA MOTTE FOUQUÉ, Caroline

See FOUQUÉ, Caroline de la Motte

LA MOTTE FOUQUÉ, Friedrich

See FOUQUÉ, Friedrich de la Motte

LA ROCHEFOUCAULD, François

Born: Paris, France, 15 September 1613. **Family:** Married Andrée de Vivonne in 1628; eight children. **Career:** Chief of staff, 1629, served in Italy, Netherlands, 1635–36, Rocroi, 1643, and Gravelines, 1644; took part in Louis XIV's Dutch campaign, 1667–68; participated in the Frondes, 1648–52; intrigues against Richelieu; severely wounded in fighting in Paris, 1652; imprisoned by Richelieu for eight days, then banished to Verteuil for two years. Lived in retirement among a small intellectual circle including Mme. de Sablé, Mme. de Sévigné, and Mme. de Lafayette. **Died:** 17 March 1680.

PUBLICATIONS

Collections

Oeuvres. 1818.
Oeuvres complètes. 1825.
Oeuvres inédites. 1863.
Oeuvres complètes, edited by D.L. Gilbert and J. Gourdault. 4 vols., 1868–83.
Oeuvres complètes, edited by A. Chassang. 2 vols., 1883–84.
Oeuvres complètes, edited by Louis Martin-Chauffier and Jean Marchand. 1935; revised editions, 1957, 1964.

Works

Portrait de La Rochefoucauld par lui-même. 1659.
Mémoires. 1662.
Sentences et maximes de morale (pirate edition). 1664; as *Réflexions; ou, Sentences et maximes morales.* 1665; 5th edition, 1678; enlarged edition as *Nouvelles réflexions ou sentences et maximes morales*, 1693; as *Maximes*, edited by Robert L. Cru, 1927, Henry A. Grubbs, 1929, F.C. Green, 1945, Roland Barthes, 1961, Jean Starobinski, 1964, Dominique Secretan, 1967, and by Jacques Truchet, 1967; as *Maximes*, translated by Aphra Behn 1685; also translated by A.S. Bolton, 1884; F.C. Stevens, 1939; Constantine Fitzgibbon, 1957; Louis Kronenberger, 1959; Leonard W. Tancock, 1959; as *Maxims*, translated by Stuart D. Warner and Stéphane Dovard, 2001.
Mémoires du duc de L.R. 1664.
La Justification de l'amour (attributed to La Rochefoucauld), edited by J.D. Hubert. 1971.
A Frenchman's Year in Suffolk, edited and translated by Norman Scarfe. 1988.
Innocent Espionage: The La Rochefoucauld Brothers' Tour of England in 1785, edited and translated by Norman Scarfe. 1995.

*

Bibliography: *Bibliographie générale raisonnée de La Rochefoucauld* by Jean Marchand, 1948; *François de la Rochefoucauld* by Edith Mora, 1965.

Critical Studies: *Le Vrai visage de la Rochefoucauld* by Emile Magne, 1923: *The Originality of La Rochefoucauld's Maxims* by H.A. Grubbs, 1929: *The Life and Adventures of La Rochefoucauld* by Maurice Bishop, 1951; *New Aspects of Style in the Maxims of La Rochefoucauld* by Mary F. Zeller, 1954; *The Concept of Love in the Maxims of La Rochefoucauld* by May W. Butrick, 1959; *La Rochefoucauld: His Mind and Art* by Will G. Moore, 1969; *Vauvenargues and La Rochefoucauld* by Peter M. Fine, 1974; *La Rochefoucauld: The Art of Abstraction* by Philip E. Lewis, 1977; *Two French Moralists: La Rochefoucauld and La Bruyère* by Odette de Mourgues, 1978; *Collaboration et originalité chez La Rouchefoucauld* by Susan Read Baker, 1980; *La Rochefoucauld and the Seventeenth Century Concept of the Self* by Vivien Thweatt, 1980; *Images de La Rochefoucauld: Acres du tricentenaire, 1680–1980* edited by Jean Lafond and Jean Mesnard, 1984; *Procès à La Rochefoucauld et à la maxime* by Corraso Rosso, 1986; *La Rochefoucauld and the Language of Unmasking in Seventeenth-Century France* by Henry C.

Clark, 1994; *La Rochefoucauld: Maximes* by D.J. Culpin, 1995; *Falsehood Disguised: Unmasking the Truth in La Rochefoucauld* by Richard G. Hodgson, 1995; *Concordance to the Maximes of La Rochefoucauld*, edited by Robyn Holman and Jacques Barchilon, 1996.

* * *

The 17th-century French ideal of the *honnête homme* was epitomized in the later life of François, duc de La Rochefoucauld, and is immortalized in his famous *Réflexions; ou, Sentences et maximes morales* (*Maxims*). His views on man and life were determined in large measure by the failure of his political ambitions and by his active role in the armed rebellion against the crown in the civil wars (the Frondes, 1648–52) in which he was seriously wounded. Deceived by his mistress, the duchesse de Longueville, La Rochefoucauld became bitter and disillusioned, retiring from public life at the age of 40. In 1659, he was allowed to resume residence in Paris, where he regularly attended the brilliant salon of Mme. de Sablé. In this cultured, sophisticated society, La Rochefoucauld displayed and honed his ideas and his literary skills. The art of conversation was highly valued among the habitués of literary salons, and their influence on language, attitudes, and ideas was profound. The nature of man and his behaviour were among the most discussed subjects in salon society. La Rochefoucauld asserted that man was not always a rational being but was governed by his "humeurs" or temperament. In humankind *amour-propre* (self-love) was the motivating factor, the well-spring of all actions. He saw a world in which men lied and cheated, and were devoid of honour and gratitude. Only man's natural tendency to *la paresse* (indolence; laziness) prevented him from acting intemperately; moderation in pursuit of virtue or vice was due to indifference and innate dullness. This grim portrait of humanity was widely held by many thoughtful people at the time, and their opinion of the common masses was even more disparaging.

La Rochefoucauld's writings reflect these pessimistic views of man and society, but he also held firmly to the masculine ideal of the age, that of the cultured gentleman; birth and breeding, manners and social graces were distinguishing features of an élite class. Openmindedness, *bienséance* (decorum; decency), and wit were to be cultivated among men of rank. La Rochefoucauld embodied these aristocratic characteristics of the gentleman who avoided pedantry, offending others, or trying to improve one's fellow men through moral exhortation; but the reality was that "we give nothing so liberally as our advice," according to La Rochefoucauld.

In La Rochefoucauld's *Portrait de La Rochefoucauld par luimême* (Potrait of La Rochefoucauld by Himself) one finds a degree of idealization as the author measures himself against the notion of the *honnête homme*. It reveals a self-sufficient man, aloof, proud, and conscious of his aristocratic rank. He claims a melancholic temperament, prone to depression, reserved, and even secretive. Moderation and self-control, intelligence, retentive memory, and "fluent tongue" are cited among his more notable qualities in the *Portrait de La Rochefoucauld par lui-même*. Further, he claims that he was "right thinking and naturally inclined towards good . . . ," fond of his friends, but not overtly demonstrative. The portrait is a kind of manifesto by which the author hoped to be judged favourably by his contemporaries. Appearance was of prime importance in French society, to the people of quality, as La Rochefoucauld would have put it. His self-portrait may have been idealized to some degree, but one can recognize the same sombre, irresolute man pictured in the Cardinal de Retz's pen-portrait of La Rochefoucauld.

Numerous pen-portraits are the most salient feature of La Rochefoucauld's *Mémoires*. Sketches of his contemporaries reveal the attitudes and ideals of the French upper classes, the fostering of *honnêteté* (civility), self-discipline, and social order. Unpleasant characteristics, physical or moral, are seldom mentioned—a gentleman avoided deliberately giving offence. The *Mémoires* are not in the modern sense autobiographical. Indeed, they reveal more about La Rochefoucauld's social milieu and the culture of the age of Louis XIV than about the memoirist.

On the other hand, La Rochefoucauld's deservedly famous maxims reveal a great deal about the personality and ideas of the writer as he probes human nature, motives, and conduct. The ideal of the *honnête homme* is counterpoised to reality; the *Maxims* describe man as he is, not as he ought to be. One can discern a definite point of view, one that is often harsh, bitter, cynical, and pessimistic. La Rochefoucauld's likes and dislikes, and those of his aristocratic peers, are evident as he deals with subjects such as love, friendship, old age, death, women, and human virtues and vices. His attitude towards women is particularly striking: "Most virtuous women are hidden treasures, safe only because no one is looking for them." And about love he declares: "Nothing is more natural or deceptive than to believe one is loved." The moral and ethical standards found in the *Maxims* generally reflect those commonly held by upper-class 17th-century society: man is by nature weak and irrational, motivated by *amour-propre* but just as frequently immobilized by *la paresse*, which renders him indecisive and impassive. However, La Rochefoucauld's own experiences undoubtedly influenced his ideas, especially those relating to women, love, self-interest, mistrust, and ingratitude. Betrayed by the woman he loved, denied a post at Court, censured for rebellion against his monarch, and forever labelled a "frondeur," La Rochefoucauld became disenchanted with his fellow men and with the pursuit of worldly power and position.

La Rochefoucauld was an astute observer, a recorder of human follies and foibles. His intention was to inform, not to reform, mankind, and he avoided dogmatic statements and the appearance of preaching. He accepts that man's nature is what it is; one's conduct is often restrained only by the need to be socially accepted. Without question, the *Maxims* are universally applicable, unrestricted by time or place. In these timeless aphorisms that speak to all, the language employed is markedly neutral, avoiding words that would evoke an emotional rather than a rational reaction. The carefully crafted sentences are notable for their terseness, precise phrasing, and minimal vocabulary. They are immediately understandable, devoid of esoteric allusions, metaphors, and other scholarly devices. The highly polished style of La Rochefoucauld's sentences is due in large part to years of refining and honing of ideas and language in the Paris salons. Creating pithy proverbs, witticisms, and maxims was a popular "parlour-game" among French sophisticates; their search for principles of universal validity was taken seriously and led these perceptive *salonniers* to accept that "we find few sensible people, except those who are of our way of thinking." In Mme. de Sablé's salon, men and women discussed, analyzed, and criticized both the form and the content of ideas, stressing clarity, precision, and simplicity. The *Maxims* also mirror the 17th-century tendency to self-examination, the inward-looking, reflective nature of the French upper classes. The harsh, cynical sentiments expressed in the *Maxims* were softened in later editions, most likely through the influence of La Rochefoucauld's closest women friends, Mme. de Lafayette and Mme. de Sévigné. La Rochefoucauld's *Maxims*, according to Voltaire, helped to shape the

French taste for precision and accuracy, attributes which still set the standards for their thought and writing.

—Jeanne A. Ojala

See the essay on *Maxims*.

LACLOS, (Pierre Ambroise Francois) Choderlos de

Born: Amiens, France, 18 October 1741. **Education:** Educated at École d'Artillerie de la Fère, 1759–63. **Military Service:** 2nd lieutenant, 1762; served in Toul, 1763–66; Strasbourg, 1766–69; Grenoble, 1769–75; Besançon, 1775–76; Valence, 1776–78; l'Île d'Aix, 1778–88; left the army for a brief period as politician; rejoined army as Maréchal de camp, 1792; general of the artillery in the army of Naples, 1800. **Family:** Married Marie-Soulange Duperré in 1786. **Career:** Editor, *Journal des Amis de la Constitution*, 1790–91. **Died:** 5 September 1803.

PUBLICATIONS

Collections

Oeuvres complètes, edited by Maurice Allem. 1944; revised edition, edited by Laurent Versani, 1979.

Fiction

Les Liaisons dangereuses. 1782; edited by René Pomeau, 1981; as *Dangerous Connections*, 1784; as *Dangerous Acquaintances*, translated by Richard Aldington, 1924; as *Les Liaisons dangereuses*, translated by P.W.K. Stone, 1961; also translated and adapted by Christopher Hampton, 1985; translated and edited by Douglas Parmée, 1995; translated by Ernest Dowson, 1998.

Plays

Ernestine, music by Saint-Georges, from a novel by Mme. Riccoboni (produced 1777).

Verse

Poésies, edited by Arthur Symons and Louis Thomas. 1908.

Other

Lettre à M.M. de l'Académie française. 1786.
La Galerie des États-Généraux, with others. 1789.
La Galerie des dames françaises. 1789.
Causes secrètes de la révolution. 1795.
De l'éducation des femmes, edited by Édouard Champion. 1903.
Lettres inédites, edited by Louis de Chauvigny. 1904.

*

Bibliography: *Choderlos de Laclos: The Man, His Works and His Critics: An Annotated Bibliography* by Colette Verger Michael, 1982.

Critical Studies: *Laclos and the Epistolary Novel* by Dorothy R. Thelander, 1963; *The Novel of Worldliness: Crébillon, Marivaux, Laclos, and Stendhal* by Peter P. Brooks, 1969; *Laclos: Les Liaisons dangereuses* by Philip Thody, 1970, revised edition, 1975; *Critical Approaches to Les Liaisons dangereuses* edited by Lloyd R. Free, 1978; *Intimate, Intrusive and Triumphant: Readers in the "Liaisons dangereuses"* by Peter V. Conroy, 1987; *Laclos: Les Liaisons dangereuses* by Simon Davies, 1987; *The Seducer as Mythic Figure in Richardson, Laclos and Kierkegaard* by Betty Becker-Theye, 1988; *Strategies of Resistence in Les Liaisons dangereuses: Heroines in Search of "Author-ity"* by Ann-Marie Brinsmead, 1989; *Les Liaisons dangereuses: A Study of Motives and Moral* by Patrick W. Byrne, 1989; *Resistance to Culture in Molière, Laclos, Flaubert, and Camus: A Post-modernist Approach* by Larry W. Riggs, 1992; *Terrible Sociability: The Text of Manners in Laclos, Goethe, and James* by Susan Winnett, 1993; *Virtue, Gender, and the Authentic Self in Eighteenth-century Fiction: Richardson, Rousseau, and Laclos* by Christine Roulston, 1998.

* * *

Choderlos de Laclos is a man of one book, *Les Liaisons dangereuses*, an impeccably constructed epistolary novel describing and analysing the sexual immorality which is said to have characterized certain members of the French aristocracy in the years immediately preceding the Revolution of 1789. But the novel is not the endorsement of promiscuity it was considered to be in the 19th century, any more than it is the transference into fiction of Laclos's own exploits and world view, or a realistic novel in the sense of one based on actual events. Indeed, recent historical research has revealed how the principal male character, the Vicomte de Valmont, far from being drawn from life, served rather as a model to would-be seducers who wished to follow his example after reading the novel. Laclos himself, unlike Valmont, was a very minor nobleman, whose dislike of the top aristocracy of the day may well have stemmed from the slowness with which, as a professional soldier, he obtained promotion in the artillery in the *ancien régime*. *Les Liaisons dangereuses* can thus be seen as a socially committed novel written by a man sympathetic to the revolutionary and moralistic views of Rousseau, and intended to show, by contrast, the superiority of the more modest but increasingly self-confident middle-class. Laclos's own marriage, to a girl who was 17 when he married her at the age of 45, was a very happy one. Indeed, a letter exists, written to her while he was on active service with the Revolutionary armies in the 1790s, telling her of his ambition to write a novel proving that "true happiness can be found only in the Family."

The plot of *Les Liaisons dangereuses* can certainly be interpreted as a criticism of how Valmont and his female accomplice, the Marquise de Merteuil, behave in their sexual relationships to other people and to each other, and it is also possible to see the extremely intelligent and somewhat terrifying Marquise as a very conscious warning of how feminism can go sour. For Laclos, as an essay published long after his death revealed, held views on the equality of women and men which are advanced even by modern standards ("Learn," he wrote, "that one escapes from slavery only by a great revolution"), and Madame de Merteuil is the strongest willed, the most intellectual, the most interesting, and the least successful of all French fictional heroines. *Les Liaisons dangereuses* is nevertheless too complex and ambiguous a novel to be interpreted in only one light. It deserves its place as the best novel written in France in the

18th century, and one of the best studies ever published of evil, of sexual aggression and of the lust for power. There is also an intriguing contrast between the perfection of its formal finish and the endlessly interesting questions to which it gives rise.

—Philip Thody

See the essay on *Les Liaisons dangereuses*.

LAFAYETTE, Madame de

Born: Marie-Madeleine Pioche de la Vergne, in Paris, France, in 1634. **Family:** Married François, Comte de Lafayette, in 1655 (died 1683), two sons. **Career:** Grew up in Paris, and after a period of life in her husband's château of Nades, lived in Paris after 1659; friend of Henriette d'Angleterre, wife of Louis XIV's brother, of Mme. de Sévigné, and the duc de La Rochefoucauld *q.v.* **Died:** 25 May 1693.

PUBLICATIONS

Collections

Oeuvres, edited by Robert Lejeune. 3 vols., 1925–30.
Romans et nouvelles, edited by Emile Magne. 1958.
Secret History of Henrietta, Princess of England: First Wife of Philippe, duc d'Orléans; Together with, Memoirs of the Court of France for the Years 1688–1689, translated with an introduction by J.M. Shelmerdine. 1993.

Fiction

La Princesse de Montpensier. 1662; as *The Princess Montpensier*, translated anonymously, 1666; also translated by Anthony Bonner, 1805; edited and translated by Terence Cave, with *The Princesse de Clèves* and *The Comtesse de Tende*, 1992; edited with translation by John D. Lyons, 1994; translated by Michael G. Paulson and Tamara Alvarez-Detrell, 1995.
Zaïde. 1669–70; as *Zayde: A Spanish History*, translated by P. Porter, 1678.
La Princesse de Clèves. 1678; edited by Emile Magne, 1950; also edited by Peter H. Nurse, 1971; as *The Princess of Cleves*, translated anonymously, 1679; also translated by Thomas Segeant Perry, 1777; Nancy Mitford, 1950; Walter J. Cobb, 1961; Robin Buss, 1992; edited and translated by Terence Cave, with *The Princesse de Montpensier* and *The Comtesse de Tende*, 1992.
La Comtesse de Tende. 1724; edited and translated by Terence Cave, with *The Princesse de Montpensier* and *The Princesse de Clèves*, 1992.

Other

Histoire d'Henriette d'Angleterre. 1720; edited by Gilbert Sigaux, 1965; as *Fatal Gallantry*, translated anonymously, 1722.
Mémoires de la cour de France. 1731; edited by Gilbert Sigaux, 1965.
Correspondance, edited by A. Beaunier. 2 vols., 1942.

*

Bibliography: *Madame de Lafayette: A Selected Critical Bibliography* by James W. Scott, 1974.

Critical Studies: *Moral Perspective in "La Princesse de Clèves"* by Helen Kaps, 1968; *Madame de Lafayette* by Stirling Haig, 1970; *Classical Voices: Studies of Corneille, Racine, Moliere, Madame de Lafayette* by Peter H. Nurse, 1971; *Madame de Lafayette and "La Princesse de Clèves"* by Janet Raitt, 1971; *La Princesse de Clèves: The Tension of Elegance* by Barbara R. Woshinsky, 1973; *Narrative Strategies in La Princesse de Clèves* by Donna Kuizenga, 1976; *A Structural Analysis of "La Princesse de Clèves"* by Susan W. Tiefenbrun, 1976; *Madame de Lafayette: La Princesse de Clèves* by J.W. Scott, 1983; *Order in the Court: History and Society in La Princesse de Clèves* by Laurence A. Gregorio, 1986; *Une amitié parisienne au Grand siècle: Mme. de Lafayette et Mme. de Sévigné 1648–1693* by Denis Mayer, 1990; *A Critical Analysis of de Lafayette's La Princess de Clèves as a Royal Novel: Kings, Queens and Splendor* by Michael G. Paulsson, 1991; *An Inimitable Example: The Case for the Princess de Clèves*, edited by Patrick Henry, 1993; *The Princess of Clèves: Contemporary Reactions, Criticism*, edited with a revised translation by John D. Lyons, 1994; *Privileged Anonymity: The Writings of Madame de Lafayette* by Anne Green, 1996; *Approaches to Teaching Lafayette's The Princess of Clèves*, edited by Faith E. Beasley and Katherine Ann Jensen, 1998.

* * *

As a member of the nobility, Madame de Lafayette was an amateur writer, and was reluctant to admit authorship of her novels. Indeed, she wrote them to a certain extent in collaboration with male friends, particularly Gilles Ménage and La Rochefoucauld. But they are unquestionably her creation and bear the stamp of her particular if somewhat narrowly focused genius. Her works have survived because one of them, *La Princesse de Clèves* (*The Princess of Cleves*), ranks among the finest psychological novels ever written. Her other books, however, are of interest primarily to the literary historian.

She left four works of fiction. All are variations on the same theme—a love story in the form of a pseudo-historical romance. *La Comtesse de Tende* is a slight novella about an adulterous wife, the countess of the title, who nobly repents before her death. *Zaïde* (*Zayde*) is a "Spanish history" very much in the taste of the time, replete with digressions, adventures, and discourses on the finer points of amorous activity, and needless to say describes love's tribulations at generous length. *La Princesse de Montpensier* (*The Princess Montpensier*) is a more solid effort, which argues, as does the Comtesse de Tende's story, that women can be sure of attaining happiness only if both prudence and virtue govern their actions; but they find that rather difficult, and most of them allow men to make a mess of their lives.

A somewhat mechanistic psychology allied with a platitudinous morality considerably reduces the interest of these works for the modern reader. It is all the more remarkable, then, that using the same ingredients Madame de Lafayette produced one novel that is a masterpiece. *The Princess of Cleves* is set in the 16th century (the material is lifted, with some changes as was her wont, from the candid memoirs of Pierre de Brantôme). It tells of a beautiful young woman who arrives at the French court and is soon married to the Prince of Cleves. She likes and respects him, but is not sexually attracted to him. When the Duc de Nemours appears at court, however, this handsome and seductive creature steals her heart. For a long time she conceals her violent feelings from Nemours, and indeed from everyone else except her own stern mother, but eventually she betrays herself when she experiences acute jealousy over a love letter that she assumes (wrongly) has been sent to Nemours by another woman. When her mother dies she turns for comfort to exactly the wrong person: her husband. Her famous ''avowal'' of her feelings for a rival poisons his life, and he dies not long afterwards of a broken heart. She is now, paradoxically, free to marry the man she loves, but she decides not to do so. This is partly out of remorse at having precipitated her husband's death, but mainly because she fears Nemours will be unfaithful to her once he has made her his wife. So she sacrifices her love on the altar of her peace of mind, and dies not long afterwards, an unattached and virtuous woman. This early blow for feminism, coupled with precise insight into the painful ecstasies of erotic attraction, has ensured the survival of this at first sight unlikely classic.

—John Fletcher

LAFORGUE, Jules

Born: Montevideo, Uruguay, 16 August 1860. Moved to France with his family, 1866. **Education:** Educated at Tarbes from 1866: Collège Impérial, 1869–76; Lycée Condorcet, Paris, 1876–77. **Family:** Married Leah Lee in 1886. **Career:** First poems published in magazines in Tarbes and Toulouse, 1879; part-time assistant to Charles Ephrussi, art historian and editor, 1881; French reader to Empress Augusta of Germany, in Berlin and travelling, 1881–86. **Died:** 21 August 1887.

PUBLICATIONS

Collections

Poésies complètes. 1894.
Oeuvres complètes, edited by G. Jean-Aubry. 6 vols., 1922–30.
Poésies complètes, edited by Pascal Pia. 2 vols., 1979.
Oeuvres complètes. 1988.
Selected Poems, translated with introduction and notes by Graham Dunstan Martin. 1998.
Poems of Jules Laforgue, translated and introduced by Peter Dale. 2001.

Verse

Les Complaintes. 1885; edited by Michael Collie, 1977; also edited by Pierre Reboul, 1981.
L'Imitation de Notre-Dame la Lune. 1886; edited by Pierre Reboul, 1981.
Le Concile féerique. 1886.
Les Derniers Vers. 1890; edited by Michael Collie and J.M. L'Heureux, 1965; as *The Last Poems*, edited by Madeleine Betts, 1973.
Poems, translated by Patricia Terry. 1958.
Poems, translated by Peter Dale. 1986.

Fiction

Moralités légendaires. 1887; edited by Daniel Grojnowski, 1980; as *Moral Tales*, translated by William J. Smith, 1985.

Other

Hamlet; or, The Consequences of Filial Piety, translated by Gustave Leopold van Roosbroeck. 1934.
Lettres à un ami 1880–86. 1941.
Stéphane Vassiliew. 1946.
Selected Writings, edited and translated by William Jay Smith. 1956.
Translator, *Oeuvres choisies*, by Walt Whitman. 1918.

*

Critical Studies: *Laforgue and the Ironic Inheritance* by Warren Ramsey, 1953, and *Laforgue: Essays on a Poet's Life and Work* edited by Ramsey, 1969; *Laforgue*, 1963, and *Jules Laforgue*, 1977, both by Michael Collie; *Looking for Laforgue: An Informal Biography* by David Arkell, 1979; *Jules Laforgue: Poet of His Age* by Laurence J. Watson, 1980; *Exiles and Ironists: Essays on the Kinship of Heine and Laforgue* by Ursula Franklin, 1988; *Parody and Decadence: Laforgue's Moralités Légendaires* by Michele Hannoosh, 1989; *Jules Laforgue and Poetic Innovation* by Anne Holmes, 1993.

*   *   *

Jules Laforgue helped liberate and rejuvenate French prosody by means of a series of bold, iconoclastic, but highly original verse experiments that had the effect of establishing free verse as a legitimate and viable poetic mode not only in France, but also in Britain and the United States. Though disguised as a dilettante, Laforgue was devoted to literature; though a fashionable dandy, he worked through the night and in a short career was extremely productive. His early poems, *Le Sanglot de la terre* [The Sob of the Earth], he himself suppressed, realizing they were derivative, tendentious, verbally flat, and technically uninspired. Two other volumes, *L'Imitation de Notre-Dame la Lune* [Imitation of Our Lady of the Moon] and *Le Concile féerique*, are distinctly modish and lightweight, though some of the Pierrot poems in the first of these show a pleasing cleverness in the dramatization of the clown's anguish. Laforgue's reputation, however, rests chiefly on two volumes of great historical as well as intrinsic importance: *Les Complaintes* and *Les Derniers Vers* (*The Last Poems*).

In these two volumes he challenged not just traditional, middle-class ideas about institutions such as marriage and the church, but also the stability of language itself. Standard usage and normal meanings are in both books ironically subverted by puns and neologisms; by disruptive, unconventional rhymes; by a vigorous, but controlled disturbance of metrical expectation; and by the invention, or at least adoption of new forms. A reader brought up on Lamartine and Hugo could only be shocked by Laforgue's rejection of traditional poetic rhetoric. The witty poems in *Les Complaintes* are remarkably inventive, superbly sophisticated verbal confections presented in the demotic guise of reworked street tunes and popular ballads, confections, one can say, because of their artificiality and high-spiritedness, but none the less in many cases brilliantly imaginative as well (e.g., ''Complainte du pauvre chevalier-errant'' and ''Complainte d'une convalescence en Mai''). The 12 poems of *The Last Poems* constitute a further advance in lexical and prosodic experimentation. Influenced, as he acknowledged himself, both by the theory of Impressionist painting and by the music of Wagner, Laforgue wrote a set of free-verse tone poems whose emphasis and impact were artistic, in the *fin-de-siècle* art-for-art's-sake sense, rather than moral. He interested himself in anything that was different, modern, untraditional: photography, for example, and contemporary sculpture. In Paris he had seen the work of Monet, Sisley, and Pissarro. In Germany he had heard the music of Wagner. He had read about these, and other artists, in avant-garde journals like *La Vogue* and *La Revue Wagnérienne*. He had studied and translated Whitman. Thoroughly imbued with a nihilistic, but technically innovative, modern spirit, he proceeded right at the end of his short life to produce *The Last Poems*, the poetic *tour de force* that first established free-verse as an exciting extension of what was possible in French, and then later exerted a strong influence on English and American writers, most notably T.S. Eliot.

Laforgue's nihilism was that of the late 19th-century *flâneur* whose mind, like Ibsen's, was dominated by the imagined reality of biological determinism. In that post-Darwinian intellectual climate no man acted freely; all men were helpless pawns in a meaningless biological game; women were despised because seemingly ignorant of their merely sexual role; and the individual's only hope of personal integrity was not to participate in other people's normal activities. Experience was a kaleidoscope of impressions; nothing whatsoever could be trusted absolutely. In highly crafted poems like "Dimanches," "Solo de Lune," and "L'Hiver qui vient" Laforgue gave expression to the sensations of disbelief, the psychology of alienation, the loneliness in a world where "il n'y plus de raison" and where the subjunctive and the conditional must necessarily have greater appeal than either the present or the future tense. "J'eusse été le modèle des époux," said Laforgue; "your heart would have responded/Gaily" said T.S. Eliot some years later in imitation of him. Whatever one may think, ultimately, about Laforgue's tantalizing amalgam of irony and sentiment—his cynicism fretted with nostalgia—there seems no doubt that the poems of *The Last Poems* are one of the landmarks of 19th-century French poetry, marking the point at which freedom from conventional rhetoric had been fully achieved.

The same ironic, nihilist sensibility was given expression in a collection called *Moralités légendaires* (*Moral Tales*). Laforgue amused himself by giving popular stories or myths an extravagantly anti-romantic treatment, negating the idealism of the original and poking fun at out-moded heroism. The flippancy and ebullience of these stories can still be enjoyed, as can their affected decadent prose, even though the underlying tone is remorselessly negative. Nor need one be too severe in judging these nihilistic contrivances; Laforgue died at the age of 27, with his great talent denied its full expression.

—Michael Collie

See the essay on *The Last Poems*.

LAGERKVIST, Pär (Fabian)

Born: Växjö, Sweden, 23 May 1891. **Education:** Educated at the University of Uppsala, 1911–12. **Family:** Married 1) Karen Dagmar Johanne Sørenson in 1918 (divorced 1925); 2) Elaine Luella Hallberg in 1925. **Career:** Theatre critic, *Svenska Dagbladet*, Stockholm, 1919. **Awards:** Samfundet De Nio prize, 1928; Bellman prize, 1945; Saint-Beuve prize, 1946; Foreign Book prize (France), 1951; Nobel prize for literature, 1951. Honorary degree: University of Gothenburg, 1941. **Member:** Swedish Academy of Literature, 1940. **Died:** 11 July 1974.

PUBLICATIONS

Fiction

Människor [People]. 1912.

Två sagor om livet [Two Tales about Life]. 1913.

Järn och människor. 1915; as *Iron and Men*, translated by Roy Arthur Swanson, in *Five Early Works*, 1989.

Det eviga leendet. 1920; as *The Eternal Smile*, translated by Denys W. Harding and Erik Mesterton, 1934, and in *Guest of Reality*, 1936; also translated by Alan Blair, in *The Eternal Smile and Other Stories*, 1954.

Onda sagor [Evil Tales]. 1924.

Gäst hos verkligheten. 1925; as *Guest of Reality*, translated by Denys W. Harding and Erik Mesterton, 1936; also translated by Robin Fulton, in *Guest of Reality and Other Stories*, 1989.

Kämpande ande [Struggling Spirit]. 1930; translated in part as *Masquerade of Souls*, 1954.

Bödeln. 1933; as *The Hangman*, in *Guest of Reality*, translated by Denys W. Harding and Erik Mesterton, 1936; as *The Executioner*, translated by David O'Gorman, in *The Eternal Smile and Other Stories*, 1971.

I den tiden [In That Time]. 1935.

Guest of Reality (includes *Guest of Reality; The Eternal Smile; The Hangman*), translated by Denys W. Harding and Erik Mesterton. 1936.

Dvärgen. 1944; as *The Dwarf*, translated by Alexandra Dick, 1945.

Barabbas. 1950; as *Barabbas*, translated by Alan Blair, 1951.

The Eternal Smile and Other Stories, translated by Alan Blair and others. 1954.

The Marriage Feast and Other Stories, translated by Alan Blair and Carl Eric Lindin. 1955.

Sibyllan. 1956; as *The Sibyl*, translated by Alexandra Dick, 1953; also translated by Naomi Walford, 1958.

Pilgrimen [The Pilgrim] (trilogy). 1966.

    Ahasverus död. 1960; as *The Death of Ahasuerus*, translated by Naomi Walford, 1962.

    Pilgrim på hayet. 1962; as *Pilgrim at Sea*, translated by Naomi Walford, 1964.

    Det heliga landet. 1964; as *The Holy Land*, translated by Naomi Walford, 1966.

Mariamne. 1967; as *Herod and Mariamne*, translated by Naomi Walford, 1968; as *Mariamne*, translated by Walford, 1968.

The Eternal Smile and Other Stories (includes *The Eternal Smile; Guest of Reality; The Executioner*), translated by Erik Mesterton, Denys W. Harding, and David O'Gorman. 1971.

Den svåra resan (selected stories). 1985.

Guest of Reality and Other Stories, translated by Robin Fulton. 1989.

Verse

Motiv [Motifs]. 1914.

Ångest [Angst]. 1916.

Den lyckliges väg [The Happy One's Road]. 1921.

Hjärtats sånger [Songs of the Heart]. 1926.

Vid lägereld [By the Campfire]. 1932.

Genius. 1937.

Sång och strid [Song and Battle]. 1940.

Dikter [Verse]. 1941; revised edition, 1958, 1974.

Hemmet och stjärnan [The Home and the Stars]. 1942.

Aftonland. 1953; as *Evening Land*, translated by W.H. Auden and Leif Sjöberg, 1977.

Valda dikter [Selected Poems]. 1967.

Plays

Sista Mänskan. 1917; as *The Last Man*, translated by Roy Arthur Swanson, in *Five Early Works*, 1989.

Den svåra stunden (three one-act plays; produced 1918). In *Teater*, 1918; as *The Difficult Hour I–III*, translated by Thomas R. Buckman, in *Modern Theatre: Seven Plays and an Essay*, 1966.

Himlens hemlighet (produced 1921). In *Kaos*, 1919; as *The Secret of Heaven*, translated by Thomas R. Buckman, in *Modern Theatre: Seven Play's and an Essay*, 1966.

Den osynlige [The Invisible One] (produced 1924). 1923.

Han som fick leva om sitt liv (produced 1928). 1928; as *The Man Who Lived His Life Over*, translated in *Five Scandinavian Plays*, 1971.

Konungen (produced 1950). 1932; as *The King*, translated by Thomas R. Buckman, in *Modern Theatre: Seven Plays and an Essay*, 1966.

Bödeln, from his own novel (produced 1934). In *Dramatik*, 1946; as *The Hangman*, translated by Thomas R. Buckman, in *Modern Theatre: Seven Plays and an Essay*, 1966.

Mannen utan själ (produced 1938). 1936; as *The Man Without a Soul*, translated by Helge Kökeritz, in *Scandinavian Plays of the Twentieth Century 1*, 1944.

Seger i mörker [Victory in Darkness] (produced 1940). 1939.

Midsommardröm i fattighuset (produced 1941). 1941; as *Midsummer Dream in the Workhouse*, translated by Alan Blair, 1953.

Dramatik [Plays]. 1946; revised edition, 1956.

Den vises sten (produced 1948). 1947; as *The Philosopher's Stone*, translated by Thomas R. Buckman, in *Modern Theatre: Seven Plays and an Essay*, 1966.

Låt människan leva (produced 1949). 1949; as *Let Man Live*, in *Scandinavian Plays of the Twentieth Century 3*, translated by Henry Alexander and Llewellyn Jones, 1951.

Barabbas, from his own novel (produced 1953). 1953.

Modern Theatre: Seven Plays and an Essay (includes *The Difficult Hour I–III; The Secret of Heaven; The King; The Hangman; The Philosopher's Stone;* the essay "Points of View and Attack"), translated by Thomas R. Buckman. 1966.

Other

Ordkonst och bildkonst. 1913; as *Literary Art and Pictorial Art: On the Decadence of Modern Literature—On the Vitality of Modern Art*, translated by Roy Arthur Swanson and E.M. Ellestad, 1991.

Kaos [Chaos]. 1919.

Det besegrade livet [The Conquered Life]. 1927.

Skrifter [Writings]. 3 vols., 1932.

Den knutna näven. 1934; as *The Clenched Fist*, translated by Roy Arthur Swanson, in *Five Early Works*, 1989.

Den befriade människan [Liberated Man]. 1939.

Prosa. 5 vols., 1945; revised edition, 1949.

Antecknat [Noted] (diary), edited by Elin Lagerkvist. 1977.

Five Early Works (includes *Iron and Men; The Last Man; The Expectant Guest; The Morning; The Clenched Fist*), translated by Roy Arthur Swanson. 1989.

*

Bibliography: *Pär Lagerkvists bibliografi* by U. Willers, 1951; *Pär Lagerkvist in Translation: A Bibliography* by A. Ryberg, 1964; *Pär Lagerkvists kritiker: En recensionsbibliografi* by R. Yrlid, 1970.

Critical Studies: *Pär Lagerkvist: An Introduction* by Irene Scobbie, 1963, and "Lagerkvist," in *Aspects of Swedish Literature*, edited by Scobbie, 1988; *Pär Lagerkvist: A Critical Essay* by Winston Weathers, 1968; Lagerkvist supplement, in *Scandinavica*, 1971; *Pär Lagerkvist* by Robert Spector, 1973; *Pär Lagerkvist* by Leif Sjöberg, 1976; *Pär Lagerkvist in America* by Ray Lewis White, 1979; *Som är från evighet* by Willy Jönsson, translated by I. Nettervik, 1991.

* * *

As lyric poet, dramatist, satirist, and novelist Pär Lagerkvist was an innovator and one of Sweden's most influential writers of the 20th century. The autobiographical prose work *Gäst hos verkligheten* (*Guest of Reality*) shows his deep affection for his pious parents and a yearning for a faith but an inability to accept their god. The resultant spiritual void and a fevered reaction to the bloodshed of World War I led to an overwhelming angst conveyed in his poems *Ångest* [Angst] and the plays *Sista Mänskan* (*The Last Man*), *Den svåra stunden* (*The Difficult Hour*), and *Himlens hemlighet* (*The Secret of Heaven*), in which he emerged as Sweden's leading expressionist writer. The prose fantasy *Det eviga leendet* (*The Eternal Smile*) reflects a newly found resignation, an appreciation of the beauty of the world and a tentative belief in humanity. Two of his best cycles of poems included in *Hjärtats sånger* [Songs of the Heart] also suggest an inner harmony. This was dispelled as totalitarian regimes took control in Europe. In 1933 Lagerkvist published *Bödeln* (*The Hangman*), where the role of the symbolic central character is examined in a medieval and then contemporary setting. Modern man's propensity for evil clearly surpasses the superstitious crudities of the Middle Ages. A further powerful symbol of evil is the title figure in *Dvärgen* (*The Dwarf*), a masterly novel in diary form set in an Italian Renaissance court. We all have a dwarf within us which when unleashed exults in destruction. The dwarf is in chains in the final chapter but is certain of eventual release.

In *Barabbas*, largely instrumental in his winning the Nobel prize for literature, Lagerkvist makes the biblical robber and insurgent an existentialist figure searching for a belief. Born into a world of violence and hatred, he cannot accept the Christian message, but having met Christ, he cannot shake off his influence. Afraid of death, unable to believe in an afterlife, he remains a lonely, moving representative of modern man. Man's relation to God is explored further in a series of symbolic novels. For the Pythia in *Sibyllan* (*The Sibyl*) the god can be both wonderful and terrible but her life without him would have been nothing; the Wandering Jew in *Ahasverus död* (*The Death of Ahasuerus*) bears God's curse and achieves death only by turning his back on religion; in *Pilgrim på havet* (*Pilgrim at Sea*) and *Det heliga landet* (*The Holy Land*) the struggling pilgrim finally finds reconciliation with God and man. In *Mariamne* (*Herod and Mariamne*) evil in man is embodied in the symbolic figure of Herod. It is a desolate book, for Herod has Mariamne the Good killed, but it ends in hope—the Magi have found their way to a new-born babe.

Lagerkvist's last cycle of poems, *Aftonland* (*Evening Land*), contains beautifully expressed reminiscences and an indication of his unsolved paradox: "The non-existing god/he has set my soul in flames." In his early twenties Lagerkvist wrote numerous articles on Cubism and other forms of modern art. He subsequently endeavoured to apply the Cubists' method of composition to his creative writing. Even at its most feverishly inspired his work is carefully constructed, his novels particularly having an almost architectural structure.

—Irene Scobbie

LAGERLÖF, Selma (Ottiliana Lovisa)

Born: Mårbacka, Värmland, Sweden, 20 November 1858. **Education:** Lame from age 3, and educated at home; studied at Teachers' Seminary, Stockholm, 1882–85. **Career:** Taught in a school in Landskrona until 1895, then writer: lived in Falun and, after she bought back her birthplace, Mårbacka. **Awards:** *Idun* magazine prize, 1895; travelling fellowship, 1895; Swedish Academy gold medal, 1904; Nobel prize for literature, 1909. Ph.D.: Uppsala University, 1907. **Member:** Swedish Academy, 1914. **Died:** 16 March 1940.

PUBLICATIONS

Collections

Skrifter. 12 vols., 1949–56.
Girl From the Marsh Croft and Other Stories, selected and edited by Greta Anderson, 1996.

Fiction

Gösta Berlings Saga. 1891; as *Gösta Berling's Saga*, translated by Pauline Bancroft Flach, 1898; as *The Story of Gösta Berling*, translated by Lillie Tudeer, 1898; also translated by Robert Bly, 1982.
Osynliga länkar: Berättelser. 1894; as *Invisible Links*, translated by Pauline Bancroft Flach, 1899.
Antikrists mirakler. 1897; as *The Miracles of Antichrist*, translated by Pauline Bancroft Flach, 1899.
Drottningar i Kungahälla jämte andra berättelser. 1899; as *The Queens of Kungahälla and Other Sketches*, translated by Claud Field, 1917.
En herrgårdssägen. 1899; as *From a Swedish Homestead*, translated by Jessie Brochner, 1901; as *The Tale of a Manor and Other Sketches*, 1917.
Jerusalem I–II. 1901–02; as *Jerusalem* and *The Holy City*, translated by J. Brochner, 2 vols., 1903–18.
Herr Arnes Penningar. 1903; as *Herr Arne's Hoard*, translated by Arthur G. Chater, 1923.
Legender: Berättade [Legends: Stories]. 3 vols., 1904.
Kristuslegender. 1904; as *Christ Legends*, translated by Velma Swanston Howard, 1908.
En saga om en saga och andra sagor. 1908; as *The Girl from the Marsh Croft*, translated by Velma Swanston Howard, 1911.
Meli. 1909.
Liljecronas hem. 1911; as *Liliecrona's Home*, translated by Anna Barwell, 1913.

Körkarlen. 1912; as *The Soul Shall Bear Witness*, translated by William F. Harvey, 1921.
Astrid och andra berättelser [Astrid and Other Stories]. 1914.
Kejsarn av Portugallien. 1914; as *The Emperor of Portugallia*, translated by Velma Swanston Howard, 1916.
Silvergruvan och andra berättelser [The Silver Mine and Other Stories]. 1915.
Troll och människor [Trolls and Humans]. 1915.
Kavaljersnoveller. 1918.
Bannlyst. 1918; as *The Outcast*, translated by William Worster, 1920.
Legender i urval [Selected Legends]. 1922.
The Tale of a Manor and Other Sketches, translated by Claud Field. 1922.
The Ring of the Löwenskölds, translated by Frances Martin and Velma Swanston Howard. 3 vols., 1931; as *Löwenskölds Ring*, translated by Linda Schenck, 1991.
   Löwensköldska ringen. 1925; as *The General's Ring*, translated by Frances Martin, 1928; as *The Löwensköld Ring*, translated by Linda Schenck, 1991.
   Charlotte Löwensköld. 1925; as *Charlotte Löwensköld*, translated by Velma Swanston Howard, 1927.
   Anna Svärd. 1928; as *Anna Svärd*, translated by Velma Swanston Howard, 1931.
Mors porträtt och andra berättelser [Portrait of Mother and Other Stories]. 1930.
Julberättelser [Christmas Stories]. 1938.

Plays

Fritiofs saga [Fritiof's Story], music by E. Andrée. 1899.
Stormyrtösen [Girl from the Marshes], with Bernt Fredgren, from a story by Lagerlöf. 1913.
Dunungen [The Cygnet]. 1914.
Vinterballaden [Winter Ballad], from a play by Gerhart Hauptmann. 1919.
The Lighting of the Christmas Tree, adapted by Josephine L. Palmer and Annie L. Thorp (from *The Christmas Guest*). 1921.
Kejsarn av Portugallien, with Poul Knudsen, from the novel by Lagerlöf. 1939.

Other

Nils Holgerssons underbara resa (for children). 2 vols., 1906–07; as *The Wonderful* [and *Further*] *Adventures of Nils*, translated by Velma Swanston Howard, 2 vols., 1907–11; also translated by Richard E. Oldeburg, 1967.
Mårbacka.
   Mårbacka. 1922; as *Mårbacka*, translated by Velma Swanston Howard, 1924; as *Memories of Mårbacka*, compiled with notes by Greta Anderson, 1996.
   Ett barns memoarer. 1930; as *Memories of My Childhood*, translated by Velma Swanston Howard, 1934.
   Dagbok. 1932; as *Diary*, translated by Velma Swanston Howard, 1936.
Höst: Berättelser och tal. 1933; as *Harvest: Tales and Essays*, translated by Florence and Naboth Hedin, 1935.
Från skilda tider: Efterlämnade skrifter [Posthumous Works], edited by Nils Afzelius. 2 vols., 1943–45.

Brev 1871–1940 [Letters], edited by Ying Toijer-Nilsson. 2 vols., 1967–69.

*

Bibliography: *Lagerlöfs bibliografi originalskrifter* by Nils Afzelius, 1975.

Critical Studies: *Lagerlöf* by H.A. Larsen, 1936; *Six Scandinavian Novelists: Lie, Jacobsen, Heidenstam, Selma Lagerlöf, Hamsun, Sigrid Undset* by Alrik Gustafson, 1940; *Fact and Fiction in the Autobiographical Works of Lagerlöf* by Folkerdina Stientje de Vrieze, 1958; *Lagerlöf* (in Swedish) by Carl O. Zamore, 1958; *Lagerlöf* by Walter A. Berendsohn, 1968; *Lagerlöf: Herrn Arnwes Penningar* by Brita Green, 1977; *Selma Lagerlöf*, 1984, and *Selma Lagerlöfs litterära profil*, 1986, both by Vivi Edström; *Rediscoveries in Children's Literature* by Suzanne Rahn, 1995.

* * *

Selma Lagerlöf's childhood at Mårbacka offered a rich store of old Värmland traditions but the realistic mode of writing in the 1880s was alien to her temperament and material. Witnessing the sale of Mårbacka in 1888, she resolved to eschew current fashion and write ''in the Mårbacka manner.'' *Gösta Berlings Saga* (*Gösta Berling's Saga*) was completed in 1891. Gösta, the handsome, Byronic, defrocked parson, joins 12 ''cavaliers'' who are to run Ekeby estate for a year provided they live only for beauty and pleasure. There is much merrymaking, but Lagerlöf could not wholly accept a *carpe diem* philosophy and ends by eulogizing hard work. This novel introduces typical Lagerlöfian themes: guilt and atonement; the saving qualities of a woman's selfless love; how to combine happiness with goodness. Having betrayed his calling Gösta must purge his guilt. The magnificent Margareta Celsing, the major's wife, has broken two commandments and accepts banishment until she has expiated her sin. The supernatural is introduced when the cavaliers sell their souls to the Mephistophelian Sintram, while the elements are used both to heighten effect and to force characters' courses of action. The style ranges from rhetoric and *Sturm und Drang* tempestuousness to textbook prose, but the book bears the stamp of genius.

In *En herrgårdssägen* (*The Tale of a Manor*) Lagerlöf successfully fuses Beauty and the Beast with a Dalarna legend. Fear of losing his estate threatens Gunnar Hede's sanity but a young girl's unselfish love saves him. Within the framework of symbolic folktale Lagerlöf produces a valid psychological study of schizophrenia.

On a visit to Palestine in 1900 Lagerlöf discovered a settlement of Dalarna peasants and this inspired the novel *Jerusalem*, at the heart of which are the Ingmarssons representing such sterling qualities as loyalty to one's province, an innate sense of justice, simple faith, and moral courage. The powerful stylized characterization and the epic scope of the novel show the influence of the Icelandic saga. Acknowledged as her masterpiece, *Jerusalem* won universal acclaim. The supernatural, merely suggested in *Jerusalem*, is a major element in *Herr Arnes Penningar* (*Herr Arne's Hoard*) where a murdered girl's ghost is instrumental in bringing the murderers of Herr Arne's household to justice. Commissioned to write a school textbook Lagerlöf, influenced partly by Kipling's *Jungle Book*, wrote *Nils*

Holgerssons underbara resa (*The Wonderful Adventures of Nils*), in which Sweden's geography, flora, and fauna become part of a tale about a boy's magic journey on a goose's back.

World War I had a debilitating effect, and although Lagerlöf subsequently wrote autobiographies centred on Mårbacka and completed the Löwensköld trilogy, her creative genius was spent. Her greatest gift was that of a storyteller. She refashioned local oral tradition into powerful universal prose works reflecting her instinctive understanding of the human heart and conscience. Her attitude to miracles and religion is ambivalent but her innate sense of justice and natural order ultimately restores harmony in her works. There is nothing facile in such happy endings, however, for they are achieved by personal sacrifice and a supreme effort to overcome destructive elements in human nature.

—Irene Scobbie

See the essay on *Gösta Berling's Saga*.

LAMARTINE, Alphonse (-Marie-Louis de Prat) de

Born: Mâcon, France, 21 October 1790. **Education:** Educated at Institut Puppier, Lyons, 1801–03; Jesuit college, Belley, 1803–07. **Family:** Married Anna Eliza Birch in 1820 (died 1863); one son and one daughter; one daughter from a previous relationship with Nina de Pierreclau. **Career:** Served in Louis XVIII's Garde-du-Corps, 1814–15. Mayor of Milly, 1812; diplomat, Naples, 1820–25; embassy secretary, Florence, 1825–29; elected to the Académie française, 1830; stood for the Chamber of Deputies, (unsuccessfully 1831), elected, 1833; minister of foreign affairs, 1848; defeated in the presidential election and retired from public life, 1851. Travelled to Greece, Syria, and Palestine. **Died:** 28 February 1869.

PUBLICATIONS

Collections

Oeuvres. 2 vols., 1893.
Oeuvres. 22 vols., 1900–07.
Poésies. 1957.
Oeuvres poétiques complètes, edited by Marius-François Guyard. 1963.
Oeuvres poétiques. 1977.

Verse

Méditations poétiques. 1820; as *Poetical Meditations*, translated by Henry Christmas, 1839; also translated with introduction by Gervase Hittle, 1993; as *The Poetical Meditations*, translated by William Pulling, 1849; as *Translations from the Meditations*, translated by James T. Smith, 1852.
La Mort de Socrate. 1823; as *The Death of Socrates*, translated by Harriet Cope, 1829.
Nouvelles méditations poétiques. 1823.

Le Dernier Chant du pèlerinage d'Harold. 1825; as *The Last Canto of Childe Harold's Pilgrimage*, translated anonymously, 1827.

Epîtres. 1825.

Chant du sacre. 1825.

Harmonies poétiques et religieuses. 2 vols., 1830.

Contre la peine de mort. 1830.

Á Némesis. 1831.

Jocelyn. 2 vols., 1836; as *Jocelyn: An Episode*, translated by F.H. Jobert, 1837; also translated by Robert Anstruther, 1844; as *Jocelyn*, translated by H.G. Evans and T.W. Swift, 1868; as *Jocelyn: A Romance in Verse*, translated by Hazel Patterson Stewart, 1954.

Gethsémani, in *Souvenirs, impressions, pensées et paysages pendant un voyage en orient.* 1835; as *Gethsemane: or, the Death of Julia*, translated by I.H. Urquhart, 1838.

La Chute d'un ange. 2 vols., 1838.

Recueillements poétiques. 1839.

Premières et nouvelles méditations poétiques (selection). 1855; as *Selected Poems*, edited and translated by George O. Curme, 1888.

Poésies inédites. 1873; revised edition, 1881.

Premières méditations poétiques. 1907.

Méditations, edited by Fernand Letessier. 1968.

Fiction

Graziella. 1849; edited by Alfred T. Baker, 1904; as *Graziella; or, My First Sorrow, and Other Poems . . .* , translated by W.C. Urquhart, 1871; as *Graziella*, translated by Bertha Norwood, 1876; as *Graziella; or The History of a Broken Heart*, translated by J.B.S., 1882; also translated by Ralph Wright, 1929.

Raphaël. 1849; as *Raphaël*, translated anonymously, 1849.

Les Confidences. 1849; as *Confidential Disclosures*, translated by E. Plunkett, 1849; as *Memoirs of My Youth*, translated anonymously, 1849.

Les Nouvelles Confidences. 1851; as *The Wanderer and His Home*, translated anonymously, 1851.

Le Tailleur des pierres de Saint-Point, récit villageois. 1851; as *The Stonecutter of St-Point*, translated anonymously, 1851; as *The Stonemason of St-Point*, translated anonymously, 1851.

Geneviève: Histoire d'un servante. 1850; as *Genevieve; or, The History of a Servant Girl*, translated by A.R. Scoble, 1850; as *Genevieve; or, Peasant Love and Sorrow*, translated by Fayette Robinson, 1850: as *Genevieve: A Tale of Peasant Life*, translated by Mary Howitt, 1851.

Antoniella. 1867.

Plays

Toussaint L'Ouverture (produced 1850). 1850.

Fior d'Aliza. 1863; as *Fior d'Aliza*, translated by G. Perry, 1869.

Saül. 1879.

Other

De la politique rationnelle. 1831; as *The Polity of Reason*, translated anonymously, 1848.

Oeuvres. 4 vols., 1832.

Oeuvres complètes. 13 vols., 1834–43.

Souvenirs, impressions, pensées et paysages pendant un voyage en orient (1832–1833); ou, Notes d'un voyageur. 4 vols., 1835; as *A Pilgrimage to the Holy Land*, translated anonymously, 1835, reprinted 1978; as *De Lamartine's Visit to the Holy Land*, translated by Thomas Phipson, 1847.

Histoire des Girondins. 8 vols., 1847; as *Deux Héroïnes de la Révolution française*, edited by Mary Bentinck Smith, 1904; as *History of the Girondists*, translated by H.T. Ryde, 3 vols., 1847–48; as *Pictures of the First Revolution*, translated by J.F.S. Wilde, 1850.

Manifeste à l'Europe. 1848.

Trois Mois au pouvoir. 1848; as *Three Months in Power: A History and Vindication of My Political Conduct During the Late Revolution in France*, translated by H.T. Ryde, 1848.

Oeuvres [Souscripteurs Edition]. 14 vols., 1849–50.

Histoire de la Restauration. 8 vols., 1851–52: as *The History of the Restoration of Monarchy in France*, parts written in English by Lamartine the remainder translated by Captain Rafter, 4 vols., 1851–53.

Histoire de la révolution de 1848. 2 vols., 1849; as *History of the French Revolution of 1848*, translated anonymously, 1849; also translated by Francis Durivage and William Chase, 1849.

Nouveau voyage en orient. 1851.

Nelson. 1853.

Cromwell. 1854; as *Life of Oliver Cromwell*, translated anonymously, 1859.

Histoire des Constituants. 2 vols., 1854; as *History of the Constituent Assembly*, 4 vols., translated anonymously, 1858.

Histoire de la Turquie. 5 vols., 1854; as *History of Turkey*, 3 vols., translated anonymously, 1855–57.

Histoire de la Russie. 1855.

Cours familier de littérature. 28 vols., 1856–69.

Vie d'Alexandre le Grand. 2 vols., 1859.

Oeuvres complètes de Lamartine publiées et inédites. 41 vols., 1860–66.

Cicéron. 1863.

Christophe Colomb. 1863; as *Life of Christopher Columbus*, translated anonymously, 1859; as *The Life and Voyages of Christopher Columbus*, translated by E.M. Goldsmid, 1887.

Homère et Socrate. 1863; as *Homer and Socrates*, translated by Elizabeth Winchell Smith, 1872.

Jeanne d'Arc. 1863; as *Joan of Arc: A Biography*, translated by H.M. Grimké, 1867.

Madame de Sévigné (biography). 1864.

La France parlementaire (1834–1851), oeuvres, oratoires et écrits politiques. 6 vols., 1864–65.

Les Grands Hommes de l'Orient. 1865.

Les Hommes de la révolution. 1865.

Portraits et biographies. 1865; as *Biographies and Portraits*, translated anonymously, 1866.

Shakespeare et son oeuvre. 1865.

Vie de César. 1865.

Vie de Lord Byron. 1865; revised edition, edited by Marie-Renée Morin, 1989.

Balzac et ses oeuvres. 1866.

Jean Jacques Rousseau. 1866.

Mémoires inédits 1790–1815. 1870; as *25 Years of My Life*, translated by Lady Herbert, 2 vols., 1872.

Manuscrit de ma mère. 1871; as *Memoirs of My Mother*, translated by Lady Herbert, with *25 Years of My Life*, 2 vols, 1872; as *My Mother's Manuscript*, translated by Maria Louisa Helper, 1877.

Correspondance publiée par Mme. Valentine de Lamartine. 6 vols., 1873–1875; 4 vols., 1881–82.

Correspondance. 4 vols., 1873–74.

La Politique de Lamartine (selection). 1878.

Correspondance 1873–1875. 2 vols., 1881–82.

A. de Lamartine par lui-même (autobiography). 1892.

L'Album de Saint-Point (correspondence). 1923.

Lamartine et ses nièces (correspondence). 1928.

Un grand vigneron (correspondence). 1933.

Correspondance générale, edited by Maurice Levaillant. 2 vols., 1943–48.

Lettres inédites 1821–51, edited by Henri Guillemin. 1944.

Lettres à Clériade Vacher (1811–1818), edited by Jean Richer. 1963.

Correspondance Alphonse de Lamartine-Aymon de Virieu 1808–15, edited by Marie-Renée Morin. 2 vols., 1987.

Correspondance 1809–1858, with Henry-Roch Dupuys, edited by Marie-Renée Morin. 1989.

Mémoires de jeunesse: 1790–1815, edited by Marie-Renée Marin. 1990.

*

Critical Studies: *The Life of Lamartine* by H. Remsen Whitehouse, 2 vols., 1918; *Lamartine* by Paul Hazard, 1925; *Lamartine et la Savoie* by Georges Roth, 1927; *Les Méditations de Lamartine* by G. Fréjaville, 1931; *Lamartine et le sentiment de la nature* by Yvonne Boeniger, 1934; *Lamartine* by Louis Bertrand, 1940; *Lamartine and Romantic Unanimism* by Albert J. George, 1940; *Lamartine, l'homme et l'oeuvre* by H. Guillemin, 1940; *Les Travaux et les jours d'Alphonse de Lamartine* by Marquis de Luppé, 1942; *Lamartine* by Marius-François Guyard, 1956; *Les Amours italiennes de Lamartine, Graziella et Lena* by Abel Verdier, 1963; *Lamartine: A Revaluation* by John C. Ireson, 1969; *Lamartine; ou, l'amour de la vie* by Maurice Toesca, 1969; *La Vie sentimentale de Lamartine* by Abel Verdier, 1971; *Lamartine: Le Livre du centenaire* edited by Paul Viallaneix, 1971; *Lamartine* by Charles M. Lombard, 1973; *In Search of Eden: Lamartine's Symbols of Despair and Deliverance* by Norman Araujo, 1976; *Lamartine and the Poetics of Landscape* by Mary Ellen Birkett, 1982; *Alphonse de Lamartine: A Political Biography* by William Fortescue, 1983; *L'Auteur des Girondins; ou, Les Cent-vingt Jours de Lamartine*, 1988, and *Les Girondins de Lamartine*, 1988, both by Antoine Court; *Lamartine* by Xavier de la Fournière, 1990; *Maternal Echoes: The Poetry of Marceline Desbordes-Valmore and Alphonse de Lamartine* by Aimée Boutin, 2001.

*   *   *

It was Alphonse de Lamartine who created the image, in France, of the Romantic poet. The publication of his first collection, *Méditations poétiques* (*Poetical Meditations*), in 1820 was undoubtedly a landmark in French literature. Without radically modifying the form of French poetry, Lamartine gave it back a soft lyrical quality it had lost in the previous century. Though "Le Lac" ("The Lake") is probably the best-known poem in the volume, the opening text, "L'Isolement" ("Isolation") likewise epitomizes its plaintive tonality and illustrates the way in which the natural world cast an ambiguous spell over the poet:

Que me font ces vallons, ces palais, ces chaumières,
Vains objects dont pour moi le charme est envoié?
Fleuves, rochers, forêts, solitudes si chères,
Un seul être vous manque, et tout est dépeuplé!

(These valleys, these palaces, these cottages, what are
    they to me?
Vain objects whose charm for me has flown;
Rivers, rocks, forests, solitudes so dear,
One single being is missing and everything is empty!)

Elsewhere in the collection Lamartine meditates on religious and philosophical matters, giving voice to the thoughts and feelings of his generation. Yet even more than this first book or its sequel, the *Nouvelles méditations poétiques* [New Poetic Meditations] of 1823, the *Harmonies poétiques et religieuses* [Poetical and Religious Harmonies] of 1830 are generally recognized as Lamartine's masterpieces. The title of his work evokes almost perfectly the nature of the poems, where the recognition of both divine ubiquity and mankind's religious instinct finds expression in the mellifluous musicality of the verses. With a sense of awe and mystery Lamartine writes of "The idea of God"; with humility and wonder he composes "Eternité de la nature, brièveté de l'homme" ("Eternity of Nature, Brevity of Man"); influenced by Pascal, he conceives of "L'Infini dans les cieux" ("Infinity in the Heavens").

Having made his reputation as a lyric poet, Lamartine turned to the epic. *Jocelyn* was originally intended to form part of a greater work, but the subject-matter, the life and love of a humble priest, may have been more suitable for treatment in a different literary genre. The stature of the hero of *La Chute d'un ange* [The Fall of an Angel] was more obviously epic, but the style of the work too often bordered on the melodramatic. However, the structuring of the poem into "visions" was an imaginative solution to the problem of form.

When Lamartine turned his hand to prose, his first success came with his *Souvenirs, impressions, pensées et paysages pendant un voyage en orient* (*Visit to the Holy Land*), an impressionistic personal record, in the form of a diary, of a trip to the Near East three years earlier. In his foreword he made it clear that he was writing as a poet and a philosopher, and not as a historian or a geographer. From time to time he cannot resist the temptation to express his sentiments in verse, but many of his accounts, e.g. those of the peoples of Lebanon, are informative, and his editor gave the text a special poignancy by inserting after the evocation of Jerusalem the poem "Gethsémani," that Lamartine wrote to commemorate the death of his ten-year-old daughter Julia.

With the eight volumes of his *Histoire des Girondins* (*History of the Girondists*) he set out his stall as a historian, but although the work was a popular success it reads more like an historical novel with a very visual quality. There are inaccuracies, and the writer seems at times to seek to curry favour with contemporary voters. Other histories, of the Restoration, of the Constituent Assembly, of Russia, and of Turkey were to follow in the 1850s.

Immediately after the high point of his political career in 1849, Lamartine published *Graziella*, which fictionalized his affair in 1811 with a seductive Neapolitan girl. Also in 1849 he brought out another novel, *Raphaël*, which treated in a similar fashion his more famous love-affair with Julie Charles. With *Geneviève*, the story of a servant girl, Lamartine attempted to produce a social novel, but its realism was somewhat superficial, despite the author's evident sympathies with the ordinary people. His last attempt at fiction, *Antoniella*, again demonstrated his inability to come up with convincing plots.

Right at the start of his career Lamartine had tried to write for the theatre: he composed *Saül* in 1817, hoping—in vain—that Talma, the leading tragic actor of the day, would play the title role. Although *Toussaint L'Ouverture* was performed in 1850, its failure made him abandon thoughts of becoming a dramatist. The choice of subject, the Haitian national hero, was interesting, however, and may be related to Lamartine's freeing of the slaves in all French territories in 1848.

In an attempt to pay off his debts he published between 1856 and his death in 1869 the 28 volumes of the *Cours familier de littérature*, structured in the form of *entretiens* (conversations) of a very eclectic nature. Despite the title, the work was not confined to literature: Lamartine digressed to the other arts (considering Mozart, Michelangelo, and Cellini, for example), to religion (especially Hinduism), to science (Alexander Humboldt), and even personal reminiscences, in addition to his coverage of a wide range of writers throughout the ages.

It was within this context that Lamartine brought out his last two major poems, "Le Désert; ou, L'Immatérialité de Dieu" [The Desert; or, The Immateriality of God], 1856, and "La Vigne et la maison" [The Vine and the House], 1857. The former, heavily influenced by the Book of Job, emphasizes the importance of mystery in the relationship between man and the deity; "La Vigne et la Maison," a dialogue between the elderly poet and his soul, reveals how much he longed for happier days, but how the sight of well-loved places served only to remind him of the absence and the death of loved ones. The final address to God, however, brought the poet a kind of peace and he found his true voice once more, as a lyric poet, and one by which he should always be judged.

—Keith Aspley

LAMPEDUSA, Giuseppe Tomasi di

Also known as Duke of Palma and, from 1934, Prince of Lampedusa. **Born:** Palermo, Sicily, Italy, 23 December 1896. **Education:** Educated at Liceo-Ginnasio Garibaldi, Palermo, 1911–14; enrolled (but probably did not take classes) at University of Genoa, 1914–15; University of Rome, 1920. **Military Service:** Trained to be officer in Italian army, 1915–17; lance-corporal during World War I; taken prisoner, but succeeded in his second escape attempt, and found his way back to Italy in disguise; discharged from the army, 1920 (some sources give 1925). **Family:** Married Baroness Alessandra (Licy) von Wolff-Stomersee in 1932; one adopted son. **Career:** Largely withdrew from public life after the rise to power of Mussolini and the Fascists, and devoted himself to travelling and writing; contributor, *Le Opere e i Giorni*, Geneva, 1926–27. **Awards:** Strega prize (posthumously), 1959. **Died:** 23 July 1957.

PUBLICATIONS

Collections

The Siren and Selected Writings, translated by Archibald Colquhoun, David Gilmour and Guido Waldman. 1995.

Fiction

Il Gattopardo. 1959; as *The Leopard*, translated by Archibald Colquhoun. 1960.
Racconti (includes "I luoghi della mia prima infanzia," "Il mattino di un mezzadro," "La gioia e la Legge, Lighea"). 1961; revised and enlarged edition, 1988; as *Two Stories and a Memory* (includes "Places of My Infancy," "The Professor and the Siren," "The Blind Kittens"), translated by Archibald Colquhoun, 1962, and with *The Leopard*, 1986.

Other

Lezioni su Stendhal (criticism). 1977.
Invito alle lettere francesi del Cinquecento (criticism). 1979.
Lettere a Licy: Un matrimonio epistolare (selected letters to his wife). 1987.
Letteratura inglese. Dalle origini al Settecento (criticism). 1990.
Letteratura inglese. L'Ottocento e il Novecento (criticism). 1991.

*

Critical Studies: "Lampedusa in Sicily: The Lair of the Leopard" by Archibald Colquhoun, in *The Atlantic Extra*, February 1963; *Ricordo di Lampedusa* by Francesco Orlando, 1963; "Lampedusa's *The Leopard*" by David Nolan, in *Studies*, Winter 1966; "Lampedusa and De Roberto" in *Italica*, 47 (2), 1970, and "Ants and Flags: Tomasi di Lampedusa's *Gattopardo*" in *The Italianist*, 13, 1993, both by Tom O'Neill; *Invito alla lettura di Giuseppe Tomasi di Lampedusa* by Giancarlo Buzzi, 1972, revised editions 1976 and 1984; *Tomasi di Lampedusa* by Simonetta Salvestroni, 1973; *Il Gattopardo; I Racconti: Lampedusa* by Giuseppe Paolo Samona, 1974; "Stendhal, Lampedusa and the Limits of Admiration" by W.J.S. Kirton, in *Trivium*, 10, 1975; "Stendhal, Tomasi di Lampedusa, and the Novel," by Olga Ragusa, in her *Narrative and Drama: Essays in Modern Italian Literature from Verga to Pasolini*, 1976; "The Risorgimento and Social Change: Reflections in the Sicilian Novel" by Christopher Cairns, in *Trivium*, 13, 1978; "The Structure of Meaning in Lampedusa's *Il Gattopardo*" by Richard H. Lansing, in *Publications of the Modern Language Association*, 93, 1978; "Tomasi di Lampedusa's *Il Gattopardo*: Figure and Temporality in an Historical Novel" by Gregory L. Lucente, in *Modern Language Notes*, 1978; *Il Gattopardo o, la metafora decadente dell'esistenza* by Maria Pagliara-Giacovazzo, 1983; *I Gattopardi e le lene. Il messaggio inattuale di Tomasi di Lampedusa* by Nunzio Zago, 1983; *Sirene siciliane: L'anima esiliata in Lighea di Tomasi di Lampedusa* by Basilio Reale, 1986; *Giuseppe Tomasi di Lampedusa* (biography) by Andrea Vitello, 1987; *Giuseppe Tomasi di Lampedusa: La figura e l'opera* (includes texts and bibliography) by Nunzio Zago, 1987; *The Last Leopard: A Life of Giuseppe di Lampedusa* by David Gilmour, 1988; "Nobility and Literature: Questions on Tomasi di Lampedusa" by Edoardo Saccone, in *Modern Language Notes*, 106(1), 1991; *Tomasi di Lampedusa* by Manuela Bertone, 1995.

* * *

With the exception of three brief articles which appeared in a monthly review in Genoa in 1926–27, Giuseppe Tomasi di Lampedusa's work, essentially concentrated into the final years of his life, was published posthumously. It consists of *Il Gattopardo* (*The Leopard*), his only full-length novel and the work on which his reputation substantially rests; *Racconti* (*Two Stories and a Memory*), including "I luoghi della mia prima infanzia" ("Places of My Infancy"), important for understanding the strong autobiographical thread running through the novel, and "La gioia e la Legge, Lighea" (The Professor and the Siren'), no less important for understanding his concern with death and immortality; *Lezioni su Stendhal* [Lessons on Stendhal], which, with hindsight, tell us much about his own aspirations as a writer (in theory if not in practice: Stendhal was to him a commendably "thin" writer, while he himself was "fat"); and *Invito alle lettere francesi del Cinquecento* [Introduction to 16th-Century French Literature], a series of "lectures" on French literature from Rabelais to Montaigne. In addition, there are two substantial volumes of "lectures" (*Letteratura inglese*) on English literature, from Beowulf to Lampedusa's own days, all of which bear witness to the wide-ranging, exquisitely literary cast of a mind refined over a lifetime of aristocratic leisure.

Lampedusa's original idea in *The Leopard* was to deal, in Joyce-like fashion (*Ulysses* serving as model), with 24 hours in the life of his great-grandfather at the time of Garibaldi's landing at Marsala on 11 May 1860, which was to lead to the eventual unification of Italy under the House of Savoy. The time span of the novel, however, was extended well beyond its original 24 hours to May 1910, the 50th anniversary of the historic event. Given its extensive historical background most Italian critics assumed (not unreasonably) that the work was basically a historical novel, and not a very good one at that, since it essentially replicated Federico De Roberto's late 19th-century novel, *I vicere* (*The Viceroys*). They assumed, moreover, a total identification between the novel's protagonist, Don Fabrizio Salina, and its aristocratic author, attributing what they perceived as the novel's arch-conservative and static vision of history to Lampedusa himself: in part one there is the enigmatic remark of Fabrizio's nephew, Tancredi, as he is about to go off to join Garibaldi: "If we want things to stay as they are, things will have to change"; and, in part four, Fabrizio remarks to some English naval officers apropos Garibaldi's volunteers: "They are coming to teach us good manners . . . But they won't succeed, because we are gods." What these early readers failed to appreciate was the novel's irony, whereby the seemingly unchanged and unchanging surface nature of Sicilian society ("Thanks be to God, everything seems as usual," thinks Fabrizio in part two, on his arrival at his summer residence of Donnafugata, after Garibaldi's "revolution") is undermined by a multiplicity of symbols in the text, clearly designed to undermine the immediate impression—the dismemberment of the fortress-like rum jelly in part one, for example, "rather threatening at first sight," but in the end consisting only "of shattered walls and hunks of wobbly rubble"; or the observation at the ball, in part six, apropos its aristocratic guests, that "They thought themselves eternal; but a bomb manufactured in Pittsburgh, Penn., was to prove the contrary in 1943."

The catapulting forward in time, from 1862 to 1943 (specifically to 5 April 1943, when Allied bombs substantially damaged Palazzo Lampedusa, the author's own home since birth, as "Places of My Infancy" informs us), focuses on the importance of places rather than people in Lampedusa's life and, indeed, his work (the numerous and often minute correspondences between "Places of My Infancy" and *The Leopard* have been traced by Daniel Devoto); and the importance given to places should provide caution against an excessively political reading of Fabrizio's actions (or, more accurately, non-actions) in the novel. He is, perhaps not surprisingly, an astronomer, preferring the

world of the stars to that of men, as he muses in part six, because "they were distant, they were omnipotent and at the same time they were docile to his calculations; just the contrary to humans, always too near, so weak and yet so quarrelsome."

While much of the early fascination with the work derived from its author's sense of place, its continuing fascination lies elsewhere, for "though he is dealing with a closed, dead society, though his knowledge is esoteric," as David Nolan has observed, "the reader feels that there by the grace of Lampedusa, life has been described." The range and variety of the novel's "minor" characters confirms the truth of the observation—from Fabrizio's hysterical wife, Stella, to his stubborn eldest daughter, Concetta; from his charming, politically trimming nephew, Tancredi, to the beautiful and sensual Angelica Sedara, destined through her marriage to Tancredi to bring about the new social order incarnated in her clearly *mafioso* father, Don Calogero.

But it is the novel's protagonist, Don Fabrizio, who literally dominates from the outset ("the sudden movement of his huge frame made the floor tremble, and a glint of pride flashed in his light-blue eyes at this fleeting confirmation of his lordship over both humans and their works"). This physical presence, however, is all there is in reality, for the principal trait in his character is a deep-rooted need for peace and quiet, at any cost. The fine figure of a man is, deep down, a moral coward, and moreover one who is invariably misunderstood. In an emblematic moment in part three, the advice he gives to vote in favour of the Revolution is interpreted as being ironic by his listeners. Their self-congratulation at having penetrated his meaning casts a retrospective shadow over the accuracy of Fabrizio's own interpretation of Tancredi's earlier words in part one, and both events anticipate the moment in the novel's final section when Concetta, too, is obliged to contemplate the possibility that misinterpretation of events, of words, 50 years earlier, stunted the rest of her life. The events of history blend with the private, politics gives way to psychology, and all are subsumed in the final question, "But was it the truth?," which highlights Lampedusa's concern with enigma and myth—the qualities which perhaps give the novel its enduring appeal.

—Tom O'Neill

LAO She

Also known as Shu Sheyu. **Born:** Shu Qingchun in Beijing, China, 3 February 1899. **Education:** Attended Beijing shifan xuexiao [Beijing Normal School], Beijing, 1913–18. **Family:** Married Hu Jieqing, 1931; one son and three daughters. **Career:** Appointed headmaster, Jingshi gongli dishiqi gaodeng xiaoxuexiao [Beijing 17th Public Elementary School], 1918–20; Supervisor, Beiqu quanxuesuo [Northern Educational Section], 1920–22; Baptized, 1922; Chinese Instructor, Nankai xuexiao zhongxuebu [Nankai Middle School], Tianjin, 1922–23; worked as a staff in Beijing jiaoyuhui [Beijing Education Society] and Chinese Instructor at Diyi zhongxue [First Middle School], Beijing, 1923–24; Chinese Lecturer, London University, 1924–29; joined Wenxue yanjiuhui [Literary Studies Association], 1926; Professor and Director, Qilu daxue guoxue yanjiusuo [Institute for Chinese Studies, Qilu University], Jinan, 1930–34; Professor, Shandong daxue [Shandong University], Qingdao, 1934–36; Member of the Executive Committee and Director, Zhonghua quanguo wenyijie kangdi xiehui [General Department, All China Association of Writers and Artists against Aggression] (renamed as Zhonghua quanguo wenyijie xiehui [All China Association of Writers and Artists]), 1945, 1938–46; visited the United States, 1947–49; elected Chairman, Beijing shi wenlian [Association of Beijing Writers and Artists], 1950; elected Vice Chairman, Zhongguo zuojia xiehui [Chinese Writers' Association], 1953; visited Korea during the Korean War, 1953–54. **Awards:** Renmin yishujia [People's Artist] medal, awarded by Beijing Municipal Government, 1951. **Died:** (suicide), 24 August 1966 in Beijing.

PUBLICATIONS

Collections

Lao She youmo shiwen ji. 1934.
Lao She chuangzuo xuan. 1936.
Lao She xuanji. 1936.
Lao She xuanji. 1951.
Lao She wenji. 1981–91.

Fiction

Lao Zhang de zhexue. 1928.
Zhao Ziyue. 1928.
Maocheng ji. 1933; as *City of Cats*, translated by James E. Dew, 1964; as *Cat Country*, translated by William A. Lyell, 1970.
Lihun. 1933, as *Divorce*, translated by Evan King, 1948; as *The Quest for Love of Lao Lee*, translated by Helena Kuo, 1948.
Xiaopo de shengri. 1934.
Ganji. 1934.
Si wai. 1934.
Er Ma. 1935; as *The Two Mas*, translated by Kenny K. Huang & David Finkelstein, 1984; as *Mr. Ma & Son: A Sojourn in London*, translated by Julie Jimmerson, 1991.
Yinghai ji. 1935.
Gazao ji. 1936.
Niu Tianci zhuan. 1936, as *Heavensent*, translated by Xiong Deni, 1986.
Huoche ji. 1939.
Luotuo Xiangzi. 1939; as *Rickshaw Boy*, translated by Evan King, 1945; as *Camel Xiangzi*, translated by Shi Xiaoqing, 1981.
Wen boshi. 1940.
Huozang. 1944.
Pinxue ji. 1944.
Sishi tongtang. 1946.
Huanghuo. 1947.
Tousheng. 1947.
Wo zhe yibeizi. 1947.
Weishen ji. 1947.
Yueya ji. 1948; as *Crescent Moon and Other Stories*, 1985.
Wuming gaodi youle ming. 1955.
Lao She duanpian xiaoshuo xuan. 1956.
Yueyaer. 1959.
Jihuang. 1975.
Zheng hongqi xia. 1980; as *Beneath the Red Banner*, translated by Don J. Cohn, 1982.
Gushu yiren (translated back by Ma Xiaomi from the English translation of the original manuscript, which was lost). 1980; as *The Drum Singers*, translated by Helena Kuo, 1952.
Lao She xiaoshuo jiwaiji. 1982.

Prose

Fuxing ji. 1958.
Xiao huaduo ji. 1963.

Plays

Can wu. 1940.
Dadi longshe. 1942.
Guiqulai xi. 1943.
Guojia zhishang. 1943.
Shui xian daole Chongqing. 1943.
Zhang Zizhong. 1943.
Taoli chunfeng. 1943.
Mianzi wenti. 1945.
Lao She xiju ji. 1947.
Fang Zhenzhu. 1950.
Longxugou. 1951, as *Dragon Beard Ditch*, translated by Liao Hungying, 1956.
Xiaomie bingjun. 1952.
Qingnian tujidui. 1955.
Xiwang Changan. 1956.
Shiwu guan. 1956.
Chaguan. 1958, as *Teahouse*, translated by John Howard-Gibbon, 1980.
Hong dayuan. 1959.
Lao She juzuo xuan. 1959.
Nüdianyuan. 1959.
Qingxia danlei. 1959.
Quanjia fu. 1959.
Bao chuan. 1961.
He zhu pei. 1962.
Shenquan. 1963.

Verse

Lao She xinshi xuan. 1983.
Lao She jiutishi jizhu. 2000.

Other

Laoniu poche. 1937.
Guo xinnian. 1951.
Guanyu xiangsheng xiezuo. 1951.
He gongren tongzhi tan xiezuo. 1952.
Wenxue yuyan wenti. 1955.
Guanyu yuyan guifanhua. 1956.
Shangren. 1958.
Chukou chengzhang. 1964.
Lao She lun chuangzuo. 1980.
Lao She xiezuo shengya. 1981.
Lao She quyi wenxuan. 1982.
Lao She shenghuo yu chuangzuo zishu. 1982.

*

Bibliography: *Lao She zhuyi bianmu* by Zhang Guixing, 2000.

Critical Studies: *Lao She and the Chinese Revolution* by Ranbir Vohra, 1974; *Lao She he ta de zuopin* by Hu Jinquan, 1977; *Two Writers and the Cultural Revolution: Lao She and Chen Jo-hsi* edited by George Kao, 1980; *Lao She de hua ju yi shu,* edited by Ke Ying and Li Ying, 1982; *Lao She yanjiu lunwen ji,* edited by Meng Guanglai et al., 1983; *Lao She zuopin zhong de Beijinghua ciyu lishi* by Yang Yuxiu, 1984; *Lao She yanjiu ziliao,* edited by Wu Huaibin and Zeng Guangcan, 1985; ''Split Consciousnes: The Dialectic of Desire in *Camel Xiangzi*'' by Stephen Chan, in *Modern Chinese Literature,* vol. 2, no. 2, 1986; *Lao She juzuo yanjiu* by Ran Yiqiao and Li Zhentong, 1988; *Lao She yu Zhongguo wenhua guannian* by Song Yongyi, 1988; ''Lao She's Wartime Fiction'' by David Wang, in *Modern Chinese Literature,* vol. 5, no. 2, 1989; *Meng Guanglai lunzhu ji: Lao She yanjiu,* edited by Meng Dan, 1991; *Fictional Realism in Twentieth-Century China: Mao Dun, Lao She, Shen Congwen* by David Wang, 1992; *Lao She de xiaoshuo shijie yu dongxifang wenhua* by Wu Xiaomei and Wei Shaohua, 1992; *Lao She de yishu shijie* by Sun Junzheng, 1992; *Lao She zai Lundun* by Li Zhenjie, 1992; *Lao She huaju de yishu shijie* by Hong Zhonghuang, Ke Ying, 1993; *Lao She lungao* by Wang Huiyun et al, 1993; *Lao She wenxue sixiang de shengcheng yu fazhan* by Shi Xingze, 1993; *Lao She yu Beijing wenhua* by Gan Hailan, 1993; *Lao She chuangzuo lun* by Zhang Huizhu, 1994; *Lao She xiaoshuo yishu xinli yanjiu* by Xie Zhaoxin, 1994; *Lao She xiaoshuo xinlun* by Wang Runhua, 1995; *Lao She de yuyan yishu* by Wang Jianhua, 1996; ''Who is Yuan Ming? A Political Mystery in Lao She's *Camel Xiangxi*'' by Qiguang Zhang, in *China Information,* vol. 12, no. 3, Winter 1997–98; *Lao She yu Jinan* by Li Yaoxi and Zhou Chang feng, 1998; *Lao She ziliao kaoshi* by Zhang Guixing, 1998; *Lao She xinlun* by Wang Xiaoqin, 1999; *Jianming Lao She cidian,* edited by Shi Chengjun, 2000; *Lao She wenxue cidian,* edited by Shu Ji et al., 2000; *Lao She xiaoshuo chuangzuo bijiao yanjiu* by Cheng Mei, 2000; *Lao She yanjiu lunwen ji,* edited by Li Runxin and Zhou Siyuan, 2000; *Lao She yu dier guxiang* by Zhang Guixing, 2000; *Lao She yu ershi shiji,* edited by Zeng Guangcan, 2000; *Lao She ziliao kaoshi* by Zhang Guixing, 2000; *Lao She pingzhuan* by Guan Jixin, 2001.

* * *

Lao She was one of the most prolific novelists, playwrights, and short story writers in 20th-century China. Generally considered a realist, Lao She wrote in a way more sophisticated than is categorized. His style, influenced by both western realism and Chinese vernacular fiction, often contains melodramatic and farcical elements at the same time.

Lao She's first novel, *Lao Zhang de zhexue* [The Philosophy of Lao Zhang], excels in its grotesque and comic account of an urban villain and his vicious actions in a Dickensian manner. His art of buffoonery and burlesque develops in *Zhao Ziyue, Er Ma (The Two Mas),* and *Lihun (Divorce),* in which his satiric narratives are to be read as critiques of the ''national character,'' following the May Fourth tradition of social enlightenment. Benefited from his living experience in London, *The Two Mas* is one of the earliest in modern Chinese literature to examine the clashes between Chinese and Western cultures, a theme that continues in his later novels such as *Wen boshi* [Dr. Wen]. Unique among Lao She's writings is his *Maocheng ji (City of Cats),* an allegorical novel whose exposé of

avarice, ignorance, chaos and barbarity in the city of cats points, though indirectly, to the human world.

Luotuo Xiangzi (Rickshaw Boy) marks the peak of Lao She's literary career. Often regarded as one of the literary masterpieces in the first half of the 20th century, the novel portrays how a physically sturdy and morally innocent rickshaw puller labors, suffers and degenerates in a world of rapid economic and social change. The theme of historical change is also developed in his epic trilogy *Sishi tongtang* [Four Generations under One Roof], including *Huanghuo* [Bewilderment], *Tousheng* [Ignoble Life], and *Jihuang* [Famine], which, spanning the whole Japanese occupation period, represents the life and struggle in a typical Chinese family facing national crisis.

Lao She's short stories reflect his observations of various aspects of modern China, especially the dramatic moments against the background of social history. *Duanhun qiang* [Soul-Breaking Spear] features the marvel of traditional Chinese martial arts and laments its decline; in *Yueyaer* [Crescent], a lower-class girl is forced to become a prostitute and is sent to reformatory and finally prison; and *Lao zihao* [An Old and Established Name] shows a dismal picture of how old, disciplined mode of civilization is irretrievably replaced by the modern and somewhat flashy one.

Throughout his writing career Lao She expresses both love for, and critique of, Chinese society and culture. He is especially acclaimed for his skillful use of Beijing dialect, registering comical flavor in the specific cultural environment. His interest in folk culture also prompted his extensive writings of popular literature during the time of Japanese occupation and after the establishment of the People's Republic.

Lao She began to use drama as a form of propaganda during the Anti-Japanese War period. Under the cultural policy of the People's Republic, drama became again the major genre of Lao She's writings. Modern plays such as *Fang Zhenzhu* and *Longxugou (Dragon Beard Ditch)* were intended to glorify the ''new society'' and denounce the old one by way of stage performance. Among Lao She's most frequently performed and most celebrated plays is *Chaguan (Teahouse),* which chronicles the historical vicissitude of modern China by unfolding a series of incidents that take place in a teahouse throughout different historical moments.

Hailed as the ''master of language'' and ''master of humor,'' Lao She has a great influence on the later generations with his satirical power and sensitivity to living language. Many of his novels have been adapted into films and TV serials, which popularize his works decades after his tragic suicide.

—Xiaobin Yang

See the essay on *Rickshaw Boy.*

LAUTRÉAMONT, Comte de

Born: Isidore Lucien Ducasse in Montevideo, Uruguay, 4 April 1846. **Education:** Educated at Collège Imperial de Tarbes, France, 1859–63; Lycée de Pau, 1963–65. **Career:** Little is known of his life. Returned briefly to Montevideo, 1867; moved to Paris, 1867, where he was supported by a private income. **Died:** 24 November 1870.

Collections

Oeuvres complètes, edited by Philippe Soupault. 1927.
Oeuvres complètes. 1938.
Les Chants de Lautréamont et oeuvres complètes. 1947.
Oeuvres complètes, edited by Alfred Jarry. 1953–1977.
Oeuvres complètes, edited by Maurice Saillet. 1963.
Oeuvres complètes, edited by Marguerite Bonnet. 1969.
Oeuvres complètes, edited by Pierre Olivier Walzer. 1970.
Oeuvres complètes, edited by Herbert Juin. 1970.
Oeuvres complètes, edited by Jean Marcel and Arpad Mezei. 1971.
Poésies and Complete Miscellanea, edited and translated by Alexis Lykiard. 1978.
Maldoror and the Complete Works of the Comte de Lautreamont, translated by Alexis Lykiard, 1994.

Verse

Les Chants de Maldoror. 1868–69; revised editions, 1874, 1980; edited by Jean Cocteau, 1963, and by Philippe Sellier, 1980; as *The Lay of Maldoror*, translated by John Rodker, 1924; also translated by Guy Wernham, 1943; Alexis Lykiard, 1970; Paul Knight, 1978.
Poésies I and *II* (published privately). 1870; edited by J.L. Steinmetz, 1990.
Préface à un livre futur. 1922.
Poésies, edited by Georges Goldfayn and Gérard Legrand. 1960.

*

Critical Studies: *Lautréamont* by Gaston Bachelard, 1939, enlarged edition, 1963; *Lautréamont's Imagery: A Stylistic Approach* by Peter Nesselroth, 1969; *Isidore Ducasse, Comte de Lautréamont* by François Caradec, 1970, revised edition, 1975; *Vie de Lautréamont* by Edouard Peyrouzet, 1970; *Lectures de Lautréamont* by M. Philip, 1971; *Lautréamont et le style homérique* by Lucienne Rochon, 1971; *Lauréamont: The Violent Narcissus* by Paul Zweig, 1972; *Lautréamont* by Wallace A. Fowlie, 1973; *Nightmare Culture: Lautréamont and Les Chants de Maldoror* by Alexander H.F. de Jonge, 1973; *Lautréamont, du lieu commun à la parodie* by Claude Bouché, 1974; *Le Visage de Lautréamont: Isidore Ducasse à Tarbes et à Pau* by Jacques Lefrère, 1977; *Lautréamont et la cohérence de l'écriture: Études structurales des variantes du Chant premier des Chants de Maldoror* by Jean Peytard, 1977; *Lautréamont génie; ou, maladies mentale, suivie de Nouveau bilan psychopathologique* by Jean Pierre Soulier, 1978; *Lautréamont, le texte du vampire* by J.M. Olivier, 1981; *Lautréamont: Ethique à Maldoror* by Michel Pierssens, 1984; *La Guerre sainte, Lautréamont et Isidore Ducasse* by Liliane Durant-Dessert, 2 vols., 1988; *Lautréamont-Ducasse: Image, Theme and Self Identity* by Robert Pickering, 1990; *Isidore de Lautréamont* by Sylvain-Christian David, 1991; *Poetics of the Pretext: Reading Lautréamont* by Roland-François Lack, 1998.

*   *   *

Le Comte de Lautréamont's two works, *Les Chants de Maldoror* (*The Lay of Maldoror*) and *Poésies* [Poems], were published in comparative obscurity and for three decades received only passing attention from very few, albeit important, men of letters (Gourmont, Bloy, Fargue, and Larbaud). However, beginning in the 1920s, these texts were to provide the inspiration for a number of French avant-garde movements, from the Surrealists to the Tel Quel group of the 1960s, and were to be an object of study for some of the most original and influential French critics, including Edmond Jaloux, Roger Caillois, Gaston Bachelard, Maurice Blanchot, and Julia Kristève. As André Gide wrote in 1925, "[Lautréamont's] influence in the 19th century was nil; but . . . he has opened the flood-gates for the literature of tomorrow." Apart from the themes of iconoclasm and revolt evident in *The Lay of Maldoror*, both the works pose profound questions concerning the status of authorship, the meaning of a text, and the reception and influence of a literary work.

Far longer than the *Poésies*, *The Lay of Maldoror* reads like a parody-cum-apotheosis of all the early 19th-century literature of Romantic revolt and Gothic macabre. The hero, Maldoror, narrates or is shown in a series of scenes in which he battles with his arch-enemy God, torments a humanity he despises, and engages in acts as contrary to nature as possible. Often the latter are so much more original and extreme than anything in Romantic literature that all idea of subservience to a model is surpassed. In the second "Song," for example, Maldoror dives into the ocean to help a female shark fight off rival members of her own species; the scene concludes with Maldoror copulating with the creature in the midst of a raging tempest.

While outstripping the most "frenetic" aspects of Romanticism, the episode is indicative of a more profound theme. It begins with the words, "I sought a soul that might resemble mine, and I could not find it." The central character displays a very human need for companionship, but is able only to destroy and mutilate the human objects of his affection. Instead his need is perversely satisfied more often than not among supposedly lower forms of life. *The Lay of Maldoror* is filled with toads, snakes, leeches, lice, and all manner of insects, and Maldoror himself is not afraid to engage in or to extol metamorphosis into other members of the animal kingdom. He becomes, in Bachelard's coinage, a "superanimal" able to adopt the forms and aggressive energy of a natural world that is closer to the Marquis de Sade or to Darwin than to the Romantic sublime. The old hierarchy of creation, from beast to man to God, is turned upside down. The deity is reviled and mankind humiliated in the name of a revolt that rejoices in its own protean inventiveness.

The Romantic sources do not make *The Lay of Maldoror* any easier to classify from the point of view of genre. The text is written in prose and sometimes recalls the Gothic romance à la Maturin (the author of *Melmoth the Wanderer* is mentioned in the *Poésies*), or the serial novel of fantastic or criminal adventures as exemplified in France by Sue, Féval, and Ponson du Terrail (the final "Song," in which Maldoror murders a Parisian adolescent, is very reminiscent of the 19th-century crime novel). Yet for all that, Lautréamont's prose is highly poetic, The sentences are frequently very long, sinuous, and rhapsodic, often borrowing the lofty diction of verse and launching into grandiloquent apostrophe. At the same time the discourse frequently refers to itself or is self-mocking. The result is an absolutely unique tone, managing to combine the sublime seriousness of Romanticism with a grotesque form of parodic humour, which looks forward to French modernism of the following century. A particular feature of Lautréamont's style is the use of unsettling metaphors, and this was to be a prime attraction for the Surrealists, always fond of quoting, "He is fair . . . above all, as the chance meeting on a dissecting-table of a sewing-machine and an umbrella."

In fact, despite the use of prose, the most explicit generic model is a poetic one. The structure of the work echoes the Roman verse epic, as practised by the likes of Lamartine and Quinet, which recounted the cosmic deeds of an angel or hero in a series of cantos. Lautréamont's work does just this for Maldoror in the set of six "Songs." Yet beyond Romanticism lies the epic itself as a genre, from Homer to Dante and Milton, and the reader of *The Lay of Maldoror* seems to find multiple reminiscences working concurrently from a vast array of literary texts. Whether these are conscious sources or unconscious recreations, it is as though this one book called into play many others, and Blanchot has gone so far as to speak of a collective and impersonal level of literature. Yet *The Lay of Maldoror* simultaneously calls into question the notion and practices of literature itself. They mock and parody not only literary styles, but also narrative and descriptive devices, drawing attention to the tacit contract between the writer and the reader whereby the latter agrees to try and believe what the former strains to fabricate for him. The book opens with a warning only to carry on if one is equal to the work's ferocious savagery, while towards the end Lautréamont has the reader say, "One must give him his due. He has considerably cretinized me" (6th "Song"). At various points on the way the narrator/Maldoror talks of his struggle to write (at one point being struck by a thunderbolt in a vain attempt on God's part to prevent the writing of so blasphemous a work), of how far one can believe either supposedly real phenomena or words, and of the likely acceptability of his style to the reader. It is in this self-consciousness of literary processes and of the power and treacherousness of language that Lautréamont's revolutionary qualities lie.

The other work, *Poésies*, is entirely different in nature. It consists of two instalments of manifesto-like declarations about literature and morality that denounce explicitly the Romantic poetry of Satanic revolt and macabre exaggeration embodied by *The Lay of Maldoror*. Yet a connection remains, for his work proposes a new form of creation based on rewriting or rearranging the words of others, much of *Poésies II* being a series of aphorisms from the French 17th-century moralists turned inside out. Here, as in the *The Lay of Maldoror*, Lautréamont shows a modernist awareness of language and literature as vast systems over which individuals do not have the degree of control they believe they have, but which can be exploited as systems to transcend the limited notions of logic and of individual consciousness that had hitherto prevailed.

—J.R. Stubbs

LAXNESS, Halldór (Kiljan)

Born: Halldór Gujónsson in Reykjavík, Iceland, 23 April 1902. **Education:** Educated at a grammar school, Reykjavík; lived in Benedictine monastery, Luxembourg; Jesuit school, Champion House, Osterley, England, 1923–24. **Family:** Married 1) Ingibjörg Einarsdóttir in 1930, one son; 2) Auur Sveinsdóttir in 1945, two daughters. **Career:** Lived in Europe, from 1919, then in the United States, 1927–29, and in Iceland from 1930. **Awards:** International Peace Movement prize, 1953; Nobel prize for literature, 1955; Sonning prize, 1969. Honorary degrees: Aabo University, 1968; University of Iceland, 1972; Eberhaar-Karls University, Tübingen, 1982. Honorary member, Union of Icelandic Artists. **Died:** 8 February 1998, near Reykjavík, Iceland.

PUBLICATIONS

Fiction

Barn náttúrunnnar [Child of Nature]. 1919.
Nokkrar sögur [Several Stories]. 1923.
Undir Helgahnúk [Under the Holy Mountain]. 1924.
Vefarinn mikli frá Kasmír [The Great Weaver from Kashmir]. 1927.
Salka Valka (þu vínviður hreini, Fuglinn í fjörunni). 2 vols., 1931–32; as *Salka Valka*, translated by F.H. Lyon, 1936; revised edition, 1963.
Fótatak manna [Footsteps of Men]. 1933.
Sjálfstætt fólk. 2 vols., 1934–35; as *Independent People*, translated by J.A. Thompson, 1945.
þórður gamli halti [Old þórður the Lame]. 1935.
Heimsljós. 2 vols., 1955; as *World Light*, translated by Magnus Magnusson, 1969.
   1. *Ljós heimsins* [The Light of the World]. 1937.
   2. *Höll sumarlandsins* [The Palace of the Summerland]. 1938.
   3. *Hús skáldsins* [The Poet's House]. 1939.
   4. *Fegurð himinsins* [The Beauty of the Sky]. 1940.
Gerska æfintýri [The Russian Adventure]. 1938.
Sjö töframenn [Seven Magicians]. 1942.
Trilogy:
   1. *Íslandsklukkan* [Iceland's Bell]. 1943.
   2. *Hið ljósa man* [The Bright Maiden]. 1944.
   3. *Eldur í Kaupinhafn* [Fire in Copenhagen]. 1946.
Atómstöðin. 1948; as *The Atom Station*, translated by Magnus Magnusson, 1961.
Gerpla. 1952; as *The Happy Warriors*, translated by Katherine John, 1958.
Brekkukotsannáll. 1957; as *The Fish Can Sing*, translated by Magnus Magnusson, 1966.
Ungfrúin góða og Husi [The Honour of the House]. 1959.
Paradisarheimt. 1960; as *Paradise Reclaimed*, translated by Magnus Magnusson, 1962.
Sjöstafakverið. 1964; as *A Quire of Seven*, translated by Alan Boucher, 1974.
Kristnihald undir Jökli. 1968; translated as *Christianity at the Glacier*, 1972.
Guðsgjafaþula [A Narration of God's Gifts]. 1972.
Seiseijú, mikil ósköp [Oh Yes! By Jove]. 1977.
Dagar hjá múnkum [Day Spent with Monks]. 1987.

Plays

Straumrof [Short Circuit]. 1934.
Snæfríður Íslandssól [Snaefríur, Iceland's Sun]. 1950.
Silfurtúnglið [The Silver Moon]. 1954.
Strompleikurinn [The Chimney Play]. 1961.
Prjónastofan Sólin [The Sun Knitting Works]. 1962.
Dúfnaveislan. 1966; as *The Pigeon Banquet*, translated by Alan Boucher, 1973.
Úa. 1970.
Norðanstulkan [The Girl from the North]. 1972.

Verse

Kvaeðakver [A Sheaf of Poems]. 1930.

Other

Kapólsk viðhorf [Catholic Views]. 1925.

Althýðubókin [The Book of the Plain People]. 1929.

Í austurvegi [On the Eastern Road]. 1933.

Dagleið á fjöllum: greinar [Day's Journey in the Mountains]. 1937.

Vettvangur dagsins [Forum of the Day]. 1942.

Sjálfsagðir hlutir [Things Taken for Granted]. 1946.

Reisubókarkorn [A Little Travel Book]. 1950.

Heiman eg fór [I Left Home]. 1952.

Dagur í senn [A Day at a Time]. 1955.

Gjörningabók [Miscellany]. 1959.

Skáldatími [Poets' Time]. 1963.

Upphaf mannúarstefnu [The Origin of Humanism]. 1965.

Íslendíngaspjall [Talk of Icelanders]. 1967.

Vínlandspúnktar [Vineland Notes]. 1969.

Innansveitarkronika [A Parish Chronicle]. 1970.

Yfirskygir staðir [Overshadowed Places]. 1971.

þjóðhátiðarrolla [Book of National Celebration]. 1974.

Í túninu heima [In the Hayfields of Home]. 1975.

Úngur eg var [Young I Was]. 1976.

Sjömeistarasagan [The Story of the Seven Masters]. 1978.

Grikklandsári [The Year in Greece]. 1980.

Við heygarshornið. 1981.

N. Tryggvadóttir: Serenity and Power, with Hrafnhildur Schram. 1982.

Og árin líða [And the Years Pass]. 1984.

Af menníngarástandi [On the Cultural Situation]. 1986.

Sagan af brauði nu dýra/The Bread of Life, translated by Magnus Magnusson. 1987.

Editor, *Grettissaga* [The Saga of Grettir the Strong]. 1946.

Editor, *Laxdæla saga* [The Laxdalers' Saga]. 1973.

Translator, *Aðventa* [Advent], by Gunnar Gunnarsson. 1939.

Translator, *Alexandreis; það, Er Alexanders saga mikla* [Alexandreis; That Is, the Saga of Alexander the Great]. 1945.

Also translator of *A Farewell to Arms* and *A Moveable Feast* by Hemingway and *Candide* by Voltaire.

*

Bibliography: by Haraldur *Sigurðsson, in Landsbókasafn Íslands: Árbok*, 1971, and in *Skirnir 146*, 1972; ''Halldór Laxness and America: A Bibliography'' by Fred R. Jacobs, in *The Serif*, 10(4), 1973.

Critical Studies: *Den store vävaren*, 1954, *Skaldens hus*, 1956, *Halldór Laxness*, 1971, and ''Halldór Laxness and the Icelandic Sagas,'' in *Leeds Studies in English*, 13, 1982, all by Peter Hallberg; ''Halldór Kiljan Laxness'' by Lawrence S. Thompson, in *Books Abroad*, 28, 1954; ''Halldór Kiljan Laxness: Iceland's First Nobel Prize Winner,'' in *American-Scandinavian Review*, 44, 1956, and ''The World of Halldór Laxness,'' in *World Literature Today*, 6(33), 1992, both by Sigurur A. Magnússon; ''Christianity on the Slopes of the Glacier'' by Richard N. Ringler, in *Books Abroad*, 44, 1970; Laxness issue of *Scandinavica*, 11(2), 1972; ''Beyond *The Atom Station*'' by Hermann Pálsson, in *Ideas and Ideologies*, 1975; ''Halldór Kiljan Laxness and the Modern Scottish Novel: Some Sociolinguistic Parallels'' by Harry D. Watson, in *Scandinavica*, 21(2), 1982; ''Eldorado and the Garden in Laxness' *Paradisarheimt*'' by George S. Tate, in *Scripta Islandica*, 36, 1985; ''The Quintessence in the Novels of Halldór Laxness'' by Wilhelm Friese, in *Skandivistik*, 16(2), 1986; *Halldór Laxness die Romane: Ein Einführung* by Wilhelm Friese, 1995; *Moskvulínan: Kommúnistaflokkur Íslands og Komintern, Halldó Laxness og Sovétríkin* by Arnór Hannibalsson, 1999.

*   *   *

Halldór Laxness made his breakthrough in 1927 with the novel *Vefarinn mikli frá Kasmír* [The Great Weaver from Kashmir]. It is a conversion novel, inspired by the spirit, if not the facts, of Laxness's own conversion to Roman Catholicism. It confronts a baffling number of conflicting views of the world, and makes clear that in turning to religion, Stein Ellidi is renouncing human claims. Thus it represents an important element in Laxness's work: the problem of the individual *vis-à-vis* a monolithic authority, the claims of the individual conscience as opposed to the conformative nature of the major ideologies.

Laxness subsequently spent a period in America where under the influence of Upton Sinclair and Sinclair Lewis he developed a sense of social injustice and became a Communist. One result was the major novel *Salka Valka*, concerning the establishment of a trade union in a fishing village and its effect on the environment, and in particular on Salka Valka herself. Social novels continued with *Sjálfstætt fólk* (*Independent People*), portraying the individualist peasant who believes he is free but is in fact being exploited by society, and *Heimslljós* (*World Light*), about a visionary pauper persecuted by his peers.

In 1943–46 Laxness turned to the historical novel, beginning with *Íslandsklukkan* [Iceland's Bell], about Jón Hreggvidsson's battle with the authorities. Unjustly condemned to death, he pursues a prolonged and ultimately successful struggle against bureaucracy. There are distinct national overtones, but also a poetical element centred on the main female character. The novel can be seen as a glorification of the Icelandic character, but it also represents the individual confronted with an impersonal bureaucracy. Similar ideas are found in *Atómstöðin* (*The Atom Station*) and *Gerpla* (*The Happy Warriors*).

The national theme, though with universal overtones, appears in *Paradisarheimt* (*Paradise Reclaimed*), about a poor Icelandic farmer tempted by a Mormon bishop to emigrate to the earthly paradise of Salt Lake City. In a touching, but sometimes bitingly satirical novel, Steinar experiences the unswerving faith of an ideology, but fails to accept it fully himself, and he returns to his home in Iceland, *his* paradise.

Laxness then moved from the long epic to the more concentrated, pithy novel, closely related to the plays with which he also experimented. Outstanding is *Kristnihald undir Jökli* (*Christianity at the Glacier*), a humorous but nevertheless serious and philosophical novel about a bishop who sends an assistant to examine the state of Christianity in an outlying village. The result, when he finds a priest who cannot be bothered to bury the dead, preferring to shoe horses and offer his congregation practical help, a doctor who has given up a brilliant career to study the skies, and a pastor's wife who has been both nun and prostitute, is a picture of humankind in all its diversity.

In portraying the individual's confrontation with societies and ideologies, Laxness constantly takes the side of the individual. He examines both Catholicism and communism, but ultimately it is probably Taoism, with its demand for tolerance and humanity, that attracts him most. He weds his philosophical considerations to his intense national feeling and gives the two a universal significance.

—W. Glyn Jones

LENZ, Jakob Michael Reinhold

Born: Sesswegen, Russian Baltic Province of Livonia, 23 January 1751. Family moved to Dorpat (now Tartu), Estonia, 1759. **Education:** Educated at Latin grammar school, Dorpat; University of Königsberg, studied theology, 1768–71. **Career:** Tutor to the Kleist brothers in Strasbourg, 1771; entered literary circles, meeting Goethe, Salzmann, and others; freelance writer from 1774, supplementing income with tuition; co-founder, Deutsche Gesellschaft [German Society], Strasbourg, 1775, and contributor to its journal, *Der Bürgerfreund* [The Citizens' Friend]; travelled throughout Germany and Switzerland, 1776–77; suffered first bout of mental illness, 1777; first suicide attempt, 1778; taken by his brother to Riga, 1779; travelled to St. Petersburg, 1780, attempt to become teacher and soldier failed, and to Moscow, 1781, held a number of positions as tutor; mental health deteriorated seriously during the 1780s. **Died:** 4 June 1792.

PUBLICATIONS

Collections

Dramatischer Nachlass, edited by Karl Weinhold. 1884.
Werke und Schriften, edited by Britta Titel and Hellmut Haug. 2 vols., 1966–67.
Werke und Schriften, edited by Richard Daunicht. 1967.
Gedichte, edited by Helmut Haug. 1968.
Werke und Briefe, edited by Sigrid Damm. 3 vols., 1987.
Werke, edited by Karen Lauer. 1992.

Plays

Der Hofmeister; oder, Die Vorteile der Privaterziehung (produced 1778). 1774; edited by Michael Kohlenbach, 1986; as *The Tutor*, translated by William E. Yuill, with *The Soldiers*, 1972; also translated and adapted by Pip Broughton, 1988; Anthony Meech, in *Three Plays*, 1993.
Lustspiele nach dem Plautus (adaptations from Plautus; includes *Das Väterchen; Die Aussteuer; Die Entführungen; Die Buhlschwester; Die Türkensklavin; Die beiden Alten*). 1774.
Amor vincit omnia, from *Love's Labours Lost* by Shakespeare. With *Anmerkungen übers Theater*, 1774.
Der neue Menoza; oder, Die Geschichte des cubanischen Prinzen Tandi. 1774; as *The New Menoza*, translated by Meredith Oakes, in *Three Plays*, 1993; as *Prince Tandi of Cumba, Or, The New Mendoza*, adapted by Theresa Heskins, 1995.
Pandämonium Germanicum. 1775.
Die Soldaten (produced 1863). 1776; as *The Soldiers*, translated by William E. Yuill, with *The Tutor*, 1972; also translated by Robert David MacDonald, in *Three Plays*, 1993.
Die Freunde machen den Philosophen. 1776.
Der Engländer. 1777.
Die Sizilianische Vesper. In *Liefländisches Magazin der Lektüre*, 1782.
Myrsa Polagi; oder, Die Irrgärten. In *Liefländisches Magazin der Lektüre*, 1782.
Tantalus. 1798.

Leopold Wagner, Verfasser des Schauspiels von neuen Monaten im Walfischbauch; oder, Eine Matinee. 1828.
Der verwundete Bräutigam, edited by K.L. Blum. 1845.
Three Plays (includes *The Soldiers; The New Menoza; The Tutor*). 1993.

Verse

Die Landplagen. 1769.
Der Herr Professor Kant. 1770.
Petrarch. 1776.

Fiction

Der Landprediger. 1777.
Der Waldbruder (fragment). 1797; edited by Max von Waldberg, 1882.
Zerbin; oder, Die neuere Philosophie, edited by Alfred Gerz. 1943.

Other

Anmerkungen übers Theater. With *Amor vincit omnia*, 1774.
Tagebuch. In *Deutsche Rundschau*, 11, 1877; in book form, in *Werke und Briefe*, 1987.
Briefe von und an J.M.R. Lenz, edited by Karl Freye and Wolfgang Stammler. 2 vols., 1918.

*

Critical Studies: *J.M.R. Lenz: Moralist und Aufklärer* by R. Ottomar, 1969; "Lenz's *Hofmeister* and the Drama of Storm and Stress" by M.A. Brown, in *Periods in German Literature, 2: Texts and Kontexts*, 1970; "Structural Unity in J.M.R. Lenz's *Der Hofmeister*: A Revaluation" by Edward P. Harris, in *Seminar*, (8), 1972; *Epische Etemente in Jakob Michael Reinhold Lenzens Drama "Der Hofmeister"* by Ford B. Parkes, 1973; "Language and Politics: The Patriotic Endeavours of J.M.R. Lenz" by Allan Blunden, in *Deutsche Vierteljahresschrift für Literatur und Geschichte*, (49), 1975; *J.M.R. Lenz: The Renunciation of Heroism* by John Osborne, 1975; *J.M.R. Lenz in Selbstzeugnissen und Bilddokumenten* by C. Hohoff, 1977; "Character and Paradox in Lenz's *Der Hofmeister*" by Michael Butler, in *German Life and Letters*, (32), 1979; *Lenz: "Der Hofmeister"; "Die Soldaten"; mit Brechts "Hofmeister" Bearbeitung und Materialien* by Herbert Haffner, 1979; *Shakespeare in Deutschland: Der Fall Lenz* by Eva Maria Inbar, 1982; *Lenz and Büchner: Studies in Dramatic Form* by John D. Guthrie, 1984; *Dasein und Realität: Theorie und Praxis des Realismus bei J.M.R. Lenz* by H.G. Schwarz, 1985; *Vögel, die verkünden Land: Das Leben des Jakob Michael Reinhold Lenz* by Sigrid Damm, 1986; *Jakob Michael Reinhold Lenz: "Der Hofmeister oder Vorteile der Privatziehung": Erläuterungen und Dokumente* edited by Friedrich Voit, 1986; "Irrtum als dramatische Sprachfigur. Sozialfall und Erziehungsdebatte in J.M.R. Lenzens *Hofmeister*" by Klaus Bohnen, 1987; "A Question of Norms: The Stage Reception of Lenz's *Der Hofmeister*" by Helga Madland, 1987; *J.M.R. Lenz* by Hans-Gerd Winter, 1987; "Das Politische" in *Die Soldaten* by David Hill, 1988; *Lenz Jahrbuch* edited by M. Luserke and Christoph Weiss, 1991; *A Critique of Lenz's Art of Scenic Variation* by Edward Batley, 1993; *Space to Act: The Theater of J.M.R. Lenz* by Alan C. Leidner and

Helga S. Madland, 1994; *Image and Text: J.M.R. Lenz* by Helga Stipa Madland, 1994; *Unpopular Virtues: The Critical Reception of J.M.R. Lenz* by Alan C. Leidner and Karin A. Wurst, 1999.

* * *

Jakob Michael Reinhold Lenz was a writer of considerable talent whose major output coincided with that short but explosive period of German literature dubbed the *Sturm und Drang* (Storm and Stress). This pre-Revolutionary movement, expounding the Encyclopaedists' ideals of equality, liberty, and fraternity, as well as individual writers within it, exerted a profound influence on European literature, principally German Romanticism, Realism, Junges Deutschland, Naturalism, Expressionism, and Modernism. It laid the foundations for the development of German social drama, bourgeois and working-class, by writers such as Georg Büchner, Gerhart Hauptmann, Frank Wedekind, and Bertold Brecht. The style and content of Büchner's theatre reflects Lenz's innovative approach to the medium, while Büchner's unique psycho-analytical *Novelle* was inspired by Lenz's mental illness, his name providing its title. Brecht revived interest in Lenz with his Berlin adaptation and production of *Der Hofmeister* (*The Tutor*) in 1950 and Rolf Hochhuth's preface to his documentary play on Churchill and the bombing of Dresden, *Soldaten* (*Soldiers*) of 1967 acknowledged his indebtedness to Lenz's play of the same title. Modern German opera from Alban Berg to Bernd Alois Zimmermann showed itself particularly appreciative of his unique theatrical style and visual appeal.

However, Lenz's seminal influence generally has long been undervalued, principally for two reasons. First, his productive years were restricted almost without exception to the 1770s, while the talent which outlasted, outlived, and outshone him, Goethe, not only abandoned his former friend after his departure from Court but also caricatured him unappreciatively in his own autobiography, *Aus meinem Leben: Dichtung und Warheit* [Poetry and Truth]. Second, partly inspired by the older Goethe's rather jaundiced view of the period, the *Sturm und Drang* came to be looked on, and written off as, a period of literary excess, indulgence, and adolescence, despite the younger Goethe having been its leading light. Recent scholarship has begun the process of evaluating Lenz's works independently of the shadow which Goethe cast upon them.

In the short productive span allotted to him, Lenz wrote poetry, essays, short prose works, novels, and plays. His remarkable gift was that of being able to assimilate a wide variety of styles, from the classical and neo-classical to the popular folk traditions, and to mould them together organically. Lenz's poetry shows these characteristics too, a neo-classical and classical inheritance bound up with an ability to use language to evoke mood in a way which prefigures German Romantic poetry. Its innovative forms apart, his poetry is in this sense untypical of the *Sturm und Drang*. Lenz's poetry, essays, and prose writing are not as widely known or researched as his plays, although, with three international conferences devoted to him in 1992, 200 years after his death, these expressions of his literary activity are now being reassessed. *Der Waldbruder* [The Forest Hermit], a conscious pendant to Goethe's novel *The Sufferings of Young Werther*, satirizes his own romantic self-indulgence. *Zerbin; oder, Die neuere Philosophie* [Zerbin, or The Modern Philosophy] converts its hero to the "modern philosophy" of exploiting others for personal advantage, until Marie's execution, out of unswerving loyalty to him, leads Zerbin to despair and suicide. *Der Landprediger* [The Country Vicar], told with gentler irony, relates the story of Father Oberlin of Waldersbach, who helps members of the local farming community find salvation not in learning the catechism by rote but in reflecting on the activity of their daily lives. The vicar's method of teaching the "best way of watering meadows" is the truly Christian way to salvation.

Lenz's style of theatre is occasionally offensive: penetratingly critical of human behaviour as of society, its naturalism is as daring as Hauptmann's and its proposals for reform more tangible than Brecht's. Shot through with irony, parody, and stark realism, Lenz's work reflects his utter sincerity. He presents audiences and reading public alike not only with incisive criticisms of contemporary German society, its hypocrisy, class-consciousness, aping of French manners, snobbery, pretentiousness, indulgent sexuality, foibles, wickedness, cruelty, and weakness, but also with practical proposals for reform. He takes up issues treated in his own dramatic dialogue in serious reformatory essays. In "Die Soldatenehen" [On Soldiers Marrying] he presents persuasive spiritual, moral, economic, military, and political arguments in favour of allowing soldiers to marry, having first given the subject a public airing on the stage in his *Die Soldaten* (*The Soldiers*). Several plays remained unfinished, and some were never performed in his own lifetime. His sketch of *Pandämonium Germanicum* [The Hall of German Heroes] reflects his adulation of Goethe, his criticism of imitators, journalists, and philistines, a playful attitude towards other contemporary writers such as Wieland, Uz, Gellert, Gleim, Rabener, Lessing, and Heder, and a teasingly self-deprecating view of himself.

He is best known for three plays. *The Tutor* depicts quite uninhibitedly the wretchedness caused when a spoilt and lonely young woman is given private lessons, in her own room, by a family tutor who has no sense of purpose or vocation. The educational issue of family tuition in the home versus community education in the village school is hotly debated and also provides the central and unifying theme of a complex play which, although it contains seduction, attempted suicide, and castration, ends happily for most of the cast. *Der neue Menoza* (*The New Menoza*), a parody of the traditional comedy of revealed identities, has the sibling relationship between Prince Tandy and Wilhelmina disclosed to them only after they are married to each other, but baby swapping is finally identified as the original cause of this misinformation.

The Soldiers, set in and around Lille, depicts how a foolish and irresistibly attractive shopkeeper's daughter Marie becomes disloyal to her fiancé, involved with one officer after another before being attracted to a young Count. Although the Countess tries to reform her, Marie's degradation continues until, stripped of all the trappings of middle-class civilization, she and her father roll on the ground wrapped in each other's arms, ecstatic at being together again, and embodying for a moment the elemental society envisioned by Rousseau, one of the several writers who profoundly influenced Lenz. Lenz's translations of the comedies of Plautus and of plays by Shakespeare nourished his own *Anmerkungen übers Theater* [Notes on the Theatre] and his essays on *Hamlet* and on scene change in Shakespeare, but they are also reflected in his wholesale nonconformist yet organic style of theatre. Rejecting the barrenness of the neoclassical conventions of the unities of action, place, and time, Lenz developed a composite form of artistry which moulded together in one major unifying theme the characters and types he had created, the theatrical situations in which they found themselves, and the setting and sequencing of scenes: education in *The Tutor* the hypocrisy of middle-class German society in *The New Menoza*, and the question of whether soldiers should be allowed to marry in *The*

Soldiers. It is in the theatre above all that Lenz's artistic genius, drawn from his concept of *Anschauen* (seeing and reflecting), is acknowledged today, but there is a renaissance of interest in his poetry, prose writing, and reformist zeal which gives promise of far more comprehensive appreciation of this unique writer.

—Edward Batley

See the essay on *The Tutor*.

LENZ, Siegfried

Born: Lyck, East Prussia (now Elk, Poland), 17 March 1926. **Education:** Educated at the University of Hamburg, 1945–48. **Military Service:** Served in the navy during World War II. **Family:** Married Lieselotte Lenz in 1949. **Career:** Reporter, 1948–50, and editor, 1950–51, *Die Welt* newspaper, Hamburg; since 1951 freelance writer; visiting lecturer, University of Houston, Texas, 1969; campaign speaker for Social Democratic party, from 1965. Lives in Hamburg, Germany. **Awards:** Schickele prize, 1952; Lessing prize, 1953; Hauptmann prize, 1961; Mackensen prize, 1962; Schickele prize, 1962; City of Bremen prize, 1962; State of North Rhine-Westphalia arts prize, 1966; Gryphius prize, 1979; German Free Masons prize, 1979; Thomas Mann prize, 1984; Raabe prize, 1987; Federal Booksellers peace prize, 1988; Galinsky Foundation prize, 1989. Honorary doctorate: University of Hamburg, 1976. **Member:** Gruppe 47.

PUBLICATIONS

Fiction

Es waren Habichte in der Luft. 1951.
Duell mit dem Schatten. 1953.
So zärtlich war Suleyken (stories). 1955.
Der Mann im Strom. 1957.
Dasselbe. 1957.
Jäger des Spotts. 1958; as *Jäger des Spotts, und andere Erzählungen*, edited by Robert H. Spaethling, 1965.
Brot und Spiele. 1959.
Das Feuerschiff (stories). 1960; title story as *The Lightship*, translated by Michael Bullock, 1962.
Das Wunder von Striegeldorf: Geschichten. 1961.
Stimmungen der See. 1962.
Stadtgespräch, adapted from his play *Zeit der Schuldlosen.* 1963: as *The Survivor*, translated by Michael Bullock, 1965.
Der Hafen ist voller Geheimnisse: Ein Feature in Erzählungen und zwei masurische Geschichten. 1963.
Lehmanns Erzählungen; oder, So schön war mein Markt: Aus den Bekenntnissen eines Schwarzhändlers. 1964.
Der Spielverderber. 1965.
Begegnung mit Tieren, with Hans Bender and Werner Bergengruen. 1966.
Das Wrack, and Other Stories, edited by C.A.H. Russ. 1967.
Die Festung und andere Novellen. 1968.

Deutschstunde. 1968; as *The German Lesson*, translated by Ernst Kaiser and Eithne Wilkins, 1971.
Hamilkar Schass aus Suleyken. 1970.
Lukas, sanftmütiger Knecht. 1970.
Gesammelte Erzählungen. 1970.
So war es mit dem Zirkus: Fünf Geschichten aus Suleyken (stories). 1971.
Erzählungen. 1972.
Meistererzählungen. 1972.
Ein Haus aus lauter Liebe. 1973.
Das Vorbild. 1973; as *An Exemplary Life*, translated by Douglas Parmée, 1976.
Der Geist der Mirabelle: Geschichten aus Bollerup. 1975.
Einstein überquert die Elbe bei Hamburg. 1975.
Die Kunstradfahrer und andere Geschichten. 1976.
Heimatmuseum. 1978; as *The Heritage*, translated by Krishna Winston, 1981.
Der Verlust. 1981; as *The Breakdown*, translated by Ralph R. Read, 1986.
Der Anfang von etwas. 1981.
Ein Kriegsende. 1984.
Exerzierplatz. 1985; as *Training Ground*, translated by Geoffrey Skelton, 1991.
Der Verzicht. 1985.
Die Erzählungen: 1949–1984. 3 vols., 1986.
Das serbische Mädchen. 1987.
Geschichten ut Bollerup. 1987.
Motivsuche. 1988.
Selected Stories, edited and translated by Breon Mitchell. 1989.
Die Klangprobe. 1990.

Plays

Das schönste Fest der Welt (radio play). 1956.
Zeit der Schuldlosen; Zeit der Schuldigen (radio play). 1961; stage adaptation (in German), 1966.
Das Gesicht: Komödie (produced 1964). 1964.
Haussuchung (radio play), 1967.
Die Augenbinde; Schauspiel; Nicht alle Förster sind froh: Ein Dialog. 1970.
Drei Stücke. 1980.
Zeit der Schuldlosen und andere Stücke. 1988.

Radio Plays: *Zeit der Schuldlosen/Zeit der Schuldigen*, 1961; *Das schönste Fest der Welt.*

Other

So leicht fängt man keine Katze. 1954.
Der einsame Jäger. 1955.
Das Kabinett der Konterbande. 1956.
Flug über Land und Meer: Nordsee—Hotstein—Nordsee, with Dieter Seelmann. 1967; as *Wo die Möwen schreien: Flug über Norddeutschlands Küsten und Länder*, 1976.
Leute von Hamburg: Satirische Porträts. 1968.
Versäum nicht den Termin der Freude. 1970.
Lotte soll nicht sterben (for children). 1970; as *Lotte macht alles mit*, 1978.
Beziehungen: Ansichten und Bekenntnisse zur Literatur. 1970.
Die Herrschaftssprache der CDU. 1971.

Verlorenes Land—gewonnene Nachbarschaft: zur Ostpolitik der Bundesregierung. 1971.

Der Amüsierdoktor. 1972.

Der Leseteufel. 1972(?).

Elfenbeinturm und Barrikade: Schriftsteller zwischen Literatur und Politik. 1976.

Die Wracks von Hamburg: Hörfunk-Features. 1978.

Himmel, Wolken, weites Land: Flug über Meer, Marsch, Geest und Heide, with Dieter Seelmann. 1979.

Waldboden: Sechsunddreissig Farbstiftzeichnungen, illustrated by Liselotte Lenz. 1979.

Gespräche mit Manès Sperber und Leszek Kołakowski, edited by Alfred Mensak. 1980.

Über Phantasie: Siegfried Lenz, Gespräche mit Heinrich Böll, Günter Grass, Walter Kempowski, Pavel Kohout, edited by Alfred Mensak. 1982.

Fast einem Triumph: aus ein Album. 1982.

Elfenbeinturm und Barrikade: Erfahrungen am Schreibtisch. 1983.

Manès Sperber, sein letztes Jahr, with Manès and Jenka Sperber. 1985.

Etwas über Namen (address). 1985.

Kleines Strandgut, illustrated by Liselotte Lenz. 1986.

Am Rande des Friedens. 1989.

Editor, with Egon Schramm, *Wippchens charmante Scharmützel,* by Julius Stettenheim. 1960.

*

Critical Studies: "From the Gulf Stream in the Main Stream: Siegfried Lenz and Hemingway" by Sumner Kirshner, in *Research Studies,* 1967; "Narrowing the Distance: Siegfried Lenz's *Deutschstunde*" by Robert H. Paslick, in *German Quarterly,* 1973; "The Macabre Festival: A Consideration of Six Stories by Siegfried Lenz" by Colin Russ, in *Deutung und Bedeutung: Studies in German and Comparative Literature,* edited by Brigitte Schludermann and others, 1973; "How It Seems and How It Is: Marriage in Three Stories by Siegfried Lenz" by Esther N. Elstun, in *Orbis litterarum,* (29), 1974; "Ironic Reversal in the Short Stories of Siegfried Lenz," in *Neophilologus,* (58), 1974, and *Siegfried Lenz,* 1978, both by Brian O. Murdoch; "Siegfried Lenz's *Deutschstunde:* A North German Novel," in *German Life and Letters,* 1975, and "The 'Lesson' in Siegfried Lenz's *Deutschstunde,*" in *Seminar,* February 1977, both by Peter Russell; "Zygmunt's Follies? On Siegfried Lenz's *Heimatmuseum*" by Geoffrey P. Butler, in *German Life and Letters,* 1980; "Captive Creator in Siegfried Lenz's *Deutschstunde*: Writer, Reader, and Response" by Todd Kontje, in *German Quarterly,* (53), 1980; "The Interlocutor and the Narrative Transmission of the Past: On Siegfried Lenz's *Heimatmuseum*" by Marilyn Sibley Fries, in *Monatshefte,* 1987; "The Eye of the Witness: Photography in Siegfried Lenz's Short Stories" by Hanna Geldrich-Zeffmann, in *Modern Language Review,* 1989; *Realisme de Siegfried Lenz* by Dorothee Merchiers, 2001.

*   *   *

In his career Siegfried Lenz has long focused heart and mind on his homeland in Eastern Europe, and this is reflected in his fiction and in his critical writings as a political commentator. Born in East Prussia in 1926, he observed as an adolescent the German occupation of Poland. At the age of 17, he served in the Navy during the latter part of World War II. In the immediate and difficult post-war years he studied philosophy and literature at the University of Hamburg. That post-war atmosphere is humorously, indeed satirically portrayed in *Lehmanns Erzählungen; oder, So schön war mein Markt,* while World War II and the serious moral dilemmas confronting the fictional protagonist have continued to occupy Lenz's attention, as in *Ein Kriegsende.* Lenz's nascent interest in literature was evident already at university and was stimulated more directly by his work as a journalist and literary editor on *Die Welt.* The journalistic eye for detail and atmosphere undoubtedly helped his literary apprenticeship during which he produced his first short stories published in serial form or *in toto* in newspapers and journals.

The publication of his first novel *Es waren Habichte in der Luft* [There Were Hawks in the Sky] determined Lenz's career as a freelance writer. The story immediately points to his subsequent thematic concentration on border regions, marginal situations, on danger, flight, failure, and the inescapability of fate. The setting is Karelia just after World War I and deals with the establishment of the communist regime there. Stenkka, a teacher, is on the run, accused of murder although in reality he was only a witness to the deed. A pessimistic viewpoint is suggested by the notion of death at the border (though Erkii, a former pupil, does survive the ordeal) and the predatory hawks are symbolically ever watchful and ever present. The straightforwardness of style and language, reminiscent of Heinrich Böll and Wolfgang Borchert, in his early short stories and novels reflects incidentally the effect of *Kahlschlad* as well as an acknowledgement of Hemingway's influence.

The post-World War II setting of Hamburg harbour and the clearing of wrecks in the waters there provides the background to the novel *Der Mann im Strom* [The Man in the River]. Hinrichs is a good diver but fear of unemployment makes him falsify his real age on his papers. But there is no escape from the inevitability of events and he is eventually dismissed. Generational conflict—so redolent in Lenz's fiction—is present here in the figure of the younger diver Manfred who has been trained by Hinrichs but is then killed as a result of his own inexperience. Manfred's relationship with Hinrich's daughter Lena provides another important complicating factor in this tale of personal guilt. The end of a career and fear of failure preoccupy the thoughts of the lonely long-distance runner Bert Buchner in *Brot und Spiele* as he relives the course of his life in his last race, the European 10,000 metres. This is ultimately not a race against other competitors but against himself: his conjuring up of memories of earlier races, other experiences, his dealings with people, force him to recognize now some serious shortcomings in what had seemed to him and in fact had been a successful and popular athletics career. The theme of pursuit, be it by British soldiers in the war or subsequently competitors on the track, registers strongly in the novel. Buschner's fall before the end of the race symbolizes his position. The relationship of the protagonist and the narrator as a factor in the process of understanding and self-understanding is of importance in this novel as in other of Lenz's stories, for example in *Stadtgespräch* (The Survivor). The overcoming of the past and the question of guilt—here both individual and collective—is the thematic kernel of *The Survivor.* The story is seen through the eyes of the narrator Tobias Lund who recalls the botched attack by Resistance fighters on a visiting German general to a town in (presumably) occupied Norway during World War II. In reprisal, 44 townsmen are taken hostage and eventually killed after Daniel, leader of the Resistance fighters, has failed to surrender. Should he have given himself up? That was the question asked at the time and continually posed after the war as different people relate different aspects of the same story. Daniel, the embodiment of the idea of opposition, serves as a symbol of the moral dilemma presented.

Lenz's overall concern with getting his fictional characters to try to make sense of a situation and gain a true perspective on life is arguably best manifested in *Deutschstunde* (*The German Lesson*). Ensconced in a corrective institution for juvenile offenders that is significantly situated on an island in the river Elbe and hence distanced from society, Siggi Jepsen faces the task of writing an essay on the joys of duty. As such, it becomes a German lesson that reveals his own life story against the backcloth of Germany in the last years of World War II. Once again, a remote setting is chosen—not the lightship on the water in *Das Feuerschiff* (*The Lightship*), nor the small town set in a Norwegian fjord in *The Survivor*, but the distant north German coast near the Danish border where, though not at the hub of events, the village inhabitants are inextricably caught up in them and duly suffer from the conflicting and burdensome claims of family ties, loyalties to the state, and individual responsibilities. This is as true for Siggi's father the community policeman, and Nansen the celebrated Expressionist painter, as it is for Siggi himself. The lesson of history so often is that no one learns from it, and here within the framework setting of the institution a decade later, towards the end of Siggi's stay there, Siggi pointedly remarks that both he and Himpel, the institution's director, will each think to have won. A serious question mark must remain over whether the young offender had properly prepared himself or been prepared for future life in society. The self-questioning and the revelations of individual and societal inadequacies continue in the search by three disparate individuals for a role model to complete an educational reader in *Das Vorbild* (*An Exemplary Life*). The lives of Pundt, Heller, and Rita Süssfeldt that reflect varying generational, social, and political interests in the urban setting of Hamburg are all beset with shortcomings and even their final chosen example is revealed to be less than an ideal figure.

Like Günter Grass, Lenz has turned his eyes to his homeland in the East. The story collections *So zärtlich war Suleyken* [So Tender Was Suleyken] and *So war es mit dem Zirkus* had pointed the way in a series of anecdotes on life in his native Masurda that constitute a sympathetic and humorous recollection of a golden past (to be counterbalanced incidentally by his north German tales from Bollerup, *Der Geist der Mirabelle* [1975], where the real, bustling modern world threatens to intrude). The novel *Heimatmuseum* (*The Heritage*) returns to Masuria in a far more serious vain: in a series of flashbacks told from his hospital bed where he is recovering from burns sustained in the conflagration of the regional museum that was in his care but to which he had set fire, Zygmunt Rogalla relives the original desire to recapture and preserve past cultural traditions (not least of all carpet weaving) in the face of change that threatens first from Nazi ideological intentions and then the war itself. Flight to the West makes possible the eventual rebuilding of the folk museum in Schleswig-Holstein, only for it to become endangered once again through misuse. Fire plays an important symbolic role here as in *The German Lesson*, but in *The Heritage* an acceptance of guilt and recognition of the need for adjustment to change seems ultimately to be better understood.

Lenz professes to write stories to try to understand the world. His multifarious fictional forays underscore his stated endeavour. His tales are tightly woven (though proliferation of them in the novels in the shape of sub-plots is sometimes negatively viewed by the critics). The element of violence is often a feature in his fiction, as is

emotional and spiritual tension which can produce a dramatic effect particularly in the short works (the title piece of the collection *The Lightship* is a good example). Lenz displays a compassion for many of his characters while being equally capable of casting a sharply critical eye, and as with Böll, the moral factor features strongly in his writings. In this connection, the role of the observer-cum-narrator or interlocutor is important in as much as that character, in following the course of events befalling the protagonist, can pose questions, search for an understanding, provide another perspective—and hence serve us and for us, the readers.

In the 1960s Lenz wrote sporadically for the theatre and the radio with mixed success. *Zeit der Schuldlosen* [Time of the Innocents], on the theme of guilt and serving as a basis for the novel *The Survivor*, is widely regarded as his best dramatic work. But fiction remains his forte. He was a member of Gruppe 47, later sided openly with the SPD, and worked in political journalism and broadcasting. The association of politics and writing has never been far removed from Lenz's thinking as is suggested in *Elfenbeinturm und Barrikade: Schriftsteller zwischen Literatur und Politik*. The need to communicate, to tell stories as a means of understanding the world is what motivates Lenz. Of significance then is the novel *Der Verlust* (*The Breakdown*), where Lenz, on the heels of Wittgenstein and Handke, turns to the question of the loss of speech as the protagonist Ulrich Martens becomes more powerless to communicate. Today Lenz stands in the forefront of major German writers in the second half of the 20th century. His success and popularity may be gauged in part by the numerous translations of his works into foreign languages and the filming of several of his stories, to say nothing of the sheer frequency of editions of his books.

—Ian Hilton

See the essay on *The German Lesson*.

LEOPARDI, Giacomo

Born: Recanati, Italy, 29 June 1798; became a Count on his father's death. **Education:** Educated at home by tutors; studied privately until 1822. **Career:** Lived in Rome, 1822–23; advisor, A.F. Stella, publishers, Milan, 1825–28; lived in Bologna, Florence, and Pisa, and in Naples from 1833. **Died:** 14 June 1837.

PUBLICATIONS

Collections

Opere (includes "La ginestra"), edited by Antonio Ranieri. 6 vols., 1845–49.
Opere inedite, edited by Giuseppe Cugnoni. 2 vols., 1878–80.
Tutte le opere, edited by Francesco Flora. 5 vols., 1937–49.
Tutte le opere, edited by Walter Binni and Enrico Ghidetti. 2 vols., 1969.
A Leopardi Reader, edited by Ottavio M. Casale (bilingual edition). 1981.
Leopardi: Selected Poems, translated by Eamon Grennan. 1997.

Verse

Canzoni. 1819.

Canzone ad Angelo Mai. 1820.

Versi. 1824.

Versi, edited by Pietro Brigherti. 1826.

I canti. 1831; revised edition, 1835; edited by I. Sanesi, 1943, by Francesco Flora, 1949, and by Mario Fubini, 1970; as *Canti,* translated by J.H. Whitfield, 1962.

I Paralipomeni della Batracomiomachia. 1842; as *The War of the Mice and the Crabs,* edited and translated by Ernesto G. Caserta, 1976.

Poems, translated by Frederick Townsend. 1887.

The Poems, translated by Francis H. Cliffe. 1893.

The Poems (''Canti''), translated by J.M. Morrison. 1900.

Poems, translated by Theodore Martin. 1904.

Poems, edited by Francis Brooks. 1909.

The Poems, edited and translated by Geoffrey L. Bickersteth (bilingual edition). 1923.

[Selections], translated by R.C. Trevelyan. 1941.

Poems, translated by John Heath-Stubbs. 1946.

Poems, translated by J.-P. Barricelli. 1963.

Canti, paralipomeni, poesie varie, traduzioni, poetiche, e versi puerili, edited by C. Muscetta and G. Savoca. 1968.

Canti, edited by G. Singh, various translators. 1990.

Canti, translated by Paul Lawton. 1996.

Canti: With a Selection of His Prose, translated by J.G. Nichols. 1998.

Leopardi's Canti, translated by Joseph Tusiani. 1998.

Other

Operette morali. 1827; revised edition, 1836; edited by Cesare Galimberti, 1978; as *Essays and Dialogues,* translated by Charles Edwardes, 1882; as *Essays, Dialogues and Thoughts,* translated by Patick Maxwell, 1893, also translated by James Thomson, 1905; as *Operette Morati, Essays and Dialogues,* edited and translated by Giovanni Cecchetti, 1982; as *Moral Tales,* translated by Patrick Creagh, 1983.

Pensieri di varia filosofia e di bella letteratura [*Lo Zibaldone*]. 7 vols., 1898–1900; edited by Anna Maria Moroni, 2 vols., 1972, and by Giuseppe Pacella, 3 vols., 1991; as *Zibaldone: A Selection,* translated by Martha King and Daniela Bini, 1992.

Epistolario, edited by F. Moroncini and others. 7 vols., 1934–41.

Selected Prose and Poetry, edited and translated by Iris Origo and John Heath-Stubbs. 1966.

Poems and Prose, edited by Angel Flores (bilingual edition). 1966.

Entro dipinta gabbia, edited by Maria Corti. 1972.

Lettere, edited by Sergio and Raffaella Solmi. 1977.

Pensieri, edited and translated by W.S. Di Piero (bilingual edition). 1981.

Editor, *Rime,* by Petrarch. 1826.

Editor, *Crestomazia italiana: prosa, poesia.* 2 vols., 1827–28.

*

Bibliography: *Bibliografia leopardiana,* 3 vols., 1931–53; *Bibliografia analitica leopardiana,* 2 vols., 1963–73; *Bibliografia analitica leopardiana (1971–1980)* by Ermanno Carini, 1986; *Il labirinto leopardiano: bibliografia, 1976–1983, con una breve appendice, 1984–1985* by Emilio Giordano, 1986.

Critical Studies: *Leopardi: A Biography* by Iris Origo, 1935, revised edition, as *Leopardi: A Study, in Solitude,* 1953; *Giacomo Leopardi* by J.H. Whitfield, 1954; *The Artifice of Reality: Poetic Style in Wordsworth, Foscolo, Keats, and Leopardi* by Karl Kroeber, 1964; *Leopardi and the Theory of Poetry,* 1964, and *Leopardi e i poeti inglese,* 1990, both by G. Singh; *Night and the Sublime in Giacomo Leopardi* by Nicolas James Parella, 1970; *Giacomo Leopardi: The Unheeded Voice* by Giovanni Carsaniga, 1977; *A Fragrance from the Desert: Poetry and Philosophy in Giacomo Leopardi* by Daniela Bini, 1983; *Giacomo Leopardi* by J.-P. Barricelli, 1986; *The Aspiration toward a Lost Natural Harmony in the Work of Three Italian Writers: Leopardi, Verga and Moravia* by Foscarina Alexander, 1990; *Leopardi: A Study in Solitude* by Iris Origo, 1999.

* * *

No Italian poet—not even Dante—exemplifies with such vigour and conviction as Leopardi the validity of Coleridge's dictum that a great poet is also a profound philosopher. The union between poetry and first-hand thought—critical as well as philosophical, analytical as well as exploratory—gives Leopardi's style and language an unmistakably personal timbre which is at the same time a hallmark of universality. A contemporary of the English Romantic poets, Leopardi was not ''romantic'' in the way they were; in fact, as his essay ''Discorso di un italiano intorno alla poesia romantica'' [An Italian's Discourse on Romantic Poetry] shows, he adopted a polemical attitude to Romanticism, or to what he understood this to mean; and although a contemporary of Goethe and Hölderlin, he wasn't ''classical'' in the way they were. Similarly, although he was (like Baudelaire) a precursor of poetic modernity, his art is as different in ethos and temperament from Baudelaire's as it is from Byron's, Keats's, or Shelley's. Moreover, although he was saturated—as few poets were—in classical literature and classical learning, his poetry is refreshingly free from the weight of such learning. Ill-health and growing blindness as well as frustration in love dogged him all his life, but he managed to rise above them, transforming his joy and pain, and the vicissitudes of his uneventful but emotionally rich life, into material for poetry and philosophic contemplation which is at once rapt and deliberate, cool and impassioned. Hence his poetry, even at its most lyrical, is at bottom philosophical, and his style and diction, even at their most charged, have a philosophic calm and detachment about them. In fact, Leopardi may be said to have created a new poetic genre in Italian—the philosophic lyric—through which he interfused, to borrow Eliot's words, the man who suffers and the mind which creates.

Leopardi's poetic genius finds its supreme manifestation in the *Canti,* just as his analytical and speculative powers do theirs in his *Operette morali* (*Essays and Dialogues*). *Epistolario,* on the other hand, is a richly human document of the psychological and autobiographical side of Leopardi's personality, and *Pensieri di varia filosofia e di bella letteratura* (or *Lo Zibaldone*) [Thoughts on Various Philosophies and Great Literature]—a monumental miscellany of notes, comments, and reflections—is an encyclopedic mine of literary, philological, and cultural erudition all rolled into one. Binding all these works together as well as underlying them is a singularly gifted mind—at once creative and critical, learned and inventive, cultivated and inquisitive—with an unsurpassed mastery over prose and verse.

The English critics, together with Sainte-Beuve, were the first to recognize and critically comment on these qualities of Leopardi's art and personality. ''A man of acknowledged genius and irreproachable character,'' wrote Henry Crabb Robinson after meeting Leopardi in

Florence in 1830–31. "There have been," observed H.G. Lewes, apropos of Leopardi's patriotic odes, "no more piercing, manly, vigorous strains than those which vibrate in the organ-peal of patriotism sent forth by Leopardi." And as a poet of despair, Lewes went on, "we know of no equal to Leopardi . . . His grief is so real and so profound that it is inexhaustible in expression, to say nothing of the beauty in which he embalms it." According to Gladstone, too, Leopardi applies to his work, "with a power rarely equalled, all the resources of thought and passion, all that his introspective habit had taught him . . . and he unites to a very peculiar grace a masculine energy and even majesty of expression which is not surpassed . . . in the whole range of poetry." And as far as Leopardi's mastery over form and style is concerned, here is Matthew Arnold's testimony: Leopardi "has the very qualities which we have found wanting in Byron; he has the sense for form and style, the passion for just expression, the sure and firm touch of the true artist . . . he has a far wider culture than Wordsworth, more mental lucidity, more freedom from illusions as to the real character of the established fact and of reigning conventions; above all, this Italian, with his pure and sure touch, with his fineness of perception, is far more of the artist [than Wordsworth]." But besides being that of a stylist and an artist of such calibre, Leopardi's poetry has something perpetually modern about it, as has his theory of poetry. Leopardi jotted down his reflections on and analysed the nature of poetry, style, poetic inspiration, the language of poetry—in fact no poet in the history of Italian literature has occupied himself with the theory of poetry as much as Leopardi, and, indeed, as Maurice Bowra remarks, "few men have given so much hard thought to the matter"—so that he may be regarded justly as a worthy peer of Goethe, Wordsworth, and Coleridge. Moreover, certain aspects of his poetics—and poetry—are startlingly modern and anticipate the development of 20th-century poetry.

For although Leopardi's poetry deals with themes that are conventional—love, death, youth, nature, memory, the transience of life, etc.—what comes out of his treatment of such themes is of the very essence of modernity: modernity of thought as well as of spirit. And if his poetry has a philosophic basis, it is not because it expounds a particular philosophy, or is inspired by or dependent on a particular philosophic system as such. It is because it is firmly rooted in his perception of the truth about life as he saw it and of the illusions one needed in order to be able to bear it, since "human kind cannot bear very much reality."

Thus Leopardi's pessimism, in the *Canti* no less than in *Operette morali*, is not so much a creed based on emotional or imaginative grounds as an outcome of closely argued premises, conclusions and convictions regarding the nature of life and human destiny, which the poet-philosopher has the courage to look unflinchingly in the face. At the same time he embraces what his own experience of life and his knowledge as well as observation of the world and of man in society have taught him. From his very early life Leopardi was filled with what he himself calls "the infinite desire to know precisely," that never abandoned him. His explorations of reality were conveyed in accents of matchless lyricism with which he covered "the nudity of things." That is why his art was admired not only by a modern poet like Pound—'Leopardi splendid, and the only author since Dante who need trouble you," Pound wrote to Iris Berry—but also by a modern philosopher like Bertrand Russell. In a letter to me Russell said that he found Leopardi's poetry and philosophy "the most beautiful expression of what should be the creed of a scientist," and described "La ginestra" ("The Broom") as expressing "more

effectively than any other poem known to me my views about the universe and the human passions."

—G. Singh

See the essays on "The Broom," "The Infinite," and "To Himself."

LERMONTOV, Mikhail (Iur'evich)

Born: Moscow, Russia, 2/3 October 1814. **Education:** Educated at School for the Nobility, Moscow, 1828–30; University of Moscow, 1830–32; Junker School, St. Petersburg, 1832–34. **Career:** Cavalry cornet in Regiment of Life Guards Hussars; exiled to the Caucasus for poems on Pushkin's death, 1835–38; because of a duel, again exiled, to Tenginskii Infantry Regiment on Black Sea, 1840–41. **Died:** In duel, 15 July 1841.

PUBLICATIONS

Collections

Sochineniia [Works]. 6 vols., 1954–57.
Izbrannye sochineniia [Selected Works]. 4 vols., 1958–59.
Sobranie sochinenii [Collected Works], edited by V. Arkhipov. 4 vols., 1969.
Sochineniia [Works], edited by I.M. Andronikov. 2 vols., 1970.
Sobranie sochinenii [Collected Works], edited by I.M. Andronikov. 4 vols., 1975.
Selected Works, translated by Avril Pyman, Irina Zheleznova, and Martin Parker. 1976.
Sobranie sochinenii [Collected Works], edited by V.A. Manuilov. 4 vols., 1979.
Izbrannye sochineniia [Selected Works], edited by V. Vatsuro. 1983.
Sobranie sochinenii [Collected Works], edited by Iu. Bondarev. 4 vols., 1985.
Izbrannye sochineniia [Selected Works], edited by G.I. Belen'kii. 1987.
Sochineniia [Works], edited by G.A. Andzhaparidze. 2 vols., 1988.
Sobranie sochinenii [Collected Works], edited by G.P. Makogonenko. 4 vols., 1989.
Polnoe sobranie stikhotvorenii [Complete Collected Poetry], edited by Iu. A. Andreev. 2 vols., 1989.

Fiction

Geroi nashego vremeni. 1840; translated as *Sketches of Russian Life in the Caucasus*, 1853; as *The Hero of Our Days*, translated by T. Pulsky, 1854; as *The Heart of a Russian*, translated by J. Wisdom and M. Murray, 1912; as *A Hero of Nowadays*, translated by John Swinnerton Phillimore, 1920; as *A Hero of Our Time*, translated by Reginald Merton, 1928, also translated by Vladimir and Dmitri Nabokov, 1958; Philip Longworth, 1962; Paul Foote, 1966; Martin Parker, 1995; as *A Hero of Our Own Times*, translated by Eden and Cedar Paul, 1940.
Vadim (unfinished), in *Sochineniia*, 6. 1957; edited and translated by Helen Goscilo, 1984.

Plays

Maskarad [Masquerade]. 1836.

Verse

Pesnia pro tsaria Ivana Vasil'evicha. 1837; as *A Song about Tsar Ivan Vasilyevich,* translated by John Cournos, 1929.
Mtsyri. 1840; as *The Circassian Boy,* translated by S. Conant, 1875.
Demon. 1842; as *The Demon,* translated by A. Stephens, 1875; also translated by F. Storr, 1894; E. Richter, 1910; R. Burness, 1918; G. Shelley, 1930.
Selected Poetry. 1965.
Major Poetical Works, edited and translated by Anatoly Liberman. 1983.
Poemy i povesti v stikhakh [Narrative Verse and Stories in Verse]. 1984.
Narrative Poems by Pushkin and Lermontov, translated by Charles Johnston. 1983.
Poemy i stikhotvoreniia [Narrative Verse and Poetry]. 1985.
Poemy [Narrative Verse]. 1990.

Other

Proza [Prose]. 1941.
Proizvedeniia na kavkazskie temy [Works on the Caucasian Theme]. 1968.
Proza. Poemy. Lirika [Prose. Narrative Verse. Lyrics]. 1982.
M.Iu. Lermontov v russkoi kritike [M.Iu. Lermontov in Russian Criticism]. 1985.
M.Iu. Lermontov v vospominaniiakh sovremennikov [M.Iu. Lermontov in the Reminiscences of Contemporaries]. 1989.
Lermontov (al'bom) [Lermontov (album)]. 1991.

*

Critical Studies: *Lermontov* by Janko Lavrin, 1959; *Lermontov* by John Mersereau, Jr., 1962; *Lermontov: Tragedy in the Caucasus* by Laurence Kelly, 1977; *An Essay on Lermontov's "A Hero of Our Times"* by C.J.G. Turner, 1978; *Lermontov: A Study in Literary-Historical Evaluation* by B.M. Eikhenbaum, translated by Ray Parrott and Harry Weber, 1981; *Lermontov* by John Garrard, 1982; *A Wicked Irony: The Rhetoric of a Hero of Our Time* by Andrew Barratt and A.D.P. Briggs, 1989; *The Fey Hussar* by Jessie Davies, 1989; *Lermontov's A Hero of Our Time* by Robert Reid, 1997; *Lermontov's Narratives of Heroism* by Vladimir Golstein, 1998; *M. Iu. Lermontov: His Life and Work* by Walter N. Vickery, 2001.

* * *

Mikhail Lermontov is often thought of as Pushkin's successor in the role of Russian national poet. Lermontov was profoundly influenced by Pushkin, but an equally potent and more visible influence was that of Byron. Whereas Pushkin's ingrained classical instincts allowed him to assimilate classical influences (often ironically) without wholly succumbing to Romantic style, Lermontov must be regarded as a full-blooded representative of the Romantic movement.

During his short life Lermontov attempted most literary genres but was chiefly a lyric and narrative poet. His drama is less memorable but his single prose work of note, *Geroi nashego vremeni* (*A Hero of Our Time*), is one of the most original and influential of Russian novels.

Lermontov's lyrics are often highly subjective and reflect the isolation of the post-Decembrist poet and the search for inner consolation which eluded Lermontov more than his contemporary, Tiutchev. Lermontov also uses lyric poetry as a means of expressing his metaphysic, often symbolically. Inanimate objects in juxtaposition (a rock and a cloud; a dead leaf floating in a river) or in isolation (a mountain peak; a solitary tree) are used in an almost Ovidian way to convey the tragic helplessness of particular aspects of the human condition. Ineluctable fate is a brooding presence throughout Lermontov's work: in the short poem "Angel" (1831), the human soul is conceived as pre-existing physical birth, birth itself being the forcible removal of the soul from a state of heavenly bliss to bodily imprisonment and exile among the world's miseries.

Fate, however, is not to be accepted blindly. Lermontov's most memorable creations are those in which Sisyphus-like characters struggle heroically against insuperable forces. Early in his literary career Lermontov became fascinated by the demonic personality, which, though shunned by God, is nevertheless capable of love and passion. As well as several lyrics on this theme, Lermontov produced, in successive drafts, a narrative poem called *The Demon* in which a demon, expelled from heaven, seeks redemption through the love of a Georgian girl but is eventually thwarted by God. Undemonic, but equally heroic, the hero of *Mtsyri* (*The Circassian Boy*) is a young postulant of Circassian origin. He is brought up in a Georgian monastery, and his one wish is to return to his home in the Caucasus but, after an ill-fated attempt to escape, he is brought back to the monastery and dies.

A Caucasian setting and demonic exertion of the will against fate also dominate *A Hero of Our Time*. This work, generally thought to be Lermontov's greatest, is sometimes said by critics to show that, by the end of his life, Lermontov was forsaking Romanticism in favour of realism. Certainly Lermontov takes great pains to motivate his novel, to suggest that it has as its initial impulse a documentary rather than a fictional intention. But the hero himself is still an embittered representative of the Byronic tradition and, though at times self-deprecating, is never a vehicle for parodying or diminishing that tradition. The most remarkable feature of *A Hero of Our Time* is its architecture: five structurally autonomous but thematically intermeshed first-person narratives create the illusion of a living, multi-dimensional hero who makes himself known to the reader by the gradual accumulation of psychological detail rather than by the consecutive unfolding of plot. Lermontov's prose style in the novel, remarkably simple but capable of sustaining impressive passages of natural description, influenced later writers, particularly short-story writers such as Chekhov. The character of Pechorin, the hero, has come to epitomize "the superfluous man," the disillusioned internal exile who figures so largely in the 19th-century Russian novel.

—Robert Reid

See the essay on *A Hero of Our Time*.

LESAGE, Alain-René

Born: Sarzeau, Brittany, France, 8 May (13 December in some sources) 1668. **Education:** Educated by Jesuits in Vannes, Brittany; studied law in Paris. **Family:** Married Marie-Élizabeth Huyard in

1694; three sons, including the actor Montménil, and one daughter. **Career:** Possibly a lawyer in Paris, 1690s; wrote original plays and adaptations/translations from the Spanish for the Comédie-Française, Paris, 1700–09; broke with the Comédie-Française, and subsequently wrote farces, comic operas, *vaudevilles*, and other pieces for the Paris fairs of St. Germain and St. Laurent, often in collaboration with Louis Fuzelier, d'Orneval, and others; lived with one son, the Abbé de Lyonne, in Boulogne, from 1743. **Died:** 7 November 1747.

PUBLICATIONS

Collections

Le Théâtre de la foire; ou, L'Opéra-comique (10 vols.: two of them numbered as 9). 1721–37.
Oeuvres choisies de Lesage, edited by C.J. Mayer. 16 vols., 1810.
Oeuvres complétes. 12 vols., 1821.
Novels. 4 vols., 1821.
Oeuvres de Le Sage. 1877.
Théâtre. 1911.
Oeuvres complètes. 1935–.
Théâtre, edited by Maurice Bardon. 1948.
Il Teatro della foire. 1965.
Three French Comedies, translated with introduction by James Magruder. 1996.

Plays (adaptations and plays for the legitimate stage)

Le Traître puni, from a play by Rojas Zorilla. In *Théâtre espagnol*, 1700.
Don Félix de Mendoce, from a play by Lope de Vega. In *Théâtre espagnol*, 1700.
Le Point d'honneur, from a play by Rojas Zorilla (produced 1702). 1739.
Don César Ursin, from a play by Calderón (produced 1707). 1739.
Crispin, rival de son maître (produced 1707). 1707; revised version, in *Recueil des pièces mises au Théâtre Français*, 1738; edited by Andrew Clark, 1910, Marcello Spaziani, 1956, and by T.E. Lawrenson, 1961; as *Neck or Nothing*, translated by D. Garrick, 1766; as *Crispin, Rival of His Master*, translated by Barrett H. Clark, 1915; as *The Rival of His Master*, translated by W.S. Merwin, in *Tulane Drama Review*, 6(4), 1962.
Turcaret (produced 1709). 1709; revised version, in *Recueil des pièces mises au Théâtre Français*, 1738; edited by A. Hamilton Thompson, 1918, T.E. Lawrenson, 1969, B. Blanc, 1970, and by E. Lavielle, 1964; translated by John Norman, 1989.
La Tontine (produced 1732). In *Recueil des pièces mises au Théâtre Français*, 1738.
Les Amants jaloux (produced 1735). 1736.
Recueil des pièces mises au Théâtre Français (includes final versions of *Turcaret; Crispin, rival de son maître; La Tontine*). 1738.

Pièces forains produced at Fair of St. Germain; the dates given are those of first production: *Le Retour d'Arlequin à la foire*, 1712; *Arlequin Baron Allemand*, 1712; *Arlequin roi de Sérendib*, 1713; *Arlequin colonel*, 1714; *La Ceinture de Vénus*, 1715; *Parodie de l'opéra de Télémaque*, 1715; *Arlequin gentilhomme malgré lui*, with d'Orneval, 1716; *Le Temple d'ennui*, with Louis Fuzelier, 1716; *Le Tableau du mariage*, with Louis Fuzelier, 1716; *L'École des amants*,

with Louis Fuzelier, 1716; *L'Ombre de la foire*, with d'Orneval, 1720; *L'Île du Gougou*, with d'Orneval, 1720; *Arlequin roi des ogres; ou, Les Bottes de sept lieues*, with d'Orneval and Fuzelier, 1720; *La Queue de vérité*, with d'Orneval and Fuzelier, 1720; *Magotin*, with d'Orneval, 1721; *Prologue*, with d'Orneval and Fuzelier, 1721; *Arlequin Endymion*, with d'Orneval, 1721; *La Forêt de Dodôre*, with d'Orneval, 1721; *L'Ombre du cocher poète*, with d'Orneval and Fuzelier. 1722; *L Rémouleur d'amour*, with d'Orneval and Fuzelier, 1722; *Pierrot Romulus; ou, Le Ravisseur poli*, with d'Orneval and Fuzelier. 1722; *Arlequin barbet, pagode et médicin*, with d'Orneval, 1723; *Les Trois Comméres*, with d'Orneval, 1723; *Les Couplets en procès*, with d'Orneval, 1729; *La Reine du Barostan*, with d'Orneval, 1729; *L'Opèra-comique assiègè*, with d'Orneval, 1730; *Pièces du Thèâtre de la Foire* (includes previously uncollected plays), 1731.

Pièces forains produced at the Fair of St. Laurent; the dates given are those of first production: *Les Petits-maîtres*, 1712; *Arlequin et Mezzetin morts par amour*, 1712; *Arlequin Thétis*, 1713; *Arlequin invisible*, 1713; *La Foire de Guibray*, 1714; *Arlequin Mahomet*, 1714; *Le Tombeau de Nostradamus*, 1714; *Le Temple du destin*, 1715; *Les Eaux de Merlin*, 1715; *Colombine Arlequin; ou, Arlequin Colombine*, 1715; *Arlequin Hulta; ou, La Femme répudiée*, with d'Orneval, 1716; *La Princesse de Charizme*, 1718; *La Querelle des thêâtres*, with Joseph de Lafont, 1718; *Le Monde renversé*, with d'Orneval, 1718; *Les Amours de Nanterre*, with d'Orneval and Jacques Autreau, 1718; *Les Funérailles de la foire*, with d'Orneval and Fuzelier, 1718; *La Statue merveilleuse*, with d'Orneval, 1720; *L'Île des Amazones*, with d'Orneval, 1720; *La Fausse foire*, with d'Orneval and Fuzelier, 1721; *La Boîte de Pandore*, with d'Orneval and Fuzelier, 1721; *La Tête noire*, with d'Orneval and Fuzelier, 1721; *Le Rappel de la foire à la vie*, with d'Orneval and Fuzelier, 1721; *Le Régiment de la Calotte*, with d'Orneval and Fuzelier, 1721; *Le Jeune Vieillard*, with d'Orneval and Fuzelier, 1722; *Le Dieu du hasard*, with d'Orneval and Fuzelier, 1722; *La Force de l'amour*, with d'Orneval and Fuzelier, 1722; *La Foire des fées*, with d'Orneval and Fuzelier, 1722; *Les Captifs d'Alger*, with d'Orneval, 1724; *La Toison d'or*, with d'Orneval, 1724; *L'Oracle muet*, with d'Orneval, 1724; *La Pudeur á la foire*, with d'Orneval, 1724; *La Matrone de Charenton*, with d'Orneval, 1724; *Les Vendanges de la foire*, with d'Orneval, 1724; *L'Enchanteur Mirliton*, with d'Orneval and Fuzelier, 1725; *Le Temple du mémoire*, with d'Orneval and Fuzelier, 1725; *Les Enragés; ou, La Rage d'amour*, with d'Orneval and Fuzelier, 1725; *Les Pèlerins de la Mecque*, with d'Orneval, 1726; *Les Comédiens corsaires*, with d'Orneval and Fuzelier, 1726; *L'Obstacle favorable*, with d'Orneval and Fuzelier, 1726; *Les Amours déguisés*, with d'Orneval and Fuzelier, 1726; *Achmet et Almanzine*, with d'Orneval and Fuzelier, 1728; *La Pénélope moderne*, with d'Orneval and Fuzelier, 1728; *Les Amours de Protée*, with d'Orneval and Fuzelier, 1728; *La Princesse de la Chine*, with d'Orneval, 1729; *Les Spectacles malades*, with d'Orneval, 1729; *L'Industrie*, with d'Orneval and Fuzelier, 1730; *Zémine et Almanzor*, with d'Orneval and Fuzelier, 1730; *Les Routes du monde*, with d'Orneval and Fuzelier, 1730; *L'Indifférence*, with d'Orneval and Fuzelier, 1730; *L'Amour marin*, with d'Orneval and Fuzelier, 1730; *L'Espérance*, with d'Orneval and Fuzelier, 1730; *Roger roi de Sicile, surnommé le roi sans chagrin*, with d'Orneval, 1731; *Les Déseperés*, with d'Orneval, 1732; *Sophie et Sigismond*, with d'Orneval, 1732; *La Sauvagesse; ou, La Fille sauvage*, with d'Orneval, 1732; *Le Rival dangereux*, 1734; *Les Deux Frères*, 1734; *La Première Représentation*, 1734; *Les Mariages de Canada*, 1734; *L'Histoire de l'Opéra-Comique; ou, Les Métamorphoses de la foire*, 1736; *Le Mari préféré*, 1736; *Les Vieillards rajeunis*, with Nicolas Fromaget, 1736; *Le Neveu supposé*, 1738.

Fiction

Lettres galantes d'Aristénète. 1695.

Nouvelles aventures de l'admirable Don Quichotte de la Marche. 1704; as *The New Adventures of Don Quixote*, 1705.

Le Diable boiteux. 1707; revised editions, 1726, 1737; edited by Roger Laufer, 1970; as *The Devil Upon Two Sticks*, translated anonymously, 1708; several subsequent translations under same title; as *Asmodeus; or, the Devil Upon Two Sticks*, translated by Lesage, 1729; as *The Devil Upon Crutches*, translated by Joseph Thomas, 1841; as *The Lame Devil*, translated anonymously, 1870.

Les Mille et un jours, contes persans (satire of the Arabian Nights). 5 vols., 1710–12; translated, 1714.

Histoire de Gil Blas de Santillane. 3 vols., 1715–35; revised edition, 1747; as *The History and Adventures of Gil Blas of Santillane*, translated anonymously, 1716; as *The Adventures of Gil Blas*, translated by Tobias Smollett, 1749; several subsequent translations including by Percival Proctor, 1774, and W.H. Dilworth, 1790.

Nouvelle Traduction de Roland l'amoureux, from *Orlando inamorato* by Boiardo. 2 vols., 1717.

Histoire de Guzman d'Alfarache, from a romance by Matheo Aleman. 2 vols., 1732; as *The Pleasant Adventures of Gusman of Alfarache*, translated by A. O'Connor, 1812.

Les Aventures de Monsieur Robert Chevalier, capitaine des filibustiers dans la Nouvelle-France. 2 vols., 1732; edited by H. Kurtz, 1926; as *The Adventures of Robert Chevalier*, translated anonymously, 1747.

Une Journée des parques. 1734; as *A Day of the Fates*, translated by Adam L. Gowans, 1922.

Histoire d'Estevanille Gonzalez, surnommé le garçon de bonne humeur, from a work by Vincention Espinella. 4 vols., 1734–41; as *The History of Vanillo of Gonzales, Surnamed the Merry Bachelor*, translated anonymously, 1735; as *The Merry Bachelor*, translated anonymously, 1812.

Le Bachelier de Salamanque; ou, Les Mémoires de D. Chérubin de la Ronda. 2 vols., 1736–38; as *The Bachelor of Salamanca*, 2 vols., translated by Mr. Lockman, 1737–39; also translated by J. Townsend, 1822.

La Valise trouvée. 1740.

Other

Mélanges amusants de saillies d'esprit et de traits historiques des plus frappants. 1743.

*

Bibliography: *Essai bibliographique sur les oeuvres d'Alain-René Lesage* by H. Cordier, 1910.

Critical Studies: *Lesage et Gil Blas* by C. Dédéyan, 2 vols., 1965; *The Theatre of Alain-René Lesage* by Ardelle Striker, 1968; *Lesage; ou, Le Métier de romancier* by Roger Laufer, 1971; *The Interrelationship Between Prominent Character Types in ''Le Diable Boiteux,'' ''Gil Blas,'' and ''Le Théâtre de la Foire''* by Alain-René Lesage by Raymond Joseph Pelletier, 1977; *Lesage et le picaresque* by Francis Assaf, 1983; *L'Espagne dans la trilogie ''picaresque'' de Lesage. Emprunts littéraires, empreinte culturelle* by C. Cavillac, 2 vols., 1984; *Le Type du valet chez Moliére et ses successeurs: Regnard, Dufresny, Dancourt et Lesage* by G. Gouvernet, 1985; *Lesage: Crispin rival de son maître and Tucaret* by George Evans, 1987; *Lesage, Gil Blas* by Malcolm Cook, 1988.

* * *

Although he had already translated several Spanish plays into French, Alain-René Lesage's literary career really began in 1707 when he wrote both a successful play, *Crispin, rival de son maître* (*Crispin, Rival of His Master*) and a successful novel, *Le Diable boiteux* (*The Devil Upon Crutches*). *Crispin* is a one-act prose comedy with a complex plot involving deception and impersonation. Crispin, the valet of Valère, impersonates Damis in an attempt to make off with the dowry of Angélique, the woman whom Valère loves but who has been promised to Damis, who has secretly married another woman. The plot is foiled, the valets are forgiven, and all ends well. In its plot, use of deception, and complex love relationships, the play recalls Molière's comedies; the unscrupulous motivation of Crispin for his own gain at the expense of his master contrasts sharply with Molière's lackeys who engage in their ruses in order to help their masters.

In *Turcaret*, Lesage increases the sharpness of his satire and the comedy becomes what has been called a bitter comedy. The play presents a host of heartless, mean characters and draws its comedy from the fact that none of the victims is worthy of sympathy, but all rather deserve the punishment they receive. The plot is less complex than that of *Crispin* in that it is constructed in a series of layers of deceptions for financial gain. Lesage uses the motif of the trickster tricked, but here the trickster is no longer a likeable fellow. Turcaret, a dishonest tax farmer, has abandoned his wife, who is searching for him. In spite of his cleverness in financial matters, he has fallen under the spell of the Baronne, who is trying to dupe him; his wife in turn is being duped by her lover, the Chevalier. Both the Baronne and the Chevalier are in turn being cheated by their servants. All of the trickery is brought to a halt when Turcaret's wife arrives and he is arrested. This dénouement recalls the just punishment of Tartuffe at the close of Molière's famous comedy. The play, which was a scathing attack upon the tax farmers of the period, enjoyed enormous success in spite of the efforts of those it attacked to suppress it. *La Tontine*, also deals with the world of finance and is another comedy of manners.

In addition to these three major plays, Lesage wrote more than 100 farces. Both *Crispin* and *Turcaret* were written for the Comédie-Français; soon after the performance of *Turcaret*, Lesage quarrelled with the Comédie-Français over their acting style and associated himself with the Théâtre de la Foire, for whom he wrote his farces either alone or in collaboration.

Lesage's novels reflect the same interests and preoccupations as his plays. He is considered by many critics to be the creator of the novel of manners. *The Devil Upon Crutches* is based on the Spanish novel *Diablo conjuelo* by Guevara. Although the action takes place in Madrid, the novel is actually a satirical portrayal of 18th-century Parisian society. Asmodée, the lame devil, once he is released from the bottle in which he has been imprisoned, entertains his benefactor by lifting the roofs off the houses in Madrid (actually Paris) to reveal the activity within. The novel is at times referred to as a romance because it contains a secondary plot in which Asmodée arranges the marriage of his benefactor with Seraphina. However, the greater part of the novel is a series of anecdotes, satires of manners, and portraits.

It is in Lesage's major novel *Histoire de Gil Blas de Santillane* (*The Adventures of Gil Blas*) that we really see his development as a novelist. Lesage uses the Spanish genre of the picaresque and once again satirizes his French contemporaries under the guise of a Spanish setting. The hero experiences the traditional picaresque alternation of good and bad fortune; a whole panorama of social ranks, professions, and situations is presented. Lesage adds a moral sense to the picaresque novel for his hero Gil Blas advances not only in social rank but also in his sense of moral values. Gil Blas is both a spectator of and a participant in society, whereas the lame devil and his benefactor only observe. As Henri Coulet (*Le Roman jusqu'à la Révolution*) has stated, the novel progresses from a simple comic narration to become a work imbued with a serious realism. *Gil Blas*, unlike the typical 18th-century novel, does not depend upon the motif of love. In its panoramic portrayal of society, it foretells the novels of Balzac.

While writing *Gil Blas*, Lesage also composed two other novels: in 1732, *Histoire de Guzman d'Alfarache* (*The Pleasant Adventures of Gusman of Alfarache*), which he based heavily on the work of Mateo Aleman, and in 1734, *Histoire d'Estevanille Gonzalez* (*The History of Vanillo of Gonzales*). In 1736, he created a totally original novel (that is, no models have been found for it), *Le Bachelier de Salamanque* (*The Bachelor of Salamanca*). This novel is a delightful romp through adventure after adventure, with little concern for verisimilitude. Lesage also published *Les Aventures de Monsieur Robert Chevalier* (*The Adventures of Robert Chevalier*), in 1732, a curious novel that includes the exploits of an adventurer in the New World and several narratives treating themes used by other contemporary writers, particularly Prévost and Marivaux.

The plays and novels of Lesage were very popular during the 18th century. In the theatre, he further developed the comedy of manners and added a more satirical tone to comedy. He also contributed significantly to the development of the novel of the period, influencing many of the novelists of the time such as Marivaux and Voltaire (although Voltaire failed to acknowledge this influence). His work does, however, present certain contrasts to the body of 18th-century fiction: he turned to Spain rather than to England for his models, and he found subjects other than love for his novels.

—Shawncey J. Webb

LESSING, Gotthold Ephraim

Born: Kamenz, Saxony (then part of the Holy Roman Empire), 23 January 1729. **Education:** Educated at school of St. Afra, Meissen, 1741–46; studied theology, then medicine, at University of Leipzig, 1746–48; University of Wittenberg, 1748, 1751–52, master of arts 1752. **Family:** Married Eva König in 1776 (died 1778); one son (died in infancy). **Career:** Writer from 1748 in Berlin; editor, with Christlob Mylius, *Beiträge zur Historie und Aufnahme des Theaters*, 1750; editor, *Theatralische Bibliothek*, 1754–58, and *Briefe, die neueste Literatur betreffend (Literaturbriefe)*, 1759; official secretary to General Bogislaw von Tauentzien, Breslau, 1760–65; resident adviser to the National Theatre in Hamburg, 1767–68; librarian to the Duke of Brunswick, Wolfenbüttel, 1770–81. **Member:** Academy of Mannheim, 1776. **Died:** 15 February 1781.

PUBLICATIONS

Collections

Dramatic Works, edited and translated by E. Bell. 2 vols., 1878.
Sämtliche Schriften, edited by Karl Lachmann, revised by Franz Muncker. 23 vols., 1886–1924; reprinted 1979.
Werke, edited by Julius Petersen and Waldemar von Olshausen. 25 vols., 1925; supplement, 5 vols., 1929–35.
Werke, edited by H.G. Göpfert and others. 8 vols., 1970–79.
Werke und Briefe, edited by Wilfried Barner and others. 1985–.

Plays

Der junge Gelehrte, with others (produced 1748). In *Schriften*, 1754.
Die alte Jungfer. 1749.
Die Juden (produced 1749). In *Schriften*, 1754.
Der Freigeist (produced 1767). In *Schriften*. 1753–55.
Miss Sara Sampson (produced 1755). In *Schriften*, 1755; edited by K. Eibl, 1971; as *Miss Sarah Sampson*, translated by E. Bell, in *World Drama*, edited by Barrett Clark, 1933; as *Sara*, 1990.
Philotas (produced 1780). 1759.
Lustspiele. 2 vols., 1767.
Minna von Barnhelm (produced 1767). 1767; edited by Dieter Hildebrandt, 1969; as *The Disbanded Officer*, translated and adapted by James Johnstone, 1786; as *The School for Honor*, 1789; as *Minna von Barnhelm*, translated by F. Holcroft, 1805; also translated by W.C. Wrankmore, 1858; P. Maxwell, 1899; W.A. Steel, with *Laocoon* and *Nathan the Wise*, 1930; E. Bell, 1933; K.J. Northcott, 1972; Anthony Meech, 1990; as *The Way of Honour*, translated by E.U. Ouless, 1929; as *Minna von Barnhelm or the Soldier's Fortune: Comedy in Five Acts*, translated by Arnold P. Grunwald, 1999.
Trauerspiele. 1772.
Emilia Galotti (produced 1772). In *Trauerspiele*, 1772; as *Emilia Galotti*, translated by Benjamin Thompson, 1800; also translated by Edward Dvoretzky, 1962; F.J. Lamport, in *Five German Tragedies*, 1969; A.J.G. von Aesch, 1981.
Nathan der Weise (produced 1783). 1779; edited by P. Demetz, 1966, also edited by Renate Waack, 1979; as *Nathan the Wise*, translated by R.E. Raspe, 1781; numerous subsequent translations including by A. Reich, 1860; Robert Willis, 1868; W.A. Steel, with *Laocoon* and *Minna von Barnhelm*, 1930; Bayard Quincy Morgan, 1955; T.H. Lustig, in *Classical German Drama*, 1963; Walter F.C. Ade, 1972.

Other

Schriften. 6 vols., 1753–55; revised edition, 1771.
Fabeln. 1759; revised edition, 1777; as *Fables*, translated by J. Richardson, 1773.
Laokoon; oder, Über die Grenzen der Malerei und Poesie. 1766; as *Laocoon; or, The Limits of Poetry and Painting*, translated by W. Ross, 1836; numerous subsequent translations including by E.C. Beasley, 1853; W.B. Rönnfeldt, 1895; W.A. Steel, with *Nathan*

the Wise and *Minna von Barnhelm*, 1930; Edward Allen McCormick, 1962.

Briefe, antiquarischen Inhalts. 2 vols., 1768.

Berengarius Turonensis. 1770.

Zur Geschichte und Literatur [so-called *Wolfenbütteler Beiträge*]. 3 vols., 1773–81.

Anti-Goeze, 1–11. 1778.

Ernst und Falk. 1778–81; edited by Wolfgang Kelsch, 1981; as *Ernst and Falk*, 1854–72; as *Masonic Dialogues*, translated by A. Cohen, 1927.

Die Erziehung des Menschengeschtechts. 1780; edited by Louis Ferdinand Helbig, 1980; as *The Education of the Human Race*, translated by F.W. Robertson, 1858; also translated by H. Chadwick, in *Lessing's Theological Writings*, 1956.

Theologischer Nachlass, edited by K.G. Lessing. 1784.

Theatralischer Nachlass, edited by K.G. Lessing. 2 vols., 1784–86.

Literarischer Nachlass, edited by K.G. Lessing. 3 vols., 1793–95.

Hamburgische Dramaturgie (1767–69), edited by O. Mann. 1958; translated in *Lessing's Prose Works*, edited by E. Bell, 1897.

Lessing im Gespräch, edited by Richard Daunicht. 1971.

Briefwechsel über das Trauerspiel, edited by J. Schulte-Sasse. 1972.

Briefe aus Wolfenbüttel, edited by Günter Schulz. 1975.

Meine liebste Madam: Briefwechsel, with Eva König, edited by Günter and Ursula Schulz. 1979.

Gotthold Ephraim Lessing: A Selection of His Fables in English and German, translated by Lesley Macdonald and H. Weissenborn. 1979.

Dialog in Briefen und andere ausgewählte Dokumente zum Leben Gotthold Ephraim Lessings mit Eva Catharina König, edited by Helmut Rudolff. 1981.

Unvergängliche Prosa: die phitosophischen, theologischen und esoterischen Schriften (selections), edited by Konrad Dietzfelbinger. 1981.

Die Ehre hat reich nie gesucht: Lessing in Berlin (selections), edited by Gerhard Wolf. 1985.

*

Bibliography: *Gotthotd Ephraim Lessing* by G. and S. Bauer, 1968, revised edition, 1986; *Lessing-Bibliographie* [to 1971] by Siegfried Seifert, 1973; *Lessing-Bibliographie 1971–1985* by Doris Kuhles, 1988.

Critical Studies: *Lessing, The Founder of Modern German Literature* by Henry B. Garland, 1937, revised edition, 1962; *Lessing's Dramatic Theory* by J.G. Robertson, 1939, reprinted 1965; *G.E. Lessing: Lakoon* edited by D. Reich, 1965; *Lessing and the Enlightenment* by Henry E. Allison, 1966; *Lessing and the Language of Comedy* by M.M. Metzger, 1966, *Gotthold Ephraim Lessing* by F. Andrew Brown, 1971; *Gotthold Ephraim Lessing's Theology* by L.P. Wessell, 1977; *Lessing and the Drama* by F.J. Lamport, 1981; *Lessing's Laocoon: Semiotics and Aesthetics in the Age of Reason* by David E. Wellbery, 1984; *Minna yon Barnhelm* by Robin Harrison, 1985; *Lessing and the Enlightenment* edited by Alexej Ugrinsky, 1986; *Aesthetic Reconstructions: The Seminal Writings of Lessing, Kant and Schiller* by Anthony Savile, 1987; *The Spinoza Conversations between Lessing and Jacobi: Text with Excerpts from the Ensuing Controversy* by Gérard Vallée, 1988: *Catalyst of Enlightenment, Gotthold Ephraim Lessing: Productive Criticism of Eighteenth-Century Germany* by Edward M. Batley, 1990; *Behind the Mask: Kierkegaard's Pseudonymic Treatment of Lessing in the Concluding Unscientific Postscript* by Michelle Stott, 1993; *Lessing's Nathan the Wise and the Critics, 1779–1991* by Jo-Jacqueline Eckardt, 1993; *The Disciplines of Interpretation: Lessing, Herder, Schlegel and Hermeneutics in Germany, 1750–1800* by Robert S. Leventhal, 1994; *Absent Mothers and Orphaned Fathers: Narcissism and Abjection in Lessing's Aesthetic and Dramatic Production* by Susan E. Gustafson, 1995; *Enlightenment and Community: Lessing, Abbt, Herder and the Quest for a German Public* by Benjamin W. Redekop, 2000; *The Reconstruction of Religion: Lessing, Kierkegaard, and Niezsche* by Jan-Olav Henriksen, 2001; *Lessing's Philosophy of Religion and the German Enlightenment: Lessing on Christianity and Reason* by Toshimasa Yasukata, 2002.

*   *   *

Gotthold Ephraim Lessing is the principal literary figure of the German Enlightenment and founder of the modern German drama. Intending to follow his father into the Lutheran ministry, he made his literary debut while still a theological student with a number of comedies, for the most part conventional but in some cases (*Die Juden, Der Freigeist*) touching upon serious matters of intellectual controversy and humanitarian concern. By the time he was 25 he had also established a reputation as a trenchant critic and essayist on a wide range of topics. But the series of works upon which his lasting reputation rests begins with *Miss Sara Sampson*. This "domestic" or "middle-class" tragedy was the first successful attempt in German, indeed in European drama, at the serious and in some measure "realistic" depiction of ordinary contemporary characters, situations, and issues. This vein is continued in *Minna von Barnhelm*, a comedy of love and reconciliation in the aftermath of the Seven Years War, and the tragedy *Emilia Galotti*, a powerful amalgam of social and psychological conflict with a strong (if only implicit) note of political criticism. These works paved the way for the realistic social drama which was only to develop fully in the 19th century. Less successful was the laconic *Philotas*, a tragedy of patriotic fanaticism in a neo-classical setting. Lessing admired the Greeks, and in *Laokoon* (*Laocoon*) praised Greek art as the supreme expression of the human spirit, while attacking what he saw as perversions of the true classical tradition; similarly in the *Hamburgische Dramaturgie* (Hamburg Dramaturgy) he sought to liberate German drama from any dependence on the neo-classical style of 17th-century France. *Laocoon* also seeks to delimit the proper spheres of the various arts, attacking the doctrine "ut pictura poesis" and maintaining that while the scope of the visual arts is limited to beauty, poetry and literature should depict actions.

In the 1770s Lessing's interests returned largely to theology. Beginning with the defence of various so-called heretics and of the rights of freedom of conscience, of intellectual inquiry, and of expression, he proceeded to a number of searching examinations of the concept of religious truth. Truth itself becomes increasingly elusive, increasingly relative, but Lessing holds fast to the belief in an ultimately benevolent Providence and in the supreme importance of ethical conduct in man. This faith is proclaimed in his last play, *Nathan der Weise* (*Nathan the Wise*): here Lessing abandons his earlier realism for a kind of symbolic fairytale, in which Christian, Muslim, and Jew are ultimately revealed as members of one family. His final treatise, *Die Erziehung des Menschengeschlechts* (*The Education of the Human Race*), traces the course of human history as a dialectic between human reason and divine revelation, between developing human autonomy and a transcendent providential plan.

By his own and succeeding generations, Lessing has been regarded above all as a liberator, a champion of humanity, and an
unrelenting critic of intolerance and pretension. His major plays are
still successfully performed today; his critical writings are models of
supple and incisive German prose.

—F.J. Lamport

See the essays on *Minna von Barnhelm* and *Nathan the Wise*.

LEVI, Carlo

Born: Turin, Italy, 29 November 1902. **Education:** Educated at the
University of Turin, degree in medicine 1924. **Career:** Gave up a
brief medical practice to be a painter: exhibited first in 1923, in the
expressionist "Six Painters of Turin" exhibition, 1929, and subsequently at the Venice Bi-Annual Exhibition, where a room was
designated exclusively for his work in 1954. Active in political action
and journalism: contributor, *Giustizia e Libertà*, early 1930s; co-
editor, underground publication *Lotta politica*; arrested, 1934, exiled
in Grassano and Gagliano, both in Lucania (i.e. Basilicata), 1936,
freed under a general amnesty, 1936; resumed political activity and
emigrated to France; returned to Italy to work with the Resistance; in
Florence during conflict, 1942, re-arrested; co-editor, *La Nazione del
Popolo*, the publication of the CTLN; editor, the Action Party's
L'Italia Libera, Rome, 1945–46; frequent contributor to *La Stampa*,
Turin; independent parliamentary deputy, on the Communist Party
list, 1963–72. **Died:** 4 January 1975.

PUBLICATIONS

Fiction

L'orologio. 1950; as *The Watch*, translated by John Farrar, 1951.

Other

Cristo si è fermato a Eboli. 1945; edited by Peter M. Brown, 1965; as
    Christ Stopped at Eboli, translated by Frances Frenaye, 1947.
Paura della libertà. 1946; as *Fear and Freedom*, translated by
    Adolphe Gourevitch, 1950.
Le parole sono pietre: Tre giornate in Sicilia. 1955; as *Words Are
    Stones: Impressions of Sicily*, translated by Angus Davidson,
    1958.
Il futuro ha un cuore antico: Viaggio nell'Unione Sovietica. 1956.
La doppia notte dei tigli. 1959; as *The Linden Trees*, translated by
    Joseph M. Bernstein, 1962; as *The Two-Fold Night*, translated by
    Bernstein, 1962.
Un volto che ci somiglia: Ritratto dell'Italia. 1960.
Coraggio dei miti: Scritti contemporanei (selection), edited by Gigliola
    De Donato. 1975.
Contadini e luigini: Testi e disegni, edited by Leonardo Sacco. 1975.
Levi si ferma a Firenze (exhibition publication), edited by Carlo
    Ludovico Ragghianti. 1977.
I monotipi di Carlo Levi (catalogue). 1977.

Carlo Levi 1928–1937 (catalogue), edited by Mario De Micheli.
    1977.
Quaderni a cancelli. 1979.
Disegni 1920–1935. 1980.
In Lucania con Carlo Levi, photographs by Mario Carbone, commen-
    tary by Gino Melchiorre. 1980.
L'altro mondo è il Mezzogiorno, edited by Leonardo Sacco. 1980.
Carlo Levi e la Lucania: Dipinti del confino 1935–1936 (catalogue).
    1990.
E questo il "carcer tetro"?: Lettere dal carcere 1934–1935, edited
    by Daniela Ferraro. 1991.
Editor, *Amicizia: Storia di un vecchio poeta e di un giovane canarino*,
    by Umberto Saba. 1951.

*

Critical Studies: *Saggio su Carlo Levi* by Gigliola De Donato, 1974;
Carlo Levi by Giovanni Falaschi, 1978; *Come leggere Cristo si è
fermato a Eboli di Carlo Levi* by Mario Miccinesi, 1979; *Carlo Levi:
Dall'antifascismo al mito contadino* by Vincenzo Napolillo, 1984;
"The Politics of *Cristo si è fermato a Eboli*" by Howard Moss, in
Association of Teachers of Italian Journal, Spring 1988; *L'azione
politica di Carlo Levi* by Ghislana Sirovich, 1988; "Carlo Levi: The
Pursuit of the Essential in *Christ Stopped at Eboli*" by Vincenzo
Bollettino, in *Fusta*, 8(1), 1990; *Antifascisms: Cultural Politics in
Italy, 1943–46: Benedetto Croce and the Liberals, Carlo Levi and the
"Actionists"* by David Ward, 1996.

*   *   *

Carlo Levi was one of Italy's most prominent and influential
intellectuals of the 20th century. He trained as a doctor, receiving a
degree in medicine from the University of Turin in 1924, although he
never formally practised. He is remembered as a great humanitarian, a
painter, a writer, and a political activist, and his artistic activity was
closely allied to his socialist engagement.

Levi reached adulthood during Mussolini's Fascist regime, when
the young man's socialist ideals and Jewish heritage were not
popular. He began therefore to spend extended periods of time in
Paris with the leaders of the Italian Resistance. While in France, he
helped to found the underground organization Giustizia e Libertà
(Justice and Liberty). It was this activity which eventually led to his
arrest and exile, first in the town of Grassano and later in Gagliano.
Both villages are located in the southern Italian region of Lucania,
known today as Basilicata. It was the practice of the Fascist party to
confine political prisoners to remote areas of the peninsula in order to
separate them from other activists. (Such key cultural figures as
Antonio Gramsci, Cesare Pavese, and Leone and Natalia Ginzburg all
spent long periods of exile under Mussolini's dictatorship.) After his
release, at the end of the war, Levi was instrumental in the formulation
of the left-wing Action Party, and in the 1960s he was elected as a
senator in the independent list of the Italian Communist Party, a
position he held for almost a decade.

The principal achievement of Levi's life was undoubtedly his
campaign to achieve a greater awareness of both the gulf separating
the industrial north of Italy from the rural south, and the resultant
social problems. His political exile in Lucania was crucial for Levi, as
it placed him in direct contact with the life of local peasants—an
environment drastically different from his own upbringing in the

industrial city of Turin. The inhabitants of Lucania still lived in a feudal society, virtually ignored by the modern Italian state. The publication of *Cristo si è fermato a Eboli* (*Christ Stopped at Eboli*) resulted in a literary *cause célèbre* in post-war Italy. With a candour impossible during the years of Fascist censorship, Levi described the social conditions of the tiny village of Gagliano, presented under the fictitious name of Aliano, which became a symbol of all such forgotten towns of the south.

Like the rest of Levi's writings, the work is of a nonfictional character. Indeed, the only truly literary aspect of these documentary memoirs is to be found in the title itself, which alludes to a local popular saying. Eboli is the last major town on the road southward to Lucania, the ancient Appian Way. Christ, or rather Christianity, is a metaphor for western culture that has not made its way beyond Eboli to the wasteland of Lucania. The peasants describe themselves as less than human beings, without civilization, and cut off from the world beyond the confines of their remote region. The harsh realities of their basic existence are related by Levi in a simple, direct manner, and it is for this reason that literary critics have referred to his work as "neo-realist" in both style and content. By presenting this reality to a national audience for the first time, Levi encouraged political debate on the Southern question, a central concern in post-war Italy, and to this day not yet resolved completely. Levi's name is thus inexorably linked to his first published book and the ensuing controversy. Throughout his later life, the author worked tirelessly to promote the concerns of the inhabitants of Italy's south.

Although it may be less celebrated, one other work is actually more crucial to an understanding of Levi's philosophy. *Paura della libertà* (*Fear and Freedom*) predates *Christ Stopped at Eboli* in its date of composition, but was published in the following year, after the great success of the author's first novel. This essay, never originally intended for publication, gives us the essence of the author's philosophy. Beginning with the premise that the crisis which led to the outbreak of World War II in Europe had its origins in the soul of modern man, Levi analyses various aspects of the contemporary soul in order to demonstrate that liberty is *not* to be feared, but rather to be understood and desired as a response to the empty rhetoric of Fascist authority.

Levi's minor works are all imbued with his political philosophy, and, with one exception, are all non-fictional. The only novel written by Levi is *L'orologio* (*The Watch*), a fictionalized account of the political situation in post-World War II Italy, during the passage from the period of the Resistance under Ferruccio Parri's leadership to the Cold War and Alcide De Gasperi's government. However, for most readers, *Christ Stopped at Eboli* is considered Levi's first and foremost literary work.

—Jordan Lancaster

See the essay on *Christ Stopped at Eboli*.

LEVI, Primo

Also wrote as Damiano Malabaila. **Born:** Turin, Italy, 31 July 1919. **Education:** Educated at d'Azeglio grammar school, Turin, from 1934; Turin University, degree in chemistry (summa cum laude) 1941. **Family:** Married Lucia Morpurgo in 1947, one son and one daughter. **Career:** Participated in the Italian Resistance, 1943; captured and imprisoned first in Fossoli, then sent to Auschwitz concentration camp, 1944: freed by Russian forces, 1945; returned to Italy in 1945 after a long journey through Eastern Europe. Industrial chemist, SIVA, Turin, 1945–77: retired in order to be a full-time writer. Regular contributor to *La Stampa*, Turin. **Awards:** Campiello prize, 1963, 1982; Bagutta prize, 1967; Prato prize (for Resistance work), 1975; Strega prize, 1979; Viareggio prize, 1982; Kenneth B. Smilen award (with Saul Bellow), 1985. **Died:** Suicide, 11 April 1987.

PUBLICATIONS

Collections

Opere. 3 vols., 1987–90.
Collected Poems, translated by Ruth Feldman and Brian Swann. 1988; revised edition, 1992.
If This Is a Man; The Truce, translated by Stuart Woolf. 1996.

Fiction

Storie naturali (as Damiano Malabaila). 1966; parts translated by Raymond Rosenthal, in *The Sixth Day and Other Tales*, 1990.
Vizio di forma (stories). 1971; as *The Sixth Day*, translated by Raymond Rosenthal, in *The Sixth Day and Other Tales*, 1990.
Il sistema periodico. 1975; as *The Periodic Table*, translated by Raymond Rosenthal, 1984.
La chiave a stella (stories). 1978; as *The Monkey Wrench*, translated by William Weaver, 1986; as *The Wrench*, translated by Weaver, 1987.
Lilít e altri raconti (stories). 1981; as *Moments of Reprieve*, translated by William Weaver, 1986; also translated by Ruth Feldman, 1986.
Se non ora, quando?. 1982; as *If Not Now, When?*, translated by William Weaver, 1985.

Verse

L'osteria di Brema. 1975; as *Shema: Collected Poems*, translated by Ruth Feldman and Brian Swann, 1976.
Ad ora incerta. 1984; as *At an Uncertain Hour*, in *Collected Poems*, 1988.

Plays

Intrevista aziendale (radio play), with Carlo Carducci. 1968.
Se questo è un uomo, with Pieralberto Marché. 1966.

Other

Se questo è un uomo. 1947; as *If This Is a Man*, translated by Stuart Woolf, 1960; as *Survival in Auschwitz: The Nazi Assault on Humanity*, translated by Woolf, 1961.
La tregua. 1963; as *The Reawakening*, translated by Stuart Woolf, 1965; as *The Truce: A Survivor's Journey Home from Auschwitz*, translated by Woolf, 1965.
Abruzzo forte e gentile: Impressioni d'occhio e di cuore, edited by Virgilio Orsini. 1976.
If This Is Man; The Truce, translated by Stuart Woolf. 1979; as *Survival in Auschwitz; The Reawakening: Two Memoirs*, translated by Woolf, 1986.
La ricerca delle radici: Antologia personale. 1981.

Dialogo (dialogues), with Tullio Regge. 1984; as *Dialogo*, translated by Raymond Rosenthal, 1989; as *Conversations*, translated by Rosenthal, 1989.

L'altrui mestiere (essays). 1985; as *Other People's Trades*, translated by Raymond Rosenthal, 1989.

I sommersi e i salvati. 1986; as *The Drowned and the Saved*, translated by Raymond Rosenthal, 1988.

Racconti e saggi. 1986; as *The Mirror Maker: Stories and Essays*, translated by Raymond Rosenthal, 1989.

Autoritratto. 1987; as *Conversations with Primo Levi*, with Ferdinando Camon, translated by John Shepley. 1989.

The Voice of Memory: Interviews, 1961–87, edited by Marco Belpoliti and Robert Gordon, translated by Robert Gordon. 2001.

Translator, *Il processo*, by Kafka. 1983.

Translator, *Lo squalo da lontano*, by Lévi-Strauss. 1984.

Translator, *La via delle maschere*, by Lévi-Strauss. 1985.

*

Critical Studies: *Invito alla lettura di Primo Levi* by Fiora Vincenti, 1973, revised edition, 1990; *Primo Levi* by Giuseppe Grassano, 1981; *Prisoners of Hope: The Silver Age of the Italian Jews 1924–1974* by H. St. Hughes, 1983; "Primo Levi and the Language of Atrocity" by Adam Epstein, in *Bulletin for the Society of Italian Studies*, 20, 1987; *Il Vocabolario italiano tedesco di Se questo è un uomo di Primo Levi* by Rosemarie Wildi-Benedict, 1988; "Primo Levi's Strenuous Clarity" by Lawrence R. Schehr, in *Italica*, 66(4), 1989; *Primo Levi as Witness* edited by Pietro Frassica, 1990; *A Dante of Our Time— Primo Levi and Auschwitz* by Risa B. Sodi, 1990; *Reason and Light: Essays on Primo Levi* edited by Susan Tarrow, 1990; *Come leggere Se questo è un uomo* by Claudio Toscani, 1990; *Ascoltando Primo Levi: Organizzazione, narrazione, etica* by Giuseppe Varchetta, 1991; *Primo Levi e Se questo è un uomo* by Alberto Cavaglion, 1993; *Primo Levi: Bridges of Knowledge* by Mirna Cicioni, 1995; *Understanding Primo Levi* by Nicholas Patruno, 1995; *Primo Levi: Tragedy of an Optimist* by Myriam Anissimov, translated by Steve Cox, 1998; *Holocaust Literature: Schulz, Levi, Spiegelman and the Memory of the Offence* by Gillian Banner, 2000; *Primo Levi's Ordinary Virtues: From Testimony to Ethics* by Robert S.C. Gordon, 2001; *Primo Levi and the Politics of Survival* by Frederic D. Homer, 2001; *Memory and Mastery: Primo Levi as Writer and Witness*, edited by Roberta S. Kremer, 2001.

*   *   *

One of the most famous of contemporary Italian writers, and one of the world's best writers on the Holocaust, Primo Levi repeatedly stated that his initial motivation to write came from the need to bear witness after his deportation from Italy. He is identified, both in Italy and abroad, with his testimony on Auschwitz, which is the central theme of three of his books, and which is present to varying degrees in all his writings. However, Levi's works go far beyond mere testimony, and are characterized by the constant attempt to mediate between several different cultures and world-views.

Se questo è un uomo (*If This Is a Man*), published first in 1947, is the account of Levi's arrest, deportation, and survival in Buna-Monowitz, one of the satellite camps of Auschwitz. It stands out among Holocaust literature because of the author's determination not only to bear witness, but also to clarify and understand the "gigantic biological and social experience" of the camps. The aspect Levi

consistently stresses, as suggested in the title, is the contrast between the order of the Lager (the camp), which dehumanizes, enslaves, and finally eliminates the prisoners with "geometrical madness," and his own endeavours to ascertain "what is essential and what adventitious to the conduct of the human animal in the struggle for life." The descriptions of life, work, and death in the camp are all the more powerful because they are filtered through Levi's rigorous training as a scientist: they move inductively from particular experiences to universal reflections on what may constitute individual identity and self-awareness when everything—country, loved ones, language, name—has been forcibly removed. The numerous explicit or implicit references to Dante's *Inferno* are, rather than mere literary conceits, attempts to convey the unprecedented degradation and despair of Auschwitz through the only available analogy.

La tregua (*The Truce*) follows the survivors' eventful journey home and their gradual return to humanity from their initial utter shame and hopelessness. The survivor's odyssey through the former Soviet Union and Eastern Europe is also a quest for human contacts and co-operation, and contains, as well as constant reminders that the poison of Auschwitz is "irreparable and final, present everywhere," moments of relaxation and joy, and humorous descriptions of incongruous behaviour on the margins of civilization.

I sommersi e i salvati (*The Drowned and the Saved*), Levi's last book, written 40 years after *If This Is a Man*, is a critical re-examination of the subject matter of the first book. Its explicitly stated purpose is to ascertain "how much of the concentration camp world is dead and will not return, [and] how much is back or coming back." The title itself is problematic: through it, Levi stresses that those who survived, the "saved," did so not because of their greater worth, but because they were in some cases lucky, and in most cases aggressive and ready to co-operate with the oppressors. The "drowned," those who did not return to bear witness, were often the best people. The verbs "to know" and "to understand" recur throughout the text, highlighting the central argument: knowledge and understanding are essential, especially for those who are young 40 years after Auschwitz, because what happened once can happen again, everywhere. To keep asking questions—including uncomfortable questions about "the grey zone" of the victims who co-operated with the oppressors, and about the shame and guilt of the survivors—is emphasized as an intellectual as well as a moral duty.

The rest of Levi's creative production is characterized by the explicit desire to build a variety of bridges between different cultures. *Il sistema periodico* (*The Periodic Table*)—a collection of 21 stories, each named after an element of Dimitri Mendeleev's table, and arguably Levi's masterpiece—is at the same time a fragmentary autobiography, a history of Levi's generation, and an attempt to convey to readers of literature some aspects of the conflicts and lessons of scientific learning, specifically some aspects and meanings of the chemist's trade, which is "a particular instance, a more strenuous version of the business of living." *La chiave a stella* (*The Wrench*)—a collection of 14 stories in which a globe-trotting industrial steel-rigger recounts his humorous or dramatic successes and failures in several continents—can be read as a series of variations on the theme of skilled work, written in order to convey some of its practical and moral lessons to implied readers unfamiliar with technological processes.

Se non ora, quando? (*If Not Now, When?*)—the story of a band of Jewish guerrilla fighters who move through Nazi-occupied Eastern Europe, and finally set off from Italy for Palestine—was written with the purpose of paying homage to those Jews who had found the courage and the skills to fight back, and of explaining the cultural and ideological plurality of Jewishness, Ashkenazi Jewishness in particular, to Levi's Italian readers. It contains therefore both characters who represent diverse Jewish religious and secular ideologies, and a multiplicity of cultural references that include proverbs, songs, blessings, examples from the Talmud, folktales, and a number of carefully glossed Yiddish expressions.

The "technology-fiction" stories collected in *Vizio di forma* (*The Sixth Day*) are speculations on possible, and generally undesirable, future developments of highly industrialized capitalist societies, with an implicit continuity between the moral failings of contemporary science and the "geometric madness" of Auschwitz. The 50 or so brief essays written originally for *La Stampa*, and collected under the title *L'altrui mestiere* (*Other People's Trades*), are evidence of Levi's pleasure in extending his knowledge from the natural sciences to literature, from philology to the technology of the 1980s, and in communicating his discoveries to his readers. Levi also wrote some poetry, which ranges from the "concise and gruesome" poems written soon after his return from Auschwitz, to later meditations on individual isolation and implicit comparisons between animals and human beings.

In *The Drowned and the Saved* Levi defines an intellectual as "the person educated beyond his daily trade; whose culture is alive inasmuch as it makes an effort to renew itself, increase itself and keep up to date; and who does not react with indifference or irritation when confronted by any branch of knowledge." This clearly applies to Levi himself, and to his consistently rational and ethical production.

—Mirna Cicioni

See the essay on *The Periodic Table*.

LEZAMA LIMA, José

Born: Havana, Cuba, 19 December 1910 (some sources give 1912). Grew up in the Fort Barrancas military camp, Pensacola. **Education:** Educated at the Instituto de Havana, until 1928; University of Havana, degree in law 1938. **Family:** Married María Luisa Bautista in 1965. **Career:** Worked briefly in private law practice after graduation; official, Higher Council for Social Security, 1938–40, and from 1941; director, Department of Culture, Ministry of Education, from 1945; travelled to Mexico, 1949, Jamaica, 1950; director, Department of Literature and Publications, National Council of Culture, Havana, from 1959, and adviser, Cuban Centre for Literary Investigation. Editor or coeditor, *Verbum* (with Guy Pérez de Cisneros), 1937, *Espuela de Plata*, 1939–41, *Nadie Parecía*, 1942–44, *Orígenes*, 1944–56. One of six vice-presidents, Cuban Union of Artists and Writers (UNEAC), 1959–62. **Died:** 9 August 1976.

Publications

Collections

Obras completas, edited by Cintio Vitier. 2 vols., 1975–77.
Poesía completa. 1985.
Poesía, edited by Emilio de Armas. 1992.

Fiction

Paradiso. 1966; revised edition, edited by Julio Cortázar and Carlos Monsiváis, 1968; also edited by Eloísa Lezama Lima, 1980, and Cintio Vitier, 1988; as *Paradiso*, translated by Gregory Rabassa, 1974.
Lezama Lima (anthology). 1968.
Oppiano Licario (unfinished). 1977; edited by César López, 1989.
Juego de las decapitaciones (stories). 1982.
Relatos. 1987.

Verse

Muerte de Narciso. 1937; selection edited by David Huerta, 1988.
Enemigo rumor. 1941.
Aventuras sigilosas. 1945.
La fijeza, illustrations by René Portocarrero. 1949.
Dador. 1960.
Antología de la poesía cubana. 3 vols., 1965.
Poesía completa. 1970.
Poesía completa. 1975.
Fragmentos a su imán. 1977.

Other

Coloquio con Juan Ramón Jiménez. 1938.
La pintura de Arístides Fernández. 1950.
Arístides Fernández (essay). 1950.
Analecta del reloj (essays). 1953.
Gradual de laudes: El padre Gaztelu en la poesía. 1955.
La expresión americana (lectures). 1957.
Tratados en La Habana (essays). 1958.
Órbita (interviews and selected texts) edited by Armando Álvarez Bravo. 1966.
Los grandes todos (anthology). 1968.
Posible imagen de José Lezama Lima, edited by José Agustín Goytisolo. 1969.
Esferaimagen; Sierpe de Don Luis de Góngora; Las imágenes posibles, edited by José Agustín Goytisolo. 1970.
La cantidad hechizada (essays). 1970.
Nuevo encuentro con Víctor Manuel. 1970.
Introducción a Los vasos órficos (essays). 1971.
Algunos tratados en La Habana. 1971.
Las eras imaginarias. 1971; reprinted 1982.
Interrogando a Lezama Lima. 1972.
Cangrejos y golondrinas (stories and essays). 1977.
Cartas (1939–1976), edited by Eloísa Lezama Lima. 1979.
Imagen y posibilidad (miscellany), edited by Ciro Bianchi Ross. 1981.
El reino de la imagen (selected essays), edited by Julio Ortega. 1981.
Confluencias (essays). 1988.
La Habana, edited by Gastón Baquero. 1991.
Mi correspondencia con Lezama Lima, by José Rodríguez Feo. 1991.

*

Bibliography: "A Bibliography of the Fiction of Carpentier, Cabrera Infante, and Lezama Lima," in *Abraxas*, 1(3), 1971, and *Cuban Literature: A Research Guide*, 1985, both by David William Foster; *Sobre José Lezama Lima y sus lectores: Guía y compendio bibliográfico* by Justo C. Ulloa, 1987.

Critical Studies: *Recopilación de textos sobre José Lezama Lima* edited by Pedro Simón, 1970; *Lezama Lima: Peregrino inmóvil (Paradiso al desnudo): Un estudio crítico* by Álvaro de Villa and José Sánchez-Boudy, 1973; *Major Cuban Novelists*, 1976, and *The Poetic Fiction of José Lezama Lima*, 1983, both by Raymond D. Souza; *Novelística cubana de los años 60: Paradiso; El mundo alucinante* by Gladys Zaldívar, 1977; *José Lezama Lima: Textos críticos* edited by J.C. Ulloa, 1979; *Bajo el signo de Orfeo: Lezama Lima y Proust* by Jaime Valdiviesco, 1980; *Voces* by Cintio Vitier, 1982; *Coloquio internacional sobra la obra de José Lezama Lima* edited by A. Álvarez Bravo, 2 vols., 1984; *The American Gnosis of José Lezama Lima* by Ruben Ríos-Ávila, 1984; *El paradiso de Lezama Lima* by Carmen Ruiz Barrionuevo, 1986; *Lezama Lima* edited by E. Suárez Galbán, 1987; *José Lezama Lima; o, El hechizo de la búsqueda* by Rita V. Molinero, 1989; *José Lezama Lima's Joyful Vision: A Study of Paradiso and Other Prose* by Gustavo Pellón, 1989; *José Lezama Lima: Poet of the Image* by Emilio Bejel, 1990; *Lezama Lima. Una cosmología poética* by Lourdes Rensoli and Ivette Fuentes, 1990; *José Lezama Lima* by E. Márquez, 1991; *Assimilation/Generation/Resurrection: Contrapuntal Readings in the Poetry of José Lezama Lima* by Ben A. Heller, 1997; *From Modernism to Neobaroque: Joyce and Lezama Lima* by César Augusto Salgado, 2001.

*   *   *

The work of the Cuban writer José Lezama Lima defies classification. Poet, novelist, essayist, and one of Cuba's leading intellectuals both before and after the Revolution, he made his name in Latin America and internationally with the novel *Paradiso*. Much of Lezama Lima's work was written before 1959, but his Catholic beliefs, open discussion of homosexuality, and the more general hermeticism of his work did not make him popular with the revolutionaries. Although Lezama Lima's work was somewhat marginalized in Cuba during the 1960s and 1970s (despite his holding of a series of official posts), it has been re-assessed more recently, and he is now considered a genius and visionary by many young Cuban writers, especially after the demise of Marxism in Europe.

Lezama Lima's creative writing should be approached as an integrated, coherent corpus. His life's objectives—to plumb the mysteries of the unknown, and to search the invisible and incomprehensible world which lies beyond reality as we know it—remained constant and uncompromising throughout. From the 1930s onwards, he founded and edited a series of avant-garde literary magazines culminating in the outstanding review, *Orígenes*, which became the focal point for a new generation of Cuban writers and artists including José Rodríguez Feo, Eliseo Diego, Cintio Vitier, and Fina García Marruz. It was in *Orígenes* that Lezama Lima published the first five chapters of *Paradiso*.

Lezama Lima's poetry, which he referred to as his "dark work," was much influenced by the neo-Góngora movement of the 1920s, his early encounter with Juan Ramón Jiménez, the French avant-garde, and surrealism. His first publication, the poem *Muerte de Narciso* [Death of Narcissus], exemplifies the complex baroque style and formal rigour he was to cultivate, and is best read as a coda to his work as a whole. Narciso, the aesthete and poet, who is bedazzled by his reflected self-image, fulfils his desire to penetrate and merge with the unknown self in death. The hermetic poems of *Enemigo rumor* [Enemy Murmur], often considered his most important collection, enquire into the nature of reality beyond appearances in a profusion of oneiric and quasi-mystical images. *Aventuras sigilosas* [Discreet Adventures], more accessible and formally heterogeneous, includes poetic prose and cryptic aphorisms. *La fijeza* [Fixity] continues the quest for transcendental knowledge through art and erudition in lengthy poems, epigrammatic verse, and intensely worked poetic prose-essays. *Dador* [Donor], Lezama Lima's most extensive work of poetry, similarly exults in an outpouring of hyperbolic, esoteric imagery, while the posthumously published *Fragmentos a su imán* [Fragments to His Magnet], written during the 1970s, is less obscure. The 1985 volume of Lezama Lima's complete poetical works (dedicated in their entirety to his mother) includes poems not-previously published in books, as well as his first, hitherto unpublished collection, "Inicio y escape" [Beginning and Escape] (written 1927–32).

Poetry imbues all Lezama Lima's work. For him it was the rationality of the unreal, the cult of mystery, the revelation that conceals. According to Cintio Vitier (1958) poetry was Lezama Lima's means of penetrating reality: the image functions as axis between history and poetry, and metaphor enables the acquisition of self-knowledge through analogy. The mission of the South American poet, therefore, was to discover the nature of the image.

The key to the interpretation of Lezama Lima's prose and poetry is to be found in his collections of essays. These do not make for easy reading, but lift the essay genre to the heights of conceptual lyricism. Thematically, they are inseparable from the rest of his work and constitute further explorations into his teleology. Four collections are particularly important: *Analecta del reloj* [Analecta of the Clock], which deals with several writers including Garcilaso, Valéry, Julián de Casal, Joyce, and Mallarmé; *La expresión americana* [American Expression], where Lezama Lima posits *criollo* (Creole) art as fundamentally baroque, in as much as it is formed from the reconstitution of old myths; and *Tratados en La Habana* [Essays in Havana] and *La cantidad hechizada* [The Bewitched Quantity] which discuss poetics and aesthetics.

Lezama Lima gained international recognition with *Paradiso*, which, he claimed, could only be understood "beyond reason" by a few select readers. It was begun in the late 1940s and completed after his mother's death in 1964. To describe this masterpiece, the result of a lifetime's work, as a semi-autobiographical Bildungsroman would be to understate grossly the complex density of this unique text, referred to by Reinaldo Arenas as "the exuberant reconstruction of the life of a poet." Novel, epic, philosophical treatise, and poetic prose, *Paradiso* is usually read as an allegory or fable portraying the young hero, José Cemí (signifying "image" or "idol"), growing up and progressing through the various stages of spiritual perfection to fulfil his family destiny. The first eight chapters trace an autobiographical narrative centring on Cemí's family and childhood up to his father's death. This first half deals with the development of the embryonic man within the protective family womb dominated by the mother. The brutal sexuality of chapter eight, which describes in daring detail heterosexual and homosexual eroticism, announces the more amorphous second section of the novel. Through a series of juxtaposed anecdotes, the hero is seen to cross the intellectual quagmires presented by the philosophical disquisitions of his student companions, Fronesis and Foción (representing the positive and the negative respectively) at Upsalón (University of Havana), until he ascends out of the realms of darkness to reach the final encounter with the master himself, Oppiano Licario, in the penultimate chapter. Thus Cemí, initiated as poet and redeemed through poetry, moves towards inner growth and outer experience.

The novel is marked by a wealth of erudition and intertextual allusion, and by its exquisite language which often defies translation.

For example, from *Paradiso*: "Foción listened to him as one who watches a branch break off in relation to the stone it will cover, the tiger that it will awaken, the splash it will make in the current," or:

> After a dish of such impressive appearance, with flowing colours like those of a flambée, nearing the baroque but still gothic, owing to the baking and allegories sketched by the prawns, Doña Augusta wanted to calm the rhythm of the meal with a beet salad that had received a spatula lick of mayonnaise, crossed by Lubeck asparagus.

(translated by Gregory Rabassa)

Lezama Lima was working on the continuation of *Paradiso*, a novel entitled *Oppiano Licario*, when he died. Fragments of the novel were published posthumously in 1977 but other sections have since been discovered, and a new edition appeared in 1989. In this second novel the main characters from *Paradiso* reappear, but looming over them all is the singularly original yet paradigmatic Oppiano Licario (his name stemming from Icarus), the master and (some critics believe) the mirror-image of Lezama Lima himself. Oppiano Licario is complemented by the feminine principle, his sister Ynaca Eco who represents poetry. She infuses Cemí with divine spirituality through the sexual act, which—for Lezama Lima—was a means of reaching knowledge and of communicating with the universe.

Lezama Lima devised his impressive "poetic system" in an attempt to capture the unknown mysteries of the infinite through imagery, to express the inexpressible, and to make the invisible visible.

—Catherine Davies

LI Ang

Pseudonym for Shih Shu-tuan. **Born:** Lu-kang, Taiwan, 4 April 1952. **Education:** University of Chinese Culture, Taipei, Taiwan, B.A., 1974; University of Oregon at Eugene, M.A., 1977. **Family:** Never married; younger sister of Shih Shunü, literary critic, and Shih Shu-ch'ing, novelist. **Career:** Instructor of Dramatic Arts, University of Chinese Culture, Taipei, Taiwan. Lives in Taipei County, Taiwan. **Award:** *United Daily News* prize for fiction (Taiwan), 1983

PUBLICATIONS

Fiction

Hunsheng hechang [Mixed Chorus] (short stories). 1975.
Renjian shi [The Mundane World] (short stories). 1977.
Aiqing shiyan [Experiments in Love] (short stories). 1982.
Shafu. 1983; as *The Butcher's Wife*, translated by Howard Goldblatt, 1986; reissued as *The Butcher's Wife and Other Stories*, 1995.
Tamen de yanlei [Their Tears] (short stories). 1984.
Huaji [Flower Season] (short stories). 1985.
Anye [Dark Nights]. 1985.
Yifeng weiji de qingshu [A Love Letter Never Sent]. 1986.
Nianhua [Youthful Years]. 1988.
Miyuan [The Labyrinth]. 1991.

Beigang xianglu renren ca [Everybody Sticks Their Incense in the Beigang Burner] (novel in stories). 1997.
Zizhuan no xiaoshuo [Autobiography: A Novel]. 1999.

Other

Qunxiang [Images]. 1976.
Nüxing de yijian [A Woman's Opinion] (newspaper columns). 1984.
Waiyu [Extramarital Affairs]. 1985.
Zouchu anye [Leaving the Dark Nights] (newspaper columns). 1986.
Maomi yu qingren [Cats and Lovers] (essays). 1987.
Li Ang shuo qing [Li Ang Talks of Love] (newspaper columns). 1994.
Editor, *Ai yu zui* [Love and Sin]. 1979.
Editor, *Jing yu deng* [The Mirror and the Lamp]. 1984.

*

Bibliography: *Li Ang, Beigang xianglu renren ca*, 1997.

Critical Studies: "Sex and Society: The Fiction of Li Ang" by Howard Goldblatt, in *Worlds Apart*, 1990; "From Sexual Protest to Feminist Social Criticism: Li Ang's Works 1967–1987" by Helmut Martin, in *Chinese Literature in Southeast Asia*, 1989; "Li Ang's *The Butcher's Wife*" by Sheung-Yuen Daisy Ng, in *Modern Chinese Literature*, vol. 4, nos. 1–2, 1988; "The Labyrinth of Meaning: A Reading of Li Ang's Fiction" by Sheung-Yuen Daisy Ng, in *Tamkang Review*, vol. 18, nos. 1–4, 1988; "Li Ang's Experiments with the Epistolary Form" by Sheung-Yuen Daisy Ng, in *Modern Chinese Literature*, vol. 3, nos. 1–2, 1987; "Shapes of Darkness: Symbols in Li Ang's *Dark Night*" by Michelle Yeh, in *Modern Chinese Women Writers*, 1989; "From Utopian to Dystopian World: Two Faces of Feminism in Contemporary Taiwanese Women's Fiction" by Yingying Chien, in *World Literature Today*, vol. 68, nos. 1, 1994; "Panni yu jiushu—Li Ang guilai de xunxi" ["Rebellion and Redemption—the Message of Li Ang's Homecoming"] by Lin I-chieh, in Appendix to *Tamen de yanlei* by Li Ang, 1984; "Protest of a Woman Author against Reckless Accusations" (self-interview), by Li Ang, in *Modern Chinese Writers: Self-Portrayals*, 1992.

* * *

Li Ang has often acknowledged that she draws most of her creative inspiration from the coastal town of Lu-kang in central Taiwan, where she was born. Generally regarded as one of Taiwan's most talented and controversial writers, she began writing at the age of sixteen, when she published her first story, "Flower Season," which deals with a young woman's curiosity about sex at a time when such topics were taboo. Over the next few years, before entering college in Taipei, she published several more astonishingly mature stories, such as the Kafkaesque "Wedding Ritual" and the highly erotic "Curvaceous Dolls," all of which deal with sexual awakening and fantasies, but with a degree of authorial distance that makes these stories seem gender-neutral. Nonetheless, traditional Chinese society's aversion to the discussion of sex inevitably drew attacks to her, especially with the publication of a story titled "The Mundane World" in 1973, written while the author was still in college. Set in the environment of a public school, the author examines the tragic results of a culture-wide suppression of sexuality among the young. Interestingly, according to the author herself, not until she went to college did she actually see herself as a woman, and a more feminine tone than was apparent in her earliest works began to creep into her stories.

After returning from the University of Oregon in 1977, M.A. degree in hand, she recommenced her writing career, continuing to focus on issues of love, sexuality and, in particular, the abuse of women in a modernizing world. The latter culminated in the publication of an internationally acclaimed short novel, *Shafu* (*The Butcher's Wife*), which won Taiwan's prestigious *United Daily News* prize for fiction in 1983. Long before domestic abuse and violence against women had become a widely recognized problem, even in the United States, *The Butcher's Wife* brought the issue to the attention of Taiwanese society, which, not surprisingly, led to more attacks, many of them personal and extremely vicious. The novel centers on an abusive butcher who uses food to control his wife sexually and psychologically. The protagonist is forced to prostitute herself to her husband, while women of the neighborhood pass on moralistic judgment and scathing criticism of her. Driven by the double oppression of marital brutality and social pressures, she eventually takes up her husband's knife and butchers him in the same fashion that he slaughters pigs. Readers generally agree that this is a novel attacking the Chinese patriarchal society with the graphic descriptions of people's most basic needs—food and sex. But what has often escaped their attention is that the neighborhood women actually assist in pushing her farther into the inferno of abuses. In this sense, contrary to what many of her most severe critics have claimed, Li Ang is not attacking Chinese men, but Chinese tradition; in her own words, the novel is more about humanity than about women.

Although the issue of sexual politics in the Chinese context remains Li Ang's dominant theme, she nonetheless constantly seeks ways to broaden her scope and, more importantly, keep up with the rapid social and cultural changes in contemporary Taiwan. Her second novel, *Anye* [Dark Nights], is exemplary in this regard, although it is generally considered to be an artistically inferior, if more daring, novel. Depicting a group of middle- and upper-class men and women in the increasingly materialistic world of cosmopolitan Taipei, *Anye* attempts to capture the complexities of modern life without losing sight of the issues that concern the author most: infidelity, humiliation, and manipulation in the business world, and how women figure in the neverending struggle with men. Explicit depictions of sexual activities remain the center of controversy over this work, although Li Ang's detractors often ignore the parallels between sexual conquest and domination in the ruthless world of business.

In 1991, four years after the lifting of martial law in Taiwan, Li Ang wrote her most political novel, *Miyuan* [The Labyrinth]. As writers began to publicly explore the effects of the "White Terror" of the Chiang Kai-shek regime, Li Ang merged the dual quest of recapturing both family and national (Taiwanese) history, releasing the secrets of the past through the protagonist's relationship with a man who mediates that quest, both intellectual and sexually. Even given the warming intellectual and political climate of the time, Li Ang was forced to self-publish this explosive novel (it was later re-released by one of Taiwan's most highly respected literary presses). Li Ang's experience as a female participant in a predominantly male politic milieu prompted her to compose her next work, *Beigang xianglu renren ca* [Everybody Sticks Their Incense in the Beigang Burner], a collection of four linked stories on sex and politics. A scandal erupted when one of the stories was serialized in a leading newspaper, *The China Times*, when readers identified the characters in her story with real life political figures: a flamboyant former DPP

Chairman and the female secretary of public relations. The secretary threatened to sue Li Ang for slander, which helped increase sales of the book to an unprecedented level. Unfortunately, the controversy obscured the core issues of Li Ang's work: an exploration of the intricate connection between sex and politics in post martial-law Taiwan, an examination of the role of women in the formation of a true opposition party in Taiwan's democratization process, and an investigation of the ways in which women obtain political power. Ultimately, the work forces the reader to ponder the fundamental question of feminism, that is, whether women should empower themselves by exploiting their sexuality.

Never content to cater to her reading public or shy away from controversy, Li Ang has been a catalyst for change in bringing important social, political, and cultural issues to the Taiwanese people's attention: from her earliest work, which tackles female sexuality and fantasy, to *The Butcher's Wife*, which deals with domestic abuse and sexual politics, to *Anye*, which exposes the roles of sex and women in the business world, and finally, to her latest works, *Beigang xianglu renren ca*, and *Zizhuan no xiaoshuo* [Autobiography: A Novel], both of which focus on women and politics, with the latter adding fiction to the known facts of an early 20th century feminist and member of the Taiwan Communist Party, narrated as autobiography.

—Sylvia Li-Chun Lin

LI BAI

Also known as Li Po and Li Taibo. **Born:** Central Asia, in 701 or possibly 705; brought up in Sichuan province, China. **Family:** Married four times. **Career:** Spent a few years as a Daoist hermit in his teens, and trained as a knight-errant before the age of 25. Spent early life in wandering; was summoned to the court of Emperor Xuanzong, 742, and retained as an unofficial court poet until 745: fell victim to the intrigue of the influential court officials and left the court in disgrace; lived as wanderer again, and entered service of Prince Lin, brother of Emperor Suzong, 757, but was banished after Lin's defeat in a bid for the throne, 759. **Died:** 762.

PUBLICATIONS

Works

Li Taibai wenji (works). 1717 (based on 8th-century manuscripts); modern editions: *Sibu beiyao*, 1936—; *Li Taibai quanji* [Complete Works], edited by Wang Qi, 3 vols., 1977; selections: *Lyrics*, translated by Michitaro Hisa and William Wells Newell, 1905; "Cathay," translated by Ezra Pound, in his *Poetry*, 1915; *Lustra*, translated by Ezra Pound, 1916; *Li Po: The Chinese Poet*, translated by Shigeyoshi Obata, 1922; *Tu Fu and Li Po: Selected Poetry*, edited and translated by Arthur Cooper, 1973; *Li Po: A New Translation* (bilingual edition), translated by Sun Yu, 1982; translated by Bradford S. Miller, 1997.

Endless River: Li Po and Tu Fu, A Friendship in Poetry, edited by Sam Hamill. 1993.

Three Chinese Poets: Translations of Poems by Wang Wei, Li Bai, and Du Fu, translated by Vikram Seth. 1992.

Selected Poems of Li Po, translated by David Hinton. 1996.

*

Critical Studies: *The Poetry and Career of Li Po* by Arthur Waley, 1950; "On Li Po" by E.O. Eide, in *Perspectives on the T'ang,* edited by A.F. Wright and D. Twitchett, 1973; *The Genius of Li Po* by Wong Siu-kit, 1974; *The Poet Li Po* by Yung Teng Chia-yee, 1975; "The Lonely Journey: The Travels of Li Po" by J.W. Fenn, in *Asian Culture Quarterly,* 8, 1980; "Li Po and Tu Fu: A Comparative Study" by Huang Kuo-pin, in *Renditions,* 21–22, 1984.

* * *

No poet, except Du Fu, holds so prominent a position as Li Bai among Chinese classical poets since the Tang dynasty. He was highly praised by the poets of his time, earning the title "celestial poet." His poems, especially because of their exuberant and romantic style, were admired and imitated by later poets, and also widely read by succeeding generations.

Li Bai was born of a wealthy family and lived an extravagant life when he was young. He learned swordplay and in his early years the scope of his reading was wide. At the age of 26 he left his native place and became a poor wanderer, travelling over most of the country. He visited famous mountains and rivers, Daoist priests and temples. As his reputation spread, he was recommended to the imperial court and soon summoned by the Emperor to Chang'an, the capital. Although he wanted to become involved in the administration of state affairs and to help improve the quality of people's lives, he was employed only to write poems for the Emperor's pleasure. He despised the corrupt and treacherous court officials. (On one occasion, he forced Gao Lishi, a powerful eunuch, to take off his boots in the presence of the Emperor.) After he left the court, he went through great hardships in his later life of wandering.

His love for the beauty of nature and his legendary experiences contributed a great deal to the enduring themes and style of his poems. In many poems he described the beautiful landscape of the swift Yellow River, the precipitous mountains, and the long and wide Yangzi River. Some of these poems, such as "Viewing the Waterfall at Mount Lu," rank as masterpieces. The scene of the falls delineated in the verse: "Flying waters descending straight three thousand feet, Till I think the Milky Way has tumbled from the ninth height of Heaven" is like a beautiful picture.

He was a patriot, and his poems express his love for the country and sympathy for the sufferings of the common people. He condemned the evil war in his verse: "White bones are piling up like hills, Why should the people suffer?" Failing to fulfil his wish to save the common people and help the country out of great difficulties, he nevertheless severely criticized and mocked the debauched and treacherous court officials in his poems, while, on the other hand, he revealed his personal anguish and melancholy. From time to time he found escape from his worldly trouble in retirement and indulgence in wine: "I'm glad to talk and drink good wine, Together with my hermit friend. I'm drunk and you're merry and glad, We both forget the world is sad." As he was unsatisfied with life, he expressed in his poems his wish to withdraw from human society and seek happiness by living in seclusion. For him wine was indispensable. He said bluntly in "The Song of Wine": "I wish to drink myself drunk, never to become sober again."

Among other poems, "I Miss My Husband When Spring Comes," "Lovesick," and "The Crows Caw in the Evening" are expressive of faithful love and the grief of lovers separated by long military service.

He described in "Ballads of Four Seasons" the feeling of a woman longing for her husband to return home: "When will they put down the barbarians and my good man come home from his far campaign?" Elsewhere he showed his sympathy with women forsaken by their husbands. "Waiting in Vain," for example, exhibits grudges borne by a fair lady against her lover who has probably deserted her: "Wet stains of tears can still be seen. Who, heartless, has caused her the pain?"

Li Bai learned from his predecessors and from the folk songs and ballads (*yuefu* poetry). He inherited the traditions of Chinese poetry but developed his own style, characterized by his brilliant imagination, exquisite but not ornate language, and by delicate, vivid, yet natural descriptions. As far as aesthetic value is concerned, in the history of Chinese literature there is hardly any ancient poet of later generations who could equal him.

—Binghong Lu

See the essays on "Hard is the Road to Shu" and "Invitation to Wine."

LI PO

See LI BAI

LI TAIBO

See LI BAI

LIMA, José Lezama

See LEZAMA LIMA, José

LINNA, Väinö

Born: Urjala, Finland, 20 December 1920. **Military Service:** Served in the army during Finland's Continuation War against the Soviet Union, 1941–44. **Family:** Married Kerttu Seuri in 1945; two children. **Career:** Worked on farms and in the mill industry; factory worker, Tampere, 1938–55. **Awards:** Finnish state literature prize, 1959, 1960; Nordic prize, 1963; Finnish cultural prize, 1974. **Died:** 21 April 1992.

PUBLICATIONS

Fiction

Päämäärä [The Goal]. 1947.
Musta rakkaus [Black Love]. 1948.
Tuntematon sotilas. 1954; translated as *The Unknown Soldier,* 1957.
Täältä Pohjantähden alla [Here under the North Star]. 3 vols., 1959–62.

Other

Oheisia: esseitä ja puheenvuoroja [By the Way] (essays and addresses). 1967.
Murroksia: esseitä, puheita ja kirjoituksia [Transitions] (essays, articles, and talks). 1990.

*

Critical Studies: "Väinö Linna: A Classic in His Own Time" by Yrjö Varpio, in *Books from Finland*, 11(3), 1977; "What Do the People Sing? Singing in Väinö Linna's Novel *The Unknown Soldier*" by Jyrki Nummi, in *Proceedings of the Sixth Annual Meeting of the Finno-Ugric Studies Association of Canada*, edited by Joel Ashmore Nevis, 1989.

*　*　*

Väinö Linna's breakthrough novel, *Tuntematon sotilas* (*The Unknown Soldier*), has become a noteworthy critical and popular success. The novel has been translated into more than 20 languages, made into two films, adapted for stage performances, and has inspired the composition of an opera. The novel is often compared with Erich Maria Remarque's *Im Westen nichts Neues* (*All Quiet on the Western Front*) and Norman Mailer's *The Naked and the Dead*, invariably to *The Unknown Soldier*'s advantage. Upon its first appearance in 1954, however, the novel engendered more critical controversy in Finland than any other literary work to that date—controversy which subsequently came to be known as "the literary war." Traditionalists, in particular, saw the novel as destroying the idealistic myth about the Finnish soldier as an unselfish, ultra-nationalistic hero, a myth which the army, media, and educational institutions had been perpetuating over 30 years. Rather, *The Unknown Soldier* reflected a general change in attitudes in post-war Finland. In retrospect, it is difficult to say to what extent the general attitudes of the people influenced the novel, and the novel shaped the thoughts and attitudes of the people. For the post-war generations *The Unknown Soldier* became, besides an anti-war novel, a historical document, not in the traditional documentary sense, but in the sense that it chronicled the *experience* of Finland's 20th-century war, stripped of both varnish and rhetoric.

The Unknown Soldier describes the 1941–44 war between Finland and the (then) Soviet Union from the point of view of the ordinary rank-and-file soldier. More specifically, the central characters of the novel are a platoon of machine-gunners who belong to Finland's 11th division, troops who at the beginning of hostilities are the first to endure the enemy's firepower at its most devastating. Linna's mode of writing about the men's extraordinary physical and psychological tenacity, and their ability to adjust to the inhuman demands made on them, separates his novel from *All Quiet on the Western Front* and *The Naked and the Dead*. By showing the ability of human intelligence to carry on a dialogue with itself, to differentiate between what is valuable and what is worthless even in the midst of the worst adversity, Linna portrays bitter reality in a positive light rather than as a manifestation of all-encompassing moral decay. Moreover, each of Linna's soldiers has an exceptionally strong sense of his own worth as a human being, and it is this unshakeable sense of self that gives him his remarkable strength to endure, no matter how miserable and insignificant his existence.

Although *The Unknown Soldier* shows the utter futility and mindlessness of war, it consciously avoids utopian sentimentalism.

Moreover, Linna's opposition is not to nationalism as such, but its deterioration into ultra-nationalism which valorizes combat and attaches some kind of human value to war. His realistic treatment of his subject—a war story told at "ground-level" where the results of decisions made by those in power are experienced at their toughest; where utter misery silences rather than gives birth to jingoistic sentiments; and where fear is as much a physical as an emotional experience—searches and finds in the novel's characters what might be termed "the core human." Thus despite being a war novel, its characters ultimately affirm life and the novel retains a positive view of humanity.

Linna's soldiers are from different parts of Finland and speak in the dialects of their home regions. The idiosyncrasies of speech not only provide much of the humour in the novel, but also function to emphasize the individual personalities of the men, thus adding life to the novel. The fact that each man has his own unique way of expressing himself separates him from his comrades, however common their day-to-day experiences; hence his colloquial mode of speech becomes a principal feature of each soldier, and each turn of dialogue corresponds with the speaker's nature, resulting in living, multi-dimensional characterizations.

The soldiers are an amalgam of loggers, factory workers, and simple farmers, each with virtues and vices, who nevertheless accomplish heroic deeds which lead at times to victories. Linna's soldier is more often than not a complaining individualist with an abundant reserve of black humour, who rises above the propagandist rhetoric about war and who fights when necessary out of fear of death and out of loyalty to his comrades, not as a reflex to army discipline. In that he fights and gives his life for his country, despite his irreverent attitude, lies his greatness. The central character in the novel, the stubborn farmer, Antti Rokka, is just such a rugged individualist. In drawing his character, Linna's creative brilliance produces a Colossus, one who never learns to obey orders with which he does not agree, and yet who as a soldier is unmatched.

It has been argued that Linna's treatment not only misrepresents (if not vilifies), but certainly diminishes the glory bestowed upon the Finnish soldier by military experts familiar with the Finnish army's conduct during the so-called Winter War and the subsequent 1941–44 war. They maintain that no army could have fought as effectively without iron-fisted discipline. Military-historical arguments aside, *The Unknown Soldier* also acknowledges the size and weight of the contribution the soldiers made; this is particularly true of the second half of the novel. In his own way Linna acknowledges what is generally known, namely that it was the Finnish soldier who guaranteed Finnish independence although both wars ended in defeat for Finland.

Linna's employment of the rich variations in Finnish language, both in terms of colloquialisms and regional dialects, not only links this epic work with the Finnish prose tradition, but makes it an unusually challenging and problematic novel to translate. Much of the humour in the novel, the positive contrast to the cruelty and misery of war, becomes lost and the psychological dimensions of the characters are diminished in translation. Among foreign-language editions, the Swedish translation has been the most successful and the English-language edition perhaps the least impressive owing, in part, to arbitrary omissions and mistranslations. Nevertheless, reception of the novel has been as varied outside as within the sphere of its original language. It has run the gamut from being viewed as a source of study for military reserve officers, a chronicle of 20th-century history in part, a fascinating tale of battle between a modern David and Goliath, a documentation of the Finland-Soviet War to, finally, what *The Unknown Soldier* is above all else, a representative of the international genre of war novels. As such it is ranked among the best of its kind.

—Seija Paddon

LISPECTOR, Clarice

Born: in Tchetchelnik, Ukraine, USSR (now independent republic), 10 December 1925. Family moved to Brazil, 1925, and settled in Recife, 1927. **Education:** Educated at the Ginásio Pernambuco, 1935–36; Colégio Sílvio Leite, Rio de Janeiro, 1937; Colégio Andrews, Rio de Janeiro; National Faculty of Law, Rio de Janeiro, 1941–44, degree in law 1944. **Family:** Married Mauri Gurgel Valente in 1943 (separated 1959); two sons. **Career:** Editor and contributor, *Agência Nacional* and *A Noite*, while still a student, 1941–44; left Brazil because of her husband's diplomatic postings: lived in Europe (principally Naples and Berne), 1944–52, and in the United States, 1952–59; returned to Rio de Janeiro after separation from her husband, 1959. **Awards:** Graça Aranha Foundation prize, 1944; São Paulo Cármen Dolores Barbosa prize, 1962; Golfinho de Ouro prize, 1969; Tenth National Literary Library Competition prize, 1976. **Died:** 9 December 1977.

PUBLICATIONS

Collections

Antologia cometada, edited by Samira Youssef Campedello and Benjamin Abdalla. 1981.
Selected Cronicas, translated by Giovanni Pontiero. 1996.

Fiction

Perto do coração selvagem. 1944; as *Near to the Wild Heart*, translated by Giovanni Pontiero, 1990.
O lustre. 1946.
A cidade sitiada: romance. 1948; revised edition, 1964; translated by Giovanni Pontiero, 1995.
Alguns contos (stories). 1952.
Laços de família (stories). 1960; as *Family Ties*, translated by Giovanni Pontiero, 1972.
A maçã no escuro. 1961; as *The Apple in the Dark*, translated by Gregory Rabassa, 1967.
A Paixão Segundo G.H. 1964; edited by Benedito Nunes, 1988; as *The Passion According to G.H.*, translated by Ronald W. Sousa, 1988.
A Legião Estrangeira (stories and chronicles). 1964; as *The Foreign Legion*, translated by Giovanni Pontiero, 1986.
O mistério do coelho pensante (for children). 1967.
A mulher que matou os peixes (for children). 1968; as *The Woman Who Killed the Fish*, translated by Earl E. Fitz, in *Latin American Literary Review*, 32, July-December 1988.
Uma aprendizagem; ou, o livro dos prazeres. 1969; as *An Apprenticeship; or, The Book of Delights*, translated by Richard A. Mazzara and Lorri A. Parris, 1986.
Felicidade clandestina: contos. 1971.

Água viva. 1973; as *The Stream of Life*, translated by Elizabeth Lowe and Earl E. Fitz, 1989.
A imitação da Rosa (stories). 1973.
Onde estivestes de noite (stories). 1974; selection in *Soulstorm*, 1989.
A via crucis do corpo (stories). 1974; selection in *Soulstorm*, 1989.
A vida intima de Laura (for children). 1974.
Cont escolhidos (stories). 1976.
A hora da estrela. 1977; as *The Hour of the Star*, translated by Giovanni Pontiero, 1986.
Um sopro de vida: pulsações. 1978.
Quase de verdade (for children). 1978.
A Bela e a Fera (stories). 1979.
Soulstorm (stories), translated by Alexis Levitin. 1989.

Other

De corpos inteiro (interviews). 1975.
Seleta, edited by Renato Cordeiro Gomes and Amariles Guimarães Hill. 1975.
Visão do esplendor: impressôes leves. 1975.
Para não esquecer (essays). 1978.
A descoberta do mundo (diary). 1984; as *Discovering the World*, translated by Giovanni Pontiero, 1992.
Reading with Clarice Lispector (miscellany), edited by Hèléne Cixous, translated by Verena Andermatt Conley. 1990.
Translator, *O retrato de Dorian Gray*, by Oscar Wilde. 1974.

*

Bibliography: *Brazilian Literature: A Research Guide* by David William Foster and Walter Rela, 1990.

Critical Studies: "Existence in *Laços de família*" by Rita Herman, in *Luso-Brazilian Review*, 4(1), 1967; *Clarice Lispector* by Assis Brasil, 1969; "Lispector: Fiction and Comic Vision" by Massuad Moisés, translated by Sara M. McCabe, in *Studies in Short Fiction*, 8(1), 1971; "The Drama of Existence in *Laços de família*," in *Studies in Short Fiction*, 8(1), 1971, and "Lispector: An Intuitive Approach to Fiction," in *Knives and Angels* edited by Susan Bassnett, 1990, both by Giovanni Pontiero; *Leitura de Clarice Lispector* by Benedito Nunes, 1973; "Clarice Lispector and the Lyrical Novel: A Re-Examination of *A maça no escuro*," in *Luso-Brazilian Review*, 14(2), 1973, "The Leitmotif of Darkness in Seven Novels by Clarice Lispector," in *Chasqui: Revista de Literatura Latinoamericana*, 7(2), 1978, "Freedom and Self-Realization: Feminist Characterization in the Fiction of Clarice Lispector," in *Modern Language Studies*, 10(3), 1980, "Point of View in Clarice Lispector's *A hora da estrela*," in *Luso-Brazilian Review*, 19(2), 1982, and *Clarice Lispector*, 1985, all by Earl E. Fitz; "Narrative Modes in Clarice Lispector's *Laços de família*: The Rendering of Consciousness" by Maria Luísa Nunes, in *Luso-Brazilian Review*, 14(2), 1977; "Clarice Lispector: Articulating Women's Experience" by Naomi Lindstrom, in *Chasqui: Revista de Literatura Latinoamericana*, 8(1), 1978; *A escritura de Clarice Lispector* by Olga de Sá, 1979; "Clarice Lispector and the Clamor of the Ineffable" by Daphne Patai, in *Kentucky Romance Quarterly*, 27(2), 1980; *Clarice Lispector* edited by Samira Y. Campedello and Benjamin Abdalla, 1981; *Clarice Lispector: esboço para um possivel retrato* by Olga Borelli, 1981; *Clarice Lispector* by Berta Waldman, 1983; *O alto criador de Clarice Lispector* by Nicolino Novello, 1987; *Clarice Lispector: A Bio-bibliography*, edited by Diane E. Marting, 1993; *Passionate Fictions: Gender, Narrative, and Violence in Clarice Lispector* by Marta Peixoto, 1994; *Clarice Lispector: Spinning the Webs of Passion* by Maria José Somerlate Barbosa, 1997; *Sexuality and Being in the Poststructuralist Universe of Clarice Lispector: The Différance of Desire* by Earl E. Fitz, 2001.

*   *   *

When Clarice Lispector published her first novel, *Perto do coração selvagem* (*Near to the Wild Heart*), aged 17, the critical establishment hailed this event as a turning point in Brazilian fiction, heralding as it did the advent in Brazil of the technique of stream of consciousness first experimented with in Europe by James Joyce and Virginia Woolf. The significance of the assimilation of this formal innovation to Brazilian literature encompassed (as it had in the case of its European precursors) implications of much greater import than the purely stylistic, gesturing as it did—in the case of Brazil three decades later than in Europe—towards the beginning of the articulation of a crisis of modernity which had not truly made itself felt in that country until the period immediately following the world Depression in the 1930s. It is in the context of the emergence of a new reality demanding articulation, and of the difficulties inherent in this process of articulation, earlier confronted by the European Modernists' fragmented vision of the ruins of the old order and the uncharted territory of a post-World War I scenario, that Lispector's writing must be understood; and it is in the light of this awareness, too, that the fundamental importance in Lispector's writing of language itself as that which must at once be struggled against and drawn upon in the formulation of a new reality ought to be emphasized. In her narrative fiction, therefore, much more crucially than the social problems that underwrite the Brazilian crisis of modernity the Lispector's own vision (imminent national bankruptcy, poverty, unequal distribution of wealth, the situation of women under patriarchy), the impossibility of reaching a coherent verbal expression for these dilemmas figures as the immediate and irresolvable impasse of protagonists whose perception or gaze disintegrates the very reality they seek to understand.

It is discourse itself, therefore, and the brutal authoritarianism of a language rendered all-powerful in the face of the protagonists' existential difficulties, which rules the narrative: discourse as the demiurge of self and other, discourse as the creator, source and definer of the narrative world, discourse as the linguistic articulator, classifier, and omnipotent decision-maker concerning character, time, and place in these universes of fiction. Whether dealing with first- or third-person narration, therefore, it is language itself as the instrument of gnosis that beckons character and reader with the promise of understanding, only immediately to shatter that possibility; and it is the focus on precisely that moment of fragmentation, the moment that separates the time when knowledge, truth, and comprehension are still possible from the non-linearity and disconnection of the untimely space following the instant of breakage, that is the hallmark of Lispector's writing. She dwells repeatedly, throughout each of her novels and short stories on the process whereby the everyday, the ordinary, the linguistically, intellectually, and emotionally comprehensible is set adrift, stripped of cohesion and abandoned as the disorderly remnant of a previous, now inconceivable old order. In this new reality, the focus of narrative concern in the unfolding subjectivity of the protagonists, of the world through their eyes, the process of gazing upon an erstwhile ordinary reality unwarningly rendered imponderable; and in the process, too, the concept of "ordinary reality" becomes itself questionable, or impossible, in the face of the abrupt defamiliarization of the familiar, and its subsequent destruction.

Reading Lispector, therefore, requires the acceptance of loss on the part of the reader, loss of old points of reference, of established readership assumptions, of logic, received wisdom and expectation, and the tacit readerly agreement to flow with the language of the text, and to surrender to the disorder that this language carries in its wake, put to a use that is not now necessarily the fixation of narrative meaning, but its postponement or abolition.

In consideration Lispector's writing, the uncharted intellectual/ existential/emotional terrain that her protagonists' subjectivity opens up, and in confronting the manner in which these protagonists' dilemmas force us to ask questions concerning their participation or exclusion from reality, the tenability of previous definitions or normality and consciousness, linearity of time, circumscription of space, and the possibility of meaning, we are also, as readers, forced to entertain the hypothesis that logic, language, and meaning are not monopolies of a single origin, but are rather defined by multiplicity, plurality, and dispersal, and that pre-existent, transcendental meaning, therefore, is not inevitably grasped by the reading spectator, but is possibly elusive and may not exist as a single entity.

It is this acceptance of disruption of reader expectation, in other words of the reader's entitlement to processed and digestible meaning, which is required of Lispector's readers, and her refusal to provide plot or clear-cut character outlines is also what forces her reader to posit the likelihood that here is indeed a new language focused on a new reality, not just an old one put to (relatively) new usage. Language, in Lispector, is of the essence, while refusing essential, unambiguous meaning: language is life-giving and life-destroying. It is the workings of language itself which we witness in these narratives, allowing us as readers to observe its backstage manoeuvres, discarding the realist need for readerly suspension of disbelief and replacing it instead with an exhibition of its narrative status as language *per se*, language at play in realities in invented, rather than language as a transparent window held up to a pre-existing, comprehensible reality.

Lispector's fiction is peppered with moments of epiphany or revelation; this is not, however, the revelation of an ultimate or divine meaning or explanation, but only the realization that any meaning attained is likely to be so temporary and dispersed as to relinquish the right to the very concept of meaningfulness. In terms of plot parameters or character subjectivity, this realization, in works such as *A hora da estrela* (*The Hour of the Star*) or "A imitação da rosa" ("The Imitation of the Rose"), potentially leads to a temporary or indefinite suspension of sanity, or affirmation of madness. If, as is the case with Laura in the latter text, her madness allows us a glimpse of her immersion into a new, alternative reality, it is a reality that our language, circumscribed by the limitations of logic and reason cannot convey, being reduced instead to underpinning it through images of crazed incoherence. Madness, therefore, which becomes simply an alternative consciousness following the moment of severance with everyday reality, is a leitmotif in this writer's work. Another characteristic is the relinquishing of a social underpinning in favour of prioritizing philosophical abstraction and individual subjectivity.

The latter point elicits the question of whether or not there is a dimension of social and political concern to Lispector's work, a question all the more pertinent given her frequent choice of women or the dispossessed as central to the process of subjective fragmentation at the heart of her fiction. Several critical readings have pinpointed successfully a clear social preoccupation with both feminist and material or class issues in her writing, and a thematic constancy in her consideration of problems of human disenfranchisement as a variety of levels. Lispector remains, at all these levels, therefore, one of the essential voices of Brazilian modernism and continues to influence contemporary experimental authors and intellectuals within and outside Brazil.

—Maria Manuel Lisboa

LIVY

Born: Titus Livius in Patavium (now Padua), northern Italy, in 64 or 59 BC. **Family:** Had one daughter and one son. **Career:** Settled in Rome, c. 29 BC; came to know the emperor Augustus who expressed an interest in his work; encouraged the historical studies of the future emperor Claudius. **Died:** AD 12 or 17.

PUBLICATIONS

Works

Ab urbe condita, as *History of Rome*, edited by Charles William Stocker. 2 vols., 1838–44; also edited by W. Weissenborn, revised by Müller and Heraeus, 1887–1908; Books XXI–XXII edited by T.A. Dorey, 1971, Books XXVI–XXX by P.G. Walsh, 2 vols., 1982–86, Books XXXI–XL by J. Briscoe, 2 vols., 1991; Books I–X and XXI–XXXV edited by R.M. Ogilvie, C.F. Walters, A.H. McDonald, and others, 1919–74; also edited by J. Bayet and Paul Jal, 1947–; as *Roman History*, translated by Philemon Holland, 1600; also translated by William Gordon, 1783; J.H. Freese, A.J. Church, and W.J. Brodribb, 1898; as *History of Rome*, translated by George Baker, 6 vols., 1797, revised edition, 1864; also translated by D. Spillan, Cyrus Edmonds, and William A McDevitte, 4 vols., 1849–50; J.H. Freese and Edward Sprague Weymouth, 1892–93; William M. Roberts, 1912–24; B.O. Foster, E.T. Sage, A.C. Schlesinger, and F.G. Moore [Loeb Edition; bilingual], 14 vols., 1919–59; *The Early History of Rome* (Books I–V), 1960, and *The War with Hannibal* (Books XXI–XXX), 1965, both translated by Aubrey de Selincourt, and (Books XXI–XXX) translated by Selincourt and Betty Radice, 1970; *Rome and the Mediterranean* (Books XXXI–XLV) translated by Henry Bettenson, 1976; *Rome and Italy* (Books VI–X) translated by Betty Radice, 1982; selections as *Stories from Livy*, translated by R.M. Ogilvie, 1970, new edition, 1981; as *Stories of Rome*, translated by Roger Nichols, 1982; commentary on Books I–V by R.M. Ogilvie, 1965, on Books XXXI–XXXIII, 1973, and Books XXXIV–XXXVII, 1981, both by John Briscoe; commentary on Book VI by Christina Shuttleworth Kraus, 1994; as *The Rise of Rome: Books One to Five*, translated with introduction and notes by T.J. Luce, 1998; as *The Dawn of the Roman Empire: Books Thirty-one to Forty*, translated by J.C. Yardley, 2000.

*

Critical Studies: *Constancy in Livy's Latinity* by K. Gries, 1947; *God and Fate in Livy* by I. Kajanto, 1957; *Livy: His Historical Aims and Methods*, 1961, and *Livy*, 1974, both by P.G. Walsh; *A Concordance to Livy* by David W. Packard, 4 vols., 1969; *Livy* edited by T.A. Dorey, 1971; *Livy: The Composition of His History* by T.J. Luce, 1977; *The Prose Rhythms of Sallust and Livy* by Hans Aili, 1979; *Notes on the Manuscripts of Livy's Fourth Decade* by John Briscoe, 1980; *A Historiographical Study of Livy, Books VI–X* by J.P. Lipovsky, 1981; *Infinity of Narration in Livy: A Study in Narrative Technique* by Toivo Viljamaa, 1983; *Artistry and Ideology: Livy's Vocabulary of Virtue* by Timothy J. Moore, 1989; *Scipio Africanus and Rome's Invasion of Africa: A Historical Commentary on Titus Livius, Book XXIX* by Philip J. Smith, 1993; *Livy: Reconstructing Early Rome* by Gary B. Miles, 1995; *The Initiation of the Second Macedonian War: An Explication of Livy Book 31* by Valerie M. Warrior, 1996; *A Commentary on Livy: Books VI–X* by S.P. Oakley, 1997; *Livy's Written Rome* by Mary Jaeger, 1997; *Discourses on Livy* by Niccolò Machiavelli, translated by Julia Conaway Bondanella and Peter Bondanella, 1997; *Spectacle and Society in Livy's History* by Andrew Feldherr, 1998; *Liby and Early Rome: A Study in Historical Method and Judgement* by Gary Forsythe, 1999; *Livy's Exemplary History* by Jane D. Chaplin, 2000.

*   *   *

Although the tradition of Roman historical writing goes back to the 3rd century BC, Cicero was still able to complain in the mid-50s BC (*De oratore*) that the earlier Roman historians had no pretensions to literary embellishment and were unable to tell a properly constructed story; he wished that they had brought to their works an elegant style and not regarded brevity as the only stylistic virtue. But it was more than 20 years before a historian set out to eclipse the writers whom Cicero had criticized, and to produce the great historical work which Cicero had desired. That historian was Livy.

Livy's original plan was immensely ambitious: to tell the story of Rome from its legendary foundation to the death of Cicero (43 BC) in 120 volumes. In his preface to the work, almost certainly written before the end of the civil wars (49–31 BC), Livy expresses dismay at his own times and relishes the prospect of being able to escape from them by reliving the past in his history. It may therefore be inferred that he saw Roman history in terms of decline, thus following a tradition of Roman historiography already established in the 2nd century BC according to which the course of Roman history was seen as undergoing progressive degeneration. At the same time, however, Livy intended to lay before his readers examples, drawn from history, of the kind of behaviour which they should imitate and avoid (preface 10); evidently he did not exclude the possibility of Rome's recovering from the nadir epitomized by contemporary society.

Unfortunately only 35 of Livy's 120 volumes have survived (1–10, 21–45), but the flavour of his work can be appreciated in a story such as Tarquin's rape of Lucretia. The story is divided, like a miniature play, into four ''acts,'' each of which is subdivided into individual ''scenes''; the action is brought before the reader's eyes by means of judiciously selected detail and the use of direct speech at crucial moments; the pathos of the episode is further underlined by effective repetitions of word and phrase; and the whole drama is designed to praise Lucretia's *pudicitia* (chastity) and condemn Tarquin's *vis*, *libido*, and *superbia* (violence, lust, arrogance). Livy's achievement in this and many other passages can be gauged where we are able to compare his work with that of a predecessor. Thus earlier historians, writing 50 years or so before, described how Manlius Torquatus and Valerius Corvinus acquired their *cognomina* (surnames); but the accounts are brief and crude, written in an unambitious and inelegant style. Livy has expanded the episodes with a wealth of circumstantial detail and expressed them in a "periodic" style that is the historian's counterpart of the oratorical period of Cicero. Here, no less than in his long and patriotic treatment of the struggle against Hannibal (Books XXI–XXX), Livy convinces the reader that he is witnessing one of the glorious episodes of Rome's past history, written in an appropriately elevated style.

No doubt Livy originally intended these earlier and glorious periods of Rome's history to emphasize by contrast the degeneration which had set in subsequently and which was epitomized by the civil wars of his own lifetime; but at some unknown point he decided to extend the scope of his work by almost 35 years, bringing the history down to the death of Augustus' stepson Drusus in 9 BC. This decision radically affected the whole perspective of the work. No longer did the latest years of his history afford an unhappy comparison with the past: since the extra 22 volumes (of which none survives except in summary form) now took him midway through Augustus' reign, his revised plan meant that the latest years of his history now actually challenged the past in glory. The explanation for Livy's change of mind presumably rests with the emperor himself, with whom the historian, as mentor to the future emperor Claudius, was on personal terms and whom he came to see as the saviour of Rome. As a result, the 142 volumes of the completed enterprise constituted a monumental testimony to a nation's inherent greatness and its remarkable capacity for survival.

—A.J. Woodman

LLOSA, Mario Vargas

See VARGAS LLOSA, Mario

LO-JOHANSSON, (Karl) Ivar

Born: Ösmo, Sweden, 23 February 1901. **Education:** Self-educated. **Career:** Worked as a stonecutter, farmhand, journalist, workman in France, England, and Hungary, 1925–29; then full-time writer. **Awards:** Nio Society prize, 1941; Foundation for the Promotion of Literature Little Nobel prize, 1953; Doubloug prize, 1953, 1973; Nordic Council prize, 1979. Ph.D.: University of Uppsala, 1964. Officier de l'Ordre des Arts et des Lettres (France), 1986. **Died:** 10 April 1990.

PUBLICATIONS

Fiction

Måna är död [Måna Is Dead]. 1932.
Godnatt, jord. 1933; as *Breaking Free*, translated by Allan Tapsell, 1990.
Kungsgatan [King's Street]. 1935.
Statarna [The Estate Workers] (stories). 2 vols., 1936–37.
Bara en mor. 1939; as *Only a Mother*, translated by Robert E. Bjork, 1991.
Jordproletärerna [Proletarians of the Earth]. 1941.
Traktorn [The Tractor]. 1943.

Geniet: en roman om pubertet [The Genius: A Novel of Puberty]. 1947.
Ungdomsnoveller [Stories of Youth]. 1948.
Autobiographical Series:
    Analfabeten [The Illiterate Man]. 1951.
    Gårdfarihandlaren [The Country Pedlar]. 1953; as *Peddling My Wares*, translated with introduction by Rochelle Wright, 1995.
    Stockholmaren [The Stockholmer]. 1954.
    Journatisten [The Journalist]. 1956.
    Författaren [The Writer]. 1957.
    Socialisten [The Socialist]. 1958.
    Soldaten [The Soldier]. 1959.
    Proletärförfattaren [The Proletarian Writer]. 1960.
Lyckan. 1962; as *Bodies of Love*, translated by Allan Tapsell, 1971.
Astronomens hus [Astronomer's House]. 1966.
Elektra, kvinna år 2070 [Woman of the Year 2070]. 1967.
Passionerna: älskog [The Passions: Love]. 1968.
Martyrerna [The Martyrs]. 1968.
Girigbukarna [The Misers]. 1969.
Karriäristerna [The Careerists]. 1969.
Vällustingarna [The Lechers]. 1970.
Lögnhalsarna [The Liars]. 1971.
Vishetslärarna [Teachers of Wisdom]. 1972.
Orders makt: historien om språket [The Power of Words]. 1973.
Nunnan i Vadstena: sedeskildringar [The Nun of Vadstena: Moral Stories]. 1973.
Folket och herrarna [The People and the Masters]. 2 vols., 1973.
Furstarna: en krönika från Gustav Vasa till Karl XII [The Rulers]. 1974.
Lastbara berättelser [Stories of Vice]. 1974.
Passionsnoveller I–II [Stories of Passion] (selection). 2 vols., 1974.
En arbetares liv: proletärnoveller [A Worker's Life: Proletarian Stories]. 1977.

Verse

Ur klyvnadens tid [The Splitting Time]. 1958.

Other

Vagabondliv i Frankrike [Vagabond Life in France] (travel writing). 1927.
Kolet i våld [The Coal's Power]. 1928.
Statarliv [Farm Labourer's Lives]. 1941.
Stridsskrifter [Polemical Pamphlets]. 1946.
Statarna i bild [Estate Workers], illustrated by Gunnar Lundh. 1948.
Monism. 1948.
Ålderdom [Old Age], illustrated by Sven Järlås, 1949.
Vagabondliv [Vagabond Life]. 1949.
Ålderdoms-Sverige [Sweden for the Aged]. 1952.
Okänt Paris [Unknown Paris], illustrated by Tore Johnson. 1954.
Zigenarväg [Gypsy Ways], illustrated by Anna Riwkin-Brick. 1955.
Att skriva en roman [Writing a Novel]. 1957.
Zigenare [Gypsies]. 1963.
Statarnas liv och död [The Lives and Deaths of the Estate Workers] (selection). 1963.
Statarskolan i litteraturen [The School of Literature of the Estate Workers]. 1972.
Dagbok från 20-talet I–II [Diary from the Twenties]. 1974.
Stridsskrifter I–II [Polemical Pamphlets]. 1974.

Dagar och dagsverken: debatter och memoarer [Days and Day's Work]. 1975.
Under de gröna ekarna i Sörmland [Under the Green Oaks in Sörmland]. 1976.
Passioner i urval [Passions] (selection). 1976.
Den sociala fotobildboken [The Social Photograph Book]. 1977.
Pubertet [Puberty] (memoirs). 1978.
Asfalt [Asphalt] (memoirs). 1979.
Att skriva en roman, en bok om författeri [Writing a Novel, a Book on Writing] (selected articles). 1981.
Tröskeln [The Threshold] (memoirs). 1982.
Frihet [Freedom] (memoirs). 1985.
Till en författare [To an Author]. 1988.

*

Critical Studies: Ivar Lo-Johansson: Crusader for Social Justice' by Jan-Anders Paulsson, in *American-Scandinavian Review*, 59(1), 1971; "Ivar Lo-Johansson" by Peter Graves and Philip Holmes, in *Essays on Swedish Literature from 1880 to the Present Day*, edited by Irene Scobbie, 1978; "Ivar Lo-Johansson and the Passions" by Peter Graves, in *Proceedings of the Conference of Scandinavian Studies in Great Britain and Northern Ireland*, 1983; Lo-Johansson issue of *Swedish Book Review*, supplement, 1991; "Dream and Dream Imagery in Ivar Lo-Johansson's *Godnatt, jord*" by Rochelle Wright, in *Scandinavian Studies*, 64(1), 1992.

* * *

Ivar Lo-Johansson forms, together with Jan Fridegård and Moa Martinsson, the *statareskolan* in Swedish literature. All three come from the lowest class of agricultural workers, the estate workers (*statare*) who were tied to the big estates, being paid in kind and enduring substandard living conditions, and for all practical purposes not "free." It is remarkable that a social class where illiteracy was the norm produced three of Sweden's foremost writers.

Lo-Johansson is credited with opening the eyes of politicians and Swedes in general to the poverty and suffering of the *statare* through his fiction, thus contributing greatly to improving their tot and dismantling the system. His novel *Godnatt, jord (Breaking Free)* depicts a young man, Mikael, in his struggle for freedom. His dream world and his feelings for nature and beauty stand in sharp contrast to the reality of the conformist, subservient estate workers in their tedious work. They all, however, dream of freedom from their oppressive reality, but only Mikael is able to achieve it.

Probably better known is *Bara en mor (Only a Mother)*, about a beautiful young woman, Rya-Rya, who swims nude in an isolated lake on a hot summer day and is branded by the conservative estate workers as a fallen woman. Defiantly, she marries a weak, irresponsible worker and produces one child after another, like the rest of the women. This gradually weakens her physically, while her social standing as a worker who can choose the work she does declines with her increasing alienation from her husband. He mistreats her in a feeble attempt to feel powerful, although he is, in fact, a miserable failure even as an estate worker. There is no question that Rya-Rya is the stronger and the more competent, but she is a woman and trapped in a life of repression while lacking the ability to change it. Only as a mother can she realize some of her strength, but she dies young and overworked. Rya-Rya's fate is a comment on the hypocritical Swedish attitude to a natural sensuality, expressed in her nude swimming, which is punished for life.

Lo-Johansson's other works dealing with the plight of the *statare* include *Statarna* [The Estate Workers], *Jordproletärerna* [Proletarians of the Earth], and *Traktorn* [The Tractor], which features a machine as the main character.

Contributing to the success of his *statare*, work was a keen eye for documentary details. He believed that literature should have a definite social function which is best met through realistic journalistic methods. In fact his first published work was a series of travel books, *Vagabondliv i Frankrike* [Vagabond Life in France], where adventure is mixed with social commentary.

Lo-Johansson is also one of Sweden's foremost writers on the erotic and human (male) sexuality. Early on, he scandalized the Swedes by arguing that young men should have access to young women as a natural outlet for their sexuality. His first novel, *Måna är död* [Måna Is Dead], deals with a young man's problems in combining his erotic yearnings with his work. *Kungsgatan* [King's Street] deals with a farm boy's life in a big city. Here Lo-Johanson describes prostitution and venereal disease with a frankness new for the times.

Lo-Johansson's fascination with love and sex, human vices and sins is also expressed in seven volumes of stories of passion published between 1968 and 1972, and dealing with the forces that drive people to abandon reason and will in their actions. Each volume is devoted to a particular human weakness, as indicated in their titles—for example *Girigbukarna* [The Misers], *Vällustingarna* [The Lechers], and *Lögnhalsarna* [The Liars].

A third major focus of his writing is autobiographical. In the 1950s he published eight autobiographical novels, beginning with *Analfabeten* [The Illiterate Man], a touching and loving portrayal of his father, and a masterpiece in Swedish literature. His father was a man of few words and great integrity, whose life and people around him are perceived with much humour. Through the other novels in the series we follow Lo-Johansson's career from *Gårdfarihandlaren (Peddling My Wares)* to *Författaren* [The Writer] and *Proletärförfattaren* [The Proletarian Writer]. His fellow writers were identified in these books by their initials, which engaged his readers in popular deciphering games.

Another series of autobiographical writings was published from 1978 to 1985, starting with *Pubertet* [Puberty], for which he received the Nordic Council literary prize in 1979. This was not his first distinction. In 1941 he had received the Nio Society prize for *Only a Mother* and in 1953 the so-called Little Nobel prize from the Foundation for the Promotion of Literature. His last award came from France where he was made Officier de l'Ordre des Arts et des Lettres de France in 1986.

Lo-Johansson was a major modern writer who produced over 50 volumes dealing with basic human questions about love, sex, vice, and sin. His characters are multi-dimensional and show a deep insight into what makes a human being human. He translated social consciousness and compassion into great literature and created many unforgettable characters. His language is rich and powerful, poetic and realistic, entertaining and captivating.

—Torborg Lundell

LONGINUS

See ON THE SUBLIME

LÖNNROT, Elias

See KALEVALA

LOPE DE VEGA CARPIO

See VEGA CARPIO, Lope de

LORCA, Federico García

See GARCÍA LORCA, Federico

LORRIS, Guillaume de

See ROMANCE OF THE ROSE

LU XUN

Also known as Lu Hsün. Pseudonym for Zhou Shuren. **Born:** Shaoxing, Zhejiang province, China, in 1881. **Education:** Educated at Jiangnan Naval Academy, Nanjing, 1898–99; School of Railways and Mines, Nanjing, 1899–1902; studied Japanese language in Japan, 1902–04, and medicine at Sendai Provincial Medical School, Japan, 1904–06; continued private studies in Japan, 1906–09. **Career:** Teacher in Shaoxing, 1910–11; served in the Ministry of Education, Beijing, 1912–26, and taught Chinese literature at National Beijing University, 1920–26; taught at Xiamen (Amoy) University, 1926, and University of Canton, 1927; then lived in international settlement of Shanghai: editor, *Benliu* [The Torrent], 1928, and *Yiwen* [Translation], 1934. Translated many works by Russian, German, and Japanese authors. Also a draughtsman. **Died:** 19 October 1936.

PUBLICATIONS

Collections

Lu Xun xiansheng quanji [Complete Works]. 20 vols., 1938; revised edition, 1973; supplements edited by Tang Tao, 2 vols., 1942–52; his original works republished as *Lu Xun quanji*, 10 vols., 1956–58.
Selected Works, translated by Yang Hsien-yi and Gladys Yang. 4 vols., 1956–60.

Fiction

Nahan (stories). 1923; as *The War Cry* (bilingual edition), edited and translated by Jörgenson. 1949.
A Madman's Diary (stories; bilingual edition). 1924(?).
Panghuang (stories). 1926; as *P'anghuang/Hesitation*, edited and translated by Jörgenson, 1946.

The True Story of Ah Q, translated by George Kin Leung. 1926, bilingual edition, 1949; also translated by Yang Hsien-yi and Gladys Yang, 1960.
The Tragedy of Ah Qui and Other Modern Chinese Stories, edited by J. Kyn Yn-yu. 1930.
Gushi xinbian (stories). 1935; as *Old Tales Retold*, translated by Yang Hsien-yi and Gladys Yang, 1961.
Stories (includes *Benediction; Divorce; Kites; Kung Yiji; A Little Incident; Medicine; Mother's*), edited by Edgar Snow and Yao Hsinnung. 1936.
Ah Q and Others: Selected Stories, translated by Chi-chen Wang. 1941.
Selected Stories (in English). 1954.
Selected Stories, translated by Yang Hsien-yi and Gladys Yang. 1960.
Wild Grass (prose poems). 1974.
K'ung I-chi (stories; bilingual edition). 1975.

Verse

Selected Poems, translated by W.J.F. Jenner. 1982.

Other

Zhongguo xiaoshuo shilüe. 1924; as *A Brief History of Chinese Fiction*, translated by Yang Hsien-yi and Gladys Yang, 1959.
Lu Xun Shuxinji [Letters]. 1946; revised edition, 3 vols., 1976; selection translated as *Letters*, 1973.
Lu Xun riji [Diary]. 1951; revised edition, 3 vols., 1976.
Chun feng yüeh t'an (essays). 1954.
Selected Works. 1956.
A Lu Hsun Reader (Chinese text), edited by William A. Lyell, Jr. 1967.
Silent China: Selected Writings, edited and translated by Gladys Yang. 1973.
Extracts of Speeches on Criticism of the Doctrines of Confucius and Mencius (Chinese text). 1974.
Dawn Blossoms Plucked at Dusk, translated by Yang Hsienyi and Gladys Yang. 1976.
Love-letters and Privacy in Modern China: The Intimate Lives of Lu Xun and Xu Guangping, translated by Bonnie S. McDougall. 2002.

*

Critical Studies: *Lu Hsün and the New Culture Movement of Modern China* by Huang Sung-k'ang, 1957; *Gate of Darkness* by T.A. Hsia, 1974; *The Social Thought of Lu Hsün 1881–1936: A Mirror of the Intellectual Current of Modern China* by Pearl Hsia Chen, 1976; *Lu Hsün's Vision of Reality* by William A. Lyell, 1976; *The Style of Lu Hsun* by Raymond S.W. Hsu, 1980; *Lu Xun: A Biography* by Shiqing Wang, 1984; *Lu Xun and his Legacy*, 1985, and *Voices from the Iron House: A Study of Lu Xun*, 1987, both by Leo Ou-fan Lee; *Lu Xun: A Chinese Writer for All Times* by Ruth F. Weiss, 1985; *A Selective Guide to Chinese Literature 1900–1949: Volume 2: The Short Story*, edited by Zbigniew Slupski, 1988; *Lu Xun as Translator: Lu Xun's Translation and Introduction of Literature and Literary Theory, 1903–1936* by Lennart Lundberg, 1989; *The Lyrical Lu Xun: A Study of His Classical-style Verse* by Jon Eugene von Kowallis, 1996; *Lu Xun and Evolution* by James Reeve Pusey, 1998; *Children's Literature in China: From Lu Xun to Mao Zedong* by Mary Ann Farquhar, 1999.

* * *

Lu Xun, whose real name was Zhou Shuren, has been regarded as one of the greatest modern Chinese writers. The first to compose Western-style fiction, he was also in the vanguard of the colloquial language movement starting in 1918. A Communist sympathizer from about 1929, he died in 1936 before the Revolution, and has since been praised as a cultural hero in the Peoples' Republic of China.

He decided upon a writing career after formative experiences during his studies in Japan from 1902 to 1909. From the start his goal was polemical—to take China to task for its traditionalism and its refusal to adjust to the modern world. But he produced only mediocre essays and one story in the classical language until 1918, when he wrote the first Western-style story in China, "The Diary of a Madman." Based on a tale by Nikolai Gogol', the story is about a man who concludes that all around him intend to kill and eat him, and that such cannibalism is an inevitable result of hypocritical moral teachings of ancient China.

"The Diary of a Madman" and other stories were published in a collection called *Nahan* (*The War Cry*) in 1923. Of these the most famous is *The True Story of Ah Q*, which has received international acclaim. The character of Ah Q is the composite of all weak and lowly qualities of the Chinese national character, especially at the time in history when China was pathetically subservient to nations of greater physical and moral strength. He is the epitome of the individual who lacks self-knowledge, a condition that leads to absurd acts of self-abuse and accommodation to the external world. Although Ah Q is a composite and symbolic character, each detail of his behaviour, however grotesque or absurd, might as well be taken as a representation of what Lu Xun saw in actual life—for example, Ah Q's attempt to outdo someone else by searching his own body for lice and cracking them loudly between his teeth.

Panghuang (translated as *Hesitation*) is Lu Xun's second story collection, published in 1926. In general it is bleaker in tone than *Nahan* and is more mature and incisive, as Lu Xun himself asserted. As in all his works, the themes are topical and deal with various traditional evils. However, the stories in *Hesitation* are rarely lost on moral or polemical points and show how Lu Xun has mastered a technique of stark and essential portrayal. "Regret for the Past," for example, is a concise and ironic story of a "modern" love affair. It begins with a period of idyllic attachment but then evolves to a state in which that beginning becomes history, only to be reinvoked in the form of a sort of sustaining ritual. It ends when neither can any longer play their original roles.

Lu Xun's stories have rightly been compared to those of James Joyce's *Dubliners* and also resemble the 19th-century fiction of Gogol' or Dostoevskii. His characters are mostly petty but nevertheless real and sympathetic individuals, who are caught in a general condition of apathy, brutality, superstition, and hypocrisy.

In addition to writing stories, Lu Xun also composed a volume of prose poetry, *Ye cao* (*Wild Grass*), and a volume of childhood memories, *Dawn Blossoms Plucked at Dusk*. After 1926 he mainly wrote polemical essays, his only stories being those of *Gushi xinbian* (*Old Tales Retold*), in which he satirically revised the accounts of various ancient heroes. In his essays, besides repeatedly attacking wrong-headed contemporaries, he also sought to expose what he saw as an accumulated and collective national lethargy. He viewed the Chinese nation as a "dish of loose sand" in which individuals were separate and "oblivious to each other's sufferings" ("Silent China," 1927). Moreover, he saw hierarchy as so ingrained that, as he literally

demonstrated in Ah Q, "a hand cannot help but look down upon a foot" (his preface to the Russian translation of *The True Story of Ah Q*, 1925). Lu Xun must be counted among the sharpest and most astute critics and defenders of China that modern times have witnessed.

—Keith McMahon

LUCAN

Born: Marcus Annaeus Lucanus in Corduba (now Cordoba), Spain, 3 November AD 39. Grandson of Seneca the Elder and nephew of Seneca the Younger, *q.v.* **Education:** Studied in Rome and Athens. **Career:** Became a favourite of the emperor Nero, who made him financial administrator (*quaestor*) and augur; won the poetry contest in the Neronian games in AD 60, but fell out of favour and committed suicide under compulsion when his part in Piso's conspiracy against Nero was discovered. **Died:** 30 April AD 65.

PUBLICATIONS

Works

Civilis libri decem, edited by Alfred E. Housman. 1926; as *De bello civili*, edited by D.R. Shackleton Bailey, 1988; Book I edited by R.J. Getty (with commentary), 1940, corrected edition, 1955; Book VII edited by J.P. Postgate, 1913, revised by O.A.W. Dilke, 1960; Book VIII edited by J.P. Postgate, 1917, and R. Mayer, as *Civil War III*, 1981; as *Pharsalia*, translated by Sir A. Gorges, 1614; also translated by Nicholas Rowe (verse), 1713; Edward Ridley (verse), 1896; J.D. Duff [Loeb Edition], 1928; Robert Graves, 1956; Douglas Little (verse), 1989; Jane Wilson Joyce, 1994; as *Civil War*, translated by P.F. Widdows (verse), 1988; also translated by S.H. Braund, 1992; as *Pharsalia*, translated with introduction by Jane Wilson Joyce, 1993.

*

Bibliography: by Rudolf Helm, in *Lustrum*, 1, 1956, and by Werner Rutz, in *Lustrum*, 9, 1964, and *Lustrum*, 26, 1984.

Critical Studies: *Nicholas Rowe's Translation of Lucan's Pharsalia, 1703–1718: A Study in Literary History* by Alfred W. Hesse, 1950; *The Poet Lucan* by Mark P.O. Morford, 1967; *Lucan: An Introduction* by Frederick M. Ahl, 1976; *Momentary Monsters: Lucan and His Heroes* by W.R. Johnson, 1987; "Lucan/The Word at War" by J. Henderson, in *The Imperial Muse*, edited by A.J. Boyle, 1988; *Poetry and Civil War in Lucan's Bellum Civile* by Jamie Masters, 1992; *M. Annaeus Lucanus Bellum Civile Book III: A Commentary* by Vincent Hunink, 1992; *Ideology in Cold Blood: A Reading of Lucan's Civil War* by Shadi Bartsch, 1997; *Lucan: Spectacle and Engagement* by Matthew Leigh, 1997.

* * *

Lucan's poem *De bello civili* (popularly known as the *Pharsalia*) is an epic poem in hexameters, of which nine complete books and an incomplete tenth survive. Its subject is the civil war fought between Pompey and Caesar and it covers events from Caesar's crossing of the

Rubicon in 49 BC (Book I) through the battle of Pharsalus (Book VII) and Pompey's death in Egypt in 49 BC (Book VIII). It was probably planned to end with the suicide of Cato at Utica after the battle of Thapsus in 46 BC. The poem has none of the glamour of mythological epic, such as Virgil's *Aeneid*, but sets out to present a stark condemnation of civil war. It achieves this by subverting and inverting the conventions of mythological epic. Thus none of the three protagonists can be called "the hero" in any meaningful sense. Caesar, the most prominent character, is presented as a terrifying, destructive, and irresistible force with superhuman powers. Pompey is presented much more sympathetically in human terms but as a man past his prime and weak, indecisive, and insecure. Cato, who in Book IX takes over the leadership of the Republican forces after Pompey's murder, is the austere embodiment of Stoic principles with no softening human qualities.

Lucan abandons the traditional divine machinery of anthropomorphic deities in favour of the impersonal Stoic concepts of Fate and Fortune in order to focus attention on human responsibility and culpability for the horrors of the civil war. He nonetheless makes telling use of the supernatural in the form of dreams and visions, portents and prophecies which enhance the macabre atmosphere. Appius' consultation of the Delphic oracle in Book V and the necromancy performed by the witch Erichtho in Book VI illustrate Lucan's virtuoso powers. In this and many other respects he reflects the tastes and interests of his contemporaries. His own literary, moral, and rhetorical training emerges in his use of historical *exempla* (Hannibal in Book I, Marius and Sulla in Book 2), his incorporation of mythological episodes (Hercules in Book IV), and his scientific discussions of geography, astrology, astronomy, and natural phenomena (concentrated in Books IX and X). He is clearly an educated man writing for an educated audience.

Lucan's treatment of warfare shows most clearly his condemnation of civil war. He incorporates many of the episodes that are "standard" in martial epic but gives them paradoxical or extreme treatment. For example, in Book VI Caesar's centurion Scaea makes an incredible single-handed stand (*aristeia*) against Pompey's troops and prevents them from breaking out of the blockade, and in Book III the sea battle off Marseilles is said to resemble a land battle once Caesar's ships have been rammed. Lucan takes every opportunity to describe bizarre forms of death, most of which are striking for their strangeness, suddenness, and lack of dignity and heroism. The horror of civil war—of Roman fighting Roman, brother fighting brother, father fighting son—is presented starkly with an unheroized spilling of blood and a strikingly large number of unburied bodies and headless corpses, of which the most memorable is that of Pompey himself.

On the basis of his novel treatment of many of the conventions of mythological epic poetry, Lucan's poem may be regarded as an anti-Virgilian poem, although not in the sense of an antipathy towards Virgil. His essentially pessimistic poem reworks some of the stirring, patriotic episodes of the *Aeneid* into shocking, black scenes which seem to require contemplation of the crime of civil war. The most obvious example is Aeneas and the Sibyl in the Underworld in Book VI, evoked by the necromancy in *Civil War* Book VI.

The same anti-Virgilian strain is true of his style. His use of the hexameter is repetitive, even monotonous, in contrast with Virgil's musical hexameter. Similarly, his diction is prosaic and unembellished. The poem has been called a "predominantly monochrome epic" (Bramble) in which black, grey, and white are the predominant colours, followed by the red of the blood spilled. Key words and images which recur throughout the poem indicate disintegration and destruction, on the level of the individual, the state, and the cosmos—words like *ruina* (collapse), *viscera* (guts), *tabes* (decay), and *sanguis* (gore). Lucan characteristically dwells on an idea, reiterating it to make the audience stop and confront the issue. He often uses arresting maxims (*sententiae*), antitheses, and paradoxes for the same purpose, of which the most memorable is "they abandon Rome and flee towards war." This also explains the marked disproportion between narrative and speeches in the poem: narrative of the events of the war, with which his original audience was familiar, is kept to a minimum and often punctuated by exclamations or condemnatory outbursts from the poet. Instead, Lucan supplies emotive scenes that have no actual impact on the events of the war, such as Caesar's battle with the storm in Book V and the necromancy in Book VI, together with many long speeches which set the emotional tone. Particularly striking is Lucan's use of apostrophe, when he enters the poem as an unnamed character in order to address one of the actors. This technique, perhaps above all, invites us to pause and comprehend the horror of the events of civil warfare.

Some readers find Lucan's stark portrayal of the suicide of a powerful nation not to their taste. This could be because the poem is too uncomfortable and too disconcerting. If so, it is salutary to remember that many poets and scholars of medieval, Renaissance, and modern times had a high regard for Lucan. In Dante's view, Lucan ranked with Homer, Horace, Ovid, and Virgil as an exponent of elevated poetry.

—S.H. Braund

LUCIAN

Born: Samosata, Syria (now Samsat, Turkey), c. AD 120. Probably not Greek. **Family:** Married; one son. **Career:** Apprenticed to a sculptor; then received an education in rhetoric, and became a pleader, then a travelling lecturer, practising sophistic rhetoric in Gaul; moved to Athens about age 40; may have accompanied the Emperor Verus to Antioch in 162; chief court usher (*archistator*) with the Roman administration in Alexandria in early 170s. **Died:** After AD 180.

PUBLICATIONS

Collections

[Works], edited by M.D. MacLeod. 4 vols., 1972–87; also edited by John Dryden, various translators, 4 vols., 1711, and J. Sommerbrodt, 5 vols., 1886–99; translated by F. Spence, 5 vols., 1684–85; also translated by Thomas Francklin, 2 vols., 1780; William Tooke, 1820; H.W. and F.G. Fowler, 4 vols., 1905; A.M. Harmon (vols. 1–5), K. Kilburn (vol. 6), and M.D. MacLeod (vols. 7 and 8), 8 vols. [Loeb Edition], 1913–67; selections edited and translated by Emily James Smith, 1892; B.P. Reardon, 1965; Keith C. Sidwell, 1985; M.D. MacLeod (with commentary), 1990.

Works

Charon, Vita and Timon, translated by D.S. Smith. 1865.

Dialogues, translated by Jasper Mayne. 1638; also translated by John Dryden, 1739; William Maginn, 1856; H. Williams, 1888; R. Mongan and J.A. Prout, with *Somnium*, 1890; William Tooke, 1930; selection translated by "J.P.P.," 1845; *Six Dialogues*, translated by S.T. Irwin, 1894; *Dialogues and Stories*, translated by W.D. Sheldon, 1901; *Seventy Dialogues*, edited by H.L. Levy, 1977.

Somnium, with *The Dialogues*, translated by R. Mongan and J.A. Prout. 1890; also translated by William Armour, 1895.

Tragodopodagra, as *The Trago-Podagra, or Gout Tragedy*, translated by Rev. Symeon T. Bartlett. 1871.

Vera Historia [True Story], translated by Francis Hickes. 1634, reprinted 1925; also translated by Emily James Smith, 1892; J.A. Prout, 1901; selection as *Trips to Wonderland*, translated by Francis Hickes, 1905; as *Lucian Goes A-Voyaging*, translated and adapted by Agnes Carr Vaughan, 1930.

Cyprian Masques, translated by Ruby Melvill. 1929.

Satirical Sketches, translated by Paul Turner. 1961.

Selected Satires, edited by Lionel Casson. 1962.

*

Critical Studies: *Lucian, Satirist and Artist* by F.G. Allinson, 1926; *The Translations of Lucian by Erasmus and Thomas More* by C.R. Thompson, 1940; *Literary Quotation and Allusion in Lucian* by F.W. Householder, 1941; *The Sophists in the Roman Empire* by Glen W. Bowersock, 1969; *Studies in Lucian* by Barry Baldwin, 1973; *Studies in Lucian's Comic Fiction* by Graham Anderson, 1976; *Ben Jonson and the Lucianic Tradition* by Douglas Duncan, 1979; *Lucian and His Influence in Europe* by Christopher Robinson, 1979; *Prolegomena to a New Text of Lucian's Vitarum Auctio and Piscator* by Joel B. Itzkowitz, 1986; *Culture and Society in Lucian* by C.P. Jones, 1986; *Unruly Eloquence: Lucian and the Comedy of Traditions* by R. Bracht Branham, 1989; *Lucian of Samosata in the Two Hesperias: An Essay in Literary and Cultural Translation* by Michael O. Zappala, 1990; *Lucian and the Latins: Humor and Humanism in the Early Renaissance* by David Marsh, 1998.

* * *

Literal-minded Byzantines saw Lucian as an anti-Christ; Lord Macaulay dubbed him the Voltaire of antiquity. He deserves neither title. Lucian is best regarded as a journalist-cum-intellectual, unscrupulously versatile.

Least popular now are his occasional pieces on various rhetorical themes. One or two deserve attention, notably his essay on Slander which describes a Greek painting that inspired Botticelli's *La Calunnia*. Lucian is one of a relatively small number of ancient writers on art, which should commend him to modern counterparts.

As is ever the case with intellectuals, Lucian was frequently embroiled in controversies; several pamphlets commemorate these in vicious terms. Their contemporary bite has naturally staled, but two stand out. The *Peregrinus* lambasts its eponymous villain who, after flirting with Christianity and cynicism, immolates himself at the Olympic Games. Some mild comments on Christian credulity earned Lucian a place on the Catholic index of Forbidden Books. But Christians get a better press in his *Alexander* where, along with the Epicureans and Lucian himself, they oppose a trendy religious charlatan.

Lucian was also capable of appreciation, and wrote some admiring obituaries, notably the *Demonax*, commemorating a witty philosopher and preserving a large collection of his jokes. He also tried his hand at verse. Fifty or so epigrams attributed to him in the *Greek Anthology* are unremarkable. But his *Tragodopodagra* (*Gout Tragedy*) is a delicious parody of Greek drama, comparable to Housman's immortal *Fragment of a Greek Tragedy*.

Perhaps most congenial is the prose *Vera Historia* [True Story], at one level a parody of travellers' tall tales, but also enjoyable as early science fiction with monsters and adventures worthy of 20th-century inventions.

However, Lucian himself prized his satirical dialogues, a genre he revived and perfected. Some pass social comments on wealth and poverty that might endear him to the modern left, but which were politically safe in his own relatively enlightened age—Lucian was no martyr. His main targets are the absurdities of mythology, as well as the illogical and often hypocritical representatives of the philosophical schools. Typical pieces include *Descent into Hell, Dialogues of the Dead, Philosophies for Sale*—all much imitated in later times.

Lucian was no deep thinker, and had no obvious influence on his own times. His fame was in the future. He was a professional entertainer in a crowded and competitive field, and it is probably fair to suppose that his works survived because they were superior in elegance and wit to those that did not.

—Barry Baldwin

LUCRETIUS

Born: Titus Lucretius Carus, c. 99–94 BC. His work is dedicated to C. Memmius Gemellus, the friend of Catullus and Cinna; may have been acquainted with Cicero; otherwise nothing is known of his life. **Died:** c. 55 BC.

PUBLICATIONS

Verse

De rerum natura, edited by Joseph Martin. 1953; also edited by William Ellery Leonard and Stanley Barney Smith, 1961, Alfred Ernout, 2 vols., 1964–66, and K. Müller, 1975; selections: edited and translated by Cyril Bailey, 1922, 1947, revised edition, 1977, and W.H.D. Rouse [Loeb Edition], 1928, revised by M.F. Smith, 1975; as *On Matter and Man* (Books I, II, IV, and V; in Latin), edited by A.S. Cox, 1967, Book III edited by E.J. Kenney, 1977, Book I edited by P.M. Brown, 1984, Book V edited by C.D.N. Costa, 1984, Book IV, 1986, and Book VI, 1991, both edited and translated by John Godwin; as *On the Nature of Things*, translated by J.S. Watson and J.M. Good, 1848; also translated by C.F. Johnson, 1872; H.A.J. Munro, 1907; Cyril Bailey, 1910; Robert Allison, 1919; R.C. Trevelyan, 1937; J.H. Maitland, 1965; Frank Copley, 1977; as *The Way Things Are*, translated by Rolfe Humphries, 1968; as *The Poem on Nature*, translated by C.H. Sisson, 1976; also translated in prose by Ronald Latham, 1951; R. Geer, 1965; M.F. Smith, 1969; Book I as *De Rerum Natura*, translated by J. Evelyn, 1656; *Selections*, translated by Henry, S. Salt, 1912; *Selections*, edited by G. Benfield and R.C. Reeves, 1967; Book IV translated by Robert D. Brown, in *Lucretius on*

Love and Sex, 1987; as *The Nature of Things*, edited and translated by Anthony M. Esolen, 1995; as *Lucy Hutchinson's Translation of Lucretius De rerum natura*, edited by Hugh de Quehen, 1996; as *On the Nature of the Universe*, with introduction and explanatory notes by Don and Peta Fowler, 1997; as *Selections from De rerum natura*, edited by Bonnie A. Catto, 1998.

*

Bibliography: *A Bibliography of Lucretius* by Cosmo A. Gordon, 1962, 2nd edition, revised by E.J. Kenney, 1985. Critical Studies: *Three Philosophical Poets: Lucretius, Dante, and Goethe* by George Santayana, 1910; *Lucretius and His Influence* by George D. Hadzsits, 1935; *Lucretius* by E.E. Sykes, 1936; *Lucretius' Imagery* by G.J. Sullwood, 1958; *Philosophy of Poetry: The Genius of Lucretius* by Henri Bergson, 1959; *Lucretius and English Literature, 1680–1740* by Wolfgang B. Fleischmann, 1964; *Lucretius* edited by Donald R. Dudley, 1965; *The Lyre of Science: Form and Meaning in Lucretius' De Rerum Natura* by Richard Minadeo, 1969; *The Imagery and Poetry of Lucretius* by David A. West, 1969; *Epicurean Political Philosophy: The De Rerum Natura of Lucretius* by James Hunt Nichols, 1976; *Lucretius and the Diatribe Against the Fear of Death: De Rerum Natura III, 830–1094* by Barbara Price Wallach, 1976; *Lucretius* by E.J. Kenney, 1977; *Mode and Value in the De Rerum Natura: A Study in Lucretius' Metrical Language*, 1978, and *Lucretius and the Late Republic: An Essay in Roman Intellectual History*, 1985, both by John Douglas Minyard; *Lucretius and the Transpadanes* by Louise Adams Holland, 1979; *Puns and Poetry in Lucretius' De Rerum Natura* by Jane McIntosh Snyder, 1980; *Lucretius and Epicurus* by Diskin Clay, 1983; *Lucretius on Love and Sex: A Commentary on De Rerum Natura IV, 1030–1287 with Prolegomena, Text and Translation*, 1987, and *Lucretius on Love and Sex*, 1989, both by Robert D. Brown; *Lucretius on Death and Anxiety: Poetry and Philosophy in De Rerum Natura* by Charles Segal, 1990; *The Song of the Swan: Lucretius and the Influence of Callimachus* by Harold Donohue, 1993; *Myth and Poetry in Lucretius* by Monica R. Gale, 1994; *Philodemus and Poetry: Poetic Theory in Lucretius, Philodemus, and Horace*, edited by Dirk Obbink, 1995; *The Criticism of Didactic Poetry: Essays on Lucretius, Virgil, and Ovid* by Alexander Dalzell, 1996; *Lucretius and the Transformation of Greek Wisdom* by David Sedley, 1998; *Lucretius and the Modern World* by W.R. Johnson, 2000; *Lucretius and the Didactic Epic* by Monica R. Gale, 2001.

*   *   *

Little is known about the Roman poet Lucretius apart from what may be inferred from his work and the probably apocryphal tale that he committed suicide after suffering the shattering effects of a love potion. Only *De rerum natura* (*On the Nature of Things*) survives, a long philosophical poem in six books of over 7,400 lines of Latin hexameters. The work itself proposes the modest task of liberating humankind from fear and superstition by explaining everything. Underlying this is the premise that fear derives from ignorance or uncertainty, especially in relation to the arbitrary actions of the gods and to the fate of the soul after death. By showing that the order of things is the result of orderly and predictable mechanical processes, Lucretius hoped to dissolve all mysteries, thereby eliminating all uncertainty and fear.

Lucretius saw his task as essentially didactic, expounding the ethical and mechanical theories of the Greco-Roman philosopher Epicurus, "the first to break the close bars of nature's portals" (1.71). In turn, Epicurus had adopted and developed the implications of the Atomists Leucippus and Democritus. Thus, for Lucretius, Epicurus, and the Atomists, all reality was composed of two basic elements, atoms or particles and void. They viewed reality as we know it as nothing more than elaborate configurations of atoms and void existing in a state of constant motion, a view that anticipates to some degree Galileo's theory of atoms, Descartes's corpuscles, and even some aspects of the modern atomic theory.

As Lucretius proceeds through his six books, he follows the basic metaphysical project of starting with the most fundamental, and showing how he can build on that to account for the cosmos as a whole. Thus he moves from the derivation of the basic elements to an account of life, mind, and reproduction, through larger structures and finally to an account of terrestrial and celestial phenomena. The observation of change in the world, of generation and decay, nutrition and growth, the cycles of the season, and even the larger cycles of the cosmos, is nothing more than the expression of the perpetual rearrangements of the basic constituent particles in the void. In this way, Lucretius attempts to account for the mutability of the world while defending the fundamental postulate that "nothing can be produced from nothing," and its corollary, that "nothing is ever reduced to nothing."

These postulates are crucial to Lucretius' project of dispelling religious superstition, for they entail the principle that the gods are bound to the laws of nature, unable to act in an arbitrary, unreasonable, or unpredictable manner. Any fortune or disaster that might befall people is the result of predictable natural laws and not the caprice of Apollo or Jupiter. As such, Lucretius posits a responsibility for individuals to exercise reasonable caution, for within the limits of nature, their fates are in their own hands. Lucretius' theory is most important, however, when applied to dispelling fear of death.

As with superstition and fear in general, Lucretius suggests that the fear of death is related to a fear of the unknown, and especially the prospect of some torment or retribution that the soul might encounter after death. In Book III, he argues why he believes such fears to be groundless. In effect, Lucretius argues that mental and vital processes, like any other natural phenomena, are a function of the motion of particles, in this case an especially fine grade of particles, but particles nonetheless. "It must therefore necessarily be the case," he argues, "that the whole soul consists of extremely small seminal atoms, connected and diffused throughout the veins, and viscera, and nerves." This being so, there is no substantive difference between the soul and the body. Accordingly, the death of the body also entails the death of the soul. In other words, insofar as death and decay of the body represent a dissociation and reconfiguration of the constituent particles, so they represent the same for the soul. The collection and configuration of atoms that combine to form one's unique self and identity diffuse into the whole. Since the soul is inseparable from the body, the only way that a person might suffer after death is if all of the specific particles that formed the person were able to recombine in their original configuration. Since that is effectively impossible, Lucretius concludes that there is no after-life to anticipate.

> We may be assured that in death there is nothing to be dreaded by us; that he who does not exist, cannot become miserable; and that it makes not the least difference to a man, when immortal death has ended his mortal life, that he was ever born at all.

Thus Lucretius offers the cold comfort that the life people live is the only life they have and may expect, and that since death is complete annihilation, they have nothing to fear.

On the Nature of Things proved an important vehicle for Epicurean thought, both in the Roman world and later with Voltaire and other figures of the Enlightenment who were drawn to his material vision of the cosmos and his ethics of the garden. At the same time, Lucretius' flights of lyricism made his poem widely read and appreciated among those influenced by Latin literature. However, the enduring quality stems from Lucretius' regard for the perennial problem of human mortality and the meaning of human existence: what philosopher George Santayana termed the ''art of accepting and enjoying what the conditions of our being afford.'' Because of this, *On the Nature of Things* may be classed among the great philosophical poems in the Western tradition, comparable with Dante's *Divine Comedy*, Wordsworth's *Prelude*, or Goethe's *Faust*.

—Thomas L. Cooksey

LUTHER, Martin

Born: Eisleben, Thuringia, 10 November 1483. **Education:** Educated at the University of Erfurt, B.A. 1502, M.A. 1505. **Family:** Married Katherine von Bora in 1525; three sons and three daughters. **Career:** Entered Augustinian monastery, Erfurt, 1505; installed as professor of moral philosophy, University of Wittenberg, 1508: doctor of theology 1512; visited Rome, 1511; published 95 Theses against the sale of indulgences, 1517, and thereafter drawn into Reformation controversies: excommunicated, 1520, tried at Imperial Diet of Worms in 1521 and outlawed; kept in hiding at the Wartburg, 1521–22; spent most of the remainder of his life in Wittenberg, teaching, preaching, writing, and overseeing the emergence of reformed, Lutheran institutions. **Died:** 18 February 1546.

PUBLICATIONS

Werke [Weimar Edition], edited by J.C.F. Knaake and others, 110 vols., 1883–.
Works [American Edition], edited by Jaroslav Pelikan and Helmut T. Lehmann. 55 vols., 1955–.
Selections, edited by J. Dillenberger. 1961.
Selected Political Writings, edited by J.M. Porter. 1974.
Luther's Theological Testament: The Schmalkald Articles, translated by William R. Russell. 1995.
Sermons of Martin Luther: The House Postils, edited and translated by Eugene F.A. Klug. 1996.
The 1529 Holy Week and Easter Sermons of Dr. Martin Luther, translated by Irving L. Sandberg. 1999.

*

Bibliography: *Annotated Bibliography of Luther Studies, 1967–1976* by John E. Bigane, 1977; by Mark U. Edwards, in *Reformation Europe: A Guide to Research* edited by Steven Ozment, 1982.

Critical Studies: *Here I Stand: A Life of Martin Luther* by Roland Bainton, 1950; *Luther and His Times* by E.C. Schwiebert, 1950; *Martin Luther: Road to Reformation* by Heinrich Boehmer, translated by W. Doberstein and Theodore G. Tappert, 1957; *Martin Luther: A Biographical Study* by John M. Todd, 1964; *Martin Luther and the Reformation* by A.G. Dickens, 1967; *Luther: An Introduction to His Thought* by Gerhard Ebeling, 1970; *The German Nation and Martin Luther* by A.G. Dickens, 1974; *Martin Luther and the Drama* by Thomas I. Bacon, 1976; ''Luther and Literacy,'' in *Publications of the Modern Language Association of America 91*, 1976, and *Luther: An Experiment in Biography*, 1980, both by H.G. Haile; *Martin Luther: An Illustrated Biography* by Peter Manns, translated by Michael Shaw, 1982; *Luther in Mid-Career 1521–30* by Heinrich Bornkamm, translated by Theodore Bachmann, 1983; *Martin—God's Court Jester: Luther in Retrospect* by Eric Walter Grilsch, 1983; *Martin Luther: The Man and the Image* by Herbert David Rix, 1983; *The Political Thought of Martin Luther* by W.O.J. Cargil Thompson, 1984; *Luther and Learning* edited by Marilyn J. Harran, 1985; *Martin Luther and the Modern Mind: Freedom, Conscience, Toleration, Rights* edited by Manfred Hoffmann, 1985; *Martin Luther: His Road to Reformation 1483–1521* by Martin Brecht, translated by James L. Schaaf, 1985; *Luther the Reformer: A Story of the Man and His Career* by James M. Kitelson, 1986; *Luther in Context* by David C. Steinmetz, 1986; *Martin Luther: An Introduction to His Life and Works* by Bernhard Lohse, translated by Robert C. Schultz, 1987; *Martin Luther in the American Imagination* by Hartmut Lehmann, 1988; *Luther: Man between God and the Devil* by Heiko A. Oberman, translated by Eileen Walliser-Schwarzbart, 1989; *Martin Luther* by Gerhard Brendler, 1992; *The Assurance of Faith: Conscience in the Theology of Martin Luther and John Calvin* by Randall C. Zachman, 1993; *Martinus Noster: Luther in the German Reform Movement, 1518–1521* by Leif Grane, 1994; *Luther's Legacy: Salvation and English Reformers, 1525–1556* by Carl R. Trueman, 1994; *Printing, Propaganda, and Martin Luther* by Mark U. Edwards, Jr., 1994; *Baptism in the Theology of Martin Luther* by Jonathan D. Trigg, 1994; *In Martin's Footsteps* by Matthias Gretzschel and Toma Babovic, 1996; *Luther and German Humanism* by Lewis W. Spitz, 1996; *True Faith in the True God: An Introduction to Luther's Life and Thought* by Hans Schwarz, translated by Mark William Worthing, 1996; *Luther* by Hans-Peter Grosshans, 1997; *Proverbs and Proverbial Expressions in the German Works of Martin Luther* by James C. Cornette, Jr., 1997; *Union with Christ: The New Finnish Interpretation of Luther*, edited by Carl E. Braaten and Robert W. Jenson, 1998; *The Trinity and Martin Luther: A Study on the Relationship between Genre, Language and the Trinity in Luther's Work (1523–1546)* by Christine Helmer, 1999; *Martin Luther's Theology: Its Historical and Systematic Development* by Bernhard Lohse, translated and edited by Roy A. Harrisville, 1999; *Martin Luther and John Wesley on the Sermon on the Mount* by Tore Meistad, 1999; *Martin Luther: The Christian between God and Death* by Richard Marius, 1999; *Martin Luther, German Saviour: German Evangelical Theological Factions and the Interpretation of Luther, 1917–1933* by James M. Stayer, 2000; *Renaissance Humanism in Support of the Gospel in Luther's Early Correspondence: Taking All Things Captive* by Timothy P. Dost, 2001; *Luther's Lives: Two Contemporary Accounts of Martin Luther*, translated and annotated by Elizabeth Vandiver, Ralph Keen, and Thomas D. Frazel, 2002.

* * *

At the centre of all Martin Luther's activities lay a profound faith in the redemptive personal experience of Christ, the Word of God to mankind, and he always regarded his writing and teaching as forms of preaching, in continuation of the saving work of God, the supreme poet. Trained in scholastic and humanistic studies alike, he used them merely as skills which aided his ''preaching.'' While not subscribing to the humanists' literary aestheticization of spiritual matters, Luther none the less aspired to the fitting and effective use of language to give expression to truth as he saw it revealed. This is one reason why he embarked upon the composition of a liturgy and hymns in German, for the initial efforts of his arch rival, the radical Thomas Müntzer, seemed wooden and unsatisfactory. Equally fluent in Latin and German, he employed the vernacular increasingly after 1515 to impart his Reformation precepts to the people, setting clarity and simplicity as goals. He was no systematic theologian: his writings have the character of dialogue or polemic (often virulent) about them; most of his main ideas were formulated in response to an adversary. His thinking is strongly antithetical, he worked in terms of polar opposites: Letter and Spirit, Faith and Works, Freedom and Bondage, God and Man. His output was prolific: for 30 years after 1516 he published almost one title per fortnight. In numerous works on controversial matters of theology, church polity, and social order, he gave articulated theoretical foundation to traditional national grievances: his tract *An den Christlichen Adel deutscher Nation* [To the Christian Rulers of Germany] of 1520 ran to 13 editions within five months and quickened the pace of political debate and literary agitation in Germany.

Luther began his translation of the Bible in 1521 in order to promote his theological principle of the priesthood of all believers by making the Scriptures accessible in the vernacular to all estates of men, and revised the work constantly up to his death. Of this translation over half a million whole or part-bibles were sold (for a population of some 15 million). Luther's oeuvre includes devotional works, prayers, and *ars moriendi* (books of comfort for the dying), tracts on catechism and sacraments, about 2,000 sermons, programmatic tracts on matters of ecclesiastical and social controversy, and exegesis; he also wrote fables, hymns, and hundreds of letters; moreover, his table talk was transcribed and recorded for posterity. The outer forms of his writings are usually simple, the language clear, occasionally crude. Frequently, however, as in *Von der Freyheyt eyniss Christen menschen* [The Freeedom of a Christian], plain and direct language couches a profoundly logical dialectic argument in which the precepts of classical rhetoric are deployed. Literature, in the sense of the written word being read or listened to and taken seriously by a significant proportion of the population, was virtually brought into existence for Germany by Luther. Almost single-handed during the Reformation (and especially in the period 1520–25) he created public opinion as an effective power in the land, and the leaders of both movements which rose in rebellion and failed in these years— the Imperial Knights and the Peasants—adduced Luther's writings in their cause.

Luther used to be solely credited with creating a national unified German language; it is acknowledged currently that he made few innovations of syntax or phonology, but did, however, succeed decisively in reinforcing existing trends in the language. His home territory—Saxony and Thuringia—was the dialect area of East Central German, which embraced features of diverse dialects from the old German ''heartlands'' in north, west, and south-west; moreover it straddled the linguistic boundary between Lower and Upper (north and south) German dialects. Luther employed the synthetic scribal language of the Saxon chancellory, an official language which was by assimilation comprehensible in most of the German lands. In his German Bible he imbued the stilted official language with the colour, idiom, flexibility—in short, life—of spoken German. His aim was to translate the matter of Scripture faithfully, but to do so in keeping with the inherent principles of the German language: in the *Sendbrieff von Dolmetzschenn* [Open Letter on Translation] he states his aim to write what he ''heard,'' from ''the mother in the house, the child in the street, the man in the market place.'' In particular, his striking innovations of vocabulary gave his German Bible a unifying cultural significance for the nation comparable to that of the King James Bible in England, and he was sometimes aware of his command of the German language claiming that even his adversaries had to learn from him.

Luther's hymns are possibly the most powerful manifestation of his theology, and it is a major achievement of his Reformation that the vernacular hymn has so central a role in Church worship; Luther's love of music—he composed several tunes himself—contrasts with the stance of other reformers (Zwingli, Calvin). He wrote hymns as part of his vernacular liturgy, in a 12-month creative outpouring in 1523–24 he completed 23, and out of his total of 36 some 30 survive in current hymnals. For Luther ''the notes give life to the text,'' and hymns lent unity, and—memorable for being set to music—implanted theological principles in the minds of the congregation. Luther drew heavily on traditions; most hymns are adaptations, of Biblical or sacramental material: ''Christ unser Herr zum Jordan kam'' [Christ Our Lord to Jordan Came], ''Aus tieffer Not. De Profundis'' [Out of the Depths, O Lord]. Others derive from Latin hymns: ''Mitten wyr ym leben sind'' [In the Midst of Life We Are in Death] from the antiphonal ''Media vita in morte sumus,'' while a few spring from German folksongs: ''Vom himel hoch da kom ich her'' [From Heaven Above] adapts an old traveller's song as children's Nativity story. The most famous, ''Ein feste Burg'' [A Mighty Fortress], portrays in pugnacious monosyllables and stark antitheses the cosmic battle between God and the devil in which impotent man is saved by alliance with Christ alone in faith and trust: truths central to Luther's Reformation.

—Lewis Jillings

See the essay on ''Ein feste Burg.''

M

MACHADO, (Ruiz) Antonio

Born: Seville, Spain, 1875. Family moved to Madrid, 1883. **Education:** Educated at the Institución Libre de Enseñanza, Madrid, 1883–89; Instituto de San Isidro, Madrid, 1889; Instituto Cardenal Cisneros, Madrid, from 1890, degree 1900; Central University, Madrid, 1915–16, Ph.D, 1916. **Family:** Married Leonor Izquierdo Cuevas in 1909 (died 1912). **Career:** Regular collaborator, *La Caricatura*, 1892–93; translator, Garnier, publishers, Paris, 1899; contributed to various periodicals from 1903, including *Helios, Alma Expañola, Blanco y Negro, Renacimiento Latino*, and *La República de las Letras*; professor of French, 1907–08, deputy director, 1908–12, Instituto de Soria; undertook research on French philology and attended classes at Collège de France, Paris, 1911; professor of French, 1912–15, deputy director, 1915–19, Instituto de Baeza, Madrid; professor of French, Instituto de Segovia, 1919–31, and Instituto Calderón de la Barca, Madrid, 1932–36; contributor to *La Plums* and *Los Lunes de Imparcial*, from 1920, *La Revista de Occidente*, from 1923, *Diario de Madrid*, from 1934, and *El Sol*; on the outbreak of the Spanish Civil War, supported the Republic through journalism and involvement in cultural events: contributor to *La Hora de España*, from 1937; lived in Rocafort, Valencia, 1936–38, and Barcelona, 1938–39; left Barcelona with his mother and younger brother Juan, and crossed into France, January 1939. **Died:** 22 February 1939.

Publications

Collections

Obras. 1940.
Obras completas, with Manuel Machado. 1947; reprinted 1984.
Obras: Poesía y prosa, edited by Aurora de Albornoz and Guillermo de Torte. 1964.
Poesías completas, edited by M. Alvar. 1975.
Obra completa. 2 vols., 1988.
Obra completa. 4 vols., 1989.
Poesía y prosa, edited by Oreste Macrí and Gaetano Chiappini. 4 vols., 1989.
Verso y prosa, edited by Jesús Toboso. 1990.
Roads Dreamed Clear Afternoons: An Anthology of the Poetry of Antonio Machado, translated by Carl W. Cobb. 1994.

Verse

Soledades. 1903; edited by Rafael Ferreres, 1968.
Soledades, Galerías y otros poemas. 1907; revised edition, 1919; edited by Geoffrey Ribbans, 1973.
Campos de Castilla. 1912; revised and enlarged edition, 1917; edited by José Luis Cano, 1967, and by Rafael Ferreres, 1970; also translated by Robert Harvard, 1997; selection in *Spanish Prose and Poetry*, translated by Ida Farnell, 1920; as *The Castilian Camp*, translated by J.C.R. Green, 1982.
Páginas escogidas. 1917.

Poesías completas. 1917; revised and enlarged editions, 1928, 1933, 1936.
Nuevas canciones. 1924; edited by José María Valverde, with *De un cancionero apócrifo*, 1971; as *Canciones*, translated by Robert Bly, 1980.
De un cancionero apócrifo. 1926; edited by José María Valverde, with *Nuevas canciones*, 1971.
La guerra. 1937.
La tierra de Alvargonzález y Canciones del Alto Duero, illustrated by José Machado. 1938; *La tierra de Alvargonzález* as *The Legend of Alvargonzález*, translated by Denis Doyle, 1982.
Poesías completas. 1943.
La voz de Antonio Machado (selection). 1947.
Poesías escogidas, edited by Federico C. Sainz de Robles. 1947.
Zero (bilingual edition), translated by Eleanor L. Turnbull. 1947.
Sea of San Juan: A Contemplation, translated by Eleanor L. Turnbull. 1950.
Eighty Poems of Antonio Machado (bilingual edition), translated by Willis Barnstone. 1959.
Poesías de guerra, edited by Aurora de Albornoz. 1961.
Castilian Ilexes: Versions from Antonio Machado, 1875–1939, translated by Charles Tomlinson and Henry Gifford. 1963.
Poesías completas. 1964.
Antología poética, edited by José Hierro. 1968.
Poesía, edited by M.P. Palomo. 1971.
Sunlight and Scarlet: Selected Poems (bilingual edition), translated by Ivor Waters. 1973.
Poemas: Antología de urgencia, edited by L. Izquierdo. 1976.
Selected Poems, translated by Betty Jean Craige. 1978.
I Never Wanted Fame, translated by Robert Bly. 1979.
Poesías, edited by Jorge Campos. 1979.
The Dream below the Sun: Selected Poems, translated by Willis Barnstone. 1981.
Antología poética; Biografía, edited by José Luis Cano. 1982.
Selected Poems (bilingual edition), edited and translated by Alan S. Trueblood. 1982.
Times Alone: Selected Poems (bilingual edition), edited and translated by Robert Bly. 1983.
Poesía (selection), edited by Roque Esteban Scarpa. 1986.
Poesía de guerra y de postguerra (selection), edited by Miguel d'Ors. 1992.

Plays

El condenado por desconfiado, with J. López Pérez Hernández, from a play by Tirso de Molina (produced 1924). In *La Farsa*, 1924.
Hernani, with Manuel Machado and Francisco Villaespesa, from a play by Hugo (produced 1925). In *La Farsa*, 1924.
Hay verdades que en amor . . . , from a play by Lope de Vega (produced 1925).
La niña de plata, with Manuel Machado and J. López Pérez Hernández, from a play by Lope de Vega (produced 1926). In *La Farsa*, 1926.
Desdichas de la fortuna o Julianillo Valcárcel, with Manuel Machado (produced 1926). 1926.
Juan de Mañara, with Manuel Machado (produced 1927). 1927.

Las adelfas, with Manuel Machado (produced 1928). In *Teatro completo*, 1932.

La Lola se va a los puertos, with Manuel Machado (produced 1929). 1930.

El perro del hortelano, with Manuel Machado and José López Pérez Hernández, from a play by Lope de Vega (produced 1931).

La prima Fernanda, with Manuel Machado (produced 1931). In *La duquesa de Benamejí, La prima Fernanda y Juan de Mañara*, 1942.

Teatro completo (includes *Desdichas de la fortuna; Juan de Mañara; Las adelfas*), with Manuel Machado. 2 vols, 1932.

La duquesa de Benamejí, with Manuel Machado (produced 1932). 1932.

Desdichas de la fortuna o Julianillo Valcárcel; Las adelfas; La Lola se va a los puertos. 1940.

El hombre que murió en la guerra, with Manuel Machado (produced 1941). With *Las adelfas*, 1947.

La duquesa de Benamejí, La prima Fernanda y Juan de Mañara. 1942; revised edition, 1944.

Other

Juan de Mairena: Sentencias, donaires, apuntes y recuerdos de un profesor apócrifo (poetry, essays, and sketches). 1936; edited by José María Valverde, 1972, Pablo del Barco, 1981, and by Antonio Fernández Ferrer, 1986; as *Juan de Mairena: Epigrams, Maxims, Memoranda, and Memoirs of an Apocryphal Professor, with an Appendix of Poems from the Apocryphal Songbooks*, translated by Ben Belitt, 1963.

Abel Martin; Cancionero de Juan de Mairena; Prosas varias. 1943.

Antología de guerra. 1944.

Cuaderno de Literatura, Baeza 1915, edited by Enrique Casamayor. 1952.

Los complementarios y otros prosas póstumas, edited by Guillermo de Torre. 1957; *Los complementarios*, edited by Domingo Ynduráin, 2 vols., 1972, and by Manuel Alvar, 1982.

Antología, edited by José Luis Cano. 1961.

Prosas y poesías olvidadas, edited by Ramón Martínez-López and Robert Marrast. 1964.

Antología de su prosa, edited by Aurora de Albornoz. 4 vols., 1970–72.

Cartas a M. de Unamuno; Seis poemas inéditos; Papeles póstumos; Ideario; Esbozo biográfico. 1975.

La guerra: Escritos 1936–1939, edited by Julio Rodríguez Puértolas and Gerardo Pérez Herrero. 1983.

Proyecto del discurso de ingresso en la Real Academia de la Lengua. 1986.

*

Critical Studies: *Antonio Machado: Poeta y filósofo* by Santiago Monserrat, 1940; *Antonio Machado* by Arturo Serrano Plain, 1944; *Vida de Antonio Machado y Manuel* by Miguel Pérez Ferrero, 1947; *Antonio Machado* by J.B. Trend, 1953; *Antonio Machado: Su mundo y su obra* by Segundo Serrano Poncela, 1954; *La poesía de Antonio Machado* by Ramón de Zubiría, 1955, 3rd edition, 1973; *Las secretas galerías de Antonio Machado*, 1958, and *Una poética para Antonio Machado*, 1970, both by Ricardo Gullón, and *Antonio Machado* edited by Gullón and Allen W. Phillips, 1973; *Ultimas soledades del poeta Antonio Machado* by José Machado, 1958; *Estudios sobre Unamuno y Machado*, 1959, *Los poemas de Antonio Machado*, 1967, revised 4th edition, 1981, and *El pensamiento de Antonio Machado*, 1974, all by Antonio Sánchez Barbudo; *Antonio Machado: Poeta de Soria* by María Concepción Pérez Zalabardo, 1960; *Antonio Machado en el camino* by Emilio Orozco Díaz, 1962; *Humor y pensamiento de Antonio Machado en la metafísica poética* by Pablo de A. Cobos, 1963; *Antonio Machado y Guiomar* by Justina Ruiz de Conde, 1964; *The Victorious Expression: A Study of Four Contemporary Spanish Poets: Miguel de Unamuno, Antonio Machado, Juan Ramón Jiménez, Federico García Lorca* by Howard T. Young, 1964; *La Naturaleza y Antonio Machado* by Adela Rodríguez Forteza, 1965; *Antonio Machado* by Alberto Gil Novales, 1966; *Antonio Machado: Poeta del pueblo* by Manuel Tuñón de Lara, 1967; *La presencia de Miguel de Unamuno en Antonio Machado* by Aurora de Albornoz, 1968; *Poesía y prosa en Antonio Machado* by Rafael Gutierrez-Girardot, 1969; *Machado: A Dialogue with Time* by Norma Louise Hutman, 1969; *El pensamiento de Antonio Machado en Juan de Mairena* by Pablo de A. Cohos, 1971; *El intimismo en Antonio Machado* by Marta Rodríguez, 1971; *Antonio Machado: Poeta simbolista* by J.M. Aguirre, 1973; *Antonio Machado: Campos de Castilla* (in English) by Arthur Terry, 1973; *Palabra en el tiempo: Poesía y filosofía en Antonio Machado* by P. Cerezo Galán, 1975; *Ideas recurrentes en Antonio Machado* by Domingo Ynduráin, 1975; *Guía popular de Antonio Machado* by Andreas Sorel, 1975; *El simbolismo en la poesía de Antonio Machado* by Frank Pino, 1976; *Antonio Machado: Ejemplo y lección* by Leopoldo de Luis, 1975; *Antonio Machado, 1875–1939* by Antonio Campoamor González, 1976; *Estudios sobre Antonio Machado* edited by José Ángeles, 1977; *Guerra de ideas y lucha social en Machado* by D. Gomez Molleda, 1977; *Guiomar, un amor imposible de Machado* by José María Moreiro, 1980, revised edition, 1982; *El pensamiento religioso y filosófico de Antonio Machado* by Armand F. Baker, 1985; *La libra mecánica: En torno a la prosa de Antonio Machado* by Edward Baker, 1986; *La Naturaleza en la obra de Antonio Machado* by Carlos López Bustos, 1989; *Antonio Machado: El poeta y su doble* (University of Barcelona symposium), 1989; *Antonio Machado y la filosofía* by José Luis de la Iglesia and others, 1989; *Entorno a Antonio Machado* edited by Francisco López, 1989; *Antonio Machado: Soledad, infancia y sueño* by Joaquín Verdu de Gregorio, 1990; *Antonio Machado Hoy* (proceedings of the international conference, on the 50th anniversary of Machado's death), 4 vols., 1990; *Estelas en la mar: Essays on the Poetry of Antonio Machado (1875–1939)* edited by D. Gareth Walters, 1992; *Antonio Machado's Writings and the Spanish Civil War* by James Whiston, 1996; *Power of Paradox in the Work of Spanish Poet Antonio Machado: 1875–1939* by Philip G. Johnston, 2002.

*   *   *

Grandson of a governor of Seville and son of a noted folklorist, Antonio Machado was born ten months after his brother Manuel, his partner in numerous literary ventures. After youthful teamwork on a satiric series of caricatures, they translated for a French publisher, then became modernist poets. Later in life they collaborated on plays. Manuel, a pretentious aristocratic playboy, initially overshadowed Antonio, a sober democratic educator, who was unassuming, altruistic, quiet, and shy. Growing political divergences placed them on opposite sides during the Spanish Civil War.

Although Machado's literary production is small, its quality and density are unsurpassed. He began writing poetry in the 1890s, but destroyed his early post-romantic efforts. *Soledades* [Solitudes], employs modernist metrics, Parnassian plastic elements, and self-conscious aesthetics. But Machado's austere noble spirit found modernist sensibilities ultimately alien, and even this early poetry (expanded as *Soledades, Galerías y otros poemas* [Solitudes, Galleries and Other Poems]), evinces spiritual and ethical concerns uncommon in modernist writing. Compared with contemporaries of the Generation of 1898, Machado addresses the majority, while Jiménez writes for a limited minority. Unamuno's theatrical existential anguish waxes melodramatic, while Machado's art maximizes understatement. Jiménez influenced the Generation of 1927 while Unamuno, and especially Machado, influence post-war generations. Machado's humane fraternalism contrasts with his generation's rampant egomania.

Machado's lyrics comprise three distinct styles or manners, and three corresponding chronological periods. Poems written from 1897–1907 (*Soledades* and subsequent augmented editions), subjective and introspective, exhibit modified modernism, increasingly attenuated. Machado's admiration for Unamuno, who emphasized feeling and spiritual activity, exercises a deepening influence. Self-isolation while studying for *oposiciones* (competitive teachers' examinations) distanced Machado from his modernist associates. The second period (1907–17), more objective and outward-looking, comprises years in Soria expressing the Castilian spirit at its purest—*Campos de Castilla* (*The Castilian Camp*). Subsequently, Machado's preoccupations become increasingly metaphysical, although poems written in Baeza (1912–17) voice the concerns of the Generation of 1898: Spain's decline, national problems, "national character," and history.

Poesías completas closes the second period. Theatrical activity then partially fills a poetic hiatus (1919–31). The later poems (1924–36) are philosophical, ironic, pithy, aphoristic, and gnomic, sometimes deceptively prosaic. Machado also wrote love poetry ("Songs for Guiomar"), inspired by a late-life secret passion.

Soledades enjoyed moderate success but contained much that was imitative (Bécquer, Darío, and Verlaine are significant models), despite poems revealing Machado's own authentic voice. Personal themes include: the power of memory, time, reverie, death, loss of faith, dreams (with the related symbols of mirrors and galleries), temporal existence (symbolized by river, road, and fountain), nature (twilight, quiet countryside, and lonely roads), childhood in Seville, the evanescence of youth, a desperate seeking for love, the inseparability of passion and pain, melancholy, yearning disillusionment, hope, and remembrance.

The Castilian Camp contains several distinct thematic groups: Spain's decadence and destiny; poetic homages to admirable cultural figures; love for Leonor, her illness, and Machado's hope and despair; poems inspired by popular forms; and the "Proverbs and Songs" anticipating his philosophical period. Machado's masterpiece, *The Castilian Camp*, differs significantly from all his other works. Abandoning the modernist quest for ideal (and somewhat artificial) beauty, Machado discovered unadorned reality. Contemplating the arid, exhausted farmlands, stark plateaux, impoverished villages with their starving greyhounds and crumbling vestiges of former days, the poet harboured no illusions, yet looked with love to see beyond, to the flawless sky and endless horizon, the landscape flooded with moonlight. Where others saw emptiness and misery, Machado found tiny yellow flowers, wild herbs, a lone shepherd, distant mountains where eagles nest—not just a dun-coloured expanse, but shades of mauve

and ochre, gold and tan. The Roman bridge across the timeless Duero, ruins of prehistoric Numancia, and remains of Soria's medieval castle compose a panorama where history is palpable, and time visible and tangible. Love and loss, time and death, faith and doubt—eternal, universal themes of all great poetry—were no poetic pretext: Machado lived them with maximum intensity, yet in absolutely unassuming fashion, and captured them in his lyrics.

The Machados' initial theatrical efforts, adaptations of 17th-century dramatists Lope de Vega and Tirso de Molina, updated the originals through compressing, deleting, and shifting scenes; and their first original play imitated Golden Age formulas. *Desdichas de la fortuna o Julianillo Valcárcel* [The Workings of Fate; or, Julianillo Valcárcel] re-creates 17th-century political intrigues of the Count-Duke of Olivares: his illegitimate son, Julianillo Valcárcel, forcibly separated from his lower-class lover and obliged to marry the Count-Duke's cousin, pines away romantically and dies. *Juan de Mañara* revivifies one historical antecedent for the legend of Don Juan. The Machados' version stresses ethical values: Don Juan loses his seductive essence, choosing charity and a severely religious life. *Las adelfas* [Bitter Oleander] attempts modern psychological drama, notwithstanding a soap-opera plot. The brothers' greatest dramatic success presents a Flamenco singer in *La Lola se va a los puertos* [Lola Goes to Sea]: Lola is courted by several men representing different ages and social classes, but elects to become a symbol of her art. *La prima Fernanda* [Cousin Fernanda], a modern satiric comedy, targets high finance and power politics. *La duquesa de Benamejí* [The Duchess of Benamejí], their last major play, resuscitates 19th-century romanticism with the Duchess and an upper-class officer in tangled love affairs involving a gypsy girl and a Robin-Hood-style bandit. *El hombre que murió en la guerra* [The Man Who Died in the War], written in 1928, was unknown until after Antonio's death, when Manuel (ignoring political implications) had it produced. The brothers' only play in prose, it presents Antonio's ideal contemporary man, young, intelligent, liberal, and progressive, devoted to creating a new world and social order.

Nueves canciones [New Songs], *De un cancionero apócrifo* [From an Apocryphal Songbook], and *Juan de Mairena* contain Machado's ontological speculation. His heteronyms, Juan de Mairena and Abel Martín, poetic personae or masks, facilitate philosophical discussion and autocriticism. Antedating existentialism, Machado recognized the significance of his thought, pointing out that he had published certain concepts before Heidegger. The poet's final writings, *Los complementarios* [The Complementaries] (heterogeneous notebooks) and pro-Republican propaganda, cannot be considered as artistic work.

Machado's sensitivity, intensity, and emotional strength are transmitted—distilled and undiluted—through his poetry. His lyrics are neither rhetoric nor artifice; their power derives from the poet's absolute conviction, their self-evident reality and veracity, and condensation. Machado uncovers the beauty of small, humble things, but nothing he says is trivial. His death as a refugee *en route* to exile after the Civil War, and the silencing of his name by the Franco regime, failed to prevent homage by the poets who remained and those who came later. More than a decade after the dictator's death, the democratic government—belatedly, insufficiently—erected a statue honouring Machado as "one of the glories of Spain."

—Janet Pérez

MACHADO DE ASSIS, Joaquim Maria

Born: Rio de Janeiro, 21 June 1839. **Family:** Married Carolina de Novaes in 1869 (died 1904). **Career:** Journalist from age 15: proofreader, typesetter, writer, and editor; editor and columnist, *Diário do Rio de Janeiro*, and *A Semana Ilustrada*, 1860–75. Clerk, then director of accounting division, Ministry of Agriculture, Commerce, and Public Works, 1874–1908. **Awards:** Order of the Rose, 1888.**Member:** and censor, 1862–64, Conservatório Dramático Brasilerio; founding president, Academia Brasileira de Letras, 1897–1908. **Died:** 29 September 1908.

PUBLICATIONS

Collections

Obras completas. 31 vols., 1937–42.
Obra completa, edited by Afrânio Coutinho. 3 vols., 1959–62.

Fiction

Contos fluminenses. 1872.
Resurreição. 1872.
Histórias da Meia-Noite. 1873.
A mão e a luva. 1874; as *The Hand and the Glove*, translated by Albert I. Bagby, Jr., 1970.
Helena. 1876; as *Helena*, translated by Helen Caldwell, 1984.
Yayá Garcia. 1878; translated as *Yayá Garcia*, translated by Albert I. Bagby, Jr., 1977.
Memórias póstumas de Bráz Cubas. 1881; as *The Posthumous Memoirs of Braz Cubas*, translated by William Grossman, 1951; as *Epitaph of a Small Winner*, translated by Grossman, 1952; as *Posthumous Reminiscences of Braz Cubes*, translated by E. Percy Ellis, 1955; translated by Gregory Rabassa, 1997.
Papéis avulsos. 1882.
Histórias sere data. 1884.
Quincas Borba. 1891; as *The Heritage of Quincas Borba*, translated by Clotilde Wilson, 1954; as *Philosopher or Dog?*, translated by Wilson, 1954; as *Quincas Borba: A Novel*, translated by Gregory Rabassa, 1998.
Várias histórias. 1896.
Páginas Recolhidas. 1899.
Dom Casmurro. 1899; as *Dom Casmurro*, translated by Helen Caldwell, 1953; translated by R.L. Scott Buccleuch, 1992; also translated by John Gledson, 1997.
Esaú e Jacó. 1904; as *Esau and Jacob*, translated by Helen Caldwell, 1966.
Relíquias de Casa Velha. 1906.
Memorial de Ayres. 1908; as *Counselor Ayres' Memorial*, translated by Helen Caldwell, 1972; as *The Wager: Aires' Journal*, translated by R.L. Scott Buccleuch, 1990.
The Psychiatrist and Other Stories, translated by H.C. and William L. Grossman. 1963.
Casa Velha. 1968.
The Devil's Church and Other Stories, edited and translated by Jack Schmitt and Lorie Ishimatsu. 1977.

Plays

Pipelet, from the novel *Los Mystéres de Paris* by Eugéne Sue (produced 1859).
As bodas de Joaninha, with Luíz Olona, music by Martin Allu (produced 1861).
Desencantos: Phantasia dramatica. 1861.
O caminho da porta (produced 1862). In *Teatro*, 1863.
O protocolo (produced 1862). In *Teatro*, 1863.
Gabriella (produced 1862).
Quase ministro (produced 1863). 1864(?).
Montjoye, from a play by Octave Feuillet (produced 1864).
Suplício de uma mulher, from a play by Emile de Girardin and Dumas fils (produced 1865). In *Teatro*, 1937.
Os douses de casaca (produced 1865). 1866.
O barbeiro de Sevilha, from a play by Beaumarchais (produced 1866).
O anjo de Meia-Noite, from a play by Théodore Barriére and Edouard Plouvier (produced 1866).
A família Benoiton, from a play by Victorien Sardou (produced 1867).
Como elas são todas, from a play by Alfred de Musset (produced 1873).
Tu só, tu, puro amor (produced 1880). 1881.
Náo consultes médico (produced 1896). In *Teatro*, 1910.

Verse

Chrysálidas. 1864.
Phalenes. 1870.
Americanas. 1875.
Poesies completes. 1901.

Other

Correspondência, edited by Fernando Nery. 1932.
Adelaide ristori. 1955.
Translator, *Os trabalhadores do mar*, by Victor Hugo. 1866.

*

Bibliography: *Bibliografía de Machado de Assis* by J. Galante de Sousa, 1955.

Critical Studies: *The Brazilian Othello of Machado de Assis: A Study of Dom Casmurro, 1960*, and *Machado de Assis: The Brazilian Master and His Novels*, 1970, both by Helen Caldwell; *The Craft of an Absolute Winner: Characterization and Narratology in the Novels of Machado de Assis* by Maris Luisa Nunes, 1983; *The Deceptive Realism of Machado de Assis: A Dissenting Interpretation of "Dom Casmurro"* by John Gledson, 1984; *The Poetry of Machado de Assis* by Lorie Chieko Ishimatsu, 1984; *Machado de Assis: The Brazilian Pyrrhonian* by José Raimundo Maia Neto, 1994; *Machado de Assis and Feminism: Re-reading the Heart of the Companion* by Maria Manuel Lisboa, 1996; *Machado de Assis: Reflections on a Brazilian Master Writer*, edited by Richard Graham, 1999.

*   *   *

Had Machado de Assis not written in the Portuguese language—so often described as "the cemetery of literature"—there is no doubt that he would today be universally regarded as one of the greatest 19th-century writers of prose fiction. Brazil did not possess a strong novelistic tradition—the genre developed there during Machado's own lifetime—and he therefore felt free to experiment with forms and techniques which seem far closer to Kafka or Borges than to Dickens or Flaubert. While the surface texture of Machado's novels and stories is carefully realistic, providing a Balzacian panorama of Brazilian society, the universe of his fiction is an artificial, created reality of improbabilities, of egregiously unreliable narrators who speculate at length about the process of writing, of texts layered within texts.

Machado's technically traditional early novels show his intense interest in the social and psychological effects of upward mobility. This preoccupation is understandable, for Machado's own biography—the poor and dependent mulatto who attained great prestige among a white élite that came to perceive him as equally white—represents the most extreme case of upward social mobility within the hierarchical rigidity of imperial Brazil.

With *Memórias póstumas de Bráz Cubas* (*The Posthumous Memoirs of Braz Cubas*), Machado freed himself from all constraints of tradition, although his obsessive interest in social change continued. Braz Cubas's autobiographical narrative—not merely published after his death, but composed posthumously as well—is at once hilariously funny and pathetically moving. The evasive and unreliable omniscient third-person narrator of *Quincas Borba* (*The Heritage of Quincas Borba*) presents his text as the exemplification of a comprehensive theory of human behaviour—in fact a brilliant parody of Positivism and Social Darwinism—which both explains and justifies the vast network of mutual aggression and humiliation Machado saw in society; the story the narrator relates, as Machado structures it, forces us instead to reject that theory and to confront our common inhumanity.

The third of Machado's major novels, *Dom Casmurro*, is the most technically complex of all. The narrator recounts his marriage to Capitu and her infidelity, marshalling all the incriminating evidence. Half hidden within Dora Casmurro's narrative, however, is another story entirely, a mirror image of the explicit text—Capitu's story of innocence and fidelity betrayed by her husband's insane jealousy; we, as readers, must write this story for ourselves, discovering and ordering the hints and details Dora Casmurro lets slip. In the final analysis, both these absolutely irreconcilable narratives are equally valid; we cannot logically choose between them. And this is, perhaps, Machado's ultimate assault upon the traditional novel and its most basic postulate: that human experience can be arranged into meaningful and comprehensible patterns.

Machado's fiction implies two quite different possible theories: either human lives and emotions are simply too complex and illogical to be understood; or the reality of human existence is so blinding in its utter amorality and meaninglessness that we cannot bear to look upon it without the tinted lenses of our pitiable and improbable illusions—one of which is the form we call the novel.

—David T. Haberly

See the essays on *Dom Casmurro* and *The Posthumous Memoirs of Braz Cubas*.

MACHAUT, Guillaume de
See GUILLAUME DE MACHAUT

MACHIAVELLI, Niccolò (di Bernardo dei)

Born: Republic of Florence, 3 May 1469. **Family:** Married Marietta Corsini in 1501, five children. **Career:** Probably involved in overthrowing the Savonarolist government, 1498; appointed to head the new government's Second Chancery, 1498, and secretary of an agency concerned with warfare and diplomacy, 1498–1512: some 6,000 surviving documents record his unceasing activity, including trips to visit Caterina Sforza, 1499, Cesare Borgia, 1502, Rome, 1503 and 1506, France, 1504 and 1510, and Germany, 1507–08; helped to set up a standing army (which reconquered Pisa, 1509); the Florentine Republic ended with the return to power of the Medici family (under Piero dei Medici), 1512: Machiavelli was suspected of complicity in plotting against the Medici, and was jailed and exiled to Sant'Andrea in Percussina where he spent his remaining years in retirement, though he was given a few diplomatic or writing jobs. **Died:** 21 June 1527.

PUBLICATIONS

Collections

Tutte le opere. 1550(?). *The Works of the Famous Nicolas Machiavel* (includes *History of Florence; The Prince; Guelfs and Ghibilins; Life of Castruccio Castracani; Murther of Vitelli; State of France; State of Germany; Discourses on Livy; Art of War; Marriage of Belphegor; Letter in Vindication of Himself and His Writings*), translated by Henry Nevile. 1675.

Opere inedite, edited by Giovanni Maria Lampredi. 1760.

Opere inedite in prosa e in verso. 1763.

Opere, edited by Pietro Fanfani, Gaetano Milanesi, and Luigi Passerini Orsini de Rilli. 6 vols., 1873–77.

Opere letterarie, edited by Luigi Blasucci. 1964.

The Chief Works and Others, translated by Allan H. Gilbert. 3 vols., 1965, reprinted 1989.

Opere, edited by Sergio Bertelli and others. 4 vols., 1968–89.

Tutte le opere, edited by Mario Martelli. 1971.

The Portable Machiavelli, edited and translated by Peter E. Bondanella and Mark Musa. 1979.

Selected Political Writings, edited and translated by David Wootton. 1994.

The Other Machiavelli: Republican Writings by the Author of "The Prince", edited by Quentin P. Taylor. 1998.

The Ruthless Leader: Three Classics of Strategy and Power, edited by Alistair McAlpine. 2000.

Prose

Discorso dell'ordinare lo stato di Firenze alle armi. 1507(?).

Dell'arte della guerra. 1521; as *The Art of War*, translated by Peter Whitehorne, 1560; also translated by Ellis Farneworth, 1990.

Discorsi sulla prima deca di Tito Livio. 1531; as *The Discourses on Livy*, translated by Edward Dacres, 1636, translation edited by Bernard Crick, 1971; also translated by Christian E. Detmold, in *The Historical, Political and Diplomatic Writings*, 1882; as *Ten Discourses of Livy*, translated by Allan H. Gilbert, 1946; as *Discourses on Livy*, translated with introduction by Julia Conaway Bondanella and Peter Bondanella, 1997.

Discorsi. 1531; as *The Discourses*, translated by Leslie J. Walker, 2 vols., 1950, revised by Brian Richardson, 1971.

Il principe. 1532; edited by Luigi Firpo, 1974, and by Brian Richardson, 1979; translated as *The Prince*, 1560; numerous subsequent translations including, by Edward Dacres, 1640, reprinted 1968; Voltaire, 1741; J. Scott Byerley, 1810; Christian E. Detmold, in *The Historical, Political and Diplomatic Writings*, 1882; Ninian Hill Thomson, 1882; Luigi Ricci, 1903; W.K. Marriott, 1908, reprinted 1992; Allan H. Gilbert, 1946; George Bull, 1961; Daniel Donno, 1966; Peter E. Bondanella and Mark Musa, 1984; Harvey Claflin Mansfield, 1985; Russell Price, 1988; Robert M. Adams, 1977, revised edition, 1992; edited and translated by Bruce Penman, in *The Prince and Other Political Writings*, 1981; as *The Ruler*, translated by Peter Rodd, 1954; translated by David Wootton, 1995; translated by Paul Sonnino, 1996.

Istorie fiorentine. 1532; as *Florentine History*, translated by Thomas Bedingfield, 1595; also translated by "M.K.," 1674; and W.K. Mariott, 1909; as *The History of Florence*, translated by Henry Nevile, 1675; also translated by Christian E. Detmold, in *The Historical, Political and Diplomatic Writings*, 1882; and Ninian Hill Thomson, 2 vols., 1906; as *The Florentine Histories*, translated by C. Edwards Lester, 1845; as *History of Florence and of the Affairs of Italy*, translated anonymously, with *The Prince*, 1847; as *Reform in Florence*, translated by Allan H. Gilbert, 1946.

La vita di Castruccio Castracani da Lucca. 1532; edited by Riekie Brakkee, 1986; as *The Life of Castruccio Castracani*, translated by Henry Nevile, in *The Works of the Famous Nicolas Machiavel*, 1675; as *Castruccio Castracani*, translated by Allan H. Gilbert, 1946.

Lettere, edited by F. Fossi. 1767.

Scritti inediti (letters), edited by Giuseppe Canestrini. 1857.

The Historical, Political and Diplomatic Writings (includes *The History of Florence; The Prince; Discourses on Livy; Thoughts of a Statesman; Missions*; miscellaneous papers), translated by Christian E. Detmold. 4 vols., 1882.

The Prince and Other Pieces, edited by Henry Morley and translated by Henry Nevile. 1883.

Lettere familiari, edited by Edoardo Alvisi. 1883; as *Familiar Letters*, translated by Allan H. Gilbert, 1965.

The Private Correspondence, translated by Charles H. Moore. 1929.

The Living Thoughts of Machiavelli (includes *Discourses on Livy; The Prince; Private Letters*), edited by Count Carlo Sforza; translated by Sforza and Arthur Livingston. 1940.

The Prince; Reform in Florence; Castruccio Castracani; On Fortune; Letters; Ten Discourses of Livy, translated by Allan H. Gilbert. 1946.

Letters, translated by Allan H. Gilbert. 1946.

Corrispondenza con Francesco Vettori (1513–1515), edited by Alfredo Moretti. 1948.

Discorso o dialogo intorno a la nostra lingua, as *A Dialogue on Language*, translated by John R. Hale, in *The Literary Works*. 1961.

The Literary Works (includes *Mandragola; Clizia; Belfagor; A Dialogue on Language*), translated by John R. Hale. 1961.

Lettere, edited by Franco Gaeta. 1961.

Letters: A Selection, edited and translated by Allan H. Gilbert. 1961.

Legazioni, commissarie, scritti di governo, edited by Fredi Chiappelli. 1971–.

The Prince and Other Political Writings, edited and translated by Bruce Penman. 1981.

Fiction

Novella di Belfagor arcidiavolo. 1545; as *A Caveat for Wives to Love Their Husbands, or, Pleasant News from Hell*, 1660; as *The Marriage of Belphegor*, translated by Henry Nevile, 1675; as *The Marriage of Belfager*, 1719; as *Belfagor*, translated by John R. Hale, in *The Literary Works*, 1961.

Plays

La mandragola (produced c. 1518–20). c. 1518–24; edited by Roberto Guicciardini, 1977, and by R. Raimondi, with *Clizia*, 1984; as *Mandragola*, translated by Stark Young, 1927; also translated by Ashley Dukes, 1940; John R. Hale, 1956; Bruce Penman, in *Five Renaissance Comedies*, 1978; as *The Mandrake*, translated by Frederick May and Eric Bentley, in *Classic Theatre 1*, 1958; also translated by David Sices and James B. Atkinson, in *Comedies*, 1985.

La Clizia (produced 1525). 1532; edited by Guido Davico Bonino, 1977, and by R. Raimondi, with *Mandragola*, 1984; as *Clizia*, translated by John R. Hale, in *The Literary Works*, 1961; and translated by David Sices and James B. Atkinson, in *Comedies*, 1985.

Andria, from the play by Terence. In *Opere inedite in prosa e in verso*, 1763; and in *Teatro*, 1979; as *The Woman from Andros*, translated by David Sices and James B. Atkinson, in *Comedies*, 1985.

Tutto il teatro, edited by Bruno Cagli. 1975.

Teatro (includes *Andria; Mandragola; Clizia*), edited by Guido Davico Bonino. 1979.

The Comedies (includes *The Woman from Andros; The Mandrake; Clizia*), edited and translated by David Sices and James B. Atkinson (bilingual edition). 1985.

Verse

Decennale Primo. 1504(?).

Lust and Liberty, translated by Joseph Tusiani. 1963.

*

Bibliography: *Bibliografia machiavelliana* by S. Bertelli and P. Innocenti, 1979.

Critical Studies: *The Life and Times of Niccolò Machiavelli* by Pasquale Villari, 1892, revised edition, 2 vols., 1982; *Machiavelli and the Modern State* by Louis Dyer, 1904; *Machiavelli's Prince and Its Forerunners* by Allan H. Gilbert, 1938; *Machiavelli*, 1947, and *Discourses on Machiavelli*, 1969, both by J.H. Whitfield; *Machiavelli and the Renaissance* by Frederick Chabod, translated by David Moore, 1958; *Thoughts on Machiavelli* by Leo Strauss, 1958; *Machiavellism: The Doctrine of Raison d'État and Its Place in Modern History* by Friedrich Meinecke, translated by Douglas Scott, 1959; *Machiavelli and Renaissance Italy* by J.R. Hale, 1961; *The Life of Machiavelli* by Roberto Ridolfi, 1963; *The English Face of Machiavelli: A Changing Interpretation 1500–1700* by Felix Raab, 1964; *Machiavelli and Guicciardini: Politics and History in Sixteenth-Century Florence* by Felix Gilbert, 1965; *Studies on Machiavelli* edited by Myron P. Gilmore, 1965; *Notes on Machiavelli's Prince* by Luisa Vergani, 1967; *Fortune's Circle: A Biographical Interpretation of Niccolò Machiavelli* by C.D. Tarleton, 1970; *The Political*

Calculus: Essays on Machiavelli's Philosophy, 1972, and *The Machia-vellian Cosmos*, 1992, both by Anthony Parel; *Machiavelli and the Art of Renaissance History* by Peter E. Bondanella, 1974; *The Machiavellian Moment: Florentine Political Thought and the Atlantic Republican Tradition* by J.G.A. Pocock, 1975; *Machiavelli to Marx: Modern Western Political Thought* by Dante Germino, new edition, 1979; *Machiavelli's New Modes and Orders: A Study of the Discourses on Livy* by Harvey Claflin Mansfield, 1979; *Machiavelli* by Quentin Skinner, 1981; *Politics and Ethics: Machiavelli to Niebuhr* by Erwin A. Gaede, 1984; *Machiavelli and the History of Prudence* by Eugene Garver, 1987; *Machiavelli and Mystery of State* by Peter S. Donaldson, 1989; *Machiavelli in Hell* (biography) by Sebastian De Grazia, 1989; *Niccolò Machiavelli* by Sylvia Ruffo-Fiore, 1990; *Machiavelli and Republicanism* by Gisela Bock and others, 1991; *Machiavelli and the Discourse of Literature*, edited by Albert Russell Ascoli and Victoria Kahn, 1993; *Between Friends: Discourses of Power and Desire in the Machiavelli-Vettori Letters of 1513–1515* by John M. Najemy, 1993; *Hegemony and Power: On the Relation Between Gramsci and Machiavelli* by Benedetto Fontana, 1993; *Machiavellian Rhetoric: From the Counter-Reformation to Milton* by Victoria Kahn, 1994; *Niccolò Machiavelli's The Prince: New Interdisciplinary Essays*, edited by Martin Coyle, 1995; *Machiavelli's Three Romes: Religion, Human Liberty, and Politics Reformed* by Vickie B. Sullivan, 1996; *Machiavelli's Virtue* by Harvey C. Mansfield, 1996; *Machiavelli, Leonardo, and the Science of Power* by Roger D. Masters, 1996; *Hypocrisy and Integrity: Machiavelli, Rousseau, and the Ethics of Politics* by Ruth W. Grant, 1997; *A Case for Freedom: Machiavellian Humanism* by Adam D. Danél, 1997; *The Machiavellian Legacy: Essays in Italian Political Thought* by Joseph V. Femia, 1998; *Machiavelli* by Maurizio Viroli, 1998; *Machiavelli Redeemed: Retrieving His Humanist Perspectives on Equality, Power, and Glory* by Robert A. Kocis, 1998; *Machiavelli and Us* by Louis Althusser, translated by Gregory Elliot, 1999; *The Swarm of Heaven: A Renaissance Mystery Being Certain Incidents in the Life of Niccolo Machiavelli* by Derek Wilson, 1999; *The Machiavellian Enterprise: A Commentary on The Prince* by Leo Paul S. de Alvarez, 1999; *Niccolò's Smile: A Biography of Machiavelli* by Maurizio Viroli, translated by Antony Shugaar, 2000; *The Comedy and Tragedy of Machiavelli: Essays on the Literary Works*, edited by Vickie B. Sullivan, 2000; *Well-ordered License: On the Unity of Machiavelli's Thought* by Markus Fischer, 2000.

* * *

Niccolò Machiavelli's talents were so varied that it is difficult to classify him. Public servant, diplomat, poet, playwright, satirist, historian, he is best known as a political theorist. Yet his most celebrated work, *Il principe* (*The Prince*), does not fit easily into the category of political theory. It belongs rather to the literature of political practice.

Machiavelli's ideas on government are best represented in his *Discorsi sulla prima deca di Tito Livio* (*Discourses on Livy*). In 1513, out of favour with the Medici, he turned his mind to the question of stability in politics. Commenting on Livy's history of Rome, he accepts the cyclical theory of successive changes but suggests that they can be arrested by a modern form of mixed government, similar to a constitutional monarchy, the nearest possible to his ideal of a republic. A second-best solution was the absolute rule of a prince. Becoming interested in the problems of establishing and securing a principality, he broke off work on the *Discorsi* and wrote *The Prince*.

The Prince is based, the author claims, on long experience of modern affairs and a continual study of the past. In this it differs from earlier works on government, which describe ideal republics and principalities. Machiavelli intends to show how things really are. A ruler who tries to follow moral precepts instead of pragmatic considerations is bound to fail, for men are ungrateful, untrustworthy, cowardly, and greedy for gain. He admires Cesare Borgia for his ruthlessness and his ability to conquer by force or fraud. When dealing with opponents, half-measures are dangerous, but cruelty should not be used unnecessarily. If a prince cannot avoid being feared he can at least avoid being hated, above all by respecting the property of his subjects, "for men sooner forget the death of a father than the loss of their property."

Statements like these made *The Prince* notorious. Machiavelli was held to be the embodiment of guile and lack of scruple. Yet the literature of political practice (memoirs, reports of ambassadors, letters of statesmen) abounds in similar recommendations and comments. The impact made by *The Prince* was exceptional. This was due not so much to the novelty of Machiavelli's method as to his superb skill as a writer of lucid, trenchant, remorselessly logical prose.

The same skill is found in his *Istorie fiorentine* (*The History of Florence*). He is at his best when relating events involving suspense, such as the Pazzi conspiracy against the Medici in 1478.

His comedy, *La mandragola* (*The Mandrake*) is a perfect combination of classical form and contemporary satire. The play is a sharp and shrewd comment on hypocrisy and corruption, with superb moments of farce. Machiavelli also wrote a short story, *Novella di Belfagor arcidiavolo* (*Belfagor*), in which an archdevil is commanded to take human form on earth, choose a wife, and report back after ten years. Pretending to be a wealthy man, he chooses the most beautiful among the many women eager to marry him. He is ruined by her extravagance and takes refuge with a peasant, whom he enriches by tricks of exorcism. The peasant proves ungrateful and tricks him into believing that his wife has come to claim him. Terrified, Belfagor scuttles back to Hell. The tale, told in lively satirical style, and aimed at superstition as well as marriage, has been compared to *The Decameron*.

—Barbara Reynolds

See the essays on *The Mandrake* and *The Prince*.

MAETERLINCK, Maurice

Born: Mauritius Polydorus Maria Bernardus Maeterlinck in Ghent, Belgium, 29 August 1862. **Education:** Educated at a convent school in Ghent, age 6–7; Institut Central, Ghent, age 7–11; Jesuit Collège de Sainte-Barbe, 1874–81; studied law at University of Ghent, 1881–85, Doctor of Law, 1885, and registered as barrister, 1885. **Family:** Lived with Georgette Leblanc, 1896–1918; married Renée Dahon in 1919. **Career:** Practised law in Ghent, 1886–89; lived in Parks, 1896–1906, Grasse, 1906–11, Nice, 1911–39, Portugal, 1939–40, United States, 1940–47, and Nice again, after 1947. **Awards:** Nobel prize for literature, 1911; medal of the French Language, 1948. Honorary degrees: Glasgow University, 1919; University of Brussels, 1920; Rollins Park College, Florida, 1941. Created Count of Belgium, 1932.

Member: Belgian Royal Academy, 1920. Grand Officier, 1912, and Grand Croix, 1920, Order of Leopold; Order of St. James of the Sword, Portugal, 1939. **Died:** 6 May 1949.

PUBLICATIONS

Collections

Serres chaudes: Chansons complètes. 1955.
Poésies complètes, edited by Joseph Hanse. 1965.
Pelléas et Mélisande; Les aveugles; L'intruse; Intérieur, edited with introduction and notes by Leighton Hodson. 1999.

Plays

La Princesse Maleine. 1889; as *The Princess Maleine*, 1890; also translated by Gérard Harry, with *The Intruder*, 1892.
Les Aveugles (produced 1891). 1890; as *The Blind*, translated by Mary Vielé, with *The Intruder*, 1891; also translated in *A Miracle of St. Anthony and Five Other Plays*, 1917; as *The Sightless*, translated by Charlotte Porter and Helen A. Clarke, with *Pelleas and Melisande*, 1893; also translated by Laurence Alma Tadema, with *Pelléas and Mélisanda*, 1895; also translated as *The Blind* in *Three Pre-surrealist Plays*, translated by Maya Slater, 1997.
L'Intruse (produced 1891). 1890; as *The Intruder*, translated by Mary Vielé, with *The Blind*, 1891; also translated by W. Wilson, with *The Princess Maleine*, 1892; Haskell M. Block, 1962.
Les Sept Princesses (produced 1893). 1890; as *The Seven Princesses*, translated by William Metcalfe, 1909.
Pelléas et Mélisande (produced 1893). 1892; as *Pelleas and Melisande*, translated by Charlotte Porter and Helen A. Clarke, with *The Sightless*, 1893; also translated by Hugh Macdonald, 1982; as *Pelléas and Mélisande*, translated by Erving Winslow, 1894; Laurence Alma Tadema, with *The Sightless*, 1895; and in *A Miracle of St. Anthony and Five Other Plays*, 1917.
Trois petits drames pour marionnettes (includes *Alladine et Palomides; Intérieur; La Mort de Tintagiles*). 1894; as *Alladine and Palomides; Interior; The Death of Tintagiles*, translated by Alfred Sutro and William Archer, 1899; as *Three Little Dramas*, translated by Sutro and Archer, 1915.
Intérieur (produced 1895). In *Trois petits drames*, 1894; as *Home*, translated by Richard Hovey, in *Plays*, 1894–96; as *Interior*, translated by William Archer, in *Alladine and Palomides; Interior; The Death of Tintagiles*, 1899; also translated in *A Miracle of St. Anthony and Five Other Plays*, 1917.
Alladine et Palomides (produced 1896). In *Trois petits drames*, 1894; as *Alladine and Palomides*, translated by Charlotte Porter and Helen A. Clarke, 1895; also translated by Alfred Sutro, in *Alladine and Palomides; Interior; The Death of Tintagiles*, 1899; and in *A Miracle of St. Anthony and Five Other Plays*, 1917.
La Mort de Tintagiles (produced 1905). In *Trois petits drames*, 1894; as *The Death of Tintagiles* translated by Alfred Sutro, in *Alladine and Palomides; Interior; The Death of Tintagiles*, 1899; also translated in *A Miracle of St. Anthony and Five Other Plays*, 1917.
Plays (includes *Princess Maleine; The Intruder; The Blind; Seven Princesses; Alladine and Palomides; Pelléas and Mélisande; Home; Death of Tintagiles*), translated by Richard Hovey. 2 vols., 1894–96.

Annabella: 'Tis Pity She's a Whore, from the play by John Ford (produced 1894). 1895.
Aglavaine et Sélysette (produced 1896). 1896; as *Aglavaine and Selysette*, translated by Alfred Sutro, 1897.
Ariane et Barbe-Bleue; ou, La Délivrance inutile, music by Paul Dukas (produced 1907). In *Théâtre 2*, 1901; as *Ardiane and Barbe-Bleue*, translated by Bernard Miall, with *Sister Beatrice*, 1901; also translated by Alexander Teixeira de Mattos, with *The Betrothal*, 1918.
Soeur Béatrice (produced 1901). In *Théâtre 2*, 1901; as *Sister Beatrice*, translated by Bernard Miall, with *Ardiane and Barbe-Bleue*, 1901.
Théâtre. 3 vols., 1901–02, reprinted 1979.
Monna Vanna (produced 1902). 1901; as *Monna Vanna*, translated by Alexis Irénée du Pont Coleman, 1903; translated by Alfred Sutro, 1904; also translated by Alexis Irénée du Pont Coleman, 1993.
Joyzelle (produced 1903). 1903; as *Joyzelle*, translated by Clarence Stratton, 1906; also translated by Alexander Teixeira de Mattos, 1906.
Le Miracle de Saint-Antoine (produced 1903). 1919; as *A Miracle of St. Anthony* translated in *A Miracle of St. Anthony and Five Other Plays*, 1917; as *The Miracle of Saint Anthony*, translated by Alexander Teixeira de Mattos, 1918.
L'Oiseau bleu (produced 1909). 1909; as *The Blue Bird*, translated by Alexander Teixeira de Mattos, 1909; as *The Children's Blue Bird*, translated and adapted by Teixeira de Mattos (for children), 1913; adapted by Brian Wildsmith, 1977.
Macbeth, from the Play by Shakespeare (produced 1909). 1909.
Marie-Magdeleine (produced 1910). 1913; as *Mary Magdalene*, translated by Alexander Teixeira de Mattos, 1910.
Le Malheur passe (produced 1916?). 1925; as *The Cloud That Lifted*, translated by F.M. Atkinson, with *The Power of the Dead*, 1923.
A Miracle of St. Anthony and Five Other Plays (includes *A Miracle of St. Anthony; Pelleas and Melisande; Interior; The Death of Tintagiles; Alladine and Palomides; The Intruder*). 1917.
Le Bourgmestre de Stilmonde (produced 1918). With *Le Sel de la vie*, 1919; as *The Burgomaster of Stilemonde*, translated by Alexander Teixeira de Mattos, 1918.
Les Fiançailles (produced 1918). 1918; as *The Betrothal*, translated by Alexander Teixeira de Mattos, 1918; as *Tyltyl*, translated and adapted by Teixeira de Mattos (for children), 1920.
Le Sel de la vie. With *Le Bourgmestre de Stilmonde*, 1919.
Berniquel (produced 1923). 1929.
La Puissance des morts. 1926; as *The Power of the Dead*, translated by F.M. Atkinson, with *The Cloud That Lifted*, 1923.
Marie-Victoire. 1927.
Juda de Kérioth. 1929.
La Princesse Isabelle (produced 1935). 1935.
L'Abbé Sétubal (produced 1941). In *Théâtre inédit*, 1959.
Jeanne d'Arc. 1948.
Théâtre inédit (includes *L'Abbé Sétubal; Les Trois Justiciers; Le Jugement dernier*). 1959.

Fiction

Deux contes: Le Massacre des innocents, Onirologie. 1918; *Le Massacre des innocents*, as *The Massacre of the Innocents* translated by E.W. Rinder, 1895; also translated by Alfred Allinson, 1910.

Verse

Serres chaudes: Poèmes. 1889; as *Poems* (includes *Hot Houses; 15 Songs*), translated by Bernard Miall, 1915.

Album de douze chansons. 1896; as *Twelve Songs*, translated by Martin Schtütze, 1902.

Serres chaudes, suivi de quinze chansons. 1900.

Serres chaudes, quinze chansons, vers de fin. 1947.

Other

Works. 16 vols., 1894–1913; in 23 vols., 1915–21.

Le Trésor des humbles. 1896; as *The Treasure of the Humble*, translated by Alfred Sutro, 1897, excerpt reprinted as *The Inner Beauty*, 1910; also translated in *Three Essays*, 1946.

La Sagesse et la destinée. 1898; as *Wisdom and Destiny*, translated by Alfred Sutro, 1898; as *New Age and Happiness: Maurice Maeterlinck's Confession*, translated by Sutro, 1992.

La Vie des abeilles. 1901; as *The Life of the Bee*, translated by Alfred Sutro, 1901, excerpt reprinted as *The Swarm*, 1906; as *The Children's Life of the Bee*, edited and translated by Sutro and Herschel Williams, 1920.

Le Temple enseveli. 1902; as *The Buried Temple*, translated by Alfred Sutro, 1902.

Le Double Jardin. 1904; as *The Double Garden*, translated by Alexander Teixeira de Mattos, 1904, reprinted as *Old-Fashioned Flowers and Other Out-of-Door Studies*, 1905, and as *Old-Fashioned Flowers and Other Open-Air Essays*, 1906, excerpt reprinted as *Our Friend the Dog*, 1904, and *My Dog*, 1906.

L'Intelligence des fleurs. 1907; as *Life and Flowers*, translated by Alexander Teixeira de Mattos, 1907; as *Intelligence of the Flowers*, translated by Teixeira de Mattos, 1907, excerpt reprinted as *Measures of the Hours*, 1907, and another excerpt reprinted in *Hours of Gladness*, 1913.

Chrysanthemums and Other Essays, translated by Alexander Teixeira de Mattos. 1907.

News of Spring and Other Nature Studies, translated by Alexander Teixeira de Mattos, 1907; as *Hours of Gladness*, translated by Teixeira de Mattos, 1912.

Works. 14 vols., 1907–11.

La Mort. 1913; as *Death*, translated by Alexander Teixeira de Mattos, 1911; revised edition, as *Our Eternity*, 1913.

On Emerson and Other Essays, translated by Montrose J. Moses. 1912.

L'Hôte inconnu. 1917; as *The Unknown Guest*, translated by Alexander Teixeira de Mattos, 1914.

Les Débris de la guerre. 1916; as *The Wrack of the Storm*, translated by Alexander Teixeira de Mattos, 1916.

The Light Beyond (essays; selections from *Our Eternity; Unknown Guest; Wrack of the Storm*), translated by Alexander Teixeira de Mattos. 1917.

Les Sentiers dans la montagne. 1919; as *Mountain Paths*, translated by Alexander Teixeira de Mattos, 1919.

Le Grand Secret. 1921; as *The Great Secret*, translated by Bernard Miall, 1922.

En Égypte: Notes de voyage. 1928; as *Ancient Egypt*, translated by Alfred Sutro, 1925.

En Sicile et en Calabre. 1927.

La Vie des termites. 1927; as *The Life of the White Ant*, translated by Alfred Sutro, 1927.

La Vie de l'espace. 1928; as *The Life of Space*, translated by Bernard Miall, 1928.

La Grande Féerie: Immensité de l'univers, notre terre, influences sidérales. 1929; as *The Magic of the Stars*, translated by Alfred Sutro, 1930.

La Vie des fourmis. 1930; as *The Life of the Ant*, translated by Bernard Miall, 1930.

L'Araignée de verre. 1932; excerpts as *Pigeons and Spiders: The Water Spider; The Life of the Pigeon*, translated by Bernard Miall, 1934.

La Grande Loi. 1933; as *The Supreme Law*, translated by K.S. Shelvankar, 1934.

Avant le grand silence. 1934; as *Before the Great Silence*, translated by Bernard Miall, 1935; as *Silence*, translated in *Three Essays*, 1946.

Le Sablier. 1936; as *The Hour-Glass*, translated by Bernard Miall, 1936.

L'Ombre des ailes. 1936.

Devant Dieu. 1937.

La Grande Porte. 1939.

L'Autre Monde; ou, Le Cadran stellaire. 1942; as *The Great Beyond*, translated by Marta K. Neufeld and Renée Spodheim, 1947.

Three Essays (includes *The Inner Beauty; Silence; The Invisible Goodness*). 1946.

Bulles bleues: Souvenirs heureux. 1948.

Le "Cahier bleu," edited by Joanne Wieland-Burston. 1977.

Translator, *L'Ornement des noces spirituelles*, by Jan van Ruysbroeck. 1891; as *Ruysbroeck and the Mystics*, 1894.

Translator, *Les Disciples à Saïs*, by Novalis. 1895.

*

Bibliography: *Bibliographie de Maeterlinck: Littérature, science, philosophie* by Maurice Lecat, 1939, revised edition, in *Le Maeterlinckisme*, 2, 1941; *L'Oeuvre et son audience: Essai de bibliographie 1883–1960* by R. Brucher, 1972, supplement in *Annales de la Fondation Maurice Maeterlinck*, 18–19, 1972–73.

Critical Studies: *Maeterlinck's Symbolism: The Blue Bird and Other Essays*, 1910, and *On Maeterlinck*, 1911, reprinted 1982, both by Henry Rose; *Interpreters of Life and the Modern Spirit* by Archibald Henderson, 1911; *Maurice Maeterlinck* by Edward Thomas, 1912, reprinted 1982; *The Life and Writings of Maurice Maeterlinck* by Jethro Bithell, 1913; *The Bird That Is Blue: A Study of Maeterlinck's Two Fairy Plays* by Florence G. Fidler, 1928; *Maeterlinck and I* by Georgette Leblanc, translated by Janet Flanner, 1932, reprinted as *Souvenirs 1895–1918: My Life with Maeterlinck*, 1977; *Maeterlinck and America* by Françoise Dony Cartwright, 1935; *The Magic of Maeterlinck*, 1951, and *Maurice Maeterlinck, Mystic and Dramatist* (biography), 1984, both by Patrick Mahoney; *Maeterlinck: A Study of His Life and Thought* by W.D. Halls, 1960; *Maeterlinck's Symbolic Drama: A Leap Into Transcendence* by Miroslav John Hanak, 1974; *Maeterlinck* by Bettina Knapp, 1975; *Maeterlinck* by Auguste Bailly, 1982; *Maeterlinck's Plays in Performance* by Katharine Worth, 1985; *Modern Drama as Crisis: The Case of Maurice Maeterlinck* by Linn Bratteteig Konrad, 1986; *Maurice Maeterlinck and the Making of Modern Theatre* by Patrick McGuinness, 2000.

* * *

Maurice Maeterlinck's entire literary production can be seen as a lifelong quest better to understand the human condition, its essential enigma being death in his view. An extraordinary sensitivity as well as thirst for liberation from a narrow and stifling reality through a greater spiritual dimension characterize his early poetry. The title of his first collection, *Serres chaudes* (*Hot Houses*), refers to the soul's imprisonment and indicates a revolt against the dominant realism of the time. The poet soon chose to explore the soul's predicament in a different mode and proceeded to create a suggestive, poetic, dramatic universe where silence and absence are more eloquent than words and physical action, and in which the overwhelming forces of death and of love are presented as tragic obstacles to freedom and creative action. The so-called "second dialogue" to which the spoken one is conducive, along with "the sublime character" (Death), conveyed by reactions of fear among the real characters of the plays and thus forcefully present in its silence and invisibility, are the most innovative and effective devices in Maeterlinck's Symbolist theatre.

The setting for this metaphysical drama is often a strange fairytale world of princes and princesses, who are helplessly groping for light, love, and understanding within medieval castles, dark forests, and above murky waters—e.g. *La Princesse Maleine* (*The Princess Maleine*), *Pelléas et Mélisande* (*Pelleas and Melisande*), *La Mort de Tintagiles* (*The Death of Tintagiles*). Fear is here the pervasive feeling. But the mysterious unknown invades and threatens life and action also in a more modern—but always vague and indefinite—dramatic environment, as in *L'Intruse* (*The Intruder*) and *Intérieur* (*Interior*). Such theatrical strategies, which create distance, connect Maeterlinck's drama to classical tragedy where moral and psychological forces reign supreme over everyday reality. Yet the reductive quality of his plays aims at revealing the most ordinary experience, in fact the seemingly insignificant aspects of our lives to which most are blind. The author himself refers to this essential dimension as "the quotidian tragic" and discusses it at length in an essay by the same title: in *Le Trésor des humbles* (*The Treasure of the Humble*).

In spite of enthusiastic response from literary colleagues in Paris, Maeterlinck's symbolic, elusive, certainly avant-garde plays did not reach a wide public. It was not until he adopted a rather naturalistic style with a historical event as dramatic plot that he won world recognition as a playwright. *Monna Vanna*, though a drama of love, can be seen also as a subtle analysis of the creative and destructive powers of language. The writer had suffered a crisis in his search for meaningful knowledge and authentic expression, evidenced by two earlier plays, *Aglavaine et Sélysette* (*Aglavaine and Selysette*) and *Ariane et Barbe-Bleue* (*Ariane and Barbe-Bleue*), which made him relinquish—although reluctantly—the symbolic mode and accept the full reality of language.

Notwithstanding returns to dramatic symbolism as in *L'Oiseau bleu* (*The Blue Bird*), which also became a worldwide success, Maeterlinck gradually relied more on prose than on poetic dialogue. His many essays, most of a philosophical nature, in which his speculations on various aspects of the human condition often take their point of departure in close observation of natural life, like that of flowers and insects, found a more positive public response than the bulk of his dramatic work. He was awarded the Nobel prize in 1911, primarily for this genre. It should be noted, however, that he continued to write plays, and that his analyses in prose demonstrate a certain dramatic quality: they often proceed in question and answer form. Although his "philosophical" reflections constitute efforts to reject

nihilism and to discover consolation for a life condemned to ignorance about its meaning and purpose, the undercurrent continues to question a tragic human destiny from which Maeterlinck could never free himself. There is therefore a solid continuity in his work. The changes from poetry, to drama, and to prose, do not constitute reversals in the author's evolution as much as decisions to explore new forms of thinking and writing, necessitated by a continual threat of despair in this heroic, wonderfully perceptive, and productive quest for certainty.

—Linn Bratteteig Konrad

See the essay on *The Blue Bird* and *The Intruder*.

MAHFOUZ, Naguib (Abdel Azīz al-Sabilgi)

Born: Gamaliya, Cairo, Egypt, 11 December 1911. **Education:** Educated at the University of Cairo, 1930–34, degree in philosophy 1934, postgraduate study 1935–36. **Family:** Married 'Atiyya 'Alla' in 1954; one son and one daughter. **Career:** Secretary, University of Cairo, 1936–38; journalist: staff member, *Al-Risāla*, and contributor to *Al-Hilāl* and *Al-Ahrām*; civil servant, Ministry of Islamic Affairs, 1939–54; director of censorship, Department of Art; director of Foundation for Support of the Cinema for the State Cinema Organization, 1959–69; consultant for cinema affairs to the Ministry of Culture, 1969–71; retired from civil service, 1971. Member of board, Dar al/Ma'āref publishing house. Lives in Cairo. **Awards:** Egyptian state prize, 1956; National prize for letters, 1970; Collar of the Republic (Egypt), 1972; Nobel prize for literature, 1988. Named to Egyptian Order of Independence and Order of the Republic.

PUBLICATIONS

Fiction

Hams al-junūn [The Whisper of Madness]. 1939.
'*Abāth al aqdār* [The Mockery of Fate]. 1939.
Rhodōpis. 1943.
Kifāh Tība [Thebes' Struggle]. 1944.
Khān al-Khalīli [Khalili Market]. 1945.
Al-Qāhira al-jadīda [New Cairo]. 1946.
Zuqāq al-Midaqq, 1947; as *Midaq Alley*, translated by Trevor Le Gassick, 1966; revised edition, 1975.
Al-sarāb [Mirage]. 1949(?)
Bidāya wa-nihāya. 1949; as *The Beginning and the End*, translated by Ramses Awad, 1985.
Al-thulāthiya [The Cairo Trilogy]:
    Bayn al-Qasrayn. 1956; as *Palace Walk*, translated by William M. Hutchins and Olive E. Kenny, 1991.
    Qasr al-shawq. 1957; as *Palace of Desire*, translated by William M. Hutchins, Lorne M. Kenny, and Olive E. Kenny, 1992.
    Al-sukkariya. 1957; as *Sugar Street*, translated by William M. Hutchins and Angele Botros Samaan, 1992.
Al-lis wa-l-kilāb. 1961; as *The Thief and the Dogs*, translated by Trevor Le Gassiek and M.M. Badawi, revised by John Rodenbeck, 1984.

Al-sammān wa-l-kharīf. 1962; as *Autumn Quail*, translated by Roger Allen, 1985.

Dunyā Allah [The World of God]. 1963.

Al-Tarīq. 1964; as *The Search*, edited by Magdi Wahba, translated by Mohamed Islam, 1991.

Al-shahhāz. 1965; as *The Beggar*, translated by Kristin Walker Henry and Narim Khales Naili al Warraki, 1986.

Bayt sayyi' al-sum'a [A House of Ill-Repute]. 1965.

Tharthara fawq al-Nīl. 1966; as *Adrift on the Nile*, translated by Frances Liardet, 1993.

Awlād hāratina. 1967; as *Children of Gebelawi*, translated by Philip Stewart, 1981; as *Children of the Alley*, translated by Peter Theroux, 1996.

Miramār. 1967; as *Miramar*, translated by Fatma Moussa-Mahmoud, 1978, revised and edited by Maged el Kommos and John Rodenbeck, 1993.

Khammārat al-qitt al-aswad [The Black Cat Tavern]. 1968.

Taht al-midhalla [Under the Awning]. 1969.

Hikāya bi-la bidāya wa-la nihāya [A Story without Beginning or End]. 1971.

Shahr al-'asal [Honeymoon]. 1971.

Al-marāya. 1972; as *Mirrors*, translated by Roger Allen, 1977.

Al-hubb tahta al-matar [Love in the Rain]. 1973.

God's World: An Anthology of Short Stories, edited and translated by Akef Abadir and Roger Allen. 1973.

Al-jarīma [The Crime]. 1973.

Al-karnak. 1974; as *Al-karnak*, translated by Saad El-Gabalawy, in *Three Contemporary Egyptian Novels*, 1979.

Hikāyāt hāratina. 1975; as *Fountain and Tomb*, translated by Soad Sobhy, Essam Fattouh, and James Kenneson, 1988.

Qalb al-layl [In the Heart of the Night]. 1975.

Hadrat al-muhtaram. 1975; as *Respected Sir*, translated by Rasheed el-Enamy, 1986.

Modern Egyptian Short Stories, with Yusuf Idrīs and Sa'd al-Khādim, translated by Saad El-Gabalawy. 1977.

Malhamat at harāfīsh [The Epic of the Riff-Raff]. 1977; as *The Harafish*, translated by Catherine Cobham, 1994.

Al-hubb fawqa Hadabat al-Haram [Love on Pyramid Mount]. 1979.

Al-shaytān ya'id [Satan Preaches]. 1979.

'Asr al-hubb [Age of Love]. 1980.

Layāli alf laylah [A Thousand and One Nights]. 1981; as *Arabian Nights and Days*, translated by Denys Johnson-Davies, 1995.

Afrāh al-qubbah. 1981; as *Wedding Song*, translated by Olive E. Kenny, revised and edited by Mursi Saad el-Dīn and John Rodenbeck, 1984.

Ra'aytu fīma yara al-na'im [I Have Seen What a Sleeper Sees]. 1982.

Bāqi min al-zaman sā'ah [One Hour Left]. 1982.

Amāma al'arsh [In Front of the Throne]. 1982.

Rihlat Ibn Fattūma. 1983; as *The Journey of Ibn Fattouma*, translated by Denys Johnson-Davies, 1992.

Al-tandhīm al-sirri [The Secret Organization]. 1984.

Al-a'ish fi al-haqīqa [Living with the Truth]. 1985.

Yawm qutila al-za'īm. 1985; as *The Day the Leader Was Killed*, translated by Malak Hashem, 1989.

Hadīth al sabāh wa-al-masā' [Morning and Evening Talk]. 1987.

Sabāh al-ward [Good Morning]. 1987.

Qushtumor. 1989.

The Time and the Place and Other Stories, edited and translated by Denys Johnson-Davies. 1991.

Akhenaten: Dweller in Truth, translated by Tagreid Abu-Hassabo. 2000.

Plays

One-Act Plays, translated by Nehad Selaiha. 1989.

Other

Nagīb Mahfuz-yatazakkar [Mahfouz Remembers], edited by Jamāl al-Ghītani. 1980.

Asdaa' al-sira al-dhatiyya. 1995; as *Echoes of an Autobiography*, translated by Denys Johnson-Davies, 1997.

*

Critical Studies: *The Changing Rhythm: A Study of Nagib Mahfuz's Novels* by Sasson Somekh, 1973; ''Reality, Allegory and Myth in the Work of Najib Mahfuz'' by Mehahern Milson, in *African and Asian Studies*, 11, 1976; ''Mahfuz's Al-karnak: The Quiet Conscience of Nassir's Egypt Revealed'' by Trevor Le Gassick, in *Middle Eastern Journal*, 31(3), 1977, and *Critical Perspectives on Naguib Mahfouz* edited by Le Gassick, 1989; *Religion, My Own: The Literary Works of Nagib Mahfuz* by Matityahu Peled, 1983; *Naguib Mahfouz, Nobel 88: Egyptian Perspectives: A Collection of Critical Essays* edited by M.M. Enani, 1989; *Naguib Mahfouz's Egypt: Existential Themes in His Writings* by Gordon Hain, 1990; *Individuals and Community in Midaq Alley: Societal Dynamics in the World of Naguib Mahfouz* by Mitsuhiro Kodama, 1991; *Studies in the Short Fiction of Mahfouz and Idris* by Mona N. Mikhail, 1992; *Naguib Mahfouz: The Pursuit of Meaning* by Rasheed El-Enamy, 1993; *Naguib Mahfouz: From Regional Fame to Global Recognition* by Michael Beard and Adnan Hayden, 1993; *Naguib Mahfouz: The Pursuit of Meaning* by Rasheed El-Enany, 1993; *The Early Novels of Naguib Mahfouz: Images of Modern Egypt* by Matti Moosa, 1994; *Three Dynamite Authors: Derek Walcott (Nobel 1992), Naguib Mahfouz (Nobel 1988), Wole Soyinka (Nobel 1986): Ten Bio-critical Essays from Their Works as Published by Three Continents Press*, edited by Donald E. Herdeck, 1995.

* * *

Crowned with the Nobel prize for literature, Naguib Mahfouz reigns over 20th-century Arabic prose literature like an influential but unassuming constitutional monarch. The current success of translations of his works in many languages is unprecedented for a modern Arab author. His novels and collections of short stories portray different strata and aspects of Egyptian society, most frequently those of contemporary Cairo, although four are pharaonic novels.

Al-thulāthiya [The Cairo Trilogy], consisting of *Bayn al-Qasrayn* (*Palace Walk*), *Qasr al-shawq* (*Palace of Desire*), and *Al-sukkariya* (*Sugar Street*), is thought by many critics to be his masterpiece. It is a massive but intimate account of the emotional and intellectual development from childhood to maturity of the hero, Kamal, and of the adventures of his parents, siblings, and—in the third volume—his nephews and nieces. Part of the fascination of the Trilogy is the mirror that the fortunes and misfortunes of this family provide for those of Egypt as a whole during the period from 1917 to 1944. In the Trilogy and elsewhere, Mahfouz has been able to reveal the universal dimensions of chance events and of eccentric characters, thus introducing outsiders to some of Cairo's secret worlds while at the same time reintroducing readers to themselves.

Known for his sympathetic portrayals of female characters, this author's most typical hero, however, is the male civil servant—whether a teacher like Kamal or an office clerk like his libidinous brother Yasin—who is making his way through life none too surely, pushed in many different directions by the demands of family, sex, ambition, religion, modernity, tradition, and idealism. He has chronicled the full range of human possibilities, including the most sexually confused (for example in *Al-sarāb* [Mirage]) or corruptly degraded, in a sympathetic way that does not seem judgemental. If Mahfouz has a typical villain, it is time.

Mahfouz is an author who may weep at the tragedies of his characters without once moderating the blows he administers to them on behalf of fate. Although his works are often flavoured with a melancholy pessimism, there is usually a life-affirming thread in the fabric. Novels by Mahfouz frequently depict the comic or pathetic attempts of human beings to make sense of those fleeting moments of consciousness that constitute our allotment of the pulsing surge of evolutionary life. Traditional conservatism and revolutionary experiments are merely rival extremes in an endless dialectic that presses humanity toward a tantalizing but unreachable synthesis. Paternalism, no matter how affectionate and benevolent, is doomed to tragic failure, but so too is liberalism, understood as surrender to sensual or intellectual appetites.

An autobiographical author, Mahfouz tends to identify not with any one character, except perhaps Kamal, but with the sum of all character traits presented. Trained as a philosopher, he has allowed his heroes to brood about deep questions, without forgetting that the job of an author is to tell stories.

Besides the Cairo Trilogy, several other works by Mahfouz have acquired many fans. In *Miramār*, thought by some to be his best work, residents of a pension that has seen better days reveal their outlook and backgrounds as they react to a beautiful woman who joins the staff. *Zuqāq al-Midaqq* (*Midaq Alley*), a racy slice of working-class life in Cairo during World War II, asks readers whether the heroine should elect to be a prostitute for British forces stationed in Cairo or the wife of a nice but dull alley barber. *Al-Qāhira al-jadīda* [New Cairo] records the exploits of some school friends, one of whom willingly sacrifices his honour to further his career. Like many of his other novels, some of which have also been successfully adapted for the stage, it has been made into a popular film. *Al-liss wa-l-kilāb* (*The Thief and the Dogs*) is a brief and grim account of a convicted felon who attempts to take revenge on the powerful man who betrayed him. *Awlād hāratina* (*Children of Gebelawi*), a book banned in Egypt, draws on the heritage of the Abrahamic religions to create an allegory about mankind's continuing search for spiritual values. In *Hikāyāt hāratina* (*Fountain and Tomb*) as in other works Mahfouz has utilized elements of Islamic mysticism, here as part of the framework for a series of lively vignettes of backstreet life.

If Mahfouz has rarely shown the stylistic brilliance in Arabic of Ibrahim Abd al-Qadir al-Mazini or the natural simplicity of Tawfiq al-Hakim, he has demonstrated an awesome and deft mastery of the Arabic language, which in its vast potential resembles an enormously complicated pipe organ. Even so, Mahfouz is more noteworthy for his psychological penetration and his ability to make even minor characters convincing and appealing, no matter how disgusting, than for the poetry of his language. In his more recent fiction, Mahfouz, who has been amazingly prolific through the years, has tended to abandon the detailed social realism that first made his reputation, favouring

instead experiments in more rapid delivery of stories stripped to their psychological core or attempts to return to a more traditional, Islamic form of storytelling. Yet from the very beginning of his career with his first historical novels set in ancient Egypt, Mahfouz has been experimenting with different literary forms. The Cairo Trilogy, for all its traditional social realism, must have seemed to him a giant experiment.

—William M. Hutchins

MAIAKOVSKII, Vladimir (Vladimirovich)

Also known as Vladimir Mayakovsky. **Born:** Bagdadi, Kutais region, now Maiakovskii, Georgia (then part of the Russian Empire), 7 July 1893. **Education:** Educated at gymnasium, Kutais, 1902–06; school in Moscow, 1906–08; Stroganov School of Industrial Arts, Moscow, 1908–09; Moscow Institute of Painting and Sculpture and Architecture, 1911–14. **Career:** Political activities led to his being jailed, 1909–10; in Futurists' circle after 1912; editor, *Seized* and *New Satyricon*, Petrograd; served in the army, 1917; reader at Poets Café, Moscow, 1918; editor, *Futurist Gazette*, 1918; film actor and writer; associated with the magazine *Art of the Commune*, 1918–19, and *Art*, Petrograd; designed posters and wrote short propaganda plays and texts for Russian Telegraph Agency (Rosta), Moscow, 1919–21; co-founder, with Osip Brik, *LEF* [Left Front], 1923–25, and *Novyi LEF* [New Left Front], 1927–28. **Died:** (suicide) 14 April 1930.

PUBLICATIONS

Collections

Polnoe sobranie sochinenii [Complete Works], edited by N.N. Aseev. 12 vols., 1939–49.
Polnoe sobranie sochinenii [Complete Works], edited by V.A. Katanian. 13 vols., 1955–61.
Complete Plays, translated by Guy Daniels. 1968.
Sobranie sochinenii [Collected Works], edited by L.B. Maiakovskaia. 6 vols., 1973.
Sobranie sochinenii [Collected Works], edited by F.F. Kuznetsov. 12 vols., 1978–79.
Selected Works, edited by Alexander Ushakov, translated by Dorian Rottenberg and others. 3 vols., 1985–87.
    1. *Poetry*. 1985.
    2. *Longer Poems*. 1986.
    3. *Plays, Articles, Essays*. 1987.
Sochineniia [Works], edited by G.P. Berdnikov. 2 vols., 1987.

Verse

Oblako v shtanakh. 1915; revised edition, 1918; as *Cloud in Trousers*, in *Mayakovsky*, 1965; as *Cloud in Pants*, translated by Dorian Rottenberg, in *Selected Works*, 2, 1986.
Fleita pozvonochnik [The Backbone Flute]. 1916.
Prostoe kak mychanie [Simple as Mooing]. 1916.
Voina i mir. 1916; as *War and the World*, translated by Dorian Rottenberg, in *Selected Works*, 2, 1986.
Chelovek [Man]. 1917.

Vse sochinennoe Vladimirom Maiakovskim [Everything Written by Vladimir Maiakovskii]. 1919.

150,000,000. 1921.

Pro eto [About This]. 1923; as *It*, translated by Dorian Rottenberg, in *Selected Works*, 2, 1986.

Lirika [Lyrics]. 1923.

Vladimir Il'ich Lenin. 1924; as *Vladimir Ilyich Lenin*, translated by Dorian Rottenberg, in *Selected Works*, 2, 1986.

Khorosho!. 1927; as *Fine*, translated by Dorian Rottenberg, in *Selected Works*, 2, 1986.

Maiakovskii and His Poetry, edited by Herbert Marshall. 1942; revised edition, 1945, 1955.

Mayakovsky (selection), edited and translated by Herbert Marshall. 1965.

Stikhotvoreniia—poemy [Poetry and Narrative Verse]. 1968.

Wi the Haill Voice (in Scottish), translated by Edwin Morgan. 1972.

Poems, translated by Dorian Rottenberg. 1972.

Stikhotvoreniia i poemy [Poetry and Narrative Verse]. 1973.

Stikhi [Poems]. 1981.

Poslushaite! [Listen]. 1983.

Poemy [Narrative Verse]. 1983.

Sila klassa, slova klassa [The Strength of the Class, the Words of the Class]. 1983.

Stikhotvoreniia [Poetry]. 1983.

Stikhi i poemy [Poems and Narrative Verse]. 1984.

Stihkotvoreniia: Poemy [Poetry: Narrative Verse]. 1986.

Listen!: Early Poems 1913–1918, translated by Maria Enzensberger. 1987.

Poemy. Stikhotvoreniia [Narrative Verse: Poetry]. 1989.

For the Voice, with El Lissitzky. 2000.

Plays

Vladimir Maiakovskii (produced 1913). 1914; as *Vladimir Mayakovsky: A Tragedy*, translated by Guy Daniels, in *Complete Plays*, 1968.

Misteriia-Buff (produced 1918; revised version, produced 1921). 1919; as *Mystery-Bouffe*, translated by G.R. Noyes and A. Kaun, in *Masterpieces of the Russian Drama*, 2, 1933; also translated by Guy Daniels, in *Complete Plays*, 1968; Dorian Rottenberg, in *Selected Works*, 3, 1987.

Klop (produced 1929). 1929; as *The Bedbug*, edited by Robert Russell, 1985; translated by Max Hayward, in *The Bedbug and Selected Poetry*, 1960; also translated by Guy Daniels, in *Complete Plays*, 1968; Kathleen Cook-Horujy, in *Selected Works*, 3, 1987.

Bania (produced 1930). 1930; as *The Bathhouse*, translated by Guy Daniels, in *Complete Plays*, 1968; as *The Big Clean-Up*, translated by Kathleen Cook-Horujy, in *Selected Works*, 3, 1987.

Other

Ia: Futur-almanakh vselenskoi samosti [Me: Futuro-Miscellany of Universal Selfhood]. 1913.

Sobranie sochinenii [Collected Works]. 4 vols., 1925.

Moe otkrytie Ameriki [My Discovery of America]. 1926.

Kino. 1937.

Pis'ma [Letters], edited by Lili Brik. 1956.

The Bedbug and Selected Poetry, edited by Patricia Blake, translated by Max Hayward and George Reavey. 1960.

How Are Verses Made? 1970; as *How Make Verse*, 1985.

Essays on Paris. 1975.

Memoirs and Essays, edited by Bengt Jangfeldt and N.A. Nilsson. 1975.

Sploshnoe serdtse [Solid Heart]. 1983.

Poemy. P'esy [Narrative Verse. Plays]. 1985.

Love Is the Heart of Everything: Love Letters of Mayakovsky To Lili Brik, edited by Bengt Jangfeldt, translated by Julian Graffy. 1985.

Proza. Dramaturgiia [Prose. Drama]. 1986.

Stikhi, poemy, materialy o zhizni i tvorchestve [Poems, Narrative Verse, Material about Life and Work]. 1988.

Nashemu iunoshestvu [To Our Youth]. 1989.

*

Bibliography: "Mayakovsky: A Bibliography of Criticism (1912–1930)" by Gerald Darring, in *Russian Literature Triquarterly*, 2, Winter 1972.

Critical Studies: *The Symbolic System of Mayakovsky* by Lawrence Leo Stahlberger, 1964; *The Life of Mayakovsky* by Wiktor Woroszylski, 1971; *Mayakovsky and His Circle* by Viktor Shklovsky, 1972; *Mayakovsky, A Poet in the Revolution* by Edward J. Brown, 1973; *Maiakovskij and Futurism 1917–1921* by Bengt Jangfeldt, 1976; *Brik and Mayakovsky* by Vahan D. Barooshian, 1978; *Vladimir Mayakovsky: A Tragedy* by A.D.P. Briggs, 1979; *I Love: The Story of Mayakovsky and Lili Brik* by Ann and Samuel Charters, 1979; *Vladimir Mayakovksy* by Victor Terras, 1983; *Voskresenie Maiakovskogo* [The Resurrection of Maiakovskii] by Iury Karabchevskii, 1985; *Mayakovsky's Cubo-Futurist Vision* by J. Stapanian, 1986; *Verse Form and Meaning in the Poetry of Vladimir Maiakovskii* by Robin Aizlewood, 1989; *Mayakovsky in Manhattan: A Love Story with Excerpts from the Memoir of Elly Jones* by Patricia J. Thompson, 1993; *The Ode and the Odic: Essays on Mandelstam, Pasternak, Tsvetaeva and Mayakovsky* by Ilya Kutik, 1994.

*   *   *

Everything in Vladimir Maiakovskii evokes either admiration or indignation: his appearance, his behaviour, his poetry. He began as a subverter of authority in life and in literature. As a Futurist he revolted against all established artistic practice. The titles of many of his works reveal his individualistic self-assertion: from "I" (1913) and "I and Napoleon" (1913) to the very last unfinished poem "Vo ves' golos" ("At the Top of My Voice," 1930). Outrageous metaphors, eccentric rhymes, rough-textured phonetics, broken sentences, and heavy inversions are the mark of his poetic style. He expressed the essence of futuristic poetics when he said: "The word, its outline, its phonetic property, myth, symbol are the concept of poetry." He emphasized "the word as such" by graphic, grammatical, and rhythmical means while creating myth out of his own "I." His whole poetry can be viewed as a huge metaphor of himself. "The poet himself is the theme of his poetry," said Pasternak about the tragedy *Vladimir Maiakovskii*. He also entertained the Futurists' cult of big industrial cities. He said: "The city must take the place of nature." He never tired of militating against all established habits of living, feeling, and thinking that is called "byt"—a short untranslatable Russian word. This is especially apparent in two of his best long poems *Oblako v shtanakh* (*Cloud in Trousers*) and *Fleita pozvonochnik* [The Backbone Flute]. Describing himself as the Thirteenth Apostle, the poet denies the old society, culture, art, religion, and declares his faith in the coming revolution: "I, / mocked by my contemporaries like a prolonged dirty joke, / I perceive what no one sees / crossing the mountains of time."

Maiakovskii is often seen as a revolutionary par excellence for his innovation in poetic language and for subordinating his talent to the "social command." "To accept or not to accept [the Revolution]— for me is no question. It is my Revolution," stated Maiakovskii in 1917. To be accepted himself took a little longer. After the revolution his great ambition was to become a poet of the masses. He considerably changed his poetic manner by introducing ordinary speech, street slang, and political slogans. But he was never able to avoid wild, emotional diction, eccentric rhymes, outrageous metaphors or to resist clashing the sublime with the ridiculous in his attempt to create "a poetry for all." His poetry remains too intricate for the masses to understand. He complained: "I must confess with some pain, that even advanced revolutionary comrades, even they . . . showered us with bewildered questions: 'But what the devil is this?' 'Please explain!'." Being his own most severe censor, he "democratized" his style even further in two of his most inferior poems, *Vladimir Il'ich Lenin* (*Vladimir Ilyich Lenin*) and *Khorosho!* (*Fine*). But they help to set up Lenin as a "mythical hero." In order to strengthen the new revolutionary art he founded the highly controversial journal *LEF* [Left Front], loudly declaring its Communist and anti-aesthetic intent. Maiakovskii had always been a kind of "anti-poet"; now with *LEF* he declared a war against poetry. In a way, his practice contradicted his theories: the irrational theme—love—was his deepest concern. As Shklovsky put it, "Maiakovskii was prisoner of his theme—revolution and love—and love apologizing for having come at the time of the Revolution." The tragic end was inevitable. Marina Tsvetaeva explained his suicide as his last revolutionary act: "For 12 years on end Maiakovskii the man killed in himself Maiakovskii the poet, in the 13th the poet arose and killed the man."

Maiakovskii's "I" dominates over all his principal themes: Love, God, Art, and Revolution. He demanded the impossible from these. He "blasphemed and screamed that there is no God" in order to take His place. He assigned his art to serve the Revolution by "stepping on the throat of his own song." Disillusioned with its outcome he called for "the third Revolution of spirit." Many times a rejected lover, he shouted out in every direction and blamed God and "byt" for love's madness and pain. This "man from the future" projected a huge image of himself in his writing: "From the tail of the years I must resemble a long-tailed monster." He strikes us, however, as a sad and lonely figure: "I am lonely as the last eye left to a man on his way to join the blind." "He inflated his talent and tortured it until it burst," wrote Isaiah Berlin. His art was forcibly propagated "like potatoes in the reign of Catherine the Great" after Stalin's pronouncement in 1935: "Maiakovskii was and remains the most talented poet of our Soviet epoch. Indifference to his memory and words is a crime." As Pasternak remarked: "That was his second death and for that he is not to blame."

—Valentina Polukhina

See the essays on *About This*, *The Bedbug*, and *Cloud in Trousers*.

MALLARMÉ, Stéphane

Born: Paris, France, 18 March 1842. **Education:** Educated at schools in Passy, 1852–56; Lycée de Sens, 1856–60. **Family:** Married Marie Christina Gerhard in 1863; one daughter and one son. **Career:** Taught English in Tournon, 1863–66, Besançon, 1866–67, Avignon, 1867–70,

Lycée Fontanes, Paris, 1871–84, and Lycée Janson de Sailly, Paris, 1884–85; appointed to the Collège Rollin, Paris, 1885, retired, 1893; editor and contributor, *La Dernière Mode*, 1874–75. **Died:** 9 September 1898.

PUBLICATIONS

Collection

Oeuvres complètes, edited by Henri Mondor and G. Jean-Aubry. 1945.

Collected Poems, translated by Henry Weinfield. 1994.

Mallarmé in Prose, edited by Mary Ann Caws, translated by Jill Anderson. 2001

Verse

L'Après-midi d'un faune: Eglogue. 1876.

Los Poésies. 1887, enlarged edition, 1899, 1913; translated by Charles Chadwick in *The Meaning of Mallarmé: A Bilingual Edition of his Poésies and Un coup de dé*, 1996.

Un coup de dés jamais n'abolira le hasard. 1914; edited by Mitsou Ronat, 1980; as *Un coup de dés jamais n'abolira le hasard*, translated by Daisy Aldan, 1956; as *Dice Thrown Never Will Annul Chance*, translated by Brian Coffey, 1965; translated by Charles Chadwick in *The Meaning of Mallarmé: A Bilingual Edition of His Poésies and Un coup de dés*, 1996.

Madrigaux. 1920.

Vers de circonstance. 1920.

Hérodiade, translated by Joseph T. Shipley. 1921.

Mallarmé in English Verse, translated by Arthur Ellis. 1927.

Poems, translated by Roger Fry. 1951.

Selected Poems, translated by C.F. MacIntyre. 1957.

Poems, translated by Keith Bosley. 1977.

Poésies, translated by Arthur Symons. 1986.

Poems, translated by Brian Coffey. 1990.

Other

Les Mots anglais. 1877.

Les Dieux antiques. 1880.

Album de vers et de prose. 1887.

Villiers de L'Isle-Adam. 1890.

Pages. 1891.

Vers et prose. 1893.

La Musique et les lettres. 1895.

Divagations. 1897.

Igitur; ou, La Folie d'Elbehnon. 1925.

Contes indiens. 1927.

Thèmes anglais. 1937.

Correspondance, edited by Henri Mondor, J.P. Richard, and Lloyd James Austin. 11 vols., 1959–85.

Selected Letters, edited and translated by Rosemary Lloyd. 1988.

Editor, *Favourite Tales for Very Young Children*, by James Stephens. 1885.

Translator, *Le Corbeau, The Raven*, by Poe. 1875.

Translator, *L'Étoile des fées*, by Mrs. W.-C. Elphinstone Hope. 1881.

Translator, *Les Poèmes d'Edgar Poe.* 1888.

Translator, *Le "Ten O'Clock,"* by J.M. Whistler. 1888.

*

Critical Studies: *Towards "Hériodade"*, 1934, and *Mallarmé's "Grand Oeuvre"*, 1962, both by A.R. Chisolm; *Mallarmé* by Wallace Fowlie, 1953; *Mallarmé and the Symbolist Drama* by Haskell M. Block, 1963; *Toward the Poems of Mallarmé*, 1965, *Mallarmé's "Un coup de dés,"* 1980, *Mallarmé Igitur*, 1981, and *Mallarmé's Prose Poems: A Critical Study*, 1987, all by Robert Greer Cohn; *Mallarmé* by Guy Michaud, 1966; *Mallarmé* by Frederick C. Saint Aubyn, 1969, revised edition, 1989; *The Anatomy of Poesis: The Prose Poems of Mallarmé* by Ursula Franklin, 1976; *The Prose of Mallarmé: The Evolution of a Literary Language* by Judy Kravis, 1976; *The Aesthetics of Mallarmé in Relation to His Public* by Paula Gilbert Lewis, 1976; *Mallarmé and the Art of Being Difficult* by Malcolm Bowie, 1979; *The Early Mallarmé* by Austin Gill, 2 vols., 1979–86; *Vers le théâtre intérieur: Elements of Mallarmé's Total Art Form* by William Carpenter, 1981; *The Death of Stéphane Mallarmé* by Leo Bersani, 1982; *Desire Seeking Expression: Mallarmé's Prose pour Des Esseintes* by Marshall C. Olds, 1983; *The Symbolist Home and the Tragic Home: Mallarmé and Oedipus* by Richard E. Goodwin, 1984; *Poésies*, edited by Rosemary Lloyd, 1984; *Mallarmé's "Divine Transposition": Real and Apparent Sources of Literary Value* by Peter Dayan, 1986; *Patterns of Thought in Rimbaud and Mallarmé* by John Porter Houston, 1986; *Mallarmé and the Sublime* by Louis Wirth Marvick, 1986; *The Dynamics of Space: Mallarmé's "Un coup de dés jamais n'abolira le hasard"* by Virginia La Charité, 1987; *The Obscure and the Mysterious: A Research in Mallarmé's Symbolist Poetry* by K.D. Sethna, 1987; *Eros Under Glass: Psychoanalysis and Mallarmé's Hérodiade* by Mary Ellen Wolf, 1987; *The Poetics of the Occasion: Mallarmé and the Poetry of Circumstance* by Marian Zwerling Sugano, 1992; *The Poem on the Edge of the Word: The Limits of Language and the Uses of Silence in the Poetry of Mallarmé, Rilke, and Vallejo* by Dianna C. Niebylski, 1993; *Performance in the Texts of Mallarmé: The Passage from Art to Ritual* by Mary Lewis Shaw, 1993; *Poetry and Painting: Baudelaire, Mallarmé, Apollinaire, and Their Painter Friends* by Alan Bowness, 1994; *Mallarmé: A Throw of the Dice* (biography) by Gordon Millan, 1994; *The Orphic Moment: Shaman to Poet-Thinker in Plato, Nietzsche, and Mallarmé* by Robert McGahey, 1994; *The Name of the Poet: Onamastics and Anonymity in the Works of Stéphane Mallarmé* by Michael Temple, 1995; *Symbolist Aesthetics and Early Abstract Art: Sites of Imaginary Space* by Dee Reynolds, 1995; *Unfolding Mallarmé: The Development of a Poetic Art* by Roger Pearson, 1996; *Unlocking Mallarmé* by Graham Robb, 1996; *Meetings with Mallarmé: In Contemporary French Culture*, edited by Michael Temple, 1998; *Mallarmé in the Twentieth Century*, edited by Robert Greer Cohn, 1998; *Mallarmé: The Poet and His Circle* by Rosemary Lloyd, 1999; *Situating Mallarmé* by David Kinloch and Gordon Millan, 2000.

* * *

Stéphane Mallarmé is a significant figure in the history of French literature, not only because his poetry is strikingly unusual and fine, but because he was a major influence on the poets of the next generation. Writers such as Paul Valéry in France, Stefan George in Germany, d'Annunzio in Italy, and Oscar Wilde in England, all acknowledge their debt to Mallarmé.

The extent of his influence seems ironic; after all, his aim to render poetry less accessible to a general readership, to "purify the language of the tribe," as the alchemist transforms dross to gold, hardly seems conducive to widespread influence. Mallarmé's poems are far from easy to read. But he was the key figure in a movement which achieved a complete transformation of French poetry. Poets such as Rimbaud and Verlaine had for some time been trying to escape the excesses of Romantic lyricism, and when, in 1884, Verlaine published *Les Poètes maudits* [The Accursed Poets], a collection that included some of Mallarmé's compositions, the public became aware for the first time that a revolution had been fermenting, and that Mallarmé was one of the leading revolutionaries. In Huysmans's *À Rebours* (*Against Nature*), the hero, not surprisingly, bears many of Mallarmé's own characteristics; Huysmans openly extols Mallarmé's work, calling it "... this condensed literature, this concentration of essence, this purification of art ...." Mallarmé, modest and reserved though he was, found himself a literary celebrity, and hailed as the leading light of the new aesthetic movement.

His own definition of poetry, as he stated it in 1885, is that "Poetry is the expression, by means of the human language restored to its essential rhythm, of the mysterious sense of certain aspects of existence; poetry thus endows our span on earth with authenticity, and constitutes our sole spiritual task ...." An investigation of Mallarmé's writings prior to this statement shows to what extent this was a summary of his own practice. As early as the year 1862 he had declared his allegiance to the new art, when he wrote in an article entitled "Hérésie artistique: L'Art pour tous" that "... everything sacred that is to remain sacred is veiled in mystery." It is the poet's task to restore the sense of religious mystery to poetry, to preserve its sanctity. The notion of a task, together with the cultivation of mystery, are at the core of Mallarmé's work.

Although the poet's mission is to purify language, the ideal of absolute purity may conflict with his vocation. The poet, in Mallarmé's words, is like "a ridiculous Hamlet who can't come to terms with his own downfall." How can the poet reconcile an imperative vocation with the inaccessibility of his ideal? The conflict is clearly expressed in an image recurring throughout Mallarmé's work, namely that of whiteness. White is both a non-colour and the synthesis of all colours; it represents at once potential (the whiteness of a virgin page to be covered with lines of poetry), and, at the same time, sterility (the clinical whiteness of hospital curtains, the "sterile winter" imprisoning the swan).

Two longer poems, the dramatic pieces *Hérodiade* and *L'Après-midi d'un faune* [The Afternoon of a Faun], again demonstrate the complexity of the conflict. The princess Herodias refuses life and its attractions for the sake of purity. Her nurse, who tries in vain to tempt her back to life, asks the crucial question:

> For whom, devoured
> By anguish, do you reserve the unknown splendour
> And the vain mystery of your being?

The Faun is Herodias's counterpart and complement. Where Herodias is sheathed in icy reserve, the Faun is all fire and desire. He sees two nymphs asleep, united in an embrace, and, witnessing their "extase d'être deux," their ecstasy at being two, he tries to possess them, bearing them away in his arms. But they awake and flee. The Faun is left alone with his memories, pondering them in the silence. Are they real, or are they merely a figment of his imagination? He is punished for attempting to divide what was once whole, for trying to sully the purity that his alter ego, Herodias, wanted to preserve at all costs.

Mallarmé was a little puzzled that Debussy should want to set *L'Après-midi d'un faune* to music—was it not already musical enough? The restoration of language "to its essential rhythm" involved the exploitation of the sound, rather than the meaning, of words, so that they would appeal, as music does, to the reader's senses before appealing to his intellect. The reader must be aware of this fact if he is to appreciate Mallarmé's poetry. In order to enhance the music of language, Mallarmé distorted conventional syntax, developed the significance of rhythm and vowel-pitch, and made extensive use of aural evocation. All these techniques present difficulties for the translator, and indeed for the reader of a translation. The sonnet "Une dentelle s'abolit" ("A Lace Curtain Stands Effaced") ends with the line "Filial on aurait pu naître," which has been translated as "Filial one might be born." It is inevitable that part of the richness of the French should be lost, and unfortunate that the aural evocation of "n'être," a negation of being, which adds a crucial ambiguity to Mallarmé's original French line, cannot be conveyed by a similar technique in English.

However, as Mallarmé stated during the composition of *Hérodiade*, he was creating a "très nouvelle poétique," a very new mode of poetic expression, whose chief aim was to "peindre, non la chose mais l'effet qu'elle produit"—to paint, not the object itself, but the effect it produces. In other words, Mallarmé relies on the sensation aroused in the reader by his words rather than on any intellectual process of analysis. If the English translation is capable of arousing similar sensations, the loss of certain nuances is only of secondary importance.

In the light of Mallarmé's encouragement of intuitive response to his works, it is something of a paradox that they should be considered "obscure." He has been accused of wilfully baffling and disconcerting the reader, of practising "hermeticism" quite deliberately. This is undoubtedly true, up to a point. Yet the motive behind the "art of being difficult" is not merely mischievous pleasure in mystification, but Mallarmé's concern to endow his work with a third dimension. In order to identify with the Mallarmean universe, the reader has to become familiar with the idiom. The attempt to find a single logical pattern of meaning among the polyvalent images is doomed to failure. Mallarmé himself said of a young follower, "he is charming, but why does he always explain my poems? Anyone would think they were obscure!"

—Sally McMullen (Croft)

See the essays on *L'Après-midi d'un faune*, *Un coup de dés jamais n'abolira le hasard*, *Hérodiade*, and *Ses purs ongles très haut dédiant leur onyx*.

MALRAUX, (Georges) André

Born: Paris, France, 3 November 1901. **Education:** Educated in Bondy; Lycée Condorcet, Paris; École Turgot, Paris, 1915–18; attended lectures at Musée Guimet and École du Louvre, 1919. **Military Service:** Served in the French army during World War II;

wounded, imprisoned, escaped, and joined resistance: Compagnon de la Libération, medal of the Resistance, Croix de Guerre, Distinguished Order. **Family:** Married 1) Clara Goldschmidt in 1921 (divorced), one daughter; had two sons by Josette Clotis; 2) Marie-Madeleine Lioux Malraux in 1948, one stepson. **Career:** Worked for René-Louis Doyon, booksellers, and in art department of Kra, publishers, Paris; archaeological expedition to Indochina, 1923: detained for stealing ancient sculptures, but case set aside; involved in political activities in Indochina: established opposition newspaper, *L'Indochine*, later *L'Indochine Enchaînée*, 1925–26; art editor, then literary editor, and director of the Pléiade series, Gallimard publishers, Paris, after 1928. Actively engaged in political activities: fought in Spain in the civil war: Colonel of the Spanish Republic; Minister of Information in de Gaulle's government, 1945–46; Minister of Culture in de Gaulle's cabinet, 1959–69. President, Charles de Gaulle Institute, 1971. **Awards:** Goncourt prize, 1933; Louis-Delluc prize, for film, 1945; Asolo film festival prize, 1973; Nehru Peace prize, 1974. Honorary degrees: Oxford University, 1967; Jyvacskylae University, Finland, 1969; Rajshahi University, Bangladesh, 1973. Officer, Légion d'honneur. **Died:** 23 November 1976.

PUBLICATIONS

Fiction

Lunes en papier. 1921.
La Tentation de l'occident. 1926; as *The Temptation of the West*, translated by Robert Hollander, 1961.
Les Conquérants. 1928; enlarged edition, 1949; as *The Conquerors*, translated by Winifred Stephens Whale, 1929; also translated by Stephen Becker, 1976.
Royaume farfelu. 1928.
La Voie royale. 1930; as *The Royal Way*, translated by Stuart Gilbert, 1935.
La Condition humaine. 1933; revised edition, 1946; as *Man's Fate*, translated by Haakon M. Chevalier, 1934; as *Storm in Shanghai*, translated by Alastair MacDonald, 1934; as *Man's Estate*, translated by MacDonald, 1948.
Le Temps du mépris. 1935; as *Days of Wrath*, translated by Haakon M. Chevalier, 1936; as *Days of Contempt*, translated by Chevalier, 1936.
L'Espoir. 1937; as *Man's Hope*, translated by Stuart Gilbert and Alastair MacDonald, 1938; as *Days of Hope*, translated by Gilbert and MacDonald, 1938.
Les Noyers de l'Altenburg. 1943; as *The Walnut Trees of Altenburg*, translated by A.W. Fielding, 1952.
Et sur la terre. . . (unpublished chapter of *L'Espoir*). 1977.

Screenplays: *Sierra de Teruel.* 1938.

Other

Le Démon de l'absolu. 1946.
Esquisse d'une psychologie du cinéma. 1946; in *Reflections on Art*, edited by Susanne Langer, 1958.
La Psychologie de l'art: Le Musée imaginaire, La Création artistique, La Monnaie de l'absolu. 3 vols., 1947–49; as *The Psychology of*

Art: Museum without Walls, The Creative Act, The Twilight of the Absolute, translated by Stuart Gilbert, 3 vols., 1949–51; revised edition, as *Les Voix du silence*, 4 vols., 1951; as *The Voices of Silence*, translated by Gilbert, 4 vols., 1953.

The Case for de Gaulle, with James Burnham. 1949.

Saturne: Essai sur Goya. 1949; revised edition as *Saturne, le destin, l'art et Goya*, 1978; as *Saturn: An Essay on Goya*, translated by C.W. Chilton, 1957.

La Musée imaginaire de la sculpture mondiale: Le Statuaire, Des Bas-reliefs aux grottes sacrées, Le Monde chrétien. 3 vols., 1952–54.

La Métamorphose des dieux:

    L'Inaccessible. 1957; revised edition, as *Le Surnaturel*, 1977; as *The Metamorphosis of the Gods*, translated by Stuart Gilbert, 1960.

    L'Irréel. 1974.

    L'Intemporel. 1975.

Brasilia, la capitale de l'espoir (multilingual edition). 1959.

Discours 1958–1965. 1966.

Le Miroir des limbes:

    Antimémoires. 1967; revised edition, 1972; as *Anti-Memoirs*, translated by Terence Kilmartin, 1968.

Le Triangle noir. 1970.

Oeuvres. 4 vols., 1970.

La Corde et les souris:

    Les Chênes qu'on abat. 1971; as *Fallen Oaks*, translated by Irene Clephane, 1972; as *Felled Oaks*, revised and edited by Linda Asher, 1972.

    La Tête d'obsidienne. 1974; as *Picasso's Mask*, translated by June and Jacques Guicharnaud, 1976.

    Lazare. 1974; as *Lazarus*, translated by Terence Kilmartin, 1976.

    Les Hôtes de passage. 1976.

Oraisons funèbres. 1971.

Paroles et écrits politiques 1947–1972. 1973.

L'Homme précaire et la littérature. 1977.

*

Critical Studies: *André Malraux and the Tragic Imagination*, 1952; revised edition, 1967, and *André Malraux*, 1974, both by Wilbur Merrill Frohock; *André Malraux: The Conquest of Dread* by Gerda Blumenthal, 1960; *André Malraux* by Geoffrey H. Hartman, 1960; *André Malraux, Tragic Humanist* by Charles D. Blend, 1963; *Malraux: A Collection of Critical Essays* edited by R.W.B. Lewis, 1964; *Malraux: An Essay in Political Criticism* by David Wilkinson, 1967; *André Malraux* by Denis Boak, 1968; *André Malraux: The Human Adventure* by Violet M. Horvath, 1969; *A Portrait of André Malraux* by Robert Payne, 1970; *André Malraux* by Cecil Jenkins, 1972; *André Malraux and the Metamorphosis of Death* by Thomas Jefferson Kline, 1973; *Malraux's Heroes and History* by James W. Greenlee, 1975; *André Malraux* by Jean Lacouture, translated by Alan Sheridan, 1975; *Malraux: Life and Work* edited by Martine de Courcel, 1976; *Malraux: A Biography*, 1976, and *Silk Roads: The Asian Adventures of Clara and André Malraux*, 1990, both by Axel Madsen; *André Malraux* by James Robert Hewitt, 1978; *Imagery in the Novels of André Malraux* by Ralph Tarica, 1980; *Malraux: La Voie royale* by Elizabeth Fallaize, 1982; *Reflections on Malraux: Cultural Founding*

in Modernity by Will Morrisey, 1984; *Witnessing André Malraux: Visions and Re-visions* edited by Brian Thompson and Carl A. Viggiani, 1984; *André Malraux: Towards the Expression of Transcendence* by David Bevan, 1986; *Malraux: The Absolute Agnostic; or, Metamorphosis as Universal Law* by Claude Tannery, 1992; *André Malraux: A Reference Guide 1940–1990* by John B. Romeiser, 1994; *André Malraux: A Biography* by Curtis Cate, 1995; *André Malraux: Politics and the Temptation of Myth* by Gino Raymond, 1995; *Shaping the Novel: Textual Interplay in the Fiction of Malraux, Hébert, and Modiano* by Constantina Thalia Mitchell and Paul Raymond Côté, 1996; *André Malraux: A Reassessment* by Geoffrey T. Harris, 1996; *Signed, Malraux* by Jean-François Lyotard, translated by Robert Harvey, 1999; *Mona Lisa's Escort: André Malraux and the Reinvention of French Culture* by Herman Lebovics, 1999; *Soundproof Room: Malraux's Anti-aesthetics* by Jean François Lyotard, translated by Robert Harvey, 2001.

*   *   *

André Malraux's theme, running through all his works, can best be summed up by a remark made by a quite different writer in an altogether different connection. It was Gore Vidal who wrote, in *Sex, Death, and Money* (1968), that "in certain human actions, in love, in violence, [man] can communicate with others, touch and be touched, act and in the act forget his fate." This sentiment lies at the heart of Malraux's humanism also; but it is a tragic humanism, as critics have clearly perceived. W.M. Frohock, for instance, remarked: "there inheres in man's fate, in spite of all the possibilities of defeat, the possibility of the power and glory of being a man."

Malraux's mythic explorations of men (women play only a subordinate role in his fiction) caught up in history, picked out for large action by destiny, probe our fate in a grandiose manner that is comparable in few other novels. Indeed, it is to the great epic writers like Zola, Melville, or Dostoevskii that we have to turn if we are to seek parallels. Malraux is admired justly for the way he has used adventure stories—in much the same way as Melville used a whaling narrative, or Conrad used tales of the merchant navy—to convey a world-view marked by a tragic humanism which is nevertheless uniquely his own.

His individuality arises from a distinctive prose style. He uses a rhetorical manner that is elevated, imposing, even grandiloquent, on the one hand, and, on the other, a utilitarian style, modelled on Céline and the American writers of the 1920s whom he admired, which is curt, economical, and firmly action-oriented. This makes him a fine writer of stories in which men are fighting for a noble cause, especially when that cause is doomed. As a result, his best books are *La Condition humaine* (*Man's Fate*), a graphic narrative of the collapse of the Communist rebellion in Shanghai in 1927, and *L'Espoir* (*Days of Hope*), an account of the Spanish civil war seen from the Republican standpoint as a moment of glory, sacrifice, and brotherhood.

Correspondingly there is not much to laugh about in Malraux's world, and where there is humour it tends to be other-directed rather than self-directed: at the buffoon Clappique in *Man's Fate*, for instance, or at grotesques like the worthies of French Guiana satirized in *Antimémoires* (*Anti-Memoirs*). His sometimes excessive fondness for aphorisms, too, can give the impression of an inflation in which the sublime teeters on the brink of the ridiculous and in which the nobility of the utterance can slide into windy rhetoric.

In politics Malraux was a kind of pessimistic radical, which accounts for his left-wing leanings before the war and his whole-hearted endorsement of Charles de Gaulle after it. All his writings—his influential art criticism and autobiographical works as well as his novels and essays—are ultimately meditations on death. In *La Tentation de l'occident* (*The Temptation of the West*) a Chinese intellectual indicts Western man for having given death "a tragic face." Not surprisingly, therefore, Malraux's finest book, *Man's Fate*, ends on the death of love and the death of hope. Nevertheless he has done much—not only as a writer, but also as a controversial minister for the arts in de Gaulle's administration in the 1960s—to promote a sense of human dignity, a recognition of the value of a man's life which, as he once eloquently put it, "is worth nothing, but which nothing can buy."

—John Fletcher

See the essay on *Man's Fate*.

MANDEL'SHTAM, Osip (Emil'evich)

Born: Warsaw, Poland (then in the Russian Empire), 15 January 1891. **Education:** Educated at Tenishev School, St. Petersburg, 1900–07; travelled to Paris, 1907–08, and to Germany, 1908–10; attended lectures at University of Heidelberg, 1909–10; studied philosophy, University of St. Petersburg, 1911. **Family:** Married Nadezhda Iakovlevna Khazina in 1919 (formally in 1922). **Career:** Not involved politically in revolution, and freelance writer in 1920s: translator of works by Upton Sinclair, Jules Romains, Charles de Coster, and others; a poem critical of Stalin in 1934 led to sentence of hard labour on White Sea canal: sentence commuted to exile in Cherdyn, later in Voronezh; exile ended in 1937, but he was arrested again in May 1938, and died in labour camp near Vladivostock. **Died:** 27 December 1938.

PUBLICATIONS

Collections

Sobranie sochinenii [Collected Works], edited by Gleb Struve. 1955.
Sobranie sochinenii [Collected Works], edited by Gleb Struve and Boris Filippov. 4 vols., 1967–81; vol. 1 revised, 1967; vol. 2 revised, 1971.
Complete Poetry, translated by Burton Raffel and Alla Burago. 1973.
Stikhotvoreniia [Poetry], edited by A.L. Dymshitz and N.U. Khardzhiev. 1974.
The Complete Critical Prose and Letters, edited by Jane Gary Harris, translated by Harris and Constance Link. 1979.
Izbrannoe [Selection], edited by P. Nerler. 1989.
Sochineniia [Works], edited by P. Nerler. 2 vols., 1990.
Sobranie sochinenii [Collected Works]. 4 vols., 1991.
Stikhotvoreniia. Izbrannaia proza [Poetry. Selected Prose]. 1991.

Sobranie proizvedenii [Collected Works], edited by S.V. Vasilenko. 1992.
The Voronezh Notebooks: Osip Mandelstam, Poems 1935–1937, translated by Richard and Elizabeth McKane. 1996.

Verse

Kamen'. 1913; revised editions, 1916, as *Pervaia kniga stikhov*, 1923, 1928; as *Stone*, translated by Robert Tracy, 1981.
Tristia. 1922; as *Vtoraia kniga* [The Second Book], 1923; as *Tristia*, translated by Bruce McClelland, 1986.
Stikhotvoreniia [Poetry]. 1928.
Selected Poems, translated by Clarence Brown and W.S. Merwin. 1973.
Selected Poems, translated by David McDuff. 1973.
Stikhotvoreniia [Poetry]. 1973.
Octets, translated by John Riley. 1976.
50 Poems, translated by Bernard Meares. 1977.
Poems, translated by James Greene. 1977; revised edition, 1980.
Otklik neba [The Response of the Sky] (with prose). 1989.
Vypriamitel'nyi vzdokh [Rectifying Deep Breath]. 1990.
The Eyesight of Wasps, translated by James Greene. 1989; revised edition, as *Selected Poems*, 1991.
Medlennyi den' [Slow Day]. 1990.
Stikhi [Poems]. 1990.
Stikhtvoreniia—Poems. 1991.
Izvozchik i Dant [The Coach Driver and Dante]. 1991.
Sokhrani moiu rech'. . . [Preserve My Speech. . .] (includes prose). 1991.
The Moscow Notebooks, translated by Richard and Elizabeth McKane. 1991.

Fiction

Shum vremeni. 1925; as *The Noise of Time*, translated by Clarence Brown, in *Prose*, 1965.
Egipetskaia marka. 1928; as *The Egyptian Stamp*, translated by Clarence Brown, in *Prose*, 1965.
Chernyi karlik [Black Dwarf]. 1992.

Other

Primus (for children). 1925.
Dva tramvaia [Two Streetcars] (for children). 1926.
Shary [Balloons] (for children). 1926.
Kukhnia [The Kitchen] (for children). 1926.
Opoezii [On Poetry]. 1928.
Puteshestvie v Armeniiu. 1933; as *Journey to Armenia*, translated by Clarence Brown, 1973.
Prose, edited and translated by Clarence Brown. 1965; revised edition, 1967; revised edition, as *The Noise of Time and Other Prose Pieces*, 1986.
Razgovor o Dante [Conversations about Dante]. 1967.
Selected Essays, edited and translated by Sidney Monas. 1977.
Voronezhkie tetradi [The Voronezh Notebooks]. 1980.
Slovoi kul'tura [The Word and Culture] (collections). 1987.
Stikhotvoreniia. Proza. Zapisnye knizhki [Poetry. Prose. Notebooks]. 1989.

I Ty, Moskva, sestra moia, legka. . . [And You, Moscow, my Sister, Light. . .] (verse, prose, memoirs, biographical material). 1990.

Stikhotvoreniia. Perevody. Ocherki. Stat'i [Poetry. Translations. Essays. Articles]. 1990.

Chelvertaia proza. Ocherki, sbornik [Fourth Prose. Essays, Note-book]. 1991.

*

Critical Studies: *Hope against Hope: A Memoir*, 1970, and *Hope Abandoned: A Memoir*, 1974, both by Nadezhda Mandel'shtam, translated by Max Hayward; *Mandelstam* by Clarence Brown, 1973; *Osip Emilievich Mandelstam: An Essay in Antiphon* by Arthur A. Cohen, 1974; *Osip Mandelstam and His Age: A Commentary on the Themes of War and Revolution in the Poetry 1913–1923* by Steven Broyde, 1975; *Mandelstam: The Later Poetry* by Jennifer Baines, 1976; *Essays on Mandelstam* by Kiril Taranovsky, 1976; *Mandelstam: The Egyptian Stamp* by Daphne M. West, 1980; *Osip Mandelstam* by Nikita Struve, 1982; *An Approach to Mandelstam* by Omry Ronen, 1983; *Substantial Proofs of Being: Osip Mandelstam's Literary Prose* by Charles Isenberg, 1986; *God's Grateful Guest: An Essay on the Poetry of Osip Mandelstam* by Ryszard Przybylski, 1987; *A Coat of Many Colors: Osip Mandelstam and His Mythologies of Self-Presentation* by Gregory Freidin, 1987; *Osip Mandelstam* by Jane Gary Harris, 1988; *The Later Poetry of Osip Mandelstam: Text and Context* by Peter Zeeman, 1988; *Mandelstam Centenary Conference* edited by Robin Aizlewood and Diana Myers, 1994; *The Ode and the Odic: Essays on Mandelstam, Pasternak, Tsvetaeva and Mayakovsky* by Ilya Kutik, 1994; *Mandelstam the Reader* by Nancy Pollak, 1995; *Osip Mandelstam and the Modernist Creation of Tradition* by Clare Cavanagh, 1995; *The Mandelstam and "Der Nister" Files: An Introduction to Stalin-Era Prison and Labor Camp Records* by Peter B. Maggs, 1996; *Mandel'shtam's Poetics: A Challenge to Postmodernism* by Elena Glazov-Corrigan, 2000.

*   *   *

Osip Mandel'shtam is regarded by many as the greatest Russian poet of the 20th century. The beginning of his brilliant poetic career is associated with the Acmeist movement, which stood for clarity and precision and rejected the Symbolists' aesthetics. The title of Mandel'shtam's first book of poems, *Kamen'* (*Stone*), suggests the Acmeists' demand that verse had to be constructed like a stone edifice. Mandel'shtam aspired to "build" his poems like Gothic Towers (see his poems "Hagia Sophia," "Notre Dame," "The Admiralty Building"): "To build," he said, "means to conquer emptiness, to hypnotize space." For the Acmeists a poet was no longer a prophet or a theurgist, but a craftsman, a master, and ". . . beauty is not the fancy of a demi-god, but the predatory eye of the simple carpenter." Hence, the abundance of architectural metaphors in Mandel'shtam's early poetry. The balance of rhythm and imagery, the classical structural organization are the hallmarks of his second collection, *Tristia*. The concreteness of the details is also balanced by their paucity. His detached view of things put a concrete detail into an abstract perspective, but he never misused philosophical terminology although he was attracted and influenced by the philosophy of

Bergson. Like Pushkin, using both the solemn archaism and the plain colloquialism, Mandel'shtam "built" the most refined lyrics of 20th-century Russian poetry. But he travelled further down its path of cultural tradition: "The silver trumpet of Catullus alarms and excites us more forcefully than any Futurist riddle" (*Slovo i kul'tura* [The Word and Culture]). Homer, Ovid, Virgil, and Dante gaze at us from every poem of the early Mandel'shtam. If *Stone* can be called his "Roman" book, *Tristia* is full of allusions to the classical world of Greece. He defined Acmeism as "the nostalgia for a world culture." World culture is given by Mandel'shtam its finest representation in the Russian language. "Such poetry does not exist in Russian. Yet, it must exist in Russian," he wrote in his essay *Slovo i kul'tura*. His poetry reflects the wholeness of our Judean—Hellenic—Latin civilization. Brodskii called him "a poet for and of civilization," others called him a bookish, erudite poet.

Reading Mandel'shtam is an endless labour (as he said of Dante), but it is also an endless pleasure. His poems are powerful and haunting. He possessed an amazing ability to reconstruct an ancient cultural heritage which he interpreted as a living active force in the contemporary world. "Mandel'shtam was a philosopher of History," wrote the critic Berkovskii. "He had to place every bird, large or small, back into the cultural nest from which it had flown." It is precisely his historical sensitivity that enabled him to comprehend the pathos of the October Revolution, "the majesty of history in the making." As he said in one of his apocalyptic poems, "The Twilight of Freedom" (1918):

> Then let us try: enormous, cumbersome,
> one screeching turn of the wheel.
> The earth is sailing. Be manful, men.

Mandel'shtam hardly ever concentrated on his own personality. The objectification of the self in his poetry reaches at times the point of obliteration: "I have forgotten the superfluous 'I'." He preferred to confront time, to celebrate life, or to redefine history. He transformed the raw materials of history—the "noise of Time"—into a cultural creation. As Sidney Monas wrote: "Mandel'shtam saw a Culture marked for death, and a new barbarism terrifying yet perhaps potentially creative, waiting at the gate." In his third and last published collection of verse, *Stikhotvoreniia* [Poetry], Hellenism has been put aside. Such poems as "The Age," "The Slate Ode," and "1 January 1924" are about the relationship between the poet and his era. Mandel'shtam found himself completely estranged from official Soviet literature. According to Nadezhda Mandel'shtam, his name was crossed out of all the Soviet periodicals after 1923. The poet was certainly aware of the increasing hostility of the new regime: "the wolf-hound age rushes onto my shoulders." Between 1925 and 1930 he wrote no poetry. Soon he fell victim to the beast. The new ideology could not accept the challenge to the very spirit of any Utopia that Mandel'shtam (and the whole of Acmeism) constituted. In 1934 he was arrested, imprisoned, and tortured. Although it was his "Epigram on Stalin" that cost Mandel'shtam his freedom and his life, he was doomed to destruction by the specific quality of his poetry and his personality. Brodskii said in his essay on Mandel'shtam: "When a man creates a world of his own, he becomes a foreign body against which all laws are aimed: gravity, compression, and annihilation. Mandel'shtam's world was big enough to invite all of these." He was deported to a small town in the Urals where he tried to commit suicide, then he was transferred to Voronezh. Some of his best poems were written during his second exile. They reveal the naked existential horror of his isolation and poverty. After having been allowed to return to Moscow (in 1937) he was rearrested (May 1938). He was moved from camp to camp until he reached the very end of Soviet territory, Vladivostok, where he died a horrible death of starvation and madness (27 December 1938). "Mandel'shtam is one of those supreme artists who convinces you that there is such a thing as poetic immortality, and that it is at one with the simplest forces of creation, so that nothing can destroy it" (C. James).

—Valentina Polukhina

MANN, Heinrich

Born: Luiz Heinrich Mann in Lübeck, Germany, 27 March 1871. Brother of the writer Thomas Mann, *q.v..* **Education:** Educated at private preparatory school, Lübeck, left 1889; apprenticed to Zahn and Jaensch, booksellers, Dresden, 1889–91. **Family:** Married 1) the actress Marie (Mimi) Kanová in 1914 (divorced 1930), one daughter; 2) Nelly Kroeger in 1939 (committed suicide 1944). **Career:** Worked for the publishers S. Fischer, Berlin, 1891–92; spent a period in a sanatorium in Switzerland suffering from tuberculosis; moved to Munich, 1894; lived in France and Italy, 1895–96, returned to Munich, 1914, moved to Berlin, 1928. Editor, *Das Zwanzigste Jahrhundert*, 1894; lecturer and journalist during the 1920s; chairman, Volksverband für Filmkunst, Berlin, 1928; president, literary section of the Prussian Academy, 1931, dismissed from office, 1933. Deprived of German citizenship; became Czech citizen in 1936. Fled to France to escape the Nazi regime, 1933–40; moved to the United States; lived in Los Angeles, 1940–49; writer, Warner Brothers film studios, Hollywood, 1940–41; accepted appointment as president of the Academy of Arts, German Democratic Republic, Berlin, 1949. **Awards:** German Democratic Republic National prize, 1949. **Died:** 12 March 1950.

PUBLICATIONS

Collections

Gesammelte Werke, edited by Alfred Kantorowicz and Sigrid Anger. 1965–.
Politische Essays, edited by Hans Magnus Enzensberger. 1968.
Gesammelte Werke. 4 vols., 1969–71.

Fiction

In einer Familie. 1894; revised edition, 1924.
Das Wunderbare und andere Novellen (stories). 1897.
Ein Verbrechen und andere Geschichten (stories). 1898.
Im Schlaraffenland. 1900; as *In the Land of Cockaigne*, translated by Axton D.B. Clark, 1929; as *Berlin: The Land of Cockaigne*, translated by Clark, 1929.
Die Göttinnen; oder, Die drei Romane der Herzogin von Assy. 1903.
Die Jagd nach Liebe. 1903.

Professor Unrat; oder, das Ende eines Tyrannen. 1905; as *Der Blaue Engel*, 1947; as *The Blue Angel*, translated anonymously, 1931, and by Wirt Williams, 1959; as *Small Town Tyrant*, translated by Williams, 1944.
Flöten und Dolche (stories). 1905.
Mnais und Ginevra (stories). 1906.
Schauspielerin (stories). 1906.
Stürmische Morgen (stories). 1906.
Zwischen den Rassen. 1907.
Die Bösen (stories). 1908.
Die kleine Stadt. 1909; as *The Little Town*, translated by Winifred Ray, 1930.
Das Herz (stories). 1910.
Die Rückkehr vom Hades (stories). 1911.
Auferstehung. 1913.
Gesammelte Romane und Novellen. 10 vols., 1917.
Die Novellen. 2 vols., 1917.
Die Armen. 1917.
Bunte Gesellschaft. 1917.
Der Untertan. 1918; as *The Patrioteer*, translated by Ernest Boyd, 1921; as *Little Superman*, translated by Boyd, 1945; as *Man of Straw*, translated by Boyd, 1947; as *The Loyal Subject*, edited by Helmut Peitsch, 1998.
Der Sohn. 1919.
Die Ehrgeizige (stories). 1920.
Die Tote und andere Novellen (stories). 1921.
Abrechnungen (stories). 1924.
Der Jüngling (stories). 1924.
Der Kopf. 1925.
Kobes. 1925.
Liliane und Paul. 1926.
Mutter Marie. 1927; as *Mother Mary*, translated by Whittaker Chambers, 1928.
Suturp. 1928.
Eugénie; oder, die Bürgerzeit. 1928; as *The Royal Woman*, translated by Arthur J. Ashton, 1930.
Der Tyrann; Die Branzilla. 1929.
Sie sind jung (stories). 1929.
Die grosse Sache. 1930.
Der Freund. 1931.
Ein ernstes Leben. 1932; as *The Hill of Lies*, translated by Edwin and Willa Muir, 1934.
Die Welt der Herzen. 1932.
Die Jugend des Königs Henri Quatre. 1935; as *Young Henry of Navarre*, translated by Eric Sutton, 1937; as *The Youth of Henri IV*, 1937; as *King Wren: The Youth of Henri IV*, translated by Sutton, 1937.
Die Vollendung des Königs Henri Quatre. 1938; as *Henri Quatre, King of France*, translated by Eric Sutton, 1938–39; as *Henry, King of France*, translated by Sutton, 1939.
Lidice. 1943.
Der Atem. 1949.
Eine Liebesgeschichte. 1953.
Empfang bei der Welt. 1956.
Das gestohlene Dokument und andere Novellen. 1957.
Die traurige Geschichte von Friedrich dem Grossen: Fragment. 1960.

Plays

Variété. 1910.
Schauspielerin. 1911.
Die grosse Liebe. 1912.
Madame Legros (produced 1917). 1913.
Brabach (produced 1919). 1917.
Drei Akte: Der Tyrann; Die Unschuldige; Variété. 1918.
Der Weg zur Macht (produced 1920). 1919.
Das gastliche Haus. 1924.
Bibi (produced 1928). 1928.
Die Unschuldige. 1929.
Das Strumpfband. 1965.

Other

Eine Freundschaft: Gustav Flaubert und George Sand (essays). 1905.
Gesammelte Werke. 4 vols., 1909.
Macht und Mensch (essays). 1919.
Diktatur der Vernunft: Reden und Aufsätze (essays). 1923.
Gesammelte Werke. 13 vols., 1925–32.
Sieben Jahre: Chronik der Gedanken und Vorgänge (essays). 1929.
Geist und Tat: Franzosen 1780–1930 (essays). 1931.
Fünf Reden und eine Entgegnung zum sechzigsten Geburtstag. 1931.
Das öffentliche Leben (essays). 1932.
Das Bekenntnis zum Übernationalen (essays). 1933.
Der Hass: Deutsche Zeitgeschichte (essays). 1933.
Der Sinn dieser Emigration (essays). 1934.
Es kommt der Tag: Deutsches Lesebuch. 1936.
Hilfe für die Opfer des Faschismus: Rede 1937. 1937.
Was will die deutsche Volksfront? 1937.
Mut (essays). 1939.
Ein Zeitalter wird besichtigt (autobiography). 1945.
Das Stelldichein; Die Roten Schuhen. 1960.
Briefe an Karl Lempke 1917 bis 1949. 1963.
Briefwechsel 1900–1949, with Thomas Mann, edited by Ulrich Dietzel. 1965; also edited by Hans Wylsing, 1968.
Briefe an Karl Lemek und Klaus Pinkus. 1965.
Verteidigung der Kultur: Antifaschistische Streitschriften und Essays. 1971.
Briefe an Ludwig Ewers 1889–1913, edited by Ulrich Dietzel and Rosmarie Eggert. 1980.
The King and His Rival: The Expanded New Edition of the Correspondence Between Thomas and Heinrich Mann, translated by Marcel Reich-Ranicki. 1985.
Letters of Heinrich and Thomas Mann: 1900–1949, edited by Hans Wysling, translated by Don Reneau. 1998.
Editor, *The Living Thoughts of Nietzsche.* 1939.
Translator, *Wer zuletzt lacht*, by Alfred Capus. 1901.
Translator, *Komödianter-Geschichte*, by Anatole France. 1904.
Translator, *Gefährliche Freundschaften*, by Choderlos de Laclos. 1905; as *Schlimme Liebschaften*, 1920; as *Gefährliche Liebschaften*, 1926.

*

Bibliography: *Heinrich-Mann-Bibliographie: Werke* by Edith Zenker, 1967; *Heinrch Mann* by Ewald Birr, 1971.

Critical Studies: *Heinrich Mann: Sein Werk und sein Leben* by Herbert Ihering, 1952; *Heinrich Mann: Eine historischkritische Einführung in sein dichterisches Werk* by Ulrich Weisstein, 1962; *Heinrich Mann* by Rolf N. Linn, 1967; *Heinrich Mann* by André Banuls, 1970; *Heinrich Mann 1871–1950: Leben und Werk in Dokumenten und Bildern* edited by Sigrid Anger, 1971; *Artistic Consciousness and Political Conscience: The Novels of Heinrich Mann 1900–1938* by David G. Roberts, 1971; *Skeptizismus, Asthetizismus, Aktivismus: Der frühe Heinrich Mann*, 1972, and *Heinrich Mann: Texte zu seiner Wirkungsgeschichte in Deutschland*, 1977, both by Renate Werner; *Heinrich Mann: Eine kritische Einführung in die Forschung* by Hugo Dittberner, 1974; *The Brothers Mann: The Lives of Heinrich and Thomas Mann 1871–1950 and 1875–1955* by Nigel Hamilton, 1978; *Heinrich Mann: Leben, Werk, Wirken* by Volker Ebersbach, 1980; *The Writer and Society: Heinrich Mann and Literary Politics in Germany 1890–1940* by David Gross, 1980; *Heinrich Mann* by Jürgen Haupt, 1980; *Heinrich Mann* by Brigitte Hocke, 1983; *Heinrich Mann's Novels and Essays: The Artist as Political Educator* by Karin Verena Gunnemann, 2002.

* * *

Four years older than his brother Thomas and with a markedly more politically-oriented perspective, Heinrich Mann was a prolific writer of prose fiction—including some 20 novels and numerous collections of short stories—and a noted essayist on cultural and political topics.

Born in Lübeck in 1871, as a teenager Mann was already writing Heinesque poetry and attempting short stories on the themes of problematic love and the despairing outsider figure. An interest in the irrational and in dream visions propelled Mann towards the increasingly popular neo-romantic mood of the day and is reflected in his first novel *In einer Familie*, though its concluding note already points to Mann's future concern with social issues. An involvement with French literature and culture generated initially during a period of recuperation from illness—plus the vantage points of abodes in both France and Italy, provided the external perspectives for Mann in his resolve now to concentrate on portraying in his fiction a Wilhelminian society he saw dominated by a decadent bourgeoisie and cynical capitalism. It was a time too when he was influenced by Nietzschean thought. His short story collections *Das Wunderbare und andere Novellen* and *Ein Verbrechen und andere Geschichten* exemplify this more positive and productive period of Mann's writing. The new satirical note of social criticism is evident in the very title of his second novel *Im Schlaraffenland* (*In the Land of the Cockaigne*). A veritable cross-section of life is presented in this novel, but the focus is on the society of "fine people" drawn into a world dominated by cynical and all-powerful financiers and businessmen, where money and possessions count for everything. Even the intellectuals and artists are not immune or excluded. The novel brought Mann recognition, but arguably his most successful and popular work is *Professor Unrat; oder, das Ende eines Tyrannen* (*The Blue Angel*). The eponymous schoolmaster-"hero" becomes infatuated with a cabaret artiste and in so doing, this rather authoritarian individual and representative of a structured society abandons himself to anarchial impulses that bring him consciously into opposition with hypocritical bourgeois standards of morality. Mann portrays the naive but positive Rosa Frühlich as epitomizing Bohemian unconventionality and generosity. The concluding message of this satire is that both individual and society are bent on self-destruction.

Important too, from 1910 onwards, were a series of essays that manifest Mann's growing political awareness and indeed a republican radicalism. The essays *Voltaire-Goethe* and *Geist und Tat* of 1910 constitute an attack against a false Germany (the *Kaiserreich*) in the search for a true *Vaterland* through French enlightenment. While Mann displayed still an intellectual approach, he found appreciation from expressionist activists such as Pfemfert and Herzog. Perhaps his most significant political essay in these years was *Zola*, 1915. The weightiest fiction is undoubtedly *Der Untertan* (*Man of Straw*), which traces the rise to power (and corresponding moral decline) of the ruthless opportunist Diederich Hessling. Once more, the theme of dominance and subservience underlies the work. So thorough was the ''exposure'' of Wilhelminian society across the broad spectrum of social, economic, political, religious, and cultural affairs that the novel could only be fully published on the downfall of the empire in 1918. Indeed its sequel and second part of a planned *Kaiserreich* trilogy of novels, *Die Armen*, was published in 1917 and seen by Mann as a work centring on the proletariat. The power of the capitalist system and of the army remains, notwithstanding the threat of strikes and the dangers of war; the workers are shown as essentially still incapable of supplanting the discredited Wilhelminian society. Mann provides a sympathetic yet critical portrayal of the worker Balrich with his individualist and idealist stance.

With an interest in the theatre too, Mann turned to political drama with plays such as *Madame Legros*, and *Der Weg cur Macht*. Everything he wrote at the time was for ''our revolution'' (e.g. the essay collection *Macht und Mensch*, 1919) and humanist and democratic became important words in his vocabulary. Yet extremist views of both right and left persuasions caused Mann to remain somewhat pessimistic, indeed sceptical. On the personal front, however, Mann's fortunes rose in every sense. The publication of *Man of Straw* in mass circulation at the end of 1918, coupled with the appearance of his collected works to date through Kurt Wolff, ensured for Mann the literary breakthrough for which he had struggled for years. He was subsequently reconciled with his brother Thomas after a lengthy bitter estrangement due to political differences (summed up, on Heinrich's part, in the *Zola* essay) and a certain literary rivalry (not least induced by Thomas's negative view of his brother's Duchess of Assy novels *Die Göttinnen*).

Mann's hopes for a greater democracy sank correspondingly as the dangers of inflation manifested themselves in Germany. The crisis is encapsulated in the essay collection *Diktatur der Vernunft* of 1923. The situation of the day is fictionally captured in the short story *Kobes*, 1925 and, also of the same year, the novel *Der Kopf*, which completed the *Kaiserreich* trilogy. This latter work traces the republican failure from 1918 and as such presents a social history of the age. There is much documentary detail that helps to make for a realistic epic, yet the theme of the bankrupting of political power and the self-destructive urge of the bourgeois intelligentsia induces savage satire from Mann's pen. The ultimate bleak prospects for the future herein presented led Mann to describe this novel as his ''saddest work.'' Mann now threw himself wholeheartedly into trying to further German-French intellectual relations (Alfred Kantorowicz argued that no one tried harder than Mann in Germany in the 20th century), and he became very much a public figure on the cultural scene. His collection of essays *Geist und Tat: Franzosen 1780–1930* reflects this affinity with France. A turning to communism had also by now

manifested itself. He called for a mass theatre that is educative; recognized the importance of talking films (the filmed version of *Professor Unrat* had just appeared under the title *Der Blaue Engel* with Emil Jannings and Marlene Dietrich and which brought Mann popular success); he further recognized the function of the popular crime detection story that would both please and at the same time present a deeper purpose—for example, *Ein ernstes Leben* (*The Hill of Lies*).

In 1931 Mann became president of the section for literature of the Prussian Academy of Arts. He became increasingly hostile towards the Nazis and an important essay in this context is *Das Bekenntnis zum Übernationalen.* With Hitler's accession to power in 1933, Mann was excluded from the Academy as a result of his political activities and fled a week later into exile in France. His continuing political commitment in the defence of culture against fascism is expressed in an essay collection of 1936, *Es kommt der Tag.* The outstanding fictional products of Mann's years in exile in France in the 1930s were the *Henri Quatre* novels—*Die Jugend des Königs Henri Quatre* (*The Youth of Henri IV*) and *Die Vollendung des Königs Henri Quatre* (*Henry, King of France*). Sixteenth-century France provides the historical backcloth to Mann's search for a greater humanity embodied in the figure of the French king. The death of Henry served to reflect the inevitable and unavoidable setbacks to be encountered on this quest. The novels betray Mann's preoccupation with the duality of ''Geist'' and ''Macht''; analogies with 20th-century Europe are not hard to find. The publication of the novel in Amsterdam attracted a very favourable response from critics.

The occupation of France drove Mann next to exile in America, where his brother Thomas was already living. The remaining years of his life were spent there in a degree of misery. His late writings do not enhance his reputation. The last novel, *Der Atem*, centres on the final hours in the life of the old aristocrat Lady Lydie Kovaisky. Her death coincides with the outbreak of World War II and symbolizes the demise of Old Europe and its cultural values. There is little action as such in the novel, much of which is given over to reflection, recollections, dreams, and inner monologues. Arguably, the most significant product of these years in America is *Ein Zeitalter wird besichtigt*, a collection of autobiographical recollections.

Mann died in 1950, a month before he was due to return to Europe to become president of the newly formed Academy of Arts in East Germany. His literary stature was assured in the Democratic Republic, where he gave his name to one of that country's most prestigious literary prizes. His work has met with a more mixed reception in the West, where critics point to the aesthetic deficiencies. Unevenness of performance in his writings is, however, almost inevitable in a writer who produced so many works over six decades. His brother Thomas described him as a ''Zivilisationsliterat'' (''cultural writer''). Undoubtedly, Heinrich Mann suffered to a degree from living in the shadow of his brother when his works were as widely known, although there were some notable exceptions. Nevertheless, Mann received, at various stages of his life, plaudits from the likes of Rilke, Musil, Benn, Schnitzler, and Brecht and remains one of the most significant literary figures in the first half of the 20th century.

—Ian Hilton

See the essay on *The Blue Angel*.

MANN, (Paul) Thomas

Born: Lübeck, Germany, 6 June 1875. Brother of the writer Heinrich Mann, *q.v.* **Education:** Educated at Dr. Bussenius's school, 1882–89; Gymnasium, Lübeck, 1889–94. **Military Service:** Military service, 1898–99. **Family:** Married Katja Pringsheim in 1905; six children, including the writers Erika and Klaus. **Career:** Worked in insurance company, Munich, 1894–95, then writer; lived in Switzerland, 1933–36 (deprived of German citizenship, 1936), Princeton, New Jersey, 1938–41, Santa Monica, California, 1941–52, and Switzerland, 1952–55. **Awards:** Bauernfeld prize, 1904; Nobel prize for literature, 1929; Goethe prize (Frankfurt), 1949; Feltrinelli prize, 1952. Honorary degree: University of Bonn (rescinded, 1936). Honorary Citizen, Lübeck, 1955. **Died:** 12 August 1955.

PUBLICATIONS

Collections

Gesammelte Werke. 14 vols., 1974.
Gesammelte Werke, edited by Peter de Mendelssohn. 1980–.
Six Early Stories, translated by Peter Constantine. 1997.
Death in Venice, Tonio Kröger, and Other Writings, edited by Frederick A. Lubich. 1999.

Fiction

Der kleine Herr Friedemann: Novellen. 1898; enlarged edition, 1909.
Buddenbrooks: Verfall einer Familie. 1900; as *Buddenbrooks: The Decline of a Family*, translated by H.T. Lowe-Porter, 1924; also translated by John E. Woods, 1993.
Tristan: Sechs Novellen. 1903.
Königliche Hoheit. 1909; as *Royal Highness: A Novel of German Court-Life*, translated by A. Cecil Curtis, 1916; revised translation by Constance McNab, 1979.
Der Tod in Venedig. 1912; as *Death in Venice*, translated by Kenneth Burke, 1925; as *Death in Venice: A New Translation, Backgrounds and Contexts, Criticism*, translated by Clayton Koelb, 1994.
Das Wunderkind: Novellen. 1914.
Herr und Hund: Ein Idyll. 1919; enlarged edition, 1919; as *Basham and I*, translated by Hermann George Scheffauer, 1923; as *A Man and His Dog*, 1930.
Wälsungenblut. 1921.
Bekenntnisse des Hochstaplers Felix Krull; Buch der Kindheit. 1922; additional chapter published as *Die Begegnung*, 1953; complete version, 1954; as *Confessions of Felix Krull, Confidence Man: The Early Years*, translated by Denver Lindley, 1955.
Novellen. 2 vols., 1922.
Der Zauberberg. 1924; as *The Magic Mountain*, translated by H.T. Lowe-Porter, 1927; also translated by John E. Woods, 1995.
Death in Venice and Other Stories, translated by Kenneth Burke. 1925.
Children and Fools, translated by Hermann George Scheffauer. 1928.
Mario und der Zauberer: Ein tragisches Reiseerlebnis. 1930; as *Mario and the Magician*, translated by H.T. Lowe-Porter, 1930.
Joseph und seine Brüder: Die Geschichten Jakobs, Der junge Joseph, Joseph in Ägypten, Joseph der Ernährer. 4 vols., 1933–43; as *Joseph and His Brothers (Joseph and His Brethren): The Tale of Jacob (Joseph and His Brothers), Young Joseph, Joseph in Egypt, Joseph the Provider*, 4 vols., translated by H.T. Lowe-Porter, 1934–44.
Nocturnes. 1934.
Stories of Three Decades, translated by H.T. Lowe-Porter. 1936; enlarged edition, as *Stories of a Lifetime*, 1961.
Lotte in Weimar. 1939; as *Lotte in Weimar*, translated by H.T. Lowe-Porter, 1940; as *The Beloved Returns*, 1940.
Die vertauschten Köpfe: Eine indische Legende. 1940; as *The Transposed Heads: A Legend of India*, translated by H.T. Lowe-Porter, 1941.
Das Gesetz: Erzählung. 1944; as *The Tables of the Law*, translated by H.T. Lowe-Porter, 1945.
Ausgewählte Erzählungen. 1945.
Doktor Faustus: Das Leben des deutschen Tonsetzers Adrian Leverkühn, erzählt von einem Freunde. 1947; as *Doctor Faustus: The Life of the German Composer, Adrian Leverkuehn, as Told by a Friend*, translated by H.T. Lowe-Porter, 1948.
Der Erwählte. 1951; as *The Holy Sinner*, translated by H.T. Lowe-Porter, 1951.
Die Betrogene. 1953; as *The Black Swan*, translated by Willard R. Trask, 1954.

Plays

Fiorenza. 1906.

Other

Bilse und Ich. 1908.
Friedrich und die grosse Koalition. 1915.
Betrachtungen eines Unpotitischen. 1918; as *Reflections of a Nonpolitical Man*, translated by Walter D. Morris, 1983.
Rede und Antwort: Gesammelte Abhandungen und kleine Aufsätze. 1922.
Von Deutscher Republik. 1922.
Okkulte Erlebnisse. 1924.
Bemühungen. 1925.
Pariser Rechenschaft. 1926.
Three Essays, translated by H.T. Lowe-Porter. 1929.
Die Forderung des Tages: Reden und Aufsätze aus den Jahren 1925–1929. 1930.
Lebensabriss. 1930; as *A Sketch of My Life*, translated by H.T. Lowe-Porter, 1930.
Goethe und Tolstoi: Zum Problem der Humanität. 1932.
Past Masters and Other Papers, translated by H.T. Lowe-Porter. 1933.
Leiden und Grösse der Meister: Neue Aufsätze. 1935.
Freud und die Zukunft: Vortrag. 1936.
Achtung, Europa! Aufsätze zur Zeit. 1938.
Dieser Friede. 1938; as *This Peace*, translated by H.T. Lowe-Porter, 1938.
Schopenhauer. 1938.
Dieser Krieg: Aufsatz. 1940; as *This War*, translated by Eric Sutton, 1940.
Order of the Day: Political Essays and Speeches of Two Decades, translated by H.T. Lowe-Porter, Agnes E. Meyer, and Eric Sutton. 1942.
Deutsche Hörer! 25 Radiosendungen nach Deutschland. 1942; as *Listen, Germany! Twenty-Five Radio Messages to the German*

649

People over BBC, translated by H.T. Lowe-Porter, 1943; enlarged edition (55 messages), 1945.

Adel des Geistes: Sechsehn Versuche zum Problem der Humanität. 1945; enlarged edition, 1956.

Leiden an Deutschland: Tagebuchblätter aus den Jahren 1933 und 1934. 1946.

Essays of Three Decades, translated by H.T. Lowe-Porter. 1947.

Neue Studien. 1948.

Die Entstehung des Doktor Faustus: Roman eines Romans. 1949; as *The Story of a Novel: The Genesis of Doctor Faustus*, translated by Richard and Clara Winston, 1961.

Goethe und die Demokratie (lecture). 1949.

Michelangelo in seinen Dichtungen. 1950.

The Thomas Mann Reader, edited by Joseph Warner Angell. 1950.

Altes und Neues: Kleine Prosa aus fünf Jahrzehnten. 1953; revised edition, 1956.

Ansprache im Schillerjahr 1955. 1955.

Versuch über Schiller. 1955.

Zeit und Werk: Tagebücher und Schriften zum Zeitgeschehen. 1956.

Nachlese: Prosa 1951–55. 1956.

Last Essays, translated by Richard and Clara Winston, Tania and James Stern, and H.T. Lowe-Porter. 1959.

Briefe an Paul Amann 1915–1952, edited by Herbert Wegener. 1959; as *Letters*, translated by Richard and Clara Winston, 1961.

Gespräch in Briefen, with Karl Kerényi, edited by Kerényi. 1960; as *Mythology and Humanism: Correspondence*, translated by Alexander Gelley, 1975.

Briefe an Ernst Bertram 1910–1955, edited by Inge Jens. 1960.

Briefe 1899–1955, edited by Erika Mann. 3 vols., 1961–65; as *Letters of Thomas Mann, 1889–1955*, edited and translated by Richard and Clara Winston, 2 vols., 1970.

Briefwechsel, with Robert Faesi, edited by Faesi. 1962.

Wagner und unsere Zeit, edited by Erika Mann. 1963; as *Pro and Contra Wagner*, translated by Allan Blunden, 1985.

Briefwechsel 1900–1949, with Heinrich Mann, edited by Hans Wysling, revised edition, edited by Ulrich Dietzel. 1968; revised edition, 1975.

Briefwechsel, with Hermann Hesse, edited by Anni Carlsson. 1968; revised edition, 1975; also edited by Hans Wysling, 1984; as *The Hesse/Mann Letters: The Correspondence of Hermann Hesse and Thomas Mann, 1910–1955*, translated by Ralph Manheim, 1975.

Das essayistische Werk, edited by Hans Bürgin. 8 vols., 1968.

Briefwechsel im Exil, with Erich Kahler, edited by Hans Wysling. 1970; as *An Exceptional Friendship: The Correspondence of Thomas Mann and Erich Kahler*, translated by Richard and Clara Winston, 1975.

The Letters to Caroline Newton, edited by Robert F. Cohen. 1971.

Briefwechse 1932–1955, with Gottfried Bermann Fischer, edited by Peter de Mendelssohn. 1973.

Briefe an Otto Grautoff 1894–1901, und Ida Boy-Ed, 1903–1928, edited by Peter de Mendelssohn. 1975.

Briefwechsel, with Alfred Neumann, edited by Peter de Mendelssohn. 1977.

Tagebücher, edited by Peter de Mendelssohn. 1977–; as *Diaries, 1918–1939*, edited by Hermann Kesten, translated in part by Richard, Clara, and Krishna Winston, 1982–.

Briefwechsel mit Autoren: Rudolf Georg Binding, edited by Hans Wysling. 1988.

Dichter oder Schriftsteller? der Briefwechsel zwischen Thomas Mann und Josef Ponten, 1919–1930, edited by Hans Wysling. 1988.

Jahre des Unmuts: Thomas Mann's Briefwechsel mit René Schickele, 1930–1940, edited by Hans Wysling and Cornelia Bernini. 1992.

Letters of Heinrich and Thomas Mann: 1900–1949, edited by Hans Wysling, translated by Don Reneau and Richard and Clara Winston. 1998.

Editor, *The Living Thoughts of Schopenhauer.* 1939.

Editor, *The Permanent Goethe.* 1948.

*

Bibliography: *Fifty Years of Thomas Mann Studies* by Klaus Werner Jonas, 1955, and *Thomas Mann Studies* by Klaus Werner and Ilsedore B. Jonas, 1967; *Das Werk Manns: Eine Bibliographie* by Hans Bürgin, 1959; *Manns Briefwerk* by Georg Wenzel, 1969; *Die Literatur über Mann: Eine Bibliographie 1898–1969* by Harry Matter, 2 vols., 1972.

Critical Studies: *Thomas Mann: An Introduction to His Fiction*, 1952, revised edition, 1962, and *From "The Magic Mountain": Mann's Later Masterpieces*, 1979, both by Henry Hatfield; *Thomas Mann: The World as Will and Representation* by Fritz Kaufmann, 1957; *The Ironic German: A Study of Thomas Mann* by Erich Heller, 1958, revised edition, 1981; *The Last Year of Thomas Mann* by Erika Mann, translated by Richard Graves, 1958; *The Two Faces of Hermes*, 1962, and *Understanding Mann*, 1966, both by Ronald D. Miller; *Essays on Thomas Mann* by Georg Lukács, translated by Stanley Mitchell, 1964; *Thomas Mann* by J.P. Stern, 1967; *Thomas Mann* by Ignace Feuerlicht, 1968; *Thomas Mann: A Chronicle of His Life* by Hans Bürgin and Hans-Otto Mayer, translated by Eugene Dobson, 1969; *Thomas Mann: Profile and Perspectives* by André von Gronicka, 1970; *Thomas Mann: A Critical Study* by R.J. Hollingdale, 1971; *Thomas Mann: The Uses of Tradition* by T.J. Reed, 1974; *Unwritten Memories* by Katia Mann edited by Elisabeth Plessen and Michael Mann, translated by Hunter and Hildegarde Hannum, 1975; *Montage and Motif in Thomas Mann's "Tristan"* by Frank W. Young, 1975; *The Devil in Thomas Mann's "Doktor Faustus" and Paul Valéry's "Mon Faust"* by Lucie Pfaff, 1976; *Thomas Mann: The Devil's Advocate* by T.E. Apter, 1978; *The Brothers Mann: The Lives of Heinrich and Thomas Mann, 1871–1950 and 1875–1955* by Nigel Hamilton, 1978; *The Preparation of the Future: Techniques of Anticipation in the Novels of Theodor Fontane and Thomas Mann*, by Gertrude Michielsen, 1978; *The Ascetic Artist: Prefigurations in Thomas Mann's "Der Tod in Venedig"* by E.L. Marson, 1979; *Thomas Mann: A Study* by Martin Swales, 1980; *Thomas Mann: The Making of an Artist 1875–1911* by Richard Winston, 1981; *Brother Artist: A Psychological Study of Thomas Mann's Fiction* by James R. McWilliams, 1983; *Myth and Politics in Thomas Mann's Joseph und seine Brüder* by Raymond Cunningham, 1985; *Thomas Mann's Recantation of Faust: "Doctor Faustus" in the Context of Mann's Relationship to Goethe* by David J.T. Ball, 1986; *Thomas Mann* edited by Harold Bloom, 1986; *Sympathy for the Abyss: A Study in the Novel of German Modernism: Kafka, Broch, Musil and Thomas Mann* by Stephen D. Dowden, 1986; *Mann the Magician; or, the Good Versus the Interesting* by Alan F. Bance, 1987; *Vision and Revision: The Concept of Inspiration in Thomas Mann's Fiction* by Karen Draybeck Vogt, 1987; *Critical Essays on Thomas Mann* edited by Inta M. Ezergailis, 1988; *Thomas Mann's Short Fiction: An Intellectual Biography* by Esther H. Léser edited by Mitzi Brunsdale, 1989; *Thomas Mann and His Family* by Marcel Reich-Ranicki, translated by Ralph Manheim, 1989; *Music, Love, Death, and Mann's Doctor Faustus* by John F. Fetzer, 1990; *Thomas Mann's Doctor*

Faustus: A Novel at the Margin of Modernism edited by Herbert Lehnert and Peter C. Pfeiffer, 1991; *Thomas Mann* by Martin Travers, 1992; *Approaches to Teaching Mann's "Death in Venice" and Other Short Fiction* edited by Jeffrey B. Berlin, 1993; *The Problematic Bourgeois: 20th-Century Criticism and Thomas Mann's Buddenbrooks and The Magic Mountain* by Hugh Ridley, 1994; *Death in Venice: Making and Unmaking a Master* by T.J. Reed, 1994; *Thomas Mann: Doctor Faustus* by Michael Beddow, 1994; *Ironic Out of Love: The Novels of Thomas Mann* by Irvin Stock, 1994; *Thomas Mann*, edited by Michael Minden, 1995; *Thomas Mann: A Life* by Donald Prater, 1995; *Thomas Mann: A Biography* by Ronald Hayman, 1996; *Being and Meaning in Thomas Mann's Joseph Novels* by Charlotte Nolte, 1996; *Changing Perceptions of Thomas Mann's Doctor Faustus: Criticism 1947–1992* by John F. Fetzer, 1996; *Thomas Mann: Eros and Literature* by Anthony Heilbut, 1996; *History, Myth, and Music: Thomas Mann's Timely Fiction* by Susan von Rohr Scaff, 1998; *Thomas Mann and Friedrich Nietzsche: Eroticism, Death, Music, and Laughter* by Caroline Joan S. Picart, 1999; *Thomas Mann's Joseph and His Brothers: Writing, Performance, and the Politics of Loyalty* by William E. McDonald, 1999; *A Companion to Thomas Mann's Magic Mountain*, edited by Stephen D. Dowden, 1999; *Mann: Der Zauberberg* by Martin Swales, 2000; *The Cambridge Companion to Thomas Mann*, edited by Ritchie Robertson, 2002.

*   *   *

Thomas Mann's origins lie unmistakably in the *fin de siècle* period of neo-Romanticism and fascination with decadence. Dominating his early stories and the precocious masterpiece, *Buddenbrooks*, is the duality of *Komik und Elend*, comedy and pathos. He shares a contemporary sense of his era as a terminal one and depicts a *Spätzeit* (latter-day age) in which neurasthenic characters, especially artist-figures, find release from the world's coarse demands only in the grand life-denying pessimism of Schopenhauer or the climax of a Wagnerian *Liebestod* (love-death, death in love), as in the episode in the story "Tristan" which recreates the *Liebestod* of the second act of Wagner's *Tristan und Isolde*, or the scene in which the young Hanno Buddenbrook, the last of his line and a doomed artist *manqué*, extemporizes a piano-fantasy whose culmination bears a strong suggestion both of death and of sexual climax. The individual is seen as incomplete, a fragment broken away from the whole, and necessarily both tragic and comic. The dualism of Life and Death which ultimately asserts its domination in "Tristan" is as remote from the tragi-comic struggles of the characters in the story as are the mountains surrounding the sanatorium which is the setting for this novella, and of the later novel *Der Zauberberg* (*The Magic Mountain*). Decadence is the cult of beauty proclaimed against a background of decline, and Mann is certainly drawn to this cult. And yet, typically, his attitude to it was a highly ambivalent one, similar to his ambivalence towards Wagner. Although it goes without saying that he was not in sympathy with the materialist and arrogant society of pre-World War I Germany, at the same time he was prevented by his solid, north German burgher inheritance from sustaining a mood of disgust with reality or retreat into decadence. The result of ambivalence is irony. This most famous aspect of his work derives in part from the critical insight of the outsider who has taken lessons from Nietzsche in the self-deceiving motivation of human conduct; and in part from a latter-day scepticism about the function of art itself in an era when the quest for form and harmony suspiciously resembles a denial of that disturbing Nietzschean insight. An illustration is provided by the artist figure, Gustav Aschenbach, in *Der Tod in Venedig* (*Death in Venice*), who, from a highly respected position as the traditional German *Dichter* (a combination of poet and pedagogue)—a position he holds, it becomes clear, only by an effort of will to deny certain painful complexities—degenerates in the course of the story to become an old *roué* whose homoerotic fixation upon a young boy leads him to "conspire" with the Venetian authorities to conceal the facts of a cholera epidemic sweeping through the tourist city. By his immoral denial of Knowledge for the sake of the pursuit of Beauty he allegorically betrays the artist's deeper duty to society, that of portraying the truth as he sees it, even at the expense of the security of social existence.

The irony of Mann's treatment of Aschenbach characteristically includes also an element of parody of his own beautifully controlled and convoluted "master-style." Equally characteristically, Mann's political sense lagged some way behind his artistic insight (it is a familiar observation in German cultural history) and in his overgrown war-time essay, *Betrachtungen eines Unpolitischen* (*Reflections of a Nonpolitical Man*), written as a defence of Germany's war-aims in terms of her separate cultural tradition, Mann even resurrects concepts he had already completely undermined in *Death in Venice*: for example, his desire to see the artist as a "warrior," just as his hero Aschenbach had done at the outset of the story. It is not surprising that after the war, in his final and permanent conversion to democracy in 1922, he uses very much the same language and authorities as he had called upon in his attack on democracy in the *Reflections*. As well as employing Novalis's metaphysics of the State to assert that the idea of a republic is a part of the German Romantic legacy, he now presents the Romantic "attraction of death" of the *Reflections* as a constituent part of "an interest in life." The central themes of his great post-war novel of education, *The Magic Mountain*, can be summarized as the need to break out from decadence. The question is a constant one in Mann: how is it possible to know and yet live, to be a man of your age, sharing in all its spiritual insecurity and scepticism, and yet be able to say "yes" to life? The answer to the question is not constant, but evolving. Art, which in Mann is set in opposition to life, in the end becomes identified with life. The vast question raised by *The Magic Mountain*, "what is life?," is answered partly that "life is increasing knowledge of life." Forming, writing, is a life-giving act in itself, a bulwark against chaos. It is true—as the earlier, Romantic Mann knew—that the insight into "first causes," the self-knowledge which informs the Romantic irony of consciousness spying upon consciousness, can paralyze the will to form; that this can even be a liberating discovery, however, a giving way to chaos, is shown in the experiences of Hans Castorp, hero of *The Magic Mountain*, in the early chapters of the novel. But the second wisdom goes further: to give shape to life reflecting upon life is a healthy adjunct to living it, overcoming on behalf of man in general the "sickly" temptation to doubt and introspection. Mann's own (always ironized) surrender to romantic aestheticism was the precondition for his renunciation of it; just as Hans Castorp's illness on the Magic Mountain had to be brought to light before it could be cured.

It was as well that Mann had resolved these issues before the chaos of the Weimar years and the emergence of totalitarianism gave a new urgency to the intellectual debate he had always incorporated in an interplay of "ideas" so tangible as to become almost the protagonists of his works. The reply to crude and regressive Nazi mythologizing was the tetralogy of Joseph-novels, *Joseph und seine Brüder* (*Joseph and His Brothers*), where the journey into the Biblical past is at once a Nazi-defying homage to the Judeo-Christian humanistic tradition, and a journey into the depths of the individual unconscious, the region where myths originate and are perpetuated. His attempt to comprehend Germany's lapse into diabolism is incorporated in *Doktor Faustus* (*Doctor Faustus*), in the story of a demonic artist, the composer Adrian Leverkühn, presented through a new version of the Faust legend. German inwardness is here brilliantly related to Germany's outward "adventures" and journey towards catastrophe.

The extraordinary range of Mann's talent is apparent in his last novel, *Bekenntnisse des Hochstaplers Felix Krull* (*Confessions of Felix Krull, Confidence Man*), which he took up again in 1953 where he had left off in 1910. A picaresque and superbly humorous book, it allows its autobiographical narrator to manipulate and parody a number of literary conventions and establish himself as the archetypal "unreliable narrator": quite appropriately, since Krull is a confidence-trickster as well as an artist of life, bringing to the fore once again Mann's early perception of the "bad conscience" of the artist who manipulates his readers' response and "simulates" for their benefit emotions which he does not feel but has cold-bloodedly observed. It is an appropriate conclusion to Mann's career: a sublimated account of the ambivalence of fiction, and yet a vindication of fiction by its very existence, without which the world would be infinitely poorer.

—Alan F. Bance

See the essays on *Buddenbrooks: The Decline of a Family*, *Confessions of Felix Krull, Confidence Man*, *Death in Venice*, *Doctor Faustus*, and *The Magic Mountain*.

MANZONI, Alessandro (Francesco Tommaso Antonio)

Born: Milan, 7 March 1785. **Education:** Educated at the Somaschian college at Merate, 1791–96, and at Lugano, 1796–98; Barnabite Collegio dei Nobili, Milan and Magenta, 1797–1801. **Family:** Married 1) Henriette Blondel in 1808 (died 1833), eight children survived infancy; 2) Teresa Borri in 1837. **Career:** Senator of the Kingdom, 1860; Honorary Citizen, Rome, 1872. **Died:** 22 May 1873.

PUBLICATIONS

Collections

Opere, edited by Riccardo Bacchelli. 1953.
Tutte le opere, edited by Alberto Chiari and Fausto Ghisalberti. 11 vols., 1957–70.
The Betrothed; and, History of the Column of Infamy, edited by David Forgacs and Matthew Reynolds. 1997.
Alessandro Manzoni: Two Plays, translated by Michael J. Curley. 2002.

Fiction

I promessi sposi. 3 vols., 1827; revised edition, 1840–42; as *The Betrothed Lovers*, translated by Charles Swan, 1828; also translated with *The Column of Infamy*, 1845; as *I promessi sposi*,
translated by G.W. Featherstonhaugh, 1834; as *The Betrothed*, translated by Daniel J. Connor, 1924; also translated by Archibald Colquhoun, 1951; Bruce Penman, 1972.
Storia della colonna infame. With *I promessi sposi*, 1842; edited by Renzo Negri, 1974; translated as *The Column of Infamy*, with *The Betrothed Lovers*, 1845; also translated by Kenelm Foster, 1964.

Plays

Il conte di Carmagnola (produced 1823). 1820.
Adelchi (produced 1822). 1822.
Tragedie, edited by Giulio Bollati. 1965.

Verse

Inni sacri. 1815; edited by Dino Brivio, 1973; as *The Sacred Hymns*, translated by Joel Foote Bingham (bilingual edition), 1904.
Del trionfo della libertà, edited by C. Romussi. 1878.

Other

Sulla morale cattolica. 1819; revised edition, 1855; edited by R. Amerio, 1965; as *A Vindication of Catholic Morality*, 1836.
Discorso sopra alcuni punti della storia longobardica in Italia. 1822.
Lettre à M. Chauvet sur les unités de temps et de lieu dans la tragédie. 1823; edited by Natalino Sapegno, 1947.
Opere varie. 1845–55.
La rivoluzione francese del 1789 e la rivoluzione italiana del 1859, edited by Pietro Brambilla. 1889.
Lettere, edited by Cesare Arieti. 3 vols., 1970.
Del romanzo storico. As *On the Historical Novel*, translated by Sandra Bermann, 1984.

*

Bibliography: *Bibliografia manzoniana* by M. Parenti, 1936; *Critica Manzoniana d'un decennio (1939–1948)* by F. Ghisalberti, 1949; *Bibliografia manzoniana 1949–1973* by Silvia Brusamolino Isella and Simonetta Usuelli Castellani, 1974.

Critical Studies: *Manzoni: Esthetics and Literary Criticism* by Joseph F. de Simone, 1946; *The Linguistic Writings of Manzoni* by Barbara Reynolds, 1950; *Manzoni and His Times* by Archibald Colquhoun, 1954; *Manzoni and the Catholic Revival* by Carlo Dionisotti Casalone, 1974; *Manzoni: The Story of a Spiritual Quest* by Stanley B. Chandler, 1974; *Manzoni's Christian Realism* by Ernesto G. Caserta, 1977; *The Reasonable Romantic: Essays on Alessandro Manzoni* by Sante H. Matte and Larry H. Peer, 1986; *La linea longobarda*, edited by Luigi Ballerini, 1996; *Manzoni and the Aesthetics of the Lombard Seicento: Art Assimilated into the Narrative of I promessi sposi* by Glenn Pierce, 1998; *Topographies of Desire: Manzoni, Cultural Practices, and Colonial Scars* by Susanna F. Ferlito, 2000.

* * *

I promessi sposi (*The Betrothed*), the work which won Alessandro Manzoni lasting fame and which occupies a place of fundamental importance in the development of both the Italian language and its literature, was written and read initially in the wake of the phenomenal European success of Sir Walter Scott's historical novels. The link with Scott has ensured continuing attention for Manzoni on the part of readers interested in the evolution of modern narrative fiction. But it has also served as a barrier to a deeper, more sensitive and unprejudiced understanding of his art. Manzoni's plumbing of the inner forces at work in individual consciences and social movements finds no parallel in Scott's lively and colourful reconstructions of a people's national past. Two early (1827) French comments on *The Betrothed* are worth noting. "All in all I prefer Manzoni to Scott. But he will not have the same success for he is religious and thoroughly Catholic," wrote Lamennais, probably France's chief Catholic apologist at the time, boldly recognizing the powerful influence of opposing beliefs and ideologies in literary judgements. As for the poet Lamartine, one of the few to praise the long historical passages (especially those on the 1630 plague in Lombardy) which most critics found prolix and digressive, he urged Manzoni "to get out of the historical novel and give us history of a new kind" instead; thus he pointed ahead to the radical solution of epistemological and aesthetic problems perceived by Manzoni himself in his attempt to reconcile the dictates of art with respect for historical truth. Indeed, Manzoni never wrote the expected second novel, but in his *Storia della colonna infame* (*The Column of Infamy*), begun as an offshoot of *The Betrothed* and eventually published as a separate work, he created the forerunner of a new genre, today's "essay in narrative reporting" (as Solzhenitsyn has called *The Gulag Archipelago*) or "documentary novel" (as Truman Capote called *In Cold Blood*).

The choice of 17th-century Lombardy under Spanish domination as the setting for *The Betrothed* was a by-product of Manzoni's highly developed historical interests that had already found expression in the two tragedies and the essays accompanying them. He was attracted to the period (as he wrote to Fauriel) because of the "extraordinary state of society" it manifested: "the most arbitrary government combined with feudal and popular anarchy; legislation that is amazing in the way it expressed a profound, ferocious, pretentious ignorance; classes with opposed interests and maxims; some little-known anecdotes, preserved in trustworthy documents; finally a plague which gave full rein to the most consummate and shameful excesses, to the most absurd prejudices, and to the most touching virtues"—in short, enough to fill a canvas.

An episode of the Thirty Years War in Lombardy, which pitted the French against the Spanish king and the latter's liege and sovereign lord the Holy Roman Emperor, provides the time-frame (1628–31) for the novel. The foreground is occupied by the "little world" of Manzoni's fictional characters in the rural landscape of the Lecco branch of Lake Como. With an unusual twist in the storytelling tradition—be it romance, fairytale, or even realistic novel—the courtship leading to the betrothal of Renzo and Lucia already lies in the past when the novel opens: this is not a story of love and passion but of tranquil affections and the founding of family life. Though they succeed in bettering their social and economic condition in an instance of upward mobility perhaps more typical of the century in which the book was written than of that in which it is set, neither Renzo nor Lucia has any other ambition than marriage within their class and environment. They are humble artisans who have not quite ceased being peasants: "nobody's people," Manzoni calls them, "without even a master," he adds, referring to their defencelessness in a society of well-organized, belligerent, corrupt, and wary factions and groups. They run foul of the petty local lord, a small-time tyrant

who on a whim makes a bet that he will succeed in seducing Lucia, and of the cowardly parish priest who once again forgets "the duties and noble aims" of his profession and permits himself to be intimidated by the lord's henchmen against performing the marriage. Forced to leave their native village, they are separated and reunited only three years later after the scourges of famine, war, pestilence, and death have devastated the land, cleared and cleansed it for a new beginning.

Increasing secularism and more recently the spread of schools of literary criticism averse to moral judgements have created a barrier of ambiguities between Manzoni and the contemporary reader. *The Betrothed* reflects Manzoni's religious belief on virtually every page. It is present in the succession of "trials," the fictional equivalent to the Christian view of life as a testing time, which the plot prepares for the characters. It is present in the judgements expressed by the author in his many different guises, from omniscient narrator to detached observer, to mediator between the reader and the anonymous writer of the supposed manuscript from which the story derives. It is present in the "portraits," the more or less elaborate presentations of the physical, psychological, and life-history particulars of the characters, both "invented" and derived from factual reality. It is present in "the moral of the tale" with which the story ends. And it is present in a distinctly disquieting manner in the intertwining of a pessimistic view of human nature with the optimistic acceptance of the ways of God to man. The overall design is providential—the ending is a happy one and as in comedy it brings the accommodation of a well-assorted marriage. But along the way, in passage upon passage, instances of violence abound: a veritable anatomy of acts of violence is built up, from the unbridled application of force in riots, duels, forced entry, kidnapping, and murder to more subtle forms of coercion in political manipulation or the imposition of one man's will upon another's. Again and again, sometimes directly, more often indirectly, the reader is invited to weigh the implications of an action, to arrive at a moral judgement whereby in the long run he will himself be judged implicitly.

By today's standards a conservative, Manzoni was in his own time liberal and in siding with the Romantics against the Classicists and in supporting the struggle for Italian independence and unity actually revolutionary. The most important intellectual events in Manzoni's life preceding the composition of *The Betrothed* were his two so-called "conversions": the return to the practice of Catholicism and the rejection of the neo-classical poetry of his youth. In *Inni sacri* (*The Sacred Hymns*) the heavily accented octosyllables of short rhyming stanzas reminiscent of popular poetry close the gap between audience and poet and make present the ever-recurrent encounter between man and God celebrated in the major festivities of the liturgical year. *Il conte di Carmagnola* [The Count of Carmagnola] and *Adelchi* mark a major innovation in the Italian theatre by breaking with the classical rules of tragedy. Their heroes are historical figures faced by problems of individual responsibility and the need to come to terms with the presence of injustice and evil. The essence of Manzoni's religious thought is found in *Sulla morale cattolica* (*A Vindication of Catholic Morality*), his major work in Italian prose before *The Betrothed*. (His most important work of literary criticism, the *Lettre à M. Chauvet sur les unités de temps et de lieu dans la tragédie*, as well as most of his correspondence, was in French.) His tone is eloquent and solemn, as with his wonted emphasis on telling particulars he details "the unity of revelation" (which is also at work in the novel):

> What is and what should be; misery and lust, and the ever living idea of perfection and order that we also find in

ourselves; good and evil; the words of divine wisdom and the vain talk of men; the watchful joy of the righteous, the sorrows and consolations of the repentant, the terror or unshakeable indifference of the wicked; the triumphs of justice and those of iniquity; men's plans brought to fruition amidst a thousand obstacles or overturned by the one unexpected one; disbelief itself—all is explained with the Gospel, all confirms it.

In an age of increasing violence, of its growing acceptance as a part of daily life, of its polarization into rival group struggles, and its frequent institutionalization into accepted norms of behaviour, Manzoni's message continues to be that of love and compassion, of a common destiny and burdens shared, of purpose in life, of the individual's capacity to will and effect change by transforming himself, by making or aiming to make himself more human through the education of his faculties of thought and feeling.

—Olga Ragusa

See the essay on *The Betrothed*.

MARECHAL, Leopoldo

Born: Buenos Aires, Argentina, 11 June 1900. **Education:** Educated at the Escuela Normal de Profesores Mariano Acosta, Buenos Aires, until 1915, teaching degree. **Family:** Married 1) María Zoraida Barreiro, two daughters; 2) Elbia Rosbaco in 1950. **Career:** Elementary schoolteacher, c. 1920–40; also journalist from 1922; travelled to Spain and France, 1926, and encountered several avant-garde artistic groups, and was friendly with Jorge Luis Borges, *q.v.*; active in pro-Peronist politics, from 1943, and held official posts during Juan Perón's regime, 1946–55, including: director-general, Ministry of Education Department of Culture, 1944–45; head, Santa Fe province education council, 1944; president, National Commission for Tradition and Folklore, 1947–55; director-general of Higher Education and the Arts, 1948–55; largely ostracized in artistic and political spheres for his Peronism, 1955–65; visited Cuba, 1967. Also journalist, including contributor to *La Nación, Sol y luna, Proa*, and *Martín Fierro*. Vice-president, Argentinian Society of Writers, 1938–39. **Awards:** Buenos Aires prize, 1929; National Poetry prize, 1940. **Died:** 26 June 1970.

PUBLICATIONS

Collections

Obras Completas. 1998.

Fiction

El niño Dios (children's stories). 1939.
Adán Buenosayres (prose poem). 1948; selection edited by Luis Gregorich and Ángel Núñez, 1965.
El banquete de Severo Arcángelo. 1966.
Megáfon; o, La guerra. 1970.

Verse

Los aguiluchos. 1922.
Días como flechas. 1926.
Odas para el hombre y la mujer. 1929.
Cinco poemas australes. 1936.
Laberinto de amor. 1935.
El centauro. 1940; as *The Centaur*, translated by Richard O'Connell and James Graham-Luján, 1944.
Sonetos a Sophía y otros poemas. 1940.
La rosa en la balanza (includes *Odas para el hombre y la mujer* and *Laberinto de amor*). 1944.
El viaje de la primavera. 1945.
Antología poética, edited by Juan Carlos Ghiano. 1950.
La poética. 1959.
La Patria. 1960.
Leopoldo Marechal (anthology). 1961.
La alegropeya. 1962.
El heptamerón. 1966.
El poema de robot. 1966.
Poemas. 1966.
Antología poética, edited by Alfredo Andrés. 1969.
Poemas de la creación. 1979.
Poesía (1924–1950). 1984.

Plays

El canto de San Martín (dramatic poem with music) (produced 1950). 1950.
Antígona Vélez (produced 1951). 1965.
Las tres caras de Venus (produced 1952). 1966.
La batalla de José Luna (produced 1967). 1970.
Don Juan (produced 1984). 1978.

Other

Historia de la calle Corrientes. 1937.
Descenso y ascenso del alma por la balleza (essay). 1939; revised edition, 1965.
Vida de Santa Rosa de Lima. 1943.
Autopsia de Creso (essays). 1965.
Cuaderno de navegación. 1966.
Palabras con Leopoldo Marechal (interview and anthology), edited by Alfredo Andrés. 1968.
La nueva literatura argentina (dialogue), with Horacio Armani and Miguel Bustos. 1970.
El beatle final y otras páginas, edited by Ángel Núñez. 1981.

*

Bibliography: "Contribución a la bibliografía de Leopoldo Marechal" by G. Coulson and W. Hardy, Jr., in *Revista Chilena de Literatura*, 5–6, 1972; "Leopoldo Marechal" in *Argentine Literature: A Research Guide* by David William Foster, 1982.

Critical Studies: *La poesía de Leopoldo Marechal* by Santiago Montero Díaz, 1943; *Leopoldo Marechal* by R. Squirru, 1961; *Leopoldo Marechal: Poeta argentino* by Daniel Barros, 1971; "Marechal's *Antígona*: More Greek Than French" by A. De Kuehne, in *Latin American Theater Review*, 9(1), 1973; *Mi vida con Leopoldo Marechal* by Elbia Rosbaco de Marechal, 1973; *Marechal: La pasión metafísica* by Graciela Coulson, 1974; *Interpretaciones y claves de Adán Buenosayres*, various authors, 1977; *Leopoldo Marechal: El espacio de los signos* by H.M. Cavallari, 1981; *Marechal, el otro: La escritura testada de Adán Buenosayres* by Valentin Cricco and others, 1985; *Catedra Marechal* by Graciela Maturo, 1986; *Narrativa argentina contemporánea: Representación de lo real en Marechal, Borges y Cortázar* by Manuel Alcides Jofre, 1991; *Ironic Apocalypse in the Novels of Leopoldo Marechal* by Norman Cheadle, 2000.

* * *

Perhaps the best introductory characterization of Leopoldo Marechal's writing, which covered all of the standard literary genres, is obtained by viewing him as an outstanding Argentinian representative of interwar modernism. Although his early comrade in literary arms, Jorge Luis Borges, is the one to enjoy an international reputation (they broke in the 1940s after Marechal's affiliation with the Peronist movement), Borges renounced his youthful vanguard enthusiasms and, indeed, today he is viewed more as a precursor of the postmodern, and his modernist writing prior to *Ficciones* (1944) is usually viewed in almost archaeological terms. By contrast, Marechal's writing in the 1940s, especially *Adán Buenosayres* [Adam Buenosaires], which he began in Paris in 1931 and published in 1948, must be taken as the high point of his career. Marechal participated actively in the vanguard renovation of Argentinian poetic expression following the first phase of cultural modernism during Argentina's *belle époque* period (which in Spanish is called *modernismo*; the second phase is customarily identified as *vanguardismo*), and his name appears in the roster of such 1920s reviews as *Martín Fierro* (taken from the name of the protagonist of the gaucho epic by José Hernández) and *Proa* [Prow]. Marechal's 1926 voyage to Spain and France also put him in contact with poetic innovations in those countries, and these influences are evident in his early collections.

However, the most significant aspect of Marechal's literary career is his identification with the populist and nationalist political movement initiated by Juan Domingo Perón (president of Argentina between 1946 and 1955). Perón's Argentinian interpretation of fascism suggested overarching nationalist interpretations of Argentinian society and culture that appealed to Marechal, and he became virtually the only major writer of the period to align himself with Peronism and to remain loyal to it throughout Perón's presidency. Marechal, who had been a secondary-school teacher, held several official appointments in the government, a circumstance which caused him to be ostracized by the literary establishment, which in general distributed itself along the more traditional political axis of Catholic conservatives or committed leftists. The Latin American literary vanguard in general had been culturally nationalistic and had seen in the aesthetic innovations of modernism a way to characterize the inner subconscious or mythic structure of Creole identity—hence the use by Marechal and others as the title of a vanguard poetic review the name of a paradigmatic gaucho hero Martín Fierro; and there are many other such echoes of cultural nationalism throughout the continent.

In Marechal's case, this feature became evident in the title of his 1948 novel, which may be variously interpreted as ''Adam in Buenos Aires,'' ''a Buenos Aires Adam,'' and ''Adamic Buenos Aires.'' Unabashedly following the lead of Joyce's Dublin Ulysses, Marechal follows his Creole Adam on a voyage of personal discovery and mythic interpretation of his society through more than 700 pages of dense prose. Yet it must be stressed that Marechal is not simply writing an Argentinian version of *Ulysses*. He is not interested in Joyce's delirious linguistic experiments, nor does he make primary use of the stream of consciousness and psychological free association that typify Joyce's narrative. What does bring the two works together is the deployment of a mythic everyman to plumb dimensions of national cultural identity. However, where Joyce's global image is that of cultural disintegration under the pressures of contemporary social forces and the specific circumstances and problem of an Irish identity, Marechal's Adam bespeaks cultural continuity despite modern alienation. It is in this sense that *Adán Buenosayres* is the literary masterpiece of Peronist culture. Perón sought to maintain the image of a unique Argentinian character, of a sustained sociocultural identity among the humble populace that contrasted with the historical betrayals of a Europeanizing oligarchy which, in expanding political definitions, included most of the literary and cultural institutions. Peronism depended very much on the efficacy of evoking, in the best fascist tradition, a Creole iconography as part of its processes of ideological legitimation. Thus, the abiding image of Marechal's Adam, an image promulgated by his novel during the apogee of the Peronist administration, is that of triumphant nationalistic cultural integration. It should be noted, however, that Marechal's novel is no facile text of cultural propaganda, and, while it may not reveal the same level of linguistic and narrative complexity as Joyce's work, it bears all the traces of its author's formation within the literary vanguard and the extension of interest from the primary domain of expression in poetry to the writing of fiction.

After the demise of Peronism, and during the period of Marechal's ostracism, which only abated toward the end of his life with the neo-Peronist resurgence, Marechal produced a number of significant works of fiction, which, in the context of profound repeated crises in Argentina and Latin America in general, as manifested by recurring authoritarian military regimes, focused on the deleterious effects of rampant capitalism (Marechal visited Cuba in 1967 at a time when that country offered a new eloquent programme of cultural reaffirmation for Latin America). Marechal continued to write dense prose texts, characterized by the use of allegorical/mythic characters and plots within narrative programmes that seek to denote the oppression of the individual in alienating societies and the tragic destruction of communal identity by unstoppable forces. It is evident that Marechal did not come to subscribe to anything like a Marxist interpretation of social history, and one ventures to say that there is the permanence in his writing of something like a fascist demiurgism, which makes them unique texts within the field of contemporary Latin American fiction.

—David William Foster

MARGUERITE DE NAVARRE

Born: D'Angoulême, France, 10 April (11 April in some sources) 1492. **Family:** Married 1) Charles, Duke of Alençon in 1509 (died 1525); 2) Henri d'Albret, King of Navarre in 1527, one daughter. **Career:** Played an important political role during the captivity of Francis I. Supported *évangélisme* and protected persecuted theologians including Lefèvre, Marot, and Calvin. **Died:** 1549.

PUBLICATIONS

Collections

Oeuvres: Comédies, edited by F. Schneegans. 1924.
Théâtre profane, edited by Verdun L. Saulnier. 1946; revised edition, 1978.
Oeuvres choisies, edited by H.P. Clive. 2 vols., 1968.
Coach; and, The Triumph of the Lamb, translated by Hilda Dale and Simone de Reyff. 1999.

Fiction

L'Heptaméron. Unauthorized and incomplete edition, as *Histoires des Amans Fortunez*, 1558–59; complete edition (72 tales), 1853–54; edited by Yves Le Hir, 1967, H.P. Clive, 1970, and by Simone de Reyff-Glasson, 1982; as *The Heptameron*, translated by A. Machen, 1904; also translated by John Smith Chartres, 1922; P.A. Chiltern, 1984.
Contes et nouvelles. 2 vols., 1698; edited by J.R. Sinne, 3 vols., 1780–81.

Verse

Le Miroir de l'âme pécheresse. 1531; as *Le Miroir de treschrestienne Princesse M. de France*, 1533; as *Le Miroir de l'âme pécheresse*, edited by J.A. Allaire, 1972, Renja Salminen, 1979, and by Joseph Allaire, 1979; as *Elizabeth's Glass: With "The Glass of the Sinful Soul" (1544) by Elizabeth I, and "Epistle Dedicatory" and "Conclusion" (1548) by John Bale* by Marc Shell, 1993.
Dialogue en forme de vision nocturne. 1533; edited, 1985.
Les Marguerites de la Marguerite des princesses. 1547; 4 vols., 1873; edited by Félix Frank, 2 vols., 1970, and by Ruth Thomas, 2 vols., 1970.
Les Dernières Poésies, edited by Abel Lefranc. 1896.
Le Navire; ou, Consolation du Roy François I à sa soeur Marguerite, edited by Robert Marichal. 1956.
Petit oeuvre dévot et contemplatif. 1960.
Chansons spirituelles, edited by Georges Dottin. 1971.
Le Coche, edited by Robert Marichal. 1971.
Les Prisons, edited by Simone Glasson. 1978; as *The Prisons of Marguerite de Navarre*, edited and translated by Claire Lynch Wade, 1989; also translated as *The Prisons* by Hilda Dale, 1989.
Le Miroir de Jésus Christ crucifié, edited by L. Fontanella. 1984.

Plays

Comédie jouée à Mont-de-Marsan en 1547. N.d.
Deux farces inédites. 1856.
Comédie de la nativité de Jésus-Christ. 1939.

Other

L'Art et usage du souverain mirouer du chrestien. 1556.
Les Mémoires de la reine Marguerite. 1628; as *Memoirs of Marguerite de Valois*, translated by Liselotte Dieckmann, 1984.
Correspondance, edited by François Génin. 2 vols., 1841–42.
Les Sept Journées de la Reine de Navarre. 1872.
Lettres de la Reine de Navarre au Pape Paul III. 1887.

Lettres de Marguerite de Valois-Angoulême, edited by Raymond Ritter. 1927.
Correspondance (1521–1524), edited by Christine Martineau, Michel Vessière, and Henry Heller. 2 vols., 1975–79.

*

Bibliography: *Répertoire analytique et chronologique de la correspondance de Marguerite d'Angoulême* by Pierre Jourda, 1930; *Marguerite de Navarre: An Annotated Bibliography* by H.P. Clive, 1983.

Critical Studies: *The Pearl of Princesses: The Life of Marguerite d'Angoulême, Queen of Navarre* by H. Williams, 1916; *Marguerite d'Angoulême, duchesse d'Alençon, reine de Navarre (1492–1549)* (includes bibliography) by Pierre Jourda, 2 vols., 1930, revised edition, 1968; *Marguerite de Navarre* by Samuel Putnam, 1936; *Bandello and the Heptameron* by Kelver Hartley, 1960; *World of Many Loves: The Heptameron of Marguerite de Navarre* by Jules Gelernt, 1966; "The "Heptaméron" Reconsidered" by A.J. Krailsheimer, in *The French Renaissance and Its Heritage* edited by D.R. Haggis, 1968; *Marguerite de Navarre's "Heptaméron": Themes, Language and Structure* by Marcel Tetel, 1973; *L'Heptaméron de Marguerite de Navarre* by Nicole Cazauran, 1976; *The Storytellers in Marguerite de Navarre's Heptaméron* by Betty J. Davis, 1978; *Marguerite de Navarre* by Marie Cerati, 1981; *Mysticism in the Poetry of Marguerite de Navarre* by Hanna Hone Leckman, 1982; *The Grammar of Silence: A Reading of Marguerite de Navarre's Poetry* by Robert D. Cotrell, 1986; *Platonic Symbolism of Marguerite d'Angoulême in the Royal Courts of France and Navarre (1492–1549)* by Yon Oria, 1986; *Marguerite de Navarre* by Jean Luc Déjean, 1987; *Celestial Ladders: Readings in Marguerite de Navarre's Poetry of Spiritual Ascent*, by Paula Sommers, 1989; *Le Vocabulaire de l'Heptaméron de Marguerite de Navarre* by Suzanne Hanon, 1990; *Rage and Writing in the Heptameron of Marguerite de Navarre* by Patricia Francis Cholakian, 1991; *Mirroring Belief: Marguerite de Navarre's Devotional Poetry* by Gary Ferguson, 1992; *New Studies of the Heptameron and Early Modern Cultures* edited by John D. Lyons and Mary B. McKinley, 1993; *Heroic Virtue, Comic Infidelity: Reassessing Marguerite de Navarre's Heptaméron*, edited by Dora E. Polachek, 1993; *Critical Tales: New Studies of the Heptameron and Early Modern Culture*, edited by John D. Lyons and Mary B. McKinley, 1993; *The Pleasure of Discernment: Marguerite de Navarre as Theologian* by Carol Thysell, 2000.

* * *

As Queen of Navarre and sister of King François I of France, Marguerite has a marked influence on French culture during the first half of the 16th century; her contribution earned her the accolade of the "Minerva of France." Described as a New Woman, the feminine counterpart to Renaissance Man, she advocated equality between men and women of rank; women shared with men a free will and minds of their own. Her writings reveal that Marguerite was deeply religious but not prudish or narrow-minded. Frank, even earthy language mingles with pious sentiments in her prose and poetry, a common feature of her social milieu.

Marguerite's work was greatly influenced by Petrarch, Dante, Boccaccio, Poggio, Masuccio, Bandelle, and others, showing her to be intelligent and well-educated. According to her critics, she was not a first-rate poet; she was a humanist but not a "femme des lettres." Arthur Tilley maintains that Marguerite had "more sympathy than originality, more quickness than depth, more sweetness than strength" as a writer. Indeed, her writing often lacks polish; rather it exhibits spontaneous outpourings of deep personal feeling and emotions. Marguerite's habit of composing while travelling in her litter, and often dictating to her women companions, may be responsible in large part for the extemporaneous, often uneven quality of her work. Marguerite was, however, a gifted and prolific writer, able to express herself in a variety of genres. Her best known and most appreciated work is *L'Heptaméron* (*The Heptameron*), a collection of tales that embody and portray the attitudes, concerns, ideas, and language of the period. She wrote eight long poems on sacred, amorous, and historical subjects that reveal much about her personal beliefs and feelings. Numerous poetic epistles were addressed to her mother, her second husband (Henri de Navarre), her only daughter, Jeanne d'Albret, and to her adored brother, the king. The latter was the object of her affection to such an extent that some critics have judged their relation to be incestuous, in thought if not in fact: "I am yours," she writes in *Les Marguerites de la Marguerite des princesses*, "and you say you are mine / Yes, I am yours . . . And would be yours for all eternity." This collection includes 33 poems on religious and secular subjects, written in a variety of metres, including the only sonnet attributed to Marguerite. Her dramatic pieces include four mystery plays, two morality plays, four *soi-disant* comedies, and three farces, none of which is memorable. These plays were written to be staged, but all are devoid of drama; the characters are mere abstractions and are nameless. Other minor works such as her rondeaux, dizains, and songs are of interest only in assessing her personal interests and her use of language.

About 1524, Marguerite wrote her first important long poem, *Dialogue en forme de vision nocturne* [Dialogue in the Form of a Nocturnal Vision], an expression in dialogue of sorrow after the death of her niece Charlotte. The 1,300 verses in *terza rima* reveal that she was strongly influenced by Dante's *Divine Comedy*. Marguerite reflects on the question of free will, on original sin and redemption, and on death as a release from life, which she describes as a prison. Death provides rest for the soul, an escape from "prison." (Marguerite frequently refers to both life and love as prisons, even, in the second case, as a "dulcet dungeon.") On the thorny topic of faith and good works, she believed man alone could do nothing, and good works alone would not assure salvation. God's grace was essential; through prayer and intercession of the saints, man grew nearer to God. Typical of Marguerite's compositions is her "Chanson faicte par M. d'Angoulême dans la litière pendant la maladie du Roy" [Song Written by M. d'Angoulême in Her Litter During the Illness of the King]. Composed in September 1525 as she journeyed to Spain to see François I, who was a prisoner-of-war of Emperor Charles V, the poem is a personal prayer, an outpouring of concern for her "ami." Marguerite risked her own safety to comfort her beloved brother and to negotiate with his captor. As in other poems, Marguerite writes of death as the liberator—undoubtedly referring to the recent death of her first husband, the duc d'Alençon, whom she had never loved. Her release from an unhappy marriage, another prison, allowed her to focus on a more "pure" love, the object of her song/poem.

Les Prisons (*The Prisons*) is one of Marguerite's most heartfelt examinations of the various stages of love. She had failed to find love or happiness in her marriages; like life itself, love had been confining,

not liberating. She uses the sun to symbolize the lover. After one has gazed directly at the sun, its bright image remains, seen everywhere one looks. The face of a loved one created the same effect. In this instance, the sun was probably Henri de Navarre, whom Marguerite loved and married, only to be disappointed again. Clearly, her view of love was both Christian and Platonic, representing the more elevated stage of *agape*. Jean Calvin, who admired some of her writings, labelled *The Prisons* as "spiritual libertinism."

Le Miroir de l'âme pécheresse [The Mirror of the Sinful Soul] appeared in 1531, written in rhymed decasyllables in an allegorical-erotic style. It opens with a notice "Au Lecteur" in which Marguerite surprisingly attributes faults of diction and composition to the fact that the writer is a woman. Critics have characterized this disclaimer as Christian humility or an effort to disarm zealous Catholics who might interpret the poem as an apologia for Protestantism. The focus is on faith and on Christ to the exclusion of the saints, the Virgin Mary, and other Catholic beliefs. Reaction from theologians at the Sorbonne was immediate and sharp; they banned the work. But direct intervention by François I led to a retraction and lifting of the ban. The poem has subsequently been cited as evidence that Marguerite held heretical ideas.

In *The Heptameron* Marguerite returns to the subject of love, marital fidelity, friendship, and human weaknesses. The characters and events depicted indicate that it was written between 1538 and 1542. Legend has it that Marguerite composed the tales in order to amuse her brother, whose health had deteriorated from years of debauchery. To hold his interest she used the exploits and misadventures of real persons in the stories: Marguerite herself appears both as Floride and Parlamente, Henri of Navarre is Hircan, and her mother, Louise of Savoy, is Oiselle. The format is modelled on Boccaccio's *Decameron*, with which Marguerite was familiar. Ten people become stranded on their way home from the baths at Cauterets in the Pyrenees. To occupy their time each *devisant* relates a story every day, for a proposed 100 stories. For some reason, only 72 tales were completed. Marguerite figures prominently in tales IV and X which are assumed to be autobiographical. Of special interest are her views on love, again based on Platonic ideals, and on religion, which reveal a strong Protestant predilection. Woman is portrayed as man's equal with a will of her own, not an object created to satisfy man's sensual pleasures. One also finds undisguised criticism of religious orders, especially the Franciscans and the Cordeliers, in tales told by Oiselle. These coincide, in fact, with sentiments Louise of Savoy expressed in her journals. As in the *Decameron*, bawdy, earthy language is employed by the noble storytellers, but Marguerite never violates the conventional rules of decorum. Each tale ends with a spiritually uplifting message. Despite this, the tales have been at times labelled risqué and consequently lacking in literary merit, particularly the pirated 1558 edition.

In that year Pierre Boaisteau published a "corrected and improved" version of the original tales under the title *Histoires des Amans Fortunez* [Tales of Happy Lovers], attributing the stories to an anonymous author. Further, he suppressed five tales and several passages that he judged heretical, and omitted the prologues. The following year Marguerite's daughter Jeanne d'Albret bought and destroyed almost the entire unauthorized, bowdlerized edition. 72 were published under her direction in 1559, and edited by Claude Gruget who gave the title *The Heptameron* to the book. This edition was not authentic, for Gruget substituted three of his own stories for three tales expunged by Boaisteau, numbers 11, 44, and 46. Only in

1853–54 was the original manuscript published (by Le Roux de Lincey), containing 72 tales and the prologues. *The Heptameron* lacks the verve and finesse of the *Decameron*, perhaps because of Marguerite's decision to base the stories on real people and events, which constrained her imagination to some extent. But according to Arthur Tilley, *The Heptameron* is "the most characteristic book of the early French Renaissance . . . which gives us the best picture of its social and intellectual atmosphere, of that curious mixture of coarseness and refinement, of cynicism and enthusiasm, of irreverence and piety, of delight in living and love of meditation on death." Despite questions regarding the authorship of the tales, most scholars attribute them to Marguerite on the grounds of similarity of style, while recognizing the uneven quality of the tales themselves.

Marguerite wrote some of her most carefully crafted poetry during the last decade of her life. Love and religious themes predominate. Two of her longest and most emotive poems concern relations between men and women, a popular subject of the day. "Les Quatre dames et les quatre gentilshommes" [Four Ladies and Four Gentlemen] and *Le Coche* [The Coach] explore this same topic at great length. Her "Triomphe de l'Agneau" [The Triumph of the Lamb] and "Oraison de l'Ame fidèle à son Seigneur Dieu" [Prayer of a Faithful Soul to Its Lord God] appeared in the 1540s. Among Marguerite's most adroitly handled themes are those which touched her deeply—love of God and of her brother, as seen in the *Chansons spirituelles* [Spiritual Songs]. In "Les Adieus" [Farewells] Marguerite again reflects on her affection for her second husband and the emotional suffering she had endured. These later poems, filled with passion and feeling, reveal the depth and breadth of Marguerite's learning. Her talent for rhyme, her experimentation with metre, and her spontaneity are often overshadowed by her profuseness and her lack of "technical skill and sense of form." However, as patroness of and contributor to the arts, Queen Marguerite de Navarre was a major influence in the French Renaissance and at the brilliant court of François I.

—Jeanne A. Ojala

MARIE DE FRANCE

Born: in France but lived in England. **Career:** Literary activity thought to date from c. 1160 to c. 1215. Fl. late 12th century. Little is known of her life; possibly was the abbess of Shaftesbury from 1181 to 1216, illegitimate daughter of Geoffrey Plantagenet.

PUBLICATIONS

Collections

Espurgatoire seint Patriz, edited by T.A. Jenkins. 1894; as *Saint Patrick's Purgatory: A Poem*, translated by Michael J. Curley, 1993.
Fables (written c. 1180), edited by Alfred Ewert and Ronald C. Johnston. 1942; *The Fables of Marie de France*, edited and translated by Mary Lou Martin, 1984; also edited and translated by Harriet Spiegel, 1987.

Graelent and Guigamor: Two Breton Lays, edited and translated by Russell Weingartner. 1985.
Lais, edited by Alfred Ewert. 1944; also edited by Jean Rycher, 1966, Pierre Jonin, 1979, and by Charles Brucker, 1991; as *Lays of Marie de France*, translated by Eugene Mason, 1911; as *The Lais of Marie de France*, translated by Harry F. Williams, 1970; also edited and translated by Joan M. Ferrante and Robert W. Hanning, 1978; Glyn S. Burgess and Keith Busby, 1986; *In Quest of Marie de France: A Twelfth-century Poet*, edited with introduction by Chantal E. Maréchal, 1992; *Le Présent de Marie* by Milena Mikhaïlova, 1996.
Oeuvres completés. 1987.

*

Bibliography: *Marie de France: An Analytical Bibliography* by Glyn S. Burgess, 1977.

Critical Studies: *Les Lais de Marie de France* by Ernest Hopffner, 1935; *The Vision of Hell: Infernal Journeys in Medieval French Literature* by D.D.R. Owen, 1970; *Marie de France* by Emanuel J. Mickel, Jr., 1974; *Narrative Technique in the Lais of Marie de France: Themes and Variations* by Judith Rice Rothschild, 1974; *Woman as Image in Medieval Literature from the Twelfth Century to Dante* by Joan M. Ferrante, 1975; *Les Lais de Marie de France: Du conte merveilleux à la nouvelle psychologique* by Edgard Sienaert, 1978; *Les Lais de Marie de France: Contes d'amour et d'aventure du moyen âge* by Philippe Ménard, 1979; *Marie de France, Lais* by Paula Clifford, 1982; *The Lais of Marie de France: Text and Context* by Glyn S. Burgess, 1987; *Oyez ke dit Marie: Étude sur les lais de Marie de France* by Claude-Henri Joubert, 1987.

* * *

Marie de France was the first woman to write successfully in the French vernacular. Little is known about her, but scholars agree that she was of French origin and lived in England at the court of the Plantagenets during the 12th century. Her literary production consists of three books, each of very different inspiration, and is usually dated between 1160 and 1190. She apparently knew Latin and English as well as French.

Her *Fables*, commissioned by a Count William and written probably around 1180, are an adaptation of an English translation of a number of Aesopic fables. She entitled her text "Esope," which became the common name for fables in the Middle Ages. Curiously, until late into the 18th century, Marie de France was primarily known as the author of the *Fables* and was considered a 13th-century author. It was only in the 19th century, thanks to the work of Karl Warnke, that she was recognized as a 12th-century author and her *Lais* (Lays), for which she is best known today, became widely available. It is in the Epilogue to the *Fables*, that her name and origin are found. "Marie ai num, si sui de France" ("Marie is my name, I am from France").

She also wrote a translation of a French version of the Latin *Tractatus de Purgatoria Sancti Patricii* which she titled *Espurgatoire seint Patriz* (*Saint Patrick's Purgatory*). The work is composed of 2,300 lines and presents a vivid description of purgatory and the suffering endured there.

Today Marie de France is best known for her *Lays*, a collection of 12 short narrative poems written in eight-syllable verse. They vary in length from 118 lines (''Chevrefoil'') to 1,184 (''Eliduc''). All are based on Breton or Celtic legends which were part of the oral literature of the Bretons. Marie, having heard them sung by the court jongleurs, turned them into written narratives. The modern reader needs to be aware that for Marie de France, a medieval author, the retelling or re-creating of a story was artistic creation, just as were her translations of the *Fables* and *Saint Patrick's Purgatory*. Throughout her work she makes references to the important role played by the author who preserves information and disseminates it. She envisioned her work as significant and worthy of praise. Her contemporaries were in agreement, as is evidenced in the comments of Denis Piramus in his prologue to *La Vie de Saint Edmund le roi* (*The Life of Saint Edmund the King*).

Marie de France wrote her *Lays* at a time when there was great literary activity in France and this literature was making its way into England. She, therefore, was acquainted with the Provençal courtly love lyric, the theories of *fin'amor*, the Arthurian and Tristan materials, and the romances of antiquity. Many scholars have spoken of the influence of the *Enéas* on her lays; ''Lanval'' is based on the legends of Arthur, and ''Chevrefoil'' uses the Tristan story. Her concept of love as portrayed in the *Lays* shares many of the ideas found in these various traditions. The power of love is irresistible and overwhelming, causing the physical illness of the lover if it is unrequited. Love is at times either pre-ordained or pre-arranged by supernatural forces, as in *Guigamar* (*Guigamor*); it often has tragic consequences and results in the death of the lovers, for it is often adulterous and in opposition to societal exigencies. Fidelity between the lovers is of the utmost importance. Marie de France's concept of love, like the other treatments of the subject popular in her time, shows little influence from the Church's concept of unmarried love as sinful. She does not condemn the adulterous or illicit love of her characters and uses dissolution of marriage to solve problems for her lovers (''Le Fresne,'' ''Eliduc'').

However, unlike love in the courtly and *fin'amor* tradition, for Marie de France love does not have to be adulterous. Several of the lays tell of love between unmarried individuals who face obstacles: an overly possessive father in ''Los Deus Amanz'' [Two Lovers], an inequality of rank in ''Le Fresne.'' For many of the lovers, the obstacles are overcome, and marriage brings about a happily-ever-after ending (''Le Fresne,'' ''Milun''). Consequently, the *Lays* may be considered unique in the body of love stories of the period.

The *Lays* portray love in a world in which reality and fantasy intermingle with ease; however, the presence of the supernatural varies from lay to lay. *Guigamor* relies heavily upon the magical: a white hind, a wound to be cured only by a woman who will suffer more than any woman has ever suffered, a magical ship without a crew. In ''Yonec,'' the hero of the same name is able to take the form of a hawk; while the hero of ''Bisclavret'' becomes a werewolf. In contrast, there are no supernatural elements in ''Los Deus Amanz,'' ''La Laustic'' [The Nightingale], or ''Chaitivel.''

It is particularly in the *Lays* that Marie de France's talent as a storyteller is apparent. Although the *Lays* are short narratives in which the action is the most important element, she demonstrates an ability to describe a character, a place, or an object, or to create an image, with notable economy of words. In spite of their brevity, her descriptions are forceful.

Marie de France's narrations exhibit many standard elements of medieval storytelling. She uses superlatives and exaggeration freely—the knights are all the most valiant, the women the most beautiful. She

is at a loss for words to do justice to the beauty or excellence of a character or object. She often intervenes in her works, especially in the prologues and epilogues, reassuring the reader that the story is true and emphasizing her role as author. The *Lays* as well as the *Fables* and the *Saint Patrick's Purgatory* attest Marie de France's serious commitment to her role as a literary author.

—Shawncey J. Webb

See the essay on *Guigamor*.

MARIVAUX

Born: Pierre Carlet de Chamblain de, in Paris, France, 4 February 1688. **Education:** Studied law in Paris, 1710–13; law degree, 1721, and practised briefly. **Family:** Married Colombe Bollogne in 1717 (died 1723), one daughter; lived with Mlle. Angelique Saint-Jean from 1744. **Career:** Contibutor, *Le Nouveau Mercure from 1717–21*; lost much of his fortune, 1720, and subsequently earned living as a professional writer; founder and publisher, *Le Spectateur français*, 1721–24, and *L'Indigent Philosophe*, 1726–27. **Member:** 1742, chancellor, 1750, and director, 1759, Académie française. **Died:** 12 February 1763.

PUBLICATIONS

Collections

Oeuvres complètes. 12 vols., 1781.
Théâtre complet, edited by Frédéric Deloffre. 2 vols., 1968.
Journaux et oeuvres diverses, edited by Frédéric Deloffre and Michel Gilot. 1969.
Oeuvres de jeunesse, edited by Frédéric Deloffre and Claude Rigault. 1972.
Plays (includes *The Double Inconstancy; The False Servant; The Game of Love and Chance; Careless Vows; The Feigned Inconstancy; Harlequin's Lesson in Love; Slave Island; The Will; A Matter of Dispute; The Constant Players*). 1988.

Plays

Le Père prudent et équitable; ou, Crispin l'heureux fourbe (produced 1712). 1712.
L'Amour et la vérité, with Chevalier Rustaing de Saint-Jory (produced 1720). In *Théâtre complet*, 1968.
Arlequin poli par l'amour (produced 1720). 1723; as *Robin, Bachelor of Love*, translated by Oscar Mandel, in *Seven Comedies*, 1968; as *Harlequin's Lesson in Love*, translated by Donald Watson, in *Plays*, 1988.
Annibal (produced 1720). 1727.
La Surprise de l'amour (produced 1722). 1723.
La Double Inconstance (produced 1723). 1723; as *Double Infidelity*, translated by Oscar Mandel, in *Seven Comedies*, 1968; as *Infidelities*, translated by David Cohen, 1980; as *The Double Inconstancy*, translated by Nicholas Wright, in *Plays*, 1988.
Le Prince travesti; ou, L'Illustre Aventurier (produced 1724). 1727.

La Fausse Suivante; ou, Le Fourbe puni (produced 1724). 1729; as *The False Servant*, translated by Michael Sadler, in *Plays*, 1988.

Le Dénouement imprévu (produced 1724). 1727.

L'Île des esclaves (produced 1725). 1725; as *Slave Island*, translated by Nicholas Wright, in *Plays*, 1988.

L'Héritier du village (produced 1725). 1729.

L'Île de la raison; ou, Les Petits Hommes (produced 1727). 1727.

La (Seconde) Surprise de l'amour (produced 1727). 1728.

Le Triomphe de Plutus (produced 1728). 1739; as *Money Makes the World Go Round*, translated by Oscar Mandel, in *Seven Comedies*, 1968.

La Colonie (as *La Nouvelle Colonie*, produced 1729; revised version, produced 1750). In *Théâtre complet*, 1968.

Le Jeu de l'amour et du hasard (produced 1730). 1730; as *Love in Livery*, translated by Harriet Ford and Marie Louise le Verrier, 1907; as *The Game of Love and Chance*, translated by Richard Aldington, in *French Comedies of the 18th Century*, 1923; also translated by Wallace Fowlie, 1962; Oscar Mandel, in *Seven Comedies*, 1968; David Cohen, 1980; edited with introduction by D.J. Culpin, 2000.

La Réunion des amours (produced 1731). 1732.

Le Triomphe de l'amour (produced 1732). 1732; translated by James Magruder in *Three French Comedies*, 1996; as *The Triumph of Love*, translated by Martin Crimp, 1999.

Les Serments indiscrets (produced 1732). 1732; as *Careless Vows*, translated by John Walters, in *Plays*, 1988.

L'École des mères (produced 1732). 1732.

L'Heureux Stratagème (produced 1733). 1733; as *The Agreeable Surprise*, translated by John Rule, in *Poetical Blossoms*, 1766; as *The Wiles of Love*, translated by Oscar Mandel, in *Seven Comedies*, 1968; as *The Feigned Inconstancy*, translated by John Bowen, in *Plays*, 1988.

La Méprise (produced 1734). 1739.

Le Petit-Maître corrigé (produced 1734). 1739.

La Mère confidante (produced 1735). 1735.

Le Legs (produced 1736). 1736; as *The Legacy*, translated by Barrett H. Clark, 1915; as *The Will*, translated by Michael Sadler, in *Plays*, 1988.

Les Fausses Confidences (produced 1737). 1738; as *The False Confessions*, in *The Classic Theatre 4*, edited by Eric Bentley, 1961; as *Sylvia Hears a Secret*, translated by Oscar Mandel, in *Seven Comedies*, 1968.

La Joie imprévue (produced 1738). 1738.

Les Sincères (produced 1739). 1739.

L'Épreuve (produced 1740). 1740; as *The Test*, translated by Oscar Mandel, in *Seven Comedies*, 1968.

La Commère (produced 1741). In *Théâtre complet*, 1968.

La Dispute (produced 1744). 1747; as *A Matter of Dispute*, translated by John Walters, in *Plays*, 1988; as *The Dispute*, translated by Neil Bartlett, 1999.

Le Préjugé vaincu (produced 1746). 1747.

La Femme fidèle (produced 1755). In *Théâtre complet*, 1968.

Les Acteurs de bonne foi (produced 1947). In *Théâtre complet*, 1968; translated as *The Constant Players*, translated by Donald Watson, in *Plays*, 1988.

Félicie (produced 1957). In *Théâtre complet*, 1968.

Seven Comedies (includes *Robin, Bachelor of Love; Double Infidelity; Money Makes the World Go Round; The Game of Love and Chance; The Wiles of Love; Sylvia Hears a Secret; The Test*), edited and translated by Oscar Mandel. 1968.

Fiction

Les Aventures de ***; ou, Les Effets surprenants de la sympathie. 5 vols., 1713–14.

La Voiture embourbée. 1714.

La Vie de Marianne; ou, Les Aventures de Mme la comtesse de ***. 11 vols., 1731–41; edited by Frédéric Deloffre, 1957; as *The Life of Marianne*, translated anonymously, 1736–42; as *The Virtuous Orphan*, translated anonymously, 1743; as *The Life and Adventures of Indiana*, translated by Mary Collyer, 1746; as *The Hand of Destiny*, translated by Sir Gilbert Campbell, 1889.

Le Paysan parvenu; ou, Les Mémoires de M. ***. 5 vols., 1735–36; edited by Frédéric Deloffre, 1959; as *The Fortunate Villager*, translated anonymously, 1765; as *The Upstart Peasant*, translated by Benjamin Boyce, 1974; as *Up from the Country*, translated by David Cohen, 1980.

Le Télémaque travesti. 1736.

Pharsamon; ou, Los Nouvelles Folies romanesques. 1737; as *Pharsamond*, translated by Joseph Lockman, 1950.

Verse

L'Homère travesti; ou, L'Iliade en vers burlesques. 2 vols., 1716.

Other

Le Spectateur français. 2 vols., 1723–24; enlarged edition, 1725.

L'Indigent Philosophe; ou, L'Homme sans souci. 1727.

Le Cabinet du philosophe. 1734.

Le Miroir. 1755; edited by Mario Matucci, 1958.

Journaux et oeuvres diverses, edited by Frédéric Deloffre and Michel Gilot. 1969.

Oeuvres de jeunesse, edited by Frédéric Deloffre and Claude Rigault. 1972.

*

Critical Studies: *Une Préciosité nouvelle: Marivaux et le marivaudage* by Frédéric Deloffre, 1955, revised edition, 1971; *The Theatre of Marivaux* by Kenneth N. McKee, 1958; *Marivaux* by E.J.H. Greene, 1965; *The Novel of Worldliness: Crébillon, Marivaux, Laclos, and Stendhal* by Peter P. Brooks, 1969; *Love in the Theatre of Marivaux* by Valenti Papadopoulou Brady, 1970; *Marivaux: Un humanisme expérimental* by Henri Coulet and Michel Gilot, 1973; *Marivaux* by Oscar A. Haac, 1973; *Marivaux's Novels: Theme and Function in Early Eighteenth Century Narrative* by Ronald C. Rosbottom, 1974; *Marivaux and Molière: A Comparison* by Alfred Girmaru, 1977; *Structuralist Perspectives in Criticism of Fiction: Essays on "Manon Lescaut" and "La Vie de Marianne"* by Patrick Brady, 1978; *Marivaux, La Vie de Marianne and Le Paysan parvenu* by David Coward, 1984; *Marivaux: Le Jeu de l'amour et du hasard and Les Fausses Confidences* by Graham E. Rodmell, 1982; *The Rococo and Eighteenth-Century French Literature: A Study Through Marivaux's Theater* by George Poe, 1987; *Face Value: Physiognomical Thought and the Legible Body in Marivaux, Lavater, Balzac, Gautier, and Zola* by Christopher Rivers, 1994; *Sites of the Spectator: Emerging Literary and Cultural Practice in Eighteenth-Century France* by Suzanne R. Pucci, 2001.

* * *

Marivaux's comedies today are the most frequently performed in France after Molière's; his two major novels are important precursors of the psychological novel; his journals, first conceived like the *Spectator* of Addison and Steele, provide a significant commentary on man's struggle to find himself. Indeed, *La Recherche de la vérité* (*The Search for Truth*), the title of a work by Nicolas Malebranche that Marivaux admired, qualifies his own literary enterprise, "grounded neither in traditional morality nor the cult of passions, but in respect for the human person" (Deloffre).

Comedy arises from paradox which makes the spectator feel wiser and smile. The "reflections" of his characters often express their misapprehensions. In *La Double Inconstance* (*The Double Inconstancy*) Silvia, the peasant girl, will not love the Prince: better poor in my village than weeping in luxury! But later she enjoys his palace and is happy there. The lighthearted style hides seduction and cruelty, as can be seen in *La Répétition* (*The Rehearsal*), the tragic reinterpretation by Jean Anouilh of *The Double Inconstancy*. Marivaux's interplay of meanings veils the truth (like Pirandello), a surprisingly modern note which lets us discover in his sparkling wit the undertones of realism or even pessimism: this is *marivaudage*.

Paradox may arise also from the contrasting meanings of a single word like *honnêteté* (honour; the code of a gentleman; simple politeness). The ambitious Marianne and Jacob, her male counterpart in the novel *Le Paysan parvenu* (*The Upstart Peasant*), are much beset by these implications, for how *honnête* must one be to make a good marriage? The Europeans, reduced to liliputian size in *L'Île de la raison*, are required to admit their faults and prejudices to recover their stature (i.e., greatness) and this is a much harder task for gentlemen and ladies than for their less complicated servants.

Characters are placed in perspective by their servants. The idealistic masters are often entrapped by convention and illusion, in striking contrast to the more basic motivation (hunger, thirst, love) of their associates who keep them in touch with reality, as Sancho Panza does for Don Quixote. For all that they are not frozen in their social positions. Just as the peasant girl may marry the Prince, Arlequin may outwit a fairy queen in *Arlequin poli par l'amour* (*Harlequin's Lesson in Love*), or master and servant may exchange roles to bring about a more dramatic victory of love in *Le Jeu de l'amour et du hasard* (*The Game of Love and Chance*). The sharply individualized portrayal of each character is all the more remarkable because their names and roles are adapted from the stock of the Comédie-Italienne, the troupe for whom he wrote most of his plays.

Marivaux is a master of language who lets everyone speak in his own particular style. Marianne's self-assured rhetoric overcomes the obstacles to her ambitions very differently than Jacob's disarming frankness. Dorante attracts Silvia by his sensitivity where Arlequin repels her with his popular mind (*The Game of Love and Chance*). Here Marivaux could have gone much further, as we can see in the battle of words between Marianne's coachman and her landlady, a washer woman (critics of the time were scandalized by this vulgarity), if the pressures of society and Marivaux's ambitions to enter the French Academy had not stood in the way. Even so, it is the variety of styles that lends dramatic perspective.

—Oscar A. Haac

See the essays on *The False Confessions, The Game of Love and Chance,* and *A Matter of Dispute.*

MÁRQUEZ, Gabriel Garcia

See GARCÍA MÁRQUEZ, Gabriel

MARQUIS DE SADE

See SADE, Marquis de

MARTÍ (PÉREZ), José (Julián)

Born: Havana, Spanish colony of Cuba (now independent), 28 January 1853. **Education:** Educated at the Municipal Boys' School, Havana, 1865–66; Instituto de Havana, 1866–69; University of Madrid, 1873; University of Zaragoza, degree in law, 1873, degree in philosophy and letters, 1874. **Family:** Married Carmen Zayas Bazán in 1876; one son. **Career:** Collaborated on the underground periodicals *El Diablo Cojuelo* and *La Patria Libre,* 1869: arrested for subversion, 1869, and sentenced to six years' hard labour, but exiled to Spain in 1871; moved to Mexico, 1875, via France and England; contributor, *Revista Universal,* 1875–76, and co-founder, Alarcón Society, both in Mexico City; visited Cuba briefly, 1877; taught languages and philosophy in Guatemala, 1876–77; returned again to Cuba: worked in a law office, and taught literature at the Liceo de Guanabaco; arrested on suspicions of anti-government activity, and deported again to Spain, 1879; travelled to France, 1879, then sailed to the United States: based in New York, 1879–95; journalist, *New York Sun,* c. 1880; travelled to Venezuela and founded the *Revista Venezolana,* Caracas, 1881; correspondent for various Spanish-American newspapers in New York, including *El Partido Liberal* (Mexico), *La Opinión Nacional* (Venezuela), from 1881, *La Nación* (Argentina), from 1882, and *La República* (Honduras), from 1886, *El Economista Americano* (New York), 1887, and *La Opinión Pública* (Uruguay), from 1889; translator, Appleton, publishers, New York, from 1882; contributing editor, *La América* (New York), from 1883; consul for Uruguay, New York, 1887–91; North American representative, Free Press Association of Argentina, from 1888; founding editor, children's magazine *La Edad de Oro* [The Golden Age], 1889; Spanish teacher, Central High School, New York, 1890; consul for Argentina and Paraguay, 1890–91; founder, *Liga de Instrucción,* Tampa, Florida, 1891; in last years deepened his involvement in Cuban revolutionary politics: co-founder, Cuban Revolutionary Party and the revolutionary journal *Patria* (both 1892), travelled incessantly throughout Central America, the Caribbean, and Florida, helped organize the invasion of Cuba, 1895 (and was named Major General of the Army of Liberation in the island). **Died:** (killed in action) 19 May 1895.

PUBLICATIONS

Collections

Obras del maestro, edited by Gonzalo de Quesada y Aróstegui and others. 16 vols., 1900–33.
Obras completas, edited by Néstor Carbonell Rivero. 8 vols., 1918–20.
Obras completas, edited by Gonzalo de Quesada y Miranda. 70 vols., 1936–47.

1–14. *Cuba*. 1936–38.
15–17. *Norteamericanos*. 1939.
18. *Hispanoamericanos*. 1939.
19–23. *Nuestra América*. 1939–40.
24. *La Edad de Oro*. 1940.
25. *Amistad funesta*. 1940.
26. *Teatro*. 1940.
27–40. *Escenas norteamericanas*. 1940–42.
41–43. *Versos*. 1942.
44–47. *Escenas europeas*. 1942.
48–50. *Escenas mexicanas*. 1942–43.
51–54. *Crítica y arte*. 1943–44.
55–56. *Viajes*. 1944.
57–61. *Traducciones*. 1944–45.
62–64. *Apuntes*. 1945–46.
65–67. *Epistolario*. 1946.
68–69. *Cartas a Mercado*. 1946.
70. *Guía para las obras de Martí*. 1947.
Obras completas, edited by M. Isidro Méndez. 2 vols., 1946.
Poesías completas, edited by Rafael Esténger. 1953.
Obras completas [Editorial de Ciencia Sociales Edition]. 27 vols., 1954; reprinted 1975.
Obras completas, edited by Francisco Baeza Pérez. 25 vols., 1961.
Obras completas [Nacional de Cuba Edition]. 28 vols., 1963–73.
Obra literaria, edited by Cintio Vitier. 1978.
Obras completas. 1983–.
Poesía completa, edited by Eliana Dávila. 1985.
José Martí Reader: Writings on the Americas, edited by Deborah Shnookal and Mirta Muñiz. 1999.
José Martí: Selected Writings, edited and translated by Esther Allen. 2002.

Prose

El presidio político en Cuba. 1871.
Artículos desconocidos. 1930.
Epistolario. 3 vols., 1930–31.
The America of José Martí: Selected Writings, edited and translated by Juan de Onís. 1953.
Obras escogidas, edited by Rafael Esténger. 1953.
Argentina y la primera conferencia panamericana, edited by Dardo Cúneo. 1955.
Páginas de José Martí, edited by Fryda Schulz de Mantovani. 1963.
Martí on the USA, edited and translated by Luis A. Baralt. 1966.
Diario de un revolucionario (letters and diaries). 1969.
Martí y Puerto Rico, edited by Carlos Alberto Montaner. 1970.
Escritos desconocidos, edited by Carlos Ripoll. 1971.
Ensayos sobre arte y literatura, edited by Roberto Fernández Retamar. 1972.
Nuestra América, edited by Roberto Fernández Retamar. 1974; also edited by Hugo Achugar, 1977.
Inside the Monster: Writings on the United States and American Imperialism, edited by Philip S. Foner, translated by Foner, Elinor Randall, and others. 1975.
Correspondencia con General Antonio Maceo. 1977.
Discursos selectos. 1977.
El Partido Revolucionario Cubano y la guerra. 1978.
On Education: Articles on Educational Theory and Pedagogy, and Writings for Children from the Age of Gold, edited by Philip S. Foner, translated by Elinor Randall. 1979.

Our America: Writings on Latin America and the Struggle for Cuban Independence, edited by Philip S. Foner, translated by Elinor Randall. 1979.
Nuevas cartas de Nueva York, edited by E. Mejía Sánchez. 1980.
On Art and Literature, edited by Philip S. Foner, translated by Elinor Randall. 1982.
Dos congresos; Las razones ocultas, edited by the Centro de Estudios Martianos. 1985.
Lectura en Steck Hall. 1985.
Martí y el Uruguay: Crónicas y correspondencia (includes correspondence with Enrique Estrázulas 1887–89). 1988.
Political Parties and Elections in the United States, edited by Philip S. Foner and translated by Elinor Randall. 1989.
Thoughts: On Liberty, Social Justice, Government, Art and Morality, translated by Carlos Ripoll. 1995.

Verse

Guatemala. 1878.
Ismaelillo. 1882.
Versos sencillos. 1891; selection as *Tuya; Other Verses*, translated by Charles Cecil, 1898; also translated by Manuel A. Tellechea, 1997.
Versos libres. 1913.
Poesías, edited by Juan Marinello. 1928.
Versos de amor (inéditos), edited by Gonzalo de Quesada y Miranda. 1930.
Flores del destierro (versos inéditos), edited by Gonzalo de Quesada y Miranda. 1933.
Major Poems (bilingual edition), edited by Philip S. Foner, translated by Elinor Randall. 1982.
Antología poética, edited by Maria Esther Cantonnet. 1987.

Fiction

Amistad funesta (as Adelaida Ral). 1885.
Lucía Jerez y otras narraciones (for children), edited by Mercedes Santos Moray. 1975.

Plays

Amor con amor se paga (produced 1875). 1876; as *Love Is Repaid by Love*, translated by Willis K. Jones, in *Archivos de José Martí 2*, 1947.
Adúltera: Drama inédito. 1935.
Translator, *Antigüedades clásicas 1: Antigüededas griegas*, by J.S. Mahafy. 1883.
Translator, *Antigüedades clásicas 2: Antigüededas romanas*, by A.S. Wilkins. 1883.
Translator, *Mistero . . . (Called Back)*, by Hugh Conway. 1886.
Translator, *Nociones de lógica*, by William Stanley Jevons. 1886.
Translator, *Ramona, novela americana*, by Helen Hunt Jackson. 1888.

*

Bibliography: *Fuentes para el estudio de José Martí* by Manuel Pedro González, 1950; *Bibliografía martiana (1853–1953)*, by Fermín Peraza Sarausa, 1954, supplemented with *Bibliografía martiana*

(1954–63), by Celestino Blanch y Blanco, 1965; *Archivo José Martí* (on Martí criticism), 1971, and *Índice universal de la obra de José Martí*, 1971, both by Carlos Ripoll.

Critical Studies: *Martí su obra literaria* by Raimundo Lazo, 1929; *Vida de Martí* by Rafael Esténger, 1934; *La lengua de Martí* by Gabriela Mistral, 1934; *Archivo José Martí*, 6 vols., 1940–53; *Vida y pensamiento de Martí*, 2 vols., 1942; *Martí, el apóstol*, 1942, and *El espíritu de Martí*, 1952, both by Jorge Mañach; *Martí, carne y espíritu* by Néstor Carbonell, 2 vols., 1951–52; *Martí, escritor* by Andrés Iduarte, 1951; *José Martí: Epic Chronicler of the United States in the Eighties* by Manuel Pedro González, 1953, and *Antología crítica de José Martí*, 1960, and *Indagaciones martianas*, 1961, both edited by González; *Memoria del Congresso de Escritores Martianos*, 1953; *Pensamiento y acción de José Martí*, 1953; *José Martí, escritor americano: Martí y el modernismo*, 1958, and *Once ensayos martianos*, 1964, both by Juan Marinello; *Símbolo y color en la obra de José Martí*, 1960, and *Martí, Darío y el modernismo*, 1969, both by Ivan Schulman, and *José Martí: Esquema ideológico* by Schulman and Manuel Pedro González, 1961; *José Martí: Cuban Patriot* by Richard B. Gray, 1962; *Martí: El héroe y su acción revolucionaria* by Ezequiel Martínez Estrada, 1966; *José Martí* by Juan Carlos Ghiano, 1967; *Genio y figura de José Martí* by Fryda Schultz de Mantovani, 1968; *Anuario martiano*, 4 vols., 1969–78; *Los versos de Martí* by Cintio Vitier, 1969, and *Temas martianos* by Vitier and Fina García Marruz, 1969; *Algunas ideas de José Martí en relación con la clase obrera y el socialismo* by José Cantón Navarro, 1970; *Martí* by R. Fernández Retamar, 1970; *Martí y su concepción del mundo* by Roberto Agramonte, 1971; *En torno a José Martí* edited by Noel Salomán, 1974; *El ideario y estético de José Martí* by H.O. Dill, 1975; *Anuario del Centro de Estudios Martianos*, 1978–; *Atlas histórico-Biográfico José Martí*, 1983; *José Martí: Poesía y existencia* by José Olivio Jiménez, 1983; *José Martí: Mentor of the Cuban Nation* by John M. Kirk, 1983; *Estudios sobre Martí* by R. Rexach, 1985; *José Martí: Revolutionary Democrat* by Christopher Abel and Nissa Torrents, 1986; *Re-reading José Martí (1853–1895): One Hundred Years Later*, edited with introduction by Julio Rodríguez-Luis, 1999; *American Chronicles of José Martí: Journalism and Modernity in Spanish America* by Susana Rotker, translated by Jennifer French and Katherine Semler, 2000.

* * *

Much of José Martí's writing expresses the sentiment voiced in his poem "My son" from *Ismaelillo:* "I have faith in human betterment, in a future life, in the usefulness of virtue . . . ." This conviction is less evident in his drama and novels, genres he abandoned early in his career, and is most in evidence in the journalistic essays which comprise the bulk of his collected works. In them, he records his observations: on the cultures of countries where he sojourned during his exile; on art, literature, and literary figures; on pedagogy; and on patriotic reflections about Cuba's struggle for independence. Martí's preference for the essay puts him closer to Latin America's essayists of the 19th century than to his contemporaries, the aestheticist initiators of modernism.

His journalistic essays display a very personal style. They are, for the most part, pragmatic, meant to persuade his reader to share his ideals and ideas; consequently, his prose often resembles persuasive orations or horatory sermons. His proselytizing is made more palatable by a musicality of language reminiscent of the spoken word. The richness of his literary language is due to a synthesis which, while embracing elements of the contemporary popular speech of Cuba and other Latin American countries, as well as archaic vocabulary and turns of phrase, nevertheless observes the academically established linguistic norms of the Spanish language. Another of Martí's important contributions to the language of Latin America is found in the neologisms he coined, most of which were verbs that increased the dynamism of his texts.

Although he was not a slavish imitator of any of the masters he admired, Martí nevertheless allowed them to influence his writing. The influence of Spanish classics is discernible in the tendency toward a baroqueness of style in both his prose and his poetry. The hyperbaton is ubiquitous; and extended, complex sentences, which set, develop, and illustrate his ideas, mingle and contrast with brief, simple sentences, which state a premise or synthesize an argument. Paragraphs become lengthy as his initial thought unfolds in its varied aspects. To maintain clarity in these protracted, complex paragraphs, Martí made systematic, logical, and innovative use of punctuation.

Martí disapproved of, and spoke out against, the aestheticism, the imitative tendencies, and the notion of art for its own sake popular in his time. In his own writing, he managed to transcend these trends, thus contributing significantly to the creation of an autochthonous, Latin American form of literary expression. Without turning his back on the classics of the Spanish tradition, he rejected the shame and humiliation of colonialism, instead searching for the pride of independent American existence, thought, and expression.

A different facet of Martí's prose is found in the pages of *La Edad de Oro* [The Golden Age], a children's periodical he published. In that journal he adapted his language and ideas to a more infantile level of understanding in order to reach his young readers' minds. Martí's characteristic didactic intention can be detected in "Tres héroes" ("Three Heroes"), an essay in praise of Latin American patriots, which counsels that "every American should love Bolívar as a father—Bolívar and all the soldiers who fought as he did so that America would belong to Americans."

He also published children's short stories, like "La muñeca negra" ("The Black Doll"), which, while charged with fantasy, nevertheless teaches about love and the equality of the races. His children's poetry was edifying too. "Dos patrias" ("The Two Princes"), for instance, discusses the inherent equality of all persons, regardless of class, and "Los zapaticos de rosa" ("The Rose-Coloured Slippers") reveals the beauty of selfless giving.

Critics have understandably lavished attention on Martí's poetry, for it tilled the ground on which modernism was able to thrive. He threw off the yokes imposed by the principles of traditional Spanish versification, explored innovative rhythms and metres, used symbolism and colour with originality, and introduced free verse, thus liberating poetic language from the strictures of form and rhyme.

The poems of *Ismaelillo*, written while he was in exile, are tender, loving words written for his toddler son, whom he evokes as that "floating child" riding "joyously astride / The humble neck" of his absent father. *Versos sencillos* [Simple Poetry] is a collection of poems best described by their title. In them, Martí uses the eight-syllable line of traditional, popular, Spanish poetry and both consonant and assonant rhyme in traditional rhyme schemes. These poems explore Martí's ideals, ethics, and literary principles. In poem "V" he describes his verse as "a hill of foam" and as "daggers / Sprouting blossoms from the hilts," and reveals his dual purpose in writing—the creation of simple beauty and the exhortation of the patriot.

The poems of *Versos libres* [Free Verse], Martí claimed, were written in his twenties, but not published until his forties. Rather than ''trimming'' these poems, as he notes in the preface, he allowed them to remain as they came to him, ''as tears leave the eyes and blood bubbles out of a wound.'' They, like the poems of *Flores del destierro* [Flowers of Exile], are deeply-felt, honest, and personal poems, which speak of his suffering in prison and in exile, and of his nostalgia and aspirations for his homeland. The title, *Flores del destierro*, applies as well to Martí's patriotic sentiments as to his poetic form—free and innovative, paving the way for modernism.

Martí's idealism is manifest in his trail-blazing works—in respect of the commitment to Cuba's independence expressed in them, his poetic language, with which he revitalized the form, and the literary forms he liberated.

—Oralia Preble-Niemi

MARTIAL

Born: Marcus Valerius Martialis in Bilbilis (now Calatayud, Spain), 1 March AD 38–41. **Education:** Educated in Spain; went to Rome in AD 64; associated with Seneca, Lucan, Juvenal, Quintilian, *qq.v.*, Pliny the Younger, and L. Calpurnius Piso; granted honorary military tribuneship, and *ius trium liberorum* (marriage legislation granting privileges to those with three or more children) although he never married; his return to Spain c. AD 99 was subsidized by Pliny the Younger. **Died:** c. AD 104.

PUBLICATIONS

Verse

[Epigrams], edited by W.M. Lindsay. 1903, revised edition, 1929; also edited by W. Heraeus, 1925, revised by I. Borovskij, 1976, H.J. Izaac, 1930–33, and D.R. Shackleton Bailey, 1990; edited and translated by Walter C.A. Ker [Loeb Edition], 2 vols., 1919–20, revised edition, 1968, and by D.R. Shackleton Bailey [Loeb Edition], 3 vols., 1993; edited in English by H.G. Bohn, 1860, and by J.P. Sullivan and Peter Whigham (translated by Dryden and others), 1987; translated by R. Fletcher, in *Ex otio negotium*, 1656; also translated by Henry Killigrew, 1689; James Elphinston, 1782; Paul Nixon, in *A Roman Wit*, 1911; A.L. Francis and H.F. Tatum, 1924; J.A. Pott and F.A. Wright, 1924; Rolfe Humphries, 1963; R. Marcellino, 1968; Peter Whigham, 1983; as *Twelve Books of Epigrams*, translated by J.A. Pott and F.A. Wright, 1924; selections translated by Thomas May, 1629; William Hay, 1755; Andrew Amos, in *Martial and the Moderns*, 1858; James Michie, 1972; other selections as: *Martial and His Times: Selections from the Epigrams of Martial*, edited by K.W.D. Hall, 1967; *Selections* (with Pliny), edited by Eberhard Christopher Kennedy, 1984; *Letter to Juvenal: 101 Epigrams from Martial*, translated by Peter Whigham, 1985; commentaries by Mario Citroni (Book I), 1975, Peter Howell (Book I), 1980, and N.M. Kay (Book VI), 1984 and (Book XI), 1985; as *Selections from Martial's Epigrams*, edited with introduction by A. Dwight Castro, 1993; as *Mortal City: 100 Epigrams of Martial* by William Matthews, 1995; as *Martial Book XIV: The Apophoreta*, with introduction and commentary by T.J. Leary, 1996; as *Martial in*

English, edited by John Sullivan and Anthony Boyle, 1996; as *Martial, Book IX: A Commentary* by Christer Henriksén, 1998–1999; as *Book XIII: The Xenia*, with introduction and commentary by T.J. Leary, 2001; as *Martial, Book VII: A Commentary* by Guillermo Galán Vioque, translated by J.J. Zoltowski, 2002.

*

Critical Studies: *Martial the Epigrammatist, and Other Essays* by Kirby F. Smith, 1920; *Martial and the English Epigram from Sir Thomas Wyatt to Ben Jonson* by Thomas K. Whipple, 1925; *Martial and the Modern Epigram* by Paul Nixon, 1927; *Martial: Realism and Sentiment in the Epigram* by John W. Duff, 1929; *The Obituary Epigrams of Martial* by Skuli Johnson, 1952; *Aspects of Martial's Epigrams* by A.G. Carrington, 1960; *Martial: The Unexpected Classic: A Literary and Historical Study* by J.P. Sullivan, 1991.

*   *   *

Martial commenced writing epigrams on relatively limited themes before developing a wider range of subject matter and techniques. Earliest was his *Liber spectaculorum* [Book of the Spectacles], a collection of about 30 brief poems written to celebrate the opening of the Colosseum by the Emperor Titus in AD 80. The poems reflect the extravagance of the Games staged on that occasion, describing with wonder and enthusiastic expressions of loyalty to the emperor the ''spectacles'' provided by men and beasts.

Next to appear, in around AD 84, were his two books of two-line poems or mottoes ostensibly designed to accompany presents, the *Xenia* [Guest-Gifts] and *Apophoreta* [Take-Away Gifts], numbered Books XIII and XIV. Martial suggests that these poems may be sent in place of gifts.

Then from AD 86 onwards appeared Martial's books of epigrams, at a rate of approximately one per year. Books I–IX (AD 86–96) were written and published under Domitian, the last of the Flavian emperors; Books X and XI (AD 97) were produced under the new emperor Nerva, and Martial published his last book, XII, in AD 101, under the Emperor Trajan, after his return to Spain in AD 98. Whoever the emperor, Martial's voice is full of adulation; his poetry is typical, in this respect, of the poetry of court circles at this time.

The genre of epigram was lowly and minor, proclaiming no great literary pretensions. It provided light yet cultured entertainment for wealthy gentlemen of leisure, both as audience and as poets themselves. According to the convention expressed by Martial like this—''my page is lascivious, my life without rebuke''—writing epigrams in no way detracted from a man's moral integrity.

Among his literary forerunners and models, Martial names Catullus (Preface to Book I): in form, matter, and manner, Catullus' influence on Martial is obvious. Martial exhibits Catullus' range of metres in his poems: elegiacs, hendecasyllables, scazons, hexameters, and iambics. His range of subject matter is similar too. There are poems about poetry—his own and others'—and the prose prefaces (to Books I, II, VIII, IX, and XII) contain literary apologia and polemic. Many epigrams have as their theme decorum and moderation in social and sexual behaviour; obscenity and invective abound here. Sometimes Martial attempts longer poems on non-satiric themes—the praise of places, buildings, or works of art—highly reminiscent of Statius' occasional poetry in the *Silvae*.

Finally, and most important, Martial's manner. Martial takes over Catullus' stress on *urbanitas:* polish and sophistication in the presentation of poems. Careful structure through repetition, balance, and chiasmus are intrinsic to the epigrams of both poets. But the special and most influential feature of Martial's epigrams is ''point'': in his poems, the reader's enjoyment frequently resides in a final pun, surprise, antithesis, or paradox towards which the entire poem has been building. With a deft word or phrase, often rude or shocking, usually witty, Martial pulls the rug from under his victim's feet: this moment of deflation is often the only rationale for the poem. At this moment, we, the audience, experience a sense of satisfaction and complicity with the author resulting from superiority over the victim. This was probably still more vivid for Martial's original audience: it seems apparent that the books were published for an ''in-crowd'' of *cognoscenti*—the leading intellectuals of the day such as Silius Italicus, Valerius Flaccus, Pliny the Younger, and Quintilian—who were in a position to appreciate Martial's jokes. And while it may not be to the modern taste to read a book of Martial's epigrams from start to finish, yet they are arranged so as to provide maximum possible variation, of form and content and manner: quite a *tour de force* in a minor and limited genre.

—S.H. Braund

See the essay on ''Epigrams.''

MARTIN DU GARD, Roger

Born: Neuilly-sur-Seine, 23 March 1881. **Education:** Educated at École Fénelon, Paris, 1892; Lycée Condorcet; studied under Louis Mellerio in Passy, 1896, baccalauréat, 1897; Lycée Janson-de-Sailly, 1897, baccalauréat, 1898; the Sorbonne, 1899, failed exams, 1899; École des Chartes, 1900–05, certificate of historiography and paleography, 1905. **Military Service:** Infantry, 39th Regiment in Rouen. **Family:** Married Hélène Foucault in 1906 (died 1949); one daughter. **Career:** Worked with Jacques Copeau at the Théâtre du Vieux-Colombier, Paris, 1913–14, and 1918–20. Closely associated with André Gide *q.v.* during the 1920s. Travelled in Italy and France; visited Martinique, 1939. **Awards:** Grand Prix Littéraire de la Ville de Paris, 1937; Nobel prize for literature, 1937. **Died:** 22 August 1958.

PUBLICATIONS

Collections

Oeuvres complètes. 2 vols., 1969–72.

Fiction

Devenir!. 1909.
Jean Barois. 1913; as *Jean Barois,* translated by Stuart Gilbert, 1949.
Les Thibaults. 1922–40; parts translated in *The World of the Thibaults,* by Madeleine Boyd, 1926; *The Thibaults,* by Stephen Hayden Guest and Stuart Gilbert, 1933–34, and by Gilbert, 1939–40.
  Le Cahier gris. 1922; as *The Grey Notebook,* translated by Madeleine Boyd, 1926; also translated by Stephen Hayden Guest, 1933; Stuart Gilbert, 1939.

  Le Pénitencier. 1922; as *The Penitentiary,* translated by Madeleine Boyd, 1926; as *The Reformatory,* translated by Stephen Hayden Guest, 1933; as *Le Pénitencier,* translated by Stuart Gilbert, 1939.
  La Belle Saison. 2 vols., 1923; as *The Springtime of Life,* translated by Madeleine Boyd, 1926; as *High Summer,* translated by Stephen Hayden Guest, 1933; as *La Belle Saison,* translated by Stuart Gilbert, 1939.
  La Consultation. 1928; as *The Consulting Day,* translated by Stuart Gilbert, 1934.
  La Sorellina. 1928; as *La Sorellina,* translated by Stuart Gilbert, 1939.
  La Mort du père. 1929; as *La Mort du père,* translated by Stuart Gilbert, 1939.
  Eté 1914. 1936; as *Summer 1914,* translated by Stuart Gilbert, 1939.
  Epilogue. 1940; as *Epilogue,* translated by Stuart Gilbert, 1940.
Confidence africaine. 1931; as *Confidence Africaine,* translated by Austryn Wainhouse, 1983.
Vieille France. 1933; as *The Postman,* translated by John Russell, 1954.
Le Lieutenant-Colonel de Maumort (unfinished), edited by André Daspre. 1983; translated by Luc Brébion and Timothy Crouse, 1999.

Plays

Le Testament du père Leleu (produced 1914). 1920; as *Le Testament du père Leleu,* translated by Victor MacClure, 1921.
La Gonfle. 1928.
Un Taciturne (produced 1931). 1932; revised by Martin de Gard, 1948.

Other

L'Abbaye de Jumiège (on architecture). 1909.
L'Une de nous. 1910.
Témoignage. 1921.
Noizemont-les-Vierges. 1928.
Dialogue. 1930.
Le Voyage de Madagascar. 1934.
Notes sur André Gide (1913–1951). 1951; as *Notes on André Gide,* translated by John Russell, 1953; as *Recollections of André Gide,* translated by Russell, 1953.
Oeuvres complètes. 2 vols., 1955.
Correspondance, with André Gide. 2 vols., 1968.
Correspondance, with Jacques Copeau, edited by Claude Sicard. 2 vols., 1972.
Correspondance générale, edited by Maurice Rieuneau, André Daspre and Claude Sicard. 5 vols., 1980–88.
Eugène Dabit, Roger Martin du Gard, correspondance (1927–1936), edited by Pierre Bardel. 2 vols., 1986.
Témoins d'un temps troublé: Roger Martin du Gard, Georges Duhamel, correspondance 1919–1958, edited by Arlette Lafay. 1987.
Lettres de confiance à Jean Morand: 1938–1957. 1991.
Translator, *Olivia,* by Dorothy Bussy. 1949.

*

Critical Studies: *Roger Martin du Gard* by René Lalou, 1937; *Roger Martin du Gard and the World of the Thibaults* by Howard C. Rice,

1941; *Roger Martin du Gard* by Clemont Borgal, 1957; *Réflexions sur la méthode de Roger Martin de Gard* by Pierre Daix, 1957; *The World of Roger Martin du Gard* by Edwin Grant Kaiser, 1957; ''The Function of Irony in Roger Martin du Gard'' by Léon Roudiez in *Romanic Review*, 48, 1957; Roger Martin du Gard issue of *Nouvelle Revue Française* December 1958; *Martin du Gard* by Jacques Brenner, 1960; *Roger Martin du Gard* by Robert Gibson, 1961; *Roger Martin du Gard*, by Denis Boak, 1963; *Roger Martin du Gard et la religion* by Réjean Robidoux, 1964; *Roger Martin du Gard: The Novelist and History* by David Schalk, 1967; *Roger Martin du Gard* by Catharine Savage, 1968; *The Quest for Total Peace: The Political Thought of Roger Martin du Gard* by R. Jouejati, 1971; *Index de la correspondance André Gide-Roger Martin du Gard* by Susan M. Stout, 1971; *Martin du Gard: Jean Barois* by Michael John Taylor, 1974; *Roger Martin du Gard: Les Années d'apprentissage littéraire 1881–1910* by Claude Sicard, 1976; Martin du Gard issue of *Folio*, 13, 1981; *Roger Martin du Gard; ou, De l'intégrité de l'être à l'intégrité du roman* by P.M. Cryle, 1984; *Roger Martin du Gard: Études sur son oeuvre* edited by André Daspre and Jochen Schlobach, 1984; *L'Art de Roger Martin du Gard* by Renée Fainas Wehrmann, 1986; *Martin du Gard, romancier* by Bernard Alluin, 1989.

* * *

Roger Martin du Gard's artistic aim was to render reality as accurately and thoroughly as possible; he is thus one of the principal heirs of the 19th-century French Realists, although, unlike the Naturalists, he did not confine his attention to the lower classes and the sordid aspects of existence. His historian's training prepared him well for his mimetic project; he took voluminous notes and based his work on observation and careful research. He handled his material with an exemplary craftsmanship. He did not, however, lack the imagination that allows a writer to create convincing characters different from himself and treat topics foreign to his experience; he also had a powerful visual imagination, which he used to convey an intense impression of life. Moreover, his artistic discipline was tempered by strong emotions, and his conservatism of personal habit did not prevent his treating aberrant behaviour and controversial topics such as incest and homosexuality. It should not be supposed, therefore, that his work has the tedious and unimaginative quality of writing that merely records the mundane.

Martin du Gard worked chiefly in fiction and preferred the full-length novel, even the *roman-fleuve* (series novel), which he illustrated exceptionally well in *Les Thibaults* (*The Thibaults*). With the exception of the novella *Confidence africaine* [African Confession], he turned away from the classical French *récit* and worked instead with several plots and characters, often arranged in pairs. In the plays *Le Testament du père Leleu* [Daddy Leuleu's Will] and *La Gonfle* [Dropsy], and the satirical sketches *Vieille France* (*The Postman*), peasant language is used to effect. Elsewhere he combined an unobtrusive but flexible and sensitive style, whose aim was to convey truth clearly, with careful composition, in the tradition of Flaubert and Maupassant; he was also influenced by Tolstoi. Most of his fiction is narrated by an implied third-person omniscient narrator, but other narrative modes appear; *Jean Barois* is written almost entirely in dialogue, *Confidence africaine* has two first-person narrators, *La Sorellina* contains a story-within-a-story, and the *Epilogue* to *The Thibaults* is narrated in first and third persons, from one character's point of view. To create narrative rhythm and deal economically with the large amount of material in the series novel, description and summary are alternated skilfully with scenes, built around superb dialogue. The importance of perspective is underlined by showing events occasionally from more than one viewpoint.

Martin du Gard's fiction is concerned primarily with the dramatic interactions between individual and society in the period between the 1890s and 1918. His insights into these relationships and into social dynamics and structures, especially those of the bourgeoisie, to which he belonged, have been praised by Marxist critics such as Georg Lukacs. Rebellious young heroes are contrasted with the families and institutions against which they revolt. Conversely, the claims of individualism as understood by the Third Republic—the rights to wealth, to capitalism—are qualified by socialist views of the rights of the collectivity. Truths such as those concerning the conviction of Dreyfus are weighed against the need for social order. In most cases, the author refrains from interjecting his position directly into the text. Moreover, for each spokesman for a position or institution—Socialism, Rationalism, family—there is someone who expresses the opposite view; although most believers are shown as simple-minded or hypocritical, even religion has a persuasive defender. Unlike thesis novels, there is no explicit resolution of the debates.

However, despite the author's narrative and stylistic objectivity, attentive reading reveals authorial preferences. An early work in which a failed artist becomes a dull, conventional country squire suggests authorial blame for the hero's surrender of his idealism. In *Jean Barois*, the author shows preference for the partisans of Dreyfus and for rationalism as opposed to belief. In *The Thibaults* the novelist's sympathy seems to go to the rebellious Jacques, although the moderate positions of his brother Antoine are expressed convincingly. The author's views on war are particularly perceptible. Although the historical plot line of *Eté 1914* (*Summer 1914*) moves toward the outbreak of war—Europe was approaching war as the work was being written—he clearly sympathizes with individual efforts to prevent conflict. His pacifism is, however, qualified somewhat in *Le Lieutenant-Colonel de Maumort*, his unfinished posthumous novel.

Another major topic in his plays and fiction is the seemingly doomed nature of human relationships. Passion is destructive, as in *Un Taciturne* [A Quiet Man], where the hero shoots himself, and *The Thibaults*, when Jérôme de Fontanin destroys his marriage through philandering, and Rachel, the beautiful woman Antoine loves, returns to her sadistic lover in Africa. Friendship is often built on misunderstanding; family ties do not suffice for communication, and often interfere with it, as siblings develop differently and sons struggle to establish their individuality. The darkest element in Martin du Gard's work may be, however, the self, in which reason struggles with passion, practical compromise with idealism, and the will to live with the urge to destroy inner demons.

These features and others point to a strong vein of determinism, which may reflect the scientific positivism of the late 19th century in France, the author's study of psychiatry, or deep personal pessimism. As in Zola's work, heredity plays a major role, presiding over destinies like Greek fate. There is also a collective, historical determinism, which makes Martin du Gard's world view resemble somewhat that of Hegel and Marx, although he was not a Marxist. Historical irony is abundant, as individual efforts during the *belle époque* to prevent the cataclysm of war are powerless before the momentum of historical event. Even works marked by vitality have a sombre, crepuscular, or cruel element.

While considered uninteresting by partisans of experimental literature, Martin du Gard's work has worn well, thanks doubtless to its psychological and social truth and its superb craftsmanship. As a mirror of the society it treats and the human, even metaphysical problems it wrestles with, it retains great pertinence.

—Catharine Savage Brosman

MASAOKA Shiki

Born: Masaoka Tsunenori in Matsuyama, Iyo Province (now Ehime Prefecture), 14 October 1867. **Education:** Tutored privately in Sino-Japanese and the Chinese classics while attending elementary school and Matsuyama Middle School; attended Kyōritsu Middle School, University Preparatory School, Tokyo, 1883–90; entered Imperial University (now Tokyo University), 1890; failed final exams, 1892; withdrew from university, 1893. **Career:** After short-lived ambitions to become, successively, politician, philosopher, and novelist, he resolved to become a poet and began his haiku reform, 1892. Haiku editor of newspaper Nippon, 1892–1902 except for six months tenure as editor-in-chief of the short-lived Shōnippon, 1894; war correspondent for Nippon in China, one month, 1895; on return trip, had severe lung hemorrhage and almost died; supervised editing of Hototogisu, literary magazine edited by his disciples, 1897–1902. Bedridden and in constant pain by 1897, but continued his literary activities unabated. Formed group to study haiku of Yosa Buson, 1898, then the Negishi Tanka Society, 1899, and the Mountain Society for sketch from life prose, 1901. **Died:** From tuberculosis in Tokyo, 19 September 1902.

PUBLICATIONS

Collections

Shiki Zenshū. 25 vols. 1975–78.

Poetry

Takenosato Uta. 1904; as *Songs from a Bamboo Village: Selected Tanka from Takenosato Uta*, partly translated by Sanford Goldstein and Seishi Shinoda, 1998.
Kanzan Rakuboku. 1924–25.
Haiku Kō. 1925.

Literary Criticism

Dassai Sho-oku Haiwa. 1892.
Bunkai Yatsu Atari. 1893.
Bashō Zatsudan. 1893.
Haikai Taiyō. 1895.
Haijin Buson. 1897.
Utayomi ni Atauru Sho. 1899.

Diaries

Bokujū Itteki. 1901; as "Masaoka Shiki's *A Drop of Ink*," partly translated by Janine Beichman, in *Monumenta Nipponica*, vol. 30, 1975.
Byōshō Rokushaku. 1902.
Gyōga Manroku. 1901–1902.

Other

Shōen no Ki (essays). 1898; as "Record of the Little Garden," translated by Janine Beichman, in *Masaoka Shiki: His Life and Works*, 2002.
Shigo (essays). 1901.
Bunrui Haiku Zenshū. 12 vols. 1928–29; as *Bunrui Haiku Taikan*, reprinted, 1992.

*

Bibliography: *Masaoka Shiki no Kenkyū*, vol. 2., by Matsui Toshihiko, 1976; "Kokusaiteki na Shiki Kenkyū" by Janine Beichman, in *Kinsei Bungaku Ronkō—Kenkyu to Shiryō*, edited by Matsuo Haruaki, 1985.

Critical Studies: "Masaoka Shiki and Tanka Reform" by Robert H. Brower, in *Tradition and Modernization in Japanese Culture*, edited by Donald H. Shively, 1971; "Shiki and Takuboku" by Donald Keene, in *Landscapes and Portraits: Appreciations of Japanese Culture*, 1971; *Masaoka Shiki* by Janine Beichman, 1982 (reprinted as *Masaoka Shiki: His Life and Works*, 2002); "Masaoka Shiki" by Makoto Ueda, in *Modern Japanse Poets and the Nature of Literature*, 1983; "The Diaries of Masaoka Shiki" by Donald Keene, in *Modern Japanese Diaries*, 1995.

* * *

Masaoka Shiki, who famously declared "Haiku is literature," was the most influential poet and critic in the revival and modernization of the haiku at the turn of the 19th century in Japan. By applying Western ideas of literature and realism to this traditional 17-syllable poetic form, he renewed its literary potential at a time when most Japanese poets were ready to abandon it in favor of longer forms inspired by Western models. In his first major critical work, *Dassai Sho-oku Haiwa* [Talks on Haiku from the Otter's Den], Masaoka used the mathematical theory of permutations to buttress his sensational prediction that the haiku and the tanka, because they were so short and so limited in theme and vocabulary, were both doomed to extinction. What gave him the way out of this cul de sac was his own theory of shasei, or the sketch from life. In *Haikai Taiyō* [The Elements of Haiku], Masaoka wrote that the sketch from life promised an unlimited source of new material and themes, as varied as reality itself. If one observed from multiple points of view, near and far, high and low, then subjects for numerous haiku poems could be found everywhere, even in a small garden. Thus, Masaoka made the observation of reality into a strict discipline, the most fundamental exercise in the poet's training.

Once his haiku reform was well established, Masaoka turned to the tanka. He initiated his efforts with *Utayomi ni Atauru Sho* [Letters to a Tanka Poet], which challenged the pre-eminence of the 10th century *Kokinshū*, and exalted the earlier *Man yōshū*, whose frank expression of feeling seemed closer to realism. Masaoka turned to the personal essay at around the same time as the tanka. His sketch from life essays were written in a fluid colloquial style completely different from the stiff Sino-Japanese of his early prose, and are thought to have influenced a number of Japanese novelists.

The full flowering of Masaoka's talent, paradoxically enough, came in a genre that he did not consciously seek to reform: the diary, specifically *Bokujū Itteki* [A Drop of Ink], and *Byōshō Rokushaku* [A Sixfoot Sickbed], the two sickbed diaries that he published daily during the last two years of his life in the newspaper *Nippon*. The ostensible aim of both works was to solace his boredom as he lay in bed, mortally ill and in constant pain. On the surface each diary was a sparkling tapestry of comments on daily affairs, conversations with visitors, retellings of his dreams and fantasies, as well as the occasional poem. Beneath this colorful variety, however, one feels a tragic counterpoint, for Masaoka was working out his relation to the world as he prepared to leave it, moving from resistance to reconciliation, and the diaries were, in a sense, his farewell to the world. Masaoka's accomplishments as a critic and poet changed the course of modern Japanese literature and have played a significant role in the world haiku movement outside Japan, but as human documents it may be his diaries that have the deepest and most universal appeal.

—Janine Beichman

MAUPASSANT, (Henri René Albert) Guy de

Born: the Château de Miromesnil, near Rouen, France, 5 August 1850. **Education:** Educated at Lycée Impérial Napoléon, Paris, 1859–60; Institution Ecclésiastique, Yvetot, 1863–68; Lycée Pierre Corneille, Rouen, 1868–69; studied law, University of Paris, 1869–70. **Military Service:** Messenger, then orderly, in the army, 1870–71. **Career:** Clerk in Ministry of the Navy: in library, 1872–73, and in Department for the Colonies, 1873–77; transferred to Ministry of Education, 1878–82. Also writer, especially for *Gaulois* and *Gil-Blas* newspapers; introduced by Flaubert to Zola and other Naturalist writers. Attempted suicide, January, 1892; confined to insane asylum, Passy, 1892. **Died:** 6 July 1893.

PUBLICATIONS

Collections

Works (in English). 1909–.
Complete Works, translated by Alfred de Sumichrast. 9 vols., 1910.
Collected Novels and Stories, edited and translated by Ernest Boyd. 18 vols., 1922–26.
Works, translated by Marjorie Laurie. 10 vols., 1923–29.
Oeuvres complètes. 29 vols., 1925–47.
Novels and Tales. 18 vols., 1928–.
Contes et nouvelles, edited by Albert-Marie Schmidt. 2 vols., 1956–57.
Romans, edited by Albert-Marie Schmidt. 1959.
Complete Short Stories. 3 vols., 1970.
Contes et Nouvelles, edited by Louis Forestier. 2 vols., 1974–79.
Romans, edited by Louis Forestier. 1987.
A Parisian Bourgeois' Sundays, and Other Stories, translated by Marlo Johnston. 1997.

Fiction

La Maison Tellier (stories). 1881.
Mademoiselle Fifi (stories). 1882.
Une vie. 1883; as *A Woman's Life*, translated anonymously, 1888; numerous subsequent translations including by Marjorie Laurie, 1942, Antonia White, 1959, and H.N.P. Sloman, 1965; as *Une Vie*, translated by Katharine Vivian, 1981; as *A Life: The Humble Truth*, translated by Roger Pearson, 1999.
Contes de la Bécasse (stories). 1883.
Miss Harriet (stories). 1883.
Clair de lune. 1884.
Les Soeurs Rondoli (stories). 1884.
Tyette. 1885.
Bel-Ami. 1885; as *Bel-Ami*, translated 1891; several subsequent translations including by Eric Sutton, 1948, Brian Rhys, 1958, H.N.P. Sloman, 1961, and Douglas Parmée, 1975; also translated by Margaret Mauldon, 2001.
Contes et nouvelles. 1885.
Contes du jour et de la nuit (stories). 1885.
Monsieur Parent (stories). 1885.
Toine. 1886.
La Petite Roque. 1886.
Mont-Oriol. 1887; as *Mont-Oriol*, translated 1891; edited by Ernest Boyd and translated by Storm Jameson, 1924; translated by Marjorie Laurie, 1949.
Le Horla. 1887; as "The Horla," translated by Jonathan Sturges, in *Modern Ghosts*, edited by G.W. Curtis, 1890; also translated by Ernest Boyd and Storm Jameson, in *Eighty-Eight More Stories*, 1932; Ronald de Levington Kirkbride, in *The Private Life of Guy de Maupassant*, 1961.
Pierre et Jean. 1888; as *Pierre and Jean*, translated by Clara Bell, 1890; also translated by Hugh Craig, 1890; Leonard Tancock, 1979; translated by Lowell Bair, 1994; translated by Julie Mead, 2001.
Le Rosier de Madame Husson (stories). 1888.
La Main gauche. 1889.
Fort comme la mort. 1889; as *Strong as Death*, translated by Teofilo E. Combs, 1899; as *The Master Passion*, translated by Marjorie Laurie, 1958.
L'Inutile Beauté (stories). 1890.
Notre coeur. 1890; as *Notre Coeur (The Human Heart)*, translated by Alexina Loranger Donovan, 1890; also translated by Marjorie Laurie, 1929.
Eighty-Eight Short Stories, translated by Fanny Rousseau-Wallach. 1909; also translated by Ernest Boyd and Storm Jameson, 1928.
Eighty-Eight More Stories (includes "The Horla"; "Boule de Suif"; "Mlle. Fifi" and others), translated by Ernest Boyd and Storm Jameson. 4 vols., 1932.
Miss Harriet and Other Stories, translated by H.N.P. Sloman. 1951.
The Diamond Necklace and Four Other Stories. 1967.
Tales of Supernatural Terror, edited and translated by Arnold Kellett. 1972.
The Diary of a Madman and Other Tales of Horror, translated by Arnold Kellett, 1976; as *The Dark Side of Guy de Maupassant*, 1989; as *Dark Side: Tales of Terror and the Supernatural*, translated by Arnold Kellett, 1997.
A Day in the Country and Other Stories, translated by David Coward. 1990.

Mademoiselle Fifi and Other Stories, edited and translated by David Coward. 1992.

Plays

Une répétition. 1879.
Histoire du vieux temps (produced 1879). In *Des vers*, 1880.
Musotte, with Jacques Normand, from a story by Maupassant (produced 1891). In *Oeuvres complètes illustrées*, 1904.
La Paix du ménage, from his own story (produced 1893).

Verse

Des vers. 1880.

Other

Au soleil. 1884.
Sur l'eau. 1888; as *Afloat*, translated by Laura Ensor, 1889; also translated by Marlo Johnston, 1995.
La Vie errante. 1890.
Correspondance, edited by Jacques Suffel. 3 vols., 1973.
Correspondance, with Gustave Flaubert, edited by Yvan Leclerc. 1994.
Selection of the Political Journalism: With Introduction and Notes, edited by Adrian C. Ritchie. 1999.
Selections of the Chroniques (1881–87), edited with introduction and notes by Adrian C. Ritchie. 2002.

*

Bibliography: *Maupassant Criticism in France 1880–1940* by Artine Artinian, 1941; *Maupassant Criticism: A Centennial Bibliography 1880–1979* edited by Robert Willard Artinian, 1982.

Critical Studies: *Maupassant: A Biographical Study* by Ernest Bond, 1928; *Maupassant: A Lion in the Path* by Francis Steegmuller, 1949; *Maupassant the Novelist*, 1954, and *Maupassant: The Short Stories*, 1962, both by Edward D. Sullivan; *The Private Life of Guy de Maupassant* by R. de L. Kirkbridge, 1961; *The Paradox of Maupassant* by Pál Ignotus, 1967; *Illusion and Reality: A Study of the Descriptive Techniques in the Works of Guy de Maupassant* by John R. Dugan, 1973; *Maupassant* by Albert H. Wallace, 1973; *Maupassant* by Michael G. Lerner, 1975; *Maupassant: Pierre et Jean* by Robert Lethbridge, 1984; *A Woman's Revenge: The Chronology of Dispossession in Maupassant's Fiction* by Mary Donaldson-Evans, 1986; *Style and Vision in Maupassant's Nouvelles* by Matthew MacNamara, 1986; *Love and Nature, Unity and Doubling in the Novels of Mauspassant* by Bertrand Logan Ball, 1988; *Guy de Maupassant: Boule de suif* by P.E. Chaplin, 1988; *Bel-Ami: Maupassant* by Christopher Lloyd, 1988; *Maupassant in the Hall of Mirrors* by T.A. Le V. Harris, 1990; *Struggling Under the Destructive Glance: Androgyny in the Novels of Guy de Maupassant* by Rachel Mildred Hartig, 1991; *Comme Maupassant* by Philippe Bonnefis, 1993; *Rhetoric of Pessimism and Strategies of Containment in the Short Stories of Guy de Maupassant* by David Bryant, 1993; *Maupassant and the American Short Story: The Influence of Form at the Turn of the Century* by Richard Fusco, 1994; *The Art of Rupture: Narrative Desire and Duplicity in the Tales of Guy de Maupassant* by Charles J. Stivale, 1994; *Possible Worlds of the Fantastic: The Rise of the Paranormal in Fiction* by Nancy H. Traill, 1996; *Guy de Maupassant* by Jean-Marie Dizol, 1997.

*   *   *

Guy de Maupassant's literary apprenticeship ended in 1880 with the appearance of "Boule de suif" ("Ball-of-Fat"). His literary preceptor and friend, Gustave Flaubert, rightly characterized the work as evidence of the arrival of a new master of the short story. Flaubert's death that same year firmed the young writer's resolve to be, at whatever cost, a worthy disciple of his dear friend. For about eight years Maupassant dedicated himself totally to his work, a tribute to Flaubert's influence, and also possibly because of a premonition of how especially desperate was his own race with time.

The great stream of stories, novels, travel accounts, and essays that flowed from his pen is astonishing for its high quality. The mediocre offerings, substantial in number in the vast outpouring, seem proportionately insubstantial when measured against the accomplishments, and pose no threat to the high place he occupies among 19th-century writers.

He has attracted a large and appreciative audience among general readers and critics with his highly developed powers of observation. They are a result of Flaubert's insistence that the artist observe his subject until he can distinguish in it the one feature that sets it apart from all similar subjects. Then he must represent this feature with the exact language that only it calls into use. Maupassant did not approach the latter ideal as closely as did his master, but he demonstrated the ability to penetrate the meaning of his subject by observation to a degree that few other writers have.

Maupassant had little fondness for the unaccomplished individuals who are his subjects. His popularity among this group certainly does not derive from flattering suggestions of some great redeeming virtue in their kind. The privileged class was affronted that those it scorned and cast out were the very ones Maupassant depicted in a favourable light. He is saying that real virtue is something people have; it is not something they talk about. Elizabeth Rousset ("Ball of Fat"), Irma ("Bed 29") and Rachel ("Mademoiselle Fifi"), prostitutes to whom it would never occur to define courage, have it when it alone will serve. Maupassant was contemptuous of social institutions whose product was more often than not fruitless talk; doubtless this attitude contributes to his popular following. It offended many of his contemporaries who saw it as a narrowly unfair and prejudiced attack on the system.

Heroic efforts are monopolized by women characters in Maupassant's stories. It was evident to him that conventional morality was shaped in such a way as to suppress the female in favour of the male. The struggle of women in society produced the dramatic and courageous defiance that Maupassant wished to portray. With considerable understanding he depicts the situation of the unhappy and unfulfilled married woman. For her, unlike her husband, the discovery of her unhappiness means the end of the prospect that her life might have meaning; she is trapped. Defiance is the only way out. Merely the courage to defy convention is not enough in the case of Mme. Roland in *Pierre et Jean* (*Pierre and Jean*)—she needs, not just a lover, but one who satisfies the ideal she had hoped to find in marriage, for the severe consequences of being found out far outweigh the temporal satisfactions of a mediocre affair. Maupassant depicts the husband in such a way that the reader is rather pleased to see him cuckolded: trust in one's wife is no virtue if it is merely a manifestation of vanity. Though Maupassant more generally breaks with tradition in his depiction of adulteresses and prostitutes, occasionally he presents the conventional image of her as the corrupter of the species. In his personal life he had the reputation for being a misogynist. But the real Maupassant is to be found in his writing which treats cuckoldry as a situation that is not at all amusing.

Most of his characters are Norman peasants, Parisian bureaucrats, soldiers, and sailors. All have a diminished belief in a Higher Order and in their dreams. But on their holidays and weekends they resurrect these dreams as if reality had never marked them for death. The consequences of these momentary delusions run the gamut from the amusingly petty to the soberingly tragic. He has no favourite ending, for life has none. He merely chooses one from the possible endings that reality imposes and which he has verified by observation. The presentation of a distinct image of what he has seen with his eyes is his first purpose. If what a character does cries out for a reason hidden in his mind, then, and only then, does Maupassant entangle himself in the web of psychological speculation.

Pathological behaviour calls for psychological explanations. Maupassant wrote stories about madness with tragic authority. ''Le Horla'' (''The Horla''), ''Lui?'' (''Him?''), and ''Qui sait?'' (''Who Knows?''), with heroes subject to autoscopic hallucinations, pathological loneliness, and suicidal tendencies, reflect some of the pain of his own struggle with the fatal malady. The anguished conviction that existence was pointless evidences itself progressively in his work until it becomes a crushing presence. In *La Vie errante* [In Vagabondia] he is continually troubling himself with the question of why mind was given dominion over its own futility, just as the hero of the masterpiece, *Pierre and Jean*, troubles himself over the absurdity of being forced to accept the unacceptable. Such, for Maupassant, was the profit of giving thought to the meaning of life. That is why he preferred to observe and present what could be seen with the eye.

—Albert H. Wallace

See the essays on ''L'Abondonné,'' ''The Necklace,'' and *Pierre and Jean*.

MAURIAC, François (Charles)

Born: Bordeaux, France, 11 October 1885. **Education:** Educated at Collège des Marianites, Grand-Lebrun; University of Bordeaux, licence ès lettres; École Nationale des Chartes, Paris. **Family:** Married Jeanne Lafon in 1913; two sons, including the writer Claude Mauriac, and two daughters. **Career:** Freelance writer in Paris from 1906; served as hospital orderly in Salonika, 1916–17; columnist (''Bloc-Notes''), *L'Express*, 1954–61; contributor, *Figaro Littéraire*, after 1961. **Awards:** Heinemann prize, 1925; Académie française Grand prize for novel, 1926; Nobel prize for literature,

1952. D.Litt.: Oxford University. President, Société des Gens de Lettres, 1932–70. Grand Cross, Légion d'honneur. **Member:** Académie française, 1934; Honorary Member, American Academy. **Died:** 1 September 1970.

PUBLICATIONS

Collections

Oeuvres romanesques et théâtrales complètes, edited by Jacques Petit. 3 vols., 1978–81.

Fiction

L'Enfant chargé de chaînes. 1913; as *Young Man in Chains*, translated by Gerard Hopkins, 1961.
La Robe prétexte. 1914; as *The Stuff of Youth*, translated by Gerard Hopkins, 1960.
La Chair et le sang. 1920; as *Flesh and Blood*, translated by Gerard Hopkins, 1954.
Préséances. 1921; as *Questions of Precedence*, translated by Gerard Hopkins, 1958.
Le Baiser au lépreux. 1922; as *A Kiss to the Leper*, translated by James Whitall, 1923; as *The Kiss for the Leper*, translated by Gerard Hopkins, 1950.
Le Fleuve de feu. 1923; as *The River of Fire*, translated by Gerard Hopkins, 1954.
Génitrix. 1923; as *Genetrix*, translated by Gerard Hopkins, in *The Family*, 1930.
Le Désert de l'amour. 1925; as *The Desert of Love*, translated by Samuel Putnam, 1929; also translated by Gerard Hopkins, 1949.
Fabien. 1926.
Thérèse Desqueyroux. 1927; as *Thérèse*, translated by Eric Sutton, 1928; as *Therese: A Portrait in Four Parts*, translated by Gerard Hopkins, 1947.
Le Démon de la connaissance. 1928.
Destins (includes *Coups de couteau* and *Un homme de lettres*). 1928; as *Destinies*, translated by Eric Sutton, 1929; as *Lines of Life*, translated by Gerard Hopkins, 1957.
La Nuit du bourreau de soi-même. 1929.
Trois récits. 1929.
Ce qui était perdu. 1930; as *Suspicion*, 1931; as *That Which Was Lost*, translated by J.H.F. McEwan, with *Dark Angels*, 1951.
Le Noeud de vipères. 1932; as *Vipers' Tangle*, translated by Warre B. Welles, 1933; as *Knot of Vipers*, translated by Gerard Hopkins, 1951.
Le Mystère Frontenac. 1933; as *The Frontenac Mystery*, translated by Gerard Hopkins, 1952.
La Fin de la nuit. 1935; as *The End of the Night*, translated by Gerard Hopkins, in *Therese: A Portrait in Four Parts*, 1947.
Le Mal. 1935; as *The Enemy*, translated by Gerard Hopkins, with *The Desert of Love*, 1949.
Les Anges noirs. 1936; as *The Dark Angels*, translated by Gerard Hopkins, with *That Which Was Lost*, 1951; as *The Mask of Innocence*, translated by Hopkins, 1953.
Plongées. 1938.
Les Chemins de la mer. 1939; as *The Unknown Sea*, translated by Gerard Hopkins, 1948.

La Pharisienne. 1941; as *A Woman of the Pharisees*, translated by Gerard Hopkins, 1946.

Le Sagouin. 1951; as *The Little Misery*, translated by Gerard Hopkins, 1952; as *The Weakling*, translated by Hopkins, 1952.

Galigaï. 1952; as *The Loved and the Unloved*, translated by Gerard Hopkins, 1952.

L'Agneau. 1954; as *The Lamb*, translated by Gerard Hopkins, 1955.

A Mauriac Reader, edited by Wallace Fowlie, translated by Gerard Hopkins. 1968.

Un adolescent d'autrefois. 1969; as *Maltaverne*, translated by Gerard Hopkins, 1970.

Plays

Asmodée (produced 1937). 1938; as *Asmodee; or, The Intruder*, translated by Basil Bartlett, 1939; also translated by Beverly Thurman, 1957.

Les Mal-aimés (produced 1945). 1945.

Passage du Malin (produced 1947). 1948.

Le Feu sur la terre (produced 1950). 1951.

Le Pain vivant. 1955.

Screenplays: *Thérèse*, with Claude Mauriac and Georges Franju, 1963.

Verse

Les Mains jointes. 1909.

L'Adieu à l'adolescence. 1911.

Orages. 1925; revised edition, 1949.

Le Sang d'Atys. 1940.

Other

De quelques coeurs inquiets: Petits essais de psychologie religieuse. 1920.

La Vie et la mort d'un poète (on André Lafon). 1924.

Le Jeune Homme. 1926.

Le Tourment de Jacques Rivière. 1926.

Les Beaux Esprits de ce temps. 1926.

Proust. 1926.

La Province. 1926.

Bordeaux. 1926.

Le Rencontre avec Pascal. 1926.

Conscience, instinct divin. 1927.

Dramaturges. 1928.

Supplément au Traité de la concupiscence de Bossuet. 1928.

Divagations sur Saint-Sulpice. 1928.

La Vie de Jean Racine. 1928.

Le Roman. 1928.

Voltaire contre Pascal. 1929.

Dieu et Mammon. 1929; as *God and Mammon*, translated anonymously, 1936.

Mes plus lointains souvenirs. 1929.

Paroles en Espagne. 1930.

Trois grands hommes devant Dieu. 1930.

L'Affaire Favre-Bulle. 1931.

Blaise Pascal et sa soeur Jacqueline. 1931.

Le Jeudi saint. 1931; as *Maundy Thursday*, translated by Harold F. Kynaston-Snell, 1932; as *The Eucharist: The Mystery of Holy Thursday*, translated by Marie-Louise Dufrenoy, 1944.

Souffrances et bonheur du chrétien. 1931; as *Anguish and Joy of the Christian Life*, translated by Harold Evans, 1964.

René Bazin. 1931.

Pèlerins. 1932; as *Pèlerins de Lourdes*, 1933.

Commencements d'une vie. 1932.

Le Drôle (for children). 1933; as *The Holy Terror*, translated by Anne Carter, 1964.

Le Romancier et ses personnages. 1933; reprinted in part as *L'Éducation des filles*, 1936.

Journal. 5 vols., 1934–53.

Vie de Jésus. 1936; as *Life of Jesus*, translated by Julie Kerman, 1937.

Les Maisons fugitives. 1939.

Le Cahier noir. 1943; as *The Black Note-Book*, translated anonymously, 1944.

La Nation française a une âme. 1943.

Ne pas se renier. . . 1944.

Sainte Marguerite de Cortone. 1945; as *Saint Margaret of Cortona*, translated by Bernard Frechtman, 1948.

La Rencontre avec Barrès. 1945.

Le Bâillon dénoué, après quatre ans de silence. 1945.

Du côté de chez Proust. 1947; as *Proust's Way*, translated by Elsie Pell, 1950.

Mes grands hommes. 1949; as *Men I Hold Great*, translated by Elsie Pell, 1951; as *Great Men*, translated by Pell, 1952.

Terres franciscaines. 1950.

Oeuvres complètes. 12 vols., 1950–56.

La Pierre d'achoppement. 1951; as *The Stumbling Block*, translated by Gerard Hopkins, 1952.

La Mort d'André Gide. 1952.

Lettres ouvertes. 1952; as *Letters on Art and Literature*, translated by Mario Pei, 1953.

Écrits intimes. 1953.

Paroles catholiques. 1954; as *Words of Faith*, translated by Edward H. Flannery, 1955.

Bloc-Notes 1952–1967. 5 vols., 1958–71.

Trois écrivains devant Lourdes, with others. 1958.

Le Fils de l'homme. 1958; as *The Son of Man*, translated by Bernard Murchland, 1958.

Mémoires intérieures. 1959; as *Mémoires Intérieures*, translated by Gerard Hopkins, 1960.

Rapport sur les prix de vertu. 1960.

Second Thoughts: Reflections on Literature and Life, translated by Adrienne Foulke. 1961.

Ce que je crois. 1962; as *What I Believe*, translated by Wallace Fowlie, 1963.

Cain, Where Is Your Brother?, translated anonymously. 1962.

De Gaulle. 1964; as *De Gaulle*, translated by Richard Howard, 1966.

Nouveaux mémoires intérieures. 1965; as *The Inner Presence: Recollections of My Spiritual Life*, translated by Herma Briffault, 1968; as *More Reflections from the Soul*, translated with introduction by Mary Kimbrough, 1991; *Mauriac et le symbolisme* by Bernard C. Swift, 2000.

D'autres et moi. 1966.

Mémoires politiques. 1967.

Correspondance 1912–1950, with André Gide, edited by Jacqueline Morton. 1971.

Laçordaire, edited by Keith Goesch. 1976.

Correspondance 1916–1942, with Jacques-Émile Blanche, edited by Georges-Paul Collet. 1976.

Mauriac avant Mauriac (early writings), edited by Jean Touzot. 1977.

Chroniques du Journal de Clichy, with Paul Claudel (includes Claudel-Fontaine correspondence), edited by François Morlot and Jean Touzot. 1978.

Lettres d'une vie (1904–1969), edited by Caroline Mauriac. 1981.

Editor, *Les Pages immortelles de Pascal.* 1940; as *Living Thoughts of Pascal*, 1940.

Editor, with Louise de Vilmorin, *Almanach des Lettres 1949.* 1949.

*

Bibliography: *Mauriac: Essai de bibliographie chronologique 1908–1960* by Keith Goesch, 1965.

Critical Studies: *Mauriac* by Elsie Pell, 1947; *Mauriac* by Martin Jarret-Kerr, 1954; *Faith and Fiction: Creative Process in Greene and Mauriac* by Philip Stratford, 1964; *Mauriac* by Cecil Jenkins, 1965; *Mauriac* edited by A.M. Caspary, 1968; *A Critical Commentary on Mauriac's "Le Noeud de vipères,"* 1969, and *Intention and Achievement: An Essay on the Novels of Mauriac*, 1969, both by John Flower, and *François Mauriac: Visions and Reappraisals* by Flower and Bernard C. Swift, 1989; *François Mauriac: A Study of the Writer and the Man* by Robert Speaight, 1976; *Mauriac: The Politics of a Novelist* by Malcolm Scott, 1980; *Mauriac: Le nœud de vipères* by Kathleen M. McKilligan, 1993; *François Mauriac Revisited* by David O'Connell, 1995.

* * *

Saurai-je jamais rien dire des êtres ruisselants de vertu et qui ont le coeur sur la main? Les "coeurs sur la main" n'ont pas d'histoire; mais je connais celle des coeurs enfouis et tout mêlés à un corps de boue.

(Will I ever have anything to say about the virtuous and open-hearted? The open-hearted have no story. But those whose hearts are buried deep, and mingle with the vile flesh, their story I know.)

(From *Thérèse Desqueyroux*)

François Mauriac wrote as a moralist and a Roman Catholic, the essence of whose Catholicism lay in a sense of sin. Avarice and greed, selfishness and self-congratulation, sham piety and canting respectability are the very stuff of his novels. His characters are extreme, in the grip of powerful passions. Each craves an absolute, each fashions a "religion" after his own heart—be it mysticism, sensuality, or veneration for the land and the accumulation of property.

At the centre of Mauriac's novels is the family: a sacrosanct institution which seals itself in with prejudice, casts out justice and humanity, and imprisons the individual. The family ordains marriage and values procreation for the sake of inheritance, alone, and the preservation of its name: Thérèse Desqueyroux marries into a family who revere her as "a sacred vessel, the receptacle of their progeny." The majority of Mauriac's characters are so engulfed in materialism that they go through life like sleepwalkers—neither seeing, hearing, thinking, nor understanding. Lacking the ability to "go beyond themselves" in empathy or love for another human being, they are unreceptive to suffering and, therefore, hopeless of salvation.

Mauriac sees no easy way to atonement. Mere confession may not buy it, nor may mystical exaltation, tainted—as Pierre Gornac's in *Destins* (*Lines of Life*)—with a blind and selfish pride. Only where a

human being plumbs the depths of humiliation and despair does Mauriac offer us a glimmer of hope. Solitude and emotional asphyxiation drive Thérèse Desqueyroux to commit a monstrous crime—the attempted poisoning of her husband; and yet Thérèse, of all Mauriac's many sinners, is portrayed with great compassion and is one of his most powerful and sympathetic creations.

Mauriac's sympathy lies clearly with his victims and his lovers. And yet the problem of sin and atonement remains a complex and ambivalent one. Had Robert Lagave in *Lines of Life* lived, could his "simple love" have saved him from degeneracy? Should one see in his horrific death an atonement for sins committed in this life? Elisabeth Gornac wakes from moral stupour to catch a glimpse of the eternal in human love; for the first time she truly "sees" another human face. And yet she can never rise above a love of the senses, but slips back into the sluggish current of "death-in-life."

The very heat and torpor of Mauriac's Landes evoke the aridity of human passion; the fire ever threatening to consume the pines symbolizes its destructiveness. Mauriac's characters are isolated, without grace, in a desert as bleak as the wind-blown dunes and marshes that stretch endlessly to the sea. Theirs is a world governed by fatality—for Mauriac is both playwright and *dramatic* novelist. Robert Lagave is doomed to debauchery by his physical beauty; lack of maternal affection drives Pierre Gornac towards a warped mysticism; Thérèse is drawn into her crime almost unconsciously—like a sleepwalker.

These psychological dramas have an extraordinary intensity, and an economy and vigour of style—the style of the dramatist. In this lies Mauriac's striking originality as a novelist, as in his powerful evocation of the landscape of his native Landes, which goes beyond realistic description to become symbol.

—Ruth Shaman

See the essay on *Thérèse*.

MAWLANA

See RUMI, Jalalu'd-Din

MEMMI, Albert

Born: Tunis, Tunisia, 15 December 1920; naturalized French citizen, 1960. **Education:** Attended French Lycée Carnot, Tunis; University of Algiers, degree in philosophy, 1943; University of Paris, Sorbonne, Doctor es lettres, 1970. **Military Service:** Interned in a Nazi labor camp in Tunisia toward the end of World War II. **Family:** Married Germaine Dubach; three children. **Career:** Taught high school philosophy, Tunis, 1953–56; director, Center for Educational Research, Tunis, 1953–57; researcher, National Center of Scientific Research, Paris, 1958–60; assistant professor, Ecole practique des hautes études, 1959–66, and social psychology, 1966–70, University of Paris, Sorbonne; professor of sociology, then professor emeritus University of Paris, Nanterre, 1970–; Walker Ames Professor of Sociology, University of Washington, 1972; faculty member, International Institute for Secular Humanistic Judaism. Lives in Paris, France. **Awards:** Commander of Ordre de Nichan Iftikhar (Tunisia); Legion of Honor; Officer of Tunisian Republic; Officier des Arts et des Lettres; Officier des Palmes Academiques; Prix Carthage (Tunisia), 1953; Prix Fénéon (Paris), 1954; Prix Simba (Rome). Honorary doctorate, Ben-Gurion University, Beersheba, Israel. **Member:** Chair of Association pour Judaisme Laique et Humaniste; Society of Gens de Lettres; PEN Club; Academie des Sciences d'Outremer; honorary member, advising board for the Institute for Advanced Studies, Princeton University, United States.

PUBLICATIONS

Fiction

La Statue de sel. 1953; as *The Pillar of Salt*, translated by Edouard Roditi, 1955.

Agar, roman. 1955; as *Strangers*, translated by Brian Rhys, 1960.

Le Scorpion; ou, la Confession imaginaire. 1969; as *The Scorpion; or, The Imaginary Confession*, translated by Eleanor Levieux, 1971.

Le Desert; ou, La vie et les aventures de Jubair Oulai El-Mammi. 1977.

Pharaon: roman. 1988.

Le Nomade immobile: récit. 2000.

Verse

Le Mirliton du ciel. 1990.

Other

Portrait du colonisé, précédé du Portrait du Colonisateur. 1957; as *The Colonizer and the Colonized*, translated by Howard Greenfeld, 1965.

Portrait d'un Juif. 1962; as *Portrait of a Jew*, translated by Elisabeth Abbott, 1962.

La liberation du Juif. 1966; as *The Liberation of the Jew*, translated by Judy Hyun, 1966.

L'Homme domine. 1968; as *Dominated Man: Notes toward a Portrait* (translator unknown), 1968.

Juifs et Arabes. 1974; as *Jews and Arabs*, translated by Eleanor Levieux, 1975.

Personnage de Jeha dans la littérature orale des Arabes et des Juifs. 1974.

Albert Memmi: un entretien avec Robert Davies suivi de Itinéraire de l'expérience vécue à la théorie de la domination. 1975.

Le terre interieure: entretiens avec Victor Malka. 1976.

La dependance: esquisse pour un portrait du dependant. 1979; as *Dependence: A Sketch for a Portrait of the Dependent*, translated by Philip A. Facey, 1984.

Le Racisme: description, définition, traitement. 1982; as *Racism*, translated by Steve Martinot, 2000.

Albert Memmi: écrivain de la dechirure, edited by Guy Dugas. 1984.

Ce que je crois. 1985.

Ecriture colorée, ou, Je vous aime en rouge: essai sur une dimension nouvelle de l'écriture, la couleur. 1986.

Bonheurs: 52 semaines. 1992.

A contre-courants. 1993.

Ah, quel bonheur!; précédé de L'exercice du bonheur. 1995.

Le juif et l'autre, with Maurice Chavardès and François Kasbi. 1995.

Le Buveur et l'amoureux: le prix de la dépendance. 1998.

Editor, *Poésie algérienne de 1830 à nos jours; approaches socio-historiques* by Jean Déjeux, 1963.

Editor, *Anthologie des écrivains maghrebins d'expression francaise.* 1965.

Editor, *Biliographie de la litterature nord-africaine d'expression francaise, 1945–1962.* 1965.

Editor, *Écrivains francophones du Maghreb: Anthologie.* 1985.

*

Critical Studies: ''Albert Memmi et 'l'homme domine''' by Madeleine Akselrad, in *L'Afrique Litteraire*, 4, 1969; ''Interview with Albert Memmi: Propos recueillis par Jacqueline Leiner'' by Jacqueline Leiner, in *Presence Francophone: Revue Litteraire*, 6, 1973; ''Albert Memmi: The Syndrome of Self-exile'' by Isaac Yetiv, in *International Fiction Review*, 1, 1974; ''Le probleme du langage chez Frantz Fanon, Malek Haddad et Albert Memmi'' by Jacqueline Leiner, in *Presence Francophone: Revue Litteraire*, 8, 1974; ''Albert Memmi, defenseur et illustrateur de l'homme francophone'' by Alex Maugey, in *Culture Francaise*, 29 (3), 1980; ''Albert Memmi ou le cul-de-sac et l'ecriture'' by Esther Benaim-Ouaknine and Robert Elbaz, in *Presence Francophone: Revue Litteraire*, 23, 1981; ''Albert Memmi'' by Giuliana Toso Rodinis, in *Le rose del deserto*, II, 1982; ''Memmi's Introduction to History: Le Desert as Folktale, Chronicle and Biography'' by Judith Roumani, in *Philological Quarterly*, 61 (2), 1982; ''L'Oeuvre romanesque d'Albert Memmi, ou le plaisir des yeux'' by Guy Dugas, in *Revue Celfan*, 4(2) 1985; ''Ethics and Esthetics in Memmi's *Le Scorpion*'' by Isaac Yetiv, in *Interdisciplinary Dimensions of African Literature*, edited by K. Anyidoho, A.M. Porter, D. Racine, and J. Spleth, 1985; ''Albert Memmi: Conversation'' by Najwa Tlili, in *Europe-Revue Litteraire Mensuelle*, 702, 1987; ''Acculturation, alienation et emancipation dans les oeuvres d'Albert Memmi et de Cheikh Hamidou Kane'' by Isaac Yetiv, in *Presence Francophone: Revue Litteraire*, 34, 1989; ''Albert Memmi and Alain Finkielkraut: Two Discourses on French Jewish Identity'' by Judith Morganroth Schneider, in *Romanic Review*, 81 (1), 1990; ''La Lecon hermeneutique du Scorpion d'Albert Memmi'' by Odette Mercure, in *Revue Francophone de Louisiane*, 7 (1), 1992; ''Albert Memmi: Du roman a l'essai, d'*Agar* au *Portrait du colonise*'' by Joelle Strike, in *French Studies in Southern Africa*, 24, 1995; ''Albert Memmi: L'Exil, le desert, l'ecriture'' by Amy Dayan-Rosenman, in *Pardes*, 21, 1995; ''Deracinement et gommages de l'identite: Le 'passe entre parentheses' dans Europa, Europa et *La Statue de sel* d'Albert Memmi'' by Peter Schulman, in *Romance Notes*, 39 (1), 1998; ''Colonialism, Psychoanalysis, and Cultural Criticism: The Problem of Interiorization in the Work of Albert Memmi'' by Suzanne Gearhart, in *'Culture' and the Problem of the Disciplines*, edited by J.C. Rowe, 1998; *Postcolonialisme et Autobiographie: Albert Memmi, Assia Djebar, Daniel Maximin*, edited by A. Hornung and E. Ruhe, 1998; ''Eclats de sourire: De la fragmentation dans l'oeuvre d'Albert Memmi'' by Joelle Strike, in *French Studies in Southern Africa*, 30, 2001.

* * *

As one of Africa's greatest intellectuals, Albert Memmi has continued to write and lecture on the problems of difference and racism for nearly half a century. Although sympathetic to the Arab cause in the country where he was born and raised, Tunisia, Memmi was, however, disconcerted by the religious character of the new state. He left Tunisia a year after its 1956 independence to settle in France. The question of homeland, never fully resolved in Memmi's personal life, appears repeatedly throughout his writings. As a Jew, Memmi supports the state of Israel, although he promotes non-religious, cultural Judaism. While he is an unapologetic secular Zionist, Memmi has never seriously considered living in Israel. He raises the problem of Arab-Jewish relations in his works *Le Statue de sel* (*The Pillar of Salt*) and *Juifs et Arabes* (*Jews and Arabs*). Pacifists and socialist groups have nonetheless criticized Memmi for his support of Israel, especially after Israel's victorious Six-Day War of 1967. What Memmi does want to avoid is Israel's current focus on the Old Testament and the Holocaust, which, in Memmi's view, limits Jewish cultural development. Memmi's first novel, *The Pillar of Salt*, appeared in 1953. Its balanced portrayal of the young hero's growing sense of alienation from his native Jewish-Tunisian milieu and from the French quickly won Memmi a place in the liberal French intellectual community.

Like fellow Francophone intellectuals Frantz Fanon and Aime Cesaire, Memmi has a deeply personal relationship to the questions of inter-ethnic violence. During World War II, Tunis suffered pogroms against the Jewish population; later, under Vichy rule, Jews, including Jewish teachers, were dismissed from their positions. After the war, France's equivocal relationship toward Jews inspired mistrust and resentment, not only in France, but in the colonies as well. Memmi, despite not having overcome his mixed feelings toward the French authorities, moved to France permanently in 1957.

Agar (*Strangers*), Memmi's second novel, treats mixed marriages from the point of view of a Tunisian Jew who marries a Frenchwoman from the Alsace, a story similar in some particulars to Memmi's own. The English-language title, *Strangers*, also recalls Albert Camus' famous 1942 novel *L'Étranger*. For the unnamed protagonist, a sort of "everyman," the tensions between the new conservative state of Tunisia, Sephardic Jewish tradition, and his French secular-scientific education play a dramatic psychological role. Memmi shows that the kernel of the problem is the hero's position half-way between his native Tunisian culture and that of the European colonials. His own ambivalence toward his people and country is thus reflected, magnified, and exacerbated by his French wife, leading to conflict and mutual blame in their household. The novel ends with the disintegration of the hero's marriage and the wife's abortion of their second child. The abortion, as the narrator of a later novel explains, symbolizes the impossibility of a fusion between the husband's Tunisian and the wife's French worlds.

Yet it was not until the 1957 publication of *Portrait du colonisé, précédé du Portrait du Colonisateur* that Memmi truly caught the world's attention. Translated as *The Colonizer and the Colonized*, the book became a handbook for national liberation, and was subsequently confiscated from North African prisons for that reason. Memmi argues that colonization is a "historical misfortune"; it separates both the colonizer and the colonized from their true selves. Although Memmi calls for a rejection of the colonial system, he at first had no plans to reject Europe in its entirety. After all, even this work denouncing France's position in Africa and in the Caribbean was written in French; Memmi's wife, Germaine Dubach, is French. Optimistic about the possibilities for the cultural renewal of colonized peoples, *The Colonizer and the Colonized* is an idealistic work that continues to be influential in post-colonial thought. Jean-Paul Sartre's introduction and the recent foreword by post-colonial theorist Homi Bhabha attest to the book's continuing relevance within an international academic community.

The Colonizer and the Colonized attempts to analyze the destructive effect of colonization of the colonized people's psyche. Colonization is harmful because it undermines the colony's native institutions and replaces them with those of the colonizer; it relegates native languages and customs to a secondary status; it requires that those who hope to succeed in the colonial system master the colonizer's language in order to progress in education and employment. All of these impositions inspire in the colonized people a feeling of inferiority. Memmi then outlines a plan for the reclamation of the colonized people's autonomy and dignity after the overthrow of a colonial government. Yet even in this highly political work, Memmi shows his sympathy and understanding of human complexity.

Due to the highly personal nature of his writing, it can be difficult to assign a genre to Memmi's works. His works are self-conscious and self-referential; action and devices developed in one book may be discussed elsewhere. Characters are carried from one work to another. *Le Scorpion* (*The Scorpion*) even lays bare this technique by having the narrator questioning the fictionalized novelist's memory and judgment in his particular portrayals of characters. This multi-layered semi-autobiographical novel combines religion, folklore, historical analysis, and theory in a joyous, postmodern amalgam. In the novel, a physician is asked by his sister-in-law to sort his brother's papers. *Le Scorpion* is thus a novel within a novel: it presents not only the brother's unfinished manuscript, but also his journal, quotations from other sources, and the physician's notes and commentary on the entire text. Printed with four different typefaces, *Le Scorpion* deconstructs the illusion of a single dimension within memory; likewise identity is multifaceted, a complex of roles and points of view, some of which are mutually exclusive. Yet from this confusion evolves the uniqueness of an individual's experience.

Le Racisme (*Racism*), originally published in 1982, has only recently been translated into English. This book, addressed especially to the Western liberal establishment, is an examination in three parts (description, definition, and treatment) of the dynamics of racism and how it can be overcome. The root of racism is the social attribution of difference. Difference is a fact; but difference does not have an inherent value, good or bad. Naturally humans respond to difference, but it is when they begin to generalize conclusions based on their observations of difference that "heterophobia" begins. To counteract this human tendency, Memmi promotes socially responsive education as treatment for racism. Memmi also betrays his own universalist tendencies in his expressed hopes for universalism to mitigate the effects of xenophobia, superstition, and simple fear. Best known in the West for his condemnation of colonization, Albert Memmi continues to be active in struggles against racial discrimination and religious bigotry.

—Natalie Smith

See the essay on *The Pillar of Salt*.

MENANDER

Born: Of an Athenian family, c. 342–41 BC. **Career:** Associated with the philosopher Theophrastus, *q.v.*, and with Demetrius of Phalerum, ruler of Athens, 317–07 BC. First play to be produced was *Orge* [*Anger*], 321 BC; won eight prizes; titles of more than 100 of his plays are known, though some might be alternative titles. **Died:** (possibly by drowning) 293–289 BC.

PUBLICATIONS

Collections

[Plays], edited by F.H. Sandbach. 1972; revised edition, 1976; translated by W. Geoffrey Arnott [Loeb Edition], 1979–.

Fragments (*The Litigants; The Lady with the Shorn Locks; The Woman of Samos; The Hero*) (includes translations), edited by J.S.P. Harberton. 1909.

Principal Fragments [Loeb Edition], translated by Francis G. Allinson. 1921.

[*Fragments*], edited by A. Körte and A. Thierfelder. 1959.

Plays and Fragments, translated by Philip Vellacott. 1967.

The Plays (includes *The Grouch; The Woman of Samos; The Shield; The Arbitration; She Who Was Shorn*), edited and translated by Lionel Casson. 1971.

Plays and Fragments (includes *Old Cantankerous; The Girl from Samos; The Arbitration; The Rape of the Locks; The Shield; The Sikyonian*; fragments), translated by Norma Miller. 1987.

Menander, edited by David R. Slavitt and Palmer Bovie. 1998.

Plays

Dyskolos (produced 316 BC). Edited by H. Lloyd-Jones, 1960; revised edition, 1970; also edited by Jean Bingen, 1960, J.M. Jacques, 1963, Eric W. Handley (with commentary), 1965, and Warren B. Blake (includes translation), 1966; as *Dyskolos*, translated by W. Geoffrey Arnott, 1960; as *The Bad-Tempered Old Man*, translated by Philip Vellacott, 1960; as *The Cross Old Devil*, translated by H.C. Fay, in *Three Classical Comedies*, 1967; as *The Grouch*, translated by Lionel Casson, in *The Plays*, 1971; as *The Feast of Pan*, translated by R.N. Benton, 1977; as *Old Cantankerous*, translated by Norma Miller, in *Plays and Fragments*, 1987.

Samia (produced 315–09 BC). Edited by Edward Capps, in *Four Plays*, 1910; also edited by Colin Austin, 1969; edited and translated by David M. Bain, 1983; as *The Woman of Samos*, translated in *Fragments*, edited by J.S.P. Harberton, 1909; also translated by Lionel Casson, in *The Plays*, 1971; as *The Girl from Samos*, translated by L.A. Post, in *Three Plays*, 1929; also translated by Ida Lublenski Ehrlich, 1955; Eric G. Turner, 1972; Norma Miller, in *Plays and Fragments*, 1987; as *The Samia*, translated by J.M. Edmonds, 1951.

Perikeiromene (produced c. 310 BC). Edited by Edward Capps, in *Four Plays*, 1910; as *The Lady with the Shorn Locks*, translated in *Fragments*, edited by J.S.P. Harberton, 1909; as *The Shearing of Glycera*, translated by L.A. Post, in *Three Plays*, 1929; as *The Rape of the Locks*, translated by Gilbert Murray, 1942; Norma Miller, in *Plays and Fragments*, 1987; as *She Who Was Shorn*, translated by Lionel Casson, in *The Plays*, 1971.

Aspis (fragmentary text), edited by Colin Austin. 1969; as *The Shield*, translated by Lionel Casson, in *The Plays*, 1971; also translated by Norma Miller, in *Plays and Fragments*, 1987.

Epitrepontes (fragmentary text), edited by Edward Capps, in *Four Plays*. 1910; also edited by Ulrich von Wilamowitz-Möllendorff, 1925, and Henry Bertram Lister, 1937; as *The Arbitration*, translated by L.A. Post, in *Three Plays*, 1929; also translated by Gilbert

Murray, 1945; Lionel Casson, in *The Plays*, 1971; Norma Miller, in *Plays and Fragments*, 1987.

Heros (fragmentary text), as *The Hero*, edited by Edward Capps, in *Four Plays*. 1910; translated in *Fragments*, edited by J.S.P. Harberton, 1909.

Sikyonios (fragmentary text), edited by R. Kassel. 1965; as *The Sikyonian*, translated by Norma Miller, in *Plays and Fragments*, 1987.

Four Plays (includes *The Hero; Epitrepontes; Perikeiromene; Samia*) (in Greek), edited by Edward Capps. 1910.

Three Plays (includes *The Girl from Samos; The Arbitration; The Shearing of Glycera*), translated by L.A. Post. 1929.

*

Critical Studies: *Studies in Menander*, 1950, revised edition, 1960, and *An Introduction to Menander*, 1974, both by T.B.L. Webster; *Notes on the Dyskolos of Menander* by H.J. Quincey and others, 1959; *New Fragments of the Misoumenos of Menander*, 1965, and *The Lost Beginnings of Menander's Misoumenos*, 1978, both by Eric G. Turner; *Menander, Plautus, and Terence* by W. Geoffrey Arnott, 1968; *Menander and Plautus: A Study in Comparison* by Eric W. Handley, 1968; *Menander: A Commentary* by F.H. Sandbach and Arnold W. Gomme, 1973, and *The Comic Theatre of Greece and Rome* by Sandbach, 1977; *Tragic Patterns in Menander* by Andreas G. Katsouris, 1975; *Menander and the Monologue* by John Blundell, 1980; *The Making of Menander's Comedy* by Sander M. Goldberg, 1980; *Menander's Courtesans and the Greek Comic Tradition* by Madeleine Mary Henry, 1985; *The New Comedy of Greece and Rome* by R.L. Hunter, 1985; *Exits and Entrances in Menander* by K.B. Frost, 1988; *The Masks of Menander* by David Wiles, 1991; *Menander: Dyskolos, Samia and Other Plays: A Companion to the Penguin Translation of the Plays of Menander by Norma Miller* by Stanley Ireland, 1992; *Ancient Comedy: The War of the Generations* by Dana F. Sutton, 1993; *Comedy of Menander: Convention, Variation, and Originality* by Netta Zagagi, 1995; *Menander and the Making of Comedy* by J. Michael Walton and Peter D. Arnott, 1996; *Oxford Readings in Menander, Plautus, and Terence*, edited by Erich Segal, 2002.

* * *

In the course of the 4th century BC, the boisterous political and social fantasies of Aristophanes gave way to a more sedate comedy of character and manners, which reflected the concerns of everyday life among the Athenian middle classes. Many of our most familiar comic figures and plot devices can be traced back to these developments, but, until recently, the greatest writer of this Greek New Comedy was little more than a name to us. Ancient critics had ranked Menander with Homer and preferred his refined style to Aristophanes' more vigorous one, but a combination of changing tastes and bad luck conspired against him. Menander lost his readership in late antiquity. Without readers, his plays were neglected, and the old books that contained them eventually perished. All that remained for modern readers then were short quotations by later authors, a collection of epigrams (many of doubtful authenticity), and Latin adaptations of his plays by Plautus and Terence. The situation, however, is now very different, and the history of Western comedy has been able to add a new chapter. In 1905, excavations in Egypt uncovered a papyrus book from the 3rd century BC that contained large fragments of five Menandrean plays, and since 1959 much further material has come to light on additional papyri. We now possess one play complete: *Dyskolos* (*The Grouch*), one that is almost complete: *Samia* (*The Woman of Samos*), and substantial portions of several more, The literary appraisal of these discoveries is still in its infancy, but several things are rapidly becoming clear.

Though the Roman poet Ovid once claimed that no play of Menander was without "pleasant love" (*iucundus amor*), we can now see just how limited that truth is and how deliberately unfaithful were Menander's Roman copyists. We can no longer treat Greco-Roman comedy as a single genre. All Menander's plays do in fact have a clear romantic component, but it is rarely the true focus of the dramatist's interest. Though *The Woman of Samos* has a young man desperate to marry, it concentrates attention on the fragility of trust between that young man and his adoptive father. *Perikeiromene* (*She Who Was Shorn*) depicts a soldier's difficulty in adjusting to the restrictions of civilian society; his love for Glykera is but the means for testing and tempering his character. *Epitrepontes* (*The Arbitration*) explores the foolishness and vanity of moral pretensions. Even *The Grouch*, whose plot probably comes closest to the romantic stereotype, derives its point not from the pratfalls of its rather hapless Lothario, but from the dilemma of an old misanthrope forced to confront his social responsibilities. Menander's comedies all tend to have a serious core, and so do his characters. He treats them with an amused and affectionate sympathy that not only displays their foibles and frailties, but also provides means for their moral improvement. An expository prologue—the device was perhaps learned from Euripides—normally tells the audience more than the characters know and hints at a divine order behind the human confusion. The audience can then enjoy the turns of plot that bring these characters to a better understanding of themselves and their circumstances, and the result is a sense not just of amusement, but of significant lessons well learned.

Considerable technical skill underlies the plays. Menander's iambic and trochaic verse patterns capture the freshness of colloquial speech without excessive stylization, and major characters display speech mannerisms and other idiosyncrasies that make memorable individuals from the stock figures of his tradition. Thus, while some minor figures such as cooks remain broad and familiar figures of fun who raise laughter with the same old jokes and stage antics, no two old men are ever quite alike and no two young ones ever face their moral dilemmas in quite the same way. Menander's plots are equally varied. Stock contrasts—rich versus poor, city versus country, Athenian versus foreign—are discernible in the background, but the twists of a Menandrean plot originate in the characters themselves, not in their external circumstances. These dramatic actions are not the product of blatant manipulation. Nor are they unnecessarily complex. Plots are carefully built around a five-act structure marked by unrelated choral interludes (labelled simply "choral song" in our manuscripts) to pace the action. Exits and entrances are carefully orchestrated, but there are no true double plots or any of the contrived coincidences or convoluted intrigues familiar from Plautus. The ubiquitous birth tokens and other devices for recognition are but the exceptions that prove the rule: Menander cares more for the psychological shock of recognition than for the mechanism that brings it about. The plays' richness comes more from their skilful depiction of common dilemmas and sympathetic characters than from elaborate

stage action. "Menander and Life," wondered an ancient critic, "which of you really imitated which?" It is a fair question, and not easily answered.

—Sander M. Goldberg

See the essay on *The Grouch*.

MÉRIMÉE, Prosper

Born: Paris, France, 28 September 1803. **Education:** Educated at Lycée Napoleon (formerly Lycée Henri IV), baccalauréat 1819; studied law, University of Paris, graduated 1823. **Military Service:** Exempted from military service. **Career:** Inspector general of historical monuments, 1834–60, travelled throughout France classifying important buildings and writing reports on the need for preservation; prominent figure in Court of Napoleon III. Associated with Stendhal, *q.v.* His left arm was injured in a duel with Félix Lacoste, husband of Mérimée's lover, Émilie. **Awards:** Chevalier, Légion d'honneur, 1831. **Died:** 23 September 1870.

PUBLICATIONS

Collections

The Writings. 1905.
Oeuvres complètes, edited by Pierre Trahard and Edouard Champion. 12 vols., 1927–35.
Romans et contes, edited by H. Martineau. 1951.
Romans et nouvelles, edited by Maurice Parturier. 2 vols., 1967.
Nouvelles complètes, edited by Pierre Josserand. 2 vols., 1973–74.
Théâtre de Clara Gazul, romans, nouvelles [Pléiade Edition], edited by Jean Mallion and Pierre Salomon. 1978.
Nouvelles, edited by Michel Crouzet. 2 vols., 1987–88.

Fiction

Chronique du règne de Charles IX. 1829; revised edition, with "1572" prefixed, 1832; edited by Alfred Baker, 1947; as *A Chronicle of the Reign of Charles IX*, translated by A.R. Scoble, 1853; also translated by G. Saintsbury, 1890; Diane de Turgis, 1925.
Mosaïque (stories: includes *Mateo Falcon; Tamango; La Partie de trictrac*). 1833; as *Mosaica*, 1903; as *The Pearl of Toledo*, translated by Colin Fenton, 1966.
Colomba (stories). 1840; edited by Theodora de Selincourt, 1910, and Pierre Jourda, 1947; as *Colomba: A Corsican Story*, translated by A.R. Scoble, 1853; also translated by J.A. Prout, 1896; Edward Marielle, 1965.
Carmen. 1846; edited by N. Scarlyn Wilson, 1962; as *Carmen*, translated by Edmund H. Garrett, 1896; also translated by A.E. Johnson, 1916; Lady Mary Lloyd, 1941; Michael J. Tilby, 1981.
Nouvelles. 1852.
Dernières nouvelles. 1873.
Short Stories, translated by George Burnham Ives. 1909.

The Slave Ship, translated by Eliot Fay. 1934. *Carmen and Other Stories*, translated by Alec Brown, 1960; also translated by Edward Marielle, 1965; Guy Chapman, 1966; Nicholas Jotcham, 1989.

The Venus of Ille and Other Stories, translated by Jean Kimber. 1966.

Verse

La Guzla. 1827; edited by Eugène Marsan, 1928.

Plays

Le Théâtre de Clara Gazul, comèdienne espagnole (includes *Les Espagnols en Danemarck; Une femme est un diable; L'Amour africain; Inès Mendo ou Le Préjugé vaincu; Inès Mendo ou Le Triomphe du préjugé; Le Ciel et l'enfer*). 1825; revised edition (includes *Le Carosse du Saint-sacrement* and *L'Occasion*), 1830; revised edition, 1842; edited by Pierre Salomon, 1968;.

Les Espagnols en Danemarck. In *Le Théâtre de Clara Gazul, comèdienne espagnole*, 1825; also translated by Oscar Mandel in *The Spaniards in Denmark; And, The Rebels of Nantucket*, 1996.

Une femme est un diable. In *Le Théâtre de Clara Gazul, comèdienne espagnole*, 1825.

L'Amour africain (produced 1827). In *Le Théâtre de Clara Gazul, comèdienne espagnole*, 1825.

Inès Mendo ou Le Préjugé vaincu. In *Le Théâtre de Clara Gazul, comèdienne espagnole*, 1825.

Inès Mendo ou Le Triomphe du préjugé. In *Le Théâtre de Clara Gazul, comèdienne espagnole*, 1825.

Le Ciel et l'enfer. In *Le Théâtre de Clara Gazul, comèdienne espagnole*, 1825.

La Jacquerie, scènes féodales. 1828.

La Famille de Carvajal. 1828.

L'Occasion. 1829; in *Le Théâtre de Clara Gazul, comèdienne espagnole*, revised edition, 1830.

Le Carosse du Saint-Sacrement (produced 1850). 1829; in *Le Théâtre de Clara Gazul, comèdienne espagnole*, revised edition, 1830.

La Chambre bleue. 1873.

Les Deux Héritages. 1876.

The Conspirators: A Play, translated and adapted by Paul Vaughan. 1997.

Other

La Double Méprise. 1833; as *A Slight Misunderstanding*, translated by Douglas Parmée, 1959.

Notes d'un voyage dans le midi de la France. 1835.

Notes d'un voyage dans l'ouest de la France. 1836.

Notes d'un voyage en Auvergne. 1838.

Notes d'un voyage en Corse. 1840.

Essai sur la guerre sociale. 1841.

Études sur l'histoire romain. 2 vols., 1844.

Notice sur les peintures de l'église de Saint-Savin. 2 vols., 1845.

Vézelay. 1847.

Histoire de don Pèdre I, roi de Castille. 1848.

Histoire du règne de Pierre le Grand, suivie de l'histoire de la fausse Elizabeth II. 1848; as *The History of Peter the Cruel*, translated anonymously, 2 vols., 1849; also translated by James Pearse Peachey, 1851.

Épisode de l'histoire de Russie—Le Faux Démétrius. 1852; as *Demetrius the Impostor: An Episode in Russian History*, translated by A.R. Scoble, 1853.

Mélanges historiques et littéraires. 1855.

Architecture gallo-romaine et architecture du Moyen Âge, with Albert Lenoir, Auguste Leprévost and Lenormant. 1857.

Lettres à une inconnue. 2 vols, 1874; as *Prosper Mérimée's Letters to an Incognita*, translated by R.H. Stoddard, 3 vols., 1874; as *Letters to an Unknown*, translated by H. Pène du Bois, 1897; as *The Love Letters of a Genius*, translated by E.A.S. Watt, 1905.

Portraits historiques et littéraires. 1874.

Lettres à une autre inconnue. 1875.

Lettres à M. Panizzi. 2 vols., 1881; as *Letters to M. Panizzi*, translated by H.M. Dunstan, 2 vols., 1881.

La Passion d'un auteur. 1889; as *An Author's Love*, 1889.

Une correspondance inédite. 1897.

Lettres inédites. 1900.

Lettres aux Lagrené (1840–1870). 1904.

Lettres d'Espagne. 1913.

Lettres aux Grasset. 1929.

Lettres de Prosper Mérimée à la comtesse de Montijo. 2 vols., 1930; edited by Pierre Josserand, 1936.

Lettres de Mérimée à la famille Delessert. 1931.

Lettres de Prosper Mérimée à la comtesse de Boigne. 1933.

Lettres à Ludovic Vitet. 1934.

Lettres à Madame de Beaulaincourt 1866–1870. 1936.

Lettres de Mérimée (selection), edited by Jean Mallion. 1937.

Lettres aux antiquaires de l'ouest 1836–1869. 1937.

Lettres à Fanny Lagden (bilingual edition). 1937.

Lettres à la duchesse de Castiglione-Colonna. 1938.

Mérimée inconnu (selection), edited by Ferdinand Bac. 1939.

Correspondance générale, edited by Maurice Parturier. 17 vols., 1941–64.

Lettres à Edward Ellice 1857–1863, edited by Marianne Cermakian and France Achener. 1963.

Études sur les arts du Moyen Âge. 1967.

Notes sur voyages, edited by Pierre-Marie Auzas. 1971.

Editor, *Aventures du baron de Foeneste*, by Th.-A. d'Aubigné. 1855.

Translator, *La Dame de pique*, by Pushkin. 1849.

Translator, *Le Coup de pistolet*, by Pushkin. 1852.

Translator, *L'Inspecteur général*, by Gogol. 1853.

*

Bibliography: *Bibliographie des oeuvres de Prosper Mérimée* edited by Pierre Trahard and Pierre Josserand, 1929; *A Half-Century of Mérimée Studies* by Louise Dupelty, 1976.

Critical Studies: *Prosper Merimée: A Face and a Mask* by G.H. Johnstone, 1927; *The Life and Times of Prosper Mérimée* by Sylvia Lyon, 1948; *Prosper Mérimée: Heroism, Pessimism and Irony* by Frank Paul Bowman, 1962; *The Poetics of Prosper Mérimée* by Robert C. Dale, 1966; *Prosper Mérimée* by Alan W. Raitt, 1970; *Prosper Mérimée* by M.A. Smith, 1972; *Prosper Mérimée: Écrivain, archéologue, homme politique* by Jean Autin, 1982; *Pushkin and Mérimée as Short Story Writers: Two Different Approaches to Description and Detail* by Karl-Heinrich Barsch, 1983; *L'Autre Moi: Fantasmes et fantastiques dans les Nouvelles de Mérimée* by Jacques Chabot, 1983; *Le Cosmopolitisme dans les textes courts de Stendhal* *et Mérimée* by Muriel Augry-Merlino, 1990; *The Fate of Carmen* by Evlyn Gould, 1996.

* * *

Prosper Mérimée's fate is to be remembered above all for one book, *Carmen*, and there is some force in the argument that what has given this thrilling novella its almost universal popular fame is in fact the operatic version which was set to music by Georges Bizet and premiered in Paris only shortly before the composer's death in 1875 and whose libretto, by Henri Meilhac and Ludovic Halévy, is a rather free adaptation of the original work. Yet, even if it is hard to think of *Carmen* without hearing ringing in one's ears the pounding rhythms of the "March of the Toreadors" or the seductive rhythms and sensuous chromaticism of the heroine's *habañera*, the fact remains that in the depiction of overwhelming passions and of the devastating inescapability of their cruel consequences in exotic settings there is much, though not all, of the essential Mérimée. Traditionally Spain had figured in the French literary imagination as the land where passions ran high and the rival claims of love and honour led to violent, usually tragic, conflict.

Carmen came, however, relatively late in Mérimée's career. Born into a fairly prosperous family, he had a good education. The first indication of an interest in literature was a historical drama about Cromwell. The style and theme of this play, which was never performed and of which the text has not survived, were, in the early 1820s, clear signals of Romantic affiliations. Mérimée turned next to Spanish drama, first publishing a number of articles and then bringing out, in 1825, a work bearing the title *Le Théâtre de Clara Gazul*. A prefatory note assures us that it was in Spain in 1813 that Joseph L'Estrange, the translator of the texts, had met the 14-year-old Clara. But this was just a hoax transparent in fact to virtually everybody from the outset, and what we have here are half a dozen Romantic playlets, not really intended for performance. Mérimée could not resist yet another hoax and in 1827 brought out *La Guzla*, a collection of alleged translations from the work of the Illyrian poet, "Hyacinthe Maglanowich," which bears witness not only to a certain taste for mystification but also to the Romantic passion for folksong and national literature more generally. Two years later, under the influence of Sir Walter Scott, whose impact can also clearly be seen in Victor Hugo's *Notre-Dame de Paris* (*The Hunchback of Notre-Dame*) which was completed at virtually the same time, Mérimée turned to the historical novel. *Chronique du règne de Charles IX* (*A Chronicle of the Reign of Charles IX*) is set in the France of the second part of the 16th century, an exciting and colourful period especially favoured by the French Romantics. Despite a genuine effort to achieve factual accuracy, the novel cannot be regarded as entirely successful.

The appearance of *Mosaïque* (*Mosaica*), which brought together into a single volume a number of tales that had been offered originally to the public in such magazines as the *Revue de Paris*, revealed that Mérimée had, after these various experiments, at last discovered in the short story the form that suited his talents best. "Charles XI's Vision," set in Stockholm, reveals an abiding interest in the supernatural, and the reader is all the more enthralled by the deft interweaving of realistic detail in this tale of the uncanny. "Mateo Falcone" is one of the world's great short stories. The scene is the hard landscape of Corsica, which Mérimée knew at the time only from his reading, and the background is the rigorous code of honour that inspires Mateo. He has only one son, a ten-year-old to whom he is devoted, but

affection counts for nothing in the face of an ignoble act. The conclusion is all the more heart-rending because Mérimée recounts dreadful deeds in the most impassive of styles, leaving it to his readers to make what sense they can of a great disproportion between event and expression that must have been especially evident in the first half of the 19th century, when many writers were uninhibited in their endeavours to give full expression to emotion. "Tamango" is another striking tale. Perhaps partly inspired by contemporary efforts to suppress the slave trade, this is an account of an African who sells to a rascally sea captain a number of his fellow countrymen, including even his wife. Our sympathies are pulled in one direction, then another, as Tamango is next captured, manages to break free from his shackles, and takes command of the ship only to lead his companions in misfortune from one disaster to another. The conclusion, after a great accumulation of horrors, is ironic: rescued by a British frigate, Tamango is taken to Jamaica, where he ends his days playing the cymbals in a military band.

With "La Vénus d'Ille," Mérimée produced one of his most powerful essays in the uncanny and then, after a trip to Corsica, he published *Colomba*. Longer than his short stories, but written with the same economy of style and similar impassivity, it is again a tale of banditry and revenge in a wild environment. *Carmen* dates from 1845, and though Mérimée continued to write stories, his reputation now was made.

—Christopher Smith

METASTASIO, Pietro

Born: Pietro Antonio Domenico Bonaventura Trapassi in Rome, Papal States, 3 January 1698. **Education:** Studied Greek and Latin under his patron, the dramatist, critic, and founding member of the Arcadian Academy, Gian Vincenzo Gravina, who Hellenized Trapassi's name to Metastasio; travelled to Scalèa, in Calabria, to study cartesian philosophy, 1712. **Family:** Married Rosalia Gasparini in 1719. **Career:** Inherited the greater part of Gravina's fortune on his death in 1718; admitted to the Arcadian Academy (under the pastoral name Artino Corasio), 1718; lived in Naples, 1719–24; settled in Rome, 1727–30; succeeded Apostolo Zeno as imperial poet in Vienna, then capital of the Hapsburg Holy Roman Empire, spent most of the rest of his life writing for the Emperor, Charles VI, and his daughter Maria Teresa: his works produced mostly in the imperial theatres or at court, to celebrate royal occasions; wrote only in prose after 1772. **Died:** 12 April 1782.

PUBLICATIONS

Collections

Opere postume, edited by S. D'Ayala. 3 vols., 1795.
Opere, edited by Fausto Nicolini. 4 vols., 1912–14.
Opere, edited by Bruno Brunelli. 5 vols., 1943–54.
Teatro, edited by R. Bracchelli. 1962.
Opere scelte, edited by F. Gavazzeni. 1968.
Opere, edited by Mario Fubini and Ettore Bonora. 1968.
Teatro, edited by Mario Fubini. 1977.
Opere, edited by Franco Mollia. 1979.

Plays

The following list includes melodramas, sacred dramas, and other selected works, along with the original musical collaborators. First publication dates of Italian works are not given; the first full edition is the 12-volume *Opere* of 1780–82 listed below.

Gli orti esperidi, music by Nicola Porpora (produced 1721).

Endimione (produced 1721). As *Endimione* (bilingual edition), 1758.

Galatea (produced 1721/22).

Angelica, music by Nicola Porpora (produced 1722). As *Angelica e Medoro* (bilingual edition), 1739.

Didone abbandonata (melodrama), music by Domenico Sarro (produced 1724). As *Didone abbandonata* (bilingual edition), 1748; as *Dido Forsaken*, translated by Joseph G. Fucilla, 1952; as *Dido Abandoned*, translated by Fucilla, in *Three Melodramas*, 1981.

Siface, music by Nicola Porpora, from an anonymous work (produced 1726).

Siroe, re di Persia (melodrama), music by Leonardo Vinci (produced 1726). As *Siroe, re di Persia*, translated and abridged by N.F. Haym, 1728; also translated 1736 (bilingual edition), and 1755.

Per la festività del SS. Natale, music by Gian Battista Costanzi (produced 1728).

Catone in Utica (melodrama), music by Leonardi Vinci (produced 1728). As *Catone* (bilingual edition), 1732.

Ezio (melodrama), music by Pietro Auletta (produced 1728). As *Ezio* (bilingual edition), 1732.

Semiramide riconosciuta (melodrama), music by Leonardo Vinci (produced 1729). As *Semiramide riconosciuta* (bilingual edition), 1733; as *Semiramide riconosciuta; or, Semiramis Discovered*, adapted by G.G. Bottarelli, 1771.

La contesa de' Numi (festival piece), music by Leonardo Vinci (produced 1729).

Alessandro nelle Indie (melodrama), music by Leonardo Vinci (produced 1729). As *La generosità d'Alessandro* (bilingual edition), 1790.

Artaserse (melodrama), music by Leonardo Vinci (produced 1730). As *Artaxerxes* (bilingual edition), translated by Thomas Arne, 1734; also translated in *Works*, 1767; as *Artaserse* (bilingual edition), 1754.

La passione di Cristo (sacred drama), music by Antonio Caldara (produced 1730).

Sant'Elena al Calvario (oratorio), music by Antonio Caldara (produced 1731).

Enea negli Elisi; ovvero, Il Tempio dell'Eternità (festival piece), music by Giovanni Fux (produced 1731).

Demetrio (melodrama), music by Antonio Caldara (produced 1731). As *Demetrius* (bilingual edition), 1737; also translated in *Works*, 1767, and in *Three Melodramas*, 1981; as *Alceste*, translated by P.A. Rolli, 1744.

L'Issipile (melodrama), music by Francesco Conti (produced 1732). As *Hypsipile*, 1735; also translated in *Works*, 1767; as *L'Issipile* (bilingual edition), 1758.

La morte di Abele (sacred drama), music by Giorgio Reuter (produced 1732). As *The Death of Abel*, with *Morning Hymn from Paradise* by Milton, 1768.

L'asilo d'amore, music by Antonio Caldara (produced 1732). As *L'asilo d'amore* (bilingual edition), 1757.

Adriano in Siria (melodrama), music by Antonio Caldara (produced 1732). As *Adrian in Siria* (bilingual edition), 1735.

Giuseppe riconosciuto (sacred drama), music by Giuseppe Porsile (produced 1732).

L'Olimpiade (melodrama), music by Antonio Caldara (produced 1733). As *Merope ovvero L'Olimpiade*, translated by P. Rolli, 1742; also translated as *L'Olimpiade* (bilingual edition), 1756; as *The Olympiad*, in *Works*, 1767, and in *Three Melodramas*, 1981.

Demofoonte (melodrama), music by Antonio Caldara (produced 1733). As *Demofoonte* (bilingual edition), 1755; as *Demophoon*, in *Works*, 1767; as *The Innocent Usurper*, translated by "J.W.S.," 1819.

Opere drammatiche. 4 vols., 1733–77.

Betulia liberata (sacred drama), music by Giorgio Reuter (produced 1734). As *The Deliverance of Bethulia* (bilingual edition), 1768.

La clemenzia di Tito (melodrama), music by Antonio Caldara (produced 1734). As *Titus Vespasian*, 1755; as *La clemenzia di Tito* (bilingual edition), 1760; also translated by S. Buonaiuti, 1806; as *Titus*, in *Works*, 1767, and 1841; as *Conspiracy: A Tragedy*, adapted by R. Jephson, 1796; as *The Clemency of Titus*, translated anonymously, 1812.

Le Cinesi (ballet libretto), music by Giorgio Reuter (produced 1735; expanded version produced 1753).

Gioas re di Giuda (sacred drama), music by Giorgio Reuter (produced 1735).

Le grazie vendicate, music by Antonio Caldara (produced 1735).

Il Palladio conservato, music by Giorgio Reuter (produced 1735).

Il sogno di Scipione, music by Luc'Antonio Predieri (produced 1735). As *The Dream of Scipio*, translated by T. Olivari, in *Three Dramatic Pieces*, 1797.

Achille in Sciro (melodrama), music by Antonio Caldara (produced 1735).

Il Ciro riconosciuto (melodrama), music by Antonio Caldara (produced 1736). As *Il Ciro riconosciuto* (bilingual edition), 1759.

Temistocle (melodrama), music by Antonio Caldara (produced 1736). As *Il Temistocle* (bilingual edition), 1742; as *The Patriot*, adapted by C. Hamilton, 1784.

Il Parnaso accusato e difeso, music by Giorgio Reuter (produced 1738).

La pace fra la virtù e la bellezza, music by Luc'Antonio Predieri (produced 1738).

Astrea placata; ovvero, La felicità della terra, music by Luc'Antonio Predieri (produced 1739). As *Astrea Appeased*, translated by T. Olivari, in *Three Dramatic Pieces*, 1797.

La Canzonetta (ballet libretto), music by Giuseppe Bonno (produced 1740).

Isacco figura del Redentore (sacred drama), music by Luc' Antonio Predieri (produced 1740).

Zenobia (melodrama), music by Luc'Antonio Predieri (produced 1740).

Il natale di Giove, music by Giuseppe Bonno (produced 1740). As *The Birth of Jupiter*, translated by T. Olivari, in *Three Dramatic Pieces*, 1797.

L'amor prigioniero, music by Giorgio Reuter (produced 1741).

Il vero omaggio, music by Giuseppe Bonno (produced 1743).

Ipermestra (melodrama), music by Giovanni Adolfo Haase (produced 1744).

Antigono (melodrama), music by Giovanni Adolfo Haase (produced 1744). As *Antigono* (bilingual edition), 1757.

La danza (cantata), music by Giuseppe Bonno (produced 1744).

Attilio Regolo (melodrama), music by Giovanni Adolfo Haase (produced 1750).

La rispettosa tenerezza (musical dialogue), music by Giorgio Reuter (produced 1750).

Il re pastore (melodrama), music by Giuseppe Bonno (produced 1751). As *Il re pastore* (bilingual edition), 1757; also translated by F. Bottarelli (bilingual edition), 1778; as *The Royal Shepherd*, adapted by R. Rolt, 1764; as *La passione*, translated by John S. Allitt, 1970.

L'eroe cinese (melodrama), music by Giuseppe Bonno (produced 1752). As *L'eroe cinese* (bilingual edition), 1782.

L'isola disabitata, music by Giuseppe Bonno (produced 1753). As *L'isola disabitata* (bilingual edition), 1760; as *The Desert Island*, translated by Arthur Murphy, 1760.

La gara, music by Giorgio Reuter (produced 1755).

Nitteti (melodrama), music by Niccolò Conforti (produced 1756). As *La Nitteti* (bilingual edition), 1774.

Alcide al bivio, music by Giovanni Adolfo Haase (produced 1760).

Il trionfo di Clelia (melodrama), music by Giovanni Adolfo Haase (produced 1762).

Egeria, music by Giovanni Adolfo Haase (produced 1764).

Il Parnaso confuso, music by Gluck (produced 1765).

Romolo ed Ersilia (melodrama), music by Giovanni Adolfo Haase (produced 1765).

Partenope, music by Giovanni Adolfo Haase (produced 1767).

Works, translated by John Hoole. 2 vols., 1767; as *Dramas and Other Poems of the Abbè Metastasio*, 3 vols., 1800.

Ruggiero; ovvero, L'eroica gratitudine (melodrama), music by Giovanni Adolfo Haase (produced 1771).

Three Dramatic Pieces (includes *The Dream of Scipio; The Birth of Jupiter; Astrea Appeased*), translated by T. Olivari. 1797.

Teatro scelto (includes *Didone abbandonata; Demetrio; L'olimpiade; Attilo Regolo*). 1974.

Three Melodramas (includes *Dido Abandoned; Demetrius; The Olympiad*), translated by Joseph G. Fucilla. 1981.

Verse

Poesie (includes tragedy *Giustino*). 1717.

Poesie, edited by R. de' Calsabigi. 10 vols., 1755–69.

La pubblica felicità per la restaurata salute dell'Imperatrice Regina nel 1767. 1767.

Translations from the Italian of Petrarch and Metastasio, translated by Philip Bracebridge Homer. 1790.

Solitude and Other Poems, translated anonymously. 1830(?).

Other

Lettere. 5 vols., 1768–87; 2 vols., 1795.

Opere, edited by G. Pezzana. 12 vols., 1780–82.

Memoirs of the Life and Writings of the Late Abate Metastasio in Which Are Incorporated Translations of His Principal Letters, translated by Charles Burney. 3 vols., 1796.

Select Airs from Metastasio, translated by "J.G." 1818.

Alcune lettere inedite. 1876.

Lettere disperse e inedite, edited by C. Antona Traversi. 1886.

Pagine metastasiane (selection), edited by A. Costa. 1923.

*

Critical Studies: *Pietro Metastasio* by Angelo De Gubernatis, 1910; *Metastasio* by Mario Apollonio, 1930; *Pietro Metastasio* by Mario Fubini, in *I classici italiani* edited by Luigi Russo, 1940; *Metastasio* by Luigi Russo, 1945; *Saggio sul Metastasio* by C. Varese, 1950; *L'Arcadia e il Metastasio* by W. Binni, 1963; *Studi metastasiani* by Franco Gavazzeni, 1964; *Haydn, Mozart, and Metastasio* by Marie Henri Beyle, 1972; *Metastasio* by Maria Luisa Astaldi, 1979; *Metastasio e il teatro del primo Settecento* by Guido Nicastro, 1982; *Metastasio: ideologia, drammaturgia, spettacolo* by Elena Sala Di Felice, 1983; *Metastasio e la tragedia* by Gian Piero Maragoni, 1984; *Metastasio e il melodramma* edited by Elena Di Felice and Laura Sannia Nowé, 1985; *Metastasio: Acts of the Conference Held for the Bicentenary of Metastasio's Death*, 1985; "Betulia liberata: Pietro Metastasio's Melodramatic Oratorio" by David C. Bradley, in *Italian Culture*, 28(108), 1987; *Pietro Metastasio da poeta di teatro a "virtuoso di poesia"* by Rosy Candiani, 1998; *Esilio di Metastasio: Forme e riforme dello spettacolo d'opera fra Sette e Ottocento* by Andrea Chegai, 1998.

* * *

Pietro Metastasio's literary career can be said to have begun with the publication in 1718 of *Giustino*, a tragedy influenced in content and structure by the 16th-century Italian writers Trissino, Tasso, and Guarini, together with occasional rhymes whose importance lies not as much in their intrinsic literary value as in their promise of potential still to be realized. The successful performance in Naples between 1721 and 1722 of four dramatic pieces (*Galatea, Endimione, Gli orti esperidi* [The Garden of the Hesperides], *Angelica*), set to music by Nicola Porpora and Domenico Sarro, and featuring Marianna Benti Bulgarelli, the young poet's friend and protector, was followed in 1724 by the triumphant staging of *Didone abbandonata* (*Dido Abandoned*), once again with music by Sarro and interpreted by Bulgarelli. This melodrama contains almost all the typical characteristics of Metastasio's subsequent works, elaborated around a no less typical structure of love unrequited and renounced. It was with this melodrama, arguably Metastasio's most celebrated, that the poet established his reputation as the inaugurator of a new art form and a new kind of theatrical genre.

Between 1726 and 1730, Metastasio, famous throughout Europe, composed a further six melodramas (*Siroe, Catone in Utica, Ezio, Alessandro nelle Indie, Semiramide riconosciuta, Artaserse*), staged in Rome, Naples, and Venice, with music by the foremost composers of the time. In *Siroe* Metastasio experimented for the first time with a happy ending, and with *Catone in Utica* he began a series of melodramas based on Roman history and tragic models. As with the earlier *Dido Abandoned*, these works offered musicians libretto of indisputable literary value and intrinsic musicality. For the first time in the history of melodrama, the literary text commanded at least as much attention from the public as the music to which it was set.

Between 1730 and 1740, at the Viennese court of Emperor Charles VI, Metastasio composed 11 further melodramas, together with numerous other dramatic pieces and oratorios, staged at court to celebrate such events as births and weddings. The melodramas of this second period, including *L'Olimpiade* (*The Olympiad*) with its happy ending and conflict between love and friendship, and *Attilio Regolo* with its noble characters torn between love and duty, are generally held by critics to be among Metastasio's finest. The following 26 years saw a reduction in both the quantity and quality of Metastasio's literary output. The death, in 1751, of his second friend and protector,

Marianna Pignatelli Althann, the poet's own fluctuating health, the unsettling repercussions in the Viennese court of the War of Succession, and the demands made on librettists by the music of Gluck and Mozart, all contributed to the deterioration, evident in the eight melodramas of this third period, of which the poet himself was well aware. These later works are marred by a certain repetitiveness, a lack of originality, as Metastasio takes up motifs already elaborated in previous melodramas. Metastasio sought to elevate the libretto from being merely an accessory to the music and spectacle, which had largely been its lot until Apostolo Zeno laid the foundations for the reform of the genre. Metastasio turned his literary talents to composing librettos that could be read as pure literature or enacted as dramas without the musical interpretation of their parts. With very few exceptions, Metastasio drew upon Greek, Roman, and Oriental history and legend for his subject matter, and his dramas usually focus on an internal conflict (for example, love versus duty in *Dido*; love versus friendship in *The Olympiad*). His best protagonists are psychologically credible, particularly his female ones, and love, characteristic of most Arcadian poetry, is the unifying motif of his works.

A number of critics have commented on a comic element perceptible in some of the melodramas, viewing it as unintended and thus a weakness (tragic art that induces laughter). Other critics, such as Guido Nicastro, see Metastasio's comicality as anything but involuntary, considering it instead an element used wittingly so as to overcome the rigid barriers between different genres, much the same as contemporary dramatists were doing with the *comédie larmoyante*.

Besides his melodramas, Metastasio wrote numerous poems, *azioni sacre* or oratories, and mythological idylls: occasional works that he composed throughout his career, of limited importance (according to Nicastro), and serving a precise encomiastic end. Of likewise little value are his sacred *azioni* (1727–40), his 34 *cantate*, written mostly in Vienna, and his sonnets, almost all commissioned. Apart from his melodramas, his best works of the Viennese period (according to Fucilla) are his *canzonette*: "La libertà" [Freedom], 1733; "Palinodia"; and "La partenza" [The Departure], 1746— all evidence of his noteworthy poetic talent. His poetics are well documented by his late commentaries, on Aristotle's *Poetics*, on Greek theatre, and on Horace's *Ars Poetica* (*Art of Poetry*), published posthumously.

Invaluable for the light they cast on Metastasio as a man and artist are his voluminous letters (2,645 in the Brunelli edition of Metastasio's works), which also have artistic value in that they reveal a brilliant and controlled prose writer (according to Nicastro), a perceptive and lucid witness to contemporary life and history.

Criticism of Metastasio's works in the 18th century was on the whole positive, while 19th-century critics (such as Leopardi, Schlegel, and Stendhal) were more negative, as were also many of the early critics of the 20th century (Flora, Croce, Fubini). More recent scholars (Varese, Binni, Gavazzeni), however, have acknowledged Metastasio's worth as a fine lyric poet.

—Nicole Prunster

MEUNG, Jean de

See ROMANCE OF THE ROSE

MEYER, Conrad Ferdinand

Born: Zurich, Switzerland, 11 October 1825. **Education:** Educated at the Gymnasium, Zurich, 1837–44; studied law at the University of Zurich, 1844–45. **Family:** Married Luise Ziegler in 1875. **Career:** Developed a recurring mental condition which was to trouble him throughout his life; suffered a mental breakdown in 1852 and spent several months in the clinic Prèfargier near Neuchâtel; received a legacy in mid-1850s which left him financially independent; took private studies in literature, history, and art; visited Paris and Munich, 1857, Rome, 1858, Lausanne, 1860, Verona and Venice, 1871–72; spent time in an asylum in Königsfelden, 1892. **Died:** 28 November 1898.

PUBLICATIONS

Collections

Sämtliche Werke, edited by Hans Zeller and Alfred Zäch. 1958–.
Werke, edited by Gerhard Stenzel. 2 vols., 1965–67.
Werke, edited by Heinz Schöffer. 2 vols., 1967.
Werke, edited by Helmut Brandt. 2 vols., 1970.
The Complete Narrative Prose of Conrad Ferdinand Meyer, translated by George F. Folkers, David B. Dickens, and Marion W. Sonnenfeld. 2 vols., 1976.
Gesammelte Werke, edited by Wolfgang Ignée. 1985.

Verse

Zwanzig Balladen von einem Schweizer. 1864.
Balladen. 1867.
Romanzen und Bilder. 1869.
Huttens Letzte Tage. 1871.
Engelberg. 1872.
Gedichte. 1882.

Fiction

Das Amulet. 1873; as *The Amulet*, translated by George F. Folkers, in *The Complete Narrative Prose*, 1976.
Georg Jenatsch. 1876; as *Jürg Jenatsch*, 1882; as *Jürg Jenatsch*, translated by David B. Dickens, in *The Complete Narrative Prose*, 1976.
Der Schuss von der Kanzel. 1877; as *The Shot from the Pulpit*, translated by George F. Folkers, in *The Complete Narrative Prose*, 1976.
Der Heilige. 1880; as *Thomas à Beckett*, translated by M. von Wendheim, 1885; as *The Chancellor's Secret*, translated by Mary J. Taber, 1887; as *The Saint*, translated by Edward Franklin Hauch, 1930; also translated by George F. Folkers, in *The Complete Narrative Prose*, 1976; W.F. Twaddell, 1977.
Plautus im Nonnenkloster. 1881; as *Plautus in the Convent*, translated by William Guild Howard, with *The Monk's Marriage*, 1965.
Gustav Adolfs Page. 1882.
Das Leiden eines Knaben. 1883; as *The Tribulations of a Boy*, translated by E.M. Huggard, 1949.

Die Hochzeit des Mönchs. 1884; as *The Monk's Wedding*, translated by S.H. Adams, 1887; as *The Monk's Marriage*, translated by William Guild Howard, with *Plautus im Nonnenkloster*, 1965.
Die Richterin. 1885.
Die Versuchung des Pescara. 1887; as *The Tempting of Pescara*, translated by Clara Bell, 1890.
Angela Borgia. 1891.

Other

Louise von François und Conrad Ferdinand Meyer: Ein Briefwechsel, edited by Anton Bettelheim. 1905; revised edition, 1920.
Briefwechsel zwischen Conrad Ferdinand Meyer und Gottfried Keller. 1908.
Briefe Conrad Ferdinand Meyers nebst seinen Rezensionen und Aufsätzen, edited by Adolf Frey. 2 vols., 1908.
Conrad Ferdinand Meyer und Julius Rodenberg: Ein Briefwechsel, edited by August Langmesser. 1918.
Briefe von Conrad Ferdinand Meyer, Betsy Meyer, und J. Hardmeyer-Jenny, edited by Otto Schulthess. 1927.
Johanna Spyri, Conrad Ferdinand Meyer: Briefwechsel 1877–1897, edited by Hans and Rosemarie Zeller. 1977.
Translator, *Erzählungen aus den merowingischen Zeiten mit einleitenden Betrachtungen über die Geschichte frankreichs,* by Augustin Thierry. 1855.

*

Critical Studies: *The Poetry of Conrad Ferdinand Meyer* by Heinrich Henel, 1954; *The Stories of C.F. Meyer* by William D. Williams, 1962; *Conrad Ferdinand Meyer in Selbstzeugnissen und Bilddokumenten* by D.A. Jackson, 1975; *Conrad Ferdinand Meyer* by Marianne Burckhard, 1978; *Imagery in Conrad Ferdinand Meyer's Prose Works: Form Motifs and Functions* by Tiiu V. Lanne, 1983; *Meyer or Fontane?: German Literature after the Franco-Prussian War 1870–71* by John Osborne, 1983; *States of Consciousness in Three Tales by C.F. Meyer* by Dennis McCort, 1988; *Ambiguity as Narrative Strategy in the Prose Work of C.F. Meyer* by Deborah S. Lund, 1990.

* * *

Born in 1825 into a patrician Zurich family, Conrad Ferdinand Meyer lost his father in his youth. Rebellion against his mother's pietistic, evangelical Protestantism and against family expectations ended with him becoming a recluse. In 1852 he spent time in a mental asylum. After his mother's suicide he lived as a rentier with his sister Betsy till his marriage in 1875. Literary recognition came in 1870–71. Between then and 1892 he wrote a novel, some ten novellas, a verse cycle, and a verse epic. In 1892 insanity overtook him. He died in Kilchberg in 1898.

Meyer's work has often been disparaged. As the delicate, neurotic scion of an exhausted line, he was perpetually torn between a craving for power and passion and equally strong ingrained moral notions. He thus both indulged and censured his longings in his works, juxtaposing amoral, aesthetic Latin values with ethical, Germanic ones. In short, Renaissance was pitted against Reformation. The charge of sterile aestheticism, of art feeding off art, has also often been levelled against him. Supposedly he was too obsessed with his inner problems for social, political, or economic problems to impinge seriously upon

his attention. Post-war critics have even recommended writing off his prose works to concentrate solely on his Symbolist poems.

Such negative and narrow views of Meyer's achievement are harsh. His works are intellectually satisfying responses to many of the major issues of his time. From the 1840s to the early 1890s they grapple with social and political issues. Similarly, they reflect a life-long concern with scrutinizing religious beliefs and moral categories. Formal complexity and subtlety of content go hand in hand.

The nature of German unification under Bismarck and the ideological revisions which came in its wake sorely tested Meyer's confidence that in every area Enlightenment was conquering darkness and that a peaceful Europe of liberal nation states was emerging. Ironically, however, he depended at this time on pro-Prussian German patrons in Zurich who in 1870 insisted that he renounce all French sympathies and publicly espouse the German cause. Henceforth the patron-protégé relationship and the problem of articulating criticism of institutions and ideologies without alienating patrons and public would be at the heart of Meyer's fictions. Other taboo topics, too, could only be treated in camouflaged form.

Historically subjects provided a mask behind which he could present both personal experiences and wider contemporary issues. The verse cycle *Huttens Letzte Tage* thus captures both intimate feelings and Meyer's liberal-enlightenment view of politics and history. In the novella *Das Amulet* (*The Amulet*), which is based on Prosper Merimée's novel *Chronique du règne de Charles IX* (*A Chronicle of the Reign of Charles IX*), the pattern of significances is cleverly constructed so as to destroy the interpretation of events offered by the fictional narrator, the dogmatic Calvinist Schadau. In the novel *Georg Jenatsch* (*Jürg Jenatsch*), Meyer created a political novel which deftly criticizes its "hero" and the *Realpolitik* he espouses.

Der Heilige (*The Saint*) depicts the struggle between Thomas à Becket and Henry II. It explores the genealogy of religious and moral ideals. Developing ideas found in Thierry, Taine, Sainte-Beuve, and the Social Darwinists, Meyer anticipates Nietzsche in suggesting that Christian values may be rooted in the impotent hatred of the weak and oppressed for their brutal, physically vital masters. Behind the Saxon-Norman antithesis stands the Jewish-Roman one; behind Becket, Jesus Christ. In order to avoid exposing himself to possible scandal by being too explicit, Meyer employs a fictional narrator whom the full significance of events escapes.

Meyer's *Gedichte* [Poems] appeared in 1882. Much recent attention has justifiably focused on those poems which show Meyer to be a precursor of the Symbolist movement. Heinrich Henel (*The Poetry of Conrad Ferdinand Meyer*) argued that he sought "themes" for a small number of essential "motifs." Thanks to the critical edition we can study the complicated fates of individual motifs and poems over decades. However, it would be wrong to ignore Meyer's non-Symbolist poems or to assume that he was only interested in "the inner dream life, detachment, the rest without death" (Henel).

The novellas of the early 1880s illustrate superbly his ability to combine penetrating ruminations on his experiences with subtle diagnoses of contemporary problems. In *Das Leiden eines Knaben* (*The Tribulations of a Boy*), Louis XIV's physician, Fagon, attempts to confront the King with some of the grim realities of his realm. However, the text suggests that literature's impact on the powerful will be slight. Meyer drew on his own distressing youth in his depiction of the trials of his hero, the mentally slow Julian Boufflers. In *Die Hochzeit des Mönchs* (*The Monk's Wedding*), Dante, appalled by the autocratic Cangrande and the moral laxity of his court, relates a would-be salutary tale. Mindful that as a political refugee he cannot afford to antagonize Cangrande, he disclaims any intention of basing his fiction on his actual audience—before doing just that. Meyer's mastery of the framework technique is here at its height. The text cleverly suggests that Dante misinterprets the behaviour of the monk Astorre in whom celibacy generates sado-erotic fantasies. It also intimates that the Christian cult of suffering may cater for similar urges. In *Die Richterin* [The Judge], which fascinated Sigmund Freud, Meyer explored an even more sensitive topic, his incestuous feelings for his sister Betsy. But he also used the medieval story to challenge Rousseauesque ideas put forward by Tolstoi in *V chem moia vera?* (*My Religion*), about abolishing oaths, armies, and law courts and instead turning the other cheek.

Meyer's late fiction oscillates between Cassandra-like evocations of impending disaster and utopian hopes that a conservative solution might yet be found to the social problem. In *Die Versuchung des Pescara* (*The Tempting of Pescara*), Renaissance Italy is condemned to atone for its machiavellian *Realpolitik* and hedonism with suffering, death, and destruction. The military commander Pescara, who is ennobled and placed beyond temptation by his own fatal wound, becomes the Christ in judgement depicted in Michelangelo's Sistine frescoes. Modern Europe, too, Meyer feared, might have to endure a similar fate. As his health worsened, he himself had a desperate need to hope that death the reaper would be equally kind to him. It proved to be a vain hope.

—David Jackson

MICHAUX, Henri

Born: Namur, Belgium, 24 May 1899; French citizenship, 1955. **Education:** Educated at Putte-Grasheide, 1906–11; Jesuit College, Brussels, 1911–17; studied medicine in Brussels, 1919. **Family:** Married Marie Louise Ferdière in 1941 (died 1948). **Career:** Ship's stoker in French merchant marines, in Europe and North and South America, 1920–21; freelance writer, Brussels, 1922–24; painter, in Paris, from 1924; numerous individual exhibitions, from 1937, including retrospectives at Musée d'Art Moderne, Paris, 1978, and Guggenheim Museum, New York, 1978; editor, *Hermès* review, Paris, 1937–39. **Awards:** Einaudi prize 1960; he refused the National Grand prize for letters (France), 1965. **Died:** 17 October 1984.

PUBLICATIONS

Collections

Darkness Moves: An Henri Michaux Anthology, 1927–1984, edited and translated by David Ball. 1994.

Verse

Qui je fus. 1927.
Mes propriétés (includes prose). 1929.
Trois nuits. 1930.
Une certaine Plume. 1930.
La Nuit remue. 1935; revised editions, 1967, 1985.
La Ralentie. 1937.

Plume, précédé de Lointain intérieur. 1938; revised editions, 1967, 1984.
Au Pays de la magie (includes prose poems). 1941; edited by Peter Broome, 1977.
Je vous écris d'un pays lointain. 1942.
Épreuves, exorcismes 1940–44. 1945.
Liberté d'Action. 1945.
Apparitions, illustrated by Michaux. 1946.
Ici Poddema. 1946.
Ailleurs (includes *Voyage en Grande Garabagne; Au pays de la magie; Ici Poddema*). 1948; revised editions, 1967, 1984.
La Vie dans les plis. 1949; revised editions, 1972, 1979, 1989.
Poésie pour pouvoir. 1949.
Passages 1937–1950. 1950; revised edition, 1963.
Mouvements, illustrated by Michaux. 1951.
Face aux verrous. 1954; revised edition, 1967.
Paix dans les brisements, illustrated by Michaux. 1959.
Vers la complétude (Saisie et dessaisies). 1967.
Poems, translated by Teo Savory. 1967.
Moments: Traversées du temps. 1973.
Vers les icebergs (includes prose). 1973.
Choix de poèmes (selection). 1976.
Jours de silence. 1978.
Par des traits (includes prose). 1984.
Déplacements, Dégagements (includes prose). 1985; as *Spaced, Displaced*, edited and translated by David and Helen Constantine, 1991.

Fiction

Voyage en Grande Garabagne. 1936.

Plays

Quand tombent les toits. 1973.

Screenplays: *Images du monde visionnaire*, with Eric Duvivier, 1963.

Other

Fables des origines. 1923.
Les Rêves et la jambe. 1923.
Ecuador: Journal de voyage. 1929; revised editions, 1968, 1980, 1990; as *Ecuador: A Travel Journal*, translated by Robin Magowan, 1968.
Un barbare en Asie. 1933; revised edition, 1967; as *A Barbarian in Asia*, translated by Sylvia Beach, 1949.
Entre centre et absence, illustrated by Michaux. 1936.
Sifflets dans le temple. 1936.
Peintures. 1939.
Arbres des tropiques, illustrated by Michaux. 1941.
Exorcismes, illustrated by Michaux. 1943.
Tu vas être père (published anonymously, privately printed). 1943.
Labyrinthes, illustrated by Michaux. 1944.
Le Lobe des monstres, illustrated by Michaux. 1944.
L'Espace du dedans. 1945; revised editions, 1966, 1977; as *Selected Writings: The Space Within*, translated by Richard Ellmann, 1951.
Peintures et dessins. 1946.
Arriver à se réveiller. 1947.
Nous deux encores. 1948.

Meidosems, illustrated by Michaux. 1948; as *Meiclosems: Poems and Lithographs*, translated by Elizabeth R. Jackson, 1993.

Lecture, illustrated by Zao-Wou-Ki. 1950.

Tranches de savoir; suivi du Secret de la situation politique. 1950.

Veille. 1951.

Nouvelles de l'étranger. 1952.

Quatre cents hommes en croix, illustrated by Michaux. 1956.

Misérable miracle, illustrated by Michaux. 1956; revised edition, 1972; as *Miserable Miracle: Mescaline*, translated by Louise Varèse, 1963.

L'Infini turbulent, illustrated by Michaux. 1957; revised edition, 1964; as *Infinite Turbulence*, translated by Michael Fineberg, 1975.

Vigies sur cible. 1959.

Connaissance par les gouffres. 1961; revised edition, 1984; as *Light Through Darkness: Explorations Through Drugs*, translated by Haakon Chevalier, 1963.

Vents et poussières 1955–1962, illustrated by Michaux. 1962.

Les présences qui ne devraient pas être là. 1965.

Les Grandes Épreuves de l'esprit et les innombrables petites (autobiography). 1966; as *The Major Ordeals of the Mind and Countless Minor Ones*, translated by Richard Howard, 1974.

Parcours, edited by René Bertelé. 1967.

Façons d'endormi, façons d'éveillé. 1969.

Poteaux d'angle. 1971; revised edition, 1981.

Emergences-Résurgences, illustrated by Michaux. 1972.

En rêvant à partir de peintures énigmatiques. 1972.

Bras cassé. 1973.

Par la voie des rythmes. 1974.

Moriturus. 1974.

Coups d'arrêt. 1975.

Face à ce qui se dérobe. 1975.

Idéogrammes en Chine. 1975; as *Ideogrames in China*, translated by Gustaf Sobin, 1984.

Les Ravagés. 1976.

Jours de silence. 1978.

Henri Michaux: A Selection, translated by Michael Fineberg. 1979.

Saisir. 1979.

Une voie pour l'insubordination. 1980.

Comme un ensablement. 1981.

Affrontements (selection). 1981.

Chemins cherchés, Chemins perdus, Transgressions. 1981.

En appel de visages, illustrated by Michaux. 1983.

Le Jardin exalté. 1983.

Par surprise. 1983; as *By Surprise*, translated by Randolph Hough, 1987.

Les Commencements: dessins d'enfants, essais d'enfants. 1983.

*

Critical Studies: *Découvrons Henri Michaux* by André Gide, 1941; *Michaux* by René Bertelé, 1946, revised edition, 1980; *Michaux* by Robert Bréchon, 1959; *Henri Michaux; ou, Une Mesure de l'être* by Raymond Bellour, 1965; *Henri Michaux* by Kurt Leonhard, 1967; *Michaux: A Study of His Literary Works* by Malcolm Bowie, 1973; *Henri Michaux peintre* by Geneviève Bonnefoi, 1976; *Ruptures sur Henri Michaux* by Roger Dadoun, 1976; *Henri Michaux* by Peter Broome, 1977; *Henri Michaux* by Virginia La Charité, 1977; *Creatures Within: Imaginary Beings in the Work of Henri Michaux* by Frederic Shepler, 1977; *From the Gloom of Today to New Greatness of Man: Itinerary by Henri Michaux, Builder of New Poetry* by L.A. Velinsky, 1977; *Le Fantasmagorie dans l'oeuvre d'Henri Michaux* by James Burty David, 1981; *Michaux: Passager clandestin* by Jean-Michel Maulpoix, 1984; *Le Darçana d'Henri Michaux* by Gabriel Bounoure, 1985; *Improvisations sur Henri Michaux* by Michel Butor, 1985; *Henri Michaux and the Poetics of Movement* by Laurie Edson, 1985; *Passages et langages de Henri Michaux* edited by Jean-Claude Mathieu and Michel Collot, 1987; *Signs in Action: The Ideograms of Ezra Pound and Henri Michaux* by Richard Sieburth, 1987; *Henri Michaux: Qui êtes-vous?* by Brigitte Ouvry-Vial, 1989; *Michaux: The Poet of Supreme Solipsism* by Lawrence Durrell, 1990; *Henri Michaux* by Jean-Dominique Rey, 2001.

*   *   *

Henri Michaux, rebel against literary stereotypes and clichés of vision, ruthless explorer of his own restless and deceptive inner movements, dark and disturbing artist of a poetics of the metamorphic and the imperfect, ingenious technician in the seams of the unconscious, penetrating humourist deft at exposing the absurdities of human behaviour, and stylist of an uncanny balance poised between the lucid and the hallucinatory, the harmless and the horrific, the controlled and the uncontrollable, has stamped himself as one of the great original spirits of 20th-century French writing.

The title of Michaux's first collection, *Qui je fus* [Who I Was], touches the theme of the divisions and the disperion of the self: a moving round of enigmas, oddities, and threatening contradictions. It was followed in 1929 by *Mes propriétés* [My Properties], where a groping protagonist, precursor of Beckett's alienated derelicts, seeks to appropriate the intractable and senseless matter of reality; where the author, by a quirkish humour and a private psychological magic, grapples with the unpredictabilities of a hostile or unaccommodating world. This humour of the absurd takes full flight in *Un certain Plume* [A Certain Plume] in the creation of the character Plume, a featherweight *étranger* in the family of Kafka's K. or Camus's Meursault, embodying what Camus calls the "divorce between the actor and his decor, man and his life," but rebounding, Chaplin-like, through the caprices and incomprehensibilities of a foreign order.

One of the century's most wilful *déracinés*, Michaux has been tempted by the disruptive trajectories of travel. His travel journal *Ecuador: Journal de voyage* (*Ecuador: A Travel Journal*), spasmodically charting a year's arduous descent from the Andes to the Amazon estuary, is an abrasive antidote to romanticism and exoticism: curt, unillusioned, denuded. The travelogue which followed, *Un barbare en Asie* (*A Barbarian in Asia*), is by contrast receptive, effervescent, and stylistically provocative as it flits dextrously and with probing analysis through the mentality and idiosyncrasies of the Indians, Malays, Chinese, Indonesians, and Japanese. Their conclusion, however, is the same: that the answer lies not in the outside world or external movement, but in the infinite mobility and unexplored expanses of the *lointain intérieur*, that *espace du dedans* which gives its title to the major collective anthology of Michaux's work.

Just as the displaced person Plume was already a buffer-character wedged comically between hostile powers, so the imaginary lands, Grande Garabagne, the Pays de la Magie, and Poddema, depicted in Michaux's great trilogy *Ailleurs*, are described by the author as "buffer-states," situated disconcertingly between external observation and inner obsession, the enchanting and the grotesque, entertaining fancy and the most biting satirical and moral diagnosis. Here, in weird utopias reminiscent of Jonathan Swift's *Gulliver's Travels*,

Samuel Butler's *Erewhonor*, or Aldous Huxley's *Brave New World*, the author and the world, the real and the ideal, play out a balance of power in a no-man's land which is fascinating and at times unnerving.

Michaux's "resistance" poetry of World War II is collected in *Épreuves, exorcismes 1940–44* [Ordeals, Exorcisms 1940–44], famous for its idiosyncratic definition of poetry as exorcism and notable for its resourceful counter-measures against institutions and nightmares of monstrosity.

La Vie dons les plis and *Face aux verrous* invite us into the full display of the ingenuities of the poet's inner workshop; philosophical maxims that freeze, long poems whipping up ungovernable energies, tongue-in-cheek analyses that hold reality in check, turn it topsy-turvy or twist its neck, strange metaphorical configurations depicting the deepest dualities of human nature, flexible lyrical forays into zones of spriritual movement that defy identification. These texts lead in turn to Michaux's vast explorations, in the wake of De Quincey, Baudelaire, and Aldous Huxley, of the furthermost reaches of the human mind as revealed through drugs: its rhythms and tempos, its visions and blanks, its incurable ambivalences, its dazzling captures and clumsy impotences, its euphoric joys and unbearable tortures, as evoked in *Misérable miracle* (*Miserable Miracle: Mescaline*), *L'Infini turbulent* (*Infinite Turbulence*), *Connaissance par les gouffres* (*Light Through Darkness: Explorations Through Drugs*), or *Les Grandes Épreuves de l'esprit et les innombrables petites* (*The Major Ordeals of the Mind and Countless Minor Ones*). One should mention, finally, the remarkable poetry of a collection such as *Moments: Traversées du temps* [Moments: Travels in Time]: transcendental intuitions of a cleansing purity, precariously held in space and almost beyond expression, which act as a reminder that Michaux, endlessly inventive, has never ceased to shape new definitions of poetic language.

—Peter Broome

MICKIEWICZ, Adam (Bernard)

Born: Zaosie, near Nowogródek, Lithuania, 24 December 1798. **Education:** Educated at a secondary school in Nowogródek, graduated 1815; University of Wilno (Vilnius), 1815–19. **Family:** Married Celina Szymanowska; two sons and two daughters. **Career:** Teacher at a gymnasium, Kowno, 1819–23; arrested for membership in the literary group Philomaths, considered conspiratorial and anti-Russian, 1823: exiled to Russia, 1824; lived in St. Petersburg, 1824, and 1827–29; high school teacher, Odessa, 1824–26; lived in Moscow, 1826, where he became friends with Pushkin, *q.v.*; travelled in Europe, 1829–32; settled in Paris, 1832; editor, *The Pilgrim*, 1833; professor of Latin, Collège de Lausanne, 1839–40; professor of Slavonic languages and literatures, Collège de France, Paris, 1840–44; attempted to raise a Polish military unit, 1848; editor, *La Tribune des peuples*, Paris, 1849; librarian, Arsenal Library, Paris, 1852. **Died:** 26 November 1855, of cholera in Constantinople while attempting to help Poles in Crimean War.

PUBLICATIONS

Collections

Dziela (includes letters), edited by Leon Płoszewski. 16 vols., 1948–55.

Sun of Liberty: Bicentenary Anthology, 1798–1998: Polish-English Edition, edited and translated by Michael J. Mikós. 1998.
Treasury of Love Poems by Adam Mickiewicz: In Polish and English, compiled and edited by Krystyna S. Olszer. 1998.

Verse

Poezje 1–2 [Poetry]. 2 vols., 1822–23.
Grażyna. 1823; as *Grazyna*, translated by Irene Suboczewski, with *Konrad Wallenrod*, 1989.
Sonety [Sonnets]. 1826.
Sonety krymskie. 1826; as *Sonnets from Crimea*, translated by Edna Worthley Underwood, 1917.
Konrad Wallenrod. 1828; as *Konrad Wallenrod*, translated by M.A. Biggs (verse), 1882; also translated by G.R. Noyes and Dorothea Prall Radin, in *Konrad Wallenrod and Other Writings*, 1925; Irene Suboczewski, with *Grazyna*, 1989.
Pan Tadeusz. 1834; as *Master Thaddeus; or, The Last Foray in Lithuania*, translated by M.A. Biggs, 2 vols., 1885; as *Pan Tadeusz*, translated by G.R. Noyes (prose), 1917, revised edition, 1930; also translated by Watson Kirkconnell (verse), 1962; Kenneth R. Mackenzie (verse), 1964.
Selected Poems, translated by W.J. Linton. 1881.
Gems of Polish Poetry (selection), translated by Frank H. Fortey. 1923.
Abdication of the Sun (includes passages from *Forefathers*), translated by Count Potocki of Montalk. 1938.
The Lilies, Twardowski's Wife, and Religious Poems, translated by Dorothea Prall Radin. 1938.
Poems, edited by G.R. Noyes, various translators. 1944.
Mickiewicz in Music: Twenty Five Songs to Poems of Mickiewicz, edited by Arthur P. and Marion M. Coleman. 1947.
Twenty Five Poems (in English), edited by Arthur P. and Marion M. Coleman, various translators. 1955.
Selected Poems and New Selected Poems, edited by Clark Mills, various translators. 2 vols., 1956–57.
Poems, translated by Jack Lindsay. 1957.

Plays

Dziady (dramatic poem). 2 vols., 1823–32; as *Forefathers' Eve*, edited by G.R. Noyes, translated by Dorothea Prall Radin, 1925; translated as *Forefathers*, in *Poems*, edited by G.R. Noyes, 1944; *Forefathers' Eve* (part III), translated by Count Potocki of Montalk, 1946; also translated by Harold B. Segel, in *Polish Romantic Drama*, 1977; selections translated by Count Potocki, in *Abdication of the Sun*, 1938.

Other

Księgi narodu i pielgrzymstwa polskiego [The Books of the Polish Nation and Polish Pilgrimage]. 1832.
L'Église officielle et le Messianisme, L'Église et le Messie (lectures). 1845.
Konrad Wallenrod and Other Writings, edited by G.R. Noyes, translated by Jewell Parish, Dorothea Prall Radin, and G.R. Noyes. 1925.
Selected Poetry and Prose, edited by Stanislaw Helsztynski, various translators. 1955.
Translator, *Giaour*, by Byron. 1833.

*

Bibliography: *Mickiewicz: His Life and Work in Documents, Portraits, and Illustrations* by Marie Kapuścieńska and Wanda Markowska, 1956; *Bibliografia utworów: Adama Mickiewicza* by Aleksander Semkowicz, 1958.

Critical Studies: *Adam Mickiewicz: The National Poet of Poland* by Monica M. Gardner, 1911; *Mickiewiczana: Articles, Translations and Bibliographies of Interest to Students of Mickiewicz* edited by Arthur P. and Marion M. Coleman, 1946; *Adam Mickiewicz: The Life Story of the Greatest Polish Poet* by Ksawery Pruszynski, 1950; *Adam Mickiewicz, Poet of Poland: A Symposium* edited by Manfred Kridl, 1951; *Adam Mickiewicz in English*, 1954, and *Young Mickiewicz*, 1956, both by Marion M. Coleman; *The Poetry of Mickiewicz*, 1954, and *Literature as Prophecy: Scholarship and Martinist Poetics in Adam Mickiewicz' Parisian Lectures*, 1959, both by Wiktor Weintraub; *Mickiewicz 1798–1855: In Commemoration of the Centenary of His Death*, 1955; *Adam Mickiewicz* by Mieczysław Jastrun, 1955; *Mickiewicz in World Literature: A Symposium* edited by Waclaw Lednicki, 1956; *Adam Mickiewicz* by David Welsh, 1966; *Pushkin, Mickiewicz and the Overcoming of Romanticism* by Monika A. Dudli, 1976; *Country of the Mind: An Introduction to the Poetry of Adam Mickiewicz* by Anita Debska, 2000; *The Poetics of Revitalization: Adam Mickiewicz between Forefathers' Eve, Part 3, and Pan Tadeusz*, by Roman Robert Koropeckyj, 2001.

*   *   *

Few writers have had quite the impact on their own nation as Adam Mickiewicz. Hailed after the publication of his first volume of verse in 1822 as an innovator, Mickiewicz continually surprised his readers with experiments and changes in form and content, much like Chopin, his contemporary, in another medium. Mickiewicz's legacy is not merely represented by an "oeuvre complète"—it must also include what may be termed his contribution to a nation's mentality: the association of historical past to prophetic future, patriotic cause to spiritual aspiration, and national to personal despair.

That first collection of poems, based on peasant song and local legend, is indebted to the precedents and theories of German Romanticism, and emphasizes emotionality and authenticity. Mickiewicz's next artistic success, more formal and conventional, was with two sets of sonnets. One, entitled simply *Sonety* [Sonnets], deals with lovers' emotional games, the ennuis of the fashionable salons, and impressions of nature. The other set, *Sonety krymskie* (*Sonnets from Crimea*), is Mickiewicz's finest poetic achievement. They are intricate and delicate as miniatures; the language is inventive and captivating, and the style exotic, all intensified by the sonnet form. Mickiewicz the poet-pilgrim travels through a landscape that is wild, rich, and mystical, and momentarily finds himself a home. Yet his sense of nationality overpowers him as he ponders his isolation, and the Oriental environment only exaggerates his contradictory feelings of impotence, commitment, and spirituality.

The *Dziady* (*Forefathers' Eve*) series of dramatized poems, completed by 1832, and inspired by the very real but very unsuccessful November Uprising of 1830, blends history and soteriology, student plots and superstition, horror and comedy. It is a vital stage of Mickiewicz's self-revelatory voyage through the Polish national consciousness, and is still the most formative and informative source of a national historiosophy (Polish Messianism) ever written, influencing all generations that followed. Konrad, the hero of the crucial

third part of *Forefathers' Eve* (*Część III*), is portrayed as the poet-battleground for the opposing forces of Good (Poland/Catholicism) and Evil (the Tsar/Lucifer/Russia). Improvisation, ritual, visions, and historical events merge as Lucifer's Russian lackeys contrive the downfall and possession of Konrad. Exorcized of these forces, Konrad, as the horseman of apocalyptic national liberation, goes forth for the cause. The sequel showing how this liberation would come about was never written, but the result was that Mickiewicz had created a new stereotype: a nationalized poet with Catholicized patriotism instilled.

Pan Tadeusz, written not long after *Forefathers' Eve*, seems different yet again. Mickiewicz's last significant work, it is an "autobiographical" epic poem recounting the euphoria of his adolescence, when in 1811–12 Napoleon's troops liberated Poland and Lithuania en route to Moscow. Superficially a superior satire on the lifestyle of the Lithuanian gentry, *Pan Tadeusz* is also a subtle compilation of most of the themes in previous works in an idealized setting. Here the "old country's" virtues and vices are paraded, highlighting the xenophobic, anarchistic attitudes that led to the Partitions of 1795, remaining at the same time a sentimental portrayal of the characters concerned. The poem charts how the bumbling gentry replaces personal concerns with national cause, and selfishness with self-sacrifice. This Catholic morality is the real tenor of the work: the blinding faith exemplified by the saint-hero in monk's clothing, Jacek Soplica (expiating before God and country his youthful treason), is matched by the patriotic fervour of his son Tadeusz (thus abandoning the delights of adolescent innocence). As Mickiewicz bitterly admitted in his Epilogue to the work, such zeal led nowhere. In recounting his vision of the past and its truth, the historical detail and depiction of traditional social graces alone make *Pan Tadeusz* a masterpiece. Like *Forefathers' Eve* it was read by a nation in geographical exile as a true picture of its origins and aspirations, a Messianic covenant of national identity.

Mickiewicz wrote through the prism of his own experiences. His poetic output reflects the changes in and around him, in his culture and his fellow Poles, but does not reflect the enormous contribution Mickiewicz made to that nation and its people.

—Donald Peter Alexander Pirie

See the essay on *Pan Tadeusz*.

MIŁOSZ, Czesław

Born: Szetejnie, Lithuania, 30 June 1911; naturalized American citizen, 1970. **Education:** Educated at the high school in Wilno (Vilnius); University of Stefan Batory, Wilno, M. Juris 1934; studied in Paris, 1934–35. **Career:** Co-founder of the literary periodical *Żagary* [Charred Wood], 1931; programmer, Polish National Radio, 1935–39; took part in the Polish Resistance during World War II; member of editorial group of monthly journal *Twórczość* [Creativity], 1945; member of the Polish Diplomatic Service, Washington, DC, 1945–49, and Paris, 1950; defected to the West, 1951; freelance writer in Paris, 1951–60; visiting lecturer, 1960–61, professor of Slavic languages and literatures, 1961–78, and professor emeritus, from 1978, University of California, Berkeley. Lives in the United States. **Awards:** European literary prize, 1953; Kister award, 1967; Jurzykowski Foundation award, 1968; Creative Arts fellowship,

1968; Polish PEN Club award for translation, 1974; Guggenheim fellowship, 1976; Neustadt international prize, 1978; Nobel prize for literature, 1980; Bay Area Book Reviewers prize, 1985; National Medal of Arts (United States), 1989. Litt.D.: University of Michigan, Ann Arbor, 1977; honorary doctorate: Catholic University, Lublin, 1981; Brandeis University, Waltham, Massachusetts, 1983; Harvard University, Cambridge, Massachusetts, 1989; Jagiellonian University, Cracow, 1989; University of Rome, 1992.

PUBLICATIONS

Verse

Poemat o czasie zastygłym [A Poem on Time Frozen]. 1933.
Trzy Zimy [Three Winters]. 1936.
Wiersze [Poems] (as J. Syruć). 1940.
Ocalenie [Rescue]. 1945.
Światło dzienne [Daylight]. 1953.
Traktat poetycki [Treatise on Poetry]. 1957.
Kontynenty [Continents]. 1958.
Król Popiel i inne wiersze [King Popiel and Other Poems]. 1962.
Gucio zaczarowany [Bobo's Metamorphosis]. 1965.
Wiersze [Poems]. 1967.
Lied vom Weltende [Song for the End of the World]. 1967.
Miasto bez imienia [City Without a Name]. 1969.
Selected Poems. 1973; revised edition, 1981.
Gdzie wschodzi słońce i kiedy zapada [From Where the Sun Rises to Where It Sets]. 1974.
Utwory poetyckie [Selected Poems]. 1976.
Bells in Winter, translated by Miłosz and Lillian Vallee. 1978.
Poezje [Poems]. 1981.
Moja wierna mowo [My Faithful Tongue]. 1981.
Wiersze wybrane [Selected Poems]. 1981.
Traktat moralny [A Moral Treatise]. 1981.
Hymn o perle [Hymn to the Pearl]. 1982.
Poezje [Poems]. 1982.
Wiersze [Poems]. 1983.
The Separate Notebooks, translated by Robert Hass and Robert Pinsky. 1984.
Nieobjęta ziemia. 1984; as *The Unattainable Earth*, translated by Robert Hass, 1986.
Wiersze [Poems]. 1985.
The View, translated by Miłosz and Lillian Vallee. 1985.
Dziewięć wierszy [Nine Poems], with Karl Dedecius. 1987.
Kroniki [Chronicles]. 1987.
The Collected Poems 1931–1987. 1988.
Świat/The World (bilingual edition), translated by Miłosz. 1989.
Provinces: Poems 1987–1991, translated by Miłosz and Robert Haas. 1991.
Facing the River: New Poems, translated by Miłosz and Robert Haas. 1995.

Fiction

Zdobycie Władzy (first published in French as *La Prise du pouvoir*, translated by Jeanne Hersch, 1953). 1955; as *The Seizure of Power*, translated by Celina Wieniewska, 1955; as *The Usurpers*, translated by Wieniewska, 1955.

Dolina Issy. 1955; as *The Issa Valley*, translated by Louis Iribarne, 1981.

Other

Zniewolony umysł (essays). 1953; as *The Captive Mind*, translated by Jane Zielonko, 1953.
Praca i jej gorycze [Work and Its Discontents]. 1957.
Rodzinna Europa (essays). 1959; as *Native Realm: A Search for Self-Definition*, translated by Catherine S. Leach, 1968.
Człowiek wśród skorpionów: Studium o Stanisławie Brzozowskim [A Man among Scorpions: A Study of Stanisław Brzozowski]. 1962.
The History of Polish Literature. 1969; revised edition, 1983.
Widzenia nad Zatok San Francisco. 1969; as *Visions from San Francisco Bay*, translated by Richard Lourie, 1982.
Prywatne obowizki [Private Obligations] (essays). 1972.
Mój wiek: pamiętnik mówiony [My Century: An Oral Diary] (interview with Alexander Wat), edited by Lidia Ciołkoszowa. 2 vols., 1977.
Emperor of the Earth: Modes of Eccentric Vision. 1977.
Ziemia Ulro. 1977; as *The Land of Ulro*, translated by Louis Iribarne, 1984.
Ogród nauk [The Garden of Knowledge]. 1980.
Nobel Lecture. 1981.
Swiadectwo poezji: sześć wykładów o dotkliwości naszego wieku (lectures). 1983; as *The Witness of Poetry*, 1983.
Dzieła zbiorowe [Collected Works]. 12 vols., 1984–85.
Poszukiwania: wybór publicystyki rozproszonej 1931–1983 [Search: Selection of Essays from 1931–1938]. 1985.
Zaczynajac od moich ulic. 1985; as *Beginning with My Streets: Baltic Reflections*, translated by Madeline G. Levine, 1992.
Conversations with Czesław Milosz, with Ewa Czarnecka and Aleksander Fiut. 1987.
Czesława Miłosza autoportret przekorny [Czesław Miłosz's Wilful Self-Portrait] (interviews), with Aleksander Fiut. 1988.
Exiles, photographs by Josef Koudelka. 1988.
Metafizyczna pauza [Metaphysical Intervals]. 1989.
Rok myśliwego. 1990; as *A Year of the Hunter*, translated by Madeline G. Levine, 1994.
Listy [Letters], with Thomas Merton. 1991.
Listy do Czesława Miłosza, 1952–1979 [Letters], edited by Renata Gorczyńska. 1992.
Szukanie ojczyzny. 1992.
Editor, with Zbigniew Folejewski, *Antologia poezji spol; asecznej* [Anthology of Social Poetry]. 1933.
Editor, *Pieśń niepodległa* [Invincible Song]. 1942.
Editor and Translator, *Drogami klęski* [On the Roads of Defeat], by Jacques Maritain. 1942.
Editor and Translator, *Polityka i rzeczywistość* [Politics and Reality], by Jeanne Hersch. 1955.
Editor and Translator, *Praca i jej gorycze* [Work and Its Discontents], by Daniel Bell. 1957.
Editor and Translator, *Wybór pism* [Selected Works], by Simone Weil. 1958.
Editor, *Kultura masowa* [Mass Culture]. 1959.
Editor, *Węgry* [Hungary]. 1960.
Editor and Translator, *Postwar Polish Poetry: An Anthology.* 1965; revised edition, 1983.
Editor, *Lettres inédites de O.V. de L. Milosz à Christian Gauss.* 1976.

Editor and Translator, *Mediterranean Poems*, by Alexander War. 1977.

Editor and Translator, with Leonard Nathan, *With the Skin: The Poems of Aleksander Wat*. 1989.

Editor and Translator, *Haiku*. 1992.

Translator, with Peter Dale Scott, *Selected Poems*, by Zbigniew Herbert. 1968.

Translator, *Ewangelia według św. Marka* [The Gospel According to St. Mark]. 1978.

Translator, *Księga Hioba* [The Book of Job]. 1980.

Translator, *Ksiega psalmów* [Psalms]. 1980.

Translator, *Księgi pięciu megilot*. 1984.

Translator, with Leonard Nathan, *Happy as a Dog's Tail*, by Anna Swir. 1985.

Translator, *Mowa wizana* [Poetry Language]. 1986.

*

Critical Studies: Miłosz issues of *World Literature Today*, 52, Summer 1978, and *Ironwood*, 18, 1981; *Czesław Miłosz and the Insufficiency of Lyric* by Donald Davie, 1986; *Between Anxiety and Hope: The Poetry of Czesław Miłosz*, edited by Edward Mozejko, 1988; *The Eternal Moment: The Poetry of Czesław Miłosz* by Aleksander Fiut, translated by Theodosia S. Robertson, 1990; *The Poet's Work: An Introduction to Czesław Miłosz* by Leonard Nathan and Arthur Quinn, 1991; *Dynamics of Being, Space, and Time in the Poetry of Czesław Miłosz and John Ashbery* by Barbara Malinowska, 2000.

*   *   *

Czesław Miłosz is an outstanding figure of 20th-century Polish literature. In his youth he belonged to the so-called "Second Vanguard," the poetry of which was characterized by neo-symbolistic tendencies of a "catastrophist" kind. Miłosz's poetry before World War II suggests the nearness of some kind of a cataclysm; there is a "thorn of prophecy" in these otherwise carefully structured, distant, and allusive poems. During the war the poet's perception of reality and with it his poetic language underwent a substantial change—in the cycle *Świat* (*The World*) and even more so in the collection *Ocalenie* [Rescue], he dropped many of his poetic adornments of the 1930s and tried to redefine the world in terms of compassion and hope. At the same time he was profoundly disturbed by the brutality of totalitarianism and the savagery of war, as in "Dedication":

What is poetry which does not save
Nations or people?
A connivance with official lies,
A song of drunkards whose throats
will be cut in a moment.

The antinomies of Miłosz's poetry are between "immoral" beauty and "moral" truth, between chaos and order, nature and civilization. His poetry is pervaded by a strong historicism and a constant awareness of transience, and the poet himself seems to oscillate between his "private cares" and contemplations and his historical, even social preoccupations. This is reflected by the "polyphony" of Miłosz's poetic voices, stressed by Jan Blonski in his essay in *World Literature Today* (Summer 1978); he sometimes speaks with different voices within the same poem. Nevertheless, his longer poems *Traktat moralny* [A Moral Treatise] and *Traktat poetycki* [Treatise on Poetry] are didactic in a way that has not been attempted since Cyprian Norwid. *Traktat poetycki* is a multi-faceted, ironic survey of Polish literature since the end of the 19th century.

In California Miłosz's poetry became more introspective and absorbed elements of surrealism in poems such as "Album snów" [Album of Dreams] and "Po ziemi naszej" [Throughout Our Lands]. The most representative piece of his Californian period, the long polyphonic poem *Gdzie wschodzi słońce i kiedy zapada* [From Where the Sun Rises to Where It Sets] blends memories of the poet's childhood and youth with the imagery of American nature and with eschatological expectations of the Last Judgement.

Miłosz's reputation as a writer of fiction rests on a number of novels of which the compelling *Dolina Issy* (*The Issa Valley*), a Manichean tale of the poet's childhood in densely wooded Lithuania, is the most accomplished. *Rodzinna Europa* (*Native Realm*) is also written in the autobiographical vein but with the purpose of tracing the author's intellectual development from his university years in Wilno (through Paris) to his settling down in Warsaw. None the less, it was *Zniewolony umysł* (*The Captive Mind*) that made Miłosz best known outside Poland. Written soon after his break with the Communist Polish authorities in 1951, this book is an incisive and rather pessimistic analysis of the intricate mechanism of the Polish intelligentsia's adaptation to Communist ideology. Miłosz has also written several books of essays on Polish and American themes—of these *Widzenia nad Zatok San Francisco* (*Visions from San Francisco Bay*), written "to exorcize the evil spirit of contemporary times," should have the greatest appeal to the general reader.

Miłosz is the author of a comprehensive and challenging history of Polish literature, *The History of Polish Literature*, and an excellent translator. He has translated into Polish among other things the writings of T.S. Eliot and Simone Weil, and has published an anthology of Polish poetry in English translation, *Postwar Polish Poetry*. In recent years his most interesting prose publication has been the "literary diary" of *Rok myśliwego* (*A Year of the Hunter*), which records Miłosz's thoughts, memories, comments, and travels throughout the year 1987–88. It shows that advancing age has impaired neither Miłosz's critical judgement nor his ability to assist in the political transformation for which Central- and East-European intellectuals have been striving.

—George Gömöri

MĪRĀ BĀĪ

Also known as Mirabai. **Born:** Into a leading family of the Rajput (warrior caste) in Kuraki, Rajasthan (now Karachi, Pakistan), 1498. After death of her mother in childhood, probably brought up by Rathore Rao Dūdā (who may have been her grandfather). **Family:** Married Kumvar Bhojrāj in 1516 (died 1522). **Career:** After her husband's death, started composing verses in praise of Kṛṣṇa in a mixture of the Rajasthani and Brajbhāṣā languages; left marital home at Chittor and made a pilgrimage around Northern India, 1534, settling in Dwarka, Gujurat. Several works supposedly by her are of questionable attribution. **Died:** in 1546/47 (some sources give 1563/65).

PUBLICATIONS

Works

Padāvalī, as *Sangīt-Rāg-Kalpadruma* (includes 43 poems), edited by K.D. Vyās, 1842; also edited by G.M Kārlekar, in *Bhajan bhaṇḍār* (includes 352 poems), 1922, B. Miśra Mādhava, in *Mīrā ki premsādhanā* (126 poems), 1934, Rāmalochana Ṣarmā, in *Mīrāṁ-kī prema-vāṇī* , 1945, Padmāvatī Śabanam, in *Mīrābrhat pad sangraha* (590 poems), 1952, Brajratnadās, in *Mīrā-mādhurī* (469 poems), 1956, A. Svarūp, in *Mīrāsudhāsindhu* (1,312 poems), 1957, Paraśūram Caturvedī in *Mīrābāī kī Padāvalī* 1973; selections as: *Songs of Mirabai*, translated by Ram Chandra Tandan, 1934; *Three Mughal Poets: Mir, Sauda, Mir Hasan*, translated by Ralph Russell and Khurshidul Islam, 1968; *Devotional Poems*, translated by Shreeprakash Kurl, 1973; *Songs of Mirabei*, translated by Pritish Nandi, 1975; *Mira the Divine Lover*, translated by V.K. Sethi, 1979; *Devotional Poems*, translated by A.J. Alston, 1980; *Mirabei Versions*, adapted by Robert Bly, 1980; *For Love of the Dark One: Songs of Mirabai*, translated by Andrew Schelling, 1993; *In the Dark of the Heart: Songs of Meera*, translated by Shama Futehally, 1994; *Mīrābāī and Her Padas*, translated by Krishna P. Bahadur, 1998; *Mira: The Call of the Heart: Mira bhajans*, translated by Sushil Rao, 2000.

*

Critical Studies: *A Monograph on Mirabai, the Saint of Mewad* by Sambhuprasad Sivaprasad Mehtā, 1920; *Mirabai: Saint and Singer*, by Vasu Anātha-Nātha, 1934; *Mira Bai: Her Life and Times* by Hermann Goetz, 1966; *Mira Bai* by U.S. Nilsson, 1969; *Mīrāṁbāī kā jīvanvṛtt evaṁ kāvya* [On the Life and Works of Mīrā Bāī] (includes text of previously unpublished *Padas*) by K. Śekhāvat, 1974; "Mīrā Bāī", in *History of Rajasthani Literature* by Hiralal Maheshwari, 1980; *Saint Mira Bai, the Gopi Incarnate* by Srila Gurudev Gopal Gosvami, 1986; *Upholding the Common Life: The Community of Mirabai* by Parita Mukta, 1994; *Sweet on My Lips: The Love Poems of Mirabai* by Louise Landes Levi, 1997.

* * *

The celebrated poet-saint of medieval India, Mīrā Bāī, was born in 1498 to one of the most illustrious Rajput (warrior caste) families. In 1516 she married but became a widow a few years later. The task she faced was an uphill one, since the rigid conventions and traditions of conduct imposed upon her by the Rajput aristocracy to which she belonged made her life extremely difficult. A second marriage being out of the question, she tried to achieve self-realization on an altogether different plane: that of devotion to Kṛṣṇa, incarnation of the Hindu god, Viṣṇu. It is related that, when a child, she was one day watching a marriage procession from the balcony of her palace and asked her mother who the man riding on the horse was. When told he was the bridegroom, she asked who was *her* bridegroom. Pointing to a statue of Kṛṣṇa in the palace, her mother said that he was her bridegroom. After that, Mīrā became a devotee of Kṛṣṇa. What the name and figure of Kṛṣṇa signified became the *raison d'être* of her life, the goal of all goals. This brought her into conflict with the manner in which she, as a royal widow, was expected to behave. However, neither her social and family background, nor the inflexible caste ethos could bend her will; in fact, they strengthened it all the more.

The circumstances and restraints in her life are reflected in her poetry, even though it is largely concerned with Mira's love for Kṛṣṇa, something at once mystical and religious, but treated in terms of human and earthly love:

Mother, I have bought Śyām.
Some say I bought him secretly,
some say openly, but
I bought him by beat of drum.
Some say I bought him dearly,
some say cheaply, but
I bought him by weighing him in a balance.
Some say he's dark,
some say he's fair,
but I took him with my eyes open.
The only price I paid
is that of love which knows no price.

Mīrā lived in an epoch that saw the flowering of *Vishnuism*—the transformation of the Vedic Creator, the Impersonal God without attributes, qualities, form, beginning, end, as expounded by the philosophy of Vedantism and by its greatest exponent Śaṅkarāchārya (788–820)—into a personal god, Viṣṇu, who is at once friend and lover, and whose transcendental qualities are manifested in terms of human love and personal relationship. In Mīrā's poetry, however, there are traces of many other forms and cults of religious devotion, including yoga. Well-versed in the *Bhagavadgītā* , Mīrā knew about the three forms of yoga that Kṛṣṇa expounds—three paths through which self-realization, perfection, and salvation can be achieved: the *jñāna* yoga (the yoga of knowledge); the *karma* yoga (the yoga of action), and the personal *bhakti* yoga (the yoga of love and devotion). Mīrā, not merely because of her personal circumstances, chose the last form of yoga through which to realize herself and to become "a harmonized soul."

A deep-seated joy and an imperturbable serenity of spirit pervade Mīrā's poetry, not only when she hopes and has faith ("Soon the fruit of my joy supreme will grow"), but also when she doubts and despairs ("The palace of love / is both too high and too low / for my tottering feet"), when the fever of the yearning for Śyām consumes her day and night, when "the thunder of the clouds" and "the fear of the hereafter" frighten her, or when her heart behaves "like a mad elephant" which none can dominate. In her songs she calls God by different names, among which the most recurrent are Giridhar (sustainer of the mountain), Śyām (literally meaning "dark skinned" but metaphorically also "lover"), Gopāla (protector of the cows), Hari (epithet of Kṛṣṇa, meaning "the destructor of sin"). However, in so far as the object of Mīrā's divine love (or *bhakti*) is conceived, invoked, interrogated, and supplicated, her impassioned lyricism acquires a sensuous and sentimental corporeality not found—or not in the same degree—in other poets of the *bhakti* school, including such giants as Tulsīdās, Sūrdās, Keśavdās, and Raskhāna.

The God invoked by Mīrā, however, is none other than the impersonal Vedic god; i.e. God that is *nirguṇa* (without attributes) transformed into God that is *saguṇa* (with attributes), or God that is *nirākār* (without form) having become, in the mystical fantasy and devotion of Mīrā, God who is *sākāra* (with form), and conceived by the devotee as a lover who is at once human and divine:

> Stay firm before my eyes,
> don't let me slip from your mind.
> The waves of life are dragging me
> far, be quick and bring me
> to the shore, and our encounter
> will be one that knows no end.

Mīrā's devotion to such a god takes the form of the drama of love (love for Kṛṣṇa with its vicissitudes), hope and disappointment, joy and anguish, union and separation, reflected in the very language of her poetry with its openness, directness, and lyrically charged simplicity:

> Such a lover
> you must never let go;
> must give him everything
> —body, heart and riches—
> and make him live within you.
> You must drink your happiness just
> by looking into his eyes,
> and give him every enjoyment
> he wants, which will be
> the token of your greatest bliss.

Mīrā celebrates in her songs "the joy supreme" of her union with the object of her love and devotion; the pangs of separation between lovers who are "for centuries apart," because of which she wastes her life like "a tree without roots." Other themes of her poetry include: the illusion, which nourishes yet destroys love, of possessing the lover in a dream, and the inevitable shock of realizing that he cannot be possessed; love that derives from absolute trust in the lover, as if such a love has been bought "with the sound of drum," and that obtains the offerings of sacrifice, total surrender, and devotion; rejection rather than abnegation of this false and transient world, which is compared to a game of chess "which ends when evening comes"; and the concept of a spouse "who never dies."

Thus, even though the object of her love is One who knows no beginning and no end, was never born and can never die, and who is above the cycle of birth, death, and rebirth, Mīrā's heart beats for him with the same vigour, and she feels with the same degree of intensity as if she had been in love with a human being. That is why her joys and sufferings have a profoundly human as well as artistic appeal, and why her poetry still enjoys an undisputed popularity throughout India.

—G. Singh

MISHIMA Yukio

Born: Hiraoka Kimitake in Tokyo, Japan, 14 January 1925. **Education:** Educated at Peers School and College, graduated 1944; Tokyo University, degree in jurisprudence 1947. **Family:** Married Sugiyama Yoko in 1958; one daughter and one son. **Career:** Civil servant, Finance Ministry, 1948; then freelance writer; also film director, designer, and stage producer and actor. **Awards:** Shincho prize, 1954; Kishida Drama prize, 1955; Yomiuri prize, 1957, 1961; Mainichi prize, 1965. **Died:** (suicide) 25 November 1970.

PUBLICATIONS

Collections

Zenshū [Collected Works], edited by Shoichi Saeki and Donald Keene. 36 vols., 1973–76.
My Friend Hitler and Other Plays of Mishima Yukio, translated by Hiroaki Sato, 2002.

Fiction

Hanazakari no mori [The Forest in Full Bloom]. 1944.
Misaki nite no monogatari [Tales at a Promontory]. 1947.
Yoru no shitaku [Preparations for the Night]. 1948.
Tozoku [Thieves]. 1948.
Shishi [Lion]. 1948.
Kamen no kokuhaku. 1949; as *Confessions of a Mask*, translated by Meredith Weatherby, 1958.
Hoseki baibai [Precious-Stone Broker]. 1949.
Magun no tsuka [Passing of a Host of Devils]. 1949.
Ai no kawaki. 1950; as *Thirst for Love*, translated by Alfred H. Marks, 1970.
Kaibutsu [Monster]. 1950.
Janpaku no yoru [Snow-White Nights]. 1950.
Ao no jidai [The Blue Period]. 1950.
Kinjiki; Higyo. 2 vols., 1951–53; as *Forbidden Colours*, translated by Alfred H. Marks, 1968.
Natsuko no boken [Natsuko's Adventures]. 1951.
Manatsu no shi. 1953; as *Death in Midsummer*, translated in *Death in Midsummer and Other Stories*, 1966.
Nipponsei [Made in Japan]. 1953.
Shiosai. 1954; as *The Sound of Waves*, translated by Meredith Weatherby, 1957.
Shizumeru taki [The Sunken Waterfall]. 1955.
Kinkakuji. 1956; as *The Temple of the Golden Pavilion*, translated by Ivan Morris, 1959.
Kofuku go shuppan. 1956.
Bitoku no yorimeki [The Tottering Virtue]. 1957.
Hashizukushi [A List of Bridges]. 1958.
Kyoko no ie [Kyoko's House]. 1959.
Utage no ato. 1960; as *After the Banquet*, translated by Donald Keene, 1963.
Suta [Movie Star]. 1961.
Nagasugita haru [Too Long a String]. 1961.
Utsukushi hoshi [Beautiful Star]. 1962.

Gogo no eikō. 1963; as *The Sailor Who Fell from Grace with the Sea*, translated by John Nathan, 1966.

Ken [The Sword]. 1963.

Nikutai no gakko [The School of Flesh]. 1964.

Kinu to meisatsu [Silk and Insight]. 1964; as *Silk and Insight: A Novel*, translated by Hiroaki Sato, 1998.

Han-teijo daigaku [College of Unchasteness]. 1966.

Eirei no koe [Voices of the Spirits of the War Dead]. 1966.

Death in Midsummer and Other Stories, various translators. 1966.

Fukuzatsuma kare [A Complicated Man]. 1966.

Yakaifuku [Evening Dress]. 1967.

Taiyo to tetsu. 1968; as *Sun and Steel*, translated by John Bester, 1971.

Hōjō no umi, as *The Sea of Fertility*. 1985.

    1. *Haru no yuki.* 1969; as *Spring Snow*, translated by Michael Gallagher, 1972.

    2. *Homba.* 1969; as *Runaway Horses*, translated by Michael Gallagher, 1973.

    3. *Akatsuki no tera.* 1970; as *The Temple of Dawn*, translated by E. Dale Saunders and Cecilia Segawa Seigle, 1973.

    4. *Tennin gosui.* 1971; as *The Decay of the Angel*, translated by Edward Seidensticker, 1974.

Kemono no tawamure [The Play of Beasts]. 1971.

Acts of Worship: Seven Stories, translated by John Bester. 1989.

Plays

Kataku [Burning Houses] (produced 1949). In *Ningen*, 1948.

Tōdai [Lighthouse] (produced 1950). 1950.

Kantan (produced 1950). In *Kindai Nōgakushū*, 1956; as *Kantan*, translated by Donald Keene, in *Five Modern No Plays*, 1957.

Seijo [Saintess]. 1951.

Aya no tsuzumi (produced 1952). 1953; as *The Damask Drum*, translated by Donald Keene, in *Five Modern No Plays*, 1957.

Sotoba komachi (produced 1952). In *Kindai Nōgakushū*, 1956; as *Sotoba komachi*, translated by Donald Keene, in *Five Modern No Plays*, 1957.

Yoru no himawari (produced 1953). 1953; as *Twilight Sunflower*, translated by Shigeho Shinozaki and Virgil A. Warren, 1958.

Wakodo yo yomigaere [Young Man Back to Life] (produced 1955). 1954.

Aoi no ue (produced 1955). In *Kindai Nōgakushū*, 1956; as *The Lady Aoi*, translated by Donald Keene, in *Five Modern No Plays*, 1957.

Shiroari no su [Nest of White Ants] (produced 1955). 1956.

Fuyo no Tsuyu Ouchi Jikki [True History of the House of Ouchi] (produced 1955).

Kindai Nōgakushū. 1956; as *Five Modern No Plays*, translated by Donald Keene, 1957.

Yuya (produced 1957). In *Kindai Nōgakushū*, 1956.

Rokumeikan [Rokumei Mansion] (produced 1956). 1957.

Hanjo (produced 1957); as *Hanjo*, translated by Donald Keene, in *Five Modern No Plays*, 1957.

Bara to kaizoku [Rose and Pirates] (produced 1958). 1958.

Nettaiju (produced 1961). In *Koe*, 1960; as *Tropical Tree*, translated by Kenneth Strong, in *Japanese Quarterly*, 11(2), 1964.

Toka no kiku [Late Flowering Chrysanthemum] (produced 1961).

Kurotokage [Black Lizard], from a story by Edogawa Rampo (produced 1962).

Gikyoku zenshū [Collected Plays]. 1962.

Yorokobo no Koto [Koto of Rejoicing] (produced 1964).

Sado koshaku fujin (produced 1965). 1965; as *Madame de Sade*, translated by Donald Keene, 1968.

Suzaku-ke no metsubo [Downfall of the Suzaku Family] (produced 1967). 1967.

Waga tomo Hitler [My Friend Hitler] (produced 1968). 1968.

Raio no terasu [Terrace of the Leper King] (produced 1969). 1969.

Chinsetsu yumiharizuki [The Strange Story of Tametomo] (produced 1969). 1969.

Screenplays: *Yukoku*, 1965; as *Patriotism*, translated by Geoffrey W. Sargent, 1995.

Other

Kari to emono [The Hunter and His Prey]. 1951.

Aporo no sakazuki [Cup of Apollo]. 1952.

Sakuhin-shu [Works], 6 vols., 1953–54.

Koi no miyako [City of Love]. 1954.

Megami [Goddess]. 1955.

Seishun o do ikiru ka [How to Live as a Young Man]. 1955.

Senshu [Selected Works]. 19 vols., 1957–59.

Gendai shosetsu wa koten tari-uru ka [Can a Modern Novel Be a "Classic"?]. 1957.

Fudotoku kyoiku koza [Lectures on Immoralities]. 1959.

Hayashi Fusao Ron [Study of Hayashi Fusao]. 1963.

Watashi no henreki jidai [My Wandering Years]. 1964.

Tampen zenshū [Short Pieces]. 1964.

Mikuma no Mode [Pilgrimage to the Three Kumano Shrine]. 1965.

Hyoron zenshū [Collected Essays]. 1966.

Hagakure nyūmon. 1967; as *The Way of the Samurai: Mishima on Hagakure in Modern Life*, translated by Kathryn Sparling, 1977; as *Hagakure: The Samurai Ethic and Modern Japan*, translated by Sparling, 1977.

Taidan, ningen to bungaku [Dialogues on Human Beings and Literature], with Mitsuo Nakamura. 1968.

Wakaki samurai no tame no seishin kōwa [Spiritual Lectures for the Young Samurai]. 1968.

Bunka boeiron [Defence of Culture]. 1969.

Yukoku no genri [The Theory of Patriotism]. 1970.

Sakkaron [Essays on Writers]. 1970.

Gensen no kanjo [The Deepest Feelings]. 1970.

Kodogaku nyūmon [An Introduction to Action Philosophy]. 1970.

Shobu no kororo [Heart of Militarism]. 1970.

Waga shishunki [My Adolescence]. 1973.

Editor, *Rokusei nakamura utaemon.* 1959.

Editor, with Geoffrey Bownas, *New Writing in Japan.* 1972.

                           *

Critical Studies: *Accomplices of Silence: The Modern Japanese Novel* by Masao Miyoshi, 1974; *Mishima: A Biography* by John Nathan, 1974; *The Life and Death of Yukio Mishima* by Henry Scott-Stokes, 1974; *The Moon in the Water: Understanding Tanizaki, Kawabata, and Mishima* by Gwenn Boardman Petersen, 1979; *Mishima: A Vision of the Void* by Marguerite Yourcenar, translated by Alberto Manguel, 1985; *Escape from the Waste: Romanticism and Realism in the Fiction of Mishima Yukio and Oe Kenzaburo* by Susan J. Napier, 1991; *Deadly Dialectics: Sex, Violence, and Nihilism in the World of Yukio Mishima* by Roy Starrs, 1994; *Forbidding Colors: Essays on Body and the Mind in the Novels of Mishima Yukio* by Noriko Thunman, 1999.

* * *

The brilliant literary career of Mishima was cut short by his own hands on 25 November 1970. He killed himself in a traditional "samurai" style within the compounds of the Ground Self-Defence Force (Ichigaya, Tokyo). He planned a military *coup d'état*, and put it into practice; it turned out, of course, to be a total failure. We cannot be sure how seriously devoted he was to this fantastic scheme, and it might be surmised that he had been carried away by his literary imagination and driven to realize his imaginary vision in action.

Mishima made a dazzling literary début as a teenage prodigy. His first book, *Hanazakari no mori* [The Forest in Full Bloom], was published in 1944, when the Pacific War was approaching its dismal close. It was a genuine *tour de force*, in its rich evocativeness, and clever—too clever for the 19-year-old author—pastiche of decorative classical prose. Even fastidious critics could not help admiring Mishima's extraordinary talent, but the book was just too romantic and precious. His first real achievement as novelist was *Kamen no kokuhaku* (*Confessions of a Mask*), which was lucid in its rich details, and challenging in its theme. He described the physical and psychological process by which the hero ("I") is led to the inevitable realization that he is a homosexual; the title suggested it should be taken as a "confessional" novel. In the late 1940s, homosexuality was not a popular theme at all. Young Mishima admired Oscar Wilde, and Wildean pose and tastes are certain to have influenced him. His essay on Wilde (1950) was full of revealing insights, on both Wilde and Mishima himself. We can even get an ominous premonition of his provocative "suicide," which seems to have been a curious mixture of exhibitionism and an irresistible impulse toward self-destruction.

Mishima proved himself even more versatile than Wilde: certainly his contribution as novelist surpasses Wilde's. *Kinjiki; Higyo* (*Forbidden Colours*), *Shiosai* (*The Sound of Waves*), *Kinkakuji* (*The Temple of the Golden Pavilion*), *Utage no ato* (*After the Banquet*), *Gogo no eikō* (*The Sailor Who Fell from Grace with the Sea*), and the *Hōjō no umi* (*The Sea of Fertility*) tetralogy (completed just before his death), should be sufficient to secure his position as one of the major novelists of the 20th century. His range is wide indeed: *The Sound of Waves* is an idyllic evocation of innocent love in a remote fishing village; *The Temple of the Golden Pavilion* probes the morbid impulses of a young incendiary who destroys one of the traditional treasures of Japanese architecture; *After the Banquet* provides a satirical picture of the Japanese political scene and of the amorous behaviour of an elder statesman and his new wife; *The Sailor Who Fell from Grace with the Sea* describes youthful hero-worship, which, once bitterly disappointed, turns vindictive and destructive. Mishima was amazingly prolific, and wrote short stories, plays, literary criticism, travelogues, and political articles. His modern Nō plays are remarkable for their fusion of a refined sense of form, derived from traditional Nō drama, and vulgar realistic details in contemporary scenes and characters. *Sado koshaku fujin* (*Madame de Sade*), in which the real hero of the play does not appear on the stage at all, is another *tour de force*, which, while adhering strictly to the classical unities, is sensual and sharp in its touch.

The Sea of Fertility, Mishima's last major work, is a tantalizing achievement. Its central theme is based on the Buddhist concept of the metamorphosis of the human soul. The underlying mystic system may not be wholly convincing, but the consecutive appearances or incarnations of "the eternal spirit" as the four main characters make for fascinating stories. This tetralogy might be taken as Mishima's gigantic bid for immortality, and, at the same time, as symbolic expression of his impulse toward annihilation.

—Shoichi Saeki

MISTRAL, Gabriela

Born: Lucila Godoy Alcayaga in Vicuña, Chile, 7 April 1889. Grew up in Montegrande, Vicuña, and (from 1901) La Serena. **Education:** Educated at Vicuña state secondary school, 1898–1901, then in La Serena; Escuela Normal, Santiago, secondary-level teaching certificate, 1910. **Family:** Adopted her half-brother's son in 1926. **Career:** Teaching assistant, elementary school, La Serena, 1905–06; secretary, La Serena secondary school, 1906–08; director, elementary school, La Cantera, 1908–09; teacher, Barrancas, 1910–11, Traiguén, 1911, and Antofagasta secondary schools, 1911–12; teacher and inspector, Los Andes secondary school, 1912–18; headteacher and Spanish lecturer, Punta Arenas girls' secondary school, 1918–20; headteacher, secondary school, Temuco, 1920, and "Number 6" secondary school, Santiago, 1921–22; joined the Mexican government's educational reform programme, 1922; travelled throughout the United States and Europe, 1924; visiting professor in the United States, 1929–30, at Mills College, Oakland (California), Vassar College, Poughkeepsie (New York), Middlebury College, Middlebury (Vermont), and Barnard College, New York City; also lectured in Puerto Rico, Havana, Guatemala, El Salvador, all 1931. Received pension from Chilean government, 1925, and subsequently pursued career as diplomat and Chilean representative at international organizations: delegate, 1926, literary director, League of Nations Institute for Intellectual Co-Operation, 1927–30, in Paris and Rome; executive member, Institute for Cinematography in Education, Rome, until 1930; delegate, International Congress of University Women, Spain, 1928; consul, 1932–35, and designated Consul for Life, from 1935, in: Guatemala and France, 1932–33, Madrid, 1933–35 (honorary position), Lisbon, 1935–37, Paris, 1937–38, Veracruz (Mexico), 1938–40 and 1948, Brazil, 1940–44, Los Angeles, 1945, Naples, 1951, Long Island (New York), 1953; travelled through Sweden, France, and Italy, 1945; lived in Monrovia, 1946, Santa Barbara, 1947–50, Veracruz, 1948. Also actively involved in UNICEF. Contributor to numerous publications, including: *El Coquimbo* and *La Vox de Elqui* (both in Vicuña), from 1904; *Penumbras*, 1907; and began using the pseudonym Gabriela Mistral in 1908, *Elegancias*, 1913; *Norte y Sur*, 1913; *Nueva Luz*, 1913; *Revista de Educación*, 1913–15; *Zig-Zag*, 1915; *Primrose*, 1915–16; *Libro de lectura* textbooks, 1916–17; *Los Diez*, 1917; *Selva Lírica*, 1917–18; *Cervantes*, 1917–20; *Pacífico Magazine*, 1919; *Renacimiento*, 1919; *Repertorio Americano*, from 1921; *Chile Magazine*, 1921–22; and in later years, *El Mercurio* (Santiago), *La Nación* (Buenos Aires, Argentina), *El Universal* (Caracas, Venezuela), and *El Tiempo* (Bogotá, Colombia). Named honorary professor of Spanish, University of Santiago, 1923. **Awards:** Golden Orchid prize for literature (Panama), 1932; Nobel prize for literature, 1945; Academy of American Franciscan History Serra prize, 1950; Chilean National prize for literature, 1951. Honorary doctorates: Mills College, Oakland, California, 1947; Columbia University, New York, 1954; University of Chile, Santiago, 1954. **Died:** 10 January 1957.

PUBLICATIONS

Collections

Poesías completas, edited by Margaret Bates. 1958; 3rd edition, 1966.
A Gabriela Mistral Reader, translated by Maria Giachetti, edited by Marjorie Agosin. 1993.
Women, edited by Marjorie Agosín and Jacqueline C. Nanfito, translated by Jacqueline C. Nanfito. 2000.
Poesías completas, with notes by Jaime Quezada. 2001.
Selected Prose and Prose-poems, edited and translated by Stephen Tapscott. 2002.

Verse

Desolación. 1922; revised editions, 1923, 1926.
Ternura. 1924; enlarged edition, 1945; edited by Jaime Quezeda, 1989.
Nubes blancas. 1926.
Los mejores poemas. 1936.
Tala. 1938; edited by Alfonso Calderón, 1979.
Antología: Selección de la autora. 1941.
Antología. 1947.
Poemas de las madres (prose poems). 1950.
Lagar. 1954.
Selected Poems, translated by Langston Hughes. 1957.
Motivos de San Francisco (prose poems), edited by César Díaz-Muñoz Cormatches. 1965.
Antología, edited by Emma Godoy. 1967.
Poema de Chile, edited by Doris Dana. 1967.
Poesías, edited by Eliseo Diego. 1967.
Todas íbamos a ser reinas. 1971.
Crickets and Frogs: A Fable, translated by Doris Dana. 1972.
Antología poética, edited by Alfonso Calderón. 1974.
El niño en la poesía de Gabriela Mistral (selection), edited by Roque Esteban Scarpa. 1979.
Elogio de las cosas de la tierra, edited by Roque Esteban Scarpa. 1979.
Selected Poems, edited and translated by Doris Dana. 1979.
Reino, edited by Gastón von dem Bussche. 1983.
Lagar II. 1991.

Other

Lecturas para mujeres. 1923.
Breve descripción de Chile. 1934.
La lengua de Martí. 1934.
Versos sencillos: Estudio. 1939.
Palabras para la Universidad de Puerto Rico. 1948.
Obras selectas. 6 vols., 1954.
El sentido de la profesión. 1956.
Cartas a Eugenio Labarca, edited by Raúl Silva Castro. 1957.
Croquis mexicanos: Gabriela Mistral en México. 1957.
Recados contando a Chile (letters and articles), edited by Alfonso M. Escudero. 1957.
Canto a San Francisco. 1957.
Páginas en prosa, edited by José Pereira Rodríguez. 1962.
Gabriela Mistral y el Brasil. 1963.
Cartas de amor, edited by Sergio Fernández Larraín. 1978.

Gabriela Mistral en el repertorio americano (essays), edited by Mario Céspedes. 1978.
Gabriela piensa en. . . , edited by Roque Esteban Scarpa 1978.
Materias: Prosa inédita, edited by Alfonso Calderón. 1978.
La prosa religiosa, edited by Luis Vargas Saavedra. 1978.
Grandeza de los oficios, edited by Roque Esteban Scarpa. 1979.
Magisterio y niño, edited by Roque Esteban Scarpa. 1979.
Gabriela Mistral (anthology), edited by Pedro Bravo Elizondo. 1983.
Poesía y prosa, edited by Floridor Pérez. 1984.
El otro suicida de Gabriela Mistral, edited by Luis Vargas Saavedra. 1985.
Gabriela presente, edited by Inés Moreno Mistral. 1987.
Cartas a Lydis Cabrera. 1988.
Epistolario de Gabriela Mistral y Eduardo Barrios, edited by Luis Vargas Saavedra. 1988.
Gabriela Mistral y Joaquín García Monge: Una correspondencia inédita, edited by Magda Arce and Eugenio García Carrill. 1989.
Memorias (1911–1934) y correspondencia con Gabriela Mistral y Jacques Maritain, edited by Eduardo Frei Montalva. 1989.
Vendré olvidada o amada (selection), edited by Alfonso Calderón. 1989.

*

Bibliography: *Gabriela Mistral: Vida y obra: Bibliografía; Antología* by Jorge Mañach and others, 1936; *Bibliografía crítica sobre Gabriela Mistral* by Norberto Pinilla, 1940; *Compendio bibliográfico de Gabriela Mistral* by Betty Jorquera Toro, 1985.

Critical Studies: *La divina Gabriela* by Virgilio Figueroa, 1933; *Estudios sobre Gabriela Mistral*, 1935, and *Producción de Gabriela Mistral de 1912 a 1918*, 1957, both by Raúl Castro Silva; *Modern Women Poets of Spanish America* by Sidonia C. Rosenbaum, 1945; *Biografía de Gabriela Mistral* by Norberto Pinilla, 1946; *Gabriela Mistral: Su vida y su obra* by Julio Saavedra Molina, 1947; *Gabriela Mistral y el modernismo en Chile* by Augusto Iglesias, 1950; *Gabriela Mistral: Fuerza y ternura de América*, 1951, and *De la vida y la obra de Gabriela Mistral*, 1959, both by Gastón Figueira; *Santa Gabriela Mistral* by Benjamin Carrión, 1956; *Gabriela Mistral, rebelde magnífica* by Matilde Ladrón de Guevara, 1957; *La voz de Gabriela Mistral* by Cintio Vitier, 1957; *Homenaje a Gabriela Mistral* edited by Salvador de Madariaga, 1958; *Aspectos del estilo en la poesía de Gabriela Mistral* by Cora Santandreu, 1958; *Gabriela Mistral: Biografía emotiva* by Efraín Szmulewicz, 1958, enlarged edition, 1974; *El sentido de la vida en algunas imágenes de Gabriela Mistral* by Luis V. Anastasía Sosa, 1961; *Gabriela Mistral* by Arturo Torres-Rioseco, 1962; *Gabriela Mistral: The Poet and Her Work* (from the Spanish) by Margot Arce de Vásquez, 1964; *Genio y figura de Gabriela Mistral* by Fernando Alegría, 1966; *Vida y obra de Gabriela Mistral* by L. Silva, 1967; *Gabriela Mistral íntima* by Ciro Alegría, 1968; *Gabriela Mistral: The Chilean Years* by Margaret T. Rudd, 1968; *Gabriela Mistral's Religious Sensibility* by Martin C. Taylor, 1968; *Mysticism in Gabriela Mistral: A Clarification* by E.M. Camaino, 1969; *Gabriela Mistral* by Carmen Conde, 1970; *Vida y personalidad de Gabriela Mistral* by Marie-Luise Gazarian-Gautier, 1971, as *Gabriela Mistral: Teacher from the Valley of Elqui*, 1975; *Una mujer nada de tonta*, 1976 and *La desterrada en su patria*, 2 vols., 1977, both by Roque Esteban Scarpa; *Gabriela Mistral en Antofagasta: Años de forja y valentía* by Mario Bahamonde, 1980; *Beauty and the Mission for the Teacher: The Life of Gabriela Mistral* by William J. Castleman, 1982; *La crítica literaria en la obra de Gabriela Mistral* by Onilda A. Jiménez, 1982; *Gabriela Mistral* by Jaime Concha, 1987; *El otro suicido de Gabriela Mistral* by Luis Vargas Saavedra, 1987; *El último viaje de Gabriela Mistral* by Santiago Daydi-Tolson, 1989; ''Matrilineage, Matrilanguage: Gabriela Mistral's Audience of Women'' by E.R. Moran, in *Revista Canadiense de Estudios Hispánicos*, 14(3), 1990; *Gabriela Mistral: An Artist and Her People* by Elizabeth Horan, 1994; *Critical Acts: Latin American Women and Cultural Criticism* by Elizabeth A. Marchant, 1999.

*   *   *

Gabriela Mistral is one of the greatest poets of Latin America, but, although she was awarded the Nobel prize for literature, her works have not received the attention they deserve in the English-speaking world, and have not been widely translated. From humble beginnings in rural Chile, and a lonely childhood following the departure of her father when she was only three years old, she came to be a figure whose writing and willingness to speak out for those who had no voice earned her respect throughout Latin America. She has often been compared to her compatriot Pablo Neruda, who also combined poetry, diplomacy, and a passionate commitment to socialist ideals, though unlike him she found the subject of much of her poetry in the pain of lost love, of childlessness, of exile from happiness.

Desolación [Desolation], her first collection, in which she claimed to write from her own ''bleeding past,'' followed soon after the suicide of the man she loved, and the death of her beloved mother in 1929 inspired some of the poems included in *Tala*. The scholar Jaime Concha claims that *Tala* is her greatest work, and points out that by this time Mistral had come under the influence of other great avant-garde poets. Her friendship with Victoria Ocampo brought her into contact with the literary milieu of *Sur* [South], the journal that introduced so many writers to Latin America, and the unlikely relationship between the Argentinian feminist intellectual and the Chilean peasant poet was a rewarding one for both women.

Mistral's poetry returns constantly to certain key themes—the theme of loss, through death, abandonment, childlessness, or exile; the theme of belonging, especially to a particular place, or to the soil itself; the theme of American/Chilean identity, what the Conquest means in terms of the history of a people, how the arrival of the military and religious might of the colonizers changed irrevocably the pattern of native American cultures.

Although she was a deeply spiritual woman, Mistral found little consolation in religion. In one of the poems in *Desolación* she asks bluntly, ''Our Father who art in heaven / why hast thou forgotten me?,'' while in her famous ''Poema del hijo'' [Poem for a Son], which she said was her most deeply felt poem, she reflects on the contrast between the fecundity of nature and her own sterility. At times she portrays the earth as a mother, even going so far as to see God as a mother-figure. There can be few poets who have written with such power, deriving from an inner source of constant pain, about the meaning of childlessness for a woman who saw maternity as essential to her femininity.

From the unborn child in *Desolación* to the lost mother in *Tala*, Mistral's poetry focuses on images of women, and her later collections offer a wide variety of female portraits. Her beautiful lyric poem ''La extranjera'' [The Foreign Woman], also from *Tala*, depicts a woman whose lifetime has been spent in an alien culture and whose heart still belongs with her lost roots. ''La bailarina'' [The Dancer], from *Lagar* [Wine Press], starts with a single image and progresses outwards:

> Now the dancer is dancing
> the dance of losing all she had.
> She lets fall everything she held
> fathers and brothers, gardens and farmland,
> the sound of her own stream, her pathways,
> the story of her hearth, her own face
> and her name, and her childhood games.

Women in Mistral's poetry suffer, but are strong. They resist the pain and fight on in the eternal battle of survival. Depicting that struggle, her technique is to combine the physical and the metaphysical in ways that create powerfully evocative images. In many respects, her poetry is similar to the poetry of Anna Akhmatova or Marina Tsvetaeva in Russia, or of Ann Sexton or Sylvia Plath whose works she can never have known, yet all of whom transformed their personal anguish into psychic landscapes of extraordinary poignancy. So her poem ''País de la Ausencia'' [The Land of Absence], for example, opens with a verse describing the strange land that has always existed, never knowing happiness, and goes on to say:

> No pomegranates grow
> no jasmine blooms,
> there are no skies
> or indigo seas,
> Its name is a name
> that I never heard,
> and in that nameless land
> I shall go to die.

When one reads Mistral's poetry today, what comes across is not only her ability to handle language in ways that combine extraordinary simplicity with great depth and richness, but the genuinely authentic voice of a woman who had much love to give, yet was continually thwarted in her efforts to bestow it upon someone. Deprived of her father, then of her lover and her adored mother, and denied a child, she transformed her pain into poetry and into passion for humanity.

—Susan Bassnett

MIYAZAWA Kenji

Also know as Miyazawa Kenzi. **Born:** Hanamaki, 27 August 1896. **Education:** Kajō Primary School, Hanamaki, 1903–09, Morioka Middle School, 1909–14; studied agriculture and soil science at the Morioka Kōtō Nōrin Gakkō (later the Agricultural School of Iwate University), 1915–18. **Family:** Unmarried, lived most of his life in his parents' home. **Career:** After his graduation in 1918 served intermittently as research assistant at the agricultural school in Morioka, officially giving up the post in 1920; during this time, as eldest son, he struggled with his parents' wish for him to manage the family pawnshop business, a role he resisted; wrote children's stories and free verse poems, 1918–; taught at the Hanamaki Agricultural School, 1921–26; farmed family-owned land near Hanamaki while working to improve local farming conditions, 1926–28; increasingly troubled by lung disease, from 1928; worked briefly as engineer and salesman for local lime works but forced to quit due to poor health, 1931. **Died:** Of tuberculosis in Hanamaki, 21 September 1933.

PUBLICATIONS

Collections

Chūmon no ōi no ryōriten (nine children's stories). 1922.
Miyazawa Kenji zenshū [Complete works]. 3 vols. 1934–35.
Miyazawa Kenji zenshū [Complete works]. 7 vols. 1939–44.
Miyazawa Kenji zenshū [Complete works]. 11 vols. 1956–58.
Kōhon Miyazawa Kenji zenshū [Variorum edition of complete works]. 15 vols. 1973–77.
Shinshū Miyazawa Kenji zenshū [Newly edited complete works]. 17 vols. 1979–80.

Fiction

Ginga tetsudō no yoru (novella). Probably written 1924–33; as *Night Train to the Stars* translated by John Bester, 1987; as *Night of the Milky Way Railway* translated by Sarah Strong, 1991; also translated by Roger Pulvers, 1996, and Seigrist and Stroud, 1998.
Kaze no Matasaburō (novella). Probably written 1923–33; as *Matasaburō the Wind Imp*, translated by John Bester, 1992.
Gusuko Budori no denki (novella). 1932.
"Futago no hoshi" (children's story). Probably written 1918; as "The Twin Stars" translated by Sarah Strong 1998.
"Kumo to namekuji to tanuki" (children's story). Probably written 1918; as "The Spider, the Slug and the Racoon" translated by John Bester in *Once and Forever*, 1994.
"Yukiwatari" (children's story). 1921; as "Crossing the Snow" translated by Karen Colligan-Taylor, 2000.
"Kai no hi" (children's story). Probably written 1922; as "The Fire Stone" translated by John Bester in *Winds from Afar*, 1972; as "Gem Fire" translated by Sarah Strong, 1997.
"Yamanashi" (children's story). Probably written 1923; as "The Wild Pear" translated by John Bester, in *Once and Forever*, 1993.
"Chūmon no ōi ryōriten" (children's story). 1924; as "The Restaurant of Many Orders" translated by John Bester in *Winds and Wildcat Places*, 1967.
"Donguri to yamaneko" (children's story). 1924; as "Wildcat and the Acorns" translated by John Bester in *Winds and Wildcat Places*, 1967; translated by Sarah Strong 2000.
"Shishi odori no hajimari" (children's story). 1924; as "The First Deer Dance" translated by John Bester in *Winds and Wildcat Places*, 1967.
"Suisengetsu no yokka" (children's story). 1924; as "The Red Blanket" translated by John Bester in *Winds and Wildcat Places*, 1967; as "On the Fourth Day of the Narcissus Month" translated by Sarah Strong, 1997.
"Tsukiyo no denshinbashira" (children's story). 1924; as "March by Moonlight" translated by John Bester in *Once and Forever*, 1993; translated as "The Telegraph Poles on a Moonlit Night" by Sarah Strong, 2000.
"Yamaotoko no shigatsu" (children's story). 1924; as "The Man of the Hills" translated by John Bester in *Once and Forever*, 1993.
"Hikari no suashi" (children's story). Probably written 1920s; as "The Shining Feet" translated by Sarah Strong, 1997.
"Ichō no mi" (children's story). Probably written 1920s.
"Kenjū kōen rin" (children's story). Probably written 1920s; as "Kenju's Wood" translated by John Bester in *Once and Forever*, 1993; as "The Kenju Park Grove" translated by Karen Colligan-Taylor, 1999.

"Nametoko yama no kuma" (children's story). Probably written 1920s; as "The Bears of Mt. Nametoko" translated by John Bester in *Winds from Afar*, 1972; also translated by Karen Colligan-Taylor, 1998.
"Sero-hiki no Gōshu" (children's story). Probably written 1920s; as "Gorsh the Cellist" translated by John Bester in *Winds from Afar*, 1972.
"Yodaka no hoshi" (children's story). Probably written 1920s; as "The Night Hawk Star" translated by John Bester in *Winds and Wildcat Places*, 1967.
"Hokushu Shōgun to sannin kyōdai no ishi" (children's story). 1931; as "General Son Ba-yu and the Three Physicians" translated by John Bester in *Winds from Afar*, 1972.

Verse

Haru to shura (free verse collection). 1924. Many poems from this volume translated by Hiroaki Sato in *Spring & Asura*, 1973 and *A Future of Ice*, 1989.
Haru to shura Vol. II (free verse collection). 1924–26. Many poems from this volume translated by Hiroaki Sato in *Spring & Asura*, 1973 and *A Future of Ice*, 1989.
Haru to shura Vol. III (free verse collection). 1926–27. Many poems from this volume translated by Hiroaki Sato in *Spring & Asura*, 1973 and *A Future of Ice*, 1989.
"Eiketsu no asa." 1924; as "The Last Farewell" translated by Hiroaki Sato, 1973.
"Matsu no ha." 1924; as "Pine Needles" translated by Hiroaki Sato, 1973.
"Musei dōkoku." 1924; as "Voiceless Lament" translated by Hiroaki Sato, 1973.
"Jūichi gatsu mikka/Ame ni mo makezu." 1931; as "November 3rd" translated by Hiroaki Sato, 1973.

Plays

Banana Taishō (musical; performed 1923).
Porano no hiroba (musical; performed 1924).
Taneyama-ga-hara no yoru (musical; performed 1924).

Other

Nōmin geijutsu gairon kōyō (treatise). Written 1926.

*

Bibliography: Published annually in *Miyazawa Kenji kenkyū Annual* vols. 1–, Miyazawa Kenji Gakkai Iihatōbu Centaa, ed., 1991–; "Miyazawa Kenji kenyū mokuroku" in *Shinshū Miyazawa Kenji zenshū bekkan*, Kusano Shimpei, ed. 1980; "Works on Miyazawa Kenji Published in Japan" in "Miyazawa Kenji: His Stories, Characters and World View," Ph.D dissertation by Kerstin Vidaeus, 1994.

Critical Studies: *Hyōden Miyazawa Kenji* by Sakai Tadaichi (also, Chūichi), 1968; *Tōgi: Ginga tetsudō no yoru to wa nani ka* by Irisawa Yasuo and Amazawa Taijirō, 1976 (new edition, 1990); *Miyazawa Kenji ron*, 3 vols. by Onda Itsuo, 1981; *Miyazawa Kenji ron shū*, 3 vols. by Ozawa Toshirō 1987; *Miyazawa Kenji: Yojigenron no tenkai* by Saitō Bun'ichi, 1991; "The Ideals of Miyazawa Kenji," Ph.D. dissertation by Mallory Blake Fromm, 1980; "The Poetry of Miyazawa Kenji," Ph.D. dissertation by Sarah Strong, 1984; "The Theme of

Innocence in Miyazawa Kenji's Tales,'' Ph.D. dissertation by Takao Hagiwara, 1986; ''Miyazawa Kenji and the Lost Gandharan Painting'' by Sarah Strong in *Monumenta Nipponica*, 1986; ''Innocence and the Other World: The Tales of Miyazawa Kenji'' by Takao Hagiwara in *Monumenta Nipponica*, 1992; ''The Bodhisattva Ideal and the Idea of Innocence in Miyazawa Kenji's Life and Literature'' by Takao Hagiwara, in *Journal of the Association of Teachers of Japanese*, 1993; ''Miyazawa Kenji: His Stories, Characters, and World View,'' Ph.D. dissertation by Kerstin Vidaeus, 1994.

* * *

While virtually unknown during his lifetime, Miyazawa Kenji became a highly recognized writer in Japan with the publication of his collected works shortly after his death in 1933. His popularity since has remained strong, becoming nothing short of phenomenal in the last three decades of the 20th century as more and more popular and scholarly studies of his works appeared, feature films based on his stories and biography played in cinemas and on television, and tourists flocked to the memorial museum in his hometown of Hanamaki in northern Japan's Iwate Prefecture.

Most of the popular enthusiasm for Miyazawa's works is based on his children's stories and on his longer novellas, which also were written for a youthful audience. Despite their designation as being for children, these stories have always attracted a wide adult readership and are the subject of extensive critical and scholarly study. While different readers are drawn to different aspects of Miyazawa's tales, many report being attracted to their imaginative richness, to their vivid depiction of the natural world of early 20th-century rural Iwate Prefecture, to their often luminous reflection of Miyazawa's Buddhist worldview and values, and to the humor and compassion with which the author depicts the foibles of both human and animal behavior.

While most of Miyazawa's stories are to varying degrees fantasies, they cover a wide range of subject matter and style. Some, such as ''Donguri to yamaneko'' (''Wildcat and the Acorns''), ''Kai no hi'' (''The Fire Stone''), and ''Kumo to namekuji to tanuki'' (''The Spider, the Slug and the Racoon''), involve talking animal characters within a clear narrative plot. It has been remarked that while Miyazawa's animal characters are not without human aspects, they retain much more of their animal nature than do the talking beasts in such western stories as Aesop's fables. It is not only animals that talk in these tales; some of Miyazawa's most evocative pieces involve plants as speaking subjects. In ''Ichō no mi'' and ''Yamanash'' (''The Wild Pear''), for example, the reader is invited to listen in on the poignant conversations of ginkgo nuts and wild pears registering a dawning awareness of their individual impermanence within the cycle of life.

Some of Miyazawa's most moving stories involve characters from very poor, up-land rural families whose members draw their living from the hills by making charcoal, hunting bear, pasturing horses, etc. ''Hikari no suashi'' (''The Shining Feet''), ''Suisengetsu no yokka'' (''The Red Blanket''), ''Nametoko yama no kuma'' (''The Bears of Mt. Nametoko''), and the novella *Kaze no Matasaburō* (*Matasaburō the Wild Imp*) are good examples of such tales. The characters in them, whether children or adults, always speak in the rural Iwate dialect. Despite the harsh circumstances of the lives depicted, many contemporary readers value the regionalism Miyazawa successfully captures in these stories.

Miyazawa probably first began writing stories in 1918 with his production increasing dramatically in 1921. Only a few of the stories

he poured out in the early 1920s and continued to write and to rewrite until his death in 1933, were published during his lifetime. The vast majority were found in manuscript form after his death, most in a confused state of multiple drafts and rewrites with occasional gaps and illegible passages. Immediately after the writer's death, Miyazawa's brother, Seiroku, began to work to see that these manuscripts were put in order and published. The effort took time and progressed by stages, but by the 1970s, aided by Miyazawa's growing popularity and the detailed textual scholarship of Amazawa Taijirō, Irisawa Yasuo and others, Seiroku, succeeded in publishing literally all of this brother's surviving manuscripts.

This unusual history of literary production and publication means that that reader of any one of Miyazawa's stories is presented with a work in progress. Many works exist in two or more fairly distinct versions. One of Miyazawa's most beloved tales is *Ginga tetsudō no yoru* (*Night of the Milky Way Railway*). This novella-length fantasy of a journey along the celestial railway of the Milky Way is an example of a story with more than one version. While the latest rendering is arguably more developed as a narrative, many readers prefer the earlier version with its mysterious Professor Bulcaniro, a telepathic figure whose mental ''experiment'' becomes the source of the fantastic journey.

In addition to his children's stories and novellas, Miyazawa is also known for his free-verse poems. As a schoolboy and young man Miyazawa wrote poems in the traditional 31-syllable *tanka* form. By 1921 he had begun to experiment with free verse written in a unique stream of consciousness style that he called ''the mental sketch.'' In these sketches he uses indentation to indicate varying levels of interiority with the most objective thoughts and observations left unindented. While this strategy indicates an awareness of western, psychoanalytic notions of the structure of the psyche, Miyazawa's mental sketches are also influenced by Buddhist concepts of consciousness. The acts of consciousness that Miyazawa ''sketches'' in his poems, while linked to particular settings and moments in time, are intellectually sophisticated. Among other things, the poet brings his knowledge of early 20th-century science as well as Buddhist scripture to his verse, at times blending these seemingly disparate forms of knowledge within a single reflection.

Miyazawa published *Haru to shura*, a collection of 69 mental sketch poems, in 1924. While little noticed at the time, the volume eventually won high critical acclaim. Much of the artistic success of *Haru to shura* rests in the emotional intensity of the poems Miyazawa wrote about the death of his sister Toshiko in November 1922 and his subsequent mourning for her. They are ranked among the most moving free-verse poems in Japanese.

Miyazawa went on to compile two additional volumes of mental sketch poems under the *Haru to shura* title. But even more than these volumes of complex, stream of consciousness verse, Miyazawa's name as a poet is deeply associated with the simple, declarative lines of a notebook entry he made on 3 November 1931 at a time when he was travelling alone and very ill. Popularly known by its opening line, ''Ame ni mo makezu'' (undaunted by the rain), the poem expresses Miyazawa's altruistic wish to live a life of service to the rural poor.

The desire for service and self-sacrifice expressed in ''Ame ni mo makezu'' and elsewhere in Miyazawa's works resonated with values of individual renunciation promoted during Japan's war years. The initial reputation for ''saintliness'' he acquired at this time continued through the post-war period. In the 1970s however, studies emerged that called for a more complex assessment of Miyazawa's life and work, a pattern of critical reception that continues to this day. Given Miyazawa's enormous popularity in Japan and the imaginative power of his stories and poems, with their close attention to the natural world and their fusion of Buddhist and scientific world views, he merits more international attention than he has yet received.

—Sarah M. Strong

MO Yan

Born: Guan Moye in Gaomi County, Shandong Province, China, 5 March, 1956. **Education:** Attended Jiefangjun wenyi xueyuan [PLA College of Arts], Beijing, 1984–86; Beijing shifan daxue Lu Xun wenxueyuan [Lu Xun Literary Institute, Beijing Normal University], Beijing, 1989–91, M.A. degree, 1991. **Military Service:** Served between 1976–84. **Family:** Married in 1974; one daughter. **Career:** Worked in the County Cotton Oil Plant, 1973; served in People's Liberation Army, 1976–79; staff, instructor and librarian, Headquarters of the General-Staff of PLA, 1979–; writing staff, Headquarters of the General-Staff of PLA, 1986–89, 1991–97; *Jiancha ribao* [Daily Procuratorial], 1997–present. Lives in Beijing, China. **Awards:** 1985–86 Quanguo zhongpianxiaoshuo jiang [1985–86 National award in Novellas] (for the novella *Hong Gaoliang*), 1986; Dajia wenxue jiang [Dajia prize in literature] (for the novel *Fengru feitun*), 1997.

PUBLICATIONS

Collections

Mo Yan wenji (included *Hong gaoliang, Mingding guo, Zai baozha, Xian nüren,* and *Dao shenpiao*). 5 vols. 1995.
Bingxue meiren (included short stories and a play, *Bawang bieji*). 2001.

Fiction

Touming de hongluobo. 1986.
Hong gaoliang jiazu. 1987; as *Red Sorghum: A Novel of China,* translated by Howard Goldblatt, 1993.
Tiantang suantai zhi ge. 1988; as *The Garlic Ballads,* translated by Howard Goldblatt, 1995.
Baozha. 1988; as *Explosions and Other Stories,* edited by Janice Wickeri, 1991.
Huanle shisan zhang. 1989.
Shisan bu. 1989.
Bai mianhua. 1991.
Jiuguo. 1992; as *The Republic of Wine,* translated by Howard Goldblatt, 2000.
Fennu de suantai. 1993.
Huaibao xianhua de nüren. 1993.
Jinfa ying'er. 1993.
Shenliao. 1993.
Shicao jiazu. 1993.
Maoshi huicui. 1994.
Mengjing yu zazhong. 1994.

Fengru feitun. 1995; as *Big Breasts and Wide Hips,* translated by Howard Goldblatt, 2002.
Chuanqi Mo Yan. 1998.
Hong erduo. 1998.
Chang'an dadao shang de qilü meiren. 1999.
Hong shulin. 1999.
Weiqing qiyue. 1999.
Cangying menya. 2000.
Chulian shenpiao. 2000.
Laoqiang baodao. 2000.
Shifu yuelaiyue youmo. 2000; as *Shifu, You'll Do Anything for a Laugh,* translated by Howard Goldblatt, 2002.
Lengao de qingren. 2001.
Sheng pu de zuxian men. 2001.
Tan xiang xing. 2001.
Zhanyou chongfeng. 2001.

Prose

Hui changge de qiang. 1998.
Mo Yan sanwen. 2000.

Other

Hong gaoliang. 1987.
Meng duan qinglou. 1994.
Taiyang you er. 1994.
Gege men de qingchun wangshi. 1997.
Hong shulin. 1998.

*

Critical Studies: *Mo Yan lun* by Zhang Zhizhong, 1990; *Guaicai Mo Yan* by He Lihua, 1992; *Mo Yan yanjiu ziliao,* edited by He Lihua and Yang Shousen, 1992; *Mo Yan xiaoshuo: "Lishi" de chonggou* by Zhong Yiwen, 1997.

* * *

Mo Yan is one of the leading novelists and short story writers in post-Maoist China, highly acclaimed by both critics and readers. His earliest fame arose from his 1985 short novella *Touming de hong luobo* [A Translucent Carrot], a narrative built upon extraordinarily rich and often anomalous sensibilities of a village boy. It is perceivable that Garcia Marquez, or magic realism in general, was an immense influence on Mo Yan's writing, which is distinguished by unsurpassable imaginations and vagaries. Mo Yan's stylistic peculiarity developed in the short novella *Hong gaoliang* [Red Sorghum], which immediately became controversial, not exclusively for its glorification of wild passion and love, but more for its unconstrained and at times barbarous descriptions of the atrocities in the Sino-Japanese War. Its popularity reached a peak after being adapted into the Zhang Yimou film with the same title (Mo Yan co-authored the screenplay) that won the Golden Bear award at the 1988 Berlin International Film Festival.

Although it is easy to categorize *Hong gaoliang* within the "root-seeking" movement in the mid-1980s that endorses primitive vigor and native culture, its contribution to the history of modern Chinese literature lies also in rewriting modern history from a sensualistic and thus morally ambivalent perspective, which challenges the mainstream historiography.

Based on a real event, *Tiantang suantai zhi ge* (*The Garlic Ballads*) is unique among Mo Yan's works for its nearly documentary exposure of a corruptive world and the social opposition to it. Beyond the level of social critique, the novel shows the power of a blind minstrel's ballads that tie together all chapters. Mo Yan's enduring interest in folk literature/performance is reflected also in his early short story "Minjian yinyue" ["Folk Music"] through his novel *Tanxiang xing* [Sandalwood Torture].

A central theme that runs throughout Mo Yan's oeuvre is the contrast between the violent/potent past and the troubled/effete present. Inspired by Faulkner's Yoknapatawpha series, Mo Yan sets almost all his stories in his hometown, Northeast Gaomi Village. *Hong gaoliang* later expanded into the novel *Hong gaoliang jiazu* (*Red Sorghum*), initiated Mo Yan's legendary account of the grandparental generation. His *Shicao jiazu* [The Herbivorous Family] was assembled from a series of short stories and novellas, including *Honghuang* [Red Locusts] and *Meigui meigui xiangqi pubi* [Rose, Rose, Pungent Aroma], all unfolding surreal events about the miraculous and defiant deeds of grandparents, uncles and aunts decades ago.

In the late 1980s, Mo Yan's exploration of new modes of writing is exemplified by his *Shisan bu* [Thirteen Steps], which marked not a departure from his outrageously extravagant style in the mid-1980s but a radical development of that style into ironic and farcical sophistication.

Mo Yan is one of the few writers who continued to develop narrative innovation after 1989. *Jiuguo* (*The Republic of Wine*), a masterpiece that was ignored within the first few years of its publication, touches again upon the theme of social corruption (excessive eating to the extent of cannibalism), but within a narrative framework that at the same time questions the narrator himself. A social critique that involves self-deconstruction marks Mo Yan's transition from modernism (*Red Sorghum* being a model) to postmodernism.

Mo Yan's latest novels, however, invalidate any categorization, even though magic realism remains a dominant influence. Both *Fengru feitun* (*Big Breasts and Wide Hips*) and *Sandalwood Torture* deal partly with a postcolonial theme, and partly with a post-traditional theme, in which resistance to the historical oppression involves more complexities than has been imagined. To a great extent, his later works undermine the idealistic vision of élan vital by exposing the infantile mentality in primitivism and the multifarious and heterogeneous features—inhumanity, carnality, aestheticism, heroism, ignorance—in native Chinese culture.

Exemplified by *Shifu yuelaiyue youmo* (*Shifu, You'll Do Anything for a Laugh*), which became popular for being adapted into another Zhang Yimou film, Mo Yan's recent short stories provide comical critique of contemporary Chinese society. Mo Yan is in every sense the most prolific, creative and powerful novelist of China today. He has also established his international reputation with his works widely translated into different languages in recent years.

—Xiaobin Yang

MOLIÈRE

Born: Jean-Baptiste Poquelin in Paris, France, 15 January 1622. **Education:** Educated at Collège de Clermont, to 1641; studied law at University of Orléans, law degree 1642. **Family:** Married Armande Béjart in 1662; two sons (died in infancy) and one daughter. **Career:** Inherited father's post as Tapissier du Roi [Royal Upholsterer], and accompanied court to Narbonne, 1642–43; co-founder, with the Béjart family and others, Illustre Théâtre, Paris, 1643; adopted the stage name Molière, 1643; member, 1645–58, and director, from c. 1650, Dufresne's touring theatre troupe, toured in French provinces, 1645–58, then in hall of the Petit-Bourbon, Paris, under the protection of the Duc d'Orléans, Louis XIV's brother, 1658–60; some court opposition after the production of *L'École des femmes*, 1662; Louis XIV replaced the Duc d'Orléans as his patron in 1665, and the company was established at the Palais Royal. **Died:** 17 February 1673.

PUBLICATIONS

Collections

Oeuvres complètes, edited by E. Despois and Paul Mesnard. 14 vols., 1873–1900.
Plays (bilingual edition), edited and translated by A.R. Waller. 8 vols., 1926.
Comedies. 2 vols., 1929.
Oeuvres complètes [Pléaide Edition]. 2 vols., 1933; revised editions, 1959, 1971.
Oeuvres complètes, edited by Maurice Rat. 2 vols., 1956; revised by Georges Coutin, 2 vols., 1971.
The Miser and Other Plays, translated by John Wood and David Coward. 2000.
The Miser; The Idiot, translated by Ranjit Bolt. 2001.
The Misanthrope, Tartuffe and Other Plays, translated with introduction by Maya Slater. 2001.

Plays

Le Médecin volant (attributed to Molière; produced on tour before 1655). 1819; as *The Flying Doctor*, translated by Allan Clayson, in *Four Short Farces*, 1969.
La Jalousie du barbouillé (attributed to Molière; produced on tour before 1655). 1819.
L'Etourdi; ou, Les Contre-temps (produced 1655?). 1663; as *The Blunderers*, translated by Samuel Foote, 1762.
Le Dépit amoureux (produced 1656). 1663; as *The Amorous Quarrel*, 1762; as *Lovers' Quarrels*, translated by A.R. Waller, in *Plays*, 1926; as *The Love Tiff*, translated by Frederic Spencer, 1930.
Les Précieuses ridicules (produced 1659). 1660; as *The Conceited Young Ladies*, translated by Samuel Foote, 1762; as *The Affected Young Ladies*, translated by Barrett H. Clark, 1913; as *The Precious Damsels*, translated by Morris Bishop, in *Eight Plays*, 1957; as *The Pretentious Young Ladies*, translated by Herma Briffault, 1959; as *The Ridiculous Précieuses*, translated by Donald Frame, in *Tartuffe and Other Plays*, 1967.
Sganarelle; ou, Le Cocu imaginaire (produced 1660). 1660; as *The Picture*, 1745; as *Sganarelle*, translated by A.R. Waller, in *Plays*, 1926.
Don Garcie de Navarre; ou, Le Prince jaloux (produced 1661). In *Oeuvres posthumes*, 1684; as *Don Garcie de Navarre*, translated by A.R. Waller, in *Plays*, 1926.
L'École des maris (produced 1661). 1661; as *The School for Husbands*, translated by A.R. Waller, in *Plays*, 1926; several subsequent translations including by Richard Wilbur, 1992; also translated by Ranjit Bolt, 1997.

Les Fâcheux (produced 1661). 1662; as *The Impertinents*, 1732; as *The Boors*, translated by A.R. Waller, in *Plays*, 1926.

L'École des femmes (produced 1662). 1663; as *The School for Wives*, translated by Morris Bishop, in *Eight Plays*, 1957; several subsequent translations including by Richard Wilbur, 1971, Eric M. Steel, 1971, and Robert David Macdonald, 1987.

La Critique de L'École des femmes (produced 1663). 1663; as *The Critique of the School for Wives*, translated by Morris Bishop, in *Eight Plays*, 1957; also translated by Donald Frame, in *Tartuffe and Other Plays*, 1967.

L'Impromptu de Versailles (produced 1663). In *Oeuvres posthumes*, 1684; as *The Versailles Impromptu*, translated by Morris Bishop, in *Eight Plays*, 1957; also translated by Donald Frame, in *Tartuffe and Other Plays*, 1967.

Le Mariage forcé (produced 1664). 1664; as *The Forced Marriage*, 1762.

La Princesse d'Élide (produced 1664). 1674.

Tartuffe; ou, L'Imposteur (produced 1664; revised version, produced 1664). 1669; as *Tartuffe*, 1670; several subsequent translations including by Curtis Hidden Page, 1908, Haskell M. Block, 1958, Renée Waldinger, 1959, Richard Wilbur, 1963, and Christopher Hampton, 1984.

Les Plaisirs de l'île enchantée (produced 1664). 1664.

Dom Juan; ou, Le Festin de pierre (produced 1665). 1683; as *Don Juan*, translated by A.R. Waller, in *Plays*, 1926; several subsequent translations including by George Graveley and Ian Maule, in *Don Juan and Other Plays*, edited by Ian Maclean, 1989.

L'Amour médecin (produced 1665). 1666; as *The Quacks*, 1705; as *Doctor Love*, translated by Barrett H. Clark, 1915; as *Love Is the Best Remedy*, translated by Allan Clayson, in *Four Short Farces*, 1969.

Le Misanthrope (produced 1666). 1667; as *The Misanthrope*, 1762; several subsequent translations including by Richard Wilbur, 1955, and Bernard Grebanier, 1960; as *The Man-Hater*, 1770; translated by Tony Harrison, 1973; translated by Jonathan Mallinson, 1996; translated by Martin Crimp, 1996; also translated by Ranjit Bolt, 1998.

Le Médecin malgré lui (produced 1666). 1667; as *The Dumb Lady*, 1672; as *Love's Contrivance*, 1703; as *The Mock Doctor*, translated by Henry Fielding, 1732; as *The Faggot-Binder*, 1762; as *The Doctor in Spite of Himself*, translated by Barrett H. Clark, 1914; also translated by Albert Bermel, 1987; as *The Unwilling Doctor*, translated by Lisl Beer, 1962.

Mélicerte (produced 1666). In *Oeuvres posthumes*, 1684; as *Mélicerte*, translated by A.R. Waller, in *Plays*, 1926.

La Pastorale comique, music by Lully (produced 1666). In *Théâtre*, 1888–93.

Le Sicilien; ou, L'Amour peintre (produced 1667). 1668; as *The Sicilian*, 1732; also translated by John Wood, 1959.

Amphitryon (produced 1668). 1668; translated as *Amphitryon*, 1690.

George Dandin; ou, Le Mari confondu (produced 1668). 1669; as *George Dandin; or, The Husband Defeated*, translated anonymously, 1732.

L'Avare (produced 1668). 1669; as *The Miser*, 1672; several subsequent translations including by Wallace Fowlie, 1964, and Jeremy Sams, 1991.

Monsieur de Pourceaugnac (produced 1669). 1670; as *The Cornish Squire*, 1734; as *Monsieur de Pourceaugnac*, translated by A.R. Waller, in *Plays*, 1926.

Les Amants magnifiques (produced 1670). In *Oeuvres posthumes*, 1684; as *The Courtly Lovers*, translated by A.R. Waller, in *Plays*, 1926.

Le Bourgeois Gentilhomme (produced 1670). 1670; as *The Citizen Turned Gentleman*, 1672; as *The Merchant Gentleman*, translated by Margaret Baker, 1915; as *The Prodigious Snob*, 1952; as *The Would-Be Gentleman*, translated by John Wood, in *Five Plays*, 1953; as *The Self-Made Gentleman*, translated by George Graveley, in *Six Prose Comedies*, 1956; as *The Proper Gent*, translated by Henry S. Taylor, 1960; as *The Bourgeois Gentleman*, translated by Albert Bermel, 1987; as *The Bourgeois Gentilhomme*, translated by Nick Dear, 1992; also translated by Bernard Sahlins, 2000.

Psyché, with Corneille and Philippe Quinault, music by Lully (produced 1671). 1671.

Les Fourberies de Scapin (produced 1671). 1671; as *The Cheats of Scapin*, 1677; as *Scapin the Scamp*, translated by George Gravely, in *Six Prose Comedies*, 1956; as *That Scoundrel Scapin*, translated by John Wood, in *Five Plays*, 1953; as *The Rogueries of Scapin*, 1968; as *Scapin*, translated by Gerard Murphy, 1998.

La Comtesse d'Escarbagnas (produced 1671). In *Oeuvres posthumes*, 1684; as *The Countess of Escarbagnas*, translated by A.R. Waller, in *Plays*, 1926.

Les Femmes savantes (produced 1672). 1673; as *The Female Virtuosos*, 1693; as *Blue-Stockings*, 1884; as *The Learned Ladies*, translated by Renée Waldinger, 1957; also translated by Richard Wilbur, 1978; Freyda Thomas, 1991; as *The Sisterhood*, translated and adapted by R.R. Bolt, 1989.

Le Malade imaginaire (produced 1673). 1673–74; as *Doctor Last in His Chariot*, 1769; as *The Imaginary Invalid*, 1925; as *The Would-Be Invalid*, translated by Morris Bishop, 1950; as *The Hypochondriac*, in *Three Great French Plays*, 1961; translated by Alan Drury, 1982; also translated by Gerard Murphy, 1998.

Oeuvres posthumes (includes *Don Garcie de Navarre; ou, Le Prince jaloux; L'Impromptu de Versailles; Mélicerte; Les Amants magnifiques; La Comtesse d'Escarbagnas*). 1684.

Five Plays, translated by John Wood. 1953; as *The Miser and Other Plays*, 1960.

Six Prose Comedies, translated by George Gravely. 1956.

Eight Plays, translated by Morris Bishop. 1957.

The Misanthrope and Other Plays, translated by John Wood. 1959.

One-Act Comedies, translated by Albert Bermel. 1964.

Tartuffe and Other Plays, translated by Donald Frame. 1967.

Four Short Farces, translated and adapted by Allan Clayson. 1969.

Five Plays, translated by Richard Wilbur and Alan Drury. 1981.

Four Comedies, translated by Richard Wilbur. 1982.

*

Bibliography: *Cent ans de recherches sur Molière* by M. Jurgens and M. Maxfield-Miller, 1963.

Critical Studies: *Molière: A Biography* by H.C. Chatfield-Taylor, 1905; *Molière: A New Criticism* by W.G. Moore, 1949, revised edition, 1968; *Molière: The Man through His Plays* by Ramon Fernandez, 1958; *Molière: The Comic Mask* by D.B. Wyndham Lewis, 1959; *Molière and the Comedy of Intellect* by Judd Hubert, 1962; *Men and Masks: A Study of Molière* by Lionel Gossman, 1963; *Molière: A Collection of Critical Essays* by Jacques Guicharnaud, 1963; *The Spirit of Molière* edited by Percy Addison Chapman, 1965; *Molière: The Comedy of Unreason* by F.L. Lawrence, 1968; *Molière* by Hallam Walker, 1971; *Molière as Ironic Contemplator* by Alvin

Eustis, 1973; *Molière: Stage and Study* edited by W.D. Howarth and M. Thomas, 1973, and *Molière: A Playwright and His Audience* by Howarth, 1982; *Molière. Tradition in Criticism: 1906–1970* by Laurence Romero, 1974; *Molière: An Archetypal Approach*, 1976, and *The Triumph of Wit: Molière and Restoration Comedy*, 1988, both by Harold C. Knutson; *Marivaux and Molière: A Comparison* by Alfred Girmaru, 1977; *Molière's Tartuffe and the Traditions of Roman Satire* by Jerry Lewis Kasparek, 1977; *The Sceptical Vision of Molière: A Study in Paradox* by Robert McBride, 1977; *The Original Casting of Molière's Plays* by Roger W. Herzel, 1981; *Molière: Le Malade imaginaire* by H.T. Barnwell, 1982; *Molière: L'École des femmes, and Le Misanthrope* by J.H. Broome, 1982; *From Gesture to Idea: Esthetics and Ethics in Molière's Comedy* by Nathan Gross, 1982; *On the Structure of Molière's comédies-ballets* by Claude Abraham, 1984; *Social Structures in Molière's Theater* by James F. Gaines, 1984; *Comedy in Context: Essays on Molière*, 1984, and *Molière's Le Bourgeois Gentilhomme: Context and Stagecraft*, 1990, both by Hugh Gaston Hall; *Molière: Les Précieuses ridicules* by David Shaw, 1986; *L'Avare: Molière* by G.J. Mallinson, 1988; *Molière's "L'École des femmes"* by N.A. Peacock, 1988; *Molière's Theatrical Bounty: A New View of the Plays* by Albert Bermel, 1989; *Tarte à la crème: Comedy and Gastronomy in Molière's Theatre* by Ronald W. Tobin, 1990; *Molière and the Comic Spirit* by Peter H. Nurse, 1991; *Molière, Le Misanthrope* by David Whitton, 1991; *Triumph of Ballet in Molière's Theatre* by Robert McBride, 1992; *Molière in Scotland: 1945–1990* by Noël Peacock, 1993; *Molière: The Theory and Practice of Comedy* by Andrew Calder, 1993; *Music, Dance, and Laughter: Comic Creation in Molière's Comedy-Ballets* by Stephen H. Fleck, 1995; *Intruders in the Play World: The Dynamics of Gender in Molière's Comedies* by Roxanne Decker Lalande, 1996; *The Public Mirror: Molière and the Social Commerce of Depiction* by Larry F. Norman, 1999; *Molière*, edited with introduction by Harold Bloom, 2002.

* * *

Molière is one of the world's greatest dramatists, a man whose originality and importance puts him in the same league as Sophocles, Shakespeare, and Ibsen. Like Shakespeare, he was very much a professional man of the theatre, a busy actor-manager who wrote plays for performance by his own company, and like Ibsen his work translates easily and so ensures his acceptance abroad, a distinction denied, for instance, to Molière's illustrious contemporary Racine, who has never been widely appreciated outside France.

Because neo-classical conventions under which Molière worked—and, indeed, readily accepted—insisted on the strict segregation of dramatic categories, all his works are technically comedies, which means in practice that they have happy endings and deal with ordinary middle-class people rather than the kings and princes of tragedy. His plots are usually quite conventional, featuring for the most part young star-crossed lovers whose plans for married happiness are temporarily thwarted by older people, and they derive from the Roman comedies that Molière was happy to imitate since it was expected of him by the all-powerful critics of his age. He wrote for the most part five-act plays in verse, and in all other respects conformed to the tastes of his time such as a decided preference for the "three unities" of place, time, and action, and the avoidance of coarse expressions or bawdy situations on stage.

The remarkable thing, therefore, is that he was able to transcend the restrictions imposed upon him and create works of universal

appeal. His early plays, produced on tour in the provinces before he found a theatre of his own in Paris, are fairly crude pieces imitated from the *commedia dell'arte*, but he found his own voice in *Les Précieuses ridicules* (*The Conceited Young Ladies*), a rumbustious send-up of a contemporary affectation, that of excessively refined speech reflecting impossibly exalted sentiments. This vein of social satire proved a rich one for Molière, and he made the most of it in the dozen or so years he had left to live. *L'École des femmes* (*The School for Wives*), in some respects his most characteristic comedy, concerns a man who plans to keep his future wife faithful by bringing her up in uneducated innocence, but the scheme misfires when a much more attractive younger man enters her life and, after several hilarious setbacks, carries her off for himself. This theme was to be taken up a decade or so later by Wycherley in his much coarser version, *The Country Wife*.

More complex is *Tartuffe*, a play in which things nearly go wrong and happiness is restored only by a *deus ex machina*. It also caused a serious controversy about supposed immorality in Molière's work. Tartuffe is a religious hypocrite who is unmasked at the eleventh hour, but not before he has nearly ruined his gullible benefactor and come close to raping the man's loyal wife. Satire of this kind cut too near the bone for many people in that still largely devout age, and Molière escaped punishment only thanks to royal protection.

Le Misanthrope (*The Misanthrope*) is usually considered his masterpiece, largely because the comedy is ambiguous, and the play even subtler than *Tartuffe*. Alceste and Célimène—the names, as so often in Molière, are purely conventional—are expected to marry soon, but his acerbic temperament and her flightiness make this an improbable match. He rails at the hypocrisy of the age; she is a normal social being for whom tact and discretion are considerable virtues. After much friction, he insists, as a test of her loyalty, that she leave Paris with him for ever. Her response is quite predictable. In Tony Harrison's inspired translation, "I'm only twenty! I'd be terrified!" she gasps: "Just you and me, and all that countryside!" Alceste storms out in embittered despair. In one sense he is an antisocial buffoon; in another, he is a penetrating critic of a corrupt and cynical milieu. Molière shrewdly leaves the question open.

An equally serious situation is explored in *L'Avare* (*The Miser*), a probing treatment of that most dismal of human vices, avarice, and in *Le Bourgeois Gentilhomme* (*The Bourgeois Gentleman*), a shrewd analysis of social snobbery and human gullibility. The last two plays Molière wrote in a way sum up his whole career. *Les Femmes savantes* (*The Learned Ladies*) is social satire, mocking the pretensions of women who aspire to be intellectuals and whose vanity is exploited by the unscrupulous. *Le Malade imaginaire* (*The Hypochondriac*) takes the scalpel of comedy to hypochondria, and Molière no doubt savoured the irony which decreed that his own death took place as he acted the part of the imaginary invalid himself.

Molière exerted a considerable influence on his contemporaries, the Restoration dramatists in England, who imitated him without always understanding him, but otherwise he had few immediate followers. He has been successfully translated and produced on the modern stage and on television. His situations are so straightforward and universal that it is not difficult for directors to update him without in any way distorting his meaning. *The Misanthrope*, for instance, has been effectively staged as a satire on Paris high society under General de Gaulle's administration, and as a shrewd comment on the "jazz age'' of F. Scott Fitzgerald's characters. As a true professional himself, Molière would be gratified by the fact that today's actors have no difficulty in bringing his characters to life in modern dress. Religious hypocrisy may no longer be a threat in our society, but Tartuffe stands for any kind of cynical deception practised on the susceptibility of human beings to flattery, just as Alceste is the eternal boor, high on the egoism of the self-righteous, the very personification of negativity and destructiveness. And the miracle is, that in spite of being so serious, it is all so helplessly funny.

—John Fletcher

See the essays on *The Conceited Young Ladies*, *Don Juan*, *The Hypochondriac*, *The Misanthrope*, *The Miser*, and *Tartuffe*.

MOLINA, Tirso de

See TIRSO DE MOLINA

MOLNÁR, Ferenc

Born: Ferenc Neumann in Budapest, Hungary (then in the Austro-Hungarian Empire), 12 January 1878; naturalized United States citizen, 1947. **Education:** Educated at Református Gimnázium, Budapest, 1887–95; studied law in Budapest and Geneva, 1895. **Family:** Married 1) Margit Vészi in 1906 (divorced 1910), one daughter; 2) the actress Sári Fedák in 1922 (divorced 1924); 3) the actress Lili Darvas in 1926 (separated c. 1932). **Career:** Journalist with *A Hét* [The Week], *Új Idők* [New Times], and *Pesti Hírlap* [Pest News]; changed his name to Molnár, 1896; correspondent, *Budapesti Napló* [Budapest Diary], from 1906; war correspondent in Galicia, 1914–15; travelled to the United States, 1927, travelled in Europe, 1932, and with his companion Wanda Bartha, 1934–36; left Budapest, 1937, travelled to France and Switzerland and settled in New York, 1940; converted to Christianity in later life. **Member:** Elected to Petőfi Society, 1908, and Kisfaludy Society, 1911. **Awards:** Vionits prize (Hungary), 1916. Order of Franz Josef, 1916; Légion d'honneur (France), 1927. **Died:** 1 April 1952.

PUBLICATIONS

Collections

Plays of Molnár (includes *The Lawyer; The Devil; Liliom; The Guardsman; The Tale of the Wolf; The White Cloud; Carnival; Fashions for Men; The Swan; A Prologue to ''King Lear''; Marshal; The Violet; Heavenly and Earthly Love; Mima; The Glass Slipper; Riviera; Still Life; The Play's the Thing; The Witch; Olympia*), edited by Louis Rittenberg, translated by Benjamin F. Glazer. 1929; as *All the Plays of Molnár*, 1937.
Válogatott művei [Selected Works]. 1958.
Színház [Theatre] (selected works). 1961.

Plays

A doktor úr (produced 1902). 1902; as *The Lawyer*, translated by Benjamin F. Glazer, in *Plays of Molnár*, 1929.
Józsi [Jozsi] (produced 1904). 1902.
Az ördög (produced 1907). 1907; as *The Devil*, translated by Oliver Herford, 1908; also translated by Benjamin F. Glazer, in *Plays of Molnár*, 1929.
A vacsora (produced 1915). 1909; translated as *Dinner*, in *Smart Set*, 67, 1922; as *The Host*, in *One-Act Plays for Stage and Study*, 1925; as *Anniversary Dinner*, in *Romantic Comedies*, 1952.
Liliom (produced 1909). 1910; as *Liliom*, translated by Benjamin F. Glazer, 1921, and in *Plays*, 1927; as *Carousel* (musical comedy), adapted by Glazer, 1956; as *Liliom*, translated by Benjamin F. Glazer, 1999.
A testőr (produced 1910). 1910; as *The Guardsman*, translated by Grace I. Cobron and Hans Bartsch, 1924; also translated by Frank Marcus, 1978.
A farkas (produced 1912). 1912; as *The Tale of the Wolf*, translated by Benjamin F. Glazer, in *Plays of Molnár*, 1929; as *The Wolf*, translated by Henric Hirsch and Frank Hauser, 1975.
A fehér felhő (produced 1916). 1916; as *The White Cloud*, translated by Benjamin F. Glazer, in *Plays of Molnár*, 1929.
Farsang (produced 1916). 1917; as *Carnival*, translated by Benjamin F. Glazer, in *Plays of Molnár*, 1929.
Úridivat (produced 1917). 1917; as *Fashions for Men*, translated by Benjamin F. Glazer, 1922, and in *Plays*, 1927, and *Plays of Molnár*, 1929.
A hattyú (produced 1920). 1921; as *The Swan*, translated by Benjamin F. Glazer, 1922, and in *Plays*, 1927, and *Plays of Molnár*, 1929; also translated by Melville P. Baker, 1929.
Színház [Theatre] (one act plays; produced 1921). 1923.
    Előjáték Lear királyhoz, as *A Prologue to ''King Lear,''* translated by Benjamin F. Glazer, in *Plays of Molnár*. 1929.
    Marsall, as *Marshal*, translated by Benjamin F. Glazer, in *Plays of Molnár*. 1929; as *Actor from Vienna*, in *Romantic Comedies*, 1952.
    Az ibolya, as *The Violet*, translated by Benjamin F. Glazer, in *Plays of Molnár*. 1929.
Égi és földi szerelem (produced 1923). 1922; as *Heavenly and Earthly Love*, translated by Benjamin F. Glazer, in *Plays of Molnár*, 1929.
A vörös malom [The Red Mill] (produced 1922). 1923; as *Mima*, translated by Benjamin F. Glazer, in *Plays of Molnár*, 1929.
Az üvegcipő (produced 1924). 1924; as *The Glass Slipper*, translated by Benjamin F. Glazer, in *Plays of Molnár*, 1929.
Riviera (produced 1925). 1926; as *Riviera*, translated by Benjamin F. Glazer, in *Plays of Molnár*, 1929.
Csendélet (produced 1925). As *Still Life*, translated by Benjamin F. Glazer, in *Plays of Molnár*, 1929.
Játék a kastélyban (produced 1926). 1926; as *The Play's the Thing*, translated by P.G. Wodehouse, 1927; also translated by Benjamin F. Glazer, in *Plays of Molnár*, 1929; adapted by Tom Stoppard as *Rough Crossing*, 1985.
Plays (includes *Liliom; Husbands and Lovers; Fashions for Men; The Swan*), translated by Benjamin F. Glazer. 1927.
A boszorkány (produced 1927). As *The Witch*, translated by Benjamin F. Glazer, in *Plays of Molnársr*, 1929.
Olympia (produced 1928). 1928; as *Olympia*, translated by Sydney Howard, 1928; also translated in *Plays of Molnár*, 1929.

Egy, kettő, három [One, Two, Three] (produced 1929). 1929; translated as *President*, in *Romantic Comedies*, 1952.

A jó tündér (produced 1930). 1930; as *The Good Fairy*, translated by Jane Hinton, 1932; also translated in *Romantic Comedies*, 1952.

Valaki [Somebody] (produced 1932). 1932; translated as *Arthur*, in *Romantic Comedies*, 1952.

Harmónia [Harmony] (produced 1932). 1932.

Csoda a hegyek között [Miracle in the Mountains] (produced 1936). 1933.

Az ismeretlen lány [The Unknown Girl] (produced 1934). 1934.

A cukrászné [The Confectioner's Wife] (produced 1935). 1934; as *Delicate Story*, translated by Gilbert Miller, 1941.

Nagy szerelem [Great Love] (produced 1935). 1935.

Delila (produced 1937). 1937; translated as *Delilah*, 1947; as *Blue Danube*, in *Romantic Comedies*, 1952.

Panoptikum, from the play *Merciless Mrs Roy* (produced 1948). 1941; as *Waxworks*, translated by Arthur Richman, in *Romantic Comedies*, 1952.

The King's Maid (produced in English 1941).

A császár [The Emperor] (produced 1946).

Pit-a-Pat (produced 1971). As *Game of Hearts*, in *Romantic Comedies*, 1952.

Romantic Comedies (includes *Actor from Vienna; President; Waxworks; Arthur; Blue Danube; The Good Fairy; Anniversary Dinner; Game of Hearts*). 1952.

Fiction

"Magdolna" és egyéb elbeszélések ["Magdalena" and Other Stories]. 1898.

"A csókok éjszakája" és egyéb elbeszélések ["The Night of Kisses" and Other Stories]. 1899.

Az éhes város [The Hungry City]. 1901.

Egy gazdátlan csónak története. 1901; as *The Derelict Boat*, translated by Emil Lengyel, with *Eva*, 1924.

Eva. 1903; as *Eva*, translated by Emil Lengyel, with *The Derelict Boat*, 1924.

Egy pesti leány története [The Story of a Girl from Pest]. 1905.

A Pál utcai fiúk. 1907; as *The Paul Street Boys*, translated by Louis Rittenberg, 1927; also translated by Louis Rittenberg, 1994.

Rabok. 1908; as *Prisoners*, translated by Joseph Szebenyei, 1925.

Muzsika [Music] (stories). 1908.

"Báró Márczius" éss egyéb elbeszélések ["Baron Marczius" and Other Stories]. 1913.

Kis hármaskönyv [Three in One] (stories). 1914.

"Az óriás" és egyéb elbeszélések ["The Giant" and Other Stories]. 1917.

Széntolvajok [Coal Thieves]. 1918.

Andor [Andor]. 1918.

A gőzoszlop. 1926; as *The Captain of St. Margaret's*, translated by Barrows Mussey, 1945; as *Captain Magnificent*, translated by Mussey, 1946.

"A csók" és egyéb elbeszélések ["The Kiss" and Other Stories]. 1927.

A zenélő angyal. 1933; as *Angel Making Music*, translated by Victor Katona and Peggy Barwell, 1934.

A zöld huszár [The Green Hussar]. 1937.

Oszi utazás [Autumn Journey]. 1939.

The Blue Eyed Lady (stories). 1942; as *A kékszemű*, 1958.

Farewell My Heart. 1945; as *Isten veled szívem*, 1947.

Other

"Józsi" és egyéb kis komédiák ["Józsi" and Other Small Comedies]. 1902.

Gyerekek [Children]. 1905.

Ketten beszélnek (sketches). 1909; translated as *Stories for Two*, 1950.

Pesti erkölcsök [Metropolitan Morals]. 1909.

Hétágú sip [Pipes of Pan]. 1911.

Ma, tegnap, tegnapelőtt [Today, Yesterday, The Day Before Yesterday]. 1912.

Egy haditudósító emlékei [The Memoirs of a War Correspondent]. 1916.

"Az aruvimi erdő titka" és egyéb szatirák ["The Secret of the Aruwim Forest" and Other Satires]. 1917.

Ismerősök [Acquaintances]. 1917.

Vacsora és egyéb jelenek [Dinner and Other Scenes]. 1917.

Toll [Pen]. 1921.

Husbands and Lovers (includes sketches and dialogues), translated by Benjamin F. Glazer. 1924.

Művei [Collected Works]. 20 vols., 1928.

Companion in Exile: Notes for an Autobiography, translated by Barrows Mussey. 1950; as *Utitárs a száműzetésben*, 1958.

Szülőfalum, Pest (miscellany). 1962.

*

Bibliography: *Hungarian Authors: A Bibliographical Handbook* by Albert Tezla, 1970; *Ferenc Molnár: A Bibliography* by Elizabeth M. Rajec, 2 vols., 1986; *A magyar irodalomtörténet bibliográfiája, 1905–1945* by Ferenc Botka and Kálmán Vargha, 2 vols., 1989.

Critical Studies: *Ferenc Molnár: The Man Behind the Monacle* by George Halasz, 1929; *Hungarian Drama in New York* by Emro J. Gergely, 1947; *Molnár* by Delfino Tinelli, 1967; *Ferenc Molnár* (in English) by Clara Györgyey, 1980; *Der Drammatiker Ferenc Molnár* by Georg Köváry, 1984; "Names of Characters in Plays by Molnár" by Elizabeth M. Rajec, in *Literary Onomastics Studies*, 12, 1985; *Ferenc Molnár and the Austro-Hungarian "Fin de Siécle"* by István Várkonyi, 1992; *Romantic Comedy of Ferenc Molnár*, edited by Joel A. Smith and Michael Bigelow Dixon, 1995.

* * *

Ferenc Molnár began his career as a journalist and excelled both as prose writer and playwright. Because his works have been so widely translated, he has become Hungary's best-known writer abroad. Drawing on his intimate knowledge of city life, his writings depict unsuccessful human relations in a tone which ranges from the playful to the satirical, frequently containing elements of nostalgia or pure sentimentalism. He treats absurd situations in which characters violate social conventions and thus uncover their arbitrary and ridiculous nature. All his writings, in addition to being well-made, show great psychological subtlety. Molnár was a highly prolific writer and the pieces discussed here characterize all aspects of his literary output.

Two of his novels, *Egy gazdátlan csónak története* (*The Derelict Boat*) and *A Pál utcai fiúk* (*The Paul Street Boys*), capture life in Budapest, the expanding Hungarian metropolis at the time of the Dual Monarchy in the 1900s, with a freshness of sensory impression unique to Molnár. Both novels treat the problems of adolescence with profound insight in which empathy and gentle irony blend almost imperceptibly. Molnár's protagonists are marginal in their environment in both novels. In *The Derelict Boat*, 15-year-old Pirkó stands out for her intellectual superiority and maturity: she wants to preserve her independence and pursue a professional career, Sándor, a grammar-school boy, loves her hopelessly but she, in turn, falls in love with a 32-year-old journalist. He flirts with her but treats her with condescension. A novella-like peripeteia occurs when Pirkó realizes that her real rival is her own mother, prompting her to drown herself in the flooding Danube.

The Paul Street Boys concerns teenage grammar-school boys. The setting, however, differs considerably from that of *The Derelict Boat*. While the latter takes place on Margaret Island during the summer holidays and the adolescent protagonist is surrounded by the world of upper-middle-class adults, the Paul Street boys go to school in the lower-middle-class district of Pest. After lessons they play in their beloved playground where military order prevails. The protagonist, a boy called Ernő Nemecsek, is a marginal figure: he is the smallest, weakest, and probably poorest. However, when a group of boys from another school want to take their playground, a vacant lot already destined for the construction of a block of flats, Nemecsek distinguishes himself with true heroism. As a result of selfless devotion to his friends, he catches pneumonia and dies. This novel is the most popular piece of juvenile literature in Hungarian, and with good reason: the relationship between the children, their devotion to their playground, and their interactions with the world of adults are depicted simultaneously from their own perspective and from that of mature readers. This accomplishment is complemented by the sophisticated narrative voice which strikes a fine balance between irony and pity.

Both texts recreate the atmosphere of the city. The successful rendering of smells, sound, and a variety of visual and auditory effects capture impressionistic glimpses of Budapest and its people. Molnár's ability to grasp the typical comes out best, however, in the characters he creates. The journalist, the mediocre actress, and the "society" woman in *The Derelict Boat*, and the poor parents of a dying child or the teachers of an Austro-Hungarian grammar school in *The Paul Street Boys*, already point to Molnár the dramatist.

Dramatic dialogues and well-drawn characters arranged in a novella replete with all the characteristic accoutrements of that genre make *Széntolvajok* [Coal Thieves] one of the best Hungarian short stories. The setting on Margaret Island allows Molnár to juxtapose the permanence of nature with human transitoriness and the grotesque ways of society. Working-class people, the lower-middle classes, and the police have similar interests, but occupy mutually antagonistic positions in the social hierarchy. The story, is very simple: the delivery men steal coal, a socially ambitious porter reports them to an off-duty policeman and the carters face arrest and prosecution. In the meantime, an old bourgeois lady is leaving the hotel on her way to the city where death awaits her. The stylized narrative recreates the social milieu of the characters. Their banal world of poverty and exploitation contrasts sharply with the refined beauty of the island whose image is reminiscent of an impressionistic painting.

Visual and auditory effects, however, found their most eloquent expression in Molnár's theatrical works. He earned significant international recognition with his plays after World War I. The musical comedy *Carousel*, well-known in the English-speaking world, is based on his play in seven scenes, *Liliom*. The title bears the name of the protagonist, a fairground operator in the open-air amusement area of Budapest in Varosliget. This is the world of off-duty domestic servants and soldiers, and of thieves and other criminals. Liliom and a servant girl, Juli, fall in love. Their decision to move in together results in the loss of their respective jobs. Having made Juli pregnant, Liliom becomes involved in an attempted robbery with murder, and upon his arrest he commits suicide. Through supernatural insight, the play depicts Liliom as his "fate" in an "afterlife" is being determined. As in his life, so in his death, this rough yet caring rascal is too ashamed to admit that he loves Juli. His habits carry over to his death unchanged. Ironically, the court where people are forwarded to Heaven, Purgatory, or Hell contains the same social structures and conventions as the Budapest of the 1900s and appears just as corrupt and trivial.

Throughout the play, we see the progress of Juli's more conventional friend, Mari, another servant girl, who marries a hard-working, ambitious, and boring porter. They become relatively wealthy and join the ranks of the lower-middle class, even as Juli faces a life of hardship raising her fatherless daughter. *Liliom* contains some brilliantly stylized dialogue and evocative musical effects on the stage: we hear the hurdy-gurdy, whistles, songs and bells. Some gushingly sentimental scenes and the author's bowing to convention prevent him from making use of some excellent dramatic possibilities: he fails to come to conclusions about outrageous injustice and he also avoids considering existential questions about a world in which death continues to be as unbearable as life.

In the play *A hattyú* (*The Swan*) we find similar shortcomings and virtues. Witty and scintillating dialogues mark the social conflict between an aristocratic family and the middle-class tutor employed to educate the children. While the family treats him insensitively and he, in turn, gives them a rather didactic lecture about social equality, the play concludes disappointingly, restoring the "order" that, in reality, never was. The play is cleverly staged: dialogues have several levels of meaning and people talk over each other's heads in a Chekhovian fashion.

Molnár was a gifted writer who has remained popular in Hungary in spite of his cosmopolitanism, which made him suspect to fascists and Communists alike. While he caters to the intellectual tepidity of his socially "fashionable" audience and seeks safe, if unconvincing, resolutions to conflicts, he introduces issues with great psychological insight and social accuracy. His best writings about city life and conflicts between social classes strongly remind readers of such authors as Oscar Wilde, Noël Coward, Guy de Maupassant, Arthur Schnitzler, and Robert Musil, whose Hungarian equivalent Molnár undoubtedly was.

—Peter I. Barta

MONTAIGNE, Michel (Eyquem) de

Born: 1533. **Education:** Educated at home (learned Latin as native tongue); Collège de Guienne, Bordeaux, 1540–46; probably studied law, possibly in Toulouse. **Family:** Married Françoise de la Chassaigne in 1565. **Career:** Entered Cour des Aides of Périgueux as magistrate, 1554; transferred his magistracy to Bordeaux, 1557; at Bar-le-Duc at court of Francis II, 1559, and at Rouen for majority of Charles IX, 1560; friend of Henry of Navarre, and legal messenger for state duties; retired to country life and resigned his magistracy after his father's death, 1568; mayor of Bordeaux, 1581, and re-elected, 1583. **Died:** 13 September 1592.

PUBLICATIONS

Collections

Complete Works, translated by Donald M. Frame. 1948.
Oeuvres completes, edited by Albert Tribaudet and Maurice Rat. 1962.
The Complete Essays, translated by M.A. Screech. 1991.

Works

Essais. 2 vols., 1580; revised editions, 1582, 1588; edited by Marie de Gournay, 1595; as *Essays*, translated by John Florio, 1603; also translated by Charles Cotton, 3 vols., 1913–30; E.J. Trenchman, 2 vols., 1927; J.M. Cohen, 1958; as *Complete Essays*, translated and edited by M.A. Screech, 1993; as *Montaigne Entire and Entirely Naked: An Anthology of the Essays*, selected, presented and commented by Pierre Leschemelle, translated by William J. Beck, 2001.
Journal de voyage en Italie par la Suisse et l'Alltemagne en 1580 et 1581. 1774; translated by W.C. Hazlitt, in *Complete Works*, 1842; as *Diary of the Journey to Italy, 1580–81*, translated by E.J. Trechmann, 1929; also translated by Donald Frame, 1957.
Autobiography of Michel de Montaigne, selected, edited and translated by Marvin Lowenthall. 1999.
Editor, *Vers français*, by Étienne de la Boëtie. 1572.
Editor, *Discours sur la servitude volontaire*, by Étienne de la Boëtie. 1574; translated by Malcolm Smith (includes *On Friendship*), 1988.
Translator, *La Théotogie naturelle*, by Raymond Sebond. 1569.

*

Bibliography: *A Descriptive Bibliography of Montaigne's Essais, 1580–1700* by Richard A. Sayce, 1983.

Critical Studies: *Montaigne's Discovery of Man*, 1955, and *Montaigne: A Biography*, 1965, both by Donald M. Frame; *The Essays of Montaigne*, by Richard A. Sayce, 1972; *Montaigne's Deceits* by Margaret McGowan, 1974; *Montaigne and the Introspective Mind* by Glyn P. Norton, 1975; *Montaigne's Self-Portrait and its Influence in France 1580–1630* by Ian J. Winter, 1976; *Montaigne and Feminism* by Ceale Insdorf, 1977; *The Matter of My Book: Montaigne's "Essais" as the Book of the Self* by Richard L. Rogosin, 1977; *The Use of Metaphor: Studies in the Imagery of Montaigne's Essais* by B. Clark, 1978; *Montaigne* by Peter Burke, 1981; *Montaigne and His Age* edited by Keith Cameron, 1981; *Sexuality/Textuality: A Study of the Fabric of Montaigne's Essais* by Robert Duane Cottrell, 1981; *Words in a Corner: Studies in Montaigne's Latin Quotations* by Mary B. McKinley, 1981; *Montaigne and the Roman Censors* by Malcolm Smith, 1981; *Lectures on Montaigne* by Jules Brody, 1982; *Montaigne: Essays in Memory of Richard Sayce* edited by I.D. McFarlane and Ian Maclean, 1982; *Essaying Montaigne: A Study of the Renaissance Institution of Writing and Reading* by John O'Neill, 1982; *Montaigne, Essais*, 1983, and *Contextual and Thematic Interference in Montaigne's Essais*, 1983, both by John Holyoake; *Montaigne and Melancholy:*

The Wisdom of the Essays by M.A. Screech, 1983; *Arms Versus Letters: The Military and Literary Ideals in the Essais of Montaigne* by James J. Supple, 1984; *Montaigne in Motion* by Jean Starobinski, translated by Arthur Goldhammer, 1985; *Montaigne's Essais* by Dorothy Coleman, 1987; *Montaigne in Dialogue, Censorship and Definitive Writing, Architecture and Friendship, the Self and the Other* by Patrick Henry, 1987; *The Discipline of Subjectivity: An Essay on Montaigne* by Ermanne Bencivenga, 1990; *Montaigne: A Collection of Essays: A Five Volume Anthology of Scholarly Articles*, edited by Dikka Berven, 1995; *Publication History of the Rival Transcriptions of Montaigne's Essays* by Ken Keffer, 2001.

*   *   *

The "essay" is now a well-established and flourishing literary genre in its own right, but when Michel de Montaigne coined the word in 1580 he used it to suggest that his collection of discursive musings represented little more than "try-outs" or "attempts" at reaching an understanding of things by writing about them. His short preface is disarmingly limited in its objectives; he makes it clear that the book was originally conceived for strictly private (in his words, for a few "relations and friends") use, and that it is the work of a gentleman, not of a professional philosopher. Which is why he has no qualms about making himself the "subject matter of [my] book." He goes on to imply that his true significance is in that—like most of his readers—he is ordinary and imperfect. The self-disparagement of this opening is in part a ploy (there is an element of provocation, too, in warning your reader not to waste his time on so "frivolous and vain" a subject) which allows him to refer his critics back to the unpretentiousness of his preface should his erudition or reasoning be found wanting. But throughout his writings one finds a prickly defensiveness whenever the question of academic expertise comes up, and Montaigne rarely misses an opportunity of deriding "pedants." In his chapter (I,26) on the education of children, he claims to prefer an accomplished (*habile*) man to a scholarly (*sçavant*) one, a sound head to a well-filled one. In Montaigne's eyes morals and judgement are more important than mere learning.

The getting of this wisdom is one of the major preoccupations of the *Essais* (*Complete Essays*). Like the Delphic oracle, he would have us know ourselves. Our first duty is to admit the limits of our knowledge, for "to recognize one's ignorance is one of the best and surest signs of judgement I know" ("On Books," II,10). Flexibility of mind is the surest remedy for dogmatism, which he abhorred. As early as the very first chapter of the first book, we see him stressing man's inconsistency ("vain, divers et ondoyant" as he puts it) and deciding that universally binding laws of behaviour cannot be drawn up. This "relativism" inevitably weakened his early allegiance to Stoicism and made him lean towards scepticism. In 1576 he had a medallion struck with the motto "Que sçay je?" to indicate his state of uncertainty. Along with other sceptics he wonders just what he knows, or can know. It has often been said that Montaigne evolved from Stoicism to scepticism before reaching a personal variation on Epicureanism, but this categorization is nowadays considered an over-simplification. Certainly his growing affection for Sextus Empiricus did not mean that he turned his back completely on Seneca and Plutarch and, as we have seen, he possessed an innate scepticism that never left him.

Montaigne's awareness of the wide variety of men's experience sharpened his interest in the New World, and his chapter "On Cannibals" (I, 31) is a fine example of open-mindedness and tolerance. He argues that the so-called cannibals are not "barbaric" or "savage," as they are usually thought, but merely different, and remarks that "everyone calls barbaric things which are not part of their habits." In an endeavour to break down what he termed elsewhere the "barrier of custom" (I, 36), he himself interviewed a indigenous Brazilian and tried to see his own world through their eyes. He tackles the problem of witchcraft in a similarly level-headed fashion (III, 11). Unlike most commentators of his day, Montaigne gives little credence to the self-confessed witches appearing—or being made to appear—in increasing numbers, refuses to believe stories about broomsticks or people disappearing up chimneys, and proposes to treat them as sick rather than evil. He is much harsher in the event on those who presume to punish these poor wretches with the utmost severity than on the "witches" themselves. In this case doubt becomes a positive virtue and, in the later chapters in particular, Montaigne frequently exploits the potentiality of doubt as a method of thinking and being. He comes to rejoice in the very diversity of experience and opinion he sees around him. The *Essays* started out as a sort of commonplace book, not unlike the *Adages* of Erasmus or, on a more mundane level, a collection of "Memorable Sayings" such as Gilles Corrozet's, favouring topics such as sadness or the fear of death, but they developed into "essays" in self-acceptance. Revelling in polyvalence and ambiguity, Montaigne discovers that his attempts to circumscribe life's mysteries have led him to a deeper enjoyment of them. Indeed, the beautifully serene chapter which brings the *Essays* to a close, "On Experience" (III, 13), is a hymn to life, kidney stones and all: "Our great and glorious masterpiece is to live properly." By "properly"—in the original "*à propos*"—he means coming to terms with ourselves as we are. At the end of the same chapter he uses *loiallement* in a similar sense, affirming that it is "absolute perfection, and almost divine, to know how to enjoy loyally one's being." Self-knowledge increases self-enjoyment and, by the end of his *Essays*, Montaigne seems able simply to be.

—Michael Freeman

See the essays on "Apology for Raymond Sebond," "On the Power of the Imagination," and "On Vanity."

MONTALE, Eugenio

Born: Genoa, Italy, 12 October 1896. **Education:** Educated at schools in Genoa to age 14; studied opera singing under Ernesto Sivori. **Military Service:** Served in the Italian army, 1917–19: infantry officer. **Family:** Married Drusilla Tanzi (died 1963). **Member:** Founder, with others, *Primo Tempo* literary journal, Turin, 1922; staff member, Bemporad, publishers, Florence, 1927–28; curator, Vieusseux Book Collection, Florence, 1928–38; poetry critic, *La Fiera Letteraria*, 1938–48, director, *Il Mondo*, 1945–48, literary editor, *Corriere della Sera*, from 1948, and music critic, *Corriere d'Informazione*, 1955–67, all Milan. Life member of the Italian

Senate, 1967. **Awards:** Antico Fattore prize, 1932; Marzotto prize, 1956; Feltrinelli prize, 1962; Gulbenkian prize, 1971; Nobel prize for literature, 1975. Honorary degrees: Cambridge University, 1967; universities of Basle, Milan, and Rome. **Died:** 12 September 1981.

PUBLICATIONS

Verse

Ossi di seppia. 1925; revised edition, 1926, 1948; as *The Bones of Cuttlefish*, translated by Antonio Mazza, 1983; as *Cuttlefish Bones*, translated by William Arrowsmith, 1990.

La casa dei doganieri e altre poesie. 1932; as *The Coastguard's House*, translated by Jeremy Reed, 1990.

Le occasioni. 1939; as *The Occasions*, translated by William Arrowsmith, 1987.

Finisterre. 1943.

Poesie. 3 vols., 1948–57.

La bufera e altro. 1956.

Poems, translated by Edwin Morgan. 1959.

Poesie di Montale (bilingual edition), translated by Robert Lowell. 1960.

Accordi e pastelli. 1963.

Poesie: Poems, edited and translated by George Kay (bilingual edition). 1964; as *Selected Poems* (English translations only), 1969.

Selected Poems, edited by Glauco Cambon. 1965.

Il colpevole. 1966.

Satura. 1966; revised edition, 1971; as *Satura: Five Poems*, translated by Donald Sheehan and David Keller (bilingual edition), 1969; as *Satura: 1962–1970*, translated with notes by William Arrowsmith, 1998.

Xenia. 1966; as *Xenia*, translated by G. Singh, 1970; also translated by K. Hughes, in *Xenia and Motets*, 1980.

Provisional Conclusions: A Selection of the Poetry of Montale 1920–1970, translated by Edith Farnsworth. 1970.

Trentadue variazioni. 1973.

Diario del '71 e del '72. 1973.

Mottetti (bilingual edition), translated by Lawrence Kart. 1973; as *Motets*, translated by K. Hughes, in *Xenia and Motets*, 1980; as *The Motets: Twenty Love Poems*, translated by Dana Gioia, 1987.

Selected Poems (in Italian), edited by G. Singh. 1975.

New Poems: A Selection from Satura and Diario del '71 e del '72, translated by G. Singh. 1976.

Tutte le poesie. 1977.

Quaderno di quattro anni. 1977; as *It Depends: A Poet's Notebook*, edited and translated by G. Singh, 1980.

The Storm and Other Poems, translated by Charles Wright. 1978.

L'opera in versi, edited by Rosanna Bettarini and Gianfranco Contini. 2 vols., 1980.

Altri versi e poesie disperse. 1981.

The Storm and Other Things, translated by William Arrowsmith. 1985.

Satura: 1962–1970, edited by Rosanna Warren. 1998.

Collected Poems: 1920–1954, translated by Jonathan Galassi. 2000.

Fiction

La farfalla di Dinard. 1956; revised edition, 1960; as *The Butterfly of Dinard*, translated by G. Singh, 1970.

Other

La solitudine dell' artista. 1952.

Lettere: Montale-Italo Svevo. 1966.

Auto da fé: Cronache in due tempi. 1966.

Fuori di casa. 1969.

La poesia non esiste. 1971.

Nel nostro tempo. 1972; as *Poet in Our Time*, translated by Alastair Hamilton, 1976.

Sulla poesia, edited by Giorgio Zampa. 1976.

Selected Essays, edited and translated by G. Singh. 1978.

Prime alla Scala. 1981.

Lettere a Salvatore Quasimodo, edited by Sebastiano Grasso. 1981.

The Second Life of Art: Selected Essays, edited by Jonathan Galassi. 1982.

Posthumous Diary: Diario Postumo, translated by Jonathan Galassi. 2001.

Translator, *La battaglia*, by John Steinbeck. 1940.

Translator, *La storia di Billy Budd*, by Melville. 1942.

Translator, *Il mio mondo è qui*, by Dorothy Parker. 1943.

Translator, *Strano interludio*, by Eugene O'Neill. 1943.

Translator, *Al Dio sconosciuto*, by John Steinbeck. 1946.

Translator, *La commedia degli errori, Racconto d'inverno, Timone d'Atene*, by Shakespeare. 3 vols., 1947.

Translator, with Luigi Berti, *Il volto di pietra*. 1947.

Translator, *Quaderno di traduzioni*. 1948; revised edition, 1975.

Translator, *Amleto, principe di Danimarca*, by Shakespeare. 1949.

Translator, *La tragica storia del dottor Faust*, by Marlowe. 1951.

Translator, *Proserpina e lo straniero*, by Omar Del Carlo. 1952.

Translator, *La cicuta e dopo*, by Angus Wilson. 1956.

Translator, (Selections), by T.S. Eliot. 1958.

Translator, *Il Cid*, by Corneille, in *Teatro francese del grande secolo*, edited by G. Macchia. 1960.

*

Bibliography: *Bibliografia montaliana* by Laura Barile, 1977.

Critical Studies: *Montale and Dante* by Arshi Pipa, 1968; *Three Modern Italian Poets: Saba, Ungaretti, Montale* by Joseph Cary, 1969; *Montale*, 1973, and *Montale's Poetry: A Dream in Reason's Presence*, 1982, both by Glauco Cambon; *Eugenio Montale: A Critical Study of His Poetry, Prose and Criticism*, 1973, and *The Achievement of Eugenio Montale*, 1974, both by G. Singh; *Eugenio Montale: The Private Language of Poetry* by Guido Almansi and Bruce Merry, 1977; *Reading Out Poetry; Eugenio Montale: A Tribute* by F.R. Leavis, 1979; *Eugenio Montale: Poet on the Edge* by Rebecca J. West, 1981; *Montale and the Occasions of Poetry* by Claire de C.L. Huffman, 1983; *Montale, Debussy and Modernism* by Gian-Paolo Biasin, 1989; *Montale's Mestiere Vile: The Elective Translations from English of the 1930s and 1940s* by George Talbot, 1995; *Eugenio Montale: The Poetry of the Later Years* by Éanna Ó Ceallacháin, 2001; *Expression of the Inexpressible in Eugenio Montale's Poetry: Metaphor, Negation, and Silence* by Clodagh J. Brook, 2002.

* * *

Eugenio Montale is generally considered Italy's greatest poet of the 20th century. Much admired by writers and intellectuals of a variety of ideological persuasions, he has been a kind of stabilizing force on the Italian literary scene for more than 50 years—beginning in 1925, when he signed Croce's Manifesto of anti-Fascist Intellectuals and published his first book of poetry, to 1975, when he won the Nobel prize for literature, to his death in 1981. This widespread esteem is perhaps somewhat surprising, for Montale is an austere, highly moral, and "difficult" poet whose work requires careful re-reading and reflection before it will begin to yield its meaning. In part this is because for Montale poetry is a means of understanding rather than of representation. Unabashedly (and sometimes mischievously) metaphysical, his work frequently seeks to capture the conjunction of (as he puts it) the miraculous with the necessary, the transcendent with the immanent.

To the tradition of Italian verse that he inherited, Montale brought new and more dissonant harmonies, a broader and more eclectic poetic lexicon, and—above all—a new poetic stance of doubt, scepticism, and extreme self-reflexivity. Many of his poems are concerned with the hesitations, anxieties, and small personal defeats of everyday life. At a time in Italy's political history when official rhetoric was trumpeting the mostly spurious victories of the Fascist State, his lowered, ironic, and deliberately unheroic voice seemed a singular guarantee of the authenticity that has come to be associated with his writing ever since. Much of Montale's earliest work is set in the spare, seaside landscape of Liguria; but in *Le occasioni* (*The Occasions*) of 1939 and *La bufera e altro* [The Storm and Other Things] of 1956, the focus widens to include a variety of European settings, as historical forces tragically irrupt into the poet's intimate world of metaphysical and existential meditation. There is thus a kind of dramatic progression that accompanies his poetic development. In the *Ossi di seppia* (*Cuttlefish Bones*) such personal considerations as memory, identity, and the relation of the self with the outside world are paramount, while in the later volumes these same concerns are viewed in the more complex historical context of the threat to civilized values posed by the brutal forces of war and fascism. A saving constant for the poet in this period and a compelling presence in much of his poetry is that of the woman he usually calls "Clizia," a figure strikingly reminiscent of Dante's Beatrice and perhaps the most vivid and important poetic "lady" in Italian poetry since Petrarch's Laura. Opposed by her very nature to the forces of darkness that threaten not only a lover's affection but also the survival of all the accomplishments that previous centuries of civilization have amassed, she is a numinous presence frightening in her splendour, a miraculous reminder of the potency of love, and a tantalizing hint at the existence of something more than human at large in the cosmos.

With the "fourth phase" of Montale's work after "The Storm" there is a change of tone, as the sometimes exalted language of the earlier production gives way to a more informal, even offhand manner in verse that can seem little more than wry jottings or entries in a day-book, but has sufficient resilience to treat issues of importance with wit and insight. The same gentle humour and delight in the unusual and paradoxical that characterize these poems also permeate the far from negligible prose produced mostly on commission for newspapers and other periodicals.

—Charles Klopp

See the essays on *Cuttlefish Bones* and "The Storm."

MORANTE, Elsa

Born: Rome, Italy, 18 August 1912. **Family:** Married the writer Alberto Moravia, *q.v.*, in 1941 (divorced 1962). **Career:** Contributor to several important periodicals, including *Oggi*, from 1935; lived in Anacapri (on Capri), 1941–43; after the German invasion of Italy, went into hiding with Moravia, in Fondi, near Cassino, from 1943 until the Allied Liberation; returned to Rome, 1944; travelled to Britain, 1948; collaborated with RAI as film critic for *Cronache del cinema*, 1950–51; contributor, *Il Mondo*, from 1951; travelled extensively after 1957, including trips to Iran, India, USSR, China, and the United States. **Awards:** Viareggio prize, 1948; Strega prize, 1957; Séguier prize, 1977; Médicis Foreign Book prize (France), 1984; Zafferana prize, 1968. **Died:** 25 November 1985.

PUBLICATIONS

Collection

Opere, edited by Carlo Cecchi and Cesare Garboli. 2 vols., 1988–90.

Fiction

Le bellissime avventure di Caterì dalla trecciolina (for children). 1941; revised edition, as *Le straordinarie avventure di Caterina*, 1959.
Il gioco segreto (stories). 1941.
Menzogna e sortilegio. 1948; abridged translation, as *House of Liars*, translated by Adrienne Foulke, 1951.
L'isola di Arturo. 1957; as *Arturo's Island*, translated by Isabel Quigly, 1959.
Botteghe oscure. 1958.
Lo scialle andaluso (stories). 1963.
La storia. 1974; as *History: A Novel*, translated by William Weaver, 1977.
Aracoeli. 1982.

Verse

Alibi. 1958.
Il mondo salvato dai ragazzini e altri poemi (includes prose). 1968.
The Coastguards House, translated by Jeremy Reed. 1990.

Other

Translator, *Il libro degli appunti*, by Katherine Mansfield. 1945; as *Quaderno appunti*, 1979.
Translator, with Marcella Hannau, *Il meglio di Katherine Mansfield*. 1957.

*

Critical Studies: *Struttura e stile nella narrativa di Morante* by A.R. Pupino, 1968; *Invito alla lettura di Elsa Morante* by C. Sgorlow, 1972; *Elsa Morante* (in Italian) by Gianni Venturi, 1977; *Scrittura e follia nei romanzi di Elsa Morante* by Donatella Ravanello, 1980; "Scrivere o fare . . . o altro" by Gregory L. Lucente, in *Italica*, 61, 1984; "The Experience of Separation: The Novels of Elsa Morante" by Tim Parks, in *PN Review*, 14, 1988; "Elsa Morante's *Aracoeli*: The End of a Journey" by Rocco Capozzi, in *Women in Italian*

Culture edited by Ada Testaferri, 1989; "Elsa Morante: The Trauma of Possessive Love and Disillusionment" by Rocco Capozzi, in *Contemporary Women Writers in Italy* edited by Santo L. Aricò, 1990; "Elsa Morante's Use of Dream" by Paola Blelloch, in *Fusta*, Spring-Fall, 1990; "Cassandra's Daughters: Prophecy in Elsa Morante's *La storia*" by Susan Briziarelli, in *Romance Languages Annual*, 1990; *Per Elise: Studi su Menzogna e sortilegio* (essay collection), 1990; "The Bewitched Mirror: Imagination and Narration in Elsa Morante" by Sharon Wood, in *Modern Language Review*, 86(2), 1991; *The Theme of Childhood in Elsa Morante* by Grace Zlobnicki Kalay, 1996.

* * *

Elsa Morante is considered one of Italy's most prominent writers of the 20th century. Her artistic career unfolds around the obsessive need to redefine the concept of reality. Morante's novels and short stories explore the conflict between dream or illusion and ordinary life: "For years, my expressed intention has been to represent reality not on the surface, but in its profound truth. To me this is poetry." Morante's central themes speak the language of enchantment, betrayal, solipsism, escapism, and memory. Her protagonists, usually isolated young individuals, struggle against social structures and often find, in the family, the sole means of survival. They inhabit a universe of metaphors, myths, legends, and fables; they undertake journeys to self-discovery in a state of manic divination. Morante's cult of the imagination has brought some critics to regard her style as "magic realism," after the avant-garde narrative mode associated with Massimo Bontempelli in the 1920s. Morante's work incorporates a perfect blend of descriptive detail and visionary allusion; imagination is invested with the power to evoke the invisible shadows of the unconscious, the only way man can perceive and experience the objective world.

Morante's first novel, *Menzogna e sortilegio* (*Houses of Liars*), relates the story of Elisa, the 25-year-old narrator, who decides to retrace her family lineage after the death of her parents. Beginning with her maternal grandmother, who was unhappily married to a degenerate nobleman, Elisa tries to exorcize the hallucinations of her past in order to overcome her frustration and loneliness. In the process, she discloses a terrain of obsession, madness, lies, and rivalry. The narrator's chronicle relies on both memory and history, evocation and recollection. The external setting (the Sicilian landscape) is nothing but a projection of the character's state of consciousness; story-telling becomes a cathartic device to exorcize childhood traumas. As in earlier collections of stories, such as *Il gioco segreto* [The Secret Game], Morante appears to be following the realist tradition of the 19th century, but the psychological investigation into Elisa's paralysis is startlingly contemporary. *House of Liars* was a stunning debut, full of promise for what Morante had to offer in the future.

Published between 1957 and 1958, the short story "Lo scialle andaluso" [The Andalusian Shawl] and *L'isola di Arturo* (*Arturo's Island*) introduce the Freudian scheme of the possessive love of a male character for his absent mother, a theme that was to be central to Morante's final novel, *Aracoeli*. Set on the island of Procida, near Naples, Arturo's story emphasizes repression and the vast displacements occasioned by society's coming of age. Desperately seeking love and attention, the adolescent protagonist reappropriates his childhood memories to confront, as Elisa did, an overwhelming sense of emptiness in the present. In Morante's work, childhood represents a stage of legendary life; it is not a dramatic overture to adulthood. Arturo is an imaginative boy, whose passivity and worship of his father, Wilhelm, a kind of fairytale hero, is broken when Wilhelm brings home a much younger wife. Eventually, Arturo will struggle to possess his surrogate mother, a re-enactment of primal exclusion. Rejected once again, he leaves his phantasmagoric island only to find out that Wilhelm's journeys were no more than short trips to Naples' slums. Arturo's departure is an initiation into the realms of external reality.

Morante's most ambitious and controversial work, *La storia* (*History: A Novel*), elaborates a moral definition of history in a style that reproduces the failures of an illusion: inflated rhetoric, social pretension and deception embody the collapse of Mussolini's ideals from 1941 to 1947. *History* centres on the life of Useppe, a visionary child of war, whose mother Ida, a widowed schoolteacher, has been raped during the German occupation of Rome. Of Jewish descent, Ida also fears for her eldest son, Nino, a Fascist turned partisan. Each section of the novel is prefaced by a summary of the historical events which complement the narrative of the characters' private domain. Useppe's short life is a witness to starvation, destruction, and racial discrimination. When he dies of epilepsy (a predisposition inherited from his mother) at the age of six, Ida falls into despair, and is to be confined to an asylum. According to Morante, "a writer always tries to express his concept of the universe . . . Using the pretext of fictional events and characters, he aims at transposing, in his novel, the utmost of his experience, his ultimate idea of life." Morante's view of history is that all power is violent and evil. Ordinary people are the victims of the indifferent forces of history. As Stephen Spender has said, *History* is about the "inability of men to make politics human" (*New York Review of Books*, 1977).

Set in 1975, *Aracoeli* recounts the journey of the disillusioned 43-year-old Emanuele to Andalusia, the birthplace of his mother who died when he was six. Emanuele's father, an officer in the Italian Navy, met the peasant girl Aracoeli while in Spain, and brought her to Rome. Frustrated by an alien bourgeois environment, Aracoeli gradually slides into depression and, at the death of her second child, escapes into a life of prostitution. The novel culminates with Emanuele's attempt to recapture a pre-verbal level of existence. His journey is structured around hallucinations, flashbacks, "visionary, remote and fictional reconstructions," "apocryphal memories," all of which could be entirely invented by him. Morante explores the depths of a psychological reality definable within this liminal relationship with imagination. The distinction is made clear in the episode of the mirror, in which she identifies the primary alienation of the infant from himself, and the perceptual relationship of the son to his mother as Other. The narrator's neurosis, caused by his sense of irreplaceable loss, confines him to a state of amnesia and sleep. Whether we read *Aracoeli* as a political allegory (in the decomposition of the mother's body) or we read it in light of the pre-Oedipal stage of the Lacanian concept of the imaginary, Morante's final novel departs from her previous work because of its ironic force, and its mode of consciousness which signals final disintegration.

Morante is an extraordinary writer who avoided the baroque artifices so common to Italian prose. Her retreat into the world of the child is a strategy for recapturing mankind's lost innocence. In *Il mondo salvato dai ragazzini* [The World Saved By the Children], a collection of poems, prose, and drama, Morante divides the world into the "happy few" and the "unhappy many." She categorizes the childlike artist in the first group. One would like to think, with Pier Paolo Pasolini, that Morante herself was a "grandmother-child,"

capable of saying extraordinary things about society, and yet able to lead us to an imaginative return to unity.

—Gaetana Marrone

See the essay on *House of Liars*.

MORAVIA, Alberto

Born: Alberto Pincherle in Rome, Italy, 28 November 1907. **Education:** Educated privately; received high school equivalency diploma 1967. Contracted tuberculosis in 1916 and spent much time in sanatoriums over the next nine years. **Family:** Married 1) the writer Elsa Morante, *q. v.*, in 1941 (divorced 1962; died 1985); 2) Dacia Maraini in 1963; 3) Carmen Llera in 1986. **Career:** Foreign correspondent, *La Stampa*, Milan, and *Gazzetta del Popolo*, Turin, in the 1930s, travelled extensively, with long periods in France, Britain, United States, Mexico, Greece, and China; lived in Anacapri (on Capri), 1941–43; after the German invasion of Italy, went into hiding with Morante, in Fondi, near Cassino, from 1943 until the Allied Liberation; film critic, *La Nuova Europa*, 1944–46; co-editor, with Alberto Carocci, *Nuovi Argomenti*, Milan, from 1953; film critic, *L'Espresso*, Milan, from 1955; State Department lecturer in the United States, 1955; travelled extensively throughout the world, 1958–70; co-editor with Leonardo Sciascia, *q. v.*, and Enzo Siciliano, *Nuovi Argomenti*, 1982. President, International PEN, 1959. **Awards:** Corriere Lombardo prize, 1945; Strega prize, 1952; Marzotto prize, 1954; Viareggio prize, 1961. Honorary member, American Academy; chevalier, 1952, and commander, 1984, Légion d'honneur. **Died:** 26 September 1990.

PUBLICATIONS

Fiction

Gli indifferenti. 1929; as *The Indifferent Ones*, translated by Aida Mastrangelo, 1932; as *The Time of Indifference*, translated by Angus Davidson, 1953; as *The Time of Indifference*, translated by Tami Calliope, 2000.

Le ambizioni sbagliate. 1935; as *The Wheel of Fortune*, translated by Arthur Livingston, 1937; as *Mistaken Ambitions*, translated by Livingston, 1955.

La bella vita. 1935.

L'imbroglio. 1937.

I sogni del pigro. 1940.

La mascherata. 1941; as *The Fancy Dress Party*, translated by Angus Davidson, 1947.

L'amante infelice. 1943.

L'epidemia: Racconti surrealistici e satirici. 1944.

Agostino. 1945; as *Agostino*, translated by Beryl de Zoete, 1947.

Due cortigiane; Serata di Don Giovanni. 1945.

La romana. 1947; as *The Woman of Rome*, translated by Lydia Holland, 1949; updated and revised edition by Tami Calliope, 1999.

La disubbidienza. 1948; as *Disobedience*, translated by Angus Davidson, 1950; as *Luca*, translated by Davidson, in *Five Novels*, 1955.

L'amore coniugale e altri racconti (stories). 1949; selection as *Conjugal Love*, translated by Angus Davidson, 1951, and in *Five Novels*, 1955.

Two Adolescents: The Stories of Agostino and Luca (includes *Agostino* and *Disobedience*), translated by Beryl de Zoete and Angus Davidson, 1950.

Il conformista. 1951; as *The Conformist*, translated by Angus Davidson, 1951; as *Conformist: A Novel*, translated by Tami Calliope, 1999.

I racconti. 1952; as *I racconti 1927–1951*, 2 vols., 1983; selection as *Bitter Honeymoon and Other Stories*, translated by Bernard Wall, Frances Frenaye, and Baptista Gilliat Smith, 1954, and *The Wayward Wife and Other Stories*, translated by Angus Davidson, 1960.

Racconti romani (stories). 1954; selection as *Roman Tales*, translated by Angus Davidson, 1956.

Il disprezzo. 1954; as *A Ghost at Noon*, translated by Angus Davidson, 1955; as *Contempt*, translated by Angus Davidson, 1999.

Five Novels (includes *Mistaken Ambitions; Agostino; Luca; Conjugal Love; A Ghost at Noon*), translated by Arthur Livingston, Beryl de Zoete, and Angus Davidson. 1955.

La ciociara. 1957; as *Two Women*, translated by Angus Davidson, 1958; updated and revised edition by Ann McGarrell, 2001.

Nuovi racconti romani (stories). 1959; selection as *More Roman Tales*, translated by Angus Davidson, 1963.

La noia. 1960; as *The Empty Canvas*, translated by Angus Davidson, 1961; as *Boredom*, translated by Angus Davidson, 1999.

L'automa. 1962; as *The Fetish and Other Stories*, translated by Angus Davidson, 1964; as *The Fetish: A Volume of Stories*, translated by Davidson, 1964.

Cortigiana stanca. 1965.

L'attenzione. 1965; as *The Lie*, translated by Angus Davidson, 1966.

Una cosa è una cosa. 1967; selection as *Command and I Will Obey You*, translated by Angus Davidson, 1969.

Il paradiso (stories). 1970; as *Paradise and Other Stories*, translated by Angus Davidson, 1971; as *Bought and Sold*, translated by Davidson, 1973.

Io e lui. 1971; as *Two: A Phallic Novel*, translated by Angus Davidson, 1972; as *The Two of Us*, translated by Davidson, 1972.

Un'altra vita. 1973; as *Lady Godiva and Other Stories*, translated by Angus Davidson, 1975.

Boh. 1976; as *The Voice of the Sea and Other Stories*, translated by Angus Davidson, 1978.

La vita interiore. 1978; as *Time of Desecration*, translated by Angus Davidson, 1980.

1934. 1982; as *1934*, translated by William Weaver, 1983. *La cosa e altri racconti.* 1983; as *Erotic Tales*, translated by Tim Parks, 1985.

Storie della preistoria: Favole. 1983.

L'uomo che guarda. 1985; as *The Voyeur*, translated by Tim Parks, 1986.

Il viaggio a Roma. 1988; as *Journey to Rome*, translated by Tim Parks, 1990.

Plays

Gli indifferenti, with Luigi Squarzini, from the novel by Moravia (produced 1948). In *Sipario*, 1948.

Il provino (produced 1955).

Non approfondire (produced 1957).

Beatrice Cenci. In *Teatro*, 1958; as *Beatrice Cenci*, translated by Angus Davidson, 1965.

La mascherata, from his own novel. In *Teatro*, 1958.

Il mondo è quello che è (produced 1966). 1966.

Il dio Kurt (produced 1969). 1968.

La vita è gioco (produced 1970). 1969.

Screenplays: *Un colpo di pistola*, 1941; *Zazà*, 1942; *Ultimo incontro*, 1951; *Sensualità*, 1951; *Tempi nostri*, 1952; *La provinciale* (*The Wayward Wife*), 1952; *Villa Borghese*, 1953; *La donna del fiume*, 1954; *La romana* (*The Woman of Rome*), 1955; *Racconti romani* (*Roman Tales*), 1956; *Racconti d'estate* (*Love on the Riviera*), 1958; *I delfini* (*The Dauphins*), 1960; *La giornata balorda* (*From a Roman Balcony*), 1960; *Una domenica d'estate*, 1961; *Agostino*, 1962; *Ieri oggi domani* (*Yesterday, Today, and Tomorrow*), 1963; *Le ore nude*, 1964; *L'occhio selvaggio* (*The Wild Eye*), 1967.

Other

La speranza: Ossia cristianesimo e comunismo. 1944.

Opere complete. 16 vols., 1952–76.

Un mese in U.R.S.S. 1958.

I moralisti moderni, with Elemire Zolla. 1960.

Women of Rome, photographs by Sam Waagenaar. 1960.

Un'idea dell'India. 1962.

Claudia Cardinale. 1963.

L'uomo come fine e altri saggi. 1964; as *Man as an End: A Defense of Humanism*, translated by Bernard Wall, 1965.

La rivoluzione culturale in Cina ovvero il convitato di pietra. 1967; as *The Red Book and the Great Wall: An Impression of Mao's China*, translated by Ronald Strom, 1968.

A quale tribù appartieni?. 1972; as *Which Tribe Do You Belong To?*, translated by Angus Davidson, 1974.

Al cinema: Centoquarantotto film d'autore. 1975.

La mutazione femminile: Conversazione con Alberto Moravia sulla donna, with Carla Ravaiola. 1975.

Intervista sullo scrittore scomodo, edited by Nello Ajello. 1978.

Quando Ba Lena era tanto piccola, illustrations by Diana Saputi. 1978.

Cosima e i briganti. 1980.

Impegno controvoglia: Saggi, articoli, interviste, edited by Renzo Paris. 1980.

Lettere del Sahara. 1981.

Lettere, with Giuseppe Prezzolini. 1982.

Storia della preistoria, illustrations by Flaminia Siciliano. 1982.

Passeggiate africane. 1987.

Io e il mio tempo: Conversazioni critiche con Ferdinando Camon. 1988.

Life of Moravia, with Alain Elkann, translated by William Weaver. 2000.

Editor, with Elemire Zolla, *Saggi italiani*. 1960.

*

Bibliography: *An Annotated Bibliography of Moravia Criticism in Italy and in the English-Speaking World (1929–1975)* by Ferdinando Alfonsi, 1976.

Critical Studies: *Moravia* (in English) by Giuliano Dego, 1966; *Three Italian Novelists* by Donald W. Heiney, 1968; *Moravia* by Fulvio Longobardi, 1969; *The Existentialism of Moravia* by Joan

Ross and Donald Freed, 1972; *Invito alla lettura di Moravia* by Giancarlo Pandini, 1973; *Alberto Moravia* by Jane E. Cottrell, 1974; *Come leggere Gli indifferenti* by Marinella Mascia Galateria, 1975; *Alberto Moravia: Introduzione e guida* by Roberto Tessari, 1975; *Moravia desnudo* by Sergio Savaiane, 1976; *Il sistema dell'in/differenza: Moravia e il fascismo* by Roberto Esposito, 1978; *Le cose e le figure negli Indifferenti di Moravia* by Lucia Strappini, 1978; *L'ossessione e il fantasma: Il teatro di Pasolini e Moravia* by Enrico Groppali, 1979; *Alberto Moravia: Vita, parole e idee di un romanziere* by Enzo Siciliano, 1982; *Il punto su Moravia* by Cristina Benussi, 1987; *La magia della scrittura: Moravia, Malerba, Sanguineti* by Armando La Torre, 1987; ''For Better, for Worse: Elements of Irony and Reversal in Alberto Moravia's *L'Amore coniugale*,'' in *Italianist*, 7, 1987, ''Gender and Structure in Moravia's *1934*,'' in *Bulletin of the Society for Italian Studies*, 20, 1987, ''Crossing Frontiers: Some Reflections on Moravia,'' in *Association of Teachers of Italian Journal*, 52, 1988, ''Religion, Politics and Sexuality in Moravia's *Il conformista*,'' in *Italian Studies*, 44, 1989, and *Women as Object: Language and Gender in the Work of Alberto Moravia*, 1989, all by Sharon Wood; *Moravia ''Art Deco''* by Joseph Venturini, 1988; ''The Forensics of Freedom: Dialogues and Dialectics in Moravia's Seventies Novels'' by William Slaymaker, in *Italian Culture*, 66(2), 1989; *The Aspiration Toward a Lost Natural Harmony in the Work of Three Italian Writers: Leopardi, Verga and Moravia* by Foscarina Alexander, 1990; *Discorrendo di Alberto Moravia* by Memy Piccinonno, 1992; *Homage to Moravia*, edited by Rocco Capozzi and Mario B. Mignone, 1993; *Alberto Moravia* by Thomas Erling Peterson, 1996; *Self and Self-compromise in the Narratives of Pirandello and Moravia* by M. John Stella, 1999.

*   *   *

Alberto Moravia made his fortune with his very first novel, *Gli indifferenti* (*The Time of Indifference*), written when he was only 22. It captured the spirit of the times both in Italy and elsewhere in Europe, depicting in a provocatively realistic, rather than an evocatively suggestive, way the malaise of society, the existential crisis of man, and the dramatic transvaluation of moral, social, and political values. Sartre, de Beauvoir and Camus admired the novel, and perhaps owed something to it. Such a *succès d'estime* Moravia himself was never to repeat in his long literary career. His other famous works include the novels *Agostino*, *La romana* (*The Woman of Rome*), *La ciociara* (*Two Women*), *La noia* (*The Empty Canvas*), the short-story collections *I racconti*, *Racconti romani* (*Roman Tales*), and *Nuovi racconti romani* (*More Roman Tales*).

Moravia's main strength as a novelist lies in his ability to combine the true and the realistic in a satirical vein, and apply them to his critique of man and society. Sometimes, however, his diagnostic analysis of the various ills of society is lost in gratuitous description—description whose sole motivation seems to be the desire to shock. Hence, some of his work—for instance, the short story ''Il Paradiso'' (''Paradise'')—gives the impression of Italian society as a whole being a kind of lunatic asylum. The same criticism may be levelled against Moravia's obsession, particularly in his later works, with sex.

At times even the satirical-polemical vein in Moravia, for all his professed objectivity and disinterestedness, gets the better of him, and he appears one of the most *engagé* and ideologically obsessed writers of the 20th century. His obsession with sex manifests itself through an extreme form of realism, sometimes bordering on the obscene and the morbid. Nevertheless, his inventiveness of plot and character, his linguistic verve, psychological insight, and graphic vividness of detail make his criticism of the corruptions, malaise, and decadence of modern society all the more telling.

It is not as a moralist, but as a pathologist that Moravia largely presents himself in his work. Behind an acquired mask of cold clinical detachment, his burning passion is not so much that of a reformer, as that of chronicler and caricaturist. Diagnosis for the sake of diagnosis, castigating the ills of modern society and civilization for the mere pleasure of doing so is a tendency from which Moravia, in his long literary career, was never able to free himself. These aspects of his work make him not moralistic, but essentially amoral; even behind his urge to write and to create, there is something calculated mechanically.

Moravia's commitment to a political ideology—he was a member of the Communist Party—seems to have been little more than a strategy. For all his professed communism, for instance, he was not prevented from writing in the Milanese daily *Il Corriere della Sera* with its rather right-wing sympathies.

It is, however, as one of the major Italian novelists of this century, as well as an essayist, that Moravia must be judged. His first and, in many respects, most important novel, *The Time of Indifference*, is considered to be the first existentialist novel that sets out not only to castigate the decadent Italian bourgeoisie, a society of depraved and unhappy but materially rich people, but also exposes the domineering role that sex and money play in it. These themes were to dominate many of Moravia's subsequent novels, for instance in *Agostino*, where the discovery of sexuality on the part of an adolescent is the leitmotif, in *The Woman of Rome*, where the novelist portrays the life of a prostitute, with its misery, hardships, but also with a certain degree of satisfaction and self-complacency, and in *Io e lui* (*Two: A Phallic Novel*), where the narrator is conversing with his penis, which is supposed to symbolize man's relation to himself as well as the conflict between flesh and spirit, the body and the soul.

In other novels, such as *The Empty Canvas* and *L'attenzione* (*The Lie*), Moravia deals with his and, in general, man's relation to reality. In *The Empty Canvas* the protagonist considers himself to be a misfit in the world, but only when he is near death does he feel himself to be ''reborn,'' and come to terms with life. In *The Lie*, the novelist tries to analyse the kind of relationship that exists between himself and the reality he wants to depict, thereby attempting to achieve an ''authentic'' realistic novel—something he cannot do, since any reality he depicts is bound to be inherently inauthentic.

As a critic of the ills and evils of modern society, as well as an articulator of the anguish, dilemmas, and essential emptiness of modern man, Moravia, among modern Italian writers, ranks with Svevo, Pirandello, Montale, and Pavese.

—G. Singh

See the essay on *The Time of Indifference*.

MORI Ōgai

Pseudonyms: Ōgai-gyoshi, Senda Sanbō Shujin, Shigure-no-ya, Kakushi-nagashi, Yume miru hito. **Born:** Mori Rintarō in Tsuwano, Iwami Province (present-day Shimane Prefecture), Japan, 19 January 1862. **Education:** Studied Chinese classics at home and at local fief school, 1867–1872; began study of Dutch language at home in 1870; moved to Tokyo and began study of German language in 1872;

falsified age by two years in order to enter Tokyo University pre-medical study program in 1874; graduated from Tokyo University medical school, 1881; sent to Germany by Japanese military to study military hygiene and public health with Franz Hoffmann, Max von Pettenkofer, Wilhelm Roth, and Robert Koch at universities in Leipzig, Munich, and Berlin, 1884–1888. **Military Service:** Joined Japanese army as lieutenant upon graduation from medical school, 1881; promoted to captain while in Germany; served in China and Taiwan during Sino-Japanese war, 1894–95; served in China and Manchuria during Russo-Japanese war, 1904–06; promoted to rank of Surgeon General, 1907; retired, 1916. **Family:** Married 1) Akamatsu Toshiko in 1889 (divorced 1890), one son; 2) Araki Shige in 1902, two daughters and two sons. **Career:** Had dual career in medicine and literature; accepted post with army medical service, 1881; began reading and collecting German literature during stay in Germany, 1884–88; instructor at army medical school, 1888; instructor of anatomy at Tokyo University for the Arts, 1889; first translations from German, 1889; first work of original short fiction, 1890; appointed Doctor of Medicine, 1891; Head of the Staff College, 1893; Chief Medical Officer for the Twelfth Division in Kokura, 1899–1902; Head of Bureau of Medical Affairs at Department of War, 1907–16; Director of Imperial Museum and Library, 1917–22. **Died:** 9 July 1922, officially of kidney disease, possibly of tuberculosis.

PUBLICATIONS

Collections

Ōgai zenshū. 35 vols., 1936–39.
Ōgai zenshū. 38 vols., 1971–75.
The Incident at Sakai and Other Stories, edited by David Dilworth and J. Thomas Rimer. 1977.
Youth and Other Stories, edited by J. Thomas Rimer. 1994.

Fiction

"Maihim." 1890; as "The Dancing Girl," translated by Richard Bowring, 1975.
"Utakata no ki." 1890; as "Utakata no ki," translated by Richard Bowring, 1974.
"Fumizukai." 1891; as "The Courier," translated by Karen Brazell, 1971.
Somechigae. 1897.
Asane. 1906.
Yūrakumon. 1907.
"Hannichi." 1909; as "Half a Day," translated by Darcy Murray, 1973.
"Tsuina." 1909; as "Exorcism," translated by John Dower, 1971.
Vita Sexualis. 1909; as *Vita Sexualis*, translated by Kazuji Ninomiya and Sanford Goldstein, 1972.
"Dokushin." 1910; as "A Bachelor," translated by James Vardaman, Jr., 1994.
Seinen. 1910; reprinted 1913; as *Youth*, translated by Shoichi Ono and Sanford Goldstein, 1994.
"Fushinchū." 1910; as "Under Reconstruction," translated by Ivan Morris, 1962.
Hanako. 1910; translated by Torao Takemoto, 1918.
"Asobi" 1910; as "Play," translated by James Vardaman, Jr., 1994.

"Chinmoku no tō." 1910; as "The Tower of Silence," translated by Helen Hopper, 1994.
"Shokudō." 1910; as "The Dining Room," translated by Helen Hopper, 1994.
"Hebi." 1911; as "Snake," translated by John Dower, 1971.
"Mōsō." 1911; as "Delusion," translated by John Dower, 1970; as "Daydreams," translated by Richard Bowring, 1994.
Ryūkō. 1911.
Shinchū. 1911.
Gan. 1911; reprinted 1915; as *The Wild Geese*, translated by Kingo Ochiai and Sanford Goldstein, 1959; as *The Wild Goose*, translated by Burton Watson, 1995.
"Hyaku monogatari." 1911; as "Ghost Stories," translated by J. Thomas Rimer, 1994.
"Ka no yō ni." 1912; as "As If," translated by G. Sinclair and Kazo Suita, 1925.
Fushigi na kagami. 1912.
Nezumizaka. 1912.
"Kaijin." 1912; as "The Ashes of Destruction," translated by James Vardaman, Jr., 1994.
"Okitsu Yagoemon no isho." 1912; as "The Last Testament of Okitsu Yagoemon," translated by Richard Bowring, 1977; translated by William Wilson, 1971.
"Abe ichizoku." 1913; as "The Abe Family," translated by David Dilworth, 1977.
Nagashi. 1913.
Sahashi Jingorō. 1913; translated by J.J. Thomas Rimer, 1977.
"Sakai jiken." 1914; as "The Incident at Sakai," translated by David Dilworth, 1977.
Yasui fujin. 1914; translated by David Dilworth and J. Thomas Rimer, 1977.
Kuriyama daizen. 1914; translated by J. Thomas Rimer, 1977.
Tenchō. 1915.
Tsuge Shirōzaemon. 1915; translated by E.R. Skrzypczak, 1977.
Sanshō dayū. 1915; translated by Tsutomu Fukuda, 1970; translated by J. Thomas Rimer, 1977.
"Jiisan baasan." 1915; as "The Old Man and the Old Woman," translated by David Dilworth and J. Thomas Rimer, 1977.
"Saigo no ikku." 1915; as "The Last Phrase," translated by David Dilworth and J. Thomas Rimer, 1977.
"Takasebune." 1916; reprinted 1918; as "The Boat on the River Takase," translated by E.R. Skrzypczak, 1977.
Kanzan jittoku. 1916; translated by David Dilworth and J. Thomas Rimer, 1971.

Plays

Tama kushige futari urashima. 1902.
Chōsokabe Nobuchika. 1903.
Nichiren shōnin tsuji seppo. 1904.
Purumura. 1909.
Kamen. 1909; as *Masks*, translated by James Vardaman, Jr., 1994.
Shizuka. 1909.
Ikutagawa. 1910.
Onnagata. 1912.

Verse

Uta nikki. 1907. Translated and original verse.
Sara no ki. 1915. Translated and original verse.

Other

Minawashū. 1892; reprinted 1906.
Kagegusa. 1897; reprinted 1911.
Ōgonhai. 1910.
Suginohara shina. 1916.
Shibue chūsai. 1916; translated in part and summarized as *The Woman in the Crested Kimono*, by Edwin McClellan, 1985.
Juami no tegami. 1916.
Izawa Ranken. 1916–17.
Tokō tahei. 1917.
Suzuki Tōkichirō. 1917.
Saiki Kōi. 1917.
Kojima Hōso. 1917.
Hōjō Katei. 1917.
Hōjō Katei. 1918–20.
Hōjō Katei shōgai no matsu ichinen. 1920.
Translator, *Omokage*, 1889.
Translator, *Shirabe wa Takashi Gitarura no Hitofushi* [*El alcalde de Zalamanca*], by Calderón de la Barca. 1889.
Translator, *Ori Bara* [*Emilia Galotti*], by G. Lessing. 1889–1892.
Translator, *Sokkyō shijin* [*Improvisatoren*], by Hans Christian Anderson. 1902.
Translator, *Jon Gaburieru Borukman* [*John Gabriel Borkman*], by Henrik Ibsen. 1909.
Translator, *Sarome*, by Oscar Wilde, 1909.
Translator, *Gyottsu* [*Götz von Berlichingen*], by Johann Wilhelm Goethe. 1912–13.
Translator, *Fausuto I*, by Johann Wilhelm Goethe. 1913.
Translator, *Fausuto II*, by Johann Wilhelm Goethe. 1913.
Translator, *Makubesu*, by William Shakespeare. 1913.
Translator, *Nora* [*Et Dukkehjem*], by Henrik Ibsen. 1913.
Translator, *Perikan*, by A. Strindberg. 1916.

*

Critical Studies: *Mori Ōgai ronkō* by Hasegawa Izumi, 1962; *Wakaki hi no Mori Ōgai* by Kobori Keiichirō, 1969; "Mori Ōgai" by Hasegawa Izumi, 1965; "Mori Ōgai's Response to Suppression of Intellectual Freedom 1909–1912" by Helen Hopper, 1974; *Accomplices of Silence* by Masao Miyoshi, 1974; *Mori Ōgai* by J. Thomas Rimer, 1975; *Mori Ōgai and the Modernization of Japanese Culture* by Richard Bowring, 1979; *Mori Ōgai: bungyō kaidai* by Kobori Keiichirō, 1982; *The Historical Fiction of Mori Ōgai* edited by David Dilworth and J. Thomas Rimer, 1991; *Paragons of the Ordinary* by Marvin Marcus, 1993.

* * *

Mori Ōgai stands with Natsume Sōseki as one of two literary giants of the Meiji (1868–1912) and Taishō (1912–1925) periods in Japan. Sustaining dual careers in both literature and medicine, he made significant contributions to the fields of poetry, fiction, drama, literary criticism, translation, historical fiction, and biography, as well as to public health and hygiene, and military health and sanitation. Ōgai helped steer Japan as it negotiated its place in the modern world, advocating modernization of both medical and literary practices while fiercely preserving what he considered the best of Japanese tradition.

Ōgai launched his careers during his four-year stay in Germany where he studied with Germany's foremost scholars on public and military health, notably Nobel laureate Robert Koch, an expert in research on cholera and other infectious diseases, and Max von Pettenkofer, a founder of epidemiology. He also read widely in European literature in German translation. Notes in his diaries and books indicate that he was profoundly moved by these works, spending much of his time away from his medical work reading. He became one of the best-informed Japanese writers of his day on the trends in European literature and philosophy.

Upon his return to Japan in 1888, Ōgai lost no time in carving a niche for himself in the literary world and soon became one of the leading figures in the Japanese literary establishment. His earliest publications were translations of a play and several short stories by authors such as Calderón, Daudet, Hoffman, and Lessing, but his first widely acclaimed translation was his 1889 collection of poetry, *Omokage* [Vestiges]. This collection, created with the help of three friends and his younger sister, Kimiko, introduced Japanese readers to Byron, Goethe, Heine, and other Romantic poets. *Omokage* appealed to Japanese readers by successfully blending the old and new, the foreign and native. The authors experimented with new verse forms and methods of translation, such as replicating meter and rhyme with syllable count and Chinese tones. Their translations introduced vocabulary and subject matter not possible in the convention-laden traditional Japanese poetry while still using classical Japanese and Chinese grammar.

Ōgai continued translating verse, and later poetry collections; he also included original and innovative poetry in traditional forms such as *waka*, *haiku*, and Chinese *kanshi*. Proceeds from the sale of *Omokage* financed *Shigarami zōshi*, the first of Ōgai's several journals devoted to publishing original and translated literature, as well as scholarly literary criticism.

Ōgai continued throughout his writing career to be a bold translator of drama, fiction, and verse. Translating nearly one hundred short stories and nearly fifty plays during his career, Ōgai introduced Japanese readers to influential and popular literature from around the world and to new ideas of romantic love, self-revelation, and personal freedom. Moreover, these translations helped resuscitate the ailing reputation of Japanese fiction: never very highly regarded, the genre had come to be seen as frivolous and incapable of exploring the depths of human experience. Ōgai showed contemporaries that fiction was highly valued in other countries as a medium of "truth."

Reading and translating foreign literature no doubt influenced Ōgai's own production of fiction. His influential 1890 short story "Maihime" ("The Dancing Girl") is often considered the first work of modern Japanese fiction and was certainly revolutionary in its subject matter and form. Structured very much like the *Novellen* Ōgai had been reading and translating, "The Dancing Girl" tells the story of young Ōta Toyotarō who falls in love with a German dancing girl while working abroad. Ōta is torn between duty to his native government and family and feelings for the young dancing girl who carries his child. He is eventually convinced to fulfill his duty and return to Japan, abandoning the girl. This story plays upon the traditional Japanese motif of conflict between duty and human feeling, and does so in traditional, almost classical, language; but Ōgai explores the theme from Ōta's point of view with a psychological depth, intensity, and honesty not to be found in Japanese writing before "The Dancing

Girl.'' Moreover, Ōgai shows the personal, human cost exacted in the very modern struggle for individualism and freedom. ''The Dancing Girl'' was followed by two other short stories set in Germany to make up Ōgai's ''German Trilogy,'' often considered the masterwork of his ''Romantic'' period.

During his posting in the remote town of Kokura (1899–1902), Ōgai produced very little literature. Upon his return to Tokyo, however, he entered one of his most productive periods. The fiction of these later years employs the very personal point of view of his German Trilogy, but the narrating voice becomes more sardonic, detached, and objective, as if Ōgai observes life as an outsider. He examines the intricacies and disappointments of domestic life in works such as ''Hannichi'' (''Half a Day'') and ''Hebi'' (''The Snake'') and explores young men's passages to self-awareness through disillusionment in works such as the decidedly unerotic *Vita Sexualis*, and his longer work about an aspiring writer, *Seinen* (*Youth*). His popular novel *Gan* (*The Wild Goose*) examines frustrated romantic love. Ōgai's later fiction defied contemporary trends toward naturalism and sordid self-revelation.

The years after Kokura also proved fruitful for Ōgai as a playwright. His stage dramas, set in both historical and modern times and in Japan and abroad, helped usher in a contemporary theater movement in Tokyo. In addition, Ōgai translated a number of influential plays, many of which were performed to great acclaim, notably his translation of Ibsen's *John Gabriel Borkman* performed by Osanai Kaoru's Free Theater. He was also active during these years in promoting theater through his contributions to and editing of the journal *Kabuki*.

The death of Emperor Meiji and subsequent ritual suicide of General Nogi and his wife in 1912 shook a nation convinced that it had entered the modern age. Ōgai, too, began to reassess his relationship to traditional Japanese values and Western modernization as he embarked on a careful exploration of Japan's history. His fiction of the last ten years of his life is almost exclusively based on traditional stories, legends, and events and examines a range of ideas—from the age-old conflict of the individual will and duty to society in ''Abe ichizoku'' (''The Abe Family'') to the lyrical exploration of family love and bittersweet reconciliation in *Sanshō dayū*.

The crowning work of Ōgai's later years is not his historical fiction but his carefully researched and written historical biographies. His best known work in this genre, *Shibue Chūsai*, examines the life of a relatively obscure Tokugawa Confucian scholar and his family. In this and other biographies, Ōgai identifies strongly with his subject and, though writing an objective tale of a life, inserts his own voice into the narrative, revealing almost as much about himself as about his subjects. Ōgai chose subjects who exemplified traditional values and ethics he thought worth preserving in Japan.

Although Ōgai began his writing career looking outside to the Western world, he ended it looking carefully into Japan's own past and traditions. Throughout his career he balanced the need for understanding the literary world beyond Japan and for innovation and reform in Japan's literature, with the recognition that Japan must also preserve its own literary traditions and values. He strove for this balance with great energy, contributing to every aspect of Japanese literary life while rising to the top of the military medical world. His works are still revered today as examples of intelligent, careful, and elegant literary production.

—Sarah Cox Smith

MÖRIKE, Eduard (Friedrich)

Born: Ludwigsburg, Germany, 8 September 1804. **Education:** Educated in Stuttgart, Urach, 1818–22; Tübinger Stift, 1822–26. **Family:** Married Margarete von Speeth in 1851 (separated 1873). **Career:** Curate, Möhringen, 1827, Plattenhardt, 1829, Owen, Ochsenwang, 1832; vicar, Cleversulzbach, 1834; worked as a journalist; pensioned in 1843; lived with his sister at Schwäbisch-Hall and from 1844 at Bad Mergentheim. **Died:** 4 June 1875.

PUBLICATIONS

Collections

Gesammette Erzaählungen. 1894.
Werke und Briefe, edited by Herbert Göpfert. 1954.
Sämtliche Werke, edited by Gerhart Baumann. 3 vols., 1954–59.
Werke und Briefe. Historisch-kritische Ausgabe, edited by Hans-Henrik Krummacher, Herbert Meyer, and Bernhard Zeller. 15 vols., 1968–86.
The Complete Poems. 1969.

Verse

Gedichte. 1838, revised editions, 1844, 1848, 1856, 1867.
Klassische Blumenlese. 1840.
Theokritos, Bion und Moschos. 1855.
Anakreon. 1864.
Poems, translated by Norah K. Cruickshank and Gilbert E. Cunningham. 1959.

Fiction

Maler Nolten. 1832.
Iris: Eine Sammlung erzählender und dramatischer dichtungen. 1839.
Idylle vom Bodensee. 1847.
Das Stuttgarter Hutzlemännlein (stories). 1853.
Mozart auf der Reise nach Prag. 1856; as *Mozart's Journey from Vienna to Prague*, translated by Florence Leonard, 1897; as *Mozart on the Way to Prague*, translated by Walter and Catherine Alison Philips, 1934; as *Mozart's Journey to Prague*, translated by Leopold von Loewenstein-Wertheim, 1957; also translated by David Luke, 1997.
Die Historie von der schönen Lau. 1873.
Lucie Gelmeroth. 1923.

Other

Mörike-Storm Briefwechsel. 1891; as *Correspondence with Storm*, edited by H.W. Rath, 1919.
Gedichte und Briefe an Seine braut Margarete V. Speeth, edited by Marie Bauer. 1903.
Eine Dichters Liebe: Eduard Mörike's Brautbriefe, edited by Walther Eggert Winbegg. 1911.

Unveröffentlichte Briefe, edited by Friedrich Seebass. 1941, revised
edition, 1945.
Traum und Tag: Sein Leben in Briefen. 1942.
Briefe, edited by Gerhart Baumann. 1960.
Briefe an seine Braut Luise Rau, edited by Friedhelm Kemp. 1965.
Editor, *Tannhaüser und der Sängerkreig auf Wartburg.* 1861.
Translator, *Römanische Lyrik.* 1946.
Translator, *Griechische Lyrik.* 1949.

*

Critical Studies: *Eduard Mörike: The Man and the Poet* by Margaret
Mare, 1957; *Eduard Mörike in Mergentheim* by Max Fischer, 1973;
Poetik des Übergangs: zu Mörikes Gedicht Göttliche Reminiszence
by Eleonore Frey, 1977; *Eduard Mörike: Die Kunst der Sünde: Zur
Geschichte des literarischen Individuums* by Gerhart von Graevenitz,
1978; *Eduard Mörike Der Letzte König von Orplid vorgelegt* by
Beatrice Funk-Schoellkopf, 1980; *Eduard Mörike's Orplid: Myth
and the Poetic Mind* by Jeffrey Todd Adams, 1984, and *Mörike's
Muses: Critical Essays on Eduard Mörike* edited by Adams, 1990;
*Lyrik im Realismus: Studien über Raum und Zeit in den Gedichten
Mörikes, der Droste und Liliencross* by Heinz Schlaffer, 1984;
*Mörikes lemurische Possen: Die Grenzgänger der schönen Künste
und ihre Bedeutung für eine dem Mahler Nolten immanente Poetik* by
Roland Ischerpel, 1985; *Eduard Mörike's Prosaerzählungen* by
Birgit Mayer, 1985; *Eduard Mörike's Reading and the Reconstruc-
tion of His Extant Library* by Hal H. Rennert, 1985; *Willkomm und
Abschied: Herzschlag und Peitschenhieb: Goethe, Mörike, Heine* by
Eckhardt Meyer-Krentler, 1987; *Der Dichter und die Dilettanten:
Eduard Mörike und die bürgerliche Geselligkeitskultur des 19.
Jahrhunderts* by Susanne Fleigner, 1991.

* * *

Eduard Mörike is known primarily for his lyric poetry, and
although he also wrote prose, he is considered one of the finest 19th-
century German lyric poets. Many of Mörike's poems have a rural,
provincial setting. Through his verse he depicts man in contact with
the natural world. For him, nature acted as a consoler and giver of
meaning to human relationships; nature is portrayed as underlining
man's essential solitude.

The freshness and apparent simplicity of his poetic voice gives the
impression that several decades of aesthetic debate and Romantic
theorizing left no trace in his verse. Several critics, however, consider
him a late Romantic because of his frequent portrayal of unhappy
love, as for example in his poem "Das verlassene Mägdlein" [The
Forsaken Maid], and because, like the Romantics, he too had a
penchant for dualisms, shadows and light, and the dark, demonic,
irrational forces as personified, for example, in the ballad "Der
Feuerreiter" [The Fire-Rider].

Some critics, however, feel that idealism, industrialism, and the
social movements of his time passed him by unconsidered. This is
especially seen in the poem "Verborgenheit" [Hidden Sorrow],
which expresses a gentle resignation and a contentment with that
which the heart has already experienced, and a renunciation or
apprehension of further turbulent emotions. The first and last stanzas
begin with the line, "Lass, O Welt, O lass mich sein" (Leave, O
world, O leave me alone). From Mörike's correspondence, it is
known that he was aware of the world with all its pleasures, desires,

and allures, but as a poet and former clergyman he resisted being
drawn into the world with its cares and controversies. Withdrawal
from the world, parting, and solitude are common themes throughout
his poetry.

Mörike's creativeness led him to portray a transformation of all
discord into harmony. It is not from some sense of aestheticism that
Mörike showed the perfect triumphing over the base, but from a
spiritual belief in the connectedness of the human and the divine. Art
for him is an expression not of the ineffable but of the world as a
creation of God. It is for that reason that he strove to overcome the
dualisms and the demons in himself and in the world, and that he
sought to find a classic calm. In that sense he has an affinity with John
Keats, who achieved a fusion of classical and Romantic worlds.

In the poem "Um Mitternacht" [At Midnight] Mörike attained
classical harmony on the basic Romantic theme of night and day, life
and death, a harmony symbolized by balanced scales. The poem
achieves simultaneously an effect of unity and of contrast by the
division into two equal parts rhythmically different, one restful,
regular iambs and the other a lively, hopping and skipping mixture of
iambs and anapaests. This interplay of light and dark, of movement
and rest, in imagery of unique suggestiveness and rhythms of great
subtlety, is also achieved in "An einem Wintermorgen" [On a
Winter's Morning] and "Vor Sonnenaufgang" [Before Sunrise].

Dualism, specifically moments of rest and flow, and pictures of
recollected experience are evident in his five short "Peregrina"
poems. The depiction of betrayal and unhappy love relates to the most
painful of Mörike's love affairs with a girl, half vagrant, half *dévotée*,
whom he met during his years as a student at the university. The cycle
of "Peregrina," consisting of five separate parts, contains a direct
evocation of the demonic, destructive forces of love. The last stanza
of Part I, for example, speaks of the poet's being handed death in a
chalice of sin ("eichst lätchelnd mir den Tod im Kelch der Sünden").
Part V, written in classical sonnet form, speaks of the "kiss of love
and hatred" and of love being bound to a stake—"Die Liebe, sagt
man, steht am Pfahl gebunden." The emotion expressed shows a
rawness which at times turns into bathos.

Humour is rare in German poetry of this period except in the form
of satire, but Mörike in his poem "Der alte Turmhahn" [The Old
Belfry] shows a certain humour born of detachment and disengagement. His poems, "Der Kehlkopf" [The Larynx] and "Die
Streichkröte" [The Rambling Toad] anticipate the work of 20th-
century writers of nonsense verse.

"Auf eine Lampe" shows Mörike at his closest to classical
serenity and perfection of form, using the stately trimeter of Greek
tragedy. The poem is constructed symmetrically in three parts of three
lines each and a single concluding line: "Was aber schön ist, selig
scheint es in ihm selbst" (Whatever is beautiful, appears blessed in
itself). This poem, like Keats's "Ode on a Grecian Urn," laments a
lost golden age of beauty and harmony, evoked by the object
contemplated. In this poem we have Mörike's major contribution to
German poetry: the presentation of the *Dinggedicht*, which later poets
were to cultivate more extensively and which anticipates Rilke.

Mörike's technical skill is exceptional in the handling of such
diverse forms as hexameters, the Sapphic ode, sonnets, alexandrines,
Knittelvers (doggerel), and free verse. He wrote with equal dexterity
in the idioms of German folk poetry, and balladry, as in "Schön
Rohtraut" [Pretty Rohtraut] or "Die Geister am Mummelsee" [The

Spirits of the Mummelsee], the latter in the form of a conversation, a dialogue with questions and answers, the speaker, however, both asking and answering the questions.

It is this wide range of lyric forms which characterizes Mörike's poetry. For example, he went back to the German Anacreontics of the 18th century and even further back still to the Greek and Roman originals. Thus he published selections from the poetry of Theocritus and Catallus and edited *Anakreon und die sogenannten anakreontischen Lieder* [Anacreon and the So-Called Anacreontic Lyrics]. This side of Mörike's work is unique in 19th-century German poetry.

Mörike also wrote novels. *Maler Nolten* (in which the "Peregrina" poem can also be found) is a balance between spirituality and sensuality, and, like his poetry, reflects his personal problems and predicaments. It is essentially a Bildungsroman or apprenticeship novel, dealing with the life of the artist Nolten, and shows the influence of Goethe's *Wilhelm Meisters Lehrjahre* (*Wilhelm Meister's Apprenticeship*) and *Die Wahlverwandschaften* (*Elective Affinities*). A later novel, *Mozart auf der Reise nach Prag* (*Mozart's Journey to Prague*), shows Mörike's spiritual affinity with Mozart and the profound emotions aroused in him by the opera *Don Giovanni*. Clearly, Mozart's journey to Prague can be seen as symbolic of life's journey with its mingling of pain and pleasure, the mundane and the spiritual, despair and creative ecstasy.

—Brigitte Edith Zapp Archibald

MOTTE FOUQUÉ, Caroline de la

See FOUQUÉ, Caroline de la Motte

MOTTE FOUQUÉ, Friedrich de la

See FOUQUÉ, Friedrich de la Motte

MULTATULI

Pseudonym for Edouard Douwes Dekker. **Born:** in Amsterdam, The Netherlands, 3 March 1820. **Education:** Educated at Latin school. **Family:** Married 1) Everdina (Tine) Huberta van Wijnbergen in 1848 (died 1874), one son; 2) Mimi Hamminck Schepel in 1874. **Career:** Lived in Dutch East Indies (now Indonesia), 1839–52: held various positions on Java and elsewhere; controller for town of Natal, west coast of Sumatra, until dismissed for mismanagement of finances, and recalled to Padang, 1844; various posts, including in Krawang, west Java, from 1845, and Menado, 1849–52; appointed assistant-resident of Lebak, west Java, 1856: transferred because of conflict with superiors, then resigned; returned to Europe: travelled through Germany as a journalist, then lived in Brussels, in poverty; alterations of novel *Max Havelaar* by publisher led to unsuccessful lawsuit, 1860; sank further into debt; left for Germany in 1866; stopped writing almost completely after J. van Vloten published a personal attack in 1875. **Died:** 19 February 1881.

PUBLICATIONS

Collections

Verzamelde werken [Collected Works], edited by M.F.C. Douwes Dekker. 10 vols., 1888–89.
Multatuliana. Verspreide en onuitgegeven stukken [Scattered and Unedited Pieces], edited by A.S. Kok. 1903.
Volledige werken [Complete Works], edited by G. Stuiveling. 12 vols., 1950.

Fiction

Losse bladen uit het dagboek van een oude man [Loose Leaves from the Diary of an Old Man]. 1841–44.
Geloofsbelijdenis [Confession of Faith]. 1859.
Max Havelaar. 1860; edition from the original manuscript, 1950; revised edition, 1990; as *Max Havelaar; or, The Coffee Auctions of the Dutch Trading Company*, translated by Alphonse Nahuis, 1868; as *Max Havelaar; or, The Coffee Sales of the Netherlands Trading Company*, translated by W. Siebenhaar, 1927; as *Max Havelaar*, translated by Roy Edwards, 1967.
Minnebrieven [Love Letters]. 1861.
De geschiedenis van Woutertje Pieterse (selection from *Ideën*). 1890; as *Walter Pieterse*, translated by Hubert Evans, 1904.

Plays

De bruid daarboven [The Bride On High]. 1866.
Aleid. Twee fragmenten uit een onafgewerkt blyspel van Multatuli [Two Fragments of an Unfinished Drama]. 1891.
Vorstenschool [School for Princes]. In *Ideën*, 7 vols., 1862–77.

Other

Indrukken van den dag [Impressions of the Day]. 1860.
Ideën [Ideas] (includes some fiction and a play). 7 vols., 1862–77; revised edition, 1879.
Over vrijen arbeid in Nederlandsch Indië, en de tegenwoordige koloniale agitatie [Concerning Free Labour in Dutch India and the Current Colonial Agitation]. 1862.
De zegen gods door Waterloo [God's Blessing through Waterloo]. 1865.
Nog-eens: Vrye arbeid in Nederlandsch-Indië. 1870; as *Indonesia: Once More Free Labour*, translated by Nicolaas Steelinck, 1948.
Duizend-en-enige hoofdstukken over specialiteiten [A Thousand and One Chapters on Specialities]. 1871; edited by J. Kluiver, 1991.
Miljoenen-studiën [Million Studies]. 1872.
Brieven [Letters], edited by M.F.C. Douwes Dekker. 1890–96.
Multatuli en zijn zoon. Brieven [Letters to His Son], edited by Menno ter Braak. 1937.
Briefwisseling tusschen Multatuli en G.L. Funcke [Correspondence], edited by G.L. Funcke. 1947.

*

Critical Studies: *Het leven en de werken van Edouard Douwes Dekker* by J. Gruyter, 1920; *De man van Lebak* by C.E. Du Perron, 1937; *Erflaters van onze beschaving* by J. and A. Romein, 1940; *De* *betekenis van Multatuli voor onze Tijd* by H.A. Ett, 1947; *De structuur van Max Havelaar* by A.L. Sotermann, 1966; *Multatuli en de kritiek* by J.J. Oversteegen, 1970; *Multatuli*, 1972, and *Multatuli's Max Hardaar, Fact and Fiction*, 1987, both by Peter K. King; *De raadselachtige Multatuli* by W.F. Hermans, 1976; *K. ter Laan's Multatuli Encyclopedie* by Kornelis ter Laan, 1995.

* * *

Edouard Douwes Dekker is the author of one of the most influential and enduring works in Dutch literature, *Max Havelaar*. Born in Amsterdam in 1820, the 18-year-old Dekker left for the Dutch East Indies to pursue a career in colonial administration. A promising career received its first setback when he was suspected of embezzlement, a charge of which he was completely cleared. In 1856, however, he received an unexpected promotion to Assistant-Resident in the area of Lebak. He rejected the widespread corruption and oppression of the local population by colonial officials and the local Indonesian prince who had been appointed Regent. He took the dangerous step of making an official charge against the Regent, which was not upheld by the administration. An appeal to the Governor-General over the head of his immediate superior resulted in the offer of another administrative position, but in disgust he resigned.

After another year trying to plead his case, he returned to Europe, temporarily settling in Brussels where he wrote *Max Havelaar*, under the telling pseudonym ''Multatuli'' (I have borne much) in a period of under four weeks. On 13 October 1859 he was able to report joyously to his wife Tine van Wijnbergen that his book was finished. It was published the following year with the dubious help of Jacob van Lennep, who both toned down the political message in the book and managed to get control of its copyright until Multatuli was able to acquire it after van Lennep's death in 1875.

The book was written with a double purpose. On the one hand, Multatuli attacked colonial injustice and advocated a more enlightened colonial policy. In particular the famous *kultuurstelsel*, the system whereby local people had to grow a certain amount of prescribed products, is said to have had its demise hastened by the moral outrage the book caused. In the Dutch Parliament, the politician van Hoëvell described its effect as that of a shiver going through the country. Equally important, though, was Multatuli's goal of reinstatement to a new, high colonial post, which to his disappointment never occurred.

Perhaps to bolster these practical goals, the book has a very modern, highly literary narrative technique and style. Many critics have viewed this technique as the seduction of the unsuspecting 19th-century reader into accepting the political message. Two alternating narrators, the cynical, prosaic coffee merchant Droogstoppel and his young idealist employee Stern, are dealing with a sheaf of papers given to them by the penniless ex-colonial Sjaalman, purportedly dealing with the coffee trade. The presentation of Sjaalman's writings results in a collection of miscellaneous texts, making the book a hectic mixture of styles and genres, combining comic-realist narrative with poetry, parable, sermon, romance, political tirade, philosophical essay, even lists. Throughout, though, we see the fictionalized story of Douwes Dekker's conflict with the colonial administration, now in the shape of a highly idealized Max Havelaar. Famously, in the final pages all fictional pretence is dropped and an insistent, haranguing Multatuli addresses the Dutch political establishment directly. Still surprisingly fresh, dynamic, and modern, *Max Havelaar*'s literary influence stretches well into the 20th century.

Multatuli's later literary work continued to use the same quirky combination of genres and styles, of moralizing idealism and embittered satire. His dense and difficult *Minnebrieven* [Love Letters] again features comments on the episode of Lebak, presented as a collection of love letters, but also includes highly divergent material. In fact, J.J. Oversteegen has interpreted this book as an attempt for Multatuli to analyse the process of literary creation.

Miljoenen-studiën [Million Studies] presents a method at winning roulette, as well as the discussion of a ''reality'' that exists beyond human logic and science. Even more heterogeneous, the seven volumes of *Ideën* [Ideas] include epigrams, essays, anecdotes, stories, and ruminations on a variety of topics. Included among these is the famous short novel *De geschiedenis van Woutertje Pieterse* (*Walter Pieterse*), the semi-autobiographical story of a young idealistic boy in conflict with his society, and a play, *Vorstenschool* [School for Princes].

—Sabine Vanacker

MURAKAMI Haruki

Born: Kyoto, Japan, January 1949. **Education:** Attended Waseda University in Tokyo, 1968–75, majoring in drama. Primary training in screenwriting. **Family:** Married Takahashi Yōko in 1971. **Career:** While still attending Waseda, opened jazz club in Tokyo called ''Peter Cat'' with his wife, 1974; began writing first novel, *Kaze no uta o kike* (*Hear the Wind Sing*, published in 1979), 1978; continued to write in his spare time until 1981, when he sold the club in order to become a full time writer. Travelled to Greece and Italy in 1986, returned to Japan for one year (1990–91), then headed for the east coast of the United States, spending two and a half years in Princeton, New Jersey, and two more years in Cambridge, Massachusetts. Began to write nonfiction concerning major current events following his return to Japan in 1995. **Awards:** Gunzō prize for New Writers, 1979; Noma prize for New Writers, 1982; Tanizaki prize, 1985; Yomiuri Literary prize, 1995; Kuwabara Takeo prize, 1999.

PUBLICATIONS

Collections

Murakami Haruki zensakuhin, 1979–1989 [Complete Works of Murakami Haruki, 1979–1989]. 8 vols., 1990–91.

Fiction

Kaze no uta o kike. 1979; as *Hear the Wind Sing*, translated by Alfred Birnbaum, 1987.
1973-nen no pinbōru. 1980; as *Pinball*, *1973*, translated by Alfred Birnbaum, 1985.
Hitsuji o meguru bōken. 1982; as *A Wild Sheep Chase*, translated by Alfred Birnbaum, 1989.
Chūgokuyuki no surōbōto (short story collection). 1983.
Kangarū biyori (short story collection). 1983.
Hotaru, naya o yaku, sono hoka no tampen (short story collection). 1984.
Kaiten kiba no deddo hiito (short story collection). 1985.

Sekai no owari to hādo-boirudo wandārando. 1985; as *Hard-Boiled Wonderland and the End of the World*, translated by Alfred Birnbaum, 1991.

Pan'ya saishūgeki (short story collection). 1986.

Noruwei no mori. 1987; as *Norwegian Wood*, translated by Jay Rubin. 2000.

Dansu dansu dansu. 1988; as *Dance Dance Dance*, translated by Alfred Birnbaum. 1994.

TV piipuru (short story collection). 1989.

Kokkyō no minami, taiyō no nishi. 1992; as *South of the Border, West of the Sun*, translated by Philip Gabriel, 1999.

Nejimakidori kuronikuru. 1994–96; as *The Wind-Up Bird Chronicle*, translated by Jay Rubin, 1997.

Spūtonikku no koibito. 1999; as *The Sputnik Sweetheart*, translated by Philip Gabriel, 2001.

Kami no kodomotachi wa minna odoru. 2000; as *After the Earthquake: Stories*, translated by Jay Rubin, 2002.

Nonfiction

'The Scrap': Natsukashi no 1980-nendai. 1987.

Tōi taikō. 1990.

Yagate kanashiki gaikokugo. 1994.

Andāguraundo. 1997; as *Underground*, translated by Alfred Birnbaum and Philip Gabriel, 2001.

Wakai dokusha no tame no tampen shōsetsu annai. 1997.

Yakusoku sareta basho de: Underground 2. 1998; with above as *Underground*, translated by Alfred Birnbaum and Philip Gabriel, 2001.

Other

Translator, *Mai rosuto shitii*, by F. Scott Fitzgerald. 1981.

Translator, *Boku ga denwa o kakete iru basho*, by Raymond Carver. 1983.

Translator, *Yoru ni naru to sake wa . . .*, by Raymond Carver. 1985.

Translator, *Kuma wo hanatsu*, by John Irving. 1986.

Translator, *Wāruzu endo*, by Paul Thereaux. 1987.

Translator, *Ojiisan no omoide*, by Truman Capote. 1988.

Translator, *Sasayaka dakeredomo, yaku ni tatsu koto*, by Raymond Carver. 1989.

*

Critical Studies: "Beyond 'Pure' Literature: Mimesis, Formula, and the Postmodern in the Fiction of Murakami Haruki" by Matthew C. Strecher, in *The Journal of Asian Studies*, vol. 57, no. 2, 1998; *Dances With Sheep: The Quest for Identity in the Fiction of Murakami Haruki* by Matthew C. Strecher, 2002; *Haruki Murakami and the Music of Words* by Jay Rubin, 2002; *Haruki Murakami's The Wind-Up Bird Chronicle: A Reader's Guide* by Matthew C. Strecher, 2002; "Magical Realism and the Search for Identity in the Fiction of Murakami Haruki" by Matthew C. Strecher, in *Journal of Japanese Studies*, vol. 25, no. 2, 1999; "'Monogatari' no tame no bōken" by Kawamoto Saburō, in *Bungakukai*, vol. 39, no. 8, 1985; "Murakami Haruki: Japan's Coolest Writer Heats Up" by Matthew C. Strecher, in *Japan Quarterly*, vol. 45, no. 1, 1998; *Murakami Haruki: 90-nendai* by Yokoo Kazuhiro, 1994; *Murakami Haruki to dōjidai no bungaku* by Kuroko Kazuo, 1990; "The Other World of Murakami Haruki" by Jay Rubin, in *Japan Quarterly*, vol. 39, no. 4, 1992; "Two Murakamis and Marcel Proust: Memory as Form in Contemporary Japanese Fiction" by Stephen Snyder, in *In Pursuit of Contemporary East Asian Culture*, edited by Stephen Snyder and Xiaobing Tang, 1996; "Two Murakamis and their American Influence" by Glynne Walley, in *Japan Quarterly*, vol. 44, no. 1, 1997.

*   *   *

The emergence of Murakami Haruki on Japan's literary scene in 1979 with his 1979 Gunzō prize-winning novel *Kaze no uta o kike* (*Hear the Wind Sing*) marked the beginning of a period of transition for modern Japanese literature. Long dominated by practitioners of so-called "pure literature" (*junbungaku*), not unlike the Modernist or Formalist-oriented "serious" literature in the West, Japanese literature received much-needed energy from Murakami, who brought a sense of freshness and innovation such as the field had not seen in decades.

With a writing style that is at once simple, elegant, yet which also displays its author's familiarity with contemporary Western (especially American) fiction, Murakami Haruki has achieved something no other Japanese author has to date: he has created a Japanese literary voice that speaks to mass audiences across generations, yet appeals to literary critics and scholars; that presents a worldview recognizable to contemporary Japanese urbanites, yet is accessible and meaningful to legions of readers outside of Japan. Murakami is well known in the United States, Great Britain, and Europe; he has achieved genuine "rock star" status in South Korea and Taiwan, and even enjoys wide popularity in the People's Republic of China. Perhaps no other writer in Japanese history has managed to gather such a diverse audience, from such a diversity of cultures. Murakami is one of Japan's first truly "international" writers.

Murakami's rise to fame was coincident with the so-called "postmodern boom" in Japan during the 1980s, a time when the postmodern theories of François Lyotard and Jürgen Habermas were disseminated both to popular and intellectual audiences by intellectuals such as Asada Akira and Karatani Kōjin. Expressing a worldview that is highly resonant with the postmodern, especially in its mixture of seemingly incompatible elements (magic and realism, reality and unreality, past and present, conscious and unconscious), Murakami's timing could hardly have been better.

But there was more to Murakami's success than simply joining the latest intellectual fad (and in fact the author himself has never claimed to be part of any intellectual movement). After all, the postmodern boom in Japan passed, but Murakami's domination of contemporary literature has not. One reason for this is that his central theme, which explores the nature of individual identity and critiques the relationship between the individual and the Japanese State, remains relevant, especially among younger readers.

His initial inquiries into this individual/state relationship took the form of an introspective, often painfully nostalgic narrative about the demise of the 1960s. At an imprecise point between the fall of 1969 and the fall of 1970, the author suggests, Japan's counterculture was subsumed into mainstream Japanese society, and something of critical importance—individual identity—was lost. Desire for individual identity was then gradually supplanted by the desire to participate in Japan's increasingly consumerist social system. Indeed, as one reads through the author's works an evolving model appears in which the consumerist urge spreads throughout Japanese society like a disease, infiltrating ever deeper into enclaves once thought to be free: human emotion, the unconscious, memory, the imagination. As these areas are appropriated little by little, the world around the Murakami protagonist seems to shrink and he seeks escape, sometimes into the pastoral landscape of Hokkaido, but increasingly (especially as Hokkaido itself is gradually subsumed) he retreats to the inner spaces of his own mind, fighting desperately to preserve his own memories, his own desires, fears, and weakness. In short, he struggles to preserve his unique identity.

Clearly, the nature of identity—how it is formed, how it can be destroyed—occupies a central place in Murakami's writing. In his fictional universe, essentially a realistic one, but tinged with the bizarre and the magical, characters explore the nature of their inner selves, and discover the importance of an interactive relationship between the conscious and unconscious minds. Frequently they enter the freezing darkness of their unconscious minds, reencountering memories of those they long for and thus partially recovering them. Alternately, they may have a momentary glimpse of the object of their desire, revealed in the briefest opening of the barrier that separates the inner and outer minds, and from this they form an obsession for that object, which shortly thereafter emerges from the mind, lingers a while, then returns to its place of origin. Never, however, does any image emerge from the unconscious in any recognizable form; ultimately grounded in language, in words, these memories can appear only as images, linguistically connected to the original memory via a series of word associations.

In his explorations of identity, memory, and the unconscious Murakami utilizes a variety of styles and methods, many of which are grounded in his extensive reading of Western literature. His narrative "voice" is warm and personal, yet at times exhibits the "hard-boiled" character of American detective fiction. He acknowledges a close affinity to the work of Raymond Carver, much of whose fiction he has translated into Japanese, and has been an avid reader of John Irving, Truman Capote, Raymond Chandler, and Richard Brautigan. In his juxtapositioning of the magical and the realistic he stands together with contemporary Latin American writers such as Gabriel Garcia Marquez, Laura Esquivel, and Manuel Puig. His use of the so-called "magical realism" commonly associated with Latin American fiction is the principal method by which he permits his protagonists to enter their own inner minds, or to draw from the unconscious images of the memories with which they are obsessed.

At times Murakami also plays with literary formulas. His third work, *Hitsuji o meguru bōken* (*A Wild Sheep Chase*) is an excellent example of the author playing with the "hard-boiled" detective formula, though in the end he subverts the demands of that formula—the requirement that the mystery be clearly solved—and leaves his readers puzzled as to what is real and what merely fantasy. A similar problem attends his Tanizaki prize-winning *Sekai no owari to hādo-boirudo wandārando* (*Hard-Boiled Wonderland and the End of the World*), whose title clearly suggests Murakami's awareness of the hard-boiled genre in which he writes, but whose conclusion can hardly satisfy readers' anticipation of a "pat" ending. In *Noruwei no mori* (*Norwegian Wood*), the author plays similarly with the romance formula, with equally unorthodox results. Murakami himself, defending this subversion of the popular formula, has acknowledged his dislike for clear, satisfactory endings with no loose ends, insisting that this is not the way the real world works. One may thus conclude that his use of popular literary formulas is merely an expedient for bringing the contradictory nature of the world to the forefront.

This sense of the contradictory in Murakami's literary world places his work firmly into the realm of postmodern fiction. At the same time, one must be cautious of forcing Murakami too tightly into any specific genre or method of writing, because his work has been experimental from the beginning, and continues to be so. As he grows more comfortable with his skills as a writer, one sees him challenging himself more and more, overcoming a timid passivity (seen both in his characters and his own writing style) as he gains confidence. Now in his early fifties, it is impossible to say where Murakami Haruki will go from here, but in his constant search for new ways of expressing the crisis of identity in contemporary Japan, it is quite possible that his best work lies ahead of him. Today, one can at least say with certainty that Murakami has assured himself a central role in the history of late twentieth century Japanese literature.

—Matthew Carl Strecher

MURASAKI Shikibu

Also known as Lady Murasaki. **Born:** c. 978. **Family:** Married Fujiwara no Nobutaka in 998 (died 1001); one daughter. **Career:** Spent some years in close contact with the court at Kyoto; in the service of Empress Akiko from c. 1005. **Died:** Date of death unknown.

PUBLICATIONS

Fiction

Genji Monogatari, edited by Yamagishi Tokuhei. 5 vols., 1958–63; also edited by Abe Akio and others, 6 vols., 1970–76; translated into modern Japanese by Jun'ichiro Tanizaki, 26 vols., 1939–41; as *The Tale of Genji*, translated by Arthur Waley, 6 vols., 1925–33; also translated by Edward Seidensticker, 1976; part as *Genji Monogatari*, translated by Suyematz Kenchio, in *Persian and Japanese Literature*, 2 vols., 1900.

Other

Murasaki Shikibu: Her Diary and Poetic Memoirs , translated by Richard Bowring. 1982.
The Diary of Lady Murasaki, translated and introduced by Richard Bowring. 1996.

*

Critical Studies: *The World of the Shining Prince: Court Life in Ancient Japan* by Ivan Morris, 1964; *Murasaki Shikibu: The Greatest Lady Writer in Japanese Literature* by Sen'ichi Hisamatsu and others, 1970; *Ukifune: Love in The Tale of Genji* edited by Andrew Pekarik, 1982; *Poetic Allusion: Some Aspects of the Role Played by Kokin Wakashuu as a Source of Poetic Allusion in Genji Monogatari* by Gunilla Lindberg-Wada, 1983; *Iconography of The Tale of Genji* by Miyeko Murase, 1983; *Guide to the Tale of Genji* by W.J. Puette, 1985; *The Splendor of Longing in the Tale of Genji* by Norma Field, 1987; *The Bridge of Dreams: A Poetics of The Tale of Genji* by Hamo Shirane, 1987; *Murasaki Shikibu: The Tale of Genji* by Richard Bowring, 1988; *Noh Drama and The Tale of Genji: The Art of Allusion in Fifteen Classical Plays* by Janet Goff, 1991; *Murasaki's Genji and Proust's Recherche: A Comparative Study* by Shirley M. Loui, 1991; *Approaches to Teaching Murasaki Shikibu's The Tale of the Genji*, edited by Edward Kamens, 1993; *A Woman's Weapon: Spirit Possession in The Tale of Genji* by Doris G. Bargen, 1997;

Idealism, Protest, and The Tale of Genji: The Confucianism of Kumazawa Banzan (1619–91) by James McMullen, 1999; *Yosamo Akiko and The Tale of Genji* by G.G. Rowley, 2000; *The Tale of Genji: Legends and Paintings*, with introduction by Miyeko Murase, 2001.

* * *

Murasaki Shikibu, sometimes called Lady Murasaki, is the author of many works, including a ''diary'' which is not so much that as a discursive account of events at the Japanese court over a short expanse of time early in the 11th century; a collection of more than a hundred short lyric poems which overlaps in some measure with the diary; a scattering of poems to be found only in royally commissioned anthologies; and *Genji Monogatari* (*The Tale of Genji*).

The last, much her most important work, is a very long romance, probably finished (if it is finished—of that we cannot be sure) in the first or second decade of the 11th century. Nothing survives in her hand, and the earliest texts of the *Genji*, from almost two centuries after the probable date of composition, are fragmentary. Hence scholars will forever ask how close the texts of our day are to Murasaki's original, and the quest for a definitive text will be endless. The sensible view, supported by a large mass of scholarly writing, is that what we read today is essentially what came from the brush of a remarkable Japanese court lady early in the 11th century.

Though there are sallies and sub-plots, the story is essentially simple. The first two-thirds or so are dominated by an increasingly powerful courtier known, from his family name, as ''the shining Genji,'' and the story is of perdurable love. Genji meets the great love of his life in the fifth of the 54 chapters. She dies in the 40th, and a chapter later Genji himself disappears from the scene. The remainder of the story has to do with the less vigorous affairs, also largely amorous, of Genji's grandson and of a young man reputed to be his son but actually the grandson of his best friend.

Though the story is simple, the *Genji* is a complex work. Numbers of meanings can be abstracted from it, most of them deriving from the fact that the tone is melancholy and the general import pessimistic. Since the action covers almost three-quarters of a century, the earlier portions are set at a considerable though not precisely defined time in the past. An important implication would seem to be that the best time has passed: there once were giants, Genji pre-eminent among them, but they will not reappear. So the story is of social decline, and it may also be about metaphysical decline, a popular notion of the time being that the ''good law'' of Buddhism was about to enter the last phase before its extinction. The *Genji* certainly concerns evanescence, and it may also be about retribution. It may describe the quest for a lost parent: Genii is drawn to the ladies he believes bear resemblance to his mother, whom he cannot remember.

It may be about all that is mentioned above, but it is also something more immediate, and less abstract. The reader's attention is held, through the very great length of the tale, not by remarkable incident and suspense, but by character. Several hundred characters make their appearance, and among them perhaps 40 or 50 may be called major. They are distinguished one from another with most remarkable skill, and each is what E.M. Forster called three-dimensional—a believable individual and not merely a type or caricature.

The *Genji* is often called the first great novel in the literature of the world. The designation is controversial, but the controversy is largely a matter of definition. If by ''novel'' we mean a kind of prose narrative in which character, and not plot or incident, is the most important element, then a very strong case can be made for proclaiming the *Genji* the first superior specimen of the genre. There is nothing like it, certainly, in earlier Oriental literature.

—Edward Seidensticker

MUSIL, Robert

Born: in Klagenfurt, Austria, 6 November 1880. **Education:** Educated at a school in Steyr; military school in Eisenstadt, 1892–94, and in Mährisch-Weisskirchen, 1895–97; studied engineering at Technische Hochschule, Brno, 1898–1901; studied philosophy, University of Berlin, 1903–05, Ph.D. 1908. **Military Service:** 1901–02; served in Austrian army, 1914–16; hospitalized, 1916, then editor of army newspaper, 1916–18; bronze cross. **Family:** Married Martha Marcovaldi in 1911. **Career:** Engineer in Stuttgart, 1902–03; in Berlin until 1911; archivist, 1911–13; editor, *Die Neue Rundschau*, Berlin, 1914; in press section of Office of Foreign Affairs, Vienna, 1919–20, and consultant to Defence Ministry, 1920–23; then freelance writer in Berlin, 1931–33, in Vienna, 1933–38, and in Switzerland, 1938–42. **Awards:** Kleist prize, 1923; City of Vienna prize, 1924. **Died:** 15 April 1942.

PUBLICATIONS

Collections

Gesammelte Werke, edited by Adolf Frisé 3 vols., 1952–57; revised edition, 2 vols., 1978.

Fiction

Die Verwirrungen des Zöglings Törless. 1906; as *Young Törless*, translated by Eithne Wilkins and Ernst Kaiser, 1955.
Vereinigungen (stories). 1911.
Drei Frauen (stories; includes *Grigia; Die Portugiesin; Tonka*). 1924; as *Five Women*, translated by Eithne Wilkins and Ernst Kaiser, 1965; as *Tonka and Other Stories* (includes translation of *Vereinigungen*), 1965.
Der Mann ohne Eigenschaften, completed by Martha Musil. 3 vols., 1930–43; edited by Adolf Frisé, 1952, revised edition, 1965; as *The Man without Qualities*, translated by Eithne Wilkins and Ernst Kaiser, 3 vols., 1953–60; also translated by Sophie Wilkins, 1995.

Plays

Die Schwärmer. 1921; as *The Enthusiasts*, translated by Andrea Simon, 1982.
Vinzenz und die Freundin bedeutender Männer. 1923.

Other

Das hilflose Europa. 1922.
Nachlass zu Lebzeiten. 1936; as *Posthumous Papers of a Living Author*, translated by Peter Wortsman, 1987.
Theater: Kritisches und Theoretisches, edited by Marie-Louise Roth. 1965.

Der Deutsche Mensch als Symptom, edited by Karl Corino and Elisabeth Albertsen. 1967.

Briefe nach Prag, edited by Barbara Köpplova and Kurt Krolop. 1971.

Tagebüicher, edited by Adolf Frisé 2 vols., 1976; as *Diaries: 1899–1941*, edited with introduction by Mark Mirsky, 1998.

Texte aus dem Nachlass. 1980.

Beitrag zur Beurteilung der Lehren Machs (dissertation), edited by Adolf Frisé. 1980; as *On Mach's Theories*, translated by Kevin Mulligan, 1983.

Briefe 1901–1942, edited by Adolf Frisé. 2 vols., 1981.

Selected Writings, edited by Burton Pike. 1986.

Precision and Soul: Essays and Addresses, edited and translated by Burton Pike and David S. Luft. 1990.

*

Bibliography: *Robert-Musil-Bibliographie* by Jürgen C. Thöming, 1968; *Robert Musil-Bibliographie: Ergänzungsbibliographie 1980–1983* by Michiko Mae, 1983.

Critical Studies: *Robert Musil: An Introduction to His Work* by Burton Pike, 1961: *Femininity and the Creative Imagination: A Study of Henry James, Robert Musil, and Marcel Proust* by Lisa Appignanesi, 1973; *Musil: "Der Mann ohne Eigenschaften": An Examination of the Relationship Between Author, Narrator, and Protagonist* by Alan Holmes, 1978; *Robert Musil: Master of the Hovering Life* by Frederick G. Peters, 1978; *Robert Musil and the Crisis of European Culture 1880–1942* by David S. Luft, 1980; *Musil in Focus: Papers from a Centenary Symposium*, 1982, and *Robert Musil and the Literary Landscape of His Time: Papers of an International Symposium*, 1991, both edited by Lothar Huber and John J. White; *Robert Musil and the Ineffable: Hieroglyph, Myth, Fairy Tale, and Sign* by Ronald M. Paulson, 1982; *Robert Musil and the Culture of Vienna* by Hannah Hickman, 1984; *Proust and Musil: The Novel as Research Instrument* by Gone M. Moore, 1985; *Sympathy for the Abyss: A Study in the Novel of German Modernism: Kafka, Broch, Musil and Thomas Mann* by Stephen D. Dowden, 1986; *Robert Musil's Works, 1906–1924: A Critical Introduction*, 1987, and *Robert Musil's "The Man without Qualities": A Critical Study*, 1988, both by Philip Payne; *Robert Musil* by Lowell A. Bangerter, 1988; *Musil's Socratic Discourse in Der Mann ohne Eigenschaften* by D.J. Brooks, 1989; *Musil: Leben und Werk in Bildern und Texten* by Karl Corino, 1989; *Implied Dramaturgy: Robert Musil and the Crisis of Modern Drama* by Christian Rogowski, 1993; *Distinguished Outsider: Robert Musil and His Critics* by Christian Rogowski, 1994; *Subject without Nation: Robert Musil and the History of Modern Identity* by Stefan Jonsson, 2000; *Five Portraits: Modernity and the Imagination in Twentieth-Century German Writing* by Michael André Bernstein, 2000.

*   *   *

The Austrian novelist Robert Musil ranks with Thomas Mann and Franz Kafka among major German writers of the 20th century, but the highly essayistic nature of much of his writing makes him less of a storyteller than Mann and less of a pure modernist than Kafka. None the less, his extraordinary intelligence and his genius for metaphor allowed him to achieve in *Der Mann ohne Eigenschaften* (*The Man without Qualities*) a prose that has few equals in German literature, and no one writing in German in the 20th century has had more balanced or penetrating insight into so broad a range of issues.

The task of Musil's fiction was to invent the inner person and to extend our understanding in the realm of the soul by portraying borderline experiences of perception, sexuality, and mysticism. His first novel, *Die Verwirrungen des Zöglings Törless* (*Young Törless*), established these themes when he was only 25; this portrayal of adolescent homosexuality and political conflict is the most realistic and accessible of Musil's narrative works, but even here the emphasis is on the protagonist's inner crisis and his complex feelings about sexuality and the behaviour of those around him. In the stories of *Vereinigungen* [Unions] Musil continued to explore sexuality and ethical experience, but now from the perspective of feminine consciousness; by this time, Musil was familiar with Freud and ready for an ambitious experiment in the metaphorical representation of inwardness. In these stories, as in the aesthetically more perfected novellas of *Drei Frauen* (*Five Women*) and the play *Die Schwärmer* (*The Enthusiasts*), Musil was preoccupied with the unreal life of the feelings—not the lives we lead but the lives we feel.

What makes Musil a writer of such a high order is that he was able to deal with these psychological themes in relation to the problems of modern, technological society and the breakdown of traditional European ideologies. His scientific training and his dissertation on Ernst Mach (1908) not only established his high level of scientific sophistication, but provided him with the tools for criticizing outmoded ideologies and theories of human nature and history. Drawing on Nietzsche as well as Mach, Musil began to develop his critique of ideology and morality in the essays that he wrote for the *Neue Rundschau* and other liberal journals before World War I. But it was the war that brought his characteristic themes into focus, and the major essays of the post war period clarified his view that European civilization before 1914 had failed to create a meaningful cultural and emotional life. The realm of the spirit had failed to keep pace with the practical achievements of the age.

Musil devoted the last two decades of his life to an attempt to summarize the predicament of the individual in modern civilization. Critics differ concerning whether Musil managed to break out of the modern predicament in a decisive way, but all are agreed that his novel, *The Man without Qualities*, is a brilliant description of the situation. Ulrich, the protagonist of Musil's masterpiece, explores the possibilities for right living in the midst of the massive scale and cultural fragmentation of life in modern civilization. The setting is Austria on the eve of World War I, but the satire of old-fashioned ideologies leads on to more universal questions about the sources of ethical motivation. Ulrich's ironic voice emphasizes the critique of action, ego, and dead ideology, but the appearance of his sister Agathe opens the door on a more constructive attempt to think about morality and the world out of the condition of love. This novel is the purest expression of Musil's capacity to balance positivism and romanticism, thinking and feeling, masculinity and femininity, to think out a world in which human beings are likely to become in part highly efficient masters of practical reality and in part mystics.

—David S. Luft

See the essays on *The Man without Qualities* and *Young Törless*.

MUSSET, (Louis Charles) Alfred de

Born: Paris, France, 11 December 1810. **Education:** Educated at
Collège Henri IV, Paris, 1820–28; studied law and medicine briefly.
Family: Lived with George Sand, 1833–34; later associated with
Mlle. Aimée d'Alton and Mme. Allan-Despréaux. **Career:** Entered
Parisian literary cricles in the late 1820s; clerical worker for a heating
company, 1829–30; contributor, *Revue des deux mondes* (in which
many of his works first appeared), from 1832; librarian, Ministry of
the Interior, Paris, 1838–48, and the Ministry of Education, from
1853. **Member:** Académie française, 1852. **Died:** 2 May 1857.

PUBLICATIONS

Collections

Oeuvres complètes, edited by Paul de Musset. 10 vols., 1865–66.
Complete Writings. 10 vols., 1905; volumes 3 and 5 reprinted as *Ten
Plays*, 1987.
Oeuvres complètes. 8 vols., 1907–09.
Oeuvres complètes illustrées. 10 vols., 1927–29.
Oeuvres complètes en prose; Théâtre complet; Poésies complètes,
edited by Maurice Allem. 3 vols., 1951–58.
Oeuvres complètes, edited by Philippe Van Tieghem. 1963.
Fantasio and Other Plays, translated by Michael Feingold. 1993.
Five Plays, edited and introduced by Claude Schumacher. 1995.

Plays

La Nuit vénitienne (produced 1830). In *Un spectacle dans un fauteuil*,
1834; as *A Venetian Night*, in *Complete Writings*, 1905.
Andre del Sarto (produced 1848). In *Un spectacle duns un fauteuil*,
1834; revised version (produced 1848), 1851; as *André del Sarto*,
in *Complete Writings*, 1905.
Les Caprices de Marianne (produced 1851). In *Un spectacle dans un
fauteuil*, 1834; revised version (produced 1851), 1851; edited by
P.-G. Castex, 1979; as *A Good Little Wife*, n.d. (1847?); as *The
Follies of Marianne*, in *Complete Writings*, 1905; as *What Does
Marianne Want?* translated by David Sices, in *Comedies and
Proverbs*, 1994.
On ne badine pas avec l'amour (produced 1861). In *Un spectacle
dans un fauteuil*, 1834; edited by P.-G. Castex, 1979; as *No
Trifling with Love*, in *Comedies*, 1890; as *Love is Not to Be Trifled
With*, translated by Eirene G. Owen, 1957; as *Camille and
Perdicon*, translated by Peter Meyer, 1961; as *Don't Fool with
Love*, in *Three Plays*, 1993; as *You Can't Trifle With Love*,
translated by David Sices, in *Comedies and Proverbs*, 1994.
Fantasio (produced 1866). In *Un spectacle dans un fauteuil*, 1834;
translated as *Fantasio*, in *Comedies*, 1890; also translated by
Maurice Baring, 1927; David Sices, in *Comedies and Proverbs*,
1994.
Lorenzaccio (produced 1896). In *Un spectacle dans un fauteuil*, 1834;
edited by Paul Dimoff, in *La Genèse de Lorenzaccio*, revised
edition, 1964; translated as *Lorenzaccio*, 1907; as *The Lorenzaccio
Story*, adapted by Paul Thompson, music by Stephen Oliver, 1978.
Un caprice (produced in Russian, 1837; in French, 1843). In *Comédies
et proverbes*, 1840; as *A Caprice*, in *Poet Lore*, 33, 1922; as *A
Diversion*, translated by Peter Meyer, in *Seven Plays*, 1962; as *A

Passing Fancy*, translated by David Sices, in *Comedies and
Proverbs*, 1994.
Comédies et proverbes. 1840; enlarged and revised edition, 2 vols.,
1853; edited by Pierre and Françoise Gastinel, 4 vols., 1934,
1952–57.
Le Chandelier, in *Comédies et proverbes*. 1840; revised version
(produced 1848), 1848; as *The Candlestick*, translated by Peter
Meyer, in *Seven Plays*, 1962, and in *Three Plays*, 1993; also
translated by David Sices, in *Comedies and Proverbs*, 1994.
Il ne faut jurer de rien (produced 1848). In *Comédies et proverbes*,
1840; as *You Never Can Tell*, translated by David Sices, in
Comedies and Proverbs, 1994.
La Quenouille de Barberine, in *Comédies et proverbes*. 1840; revised
version, as *Barberine* (produced 1882), in *Comédies et proverbes*,
1853; as *Barberine*, translated by S.S. Gwynn, in *Comedies*, 1890.
Il faut qu'une porte soit ouverte ou feréde (produced 1848). 1848; as
A Door Must Be Either Open or Shut, in *Comedies*, 1890; as *A
Door Must be Kept Shut or Open*, in *Three Plays*, 1993; as *A Door
Has to Be Either Open or Shut*, translated by David Sices, in
Comedies and Proverbs, 1994.
L'Habit vert, with Émile Augier (produced 1849). 1849; as *The Green
Coat*, translated by Barrett H. Clark, 1914.
Louison (produced 1849). 1849; as *Louison*, translated by Andrew
Lang, in *Complete Writings*, 1905.
On ne saurait penser à tout (produced 1849). In *Comédies et
proverbes*, 1853; as *One Cannot Think of Everything*, translated
by Andrew Lang, in *Complete Writings*, 1905.
Bettine (produced 1851). 1851.
Carmosine (produced 1865). In *Comédies et proverbes*, 1853; trans-
lated as *Carmosine*, n.d. (1865?).
L'Âne et le ruisseau (produced 1876). In *Oeuvres posthumes*, 1860; as
All Is Fair in Love and War, adapted by "W.P.C.," 1868.
La Quittance du diable (produced 1938). 1896.
Three Plays (includes *Don't Fool with Love; The Candlestick; A
Door Must Be Kept Shut or Open*), translated by Declan Donnellan
and Peter Meyer. 1993.
Comedies and Proverbs (includes *What Does Marianne Want?;
Fantasio; You Can't Trifle With Love; The Candlestick; You
Never Can Tell; A Passing Fancy; A Door Has to Be Either Open
or Shut*), translated by David Sices. 1994.

Fiction

La Confession d'un enfant du siècle. 2 vols., 1836; as *The Confession
of a Child of the Century*, translated by Kendall Warren, 1892; as *A
Modern Man's Confessions*, translated by G.F. Monkshood, 1908.
Nouvelles. 1848; as *Tales from Musset*, 1888; as *The Two Mistresses,
etc.*, translated by Gertrude Fosdick, 1900.
Contes. 1854.
Two Fables, translated by Christopher Morley. 1925.

Verse

Les Contes d'Espagne et d'Italie. 1830; edited by Margaret Rees,
1973.
Poésies complètes. 1840.
Premières poésies, Poésies nouvelles. 2 vols., 1852.
Poésies complètes. 2 vols., 1854.
La Nuit de mai, translated by Claire N. White. 1989.

Other

Un spectacle dans un fauteuil (verse and plays). 1833; second series, 2 vols., 1834.
Lettres de Dupuis et Cotonet 1836–37. In *Oeuvres complètes*, 1866.
Mélanges de littérature et de critique (essays and criticism). 1867.
Old and New (selection), translated by Walter Herries Pollock. 1880.
Correspondance, edited by Léon Séché. 1907.
Lettres d'amour à Aimée d'Alton, edited by Léon Séché. 1910.
Oeuvres complémentaires, edited by Maurice Allem. 1911.
George Sand et Musset: Correspondance. . ., edited by Louis Évrard. 1956.

*

Bibliography: *Alfred de Musset: A Reference Guide* by Patricia Joan Siegel, 1982.

Critical Studies: *Alfred: The Passionate Life of Musset* by Charlotte Haldane, 1960; *Stage of Dreams: The Dramatic Art of Musset* by Herbert S. Gochberg, 1967; *Alfred de Musset* by Margaret A. Rees, 1971; *A Stage for Poets: Studies in the Theatre of Hugo and Musset* by Charles Affron, 1971; *Theatre of Solitude: The Drama of Musset* by David Sices, 1974; *Musset, Lorenzaccio* by Ceri Crossley, 1983; *The Poetry of Alfred de Musset: Styles and Genres* by Lloyd O. Bishop, 1987; *The Romantic Art of Confession: De Quincey, Musset, Sand, Lamb, Hogg, Fremy, Soulie, Janin* by Susan M. Levin, 1998.

* * *

Alfred de Musset is both an exemplary and a paradoxical figure of French Romanticism. The youthful disciple of Hugo and the *Cénacle* had, by the age of 20, estranged himself from the movement. His parodic collection of narrative and dramatic poems, *Les Contes d'Espagne et d'Italie* [Tales of Spain and Italy], of Byronic inspiration, showed both his independence and a precocious mastery of form, language, and rhythm; it points toward the *Poésies nouvelles*, particularly "olla" (1833) and the celebrated four "Nuits" (the "Nights" of May, December, August, and October, 1835–37), in which he attained the height of his lyric powers. Inspired in great part by his stormy love affair with George Sand, the "Nuits" present a repertory of Romantic poetic theory and practice. These dialogues between Poet and Muse turn upon the confrontation between poetry and love, art and life, expression and feeling, language and silence. Their exasperated individualism and exalted pathos spoke powerfully to and for several generations of readers.

Musset's dialogic imagination emerges most remarkably in four plays which he wrote between 1833 and 1834: *Les Caprices de Marianne* (*The Follies of Marianne*), *Fantasio, On ne badine pas avec l'amour* (*Don't Fool with Love*), and *Lorenzaccio*. The author's alter-ego protagonists engage in the "game of love and death" of a Romantic Marivaux, or, with his monumental Renaissance historical drama, *Lorenzaccio*, in a deadly, mocking duel of conscience and politics, ideal and reality. They are Protean—or splintered, as in the *Caprices*, where Coelio and Octave embody idealistic and disillusioned halves of Musset's personality. His lovers are often surrounded, or confronted, by uncomprehending puppet-figures. The plays' language is a supple, imaged, eloquent prose. Musset the dramatist has survived the rigours of time better than his more successful contemporaries, such as Hugo, Vigny, and Dumas *père*. His efforts to free dramatic form from contemporary stage practice (the works were not intended for performance) have attracted significant modern directors like Copeau, Baty, Vilar, and Krejca. His later dramas are less original and important, but several "comedy-proverbs"—*Le Chandelier* (*The Candlestick*), *Il ne faut jurer de rien* (*You Never Can Tell*), and *Il faut qu'une porte soit ouverte ou fermée* (*A Door Must Be Kept Shut or Open*)—have remained staples of the French repertory, thanks to their verbal elegance and humour.

Musset completed one novel, *La Confession d'un enfant du siècle* (*The Confession of a Child of the Century*), a fictional treatment of the Sand affair. Conceived as an apologia for his mistress, the novel—with its over-wrought rhetoric, its tone of a *mea culpa*, and the discontinuity between its apocalyptic historical prologue and the confessions which follow—has not aged well. It had a considerable *succès de scandale* at its publication, however, and elicited passionate controversy for the remainder of the century. Musset's short fiction, collected as *Nouvelles* (*Tales from Musset*) and *Contes*, was a major source of revenue but, aside from the transposed autobiography of "Le Fils du Titien," does not add significantly to his literary reputation.

Throughout his career, Musset published art and drama reviews and essays. These point up his growing literary conservatism—"classicism" in the terms of the period—yet do not constitute a major contribution to the genre, in comparison with such contemporaries as Gautier or Baudelaire. But the *Lettres de Dupuis et Cotonet 1836–37*, a satire of Romantic aesthetics, and his reviews of the actress Rachel's revival of neo-classical tragedy, 1838, were influential in the French reaction to Romanticism.

Musset's greatest influence on his century may have been as a quasi-mythic *poète damné*: the portrait of the artist as suffering lover, as self-destructive genius, and ultimately as failure. It is ironic that this apologist for the classical ethos and aesthetic should be one of the models of the Romantic, confessional artist-hero.

—David Sices

See the essay on *Lorenzaccio*.

N

NATSUME Sōseki

Born: Natsume Kinnosuke in Tokyo, Japan, 9 February 1867.
Education: Educated at schools in Tokyo; Tokyo Imperial University, 1890–93. **Family:** Married Nakane Kvoko in 1896; five daughters. **Career:** Taught at Tokyo Normal College, 1894–95; Middle School, Matsuyama, 1895–1900; lived in England, 1900–02; Professor of English, Tokyo Imperial University, 1903–07. Member of the staff, *Tetsugaku Zasshi*, 1892; associated with *Asahi* from 1907: in charge of literary columns from 1909. **Awards:** Honorary doctorate: Ministry of Education (refused). **Died:** 9 December 1916.

PUBLICATIONS

Collections

Zenshū [Complete Works], edited by Komiya Toyataka. 34 vols., 1956–59.
Zenshū. 16 vols., 1965–67.

Fiction

Rondon-Tō (story). 1905; as *The Tower of London*, translated by Peter Milward and Kii Nakano, 1992.
Wagahai wa neko de aru. 2 vols., 1905–07; as *I Am a Cat*, translated by K. Ando, 1906, revised by K. Natsume, 2 vols., 1906–09; also translated by Katsue Shibata and Motonari Kai, 1971 (vol. 1), and A. Ito and G. Wilson, 1980 (vol. 2).
Yōkyoshū [Drifting in Space] (stories). 1906.
Botchan. 1906; as *Botchan (Master Darling)*, translated by Yasotaro Morri, 1918; as *Botchan*, translated by Umeji Sasaki, 1968; also translated by Alan Turney, 1972.
Kusamakura. 1906; as *Kusamakura*, translated by Umeji Sasaki, 1927; as *Unhuman Tour*, translated by Kazutomo Takahashi, 1927; as *The Three-Cornered World*, translated by Alan Turney, 1965.
Ni hyaku toka [The Two Hundred and Tenth Day]. 1906.
Nowaki [Autumn Wind]. 1907.
Uzurakago [Basket of Quails] (includes *Botchan; Kusamakura; Ni hyaku toka).* 1907.
Gubijinso [The Poppy]. 1908.
Kofu [Miner]. 1908,
Yume jūya. 1908; as *Ten Nights' Dream*, translated by Sankichi Hata and Dofu Shirai, with *Our Cat's Grave*, 1934.
Sanshirō. 1908; as *Sanshiro*, translated by Jay Rubin, 1977.
Sorekara. 1910; as *And Then*, translated by Norma Moore Field, 1978.
Mon. 1911; as *Mon*, translated by Francis Mathy, 1972.
Higan Sugi made [Until after the Equinox]. 1912.
Kōjin. 1914; as *The Wayfarer*, translated by Beongcheon Yu, 1967; as *The Wanderer*, translated by Yu, 1967.
Kokoro. 1914; as *Kokoro*, translated by Ineko Sato, 1941; also translated by Iñeko Kondon, 1956; Edwin McClellan, 1957.

Garasudo no naka. 1915; as *Within My Glass Doors*, translated by Iwao Matsuhara and E.T. Iglehart, 1928.
Michikusa. 1915; as *Grass on the Wayside*, translated by Edwin McClellan, 1969.
Meian (incomplete). 1917; as *Light and Darkness*, translated by V.H. Viglielmo, 1971.
Ten Nights' Dream, and Our Cat's Grave, translated by Sankichi Hata and Dofu Shirai. 1934.
Ten Nights of Dream, Hearing Things, The Heredity of Taste, translated by Aiko Itō and Graeme Wilson. 1974.

Other

Eibungaku keishiki ron [Theory of Form in English Literature]. 1903.
Bungakuron [Theory of Literature]. 1907.
Bungaku hyōron [Literary Criticism]. 1909.
Kirinukicho yori [Random Recollections]. 1911.
Shakai to jibun [Society and I]. 1913.
Zen Haiku: Poems and Letters of Natsume Sōseki , translated and edited by Soiku Shigematsu. 1994.

*

Bibliography: *Ogai and Sōseki* by Naruse Masakatsu and Hashimoto Yoshiichiro, 1965.

Critical Studies: *Natsume Sōseki* by Beongcheon Yu (in English), 1969; *Two Japanese Novelists: Sōseki and Toson* by Edwin McClellan, 1969; *Essays on Natsume's Works*, 1970; *Accomplices of Silence: The Modern Japanese Novel* by Masao Miyoshi, 1974; *Natsume Sōseki as a Critic of English Literature* by Matsui Sakuko, 1975; *The Psychological World of Natsume Sōseki* by Takeo Doi, 1976; *Sōseki's Development as a Novelist until 1907: With Special Reference to the Genesis, Nature and Position in His Work of Kusa Makura* by Alan Turney, 1985; *Three Modern Novelists: Sōseki, Tanizaki, Kawabata* by Van C. Gessel, 1993; *Rereading Soseki: Three Early Twentieth-century Japanese Novels* by Reiko Abe Auestad, 1998; *Chaos and Order in the Works of Natsume Sōseki* by Angela Yiu, 1998.

* * *

One of the leading figures at the formative stage of Japan's "modern" prose fiction, Natsume Sōseki is still widely read and highly revered. Acutely aware of the nation's cultural and historical fissure that resulted from the exposure to Western hegemony, he saw the problems of a rapid change everywhere. The inherited values and customs had to be reexamined in the light of new and "rational" knowledge, but this freshly acquired modern insight, too, required authentication both for its legitimacy and adaptability. His earlier studies of English literature may have led him to believe that historical discontinuity was universal, as it was in some sense. The notion of universalism and centrality of the West was, however, not unmixed with a conviction about Japan's distinctness and orientalness. As has been the case with most serious Japanese writers since, the major motif of his work from beginning to end was a struggle to make the competing claims somehow compatible and to contain the incongruous and contradictory within the narrative form he had to forge.

Reflecting the deep cultural fracture, Natsume's form and style are both traditional and experimental. His attachment to "pre-modern" Edo culture is evident throughout his work: in the colloquialism of the dialogue, the narrator's reference to the commonplace in arts, and the choice of familiar and vulgar characters in the older quarters of Tokyo, which together serve to deflate the pompous pretentions of the newly emerging bureaucracy. Also unmistakable is his fascination with a dense verbal texture—puns, parodies, and periphrases—which he discovered in 18th-century *gesaku* (playful writing) books and their entertainment-hall descendants. This, together with his intimate knowledge of Chinese classics, foregrounds Natsume's writing in the art of eloquence. Especially in his earliest works such as *Wagahai wa Neko de aru* (*I Am a Cat*), *Botchan*, and *Kusamakura* (*The Three-Cornered World*), Natsume's still youthful buoyancy and energy are at times defined in the imagery and rhetoric of Edo fiction. Natsume, however, was also a "modern" intellectual obsessed with the crisis of alienation. Hero after hero in his works broods darkly and endlessly over his personal isolation and cultural insularity. Mr. Hirota ("Great Darkness") in *Sanshirō*, Daisuke in *Sorekara* (*And Then*), and the Sensei in *Kokoro* are such characters confronting the blind alley of bourgeois life. And in such writing, Natsume's grammar, too, takes on the vocabulary and syntax of an unidiomatic "translation style."

The sentence in *Kokoro* (meaning Heart) is dominated by the first-person pronoun. As in Conrad's *Heart of Darkness* (which Natsume is most likely to have read), the multiple narrators of the work are guides for the reader on a journey inward to glimpse the darkest core of the interior. Deaths abound, and the disrupted narrative sequence finally leads to the starting point that was already a dead end. The central character's suicide silences the story at the end.

By the time of Natsume's death Japan had been embarking on its own program of expansionism into the Asian continent. His last work, *Meian* (*Light and Darkness*), intimates a firmer will to face the national and social issues with clarity and irony. A bourgeois critic of Imperial Japan, Natsume still remains perhaps the most thoughtful of writers produced by 20th-century Japan.

—Masao Miyoshi

NAVARRE, Marguerite de

See MARGUERITE DE NAVARRE

NERUDA, Pablo

Born: Neftalí Ricardo Reyes Basoalto in Parral, Chile, 12 July 1904; Pablo Neruda became his legal name, 1946. **Education:** Educated at school for boys in Temuco, 1910–20; Instituto Pedagógico, Santiago (poetry prize, 1921), in the 1920s. **Family:** Married 1) María Antonieta Hagenaar in 1930, one daughter; lived with Delia del Carril; 2) Matilde Urrutia. **Career:** In Chilean consular and diplomatic service: consul in Rangoon, 1927, Colombo, 1928, Batavia, 1930, Singapore, 1931, Buenos Aires, 1933, Barcelona, 1933, Madrid, 1935–36; helped Spanish refugees as consul in Paris, 1939; Consul-General, Mexico City, 1940–43; elected to Chilean Senate as communist,

1945; attacked President Gonzales Videla in print, and in exile after 1947; returned to Chile after victory of anti-Videla forces, 1952; after Allende's victory in 1970, named Ambassador to France, 1971–72 (resigned because of ill health). Editor, with Manuel Altolaguirre, *Caballo Verde*, Spain, 1935–36, and *Aurora de Chile*, 1938. **Awards:** National literature prize, 1945; Stalin Peace prize, 1953; Viareggio-Versilia prize, 1967; Nobel prize for literature, 1971. Honorary doctorates: University of Michoacán, Mexico, 1941; Oxford University, 1965. Honorary fellow, Modern Language Association (United States). **Member:** World Peace Council, from 1950; president, Union of Chilean Writers, 1957–73. **Died:** 23 September 1973.

PUBLICATIONS

Verse

Crepusculario. 1923.

Veinte poemas de amor y una canción desesperada. 1924; as *The Man Who Told His Love*, translated by Patrick Bowles and adapted by Christopher Logue (bilingual edition), 1958; as *Twenty Love Poems and a Song of Despair*, translated by W.S. Merwin, 1969.

Tentativa del hombre infinito. 1926.

El hondero entusiasta 1923–1924. 1933.

Residencia en la tierra. 2 vols., 1933–35; as *Residence on Earth*, translated by Angel Flores, 1946; also translated by Donald D. Walsh (bilingual edition), 1973.

Tres cantos materiales. 1935; as *Three Material Songs*, translated by Angel Flores, 1948.

España en el corazón: Himno a las glorias del pueblo en la guerra 1936–1937. 1937; as *Spain in the Heart: Hymn to the Glories of the People at War, 1936–1937*, translated by Richard Schaaf, 1993.

Las furias y las penas. 1939.

Un canto para Bolívar. 1941.

Selected Poems. 1941.

Nuevo canto de amor a Stalingrado. 1943.

Selected Poems, translated by Angel Flores. 1944.

Obra poética. 10 vols., 1947–48.

Tercera residencia 1935–1945. 1947.

¡Que despierte el lenador! 1948; as *Let the Rail Splitter Awake!*, translated in *Let the Rail Splitter Awake and Other Poems*, translated by Samuel Sillen, 1950, also in *Peace for Twilights to Come!*, 1950.

Himno y regreso. 1948.

Dulce patria. 1949.

Canto general. 1950; in part as *The Heights of Macchu Picchu*, translated by Nathaniel Tarn, 1966; as *Poems from Canto General*, translated by Ben Belitt, 1968; as *Canto General*, translated by Jack Schmitt, 1991.

Poesías completas. 1951.

Los versos del capitán: Poemas de amor. 1952; as *The Captain's Verses*, translated by Donald D. Walsh, 1972; translated by Brian Cole, 1994.

Todo el amor (selection). 1953.

Odas elementales, Nuevas odas elementales, Tercer libro de las odas. 3 vols., 1954–57; as *Elementary Odes*, translated by Carlos Lozano, 1961; as *Elemental Odes*, translated by Margaret Sayers Peden, 1990; as *Odes to Common Things*, translated by Ken Krabbenhoft, 1994.

Las uvas y el viento. 1954.

Oda a la tipografía. 1956; as *Ode to Typography*, translated by Enrique Sacerio-Garí, 1977.

Estravagario. 1958; as *Extravagaria*, translated by Alastair Reid, 1972.

Todo lleva tu nombre. 1959.

Odas: Al libro, a las Américas, a la luz. 1959.

Navegaciones y regresos. 1959.

Cien sonetos de amor. 1959; as *One Hundred Love Sonnets*, translated by Stephen Tapscott, 1986.

Algunas odas. 1959.

Toros. 1960.

Canción de gesta. 1960; as *Epic Song*, translated by Richard Schaaf, 1998.

Las piedras de Chile. 1960; as *Stones of Chile*, translated by D. Maloney, 1990.

Los primeros versos de amor. 1961.

Selected Poems, translated by Ben Belitt. 1961.

Cantos ceremoniales. 1961; as *Ceremonial Songs*, translated by Maria Jacketti, 1996.

Plenos poderes. 1961; as *Fully Empowered*, translated by Alastair Reid, 1975.

La insepulta de Paíta. 1962.

Oceana. 1962.

Memorial de Isla Negra. 5 vols., 1964; as *Isla Negra: A Notebook*, translated by Alastair Reid, 1981; translated by Maria Jacketti, 2001.

Bestiary/Bestiario. 1966; as *Bestiary*, translated by Elsa Neuberger, 1965.

Arte de pájaros. 1966; as *Art of Birds*, translated by Jack Schmitt, 1985.

Una casa en la arena. 1966.

We Are Many, translated by Alastair Reid. 1967.

La barcarola. 1967.

Twenty Poems, translated by James Wright and Robert Bly. 1967.

Lax manos del día. 1968.

Aún. 1969.

Fin del mundo. 1969.

Early Poems, translated by David Ossman and Carlos B. Hagen. 1969.

A New Decade: Poems 1958–67, translated by Ben Belitt and Alastair Reid. 1969.

La espada encendida. 1970.

Maremoto. 1970; as *Seaquake: Poems*, translated by Maria Jacketti and Dennis Maloney, 1993.

Las piedras del cielo. 1970.

Selected Poems, edited by Nathaniel Tarn, translated by Anthony Kerrigan and others. 1970.

Neruda and Vallejo: Selected Poems, translated by Robert Bly, James Wright, and John Knoepfle. 1971.

Geografía infructuosa. 1972.

La rosa separada. 1972; as *The Separate Rose*, translated by William O'Daly, 1985.

Incitación al nixonicidio y alabanza de la revolución chilena. 1973; as *Incitation to Nixoncide and Praise for the Spanish Revolution*, translated by Steve Kowit, 1973; as *A Call for the Destruction of Nixon and Praise for the Chilean Revolution*, translated by Teresa Anderson, 1980.

El mar y las campanas. 1973; as *The Sea and the Bells*, translated by William O'Daly, 1988.

New Poems 1968–1970, translated by Ben Belitt. 1973.

Jardín de invierno. 1974; as *Winter Garden*, translated by William O'Daly, 1987.

2000. 1974; translated by Richard Schaaf, 1997.

El corazón amarillo. 1974.

Libro de las preguntas. 1974.

Elegía. 1974.

Defectos escogidos. 1974.

Five Decades: Poems 1925–1970, translated by Ben Belitt. 1974.

Selections: Poems from Canto General, translated by J.C.R. Green. 1982.

Still Another Day, translated by William O'Daly. 1984.

Late and Posthumous Poems 1968–1974, translated by Ben Belitt. 1988.

The House in the Sand: Prose Poems, translated by Dennis Maloney and Clark M. Zlotchew. 1990.

Selected Odes, translated by Margaret Sayers Peden. 1990.

Neruda's Garden: An Anthology of Odes, translated by Maria Jacketti. 1995.

Plays

Romeo and Juliet, from the play by Shakespeare (produced 1964). 1964.

Fulgor y muerte de Joaquín Murieta (produced 1967). 1967; as *Splendor and Death of Joaquín Murieta*, translated by Ben Belitt, 1972.

Fiction

El habitante y su esperanza. 1926.

Other

Prosas. 1926.

Anillos, with Tomás Lagos. 1926.

Neruda entre nosotros, with Emilio Oribe and Juan Marinello. 1939.

La crisis democrática de Chile. 1947; as *The Democratic Crisis of Chile*, 1948.

Cartas a México. 1947.

Viajes al corazón de Quevedo y pot las costas del mundo. 1947.

Pablo Neruda acusa. 1948.

Gonzáles Videla, el Laval de la América Latina. 1949.

Poesía política: Discursos políticos. 2 vols., 1952.

Cuando de Chile. 1952.

Viajes. 1955.

Obras completas. 1957; 4th edition, 3 vols., 1973.

Cuba, los obispos. 1962(?).

Comiendo en Hungría, with Miguel Ángel Asturias (verse and illustrations). 1969; as *Sentimental Journey around the Hungarian Cuisine*, translated by Barna Balogh, 1969; revised translation by Mary Arias, 1969.

Confieso que he vivido. 1974; as *Memoirs*, translated by Hardie St. Martin, 1977.

Cartas de amor, edited by Sergio Fernández Larraín. 1974.

Pablo Neruda: A Basic Anthology (in Spanish), edited by Robert Pring-Mill. 1975.

Cartas a Laura, edited by Hugo Montes. 1978.

Para nacer he nacido, edited by Matilde Neruda and Miguel Otera Sila, 1978; as *Passions and Impressions*, translated by Margaret Sayers Peden, 1983.

Correspondancia, with Héctor Eandi, edited by Margarita Aguirre. 1980.

Pablo Neruda and Nicanor Parra Face to Face: A Bilingual and Critical Edition of Their Speeches on the Occasion of Neruda's Appointment to the Faculty of the University of Chile, translated with introduction by Marlene Gottlieb. 1997.

Editor and translator, *Páginas escogidas de Anatole France*. 1924.

Translator, *44 poetas rumanos*. 1967.

*

Bibliography: *Neruda: Bibliografía* by Horacio Jorge Becco, 1975; *Pabo Neruda: An Annotated Bibliography of Bibliographical and Critical Studies* by Hensley C. Woodbridge and David S. Zubatsky, 1988.

Critical Studies: *Testimony of the Invisible Man: William Carlos Williams, Francis Ponge, Rainer Maria Rilke, and Pablo Neruda* by Nancy Willard, 1970; *The Word and the Stone: Language and Imagery in Neruda's "Canto General"* by Frank Riess, 1972; *The Poetry of Pablo Neruda* by René de Costa, 1979; *Pablo Neruda: All Poets the Poet* by Salvatore Bizzaro, 1979; *Translating Neruda: The Way to Macchu Picchu* by John Felstiner, 1981; *Earth Tones: The Poetry of Pablo Neruda* by Manuel Durán and Margery Safir, 1981; *Pablo Neruda: The Poetics of Prophecy* by Enrico Mario Santí, 1982; *Pablo Neruda* by Marjorie Agosín, 1986; *On Elevating the Commonplace: A Structuralist Analysis of the "Odes" of Pablo Neruda* by David G. Anderson, 1987; *The Late Poetry of Neruda* by Christopher Perriam, 1989; *Pablo Neruda: Absence and Presence* by Luis Poirot, translated by Alastair Reid, 1990; *An Intimate Biography* by Volodia Teitelboim, 1991; *Pablo Neruda: Chilean Poet and Diplomat* by Joe Roman, 1992; *Poet-chief: The Native American Poetics of Walt Whitman and Pablo Neruda* by James Nolan, 1994; *Neruda's Ekphrastic Experience: Mural Art and Canto General* by Hugo Méndez-Ramirez, 1999.

* * *

Pablo Neruda, sometimes called the Picasso of poetry, is a writer of many styles and many voices; his vast and varied work, spanning more than half a century, is central to every major development in Spanish and Spanish American poetry between the 1920s and the 1970s. Despite his humble beginnings (born into a working-class family and raised in a rough-and-tumble frontier town in the south of Chile), by the time he turned 20 he had come to occupy a pre-eminent place in the literature of his country.

Veinte poemas de amor y una canción desesperada (*Twenty Love Poems and a Song of Despair*) was a *succès de scandale* when it first appeared in 1924. Judged to be shamelessly erotic and faulted for its bold departure in form and style from the genteel tradition of Hispanic lyricism the book went on to become something of a bestseller, and remains so today. Its power derives from Neruda's new and unusual treatment of the age-old subject of love. Employing a dense and almost hermetic language combining the normally unarticulated level of digressive thought and the ordered level of logical discourse, each poem is a kind of monologue in which the poet speaks as though to himself and to an absent lover. Making use of a rhetoric which is not conventionally poetic (staggered repetitions, an irregular temporal exposition, and a prosaic syntax), Neruda managed to convey a quality that was often lacking in traditional love poetry: the quality of

sincerity and conviction. The result was a highly charged confessional intimacy that challenged and charmed the sensibility of its reader, creating in the process a contemporary *stil nuovo* which continues to resonate in the language of love in Spanish.

Tentativa del hombre infinito [The Infinite Man's Attempt] furthered the poet's experiments with form and placed him in the forefront of the Chilean avant-garde. In this long and difficult poem, organized in 15 cantos around the idea of a nocturnal voyage in search of the absolute, he foregoes the use of rhyme, meter, capitalization, and punctuation to attain a more concentrated literary language capable of conveying a maximum degree of subjectivity. The poem's seemingly unmediated discourse is similar in texture to that of surrealist writing but differs in that it is not the outcome of "psychic automatism," but the result of a lengthy compositional process of revision and modification, pruning relator words, connectives, and punctuation so as to enhance the run-on associative power of the imagery. Neruda, in his later years, called attention to this vanguard experiment of 1926, relating it to his hermetic poetry of the *Residencia* cycle.

Residencia en la tierra (*Residence on Earth*), when published in Spain in 1935, was hailed by García Lorca and others as "one of the most authentic realities of poetry in the Spanish language today." At the time Neruda also felt that in this work he had achieved a kind of perfection and "had passed a literary limit" hitherto thought impossible. *Residence on Earth*, which assured his international fame, is a work in two volumes, the first of which was originally published in Chile in a limited edition of 100 copies and contains poems written in the Far East where Neruda had served as a consular official from 1927 to 1931. These texts cover a diverse range of topics, from monsoons to marriage, and stand as individual testimonials of moments of heightened awareness. The discourse is quite free, unbound by logic, and despite the ample use of prosaic locutions utilizes an unprosaic reasoning process based on implied and generative associations. Although the basic discursive situation is soliloquial, as in the earlier poetry, the style is decidedly anti-lyrical, often jarring the reader's sensibility with references to the ordinary and the "unpoetic." In 1935 the book was reissued with a companion volume, *Residencia II*, containing Neruda's more recent poetry and a significant change of form and style: where once the poet had been concentrated and introspective, he had become digressive and outward. Essentially, by the mid-1930s, Neruda was beginning to write a poetry to be spoken out loud, not to be read in silence, and for the first time his discourse is addressed not to an absent personage or to the poet's inner self, but to his reader. The second *Residencia*, dealing engagingly with life's random experiences, substantiated a new kind of poetic realism. In a manifesto of the time ("On Impure Poetry"), Neruda explains this change, speaking out against his earlier hermetic writing and against the ultra-refined aestheticism of "pure poetry." His goal henceforth was a poetry that was not only sincere but also uninvented, in a word "realistic."

Tercera residencia, a collection of post-*Residencia* poems, documents Neruda's new social and political awareness. The realities of fascism and the Spanish Civil War provoked a shift in perspective, transforming his poetic realism to a more committed kind of writing. The idea was to use the persuading power of literature to make the reader share the writer's view of the socio-political realities of a world at war. Oral diction is enhanced and rendered poetic through a revival of traditional poetic forms: rhymed stanzas and metrical verses. At this point, secure in his position as a public poet, Neruda assumed a broader role, spokesman for the continent.

Canto general, the general song of America, presenting in some 500 pages and almost 20,000 verses the theme of man's struggle for justice in the New World, is by far his most ambitious work, and caused a sensation when it first appeared in 1950. Even today critics are split into two camps over the merits of this text: those who ridicule Neruda's militant politics (he joined the Communist Party in 1945) and those who find them justified. Politics aside, the work is masterful for its epic sweep and for the extraordinary variety and quantity of old and new poetic forms and voices employed to maintain reader interest and render persuasive the political message.

Odas elementales (*Elemental Odes*) continued Neruda's efforts to reach the common man, to bring poetry to the people. Political without appearing to be politicized, simple without being simplistic, it appealed to an extraordinarily wide range of readers through a seemingly artless, almost breezy series of compositions exalting the most basic things of daily existence, the plain and the ordinary, fruits and flowers, thread and bread. Since many of these poems were first published in the columns of a daily newspaper the style is simple and straightforward, the verses are short and direct, and the tone is intimate and conversational. *Estravagario* (*Extravagaria*) took the conversational mode of the odes one step further, desolemnizing poetry itself. In this book, for the first time, everything is treated irreverently, even politics—and in a sardonic tone and an everyday manner typical of what has come to be called anti-poetry.

Neruda, in his later years, tried his hand at theatre—*Fulgor y muerte de Joaquín Murieta* (*Splendor and Death of Joaquín Murieta*)—and took a more direct role in politics, serving as the Communist Party's pre-candidate to the 1970 elections which brought Salvador Allende to power. He continued to cultivate a poetry concerned with the here and now: the Cuban Revolution in *Canción de gesta* (*Epic Song*); Vietnam and the generally deplorable state of the world in *Fin del mundo* [End of the World]; and Nixon in *Incitación al nixonicidio* (*Incitation to Nixoncide*). Two volumes of memoirs and several volumes of posthumously published poetry cap this extraordinary career in the literature of our time.

—René de Costa

See the essays on "Arte Poética" and *Tentativa del hombre infinito*.

NERVAL, Gérard de

Born: Gérard Labrunie in Paris, France, 22 May 1808. **Education:** Educated at Lycée Charlemagne, Paris, 1820–28; possibly apprenticed to a printer and studied law; studied medicine to 1834. **Career:** Led a life of wandering; after inheriting money from his grandfather in 1834 founded *Le Monde Dramatique*, 1835; drama critic, *La Presse*, and contributor to other journals from 1838. Suffered first mental breakdown in 1841; hospitalized in mental clinics, 1849, 1851, 1853, 1854. **Died:** (suicide) 26 January 1855.

PUBLICATIONS

Collections

Oeuvres complètes, edited by Aristide Marie, Jules Marsan, and Édouard Champion. 6 vols., 1926–32.
Oeuvres complémentaires, edited by Jean Richer. 1959–.

Oeuvres, edited by Jean Guillaume and Claude Pichois. 3 vols., 1984–93.
Aurélia and Other Writings, translated by Geoffrey Wagner, Robert Duncan and Marc Lowenthal. 1996.
Selected Writings, translated with an introduction by Richard Sieburth. 1999.

Verse

Élégies nationales. 1826.
Les Chimères, in *Les Filles du feu*. 1854; edited by Norma Rinsler, 1973; as *The Chimeras*, translated by Andrew Hoyem, 1966; also translated by Derek Mahon, 1982; Peter Jay, 1984; translated by William Stone, 1999.
Fortune's Fool: Thirty-Five Poems, translated by Brian Hill. 1959.

Plays

Piquillo, with Alexandre Dumas *père*, music by Hippolyte Monpou (produced 1837). 1837.
Léo Burckart, with Alexandre Dumas *père* (produced 1839). 1839.
L'Alchimiste, with Alexandre Dumas *père* (produced 1839). 1839.
Les Monténégrins, with E. Alboize, music by Armand Limnander (produced 1849). 1849.
Le Chariot d'enfant, with Joseph Méry (produced 1850).
L'Imagier de Harlem, with Joseph Méry and Bernard Lopez, music by Adolphe de Groot (produced 1851). 1852.

Fiction

Le Marquis de Fayolle. 1849.
Contes et facéties. 1852.
Les Filles du feu. 1854; as *Daughters of Fire*, translated by James Whitall, 1923.
Aurélia. 1855; as *Aurelia*, translated by Richard Aldington, 1932; as *Dreams and Life*, translated by Vyvyan Holland, 1933; translated by Geoffrey Wagner, 1996; translated by Monique DiDonna, 2001.
Le Prince des Sots, edited by Louis Ulbach. 1866.

Other

Voyage en Orient. 1851; in part as *The Women of Cairo*, translated anonymously, 1929; as *Journey to the Orient*, edited by Norman Glass, 1972.
Les Illuminés; ou, Les Précurseurs du socialisme. 1852.
Lorély. 1852.
Petits châteaux de Bohême: Prose et poésie. 1853.
Promenades et souvenirs. 1854.
Selected Writings, edited by G. Wagner. 1958.
Le Carnet de Dolbreuse, edited by Jean Richer. 1967.
Editor, *Choix des poésies de Ronsard*. 1830.
Editor and translator, *Choix de poésies allemandes*. 1830.
Translator, *Faust*, by Goethe. 1828; enlarged edition, *Faust, et Le Second Faust*, 1840.

*

Bibliography: *Nerval: Essai de bibliographie* by Jean Senelier, 1959, supplements, 1968, 1982, 1991; *Nerval: A Critical Bibliography 1900–1967* by James Villas, 1968.

Critical Studies: *Nerval: L'Homme et l'oeuvre* by Léon Cellier, 1956; *Nerval par lui-même* by Raymond Jean, 1964; *Nerval and the German Heritage* by Alfred Dubruck, 1965; *Gérard de Nerval* by Norma Rinsler, 1973; *The Disinherited: The Life of Nerval* by Benn Sowerby, 1973; *The Style of Nerval's Aurélia* by William Beauchamp, 1976; *Nerval's Double: A Structural Study* by Claire Gilbert, 1979; *Gérard de Nerval's Dilemma: The Mystic's Dilemma* by Bettina L. Knapp, 1980; *There and Here: A Meditation on Gérard de Nerval* by David Miller, 1982; *Gérard de Nerval: The Poet as Social Visionary* by Kari Lokke, 1987; *Critical Fictions: Nerval's Les Illuminés* by Meryl Tyers, 1998; *Subjects of Terror: Nerval, Hegel, and the Modern Self* by Jonathan Strauss, 1998.

* * *

Gérard de Nerval, who belonged to the generation of the younger Romantics, published his first volumes of verse while still at school, and translated Goethe's *Faust* before he was 20. His precocious and graceful talent was threatened from his early thirties onwards by bouts of alternating depression and elation which led to several periods of treatment in clinics and to a widespread belief among his contemporaries that he was incurably mad. This reputation bedevilled criticism of his achievement for at least a century, since the more difficult of his works were labelled as incoherent or insane.

More recently it has become clear that late texts such as *Aurélia* (*Dreams and Life*) and "Pandora" are accounts of a mind obsessed by the search for the ideal, distracted by guilt for its human failings, but lucidly aware of the sources of its problems. Early in the 20th century, Nerval was best known as a poet; his sonnets, *Les Chimères* (*The Chimeras*), were rediscovered by the French Symbolists and acclaimed in both France and England as examples of "pure" poetry. A more judicious approach to these immensely dense and complex poems may be attempted by way of the prose pieces in *Les Filles du feu* (*Daughters of Fire*), with which they were originally published: in "Sylvie," he offers a penetrating analysis of the dilemma of the French Romantics, torn between their heritage of 18th-century rationalism, their daily experience of social and political disorder, and their frustrated idealism; the clash between religion and reason appears again in "Isis," and also in the study of "Quintus Aucler" in *Les Illuminés* [The Illuminati]. *Dreams and Life* explores the role of dream as a non-rational mode of knowledge, and Nerval concludes that reason alone is not the road to salvation. "Les Chimères" means "illusions," but illusions may be consciously preferred, may indeed be necessary; and the world of the illusory ideal is brilliantly explored both in the sonnets and in "Sylvie," where the dream-like course of the narrative mirrors the theme.

Nerval's writings are interrelated to a quite remarkable extent; almost every work finds echoes and inversions of its themes and images in other works ranging over the whole of his career. His concerns are deeply serious, but he is never solemn. Nor is he only a dreamer: fantasy, humour, and compassion are blended with sharp observation in "Les Nuits d'octobre" [October Nights], in "Angélique," in *Promenades et Souvenirs* [Excursions and Memories], and in his travel books. The sonnets are technically very interesting, using a method of juxtaposition later much favoured by the Surrealists, but creating thereby a coherent network of musical echoes and resonant images which maps a mental landscape, engaging the reader's understanding without asking for his indulgence. Difficult poetry, in the sense that they demand very close attention to syntax and to what the words are actually saying, the sonnets are

tightly organized structures which a relaxed and "lyrical" reading will fail to grasp; but dignified and approachable poetry in which, Nerval believed, he had managed to say what was most important to him, and in which he offers his account of a "descent into Hell" as a modest guide and encouragement to others. "The experience of each of us," he said, "is treasure for us all."

—Norma Rinsler

NESTROY, Johann Nepomuk (Eduard Ambrosius)

Born: in Vienna, Austria, 7 December 1801. **Education:** Educated at Gymnasium, 1811–16; studied law at the University of Vienna, 1817–21 (did not take degree). **Family:** Married Wilhelmine von Nespiesni in 1823 (separated 1827, divorced 1845), one son; lived with the singer Marie Weiler from 1827, one son and one daughter. **Career:** Actor and singer with the German Theatre of Amsterdam, 1823–25, Nationaltheater in Brünn (now Brno, Czech Republic), 1825–26, and the theatres in Graz and Pressburg, 1826–28; returned to Vienna, 1829; guest singer at Theater in der Josephstadt and Kärntnertortheater, 1829–31; with Marie Weiler, joined Karl Carl's theatre company, based at the Theater an der Wien (from 1845 at the Theater in der Leopoldstadt, which was renamed the Carl-Theater, 1847), as comic actor and writer, 1831–54, director and manager, 1854–60: dominated Vienna's commercial stage as its leading comic actor, appearing in his own plays; undertook guest seasons in various parts of Germany and Central Europe during the 1840s and 1850s. **Died:** 25 May 1862.

PUBLICATIONS

Collections

Gesammelte Werke, edited by Vincenz Chiavacci and Ludwig Ganghofer. 12 vols., 1890–91.
Sämtliche Werke, edited by Fritz Brukner and Otto Rommel. 15 vols., 1924–30.
Gesammelte Werke, edited by Otto Rommel. 6 vols., 1948–49.
Komödien, edited by F.H. Mautner. 1970.
Sämtliche Werke, edited by Jürgen Hein and Johann Hüttner. 1977–.

Plays

Zwölf Mädchen in Uniform (produced 1827). With *Ein gebildeter Hausknecht*, 1943.
Der Zettelträger Papp, from a play by Hermann Herzenskron (produced 1927). In *Sämtliche Werke*, 9, 1927.
Die Verbannung aus dem Zauberreiche; oder, Dreissig Jahre aus dem Leben eines Lumpen (produced 1828). In *Sämtliche Werke*, 1, 1924.
Der Einsilbige; oder, Ein dummer Diener seines Herrn, from a play by Franz Grillparzer (produced 1829).
Der Tod am Hochzeitstage; oder, Mann, Frau, Kind (produced 1829). In *Sämtliche Werke*, 1, 1924.
Der unzusammenhängende Zusammenhang (produced 1830).

Magische Eilwagenreise durch die Komödienwelt (produced 1830). In *Sämtliche Werke*, 9, 1927.

Zwei Schüsseln voll Faschingskrapfen (produced 1831).

Der gefühlvolle Kerkermeister; oder, Adelheid, die verfolgte Wittib (produced 1832). In *Gesammelte Werke*, 1890–91.

Nagerl und Handschuh; oder, Die Schicksale der Familie Maxenpfutsch, from a libretto by C.-G. Étienne (produced 1832). In *Gesammelte Werke*, 1890–91.

Humoristische Eilwagenreise durch die Theaterwelt (produced 1832). In *Sämtliche Werke*, 9, 1927.

Zampa der Tagdieb; oder, Die Braut von Gips (produced 1832). In *Gesammelte Werke*, 1890–91.

Der konfuse Zauberer; oder, Treue und Flatterhaftigkeit (produced 1832). In *Gesammelte Werke*, 1890–91.

Die Zauberreise in die Ritterzeit; oder, Die Übermütigen (produced 1832). In *Gesammelte Werke*, 1890–91.

Der Zauberer Februar; oder, Die Überraschungen (produced 1833). In *Sämtliche Werke*, 1, 1924.

Der böse Geist Lumpazivagabundus; oder, Das liederliche Kleeblatt (produced 1833). 1835.

Robert der Teufel (produced 1833). In *Gesammelte Werke*, 1890–91.

Der Tritschtratsch (produced 1833). In *Gesammelte Werke*, 1890–91.

Der Zauberer Sulphurelektrimagnetikophosphoratus und die Fee Walpurgiblocksbergiseptemtrionalis. . . (produced 1834). In *Gesammelte Werke*, 1890–91.

Müller, Kohlenbrenner und Sesselträger; oder, Die Träume von Schale und Kern (produced 1834). In *Gesammelte Werke*, 1890–91.

Die Gleichheit der Jahre (produced 1834). In *Gesammelte Werke*, 1890–91.

Die Familien Zwirn, Knieriem und Leim; oder, Der Welt-Untergangs-Tag (produced 1834). In *Gesammelte Werke*, 1890–91.

Die Fahrt mit dem Dampfwagen (produced 1834). In *Gesammelte Werke*, 1890–91.

Weder Lorbeerbaum noch Bettelstab (produced 1835). In *Gesammelte Werke*, 1890–91.

Eulenspiegel; oder, Schabernack über Schabernack (produced 1835). 1839.

Zu ebener Erde und erster Stock; oder, Die Launen des Glückes, from a play by C.-D. Dupeuty and Frádéric de Courcy (produced 1835). 1838.

Der Treulose; oder, Saat und Ernte (produced 1836). In *Gesammelte Werke*, 1890–91.

Die beiden Nachtwandler; oder, Das Notwendige und das Überflüssige (produced 1836). In *Gesammelte Werke*, 1890–91.

Der Affe und der Bräutigam (produced 1836). In *Gesammelte Werke*, 1890–91.

Eine Wohnung ist zu vermieten in der Stadt. . . (produced 1837). In *Gesammelte Werke*, 1890–91.

Moppels Abenteuer im Viertel unter Wiener Wald, in Neu-Seeland und Marokko (produced 1837). In *Gesammelte Werke*, 1890–91.

Das Haus der Temperamente (produced 1837). As *The House of Humors*, translated by Robert Harrison and Katharina Wilson, in *Three Viennese Comedies*, 1986.

Glück, Missbrauch und Rückkehr; oder, Das Geheimnis des grauen Hauses, from a novel by Paul de Kock (produced 1838). 1845.

Der Kobold; oder, Staberl im Feendienst (produced 1838). In *Gesammelte Werke*, 1890–91.

Gegen Torheit gibt es keine Mittel (produced 1838). In *Gesammelte Werke*, 1890–91.

Die verhängnisvolle Faschingsnacht, from a play by Holtei (produced 1839). 1842.

Der Färber und sein Zwillingsbruder, from a libretto by Adolphe de Leuven and Léon Lhérie (produced 1840). In *Gesammelte Werke*, 1890–91.

Der Erbschleicher (produced 1840). In *Gesammelte Werke*, 1890–91.

Die zusammengestoppelte Komödie (produced 1840).

Der Talisman (produced 1840). 1843; as *The Talisman*, translated by Max Knight and Joseph Fabry, in *Three Comedies*, 1967; also translated by Robert Harrison and Katharina Wilson, in *Three Viennese Comedies*, 1986.

Das Mädl aus der Vorstadt; oder, Ehrlich währt am längsten (produced 1841). 1845.

Friedrich, Prinz von Korsika (produced 1841). In *Unbekannter Nestroy*, 1953.

Einen Jux will er sich machen, from a play by John Oxenford (produced 1842). 1844; as *The Merchant of Yonkers*, translated and adapted by Thornton Wilder, 1939; as *The Matchmaker*, 1954; as *On the Razzle*, translated and adapted by Tom Stoppard, 1981.

Die Ereignisse im Gasthofe (produced 1842).

Die Papiere des Teufels; oder, Der Zufall (produced 1842). In *Gesammelte Werke*, 1890–91.

Liebesgeschichten und Heiratssachen (produced 1843). In *Gesammelte Werke*, 1890–91; as *Love Affairs and Wedding Bells*, translated by Max Knight and Joseph Fabry, in *Three Comedies*, 1967.

Das Quodlibet verschiedener Jahrhunderte (produced 1843). In *Sämtliche Werke*, 9, 1927.

Nur Ruhe! (produced 1843). In *Gesammelte Werke*, 1890–91.

Eisenbahnheiraten; oder, Wien, Neustadt, Brünn, from a play by J.-F.-A. Bayard and Victor Varin (produced 1844). In *Gesammelte Werke*, 1890–91.

Hinüber-Herüber (produced 1844). 1852.

Der Zerrissene (produced 1844). 1845; as *A Man Full of Nothing*, translated by Max Knight and Joseph Fabry, in *Three Comedies*, 1967.

Die beiden Herren Söhne (produced 1845). In *Gesammelte Werke*, 1890–91.

Das Gewürzkrämerkleeblatt; oder, Die unschuldig Schuldigen, from a play by J.-P. Lockroy and Auguste Anicet-Bourgeois (produced 1845). In *Gesammelte Werke*, 1890–91.

Unverhofft, from a play by J.-F.-A. Bayard and Philippe Dumanoir (produced 1845). 1848.

Der Unbedeutende (produced 1846). 1849.

Zwei ewige Juden für einen (produced 1846). As *Zwei ewige Juden und keiner*, in *Gesammelte Werke*, 1890–91.

Der Schützling (produced 1847). In *Gesammelte Werke*, 1890–91.

Die schlimmen Buben in der Schule, from a play by J.-P. Lockroy and Auguste Anicet-Bourgeois (produced 1847). In *Gesammelte Werke*, 1890–91.

Martha; oder, Die Mischmonder Markt-Mägde-Mietung, from a libretto by W.F. Riese and Saint-Georges (produced 1848). In *Gesammelte Werke*, 1890–91.

Die Anverwandten, from a novel by Charles Dickens (produced 1848).

Freiheit in Krähwinkel (produced 1848). 1849; as *Liberty Comes to Krähwinkel*, translated by Sybil and Colin Welch, 1961.

Lady und Schneider (produced 1849). In *Gesammelte Werke*, 1890–91.

Judith und Holofernes, from a play by Friedrich Hebbel (produced 1849). In *Gesammelte Werke*, 1890–91; as *Judith and Holofernes*, translated by Robert Harrison and Katharina Wilson, in *Three Viennese Comedies*, 1986.

Höllenangst, from a play by J.-B. d'Épagny and J.-H. Dupin (produced 1849). In *Gesammelte Werke*, 1890–91.

Sie sollen ihn nicht; oder, Der holländische Bauer (produced 1850). In *Gesammelte Werke*, 1890–91.

Karikaturen-Charivari (produced 1850). In *Gesammelte Werke*, 1890–91.

Alles will den Propheten sehen (produced 1850). In *Gesammelte Werke*, 1890–91.

Verwickelte Geschichte (produced 1850). In *Gesammelte Werke*, 1890–91.

Mein Freund (produced 1851). 1851.

Der gutmütige Teufel; oder, Die Geschichte vom Bauer und der Bäuerin (produced 1851). As *Der gemütliche Teufel*, in *Gesammelte Werke*, 1890–91.

Kampl; oder, Das Mädchen mit den Millionen und die Nähterin (produced 1852). 1852.

Heimliches Geld, heimliche Liebe (produced 1853). In *Gesammelte Werke*, 1890–91.

Theaterg'schichten durch Liebe, Intrige, Geld und Dummheit (produced 1854). 1854.

Umsonst (produced 1857).

Tannhäuser, from the libretto by Richard Wagner (produced 1857). 1857.

Lohengrin, from the libretto by Richard Wagner (produced 1859). In *Gesammelte Werke*, 1890–91.

Frühere Verhältnisse (produced 1862). In *Gesammelte Werke*, 1890–91.

Zeitvertreib (produced 1862). In *Gesammelte Werke*, 1890–91.

Häuptling Abendwind; oder, Das greuliche Festmahl, from an operetta by Jacques Offenbach (produced 1862). In *Sämtliche Werke*, 14, 1930.

Der alte Mann mit der jungen Frau (produced in revised version, as *Der Flüchtling*, 1890; original version produced 1948). In *Gesammelte Werke*, 1890–91.

Genius, Schuster und Marqueur; oder, Die Pyramiden der Verzauberung. In *Sämtliche Werke*, 1, 1924.

Der Feenball; oder, Tischler, Schneider und Schlosser. In *Sämtliche Werke*, 1, 1924.

"Nur keck!" (produced 1943). In *Sämtliche Werke*, 14, 1930.

Ein gebildeter Hausknecht. With *Zwölf Mädchen in Uniform*, 1943.

Unbekannter Nestroy (includes *Zwölf Mädchen in Uniform; Ein gebildeter Hausknecht; Friedrich, Prinz von Korsika*). 1953.

Three Comedies (includes *A Man Full of Nothing; The Talisman; Love Affairs and Wedding Bells*), translated and adapted by Max Knight and Joseph Fabry. 1967.

Three Viennese Comedies (includes *The Talisman; Judith and Holofernes; The House of Humours*), translated by Robert Harrison and Katharina Wilson, 1986.

Other

Gesammelte Briefe und Revolutionsdokumente (1831–1862), edited by Fritz Brukner. 1938.

Briefe, edited by Walter Obermaier. 1977.

*

Bibliography: *Bibliography of Criticism* by Jürgen Hein, in *Das Wiener Volkstheater*, 1978; *Johann Nepomuk Nestroy: Bibliographic zur Nestroy-forschung und -rezeption*, by G. Conrad, 1980.

Critical Studies: *Nestroy und die Nachwelt* by K. Kraus, 1912, revised edition, 1987; *Johann Nestroy und seine Kunst* by Franz H. Mautner, 1937; *Johann Nestroy: Abschätzer der Menschheit, Magier des Wortes* by O. Forst-Battaglia, 1962; *Johann Nestroy in Selbstzeugnissen und Bilddokumenten* by Otto Basil, 1967; *Die Komödie der Sprache: Untersuchungen zum Werke Nestroys* by S. Brill, 1967; *Die Dramatisierung des komischen Dialogs: Figur und Rolle bei Nestroy* by A. Hillach, 1967; *Johann Nestroy* by H. Weigel, 1967; *Johann Nepomuk Nestroy: Der Schöpfer der tragischen Posse* by Rio Preisner, 1968; *Die künstlerische Eigenständigkeit und Eigenart Nestroys* by L. Tönz, 1969; *Spiel und Satire in der Komödie Johann Nestroys* by Jürgen Hein, 1970; *Johann Nestroy; oder, der wienerische Shakespeare* by Kurt Kahl, 1970; *Nestroys dramatische Technik* by R. Koth, 1972; *Nestroy: Satire and Parody in Viennese Popular Comedy* by W.E. Yates, 1972; *The Dramatic Art of Ferdinand Raimund and Johann Nestroy* by Laurence V. Harding, 1974; *Nestroy* by Franz H. Mautner, 1974; *Johann Nestroy: Nihilistisches Welttheater und verflixter Kerl*, by B. Hannemann, 1977; *Johann Nestroy im Bild: Eine Ikonographie* by H. Schwarz, 1977; *Das wiener Volkstheater: Raimund und Nestroy*, 1978, and *Johann Nestroy*, 1990, both by Jürgen Hein; *"Bis zum Lorbeer versteig ich mich nicht": Johann Nestroy—Ein Leben* by H. Ahrens, 1982; *Nestroy and the Critics* by W.E. Yates, 1994.

* * *

Johann Nepomuk Nestroy was a philosopher and clown called by Franz Mautner "the greatest German writer" and by Fritz Martini "the Viennese Aristophanes." In spite of this, Nestroy was not truly appreciated on the international scene until after his death in 1862. During his lifetime, though, he was beloved by the common people and was played in the "Burgtheater," which was not considered to be a serious theatre the way the Staatstheater was. Hans Weigel in *Der Monat*, Germany's leading international magazine for political and intellectual life, pointed out that Nestroy was interested only in writing for the people and in creating parts for certain actors including himself (almost always the main part), and doing this for no other reason than to entertain and make money. World success was not on his mind; he had not written in the expectation that posterity would listen to him. And yet, today, Vienna has its own Nestroy Theatre which produces nothing but the works of the master.

Nestroy wrote his dramas for the masses and he gave them what they wanted: raw comedies and tear-jerkers in the heavy Viennese idiom, the Austrian version of the *le commedia dell'arte*. These plays had become stereotyped—fairytales, romantic stories, vulgar farces— but the crumbling of the class system and the emergence of a monied aristocracy broke up the stereotypes. And yet the remnants of feudalism are still in evidence in the plays. The aristocrat in his mansion is seen as the protector of the people in the village, and it is he who controls the local police. But the newly rich man can now buy the mansion and the power. Nestroy poured forth his irony against the rich, which censorship did not allow him to do against the establishment and the aristocracy. All problems are solved by money; money often comes in the crudest form: a sudden inheritance, an unforeseen treasure, an unexpected gift. The unexpected money brings about the happy ending.

With two exceptions, 50 of Nestroy's most popular works were really adaptations of novels or plays by others—often parodies. For instance, *Der Einsilbige; oder, Ein dummer Diener seines Herrn* [The Taciturn One; or, A Stupid Servant of His Lord] parodies Franz Grillparzer's *Ein treuer Diener seines Herrn* (*A Faithful Servant of His Master*); Friedrich Hebbel's *Judith* inspired Nestroy's *Judith and Holofernes*, in which Nestroy lays bare the weaknesses of Hebbel's characters. Hebbel's inhuman monster Holofernes, impelled to destroy all in his path, becomes in Nestroy's play a good-natured bourgeois lapsing into Viennese dialect. Nestroy also parodied Richard Wagner in his plays *Tannhäuser* and *Lohengrin*.

When Nestroy adapted borrowed plots, he was usually satisfied with writing juicy parts for himself and his colleagues. The parts he wrote for himself most often embody figures from the lower level of society: servants, apprentices, adventurers, and proletarian types. In creating amusing situations, Nestroy looked for opportunities to clown. The plays abound in comical disguises and primitive misunderstandings that lead to colossal and often unnecessary mix-ups: people hiding behind curtains, unlikely chance meetings, and just plain fun, even if it interferes with the plot and stops the show. In fact, that was often the purpose. Furthermore, Nestroy was skilful at transplanting foreign settings to Vienna and at pumping life into the often pale characters of the originals. In his hands even minor characters became people his Viennese public could identify with. Most characters look like prototypes of 19th-century Austrians: even the foreign types were naturalized by Nestroy's pen and have become part of Austrian folklore. So thorough was the transformation that even people who knew the original play did not recognize the characters when they saw Nestroy's version on the stage. By the same token, one of Nestroy's plays was reworked into an English musical: his *Einen Jux will er sich machen* (*The Merchant of Yonkers* and *On the Razzle*) inspired Thornton Wilder's *The Matchmaker*.

Whereas Nestroy's plots often were borrowed and his characters adapted, the dialogue was unadulterated Nestroy. His plays are sprinkled with witticisms, puns, and homespun philosophy packaged into quips which were used in the parts he wrote for himself. Indeed, the real source of Nestroy's greatness lies neither in the plots nor even in the complex and highly effective theatrical devices of his comedies, but rather in his characterizations or, more precisely, in his astonishing verbal inventiveness and virtuosity. His famous "couplets," doggerel or ballad songs, sometimes improvised before the show, are a unique mixture of the topical and the perennial, full of hidden allusions to avoid the absurd censorship of Metternich's police. Nestroy was truly a virtuoso of the German language and more particularly in combining Viennese idiom and standard High German into similes, metaphors, mixed-up proverbs, and gyrating figures of speech. His puns are often popular sayings turned inside out and parodies of archness and sententiousness. In them and in the rapid repartees of his characters, the Austrian dialect is exploited as never before. The greater part of Nestroy's verbal acrobatics is usually entrusted to the character he himself played, and hence derives a special fascination in the mouth of a character at the bottom level of society.

Der böse Geist Lumpazivagabundus [The Evil Spirit Lumpazivagabundus] was Nestroy's first great success; it made him famous and he acted in it 259 times. In this early farce, Nestroy still uses the world of magic: the king of the good fairies and the patron saint of the vagabonds (the title part) make a bet whether down-and-outs will remain down-and-outs even if they win a fortune in the lottery. The test is made on three unemployed tradesmen: a cobbler, a tailor, and a carpenter. The first two waste their money on wine, women, and song, but the carpenter becomes a thrifty family man, saved by true love. The play has three magnificent parts, plenty of antics, and one of Nestroy's most famous songs. The cobbler, an amateur astrologer, is certain that a comet will soon destroy the earth, and sings, almost yodels, the catch line, "Die Welt steht auf kein Fall mehr lang" (The world will surely not last long).

In *Der Zerrissene* (*A Man Full of Nothing*) the main character, Herr von Lips, a millionaire who doesn't know what to do with his money or his life, thinks he has drowned a jealous locksmith (who in turn thinks he has drowned the hapless Herr von Lips), and in fear of the police, flees to one of his own farms, disguised as a labourer. The farcical action turns on the curse of money, the double dealing of false friends, and rescue from adversity by the poor-but-faithful lover.

Nestroy's use of language and songs, his fertile invention of comic situations and skilful characterization, combine to reveal him as one of the most brilliant writers of farce in European literature.

—Brigitte Edith Zapp Archibald

NIETZSCHE, Friedrich (Wilhelm)

Born: in Röcken, Germany, 15 October 1844. **Education:** Educated at Domgymnasium, Naumburg, 1854–58; Pforta School, 1858–64; studied philology and theology at Bonn University, 1864–65; Leipzig University, 1865–67, Ph.D., 1869. **Career:** Met the composer Richard Wagner in Leipzig, 1868; the influential friendship later deteriorated. Chair of classical philology, University of Basle, 1869–79, retired because of ill health; volunteer in the army medical service, 1867–68; gave up Prussian citizenship, 1869; attempted to become Swiss national but did not fulfil the residential requirements for Swiss citizenship and remained stateless for the rest of his life; travelled frequently to Sils Maria, Sorrento, Genoa, Nice, and Turin, 1879–89; spent last 11 years of his life incapacitated by mental illness in Jena and Weimar. **Died:** 25 August 1900.

PUBLICATIONS

Collections

The Complete Works, edited by Oscar Levy. 18 vols, 1909–11.
Musikalische Werke, edited by Georg Göhler. 1924.
Werke des Zusammenbruchs, edited by E.F. Podach. 1961.
Werke, edited by Giorgio Colli and Mazzino Montinari. 22 vols., 1967–86.
Briefwechsel: Kritische Gesamtausgabe, edited by Giorgio Colli and Mazzino Montinaro. 16 vols., 1975–84; as *The Pre-Platonic Philosophers*, translated by Greg Whitlock, 2001.
Hammer of the Gods, compiled, edited and translated by Stephen Metcalf. 1996.

Prose

Die Geburt der Tragödie aus dem Geiste der Musik. 1872; as *Die Geburt der Tragödie; oder, Griechentum und Pessimismus*, 1886;

as *The Birth of Tragedy*, translated by William A. Haussmann, 1909; also translated by Francis Golffing; 1956; Walter Kaufmann, 1967; Shaun Whiteside, 1993; Clifton P. Fadiman, 1995; Ronald Speirs, 1999; Douglas Smith, 2000.

Die Philosophie im tragischen Zeitalter der Griechen. 1873; as *Philosophy in the Tragic Age of the Greeks*, translated by Marianne Cowan, 1962.

Unzeitgemässe Betrachtungen. 4 vols., 1873–76; as *Unmodern Observations: Thoughts Out of Season*, translated by Anthony M. Ludovici, 1909; as *Untimely Meditations*, translated by R.J. Hollingdale, 1983.

   1. *David Strauss, der Bekenner und der Schriftsteller*. 1873.

   2. *Vom Nutzen und Nachteil der Historie für das Leben*. 1874; as *The Use and Abuse of History*, translated by Adrian Collins, 1949; as *Of the Advantage and Disadvantage of History for Life*, translated by Peter Preuss, 1980.

   3. *Schopenhauer als Erzieher*. 1874; as *Schopenhauer as Educator*, translated by James W. Hillesheim and Malcolm B. Simpson, 1965.

   4. *Richard Wagner in Bayreuth*. 1876.

Menschliches, Allzumenschliches: Ein Buch für freie Geister. vol. 1, 1878; *Vermischte Meinungen und Sprüche*, vol. 2 (first part), 1879; *Der Wanderer und sein Schatten*, vol. 2 (second part), 1880; complete edition, 1886; as *Human, All Too Human: A Book for Free Spirits*, translated by Alexander Harvey, 1908; also translated by Helen Zimmern, 1909; P.V. Cohn, 1911; M. Faber, 1984; R.J. Hollingdale, 1986; as *Human, All Too Human*, translated by R.J. Hollingdale, 1996.

Morgenröte, Gedanken über die moralischen Vorurteile. 1881; as *The Dawn of Day*, translated by J.M. Kennedy, 1974; as *Daybreak: Thoughts on the Prejudices of Morality*, translated by R.J. Hollingdale, 1982.

Die fröhliche Wissenschaft. 1882, revised edition including book V, 1887; as *The Joyful Wisdom*, translated by Thomas Common, 1910; as *The Gay Science*, translated by Walter Kaufmann, 1974.

Also sprach Zarathustra: Ein Buch für Alle und Keinen. 1883–85; revised and complete edition, 1892; as *Thus Spoke Zarathustra*, translated by Alexander Tille, 1896; also translated by Thomas Common, 1898; Marianne Cowan, 1957; R.J. Hollingdale, 1961; Walter Kaufmann, 1966.

Jenseits von Gut und Böse: Vorspiel einer Philosophie der Zukunft. 1886; as *Beyond Good and Evil: Prelude to the Philosophy of the Future*, translated by Helen Zimmern, 1907; also translated by Marianne Cowan, 1955; Walter Kaufmann, 1966; R.J. Hollingdale, 1973; Robert C. Holub, 1998; Judith Norman, 2002.

Zur Genealogie der Moral. 1887; as *A Genealogy of Morals*, translated by William A. Hausemann, 1897; as *The Genealogy of Morals*, translated by Horace B. Samuel, 1910, also translated by Francis Golffing, 1956; as *On the Genealogy of Morals*, translated by Walter Kaufmann and R.J. Hollingdale, 1967; as *On the Genealogy of Morality*, translated by Carol Diethe, 1994; as *On the Genealogy of Morals: A Polemic: By Way of Clarification and Supplement to My Last Boo, Beyond Good and Evil*, translated with introduction by Douglas Smith, 1996; as *On the Genealogy of Morality: A Polemic*, translation with notes by Maudemarie Clark and Alan J. Swensen, 1998.

Der Fall Wagner: Ein Musikanten-Problem. 1888; as *The Case of Wagner*, translated by Walter Kaufmann, 1967.

Götzendämmerung; oder, Wie man mit dem Hammer philosophiert. 1889; as *Twilight of the Idols*, translated by Anthony M. Ludovici,

1911; also translated by R.J. Hollingdale, 1968; as *Twilight of the Idols: Or, How to Philosophize With the Hammer*, translated by Richard Polt, 1997; translated by Duncan Large, 1998.

Der Antichrist: Fluch auf das Christentum. 1895; as *The Anti-Christ*, translated by H.L. Mencken, 1920, reprinted 1988; also translated by P.R. Stephenson, 1928; R.J. Hollingdale, 1968; translated by Anthony M. Ludovici, 2000.

Der Wille zur Macht, edited by P. Gast and Elisabeth Fo; aurster-Nietzsche. 1901; as *The Will to Power*, translated by Anthony M. Ludovici, 1909–10; also translated by R.J Hollingdale and Walter Kaufmann, 1968.

Ecce homo: Wie man wird was man ist, edited by Raoul Richter. 1908; as *Ecce homo: How One Becomes What One Is*, translated by Anthony M. Ludovico, 1974; also translated by R.J. Hollingdale, 1979.

The Portable Nietzsche, edited by Walter Kaufmann. 1954.

Unpublished Letters, edited and translated by Kurt F. Leidecker. 1960.

A Nietzsche Reader, edited by R.J. Hollingdale. 1977.

Philosophy and Truth: Selections from Nietzsche's Notebooks of the Early 1870s, edited by Daniel Breazeale. 1979.

Selected Letters, edited by Oscar Levy. 1985.

On Rhetoric and Language, edited by Sander L. Gilman, Carole Blaire, and David J. Parent. 1988.

Verse

Dionysos-Dithyramben. 1892; as *Dithyrambs of Dionysus*, translated by R.J. Hollingdale, 1984.

Aus hohen Bergen. 1920.

Fifty Poems, edited by Earl R. Nitschke. 1965.

*

Bibliography: *International Nietzsche Bibliography* by Herbert W. Reichert and Karl Schlechta, 1960; revised edition, 1968.

Critical Studies: *A Century of Hero-Worship: A Study of the Idea of Heroism in Carlyle and Nietzsche*, 1944, as *The Cult of the Superman*, 1947, by Eric Bentley; *Nietzsche: Philosopher, Psychologist, Antichrist* by Walter Kaufmann, 1950, revised edition, 1968; *Nietzsche in the Early Works of Thomas Mann* by Roger A. Nicholls, 1955; *Young Nietzsche and the Wagnerian Experience* by Frederick R. Love, 1963; *Nietzsche: The Man and His Philosophy* by R.J. Hollingdale, 1965, revised edition, 1985; *What Nietzsche Means* by George A. Morgan, 1965; *Nietzsche: A Self-Portrait from His Letters*, edited and translated by Peter Fuss and Henry Shapiro, 1971; *Nietzsche in Anglosaxony: A Study of Nietzsche's Impact on English and American Literature* by Patrick Bridgwater, 1972; *Nietzsche and Other Exponents of Individualism* by Paul Carus, 1972; *Nietzsche's Thought of Eternal Return*, by Joan Stambaugh, 1972; *Friedrich Nietzsche's Impact on Modern German Literature: Five Essays* by Herbert W. Reichert, 1975; *Nietzschean Parody: An Introduction to Reading Nietzsche* by Sander L. Gilman, 1976; *Nietzsche's Gift* by Harold G. Alderman, 1977; *Zarathustra's Sister: The Case of Elisabeth and Friedrich Nietzsche* by H.F. Peters, 1977; *The Question of Elites: An Essay on the Cultural Elitism of Nietzsche, George and Hesse* by Stanley J. Antosik, 1978; *Nietzsche's Existential Imperative* by Magnus Bernd, 1978; *The Dissimulating Harmony: The Image of Interpretation in*

Nietzsche, Rilke, Artaud and Benjamin by Carol Jacobs, 1978; *Nietzsche: Imagery and Thought: A Collection of Essays* edited by Malcolm Pasley, 1978; *Nietzsche*, 1978, and *A Study of Nietzsche*, 1979, both by J.P. Stern; *Angels of Daring: Tightrope Walker and Acrobat in Nietzsche, Kafka, Rilke and Thomas Mann* by Marion Faber, 1979; *Nietzsche: A Critical Life* by Ronald Hayman, 1980; *Dionysian Aesthetics: The Role of Destruction in Creation as Reflected in the Life and Works of Friedrich Nietzsche*, 1981, and *Nietzsche contra Nietzsche: Creativity and the Anti-Romantic*, 1989, both by Adrian del Caro; *Heirs to Dionysus: A Nietzschean Current in Literary Modernism* by John Burt Foster Jr., 1981; *Yeats and Nietzsche: An Exploration of Major Nietzschean Echoes in the Writings of W.B. Yeats* by Otto Bohlmann, 1982; *Nietzsche and the French Moralists* by Brendan Donnellan, 1982; *Nietzsche contra Rousseau* by Keith Ansell-Pearson, 1982; *A Brief Introduction to the Genius of Nietzsche* by Richard D. Chessick, 1983; *The Great Years of Zarathustra*, edited by David Goicoechea, 1983; *Nietzsche* by Richard Schacht, 1983; *Beyond Nihilism: Nietzsche without Masks* by Ofelia Schutte, 1984; *Nietzsche: Life as Literature* by Alexander Nehamas, 1985; *Studies in Nietzsche and the Judaeo-Christian Tradition* edited by James C. O'Flaherty, Timothy F. Sellner, and Robert M. Helm, 1985; *The Poetry of Friedrich Nietzsche* by Philip Grundlehner, 1986; *Nietzsche's Teaching: An Interpretation of Thus Spoke Zarathustra* by Laurence Lampert, 1986; *Nietzsche's Moral Philosophy* by John Bernstein, 1987; *Friedrich Nietzsche* edited by Harold Bloom, 1987; *Nietzsche and Literary Values* edited by Volker Dürr, 1987; *Nietzsche's Zarathustra* by Kathleen M. Higgins, 1987; *Poetic Truth and Transvaluation in Nietzsche's Zarathustra: A Hermeneutic Study* by Ernest Joós, 1987; *Lawrence and Nietzsche: A Study in Influence* by Colin Milton, 1987; *Mask and Tragedy: Yeats and Nietzsche, 1902–10* by Frances Nesbitt Opel, 1987; *Nietzsche and Greek Thought* by Victorino Tejera, 1987; *The Beginnings of Nietzsche's Theory of Languages* by Claudia Crawford, 1988; *The Importance of Nietzsche: Ten Essays* by Erich Heller, 1988; *Exceedingly Nietzsche: Aspects of Contemporary Nietzsche Interpretation*, edited by David Farrel Krell and David Wood, 1988; *Nietzsche and Modern Literature: Themes in Yeats, Rilke, Mann and Lawrence*, 1988, and *Nietzsche and the Spirit of Tragedy*, 1990, both by Keith M. May; *Reading Nietzsche*, edited by Robert C. Solomon and Kathleen M. Higgins, 1988; *Nietzschean Narratives* by Gary Shapiro, 1989; *Nietzsche: A Frenzied Look* by Robert John Ackermann, 1990; *Character and Chaos: The Moral and Political Philosophy of Friedrich Nietzsche*, 1990, and *Nietzsche and the Origin of Virtue*, 1993, both by Lester M. Hunt; *Crossings: Nietzsche and the Space of Tragedy* by John Sallis, 1991; *Nietzsche's Philosophy of Art* by Julian Young, 1992; *Basic Writings of Nietzsche*, translated and edited by Walter Kaufmann, 1992; *Nietzsche, Feminism and Political Theory* edited by Paul Patton, 1993; *Friedrich Nietzsche: His Life and Thought* by A.J. Hoover, 1994; *Nietzsche, Biology, and Metaphor* by Gregory Moore, 2002.

*   *   *

Though Friedrich Nietzsche shared the concerns of most traditional philosophers—ethics, epistemology, metaphysics, aesthetics—many people believe that he was perhaps not a philosopher at all and, having failed to fit him neatly into a category, relegate him to a grey area between philosophy and literature. For he disappoints the usual expectations of a philosopher by being deliberately unsystematic. He came to advocate a radical scepticism that viewed systems as implying a cowardly and crippling lack of intellectual honesty. (It should be noted however that he was probably groping towards a loosely systematic presentation of his own thought when madness overtook him.) The second reason for suspicion about the seriousness of Nietzsche's philosophical enterprise may be that with its uniquely personal flavour, much of his writing lacked the objectivity traditionally seen as the hallmark of philosophy. Nietzsche was quite unashamed of his concentration on the individual self, since his radical perspectivism dictated this viewpoint. He saw himself as typical of his age, so by describing one he described the other. In testing philosophical propositions by "living through" them, by submitting himself to a process of rigorous intellectual experimentation, he was demonstrating the process he saw as central to the creative human being: how the individual "becomes what he is."

Nietzsche's first major published work *Die Geburt der Tragödie* (*The Birth of Tragedy*) drew on one of his main sources of experience and inspiration, the Greek tradition. This however cut him off from his professional colleagues; one reviewer declared the author of such an "unscholarly" work "academically dead." The Greeks, Nietzsche argued, were on the one hand uniquely capable of suffering and aware of the inherent meaninglessness of life, but also uniquely well equipped to survive this insight. The development of Greek tragic art is the synthesis of two "artistic forces" (whose ultimate origins remain obscure): the Apollonian, which is concerned with clarity, contour, form, and connected with the "principle of individuation"; the Dionysian, a darker force associated with energy, frenzy, sexual licence, intoxication, and the submergence of the individual self in the mass. The Dionysian, the older and potentially destructive force, threatened to overwhelm the Greeks, but they were able to contain and channel it creatively into tragedy, which is the "Apollonian expression in sensual form of the Dionysian insights and wisdom." The Greeks, according to Nietzsche, thus respond positively to the challenge of the essential horror of life by creating a veil of artistic illusion through which the horror becomes bearable; they achieve an acceptance of life which is both tragic and ecstatic. The final decline of Greek tragedy is brought about by the "spirit of Socrates," which seeks to banish myth and suffering in favour of the conviction that rational knowledge is a panacea for all ills. Socrates is a figure with whom Nietzsche struggled intermittently throughout his works, admiring (and often imitating) his analytical methods, yet critical of what he regarded as Socrates' fundamental hostility to myth and his over-reliance on reason. The last sections of the essay derive from Nietzsche's hope, soon abandoned, that Richard Wagner's music might lead to a rebirth of the tragic spirit of Ancient Greece in modern German culture. This aim is pursued in *Richard Wagner in Bayreuth*, the fourth of the *Unzeitgemässe Betrachtungen* (*Untimely Meditations*), published in 1876. Nietzsche envisaged a series of 12 essays casting a cool and sceptical eye on modern Germany, but completed only four. The first, *David Strauss, der Bekenner und der Schriftsteller* [David Strauss, the Confessor and Writer], attacks the modish contemporary theologian, not only for his poor literary style, but also for his continued naive adherence to Christian morality after he had helped to destroy the beliefs on which it was founded. (Nietzsche made good this omission in his own later writings.) The second essay, *Vom Nutzen und Nachteil der Historie für das Leben* (*Of the Advantage and Disadvantage of History for Life*), and the third, *Schopenhauer als Erzieher* (*Schopenhauer as Educator*), point to the potentially poisonous effects of academic pursuits in general, whether it be the study of history, with its tendency to swamp the student with excess information, or of philosophy, which, as purveyed at German universities, Nietzsche stigmatized as merely a branch of history. He speaks scathingly of the "victorious" end of the Franco-Prussian War, as marking the "extirpation of the German mind in favour of the German *Reich*," and accuses his fellow-countrymen of lacking true culture, which he defines as "unity of style in all the expressions of the life of a people." Since the "*goal of humanity* cannot lie in its end but only *in its highest exemplars*," Nietzsche had already set course on a path which was essentially ahistorical, aristocratic, and potentially undemocratic. In a way it was also apolitical, since the state was seen as hostile to the growth of the great individual.

There is a sense in which the works of Nietzsche's middle period can be seen as a continuous whole, for they are linked by format, style, and content. *Menschliches, Allzumenschliches: Ein Buch für freie Geister* (*Human, All Too Human: A Book for Free Spirits*), the three parts written between 1878 and 1880, published as a whole work in 1886; *Morgenröte, Gedanken über die moralischen Vorurteile* (*Daybreak: Thoughts on the Prejudices of Morality*), and *Die fröhliche Wissenschaft* (*The Gay Science*), 1882, but with book V added in 1887, are all collections of short passages, ranging from a sentence to two or three pages, and loosely grouped into chapters. These books have three things in common. First, a sceptical analysis of human values, morality, and psychology, from an uncompromisingly modern, scientific point of view (the influence of Darwin being particularly notable). This in turn tends to have destructive consequences— values collapse or are revealed as little more than animal cunning, or a blind will to survive (in Nietzsche's metaphor: gods are revealed as mere idols, with feet of clay into the bargain). But at the same time there is a burning desire to transcend mere man, to re-establish human (or super-human?) greatness, to discover ways in which human, all too human man can pass over into something beyond mere man—yet remain within the world of immanence. It had become apparent to Nietzsche that the notion of a Beyond of any kind, although strictly speaking susceptible to neither proof nor disproof, is a dangerous fiction, and that man's true aim must be to rediscover himself, and his natural habitat, namely the earth.

In *Also sprach Zarathustra* (*Thus Spoke Zarathustra*), which Nietzsche regarded as his chief work, we find ecstatic, if not always lucid, proclamation of the doctrines with which his name is most widely associated: the death of God; the *Übermensch* (superman or overman) and his contemptible opposite, the last man; the will to power; and the mysterious eternal recurrence. The next two books, *Jenseits von Gut und Böse* (*Beyond Good and Evil*) and *Zur Genealogie der Moral* (*The Genealogy of Morals*), are linked, in that Nietzsche regarded the latter as a supplement and explanation of the former: one of their main aims is to elucidate the question of the "natural history" of morality. Stripped of all otherworldly support and sanction, morality is seen as a cultural product, originating in instincts for survival, domination, and social cohesion. Nietzsche posits two types which must have developed long before recorded history (and are hence conveniently located in unverifiable territory): master morality, the active, vigorous expression of the naturally strong, who define their own selves as "good," and that which is beneath them as "bad," in the sense of lowly and inferior; and the slave morality of the naturally weak, who likewise define their own selves as "good" but brand others (the strong) as "evil," since they are fired by a resentful desire to be avenged on the strong and to seek domination. The weak are reactive, underhand, scheming, and dishonest; their

only effective means of attacking the strong is by demonizing them as "evil." It must be noted that Nietzsche is describing *types*, not individuals, nor even specific moral systems. Nevertheless, the idea of "slave morality" would prove a convenient label with which to stigmatize Christianity.

Nietzsche's final active year, 1888, involved a manic burst of creative activity. Two short books were directed against Wagner, whom Nietzsche now regarded largely as a charlatan surrounded by detestable toadies (Christian, anti-semitic, and nationalistic), although one of them (*Nietzsche Contra Wagner*) is merely a compilation from earlier writings. *Götzendämmerung; oder, Wie man mit dem Hammer philosophiert* (*Twilight of the Idols*) adds little that is new to Nietzsche's thinking, but is a work of breathtaking range and brilliance. The provocatively titled autobiography *Ecce homo: Wie man wird was man ist* (*Ecce Homo: How One Becomes What One Is*), with its immodest chapter headings (*Why I Am So Wise, Why I Write Such Good Books*), would have gone far towards removing the misunderstandings that Nietzsche knew his works would provoke, if his sister had not delayed its publication until 20 years later, by which point she had been able to present to the world *her* view of her by now hopelessly insane brother. She achieved this largely by releasing, in careful doses, what she claimed was her brother's *magnum opus, Der Wille zur Macht* (*The Will to Power*). The individual sections are, to be sure, all from Nietzsche's pen, but a lot are also from his wastepaper basket; the "plan" of the work was one of many that he sketched in his last year, and almost certainly one he rejected. The "work" appears as unpublished remains, in respectable editions of Nietzsche's writings. If Nietzsche did start to compile a large work assembling his mature thinking, it was *Revaluation of All Values*; its first part is *Der Antichrist: Fluch auf das Christentum* (*The Antichrist*) which he saw through the press. (His sister predictably suppressed the subtitle.) Leaning on a tradition which goes back at least to H.S. Reimarus (1694–1768), Nietzsche attacks Christianity as an essentially fraudulent enterprise, motivated by the disciples' desire for gain, fuelled by the vitriol of St. Paul (the "apostle of hatred"), and far divorced from the childlike innocence and pathological hypersensitivity of its alleged founder, Jesus of Nazareth. The metaphysics of Christianity are rejected as vacuous and damaging to existence in *this* world, while its prime virtue, compassion, is seen as weakening to the human species. It comes as no surprise that Nietzsche's final words in his autobiography are "Have I been understood? *Dionysus against the Crucified One.*" (By this point Dionysus has undergone a transformation in Nietzsche's mind; the deity of the *Birth of Tragedy* has assumed Apollonian qualities, so that what had been chaotic energy is now energy harnessed to the process of self-direction and self-creation of which Goethe is the great exponent.)

Even a century after the end of his active life, it may be too early to assess the full impact of Nietzsche's achievement. He stands alongside Marx and Freud as one of the inescapable sources (and diagnosticians) of modern man's consciousness. Although he is often popularly believed to have been a proto-Nazi, Nietzsche was neither a nationalist (the reverse if anything), nor anti-semitic, and had a boundless contempt for mass-movements. In a sense, he was quite apolitical—acutely sensitive to the individual, but frequently blind about groups and communities (and embarrassingly wrong-headed about women). Nevertheless, the violence of his language, his taste for hyperbole, his extremism—of which he was well aware—made it possible for dishonest editors, commentators, and propagandists to misuse his name and some of his more lurid utterances in the cause of German fascism.

Nietzsche's abiding greatness may well lie in his psychology. Freud, for example, acknowledged the deep insight revealed in the passage from *Beyond Good and Evil*: "'I have done that,' says my memory. 'I cannot have done that,' says my pride, and remains adamant. At last—memory yields.''

—Bruce Watson

See the essays on *The Birth of Tragedy* and *Thus Spoke Zarathustra*.

NIJHOFF, Martinus

Born: in The Hague, The Netherlands, 20 April 1896. **Education:** Studied law at the University of Amsterdam; University of Utrecht, degree in language and literature 1937. **Military Service:** Served two years as a conscript in the army. **Family:** Married 1) A.H. Nijhoff-Wind in 1916; 2) G. Hagedoorn in 1952. **Career:** Travelled widely in Europe; in hiding during World War II; literary adviser, Ministry of Education and Science, after 1945; also worked in the family firm. Wrote for various newspapers: critic for the *Nieuwe Rotterdamsche Courant*; editor and contributor to *De Gids*, 1926–33 and after World War II. **Died:** 26 January 1953.

PUBLICATIONS

Collections

Lees maar, er staat niet wat er staat [Read for Yourself: It Does Not Say What It Says] (anthology). 1959.
Verzamelde gedichten [Collected Poems]. 1978.
Verzamelde werk [Collected Work], edited by G. Borgers and G. Kamphuis. 3 vols., 1982.
Martinus Nijhoff, een geur van hoger honing [A Scent of Purer Honey], edited by W.J. van den Akker and G.J. Dorelijn. 1990.

Verse

De wandelaar [The Wayfarer]. 1916.
Pierrot aan de lantaarn [Pierrot by a Lantern]. 1919.
Vormen [Forms]. 1924.
De vliegende Hollander [The Flying Dutchman]. 1930.
Gedachten op dinsdag [Thoughts on Tuesday]. 1931.
Halewijn. 1933.
Nieuwe gedichten [New Poems]. 1934.
Het uur u. 1936; as *Zero Hour*, translated by Adriaan Barnouw, and as *Your Zero Hour*, translated by Peter K. King, both in *Dit meldt her uur u, teksten omtrent Het uur u van Martinus Nojhoff* by Dirk Kroon, 1986.
In Holland staat een huis [In Holland Stands a House]. 1937.
Het uur u gevolgd door een idylle [Zero Hour Followed by an Idyll]. 1942.
De Ster van Bethlehem [The Star of Bethlehem]. 1947.
Het heilige hout [Holy Wood]. 1950.

Other

De pen op papier, gevolgd door een vertaling van Lafontaine's Fabel van de twee duiven. 1927; as *Pen on Paper*, translated by W.C. Niewenhous, in *Harvest of the Lowlands*, 1945.
Translator, *Moer*, by André Gide. 1929.
Translator, *De Geschiedenis van de soldaat*, by Ramuz. 1930.
Translator, *Het verhaal van de vos*, by Ramuz. 1930.
Translator, *De Storm*, by Shakespeare. 1930.
Translator, *Iphigenia in Tauris*, by Euripides. 1951.
Translator, *De Cocktail partij*, by T.S. Eliot. 1951.

*

Critical Studies: *Nijhoff, de levensreiziger* by A. Donker, 1954, reprinted 1977; *Martinus Nijhoff* by J. de Poortere, 1960; *Het wonderbaarlijk lichaam: Martinus Nijhoff en de westerse poëzie* by L. Wenseleers, 1966; *''Non-Spectacular'' Modernism: Martinus Nijhoff's Poetry in Its European Context* by A.L. Sotemann, in *Nijhoff, Van Ostaijen, De Stijl: Modernism in the Netherlands and Belgium in the First Quarter of the 20th Century*, edited by Francis Bulhof, 1976; *Over ''De wandelaar'' van Martinus Nijhoff* by Arend J. Bolhuis, 1980; *Nooit zag ik Awater so nabij: Teksten omtrent ''Awater'' van Martinus Nijhoff* edited by Dirk Kroon, 1981, and *Dit meldt her uur u, teksten omtrent Her uur u van Martinus Nojhoff* by Kroon, 1986; *Een dichter schrijft niet. De poëtica van M. Nijhoff* by W.J. van den Akker, 1985.

* * *

Martinus Nijhoff's first volume, *De wandelaar* [The Wayfarer], contains 48 poems of which 36 are sonnets, the preferred form of the previous generation of Dutch poets. The title poem of six stanzas sets the tone of this and his second collection, *Vormen* [Forms]. "My lonely life wanders through the streets . . . blood no longer flows through my dead hands. . . .'' Like a medieval monk or a Renaissance artist, or a poet at the time of Baudelaire, he watches the world go by and studies the people in it.

By day among my books, by night in a café
I curse my love and dance like Salomé.
The world has its opulence and its misery.

"Empty space separates me from the world . . . which I cannot touch or hear . . . I saw a procession of images passing by, a silent mosaic without perspective.''

The process of alienation, compensation in frenzied Dionysianism, and a final tone of acceptance runs through much of the earlier poetry. More typical of the earlier mood, however, is a final note of uneasiness or even horror at the dichotomy between his true desire and the actual futility of life. Music, the medium of lyrical restraint but also of sensual abandon, and light, natural and artificial (the moon and Chinese lanterns) symbolize the ambivalence in the poet himself and in his characters such as Pierrot, Harlequin, and the clown.

Vormen, as its title suggests, casts the dilemma found in *De wandelaar* into new forms. The clearer the paradox becomes, the more painful is the discovery that he cannot himself resolve it.

Acceptance is an awareness that cannot be induced to order. Where in *De wandelaar* Nijhoff had been in the mainstream of visionaries and creators, he now finds himself in the mainstream of humanity. Why, he asks in "Tweespraak" [Dialogue], were the witnesses of Christ shepherds (at Bethlehem), fishermen (by the Sea of Galilee), and soldiers (at the Crucifixion)?

> Ah, why did the enemy
> Use a kiss to greet Him,
> And only at Emmaus
> Did His friends really meet Him?
> Ah, was that not us?
> Ah, not me? and not you?

These simple people are, by their witness to Christ, identified as innocent, and cannot the world therefore also be(come) innocent? Innocence, but also vulnerability, and implications of Christ-like simplicity are conveyed in the references to children in this collection. In "Satyr en Christofoor" [The Satyr and Christopher], the encounter with the Christ-child (whether in the purity of the water or the earthiness of the woods) creates a longing "for Christopher unreachable, for the satyr unapproachable, for me, ah, untouchable." The innocence of the child, and the home, and the mother as the place of return from the corruption of adult life, are related to the Christ child in the many Christmas poems, and in "De Kinderkruistocht" [The Children's Crusade] the theme has ontological overtones echoed later in *Het uur u* (*Zero Hour*). Here the children explicitly do not have to take their leave because they are not, in fact, leaving the innocence of their home environment. The child is a symbol of reconciliation too, because it is so vulnerable, "so outside the world and so impetuous . . . wandering without guide or money," so vulnerable to the actions of Christopher and the satyr, the shepherds, the fishing disciples, soldiers, Iscariot ("Tweespraak") that he becomes completely identified with them.

De pen op papier (*Pen on Paper*) is Nijhoff's prose account of how, having failed "to carry my soul upwards in all its intellectual essence towards what I called 'a vision of God'," he accepted the need to find salvation in earthly reality.

In *Nieuwe gedichten* [New Poems], the theme of escape and return, self-deception and confrontation, is more broadly applied to reality and ideal, to the now and the hereafter, and in a number of poems there is the reassurance that across the divide there is a bridge, ferry, or ship, to unite the here-and-now with the ideal. "Awater" in this collection is the name given to a man who "has no name. Give him all our forenames all together." It has a double association with water, since the prefix "A" is an early Germanic form of the same word. He is universal, and a universal conscience (John the Baptist) with his place in history (monk and soldier, recluse and traveller) and in every country (Arabia and Italy, with plans to continue his journey). He is conscious of time, yet aware that it is not the ultimate factor. He has an attraction for the poet, who follows him, wanting a companion replacement for his dead brother. The emanence as well as the immanence surrounding this figure is reflected in the poet's invocation, "o brother in heaven, be here too." The poet feels himself in the presence of ordinary man, but also of someone beyond mortal ken, yet a man for all: they seem to know him and have always done so. The background, specifically asphalted, paved, and shop-windowed,

is also a desert (implied in symbolism). So water in the desert is associated with the man the poet is following (at a distance), hoping to find the promised land beyond the desert. The poet's continuing distance from what begins to look like his alter ego is finally confirmed when Awater stays with a Salvation Army meeting outside the station while the poet takes his train back to a distressed world which he must face and understand on his own.

Het uur u has a title as ambiguous as its meaning: "D-day," "Zero-hour," "Your hour (of reckoning)" are all possible interpretations, as will be seen from a short summary of the poem.

On a hot summer's day a man enters an abandoned street, intensifying the silence as if it were a lull before the storm, before zero hour:

> It is a big word: panic,
> but it describes the silent fear
> that at this moment here
> gripped the empty street.

As the stranger passes the houses, their inhabitants, a general practitioner, a judge, and a loose-living woman, see themselves in their true and their redeemed light:

> Behind every window
> a person smiles into
> his own crippled portrait.

Their relief that the stranger has passed and that they can return to their old ways suddenly turns to terror when they see that the man is approaching their guileless children happily playing in the street. The group joins up to follow him, tripping along on his shadow until he disappears with them round the corner. Panic breaks out as mothers emerge, screaming for the children to come back for their meals, and as the normal sounds of life return, the children also return at last. Who is the stranger? Death? Christ? Everyman's conscience or ideal alter ego? Certainly not a kind of Pied Piper, since the children return, though their affinity with him does recall the innocent abandon of the children going off to the Crusade.

This long poem of 489 lines, Nijhoff's last, conveys a dream sequence in the most mundane and realistic terms, thus encapsulating the harmony that gradually emerged in his poetry between the actual and the unattainable, the same harmony that he discovered in surrealist painting. Indeed, as Simon Vestdijk has said, his style and language throughout speak of the same antithesis "between spirit and substance, abstract spirituality and concrete actuality, art and life, literary and conversational language, aesthetic form and direct self-expression."

—Peter King

NISHIWAKI Junzaburō

Born: Ojiya, Niigata, Japan, 20 January 1894. **Education:** Ojiya Jinjō Kōtō elementary school, 1900–06; Ojiya middle school, 1906–11;

studied painting under Fujishima Takeji and Kuroda Seiki, 1911–12; the preparatory course for the Department of Economics at Keiō University, Tokyo, 1912–14; the Department of Economics at Keiō University, Tokyo, 1914–17; New College, Oxford University, England, 1923–25 (no degree awarded). **Family:** Married 1) Marjorie Biddle in 1924 (divorced 1932); 2) Kuwayama Saeko in 1932, son. **Career:** Lecturer of English at Keiō University, 1920; went to England to study English literature, 1922; traveled Europe, 1923; appointed Professor of English at Keiō University, 1926; PhD in Literature awarded, 1949. **Awards:** Yomiuri literature prize, 1957; honorary citizen, Ojiya, 1964; Japan Cultural Service award, 1971; honorary foreign member, American Academy of Arts and Sciences, 1973. **Member:** Association of Contemporary Poets, 1957, (president, 1962); Japan Art Academy, 1961. **Died:** Of heart failure, in Ojiya, 5 June 1982; funeral attended by 1200 mourners.

PUBLICATIONS

Collections

Shishū [Poems]. 1957; 1965; 1967; 1967; 1978; 1979; 1991.
Zenshishū [Collected Poems], 1963; 1981.
Shironshū [Selected Works on Poetics]. 1964.
Zenshū [Collected Works]. 10 vols., 1971–73; 12 vols., 1982–83; 13 vols., 1993–94.
Shi to shiron [Poetry and Poetics]. 6 vols., 1975.

Poetry

Spectrum (English poems). 1925.
Poems Barbarous (French poems). 1930.
Ambarvalia. 1933; partially translated by Yasuko Claremont 1991 and Hosea Hirata, 1993.
Amubaruwaria. 1947.
Tabibito kaerazu. 1947; as "No Traveller Returns," complete translation by Hosea Hirata, 1993, partial translation by Yasuko Claremont, 1991.
Kindai no gūwa [Modern Fables]. 1953; partially translated by Yasuko Claremont, 1991.
Dai san no shinwa [The Third Myth]. 1956; partially translated by Yasuko Claremont, 1991.
Ushinawareta toki [Lost Time]. 1960; partially translated by Yasuko Claremont, 1991.
Hōjō no megami [The Goddess of Fertility]. 1962; partially translated by Yasuko Claremont, 1991.
Eterunitasu [Aeternitas]. 1962; partially translated by Yasuko Claremont, 1991; and Hosea Hirata, 1993.
Hōseki no nemuri [A Gemstone's Sleep]. 1963; partially translated by Yasuko Claremont, 1991.
Raiki [Book of Rites]. 1967; partially translated by Yasuko Claremont, 1991.
Jōka [Earth Song]. 1969; partially translated by Yasuko Claremont, 1991.
Rokumon [Lu-Men]. 1970; partially translated by Yasuko Claremont, 1991.
Jinrui [Mankind]. 1979; partially translated by Yasuko Claremont, 1991.

Other

Chōgenjitsu shugi shiron. 1929; as *Surrealist Poetics*, translated by Hosea Hirata, 1993.
Shururearisumu bungakuron [Literary Surrealism]. 1930.
Seiyō shikaron [Western Poetry]. 1932.
Yōroppa bungaku [European Literature]. 1933.
Wa no aru sekai [A World with a Ring]. 1933.
William Langland. 1933.
Gendai igirisu bungaku [Contemporary English Literature]. 1934.
Junsui na uguisu [Pure Warbler]. 1934.
Kōgo to bungo [Colloquial Language and Literary Language]. 1936.
Eibei shisōshi [English and American Intellectual History]. 1941.
Kinsei eibungakushi [Modern English Literary History]. 1948.
Kodai bungaku josetsu [An Introduction to Ancient Literature]. 1948.
Fūshi to kigeki [Satire and Comedy]. 1948.
Andoromeda [Andromeda]. 1955.
Nashi no onna [Pear Woman]. 1955.
Izakaya no bungakuron [Literary Discussions in a Pub]. 1956.
Memori to vijon [Memory and Vision]. 1956.
T. S. Eliot. 1956.
Shatō no meishin [Superstitions of a Tilting Tower]. 1957.
Azami no koromo [Garment of Thistle]. 1961.
Junsai to suzuki [Water Shield and Sea Bass]. 1969.
Shi no yorokobi [Pleasures of Poetry]. 1970.
Chromatopoiema. 1972.
Nohara o yuku [Crossing a Field]. 1972.
Zatsudan no yoake [Conversations at Dawn]. 1978.
Bashō, Shakespeare, Eliot. 1993.
Translator, *Jyoisu shishū* [Poems by Joyce], by James Joyce, 1933.
Translator, *Kantaberi monogatari* [Canterbury Tales] by Geoffrey Chaucer, 1949.
Translator, *Arechi* [The Waste Land], by T.S. Eliot, 1952.
Translator, *Sonetto shishū* [The Sonnets], by William Shakespeare, 1966.
Translator, *Mararume shishū* [Poems], by Stéphane Mallarmé, 1969.

*

Critical Studies: *Nishiwaki Junzaburō nōto* by Toshitada Iketani, 1967; *Nishiwaki Junzaburō ron* by Yukinobu Kagiya, 1971; *Nishiwaki Junzaburō kenkyū* by Shirō Murano, et al, 1971; *Nishiwaki Junzaburō no shi* by Haruhiko Kondō, 1975; *Nishiwaki Junzaburō inyu shūsei* by Toshikazu Niikura, 1982; *Nishiwaki Junzaburō no shi to shiron* by Masahiro Sawa, 1991; *Gen'ei: Selected Poems of Nishiwaki Junzaburō* by Yasuko Claremont, 1991; *The Poetry and Poetics of Nishiwaki Junzaburō: Modernism in Translation* by Hosea Hirata, 1993.

*   *   *

Nishiwaki Junzaburō is considered the father of Japanese modernist poetry. He introduced European modernist movements to Japan in the late 1920s and revolutionized the language of poetry in Japan through his innovative poetry as well as theoretical writings. A professor of English Literature at Keiō University in Tokyo from 1920 to 1967, his vast scholarship included works on Old and Middle English literature, French Symbolist poetry, T.S. Eliot, James Joyce, and a comparative linguistic study of ancient Greek and Chinese. He was also an accomplished painter.

One of the most distinguishing aspects of Nishiwaki's work is its transnational and extensive historical scope. It encompasses not only Eastern and Western literary traditions but also literatures from ancient times to the most avant-garde. For instance, one may find in a single poem by Nishiwaki references to an old Japanese *waka*, to *Divine Comedy* by Dante, to *The Vision Concerning Piers the Plowman* by William Langland, and to a poem by Mallarmé.

Since his youth, Nishiwaki was exceptionally gifted in learning foreign languages, including English, French, German, Greek, and Latin. He first began to write poems in foreign languages. After landing a job at his alma mater Keiō University as a lecturer of English, he was sent to England in 1922 to study Old and Middle English literature at Oxford University. Arriving in England too late to register at Oxford, Nishiwaki spent a carefree year among London's artistic circles where he learned of the newest currents in art and literature, including modernist poems by T. S. Eliot and a forbidden text called *Ulysses* by James Joyce.

During his three-year stay in England, Nishiwaki published his first collection of poems in English. He also tried to publish a collection of French poems in Paris but was not successful. After returning to Japan in 1925, he was appointed professor of English literature at Keiō University and began publishing some of his French poems and theoretical papers on surrealism in Keiō's literary journal. With some young poets who surrounded Nishiwaki at that time, he helped launch Japan's first Surrealist anthology in 1927. In 1929, a collection of his theoretical papers, *Chōgenjitsu shugi shiron* (*Surrealist Poetics*), appeared. When he published his first collection of poems in Japanese, *Ambarvalia*, in 1933, he was already at a mature age of thirty-nine.

It is no exaggeration to say that Nishiwaki's two early publications, *Surrealist Poetics* and *Ambarvalia*, profoundly changed the course of modern Japanese poetry. *Surrealist Poetics* contained Nishiwaki's lucid yet poetic essays, single-mindedly pursuing the impossible question of what poetry is. He was intrigued to find the essential mechanism of Surrealism—the juxtaposition of two distant realities—not only discussed at the present time by French Surrealists but also present in various forms throughout the history of poetry from ancient times. How did poetry begin? How did it develop? Where is it going? In order to respond to these questions, Nishiwaki drew a bold hypothesis: poetry is an artistic movement toward its own extinction. Poetry began as an expressive act in ancient times. In the modernist era, such an expressive mode of poetry has been reversed: it is now in an anti-expressive mode, in which a poem is, if anything, an expression of not wanting to express. If we are to extend this logic to its conclusion, the outcome becomes evident: the self-extinction of poetry, which Nishiwaki called "pure poetry."

What indeed distinguished *Ambarvalia* from previous Japanese poetry was its utter divorce from the model of poetry as an expression of the poet's inner feelings. Nishiwaki's poems offered instead a bright new world of images without familiar references, without a unifying center, such as the author or a national tradition of literature. This strange, foreign effect was constructed by a language of translation. Though not obvious to many readers, many of the poems in *Ambarvalia* were actually his own Japanese translations of poems Nishiwaki wrote originally in foreign languages. Moreover, Nishiwaki willfully utilized unnatural or ungrammatical expressions inexperienced translators might produce. The result was a strangely deformed, new Japanese poetic language, which would inspire many modern Japanese poets to follow.

After World War II, Nishiwaki's poetry began to mature, perhaps less experimental on the surface but incomparably expansive in its scope. After a self-imposed silence during the war at the age of fifty-four, Nishiwaki published a long poem *Tabibito kaerazu* ("No Traveller Returns") in 1947. For the admirers of Nishiwaki's prewar avant-gardism, this collection came as a total shock. A long text, composed of 168 short poems, repeatedly spoke of the most traditional element in Japanese classical literature: the Zen-like lamentation of impermanence. It was as if the devastating war experience had sapped his youthful poetic energy and left him aged and forlorn. But time has proven that "No Traveller Returns" remains one of the most beloved of Nishiwaki's works today. It is definitely not a product of a washed-out talent. Though seemingly a return to a traditional mode of poetry, its unique collage-like structure with hidden references to diverse literary sources, East and West, shows some definite signs of Nishiwaki going beyond mere modernist experimentations.

Like Wallace Stevens, it could be said that Nishiwaki wrote on a single topic: the impossibility of writing "pure poetry." But instead of resigning to such impossibility, Nishiwaki kept writing: after "No Traveller Returns" came ten more volumes of poetry before his death at the age of eighty-eight. Even as an old man, Nishiwaki's creative and intellectual energy were exceptional. In his seventies, much intrigued by James Joyce's *Finnegans Wake*, Nishiwaki began to write increasingly longer poems, which culminated in his longest poem "Jōka" [Earth Song], with 2,000 lines, published in 1969.

His poems are musical, often humorous due to a sudden leap of imagination. At the core of Nishiwaki's poetry, one may find a profound sense of transience echoing Zen. But his expressions of sorrow were never sentimental but concrete like some forgotten objects in a yard. As we read his immense orchestral verse, we see his traveler's spirit freely traversing linguistic boundaries and historical times: Bashō, Eliot, Dante, Shakespeare, all eating noodles at a corner take-out joint.

—Hosea Hirata

NOOTEBOOM, Cees (Cornelis Johannes Jacobus Maria)

Born: The Hague, The Netherlands, 31 July 1933. **Education:** After attending four Catholic schools in rapid succession, he went to work in a bank, continuing his secondary education in evening school in Utrecht, 1951. **Military Service:** Rejected in 1952 for military service because he was too thin. **Family:** Married Frances (Fanny) Diana Lichtveld in 1957 (divorced 1964). *Career:* Hitchhiked in Scandinavia and France, followed by a voyage to Suriname as crew member, 1953–57; staff journalist with *De Volkskrant*, 1961–68, where his reports on the Paris riots in May 1968 earn him recognition as a journalist; began partnership with photographer Simone Sassen, 1979; Regent's Lecturer, University of California (Berkeley), 1987. **Awards:** Anne Frank-prijs, 1957; Prijs voor de Dagbladjournalistiek, 1969; Pegasus prize for Literature, 1982; Literaturpreis zum 3 Oktober, 1991; Aristeion prize for European Literature, 1993. **Member:** Academie der Künste Berlin, 1992, and Bavaria, 1996; Académie Européenne de Poésie, 1996.

PUBLICATIONS

Collections

Vuurtijd, ijstijd. Gedichten 1955–1983. 1984.

Fiction

Philip en de anderen. 1955; as *Philip and the Others*, translated by Adrienne Dixon, 1988.

De ridder is gestorven. 1963; as *The Knight Has Died*, translated by Adrienne Dixon, 1990.

Rituelen. 1980; as *Rituals*, translated by Adrienne Dixon, 1983.

Een lied van schijn en wezen. 1981; as *A Song of Truth and Semblance*, translated by Adrienne Dixon, 1984.

Mokusei!. 1982; translated by Adrienne Dixon, 1985.

In Nederland. 1984; as *In the Dutch Mountains*, translated by Adrienne Dixon, 1987.

Het volgende verhaal. 1991; as *The Following Story*, translated by Ina Rilke, 1993.

Allerzielen. 1998; as *All Souls' Day*, translated by Susan Massoty, 2001.

Verse

De doden zoeken een huis. 1956.
Koude gedichten. 1959.
Het zwarte gedicht. 1960.
Gesloten gedichten. 1969.
Aanwezig, afwezig. 1970.
Open als een schelp, dicht als een steen. 1978.
Aas. 1982.
Het gezicht van het oog. 1989.
Rollende stenen, getijde. 1991.
Zo kon het zijn. 1999.
Bitterzoet. 2000.

Other

De zwanen van de Theems (play). 1959.

Een avond in Isfahan. 1978.

Nooit gebouwd Nederland. 1980; as *Unbuilt Netherlands*, translated by Adrienne Dixon. 1985.

Voorbije passages. 1981.

Waar je gevallen bent, blijf je. 1983.

Berlijnse notities. 1990; as *Berliner Notizen*, translated by Rosemarie Still, 1991.

De omweg naar Santiago. 1992; as *Roads to Santiago*, translated by Ina Rilke, 1996.

Van de lente de dauw. 1995.

De filosoof zonder ogen: Europese reizen. 1997.

Translator, *De duivelshaan* by Scan O'Cascy. 1962.

Translator, *Twaalf gezworenen* by Reginald Rose. 1963.

Translator, *De gijzelaar* by Brendan Behan. 1965.

Translator, *De grote dierentuin* by Nicolás Guillén. 1969.

Translator, *Listen to the warm. Liefde in woorden* by Rod McKuen. 1971.

Translator, *De uitvinding van Wals* by Vladimir Nabokov. 1971.

Translator, *Ode aan de typografie* by Pablo Neruda. 1989.

*

Critical Studies: *De tijd en het labyrinth. De poëzie van Cees Nooteboom* by Roger Rennenberg, 1982; *Over Rituelen van Cees Nooteboom* by Jaap Goedegebuure, 1983; *Over Cees Nooteboom. Beschouwingen en Interviews*, edited by Daan Cartens, 1984; *Cees Nooteboom. Ik had wel duizen levens en ik nam er maar één*, edited by Harry Bekkering, Daan Cartens, and Aad Meinderts, 1997.

* * *

Without translation, the audience for Cees Nooteboom's novels would be considerably reduced, for his main works have been translated into all the major European languages, and the two prize-winning novels, *Rituelen* (*Rituals*) and *Het volgende verhaal* (*The Following Story*), have appeared in many others including Japanese and Korean. Translation could be said to be responsible for Nooteboom's recognition in the country of his birth, the Netherlands, since this followed on his success abroad, particularly in Germany. These two countries, together with Spain, are featured in Nooteboom's fiction, the former representing the northern, "autistic" cultures of Europe and the latter the collective, communicative cultures of the south. He is frequently perceived as a European writer transcending national cultural boundaries and, having been prompted by *The Following Story*, one English reviewer suggested that Nooteboom represents a new genre of "eurofable."

Nooteboom's major theme is identity and its relation to place, language, and all aspects of culture. His oeuvre addresses the problem of finding a mode of existence that embraces multiple and shifting identities. The novels explore different responses to the problem; Inni Wintrop, the protagonist of *Rituals*, fails in a suicide attempt and through his confrontation with the father and son Arnold and Philip Taads, whose answer is a life of such order and ritual that it is more like death, realizes that being alive means accepting the senselessness and chaos of life. Death is nevertheless a preoccupation of Nooteboom's: Herman Mussert, the narrator of *The Following Story*, tells the story of his own "translation" from the world of the living to that of the dead. In this playful, light novel full of intertextual references, the act of dying is represented as telling the story of one's life, and this particular story shows that despite his apparently lonely existence as a travel writer and classical scholar, the core of Mussert's existence is love, both physical and spiritual. *Allerzielen* (*All Souls' Day*), is set in Berlin and Madrid and follows Arthur Daane's attempt to find a meaningful existence after the death of his wife and son in a plane crash. He cultivates the life of a loner and films elements of the world around him—feet in the street, snow, car wheels moving past—with emptiness and transit being the two constant themes. His encounter with a young woman who grew up in Spain with a drunken Dutch mother, the child of a liaison with a barman from northern Africa, is fateful and nearly fatal. Arthur is fascinated by this physically and mentally scarred girl who finds her escape by living in the distant past. He follows her to Spain, which like the girl is both attractive and dangerous to him; at one point he is viciously attacked for his camera. Finally, he rejects the romance of Spain, the girl, and the past and he heads north.

An important aspect of the distinctive world Nooteboom creates for his readers is that his central characters are always travelling without arriving at a definitive existence or identity, although there is usually a sense that the whole point of life is the journey. It is not surprising that Nooteboom himself is also a travel writer and has spent much of his adult life travelling around the world either as a journalist in the 1960s and 1970s or independently revisiting and researching some of these places, most notably Spain. This resulted in *De omweg naar Santiago* (*Roads to Santiago*) in which Nooteboom makes the genre his own: far from being a means of getting from point A to point B, travelling means meandering, being open to serendipity, communing with the spirit of a place, and giving in to the reflections this prompts. "Call it a pilgrimage or a meditation if you wish, for with all the diversions and musings my progress is slow. I am making two journeys, one in my rented car and another through the past as evoked by fortresses, castles, monasteries, and by the documents and legends I find there." In Nooteboom's intensely personal Spain, time seems frequently to be suspended on hot dusty roads, and in churches and monasteries.

The preoccupation with timelessness and time past also permeates Nooteboom's poetry, where it is part of a larger picture in which unity and fragmentation confront the poet. Far from being considered undesirable, fragmentation allows him the possibility of many selves that may provide consolation: "he, / someone, the man in pieces, / not unified, / in conversation with himself, dreaming and thinking, / present, invisible."

It would not do justice to Nooteboom as a novelist, travel writer, and poet if one did not mention his use of irony, directed at himself as well as the world around him. To write about large subjects such as life and death, time, and identity while simultaneously smiling wryly at oneself and revealing a quirky humour and sharp capacity for observation of human beings and their culture is Cees Nooteboom's most profound achievement.

—Jane Fenoulhet

NORWID, Cyprian Kamil

Born: Laskowo-Głuchy, Poland, 24 September 1821. **Education:** Gymnasiums in Warsaw 1831–37; Art classes in studios in Warsaw 1838–39 and Florence, 1843–44. **Career:** Due to increasing terror in Russian-occupied Poland, left the country in 1842, travelled extensively in Germany, Italy and Belgium; lived in Paris 1849–52; travelled to United States via Britain 1852–54; again in Paris 1854–83. **Died:** Ivry near Paris, 23 May 1883. Urn with earth from his Paris grave ceremonially transferred to Royal Chapel in Kraków, Poland, 24 September 2001.

PUBLICATIONS

Collections

Pisma wszystkie. 11 vols, 1971–74.

Verse

Poezje. As *Poems*, translated by Adam Czerniawski, 1986.
The Burning Forest, translated by Adam Czerniawski. 1988.
Poems—Letters—Drawings, translated by Jerzy Peterkiewicz, Christine Brooke-Rose and Burns Singer. 2000.

*

Bibliography: *Studia Norwidiana.* 1983–2002.

Critical Studies: "Introducing Norwid" by Jerzy Peterkiewicz, in *The Slavonic and East European Review*, 1948; *Cyprian Norwid* by George Gömöri, 1974; "Norwid and Baudelaire as Contemporaries" by Hans Jauss, in *Cross Currents*, 1983; *Norwid* by Zdzisław Łapiński, 1984; *Norwid*, edited by Bolesław Mazur and George Gömöri, 1988; *The Mature Laurel*, edited by Adam Czerniawski, 1991; *Norwid* by Janusz Maciejewski, 1992; *Norwid poeta pisma* by Wiesław Rzońca, 1995; *Sztukmistrz* by Aleksandra Melbechowska-Luty, 2001; *Archeologia wyobra_ni* by Włodzimierz Szturc, 2001; "The poet as Christian Socrates: Cyprian Kamil Norwid" by Bogdan Czaykowski, in *Metre*, 2002.

* * *

Alongside Hölderlin, Baudelaire, Rimbaud, Hopkins and Dickinson, Cyprian Kamil Norwid is one of the great 19th century poets, who gave a new direction to poetry and determined its course in the 20th century. Like them, he had difficulties with his readers, like them he had to wait for posthumous recognition. But unlike their tendency to introspection, he displays extensive interests and sympathies. His plays, narratives, essays, pamphlets and reminiscences, as well as his poetry, are rich in cultural and historical material. He is proud to proclaim that:

> My country has not risen *here*;
> My body antedates the Flood,
> My spirit soars over Chaos:
> > I pay rent to the world.
> No nation fashioned or saved me;
> I recall eternity's span;
> David's key unlocked my lips,
> > Rome called me man.

A committed Catholic, he is particularly drawn to that critical moment in history when Christianity and Judaism come to challenge the paganism of the Roman Empire. This is the theme of his longest narrative poem "Quidam," of his miniature play *Sweetness*, and, indirectly, of his short story "Ad leones." But whereas the first two are set in imperial Rome, "Ad leones" has a contemporary setting. Isaak Edgar Middlebank Jr., a wealthy American journalist, visits a sculptor's studio in Rome and is attracted to a work in progress intended to depict Christians being thrown to the lions. It gradually becomes clear that, aided by the sculptor's crass friends and the sculptor's own venality, the American is encouraged to interpret the half-realised lumps of clay as work-in-progress towards an allegorical representation of capitalism, and is therefore willing to purchase it. Norwid's Jamesian irony and nuancing of language, as well as his powers of description, provide a graphic account of the artist, his magnificent greyhound, his studio and his friends. With masterly control and economy, he portrays the gradual transformation of the sculpture and the consequential betrayal of his art by the sculptor sold on a lucrative commission.

In mid-19th century Paris, London, and New York, Norwid was keenly aware of the social changes being brought about by the industrial revolution and the pervasiveness of unbridled commercialism, and these he contrasted with Christian values, just as T.S. Eliot, half a century later, was to rely on those values as a defence against contemporary barbarism. However, Norwid's lifelong commitment to Catholicism showed none of the bigotry and intolerance that the Church has all too often manifested. His ability to empathise with those who suffer, are denied justice or are victims of uncontrollable forces, and to praise those who try to protect those victims, is applied universally. He acknowledges the age-old sufferings of the Jews, he praises a Muslim leader for defending Christians from a Muslim mob in Damascus, he commemorates the death of a Polish exile from an explosion in a factory in Manchester, he protests at the death penalty inflicted on John Brown, a white American, for his attempted armed resurrection in aid of black slaves. These people deserve sympathy and understanding simply because they are human. But there is also praise in equally very fine poems for those who in one way or another have enriched humanity: Socrates in the past, General Bem, a contemporary fighter for Polish and Hungarian independence, or Norwid's friend Frederick Chopin.

In claiming such unbounded citizenship, Norwid was also challenging the fierce nationalism endorsed by his elder contemporaries Adam Mickiewicz and Juliusz Słowacki, and readily embraced by the generality of Poles, all too eager to shed blood because of their suffering under Russian, Prussian, and Austrian occupation.

But worthy attitudes are no guarantee of great art; piety may spell artistic disaster. What ultimately matters is the way a writer handles the material. Here Norwid's achievement lies in his formal innovations. Although the author of several overly long discursive and narrative poems, Norwid in his best works is a master of the telescoped yet vivid image, of the unspoken and the half-spoken, enriched with irony. This tautness, this reliance on the reader's intelligence and perseverance, baffled his contemporaries, but have found admirers in later generations sympathetic to his insistence on liberating poetry from journalistic and didactic elements, on his preferring works which appear rough-hewn and unfinished, and therefore leave room for the reader's imaginative participation. But while Norwid has consequently at times produced elliptic poems that continue to defy interpretation, he is capable of great simplicity and directness, as in "Feelings":

> Feelings—are like a cry full of war,
> And like the current of whispering springs,
> And like a funeral march. . .
> And like a long plait of blond hair
> On which a widower wears
> A silver watch — — —

While in "Quidam" Norwid is at pains to obscure its complex narrative, the play *Pierścień wielkiej clamy* [The Grand Lady's Ring], which is poised between high comedy and tragedy, dazzles with its lucidity and effervessence. Along with Mickiewicz, Słowacki and Zygmunt Krasiński, Norwid in effect created the Polish theatre, which had little to offer before the 19th century. But whereas Mickiewicz sought to create a Polish nationalist version of Goethe's Faust, whereas Słowacki saw himself as a Polish Shakespeare, whereas Krasiński drew on grand clashes of politics and culture, both contemporaneously and in ancient Rome; Norwid's plays, while at times thematically close to Krasiński's, as in *Sweetness* and the unfinished *Kleopatra* [Cleopatra], are minimalist in terms of plot and action. Set, as in the case of *Pierścień wielkiej clamy* and *Miłość czysta u kąpieli morskich* [Clean Sea-bathing], in a contemporary salon and a fashionable resort, respectively, they chart half-articulated feelings, focus on that crucial word or phrase, that subtle

gesture. It is a theatre that abandons the heroics of Romanticism and anticipates the interiorised themes in Chekhov and Maeterlink.

—Adam Czerniawski

NOVALIS

Born: Georg Philipp Friedrich Leopold von Hardenberg in Oberwiedstedt, Thuringia, 2 May 1772. **Education:** Educated privately then at Luther-Gymnasium, Eisleben, 1790; studied at University of Jena, 1790–91; University of Leipzig, 1791–93, and University of Wittenberg, 1794; law degree, 1794; studied at Mining Academy in Freiberg, 1797–99. **Family:** Engaged to Sophie von Kühn in 1795 (died 1797); engaged to Julie von Charpentier in 1798. **Career:** Actuary for Kreisamtmann Just, Tennstedt, 1795–97; assistant in salt works, Weissenfels, 1796–97, 1799–1801; associated with Bergakademie, Freiberg, 1797–99. **Died:** 25 March 1801.

PUBLICATIONS

Collections

Schriften, edited by Ludwig Tieck and Friedrich Schlegel. 2 vols., 1802.
Werke, Briefe, Dokumente, edited by E. Wasmuth. 4 vols., 1953.
Schriften, edited by Paul Kluckhohn and Richard Samuel. 5 vols., 1960–75; revised edition, 1977–.
Werke, edited by Gerhard Schulz. 1969.
Werke, Tagebücher und Briefe Friedrich von Hardenbergs, edited by Hans-Joachim Mähl and Richard Samuel. 3 vols., 1978–87.
Pollen and Fragments: Selected Poetry and Prose, translated by Arthur Versluis. 1989.
Philosophical Writings, translated and edited by Margaret Mahony Stoljar. 1997.

Verse

Devotional Songs, edited by Bernard Pick. 1910.
Hymns to the Night (bilingual edition), translated by Mabel Cotterell. 1948; also translated by Charles E. Passage, in *Hymns to the Night and Other Selected Writings*, 1960; Dick Higgins, 1984; translated by James Thomson, in *Novalis and the Poets of Pessimism*, 1995.
Sacred Songs, translated by Eileen Hutchins. 1956.

Other

Friedrich Schlegel und Novalis: Biographie einer Romantikerfreundschaft in ihren Briefen, edited by Max Preitz. 1957.

*

Bibliography: *Novalis: Der handschriftliche Nachlass des Dichters. Zur Geschichte des Nachlasses* by Richard Samuel, 1973.

Critical Studies: *Novalis: German Poet, European Thinker, Christian Mystic* by Friedrich Hiebel, 1954; *Novalis, The Veil of Imagery: A Study of the Poetic Works of Friedrich von Hardenburg* by Bruce Haywood, 1959; *Novalis's "Fichte Studies": The Foundation of His*

Aesthetics, 1970, and *Romantic Vision, Ethical Content: Novalis and Artistic Autonomy*, 1987, both by G. von Molnár; *Bifocal Vision: Novalis's Philosophy of Nature and Disease*, 1971, and *Novalis*, 1980, both by John Neubauer; *Blake and Novalis: A Comparison of Romanticism's High Arguments* by Joachim J. Scholz, 1978; *The Boundless Present: Space and Time in the Literary Fairy Tales of Novalis and Tieck* by Gordon Birrell, 1979; *The Fichtean Dynamic of Novalis's Poetics* by Richard W. Hannah, 1981; *The Androgyne in Early German Romanticism: Friedrich Schlegel, Novalis, and the Metaphysics of Love* by Sara Friedrichsmeyer, 1983; *The Concept of Imagination in Novalis's Works* by Jaishree Kale Odin, 1984; *History and Poetry in Novalis in the Tradition of German Enlightenment* by Nicholas Saul, 1984; *Delayed Endings: Nonclosure in Novalis and Hölderlin* by Alice Kuzniar, 1987; *Novalis: A Romantic's Theory of Language and Poetry* by Kristin Pfefferkorn, 1988; *Russian Symbolism and Literary Tradition: Goethe, Novalis, and the Poetics of Vyacheslav Ivanov* by Michael Wachtel, 1994; *The Critical Fortunes of a Romantic Novel: Novalis's Heinrich von Ofterdingen* by Dennis F. Mahoney, 1994; *Novalis: Signs of Revolution* by William Arctander O'Brien, 1995; *Novalis and the Poets of Pessimism*, edited with introduction by Simon Reynolds, 1995; *The Retreat of Representation: The Concept of Darstellung in German Critical Discourse* by Martha B. Helfer, 1996; *Locating the Romantic Subject: Novalis with Winnicott* by Gail M. Newman, 1997.

* * *

Novalis, the central figure of early German Romanticism, combines strong philosophical leanings with his poetic gift. It was his view that "the separation of philosopher from poet is only apparent and to the disadvantage of both." The poet is for him both seer and scientist, priest and craftsman, whose ability to harmonize and unify intellectual and intuitive powers can overcome the divisions of human knowledge. "Blütenstaub," his early contribution to the Schlegel brothers' journal *Athenäum*, takes the form of speculative "Fragments" which display novel powers of creative thinking through the use of analogue, metaphor, conceit, and paradox. His literary beginnings reflect assiduous study of contemporary Romantic thought (Fichte, Schelling) as well as of the Mystic Jacob Böhme. Though he had studied the rationalist philosophers of the 18th century, his unsystematic, speculative form of thought inclined him to thinkers such as Hemsterhuis, Zinzendorf, and adherents of the Pietist tradition.

A highly individual form of religious mysticism informs a great part of Novalis's writings. His essay "Die Christenheit oder Europa," which looks back nostalgically to pre-Reformation times, offers an idealized image of an undivided Church and society; it became an influential document of German Romantic attitudes to Catholicism. The *Hymns to the Night*, immediately inspired by the death of his 15-year-old fiancée, Sophie von Kühn, are mystical celebrations of a love which finds its transcendental fulfilment beyond the grave. The painful consciousness of finite existence redeemed by an assurance of eternal union through love, the inversion of life and death symbolism, the fusion of eroticism and religion, are features which give these rhythmic prose poems a complex richness of texture. The mystical celebration and rapturous embracing of death as the gateway to the intenser day of transcendental life was a vision which deeply influenced Richard Wagner especially in composing *Tristan and Isolde*. Novalis rediscovered and poetically restored that intimate marriage of the bodily with the immaterial, of sensualism with spiritualism (that Heine also later addressed yet failed to resolve) which was a legacy of the mystics and the medieval hymn. The reinstitution of symbolic modes of perception in all departments of human understanding was perhaps his greatest single contribution. His profound influence on modern religious movements (theosophy, anthroposophy) is therefore understandable.

The unfinished novel *Heinrich von Ofterdingen* represents the poet's vocation in terms of a symbolic journey in search of "the blue flower" (subsequently to become the representative symbol of all Romanticism). Heinrich's various encounters with dream, fairytale, myth, nature symbolism, and poetic art represent stages in the growth of the poet's self-awareness. The goal of fulfilment towards which he securely moves is essentially a form of self-knowledge which unites elements of erotic, spiritual, and religious experience.

The Geistliche Lieder, based on the Pietist hymn tradition, are confessional in character, conveying intimate accents of Romantic yearning. The combination of mystical religiosity with Romantic sensibility and imagination places these devotional songs outside orthodoxy.

Novalis is master of the aphorism, and the greater part of his oeuvre consists of fragmentary thoughts on a vast range of subjects from experimental physics to poetics, from school philosophy to magic. His plan was to bring about a unification of disparate human knowledge into a kind of encyclopedia which he called "a scientific bible." The creation of wholeness, the reconciliation of disparities, were Romantic ideals which he strove to realize in the realm of thought. The characteristic form of most of Novalis's aphorisms involves either a synthesis which attempts to bridge the dialectical divide, or an arresting analogue which forms a connection. Among his most stimulating and fruitful contributions are his ideas on literary, aesthetic, and philosophical topics. By virtue of his paramount gift of symbolic statement Novalis was of seminal importance to the Symbolist movement in France and his influence on later 19th-century neo-Romanticism was equally important.

—Alexander Stillmark

See the essay on *Hymns of the Night*.

O

ŌE Kenzaburō

Born: Ōse village, Shikoku island, Japan, 31 January 1935. **Education:** Educated at Tokyo University, 1954–59, B.A. in French literature 1959. **Family:** Married Itami Yukari in 1960; three children. **Career:** Freelance writer. Travelled to China as member of Japan-China Literary Delegation, 1960; travelled to Eastern and Western Europe, 1961, United States, 1965, 1968, Australia, 1968, and South-East Asia, 1970; visiting professor, Collegio de México, Mexico City, 1976. Lives in Tokyo. **Awards:** May Festival prize, 1954; Akutagawa prize, 1958; Shinchōsha prize, 1964; Tanizaki prize, 1967; Noma prize, 1973; Osaragi Jirō award; Nobel prize for literature, 1994; Order of Cultural Merit (refused), 1994.

PUBLICATIONS

Fiction

Shiiku. 1958; translated as *The Catch*, in *The Catch and Other War Stories*, edited by Shoichi Saeki, 1981.

Shisha no ogori [The Arrogance of the Dead] (collection). 1958.

Miru maeni tobe [Leap Before You Look] (collection). 1958.

Memushiri kouchi. 1958; as *Nip the Buds, Shoot the Kids*, translated by Paul Mackintosh and Maki Sugiyama, 1995.

Warera no jidai [Our Age]. 1959.

Seinen no omei [The Young Man's Stigma]. 1959.

Kodoku na seinen no kyūka. 1960.

Okurete kita seinen [The Youth Who Arrived Late], in *Shinchō.* September 1960–February 1962; in book form, 1962.

Sevuntiin [17], in *Bungakukai.* January 1961.

Seiji shōnen shisu [The Death of a Political Boy], in *Bungakukai.* February 1961.

Sakebigoe [Outcries], in *Gunzō.* November 1962; in book form, 1963.

Seiteki ningen [The Sexual Man]. 1963.

Nichijō seikatsu no bōken [Adventures of Everyday Life]. 1963.

Kojinteki na taiken. 1964; as *A Personal Matter*, translated by John Nathan, 1968.

Sora no kaibutsu Aguii. 1964; as *Aghwee the Sky Monster*, translated by John Nathan, in *Teach Us to Outgrow Our Madness: Four Short Novels*, 1977.

Man'en gannen no futtobōru [Football in the First Year of the Man'en Era]. 1967; as *The Silent Cry*, translated by John Bester, 1974.

Warera no kyoki o iki nobiru michi o oshieyo. 1969; augmented edition, 1975; as *Teach Us to Outgrow Our Madness*, translated by John Nathan, in *Teach Us to Outgrow Our Madness: Four Short Novels*, 1977.

Waga namida o nuguitamū hi. 1972; as *The Day He Himself Shall Wipe My Tears Away*, translated by John Nathan, in *Teach Us to Outgrow Our Madness: Four Short Novels*, 1977.

Kōzui wa waga tamashii ni oyobi [The Flood Has Reached My Soul]. 2 vols., 1973.

Pinchiranna chōsho. 1976; as *The Pinch Runner Memorandum*, translated by Michiko N. and Michael K. Wilson, 1994.

Teach Us to Outgrow Our Madness: Four Short Novels (includes *Teach Us to Outgrow Our Madness; The Day He Himself Shall Wipe My Tears Away; Prize Stock; Aghwee the Sky Monster*), translated by John Nathan. 1977.

Dōjidai gemu [The Game of Contemporaneity]. 1979.

Gendai denkishū [Modem Tales of Wonder]. 1980.

"Ame no ki" o kiku onnatachi [Women Listening to "ain Tree"]. 1982.

Atarashi hito yo mezameyo [Rouse Up O Young Men of the New Age!]. 1983.

Natsukashii toshi e no tegami [Letters to the Lost Years]. 1986.

Chiryō no tō [The Treatment Tower]. 1990.

Shizuka na seikatsu. 1990; as *A Quiet Life*, translated by Kunioki Yanagishita and William Wetherall, 1996.

Atarashii hito yo mezameyo; 2002; as *Rouse Up, O Young Men of the New Age*, 2002.

Other

Sekai no wakamonotachi. 1962.

Hiroshima nōto [Hiroshima Notes]. 1965; translated by David L. Swain and Toshi Yonezawa, 1995.

Genshuku na tsunawatari [The Solemn Tightrope Walking]. 1965.

Ōe Kenzaburō zensakuhin [Collected Works]. 6 vols., 1966–67; 2nd series, 6 vols., 1977–.

Jizokusuru kokorozashi [Enduring Volition]. 1968.

Kowaremono to shite no ningen [Fragile Human]. 1970.

Okinawa nōto [Okinawa Notes]. 1970.

Kakujidai no sōzōryoku [The Imagination of the Nuclear Age]. 1970.

Genbakugo no ningen [Homo sapiens after the A-Bomb]. 1971.

Kujira no shimetsusuru hi [The Day the Whales Shall Be Annihilated]. 1972.

Dōjidai to shite no sengo [Post-War as the Contemporaneity]. 1973.

Jōkyō e [Toward Situations]. 1974.

Bungaku nōto [Literary Notes]. 1974.

Kotoba ni yotte: Jōkyō/Bungaku [Via Words: Situations/Literature]. 1976.

Shōsetsu no hōhō [The Method of a Novel]. 1978.

Ōe Kenzaburō dōjidaironshū [An Essay on the Contemporary Age]. 10 vols., 1981.

Shomotsu—sekai no in'yu, with Yujiro Nakamura and Masao Yamaguchi. 1981.

Chūshin to shūen, with Yujiro Nakamura and Masao Yamaguchi. 1981.

Bunka no kasseika, with Yujiro Nakamura and Masao Yamaguchi. 1982.

Hiroshima kara Oiroshima e: 82 Yōroppa no hankaku heiwa undō o miru. 1982.

Kaku no taika to "ningen" no koe [The Nuclear Conflagration and the Voice of "Man"]. 1982.

Ika ni ki o korosu ka [How to Kill a Tree]. 1984.

Nihon gendai no yumanisuto Watanabe Kazuo o yomu. 1984.

Ikikata no teigi: futatabi jokyo e. 1985.

Shōsetsu no takurami chi no tanoshimi. 1985.

Kaba ni kamareru. 1985.

M/T to mori no fushigi no monogatari. 1986.

Atarashii bungaku no tame no. 1988.

Kirupu no gundan. 1988.

Saigo no shōsetsu. 1988.

Japan, the Ambiguous, and Myself: The Nobel Prize Speech and Other Lectures. 1995.

Editor, *Itami Mansaku essei shū*, by Mansaku Itami. 1971.

Editor, *Atomic Aftermath: Short Stories about Hiroshima-Nagasaki.* 1984; as *The Crazy Iris and Other Stories of the Atomic Aftermath*, 1985; as *Fire from the Ashes: Short Stories about Hiroshima and Nagasaki*, 1985.

*

Critical Studies: "Circles of Shame: 'Sheep' by Ōe Kenzaburō" by Frederick Richter, in *Studies in Short Fiction*, 11, 1974; *The Search for Authenticity in Modern Japanese Literature*, 1978, and *Oe Kenzaburo and Contemporary Japanese Literature*, 1986, both by Hisaaki Yamanouchi; "The 'Mad' World of Ōe Kenzaburō" by Iwamoto Yoshio, in *Journal of the Association of Teachers of Japanese*, 14(1), 1979; "Toward a Phenomenology of Ōe Kenzaburō: Self, World, and the Intermediating Microcosm" by Earl Jackson, Jr., in *Transactions of the International Conference of Orientalists in Japan*, 25, 1980; "Ōe's Obsessive Metaphor, Mori the Idiot Son: Toward the Imagination of Satire, Regeneration, and Grotesque Realism" by Michiko N. Wilson, in *Journal of Japanese Studies*, 7(1), 1981; "Kenzaburo Oe: A New World of Imagination" by Yoshida Sanroku, in *Comparative Literature Studies*, 22(1), 1985; *The Marginal World of Oe Kenzaburo: A Study in Themes and Techniques* by Michiko N. Wilson, 1986; *Off Center* by Miyoshi Masao, 1991; *Escape from the Wasteland: Romanticism and Realism in the Fiction of Mishima Yukio and Oe Kenzaburo* by Susan J. Napier, 1991.

*   *   *

Ōe Kenzaburō, one of Japan's most important writers and winner of the 1994 Nobel prize for literature, is known for his works celebrating the marginal and the outcast, in often violent opposition to a central establishment. It is perhaps not surprising, therefore, that Ōe was born in a mountain village on Shikoku, the smallest and still most rural of Japan's four major islands. Although Ōe now lives and writes in Tokyo, the village in the valley and the forest surrounding it have been a major source for Ōe's fictional imagination. Works highlighting a rural background range from his early so-called "pastoral fiction," such as his 1958 Akutagawa prize-winning story *Shiiku* (*The Catch*) to his nostalgic 1986 novel *Natsukashii toshi e no tegami* [Letters to the Lost Years]. While his pastoral works were largely realistic in their treatment of the village and the valley, Ōe's later fiction increasingly began to attach a mythological significance to these places. In the 1967 *Man'en gannen no futtobōru* (*The Silent Cry*), a novel Ōe describes as "a turning point," two urban brothers return to their village in the mountains to forge new lives: the older

brother searches for a "thatched hut," a retreat away from the world, while the younger brother mixes village history and legends to empower himself as leader of the increasingly apathetic villagers.

The possibilities inherent in rural folk legends became increasingly important in Ōe's fiction in the 1970s and 1980s, leading to his controversial 1979 novel *Dōjidai gemu* [The Game of Contemporaneity], which describes a hidden mountain village's relentless opposition towards what they call the Greater Japanese Empire. *Dōjidai gemu* offers the inspiration of the folklore and legends of the village as a substitute to what Ōe considers to be the pernicious influence of the élitist myths of the Japanese emperor system.

In fact, Ōe's strong opposition to the emperor system has been another important element in his writing, often combined with the events of the summer of 1945, when Japan acknowledged defeat and the emperor admitted he was not a god. Ōe's Japanese critics have pointed to 1945 as a watershed year in the young Ōe's life, creating a bifurcation in his personal ideology between the "patriotic boy" who had loved the emperor and the "democratic boy" who believed in the liberal principles fostered by the American occupation. Many of his early novels display this bifurcation. Some range obsessively over the frightening yet attractive aspects of war and violence, while others contain protagonists who have a love-hate relationship with the emperor. Ōe's angry satire *Sevuntiin* [17], published in 1961 and based on an incident that had occurred the previous year, tells the story of a pathetic young adolescent's assassination attempt on a socialist politician in the name of the emperor.

Perhaps Ōe's most fascinating fictional comment on the emperor system is his brilliant 1970 novella *Waga namida o nuguitamū hi* (*The Day He Himself Shall Wipe My Tears Away*). Inspired by the emperor-oriented suicide of Ōe's fellow novelist and personal *bête noire* Mishima Yukio, the novella is a savage attack on both the emperor system and the insane Romanticism that lay behind Mishima's death. At the same time, however, the novella betrays a certain empathy towards that very Romanticism, suggesting that traces of the "patriotic boy" still remain in Ōe's personality, although the present-day Ōe is a committed leftwing humanist.

Indeed, Ōe's portraits of Romantic protagonists, lost in dreams of violence or escape, are among his most effective, even when they are not overtly ideological. Perhaps his most successful characterization of this sort is contained in his 1964 novel *Kojinteki na taiken* (*A Personal Matter*). A darkly humorous, yet extraordinarily affecting account of a young man's struggle to come to terms with having fathered a brain-damaged child, *A Personal Matter* contains strongly autobiographical elements. But Bird, as the young father is called, is ultimately far more than Ōe's *alter ego*. A passive dreamer who initially wants only to escape his marriage and travel to Africa, Bird grows up in the course of the book through a series of grotesque and memorable encounters that range from the erotic—a marathon sex session with an old girlfriend—to the comic—the hungover Bird's breaking down and vomiting in front of his students in an English class. *A Personal Matter* is one of Ōe's funniest and most moving novels and its hero, irritating and self-pitying though he may be, remains with the reader as one of the most brilliantly realized characters in modern Japanese fiction.

The theme of father and brain-damaged son begun in *A Personal Matter* has also remained an important element in Ōe's fiction, from the surreal fantasy *Sora no kaibutsu Aguii* (*Aghwee the Sky Monster*), in which a father is unable to overcome his guilt for having murdered his brain-damaged baby, to the carnivalesque epic *Pinchiranna chōsho* (*The Pinch Runner Memorandum*), in which a father and idiot son lead an army of marginals and grotesques against the Japanese establishment. *The Pinch Runner Memorandum* thus exemplifies some of the most important elements of Ōe's work: its opposition to the centre and to the emperor system, its privileging of the marginal in the duo of outcast father and son, and its celebration of the liberating aspects of the violent and the grotesque.

In recent years Ōe's work has continued to mine these themes, although the tone has become increasingly elegiac rather than angry. Thus, the aforementioned *Natsukashii toshi e no tegami* revolves around the protagonist's guilt-ridden acceptance that he can no longer return to the valley of his childhood except in dreams and fiction. Ōe's recent work, especially the science-fiction novel *Chiryō no tō* [The Treatment Tower], set in a dystopian future where a hidden valley exists as a final escape, suggests that his favourite themes may increasingly be combined with new departures. Whatever Ōe's next direction will be, it seems certain that he will remain committed to producing politically controversial and highly imaginative fiction, an increasing rarity in the contemporary Japanese literary scene.

—Susan J. Napier

OLESHA, Yuri (Karlovich)

Born: Elizavetgrad, Ukraine, 3 March 1899. Moved with his family to Odessa, 1902. **Education:** Educated at home; Rishelevskii Gymnasium, Odessa, 1908–17; studied law at Novorossiisk University, Odessa, 1916–18. **Military Service:** Red army volunteer, 1919, serving as a telephonist in a Black Sea naval artillery battery. **Family:** Married Olga Gustaovna Suok. **Career:** Propagandist, Bureau of Ukranian Publications, Kharkov, 1921; writer of satirical verse, under pseudonym Zubilo [Chisel], for the railway periodical *Gudok* [Whistle], Moscow, 1922; defended the need for independent literature at the First Congress of Soviet Writers, 1934; evacuated with the Odessa Film Studio to Ashkhabad, Turkmenistan, 1941–45; returned to Moscow, 1946; fell into official disfavour, and worked mainly as translator and film scenarist, 1945–56. **Died:** 10 May 1960.

PUBLICATIONS

Collections

Complete Short Stories and Three Fat Men, translated by Aimee Anderson. 1979.
The Complete Plays (includes *The Conspiracy of Feelings*; *A List of Blessings*; the screenplay *The Three Fat Men*; *A Stern Young Man*; the scenario *The Black Man*), translated by Michael Green and Jerome Katsell. 1983.

Fiction

Zavist'. 1928; edited by Marion Jordan, 1969; as *Envy*, translated by Anthony Wolfe, 1936; also translated by P. Ross, with V. Kaverin's *The Unknown Artist*, 1947; J.C. Butler, 1989.
Tri tolstiaka. 1928; as *The Three Fat Men*, translated by Fainna Glagoleva, n.d.; also translated in *Complete Short Stories and Three Fat Men*, 1963.
Vishnevaia kostochka [The Cherry Stone] (stories). 1930.
Zapiski pisatelia [Notes of a Writer] (stories). 1931.

The Wayward Comrade and the Commissars and Other Stories, translated by Andrew R. MacAndrew. 1960.
Povesti i rasskazy [Short Stories and Stories]. 1965.
Love and Other Stories, translated by Robert Payne. 1967.
Rasskazy [Stories]. 1971.
Rasskazy [Stories]. 1977.

Verse

Zubilo [Chisel]. 1924.
O Lise [About Lisa] (for children). 1948.

Plays

Zagovor chuvstv, from his novel *Zavist'* (produced 1929). In *P'esy*, 1968; as *The Conspiracy of Feelings*, in *Complete Plays*, 1983; also translated by Daniel Gerould, 2002.
Tri tolstiaka, from his story (produced 1930). In *P'esy*, 1968; as *The Three Fat Men*, in *Complete Plays*, 1983.
Spisok blagodeianii (produced 1931). 1931; as *A List of Assets*, in *Envy and Other Works*, 1967; as *A List of Blessings*, in *Complete Plays*, 1968.
Idiot [The Idiot], from the novel by Dostoevskii (produced 1958).
P'esy [Plays] (includes *Zagavor chuvstv*; *Tri tostiaka*; *Spisok blagodeianii*). 1968.

Other

Izbrannoe [Selections]. 1936.
Izbrannye sochineniia [Selected Works], edited by V. Pertsov. 1956.
Ni dnia bez strochki. 1965; as *No Day without a Line*, translated by Judson Rosengrant, 1979.
Envy and Other Works (includes stories and the ''Speech to the First Congress of Soviet Writers''), translated by Andrew R. MacAndrew. 1967.
Vospominaniia o Iurii Olesha [Reminiscences about Iurii Olesha]. 1975.

*

Critical Studies: *The Invisible Land. A Study of the Artistic Imagination of Jurij Olesha* by Elizabeth Klasty Beaujour, 1970; *Major Soviet Writers: Essays in Criticism* edited by Edward J. Brown, 1973; *The Artist and the Creative Act: A Study of Jurij Olesha's Novel Zavist* by K. Ingdahl, 1984; ''Desire and the Machine: The Literary Origins of Yury Olesha's 'Ofeliya''' by Anthony Vanchu, in *The European Foundations of Russian Modernism*, edited by Peter I. Barta, 1991; *A Graveyard of Themes: The Genesis of Three Key Works in Iurii Olesha* by Kazimiera Ingdahl, 1994; *Olesha's Envy: A Critical Companion*, edited by Rimgaila Salys, 1999.

* * *

Yuri Olesha produced poetry, short stories, novels, plays, screenplays, and biographical writings. In spite of his versatility, his creative period was short and he produced few truly great works. These, however, guarantee him a stable position among the classic writers of Russian literature. His themes and his characters often face the same existential problem as did Olesha himself: how does a well-educated person of the pre-revolutionary gentry conform to the new realities of the Soviet state?

In some works, like his agitational poems of the early 1920s, he pays lip service to the Bolshevik cause. Such is also the ideological direction of his overtly partisan children's novel of the same period, *Tri tolstiaka* (*The Three Fat Men*). Because of its well-constructed plot, it has proved very popular with young readers. As the text does not invite interpretation that would challenge its straightforward message, the Soviets turned it into a radio play; it was filmed twice, and was also adapted for the stage. The enthusiastic reception the novel received contrasts sharply with the fate of Olesha's later works. *The Three Fat Men* relates the story of a revolution in an imaginary country. The land is dictatorially ruled by the three fat men. Their supporters are the rich and their enemies the poor. The latter are brave, love children, and are committed to the cause of the revolution. The rich are greedy and objectionable in every way. As is customary in propagandistic writing of this kind, the "intellectual"—Dr. Gaspar Arnery—is totally committed to the revolution. Predictably, the revolution removes the rich from power and the children—Suok the poor child and Tutti, the heir of the Three Fat Men—face a glorious future in a problem-free world.

The coming together of people from different backgrounds is examined in a much more problematic light in the novel *Zavist'* (*Envy*), Olesha's masterpiece. Written in the late 1920s, it no longer glorifies Soviet communism but, rather, sees it as a moral problem that divides families and that allows no room for people who are not wholeheartedly at its service. The people of the old world, Nikolai Kavalerov and Ivan Babichev, feel pushed aside and ignored in a pragmatic, scientific age. Ivan's brother, Andrei Babichev, manages major projects, such as the "Quarter," which free Soviet workers from household chores and provide nutritious meals on a shoestring. Andrei's protégé, Volodia, the working-class adolescent, has no time for sentiment and feels fully at home in the new world. As Kavalerov and Ivan bemoan the loss of intimacy, fantasy, and emotions, they profoundly envy Volodia who is engaged to marry Ivan's daughter, Valia, to produce a Soviet family. Kavalerov loves Valia with all the romanticism he can muster but is shunned and ends up sharing a fat petty-bourgeois widow's sexual favours with Ivan Babichev in her disgusting bed.

The novel is clearly not weighted in favour of the unsubtle and crude man of the new age, Volodia Makarov. While *Envy* was received enthusiastically, once the ideologically ambiguous plot elicited readers' sympathy for Kavalerov instead of Volodia, the novel became politically suspect and the critical establishment had no choice but to shun it. The novel's modernist narrative also added to its disfavour. Kavalerov's highly subjective vision provides the perspective in the first-person narration of the first part of the novel. In the second part his and Ivan's consciousnesses preoccupy the third-person narrator instead of the external world of "reality" which he brazenly fails to represent in a Socialist-Realist manner.

Kavalerov sees the surrounding world with the sensitive eyes of an artist and feels uncomfortable in it. In the play *Spisok blagodeianii* (*A List of Assets*) Lelia Goncharova faces similar concerns: she is a Shakespearean actress who fears that artistic insensitivity and the harshness and vulgarity of daily life will drain her talent. Her complaints echo Olesha's own feelings about writing literature to order. Ironically, the second part of the play comes very close to just that kind of literature. Lelia is allowed to travel to Paris (an opportunity Kavalerov could merely dream of) but the depiction of life in France is as two-dimensional as the imaginary country in *The Three Fat Men*. The unemployed, the strikers, the Communists, and the Soviet embassy are "good" while the émigrés, the capitalists, and the

brutal police are evil. The émigré steals Lelia's diary, which contains lists both of the crimes and the benefits of the Bolshevik regime, and publishes only the list of Lelia's complaints. In her despair, Lelia gives tendentious speeches praising the Soviets and, unrealistically, she is shot and killed on a street barricade. While in the Soviet Union the workers appreciated her talent, in the West she found art fully commercialized, as embodied in the grotesque portrait of the theatre manager. In spite of Olesha's obvious attempt to write ideologically correct literature, the play does not fail to capture realistically the spy-mania and terror of the Soviet system.

In his best short stories, Olesha achieves the same artistic perfection as in *Envy*. "Liompa"—a brief sketch of a few hours in the lives of a little child, a dying man, and a rat—has strong Tolstoian associations. Objects from the world surrounding the child enter his consciousness even as they abandon the dying man's. The latter is entering a new and ominous realm: when he suddenly realizes that he knows the rat's name—Liompa—he knows that his dying hour has come. In "Liubov" ("Love") and *Vishnevaia kostochka* [The Cherry Stone] imagination and emotions are contrasted with the dry pragmatism of the new Soviet age. *Vishnevaia kostochka*, like *Envy*, treats unhappy love. The unfortunate hero here, however, does not lose faith. He plants the stone of a cherry received from the object of his unrequited love and knows that an unplanned tree is going to bloom amidst a giant industrial plant that is part of the "five-year plan."

The subjective imagery, indirect descriptions, and avoidance of customary accounts of the world in Olesha's best writings produce an effect of estrangement. His thematic contrasts between the spiritual and the material, the individual and the collective, the irrational and the rational, convey an impression of people torn between the Old World and the New World, thereby providing the best literary account available of the Russian intelligentsia in the Soviet Union in the 1920s.

—Peter I. Barta

See the essay on *Envy*.

OMAR KHAYYAM

Born: Nishāpūr, Persia (now Iran), 18 May 1040 (purported; possibly 1023). **Education:** Studied in geometry and astronomy. **Career:** In Samarkand, worked for the chief magistrate, Abu Taher, and the ruler of Bokhara, Shamsolmolk Nasr; later entered the service of the Saljuq Sultan Malekshah (ruled 1072–92): helped in construction of an observatory and in compiling a set of astronomical tables as the basis of a new calendar era; travelled to Mecca and Baghdad, 1045, then returned to Nishāpūr. Contemporary reputation was as a scientist, and some mathematical works have survived. **Died:** 4 December 1131 (purported; possibly 1123).

PUBLICATIONS

Verse

Rubā'iyāt, edited by M.A. Forughi and Q. Ghani. 1942; also edited by A.J. Arberry, 1949, and B.A. Rozenfeld and A.P. Yushkevish, 1961; as *The Rubaiyat of Omar Khayyam*, translated by Edward Fitzgerald, 1859, translation edited by E. Heron-Allen, 1899, and A.J. Arberry, 1959; also translated by E.H. Whinfield, 1901; A.W.

Hamilton, 1935; John C.E. Bowen, 1961; Robert Graves and Omar Ali-Shah, 1967; Parichehr Kasra, 1975; Peter Avery and John Heath-Stubbs, 1979; Ahmad Saidi, 1991; Parvine Mahmoud, 1996; Willy Pogany, 1999; as *The Mirror and the Eye*, translated by Iftikhar Azmi, 1984.

*

Bibliography: *A Bibliography of Printed Editions of the Quatrains of Omar Khayyam in Foreign Languages*, 1923, and *A Bibliography of the Rubaiyat*, 1929, both by Ambrose G. Potter.

Critical Studies: *Edward Fitzgerald and Omar Khayyam: An Essay and Bibliography* by Holbrook Jackson, 1899; *A Concordance to Fitzgerald's Translation of the Rubáiyát of Omar Khayyám* by John R. Tutin, 1900; *Life of Omar al-Khayyámi* by J.K.M. Shirazi, 1905; *Omar and His Translator* by William F. Prideaux, 1909; *Sufism: Omar Khayyam and Edward Fitzgerald* by Carl H.A. Bjerregaard, 1915; *The Symbolism of the Rubáiyát of Omar Khayyam* by J.S. Pattinson, 1921; *Critical Studies in the Ruba'iyat* by Arthur Christensen, 1927; *Lumifar: The Spiritual Interpretation of Edward Fitzgerald's Translation of the Rubaiyat of Omar Khayyam* by Janette Cooper Rutledge, 1930; *The Nectar of Grace: Omar Khayyam's Life and Works* (includes translations of some scientific works) by Swami Govinda Tirtha, 1941; *In Search of Omar Khayyam* by Ali Dashti, 1971; *The Cambridge History of Iran*, vol. 20, 1975.

* * *

The name Omar Khayyam is more accurately transliterated from its original Persian as ''Umar-i-Khayyam,'' Umar the son of the tent-maker, but since publication in 1859 of Edward Fitzgerald's brilliant English versions of the *Rubā'iyāt* (*The Rubaiyat*; literally, quatrains) attributed to this poet, he has been known to too many as Omar Khayyam for this style to be dropped. He was born in 1048 in the north-eastern Iranian city of Nishāpūr, where he died and was buried in 1131.

His times were perilous. Saljuq Turks, tribesmen from the steppes of central Asia, an environment very different from that of the sophisticated city in which Khayyam was brought up, were completing their infiltration of Iran, Mesopotamia, and Asia Minor at the time of his birth, and by the year of his death near to consolidating a great empire which extended from the River Oxus to Syria, the area where they confronted the Crusaders from Europe. One of the more remarkable of the early Saljuq Sultans was Jalalu'd-Din Malekshah, who reigned from 1072 to 1092. He figured in Khayyam's life in the latter's capacity as astronomer and mathematician.

In fact, if we followed what Khayyam's contemporaries had to say of him we should be extolling him as a mathematician and one of the most eminent philosophers of his time, not as a poet, and certainly not as composer of four-part stanzas of a markedly irreligious and sceptical kind. Before he was 30 he had produced a work on algebra that established him as the pioneer of cubic equations and is still accessible to scholars both in its original Persian and in translation. Thus in 1074 Khayyam was among the astronomers summoned by Malekshah to revise the calendar and build a new observatory. The result was the new Jalali or Maleki Era, which dated from 16 March 1079.

This practical interest in the application of astronomy indicates a pragmatic side to the Turkish warlords by whom Khayyam and his

contemporaries were ruled, but as recent converts to Islam and leaders who had prospered since becoming Muslim, the Saljuq Sultans showed a powerful proclivity to insist on a rigorously orthodox practice of religion, the more so since their empire was threatened by the Frankish knights from without and by serious heresies within. Khayyam Khayyam, the great mathematician, seems, on the other hand, to have been a man as devoutly rational as the decrees of Sultans would have had him devoutly Muhammadan. It is perhaps for this reason his contemporaries are silent about his composition of boldly irreligious quatrains, which were no doubt circulated clandestinely and anonymously. It is significant that a writer who speaks of Khayyam some 90-odd years after his death and is among the first to mention *The Rubaiyat* only does so to castigate their composer and the verses themselves as wholly evil and corrupt. Yet that Khayyam's poems should be as sceptical as they are is hardly surprising since they were the products of an age when assiduous government patronage of religion must have encourged a type of hypocrisy which would be repugnant to a thinker like Khayyam.

Materials for his biography in contemporary records are in fact sparse. One contemporary describes him somewhat unfavourably as a testy old philosopher who did not suffer fools gladly; but this description softens when the writer comes to mention the circumstances of the great teacher's death as he was quietly studying a favourite text. Another notice, by a former pupil, says that Khayyam did not believe in forecasts of the future but nevertheless foretold his own death and did so at a party of friends the nature of which proves him to have had a convivial side to his character. He also foretold that he would be buried in a spot outside his native city where almond blossom would fall on his grave each Spring. It still does, no doubt deservedly on the grave of a man whose thoughts, expressed in pithy, word-thrifty four-lined stanzas, have found an echo as widely accepted epigrams in the minds of so many.

—Peter Avery

See the essay on *The Rubaiyat*.

OSTAIJEN, Paul van

Born: Antwerp, Belgium, 22 February 1896. **Military Service:** Served in the Belgian occupation army in Germany, until 1923. **Career:** Council worker in Antwerp, 1914–18; left for Berlin because of his activism; associated with Dadaists and Expressionists; returned to Antwerp, 1921; bookseller's assistant in Antwerp; art dealer in Brussels, 1925–26; moved to Miavoye-Anthée because of tuberculosis; founder, with G. Burssens and E. Du Perron, of the magazine *Avontuur,* 1928. **Died:** 18 March 1928.

PUBLICATIONS

Collections

Verzameld werk [Collected Work], edited by Gaston Burssens. 4 vols., 1952–56; revised edition, edited by Gerrit Borgers, 3 vols., 1965–66; selection as *Patriotism, Inc. and Other Tales*, translated by E.M. Beekman, 1971.

Verse

Music-hall. 1916.
Het sienjaal [The Signal]. 1918.
Bezette stad [Occupied City]. 1921.
Gedichten [Poems], edited by Gaston Burssens. 1928; "De feesten van angst en pijn" as *Feasts of Fear and Agony*, translated by Hidde van Ameyden van Duym, 1976.
Homage to Singer [and Three Other Poems], translated by Peter Nijmeijer. 1974.
The First Book of Schmoll (selected poems 1920–28), translated by Theo Hermans, James Holmes, and Peter Nijmeijer. 1982.

Other

Het bordeel van Ika Loch [The Brothel of Ika Loch]. 1926.
Vogelvrij [Outlawed], edited by Gaston Burssens. 1928.
Intermezzo. 1929.
Krities proza [Critical Prose], edited by Gaston Burssens. 2 vols., 1929–31.
Brieven uit Miavoye [Letters from Miavoye], edited by Gaston Burssens. 1932.
De bende van de stronk [The Gang of the Stump], edited by Gaston Burssens. 1932.
Diergaarde voor kinderen van nu [Zoo for Today's Children], edited by Gaston Burssens. 1932.
Self-Defence, edited by Gaston Burssens. 1933.
De trust der vaderlandsliefde en andere grotesken, edited by Gerrit Borgers. 1966.

*

Critical Studies: *Paul van Ostaijen, zoals hij was en is* by Gaston Burssens, 1933; *Poëtiek van Paul van Ostaijen* by A.T.W. Bellemans, 1939; *Een bezoek ann het prinsengraf* by Maurice Gilliams, 1952; *Paul van Ostaijen* by J. Muls and others, 1952; *Paul van Ostaijen* by Adriaan de Roover, 1958; *Paul van Ostaijen en zijn prozas* by H. Uyttersprot, 1959; *De Kringen naar binnen* by Paul Hadermann, 1965; *Paul van Ostaijen* by P. de Vree and H.F. Jespers, 1967; *Homeopathy of the Absurd* by E.M. Beekman, 1970; *Paul van Ostaijen, de Satiricus*, 1970, and *Paul van Ostaijen en zijn satire Intermezzo*, 1971, both by R. Snoeck; *Paul van Ostaijen, een documentatie* by Gerrit Borgers, 2 vols., 1971.

* * *

One of the first committed Modernists within Dutch literature, Paul van Ostaijen was a poet of the ongoing experiment. The effects of Modernism on early 20th-century literature in Dutch were modest, centred on small journals like *Het Getij* [The Tide], 1916–24, *De Vrije Bladen* [The Free Pages], 1924–31, and the more internationally famous *De Stijl* [The Style], 1917–32. Van Ostaijen was a typical Modernist in the internationalism of his interests; his career was influenced by the American poet Walt Whitman, by French poets and writers like Apollinaire, Cocteau, and Cendrars, and by German expressionism. Typically modernist as well was his profound interest in critical theory. Numerous essays like "Inleiding tot de nieuwe verskunst" [Introduction to the New Art of Poetry] (1921) or "Proeve van parallellen tussen moderne beeldende kunst en moderne Dichtkunst" [An Attempted Definition of Parallels between Modern

Art and Modern Poetry] (1925) aimed to keep Dutch literature in close touch with the most recent movements abroad. For van Ostaijen every new collection of poetry was a new beginning, repudiating what went before.

He reacted against the impressionistic, symbolist poetry still being written in the Low Countries as a result of the revolutionary literary movement around the Dutch journal *De Nieuwe Gids* [The New Guide] in the 1880s and its Flemish, less extreme equivalent *Van Nu en Straks* [Of Now and Later]. His first shocking book of poems, *Music-hall*, presented the new poet as an urban-based, refined, superior dandy. He was already moving towards an "unpoetic" colloquial style, frequently epitomizing a melancholic irony, and echoing a *fin-de-siècle* decadence. The poetry focuses on the atmosphere of the city and modern subjects such as the cinema, the tram, and electricity. As expressed in the long title-poem "Music-hall," the modern life of the city combined at times in Ostaijen's verse with a wish for a common spirit that would unite the audience, the dancers, the jugglers, the waiters of the cabaret, in a movement influenced by Jules Romains's unanism. Already van Ostaijen's poetry was moving towards free verse, and especially in the title poem, towards the strategic positioning of independent words.

Het sienjaal [The Signal] further embraced the wish for the surrender of the individual to the warmth of a common humanity. It was the first humanitarian expressionist work in Belgium, influenced by the writings of *Der Sturm* [The Assault] and expressionists like Franz Werfel or Else Lasker-Schüler, easily obtainable in occupied Belgium. Van Ostaijen's art now became an expression of all-embracing love for humanity allowing the individual to escape from himself.

However, quite swiftly van Ostaijen was to repudiate these ideals and reject *Het sienjaal* as "lyrical preening." By the time expressionist poetry in the Low Countries was taking off, he had already moved on, towards disillusion and nihilism. Active from 1916 in the movement for Flemish emancipation (which he saw as a move towards a European ideal) he wrote for various activist Flemish papers and had a court case pending as the result of a pro-Flemish demonstration against the Belgian cardinal Mercier. Consequently, he spent the period 1918–21 in Berlin where he came into contact with Berlin Dadaism but was acquainted mainly with the painting community around *Der Sturm*, including Stuckenberg, Campendonck, and possibly even Wassily Kandinsky. The Berlin period was one of great productivity, and "De feesten van angst en pijn" ("Feasts of Fear and Agony," written 1918–21 and published posthumously) reflected loneliness, fear, sarcasm, and alienation—the result of his disillusioning experiences in Berlin, where he witnessed the failure of the 1919 Spartacus rebellion, in which a group of left-wing German radicals, the Spartacus League, participated in the Berlin workers' revolt. Once again, the nihilism and disillusion was to be rejected quite quickly as having been merely an antidote to the "O Mensch" poetry of *Het sienjaal*.

Bezette stad [Occupied City], the first book of poems to be published after *Het sienjaal*, was a veritable typographic explosion, with words in different sizes and fonts colliding all over the page to create a formal tension. The text included quotations from songs, advertisements, bill boards, and film titles. Critics described it variously as Dadaist-futuristic or chaotic-nihilist, while the Dadaist *De Stijl* editor, Theo van Doesburg, wondered why these "typographic gymnastics" were necessary in what seemed to be a realist novel about the war expressionistically cut up. These nervous poems offer a picture of the German capture and occupation of Antwerp, the quiet, cautious life under occupation, and the atmosphere in the bars and cinemas.

Van Ostaijen's final poems were to have been published under the ironic title *Het eerst boek van Schmoll* (*The First Book of Schmoll*), after a well-known piano primer, but he died of tuberculosis before their publication. They are among his best work, simple and tranquil poems, often evoking a mood rather than presenting a message. In these later stages van Ostaijen had again changed his critical perspective, now championing poetry as "*woordkunst*"—art with words. He aimed for the autonomous poem, freed from the emotions of the poet. He continued to play with typography, rhythm, and repeated sounds, as in the famous poem of quiet passivity, "Melopee." Words were grammatically loosened in order to let the sounds and content of separate words react to each other, and thus to exploit fully the tension between words. Van Ostaijen's images, too, had by now often lost their element of comparison and become images from which "the umbilical cord had been cut." Only associatively connected, this imagery suggests an atmosphere, like the mood of panic slowly suggested and then muted in "Land Avond" [Land Evening] from *Feasts of Fear and Agony*. Nevertheless, van Ostaijen's posthumous collection also contained whimsical, burlesque poems like his "Huldegedicht aan Singer," an ode to Singer sewing machines, or "Alpejagerslied," an absurd narrative describing two gentlemen, one ascending and one descending a steep street, who pass each other in front of a hat shop.

For a period after van Ostaijen's death, his poetry was undervalued, but impassioned championing of his work by friends like Maurice Gilliams or critics like Paul Hadermann and Gerrit Borgers has resulted in recognition of him as one of the great poets of the Modernist era.

—Sabine Vanacker

OVID

Born: Publius Ovidius Naso in Sulmo (now Sulmona), Abruzzi, central Italy, 20 March 43 BC. **Education:** Educated in the schools of rhetoric in Rome under Arellius Fuscus and Porcius Latro; also studied in Athens, and travelled in Greece. **Family:** Married three times; one daughter, probably from second marriage. **Career:** Held minor judicial posts, but abandoned public career for poetry. Associated with circle of Messalla; acquainted with Horace and Propertius; banished for "a book and an error" (the book was the *Ars Amatoria* [The Art of Love]; the error has never been satisfactorily explained) by the emperor Augustus, to Tomis (now Constanta, Romania) on the Black Sea, AD 8: served in the Tomis home guard during times of barbarian unrest, and wrote some poetry in the local language, Getic; repeated appeals to Augustus and later to Tiberius were ineffective. **Died:** in exile AD 17.

PUBLICATIONS

Collection

[Complete Works], edited by Rudolf Ehwald and others. 1916–85; translated by Grant Showerman and others [Loeb Edition], 6 vols., 1914–29, revised by G.P. Goold, 1977–89.

Ovid in English, edited by Christopher Martin. 1998.

Verse

Amores [Loves], edited by P. Brandt (in German; with commentary). 1911; also edited by E.J. Kenney, with *Ars amatoria* and *Remedia amoris*, 1965, and F. Munari, 1970; edited and translated by Guy Lee, 1968, and by Grant Showerman, revised by G.P. Goold, with *Heroides* [Loeb Edition], 1977; Book I edited and translated by John Barsby (with commentary), 1973, and Book II by Joan Booth, 1991; translated by Rolfe Humphries, 1957; selections translated by Horace Gregory, in *Love Poems of Ovid*, 1964; Peter Green, in *Ovid: The Erotic Poems*, 1982; A.D. Melville, in *Ovid: The Love Poems*, 1990.

Ars amatoria [Art of Love], edited by P. Brandt (in German; with commentary). 1902; also edited by E.J. Kenney, with *Amores* and *Remedia amoris*, 1965, and F.W. Lenz, 1969; Book I edited by A.S. Hollis, 1977; edited and translated by H. Mozley, in *The Art of Love and Other Poems* [Loeb Edition], 1929; translated by B.P. Moore, 1935; also translated by Rolfe Humphries, 1957; selections translated by Horace Gregory, in *Love Poems of Ovid*, 1964; Paul Turner, as *The Technique of Love*, with *Remedies for Love*, 1968; Peter Green, in *Erotic Poems*, 1982; A.D. Melville, in *Love Poems*, 1990; as *Thomas Heywood's Art of Love: The First Complete English Translation of Ovid's Ars amatoria*, edited by M.L. Stapleton, 2000.

Epistulae ex Ponto [Letters from the Black Sea], edited by S.G. Owen. 1915; also edited by Jacques André, 1977; edited and translated by A.L. Wheeler, revised by G.P. Goold, with *Tristia* [Loeb Edition], 1988.

Fasti [Calendar], edited by Franz Bömer (in German; with commentary). 2 vols., 1957–58; also edited by H. Le Bonniec, 2 vols., 1969–71, G.B. Pighi, 2 vols., 1973, and E.H. Alton and others, 1985; edited and translated by J.G. Frazer (with commentary), 5 vols., 1929, revised by G.P. Goold, 1989; translated by Betty Rose Nagle, 1995; as *Fasti: Book IV*, edited by Elaine Fantham, 1998; translated by A.J. Boyle and R.D. Woodard, 2000.

Heroides (*Epistulae heroidum*) [Heroines], edited by A. Palmer (with commentary). 1898; also edited by H. Dörrie, 1971; edited and translated by Grant Showerman, revised by G.P. Goold, with *Amores* [Loeb Edition], 1977; translated by Harold C. Cannon, 1972; also translated by Harold Isbell, 1990; D. Hine 1991; edited by Peter E. Knox, 1995; as *Heroides: XVI–XXI*, edited by E.J. Kenney, 1996.

Ibis, edited by R. Ellis. 1881; edited and translated by H. Mozley, in *The Art of Love and Other Poems* [Loeb Edition], 1929.

Medicamina faciei femineae [On Facial Treatment for Ladies] (fragment), edited by A. Kunz. 1881; as *On Painting the Face*, edited and translated by H. Mozley, in *The Art of Love and Other Poems* [Loeb Edition], 1929; translated by Peter Green, in *Erotic Poems*, 1982; as *Cosmetics for Ladies*, translated by A.D. Melville, in *Love Poems*, 1990.

Metamorphoses, edited by H. Magnus. 1914; also edited by M. Haupt and others (in German; with commentary), 2 vols., 1966, and W.S. Anderson, 1977; Book I edited by A.G. Lee, 1953, Book II by J.J. Moore-Blunt, 1977, Book VI–X by W.S. Anderson, 1972, Book VIII by A.S. Hollis, 1970, and Book XI by G.M.H. Murphy, 1972; edited and translated by D.E. Hill (Books I–IV; with commentary), 1965, (Books V–VIII) 1992; edited and translated by Frank Justus Miller, revised by G.P. Goold [Loeb Edition], 2 vols., 1984; translated by Arthur Golding, 1567; also translated by A.E. Watts, 1954; Rolfe Humphries, 1955; Mary M. Innes, 1955; Horace

Gregory, 1958; A.D. Melville, 1986; C. Boar, 1989; commentaries by F. Bömer (in German), 6 vols., 1969–86; as *The Metamorphoses of Ovid*, translated by Allen Mandelbaum, 1993; translated by David R. Slavitt, 1994; translated by Michael Simpson, 2001; as *After Ovid: New Metamorphoses*, edited by Michael Hofmann and James Lasdun, 1994.

Remedia amoris [Cures for Love], edited by E.J. Kenney, with *Amores* and *Ars amatoria*. 1965; also edited by F.W. Lenz, 1968, and A.A.R. Henderson (with commentary), 1979; edited and translated by H. Mozley, in *The Art of Love and Other Poems* [Loeb Edition], 1929; translated by Rolfe Humphries, 1957; selections translated by Horace Gregory, in *Love Poems of Ovid*, 1964; as *Remedies for Love*, translated by Paul Turner, with *The Technique of Love*, 1968; Peter Green, in *Erotic Poems*, 1982; A.D. Melville, in *Love Poems*, 1990.

Tristia [Sorrows], edited by S.G. Owen. 1915; also edited by Georg Luck (in German; with commentary), 2 vols., 1967–77; edited and translated by A.L. Wheeler, revised by G.P. Goold, with *Ex Ponto* [Loeb Edition], 1988; Book II edited and translated by S.G. Owen (with commentary), 1924; translated by L.R. Lind, 1975; as *Sorrows of an Exile*, translated by A.D. Melville, 1992.

*

Critical Studies: *Ovid, a Poet between Two Worlds* by H. Fränkel, 1945; *Ovid Recalled* by L.P. Wilkinson, 1955, abridged edition, as *Ovid Surveyed*, 1962; *The Mystery of Ovid's Exile* by J.C. Thibault, 1964; *Ovid as an Epic Poet* by Brooks Otis, 1966, revised edition, 1970; *Ovid* edited by J.W. Binns, 1973; *Changing Forms: Studies in the Metamorphoses of Ovid* by Otto Stein Due, 1974; *Ovid's Heroides* by Howard Jacobson, 1974; *Ovid's Metamorphoses: An Introduction to the Basic Aspects* by G. Karl Galinsky, 1975; *Ovid's Art of Limitation: Propertius in the Amores* by Kathleen Morgan, 1977; *Ovid* by John Barsby, 1978, revised edition, 1991, *History in Ovid* by Ronald Syme, 1978; *Chaucer and Ovid* by John M. Fyler, 1979; *The Poetics of Exile: Program and Polemic in the Tristia and Epistulae ex Ponto of Ovid* by Betty Rose Nagle, 1980; *Ovid and the Elizabethans* by Frederick S. Boas, 1982; *The Death of Procris: "Amor" and the Hunt in Ovid's Metamorphoses* by Gregson Davis, 1983; *Publica Carmina: Ovid's Poems from Exile* by Harry B. Evans, 1983; *Metaformations: Soundplay and Wordplay in Ovid and Other Classical Poets* by Frederick Ahl, 1985; *Narcissus and the Invention of Personal History* by Kenneth J. Knoespel, 1985; *Ovid's Games of Love* by M. Myerowitz, 1985; *Ovid's Metamorphoses and the Tradition of Augustan Poetry* by Peter E. Knox, 1986; *The Metamorphosis of Persephone: Ovid and the Self-Conscious Muse* by S. Hinds, 1987; *Ovid* by Sara Mack, 1987; *Feminine Rhetorical Culture: Tudor Adaptations of Ovid's Heroides* by Deborah S. Greenhut, 1988; *Ovid Renewed: Ovidian Influences on Literature and Art from the Middle Ages to the Twentieth Century* edited by Charles Martindale, 1988; *The World of Ovid's Metamorphoses* by Joseph B. Solodow, 1988; *The Pythagorean Intertext in Ovid's Metamorphoses: A New Interpretation* by Maria Maddalena Colavito, 1989; *Fictus Adulter: Poet as Actor in the Amores* by John T. Davis, 1989; *Ovid's Elegiac Festivals: Studies in the Fasti* by John F. Miller, 1991; *Shakespeare and Ovid* by Jonathan Bate, 1993; *Policy in Love: Lyric and Public in Ovid, Petrarch, and Shakespeare* by Christopher Martin, 1994; *Banished Voices: Readings in Ovid's Exile Poetry* by Gareth D. Williams, 1994; *Ovid's Causes: Cosmogony and Aetiology in the Metamorphoses* by K. Sara Myers, 1994; *Seduction and Repetition in Ovid's Ars amatoria 2* by Alison Sharrock, 1994; *Ovid and the Fasti: An Historical Study* by Geraldine Herbert-Brown, 1994; *Playing with Time: Ovid and the Fasti* by Carole E. Newlands, 1995; *Ovid: The Classical Heritage*, edited by William S. Anderson, 1995; *The Curse of Exile: A Study of Ovid's Ibis* by Gareth D. Williams, 1996; *Harmful Eloquence: Ovid's Amores from Antiquity to Shakespeare* by M.L. Stapleton, 1996; *The Poet and the Prince: Ovid and Augustan Discourse* by Alessandro Barchiesi, 1997; *Selections from Ars amatoria, Remedia amoris: Text, Commentary, Vocabulary* by Graves Haydon Thompson, 1997; *Greek Gods in Italy in Ovid's Fasti: A Greater Greece* by Hugh C. Parker, 1997; *Ovid's Literary Loves: Influence and Innovation in the Amores* by Barbara Weiden Boyd, 1997; *Poetic Allusion and Poetic Embrace in Ovid and Virgil* by R.A. Smith, 1997; *Enjoinder and Argument in Ovid's Remedia amoris* by David Jones, 1997; *The Face of Nature: Wit, Narrative, and Cosmic Origins in Ovid's Metamorphoses* by Garth Tissol, 1997; *The Erotics of Domination: Male Desire and the Mistress in Latin Love Poetry* by Ellen Greene, 1998; *Virgil: His Life and Times* by Peter Levi, 1998; *Ovidian Transformations: Essays on the Metamorphoses and Its Reception*, edited by Philip Hardie, Alessandro Barchiesi and Stephen Hinds, 1999; *The Metamorphosis of Ovid: From Chaucer to Ted Hughes* by Sarah Annes Brown, 1999; *Displaced Persons: The Literature of Exile from Cicero to Boethius* by Jo-Marie Claassen, 1999; *A Discourse of Wonders: Audience and Performance in Ovid's Metamorphoses* by Stephen M. Wheeler, 1999; *Shakespeare's Ovid: The Metamorphoses in the Plays and Poems*, edited by A.B. Taylor, 2000; *Ovid, Aratus, and Augustus: Astronomy in Ovid's Fasti* by Emma Gee, 2000; *The Rhetoric of the Body from Ovid to Shakespeare* by Lynn Enterline, 2000; *Ovid Metamorphosed*, edited by Philip Terry, 2000; *Ovid and the Renaissance Body*, edited by Goran V. Stanivukovic, 2001; *Speaking Volumes: Narrative and Intertext in Ovid and Other Latin Poets* by Alessandro Barchiesi, edited and translated by Matt Fox and Simone Marchesi, 2001; *Ancient Etymologies in Ovid's Metamorphoses: A Commented Lexicon* by Andreas Michalopoulos, 2001; *Ovid's Poetics of Illusion* by Philip Hardie, 2002.

* * *

Among the classical Latin poets Ovid stands in the highest rank. He may be inferior to Virgil in depth of feeling and in seriousness of purpose, but as a poet of wit and sensibility and of verbal and narrative skill he has no equal.

His earliest work was the *Amores* [Loves], a collection of love elegies probably written between his 18th and 25th years. This has come down to us in a later edition, reduced from five books to three, but remains essentially the work of his early period. The collection is centred upon an affair with a mistress called Corinna, who must be regarded as fictitious rather than merely pseudonymous. They are poems of the intellect, not of emotional involvement. What Ovid is doing is taking the contemporary genre of love elegy and mischievously playing with its conventions. Most of the stock themes and situations occur, but always with some sort of comic twist. In Ovid's hands the traditional lover acquires a new persona, who regards the frustrations of the genre as a challenge rather than as a source of gloom. Beneath the fun there is perhaps a serious point: Ovid is offering the Romans a new lighthearted approach to love, which avoids both the hopeless idealism of the elegists and the moral strictures of the philosophers.

Next Ovid wrote the *Heroides* [Heroines], imaginary verse epistles from mythological heroines to their faithless lovers. This collection was expanded at some later date by the addition of some "paired" letters, in which the heroine's reply is set beside a letter received from her love. The *Heroides* had no precedent in Greek or Latin literature. In inventing the genre Ovid set himself the challenge of creating variety out of a potentially repetitious set of situations. He meets this by choosing heroines whose external circumstances are different and then giving each an individual character. At the same time he contrives to provide a new slant on the particular myth in the manner of the Greek poets of the Alexandrian age, often with a humanizing or modernizing touch. There is a certain artificiality about the exercise. But there are passages of pathos and lyricism, and beneath the rhetoric Ovid does show a sympathetic understanding of female psychology, if not the psychoanalytical powers with which some modern critics have credited him.

For his next variation on the theme of love Ovid turned to the didactic genre, with his *Ars amatoria* [Art of Love] and its sequel *Remedia amoris* [Cures for Love]. Didactic poetry had a long and honourable tradition; these poems constitute a light-hearted burlesque of the genre. The *Ars* is not a pornographic or even an erotic work. Its theme is how to catch and keep a lover (men are addressed in the first two books, and women in the third), and its tone is essentially the amused detached tone of the *Amores*, where indeed a number of the precepts here given are foreshadowed. The same tone is maintained in the *Remedia*, where Ovid neatly and ironically reverses his previous stance to advise those seeking a release from love. These are cultivated poems, enlivened with some vivid vignettes of contemporary Roman life. But unfortunately for Ovid this was not the kind of cultivation that commended itself to the emperor Augustus, who was at the time trying to revive traditional Roman morality and the institution of marriage.

Whatever the emperor may have thought, Ovid had now worked out his amatory vein, and he turned to two large-scale poems, on which he seems to have worked simultaneously. *Fasti* [Calendar] is a versified calendar of Roman religious observances in six books covering the first six months of the year (it was never completed). On the surface this seems to represent a conversion from irresponsible personal poetry to patriotic Roman themes, and the work does contain in passing some contemporary Augustan propaganda. But the real inspiration behind it was the Alexandrian poet Callimachus, who had written an *Aetia* [Origins] explaining Greek customs and rites; Ovid was setting himself to write a Roman equivalent, though the spirit would still be essentially Greek. *Fasti* incorporates a large amount of religious and antiquarian lore, which Ovid serves up with a characteristic mixture of wit and sensitivity, making the most of the opportunities it offers for extended passages of narrative and description. Many of the individual stories are brilliantly told, but the work as a whole suffers from a lack of unity and continuity.

Meanwhile Ovid was writing the *Metamorphoses*, his greatest work both in size and in achievement. It is a collection of some 250 myths and legends strung together in a loosely chronological order from the Creation and Flood to the deification of Julius Caesar. As the title implies, the myths are linked by the common theme of metamorphosis; but in many cases the metamorphosis is tangential to the main story, and Ovid in fact draws on the whole corpus of Greek and Roman mythology with some Near Eastern added. The incorporation of all this material into a continuous poem of epic proportions is itself a *tour de force* involving ingenious and often audacious transitions. The great qualities of the work are its narrative brilliance and its

human interest. Ovid abandons the end-stopped elegiac couplets of his earlier works and uses the traditional epic hexameter to develop a flowing narrative style which carries the reader effortlessly along. At the same time the sheer scale of the work provides scope for some exuberant rhetorical effects—in set speeches, dramatic narrative, allegory, and description. The frequency of divine intervention (often comic or cruel) and of metamorphosis itself gives the poem an air of unreality, but neither this nor the poet's irrepressible wit destroys the human interest with which the stories are invested. Its imitation by writers and painters down the centuries is eloquent testimony to the greatness of the poem.

At the age of 51 Ovid was suddenly banished by Augustus to Tomis on the shores of the Black Sea. From here he wrote two collections of verse epistles, the *Tristia* [Sorrows] in five books and the *Epistulae ex Ponto* [Letters from the Black Sea] in four, addressed to his wife, the emperor, and various friends at Rome, describing the hardships of exile and pleading for his recall. This poetry has to be appreciated against the situation that produced it. Tomis was a barbaric outpost of the empire, where the Latin language was not even spoken; Ovid was cut off not only from family and friends but from the whole civilized culture that was his inspiration. Some of the exile poems are immediately attractive, as pieces of narrative or description or as expressions of simple emotion. If the rest end by seeming monotonous, two qualities stand out—the degree of poetic artifice which Ovid still employs, and the note of defiance by which he appeals over Augustus' head to public opinion at Rome and asserts the overriding validity of his calling as a poet. Ovid died in exile unpardoned: it was a sad end to Rome's most brilliant poet.

—John Barsby

See the essays on *The Art of Love*, *Loves*, and *Metamorphoses*.

OZ, Amos

Born: Amos Klausner in Jerusalem, British Mandated Palestine (now Israel), 4 May 1939. Grandson of Russian poet Alexander Klausner. Raised in Kerem Avraham, Jerusalem. Changed his name in rebellion against his parents. **Education:** Attended Telkemoni in Jerusalem; Hebrew University, Jerusalem, B.A. in Hebrew literature and philosophy, 1965. **Military Service:** Served in the tank corps in the Six-Day War in the Sinai desert, 1967; Yom Kippur War in the Golan Heights, 1973; promoted from staff sergeant to second lieutenant, 1975. **Family:** Married Nily; two daughters and one son. **Career:** Worked at Kibbutz Hulda, teaching high school, farming on cotton fields, and writing fiction, from 1954; worked with Peace Now, from 1977; Visiting Fellow, St. Cross College, Oxford, from 1969–70; writer-in-residence, Hebrew University, Jerusalem, 1975; instructor, University of California at Berkeley; writer-in-residence, Colorado College, 1984–85; Professor and Agnon Chair of Hebrew literature, Ben-Gurion University of the Negev. **Awards:** Prix Femina; Frankfurt Peace prize; Officer of Arts and Letters of France; Brenner prize; Holon prize; B'nai B'rith annual literary award; Friedenspries international peace prize, awarded by German President Richard von Weizsacker, 1992; full member, Academy of the Hebrew Language; French cross of the Knight of Legion d'Honneur, awarded by French President Jacques Chirac, 1997; and Israeli prize for Literature, 1998.

PUBLICATIONS

Collections

Artsot ha-tan. 1965; as *Where the Jackals Howl and Other Stories*, translated by Nicholas de Lange and Philip Simpson, 1981.

Ahavah me'uheret. 1971; as *Unto Death*, translated by Nicholas de Lange and Amos Oz, 1975.

Har ha-'etsah ha-ra 'ah. 1976; as *The Hill of Evil Counsel: Three Stories*, translated by Nicholas de Lange and Amos Oz, 1978.

Fiction

Makom aher. 1966; as *Elsewhere, Perhaps*, translated by Nicholas de Lange and Amos Oz, 1973.

Mikha'el sheli. 1968; as *My Michael*, translated by Nicholas de Lange and Amos Oz, 1972.

La-ga'at ba-mayim, la-ga'at ba-ruah. 1973; as *Touch the Water, Touch the Wind*, translated by Nicholas de Lange and Amos Oz, 1974.

Sumkhi (for children). 1978; as *Soumchi*, translated by Penelope Farmer, 1980.

Menuhah nekhonah. 1982; as *A Perfect Peace*, translated by Hillel Halkin, 1985.

Kufsah shehorah. 1987; as *Black Box*, translated by Nicholas de Lange and Amos Oz, 1988.

La-da'at ishah. 1989; as *To Know a Woman*, translated by Nicholas de Lange, 1991.

Matsav ha-shelishi. 1991; as *Fima*, translated by Nicholas de Lange, 1993.

Al tagidi laila. 1991; as *Don't Call It Night*, translated by Nicholas de Lange, 1995.

Panter Ba'martef. 1995; as *Panther in the Basement*, translated by Nicholas de Lange, 1997.

Oto Ha-Yam. 1999; as *The Same Sea*, translated by Nicholas de Lange and Amos Oz, 2001.

Non-Fiction

Beor hatkhelet ha'aza. 1979; as *Under this Blazing Light: Essays*, translated by Nicholas de Lange, 1995.

Poh ova-sham be-Erets-Yisrael bi-setaov. 1982; as *In the Land of Israel*, translated by Maurie Goldberg-Bartura, 1983.

Mi-mordot ha-Levanon: ma amarim u-reshimot. 1987; as *The Slopes of Lebanon*, translated by Maurie Goldberg-Bartura, 1989.

Sheti Kat Ha-Shamayim: Agnon Mishtomem al Elohim. 1993; as *The Silence of Heaven: Agnon's Fear of God*, translated by Barbara Harshav, 2000.

Israel, Palestine and Peace: Essays, edited by Drenka Willen. 1994.

Matchilim Sipur. 1996; as *The Story Begins: Essays on Literature*, translated by Maggie Bar-Tura, 1999.

*

Bibliography: *Amos Oz: Bibliyografyah, 1953–1981, im mivohar hashlamot ad okayits* by Joseph Jerushalmi, 1983.

Critical Studies: ''The Beast Within: Women in Amos Oz's Early Fiction'' by Esther Fuchs, in *Modern Judais*, vol. 4, no. 3; *Ben El le-ohayah: iyun bi-yetsirato shel Amos Oz* by Avraham Balaban, 1986; as *Between God and Beast: An Examination of Amos Oz's Prose*, translated by Avraham Balaban, 1993; *Voices of Israel: Essays on and Interviews with Yehuda Amichai, A.B. Yehoshua, T. Carmi, Aharon Appelfeld, and Amos Oz* by Joseph Cohen, 1990; ''Strange Fire and Secret Thunder: Between Micha Josef Berdyczewski and Amos Oz'' by Avner Holtzman, in *Prooftexts*, vol. 15, no. 2, 1995; ''The Epistolary Politics of Amos Oz's *Black Box*'' by Joshua M. Getz and Thomas O. Beebee, in *Prooftexts*, vol. 18, no. 1, 1998; ''Novellas Under this Blazing Light: Transformation in the Novella Writing of Amos Oz'' by Chaya Schacham, in *Orbis Litterarum*, vol. 53, no. 5, 1998; *Ideology and Jewish Identity in Israeli and American Literature* edited by Emily Miller Budick, 2001; *Translating Israel: Contemporary Hebrew Literature and Its Reception in America* by Alan L. Mintz, 2001; *Somber Lust: The Art of Amos Oz* by Yair Mazor, translated by Marganit Weinberger-Rotman, 2002.

*   *   *

Amos Oz is recognized as one of Israel's greatest novelists and short story writers. His first great work of fiction that garnered him fame in Israel is *Mikha'el sheli* (*My Michael*). This novel is unique in that the male author tells the story through the voice and perspective of a woman, Hannah Gonen. In an interview with Yair Mazor, Oz explains why he tells *My Michael* from the point of view of a woman: ''I was born to a woman, I have loved women, and I begot women. It seems so obvious to me, that there's nothing to explain. When I write about women, from a woman's point of view, at least while I'm writing, I do not act, think, or function as a man. My testicles are put on hold, so to speak.'' Gonen meets her husband when she accidentally falls down the stairs at the university that they attend; her husband, Michael Gonen, is a geology student and is a rather bland and unemotional but mature person. The reader might wonder initially if the two characters have enough in common to sustain a permanent romantic relationship and, as it turns out, they do not. Although some critics have compared this fine novel to Gustave Flaubert's *Madame Bovary*, perhaps a more suitable comparison would be to Charlotte Perkins Gilman's *The Yellow Wallpaper* or Doris Lessing's ''To Room Nineteen.'' An intriguing aspect of the novel is how convincingly Oz portrays the mind and the inner workings of a woman, particularly a woman who is losing her sanity. Oz employs not only the perspective and attitudes of a woman, but also her language. The dexterity with which the author delves into the heart of a woman and assumes her voice in journal form might remind some readers of Samuel Richardson's *Clarissa*. Michael studies erosion, which symbolizes the erosion of their marriage. Hannah starts to lose interest in life after sacrificing her career in literature and giving birth to a baby, Yair, whom she does not love. She retreats from a harmonious relationship with her husband into a world of sexual fantasies and illness. Hannah seems jealous of her husband's success—a success of which she had been capable of before she married Michael. She also does not like living in Jerusalem. As the novel continues, Hannah's irrational behavior and psychological disintegration increase. She eventually becomes destructive (and consequently self-destructive), and her marriage to Michael, her Michael—the title suggests power, control, or ownership—is over. Although Michael is her husband, he appears to be much more mature—in some respects a father figure. Oz links Hannah's husband and father in the text. Hannah feels great resentment toward her actual father as well as toward Michael. Although the novel can be viewed from a feminist perspective, parts of the work can also be considered from a political point of view; for instance, Hannah's fantasies concerning her friends, the Arab twins, could be making a political statement, given the situation at the time that Oz wrote the novel, as well as today.

In works such as *Makom aher* (*Elsewhere, Perhaps*), "Late Love," *Menuhah nekhonah* (*A Perfect Peace*), *La-ga'at ba-mayim, la-ga'at ba-ruah* (*Touch the Water, Touch the Wind*), and "Nomad and Viper," Oz allows the kibbutz to serve as an integral part of the story. Living at Kibbutz Hulda for several decades, and only leaving the kibbutz reluctantly because of his son's health problems, Oz manifests great affinity and affection for the kibbutz. It is not surprising, therefore, that Oz portrays the kibbutz and communal living as part of the landscape of his fiction. Oz was well known at Kibbutz Hulda, and the profits from his fiction went to the kibbutz. Although Oz exhibits great respect for the idea of the kibbutz in interviews and in his fiction, he never idealizes the kibbutz and acknowledges its imperfections. Oz's fiction demonstrates that although he has strong opinions, he is not a radical or close-minded. This holds true for his ideas about the kibbutz, as well as politics—the Israeli-Palestinian situation in particular. In *A Perfect Peace*, Oz merges his preoccupation with the kibbutz with his tendency to focus on father-son relationships. The novel takes place on a kibbutz and concerns Yonatan (Jonathan is the English equivalent), who has a very strained relationship with his overbearing father, Yolek, and with his wife, Rimona. He believes himself no longer needed on the kibbutz after the appearance of Azariah, who becomes his replacement. Oz makes a triangular connection between Yolek-Yonatan-Azariah and Saul-Jonathan-David. Yonatan leaves the kibbutz and pursues his perfect peace (death) in part because he feels responsible for the death of his unborn children. Oz describes in great detail the kibbutz and the desert through which Yonatan travels. As he looks for death, Yonatan thinks introspectively about his past, attempts to come to terms with it, and heads back home.

Having been a major part of Peace Now since 1977, Oz has worked for years for peace between the Israelis and Palestinians. He wishes for more understanding between the two groups. This desire is quite apparent in "Nomad and Viper," which appears in *Artsot ha-tan* (*Where the Jackals Howl and Other Stories*). Oz describes to his primarily Israeli audience, in great detail, the mannerisms and customs of Bedouins; for instance, he describes the behavior of the shepherd of the lazy flock of sheep. A significant part of the distrust that Israelis and Arabs have for one another derives from a lack of understanding. In "Nomad and Viper," the Jews on the kibbutz accuse the Arab nomads of stealing from them, but these accusations are not verified in the story. The elder of the Bedouins returns a few useless objects, yet denies firmly that his people have stolen anything else from the kibbutz. The Jews on the kibbutz distrust one Arab nomad in particular, believing him to be sinister because he has an "infuriatingly sly face. . . . A man with such an appearance was capable of anything." Oz, through his narrator and the use of irony, demonstrates the strong distrust, sometimes unwarranted, exhibited by Israelis toward Arabs. This suspicion and prejudice of Jews toward

Arabs (these feelings are, of course, reciprocal) inhibit the prospect for peace in the Middle East.

Oto Ha-Yam (*The Same Sea*) manifests Oz's interest in the father-child relationship, an important theme and perhaps a preoccupation, in his works (*My Michael*, for instance). Oz's personal relationship with his father was strained: his father was a Zionist whose politics were considered right wing, while Oz, found himself on the opposite side of the political spectrum. Oz even changed his cognomen in rebellion. In *The Same Sea*, Albert Danon, shortly after losing his wife to cancer, loses his son, Rico, in a metaphoric sense. Troubled by his mother's death and his relationship with her while she was alive (when he has sex with his prostitute, he asks her to pretend to be his mother), Rico leaves his father to go to Tibet. The strained relationship between Albert and Rico is reminiscent of the troubled one between David and Absalom; Oz's allusions to this relationship (1, 2 Samuel and 1 Kings) are clear. Albert wants his son to come home, yet he lusts for Dita Inbar, his son's girlfriend, which adds a new dimension to the strain in the father-son relationship. The novel suggests a pessimistic view about the nature of love—the characters all seem to be self-interested, consumed with their own happiness, even at the expense of other people. Although the novel is a work of fiction, *The Same Sea* demonstrates Oz's poetic talent; the novel is full of images and metaphors. The imagistic and poetic nature of this particular novel is reminiscent of the work of Israel's fiction writer Yoel Hoffmann. Oz's novel is self-conscious: the author makes himself a character (called the Author and the Narrator) who interacts with the other characters, becomes part of the plot, and even critiques Dita's screenplay. *The Same Sea* can be considered a novel that discusses, to some extent, the writing process. The self-consciousness of the author as well as his intrusion in the plot manifest Oz's willingness to experiment in his fiction.

Amos Oz is famous in Israel for his thought-provoking novels, many of which are political. His desire for peace between the Israelis and the Palestinians, something he has worked for during the past quarter century as a member of Peace Now, pervades his fiction as well as his non-fiction. Even works such as *My Michael*, which concerns a troubled marriage, could be interpreted as having political overtones. Oz's fiction manifests sympathy and understanding for the plight of the Palestinians and the recognition that Israel's only hope for survival is to make an enduring peace with them. Although some of his works have disturbed right-wing Israelis, he is clearly one of Israel's most successful and renowned fiction writers. Oz's allusions are complex and manifest that he has read world literature exhaustively. His fiction and non-fiction concerning the volatile political situation in the Middle East, such as the need for peace between the Israelis and Palestinians, have garnered him an international reputation as an important Israeli novelist. Unfortunately his fiction, according to Alan L. Mintz, is not as well known in the United States as it deserves to be.

—Eric Sterling

P

PAGNOL, Marcel

Born: Aubagne, near Marseilles, France, 28 February 1895. **Education:** Educated at Lycée Thiers, Marseilles; University of Montpellier, degree in letters. **Military Service:** Served with the French infantry, 1914–17, and 1940. **Family:** Married Jacqueline Bouvier in 1945; two sons. **Career:** Founder of the literary magazine, *Fortunio*, 1911 (renamed *Cahiers du Sud*, 1925); teacher of English, from 1912; appointed professor at Lycée Condorcet, Paris, 1922, resigned from teaching position after success of play *Marius*, 1929; created film company and founded magazine *Les Cahiers du Film*, 1934; opened studio in Marseilles, 1933; president of Society of French Dramatic Authors and Composers, 1944–46. **Awards:** Officer, Légion d'honneur. **Member:** Académie française, 1947. **Died:** 18 April 1974.

PUBLICATIONS

Plays

Catulle. 1922. *Les Marchands de gloire*, with Paul Nivoix (produced 1926). 1926.
Jazz (produced 1927). 1927.
Topaze (produced 1928). 1930; as *Topaze*, translated by Renée Waldinger, 1958; also translated by Anthony Rossi, 1963; Tom Van Dyke, 1966; David Coward, 1981.
Marius (produced 1929). 1931; translated by Sidney Howard, 1931; also translated by Barbara Bray, 1955.
Fanny (produced 1931). 1932.
Merlusse. 1935; edited by Lucius Gaston Moffatt, 1937.
Cigalon. 1936; edited by John Braddock Sturges, 1948.
César (produced 1945). 1937.
La Femme du boulanger. 1938.
La Fille du puisatier (screenplay). 1941.
Théâtre complet. 1949.
Oeuvres dramatiques, théâtre et cinéma. 1954.
Judas (produced 1955). 1955.
Fabien (produced 1956). 1956.
Naïs. 1977.
La Trilogie marseillaise. 1992.

Screenplays: *Marius*, 1931; *Fanny*, 1932; *Topaze*, 1933; *Un direct au coeur*, 1933; *L'Agonie des aigles*, 1933; *Tartarin de Tarascon*, 1934; *Le Gendre de Monsieur Poirier*, 1934; *Jofroi*, 1934; *L'Article 330*, 1934; *Angèle*, 1934; *Merlusse*, 1935; *Cigalon*, 1935; *César*, 1936; *Regain*, from the novel by Jean Giono, 1937; *La Femme du boulanger*, from the novel by Giono, 1938; *Le Schpountz*, 1938; *Monsieur Brotonneau*, 1939; *La Fille du puisatier*, 1940; *Naïs*, 1945; *La Belle Meunière*, 1948; *Le Rosier de Madame Husson*, 1950; *Carnival*, 1953; *Trois lettres de mon moulin*, from the novel by Daudet, 1954; *La Dame aux camélias*, 1962; *Jean de Florette*, 1986; *Manon des sources*, 1986.

Fiction

Pirouettes. 1932.
L'Eau des collines. 1962; as *The Water of the Hills: Jean de Florette and Manon of the Springs: Two Novels*, translated by W.E. van Heyningen, 1962.

Other

Le Premier amour. 1946.
Notes sur le rire. 1947.
La Belle Meunière (biography of Schubert). 1948.
La Critique des critiques. 1949.
Souvenirs d'enfance (autobiography):
    La Gloire de mon père. 1957; edited by Joseph Marks, 1962; as *My Father's Glory*, translated by Rita Barisse, in *The Days Were Too Short*, 1960.
    Le Château de ma mère. 1958; as *My Mother's Castle*, translated by Rita Barisse, in *The Days Were Too Short*, 1960.
    Le Temps des secrets. 1960; as *The Time of Secrets*, translated by Rita Barisse, 1962.
    Le Temps des amours. 1977; as *The Time of Love*, translated by Eileen Ellenbogen, 1979.
Le Masque de fer. 1964.
Les Sermons de Pagnol, edited by Robert Morel. 1968.
Oeuvres complètes. 12 vols., 1970–71.
Le Secret du masque de fer. 1973.
Cinématurgie de Paris. 1980.
Confidences (autobiography). 1981.
Inédits, edited by Jacqueline and Frédéric Pagnol. 1986.
Translator, *Hamlet*, by Shakespeare. 1953.
Translator, *Les Bucoliques*, by Virgil. 1958.
Translator, *Le Songe d'une nuit d'été*, by Shakespeare. 1970.

*

Critical Studies: *Marcel Pagnol m'a raconté* by Raymond Castans, 1975; *Marcel Pagnol* by C.E.J. Caldicott, 1977; *Il était une fois—Marcel Pagnol*, 1978, *Les Films de Marcel Pagnol*, 1982, and *Marcel Pagnol: biographie*, 1987, all by Raymond Castans; *Marcel Pagnol: Sa vie, son oeuvre*, 1980, and *Merveilleux Pagnol*, 1981, both by Georges Berni; *Marcel Pagnol; ou, Le Cinéma en liberté* by Claude Beylie, 1986; *Le Théâtre de Pagnol: Personnages et thèmes dans les oeuvres de jeunesse* by Paule Gounelle Kline, 1986; *L'Eau des collines: Jean de Florette, Manon des Sources* by David Coward, 1990; *Pagnol* by Jacques Bens, 1994; *Marcel Pagnol à l'école de Jean Giono?: Essai* by Thierry Dehayes, 2001.

* * *

Marcel Pagnol is known primarily as a dramatist and screenwriter, although he is also particularly remembered for his autobiographical writing. Whatever the genre, there are certain key elements in Pagnol's style. He writes of the place he loved and knew best,

Provence. He uses, especially in the plays, a combination of classical French and *marseillaise* idiom. His characters are simple, often naive, allowing Pagnol to portray the vicissitudes of destiny using victims who are too simple to feel the metaphysical horror of their situations. This does not mean that Pagnol's works are cynical in nature: he may recognize the existence of evil, that God is not always kind, but there is an optimistic implication in much of his work, especially the *Marius* trilogy, that everything will reach a satisfactory resolution.

Pagnol's first successful play, *Topaze*, represented an important step in naturalistic theatre. Here Pagnol showed himself to be the heir of Mirbeau and Becque. The play is a comic satire centring on the shabby schoolmaster, Topaze, who loses his job because he cannot bring himself to lie to the mother of a particularly stupid, but wealthy, pupil and because he has the audacity to pursue the headmaster's daughter. The play then follows Topaze's corruption by Castel-Benac and Suzy Courtois. As Topaze becomes wealthy through dubious deals with the council on Castel-Benac's behalf, he loses his moral sense of his wrong doing, until he reaches a point where he is able to push Castel-Benac out of his double-dealing business. In doing so it is apparent that he is likely to win Courtois. This play shows most clearly Pagnol's consciousness of the existence of evil and what might be called the tragedy of existence, particularly with reference to social injustice; as an honest academic Topaze cannot receive the medal he desires so much, but Castel-Benac can buy him one once he has gone over to the side of "evil." Pagnol's moral is clear, that money corrupts, but his satire shows that he has little pity for human weakness. At the beginning of the play he shows us the injustice of Topaze's situation, but this does not excuse his actions and by the end he himself has turned corrupter by trying to lure the honest Tamise into working with him.

Pagnol continued his success with the trilogy which begins with *Marius*. To a great extent the three plays *Marius, Fanny*, and *César* are an expression of Pagnol's cultural and educational heritage. The influence of Molière is apparent in the scenes between Fanny and Pannisse in the first play, which recall the dialogues of *L'École des femmes* (*School for Wives*), while much of the stage business in the plays is borrowed from classical farce. The trilogy depicts a tight-knit community which had vanished both geographically and sociologically by the end of World War II.

Within a year of its performance on stage, *Marius* had been adapted for the cinema. The success of the film lead to the creation of *Fanny*, also subsequently adapted for the screen and, finally *César*, which emerged first as a screenplay and was then adapted for the stage after the production of the film. Pagnol enthusiastically greeted sound cinema and argued with the defenders of silent film, saying that "if a talking film projected without the sound was still comprehensible it was a bad sound film." Pagnol's contribution to French cinema was enormous. In 1934 he founded the company Les Films Marcel Pagnol and was personally involved in the production of his films, many of which he also directed. He founded the magazine *Les Cahiers du Film* in 1935. Even when he was writing for the screen Pagnol's technique was essentially theatrical, as is demonstrated by the *Marius* trilogy, which draws on the traditions of stage melodrama and classical structure. As ever with Pagnol, the focus remains on the dialogue, his own unique blend of classical French and *marseillaise* idiom.

He returned to the theatre in 1955 with *Judas*, a psychological interpretation of the Judas tragedy in the setting of a realistic, broadly conceived environment, with Judas, not Jesus, as the victim most deserving of pity. This play represented a move away from Pagnol's usual setting of France, and perhaps in consequence was less successful than his earlier works.

It is impossible to write of Pagnol without considering his importance as a writer of memoirs, for in this genre he was best able to portray the family and the landscape he loved. Here the pure style of his writing is most apparent. There is also a symmetry to his phrases and in some of the writing, especially *Le Château de ma mère* (*My Mother's Castle*), a poetic elegance in his description of nature which is close to that of Virgil (whose *Bucolics* he translated in 1958).

Pagnol is remembered best, however, for his ability to portray a particular picture of Provence through which we get impressions of a folkloric past. Perhaps this world seems too ideal, based as it is upon simple pleasures and sufferings which are eased by a naive fatalism. Pagnol's world is characteristically a humble one, dominated by family life and a feeling for the fundamental human values.

—Louise Hopkins

PALAMAS, Kostes

Born: Patras, Greece, 13 January 1859. Parents died in childhood; brought up thereafter by uncle in Missolonghi. **Education:** Educated at the High School, Missolonghi, 1870–75; studied law at the University of Athens, from 1875. **Family:** Married Maria Valvi in 1887; two sons (younger son died 1898) and one daughter. **Career:** Worked as a journalist, 1882–97; secretary-general to the University of Athens, 1897–1928. Founder of the "new school of Athens," promoting the use of demotic Greek. **Died:** 27 February 1943.

PUBLICATIONS

Collections

Hapanta. Complete Works, edited by Palamas Foundation. 16 vols., 1960–.

Verse

Tragoudia tes patridos mou [The Songs of My Country]. 1886.
Hymnos eis ten Athenai [Hymn to Athena]. 1889.
Ta matia tes psyches mou [Eyes of My Soul]. 1892.
Iamboi kai anapaistoi. 1897; as *Iambs and Anapaests*, translated by Theodore P. Stephanides and George C. Katsimbalis, in *Selections*, 1978.
Ho taphos. 1898; as *The Grave*, translated by D.A. Michaloros, 1930.
Hoi chairetismoi tes heliogennetis. 1900; as *The Greetings of Iliogenneti, the Sun-Born*, translated by Theodore P. Stephanides and George C. Katsimbalis, in *Selections*, 1978.
He asaleute Zoe. 1904; Part I as *Life Immovable*, translated by A. Phoutrides, 1919; Part II as *A Hundred Voices and Other Poems*, translated by A. Phoutrides, 1921.

Dodekalogos tou gyftou. 1907; as *The Twelve Words of the Gypsy*, translated by Frederic Will, 1964; also translated by Theodore P. Stephanides and George C. Katsimbalis, 1974; as *The Twelve Lays of the Gypsy*, translated by George Thomson, 1969.

Ho phlogera tou vasilia. 1910; as *The King's Flute*, translated by Frederic Will, 1967; also translated by Theodore P. Stephanides and George C. Katsimbalis, 1978.

He politeia kai he monadzia [The City and the Solitude] (selected verse). 1912.

Hoi chaimoi tes limnothalasses [The Sorrows of the Lagoon] (selected verse). 1912.

Vomoi [The Altars]. 1915.

Ta parakaira [Untimely Poems]. 1919.

Ta dekatetrasticha [The 14 Lines]. 1919.

Hoi pentasyllavoi kai ta pathetika kryphomilemata [The Five Syllables and the Pathetic Whispers]. 1925.

Poems, translated by Theodore P. Stephanides and George C. Katsimbalis. 1925.

Deikoi kai sklefoi stichoi [Timid and Cruel Verses]. 1928.

Ho kyklos ton tetrastichon [The Cycle of Quatrains]. 1929.

He ksanatonismene musike [Double-Stressed Music]. 1930.

Perasmata ke kayretismoi [Passages and Greetings]. 1931.

Oi nychtes tov Phemiov [The Nights of Phemius]. 1935.

Three Poems (includes "The Palm Tree"; "The Chains"; "The Satyr or Song of Nakedness"), translated by Theodore P. Stephanides and George C. Katsimbalis. 1969.

Selections, translated by Theodore P. Stephanides and George C. Katsimbalis. 1978.

Fiction

Thanatos pallekariou (story). 1884; as *A Man's Death*, translated by A. Phoutrides, 1934.

Plays

Trisevgheni. 1903; as *Royal Blossoms: or Trisevyene*, translated by A. Phoutrides, 1923.

Other

To ergon tou Krystale [The Work of Kristallis]. 1894.

Solomos. 1901.

Pragmata [Things]. 2 vols., 1904–07.

Heroika prosopa kai keimena [Heroic Characters and Texts]. 1911.

Ta prota kritika [First Critical Essays]. 1913.

Aristoteles Valaorites. 1914.

Viksuinos kai Krystales [Viksyinos and Krystallis]. 1916.

Ioulios Typaldos. 1916.

Pos tragoudoume to thanato tes choras [How We Sing about the Death of the Country]. 1918.

Peksoi dromoi [Footpaths]. 2 vols., 1929.

E Poietike mou [My Poetics]. 1933.

*

Critical Studies: *A Study on the Palm-Tree of Kostes Palamas* by Leandros K. Palamas, 1931; *Costis Palamas: Un aperçu de sa vie et de l'oeuvre du poète* by M. Peridis, 1938; *Palamas: An Inaugural Lecture (King's College London)* by R.J.H. Jenkins, 1947; *Kostis Palamas* by Thanasis Mascaleris, 1972; "Meter and Mood in Palamas' Dodecalogue of the Gypsy" by Margaret C. Carroll, in *Annual Publication of the Center for Neo-Hellenic Studies Austin*, 3, 1978; *Kostes Palamas, a Great Modern Greek Poet* by Robin A. Fletcher, 1984.

* * *

Kostes Palamas, who described himself as a poet of his time and his nation, is the leading figure of what became known as the "Generation of 1880." A prolific writer, his posthumously published *Complete Works* comprises 16 volumes of poetry, prose, drama, critical essays, and translations, while further volumes exist containing his correspondence.

Together with other poets and writers of the "Generation of 1880," Palamas promoted the use of demotic (the language of the people) and established it as a literary language, replacing *katharevousa*, the purist imitation of ancient Greek. This change of course in Greek literature is one manifestation of an ideology which, at the beginning of the 20th century, revolved around the twofold attempt to reform Greek society and expand the Greek state. The latter attempt, known as the "Great Idea," was behind Greece's victorious participation in the two Balkan wars of 1912 and 1913, and was brought to a disastrous end by the Asia Minor débâcle of 1922.

One of the two general categories into which Palamas's poetic work may be divided, long epic poems, can only be truly understood in this context. The two most important works in this category— *Dodekalogos tou gyftou* (*The Twelve Words of the Gypsy*) and *Ho phlogera tou vasilia* (*The King's Flute*)—present two different, but related, aspects of the role of the poet. The first, published in 1907, has a historical setting: the decline of the Byzantine Empire. The speaker, the Gypsy of the title, presents himself as the individual who not only differs from everybody else, but also rejects all things sacred: pagan and Christian beliefs; respect for the ancient literary and philosophical tradition, and the idea of a national homeland. He ends by listening to the voice of nature, which tells him that Truth can only be found in the harmonization of himself with nature. If the Gypsy's "prophetic violin" is individualistic, in the sense that the poet's persona follows a controversial process and proclaims a universal role for his art only after having established his absolute independence from his environment, *The King's Flute* blows a national, and even a nationalistic, song. Set once more in the last years of Byzantium, the poem harks back to the Empire's apogee, since the resounding flute is that of the dead emperor Basil II. The King's flute relates the King's victorious deeds, before his corpse turns to dust. Its song, written by the poet in 1910, is again characterized as "prophetic," this time in the more obvious sense that the lands over which the emperor Basil II reigned are those the poet urges his compatriots to recapture during the forthcoming Balkan wars. Apart from drawing on Byzantine history, the poem draws heavily on Byzantine literary tradition, combining it with Ancient and Modern Greek literary traditions and thus realizing on the literary level the continuity of Greek history posited by the historian Konstantinos Paparregopoulos in the ideological context of the "Great Idea."

While these epics were the poems for which Palamas was best known during his lifetime, the poems that have since gained more popularity are those of the second category: short, lyric poems, which deal with love, death, and nature, draw on the folk tradition, and often, especially in the poet's later years, express doubts both about his own powers and about the effect and duration of his work. One of his best known of these is *Ho taphos* (*The Grave*), which laments the death of the poet's youngest son, Alkis, in 1898; another, "Askraios," connects Palamas with Hesiod and promotes poetry with peaceful, everyday subject matter.

Palamas's most famous prose work, *Thanatos pallekariou* (*A Man's Death*), found a later echo in Greek literature in a story by the writer Stratis Myrivilis, but neither Palamas's prose nor his play, *Trisevgheni* (*Royal Blossoms*), can equal the importance and influence of his poetry. Conversely, his critical work is of considerable importance. Palamas was the first to "discover" the 19th-century poet Andreas Kalvos and to establish him, together with the other famous Ionian Islands poet, Dionysios Solomos, as the main figures on whom 20th-century poetic tradition was founded. With his numerous essays on Greek and European writers, Palamas introduced European literary currents into Greece (a task also achieved through his translations) and sought to merge these currents into Greek literary tradition. Moreover, his essays concerning his own work, the most important of which is *E Poietike mou* [My Poetics], reveal an acute understanding of the context in which his poetry belongs, describe accurately his aims, and define as the unifying element of all his protean poetry his "passion for song."

In one of these essays, employed as the preface to *Hoi pentasyllavoi kai ta pathetika kryphomilemata* [The Five Syllables and the Pathetic Whispers], Palamas states that he belongs to the period before World War I. This is true to the extent that his poetics was formed within the historical framework of the late 19th and early 20th centuries and expressed the aspirations of that time. Nevertheless, the less bombastic productions of his later years should not be overlooked.

Apart from expressing the national aspirations of his time and introducing European poetic currents into Greece, Palamas's major contributions can be considered to be the establishment of a new poetic language, based on the demotic form and consisting of numerous metrical forms and rhyme schemes, as well as the preoccupation with a variety of subjects that have served as points of reference for subsequent literary generations.

—Elli Philokyprou

PARDO BAZÁN, Emilia

Born: La Coruña, Galicia, Spain, 16 September 1851. **Education:** Self-educated. **Family:** Married José Quiroga Pérez Pinal in 1868 (separated 1885; died 1921); two daughters and one son. **Career:** Moved to Madrid, 1886, and frequented court and artistic circles; after marriage, travelled to Paris, London, Italy, and Austria, 1871–72; contributor of stories and articles to various periodicals, including *La Ciencia Cristiana*, 1876–81, *La Revista Compostelana*, 1876–77, *Revista de España, La Época*, 1882, *La Ilustración Artística*, from 1886, and *España Moderna*, 1889–90; travelled to Paris, and met several prominent French writers, 1886; visited Portugal and Paris, 1888; founding editor, *El Nuevo Teatro Crítico*, Madrid, 1891–93; contributor, *Blanco y Negro*, 1895–1920, *La Ilustración Española*, from 1908, *La Esfera*, from 1910, and *Los Contemporáneos*, from 1914; adviser to the Ministry of Education, 1910; professor of romance literature, Central University, Madrid, 1916; contributor, *Raza española*, 1919–21; contributor, *ABC*. First female president,

literary section of the Atheneum, Madrid, 1906. **Award:** Created Countess, 1908. **Died:** 12 May 1921.

PUBLICATIONS

Collections

Obras completas. 43 vols., 1891–1926.
Obras completas (novelas y cuentos), edited by Federico Carlos Sáinz de Robles. 2 vols., 1947–58; revised edition, with additional volume edited by Harry L. Kirby, Jr., 1973.
Cuentos completos, edited by Juan Paredes Núñez. 4 vols., 1990.
"The White Horse" and Other Stories, translated by Robert M. Fedorchek, 1993.
Torn Lace and Other Stories, translated by Maria Cristina Urruela, 1996.

Fiction

Pascual López, autobiografía de un estudiante de medicina. 1879.
Un viaje de novios. 1881; edited by Mariano Baquero Goyanes, 1971; as *A Wedding Trip*, translated by Mary J. Serrano, 1891.
La tribuna. 1883; as *The Tribune of the People*, translated by Walter Borenstein, 1999.
La dama joven y otros cuentos, illustrated by M. Obiols Delgado. 1885.
El cisne de Vilamorta. 1885; as *The Swan of Vilamorta*, translated by Mary J. Serrano, 1891; as *Shattered Hope; or, The Swan of Vilamorta*, translated by Serrano, 1900.
Los pazos de Ulloa. 1886; edited by Marina Mayoral, 1986, and Nelly Clémessy, 1987; as *The Son of the Bondwoman*, translated by Ethel Harriet Hearn, 1908; as *The House of Ulloa*, translated by Paul O'Prey and Lucia Graves, 1990; also translated by Roser Caminals-Heath, 1992.
La madre naturaleza. 1887.
Insolación. 1889; as *Midsummer Madness*, translated by Amparo Loring, 1907.
Morriña. 1889; as *Homesickness*, translated by Mary J. Serrano, 1891.
Una cristiana. 1890; as *A Christian Woman*, translated by Mary A. Springer, 1891; as *Secret of the Yew Tree; or, A Christian Woman*, translated by Springer, 1900.
La prueba. 1890.
La piedra angular. 1891; as *The Angular Stone*, translated by Mary J. Serrano, 1892.
Cuentos escogidos. 1891.
Cuentos de Marineda. 1892.
Adán y Eva: Doña Milagros. 1894.
Cuentos nuevos. 1894.
Novelas ejemplares. 1895.
Arco iris. 1896.
Adán y Eva: Memorias de un solterón. 1896.
El tesoro de Gastón. 1897.
El saludo de las brujas. 1898.
Cuentos de amor. 1898.
Cuentos de la patria. 1898.
Cuentos sacro-profanos. 1899.
El niño de Guzmán. 1899.

Un destripador de antaño y otros cuentos. 1900; "Un destripador de antaño" as "The Heart Lover," translated by Edward and Elizabeth Huberman, in *Great Spanish Short Stories*, 1962.

A Galician Girl's Romance, translated by Mary J. Serrano. 1900.

Cuentos dramáticos: En tranvía. 1901.

Cuentos de Navidad y Reyes. 1902.

Cuentos antiguos. 1902.

Misterio. 1903; as *The Mystery of the Lost Dauphin (Louis XVII)*, translated by Annabel Nord Seeger, 1906.

La quimera. 1905; edited by Marina Mayoral, 1991.

Novelas ejemplares: Los tres arcos de Cirilo; Un drama; Mujer. 1906.

Cuentos del terruño. 1907.

El fondo del alma (stories). 1907.

Allenda a verdad. 1908.

La sirena negra. 1908.

Finafrol. 1909.

Sud exprés y otros cuentos. 1909.

Dulce dueño. 1911; edited by Marina Mayoral, 1989.

Belcebú: Novelas breves. 1912.

Arrastrada. 1912.

Cuentos trágicos. 1913.

Cuentos de la tierra. 1922.

Cuadros religiosos. 1925.

Short Stories, translated by Albert Shapiro and F.J. Hurley. 1935.

Pardo Bazán (selected stories), edited by Carmen Castro. 1945.

Cuentos, edited by J. de Entrambasaguas. 1952.

Cuentos (selection), edited by Juan Paredes Núñez. 1984.

Cuentos y novelas de la tierra, edited by Marina Mayoral. 1984.

Las setas y otros cuentos (selection), edited by Carmen Bravo-Villasante. 1988.

Mejores cuentos. 1990.

Verse

Jaime. 1876.

Plays

La suerte. 1904.

Cuesta abajo. 1906.

Verdad. 1906.

Teatro (includes *Verdad; Cuesta abajo; Juventad; Las raíces; El vestido de boda; El becerro de metal; La suerte*). 1909.

Other

Estudio crítico de las obras del Padre Feijoo. 1876.

San Francisco de Asís, Siglo XIII. 1882.

La cuestión palpitante (essays). 1883; edited by Carmen Bravo-Villasante, 1966, and by José Manuel González Herrán, 1988.

Folklore gallego (miscellany), with others. 1884.

La leyenda de la Pastoriza. 1887.

La revolución y la novela en Rusia. 3 vols., 1887; as *Russia, Its People and Its Literature*, translated by Fanny Hale Gardiner, 1890.

Mi romería (reminiscences). 1888.

De mi tierra (criticism). 1888.

Los pedagogos del renacimiento. 1889.

Al pie de la torre Eiffel (on the 1889 Paris Exhibition). 1889.

Por Francia y por Alemania: Crónica de la exposición. 1890.

Españoles ilustres: El P. Luis Coloma: Biografía y estudio crítico. 1891.

Los franciscanos y Colón. 1892.

Alarcón: Estudio crítico. 1892.

Polémicas y estudios literarios. 1892.

Campoamor (biography). 1893.

Los poetas épicos cristianos (criticism). 1894.

Por la España pintoresca: Viajes. 1895.

Hombres y mujeres de antaño. 1896.

Vida contemporánea. 1896.

La España de ayer y la de hoy. 1899.

El Imparcial: Cuarenta días en la exposición. 1900.

De siglo a siglo (essays). 1902.

Los franciscanos y el descubrimiento de América. 1902.

Por la Europa católica. 1902.

Goya y la espontaneidad española. 1905.

Lecciones de literatura. 1906.

Retratos y apuntes literarios. 1908.

La literatura franscesa moderna. 3 vols., 1910–14; additional volume *La decadencia*, 1961.

La cocina española antigua. 1913.

Hernán Cortés y sus hazañas (for children). 1914.

La cocina española moderna. 1916.

El porvenir de la literatura después de la guerra (lectures). 1917.

El lirismo en la poesía francesa. 1923.

Obras escogidas, edited by Federico Carlos Sáinz de Robles. 1943.

Cartas a Benito Pérez Galdós (1889–1890), edited by Carmen Bravo-Villasante. 1975.

La mujer española y otros artículos feministas (essays), edited by de Leda Schiavo. 1976.

Cartas inéditas a Pardo Bazán (letters), edited by Ana María Freire López. 1991.

Los Santos Reyes. 1992.

*

Critical Studies: *Two Modern Spanish Novelists: Pardo Bazán and Armando Palacio Valdés* by C.C. Glasnock, 1926; *Emilia Pardo Bazán: Novelista de Galicia* by Emilio González López, 1944; "Pardo Bazán and the Literary Polemics about Feminism" by Ronald Hilton, in *Romanic Review*, 44, 1953; *The Catholic Naturalism of Pardo Bazán* by Donald Fowler Brown, 1957; *Vida y obra de Emilia Pardo Bazán* (includes bibliography) by Carmen Bravo-Villasante, 1962; *Emilia Pardo Bazán: Su vida y sus obras* by Robert E. Osborne, 1964; "Observations on the Narrative Method, the Psychology, and the Style of *Los Pazos de Ulloa*" by Robert E. Lott, in *Hispania*, 52, 1969; *Emilia Pardo Bazán* by Mariano Baquero Goyanes, 1971; *Pardo Bazán* by Walter Pattison, 1971; *El naturalismo en la Pardo Bazán* by Fernando J. Barroso, 1973; *Estructuras novelísticas de Emilia Pardo Bazán* by Benito Valera Jácome, 1973; "Pardo Bazán's Pessimistic View of Love as Revealed in *Cuentos de amor*" by Thomas Feeny, in *Hispanófila*, 23, September 1978; "Feminism and the Feminine in Pardo Bazán's Novels" by Mary E. Giles, in *Hispania*, 63, 1980; *Emilia Pardo Bazán como novelista* by Nelly Clémessy, 1982; *Emilia Pardo Bazán: The Making of a Novelist*, 1983, and "Pardo Bazán and the Rival Claims of Religion and Art," in *Bulletin of Hispanic Studies*, 66(3), 1989, both by Maurice Hemingway; "The *Femme Fatale*: Emilia Pardo Bazán's Portrayal of

Evil and Fascinating Women'' by Phoebe Porter, in *La Chispa '87: Selected Proceedings* edited by Gilbert Paolini, 1987; "*La quimera* of Emilia Pardo Bazán: The Pre-Raphaelite Factor in the Regeneration of a Decadent Dandy,'' in *Hispania*, 70(4), 1987, and *La quimera de Pardo Bazán y la literatura finiscular*, 1988, both by Daniel S. Whitaker; *Emilia Pardo Bazán: Novelista de Galicia* by P. González Martínez, 1988; *The Early Pardo Bazán: Theme and Narrative Technique in the Novels of 1879–89* by David Henn, 1988; *Estudios sobre Los pazos de Ulloa* edited by Marina Mayoral, 1989; *La condición humana en Emilia Pardo Bazán* by Delfín García Guerra, 1990; *In the Feminine Mode* edited by Nöel Valis and Carol Maier, 1990; *Portrait of a Woman as Artist: Emilia Pardo Bazán and the Modern Novel in France and Spain* by Francisca González-Arias, 1992; *Cigar Smoke and Violet Water: Gendered Discourse in the Stories of Emilia Pardo Bazán* by Joyce Tolliver, 1998.

* * *

Considered by many critics to be one of Spain's finest women writers, ranking second only to the venerable St. Teresa of Ávila, Emilia Pardo Bazán is remarkable for both the quantity and the quality of her literary output. Although she may be best known as a novelist, Pardo Bazán also wrote short stories, biography, literary criticism, and history. In all areas her achievements are significant: her stories number in the hundreds; leading journals of the day published her essays on literature and culture; she founded, and was the sole contributor to, the monthly journal *El Nuevo Teatro Crítico* [New Critical Theatre], that appeared for over two years.

Educated and cosmopolitan, Pardo Bazán in her travels, especially to France, came into contact with vital artistic forces that attracted her intellectually. She studied seriously the literary movements she encountered, going so far as to write books on the Russian novel and modern French literature. Given her solid understanding of European literature, she bears the description of ''eclectic'' as a just tribute.

However, it is in the genre of the novel that Pardo Bazán gained most attention, particularly when she emerged as the apparent champion of the French movement of Naturalism with the publication of her critical work *La cuestión palpitante* [The Palpitating Question] in 1883. However much she lauded the realism of the French novel with its eye for detail, Pardo Bazán was reluctant to espouse the theories of Émile Zola, finding his advocacy of scientific determinism unpalatable to her Catholic tastes. Yet even her modified acceptance of Naturalism was sufficient to raise the hackles of conservatives, who attacked her position on two counts: theoretically, determinism was incompatible with Catholic teaching on free will; and personally, Pardo Bazán was a scandal to her sex and her society for writing of matters that were not proper for a lady, and that smacked of heresy as well.

Careful reading of both *La cuestión palpitante* and the novels that are associated with her Naturalism, principally *Los pazos de Ulloa* (*The House of Ulloa*) and *La madre naturaleza* [Mother Nature], shows clearly that Pardo Bazán did not subscribe wholeheartedly to the tenets of Naturalism. Although she employs the methods of Zola in the realistic depiction of people, scenes, and events, detailing the interiors of buildings and her characters' physical appearance with exactitude, and bringing landscapes to the forefront in descriptions that may extend for several pages, there is nothing of the determinist in her approach to characterization. True, the force of the environment

is strong, but the grinding pessimism and failure of will that typify a Zola novel are absent in Pardo Bazáin's writing.

Modified Naturalism characterizes only a portion of Pardo Bazán's novelistic corpus, from the appearance of her first novel, *Pascual López*, in 1879, through that of *Morriña* (*Homesickness*) in 1889. The following year saw the publication of a two-part novel, *Una cristiana* (*A Christian Woman*) and *La prueba* [The Test], in which the spiritual dimensions that had been obvious, although secondary, in the naturalistic writings now dominate. After a second period in which the spiritual and naturalist notes strike the balance of traditional Spanish realism, Pardo Bazán gave full voice to spirituality in *La quimera* [The Chimera], *La sirena negra* [The Black Siren], and *Dulce dueño* [Sweet Master].

The periods into which the novels of Pardo Bazán fall coincide with literary movements in Europe. Thus, when the French theorists and novelists advanced a novel that was founded on the determinism of environment and heredity, Pardo Bazán imitated their taste for exact description, but without subscribing to the moral significance of the environment that was the subject of description. When *fin de siècle* writers turned inward in pursuit of psychological and spiritual meaning, so did Pardo Bazán, giving shape in her last novels to the spiritual inclination that informed all of her writing to some degree.

That Pardo Bazán was influenced by these movements does not mean that she was without an aesthetic centre of her own. Evidence lies in her development of spiritual themes. Early in her career she wrote *Los poetas épicos cristianos* [Christian Epic Poets] and *San Francisco de Asís* [Saint Francis of Assisi], studies that appear have to have been generated out of her own religious and spiritual proclivities, The study of St. Francis is especially important for understanding such figures as the priest Julian in *The House of Ulloa*, while Pardo Bazán's grounding in Christian mysticism is a key to the characterization of Nucha, from the same novel, and Carmen in *A Christian Woman* and *La prueba*. These characters prefigure the protagonists of the last three novels, whose narratives of religious conversions qualify as mystical journeys of purgation, illumination, and union. Mysticism may have been fashionable as a literary theme when Pardo Bazán wrote these novels, but her reasons for writing in this mode had more to do with a much-documented inclination for the tradition of Christian mysticism than with the vagaries of literary fashion.

Richly textured, Pardo Bazán's writings, especially her novels, have attracted the attention of literary critics for over a century. In her time, critical questions centred on her identity as a woman, a Christian, and a Spaniard. In the 20th century, earlier generations of critics applied biographical and historical methodologies to assess her contribution to the development of the Spanish novel, and to see in her female characters the manifestation of feminism for which the author was both praised and attacked. Under the urgings of the New Criticism, questions of style, narrative structure, coherence, and descriptive technique claimed centre stage. Recent scholarship relies on feminist criticism and psychological insights to illuminate the centrality of her female characters, and to cast Pardo Bazán as a model for women writers today. Just as she developed as a writer through identifiable stages, so has the scholarship surrounding her work been subject to a process of analysis by which new perspectives bring new understanding and renewed appreciation for a writer of noteworthy accomplishment in many areas.

—Mary E. Giles

PASCAL, Blaise

Born: Clermont-Ferrand, Auvergne, France, 19 June 1623. Moved with family to Paris, 1632, then to Rouen, 1640. **Education:** Educated mostly at home by his father; attended meetings at Académie Mersenne 1639, 1648–54, members included Roberval, Desargues, Mydorge, and Gassendi. **Career:** Scientist and mathematician; developed first calculating machine, *"la pascaline,"* 1642–45; conducted early experiments in connection with problem of the vacuum, 1646–48; developed system of cheap public transport in Paris, 1660–62, opened in 1662. Converted to Jansenism, 1646; returned to Paris on father's second retirement, 1647; second conversion—called his *nuit de feu*—23 November 1654. Lived in Paris for latter part of life, with occasional visits to Jansenist community of Port-Royal des Champs. **Died:** 19 August 1662.

PUBLICATIONS

Collections

Oeuvres complètes, edited by Léon Brunschvig. 14 vols., 1904–14.
Oeuvres complètes, edited by Jacques Chevalier. 1957.
Textes inédits, edited by Jean Mesnard. 1962.
Oeuvres complètes, edited by Louis Lafuma. 1963.
Oeuvres complètes, edited by Jean Mesnard. 2 vols., 1964–70.
Album Pascal, edited by Bernard Dorival. 1978.
The Mind on Fire (selection; includes *Pensées* and *Lettres provinciales*), edited by James Houston. 1989.
Pensées and Other Writings, translated by Honor Levi. 1999.

Works

Essai pour les coniques (on projective geometry). 1640.
Expériences nouvelles. 1648.
Lettres provinciales (published pseudonymously). 1656–57; edited by Louis Cognet, 1965; *as The Provincial Letters*, translated by William Andrews, 1744; also translated by W.F. Trotter and Thomas M'Crie, 1847; A.J. Krailsheimer, 1966.
Traitez de l'équilibre des ligneurs et de la pesanteur de la masse de l'air. 1663; as *The Physical Treatises of Pascal: The Equilibrium of Liquids and the Weight of the Mass of the Air*, translated by J.H.B. and A.G.H. Spiers, 1937.
Traité du triangle arithmétique. 1665.
Pensées. 1670; edited by Etienne Périer, 1670, revised edition, 1684; also edited by Charles Bossut, 1779, A.P. Faugère, 1844, Georges Brunet, 1956, Louis Marin, 1969, and by P. Sellier, 1976; as *Pensées sur la religion, et sur quelques autres sujets*, edited by Louis Lafuma, 3 vols., 1948; translated by J. Walker, 1688; also translated by Basil Kennet, 1704; E. Craig, 1825; Isaac Taylor, 1905; H.F. Stewart, 1950; John Warrington, 1960; J.M. Cohen, 1961; Martin Turnell, 1962; W.F. Trotter, 1965; A.J. Krailsheimer, 1966; John Cruickshank, 1983.
Abrégé de la vie de Jésus-Christ. 1846; as *Short Life of Christ*, translated by Émile Cailliet and John C. Blankenagel, 1950.
Opuscules philosophiques. 1864.
Nouvelle collection d'ouvrages philosophiques. 1875.
Discours sur les passions de l'amour (attributed to Pascal). 1881, edited by G. Michaut, 1900.

De l'esprit géométrique. 1886; translated by Richard Scofield, in *Pascal: Great Books of the Western World*, 33, edited by R.M. Hutchins and M.J. Adler, 1952.
Pensées et opuscules, edited by Léon Brunschvicg. 1897.
Discours de la condition de l'homme. 1948.
Great Shorter Works of Pascal, translated by E. Cailliet and John C. Blankenagel. 1948.

*

Bibliography: *Bibliography Blaise Pascal (1960–1969)* by Lane M. Heller and Thérèse Goyet, 1989.

Critical Studies: *Pascal: The Revival of Pascal: A Study of His Relation to Modern French Thought* by Dorothy M. Eastwood, 1936; *A Short Introduction to a Study of the Pensées* by Philip G. Holden, 1951; *Pascal's Unfinished Apology: A Study of His Plan* by Marie-Louise Hubert, 1952; *Discours sur les passions de l'amour de Pascal* by A. Ducas, 1953; *Blaise Pascal: The Life and Work of a Realist* by Ernest Mortimer, 1959; *The Prejudices of Pascal* by Malcolm Vivian Hay, 1962; *The Hidden God: A Study of Tragic Vision in the Pensées of Pascal* by Lucien Goldmann, 1964; *Pascal* by Jack H. Broome, 1965; *Pascal* by Jean Mesnard, 1965, translated by Claude and Marcia Abraham, 1969; *Pascal's Recovery of Man's Wholeness* by Albert N. Wells, 1965; *Pascal for Our Time* by R. Guardini, 1966; *The Rhetoric of Pascal* by P.M. Topliss, 1966; *Pascal and Theology* by Jean Miel, 1969; *La Bible selon Pascal* by A. Gounelle, 1970; *Pascal et Montaigne: Étude des réminiscences des Essais dans l'oeuvre de Pascal* by Bernard Croquette, 1974; *Blaise Pascal: The Genius of His Thought* by Roger Hazelton, 1974; *Studies in Pascal's Ethics* by A.W.S. Baird, 1975; *Strange Contrarieties: Pascal in England During the Age of Reason* by John Barker, 1975; *La critique du discours: sur la "Logique de Port-Royal" et les "Pensées" de Pascal* by Louis Marin, 1975; *Du Vide à Dieu: essai sur la physique de Pascal* by Pierre Guenancia, 1976; *Pascal's "Provincial Letters": An Introduction* by Walter Rex, 1977; *Humor in Pascal* by Olga Wester Russell, 1977; *The Origins of Certainty: Means and Meanings in Pascal's "Pensées,"* 1979, and *Blaise Pascal*, 1983, both by Hugh M. Davidson; *Pascal* by A.J. Krailsheimer, 1980; *Pascal; ou, Le Risque de l'espérance* by Pierre-Alain Cahné, 1981; *Pascal: Adversary and Advocate* by Robert J. Nelson, 1981; *L'Écriture et le reste: The Pensées of Pascal in the Exegetical Tradition of Port-Royal* by David Wetsel, 1981; *Blaise Pascal: Une biographie spirituelle* by Henri Schmitz du Moulin, 1982; *Pascal: Pensées* by John Cruickshank, 1983; *Pascal et la raison du politique* by Gérard Ferreyrolles, 1984; *Pascal entre Eudoxe et Cantor* by Jean-Louis Gardies, 1984; *The Composition of Pascal's Apologia* by Anthony R. Pugh, 1984; *Pascal; ou, La Simplicité* by Ivan Gobry, 1985; *Neither Angel nor Beast: The Life and Work of Blaise Pascal* by Francis X. J. Coleman, 1986; *Blaise Pascal: Conversion et apologétique* by Henri Gouhier, 1986; *Blaise Pascal 1623–1662* by Hans Loeffel, 1987; *Portraits of Thought: Knowledge, Methods and Styles in Pascal* by Buford Norman, 1988; *Le Problème herméneutique chez Pascal* by Pierre Force, 1989; *Pascal's "Lettres Provinciales"* by Richard Parish, 1989; *Pascal: La Clé du chiffre* by Pierre Magnard, 1991; *The Rehabilitation of the Body as a Means of Knowing in Pascal's Philosophy of Experience* by Jennifer Yhap, 1991; *Gambling on God: Essays on Pascal's Wagner*, edited by Jeff Jordan, 1993; *"Infini rien": Pascal's Wager and the Human Paradox* by Leslie Armour, 1993; *Pascal and the Arts of the Mind* by Hugh M. Davidson, 1993;

Pascal and Disbelief: Catechesis and Conversion in the Pensées by David Wetsel, 1994; *Playing with Truth: Language and the Human Condition in Pascal's Pensées* by Nicholas Hammond, 1994; *Pascal: The Man and His Two Loves* by John R. Cole, 1995; *God Owes Us Nothing: A Brief Remark on Pascal's Religion and On the Spirit of Jansenism* by Leszek Kolakowski, 1995; *Blaise Pascal: Mathematician, Physicist, and Thinker about God* by Donald Adamson, 1995; *Blaise Pascal: Reasons of the Heart* by Marvin R. O'Connell, 1997.

* * *

Blaise Pascal was a unique blend of mathematician, physicist, and man of letters, equally important in his contributions to science and to the arts. He lived during the time of the great flowering of scientific studies in the 17th century, belonging to the generation which succeeded Galileo, Cavalieri, and Torricelli; he was a contemporary of Descartes, Fermat, Huygens, and Sir Christopher Wren. Renowned as both mathematician and physicist, he numbers among his scientific achievements a treatise on conic sections, the final irrefutable proof of the existence both of barometric pressure and of vacuums, work on the theory of probability, and an intensive study of the properties of the cycloid curve.

Whereas his scientific writings were written for the most part in Latin, his literary ones were in French. All his nonscientific writings concern human life in its religious and philosophical aspects, whether he wrote as the partisan of a particular sectarian point of view, or as an apologist for the Christian religion generally, or as the author of miscellaneous treatises.

His first great literary work was *Lettres provinciales* (*The Provincial Letters*). These 18 letters are some of the most outstanding examples of invective that the world has seen. In them Pascal takes the part of the Jansenists against the Jesuits, combating the Society of Jesus first in terms of dogmatic theology (the doctrine of grace) and then (on a firmer premise) from the standpoint of moral theology. He argues that the permissiveness of their approach to the sacrament of penance will give rise within human society to a terrifying moral laxity. He seeks to demonstrate that the full extent of this permissiveness will include acts of fornication by monks, unduly lenient treatment of bankrupts, and even murder.

Pascal cunningly constructed *The Provincial Letters* in such a way as to be almost beyond reproach, and yet the fact remains that he was unduly harsh towards the Jesuits. His device of letters written to a friend (later to be imitated by Montesquieu and Voltaire) allows him to assume the persona of an intelligent but uncommitted man of the world, unversed in theological controversy. Thus the issues at stake between the parties are comically oversimplified. The man of the world displays a freshness and simplicity of outlook which entirely subverts conventional ways of looking at things, foreshadowing in this respect a technique of Voltaire's short stories. Moreover, by means of his invention of the "Jesuit father" (the protagonist of Letters 4–10) Pascal can greatly overstate the excesses of probabilism: all that the Jesuit priest says *may* happen undoubtedly may do so, but this does not mean that it often will. Pascal's quotations from Jesuit moral theologians are so chosen and arranged as to convey a much more ominous impression of the Society of Jesus than was actually justified.

In *Pensées* [Thoughts] he turns from fierce invective to the art of more gentle persuasion, though all tones and moods find expression in the work. He addresses the atheist and agnostic (but particularly the latter): this unbeliever is a gentleman of some culture and intellect. As a work of religious apologetics, *Pensées* stands equal to the writings of St. Augustine, Tertullian, Kierkegaard, and Newman. A great part of its appeal to the reader lies precisely in the aura of mystery which surrounds it—no one being at all sure what eventual form the book would have taken. It is clear, however, that it would have had two main thrusts: first, as an analysis of the fallibility of human nature; and later, as an attempt to complete the conversion by means of copious reference to the Scriptures. The connecting link between these two lines of argument would have been the thought on the Wager, which urges the unbeliever to gamble on the possibility of a Christian afterlife.

Pascal bases his explanation of human fallibility upon the doctrine of original sin. He denies that a man's sensuality can be perfectly fulfilled by hedonism or that his mind can be wholly satisfied by the so-called certainties of human knowledge. But, he argues, the passionate nature of man must be subdued before he is ready to face up to the ultimate truth of life (and death) and all that may arise from it; and even when searching in the Scriptures for proofs of the certainty of the Christian religion, man must accept that at the heart of the religion there is a Hidden God.

Pascal writes with vibrant, relentless urgency. In his wide-ranging vocabulary he is the very opposite of Racine; but he is at one with his fellow Jansenist in underlining the tragic aspects of human life. With pathos, he evokes a graveside scene; lyrically, he invokes the waters of Babylon; epically, he surveys the cosmos and the wide sweep of human history; dramatically, he puts words into the mouth of the Jesuit priest or assails his agnostic interlocutor with arguments concerning the Wager. In his denunciation of the Jesuits he is a master of invective, the equal of Demosthenes, Juvenal, and Swift. In the 12th *Provincial Letter* he proves to be a master of the syllogism; in *Abrégé de la vie de Jésus-Christ* (*Short Life of Christ*), a devotional meditation on Jesus Christ the Logos, he is a writer of poetic mysticism. But, above all, he resembles the ancient Greek authors in that he calls a spade a spade, seemingly reaching out to the true nature of things rather than refracting that truth through the prism of a conventional rhetoric.

The *Pensées* often favour a terse, staccato style compounded of vivid imagenery, anacoluthon, apostrophe, and ellipsis. By such means Pascal strives to reflect the paradoxes and dilemmas of man and to reveal the world in a new light. Yet, idiosyncratic though his style was by the very nature of its origin and purpose, it nevertheless laid the foundations of modern French prose.

—Donald Adamson

PASOLINI, Pier Paolo

Born: Bologna, Italy, 5 March 1922. **Education:** Educated at Reggio Emiliale Galvani school, Bologna, until 1937; University of Bologna, until 1943, Ph.D. **Military Service:** Served in the Italian army, 1943; regiment taken prisoner by Germans following the Italian surrender, escaped and took refuge with family in Casara. **Career:** Writer, film director, and actor. Founder, Academy of Friulian Language, 1944; secretary of Communist Party cell in Casara, 1947; accused of corrupting minors, sacked from teaching post, moved to Rome, 1949; teacher in Ciampino, suburb of Rome, early 1950s; following publication of *Ragazzi di vita*, indicted for obscenity, 1955; editor, *Officina*,

Bologna, 1955–58; columnist, *Tempo Illustrato*; prosecuted for "vilification of the Church" for directing "La ricotta" episode of *Ro Go Pag*, 1963. **Awards:** (for films): Karlovy Vary Festival award, 1962; Silver Bear award 1971; Golden Bear award, 1972; Cannes special jury award, 1974; (for verse): Viareggio prize, 1958. **Died:** (murdered) 2 November 1975.

PUBLICATIONS

Collection

Opere. 1978–.

Fiction

Ragazzi di vita. 1955; as *The Ragazzi*, translated by Emile Capouya, 1968.
Una vita violenta. 1959; as *A Violent Life*, translated by William Weaver, 1968.
Il sogno di una cosa. 1962; as *A Dream of Something*, translated by Stuart Hood, 1988.
Alì dagli occhi azzurri. 1965.
Roman Nights and Other Stories, translated by J. Shepley. 1965.
Teorema. 1968; as *Theorem*, translated by Stuart Hood, 1992.

Plays

Accattone (screenplay). 1961.
Il Vangelo Secondo Matteo (screenplay). 1964.
Uccellacci e uccellini (screenplay). 1966.
Orgia (produced 1968). In *Porcile, Orgia, Bestia da stile*, 1979.
Affabulazione: Pilade (produced 1969). 1973.
Medea (screenplay). 1970.
Ostia (screenplay). 1970.
Oedipus Rex (translation of screenplay), translated by John Mathews. 1971, revised edition, 1984.
Calderon. 1973.
Trilogia della vita (screenplays; includes *Il decameron, I racconti di Canterbury, Il fiore delle mille e una notte*). 1975. *San Paolo* (film project). 1977.
Porcile, Orgia, Bestia da stile. 1979.

Screenplays (with others): *La donna del Fiume*, 1954; *Le notti di Cabiria* (*The Nights of Cabiria*), 1956; *Marisa la civetta*, 1957; *Giovani mariti*, 1958; *La notte brava*, 1959; *Il bell'Antonio* (*Bell'Antonio*), 1960; *Morte di un amico*, 1960; *La lunga notte del '43*, 1960; *La giornata balorda* (*From a Roman Balcony*), 1960; *Il carro armato dell '8 settembre*, 1960; *La ragazza in vetrina*, 1961; *La commare secca*, 1962; (by Pasolini only): *Accattone*, 1961; *Mamma Roma*, 1962; "La ricotta" episode of *Ro Go Pag*, 1962; *Sopraluoghi in Palestina* (documentary), 1964; *Il Vangelo Secondo Matteo* (*The Gospel According to St. Matthew*), 1964; *Comizi d'amore* (documentary), 1965; *Uccellacci e uccellini* (*The Hawk and the Sparrows*), 1966; "La terra vista dalla luna" episode of *Le streghe* (*The Witches*), 1967; *Edipo Re* (*Oedipus Rex*), 1967; "Che cosa sono le nuvole" episode of *Capriccio all'italiana*, 1968; *Appunti per un film indiano*, 1968; *Teorema*, 1968; "La sequenza del fiore di carta" episode of *Amore e rabbia* (*Vangelo 70, Love and Anger*), 1969; *Porcile* (*Pig Pen*), 1969; *Medea*, 1969; *Appunti per un' Orestiade africano*, 1969; *Il decameron* (*The Decameron*), 1971; *I muri di sano,*

1971; *I racconti di Canterbury* (*The Canterbury Tales*), 1972; *Il fiore delle mille e una notte* (*A Thousand and One Nights/The Arabian Nights*), 1974; *Salò; o, Le centoventi giornate di Sodoma* (*Salo: The 120 Days of Sodom*), 1975; *Orestiade africano*, 1976; *La ricotta*, 1976.

Verse

Poesia a Casarsa. 1942.
La meglio gioventù: Poesia friulane. 1954.
Il canto popolare. 1954.
Le ceneri di Gramsci. 1957; as *The Ashes of Gramsci*, translated by David Wallace, 1982.
L'usignolo della chiesa cattolica. 1958.
Roma 1950: Diario. 1960.
La religione del mio tempo. 1961.
Poesia in forma di rosa 1961–1964. 1964.
Poesia dimenticate. 1965.
Potentissima signora, with Laura Betti. 1965.
Poesia. 1970.
Trasumanar e organizzar. 1971.
Tal cour di un frut: Nel cuore di un fanciullo. 1974.
La nuova gioventù: Poesie friulane 1941–1974. 1975.
Poesie e pagine ritrovate, edited by Andrea Zanzotto and Nico Naldini. 1980.
Selected Poems (bilingual edition), translated by Norman McAfee and Luciano Martinengo. 1982.
Roman Poems, translated by L. Ferunghetti and F. Valente. 1986.

Other

Passione e ideologia 1948–1958. 1960.
L'odore dell'India. 1962; as *The Scent of India*, translated by David Price, 1984.
Pasolini on Pasolini, edited by Oswald Stack. 1969.
Entretiens avec Pasolini, with Jean Duflot. 1970.
Empirismo eretico. 1972; as *Heretical Empiricism*, edited by Louise K. Barnett, translated by Barnett and Ben Lawton, 1988.
Il padre selvaggio. 1975; as *The Savage Father*, translated by Pasquale Verdicchio, 1999.
La divina mimesis. 1975.
Scritti corsari. 1975.
Lettere agli amici, edited by Luciano Serra. 1976.
Pasolini in Friuli 1943–1949. 1976.
Lettere luterane. 1976; as *Lutheran Letters*, translated by Stuart Hood, 1983.
Con Pasolini (interview), edited by Enrico Magrelli. 1977.
La belle dandiere: Dialoghi 1960–1965, edited by Gian Carlo Ferretti. 1977.
Pasolini e "Il Setaccio" 1942–1943, edited by Mario Ricci. 1977.
I disegni 1941–1975, edited by Giuseppe Zigaina. 1978.
Il caos, edited by Gian Carlo Ferretti. 1979.
Lettere 1940–1954, edited by Nico Naldini. 1986; as *Letters 1940–1954*, translated by Stuart Hood, 1992.
Lettere 1955–1975, edited by Nico Naldini. 1988; as *Letters 1955–1975*, 1991.
Editor, with M. dell'Arco, *Poesia dialettale del novecento.* 1952.
Editor, *La poesia popolare italiana.* 1960.
Editor, *Canzoniere italiano.* 2 vols., 1972.
Translator, *Orestiade*, by Aeschylus. 1960.
Translator, *Il vantone*, by Plautus. 1963.

*

Bibliography: *Pasolini: A Guide to References and Resources* by Ben Lawton, 1980.

Critical Studies: *Pasolini: Materiali critici* edited by Alfredo Luzi and Luigi Martellini, 1973; *Challenging the Norm: The Dialect Question in the Works of Gadda and Pasolini* by Laurie Jane Anderson, 1977; *Pasolini* edited by Paul Willemen, 1977; *Pier Paolo Pasolini* by Stephen Snyder, 1980; *Pasolini: A Biography* by Enzo Siciliano, translated by Paul Bailey, 1982, translated by J. Shepley, 1987; *Pier Paolo Pasolini* by Pia Friedrich, 1982; *Pier Paolo Pasolini: Cinema as Heresy* by Naomi Green, 1990; *The Passion of Pier Paolo Pasolini* by Sam Rohdie, 1995; *A Certain Realism: Making Use of Passolini's Film Theory and Practice* by Maurizio Viano, 1993; *Pier Paolo Pasolini: Contemporary Perspectives*, edited by Patrick Rumble and Bart Testa, 1994; *A Poetics of Resistance: Narrative and the Writings of Pier Paolo Pasolini* by David Ward, 1995; *Pasolini: Forms of Subjectivity* by Robert S. C. Gordon, 1996; *Allegories of Contamination: Pier Paolo Pasolini's Trilogy of Life* by Patrick Rumble, 1996; *Pasolini Old and New: Surveys and Studies*, edited by Zygmunt G. Baranski, 1999; *Autobiographical Representation in Pier Paolo Pasolini and Audre Lorde* by Gabriella Ricciardi, 2001.

*   *   *

Some of Pier Paolo Pasolini's earliest writings are poems in the Friulan dialect and he later depicts the peasantry of this region in *Il sogno di una cosa* (*A Dream of Something*). This novel describes traditional rural life as a flawed utopia: full of vitality but riddled with the political and sexual tensions that stem from oppression.

Pasolini's admiration for the Friulan peasants' protests led him to join the Italian Communist Party. Although he was expelled because of his homosexuality he retained a lifelong attachment to the party and considered himself a heretical communist. He loathed the institution of the Catholic church—although he had a keen religious sense—and the Christian Democrats who governed Italy.

His best-known poem, *Le ceneri di Gramsci* (*The Ashes of Gramsci*), displays his ambiguous attitude towards the Communists. While applauding them as the champions of social protest, he proclaims his own attachment to working-class life as it is, to the warm human contacts that survive amid poverty. *Poesia in forma di rosa 1961–1964* [Poetry in the Shape of a Rose] proclaims his joyous identification with working-class boys, Third World peasants, and outsiders of all kinds. A strong erotic drive marks these poems which oscillate between loneliness and that sympathy for everything human which is Pasolini's special trait.

Two novels, *Ragazzi di vita* (*The Ragazzi*) and *Una vita violenta* (*A Violent Life*), delve into the Rome subproletariat, a world left outside the new, prosperous Italy. Although Pasolini uses the slang of this world, his novels are not studies of low-life. Their complex structure allows him to depict characters who struggle against dehumanization and know moments of tenderness and of political awareness.

Outside Italy Pasolini is best known for his films. The cinema seemed to him a more direct art form than writing but his films offer a blend of realism and fantasy. Thus *Accattone* is set in the Rome slums but has a religious dimension, while *Il Vangelo Secondo Matteo* (*The Gospel According to St. Matthew*) resets Christ's life amid the southern Italian peasantry. *Il fiore delle mille e una notte* (*A Thousand and One Nights*) is a utopia of sexual liberation, but Pasolini's last film, *Salò; o, Le centoventi giornate di Sodoma* (*Salo: The 120 Days*

of Sodom), based on a work by the Marquis de Sade, is a gruesome depiction of cruelty.

Within Italy he was known also as a polemicist whose newspaper articles have been collected in such volumes as *Lettere luterane* (*Lutheran Letters*). The stands he took were resolutely controversial, and in his last years he denounced the young protestors of 1968 and declared his opposition to abortion. He was especially harsh on the consumer society which he saw emerge in Italy and which he considered to be, behind its false tolerance and prosperity, a form of total alienation. Frequently denounced as a reactionary but still disliked by the right, Pasolini is best seen as a scandal-bringer who chose to tell the most unpleasant truths.

—Patrick McCarthy

PASTERNAK, Boris (Leonidovich)

Born: Moscow, Russia, 29 January 1890. **Education:** Educated at Moscow Fifth Gymnasium, 1901–08; University of Moscow, 1909–13; also studied at University of Marburg, 1912. **Family:** Married 1) Evgeniia Vladimirovna Lourie in 1922 (dissolved 1931), one son; 2) Zinaida Nikolaevna Neigauz in 1934, one son. **Career:** Tutor; worked in management in chemical factories in the Urals, 1915–17; librarian, Soviet Ministry of Education, 1918; official duties for Union of Writers from 1932, but expelled, 1958. **Awards:** Medal for Valiant Labour, 1946; Nobel prize for literature (refused), 1958. **Died:** 30 May 1960.

Publications

Collections

Sochineniia [Works], edited by Gleb Struve and Boris Filippov. 3 vols., 1961.

Stikhotvoreniia i poemy [Poetry and Narrative Verse], edited by L.A. Ozerov. 1965.

Stikhi [Poems], edited by Z. and E. Pasternak. 1966. *Izbrannoe* [Selection], edited by E.V. and E.B. Pasternak. 2 vols., 1985.

Sobranie sochinenii [Collected Works], edited by E.B. Pasternak and K.M. Polivanova. 5 vols., 1989–92.

Izbrannye proizvedeniia [Selected Works], edited by E.B. Pasternak. 1991.

Fiction

Detstvo Liuvers. 1922; as *Childhood*, translated by Robert Payne, 1941; as *The Childhood of Luvers*, in *Collected Prose Works*, 1945.

Rasskazy [Stories]. 1925; as *Vozdushnye puti* [Aerial Ways], 1933.

Povest' [A Tale]. 1934; as *The Last Summer*, translated by George Reavey, 1959.

Doktor Zhivago. 1957; as *Doctor Zhivago*, translated by Max Hayward and Manya Harari, 1958.

Zhenia's Childhood and Other Stories (includes ''The Childhood of Luvers''; ''Il Tratto di Apelle''; ''Letters from Tula''; ''Ariel Routes''), translated by Alec Brown. 1982.

Vozdushnye puti: Proza raznykh let [Aerial Ways: Prose of Various Years], edited by C.B. and E.V. Pasternak. 1982.

Verse

Bliznets v tuchakh [Twin in the Clouds]. 1914.

Poverkh bar'erov [Over the Barriers]. 1917.

Sestra moia zhizn': Leto 1917 goda. 1922; as *Sister My Life: Summer, 1917* (bilingual edition), translated by P.C. Flayderman, 1967; complete version, as *My Sister-Life*, translated by Mark Rudman and Bohdan Boychuk, 1983.

Temy i variatsii [Themes and Variations]. 1923.

Deviat'sot piaty god. 1927; as *The Year Nineteen Five* (bilingual edition), translated by Richard Chappell, 1989.

Spektorskii. 1931.

Vtoroe rozhdenie [Second Birth]. 1932.

Stikhotvoreniia [Poetry]. 1933; revised edition, 1935–36.

Poemy [Narrative Verse]. 1933.

Stikhotvoreniia [Poetry]. 1935.

Na rannikh poezdakh [On Early Trains]. 1943.

Zemnoi prostor [Earth's Vastness]. 1945.

Selected Poems, translated by J.M. Cohen. 1946.

Stikhi o Gruzii [Poems about Georgia]. 1958.

Poems, translated by Eugene M. Kayden. 1959.

The Poetry of Boris Pasternak 1914–1960, translated by George Reavey. 1960.

Poeziia [Poetry]. 1960.

Poems 1955–1959, translated by Michael Harari. 1960; reprinted with *An Essay in Autobiography*, 1990.

Stikhotvoreniia i poemy [Poetry and Narrative Verse]. 1961.

In the Interlude: Poems 1945–1960, translated by Henry Kamen. 1962.

Fifty Poems, translated by Lydia Pasternak Slater. 1963.

The Poems of Doctor Zhivago, translated by Donald Davie. 1965.

Stikhi [Poems]. 1966.

Poemy [Narrative Verse]. 1977.

Selected Poems, translated by Jon Stallworthy and Peter France. 1983.

Svobodnyi krugozor [Free Horizon]. 1987.

Kogda razguliaetsia [When It's on the Loose]. 1989.

Stikhotvoreniia; Poemy; Perevody [Poetry; Narrative Verse; Translations]. 1989.

Poems (in translation), edited by Evgenii Pasternak. 1990.

Stikhotvoreniia i poemy [Poetry and Narrative Verse]. 2 vols., 1990.

Second Nature: Forty-Six Poems, translated by Andrei Navrozov. 1990.

Plays

Slepaia krasavitsa, edited by Christopher J. Barnes and Nicholas J. Anning. 1969; as *The Blind Beauty*, translated by Max Hayward and Manya Harari, 1969.

Other

Karusel [The Carousel] (for children). 1925.

Zverinets [The Menagerie] (for children). 1929.

Okhrannaia gramota. 1931; as *The Safe Conduct*, in *Collected Prose Works*, 1945.

Knizhka dlia detei [Little Book for Children]. 1933.

Izbrannie perevody [Selected Translations]. 1940.

Collected Prose Works, edited by Stefan Sehimanski, translated by Beatrice Scott and Robert Payne. 1945.

Gruzinskie poety [Georgian poets] (collection of translations). 1947.

Selected Writings. 1949.

Vil'iam Shekspir v perevode Borisa Pasternaka [William Shakespeare in Translation]. 1949.

Safe Conduct: An Early Autobiography, and Other Works, edited by Robert Payne, translated by Payne, Beatrice Scott, and C.M. Bowra. 1949.

Prose and Poems, edited by Stefan Schimanski. 1959.

An Essay in Autobiography, translated by Manya Harari. 1959; as *I Remember*, edited and translated by David Magarshack, 1959; partial Russian text, as *Liudi i polozheniia*, in *Novyi mir*, January 1967.

Letters to Georgian Friends, edited and translated by David Magarshack. 1968.

Boris Pasternak: Voices of Prose, edited by C.J. Barnes. 1977.

Marina Cvetaeva, Boris Pasternak, Rainer Maria Rilke: Lettere 1926, edited by Yevgeny Pasternak, Yelena Pasternak, and Konstantin M. Azadovsky. 1980; as *Letters, Summer 1926: Correspondence Between Boris Pasternak, Marina Tsvetaeva and Rainer Maria Rilke*, translated by Margaret Wettlin and Walter Arndt, 1985.

Perepiska s Olga Freidenberg [Sketches with Olga Freidenberg], edited by Elliott Mossman. 1981; as *Correspondence with Olga Freydenberg*, translated by Mossman and Margaret Wettlin, 1982.

Pasternak on Art and Creativity, edited by Angela Livingstone. 1985.

Zarubezhnaia poeziia v perevodakh B.L. Pasternaka [Foreign Poetry Translated by B.L. Pasternak]. 1990.

Selected Writings and Letters, translated by Catherina Judelson. 1990.

Iz pisem raznykh let [Letters from Various Years]. 1990.

Ob iskusstve [On Art]. 1990.

Perepiska Borisa Pasternaka [Sketches of Boris Pasternak]. 1990.

Moi vzgliad na iskusstvo [My View on Art]. 1990.

Ne ia pishu stikhi. . . [I Don't Write Poetry . . .]. 1991.

Translator, *Gamlet prints datskii* [Hamlet], by Shakespeare. 1941.

Translator, *Romeo i Dzhul'etta* [Romeo and Juliet], by Shakespeare. 1943.

Translator, *Antonii i Kleopatra* [Antony and Cleopatra], by Shakespeare. 1944.

Translator, *Otello, venetsii anskii maur* [Othello], by Shakespeare. 1945.

Translator, *Genrikh chetverty* [Henry IV, Parts I and II], by Shakespeare. 1948.

Translator, *Stikhotvoreniia*, by N.M. Baratashvili. 1948.

Translator, *Korol' Lir* [King Lear], by Shakespeare. 1949.

Translator, *Faust* (Part One), by Goethe. 1950; complete version, 1953.

Translator, *Vitiaz ianoshch*, by Sándor Petöfi. 1950.

Translator, *Makbet* [Macbeth], in *Tragedii*, by Shakespeare. 1951.

Translator, *Mariia Stiuart*, by Schiller. 1958.

Translator, *Zvezdnoe nebo.* 1966.

Editor and translator, with Nikolai Tikhonov, *Gruzinskie liriki.* 1935.

*

Critical Studies: *Pasternak's Lyric: A Study of Sound and Imagery* by Dale L. Plank, 1966; *Pasternak's Doctor Zhivago* by Mary F. and Paul Rowland, 1967; *Pasternak: Modern Judgements* edited by

Donald Davie and Angela Livingstone, 1969, and *Boris Pasternak: Doctor Zhivago* by Livingstone, 1989; *Pasternak* by J.W. Dyck, 1972; *The Poetic World of Pasternak* by Olga R. Hughes, 1974; *Themes and Variations in Pasternak's Poetics* by Krystyna Pomarska, 1975; *Boris Pasternak: A Critical Study* by Henry Gifford, 1977; *Meetings with Pasternak: A Memoir* by Aleksandr Gladkov, 1977; *Pasternak: A Collection of Critical Essays* edited by Victor Erlich, 1978; *Boris Pasternak's Translations of Shakespeare* by Anna Kay France, 1978; *A Captive of Time: My Years with Pasternak* by Olga Ivinskaya, 1978; *Boris Pasternak: His Life and Art* by Guy de Mallac, 1981; *Pasternak: A Biography* by Ronald Hingley, 1983; *Pasternak's Novel: Perspectives on Doctor Zhivago* by Neil Cornwell, 1986; *Boris Pasternak's "My Sister-Life": The Illusion of Narrative* by Katherine Tiernan O'Connor, 1988; *Boris Pasternak: A Literary Biography, Vol. I: 1890–1928* by Christopher Barnes, 1989; *Boris Pasternak: The Poet and His Politics* by Lazar Fleishman, 1990; *Pasternak: A Biography* by Peter Levi, 1990; *Boris Pasternak: The Tragic Years, 1930–1960* by Evgenii Pasternak, translated by Michael Duncan, 1990; *Pasternak's Poetics* by Anna Majmieskulow, 1990; *Boris Pasternak, Bibliographicheskii ukazatel'* by G. Zlenko, 1990; *Boris Pasternak: 1890–1990: A Centennial Symposium* edited by Lev Loself, 1991; *The Ode and the Odic: Essays on Mandelstam, Pasternak, Tsvetaeva and Mayakovsky* by Ilya Kutik, 1994; *Pasternak's Short Fiction and the Cultural Vanguard* by Larissa Rudova, 1994; *Boris Pasternak: A Reference Guide* by Munir Sendich, 1994; *Doctor Zhivago: A Critical Companion*, edited by Edith W. Clowes, 1995; *Boris Pasternak and the Tradition of German Romanticism* by Karen Evans-Romaine, 1997; *Understanding Boris Pasternak* by Larissa Rudova, 1997; *Poetry and Revolution: Boris Pasternak's My Sister Life*, edited by Lazar Fleishman, 1999; *Creating Creation: Readings of Pasternak's Doctor Zhivago* by Susanna Witt, 2000.

* * *

For many years Boris Pasternak "held undisputed sway over Russian poetry," but remained unknown outside the literary world until October 1958, when he was awarded the Nobel prize for literature. In a few days' time the situation had been reversed: he was expelled from the "literary world" (the Union of Soviet Writers) and became "the story on everyone's lips." The poet who had been almost allergic to politics and publicity was turned into a public figure on the political stage. The crowning paradox in the paradox-ridden Soviet reality was that Khrushchev had succeeded where Stalin had failed in staging Pasternak's public execution. Yet, the novel *Doktor Zhivago* (*Doctor Zhivago*), which produced such an explosion of political passion only became available to the Soviet reader to whom it was addressed in 1989. Pasternak, the modernist poet of startling originality, had written a traditional novel because there was no room in his poetry for the tragic events of his age.

For him, poetry and politics were incompatible with each other. In 1917 he pictured himself shouting through the window of his study: "What millennium is it out there?" Despite the world being "turned upside down" he wrote about love, nature, and life. As Andrei Siniavskii said: "Wonder at the miracle of existence is the attitude in which Pasternak is fixed—always bewitched by his discovery, that it is Spring again." Pasternak's love of life is the principal idea of his work, including *Doctor Zhivago*. The title of his third volume of verse, *Sestra moia zhizn'* (*My Sister-Life*), expresses Pasternak's credo of life and art. He made an effort to depict the revolutionary reality in his long poems (1924–31), but it is not these works that

account for Pasternak's greatness as a poet. He saw himself as a vessel through which nature creates its own poems. Marina Tsvetaeva put it well: "His verse was written before the sixth day, when God created man . . . it lacks human beings." Pasternak felt at the time that his poems had not been written by him, but by some mysterious outside force, as if "the world became language." This feature accounts for certain obscure and impressionistic qualities in his poetry. He introduced a complex, dynamic syntax which is, in Mandel'shtam's words, "poetry's circulatory system." He omits words, interrupts himself, speaks not in lines, but in whole stanzas. Conversely, he uses very brief sentences thereby creating an additional rhythmical division. All his rhythmical varieties are achieved by means of classical metrics. The wealth of the sound structure of his poetry is so great that it enables him to use imprecise rhymes that are often dazzling and unexpected. The phonetic links between the words allow a transformation of meaning, as happens with metaphors. Pasternak's imagery is notoriously difficult; it reflects his belief that the world is a "moving entirety."

Like the hero of his novel, Pasternak strove throughout his life towards Pushkinian simplicity. He rewrote half of his early poems in order to make them "clearer." He succeeded only in making them ordinary. He achieved a synthesis between simplicity and complexity in the poems of Iurii Zhivago, with which the novel ends. These poems create an inner harmony from the novel's otherwise episodic structure by comprising a vast range of ideas. In its inferiority to the poetry, the novel is far from straightforward. By telling the story of Zhivago in a highly poetic style, with especial reference to the concept of the poet as a Christ-figure, Pasternak sought to integrate history, religion, and the individual. He gives an intensely personal view of history. Like one of his characters, he "quarrels with history," focusing on those matters uppermost in his mind: love, nature, and the enigma of death. The novel is not apolitical, since it exposes the inner essence of the revolution. Zhivago himself is not so much a man of life, as many critics think, but a man of meaning. His world is a world of bold thinking and original art. When "the iron broom" of ideology has finished with the value of personal opinions as well as with justice and the freedom to create, life has lost its meaning for Zhivago. In the suffocating atmosphere of political dogma, Zhivago is unable to immerse himself in life. In this sense, he is not Pasternak's *alter ego*, since for Pasternak everything in life preserved its depth of meaning till the very end. If Pasternak was ever in conflict with life it was not the revolution or Soviet authority, it was "something higher, bigger, and more profound" than ideology (V. Asmus).

—Valentina Polukhina

See the essay on *Doctor Zhivago*.

PAVESE, Cesare

Born: Santo Stefano Belbo, Italy, 9 September 1908. **Education:** Educated at a Jesuit school, Turin; Ginnasio Moderno, Turin; Liceo Massimo d'Azeglio, 1924–27; University of Turin, 1927–30, degree in letters, 1930. **Career:** Translator and teacher in the early 1930s; editor, *La Cultura* review, Turin, 1934–35; confined for association with communists to Brancaleone Calabro for 8 months, 1935–36;

staff member, Einaudi, publishers, Turin, from 1942. **Awards:** Strega prize, 1950. **Died:** (suicide) 27 August 1950.

PUBLICATIONS

Collections

Opere. 16 vols., 1960–68.
Poesie edite e inedite, edited by Italo Calvino. 1962.
Selected Works (includes *The Beach; The House on the Hill; Among Women Only; The Devil in the Hills*), edited and translated by R.W. Flint. 1968.
Disaffections: Complete Poems 1930–1950, translated by Geoffrey Brock. 2002.

Fiction

Paesi tuoi. 1941; as *The Harvesters,* translated by A.E. Murch, 1962.
La spiaggia. 1942; as *The Beach,* translated by W.J. Strachan, with *A Great Fire,* 1963; also translated by R.W. Flint, in *Selected Works,* 1968.
Feria d'agosto. 1946; in part as *Summer Storm and Other Stories,* translated by A.E. Murch, 1966.
Dialoghi con Leacò. 1947; as *Dialogues with Leucò,* translated by William Arrowsmith and D.S. Cane-Ross, 1965.
Il compagno. 1947; as *The Comrade,* translated by W.J. Strachan, 1959.
Prima che il gallo canti (includes *Il carcere* and *La casa in collina*). 1949; *Il carcere* as *The Political Prisoner,* translated by W.J. Strachan, with *The Beautiful Summer,* 1955; *La casa in collina* as *The House on the Hill,* translated by W.J. Strachan, 1956; also translated by R.W. Flint, in *Selected Works,* 1968.
La bella estate (includes *La bella estate; Il diavolo sulle colline; Tra donne sole*). 1949; *La bella estate* as *The Beautiful Summer,* translated by W.J. Strachan, with *The Political Prisoner,* 1955; *Il diavolo sulle colline* as *The Devil in the Hills,* translated by D.D. Paige, 1954; also translated by R.W. Flint, in *Selected Works,* 1968; *Tra donne sole* as *Among Women Only,* translated by D.D. Paige, 1953; translated by R.W. Flint, in *Selected Works,* 1968.
La luna e i faló. 1950; as *The Moon and the Bonfires,* translated by Louise Sinclair, 1952.
Notte di festa. 1953; as *Festival Night and Other Stories,* translated by A.E. Murch, 1964.
Fuoco grande, with Bianca Garufi. 1959; as *A Great Fire,* translated by W.J. Strachan, with *The Beach,* 1963.
Racconti. 1960; as *Told in Confidence and Other Stories,* edited and translated by A.E. Murch, 1971.
Ciau Masino. 1969.
The Leather Jacket: Stories, edited by Margaret Crosland, translated by A.E. Murch. 1980.

Verse

Lavorare stanca. 1936; revised edition, 1943; as *Hard Labor,* translated by William Arrowsmith, 1979.
Verrà la morte e avrà i tuoi occhi (includes *La terra e la morte*). 1951.
A Mania for Solitude: Selected Poems 1930–1950, edited and translated by Margaret Crosland. 1969; revised edition as *Selected Poems,* 1971.

Other

La letteratura americana e altri saggi. 1951; as *American Literature: Essays and Opinions,* translated by Edwin Fussell, 1970.
Il mestiere di vivere: Diario 1935–1950. 1952; as *This Business of Living,* translated by A.E. Murch, 1961; as *The Burning Brand: Diaries 1935–1950,* translated by A.E. Murch, 1961.
8 poesie inedite e quattro lettere a un'amica. 1964.
Lettere 1924–50, edited by Lorenzo Mondo and Italo Calvino. 2 vols., 1966; as *Selected Letters 1924–1950,* edited and translated by A.E. Murch, 1969.
Lettere 1945–1950, edited by Italo Calvino. 1966.
Vita attraverso le lettere, edited by Lorenzo Mondo. 1973.
Translator, *Il nostro signor Wrenn,* by Sinclair Lewis. 1931.
Translator, *Moby Dick,* by Herman Melville. 1932.
Translator, *Riso nero,* by Sherwood Anderson. 1932.
Translator, *Dedalus,* by James Joyce. 1934.
Translator, *Il 42° parallelo,* by John Dos Passos. 1935.
Translator, *Un mucchio di quattrini,* by John Dos Passos. 1937.
Translator, *Autobiografia di Alice Toklas,* by Gertrude Stein. 1938.
Translator, *Moll Flanders,* by Daniel Defoe. 1938.
Translator, *David Copperfield,* by Charles Dickens. 1939.
Translator, *Tre esistenze,* by Gertrude Stein. 1940.
Translator, *Benito Cereno,* by Herman Melville. 1940.
Translator, *La rivoluzione inglese del 1688–89,* by G.M. Trevelyan. 1941.
Translator, *Il cavallo di Troia,* by Christopher Morley. 1941.
Translator, *Il borgo,* by William Faulkner. 1942.
Translator, *Capitano Smith,* by R. Henriques. 1947.

*

Critical Studies: *The Smile of the Gods: A Thematic Study of Pavese's Works* by Gian-Paolo Biasin, 1968; *Three Italian Novelists: Moravia, Pavese, Vittorini* by Donald W. Heiney, 1968; *The Narrative of Realism and Myth: Verga, Lawrence, Faulkner, Pavese* by Gregory L. Lucente, 1981; *Cesare Pavese: A Study of the Major Novels and Poems* by Doug Thompson, 1982; *An Absurd Vice: A Biography of Pavese* by Davide Lajolo, 1983; *Pavese* by Áine O'Healy, 1988.

* * *

Cesare Pavese was known in the 1930s as an Americanist. Having written his university thesis on Walt Whitman, he translated works by several major American authors to whom Italians were looking because of the dearth of relevant writers in their own language. He also wrote essays on Sherwood Anderson, Gertrude Stein, and Sinclair Lewis for Leone Ginzburg's *La cultura.* Part of the attraction of American literature was that it dealt with the everyday problems of ordinary people, whereas Italian literature was still remote from the man in the street or the fields and was forced to remain so because of censorship.

Pavese was particularly attracted to the colloquial language and even slang used by American writers. His first experiment with prose fiction was a collection of short stories, *Ciau Masino,* about a Piedmontese tramp. At the same time he wrote poetry in which he tried to combine verse and story, capturing the rhythms of narrative and speech in long 13-syllable lines. The first poem in *Lavorare stanca (Hard Labor),* ''I mari del Sud'' [The Southern Seas], about the return of his cousin to the Langhe hills, contains nearly all the themes that Pavese explored throughout his 20 adult years: the escape of the young lad, country versus town, the return to one's roots, work, city night-life, misogyny, and solitude. Some of the poems were written in *confino*, where he was sent because of links with a communist girlfriend. Unlike Carlo Levi (confined in Lucania) Pavese turned inwards to try to come to terms with this experience. "Lo stradduzza" ("The Morning Star") of 1936 expresses his sense of futility with this experience.

Il carcere (*The Political Prisoner*) and *Il compagno* (*The Comrade*)—both published after the war—also reflect his experiences in prison and in *confino*. Another product of this experience was his diary, *Il mestiere di vivere: Diario 1935–1950* (*This Business of Living*), which he kept until his suicide in 1950. This provides striking insights into his creative processes and his states of mind. *Paesi tuoi* (*The Harvesters*), written in 1939, describes in almost Lawrentian terms the return to the land of two prisoners. His own favourite book was *Dialoghi con Leucò* (*Dialogues with Leucò*) which represents the culmination of his thinking about the nature of myth, and his Leopardian exploration of a number of classical myths. It is a product of Pavese's retreat into the hills during the last period of the war, when he was apolitical and preferred not to participate but turned inwards again to contemplate eternal truths. After the war, with the unmuzzling of the Left, Pavese tried to commit himself to the communist cause and wrote several articles attempting to find a more open intellectual and cultural position. These are now included in *La letteratura americana e altri saggi* (*American Literature: Essays and Opinions*), along with others that look back over the 1930s infatuation with things American.

La luna e i falò (*The Moon and the Bonfires*) is Pavese's best novel. It tells of the return of an emigrant from America to the Langhe, where he had been fostered in a well-to-do family alongside the family's three daughters. Gradually the lives of these three girls are pieced together until one has a sense of the local community during the Fascist period. The title refers to local agricultural myths of death and renewal which finally involve in their mysteries the partisans, the German soldiers, and the youngest girl who has fallen foul of both. The whole is told in a spare but lyrical language which makes for an elegiac, distancing tone.

Pavese's last poems, *Verrà la morte e avrà i tuoi occhi* [Death Will Come and Will Have Your Eyes], were published posthumously. The collection reflects Pavese's last unhappy love for an American film star, Constance Dowling. Here, and in *La terra e la morte* [Earth and Death], Pavese reverted to a lyrical and personal poetry, very finely chiselled and totally without hope. It is difficult to separate Pavese from his suicide, if only because it was a theme that preoccupied him throughout his life. With all his personal obsessions, however, he did give voice to the alienation and frustration felt by many of his generation in Italy.

—Judy Rawson

See the essay on *The Moon and the Bonfires*.

PAVIĆ, Milorad

Born: Belgrade, 15 October 1929. **Education:** University of Belgrade, Bachelor of Arts 1961; University of Zagreb, Ph.D. 1966. **Career:**

Professor, University of Novi Sad and University of Belgrade; freelance writer.

PUBLICATIONS

Collections

Sabrana dela. 7 vols., 1991.

Fiction

Gvozdena zavesa. 1973.
Konji svetoga Marka. 1976.
Ruski hrt. 1979.
Nove beogradske priče. 1981.
Hazarski rečnik. Roman leksikon u 100,000 reči. 1984; as *Dictionary of the Khazars*, translated by Christina Pribićević Zorić, 1988.
Predeo slikan čajem. 1988; as *Landscape Painted with Tea*, translated by Christina Pribićević Zorić, 1990.
Izvrnuta rukavica. 1989.
Unutrašnja strana vetra ili roman o Heri i Leandru. 1991; as *The Inner Side of the Wind*, translated by Christina Pribićević Zorić, 1992.
Poslednja ljubav u Carigradu. Priručnik za gatanje. 1994; as *Last Love in Constantinople*, translated by Christina Pribićević Zorić.
Šešir od riblje kože. Ljubavna priča. 1996.

Verse

Palimpsesti. 1967.
Mesečev kamen. 1971.
Duše se kupaju poslednji put. 1982.

Plays

Krevet za tri osobe. 1975.
Zauvek i dan više. 1993; as *Forever and a Day: A Theatre Menu*, translated by Christina Pribićević Zorić, 1997.

Other

Istorija srpske književnosti baroknog doba. 1970.
Vojislav Ilić i evropsko pesništvo. 1971.
Gavril Stefanović Venclović. 1972.
Vojislav Ilić, njegovo vreme i delo. 1972.
Jezičko pamčenje i pesnički oblik. 1976.
Istorija srpske književnosti klasicizma i predromantizma. 1979.
Radjanje nove srpske književnosti. 1983.
Istorija, stalež i stil. 1985.
Kratka istorija Beograda. 1990; as *A Short History of Belgrade*, translated by Christina Pribićević Zorić, 1990.
Istorija srpske književnosti. 1991.

*

Bibliography: *Prilog za bibliografiju Milorada Pavića* by Jasmina Mihajlović, 1991.

Critical Studies: *Hazarska prizma* by Jovan Delić, 1991; *Priče o duši i telu* by Jasmina Mihajlović; several articles in *The World and I*, 1988; several articles in *The Review of Contemporary Fiction*, 1988.

* * *

Milorad Pavić started as a poet and later turned to fiction. Already in his early works he showed traits that would become his trademarks: a meditative and erudite bend in poetry, and a successful merging of fantasy and realism, bolstered by an impeccable and controlled style.

Pavić's first novel, *Hazarski rečnik* (*Dictionary of the Khazars*), invites speculations about the separation of reality from fantasy. The Khazar dictionary was allegedly printed in 1691 by an obscure printer in 17th century Prussia. There was no such dictionary and the author uses it only as a pretext for writing the novel, replete with intricate myths, legends, stories, quasi-historical documents, and a 1001-night's revelry. To understand the author's motives, the novel's philosophical, religious, cultural and aesthetic underpinnings are crucial. There is no distinct line between reality and fantasy. Characters change their appearance and reappear; some characters have their doubles, even triples. Dreams are "a garden of devils, and all dreams in this world were dreamed long ago. Now they are simply interchanged with equally used and worn reality." At least half of the novel takes place either in dreams or dream-like hallucinations. Pavić stresses our inability to acquire the historical truth because fact and legend are intertwined with equal validity. The uncertainty about the actual fate of the Khazars is the best argument for Pavić's contention that historical facts often elude us. The lines between the past, present, and future are also blurred. The characters move from one century and geographical region to another, not only in imagination or in dreams, but matter-of-factly.

Pervasive relativity is an all-important aspect of the *Dictionary of the Khazars*. Few things are as they seem to be. The very fact that the story is presented in three versions—the Christian in the Red book, the Islamic in the Green, and the Hebrew in the Yellow—speaks for the three points of view on the Khazar question. One has to accept the author's belief that many other questions, be they historical, philosophical, or ethical, can be approached from several angles. The author suggests that the novel can be read any way, horizontally or vertically, from the beginning or from the end, even diagonally, which speaks for the omnipresent relativity of Pavić's world. Through all this, he poses the age-old questions: What is the truth and how can it be obtained, if at all? He does not pretend to give definitive answers; instead, he uses the centuries-old dilemma of the Khazars' disappearance as a food for thought. By blending philosophical, historical, and cultural issues with a suspenseful yarn and modernistic narrative techniques, Pavić has created what one critic calls "the first novel of the 21st century."

Branded by the author as "a novel for the lovers of crossword puzzles," Pavić's second novel, *Predeo slikan čajem* (*Landscape Painted with Tea*), is more rooted in our time and place. It follows the fortunes and misfortunes of Atanasije Svilar, a Serb of Serbian-Russian parentage. Like his other works, it contains many puzzles; Pavić even includes instructions on "how to solve this book" as for a crossword puzzle. Svilar joins the ancient Serbian monastery of Khilandar on Mount Athos, where he hopes to lead a solitary life in prayer. There he discovers that he cannot live he monastic life and leaves for America, adopts the English language, and achieves financial success. Toward the end of his life, however, he yearns for his homeland and for the happiness of his youth, a yearning symbolized by his three notebooks adorned with landscapes painted with tea.

He visits his homeland but returns to America. The notebooks with the landscapes represent Svilar's enduring Serbian roots, underscoring the basic split in his personality, which he first experienced at Mount Athos. The symbolic function of the landscapes holds the novel together. The novel has many riddles, traps, and ambiguities and, again, has two possible endings, the male and the female, depending on the reader's sensibilities. Among the riddles are the Serbian-Russian-American connection, allusions to Tito, the stories within the novel, the meaning of the names, the role of the devils, and the solution of the crossword puzzle. The novel's ending is typical of Pavić—inconclusive and open to interpretations.

Milorad Pavić's next novel, *Unutrašnja strana vetra* (*The Inner Side of the Wind*), follows the earlier trends. The innovation in this work consists of two different halves, starting from different ends of the book and paginated separately, that can be read in any order. The two lovers, Hera and Leander, are from different centuries and countries, and the two "different" novels are actually one but presenting two angles of the same story. Hera and Leander were united upon his drowning while swimming across the Hellespont to see her and her subsequent leaping into the sea and drowning out of grief. By using an ancient myth, Pavić spans centuries and continents, resurrecting the myth and making it alive and relevant today. His other important novel, *Poslednja ljubav u Carigradu* (*Last Love in Constantinople*), employs the mysteries of tarot reading as a tool for deciphering human destiny. Milorad Pavić has also excelled as a literary historian and essayist, writing on important Serbian literary periods and bringing to closer scrutiny some neglected writers from the baroque period. Most importantly, he has enriched Serbian literature with post-modernistic writing, including a recent endeavor—an electronic short novel.

—Vasa D. Mihailovich

PAVLOVIĆ, Miodrag

Born: Novi Sad, Yugoslavia, 28 November 1928. **Education:** Attended schools in Belgrade; University of Belgrade Medical School, 1947–54. **Career:** Practiced medicine; after a few years devoted his life to literature; director of National Theater, Belgrade, 1960; editor in the publishing house Prosveta, 1960–80; freelance writer; member of the Serbian Academy of Arts and Sciences; traveled in Europe, United States, Asia, Africa, Australia. **Awards:** Golden Wreath, Struga, 1970; October award, Belgrade, 1991; Golden Key, Smederevo; Zmaj award; Branko Miljković award, Rade Drainac award, Todor Manojlović award, Desanka Maksimović award, Jovan Dučić award, and Djordje Jovanović award; European award for Poetry, Vršac.

PUBLICATIONS

Collections

Izabrana dela. 4 vols., 1981.
Sabrana dela. 10 vols., 1999.

Verse

87 pesama. 1952.
Stub sećanja. 1953.
Oktave. 1957.
Mleko iskoni. 1963.
Velika Skitija. 1969.
Nova Skitija. 1970.
Hododarje. 1971.
Svetli i tamni praznici. 1971.
Zavetine. 1976.
The Conqueror in Constantinople, translated by Joachim Neugroschel. 1976.
Karike. 1977; as *Links*, translated by Bernard Johnson. 1989.
Pevanja na viru. 1977; as *Singing at the Whirlpool*, translated by Barry Callaghan, 1983.
Bekstva po Srbiji. 1979.
Vidovnica. 1979.
Divno čudo. 1982.
Sledstvo. 1985.
The Slavs beneath Parnassus, translated by Bernard Johnson. 1985.
A Voice Locked in Stone, translated by Barry Callaghan. 1985.
Svetogorski dani i noći. 1987.
Knjiga staroslovna. 1989.
Pesme o detinjsvu i ratovima. 1992.

Fiction

Most bez obala. 1956.
Bitni ljudi. 1995.

Plays

Igre bezimenih. 1963.
Koraci u podzemlju. 1991.

Essays

Rokovi poezije. 1958.
Osam pesnika. 1964.
Dnevnik pene. 1972.
Poezija i kultura. 1974.
Poetika modernog. 1978.
Ništitelji i svadbari. 1979.
Poetika žrtvenog obreda. 1987.
Hram i preobraženje. 1989.
Eseji o srpskim pesnicima. 1992.
Ogledi o narodnoj i staroj srpskoj poeziji. 1993.

Other

Antologija moderne engleske poezije. 1957.
Antologija srpskog pesništva od XIII do XX veka. 1964.
Pesništvo evropskog romantizma. 1969.
Antologija lirske narodne poezije. 1982.
Kina—oko na putu. 1982.
Putevi do hrama. 1991.
Otvaraju se hilandarske dveri. 1997.
Uzurpatori neba. 2000.

*

Bibliography:

Critical Studies: "The Poetry of Miodrag Pavlović" by Vasa D. Mihailovich, in *Canadian Slavonic Papers*, 1978; *Epski rasponi Miodraga Pavlovića* by Bogdan A. Popović, 1985; "Poetry of Miodrag Pavlović" by Bernard Johnson, in *Relations*, 1986; "The Magic of Pavlović's Unriddling of the Spiritual Heritage of Serbia" by Žarko Trebješanin, in *Relations*, 1989.

* * *

Miodrag Pavlović has written in several genres, but it is in poetry that he excels. Together with Vasko Popa, he ushered in a new era in Serbian poetry in the 1950s, when war literature was decreasing in popularity and Yugoslav writers became aware of the outside world. In retrospect, the advent of these two writers was one of the decisive factors in Yugoslavia's re-entrance into the mainstream of world literature.

Pavlović's contribution can be measured in many ways. Of great significance is his emphasis on a distinctly Anglo-Saxon way of conceiving, writing, and appreciating poetry. He was one of the first to heed the call for regeneration and to lead Serbian poetry away from romanticism toward a disciplined, analytical, and intellectual approach, emphasizing T.S. Eliot's view that literature should be as depersonalized and unemotional as possible. A longtime student of Eliot and other English and American poets, Pavlović implemented their views and ideas in his poetry, adding his own approach. His appearance coincided with the struggle between the modernist and realist tendencies in Yugoslav literature during the early 1950s, contributing significantly to the victory of modernism.

Pavlović's poetry reveals doubts about, and a revulsion against, existence, caused by the horrors of the war he had witnessed. Images of horror and despair can be found in many of his poems. Later he moved from a big city ravaged by war and man's inhumanity to man, through a countryside rife with riddles and questions, back to prehistoric times and Greek antiquity, to the Hellenic world, Southern Slavs, and West European civilization. His erudite mind sees them as members of the same large family in their cyclic development. He found his roots and the meaning of existence in the brotherhood of mind and spirit in all civilizations and in pronounced religious poems. Though an intellectual and reflective poet, he is not devoid of emotions: they are hidden and subjected to the main objectives of his poetry. He is an aloof but not an impassive observer, so that a certain cool passion emanates from his poems, raising his voice from his earliest poems against the horrors of existence and searching for explanations of life's riddles. But because he is against romantic emotionalism and for an intellectual approach to poetry, he offers rational solutions.

Another feature of Pavlović's poetry is the universal scope of his entire outlook. Even when he speaks of ancient Greece, the old Slavic territories, the West, or his city, he always speaks for all humankind. Many of his poems depict a conflict, show the consequences of a war, or deal with a heresy—themes which humanity has held in common from time immemorial. Still, all people have a common origin. Universality has given Pavlović's poetry a dimension that has greatly enhanced his appeal among poets and critics abroad.

Pavlović's predilection for the bleak, almost tragic side of life lessened as he developed and his hope intensified. He also realized that humans are the only hope for one another. He even goes so far as to name the solidarity of men as the only salvation: The realization of the possibility of salvation is undoubtedly the result of Pavlović's constant search for the meaning and purpose of existence, which is another distinct feature of his poetry. After many probings on his journey toward the truth, he finds it in the solidarity of all humanity and in human creativity.

Pavlović's poetry shows great accomplishments in form as well. The significance of his appearance in the early 1950s lies not only in a new approach to poetry and in new themes, but also in formal innovations. There is a great variety of form ranging from the sketchy, concise, almost laconic early poems to longer poems and verses; and from the inner monologue and confessional style of the early poems to narrative, descriptive, and dramatic scenes and pictures of the later periods. Pavlović is a great experimenter, and many of his poems exemplify boldness and a fresh approach.

The use of five senses is extremely developed in his poetry to the point that, at times, the entire poem is little more than an expression of sensual perceptions of one sort or another. The poet himself is absent, yet he is always present as a cool observer voicing his observations through the senses. Pavlović's language is rich, economical, and precise. Original, striking metaphors are often hyperboles or allegories. He likes to break up logic with unexpected, shocking references. These predilections may reflect the influence of the prewar Surrealist poets.

With his protest against the senselessness and injustice of existence, untiring quest for truth and for roots, elevation of poetry to the level of excellence, high-mindedness, and spiritual richness, Miodrag Pavlović has ploughed a deep furrow in Serbian and world poetry.

—Vasa D. Mihailovich

PAZ, Octavio

Born: Mexico City, Mexico, 31 March 1914. **Education:** Educated at the National Autonomous University of Mexico, Mexico City. **Family:** Married 1) the writer Elena Garro in 1937 (divorced), one daughter; 2) Marie José Tramini in 1964; one daughter. **Career:** Founder or editor of literary reviews *Barandal*, 1931, *Cuadernos del Valle de Mexico*, 1933, *El Popular*, 1938, *Taller*, 1938–41, *El Hijo Pródigo*, 1943–46, and *Plural*, later called *Vuelta*, 1971–75. Secretary, Mexican Embassy, Paris, 1945–51; chargé d'affaires, 1951, later posted to Secretariat for External Affairs, Mexican Embassy, Tokyo, 1953–58; Mexican Ambassador to India, 1962–68 (resigned). Visiting professor of Spanish American literature, University of Texas, Austin, and Pittsburgh University, 1968–70; Simón Bolívar professor of Latin American studies, 1970, and fellow of Churchill College, 1970–71, Cambridge University; Charles Eliot Norton professor of poetry, Harvard University, Cambridge, Massachusetts, 1971–72; Regent's fellow, University of California, San Diego. **Awards:** Guggenheim fellowship, 1944; Grand Prix International de Poésie (Belgium), 1963; City of Jerusalem prize, 1977; Critics' prize (Spain), 1977; National prize for letters, 1977; Grand Aigle d'Or (Nice), 1979; Yoliztli prize, 1980; Cervantes prize (Spain), 1981–82; Neustadt International prize, 1983; Heinse medal (Gemany), 1984; Federation of German Book Trade Peace prize, 1984; Gran Cruz de Alfonso X el Sabrio, 1986; Ingersoll Foundation T.S. Eliot award, 1987; Institute de France De Toqueville prize, 1988; Nobel prize for literature, 1990. **Member:** Honorary member, American Academy of Arts and Letters, 1972. **Died:** 19 April 1998.

PUBLICATIONS

Collection

The Collected Poems 1957–87, edited by Eliot Weinberger, translated by Weinberger and others. 1987.

Verse

Luna silvestre. 1933.
¡No pasarán! 1936.
Raíz del hombre. 1937.
Bajo tu clara sombra y otros poemas sobre España. 1937; revised edition, 1941.
Entre la piedra y la flor. 1941.
A la orilla del mundo y primer día: Bajo tu clara sombra, Raíz del hombre, Noche de resurrecciones. 1942.
Libertad bajo palabra. 1949.
¿Aguila o sol? 1951; as *Eagle or Sun?*, translated by Eliot Weinberger, 1970, revised version, 1976.
Semillas para un himno. 1954.
Piedra de sol. 1957; as *Sun Stone*, translated by Muriel Rukeyser, 1963, and by Peter Miller, 1963; as *Piedra de Sol: The Sun Stone*, translated by Donald Gardner, 1969.
La estación violenta. 1958.
Agua y viento. 1959.
Libertad bajo palabra: Obra poética 1935–1958. 1960; revised edition, 1968.
Homenaje y profanciones. 1960; as *Homage and Desecrations*, translated by Eliot Weinberger, 1987.
Salamandra 1958–1961. 1962.
Selected Poems, translated by Muriel Rukeyser. 1963.
Viento entero. 1965.
Vrindaban, Madurai. 1965.
Blanco. 1967; as *Blanco*, translated by Eliot Weinberger, 1974.
Disco visuales. 1968.
Ladera este (1962–1968). 1969.
La centana: Poemas 1935–1968. 1969.
Configurations, translated by G. Aroul and others. 1971.
Topoemas. 1971.
Renga, with others. 1971; as *Renga*, translated by Charles Tomlinson, 1972.
Early Poems 1935–1955, translated by Muriel Rukeyser and others. 1973.
El mono gramático (prose poem). 1974; as *The Monkey Grammarian*, translated by Helen Lane, 1981.
Pasado en claro. 1975.
Vuelta. 1976.

A Draft of Shadows and Other Poems, edited by Eliot Weinberger, translated by Weinberger, Elizabeth Bishop, and Mark Strand. 1979.

Selected Poems, translated by Charles Tomlinson. 1979.

Poemas 1935–1975. 1979; updated edition, as *Obra poética (1935–1988)*, 1990.

Airborn/Hijos del aire, with Charles Tomlinson. 1981.

Poemas recientes. 1981.

Instante y revelación, photographs by Manuel Alvarez Bravo. 1982; bilingual edition, 1985.

Obsidian Butterfly, translated by Eliot Weinberger. 1983.

Selected Poems, edited and translated by Eliot Weinberger. 1984.

Cuatro chopos/The Four Poplars, translated by Eliot Weinberger. 1985.

Ninteen Ways of Looking at Wang Wei, with Eliot Weinberger. 1987.

Arbol adentro. 1987; as *A Tree Within*, translated by Eliot Weinberger, 1988.

Le mejor de Octavio Paz: El fuego de cada día. 1989.

Eight Poems. 1993.

A Tale of Two Gardens: Poems from India, 1952–1995, translated by Eliot Weinberger and Elizabeth Bishop, 1997.

Plays

La hija de Rappaccini, from the story by Nathaniel Hawthorne (produced 1956). In *Primera antología de obras en un acto*, edited by Maruxa Vilalta, 1959.

Other

El laberinto de la soledad. 1950; revised edition, 1959; as *The Labyrinth of Solitude*, translated by Lysander Kemp, 1961, enlarged edition, 1985.

El arco y la lira: El poema, la revelación poética, poesía e historia. 1956; revised edition, 1967; as *The Bow and the Lyre: The Poem, The Poetic Revelation, Poetry and History*, translated by Ruth L.C. Simms, 1973.

Las peras del olmo. 1957.

Tamayo en la pintura mexicana. 1959.

Cuadrivio (on Darío, López Velarde, Pessoa, Cernuda). 1965.

Los signos en rotación. 1965.

Puertas al campo. 1966.

Claude Lévi-Strauss; o, El nuevo festín de Esopo. 1967; as *Claude Lévi-Strauss: An Introduction*, translated by J.S. and Maxine Bernstein, 1970.

Corriente alterna. 1967; as *Alternating Current*, translated by Helen Lane, 1973.

Marcel Duchamp; o, El castillo de la pureza. 1968; as *Marcel Duchamp; or, The Castle of Purity*, translated by Donald Gardner, 1970.

Conjunciones y disyunciones. 1969; as *Conjunctions and Disjunctions*, translated by Helen Lane, 1974.

México: La última decada. 1969.

Posdata. 1970; as *The Other Mexico: Critique of the Pyramid*, translated by Lysander Kemp, 1972.

Las cosas en su sitio: Sobre la literatura española del siglo XX, with Juan Marichal. 1971.

Los signos en rotación y otra ensayos, edited by Carlos Fuentes. 1971.

Traducción: Literatura y literalidad. 1971.

Apariencia desnuda: La obra de Marcel Duchamp. 1973; as *Marcel Duchamp: Appearance Stripped Bare*, translated by Rachel Phillips and Donald Gardner, 1979.

El signo y el garabato. 1973.

Solo a dos voces, with Julián Ríos. 1973.

La búsqueda del comienzo. 1974.

Teatro de signos/transparencias, edited by Julián Ríos. 1974.

Los hijos del limo: Del romanticismo a la vanguardia (lectures). 1974; as *Children of the Mire: Modern Poetry from Romanticism to the Avant-Garde*, translated by Rachel Phillips, 1974, revised edition, 1991.

The Siren and the Seashells and Other Essays on Poets and Poetry, translated by Lysander Kemp and Margaret Seyers Peden. 1976.

Xavier Villaurrutia en persona y en obra. 1978.

El ogro filantrópico: Historia y política 1971–1978. 1979.

Rufino Tamayo: Myth and Magic, with Jacques Lassaigne. 1979.

Sor Juana Inés de la Cruz, o, Las trampas de la Fe (biography). 1982; as *Sor Juana; or, The Traps of Faith*, translated by Margaret Sayers Peden, 1988; as *Sor Juana: Her Life and World*, translated by Peden, 1988.

Tiempo nublado. 1983; as *One Earth, Four or Five Worlds: Reflections on Contemporary History*, translated by Helen Lane. 1985.

Sombras de obras: Arte y literatura. 1983.

Günter Gerzo (in Spanish, English, and French), with John Golding. 1983.

Hombres en su siglo y otros ensayos. 1984; as *On Poets and Others*, translated by Michael Schmidt. 1986.

De una palabra a otra (commentaries on three poems). 1985; as *One Word to the Other*, translated by Amelia Simpson, 1992.

Convergences: Selected Essays on Art and Literature, translated by Helen Lane. 1987.

Primeras letras (1931–1943), edited by Enrico Mario Santí. 1988.

Pasión crítica: Conversationes con Octavio Paz, edited by Hugo J. Verani. 1985.

The Labyrinth of Solitude: The Other Mexico, Return to the Labyrinth of Solitude, Mexico and the United States, and the Philanthropic Ogre. 1985.

Convergences: Essays on Art and Literature. 1987.

Generaciones y semblanzas: Escritores y lettras de Mexico. 1987.

El pelegrino en su patria: Historia y política de México. 1987.

Los privilegios de la vista: Arte de México. 1987.

Primeros letras, 1931–1943, edited by Enrico Mario Santí. 1988.

Poesía, mito, revolución. 1989.

La otra voz: Poesía y fin de siglo. 1990; as *The Other Voice: Poetry and the Fin-de-siècle*, translated by Helen Lane. 1992.

Essays on Mexican Art, translated by Helen Lane. 1993.

La llama double: amor y erotismo. 1994; as *The Double Flame: Love and Eroticism*, translated by Helen Lane, 1995.

Vislumbres de la India. 1995; as *In Light of India*, translated by Eliot Weinberger, 1997.

Itinerary: An Intellectual Journey, translated by Jason Wilson, 1999.

Editor, *Voces de España*. 1938.

Editor, with others, *Laurel: Antología de la poesía moderna en lengua española*. 1941.

Editor, *Anthologie de la poésie mexicaine.* 1952; as *Anthology of Mexican Poetry*, translated by Samuel Beckett, 1958.

Editor, *Antología poética.* 1956.

Editor, *Tamayo en la pintura mexicana.* 1959.

Editor, *Magia de la risa.* 1962.

Editor, *Antología*, by Fernando Pessoa. 1962.

Editor, with Pedro Zekeli, *Cuatro poetas contemporáneos de Suecia: Martinson, Lundkvist, Ekelöf, y Lindegren.* 1963.

Editor, with others, *Poesía en movimiento: México 1915–1966.* 1966; as *New Poetry of Mexico*, edited by Mark Strand, 1970.

Editor, with Roger Caillois, *Remedios varo.* 1966.

Editor, *Antología*, by Xavier Villaurrutia. 1980.

Translator, with E. Hayashiya, *Sendas de Oku*, by Basho. 1957.

Translator, *Veinte poemas*, by William Carlos Williams. 1973.

Translator, *Versiones y diversiones* (poetry selection). 1974.

Translator, *15 poemas*, by Apollinaire. 1979.

*

Bibliography: *Bibliografía selecta y crítica de Octavio Paz* by Juan O. Valencia and Edward Coughlin, 1973; *Octavio Paz: Bibliografía crítica* by Hugo J. Verani, 1983; in *Mexican Literature: A Bibliography of Secondary Sources* by David William Foster, 1992.

Critical Studies: *The Poetic Modes of Octavio Paz* by Rachel Phillips, 1972; *The Perpetual Present: The Poetry and Prose of Paz* edited by Ivar Ivask, 1973; *Octavio Paz: A Study of His Poetics*, 1979, and *Octavio Paz*, 1986, both by Jason Wilson; *Octavio Paz: Homage to the Poet* edited by Kosrot Chantikian, 1980; Paz issue of *World Literature Today*, 56, 1982; *Octavio Paz: The Mythic Dimension* by Frances Chiles, 1986; *Toward Octavio Paz: A Reading of His Major Poems 1957–1976* by John M. Fein, 1986; *Understanding Octavio Paz* by Jose Quiroga, 1999; *From Art to Politics: Octavio Paz and the Pursuit of Freedom* by Yvon Grenier, 2001.

*   *   *

Within the intellectual landscape of the 20th century, in an increasingly specialized and divided world, Octavio Paz is a writer of exceptional and diverse interests, of prodigious versatility, unusual erudition and imagination, recognized as one of the major poets of our time and as a lucid interpreter of modernity. His critical thought includes a bewildering number of fields of human activity—art, aesthetics, philosophy, Oriental religion, anthropology, psychology, political ideology. The preoccupations that cross Paz's writing—the search for lost unity and the reconciliation of man with himself and the universe, the celebration of love and of freedom of thinking, the merging of contraries, the reviving of the poetic work—converge in the reflexive prose of his essays and in a poetry that assumes the form of self-criticism and incessant interrogation, two sides of an organic whole of inseparable unity in its diversity, that constitutes an uncommon and passionate testimony of humanity.

Paz is primarily a poet, considered (along with Neruda and Vallejo) as one of the truly outstanding Spanish-American poets of the 20th century. Paz sees poetry as a path towards the revelation of man, as a means to restore authenticity. Poetic creation and erotic love are the only ways to reconcile the opposing forces of the world, the only ways to transcend solitude and reach spiritual fulfilment.

During the five years that Paz lived in France (1946–51), he participated in the surrealist movement and developed a lifelong affinity with its tenets. Paz sees surrealism as an activity of the human spirit based on the idea of rebellion, love, and freedom, as a total subversion, as a movement to recapture the natural innocence of man. The conjunction of ancient Mexican mythology and surrealism (''telluric surrealism'' as termed by Benjamin Péret) guides his quest for eternal values, his desire to transcend the contradictions of humanity. ''Hymn Among the Ruins'' and, above all, *Piedra de sol* (*Sun Stone*) are the masterpieces of this period of his poetry. His stay in India, as ambassador of his country (1962–68), profoundly affected his vision of the world and his approach to poetry. Many concepts of Oriental thought were incorporated into his poetics: detachment from the outside world, the illusory nature of the world, the stress on natural man, the illusion of the ego, sudden illumination, transcendence through the senses, rebellion against all systems. *Ladera este* and *Blanco* include the major poems of this period.

After the early 1960s the most significant constants of Paz's poetic work are experimentation with space and the use of visual effects. The most important poems of the 1960s (''Whole Wind,'' *Blanco*) are constellations of juxtaposed fragments and of voices in perpetual rotation in which the simultaneity of times and spaces is the point of confluence in an inexhaustible net of relations that enrich the analytical reading of the text. In his poetry the spatial-temporal markings disappear, and all ages converge in a privileged moment, in that evanescent and fleeting, atemporal and archetypal present. Paz liberates language from the illusion of representing an empirical reality: spaces, times, and distant cultures interweave without explicit transition and give the poem a plural meaning.

Paz is also a major essayist. Few Spanish-American writers, if any, have developed a critical system that encompasses the main intellectual currents of modern times. During almost half a century Paz has adhered to two fundamental premises: the questioning of all established truths and, above all, the passionate search for human dignity and the defence of the freedom of the human being, principles whose aim is always in Paz a recovery of the essential values of humanism.

—Hugo J. Verani

See the essay on *Sun Stone*.

PEREC, Georges

Born: Paris, France, 7 March 1936. **Education:** Secondary schooling at the Collège d'Etampes; university studies in history at the Sorbonne, and in sociology at the University of Tunis. **Military Service:** Served in French Army, 1958. *Family:* Married Paulette Pétras in 1960. *Career:* Worked as an archivist in a medical neurophysiology laboratory in the Centre National de Recherche Scientifique, 1961–1978. Thereafter, and until his death, he was put on salary by his publisher. **Awards:** Renaudot prize, 1965; Médicis prize, 1978. **Member:** Ouvroir de Littérature Potentielle (Oulipo). **Died:** Of cancer, in Paris, 3 March 1982.

PUBLICATIONS

Fiction

Les Choses: Une histoire des années soixante. 1965.
Quel petit vélo à guidon chromé au fond de la cour? 1966.
Un Homme qui dort. 1967.
La Disparition. 1969.
Les Revenentes. 1972.
W ou le souvenir d'enfance. 1975.
La Vie mode d'emploi. 1978.
Un Cabinet d'amateur. 1979.
"53 Jours." 1989.
Le Voyage d'hiver. 1993.

Verse

Ulcérations. 1974.
Alphabets. 1976.
La Clôture et autres poèmes. 1980.
Epithalames. 1982.
Beaux Présents belles absentes. 1994.

Plays

Die Maschine. 1972.
Théâtre I. 1981.

Other

La Boutique obscure: 124 rêves. 1973.
Espèces d'espaces: Journal d'un usager de l'espace. 1974.
Tentative d'épuisement d'un lieu parisien. 1975.
Je me souviens. 1978.
Les Mots croisés. 1979.
Récits d'Ellis Island: Histoires d'errance et d'espoir. 1980.
Penser/Classer. 1985.
Les Mots croisés II. 1986.
L'Infra-ordinaire. 1989.
Je suis né. 1990.
Cantatrix sopranica L. et autres écrits scientifiques. 1991.
L.G.: Une aventure des années soixante. 1992.
Jeux intéressants. 1997.
Perec/rinations. 1997.
Nouveaux jeux intéressants. 1998.
Contributor, *Petit Traité invitant à la découverte de l'art subtil du go.* 1969.
Contributor, *Oulipo: La littérature potentielle: Créations, re-créations, récréations.* 1973.
Contributor, *Atlas de littérature potentielle.* 1981.
Contributor, *What A Man!* 1996.
Translator, *Les Verts Champs de moutarde de l'Afghanistan,* by Harry Mathews. 1974.
Translator, *Le Naufrage du Stade Odradek,* by Harry Mathews. 1981.

*

Bibliography: *Tentative d'inventaire pas trop approximatif des écrits de Georges Perec* by Bernard Magné, 1993.

Critical Studies: *The Poetics of Experiment: A Study of the Work of Georges Perec* by Warren Motte, 1984; *Perec ou les textes croisés* by John Pedersen, 1985; *Pour un Perec lettré, chiffré* by Jean-Michel Raynaud, 1987; *Georges Perec* by Claude Burgelin, 1988; *Georges Perec: Traces of His Passage* by Paul Schwartz, 1988; *Perecollages 1981–1988* by Bernard Magné, 1989; *La Mémoire et l'oblique: Georges Perec autobiographe* by Philippe Lejeune, 1991; *Georges Perec: A Life in Words* by David Bellos, 1993; *Georges Perec: Ecrire pour ne pas dire* by Stella Béhar, 1995; *Georges Perec* by Bernard Magné, 1999.

*   *   *

A novelist, poet, playwright, essayist, screenwriter, librettist, and translator, Georges Perec distinguished himself among his contemporaries by his originality and his desire to approach each of his works afresh. He was an accomplished writer in a broad variety of literary genres, and he will undoubtedly be recognized as a major figure of his time. Perec was quite frank about his desire to experiment in literature. In an interview conducted in 1978, he characterized that desire in the following terms: "My ambition as a writer would be to traverse all of contemporary literature, without ever feeling that I am retracing my own steps or returning to beaten ground, and to write everything that someone today can possibly write: big books and small books, novels and poems, plays, opera librettos, detective novels, adventure novels, science fiction, serial novels, children's books." He suggested moreover that four major concerns animate his writing. First, an interest in everyday life and a wish to make apparent details of everyday life that generally go unnoticed. Second, a tendency toward personal confession and autobiography. Third, an interest in formal innovation and a will to incorporate difficult principles of literary structure in his work. Finally, a desire to write stories that "read" fluently and hold their reader spellbound.

Perec's first book, *Les Choses: Une histoire des années soixante* [Things: A Story of the Sixties], was awarded the coveted Renaudot prize, assuring a readership far broader than that of most first novels. Telling the story of a young couple and their dissatisfaction with contemporary consumer culture, *Les Choses* was praised as a "sociological novel." More fiction quickly followed. *Quel petit vélo à guidon chromé au fond de la cour?* [What Little Bike with Chrome Handlebars at the End of the Courtyard?] is the mock-heroic story of a group's efforts to prevent one of its members from being drafted; *Un Homme qui dort* [A Man Asleep] is the chronicle of a young man's struggles with depression and alienation. *La Disparition* [A Void] is a kind of detective story whose central conceit is the disappearance of the letter E from the alphabet—and indeed the letter E appears not once in the 300 pages of the novel. *Les Revenentes* [Ghosts] reads like the negative image of *La Disparition*, insofar as E is the only vowel used in the novel. *W ou le souvenir d'enfance* [W or the Memory of Childhood] is a hybrid work mixing fiction and autobiography. Both of Perec's parents were Polish Jews who had emigrated to France, and both of them died during the years of World War II. Perec's father was killed in French uniform at the front in 1940, and his mother was arrested in Paris in 1943 and deported to Auschwitz, from whence she did not return. Meditating on his childhood, Perec uses the fictional narrative in *W* to say what is clearly too painful to say in the autobiographical narrative. *La Vie mode d'emploi* [Life: A User's Manual] is a vast novel about the life of an apartment building in Paris, and many critics consider it to be Perec's most accomplished work. *Un Cabinet d'amateur* [A Collector's Room] and *Le Voyage d'hiver* [The Winter's Trip] are shorter works based on innovative formal principles; and *"53 Jours"* ["53 Days"] is the novel that Perec left unfinished when he died.

Almost all of Perec's poetry was composed according to systems of formal constraint. The long poem *Ulcérations* [Ulcerations], for instance, uses only the eleven most common letters of the alphabet; and a similar principle is at work in the collection *Alphabets*. The wedding poems in *Epithalames* [Epithalamia] were written using only the alphabetical letters figuring in the names of the bride and the groom. Much of Perec's constraint-based writing was inspired by the Ouvroir de Littérature Potentielle, or Oulipo, a group of mathematicians and writers based in Paris that he joined in 1967. Perec found a home in the Oulipo, and the Oulipo found in Perec one of its most tireless and productive members. More generally speaking, Georges Perec found a home in literature. His work taken as a whole moreover, in its astonishing diversity and originality, can be read as a sustained reflection upon literature's vigor as a cultural mode, and as a compelling demonstration of the vastness of its possibilities.

—Warren Motte

See the essay on *Life: A User's Manual*.

PÉREZ DE AYALA, Ramón

Born: Oviedo, Asturias, Spain, 9 August 1880. **Education:** Educated at the Jesuit Colegio de San Zoil, Camión de los Condes, 1888–90; Jesuit Colegio de la Inmaculada, Gijón, 1890–94; University of Oviedo, Faculty of Law, 1899–1902, degree in law. **Family:** Married Mabel Rick in 1913; two sons. **Career:** Moved to Madrid, 1902; contributor to *Helios*, 1903–04; correspondent for the Madrid *El Imparcial* in London, 1907; travelled to Germany, 1912, United States, 1913; war correspondent for the Buenos Aires *La Prensa*, 1916; in United States, writing articles for Madrid newspapers, 1919–20; co-founder, with José Ortega y Gasset and Gregorio Marañón, Association for the Defence of the Republic, 1931; Spanish ambassador in London, 1931–36: resigned; lived in Biarritz and Paris, 1936–39, and returned to Spain at the end of the Civil War, 1939; lectured in South America and settled in Buenos Aires, Argentina, 1940–54: earned living as lecturer and journalist, and was later appointed to the staff of the Spanish Embassy; visited France and Spain, 1949, and returned to Spain, 1954; regular contributor, *ABC*, Madrid, 1954–62. **Awards:** Mariano de Cavia prize (for journalism), 1922; National literature prize, 1926; Spanish Society of New York medal (co-winner); Juan March prize, 1960. Honorary doctorate: University of London, 1936. **Member:** Member-elect, Royal Spanish Academy, 1928. **Died:** 5 August 1962.

PUBLICATIONS

Collection

Obras completas, edited by José García Mercadal. 4 vols., 1964–69.

Fiction

Tinieblas en las cumbres. 1907; edited by Andrés Amorós, 1971.
Sonreía. 1909.
A.M.D.G.. 1910; edited by Andrés Amorós, 1983.
La pata de la raposa. 1912; edited by Andrés Amorós, 1970; as *The Fox's Paw*, translated by Thomas Walsh, 1924.
La araña (stories). 1913.
Troteras y danzaderas. 1913; edited by Andrés Amorós, 1972.
Prometeo; Luz de domingo; La caída de los Limones (poetic novellas). 1916; as *Prometheus; The Fall of the House of Limón; Sunday Sunlight*, translated by Alice P. Hubbard and Grace Hazard Conkling, 1920.
Belarmino y Apolonio. 1921; edited by Andrés Amorós, 1976; as *Belarmino and Apolonio*, translated by Murray Baumgarten and Gabriel Berns, 1971.
Luna de miel, luna de hiel; Los trabajos de Urbano y Simona. 2 vols., 1923; edited by Andrés Amorós, 1969; as *Bitter Honeymoon*, translated by Barry Eisenberg, 1972; as *Honeymoon, Bittermoon*, translated by Eisenberg, 1990.
El ombligo del mundo (poetic novellas). 1924.
Bajo el signo de Artemisa (novellas). 1924.
Tigre Juan; El curandero de su honra. 2 vols., 1926; edited by Andrés Amorós, 1980; as *Tiger Juan*, translated by Walter Starkie, 1933.
Justicia. 1928.
El Raposín (stories). 1962.

Verse

La paz del sendero. 1903.
El sendero ennumerable. With *La paz del sendero*, 1916.
El sendero andante: Momentos; Modos; Ditirambos; Doctrinal de vida y naturaleza. 1921.
Ramoneo. 1935.
Poesías completas. 1944 (3rd edition).

Plays

Sentimental Club. 1909; as *La revolución sentimental*, in *Obras completas*, 2, 1965.

Other

Hermann, encadenado (war essays). 1917.
Las máscaras (theatre criticism). 2 vols., 1917–19.
Política y toros (essays). 1918.
Éxodo (travel writing). 1923.
Obras completas. 19 vols., 1923–28.
El libro de Ruth: Ensayos en vivo. 1928.
Selections from Pérez de Ayala, edited by N.B. Adams and S.A. Stoudemire. 1945.
Obras selectas (novels and essays). 1957; revised edition, 1962.
Principios y finales de la novela (essays). 1958.
Divagaciones literarias (essays). 1958.
El país del futuro: Mis viajes a los Estados Unidos, 1913–1914, 1919–1920. 1959.

Más divagaciones literarias (essays), edited by José García Mercadal. 1960.

Amistades y recuerdos (essays). 1961.

Fábulas y ciudades (essays). 1961.

Tabla rasa (essays). 1963.

Pequeños ensayos, edited by José García Mercadal. 1963.

Tributo a Inglaterra (essays), edited by José García Mercadal. 1963.

Ante Azorín (essays), edited by José García Mercadal. 1964.

Nuestro Séneca, y otros ensayos, edited by José García Mercadal. 1966.

Escritos políticos, edited by P. Garagorri. 1967.

Viaje entretenido al país del ocio: Reflexiones sobre la cultura griega. 1975.

Las terceras de ABC, edited by José Luis Vázquez-Dodero. 1976.

Apostillas y divagaciones. 1976.

Cincuenta años de cartas íntimas, 1904–1956, with Miguel Rodríguez-Acosta, edited by Andrés Amorós. 1980.

Antología asturiana de Pérez de Ayala, edited by Elias García Domínguez. 1980.

Recuerdos asturianos de Ramón Pérez de Ayala, edited by Manuel Fernández Avelló. 1980.

Crónicas londinenses, edited by Agustín Coletes Blanco. 1985.

Trece dioses: Fragmentos de las memorias de Florencio Flórez, edited by Geraldin M. Scanlon. 1989.

*

Bibliography: "Ramón Pérez de Ayala: Bibliografía crítica" by Pelayo H. Fernández, in *Hispanófila*, 55, 1975; *Ramón Pérez de Ayala: An Annotated Bibliography of Criticism* by Marigold Best, 1980.

Critical Studies: *Ramón Pérez de Ayala: Su vida y obras* by Francisco Agustín, 1927; *Algunos aspectos literarios y lingüísticos de la obra de Don Ramón Pérez de Ayala* by Kasper Willem Reinink, 1959; *De Troteras a Tigre Juan: Dos grandes temas de Ramón Pérez de Ayala* by Norma Urrutia, 1960; *Perspectivo y contraste de Cadalso a Pérez de Ayala* by Mariano Baquero Goyanes, 1963; *The Literary Perspectivism of Ramón Pérez de Ayala* by Frances Wyers Weber, 1966; *Los senderos poéticos de Ramón Pérez de Ayala* by Victor G. Concha, 1970; *Pérez de Ayala y la niebla*, 1970, *El anticlericalismo de Pérez de Ayala*, 1975, and *Recuerdos asturianos de Ramón Pérez de Ayala*, 1980, all by Manuel Fernández Avelló; *Ramón Pérez de Ayala* (in English) by Marguerite C. Rand, 1971; *La novela intelectual de Ramón Pérez de Ayala*, 1972, and *Vida y literatura en Troteras y danzaderas*, 1973, both by Andrés Amorós; *Ramón Pérez de Ayala: Tres novelas analizadas*, 1972, and *Estudios sobre Ramón Pérez de Ayala*, 1978, both by Pelayo H. Fernández; *Ramón Pérez de Ayala* by Miguel Pérez Ferrero, 1973; *Contra el honor: Las novelas normativas de Ramón Pérez de Ayala* by Julio Matas, 1974; *Análisis de Belarmino y Apolonio* by Sara Suárez Solís, 1974; *La prosa de Ramón Pérez de Ayala* by José González Calvo, 1979; *Ramón Pérez de Ayala: Tigre Juan and El curandero de su honra* (in English), 1980, and *The Window and the Garden: The Modernist Fictions of Ramón Pérez de Ayala*, 1988, both by John J. Macklin; *En torno a la obra narrativa de Ramón Pérez de Ayala* by Casiano E. Fernández, 1982; *Del relato modernista a la novela poemática: La narrativa breve de Ramón Pérez de Ayala* by Miguel Ángel Lozano Marco, 1983; *La novela más popular de Pérez de Ayala: Anatomía de A.M.D.G.* by Victoriano Rivas Andrés, 1983; *Gran Bretaña y los Estados Unidos en la vida de Ramón Pérez de Ayala*, 1984, and *La huella anglonorteamericana en la novela de Pérez de Ayala*, 1987, both by Agustín Coletes Blanco; *The Paternal Orientation of Ramón Pérez de Ayala* by Thomas Feeny, 1985; *Dualism and Polarity in the Novels of Ramón Pérez de Ayala* by Margaret Pol Stock, 1988; *Etica y estética: las novelas poemáticas de la vida española de Ramón Pérez de Ayala* by José Ramón González García, 1992; *Cómo leer a Ramón Pérez de Ayala* by José Ramón González, 1993; *Mundo helénico en la obra de Ramón Pérez de Ayala* by Margarita de Hoyos González, 1994; *Pérez de Ayala: Bajo el signo de Britannia* by Agustín Coletes Blanco, 1997.

*   *   *

Novelist, critic, essayist, and poet, a disciple of philosopher José Ortega y Gasset and a member of the cosmopolitan "novecentista" group, Ramón Pérez de Ayala was by turns a journalist, war correspondent, theatre critic, political activist, diplomat, and exile, scholar of the classics, modernist theorist (and practitioner), and satiric observer of his times. Best known for his novels, he was a prolific essayist and journalistic articles, and like members of the "Generation of 1898" with which some literary histories include him, often incorporated essays in his fiction (*El libro de Ruth* [The Book of Ruth] comprises essays extracted from his novels). Social criticism appears in *Política y toros* [Politics and Bulls], in which the author indicts the national tendency to produce self-styled experts on everything, especially the topics named in the title. Theatrical criticism, sometimes rather arbitrary and caustic, appears in *Las máscaras* [The Masks], probably the most famous and often studied of Ayala's essays; the collection incorporates his reactions to plays and playwrights as well as his theory of tragedy. His aesthetics of the novel appear in *Principios y finales de la novela* [Beginnings and Ends (also, Principles and Goals) of the Novel], a key theoretical tool for understanding his later narratives. A large percentage of the numerous volumes of Pérez de Ayala's essays have been issued posthumously, compiled by various literary scholars who have collected essays on specific topics from the hundreds (and perhaps thousands) of articles Pérez de Ayala wrote during the course of a long and prolific journalistic career. Additional literary criticism, most often originally published in Spanish or Latin American newspapers and periodicals, has been collected in book form under such titles as *Divagaciones literarias* [Literary Ramblings], *Más divagaciones literarias* [More Literary Ramblings], *Amistades y recuerdos* [Friendships and Recollections (i.e. of other writers)], *Pequeños ensayos* [Little Essays], *Ante Azorín* [Facing Azorin] and *Apostillas y divagaciones* [Annotations and Musings].

Widely travelled, Pérez de Ayala also published numerous travel articles and reactions to his journeys abroad, including *Exodo* [Exodus], *El país del future: Mis viajes a los Estados Unidos, 1913–1914, 1919–1920* [The Country of the Future: My Trips to the United States], *Fábulas y ciudades* [Fables and Cities], *Tributo a Inglaterra* [Tribute to England], *Crónicas londinenses* [Chronicles of London], and *Viaje entretenido al país del ocio* [Amusing Voyages to the Land of Leisure], subtitled Reflexions on Greek Culture. Reflections on the homeland of his youth, the small northern province of Asturias, appear in two collections commemorating the centennial of the author's birth, *Antología asturiana de Pérez de Ayala* [Asturian Anthology] and *Recuerdos asturianos de Ramón Pérez de Ayala* [Asturian Memories]. Pérez de Ayala's essays on other topics include classical philology and philosophy, as seen in *Neustro Séneca* [Our Seneca] and *Tabla rasa* [Black Tablet].

Ayala achieved only minor significance in the theatre (see for example, *La revolución sentimental* (*Sentimental Club*) and as a poet. His first three books of poetry have a vague unifying motif consisting of the path or road found in each title. *La paz det sendero* [The Path of Peace], comprising poems of the earth, contains elements of the modernist lyric, while *El sendero ennumerable* [The Infinite Path] contains poems of the sea, considered his best poetry technically. In *El sendero andante* [The Moving Path], the author's unifying theme is rivers, again in a modernist vein.

Pérez de Ayala was at his best in the novel form, and his mature fiction secured his reputation as a writer during his lifetime. A definite separation exists between his first four novels, published between 1907 and 1912, representing a vaguely post-naturalist Galdosian realism, and the next five, published in rapid succession following a decade's hiatus, from 1921 until 1926, when the author won the National prize for literature and abruptly, inexplicably suspended his career as a novelist. A common thread (consisting of repeated characters and continuing anecdotes) runs through the first four works, uniting them in the manner of Galdós or of Balzac's *Comédie humaine*. *Tinieblas en las cumbres* [Darkness on the Summits] was published under the Neoplatonic pseudonym "Plotino Cuevas" (Plotinus Caves); via the narrative of playboys and libertines who hire a prostitute to accompany them to witness an eclipse on a mountain top, the work presents an allegory of man's blindness to ultimate reality and life's profundities. *A.M.D.G.* [To the Greater Glory of God] the title named after the motto of the Jesuits, with whom Pérez de Ayala studied, recreates in bitter, polemic fashion his traumatized recollection of boarding-school days and indictment of religious education in Spain. Its sequel, *La pata de la raposa* (*The Fox's Paw*), which was eagerly anticipated since its predecessor had caused a scandal, was banned; the protagonist, seen in later life, exhibits the crippling effects of early ideological indoctrination and sexual (mis)education.

Greater maturity appears in the linked novels *Luna de miel, luna de hiel* (*Honeymoon, Bittermoon*) and its sequel, *Los trabajos de Urbano y Simona* [The Labours of Urbana and Simona], indicting Spain's puritanical morality and failure to provide sex education. Generally considered his masterpiece, *Belarmino y Apolonio* (*Belarmino and Apolonio*) pits the worldview of classicism against that of romanticism, Apollonian against Dionysian, and Catholic dogma against human lives sacrificed to religious fanaticism in a tragicomic allegory of archetypal characters with implications for the conflict of science and religion, doubt and faith, intolerance and humanism. *Tigre Juan* (*Tiger Juan*) and its sequel, *El curandero de su honra* (*The Healer of his Honour*), burlesquing the Spanish codes of "machismo" or Don Juanism and Calderonian honour, solidified the author's fame.

Pérez de Ayala also wrote short fiction, including novellas and short story collections, such as his last short novel *Justicia* [Justice], and the three important "poematic novels": *Prometeo, Luz de domingo* and *La caída de los Limones* (*Prometheus, Sunday Sunlight,*

and *The Fall of the House of Limón*), all featuring interpolated poems. *Prometheus*, with aspects of the thesis novel, ridicules the concept of selective breeding or choosing a mate to produce a super-offspring. Much of the writer's fiction, set in the fictitious city of Pilares, parodies the real-life model (the Asturian city of Oviedo where Pérez de Ayala was born and educated). Self-centred, narrow, provincial attitudes are satirized in his collection, *El ombligo del mundo* [The World's Navel].

An exceptionally intelligent and accomplished novelist, Pérez de Ayala is much-praised as a polished and original stylist who excels in the depiction of ideologies, usually found at the centre of his narrative conflicts. Belonging to a transitional group that bridges the period between the famed "Generation of 1898" and the vaunted poets of the "Generation of 1927," he shares significant preoccupations of the earlier group and functions as an important link to European modernism and the vanguard. While his extensive lexicon and heightened intellectualism make him a challenging novelist, his sparkling humour and subtle satire amply reward the reader's efforts.

—Janet Pérez

PÉREZ GALDÓS, Benito

Born: Las Palmas, Grand Canary Island, 10 May 1843. **Education:** Educated at an English school, Las Palmas; Colegio de San Agustin, 1856–62; studied law at the University of Madrid, 1862–65. **Career:** Staff member, *La Nación* from 1865, and associated with *La Revista de España* from 1870; abandoned journalism for writing and travel, 1873; Liberal deputy for Puerto Rico, 1886–90; Republican deputy for Madrid, from 1907. Blind after about 1912. **Member:** Spanish Academy, 1897. **Died:** 4 January 1920.

PUBLICATIONS

Collections

Obras inéditas, edited by Alberto Ghiraldo. 11 vols., 1923–33.
Obras completas, edited by F.C. Sáinz de Robles. 6 vols., 1942–45.

Fiction

La fontana de oro. 1870; as *The Golden Fountain Cafe*, translated by Walter Rubin, 1989.
La sombra. 1871; edited by Rodolfo Cardona, 1964; as *The Shadow*, translated by Karen O. Austin, 1980.
El audaz: Historia de un radical de antaño. 1871.
Doña Perfecta. 1876; edited by Rodolfo Cardona, 1965; as *Lady Perfecta*, 1883; also translated by Mary Wharton, 1894; as *Doña Perfecta*, 1883; also translated by Mary J. Serrano, 1895; Harriet de Onís, 1960; as *Dona Perfecta*, translated by Alexander R. Tulloch, 1999.

Gloria. 1876–77; edited by Alexander H. Krappe, 1927; as *Gloria*, translated by Nathan Wetherell, 1879; also translated by Clara Bell, 1882.

Marianela. 1878; as *Marianela*, translated by Clara Bell, 1883; also translated by Helen W. Lester, 1892; Mary Wharton, 1893.

La familia de León Roch. 1878; as *The Family of Leon Roch*, translated by Clara Bell, 1886; as *Leon Roch*, translated by Bell, 1888.

La desheredada. 1881; as *The Disinherited Lady*, translated by Guy E. Smith, 1957; as *The Disinherited*, translated by Lester Clark, 1976.

El amigo Manso. 1882; as *Our Friend Manso*, translated by Robert Russell, 1987.

El doctor Centeno. 1883.

Tormento. 1884; edited by Eamonn J. Rodgers, 1977; as *Torment*, translated by J.M. Cohen, 1952; as *Inferno*, translated and edited by Abigail Lee Six, 1998.

La de Bringas. 1884; as *The Spendthrifts*, translated by Gamel Woolsey, 1951; translated and edited by Catherine Jagoe, 1996.

Lo prohibido. 1884–85; commentary by James Whiston, 1983.

Fortunata y Jacinta. 1886–87; as *Fortunata and Jacinta*, translated by Lester Clark, 1973; also translated by Agnes Moncy Gullón, 1986.

Miau. 1888; as *Miau*, translated by J.M. Cohen, 1963.

La incógnita. 1889; as *The Unknown*, translated by Karen O. Austin, 1991.

Torquemada en la hoguera, Torquemada en la cruz, Torquemada en el purgatorio, Torquemada y San Pedro. 4 vols., 1889–95; as *Torquemada*, translated by Frances M. López-Morillas, 1986; *Torquemada en la hoguera* as *Torquemada in the Fire*, translated by Nicholas G. Round, 1985.

Realidad. 1889; edited by Lisa Pauline Condé, 1993; as *Reality*, translated by Karen O. Austin, 1992.

Ángel Guerra. 1890–91; as *Ángel Guerra*, translated by Karen O. Austin, 1990.

Tristana. 1892; as *Tristana*, translated by R. Selden Rose, 1961.

La loca de la casa. 1892; as *La loca de la casa*, translated by Frances Exum, 1963.

Nazarín. 1895; as *Nazarin*, translated by Robert S. Rudder and Gloria Arjona, 1997.

Halma. 1895.

Misericordia. 1897; edited by Ángel del Río and McKendree Petty, 1946; as *Compassion*, translated by Toby Talbot, 1962; also translated by Joan MacLean, 1966; translated by Charles de Salis, 1995.

El abuelo. 1897.

Casandra. 1905.

El caballero encantado. 1909.

La razón de la sinrazón. 1915.

Fiction: *Episodios Nacionales* series

Trafalgar. 1873; edited by F.A. Kirkpatrick, 1905; as *Trafalgar*, translated by Clara Bell, 1884.

La Corte de Carlos IV. 1873; as *The Court of Charles IV*, translated by Clara Bell, 1888.

El 19 de marzo y el 2 de mayo. 1873.

Bailén. 1873.

Napoleón en Chamartín. 1874.

Zaragoza. 1874; edited by John Van Home, 1926; as *Saragossa*, translated by Minna Caroline Smith, 1899.

Gerona. 1874; as *Gerona*, translated by G.J. Racz, 1993.

Cádiz. 1874.

Juan Martín, el Empecinado. 1874.

La batalla de los Arapiles. 1875; as *The Battle of Salamanca*, translated by Rollo Ogden, 1895.

El equipaje del Rey José. 1875.

Memorias de un cortesano de 1815. 1875.

La segunda casaca. 1876.

El Grande Oriente. 1876.

El 7 de julio. 1876.

Los Cien Mil Hijos de San Luis. 1877.

El terror de 1824. 1877.

Un voluntario realista. 1878.

Los apostólicos. 1879.

Un faccioso más y algunos frailes menos. 1879.

Zumalacárregui. 1898.

Mendizábal. 1898.

De Oñate a La Granja. 1898.

Luchana. 1899.

La campaña del Maestrazgo. 1899.

La estafeta romántica. 1899.

Vergara. 1899.

Montes de Oca. 1900.

Los Ayacuchos. 1900.

Bodas reales. 1900.

Las tormentas del 48. 1902.

Narváez. 1902.

Los duendes de la camarilla. 1903.

La revolución de julio. 1904.

O'Donnell. 1904.

Aita Tettauen. 1905.

Carlos VI en La Rápita. 1905.

La vuelta al mundo en la Numancia. 1906.

Prim. 1906.

La de los tristes destinos. 1907.

España sin Rey. 1908.

España trágica. 1909.

Amadeo I. 1910.

La primera República. 1911.

De Cartago a Sagunto. 1911.

Cánovas. 1912.

Plays

Realidad, from his own novel (produced 1892). 1892; edited with introduction and notes by Lisa Pauline Condé, 1993.

Gerona, from his own novel (produced 1893). 1893.

La loca de la casa, from his own novel (produced 1893). 1893; edited by J. Warshaw, 1924.

La de San Quintín (produced 1894). 1894; as *The Duchess of San Quentin*, in *Masterpieces of Modern Spanish Drama*, edited by Barret H. Clark, 1928.

Las condenados. 1894.

Voluntad (produced 1895). 1895.

Doña Perfecta, from his own novel (produced 1896). 1896. *La fiera*. 1896.

Teatro. 5 vols., 1897–1918.

Electra (produced 1901). 1901; as *Electra*, 1901; also translated by Charles Alfred Turrell, 1919; and in *Modern Continental Plays*, edited by S.M. Tucker, 1929.

Alma y vida (produced 1902). 1902.

Mariucha (produced 1903). 1903.

El abuelo, from his own novel (produced 1904). 1904; as *The Grandfather*, translated by Elizabeth Wallace, 1910.

Bárbara (produced 1905). 1905.

Amor y ciencia. 1905.

Pedro Minio. 1908.

Casandra, from his own novel (produced 1910). 1910.

Celia en los infiernos (produced 1913). 1913.

Alceste. 1914.

Sor Simona (produced 1915). 1915.

El tacaño Salomón. 1916.

Santa Juana de Castilla (produced 1918). 1918.

Un joven de provecho, edited by H.C. Berkowitz, in *Publications of the Modern Language Association*, September 1935.

Other

Memoranda. 1906.

Cartas a Mesonero Romanos, edited by E. Varela Hervías. 1943.

Madrid, edited by J. Pérez Vidal. 1955.

Cartas a Galdós, edited by Soledad Ortega. 1964.

Cartas del archivo de Galdós, edited by Sebastián de la Nuez and Joseph Schraibman. 1967.

Las cartas desconocidas en "La Prensa" de Buenos Aires, edited by William H. Shoemaker. 1973.

Los artículos políticos en la "evista de España," 1871–1872, edited by Brian J. Dendle and Joseph Schraibman. 1982.

*

Bibliography: *Pérez Galdós: An Annotated Bibliography* by Theodore A. Sackett, 1968; *Bibliografía de Galdós I* by Manuel Hernández Suárez, 1972; *Pérez Galdós: A Selective Annotated Bibliography* by Hensley C. Woodbridge, 1975.

Critical Studies: *Pérez Galdós and the Spanish Novel of the Nineteenth Century* by Leslie B. Walton, 1927; *Pérez Galdós, Spanish Liberal Crusader* by H.C. Berkowitz, 1948; *The Novels of Pérez Galdós* by S.H. Eoff, 1954; *Benito Pérez Galdós and the Creative Process*, 1954, and *Benito Pérez Galdós*, 1975, both by Walter T. Pattison; *An Introduction to the "Episodios Nacionales" of Galdós* by Alfredo Rodríguez, 1967; *Humour in Galdós: A Study of the Novelas contemporáneas* by Michael Nimetz, 1968; *Gatdós Studies I* edited by J.E. Varey, 1970, and *Pérez Galdós: Doña Perfecta* by Varey, 1971; *The Tragic Import in the Novels of Pérez Galdós* by Joaquín Santaló, 1973; *Galdós Studies II* edited by Robert J. Weber, 1974; *Galdós and Beethoven: Fortunata y Jacinta: A Symphonic Novel* by Vernon A. Chamberlin, 1977; *Pérez Galdós, Fortunata y Jacinta*, 1977, *Reality Plain or Fancy?: Some Reflections on Galdós's Concept of Realism*, 1986, and *History and Fiction in Galdós's Narratives*, 1993, all by Geoffrey Ribbans; *Pérez Galdós, Miau*, 1978, and *From Enlightenment to Realism: The Novels of Galdós 1870–1887*, 1987, both by Eamonn Rodgers; *The Jew in the Novels of Benito Pérez Galdós* by Sara E. Schyfter, 1979; *Galdós: The Mature Thought*, 1980, and *Galdós: The Early Historical Novels*, 1987, both by Brian J. Dendle; *Pérez Galdós, La de Bringas*, 1981, *Galdós's Novel of the Historical Imagination: A Study of the Contemporary Novels*, 1983, *Vision and the Visual Arts in Galdós: A Study of the Novels and Newspaper Articles*, 1986, and *Pérez Galdós, Nazarín*, 1991, all by Peter A. Bly; *Galdós and the Art of the European Novel 1867–1887* by Stephen Gilman, 1981; *Galdós and the Irony of Language*, 1982, and *The Novel Histories of Galdós*, 1989, both by Diane Faye Urey; *Galdós and His Critics* by Anthony Percival, 1985; *Psychology, Religion and Ethics in Galdós Novels: The Quest for Authenticity* by A.M. Penuel, 1988; *Pérez Galdós: Marianela* by Geraldine M. Scanlon, 1988; *Stages in the Development of a Feminist Consciousness in Pérez Galdós 1843–1920: A Biographical Sketch*, 1990, and *Women in the Theatre of Galdós: From Realidad (1892) to Voluntad (1895)*, 1991, both by Lisa P. Condo; *Images of the Sign: Semiotic Consciousness in the Novels of Benito Pérez Galdós* by Akiko Tsuchiya, 1990; *Galdós' House of Fiction: Papers Given at the Birmingham Galdós Colloquium* edited by A.H. Clarke and others, 1991; *Benito Pérez Galdós: Fortunata and Jacinta* by Harriet S. Turner, 1992; *Tristana: Buñuel's Film and Galdós' Novel: A Case Study in the Relation Between Literature and Film* by Colin Partridge, 1995; *Conflicts and Conciliations: The Evolution of Galdós's Fortunata y Jacinta* by Geoffrey Ribbans, 1997; *Galdós's Segunda Manera: Rhetorical Strategies and Affective Response* by Linda M. Willem, 1998; *Cervantes and Galdos in Fortunata y Jacinta: Tales of Impertinent Curiosity* by Kevin S. Larsen, 1999; *Dickens in Galdós* by Timothy Michael McGovern, 2000; *Pérez Galdós: Tristana* by Lisa Pauline Condé, 2000.

* * *

As he began his literary career, around 1870, Benito Pérez Galdós was uncomfortably aware that Spain, the country of Cervantes, had produced, in the 19th century, no works of prose fiction to rival the achievements of Dickens and Balzac. The remedy, however, could not consist merely in a slavish imitation of foreign models, for although Pérez Galdós was more open to European trends than his conservative Catholic contemporaries, he was still influenced by the cultural nationalism which was one of the keynotes of Spanish literary life. In seeking, therefore, to provide a counterpart to Balzac's encyclopedic view of French society in *La Comédie humaine*, Pérez Galdós preferred to choose as models Spanish writers such as Cervantes and Quevedo, who represented a tradition of realism that was humorous, satirical, and moralistic.

This moralistic element sometimes gives rise to a certain polemical quality, especially in novels like *Doña Perfecta* (*Lady Perfecta*), which portrays contemporary religious and political conflict in the aftermath of the Revolution of 1868. However, the novels of the 1870s do not represent Pérez Galdós's most characteristic mode. By 1881, some of the tensions in post-revolutionary society had become less acute, and this is reflected in a more sober, complex, and detached presentation of contemporary reality in Pérez Galdós's novels. Nevertheless, the primary focus of interest in his work remains ethical: his major themes are social pretence, self-deception, vanity, and egoism. The treatment of these themes, however, is by no means schematic or theoretical, for Pérez Galdós's depiction of the context in which moral choices have to be made gives rise to a vivid and detailed recreation of the atmosphere of Madrid society in the last quarter of the century. For example, *El amigo Manso* (*Our Friend Manso*) is the story of a professor of philosophy who, at the very beginning of the novel, asserts that he exists only as a fictional being, and who spends his life unsuccessfully pursuing the ideal of perfect balance between reason and feeling, and between abstract principle and concrete action. Yet by portraying in detail the various social relationships in which Manso is involved, the novel also immerses the reader in the spheres of politics, fashion, the theatre, family life, and amorous intrigue. In one very characteristic scene, for instance, the philosopher is shown trying to assess the qualifications of various peasant women for the position of wet-nurse to his nephew.

This vivid quotidian realism places Pérez Galdós firmly within the broad tradition of the 19th-century European novel. At the same time, however, his links with his native literary traditions give his writings a characteristically Spanish flavour which goes beyond mere local colour. Moreover, his work is informed throughout by the desire to re-educate his contemporaries to a true understanding of their experience. This is particularly obvious in the series of historical novels, the *Episodios Nacionales*, which Pérez Galdós composed at various times between 1873 and 1912, and which trace the history of Spain from the Battle of Trafalgar (1805) to the restoration of the Bourbon monarchy (1875). This sense of educational and moral mission gives his work a tone of civic seriousness tempered by humour which is perhaps his most characteristic contribution to world literature.

—Eamonn Rodgers

PERRAULT, Charles

Born: Paris, France, 12 January 1628. **Education:** Educated at Collége de Beauvais, Paris, 1636–44; licentiate in law, 1651. **Family:** Married Marie Guichon in 1672 (died 1678); three sons. **Career:** Clerk for his brother Pierre; tax collector, Paris; adviser to Colbert, Louis XIV's finance minister; appointed by Colbert as the founder member of the Little Academy of Inscriptions and Medals, 1663 (expelled 1683); first clerk of buildings, 1668, supervising contruction at Versailles and other royal palaces. His poem, *Le Siècle de Louis le Grand* [The Age of Louis the Great], outraged the Académie française and provoked the outbreak of the Quarrel of the Ancients and Moderns, 1687. **Member:** Académie française, from 1671, instigated a series of major reforms; chancellor, 1673; director, 1681. **Died:** 15 May 1703.

PUBLICATIONS

Collections

Oeuvres diverses. 1757.
Oeuvres choisies, edited by M. Collin de Plancy. 1826.
Oeuvres complètes, edited by Jean-Jacques Pauvert. 3 vols., 1969–70.

Fiction

Contes de ma mère l'Oye. 1697; as *Fairy Tales*, translated by Robert Samber, 1729; also translated by Guy Miège and Robert Samber, 1785; as *The Tales of Mother Goose*, translated by C. Welsh, 1903; as *The Authentic Mother Goose Fairy Tales and Nursery Rhymes*, translated and edited by Jacques Barchilon and Henry Pettit, 1960.
Histoires; ou, Contes du temps passé avec des moralités. 1697; edited by Daniel Conty, 1978, Roger Zuber, 1987, Marc Soriano, 1989, and by Catherine Magnien, 1990; as *Histories or Tales of Past Times*, translated by Guy Miège and Robert Samber, 1729.

Contes des fées. 1724; edited by M. le Bon Walkenaer, 1836; also edited by C. Giraud, 1864, revised edition, 1865; A. Lefèvre, 1875; Jacques Barchilon, 1956 and 1980; Gilbert Rouger, 1967; J.P. Collinet, 1981; Roger Zuber, 1987; Catherine Magnien, 1990; as *Perrault's Popular Tales*, translated and edited by Andrew Long, 1888; as *Fairy Tales*, translated by Norman Denny, 1950; also translated by Geoffrey Brereton, 1957; Anne Carter, 1967; A.E. Johnson, 1969; Angola Carter, 1977; Anne Lawrence, 1989.

Verse

Le Siècle de Louis le Grand. 1687.
Adam; ou, La Création de l'homme. 1697.

Other

Los Murs de Troie; ou, L'Origine du burlesque. 1653.
Dialogue de l'amour et de l'amitié. 1660.
Carrousel; ou, Courses de tête et de bague. 1670.
Recueil de divers ouvrages en prose et en vers. 1675.
Labyrinthe de Versailles. 1677.
Banquet des dieux pour la naissance du duc de Bourgogne. 1682.
Saint Paulin, évêque de Nole. 1686.
Parallèle des anciens et des modernes. 4 vols., 1688–1697; revised edition, 2 vols., 1693; edited by H. Jauss and M. Imdahl, 1964.
A Mgr le Dauphin sur la prise de Philisbourg. 1688.
A l'Académie française. 1690.
Le Cabinet des Beaux-Arts. 1690.
A M. le Président Rose. 1691.
Au Roi, sur la prise de Mons. 1691.
La Chasse. 1692.
Ode au Roi: Lettre à M. D*** touchant la préface de son Ode sur la prise de Namur. 1692.
L'Apologie des femmes. 1694; as *The Vindication of Wives*, translated by Roland Gant, 1954.
Le Triomphe de sainte Geneviève. 1694.
Réponse aux Réflexions critiques de M. D*** sur Longin. 1694.
Les Hommes illustres qui ont paru en France pendant ce siècle. 2 vols., 1696–70; reprinted 1970; as *Characters Historical and Panegyrical of the Greatest Men that Have Appeared in France During the Last Century*, translated by J. Ozell, 2 vols., 1704–05.
Portrait de Messire Benigne Bossuet. 1698.
Pour le roi de Suède. 1702.
L'Oublieux. 1868.
Mémoires de ma vie, edited by Paul Bonnefon. 1909; as *Memoirs of My Life*, edited and translated by Jeanne Morgan Zarucchi, 1989.
Pensées chrétiennes, edited by Jacques Barchilon and C. Velay-Vallantin, 1987.
Translator, *Portrait de Messire Benigne Bossuet*, by F. Boutard. 1698.
Translator, *Fables de Faërne.* 1699.

*

Bibliography: *Perrault à travers la critique depuis 1960* by C.L. Malarte, 1989.

Critical Studies: *Les Perrault* by André Hallays, 1926; *Les Contes de Perrault: Culture savante et traditions populaires*, 1968, and *Le Dossier Perrault*, 1972, both by Marc Soriano; *A Concordance to Charles Perrault's Tales* by Jacques Barchilon, E. Flinders and J.

Foreman, 2 vols., 1977–79, and *Charles Perrault* (in English), 1981, by Barchilon and Flinders; *Perrault's Morals for Moderns* by Jeanne Morgan Zarucchi, 1985; *Fairytale Romance: The Grimms, Basile and Perrault* (includes bibliography) by James M. McGlathery, 1991; *Seeing Through the Mother Goose Tales: Visual Turns in the Writings of Charles Perrault* by Philip Lewis, 1996.

* * *

Charles Perrault achieved world-renowned status in a context that ironically deprived him of an original literary identity. *Histoires; ou, Contes du temps passé avec des moralités* (*Histories or Tales of Past Times*) came to be among the world's most famous stories, transmitted orally and in print from generation to generation; the eight tales included were "La Belle au bois dormant" ("Sleeping Beauty"), "Le Petit Chaperon rouge" ("Little Red Riding Hood"), "La Barbe bleue" ("Bluebeard"), "Le maître Chat, ou Le Chat botté" ("Puss in Boots"), "Les Fées" ("The Fairies"/"Diamonds and Toads"), "Cendrillon, ou La Petite Pentoufle de verre" ("Cinderella"), "Riquet à la hoppe" ("Ricky with the Tuft"), and "Le Petit Pouçet" ("Little Thumbkin"/"Tom Thumb"). Perrault became immortalized as the father of French children's literature; as the legend of the tales grew, however, his authorship became a problematical issue. In the sweep of 19th-century nostalgia for the origins of "national" folk culture, Perrault's own role in the tales' composition was reduced by scholars to that of an unwitting precursor of the Grimm brothers, transcribing the tales for the presumed entertainment of his children.

In their original versions, however, the tales are moral commentaries upon 17th-century adult behaviour, with satirical allusions to literary and social practices of the time. Each prose tale is followed by one or two "morals" in verse, a witty coda that often ignores or undermines the apparent lesson conveyed by the tale. For many critical scholars, the prose/verse dichotomy presented a contradiction that could only be resolved by attributing the authorship of the prose tales to Perrault's son, and acknowledging Perrault himself only as the author of the sophisticated verse morals.

Recent criticism, however, attributed sole authorship to Perrault on several grounds. First, the apparent simplicity of the prose tales belies a complex structure in which elements evocative of oral tradition are deliberately juxtaposed with tongue-in-cheek authorial commentary. In "Little Red Riding Hood": when instructed to jump into bed with the wolf "she was very surprised to see how her Grandmother looked in a state of undress." And in "Bluebeard": after participating in a round of lavish entertainments, "the youngest daughter began to think that the owner's beard was not really so very blue."

Second, the tales' stylistic traits are compatible with those of numerous other works of prose and poetry by Perrault, most importantly the three tales-in-verse: "Griselidis," "Les Souhaits ridicules" ("The Ridiculous Wishes"), and "Peau d'Ane" ("Donkeyskin"). In these poems, a folkloric subject is given a sophisticated stylistic treatment, in a manner analogous to that of the later tales in prose.

Third, and most significantly, the tales are now recognized to be part of a large body of work that Perrault produced as an outgrowth of his other principal literary contribution: as a proponent of the Modernist cause in the literary "Quarrel of the Ancients and Moderns." This ongoing intellectual debate, over the merits of classical antiquity versus modern progress, took a distinctive turn in 1687, when Perrault composed *Le Siècle de Louis le Grand*, a poem celebrating the age of Louis the Great as an epoch in which the French nation under Louis XIV surpassed the accomplishments of all preceding history.

The reaction of Perrault's colleagues in the Académie française was extreme, including an exclamation of outrage by his longstanding rival Boileau. While advances in science and technology seemed unarguable, the claim that modern French writers had eclipsed the sublimity of Homer and Virgil was a shocking assault upon the canon. In response to this criticism, Perrault produced a series of works specifically elevating the merits of "modern" invention over the "naive" notions of the past.

Perrault's most important overtly polemical works on this subject were the *Parallèle des anciens et des modernes* [Parallel of the Ancients and the Moderns] and *Les Hommes illustres qui ont paru en France pendant ce siècle* (*Characters Historical and Panegyrical of the Greatest Men that Have Appeared in France During the Last Century*). In the *Parallèle*, a series of imagined conversations take place between an opinionated conservative (the "judge"), a social gadfly ("the nobleman"), and an intelligent, rational philosopher (the "clergyman"); the Modernist viewpoint is inevitably argued with logical persuasion by the clergyman. The *Parallèle* is now viewed as the most important literary document of the Quarrel, the intellectual debate which opened the way for the notion of "enlightenment" in the next century.

Other works echo the Modernist cause in more subtle fashion. *L'Apologie des femmes* (*The Vindication of Wives*) was written in 1694 to counter Boileau's misogynist tenth satire, and in his poetic rebuttal, Perrault declared that only the primitive morals of ancient times could explain such ignorant anti-feminism, and that the slavish imitation of that classical model (by Boileau) was indefensible.

Most importantly, Perrault's *Tales* represent a new literary genre of non-classical inspiration. Like the classical fable, they are intended to serve a moral instructional purpose, but as Perrault argued, because of the greater sophistication of the modern age, their messages are more complex and, he believed, more worthy of praise. Fables of dubious moral virtue such as "The Matron of Ephesus" and "Cupid and Psyche" (both of which were recounted by La Fontaine, a proponent of the Ancients) were condemned by Perrault as having far less value than "the tales which our ancestors invented." The folkloric authenticity of the tales may be in doubt, since some parallel but not identical versions have been traced to the Italian writers Basile and Straparola, and other tales, notably "Little Red Riding Hood," have no known direct antecedents. Perrault wished, however, for the tales to be accepted by the reader as "modern" inventions, distinguished from their classical counterparts by the incorporation of a praiseworthy moral.

The principal literary achievement of the *Tales*, aside from their role in the Modernist polemic, is that the text is both accessible and meaningful on multiple levels. Moral commentary is presented in a style of such apparent limpidity that the subtle messages may not be apparent at first glance. As Perrault stated, they contain "a Moral which reveals itself more or less, according to the degree of penetration of the readers," a stylistic achievement that allows a child to derive pleasure and instruction from one message, whereas an adult may derive another set of messages entirely. Perrault's masterful command of what 17th-century rhetoric identified as "simple" style resulted in his historical disappearance as the text's real author, and only the critical reappraisal of the late 20th century has finally placed him in the ranks of the great moralists of 17th-century France.

—Jeanne Morgan Zarucchi

PERSE, Saint-John

See SAINT-JOHN PERSE

PERSIUS

Born: Aulus Persius Flaccus in Volaterra (Volterra), Etruria (now part of Italy), AD 34. **Education:** Educated in Rome, where he was a pupil of the Stoic philosopher Cornutus, who edited his poems for posthumous publication. **Died:** AD 62.

PUBLICATIONS

Works

[Satires] (with satires by Juvenal), edited by W.V. Clausen. 1959; revised edition, 1992; also edited by Domenicus Bo, 1969; edited and translated by G.G. Ramsey [Loeb Edition], 1918, revised edition, 1940, J.R. Jenkinson, 1980, and William Barr and Guy Lee, 1987; translated by Barten Holyday, 1616; also translated by John Dryden, 1693 and with others (with satires by Juvenal), 1735, reprinted 1979; John Conington, 1874, 3rd edition, 1893, reprinted 1987; W.S. Merwin, 1961; Niall Rudd (with satires by Horace), 1973, revised edition, 1979; commentaries by John Conington and H. Nettleship, 1893, and R.A. Harvey, 1981; as *Persius Satires*, translated by John Conington, 1998.

*

Bibliography: *A Bibliography of Persius*, by M.H. Morgan, 1909.

Critical Studies: *Roman Satire* by J.W. Duff, 1937; *The Poet Persius, Literary and Social Critic* by William H. Semple, 1961; *Persius and the Programmatic Satire* by J.C. Bramble, 1974; *Roman Satire* by M. Coffey, 1976; *Essays on Roman Satire* by William S. Anderson, 1982; *Persius* by Mark Morford, 1984; *Themes in Roman Satire* by Niall Rudd, 1986; *The Satiric Voice: Program, Form and Meaning in Persius and Juvenal* by William Thomas Wehrle, 1992; *The Knotted Thong: Structures of Mimesis in Persius* by D.M. Hooley, 1997; *Satires of Rome: Threatening Poses from Lucilius to Juvenal* by Kirk Freudenburg, 2001.

*   *   *

Aulus Persius Flaccus is the third of the four Roman satirists to have come down to us from antiquity. He was preceded in the genre, which Quintilian labels the Romans' own contribution to ancient literature, by Lucilius, of whom we have but fragmentary remains, and Horace, with whose work he shows a profound familiarity. Juvenal rounds out the genre, as we know it. Roman "satire" or *satura* (a word which refers to a type of sausage or haggis) represents a kind of literary allusion in which poets would mix together observations on society, exhortations derived from the philosophical schools and popular morality, a biting wit, and a kind of salty, unpoetic language reminiscent of conversational speech. By the end of Lucilius' career it was standard that satires be written in dactylic hexameters.

In many ways, Persius' satires are the least characteristic of all. Firstly, his *oeuvre* is by far the shortest. Published posthumously by the poet Caesius Bassus, to whom Satire Six is dedicated, Persius' poems make up one slim volume of 664 lines. Secondly, his satires are the only ones to espouse a consistent ideological and moral position based on the teachings of a single philosophical school, the late Stoa. Thus according to the ancient "Life of Persius," the poet at the age of 16 entrusted himself to the Stoic philosopher Cornutus, whom he describes in his fifth satire as providing both moral and aesthetic guidance. Yet by far the most unusual characteristic of Persius' satires is his use of language. Where Lucilius wrote in a loose, conversational style, which Horace refined into a sophisticated literary instrument, and where Juvenal offers mock-epic grandeur, Persius eschews the grand style, writing in an idiosyncratic Latin, far removed from daily conversation (see William S. Anderson, "Persius and the Rejection of Society," *Essays on Roman Satire*, 1982). He frequently uses little-known words, forms neologisms, or takes common words and gives them a sharp new turn. He creates a demanding style of diction which defies translation and which in large part accounts for why he is so little read today. Thus, although Persius' work remained popular throughout the Middle Ages and Renaissance because of its consistent moral message, from ancient times commentators have remarked on his obscurity.

Persius' practice of linguistic invention, in fact, is part of a deliberate and programmatic rhetorical strategy. Thus, in the opening of Satire Five, Cornutus admonishes his young charge, "verba togae sequeris iunctura callidus acri" (You stick to the words of the toga, clever at the sharp juxtaposition). This line is at once an explanation and instantiation of Persius' style. If we examine the initial half of the phrase first, our most difficult task is to unfold what is meant by "the words of the toga." On the one hand, it appears to refer to a preference for pure Latin diction. The toga could only be worn by Roman citizens. Hence "sticking to the words of the toga" would denote a rejection of the common practice in Neronian poetics of using a highly artificial, Greek-influenced vocabulary, for which Persius criticizes his contemporaries in Satire One. In that same first satire, the poet also makes an equivalence between poetic style and personal character, so that the poets who write in this artificial, Greek style are portrayed as morally soft and sexually perverse. Consequently, Persius' refusal of what he deems an overrefined and unnatural Greek poetic diction in turn implies the rejection of a decadent lifestyle associated with the Hellenistic East in favour of the rough and ready virtues of the traditional Roman in the mould of Cato. The toga, nonetheless, was not the everyday dress of the soldier or farmer, but that worn on formal and official occasions. Associated with it are the qualities of solemnity, seriousness, and the class consciousness of the ruling strata of Roman society (Persius in Satires Three, Four, and Five shows his low regard for the uneducated masses). Thus we are not talking about just common or moral speech, but also weighty, and by implication, educated speech. The moral gravity of this refined plain speech is portrayed in deliberate contrast to the inflated diction and hollow subject matter Persius associates with contemporary poetic style in Satires One and Five.

The fact that so much can be extracted from this careful placement of two ordinary words in turn functions as a precise illustration of the second half of the line under examination, "clever at the sharp juxtaposition." The phrase itself represents a reworking of a passage from Horace's *Ars poetica*, "You will have spoken distinctively, if clever juxtaposition will have made a known word new." Persius thus both practises and advocates the use of a poetic style which is self-consciously intertextual and possessed of a keen cutting edge. He both imitates Horace and sharpens him. Such a style is appropriate for a corpus whose primary aim is to attack vice and promote virtue. Thus, as we have already noted, Satire One attacks contemporary poetic style. Satire Two exposes the foolish and often evil requests people make in prayer. The third satire begins by lampooning the slovenly habits of a young philosophy student (thought to be Persius himself) who oversleeps on account of the previous evening's debauchery, and finishes with a sermon on the medicinal value of philosophy for diseases of the soul. Satire Four begins with a dialogue in which Socrates admonishes Alcibiades for his vanity and ends with a diatribe on the virtue of self-knowledge. Satire Five begins with Persius' praise of Cornutus, and then defends the Stoic thesis that only the wise man is free, while Satire Six advocates the Horatian position that one should enjoy one's wealth and not worry about his or her heirs. In each case, there is a clear target at which Persius' satiric venom is aimed and the "sharp juxtaposition" is his weapon of choice. Moreover, this imagery of the sharp, the keen, and the cutting is part of a continuing thematics found throughout the corpus. One of the most common words in the satires is the verb *radere* (to shave or scrape), referring to the healthy abrasive function of both philosophy and satire on the human soul. In contrast, those poets of whom the satirist disapproves are described as "soft," "fluid," "effeminate," or "trivial." Thus both in terms of style and content, Persius values the hard over the soft, the rough over the smooth, the penetrating over the pointless.

A good example of Persius' style and content may be found in the opening prologue in iambic metre. The poem begins with a rejection of the Greek mythological trappings used to describe poetic inspiration and finishes with the claim that poets only write to feed their bellies. The first line features the phrase "fons caballinus" or "nag's spring," an irreverent translation of the Greek *Hippocrene*, the sacred spring of the muses. By using the vulgar Latin *caballinus*, Persius shows his contempt for those who ape the Greek tradition, even as he demonstrates his knowledge of it. His use of a low level of diction opposes him to his overrefined contemporaries, but his erudition lifts him above the masses. Five lines later, he claims to be a "semipaganus," a "half rustic." The word itself is a neologism coined specially for the occasion and so should not be taken too literally. For even as it proclaims the poet's lack of sophistication, it demonstrates his wit. Persius may be half rustic, but in matters that count (virtue, honesty, philosophical penetration) he far surpasses his rivals.

Persius' satires make great demands on the reader. His work cannot be simply browsed through, but requires focused, self-conscious participation. His rhetoric forces our active engagement in the creation of meaning. It scrapes away our illusions of self-mastery and sophistication and forces us to see the world anew through the sharpened lens of Stoic philosophy.

—Paul Allen Miller

PESSOA, Fernando (António Nogueira)

Born: Lisbon, Portugal, 13 June 1888. **Education:** Educated at an Irish convent school in Durban, South Africa; Durban High School, 1899–1905; University of Lisbon, 1906–07. **Career:** Owner, Emprêsa Ibis, publishers, Lisbon, 1907; freelance translator, into French and English, for commercial firms, Lisbon, 1907–34; involved in several literary movements, especially *Renascença portuguêsa*; co-founder, *Orfeu* magazine, 1915. Wrote in Portuguese, English, and French. **Died:** 30 November 1935.

PUBLICATIONS

Collections

Obras completas. 1952–.
Poesias, edited by Maria Aliete Galhoz. 1942, reprinted as *Obra poética*, 1960.
Obra poética e em prosa, edited by António Quadros and Dalila Pereira da Costa. 3 vols., 1986.
Fernando Pessoa and Co.: Selected Poems, edited and translated by Richard Zenith. 1998.

Verse

Antinous, 35 Sonnets (in English). 2 vols., 1918.
English Poems: Antinous, 35 Sonnets, Epithalamium. 3 vols., 1921.
Mensagem. 1934; as *Message* (bilingual edition), translated by Jonathan Griffin, 1992.
Alberto Caeiro, Ricardo Reis, Alvaro de Campos, Fernando Pessoa, edited and translated by Jonathan Griffin. 4 vols., 1971.
Selected Poems, edited and translated by Peter Rickard. 1971.
Selected Poems, edited and translated by Edwin Honig. 1971.
Sixty Portuguese Poems, edited and translated by F.E.G. Quintanilha. 1971.
Selected Poems, edited and translated by Jonathan Griffin. 1974; revised edition, with supplement, 1982.
Stations of the Cross, translated by J.C.R. Green. 1976.
Poesias inéditas, edited by Vitorino and Jorge Nemésio. 1978.
Novas poesias inéditas, edited by Maria do Rosário Marques Sablo and Adelaide Mariam Monteiro Sereno. 1979.
The Surprise of Being: Twenty Five Poems, translated by J.C.R. Green and Clara de Azevedo Mafra. 1986.
Poems, translated by Edwin Honig and Susan Brown. 1989.

Other

Cartas a Armando Côrtez-Rodrigues, edited by Joel Serrão. 1945; revised edition, 1959.
Páginas de doutrina estética, edited by Jorge de Sena. 1946.
Cartas a João Gaspar Simões, edited by Simões. 1957.
Cartas a Fernando Pessoa (includes some works by Pessoa), by Mário Sá-Carneiro, edited by Helena Cidade Moura. 2 vols., 1958–59.
Páginas íntimas e de auto-interpretação, edited by J. do Prado Coelho and G.R. Lind. 1966.
Textos filosóficos, edited by A. de Pina Coelho. 2 vols., 1968.
Obras em prosa, edited by J. Bernardinelli. 1974.
Cartas de amor (selected letters), edited by David Mourão-Ferreira. 1978.
Always Astonished (selected prose), edited and translated by Edwin Honig. 1988.
Livro do desassossego por Bernardo Soares (selected prose), as *The Book of Disquiet*, edited by Maria José de Lancastre, translated by Margaret Jull Costa, 1991; also translated by Iain Watson, 1991; as *The Book of Disquietude*, translated by Richard Zenith, 1991; as *The Book of Disquiet*, translated by Alfred Mac Adam, 1998.

*

Critical Studies: *Three Twentieth-Century Portuguese Poets* by J.M. Parker, 1960; *Cuadrivio* (on Darío, López Velarde, Pessoa, Cernuda) by Octavio Paz, 1965; *Fernando Pessoa: The Genesis of the Heteronyms* by J.C.R. Green, 1982; *The Man Who Never Was: Essays on Pessoa* edited by George Monteiro, 1982; ''Pessoa Issue'' of *Numbers*, 4, 1988; *Fernando Pessoa: Voices of a Nomadic Soul* by Zbigniew Kotowicz, 1996; *Modern Art in Portugal: 1910–1940: The Artist Contemporaries of Fernando Pessoa*, translated by John S. Southard, 1998; *An Introduction to Fernando Pessoa: Modernism and the Paradoxes of Authorship* by Darlene J. Sadlier, 1998; *The Presence of Pessoa: English, American, and Southern African Literary Responses* by George Monteiro, 1998; *Fernando Pessoa and Nineteenth-Century Anglo-American Literature* by George Monteiro, 2000.

* * *

Fernando Pessoa is the greatest Portuguese poet since Camões, and one of the most complex and astonishing figures of 20th-century literature. At the time of his death at the age of 47, Pessoa had published very little; his reputation, even within Portuguese literary circles, was quite limited. Pessoa left behind a vast collection of unpublished works—some 25,000 texts and fragments. As these works have been organized and edited, Pessoa's uniqueness has been revealed; his posthumous influence on Portuguese and Brazilian letters has been profound, and numerous translations into other European languages have begun to establish his international reputation as a major writer and as an icon of the modern crisis of identity.

Pessoa's crisis of identity was at once personal and literary. Most of his poetry before 1909 was written in English; at that point, just as Pessoa began to shift into Portuguese, he became aware of a very broad range of foreign literary movements—everything from French symbolism to Italian futurism—which arrived almost simultaneously in Lisbon. Pessoa, like his contemporaries, struggled to make sense of these new and discordant voices; unlike his contemporaries, he was also obsessed with doubts about his own sanity, about his sexual orientation, and about the meaning of what now appears to have been a strongly repressed tendency towards multiple personalities.

Pessoa's solution to these crises began to take form in 1914: the creation, or liberation, of a number of distinct and separate literary personalities he called heteronyms. These are not pseudonyms, but discrete individuals—possessed of biographies and coherent and independent philosophies and literary styles. We now know of at least 20 heteronyms and semi-heteronyms. The four most complete identities, however, are Alberto Caeiro, Álvaro de Campos, Ricardo Reis, and the orthonym, Fernando Pessoa, whom the poet insisted was neither more nor less real than the others. Pessoa is an esoteric neo-symbolist poet of traditional forms, preoccupied with religious and patriotic myths. Caeiro, the happy survivor of a lost Golden Age, is a pastoralist whose forms and diction reflect his relative lack of education; he believes only in the simple objects which surround him and the simple joys his senses perceive. Reis, Caeiro's disciple, is also within the classical tradition; but Reis is Horace to Caeiro's bucolic Virgil, and his complex and perfect formal odes are intensely intellectual creations designed to communicate his weariness of emotion and mortality. Álvaro de Campos, Reis's mirror image, is a passionate, dynamic child of our own century—the creature of Whitman and of Marinetti, delightedly obsessed with the machines he tends as first engineer on a tanker; his formless free verse is violent and exclamatory, filled with a dead-end existentialism born before its time.

Taken as a whole, the writings of Pessoa and his heteronyms and semi-heteronyms form a document, unique to literature if not to psychoanalysis, which is also a vibrant one-man show that simultaneously exhibits a full range of literary reactions to the human condition from Theocritus to Sartre.

—David T. Haberly

PETŐFI, Sándor

Born: Kiskoőrös, Hungary, 1 January 1823. **Education:** Educated at various elementary schools in Kiskoőrös, Félegyháza, Kecskemét, Szabadszállás, and Sárszentlőrinc; Evangelical and Piarist gymnasiums in Pest, and at Evangelical Gymnasium in Aszód, 1835–38; Evangelical Lyceum in Selmec, 1838–39; high school in Pápa, from 1841. **Military Service:** Joined army in 1839: discharged because of ill health in 1841; entered military service again as captain in September 1848: died on the battlefield within a year, his body never found. **Family:** Married Júlia Szendrey in 1847; one son. **Career:** Worked as actor; translator, 1842–43; assistant editor of *Pesti Divatlap* [Pest Fashion Journal], 1844–45. One of the key figures of the Hungarian Revolution of March 1848. **Died:** Last seen on the battlefield on 31 July 1849.

PUBLICATIONS

Collections

Vegyes művei 1838–1849 [Miscellaneous Works], edited by Pál Gyulai. 3 vols., 1863.
Összes művek [Collected Works], edited by Adolf Havas. 6 vols., 1892–96.
Munkái [Works], edited by Ferenc Badics. 4 vols., 1906.
Összes költeményei [Collected Verse], edited by Géza Voinovics. 2 vols., 1921.
Összes művei [Collected Works]. 7 vols., 1951–64.
Összes művei [Collected Works], edited by Pál Pándi. 3 vols., 1955.
Összes költeményei. 2 vols., 1959.
Összes prózai művei és levelezése, edited by Pál Pándi. 1960.
Összes művei [Collected Works], edited by József Kiss. 1973–.

Verse

Versek. 1842–1844 [Poems]. 1844.
A helység kalapácsa [The Village Blacksmith]. 1844.
Czipruslombok Etelke sírjáról. 1845; as *Cypress Leaves from the Grave of Dear Ethel*, translated by William N. Loew, 1912.
János vitéz. 1845; as *John the Hero*, translated by Ferenc Pulszky, in *Tales and Traditions of Hungary*, 3 vols., 1851; as *Childe John*, translated by William N. Loew, 1912.
Szerelem gyöngyei [The Pearls of Love]. 1845.
Versek. 1844–1845 [Poems]. 1845.
Felhők [Clouds]. 1846.
Összes költeményei [Collected Verse]. 1847.

Az apostol. 1848; as *The Apostle*, translated by William N. Loew, 1912; also translated by Victor Clement, 1961.

Újabb költeményei 1847–1849 [New Poems]. 1851.

Translations from Alexander Petőfi, the Magyar Poet, translated by John Bowring. 1866.

[Selection], translated by Frederic Walter Fuller, in *Evadne and Other Poems*. 1894.

The Apostle; Childe John; Simple Steve; Cypress Leaves from the Grave of Dear Ethel, translated by William N. Loew. 1912.

[Selection], translated by Henry d'A. Blumberg, in *Prose and Poetry*. 1934.

Sixty Poems, edited and translated by Eugénie Bayard Pierce and Emil Delmár. 1948.

Rebel or Revolutionary? (selection; includes letters and pamphlets), edited by Béla Köpeczi, translated by Edwin Morgan and G.F. Cushing. 1974.

Fiction

A hóhér kötele [The Hangman's Rope]. 1846.

Plays

Tigris és hiéna [The Tiger and the Hyena] (produced 1883). 1847.

Other

Translator, *Histoire d'une femme de quarante ans*, by Charles Bernard. 1843.

Translator, *Robin Hood*, by George James. 1844.

Translator, *Coriolanus*, by William Shakespeare. 1848.

*

Bibliography: *Sándor Petőfi* by József Szinnyei, 1905; *Petőfi napjai a magyar irodalomban 1842–1849* [Petőfi's Days in Hungarian Literature] edited by Sándor Endrődi, 1911; *Hungarian Authors: A Bibliographical Handbook* by Albert Tezla, 1970; *A magyar irodalom bibliográfiája, 1772–1849* by György Kókay, 1975.

Critical Studies: *Petőfi Sándor életrajza* by Zoltán Ferenczi, 3 vols., 1896; *Alexander Petőfi: Poet of the Hungarian War of Independence* by Arthur B. Yolland, 1906; *Petőfi Sándor* by János Horváth, 1922; *Petőfi Sándor* by Frigyes Riedl, 1923; *Petőfi* by Gyula Illyés, 1936; *Le Jean le Preux d'Alexandre Petoefi* by Guy Turbet-Delof, 1954; *Five Hungarian Writers* by D. Mervyn Jones, 1966; *Így élt Petőfi* by Lajos Hatvany, 2 vols., 1967; "János Vitéz: The People's Epic" by Lóránt Czigány, in *Mosaic*, 6, 1973; *Sándor Petőfi* by Enikő Molnár Basa, 1980.

* * *

In Hungary the name Sándor Petőfi is a synonym for poetry; his name is known everywhere to everybody. The position he occupies in his fellow-countrymen's imagination is similar to Shakespeare's ranking in the English-speaking world.

Sándor Petőfi appeared on the literary scene like a comet, suddenly and out of nowhere. His brief presence radically altered prevailing literary taste and influenced not only his contemporaries (who did not always manage to escape the temptation to imitate him),

but also some modern poets (including Gyula Illyés) who came into their own only after setting out in his footsteps.

Petőfi's restless genius created a new world of poetry, which hardly resembled the restrained classicism and studiously elevated style of his older contemporaries in Hungary. His poetic attitude likens him to the Lake Poets (Wordsworth, Coleridge, Southey) who decided to bring poetic diction close to the natural spoken language. The stunning simplicity and immediacy of Petőfi's idiom had no familiar antecedents except, perhaps, in the unwritten songs of the people. In addition he proved successfully that any subject, no matter how insignificant or unpoetic, can be handled with natural ease by an exceptional talent. The ingredients of his world-view are also simple: the Romantic cult of the self coupled with fiery patriotism and the cherished ideas of the French Revolution, which led him to form his notion of *világszabadság* (freedom for all peoples), for which he was prepared to die. His untimely death did indeed take place on the battlefield—he perished in the Hungarian War of Independence.

This Romantic image of Petőfi as a champion of the oppressed, making the ultimate sacrifice for their cause, is still predominant today, in spite of the varied *oeuvre* he produced within seven short years of creative activity. When in 1989 archaeologists claimed to have found his remains in a Siberian cemetery, leading to speculations that he may after all have died as a POW captured by the Russians, the news, based on inconclusive evidence, was received with an indignant public outcry proving beyond any doubt how deep-seated his reputation as a fallen champion of freedom had been.

Petőfi is one of the few Hungarian poets who has been translated into all major languages; in England he was introduced by the polyglot Sir John Bowring. His first collection of poems, *Versek. 1842–1844* [Poems], contains few traces of contemporary mannerism and embellishments; he writes about first-hand experiences in simple yet effective forms.

His first longer narrative piece, *A helység kalapácsa* [The Village Blacksmith], was a mock-heroic poem prompted by the current literary debate about whether epic poetry was obsolete. Petőfi uses all the standard literary devices employed in classical epics, but it is clear from the first instance that the author sets out to make fun of pomposity. Written in fragments of hexameters, the parody focuses on inane conception and inept execution; Petőfi blends sublimity with the grossest bathos and employs endless retardation by fatuous description and constant digression.

Having burst the contemporary bubble of expectations about epic poetry Petőfi showed in *János vitéz* (*John the Hero*) what the subject matter of a truly contemporary epic poem should be. It is a love story of a foundling, Jancsi, and Iluska, an orphan. When Jancsi is driven out of his home by his stepfather he sets forth into the wide world (*világgá megy*) as in a folktale, but resolute to be reunited with his sweetheart. Jancsi's adventures start in the real world with real obstacles but the charming tale gradually leads the hero and the reader first to the world of folktales peopled by giants and dragons and then into an imaginary fairyland where the hero is finally united with his beloved and they are crowned King and Queen of the Fairies. The transition to different levels of reality is always smooth, and artistic unity is achieved by Jancsi's consistency. He moves towards his final triumph, overcoming his despair by the strength of his love for Iluska.

Petőfi himself experienced a series of romantic love affairs all ending in disappointment but resulting in fine poetry. The death of his beloved is mourned in *Czipruslombok Etelke sírjáról* (*Cypress Leaves from the Grave of Dear Ethel*) and a period of all-pervading gloom is recorded in *Felhők* [Clouds] reaching frightening intensity in "Az őrült'' [The Madman], a poem in which he questions all accepted values. Petőfi was also a discoverer—he described the barren beauty of his native *puszta* in ''Az Alföld'' [The Lowland], the natural habitat of *betyárs* (highwaymen) and simple countryfolk.

By 1847 he envisioned the role of the poet in society as a saviour who delivers the oppressed from their oppressors, described in *Az apostol* (*The Apostle*). His forebodings about the sacrifice he had to make was given an outlet in ''Egy gondolat bánt engem'' [Tormented by Only One Thought]. The poem is divided into short sections with galloping rhythm culminating in the final vision in which the poet dies for *világszabadság*, forecasting his own fate.

His love poetry, reaching its peak in a series of poems addressed to his wife, Júlia, includes ''Szeptember végén'' [At the End of September] and ''eszket a bokor'' [The Bush Quivers]. Life and literature unavoidably mixed in his short life of intense activity and prolific productivity, which included, besides his poetry, translations, a brilliant travel diary, and an overtly romantic novel. By the time of his disappearance on the battlefield his reputation was firmly established and his stirring ''Nemzeti dal'' [National Song] remained a focal point of revolutionary *élan* even in the 1956 uprising.

—Lóránt Czigány

PETRARCH (Francesco Petrarca)

Born: Arezzo (where his father was in political exile from Florence), 20 July 1304. **Education:** Educated in Carpentras, France, from 1312; studied law in Montpellier, 1316–20, and Bologna, 1320–26. **Family:** Had two illegitimate children. **Career:** Lived in Avignon from 1326; possibly took minor orders; in service of the Colonna family, 1330–37; held several canonries from 1335; diplomat and traveller: lived in Vaucluse, 1337–47, Milan, 1353–61, Venice, 1362–68, and Arquà, near Padua, 1369–74. **Awards:** Crowned poet laureate in Rome, 1341. **Died:** 18 July 1374.

PUBLICATIONS

Collections

Opera omnia. 1544.
Rime, trionfi, e poesie latine, edited by F. Neri and others. 1951.
Prose, edited by G. Martellotti and others. 1955.
Opere, edited by Giovanni Ponte. 1968.

Verse

Rerum vulgarium fragmenta [Fragments of Vulgar Matters] (includes *Rime in vita di Laura* and *Rime in morte di Laura*; also known as *Canzoniere* or *Rime*), edited by F. Neri, in *Rime, trionfi, e poesi latine.* 1951; also edited by Ezio Chiorboli, 1924; as *Sonnets and Stanzas*, translated by C.B. Cayley, 1879; as *Sonnets and Songs*, by A.M. Armi, 1946; as *Canzoniere in the English Renaissance*, edited by Anthony Mortimer (bilingual edition), 1975; as *Lyric Poems: The Rime Sparse and Other Lyrics*, edited and translated by Robert M. Durling, 1976; selections as *Sonnets*, translated by Joseph Auslander, 1931; as *Love Rhymes*, by Morris Bishop, 1932; in *Selected Sonnets, Odes, and Letters* edited by Thomas G. Bergin, 1966; as *Selected Poems*, by A. Mortimer, 1977; and as

Selections from the Canzoniere and Other Works (includes *Letter to Posterity; The Ascent of Mount Ventoux; Selections from the Canzioniere*), translated by Mark Musa, 1985.
Epistolae metricae [Metrical Letters], in *Poemata minora*, edited by D. Rossetti. 1829–34; selection in *Petrarch at Vaucluse*, translated by E.H. Wilkins, 1958.
I Trionfi, edited by F. Neri, in *Rime, trionfi, e poesie latine.* 1951; as *Triumphs*, translated by Lord Morley, 1554; also translated by E.H. Wilkins, 1962.
Bucolicum carmen [Eclogues], edited by A. Avena. 1906; as *Bucolicum carmen*, translated by Thomas G. Bergin, 1974.
Africa (in Latin), edited by N. Festa. 1926; as *Africa*, translated by Thomas G. Bergin and Alice S. Wilson, 1977.
Sonnets for Laura, translated by G.R. Nicholson. 1979.
Love Rimes of Petrarch, translated by M. Bishop. 1980.
Songs and Sonnets from Laura's Lifetime, edited and translated by Nicholas Kilmer. 1980.
For Love of Laura: Poetry of Petrarch, translated by M. Shore. 1987.
Rime disperse, edited and translated by Joseph A. Barber. 1991.
The Revolution of Cola Di Rienzo, translated by M.E. Cosenza. 1991.

Other

De remediis contra utriusque fortunae, as *Physic Against Fortune*, translated by Thomas Twyne. 1579; as *Remedies for Fortune Fair and Foul*, edited and translated by Conrad H. Rawski, 5 vols., 1992.
Letters to Classical Authors, translated by Mario Emilio Cosenza. 1910.
Secretum meum, as *Petrarch's Secret; or, The Soul's Conflict With Passion*, translated by William H. Draper. 1911.
De vita solitaria, as *The Life of Solitude*, translated by Jacob Zeitlin. 1924.
Epistolae familiarium, edited by V. Rossi and U. Bosco. 4 vols., 1933–42; as *Rerum familiarum* and *Letters on Familiar Matters*, translated by Aldo S. Bernardo, 2 vols., 1975–82; as *Letters* (selection), edited and translated by Morris Bishop, 1966.
De sui ipsius et multorum ignorantia, as *On His Own Ignorance and That of Many Others*, translated by Hans Nachod, in *The Renaissance Philosophy of Man*, edited by Ernst Cassirer. 1948.
Invectiva contra quendam magni status hominem. . . , edited by P.G. Ricci. 1949.
Invectivarum contra medicum [Invective against a Doctor], edited by P.G. Ricci and D. Silvestri. 1950.
Petrarch's Testament, edited and translated by Theodor E. Mommsen. 1957.
De otio religioso [On Religious Idleness], edited by G. Rotondi. 1958.
Petrarch: A Humanist Among Princes (letters and selections), edited and selection translated by David Thompson. 1971.
Liber sine nomine, as *Book Without a Name*, translated by Norman P. Zacour. 1973.
Petrarch in England: An Anthology of Parallel Texts from Wyatt to Dryden, edited by Jack D'Amico. 1979.
Letters of Old Age: Rerum Senilium Libri I–XVIII, translated by Aldo S. Bernardo, Saul Levin, and Reta A. Bernardo. 2 vols., 1992.

*

Bibliography: *Catalogue of the Petrarch Collection Bequeathed by Willard Fiske* edited by Mary Fowler, 1916, supplement, 1973; *The*

Present State of Scholarship in Fourteenth Century Literature by Thomas D. Cooke, 1982.

Critical Studies: *The Making of the "Canzoniere" and Other Petrarchan Studies*, 1951, *Studies in the Life and Works of Petrarch*, 1955, *Petrarch's Eight Years in Milan*, 1958, *Petrarch's Later Years*, 1959, *The Life of Petrarch*, 1961, and *Studies on Petrarch and Boccaccio*, 1978, all by E.H. Wilkins; *Petrarch, Scipio, and the "Africa,"* 1962, *Petrarch, Laura, and the "Triumphs,"* 1974, and *Francesco Petrarch, Citizen of the World*, 1980, all by Aldo S. Bernardo; *Petrarch and His World* by Morris Bishop, 1963; *The Icy Fire: Five Studies in European Petrarchism* by Leonard Forster, 1969; *Petrarch* by Thomas G. Bergin, 1970; *Petrarch to Pirandello: Studies in Italian Literature in Honour of Beatrice Corrigan*, edited by Julius A. Molinaro, 1973; *Petrarch and Garcilaso: A Linguistic Approach to Style* by Sharon Ghertman, 1975; *Petrarch: Six Centuries Later* edited by Aldo Scaglione, 1975; *Petrarch's Visions and Their Renaissance Analogues* by J.C. Bondanella, 1978; *The Poet as Philosopher: Petrarch and the Formation of Renaissance Consciousness* by Charles Trinkaus, 1979; *Petrarch and Petrarchism: The English and the French Traditions* by Stephen Minta, 1980; *Hieroglyph of Time: The Petrarchan Sestina* by Marianne Shapiro, 1980; *Petrarch's Poetics and Literary History* by Marguerite R. Waller, 1980; *Irenic Apocalypse: Some Uses of Apocalyptic in Dante, Petrarch and Rabelais* by Dennis Costa, 1981; *Dante, Petrarch, Boccaccio: Studies in the Italian Trecento in Honor of Charles S. Singleton*, 1983; *Petrarch, the Augustan Poets, the Italian Tradition and the Canzoniere* by Jennifer Petrie, 1983; *Petrarch: Poet and Humanist* by Kenelm Foster, 1984; *Petrarch* by Nicholas Mann, 1984; *Petrarch's "Secretum": Its Making and Its Meaning* by Hans Baron, 1985; *Petrarch's Metamorphoses: Text and Subtext in the Rime Sparse* by Sara Sturm-Maddox, 1985; *The Sonnet over Time: A Study in the Sonnets of Petrarch, Shakespeare and Baudelaire* by Sandra L. Bermann, 1988; *Petrarch the Poet: An Introduction to Return Vulgarium Fragmentum* by Peter Hainsworth, 1988; *Petrarch and the English Sonnet Sequences* by Thomas P. Roche, 1989; *Petrarch's Genius: Pentimento and Prophecy* by Marjorie O'Rourke Boyle, 1992; *The Worlds of Petrarch* by Giuseppe Mazzotta, 1994; *A Concordance to the Familiares of Francesco Petrarch* by Aldo S. Bernardo with Reta A. Bernardo, 1994; *Authorizing Petrarch* by William J. Kennedy, 1994; *Echoes of Desire: English Petrarchism and Its Counterdiscourses* by Heather Dubrow, 1995; *The Structure of Petrarch's Canzoniere: A Chronological, Psychological, and Stylistic Analysis* by Frederic J. Jones, 1995; *The Iconography of Petrarch in the Age of Humanism* by J.B. Trapp, 1996; *Modelling the Individual: Biography and Portrait in the Renaissance*, edited by Karl Enenkel, Betsy de Jong-Crane, and Peter Liebregts, 1998; *Rereading the Renaissance: Petrarch, Augustine, and the Language of Humanism* by Carol Everhart Quillen, 1998; *Ronsard, Petrarch and the Amours* by Sara Sturm-Maddox, 1999; *Petrarchan Love and the Continental Renaissance* by Gordon Braden, 1999.

* * *

By the time he had reached middle age Petrarch had attained to a state of eminence unique for a man of letters in the Europe of his times, and indeed unparalleled in all the centuries that had followed the collapse of the Roman Empire. He has been well called "the first modern man of letters." His fame was assured by his works as a scholar and a poet, but it is apparent too that his personality, outgoing, affable, and winning, had much to do with it. He made friends easily, as he admits with some complacency in his autobiographical "Letter to Posterity"—and useful friends for the most part. Rich and powerful patrons sought him out and willingly subsidised him. By the end of his life he had reached a point where he no longer needed patronage and was able to own his own house and to enjoy the library which he had collected with persistent zeal. Such an achievement for a man of letters was unheard of before the invention of printing. To his credit, the poet-scholar had won his independence without seriously compromising his principles, although his acceptance of the hospitality of the Visconti, despots of Milan, disturbed his younger friend Boccaccio.

Petrarch made good use of the comfortable life and leisure provided for him by his protectors. His works are numerous and substantial, and reveal an alert and enquiring mind and keen interest in the world around him and in his own personality. In the vernacular he composed only two works: *I Trionfi* (*Triumphs*) and the collection of lyrics (mostly sonnets, a form to which he brought a new and unsurpassed grace), which with affected modesty he called *Rerum vulgarium fragmenta* [Fragments of Vulgar Matters] but which is commonly known as the *Canzoniere*. This lyric account of a lifetime's unrequited love has had an enduring resonance. It is divided into two parts, the first consisting of items written during Laura's life and the second made of poems of mourning for her death. It is uncertain whether Laura really existed or is merely a creation of the poet's wistful fancy; the tone of the second part at least suggests that his grief is real and his tears are shed for a woman of flesh and blood. For many years critics have been in general content to identify her with the Avignon lady Laurette de Sade, who died in the plague of 1348. Except to record the date and place of his enamorment Petrarch tells us little about her, save that she had golden hair—and never yielded to his entreaties. But his verses in praise of her are so skilfully woven, so musical in tone and elegant in style, that they charm a reader of today as compellingly as they did the poet's contemporaries. Not all the items in the *Canzoniere* deal with the beloved; occasionally the poet puts aside his obsession and writes on other topics, addressing his words to friends or patrons. The short sequence on the corruption of the Avignon papacy is notable for its scorching invective, and his ode to the discordant Italian princes has a convincing patriotic fervour. But it is Laura to whom his thoughts and his longings constantly return. The worship of the unattainable lady is hardly new in European letters: it had been the central motif of the Provençal lyric. One might even see in Laura a kind of regression: unlike Dante's Beatrice she carries no evident suggestion of ethical or theological nature though the poet himself hints that her name is suggestive of the laurel wreath signifying fame. On the literal level 20 years of unrequited courtship might seem a little absurd (Gibbon has his fun with it), but if the background is contrived and the posturing sometimes tedious, yet the drama is real, for it is evident that Petrarch is recording and analysing a spiritual-emotional condition which is truly human and very moving. In this sense the sincerity of the *Canzoniere* is beyond question. The tension within the poet's heart cannot be doubted; it becomes especially clear in the poems written after Laura's death that whatever the beloved signifies (carnal love, thirst for fame, earthly pleasures) it is something at war with what should be the first concern of a Christian, the salvation of his soul. To this unending conflict, which is of the essence of our earthly pilgrimage, Petrarch gave eloquent and convincing expression. The forms—sonnets, odes, sestinas—he employs are no more his invention than the substance of his song, but with his mastery of cadence, rhyme, and musical verbal patterns he endowed them with a grace and polish never known before and hardly rivalled since.

If the vernacular Petrarch reveals new areas of sensibility and new secrets of technique to poets yet to come, the Latin Petrarch is no less significant in the field of letters. Collectively the Latin works display the same range of conflicting concerns that we find in the *Canzoniere*. The *Letters*, whether in prose or verse, are at once a shrewd commentary on the passing scene and the *autoritratto* of a man of sincere faith, aware of the transience of the things of this fascinating world and uneasy about his spiritual condition. Both aspects of this articulate man are apparent in other Latin writings. The *Secretum meum* (*Petrarch's Secret*) is a moving if somewhat stylized examination of conscience, the essay *De vita solitaria* (*The Life of Solitude*) exemplifies the author's penchant for meditation and seclusion, while the record of *Epistolae familiarium* (*Letters on Familiar Matters*) shows us an avid "sight-seer." (Petrarch loved travel and enjoyed meeting people.) The *Bucolicum carmen*, with its description of wars and plagues and its concomitant strain of melancholy, offers, in not contemptible hexameters, the same very human melange that we find in the *Letters* and to some degree in the *Canzoniere*. Much of Petrarch's Latin is mannered, patently in emulation of Latin authors, particularly Cicero, yet it is *au fond* effective and often vivid (witness for example the uninhibited mordancy of his *Invectiva* [Invectives]). But more important for Western culture than the Latin works themselves is Petrarch's fresh and sympathetic approach to the classics: he saw the Latin writers not as remote prophets but as men like himself, greater perhaps in stature but recognizably kin. In this sense he is rightly called the father of humanism. A century later scholars would learn how to write smoother Latin than Petrarch's, and his Latin works were overshadowed. In the days of the High Renaissance "Petrarch" meant the *Canzoniere* and "petrarchismo." But in more recent times the role of the Latin Petrarch has won perceptive appreciation, as is attested by the number of editions, translations, and studies that have appeared. Conceding that the Latin works lack the compelling emotional appeal of the *Canzoniere*, they yet remain an invaluable legacy. It is difficult to imagine the course of European letters without the contribution of Laura's lover—and likewise without the labours of Cicero's disciple.

—Thomas G. Bergin

See the essay on "Sonnet 90."

PETRONIUS

Also called Petronius Arbiter. **Career:** Identified by most scholars with Titus (or possibly Gaius) Petronius Niger, a close associate of Nero who called him "arbiter elegantiae" (director of elegance): proconsul of province of Bithynia; consul, AD 62; denounced as being involved in an assassination conspiracy against Nero, and committed suicide. **Died:** AD 66.

PUBLICATIONS

Collections

Satyrical Works in Prose and Verse, translated by Messrs. Wilson, Burnaby, Blount, Brown, Capt. Ayloff, and others. 1708.
Works in Prose and Verse, translated by Addison. 1736.

Complete Works, translated by Jack Lindsay. 1927; also translated by W.H.D. Rouse [Loeb Edition], with *Apocolocyntosis* by Seneca, 1936.

Works

Satyricon, edited by Alfred Ernout. 4th edition, 1958; also edited by K. Müller, 1961, revised edition by K. Müller and W. Ehlers, 1965, and Carlo Pellegrino, 1975; *Selections from the Satiricon*, edited by Gilbert Lawall, 1975; as *The Satyr*, translated by "Mr. Burnaby and another hand," 1694, reprinted 1923; translated as *Satyricon*, in *Propertius and Petronius*, edited by W.K. Kelly, 1854; also translated by Sebastian Melmoth, 1902; Michael Heseltine [Loeb Edition], 1913; Paul Dinnage, 1953, revised edition, 1971; William Arrowsmith, 1959; John Sullivan, 1965, revised edition, 1986; Paul Gillette, 1970; as *Petronius, Leader of Fashion*, translated by J.M. Mitchell, 1922, as *Satyricon*, 1923; as *Satyrica*, translated by R. Bracht Branham and Daniel Kinney, 1996; as *The Satyricon*, translated by P.G. Walsh, 1996; also translated by Sarah Ruden, 2000.
Cena Trimalchionis (extract from *Satyricon*), edited by W.B. Sedgwick. 1925; also edited by Martin S. Smith, 1982; as *Trimalchio's Dinner*, translated by Harry J. Peck, 1898; as *Cena Trimalchionis*, translated by W.D. Lowe, 1905; also translated by Michael J. Ryan, 1905, as *Trimalchio's Banquet*, 1910; as *Dinner at Trimalchio's*, translated by G.J. Acheson, 1950.
De mutatione Republicae Romanae, translated as *The Change of the Roman Empire* (bilingual edition), in *Original Letters, Dramatic Pieces and Poems*, edited by Benjamin Victor. 13 vols., 1776.

*

Bibliography: "The Bibliography of Petronius" by Stephen Gaselee, in *Transactions of the Bibliographical Society*, 10, 1909, supplement by M. Stirling, 1931; *A Bibliography of Petronius* by Gareth L. Schmeling, 1977.

Critical Studies: *The Age of Petronius* by Charles Beck, 1856; *Petronius in Italy from the Thirteenth Century to the Present Time* by Anthony Rini, 1937; *The Vocabulary of Mental Aberration in Roman Comedy and Petronius* by Dorothy M. Paschall, 1939; *Some Ancient Novels: . . . The Satyricon* by Frederick A. Todd, 1940; *Arbiter of Elegance: A Study of the Life and Works of C. Petronius* by Gilbert Bagnani, 1954; *A Formal Analysis of Petronius' Vocabulary* by D.C. Swanson, 1963; *The Satyricon of Petronius: A Literary Study* by John Sullivan, 1968, *Aspects of the Ancient Romance and Its Heritage: Essays on Apuleius, Petronius, and the Greek Romances* edited by Alexander Scobie, 1969; *Petronius* by Philip B. Corbett, 1970; *The Roman Novel: The Satyricon of Petronius and the Metamorphoses of Apuleius* by P.G. Walsh, 1970; *Petronius the Artist: Essays on the Satyricon and Its Author* by Herbert D. Rankin, 1971; *The Date and Author of the Satyricon* by Kenneth C. Rose, 1971; *Petronius the "Ancient": His Reputation and Influence in Seventeenth Century England* by Johanna H. Stuckey, 1972; *Petronius* by Andrew Lothian, 1988; *Reading Petronius* by Niall W. Slater, 1990; *The Language of the Freedmen in Petronius' Cena Trimalchionis* by Bret Boyce, 1991; *Reading and Variant in Petronius: Studies in the French Humanists and Their Manuscript Sources* by Wade Richardson, 1993; *Petronius the Poet: Verse and Literary Tradition in the Satyricon* by Catherine Connors, 1998; *Laughter and Derision in Petronius' Satyrica: A*

Literary Study by Maria Plaza, 2000; *A Companion to Petronius* by Edward Courtney, 2001.

* * *

Little is known for certain about the Roman author Titus Petronius Niger, often referred to as Petronius Arbiter. The few pieces of biographical information available to us come from the Roman historian Tacitus, who briefly summarizes Petronius' life and death under the emperor Nero (54–68) in Book XVI of the *Annales*. Unfortunately, Tacitus is more interested in Petronius as a personality than as a writer, and affords us little help in understanding Petronius' only remaining work, the *Satyricon*. In many ways the most puzzling piece of Roman literature to survive into the modern era, the *Satyricon* has long fascinated and frustrated scholars, who must struggle with the extremely fragmentary text, the apparent absence of any unifying theme or literary model, and the startling conjunction of the fantastic with the realistic. This has led to widely divergent theories on the fundamental nature and purpose of the work.

The extant text of the *Satyricon* is composed of approximately 140 pages of Latin, generally supposed to comprise parts of Books XIV, XV, and XVI of the original work. Since so much of the text has been lost, however, it is difficult to know how much narrative came before, and impossible to know how much came after, the surviving text. The plot in what remains is the story of the journeyings of the hapless narrator, Encolpius, and his various companions, most notably the boy Giton, whose sexual promiscuity provides a constant source of friction between Encolpius and his fellow travellers.

It has been noted that Encolpius' adventures in some ways reflect those of another, more famous, ancient traveller, namely Homer's Odysseus. Some (see Klebs, ''Zur Komposition von Petronius' Satirae,'' *Philologus*, 47, 1889) have speculated that the entire work is a sort of comic *Odyssey*, with Encolpius pursued by the wrath of Priapus (the Roman god of fertility) instead of Poseidon. Unlike the *Odyssey*, however, the *Satyricon* is almost entirely prose, with short poetic ''interruptions,'' ranging in style from epic to epigram. Moreover, although Encolpius appears to spend a lot of time being driven over land and sea, the central part is a long account of a dinner party, occupying more than a third of the surviving text. During this so-called ''dinner of Trimalchio,'' not only is the feverish movement from place to place of the rest of the text suspended, but the focus of the narrative moves from the narrator and his companions to settle on characters who appear here for the first and only time.

Thus it is obvious that the adventures of Petronius' narrator are not limited to what Odysseus experienced before him. Again, the *Satyricon* differs from the *Odyssey* in that it is a highly sexual work: Encolpius' misadventures centre, during the first part of the text, upon his continuing struggle for the affections of his travelling companion, the boy Giton, and during the final part, upon his inability to conquer the impotence which has beset him. In this sense, the work most clearly recalls the later genre of the Greek romantic novel, which records the trials and tribulations of a lover or lovers. Indeed, the *Satyricon* is often called a Roman novel, and grouped with the *Metamorphoses* of Apuleius, written in the 2nd century AD.

Petronius, however, continues to defy classification. Although the *Satyricon* superficially resembles the Greek novel, as well as the *Odyssey*, there is no genre which parallels Petronius exactly. The text is unique in its strange combination of prose and poetry (recently also found in a new papyrus fragment of a Greek novel; see P.J. Parson,

''A Greek *Satyricon*?,'' *Bulletin of the Institute of Classical Studies*, 18, 1971), and in the complexity of the world it presents. Often praised for its realism, the *Satyricon* also contains passages of high melodrama. Balanced against characters who speak as close to vernacular Latin as is to be found in any ancient text, are others who are so tangled in rhetorical figures that they cannot express themselves clearly. The humour of certain passages rivals that of the best stage comedies, ancient or modern, yet there are recurrent images of death which pervade the entire work. Petronius and the *Satyricon* are puzzles to which there are no easy answers. Froma Zeitlin offers one solution to both the question of genre and that of theme in ''Petronius as Paradox: Anarchy and Artistic Integrity,'' *Transactions of the American Philological Association*, 102, 1971, in which she argues that Petronius is presenting a portrait of Nero's Rome, a world in chaos, and so deliberately chooses a chaos of genres to represent it. There is, however, much room for further study, and the *Satyricon* remains one of the most fascinating texts to have emerged from antiquity.

—Kristina Milnor

PIL'NIAK, Boris

Also known as Boris Pilnyak. **Born:** Boris Andreevich Vogau in Mozhaisk, Moscow Province, Russia, 11 October 1894. **Education:** Educated in schools in Saratov and Bogorodsk; Nizhnii Novgorod Academy of Modern Languages, 1913; University of Kolomna; Moscow Commercial Institute, degree in economics, 1920. **Family:** Married 1) Maria Sokolova in 1917, one son (deceased) and one daughter; 2) Olga Scherbinovskaia in 1925; 3) the actress Kira Andronikashvili in 1933, one son. **Career:** Started writing stories regularly from 1915 (adopted pen name in the same year); chairman, Krug publications, 1923; travelled widely in Europe, the Arctic, United States, Middle East, and Far East, 1922–34. Accused of publishing ''anti-Soviet'' work abroad, 1929; a ''campaign'' against him demanded his resignation as President of the Moscow branch of the All-Russian Writer's Union, 1929. Arrested and disappeared, 6 October 1937. **Died:** 21 April 1938.

PUBLICATIONS

Collections

Izbrannye proizvedeniia [Selected Works], edited by V. Novikov. 1976.
Rasskazy, povesti, romany [Sovetskii pisatel' Edition] (includes complete version of *Solianoi ambar*). 1990.
Récits anglais [Short Stories], edited by Florence Clerc. 1993.

Fiction

S poslednim parokhodom i drugie rasskazy [With the Last Steamer and Other Stories]. 1918.
Ivan-da-Mar'ia [Ivan and Mary] (stories). 1922.
Byl'e [Bygones] (stories). 1922.

Golyi god. 1922; as *The Naked Year*, translated by Alec Brown, 1928; also translated by A.R. Tulloch, 1975.

Nikola-na-Posadiakh [As It Was] (stories). 1923.

Povesti o chernom khlebe [Stories about Black Bread]. 1923.

Mashiny i volki [Machines and Wolves], 1923–24.

Mat' syra zemlia [Mother Earth]. 1924.

Angliiskie rasskazy [English Tales]. 1924.

Tales of the Wilderness (includes "The Snow"; "A Year of Their Lives"; "A Thousand Years"; "Over the Ravine"; "Always on Detachment"; "The Snow Wind"; "The Forest Manor"; "The Bielokonsky Estate"; "Death"; "The Heirs"; "The Crossways"), translated by F. O'Dempsey. 1925.

Speranza. 1927.

Rasskazy [Short Stories]. 1927; revised editions, 1929, 1933.

Povest' nepogashennoi luny. 1927; as *The Tale of the Unextinguished Moon*, translated by Beatrice Scott, 1967.

Kitaiskaia sud'ba cheloveka, with A. Rogozina. 1927; as *Chinese Story and Other Tales*, translated by Vera T. Reck and Michael Green, 1988.

Ivan-Moskva. 1927; as *Ivan Moscow*, translated by A. Schwartzman, 1935.

Raplesnutoe vremia. Rasskazy [Spilled Time: Stories]. 1927, reprinted 1966.

Krasnoe derevo (novella). 1929; as "Mahogany," in *Mother Earth and Other Stories*, 1968.

Shtoss v zhizn' [A Chance on Life]. 1929.

Volga vpadaet v Kaspiiskoe more. 1930; as *The Volga Falls to the Caspian Sea*, translated by Charles Malamuth, 1931; as *The Volga Flows to the Caspian Sea*, translated by Malamuth, 1932.

Rasskazy [Stories]. 1932.

Rozhdenie cheloveka [The Birth of Man] (novella). 1935.

Izbrannye rasskazy [Selected Stories]. 1935.

Sozrevanie plodov [The Ripening of Fruit]. 1936.

Mother Earth and Other Stories, translated by Vera T. Reck and Michael Green. 1968.

Dvoiniki [Doubles]. 1983.

Romany [Novels]. 1990.

Zashtat [Back of Beyond]. 1991.

Other

Sobranie sochinenii [Collected Works]. 3 vols., 1923.

Korni iaponskogo solntsa [Roots of the Japanese Sun] (travel writing). 1926.

Kamni i korni [Stones and Roots]. 1927.

Sobranie sochinenii [Collected Works]. 8 vols., 1929–30.

O'kei: amerikanskii roman [OK: An American Novel]. 1932.

Tselaia zhizn': Izbrannaia proza [A Whole Life: Selected Prose]. 1988.

Chelovecheskii veter [Human Wind]. 1990.

Tret'ia stolitsa [The Third Capital]. 1992.

*

Critical Studies: *Boris Pilniak: A Soviet Writer in Conflict with the State* by Vera T. Reck, 1975; *Nature as Code: The Achievement of Boris Pilnjak 1915–1924* by Peter Alberg Jensen, 1979; *Boris Pilniak: Scythian at a Typewriter* by Gary Browning, 1985; "A New Soviet Novel for a New Soviet Man?," in *Irish Slavonic Studies*, 8, 1987, and "*Solyanoi ambar*: Pilnyak's Great Soviet Novel?," in *Irish Slavonic Studies*, 14, 1993, both by Michael Falchikov; "Boris Pil'niak and Modernism: Redefining the Self," in *Slavic Review*, 2, 1991, and "Pil'niak on Writing," in *Slavonic and East European Review*, 2, 1993, both by Mary A. Nicholas.

* * *

Boris Pil'niak belongs to that transitional generation of Russian writers whose work and life were fundamentally determined by the Bolshevik Revolution and its outcome. Born into the radical intelligentsia and brought up in central Russian provincial towns, Pil'niak's earliest influences were the mystical modernists Belyi and Remizov and, more distantly, Dostoevskii and Leskov. Pil'niak was published first in 1915, but achieved real fame with the 1922 publication of his Civil War novel *Golyi god* (*The Naked Year*). The striking features of *The Naked Year* are its verbal and stylistic inventiveness and its extraordinary atmosphere of both youthful enthusiasm and horror and suffering. There is little plot and no obvious heroic figure—unless it is Russia (Rus'). At the end of the work the forest stands tall, as the revolution slowly impinges on Russia's provincial backwaters, and society and morals fall apart.

The Naked Year was perhaps Pil'niak's greatest achievement. He published prolifically during the 1920s, however, when his principal theme—as in *Mashiny i volki* [Machines and Wolves] and *Ivan-Moskva* (*Ivan Moscow*)—remained the contrast between the unchanging nature of provincial Russia and the grand Bolshevik vision of a new technically advanced urban society. Sometimes, too, as in *Tret'ia stolitsa* [The Third Capital], he reasserts a "pre-Petrine" Russia, against the hostility of the West. Yet alongside his Russian nationalism and his fascination for folk-customs and obscure religious sects, Pil'niak was an inveterate and enthusiastic traveller, visiting, among others, western Europe, the Far East, the United States, Spitzbergen, and remoter parts of the Soviet Union between 1922 and 1934. Travel writing, or fiction with a "travelogue" element, bear witness to this enthusiasm, even though he was sometimes forced into politically acceptable conclusions.

Gregarious, self-confident and somewhat injudicious, Pil'niak got into trouble several times in his career. The first brush with authority came with *Povest' nepogashennoi luny* (*The Tale of the Unextinguished Moon*), about a military leader who submits to an operation, apparently for the good of the Party, and dies under the knife. The conflict between science and nature is an important theme in this story, but most critics detected a thinly-fictionalized account of the circumstances surrounding the death of army commander M.F. Frunze, widely rumoured to be the Stalin regime's first "medical murder." Pil'niak denied any connection, but it seemed an odd theme to choose. To the present-day reader, however, *The Tale of the Unextinguished Moon* is a well-constructed and touching tale of a man's life, friendships, and tragic death.

In 1929, worse trouble ensued. In this year, Stalin's plan for rapid industrialization and collectivization of agriculture took off, heralding even more profound changes than in 1917. Writers were pulled into this process, visiting construction sites and collectivized villages to describe the epic struggle to build the new society. In the midst of this turbulence, Pil'niak produced the novella *Krasnoe derevo* ("Mahogany"). Set in provincial Russia, "Mahogany" presents various "survivals of the past," for example, a primitive commune and two brothers who journey around the countryside buying and restoring antique mahogany furniture from impoverished families. The story conveys the stagnant atmosphere of small-town Russia and the image of the "dying bells"—a reference to the anti-religious campaign that saw the demise of many churches and monasteries. Although these themes were indeed topical, Pil'niak's nostalgic, lyrical manner was hardly in tune with the times. Moreover, "Mahogany" was published in Berlin before being cleared for domestic publication. Pil'niak was accused of "anti-Soviet activities" but claimed that he had already decided to incorporate "Mahogany" into a larger work, more in keeping with the demands of the Five-Year Plan. This was *Volga vpadaet v kaspuiiskoe more* (*The Volga Falls to the Caspian Sea*), a long, dense novel about the construction (and attempted sabotage) of a major dam project and the lives of the disparate group of people (intelligentsia and workers, male and female) engaged in its development. Some of the characters and themes from "Mahogany" reappear—but chiefly as a negative contrast to the positive aspects of the dam project. Although *The Volga Falls to the Caspian Sea* did not fully satisfy the authorities, in 1931 Pil'niak was nevertheless permitted his most ambitious journey—a six-month trip through the United States, which included an abortive attempt to collaborate on a Hollywood script. The outcome was the travelogue *O'kei: amerikanskuii roman* (*OK: An American Novel*). His good standing restored, Pil'niak returned to the Far East and another piece of travel-inspired writing ensued: *Kamni i korni* [Stones and Roots].

The 1930s, until his tragic arrest, were as productive for Pil'niak as the 1920s, the variety and quality of his work refuting the idea that after "Mahogany" he had little left to say. From *Volga* onwards he certainly sought to come to terms with the new society and its demands on the writer—this meant modifying his impressionistic, extravagant style to a more sober realism and resolving the persistent conflict between instinct and reason. This conflict appears in *Dvoiniki* [Doubles], centring upon the lives of two brothers, one a heedless, sensual artist, the other a disciplined ascetic revolutionary. *Dvoiniki* did not appear (except in a Polish translation) for 50 years, but it can be seen now as reflecting an overall theme which permeated much Soviet writing of the 1930s—that of the re-education or transformation of the human personality under communism, the emergence of New Soviet Man. This strikes a very personal note in Pil'niak's penultimate novel *Sozrevanie plodov* [The Ripening of Fruit], much of which is autobiographical and mirrors the author's new-found happiness with his third wife, the actress Kira Andronikashvili.

Pil'niak was arrested during the Stalin purges in October 1937. He had just completed a new novel, *Solianoi ambar* [The Salt Barn], which unfolds a panoramic view of provincial Russia from the turn of the century to 1917. Written on more orthodox, realistic lines, there are many fine passages that evoke the earlier Pil'niak, but its historico-political conclusions suggest that the author had come to terms with all that had happened since 1917. *Solianoi ambar* was preserved in manuscript and known to only a few people. It was finally published in 1990 as part of a comprehensive re-publication of Pil'niak's work.

—Michael Falchikov

PILNYAK, Boris

See PIL'NIAK, Boris

PINDAR

Born: Cynoscephalae, Boeotia, central Greece, in 518 (or possibly 522) BC. Probably from an aristocratic family. **Education:** Studied in Athens under Apollodorus and Agathocles. **Family:** Married. **Career:** Earliest known poem dates from 498 BC. In Sicily at courts of Theron of Acragas and Hieron I of Syracuse, 476–74 BC; by 468 BC had several patrons throughout Greece. **Died:** 438 (or possibly 446) BC.

PUBLICATIONS

Verse

[Verse], edited by Bruno Snell. 2 vols., 1953–64, revised by Hervicus Maehler, 2 vols., 1971; also edited by O. Schroeder, 1923, C.M. Bowra, 1947, and Alexander Turyn, 1948; translated by J.E. Sandys [Loeb Edition], 1915; also translated by Lewis Richard Farnell, 1930–32, reprinted 1965; Richmond Lattimore, 1947, revised edition, 1976; C.M. Bowra, 1969; Geoffrey Conway, 1972; R.A. Swanson, 1974; commentaries: *The Olympian and Pythian Odes* by B.L. Gildersleeve, 1885, reprinted 1964; *Nemean Odes* (bilingual edition), 1890, reprinted 1970, and *Isthmian Odes*, 1892, by J.B. Bury; *Seventh Olympic Ode* by Willem Jacob Verdenius, 1972; *Commentaries* (includes Olympian Odes 1, 3, 7, 10, 11, 12, 14, Nemean Ode 11, and Isthmian Ode 2) by Willem Jacob Verdenius, 2 vols., 1987; *Fourth Pythian Ode* by Bruce Karl Braswell, 1988.

Ode on Fame; First Pythian Ode, translated by Henry Flood. 1775.

The Pythian, Nemean and Isthmian Odes, translated by E.B. Greene. 1778.

Pindar and Themistocles: Aegina and Athens [Eighth Nemean Ode], translated by W.W. Lloyd (prose). 1862.

The Golden Fleece (fourth Pythian ode), translated by Henry Birkhead. 1929.

Carmina cum Fragmentis, edited by C.M. Bowra. 1947.

Selected Odes, translated by Carl A.P. Ruck and William H. Matheson. 1968.

Victory Ode, edited and translated by Mary R. Lefkowitz. 1976.

Victory Songs, translated by Frank J. Nisetich. 1980.

Selected Odes: Olympian One, Pythian Nine, Nemeans Two and Three, Isthmian One, translated and edited by Stephen Instone. 1996.

*

Bibliography: *A Bibliography of Pindar 1513–1966* by Douglas E. Gerber, 1969.

Critical Studies: *The Odes of Pindar* by F.A. Paley, 1868; *Pindar: The Olympian and Pythian Odes* by C.A.M. Fennell, 1879; *Pindar* by G. Norwood, 1956; *Studia Pindarica I* and *II* by E.L. Bundy, 1962; *Pindar's Pythian Odes* by Reginald W.B. Burton, 1962; *Pindar* by C.M. Bowra, 1964; *Folktale Motifs in the Odes of Pindar* by Mary A. Grant, 1967; *Studies in Pindar with Particular Reference to Paean VI and Nemean VII* by Staffan Fogelmark, 1972; *Epinikion: General Form in the Odes of Pindar* by Richard Hamilton, 1974; *Pindar's Odes* by R.A. Swanson, 1974; *Pindar's Vision of the Past* by George Huxley, 1975; *The Victory Ode*, 1976, and *First Person Fictions:*

Pindar's Poetic "I," 1991, both by Mary R. Lefkowitz; *The Structure of Pindar's Epinician Odes* by Carola Greengard, 1980; *Song and Action: The Victory Odes of Pindar* by Kevin Crotty, 1982; *Pindar's Olympian One* by Douglas E. Gerber, 1982; *Choreia: Pindar and Dance* by William Mullen, 1982; *Pindar's Art, Its Tradition and Aims* by John Kevin Newman, 1984; *Pindar* by D.S. Carne-Ross, 1985; *The Pindaric Mind: A Study of Logical Structure in Early Greek Poetry* by Thomas K. Hubbard, 1985; *The Measures of Praise: Structure and Function in Pindar's Second Pythian and Seventh Nemean Odes* by Glenn W. Most, 1985; *Pindar* by William H. Race, 1986; *Pindar's Mythmaking: The Fourth Pythian Ode* by Charles Segal, 1986; *The Crown of Song: Metaphor in Pindar* by Deborah Steiner, 1986; *Agonistic Poetry: The Pindaric Mode in Pindar, Horace, Hölderlin, and the English Ode* by William Fitzgerald, 1987; *Commentaries on Pindar* by W.J. Verdenius, 2 vols., 1987; *Pindar and Homer* by Frank J. Nisetich, 1989; *Pindar's Homer: The Lyric Possession of an Epic Past* by Gregory Nagy, 1990; *The Aggelia in Pindar* by Laura L. Nash, 1990; *Pindar and Greek Family Law* by Robert Stoddart, 1990; *Lying and Poetry from Homer to Pindar: Falsehood and Deception in Archaic Greek Poetics* by Louise H. Pratt, 1993; *Mind, Body, and Speech in Homer and Pindar* by Hayden Pelliccia, 1995; *A Commentary on Pindar Nemean Nine* by Bruce Karl Braswell, 1998; *Aglaia: The Poetry of Alcman, Sappho, Pindar, Bachylides, and Corinna* by Charles Segal, 1998; *Pindar and the Renaissance Hymn-Ode: 1450–1700* by Stella P. Revard, 2001; *Pindar's Paeans: A Reading of the Fragments with a Survey of the Genre* by Ian Rutherford, 2001.

* * *

For the ancients, Pindar was the greatest of the lyric poets; for us, he is the only Greek lyric poet whose work survives in something more than fragments. We have a total of 45 complete poems from four of his books, along with numerous fragments from 13 books that were lost.

The surviving poems are choral odes written to be sung and danced by a chorus in celebration of victory in the Greek athletic festivals. The choreography and musical accompaniment Pindar devised for them have perished. Worse still, the principles governing the metres in which the odes are composed were forgotten even in antiquity, with the result that Pindar, whose lines we now know obey rigorous rules, came to be regarded as an exponent of free verse. But the greatest distortion of all resulted from loss of appreciation for the conventions of the genre in which Pindar worked.

The main business of Pindar's poetry is praise, but praise is difficult to carry off. It was especially difficult in Pindar's day, when men believed that happiness was a divine prerogative, something the gods would resent seeing mortal men claim for themselves. The poet must praise his patron, but he must also secure divine favour for him and for himself. He must balance enthusiasm with caution. These conflicting needs resulted in the creation of a complex poetic genre that reached its highest development in Pindar and ceased to be cultivated almost immediately after; its unique conventions, the special devices evolved for the task of praise, were rapidly misunderstood. Until Bundy's work began the process of recovering their meaning, we have had to take Pindar's greatness on authority.

Several factors contribute to that greatness, not least the prestige that poetry enjoyed in Pindar's day. His poems do not in the first instance express his personal feelings and opinions, as was thought before; they speak rather to and for an entire society that looks upon him as the representative of Apollo and the Muses. "Prophesy, Muse, and I will be your voice," he says in one of his fragments (150 Snell). This confidence in his divine mission and genius is one of his most noticeable traits; it exerted a major influence on the creation of Pindar's traditional image as the poet *par excellence*, who owes allegiance only to the spirit that moves him and who often soars where he cannot be followed. So Horace pictured him in Odes IV.2, and so also he appears in Longinus' treatise *On the Sublime*. The careful reader, however, will perceive that Pindar's celebrations of poetic genius, like the brilliant myths that he tells, are closely bound up with the execution of his task. His poems do not for that matter amount to a simple hurrah; on the contrary, they are shot through with gleams of a tragic vision.

It has been said that Pindar's art cannot be appreciated at all in translation. This would be true if it had no theme of universal interest and importance, but it does: it deals with the springs of human motivation. Measuring hope, effort, and achievement against the ultimate failure of death, it ends by affirming the individual's longing for distinction: "Creatures of a day! What is someone? What is no one? Man: a shadow's dream. But when godgiven glory comes, a bright light shines upon us and our life is sweet" (*Pythian* 8, end).

—Frank J. Nisetich

See the essays on "Olympian One" and "Pythian Odes Four and Five."

PIRANDELLO, Luigi

Born: Agrigento, Sicily, 28 June 1867. **Education:** Educated at schools in Agrigento to 1882, and Palermo to 1886; University of Palermo, 1886–87; University of Rome, 1887–89; University of Bonn, 1889–91, Ph.D. **Family:** Married Antonietta Portulano in 1894 (she was committed to a mental clinic from 1919), two sons and one daughter. **Career:** Writer in Rome from 1891; teacher, Regio Istituto Superiore di Magistero Femminile, 1897–1922; co-editor, *Ariel*, 1898; financial disaster in 1903 forced him to increase his income by tutoring and working as travelling examination commissioner; became more involved in the theatre during World War I; director, with Nino Martoglio, Teatro Mediterraneo troupe, Rome, 1919; co-founder, Teatro d'Arte di Roma, 1924–28; lived outside Italy, mainly in Berlin and Paris, 1928–33. **Awards:** Nobel prize for literature, 1934; Légion d'honneur (France). **Member:** Joined Fascist Party, 1924, but his relations with it were strained; Italian Academy. **Died:** 10 December 1936.

PUBLICATIONS

Collections

Opere. 6 vols., 1956–60.
One-Act Plays (includes *The Vise; Sicilian Limes; The Doctor's Duty; The Jar; By Judgement of the Court; Chee-Chee; The Imbecile; At the Gate; The House with the Column; The Man with the Flower in His Mouth; Our Lord of the Ship*), edited by Arthur

Livingston, translated by Livingston, Elisabeth Abbott, and Blanche V. Mitchell. 1928.

One-Act Plays (includes *The Vise; Sicilian Limes; The Doctor's Duty; The Jar; The License; Chee-Chee; At the Exit; Imbecile; The Man with the Flower in His Mouth; The Other Son; The Festival of Our Lord of the Ship; Bellavita; I'm Dreaming, But Am I?*), translated by William Murray. 1970.

The Collected Plays, edited by Robert Rietty, various translators. 3 vols., 1987–92.

Plays

L'epilogo. 1898; as *La morsa* (produced 1910), 1926; as *The Vise*, translated in *One-Act Plays*, 1928; also translated by William Murray, in *One-Act Plays*, 1970.

Scamandro (produced 1928). 1909.

Lumie di Sicilia (produced 1910). 1911; as *Sicilian Limes*, translated in *One-Act Plays*, 1928; also translated by William Murray, in *One-Act Plays*, 1970; as *Limes from Sicily*, translated by Robert Rietty, 1967, and in *The Collected Plays*, 2, 1988.

Il dovere del medico (produced 1913). 1912; as *The Doctor's Duty*, translated in *One-Act Plays*, 1928; also translated by William Murray, in *One-Act Plays*, 1970.

Se non così (produced 1915). 1915; revised version, as *La ragione degli altri*, 1921.

L'aria del continente, with Nino Martoglio (produced 1916).

Pensaci Giacomino! (produced 1916). 1917.

Il berretto a sonagli (produced 1916). 1918; as *Cap and Bells*, in *Sicilian Comedies*, 1987.

Liolà (produced 1916). 1917; revised version, music by Giuseppe Mule (produced 1935); as *Liola*, translated by Eric Bentley and Gerardo Guerrieri, in *Naked Masks*, 1952.

La giara (produced 1917). 1925; as *The Jar*, translated in *One-Act Plays*, 1928; also translated by Frederick May, in *Four Continental Plays*, 1964; and William Murray, in *One-Act Plays*, 1970.

'A vilanza, with Nino Martoglio (produced 1917).

Così è (si vi pare) (produced 1917). 1918; as *Right You Are (If You Think So)*, translated by Arthur Livingston, in *Three Plays*, 1922; also translated by Frederick May, with *All for the Best* and *Henry IV*, 1962; as *It Is So! (If You Think So)*, translated by Arthur Livingston, in *Naked Masks*, 1952; as *Right You Are (If You Think You Are)*, translated by Bruce Penman, in *The Collected Plays*, 1, 1987.

Il piacere dell'onestà (produced 1918). 1918; as *The Pleasure of Honesty*, translated by Arthur Livingston, in *Each in His Own Way and Two Other Plays*, 1923; also translated by William Murray, in *To Clothe the Naked and Two Other Plays*, 1962.

Il giuoco delle parti (produced 1918). 1919; as *The Rules of the Game* translated by Robert Rietty, in *Three Plays*, 1959; also translated by William Murray, 1960, and in *To Clothe the Naked and Two Other Plays*, 1962; as *The Rules of the Game*, translated and adapted by David Hare, 1993.

Ma non è una cosa seria (produced 1918). 1919.

La patente (produced 1919). 1918; as *By Judgement of the Court*, translated in *One-Act Plays*, 1928; as *The License*, translated by William Murray, in *One-Act Plays*, 1970.

L'uomo, la bestia, e la virtù (produced 1919). 1922; as *Man, Beast and Virtue*, in *Sicilian Comedies*, 1987; also translated by C. Wood, 1989.

'U ciclopu, from *Cyclops* by Euripides (produced 1919). 1967.

L'innesto (produced 1919). 1921; as *Grafted*, translated by Robert Rietty, in *The Collected Plays*, 3, 1992.

Come prima, meglio di prima (produced 1920). 1921.

Tutto per bene (produced 1920). 1920; as *All for the Best*, translated by Henry Reed, 1962, and in *The Collected Plays*, 2, 1988; also translated by Frederick May, with *Right You Are! If You Think So* and *Henry IV*, 1962.

La signora Morli, una e due (produced 1920). 1922.

Cecè (produced 1920). 1926; as *Chee-Chee*, translated in *One-Act Plays*, 1928; also translated by William Murray, in *One-Act Plays*, 1970.

Sei personaggi in cerca d'autore (produced 1921). 1921; as *Six Characters in Search of an Author*, translated by Edward Storer, in *Three Plays*, 1922; several subsequent translations including by Frederick May, 1954; John Linstrum, 1979; Robert Brustein and The American Repertory Theatre Company, 1998; adapted by David Harrower, 2001.

Enrico IV (produced 1922). 1921; as *Henry IV*, translated by Edward Storer, in *Three Plays*, 1922; several subsequent translations including by Frederick May, with *Right You Are! (If You Think So)* and *All for the Best*, 1962; Julian Mitchell, 1979; as *Enrico Four* translated by R.D. MacDonald, 1990.

Vestire gl'ignudi (produced 1922). 1923; as *Naked*, translated by Arthur Livingston, in *Each in His Own Way and Two Other Plays*, 1923; as *To Clothe the Naked*, translated by William Murray, in *To Clothe the Naked and Two Other Plays*, 1962; as *Clothe the Naked*, translated by Diane Cilento, in *The Collected Plays*, 2, 1988; as *Naked*, translated by Gaynor McFarlane, version by Nicholas Wright, 1998.

Three Plays (includes *Right You Are (If You Think So); Henry IV; Six Characters in Search of an Author*), translated by Arthur Livingston and Edward Storer. 1922.

L'imbecille (produced 1922). 1926; as *The Imbecile*, translated in *One-Act Plays*, 1928; also translated by William Murray, in *One-Act Plays*, 1970.

All'uscita (produced 1922). 1926; as *At the Gate*, translated in *One-Act Plays*, 1928; as *At the Exit*, translated by William Murray, in *One-Act Plays*, 1970.

Cappiddazzu paga tuti, with Nino Martoglio. In *Teatro dialecto siciliano 7*, by Martoglio, 1922.

Each in His Own Way and Two Other Plays (includes *Each in His Own Way; Naked; The Pleasure of Honesty*), translated by Arthur Livingston. 1923.

La vita che ti diedi (produced 1923). 1924; as *The Life I Gave You*, translated by Frederick May, in *Three Plays*, 1959.

L'altro figlio (produced 1923). 1925; as *The House with the Column*, translated in *One-Act Plays*, 1928; as *The Other Son*, translated by William Murray, in *One-Act Plays*, 1970.

L'uomo dal fiore in bocca (produced 1923). 1926; as *The Man with the Flower in His Mouth*, translated in *One-Act Plays*, 1928; also translated by Frederick May, 1959; William Murray, in *One-Act Plays*, 1970; Gigi Gatti and Terry Doyle, 1983, and in *The Collected Plays*, 1, 1987.

Ciascuno a suo modo (produced 1924). 1924; as *Each in His Own Way*, translated by Arthur Livingston, 1923.

La sagra del signore della nave (produced 1925). 1925; as *Our Lord of the Ship*, translated in *One-Act Plays*, 1928; as *The Festival of Our Lord of the Ship*, translated by William Murray, in *One-Act Plays*, 1970.

Diana e la Tuda (produced 1926). 1927; as *Diana and Tuda*, translated by Marta Abba, 1950.

L'amica delle mogli (produced 1927). 1927; as *The Wives' Friend*, translated by Marta Abba, 1960.

Bellavita (produced 1927). 1937; as *Bellavita*, translated by William Murray, in *One-Act Plays*, 1970.

La nuova colonia (produced 1928). 1928; as *The New Colony*, translated by Marta Abba, in *The Mountain Giants and Other Plays*, 1958.

Lazzaro (produced 1928). 1929; translated as *Lazarus*, 1952; also translated by Frederick May, in *Three Plays*, 1959.

La salamandra, music by Massimo Bontempelli (produced 1928).

O di uno o di nessuno (produced 1929?). 1929.

Questa sera si recita a soggetto (produced 1930). 1930; as *Tonight We Improvise*, translated by Samuel Putnam, 1932; also translated by Marta Abba, 1960.

Come tu mi vuoi (produced 1930). 1930; as *As You Desire Me*, translated by Samuel Putnam, 1931; also translated by Marta Abba, 1948.

Sogno (ma forse no) (produced 1931). 1936; as *I'm Dreaming, But Am I?*, translated by William Murray, in *One-Act Plays*, 1970.

Trovarsi. 1932; as *To Find Oneself*, translated by Marta Abba, 1943.

Quando si è qualcuno (produced 1933). 1933; as *When Someone Is Somebody*, translated by Marta Abba, in *The Mountain Giants and Other Plays*, 1958.

La favola del figlio cambiato, music by Malpiero (produced 1934). 1938.

Non si sa come (produced 1934). 1935; as *No One Knows How*, translated by Marta Abba, 1963.

I giganti della montagna (unfinished; produced 1937). 1938; as *The Mountain Giants*, translated by Marta Abba, in *The Mountain Giants and Other Plays*, 1958; as *The Mountain Giants* by Charles Wood, 1993.

Naked Masks: Five Plays (includes *Liola; Six Characters in Search of an Author; Henry IV; It Is So! (If You Think So); Each in His Own Way*), edited by Eric Bentley, translated by Bentley, Gerardo Guerrieri, Edward Storer, and Arthur Livingston. 1952.

The Mountain Giants and Other Plays (includes *The Mountain Giants; The New Colony; When Someone Is Somebody*), translated by Marta Abba. 1958.

Three Plays (includes *The Rules of the Game; The Life I Gave You; Lazarus*), edited by E. Martin Browne, translated by Frederick May and Robert Rietty. 1959.

Right You Are! (If You Think So); All for the Best; Henry IV, edited by E. Martin Browne, translated by Frederick May and Henry Reed. 1962.

Henry IV; The Rules of the Game; Right You Are! (If You Think So), edited by E. Martin Browne and translated by Frederick May and Robert Rietty. 1969.

Three Plays (in Italian; includes *Sei personaggi in cerca d'autore; Enrico IV; La giara*), edited by Felicity Firth. 1969.

Three Plays (includes *Rules of the Game; Six Characters in Search of an Author; Henry IV*), edited by John Linstrum, translated by Linstrum, Robert Rietty, and Julian Mitchell. 1985.

Sicilian Comedies: Cap and Bells; Man, Beast and Virtue, edited by Olga Ragusa, translated by N.A. Bailey and R.W. Oliver. 1987.

Screenplays: *Pantera nera*, with Arnaldo Frateili, 1920; *Acciaio*, with Stefano Landi, 1933; *Pensaci Giacomino!*, with others, 1935.

Fiction

Amori senza amore. 1894.

L'esclusa. 1901; as *The Outcast*, translated by Leo Ongley, 1925.

Beffe della morte e della vita. 2 vols., 1902–03.

Quand'ero matto . . . . 1902.

Il turno. 1902.

Il fu Mattia Pascal. 1904; revised edition, 1921; as *The Late Mattia Pascal*, translated by Arthur Livingston, 1923; also translated by Nicoletta Simborowski, 1987; William Weaver, 1988.

Bianche e nere. 1904.

Erma bifronte. 1906.

La vita nuda. 1910; as *The Naked Truth*, translated by Arthur and Henrie Mayne, 1934.

Suo marito. 1911; as *Giustino Roncella nato Boggiolo*, 1953; as *Her Husband*, translated by Martha King and Mary Ann Frese Witt, 2000.

Terzetti. 1912.

I vecchi e i giovani. 2 vols., 1913; as *The Old and the Young*, translated by C.K. Scott Moncrieff, 2 vols., 1928.

Le due maschere. 1914; as *Tu Ridi*, 1920.

La trappola. 1915.

Erba del nostro orto. 1915.

Si gira . . . . 1916; as *Quaderni di Serafino Gubbio, operatore*, 1925; as *Shoot! Si gira . . . The Notebooks of Serafino Gubbio, Cinematograph Operator*, translated by C.K. Scott Moncrieff, 1927.

E domani, lunedi. 1917.

Un cavallo nella luna. 1918; as *The Horse in the Moon*, translated by Samuel Putnam, 1932.

Berecche e la guerra. 1919.

Il carnevale dei morti. 1919.

Novelle per un anno. 15 vols., 1922–37(?), vols. 1 and 2 revised 1956–57; selection (from revised edition) edited by C.A. McCormick, 1972.

Uno, nessuno, e centomila. 1926; as *One, None and a Hundred Thousand*, translated by Samuel Putnam, 1933; also translated by William Weaver, 1989.

Better Think Twice About It, and Twelve Other Stories, translated by Arthur and Henrie Mayne. 1933.

The Naked Truth and Eleven Other Stories (selection from *Novelle per un anno*), translated by Arthur and Henrie Mayne. 1933.

A Character in Distress (stories), translated anonymously. 1938.

Four Tales, translated by V.M. Jeffery. 1939; as *Limes from Sicily and Other Stories*, translated by Jeffrey, 1942.

Short Stories, edited and translated by Frederick May. 1965.

Tales of Madness: A Selection from "Short Stories for a Year," translated by Giovanni R. Bussino. 1984.

Tales of Suicide: A Selection from "Short Stories for a Year," translated by Giovanni R. Bussino. 1988.

Verse

Mal giocondo. 1889.

Pasqua di Gea. 1891.

Pier Gudrò. 1894.

Elegie renane. 1895.

Zampogna. 1901.

Fuori di chiave. 1912.

Other

Laute und Lautentwicklung der Mundart von Girgenti. 1891; as *The Sounds of the Girgenti Dialect and Their Development*, translated by Giovanni R. Bussoni (bilingual edition: German and English), 1992.

Arte e Scienza. 1908.

L'umorismo. 1908; as *On Humor*, edited and translated by Antonio Illiano and Daniel P. Testa, 1974.

Pirandello in the Theatre: A Documentary Record, edited by Jennifer Lorch and Susan Bassnett. 1988.

Pirandello's Love Letters to Marta Abba, edited and translated by Benito Ortolani. 1994.

Translator, *La filologia romanza*, by F. Neumann. 1893.

Translator, *Elegie romane*, by Goethe. 1896.

*

Bibliography: *Bibliografia di Pirandello* by Manlio Lo Vecchio-Musti, 1952; *Bibliografia della critica pirandelliana 1889–1961* by Alfredo Barbina, 1967; *Bibliografia della critica pirandelliana 1962–1981* by Corrado Donati, 1986.

Critical Studies: *Luigi Pirandello* by Walter Starkie, 1929; *The Drama of Pirandello* by D. Vittorini, 1935; *The Age of Pirandello* by Lander McClintock, 1951; *Pirandello and the French Theatre* by Thomas Bishop, 1960; *The Drama of Chekhov, Synge, Yeats and Pirandello* by F.L. Lucas, 1963; *Pirandello* by Oscar Büdel, 1966; *Pirandello: A Collection of Critical Essays* edited by Glauco Cambon, 1967; *The Structural Patterns of Pirandello's Work* by Jørn Moestrup, 1972; *Petrarch to Pirandello: Studies in Italian Literature in Honour of Beatrice Corrigan* edited by Julius A. Molinaro, 1973; *The Pirandellian Mode in Spanish Literature from Cervantes to Sastre* by Wilma Newberry, 1973; *Pirandello and Picasso: A Pragmatic View of Reality* by Victor Carrabino, 1974; *Pirandello's Theatre: The Recovery of the Modern Stage for Dramatic Art* by Anne Paolucci, 1974; *Pirandello: A Biography* by Gaspare Giudice, translated by Alastair Hamilton, 1975; *The Mirror of Our Anguish: A Study of Luigi Pirandello's Narrative Writings* by Douglas Radcliff-Umstead, 1978; *Dreams of Passion: The Theater of Luigi Pirandello* by Roger W. Oliver, 1979; *Luigi Pirandello: An Approach to His Theatre* by Olga Ragusa, 1980; *Yearbook of the British Pirandello Society*, 1981–; *Luigi Pirandello, Director: The Playwright in the Theatre* by A. Richard Sogliuzzo, 1982; *Luigi Pirandello* by Susan Bassnett, 1983, and *File on Pirandello* edited by Bassnett, 1989; *The Pirandello Commentaries* by Eric Bentley, 1985; *Luigi Pirandello* by Renate Matthaei, 1985; *An Introduction to Pirandello's "Sei personaggi in cerca d'autore"* by Doug Thompson, 1985; *Pirandello and the Crisis of Modern Consciousness* by Anthony Francis Caputi, 1988; *Luigi Pirandello: The Humorous Existentialist* by Madeleine Strong Cincotta, 1989; *Pirandello in Cinema* by Sergio Micheli, 1989; *Pirandello's Naked Prompt* by Jennifer Stone, 1989; *Pirandello in Performance* (book and slide set) by Felicity Firth, 1990; *A Companion to Pirandello Studies* edited by John Louis DiGaetani, 1991; *Painting Literature: Dostoevsky, Kafka, Pirandello, and Gabriel García Márquez, in Living Color* by Constance A. Pedoto, 1993; *Patriarchal Representations: Gender and Discourse in Pirandello's Theatre* by Maggie Günsberg, 1994; *Contemporary Italian Filmmaking: Strategies of Subversion: Pirandello, Fellini, Scola, and the Directors of the New Generation* by Manuela Gieri, 1995; *Pirandello and Film* by Nina da Vinci Nichols and Jana O'Keefe Bazzoni, 1995; *Understanding Luigi Pirandello* by Fiora A. Bassanese, 1997; *Pirandello and His Muse: The Plays for Marta Abba* by Daniela Bini, 1998; *Characters and Authors in Luigi Pirandello* by Ann Hallamore Caesar, 1998; *Luigi Pirandello: Contemporary Perspectives*, edited by Gian-Paolo Biasin and Manuela Gieri, 1999.

*   *   *

Luigi Pirandello is one of the most distinguished authors in the history of modern Italian literature. Outside Italy he is known primarily for his drama, but by the time Pirandello received the Nobel prize in 1934, he had also written poetry, essays, and novels as well as several hundred short stories. Like most European writers who came of age in the late 19th century, Pirandello was influenced heavily by the aesthetics of realism (an influence that was perhaps heightened by his friendship in Rome with his fellow Sicilian, Luigi Capuana, one of the original standard-bearers of Italian *verismo*). This realist slant is especially apparent in Pirandello's early stories and in his historical novel set in 19th-century Sicily, *I vecchi e i giovani* (*The Old and the Young*). It is evident, too, in many of the one-act plays of the period 1910–20 that were drawn from previous short stories, such as *Lumìe di Sicilia* (*Sicilian Limes*), *Pensaci Giacomino!* [Think about it, Giacomino!], and *La giara* (*The Jar*).

As Pirandello's thought developed, however, he moved away from the realist depiction of the surface of everyday life toward examination of the turbulent phenomena underneath. In Pirandello's theatre, this shift in interest and this increasing complexity can be detected as early as *Liolà*, in which society's dependence on passion and fantasy as well as on order and control is examined through the play's presentation of the sexual intrigues of its clever but feckless title character. Pirandello's concern for the truth lying beneath the mask of reality—a truth that is, however, always relative and that therefore cannot be understood totally or explained—is even clearer in *Così e (si vi pare)* (*Right You Are (If You Think You Are)*). By means of a series of dramatic discussions, Pirandello reveals the emotional trials that have made up the lives of a seemingly ordinary, middle-class family. At the play's conclusion, the group of questioners on stage is challenged to choose between competing versions of the family's story and at the same time cautioned against making any such choice. Because the audience, by implication, participates in this same challenge and warning, *Right You Are* serves as a transition from Pirandello's dramas of bourgeois life to his trilogy of plays dealing with one of his favourite topics, the "theatre in the theatre."

The trilogy comprises three of Pirandello's most highly regarded plays, *Sei personaggi in cerca d'autore* (*Six Characters in Search of an Author*), *Ciascuno a suo modo* (*Each in His Own Way*), and *Questa sera si recita a soggetto* (*Tonight We Improvise*). The first and most innovative piece among them, *Six Characters*, is also the best known of all of Pirandello's works. The play portrays a family of characters who are looking for an author to write out the events of their lives. Through their story of familial jealousy, competition, lust, and tragic violence—and the characters' presentation of the story before the uncomprehending stage company and director—Pirandello probes both the relation between art and life and that between appearance and reality. Together with *Enrico IV* (*Henry IV*), Pirandello's forceful drama of rivalry, madness, and aggression, the trilogy demonstrates Pirandello's concern, one might also say his obsession, with self-reflection in art and with the limitations of reason in coming to terms with human nature, which, by definition, contains irrational as well as rational components.

These questions of human perception, will, and understanding, all of which are basic to Pirandello's developing view of individual and social life, were already at work in his first mature novel, *Il fu Martin Pascal* (*The Late Mattia Pascal*). These and related issues are treated in expository fashion, moreover, in one of Pirandello's roughly contemporaneous essays, *L'umorismo* (*On Humor*). For Pirandello, *umorismo* is more than an attribute solely of wit or of emotion; rather, it is an all-encompassing perspective on life. According to the essay, the primary characteristics of this typically Pirandellian perspective are: first, the individual's "perception" of the comic, that something runs contrary to the normal expectations of daily life; second, the individual's emotional reaction to this perception, or the internal "sentiment" of the comic, experienced in the characteristic passage from perception to sentiment; third, the ever-present activity of reflection—including self-reflection—from which this sentiment arises and which it then further stimulates; and fourth, the constant tendency to decompose ("scomporre") the form of experience into its constituent elements so that they may be considered both separately and in relation to one another and, if possible (though for the full-fledged *umorista* such a feat is never really possible), reassembled in a workable and more liveable fashion, in a new fusion of what the essay terms life and form, "vita" and "forma."

The story of the "late" Mattia Pascal is in many respects the story of his development as an *umorista*. In essence, the plot of the novel is based on the standard anecdote of the man who dies (complicated here by a crucial instance of mistaken identity) and who then returns to this world from beyond with the uncanny knowledge of his own death. It is this special knowledge, the peculiarly distanced view of life, that lends Mattia's story the characteristic perspective of *umorismo*. That Mattia's narrative is told in the first-person by the mature, or literally "late," narrator only heightens its self-reflexive quality.

This perspective is also fundamental to one of Pirandello's novels of his middle period, *Si gira. . .* (*Shoot!*); but its fullest expression is contained in Pirandello's last and in many respects his most problematic novel, *Uno, nessuno, e centomila* (*One, None, and a Hundred Thousand*). Whereas *The Late Mattia Pascal* represents the discovery of psychological and artistic reflexivity, *One, None, and a Hundred Thousand* is a programmatic exposition not only of the process but also of the consequence of such discoveries. The novel's plot is made up of Vitangelo Moscarda's attempts to see himself as others see him. He carries out this project by gradually discarding all of those particular attributes (his wife, his reputation, his profession as a banker) that have come together to compose his identity in society. Vitangelo's social "suicide" eventually leads to a critical impasse, at which point he gives up on his project and leaves life in society altogether. At the novel's conclusion, disgusted with his former existence and with all those who were part of it, Vitangelo retires from the town in which he has spent his life in order to establish a new, totally non-reflective form of day-to-day existence at a hospice in the countryside.

Although at the beginning of the novel Vitangelo sounds a good deal like Pirandello's other highly rationalistic, sceptical, and self-involved characters, the novel's conclusion shows him in a very different light. Vitangelo's story was Pirandello's most extreme statement of the philosophy of *umorismo*, which derived both from earlier European intellectual philosophy and from the then influential views of Henri Bergson. But the novel also represented a turning point in Pirandello's thought, the completion of one line of investigation and the beginning of another. This new set of interests had been implicit in Pirandello's work for some time, but it became dominant

only in such later, socially oriented plays as *La nuova colonia* (*The New Colony*), *Lazzaro* (*Lazarus*), and the unfinished (and pointedly pessimistic) *I giganti della montagna* (*The Mountain Giants*). Generally speaking, this final shift in Pirandello's interests was from the rational powers of the self-reflective, alienated individual to the communal truth of myth. Although Pirandello did not live to carry this line of artistic and social enquiry to its conclusion, his last plays indicate that, even at his death, Pirandello had once again found the pulse of the future.

In the decades since his death, and particularly since the close of World War II, there have been many studies of Pirandello's relationship with the Fascist government in Rome. It should be noted, however, that even though Pirandello's ties with the regime were close until the very end of his career, in all of the various phases of his thought—whether realistic, rationally self-reflexive, or mythic—his work regularly manifested an iconoclastic aversion to absolute authority that set it apart from the standard political doctrines of the time in Italian social and intellectual life (and perhaps most distinctly from the work of his well-known contemporary, Gabriele D' Annunzio). The body of criticism dealing with Pirandello continues to grow at an exceptional rate in America as well as in Europe, but despite the extraordinary variety of critical treatments that his work has received, Pirandello's importance and his influence on subsequent writers both inside and outside Italy have remained beyond dispute.

—Gregory L. Lucente

See the essays on *Henry IV* and *Six Characters in Search of an Author*.

PLATO

Born: Athens (possibly in Aegina), c. 429–27 BC. **Career:** A disciple of Socrates (first met c. 407 BC); when Socrates was executed in 399 BC, Plato retired with other Socratics to Megara, then travelled for the next 12 years: visited Egypt; Sicily, 390–88 BC, where he met Dionysius I of Syracuse; and Italy, where he met Archytas of Tarentum; began teaching near the grove of Academus outside Athens in 388 BC and continued for his remaining 40 years: his pupils included Aristotle, *q.v.*; summoned to court of Dionysius II of Syracuse by Dion, the ruler's uncle, 366–65 BC, and by Dionysius II himself, 362–61 BC. **Died:** 347 BC.

PUBLICATIONS

Collections

Works (includes 55 dialogues and 12 epistles), translated by Thomas Taylor and Floyer Sydenham. 1804.
[Dialogues], edited by John Burnet. 5 vols., 1900–07; edited and translated by R.E. Allen, 2 vols., 1985–91; translated by Benjamin Jowett, 4 vols., 1868–71; also translated by Henry Cary, 1900; H.N. Fowler and others [Loeb Edition], 12 vols., 1914–29; *Collected Dialogues* (including *Letters*), edited by Edith Hamilton and Huntington Cairns, translated by Lane Cooper and others, 1961.

Complete Works, edited with introduction and notes by John M. Cooper. 1997.

Dialogues (in chronological order)

Hippias minor, edited by George Smith. 1895; as *Hippias minor*, translated by F. Sydenham, in *Dialogues*, 1767; also translated by Robin Waterfield, in *Early Socratic Dialogues*, 1987.

Laches, edited by M.T. Tatham. 1888, reprinted 1966; also edited by F.G. Plaistowe, translated by T.R. Mills, 1898; as *Laches*, translated by J. Gibson, with *Euthyphron*, 1892; also translated by W.R.M. Lamb, with *Meno; Protagoras; Euthydemus* [Loeb Edition], 1924; Rosamund Kent Sprague, 1973; Iain Lane, in *Early Socratic Dialogues*, 1987.

Charmides, edited by Richard F. Hipwell. 1951; as *Charmides*, translated by Rosamund Kent Sprague, 1973; also translated by T.G. and G.S. West, 1986; Donald Watt, in *Early Socratic Dialogues*, 1987.

Ion, edited by George Smith. 1895; also edited by St George Stock, 1909, and J.M. Macgregor, 1912; as *Ion*, translated by F. Sydenham, in *Dialogues*, 1767; also translated by Percy Bysshe Shelley, in *The Banquet of Plato and Other Pieces*, 1887; W.R.M. Lamb [Loeb Edition], 1925; Lane Cooper, 1938; W.H.D. Rouse, 1956; Paul Woodruff, 1983; Trevor J. Saunders, in *Early Socratic Dialogues*, 1987.

Protagoras, edited by James and A.M. Adam. 1981; as *Protagoras*, translated by Henry Carey, 1888; also translated by W.R.M. Lamb, with *Laches; Meno; Euthydemus* [Loeb Edition], 1924; Benjamin Jowett, in *The Portable Plato*, 1948; W.K.C. Guthrie, with *Meno*, 1956; C.C.W. Taylor, 1976; B.A.F. Hubbard, 1982; Patrick Coby, 1987; Stanley Lombardo and Karen Bell, 1992.

Euthyphro, edited and translated by T.R. Mills, with *Menexenus*. 1902; also edited by John Burnet, 1924, C.E. Graves, revised edition, 1935, and C.J. Emlyn-Jones, 1991; as *Euthyphron*, translated by F.J. Church, in *The Trial and Death of Socrates*, 1880; also translated by J. Gibson, with *Laches*, 1892; as *Euthyphro*, translated by F.M. Stawell, with *Apology* and *Crito*, 1906; also translated by Lane Cooper, in *On the Trial and Death of Socrates*, 1941; Basil Wrighton, in *The Death of Socrates*, 1948; W.D. Woodhead, in *Socratic Dialogues*, 1953; John Warrington, in *The Trial and Death of Socrates*, 1963; R.E. Allen, 1970; G.M.A. Grube, in *Five Dialogues*, 1986.

Apologia (not a dialogue), edited by A.M. Adam. 1914; also edited by Edward Henry Blakeney, 1929, Robin Barrow, 1977, and John Burnet, 1977; as *Apology of Socrates*, translated by Dr. Charleton, with *Phaedo*, 1675; also translated by J.A. Giles, 1860; as *The Apology*, translated by Joseph Mills, 1775; also translated by C.S. Stanford, with *Crito* and *Phaedo*, 1835; J. Eccleston and R. Mongan, with *Crito* and *Phaedo*, 1865; W.W. Godwin, in *Socrates*, 1879; F.J. Church, in *The Trial and Death of Socrates*, 1880; Benjamin Jowett, in *Socrates*, 1882; Henry Carey, 1888; J.A. Nicklin, 1897; D.F. Nevill, 1901; F.M. Stawell, with *Euthyphro* and *Crito*, 1906; Charles L. Marson (bilingual edition), with *Crito*, 1912; E.H. Blakeney, 1929; R.W. Livingstone, in *Portrait of Socrates*, 1938; Lane Cooper, in *On the Trial and Death of Socrates*, 1941; Basil Wrighton, in *The Death of Socrates*, 1948; W.D. Woodhead, in *Socratic Dialogues*, 1953; Hugh Tredennick, in *The Last Days of Socrates*, 1954; W.H.D. Rouse, 1956; John Warrington, in *The Trial and Death of Socrates*, 1963; Thomas G.

West, 1979; R.E. Allen, in *Socrates and Legal Obligation*, 1980; G.M.A. Grube, in *Five Dialogues*, 1986; as *Socrates on Trial*, translated by Thomas C. Brickhouse, 1989; as *Apology of Socrates*, translation by Michael C. Stokes, 1997.

Crito, edited by John Burnet. 1977; also edited by James Adam, 1988; as *Crito*, translated by C.S. Stanford, with *Apology* and *Phaedo*, 1835; also translated by J.A. Giles, 1860; J. Eccleston and R. Mongan, with *Apology* and *Phaedo*, 1865; W.W. Godwin, in *Socrates*, 1879; F.J. Church, in *The Trial and Death of Socrates*, 1880; Benjamin Jowett, in *Socrates*, 1882; Henry Carey, 1888; F.M. Stawell, with *Euthyphro* and *Apology*, 1906; Charles L. Marson (bilingual edition), with *Apology*, 1912; R.W. Livingstone, in *Portrait of Socrates*, 1938; Lane Cooper, in *On the Trial and Death of Socrates*, 1941; Basil Wrighton, in *The Death of Socrates*, 1948; W.D. Woodhead, in *Socratic Dialogues*, 1953; Hugh Tredennick, in *The Last Days of Socrates*, 1954; W.H.D Rouse, 1956; John Warrington, in *The Trial and Death of Socrates*, 1963; A.D. Woozley, 1979; R.E. Allen, in *Socrates and Legal Obligation*, 1980; G.M.A. Grube, in *Five Dialogues*, 1986.

Phaedo, edited by C.J. Rowe. 1994; as *Phaedo*, translated by Dr. Charleton, with *Apology of Socrates*, 1675; also translated by Thomas Taylor, with *Cratylus; Parmenides; Timaeus*, 1793; C.S. Stanford, with *Apology* and *Crito*, 1835; J. Eccleston and R. Mongan, with *Apology* and *Crito*, 1865; W.W. Godwin, in *Socrates*, 1879; F.J. Church, in *The Trial and Death of Socrates*, 1880; Benjamin Jowett, in *Socrates*, 1882, and in *The Portable Plato*, 1948; Henry Carey, 1888; R.W. Livingstone, in *Portrait of Socrates*, 1938; Lane Cooper, in *On the Trial and Death of Socrates*, 1941; Basil Wrighton, in *The Death of Socrates*, 1948; W.D. Woodhead, in *Socratic Dialogues*, 1953; R. Hackforth, 1972; David Gallop, 1975; G.M.A. Grube, 1977, and in *Five Dialogues*, 1986; John Burnet, 1979; R. Larson, 1980.

Gorgias, edited by E.R. Dodds. 1959; revised edition, 1990; as *Gorgias* [Loeb Edition], translated by W.R.M. Lamb, 1932; also translated by Lane Cooper, 1938; W.D. Woodhead, in *Socratic Dialogues*, 1953; W. Hamilton, 1960; Terence Irwin, 1980; D.J. Zeyl, 1986; James H. Nichols, Jr., 1998.

Meno, edited by R.S. Bluck. 1961; also edited by A. Sesonske and N. Fleming, 1965; as *Meno*, translated by R.W. Mackay, 1869; also translated by St George Stock, 1887; W.R.M. Lamb, with *Laches; Protagoras; Euthydemus* [Loeb Edition], 1924; W.K.C. Guthrie, with *Protagoras*, 1956; W.H.D. Rouse, 1956; John E. Thomas, in *Musings on the Meno*, 1980; R.W. Sharpies, 1985; G.M.A. Grube, in *Five Dialogues*, 1986.

Lysis, as *Lysis*, translated by K.A. Matthews. 1930; also translated by W.R.M. Lamb [Loeb Edition], 1932; David Bolotin, in *Plato's Dialogue on Friendship*, 1979; Donald Watt, in *Early Socratic Dialogues*, 1987; Benjamin Jowett and E. O'Connor, in *On Homosexuality*, 1991.

Menexenus, edited and translated by T.R. Mills, with *Euthyphro*. 1902; as *Menexenus*, translated by Gilbert West, in *Odes of Pindar*, 1749; also translated by T. Broadhurst, 1811; Percy Bysshe Shelley, in *The Banquet of Plato and Other Pieces*, 1887; A.S. Way, 1934.

Euthydemus, edited by G.H. Wells. 1881; also edited by E.H. Gifford, 3 vols., 1905; as *Euthydemus*, translated by W.R.M. Lamb, with *Laches; Meno; Protagoras* [Loeb Edition], 1924; also translated by Rosamund Kent Sprague, 1972; Robin Waterfield, in *Early Socratic Dialogues*, 1987; *Commentary on Plato's Euthydemus* by R.S.W. Hawtrey, 1981.

Cratylus, edited by G. Pasquali. 1908; as *Cratylus*, translated by Thomas Taylor, with *Phaedo; Parmenides; Timaeus*, 1793.

Symposium, edited by R.G. Bury. 1973; also edited by K.J. Dover, 1980; edited and translated by Robin Waterfield, 1994; as *The Symposium*, translated by F. Sydenham, in *Dialogues*, 1767; also translated by W.R.M. Lamb [Loeb Edition], 1932; Lane Cooper, 1938; Benjamin Jowett, in *The Portable Plato*, 1948, and in *On Homosexuality*, 1991, revised by Hayden Pelliccia, 1996; W. Hamilton, 1951; W.H.D. Rouse, 1956; S.Q. Groden, 1970; R. Larson, 1980; Tom Griffith, 1986; A. Nehamas and Paul Woodruff, 1989; R.E. Allen, 1991; as *Fine Talk at Agathon's*, translated by H.A. Mason, 1992; translated by William S. Cobb in *The Symposium; and, The Phaedrus: Plato's Erotic Dialogues*, 1993; Avi Sharon, 1998; Christopher Gill, 1999; Seth Benardete, 2001.

Republic, edited by James Adam, revised by D.A. Rees. 2 vols., 1963; also edited by Allan Bloom, 1968; as *The Republic* [Loeb Edition], translated by P. Shorey, 2 vols., 1930–35; also translated by A.D. Lindsay, 1935, reprinted 1993; Francis M. Cornford, 1941; Benjamin Jowett, in *The Portable Plato*, 1948; H.D.P. Lee, 1955; W.H.D. Rouse, 1956; I.A. Richards, 1966; G.M.A. Grube, 1974, revised by C.D.C. Reeve, 1992; Richard W. Sterling and William C. Scott, 1985; Robin Waterfield, 1993; as *Republic 5*, translated by S. Halliwell, 1993; as *Plato's Republic for Readers: A Constitution* by George A. Blair, 1998.

Parmenides, as *Parmenides*, translated by Thomas Taylor, with *Phaedo; Cratylus; Timaeus*. 1793; also translated by A.E. Taylor, 1934; Francis M. Cornford, 1939; John Warrington, 1961; R.E. Allen, 1983; Glenn R. Morrow and John M. Dillon, 1987; Mary Louise Gill, 1996; as *The Parmenides and Plato's Late Philosophy*, translated with commentary by Robert G. Turnbull, 1998.

Theaetetus, edited by Lewis Campbell. 2nd edition, 1883; as *Theaetetus*, translated by H.N. Fowler, in *Dialogues* [Loeb Edition], 1921; also translated by M.J. Levett, 1928; John Warrington, 1961; Tayler Lewis, 1963; John McDowell, 1973; Seth Benardete, 1986; Robin Waterfield, 1987; as *Plato's Theory of Knowledge*, translated by Francis M. Cornford, 1935.

Phaedrus, edited by W.H. Thompson. 1868; as *Phaedrus*, translated by Lane Cooper, 1938; also translated by R. Hackforth, 1952; Benjamin Jowett, 1963, and in *On Homosexuality*, 1991; Richard and Clara Winston, 1965; Walter Hamilton (with *Letters VII and VIII*), 1973; Michael J.B. Allen, 1981; Robin Waterfield, 1982; C.J. Rowe, 1986; commentary by G.J. de Vries, 1969; translated by Alexander Nehamas and Paul Woodruff, 1995.

Sophist, as *Sophist*, translated by H.N. Fowler, in *Dialogues* [Loeb Edition]. 1921; also translated by Francis M. Cornford (includes commentary), 1935; A.E. Taylor, with *Statesman*, 1961; John Warrington, 1961; Seth Benardete, 1986; commentary by Gordon C. Neal, 1975; translated by Nicholas P. White, 1993.

Statesman, translated by H.N. Fowler, in *Dialogues* [Loeb Edition]. 1925; also translated by A.E. Taylor, with *Sophist*, 1961; John Warrington, 1961; Seth Benardete, 1986; as *Politicus*, translated by J.B. Skemp, 1952; translated by C.J. Rowe, 1995.

Philebus, as *Philebus*, translated by F. Sydenham, in *Dialogues*. 1767; also translated by R. Hackforth, in *Plato's Examination of Pleasure*, 1945; A.E. Taylor, 1956; J.C.B. Gosling, 1975; Robin Waterfield, 1982; Dorothea Frede, 1993; Seth Benardete, 1993.

Timaeus, edited by Christopher Gill. 1980; as *Timaeus*, translated by Thomas Taylor, with *Phaedo; Cratylus; Parmenides*, 1793; also translated by R.G. Bury [Loeb Edition], 1929; A.E. Taylor, 1929;

H.D.P. Lee, 1965; John Warrington, 1965; as *Plato's Cosmology: The Timaeus*, translated by Francis M. Cornford (includes commentary), 1937; commentary by A.E. Taylor, 1928.

Critias, edited by C. Gill, in *Atlantis Story*. 1981; as *Critias*, translated by A.E. Taylor, 1929; also translated by H.D.P. Lee, 1971.

Laws, edited by E.B. England. 2 vols., 1921; as *Laws* [Loeb Edition], translated by R.G. Bury, 2 vols., 1926; also translated by A.E. Taylor, 1934; Trevor S. Saunders, 1970; Thomas L. Pangle, 1988.

Dialogues (includes *Ion*; *Hippias minor*; *Hippias major*; *Symposium*; *Alcibiades* I and II; *Philebus*), translated by F. Sydenham. 1767.

Dialogues (includes *Euthyphro*; *Apology of Socrates*; *Crito*; *Phaedo*), translated by W. Whewell. 1860.

Socrates (includes *Apology*; *Crito*; *Phaedo*), translated by W.W. Godwin. 1879.

The Trial and Death of Socrates (includes *Euthyphron*; *Apology*; *Crito*; *Phaedo*), translated by F.J. Church. 1880.

Socrates (includes *Apology*; *Crito*; *Phaedo*), translated by Benjamin Jowett. 1882.

Dialogues (includes *Apology*; *Crito*; *Phaedo*; *Protagoras*), translated by Henry Carey. 1888.

Selections, edited by T.W. Rolleston, translated by Thomas Taylor and F. Sydenham. 1892.

The Martyrdom of Socrates (includes *Apology*; *Crito*; selections from *Phaedo*), edited and translated by F.C. Doherty. 1923.

Phaedrus, Ion, Gorgias and Symposium, with Passages from the Republic and Laws, translated by Lane Cooper. 1938.

On the Trial and Death of Socrates (includes *Euthyphro*; *Apology*; *Crito*; *Phaedo*), translated by Lane Cooper. 1941.

Four Dialogues (includes *Protagoras*; *Phaedrus*; *Gorgias*; *Apology of Socrates*), edited by Ruth Borchard, translated by John Stuart Mill. 1946.

The Portable Plato (includes *Protagoras*; *Symposium*; *Phaedo*; *The Republic*), translated by Benjamin Jowett. 1948; edited by Scott M. Buchanan, 1977.

The Death of Socrates: An Interpretation of the Platonic Dialogues: Euthyphro, Apology, Crito and Phaedo, translated by Basil Wrighton. 1948.

Socratic Dialogues (includes *Euthyphro*; *Apology*; *Crito*; *Phaedo*; *Gorgias*), edited and translated by W.D. Woodhead. 1953.

Great Dialogues of Plato, edited by Eric H. Warmington and Philip G. Rouse, translated by W.H.D. Rouse. 1967; revised edition, 1970.

Five Dialogues: Euthyphro; Apology; Crito; Meno; Phaedo, translated by G.M.A. Grube. 1986.

Early Socratic Dialogues (includes *Ion*; *Laches*; *Lysis*; *Charmides*; *Hippias major*; *Hippias minor*; *Euthydemus*; fragments of *Aeschines* and *Spettus*), edited by Trevor J. Saunders, translated by Saunders, Iain Lane, Donald Watt, and Robin Waterfield. 1987.

The Roots of Political Philosophy: Ten Forgotten Socratic Dialogues, edited and translated by Thomas L. Pangle. 1987.

Plato on Poetry, edited by Penelope Murray. 1995.

The Plato Reader, edited by Tim Chappell. 1996.

Plato on Rhetoric and Language: Four Key Dialogues, introduced by Jean Nienkamp. 1999.

Doubtful works: *Hippias major*, edited by Dorothy Tarrant (includes commentary). 1928; translated by F. Sydenham, in *Dialogues*, 1767; also translated by Paul Woodruff (includes commentary), 1982; Robin Waterfield, in *Early Socratic Dialogues*, 1987; *Epinomis*, translated by J. Harward. 1928; also translated by A.E. Taylor, 1956;

Letters, in *Collected Dialogues*, edited by Edith Hamilton and Huntington Cairns. 1961; as *Epistles*, translated by Thomas Taylor, in *Works*, 1839; also translated by L.A. Post, 1925; J. Harward, 1932; Glenn R. Morrow, 1935.

*

Bibliography: *A Bibliography on Plato's "Laws," 1920–1970, with Additional Citations through May 1975* by Trevor J. Saunders, 1975; *Plato and Socrates: A Comprehensive Bibliography, 1958–1973* by Richard D. McKirahan, 1978.

Critical Studies: *The Political Thought of Plato and Aristotle* by Ernest Barker, 1906; *What Plato Said* by Paul Shorey, 1933; *Plato's Theory of Ideas* by David Ross, 1951; *Plato's Earlier Dialectic* by Richard Robinson, 2nd edition, 1953; *Aristotle's Criticism of Plato's Timaeus* by G.S. Claghorn, 1954; *The Open City: The Spell of Plato* by Karl Popper, 1957; *Plato* by Paul Friedlander, 3 vols., 1958–69; *An Approach to the Metaphysics of Plato Through the Parmenides* by William F. Lynch, 1959; *Religion in Plato and Cicero* by John E. Rexine, 1959; *Plato's Cretan City: A Historical Interpretation of the Laws* by Glenn R. Morrow, 1960; *Definition in Plato's Meno* by Laura Grimm, 1962; *An Examination of Plato's Doctrines* by I.M. Crombie, 2 vols., 1962–63; *Preface to Plato* by E.A. Havelock, 1963; *Plato's Republic: A Philosophical Commentary* by A.D. Woozley and R.C. Cross, 1964, and *Law and Obedience: The Arguments of Plato's Crito* by Woozley, 1979; *New Essays on Plato and Aristotle* edited by R. Bambrough, 1965; *Love and Inspiration: A Study of Plato's Phaedrus* by Josef Pieper, translated by Richard and Clara Winston, 1965; *Love, Knowledge and Discourse in Plato: Dialogue and Dialectic in Phaedrus, Republic, Parmenides* by Herman L. Sinako, 1965; *Plato's Progress* by Gilbert Ryle, 1966; *On the Semantic of Time in Plato's Timaeus*, 1970, and *Studies in Plato's Theory of Forms in the Timaeus*, 1970, both by Erkka Maukla; *Plato: A Collection of Critical Essays* edited by Gregory Vlastos, 1971, and *Platonic Studies*, 1973, and *Plato's Universe*, 1975, both by Vlastos; *Plato and Modern Morality* by P.M. Huby, 1972; *Notes on the Laws of Plato* by Trevor J. Saunders, 1972; *Plato* by J.C.B. Gosling, 1973; *The Unity of the Platonic Dialogue* by R.H. Weingartner, 1973; *Plato: The Written and Unwritten Doctrine*, 1974, and *Plato and Platonism: An Introduction*, 1978, both by J.N. Findlay; *Knowledge and Reality in Plato's Philebus* by Roger A. Shiner, 1974; *Plato's Ideas on Art and Education* by E.J.F. James, 1975; *The Argument and the Action of Plato's "Laws"* by Leo Strauss, 1975; *Miscellaneous Notes on Plato* by G.J. de Vries, 1975; *Plato and Education* by Robin Barrow, 1976; *Plato* by J.B. Skemp, 1976; *Plato on Knowledge and Reality*, 1976, and *A Companion to Plato's Republic*, 1979, both by Nicholas P. White; *The Structure of Plato's Philosophy* by Jerry S. Clegg, 1977; *Plato's Moral Theory: The Early and Middle Dialogues* by Terence Irwin, 1977; *Plato's Trilogy: Theaetetus, the Sophist, and the Statesman* by Jacob Klein, 1977; *The Fire and the Sun: Why Plato Banished the Artists* by Iris Murdoch, 1977; *Interpreting Plato* by Eugene Napoleon Tigerstedt, 1977; *Character, Plot and Thought in Plato's Timaeus-Critias* by Warman Welliver, 1977; *Plato's "Meno": A Philosophy of Man as Acquisitive*, 1978, and *Meaning, Relation and Existence in Plato's Parmenides: The Logic of Relational Realism*, 1987, both by Robert Sternfeld; *New Essays on Plato and Aristotle* by G.E.M. Anscombe, 1979; *Plato for the Modern Age* by Robert S. Brumbaugh, 1979; *Morality and the Inner Life: A Study in Plato's "Gorgias,"* 1979, and *Philosophy and the Philosophic Life: A Study in Plato's "Phaedo,"* 1992, both by Ilham Dilman; *Plato's*

Phaedrus: A Defense of a Philosophic Art of Writing, 1980, and *The Phaedo: A Platonic Labyrinth*, 1984, both by Ronna Burger; *Dialogue and Dialectic: Eight Hermeneutical Studies on Plato*, translated by C.P. Smith, 1980, and *Plato's Dialectical Ethics: Phenomenological Interpretations Relating to the Philebus*, 1991, both by Hans-Georg Gadamer; *Plato's Thought* by G.M.A. Grube, 1980; *Plato* by Robert W. Hall, 1980; *The Philosopher in Plato's Statesman*, 1980, and *Plato's Parmenides: The Conversion of the Soul*, 1986, both by Mitchell H. Miller, 1986; *An Introduction to Plato's Republic* by Julia Annas, 1981; *The Death Day of Socrates: Living, Dying and Immortality—The Theater of Ideas in Plato's Phaedo* by Jerome Eckstein, 1981; *The Virtue of Philosophy: An Interpretation of Plato's Charmides* by Drew A. Hyland, 1981; *Plato on Punishment* by Mary Margaret Mackenzie, 1981; *Plato's Theory of Understanding* by Jon Moline, 1981; *The Development of Plato's Metaphysics*, 1981, and *Socratic Education in Plato's Early Dialogues*, 1986, both by Henry Teloh; *Platonic Myth and Platonic Writing* by Robert Zaslavsky, 1981; *Plato's Phaedo: An Interpretation* by Kenneth Dorter, 1982; *Plato* by R.M. Hare, 1982; *Plato's Arguments for Forms* by Robert William Jordan, 1983; *Plato's Sophist: The Drama of Original and Image* by Stanley Rosen, 1983; *The Laborious Game: A Study of Plato's Parmenides* by Viggo Rossvaer, 1983; *Plato's Late Ontology: A Riddle Resolved* by Kenneth M. Sayre, 1983; *An Introduction to Plato's Laws* by R.F. Stalley, 1983; *Plato's Defence of Poetry* by Julius A. Elias, 1984; *For Images: An Interpretation of Plato's Sophist* by A. Chadwick Ray, 1984; *Plato* by Christopher Rowe, 1984; *The Charmides of Plato: Problems and Interpretations* by N. van der Ben, 1985; *The Education of Desire: Plato and the Philosophy of Religion* by Michel Despland, 1985; *The Platonic Cosmology* by Richard D. Mohr, 1985; *Plato's Parmenides: The Critical Moment for Socrates* by Harrison J. Pemberton, 1985; *Unity and Development in Plato's Metaphysics* by William J. Prior, 1985; *The Republic: Notes* by Robin Sowerby, 1985; *Plato's Phaedo*, 1986, and *Plato's Theaetetus*, 1988, both by David Bostock; *Self-Knowledge in Plato's Phaedrus* by Charles L. Griswold, 1986; *The Development of Plato's Political Theory* by George Klosko, 1986; *Plato's Sophist: A Philosophical Comedy* by L.M. de Rijk, 1986; *Philo of Alexandria and the Timaeus of Plato* by David T. Runia, 1986; *Being and Logos: The Way of Platonic Dialogue* by John Sallis, 1986; *Plato's Socratic Conversations: Drama and Dialectic in Three Dialogues* by Michael C. Stokes, 1986; *Women and the Ideal Society: Plato's Republic and Modern Myths of Gender* by Natalie Harris Bluestone, 1987; *Listening to the Cicadas: A Study of Plato's Phaedrus* by G.R.F. Ferrari, 1987; *Political Philosophy and Time: Plato and the Origins of Political Vision* by John G. Gunnell, 1987; *Plato on Justice and Power* by Kymon Lycos, 1987; *Understanding Plato* by David J. Melling, 1987; *Diaeresis and Myth in Plato's Statesman* by Harvey Ronald Scodel, 1987; *Plato's Theory of Explanation: A Study of the Cosmological Account in the Timaeus* by A. Freire Ashbaugh, 1988; *A Guided Tour of Five Works by Plato: Euthyphro; Apology; Crito; Phaedo (Death Scene); Allegory of the Cave* by Christopher Biffle, 1988; *The Textual Tradition of Plato's Republic* by Gerard Boter, 1988; *Justice, Law and Method in Plato and Aristotle* edited by Spiro Panagiotou, 1988; *A Friendly Companion to Plato's Gorgias* by George Kimball Plochmann, 1988; *Plato's Metaphysics of Education* by Samuel Scolnicov, 1988; *Rethinking Plato and Platonism* by Cornelia J. de Vogel, 1988; *Socrates' Second Sailing: On Plato's Republic*, 1989, and *The Rhetoric of Morality and Philosophy: Plato's Gorgias and Phaedrus*, 1991, both by Seth

Benardete; *Forms in Plato's Philebus* by E.E. Benitez, 1989; *Names, Reference and Correctness in Plato's Cratylus* by Michael D. Palmer, 1989; *Love and Friendship in Plato and Aristotle* by A.W. Price, 1989; *The Chronology of Plato's Dialogues* by Leonard Brandwood, 1990; *Plato's Theaetetus* by John M. Cooper, 1990; *Plato's Philebus* by Donald Davidson, 1990; *Plato in the Italian Renaissance* by James Hankins, 2 vols., 1990; *Plato and the English Romantics* by E. Douka Kabitoglou, 1990; *Platonic Piety: Philosophy and Ritual in Fourth-Century Athens* by Michael L. Morgan, 1990; *Parmenides, Plato and the Semantics of Not-Being* by Francis Jeffrey Pelletier, 1990; *Plato on the Self-Predication of Forms* by John Malcolm, 1991; *Plato's Invisible Cities: Discourse and Power in the Republic* by Adi Ophir, 1991; *Tragedy of Reason: Toward a Platonic Conception of Logos* by David Roochnik, 1991; *Plato Prehistorian: 10,000–5,000 BC. Myth, Religion, Archaeology* by Mary Settegast, 1991; *Acquiring Knowledge of the Ideas: A Study of Plato's Methods in the Phaedo, the Symposium and the Central Books of the Republic* by Ludwig C.H. Chen, 1992; *Methods of Interpreting Plato and his Dialogues* edited by James C. Klagge and Nicholas D. Smith, 1992; *Plato's Political Philosophy: Prudence in the Republic and the Laws* by Zdravko Planinc, 1992; *Plato's Meno in Focus*, edited by Jane M. Day, 1994; *Plato and the Socratic Dialogue: The Philosophical Use of a Literary Form* by Charles H. Kahn, 1996; *Of Art and Wisdom: Plato's Understanding of Techne* by David Roochnik, 1996; *The Stance of Plato* by Albert Cook, 1996; *Form and Argument in Late Plato*, edited by Christopher Gill and Mary Margaret McCabe, 1996; *Postmodern Platos* by Catherine H. Zuckert, 1996; *Plato Rediscovered: Human Value and Social Order* by T.K. Seung, 1996; *Genres in Dialogue: Plato and the Construct of Philosophy* by Andrea Wilson Nightingale, 1996; *Plato's Craft of Justice* by Richard D. Parry, 1996; *Towards a New Interpretation of Plato* by Giovanni Reale, translated and edited by John R. Catan and Richard Davies, 1997; *Plato's Sophist* by Martin Heidegger, translated by Richard Rojcewicz and André Schuwer, 1997; *Aristotle's Criticism of Plato's Republic* by Robert Mayhew, 1997; *The Great Tradition: Further Studies in the Development of Platonism and Early Christianity* by John M. Dillon, 1997; *Plato on the Human Paradox* by Robert J. O'Connell, 1997; *The Truest Tragedy: A Study of Plato's Laws* by Angelos Kargas, 1998; *Plato: The Invention of Philosophy* by Bernard Williams, 1998; *Plato: Critical Assessments*, edited by Nicholas D. Smith, 1998; *Plato the Myth Maker* by Luc Brisson, translated and edited by Gerard Naddaf, 1998; *Method and Politics in Plato's Statesman* by M.S. Lane, 1998; *Plato's Symposium: Eros and the Human Predicament* by Jamey Hecht, 1999; *Plato*, edited by Gail Fine, 1999; *Symposia: Plato, the Erotic, and Moral Value* by Louis A. Ruprecht, Jr., 1999; *Plato's Dialogues One by One: A Dialogical Interpretation* by Victorino Tejera, 1999; *Plato's Reception of Parmenides* by John A. Palmer, 1999; *Platonic Ethics, Old and New* by Julia Annas, 1999; *Plato's Dream of Sophistry* by Richard Marback, 1999; *Plato and the Hero: Courage, Manliness, and the Impersonal Good* by Angela Hobbs, 2000; *Plato's Philosophy of Science* by Andrew Gregory, 2000; *Plato's "Laws": The Discovery of Being* by Seth Benardete, 2000; *Images of Persons Unseen: Plato's Metaphors for the Gods and the Soul* by E.E. Pender, 2000; *Who Speaks for Plato?: Studies in Platonic Anonymity*, edited by Gerald A. Press, 2000; *Women in the Academy: Dialogues on Themes from Plato's Republic* by C.D.C. Reeve, 2001; *Plato's Introduction to the Questions of Justice* by Devin Stauffer, 2001; *Of Myth, Life and War in Plato's Republic* by Claudia Baracchi, 2002.

* * *

Plato is not, as Sir Karl Popper taught the 20th century to believe in *The Open Society and Its Enemies*, the father of modern totalitarian political ideology. No writer has ever condemned the tyrant more powerfully than Plato did in *The Republic*, not even the Greek tragic dramatists with their scathing indictments of the rule of the "great men." Nor was Plato an enemy to tolerance. He recommended the reading of Aristophanes to his pupil Dionysius, even though the comic dramatist had handled his master Socrates roughly, and might have been held indirectly responsible for his later trial and death. "It is never required of us that we know the truth, only that we never knowingly accept error." Popper, speaking for modern "realism," assumes that all idealists must be intolerant. But *Areopagitica* was written by Plato's greatest discile in English, John Milton, and not by Bacon or Hobbes, precursors of modern scepticism.

Alfred North Whitehead once described Western philosophy as "a series of footnotes to Plato." Plato has suffered the fate of being assigned to the domain of university departments of philosophy. Renaissance neoplatonists were probably more correct in viewing him as the Poet whose philosophical ideas were secondary to his imaginative creations. And any appraisal of Plato must transcend his contribution to the epistemological debate, started by his pupil Aristotle, as to whether there is laid up in heaven the perfect ideal of any earthly chair. Plato was far more concerned with achieving justice in human society, and whether or not there is an ideal for the just society is a far more important, and more practical, question than that concerning the chair.

The Republic is the first, and probably the greatest, of all contributions to political thought. As the word itself indicates, politics is as much a Greek invention as philosophy. Humans can only find their fulfilment as members of a *polis*. One who is not a member of such a community is either a wild beast or a god. This idea was subsequently Christianized; the person found salvation as member of the *ecclesia* (the assembly of citizens of the *polis*). But by divorcing the *ecclesia* from time and space, in effect morality was divorced from politics, to the damage of both. No task of modern thought is more urgent than to again unite politics and morality.

The crisis event in Plato's life was the trial and death of Socrates, analogous in every respect to the crucifixion for the disciples. With one great difference: Plato did not believe in a personal resurrection, and for him the task was to build a human society that would not execute those who should be the moral leaders. This was not a problem for Christian thought, since Jesus was historically unique. There could be a future Socrates. In Christian thought justice would be achieved by the return to earth of the triumphant Messiah. Plato had to take a more earthly route. *The Republic* is Plato's attempt to build a society that will honour its moral leaders, not destroy them. Plato never expected that such a society would exist, but he knew that humanity must never cease trying to build it. It is a foolish modern error to equate idealism with optimism. The great idealists have been great pessimists. Plato understood the terrible effects of power: "Power must never be given to those who want power." No modern political treatise recognizes that problem, let alone resolves it. Plato was profoundly doubtful that democracy would solve the problem, and his doubts seem justified. The "Great Beast" (the state) rewards those who flatter it; it will destroy those who oppose it. Each democracy has executed its own Socrates. Nor does *The Republic* ignore economic issues. "You cannot have a society with great extremes of wealth and poverty. For then you will have two societies, and they will be at war with each other.'' Modern political theory, descending from Machiavelli and Hobbes, simply ignores the problems Plato raised. We are further than ever from solving them.

As Werner Jaeger recognized in his *Paideia*, Plato also originated theology. When he exiled the poets from the Republic because they did not tell the truth about the gods, he began the study of the nature of those gods. From Plato these speculations migrated to the early Christian thinkers, who proceeded to turn the Jewish Jehovah into the Christian *Deus* (simply Latin for Zeus). It is worth noting that the early Christians, including Jesus himself, lived in bilingual areas and were drenched in Greek thought. The New Testament is a work in Greek literature.

As the Renaissance Platonists realized, Plato is the father of love. Every modern treatment descends from his *Symposium* and *Phaedrus*. All love poetry is Platonist. Interestingly, in its origin love is homosexual. Modern notions of heterosexual love are perversions of homosexual love. Testimony to this fact is provided by the unsuccessful attempt to link romantic love with marriage. The resulting mix would have brought smiles to Plato, who discussed the two incompatible horses to which the human chariot was yoked.

Plato is also the inventor of the university. His Academy was the prototype of all others. He admitted women as full equals, an achievement not again duplicated until Oberlin College was founded as a co-educational institution in the 19th century. Plato was also the first to call for full sexual equality. Women trained with men on terms of total equality as guardians of the Republic, and would in turn become the philosopher-kings. Plato's idealism was to dominate the university until in modern times Bacon turned its interests in the direction of research. Plato's Academy was to train the leadership for his ideal *polis*. Only those with an ideal of justice could hope to move the human city in the direction of achieving it.

But Plato's greatest contribution was a poetic one, the creating of his Socrates. Philip Sidney in the Renaissance had said that the essential function of the poet was "to feign notable images of virtues," and only the Jesus of the New Testament writers has rivalled Plato's Socrates as the ideal of virtue. That this was Plato's creation and not just the historical Socrates is demonstrated by the different figure in Xenophon. Prior to Plato the Greek ideal had been the *arete* of Achilles in *The Iliad*, or the shrewdness of Odysseus, the man "never without an apt word or a clever plan." Odysseus might be clever like the fox; the wisdom of Socrates was of an altogether higher order. The world after Plato could never go back to Homer; it had no choice but to go on to Christianity. To the extent that the world has been able to admire those who suffer for truth's sake, and to turn away from the "destroyers of cities," that debt in great measure is owed to Plato. Not one of the problems he raised has been solved, or will be solved. But once he had written, there was hope, and no reason for the best to lack all conviction. That is his legacy to us.

—Myron Taylor

See the essays on *Phaedrus*, *The Republic*, and *The Symposium*.

PLAUTUS

Born: Titus Maccius Plautus, possibly in Sarsina, Umbria, central Italy, c. 254 BC. **Career:** Active c. 195–184 BC; more than 130 scripts

of plays were passed under his name, but Varro listed only 21 plays as genuine, though believed other plays provided stylistic evidence for his authorship. **Died:** c. 184 BC.

PUBLICATIONS

Collections

[Plays], edited by Friedrich Leo. 2 vols., 1895–96; also edited by Wallace M. Lindsay, 2 vols., 1904–05, Alfred Ernout, 7 vols., 1932–40, Giuseppe Augello, 3 vols., 1968–72, and Ettore Paratore, 5 vols., 1976; translated by Bonnell Thronton, Richard Warner, and George Colman, 5 vols., 1767–74; also translated by Henry Thomas Riley, 2 vols., 1852; Paul Nixon [Loeb Edition], 5 vols., 1916–38; in *Complete Roman Drama*, edited by George Duckworth, 2 vols., 1942.

Plays

Amphitryo, edited by A. Palmer. 1890; also edited by W.B. Sedgwick, 1960, and Thomas Cutt, 1970; as *Amphitryon*, translated by Laurence Echard, in *Comedies*, 1694; also translated by Edward H. Sugden, in *Comedies*, 1893; Robert Allison (verse), in *Five Plays*, 1914; Lionel Casson, in *Six Plays*, 1960; Paul Roche, 1968; James H. Mantinband, 1974; as *Amphitruo*, translated 1746; as *Amphitryo*, translated by E.F. Watling, in *The Rope and Other Plays*, 1964; edited by David M. Christenson, 2000.

Asinaria, edited by F. Bertini. 2 vols., 1968; as *Asinaria*, translated by Edward H. Sugden, in *Comedies*, 1893; as *The Comedy of Asses* [Loeb Edition], translated by Paul Nixon, 1916.

Aulularia, edited by Walter Stockert. 1983; as *Aulularia*, translated by G.S. Cotter, in *Seven Comedies*, 1827; also translated by Edward H. Sugden, in *Comedies*, 1893; as *The Pot of Gold*, translated by Robert Allison (verse), in *Five Plays*, 1914; also translated by Lionel Casson, in *Six Plays*, 1960; E.F. Watling, in *The Pot of Gold and Other Plays*, 1965; P.D. Arnott, 1967; as *The Crock of Gold*, translated by H. Lionel Rogers, in *Three Plays*, 1925.

Bacchides, edited by C. Questa. 1975; as *Bacchides*, translated by Edward H. Sugden, in *Comedies*, 1893; also translated by James Tatum, in *The Darker Comedies*, 1983; edited and translated by John Barsby, 1984; as *The Two Bacchises* [Loeb Edition], translated by Paul Nixon, 1916.

Captivi, edited by W.M. Lindsay, revised edition. 1921; as *Captivi*, translated by Edward H. Sugden, in *Comedies*, 1893; also translated by A.D.C. Amos, 1903; C.W. Parry, in *Three Comedies*, 1954; as *The Captives*, translated by H.A. Strong, 1889; also translated by Robert Allison (verse), in *Five Plays*, 1914; as *The Prisoners*, translated by E.F. Watling, in *The Pot of Gold and Other Plays*, 1965; also translated by Paul Roche, 1968; A.G. Gillingham, 1968; as *Prisoners of War*, translated by H.C. Fay, in *Three Classical Comedies*, 1967.

Casina, edited by W.T. MacCary and Malcolm M. Willcock. 1976; translated by Lionel Casson, in *Six Plays*, 1960; also translated by Christopher Stace, 1981; James Tatum, in *The Darker Comedies*, 1983.

Cistellaria, as *The Casket Comedy* [Loeb Edition], translated by Paul Nixon. 1917.

Curculio, edited by G. Monaco. 1969; also edited by John Wright, 1981; as *The Weevil*, translated by A.G. Gillingham, 1968; as *Curculio*, translated by J.B. Poynton (verse), in *Five Plays*, 1973; also translated by Christopher Stace, 1981.

Epidicus [Legally Liable], edited by George Duckworth. 1940; as *Epidicus*, translated by Laurence Echard, in *Comedies*, 1694; also translated by G.S. Cotter, in *Seven Comedies*, 1827.

Menaechmi, edited by J. Brix, O. Niemeyer, and F. Conrad. 1929; also edited by Mason Hammond, 1933; Gilbert Lawall and Betty Nye Quinn, 1978; Frances Muecke, 1987; A.S. Gratwick, 1993; as *Menaechmi*, translated by William Warner, 1779, this translation edited by W.H.D. Rouse, 1912; also translated by G.S. Cotter, in *Seven Comedies*, 1827; B.B. Rogers (verse), 1907; Richard W. Hyde and Edward C. Weist, 1930; Samuel Lieberman, 1964; as *The Twin Brothers*, translated by Robert Allison (verse), in *Five Plays*, 1914; as *The Twins*, translated by Barrett H. Clark, 1914; as *The Two Menaechmuses* [Loeb Edition], translated by Paul Nixon, 1917; as *The Menaechmus Twins*, translated by Lionel Casson, in *Six Plays*, 1960; as *The Menaechmi Twins*, in *Roman Drama*, edited by Samuel Lieberman, 1964; also translated by J.B. Poynton (verse), in *Five Plays*, 1973; as *The Brothers Menaechmus*, translated by E.F. Watling, in *The Pot of Gold and Other Plays*, 1965; also translated by Erich Segal, in *Three Comedies*, 1969.

Mercator, edited by P.J. Enk. 2 vols., 1966; as *Mercator*, translated by G.S. Cotter, in *Seven Comedies*, 1827; also translated by J.B. Poynton (verse), in *Five Plays*, 1973; as *The Merchant* [Loeb Edition], translated by Paul Nixon, 1924.

Miles gloriosus, edited by Mason Hammond, Arthur W. Mack, and Walter Moskalew. 1970; as *The Braggart Warrior* [Loeb Edition], translated by Paul Nixon, 1924; as *The Braggart Soldier*, translated by Erich Segal, in *Three Comedies*, 1965; also translated by S. Allot, 1967; Paul Roche, 1968; as *The Swaggering Soldier*, translated by E.F. Watling, in *The Pot of Gold and Other Plays*, 1965; Neil King, in *Classical Beginnings*, 1984; as *Miles Gloriosus*, translated by Peter L. Smith, in *Three Comedies*, 1991.

Mostellaria, edited by J. Collart. 1970; also edited by F. Bertini, 1970; as *The Haunted House*, translated by H.A. Strong, 1872; also translated by S. Allot, 1967; A.G. Gillingham, 1968; Erich Segal, in *Three Comedies*, 1969; as *The Ghost*, translated by E.F. Watling, in *The Rope and Other Plays*, 1964; as *Mostellaria*, translated by J.B. Poynton (verse), in *Five Plays*, 1973.

Persa, edited by Erich Woytek. 1982; as *The Persian* [Loeb Edition], translated by Paul Nixon, 1924.

Poenulus [Loeb Edition], edited by G. Maurach. 1975; as *The Little Carthaginian*, translated by Paul Nixon, 1932.

Pseudolus, edited by Edgar H. Sturtevant. 1932; also edited by Malcolm M. Willcock, 1987; as *Pseudolus*, translated by G.S. Cotter, in *Seven Comedies*, 1827; also translated by Lionel Casson, in *Six Plays*, 1960; E.F. Watling, 1965; Peter L. Smith, in *Three Comedies*, 1991; as *The Trickster*, translated by H. Lionel Rogers, in *Three Plays*, 1925.

Rudens, edited by F. Marx. 1928; also edited by H.C. Fay, 1969; as *Rudens*, translated by Laurence Echard, in *Comedies*, 1694; also translated by G.S. Cotter, in *Seven Comedies*, 1827; C.W. Parry, in *Three Comedies*, 1954; Christopher Stace, 1981; Peter L. Smith, in *Three Comedies*, 1991; as *The Slip Knot*, translated by F.A. Wright, in *Three Plays*, 1925; as *The Rope*, translated by Lionel

Casson, in *Six Plays*, 1960; E.F. Watling, in *The Rope and Other Plays*, 1964; S. Allot, 1967; J.B. Poynton (verse), in *Five Plays*, 1973; as *A Villa at Cyrene*, translated by R.N. Benton, 1981.

Stichus, edited by H. Petersmann. 1973; as *The Tempest*, translated by Robert Allison (verse), in *Five Plays*, 1914; as *Stichus* [Loeb Edition], translated by Paul Nixon, 1938.

Trinummus, edited by J. Brix and O. Niemeyer. 1907; as *Trinummus*, translated by G.S. Cotter, in *Seven Comedies*, 1827; also translated by H.O. Sibley (verse), 1895; A.D.C. Amos, 1897; C.W. Parry, in *Three Comedies*, 1954; as *Trinummus, or Three Bob Day* [Loeb Edition], translated by Paul Nixon, 1938; as *A Three-Dollar Day*, translated by E.F. Watling, in *The Rope and Other Plays*, 1964; as *Thirty Bob*, translated by H.C. Fay, in *Three Classical Comedies*, 1967.

Truculentus [Churl], edited by P.J. Enk. 2 vols., 1953; as *Truculentus* [Loeb Edition], translated by Paul Nixon, 1938; also translated by James Tatum, in *The Darker Comedies*, 1983.

Vidularia [The Rucksack Play] (fragment). As *Vidularia* [Loeb Edition], translated by Paul Nixon, 1938.

Comedies (includes *Amphitryon; Epidicus; Rudens*), translated by Laurence Echard. 1694.

Seven Comedies (includes *Aulularia; Epidicus; Menaechmi; Mercator; Pseudolus; Trinummus; Rudens*), translated by G.S. Cotter. 1827.

Comedies (includes *Amphitryon; Asinaria; Aulularia; Bacchides; Captivi*), translated by Edward H. Sugden. 1893.

Five Plays (includes *The Pot of Gold; The Captives; The Twin Brothers; The Tempest; Amphitryon*), translated by Robert Allison (verse). 1914.

Three Plays (includes *The Slip Knot; The Crock of Gold; The Trickster*), translated by F.A. Wright and H. Lionel Rogers. 1925.

Three Comedies (includes *Trinummus; Captivi; Rudens*), translated by C.W. Parry. 1954.

Six Plays (includes *Amphitryon; The Pot of Gold; Casina; The Menaechmus Twins; Pseudolus; The Rope*), translated by Lionel Casson. 1960.

The Rope and Other Plays (includes *The Rope; The Ghost; A Three-Dollar Day; Amphitryo*), translated by E.F. Watling. 1964.

The Pot of Gold and Other Plays (includes *The Pot of Gold; The Prisoners; The Brothers Menaechmus; The Swaggering Soldier*), translated by E.F. Watling. 1965.

Three Classical Comedies (includes *Thirty Bob; Prisoners of War; The Cross Old Devil* by Menander), translated by H.C. Fay. 1967.

Three Comedies (includes *The Braggart Soldier; The Brothers Menaechmus; The Haunted House*), translated by Erich Segal. 1969.

Five Plays (includes *Curculio; The Menaechmi Twins; Mercator; Mostellaria; Rudens*), translated by J.B. Poynton (verse). 1973.

The Darker Comedies (includes *Bacchides; Casina; Truculentus*), translated by James Tatum. 1983.

Three Comedies (includes *Miles Gloriosus; Pseudolus; Rudens*), translated by Peter L. Smith. 1991.

Three Comedies, translated by Robert Wind. 1994.

Four Comedies, translated by Erich Segal. 1996.

*

Bibliography: *A Bibliography of Scholarship on Plautus* by J. David Hughes, 1975; ''Scholarship on Plautus 1965–76'' by Erich Segal, in *Classical World*, 74(7), 1981.

Critical Studies: *The Divisions in the Plays of Plautus and Terence* by Frederick M. Foster, 1913; *Plautinisches im Plautus* by E. Fraenkel, 1922; *A Chronology of the Plays of Plautus* by Charles H. Buck, 1940; *The Nature of Roman Comedy* by George Duckworth, 1952; *Plautus and Terence* by G. Norwood, 1963; *Menander, Plautus, and Terence* by W.G. Arnott, 1968; *Menander and Plautus: A Study in Comparison* by Eric W. Handley, 1968; *Roman Laughter: The Comedy of Plautus,* by Erich Segal, 1968; *Dancing in Chains: The Stylistic Unity of the Comoedia Palliata* by John H. Wright, 1974; *Roman Comedy* by Kenneth McLeish, 1976; *The Comic Theatre of Greece and Rome* by F.H. Sandbach, 1977; *Tradition and Originality in Plautus: Studies of the Amatory Motifs in Plautine Comedy* by Netta Zagagi, 1980; *Roman Comedy* by David Konstan, 1983; *The New Comedy of Greece and Rome* by R.L. Hunter, 1985; *The Comic Theatre of Greece and Rome* by F.H. Sandbach, 1985; *Plautus in Performance: The Theatre of the Mind* by Niall W. Slater, 1985; *Plautus, Shakespeare and the Humanist Tradition* by Wolfgang Riehle, 1991; *Barbarian Play: Plautus' Roman Comedy* by William S. Anderson, 1993; *Ancient Comedy: The War of the Generations* by Dana F. Sutton, 1993; *Shakespeare and Classical Comedy: The Influence of Plautus and Terence* by Robert S. Miola, 1994; *The Theatre of Plautus: Playing to the Audience* by Timothy J. Moore, 1998; *Slaves, Masters, and the Art of Authority in Plautine Comedy* by Kathleen McCarthy, 2000.

* * *

Plautus, whose comedies are much the earliest works of Latin literature that have survived entire, began producing in the later years of the Hannibalic war, when the number of festivals at which dramas were presented had increased to seven or eight each year. Plautus probably wrote original plots situated in Italian towns, but the plays we have are all adaptations of Greek originals by Menander and his contemporaries, the composers of Greek New Comedy. New Comedy was domestic drama, concentrating largely on the vicissitudes of young men's romantic infatuation with modest girls or clever courtesans. The style was one of artful naturalism, and this Plautus transformed into an exuberant dazzle of puns, neologisms, strings of alliteration so dear to Roman taste, fanciful figures and tropes like oxymoron and the unexpected twist at the end of a phrase, and an operatic variety of rhythms in the *cantica,* or songs, for which there was no counterpart in his models. This vivacity of style and diction was matched by Plautus' handling of plot, where he trimmed or expanded or at times conflated his models with a view to enlivening the action and emphasizing the roles of pert and farcical characters like the wily slaves who engineer liaisons and the greedy brothel-keepers or pompous mercenaries who obstruct them.

While Plautus delighted in the comic license of representing slaves riding piggy-back on their young masters in *Asinaria (The Comedy of Asses),* or taunting their elder masters as they sputter gruesome but quite realistic threats of punishment in *Mostellaria (The Haunted House),* he was sensitive as well to the themes of the comedies he adapted, sometimes highlighting them by reference to a Roman practice or by the use of significant names for his characters. The twin courtesans who seduce a pair of friends and their fathers are called Bacchis in a play that is liberal with allusions to the worship of Dionysus, which was at the time a matter of concern to the Roman senate; a miser who refuses all commerce with his neighbours in order to hoard his gold prohibits his housekeeper from lending anyone fire

or water, an interdiction reminiscent of the Roman formula for banishment, in *Aulularia (The Pot of Gold).* The miser is duly humbled. In *Captivi (The Prisoners),* a father who unwittingly holds his own son hostage as a prisoner of war affords a glimpse into the paradoxes of strife and enslavement among the Greek city-states which may have had special meaning to the Romans as they reconquered Italy from the retreating Carthaginian armies. In *Rudens (The Rope),* an old man, in exile from Athens, is reunited with his daughter on a distant shore in a kind of pastoral affirmation of the community of men, gods, and nature. With its limited cast of characters and conventional narrative repertory of outwitted parents and improbable recognitions, New Comedy touched the anxious issues of class, status, authority, and community in Hellenistic civic life. Plautus developed the spirit of farce or vaudeville in these performances without entirely sacrificing their seriousness and refinement. With the recovery of the New Comic tradition in the Renaissance, both sides of Plautus were there to be imitated and exploited (e.g. *Ralph Roister Doister* and *The Comedy of Errors*). Their co-existence in the theatre of Plautus endows his best comedies with the permanent appeal of high entertainment.

—David Konstan

See the essays on *Amphitryo, The Brothers Menaechmus,* and *The Pot of Gold.*

PLUTARCH

Born: Lucius(?) Mestrius Plutarchus in Chaeronea, Boeotia, central Greece, c. AD 46. **Education:** Studied in Athens in mid-60s AD. **Family:** Married Timoxena; at least four sons and one daughter. **Career:** Lectured in Rome and visited Egypt; a priest at Delphi, and helped revive the shrine there; held numerous municipal posts in Chaeronea; possibly made a procurator by the emperor Hadrian. **Died:** After AD 120.

PUBLICATIONS

Collection

[Works], edited by Daniel A. Wyttenbach. 8 vols., 1795–1830.

Works

Moralia, edited by H. Wegehaupt and others. 1925–; translated by Frank G. Babbitt and others [Loeb Edition; bilingual], 15 vols., 1927–69; also translated by Harold Cherniss, 1976; as *The Philosophie,* translated by Philemon Holland, 1603; as *Morals,* various translators, 5 vols., 1684–94, revised by W.W. Goodwin, 5 vols., 1874–78; part as *De Iside et Osiride,* edited and translated by J. Gwyn Griffiths (with commentary), 1970; selections translated by T.G. Tucker and A.O. Prickard, 2 vols., 1913–18; Rex Warner, 1971; Robin A.H. Waterfield, 1992; Donald Russell, 1993.

Vitae parallelae [Parallel Lives], edited by K. Ziegler and C. Lindskog. 8 vols., 1926–39, revised edition, 4 vols., 1957–80; also edited by Robert Flacelière and others, 1957–; as *Lives*, translated by Thomas North, 1579; edited in translation by John Dryden, 5 vols., 1683–86, revised by A.H. Clough, 1900; also translated by Oliver Goldsmith and Joseph Collyer, 5 vols., 1762 (abridged version); J. and W. Langhorne, 6 vols., 1770; Bernadotte Perrin [Loeb Edition], 11 vols., 1914–26; selections translated by G. Long, in *The Civil Wars of Rome: Select Lives*, 5 vols., 1844–48; also translated by W.R. Frazer, 1906; Aubrey Stewart and G. Long, 1906; C.E. Byres, 1907; *Select Essays*, translated by T.G. Tucker, 1913; *On Love, the Family and the Good Life*, translated by Moses Hadas, 1957; *Fall of the Roman Republic* (6 lives) translated by Rex Warner, 1958, revised edition, 1972; *The Rise and Fall of Athens* (9 lives), 1960, *Makers of Rome* (9 lives), 1965, and *The Age of Alexander* (9 lives), 1973, all translated by Ian Scott-Kilvert; *On Sparta* (3 lives), translated by Richard J.A. Talbert, 1988; *Greek Lives: A Selection of Nine Greek Lives*, translated by Robin Waterfield, 1998; *Life of Themistocles*, translated by J.L. Marr, 1998.

*

Critical Studies: *Plutarch as a Source of Information on the Greek Theatre* by Roy C. Flickinger, 1904; *Plutarch* by Rudolf Herzel, 1912; *Plutarch in Renaissance England* by Martha Hale Shackford, 1929; *Plutarchos von Chaironeia* by Konrat Ziegler, revised edition, 1964; *Plutarch's Historical Method*, 1965, *A Commentary on Plutarch's Pericles*, both by Philip A. Stadter, 1989, and *Plutarch and the Historical Tradition*, edited by Stadter, 1992; *Plutarch and His Times* by Reginald H. Barrow, 1967; *Shakespeare's Plutarch* edited by Terence J.B. Spencer, 1968; *Plutarch* by Constantine C. Gianakaris, 1970; *Plutarch and Rome* by Christopher P. Jones, 1971; *Plutarch* by Donald Russell, 1972; *Plutarch's Lives* by Alan Wardman, 1974; *Plutarch's Ethical Writings and Early Christian Literature* by Hans Dieter Betz, 1975; *In Mist Appareled: Religious Themes in Plutarch's Moralia and Lives* by F.E. Brenk, 1977; *Plutarch's Themistocles* by Frank J. Frost, 1980; *Plutarch: Life of Pericles—A Companion to the Penguin Translation* by A.J. Podlecki, 1987; *A Commentary on Plutarch's Table Talks* by Sven-Tage Teodorsson, 1989; *Plutarch: Lives of Pompey, Caesar and Cicero—A Companion to the Penguin Translation* by M. Edwards, 1992; *Plutarch's Sertorius: A Historical Commentary* by C.F. Konrad, 1994; *Essays on Plutarch's Lives*, edited by Barbara Scardigli, 1995; *Plutarch's Pelopidas: A Historical and Philological Commentary* by Aristoula Georgiadou, 1997; *Plutarch and His Intellectual World: Essays on Plutarch*, edited by Judith Mossman, 1997; *Plutarch's Advice to the Bride and Groom; and A Consolation to His Wife: English Translations, Commentary, Interpretive Essays, and Bibliography*, edited by Sarah B. Pomeroy, 1999; *Plutarch's Lives: Exploring Virtue and Vice* by Tim Duff, 1999.

*   *   *

Plutarch has left us the second largest corpus of works to have been preserved from classical antiquity. The prize goes to the philosopher-physician Galen, but while Galen's books slumber peacefully on the shelves of the few libraries that possess the only complete edition, Plutarch has been eagerly read by everyone with an interest in the ancient world since his works were rediscovered during the Renaissance. It would be difficult to imagine a writer better qualified to reflect every aspect of the culture of the Greco-Roman world during the *Pax Romana*. His education was the finest a wealthy family could provide, as measured by the thousands of citations from the entire legacy of classical literature scattered throughout his works, many from authors now lost. Although he trifled with rhetoric as a young man (*Fame of the Athenians, Fortune of Alexander*, etc.), he developed quickly into a philosopher in the literal sense: a lover of all wisdom. He claimed Plato and the Academy as his school, but his writings show his personal philosophical outlook to have been quite eclectic, being in general positive, optimistic, humanist, and philanthropic. He was convinced of the possibility of human progress and believed that reason was the best guide to such progress. The *Vitae parallelae* [Parallel Lives] of notable Greeks and Romans were designed to educate; he never seems to have doubted that if young men were shown good examples they would follow them.

Plutarch was not a brilliant scientist, an elegant stylist, a critical historian, or a profound thinker, but he had read and absorbed the works of those who were and was able, with an easy familiarity, to convey their wisdom to a larger audience. "He had that universal sympathy with genius which makes all its victories his own," said Emerson in the introduction to the complete Boston edition of 1870. Plutarch was a popularizer of scientific and religious thought, even the most complex (*On the Face in the Moon, De Iside et Osiride*). As an essayist he was fluent and productive, if sometimes verbose and perfunctory. He wrote on a surprising variety of topics—*On Superstition, On Fate, On Exile*; the *Cleverness of Animals* and the advantages of a mature wife (*Amatorius*); even a curious attack on the Father of History himself (*Malignity of Herodotus*), just to name a few examples. The popularity of Plutarch's biographies rests neither on literary style nor on historical insight but on his skill as a superb storyteller, whether describing epic battles (*Aristeides, Fabius*), thrilling escapades (*Aratus, Demetrius, Sulla*), virtue triumphant (*Timoleon, Pericles*), or the tragedy of thwarted idealism (*Cleomenes, Sertorius*). His sense of plot and narrative did not escape later writers, as Shakespeare's *Coriolanus, Julius Caesar*, and *Antony and Cleopatra* remind us.

Higher criticism, particularly German, in the late 19th century attempted to portray Plutarch as a second-rate compiler, stitching together his essays and biographies from the real scholarship of creative predecessors (whose works have conveniently disappeared). But since World War II there has been a revival of appreciation for Plutarch as writer and thinker. The originality of his scholarship is now generally accepted and his liberal humanism makes him one of the more attractive and illuminating spokesmen for all of Greco-Roman antiquity.

—Frank J. Frost

See the essay on *Lives of Lysander and Sulla*.

PO CHÜ-I

See BAI JUYI

POLYBIUS

Born: Megalopolis, in the Greek Peloponnese, c. 200 BC. **Career:** Appointed envoy to Egypt in 180 BC; sent as detainee to Rome, 169 BC, and befriended by the Scipios; joined Scipio Aemilianus for his African campaign, and was present during destruction of Carthage in 146 BC; returned to Greece after the Romans took Corinth in 146 BC; travelled widely in Gaul, Spain, Libya, and elsewhere. **Died:** After 118 BC.

PUBLICATIONS

Works

Historiae, edited by F. Hultsch. 4 vols., 1867–71; also edited by L. Dindorf, revised by T. Büttner-Wobst, 5 vols., 1882–1904, and P. Pédech and others [Budé Edition], 9 vols. (to 1994), 1961–; as *Histories* [Loeb Edition], edited and translated by W.R. Paton, 6 vols., 1922–27; as *The Histories*, translated by Christopher Watson, 1568; also translated by James Hampton, 1756; E.S. Shuckburgh, 2 vols., 1889, reprinted 1962; selection as *The Rise of the Roman Empire*, edited by Frank W. Walbank, translated by Ian Scott-Kilvert, 1979.

*

Critical Studies: *Ancient Greek Historians* by J.B. Bury, 1909; "Polybius" by Terror R. Glover, in *Cambridge Ancient History*, vol. 8, 1930; *Polybios-Lexikon* by A. Mauersberger, 1956–; *A Historical Commentary on Polybius*, 3 vols., 1957–1979, and *Polybius*, 1972, both by Frank W. Walbank; *La Méthode historique de Polybe* (in French) by P. Pédech, 1964; *The Manuscript Tradition of Polybius* by J.M. Moore, 1965; *Polybe* (lectures with commentary), edited by E. Gabba, 1974; *Polybius on the Writing of History* by Kenneth Sacks, 1981; *The Res Graeciae in Polybius: Four Studies* by David Golan, 1995; *Moral Vision in the Histories of Polybius* by Arthur M. Eckstein, 1995; *Roman Republican Castrametation: A Reappraisal of Historical and Archeological Sources* by John Pamment Salvatore, 1996.

*   *   *

During the years 167 to 150 BC, the Achaean statesman Polybius was a detainee in Rome. Already the author of several minor works, including one on military tactics, he was now inspired to embark upon a major enterprise, his *Historiae* (*Histories*). The theme of this work was to be the rise of Rome to world dominion in under 53 years, from the outbreak of the Hannibalic War in 220 BC to the end of the Macedonian kingdom in 167 BC, and his purpose was to explain to his primarily Greek readers how, and by virtue of what form of constitution, the Romans had brought this about. Originally planned to occupy 30 books (two introductory and the last a type of index), the work was later increased to 40 and extended to the destruction of Carthage and Corinth in 146 BC. Books XXXI–XL were probably published after the death of Polybius' friend and patron, Scipio Aemilianus, in 129 BC.

For the first decades of his history Polybius used earlier sources. For the later years, however, he drew on his own knowledge and that of contemporaries. In Rome he had access to published speeches and could consult libraries and public records. Thus he quotes the series of Romano-Carthaginian treaties and also an inscription giving the numbers of forces Hannibal had set up in a temple in southern Italy.

Polybius' *Histories* were to serve both a political and a moral purpose, instructing politicians and also assisting readers of all kinds to bear the vicissitudes of Fortune. However, as he recognizes, not everyone is out to learn. A historian may properly entertain as well as educate his readers, although utility should come first. Polybius claims to write "pragmatic history" meaning "political and military history," with perhaps the suggestion of a didactic purpose. Austere and factual, pragmatic history reacts against the dramatic sensationalism exemplified by Phylarchus, who titillated his readers' emotions by describing highly coloured and pathetic incidents. Polybius associates such writing especially with monographs, whose authors thus sought to compensate for their restricted field and limited material. He, in contrast, was writing universal history. Only from universal history, he argued, could one comprehend the part Fortune played in human affairs. Moreover, only universal history could do justice to an age in which, thanks to Rome, world events had come together in an organic whole. Thus his theme, and by implication his work itself, surpassed anything that had gone before.

Polybius expatiates upon the techniques of his craft. The historian must familiarize himself with cities, districts, rivers, harbours, and the terrain generally. Above all, he must have political and military experience. The mainspring of his writing must be to ascertain the truth, for without truth the political and moral aims of history cannot be achieved. Polybius' two concessions are to religion and patriotism. "Where such statements contribute to maintaining piety towards the gods among the masses," he remarks, "we should excuse writers for recording marvels and wonder-stories—provided that they do not go too far." And "authors should show partiality towards their own country, but they should not make statements about it that are false." In fact, Polybius displays some bias against enemies of his native Achaea, particularly Aetolia. Mostly, however, he lives up to his own strict criteria for truth and honesty.

One problematic feature of Polybius' *Histories* is his use of Fortune (*Tyche*), a concept popular among Hellenistic Greeks, who often personified *Tyche* as a goddess. Polybius employs the word in a variety of senses. Sometimes it merely indicates that something happened. Elsewhere, and often in relation to unforeseen but important events, he uses it to mean "chance." In one important passage he restricts its use as a historical explanation for such events as floods, famine, and drought, for which there is no patent cause, or to human behaviour that he considers irrational. In some passages, however, *Tyche* suggests an external power, occasionally well-disposed, but more often retributive, malevolent, or capricious. There are yet others, in particular those in which Polybius refers to his main theme, and attributes Roman imperial success to *Tyche*, where the word approaches later notions of Providence. That such a power can play a major part in human affairs militates against Polybius' claim that history can offer sure guidance in politics and in resolving moral dilemmas.

At the outset of his *Histories* Polybius emphasized the importance of the city's constitution for Roman success. Much of Book VI is devoted to an account of the Roman "mixed constitution," in which power is shared between the consuls, the senate, and the people, representing respectively the monarchic, aristocratic, and democratic elements within the state. Thanks to this constitution Rome had escaped from the cyclical track through a succession of constitutional forms (and their perversions) to which most other states were condemned. In Book VI Polybius compares the Roman constitution with other highly regarded ones. There is also an important account of the army, the instrument of Roman successes. Over the centuries Book VI, more than any other, has influenced philosophers, constitution-makers, and generals.

Of Polybius' 40 books only 1–5 survive complete. Five others were already lost by the 9th century AD. In the 10th century the Byzantine emperor, Constantine VII, had Polybius' *Histories* divided under such rubrics as "On Embassies," and "On Vice and Virtue," and these extracts discouraged the use of the original text. Unfortunately, only a handful of Constantine's sections (along with other fragments) has survived. What we possess amounts to not quite a third of the original. Nevertheless, Polybius' *Histories* are the indispensable primary narrative source for the period in which Rome acquired much of her overseas empire. "The books of Polybius," wrote the German historian Theodor Mommsen, "are like the sun shining on the field of Roman history; where they open, the mists which shroud the Samnite and Pyrrhic wars are lifted, and where they end a perhaps even more vexatious twilight descends." After Herodotus and Thucydides, Polybius can rightly claim to be considered the third great Greek historian.

—Frank W. Walbank

PONGE, Francis

Born: Montpellier, France, 27 March 1899. **Education:** Educated at Lycée Malherbe, Caen, 1909–16, baccalauréat, 1916; Lycée Louis-le-Grand, Paris, 1916–17; studied philosophy at the Sorbonne and law at École de Droit, Paris, 1917–18. **Military Service:** 1918–19. **Family:** Married Odette Chabanel in 1931; one child. **Career:** Secretary, Gallimard, publishers, Paris 1923; secretary, Hachette, publishers, Paris, 1931–37; insurance salesman, 1937–39; staff member of Resistance paper, *Progrès de Lyon*, Bourg-en-Bresse, 1942; worked for National Committee of Journalists, 1942–44; literary and artistic director of the communist weekly, *L'Action*, 1944–46; taught at Alliance française, Paris, 1952–64; Gildersleeve visiting professor, Barnard College and Columbia University, New York, 1966–67; lectured in the UK, 1971. Closely associated with Aragon, *q.v.*, and Éluard, *q.v.* **Awards:** International poetry prize, 1959; Ingham Merrill Foundation award, 1972; Neustadt International prize, 1974; French National Poetry prize, 1981. Officer, Légion d'honneur. **Member:** Communist Party, 1937–47; corresponding member, Bavarian Academy, 1969. **Died:** 6 August 1988.

PUBLICATIONS

Collections

Nouveau, nouveau recueil, edited by Jean Thibaudeau. 3 vols., 1992.

Selected Poems, translated by C.K. Williams, John Montague and Margaret Guiton. 1994.

Verse

Douze petits écrits. 1926.
Le Parti pris des choses. 1942; revised edition (includes *Proêmes*, 1949; edited by Ian Higgins, 1979; as *The Voice of Things;* edited and translated by Beth Archer, 1972.
L'Oeillet, la guêpe, le mimosa. 1946.
Le Carnet du bois de pins. 1947.
Liasse: Vingt-et-un textes suivis d'une bibliographie. 1948.
Le Peintre à l'étude. 1948.
Proêmes. 1948.
La Crevette dans tous ses états. 1948.
Cinq sapates, illustrated by Georges Braque. 1950.
Des Cristaux naturels. 1950.
La Seine. 1950.
L'Araignée. 1952.
La Rage de l'expression. 1952.
Pièces. 1962.
Francis Ponge, ou la raison à plus haut prix (selection), edited by Philippe Sollers. 1963.
Tome premier (includes *Douze petits écrits; Le Parti pris des choses; Proêmes; La Rage de l'expression; Le Peintre l'étude; La Seine*). 1965.
Ponge (selection), edited by Jean Thibaudeau. 1967.
Le Savon. 1967; as *Soap*, translated by Lane Dunlop, 1969.
Two Prose Poems, translated by Peter Hoy. 1968.
Rain: A Prose Poem, translated by Peter Hoy. 1969.
Ici haute. 1971.
Things (selection), translated by Cid Corman. 1971.
Ponge: Inventeur et classique. 1977.
The Sun Placed in the Abyss and Other Texts, edited by Serge Gavronsky. 1977.
The Power of Language: Texts and Translations, edited and translated by Serge Gavronsky. 1979.
La Table. 1981; revised and edited by Jean Thibaudeau, 1990.
Vegetation, translated by Lee Fahnestock. 1987.

Other

Le Verre d'eau, with Eugène de Kermadec. 1949.
Le Grand Receuil: Lyres, Méthodes, Pièces. 3 vols., 1961; revised edition 1976–78.
A la rêveuse matière. 1963. *Pour un Malherbe.* 1965; revised edition, 1977.
De la nature morte et de Chardin. 1967.
Nouveau recueil. 1967.
Entretiens de Ponge avec Philippe Sollers, edited by Philippe Sollers. 1970.
La Fabrique du "pré." 1971; as *The Making of the "Pré,"* translated by Lee Fahnestock, 1979.
Méthodes. 1971.
Georges Braque, de Draeger, with Pierre Descargues and André Malraux. 1971; as *Georges Braque*, translated by Richard Howard and Lane Dunlop, 1971.
Picasso de Draeger, with Pierre Descargues and Edward Quinn. 1974.
L'Atelier contemporain. 1977.

Comment une figue de paroles et pourquoi, edited by Jean Ristat. 1977.
L'Écrit Beaubourg. 1977.
Pièces. 1977.
Nioque de l'avant-printemps. 1983.
Petite suite vivaraise. 1983.
Pratiques d'écriture; ou, L'Inachèvement perpétuel. 1984.
Correspondance 1923–1968, with Jean Paulhan, edited by Claire Boaretto. 2 vols., 1986.

*

Critical Studies: *La part du feu* by Maurice Blanchot, 1949; *Francis Ponge and the New Problem of Epos* by Antoine Denat, 1963; *Francis Ponge* by Philippe Sollers, 1963; *Testimony of the Invisible Man: William Carlos Williams, Francis Ponge, Rainer Maria Rilke, Pablo Neruda* by Nancy Willard, 1970; *Francis Ponge* by Marcel Spada, 1974; *Ponge* by Ian Higgins, 1979; *L'objet du texte et le texte-objet: La Chèvre de Francis Ponge* by Thomas Aron, 1980; *Francis Ponge* by Martin Sorrell, 1981; *Signéponge = signsponge* by Jacques Derrida, 1984; *Francis Ponge cinq fois* by Jean Tortel, 1984; *Francis Ponge: La Poétique du figural* by Annette Sampon, 1988; *Poétique de Francis Ponge: Le Palais/Diaphane* by Bernard Beugnot, 1990; *Francis Ponge* by Claude Evrard, 1990; *Francis Ponge: Entre roots et choses* by Michel Collot, 1991; *The Art Criticism of Francis Ponge* by Shirley Ann Jordan, 1994; *Francis Ponge and the Nature of Things: From Ancient Atomism to a Modern Poetics* by Patrick Meadows, 1997; *Poetry and Cosmogony: Science in the Writing of Queneau and Ponge* by Chris Andrews, 1999.

* * *

Francis Ponge's work constitutes one of the most individual contributions to 20th-century French literature. His *oeuvre*, of over 100 titles, has a unity of style (despite certain apparent contradictions) and is justly considered to be pivotal in relation to the literary trends of his time. His second collection of poems, *Le Parti pris des choses (The Voice of Things)*, is perhaps the finest example of the invariable aim of his work: to celebrate the mundane.

The importance of prose poetry, and its place in French literature, was established by Ponge's predecessors, Baudelaire, Rimbaud, and Mallarmé. When Ponge's first volume, *Douze petits écrits* [Twelve Short Pieces] was published in 1926, his reputation as an exponent of the genre—along with Max Jacob, Paul Reverdy, André Breton, and Henri Michaux—began. Ponge occasionally composed pieces in verse, but all his most typical and successful achievements ("Le Galet" [Pebble], "Le Verre d'eau" [Glass of Water], "La Terre" [Earth], and "Le Savon" [Soap]) can be categorized as poems in prose. Ponge succeeded in performing the roles of poet, theorist, and critic simultaneously when he discussed the reasons for (and against) regarding this work as "prose poetry" in many of his later texts.

The second half of *The Voice of Things*, added to the revised edition, is entitled *Proêmes*. At first sight the title suggests a neologism combining both "prose" and "poems," but it is also the plural of a term used in classical rhetoric to indicate the preface, or exordium, to a discourse. In numerous exegetical studies of Ponge's work, critics make constant reference to the term "rhetoric." One of the *proêmes*, entitled "hétorique," expounds the notion of "the art of resisting words" and concludes by declaring that teaching everyone the art of founding their own rhetoric would be an act of great public benefaction.

During a visit to Algeria in the late 1940s, Ponge kept a kind of diary, ironically given an English title, *My Creative Method*, which was published in *Le Grand Receuil* [The Great Collection] in 1961. It begins with the avowal that "Les idées ne sont pas mont fort" ["ideas are not my strength"], yet manages to explore a number of ideas regarding the nature of rhetoric, the deficiencies of Plato in particular, and of philosophy in general. Ponge also discusses the importance of dictionaries—and by implication etymology—to his work. *My Creative Method* ends with the proclamation that Ponge's chief desire was not to be simply a poet but to make use of what he calls "le magma poétique" ["poetic lava"] in order to produce clear, yet impersonal, formulae.

Ponge was, for over 25 years, a close friend of Jean Paulhan, the critic, essayist, editor of *Nouvelle Revue française*, and a great impressario of mid-20th-century French writing. Renowned for his dedication to clarity of language and thought, Paulhan was the first to appreciate Ponge's special gift, and for many years encouraged, criticized, and corresponded with him. Among several texts devoted to *éloges* [eulogy], Ponge wrote four pages on Paulhan, which ended: "Co grammarien est un maitre de vie," He had long regarded Paulhan as his ideal reader, although other writers, including Malherbe, Mallarmé, Claudel, and (unexpectedly) Jules Remain, became the subjects of Ponge's chiselled encomiums. A piece in praise of the sculptress Germaine Richier bears the title "Scvlptvre," evoking the inscriptions of the Roman ruins at Nîmes, where Ponge and Paulhan spent their youth. Ponge attempted to infuse all his writing with the sense of immortality inherent in such inscription, and, for emphasis, ended some of his best-known poems with passages printed in capital letters.

Careful deliberation of composition seems wholly at odds with automatic writing, so it came as a surprise to find Ponge's name amongst the 20 signatories of Breton's *Second manifeste du surréalisme* (Second Manifesto of Surrealism) in 1930. His brief solidarity with the movement can be accounted for by his general sympathies with the twofold aims of surrealism: to promote revolutionary change at the level of society as well as at the level of consciousness. As a young man Ponge had been employed by the publishers, Hachette, in Paris, and never forgot the harsh working conditions his fellow workers had endured, which led to his involvement in syndicalism and strikes. Though his writing appears completely apolitical on the surface, he was nevertheless an active socialist, and for a while a member of the Communist Party. Following his zealous, but unarmed, participation in the Resistance, Ponge became literary editor of the Communist weekly *L'Action* in 1944, publishing Aragon, Éluard, Paulhan, Sartre, and Queneau. He finally broke away from the Communist party in 1947.

The title of his poem, "La Poétique, c'est l'objet" [Poetics Is an Object], is not simply one more statement of Ponge's literary attitude, but a quotation from Georges Braque, whom Ponge regarded as the most exemplary of the many artists and sculptors about whom he had written. To transmute commonplace objects by a process of replacing inattention with contemplation was Ponge's way of heeding Ezra Pound's edict: "Make it new." His ever-renewed attempts to celebrate objects of everyday experience in a language enlivened by puns and complex words, with onomatopoeia, and the calligrammatic, were not a restless search for novelty but rather a way of transcending "modernity" and restoring a Wordsworthian appreciation of the simple things in life: slate, the Seine, asparagus, and tables. An epicurean of language, Ponge resisted all accusations of elitism. He addressed himself to the common reader in the hope of persuading us that poetry is not merely a preoccupation of the idle and overeducated.

His work has been described as "one of the most considerable attempts of this time to reconcile man with the world." However, Ponge spent his last 30 years in virtual recluse at his country retreat, the Mas des Vergers, where he suffered from frequent periods of nervous exhaustion and psychosomatic illness. His last text, *La Table* [Table], was published posthumously in 1981. Unfinished at his death, it reflects what was Ponge's undying, and increasingly obsessional, quest for *le mot juste*. Its final sentence reads: "O Table, ma console et ma consolatrice, table qui me console, où je me consolide." For Ponge, his final subject was his writing table, which had in fact by then become his entire world.

—David Gascoyne

See the essay on *The Voice of Things*.

POPA, Vasko

Born: Grebenac, Vojvodina, Serbia (then part of Yugoslavia), 29 July 1922. **Education:** Educated at the universities of Vienna, Bucharest, and Belgrade, degree in French literature 1949. **Military Service:** Served in Tito's partisan forces during World War II. **Career:** Editor, Nolit Publishing House, Belgrade, from 1949; from 1952, devoted himself mainly to writing verse. **Awards:** Branko Radičević prize, 1953; Zmaj prize, 1956; Lenau prize (Austria), 1967. **Member:** Serbian Academy of Arts and Sciences, from 1972, and Mallarmé Academy, from 1977. **Died:** 5 January 1991.

PUBLICATIONS

Verse

Kora [Bark]. 1953.
Nepočin-polje [Unrest Field]. 1956.
Pesme [Songs]. 1965.
Sporedno nebo [Secondary Heaven]. 1968.
Selected Poems, translated by Anne Pennington. 1969.
The Little Box (selection), translated by Charles Simic. 1970.
Uspravna zemlja. 1972; as *Earth Erect*, translated by Anne Pennington, 1973.
Živo meso [Raw Flesh]. 1974.
Vučja so [Wolf Salt]. 1975.
Kuć nasred druma [The House on the Highroad]. 1975.
Izabrane pesme [Selected Poems]. 1975.
Collected Poems 1943–76, translated by Anne Pennington. 1978.
Homage to the Lame Wolf: Selected Poems 1956–75, edited and translated by Charles Simic. 1979; revised, enlarged edition, 1987.
Rez [Cut]. 1981.
Midnight Sun, edited by Stanley H. Barkan, translated by Branko Mikasinovich. 1992.

Other

Editor, *Od zlata jabuka: Rukovet narodnih umotvorina* [The Golden Apple: A Collection of Folk Literature]. 1958; selection as *The Golden Apple*, edited and translated by Anne Pennington and Andrew Harvey, 1980.
Editor, *Urnebesnik: Zbornik pesničkog humora* [Bawler: A Collection of Poetic Humour]. 1960.
Editor, *Ponočno sunce: Zbornik pesničkih snovidenja* [Midnight Sun: A Collection of Poetic Dreams]. 1962.

*

Critical Studies: "The Poetry of Popa" by Ted Hughes, in *Critical Survey*, 2, 1966; "Popa: The Poetry of Things in a Void" by V.D. Mihailovich, in *Books Abroad*, 43, 1969; "Fertile Fire: The Poetry of Popa" by B. Johnson, in *Journal of British-Yugoslav Society*, 2, 1979; *The Structure of Vasko Popa's Poetry* by Ronelle Alexander, 1985; *Quest for Roots: The Poetry of Vasko Popa* by Anita Leki'c, 1993.

*   *   *

Vasko Popa, the most celebrated post-war Yugoslav poet, shares many of the characteristics of others of his generation from Eastern Europe. The family resemblance is there in the spareness and precision of his diction, its solidity, and in the poet's lack of sentimentality. Ted Hughes, in his introduction to Anne Pennington's translations, however, tries also to define what distinguishes Popa's work from that of his contemporaries when he talks of a "primitive pre-creation atmosphere . . . as if he were present where all the dynamisms and formulae were ready and charged, but nothing created—or only a few fragments." Hughes makes a telling distinction between literary surrealism, whose influences can be seen in Popa's earlier work, and "the surrealism of folklore," which characterizes much of his *oeuvre*, "always urgently connected with the business of trying to manage practical difficulties so great that they have forced the sufferer temporarily out of the dimension of coherent reality into that depth of imagination where understanding has its roots and stores its X-rays." Charles Simic, in his introduction to his own translations of Popa in *The Little Box*, also speaks of the poet's "elemental surrealism."

It is certainly possible to discern a larger scheme or vision operating here. Many commentators have speculated about Popa's habit of writing in interrelated or interactive cycles. An epic quality, albeit fragmentary, is discernible in that the poet's universe embraces not only the "primitive," the "precreation" elements, but also the real and legendary history of his native Serbia, his personal history also finding a place within this larger context. The Yugoslav poet and critic Miodrag Pavlović has spoken of Popa's "progress towards a new form of modern mythic-philosophical epic poetry." "Each cycle," says Simic, "is like a spoke of a wheel reaching from a different cycle towards a common centre, in which the poet's entire conception of the world lies. The impulse is towards the epic." What Simic, Hughes, and others sense, Ronelle Alexander tries to show, in an analysis of Popa's *oeuvre* (*The Structure of Vasko Popa's Poetry*), examining the symmetrical organization of his entire poetic material, from thematically related books, through individual cycles, to individual poems within each cycle. The seamlessness of this *oeuvre*, of course, makes extracting from it difficult.

Popa's first book, *Kora* [Bark], is imbued with a grim and desolate humour. In "Echo," the speaker is held hostage by an empty room which demands to be fed. It is himself he feeds it, bone by bone. Finally:

The empty room begins to howl
and I myself empty
Without a single bone

Turn into a hundred fold
Echo of the howling

And echo echo
Echo.

(translated by Anne Pennington)

By contrast he is also capable of great tenderness. In the love cycle "From Far Within Us," for instance, he wonders, "Shall I be able / on this unrest-field / To set up a tent of my hands for you?" A rhapsodic note enters:

The streets of your glances
Have no ending

The swallows from your eyes
Do not migrate south

From the aspens in your breasts
The leaves do not fall

In the sky of your words
The sun does not set.

(translated by Anne Pennington)

Already, the folkloristic as well as surrealistic influence can be heard. With the publication of *Od zlata jabuka* [The Golden Apple], an anthology drawn from Serbo-Croatian folklore, again arranged in cycles, Popa was to make this connection explicit (e.g. "Eyes: Two pillars hitting the sky").

In *Nepočin-polje* [Unrest Field], perhaps his grimmest book, Popa presents us with literally the bare bones of human relationships and feelings. It is, indeed, as if, in Ted Hughes's words, "all the dynamisms and formulae were ready and charged, but nothing created . . . ." In "The Seed" from the cycle "Games," for example:

Someone sows someone
Sows him in his head
Stamps the earth down well

Waits for the seed to sprout

The seed hollows out his head
Turns it into a mouse hole
The mice eat the seed

There they lie dead

The wind comes to live in the empty head
And gives birth to fickle breezes

(translated by Anne Pennington)

In 1968 Popa published *Sporedno nebo* [Secondary Heaven]. Here the mythmaker takes over. His verse which, however recondite, is never less than precise, is raised to a cosmological level. In *Uspravna zemlja* (*Earth Erect*) and *Vučfa so* [Wolf Salt], on the other hand, the poet returns to earth in a very specific manner. He journeys into the

historic past, visiting the traumatic Blackbird's Field where in 1389 the Serbs were routed by the Ottoman Turks, and into the legendary past, following St. Sava, patron saint of the Serbs, also known as the Wolf Shepherd. The wolf is moreover an animal with which Popa identifies closely. Thus, in *Živo meso* [Raw Flesh], the poet, with eerie prescience, observes in "Eyes of a Wolf":

Before they christened me
They gave me in the interim
The name of a brother suckled by a shewolf

A long as she lives my grandmother
Will call me Little Wolf
In her linen-like Walachian tongue

On the sly she would feed me
Raw meat so I would grow up
To lead the pack some day

I believed
My eyes would start to glow
In the dark

My eyes don't glow
Perhaps because the real night
Hasn't yet begun to fall.

(translated by Charles Simic)

In these poems and in *Kuća nasred druma* [The House on the Highroad] and *Rez* [Cut], the poet writes in a far more autobiographical vein than hitherto. Francis Jones, who continued Anne Pennington's translation work, has remarked: "Many readers . . . miss the blaze of atavistic image . . . ." However, this was not to be Popa's last word. He returned to the mythic, completing the "Little Box" cycle, which was to be the focus of his next work, *Iron Garden*, planned but never finished.

Though methodologically unique among his European peers, Popa joins them in an essential enterprise of recovery. That he did not live to witness the chaotic disintegration of his own country is perhaps a blessing, but that this sane, powerful voice is now silent is a great loss at such a critical juncture.

—Daniel Weissbort

PRATOLINI, Vasco

Born: Florence, Italy, 19 October 1913. **Education:** Educated formally to age 12. **Family:** Married Cecilia Punzo in 1941, one daughter. **Career:** At work from age 12, as shop assistant, printer's apprentice, factory hand, street vendor, hotel porter, travelling salesman, all in Florence, 1925–35, and attended French lessons intermittently; gave up fulltime work to undertake private study and journalism; confined in tuberculosis sanatoriums, 1935–37; contributor, *Il Bargello*, Florence, 1937; co-founder, with Alfonso Gatto, Campo di Marte magazine, 1939 (closed down within the year by the Fascist authorities); moved to Rome, 1939, and obtained position in the department of education; contributor, *Primato, La Ruota,*

L'Ambrosiano, Il Mattino, Il Popolo di Roma, from 1939; during World War II continued working as film and art critic, and participated in the Italian Resistance (under the code-name Rodolfo Casati) in Rome, taking responsibility for the area of the Ponte Milvio; after the Liberation, spent periods in Milan and Naples; settled in Rome, 1951–54, collaborated on several screenplays, and wrote theatre and art criticism. **Awards:** *Libera Stampa* prize, 1947; Foreign Book prize (France), 1950; Viareggio prize, 1955; Feltrinelli prize, 1957; Accademia dei Lincei national prize, 1957; Veillon prize, 1961; Marzotto prize, 1963. **Died:** 12 January 1991.

PUBLICATIONS

Fiction

Il tappeto verde (novellas). 1941.
Via de' Magazzini. 1942.
Le amiche. 1943.
Il Quartiere. 1944; as *The Naked Streets*, translated by Peter and Pamela Duncan, 1952; as *A Tale of Santa Croce*, translated by the Duncans, 1952.
Cronaca familiare. 1947; as *Two Brothers*, translated by Barbara Kennedy, 1962; as *Family Chronicle*, translated by Martha King, 1988.
Cronache di poveri amanti. 1947; as *A Tale of Poor Lovers*, translated anonymously, 1949.
Mestiere da vagabondo. 1947.
Un eroe del nostro tempo. 1949; as *A Hero of Today*, translated by Eric Masbacher, 1951; as *A Hero of Our Time*, translated by Masbacher, 1951.
Le ragazze di San Frediano. 1952.
Il mio cuore a Ponto Milvio: Vecchie carte (stories). 1954.
Una storia italiana:
　Metello. 1955; as *Metello*, translated by Raymond Rosenthal, 1968.
　Lo scialo. 1960; revised edition, 1976.
　Allegoria e derisione. 1966; revised edition, 1983.
Diario sentimentale (includes *Via de' Magazzini; Le amiche; Mestiere da vagabondo; Gli uomini che si voltano; Il mio cuore a Ponte Milvio*). 1957.
La costanza della ragione. 1963; as *Bruno Santini*, translated by Raymond Rosenthal, 1965.
Opere (includes *Il quartiere; Cronaca familiare; Cronache di poveri amanti; Le ragazze di San Frediano; Metello*). 1981.

Verse

La città ha i miei trent'anni. 1967.
Calendario del '67. 1978.
Il mannello di Natascia (1930–1936). 1980.
Il mannello di Natascia e altre cronache in versi e in prosa (1930–1980). 1985.

Plays

La domenica della buona gente　(radio play), with Giandomenica Giagni, in *Sipario 76.* 1952.
Lungo viaggio di Natale, from his own story, in *Teatre d'oggi 11–12.* 1954.

Other

Gli uomini che si voltano: Diario di Villa Rosa. 1952.
La lunga attesta: Lettere a Romano Bilenchi 1935–1972, edited by Paola Mazzucchelli. 1989.
Il mio cuore da Via de'Magazzini a Ponte Milvio: Vasco Pratolini tra immagini e memorie. 1992.
Editor, *L'eredità* by Mario Pratesi. 1965.
Editor, with Carlo Bernari, *Il confine*, by Giandomenico Giagni. 1976.

*

Critical Studies: *Vasco Pratolini* by A. Asor Rosa, 1958; *Francesco Jovine; Carlo Bernari; Vasco Pratolini* by Walter Mauro, 1963; *Vasco Pratolini* by F. Longobardi, 1964, enlarged edition, 1984; *Vasco Pratolini: The Development of a Social Novelist* by Frank Rosengarten, 1965; *Vasco Pratolini* by N. Amendola, 1966; *Pratolini* by Nino Betta, 1972; *Il romanzo italiano del dopoguerra* by Giorgio Pullini, 1972; *Invito all lettura di Vasco Pratolini* by C. Villa, 1973, revised edition, 1983; *Come leggere Metello* by Mario Razetti, 1975; *Vasco Pratolini* by Francesco Paolo Memmo, 1977, revised edition, 1982; *Il caso Pratolini: Ideologia e romanzo nella letteratura degli anni Cinquanta* edited by Mirko Bevilacqua, 1982; *Apprendistato e arte di Vasco Pratolini* by Anthony G. Constanti, 1986; *Vasco Pratolini* edited by Luciano Liusi, 1988; *Vasco Pratolini: Introduzione e guida* by Fabio Russo, 1989.

* * *

Vasco Pratolini, Italian novelist, was born into a poor Florentine family. He was self-taught, and his many jobs included that of a printer. He started writing early, and his first two books, *Il tappeto verde* [The Green Carpet] and *Via de' Magazzini* [Magazzini Street] (the name of the street where he was born), are autobiographical accounts of his Florentine childhood, in which we get glimpses of daily life in the humble strata of Italian society, with all its worries and stresses as well as human warmth and sincerity of feeling. The nostalgic tenderness with which Pratolini recaptures his past seldom borders on the sentimental, partly because of his sense of realism and his use of the humdrum details of everyday life. His manner of reminiscing is at once evocative and matter of fact, functional and poetic, which is why his prose has a poetic quality. His vivid grasp of topographical detail is also of great value in depicting not only his characters, especially the female ones, as in *Le amiche* [The Girl Friends], but also in evoking particular streets and quarters of Florence, such as Santa Croce, San Frediano and Piazza Signoria.

These two earlier works have some intrinsic literary merit, including their semi-poetic prose, but they also have considerable sociological and documentary value, giving us an insight into Pratolini's development as a novelist. They do not, however, represent the narrative mastery and maturity achieved in his later works. The first such mature work is *Il Quartiere* (*The Naked Streets*). Valerio, its protagonist, is a young worker, and relates in the first person his experiences of wartime Resistance, as well as of the transitional period of his life between adolescence, when he was immersed in the life of the quarter where he lived, and manhood with its moral and social problems and responsibilities as well as political commitments. Precisely because Pratolini's other characters, like Valerio, are also working-class people, his novels convey the sense of political and social conscience at a more realistic, more factual, and concrete level; and precisely because they are patently lacking in literary veneer or social sophistication, there is greater degree of artistic efficacy in his style and language.

In his best-known and most popular novel, *Cronache di poveri amanti* (*A Tale of Poor Lovers*), and well as in *Le ragazze di San Frediano* [The Girls of San Frediano], both the theme and the ethos that were already present in *The Naked Streets* are treated with a greater moral and psychological depth, and in a more complex form, so that the poor lovers' experiences and vicissitudes epitomize the proletarian condition. The pathos and the humanity of the characters in question are so vividly presented, and so subtly exploited, that they become symbols of political and social values, without ceasing to be movingly human as individuals.

In the later novels—*Un eroe del nostro tempo* (*A Hero of Our Time*) and the trilogy *Una storia italiana*, consisting of *Metello, Lo scialo* [The Waste], and *Allegoria e derisione* [Allegory and Derision]—Pratolini's interest in the problems of the working class finds a new social and political climate, post-war Italy, as well as new themes such as workers' unionization, the conflict between the capitalist class and the proletariat class, the connection between the morally degenerate bourgeoisie in Italy and the rise of the Fascists, and so on. Political ideology and social and moral dilemmas thus intermingle in Pratolini's fiction to form a meaningful context in which the conflicts between history and the poetry of everyday life, collective truth and individual truth, are explored. For this reason alone Pratolini may well be called "the laureate of the working class."

—Gabrielle Barfoot

PRÉVERT, Jacques (Henri Marie)

Born: Neuilly-sur-Seine, France, 4 February 1900. **Education:** Educated in Paris. **Military Service:** Stationed in Saint-Nicolas-de-Port, near Lunéville, 1920–21. **Family:** Married 1) Simone Dienne in 1925; 2) Janine Tricotet in 1947. **Career:** Worked in Bon Marché and other stores in Paris, 1915–20; worked for *Argus de la Presse*, 1921; *Courrier de la Presse*, 1922; acted in *Les Grands* (film by Henri Fescourt), 1923; worked for publicity agency Damour, 1930; writer and actor with the theatre company, *Groupe Octobre*, from 1932; collaborated with the film director Marcel Carné 1936–46. Visited Moscow, 1933, and the United States, 1938. Associated with Breton. *q.v.*, and Aragon, *q.v.* **Awards:** Grand prix, Société des Auteurs et Compositeurs Dramatiques, 1973; *Cinema* National Grand prize, 1975. **Died:** 11 April 1977.

PUBLICATIONS

Collections

Oeuvres, edited by Arnaud Laster and Daniéle Gasiglia-Laster. 4 vols., 1983.
La Cinquième Saison (collected verse, screenplays, stories). 1984.
Oeuvres complétes, edited by Daniéle Gasiglia-Laster and Arnold Laster. 1992.

Verse

Paroles. 1945; revised edition, 1947; as *Selections from "Paroles,"* translated by Lawrence Ferlinghetti, 1958; revised edition, 1990.
Histoires, with André Verdet. 1946.
C'est à Saint-Paul-de-Vence. . . , with André Verdet. 1949.
Grand Bal du printemps. 1951; with *Charmes de Londres*, 1976.
Spectacle. 1951.
Charmes de Londres. 1952; with *Grand Bal du printemps*, 1976.
La Pluie et le beau temps. 1955.
Lumières d'hommes. 1955.
Images. 1957.
Poèmes, edited by J.H. Douglas and D.J. Girard. 1961.
Prévert vous parle: 18 poèmes, edited by Andrée Bergens and David Noakes. 1968.
Poésies. 1971.
Words for All Seasons (selection), translated by Teo Savory. 1979.
Couleurs, illustrated by Braque, Calder and Miró. 1981.
Chanson des cireurs de souliers. 1985.
Chanson pour chanter à tue-tête et á cloche-pied. 1985.
Blood and Feathers: Selected Poems, translated by Harriet Zinnes. 1987.
Chanson des escargots qui vont á l' enterrement. 1988.
Rue Jacques Prévert, photographs by Robert Doisneau. 1992.

Plays

Le Rendez-vous (ballet scenario). 1945.
Les Visiteurs du soir (screenplay). 1947.
Les Amants de Verone (screenplay). 1948.
L'Opéra de la lune. 1952.
A United Family, translated by J.D. Allen. In *Let's Get a Divorce! and Other Plays*, edited by Eric Bentley, 1958.
Le Jour se lève, with Marcel Carné (screenplay). In *Avant-Scène*, 1965; as *Le Jour se lève*, translated by Dinah Brooke and Nicola Hayden, 1970.
Les Enfants du Paradis (screenplay). 1968; as *Children of Paradise*, translated by Dinah Brooke, 1968.
Drôle de drame (screenplay). 1974.
Le Quai des brumes (screenplay). In *Avant-Scène*, 1979.
La Fleur de l'âge (screenplay). 1988.
Jenny (screenplay). 1988.
Le Crime de M. Lange/Les Ports de la nuit (screenplays). 1990.

Screenplays: *Souvenirs de Paris; ou, Paris-express*, 1928; *L'Affaire est dans le sac*, 1932; *Ciboulette*, 1933; *Comme un carpe*, 1933; *La Pomme de terre*, with Pierre Prévert and Yves Allegret, 1933; *L'Hotel du Libre-Échange*, 1934; *La Pêche à la baleine*, 1934; *Jeunesse d'abord*, 1935; *Taxi de minuit*, 1935; *Un Oiseau rare*, 1935; *Le Crime de Monsieur Lunge*, 1936; *My Partner Mr. Davis*, 1936; *Jenny*, 1936; *Moutonnet*, 1936; *Prisons de velours*, 1936; *L'Affaire du courrier du Lyon*, 1937; *Drôle de drame*, 1937; *C'était moi*, 1938; *Quai des brumes*, 1938; *Les Disparus de Saint-Agil*, 1938; *Ernest le rebelle*, 1938; *Le Jour se léve*, 1939; *Soleil a toujours raison*, 1941; *Une femme dans la nuit*, 1941; *Remorques*, with Roger Vercel and Charles Spaak, 1941; *Les Visiteurs du soir*, 1942; *Lumiére d'été*, with Pierre Laroche, 1943; *Adieu Léonard*, with Pierre Prévert, 1943; *Sortilèges*, 1944; *Les Enfants du paradis*, 1945; *Les Portes de la nuit*, 1946; *Voyage-Surprise*, 1946; *La Bergère et le remoneur*, with Paul Grimault, 1947; *L'Arche de Noé*, with Pierre Laroche, 1947; *Le Petit Soldat,*

1947; *Les Amants de Vérone*, 1949; *La Marie du port*, 1949; *Souvenirs perdus*, 1950; *Notre-Dame de Paris*, 1956; *La Faim du monde*, with Paul Grimault, 1957; *Paris la belle*, 1959; *Les Amours célèbres*, 1961; *Le Petit Claus et le grand Claus*, 1964; *La Maison du passeur*, 1965; *A la belle étoile*, 1966; *Le Diamant*, with Paul Grimault, 1970; *Le Roi et l'oiseau*, 1980.

Other

Quai de brumes. 1938.
La Responsibilité pharmaceutique. 1940.
Enfants. 1945.
Le Cheval de Troie, with André Verdet and André Virel. 1946.
D'autres chansons. 1947.
Le Petit Lion (for children). 1947.
Contes pour enfants pas sages (for children). 1947.
21 Chansons, with Joseph Kosma. 1947.
Des Bêtes (for children). 1950.
Bim, le petit âne, with Albert Lamorisse (for children). 1951; as *Bim, the Little Donkey*, translated by Bette and Harvey Swado, 1957.
Guignol (for children). 1952.
Lettres des îles Baladar. 1952.
Miró, with Georges Ribemont-Dessaignes. 1956.
Portrait de Picasso. 1959.
Diurnes, illustrated by Picasso and André Villiers. 1962.
Histoires, et d'autre histoires. 1963.
Les Chiens ont soif, with Max Ernst. 1964.
Le Cirque d'Izis, illustrated by Marc Chagall. 1965.
Fatras. 1966; as *Fatras*, illustrated by Miró, 1978.
Prévert, translated by Teo Savory. 1967.
Prévert II, translated by Teo Savory. 1967.
Arbres. 1968.
Varengeville. 1968.
Imaginaires. 1970.
Fêtes, with Alexander Calder. 1971.
To Paint the Portrait of a Bird, translated by Lawrence Ferlinghetti. 1971.
Choses et autres. 1972.
Hebdomadaires (interviews), with André Pozner. 1972; revised edition, 1982.
Images de Jacques Prévert, with René Bertelé. 1973.
Chansons, with Joseph Kosma. 1976.
Soleil de nuit (collection), edited by Arnaud Luster. 1980.
Anthologie Prévert, edited by Christiane Mortelier (poems and songs). 1981.
Collages, with André Pozner. 1982.

*

Critical Studies: *Jacques Prévert* (in English) by William E. Baker, 1967; *Jacques Prévert's Word Games* by Anne Hyde Greet, 1968; *Jacques Prévert* by Andrée Bergens, 1969; *Paroles-Prévert* by Arnaud Laster, 1972; *Paroles de Jacques Prévert* by Christiane Mortelier, 1976; *Le Groupe octobre* by Michel Fouré, 1977; *Jacques Prévert* by Michel Rachline, 1981; *Jacques Prévert* by Daniéle Gasiglia-Laster, 1986; *Jacques Prévert: Popular French Theatre and Cinema* by Claire Blakeway, 1990; *Des mots et merveilles, Jacques Prévert* by René Gilson, 1990.

* * *

Jacques Prévert occupies a niche of his own in the history of French poetry, achieving fame for one collection, *Paroles*, which was published in 1945, in the immediate aftermath of World War II. He had a distinctive voice, and though some critics questioned his achievement, the public responded warmly to the human values that he presented clearly in an attractively unorthodox style. In an age in which poetry has tended to become a minority interest, Prévert could claim to be the best selling French poet since Victor Hugo.

Prévert left school at the age of 14 and drifted from job to job until drafted for compulsory military service. In the 1920s he began to make contacts with surrealist writers in Paris, and towards the end of the decade his first poems were published in a variety of little magazines. He then turned towards the theatre and, with considerably more success, towards the cinema, which was entering an exciting phase of its evolution in France with the introduction of the talkies. He became an actor in the Groupe Octobre theatre company, often taking roles in his own plays.

Among the most successful of Prévert's screenplays in the late 1930s was *Le Quai des brumes* (released in the United States as *Port of Shadows*), his skilful version of the prize-winning novel by Pierre MacOrlan. Working with Jacques Viot, Prévert also wrote the script for Marcel Carné's *Le Jour se lève* [Daybreak], which was hailed as a masterpiece of French poetic realism on its release in 1939. Continuing in films throughout World War II, Prévert won an Academy award nomination for the scenario for Carné's *Les Enfants du Paradis* (*Children of Paradise*), an evocation of Parisian theatrical life in the 1840s that many critics rate the finest French film ever.

After the Liberation, Prévert continued to write for both stage and screen and mounted exhibitions of his collages and photographs. But it was with *Paroles*, his first collection of poetry, that he leapt to fame. No doubt his image helped; for, with his cigarettes and bohemian appearance, he seemed to be a man of the people, more at home in a dingy café with its strident-voiced singers of satirical ballads, than in a society drawing-room with its snobbish concern for high culture. The style seemed to reflect the man. Perhaps inspired to some degree by his experience of the cinema, Prévert knew how to give poignancy to the most everyday of experiences. In "Déjeuner du matin," for instance, we watch with mesmerized attentiveness a man at breakfast time methodically pouring out a cup of coffee, drinking it, and then smoking a cigarette before leaving. Suddenly the angle is reversed, to reveal for a moment his companion, who bursts into tears. Apparently nothing could be simpler, and no expert knowledge of the wider world of literature is needed for making sense of this scene. Closer analysis reveals, however, a precisely calculated pattern of repetition that creates tensions that are all the more unbearable because there is no punctuation and so the reader is forced at every stage to make impossible decisions about the way fraught situations are to be structured. At first glance, Prévert's poetry can appear to be naive, but his verbal dexterity reveals that he knew the meaning of the old adage that the truest art is artistry concealed. He would play with words, revelling in puns and paradoxes, presenting familiar sights in a fresh light. He turned away from traditional rhyme and conventional versification, as from difficult imagery and elegant expression, sensing that his post-war public was weary of the grand manner and poetry that smacked of officialdom and academic pomposity.

His themes, when they are not just basically humanitarian, were left-wing and anti-authoritarian. They were in tune with the times as France came out from the trauma of a disastrous war in which the

Vichy government had compounded the disgrace of defeat by collaborating with the German invaders and which ended with a deeply fissured society. Many felt that the Left had been cheated after the Liberation, and there was a considerable audience, of intellectuals as well as members of the working class, ready to assuage its disappointments by listening to subversive opinions presented with verve and humour.

Though severely injured after a fall in the Paris offices of Radiodiffusion in 1948, Prévert was eventually able to resume his career, writing a number of books for children. *Spectacle*, like *Paroles* a collection of work written over quite a long period of time, was published in 1951, and *La Pluie et le beau temps* [Rain and Fine Weather] came out four years later. Both contain delightful pieces and sold well. However, it seems likely that they owed a fair amount of their success to the fact that they were written by the author of *Paroles*.

—Christopher Smith

PRÉVOST, Abbé (Antoine-François Prévost d'Exiles)

Born: Hesdin, France, 1 April 1697. **Education:** Probably educated at a college in Hesdin; College d'Harcourt, Paris; studied for the priesthood at La Fléche: novice, Society of Jesus, 1713. **Career:** Joined the army and led a dissolute life for five years; joined community of Benedictines at Saint-Maur, 1719; ordained a priest, 1721; preacher and teacher until 1728; another spell of worldly life, often in exile in Holland and London: founded periodical *Le Pour et le contre* in London, 1733–40; again reconciled with the Benedictines: almoner and secretary, 1736; editor, *Le Journal Étranger*, 1755. **Died:** 23 November 1763.

PUBLICATIONS

Collections

Oeuvres choisies. 39 vols., 1783–85.
Oeuvres, edited by Pierre Berthiaume and Jean Sgard. 1978–.

Fiction

Les Aventures de Pomponius, chevalier romain; ou, L'Histoire de notre temps. 1724.
Mémoires et aventures d'un homme de qualité qui s'est retiré du monde. 7 vols., 1728–31; revised edition, 1756; as *Memoirs of a Man of Quality*, 1938.
Le Philosophe anglais; ou, Histoire de Monsieur Cleveland, fils naturel de Cromwell. 7 vols., 1731–39; as *The Life and Adventures of Mr. Cleveland*, translated anonymously, 1734.
Histoire du chevalier Des Grieux et de Manon Lescaut. 1733 (originally constituted the last volume of *Mémoires et aventures d'un homme de qualité);* edited by Frédéric Deloffre and Raymond Picard, 1965; as *Manon Lescaut*, translated by Charlotte Smith, 1738; also translated by Leonard Tancock, 1949; Donald Frame, 1961; edited by Patrick Byrne, 1999.

Le Doyen de Killerine: Histoire morale composée sur les mémoires d'une illustre famille d'Irlande. 6 vols., 1735–40; as *The Dean of Coleraine*, translated by C. Davis, 1742–43.
Histoire d'une grecque moderne. 2 vols., 1740; as *The History of a Fair Greek*, translated anonymously, 1755.
Histoire de Marguerite d'Anjou, Reine d'Angleterre. 1740; as *The History of Margaret of Anjou, Queen of England*, translated anonymously, 1755.
Campagnes philosophiques; ou, Mémoires de M. de Montéal. 4 vols., 1741.
Mémoires pour servir à l'histoire de Malte; ou, Histoire de la jeunesse du commandeur de ***. 2 vols., 1741.
Histoire de Guillaume le Conquérant, duc de Normandie, et roi d'Angleterre. 1741–42.
Voyages du capitaine Robert Lade. 2 vols., 1744.
Mémoires d'un honnête homme. 4 vols., 1745.
Le Monde moral; ou, Mémoires pour servir à l'histoire du coeur humain. 2 vols., 1760–64.

Other

Le Pour et le contre. 20 vols., 1733–40.
Le Critique français. 1734.
Histoire générale des voyages. 15 vols., 1746–59; continued by others: 80 vols., 1749–89.
Manuel lexique; ou, Dictionnaire portatif des mots français. 2 vols., 1750.
Editor, *Histoire métallique des XVII provinces des Pays-Bas*, by Gerard Van Loon. 2 vols., 1732.
Editor and translator, *Lettres de Cicéron à M. Brutus et de M. Brutus à Cicéron.* 1744.
Editor and translator, *Lettres de Cicéron.* 5 vols., 1745–47.
Translator, with others, *Histoire universelle*, by J-A. de Thou. 16 vols., 1733–34.
Translator, *Tout pour l'amour; ou, Le Monde bien perdu*, by John Dryden. 1735.
Translator, *Paméla; ou, La Vertu récompensée*, by Samuel Richardson. 4 vols., 1742.
Translator, *Histoire de Cicéron*, by Conyers Middleton. 4 vols., 1743–44.
Translator, *Lettres à Brutus*, by Cicero. 1744.
Translator, *Lettres familières.* 5 vols., 1745–47.
Translator, *Lettres anglaises; ou, Histoire de Miss Clarisse Harlowe*, by Samuel Richardson. 12 vols., 1751.
Translator, *Nouvelles lettres anglaises; ou, Histoire du chevalier Grandisson*, by Samuel Richardson. 6 vols., 1755–58.
Translator, *Histoire de la maison de Stuart sur le trône d'Angleterre*, by Hume. 3 vols., 1760.
Translator, *Almoran et Hamet: Anecdote orientale*, by J. Hawkesworth. 1763.
Translator, *Lettres de Mentor à un jeune seigneur.* 1764.

*

Bibliography: *Prévost: An Analytical Bibliography of Criticism to 1981* by Peter Tremewan, 1984.

Critical Studies: *The Abbé Prévost and English Literature* by G.R. Havens, 1921; *The Art of French Fiction* by Martin Turnell, 1959; *Prévost, romancier*, 1968, and *Prévost: Labyrinthes de la mémoire*, 1986, both by Jean Sgard; *Prévost: Manon Lescaut* by Vivienne

Mylne, 1972; *Structuralist Perspectives in Criticism of Fiction: Essays on "Manon Lescaut" and "La Vie de Marianne"* by Patrick Brady, 1978; *The Romantic Manon and Des Grieux: Images of Prévost's Heroine and Hero in Nineteenth-Century French Literature* by James P. Gilroy, 1980; *The Unintended Reader, Feminism and Manon Lescaut* by Naomi Segal, 1986; *The Abbé Prévost First-Person Narrators* by R.A. Francis, 1993; *Prévost: Manon Lescaut* by R.A. Francis, 1994; *Manon Lescaut and Her Representation in Nineteenth-Century Literature, Criticism and Opera* by Dina Grundemann Foster, 1998.

* * *

Like Choderlos de Laclos, Abbé Prévost is a man known to the modern reader for only one book, though for very different reasons than the author of *Les Liaisons dangereuses*. For although the book that has ensured literary immortality for Prévost, *Histoire du chevalier Des Grieux et de Manon Lescaut* (*Manon Lescaut*), contains no more than 300 pages, it is part of a very much longer but now rarely read novel entitled *Mémoires et aventures d'un homme de qualité* (*Memoirs of a Man of Quality*). Prévost continued to occupy himself during his long life with a series of other compositions, but never again encountered the success immediately won for him by this account of how a young man of 17 falls in love with a girl of 16 and proceeds to ruin all his chances of future happiness by his devotion to someone who, in spite of her love for him, is totally incapable of fidelity the moment she runs short of money. This devotion is indeed the central theme of a novel that is generally if inappropriately shortened to *Manon Lescaut* or even, in the case of Massenet's opera, to *Manon*. For although the attention of readers has always gone to the irresistible Manon, it is the paradox of the moralistic and monogamous man attached to the polygamous and amoral woman which gives the book its originality and inexhaustible fascination. For although Des Grieux loves Manon with an exclusive and all-devouring passion, he rapidly learns that there is nothing he can do to prevent her from going to bed with the nearest rich admirer as soon as he can no longer support her in the luxurious style of living without which she cannot be happy. Yet he is never able to move away from this knowledge to a position where he can do without Manon and her charms, and one result of this has been to lead critics to see Des Grieux—and, through him, his creator—as continuing the Jansenist theme of "Video meliora proboque; deteriora sequor" [I see the best and approve of it; but I follow the worst] which informs the tragic vision of Racine.

Yet there is nothing of the tragic grandeur of Racine in this story of what one hostile contemporary critic referred to as "the adventures of a crook and his whore," and Prévost's account of Paris in the Regency of Louis XV, with its tricksters, gambling dens, prostitutes, shady financiers, and cheap lodging houses looks forward to the realist novel of the 19th century. Indeed, in 1950, the story, was made into an interesting film in which the Paris of the 1720s was replaced by the comparably sordid and ambiguous period of the German Occupation of the 1940s, and the final shipping off of Manon to the Louisiana of the early 18th century was replaced by her being sent to Israel at the difficult time of the 1948 war. In both novel and film she dies in the desert and is buried by Des Grieux, who then returns to tell the story to the "Homme de Qualité," who adopts towards him the same moralizing and moralistic tone that characterizes Prévost's preface to the novel. Yet it is very difficult to accept Prévost's claim that the story of

Manon and Des Grieux is "a moral treatise agreeably reduced to an exercise." Neither Prévost nor the narrator has any real set of values to set by the side of the "world well lost for love" theme which inspires the two principals, and Prévost shows such a lack of awareness of how amoral society is in general that Manon's sexual infidelities seem relatively venial sins in comparison.

—Philip Thody

See the essay on *Manon Lescaut*.

PROPERTIUS, Sextus

Born: Asisium (Assisi), Umbria, central Italy, between 57 and 50 BC. **Education:** Educated in rhetoric. **Family:** May have married. **Career:** Spurned a legal career in favour of poetry. Associated with the patron Maecenas. **Died:** Probably c. 16 BC.

PUBLICATIONS

Verse

[Works], edited by H.E. Butler and E.A. Barber (with commentary). 1933; also edited by E.A. Barber, 1960, and W.A. Camps (with commentary), 4 vols., 1961–67; edited and translated by G.P. Goold [Loeb Edition; bilingual], 1990; translated by Peter J.F. Gantillon, John Nott, and Sir Charles A. Elton, 1854; also translated by F.A. Paley, 1866; C.R. Moore, 1870; J. Cranstoun, 1875; Seymour G. Tremenheere, 1899; J.S. Phillimore, 1906; H.E. Butler [Loeb Edition], 1912; E.H.W. Meyerstein, 1935; Arthur S. Way, 1937; A.E. Watts, 1961, revised edition, 1966; Ronald Musker, 1972; J. McCulloch, 1972; J. Warden, 1972; W.G. Shepherd, 1985; A.G. Lee, 1994; Vincent Katz, 1995.

*

Bibliography: *A Bibliography to Propertius* by Hermann Harrauer, 1973; *Bibliografia properziana 1946–1983* by P. Fedeli and P. Pinotti, 1985.

Critical Studies: *Latin Elegiac Verse: A Study of the Metrical Usages of Tibullus, Propertius, and Ovid* by Maurice Plautnauer, 1951; *The Latin Love Elegy* (with some translations) by G. Luck, 1969; *Propertius* (including poems with translations) by Margaret Hubbard, 1974; *Propertius: A Critical Introduction* by J.P. Sullivan, 1976; *The Latin Love Poets from Catullus to Horace* (with some translations) by R.O.A.M. Lyne, 1980; *Propertius: "Love" and "War," Individual and State under Augustus* by Hans-Peter Stahl, 1985; *Propertius: A Hellenistic Poet on Love and Death* by T.D. Papanghelis, 1987; *Augustan Propertius: The Recapitulation of a Genre* by John Kevin Newman, 1997; *The Politics of Desire: Propertius IV* by Micaela Janan, 2001.

* * *

Sextus Propertius is one of the extant trio of Augustan love elegists, along with Tibullus and Ovid. His four books show his interests gradually widening and his literary ambition growing, as poems portraying what are supposed to be his own love experiences become outnumbered by those on antiquarian, political, literary-polemical, and non-personal amatory themes.

Book I (c. 30 BC), which seems to have circulated separately, before the rest of Propertius' *oeuvre*, is almost exclusively personal, most of its 22 poems being devoted to his stormy love affair with a woman he calls Cynthia. The name is fictitious, and it was doubtless chosen for its associations with poetry, "Cynthian" being a cult title of Apollo, god of poetry (after Mt. Cynthus on his native Delos). Thus when Propertius begins Book I, "Cynthia first captured wretched me with her eyes," he is conceivably proclaiming his love affair with poetry as well as with a woman. Moreover, he endows Cynthia herself with literary discernment no less than beauty (II. 3). He depicts a relationship with her that is full of lively tensions, perceptible both within and between individual poems. He is inexorably drawn to her but, because she does not respond, he longs to be free (1); he poses both as one who is self-assured enough to advise others and one helpless in Cynthia's power; torn between presenting his love as either typical or unique (e.g. 4, 5, 7, 10, 13), he professes to be sure of her fidelity, but also reveals his fear through (e.g. 2, 11, 19). Although he does not want her to desert him (8, 11) or deceive him (15), *he* deserts her (17, 18), even hinting at his own infidelity (3); and he goes from the heights of jubilation (8.27–46) to the depths of despair (12).

The linking of separate elegies by subject matter and/or by addressee helps to unify the book. But whether Propertius sought to achieve the formal structural pattern some scholars detect (see Goold, 1990, pp. 6–9) is debatable. There are in any case three non-Cynthia poems at the end of the book which stand awkwardly outside any schema: 20 (to Gallus) mainly recounts in the most elaborate and esoteric Alexandrian manner the rape of Hercules' boyfriend Hylas; 21 is spoken by a kinsman of Propertius who apparently died during the siege of Perusia in 41 BC; and 22 (to Tullus) is Propertius' "biographical note" on himself. Although Propertius combatively states his preference for the life of love rather than the life of action, and for love poetry rather than war poetry, he does not at this stage direct his remarks to Maecenas, the personal friend and unofficial "cultural attaché" of Augustus. Presumably he was not at this stage part of Maecenas' literary circle, which also included Virgil and Horace.

The second book (c. 26 BC) in its surviving form is almost certainly a somewhat chaotic conflation of two originals (34 poems as it stands, but the poem division in the manuscript is unreliable). It is again Cynthia-orientated, displaying many of the same hopes, fears, and tensions, although Propertius is on the whole even less sanguine about the relationship than in Book I (see poems 5, 6, 8, 9, 17, 24, 31, 32). He begins, however, to write longer and more dramatically structured elegies (e.g. 28) together with the odd amatory piece in the playful manner of the Hellenistic epigram (e.g. 12). There are signs that he is becoming conscious of pressure of various kinds from the Augustan establishment: in 7 a clash with the moral legislation designed to force Roman citizens like himself to marry, in 1 a polite rejection (addressed to Maecenas) of lofty epic and nationalistic themes on grounds of insufficiency of talent, and in 10 a rash promise to attempt precisely such themes in the future in a poem on the wars of Augustus.

Book III (c. 23 BC) marks the watershed in Propertius' drift away from the personal love elegy. It begins with his explicit declaration of allegiance to the poetic principles of the Alexandrian Greeks Callimachus and Philetas and a confident assertion of his own poetic genius (1 and 2). Epic is again rejected in favour of love poetry, by

way of a Callimachean motif in 3 and a tactful address to Maecenas in 9. Propertius claims to have plans to study science (5) and philosophy (21), but the range of his poetry has already widened in this book to include mythological narrative, such as the story of Dirce (15), funeral elegies for Paetus (7) and Marcellus (18); reproach of a soldier for leaving a loving wife (12); praises of Bacchus (17) and of Italy (22), and a moralizing disquisition on the admirable ways of Sparta's women (14). There are still some Cynthia poems (6, 8, 10, 16), but their tone is much less intense. Poem 6, as a bold experiment with dramatic format, is perhaps the most interesting of them. The last two poems of the book (24 and 25) constitute a formal renunciation of Cynthia (and thus of the sort of poetry she inspired), with Propertius admitting to the unworthiness of his past obsession with her.

Propertius' ventures into territory beyond Cynthia culminate in the much longer elegies of Book IV (c. 16 BC). In an ambitious opening poem (or poems; what the manuscripts present as Poem 1 may in fact be two separate pieces) he announces his intention to write narrative elegies on Roman themes, boldly styling himself the "Roman Callimachus," but he is then warned by an astrologer that he is destined for a lowlier poetic future as a love elegist. The ten poems which follow complement these notions, for they comprise mainly a mixture of amatory elegies, both personal and non-personal, and Roman "aetiological" pieces: i.e. attempts to account for some name, cult, practice, or phenomenon (such is the basic subject matter of Callimachus' *Aetia* [Origins]). The most successful of the aetiological pieces (2, 4, 9, 10) is perhaps the story of the errant Vestal Virgin Tarpeia (4), and as a group these poems pave the way for Ovid's full-length Roman aetiological poem, the *Fasti* [Calendar]. The non-personal amatory elegies, too, are of interest for the influence they may have had on Ovid. It is tempting to see the germ of the *Heroides* in the imaginary letter of a deserted wife to her soldier husband (3) and the inspiration for *Amores* (I, 8) in the vitriolic portrait of an unscrupulous procuress (5). At the centre of the book (6) is Propertius' most explicitly political poem, a celebration of Augustus' victory over Antony and Cleopatra at the battle of Actium (31 BC). Its tone, however, is elusive, and it would be interesting to know what Augustus made of it. The last poem, 11, is a defence before the gods of the dead of her life by the aristocratic Cornelia, a paragon among Roman wives. This has often been thought to be Propertius' best and most nobly Roman poem, but some find its sentiments too austerely correct for comfort. Even in this book there are two Cynthia poems: in 7 her cremation-charred ghost visits Propertius in his sleep and chides him for his past neglect of her, and in 8 she comes to life again (in literary terms at least) as a superbly comic virago who bursts in on an insouciant Propertius enjoying a roistering evening with two prostitutes. His emancipation from her now indeed seems to be complete!

Propertius' elegy is in almost every respect more flamboyant and brightly toned than that of his slightly older contemporary Tibullus, who nevertheless probably had some influence upon him. In his earlier books especially he prefers poems on single themes, with a specific addressee often used as a sounding post. One of his abiding interests is in connecting love with the prospect and rituals of death (as emphasized by Papanghelis, 1987). Linguistically he is ever adventurous, and is much given to mythological allusion in the learned and esoteric Alexandrian manner. Yet his use of myth is almost never otiose, often subtly undercutting some of his more exaggerated attitudes (e.g. in I. 3); and in many of the love poems self-mockery lies just beneath the surface (e.g. I. 16). Quintilian is equivocal about Propertius' greatness as an elegist, and it is perhaps therefore fitting that he has inspired one of the most controversial modern imitations of any classical poet: Ezra Pound's *Homage to Sextus Propertius* (1917).

—Joan Booth

PROUST, Marcel

Born: Auteuil, Paris, France, 10 July 1871. **Education:** Educated at Lycée Fontanes (renamed Lycée Condorcet, 1883) Paris, 1882–89; the Sorbonne, Paris, 1891–93, bachelor of law 1893. **Military Service:** Served 1889–90. **Career:** Active in society in the 1890s, co-founder, with Fernand Gregh, of the review *Le Banquet*, 1892; occasional contributor to newspapers and journals, but gradually became a recluse. **Awards:** Goncourt prize, 1919. Chevalier, Légion d'honneur, 1920. **Died:** 18 November 1922.

PUBLICATIONS

Collection

Oeuvres complètes. 10 vols., 1929–36.

Fiction

À la recherche du temps perdu. 1913–27; edited by Pierre Clarac and André Ferré, 1954, also edited by Jean-Yves Tadié, 2 vols., 1987, Jean Milly, 10 vols., 1987, and by Bernard Raffalli, 3 vols., 1987; as *Remembrance of Things Past*, 1922–31, translated by C.K. Scott Moncrieff, this translation revised by Scott Moncrieff and Terence Kilmartin, 3 vols, 1981; adapted by Harold Pinter and Di Trevis, 2000; as *In Search of Lost Time*, revised translation by D.J. Enright, 5 vols., 1992.

Du côté de chez Swann. 1913; as *Swann's Way*, translated by C.K. Scott Moncrieff, 2 vols., 1922, revised translation by D.J. Enright, 1992; as *Combray*, edited with notes by Leighton Hodson, 1996.

À l'ombre des jeunes filles en fleurs. 1919; as *Within a Budding Grove*, translated by C.K. Scott Moncrieff, 1924, revised translation by D.J. Enright, 1992.

Le Côté de Guermantes. 1920–21; as *The Guermantes Way*, translated by C.K. Scott Moncrieff, 2 vols., 1925, revised translation by D.J. Enright, 1992.

Sodome et Gomorrhe. 1921–22; as *Cities of the Plain*, translated by C.K. Scott Moncrieff, 2 vols., 1927; as *Sodom and Gomorrah*, revised translation by D.J. Enright, 1992.

La Prisonnière. 1923; as *The Captive*, translated by C.K. Scott Moncrieff, 1929, revised translation by D.J. Enright, 1992.

Albertine disparue. 1925; as *The Sweet Cheat Gone*, translated by C.K. Scott Moncrieff, 1930; as *The Fugitive*, translated by Scott Moncrieff and Terence Kilmartin, 1981, revised translation by D.J. Enright, 1992; as *Albertine Gone*, translated by Kilmartin, 1989.

Le Temps retrouvé. 1927; as *Time Regained*, 1931; as *The Past Recaptured*, translated by Frederick A. Blossom, 1932.

Jean Santeuil. 1952; as *Jean Santeuil*, translated by Gerard Hopkins, 1955.

Matinée chez la princesse de Guermantes, edited by Henri Bonnet and Bernand Brun. 1982.

Bricquebec: Prototype d'À l'ombre des jeunes filles et fleurs', edited by Richard Bales. 1989.

Verse

Poèmes, edited by Claude Francis and Fernande Gontier. 1982.

Other

Les Plaisirs et les jours. 1896; as *Pleasures and Regrets*, translated by Louise Varèse, 1948.

Pastiches et mélanges. 1919.

Chroniques. 1927.

Correspondance générale. 6 vols., 1930–36; selection, as *Letters*, edited by Mina Curtiss, 1950.

A Selection, edited by Gerald Hopkins. 1948.

Letters of Marcel Proust, edited and translated by Mina Curtis. 1949.

Correspondance avec sa mère, edited by Philip Kolb. 1953; as *Letters to His Mother*, edited and translated by George D. Painter. 1957.

Contre Sainte-Beuve, edited by Bernard de Fallois. 1954; as *On Art and Literature 1896–1919*, translated by Sylvia Townsend Warner, 1958; as *By Way of Sainte-Beuve*, translated by Townsend Warner, 1958; as *Against Sainte-Beuve and Other Essays*, translated by John Sturrock, 1988.

Textes retrouvés, edited by Philip Kolb and Larkin B. Price. 1968, revised edition, 1971.

Correspondance, edited by Philip Kolb. 21 vols., 1970–93.

Le Carnet de 1908, edited by Philip Kolb. 1976.

Correspondance Proust-Copeau, edited by Michael Raimond. 1976.

Correspondance, with Jacques Rivière, edited by Philip Kolb. 1976.

L'Indifférent. 1978.

Selected Letters 1880–1903, edited by Philip Kolb, translated by Ralph Manheim. 1983.

Correspondance 1912–1922, with Gaston Gallimard, edited by Pascal Fouché. 1989.

Selected Letters 1904–09, and *1910–17*, edited by Philip Kolb, translated by Terence Kilmartin. 2 vols., 1989–92.

Mon cher petit: Lettres à Lucien Daudet, edited by Michel Bonduelle. 1992.

Translator, *La Bible d'Amiens*, by Ruskin. 1904.

Translator, *Sésame et le lys*, by Ruskin. 1906; Proust's preface as *On Reading*, edited by Jean Autret and William Burford, 1972; also edited by Phillip J. Wolfe, 1987.

*

Bibliography: *Bibliographie des études sur Proust et son oeuvre* by Victor E. Graham, 1976; *Marcel Proust and His Contexts: A Critical Bibliography of English-Language Scholarship* by Elizabeth Russell Taylor, 1981.

Critical Studies: *Proust, His Life and Work* by Léon Pierre-Quint, translated by Hamish and Sheila Miles, 1927; *Proust* by Samuel Beckett, 1931; *Proust's Way* by François Mauriac, 1950; *Proust and Literature: The Novelist as Critic* by Walter A. Strauss, 1957; *Proust:*

A Biography by George D. Painter, 2 vols., 1959–65, revised edition, 1989; *Proust's Nocturnal Muse* by William Stewart Bell, 1962; *Proust: A Collection of Critical Essays* edited by René Girard, 1962; *The Magic Lantern of Marcel Proust* by Howard Moss, 1963; *Proust's Binoculars: A Study of Memory, Time and Recognition in "À la recherche du temps perdu,"* 1963, and *Marcel Proust*, 1974, both by Roger Shattuck; *Marcel Proust: The Fictions of Life and Art* by Leo Bersani, 1965; *Proust's Narrative Techniques* by Brian G. Rogers, 1965; *The World of Marcel Proust* by Germaine Brée, 1966; *The Imagery of Proust* by Victor Graham, 1966; *Marcel Proust 1871–1922: A Centenary Volume* edited by Peter Quennell, 1971; *Marcel Proust and the Creative Encounter* by George Stambolian, 1972; *Proust and Signs* by Gilles Deleuze, 1973; *Marcel Proust: A Critical Panorama* edited by L.B. Price, 1973; *Proust* by William Sansom, 1973; *A Reading of Proust* by Wallace Fowlie, revised edition, 1975; *A Reader's Handbook to Proust: An Index Guide to Remembrance of Things Past* by P.A. Spalding, revised by R.H. Cortie, 1975; *The Color-Keys to "À la recherche du temps perdu"* by Allan H. Pasco, 1976; *Proust* by Patrick Brady, 1977; *Proustian Space* by Georges Poulet, translated by Elliott Coleman, 1977; *Proust's Additions: The Making of "À la recherche du temps perdu"* by Alison Winton, 2 vols., 1977; *Proust, Jealousy, Knowledge*, 1978, and *Freud, Proust and Lacan: Theory as Fiction*, 1987, both by Malcolm Bowie; *Metaphoric Narration* by Inge Karalus Crosman, 1978; *Humour in the Works of Marcel Proust* by Maya Slater, 1979; *Chronology and Time in À la recherche du temps perdu* by Gareth H. Steel, 1979; *Marcel Proust and the Strategy of Reading* by Walter Kasell, 1980; *Proust and the Art of Love: The Aesthetics of Sexuality in the Life, Times, and Art of Marcel Proust* by J.E. Rivers, 1980; *The Maladies of Marcel Proust: Doctors and Disease in His Life and Work* by Bernard Straus, 1980; *Proust's Recherche: A Psychoanalytic Interpretation* by Randolph Splitter, 1981; *A Proust Dictionary* by Maxine Arnold Vogely, 1981; *Proust: Collected Essays on the Writer and His Art* by J.M. Cocking, 1982; *The Shape and Style of Proust's Novel* by John Porter Houston, 1982; *Marcel Proust: A Study in the Quality of Awareness* by Edward J. Hughes, 1983; *A Guide to Proust* by Terence Kilmartin, 1983, revised by Joanna Kilmartin, 1992; *Proust* by Derwent May, 1983; *Thresholds: A Study of Proust* by Gerda Blumenthal, 1984; *The Reading of Proust* by David R. Ellison, 1984; *Proustian Optics of Clothes: Mirrors, Masks and Mores* by Diana Festa-McCormick, 1984; *The Quest for Proust* by André Maurois, 1984; *Proust and Musil: The Novel as Research Instrument* by Gene M. Moore, 1985; *Proust: Human Separateness and the Longing for Union* by Ilham Dilman, 1986; *Writing and Fantasy in Proust: La Place de la Madeleine* by Serge Doubrovsky, 1986; *Marcel Proust* edited by Barbara J. Bucknall, 1987; *The Oak in the Acorn: On Remembrance of Things Past, and on Teaching Proust, Who Will Never Learn* by Howard Nemerov, 1987; *The Birth of À la recherche du temps perdu* by Anthony Pugh, 1987; *Marcel Proust* by Philip Thody, 1987; *Beckett and Proust* by Nicholas Zurbrugg, 1988; *Proust and Venice* by Peter Collier, 1989; *Proust: The Critical Heritage* edited by Leighton Hodson, 1989; *Proust as Musician* by Jean-Jacques Nattiez, translated by Derrick Puffett, 1989; *Proust: Swann's Way* by Sheila Stern, 1989; *The Book of Proust* by Philippe Michel Thiriet, 1989; *Proust: The Creative Silence* by Angelo Caranfa, 1990; *The Invisible Middle Term in Proust's À la recherche du temps perdu* by Roxanne Hanney, 1990; *Proust: A Biography* by Ronald Hayman, 1990; *Proust and the Text as Macrometaphor* by Lois Marie Jaeck, 1990; *Around Proust* by Richard E. Goodkin, 1991; *The Proustian Fabric: Associations of Memory* by Christine McDonald, 1991; *The Proustian Quest* by William C. Carter, 1992; *Proust: Philosophy of the Novel* by Vincent Descombes, 1993; *Postmodern Proust* by Margaret E. Gray, 1993; *Present Past: Modernity and the Memory Crisis* by Richard Terdiman, 1993; *Proust and the Sense of Time* by Julia Kristeva, translated by Stephen Bann, 1993; *History and Ideology in Proust: A la recherche du temps perdu and the Third French Republic* by Michael Sprinker, 1994; *The Morality of Proust: An Inaugural Lecture Delivered before the University of Oxford on 25 November 1993* by Malcolm Bowie, 1994; *Marcel Proust: A l'ombre des jeunes filles en fleurs* by Leighton Hodson, 1994; *Reading Proust: In Search of the Wolf Fish* by Maria Paganini, translated by Caren Litherland with Kathryn Milun, 1994; *Proust and the Victorians: The Lamp of Memory* by Robert Fraser, 1994; *Proust: A la recherche du temps perdu* by Richard Bales, 1995; *Proust's Self-reader: The Pursuit of Literature as Privileged Communication* by Phillip Bailey, 1997; *The Year of Reading Proust: A Memoir in Real Time* by Phyllis Rose, 1997; *Processes of Literary Creation: Flaubert and Proust* by Marion Schmid, 1998; *Proust among the Stars* by Malcolm Bowie, 1998; *The Translation of Memories: Recollections of the Young Proust* by P.F. Prestwich, 1999; *Marcel Proust* by Edmund White, 1999; *Proust's Lesbianism* by Elisabeth Ladenson, 1999; *Proust: The Body and Literary Form* by Michael R. Finn, 1999; *Marcel Proust* by Jean-Yves Tadié, translated by Euan Cameron, 2000; *Proustian Passions: The Uses of Self-justification for A la recherche du temps perdu* by Ingrid Wassenaar, 2000; *Proust and Signs: The Complete Text* by Gilles Deleuze, translated by Richard Howard, 2000; *Proust's Gods: Christian and Mythological Figures of Speech in the Works of Marcel Proust* by Margaret Topping, 2000; *Science and Structure in Proust's A la recherche du temps perdu* by Nicola Luckhurst, 2000; *Proust's Way: A Field Guide to In Search of Lost Time* by Roger Shattuck, 2000; *Marcel Proust: A Life* by William C. Carter, 2000; *Proust in the Power of Photography* by Brassaï, translated by Richard Howard, 2001; *The Writings of the Young Marcel Proust (1885–1900): An Ideological Critique* by Frank Rosengarten, 2001.

*   *   *

To some of his earliest critics, Marcel Proust appeared as the novelist-heir of Balzac, as the artist bent upon painting the huge fresco of an age in French history. Today the literary ancestors appear more numerous, and the critics are beginning to estimate how much he owes to Chateaubriand, Nerval, Baudelaire, and Mallarmé. These would seem to be the writers who taught Proust something concerning the art of transfiguring objects and human beings, the art of selecting and magnifying, which is the art of transfiguration.

By comparison with the traditional 19th-century novel, *À la recherche du temps perdu* (*Remembrance of Things Past* or *In Search of Lost Time*) seems a new form in which the psychological analysis is far more developed, but is not conclusive, not dogmatic. The patterns of human existence are not clear in Proust. So many mysteries remain after the psychological exploration of the characters, that they end by bearing some resemblance to allegories. Proust is a secretive writer. Despite the elaborate analysis of scenes and characters, we never learn his complete thought about the significance of a scene or his complete understanding of a personality. The novel as a whole is esoteric, and the countless critics of Proust tend to be exegetes in their effort to explain the allegory, to pierce the secret of Proust and of his work.

Proust believed that the self a man exhibits in his daily habits, in his social life, in his vices, is artificial and even false. His real self is not easily exhibited. It is inner and concealed. If the man is a writer, it will be exhibited in his books. Far more than in the labourious and repetitious biographies of Marcel Proust, he is visible in his own novel. His real self is meticulously described in the three major cycles of the novel, all of which engage in different ways the personality of the protagonist Marcel: the cycle of Swann, first, where we see the boy as an admirer of Swann the aesthete, the connoisseur of art, and the father of Gilberte. Marcel the social being is portrayed in the cycle of the Guermantes, especially in his relationship with the duchesse Oriane and the baron Charlus. The third cycle, that of Albertine, is Marcel in love, going through all the tortured phases of love we associate with Proust.

Through the years of more than a half century, the main character of Proust, this Marcel, has taken on the dimensions of a hero, of an initiate whom we watch being submitted to trials and to tests. The hierarchy of society, the various circles of the Guermantes world, are temptations of social power, tests of endurance and skill, related to all the pleasures of worldliness. One after the other, Marcel savours each, is disillusioned, and passes on to the next. Before he leaves it, he sees its moral defects and its trivialities. In his quest for love, Marcel also passes through a series of tests and disillusionments. His love as a boy for the young girl Gilberte, his love as an adolescent for the older woman Oriane, his infatuation for Mlle. Stermaria, and finally his long painful suffering and jealousy over Albertine, represent initiatory degrees of love and passion. Here there is no real triumph for the initiate. The Proustian hero in love is either vanquished, or simply outlives his love, as in the case of Gilberte.

These tests, the initiations to the world and to love, are the great scenes in Proust's novel, when Marcel discovers the key to the one blessing in which he can believe. The title of the last volume, *Le Temps retrouvé (Time Regained)*, is in reality the recapturing of a lost vocation. It is the writer's vocation we learned of in "Combray," when Marcel's father discouraged his son from thinking of such a vocation, when Norpois, his father's dinner guest, encouraged him, and when Bergotte, encountered a bit later at Mme. Swann's luncheon, incited him to reconsider the vocation.

In the careful choice he made of themes and episodes, Proust was able to construct an entire world, namely the world encompassed by the sentiments of Marcel. We are present at the genesis of a sentiment and then we watch it rise up and develop, slowly diminish, and finally die. The ego of Marcel is a series of successive egos: Marcel in love with Gilberte is one self; Marcel infatuated with the duchesse de Guermantes is another being. He is a son, a grandson, a friend of Bergotte, an admirer of Mme. Swann, a friend of Elstir, a friend of Robert de Saint-Loup, a young friend of Charlus, an intimate friend of the duc and duchesse de Guermantes. He is especially described as the unhappy lover of Albertine. Time is consumed and lost as Marcel plays each of these roles.

Through him we watch the disappearance of love and social intercourse and time. In Marcel's sentimental life we feel the uselessness of everything that time stamps with its death. A sentiment, by its very nature, cannot be fixed outside of time. It is characterized by an inexplicable beginning, by development, and by dissolution.

The universe of Proust is the analysis of these sentiments, of Marcel living through various states of being, of enacting a series of selves in which as hero he is despondent. He is unable to hold on to any sentiment or any being because of whom the sentiment has

deepened. In this sense, Marcel is the victim of an abiding pessimism. But this pessimism about life in the deaths and resurrections of its metamorphoses, is contradicted by the optimism of Marcel the narrator and by Proust the writer. The narration of the book is a transfiguration. It is the immobilization of what changes. Life, as described by Marcel, is proliferation, both continuous and mortal. But this proliferation, in the hands of an artist, has a second life.

The temperament of Proust is everywhere visible in his book: the man's intensity of feeling, his subjectivism, his own personal adventure on this earth. But Proust the writer was the technician who adapted all of that to the laws and the architecture of the work. His depiction of society and his analysis of the heart were revealed to him not as the man living in society and suffering from his sentiments, but as the writer who, alone in his room, filled the large *cahiers* with the writing that constituted his search for the absolute beyond time.

—Wallace Fowlie

See the essays on *Against Sainte-Beuve* and *Remembrance of Things Past*.

PRUDENTIUS, Aurelius Clemens

Born: Calagurris (Calahorra), northern Spain, in AD 348. **Career:** Variously a soldier, lawyer, and judge, then high official at the court of the Emperor; abandoned his successful administrative career to write Christian poetry. **Died:** After AD 405.

PUBLICATIONS

Collections

[Works], edited by J. Bergman, in *Corpus Scriptorum Ecclesiasticarum Latinarum*, vol. 61. 1926; also edited by M.P. Cunningham, in *Corpus Christianorum Series Latina*, vol. 126, 1966; edited and translated by H.J. Thomson [Loeb Edition], 2 vols., 1949–53, and M. Lavarenne [Budé Edition], 4 vols., 1955–63.

Works

Liber Cathemerinon [Hymns for the Day], as *Hymns of Prudentius*, translated by R.M. Pope. 1905.
Hamartigenia [The Origin of Sin], translated by J. Stam. 1940.
[Selected Poems], translated by Jack Lindsay, in *Song of a Falling World*. 1948.
The Poems, translated by Sister M. Clement Eagan. 1965.
Hymns of Prudentius: The Cathemerinon, or, The Daily Round, translated by David R. Slavitt. 1996.

*

Critical Studies: *Vergil in the Works of Prudentius* by Albertus Mahoney, 1934; *The Poet Prudentius* by Bernard M. Peebles, 1951; *Prudentius' Psychomachia: A Reexamination* by Macklin Smith, 1976; *Deified Virtues, Demonic Vices and Descriptive Allegory in*

Prudentius's Psychomachia by Kenneth R. Haworth, 1980; *Allegory and Poetics: The Structure and Imagery of Prudentius's Psychomachia* by S. Georgia Nugent, 1985; *A Poetics of Transformation: Prudentius and Classical Mythology* by M. Malamud, 1989; *Prudentius on the Martyrs* by Anne-Marie Palmer, 1989; *Poetry and the Cult of the Martyrs: The Liber Peristephanon of Prudentius* by Michael Roberts, 1993.

*   *   *

Prudentius, the most prolific and enigmatic of the Latin poets of the 4th century, has always held a place in the classical canon, due to his superior metrical skills (ranking on this score with Catullus and Horace) and his comprehensive engagement of the classical tradition. However, he has most often been viewed, in the context of classical poetry, as a vestige of classicism's decline and a symbol of the deadening effect Christianity had upon literary art in the West. Needless to say, such views are aberrant in that they apply anachronistic standards to Prudentius' poetry, which, when examined, reveals a radical, even experimental poet, testing the limits of his craft in rapidly changing literary and cultural milieux.

A general sense of the status Prudentius would assign to poetry is articulated in his autobiographical "Praefatio" ("Preface"), written in AD 404–05 to introduce an edition of his poems. In it, Prudentius concludes his life's résumé with an injunction to his soul to renounce foolishness. There follows the means by which such a renunciation can be achieved, a description of his various poetic works, each of which, taking up a different aspect of Christian life, forms the counterpart to his own life as recounted. His soul's liberation will be achieved not only through Christian piety, Prudentius asserts, but also through the power of writing to redeem him. This is adumbrated in the final lines of the "Preface," where a pun on the word "free" (*liber*), which can also mean "book" in Latin if pronounced with a short "i," affirms this position in playful terms. Given the debates that raged in the 4th century over the status accorded to writing (one thinks of Paulinus of Nola's attitudes towards poetry and Augustine's consideration of the plurality of meaning in Confessions 12), Prudentius' "Preface" represents the poet's first salvo in a coherent poetic project that articulates the role and status of poetry in the larger fabric of Christian culture, then still in formation.

If his "Preface" is bold in the ways it asserts the power of poetry, Prudentius' *Liber Cathemerinon* [Hymns for the Day] (AD 404), strikes out in other directions. Many of the hymns are extraordinary examples of poetic texturing and give expression to the ways in which late antique poets were interested in expanding and sometimes challenging generic distinction. In them, a panoply of classical poets are adduced verbally, their voices, now lyric, now epic, now elegiac, merged into a hybrid Christian lyricism. Owing to their length, these hymns are less likely to have been performed than read, heightening their generic interest and constituting the bold advancement of hymnody into the mainstream of Christian lyric.

Bold, too, are the poet's personal visions revealed in the dialogues he imagines in these lyrics. In the "Hymnus ad Galli Cantum" ("Hymn at Dawn"), for example, the distance of God's exalted divinity is mediated through the poet's depiction of nature's soft rhythms and recurring patterns. The mediation of symbols in the normal sense is challenged, however, for when the poem declares that the voice of the rooster, the rising of the sun, and the spreading of the warm rays of fresh light are not symbols but "truth itself," the consonance of Christ's humanity and divinity are asserted in the life of the poet who would celebrate them. As the lyricist's articulation is affirmed, the distinction between the symbols of his poetry and the presence of his God grows evanescent.

Seemingly more theological than poetical in orientation, the *Apotheosis* [Divinity of Christ] (AD 404), a consideration of heretical doctrines offered in the context of Catholic orthodoxy, and the *Hamartigenia* [The Origin of Sin] (AD 404), a discourse on the nature of sin, are both supremely accomplished in their metre and command of classical Latinity. Seldom analysed in the larger context of Prudentius' poetry, the *Apotheosis* still awaits its modern critic. It has, however, been demonstrated (by M. Malamud, *A Poetics of Transformation*), that the *Hamartigenia* manipulates Roman mythology in subtle, profoundly original, and sometimes subversive ways, and that it, like the "Preface," contains at its conclusion a bold statement of poetic priority, helping to make a case for poetry's place in Christianity's ongoing effort to invent for itself a culture.

One of the ways in which poetry had been used in the past to serve its culture was to praise or blame politicians. Prudentius' epical *Contra orationem Symmachi* [Against the Speech of Symmachus] (AD 404) readily adopts this poetical function for the Christian tradition by taking on the cause of defending the removal of the Altar of Victory from the Roman Senate House, a relic whose privileges had been recently defended by Symmachus, the scion of an eminent patrician family. The debate that raged over the propriety of allowing the Altar of Victory to remain in the Senate sounds modern to the late 20th century, with Catholic zealots defending a unilateral orthodoxy that could brook no difference of opinion, as against the more tolerant pagans, whose eclectic attitude toward faith is best expressed in Symmachus' assertion that "there is more than one way to arrive at the grand secret of God." Many of the most vivid moments in this scathing attack on Roman culture occur when Prudentius uses pagan iconography to its worst advantage in defence of Catholic positions. Near the end of this lengthy poem, for example, a description of the Vestal Virgins, deciding the fate of victims with the turn of their thumbs, links verbally with a moment in Ovid's *Amores* when Ilia rends her hair with the turn of her own thumb. The link with Ovid, evoking Ilia's rape and other morally suspect events in the constellation of her mythology, reinforces the morally questionable bases of Roman culture.

The ways in which Christianity depicted itself in the larger fabric of human experience is given its finest late antique articulation in Prudentius' *Psychomachia* [The War of the Soul] (AD 404), an allegorical epic in which the virtues and vices battle for supremacy. While the adumbration of medieval allegories is an important contribution of this stunning poem, it is also important in the ways it questions the heroes it puts forward through a careful programme of allusion to classical material. Much attention has been paid to this poem, and its superficial consonances have been effectively challenged by a careful attention to the poetry, as opposed to the theology, of its lines (as in S. Georgia Nugent's *Allegory and Poetics*).

The longest of Prudentius' works, *Peristephanon Liber* [Book of Martyrs] (written AD 404), celebrates Christian heroism and mediates many of the thematic concerns of his other poems. Vivid in their descriptions of torture, ritual, sacrifice, and translation from corporal bonds to heavenly bliss, these 14 poems also contain a rich engagement of classical images, themes, and vocabulary, which form the backdrop against which Prudentius conceives of Christian martyrdom. Of many superb moments in these masterpieces, the vivid verbal acknowledgements to Euripides in Poem 14, the "Passio Agnetis" ("Passion of Agnes"), indicate to his students how little they know about the poetic interests, the literary context, or aesthetic practices of a poet whose reputation seems assured, but for reasons that do little justice to the brilliance of the poetic project he would seem to have set for himself or the glorious ways in which he would seem to have achieved it.

—Joseph Pucci

PRUS, Bolesław

Born: Aleksander Głowacki, near Hrubieszów, Poland, 20 August 1847. **Education:** Educated in Lublin, 1856, and in Siedlce and Kielce, from 1861; after uprising finished school in Lublin, 1866; studied mathematics and physics at Szkola Głowna in Warsaw, two years. **Family:** Married his cousin Oktawia Trembińska in 1875. **Career:** Took part in uprising, 1863; injured in battle between Siedlce and Lublin; imprisoned in Lublin; later freed because of youth. Wrote weekly chronicles in *Kurier Warszawski*, from 1874; editor of daily newspaper, *Nowiny*, 1882–83; *Kurier Warszawski* and *Kurier Codzienny*, from 1886; literary journalist, 1884–87; travelled abroad for the first time to Germany, Switzerland, and France in 1895. **Died:** 19 May 1912.

PUBLICATIONS

Collections

Pisma [Writings], edited by Z. Szweykowski. 29 vols., 1948–52.
Kroniki [Chronicles], edited by Z. Szweykowski. 20 vols., 1953–70.
The Sins of Childhood and Other Stories, translated by Bill Johnston. 1996.

Fiction

To i owo [This and That]. 1873.
Kłopoty babuni [Granny's Troubles]. 1874.
Pałac i rudera [The Palace and the Ruin]. 1874.
Dusze w niewoli [Souls in Captivity]. 1877.
Anielka. 1880.
Michałko. 1880.
Antek. 1881.
Katarynka [Organ Grinder]. 1881.
Pierwsze opowiadania [First Stories]. 1881.
Kamizelka [The Waistcoat]. 1882.
Grzechy dzieciństwa [Childhood Sins]. 1883.
Omyłka [The Error]. 1884.
Szkice i obrazki [Etchings and Pictures]. 1885.
Placówka. 1885; translated as *The Outpost*, 1886; also translated by Else Benecke, 1921; as *Ten Morgs of Land*, translated by Christina Rockover Eatus, 1957.
Lalka. 1890; as *The Doll*, translated by David Welsh, 1972, revised by Dariusz Tolczyk and Anna Zaranko, 1996. *Drobiazgi* [The Little Things]. 1891.
Emancypatki [The Emancipated Women]. 1893.
Opowiadania wieczorne [Evening Stories]. 1895.

Faraon. 1897; as *The Pharaoh and the Priest: An Historical Novel of Ancient Egypt*, translated by Jeremiah Curtin, 1910; as *Pharaoh*, translated by Christopher Kasparek, 1991.
Dzieci [Children]. 1908.

*

Critical Studies: *"Lalka" Bolesława Prusa* ["The Doll" of Bolesław Prus] by H. Markiewicz, 1967; *Twórczość Bolesława Prusa* [The Works of Bolesław Prus] by Z. Szweykowski, 2 vols., 1972; *Mlodość Bolesława Prusa* by Krystyna Tokarzówna, 1981; *Studium o "Antku" Prusa, recepcja, konstrukca, konteksty* by Aleksander Wit Labuda, 1982; *To samo ramie* by Zbigniew Wróblewski, 1984; *Nad twórczości a Boleslawa Prusa* by Edward Pieścikowski, 1989.

*   *   *

Bolesław Prus is the most accomplished Polish novelist of the 19th century. His misleadingly simple narrative art has often given rise to serious misunderstanding. Prus was forced by circumstances to interrupt his academic studies, but, through intensive self-education, he became a writer of remarkable erudition and consistency, well-grounded in contemporary philosophy and social science. As a follower of the "organic theory," advocated by the Polish Positivists and modelled on J.S. Mill and Herbert Spencer, he believed in communal welfare, based on economic and scientific progress and cooperation between all social groups. He was consequently hostile to everything that disrupted this evolutionary process, such as national uprisings and radical socialism.

Prus was also a self-conscious novelist and treated writing with considerable concern. This is reflected in his private notes on the craft of fiction and in his literary criticism. His theory of novelistic style, stressing the governing role of concrete words, and the explication of humour as a mode of portraying things simultaneously from two points of view, are among his highly acute observations. Despite close links with the aesthetic positivism of Hippolyte Taine and realistic principles, Prus was fascinated by Romantic individualism, mystery, and attention paid to the coercive force of literary stereotypes. Genuinely committed to factual wisdom, he was also interested in parapsychology and in the power of fear and irrational, subconscious impulses, which precede reasoning and intelligent actions. When, at a later stage, he sought scientific arguments to confirm the existence of Providence, it was a symptomatic attempt to reconcile those diverse inclinations.

Prus was primarily a journalist, well-known for his reports on current affairs in the Polish Kingdom, published throughout his life as the "Weekly Chronicles." These reflected better than fiction his commitment to the social ideas of positivism. His early literary works, commissioned by comic magazines *Mucha* and *Kolce*, consist of facetious sketches and jocular poems. Written under the compelling need for subsistence, they seldom represent great artistic ambitions. Even worse, the image of frivolous entertainer has attached to Prus, obstructing the reception of his serious message. Some of the initial short stories and novellas postulated the ideas of the positivistic "work at the foundation" (*Antek, Michałko*), but this was swiftly expanded into a less didactic and broader approach, which demonstrated a singular combination of humour and sadness, compassion and narrative distance, mystery and everyday detail (*Kamizelka* [The Waistcoat], *Grzechy dzieciństwa* [Childhood Sins]). Prus's emotional involvement, particularly in the case of suffering children (*Katarynka* [Organ Grinder]), has often been compared with that of Charles Dickens.

His first important novel, *Placówka* (*The Outpost*), close to French naturalism in its narrative structure, portrays the stubborn resistance of a Polish peasant to German settlers seeking to buy his land. The author is far removed from the naive idealization of peasantry, which is described with humour and in a satirical vein. Nevertheless, he makes it clear that while the nobility sold their property to foreigners without hesitation, the peasants' religious and conservative attachment to the land of their ancestors became the only "outpost" of Polishness.

Prus's most celebrated novel, *Lalka* (*The Doll*), combines the panoramic picture of Polish society with a love story that reworks the old fable about illusion and disillusion, familiar from Miguel de Cervantes's *Don Quixote* and later reprised by some Polish Romantics. The protagonist, Wokulski, lives in a constant struggle between the idealized vision of his beloved, invigorated by Romantic poems, and the much more sober assessment of the real woman of his admiration. The cyclic course of events, along with skilful manipulation of the point of view, eventually leads to the uncharacteristic open ending. The main hero, as a man of imagination and great emotion, resembles Romantic individuals and like them is opposed to the surrounding mediocrity of human marionettes, similar to Thackeray's "puppets" in *Vanity Fair*. Broader concerns for the future of modern civilization in a world of disappearing values and growing materialism offers *The Doll* another universal dimension.

Emancypatki [The Emancipated Women] is the longest of all Prus's novels. Its episodic structure leads to the relative independence of the four major parts. The way the author portrays women's attempt to equal men in society discloses his hostility towards their emancipation, based on the traditional conviction that femininity depends on compassion and motherhood and, consequently, involves a different role. While the "angelic" icon of Miss Brzeska, the heroine, is hardly convincing, Prus once again shows his mastery of social satire, providing a new gallery of human marionettes, who, even more than in *The Doll*, are distressing rather than entertaining in their selfishness and hatred of anything that exceeds mediocrity.

Faraon (*The Pharaoh and the Priest*) is Prus's only historical novel. Set in the ancient Egypt of the legendary Ramses XIII, it portrays the state mechanism in action and poses questions about the nature of historical progress. This accounts for some of the novel's anachronism, but it is also the result of the inadequacy of Egyptology at that time and the author's own mistakes. The overall structure of the Bildungsroman allowed Prus to compose the history of a prince whose genuine compassion and great natural talent was not matched by rational assessment and proper learning; therefore he lost a battle with his powerful opponents, the priests. They implemented his courageous project of social reform but, on their way forward, trampled upon an honest and well-intentioned individual. Prus's vision of historical progress is therefore depressing. His study of Egyptian society is less original. He simply followed the positivistic principle of the organic work and of mutual cooperation between all social groups. This sober analysis exists alongside, however, the Romantic atmosphere of mystery and adventure, the human passions, follies and failings, which constitute this compelling story.

Prus's last novel, *Dzieci* [Children], presents a somewhat naive assessment of the Russian Revolution of 1905, and its journalistic zeal hardly matches the complexities of his previous novels. Those novels, however (*The Doll* in particular), account for the writer's

exceptional position in the history of Polish fiction. Transforming the traditional art of realism, he played for Poland the role of Flaubert.

—Stanislaw Eile

PUIG, Manuel

Born: General Villegas, Argentina, 28 December 1932. Moved to Buenos Aires, 1946. **Education:** Educated at an American boarding school, Buenos Aires, from 1946; studied architecture, 1950, then philosophy, from 1951, at the University of Buenos Aires; studied film directing, with Vittorio De Sica, and screenwriting at the Centro Sperimentale di Cinematografia, Rome, 1956. **Career:** Travelled and undertook various jobs in Europe, 1956–63: translator and teacher of English and Spanish, London and Rome, 1956–57, dishwasher and language tutor, London and Stockholm, 1958–59, assistant film director and sub-title translator, Rome (Cinecittà), Paris, and Buenos Aires, 1957–61; moved to New York, 1963, and obtained post as clerk for Air France, 1963–67; returned to Buenos Aires, 1967; visiting lecturer, Columbia University, New York; based in Brazil, 1973–75, New York, 1976–80, in New York and Rio de Janeiro, 1980–89; settled in Cuernavaca, Mexico, 1989. **Awards:** Curzio Malaparte prize (Italy), 1966; San Sebastian Festival jury prize, 1978. **Died:** 22 July 1990.

PUBLICATIONS

Fiction

La traición de Rita Hayworth. 1968; as *Betrayed by Rita Hayworth*, translated by Suzanne Jill Levine, 1971.
The Buenos Aires Affair, translated by Suzanne Jill Levine. 1968; *The Buenos Aires Affair* (in Spanish), 1973.
Boquitas pintadas. 1969; as *Heartbreak Tango: A Serial*, translated by Suzanne Jill Levine, 1973.
El beso de la mujer araña. 1976; as *Kiss of the Spider Woman*, translated by Thomas Colchie, 1979; translated by Allan Baker and Ronald Christ in *Kiss of the Spider Woman and Two Other Plays*, 1994.
Pubis angelical. 1979; as *Pubis angelical*, translated by Elena Brunet, 1986.
Maldición eterna a quien lea estas páginas. 1980; as *Eternal Curse on the Reader of These Pages*, translated anonymously, 1982.
Sangre de amor correspondido. 1982; as *Blood of Requited Love*, translated by Jan L. Grayson, 1984.
Cae la noche tropical. 1988; as *Tropical Night Falling*, translated by Suzanne Jill Levine, 1991.

Plays

Farsa del poeta loco. 1965.
Bajo un manto de estrellas. With *El beso de la mujer araña*, 1983; as *Under a Mantle of Stars*, translated by Ronald Christ, 1985; revised translation, 1993.
El beso de la mujer araña, from his own novel. With *Bajo un manto de estrellas*, 1983; as *Kiss of the Spider Woman*, translated by

Michael Feingold, in *Drama Contemporary: Latin America*, edited by George W. Woodyard and Marion Peter Holt, 1986; also translated by Allan Baker, 1987.

La cara del villano; Recuerdo de Tijuana (screenplays). 1985.

Misterio del ramo de rosas (produced in English, 1987). 1987; as *Mystery of the Rose Bouquet*, translated by Allan Baker, 1988.

Screenplays: *Boquitas Pintadas* (adaptation), 1974; *El lugar sin limites* (adaptation), 1978; *La cara del villano*, 1985; *Recuerdo de Tijuana*, 1985.

Other

Buenos Aires, cuándo será el día que me quieras: Conversaciones con Manuel Puig, with Armando Almada Roche. 1992.

*

Critical Studies: "Manuel Puig's Chronicles of Provincial Life" by Alfred J. MacAdam, in *Revista Hispánica Moderna*, 36, 1970–71; "Manuel Puig and the Uses of Nostalgia" by David William Foster, in *Latin American Literary Review*, 1(1), 1972; "Dynamic Correlations in *Heartbreak Tango*" by Judith Weiss, in *Latin American Literary Review*, 3(5), 1974; "Castration: Artifices: Notes on the Writing of Manuel Puig" by Alicia Bronsky, in *Georgia Review*, 29, 1975; *Espejos: La textura cinemática en La traición de Rita Hayworth* by René A. Campos, 1981; "Manuel Puig's *Heartbreak Tango*: Women and Mass Culture" by Ellen McCraken, in *Latin American Literary Review*, 18, 1981; *La narrativa de Manuel Puig* by Juan Manuel Garcia Ramos, 1982; "For a New (Psychological) Novel in the Works of Manuel Puig" by Stephanie Merrim, in *Novel*, 17(2), 1984; *Manuel Puig: Montaje y alteridad del sujeto* by Roberto Echavarren and Enrique Giordano, 1986; *Suspended Fictions: Reading Novels by Manuel Puig* by Lucille Kerr, 1987; *El discurso utópico de la sexualidad en Manuel Puig* by Elías Miguel Muñoz, 1987; *The Necessary Dream: A Study of the Novels of Manuel Puig*, 1988, and *Impossible Choices: The Implications of the Cultural References in the Novels of Manuel Puig*, 1993, both by Pamela Bacarisse; *Mitos personales y mitos colectivos en las novelas de Manuel Puig* by J. Corbatta, 1988; *Pop Culture into Art: The Novels of Manuel Puig* by Norman Layers, 1988; *Manuel Puig: Un renovador de la novela argentina* by Olga Steinberg de Kaplan, 1989; *Manuel Puig* edited by Juan Manuel García-Ramos, 1991; *A Marxist Reading of Fuentes, Vargas Llosa and Puig* by Victor Manuel Durán, 1993; *Manuel Puig* by Jonathan Tittler, 1993; *Manuel Puig and Spider Woman: His Life and Fictions* by Suzanne Jill Levine, 2000.

*   *   *

The themes of Manuel Puig's novels include the debilitating effects of stereotyped sexual roles, the psychological influence of the language of popular culture (films, songs, soap operas, serial novels), the gap between the illusion presented in these forms and the reality of institutionalized domination, and the inadequacy of the two major intellectual theories of the 20th century (psychoanalysis and Marxism) to provide an adequate framework for an individualized pursuit of happiness. Above all, Puig shows how language, in its various established structures, controls and inhibits freedom of thought and understanding.

Puig's discomfort with the potentially manipulative effects of third-person narration led to his innovative use in his novels of unattributed dialogue, monologue, letters, and the second-hand language of mass culture. The effect of the absent narrator is that the process of reading is emphasized as the reader attempts to interpret and evaluate characters without the aid of the narrator's guiding voice. The characters are generally involved in psychologically realistic situations and the reader's own attitudes and worldview become part of the interpretive process. In *La traición de Rita Hayworth* (*Betrayed by Rita Hayworth*), Hollywood films of the 1930s provide an escape for a mother and her "different" son from the unrelieved machismo of the Argentinian pampa. The novel is constructed around a series of seemingly overheard voices, in which family life is portrayed as confining for both miles and females. The movies portray an idyllic male/female relationship that is non-existent in the characters' surroundings, who ultimately feel betrayed by this by promise of perfection.

Boquitas pintadas (*Heartbreak Tango*) imitates the conventions of the serial romance: it is written in melodramatic episodes which end in suspense, and characters' dialogue is followed by their own thoughts printed in italics. The story centres on the influence of a Don Juan-type character on the various women for whom they sacrifice themselves. This Don Juan, however, is dying of tuberculosis, and he and the other characters are not the idealized types of the romance, but rather more akin to the readers of this kind of fiction. The inspiration they draw from the words of tangos and boleros causes them to misread reality and make the wrong choices in their lives. The imagery of disease (tuberculosis, cancer, polio) runs through the novel.

The Buenos Aires Affair, originally banned in Spain and Argentina, is a parody of a detective novel. A woman disappears; she turns up bound and gagged; the police receive a phone call. But instead of there being a crime, a man and the woman are enjoying a sado-masochistic game. Reader expectations are overturned as the concept of restored order usual to a detective novel is replaced by the idea of society's intrusion in the private sexual lives of its citizens.

In *El beso de la mujer araña* (*Kiss of the Spider Woman*), a prison cell is the setting for a difficult relationship between a homosexual hedonist and a Marxist revolutionary. Because at first they share little common ground, the homosexual narrates films to the Marxist in an attempt to pass the long hours of confinement, who at first resists, but then becomes increasingly involved in the stories. As the characters identify with and judge the film characters, the reader does the same with the characters in the novel.

In *Pubis angelical* Puig uses the conventions of romantic adventure and science fiction to expose the sexual exploitation of three women (who all physically resemble the film star, Hedy Lamarr) from three different periods. "The Mistress" is a film star of the 1930s, whose life closely resembles that of the real actress; Ana is a contemporary middle-class Argentinian who is dying of cancer, and whose revolutionary lover wants her to risk her life for his cause; W218 is the same archetypal woman in the future—she has sex with elderly men as a service to the State. The *pubis angelical* is the image of an unsexed angel whose appearance ends man's struggle for dominance over woman's body.

In *Maldición eterna a quien lea estas páginas* (*Eternal Curse on the Reader of These Pages*), a disillusioned young North American leftist cares for a wheelchair-bound prison escapee from Argentina. The public and private, personal and political spheres converge as a father-son relationship develops between the two characters. As in *Kiss of the Spider Woman*, this novel questions the nature of political commitment and its relationship to unresolved psychological conflicts.

Sangre de amor correspondido (*Blood of Requited Love*) is set in rural Brazil ten years after two young lovers of unequal social status have been separated by their parents. The narrator who seems at first to be an omniscient third person, turns out to be the young man, Josemar, telling his own story in an unreliable third-person form. The reader, then, has to decide when he is telling the truth and when he is inventing himself and reality using a stock of societal cliches. Other versions of events are presented through the consciousness of the woman. Ultimately the reader sees that both characters have been victimized by the values and images of their society.

Cae la noche tropical (*Tropical Night Falling*) also takes place in Brazil. Two elderly Argentinian sisters converse, and then, when one moves away, correspond about their families and neighbours, At first they seem to fit the stereotype of interfering gossips. As the novel progresses, however, their generosity and true concern about others makes them seem almost saintly. Themes include obsessive love, life in exile, social responsibility, illness, and death.

Puig said that his novels were a direct reconstruction of reality. The second-hand discourses of his characters show that "reality" is often a partial view represented in an ideological construct that may not reflect the inner self. In other words, language may possess us rather than the other way around.

—Barbara P. Fulks

See the essay on *Kiss of the Spider Woman*.

PUSHKIN, Aleksandr (Sergeevich)

Born: Moscow, Russia, 26 May 1799. **Education:** Educated at home, and at Imperial lycée in Tsarskoe Selo, near St. Petersburg, 1811–17. **Family:** Married Natalia Goncharova in 1831. **Career:** Civil servant, St. Petersburg, 1817–20; exiled in southern Russia and Pskov province for his unpublished political poems, 1820–26; returned to St. Petersburg, 1826; fought with the Russian army against the Turks, in Transcaucasia, 1829; editor, *Sovremennik* [The Contemporary], 1836–37. **Died:** (in duel) 29 January 1837.

PUBLICATIONS

Collections

The Works: Lyrics, Narrative Poems, Folk Tales, Prose, edited by Avrahm Yarmolinsky. 1939.
Complete Prose Tales, translated by Gillon R. Aitken. 1966; revised edition, 1978.
Sobranie sochinenii [Collected Works]. 6 vols., 1969.
Selected Works, translated by Irina Zheleznova and others. 1974.
Polnoe sobranie sochinenii [Complete Works], edited by B.V. Tomachevskim. 10 vols., 1977–79.
Izbrannye sochineniia [Selected Works], edited by G. Makogonenko. 2 vols., 1978.
Complete Prose Fiction, edited and translated by Paul Debreczeny. 1983.
Collected Narrative and Lyrical Poetry, translated by Walter Arndt. 1984.

Izbrannye sochineniia [Selected Works], edited by G.I. Belen'kii, and others. 1990.
Izbrannye sochineniia [Selected Works], edited by V.A. Popov. 1992.
Tales of Belkin and Other Prose Writing, translated by Ronald Wilks. 1998.
The Little Tragedies, translated by Nancy K. Anderson. 2000.

Verse

Stikhotvoreniia [Poetry]. 1826; revised edition, 4 vols., 1829–35, and later editions.
Evgenii Onegin. 1831; translated as *Eugene Onegin*, 1881; also translated by Vladimir Nabokov, 1964, revised editions, 1976, 1981; Charles Johnston, 1977; Walter Arndt, revised edition, 1981; S.D.P. Clough (bilingual edition), 1988; James E. Falen, 1990; A.D.P. Briggs, 1992.
Selections from the Poems, edited by Ivan Panin. 1888; as *Poems*, 1888.
Pushkin Threefold: Narrative, Lyric, Polemic, and Ribald Verse, translated by Walter Arndt. 1972.
The Bronze Horseman: Selected Poems, translated by D.M. Thomas. 1982.
Narrative Poems by Pushkin and Lermontov, translated by Charles Johnston. 1983.
Epigrams and Satirical Verse, edited and translated by Cynthia Whittaker. 1984.
Bakhchisaraiskii fontan, as *The Bakchesarian Fountain*, translated by William D. Lewis. 1987.

Plays

Boris Godunov (produced 1870). 1831; translated as *Boris Godunov*, in *Translations from Pushkin*, 1899; also translated and adapted by D.M. Thomas, 1985.
Motsart i Sal'eri (produced 1832). 1831; as *Mozart and Salieri*, in *Translations from Pushkin*, 1899; also translated by Charles Johnston, 1982; Antony Wood, in *Mozart and Salieri: The Little Tragedies*, 1983; also translated by Rebecca Scott in *Little Russian Classics: Karamzin, Pushkin and Turgenev*, 1993.
Pir vo vremia chumy (produced 1899). 1832; as *The Feast During the Plague*, in *The Little Tragedies*, 1946.
Skupoi rytsar' (produced 1832). 1836; as *The Covetous Knight*, in *The Works*, 1939; as *The Miserly Knight*, translated by Antony Wood, in *Mozart and Salieri: The Little Tragedies*, 1983.
Kamennii gost' (produced 1847). 1839; as *The Statue Guest*, in *Translations from Pushkin*, 1899; as *The Stone Guest*, in *The Works*, 1939; also translated by Antony Wood, in *Mozart and Salieri: The Little Tragedies*, 1983.
Mozart and Salieri: The Little Tragedies (includes *Mozart and Salieri; The Miserly Knight; The Stone Guest; The Feast During the Plague*), translated by Antony Wood. 1983; revised edition, 1987.

Fiction

Povesti pokoinogo I.P. Belkina. 1830; as *Tales of P. Bielkin*, translated by Evgenia Schimanskaya and M. Elizabeth Gow, 1947; as *The Tales of Belkin, and The History of Goryukhino*, translated by Gillon R. Aitken and David Budgen, 1983.
Pikovaia dama. 1834; as *The Queen of Spades*, with *The Captain's Daughter*, 1858; also translated by Mrs Sutherland Edwards,

1894; J.E. Pouterman and C. Breurton, 1929; Alan Myers in *The Queen of Spades, and Other Stories*, 1997.

Kapitanskaia dochka. 1836; as *The Captain's Daughter*, translated by G.C. Hebbe, 1846; as *Marie: A Story of Russian Love*, translated by M. Zielinska, 1877.

Dubrovskii (fragment). 1841.

Russian Romances. 1875.

The Captain's Daughter and Other Stories (includes ''The Captain's Daughter''; ''The Queen of Spades''; ''Dubrovsky''; ''Peter the Great's Negro''; ''The Station-Master''), translated by Natalie Duddington. 1933.

The Queen of Spades and Other Stories (includes ''The Queen of Spades''; ''The Negro of Peter the Great''; ''Dubrovsky''; ''The Captain's Daughter''), translated by Rosemary Edmonds. 1962.

The Golden Cockerel and Other Stories, translated by James Reeves. 1969.

Pushkin's Fairy Tales, translated by Janet Dalley. 1978.

Two Pushkin Tales (includes ''Dubrovsky''; ''History of the Village of Goryukhino''), translated by S.D.P. Clough. 1985.

Russian Tales, translated by Peter Tempest, Avril Pyman, and Louis Zellikov. 1990.

The Captain's Daughter and Other Stories (includes ''The Captain's Daughter''; ''The Blackamoor of Peter the Great''; ''The Tales of the Late Ivan Petrovich''; ''Dubrovskii''; ''Egyptian Nights''; ''The Queen of Spades''), translated by Paul Debreczeny. 1992.

Other

Puteshestvie v Arzrum [The Journey to Arzrum]. 1836.

Letters, translated by J. Thomas Shaw. 3 vols., 1963.

Letters. 1964.

The Critical Prose, edited and translated by Carl R. Proffer. 1970.

Pushkin on Literature, edited by Tatiana Wolff. 1971.

Secret Journal 1836–1837. 1986.

The Complete Collection of Drawings, edited by S. Fomichev. 1999.

The History of Pugachev, translated by Earl Sampson. 2001.

*

Critical Studies: *Pushkin and Russian Literature* by Janko Lavrin, 1947; *Pushkin's Bronze Horseman: The Story of a Masterpiece* by W. Lednecki, 1955; *Pushkin* by E.J. Simmons, 1964; *Pushkin: A Biography* by David Magarshack, 1967; *Pushkin* by Walter Vickery, 1970; *Pushkin: A Comparative Commentary* by John Bayley, 1971; *Pushkin* by Henri Troyat, 1974; *Pushkin and His Sculptural Myth* by Roman Jakobson, 1975; *Pushkin, Mickiewicz and the Overcoming of Romanticism* by Monika A. Dudli, 1976; *Russian Views of Pushkin* edited and translated by D.J. Richards and C.R.S. Cockrell, 1976; *Pushkin: A Critical Study*, 1982, and *Eugene Onegin*, 1992, both by A.D.P. Briggs; *The Sacred Lyre: Essays on the Life and Work of Alexander Pushkin* by D.D. Blagoi, 1982; *Pushkin and Mérimée as Short Story Writers: Two Different Approaches to Description and Detail* by Karl-Heinrich Barsch, 1983; *The Other Pushkin: A Study of Alexander Pushkin's Prose Fiction* by Paul Debreczeny, 1983; *Pushkin's Egyptian Nights: The Biography of a Work* by Leslie O'Bell, 1984; *Ice and Flame: Aleksandr Pushkin's Eugene Onegin* by J. Douglas Clayton, 1985; *The Contexts of Alexandr Pushkin* edited by Peter I. Barta and Ulrich Goegel, 1988; *Distant Pleasures: Pushkin and the Writing of Exile* by Stephanie Sandler, 1989; *Strolls with Puskin* by Abram Tertz, translated by Catharine Theimer Nepomnyashchy and

Slava I. Yastremski, 1993; *Puskin's The Queen of Spades* by Neil Cornwell, 1993; *Puskin Today*, edited by David M. Bethea, 1993; *Pushkin and Romantic Fashion: Fragment, Elegy, Orient, Irony* by Monika Greenleaf, 1994; *Pushkin: The Man and His Age* by Robin Edmonds, 1995; *Pushkin's Mozart and Salieri: Themes, Character, Sociology* by Robert Reid, 1995; *The Myth of A.S. Pushkin in Russia's Silver Age: M.O. Gershenzon, Pushkinist* by Brian Horowitz, 1996; *A Lemmatized Concordance to ''The Captain's Daughter'' of A.S. Pushkin*, edited by Yasuo Urai, 1997; *Pushkin's Evgenii Onegin* by S. Dalton-Brown, 1997; *Social Functions of Literature: Alexander Pushkin and Russian Culture* by Paul Debreczeny, 1997; *Pushkin* by Elaine Feinstein, 1998; *Realizing Metaphors: Alexander Pushkin and the Life of the Poet* by David M. Bethea, 1998; *Pushkin's The Bronze Horseman* by Andrew Kahn, 1998; *Pushkin and the Creative Process* by Brett Cooke, 1998; *Pushkin's Tatiana* by Olga Peters Hasty, 1999; *Pushkin's Historical Imagination* by Svetlana Evdokimova, 1999; *Wave and Stone: Essays on the Poetry and Prose of Alexander Pushkin* by J. Douglas Clayton, 2000.

*   *   *

The protean talent of Aleksandr Pushkin gave Russian literature its first firm foothold in the wider arena of European letters. Pushkin developed and refined the literary language into a graceful, economical vehicle of expression, putting it on display in a broad range of genres. The innovations he brought to poetry, drama, fiction, and journalism were so varied and fruitful that at least a century of Russian literature was occupied with developing the forms that he had introduced.

Pushkin's writing career began early while he was still a schoolboy at Tsarskoe Selo, Aleksandr I's newly-established lycée for aristocratic youth. His early poems, though hardly memorable for their themes, exhibited the clarity and concision that became the hallmark of his later verse. Pushkin's nascent talent was well-known among his close friends and fellow writers, but he first won wide acclaim with the publication in 1820 of his narrative poem ''Ruslan and Liudmila.'' A light romance sprinkled with folk motifs, ''Ruslan and Liudmila'' is at once a move away from the stylistic strictures of classicism and a parodic poke at German Romanticism and its chief Russian practitioner, Aleksandr Zhukovskii. The transcendental ideals and lofty language of the Romantic ballad are replaced in Pushkin's poem by a gutsy earthiness and more colloquial diction.

The artistic playfulness of ''Ruslan and Liudmila'' is counterbalanced in these post-lycée years by more serious political verses that circulated among educated circles in Petersburg. Having been nurtured at Tsarskoe Selo on the values of the 18th-century French Enlightenment, Pushkin's political views were at best questionable in the eyes of the government authorities. His liberal perspective was clear in such works as: the ode ''Freedom'' (1817), in which he admonishes emperors to remember that their rule is grounded in law, not divine right; the elegy ''The Village'' (1819), which decries serfdom; and a number of epigrams mocking some of the leaders of the Tsarist regime. Eager to be rid of this brilliant gadfly, Aleksandr I exiled Pushkin to the south of Russia.

Inspired by the exotic landscapes of Bessarabia and the Crimea and a new enthusiasm for Byron, Pushkin essayed a number of narrative poems in the Byronic style. ''Kavkazskii plennik'' (''The Prisoner of the Caucasus,'' 1823) and *Bakhchisaraiskii fontan* (*The Bakchesarian Fountain*), were completed in the South, while ''Tsygany'' (''The Gypsies,'' 1824)—given special attention by

Dostoevskii in his famous "Pushkin Speech"—was completed after arriving at his family's estate at Mikhailovskoe, where his exile continued until 1826. Like Byron, Pushkin situates his dramatic action in an exotic region, but, unlike the English bard, he brings those landscapes more sharply into focus. Pushkin's style is more controlled and less flamboyant than is Byron's, and his heroes have none of the demonic dimensions of their English prototypes. While the two earlier works became models for the Russian romantic narrative poem, "The Gypsies" remains the most memorable of the "Southern poems." Lacking the consistent lyricism of the earlier works, its portrayal of the hero's abortive search for absolute freedom among the gypsies presents a philosophical problem with power and grace.

Pushkin began his most original and influential work, *Evgenii Onegin* (*Eugene Onegin*), in the South, but completed it eight years later, in 1831. From the outset Pushkin distinguished *Eugene Onegin* from his other narrative poems by declaring it a "novel-in-verse," an apt designation for the work that prepared the way for his transition to prose. In fact, the work is a microcosm of Pushkin's artistic development during the eight years of its genesis. In *Eugene Onegin* Pushkin parodies Byronism as a worldview and a literary style and announces the passing of his youthful Romanticism. His descriptions of Petersburg high society as well as the gentry on their provincial estates introduced details of everyday life that heralded a new realism in Russian literature. But Pushkin was never a naive realist. The touchstone of his complex vision is the figure of the narrator: beginning as an enthusiastic participant in the Petersburg world in which his hero travels, he becomes by the end of *Eugene Onegin* separated from his fictive world—the self-conscious author who frustrates any simple identification of art and life.

Both hero and heroine became prototypes for later fiction. Onegin is a vivid exemplar of the "superfluous man," a type that figured prominently not only in the literary but also in the sociological imagination of 19th-century Russia: upon finding that the world fails to respond to his talents, the "superfluous man" retreats into inertia or dilettantism. Tat'iana provides the model for the strong-willed heroines who grace the pages of Turgenev, Tolstoi, and Dostoevskii, among others.

By the time Pushkin completed *Eugene Onegin*, he had already published his first complete prose work, *Povesti pokoinogo I.P. Belkina* (*The Tales of Belkin*). Paradoxically, Pushkin's style displays more flexibility in his novel-in-verse, where the demands of versification would seem to militate against this very quality, than in his prose, a model of classical restraint, *The Tales of Belkin* are lighthearted parodies of some of the popular genres of the time, and as such are formal experiments through which Pushkin tested the limits of the early prose tradition in Russia.

After returning from exile, Pushkin turned his attention increasingly to prose fiction, which was becoming popular with the reading public. He also busied himself with journalism, carrying on heated literary, polemics on the pages of *Literaturnaia gazeta* [The Literary Gazette] and later editing and writing articles for his own journal, *Sovremennik* [The Contemporary], which began publication in 1836. His journalistic prose reflects his lucid and energetic habit of mind, and was often laced by his characteristic wit.

The list of Pushkin's completed prose works is brief, but numerous fragments were quite developed. They bear witness to a lively quest into a variety of forms, from the society tale to the epistolary novel. Of his completed works, *Pikovaia dama* (*The Queen of Spades*) and *Kapitanskaia dochka* (*The Captain's Daughter*) are the most famous. The former is a masterly short story, whose contemporary Petersburg setting and monomaniacal hero influenced Dostoevskii when he set out to create the ultra-rational hero verging on madness. Its style is terse and bare despite the Romantic trappings of its subject. *The Captain's Daughter*, a historical novel in the style of Walter Scott, is a fast-moving adventure that examines the meaning of honour in a world confused by partisan allegiances. Published posthumously, the novel grew out of Pushkin's historical treatise on the Pugachev rebellion, the 18th-century peasant revolt.

The fascination with history that dominated the last years of Pushkin's life had in fact surfaced earlier, most notably in *Boris Godunov*. In that play, written in the style of Shakespeare's historical drama, Pushkin relied on Karamzin's *History of the Russian State* for his interpretation of the Time of Troubles; his later historical works were products of his own research in the State Archives. He never completed his first project, a study of Peter the Great, but his developing historical insight powerfully informs the narrative poem *Medny vsadnik* (*The Bronze Horseman*). Juxtaposed with the encomium to Peter and his accomplishments, which opens the poem, is the story of how an autocratic vision, no matter how glorious, can oppress the average Russian's dreams. The Petersburg clerk Eugene loses his fiancée and finally his mind in the aftermath of the 1824 flood, which is nature's revenge on Peter's hubristic plan to introduce a note of modernity into an inhospitable cultural and physical landscape. When Dostoevskii referred to Petersburg as "the most rational city in the world," or when the Symbolist writer Andrei Belyi built an entire novel on the "Petersburg myth," they traced their understanding back to Pushkin's blend of history and imagination.

While experimenting with prose and historical topics, Pushkin never ceased writing in the traditional poetic genres with which he began his writing career. The period of his most fruitful poetic activity was from 1825 to 1831, when he wrote some of the most beautiful and memorable lyrics in the language. The subjects of the poems are varied; many were written in response to specific incidents in Pushkin's life; but all rise above the purely personal to make statements that are universal in their appeal. Friendship, nature, and the role of the poet are recurring topics, but it is love that inspired a good number of Pushkin's best-known verses. The inimitable style of Pushkin's poetry resists both classification and translation; its classical precision, measure, and fine sense of cadence finally derive from an exquisite understanding of all the potentialities of the Russian language. Pushkin stands at the centre of Russia's Golden Age of poetry, developing and perfecting the power of poetic expression to a level often aspired to but rarely equalled.

—Nancy Kanach Fehsenfeld

See the essays on *The Bronze Horseman* and *Eugene Onegin*.

Q

QUASIMODO, Salvatore

Born: Modica, Sicily, Italy, 20 August 1901. **Education:** Educated at intermediate school, Palermo, 1912–16; A.M. Jaci Technical Institute, Messina, 1916; Faculty of Engineering, Rome Polytechnic, 1919–20, studies not completed. **Family:** Married 1) Bice Donetti in 1921(?) (died 1946); 2) Maria Cumani in 1948 (separated 1960), one son before marriage; also had one illegitimate daughter during first marriage. **Career:** Technical designer, assistant in hardware store, and clerk, 1919–26; surveyor extraordinary, Italian Department of Public Works in Calabria, 1926–31, on a military highway project in Imperia, near San Remo, 1931–33, in Sardinia, and in Milan, 1934–38. Contributor to literary periodicals, from 1921; invited to Florence by his brother-in-law, the writer Elio Vittorino, *q.v.*, in 1929, where he met members of the *Solaria* artistic circle, and began publishing his poetry in their journal; contributor, *Circoli* magazine, from 1931; secretary to Cesare Zavattini, director of Mondadori, publishers, 1938–39; literary editor, *Il Tempo*, from 1939; professor of Italian literature, Giuseppe Verdi Conservatory of Music, Milan, 1940–68; accused by *La voce Republicana* of harbouring fascist sympathies, 1944; theatre critic, *Omnibus*, 1948–50; travelled to Greece, 1956, USSR, 1958; moved to Rome with his son, 1960; visited Spain, 1961, Berlin, London, Dublin, Norway, and Yugoslavia, all in 1962, Paris, Bulgaria, and Mexico, in 1964. **Awards:** San Babila prize, 1950; Etna-Taormina prize (with Dylan Thomas), 1953; Viareggio prize, 1958; Nobel prize for literature, 1959. Honorary degrees: University of Messina, 1960; University of Oxford, 1967. **Died:** 14 June 1968.

PUBLICATIONS

Collections

Complete Poems, translated by Jack Bevan. 1983.

Verse

Acque e terre. 1930.
Oboe sommerso. 1932.
Odore di eucalyptus e altri versi. 1933.
Erato e Apolliòn. 1936.
Poesie. 1938.
Ed è subito sera. 1942.
Con il piede straniero sopra al cuore. 1946.
Giorno dopo giorno. 1947.
La vita non è sogno. 1949.
Il falso il vero verde, con un discorso sulla poesie. 1953; revised edition, 1956.
La terra impareggiabile. 1958.
Poesie scelte, edited by R. Sanesi. 1959.

"Thirty Poems by Quasimodo," translated by Charles Guenther. In *Literary Review*, 3, 1960.
Selected Poems, translated by Jack Bevan. 1963.
Tutte le poesie. 1960.
Complete Poetical Works. 1960.
Dare e avere, 1959–1965. 1966; as *Debit and Credit*, translated by Jack Bevan, 1972; as *To Give and to Have, and Other Poems*, translated by Edith Farnsworth, 1975.

Plays

Billy Bud (libretto). 1949.
L'amore di Galatea (libretto). 1964.

Other

Petrarca e il sentimento della solitudine. 1941.
Lirica d'amore italiana dalle origini ai nostri giorni. 1957.
Poesia italiana del dopoguerra. 1958.
Orfeo—Anno Domini MCMXLVII. 1960.
Il poeta e il politico e altri saggi. 1960; as *The Poet and the Politician and Other Essays*, translated by Thomas G. Bergin and Sergio Pacifici, 1964.
Selected Writings, translated by Alan Mandelbaum. 1960.
Scritti sul teatro. 1961.
Milano in inchiostro di china, illustrations by Attilio Rossi. 1963.
Quasimodo per Luther King. 1968.
Un anno di Quasimodo. 1968.
Le lettere d'amore. 1969.
Poesie e discorsi sulla poesia, edited by Gilberto Finzi. 1971.
Lettere d'amore a Maria Cumani (1936–1959). 1973.
Per conoscere Quasimodo (anthology), edited by Rosalina Salina Borello. 1973.
A colpo omicida e altri scritti, edited by Gilberto Finzi. 1977.
Carteggio (correspondence), edited by Alessandro Quasimodo. 1980.
A Sibilla (correspondence). 1983.
Translator, *Lirici greci.* 1940.
Translator, *Il fiore delle Georgiche.* 1942.
Translator, *Catulli Veronensis carmina.* 1945.
Translator, *Dall'Odissea*, by Homer. 1945.
Translator, *Il Vangelo secondo Giovanni.* 1946.
Translator, *La Bibbia d'Amiens*, by John Ruskin. 1946.
Translator, *Edipo re*, by Sophocles. 1947.
Translator, *Romeo e Giulietta*, by Shakespeare. 1948.
Translator, *Le Coefcre*, by Aeschylus. 1949.
Translator, *Riccardo III*, by Shakespeare. 1952.
Translator, *Macbeth*, by Shakespeare. 1952.
Translator, *Poesie*, by Pablo Neruda. 1952.
Translator, *Elettra*, by Sophocles. 1954.
Translator, *Canti di Catullo.* 1955.
Translator, *La tempesta*, by Shakespeare. 1956.
Translator, *Tartufo*, by Molière. 1957.
Translator, *Il fiore dell'Antologia Palatina.* 1957; as *Dall'Antologia Palatina*, 1968.

Translator, *Poesie scelte*, by E.E. Cummings. 1958; as *Da Aiken e Cummings*, 1968.

Translator, *Otello*, by Shakespeare. 1959.

Translator, *Dalle Metamorfosi*, by Ovid. 1959.

Translator, *Mutevoli Pensieri*, by Conrad Aiken. 1963.

Translator, *Ecuba*, by Euripides. 1963.

Translator, *Poesie*, by T. Arghezi. 1966.

Translator, *Eracle*, by Euripides. 1966.

Translator, *Antonio e Cleopatra*, by Shakespeare. 1966.

Translator, *Il gioco degli astragali*, by Yves Lecomte. 1968.

Translator, *Iliade: Episodi scelti*, by Homer. 1968.

Translator, *Leonida di Taranto*. 1969.

Translator, *Donner à voir*, by Paul Éluard. 1970.

*

Critical Studies: *Quasimodo* by Mario Stefanile, 1943; *Salvatore Quasimodo e la condizione poetica del nostro tempo*, 1959, and *L'isola impareggiabile: Significati e forme del mito di Quasimodo*, 1977, both by Natale Tedesco; "Quasimodo" by Glauco Cambon, in *Chelsea*, 6, 1960; "Quasimodo and Modern Italian Poetry" by Chandler B. Beall, in *Northwest Review*, 4, 1961; *La poesia di Quasimodo e altri studi* by Ermanno Circeo, 1963; *Salvatore Quasimodo* by Pietro Mazzamuto, 1967; *Quasimodo* by Giuseppe Zagarrio, 1969; *Salvatore Quasimodo* by Michele Tondo, 1970; *Invito alla lettura di Quasimodo* by Gilberto Finzi, 1972, and *Quasimodo e la critica* edited by Finzi, 1975; *Quasimodo: Poeta del nostro tempo* by Gaetano Munafò, 1973; *La critica e Quasimodo* edited by Mirko Bevilacqua, 1976; *Presenza e metamorfosi del mito di Orfeo in Salvatore Quasimodo* by Pietro Pelosi, 1978; *Salvatore Quasimodo: L'uomo e il poeta* edited by Rosa Brambilla, 1983; *Salvatore Quasimodo* by Elena Salibra, 1985.

* * *

Salvatore Quasimodo's poetry represents a happy amalgam of the classical lyric tradition, of the Leopardian kind, and the modern, critical, and corrosive tradition as exemplified by the poetry of his senior contemporaries Saba, Ungaretti, Campana, and Montale. Solmi refers to the element of "uncorrupted primitivism" in Quasimodo's poetry co-existing not only with the already mentioned authentic vein of contemporaneity, but also with a "transcendental imagism" as illustrated by such verses as: "Chi non sa / che vento profondo m'ha cercato" [Who doesn't know / that the deep wind has sought me] from "Vento a Tindari"; "Un oboe gelido risillaba / gioia di foglie perenni, / non mie, e smemora" [An icy oboe risyllabises / the joy of perennial leaves, / not mine, and forgets] from *Oboe sommerso* [Sunken Oboe]; "Un sole rompe gonfio nel sonno / e urlano alberi" [A swollen sun bursts in sleep / and the trees yell], from "Alla mia terra"; and "Da secoli l'erba riposa / il suo cuore con me" [For centuries the grass has reposed / its heart with me] from "Riposo dell'erba."

A hallucinatingly vivid imagery and an evocatively luminous diction combine to make Quasimodo's poetry, at its best, a creative record of his neo-idyllic world of Sicily, his inner world of memories, desires, and disillusions, and his existential world of everyday experience, rendered with a semi-allegorical realism. "Camminano angeli,

muti / con me" [The angels walk mutely / with me], the poet tells us in "Alla notte," "non hanno respiro le cose: / in pietra mutata ogni voce, / silenzio di cieli sepolti" [things don't breathe: / each voice turned into stone, / the silence of buried skies]. The poet's efforts at defining his moral, as well as poetic, self are themselves triumphs of creative transformation of that which is personal and subjective into something impersonal: "I morti maturano, / il mio cuore con essi . . . / il mio volto è loro primavera" [The dead grow mature, / and my heart with them . . . / my face is their spring], he writes in "Metamorfosi nell'urna del santo." Through an imaginative sympathy with all that is alive, the poet becomes a transformer, too, of whatever is dead: "Nessuna cosa muore, / che in me non viva" [Nothing dies / but it lives in me], from "Seme."

Unlike Saba, Ungaretti, and Montale, Quasimodo did not contribute anything particularly notable to the "modernization" of Italian poetry; but by virtue of what he did achieve in creative terms, and the kind of authentic lyricism that is undoubtedly and unmistakably his own, he occupies an interesting and important place in the history of 20th-century Italian poetry.

—G. Singh

QUEIRÓS, José Maria de Eça de

See EÇA DE QUEIRÓS, José Maria de

QUEIROZ, Rachel de

Born: Fortaleza, Ceará, Brazil, 17 November 1910. **Education:** Educated at the Colégio da Imaculada Conceição, Fortaleza, 1921–25; completed training as a primary school teacher at age 15. **Family:** Married. **Career:** Teacher, 1925–30; contributor, from 1927, and later editor, *O Ceará*; weekly newpaper and magazine columnist from 1930, including *Diário de Notícias, O Cruzeiro* (editor, from 1946), *O Jornal, Ultima Hora, Jornal do Commercio, Folha Carioca,* and *A Cigarra*; translator of Russian and English literary works for Livraria José Olympio Editora, Rio de Janeiro, from early 1940s; Brazilian delegate to the United Nations General Assembly and its Human Rights Commission, 1966. Lives in Rio de Janeiro. **Awards:** Graça Aranha Foundation prize, 1931; Felipe d'Oliveira Society prize; *O Estado de São Paulo* Saci prize, 1953; Brazilian Academy Machado de Assis prize, 1957; National Book Institute theatre prize, 1959; Paula Brito prize, 1959; Roberto Gomes prize, 1959. **Member:** Brazilian Communist Party, 1931–33: expelled; First woman member, Brazilian Academy of Letters, 1977.

PUBLICATIONS

Fiction

O quinze. 1930.

João Miguel. 1932.

Caminho de pedras. 1937.

As três Marias. 1937; as *The Three Marias,* translated by Fred P. Ellison, 1963.

Brandão entre o mar e o amor, with Jorge Amado, José Lins do Rêgo, Graciliano Ramos, and Anibal M. Machado. 1942.

O galo de ouro. 1950.

Três romances (includes *O quinze; João Miguel; Caminho de pedras*). 1948; enlarged edition, as *Quarto romances* (also including *As três Marias*), 1960.

Luiz e Maria, with Marion Vilas Boas. 1971.

Dôra, Doralina. 1975.

Plays

Lampião (produced 1953). 1953.

A beata Maria do Egito (produced 1958). 1958.

O Padrezinho Santo (produced 1959). Parts in *Seleta,* 1973.

Other

A Donzela e a Moura Torta: crônicas e reminiscências. 1948.

Nova elas são, with others. 1957.

100 crônicas escolhidas. 1958.

O brasileiro perplexo: historías e crônicas. 1963.

O caçador de tatu (selection of *crônicas*), edited by Herman Lima. 1967.

O menino mágico (for children), illustrated by Gian Calvi. 1969.

A princesa dos escravos (for children). 1970.

Elenco de cronistas modernas, with others. 1972.

Meu livro de Brasil, with Nilda Bethlem. 1973.

Seleta (anthology), edited by Paulo Rónai and Renato Cordeiro Gomes. 1973.

As menininhas e outras crônicas. 1976.

O jogador de sinuca e mais historinhas (includes stories). 1980.

Cafute & Pena-de-prata (for children). 1986.

Mapinguari: crônicas. 1989.

Memorial de Maria Moura. 1992.

Tantos anos, with Maria Luíza de Queiroz. 1998.

O Não Me Deixes: Suas histórias e sua cozinha, with Maria Luíza de Queiroz. 2000.

Translator, *Náufragos,* by Erich Maria Remarque. 1942(?).

Translator, *Oroteiro das gaivotas,* by Daphne du Maurier. 1943.

Translator, *Fúria no céu,* by James Hilton. 1944.

Translator, *Memórias, infância, adolescência, juventude . . . ,* by Tolstoi. 1944.

Translator, *Recordações da casa dos mortos,* by Dostoevskii. 1945.

Translator, *A promessa,* by Pearl S. Buck. 1946.

Translator, *A crônica dos Forsyte,* by John Galsworthy. 3 vols., 1946.

Translator, *Cranford,* by Elizabeth Gaskell. 1946.

Translator, *Vida de Santa Teresa de Jesus,* by St. Teresa. 1946.

Translator, *Anos de Ternura,* by A.J. Cronin. 1947.

Translator, *A mulher de trinta anos,* by Balzac. 1948.

Translator, *Os dois amores de Grey Manning,* by Forrest Rosaire. 1948.

Translator, *A conquista da torre misteriosa,* by Germaine Verdat. 1948.

Translator, *Os demônios,* by Dostoevskii. 3 vols., 1951.

Translator, *Humilhados e ofendidos,* by Dostoevskii. 1951.

Translator, with Maria Luiza de Queiroz, *O doutor meu marido: confissões da esposa de um médico,* by Mary Bard. 1952.

Translator, *Mulher imortal,* by Irving Stone. 1953.

Translator, *Os irmãos Karamázovi,* by Dostoevskii. 3 vols., 1955.

Translator, *O Morro dos Ventos Uivantes,* by Emily Brontë. 1957.

Translator, *Mansfield Park,* by Jane Austen. 1958.

Translator, *Os Carolinos,* by Verner von Heidenstam. 1963.

Translator, *A exilada, retrato de uma mãe americana . . . ,* by Pearl S. Buck. 1964.

Translator, *O romance da mumia: um romance do tempo dos faraões,* by Théophile Gautier. 1972.

Translator, *O lobo do mar,* by Jack London. 1972.

Translator, *Miguel Strogoff, o correio do Czar,* by Jules Verne. 1972.

Translator, *O castelo do homem sem alma,* by A.J. Cronin. 1985(?).

Translator, *A mulher diabolica,* by Agatha Christie. 1985.

Translator, *Uma razão por dia para ser feliz,* by Laura Archera Huxley. 1988.

Translator, *Tempestades d'alma,* by Phyllis Bottome. N.d.

*

Bibliography: *Brazilian Literature: A Research Guide* by David William Foster and Walter Rela, 1990.

Critical Studies: *Brazil's New Novel: Four Northeastern Masters* by Fred P. Ellison, 1954; "Three Contemporary Brazilian Novels: Some Comparisons and Contrasts" by G.D. Schade, in *Hispania,* 39, 1956; "The Art of Rachel de Queiroz" by Benjamin M. Woodbridge, Jr., in *Hispania,* 40(2), 1957; "The Santa María Egipciaca Motif in Modern Brazilian Letters" by C.R. Reynolds, in *Romance Notes,* 13, 1971; "*A beata Maria do Egito*: Anatomy of Tyranny" in *Chasqui,* 13(2–3), 1984, "The Problematic Heroine in the Novels of Rachel de Queiroz" in *Luso-Brazilian Review,* 22(2), 1985, and "*Dôra, Doralina*: The Sexual Configuration of Discourse" in *Chasqui: Revista de Literatura Latinoamericana,* 20(1), 1990, all by Joanna Courteau; *Rachel de Queiroz* by Haroldo Bruno, 1977; "The Singular Encounter" by James Dauphiné, in *Romanian Review,* 40(2), 1986; "A Woman's Place: Rachel de Queiroz's *Dôra, Doralina*" by Renata R. Mautner Wasserman, in *Brasil/Brazil,* 2, 1989.

* * *

A metaphor used frequently by professors of Brazilian literature is perhaps the best statement on the place of Rachel de Queiroz in Brazilian letters: if José Américo de Almeida were the St. John the Baptist of the 1930s novel of social protest, de Queiroz was its Virgin Mary. The appearance of her *O quinze* [The Year Fifteen] in 1930, rather than the publication of *A bagaceira* [Trash] by Almeida in 1928, is considered to be the starting point for what Fred P. Ellison has called "Brazil's new novel."

O quinze lays out all the major elements that the Brazilian novel will explore in the decade: the Northeastern *sertão* or "backlands" as the setting; the rural masses—especially the *retirante* who is victimized by the drought of the Northeastern region—as the collective character; the social conditions in the region—with degrading imbalance of wealth distribution and chronic cultural backwardness—and the need for social reform, which functions as the central motif for many of the novels. A strong memorialistic presence is also evident, whose temporal settings often correspond to the rural childhood of the authors. Regional fiction, with noticeable roots in 20th-century writers like Alfonso Arinos, is resumed at a different level of intention, with the ideological replacing the descriptive. De Queiroz is unique among writers of this period in that her story plots centre on strong women protagonists.

Stylistically, *O quinze* sets the tone for the prose writing of the period. The trendy experimentation of the historical avant-garde that dominated the 1920s is abandoned and an earlier tradition of direct and natural expression is resumed. Colloquial language—a conquest of the avant-garde—is adapted by the young author to serve a more sober, almost humourless manner.

With *João Miguel* de Queiroz expands the feminine presence. Although the title indicates that the main character is a man, who has been jailed for a common crime, the narrative point of view displaces the focus of interest to the woman who visits the prisoner, her lover. As the character's needs grow, and she matures into awareness, the social and economic problems of the Brazilian Northeastern region become no more than a backdrop for an extended analysis the author makes of the female condition.

In *Caminho de pedras* [Road of Stones] de Queiroz continues to explore the female presence in the Northeast. This novel, whose reception at the time of publication was lukewarm, and which continues to be the least successful of her major works, shifts from rural Brazil to the city. Working primarily with autobiographical material, the author emphasizes political activism as its theme and female independence as its goal. Its basic failure comes from a technical flaw: the lack of distance in the narration gives way to a sentimental tone less compelling than the starkness of her previous narratives.

With her fourth novel, *As três Marias* (*The Three Marias*), de Queiroz fuses her personal experiences with her observations on the plight of women in Brazil. The struggle of middle-class women to find independence within the boundaries of a traditional society is portrayed in three parallel stories. Their different endings, although encompassing only a very limited range of possibilities, imply the existence of change and improvement in the female condition. By using first-person narration, and by creating a character who serves the double purpose of actor and observer, the author issues a strong indictment of the social prejudices against women. Critics have been unanimous in considering *The Three Marias* her best work.

The Three Marias closes the first cycle of de Queiroz's literary life as a novelist. She returned to writing novels sporadically—as, for example, with her attempt at popular literature, *O galo de ouro* [The Golden Rooster], set in the urban context of Rio de Janeiro's slums; and with *Dôra, Doralina*, in which she tries to resuscitate the themes of female identity and liberation. Neither of these novels was well-received by the critics. Despite their attempts to deal with some of the issues present in her previous novels, they suffer from a "journalistic" style of writing that has little aesthetic preoccupation.

De Queiroz also wrote several short stories, which have been published in the collection *O jogador de sinuca* [The Snooker Player]. They neither add to nor detract from the rest of her fictional work: the themes are similar, as are the settings and the language.

After 1939, journalism and theatre became her major literary concerns. She became one of the best-known writers of *crônicas*, a literary genre akin to the newspaper column but with a broader range of artistic interest. She brings to the *crônica* much of her experience as a novelist, and together with fellow *cronistas* Rubem Braga and Carlos Drummond de Andrade, she helped to elevate the form to an accepted literary genre in contemporary Brazilian literature. As with her novels, the Northeast and the female condition are favourite themes in her *crônicas*.

It is, however, as a playwright that de Queiroz best followed up the success of her earlier novels. *Lampião* is a forceful portrayal of banditry in rural Brazil. By stressing psychological instead of political interplay, she creates one of the most powerful roles in contemporary Brazilian theatre. Her views on religious fanaticism in the Northeastern region, as represented by *A beata Maria do Egito* [The Pious Mary of Egypt], combines her concern with social problems and the female experience. Both plays use the same stark, colloquial language found in her earlier novels.

In the broad picture of Brazilian letters, de Queiroz is a major figure by virtue of the range of her output, the influence of her writing on others, and the originality of her approach. She continues and enlarges the tradition of Júlia Lopes de Almeida, and opens the path for Clarice Lispector.

—Heitor Martins

QUENEAU, Raymond

Pseudonym: Sally Mara. **Born:** Le Havre, France, 21 February 1903. **Education:** Educated at a lycée in Le Havre; the Sorbonne, Paris, from 1920, degree in philosophy. **Military Service:** Served 1925–27; served in World War II, 1939–40. **Family:** Married Janine Kahn in 1928 (died 1972); one son. **Career:** Worked in a bank in Paris, from 1927; columnist ("Connaissez-vous Paris?"), *L'Intransigeant*, Paris, 1936–38; reader, 1938–39, secretary-general from 1941, and director of the *Encyclopédie de la Pléiade*, 1955–75, Gallimard, publishers, Paris. Also a painter. **Member:** Académie Goncourt, 1951. **Died:** 25 October 1976.

PUBLICATIONS

Collections

Oeuvres complètes [Pléade Edition], edited by Claude Deban. 1989–.

Fiction

Le Chiendent. 1933; as *The Bark-Tree, translated* by Barbara Wright, 1968.

La Gueule de pierre. 1934, revised edition, with *Les Temps mêlés*, 1941; as *Saint Glinglin*, 1948.

Les Derniers Jours. 1935; as *The Last Days*, translated by Barbara Wright, 1990.

Odile. 1937; as *Odile*, translated by Carol Sanders, 1988.

Les Enfants du Limon. 1938; as *Children on Clay*, translated by Madeleine Velguth, 1998.

Un rude hiver. 1939; as *A Hard Winter*, translated by Betty Askwith, 1948.

Les Temps mêlés. 1941; as *Saint Glinglin*, with *La Gueule de Pierre*, 1948.

Pierrot mon ami. 1942; as *Pierrot*, translated by Julian MacLaren-Ross, 1950; as *Pierrot mon ami*, translated by Barbara Wright, 1987.

Loin de Rueil. 1944; as *The Skin of Dreams*, translated by H.J. Kaplan, 1948.

On est toujours trop bon avec les femmes (as Sally Mara). 1947; as *We Always Treat Women Too Well*, translated by Barbara Wright, 1981.

Une trouille verte. 1947; as *A Blue Funk*, translated by Barbara Wright, 1968.

À la limite de la forêt. 1947; as *At the Edge of the Forest*, translated by Barbara Wright, with *The Trojan Horse*, 1954.

Le Cheval troyen. 1948; as *The Trojan Horse*, translated by Barbara Wright, with *At the Edge of the Forest*, 1954.

Saint-Glinglin (includes revised versions of *La Gueule de Pierre* and *Les Temps mêlés*). 1948; as *Saint Glinglin*, translated by James Sallis, 1994.

Journal intime (as Sally Mara). 1950.

Le Dimanche de la vie. 1951; as *The Sunday of Life*, translated by Barbara Wright, 1976.

Zazie dans le métro. 1959; as *Zazie*, translated by Barbara Wright, 1960.

Les Oeuvres complètes de Sally Mara. 1962.

Les Fleurs bleues. 1965; edited by Barbara Wright, 1971; as *Between Blue and Blue: A Sort of Novel*, translated by Barbara Wright, 1967, as *The Blue Flowers*, translated by Wright, 1967.

Un conte à votre façon. 1967; as *Yours for the Telling*, translated by John Crombie, 1982.

Le Vol d'Icare. 1968; as *The Flight of Icarus*, translated by Barbara Wright, 1973.

Contes et propos (short fiction). 1981.

Plays

En passant. 1944.

Screenplays: *Monsieur Ripois* (*Knave of Hearts; Lovers, Happy Lovers*), with René Clement and Hugh Mills, 1953; *La Mort en ce jardin* (*Gina; Death in the Garden*), with Luis Buñuel and Luis Alcoriza, 1956; *Un couple*, with others, 1960; *Le Dimanche de la vie*, 1967.

Verse

Chêne et chien (novel in verse). 1937.

Les Ziaux. 1943.

Bucoliques. 1947.

L'Instant fatal. 1948.

Petite cosmogonie portative. 1950.

Si tu t'imagines 1920–1951. 1952, revised edition, 1968.

Sonnets. 1958.

Le Chien à la mandoline. 1958, revised edition, 1965.

Cent mille milliards de poèmes. 1961; as *One Hundred Million Million Poems*, translated by John Crombie, 1983.

Courir les rues. 1967.

Battre la campagne. 1968.

Fendre les flots. 1969.

Poems, translated by Teo Savory. 1970.

Bonjour, Monsieur Prassinos. 1972.

Morale élégmentaire. 1975.

Pounding the Pavements; Beating the Bushes, and Other Pataphysical Poems, translated by Teo Savory. 1985.

Other

Exercices de style. 1947, revised and enlarged edition, 1963; as *Exercises in Style*, translated by Barbara Wright, 1958.

Monuments. 1948.

Bâtons, chiffres, et lettres. 1950, revised edition, 1965.

Lorsque l' esprit. 1956.

Le Déclin du romantisme: Edgar Poe. 1957.

Entretiens, with Georges Charbonnier. 1962.

Bords: Mathématiciens, précurseurs, encyclopédistes. 1963.

Une histoire modèle. 1966.

Queneau en verve, edited by Jacques Bens. 1970.

De quelques langages animaux imaginaires . . . . 1971.

Le Voyage en Grèce. 1973.

La Littérature potentielle. 1973.

Correspondance, with Elie Lascaux. 1979.

Une correspondance: Raymond Queneau-Boris Vian. 1982.

Journal 1939–1940, edited by A.I. Queneau and J.-J. Marchand. 1986.

Editor, *Anthologie des jeunes auteurs.* 1955.

Editor, *Histoires des littératures.* 3 vols., 1955–58.

Translator of works by Maurice O'Sullivan, Sinclair Lewis, George du Maurier, and Amos Tutuola.

*

Bibliography: *Queneau: Bibliographie des études sur l'homme et son oeuvre* by Wolfgang Hillen, 1981.

Critical Studies: *Queneau* by Jacques Bens (in French), 1962; *Queneau* by Andrée Bergens (in French), 1963; *Queneau* by Jacques Guicharnaud (in French), 1965; *Les Poèmes de Queneau* by Renée Baligand, 1972; *Queneau* by Richard Charles Cobb, 1976; *Queneau: Zazie dans le métro* by Walter D. Redfern, 1980; *The Flower of Fiction: Time and Space in Raymond Queneau's Les Fleurs bleues* by Vivian Kogan, 1982; *Queneau's Fiction: An Introductory Study* by Christopher Shorley, 1985; *Raymond Queneau* by Allen Thiher, 1985; *Raymond Queneau* (in French) by Jacques Jouet, 1988; *The Lyric Encyclopedia of Queneau* by Jane Alison Hale, 1989; *Les Fleurs bleues* (in French) by Jean-Yves Pouilloux, 1991; *Raymond Queneau* (in French) by Emmanuë Souchier, 1992; *Raymond Queneau: Exercices de style* by Teresa Bridgeman, 1995; *Poetry and Cosmogony: Science in the Writing of Queneau and Ponge* by Chris Andrews, 1999; *Naming and Unnaming: On Raymond Queneau* by Jordan Stump, 1999.

*   *   *

Not long before Raymond Queneau's death, *Le Monde* referred to him as "one of the most universal minds of our time." A justified accolade. Though primarily a novelist and poet, Queneau also wrote on philosophy, science, history, and mathematics. He was also the general editor of the Gallimard *Encyclopédie de la Pléiade*.

In the field of "pure" literature, Queneau always said he could see no difference between poetry and prose, and all his novels are infused with poetry—taking the word in its widest sense. They are also infused with humour, and for a long time this prevented critics from regarding Queneau as anything but a joker. This was particularly the case with *Pierrot mon amie* (*Pierrot*) and *Zazie dans le métro* (*Zazie*). Martin Esslin, however, in *The Novelist as Philosopher* (1962), said of *Pierrot:* ''It is only the effortless simplicity of the telling of the story that hides the delicacy of its construction and the depth of its thought. *Pierrot mon ami* is a poem on chance and destiny . . . .'' Of *Zazie* he said: ''Critics did not notice the brilliant philosopher-poet behind the clowning.''

Queneau's novels are all highly structured, none more so than his first, *Le Chiendent* (*The Bark-Tree*), which was actually based on mathematical principles. Robbe-Grillet called *The Bark-Tree* ''the new novel 20 years ahead of its time.'' Queneau said he hoped no one would notice its structure, its ''scaffolding,'' and no one did, until he himself wrote about it. This first book contains all the elements that preoccupied Queneau throughout his life: his predilection for humble characters and for the unacknowledged philosophical implications of their everyday lives; his humour (sometimes sardonic); his surrealistic inclinations; and, very particularly, his love of language. James Joyce, Faulkner, and Conrad were the only literary influences Queneau recognized. Anglo-Saxon writers, he said, were free to write as they chose, whereas French writers were strait-jacketed by what the Académie française decreed to be ''correct.''

In liberating the French language, Queneau used poetically heightened representations of the speech of the ordinary Frenchman, he interwove puns and word play with classical references, he ran words together, he coined neologisms. Thus he created books which can be read—and reread—on many levels, and always with enjoyment.

This approach, these elements, also permeate Queneau's poetry. Even at its most serious—or melancholy—it is often playful. Many of his poems were made famous during the heyday of the cabarets in St-Germain-des-Prés by artists like Juliette Greco. His extraordinary *Cent mille milliards de poèmes* (*One Hundred Million Million Poems*) is a supreme example of the fusion of mathematics with poetry. Ten sonnets are printed on pages consisting of 14 loose strips, making it possible for the reader to construct 10^{14} intelligible poems.

A further extension of such experimentation is to be found in the *OuLiPo*, or *Ouvroir de Littérature Potentielle* (Workshop of Potential Literature), of which Queneau was a co-founder. *Time* wrote that this ''lunatic fringework'' is ''yet another proof that the gap between science and art can still be bridged.''

—Barbara Wright

See the essays on *The Blue Flowers* and *Zazie*.

QUINTILIAN

Born: Marcus Fabius Quintilianus in Calagurris (Calahorra), northern Spain, c. AD 35. **Education:** Studied rhetoric in Rome; acquainted with the orator Domitius Afer. **Family:** Married (wife died); two sons (died age 5 and 9). **Career:** Travelled to Spain but returned to Rome in AD 68; taught advocacy for 20 years: pupils included the young Hadrian and Pliny the Younger; appointed tutor to Domitian's two great-nephews; granted *ornamenta consularia* (magisterial rank). **Died:** probably c. AD 100.

PUBLICATIONS

Works

Institutionis oratoriae, edited (with *Declamationes*) by Edward Bonnell. 2 vols., 1882–89; also edited by Michael Winterbottom, 2 vols., 1970; as *The Institutio Oratoria*, edited by Eugene Tavenner, 1951; as *Institutes of Eloquence*, translated by W. Guthrie, 1756; also translated by J. Patsall, 1774; as *Institutes of Oratory*, translated by J.S. Watson, 2 vols., 1856; as *The Institutio Oratoria* [Loeb Edition], translated by H.E. Butler, 4 vols., 1920–22; also translated by Charles Edgar Little, 1951; selections as *Quintilian on Education*, translated by William M. Small, 1938; as *Quintilian as Educator: Selections from the Institutio Oratorio*, translated by H.E. Butler, 1974; commentary in *Selections*, edited by D.M. Gaunt, 1952; as *The Orator's Education*, edited and translated by Donald Russell, 2001.

Declamationes Majores (attributed), edited by Georg Lehnert. 1905; also edited by Constantin Ritter, 1965; as *The Declamations*, translated by John Warr, 1686; as *The Major Declamations Ascribed to Quintilian*, translated by Lewis A. Sussman, 1987.

Declamationes Minores (attributed), edited by Constantin Ritter. 1884, reprinted 1965; as *The Minor Declamations*, edited by Michael Winterbottom, 1984.

*

Critical Studies: *Études sur Quintilien* by J. Cousin, 1936; *Quintilian* by George A. Kennedy, 1969; *Problems in Quintilian*, edited by M. Winterbottom, 1970; *An Ideal Critic: Ciceronian Rhetoric and Contemporary Criticism* by K. Hvidtfelt Nielsen, 1995.

*   *   *

By far the most important of Quintilian's works is the *Institutionis oratoriae* (*The Institutio Oratorio*). One of his early published speeches, *In Defence of Naevius Arpinianus*, and also an essay *De causis corruptae eloquentiae* [On the Causes of Corrupt Eloquence], castigating extravagant and pretentious style, do not survive. Two collections of *Declamationes* (*Declamations*), attributed to Quintilian, survive, although their authenticity has been disputed.

At first sight it seems strange that Quintilian's treatise, on the training of advocates to plead cases in the Roman law courts, should enjoy worldwide prestige. Such a topic seems narrow in scope and certainly the book contains much technical detail. Quintilian, however, took a broad view of his subject, seeing the training of an orator as part of a wider educational process. He discussed literary study in relation to the writing of speeches. His ideal orator, a man of competence and integrity, has a role beyond the law courts, namely in public affairs. Moreover, Quintilian claims that the art of speaking effectively is just as important in day-to-day private life as in the law courts or public affairs. His work therefore has something to offer anybody engaged in speaking, reading, writing, or teaching.

The treatise is organized around the five traditional parts of rhetoric: invention, disposition, style, memory, and delivery. These were the skills required for composing a speech, memorizing it, and delivering it before an audience. Rhetoric was the art of persuasion. In following this plan Quintilian expands in appropriate places upon the issues raised by his theme. He outlines this conception in his preface:

"I propose to mould the studies of my orator from infancy on the assumption that his whole education has been entrusted to my charge."

Books I and II deal with elementary education, grammar, and rhetorical exercises for children. These chapters are interspersed with recommendations on teaching methods. Books III to VII deal with invention, under which is included disposition; Books VIII to XI are assigned to eloquence, which includes memory and delivery; whilst the final Book XII offers a portrait of the complete orator. This is how Quintilian himself explains the structure of his work, but it does not give a clear picture of the shape of the treatise. A better understanding of his rather individual manner of expounding the art of rhetoric emerges from considering the contents of each book.

Oratory is defined in the latter part of Book II and the three types of oratory—epideictic, deliberative, and judicial—are explained in Book III. Book IV describes the beginning and middle parts of a speech—exordium, narration, and digression—and these topics are amplified in Book V by discussion of proofs and arguments. The final part of a speech, the peroration, is the theme of Book VI and this leads to consideration of ways of arousing emotion and gaining the good will of judges. Book VII returns to aspects of disposition—conjecture, points of law, contradictory laws, syllogism, and ambiguity. Style occupies the next three books and is approached from different angles: ornament, amplification, diminution, and tropes (Book VIII); figures of thought and speech (Book IX); the merits of various literary works as aids to style in Book X. The later sections of this celebrated book broach the topic of delivery, which is treated again in Book XI after a discussion of memory. Thus Quintilian avoids an over-systematic exposition of rhetoric by treating the same topics in different contexts and from different angles.

For the most part, Quintilian's art of rhetoric follows earlier writers, but on some points he claims originality or fuller treatment, in particular in his stress on practical needs as opposed to theory. In treating the beginning of a speech he states: "It is not sufficient to explain the nature of the exordium to our pupils, we must also consider the easiest method of composing it . . . The best test of the appropriateness of a point to any part of a speech is to consider whether it would lose effect by being placed elsewhere." Arising from his practical experience in the law courts he discusses more fully than other writers the examination of witnesses and the altercation or rapid debate, stressing the importance of quick thinking and a mastery of the details of the issues at hand.

Many of the recommendations concerning educational methods occur in the first two books. Quintilian compares the merits of public and private education and reflects on how pupils should be treated: "Some boys are slack unless spurred on; others resent control; some can be restrained by fear; others are paralysed by it." Later he discusses in more detail the different methods required for pupils of different aptitudes. He considers that teacher and pupil have mutual obligations, and that the teacher should regard himself in the place of a parent. He lays great stress on decorousness and the avoidance of vulgarity.

Of special interest to later generations has been his survey of Greek and Latin writers in Book X. He gives brief judgements on most major classical writers and on many whose works are lost. Homer is given pride of place and eulogized both for his poetic and oratorical powers. The survey ends with some criticism of Seneca's unnatural expressions and epigrammatic brevity. Quintilian then proceeds to describe various ways in which students can benefit from the study of literary works, such as imitation, translation, or paraphrase.

When he comes to describe the ideal orator in Book XII Quintilian rejects the notion that the orator is merely someone hired to plead in the law courts; rather he is a "man who to extraordinary natural gifts has added a thorough mastery of all the finest branches of knowledge, a man sent by heaven to be the blessing of mankind, one to whom all history can find no parallel, uniquely perfect in every detail and utterly noble in both thought and speech." As George Kennedy has observed, "It is difficult to think that Quintilian's great orator in the fullest sense can be anyone other than some future emperor . . . As Plato had longed for a philosopher-king, so Quintilian longs for an orator-emperor." The complete text of *The Institutio Oratoria* was discovered by Poggio in 1416 and exercised its greatest influence during the Renaissance and Reformation. Many of Quintilian's concerns are still shared by educationalists and public speakers today.

—David Maskell

R

RABELAIS, François

Born: 1484(?). **Education:** Possibly studied law, 1500–10, in Bourges, Angers, or Poitiers; became a Franciscan in 1520s; studied medicine, possibly in Paris, then in Montpellier; Bachelor of medicine, 1530; Doctor of medicine, 1537. **Family:** Had three illegitimate children (two surviving children later formally legitimated). **Career:** Lectured in medicine, Montpellier, 1531; practiced in southern France; physician at Hôtel-Dieu, Lyons, 1532; visited Italy as personal doctor of Bishop, later Cardinal, Jean Du Bellay, 1534, and later visits with Guillaume Du Bellay; Canon at Benedictine Abbey of Saint Maurtes-Fossés, 1536; given benefices at Meudon and Jambet, 1551 (resigned them, 1553). **Died:** 9 April(?) 1553.

PUBLICATIONS

Collections

Oeuvres, edited by Abel Lefranc and others. 6 vols., 1912–55.
Works, edited by Albert Jay Nock and Catherine Rose Wilson. 2 vols., 1931.
Oeuvres complètes, edited by Pierre Jourda. 2 vols., 1962.
Complete Works, translated by Donald M. Frame. 1992.

Fiction

Gargantua and Pantagruel, translated by Thomas Urquhart, 1653, continuation by P.A. Motteux, 1694; also translated by J.M. Cohen, 1955; Burton Raffel, 1990.
Pantagruel. 1532; edited by V.L. Saulnier, 1965.
Gargantua. 1534(?) (now usually printed as first book); edited by R.M. Calder and M.A. Screech, 1970.
Tiers Livre . . . Pantagruel. 1546; edited by M.A. Screech, 1964.
Quart Livre . . . Pantagruel. 1552; edited by Robert Marichal, 1947.

Other

Pantagruéline prognostication. 1533; edited by M.A Screech, 1974.
The Portable Rabelais (selection), edited and translated by Samuel Putnam. 1946.
Editor, [Works], by Hippocrates and Galen. 1532.
Editor, *Aphorismorum*, by Hippocrates. 1532.
Editor, *Typographia antiquae Romae*, by J.B. Marlianus. 1534.

*

Bibliography: *A New Rabelais Bibliography: Editions of Rabelais Before 1624* by Stephen Rawles, 1987.

Critical Studies: *The Rabelaisian Marriage: Aspects of Rabelais's Religion, Ethics, and Cosmic Philosophy*, 1958, and *Rabelais*, 1979, and *Looking at Rabelais*, 1988, all by M.A. Screech; *Rabelais: A Critical Study in Prose Fiction* by Dorothy Gabe Coleman, 1971; *The Age of Bluff: Paradox and Ambiguity in Rabelais and Montaigne* by B.C. Bowen, 1972; *The Wine and the Will: Rabelais's Bacchic Christianity* by F.M. Weinberg, 1972; *Rabelais and Panurge: A Psychological Approach to Literary Character* by Mary E. Ragland, 1976; *Rabelais: A Study* by Donald M. Frame, 1977; *Rabelais, homo logos* by Alice Fiola Berry, 1979; *Recreation, Reflection and Recreation: Perspectives on Rabelais's Pantagruel*, 1980, and *Rabelais's Incomparable Book: Essays on his Art*, 1986, both by Raymond C. La Charité; *Rhetoric at Play: Rabelais and Satirical Eulogy* by Deborah N. Losse, 1980; *Irenic Apocalypse: Some Uses of Apocalyptic in Dante, Petrarch and Rabelais* by Dennis Costa, 1981; *The Countervoyage of Rabelais and Ariosto* by Elizabeth A. Chesney, 1982; *The Problem of Unbelief in the Sixteenth Century: The Religion of Rabelais* by Lucien Febvre, 1982; *The Vulgar Rabelais* by Carol A. Clark, 1983; *Rabelais at Glasgow: Proceedings of the Colloquium Held at the University of Glasgow in December 1983*, 1984; *Pantagruel in Canada* by Marius Barbeau, 1984; *Every Man for Himself: Social Order and its Dissolution in Rabelais* by Richard M. Berrong, 1985; *Rabelais's Carnival: Text, Context, Metatext* by Samuel Kinser, 1990; *Irony and Ideology in Rabelais: Structures of Subversion* by Jerome Schwartz, 1990; *The Design of Rabelais's Pantagruel* by Edwin M. Duval, 1991; *Rabelais Revisited* by Elizabeth Chesney Zagora and Marcel Tetel, 1993; *Rabelais, Tiers livre, Quart livre, Ve livre* by Ian R. Morrison, 1994; *François Rabelais: A Reference Guide, 1950–1990* by Bruno Braunrot, 1994; *François Rabelais: Critical Assessments*, edited by Jean-Claude Carron, 1995; *Rabelais* by Michael J. Heath, 1996; *The Rabelaisian Mythologies* by Max Gauna, 1996; *Enter Rabelais, Laughing* by Barbara C. Bowen, 1998; *Imagining Rabelais in Renaissance England* by Anne Lake Prescott, 1998; *The Charm of Catastrophe: A Study of Rabelais's Quart livre* by Alice Fiola Berry, 2000.

*   *   *

François Rabelais's reputation has been fashioned largely by people who have never read a word he wrote. "Rabelaisian" is often used as a synonym for smutty, while many who have never thought to read the book like to pride themselves on their gargantuan appetites. The image goes back a long way: as early as the middle of the 16th century, Ronsard wrote an epitaph to Rabelais in which he asked passers-by to throw sausages and sides of ham, instead of flowers, on the dead author's grave. But practitioners of learned wit from Swift to Joyce and Robertson Davies have read and admired him, and Laurence Sterne swore by the "ashes of my dear Rabelais."

Rabelais is unique. His particular brand of encyclopedic humour has its origins in his theological training, his vast erudition (he was perfectly at home in Latin and Greek and conversant with most of the major classical authors), and in his expertise in the spheres of medicine, law, and popular culture. To say that he is an Evangelical Christian humanist of Neo-Platonic and Stoic inclinations is to provide the prospective reader with a map of Rabelais country; to get the feel of the landscape you have to plunge into the works themselves with as open a mind as you can. The going will never be easy, for the way is strewn with private jokes and a network of allusions which only a reader armed with a fully annotated edition can hope to understand, but the reward for perseverance will be not only a good deal of healthy laughter but admission to a world imagined by a wordsmith and storyteller of genius.

Recent years have seen Rabelais rescued from the writers of wine catalogues and restored to his rightful place as a great creative writer living in an age dominated by ideas. Yet generalizations (however complimentary) about him are rarely helpful, for the four books of *Gargantua and Pantagruel* (the posthumous fifth book is probably only partly by him) were written at different dates and in very different circumstances, when the world around him and his reaction to it had undergone great changes.

When Rabelais wrote *Pantagruel* in 1532, he was in his late forties with a couple of quite separate careers already behind him. This first excursion into prose fiction may well have been written for money (he himself suggests as much in his prologue), but it also released a side of his personality which the learned doctor had hitherto kept in check. Using the easily decipherable pseudonym of Alcofrybas Nasier, he lets the genie out of the bottle and indulges in that archetypal lord of misrule Panurge.

Whereas *Pantagruel* is a chronicle of mischief, its sequel, *Gargantua*, has a very different tone, even though the structure and subject-matter are similar. The doings of the family of giants become less important than the ideas they embody. Gargantua's mother eats vast quantities of tripe, the young giant urinates over 274,418 Parisians, and steals the bells of Notre-Dame, but, notwithstanding these episodes, one senses that he is increasingly the vehicle for Rabelais's ideas. The book divides conveniently into three distinct sections. In the first 24 chapters, devoted to the childhood of Gargantua, he expounds the sort of ideas of education which had been current for some years among "progressive" educationalists. Rabelais's debt to Erasmus and Vivès is obvious, and he is swimming with the same tide as Sir Thomas Elyot and, in his praise of discreet elegance, Castiglione. With its emphasis on courtly attributes, this part of the book is very, much a "mirror for princes" and, despite the jokes, quite removed from the spirit of much of *Pantagruel*. The narrative switches abruptly to the countryside around the author's native Chinon in which he sets the Picrocholean War between the giants and an irascible neighbour. This "war" allows Rabelais to air his views (once again strongly influenced by Erasmus) on the moral limits of military might, and the need for Christians to outlaw wars of aggression. Finally, in the third section of the book, Rabelais builds for his conquering heroes an abbey to their liking, an anti-monastery very different from any existing religious institution. This "Abbey of Thelema" (New Testament Greek for "will") is a palatial refuge from an imperfect world where those whose lives are guided by selflessness and a sense of honour learn to live together, in preparation perhaps for carrying their message beyond the abbey's walls. The famous motto "Do as you wish" must be seen in context: it is definitely not a recipe for a free-for-all.

This reflective mood continues in the *Tiers Livre* (*Third Book*), published in 1546. Panurge, who had not figured in the *Gargantua*, returns—almost, one feels, by popular demand—to overshadow the giants themselves, but is now portrayed as less a frolicsome hero than a confused and somewhat pathetic figure, an ageing lecher who is unable to make up his mind as to whether or not he should marry. Attracted by marriage for its physical benefits, he is nevertheless haunted by the fear of being made a cuckold. The book provides Rabelais with an excuse for making a contribution to the topical "*querelle des amies*", a variation on the everpopular "battle of the sexes" theme, and one to which, one would have thought, the

ecclesiastical authorities could not have taken exception. But they had their man in their sights, and, like its predecessors, the *Third Book* was banned. For this reason perhaps Rabelais returns to his old hobby-horses in the *Quart Livre* (*Fourth Book*), the final version of which came out in 1552. It contains a streak of bitter satire which was not much in evidence before, and some of his attacks (on Calvin, for example) are a treat for connoisseurs of invective. Of all Rabelais's works, the *Fourth Book* is the most linguistically inventive, and a high proportion of the jokes and anecdotes still come off. The delightfully ambiguous Brother John, who had been so important in *Gargantua*, is once more playfully to the fore, his muscular Christianity contrasting with Panurge's pusillanimity. As our heroes sail in search of the oracle of the bottle, each port of call presents them with a different aspect of human life. The model for this technique was Lucian's *Vera Historia* (*True History*), but Rabelais's vision is his own. It is summed up by that *mediocrité*, his version of Horace's *aurea mediocritas* or golden mean, which came to dominate his thinking in these last years of his life. He speaks out against sectarianism, rails at being caught between the "hammer and the anvil," and makes great play with human folly in all its variety. But parts of the *Fourth Book* lead one to suspect that the author's spirits were low, and that his advice to his reader to keep a "certain gaiety of mind full of contempt for the accidents of life" was meant as much for himself. While some episodes are pure fun, others—notably the moving chapter on the death of heroes—are tinged with sadness. Taken as a whole, though, Rabelais's work stands out as one of the great comic masterpieces of world literature. Rabelais is indeed a doctor of laughter whose books remain, in our very different world, a perfect cure of melancholy.

—Michael Freeman

See the essay on *Gargantua and Pantagruel*.

RACINE, Jean

Born: La Ferté-Milon, France, 22 December 1639. **Education:** Educated by Jansenists at Convent of Port Royal, Paris; Collège d'Harcourt, Paris, 1658–59; studied theology with his uncle at Uzès, Languedoc, 1661–63. **Family:** Married Cathérine de Romanet in 1677; five daughters and two sons. **Career:** Molière's troupe performed his first two plays at the Palais Royal, Paris, 1664; broke with Molière *q.v.*, 1665; plays produced at the Hôtel de Bourgogne, Paris, 1667–77; wrote no plays 1677–89; wrote his last two plays for the girls' school at Saint-Cyr, patronized by Madame de Maintenon; appointed historiographer (with Boileau) by Louis XIV, 1677. **Member:** Académie française, 1673. **Died:** 21 April 1699.

PUBLICATIONS

Collections

Oeuvres complètes, edited by Paul Mesnard. 8 vols., 1865–73, revised edition, 10 vols., 1885.
Oeuvres complètes, edited by Raymond Picard. 2 vols., 1950–52.
Complete Plays, translated by Samuel Solomon. 2 vols., 1967.
Oeuvres complètes, edited by Jacques Morel and Alain Viala. 1980.

Plays

La Thébaïde; ou, Les Frères ennemis (produced 1664). 1664; edited by Michael Edwards, 1965; as *The Fatal Legacy*, translated 1723; as *The Theban Brothers* translated by Samuel Solomon, in *Complete Plays*, 1967.

Alexandre le grand (produced 1665). 1666; edited by M. Hawcroft and V. Worth, 1990; as *Alexander the Great*, translated by J. Ozell, 1714; also translated by Samuel Solomon, in *Complete Plays*, 1967.

Andromaque (produced 1667). 1668; edited by R.C. Knight and H.T. Barnwell, 1977; as *Andromache*, 1675, several subsequent translations, including by Kenneth Muir, 1960, Richard Wilbur, 1982, and Douglas Dunn, 1990; as *The Distressed Mother*, 1712; as *"1953": A Version of Racine's Andromaque*, translated by Craig Raine, 1990.

Les Plaideurs (produced 1668). 1669; as *The Litigants*, translated by J. Ozell, 1715; also translated by W.R. Dunston, 1928; as *The Suitors*, translated anonymously, 1862; also translated by Irving Brown, 1871.

Britannicus (produced 1669). 1670; edited by Philip Butler, 1967; as *Britannicus*, 1714; several subsequent translations, including by Kenneth Muir, 1960, and C.H. Sisson, with *Phaedra* and *Athaliah*, 1987; translated by Robert David MacDonald, 1998.

Bérénice (produced 1670). 1671; edited by W.S. Maguinness, 1929, C.L. Walton, 1965, and L. Lejalle, 1971; as *Titus and Berenice*, translated by Thomas Otway, 1677; also translated by John Masefield, 1922; several subsequent translations as *Bérénice*, including by Kenneth Muir, 1960, and John Cairncross, 1967; translated by R.C. Knight, 1999.

Bajazet (produced 1672). 1672; as *The Sultaness*, translated anonymously, 1717; as *Bajazet*, translated by V.M. Martin, 1964; also translated by Alan Hollinghurst, 1991.

Mithridate (produced 1673). 1673; as *Mithridates*, translated by Howard Davis Spoerl, 1926.

Iphigénie (produced 1674). 1675; as *Achilles; or, Iphigenia in Aulis*, 1700; as *The Victim*, 1714; as *Iphigenia*, 1861; several subsequent translations including by R.C. Knight, 1982.

Phèdre (produced 1677). As *Phèdre et Hippolyte*, 1677; edited by J.L. Barrault, 1946; as *Phaedre and Hippolytus*, 1756; several subsequent translations as *Phaedra*, including by Bernard D.N. Grebanier, 1958, Richard Wilbur, 1986, and C.H. Sisson, with *Britannicus* and *Athaliah*, 1987; as *Phedra*, translated by Robert David MacDonald, 1985; as *Racine's Phaedra*, translated by Derek Mahon, 1996; in a new version by Ted Hughes, 1998.

L'Idylle de la paix, music by Lully (produced 1685). 1685.

Esther (produced 1689). 1689; as *Esther*, 1715.

Athalie (produced 1691). 1691; edited by Peter France, 1966; as *Athaliah*, 1722; as *Athalia*, translated by R.C. Knight, in *Four Greek Plays*, 1982; and C.H. Sisson, with *Britannicus* and *Phaedra*, 1987; as *Athalie*, translated by Kenneth Muir, 1960.

Five Plays (includes *Andromaque; Britannicus; Bérénice; Phèdre; Athatie*), translated by Kenneth Muir. 1960.

Three Plays (includes *Andromache; Britannicus; Phaedra*), translated by George Dillon. 1961.

Iphigenia; Phaedra; Athaliah, translated by John Cairncross. 1963.

Jean Racine: Andromache and Other Plays, translated by John Cairncross. 1967.

Four Greek Plays (includes *Andromache; Iphigenia; Phaedra; Athaliah*), translated by R.C. Knight. 1982.

Britannicus; Phaedra; Athaliah, translated by C.H. Sisson. 1987.

Verse

La Nymphe de la Seine. 1660.

Ode sur la convalescence du Roi. 1663.

Cantiques spirituels. 1694.

Campagne de Louis XIV, with Boileau. 1730; as *Éloge historique du Roi, Louis XIV*, 1784.

Poésies sacrées. 1914.

Poésies, edited by Gonzague Truc. 1936.

Poésies religieuses inconnues. 1954; as *Confessions: Unpublished Sonnets*, translated by Walter Roberts, 1956.

Other

Abrégé de l'histoire de Port-Royal. 1742.

*

Bibliography: *Jean Racine's Andromaque: An Annotated Bibliography* by June Moravcevich, 1984.

Critical Studies: *The Classical Moment*, 1947, and *Jean Racine, Dramatist*, 1972, both by Martin Turnell; *Racine: Convention and Classicism* by R.C. Knight, 1952, and *Racine: Modern Judgements* edited by Knight, 1969; *Aspects of Racinian Tragedy* by John C. Lapp, 1955, revised edition, 1964; *The Art of Jean Racine* by Bernard Weinberg, 1963; *Racine's Rhetoric*, 1965, and *Racine: Andromaque*, 1977, both by Peter France; *Racine; or, The Triumph of Relevance* by Odette de Mourgues, 1967; *Racine: Myths and Renewal in Modern Theatre* by Bettina Knapp, 1971; *Racine* by Lucien Goldman, 1973; *Corneille and Racine: Problems of Tragic Form* by Gordon Pocock, 1973; *Racine: A Study* by Philip Butler, 1974; *Racine, "Britannicus"* by Will Grayburn Moore, 1975; *Jean Racine* by C. Abraham, 1977; *Racine's Theatre* by W.J. Cloonan, 1977; *Toward a Freudian Theory of Literature, with an Analysis of Racine's "Phèdre"* by Francesco Orlando, 1978; *Racine* by Philip John Yarrow, 1978; *The Mannerist Aesthetic: A Study of Racine's Mithridate* by Michael O'egan, 1980; *Racine's La Thébaïde: Political, Moral, and Aesthetic Dimensions* by Robert L. Myers, 1981; *The Tragic Drama of Corneille and Racine: An Old Parallel Revisited* by H.T. Barnwell, 1982; *Jean Racine: Meditations on his Poetic Art* by Norah K. Drown, 1982; *Racine, Phèdre* by J.P. Short, 1983; *Dramatic Narrative: Racine's Recits* by Nina C. Ekstein, 1986; *Racine's Bérénice* by James J. Supple, 1986; *Illusions and Erkenntnis in Racine's Phèdre* by Astrid Bernhard, 1988; *Britannicus* by John Campbell, 1990; *Racine, Mithridate*, 1990, and *Racine: Appraisal and Reappraisal*, 1991, both by Henry Phillips; *Racine: A Theatrical Reading* by David Maskell, 1991; *Word as Action: Racine, Rhetoric and Theatrical Language* by Michael Hawcroft, 1992; *Racine: The Limits of Tragedy* by Richard Parish, 1993; *Racine: Athalie* by J. Dryhurst, 1994; *In the Grip of Minos: Confessional Discourse in Dante, Corneille, and Racine* by Matthew Senior, 1994; *Racine: Phèdre* by E.D. James and G. Jondorf, 1994; *La gloire: The Roman Empire of Corneille and Racine* by Louis Auchincloss, 1996; *Towards a Cultural Philology: Phèdre and the Construction of "Racine"* by Amy Wygant, 1999; *Jean*

Racine Revisited by Ronald W. Tobin, 1999; *Racine: The Power and the Pleasure*, edited by Edric Caldicott and Derval Conroy, 2001.

* * *

Probably France's greatest tragic playwright, arguably its best dramatic poet, and certainly the writer who observed the rules of the neo-classical drama with the greatest ease and success, Jean Racine is rightly regarded as the perfect embodiment of the French genius for psychological analysis and the accurate use of language. He solved the problem of how to write a play which conformed to the three unities of time, place, and action by the simple device of taking an emotional situation at the very moment it is about to explode. In his first great success, *Andromaque* (*Andromache*), it is the arrival of Orestes to demand that Pyrrhus hand over Hector's son Astyanax to the Greeks that sets the tragedy into motion, and it is wholly convincing that, within 24 hours, Orestes himself should then kill Pyrrhus at the instigation of Hermione and go mad, while Hermione herself commits suicide, and the widowed Andromache is left in sole command at Epirus. For beneath the perfect finish of his 12-syllable Alexandrines—Racine wrote out his plays in prose before putting the final version into verse—there is an immensely powerful world of violent, passionate emotions, and it is the contrast between this primitive world and the classical form of his plays that has made Racine one of the most admired and studied of all French 17th-century authors.

Like the mathematician and philosopher Blaise Pascal, Racine had strong links with the belief system known as Jansenism, and seems to have shared the neo-Augustinian view that man was an irredeemably fallen creature who was doomed to damnation unless saved by the gratuitous intervention of a Divine Grace which he could do nothing to deserve by his own efforts. The eponymous heroine of his most famous play, *Phèdre* (*Phaedra*), seems in this respect almost the epitome of the sinner who wishes to be virtuous but is refused the Grace which alone makes this possible, and the fact that Racine gave up writing for the profane theatre after 1677 has been interpreted as a sign that it was his own spiritual anguish and feelings of guilt that inspired this play. The continuity and intensity of his appeal to a 20th-century audience nevertheless lies more in the wider metaphysical overtones of Jansenist theology, and the edifying Christian plays that he wrote on his return to the theatre, *Esther* and *Athalie*, strike a rather strange note on the modern stage. His vision of mankind as unable to control or escape its destiny, doomed to destruction in an absurd universe in which the only sign of the Gods is their remorseless cruelty, has obvious associations with Sartre or Beckett, though his plays are far superior theatrically to anything in French other than the very best of Corneille or Molière, His female roles, especially, offer some of the best acting parts in the whole classical repertory, and Aldous Huxley's remark about the ''somewhat featureless males who serve as a pretext to their anguish'' does not really fit the demands and potentialities of roles such as Pyrrhus in *Andromache*, Acomat in *Bajazet*, or Thésée in *Phaedra*.

As a man, Racine seems to have had little of the humanity and generosity of spirit which made Molière so attractive, and he was as ruthless in promoting his own career as he was scathing in his remarks about his rivals. There is also something odd about a man who created the most passionate tragic heroines in French literature but who married a woman who never went to the theatre and is said never to have read a single one of his plays. The apparently effortless perfection of Racine's versification is partially explicable by the fact that he wrote the second line of each rhyming couplet first in order to avoid any impression of artificiality, but may also be linked to his excellence as a classical scholar. He was unusual among French 17th-century writers in reading the Greek dramatists in the original, and the atmosphere of ''Jansenist perdition'' so frequently detected in his plays might equally well stem from the influence of Euripides, the classical playwright whom he most admired. His own aesthetic was very much based on classical models, and only one of his tragedies—*Bajazet*, which takes place in Turkey—has a contemporary setting. He himself justified this by arguing that distance in space could compensate for proximity in time. Among his other plays, only the comedy *Les Plaideurs* (*The Litigants*) takes place in the 17th century, and he fully accepted the classical notion that we ''see the heroes of tragedy with a different eye'' because they are so far away from us in time.

The celebrated parallel with Corneille enshrined in La Bruyère's comment that ''Corneille depicts men as they should be, Racine as they are'' can also be explained by historical reasons. By the time Racine began his career, the self-confident and turbulent nobility depicted in Corneille's earlier tragedies had been defeated in the civil war of the 1650s known as *La Fronde* and domesticated into the court life at Versailles. There, they tended to fill their enforced leisure by the analysis of their own amorous intrigues, and were thus ready to appreciate the detailed account that Racine provided of political impotence coupled with intense if frustrated passion. Much of the 19th century's enthusiasm for Racine stemmed from this view of him as a superb analyst of the human heart, though he was naturally also used in the defence of Classicism against Romanticism as the embodiment of the classical writers of moderation, rationality, and verisimilitude as contrasted with ''vigorous barbarism'' of Shakespeare. The vision of Racine as a periwig-pated practitioner of the duller literary virtues did much to hinder an appreciation of his work in England and America, though it should be said that no other great French writer loses more in translation. From a deliberately limited, conventional vocabulary, less than 2,000 words, he produces the most extraordinary poetic effects, and no playwright has depicted sexual aggression and sexual jealousy with greater accuracy and force. While the English reader will find him inferior to Shakespeare in the narrowness of his range, abstention from speculation, and reluctance to depict the complexity of human life, compensation can be found in the concentration of his vision, unity of aesthetic creation, and constant attention to the emotions immediately under analysis.

—Philip Thody

See the essays on *Athalie*, *Bajazet*, *Bérénice*, and *Phaedra*.

RADIGUET, Raymond

Born: Parc Saint-Maur, Paris, France, 18 June 1903. **Education:** Educated at Lycée Charlemagne, Paris. **Career:** Regular contributor to numerous newspapers and journals including *Le Canard enchaîné*, *Sic*, *L'Heure*, *L'Eveil*, *Littérature*, and *Le Coq*, Paris, 1918–20; editorial secretary, *Le Rire*, Paris, c. 1918. Met Max Jacob, *q.v.*, who became an influential force on his writing. Closely associated with Jean Cocteau, *q.v.*, with whom he had an affair. **Died:** Of typhus, 12 December 1923.

PUBLICATIONS

Collections

Textes inédits, edited by Henri Massis. 1927.
Oeuvres complètes. 1952.
Oeuvres complètes, edited by Simone Lamblin. 2 vols., 1959.
Oeuvres complètes, edited by Chloé Radiguet and Julien Cendres. 1993.

Fiction

Le Diable au corps. 1923; as *The Devil in the Flesh*, translated by Kay Boyle, 1932; also translated by Alan M. Sheridan Smith, 1968; Robert Baldick, 1971.
Le Bal du comte d'Orgel. 1924; as *Ball at Count d'Orgel's*, translated by Malcolm Cowley, 1929; as *Count d'Orgel Opens the Ball*, translated by Violet Schiff, 1952; as *Count d'Orgel* translated by Alan Sheridan Smith, 1969.
Denise (story), illustrated by Juan Gris. 1926.

Verse

Les Joues en feu I. 1920; revised and enlarged edition, 1925; as *Cheeks on Fire: Collected Poems*, translated by Alan Stone, 1976.
Devoirs de vacances. 1921.
Vers libres. 1925; with *Jeux innocents*, 1988.
Jeux innocents. 1926; with *Vers libres*, 1988.

Plays

Les Pélicans (produced 1921). 1921; as *The Pelicans*, edited and translated by Michael Benedikt and George Wellworth, in *Modern French Plays*, 1964.
Paul et Virginie (opera libretto), with Jean Cocteau. 1967.

*

Critical Studies: *Raymond Radiguet: Étude biographique* by Keith Goesch, 1955; *Radiguet*, 1969, and *Raymond Radiguet: la nostalgie*, 1991, both by Clément Borgal; *Raymond Radiguet* by David Noakes, 1969; *Un Maître de 17 ans, Raymond Radiguet* by Gabriel Boillat, 1973; Raymond Radiguet issue of *Cahiers Jean Cocteau*, 4, edited by Pierre Chanel, 1973; *Los Années folles de Raymond Radiguet* (includes bibliography) by Nadia Odouard, 1974; *Raymond Radiguet: A Biographical Study with Selections from His Work* by Margaret Crosland, 1976; *Radiguet, Cocteau, "Les Joues en feu"* by Jean-Louis Major, 1977; *Radiguet* by James P. McNab, 1984; *L'Imaginaire dans les romans de Raymond Radiguet* by Calogero Giardina, 1991; *Cocteau et Radiguet; Étude comparée de leur crdation romanesque parallèle* by Damien François, 1992.

* * *

Raymond Radiguet enjoyed a literary career that in many ways imitated that of the poet Arthur Rimbaud: brief, precocious, and meteoric. However, unlike Rimbaud, who simply renounced writing around the age of 21, Radiguet certainly intended to pursue his literary career, and indeed one of the most fascinating questions in the history of 20th-century French literature is the way in which his *oeuvres* would have developed had typhoid not killed him at the age of 20. His reputation rests on two novels, *Le Diable au corps* (*The Devil in the Flesh*) and *Le Bal du Comte d'Orgel* (*Count d'Orgel Opens the Ball*), and a collection of poetry, *Les Joues en feu* (*Cheeks on Fire*). His most distinctive achievement is in the use of delicate, psychological analysis and classical restraint of style to surprise and, frequently, to shock. His writing displays adolescent intensity and disillusion in equal proportions, and holds up the mirror to a society shaken to the core by the events of World War I and unable to accommodate itself to the post-war era.

Radiguet spent his childhood in Saint-Maur-sur-Marne, on the outskirts of Paris. His father, an impoverished cartoonist whose work was published weekly in *L'Intransigeant*, tried to supplement his son's education by teaching him Greek and Latin. Although not wholly successful in this, his influence induced Radiguet to read widely in the French classics, reading that was soon supplemented by contemporary works, notably those of Cocteau, Jacob, and Apollinaire.

His formal education was somewhat perfunctory, the war creating a climate which facilitated regular truancy, At the age of 15, Radiguet more or less left home to live in Paris, where contacts with his father's publishers enabled him to publish some of his poems. He gained quickly an entrée into the avant-garde of Parisian cultural life. Cocteau became his patron and lover, introducing him to Jacob and Breton, and to Picasso and other Cubist painters. His circle of friends extended to musicians, notably the Group of Six and Erik Satie, with whom, in 1920, he produced the comic opera *Paul et Virginie*.

In the same year, he published the collection of poems *Cheeks on Fire*, characterized by striking comparisons and clever rhymes, yet focusing on the everyday, even to the extent of deliberate banality ("Strive to be banal," was on injunction contained in his article, "Advice to Great Poets"). There is an apparent paradox in this attempt to write like everyone else in an era that prioritized the cult of the individual, but Radiguet's originality lies in the classical precision of both his style and his analysis of feelings. These qualities were honed still further when he published his only play *Les Pélicans* (*The Pelicans*).

During the summer of 1921, he started writing his most notable work, *The Devil in the Flesh*, while on holiday on the Atlantic coast of France with Cocteau. The English rendering of the title is unsatisfactory, for it simply conveys lust rather than an impatience to grow up in order to relish the joys of adulthood. Inevitably, much of the novel is autobiographical, the story of an adolescent who grabs the opportunities for freedom that wartime offers. The narrator, a boy of 15, consciously falls in love with an older woman, Marthe, whose husband Jacques is away fighting at the front. The affair is recounted with astonishing lucidity, from the first tentative efforts at seduction, through his initiation by Marthe in a relationship in which sensuality, cruelty, and tenderness all play their part. The small town in which the couple live is scandalized, but their passion feeds on the flouting of convention and the risk of discovery by Jacques. Eventually, Marthe dies in childbirth, but the narrator's sorrow is perversely diminished by the discovery that Marthe has named her son after him. When the book was published in 1923 it enjoyed immediate success.

Count d'Orgel Opens the Ball was written the following year and Radiguet was still working on the proofs when he died. Narrated this time in the third person (this created certain problems for Radiguet, as at times authorial intervention into the narrative becomes obtrusive), the novel is closely modelled on the 17th-century psychological novel, Madame de Lafayette's *La Princesse de Clèves* (*The Princess of Clèves*). Mme. d'Orgel falls in love with François de Séryeuse, and although they eventually discover that their love is reciprocal, the pair never meet. Mme. d'Orgel confesses her love to her husband who, insisting that outward appearances must be maintained at all costs, invites François to his ball. Conscious echoes of the medieval Romance novel and rigorous analysis of emotions serve to create a highly literary work in which, to quote Radiguet, "only the psychology is romantic."

Three days before he died, on 12 December 1923, Radiguet told Cocteau: "Listen to something dreadful. In three days I shall be shot by the soldiers of God." Cocteau supervised the final proofs of *Count d'Orgel Opens the Ball*, published the following year, though he did not attend his friend's funeral service, arranged by Coco Chanel.

Radiguet's output may have been slight, but his renewal of the psychological novel, his concision, his humour, and above all his lucidity have exerted a continuing fascination upon later generations of readers.

—Jane McAdoo

See the essay on *The Devil in the Flesh*.

RADNÓTI, Miklós

Born: Budapest, Hungary, 5 May 1909. Mother died when he was born, his father when he was 12; thereafter brought up by relatives. **Education:** Completed studies in business school in 1927; studied textile manufacturing in Liberec, then Czechoslovakia, 1927–28; completed high school education in 1929; studied Hungarian and French at University of Szeged, 1930–34. **Family:** Married Fanni Gyarmati in 1934. **Career:** Clerk in private office, 1928–29; literary work confiscated in 1931: suspended sentence for "defamation of religion"; visited Paris several times in the 1930s; served in forced labour camp in Transylvania, 1940, and near Bor, Yugoslavia, 1944. Shot with 22 others by guards and buried in mass grave near the village of Abda, Hungary: his body, with last poems, recovered in 1946. **Awards:** Baumgarten prize, 1937. **Died:** (shot) 1944.

PUBLICATIONS

Collections

Versei [Poems], edited by Imre Trencsényi-Waldapfel. 1948.
Tanulmányok, cikkek [Essays, Articles], edited by Pál Réz. 1956.
Sem emlék, sem varázslat. Összes versei [Neither Memory, nor Magic: Complete Poems]. 1961.
Összes versei és műfordításai [Complete Poetry and Translations], edited by Pál Réz. 1966.
Összes versei és műfordításai [Complete Poetry and Translations], edited by Sándor Koczkás. 1969.
Művei [Works], edited by Pál Réz. 1979.
Forced March: Selected Poems, edited and translated by Clive Wilmer and George Gömöri. 1979.
The Complete Poetry, edited and translated by Emery George. 1980.

Foamy Sky: The Major Poems of Miklós Radnóti, edited and translated by Zsuzsanna Ozsváth and Frederick Turner. 1992.
33 Poems, translated by Thomas Ország-Land. 1992.

Verse

Naptár. 1924; as *Calendar*, translated by Emery George, in *The Complete Poetry*, 1980.
Pogány köszöntő. 1930; as *Pagan Salute*, translated by Emery George, in *The Complete Poetry*, 1980.
Újmódi pásztorok éneke. 1931; as *Song of Modern Shepherds*, translated by Emery George, in *The Complete Poetry*, 1980.
Lábadozó szél. 1933; as *Convalescent Wind*, translated by Emery George, in *The Complete Poetry*, 1980.
Ének a négerről, aki a városba ment. 1934; as *Song of the Black Man Who Went to Town*, translated by Emery George, in *The Complete Poetry*, 1980.
Újhold. 1935; as *New Moon*, translated by Emery George, in *The Complete Poetry*, 1980.
Járkálj csak, halálraítélt! 1936; as *Walk On, Condemned!*, translated by Emery George, in *The Complete Poetry*, 1980.
Meredek út. 1938; as *Steep Road*, translated by Emery George, in *The Complete Poetry*, 1980.
Válogatott versek 1930–1940 [Selected Poems]. 1940.
Tajtékos ég. 1946; as *Clouded Sky*, translated by Steven Polgar, Stephen Berg, and S.J. Marks, 1972; as *Sky with Clouds*, translated by Emery George, in *The Complete Poetry*, 1980.
Bori notesz [Notebook of Bor]. 1971.
Subway Stops: Fifty Poems, edited and translated by Emery George. 1977.
The Witness: Selected Poems, translated by Thomas Orszag-Land. 1977.

Other

Kaffka Margit művészi fejlődése [The Artistic Development of Margit Kaffka]. 1934.
Ikrek hava (autobiographical sketch). 1940; as *Under Gemini* (includes poems), translated by Kenneth and Gita McRobbie and Jascha Kessler, 1985.
Karunga, a holtak ura: Néger népmesegyűjtemény [Karunga, Lord of the Dead: Collection of Black Folk-Tales]. 1944.
Napló [Diary], edited by Tibor Melczer. 1989.
Translator, with István Vas, *Selected Poems*, by Apollinaire. 1940.
Translator, *Huizinga válogatott tanulmányai*, by Jan Huizinga. 1943.
Translator, *Selected Tales*, by Jean de La Fontaine. 1943.
Translator, with Géza Képes, Ferenc Szemlér, and István Vas, *Orpheus nyomában* [In the Footsteps of Orpheus] (verse anthology). 1943.
Also editor and translator of *Don Quixote* by Cervantes.

*

Bibliography: *Radnóti Miklós. Bibliográfia* [Bibliography of Miklós Radnóti] by István Vasvári, 1966; *Hungarian Authors: A Bibliographical Handbook* by Albert Tezla, 1970; *Radnóti Miklós. Bibliográfia* [Bibliography of Miklós Radnóti], 1989.

Critical Studies: "Miklós Radnóti, a Twentieth-Century Poet" by István Sőtér, in *New Hungarian Quarterly*, 1965; *Kortárs útlevelére.*

Radnóti Miklós 1909–1935 [In a Contemporary's Passport: Miklós Radnóti 1909–1935] by Dezső Baróti, 1977; *Radnóti Miklós* by Pomogáts Béla, 1977; *Radnóti Miklós költői nyelve* [The Poetic Language of Miklós Radnóti] by István Nemes, 1979; *The Life and Poetry of Miklós Radnós: Essays*, edited by George Gömöri and Clive Wilmer, 1999; *In the Footsteps of Orpheus: The Life and Times of Miklós Radnóti* by Zsuzsanna Oszváth, 2000.

* * *

Miklós Radnóti, the Hangarian poet and translator, lost his mother at birth and his father at the age of 12, and was brought up by relatives. Many years later he recalled these facts and the emotional trauma resulting from them in the moving autobiographical sketch *Ikrek hava* (*Under Gemini*). His first book of poetry, *Pogány köszöntő* (*Pagan Salute*), published while he was a student at the University of Szeged in southern Hungary, was strongly influenced by German and French expressionism and described the poet's joyous exultation over life as well as being a protest against social injustice. At the time Radnóti was a "Romantic" socialist and although he established some ties with the tiny, clandestine Communist Party, he was politically active only during his student years. In 1931 his book of verse *Újmódi pásztorok éneke* (*Song of Modern Shepherds*) was confiscated by the public prosecutor and the poet was given a light, suspended jail sentence for his alleged "defamation of religion."

By the mid-1930s Radnóti's poetry had lost its shrill, provocative edge and occasional mannerisms. This was connected with the poet's return to classical forms, a discipline which provided a refuge against the irrationality and wild rhetoric of European fascism. As a frequent contributor to the literary review *Nyugat*, Radnóti won the prestigious Baumgarten prize with his collection *Járkálj csak, halálraítélt!* (*Walk On, Condemned!*). Here he spelled out for the first time his recurring and increasingly dominant vision: the inevitability of violent death in the next war. After a visit to Paris, the Spanish Civil War and Federico García Lorca's death appeared to him as a kind of memento and gained symbolic meaning in his personal mythology. He wrote in "Eclogák I" ("The First Eclogue"):

Still, I keep writing in this frenzied world
As that oak over there: it knows it will be cut down and
  already
Is marked with a white cross showing that there, tomorrow,
The woodcutter begins. Yet, as it waits, it puts forth a
  new leaf.

(translated by Clive Wilmer and George Gömöri)

During the last eight years of his life Radnóti made a determined effort to find meaning in his expected martyrdom. Roman Catholicism, which the Jewish-born Radnóti had embraced inwardly years before his actual conversion during World War II, provided consolation and hope for the future. Greek and Western literary models, on the other hand, offered cultural shelter: Radnóti's last, posthumously published book of verse, *Tajtékos ég* (*Sky with Clouds*), contains dramatic eclogues contrasting the horrors of war with an Arcadia of the soul, odes and poetic letters to his beloved wife, and meditative elegies written in a rich and mellow but at the same time clear and serene idiom. His mature verse is informed by a noble brand of rhetoric in which the traditions of the *Nyugat* poets blend with the innovations of Georg Trakl and Guillaume Apollinaire. The poet in

this period can be justifiably called a "Christian Stoic," though, paradoxically, he eventually lost his life as a Jew. In 1944, after Hungary's occupation by German forces, Radnóti was sent to a labour camp near Bor in Yugoslavia from where, some months later, his unit was escorted on foot towards Germany. One of the most dramatic and beautiful poems of the last period, "Erőltetett menet" [Forced March], describes this event and the poet's still unbroken will to live. Soon afterwards, near the western Hungarian village of Abda, Radnóti and some of his comrades were shot by their guards and buried in a mass grave. When the bodies were exhumed in 1946, the poet's body was identified by a small notebook full of poems, found in his raincoat pocket. He is regarded now as the best Hungarian poet of the war years, his tragic death validating his literary achievement in a compelling manner.

Radnóti was also a noted translator of foreign poetry. His single collection of verse translations, *Orpheus nyomában* [In the Footsteps of Orpheus], which includes Latin poets such as Propertius and Tibullus, French poets such as Pierre de Ronsard and Apollinaire, as well as numerous English and German poets, is the result of inspired and conscientious craftsmanship.

—George Gömöri

REMARQUE, Erich Maria

Born: Erich Paul Remark in Osnabrück, Germany, 22 June 1898. Changed his name in 1923. Naturalized United States citizen. 1947. **Education:** Educated at Johannisschule, 1908–12, Osnabrück, Catholic preparatory school, 1912–15; Catholic teacher's seminary, Osnabrück, 1915–16, 1919. **Military Service:** Served in the German army, 1916–18; wounded twice. **Family:** Married 1) the actress Jutta Ilse Zambona in 1925 (divorced 1930, remarried in 1932, divorced 1951); 2) the actress Paulette Goddard in 1958. Had relationships with the actress Marlene Dietrich, 1939–48, and the actress Greta Garbo. **Career:** Teacher, Lohne, County Bentheim, Klein-Bersen Hümmling, and Nahne, 1919–20; had a variety of jobs including salesman, organist in a mental institution, and advertising copywriter, Hanover, 1920–25; critic, *Osnabrücker Landeszeitung*, 1921; editor, *Sport im Bild*, Berlin, 1925. Emigrated to Switzerland to escape the Nazi regime, 1931; lived in Switzerland and France, 1931–38, deprived of German citizenship, 1938; moved to the United States, 1939, lived in Hollywood, 1939–42, and in New York from 1942. Spent much time in Switzerland and Italy from 1960 for health reasons. **Awards:** Great Order of Merit, Federal Republic of Germany, 1967. **Member:** Corresponding member, German Academy for Language and Literature, 1968. **Died:** 25 September 1970.

PUBLICATIONS

Collections

Leben und Werke. 5 vols., 1985.

Fiction

Die Traumbude. 1920.

Im Westen nichts Neues. 1929; as *All Quiet on the Western Front*, translated by A.W. Wheen, 1929; also translated by Brian Murdoch, 1994.

Der Weg zurück. 1931; as *The Road Back*, translated by A.W. Wheen, 1931.

Three Comrades, translated by A.W. Wheen. 1937; as *Drei Kameraden*, 1938.

Flotsam, translated by Denver Lindley. 1941; as *Liebe deinem Nächsten*, 1941.

Arch of Triumph, translated by Denver Lindley and Walter Sorrell. 1945; as *Arc de Triomphe*, 1946.

Der Funke Leben. 1952; as *The Spark of Life*, translated by James Stern, 1952.

Zeit zu leben und Zeit zu sterben. 1954; as *A Time to Love and a Time to Die*, translated by Denver Lindley, 1954.

Der schwarze Obelisk. 1956; as *The Black Obelisk*, translated by Denver Lindley, 1957.

Der Himmel kennt keine Günstlinge. 1961; as *Heaven Has No Favourites*, translated by Richard and Clara Winston, 1961; as *Bobby Deerfield*, 1977.

Die Nacht von Lissabon. 1962; as *The Night in Lisbon*, translated by Ralph Manheim, 1964.

Schatten im Paradies. 1971; as *Shadows in Paradise*, translated by Ralph Manheim, 1972.

Plays

Die letzte Station (produced 1956). 1958; as *Full Circle*, translated by Peter Stone, 1974.

Screenplays: *Der letzte Akt*, with Fritz Habeck, 1955; *Zeit zu leben und Zeit zu sterben*, 1957.

Radio Plays: *Die letzte Station*. 1958.

*

Bibliography: *Erich Maria Remarque: A Critical Bio-Bibliography* by C.R. Owen, 1984; *Erich Maria Remarque Bibliographie: Quellen Marterialien, Dokumente* by Tilman Westphalen and others, 2 vols., 1988.

Critical Studies: *E.M. Remarque* by Franz Baummer, 1976; *Erich Maria Remarque* by Christine R. Barker and Rex Williams Last, 1979; *Erich Maria Remarque: Leben und Werk* by Alfred Antkowiak, 1983; *Erich Maria von Remarque: A Literary and Film Biography* by Harley U. Taylor, Jr., 1989; *Understanding Erich Maria Remarque* by Hans Wagener, 1991; *All Quiet on the Western Front: Literary Analysis and Cultural Context* by Richard Arthur Firda, 1994; *Opposite Attraction: The Lives of Erich Maria Remarque and Paulette Goddard* by Julie Gilbert, 1995.

*   *   *

Erich Maria Remarque was born Erich Paul Remark in Osnabrück in 1898 in reduced circumstances. The way in which he changed his name, in particular the addition of the French "tail," underlines a streak of sentimentality which intrudes in much of his work as well as pointing out his ambitions towards a flamboyant lifestyle, which the success of *Im Westen nichts Neues* (*All Quiet on the Western Front*)

and other works certainly brought him, and which he further enjoyed in his exile years in America and through his marriage to Paulette Goddard.

After working as a journalist in Weimar Germany, and a rather unfortunate *Jugendstil* sentimental venture into fiction, he gained instant fame and recognition with the publication of *All Quiet on the Western Front* (helped along by a clever advertising campaign on the part of the publishers).

In the late 1920s, the battle lines were clearly being drawn between those who regarded World War I as a disaster which destroyed a whole generation, and the growing forces of National Socialism, which perceived that conflict as a kind of platonic "foundation myth" for the coming of a new Reich, in which the spirit of the front line fighting forces with their blood and iron laid the foundations for the Darwinian struggle of the German nation to rise up again and be a power to be reckoned with.

All Quiet on the Western Front was published at the height of this debate and was an instant international bestseller. Written in autobiographical mode in the present tense, it depicts the lives and deaths of eight front-line soldiers in the trenches of World War I. It contains many of the themes which Remarque was to pursue with great consistency throughout the rest of his novels, with varying degrees of success.

The novel is based on a number of antitheses which underline the lack of organic growth and continuity in German society in the 20th century. The soldiers are depicted as the "lost generation," for whom the world of childhood, school, and parents now has no meaning. They have been cut off from their roots by the traumatic experiences of war, and have been stripped of their youth: "Iron youth? We are young old men."

The experiences of war have created an unbridgeable gulf between the younger soldiers and their elders and supposedly betters: "While they were still writing and speechifying, we saw field hospitals and dying men . . . And we saw that of their world, nothing remained." More than that, though, the war has cut them off from the values of a cultured civilization, reducing them to animals with nothing to exist for but the present moment, and no philosophy save that of pure chance, which determines from one moment to the next whether or not they survive. They are fired with a directionless Bergsonian "life force" which in later novels shades into hope for the future, and which, like that hope, is ultimately brought down and destroyed.

The novel polarized German society. On the one hand, supporters claimed that "he has written for us all," but those opposed to it claimed that it constituted a massive libel against the spirit of the brave fighting forces in the trenches. The debate was exacerbated by one of the novel's great qualities, which characterizes most of Remarque's work: his ability to write about a situation as if he had personally experienced it and to draw the reader into that *trompe l'oeil* reality. Remarque had never himself seen front line fighting, and particular incidents which he describes in the novel were attacked for their factual deficiencies as much as for the way in which they deflated the National Socialist's glorification of front-line battle.

Apart from the strand of sucrose sentimentality, a more effective aspect of his writing was the strong element of irony which pervades not only the title of *All Quiet on the Western Front* (words culled from a general's report on the battle scene), but its sequel, *Der Weg zurück* (*The Road Back*). It becomes clear that there is no road back for those young soldiers who have physically survived the war, and the impossibility ever of returning to a past situation, particularly the idyll of childhood or lost love, constitutes another of the central themes of Remarque's work.

It finds its most poignant expression in the novels about emigration—one further disruption of the lives of Germans in the National Socialist years arising from political affiliations or race. Remarque himself was forced to emigrate (and was particularly bitter after the war at the attitude of the West German government to exiles like himself). To the sense of loss at being uprooted and separated from family, work, and the dignity of an independent existence was added the theme of revenge, which had always been present in his work, and which is most powerfully expressed in *Arc de Triomphe* (*Arch of Triumph*), perhaps his best novel, which tells of a painful love affair between an émigré doctor, Ravic, and Joan, whom he fears to lose and who ultimately dies. The life of the émigré is depicted as very similar to that of the World War I soldier: surviving by chance from one moment to the next, hanging grimly on to shreds of hope for the future.

Two novels of World War II are of particular note: *Zeit zu leben und Zeit zu sterben* (*A Time to Love and a Time to Die*) is a poignant account of war reaching into the lives of civilians and of the political corruption of National Socialism destroying the fabric of society. Once again, as in Remarque's other works, the decent individuals die while others prosper. Most bitter of all, though, is the searing and utterly credible account of concentration camp existence, *Der Funke Leben* (*The Spark of Life*), in which a man and a woman fix their hopes for the future on a white house they can see on a hillside outside the camp. When, finally, they are released, they go up to the house and find that ''a bomb had fallen at the back of it . . . Only the house front remained undamaged.'' Remarque's last novel, *Schatten im Paradies* (*Shadows in Paradise*), also speaks of shattered illusions, of the émigrés who arrive in the ''paradise'' of the United States, only to find that they cannot adjust to the new world. As one character, who could have come straight from the pages of *All Quiet on the Western Front*, expresses it: ''We are spoilt for normal life . . . We are ruined . . . There is no way back, nothing stands still.''

—Rex Last

See the essay on *All Quiet on the Western Front*.

RENDRA

Also known as Raden Mas Willibrordus Surendra Broto; W.S. Rendra. **Born:** Solo, Central Java, 7 November 1935. **Education:** Catholic primary and secondary (St. Joseph High School) schools in Solo; Gajah Mada University, Yogyakarta, B.A.; American Academy of Dramatic Arts, 1964–67. **Family:** Married 1) Sitoresmi Suwandi (divorced); 2) Sitoresmi Prabuningrat, 1970 (divorced); 3) Ken Zuraida. **Career:** Lived as a poet and dramatist, in a community with his Bengkel Teater (Theatre Workshop) group, first founded in 1961, located in Jakarta after 1993. His work met with government resistance a number of times: arrested briefly in 1970; banned from performing in his hometown Yogyakarta 1973–78; and arrested again after a poetry reading in Jakarta on 28 April 1978, detained until the beginning of October 1978. Lives in Indonesia. **Awards:** Badan

Musyawarah Kebudayaan Nasional, poetry, 1957; Anugerah Seni, Indonesian Ministry of Education, 1970; Akademi Jakarta, 1975; Adam Malik award, 1989; Wertheim award, 1989; SEA Write award, Thailand, 1996.

PUBLICATIONS

Collections

Rendra: Ballads and Blues. 1974; poems from *Ballada Orang-orang Tercinta*, *Empat Kumpulan Sajak*, *Blues Untuk Bonnie*, and *Sajak-sajak Sepatu Tua*, translated by Burton Raffel, Harry Aveling, and Derwent May.
Puisi-puisi Rendra. 1992.

Verse

Ballada Orang-orang Tercinta. 1957.
Empat Kumpulan Sajak. 1961.
Blues Untuk Bonnie. 1971.
Sajak-sajak Sepatu Tua. 1972.
Nyanyian Orang Urakan. 1985.
Disebabkan oleh Angin. 1993.
Potret Pembangunan dalam Puisi. 1993; as *State of Emergency*, by Swami Anand Haridas (Harry Aveling), 1980.
Orang-orang Rangkasbitung. 1993.
Mencari Bapa. 1996.
Perjalanan Aminah. 1997.

Plays

Orang-orang di Tikungan Jalan. 1954.
Selamatan Anak Cucu Suleiman. 1967.
Mastadon dan Burung Kondor. 1972; as *The Mastadon and the Condors*, translated by Harry Aveling, 1981.
Kisah Perjuangan Suku Naga. 1975; as *The Struggle of the Naga Tribe*, translated by Max Lane, 1979.
SEKDA. 1977.
Panembahan Reso. 1986.
Tuyul Anakku. 2000.

Fiction

Ia Sudah Bertualang. 1963.

Other

Tentang Bermain Drama. 1976.
Mempertimbangkan Tradisi. 1983.
Seni Drama untuk Remaja. 1993.
Agenda Reformasi Seorang Penyair. 1998.
Memberi Makna pada Hidup yang Fana. 1999.
Deklarasi Agustus. 1999.
Rakyat belum Merdeka. 2000.
Megatruh. 2001.
Penyair dan Kritik Sosial. 2001.

* * *

Rendra is both a poet and a man of the theatre—an actor, director, and playwright. His poetry is highly theatrical, his theatre work highly poetical. Behind both lies a highly formed social conscience.

His first volume of poetry, *Ballada Orang-orang Tercinta*, (*Ballads of Dear Ones*), deals with the lives of the rural poor after the Indonesian Revolution (1945–49). The language of these poems is rich and vibrant, with some possible influence of the Spanish poet García Lorca, who had recently been translated into Indonesian by Ramadhan K.H. As ballads, the stories the poems tell are dramatic and moving and tend to focus on the suffering and deaths of their main protagonists.

Rendra's second volume, *Empat Kumpulan Sajak* [Four Collections of Verse], was a much more personal volume whose major focus rests with his courtship of, and marriage to, his first wife, Sunarti. The language is playful and highly evocative, as exemplified in Burton Raffel's translation of "Surat Cinta": "I write this letter," the collection begins, "while the rain drizzles like a toy / drum played by magic children / in some magic world. . ." This volume too had it share of the suffering of the dispossessed. As in the *Ballada*, their lives are often criminal, certainly always immoral, but Rendra's sympathy is always strongly with them. In almost every case, their choices are inevitable given the difficulty of their social circumstances.

Rendra's Catholicism, which was central to the *Ballada*, took a more mystical, pantheistic hue in his third volume, *Sajak-sajak Sepatu Tua* [Poems of Old Shoes]. "I will sleep in your eyes," the poem "Doa Malam" [Evening Prayer] affirmed, "which are full of the rainbow / and the valleys which are soft mattresses." The saint in "Amsal Seorang Santu" [Parable of a Saint] is a poor man, a known sinner, "a foolish man from a drought ravaged village," who is crucified by the sins of the world. In "Sebuah Dunia Yang Marah" [An Angry World], "God weeps and understands. / God always weeps and understands. / Is always stabbed. Always betrayed."

During the mid-1960s, Rendra spent three years studying at the American Academy of Dramatic Arts in New York. This had a profound effect on both his poetry and his theatre. In poetry, he henceforth dispensed with the glittering images he had previously used and wrote, instead, in a style which many considered to be that of the newspapers. With the change of regime in Indonesia after 1966, after Suharto replaced Sukarno in the presidency, the poor and suffering in Rendra's poetry became the explicit victims of the earlier, corrupt and hypocritical political elite. For the first time, Rendra called on the oppressed to stand up for themselves.

In the theatre, Rendra turned from well-crafted scripts and introduced a new, improvisational style, based on continuous fluid movement and melodious, meaningless sound, which was dubbed "bip-bop theatre." This quickly gave way, throughout the 1970s, to a series of plays, written by Rendra himself, which were openly critical of the developmentalism of the "New Order" government. The plays were set in some distant Central American state, but the references to Indonesia were unmistakable. The same criticisms of the indifference of the government towards the poor, the excessive wealth of the cities, the destructive effects of industrialisation and tourism, and the barrenness of education, marked his *Potret Pembangunan dalam Puisi* (*State of Emergency*) as well. (The volume was published in English translation in 1980 but did not appear in Indonesia until 1993).

Although Rendra has continued to write poetry and direct his theatre group, Bengkel Teater (Theatre Workshop), his major publications since the mid-1990s have been in the field of the essay. Many of these essays expand his concern for Indonesia. They deal with the problems of low living standards, overpopulation, as well as the domination of the Indonesian economy by foreign capitalism and political policies. Rendra has consistently argued that the duty of the artist is to provide a creative and spiritual balance to the physical life of society. He has aimed to encourage an awareness of the human potentiality for living a fuller life, one that is more natural, more just and more intelligent. In his *Rakyat belum Merdeka*, Rendra remains concerned that, despite the Declaration of Indonesian Independence on 17 August 1945, "the people are still not yet free."

—Harry Aveling

RHODES, Apollonius of

See APOLLONIUS OF RHODES

RILKE, Rainer Maria

Born: René Karl Wilhelm Johann Josef Maria Rilke, in Prague, Austro-Hungarian Empire, 4 December 1875. **Education:** Educated at Piarist School, Prague, 1882–84; military schools of St. Pölten and Mährisch-Weisskirchen, 1886–91; school of commerce, Linz; a period of study preparing for university studies in Prague, 1895–96, Munich, 1896–97, and Berlin, 1897–98. **Military Service:** Served in Military Records Office, Vienna, 1916. **Family:** Married Clara Westhoff in 1901; one daughter. **Career:** Travelled throughout Europe during his life: in a painters' colony at Worpswede, 1901–02; associated with Rodin in Paris, 1902–03, 1905–06; residence in Italy and Sweden; friendships with a series of wealthy patrons; happy relationship with the generous publisher Kippenberg from 1908; patronized particularly by Princess Marie von Thurn und Taxis from 1910; lived in Chateau de Muzot, Switzerland, after 1921. **Died:** 29 December 1926.

PUBLICATIONS

Collections

Selected Works, translated by G. Craig Houston and J.B. Leishman. 2 vols., 1954–60.

Sämtliche Werke, edited by Ruth Sieber-Rilke and Ernst Zinn. 6 vols., 1955–66; revised edition, 1980.

Werke, edited by Horst Nalewski. 3 vols., 1978.

The Best of Rilke (bilingual edition), translated by Walter Arndt. 1989.

Selected Poems of Rainer Maria Rilke: The Book of Fresh Beginnings, translated with introduction by David Young. 1994.

Verse

Leben und Lieder. 1894.
Larenopfer. 1896.
Traumgekrönt. 1897.
Advent. 1898.
Mir zur Feier. 1899; revised edition, as *Die frühen Gedichte,* 1909.
Das Buch der Bilder. 1902; revised edition, 1906; translated in part as *The Voices,* by Robert Bly, 1977; as *The Book of Images,* translated by Edward Snow, 1991.
Das Stunden-Buch. 1905; as *Poems from the Book of Hours,* translated by Babette Deutsch, 1941; as *The Book of Hours,* translated by A.L. Peck, 1961; also translated by Stevie Krayer, 1995; as *The Book of Hours: Prayers to a Lowly God,* translated with introduction and notes by Annemarie S. Kidder, 2001.
Die Weise von Liebe und Tod des Cornets Christoph Rilke. 1906; edited by Walter Simon, 1974; as *The Story of the Love and Death of Cornet Christopher Rilke,* translated by B.J. Morse, 1927; as *The Tale of the Love and Death of Cornet Christopher Rilke* translated by M.D. Herter Norton, 1932; as *The Lay of the Love and Death of Cornet Christoph Rilke,* translated by Leslie Phillips and Stefan Schimarski, 1948, also translated by M.D. Herter Norton, 1959, and Stephen Mitchell, 1983; as *The Cornet,* translated by Constantine FitzGibbon, 1958.
Neue Gedichte. 2 vols., 1907–08; as *New Poems,* translated by J.B. Leishman, 1964; as *New Poems (1907),* 1985, and *New Poems (1908): The Other Part,* 1987, both translated by Edward Snow; also translated by Stephen Cohn, 1991.
Requiem. 1909.
Das Marien-Leben. 1913; as *The Life of the Virgin Mary,* translated by R.G.L. Barrett, 1921; also translated by C.F. MacIntyre, 1947; Stephen Spender, 1951; N.K. Cruickshank, 1952.
Fünf Gesänge. 1915.
Duineser Elegien. 1923; as *Duineser Elegien: Elegies from the Castle of Duino,* translated by Vita and Edward Sackville-West, 1931; as *Duino Elegies,* translated by J.B. Leishman and Stephen Spender, 1939, revised edition, 1948, 1963; also translated by Nora Wydenbruck, 1948; Harry Behn, 1957; Stephen Garmey and Jay Wilson, 1972; Elaine E. Boney, 1975; David Young, 1978; Stephen Cohn, 1989; David Young, 1993; Leslie Norris and Alan Keele, 1993; Patrick Bridgwater, 1999; Edward Snow, 2000; as *Rilke's Duino Elegies: Cambridge Readings,* edited by Roger Paulin and Peter Hutchinson, 1996.
Die Sonette an Orpheus. 1923; as *Sonnets to Orpheus,* translated by J.B. Leishman, 1936; also translated by M.D. Herter Norton, 1942; David Young, 1987; Leslie Norris and Alan Keel, 1989; translated by Stephen Cohn in *Sonnets to Orpheus, with Letters to a Young Poet,* 2000.
Späte Gedichte. 1934; as *Later Poems,* translated by J.B. Leishman, 1938.
Requiem and Other Poems, translated by J.B. Leishman. 1935.
Fifty Selected Poems, translated by C.F. MacIntyre. 1940.
Selected Poems, translated by J.B. Leishman. 1941.
Thirty-One Poems, translated by Ludwig Lewisohn. 1946.
Poems 1906–1926, translated by J.B. Leishman. 1957.
Angel Songs, translated by Rhoda Coghill. 1958.
Poems, edited and translated by G.W. McKay. 1965.
Visions of Christ: A Posthumous Cycle of Poems, edited by Siegfried Mandel, translated by Aaron Kramer. 1967.
Selected Poems, edited by Frank M. Fowler. 1969.

Holding Out, translated by Rika Lesser. 1975; as *Rilke: Between Roots,* 1986.
Possibility of Being: A Selection of Poems, translated by J.B. Leishman. 1977.
The Rose and the Windows, translated by A. Poulin, Jr. 1979.
Selected Poems, translated by Robert Bly. 1981.
Requiem for a Woman and Selected Lyric Poems, translated by Andy Gaus. 1981.
An Unofficial Rilke: Poems 1912–1926 (bilingual edition), edited and translated by Michael Hamburger. 1981.
Selected Poetry (bilingual edition), edited and translated by Stephen Mitchell. 1982.
The Unknown Rilke: Selected Poems, translated by Franz Wright. 1983; enlarged edition, 1990.
Rainer Maria Rilke: Translations from His Poetry, by Albert Ernest Flemming. 1983.
The Migration of Powers: The French Poems, translated by A. Poulin, Jr. 1985.

Plays

Im Frühfrost (produced 1897). In *Aus der Frühzeit,* 1921; as *Early Frost,* in *Nine Plays,* 1979.
Ohne Gegenwart. 1898; as *Not Present,* in *Nine Plays,* 1979.
Die weisse Fürstin. 1899; revised version, in *Die frühen Gedichte,* 1909; as *The White Princess,* in *Nine Plays,* 1979.
Das tägliche Leben (produced 1901). 1902; as *Everyday Life,* in *Nine Plays,* 1979.
Nine Plays, translated by Klaus Phillips and John Locke. 1979.

Fiction

Am Leben hin. 1898.
Zwei Prager Geschichten. 1899; as *Two Stories of Prague: King Bohush; The Siblings,* translated by Angela Esterhammer, 1994.
Vom lieben Gott und Anderes. 1900; revised edition, as *Geschichten vom lieben Gott,* 1904; as *Stories of God,* translated by Nora Purtscher-Wydenbruck and M.D. Herter Norton, 1932.
Die Letzten. 1902.
Die Aufzeichnungen des Malte Laurids Brigge. 1910; as *Journal of My Other Self,* translated by John Linton, 1930; as *The Notebook of Malte Laurids Brigge,* translated by Linton, 1930; as *The Notebooks of Malte Laurids Brigge,* translated by Stephen Mitchell, 1983.
Ewald Tragy. 1929; translated as *Ewald Tragy,* 1929.

Other

Worpswede. 1903.
Auguste Rodin. 1903; revised edition, 1907; as *August Rodin,* translated by Jesse Lemont and Hans Trausil, 1919; as *Rodin,* translated by Robert D. Firmage, 1979.
Aus der Frühzeit: Vers, Prosa, Drama 1894–1899, edited by Fritz Adolf Hünich. 1921.
Briefe an Auguste Rodin. 1928.
Briefe an einen jungen Dichter. 1929; as *Letters to a Young Poet,* translated by M.D. Herter Norton, 1934; also translated by K.W. Maurer, 1943; Reginald Snell, 1945; Stephen Mitchell, 1984.
Briefe und Tagebücher, edited by Ruth Sieber-Rilke and Carl Sieber. 7 vols., 1929–37; revised edition of *Briefe,* as *Gesammelte Briefe,* 6 vols., 1936–39.

Briefe an eine junge Frau, edited by Carl Sieber. 1931; as *Letters to a Young Woman*, translated by K.W. Maurer, 1945.

Tagebücher aus der Frühzeit, edited by Ruth Sieber-Rilke and Carl Sieber. 1942; translated and annotated by Edward Snow and Michael Winkler, 1997.

Letters 1892–1926, translated by Jane Bannard Greene and M.D. Herder Norton. 2 vols., 1945; *Selected Letters, 1902–1926*, translated by R.F.C. Hull, 1946.

Freundschaft mit Rilke, by Elya Maria Nevar. 1946.

La Dernière Amitié: Lettres à Madame Eloui Bey, edited by Edmond Jaloux. 1949; as *Rainer Maria Rilke: His Last Friendship. Unpublished Letters to Mrs. Eloui Bey*, translated by William H. Kennedy, 1952.

Briefe an Gräfin Sizzo 1921–1926, edited by Ingeborg Schnack. 1950; revised edition, 1977.

Briefwechsel in Gedichte, with Erika Mitterer. 1950; as *Correspondence in Verse*, translated by N.K. Cruickshank, 1953.

Briefwechsel, with Benvenuta, edited by Magda von Hattingberg. 1954; as *Letters to Benvenuta*, translated by Heinz Norden, 1951; as *Rilke and Benvenuta: An Intimate Correspondence*, translated by Joel Agee, 1987.

Briefwechsel, with Marie von Thurn und Taxis, edited by Ernest Zinn. 2 vols., 1951; as *The Letters of Rainer Maria Rilke and Princess Marie von Thurn and Taxis*, translated by Nora Wydenbruck, 1958.

Briefe über Cézanne, edited by Clara Rilke. 1952; as *Letters on Cézanne*, translated by Joel Agee, 1985.

Briefwechsel, with Lou Andreas-Salomé, edited by Ernst Pfeiffer. 1952; revised edition, 1975.

Correspondance 1909–1926, with André Gide, edited by Renée Lang. 1952.

Briefe an Frau Gudi Nölke, edited by Paul Obermüller. 1953; as *Letters to Frau Gudi Nölke during His Life in Switzerland*, translated by Violet M. Macdonald, 1955.

Briefwechsel, with Katharina Kippenberg, edited by Bettina von Bomhard. 1954.

Correspondance 1920–1926, with Merline, edited by Dieter Bassermann. 1954; as *Letters to Merline*, translated by Violet M. Macdonald, 1951; also translated by Jesse Browner, 1989.

Rilke, Gide, et Verhaeren: Correspondance inédite, edited by C. Bronne. 1955.

Lettres milanaises 1921–1926, edited by Renée Lang. 1956.

Briefwechsel, with Inga Junghanns, edited by Wolfgang Herwig. 1959.

Selected Letters, edited by Harry T. Moore. 1960.

Briefe an Sidonie Nadherny von Borutin, edited by Bernhard Blume. 1973.

Rilke on Love and Other Difficulties, edited by John J.L. Mood. 1975.

Briefwechsel 1910–1925, with Helene von Nostitz, edited by Oswalt von Nostitz. 1976.

Gesammelte Erinnerungen, 1926–1956, edited by Klaus E. Bohnenkamp. 1976.

Briefe an Nanny Wunderly-Volkart, edited by Niklaus Bigler and Rätus Luck. 2 vols., 1977.

Briefwechsel 1899–1925, with Hugo von Hofmannsthal, edited by Rudolf Hirsch and Ingeborg Schnack. 1978.

Where Silence Reigns: Selected Prose, translated by G. Craig Houston. 1978.

Briefe an Axel Juncker, edited by Renate Scharffenberg. 1979.

Briefwechsel, with Rolf Freiherrn von Ungern-Sternberg, edited by Konrad Kratzsch. 1980.

Marina Cvetaeva, Boris Pasternak, Rainer Maria Rilke: Lettere 1926, edited by Yevgeny Pasternak, Yelena Pasternak, and Konstantin M. Azadovsky. 1980; as *Letters, Summer 1926*, translated by Margaret Wettlin and Walter Arndt, 1985.

Briefwechsel, with Anita Forrer, edited by Magda Kérényi. 1982.

Rodin and Other Prose Pieces, translated by G. Craig Houston. 1986.

Schweizer Vortragsweise, 1919, edited by Rätus Luck. 1986.

Rilke und Russland: Briefe, Erinnerungen, Gedichte, edited by Konstantin Asadowski. 1986.

Briefe an Ernst Norlind, edited by Paul Åström. 1986.

Die Briefe an Karl und Elisabeth von der Heydt, 1905–1922, edited by Ingeborg Schnack and Renate Scharffenberg. 1986.

Briefwechsel, with Regina Ullmann and Ellen Delp, edited by Walter Simon. 1987.

Briefwechsel mit den Brüdern Reinhart, 1919–1926, edited by Rätus Luck and Hudo Sarbarch. 1988.

Briefe und Dokumente, with Stephan Zweig, edited by Donald A. Prater. 1988.

Briefe an Tora Vega Holmström, edited by Birgit Rausing and Paul Åström. 1989.

Translator, *Sonette nach dem Portugiesischen*, by Elizabeth Barrett Browning. 1908.

Translator, *Der Kentauer*, by Maurice de Guérin. 1911.

Translator, *Die Liebe der Magdalena*. 1912.

Translator, *Portugiesische Briefe*, by Marianna Alcoforado. 1913.

Translator, *Die Rückkehr des verlorenen Sohnes*, by André Gide. 1914.

Translator, *Die vierundzwanzig Sonette der Louïze Labé*. 1918.

Translator, *Gedichte*, by Paul Valéry. 1925.

*

Bibliography: *Rainer Maria Rilke Bibliographie* by Walter Ritzer, 1951.

Critical Studies: *Rainer Maria Rilke* by E.M. Butler, 1941; *Rilke, Man and Poet: A Biographical Study* by Nora Wydenbruck, 1949; *Rainer Maria Rilke: His Life and Work* by F.W. van Heerikhuizen, translated by Fernand G. Renier and Ann Cliff, 1951; *Rilke: A Study of His Later Poetry*, 1952, and *Portrait of Rilke*, 1971, both by H.E. Holthusen; *Phases of Rilke* by Norbert Fuerst, 1958; *Rilke: The Ring of Forms* by F.H. Wood, 1958; *Rilke: Masks and the Man* by H.F. Peters, 1960; *Rilke, Europe, and the English-Speaking World*, 1961, and *Rilke*, 1963, both by Eudo C. Mason; *Creativity: A Theme from Faust and the Duino Elegies* by E.L. Stahl, 1961; *Rainer Maria Rilke: The Years in Switzerland; A Contribution to the Biography of Rilke's Later Life*, by Jean Randolphe de Salis, translated by N.K. Cruikshank, 1964; *Rilke and France: A Study in Poetic Development* by K.A.J. Batterby, 1966; *Rilke's Last Year* by George C. Schoolfield, 1969; *Rilke in Transition: An Exploration of His Earliest Poetry* by James Rolleston, 1970; *Portrait of Rilke: An Illustrated Biography* by Hans Egon Holthusen, translated by W.H. Hargreaves, 1971; *Rilke* by Arnold Bauer, 1972; *The Symbolism of Space and Motion in the Works of Rilke* by Richard Jayne, 1972; "Rilke and Nietzsche" in *The Disinherited Mind* by Erich Heller, revised edition, 1975; *Rainer Maria Rilke: A Centenary Essay* by Timothy J. Casey, 1976; *The Elegaic Mode in Milton and Rilke: Reflections of Death* by Dan Latimer, 1977; *Rainer Maria Rilke and Jugendstil: Affinities, Influences, Adaptations* by K.E. Webb, 1978; *Stone into Poetry: The*

Cathedral Cycle in Rainer Maria Rilke's "Neue Gedichte" by Ernest M. Wolf, 1978; *Figures of Transformation: Rilke and the Example of Valéry* by Richard Cox, 1979; *Rilke: The Alchemy of Alienation* edited by Frank Baron, Ernst S. Dick, and Warren R. Maurer, 1980; *Landscape and Landscape Imagery in Rilke* by John Sandford, 1980; *The Sacred Threshold: A Life of Rainer Maria Rilke* by J.F. Hendry, 1983; *Russia in the Works of Rainer Maria Rilke*, 1984, and *Rainer Maria Rilke*, 1988, both by Patricia Pollock Brodsky; *Rilke: A Life* by Wolfgang Leppmann, translated by Russell M. Stockman, 1984; *Finding the Absent Flowers in Rilke's Malte* by Doris T. Wight, 1985; *A Ringing Glass: The Life of Rainer Maria Rilke* by Donald Prater, 1986; *The European Heritage of Rose Symbolism and Rose Metaphor in View of Rilke's Epitaph Rose* by Beatrice Susanne Bullock-Kimbal, 1987; *Transcending Angels: Rainer Maria Rilke's Duino Elegies* by Kathleen L. Komar, 1988; *Negative Spring: Crisis Imagery in the Works of Brentano, Lenau, Rilke and T.S. Eliot* by David B. Dickens, 1989; *Rilke and Russia: A Re-evaluation* by Dana A. Reshetylo-Rothe, 1990; *The Beginning of Terror: A Psychological Study of Rainer Maria Rilke's Life and Work* by David Kleinbard, 1993; *A Different Poem: Rainer Maria Rilke's American Translators Randall Jarrell, Robert Lowell, and Robert Bly* by Hartmut Heep, 1996; *Life of a Poet: Rainer Maria Rilke* by Ralph Freedman, 1996; *Rilke through a Glass Darkly: Poetry of R.M. Rilke and Its English Translations: A Critical Comparison* by Roy Woods, 1996; *The Integrative Vision: Poetry and the Visual Arts in Baudelaire, Rilke and MacDiarmid* by Tom Hubbard, 1997; *Dear Friend: Rainer Maria Rilke and Paula Modersohn-Becker* by Eric Torgersen, 1998; *Rilke, Modernism and Poetic Tradition* by Judith Ryan, 1999; *A Reader's Guide to Rilke's Sonnets to Orpheus* by Timothy J. Casey, 2001; *A Companion to the Works of Rainer Maria Rilke*, edited by Erika A. Metzger and Michael M. Metzger, 2001.

* * *

Rainer Maria Rilke is unquestionably one of the greatest individualists among poets of the German language; his internationally wide appeal might seem incompatible with his oblique poetic diction, which resists translation, his frequently idiosyncratic turn of mind, and a generally unyielding attitude towards his reader. His work has been subjected to every conceivable treatment, from the manifestly uncritical admiration of many biographies and personal reminiscences, through every shade of theological, ethical, and philosophical interpretation, to claims that his aesthetic aristocratism was but thinly veiled fascism.

Rilke made little attempt to maintain any clear distinction between his public and his private persona and was disinclined to commit himself to any particular allegiances. His copious correspondence can justifiably be considered part of his creative production; read with due circumspection, the letters illuminate many aspects of his literary works, though scattered comments on social and political affairs are too non-committal and self-contradictory to be of any great relevance to his poetry.

One of the greatest cosmopolitans of modern literature, Rilke continually assimilated and processed material from his ceaseless travels. Above all, the homelessness which characterized his life (his marriage was "suspended" in the interests of the freedom and solitude he considered essential to his art)—that loneliness among men which he shared with Nietzsche—became the supreme metaphor for the rootlessness and transitoriness which are major themes of his work.

From a posture of inward exile—Hölderlin was his poetic ancestor—Rilke's work gives utterance, not simply to private agonies of spirit, but to the spiritual and intellectual impoverishment of his age: to the crisis of idioms and values which threatened Western culture as a whole, exposing man in all his vulnerability to the plurality, disjunction, and fortuitousness of a universe no longer structured around reliable concepts of religious faith, moral principle, or historical relevance. The cry of the poet *in extremis* is simultaneously a lament for an entire generation of "Enterbten" (disinherited), defenceless on the outer frontiers of human experience. The "City of Pain" of the Tenth Duino Elegy forms a counterpart to T.S. Eliot's "Waste Land."

The derivative, *fin de siècle* sentimentality of Rilke's earliest verse reveals nothing of the poet's ultimate stature, though various themes of the later work are adumbrated. His abortive essays on the dramatic form are interesting primarily for their Neo-Romantic and *Jugendstil* characteristics; Maeterlinck's influence is apparent here. The quasi-mystical religiosity which marks *Das Stunden-Buch* (*Poems from the Book of Hours*) has prompted some over-confident "theological" interpretations; the association of the divine with the sphere of darkness is an early example of the dramatic "reversals" that were to figure in later works, while the glorification of poverty pre-figures the presentation of social outcasts as "aristocrats of inwardness" in *Die Aufzeichnungen des Malte Laurids Brigge* (*The Notebooks of Malte Laurids Brigge*).

The *Neue Gedichte* (*New Poems*), product of his Paris years, represent the first real peak of Rilke's artistic development. Inspired by the techniques of Rodin and Cézanne, he developed the concept of the *Dinggedicht*: each poem represents a separate object in such total self-sufficiency that its intangible qualities become concrete, its outward features interiorized—its essence is made visible. However, the perfect self-containment of the object exposes the existential inadequacy of the onlooker-poet: much later, in "Turning-Point" (1914), Rilke wrote "For looking, you see, has a limit. / And the more looked-at world / wants to be nourished by love. / . . . now practise heart-work . . . ."

The reciprocity of inwardness and outwardness is central to the *Notebooks*. This episodic journal-novel is of seminal importance in the development of the modern novel, inviting comparisons with Proust, Kafka, Musil, and Sartre (*La Nausée*). The reader is powerfully aware of the presence of Baudelaire in Malte's quest for authentic experience amid the soulless, materialistic horror of urban existence. The theme of a "personal death" is taken from the Danish poet and novelist J.P. Jacobsen, whose work greatly influenced Rilke. Invaded by impressions of his physical surroundings, the hypersensitive narrative persona becomes as much object as subject: the inner world breaks out into the outer world. Besides the themes of Angst, loneliness, death, and the poet's struggle for authenticity of expression, the novel develops the idea of "intransitive love," ending with a reversal of the parable of the Prodigal Son, in which all hope of salvaging an authentic individual existence is seen to lie in immunity from the love of others.

The 12 silent years which elapsed between the completion of the *Notebooks* and the publication of the *Duineser Elegien* (*Duino Elegies*) were not as barren as is often implied, although it was no coincidence that Rilke's "crisis years" were years of cultural and political upheaval in Europe as a whole. Rich in ambiguities and contradictions, the *Elegies* are open to radical objections and infinite misinterpretations. They can ultimately be interpreted only in Rilke's own terms, and in his consciousness "that we don't feel very securely at home in this interpreted world." It is in the *Elegies* that the most radical reversal (*Umschlag*) occurs: the transition from negation to affirmation. Acute awareness of the irrevocability of human existence becomes a positive incentive to the creation of a new order of existence. Through *Verwandlung* (transformation) a final, radical revision of the frontiers within human experience is achieved, and the antitheses of life/death, joy/suffering, love/separation, terror/bliss, immanence/transcendence are resolved into "pure contradiction." The Angel to whom the Elegies are addressed is not that of the Christian heaven, but a symbolic transcendental being "who vouches for the recognition of a higher degree of reality in the invisible."

Only in *Die Sonette an Orpheus* (*Sonnets to Orpheus*), however, does the artist emerge as the ultimate agent of re-integration, poetry as a means of salvation from the impossibility of living with the truth—another echo of Nietzsche. The final transformation, from *Klage* (Lament) to *Rühmung* (Praise) is accomplished: "Song Is Existence," and man can pass into "the other relation."

The *Sonnets*, with their serene tone and structural formality, were not Rilke's final word. The poetry of his last years continued to challenge the fundamental contradictions of human destiny and thus to reinforce the timeless pertinence of his message.

—Andrea C. Cervi

See the essays on the seventh *Duino Elegy* and *Sonnets to Orpheus*.

RIMBAUD, (Jean Nicolas) Arthur

Born: Charleville, France, 20 October 1854. **Education:** Educated at local schools to age 16. **Career:** Ran away from home several times, 1870–71; left to join Paul Verlaine, *q.v.*, with whom he was romantically involved, in Paris; lived in France, Belgium, and England, to 1873; Verlaine jailed for two years for shooting him, 1873. Taught briefly in Reading, Berkshire, 1874; lived and worked in various parts of Europe to 1878; lived in Cyprus, Egypt, and worked as a trader, in Aden and Abyssinia, from 1878. Returned to France, because of illness, 1891; leg amputated, May 1891. **Died:** 10 November 1891.

PUBLICATIONS

Collections

Poésies complètes, edited by Paul Verlaine. 1895.
Complete Works, Selected Letters, edited by Wallace Fowlie. 1966.
Oeuvres complètes, edited by Antoine Adam. 1972.
Oeuvres, edited by Suzanne Bernard and André Guyaux. 1981.
A Season in Hell and Illuminations, translated by Mark Treharne. 1998.
Complete Works, translated by Paul Schmidt. 2000.

Verse and Prose

Une saison en enfer. 1873; as *A Season in Hell*, translated by Delmore Schwartz, 1939; also translated by Louise Varèse, 1945; Norman Cameron, 1949; Enid Rhodes Peschel, 1973; Bertrand Mathieu, 1992.
Illuminations, edited by Paul Verlaine. 1886; edited by Albert Py, 1967; also edited by Nick Osmond, 1976; as *Les Illuminations*,

translated by Louise Varèse, 1946; also translated by Enid Rhodes Peschel, 1973.
Le Reliquaire, edited by L. Genonceaux. 1891.
Les Stupra. 1923.
Selected Verse Poems, translated by Norman Cameron. 1942.
Poems of the Damned, translated by Jacques Le Clercq. 1960.
Selected Verse, translated by Oliver Bernard. 1962.
Drunken Boat, translated by Samuel Beckett, edited by James Knowlson and Felix Leakey. 1977.

*

Critical Studies: *Rimbaud* by Wallace Fowlie, 1946, revised edition, 1965; *The Time of the Assassins: A Study of Rimbaud* by Henry V. Miller, 1956; *Rimbaud*, 1957, and *Rimbaud: A Critical Introduction*, 1981, both by C.A. Hackett; *Rimbaud* by Enid Starkie, 1961; *Rimbaud's Poetic Practice* by W.M. Frohock, 1963; *The Design of Rimbaud's Poetry*, 1963, and *Patterns of Thought in Rimbaud and Mallarmé*, 1986, both by John Porter Houston; *L'Alchimie du verbe de Rimbaud* by Jean Richer, 1972; *The Poetry of Rimbaud* by Robert Greer Cohn, 1973; *Rimbaud* by F.C. St. Aubyn, 1975, revised edition, 1988; *Flux and Reflux: Ambivalence in the Poems of Arthur Rimbaud* by Enid Rhodes Peshchel, 1977; *Rimbaud* by C. Chadwick, 1979; *Rimbaud, Illuminations* by Roger Little, 1983; *Rimbaud: Visions and Hesitations* by Edward J. Ahearn, 1984; *The Subject in Rimbaud: From Self to "Je"* by Karin J. Dillman, 1984; *Exploding Poetry: Baudelaire/Rimbaud* by Georges Poulet, 1984; *Patterns of Thought in Rimbaud and Mallarmé* by John Porter Houston, 1986; *Rimbaud* by Pierre Petitfils, 1987; *The Emergence of Social Space: Rimbaud and the Paris Commune* by Kristin Ross, 1988; *Delerium: An Interpretation of Arthur Rimbaud* by Jeremy Reed, 1991; *Rimbaud's Theatre of the Self* by James R. Lawler, 1992; *Rimbaud and Jim Morrison: The Rebel as Poet* by Wallace Fowlie, 1994; *Mis-reading the Creative Impulse: The Poetic Subject in Rimbaud and Claudel, Restaged* by Adrianna M. Paliyenko, 1997; *Somebody Else: Arthur Rimbaud in Africa 1880–91* by Charles Nicholl, 1997; *Arthur Rimbaud* by Benjamin Ivry, 1998; *Rimbaud* by Graham Robb, 2000.

*   *   *

Arthur Rimbaud's career as a poet began early in 1870, shortly after his 15th birthday, and was over by 1875, before he was 21, and yet, in the space of those few adolescent years, he produced work of a quite exceptional power and originality.

Although his earliest poems were orthodox enough, his poetry soon began to reveal the first stirrings of his revolutionary ideas as regards both content and form. A vehemently anti-Christian attitude is apparent in such poems as "Soleil et Chair," "Le Mal," and "Les Premières Communions," and a no less vehement political commitment in his fiercely pro-Republican poems such as "Le Forgeron" and in his vicious attacks on Napoleon III in "L'éclatante victoire de Sarrebruck" and "ages des Césars." Even in its minor manifestations authoritarianism was intolerable to Rimbaud with the result that customs officers, librarians, and his domineering mother provoked his contempt and derision in "Les Douaniers," "Les Assis," and "Les Poètes de sept ans." But, as an alternative reaction to his refusal to conform, Rimbaud also sought refuge with equal fervour in the consoling world of his imagination and it was this that gave rise to what is no doubt his best-known poem, "Le Bateau ivre," in which the drunken boat of the title revels in the exhilarating experience of drifting wildly out of control through fantastic seas.

This rebellion against all authority and desire for total freedom soon spread to the form as well as the content of Rimbaud's poetry. In May 1871 he wrote his celebrated "Lettre du voyant" [Letter of the seer] in which he contended that the poet's function is simply to note down his disordered sensations without exercising any conscious control over their presentation. "JE est un autre," he wrote, amplifying this statement by comparing the poet to a violin or a trumpet on which some outside force plays. To thus act merely as a passive instrument was easier said than done for an inexperienced poet of 16, but even in such conventionally structured poems as "Le Bateau ivre" and "Les Voyelles" the way in which images are piled pellmell one on top of the other suggests that the balance between the orderly control of the intellect and the free play of the imagination is already shifting towards the latter.

This balance was to shift still further once Rimbaud, after several abortive attempts, finally escaped from the provincial backwater of his home town of Charleville to Paris in September 1871. There he came under the influence of a poet ten years his senior, Paul Verlaine, who had already experimented with unconventional versification. In a group of poems written in the summer of 1872 Rimbaud soon outdistanced his mentor in freedom of form, and in such poems as "Larme" and "Bonne Pensée du matin" he dispensed with rhyme in places and departed from a regular rhythmic pattern. He was soon to take the final step of moving from verse to prose in the *Illuminations* which he began to write later in 1872 and from which almost all trace of regular rhyme and uniform rhythm has disappeared. Instead, Rimbaud achieves his poetic effects by piling brilliant and unexpected images one on top of the other even more so than he had done in "Le Bateau ivre" and "Les Voyelles" and by creating flexible rhythmic patterns that extend much further the relatively modest innovations of "Larme" and "Bonne Pensée du matin."

The encounter with Verlaine had a similar liberating effect on Rimbaud's ideas. Both of them had a homosexual element in their make-up and Rimbaud gave to the intense emotional relationship that grew up between them in 1872 and the first half of 1873 an intellectual justification by seeing it as a rebellion against yet another constraint imposed by society. So along with the continuing themes of the destruction of the real world and the creation of a different, fantasy world, the theme of "le nouvel amour" is introduced into the *Illuminations* in such passages as "Conte" and "oyauté," as well as the wider theme, in "Matinée d'ivresse" and "Génie," for example, of the creation of an amoral society in which the Christian concepts of good and evil will no longer exist.

Many of the 45 passages of the *Illuminations* dealing with these themes are full of optimistic fervour, but there are others, such as "Angoisse" and "Barbare," in which a sense of disappointment and disillusion can be detected, heralding the tone which prevails throughout Rimbaud's next and probably last work, *Une saison en enfer* (*A Season in Hell*), which he wrote between April and August 1873. The significance of the title resides in the fact that Rimbaud had at first viewed his months with Verlaine as a season in heaven when, with the help of his disciple, he was to achieve his goal of total freedom. But instead of complementing each other, their widely different temperaments soon became a source of conflict and the final painful break-up of their relationship in July 1873 led Rimbaud to doubt the validity of the concepts that their union was to have expressed and furthered. "Délires," the central chapter of *A Season in Hell*, is divided into two sections, the first of which is a disenchanted account

of what is now dismissed as a "drôle de ménage" and the second an equally disenchanted account of what he now regards as a foolish excursion into "verbal alchemy," as he describes it. The remaining chapters of *A Season in Hell* acknowledge the failure of other aspects of Rimbaud's revolt. "Nous sommes à l'Occident," he writes, "je suis esclave de mon baptême," recognizing that if one is born into Christian, western society one can neither refuse to adapt to its values nor erase those values from one's mind.

Some critics believe that immediately after *A Season in Hell* Rimbaud abandoned poetry. This certainly seems the logical consequence of his changed ideas, but other critics believe nonetheless that some of the *Illuminations* date from 1874 and were written as a kind of post-script to *A Season in Hell*. But, whatever the precise date, Rimbaud certainly did give up writing poetry by 1875 and thereafter opted out of society not through the medium of his imagination but in reality. He turned his back on Europe and, like his own "bateau ivre," drifted first out to the Far East and then to the Middle East and finally down the Red Sea to live from 1880 until his death in 1891 as a trader first in Aden and then in Abyssinia, totally uninterested in his growing reputation as one of the major figures in late 19th-century French literature.

—C. Chadwick

See the essays on "Alchimie du verbe," "Le Bateau ivre," and "Fleurs."

RITSOS, Yannis

Born: Monemvasía, Greece, 1 May 1909. **Family:** Married Fallitasa Georgiades in 1954; one daughter. **Career:** Law clerk, Angepoulos law firm, Athens, 1925; clerk, Mitsopoulos-Oeconomopoulos, notaries, Athens, 1925–26; assistant librarian, Lawyers Association, Athens, 1926; in a tuberculosis sanatorium, 1927–31; worked for a musical theatre in the 1930s; member of the Chorus of Ancient Tragedies, National Theatre of Greece, 1938–45, and actor and dancer for Athens Opera House; editor and proofreader, Govostis, publishers, Athens, 1945–48, 1952–56; full-time writer, from 1956. **Awards:** Greek state prize, 1956; International grand prize for poetry, 1972; Dimitroff international prize (Bulgaria), 1974; de Vigny prize (France), 1975; Etna-Taormina prize (Italy), 1976; Seregno-Brianza international prize, 1976; Lenin prize, 1977; Mondello prize (Italy), 1978. Honorary doctorate: Salonica University, 1975; University of Birmingham, 1978. **Died:** 11 November 1990.

PUBLICATIONS

Verse

Trakter [Tractors]. 1934.
Pyramides [Pyramids]. 1935.
Epitafios [Funeral Song]. 1936; edited by A. Tassos, 1979.
To tragoudi tes adelfis mou [The Song of My Sister]. 1937.
Earini Symfonia [Spring Symphony]. 1938.
To emvatirio tou okeanou [The March of the Ocean]. 1940.

Palia mazurka se rythmo vrohis [An Old Mazurka in the Rhythm of the Rain]. 1943.

Dokimasia [Trial]. 1943.

O syntrofos [Our Comrade]. 1945.

O anthropos me to garyfallo [The Man with the Carnation]. 1952.

Agrypnia [Vigil] (includes *Romiossini*). 1954.

Proino astro [Morning Star]. 1955.

He sonata tou selenofotos. 1956; as *The Moonlight Sonata*, translated by John Stathatos, 1975.

Chroniko [Chronicle]. 1957.

Hydria [The Urn]. 1957.

Apoheretismos [Farewell]. 1957.

Cheimerine diavgeia [Winter Limpidity]. 1957.

Petrinos Chronos [Stony Time]. 1957.

He geitonies tou kosmou [The Neighbourhoods of the World]. 1957.

Otan erchetai ho xenos [When the Stranger Comes]. 1958.

Ani otachti politeia [Unsubjugated City]. 1958.

He architectoniki ton dentron [The Architecture of the Trees]. 1958.

Hoi gerontisses kai thalassa [The Old Women and the Sea]. 1959.

To parathyro [The Window]. 1960.

He gefyra [The Bridge]. 1960.

Ho mavros hagios [The Black Saint]. 1961.

Poiemata [Poems]. 4 vols., 1961–75.

To nekro spiti [The Dead House]. 1962.

Kato ap'ton iskio tou vounou [Beneath the Shadow of the Mountain]. 1962.

To dentro tis fylakis kai he gynaikes [The Prison Tree and the Women]. 1963.

Martyries [Testimonies]. 2 vols., 1963–66.

Dodeka poiemata gia ton Kavafe [Twelve Poems for Cavafy]. 1963.

Paichnidia t'ouranou kai tou nerou [Playful Games of the Sky and the Water]. 1964.

Philoctetes. 1965.

Orestes. 1966.

Ostrava. 1967.

He Romiosyne [Romiossini: The Story of the Greeks]. 1969; as *Romiossini*, translated by Elena Paidoussi, in *Romiossini and Other Poems 1968–1970.*

Poems, translated by Alan Page. 1969.

Romiossini and Other Poems, translated by Dan Georgakas and Eleni Paidoussi. 1969.

Gestures and Other Poems 1968–1970, translated by Nikos Stangos. 1971; *Gestures* as *Cheironomies* (Greek edition), 1972.

Petres, Epanalepseis, Kinglidoma [Stones, Repetitions, Railings]. 1972.

He epistrofe tes Iphigeneias [The Return of Iphigenia]. 1972.

He Helene [Helen]. 1972.

Tetarte diastase. 1972; as *The Fourth Dimension*, translated by Peter Green and Beverly Bardsley, 1993.

Chrysothemis. 1972.

Ismene. 1972.

Dekaochto lianotragouda tes pikres patridas. 1973; as *Eighteen Short Songs of the Bitter Motherland*, translated by Amy Mims, 1974.

Diadromos kai skala. 1973; as *Corridor and Stairs*, translated by Nikos Germanacos, 1976.

Contradictions, translated by John Stathatos. 1973.

Graganda. 1973.

Ho afanismos tis Milos [The Annihilation of Milos]. 1974.

Hymnos kai threnos gia tin Kypro [Hymn and Lament for Cyprus]. 1974.

Kapnismeno tsoukali [The Soot-Black Pot]. 1974.

Kodonostasio [Belfry]. 1974.

Ho tikhos mesa ston kathrefti [The Wall in the Mirror]. 1974.

Chartina [Papermade]. 1974.

Selected Poems, translated by Nikos Stangos. 1974.

He kyra ton Ambelion. 1975; as *The Lady of the Vineyards*, translated by Apostolos N. Athanassakis, 1978.

Ta Epikairika 1945–1969 [Topical Verse]. 1975.

He teleftea pro anthropou hekatontaeia [The Last Century Before Man]. 1975.

Hemerologhia exorias [Diaries in Exile]. 1975.

To hysterografo tis doxas [The Postscript of Glory]. 1975.

Mantatoforos [The Messenger]. 1975.

To thyroreio [Conciergerie]. 1976.

The Fourth Dimension: Selected Poems, translated by Rae Dalven. 1976.

To makrino [Remote]. 1977.

Gignesthai [Becoming]. 1977.

Epitome (selection), edited by G. Veloudis. 1977.

Chronicle of Exile, translated by Minas Savvas. 1977.

Loipon? [Well Then?]. 1978.

Volidoskopos [Sounding Lead]. 1978.

Toichokolletes [Bill Poster]. 1978.

To soma kai to haima [Body and Blood]. 1978.

Trochonomos [The Traffic-Regulator]. 1978.

He pyle [The Gate]. 1978.

Monemvassiotisses. 1978; as *Monovassia and the Women of Monemvasia*, translated by Kimon Friar and Kostas Myrsiades, 1987.

To teratodes aristourghima [The Monstrous Masterpiece]. 1978.

Phaedra. 1978.

To roptro [The Knocker]. 1978.

Mia pygolampida fotizei ti nychta [A Firefly Lights up the Night]. 1978.

Grafe typhlou [Scripture of the Blind]. 1979.

Ritsos in Parenthesis, translated by E. Keeley. 1979.

Scripture of the Blind (selected verse), translated by Kimon Friar and Kostas Myrsiades. 1979.

Subterranean Horses, translated by Minas Savvas. 1980.

'Oneiro kalokerinou messimeriou [A Midsummer's Noon Dream]. 1980.

Diafaneia [Transparency]. 1980.

Parodos [Parody]. 1980.

Monochorda. 1980.

Ta erotica [Love Poems]. 1981.

Syntrofica tragoudia [Comradeship Songs]. 1981.

Hypokofa [Muffled]. 1982.

Italiko triptycho [Italian Tryptich]. 1982.

Erotica: Small Suite in Red Major, Naked Body, Carnal Word, translated by Kimon Friar. 1982.

Selected Poems, translated by Edmund Keeley. 1983.

To choriko ton sfougarhadon [The Sponge-Divers' Chorale]. 1983.

Teiresias. 1983.

Ochi monacha gia sena [Not Only for You]. 1985.

Exile and Return: Selected Poems 1967–74, translated by Edmund Keeley. 1985.

Ho Ariostos arneitai na ginei hagios [Ariosto Refuses to Become a Saint]. 1986.

Ho gerontas me tous chartaitous [The Old Man with the Kites]. 1986.

Ligostevoun hoi eroteseis [The Questions Are Becoming Fewer]. 1986.

Sphragismena me hena chamogelo [Sealed with a Smile]. 1986.

3 x 111 tristicha. 1987.

Selected Poems, 1938–1988, edited and translated by Kimon Friar, Kostas Myrsiades, and others. 1989.

Repetitions, Testimonies, Parentheses, translated by Edmund Keeley. 1991.

Late Into the Night: The Last Poems of Yannis Ritsos, translated by Martin McKinsey. 1995.

Prison Poems: The Moonlight Sonata: The Prison Tree and the Women: Farewell, translated by Marjorie Chambers. 2001.

Yannis Ritsos: A Voice of Resilience and Hope in a World of Turmoil and Suffering: Selected Poems (1938–1989), translated by George Pilitsis. 2001.

Plays

Pera ap'ton iskio ton Kyparission [Beyond the Shadow of the Cypress Trees] (produced 1959). 1958.

Mia gynaika plai sti thalassa [A Woman by the Sea] (produced 1959). 1959.

Ho lophos me to syntuvani [The Hill with the Fountain]. 1990.

Ta ravdia ton typhlon [The Roads of the Blind]. 1990.

Other

Meletemata [Essays]. 1974.

Ariostos ho prosechtikos afhighite stigmes tou viou tou kai tou hypnou tou [Ariosto, the Careful One, Tells of Moments of His Life and of His Sleep]. 1982.

Ti paraxena pragmata [Strange Things]. 1983.

Antapokriseis [Correspondence]. 1987.

*

Critical Studies: *Ritsos: Étude, choix de texte, et bibliographie* by Chrysa Papandréou, 1968; "Ritsos' *Romiossini*: Style as Historical Memory" by W.V. Spanos, in *American Poetry Review*, September-October 1973; *Three Generations of Greek Writers: Introductions to Cavafy, Kazantzakis, Ritsos* by Peter Bien, 1983.

* * *

Yannis Ritsos is widely hailed as the foremost poet of the Greek Left. He was also one of the most prolific poets in any language, with more than 2,000 pages of published verse to his name. Two strands run through all his work—his Marxist commitment and a vein of pessimistic introspection. In Ritsos's earliest collections of poetry, such as *Trakter* [Tractors], we find poems which explore personal grief alongside others stridently proclaiming the future liberation of the masses. The first poem in which these two moods are combined constructively into a synthesis is *Epitafios* [Funeral Song], a lyrical

lament for a young man shot down by police at a demonstration, in which, however, the lamentation is not that of the poet himself but is dramatically projected: it is the victim's mother who speaks. By this means Ritsos was able to subordinate his talent for expressive grief within a poetic structure in which a harsh optimism prevails.

Ill-health and frequent imprisonment for his political beliefs combined to keep Ritsos at a distance from public life, and for a time in the 1940s and early 1950s, in the aftermath of the Greek civil war, he was unable to publish freely. He wrote prolifically throughout this period, however, and in 1954 published as part of the collection *Agrypnia* [Vigil] his best-known poem, "Romiossini," a long poem celebrating the historical essence of the Greek identity (the *romiosíni* of the title) as an age-old struggle against the harsh elements that comprise the Greek landscape, but still more against human oppressors. From this time on the political optimism of Ritsos's early poems was subsumed into a political and universal sense of tragedy. These poems affirm a deep faith, not so much directly in the outcome of the political struggle, but rather in the ultimate triumph of the noble and free in human nature.

In the 1950s and 1960s, Ritsos's output was characterized by the juxtaposition of long poems with very short poems. In both, the mood of introspection continues to appear, but by this time it was either placed in a dramatic context, as it is in the long poems, or refined by an ironic sharpness of detail that in the short poems converts a natural melancholy into epigrammatic surprise. Although his political commitment remained unchanged, Ritsos here depicted life as tragic, but at the same time containing heroic hope in face of the odds, and with its own beauty, even in defeat. It has often been pointed out that Ritsos was a gifted painter, and that many of his short poems, in particular, reveal the painter's eye: the poem is a juxtaposition of colours, perhaps, or of shapes. In contrast to these very short poems, with the tight structure of an epigram or of an artist's miniature, Ritsos's long poems are discursive, loosely constructed pieces. Their long, strongly rhythmical free-verse lines allow the poet to explore changing moods and to develop a theme, not consequentially, but in extended form—again rather as a painter works, but this time on a large canvas.

Many of Ritsos's poems have achieved wide popularity through being set to music by popular composers such as Mikis Theodorakis, and much of his later production seemed to be directed towards this outlet.

—Roderick Beaton

ROBBE-GRILLET, Alain

Born: Brest, France, 18 August 1922. **Education:** Educated at Lycée de Brest; Lycées Buffon and St. Louis, Paris; National Institute of Agronomy, Paris, diploma 1944. **Military Service:** Sent to work in German tank factory during World War II. **Family:** Married Catherine Rstakian in 1957. **Career:** Engineer, National Statistical Institute, Paris, 1945–49, and Institute of Colonial Fruits and Crops, Morocco, French Guinea, and Martinique, 1949–51; then full-time writer; literary consultant, Editions de Minuit, Paris, since 1955. Légion d'honneur. Lives in Neuilly-sur-Seine, France. **Awards:**

Fénéon prize, 1954; Critics prize, 1955; Louis Delluc prize, 1963; Berlin festival prize, for screenplay, 1969; Mondello prize, 1982. Officer, Order of Merit; chevalier.

PUBLICATIONS

Fiction

Les Gommes. 1953; as *The Erasers,* translated by Richard Howard, 1964.
Le Voyeur. 1955; as *The Voyeur,* translated by Richard Howard, 1958.
La Jalousie. 1957; as *Jealousy,* translated by Richard Howard, 1959.
Dans le labyrinthe. 1959; as *In the Labyrinth,* translated by Richard Howard, 1960; also translated by Christine Brooke-Rose, 1967.
L'Année dernière à Marienbad. 1961; as *Last Year at Marienbad,* translated by Richard Howard, 1962.
Instantanés. 1962; as *Snapshots,* translated by Barbara Wright, with *Towards a New Novel,* 1965; also translated by Bruce Morisette, 1968.
L'Immortelle. 1963; as *The Immortal One,* translated by A.M. Sheridan Smith, 1971.
La Maison de rendez-vous. 1965; as *Le Rendez-vous,* 1981; edited by David H. Walker, 1987; as *La Maison de Rendez-vous,* translated by Richard Howard, 1966; as *The House of Assignation,* translated by Howard, 1970.
Projet pour une révolution à New York. 1970; as *Project for a Revolution in New York,* translated by Richard Howard, 1972.
Glissements progressifs du plaisir. 1974.
Topologie d'une cité fantôme. 1976; as *Topology of a Phantom City,* translated by J.A. Underwood, 1977.
Souvenirs du triangle d'or. 1978; as *Recollections of the Golden Triangle,* translated by J.A. Underwood, 1984.
Un régicide. 1978.
Djinn. 1981; as *Djinn,* translated by Yvone Lenard and Walter Wells, 1982.

Plays

Screenplays: *L'Année dernière à Marienbad,* 1961; *L'Immortelle,* 1963; *Trans-Europ-Express,* 1967; *L'Homme qui ment,* 1968; *L'Eden et après,* 1970; *Glissements progressifs du plaisir,* 1973; *Le Jeu avec le feu,* 1975; *La Belle captive,* 1983.

Other

Pour un nouveau roman. 1963, revised edition, 1970; as *Towards a New Novel,* translated by Barbara Wright, with *Snapshots,* 1965; as *For a New Novel: Essays on Fiction,* translated by Richard Howard, 1966.
Rêves de jeunes filles, photographs by David Hamilton. 1971; as *Dreams of a Young Girl,* translated by Elizabeth Walter, 1971, as *Dreams of Young Girls,* translated by Walter, 1971.
Les Demoiselles d'Hamilton, photographs by David Hamilton. 1972; as *Sisters,* translated by Martha Egan, 1973.
Construction d'un temple en ruines à la déesse Vanadé, illustrated by Paul Delvaux. 1975.
La Belle Captive, with René Magritte. 1976; translated with essay by Ben Stoltzfus, 1995.
Temple aux miroirs, with Irina Ionesco. 1977.

Le Miroir qui revient. 1984; as *Ghosts in the Mirror,* translated by Jo Levy, 1988.
Angélique; ou, l'Enchantement. 1987.
George Segal, invasion blanche. 1990.

*

Bibliography: *Robbe-Grillet: An Annotated Bibliography of Critical Studies 1953–1972* by Dale W. Fraizer, 1973.

Critical Studies: *Alain Robbe-Grillet and the New French Novel,* 1964, *Alain Robbe-Grillet: The Body of the Text,* 1985, and *Alain Robbe-Grillet: Life, Work and Criticism,* 1987, all by Ben Frank Stoltzfus; *The French New Novel: Claude Simon, Michel Butor, Robbe-Grillet* by John Sturrock, 1969; *Narrative Consciousness: Structure and Perception in the Fiction of Kafka, Beckett, and Robbe-Grillet* by G.H. Szanto, 1972; *The Novels of Alain Robbe-Grillet,* 1975, and *Intertexual Assemblage in Robbe-Grillet from Topology to the Golden Triangle,* 1979, both by Bruce Morrissette; *Realism, Reality, and the Fictional Theory of Alain Robbe-Grillet and Anais Nin* by Patricia A. Deduck, 1982; *Robbe-Grillet, Les Gommes and Le Voyeur* by B.G. Garnham, 1982; *Robbe-Grillet* by John Fletcher, 1983; *Opacity in the Writings of Robbe-Grillet, Pinter and Zach: A Study in the Poetics of Absurd Literature* by Yoseph Milman, 1991; *Robbe-Grillet and Modernity: Science, Sexuality and Subversion* by Raylene L. Ramsay, 1992; *Robbe-Grillet and the Fantastic: A Collection of Essays,* edited by Virigina Harger-Grinling and Tony Chadwick, 1994; *The French New Autobiographies: Sarraute, Duras, and Robbe-Grillet* by Raylene L. Ramsay, 1996; *Inventing the Real World: The Art of Alain Robbe-Grillet* by Marjorie H. Hellerstein, 1998; *Intersexual Rivalry: A "Reading in Pairs" of Marguerite Duras and Alain Robbe-Grillet* by Julia Waters, 2000; *Understanding Alain Robbe-Grillet* by Roch C. Smith, 2000.

* * *

The best-known of the so-called *nouveaux romanciers* in France, Alain Robbe-Grillet began life as an agricultural scientist, and turned to literature only after illness brought his research career to an end. He thus comes from a background that is different to that of the regular French person of letters, and explains to some extent the iconoclastic impact he made on the literary scene when his second novel, *Les Gommes (The Erasers),* was published in Paris in 1953 (his first novel, *Un régicide,* appeared only in 1978).

The Erasers is a detective story based on the legend of Oedipus, a complex, enigmatic novel. In *Le Voyeur (The Voyeur),* the next book, a travelling salesman visits the offshore island of his birth and (perhaps) commits a sadistic rape and murder before leaving scot-free some days later; but the crime may have been enacted in the protagonist's sick mind only. In *La Jalousie (Jealousy),* the workings of the sick mind of the protagonist now actually become the text, so that the novel itself constitutes a fit of jealousy in which the narrator watches his wife obsessively as she plans (or so he believes) a night away from home in the company of a neighbouring planter. The jealous frenzy subsides—and the novel ends—only with the return of the (errant?) wife and the (apparent) discomfiture of the neighbour.

Robbe-Grillet has declared on a number of occasions how much he owes to Kafka, and so it is not surprising that *Dans le labyrinthe (In the Labyrinth*) should be Kafkaesque in inspiration. A soldier is wandering in a snow-covered town looking for a man to whom he wants to deliver the effects of a dead comrade after a major military disaster, and he ends up dying from wounds himself. What is not clear is how far the whole story is elaborated by the narrator on the basis of a picture called "The Defeat at Reichenfels," that is to what extent, like jealousy in the previous novel, it is a construct of the fantasizing consciousness.

During the next few years Robbe-Grillet concentrated on making or helping to make a number of films, of which the best-known is *L'Année dernière à Marienbad* (*Last Year at Marienbad*)—directed by Alain Resnais—the story of a man who succeeds in persuading a woman that agreed, the year before in Marienbad, to meet him in the resort where they presently are staying and leave her husband for him. He returned to the novel in *La Maison de rendez-vous* (*The House of Assignation*), a witty parody of James Bond stories set in an exotic Hong Kong where women's flesh "plays a large part" in the protagonist's dreams, and *Projet pour une révolution à New York* (*Project for a Revolution in New York*), a more self-indulgently sadistic fantasy about an imaginary wave of terrorism in Manhattan. Since then the preoccupation with sadism and voyeurism has become almost totally obsessive. It is now clear that his best work is contained in the three mature novels of his middle period, *The Voyeur, Jealousy*, and *In the Labyrinth*, works which will remain important in the history of 20th-century literature long after the polemics which surrounded their publication have been forgotten.

—John Fletcher

See the essays on *In the Labyrinth* and *The Voyeur*.

ROCHA, Adolfo Correia da

See TORGA, Miguel

ROCHEFOUCAULD, François La

See LA ROCHEFOUCAULD, François

RODRIGUES, Nélson

Born: Recife, Pernambuco, Brazil, 23 August 1912. Moved to Rio de Janeiro, 1916. **Career:** Wrote articles on crime for his father's newspaper *A Mañha*, from the age of 14, and subsequently worked as professional journalist. **Died:** 22 December 1980.

PUBLICATIONS

Collections

Teatro completo, edited by S. Magaldi. 4 vols., 1981–84.

Plays

Vestido de noiva (produced 1943). In *Anjo negro . . .* , 1948; revised version, in *Teatro*, 1959–60.
A mulher sem pecado (produced 1945). In *Anjo negro . . .* , 1948.
Anjo negro; Vestido de noiva; A mulher sem pecado. 1948.
Senhora dos afogados (produced 1945). In *Teatro*, 1959–60.
Dorotéia (produced 1949). In *Teatro*, 1959–60.
A valsa n.6 (produced 1950). In *Teatro*, 1959–60.
A falecida (produced 1955). In *Teatro*, 1959–60.
Perdoa-me por me traíres (produced 1957). In *Teatro*, 1959–60.
Viúva, porém honesta (produced 1957?). In *Teatro*, 1959–60.
Os sete gatinhos (produced 1959). In *Teatro*, 1959–60.
Teatro. 2 vols., 1959–60.
Álbum de família (produced 1981). In *Teatro*, 1959–60.
Boca de ouro (produced 1960). In *Teatro*, 1959–60.
O beijo no asfalto. 1961.
Teatro quase completo (includes all plays previously published, and *Toda nudez será castigada* and *Bonitinha, mas ordinária*). 4 vols., 1965–66.
Toda nudez será castigada (produced 1967). In *Teatro quase completo*, 1965–66.
O antí-Nélson Rodrigues (produced 1974?). In *Teatro completo*, 1980–84.
A serpente. 1980.

Fiction

100 contos escolhidos; A vida como ela é (stories). 1961.
Meu destino é pecar (as Suzanna Flag). 1982.

Other

O obvio ululante (articles). 1968.
O reacionario. 1977.
Á sombra das chuteiras imortais: crônicas de futebol. 1993.

*

Bibliography: *Brazilian Literature: A Research Guide* by David William Foster and Walter Rela, 1990.

Critical Studies: *Nélson Rodrigues e o fundo falso* by Maria F. Suskind, 1977; *O teatro de Nélson Rodrigues: uma realidade em agonia* by Ronaldo L. Lins, 1979; *Nélson Rodrigues, meu irmão* by Stella Rodrigues, 1986; *Nélson Rodrigues: dramaturgia e encenações* by José M. Sábato Rodríguez, 1987; *Impermanent Structures: Semiotic Readings of Nélson Rodrigues's Vestido de noiva, Álbum de família and Anjo negro* by Fred M. Clark, 1991; *The Modern Brazilian Stage* by David George, 1992; *Nélson Rodrigues: Trágico, Entáo Moderno* by Angela Leite Lopes, 1993; *Teatro de Nelson Rodrigues: Uma leitura psicanalítica* by Carmine Martuscello, 1993; *Nélson Rodrigues: Evangelista* by Francisco Carneiro de Cunha, 2000; *Nélson: Feminino e masculino* by Irã Salomão, 2000.

* * *

Nélson Rodrigues wrote 17 plays that gained him a reputation as the most powerful Brazilian playwright ever. Today he is the most admired dramatist in Brazil, and his plays are among the most often translated into other languages. On the cover of the first volume of Rodrigues's *Teatro quase completo* [Almost Complete Works],

Prudente de Morais Neto compares the playwright's artistic contribution to the Brazilian theatre to that of Hector Villa-Lobos in music, Cândido Portinari in painting, Carlos Drummond de Andrade in poetry, and Oscar Niemeyer in architecture. His plays were classified thematically by a Brazilian critic, Sábato Magaldi, as "psychological," "mythical," and "*tragédias cariocas*" (tragedies from Rio de Janeiro).

Rodrigues also wrote novels, a volume of short stories, and numerous articles for newspapers. His experience as a journalist (he began to work as a reporter for a crime column at the age of 14) had an impact on his approach to theatre. His "journalistic style," consisting of short, often abrupt dialogues, use of colloquialisms and slang expressions, as well as his predilection for "street-wise" types as characters, is evident in the later plays, the "*tragédias cariocas*". Even though these plays were not intended as, and cannot be perceived as, realistic, the characters and situations used in the "*tragédias cariocas*" are modelled on those from Rio's poor neighbourhoods of Zona Norte, which Rodrigues became familiar with when working as a reporter.

As for style, the author himself wrote in his memoirs *O reacionario* [The Reactionary]: "Plays can be divided into 'interesting' and 'vital'. Giraudoux wrote "interesting" texts. The melody of his prose is a glamorous disguise for his creative impotence. All 'vital' plays belong to 'unpleasant theatre'." Rodrigues perceived his own plays as "vital," and the term "unpleasant theatre" is one most often used by critics to comment on Rodrigues's work.

The term "unpleasant theatre" was coined a few years after the successful staging of *Vestido de noiva* [Wedding Dress], and referred mainly to three plays that Magaldi calls "mythical": *Álbum de família* [Family Album], *Anjo negro* [The Black Angel], and *Senhora dos afogados* [Our Lady of the Drowning]. Rodrigues's "revolutionary" approach to archetypes and primitive unconsciousness in these texts, the introduction of such themes as incest, homicide, and madness, caused an immediate reaction from the censors: *Álbum de família* was banned from the Brazilian stages until 1965. The other two plays were also forbidden, though for a much shorter period of time.

A mulher sem pecado [A Woman without Sin] and *Vestido de noiva*, classified by Magaldi as "psychological," were received enthusiastically by the critics. With these two works Rodrigues gained his reputation as an innovator of the Brazilian stage. In both works he abandoned the "exterior" world in order to explore the secrets of the mind and, equally importantly, he found an adequate stage language to express these concerns.

In his "mythical" tragedies, Rodrigues explored the most obscure aspects of the human mind. In spite of the negative reception from the critics and the audience, these were also his favourite plays, and he felt more accomplished artistically writing them than any of his previous or subsequent works. Each of these purposely disturbing and highly symbolic dramas—where the graphic reality presented is only a pretext to explore, in a poetic manner, more universal truths about the absurdity of human existence—are regarded by some critics as similar in mode to the theatre of Eugene O'Neill. These are also the plays in which Rodrigues, like O'Neill, uses masks. In *Dorotéia* [Dorothy], his last play from the "mythical" cycle, Rodrigues uses the mask as a device to tell the ultimate truth about the characters.

The playwright's fondness for the "mythical" plays, which belong to the "unpleasant theatre," can be explained in the context of his remarks in *O reacionario* about Glauber Rocha's film *A terra em transe* [The Earth in Trance]: "*Terra em transe* is Brazil. All these guys dancing their hideous dances represent us. We wanted to see the tables covered with nice tablecloths, with plates and silverware in the right places, like in a commercial ad in *Manchete*. Instead, Glauber Rocha offered us triumphal vomit. *Os sertões* [The Back Country] by Euclides da Cunha was also a vomited Brazil. Any work of art in order to have meaning in Brazil needs to be hideous." As for the condition of the true artist, Rodrigues wrote about Glauber Rocha in the same book of memoirs: "There are many things that I like about Glauber Rocha, including the following: he is a neurotic; he is on the verge of madness, and this vicinity, in my opinion, is vital for the work of art."

After several years of silence, caused by the negative reception of his "mythical" plays, Rodrigues wrote *A falecida* [The Deceased], a play which opened a new phase in his writing, called by Magaldi "*tragédias cariocas*." The last play from this cycle, *A serpente* [The Snake], was also the last play written by Rodrigues. Even though most of the eight tragedies in this group sythesize some of the disturbing themes from the "mythical" and "psychological" plays, they introduce an additional social dimension, as they deal with everyday life in Rio de Janeiro. The social problems, however, are not introduced in a direct, realistic manner, nor is the author's intention ideological. The author opted for more common types and situations, with which the audience could identify, in order to proceed with his exploration of the subconscious. Some of the motifs that appear in these plays are unnatural death (caused by either murder or suicide), incest, madness, physical disability, machismo, and homosexuality.

In most of Rodrigues's plays, the climate of fatalism, the irrationality of the characters' situation, and the characters' tendency towards self-destruction suggests some parallels with the Expressionist theatre. As in plays by Georg Kaiser, the characters in Rodrigues's "mythical" plays and in his "*tragédias cariocas*" are possessed by dangerous forces, over which they have no control. It is doubtful that Rodrigues had read or seen the plays of the German Expressionists. He was able, however, to read the works of O'Neill and become familiar with the expressionistic cinema of the 1920s.

Cinema had probably the greatest influence on Rodrigues's artistic formation, and psychoanalysis was another phenomenon that influenced Rodrigues in the structuring of the dramatic discourse. Both phenomena suggested to Rodrigues a possibility of breaking away from a one-dimensional, linear type of theatrical narrative. In most of his works, without repeating the same pattern, the narrative is used to project on stage the inner worlds of the characters. This projection is carried out through visual as well as verbal means. Cinematic flashbacks are among his most used devices; they allow the characters to move freely from one plane to another, from the present to the past, from the real to the subconscious, and so on. The influence of cinema in Rodrigues's theatre can also be found in the author's rejection of the decorativeness and literariness ascribed for centuries to dramatic dialogue, as well as in his denial of dialogue's theatrical supremacy.

—Elzbieta Szoka

ROJAS, Fernando de

Born: La Puebla de Montalbán, Spain, c. 1475. **Education:** Received Bachelor of Law degree from University of Salamanca, c. 1498. **Family:** Married Leonor Álvarez; four sons and three daughters.

Career: Practised law in Talavera de la Reina from c. 1507, and served as mayor of the town. **Died:** April 1541.

PUBLICATIONS

Play

Comedia de Calisto y Melibea (16 acts). 1499; as *Tragicomedia* (21 acts), 1502; as *La Celestina*, edited by M. Criado de Val and G.D. Trotter, 1958, 3rd edition, 1970, Dorothy S. Severin, 1969, Miguel Marciales, 1977, and by Peter Russell, 1991; manuscript edited by Guadalupe Martínez Lacalle, 1972; translated by J. De Lavardin, 1578, this translation edited by Denis L. Drysdall, 1975; as *The Spanish Bawd*, translated by James Mabbe, 1631, this translation edited (as *La Celestina*) by Dorothy S. Severin, 1987; as *La Celestina*, translated by L.B. Simpson, 1954; also translated by M.H. Singleton, 1958; Phyllis Hartnoll, 1959; Eric Bentley, 1959; J.M. Cohen, 1964; J. Clifford, 1989.

*

Bibliography: *La Celestina Studies: A Thematic Survey and Bibliography 1824–1970* by Adrienne Schizzano Mandel, 1971; *Celestina by Fernando de Rojas: An Annotated Bibliography of World Interest, 1930–1985* by Joseph T. Snow, 1985.

Critical Studies: *The Art of La Celestina*, 1956, and *The Spain of Fernando de Rojas*, 1972, both by Stephen Gilman; *The Petrarchan Sources of La Celestina* by Alan D. Deyermond, 1961; *Two Spanish Masterpieces: The Book of Good Love and the Celestina* by Maria R. Lida de Malkiel, 1961; *Memory in La Celestina*, 1970, and *Tragicomedy and Novelistic Discourse in Celestina*, 1989, both by Dorothy S. Severin; *Love's Fools: Aucassin, Troilus, Calisto, and the Parody of the Courtly Lover* by June H. Martin, 1972; *Fernando de Rojas* by Peter N. Dunn, 1975; *Concordance to the "Celestina"* by Lloyd Kasten and Jean Anderson, 1976; *Seneca and "Celestina"* by Louise Fothergill-Payne, 1988; *Celestina: Genre and Rhetoric* by Charles F. Fraker, 1990; *Calisto's Dream and the Celestinesque Tradition: A Rereading of Celestina* by Ricardo Castells, 1995; *Vision, the Gaze, and the Function of the Senses in Celestina* by James F. Burke, 2000; *Fernando de Rojas and the Renaissance Vision: Phantasm, Melancholy, and Didacticism in Celestina* by Ricardo Castells, 2000.

*   *   *

La Celestina, or to give the work its full title, the *Comedia de Calisto y Melibea*, is variously considered the last work of the Spanish Middle Ages or the first work of the Spanish Renaissance. Its author, Fernando de Rojas, claimed to have found the long first act of this dialogue novel (or extended humanistic tragicomedy) at Salamanca where he studied law, and to have added the next 15 acts, which were printed no later than 1499. A revised version of the original *Comedia de Calisto y Melibea* was published no later than 1502 and renamed a *Tragicomedia*, with five additional acts and a new Prologue.

The work is a generic hybrid, neither play nor novel, and tells the tragic story of the young nobleman Calisto, who enlists the services of a procuress and witch, Celestina, to seduce Melibea, the virgin daughter of a wealthy merchant, Pleberio. The action takes place at the houses of Calisto, Celestina, and Pleberio and in the streets of an unnamed town. Calisto succeeds in his suit, but not before the scheming servants Pármeno and Sempronio have killed Celestina in a brawl over her fee, and have been killed in turn. Calisto too meets a tragic end when he falls off a ladder after a visit to Melibea's garden, and Melibea then commits suicide. Pleberio is left alone to lament the fate of his daughter.

Curiously, despite the tragic denouement, the work is essentially comic. The manipulative witch Celestina is a creation of comic and diabolic genius. The reading public eventually renamed the work after her. She dominates the action with her manipulation of rhetoric and aphorisms, and in the course of the work seduces not only Melibea but also the hapless servant Pármeno, who spent his childhood in Celestina's household. Pármeno attempts to remain faithful to his master Calisto, but succumbs to the charms of the whore Areúsa.

Essentially, Rojas transforms a variety of literary genres through the use of parody and satire. Calisto is a parody of the courtly lover of the late 15th-century sentimental romance, and is a frankly comic figure in his cloying and excessive courtly postures. Celestina represents the ironic skewing of received wisdom to an evil end. Melibea fancies herself a heroine of popular ballads, and has had her head turned by reading stories from classical antiquity. Sempronio and Pármeno parody the facile wisdom of the medieval university. And even Pleberio misreads Petrarchan neostoicism, which fails him when he is faced by a genuine tragedy.

Witchcraft is another concern in *La Celestina*. Although at one level Celestina is merely an enchantress and procuress, she invokes the devil in a magic ritual and in ensuing scenes the spell is shown to be effective. Melibea's mother Alisa forgets about Celestina's reputation when the old bawd visits her house. Alisa is then called away to a family emergency and leaves Melibea in Celestina's clutches. Although there is scant textual evidence that Celestina has sold her soul to the Devil, she does call up an evil force which then takes on an autonomous power and destroys all the members of the cast. Because of Rojas's background as son of a *converso* family, converts from Judaism, there is little Christian-didactic sentiment in the book, but there is a strong moralistic and pessimistic flavour to the disastrous tragic story. There is also a quantity of anti-clerical satire in the work: at a servants' banquet Celestina recounts the good old days of her ascendancy, when she ran a large house of ill-repute and all the clerics in town paid her homage, in a passage that is a parody of the mass. Her change of fortune seems to correspond to a historical fact in the Spain of the Catholic Monarchs: in the 1490s bordellos began to be run by town councils and private enterprises were closed down. Celestina's house of ill-repute has been reduced to the services of one girl, her companion Elicia, who is also Sempronio's girlfriend.

The other female character besides Celestina who shows genuine depth of character is Melibea. In the course of the work she is transformed from a reticent virgin to a liberated woman who declares to her maidservant Lucrecia that she would prefer to elope with Calisto rather than be made to marry someone else against her will. Although in their first love scene she is physically forced by Calisto, whose moments of nobility alternate with moments of coarseness and cowardice, the second love scene, added to the *Tragicomedia*, is genuinely affecting. It includes a fine love song sung by Melibea and Lucrecia, an *alborada* or lovers' dawn meeting.

The lovers' sudden deaths at the end of the work bring a long lament spoken by Pleberio, the survivor of the wreckage. It takes the *planctus*'s traditional form, but the bereaved father never rails against death; instead he blames the world, fortune, and above all, love, for the disaster. Love replaces death and is accused of leading its victims in a dance of despair. The Petrarchan remedies against both fortunes, good and bad, fail Pleberio, who cannot find consolation in the stories of antiquity that might provide exemplary parallels. Rojas's own position is highly ambiguous and ambivalent; the authorial voice cannot be exactly identified with that of Pleberio, and even the final words, *in hac lachrymarum valle*, are a quote from the *Salve Regina* and can be read either as a pessimistic ending or as a note of hope "in this vale of tears."

—Dorothy S. Severin

ROLLAND, Romain

Born: Romain Edmé Paul Émile Rolland in Clamecy, Nièvre, France, 29 January 1866. **Education:** Educated at Collège de Clamecy, 1873–80; Lycée Saint-Louis, Paris, 1880–82; Lycée Louis-le-Grand, Paris, 1882–86, agrégation in history; École Normale Supérieure, 1886–89; École Française d'Archéologie, Rome, 1889–91, Ph.D., 1895. **Family:** Married 1) Clotilde Bréal in 1892 (divorced 1901); 2) Marie Koudacheva in 1934. **Career:** Teacher, Lycée Henri IV, Paris, 1893, Lycée Louis-le-Grand, Paris, 1894–95, École Jean-Baptiste Say, Paris, 1894–95; École Normale Supérieure, Paris, 1895–1903, and École des Hautes Études Sociales, Paris, 1902–11; lecturer, the Sorbonne, 1903–12, retired because of ill health, 1912. Moved to Switzerland, 1912; worked for International Red Cross, Geneva, 1914–15; International Agency of Prisoners of War, 1914–44; co-founder of the review, *Europe*, 1923; initiator, with Henri Barbusse, *q.v.*, of World Congress Against Imperialist War, 1932. **Awards:** Vie Heureuse prize, 1905; Académie française grand prize for literature, 1913; Nobel prize for literature, 1915; officer, Légion d'honneur, 1909; member of honour, Academy of Sciences, USSR, 1932; Goethe medal (refused), 1933; appointed President of Honour, International Anti-Fascist Committee, 1933. **Died:** 30 December 1944.

PUBLICATIONS

Collection

Chefs d'Oeuvres. 26 vols., 1971–72.

Fiction

Jean-Christophe. 10 vols., 1904–12; as *John Christopher*, translated by Gilbert Cannan, 4 vols., 1910–13; introduced by Louis Auchincloss, 1996.
Colas Breugnon. 1919; as *Colas Breugnon*, translated by Katherine Miller, 1919.
Pierre et Luce, illustrated by Frans Masereel. 1920; as *Pierre and Luce*, translated by Charles de Kay, 1922.
Clérambault: Histoire d'une conscience libre pendant la guerre. 1920; as *Clerambault: The Story of an Independent Spirit During the War*, translated by Katherine Miller, 1921; as *Clerambault; or, One Against All*, also translated Miller, 1933.
L'Âme enchantée. 4 vols., 1934; as *The Soul Enchanted*, translated by Eleanor Stimson, Van Wyck Brooks and Amalia de Alberti, 1925–35.
   Annette et Sylvie. 1922; as *Annette and Sylvie*, translated by Ben Ray Redman, 1925.
   L'Été. 1923; as *Summer*, translated by Eleanor Stimson and Van Wyck Brooks, 1925.

   Mère et fils. 2 vols., 1927; as *Mother and Son*, translated by Van Wyck Brooks, 1927.
   L'Annonciatrice (includes *La Mort d'un monde; L'Enfantement; Via sacra*) 3 vols, 1933; volumes translated by Amalia De Alberti, as *The Death of a World*, 1933, and *A World in Birth*, 1934; *A World in Birth* published in two volumes as *The Combat*, 1935, and *Via sacra*, 1935.

Plays

Saint-Louis. In *Les Tragédies de la foi*, 1897.
Les Tragédies de la Foi (includes *Saint-Louis; Aërt; Le Triomphe de la raison*). 1897.
Aërt (produced 1898). In *Les Tragédies de la Foi*, 1897; published separately, 1898.
Les Loups (produced as *Morituri* 1898). 1898; as *The Wolves*, translated by Barrett H. Clark, 1937; as *The Hungry Wolves*, edited by Michael Marland and translated by John Holmstrom, 1966.
Le Triomphe de la raison (produced 1899). In *Les Tragédies de la Foi*, 1897; published separately, 1899.
Danton (produced 1901). 1900; as *Danton*, translated by Barrett H. Clarke, in *The Fourteenth of July*, 1919.
Le Quartorze juillet (produced 1902). 1902; as *The Fourteenth of July*, translated by Barrett H. Clarke, in *The Fourteenth of July and Danton*, 1919.
Le Temps viendra. 1903.
La Montespan. 1904; as *The Montespan*, translated by Helena van Brugh De Kay, 1923.
Les Trois amoureuses. 1906.
Théâtre de la Révolution (includes *Danton; Le Quartorze juillet; Les Loups*). 1909.
Liluli: Farce lyrique. 1919; translated as *Liluli*, 1920.
Les Vaincus (unfinished). 1922.
Le Jeu de l'amour et de la mort (produced 1928). 1925; as *The Game of Love and Death*, translated by Eleanor Stimson, 1926.
Pâques fleuris. 1926; as *Palm Sunday*, translated by Eugene Löhrke, 1928.
The Plays, translated by Helena van Brugh de Kay. 1927.
Les Léonides. 1928; as *Les Léonides*, translated by Eugene Löhrke, 1929.
Robespierre. 1939.

Other

Les Origines du théâtre lyrique moderne. 1895.
Cur ars picturae apud Italos XVI saeculi deciderit. 1895.
François Millet, translated by Miss Clementina Black. 1902.
Vie de Beethoven (biography). 1903; as *Beethoven*, translated by F. Rothwell, 1907; also translated by B. Constance Hull, 1917.
Le Théâtre du peuple. 1903; as *The People's Theater*, translated by Barrett H. Clark, 1919.
La Vie de Michel-Ange. 2 vols., 1905–06; as *Michelangelo*, translated by Frederic Lees, 1912.
Musiciens d'aujourd'hui. 1908; as *Musicians of To-Day*, translated by Mary Blaiklock, 1914.
Musiciens d'autrefois. 1908; as *Some Musicians of Former Days*, translated by Mary Blaiklock, 1915.
Haendel (biography). 1910; as *Handel*, translated by A. Eaglefield Hull, 1916.

La Vie de Tolstoï (biography). 1911; as *Tolstoy*, translated by Bernard Miall, 1911.

Au-dessus de la mêlée. 1915; as *Above the Battlefield*, translated by C.K. Ogden, 1916.

Aux peuples assassinés. 1917.

Salut à la Révolution russe, with P.J. Jouve, H. Guilbeaux, and F. Masereel. 1917.

Empédocle d'Agrigente et l'âge de la haine. 1918.

Les Précurseurs (articles). 1919; revised edition, 1923; as *The Forerunners*, translated by Eden and Cedar Paul, 1920.

Voyage musical aux pays du passé. 1919; as *A Musical Tour through the Land of the Past*, translated by Bernard Miall, 1922.

La Révolte des machines; ou, La Pensée déchaînée. 1921; as *The Revolt of the Machines; or, Invention Run Wild*, translated by William A. Drake, 1932.

Mahatma Gandhi. 1924; as *Mahatma Gandhi: The Man who Became One with the Universal Being*, translated by Catherine D. Groth, 1924.

Goethe et Beethoven. 1927; as *Goethe and Beethoven*, translated by G.A. Pfister and E.S. Kemp, 1931.

Beethoven: Les Grandes Époques créatrices. 7 vols., 1928–45; as *Beethoven the Creator*, translated by Ernest Newman, 1929.

De L'Héroïque à l'Appassionata. 1928.

Essai sur la mystique et l'action de l'Inde vivante. 2 vols., 1929–30:
    La Vie de Ramakrishna. 1929; as *The Life of Ramakrishna*, translated by E.F. Malcolm-Smith, 1929, republished as *Prophets of the New India*, 1930.
    La Vie de Vivekananda et l'évangile universelle. 1930; as *The Life of Vivekananda and the Universal Gospel*, translated by E.F. Malcolm-Smith, 1931.
    Souvenir d'enfance. 1930.

Letters 1890–1891, translated by Thomas J. Wilson. 1933.

Par la Révolution, la paix (articles). 1935.

Quinze ans de combat: 1919–1934 (articles). 1935; as *I Will Not Rest*, translated by K.S. Shelvankar, 1935.

Comment empêcher la guerre. 1936.

Compagnons de route (essays). 1936.

Valmy. 1938.

Les Pages immortelles de Rousseau. 1939.

Le Voyage intérieur. 1942, revised, 1959; as *Journey Within*, translated by Elsie Pell, 1947.

Péguy. 2 vols., 1944.

Le Seuil, précédé du Royaume du T. 1945.

De Jean-Christophe à Colas Breugnon (journal). 1946.

Le Périple (essays). 1946.

Lettres de Romain Rolland à un combattant de la Résistance. 1947.

Souvenirs de jeunesse (1866–1900). 1947.

Choix de lettres à Malwida von Meysenburg. 1948.

Souvenirs sur Richard Strauss. 1948.

Correspondance entre Louis Gillet et Romain Rolland. 1949.

Inde: Journal 1915–1943. 1951; revised edition, 1960; translated, 1960.

Journal des années de guerre 1914–1918. 1952.

Le Cloître de la Rue d'Ulm: Journal de Romain Rolland dà l'École Normale, 1886–1889. 1952.

Printemps romain: Choix de lettres de Romain Rolland à sa mère, 1889–1890. 1954.

Mémoires et fragments du journal. 1956.

Retour au Palais Farnèse: Choix de lettres de Romain Rolland à sa mère, 1890–1891. 1956.

Romain Rolland, Lugné-Poe: Correspondance 1894–1901, edited by Jacques Robichez. 1957.

Chère Sofia (correspondence). 1959.

Rabindranath Tagore et Romain Rolland: Lettres et autres écrits. 1961.

Histoire d'une amitié: Textes inédits de Romain Rolland et d'Alphonse de Châteaubriant. 1962.

Deux hommes se rencontrent (correspondence, with Jean-Richard Bloch). 1964.

Fräulein Elsa. Lettres de Romain Rolland à Elsa Wolff, edited by René Cheval. 1964.

Romain Rolland et le mouvement florentin de La Voce (correspondence and journal extracts), edited by Henri Giordan. 1965.

Richard Strauss and Romain Rolland: Correspondence, edited by Rollo Meyers. 1968.

Correspondance de Romain Rolland avec Heinz Haeberlin, de 1926 à 1940, et Adolphe Ferrière, de 1915 à 1944. 1969.

D'une rive à l'autre (correspondence). 1972; as *Herman Hesse and Romain Rolland: Correspondence, Diary Entries and Reflections, 1915–1940*, translated by M.G. Hesse, 1978.

Romain Rolland and Gandhi: Correspondence (includes journal), translated by R.A. Francis. 1976.

Bon voisinage: Edmond Privat et Romain Rolland: Correspondance, edited by Pierre Hirsch. 1977.

Monsieur le Comte: Romain Rolland et Léon Tolstoy: Textes, edited by Marie Romain Rolland. 1978.

En plein vol: Jean Saint-Prix et Romain Rolland lettres 1917–1919. 1980.

L'Un et l'autre: Correspondance entre Romain Rolland et Alphonse de Chateaubriant (correspondence). 1983.

Ernest Bloch, Romain Rolland: Lettres 1911–1933. 1984.

Correspondance Intégrale Panaït Istrati—Romain Rolland (1919–1935), edited by Alexandre Talex. 1987.

Au seuil de la dernière porte: Correspondances et inédits 1936–44, edited by Bernard Duchatelet. 1989.

Romain Rolland et la NRF: Correspondances avec Jacques Copeau (et al), edited by Bernard Duchatelet. 1989.

Selected Letters, edited and translated by Francis Doré and Marie-Laure Prévost. 1990.

Correspondance Romain Rolland-Maxime Gorki 1916–1936, edited by Jean Pérus. 1991.

Voyage à Moscou: Juin-juillet 1935, edited by Bernard Duchatelet. 1992.

*

Bibliography: *A Critical Bibliography of the Published Writings of Romain Rolland* by William T. Starr, 1950; *Romain Rolland: Index bio-bibliographique* by M.N. Vaksmakher et al, 1959.

Critical Studies: *The Formation of the Esthetic of Romain Rolland* by William H. Beckwith, 1936; *The Tragedy of Romain Rolland* by Georges A. Connes, 1948; *Romain Rolland* by Jacques Robichez, 1961; *Harmony of Contrasts: Music and the Musician in "Jean-Christophe"* by David Sices, 1968; *Romain Rolland* by Pierre Sipriot, 1968; *Romain Rolland, One Against All* by William T. Starr, 1971; *Romain Rolland* by Jean-Bertrand Barrère, 1978; *Romain Rolland* by Helene M. Kastinger Riley, 1979; *Répertoire chronologique des lettres publiées de R. Rolland* by Bernard Duchatelet, 1981; *Romain*

Rolland and the Politics of Intellectual Engagement by David James Fisher, 1988; *Romain Rolland* by R.A. Francis, 1999.

* * *

Romain Rolland remains one of the towering figures of the first half of the 20th century, although his principal literary works now seem dated, and his unswerving public allegiance to the Soviet revolution is questioned today. He left his mark on his times as both author and political figure, embodying the idea of the "fellow traveller" in the latter context—in resonance with one of his collections of essays *Compagnons de route* [Fellow Travellers]—and initiating the *roman fleuve* (literally "river novel"), but figuratively a saga like those of Galsworthy, Martin du Gard, and Jules Romains that followed it—by the length of *Jean-Christophe* (*John Christopher*) and its use of the river as dominant metaphor. For both his moral example in the pre-war period and the qualities and international renown of his novel he was awarded the 1915 Nobel prize for literature.

Rolland was born in Clamecy and died in nearby Vézelay, both of them in the heart of Burgundy; but this belies the pan-European, indeed worldwide dimensions of his life and career. His family left the provinces and went to Paris when he was 14 for the express purpose of enhancing his academic opportunities. Studies at the Lycée Saint-Louis, the Lycée Louis-le-Grand, and the École Normale Supérieure were intended to lead to a teaching career at the university; he did occupy the first chair in history of music at the Sorbonne, and all his writing was marked by his training as an historian. But his dislike of academia led him to abandon the profession as soon as *John Christopher's* success gave him financial independence. The outbreak of World War I found Rolland on vacation in Switzerland, and he stayed there more or less continuously for the next 25 years. His essays pleading for intellectual and moral understanding among the combatants, published in 1915 as *Au-dessus de la mêlée* (*Above the Battlefield*) gave him perhaps unwarranted notoriety as a pacifist. Rolland's literary works and essays between the two World Wars trace his political and moral evolution from pan-European individualism, to Gandhi-inspired non-violent internationalism, to Soviet communism, although he never joined the Party. Rolland's most extensive actual journey, the fellow-traveller's canonical trip to the Soviet Union in 1935, confirmed his adherence to the ranks of the procommunists and his abandonment of previous political stances; but the non-intervention pact between Stalin and Hitler in 1939 dealt a serious blow to his support of Soviet communism, which was based in great part on strong anti-fascist sentiments dating back to Mussolini's accession to power in Italy in 1922.

Rolland's literary creation is divided among drama, the novel, biography, and the essay; he was also a co-founder of the important literary and political review, *Europe*, in 1923. Eleven of his early plays, written between 1890 and 1897, for the most part reflect historical and philosophical interests; many of them are set in the Italian Renaissance. Somewhat later, under the influence of the popular theatre movement as well as in accordance with his own evolving political sentiments, he wrote the eight plays (out of a projected 11) of his *Théâtre de la Révolution* [Drama of the Revolution], of which *Les Loups* (*The Wolves*) and *Le Jeu de l'amour et de la mort* (*The Game of Love and Death*) achieved the greatest success. Another play, the anti-war allegory *Liluli*, also had numerous performances.

Although Rolland wrote several shorter novels, including *Colas Breugnon*, *Clérambault* and *Pierre et Luce* (*Pierre and Luce*), he is no doubt best remembered for his two *romans fleuves*, *John Christopher* and *L'Âme enchantée* (*The Soul Enchanted*). The former is the story of a German musician, whose early life and general character are reminiscent of Beethoven, and who spends the greater part of his adult creative life in Paris. Like the later work, it is flawed by its creator's tendency to sermons and diatribes, but it paints a stirring picture both of the musician-hero and of the pre-World War I Parisian artistic scene. *The Soul Enchanted* focuses on its heroine, Annette Rivière, a single mother courageously raising her son, to analyse and criticize French political life after the war. Because of the extended period of its writing, this novel reflects the evolution of its author's own views toward communism.

Rolland also gained renown for his biographies. His first significant work in this genre, *Vie de Beethoven* (*Beethoven*), initiated a projected series of "Vies de hommes illustres" [Lives of Illustrious Men] inspired by Plutarch and Carlyle. It combined Rolland's lifelong veneration for the great German composer with his desire to provide a heroic moral example for his generation, in which he proved highly successful. Later biographies included his *La Vie de Michel-Ange* (*Michelangelo*), *Haendel* (*Handel*), *La Vie de Tolstoï* (*Tolstoy*), *Empédocle d'Argrigente* [Empedocles], *Beethoven: Les Grandes Époques créatrices* (*Beethoven the Creator*), lives of Ramakrishna and Vivekananda, and *Péguy*.

The list of Rolland's published essays, embracing musical, politico-social, and autobiographical themes, is a lengthy one. Principal among the first category are *Musiciens d'aujourd'hui* (*Musicians of To-day*), *Musiciens d'autrefois* (*Some Musicians of Former Days*), and *Voyage musical aux pays du passé* (*A Musical Tour through the Land of the Past*); among the second are *Le Théâtre du peuple* (*The People's Theater*), *Above the Battlefield*, *Quinze Ans de combat* (*I Will Not Rest*), and *Compagnons de route*; among the third are *Le Voyage intérieur* (*Journey Within*) and several volumes of memoirs published posthumously, including, *Inde: Journal 1915–1943* [India: A Diary, 1915–1943], *Journal des années de guerre* [Diary of the War Years], and *Mémoires*. Between 1948 and 1982, 24 volumes of correspondence, diaries, and memoirs were published in the *Cahiers Romain Rolland* by the Association des Amis de Romain Rolland.

—David Sices

RONSARD, Pierre de

Born: Château de la Possonière, near Couture, France, 10/11 September 1524. **Education:** Educated at Collège de Navarre, Paris, 1533–34; Royal Riding School, Paris 1539. **Career:** Page at French Court, 1536; accompanied Madeleine (the daughter of Francis I) to Scotland on her marriage to James V, 1537, and again in Scotland, 1538–39; in service of the diplomat Lazare de Baïf, 1540; lived on his family estate to recover his health, 1540–43; took minor orders, 1543; studied under Jean Dorat, 1544–47, with Du Bellay at Collège du Coqueret, Paris, 1547, and at the Collège de Boncourt, Paris; given ecclesiastical appointment, Evaillé, 1555; named almoner and counsellor to the king, 1559; Canon of St. Julien, Le Mans, 1560; Prior of St. Cosme des Tours, 1565; exchanged Evaillé appointment for prebendary of St. Martin, Tours, 1566; Prior of Croixval, 1566. **Died:** 27/28 December 1585.

PUBLICATIONS

Collections

Oeuvres complètes, edited by Paul Laumonier, completed by Raymond Lebègue and Isidore Silver. 18 vols., 1914–67.
Oeuvres complètes (text of 1584), edited by Gustave Cohen. 2 vols., 1950.
Oeuvres (text of 1587), edited by Isidore Silver. 4 vols., 1966–70.
Selected Poems, edited by Christine M. Scollen-Jimack. 1995.

Verse

Quatre premiers livres des odes. 1550; *Odes*, 1550, enlarged edition, 1553, revised edition, 1555; complete edition, as *Les Odes*, edited by Charles Guerin, 1952.
Le Premier Livre des amours, le Cinquième des Odes. 1552, revised edition, 1553; *Continuation des amours*, 1555; *La Nouvelle Continuation des amours*, 1556; complete edition, as *Les Amours*, edited by Albert-Marie Schmidt, 1974.
Livret de folastries. 1553.
Mélanges. 1555; *Second Livre de mélanges*, 1559.
Hymnes. 2 vols., 1555–56; edited by Albert Py, 1978.
Sonets à Sinope. 1559.
Mélanges et Chansons. 1560.
Oeuvres. 1560, revised editions, 1567, 1571, 1573, 1578, 1584, 1587.
Institution pour l'adolescence du Roy Charles IX. 1562.
Discours sur les misères de ce temps. 1562.
Remonstrance au peuple de France. 1563.
Recueil de trois livres de nouvelles poésies. 1563.
Réponse aux injures et calomnies. 1563.
Elégies, mascarades, et bergeries. 1565.
VIe et VIIe Livres des poèmes. 1569.
Franciade. 1572.
Tombeau de Charles IX. 1574.
Tombeau de Marguerite de France. 1575.
Derniers vers. 1586.
Lyrics, translated by W. Stirling. 1956.
[Selections], translated by Grahame Castor and Terence Cave. 2 vols., 1975–77.
Poems, translated by Nicholas Kilmer. 1979.

Other

Abrégé de l'art poétique français. 1565.

*

Critical Studies: *Spenser, Ronsard, and Du Bellay* by Alfred W. Satterthwaite, 1960; *Ronsard and the Hellenic Renaissance in France*, 1961, *The Intellectual Evolution of Ronsard: The Formative Influences*, 1969, *Three Ronsard Studies*, 1978, and *Ronsard and the Grecian Lyre*, 1981, all by Isidore Silver; *Ronsard, Poet of Nature* by D.B. Wilson, 1961; *Ronsard's Sonnet Cycles* by Donald Stone, Jr, 1966; *Ronsard and the Age of Gold* by Elizabeth Armstrong, 1968; *Ronsard* by K.R.W. Jones, 1970; *Ronsard the Poet* edited by Terence Cave, 1973; *Love Elegies of the Renaissance: Marot, Louise Labé, and Ronsard* by Gertrude S. Hanisch, 1979; *Ronsard's Successful Epic Venture: The Epyllion* by Bruce R. Leslie, 1979; *Ronsard's*

Ordered Chaos: Visions of Flux and Stability in the Poetry of Ronsard by Malcolm Quainton, 1980; *Ronsard and the Biblical Tradition* by Joyce Main Hanks, 1982; *Ideal Forms in the Age of Ronsard* by Margaret M. McGowan, 1985; *Ronsard in Cambridge: Proceedings of the Cambridge Ronsard Colloquium 10–12 April, 1985* edited by Philip Ford and Gillian Jondorf, 1986; *Invention, Death and Self-Definition in the Poetry of Pierre de Ronsard* by Ullrich Langer, 1986; *Ronsard's Mercury: The Arcane Muse* by Barbara L. Welch, 1986; *Theme and Version: Plath and Ronsard*, edited by Anthony Rudolf, 1995; *Ronsard's Hymnes: A Literary and Iconographical Study* by Philip Ford, 1997; *Ronsard's Contentious Sisters: The Paragone Between Poetry and Painting in the Works of Pierre de Ronsard*, 1998; *Ronsard, Petrarch and the Amours* by Sara Sturm-Maddox, 1999.

*   *   *

The undisputed ''prince of poets'' in 16th-century France, Pierre de Ronsard achieved what he and Joachim Du Bellay had set out to do in their early theoretical writings, namely change the whole course of French poetry. Insisting on the need to create a distinctly poetic language and make a complete break with the ''monstrous error'' of the past, he was a considerable innovator, bringing into the French tradition the ode and the ''hymne'' and making the love sonnet more widely accepted.

His range was both deep and wide. He is now known to the poetry-reading public mainly as a poet of love—unrequited and intellectualized in the Petrarchist sonnets to Cassandre and to Hélène, joyful and uncomplicated in those to Marie—but his stylistic register goes from the Rabelaisian frolics of the *Livret de folastries* to the serious and sometimes pedantic erudition of his Pindaric odes. What is more, he accustomed his public to the notion of the poem as a vehicle for ideas. Ronsard was never shy of philosophizing in verse. He wrote consciously (occasionally arrogantly) for a social and intellectual elite but he was not above involving himself in bruising conflicts with other poets on religions and political issues. His apotheosis as a poet—the publication of his collected works in 1560—coincided with the outbreak of the Wars of Religion, and his later life was overshadowed as much by the political upheavals of the time as by the ill-health which dogged him and of which he complained in his verses. A poet through and through, Ronsard felt to the very end of his life the need to write about even his most intimate experiences; lying on his deathbed and physically unable to put pen to paper, he managed to dictate nine final poems, published posthumously as the *Derniers vers* [Last Poems], in which he describes in poignant detail his sufferings and calls for release through death. The thought of his imminent demise is made more bearable by the certainty of that immortality which alone justifies the poet's vocation. Already, in a famous sonnet to Hélène de Surgères reminding her that she will grow old (''Quand vous serez bien vieille, au soir à la chandelle''), he had remarked that one day she will marvel at the fact that no less a poet than Ronsard had admired her youthful beauty. Thanks to his genius, he implies, the name of an otherwise unexceptional young woman will thus live as long as men have pen and ink.

Enormously prolific, immensely learned, and endowed with enviable facility, Ronsard was without doubt the colossus his contemporaries acclaimed. Today, when much of his philosophical and religious poetry has inevitably lost its accessibility, he remains the greatest French exponent of the theme of *carpe diem* and the transience of life, and at a distance of more than four centuries he is still able to make the reader delight in the freshness of a May morning and shed a tear for the dying of a rose.

—Michael Freeman

See the essays on "Hymn to Autumn," "Ode to Michel de l'Hospital," and "Quand vous serez bien vieille . . . ."

ROSA, João Guimarães

See GUIMARÃES ROSA, João

ROSTAND, Edmond (-Eugène)

Born: Marseilles, France, 1 April 1868. **Education:** Educated at Thedanat School, Marseilles; lycée, Marseilles, 1878–84; Collège Stanislas, Paris, 1884–86. **Family:** Married Rosemonde Gérard in 1890; several children. **Career:** Poet and playwright based in Paris, from the late 1880s; retired to Cambo-les-Bains, in the Basque country, because of ill health, 1900. **Award:** Légion d'honneur, 1900. **Member:** Elected to the Académie française, 1901. **Died:** 2 December 1918.

PUBLICATIONS

Collections

Oeuvres complètes. 5 vols., 1910–11; supplementary volume, 1925.
Oeuvres complètes illustrées, edited by Émile Faguet. 7 vols., 1910–30.
Plays, translated by Henderson D. Norman. 2 vols., 1921.

Plays

Le Gant rouge, with Henry Lee (produced 1888).
Les Deux Pierrots. 1891.
Les Romanesques (produced 1894). 1894; as *The Romancers,* translated by Mary Hendee, 1899; also translated by Barrett H. Clark, 1915; as *The Fantasticks,* translated by G. Fleming, 1900; as *The Romantics,* translated by Henderson D. Norman, in *Plays 1,* 1921.
La Princesse lointaine (produced 1895). 1895; as *The Princess Far Away,* translated by Henderson D. Norman, in *Plays 1,* 1921; also translated by Anna Emilia Bagstad, 1925; as *The Far Princess,* translated by John Heard, 1925.
La Samaritaine (produced 1897). 1897; as *The Woman of Sumaria,* translated by Henderson D. Norman, in *Plays 1,* 1921.
Cyrano de Bergerac (produced 1897). 1898; edited by Edward A. Bird, 1968, Oscar Kuhns and Henry Ward Church, 1968, Jean-François Ménard, 1990, Willy de Spens, 1990, and by Jean-François Grimaud-Lebeaux, 1992; as *Cyrano de Bergerac,* translated by Henderson D. Norman, in *Plays 1,* 1921; also translated by Brian Hooker, 1924; Humbert Wolfe, 1937; James Forsyth, 1968; Christopher Fry, 1975; Anthony Burgess, 1985; edited by Geoff Woollen, 1994; adapted by Jatinder Verma, rendered into verse by Ranjit Bolt, 1995; translated by John Murrell, 1995; translated by Christopher Fry, 1996.
L'Aiglon (produced 1900). 1900; edited by Patrick Besnier, 1986; as *L'Aiglon,* translated by Louis Parker, 1900; also translated by

Basil G. Davenport, 1927; as *The Eaglet,* translated by Henderson D. Norman, in *Plays 1,* 1921.
Le Bois sacré (pantomime; produced 1910). 1908.
Chantecler (produced 1910). 1910; as *Chantecler,* translated by Gertrude Hall, 1910; also translated by Kay Nolte Smith, 1987; as *Chanticleer,* translated by Henderson D. Norman, in *Plays 2,* 1921.
La Dernière Nuit de Don Juan (produced 1922). 1921; as *The Last Night of Don Juan,* translated by T. Lawrason Riggs, 1929; also translated by Dolores Bagley, 1963.

Verse

Les Musardises. 1890; as *Les Musardises 1887–1893,* 1911.
Pour la Grace. 1897.
Un soir à Hernani. 1902.
Le Vol de la Marseillaise. 1919.
Le Cantique de l'aile. 1922.
Choix de poésies. 1925.

Other

Discours de réception à l'Académie française. 1903.

*

Critical Studies: *Edmond Rostand* by G. Haraszti, 1913; *Le Théâtre d'Edmond Rostand: Étude critique* by Jean Suberville, 1919; *Vingt ans d'intimité avec Edmond Rostand* by Paul Faure, 1928; *La Vie profonde d'Edmond Rostand* by Pierre Apesteguy, 1929; *L'Oeuvre dramatique d'Edmond Rostand* by J.W. Grieve, 1931; *L'Esprit français dans le théâtre d'Edmond Rostand* by E. Katz, 1934; *The Sources of the Play "Cyrano de Bergerac"* by Hobart Ryland, 1936; *Edmond Rostand: Cyrano de Bergerac* by Mary L. Engel, 1969; *Les Rostand* by Marcel Migeo, 1973; *Edmond Rostand* by Alba della Fazia Amoia, 1978; *Edmond Rostand: Le Panache et la gloire* by Marc Andry, 1986; *Readings on Cyrano de Bergerac,* edited by Crystal R. Chweh, 2001.

* * *

Edmond Rostand, who sprang to fame with his brilliant *Cyrano de Bergerac* in 1897 and followed up that success with another, the heart-rendingly sentimental *L'Aiglon* (*The Eaglet*), three years later, occupies an interesting niche in the history of the French theatre. Austere critics have always tended to disapprove of the overt emotionalism of his plays. But the public of his day welcomed his theatricality and his lively characterization, and audiences still respond to the powerful situations and surging passions that he presents in glamorous settings and glittering verse. Not for Rostand the rather glum portrayal of humanity in decay that is characteristic of the influential drama of Ibsen and of such naturalistic French dramatists as Henri Becque or the witty, but essentially trivial concerns of the deftly crafted well-made play that was the staple of the 19th-century theatre. Instead, belatedly, he brought before the public a last gorgeous flowering of the reinvigorated French drama that had been begun by Dumas *père* and Victor Hugo in the 1820s and 1830s. At that time their success had been contested, and it was not until the late 1860s, in the last years of Napoleon III's reign, that Hugo's verse historical dramas had been revived, in part as a gesture of defiance against the regime. Victorien Sardou was inspired to move from well-made plays to grand historical spectacles, but it was left to Rostand to replace the distressing moral pessimism found in Sardou's melodramas with more uplifting sentiments, and to substitute for his pedestrian prose cleverly phrased verse capable of transporting the public to a more inspiriting sphere of experience.

Rostand's delightful and artificial comedy *Les Romanesques* (*The Romantics*) and *La Princesse lointaine* (*The Far Princess*), with its subject borrowed from France in the medieval period, give no more than some promise of what he was to achieve later. *La Samaritaine* (*The Woman of Sumaria*) is based on the episode recounted in the fourth chapter of the Gospel according to St. John. In much the same spirit that inspired Hugo's retelling of stories from Scripture in his *La Légende des siècles* (*The Legend of the Centuries*), Rostand brings out all the rich human interest of the situations he evokes, in patriarchal settings that seem far removed from the bustle of 19th-century Paris.

Cyrano de Bergerac also transports the audience to a period in the past that seems beguilingly different from the present. The Romantic movement had stressed that France in the 17th century, previously seen as the Age of Absolutism in politics and of classicism in literature, was in fact an exciting time when flamboyant characters flourished. Dumas *père* had responded with, for instance, his *Les Trois Mousquetaires* (*The Three Musketeers*), and then more than 50 years later, Rostand took the fairly insignificant literary figure Cyrano de Bergerac and turned him into last of the great flawed heroes of romanticism. His Cyrano is a dashing swashbuckler, a talker and poet whose volubility is outstanding even by the exceptional standards of his native Gascony, and a human being who holds firm to the highest standards of conduct in an age when many were departing from them as they clung to the great in the hope of advancement. But Cyrano, for all those positive qualities, is ugly, with a nose whose description beggars all the resources of the French language. The result is unhappiness in love, and a drama which begins in tearing high spirits ends in touching pathos.

Brilliant settings, traditional French verse—12-syllable rhyming alexandrines—handled with exceptional verve and daring extravagance, entrusting the role of Cyrano to Coquelin, the greatest actor of the time all helped make *Cyrano* a breath-taking success. *The Eaglet* almost achieved the feat of repeating it. The basis is the sad story of the Emperor Napoleon I's only son. Known to history variously as the King of Rome and the Duke of Reichstadt, he is aptly called "l'aiglon," the "young eagle" that did not fly from the nest to soar upwards like his father, for he never reigned but had the frustration of growing up at the Austrian court where he died shortly after his 21st birthday. From this material Rostand fashioned a six-act drama that is both patriotic and sentimental. The climax, in a scene that some find moving but that can offend others in its overt exploitation of religion for theatrical purposes, is the scene in which holy communion is administered to the dying prince in the presence of his family. Less controversial was the decision to entrust the lead not to a young male actor but to Sarah Bernhardt who, at the ripe age of 55, scored in *The Eaglet* yet another triumph in the breeches roles in which she specialized.

Though Rostand was elected to the Académie française after the success of *The Eaglet* he was in poor health and it was to be ten years before his next play was performed. *Chantecler* marked a new direction as Rostand moved from historical drama to transparent allegory for the presentation of idealism. His last play, published three years after his death, was *La Dernière Nuit de Don Juan* (*The Last*

Night of Don Juan). It was a complete failure, perhaps at least in part because the public was hoping for yet another play in the style of *Cyrano de Bergerac*.

—Christopher Smith

See the essay on *Cyrano de Bergerac*.

ROTH, Joseph

Born: Brody, Galicia, Austria (now in the Ukraine), 2 September 1894. **Education:** Educated at Baron-Hirsch-Schule, Brody, 1901–05; Imperial-Royal Crown Prince Rudolph Gymnasium, 1905–13; University of Lemberg, Vienna, 1913; studied German literature, University of Vienna, 1914–16. **Family:** Married Friederike Reichler in 1922 (died 1940). **Career:** Served in the Austrian army, 1916–18: claimed to have been prisoner of war in Russia. Journalist, Vienna, 1919–23; staff member, Berlin, 1923–25, and cultural correspondent, Paris, 1925, Soviet Union, 1926, Albania, 1927, and Poland, 1928, for the *Frankfurter Zeitung*; emigrated to Paris to escape the Nazi regime, 1933; travelled to Poland, 1933 and 1937, on lecture tour for PEN. Suffered from poor health for most of his life. **Died:** 27 May 1939.

PUBLICATIONS

Collections

Werke, edited by Hermann Kesten. 3 vols., 1956; revised edition, 4 vols., 1975–76.
Werke. 6 vols., edited by Klaus Westermann and Fritz Hackert. 1989.
Collected Stories of Joseph Roth, translated with introduction by Michael Hofmann. 2002.

Fiction

Hotel Savoy. 1924; translated by John Hoare, in *Hotel Savoy; Fallmerayer the Stationmaster; The Bust of the Emperor*, 1986.
Die Rebellion. 1924; as *Rebellion*, translated by Michael Hofmann, 1999.
April: Die Geschichte einer Liebe. 1925.
Der blinde Spiegel. 1925.
Zipper und sein Vater. 1928; as *Zipper and His Father*, translated by John Hoare, with *The Spider's Web*, 1988.
Rechts und Links. 1929; as *Right and Left*, translated by Michael Hofmann, 1991.
Hiob: Roman eines einfachen Mannes. 1930; as *Job: The Story of a Simple Man*, translated by Dorothy Thompson, 1931.
Radetzkymarsch. 1932; as *The Radetzky March*, translated by Geoffrey Dunlop, 1933; translated by Eva Tucker, 1974; also translated by Joachim Neugroschel, 1995.
Tarabas: Ein Gast auf dieser Erde. 1934; as *Tarabas: A Guest on Earth*, 1934; also translated by Winifred Katzin, 1987.
Die Büste des Kaisers. 1964; as *The Bust of the Emperor*, translated by John Hoare, in *Hotel Savoy; Fallmerayer the Stationmaster; The Bust of the Emperor*, 1986.
Der Antichrist. 1934; as *Antichrist*, translated by Moray Firth, 1935.

Die hundert Tage. 1936; as *The Ballad of the Hundred Days*, translated by Moray Firth, 1936; as *The Story of the Hundred Days*, 1936.

Beichte eines Mörders, erzählt in einer Nacht. 1936; as *Confession of a Murderer, Told in One Night*, translated by Desmond L. Vesey, 1938.

Das falsche Gewicht. 1937; as *Weights and Measures*, translated by David Le Vay, 1982.

Die Kapuzinergruft. 1938; as *The Emperor's Tomb*, translated by John Hoare, 1984.

Die Geschichte von der 1002. Nacht. 1939; as *The Tale of the 1002nd Night*, translated by Michael Hofman, 1999.

Die Legende vom heiligen Trinker. 1939; as *The Legend of the Holy Drinker*, translated by Michael Hofmann, 1989.

Der Leviathan. 1940.

Romane, Erzählungen, Aufsätze. 1964.

Der stumme Prophet. 1966; as *The Silent Prophet*, translated by David Le Vay, 1979.

Das Spinnennetz. 1967; as *The Spider's Web*, translated by John Hoare, with *Zipper and His Father*, 1988.

Die Erzählungen. 1973.

Other

Für Gott und Vaterland. 1925.

Juden auf Wanderschaft (essays). 1927; as *The Wandering Jews*, translated by Michael Hofmann, 2001.

Die Flucht ohne Ende. 1927; as *Flight Without End*, translated by Ida Zeitlin, 1930; also translated by David Le Vay and Beatrice Musgrave, 1977.

Das Moskauer Jüdische Akademische Theater. 1928.

Panoptikum: Gestalten und Kulissen (essays). 1930.

Zwischen Lemberg und Paris, edited by Ada Erhart. 1961.

Briefe 1911–1939, edited by Hermann Kesten. 1970.

Der neue Tag: Unbekannte politische Arbeiten 1919 bis 1927, Wien, Berlin, Moskau, edited by Ingeborg Sültemeyer. 1970.

Perlefter: Die Geschichte eines Bürgers, edited by Friedemann Berger. 1978.

Berliner Saisonbericht: Unbekannte Reportagen und journalistische Arbeiten 1920–39, edited by Klaus Westermann. 1984.

*

Bibliography: by David Bronsen, 1974.

Critical Studies: *Joseph Roth: Leben und Werk: Ein Gedächtnisbuch* edited by Hermann Linden, 1949; *Joseph Roth: Eine Biographie*, 1974, and *Joseph Roth und die Tradition*, 1974, both by David Bronsen; *Joseph Roth, 1894–1939: Eine Ausstellung der Deutschen Bibliothek Frankfurt am Main* edited by Günther Pflug, revised edition, 1979; *Joseph Roth in Selbstzeugnissen und Bilddokumenten* by Helmuth Nürnberger, 1981; *Joseph Roth* by Rudolf Koester, 1982; *Ambivalence and Irony in the Works of Joseph Roth* by Celine Mathew, 1984; *Understanding Joseph Roth* by Sidney Rosenfeld, 2001.

* * *

Joseph Roth had a stellar literary career in inter-war Germany which ended in the obscurity of exile. His works reflect the fragmentation of Austrian and Jewish identity as a result of escalating anti-semitism since the end of the 19th century, despite the near complete assimilation of German-speaking Jews. Roth, an uncommonly prolific author, began his career in Austria's first republic with the novel *Das Spinnennetz* (*The Spider's Web*), published in instalments in the Viennese Socialist daily paper *Arbeiter-Zeitung*. The work deals with the collapse of social hierarchy and the moral value system in the wake of World War I, decrying the chaotic conditions which were fast becoming the breeding ground for National Socialism, whose dangers Roth recognized as early as 1923. Roth's essays, book reviews, and novels appeared in the most prestigious Austrian and German journals. His articles on literature, film, theatre, psychology, and social, political, and legal problems enjoyed great popularity. They forced him to acquire specialized knowledge which, in turn, broadened the range of his literary works. Even a novel with a provincial setting, like *Hotel Savoy*, a sketch of the milieu of displaced war veterans in a hotel in Lodz, in Poland, the atmosphere of Roth's work is cosmopolitan. He formed his opinions on world affairs through extensive travel and research. Though controversial, his writings are clearly not the work of a dilettante. He sensed that the carnage of the first technological global military conflict had produced new attitudes and mass-movements of unknown dimensions.

Throughout his career he affirmed his conviction that the demise of the Austro-Hungarian empire represented an unprecedented political and cultural tragedy. The monumental novel *Die Kapuzinergruft* (*The Emperor's Tomb*), published in 1938, is one work in which Roth examines in a large social novel the psychological disintegration of a World War I veteran of Slovenian descent. Considering the traditional oppression and intermittent persecution of von Trotta's people during the Habsburg era, he is no less unlikely than Roth, as a Jew in view of traditional Habsburg anti-semitism, to support the restoration of the monarchy. However, the dissolution and lawlessness of the inter-war period, as well as the impending National Socialist revolution, drive the descendant of the hero of Solferino, who saved the emperor's life, to such despair that he can think of only one last refuge: the imperial catacombs in Vienna. Von Trotta is a symbol of Roth's own development: despite the fact that he was a pacifist at heart, and, well aware of social injustice, he had leaned toward socialism, he admired the imperial army which he had joined as a volunteer in World War I, as a unifying organization, a leveller of nationalist aspirations, and he considered the monarchy as Austria's best bet for survival.

Roth's legendary talent as a conversationalist and his love of turn-of-the-century Viennese decadence and gossip unfold in the humorous yet nostalgic novel *Die Geschichte von der 1002. Nacht* (*The Tale of the 1002nd Night*), involving an intrigue in imperial Austria engineered by the army officer Teittinger and the prostitute Mizzi Schinagl. They succeed in duping a royal visitor, the Shah of Iran in search of an adventure with a European noblewoman, but in the end they succumb to their own schemes and obsessions. The clash of two fundamentally different cultures enables Roth to draw a subtly critical portrait of the so-called good old days, an overripe culture where opulence and misery existed side by side. Other works show Roth as a master of suspense, for example *Beichte eines Mörders, erzählt in einer Nacht* (*Confessions of a Murderer, Told in One Night*), or even of tender emotions in *April: Die Geschichte einer Liebe* [April: A Love Story].

As a likely Nazi target, Roth took National Socialism seriously from the start. He supported the House of Habsburg as the symbol of European unity for pragmatic and sentimental reasons—his literary and theoretical works reveal both, for example his reaction to the speech of the Austrian Chancellor Schuschnigg, *Victoria Victis!*. The imperial concept is the central theme of Roth's novel about Napoleon, *Die hundert Tage* (*The Story of the Hundred Days*), which uses as a historical foil, Bonaparte's unsuccessful attempt to reestablish his former power position during his interlude in Paris between the exiles in Elba and St. Helena, to assess the events of Roth's time.

Most of Roth's works are overshadowed by the melancholy and pessimism of a man suffering from alcoholism, who had lost his wife to insanity and his homelands, Germany and Austria, to the Nazis. Roth rejected Zionism and Jewish orthodoxy for political reasons and went so far as to conceal his own origins at times. Considering conversion and assimilation the most likely solutions to religious and ethnic strife, he nevertheless actively opposed anti-semitism at every phase of his career. His fascination with Eastern European Jewish culture and Jewish themes comes to the fore not only in his documentary essay *Juden auf Wanderschaft* (*The Wandering Jews*), but also in his prose works of all phases such as *Der Leviathan*, *Hiob* (*Job*), *Tarabas*, and *Die Legende vom heiligen Trinker* (*The Legend of the Holy Drinker*), at times suggesting remorse over the loss of cultural identity. The most intense characters of Roth's works are earthy Jewish country people, pedlars, bar owners, and small town craftsmen calling to mind great Yiddish narrators such as Shalom Ash. Intellectually and emotionally Roth was rooted in the Jewish experience which ultimately dictated his ostensible detachment from Jewish culture. *Die Büste des Kaisers* (*The Bust of the Emperor*) and the epic saga of the generations between 1859 and 1914, *Radetzkymarsch* (*The Radetzky March*), expound the conviction that the Catholicism of Danube monarchy and political conservatism provide the antidote to chauvinist extremism. According to Roth even the small nations survived, and, as his more idealistic passages suggest, even prospered, in the multi-nation state. For this reason he believed the resurrection of the Danube monarchy to be in the interest of the oppressed minorities. Roth felt that the royalist supra-national platform had a greater chance of success than communism.

In 1938 Roth, who never kept his ideals and actions separate, went on a desperate political mission to Vienna to promote the cause of Otto von Habsburg. This initiative, foreseeably, ended in disaster. His last work, *The Legend of the Holy Drinker*, communicates through the pathetic yet lovable figure of the pure-hearted drunkard Andrea the profound despair and nihilism of an exiled writer, whose last great hope was an easy and beautiful death—a hope which remained unfulfilled.

—Dagmar C.G. Lorenz

See the essay on *The Radetzky March*.

ROUSSEAU, Jean-Jacques

Born: Geneva, Switzerland, 28 June 1712. **Family:** Married Thérèse Levasseur in 1768; several children. **Career:** Apprenticed at age 13 to a clerk, and for five years to an engraver; ran away to Annecy, 1728, and converted to Catholicism; had various occupations, often as a teacher or copyist of music; tutor in the early 1740s; secretary to French Ambassador to Venice, 1743–44; readmitted to Calvinism, 1754; settled at Montmorency, 1756, then in Neuchâtel to 1765; renounced Geneva citizenship, 1763; lived in Bienne, Switzerland,

1765; visited England, 1766; lived near Lyon, and in Paris from 1770; moved to Ermenonville, 1778. **Died:** 2 July 1778.

PUBLICATIONS

Collections

Oeuvres complètes, edited by Bernard Gagnebin and Marcel Raymond. 4 vols., 1959–69.
The Indispensable Rousseau, edited by John Hope Mason. 1979.
Collected Writings 1, edited by Roger D. Masters and Christopher Kelly. 1989.
Social Contract; Discourse on the Virtue Most Necessary for a Hero; Political Fragments; and, Geneva Manuscript, edited by Roger D. Masters and Christopher Kelley, translated by Judith R. Bush, Roger D. Masters, and Christopher Kelly. 1994.
The Confessions; and, Correspondence, Including the Letters to Malesherbes, edited by Christopher Kelly, Roger D. Masters, and Peter G. Stillman. 1995.
Selections, edited and translated by Victor Gourevitch. 1997.
The Reveries of the Solitary Walker; Botanical Writings; and Letter to Franquières, edited by Christopher Kelly, translated by Charles E. Butterworth, Alexandra Cook, and Terence E. Marshall. 2000.

Fiction

La Reine fantasque: Conte cacouac. 1758.
Julie; ou, La Nouvelle Héloïse. 1761; as *Eloisa*, translated 1761; as *Eloisa; or, A Series of Original Letters*, translated by William Kendrick, 2 vols., 1803; as *Julie; or, The New Eloise*, translated by Judith H. McDowell, 1968.
Émile; ou, De l'éducation. 1762; as *Emilius and Sophia; or, A New System of Education*, translated by William Kenrick, 1762–63; also translated by Allan Bloom, 1979; as *Emile, or Education*, translated by Barbara Foxley, 1930.

Plays

Les Muses galantes (ballet), music by Rousseau (produced 1745). In *Oeuvres*, 1826.
Le Devin du village (opera), music by Rousseau (produced 1752). 1753; as *The Cunning Man*, 1766.
Narcisse; ou, L'Amant de lui-même (produced 1753). 1753.
Pygmalion, incidental music by Rousseau (produced 1770). 1771.

Other

Projet concernant de nouveaux signes pour la musique. 1742; as *Project Concerning New Symbols for Music, 1742*, translated by Bernard Rainbow, 1982.
Dissertation sur la musique moderne. 1743.
Discours sur les sciences et des arts. 1750; as *A Discourse on the Arts and Sciences*, translated by Richard Wynne, 1752.
Discours sur l'origine et les fondements de l'inégalité parmi les hommes. 1755; as *A Discourse on the Origin of Inequality*, translated by G.D.H. Cole, 1952, also translated by Franklin Philip, edited by Patrick Coleman, 1994; as *A Discourse on Inequality*, translated by Maurice Cranston, 1984; as *Discourse on the Origin and the Foundation of Inequality among Men*, edited and translated by Victor Gourevitch, 1986.
Oeuvres diverses. 2 vols., 1756 (and later editions).

Lettre à d'Alembert sur les spectacles. 1758; as *A Letter to M. d'Alembert*, translated anonymously, 1759; also translated by Allan Bloom, in *Miscellaneous Writings*, 1960.

Lettre à Voltaire. 1759.

Du Contrat social; ou, Principes du droit politique. 1762; as *A Treatise on the Social Compact*, translated anonymously, 1764; as *The Social Contract and the Discourses*, translated by G.D.H. Cole, 1913, translation revised by J.H. Brumfitt and John C. Hall, 1973; as *Of the Social Contract; or, Principles of Political Right; and Discourse on Political Economy*, translated by Charles M. Sherover, 1984.

À Christophe de Beaumont (letter). 1763.

Lettres écrites de la montagne. 1764.

Dictionnaire de musique. 1767; as *A Dictionary of Music*, translated by William Waring, 1770.

Works. 10 vols., 1773–74.

Rousseau juge de Jean-Jacques: Dialogues. 1780.

Considérations sur le gouvernement de la Pologne. 1782; as *The Government of Poland*, translated 1972.

Les Rêveries du promeneur solitaire. 1782; as *The Reveries of a Solitary*, translated by Gould Fletcher, 1927; as *The Reveries of a Solitary Walker*, translated by Peter France, 1979.

Les Confessions. First complete edition, 2 vols., 1782–89; as *The Confessions*, translated anonymously, 1783–91; also translated by J.M. Cohen, 1953.

Botanique des enfants. 1800; as *Letters on the Elements of Botany*, translated by T. Martyn, 1785, revised edition, 1800; as *Botany: A Study of Pure Curiosity: Botanical Letters and Notes towards a Dictionary of Botanical Terms*, translated by Kate Ottevanger, 1979.

Correspondance, edited by R.-P. Plan. 20 vols., 1924–34.

A Project of Perpetual Peace, translated by Edith M. Nuttall. 1927.

Jean-Jacques Rousseau: His Educational Theories Selected from Émile, Julie and Other Writings, edited and translated by R.L. Archer. 1964.

Correspondance, edited by R.A. Leigh. 49 vols., 1965–89. *On the Origin of Languages*, translated by John A. Moran and Alexander Gode. 1967.

The Essential Rousseau, translated by Lowell Bair. 1974.

Essai sur l'origine des langues, edited by Charles Porset. 1976.

The First and Second Discourse Together with the Replies to Critics; and Essay on the Origins of Languages, edited and translated by Victor Gourevitch. 1986.

Rousseau: Selections, edited and translated by Maurice Cranston. 1988.

Rousseau's Political Writings: New Translations, Interpretive Notes, Backgrounds, Commentaries, edited by Alan Ritter and Julia Conaway Bondanella and translated by Bondanella. 1988.

Rousseau on International Relations, edited by Stanley Hoffmann and David P. Fiddler. 1991.

Essay on the Origin of Languages and Writings Related to Music, translated and edited by John T. Scott. 1998.

*

Bibliography: *Bibliographie générale des oeuvres de Rousseau* by Jean Senelier, 1949; *Bibliography of the Writings of Rousseau to 1800, Vol. 2: Émile* by Jo-Ann E. McEachern, 1989.

Critical Studies: *Rousseau and the French Revolution 1762–1791* by Joan McDonald, 1965; *Rousseau in Staffordshire* by J.H. Broome,

1966; *Rousseau* by Jean Guéhenno, 1966; *Rousseau and His Reader* by Robert J. Ellrich, 1969; *Rousseau: A Study in Self-Awareness*, 1969, and *Jean-Jacques Rousseau*, 1983, both by Ronald Grimsley; *Men and Citizens: A Study of Rousseau's Social Theory* by Judith N. Shklar, 1969; *Rousseau in America 1760–1809* by Paul Merrill Spurlin, 1969; *Rousseau and His World* by Sir Gavin de Beer, 1972; *The Extravagant Shepherd: A Study of the Pastoral Vision in Rousseau's Nouvelle Héloïse* by Christie M. Vance, 1973; *Jean-Jacques Rousseau on the Individual and Society* by Merle L. Perkins, 1974; *Rousseau as Educator* by Mabel Lewis Sahakian, 1974; *Rousseau's Political Philosophy: An Interpretation from Within* by Stephen Ellenburg, 1976; *The Making of a Saint: the Tragi-Comedy of Jean-Jacques Rousseau* by Jakob Herman Huizinga, 1976; *The Political Philosophy of Rousseau* by Roger Davis Masters, 1976; *Rousseau and the Concept of the General Will* by Frank Thakurdas, 1976; *Rousseau's Socratic Aemilian Myths* by Madeleine B. Ellis, 1977; *Rousseau's Political Philosophy: An Exposition and Interpretation* by Ramon M. Lemos, 1977; *Rousseau and Marx* by Galvano Della Volpe, 1978; *Rousseau in England* by Edward Duffy, 1979; *Rousseau's Theory of Literature* by James F. Hamilton, 1979; *Rousseau and the Problem of Tolerance in the Eighteenth Century*, 1979, *Rousseau, His Publishers and The Social Contract*, 1984, and *Unsolved Problems in the Bibliography of Jean-Jacques Rousseau*, 1986, all by R.A. Leigh; *Rousseau's State of Nature* by Marc F. Plattner, 1979; *Reappraisals of Rousseau* edited by Simon Harvey and others, 1980; *Rousseau After Two Hundred Years: Proceedings of the Cambridge Bicentennial Colloquium*, 1982; *Jean-François DeLuc of Geneva and his Friendship with Jean-Jacques Rousseau* by Douglas G. Creighton, 1982; *Jean-Jacques: The Early Life of Jean-Jacques Rousseau 1712–1754*, 1983, and *The Noble Savage: Jean-Jacques Rousseau, 1754–1762*, 1991, both by Maurice Cranston; *Rousseau's Social Contract: The Design of the Argument* by Hilail Gildin, 1983; *The Modern Self in Rousseau's Confessions: A Reply to St. Augustine* by Ann Hartle, 1983; *Rousseau, Emile* by Peter Jimak, 1983; *Rousseau and his "Emile"* by Ossian M. Lang, 1983; *The Changing Face of Nature in Rousseau's Political Writings* by R.D. Miller, 1983; *Rousseau and Romantic Autobiography* by Huntington Williams, 1983; *Rousseau's Political Imagination: Rule and Representation in the Lettre à d'Alembert* by Patrick Coleman, 1984; *Rousseau: Dreamer of Democracy* by James Miller, 1984; *Jean-Jacques Rousseau's Doctrine of the Arts* by Philip E.J. Robinson, 1984; *The Sexual Politics of Jean-Jacques Rousseau* by Joel Schwartz, 1984; *Seeing and Observing: Rousseau's Rhetoric of Perception* by John C. O'Neal, 1985; *Rousseau and the Republic of Virtue: The Language of Politics in the French Revolution* by Carol Blum, 1986; *Rousseau: Julie; ou, La nouvelle Héloïse* by R.J. Howells, 1986; *Rousseau and the Problem of War* by Christine Jane Carter, 1987; *Rousseau, Confessions* by Peter France, 1987; *Rousseau, Nature and History* by Asher Horowitz, 1987; *Writing the Truth: Authority and Desire in Rousseau* by Thomas M. Kavanagh, 1987; *Rousseau's Exemplary Life; The Confessions as Political Philosophy* by Christopher Kelly, 1987; *Social Thought of Jean-Jacques Rousseau* by Robert Wokler, 1987; *Self-Direction and Political Legitimacy: Rousseau and Herder* by F.M. Barnard, 1988; *Rousseau's Response to Hobbes* by Howard R. Cell, 1988; *Rousseau: An Introduction to his Psychological, Social and Political Theory* by N.J.H. Dent, 1988; *Rousseau: Transparency and Obstruction*, by Jean Starobinski, 1988; *Jean-Jacques Rousseau and the "Well-Ordered Society"* by Maurizio Viroli, 1988; *The Question of Rousseau* by Ernst Cassirer, edited by Peter Gay, 1989; *The Natural Goodness of Man: On the System of*

Rousseau's Thought by Arthur M. Melzer, 1990; *Language, Subjectivity and Freedom in Rousseau's Moral Philosophy* by Richard Noble, 1991; *Rousseau's Occasional Autobiographies* by Susan K. Jackson, 1992; *Gendered Community: Rousseau, Sex, and Politics* by Penny A. Weiss, 1993; *Making Citizens: Rousseau's Political Theory of Culture* by Zev M. Trachtenberg, 1993; *Justice and Difference in the Works of Rousseau: Bienfaisance and Pudeur* by Judith Still, 1993; *Modernity and Authenticity: A Study in the Social and Ethical Thought of Jean-Jacques Rousseau*, 1993; *Rousseau's Art of Persuasion in "La nouvelle Héloïse"* by Santo L. Aricò, 1994; *The Autocritique of Enlightenment: Rousseau and the Philosophes* by Mark Hulliung, 1994; *Mass Enlightenment: Critical Studies in Rousseau and Diderot* by Julia Simon, 1995; *Romanticism and the Heritage of Rousseau* by Thomas McFarland, 1995; *Rousseau's Legacy: Emergence and Eclipse of the Writer in France* by Dennis Porter, 1995; *Jean-Jacques Rousseau: Music, Illusion, and Desire* by Michael O'Dea, 1995; *Rousseau* by Robert Wokler, 1995; *Rousseau and the Politics of Ambiguity: Self, Culture, and Society* by Mira Morgenstern, 1996; *Jean-Jacques Rousseau and Political Literature in Colonial America* by Frederick William Dame, 1996; *Jean-Jacques Rousseau and the Sources of the Self*, edited by Timothy O'Hagan, 1997; *The Solitary Self: Jean-Jacques Rousseau in Exile and Adversity* by Maurice Cranston, 1997; *The Legacy of Rousseau*, edited by Clifford Orwin and Nathan Tarcov, 1997; *Domesticating Passions: Rousseau, Woman, and Nation* by Nicole Fermon, 1997; *Rousseau's Economic Philosophy: Beyond the Market of Innocents* by Bertil Fridén, 1998; *Jean-Jacques Rousseau* by Peter V. Conroy, 1998; *Theories on Music and Writing: The Legacy of Jean-Jacques Rousseau in French Letters in The Late Eighteenth Century* by Daniel Clarence Johnson, 1998; *Rousseau, Nature, and the Problem of the Good Life* by Laurence D. Cooper, 1999; *Instinct and Intimacy: Political Philosophy and Autobiography in Rousseau* by Margaret Ogrodnick, 1999; *Rousseau* by Timothy O'Hagan, 1999; *The Autobiography of Philosophy: Rousseau's The Reveries of the Solitary Walker* by Michael Davis, 1999; *The Romantic Subject in Autobiography: Rousseau and Goethe* by Eugene L. Stelzig, 2000; *Rousseau's Republican Romance* by Elizabeth Rose Wingrove, 2000; *On Jean-Jacques Rousseau: Considered as One of the First Authors of the Revolution* by James Swenson, 2000; *The Cambridge Companion to Rousseau*, edited by Patrick Riley, 2001; *Rousseau and Nietzsche: Toward an Aesthetic Morality* by Katrin Froese, 2001; *Rousseau's Garden* by Ann Charney, 2001.

* * *

Among the intellectuals of the French Enlightenment, Jean-Jacques Rousseau is the one whose writings have had the greatest influence outside his country and period. He was a profound and in many respects original and contentious thinker, and his major works raised fundamental questions in the fields of ethics, education, politics, and aesthetics.

Rousseau's literary career began in the 1740s with a series of minor works, now largely forgotten, which earned him a reputation principally as a composer and writer on music. In 1750 his *Discours sur les sciences et des arts* (*A Discourse on the Arts and Sciences*) won a prize offered by the Dijon Academy on the topic "Has the restoration of the Arts and Sciences had a purifying effect upon

morals?" The view Rousseau took was that, on the evidence he saw around him, the renascence of culture had enfeebled and depraved humanity. Rousseau's thesis was singularly at variance with the views of the time, and especially with Voltaire's, whose "Le Mondain," a poem in praise of luxury, had appeared in 1736. Rousseau submitted his *Discours sur l'origine et les fondements de l'inégalité parmi les hommes* (*A Discourse on Inequality*) for the 1755 Dijon prize, which it did not win—for one thing, it exceeded the required length. Here, he developed the view that contemporary civilization had denatured humanity, and he saw the institution of property as mainly responsible for this. The gradual development of the differential possession of property had, he argued, brought with it social and legal inequality. Men had come to be socially valued in consequence of what they possessed rather than of their moral worth. Civil law, which protects property, had therefore usurped the place of Natural Law. While Rousseau was not so naive as to propose a return to "primitive nature," he assumed that human nature, having changed once, for the worse, could therefore be changed again for the better. In order to reform the social machine, a new type of man, with a different moral outlook, was needed.

It was in this belief that Rousseau composed his treatise on education, *Émile* (*Emile*). Though Rousseau's practical experience as a tutor was limited and unsuccessful, the theoretical basis of *Emile* has made it one of the most influential works in the history of educational theory. Emile is brought up in a one-to-one relationship with his tutor, who introduces him to experience in carefully calculated steps which correspond to the increasing capacity of Emile, as he grows up, to respond and use it. Thus he will develop the moral and intellectual self-reliance which would enable him, as an adult, to fit into virtually any society. The education Rousseau proposed was essentially child-based, and, though the programme followed by the fictitious Emile would be impossible to put into practice, it was this conception of the educational process that influenced subsequent educationalists including Froebel and Dewey. *Emile* was banned in France and Switzerland, largely because of the emotional deism of the Savoyard curate's profession of faith, included in the fourth book.

There is a conceptual link between the type of self-disciplined and self-reliant individual whom Rousseau seeks to form in *Emile* and the nature of the political institution envisaged in *Du Contrat social* (*The Social Contract*), published a month or so previously (April 1762), and banned in Geneva shortly afterwards. Taking men as they are, Rousseau sought to define a political system that would restore to them the freedom that they had lost in the way he had outlined in his two early discourses. In Rousseau's scheme, each citizen is under an obligation to enhance the welfare of the state. When he acts with that obligation in mind, he contributes to the General Will of that society. The General Will is seen as taking into account only the common interest of the citizens, not private interests, and it is this that distinguishes it, Rousseau argues, from what he calls the Will of All. If a man acts selfishly or in the interest of a faction within the state, he contributes nothing to the General Will. The General Will, according to Rousseau, constitutes real sovereignty and cannot be relinquished or delegated. Since it emanates from the whole community, the whole community is sovereign. It is this formulation that has, in the view of some commentators, made Rousseau a great democratic theorist. But Rousseau believed that the General Will of the whole community could more easily find expression, unimpaired by the effects of sectional interests, if partial societies within the state did not exist and if each citizen thought independently. This monolithic political structure, lacking the pluralism that western societies see as a fundamental prerequisite of a free state, and incorporating a religious system based on the requirement that citizens should have "social sentiments without which a man could not be a good citizen or a faithful subject" (on pain of banishment), has also been seen as a totalitarian nightmare.

In 1757 d'Alembert's article "Geneva" appeared in volume VII of Diderot's *Encyclopedia*. Although drama figured in Rousseau's works, he reacted against d'Alembert's suggestion, prompted by Voltaire, that a theatre should be allowed in Geneva, where it was at the time forbidden. Rousseau's reaction was the *Lettre à d'Alembert sur les spectacles* (*A Letter to M. d'Alembert*), in which he argued that plays were immoral and useless, encouraged the passions and led people into temptation. (The age-old argument over the moral value of the theatre had intensified since the writings of Caffaro in 1694.) Rousseau's *Letter* marks the final breakdown in the already strained relations between himself and Voltaire, Diderot, and D'Alembert.

Early in 1761 Rousseau published *Julie; ou, La Nouvelle Héloïse* (*Julie; or, The New Eloise*) translating into a novel of passion and duty his thwarted love for Mme. D'Houdetot. Its success was instantaneous, and it ran into more editions than any other 18th-century French novel. It tells the story of Julie d'Étanges, who falls passionately in love with her tutor, Saint-Preux. Her father refuses to let her marry him, and instead she is married to Monsieur de Wolmar. A model wife and mother, she tells her husband of her love for Saint-Preux, and he invites the former tutor to stay with them. Julie and Saint-Preux realize their love still exists, but, with much agonizing, duty and virtue prevail. Julie eventually dies of a chill, contracted while rescuing her son from drowning. Though the slow unfolding of the digressive and improbable plot hardly appeals to the modern reader, the importance of the work lies in its new Romantic sensibility and the appeal of virtue discovered in a simple, rural life lived in a natural and harmonious environment.

By 1760 Rousseau had parted company with most of the influential French intellectuals of the day. His social clumsiness, his rejection of polite society, his austerity and eccentricity, as well as his differing views on many important topics, all served to isolate him. Those with whom he came into contact saw him as quarrelsome and discerned what they took for hypocrisy. He had written plays and operas, and he had written a treatise condemning the theatre. He had denigrated culture and deplored intellectualism, and yet he had published a novel and submitted philosophical treatises for academic prizes. A failed tutor, he had put his five children in a foundlings' home, and gone on to publish a treatise on education. Rousseau, for his part, came increasingly to see others' indifference or dislike as evidence of a universal plot to blacken and ostracize him. From 1767 Rousseau, who could not understand why he, who saw himself as basically good and well-meaning, should be the object of hostility, devoted most of his energies as a writer to works of self-justification. By making himself vulnerable, showing himself in detail in an often unfavourable light, he hoped that the world would come to pardon him and accept him as a good man, and thus he would be able finally to forgive himself for all the actions that had imposed on him a lifelong burden of guilt. The best-known and most readable of these late works is *Les Confessions* (*The Confessions*), which give an account of Rousseau's

life from 1712 to 1765. They contain, as one would expect, errors of detail, but their importance lies in their recording of the author's feelings and in the novelty of the frank self-examination they contain. New of their kind, they were to influence later generations of writers throughout Europe.

A more insistent attempt at self-justification marks the *Dialogues*, written between 1772 and 1776. This period was followed by one of calm resignation to being misunderstood, recorded by the *Les Rêveries du promeneur solitaire* (*The Reveries of a Solitary*). Rousseau claimed that these essays were written in order to enable him to recall and reactivate past pleasures, and to console him in his isolation. From then on, he was to be self-sufficient. However, the elegant and harmonious prose in which they are written, and the frequent references to the injustice of Rousseau's enemies raise doubts both about his psychic self-sufficiency and about his intention never to publish them.

A widespread cult of sensibility, inspired by Rousseau's work, arose during the writer's lifetime and characterizes much late 18th-century French literature.

—John Dunkley

See the essays on *The Confessions, Emile, The Reveries of a Solitary*, and *The Social Contract*.

ROY, Claude

Born: Claude Orland in Paris, 28 August 1915. **Education:** Secondary schooling at Lycée Montaigne, Paris; baccalaureate degree, Angoulême Lycée; attended the University of Paris and studied law at the University of Bordeaux. **Military Service:** Enlisted in French army at outset of World War II: awarded Croix de Guerre for extraordinary heroism. Captured by the Germans and imprisoned in their military camp near Metz; successfully escaped and fled to the Free Zone in southern France; actively participated in the French Resistance movement and also served as war correspondent and liaison officer between First French and First American Armies. **Family:** Married 1) Claire Vervin, 1945 (divorced 1958); one son; 2) the well-known playwright Loleh Bellon, 1962. **Career:** Writer, publishing one or two books per year; during his final years, served as a member of the Committee of Readers of the well-known publishing firm, Gallimard. **Awards:** Goncourt prize for Poetry, 1985; Grand Prix de la Maison de Poesie, 1988; Prix France-Culture for the totality of his works, 1990; many other lesser literary awards. **Died:** In Paris, December 1997.

PUBLICATIONS

Poetry

Le Poète mineur. 1949.
Un seul poème. 1955.
Poésies. 1970.
Enfantasques, poèmes et collages. 1974.
Nouvelles Enfantasques, poèmes et collages. 1978.

Sais-tu si nous sommes encore loin de la mer? Epopée cosmonique, géologique, hydraulique, philosophique, en douze chants et en vers. 1979.
Le voyage d'automne: poèmes. 1987.
Le Noir de l'aube. 1990.
Les Pas du silence et Poèmes en amont. 1993.
Poèmes à pas de loup: 1992–1996. 1996.

Fiction

La Nuit est le manteau des pauvres. 1949.
A Tort ou à raison. 1955.
Le Soleil sur la terre. 1956.
Le Malheur d'aimer. 1958; as *The Agony of Love*, translated by Peter Wiles, 1959.
Léonie et les siens. 1963.
La Dérobée. 1968.
La Nuit est le manteau des pauvres. New editions in 1969 and 1976.
La Traversée du Pont des Arts. 1979.
L'Ami lointain. 1987; as *The Distant Friend*, translated by Hugh A. Harter, 1990.

Plays

Le Chariot de terre cuite. 1969.

Criticism

Aragon. 1945.
Lire Marivaux. 1947.
Descriptions critiques. 1950.
Stendhal par lui-même. 1952.
Le Commerce des classiques. 1953.
L'Amour de la peinture. 1955; revised edition, 1992.
L'Amour du théâtre. 1956.
La Main heureuse. 1957.
Arts sauvages. 1957; as *The Art of the Savages*, translated by Eh. S. Seldon, 1958.
L'Homme en question. 1960.
Gérard Philipe, with Anne Philipe. 1960.
Arts fantastiques. 1961.
Arts baroques. 1963.
Supervielle. 1964.
Arts premiers. 1967; revised edition, 1992.
Jean Vilar. 1968.
Défense de la littérature. 1968.
Les Soleils du romantisme. 1974.
Le Voleur des poèmes: Chine. 1991.
L'Art à la source. 2 vols., 1992.
Pierre Lesieur. 1992.
Le Travail du poète, 1993.
Balthus. 1996; translated by Ann Sautier-Greening, 1996.
Picasso, la guerre et la paix. 1997.

Other

Clefs pour l'Amérique (travel writings). 1949.
La France de profil (travel writings). 1952.

Clefs pour la Chine (travel writings). 1953; as *Into China*, translated by Mervyn Savill, 1955.
La Chine dans un miroir (travel writings). 1954.
La Famille Quatre Cents Coups, texte et collages (children). 1954.
Le Journal des voyages (travel writings). 1960.
C'est le bouquet (children). 1964.
Moi je (autobiographical). 1968.
Nous (autobiographical). 1972.
Somme toute (autobiographical). 1976.
La Maison qui s'envole (children). 1977.
Nouvelles enfantasques (children). 1978.
Le Chat qui parlait malgré lui (children). 1982.
Permis de séjour: 1977–1982 (autobiographical). 1983.
Temps variables avec éclaircies (travel writings). 1984.
La Fleur du temps: 1983–1987 (autobiographical). 1988.
L'Etonnement: 1987–1989 (autobiographical). 1990.
La Cour de récréation (children). 1991.
Le ravage des jours: 1990–1991 (autobiographical). 1992.
L'Ami qui venait de l'an mil (travel writings). 1995.
Les rencontres des jours: 1992–1993 (autobiographical). 1995.
Chemins Croisés: 1994–1995 (autobiographical). 1997.

*

Critical Studies: ''Claude Roy,'' in *Littérature de Notre Temps, Recueil III* by Louis Perche, 1967; ''Les Memoires de Claude Roy'' by Roger Grenier in *Réalités*, no. 283, August 1969; *Claude Roy, Une Etude* by Roger Grenier, 1971; ''Entretien avec Claude Roy'' by Catherine Arfand, in *Lire*, May 1974; *Claude Roy: Un Poète* by Serge Koster, 1985; ''Introduction to Claude Roy'' by Jack Kolbert, in *The Distant Friend* by Claude Roy, translated by Hugh Harter, 1990.

* * *

The presence of Claude Roy has been a most ubiquitous one within the richly profuse world of French literature after World War II, a period when the literary world of Paris seemed to reign over the literature of the western world. In every book dealing with the history of French literature during the second half of the 20th century, one encounters the name of Roy. That he wrote so abundantly and produced books in virtually every medium of literature imaginable— fiction, poetry, biography, autobiography, drama, children's literature, travel books, literary and art criticism, essays—is a fact of contemporary literary life in France. As a member of the Committee of Readers of one of his country's most prominent publishing firms, the House of Gallimard, he played a crucial role in determining not only his own literary destiny but also that of many other writers from around the world. A friend of almost every major writer, painter, and composer of his era, he played a commanding role in the intellectual life of his nation. A prominent voice in the Francophone world, he was warmly received throughout Europe, Africa, Asia, and America. Only in America did he fail to receive the recognition that he merited. Relatively few of his books were translated into English, and Americans are notoriously monolingual. But among those Americans who could read French, he was warmly appreciated.

What are Roy's strengths and weaknesses? In his otherwise polished literary art one encounters, ironically, what some might regard as a flaw. Roy displayed such a remarkable facility as a *pasticheur* of the literary styles of other writers that he seemed able easily to step into the shoes of virtually every writer of every movement and period as he emulated them in their personal art of writing. He could effortlessly write in the manner of a Proust, a Stendhal, an Eluard, a Victor Hugo! His unusual talent for imitating the style of others often concealed his own unique gifts, so much so that it is difficult to discern in his prose and poetry the essential traits that would characterize his own mode of self-expression. It is not easy to identify his own personal presence in some of his texts. Because he possessed so much fluidity and suppleness as a writer, some of his texts seem almost too perfect, too flawless, and often remind the reader of someone else's style. One is tempted to ask, where is the real Roy?

Despite—or maybe because of—his unusual facility with verbal style and syntactic constructions, his works are eminently readable, glistening with a broad variety of styles, themes, and moods. Among his many virtues is the fact that he was foremost a poet, even when he expressed himself in prose. He viewed the world through the prism of poetry; he manipulated metaphors, verbal sonorities, rhythmic combinations of words, assonances and consonances, with a rare degree of ease. Extremely sensitive to the phenomena of nature, he described in the most minute detail both the tiniest and the most gargantuan creatures: insects, birds, felines, plants, flowers, clouds, even blades of grass. Because he understood so well the essence of the visual arts, he could delineate in his novels the portraits of his characters and the most complex venues in which these characters lived their lives. He could paint their feelings, passions, moods, and actions with the brush-strokes of a masterful painter. He could depict the psychological vagaries of their personality with the precision of a psychoanalyst. Thanks to his passion for traveling throughout the world, he acquired the ability verbally to reproduce a wide spectrum of venues and cosmopolitan settings—both urban and bucolic. The settings he painted in his novels are always convincing, whether he describes Paris, New York, or Buenos Aires. Roy of course knew all of these places intimately. Finally, he could not conceal his lofty regard for human beings, especially the underdogs, the oppressed, the impoverished and the hungry, the persecuted, the sickly, the mistreated. His books are for the most part a plea for a heightened degree of justice and fairness towards all people, the mighty and the feeble. In sum, Roy is both an incurable poet and an incurable humanist.

During the last years of his career he appeared to be searching for a better understanding of his own persona. One of his final lessons was the importance of human memory. He reminded his readers that the way they behaved today was shaped by what they had experienced in the past. And so he stressed that in their confrontation with the future, men and women must come to grips with their remembrance of the past.

—Jack Kolbert

ROY, Gabrielle

Born: St. Boniface, Manitoba, Canada, 22 March 1909. **Education:** Educated at St. Joseph Academy, St. Boniface; Teachers Training School, Winnipeg, Manitoba. **Family:** Married Marcel Carbotte in 1947. **Career:** Teacher in a village school, 1928–29, and in St. Boniface, 1929–37; associated with newspapers and magazines in Quebec and France, especially *Le Jour*, 1939–40, and *Bulletin des Agriculteurs*, 1940–45. **Awards:** Académie Canadienne-Francaise award, 1946; Prix Fémina, 1947; Lorne Pierce medal, 1948; Governor-General's award, 1948, 1958, 1977; Prix Duvernay, 1956; Canada Council medal, 1968; Prix David, 1971; Molson award, 1977. Fellow, Royal Society of Canada, 1947. Honorary Doctorate: University of Laval, Quebec, 1968. Companion, Order of Canada, 1967. **Died:** 13 July 1983.

PUBLICATIONS

Fiction

Bonheur d'occasion. 1945, revised edition, 1947; as *The Tin Flute*, translated by Hannah Josephson, 1947; also translated by Alan Brown, 1980.
La Petite Poule d'eau. 1950; as *Where Nests the Water Hen*, translated by Harry Lorin Binse, 1951.
Alexandre Chenevert, caissier. 1954; as *The Cashier*, translated by Harry Lorin Binse, 1955.
Rue Deschambault. 1955; as *Street of Riches*, translated by Harry Lorin Binse, 1957.
La Montagne secrète. 1961; as *The Hidden Mountain*, translated by Harry Lorin Binse, 1962.
La Route d'Altamont. 1966; as *The Road Past Altamont*, translated by Joyce Marshall, 1966.
La Rivière sans repos. 1970; as *Wildflower*, translated by Joyce Marshall, 1970.
Cet été qui chantait. 1972; as *Enchanted Summer*, translated by Joyce Marshall, 1976.
Un jardin au bout du monde. 1975; as *Garden in the Night*, translated by Alan Brown, 1977.
Ces enfants de ma vie. 1977; as *Children of My Heart*, translated by Alan Brown, 1979.
Courte-Queue. 1979; as *Cliptail*, translated by Alan Brown, 1980.
La Pékinoise et l'Espagnole. 1987.

Other

Ma vache Bossie (for children). 1976.
Fragiles lumières de la terre: Écrits divers 1942–1970. 1978; as *The Fragile Lights of Earth: Articles and Memories, 1942–1970*, translated by Alan Brown, 1982.
De quoi t'ennuies-tu, Eveline?. 1982, enlarged edition, 1984.
La Détresse et l'enchantement. 1984; as *Enchantment and Sorrow: The Autobiography of Gabrielle Roy*, translated by Patricia Claxton, 1987.

*

Bibliography: ''Gabrielle Roy: An Annotated Bibliography'' by Paul Socken, in *The Annotated Bibliography of Canada's Major Authors 1* edited by Robert Lecker and Jack David, 1979.

Critical Studies: *La Création romanesque chez Roy* by Monique Genuist, 1966; *Roy* by Phyllis M. Grosskurth, 1969; *Visages de Roy* by Marc Gagné 1973; *Three Voices: The Lives of Margaret Laurence, Gabrielle Roy, and Frederick Philip Grove* by Joan Hind-Smith, 1975; *Roy* by Francois Ricard (in French), 1975; *Gabrielle Roy* by M.G. Hesse, 1984; *The Literary Vision of Gabrielle Roy: An Analysis of Her Works* by Paula Gilbert Lewis, 1984; *The Play of the Language and Spectacle: A Structural Reading of Selected Texts by Gabrielle Roy* by Ellen Babby, 1985; *Myth and Reality in Atexandre Chenevert by Gabrielle Roy* by Paul G. Sakeis, 1987; *The Limits of Sympathy: Gabrielle Roy's The Tin Flute* by Patrick Coleman, 1993; *Gabrielle Roy: Creation and Memory* by Linda M. Clemente and William A. Clemente, 1997.

* * *

Gabrielle Roy is perhaps the first truly *Canadian* author. Her novels and short stories, written in French, render not only the complex reality of her adopted province of Quebec—*Bonheur d'occasion (The Tin Flute)*, which earned her the prestigious French Prix Fémina in 1947, and *Alexandre Chenevert (The Cashier)*—as well as of her native St. Boniface in Manitoba—among others, *La Petite Poule d'eau (Where Nests the Water Hen)*—but also the world of the Inuit—*La Rivière sans repos (Wildflower)*—and of some of the typical immigrant groups that make up the rich texture of Canadian life, such as the Doukhobors, the Chinese, the Poles—*Un jardin au bout du monde (Garden in the Night)*.

The Tin Flute is very traditional in form, a characteristic it may owe to Roy's previous career as a journalist; it is an excellent social document and the first novel in French to chart a major crisis in the history of Quebec: the transition from a rural to an urban society—Montreal—dominated by an English-speaking Establishment, during the great economic upheaval preceding World War II.

Although Roy was never again to tackle this kind of large-scale endeavour, the loving sympathy with which she here portrays even her weakest characters and this same theme of change, of its impact on ordinary people, particularly women, are characteristic of almost all her writing. Roy's own constant oscillation between stories of her early years in Manitoba and portrayals of life elsewhere reflects not only the changes she herself knew but also her need to "touch base" periodically in order to accept new challenges, a need with which she could then sympathize in others.

Indeed, there is, in her writing, a clear division between those who can go back to their roots, however temporarily, and those who are condemned to a complete break with the past. The latter are the immigrants, the Chinese, the Poles, and the Doukhobors of *Garden in the Night*. The former are the natives of Canada like Elsa in *Wildflower* who, when threatened by the white man's power, retreats into the Inuit traditions, or Alexander Chenevert, a victim of the social and spiritual upheavals of 1940s, who undertakes a pilgrimage into the past of Quebec. But change, however unpleasant, is inevitable; there can be no permanent return, no stopping the clock. Stasis is death, as Alexandre Chenevert suspects during his journey in *The Cashier* and as Pierre, the artist, discovers at the end of his in *La Montagne secrète (The Hidden Mountain)*.

There are those who regret Roy's progressive abandoning of the major in favour of the minor key. In so doing, however, she developed a clarity of style and a mastery of the cameo that are missing from her early writings.

—Maïr Verthuy

RÓŻEWICZ, Tadeusz

Born: Radomsko, Poland, 9 October 1921. **Education:** Graduated from a gymnasium in 1938; studied fine arts, Jagiellonian University, Kraków, 1945–49. **Military Service:** Trained, 1942, and served, June 1943 to November 1944, in the Polish underground Home Army. **Family:** Married Wiesława Kozłowska, a fellow soldier of the underground army, 1949; two sons. **Career:** Writer; contributed to various literary journals; collaborated with brother Stanisław Różewicz, a film director, on a number of film scripts (including *Miejsce na ziemi*, *Świadectwo urodzenia*, *Głos z tamtego świata*, *Echo*, *Samotność we dwoje*, and *Drzwi w murze*). **Awards:** K.K. Baczyński's stipend, 1948; State prize and the Fifth World Youth Festival award for *Równina*, 1955; literary award of the city of Kraków, 1959; Jurzykowski Foundation award, 1966; State prize, 1966; ''Odra'' award, 1970; literary award of the city of Wrocław, 1973; Golden Poetic Laurel, Yugoslavia, 1987; Pen Club's Parandowski award, 1998; NIKE prize, 2000, for *Matka odchodzi*.

PUBLICATIONS

Collections

Poezje zebrane. 1957.
Proza. 1973.
Poezja. 2 vols., 1988.
Teatr. 2 vols., 1988.
Proza. 2 vols., 1990.

Poetry and Drama in English Translation

Faces of Anxiety, translated by Adam Czerniawski. 1969.
Selected Poems, translated by Adam Czerniawski. 1976.
The Survivor and Other Poems, translated by M.J. Krynski and R.A. Maguire. 1977.
Conversations with the Prince and Other Poems, translated by Adam Czerniawski. 1982.
Mariage Blanc; and The Hunger Artist Departs: Two Plays, translated by Adam Czerniawski. 1982.
Selected Poems/Poezje wybrane, translated by Adam Czerniawski. 1991.
They Came to See a Poet, translated by Adam Czerniawski. 1991.
Tadeusz Różewicz's Bas-Relief and Other Poems, translated by Edward J. Czerwiński. 1991.
Tadeusz Różewicz: Forms in Relief and Other Poems, translated by Richard Sokoloski. 1994.
The Trap, translation by Adam Czerniawski. 1997.
Reading the Apocalypse in Bed: Selected Plays and Shorter Pieces, translations by Czerniawski, Barbara Plebanek, and Tony Howard. 1998.
Recycling, translated by Tony Howard and Barbara Plebanek. 2001.

Poetry

Echa leśne (clandestine publication under the pen-name "Satyr").
1944.
Niepokój. 1947.
Czerwona rękawiczka. 1948.
Pięć poematów. 1950.
Czas który idzie. 1951.
Wiersze i obrazy. 1952.
Równina. 1954.
Srebrny kłos. 1955.
Poemat otwarty. 1956.
Formy. 1958.
Rozmowa z księciem. 1960.
Et in Arcadia Ego. 1961.
Zielona róża. 1961.
Głos Anonima. 1961.
Nic w płaszczu Prospera. 1962.
Twarz. 1964.
Twarz trzecia. 1968.
Regio. 1969.
Opowiadanie traumatyczne. 1979.
Płaskorzeźba. 1991.
Zawsze fragment. 1996.
Zawsze fragment. Recycling. 1998.
Nożyk profesora. 2001.

Plays

Kartoteka. 1960.
Grupa Laokoona. 1961.
Świadkowie albo nasza mała stabilizacja. 1962.
Śmieszny staruszek. 1964.
Akt przerywany. 1964.
Spaghetti i miecz. 1964.
Wyszedł z domu. 1964.
Pogrzeb po polsku. 1971.
Przyrost naturalny. Biografia sztuku teatralnej. 1968.
Stara kobieta wysiaduje. 1968.
Teatr niekonsekwencji. 1970.
Na czworakach. 1971.
Białe małżeństwo. 1974.
Odejście głodomora. 1976.
O wojnę powszechną za wolność ludów prosimy Cię, Panie. 1977.
Do piachu. 1979.
Pułapka. 1982.
Kartoteka rozrzucona. 1992.

Prose and Essays

Kartki z Węgier. 1953.
Opadły liście z drzew. 1955.
Przerwany egzamin. 1960.
Wycieczka do muzeum. 1966.
Śmierć w starych dekoracjach. 1970.
Przygotowanie do wieczoru autorskiego. 1971.
Duszyczka. 1977.
Matka odchodzi. 1999.

Other

Języki teatru, with Kazimierz Braun. 1989.

*

Bibliography: "Bibliografia edycji książkowych Tadeusza Różewicza" by Joanna Kisielowa, in *Świat integralny: pół wieku twórczości Tadeusza Różewicza*, edited by Marian Kisiel, 1994.

Critical Studies: *Poeci i inni* by Jan Błoński, 1956; *Różewicz parokrotnie* by Kazimierz Wyka, 1977; *Teatr Różewicza* by Stanisław Gębala, 1978; *Tadeusz Różewicz* by Stanisław Burkot, 1987; *Walka o oddech: o pisarstwie Tadeusza Różewicza* by Tadeusz Drewnowski, 1990; *Laboratory of Impure Forms: The Plays of Tadeusz Różewicz* by Halina Filipowicz, 1991; *Dlaczego Różewicz: wiersze i komentarze*, edited by Jacek Brzozowski and Jerzy Poradecki, 1993; *Język małych form teatralnych Tadeusza Różewicza* by Anna Jakubczak, 1993; *Poezja jak otwarta rana: czytając Różewicza* by Majchrowski Zbigniew, 1993; *Słowo za słowo: szkice o twórczości Tadeusza Różewicza*, edited by Marian Kisiel and Włodzimierz Wójcik, 1998; *Oko poety: poezja Tadeusza Różewicza wobec sztuk* by Robert Cieślak, 1999; *Spojrzenia: szkice o poezji Tadeusza Różewicza* by Tadeusz Kłak, 1999; *Światy Tadeusza Różewicza: materiały konferencji naukowej*, 2000; *Różewicz* by Zbigniew Majchrowski, 2002.

* * *

Tadeusz Różewicz is one of the most important and versatile of postwar Polish writers. First and foremost a poet, he is also a major playwright and an accomplished prose writer. Różewicz published his first poems in 1938 but earned his reputation with his two postwar volumes: *Niepokój* [Anxiety] and *Czerwona rękawiczka* [The Red Glove], in which he revolutionized the form and language of 20th-century Polish poetry. The publication of his *Poezje zebrane* [Collected Poems] in 1957 established Różewicz as a classic who, whether admired, imitated, or scorned, has remained a classic nonetheless. His dramatic debut, *Kartoteka* (*The Card Index*), closely reflected the same moral anxiety—and the imperative of being a witness—as his poetry of the time, and was characterized by similar formal experimentation. There followed a series of over twenty experimental plays, which concluded with the rewriting of his dramatic debut as *Kartoteka rozrzucona* [The Card Index Scattered]. Such recycling of substance, style, and image became a distinctive mark of his creative method in the 1990s, culminating in the publication of a long poem *Zawsze fragment. Recycling*. The close affinity between his poetry and drama has remained a hallmark of his originality.

Bearing witness was an important starting point for works written in the name of a whole lost generation who, like Różewicz's own brother, Janusz, perished during the war (*Świadkowie albo nasza mała stabilizacja* [*The Witnesses*]). Różewicz's initial attitude to the world and to his writing was shaped not only by his experience of the war, of two totalitarian systems and their atrocities, but also by the failure of European culture and civilization to prevent them. In his famous poem, "The Survivor," the poet states matter-of-factly: "The way of killing men and beasts is the same / I've seen it: / truckfuls of chopped-up men / who will not be saved." With time Różewicz—the ironic moralist who diagnoses the irreparable loss of innocence, the spiritual emptiness, and the death of poetry in the postwar world ("the man of today / falls in all directions / simultaneously" from "Falling or Concerning Vertical and Horizontal Elements in the Life of Man Today," 1963)—has become a writer who patiently tries to regain his trust in words by borrowing them from silence, and who cautiously rebuilds the difficult belief in the existence of the sacred. As he put it in the poem, "Without": "life without god is possible / life without god is impossible."

In his later work artistic, existential, philosophical, and civilizational concerns overshadow his earlier trauma. Różewicz assesses the various aesthetic revolutions of the 20th century, which have been striving for originality at all costs, and proclaims himself the guardian of the ordinary, of common sense and the commonplace. His critique of the myths of "Art" and "Beauty" and particularly of the special status of poets is relentless, as in *Na czworakach* [On All Fours], and *Pułapka* (*The Trap*). He probes the limits of poetry ("Upon the Departure of a Poet and a Passenger Train") and of the theater and searches for new forms and a new language for both. His rejection of the supremacy of beauty in poetry, of rhetoric and metaphor, and his preference for "impure forms," have led him to anti-poetry: stern, spare, transparent, and concerned with truth, however painful, not beauty. About Keats' formula equating beauty and truth, Różewicz has written: "one needs courage / to write such a thing . . . / Keats did have the courage / but I'd rather / he hadn't said it" ("Just Imagine Such a Thing"). He respects the theater as a place in which dramatic texts become complete, but rejects conventional stage practices and sets new tasks for staging in his so-called "literary plays" and his performance scores, which are both a challenge to the theater and to theoretical statements about it. Hence his fascination with "open theatre" and postmodern poetics, including its fragmentary narrative, intertextuality, parody, and playfulness *Białe małżeństwo* (*Mariage Blanc*). Różewicz has a profound understanding of the tragic fragility of human existence, both physical and spiritual, particularly after it had lost its grounding in traditional metaphysics and theodicy and has had to struggle against all-encompassing nothingness. In his philosophical quest he probes the sources of evil and yearns for the sacred. His later works express a profound revulsion for the garbage-producing consumerism (as in *Stara kobieta wysiaduje* translated as *An Old Woman Broods*), dehumanization of culture, and worship of immoral scientism of contemporary civilization.

This "inhabitant of a small town in the North" (as he called himself in "Mask"), fully aware of the provincialism of his existence, has been deconstructing European culture, political and aesthetic doctrines, and the cherished assumptions of Western traditions with intellectual honesty, ethical courage, and profound insight. What has made Różewicz confront the most important problems of modernity and its aporias is his relentless reexamination of European history, philosophy, and culture. His reading of Wittgenstein and Russell, his formal studies of fine arts, and his life-long interest in the visual sphere of culture have created a lasting frame of reference and inspiration for his poetry and drama. Różewicz is fascinated with the major figures of the modernist period, such as Kafka, Chekhov, Joyce, Conrad, Beckett, and Tolstoy. But this inveterate individualist, who has remained aloof from politics, ideology, and literary fashions, recognizes that the paradigm of modernist individualism is now inaccessible to the artist. It can be recalled, nostalgically or critically, but it cannot be realized in good faith. A postmodern artist can find a sense of his craft only in a shared predicament with others, in the repeated gestures of relating to the world in its concreteness, and in the attempts to order this world anew the best he can.

—Tamara Trojanowska

RULFO (VISCAÍNO), Juan (Nepomuceno Carlos Pérez)

Born: Apulco, near Sayula, Mexico, 16 May 1918. Family moved to San Gabriel, c. 1919–28; both parents dead by 1927. **Education:** Educated at the Luis Silva school for orphans, Guadalajara, 1928–32; seminary and secondary school, Guadalajara, 1932–c. 34; studied law at the National University, Mexico City, 1934–35: studies abandoned. **Family:** Married Clara Aparicio in 1947, four children. **Career:** Worked for the government immigration service, in Mexico City, Tampico, Guadalajara, and Veracruz, 1935–46; co-founder, *Pan*, 1944; worked as an impounder of German and Italian ships during World War II; salesman, Goodrich-Euzkadi rubber company, 1947–54; staff member, publishing section of the Papaloapan Commission for land development, Veracruz, 1955–56; writer of screenplays, Mexico City, c. 1956–59; worked in television, Guadalajara, 1959–62; staff member, from 1962, then director of the editorial department until 1986, Instituto Nacional Indigenista (National Institute for Indigenous Studies), Mexico City. Adviser, and fellow, Centro Mexicano de Escritores. **Awards:** Mexican Writers' Centre fellowship, 1952; Rockefeller fellowship, 1954; National literature prize (Mexico), 1970; Prince of Asturias prize (Spain), 1983. **Member:** Mexican Academy of Letters, 1980. **Died:** 7 January 1986.

PUBLICATIONS

Collections

Obras. 1987.
Toda la obra, edited by Claude Fell. 1991.
Obra completa, edited by Carlos Montemayor. 1991.

Fiction

El llano en llamas y otros cuentos (stories). 1953; revised edition, 1970; edited by Luis Leal 1970, and Hugo Rodríguez Alcalá and Ray A. Verzasconi, 1973; as *The Burning Plain and Other Stories*, translated by George Schade, 1967.
Pedro Páramo. 1955; edited by José Carlos González Boixo, 1983; as *Pedro Páramo*, translated by Lysander Kemp, 1959; also translated by Margaret Sayers Peden, 1994.
Antología personal. 1978.

Plays

El gallo de oro, y otros textos para cine (screenplays: includes *Et despojo* and *La fórmula secreta*), edited by Jorge Ayula Blanco. 1980.

Screenplays: *El despojo*, 1960; *Paloma herida*, with Emilio Fernández, 1962; *El gallo de oro*, 1964; *La fórmula secreta*, 1964; *Pedro Páramo (El hombre de la Media Luna)*, with José Bolaños, 1976.

Other

Autobiografía armada, edited by Reins Roffé. 1973.
Obra completa, edited by Jorge Ruffinelli. 1977.
Rulfo en llamas. 1981; corrected edition, 1988

Juan Rulfo: Homenaje nacional, photographs by Rulfo (commentary by various authors). 1980; as *Inframundo: El México de Juan Rulfo*, edited by Juan J. Bremer, 1983; as *Inframundo: The Mexico of Juan Rulfo*, translated by Frank Janney, 1983.

*

Bibliography: "Hacia una bibliografía de y sobre Juan Rulfo" by Arthur Ramírez, in *Revista Iberoamericana*, 40(86), 1974, supplemented with "Continuación de una bibliografía. . ." by E. Kent Lioret, in *Revista Iberoamericana*, 40(89), 1974; *Bibliografía Juan Rulfo* by Ramiro Villaseñor y Villaseñor, 1986; "Juan Rulfo" in *Mexican Literature: A Bibliography of Secondary Sources* by David William Foster, 1992 (2nd edition).

Critical Studies: *El arte de Rulfo: Historios de vivos y difuntos* by Hugo Rodríguez Alcalá, 1965; *After the Storm* by Joseph Sommers, 1968; *Recopilación de textos sobre Juan Rulfo* edited by A. Benitez Rojo, 1969; *Valoración de la obra de Juan Rulfo* by Marcelo Coddou, 1970; *Paradise and Fall in Rulfo's Pedro Páramo* by George Ronald Freeman, 1970; *The Mexican Novel Comes of Age* by Walter M. Langford, 1971; *El laberinto mexicano en/de Juan Rulfo* by Manuel Ferrer Chivite, 1972; *Tríptico mexicano: Juan Rulfo, Carlos Fuentes, Salvador Elizondo* by Manuel Durán, 1973; *Juan Rulfo: autobiografía armada* by R. Roffé, 1973; *La narrativa de Juan Rulfo: Interpretaciones críticas*, 1974; *Homenaje a Juan Rulfo* edited by Helmy F. Giacoman, 1974; *Los cuentos de Juan Rulfo* by Donald K. Gordon, 1976; *Lo fantástico y lo real en la narrativa de Juan Rulfo y Guadalupe Dueñas* by Rose S. Minc, 1979; *Claves narrativas de Juan Rulfo* by José Carlos González Boixo, 1980; *El lugar de Rulfo y otros ensayos* by Jorge Ruffinelli, 1980; *Análisis semiológico de Pedro Páramo*, 1981, and *Rulfo: Dinámica de la violencia*, 1984, both by Marta Portal; *Yáñez, Rulfo y Fuentes: El tema de la muerte en tres novelas mexicanas* by K.M. Taggart, 1982; *Juan Rulfo* (in English) by Luis Leal, 1983; *El cuento mexicano contemporáneo: Rulfo, Arreola y Fuentes* by Bertie Acker, 1984; *Expresión y sentido de Juan Rulfo* by Luis Ortega Galindo, 1984; *El texto en llamas: El arte narrativo de Juan Rulfo* by Terry J. Peavler, 1985; *Utopía, paraíso e historia: Inscripciones del mito en García Márquez, Rulfo y Cortázar* by Lida Beatriz Aronne-Amestoy, 1986; *Rulfo, la palabra redentora* by Roland Forgues, 1987; *Rulfo: El llano en llamas* by William Rowe, 1987; *Juan Rulfo: Un mosaico crítico*, 1988; *Homenaje a Juan Rulfo* edited by Dante Medina, 1989; *Juan Rulfo: Del Páramo a la esperanza* by Yvette Jiménez de Báez, 1990; *Rulfo y el dios de la memoria* by Abel Ibarra, 1991; *El laberinto y la pena: Ensayo sobre la cuentística rulfiana* by Rafael José Alfonzo, 1992; *Home as Creation: The Influence of Early Childhood Experience in the Literary Creation of Gabriel García Márquez, Agustín Yáñez, and Juan Rulfo* by Wilma E. Detjens, 1993; *El arriero en el Danubio: Recepción de Rulfo en el ámbito de la lengua alemana* by Alberto Vital, 1994; *Por el camino de Juan* by Fabiola Ruiz, 1995; *Juan Rulfo: La naturaleza hostil* by Antonio Aliberti, 1996; *Ensayos sobre la obra de Juan Rulfo* by Gustavo Fares, 1998; *La sociedad en la obra de Juan Rulfo* by Magdalena González Casillas, 1998; *Rulfo en su lumbre: Y Otros Temas latinoamericanos* by Jaime Mejía Duque, 1998.

* * *

Juan Rulfo is a leading candidate both for the title of Latin America's greatest writer of prose fiction and for that of the author of the slimmest body of published work. His accomplishment, quite simply, is to have wrought one novel, *Pedro Páramo*, and one collection of short tales, *El llano en llamas y otros cuentos* (*The Burning Plain and Other Stories*), of inexhaustible depth, complexity, and creative beauty, whose startlingly melancholy portrayal of Mexico, Latin America, and life itself places Rulfo at the very pinnacle of world authors.

Rulfo could aptly be described as a metaphysical Naturalist. An ascetic vision permeates Rulfo's stark prose in its style, structure, and themes. Hope, in the hellish world he brings forth, is foolish illusion; reality is inevitably but a cycle of frustration and failure; humanity's lot is to endure the pains of the Inferno while yet alive in a final, total stasis wherein not even death itself produces release, as in "Luvina," *Pedro Páramo*, and (possibly) "El hombre" ("The Man").

Socio-political systems (the chaos and failures of the Mexican Revolution of 1910–20), as in "El llano en llamas" ("The Burning Plain") and "Nos han dado la tierra" ("They Gave Us the Land"), family heritage in "Talpa" and "The Man," personal flaws in "No oyes ladrar los perros" ("No Dogs Bark"), the deeds of others (especially the cycle of family vengeance), and original sin all join forces to trap the struggling and anguished individual in an existential void. Indeed, in Rulfo's stories time, personal identity, and space all lose their customary meanings and functions. In the total absence of salvation, love, and hope, the future is distinguishable from past and present only as an inevitable spiral to final and immobile nothingness, and local reality exists only because of the spiteful and violent *cacique* (local dictator or strongman). Rulfo's stories, then, are full of journeys which go either nowhere or to final destruction, and movement is yet another illusion of time and space (as in "Talpa," "No Dogs Bark," "The Man"). The young narrator of "Es que somos may pobres" ("We're Very Poor") simply states the only rule of life in the cosmos that Rulfo creates: "Everything is going from bad to worse here." Finally, in the absence of the potentially life-giving functions of time (now annihilated), space (now falsified, illusory) and identity (one is, in Rulfo's world, the product of uncontrollable outside forces as much as, or more than, individual acts), we are left only with words.

Words, indeed, are always the essence of literary art; yet Rulfo has left his narrative creation with, quite literally, nothing else. To his destruction of normal categories of "objective reality" we must add a series of extraordinary stylistic and technical devices, which further undermine our, and his protagonists', customary expectations: darkness is near-constant in these narratives, and the characters are often blinded; cause and effect are rent asunder so that evil cannot be undone; sense-perceptions are muted and blurred, and thought and speech often become indistinguishable; memory fails to explain even the past, much less illuminate present and future. These characteristics are effective individually, and stunningly powerful in their total effect.

"Macario" is the opening story of *The Burning Plain* and representative of the collection as a whole. The mentally retarded protagonist exemplifies both the suffering of all humankind, and the inability to rectify unending pain on a personal level: he is an innocent victim who assumes sins of which he has no awareness (if Godmother and the priest say he is damned, then he must be). His incipient sexual feelings are displaced and mingled with a pathetically understandable desire to escape back to infancy, for Macario is merely another impotent victim of the certain triumph of the world as it is over what it should be. His only "escape" is in the pain he inflicts on himself to drown out the cries of souls in Purgatory, the frogs that keep Godmother from sleeping, and the ache in his own spirit.

In Rulfo, the Church's real role is not to bring hope, but to affirm suffering by promising an ever-illusory, and even impossible, salvation as in "Talpa," or as represented by Father Rentería in *Pedro Páramo*. The state in Rulfo's narratives is largely ineffective, even in its exploitation and corruption; it is the *cacique* who defines local reality, ruling with an iron hand made more unforgiving, in the figure of Páramo, because of the wounds of a love forever unrequited. Church and state, then, are merely additional instruments of an inhumane reality, and love may be the greatest crime of all.

Numerous melancholy, and even bitter, portrayals of life can be found—Dostoevskii, Baudelaire, García Márquez, Sartre, Faulkner, Kafka: Rulfo's astounding language and imagery stand up quite well to such lofty comparisons. In his prose, plants and animals, personified, seem to become more human than his characters in their situational desperation; the arid, sterile, and rugged terrain forms, burdens, and hardens the individual; Rulfo's characters' speech reflects, in its pauses, repetitions, and reiterations, the stasis of their lives. Yet, there is a beauty in the way Rulfo portrays horror: his very lyricism, at times highly poetic, is never escapist. On the contrary its very beauty serves to intensify powerfully the horror of the world his words create.

Two additional aspects of Rulfo's work must be mentioned. One of Rulfo's greatest achievements is his creation of a narrative art of the greatest kind using a language closely based on the daily speech patterns of a rather small part of the world (his native state of Jalisco), so much so that he claimed to "have no technique" in his writing. What this should be taken to mean is that Rulfo's art constitutes one of the earliest breakthroughs in utilizing the normal daily language of "real" people—illiterate rural peasants, minor local figures—to achieve great literary art. He proves, and early on, that literature need not be derived from elitist social strata or foreign inspirations, and he creates for Latin American literature one of its first authentic voices.

Lastly, it must be observed that two short stories escape the Rulfian norm: "El día del derrumbe" ("The Day of the Landslide," not included in the Schade translation) and "Anacleto Morones" are, almost unbelievably, highly humorous. Satires on local types, they parody delightfully the regional politician ("Landslide") and the wilful discarding of sexual norms under the guise of religion (see too "Matilde Arcángel," also not in Schade's version). While the tone of these tales is assuredly different from that of the "canonical" Rulfo, they otherwise form a continuum with the other narratives, for while humour is used as a veneer, the underlying themes are similar.

Rarely have two volumes, especially ones so slim, rendered more masterfully a particular vision of reality than *Pedro Páramo* and *The Burning Plain*. In them, Rulfo established himself as a world-class creator of narrative fiction. His is an art of, and for, his native Mexico, yet also of, and for, all times and places, and it will surely endure the test of time.

—Paul W. Borgeson, Jr

RUMI, Jalalu'd-Din Muhammad

Also known as Mawlana. **Born:** Balkh (now in Afghanistan), 30 November 1207. Moved with his father to Byzantium, Asia Minor (now Turkey), c. 1217, and then to Konya, c. 1228. **Family:** Married Gowhar Khatun in 1226. **Career:** Succeeded his father as a theologian and teacher in 1230 or 1231; came under the influence of Shamsu'd-Din Tabrizi and other Sufi mystics from c. 1244; revered by his pupils and followers as Mawlana ("our master") and as founder of the Mawlaviyya, known in the West as the "whirling Dervishes." **Died:** 17 December 1273.

PUBLICATIONS

Verse

Divan-i Shams-i Tabrizi, edited by Badi Furuzanfar. 10 vols., 1957; *Selections from the Drīvāni Shamsi Tabr'z*, edited and translated by R.A. Nicholson, 1898; selections: in *The Festival of Spring from the Divan of Jelaleddin* (from German), translated by W. Hastie, 1903; *The Rubâiyât of Jalâl al-Din Rûmi*, translated by A.J. Arberry, 1949; *Sun of Tabriz: A Lyrical Introduction to Higher Metaphysics*, translated by Colin Garbett, 1956; *Where Two Oceans Meet: A Selection of Odes from The Divan of Shems of Tabrizi*, translated by James G. Gowan, 1992; as *Selected Poems from the Divan-i Shams-i Tabrizi*, translated and edited by Reynold A. Nicholson, 1994; as *Divan-e-Shams*, selected and translated by Zahra Partovi, 1996; as *The Divan of Shems of Tabriz: Selected Odes* by James G. Cowan, 1997; as *The Glance: Songs of Soul-meeting*, translated by Coleman Barks with Nevit Ergin, 1999.

Masnavi-ye Ma'navi, as *Mathnavi of Jalalu'ddin Rumi*, edited and translated by R.A. Nicholson. 8 vols., 1925–40, reprinted with commentary, 1960; as *The Masnavi*, translated by C.E. Wilson, 1910; selections in *Tales from the Masnavi*, 1961, and *More Tales from the Masnavi*, 1963, both translated by A.J. Arberry; as *Tales of Mystic Meaning*, translated and introduced by Reynold A. Nicholson, 1995.

Mystical Poems of Rumi, translated by A.J. Arberry. 1968.

The Hundred Tales of Wisdom, edited and translated by Idries Shah. 1989.

Rumi and Daylight: A Daybook of Spiritual Guidance, translated by Camille and Kabir Helminski. 1990.

Look! This Is Love: Poems of Rural, translated by Annemarie Schimmel. 1991.

One-handed Basket Weaving: Twenty Poems on the Theme of Work, translated by Coleman Barks. 1993.

Rending the Veil: Literal and Poetic Translations of Rumi by Shahram Shiva. 1995.

Light Upon Light: Inspirations from Rumi, translated and adapted by Andrew Harvey. 1996.

Rumi, edited by Robert Van de Weyer. 1998.

The Love Poems of Rumi, translated by Deepak Chopra and Fereydoun Kia. 1998.

Rumi: Whispers of the Beloved: Quatrains, selected and translated by Azima Melita Kolin and Maryam Mafi. 1999.

Hush, Don't Say Anything to God: Passionate Poems of Rumi by Shahram Shiva. 2000.

Other

Majalis-i Sab'a-yi Mawlana (prose works). 1937.

Maktubat-i Mawlana Jalal-al-Din (prose works), edited by Ahmad Remzi Akyuaurek. 1937; also edited by Yusuf Jamshidipur, 1956.

The Discourses of Rumi, translated by A.J. Arberry. 1961.

The Way of Passion: A Celebration of Rumi by Andrew Harvey. 1994.

Signs of the Unseen: The Discourses of Jalaluddin Rumi, translated by W.M. Thackston, Jr. 1994.

The Essential Rumi, translated by Coleman Barks, John Moyne, A.A. Arberry, Reynold Nicholson. 1995.

Ruminations: Quotations from the Writings of Jalaluddin Mohammad Rumi, translated by Zahra Partovi. 1998.

Drops from an Ocean, edited by Abdassamad Clarke. 1999.

The Illustrated Rumi: A Treasury of Wisdom from the Poet of the Soul: A New Translation by Philip Dunn, Manuela Dunn Mascetti, and R.A. Nicholson. 2000.

*

Critical Studies: *The Persian Mystics: Jalalud-Din Rumi* by F. Hadland Davis, 1907; *Rumi, Poet and Mystic* by R.A. Nicholson, 1951; *The Life and Thought of M.J. Rumi* by Afzal Iqbal, 1955; *Jalaluddin Rural: Songbird of Sufism* by R.C. Delamotte, 1980; *The Triumphal Sun: A Study of Jalaloddin Rumi*, 2nd edition, 1980, and *I Am Wind, You Are Fire: The Life and Work of Rumi*, 1992, both by Annemarie Schimmel; *The Sufi Paths of Love: The Spiritual Teachings of Rumi* by William C. Chittick, 1983; *The Sufism of Rum* by K. Khosla, 1987; *The Hundred Tales of Wisdom: Life, Teachings and Miracles of Jalaludin Rumi from Aflaki's Munagib* (includes translations) by Idries Shah, 1989; *All the King's Falcons: Rumi on Prophets and Revelation* by John Renard, 1994; *Poetry and Mysticism in Islam: The Heritage of Rumi*, edited by Amin Banani, Richard Hovannisian, and Georges Sabagh, 1994; *Rumi and the Sufi Tradition: Essays on the Mowlavi Order and Mysticism* by John A. Moyne, 1998; *Reading Mystical Lyric: The Case of Jalal al-Din Rumi* by Fatemeh Keshavarz, 1998; *Rumi: A Spiritual Biography* by Leslie Wines, 2000.

* * *

Jalalu'd-Din Rumi, known as Mawlana, Our Lord or Master, was, besides being the world's most prolific mystical poet, the founder of an order of mystics, which still exists in Anatolia—the Mawlawiyya (in Turkish, Mevleviyya): the Mevlevi Dervishes. The order is centred on Rumi's burial place, Konya, where he was taken by his father, Bahau'd-Din Walad, in 1228. Rumi's founding of a Sufi order has ensured that records of the main dates and events of his life have been kept. He was born in 1207 in Balkh, in what is now northern Afghanistan, and died in 1273. Owing to disagreement, apparently on doctrinal grounds, between the poet's father, a learned preacher with above-average spiritual insight, and the local ruler and his protégé the philosopher-theologian Fakhr al-Din Razi, Bahau'd-Din Walad left Balkh for Asia Minor when his son was nine or ten years old. Hence the poet grew up in the West, in what had been Byzantium, *Rum*, so he is known as *Rumi*.

The family moved to Konya some 11 years after leaving Balkh. Rumi followed his father as a theologian and teacher in the seminaries, where he seems to have achieved eminence, until a remarkable encounter in 1244 with an itinerant dervish, a world-renouncer named Shamsu'd-Din from Tabriz in north-western Iran, changed the whole course of his life. In the words of one of Rumi's own quatrains, this made him ''a singer of songs,'' a ''sot,'' and the ''butt of boys in the street.'' The man, with whom in a passionate but spiritual sense he fell in love, seeing in him the beauty of the Divine, taught Rumi to abandon book-learning and a professor's guise. Thus man's literary and spiritual heritage acquired an unparalleled collection of lyrics chiefly in the name of Shams and called the *Divan-i Shams-i Tabrizi*, the ''great Divan'' (*divan* means a poet's collected verses), songs of love and yearning, and the *Masnavi-ye Ma'navi (The Masvani)*, a work of 25,700 rhyming couplets. *The Masnavi* describes, with many religious and folk anecdotes, man's every conceivable spiritual ascent and failure, with the wide-ranging psychological insight such comprehension required.

As R.A. Nicholson says, in the Introduction to the first book of this great poem, which he edited and translated into English for publication in 1925: ''To those interested in the history of religion, morals, and culture, in fables and folklore, in divinity, philosophy, medicine, astrology, and other branches of medieval learning, in Eastern poetry and life and manners and human nature, the *Mathnawī* should not be a sealed book . . . .''

The work was originally dedicated to Husamu'd-Din Chelebi, one of Shams's successors as ''surrogate'' for the Divine in Rumi's life. Shams had been murdered in 1247 by a group of Rumi's jealous disciples and his son, in order to excite grief in the Master. The body had been thrown into a well, but was later buried. The tomb has recently been found in Konya. Rumi had another son, Sultan Walad, who was as loyal to Shams as his father, and on one occasion, when in 1246 Shams fled to Damascus, had followed him and persuaded him to return to his ''pupil'' in the Spiritual Way. During such an absence (Shams's wanderings earned him the nickname *parandeh*, ''the flyer''), Rumi possibly composed such verses as these:

> Go, comrades, draw back our friend:
> Bring me again the run-away idol.
> With sweet ditties, golden excuses,
> Entice back to the house the sweet-faced moon.
> And if with promises he says, ''I'll come another time,''
> All the promises will be false: he'll be deceiving you.

Shams taught Rumi love; this meant life, of which (for the Sufi) the essence and purpose is love of God and realization of Him through love. The *ghazals* (lyrics) of the *Divan* consist of love poetry expressing the lover's agonies in longing for the Beloved and his demonstration, through description of its lack's painfulness, of the ineffable delight of union when through grace it is granted. The style is passionate and the diction manifests the art of great Persian lyrical poetry, lifting the cadences and expressions of everyday colloquial speech seemingly effortlessly to the level of exalted literature. The colloquial flavour is perfectly consonant, indeed inevitable, with the intensity of the universal human experience with which the poems are concerned. Similarly, *The Masnavi*'s unvaried rhyming couplets are racy and as spontaneous as might be expected from a poet so dedicated to man's spiritual fulfilment in the rejection of materialism and known to decry rules of formal rhetoric. His opening prescribes listening to the reed's lament for separation from the reed-bed and his message is summed up in the anecdote of the man who knocked at a friend's door. When asked who was there, he answered ''It is I.'' Sent away, he suffered burning separation for a year. He then knocked again. This time he answered, ''It is you, o snatcher of hearts,'' and was invited in, where there was room for only one ''I.''

—Peter Avery

RUZZANTE [OR RUZANTE]

Born: Angelo Beolco in Padua, territory of Venetian Republic, c. 1495–96. Illegitimate son of a nobleman. **Education:** Trained in law. **Family:** Married Giustina Palatino, c. 1526. **Career:** Actor, from c. 1515–18, and performed, under the stage name Il Ruz(z)ante, in carnival plays in Venice and Padua from c. 1520; in the service of Alvise Cornaro, from 1525; received modest inheritance following his father's death, 1526, and later received power-of-attorney for his half-brothers' shares in their father's estate, dividing it in 1540; banished to Ferrara, 1539. **Died:** c. 17 March 1542.

PUBLICATIONS

Collections

Tutte le opere, edited and translated by Ludovico Zorzi and G. De Bosnio. 1951– (incomplete; 3 vols. issued to 1955).
Il Ruzzante: Angelo Beolco, edited by G.A. Cibotto. 1958.
Teatro, edited by Ludovico Zorzi. 1967.

Plays

Parlamento de Ruzante che iera vegnú de campo (produced c. 1515?). In *Due dialoghi di Ruzante in lingua rustica*, 1551; as *Ruzzante Returns from the Wars*, translated by Angela Ingold and Theodore Hoffman, in *The Classic Theatre 1*, edited by Eric Bentley, 1958.
La pastorale (produced 1517?). 1951; edited by Emilio Lovarini, 1951.
La Betìa (produced 1523?). Fragment in *Antichi testi di letteratura pavana*, edited by E. Lovarini, 1894; complete, in *Teatro*, 1967.
Dialogo facetissimo (produced 1525?; definitely produced 1529). 1554.
La fiorina (produced 1531–32?). 1548; edited by Emilio Lovarini, with *Moscheta*, 1941.
La moscheta (produced c. 1532). 1551; edited by Emilio Lovarini, with *Fiorina*, 1941; as *Posh Talk*, translated by Ronnie Ferguson, in *Three Renaissance Comedies*, edited by Christopher Cairns, 1991; also translated by Antonio Franceschetti and Kenneth R. Bartlett, 1993.
La piovana (produced 1532). 1548.
La vaccaria, from a play by Plautus (produced 1533). 1551.
L'anconitana. 1551; as *The Woman from Ancona*, translated with introduction and notes by Nancy Dersofi, 1994.
Bilora. In *Due dialoghi di Ruzante in lingua rustica*, 1551; as *Bilora*, translated by Babette and Glen Hughes, in *World Drama 2*, edited by Barrett H. Clark, 1933, and in *Masterworks of World Drama 3*, edited by Anthony Caputi, 1968.
Due dialoghi di Ruzante in lingua rustica. 1551; edited by Ludovico Zorzi, 1968.
Tre orazioni. 1551.
Il reduce; Bilora; Menego, edited by Emilio Lovarini. 1940.
Dialoghi (Italian versions from Venetian dialect), translated by G.A. Cibotto. 1953.
Commedie del Cinquecento 2 (includes *La pastorale; Moschetta; Fiorina*), edited by Aldo Borlenghi. 1959.
La pastorale; La prima oratione; Una lettera giocosa, edited by Giorgio Padoan. 1978.

I dialoghi; La seconda oratione; I prologhi alla Moschetta, edited by Giorgio Padoan. 1981.

*

Bibliography: "Vent'anni di critica ruzantesca (1966–1985)" by Emilio Lippi, in *Quaderni Veneti*, 2–3, 1985–86.

Critical Studies: *Angelo Beolco detto il Ruzzante* by G. Baldrin, 1924; *Il Ruzzante* by A. Cataldo, 1933; *Ruzzante* by Carlo Grabher, 1953; *Studi sul Ruzzante e la letteratura Pavana* 1965, and *Ruzzante*, 1988, both by Emilio Lovarini; *Tre studi sul teatro: Ruzzante, Aretino, Goldoni* by M. Baratto, 1966; *Angelo Beolco nominato Ruzante* by Mario Prosperi, 1970; "An Introduction to the Theatre of Angelo Beolco" in *Renaissance Drama*, 6 (new series), 1973, and "Ruzante's 'Atavistic' Memory," in *Interpreting the Italian Renaissance: Literary Perspectives* edited by Antonio Toscana, 1991, both by Franco Fido; *Arcadia and the Stage* by N. Dershofi, 1978; *Language and Dialect in Ruzzante and Goldoni*, 1981, "Ruzante's Early Adaptations from More and Erasmus," in *Italica*, 66(1), 1989, and *Angelo Beolco (Il Ruzzante)* (in English), 1990, all by Linda L. Carroll; "Observing Italian Theatre" by Richard Andrews, in *University of Leeds Review*, 29, 1986–87; *The Theatre of Angelo Beolco (Ruzante): Text, Context and Performance* by Ronnie Ferguson, 2000.

* * *

From the world of the humanistic comedy of Terentian and Plautine derivation, with its Aristotelian rules and scripted text, which the early comedies of Ariosto, Machiavelli, and Bibbiena represent, but also from that particularly Venetian brand of impromptu vulgar farce, perhaps improvised wholly or in part, with its salacious content and earthy humour, comes Ruzzante, with his unique mixture of these two apparently separate traditions. His comedies, scripted in the Paduan dialect, echo the low-life realities of peasant life, and project the image of the author also as actor. Modern scholarship sees these two traditions intermingling and cross-fertilizing in the early years of the 16th century (1520–26), and pointing forward to the innovations of Aretino's comedies of life, or the Venetian dialect comedies of Andrea Calmo and others later in the century—and ultimately to the *commedia dell'arte*.

Far from being the ragged and uncultured bohemian that subsequent romantics imagined, Angelo Beolco came from respectable middle-class origins, an intellectual of means, who married into money. He cultivated successfully the protection and support of the wealthy patrician Alvise Cornaro (1475–1566), whose patronage extended to philosophers, artists, and scientists in his native Padua, and in the garden of whose sumptuous villa Ruzzante staged his comedies, directing and acting in them himself until his fame attracted invitations to Venice and the court of Ferrara, where Ariosto's comedies were being staged. Author of two comedies in verse, five in prose, and two "dialogues," Ruzzante turns the conventional expectations of genre on their heads for parodistic ends, as in the travesty of a rustic eclogue *La pastorale*, or *La Betìa*, which sends up the conventional marriage farce to give primacy to the main ingredients in the life of the country peasant: sex, the fear of hunger, and the awe of death constitute his universe. *La Betìa* also has transparent parody of the refined utterances of more intellectual (humanistic) authors like the Neoplatonic Pietro Bembo, and deliberate betrayal of the marriage-as-consummation principle of *commedia erudita* in the worldly pact between lovers with which the play ends.

The one-act dialogues, the *Parlamento de Ruzante che iera vegnú de campo* (*Ruzante Returns from the Wars*) and *Bilora*, followed, the first of which depicts the disillusionment of a soldier returning from the wars and the dichotomy between rustic life and the city-centred power base. In *Bilora*, misery afflicts the rustic whose wife has fled with an old, rich, middle-class rival, and he can respond only by murdering the rival. *La moscheta* (*Posh Talk*) reduces the life of the rustic to the fundamentals of hunger and sex, yet introduces the question of language as a class determinant, as the protagonist mimics an upper-class accent (the *moscheta* of the title). Further comedies, *La vaccaria* and *La piovana*, are datable to the period 1532–33, and show Ruzzante reverting to something closer to the structure and form of the humanist-inspired *commedia erudita*. In *La piovana*, "classical" (high-flown) elements (from the Plautine *Rudens* and *Asinaria*) seem to have been absorbed by Ruzzante's peasant community from the Venetian countryside, while in the *La vaccaria* the same process continues in the city; the characters speak cultivated Italian (masters), and dialect (servants), all of which again prefigures the linguistic virtuosity and stereotyping of the (later) *commedia dell'arte*.

Finally, *L'anconitana* (*The Woman from Ancona*) continues the process of breakdown of the formal five-act structure, reducing it almost to a cabaret-like entertainment which contains a *tour de force* of different theatrical approaches, from the erudite comedy of humanist inspiration, through the rustic farce of Ruzzante's earlier days, to the stand-up comedy (to translate it into modern terms) of mimes and buffoons (which our earliest documents relating to the Venetian theatre mention in the occasional references to performances by such as Cherea and Cimador, and of which the *Diarii* of Marin Sanudo are such eloquent, if scattered, testimony in the first quarter of the century).

The Paduan-dialect theatre of Ruzzante, therefore, standing apart from the mainstream of humanist-inspired comedies of Bibbiena, Ariosto, and Machiavelli, and possibly prefiguring some linguistic variation in the later comedies of Aretino, also provides a counterpart to the concentration of theatre on cultivated Italian, and is of crucial importance to the later development of dialect theatre by such as Calmo and Giancarli in Venice, to the future emergence of the author/actor, and to the fusion of such apparently contrary "cultural" and "life-related" elements in the *commedia dell'arte*. Ruzzante's theatre runs the full course from the street theatre of buffoons and charlatans to the conservatism of classicism, from the realism of dialect to the Italian of the academies, and perhaps would have come full circle in his appearance as an actor in tragedy in Ferrara in 1542, had his death not robbed him of the opportunity to develop his career.

—Christopher Cairns

S

SABA, Umberto

Born: Umberto Poli in Trieste, Croatian region of the Austro-Hungarian Empire (now in Italy), 9 March 1883; legally changed name to Umberto Saba in 1920. **Education:** Educated at the Ginnasio Dante Alighieri, Trieste; Imperial Academy of Commerce and Nautical Science; University of Pisa, 1903–04. **Military Service:** Infantry regiment, Salerno. **Family:** Married Carolina (''Lina'') Woelfler in 1909 (died 1957), one son and one daughter. **Career:** Briefly a businessman; secretary, Taverna Rossa cabaret, Milan; assigned briefly to the Ministry of War, Rome, 1916; technical official, Taliedo airport, 1917; publicity writer, Leoni films, Trieste, 1919; owner and manager, Libreria Antiquaria bookshop, Trieste, 1919–40, financed the publishing of his *Il canzioniere*, 1921; member, *Solaria* artistic circle, from 1926; fled Trieste with his family, September 1943, first to Paris, and then lived in hiding in Florence, 1944; after the Allied Liberation, moved to Rome, then Milan, before returning to Trieste in the last years of his life. **Awards:** Taormina prize, 1951; Novaro Foundation prize, 1951; Viareggio prize, 1951. Honorary degree: University of Rome, 1953. **Died:** 25 August 1957.

PUBLICATIONS

Collections

Tutte le opere. 6 vols., 1949–59.
Tutte le poesie, edited by Arrigo Stara. 1988.
Stories and Recollections of Umberto Saba, translated by Estelle Gilson. 1993.

Verse

Il mio primo libro di poesie. 1903; as *Poesie*, 1911.
Coi miei occhi. 1912; edited by Claudio Milanini, 1981.
Cose leggere e vaganti. 1920.
La serena disperazione. 1920.
L'amorosa spina. 1921.
Il canzoniere (1900–1921). 1921; first revised and enlarged edition, as *Il canzoniere (1900–1945)*, 2 vols., 1945; second revised and enlarged edition, as *Il canzoniere (1900–1947)*, 2 vols., 1948; complete edition, as *Il canzoniere (1900–1954)*, 1961, corrected 1965; original edition, as *Il canzoniere 1921*, edited by Giordano Castellani, 1981; as *Songbook: Selected Poems from the Canzoniere*, translated and introduced by Stephen Sartarelli, 1998.
Preludio e canzonette. 1923.
Autobiografia. 1924.
I prigioni. 1924.

Figure e canti (includes ''Preludio e canzonette,'' ''Autobiografia,'' ''I prigioni,'' ''La vetrina,'' ''Fanciulle,'' ''Cuor morituro''). 1926.
Preludio e fughe. 1928.
Tre poesie alla mia balia. 1929.
Ammonizione ed altre poesie (1900–1910). 1932.
Tre composizioni. 1933.
Parole. 1934.
Ultime cose. 1944.
Mediterranee. 1947.
Poesie dell'adolescenza e giovanili 1900–1910. 1949.
Uccelli; Quasi un racconto. 1950.
Trieste e una donna. 1950.
Epigrafe; Ultime prose. 1959.
Il piccolo Berto 1929–1931. 1961.
Parole ultime cose 1933–1943. 1961.
Thirty-One Poems, translated by Felix Stefanile. 1980.
The Dark of the Sun: Selected Poems, translated by Christopher Millis. 1994.

Fiction

Ernesto. 1975; as *Ernesto*, translated by Mark Thompson. 1987.

Other

Scorciatoie e raccontini. 1946.
Storia e cronistoria del Canzoniere. 1948; as *History and Chronicle of the Songbook*, translated by Stephen Sartarelli, 1998.
Amicizia: Storia di un vecchio poeta e di un giovane canarino (letters to Quarantotti Gambini), edited by Carlo Levi. 1951; as *Il vecchio e il giovane: Carteggio 1930–1957*, edited by Linuccia Saba, 1965.
Ricordi-racconti. 1956.
Quello che resta da fare ai poeti (Trieste-febbriao 1911), edited by Anita Pittoni. 1959.
Prose, edited by Linuccia Saba. 1964.
Lettere a un'amico (letters to Nora Baldi). 1966.
Saba, Svevo, Comisso: Lettere inedite. 1969.
L'adolescenza del Canzoniere, e undici lettere. 1975.
Lettere a un amico vescovo (letters to Giovanni Fallani), edited by Rienzo Colla. 1980.
Per conoscere Saba (anthology), edited by Mario Lavagetto. 1981.
La spada d'amore: Lettere scelte 1902–1957, edited by Aldo Marcovecchio. 1983.

*

Critical Studies: *Umberto Saba* by Folco Portinari, 1963; *Lettura e storia di Saba* by E. Caccia, 1967; *Three Modern Italian Poets: Saba, Ungaretti, Montale* by Joseph Cary, 1969; *Saba e la psicoanalisi* by Renato Aymone, 1971; *La gallina di Saba* by Mario Lavagetto, 1974; *Umberto Saba* by Antonio Pinchera, 1974; *Invito alia lettura di Saba* by Piero Raimondi, 1974; *La poesia di Saba* by Nicola Francesco Cimmino, 1976; *La critica e Saba* edited by Francesco Múzzioli, 1976; *Umberto Saba* by Gennaro Savarese, 1976; *La prosa di Umberto Saba: Dai racconti giovanili a Ernesto* by Elvira Favretti, 1982; *Immagini per Saba* by Nora Baldi, 1983; *Umberto Saba e dintorni* by Giorgio Baroni, 1984; *Il punto su Saba* by Elvio Guagnini, 1987; *Storia di Umberto Saba* by Stelio Mattioni, 1989.

* * *

Umberto Saba, together with Ungaretti and Montale, is considered one of the most important Italian poets of the first half of the 20th century. Born of a Jewish mother and a non-Jewish father who abandoned his wife even before Saba was born, he was largely self-educated. At 20, he enlisted in an infantry regiment, in which he served for several years. At the end of World War I, when Trieste was returned to Italy, Saba returned there and started an antiquarian bookshop that was to become a lifelong preoccupation. In the last decade of his life he received several literary awards and honours, including the coveted Viareggio prize.

The one conspicuous feature of Saba's poetry is its prosaic quality, which distinguishes it from the D'Annunzian diction on the one hand, and from the Crepuscular or Hermetic one on the other. To some extent, in terms of his origins, influences, and development, Saba may be considered to be, like Ungaretti, something of an outsider, belonging more to the periphery than to the centre of the Italian poetic tradition. Hence, he brought to modern Italian poetry an altogether new tone and timbre, as well as a new ethos. In his best and most characteristic poems, especially in *Trieste e una donna* [Trieste and a Woman], emotional tension and intensity of feeling co-exist with the psychological complexity and moral depth of his thought, and both are expressed in a language characterized by a prosaic familiarity and relaxed intimacy of tone and inflexion. Though rooted in the culture, history, topography, and atmosphere of his native Trieste, Saba, nevertheless, conveys a sense of rootlessness and alienation in a touchingly simple way partly by virtue of his Jewish background. His poetry is singularly free from metaphysical themes or preoccupations; and there is nothing dramatically impassioned or exuberant about its subject-matter. Feeling quite at home with, and often making poetical capital out of, that which is normal, commonplace, and even banal, he achieves a lyricism which, by virtue of its spontaneity and naturalness, as well as by its apparent ingenuousness, is both subdued and subjective. His use of language corroborates Coleridge's dictum that there is essentially no difference between the language of prose and the language of verse.

Perhaps partly as a result of this approach, Saba tends to be prolix, his sense of self-discipline as a creative artist often giving way to self-indulgence. Hence, in his case, more than in that of any other major Italian poet of the first half of the 20th century, a drastic selection of his work has to be made to appreciate Saba at his best.

Much of the best of Saba's poetry has for its subject matter personal experiences and domestic and family ties. Saba himself considered the poems he collected in the 1921 volume *Il canzioniere* as expressing the history of a life outwardly poor, but inwardly rich, as well as rich in terms of the people he had loved in the course of his long life. Even the titles of some of his books of poetry are indicative of their autobiographical character—titles like *Poesie dell'adolescenza e giovanili* [Poems of Adolescence and Youth], *Trieste e una donna*, and *Autobiografia*.

Qualities such as the spontaneity of feeling and sentiment, as well as directness and naturalness of language and imagery characterize Saba's poetry, including his best-known book *Trieste e una donna*, where love, affection, and loyalty to his wife as well as to his native city Trieste are the dominant themes. In this volume, Saba displays that masterly ease and unobtrusive intensity of feeling, that creative union between the cadences of prose and those of poetry, which are the hallmark of his particular lyricism, and for which there is no parallel in modern Italian poetry until we come to Montale's *Xenia*. "You are like a swallow," the poet tells his wife:

> who comes back in spring.
> But in autumn leaves again;
> You do not know this art.
> But you have one thing in common with the swallow:
> the nimble movements;
> which to me, who felt old,
> and was old,
> announced another spring.

Subtlety of thought, or any form of intellectualism, is generally alien to Saba's poetry, whereas genuine feelings and emotions, in their simplicity and spontaneity, are the very stuff of which his verse is made. No wonder he prized the qualities of the heart more than those of the intellect (or indeed anything else). "Intelligence," he tells us, "as an intellectual mechanism is to be found in every corner (many imbeciles are very intelligent): but to find a heart is more rare than difficult." This assertion is at the very core of Saba's poetic inspiration, especially in his masterpiece, *Trieste e una donna*. Another characteristic note Saba strikes here, and which has inspired some of his most touching poems, is that of melancholy and solitude; this equality adds to Saba's poetry both lyric intensity and moral depth; "I know," he tells us, "how to turn a long winter into spring; / and where the street in the sun is a gilded streak, I say good evening to myself."

In *Autobiografia*, Saba deals, not so much with the external events of his life, but with what Browning would call "incidents in the development of the soul"—in his experience as a child whose mother was deserted by his father ("the only son whose father is away"), in the racial difference between the two parents ("the two races in old conflict"), in his lonely childhood ("childhood . . . poor and blest by few friends, and a few animals"), in his adolescent love for Lina who was to become his wife ("for whom I wrote my book with its most daring sincerity"), in his experience as a soldier ("bad poet, good soldier"). Saba calls his muse "my Muse in plain clothes"—but his is the plainness and simplicity of a true, at times even great, poet, especially when he manages to convey with the utmost succinctness and with an extraordinary clarity of thought and meaning his saddest and deepest feelings: "Ashes / of things dead, of evils / wasted, of ineffable contacts / of mute sighs."

The definitive collection of Saba's poems *Il canzoniere*, published after his death in 1961, ends with an epigraph: "When living I talked to a nation of the dead. / Now dead, I refuse laurels, and ask for oblivion." Both the sense and the style of this epigraph throw valuable light on the kind of poetic originality Saba believed he had achieved—an originality that needed a new poetic taste and new critical criteria, whereby it could not be appreciated and which he, rightly or wrongly, thought were not available in his time.

—G. Singh

SACHS, Hans

Born: Nuremberg, Germany, 5 November 1494. **Education:** Educated at a local school. **Family:** Married 1) Kunigunde Kreutzer in 1519 (died 1560), seven children; 2) Barbara Harscher in 1561. **Career:** Apprentice shoemaker, 1508–10; travelling journeyman to numerous towns including Vienna, Frankfurt am Main, Lübeck, and Osnabrück, 1511–16, returned to Nuremberg as master cobbler, 1516; trained in the art of the mastersingers as a teenager; member of the guild of mastersingers; helped to run the singing school in Munich and directed other schools in the towns he visited; joined Lutheran reform movement writing poetry and prose in support of the cause, after the publication of an anti-papist work in 1527 was threatened with a ban from publishing; prolific writer of *Meisterlieder, Schwänke*, and *Fastnachtspiele*. **Died:** 19 January 1576.

PUBLICATIONS

Collections

Sämtliche Werke, edited by Adalbert von Keller and Edmund Götze. 26 vols., 1870–1908; reprinted 1964.
Sämtliche Fastnachtspiele, edited by Edmund Götze. 7 vols., 1880–87.
Sämtliche Fabeln und Schwänke, edited by Edmund Götze and Carl Drescher. 6 vols., 1893–1913.
Ausgewählte Werke, edited by Paul Merker and Reinhard Buchwald. 2 vols., 1911; reprinted 1961.
Gedichte, edited by Paul Merker and Reinhard Buchwald. 1920.
Fastnachtspiele (selection), edited by Theo Schumacher. 1957.
Werke, edited by K.M. Schiller. 2 vols., 1960.
Meistergesänge, Fastnachtsspiele, Schwänke, edited by Eugen Geiger. 1963.
Prosadialoge, edited by Ingeborg Spriewald. 1970.
Selections, edited by Mary Beare. 1983.
Werke, edited by Reinhard Hahn. 1992.

Plays (selection)

Das Hoffgsindt Veneris. 1517.
Lucretia. 1527.
Von dem Tobia und seinem Sohn. 1533.
Der Teufel mit dem alten Weib. 1545.
Griselda. 1546.
Tragödie von der Schöpfung. 1548.
Der Fährende Schüler ins Paradies. 1550; as *The Wandering Scholar*, translated by E.U. Ouless, 1930; as *The Strolling Clerk from Paradise*, translated by Philip Wayne, 1935; as *The Scholar Bound for Paradise*, translated by Bayard Quincy Morgan, in *Three Shrovetide Comedies*, 1937; as *The Wandering Scholar in Paradise*, translated by S. Eliot, in *Poetic Drama*, edited by A. Kreymborg, 1941.
Der böse Rauch. 1551.
Die Judith. 1551.
Der fahrende Schüler mit dem Teufel. 1551; as *Raising the Devil*, translated by W.H.H. Chambers, in *The Drama: Its History, Literature and Influence on Civilization*, edited by A. Bates, 1903–04.

Das heisse Eisen. 1551; as *The Hot Iron*, translated by Bayard Quincy Morgan, in *Three Shrovetide Comedies*, 1937.
Der Wüterich Herodes. 1552.
Die Maccabäer. 1552.
Der Bauer im Fegfeuer. 1552; as *The Farmer in Purgatory*, translated by Henry Gibson Adams, 1926.
Die ungleichen Kinder Evä wie sie Gott der Herr an redt. 1553; as *The Children of Eve*, translated by E.U. Ouless, 1934.
Der Rossdieb zu Fünsing. 1553; as *The Horse Thief*, translated by E.U. Ouless, 1930; also translated by W. Leighton, in *Adventures in World Literature*, edited by R.B. Inglis and W.K. Stewart, 1936.
Die mörderisch Königin Klitemnestra. 1554.
Der Krämmerskorb. 1554(?); as *The Merchant's Basket*, translated by Bayard Quincy Morgan, in *Three Shrovetide Comedies*, 1937.
Sanct Peter mit der Gais. 1555
Die getreu Fürstin Alcestis. 1555.
Komödie vom verlorenen Sohn. 1556.
Tragödie König Sauls. 1557.
Der hürnen Seugfried. 1557; edited by Edmund Götze, 1967.
David mit Batseba. 1557.
Tragödie der ganz Passio. 1558.
Tragödie von Alexandro Magno. 1558.
Tragödie des jüngsten Gerichts. 1558.
Die Komödie der Königin Esther. 1559.
Die junge Witwe Franzisca. 1560.
Andreas der ungerisch König mit Bancbano seinem getrewen Statthalter. 1561.
Seven Shrovetide Plays, translated by E.U. Ouless. 1930–34.

Verse

Die wittembergisch Nachtigall. 1523; edited by G.H. Seufert with *Vier Reformationsdialoge und das Meisterlied Das Walt Got*, 1974.
Das Schlauraffen Landt. 1530.
Gespräch Sanct Peters mit den Landsknechten. 1556.
Schwänke von dem frommen Adel. 1562.
Der Schneider mit dem Pannier. 1563.
Summa all meiner Gedichte, 1576; as *Valete.* 1576.
Das Walt Got: A Meisterlied, edited and translated by Frances Hankemeier Ellis. 1941.
The Early Meisterlieder of Hans Sachs, edited by Frances H. Ellis. 1974.

Other

Disputation zwischen einem Chorherren und Schuhmacher. 1524; as *A Goodly Disputation between a Christian Shoemaker, and a Popish Parson*, translated by Anthony Scoloker, in *Three Tudor Dialogues*, 1974.

*

Critical Studies: *Hans Sachs and Goethe: A Study in Meter* by Mary C. Burchinal, 1912; *Medieval Civilization as Illustrated in the Fastnachtspiele of Hans Sachs* by Walter French, 1925; *The Literary History of the Meistergesang* by Archer Taylor, 1937; *Der Meistergesang des Hans Sachs* by Eugen Geiger, 1956; *Meistersang* by Bert Nagel, 1962, 2nd edition, 1971; *The Tristan Romance in the Meisterlieder of Hans Sachs* by Eli Sobel, 1963; *Fastnachtspiel by*

Eckehard Catholy, 1966; *Hans Sachs* by Barbara Könneker, 1971; . . . *was ein singer soll singen: Untersuchung zur Reformationsdichtung des Meistersängers Hans Sachs* by Manfred Dutschke, 1985; *Der Poet der Moralität* by Maria E. Müller, 1985; *Bildung und Belehrung: Untersuchungen zum Dramenwerk des Hans Sachs* by Dorothea Klein, 1988; *Hans Sachs and Folk Theatre in the Late Middle Ages: Studies in the History of Popular Culture*, edited by Robert Aylett and Peter Skrine, 1995.

*   *   *

Quantity rather than quality is the hallmark of Hans Sachs's immense *oeuvre*. Almost no specific works demand individual mention and our interest derives rather from the insights they offer into the 16th century.

The Free Imperial City of Nuremberg was enjoying its heyday during Sachs's lifetime, thanks to its economic, cultural, and intellectual pre-eminence, and its importance for his writing cannot be overstressed. However, it would be quite wrong to suggest that Sachs had any kind of direct access to the city's humanist élite. His writings clearly reveal him as largely self-taught, hence the importance of our knowledge of the extent of his library. The total number of Sachs's known works approaches 6,200, and almost all are extant. In his own manuscript collection of his works, the *Meisterlieder* (mastersongs) are kept separate; they were never "published" in the 16th century and the vast majority remain unedited still today. They were composed for sung performance at regular private meetings of the mastersingers. The tripartite metrical scheme was considered more important than the text; one became a master by composing what was considered to be an acceptable new melody or *Ton*. How to obey the complicated sets of rules, called *Tabulatur*, relating to both words and melodies, was to be learned in singing schools, *Singschulen*. Performances were divided into two parts: the main sessions, *Hauptsingen*, at which chiefly religious and certainly only serious topics were dealt with; and the ensuing drinking sessions, *Zechsingen*, at which lighter topics took over. Correspondingly, the subject matter of the 4,000 or so mastersongs which Sachs produced in his lifetime ranged through the Nativity, the Passion, and the Resurrection of Christ; the Creed and the Ten Commandments; and renderings of large sections of the Old and New Testaments based on Luther's translation; while for the *Zechsingen* he also produced witty anecdotes and earthy stories.

This range of content applies to all Sachs's verse writings; he did not understand the notion that some topics might best be reserved for specific forms. This is in large measure the reason why commentators disagree about the categories into which Sachs's writings should be divided; it is unclear what different categories he himself recognized, apart from the separateness of the mastersongs. The remainder of the verse writings are all in rhymed couplets; their length ranges from under 20 to several hundred lines. The only clear division is between the dramatic and the non-dramatic; and the question as to whether certain dialogues can be considered dramatic blurs even this distinction.

The dramatic writings divide between shrovetide plays (or carnival plays or carnival comedies), *Fastnacht(s)spiele*, comedies, and tragedies. The shrovetide plays continue a Nuremberg tradition from the previous century, but Sachs transforms their impact to imbue them with the same morality which pervades all his work. Apart from a few early examples such as *Das Hoffgsindt Veneris* [The Court of Venus], the majority of the 85 plays Sachs himself attributes to this group date from the period 1550–54. They are the only strand of his writings which can be considered in any sense alive today, as they are regularly

produced in the Nuremberg area and a few have been performed in English translation in Britain and North America.

The comedies and tragedies constitute the "Mastersinger Dramas," performed by the mastersingers before a paying audience in the secularized church of St. Martha in Nuremberg, usually between Epiphany and Shrove Tuesday. In the decade after 1561, Sachs himself was in charge of the performances and also performed. These plays represent the first important attempt to present in the vernacular the humanist drama which had been produced by Reuchlin, Celtis, and Locher. Sachs's plays include a *Jocasta*, a *Clitimnestra*, and an *Alcestis*. What separates the "Comedia" from the "Tragedia" is largely whether the central figure survives the action; Sachs has no sense of tragedy or comedy. About one-third of these plays are on Biblical themes; the other two-thirds are also given a Christian moralizing interpretation, which is made explicit in the prologues and epilogues as well as in the interspersed moralizing observations from the servant characters. What the modern reader perceives as a chasm between material and treatment can be exemplified from the "Clitimnestra" figure. From the epilogue to the play we learn the intended moral regarding the fallibility of woman when released from the strict control of her husband, which leads her to amorous exploits (*bulerey*); such a Clytemnestra cannot have anything remotely like tragic greatness and thus there is a kind of logic in portraying her as an average 16th-century German bourgeoise.

Sachs divides his plays into "acts," often three or five in number, though later plays quite often have seven, occasionally four or six, and exceptionally nine or ten.

All Sachs's non-dramatic verse writings apart from the mastersongs can be grouped together under the heading *Sprüche*. Besides being the generic term this is the label used for any poem where a more precise definition is not used. As indicated above, their content ranges from serious moralizing to the bawdy.

As contrasting examples one may cite *Das Schlauraffen Landt* [Fools' Paradise or Topsy-turvey Land], about a place "three leagues beyond Christmas," and Sachs's single most influential work, the allegorical poem *Die wittembergisch Nachtigall* [The Nightingale of Wittenberg], 1523, which expresses the author's early support of Luther's reforms: the night of oppression by the papal lion and its pack of ravenous wolves, who "fleece, milk, flay and eat" the sheep, is now being ended by this nightingale.

The only extant prose works by Sachs are six dialogues, four of which date from 1524 and belong to the sudden wave of such works concerning the Reformation which appeared in that year. The best known is the *Disputation zwischen einem Chorherren und Schuhmacher* (*A Goodly Disputation between a Christian Shoemaker, and a Popish Parson*), printed 11 times that year. The two later dialogues also deal with matters of immediate contemporary concern, such as Sachs was also writing about in verse at the same time.

—John E. Tailby

See the essay on *The Wandering Scholar in Paradise*.

SACHS, Nelly

Born: Berlin, Germany, 10 December 1891. Naturalized Swedish citizen 1952. **Education:** Educated at school in Berlin, 1897–1900; privately, 1900–03; Aubertschule, 1903. **Career:** Corresponded with

Selma Lagerlöf (*q.v.*) for many years; suffered from severe depression due to the Holocaust; emigrated to Sweden with Lagerlöf's help in 1940 and lived there for the rest of her life. **Awards:** Peace prize, 1965; Nobel prize for literature, 1966. **Died:** 12 May 1970.

PUBLICATIONS

Collection

Gedichte, edited by Hilde Domin. 1977.

Verse

In den Wohnungen des Todes. 1947.
Sternverdunkelung. 1949.
Und niemand weiss weiter. 1957.
Flucht und Verwandlung. 1959.
Fahrt ins Staublose. 1961.
Die Gedichte. 2 vols., 1961–71.
Ausgewählte Gedichte. 1963.
Glühende Rätsel. 1964.
Späte Gedichte. 1965.
Die Suchende. 1966.
O the Chimneys: Selected Poems, Including the Verse Play, Eli, translated by Michael Hamburger, Christopher Holme, and others. 1967; as *Selected Poems,* 1968.
The Seeker and Other Poems, translated by Ruth Mead, Matthew Mead, and Michael Hamburger. 1970.
Teile dich Nacht, Die letzten Gedichte, edited by Margaretha and Bengt Holmqvist. 1971.

Fiction

Legenden und Erzählungen. 1921.

Plays

Eli. 1951.
Zeichen im Sand. 1962.
Simson fällt durch Jahrtausende und andere szenische Dichtungen. 1967.
Verzauberung: Späte szenische Dichtungen. 1970.

Other

Das Buch der Nelly Sachs, edited by Bengt Holmqvist. 1968.
Briefe, edited by Ruth Dinesen and Helmut Müssener. 1984.
Briefregister, edited by Ruth Dinesen. 1989.
Paul Celan, Nelly Sachs: Correspondence, translated by Christopher Clark. 1995.
Editor and translator, *Von Welle und Granit: Querschnitt durch die Schwedische Lyrik des 20. Jahrhunderts.* 1947.
Editor and translator, *Aber auch die Sonne ist heimatlos. Schwedische Lyrik der Gegenwart.* 1956.
Editor and translator, *Der Schattenfischer,* by Johannes Edfelt. 1958.
Editor and translator, *Weil unser einziges Nest unsere Flügel sind,* by Erik Lindegren. 1963.
Editor and translator, *Schwedische Gedichte.* 1965.
Translator, *Poesie,* by Gunnar Ekelöf. 1962.
Translator, *Poesie,* by Karl Vennberg. 1965.

*

Bibliography: by Paul Kersten, 1969.

Critical Studies: *Poetik des modernen Gedichtes: Zur Lyrik von Nelly Sachs* by Gisela Bezzel-Dischner, 1970; *Die Metaphorik in der Lyrik von Nelly Sachs* by Paul Kersten, 1970; *Nelly Sachs: Einführung in das Werk der Dichterin jüdischen Schicksals* by Walter A. Berendsohn, 1974; *Nelly Sachs* by Ehrhard Bahr, 1980; *Religion und Religiosität in der Lyrik von Nelly Sachs* by Ulrich Klingmann, 1980; *Nelly Sachs and the Kabbala* by Burghild O. Holzer, 1983; *Nelly Sachs* by Henning Falkenstein, 1984; *Post-Shoa Religious Metaphors: The Image of God in the Poetry of Nelly Sachs* by Ursula Rudnick, 1995; *Jewish Writers, German Literature: The Uneasy Examples of Nelly Sachs and Walter Benjamin,* edited by Timothy Bahti and Marilyn Sibley Fries, 1995; *Ethics and Remembrance in the Poetry of Nelly Sachs and Rose Ausländer* by Kathrin M. Bower, 2000.

*   *   *

Nelly Sachs was one of the two famous German-language poets whose works focused on the Nazi genocide against the Jews (Paul Celan was the other). She was celebrated as the voice of the suffering of the Jewish people when she received the Nobel prize for literature in 1966 (together with the Israeli novelist S.Y. Agnon). Her poetry was then characterized as a representation of the "world-wide tragedy of the Jewish people," but has largely been forgotten since, while Celan's fame has lasted. This may be due to the appeal of Celan's poetry to academic criticism. Celan, who was a good friend of Sachs, was a *poeta doctus,* which Sachs, a mystic poet, was not. She was raising the issue of mystic poetry in a century averse to mysticism. Her poetry invited either celebration or rejection rather than critical reading. Nonetheless, hers is an authentic poetic voice and her achievements cannot be denied. As Marie Syrkin has said, "the literary virtue of Sachs is that she has managed to transmute personal anguish into personal vision" (*Midstream,* 8 [3], 1967).

Sachs's poetry can be divided into three periods. The poetry of the first period (1943–49) is dedicated to the memory of the victims of the Holocaust. The theme of death is at the centre of all these poems. In order to avoid any misunderstanding about the kind of death referred to, the poet avoids metaphors, and identifies the objects of the extermination camps: the fingers pointed at the victims at the selection ramps, the gas chambers deceptively constructed as showers, and the smoke stacks of the crematoria. Only victimization allows transfiguration: the poet's brothers and sisters escape on "the road for refugees of smoke," "freedom-ways for Jeremiah and Job's dust" ("O die Schornsteine").

The second period, in the 1950s, was a phase of experimentation under the influence of Jewish mysticism, especially the Kabbala. The author of the *Zohar,* one of the central 13th-century texts of the Kabbala, becomes a model. Opposing modes of existence are unified: fleeing is experienced as homecoming, exile as homeland. The poet holds, as Sachs says, "instead of a homeland / The metamorphoses of the world" ("Flucht und Verwandlung"). Metamorphosis is one of the central concepts of this period, represented most often by the butterfly.

Sachs's late poetry was written in the 1960s after a nervous breakdown and a long stay in a sanatorium. Many poems deal with experiences in hospital, showing the development of an individual language expressing a universal mysticism. The poems are often based on commonplace incidents of everyday life, interpreted in terms of their mystic message. The four-part cycle, entitled "Glühende Rätsel" ("Glowing Enigmas"), epitomizes this tendency. In their laconic brevity, the poems of this cycle represent the best of her later poetry.

Sachs's drama, which is exclusively lyric, can also be divided into three periods, with the first period around 1943, the second covering 1944–55, and the last 1956–62. The first is represented by her mystery play *Eli*, written in 1943, which deals with the persecution of an innocent child and the martyrdom of Israel. Set in the market place of a small Polish town after the Holocaust, the play begins with a few Jewish survivors trying to rebuild their houses. The plot revolves around the death of eight-year-old Eli, who was killed during the German occupation. His murderer is sought by Michael, a survivor who may be one of the 36 righteous men on whom, according to Jewish legends, the world rests. The murderer, when discovered in Germany, is destroyed by his own sense of guilt, not by the revenge of the survivors. His death by guilt marks the return of trust in good on earth.

The plays of the second period deal mostly with religious ritual, even in modern settings, while the plays of the last period are mostly pantomimes, employing dancers and even marionettes. Although Sachs considered Samuel Beckett a model, her plays never achieved a comparable success, in spite of their modernist form. Her drama never found a home on the German or international stage, partially because Sachs was first and foremost a lyric poet.

—Ehrhard Bahr

SADE, Marquis de (Donatien Alphonse-François), (Comte de Sade)

Born: Paris, France, 2 June 1740. **Education:** Educated at Collège Louis-le-Grand, Paris, 1750–54; at a military school for light cavalry, 1754: 2nd lieutenant, 1755. **Military Service:** Served in the French army during the Seven Years War: Captain, 1759; resigned commission, 1763. **Family:** Married Renée Pélagie Cordier de Launay de Montreuil in 1763 (separated 1790); two sons and one daughter. **Career:** Succeeded to the title Comte, 1767; arrested and imprisoned briefly for sexual offences, but pardoned by the king, 1763; arrested and imprisoned again until set free by the king, 1768; condemned to death for sex offences, 1772, but sentence commuted to imprisonment; held in Miolans, 1772–73 (escaped); convicted again and imprisoned in Vincennes, 1778–84, Bastille, Paris, 1784–89, and Charenton, 1789–90; liberated and joined Section des Piques, 1790: organized cavalry and served as hospital inspector; made a judge, 1793, but condemned for moderation and imprisoned, 1793–94; arrested for obscene work (*Justine*), and imprisoned in Sainte-Pélagie, 1801, and Charenton, from 1803. **Died:** 2 December 1814.

PUBLICATIONS

Collections

Oeuvres complètes. 35 vols., 1953–70.
The Complete Marquis de Sade, edited and translated by Paul J. Gillett. 2 vols., 1966.
Oeuvres complètes. 16 vols., 1966–67.

Oeuvres complètes, edited by Annie Le Brun and Jean-Jacques Pauvert. 12 vols., 1986–91.
Oeuvres, edited by Michel Delon. 3 vols., 1990–92.

Fiction

Justine; ou, Les Malheurs de la vertu (published anonymously). 2 vols., 1791; as *Justine; or, The Misfortunes of Virtue*, translated by Alan Hull Walton, 1964; also translated by Austryn Wainhouse and Richard Seaver, in *The Complete Justine*, 1965; Helen Weaver, 1966.
Aline et Valcour; ou, Le Roman philosophique. 4 vols., 1795.
La Philosophie dans le boudoir. 2 vols., 1795; as *Philosophy in the Bedroom*, translated by Austryn Wainhouse and Richard Seaver, in *The Complete Justine*, 1965.
La Nouvelle Justine; ou, Les Malheurs de la vertu. 4 vols., 1795.
La Nouvelle Justine; ou, Les Malheurs de la vertu, suivie de L'Histoire de Juliette, sa soeur [*ou, Les Prospérités du vice*]. 10 vols., 1797; second part as *Juliette*, translated by Austryn Wainhouse, 1968.
Pauline et Belval; ou, Les Victimes d'un amour criminel: Anecdote parisienne du XVIIIe siècle. 1798.
Les Crimes de l'amour: Nouvelles héroïques et tragiques. 4 vols., 1800; as *The Crimes of Love*, translated by Margaret Crosland, 1996.
Zoloé et ses deux acolytes; ou, Quelques Décades de la vie de trois jolies femmes: Histoire véritable du siècle dernier. 1800.
L'Auteur de "Les Crimes de l'amour" à Villetereque, folliculaire. 1803.
La Marquise de Ganges. 2 vols., 1813.
Dorci; ou, La Bizarrerie du sort. 1881.
Les 120 Journées de Sodome; ou, L'École du libertinage, edited by Eugen Dühren. 1904; edited by Maurice Heine, 3 vols., 1931–35; as *The 120 Days of Sodom*, translated by Pierralessandro Cassavini, 1954; also translated by Austryn Wainhouse and Richard Seaver, in *The 120 Days of Sodom and Other Writings*, 1966.
Dialogue entre un prêtre et un moribund, edited by Maurice Heine. 1926; as *Dialogue Between a Priest and a Dying Man*, translated by Austryn Wainhouse, in *The Complete Justine*, 1965.
Historiettes, contes, et fabliaux, edited by Maurice Heine. 1926; selection, as *De Sade Quartet*, translated by Margaret Crosland, 1963, this translation also published as *The Mystified Magistrate: Four Stories*, 1963.
Les Infortunés de la vertu (stories), edited by Maurice Heine. 1930.
Histoire secrète d'Isabelle de Bavière, reine de France, edited by Gilbert Lély. 1953.
Nouvelles exemplaires, edited by Gilbert Lély. 1958.
The Crimes of Love (three novellas), translated by Lowell Bair and others. 1964.
The Complete Justine, Philosophy in the Bedroom, and Other Writings, translated by Richard Seaver and Austryn Wainhouse. 1965; as *Justine, Philosophy in the Bedroom and Other Stories*, 1990.
Eugenie de Franval, and Other Stories, translated by Margaret Crosland. 1965; as *The Gothic Tales*, 1990.
The 120 Days of Sodom and Other Writings, edited and translated by Austryn Wainhouse and Richard Seaver. 1966.
The Misfortunes of Virtue and Other Early Tales, edited and translated by David Coward. 1992.

Plays

Oxtiern; ou, Les Malheurs du libertinage (produced 1791). 1800.

Other

Correspondence inédite, edited by Paul Bourdin. 1929.
L'Aigle, Mademoiselle . . . (letters), edited by Gilbert Lély. 1949.
Cahiers personnels (1803–04), edited by Gilbert Lély. 1953.
Selected Writings, edited by Margaret Crosland. 1953.
Le Carillon de Vincennes (letters), edited by Gilbert Lély. 1953.
Lettres inédites 1778–1784, edited by Gilbert Lély. 1954.
Cent Onze Notes pour La Nouvelle Justine. 1956.
Écrits politiques (includes *Oxtiern*). 1957.
Mon arrestation du 26 août: Lettre inédite, suivie des Étrennes philosophiques, edited by G. Lély. 1959.
Selected Letters, edited by Margaret Crosland, translated by W.J. Strachan. 1965.
Journal inédit, edited by Georges Daumas. 1970.
Opuscules et lettres politiques. 1979.
Lettres et mélanges littéraires, edited by Georges Daumas and Gilbert Lély. 3 vols., 1980.
Lettres inédites et documents. 1990.
Letters from Prison, translated with introduction by Richard Seaver. 1999.

*

Bibliography: *The Marquis de Sade: A Bibliography* by E. Pierre Chanover, 1973; *The Marquis de Sade: The Man, His Works and His Critics: An Annotated Bibliography* by Colette Verger Michael, 1986.

Critical Studies: *The Marquis de Sade: A Study in Algolania* by Montague Summers, 1920; *The Life and Ideas of the Marquis de Sade* by Geoffrey Gorer, 1934; *Vie du Marquis de Sade* by Gilbert Lély, 1952; *Must We Burn Sade?*, by Simone de Beauvoir, translated by Annette Michelson, 1953; *The Marquis de Sade* by Donald Thomas, 1976, revised edition, 1992; *De Sade: A Critical Biography* by Ronald Hayman, 1978; *The Sadeian Woman* by Angela Carter, 1979; *Intersections: A Reading of Sade with Bataille, Blanchot, and Klossowski* by Jane Gallop, 1981; *The Marquis de Sade* by Lawrence W. Lynch, 1984; *Soudain un bloc d'abîme, Sade* by Annie Le Brun, 1986, translated as *Sade: A Sudden Abyss*, 1990; *Sade: His Ethics and Rhetoric* by Colette V. Michael, 1989; *Of Glamor, Sex, and De Sade* by Timo Airaksinen, 1991; *Sade My Neighbour*, by Pierre Klossowski, translated by Alphonso Lingis, 1991; *Marquis de Sade: A Biography* by Maurice Lever, translated by Arthur Goldhammer, 1993; *The Marquis de Sade: A Biography and a Note of Hope* by Robert del Quiaro, 1994; *Sade's Wife: The Woman Behind the Marquis* by Margaret Crosland, 1995; *Sade and the Narrative of Transgression*, edited by David B. Allison, Mark S. Roberts and Allen S. Weiss, 1995; *The Philosophy of the Marquis de Sade* by Timo Airaksinen, 1995; *The Marquis de Sade's Elements of Style* by Derek Pell, 1996; *Writing the Orgy: Power and Parody in Sade* by Lucienne Frappier-Mazur, translated by Gillian C. Gill, 1996; *At Home with the Marquis de Sade: A Life* by Francine du Plessix Gray, 1998; *Sade: A Biographical Essay* by Laurence L. Bongie, 1998; *The Fan-Maker's Inquisition: A Novel of the Marquis de Sade* by Rikki Ducornet, 1999; *Must We Burn Sade?*, edited by Deepak Narang Sawhney, 1999.

* * *

The Marquis de Sade, like Edgar Allan Poe, is one of those writers whose importance is out of all proportion to the actual literary quality of his compositions. As a novelist Sade is a hopeless amateur: his plots are underdeveloped, his characterization is perfunctory, his settings are purely conventional, and his prose style is undistinguished. Judged solely as a writer of fiction Sade is stolidly third rate, and even the sensational nature of his subject-matter would not have ensured his survival as anything but a moderately competent pornographer were it not for the manic lucidity of his vision of man as a creature of intrinsic and irredeemable evil who—Sade argues at tedious length—must cast aside the last shreds or morality if he is to be true to himself.

In fact, Sade is a sort of inverted *philosophe*, a monstrous child of his time. Where the Encyclopedists, Voltaire, Rousseau, and others urged the basic goodness and perfectibility of mankind and advanced a faith in reason and sensibility, Sade turned their views on their heads. For him, human beings are fundamentally evil and any goodness is purely apparent or calculatedly feigned; if genuinely guided by reason and not a watered-down deism, people would be true to their basic nature and deceive, humiliate, and exploit their fellow human beings in the quest for the only thing of true value, sensual gratification of the cruellest imaginable kind. To call him a pessimist is to do Sade an injustice: far from lamenting this state of affairs, he welcomed it and celebrated it in his voluminous writings; and to a certain extent, indeed, he fulfilled his own preaching in his personal lifestyle, although whether he was actually more scandalous than the average petty libertine of the period is open to question. The evidence, such as it is, would seem to indicate that the man whose name gave rise to the term was a rather pathetic sadist in real life.

Of course, Sade did not invent sadism, but he was the first to demonstrate with graphic precision that human beings can and do draw intense erotic pleasure from making others suffer. Most of his wicked torturers are men (although not always so: Juliette is no phallocrat, for instance); since men were socially dominant in his day he tends to present them as sexually dominant too. A typical situation in his novels is that of men who can only attain orgasm when stimulated manually by one woman as they watch another being flogged with vicious cruelty so that each stroke of the whip literally brings their ejaculation to bursting point. This is unsavoury stuff, and it is not to uphold but to betray liberal values to gloss over the sheer nastiness of Sade's vision. Simone de Beauvoir once asked rhetorically whether we should burn Sade's books, and naturally one agrees with her that we should not, so long as we recognize that he catalogues and glorifies behaviour which not only the Nazis but ordinary criminals like the British ''moors murderers'' have indulged in in real earnest. Sade saw, and described, what people are capable of; therefore in a paradoxical way we owe him a debt of gratitude, but this does not mean that his books, like Hitler's *Mein Kampf*, are anything more than frightening aberrations of the human spirit.

—John Fletcher

See the essay on *Justine*.

SA'DI, Shaikh Muslih-al-Din

Born: Shiraz, southern Persia (now Iran), in 1209. **Education:** Educated locally; studied Islamic and Arabic literature at the Nizāmiyya College in Baghdad. **Career:** Travelled widely throughout the Middle East, North Africa, and South Asia, 1226–56, then returned to Shiraz to write of his adventures. **Died:** 1292.

PUBLICATIONS

Verse

Būstān [The Orchard], as *Bustan*, translated by H. Wilberforce Clarke (prose). 1879, reprinted 1985; also translated by G.S. Davie (verse), 1882; as *The Bustan of Sadi*, translated by A. Hart Edwards, 1911; as *Morals and Tales Adorned: The Bustan of Sa'di*, translated by G.M. Wickens, 1974; selections in *Stories From Sadi's Bustan and Gulistan*, translated by R. Levy, 1928.

Gulistān, edited by Ghulām Husayn Yūsufī. 1989; as *Gulistan*, translated by Francis Johnson, 1863; also translated by J.T. Platt, 1873; as *Gulistan or Rose Garden of Sa'di*, translated by E. Retiatsek, 1964; selections in *Tales from the Gulistan or Rose Garden of Sheikh Sa'di of Shiraz*, translated by Richard Burton, 1888; in *Stories from Sadi's Bustan and Gulistan*, translated by R. Levy, 1928; part as *Kings and Beggars*, translated by A.J. Arberry, 1945.

Kulliyāt, edited by J.A. Harrington. 2 vols., 1791–95; also edited by M.A. Furughi, 1941; selections, as *Badāyi': The Odes of Sheik Muslihud-Din Sa'di Shiraz*, 1905, and *Tayibāt*, 1926, both edited and translated by Lucas White King.

*

Critical Study: *The Poet Sa'di: A Persian Humanist* by John D. Yohannan, 1987.

*   *   *

Shaikh Muslih al-Din Sa'di of Shiraz, known as Sa'di, is one of the greatest poets of classical Persian literature. He was born in 1209 in Shiraz, southern Persia, finished his elementary education in Shiraz, and then went to Nizāmiyya College in Baghdad, known as the most important centre of education in the Islamic world. Sa'di was well educated, and was familiar with the Qur'ānic tradition, Islamic law, history, and Arabic and Persian literature. He travelled widely and visited many people and places, including India, Syria, Hijaz, Asia Minor, Balkh, Yemen, Mecca, and North Africa. During one of his travels he was captured by the Crusaders and was put to digging trenches in Tripoli. He spent almost 30 years travelling, starting in 1226, and his encounter with different people and cultures gave him a breadth of knowledge that can be best seen in his works. In 1256 he returned to Shiraz where, under the protection of the ruler of Fars, Attābak Abu Sa'd ibn Zangi, and at the request of his friends, he wrote down the results of his extensive travels in two books, *Būstān* (*Bustan*; literally "The Orchard"), completed in 1257, and *Gulistān* (*Rose Garden*) completed in 1258.

Sa'di the poet is an educator and an admonisher. He admonishes kings, dervishes, the rich and the poor alike. A humanist striving to establish justice, ethical virtues, and moral conduct in society, he used his literary talent in the service of man's moral education. In his work he traces the origin of all human beings to Adam and compares them to various limbs of a single body. A pain in a limb will affect the whole body; therefore men must treat each other with affection and compassion. Story-telling becomes a means with which Sa'di conveys his humanistic and ethical messages. From every story he draws a moral point. He advocates virtues such as righteousness, patience, charity, justice, contentment, and compassion, and condemns selfishness, miserliness, greed, and gluttony. All types of characters can be seen in his works, including kings, viziers, ascetics, slaves, merchants, craftsmen, soldiers, beasts, and birds. There are young, old, generous, hypocritical, and compassionate characters. Sa'di's extensive travels provided him with a deep insight into man's nature, and make his descriptions vivid and realistic.

Sa'di was also a great stylist and poet who produced literary masterpieces in both prose and verse. His style is eloquent, elegant, and simple and he has a talent for putting the most boring ethical principles into a lively and charming language. His language, being close to the spoken language, seems deceptively simple, but a second reading shows Sa'di's unrivalled rhetoric. His images, metaphors, and symbols are simple but expressed in a delicate and charming language. His language flows naturally with no signs of artificiality. His rhetoric is, in fact, a sharp break from the sophisticated and difficult rhetoric of his predecessors. Many of his phrases have become maxims and proverbs in Persian.

An outline of Sa'di's major works will illustrate his basic humanitarian philosophy and literary achievement. *Bustan*, Sa'di's major work in verse, contains over 4,000 rhyming couplets divided into ten chapters. It is a didactic work which illustrates Sa'di's humanitarian and sublime literary style at its best. It is a mixture of practical wisdom, political advice, and ethics. The moral point is usually conveyed by means of an anecdote, sometimes in dialogue form. Sa'di's first-person narrator in *Bustan* is not always autobiographical, and usually represents man in general. Each chapter contains anecdotes thematically related to a topic. The work deals with a range of themes and topics, including justice, beneficence, love, humility, contentment, education, gratitude, and repentance. The first two chapters deal mainly with monarchs and just government. The importance of justice becomes apparent when one remembers the absolute power of kings in medieval Persia. Sa'di believes that a king is like a tree with the people at its roots. No tree can survive without roots; a king depends on his subjects and his primary concern must be their welfare. In another chapter he discusses the education of children and the role of parents and teachers in nurturing moral virtues in children. According to Sa'di, worldly and moral education must be combined to ensure a better future for the next generation.

Sa'di's rhetoric in *Rose Garden* is unique in Persian literature. This book is a mixture of prose and verse, with the story usually told in prose and the moral point expressed in verse. The verses are mostly in Persian although they include a few Arabic poems as well. *Rose Garden*, like *Bustan*, is didactic, and consists of moral anecdotes, ethical advice, and practical wisdom. This book, which has eight chapters, deals with the manners of kings, the ethics of dervishes, contentment, silence, love, youth, old age, education, and conducts of life. Justice is again Sa'di's primary concern. In the first chapter he invites kings to justice by offering examples of just and caring kings, and warns them against tyranny. In the second chapter he addresses dervishes and pious men and reminds them of their spiritual responsibility. In his other chapters he elaborates on several other moral virtues.

In his panegyric poems (*qasida*), Sa'di continues his admonishment through admiring the virtues of just kings and pious men. He neither exaggerates nor falsifies the truth, for his aim was not merely to please the king; rather he encourages him to adopt ethical virtues and warns him against injustice. In fact, he never praises a cruel or selfish king. He does, however, praise the Fars' Attābak dynasty, who actually did the people of Fars a great service by negotiating with Mongol invaders, thus saving not only Fars but the literary heritage of Persia from total annihilation. In his criticism of unjust kings and corrupt religious figures Sa'di is blunt. Panegyrism becomes a means in his hands to serve a higher purpose, an invitation to practise moral virtues.

Sa'di is the unquestionable master of the *ghazal* (ode or lyric), composing over 700. Most of his *ghazals* deal with passionate and physical love, description of the beloved's beauty, and the suffering of separation. The images and similes he creates are vivid, pictorial, beautiful, and concise. Sa'di's rich symbolic language has given some scholars the impression that he is a mystical poet and that the subject of his *ghazals* is divine love. However, Sa'di is more a humanist than a mystic; he is concerned more with practical issues of life than with metaphysics. His *ghazal* is the story of a lover's emotions and feelings.

Sa'di the poet is a moralizer whose aim is to improve society by promoting moral virtues. He is a humanist who thinks that man's foremost responsibility is to understand his fellow humans' problems and needs, and that his primary duty is to help anyone he finds in trouble. Sa'di is a messenger of justice, peace, understanding, and love.

—Alireza Anushiravani

See the essay on *Rose Garden*.

SAER, Juan José

Born: Serodino, Santa Fe, Argentina, 28 June 1937. **Education:** Attended school in Santa Fe and studied Law at University of Litoral, Santa Fe, Argentina. **Family:** Married to Laurence Gueguen in a second marriage, one daughter; one son from his first marriage. **Career:** Taught at Universidad del Litoral, Argentina; moved to Paris and later on began to teach at Université de Rennes, France, where he spent most of his academic career, 1968. **Awards:** Nadal prize, for *La ocasión*, 1988.

PUBLICATIONS

Collections

Narraciones 1 y 2. 1983.

Fiction

En la zona. 1960.
Responso. 1964.
Palo y hueso. 1965.
La vuelta completa. 1966.
Unidad de lugar. 1967.
Cicatrices. 1969.
El limonero real. 1974.
La Mayor. 1976.
Nadie nada nunca. 1980; as *Nobody, Nothing, Never*, translated by Helen Lane.
El entenado. 1983; as *The Witness*, translated by Margaret Jull Costa, 1991.
Glosa. 1986.
La ocasión. 1988; as *The Event*, translated by Helen Lane, 1995.
Lo imborrable. 1993.

La pesquisa. 1995; as *The Investigation*, translated by Helen Lane, 1999.
Las nubes. 1997.
Cuentos completos. 2001.

Poetry

El arte de narrar. 1977.

Essays

El río sin orillas. 1991.
El concepto de ficción. 1997.

*

Bibliography: *Juan José Saer por Juan José Saer*, edited by Jorge Lafforgue, 1986.

Critical Studies: *Juan José Saer: El limonero real* by Graciela Montaldo, 1986; *Genealogías culturales: Argentina, Brasil y Chile en la novela contemporánea (1981–1991)* by Florencia Garramuño, 1997; *Narraciones viajeras (César Aira y Juan José Saer)* by Nancy Martínez, 2000; *El Arte de Bregar* by Arcadio Díaz Quiñores, 2000.

*   *   *

Juan José Saer is one of the most innovative voices of Latin American contemporary fiction. He was born in Serodino, a small town in Santa Fe Province, Argentina, in a family of Syrian immigrants. In 1949 his family moved to Santa Fe, the city where he developed most of his career in Argentina. He began writing poetry in the 1950s and was linked to groups of avant-garde poets like ''Adverbio'' and to the magazine *Poesía Buenos Aires*, directed by Raúl Gustavo Aguirre. In 1954 he began to publish poems, short stories, and essays in the newspaper *El Litoral* of Santa Fe. In this period he met the poet Juan L. Ortiz, a strong influence on the group of intellectuals he belonged to, along with the poet Hugo Gola, the film director Raúl Beceyro and other young writers and journalists. In 1962 he settled in Colastiné, a small town on the coast of Paraná river in Santa Fe. In those years he began teaching History of Film and Film Criticism at the Instituto de Cinematografía of the Universidad del Litoral. In 1968 he received a scholarship that allowed him to move to Paris, where he still lives. He never returned to live permanently in Argentina.

Saer never lived in Buenos Aires and, in a sense, his literature occupies a peripheral position in respect to canonical voices of Argentine literature, like Jorge Luis Borges or Julio Cortázar. He has been compared with other Argentine writers from the provinces like Antonio Di Benedetto and Héctor Tizón. His work can by identified with that of other writers that although being contemporaries of the so called Latin American Literary Boom of the 60s, adopted divergent literary forms, with a closer approach to realism. In the same manner, his position in the cultural domain is distanced from the literary market and his work has been appreciated with great interest primarily in academic circles. During a long period of time he was considered a writer to be read only by other writers. His narrative production starts in 1960, with the publication of *En la zona* [In the Zone], his first volume of short stories.

Since then Saer has been publishing with regularity literary pieces transversed by a set of constant thematic and formal interests, which have defined him as an author with a solid literary project. A great part of his narrative work can be read as a saga, which places the center of attention on a geographic region, with similarities to Santa Fe, on the banks of Paraná river, in the northeast of Argentina. In texts like *La vuelta completa*, *Cicatrices*, and *Nadie nada nunca* (*Nobody, Nothing, Never*), and *Glosa* a same group of characters—young, middle class intelectuals from the provinces—are protagonists of the argument and are the object of a sequence of passages that narrate different episodes that take place under the same scenario but under different historical circumstances. In other cases he maintains unaltered the spacial setting and varies the social status of the protagonists—such is the case of *El limonero real*, where he narrates the daily life of a group of semi-analphabetic farmers who inhabit the islands of the region— or the historical time—such is the case of *El entenado* (*Witness*). This novel has been considered one of his major pieces and focuses on an episode of the disovery of this "zone," where most of his narratives take place. Even though it is his eleventh book, in a chronological sense he describes the origins of the region that represents the basis of his narration. The argument recreates the story of a young Spaniard captured by the Colastiné Natives in times of the Conquest and Discovery of America, and his latter return to Spain, where he writes the memories of his experience. Although the novel has certain similarities with the genre of historical novels, in fact it is quite different. *Witness* belongs to a type of narrative with a complex relation with the past, that rewrites chronicles and documents from the conquest. That becomes a form of exploration and questioning, particularly in relation to the perception of others and its role in the construction of identity. More recent works, such as *La ocasión* (*The Event*) and *Las nubes*, Saer has introduced representations of the past.

The critics have observed a clear cut in his work, determined by his exile. A first juvenile period can be traced up to *Unidad de lugar*. His next book, *Cicatrices*, was published in Buenos Aires when Saer had already settled in France, and from that point onwards, a new cycle began in which two of his major concerns are highlighted, experience and perception. At least two of his books take the military dictatorship in Argentina as a subject: *Nobody, Nothing, Never* makes indirect reference to torture and the Dirty War, and *Glosa* refers to political activism, the *desaparecidos* and exile. But the central problem that runs through his literary production is representation and the capacity of verbal language to express reality. This interest, which has provoked comparisons with the French *nouveau roman* and with authors such as Alain Robbe-Grillet and Nathalie Sarraute, conforms the most persistent nucleus of his literature: a sophisticated theoretical reflection about the processes of literary construction.

Besides his narrative work, Saer has published a book of poetry, *El arte de narrar*, a long essay titled *El río sin orillas* and has written articles of literary criticism collected in *El concepto de ficción*. He has also worked as a film co-script writer in *Les Trottoirs de Saturne* (Hugo Santiago; París: 1985) and as a university professor at Université de Rennes in France. His work has been translated into French, English, German, Italian, and Portuguese.

—Alvaro Fernández Bravo

SAIGYŌ

Also lnown as Saigyō Shōnin. Other Buddhist names: En'i and Kensei Hōshi. **Born:** Satō Norikiyo, probably in Kyōto, Japan, 1118; son of samurai lord Satō Yasukiyo. **Education:** Raised in a samurai household; studied martial arts as well as traditional poetry; later, studied Buddhist texts as lay-monk. **Family:** Married; one son; according to tradition, he abandoned both when taking the tonsure. **Career:** Retainer to aristocratic Tokudaiji house beginning in mid-teens; taken into Imperial Gate Guards, 1135; entered service as personal bodyguard to Retired Emperor Go-Toba, 1137; later served Emperor Sutoku; took tonsure as a lay Buddhist monk and began life as a literatus, living in cottages in and around Kyōto, beginning in 1140; travelled to Mutsu in northeastern Honshū in mid-1140s; settled in Shingon temple complex on Mt. Kōya, Kii Province, in the fall of 1147; travelled to Sanuki Province and to various other sites along Inland Sea, including gravesite of his former patron, Emperor Sutoku, and the birthplace of Kōbō Daishi, founder of the Shingon sect of Buddhism in Japan, 1168–71; settled in Futaminoura, Ise Province, at time of Genpei War, in early 1180s; traveled to Michinoku, on subscription tour to raise money for rebuilding of Tōdaiji Temple in Nara, 1186–87; moved back to Saga, near Kyōto, 1187; moved into cottage near Hirokawa Temple, in Kawachi, 1189. **Died:** 16th day of Second Lunar Month, 1190.

PUBLICATIONS

Poetry Collections

Sankashū (manuscript). c. 1178; revised thereafter; edited by Itō Yoshio, 1947; edited by Gotō Shigeo, 1961.
Sankashinchūshū (manuscript; excerpts from *Sankashū*). c. 1178.
Mimosusogawa uta-awase (manuscript; mock poem contest with judgments by Fujiwara no Shunzei.). 1187.
Miyagawa uta-awase (manuscript; mock poem contest with judgments by Fujiwara no Teika). 1189.
Ihon sankashū (manuscript; excerpts from *Sankashū*, with additional new poems). Date uncertain.
Kikigakishū (manuscript). Dates uncertain.
Kikigaki zanshū (manuscript). Date uncertain.
Saigyō Shōnini shū (manuscript). Date uncertain.
Saigyō zenshū, edited by Kubota Jun. 1982.
Sankashinichūshū, edited by Kondo Jun'ichi. 1991.

Other

Saigyō Shōnin danshō (manuscript), with critical comments recorded by Saigyō's disciple, Ren'a. c. 1225–28.

*

Critical Studies: *Saigyō hōshi* by Kubota Utsubo, 1943; *Saigyō* by Kazamaki Keijirō, 1944; "Saigyō and the Buddhist Value of Nature" by William LaFleur in *History of Religions* 13:2, 1973, and 13:4, 1974; "The Death and Lives of Saigyō: The Genesis of a Buddhist Sacred Biography" by William LaFleur in *The Biographical Process: Studies in the History and Psychology of Religion*, 1976; *Saigyō: Mirror for the Moon, A Selection of Poems by Saigyō, 1118–1190* by William LaFleur, 1977; *Saigyō no shisōteki kenkyū* by Mezaki Tokue, 1978; *Saigyō Sankashū nyūmon* by Kubota Jun, 1978; *Saigyō waka no keisei to juyō* by Yamaki Kōichi, 1987, *Saigyō: Poems of a Mountain Home* by Burton Watson, 1991.

* * *

Saigyō is that rarity, a poet who is popular with both the general public and the most exacting of literary critics. In his own day, he was hailed by contemporaries as one of the finest practitioners of the courtly *uta* (or *waka*; the 5–7–5–7–7 syllable, five-line form that was the dominant classical genre), as evidenced by the decision of the compilers of the *Shin kokinshū*, the 8th imperial collection of the genre, to include more of his poems than those of any other poet. In later centuries his reputation remained stable, and today he is second only to Matsuo Bashō in popularity with the Japanese public.

Saigyō was born into a high-ranking military family and was trained in the martial arts as a youth. Like most other men of his class, however, he also studied poetic composition, which was considered an important accomplishment for anyone aspiring to success in the capital city of Kyōto. His mastery of poetic skills, as well as campaigning by wealthy relatives, served him well, and he began service at the imperial court in his mid-teens, first in the Gate Guards and later in the personal bodyguard of several emperors. This direct contact with the culture of the imperial court was obviously crucial in his development as a poet.

But the most pivotal event in Saigyō's career came when he gave up his court appointments and opted for the life of a lay monk, for motivations that the historical record does not make clear. Some say the reasons had to do with the loss of a friend, others with political reversals, but the only sure thing is that in his early twenties he left the world of courtly office forever. He maintained contact with many courtiers, including Fujiwara no Shunzei and other prominent poets of the day, but spent the rest of his life in various cottages and temples, living the life of what scholars call *suki*, or artistic connoisseur.

After leaving court life, Saigyō dedicated himself entirely to religious devotions and to poetry. Some clerics of the time taught that time spent in artistic pursuits was time better spent reading scripture, but Saigyō was among those who believed that the Way of poetry was as legitimate a path to enlightenment as any other. In this he reveals the influence of the Tendai Buddhist doctrine of non-duality, which sees all distinctions in a world that is essentially illusory as equally without substance and therefore recognizes any Way, if devoutly followed, as authentic.

Some of Saigyō's poems express doctrines explicitly, but more hint at them obliquely. The most constant of his themes is *mujō*, or transience, often expressed through the description of incessant change in the natural landscape. The two images that most dominate his poems—cherry blossoms and the moon—do so because they so obviously symbolize the principle that all that flourishes must decay, the cherry blossoms because they are in bloom for only a few days and the moon because it is set on a course that makes it wax and wane. The images are very much from the courtly tradition, but in his poems they are almost always put to the service of a Buddhist thematic. Even the quality of *sabi*, or loneliness, which is so often seen as the governing aesthetic ideal in his poems, is ultimately a Buddhist concept. For the stark, monochromatic landscapes that embody that courtly ideal also suggest the idea that behind the natural facade (flowering trees, the red and gold leaves of autumn, the lush greenery of summer) is the grim, gray reality of inevitable decay.

The proper response to the doctrine of mujō would of course be to shun all attachments to the world of appearances, which can only lead to sadness and frustration. But in Saigyō's poems we often encounter the persona of a monk who is not altogether able to do so—what might be called the reluctant recluse. Living in the hills in order to escape worldly entanglements, he finds himself secretly wishing for a friend; looking at failing blossoms, he realizes their essential ephemerality but also cannot deny their beauty. Even those who have cast the world and its cares aside, he suggests, still find themselves moved at times by scenes of beauty or sadness. Everywhere, the senses—as opposed to the intellect, which yields better to training—are overcome by the sheer detail of everyday experience. Saigyō was not the first to articulate this theme, nor would he be the last, but he does so with more skill than perhaps any other Japanese poet.

Although known primarily for poems of great simplicity, Saigyō was a very sophisticated poet who was in command of all the techniques of the court tradition, from the use of *kakekotoba* (''pivot words'' which serve as the end to one phrase and the beginning of another) to *jo* (the ''preface,'' an extended metaphorical entrée into a poem). Even many of his so-called ''nature'' poems were in fact written on conventional topics, which makes them treatments of ideas rather than examples of straightforward description—not depictions of what he was actually seeing before him but rather of what he imagines before him, mediated by a long poetic tradition. Likewise, some of his most famous travel poems, about famous places from the mountains of Yoshino to the rice fields of the far north, were likely written for poetry gatherings in Kyōto and elsewhere. Unlike many other court poets, however, he did actually travel a great deal, and his fame as one who knew the rigors and loneliness of life on the road is still fundamental to his reputation today. This is the primary reason why he was looked to as a model by later poets such as Sōgi, the great 15th-century master of linked verse, and the *haiku* poet Bashō, who also spent much time as itinerant literati.

Saigyō's personal anthology, which he put together in 1178, is titled *Sankashū*—the ''Mountain Home Collection.'' It contains more than 1,500 poems, some of which contain prefatory material, usually only indicating the topic of the poem, when it is known, but also occasionally giving background material useful in interpretation. As is the case with most such works, the poems are organized by thematic category, beginning with the four seasons and going on to Love and Miscellaneous topics. The fact that so many of the poems are prefaced with the comment, ''Topic Unknown,'' indicates one great difference between his practice and that of courtier poets, who nearly always composed on pre-arranged topics. But in terms of diction, syntax, imagery, and subject matter, the collection shows the influence of courtly conventions on his work. His other collections, put together as sequels to or excerpts from *Sankashū*, are similar in every way.

Although Saigyō left no critical writing of his own, a disciple named Ren'a recorded some of his teachings in a short work titled *Saigyō Shōnin danshō*—''Chats with Reverend Saigyō''—which in all show him to be less a scholar or critic than a poet. As models for style, he recommends the imperial anthologies, especially the first one, *Kokinshū* (''The Collection of Ancient and Modern Times,'' 905), which had by his time already been established as the foremost work of the native canon; and he is also conventional in stressing that the first concern of composition should be the creation of beauty—not philosophical profundity or even religious insight. In this too he shows the influence of Buddhist doctrines that praise art for its ability to ''embody'' the truth in form rather than stating it in terms of abstract propositions.

—Steven D. Carter

SAINT AUGUSTINE

See AUGUSTINE, St.

SAINT-EXUPÉRY, Antoine (Jeane-Baptiste Marie Roger) de

Born: Lyon, France, 29 June 1900. **Education:** Educated in Lyons, 1908; Notre-Dame de Saint-Crois, Le Mans, 1909–14, baccalauréat, 1917; Lycée Saint-Louis, Paris, 1917, evacuated to Lycée Lakanal, Sceaux, 1918; studied architecture at the École des Beaux-Arts, Paris. **Military Service:** Served in the French Air Force in North Africa and South America, 1921; qualified as a pilot, 1922. **Family:** Married Consuelo Suncin de Sandoval in 1931. **Career:** Director of operations for airline, Aeroposta Argentina, 1929–31; test pilot, Latécoère, Toulouse, 1932–33; public relations officer, Air France, 1934; special correspondent, *Paris-Soir*, during Spanish Civil War, Madrid, 1936–37; contributor, *L'Intransigeant*, Paris. Crash-landed during attempt to break Paris-Saigon air record, 1935; broke the New York-Paris speed record, 1939. **Awards:** Prix feminina, 1931; Grand prix, Académie française, 1939. Chevalier, Légion d'honneur, 1930. **Died:** Disappeared during a reconnaissance flight over southern France, 31 July 1944.

PUBLICATIONS

Collections

Oeuvres. 1953.
Oeuvres. 1959.
Cahiers Saint-Exupéry. 3 vols., 1980–89.
Oeuvres complètes. 7 vols., 1985–86.

Fiction

Courrier-sud. 1929; as *Southern Mail*, translated by Stuart Gilbert, 1933; revised and translated by Curtis Cate, with *Night Flight*, 1971.
Vol de nuit. 1931; edited by E.M. Bowman, 1963; as *Night Flight*, translated by Stuart Gilbert, 1932; also translated by Gilbert, in *Airman's Odyssey*, 1942; Curtis Cate, with *Southern Mail*, 1971.
Pilote de guerre. 1942; as *Flight to Arras*, translated by Lewis Galantière, 1942; also translated by Galantière, in *Airman's Odyssey*, 1942.
Airman's Odyssey (includes *Wind, Sand and Stars*; *Flight to Arras*; *Night Flight*), translated by Lewis Galantiére and Stuart Gilbert. 1942.
Lettre à un otage. 1943; as *Letter to a Hostage*, translated by John Rodker, in *French Short Stories*, 1948; also translated by Jacqueline Gerst, 1950.
Le Petit Prince. 1943; as *The Little Prince*, translated by Katherine Woods, 1945; also translated by Richard Howard, 2000.

Screenplays: *Courrier-sud*, 1937.

Other

Terre des hommes. 1939; as *Wind, Sand and Stars*, translated by Lewis Galantière, 1939; also translated by Galantière, in *Airman's Odyssey*, 1942.
Citadelle (unfinished). 1948; as *The Wisdom of the Sands*, translated by Stuart Gilbert, 1949.
Lettres de jeunesse 1923–31. 1953.
Carnets. 1953.
Lettres à sa mère. 1955; revised edition, 1984.
Un sens à la vie (articles). 1956; as *A Sense of Life*, translated by Adrienne Foulke, 1965.
Écrits de guerre, 1939–44. 1982; as *Wartime Writings: 1939–44*, translated by Norah Purcell, 1986.

*

Critical Studies: *Passion de Saint-Exupéry* by Jules Roy, 1951, as *Passion et mort de Saint-Exupéry*, 1964; *Fantasie et mythique dans ''Le Petit Prince'' de Saint-Exupéry* by Yves Le Hir, 1954; *The Winged Life* by Richard Rumbold and Margaret Steward, 1954; *Saint-Exupéry par lui-même* by Luc Estang, 1956; *Knight of the Air* by Maxwell A. Smith, 1956, revised edition, 1959; *L'Esthétique d'Antoine de Saint-Exupéry* by Carlo François, 1957; *Antoine de Saint-Exupéry* by Pierre Chevrier, 1958; *Saint-Exupéry* by Marcel Migéo, 1958, translated by Herma Briffault, 1960; *Saint-Exupéry* by R.M. Albérès, 1961; *Saint-Exupéry, mystique sans la foi* by Clement Borgal, 1964; *Saint-Exupéry* by Andre Devaux, 1965; *L'Idéal humain de Saint-Exupéry* by Serge Losic, 1965; *Saint-Exupéry, l'écriture et la pensée* by Jean-Louis Major, 1968; *Antoine de Saint-Exupéry: His Life and Times* by Curtis Cate, 1970; *Saint-Exupéry in America 1942–43: A Memoir* by Adèle Breux, 1971; *Les Relations humaines dans l'oeuvre de Saint-Exupéry* by Réal Ouellet, 1971; *Les Critiques de notre temps et Saint-Exupéry* edited by Bruno Vercier, 1971; *Saint Exupéry: Vol de nuit* by Michael T. Young, 1971; *A Students' Guide to Saint-Exupéry* by Brian Masters, 1972; *Antoine de Saint-Exupéry and David Beaty: Poets of a New Dimension* by Roberta J. Forsberg, 1975; *L'Ésotérisme du Petit Prince* by Yves Monin, 1975; *The Dialectic of ''The Little Prince''* by Edward J. Capestany, 1982; *Antoine de Saint-Exupéry* by Joy D. Marie Robinson, 1984; *Saint-Exupéry, Vol de nuit and Terre des hommes* by S. Beynon John, 1990; *Antoine de Saint-Exupéry: The Life and Death of the Little Prince* by Paul Webster, 1993; *Saint-Exupéry: A Biography* by Stacy Schiff, 1994; *The Little Prince: A Reverie of Substance* by James E. Higgins, 1996; *A Parable of Dialogue: The Little Prince Revisited* by Michel de Gigord, 1999; *Chaos, Cosmos, and Saint-Exupéry's Pilot-hero: A Study in Mythopoeia* by John R. Harris, 1999; *The Tale of the Rose: The Passion that Inspired The Little Prince* by Consuelo de Saint-Exupery, translated by Esther Allen, 2001.

* * *

Antoine de Saint-Exupéry's books were all directly inspired by his experiences as a pilot, firstly on commercial airlines over North Africa and South America and later on reconnaissance missions over France during World War II. As a graphic record of the sheer excitement of flying, they may be compared with such English classics as Cecil Lewis's *Sagittarius Rising* and Richard Hillary's *The Last Enemy* but they aspire to something higher than tales of aerial derring-do. Like other French writers of the inter-war years, most notably André Malraux, Saint-Exupéry combines narratives of extreme physical danger, often experienced at first hand, with reflections on the human condition and a quest for meaning. These features, conveyed via a relatively restricted but remarkably rich reservoir of images, give his diverse writings their impressive coherence.

Jacques Bernis, the hero of his first novel, *Courrier-sud* (*Southern Mail*) is an air-mail pilot who finds fulfilment only when flying. Down on earth, Bernis is literally out of his element: the only love of his life remains beyond his reach. The nightlife of Paris provides no more consolation than the interior of Notre-Dame, and he demands to know "What is the unknown promise that was made to me and that a hidden god does not keep?" The answer would seem to be somewhere beyond death. His plane crashes and the narrator finds his body stretched out on the desert sand beneath the stars. The epitaph he pronounces on Bernis has sometimes been applied by admirers to Saint-Exupéry himself: "Fugitive, Child, and Magician."

Saint-Exupéry's second novel, *Vol de nuit* (*Night Flight*), was much tauter and was commercially very much more successful. Once again, the action consists of commercial pilots battling against the odds, this time over the rugged landscape of South America but a crucial new figure is introduced with the character of Riviére, the charismatic director of operations whose life's mission is to will his pilots to succeed. The psychology and the responsibilities of leadership were to remain among Saint-Exupéy's recurrent preoccupations.

Terre des hommes (*Wind, Sand and Stars*), sometimes inaccurately styled a novel, recounts authentic episodes in the flying careers of Saint-Exupéry himself and of his comrades-in-arms Jean Mermoz and Henri Guillaumet. Mermoz is trapped in a cyclone over the South Atlantic; Guillaumet crashes in the Andes and wills himself to walk to safety simply because he wants his body to be found and so enable his family to claim the insurance money; Saint-Exupéry, by some way the least efficient pilot of the three, crashes in the Libyan desert while attempting to beat the Paris-Saigon record, and is rescued just in time by a wandering Bedouin. Episodes like these, together with reminiscences of his time as a special correspondent during the Spanish Civil War, lead Saint-Exupéry to stress the importance of human solidarity and make him appreciate how travelling through the air increases his love for the sights and sounds of this earth.

Pilote de guerre (*Flight to Arras*) provides a graphic account of a reconnaissance flight Saint-Exupéry made over Arras in May 1940. The mission is vividly described from first to last, from donning his pilot's kit, through briefing, then to flying over towns and villages ablaze and roads choked with refugees. Expecting to be killed, he needs to understand why. In seeking the answer, his thoughts switch from the security of childhood to the affirmation of his belief in mankind, in France, and in the civilisation of which it forms so precious a part. These values are reaffirmed in the slim booklet, *Lettre à un otage* (*Letter to a Hostage*), in which he declares his faith in the brotherhood of man and lyrically expresses his love both for his endangered friends in occupied France and for his beloved North African desert.

That same desert provides the setting for *Le Petit Prince* (*The Little Prince*), sometimes described as "a child's fable for adults." The first-person narrator, who has had to make a forced landing in the desert, meets there a little prince who has fallen to earth from Asteroid B612. Like Bernis in *Southern Mail*, the little prince is quite unimpressed by the earthly version of personal happiness, and he yearns to be reunited with the solitary rose he has left behind unprotected, and like Bernis, he has only one escape-route—death. Written when Saint-Exupéry was cut off from both the country and the people he

most loved, *The Little Prince* has been variously interpreted as a hymn of exile and a lament for lost innocence. Its abiding popularity owes much to the charm of the author's own illustrations of the little prince's aphorisms. Rejecting the narrator's consolation of a whole garden of roses, he observes, "It is the time you've lavished on your very own rose which makes that rose unique" and "One sees truly only with the heart. What's essential remains invisible to the eye."

Saint-Exupéry's fondness for aphorisms, a distinctive feature of his first book, is again apparent in his last, the massively ambitious *Citadelle* (*The Wisdom of the Sands*). It was begun in 1936 and found, far from complete, after his still unexplained disappearance on a reconnaissance flight over southern France in 1944. It is a chaotic collection of fragments and notes on the issues that preoccupied him throughout his career: how to give life dignity and meaning while you can no longer believe in God. The major character is a Berber chieftain ruling over his fortress-city or citadel in the heart of the desert. Like Rivière in *Night Flight*, he is particularly concerned with the need to combine decisive leadership with compassion; unlike Rivière, or Saint-Exupéry's air force commanders, he has no specific cause with which to unite his subordinates. *The Wisdom of the Sands* is very long on meditation but distinctly short of action. Another important character would have been the Geometer whose quest for God and distrust of pure reason is reminiscent of Pascal's *Pensées*, one of Saint-Exupéry's favourite books. The prose is uneven in quality but there is ample evidence of the Biblical cadences and poetic imagery that characterize his best work.

Because of the nature of his professional experience, Saint-Exupéry's world is dominated by virile values. Virtually without exception, his characters are men of action who need to prove themselves by surmounting fearsome obstacles. The few female characters remain peripheral, featuring as either solicitous mother-figures or goddesses to be worshipped from afar. As the evidence from contemporary history progressively undermines Saint-Exupéry's faith in the fundamental goodness of man, his later work reveals his growing awareness of a particularly painful paradox: the spiritual values he came to cherish were directly menaced by the very technology which had made manned flight possible. The crowning irony is that the aeroplanes which first gave sense to his life eventually ended it.

—Robert Gibson

See the essay on *Night Flight*.

SAINT JEROME

See JEROME, St.

SAINT JOHN OF THE CROSS

See JOHN OF THE CROSS, St.

SAINT-JOHN PERSE

Born: Marie-René Aléxis Saint-Léger Léger; near Point-à-Pitre, Guadeloupe, French West Indies, 31 May 1887; brought to France in

1899. **Education:** Educated at lycée in Pau; University of Bordeaux, 1904–10; University of Paris; degrees in law, diploma from École des Hautes Études Commerciales. **Family:** Married Dorothy Milburn Russell in 1958. **Career:** Deputy diplomat in political and commercial division, French Foreign Office, Paris, 1914–16; secretary, French Embassy, Beijing, 1916–21; worked with Foreign Minister Aristide Briand, 1921–32; with Ministry of Foreign Affairs: counsellor, 1925, Chef de Cabinet, 1925–33, minister, 1927, ambassador and secretary-general, 1933–40; deprived of citizenship because of anti-Nazi sentiments, and left France, 1940; moved to Washington, DC, 1941: consultant on French poetry, Library of Congress, 1941–45; citizenship restored, 1945; returned to France, 1957. **Awards:** American Academy award of merit medal, 1950; National grand prize, 1959; International grand prize for poetry (Belgium), 1959; Nobel prize for literature, 1960. Honorary member or fellow: American Academy of Arts and Sciences; American Academy; Modern Language Association; Bavarian Academy. Honorary degree: Yale University, New Haven, Connecticut. Commandeur de l'Ordre des Arts et des Lettres; Grand Officier, Légion d'honneur. KCVO (Knight Commander, Royal Victorian Order), 1927; GBE (Knight Grand Cross, Order of the British Empire), 1938; KCB (Knight Commander of the Bath), 1940. **Died:** 20 September 1975.

PUBLICATIONS

Collection

Selected Poems, edited and translated by Mary Ann Caws. 1982.

Verse

Éloges (as Saint-Léger Léger). 1911; as *Éloges and Other Poems*, translated by Louise Varèse (bilingual edition), 1944, revised edition, 1956.
Anabase. 1924; as *Anabasis*, translated by T.S. Eliot (bilingual edition), 1930, revised editions, 1938, 1949, 1959.
Quatre Poèmes 1941–1944. 1944; as *Exil, suivi de Poème à l'étrangère, Pluies, Neiges*, 1945, revised edition, 1946; edited by Roger Little, 1973; as *Exile and Other Poems*, translated by Denis Devlin (bilingual edition), 1949.
Vents. 1946; as *Winds*, translated by Hugh Chisholm (bilingual edition), 1953.
Oeuvres poétiques. 2 vols., 1953, revised edition, 1960; 3 vols., 1967–70.
Étroits sont los vaisseaux. 1956.
Amers. 1957; as *Seamarks*, translated by Wallace Fowlie (bilingual edition), 1958.
Chronique. 1960; as *Chronique*, translated by Robert Fitzgerald (bilingual edition), 1961.
L'Ordre des oiseaux. 1962; as *Oiseaux*, 1963; as *Birds*, translated by Robert Fitzgerald (bilingual edition), 1966.
Éloges, suivi de la Gloire des fork, Anabase, Exil. 1967.
Chanté par celle qui fut là . . . , translated by Richard Howard (bilingual edition). 1970.
Collected Poems, translated by W.H. Auden and others. 1971.
Chant pour un équinoxe. 1975; as *Song for an Equinox*, translated by Richard Howard, 1977.
Amitié du prince, edited by Albert Henry. 1979.

Other

A Selection of Works for an Understanding of World Affairs since 1914. 1943.
Briand (in English; as Alexis Leger). 1943.
La Publication française pendant la guerre: Bibliographie restreinte 1940–1945. 4 vols., n.d.
On Poetry (Nobel prize acceptance speech), translated by W.H. Auden (bilingual edition). 1961.
Pour Dante. 1965; as *Dante*, translated by Robert Fitzgerald, in *Two Addresses*, 1966.
Two Addresses: On Poetry; Dante, translated by W.H. Auden and Robert Fitzgerald. 1966.
Oeuvres complètes (includes letters). 1972.
Letters, edited and translated by Arthur J. Knodel. 1979.

*

Bibliography: *Saint-John Perse: A Bibliography for Students of His Poetry* by Roger Little, 1971, revised edition, 1982.

Critical Studies: *Saint-John Perse: A Study of His Poetry* by Arthur Knodel, 1966; *Paul Claudel and Saint-John Perse* by Ruth N. Horry, 1971; *Saint-John Perse* by René M. Galand, 1972; *Saint-John Perse* by Roger Little, 1973; *Worlds Apart: Structural Parallels in the Poetry of Paul Valéry, Saint-John Perse, Benjamin Peret, and René Char* by Elizabeth R. Jackson, 1976; *Saint-John Perse and the Imaginary Reader* by Steven Winspur, 1988.

* * *

From his earliest poems, published under the title *Éloges* in 1911, through *Anabase* (*Anabasis*), *Exil* (*Exile*), *Amers* (*Seamarks*), and *Oiseaux* (*Birds*), Saint-John Perse describes and analyses the condition and fate of man in our time. In *Anabasis*, in *Vents* (*Winds*), and in *Seamarks*, the poet attempts to express the wholeness of man, the integral forces of his life and his memory. Moreover, he seeks to project man ahead into the uncharted and the new, into a future impatient to live. Everywhere in these poems there is dramatic movement where man, in his historical and natural environment, plays out the role of his existence.

Saint-John Perse's work relates the secular and spiritual efforts of man to see himself as a part of the natural world, to tame the hostile powers of the world, to worship the endlessly renewed beauty of the world, to conjugate his ambitions and dreams with the changes and modifications of time. This becomes clear in his last long work, *Seamarks*, a massive ceremonial poem that reveals an extraordinary sensibility to historic man.

Seamarks moves far beyond the violence of man's history in order to exalt the drama of his fate, which is looked upon as a march, the march of all humanity. The poet himself, in a brief statement about his poem, calls it *la marche vers la mer*, the march toward the sea. The word sea, *la mer*, is found in the French title *amers* ("seamarks"), those signs on the land, both natural and man-made, that guide navigators as they approach the coastline.

The work of Saint-John Perse seems to be consecrated to pointing out a way to reconcile man with nature, and hence with himself. In his poems man is seen confronting various natural elements—the burning of the desert sands in *Anabasis*, the violence of the winds in *Winds*, and the violence of the sea in *Seamarks*. At the same time he praises the sky and sea, the earth and the winds, the snow and the rains.

In his speech at Stockholm, on the occasion of the Nobel prize award in 1960, Saint-John Perse emphasized the power of the adventure called poetry and claimed it is not inferior to the great dramatic adventures of science. He believed the poet's purpose is to consecrate the alliance between man and creation, with the seamarks indicating that the alliance takes place when the land recognizes its relationship of vassal to the sea.

—Wallace Fowlie

See the essay on *Seamarks*.

SALLUST

Born: Gaius Sallustius Crispus in Amiternum, central Italy, probably in 86 BC. **Career:** Tribune of the plebs, 52 BC; expelled from the Senate in 50 BC, possibly for his political activities in support of Caesar, or because of his action as tribune against Cicero in 52 BC; elected judicial officer (*praetor*) in 47 BC; served in Africa, where he remained as governor of Numidia, 46 BC; returned to Rome and charged with extortion, but escaped through Caesar's intervention; retired from politics on death of Caesar in 44 BC. **Died:** 35 BC.

PUBLICATIONS

Collections

[Works], edited by A. Eussner. 1897; also edited by A. Ernout, 1947, Alfons Kurfess, 1954, and L.D. Reynolds, 1991; edited and translated by J.C. Rolfe [Loeb Edition], 1921; translated by S.A. Handford, 1963.

Works

Bellum Catilinae, edited by Patrick McGushin. 1980; as *Catiline*, edited by T.M. Neatby and B.J. Hayes, 1908; with *Bellum Iugurthinum*, as *The Wars of Catilina and Jugurtha*, edited by Alfons Kurfess, 1957; as *The Conspiracy of Catiline*, with *The War against Jugurtha*, translated by Ian Scott-Kilvert, 1962; as *The Conspiracy of Catiline*, with *The Jugurtha*, translated by S.A. Handford, 1963; as *Bellum Catilinae*, translated by Samuel Johnson, edited by David L. Vander Meulen and G. Thomas Tanselle, 1993; commentaries by Patrick McGushin, 1977, and J.T. Ramsey, 1984.

Bellum Iugurthinum, edited by W.W. Capes. 1884; also edited by W.P. Brooke, 1902, W.C. Summers, 1902, and Leslie Watkiss, 1971; with *Bellum Catilinae*, as *The Wars of Catilina and Jugurtha*, edited by Alfons Kurfess, 1957; as *The War against Jugurtha*, with *The Conspiracy of Catiline*, translated by Ian Scott-Kilvert, 1962; as *The Jugurtha*, with *The Conspiracy of Catiline*, translated by S.A. Handford, 1963; commentary by G.M. Paul, 1984.

Epistulae, Invectivae, edited by P. Cagusi. 1958; also edited by A. Ernout, 1962, and Alfons Kurfess, 1962.

Historiae cum reliquiae (fragments; with commentary), edited by Berthold Maurenbrecher. 2 vols., 1891–93; as *Fragments of the Histories*, translated by J.M. Carter, 1978; as *The Histories*, translated by Patrick McGushin, 2 vols., 1992–94.

*

Bibliography: *A Systematical Bibliography of Sallust, 1879–1964* by Anton D. Leeman, 1965.

Critical Studies: ''The Structure of Sallust's *Historiae*'' by H. Bloch, in *Didascaliae*, 1961; *The Political Thought of Sallust* by Donald C. Earl, 1961; *Sallust* by Ronald Syme, 1964; ''Sallust'' by G.M. Paul, in *Latin Historians*, edited by T.A. Dorey, 1966; *The Prose Rhythm of Sallust and Livy*, 1979, and *Spes frustrata, a Reading of Sallust*, 1987, both by Hans Aili; *The Influence of Thucydides on Sallust* by Thomas F. Scanlon, 1980; *Rhetoric in Classical Historiography* by A.J. Woodman, 1988; *Law, Politics and Power: Sallust and the Execution of the Catilinarian Conspirators* by Andrew Drummond, 1995; *Latin Historians* by C.S. Kraus and A.J. Woodman, 1997.

*   *   *

Sallust is the first Roman historian by whom substantial works survive (through the accidents of transmission, no Roman historian's works survive in entirety). What we have are his shorter accounts of specific episodes, the conspiracy of Catiline (63 BC) and the war between Rome and the Numidian ruler Jugurtha, concluded in 105 BC. His later and most ambitious work, the *Historiae* (*Histories*), was in five books, and covered events from 78 BC onwards. This was, however, incomplete at the author's death and has survived only in short extracts. Inevitably this account will concentrate on the surviving monographs.

Sallust's predecessors in Latin mostly wrote general historical accounts of the rise of Rome, from the legendary foundation to their own times, sometimes with special attention to or expressing partisan views on the events which they had themselves witnessed. Since the historians were themselves often senators and generals, Roman (much more than Greek) history rested on experienced and informed testimony. It was also strongly moralistic; in particular, Sallust admired and imitated the censorious attitude and archaic style of the Elder Cato. On the Greek side, his writing owed most to the great 5th-century historian Thucydides (much in vogue in Rome at the time); Sallust followed him in presenting central issues through antithetical speeches by participants, and in his detailed psychological analysis of moral degeneracy during civil conflict. Thucydides' technique of moral and political generalization was also imitated by Sallust, particularly in the prologues (which deal with the moral qualities needed by a state, and the processes by which these can be corrupted), as well as in a number of moralizing digressions.

Bellum Catilinae (*The Conspiracy of Catiline*) focuses on the anti-hero of the title, presented as a figure of brilliant potential but debased by the immorality of his times. The origins and progress of the conspiracy are analysed vividly but without chronological precision or sociological detail: Sallust is far more interested in dramatic scenes and cynical comment on human weakness. The core of the work is the senatorial debate after the majority of the conspirators are imprisoned; here, Caesar and Cato argue the case for and against clemency. Cato, the advocate of execution, prevails. The conflict prefigures the later political and military clash between the two figures; Sallust's comments on these two eminent Romans emphasize their remarkable qualities and broaden the scope of the monograph beyond its ostensible subject. The work ends with a description of Catiline's defeat and death in battle.

Bellum Iugurthinum (*The War against Jugurtha*), Sallust's second work, is considerably longer and concerns a more remote period before his own lifetime. He deals here with an external war, but one which is hampered by the competition and corruption among Rome's leaders, and by Rome's moral degeneracy. The rise of the "new man" Marius, who takes over command in the war from the noble Metellus, gives an opportunity for criticism of the decadence of the privileged senatorial order (especially in Marius' powerful speech when standing for the consulship). Sallust, however, does not adopt the obvious black versus white antitheses (noble savage versus decadent civilization; corrupt *ancien régime* versus virtuous newcomer). All those involved are deficient in the qualities needed in a great city and an empire. Marius' military prowess is outstanding, but Sallust also hints at the future civil wars between Marius and Sulla, in which his gifts will be turned against his country. The Jugurthine war, of relatively small historical importance, is made into a paradigm case of wartime politics in a corrupt society.

Sallust, like other Roman historians, is a moralist first, a researcher second. His grasp of chronology is weak, his use of evidence unreliable, his descriptions of places, peoples, and battles composed for dramatic and emotive effect. He preserves information and evidence for attitudes which we are glad to have, but his deficiencies make him an untrustworthy source. His undoubted gifts as a narrator, and his terse, epigrammatic analyses of human depravity, however, make his works memorable. They were a powerful influence on Tacitus and held a central place in the educational curriculum for centuries thereafter.

—R.B. Rutherford

SAND, George

Born: Amantine Aurore Lucile Dupin in Paris, France, 1 July 1804. **Education:** Educated at Nohant, her grandmother's estate, and at Couvent des Anglaises, Paris, 1817–20. **Family:** Married Casimir Dudevant in 1822 (judicially separated 1836; died 1871), one son and one daughter; had liaisons with Jules Sandeau, Alfred de Musset, 1833–34, Chopin, 1838–47, Alexandre Manceau, 1849–65, and others. **Career:** Inherited Nohant, 1821; left her husband to live in Paris, 1831: journalist, *Le Figaro*, 1831; adopted pseudonym George (briefly Georges) Sand, 1832; contributor, *Revue des Deux Mondes*, 1832–41; co-editor, *Revue Indépendante*, 1841; contributor, *La République*, 1848; settled at Nohant, 1848; lived in Palaiseau, near Versailles, 1864–67. **Died:** 8 June 1876.

PUBLICATIONS

Collections

The Masterpieces of George Sand, translated by George Burnham Ives. 20 vols., 1900–02.
Oeuvres autobiographiques, edited by Georges Lubin. 2 vols., 1970–71.
Oeuvres complètes. 32 vols., 1978.
The Marquise and Pauline, translated by Sylvie Charron and Sue Huseman. 1999.

Fiction

Rose et Blanche, with Jules Sandeau (jointly as J. Sand). 1831.
Indiana. 1832; as *Indiana*, translated anonymously, 1850.
Valentine. 1832; as *Valentine*, translated by George Burnham Ives, in *The Masterpieces of George Sand*, 1900–02.
Lélia. 1833; revised edition, 1839; as *Lélia*, translated by Maria Espinosa, 1978.
Le Secrétaire intime (includes *Métella; La Marquise; Lavinia*). 1834; *Lavinia* as *Lady Blake's Love-Letters*, translated by Page McCarty, 1884; as *Lavinia*, translated by George Burnham Ives, in *The Masterpieces of George Sand*, 1900–02.
Jacques. 1834; as *Jacques*, translated by Anna Blackwell, 1847.
Leone Leoni. 1835; as *Leone Leoni*, translated by George Burnham Ives, in *The Masterpieces of George Sand*, 1900–02.
André. 1835; as *André*, translated by Eliza A. Ashurst, in *The Works of George Sand*, 1847.
Simon. 1836; as *Simon*, translated by Matilda M. Hays, in *The Works of George Sand*, 1847.
Mauprat. 1837; as *Mauprat*, translated by Matilda M. Hays, in *The Works of George Sand*, 1847; also translated by V. Vaughan, 1870; H.E. Miller, 1891; Stanley Young, 1902; Sylvia Raphael, 1997.
Les Maîtres mosaïstes. 1838; as *The Mosaic Workers*, translated by Eliza A. Ashurst, 1844; as *The Mosaic Masters*, translated by Ashurst, in *The Works of George Sand*, 1847; as *The Master Mosaic Workers*, translated by C.C. Johnstone, 1895.
L'Uscoque. 1838; as *The Uscoque*, translated by J. Bauer, 1850.
La Dernière Aldini. 1839; as *The Last Aldini*, translated by Matilda M. Hays, in *The Works of George Sand*, 1847; as *The Last of the Aldinis*, translated by George Burnham Ives, in *The Masterpieces of George Sand*, 1900–02.
Spiridion. 1839; as *Spiridion*, translated anonymously, 1842.
Pauline. 1840.
Le Compagnon du tour de France. 1841; as *The Companion of the Tour of France*, translated by Matilda M. Hays, in *The Works of George Sand*, 1847; as *The Journeyman Joiner*, translated by Francis G. Shaw, 1849.
Horace. 1842; translated by Zack Rogow, 1995.
Consuelo. 1843; as *Consuelo*, translated by Francis G. Shaw, 1846; also translated by Fayette Robinson, 1851; Frank H. Potter, 1889.
La Comtesse de Rudolstadt. 1844; as *The Countess of Rudolstadt*, translated by Francis G. Shaw, 1847; also translated by Fayette Robinson, 1870; Frank H. Potter, 1891.
Jeanne. 1844; edited by Simone Viernne, 1978.
Lettres à Marcie. 1844; as *Letters to Marcie*, translated by Betsy Wing, 1988.
Le Meunier d'Angibault. 1845; as *The Miller of Angibault*, translated by Edmund R. Larkin, in *The Works of George Sand*, 1847; also translated by M.E. Dewey, 1871.
Teverino. 1845; as *Teverino*, translated anonymously, 1855; as *Jealousy; or, Teverino*, translated by O.S. Leland, 1870.
Le Péché de Monsieur Antoine. 1846; as *The Sin of M. Antoine*, translated by George Burnham Ives, in *The Masterpieces of George Sand*, 1900–02.
Isidora. 1846.
La Mare au diable. 1846; as *The Devil's Pool*, translated by Francis G. Shaw, 1847; Frank H. Potter, 1890; Jane M. and Ellery Sedgwick, 1895; Hamish Miles, 1929; Antonia Cowan, 1966; as *The Haunted Marsh*, translated anonymously, 1848; as *The*

Enchanted Lake, translated by Shaw, 1850; as *Germaine's Marriage*, translated 1892; as *The Haunted Pool*, translated by Potter, 1976.

Lucrezia Floriani. 1846; as *Lucrezia Floriani*, translated by Julius Eker, 1985.

The Works of George Sand, edited by Matilda M. Hays and translated by Hays, Eliza A. Ashurst, and Edmund R. Larkin. 6 vols., 1847.

Le Piccinino. 1847; as *The Piccinino*, translated by George Burnham Ives, in *The Masterpieces of George Sand*, 1900–02.

François le Champi. 1848; as *Francis the Waif*, translated by Gustave Masson, 1889; also translated by Jane M. Sedgwick, 1894; as *The Country Waif*, translated by Eirene Collis, 1930.

La Petite Fadette. 1849; as *Little Fadette*, translated by Joseph Mazzini, 1850, also translated by Hamish Miles, 1928, and Eva Figes, 1967; as *Fadette*, translated anonymously, 1851; also translated by Jane M. Sedgwick, 1893; J.M. Lancaster, 1896; as *Fanchon the Cricket*, translated anonymously, 1863; as *Petite Fadette*, translated by F.A. Binas, 1892.

Le Chateau des déserts. 1851; as *The Castle in the Wilderness*, translated 1856.

Mont-Revêche. 1853.

La Filleule. 1853.

Les Maîtres sonneurs. 1853; as *The Bagpipers*, translated by K.P. Wormeley, 1890.

Adriani. 1854.

Le Diable aux champs. 1856.

Évenor et Leucippe. 1856; as *Les Amours de l'âge d'or*, in *Oeuvres*, 1871.

La Daniella. 1857.

Les Dames vertes. 1857; as *The Naiad: A Ghost Story*, translated by K. Berry di Zéréga, 1892.

Les Beaux Messieurs de Bois-Doré. 1857; as *The Gallant Lords of Bois-Doré*, translated by Steven Clovis, 1890.

L'Homme de neige. 1858; as *The Snow Man*, translated by V. Vaughan, 1871.

Narcisse. 1859.

Elle et lui. 1859; as *He and She*, translated by George Burnham Ives, in *The Masterpieces of George Sand*, 1900–02, this translation also published as *She and He*, 1902.

Flavie. 1859.

Jean de la Roche. 1860.

Constance Verrier. 1860.

La Ville noire. 1860; edited by Jean Courrier, 1978.

Le Marquis de Villemer. 1860–61; as *The Marquis of Villemer*, translated by R. Keeler, 1871.

Valvèdre. 1861.

La Famille de Germandre. 1861; as *The Germandre Family*, translated by George Burnham Ives, in *The Masterpieces of George Sand*, 1900–02.

Tamaris. 1862.

Antonia. 1863; as *Antonia*, translated by V. Vaughan, 1870.

Mademoiselle la Quintinie. 1863.

Laura, voyage dans le cristal. 1864; as *Journey within the Crystal*, translated Pauline Pearson-Stamps, 1992.

La Confession d'une jeune fille. 1864.

Monsieur Sylvestre. 1865; as *M. Sylvestre*, translated by Francis G. Shaw, 1870.

Le Dernier Amour. 1867.

Cadio. 1868.

Mademoiselle Merquem. 1868; edited by Raymond Rheault, 1981; as *Mademoiselle Merquem*, translated anonymously, 1868.

Pierre qui roule; Le Beau Laurence. 1870; as *A Rolling Stone; Handsome Laurence*, translated by Carroll Owen, 1871.

Malgrétout. 1870.

Césarine Dietrich. 1871; as *Césarine Dietrich*, translated by E. Stanwood, 1871.

Francia. 1872.

Nanon. 1872; as *Nanon*, translated by Elizabeth Wormeley Latimer, 1890.

Ma soeur Jeanne. 1874; as *My Sister Jeannie*, translated by S.R. Crocker, 1874.

Flamarande; Les Deux Frères. 1875.

La Tour de Percemont; Marianne. 1876; first part as *The Tower of Percemont*, translated anonymously, 1877; second part translated as *Marianne*, 1880; also translated by Siân Miles (includes letters), 1987.

Plays

Les Sept Cordes de la lyre. 1840; as *The Seven Strings of the Lyre: A Woman's Version of the Faust Legend*, translated by George A. Kennedy, 1989.

Gabriel. 1840; as *Gabriel*, translated by Gay Manifold, 1992.

Cosima (produced 1840). 1840.

François le Champi, from her own novel (produced 1849). 1849.

Claudie (produced 1851). 1851.

Le Mariage de Victorine (produced 1851). 1851.

Molière (produced 1851). 1851.

Le Démon du foyer (produced 1852). 1852.

Mauprat, from her own novel (produced 1853). 1854.

Maître Favilla (produced 1855). 1855; as *La Baronnie de Muhldorf*, n.d.

Lucie (produced 1856). 1856.

La Petite Fadette, verse parts by Michel Carré, music by Théodore Semet, from her own novel (produced 1869). 1869; as *Fanchon the Cricket*, translated by A. Waldauer, 1860; as *Little Cricket*, translated by J. Mortimer, 1878.

Les Beaux Messieurs de Bois-Doré with Paul Meurice, from her own novel. 1862.

Le Marquis de Villemer, with Dumas *fils*, from her own novel (produced 1864). 1864.

Le Drac, with Paul Meurice (produced 1864). 1865.

Cadio, with Paul Meurice (produced 1868). 1868.

Théâtre complet. 3 vols., 1879.

Other

Lettres d'un voyageur. 1837; as *Letters of a Traveller*, translated by Eliza A. Ashurst, in *The Works of George Sand*, 1847; as *Lettres d'un voyageur*, translated by Sach Rabinovitch and Patricia Thomson, 1987.

Oeuvres. 27 vols., 1837–42 (and later editions).

Un hiver à Majorque. 1841; as *Winter in Majorca*, translated by Robert Graves, 1956.

Histoire de France écrite sous la dictée de Blaise Bonnin. 1848.

Histoire de ma vie. 20 vols., 1854–55; part as *Convent Life of George Sand*, translated by Maria E. Mackaye, 1893; as *My Convent Life*, translated 1977; abridged edition, as *My Life*, edited and translated by Dan Hofstadter, 1979; abridged edition, as *Story of My Life*, edited by Thelma Jurgrau, 1991.

La Guerre. 1859.

Journal d'un voyageur pendant la guerre. 1871.

Impressions et souvenirs. 1873; as *Recollections*, translated by R.H. Stoddard, 1874; as *Impressions and Reminiscences*, translated by H.K. Adams, 1877.

Contes d'une grand-mère (for children). 2 vols., 1873–76; as *Tales of a Grandmother*, translated by Margaret Bloom, 1930; selections as *The Wings of Courage: Stories for American Boys and Girls*, translated by Marie E. Field, 1878; as *Wings of Courage*, translated and adapted by Philippa Pearce, 1982; translated by Holly Erskine Hirko, 1994.

Questions d'art et de littérature. 1878.

Questions politiques et sociales. 1879.

Letters of George Sand, translated by R. Ledos de Beaufort. 3 vols., 1886.

Correspondance de George Sand et d'Alfred de Muaset. 1904; as *Sand et Alfred de Musset: Correspondance . . .* , edited by Louis Évrard, 1956.

Journal intime, edited by Aurore Sand. 1926; as *Intimate Journal*, edited and translated by Marie J. Howe, 1929.

Letters, edited and translated by Veronica Lucas. 1930.

Correspondance inédit, with Marie Dorval, edited by Simone André-Maurois. 1953.

Lettres inédites de Sand et de Pauline Viardot 1839–1849, edited by Thérèse Marix-Spire. 1959.

Lettres à Sainte-Beuve, edited by Östen Södergård. 1964.

Correspondance, edited by Georges Lubin. 25 vols., 1964–91.

George Sand: In Her Own Words, edited and translated by Joseph Barry. 1979.

Correspondance, with Flaubert, edited by Alphonse Jacobs. 1981; as *Flaubert-Sand: The Correspondence*, translated by Francis Steegmuller and Barbara Bray, 1993.

*

Bibliography: *George Sand: Étude bibliographique sur ses oeuvres* by Vicomte Charles Spoelberch de Lovenjoul, 1914; *Bibliographie des premières publications des Romans de George Sand* by Georges Colin, 1965; "Works on George Sand, 1964–1980: A Bibliography" by Gaylord Brynolfson, in *George Sand Papers: Conference Proceedings*, edited by Natalie Datlof, 1982.

Critical Studies: *George Sand: Sa vie et ses oeuvres* by Wladimir Karénine, 4 vols., 1899–1926; *George Sand* by André Maurois (translated from the French), 1953; *George Sand* by Samuel Edwards, 1972; *Chopin and George Sand in Majorca* by Bartomeu Ferra, 1974; *George Sand: A Biography* by Curtis Cate, 1975; *George Sand Papers: Conference Proceedings*, biennial from 1976; *George Sand: A Biography* by Ruth Jordan, 1976; *Friends of George Sand Newsletter*, 1977–; *Infamous Woman: The Life of George Sand* by Joseph Barry, 1977; *George Sand and the Victorians: Her Influence and Reputation in Nineteenth-Century England* by Patricia Thomson, 1977; *The Double Life of George Sand: Woman and Writer* by Renée Winegarten, 1978; *George Sand and the Victorian World* by Paul G. Blount, 1979; *The Lioness and the Little One: The Liaison of George Sand and Frédéric Chopin* by William G. Atwood, 1980; *Turgenev and George Sand: An Improbable Entente* by Patrick Waddington, 1981; *Sand: Collected Essays* edited by Janis Glasgow, 1985; *George Sand's Theatre Career* by Gay Manifold, 1985; *Family Romances: George Sand's Early Novels* by Kathryn J. Crecelius, 1987; *George Sand: A Brave Man—The Most Womanly Woman* by Donna Dickenson, 1988; *George Sand: Writing for Her Life* by Isabelle Hoog Naginski, 1991; *The Traveler in the Life and Works of George Sand* edited by Tamara Aluarez-Detrell and Michael G. Paulson, 1994; *George Sand and the Nineteenth-Century Russian Love-Triangle Novels* by Dawn D. Eidelman, 1994; *George Sand and Autobiography* by Janet Hiddleston, 1999; *George Sand: A Woman's Life Writ Large* by Belinda Jack, 1999; *George Sand: Indiana, Mauprat* by Janet Hiddleston, 2000; *Gender in the Fiction of George Sand* by Françoise Massardier-Kenney, 2000; *While the Music Lasts: The Representation of Music in the Works of George Sand* by David A. Powell, 2001.

* * *

Like her 18th-century predecessor, Germaine de Staël, and her 20th-century equivalent, Simone de Beauvoir, George Sand (the English spelling of her assumed Christian name was her choice) showed how indissoluble the link has always been so far in Western culture between feminism and political ideas which are advanced to the point of being revolutionary by contemporary standards. Her tempestuous lifestyle, involving as it did the break-up of her early marriage with Casimir Dudevant and a series of rather ostentatious liaisons with Alfred de Musset, Fréderic Chopin, and several others, was reflected in the subject-matter of her early novels. These, and especially *Lélia*, probably her best, developed the Romantic theme of the incompatibility between sexual passion and conventional family life, were much read in her day, and are not wholly devoid of interest for the modern reader. She identified herself closely and fervently with the early socialist movement, and described working conditions in the France of her time in *Le Compagnon du tour de France* (*The Companion of the Tour of France*).

Like Victor Hugo, she disapproved strongly of the military *coup d'état* whereby Napoleon III put an end to the existence and hopes of the 1848 revolution in December 1851, and retired from public life. She lived in her native Berry, in the West of France, which she had already described in idyllic tones in *La Mare au diable* (*The Devil's Pool*) and *François le Champi* (*Francis the Waif*). These pastoral novels are still admired and read today, and provided consolation for the narrator in the first volume of Proust's *A la Recherche du temps perdu* (*Remembrance of Things Past*) on that memorable evening when his mother was allowed—and allowed herself—to calm his anguish by spending the night in his bedroom.

While disapproving strongly of her progressive ideas, Gustave Flaubert kept up a long and interesting correspondence with Sand, and she wrote voluminously to other intellectuals and men of letters of her day. Although Charles Baudelaire regarded her as the epitome of all that was most obnoxious in the optimistic humanitarianism of mid-19th-century France, her sense of human and humane values is in many ways preferable to the misanthropic pessimism which informs *Les Fleurs du mal*, as it also does *Madame Bovary*. Yet one only needs to compare her novels to those of the English 19th-century writer whom she most resembles, George Eliot, to see that the woman who was *née* Amantine Aurore Lucile Dupin lacked both the critical intelligence and the understanding of society which make *Middlemarch* a masterpiece.

—Philip Thody

See the essay on *Lélia*.

SAN JUAN DE LA CRUZ

See JOHN OF THE CROSS, St.

SANNAZARO, Jacopo

Also known as Iacopo Sannazaro. **Born:** Naples, Kingdom of Naples, 28 July 1456, 1457, or 1458. Grew up in San Piacentino, region of Salerno, but family returned to Naples by 1475. **Education:** Educated in Latin and Greek by Giuliano Maio (or Maggio), and in poetry by Lucio Crasso; also became member of the Pontano Academy (under the name Actius Sincerus), early 1480s. **Career:** Entered the service of Alfonso of Aragon, 1481; fought with Alfonso's forces against Pope Innocent VIII, 1485–86; after Alfonso's brief rule, 1494 (abdicated), served his son, Ferrandino, and went into short exile with him after the the French King Charles VII entered Naples, 1495; returned to Naples, 1495, and after Ferrandino's death, 1496, served Alfonso's younger brother, Federico, who contributed music for Sannazaro's verse and gave him the Villa of Mergellina; accompanied Federico into exile after Louis XII's occupation of Naples, 1501: travelled to Ischia, Marseilles, Milan, and Blois (where Federico was allowed refuge in exchange for renouncing his rule over Naples); following Federico's death in 1504, returned to Naples (under Spanish rule from 1502), 1505, and settled at Mergellina; in later years had two chapels and the church of Santa Maria del Porto built. **Died:** 24 April 1530.

PUBLICATIONS

Collections

Opera omnia latine scripta. 1535.
Opere latine scripta, edited by Giacomo Raillard. 1719; revised edition, edited by Jan Broukhusii, 1728.
Opere volgari. 1723.
Opere, edited by Enrico Carrara. 1952.
Opere volgari, edited by Alfredo Mauro. 1961.
The Major Latin Poems of Jacopo Sannazaro, translated by Ralph Nash. 1996.

Verse

Le eclogae piscatoriae. With *De partu virginis* and *Lamentatio de morte Christi Domini*, 1526; edited by W.P. Mustard, as *The Piscatory Eclogues of Jacopo Sannazaro*, 1914; as *Eclogues*, translated anonymously, 1726; as *Piscatorial Eclogues*, translated by Ralph Nash, with *Arcadia*, 1966.
De partu virginis. With *Eclogae piscatoriae* and *Lamentatio de morte Christi Domini*, 1526; edited by A. Altamura, 1948, and Charles Fantazzi and Alessandro Perosa, 1988.
Rime. 1530; as *Sonetti e canzoni*, 1530; revised edition, 1543.
Sannazarius on the Birth of Our Saviour, translated anonymously. 1736.
Ecloghe; Elegie; Odi; Epigrammi, edited by Giorgio Castello. 1928.

Plays

La farsa dell'ambasceria del Soldano (produced 1490). In *Il teatro italiano nei seccoli XIII, XIV, XV*, edited by F. Torraca, 1885.

Il trionfo della fama (produced 1492). In *Studi di storia letteraria napoletana*, by F. Torraca, 1884.
La presa di Granata (produced 1492). In *Il teatro italiano nei seccoli XII, XIV, XI*, edited by F. Torraca, 1885.
Farsa di Venere che cerca il figliuolo amore (produced 1488? or 1490?). In *Studi di storia letteraria napoletana*, by F. Torraca, 1884.

Other

Arcadia (prose and verse). 1502 (unauthorized edition); 1504 (authorized edition); edited by Michele Scherillo, 1888, and Enrico Carrara, 1926; as *Arcadia*, translated by Ralph Nash, with *Piscatorial Eclogues*, 1966.
The Osiers (pastoral), translated by J. Rooke. 1734.

*

Critical Studies: *Il più nobile umanista del Rinascimento* by V. Borghini, 1943; *Jacopo Sannazaro* by Antonio Altamura, 1951; *La tradizione manoscritta dei Carmina del Sannazaro* by A. Altamura, 1957; *Sannazaro en Garcilaso* by Vittore Bocchetta, 1976; *Edipo in Arcadia: Miti e simboli nell'Arcadia* by Vittorio Gajetti, 1977; *Jacopo Sannazaro and the Uses of the Pastoral* by William J. Kennedy, 1983; *Iacopo Sannazaro in Francia: Scoperte di codici all'inizio del XVI secolo* by Carlo Vecce, 1988; *Per l'eduzione dell' Arcadia* by Gianni Villani, 1989; *Sannazaro and Arcadia* by Carol Kidwell, 1993.

*   *   *

Jacopo Sannazaro was an ideal courtier and an ideal humanist, the model of a Quattrocento Renaissance man. Born in Naples, to a noble family of courtiers at the Aragonese court, he was named, as a young man, a member of the prestigious ''Accademia Pontaniana'' founded by the humanist Giovanni Pontano. It is within this organization that he took on the pseudonym ''Actius Sincerus.'' This name, derived from the Latin, means ''the honest one of the seashore,'' the location being a possible reference to his family home in the little port of Mergellina on the shores of the Bay of Naples.

Sannazaro is certainly the most important writer of the period of Neapolitan humanism, and he is also one of the most significant cultural figures of the Italian Quattrocento. Because of his masterpiece, *Arcadia*, his name is linked with the rediscovery and interpretation of the pastoral mode and its motifs. Poetry of an idyllic or bucolic nature flourished in the Renaissance as the expression of a fundamentally new civilization: man's search for grace and vital harmony in nature. Although the pastoral eclogue had been revived on a few occasions since antiquity, Sannazaro is credited with the first successful adaptation in the vernacular. His later poetry in Latin was also enriched by pastoral conventions. Sannazaro's major contribution to literary history consists, therefore, not only of his rediscovery of the pastoral genre, but also in his encouragement of a fuller understanding of classical poetry.

His first major work is also his most famous. The entirety of his pastoral romance, *Arcadia*, was composed between 1480 and 1485, with the exception of the two final chapters, which were added in a second edition published in 1504. *Arcadia* is made up of 12 prose chapters, interspersed with poetry in the form of eclogues. The first-person narrative is considered somewhat autobiographical. The protagonist is a youth called Sincero (the *alter-ego* chosen by Sannazaro for the ''Accademia Pontaniana''), who seeks refuge from an unrequited love in the simple existence of the shepherds of Arcadia. Arcadia is a mountainous region of peninsular Greece, which since antiquity was considered home of the bucolic tradition. Here Sincero partakes in the serene life of the shepherds in close harmony with nature. He experiences the simple joys of games, the hunt, songs, and poetry, a life reminiscent of the mythical golden age of humanity. According to the poets of antiquity who first portrayed Acardia as the mythical home of human happiness, it was an ideal region where bountiful sentiments of love were expressed in continuous music and song, in a beautiful communion between man and nature. Sincero is soon inspired to tell his painful love story to a shepherd, Carino, who exhorts him not to give up hope. Finally, a nymph escorts him back to Naples where he learns from two tearful maidens of the death of his beloved. The autobiographical nature of the tale is a convention of ancient pastoral poetry. The work can thus be read as an allegory of Sannazaro's love for Carmosina, beloved of the poet in his youth and the victim of an early death. The description of the mythical land of Arcadia is based on the author's early years in the countryside south of Naples.

The plot of this work is secondary to its descriptive and impressionistic passages. Hardly any situation or image is invented by the author, who has chosen instead to elaborate upon classical references, to both Greek and Latin culture, giving an almost archaeological quality to the text. Sannazaro's tone is nostalgic both in its tribute to the pastoral tradition and in the allegorical references to Sannazaro's youth and first love. His humanistic training made him the heir not only to the stylistic tradition of antiquity, but also to the prose models of the Trecento, thus further diffusing the Tuscan linguistic model in southern Italy. The hybrid nature of the text provided an ideal opportunity for linguistic experimentation, as it required an artificial literary language. One can see clearly the influence of Pietro Bembo, the great Renaissance theoretician of the Italian language. This Florentine philologist advised the stylistic imitation of Petrarch for poetry and Boccaccio for prose in the formation of a vernacular literary idiom. Although Bembo's theoretical text *(Le prose della volgar lingua)* was published in 1525, we know that it circulated earlier in the great debate on the vernacular.

The period of Sannazaro's voluntary exile in France, in the service of King Federico of Naples, coincided with a turning point in his writing style, as he chose to use Latin for the literary works of his maturity. His principal Latin work is the religious poem *De partu virginis* [The Virgin Birth], which tells the story of the birth of Christ. Once again, the pastoral mode is important for the work, in its style, setting, and motifs. It is Sannazaro's intent here to fuse the bucolic tradition with the gospel narratives. The poem is written entirely in hexameters, and is divided into three books dealing respectively with the Annunciation, the Nativity, and the Adoration of the Magi. His other significant Latin work is *Le eclogae piscatoris* (*Piscatorial Eclogues*), in which he again attempts to fuse the form of the pastoral tradition with contemporary elements. His innovation in this instance consists in the substitution of the world of the fishermen of Naples for that of shepherds.

Sannazaro regained for the pastoral mode the prestige it had lost since classical times. His major literary achievement was the fresh, innovative quality he brought to his own writings. He wove together poetry and prose, ancient and modern features, Christian and Classical traditions into an innovative whole. His masterpiece, *Arcadia*, was an immediate success, and many editions were published during the 16th century, contributing to its extensive diffusion throughout Italy and in Europe.

—Jordan Lancaster

SAPPHO

Born: Eresus or Mytilene, on Lesbos, c. 612 BC (some sources give c. 620 or 630 BC). **Family:** Married to Cercylas; one daughter. **Career:** Spent part of her life in exile in Sicily; lived most of her life in Mytilene.

PUBLICATIONS

Verse

Poetarum Lesbiorum fragmenta, with other poets, edited by Edgar Lobel and Denys Page. 1955.

Sappho and Alcaeus (bilingual edition), edited and translated by Denys Page. 1955.

[Poems], translated by Mary Barnard. 1958.

Lyrics in the Original Greek with Translations, translated by Willis Barnstone. 1965; revised edition, as *Sappho and the Greek Lyric Poets*, 1988.

Poems and Fragments, translated by Guy Davenport. 1965.

Poems, translated by Suzy Q. Groden. 1966.

Sappho et Alcaeus, edited by Eva-Maria Voigt. 1971.

The Soldier and the Lady: Poems of Archilochus and Sappho, translated by Barriss Mills. 1975.

Archilochus, Sappho, Alkman: Three Lyric Poets of the Late Greek Bronze Age, translated by Guy Davenport. 1980.

Greek Lyric: 1. Sappho [and] Alcaeus [Loeb Edition], translated by David A. Campbell. 1982.

Poems and Fragments, translated by Josephine Balmer. 1984; revised and corrected edition, 1992.

Poetic Fragments, translated by D.W. Myatt. 1986.

The Poems, translated by Terence Duquesne. 1990.

Sappho, a Garland: The Poems and Fragments of Sappho, translated by Jim Powell. 1993.

The Poems, translated with introduction by Willis Barnstone. 1998.

Sappho: Poems and Fragments, translated by Stanley Lombardo. 2002.

*

Critical Studies: *Sappho and Her Influence* by D.M. Robinson, 1924; *Sappho* by Alphonse Daudet, translated by Eithne Wilkins, 1951; *Sappho and Alcaeus: An Introduction to the Study of Ancient Lesbian Poetry* by Denys Page, 1955; *The Poetic Dialect of Sappho and Alcaeus* by Angus M. Bowie, 1981; *Three Classical Poets: Sappho, Catullus, and Juvenal* by Richard Jenkyns, 1982; *Three Archaic Poets: Archilochus, Alcaeus, Sappho* by Anne Pippin Burnett, 1983; *The Golden Lyre: The Themes of the Greek Lyric Poets* by David A. Campbell, 1983; *Love as War: Homeric Allusion in the*

Poetry of Sappho by Leah Rissman, 1983; *Fictions of Sappho, 1546–1937* by Joan DeJean, 1989; *Sappho's Immortal Daughters* by Margaret Williamson, 1995; *Sappho is Burning* by Page duBois, 1995; *Re-reading Sappho: Reception and Transmission*, edited by Ellen Greene, 1996; *Reading Sappho: Contemporary Approaches*, edited by Ellen Greene, 1996; *Sappho: Through English Poetry*, edited and introduced by Peter Jay and Caroline Lewis, 1996; *Sappho and the Virgin Mary: Same-Sex Love and the English Literary Imagination* by Ruth Vanita, 1996; *Sappho's Sweetbitter Songs: Configurations of Female and Male in Ancient Greek Lyric* by Lyn Hatherly Wilson, 1996; *Lesbian Desire in the Lyrics of Sappho* by Jane McIntosh Snyder, 1997; *Sappho: The Tenth Muse* by Nancy Freedman, 1998; *Victorian Sappho* by Yopie Prins, 1999; *Psappha: A Novel of Sappho* by Peggy Ullman Bell, 2000; *The Sappho Companion*, edited and introduced by Margaret Reynolds, 2000; *Fragments of an Elegy: Tennyson Reading Sappho* by Margaret Reynolds, 2001; *Sappho in Early Modern England: Female Same-Sex Literary Erotics, 1550–1714* by Harriette Andreadis, 2001.

* * *

The nine books of Sappho's poems edited at Alexandria did not survive the Middle Ages. All that remained of them were 120 quotations made by various writers. These were not collected into a single volume until 1733 and it was not until 1885 that all were translated and published together in English. In the past century the amount of surviving Sappho has almost doubled with the recovery of fragments of her poems preserved on papyri. In 1955 Lobel and Page edited the new together with the older fragments and produced the standard text. For all the achievements of modern scholarship, the fragmentary state of Sappho's poems remains the most powerful factor conditioning our appreciation of her.

A second factor is the nature of her eroticism. Her most famous poem, imitated by Catullus and quoted in part by Longinus, describes her feelings on seeing a girl she loves seated beside a man. The hymn to Aphrodite, Sappho's only poem to survive in its entirety, calls on the goddess to help her win the love of an unnamed girl. The situation, unambiguous in the Greek, so embarrassed English translators that they substituted a young man for the girl; it was not until 1883, in John Addington Symonds's version, that the girl was allowed back onto the page. A similar, possibly worse distortion results from the opposite tendency, overemphasis on Sappho's sexual orientation. Only one of the new (and none of the older) fragments contains a hint of physical contact between Sappho and a girl or between two girls of Sappho's circle.

Most of Sappho's poems address someone specific; others belong to a specific occasion, such as a wedding. Portions of her wedding songs, for which she was famous in antiquity, survived in quotation, but the longest specimen we now have is papyrus fragment 44 LP, a poem in which Sappho apparently compared the bride and groom to Andromache and Hector on their wedding day. Another poem in which she uses myth to highlight the present is fragment 16 LP, which opens by declaring that beauty is for each person not what others call beautiful but what each desires for himself; the point is then illustrated by the myth of Helen, who abandoned husband, home, and daughter for love of Paris. The last surviving stanza draws a parallel between Helen's ruinous passion and Sappho's own longing for Anactoria. In 94 LP we find Sappho consoling a girl for a loss she no doubt feels herself. The objectification of her emotions is the most striking feature of her art.

Sappho's reputation, high in antiquity, is so high in modern times that new discoveries can hardly enhance it. The papyrus fragments, however, have given us a fuller view of her work. We can tell that she employed a more traditional diction in her wedding poems. Her love songs cleave to the vernacular of Lesbos, combining directness of expression with rigorous metrical control. Comparison of 34 and 96 LP shows that she was not averse to using the same image twice. The word "again" recurs with remarkable frequency in her love poems, suggesting a conventionality that we could not detect before because we had so few examples. But for all the qualities that make her appealing to a contemporary audience, her conviction of her own immortality is quintessentially Greek. When she admonishes her daughter not to mourn for her death because "it is not right that there should be lamentation in the house of those who serve the Muses" (130 LP), she is looking back to Hesiod and forward to Pindar.

—Frank J. Nisetich

See the essays on "Fragment 1 [Address to Aphrodite]" and "Fragment 31 [Declaration of Love for a Young Girl]"

SARRAUTE, Nathalie

Born: Nathalie Tcherniak in Ivanovo, Russia, 18 July 1900; moved to France in 1908. **Education:** Educated at Lycée Fénelon, Paris; the Sorbonne, Paris, licence in English, 1920; Oxford University, 1921; University of Berlin, 1921–22; École de Droit, Paris, law degree, 1925. **Family:** Married Raymond Sarraute in 1925; three daughters. **Career:** Member of the French Bar, 1926–41. Since 1941, full-time writer. Lives in Paris. **Awards:** International Publishers prize, 1964; Formentor prize, 1964. Honorary doctorates: Trinity College, Dublin, 1976; University of Kent, Canterbury, 1980; Oxford University, 1991. **Died:** 19 October 1999.

PUBLICATIONS

Collections

Oeuvres Complètes, edited by Jean-Yves Tadié. 1996.

Fiction

Tropismes. 1939; revised edition, 1957; as *Tropisms*, translated by Maria Jolas, with *The Age of Suspicion*, 1963; published separately, 1967.

Portrait d'un inconnu. 1948; as *Portrait of a Man Unknown*, translated by Maria Jolas, 1958.

Martereau. 1953; as *Martereau*, translated by Maria Jolas, 1959.

Le Planétarium. 1959; as *The Planetarium*, translated by Maria Jolas, 1960.

Les Fruits d'or. 1963; as *The Golden Fruits*, translated by Maria Jolas, 1964.

Entre la vie et la mort. 1968; as *Between Life and Death*, translated by Maria Jolas, 1969.

Vous les entendez?. 1972; as *Do You Hear Them?*, translated by Maria Jolas, 1973.

"Disent les imbéciles." 1976; as *"Fools Say,"* translated by Maria Jolas, 1977.

L'Usage de la parole. 1980; as *The Use of Speech*, translated by Barbara Wright, 1983.
Tu ne t'aimes pas. 1989; as *You Don't Love Yourself*, translated by Barbara Wright, 1990.
Ici. 1995; as *Here*, translated by Barbara Wright, 1997.

Plays

Le Silence; suivi de Le Mensonge (produced 1967). 1967; as *Silence, and The Lie*, translated by Maria Jolas, 1969, and in *Collected Plays*, 1980.
Isma (produced 1973). 1970; with *Le Silence* and *Le Mensonge*, 1970; as *Izzuma*, translated by Maria Jolas, in *Collected Plays*, 1980.
C'est beau (produced 1975). 1973; in *Théâtre I*, 1978; as *It's Beautiful*, translated by Maria Jolas, in *Collected Plays*, 1980.
Elle est là (produced 1980). 1978; in *Théâtre I*, 1978; as *It Is There*, translated by Barbara Wright, in *Collected Plays*, 1980.
Théâtre I (includes *Elle est là; C'est beau; Isma; Le Mensonge; Le Silence*). 1978;
Collected Plays (includes *It is There; It's Beautiful; Izzuma; The Lie; Silence*), translated by Barbara Wright and Maria Jolas. 1980.
Pour un oui ou pour un non (produced 1986). 1982; as *For No Good Reason* (produced 1985).
Childhood, from her autobiography (produced 1984).

Other

L'Ère du soupçon (essays). 1956; as *The Age of Suspicion*, translated by Maria Jolas, with *Tropisms*, 1963.
Enfance (autobiography). 1983; as *Childhood*, translated by Barbara Wright, 1984.
Paul Valéry et l'enfant d'éléphant; Flaubert le précurseur (essays). 1986.
Nathalie Sarraute, qui êtes-vous?: conversations avec Simone Benmussa. 1987.

*

Bibliography: *Nathalie Sarraute: A Bibliography* by Sheila M. Bell, 1982.

Critical Studies: *Nathalie Sarraute* by Mimica Cranaki and Yvon Belaval, 1965; *Nathalie Sarraute* by René Micha, 1966; *Nathalie Sarraute* by Jean-Luc Jaccard, 1967; *Nathalie Sarraute* by Ruth Z. Temple, 1968; *Le Thème du masque et les banalités dans l'oeuvre de Nathalie Sarraute* by Christine B. Wunderli-Müller, 1970; *Nathalie Sarraute; ou, La Recherche de l'authenticité* by Micheline Tison-Braun, 1971; *Au delà des tropismes: Étude des romans de Nathalie Sarraute* by Elsa Vineberg, 1973; *La Vie retrouvée: Étude de l'oeuvre romanesque de Nathalie Sarraute* by Françoise Calin, 1976; *Une Poésie des discours: Essai sur les romans de Nathalie Sarraute* by A.S. Newman, 1976; *Nathalie Sarraute* by Gretchen Rous Besser, 1979; *L'Oeuvre romanesque de Nathalie Sarraute* by André Allemand, 1980; *The Nouveau Roman and the Poetics of Fiction* by Ann Jefferson, 1980; *Nathalie Sarraute and the War of the Words: A Study of Five Novels* by Valerie Minogue, 1981; *The Novels of Nathalie Sarraute: Towards an Aesthetic* by Helen Watson-Williams, 1981; Nathalie Sarraute issue of *Arc*, 95, 1984; *Sarraute: "Le Planétarium"* by Roger McClure, 1987; *Sarraute: "Portrait d'un inconnu" and "Vous les entendez?"* by Sheila M. Bell, 1988; *Sarraute Romancière. Espaces intimes* by Sabine Raffy, 1988; *Nathalie Sarraute* by Jean Pierrot, 1990; *Nathalie Sarraute* by Arnaud Rykner, 1991; *Nathalie Sarraute and the Feminist Reader: Identities in Process* by Sarah Barbour, 1993; *The French New Autobiographies: Sarraute, Duras, and Robbe-Grillet* by Raylene L. Ramsay, 1996; *Reading Nathalie Sarraute: Dialogue and Distance* by Emer O'Beirne, 1999; *Nathalie Sarraute, Fiction and Theory: Questions of Difference* by Ann Jefferson, 2000.

* * *

Nathalie Sarraute was creating the *Nouveau Roman* (New Novel) before the term was invented, linking her with authors such as Robbe-Grillet and Butor. What she shares with other "new novelists" is their rejection of those familiar conventions that allow the reader to be comfortably passive, reassured by traditional forms. What sets her apart from them is the fact that challenging new techniques never became the central focus of her attention. She needs new forms in order to express a new vision of human relationships, in which unspoken, barely perceptible inner movements lie beneath the surface of the most banal everyday events. She calls these movements "tropisms" on the analogy of the automatic responses of plants to external stimuli, for instance light.

Her first work, *Tropismes* (*Tropisms*), is not a novel but a series of short texts that simply focus on these movements, using imagery and rhythm to communicate feelings that are usually unspoken. These subtle glimpses sum up the essence of a moment, a relationship, without supplying any framework or background. In the novels Sarraute continues to focus on such tropisms, now presented in an organized structure—the term plot would be misleading—and often in a very recognizable social setting. She has always asserted that the tropisms are the only important subject for her, but her success as a novelist is due certainly in part to the fact that she is a brilliantly comic social observer. She has, in particular, a perceptive ear for dialogue, which becomes more and more important as her work develops. The novels all contain miniature dramatic scenes, and it seems quite natural that she should later have turned to the theatre in plays that relate closely to the fiction.

Portrait d'un inconnu (*Portrait of a Man Unknown*), the first novel, is the attempt of a first-person narrator to communicate his inner experience of the world, in language that reveals his doubts about the reality of what he is communicating. As Sartre points out in his preface, it is a work that questions the idea of writing a novel. A traditional novel character does appear at the end of the work, and, as Sarraute put it "stops all these tiny underground movements." This traditional character is simply an obstacle to the living movements that interest the author, who sees his arrival as producing a deathlike stillness.

Martereau has a similar structure, but now the "traditional" character, Martereau, is introduced much earlier, in the context of a family. The first part of the novel shows the narrator painfully aware of the writhing mass of emotions that underlie the simplest exchanges between himself and his family. By contrast Martereau seems to him enviably solid and stable, his world a kind of innocent paradise. When Martereau becomes involved with the family, however, his reassuring solidity begins to disintegrate. The narrator's multiple images of Martereau are never resolved into any definitive portrait, and the novel is partly about the images we create, and our attempts to find ready-made models for reality.

In *Le Planétarium* (*The Planetarium*) we find a more complex structure, and a wider range of relationships. There is a satirical view of Alain Guimier's bourgeois family, and of the Paris literary set that he tries to use as a refuge from the bourgeois vales he despises. There is no single narrator, but a frequently shifting viewpoint, giving different, often contradictory versions of the same characters, and sometimes the same incidents. The real issue in the work is the co-existence of these conflicting viewpoints, which are not simply opinions, but attempts by each individual to model the world on his desires. Such conflicts take place at the level of the innermost self, while the social surface remains an almost unruffled banality.

Alain's elderly aunt, for instance, has an ideal image of the décor for her flat, centred on an oval oak door. When the workmen install it with the wrong handle, she sees them as ruthless vandals, planting a bomb that leaves her dream in smoking ruins. The comic incongruity between the door handle and the violent image does not remove our awareness of Aunt Berthe's real distress. This kind of ambiguous comedy is typical of Sarraute's work.

Les Fruits d'or (*The Golden Fruits*) is even further removed from conventional plot and character. Its central figure is a novel, by Brehier, entitled "The Golden Fruits," but we never discover anything definite about this work. We see it through the eyes of its critics and admirers as it progresses from being the latest literary sensation to neglect. The pedlars of critical jargon are mercilessly caricatured, and readers can enjoy this novel as a witty satire on the snobbish Paris salon scene. As usual, however, Sarraute uses the superficial events in a limited society to reveal something about basic human relationships. Here she explores the question of artistic values, showing how our opinions relate to the need to defend our independence, and the conflicting need to be accepted by those around us.

The concern with writing and the power of words becomes more central in many later works. *Entre la vie et la mort* (*Between Life and Death*) takes us inside the mind of the writer. Social context has become more generalized as we experience the different conflicts and attitudes met by the writer in attempting to come to terms with his work. In *L'Usage de la parole* (*The Use of Speech*), a series of short independent texts, we are invited to examine individual, apparently banal phrases, often from earlier works, and experience their resonance, their hidden power to create reactions. *Tu ne t'aimes pas* (*You Don't Love Yourself*) consists of dialogues between different inner selves, who are concerned with the language of self-definition and so ultimately with the nature of the self.

Sarraute's theatre involves, as she says, turning her novels inside out, and she was surprised when Jean-Louis Barrault successfully staged the first of these subtle, language-based plays. The inner dialogues that play such a central part in the novels are externalized in the plays. *Le Silence* (*Silence*) and *Le Mensonge* (*The Lie*) are typical in that the "action" is an apparently trivial social incident, an embarrassing silence in the first play, a character who pretends to be poorer than she is in the second. These incidents provoke intense reactions in the characters, and it is these reactions, not the characters themselves, that are the centre of interest.

Sarraute's work is not easy. As many critics suggest, it has the qualities of poetry, and it will never appeal to the reader who is looking for a "good story." The reader who comes to it with an open mind, however, will discover some of the most original, amusing, and challenging writing of the present day.

—John Rothenberg

See the essay on *Tropisms*.

SARTRE, Jean-Paul (-Charles-Aymard)

Born: Paris, France, 21 June 1905. **Education:** Educated at Lycée Montaigne and Lycée Henri-IV, Paris, 1913–22, baccalauréat, 1922; Lycée Louis le Grand, Paris, 1922–24; École Normale Supérieure, Paris, 1924–29, agrégation in philosophy 1929. **Military Service:** Served in the French army 1929–31, and World War II: captured, 1940; escaped, 1941. **Family:** Began lifelong relationship with the writer Simone de Beauvoir, *q.v.*, in 1929; Sartre had one adopted daughter. **Career:** Professor, Lycée du Havre, 1931–32 and 1934–36; Lycée de Laon, 1936–37; Lycée Pasteur, Paris, 1937–39; Lycée Condorcet, Paris, 1941–44; travelled and lectured extensively during the 1950s and 1960s: member of Bertrand Russell's International War Crimes Tribunal, 1966. Founding editor, with de Beauvoir, *Les Temps Modernes*, from 1945; editor, *La Cause du Peuple*, from 1970, *Tout*, 1970–74, *Révolution*, 1971–74, and *Libération*, 1973–74; founder, with Maurice Clavel, Liberation news service, 1971. **Awards:** French Institute Research grant, 1933; Popular Novel prize, 1940; New York Drama Critics Circle award, 1947; Grand Novel prize, 1950; Omegna prize (Italy), 1960; Nobel prize for literature, 1964 (refused). Légion d'honneur, 1945 (refused). Honorary Degree: University of Jerusalem, 1976. **Member:** Foreign Member, American Academy of Arts and Sciences. **Died:** 15 April 1980.

PUBLICATIONS

Collection

Oeuvres romanesques, edited by Michel Contat and Michel Rybalka. 1981.

Fiction

La Nausée. 1938; as *The Diary of Antoine Roquentin*, translated by Lloyd Alexander, 1949; as *Nausea*, translated by Alexander, 1949; also translated by Robert Baldick, 1965.
Le Mur (stories). 1939; as *The Wall and Other Stories*, translated by Lloyd Alexander, 1949; as *Intimacy and Other Stories*, translated by Alexander, 1949; as *Mur*, edited by Walter Redfern, 1997.
Les Chemins de la liberté (*Paths of Freedom*):
  L'Âge de raison. 1945; as *The Age of Reason*, translated by Eric Sutton, 1947.
  Le Sursis. 1945; as *The Reprieve*, translated by Eric Sutton, 1947.
  La Mort dans l'âme. 1949; as *Iron in the Soul*, translated by Gerard Hopkins, 1950; as *Troubled Sleep*, translated by Hopkins, 1951.

Plays

Bariona; ou, Le Fils du tonnerre (produced 1940). 1962; as *Bariona; or, The Son of Thunder*, translated by Richard C. McCleary, in *The Writings 2*, 1974.
Les Mouches (produced 1943). 1943; as *The Flies*, translated by Stuart Gilbert, in *The Flies and In Camera*, 1946, also in *No Exit and The Flies*, 1947.
Huis clos (produced 1944). 1945; as *In Camera*, translated by Stuart Gilbert, in *The Flies and In Camera*, 1946; as *No Exit*, translated by Gilbert, in *No Exit and The Flies*, 1947.

The Flies and In Camera, translated by Stuart Gilbert. 1946; as *No Exit and The Flies*, translated by Gilbert, 1947.

Morts sans sépulture (produced 1946). 1946; as *Men without Shadows*, translated by Kitty Black, in *Three Plays* (UK), 1949; as *The Victors*, translated by Lionel Abel, in *Three Plays* (United States), 1949.

La Putain respectueuse (produced 1946). 1946; as *The Respectable Prostitute*, in *Three Plays* (UK), translated by Kitty Black, 1949; as *The Respectful Prostitute*, translated by Lionel Abel, in *Three Plays* (United States), 1949.

Les Jeux sont faits (screenplay). 1947; as *The Chips Are Down*, translated by Louise Varèse, 1948.

Les Mains sales (produced 1948). 1948; as *Crime Passionnel*, translated by Kitty Black, in *Three Plays* (UK), 1949; as *Dirty Hands*, translated by Lionel Abel, in *Three Plays* (United States), 1949.

L'Engrenage (screenplay). 1948; as *In the Mesh*, translated by Mervyn Savill, 1954.

Three Plays (UK; includes *Men without Shadows; The Respectable Prostitute; Crime Passionnel*), translated by Kitty Black. 1949.

Three Plays (United States; includes *The Victors; The Respectful Prostitute; Dirty Hands*), translated by Lionel Abel. 1949.

Le Diable et le bon Dieu (produced 1951). 1951; as *Lucifer and the Lord*, translated by Kitty Black, 1953; as *The Devil and the Good Lord*, in *The Devil and the Good Lord and Two Other Plays*, 1960.

Kean, from the play by Dumas *père* (produced 1953). 1954; as *Kean*, translated by Kitty Black, 1954.

Nekrassov (produced 1955). 1956; as *Nekrassov*, translated by Sylvia and George Leeson, 1957.

Les Séquestrés d'Altona (produced 1959). 1960; as *Loser Wins*, translated by Sylvia and George Leeson, 1960; translated as *The Condemned of Altona*, 1961.

The Devil and the Good Lord and Two Other Plays (includes *Kean* and *Nekrassov*). 1960.

Les Troyennes, from a play by Euripides (produced 1965). 1965; as *The Trojan Women*, translated by Ronald Duncan, 1967.

Le Scénario Freud (screenplay). 1984; as *The Freud Scenario*, edited by J.-B. Pontalis and translated by Quintin Hoare, 1985.

Screenplays: *Les Jeux sont faits* (*The Chips Are Down*), 1947; *L'Engrenage*, 1948; *Les Sorcières de Salem* (*Witches of Salem*), 1957.

Other

L'Imagination. 1936; as *Imagination: A Psychological Critique*, translated by Forrest Williams, 1962.

Esquisse d'une théorie des émotions. 1939; as *The Emotions: Outline of a Theory*, translated by Bernard Frechtman, 1948; as *Sketch for a Theory of the Emotions*, translated by Philip Mairet, 1962.

L'Imaginaire: Psychologie phénoménologique de l'imagination. 1940; as *The Psychology of the Imagination*, translated by Bernard Fechtman, 1948.

L'Étre et le néant: Essai d'ontologie phénoménologique. 1943; as *Being and Nothingness: An Essay on Phenomenological Ontology*, translated by Hazel E. Barnes, 1956.

L'Existentialisme est un humanisme. 1946; as *Existentialism*, translated by Bernard Frechtman, 1947; as *Existentialism and Humanism*, translated by Philip Mairet, 1948.

Explication de "L'Étranger." 1946.

Réflexions sur la question juive. 1947; as *Anti-Semite and Jew*, translated by George G. Becker, 1948; as *Portrait of an Anti-Semite*, translated by Erik de Mauny, 1948.

Baudelaire. 1947; as *Baudelaire*, translated by Martin Turnell, 1950.

Situations 1–10. 10 vols., 1947–76; selections as: *What Is Literature?*, translated by Bernard Frechtman, 1949; *Literary and Philosophical Essays*, translated by Annette Michelson, 1955; *Black Orpheus*, translated by S.W. Allen, 1963; *Situations*, translated by Benita Eisler, 1965; *The Communists and Peace*, translated 1965; *The Ghost of Stalin*, translated by Martha H. Fletcher and John R. Kleinschmidt, 1968 (as *The Spectre of Stalin*, translated by Irene Clephane, 1969); *Between Existentialism and Marxism*, translated by John Mathews, 1974; *Life/Situations*, translated by Paul Auster and Lynda Davis, 1977; *Sartre in the Seventies*, 1978; as *Colonialism and Neo-colonizalism*, translated by Steve Brewer, Azzedine Haddour and Terry Mc Williams, 2001.

Entretiens sur la politique, with others. 1949.

Saint Genet, Comédien et martyr. 1952; as *Saint Genet, Actor and Martyr*, translated by Bernard Frechtman, 1963.

L'Affaire Henri Martin, with others. 1953.

Critique de la raison dialectique: Théorie des ensembles pratiques. 1960; as *Search for a Method*, translated by Hazel E. Barnes, 1963; as *Critique of Dialectical Reason: Theory of Practical Ensembles*, edited by Jonathan Rée and translated by Alan Sheridan-Smith, 1976; as *The Intelligibility of History*, edited by Arlette Elkaim-Sartre and translated by Quintin Hoare, 1991.

On Cuba. 1961.

Les Mots (autobiography). 1963; as *Words*, translated by Bernard Frechtman, 1964; as *The Words*, translated by Irene Clephane, 1964.

Essays in Aesthetics, edited and translated by Wade Baskin. 1963.

Que peut la littérature?, with others. 1965.

La Transcendance de l'ego, Esquisse d'une description phénoménologique. 1965; as *The Transcendence of the Ego: An Existentialist Theory of Consciousness*, edited and translated by Forrest Williams and Robert Kirkpatrick. 1957.

The Philosophy of Sartre, edited by Robert Denoon Cumming. 1966.

Of Human Freedom, edited and translated by Wade Baskin. 1967.

Essays in Existentialism, edited and translated by Wade Baskin. 1967.

On Genocide. 1968.

Les Communistes ont peur de la révolution. 1969.

L'Idiot de la famille: Gustave Flaubert de 1821 à 1857. 3 vols., 1971–72; as *The Family Idiot: Gustave Flaubert 1821–1857*, translated by Carol Cosman, 5 vols., 1981–93.

War Crimes in Vietnam, with others. 1971.

Un théâtre de situations, edited by Michel Contat and Michel Rybalka. 1973; as *On Theatre*, translated by Frank Jellinek, 1976.

Politics and Literature, translated by J.A. Underwood and John Calder. 1973.

The Writings 2: Selected Prose, edited by Michel Contat and Michel Rybalka. 1974.

On a raison de se révolter, with others. 1974.

Les Carnets de la drôle de guerre: Novembre 1939–Mars 1940. 1983; as *War Diaries: November 1939–March 1940*, translated by Quintin Hoare, 1984; as *War Diaries: Notebooks from a Phoney War*, translated by Hoare, 1984.

Lettres au Castor et à quelques autres 1926–39 and *1940–63*, edited by Simone de Beauvoir, 2 vols., 1983; as *Witness to My Life: The Letters of Jean Paul Sartre to Simone de Beauvoir 1926–1939*, and *Quiet Moments in a War: The Letters of Jean-Paul Sartre to*

Simone de Beauvoir 1943–63, translated by Lee Fahnestock and Norman MacAfee, 1993–94.
La Mauvaise Foi, edited by Marc Wetzel. 1985.
Mallarmé, la Lucidité et sa face d'ombre. 1986; as *Mallarmé: or, the Poet of Nothingness*, translated by E. Sturm, 1988.
Vérité et existence, edited by Arlette Elkaim-Sartre. 1989.
Notebooks for an Ethics, translated by David Pellauer. 1992.
Jean-Paul Sartre: Basic Writings, edited by Stephen Priest. 2000.

*

Bibliography: *The Writings 1: A Bibliographical Life* edited by Michel Contat and Michel Rybalka and translated by Richard McCleary, 1974; *Jean-Paul Sartre: A Bibliography of International Criticism* by Robert Wilcocks, 1975; *Jean-Paul Sartre and His Critics: An International Bibliography 1938–1980* by François and Claire Lapointe, 1981.

Critical Studies: *Sartre, Romantic Rationalist* by Iris Murdoch, 1953; *Sartre: a Literary and Political Study*, 1960, and *Sartre: A Biographical Introduction*, 1971, both by Philip Thody; *Jean-Paul Sartre: A Collection of Critical Essays* edited by Mary Warnock, 1971; *Camus and Sartre: Crisis and Commitment* by Germaine Brée, 1972; *Sartre*, 1973, and *Sartre and Flaubert*, 1981, both by Hazel E. Barnes, 1981; *A Commentary of Sartre's "Being and Nothingness,"* 1974, and *A Commentary on Sartre's Critique of Dialectic Reason*, 1986, both by J. Catalano; *From Sartre to the New Novel* by Betty T. Rahv, 1974; *Critical Fictions: The Literary Criticism of Jean-Paul Sartre* by Joseph Halpern, 1976; *Jean-Paul Sartre's Existentialism in "Nausea"* by Ashok Kumar Malhotra, 1978; *Sartre* by Peter Caws, 1979; *Sartre's Theory of Literature*, 1979, and *Sartre: The Necessity of Freedom*, 1988, both by C. Howells; *Sartre's Marxism* by Mark Poster, 1979; *Sartre as Biographer* by Douglas Collins, 1980; *Sartre and Surrealism* by Marius Perrin, 1980; *The Philosophy of Jean-Paul Sartre* edited by Paul Arthur Schilpp, 1981; *Sartre: Literature and Theory* by Rhiannon Goldthorpe, 1984; *Sartre: Life and Works* by Kenneth and Margaret Thompson, 1984; *Writing Against: A Biography of Sartre* by Ronald Hayman, 1986; *Sartre's Second Critique* by Ronald Aronson, 1987; *Sartre: A Life* by Annie Cohen-Solal, translated by Anna Cancogni, 1987; *Jean-Paul Sartre: Les Mains sales* by Paul Reed, 1988; *Critical Essays on Sartre* edited by Robert Wilcocks, 1988; *Jean-Paul Sartre: Hated Conscience of His Century* by John Gerassi, 1989; *In the Shadow of Sartre* by Liliane Siegel, 1990; *Understanding John-Paul Sartre* by Philip R. Wood, 1990; *Simone de Beauvoir and Jean Paul Sartre: The Remaking of a 20th-Century Legend* by Kate and Edward Fullbrook, 1993; *Sartre*, edited and introduced by Christina Howells, 1995; *Sartre's French Contemporaries and Enduring Influences*, edited with introductions by William L. McBride, 1997; *The Bodily Nature of Consciousness: Sartre and Contemporary Philosophy of Mind* by Kathleen Wider, 1997; *Existential Fiction of Ayi Kwei Armah, Albert Camus and Jean-Paul Sartre* by Tommie Lee Jackson, 1997; *Below the Iceberg: Anti-Sartre and Other Essays* by Colin Wilson, 1998; *Jean-Paul Sartre*, edited with introduction by Harold Bloom, 2001.

* * *

Jean-Paul Sartre can be said to have made a profession of being the gadfly of France and of a sizeable portion of the Western world for some three decades following World War II. His moral authority extended far beyond the actual readership of his literary, philosophical, and political writings, although these were quite numerous and varied. Among intellectuals in the English-speaking world, only Bertrand Russell was his equal as a force in marshalling opinion on the Left, and together they created the International War Crimes Tribunal in 1966 to condemn the American war in Vietnam. Sartre's career as a writer and thinker traces a long, rather tortuous route from the radical individualism of his beginnings to spokesman for all wars of national liberation, and for proletarian causes of every sort, from the 1950s onward.

On the eve of World War II, Sartre began to emerge as a redoubtable if impetuous critic of the previous generation of French writers, in articles (on Giraudoux and Mauriac, most notably) that he contributed to the *Nouvelle Revue française*. At the same time he published a first novel, *La Nausée* (*Nausea*), that presents an atheist intellectual hero, seriously at odds with society, who undergoes a psychological crisis that threatens his very identity. He concludes ultimately that salvation is to be found only in the making of art. Antoine Roquentin, the hero of this pre-existentialist *Künstlerroman*, thus bears a marked resemblance to Proust's Marcel, and the novel has frequently been taken to represent a critical phase of development within European modernism. An early collection of short stories evidencing numerous naturalistic and ironic features *Le Mur* (*The Wall*) dates from this same period, which antedates the Sartrean notion of the writer's commitment to his time and to changing the world.

His experiences in a German prisoner of war camp from June 1940 to March 1941 had a determining effect on Sartre's notion of ethical choice. For Christmas 1940 he wrote a play on the massacre of the Innocents entitled *Bariona; ou, Le Fils de tonnerre* (*Bariona; or, The Son of Thunder*), which he produced in the prison camp. The effect of the play on his fellow prisoners moved Sartre deeply, as he was to relate much later to Jean Genet. From this experience derives a central feature of his early theatre: the conversion of a protagonist to responsible action in the name of a community with whom he henceforth recognizes a bond. This was to be the treatment he would give the Orestes myth in his first play produced commercially in occupied Paris, *Les Mouches* (*The Flies*). His second play, *Huis clos* (*No Exit*), produced a year later, in 1944, has provided two of the most memorable catch phrases of Sartrean existentialism: "You are—your life, and nothing else"; and: "Hell is—other people!".

Sartre's optimism concerning the creative writer's ability to influence others and, in particular, to jar them from complacency to a recognition that all mankind is doomed to freedom—reliance upon exterior moral values and trust in an inner life being equally reprehensible forms of "bad faith," in his view—stimulated him to formulate an austere, yet exhilarating form of the writer's commitment (*engagement*) in *L'Existentialisme est un humanisme* (*Existentialism and Humanism*) early in the post-war years. This existentialist ethos, in which the individual is obliged to make choices as though he were choosing for all mankind, owes much to Kant's categorical imperative, and possibly more to the Alsatian Protestant values of Sartre's grandfather Schweitzer, who reared him. (Despite the obvious difference in their professed thought and in their careers, Sartre and his second cousin, Albert Schweitzer, had this important element of their formative years in common.) This difficult and restless version of ethics represents Sartre's first major effort to overcome the individualist ontology of *L'Être et le néant* (*Being and Nothingness*), which belongs conceptually to Sartre's pre-war period.

Sartre had high hopes for a novelistic tetralogy published under the programmatic title, *Les Chemins de la liberté* (*Paths of Freedom*), from 1945 to 1949. As a formal experiment, it is a modification of techniques developed by the pre-war American novel. In it Sartre intended to align his notion of individual freedom with responsible political action. Possibly because Sartre wished to maintain that a fictional character is "free" of the author, the proposed synthesis of the work, projected for the fourth novel, was never completed. It is probably for a similar reason that Sartre never wrote the formal treatise on ethics that he had promised as an accompaniment to *Being and Nothingness*. Sartre was to write several more plays between the 1951 *Le Diable et le bon Dieu* (*The Devil and the Good Lord*) and the 1965 *Les Troyennes* (*The Trojan Women*), as well as three screenplays.

Les Temps Modernes, a magazine of contemporary commentary co-founded by Sartre with Simone de Beauvoir and Maurice Merleau-Ponty in 1945, rapidly took its place as the foremost moulder of opinion among readers of the non-communist Left. From the early 1950s onward, Sartre's evolution as a writer is inseparable from his relations with the French Communist Party. A series of essays prompted by the Cold War and published in English as *The Communists and Peace* appeared in *Les Temps Modernes* from July 1952. At the same time Sartre had a noisy falling-out with Camus. Seen from a sufficient distance, Sartre's political articles resemble many other pro-Soviet, anti-Atlantic Alliance positions. Their real interest, however, lies in Sartre's efforts to establish a position independent of the Party, while defending it against its enemies. The same decade of the 1950s again found Sartre thinking against a former self, the author of *Being and Nothingness*. Whereas he had initially refused Marxist historical determinism as well as the Freudian unconscious, the methodological preface to his *Critique de la raison dialectique* (*Critique of Dialectical Reason*) attempted to conciliate the two.

Still another activity that spans his existentialist and Marxist periods is that of biographer, in a series of existential psychoanalyses of Baudelaire, Genet, and, eventually, himself. The least interesting of these books is *Baudelaire*, which on existentialist principles indicts Baudelaire for making the wrong choices in his life. *Saint Genet, Comédien et martyr* (*Saint Genet, Actor and Martyr*) is richer, more sympathetic, and, although characteristically turgid at times, a better piece of writing. *Les Mots* (*The Words*) may well stand as Sartre's literary masterwork.

Sartre enjoyed a lifelong love-hate relationship with Flaubert, and, had he been able to complete the promised study of *Madame Bovary* (yet another unfinished major project), he might have given the world the most thorough critical study any major writer ever devoted to another. As it stands, in three volumes, *L'Idiot de la famille* (*The Family Idiot*) is rather the most extensive application of Sartre's new critical method as set forth in the *Critique of Dialectical Reason*.

By the time he published his autobiography, Sartre had lost confidence completely in the ability of writers to change anything in the world through their writing. Never one to avoid taking a stand, however, he refused the Nobel prize for literature that same year, on the grounds that it rewarded anti-Soviet writers. From the mid-1960s until his death, Sartre published nothing literary, aside from his work on Flaubert, and even his political writing tended progressively toward journalism. In 1969 he signed the pamphlet *Les Communistes ont peur de la révolution*, accusing the French Communist Party of conservatism. The student revolt of 1968 finally provided him with an opportunity to mount the barricades, at age 63, and exhort youth to bring about the Revolution. In 1970, consistent with these principles and to the chagrin of many former admirers, Sartre assumed the

editorship of the rabble-rousing Maoist paper, *La Cause du Peuple*. Sartre's last decade was marked by ruined health and near-blindness. On the eve of his death, near the end of his 75th year, he was arguably the best-known living writer in the world.

—A. James Arnold

See the essays on *The Age of Reason*, *The Flies*, *Nausea*, and *No Exit*.

SCARRON, Paul

Born: Paris, France, 4 July 1610. **Education:** Educated at numerous establishments. **Family:** Married Françoise d'Aubigné in 1652. **Career:** Joined the household of Charles de Beaumanoir-Lavardin, bishop of Le Mans, 1632, appointed canon, 1636, although the appointment was disputed, resolved in the ecclesiastical courts (in Scarron's favour), 1640; accompanied Alphonse de Richelieu on a visit to Rome, 1635; was renowned for his womanizing and drinking in preference to his ecclesiastical duties, but began writing during this time. Suffered from a severe disabling disease that left him paralysed and deformed, from 1638. Returned to Paris, 1641; Received pension from Anne d'Autriche until 1651, and from Foucquet, from 1653; moved to Fontenay-aux-Roses, 1659–60. **Died:** 6 October 1660.

PUBLICATIONS

Collections

Les Dernières oeuvres. 2 vols., 1668.
Oeuvres. 7 vols., 1752.
Oeuvres complètes, edited by Jean-François Bastiien. 7 vols., 1786.
Théâtre complet. 1912.
Poésies diverses, edited by Maurice Cauchie. 2 vols., 1947–61.
Oeuvres diverses. 1948–.
Oeuvres complètes. 2 vols., 1951.

Fiction

Le Roman comique (unfinished). 2 vols., 1651–57; revised by V. Fournel, 2 vols., 1857; edited by Henri Bénac, 1951, Émile Magne, 1955, Antoine Adam, 1958, and by V. Serroy, 1985; as *The Comical Romance* (second part), translated by John Balteel, 1665; also translated by Tom Brown, 1968; as *The Comic Romance*, translated by O. Goldsmith, 2 vols., 1775.
Nouvelles tragi-comiques tournées de l'espagnol en français. 5 vols., 1655–63; edited by R. Guichemerre, 1986 (includes *La Précaution inutile*; *Les Hypocrites*; *L'Adultère innocent*; *Plus d'effets que de parolles*; *Le Châtiment d'avarice*).
Scarron's Novels (includes *The Fruitless Precaution*; *The Hypocrites*; *The Innocent Adultery*; *The Judge in His Own Cause*; *The Rival-Brothers*; *The Invisible Mistress*; *The Chastisement of Avarice*), translated by John Davies. 1665.
La Foire Saint-Germain. 1665.
Plus d'effets que de parolles, as *The Unexpected Choice*, translated by John Davies. 1670.

Plays

Jodelet; ou, Le Maître valet (produced 1643). 1645; in *Théâtre du XVIIe siècle*, 1986.
Les Trois Dorothées; ou, Jodelet souffleté (produced 1646). 1646.
Les Boutades du capitaine Matamore et ses comédies. 1646.
L'Héritier ridicule; ou, La Dame intéressée (produced 1649). 1649; edited by R. Guichemerre, 1983.
Don Japhet d'Arménie (produced 1652). 1653; edited by R. Garapon, 1967.
L'Écolier de Salamanque; ou, Les Ennemis généreux. 1654.
Le Gardien de soi-même. 1655.
Le Marquis ridicule; ou, La Comtesse faite à la hâte. 1656.
La Fausse Apparence. 1662.
Le Prince corsaire. 1662.

Verse

La Suite du Cid en abrégé. 1637.
Receuil de quelques vers burlesques. 1643.
Le Typhon; ou, La Gigantomachie. 1644; as *Typhon, or, The Gyant's War with the Gods*, translated by J. Phillips, 1665; also translated by Bernard Mandewille, 1704.
Oeuvres burlesques. 3 vols., 1646–51.
Le Virgile travesti. 7 vols., 1648–52; additional volume (unfinished), 1660; edited by Jean Serroy, 1988; as *Scarronides*, 1854.
Léandre et Héro. 1656.
The Unexpected Choice, translated by John Davies. 1670.
La Ville de Paris en vers burlesques. 1973.

Other

Apologie pour M. Mairet contre le calomnies du sieur Corneille de Rouen. 1637.
Mazarinade. 1651.
Factum; ou, Requête. 1652.
Letters to Persons of the Greatest Eminence and Quality, translated by John Davies. 1677.

*

Bibliography: *Bibliographie générale des oeuvres de Scarron* by Émile Magne, 1924.

Critical Studies: *Paul Scarron's Adaptations of the Comedia* by Max Sorkin, 1938; *The Theater of Paul Scarron and the Spanish Comedia* by Raymond R. MacCurdy, 1941; *The Queen's Invalid: A Biography of Paul Scarron* by Naomi Phelps, 1951; *The Drama of Paul Scarron* by F.W. Moore, 1956; *Aspects of Literary Satire in Sorel, Scarron and Furetière* by Robert Berens, 1966; *The Four Interpolated Stories in the "Roman Comique"*, 1971, and *Paul Scarron* (in English), 1972, both by Frederick De Armas; *Paul Scarron, Homme de Lettres* by Marvin H. Cheiten, 1971; *Scarron's Roman comique: A Comedy of the Novel, A Novel of Comedy* by Joan E. De Jean, 1977; *Scarron Satirique* by Lester S. Koritz, 1977; *Menipean Elements in Paul Scarron's Roman comique* by Barbara L. Merry, 1991; *Le livre en trompe-lœ, ou, Le jeu de la dédicace: Montaigne, Scarron, Diderot* by Lorraine Piroux, 1998; *Scarron: Le malade de la reine* by Ange-Pierre Leca, 1999.

* * *

Burlesque poet, comic novelist, and playwright, Paul Scarron was essentially a humorous writer. Recognized by his contemporaries as the chief proponent of the burlesque, a comic genre defined and made popular in the period 1643 to 1657 largely through his own works, Scarron exploited every opportunity to give pleasure by amusing. His substantial output of occasional verses, composed variously from 1643 until his death, bears witness to his lifelong indigence. The need of patronage accounts for a large proportion of this poetry, which ranges from laudatory and gallant salon verses to lively descriptions of everyday activities; but always spiced with Scarron's inimitable use of low style and familiar vocabulary to comic end.

The wide range of social acquaintances enjoyed by Scarron are attested to by his verses, but there is very little if any truly "engaged" writing to his credit: his bantering often self-deprecating wit precludes bitterness or mordant satire. Exceptionally, in 1637, at the instigation of his then patron, the Comte de Delin, he wrote pamphlets attacking Corneille's *Le Cid*, so sparking off the famous literary quarrel over the play; but his sole work of political dissent—a "mazarinade" (a lampoon criticizing the prime minister, published in 1651 at the height of the Frondes), may well have been prompted more by his festering anger at Mazarin's curtailment of his royal stipend than out of any loyalty to the cause of his long-standing friend, the malcontent leader of the insurgents, Paul de Gondi, future Cardinal de Retz.

The rest of Scarron's literary works, which have better stood the test of time, are as eclectic as were his friendships. They can be separated into three main categories. Into the first category fall two long burlesque poems, the first *Le Typhon*, a parody in which he makes fun of the Olympian gods engaged futilely in cosmic battle with the giants led by Typhon; the second, *Le Virgile travesti* [Virgil Travestied], a skit on the *Aneid*. The first seven books of *Le Virgile travesti* were published between 1648 and 1653 after which time the enterprise was, for all intents and purposes, abandoned, though an uncompleted eighth book was published in 1660. These two long poems define the burlesque genre, which creates humour out of the incongruous juxtaposing of opposites; or, as Charles Perrault put it "parler bassement des choses les plus relevees" ([in speaking] basely—in low style—of the noblest of subjects). The great popularity of *Le Virgile travesti* was attributable largely to the rebellious spirit of the time. With its diametrical inversion of the classical literary canon, of which Virgil was the exemplar, it was intended at once to shock and to delight a public well-versed in the classic it parodied. Contemporary political insurrection found itself paralleled by an art form that flouted with complete irreverence accepted literary norms.

The second category includes nine full-length comedies and three unfinished ones, invariably adapted from Spanish models. The best known and most successful are *Jodelet; ou, Le Maître valet* [Jodelet; or, the Master Valet], his first play, performed in 1643 at the Marais theatre, with the renowned comic actor, Julien Bedeau (who used the stage name Jodelet) in the title role, and *Don Japhet d'Arménie* [Japhet of Armenia], the most popular of all Spanish comedy combined in varying proportions the heroic and the comic, the latter aspect being assigned to the stock character of the *gracioso*, a foolish, braggart, yet cowardly valet. Scarron adopts this formula, but fleshes out the role of the servant, allotting him the same type of witty lines and word-play as are to be found in his burlesque poetry. Historically, Scarron's brand of comedy bridges the gap between Corneille's early comedies of the 1630s and those of Molière who, indeed, drew upon Scarronian prototypes in the creation of his own stage persona. Sganarelle, and of his "imaginaire" characters, so-called because, like the Jodelet of Scarron's *Les Trois Dorothées* [The Three Dorothys], they persist in indulging in ridiculous false beliefs.

In the third category are Scarron's most important work, his unfinished episodic novel, *Le Roman comique* (*The Comic Romance*) and five short stories freely translated from variously authored Spanish short novels, collectively entitled *Nouvelles tragi-comiques tournées de l'espagnol en français* [Tragi-comic Tales Translated from Spanish Into French], the first four appearing 1655–57, the last published posthumously in 1663. The popularity of these tales is attested by the 20 editions that were published between 1657 and 1717 as well as by the increase in popularity of this genre throughout the 1600s. They combine romance with wry humour assured by the authorial narrator's comic asides. The first of the five, "La Précaution Intuile" ("The Useless Precaution"), is the main source of Molière's *L'École des femmes* (*School for Wives*), while the hypocrite, Montufar, in the second tale, textually provides the essential traits of Tartuffe.

As in the majority of his comedies and short stories, so too in his long novel, Scarron pits the romantic and the comic against each other, and it is partly to this that the title alludes. A deliberate play on words, the oxymoron "comic romance" admirably describes the novel's content, structure, and disparate tonalities, in addition to designating its genre and main characters. Set in the present, the main story portrays the life of a troupe of strolling players during a fortnight's stay in Le Mans and its environs. Duality and dislocation characterize every aspect of the narrative. The work's apparently random structure, criticized by past critics as, at best, stylistic sloppiness, at worst, incoherence, is recognized today as artfully contrived, to form a rich tapestry of echoing themes and oppositions. The main plot is the least important of the many narrative levels. In the forefront, short, comic chapters retell prefectly-timed farcical episodes involving a stereotypically short, fat, stooge character (Ragotin), or his comic counterpart, the cynical failed actor, Rancour, who is a rogue/trickster type. These alternate with much longer chapters devoted to the quite separate romantic stories of the young lead actors, the ideal lovers prototypically named Destiny and Star, or their more down-to-earth companions, Leander and Angelica; and with four autonomous mini-romances, each of which is derived from a Spanish short novel, and bears no relation to the main story. Scarron's perfect sense of timing and variation of pace, the acuity of his visual observations, and the subtle tonalities of his prose, in sum, his sheer good-hearted yet mischievous sense of fun, lend to his work a unique quality, unmatched by any of his contemporaries, and certainly lacking in the two versions of a denouement to the tale, composed by others after his death, namely, the *Sequel of Offray*, published in 1663, and Préchac's continuation of 1679.

—Patricia M. Harry

SCHEHERAZADE

See THE THOUSAND AND ONE NIGHTS

SCHILLER, (Johann Christoph) Friedrich von

Born: Marbach am Neckar, Duchy of Württemberg, 10 November 1759. **Education:** Educated at village school in Lorch; Latin school, Ludwigsburg, 1766–72. **Family:** Married Charlotte von Lengefeld in 1790; two sons and two daughters. **Military Service:** Conscripted in 1773, and studied law, later medicine, in military academy of Duke Karl Eugen of Württemberg: regimental surgeon, 1780. **Career:** His writing displeased Duke Karl Eugen of Württemberg, so he fled Württemberg in 1782, and sought refuge in the Palatinate, where he received contract to write for the Nationaltheater, Mannheim, 1783–84; editor, *Die Rheinische Thalia* (later *Die Thalia* and *Die Neue Thalia*), 1785–93; joined the Körner circle, in Leipzig, then in Dresden; in Weimar, 1787: through Goethe's help, obtained professorship of history at University of Jena, 1789–91 (resigned because of illness); refused professorship in Tübingen, 1795; lived in Weimar after 1799, and several plays produced under Goethe's direction at the Hoftheater. Ennobled by Emperor Franz II, 1802. **Died:** 9 May 1805.

PUBLICATIONS

Collections

Works [Bohn Standard Library]. 4 vols., 1846–49.
Sämtliche Werke [Säkular-Ausgabe], edited by Eduard von der Hellen. 16 vols., 1904–05.
Sämtliche Werke, edited by Otto Güntter and Georg Witkowski. 20 vols., 1910–11.
Werke [Nationalausgabe], edited by Julius Petersen and Gerhard Fricke. 1943–.
Sämtliche Werke, edited by Gerhard Fricke, H.G. Göpfert, and H. Stubenrauch. 5 vols., 1958–59.
Plays (includes *Intrigue and Love; Don Carlos; Letters on Don Carlos*), edited and translated by Walter Hinderer. 1983.
Werke und Briefe, edited by Klaus Harro Hilzinger and others. 1988–.
Essays, edited by Walter Hinderer and Daniel O. Dahlstrom. 1993.
Five Plays, translated by Robert David MacDonald. 1998.

Plays

Die Räuber (produced 1782). 1781; as *The Robbers*, translated by A.F. Tytler, 1792; several subsequent translations including by F.J. Lamport, with *Wallenstein*, 1979; Robert David MacDonald, 1995.
Die Verschwörung des Fiesko zu Genua (produced 1784). 1783; as *Fiesco; or, The Genoese Conspiracy*, translated by G.H. Noehden and J. Stoddart, 1796.
Kabale und Liebe (produced 1784). 1784; as *Cabal and Love*, 1795; as *The Minister*, translated by M.G. Lewis, 1798; as *The Harper's Daughter*, 1813; as *Love and Intrigue*, translated by Frederick Rolf, 1962.
Don Carlos (produced 1787). 1787; as *Don Carlos*, translated by G.H. Noehden and J. Stoddart, 1798; numerous subsequent translations including by James Kirkup, in *Classic Theatre 2*, edited by Eric Bentley, 1959, and James Maxwell, 1987; translated by Robert David MacDonald, 1996; in *Don Carlos; and, Mary*

Stuart, translated by Hilary Collier Sy-Quia, adapted by Peter Oswald, 1996.

Egmont, from the play by Goethe (produced 1796). 1857.

Wallenstein: Wallensteins Lager, Die Piccolomini, Wallensteins Tod (produced 1798–99). 1798–99; translated as *Wallenstein*, by S.T. Coleridge, 1800; numerous subsequent translations including by Charles E. Passage, 1958, and F.J. Lamport, with *The Robbers*, 1979.

Maria Stuart (produced 1800). 1801; as *Mary Stuart*, translated by J.C. Mellish, 1801; numerous subsequent translations including by Stephen Spender, 1959, F.J. Lamport, in *Five German Trage-dies*, 1969; Robert David Macdonald, 1987; and Jeremy Sams, 1996.

Macbeth, from the play by Shakespeare (produced 1800). 1801.

Nathan der Weise, from the play by Lessing (produced 1801).

Die Jungfrau von Orleans (produced 1801). 1801; as *The Maid of Orleans*, translated by J.E. Drinkwater, 1835; as *Joan of Arc*, translated by Robert David Macdonald, 1987.

Turandot, from the play by Gozzi (produced 1802). 1802.

Der Neffe als Onkel, from a play by Louis-Benoit Picard (produced 1803). 1842; as *The Nephew as Uncle*, translated by G.S. Harris, 1856.

Der Parasit, from a play by Louis-Benoit Picard (produced 1803). 1806; as *The Parasite*, translated by F. Simpson, 1856.

Die Braut von Messina (produced 1803). 1803; as *The Bride of Messina*, translated by G. Irvine, 1837; also translated by A. Lodge, 1841; E. Allfrey, 1876.

Wilhelm Tell (produced 1804). 1804; as *William Tell*, translated by R.L. Pearsall, 1825; numerous subsequent translations including by John Prudhoe, 1970, and William E. Mainland, 1972.

Die Huldigung der Künste (produced 1804). 1805.

Phädra, from the play by Racine (produced 1805). 1805.

Iphigenie in Aulis, from the play by Euripides. 1807.

Fiction

Der Verbrecher aus Infamie. 1786; as *Der Verbrecher aus verlorener Ehre*, 1792; as *The Dishonoured Irreclaimable*, translated by R. Holcroft, in *Tales from the German*, 1826.

Der Geisterseher (fragment). 1789; as *The Ghost Seer; or, Apparitionist*, 1795; as *The Armenian; or, the Ghost-Seer*, translated by W. Render, 1800; as *The Ghost-Seer*, translated by Henry G. Bohn, 1992.

Spiel des Schicksals. 1789.

Verse

Anthologie auf das Jahr 1782. 1782.

Gedichte. 2 vols., 1800–03.

The Poems and Ballads, translated by Edward Bulwer Lytton. 1844.

The Minor Poems, translated by J.H. Merivale. 1844.

The Poems of Schiller Complete, translated by E.A. Bowring. 1856.

Selected Poems, edited by Frank M. Fowler. 1969.

Poet of Freedom (English translations). 2 vols., 1985–88.

Other

Die Geschichte des Abfalls der vereinigten Niederlande von der spanischen Regierung. 1788; as *History of the Rise and Progress of the Belgian Republic*, translated by T. Horne, 1807; as *The History of the Defection of the United Netherlands from the*

Spanish Empire, translated by E.B. Eastwick, 1844; as *The Revolt of the Netherlands*, translated by A.J.W. Morrison and L. Dora Schmitz, 1897.

Geschichte des dreissigjährigen Krieges. 1793; as *The History of the Thirty Years War in Germany*, translated by Captain Blaquiere, 1799; also translated by A.J.W. Morrison, 1899.

Über naive und sentimentalische Dichtung. In *Die Horen*, 1795–96; as *On Simple and Sentimental Poetry*, in *Essays Aesthetical and Philosophical*, 1884; as *On the Naive and Sentimental in Litera-ture*, translated by Helen Watanabe O'Kelly, 1981.

Briefe über die ästhetische Erziehung des Menschen. In *Die Horen*, 1795; as *Upon the Aesthetic Culture of Man*, in *Philosophical and Aesthetic Letters and Essays*, 1845; as *On the Aesthetic Education of Man*, translated by Reginald Snell, 1954; also edited and translated by Elizabeth M. Wilkinson and L.A. Willoughby, 1967; as *The Aesthetic Letters*, 1967; as *On the Aesthetic Education of Man: In a Series of Letters*, translated with introduction by Reginald Snell, 1994.

Briefwechsel, with Cotta, edited by W. Vollmer. 1876.

Briefwechsel, with Goethe, edited by F. Muncker. 4 vols., 1892; edited by Siegfried Seidel, 3 vols., 1984.

Briefe, edited by Fritz Jonas. 7 vols., 1892–96.

Briefwechsel, with Körner, edited by L. Gaiger. 4 vols., 1893; edited by Klaus Berghahn, 1973.

Briefwechsel, with Wilhelm von Humboldt, edited by A. Leitzmann. 1900.

Briefe 1776–1789, edited by Karl Pörnbacher. 1969.

Friedrich Schiller: Medicine, Psychology and Literature, translated by Kenneth Dewhurst and Nigel Reeves. 1978.

Schillers Briefe, edited by Erwin Streitfeld and Viktor Žmegač. 1983.

*

Bibliography: *Schiller-Bibliographie 1893–1958* by W. Vulpius, 1959; continuation volumes by W. Vulpius, 1967, P. Wersig, 1977, and Roland Bärwinkel (and others), 1989; supplements in *Jahrbuch der Deutschen Schillergesellschaft*.

Critical Studies: *Schiller's Drama: Theory and Practice* by E.L. Stahl, 1954; *Schiller and the Ideal of Freedom*, 1959, *The Drama of Schiller*, 1963, *Interpreting Schiller: A Study of Four Plays*, 1986, and *A Study of Schiller's "Letters on the Aesthetic Education of Man,"* 1986, all by Ronald D. Miller; *A Schiller Symposium* edited by A. Leslie Willson, 1960; *Schiller's Writings on Aesthetics* by Stanley S. Kerry, 1961; *Friedrich Schiller* by Bernt von Heiseler, 1962; *Schiller, The Poet as Historian* by Walter M. Simon, 1966; *Schiller, The Dramatic Writer* by H.B. Garland, 1969; *The Theatre of Goethe and Schiller* by John E. Prudhoe, 1973; *Schiller's Dramas: Talent and Integrity*, 1974, and *Schiller, A Master of the Tragic Form*, 1975, both by Ilsa Graham; *Friedrich Schiller* by Charles E. Passage, 1975; *Friedrich Schiller and Christian Gottfried Körner: A Critical Rela-tionship* by Albert James Camigliano, 1976; *Images of Transcience in the Poems and Ballads of Friedrich Schiller* by Ronald F. Crawford, 1977; *Schiller and "Alienation"* by Vicky Rippere, 1981; *Schiller* by John D. Simons, 1981; *Schiller and the Historical Character: Presen-tation and Interpretation in the Historiographical Works and in the Historical Dramas*, 1982, and *Friedrich Schiller: Drama, Thought and Politics*, 1991, both by Lesley Sharpe; *The Philosophical Back-ground to Friedrich Schiller's Aesthetics of Living Form* by Leonard

P. Wessell, 1982; *Spirited Women Heroes: Major Female Characters in the Dramas of Goethe, Schiller and Kleist* by Julie D. Prandi, 1983; *Greek Antiquity in Schiller's Wallenstein* by Gisela M. Berns, 1985; *Friedrich Schiller and Swabian Pietism* by Arthur W. McCardle, 1986; *The Theme of Freedom in Schiller's Plays* by Marie-Luise Waldeck, 1986; *Constructing Reality: A Rhetorical Analysis of Friedrich Schiller's Letters of the Aesthetic Education of Man* by Tod Curtis Kontje, 1987; *Dynamic Stillness: Philosophical Conceptions of "uhe" in Schiller, Büchner and Heine* by Mark William Roche, 1987; *Aesthetic Reconstructions: The Seminal Writings of Lessing, Kant and Schiller* by Anthony Savile, 1987; *Friedrich von Schiller and the Drama of Human Existence* by Alexej Ugrinsky, 1988; *Maria Stuart* by Erika Swales, 1988; *Pre-Romantic Attitudes to Landscape in the Writings of Friedrich Schiller* by Sheila Margaret Benn, 1991; *Friedrich Schiller* by T.J. Reed, 1991; *Nostalgic Teleology: Friedrich Schiller and the Schemata of Aesthetic Humanism* by Constantin Behler, 1995; *Schiller's Aesthetic Essays: Two Centuries of Criticism* by Lesley Sharpe, 1995; *A Study of Schiller's Jungfrau von Orleans* by R. D. Miller, 1995; *Harmonious Tensions: The Writings of Friedrich Schiller* by Steven D. Martinson, 1996; *Nietzsche and Schiller: Untimely Aesthetics* by Nicholas Martin, 1996; *Dialectic of Love: Platonism in Schiller's Aesthetics* by David Pugh, 1997; *Images of Goethe Through Schiller's Egmont* by David G. John, 1998; *Schiller's Early Dramas: A Critical History* by David Pugh, 2000; *Schiller's Wound: The Theater of Trauma from Crisis to Commodity* by Stephanie Hammer, 2001; *Schiller's Wallenstein, Maria Stuart, and Die Jungfrau von Orleans: The Critical Legacy* by Kathy Saranpa, 2002.

* * *

Friedrich von Schiller is the principal writer, after Goethe, first of the *Sturm und Drang*, then of the classical movement in German literature. Goethe observed in 1827 that "the idea of freedom dominates all Schiller's work . . . in his youth it was physical, in his later years ideal freedom that concerned him." The three early prose plays, *Die Räuber* (*The Robbers*), *Die Verschwörung des Fiesko zu Genua* (*Fiesco; or, The Genoese Conspiracy*), and *Kabale und Liebe* (*Cabal and Love*), all depict heroes who rebel against physical and social confinement, who seek to be the architects of their own and others' earthly destinies, and who fail tragically because they seek to fly too high, to transcend the limits inherent in human nature. All begin as idealists, but Karl Moor in *The Robbers* turns into a criminal, Fiesco and on a smaller scale Ferdinand (in *Cabal and Love*) into tyrants like the corrupt rulers they oppose. Their rebellion is expressed in a dramatic style of extreme forcefulness, even violence, which is also found in Schiller's early poetry. *Don Carlos* marks the beginning of a transition. It is still concerned with "physical"—in this case social and political—freedom, and it evokes this ideal in language recalling what is probably (thanks to Beethoven) Schiller's best-known poem, *An die Freude*, the *Ode to Joy* which dates from the same period. It also shows how idealism may verge upon fanaticism (Schiller's verdict on the political idealist Marquis von Posa remains ambiguous and disputed); and the nominal hero and his friend Posa appear scarcely more tragic than their tyrannical adversary, Philip II of Spain, seen as the prisoner of history, of the Inquisition, and of the despotic system of which he himself is the head. *Don Carlos* anticipates Schiller's mature dramas in its adoption of blank verse and elevated diction, in contrast to the prose of the early plays, with their

often uneasy mixture of earthy realism and exaggerated rhetoric. But it is an over-long and unwieldy play, and did not satisfy its creator, who after it completed no more dramatic work for 13 years.

Those years were principally devoted to aesthetic, historiographical, and philosophical studies. The instinctive playwright now yielded to the theorist, concerned to define the nature and function of his own art and of art in general, the role of art and culture in human society and history. The idealistic champion of freedom and progress was shocked by the excesses of the French Revolution (though on the strength of *The Robbers* he was made an honorary citizen of the French Republic) and now sought to understand the nature of the historical process and to relate to it the ultimate freedom of the human will in which he still strove to believe. He grappled intensively with the philosophy of Kant, and sought to understand the human and artistic character of his friend Goethe, so different from his own. The great essay *Über naive und sentimentalische Dichtung* (*On the Naive and Sentimental in Literature*) sums up all these speculative concerns. Schiller's collaboration with Goethe extended to joint authorship in the case of the *Xenien*, satirical epigrams on the state of contemporary German culture, and friendly rivalry in the ballads of which both men produced notable examples in 1797.

The *Wallenstein* trilogy ushers in Schiller's dramatic maturity. The themes of self-determination, of idealism, of personal and political freedom take on new significance against a background of war and of harsh political necessity, and Schiller hints at parallels between the Thirty Years War and the revolutionary wars of his own day. True freedom is now seen to be "ideal" in the sense that it cannot be achieved in the real world, or measured by any kind of material success, but is only to be found in the acceptance of moral responsibility. This is also the theme of *Maria Stuart* (*Mary Stuart*), embodied in the contrast between the physical and political freedom achieved by Elizabeth of England at the price of her moral dignity, and the spiritual freedom achieved by Mary Queen of Scots at the price of her own death and the defeat of her political cause. These two works mark the summit of Schiller's classical phase, combining a rich and complex historical subject matter and lofty philosophical themes with a high degree of dramatic concentration and formal discipline—a synthesis, as Schiller himself defined his aim, of Shakespearian and Sophoclean drama.

His later plays are more experimental, tending in *Die Braut von Messina* (*The Bride of Messina*) to further classical concentration, in *Die Jungfrau von Orleans* (*The Maid of Orleans*, also translated as *Joan of Arc*) and *Wilhelm Tell* (*William Tell*) to a more Romantic expansiveness, with large casts and colourful spectacle. All three again show freedom to be found not in self-assertion but in the acceptance of responsibility, though in *The Maid of Orleans* and particularly in *William Tell* this moral autonomy appears as the guarantee of the ultimate possibility of national and political liberation. But if in these works Schiller appears to oppose an optimistic vision of history to the chaos of his own times, the unfinished *Demetrius*, on which he was working when he died, seems to revert to the grimmer realism of *Wallenstein*.

Schiller's later plays established the historical drama as the major serious dramatic form in German. The plays themselves, with their elevated sentiments and elevated language, have fallen somewhat out of theatrical fashion in recent years: modern taste has tended to prefer the rawness and vigour and the more direct political engagement of his earlier works. The idealism of *The Maid of Orleans* was parodied by Brecht in his *Die heilige Johanna der Schlachthöfe* (*Saint Joan of the Stockyards*), 1932, and more recently *William Tell* and *Mary*

Stuart have similarly been irreverently "demythologized" by Max Frisch and Wolfgang Hildesheimer respectively. Latterly a number of German academic critics have drawn attention to the complexity and subtlety of Schiller's vision of history; but it remains doubtful whether his mature works will receive appropriate productions in a theatre still largely dominated by the Brechtian tradition, so resolutely opposed to the view of art which he and Goethe in their classical collaboration propounded.

—F.J. Lamport

See the essays on *Don Carlos*, *Mary Stuart*, *Ode to Joy*, *Wallenstein*, and *William Tell*.

SCHLEGEL, August Wilhelm von and Friedrich von

August Wilhelm von Schlegel: **Born:** Hanover, Germany, 5 September 1767. **Education:** Educated at schools in Hanover; Göttingen University, Hanover, 1786–91. **Family:** Married 1) Caroline Böhmer (née Michaelis) in 1796 (divorced 1803); 2) Sophie Paulus in 1818. **Career:** Private tutor, Amsterdam, 1791–95; contributor to Schiller's journal *Die Horen*, 1796–1800; lecturer, 1796–98, professor, 1798–1801, University of Jena; reviewer for the *Jenaer Allgemeine Literaturzeitung*, 1796–1801; co-founder and editor with Friedrich Schlegel, *Das Athenäum*, 1798–1800; delivered a series of lectures supporting the Romantic movement, Berlin, 1801–04; employed by Madame de Staël, *q.v.* as an adviser on German literature and culture, and tutor to her children, lived in Lausanne, Switzerland with the de Staëls and made frequent trips to Italy, Austria, France, and Geneva, 1804–08; delivered a series of lectures on drama, Vienna, 1808; moved to Chaumont-sur-Loire, near Tours with the de Staëls; moved to Berne, 1810; Madame de Staël forced to leave France by Napoleon's government and Schlegel travelled with her to Vienna, Moscow, St. Petersburg, Stockholm, and London, 1812; worked in the service of the Swedish Prince and General Bernadotte as a French-speaking propagandist, Stockholm, 1812–14; joined de Staël in London and travelled with her to Paris and Italy, 1814–17; professor of literature and art history, University of Bonn, from 1818; founding editor, *Indische Bibliothek*, 1823–30. **Died:** 12 May 1845. *Friedrich von Schlegel*: **Born:** Karl Wilhelm Friedrich Schlegel in Hanover, Germany, 10 March 1772. **Education:** Educated at Göttingen University, Hanover, 1790–91; Leipzig University, 1791–94. **Military Service:** Attached to the Austrian army, 1809–10; edited the army newspaper, *Österreichische Zeitung*. **Family:** Married the writer Dorothea Veit (née Mendelssohn) in 1804. **Career:** Apprenticed to a banker in Leipzig, 1788; moved to Dresden, 1794, and Berlin, 1797; contributor, *Deutschland*, Berlin, 1797, and *Der Teutsche Merkur*; co-founder and editor, with August Wilhelm Schlegel, *Das Athenäum*, 1798–1800, the journal of the Jena Romantics, a group including Ludwig Tieck, Caroline and Dorothea Schlegel, Friedrich Schleiermacher, Novalis, the philosopher Johann Gottlieb Fichte; lecturer, University of Jena, 1800–01; lived in Paris, 1802–04; founding editor of the journal *Europa*, 1803–05; lived in Cologne, 1804–07; converted to Roman Catholicism, 1808; moved to Vienna, 1808; administrative position with the Austrian government's diplomatic service, 1809;

returned to Vienna, 1810, gave a series of lectures on modern history, 1811; co-founder and editor of the periodical *Deutsches Museum*, 1812–13; appointed by Metternich as a member of the Austrian delegation to the Bundestag, Frankfurt, 1815–18; returned to Vienna, 1818; editor of the journal, *Concordia*, 1820–23. **Died:** 12 January 1829.

PUBLICATIONS

Prose

Charakteristiken und Kritiken. 1801; edited by Hans Eichner, 1967.

PUBLICATIONS BY AUGUST WILHELM VON SCHLEGEL

Collections

Sämtliche Werke, edited by E. Böcking. 26 vols., 1846–48.
Kritische Schriften und Briefe, edited by Edgar Lohner. 7 vols., 1962–74.
Kritische Ausgabe der Vorlesungen, edited by Ernst Behler. 1989–.

Prose

Ehrenpforte und Triumphbogen für den Theaterpräsidenten von Kotzebue. 1801.
Vorlesungen über schöne Literatur und Kunst. 1801–04; edited by Jakob Minor, 1884; reprinted 1968.
Comparaison entre la Phèdre de Racine et celle d'Euripide. 1807.
Vorlesungen über dramatische Kunst und Literatur. 1809–11; edited by Giovanni V. Amoretti, 1923; as *A Course of Lectures on Dramatic Art and Literature*, translated by John Black, 1815; revised edition translated by A.J.W. Morrison, 1846.
Werke. 1812–17.
Betrachtungen über die Politik der dänischen Regierung. 1813.
Réflexions sur l'état actuel de la Norvège. 1814.
Tableau de l'état politique et moral de l'Empire français en 1813. 1814.
Lettre aux éditeurs de la bibliothèque italienne, sur les chevaux de bronze de Venise. 1816.
Rezension von Niebuhrs Römischer Geschichte. 1816.
Le couronnement de la Sainte Vierge, et les miracles de Saint-Dominique. 1817.
Observations sur la langue et la littérature provençales. 1818.
Vorlesungen über Theorie und Geschichte der bildenden Künste. 1827.
Berichtigung einiger Missdeutungen. 1828.
Kritische Schriften. 1828; edited by Emil Staiger, 1963.
Réflexions sur l'étude des langues asiatiques adressées à Sir James Mackintosh, suivies d'une lettre à M. Horace Hayman Wilson. 1832.
Essais littéraires et historiques. 1842.
Oeuvres de M. Auguste-Guillaume de Schlegel écrites en français, edited by Eduard Böcking. 1846.
Briefwechsel zwischen Wilhelm von Humboldt und August Wilhelm Schlegel, edited by Albert Leitzmann. 1908.
Briefwechsel A.W. von Schlegel, Christian Lassen, edited by W. Kirfel. 1914.
August Wilhelm Schlegels Briefwechsel mit seinen Heidelberger Verlegern, edited by Erich Jenisch. 1922.

August Wilhelm und Friedrich Schlegel im Briefwechsel mit Schiller und Goethe, edited by Josef Körner und Ernst Wieneke. 1926.

Briefe von und an Friedrich und Dorothea Schlegel, edited by Josef Körner. 1926.

Briefe von und an August Wilhelm Schlegel, edited by Josef Körner. 1930.

Editor, *Friedrich Nicolai's Leben und Sonderbare Meinungen*, by Johann Gottlieb Fichte. 1801.

Editor, *Lacrimas: Ein Schauspiel*, by Wilhelm von Schütz. 1804.

Editor, *Dramatische Spiele*, by Friedrich de la Motte-Fouqué. 1804.

Editor, *Dépeches et lettres interceptées par des partis détachés de l'armée combinée du nord de l'Allemagne*. 1814.

Editor, *Considérations sur les événements principaux de la révolution française, ouvrage posthume, publié par M. le Duc de Broglie et M. le Baron de Staël*, by Madame de Staël. 1818.

Editor, *Flore und Blanchefleur: Romantisches Gedicht in zwölf Gesängen*, by Sophie Bernhardi. 1822.

Editor, *Verzeichnis einer von Eduard Alton hinterlassenen Gemäldesammlung*. 1840.

Editor and translator, *Spanisches Theater*, by Calderón. 1803–09.

Editor and translator, *Blumensträusse italienischer, spanischer und portugiesischer Poesie*. 1804.

Editor and translator, *Bhagavad-Gita*. 1823.

Editor and translator, with Christian Lassen, *Hitopadesas, id est, Institutio salutarius*. 1829–31.

Editor and translator, *Ramayana*. 4 vols., 1829–46.

Translator, *Geheime Nachrichten zur Aufklärung der Vorfälle während des letzten Kriegs zwischen England und Holland*, by Joachim Rendorp. 1793.

Translator, *Dramatische Werke*, by Shakespeare. 9 vols., 1797–1819.

Translator, *Historische, literarische und unterhaltende Schriften*, by Horace Walpole. 1800.

Translator, *Über den Charakter und die Schriften der Frau von Staël*, by Albertine Necker de Saussure. 1820.

Verse

Gedichte. 1800.
Rom. 1805.
Poetische Werke. 1811.

Plays

Ion, adaptation of the play by Euripides (produced 1802). 1803.

PUBLICATIONS BY FRIEDRICH VON SCHLEGEL

Collection

Kritische Friedrich-Schlegel-Ausgabe, edited by Ernst Behler and others. 1958–.

Prose

Die Griechen und Römer. 1797.
Geschichte der Poesie der Griechen und Römer. 1798.
Über die Sprache und Weisheit der Indier. 1808; as "On the Language and Wisdom of the Indians," translated by E.J. Millington,

in *The Aesthetic and Miscellaneous Works of Friedrich Schlegel*, 1849.

Über die Neuere Geschichte (lectures). 1810; translated by Lyndsey Purcell and R.H. Whitelock, in *A Course of Lectures on Modern History*, 1849.

Geschichte der alten und neuen Literatur. 1812; as *Lectures on the History of Literature, Ancient and Modern*, translated by J.G. Lockhart, 1818.

Sämmtliche Werke. 10 vols., 1822–23; revised edition, 15 vols., 1845.

Die drei ersten Vorlesungen über die Philosophie des Lebens. 1827.

Philosophie des Lebens (lectures). 1827; as *The Philosophy of Life and Philosophy of Language*, translated by A.J.W. Morrison, 1847.

Philosophie der Geschichte (lectures). 1828; as *The Philosophy of History*, translated by James Burton Robertson, 1835.

Philosophische Vorlesungen insbesondere über Philosophie der Sprache und des Wortes. 1830; as *The Philosophy of Life and Philosophy of Language*, translated by James Burton Robertson, 1847.

Briefe an seinen Bruder August Wilhelm, edited by O.F. Walzel. 1890.

Krisenjahre der Frühromantik: Briefe aus dem Schlegelkreis, edited by J. Körner. 1936–58.

Literarische Notizen 1797–1801, edited by Hans Eichner. 1980.

Editor, *Florentin*, by Dorothea Schlegel. 1801.

Editor, *Geschichte der Jungfrau von Orleans.* 1802.

Editor, *Lessings Gedanken und Meinungen aus dessen Schriften.* 1804.

Editor, with Dorothea Schlegel, *Sammlung romantischer Dichtungen des Mittelalters.* 1804.

Editor, with Dorothea Schlegel, *Lother und Maller: Eine Rittergeschichte aus einer ungedruckten Handschrift.* 1805.

Editor and translator, *Geschichte der Margaretha von Valois.* 1803.

Translator, with Dorothea Schlegel, *Corinne; oder, der Italien*, by Germaine de Staël. 1807–08.

Fiction

Lucinde. 1799; edited by K.K. Polhein, 1964; as *Lucinda*, translated by Paul Bernard Thomas, in *The German Classics of the Nineteenth and Twentieth Centuries*, volume 4, 1913; as *Lucinde*, translated by Peter Firchow, with *Fragments*, 1968.

Plays

Alarcos. 1802.

Verse

Gedichte. 1809.

*

Bibliography: "Die Friedrich-Schlegel-Forschung 1945–1972" by Volker Deubel, in *Deutsche Vierteljahrsschrift*, (47), 1973.

Critical Studies: *August Wilhelm Schlegel as a Translator of Shakespeare* by Margaret E. Atkinson, 1958; *Friedrich Schlegel in Selbstzeugnissen und Bilddokumenten* edited by Ernst Behler, 1966;

Friedrich Schlegel by Hans Eichner, 1970; *Friedrich Schlegel und die Romantik* edited by Hugo Moser and Benno von Wiese, 1970; *The Literary Theories of August Wilhelm Schlegel* by Ralph W. Ewton, Jr., 1972; *Friedrich Schlegels "Transzendentalpoesie"* by Heinz-Dieter Weber, 1973; "The 'Bekenntnisse eines Ungeschickten': A Re-Examination of Emancipatory Ideas in Friedrich Schlegel's 'Lucinde'" by Richard Littlejohns, in *Modern Language Review*, (72), 1977; *Friedrich Schlegel* by Klaus Peter, 1978; *August Wilhelm Schlegel: Auffassung der Tragödie im Zusammenhang mit seiner Poetik und ästhetischen Theorien seiner Zeit* by Silke Agnes Reavis, 1978; *Das Konzept des Klassischen bei Friedrich und August Wilhelm Schlegel* by Annelen Grosse-Brockhoff, 1981; *A.W. Schlegel's Shakespearean Criticism in England, 1811–1846* by Thomas G. Sauer, 1981; *Ästhetische Hermeneutik und frühromantische Kritik: Friedrich Schlegels fragmentarische Entwürfe, Rezensionen, Charakteristiken und Kritiken (1795–1801)* by Willy Michel, 1982; *Die Zeitschriften der Brüder Schlegel: Ein Beitrag zur Geschichte der deutschen Romantik* by Ernst Behler, 1983; *The Androgyne in Early German Romanticism: Friedrich Schlegel, Novalis and the Metaphysics of Love* by Sara Friedrichsmeyer, 1983; *Friedrich Schlegels Geschichts-philosophie (1794–1808): Ein Beitrag zur politischen Romantik* by Klaus Behrens, 1984; *Friedrich Schlegels "Lucinde" als "Neue Mythologie": geschichtsphilosophischer Versuch einer Rückgewinnung gesellschaftlicher Totalität durch das Individuum* by Cornelia Hotz, 1985; *Naturpoesie und Kunstpoesie im Frühwerk Friedrich Schlegels* by Gerhard Kraus, 1985; *August Wilhelm Schlegel und die vergleichende Literaturwissenschaft* by Hilde Marianne Paulini, 1985; *Friedrich Schlegel und die Kunsttheorie seiner Zeit* edited by Helmut Schanze, 1985; *Leben wie im Roman: Untersuchungen zum ästhetischen Imperativ im Frühwerk Friedrich Schlegels (1794–1800)* by Bernd Bräutigam, 1986; *August Wilhelm Schlegel und seine Zeit: ein Bonner Leben* by Ruth Schirmer, 1986; *August Wilhelm Schlegels "Ion": Das Schauspiel und die Aufführungen unter der Leitung von Goethe und Iffland* by Georg Reichard, 1987; *The Romantic Irony of Semiotics: Friedrich Schlegel and the Crisis of Representation* by Marike Finlay, 1988; *Das Unendliche: Höchste Fülle oder Nichts: Zur Problematik von Friedrich Schlegels Geschichtsbegriff* by Ulrike Zeuch, 1991.

*   *   *

Friedrich and August Wilhelm von Schlegel's extensive study of the literature of classical antiquity was important for the development of their aesthetic theories. Friedrich Schlegel's first essay of note, "Über das Studium der griechischen Poesie" [On the Study of Greek Poetry], which bears a remarkable similarity to Schiller's *Über naive und sentamentalische Dichtung* (*On the Naive and Sentimental in Literature*), written in the same year (1795), was principally concerned with comparing modern literature, which Friedrich castigated for its self-consciousness and artificiality, unfavourably with that of the Greeks. At the same time he praised Goethe's works as the dawn of a new, genuine art. Friedrich enthused about the power of Goethe's *Faust*, and about Goethe's instinctive search for beauty and truth. In this aspect of the essay one detects the beginning of a judgement of art according to Romantic criteria.

Wilhelm Heinrich Wackenroder and Ludwig Tieck had, in 1797, published *Herzensergiessungen eines kunstliebenden Klosterbruders* (*Outpourings from the Heart of an Art-Loving Friar*), which exalted, without once using the word "romantisch," a Romantic view of

painting and music, but Friedrich Schlegel and, some would say, to a lesser degree August Wilhelm Schlegel, are to be credited with providing German Romantic literature, especially the early phase centred on Jena, Berlin, and Dresden, with its main aesthetic basis. In the short-lived literary periodical the *Athenäum*, founded and edited by the two brothers, it was Friedrich who for the first time gave the adjective "romantisch" the definition in terms of literature that one associates with German Romanticism.

In the 451 *Fragments* published in the *Athenäum* Friedrich pronounced authoritavely, but not systematically, on the nature of "romantische Poesie" (Romantic literature). Volatile and mercurial, Friedrich clearly found in the aphoristic style of writing that characterizes the *Fragments*, some of them no longer than a single sentence, a form that suited his temperament. In the famous *Fragment 116* he rejected the traditional differentiation between genres, indeed the differentiation between all forms of human expression. Influenced by the philosopher Fichte, he stressed the subjective nature of all worthwhile literature. *Fragment 116* also contains the declaration that the essence of Romantic literature is its infinite creativity, and concludes that all literature is or should be Romantic. One of the longer *Fragments*, it is typical of Friedrich's emotional, highly individual style and questionable argumentation.

In a large number of the *Fragments* Friedrich wrote on the subject of irony. Friedrich believed that literature should be a dynamic, never-ending progression in which a writer constantly found himself in the position of negating previous output. Self-parody and irony were therefore essential constituents of Romantic literature. Friedrich's pronouncements on irony were important in prompting German Romantic writers to develop the potential in irony and narrative perspective.

Closely linked to his concept of irony was the notion of "transcendental poetry." By this Friedrich understood the unending striving for aesthetic and ethical perfection that should be central to all worthwhile, i.e. Romantic literature. His concept of transcendental poetry is in many respects analogous to the "romantische Sehnsucht" (Romantic yearning) that is a feature of many German Romantic works.

In the *Fragments* and in other writings included in the *Athenäum* Friedrich had much to say about the novel, a genre regarded as inferior to lyric poetry and drama. When he said that "Ein Roman ist ein romantisches Buch" (A novel is a romantic book), he exploited the semantic link between the German word for novel (*Roman*) and the adjective "romantisch" (Romantic) to present a genre that was held at the time in low esteem as the epitome of Romanticism and so, by definition, as the supreme literary form.

August Wilhelm was a more objective, systematic writer than Friedrich. It has been argued that he merely reproduced his brother's ideas and that he lacked originality, but this does not do him justice. Whereas Friedrich interacted with and influenced his fellow German Romantics, August Wilhelm's main contribution in the early days of Romanticism was to make the aesthetics of Romanticism known to a broader public. This was the effect of his series of lectures on belles lettres and art (*Vorlesungen über schöne Literatur und Kunst*), given in Berlin.

One of the essays included in these lectures, "On the Middle Ages," glorified the triumph of Christian chivalry over the forces threatening Europe, and conveys a pride in the Germanic past (similar sentiments are to be found in Friedrich's Vienna lectures *Über die Neuere Geschichte* [*A Course of Lectures on Modern History*]). Elsewhere in the lectures August Wilhelm praised the German medieval epic, the *Nibelungenlied*, concurring entirely with another critic's suggestion that it was the "Iliad of the North." Together with Novalis's *Christianity or Europe*, 1799, these lectures encouraged the Romantic image of medieval Europe, especially of medieval Germany, as a lost Golden Age.

In these lectures on literature and art August Wilhelm also wrote on the nature of beauty and symbolism, and it is generally accepted that he made valuable contributions to this area of aesthetics.

August Wilhelm is to be credited with making German Romanticism more widely known in Europe. Initially this came about through his travels and long association with Madame de Staël. His Vienna *Vorlesungen über dramatische Kunst und Literatur* (*A Course of Lectures on Dramatic Art and Literature*) were widely translated and influenced, among others, Samuel Taylor Coleridge.

August Wilhelm is best remembered today for his translations of Shakespeare into German. Starting in 1797, and, undoubtedly attracted by the "romantic" works such as *Romeo and Juliet, A Midsummer Night's Dream*, and *The Tempest*, he translated 17 of the plays, and these formed part of the translation of the complete dramatic works (finished by Dorothea Tieck and Graf Baudissin) that resulted in Shakespeare being practically adopted as a German. The quality of August Wilhelm's translations is widely acknowledged.

Both brothers wrote poems, plays, and novels. Only one of these, Friedrich's novel *Lucinde*, is remembered today. In some respects *Lucinde* is an autobiographical presentation of his relationship with Dorothea Veit. The work can be seen as an attempt by Friedrich to put his pronouncements in the *Athenäum* into practice. As one might expect, the novel remained a fragment. Mirroring Friedrich's rejection of artificial divisions in literature, the novel is a rejection of the artificial compartmentalization of human relationships, particularly those between women and men. The mixture of styles and the irony of *Lucinde* are typical of Friedrich's Romanticism; the work can also be regarded as one of the first experimental novels. The scandal that surrounded its publication was a result mainly of the hypocrisy of the age; it certainly was not conceived as an encouragement to sexual promiscuity, as Friedrich's enemies claimed.

Friedrich's conversion to a very conservative Catholicism, his work in the service of an Austria that was becoming increasingly reactionary, and his disparagement of political and religious freedom in later life are a seeming betrayal of the Romanticism of his Jena years. Outliving his younger brother, August Wilhelm ended his days in Bonn in relative obscurity. However, this should not detract from the Schlegels' significant contribution to Romantic thought and their influence on German Romantic writers. They are also to be credited with initiating studies in comparative philology and literature.

—D.J. Andrews

SCHNITZLER, Arthur

Born: Vienna, Austria, 15 May 1862. **Education:** Educated at Akademisches Gymnasium, Vienna, 1871–79; studied medicine at the University of Vienna, 1879–85, M.D. 1885. **Family:** Married Olga Gussmann in 1903 (separated 1921); one son and one daughter. **Career:** Medical intern, 1885–88; assistant at Allgemeine Poliklinik, 1888–93, then in private practice. **Awards:** Bauernfeld prize, 1899, 1903; Grillparzer prize, 1908; Raimund prize, 1910; Vienna Volkstheater prize, 1914. **Died:** 21 October 1931.

PUBLICATIONS

Collections

Gesammelte Werke. 7 vols., 1912; enlarged edition, 9 vols., 1922.
Gesammelte Werke, edited by Robert O. Weiss. 5 vols., 1961–67.
Plays and Stories, edited and translated by Egon Schwarz. 1982.
Illusion and Reality: Plays and Stories, translated by Paul F. Dvorak. 1986.
Professor Bernhardi and Other Plays, translated by G.J. Weinberger. 1993.
Paracelsus and Other One-act Plays, translated by G.J. Weinberger. 1994.
The Final Plays, translated by G.J. Weinberger. 1996.
Arthur Schnitzler: Four Plays, translated by Carl R. Mueller. 1999.
Selected Short Fiction, translated with introduction by J.M.Q. Davies. 1999.
Casanova's Journey Home and Other Late Stories, translated with afterword by Norman M. Watt. 2001.

Plays

Das Abenteur seines Lebens (produced 1891). 1888.
Das Märchen (produced 1893). 1894.
Anatol (cycle of seven one-act plays; produced as a cycle 1910). 1893; edited by Ernst L. Offermann, 1964; as *Anatol: A Sequence of Dialogues*, translated by H. Granville-Barker, 1911; as *The Affairs of Anatol*, 1933; as *Anatol*, 1949–56; also translated by Charles Osborne, in *The Round Dance and Other Plays*, 1982; Frank Marcus, 1982; edited with introduction by William-Alan Landes, 1999.
Das Märchen (produced 1893). 1894.
Liebelei (produced 1895). 1896; as *Light-o'-Love*, translated by Bayard Quincy Morgan, 1912; as *Playing with Love*, translated by P. Morton Shand, 1914; as *Love Games*, translated by Charles Osborne, in *The Round Dance and Other Plays*, 1982; as *Flirtations*, translated by Arthur S. Wensinger and Clinton J. Atkinson, in *Plays and Stories*, 1982; as *Dalliance*, translated and adapted by Tom Stoppard, with *Undiscovered Country*, 1986.
Freiwild (produced 1897). 1898; as *Free Game*, translated by Paul Grummann, 1913.
Das Vermächtnis (produced 1898). 1899; as *The Legacy*, translated by Mary L. Stephenson, in *Poet Lore*, July-August 1911.
Der grüne Kakadu, Paracelsus, Die Gefährtin. 1899; as *The Green Cockatoo and Other Plays* (includes *Paracelsus* and *The Mate*), translated by Horace B. Samuel, 1913; *Der grüne Kakadu* also translated as *The Duke and the Actress*, by Grace Isable Colbron, in *One-Act Plays*, 1977.
Der Schleier der Beatrice (produced 1900). 1901.
Reigen (produced 1920). 1900; as *Hands Around*, translated by L.D. Edwards and F.L. Glaser, 1920; as *Couples*, translated by Lily Wolfe and E.W. Titus, 1927; as *Merry-Go-Round*, translated by Frank and Jacqueline Marcus, 1953; as *La Ronde*, translated by Eric Bentley, in *From the Modern Repertoire*, edited by Bentley, 1954; also translated by Sue Davies and adapted by John Barton,

1982; as *Dance of Love*, 1965; as *The Round Dance*, translated by
Charles Osborne, in *The Round Dance and Other Plays*, 1982.

Lebendige Stunden (includes *Die Frau mit dem Dolche; Die letzten
Masken; Literatur; Lebendige Stunden*; produced 1902). 1902; as
Living Hours: Four One-Act Plays (includes *The Lady with the
Dagger; Last Masks; Literature; Living Hours*), translated by
Paul H. Grummann, 1913.

Der einsame Weg (produced 1904). 1904; as *The Lonely Way*,
translated by Edwin Björkman, 1904; as *The Lonely Road*, 1985.

Marionetten (includes *Der Puppenspieler; Der tapfere Cassian; Zum
grossen Wurstel*). 1906; revised version of *Der tapfere Cassian*,
music by Oscar Straus, 1909; as *Gallant Cassian*, translated by
Moritz A. Jagendorf, 1914.

Zwischenspiel (produced 1905). 1906; as *Intermezzo*, translated by
Edwin Björkman, in *Three Plays*, 1915.

Der Ruf des Lebens (produced 1906). 1906.

Komtesse Mizzi; oder, Der Familientag (produced 1909). 1909; as
Countess Mizzie, translated by Edwin Björkman, in *Three Plays*,
1915; as *Countess Mitzi; or, the Family Reunion*, revised translated by Egon Schwarz, in *Plays and Stories*, 1982.

Der Schleier der Pierrette, music by Ernst von Dohnanyi (produced
1910). 1910.

Der junge Medardus (produced 1910). 1910.

The Green Cockatoo and Other Plays (includes *Paracelsus* and *The
Mate*), translated by Horace B. Samuel. 1913.

Das weite Land (produced 1911). 1911; as *Undiscovered Country*,
translated by Tom Stoppard, 1980.

Professor Bernhardi (produced 1912). 1912; as *Professor Bernhardi*,
translated by Kate A. Pohli, 1913; also translated by Hetty
Landstone, 1927; Louis Borell and Ronald Adam, 1913.

Komödie der Worte (includes *Stunde des Erkennens; Grosse Szene;
Das Bacchusfest*; produced simultaneously 1915). 1915; as *Come-
dies of Words and Other Plays* (includes *The Hour of Recognition;
The Big Scene; The Festival of Bacchus*), translated by Pierre
Loving, 1917.

Three Plays (includes *The Lonely Way; Intermezzo; Countess Mizzi*),
translated by Edwin Björkman. 1915.

Fink und Fliederbusch (produced 1917). 1917.

Die Schwestern; oder, Casanova in Spa (produced 1920). 1919; as
The Sisters; or Casanova in Spa, translated by G.J. Weinberger, in
Three Late Plays, 1992.

Komödie der Verführung (produced 1924). 1924; as *Seduction Comedy*, translated by G.J. Weinberger, in *Three Late Plays*, 1992.

Der Gang zum Weiher (produced 1931). 1926; as *The Way to the
Pond*, translated by J.G. Weinberger, in *Three Late Plays*, 1992.

Im Spiel der Sommerlüfte (produced 1929). 1930; as *Summer Breeze*,
1989.

Zug der Schatten, edited by Françoise Derre. 1970.

The Round Dance and Other Plays (includes *Anatol* and *Love
Games*), translated by Charles Osborne. 1982.

Three Late Plays (includes *The Sisters; or, Casanova in Spa; Seduction Comedy; The Way to the Pond*), translated by G.J. Weinberger.
1992.

Fiction

Sterben. 1895; as ''Dying,'' translated by Harry Zohn, in *The Little
Comedy and Other Stories*, 1977.

Die Frau des Weisen: Novelletten. 1898.

Leutnant Gustl. 1901; as *None But the Brave*, translated by Richard L.
Simon, 1926.

Frau Bertha Garlan. 1901; as *Bertha Garlan*, translated by Agnes
Jacques, 1913; also translated by J.H. Wisdom and Marr Murray,
1914; as *Berta Garlan*, translated by G.J. Weinberger, 1987.

Die griechische Tänzerin: Novellen. 1905.

Dämmerseelen: Novellen. 1907.

Der Weg ins Freie. 1908; as *The Road to the Open*, translated by
Horace B. Samuel, 1923.

Die Hirtenflöte. 1912.

Masken und Wunder: Novellen. 1912.

Frau Beate und ihr Sohn. 1913; as *Beatrice*, translated by Agnes
Jacques, 1926; as *Beatrice and Her Son*, translated by Shaun
Whiteside, 1999.

Viennese Idylls, translated by Frederick Eisemann. 1913.

Doktor Gräsler, Badearzt. 1917; as *Dr. Graesler*, translated by E.C.
Slade, 1923.

Casanovas Heimfahrt. 1918; as *Casanova's Homecoming*, translated
by Eden and Cedar Paul, 1921.

Der Mörder. 1922.

The Shepherd's Pipe and Other Stories, translated by O.F. Theis.
1922.

Fräulein Else. 1924; as *Fräulein Else*, translated by Robert A. Simon,
1925; also translated by F.H. Lyon, 1925.

Die dreifache Warnung: Novellen. 1924.

Die Frau des Richters. 1925.

Traumnovelle. 1926; as *Rhapsody: A Dream Novel*, translated by Otto
P. Schinnerer, 1927; as *Dream Story*, translated by J.M.Q. Davies,
1999.

Beatrice and Other Stories, translated by Agnes Jacques. 1926.

Spiel im Morgengrauen. 1927; as *Daybreak*, translated by William A.
Drake, 1927.

Therese: Chronik eines Frauenlebens. 1928; as *Theresa: The Chronicle of a Woman's Life*, translated by William A. Drake, 1928.

Gesammelte Schriften. 6 vols., 1928.

Little Novels, translated by Eric Sutton. 1929.

Flucht in die Finsternis. 1931; as *Flight into Darkness*, translated by
William A. Drake, 1931.

Viennese Novelettes. 1931.

Abenteuernovelle. 1937.

Vienna 1900: Games with Love and Death. 1973.

Other

Buch der Sprüche und Bedenken: Aphorismen und Fragmente. 1927.

Der Geist im Wort und der Geist in der Tat. 1927; as *The Mind in
Words and Action: Preliminary Remarks Concerning Two Dia-
grams*, translated by Robert O. Weiss, 1972.

Über Krieg und Frieden. 1939.

Briefwechsel, with Otto Brahm, edited by Oskar Seidlin. 1953;
revised edition, 1964.

Briefwechsel, with Georg Brandes, edited by Kurt Bergel. 1956.

Briefwechsel, with Hugo von Hofmannsthal, edited by Therese Nickl
and Heinrich Schnitzler. 1964.

Jugend in Wien: Eine Autobiographie, edited by Therese Nickl and
Heinrich Schnitzler. 1968; as *My Youth in Vienna*, translated by
Catherine Hutter, 1971.

Liebe, die starb vor der Zeit: Ein Briefwechsel, with Olga Waissnix,
edited by Therese Nickl and Heinrich Schnitzler. 1970.

Briefwechsel, with Max Reinhardt, edited by Renate Wagner. 1971.

Correspondence, with Raoul Auernheimer, edited by David G. Daviau and Jorun B. Johns. 1972.

Letters of Arthur Schnitzler to Hermann Bahr, edited by Donald G. Daviau. 1978.

Briefe 1875–1912, edited by Therese Nickl and Heinrich Schnitzler. 1981.

Tagebuch 1909–1912, edited by Peter M. Braunworth and others. 1981; further volumes: *1913–1916*, 1983, *1917–1919*, 1985; *1879–1892*, 1987.

Briefe 1913–1931, edited by Peter M. Braunworth and others. 1984.

Beziehungen und Einsamkeiten: Aphorismen, edited by Clemens Eich. 1987.

*

Bibliography: *An Annotated Arthur Schnitzler Bibliography: Editions and Criticisms in German, French, and English 1879–1965* by Richard H. Allen, 1966; *An Annotated Arthur Schnitzler Bibliography 1965–1977* by Jeffrey B. Berlin, 1978.

Critical Studies: *Arthur Schnitzler* by Sol Liptzin, 1932; *Studies in Arthur Schnitzler* edited by H.W. Reichart and Herman Salinger, 1963; *Arthur Schnitzler: Die späte Prosa als Gipfel seines Schaffens* by William H. Rey, 1968; *The Concept of the Physician in the Writings of Hans Carossa and Arthur Schnitzler* by Marie P. Alter, 1971; *Arthur Schnitzler: A Critical Study* by Martin Swales, 1971; *Arthur Schnitzler* by Richard Urbach, translated by Donald G. Daviau, 1973; *The Late Dramatic Works of Arthur Schnitzler* by Brigitte L. Schneider-Halvorson, 1983; *Arthur Schnitzler and His Age: Intellectual and Artistic Currents* edited by Petrus W. Tax and Richard H. Lawson, 1984; *Arthur Schnitzler and the Crisis of Musical Culture* by Marc A. Weiner, 1986; *Arthur Schnitzler* by Michaela L. Perlmann, 1987; *Arthur Schnitzler and Politics* by A.C. Robert, 1989; *Hauptmann, Wedekind and Schnitzler* by Peter Skrine, 1989; *Deadly Dishonor: The Duel and the Honor Code in the Works of Arthur Schnitzler* by Brenda Keiser, 1990; *Schnitzler's Vienna: Image of a Society* by Bruce Thompson, 1990; *Schnitzler, Hoffmansthal and the Austrian Theatre* by W.E. Yates, 1992; *Political Dimensions of Arthur Schnitzler's Late Fiction* by Felix W. Tweraser, 1998; *The Divided Rhetoric of Sentimentality: Critique and Self-definition in Wagner, Nietzsche, and Schnitzler*, 1999; *Schnitzler's Century: The Making of Middle-Class Culture, 1815–1914* by Peter Gay, 2002.

* * *

Arthur Schnitzler's reputation stood high in the Austria and Germany of his day, but until its reinstatement in the 1950s it was diminished by his close identification with one time and place, turn-of-the-century Vienna (also recently "rediscovered"), and by the Nazis' suppression of his works. Even now he is best known for one play, *Reigen* (*La Ronde*, or *Hands Around*, or *The Round Dance*), a sexually explicit series of ten seduction scenes forming a "coital circle" linking all Vienna, high and low. The subject of considerable scandal (its premiere had to wait for some years) it has found its way into more than one film version; and its notoriety never ceased to depress its author. A reputation for lack of seriousness was compounded by the limitation of his range, and by a facile association of his work with the myth of "gay Vienna," encouraged by his penchant for idle young aristocrats and their dalliance with actresses or touchingly

vulnerable shopgirls—the "süsses Mädel" of, for example, *Liebelei* (*Light-o'-Love*). It is true that Schnitzler's range is limited. He wrote only about the period that ended in August 1914; and for him the city of his birth, from which he never moved away, was a sufficient mirror of the world. Critics are agreed, too, that his limitations are most apparent in his larger works, the longer plays like *Professor Bernhardi* or the one attempt at a full-scale novel of society, *Der Weg ins Freie* (*The Road to the Open*). But the other side of the critical coin is that he is a master of the short form. He wrote some 40 novellas and about the same number of one-act plays, and within their narrow compass he evokes the existential confrontations of his characters with the basic crises of love, isolation, or death (especially death), bringing to the fore their whole mentality and psychological complexity. Freud's envy of Schnitzler's apparently effortless grasp of psychological processes is well known.

Schnitzler was, in fact, the product of a highly cultivated, almost over-refined milieu, and a member of a brilliant circle centring on the Viennese coffee-house culture epitomized by the famous Café Griensteidl, a meeting place of literati such as Hugo von Hofmannsthal, Hermann Bahr, Peter Altenberg, and Schnitzler himself. His medical training and practice gave him the stock of experience he needed to act as the vehicle for his sensitive insight. As a Jew he was well placed to explore the pathology of a society in many ways atrophied, whose upper-middle class had failed to liberalize the moribund Austrian Empire and had taken refuge in a cult of aestheticism, nuances, and ambiguities, inclining to reject all that presented itself in too uncomfortably distinct a form. If, as Schnitzler saw it, casual sex reflected the identity crisis of the individual, then anti-semitism was the social embodiment of this crisis. He considered it a symptom of a universal spiritual malaise, and presented its morphology, with the professional restraint of the medical man, in both *The Road to the Open* and *Professor Bernhardi*. But the play typically moves beyond anti-semitism to become an exposure of the very Austrian theme of the way the world distorts the individual's intentions even as he gives utterance to them. Out of Bernhardi's professional stand against religious and political interference in the running of his hospital a *cause célèbre* is created; and out of Bernhardi himself, an unwilling and, in the end, inadequate martyr. The victim of anti-semitism and dishonest politics appears just as much the victim of himself. Not that Schnitzler is inclined to pass judgement, for, as he said: "I see it as my profession to create characters, and I am out to prove nothing except the world's variety." In that variety is included, however, a good deal of Ibsen-style relation of the "lie of life," as for example in the masterly, pioneering stream-of-consciousness narrative *Leutnant Gustl* (*None But the Brave*)—published 21 years before Joyce's *Ulysses*—where the inner monologue takes us into the world of a young army officer confronted with a personal conflict in which a false concept of honour is exposed for what it is by a healthy instinct for self-preservation. (The Imperial Army took umbrage, and Schnitzler lost his reserve officer's rank.) There is no element of caricature in the portrait of Gustl, and we are even enabled to enter his world with a degree of sympathy. Schnitzler's variety also has room for a *fin de siècle* fascination with abnormal states (e.g., his last story, *Flucht in die Finsternis, Flight into Darkness*, a case of incipient insanity which becomes total), with sickness as more interesting than health; and he is very much a modern in his exploration of "the whole crisis of man's erotic experience as symptomatic of a total philosophical revaluation of the world and man's place in it" (Martin Swales).

Yet he is a Janus-faced phenomenon in that he also looks back to the Austrian baroque tradition of the *Theatrum Mundi*, or notion of the world as spectacle, a view which was influential, as he said, in "developing that basic motif of the intermingling of seriousness and play-acting, of life and theatre, of truth and mendacity . . . that moved and preoccupied me again and again, beyond any concern for the theatre and acting, indeed to a point beyond the realm of art." The seriousness of his intentions has long ceased to be in dispute, but any lingering doubts should be dispelled by his "Sprüche und Aphorismen," the collection of aphorisms which was slow to see the light of publication, but contains penetrating observations on art, religion, philosophy, and the issues of his day.

—Alan F. Bance

See the essays on *Professor Bernhardi* and *La Ronde*.

SCHULZ, Bruno

Born: Drohobycz, Ukraine, in 1892. **Education:** Educated at schools in Drohobycz; studied architecture in Lvov, 1911–14, and fine arts in Vienna. **Career:** Art teacher in gymnasium, Drohobycz, 1924–39; illustrated own works and *Ferdydurke* by Witold Gombrowicz, *q.v.* **Awards:** Polish Academy of Letters Golden Laurel award, 1938. **Died:** Shot in Drohobycz ghetto by German officer, 1942.

PUBLICATIONS

Collections

Proza, edited by Artur Sandauer and Jerzy Ficowski. 1964; revised edition, 1973.
The Complete Fiction, translated by Celina Wieniewska. 1989.
Collected Works of Bruno Schulz, edited by Jerzy Ficowski. 1998.

Fiction

Xięga balwochwalcza. 1922; as *The Booke of Idolatry*, edited by Jerzy Ficowski, translated by Bogna Piotrowska, 1988(?).
Sklepy cynamonowe. 1934; as *The Street of Crocodiles*, translated by Celina Wieniewska, 1963; as *Cinnamon Shops and Other Stories*, translated by Wieniewska, 1963; as *The Fictions of Bruno Schulz*, translated by Wieniewska, 1988.
Sanatorium pod klepsydrą. 1937; as *Sanatorium under the Sign of the Hourglass*, translated by Celina Wieniewska, 1978.
Ptaki, as *Birds: A Tale*, translated by Celina Wieniewska. 1980.

Other

Księga Listów [A Book of Letters], edited by Jerzy Ficowski. 1975.
Listy, fragmenty, wspomnienia o pisarzu [Letters, Fragments, and Reminiscences about Writing], edited by Jerzy Ficowski. 1984.
Letters and Drawings, with Selected Prose, edited by Jerzy Ficowski, translated by Walter Arndt and Victoria Nelson. 1988.
Opowiadania, wybór esejów i listów [Stories, Selections, Essays, and Letters], edited by Jerzy Ficowski. 1989.
The Drawings of Bruno Schulz, edited by Jerzy Ficowski. 1990.
Ilustracje do wlasnych utworow, edited by Jerzy Ficowski. 1992.

*

Critical Studies: "Masochistic Motives in the Literary and Graphic Art of Bruno Schulz" by Henry Wegrocki, in *Psychoanalytical Review*, 33, 1946; "Bruno Schulz's *The Street of Crocodiles*: A Study in Creativity and Neurosis" by Olga Lukashevich, in *Polish Review*, 13, 1968; "Childhood Revisited: The Writings of Bruno Schulz" by Coleen M. Taylor, in *Slavic and East European Journal*, 13, 1969; *Die Prosa von Bruno Schulz* by Elisabeth Baur, 1975; "Metamorphosis in Bruno Schulz," in *Polish Review*, 30, 1985, "Schulz's Sanatorium Story: Myth and Confession," in *Polish Perspectives*, 30, 1987, "Bruno Schulz: The Myth of Origins," in *Russian Literature*, 22, 1987, "Bruno Schulz and Franz Kafka: Servant Girls and Other Temptations," in *Germano-Slavica*, 6, 1988, "Bruno Schulz and World Literature," in *Slavic and East European Journal*, Summer 1990, and *Myths and Relatives: Seven Essays on Bruno Schulz*, 1991, all by Russell E. Brown; "Galicia in the Work of Bruno Schulz" by Bohdan Budurowycz, in *Canadian Slavonic Papers*, 28, 1986; "Bruno Schulz and the Myth of the Book" by Piotr J. Drozdowski, in *Indiana Slavic Studies*, 5, 1990; "Time in Bruno Schulz" by Theodosia S. Robertson, in *Indiana Slavic Studies*, 5, 1990; *On the Margins of Reality: The Paradoxes of Representation in Bruno Schulz's Fiction* by Krysztof Stala, 1993; *The Divine Duty of Servants: A Book of Worship Based on the Artwork of Bruno Schulz* by Rolando Perez, 1999; *Bruno Schulz: New Documents and Interpretations*, edited by Czeslaw Z. Prokopczyk, 1999; *Holocaust Literature: Schulz, Levi, Spiegelman and the Memory of the Offence* by Gillian Banner, 2000.

*   *   *

Bruno Schulz was a shy teacher, whose life in an obscure corner of Europe camouflaged an extraordinary imagination. His stories magnify the provincial characters of the predominantly Jewish town of Drohobycz to the status of epic heroes involved in magical and surreal events.

Two separate collections of stories were published in his lifetime, *Sklepy cynamonowe* (*The Street of Crocodiles*) and *Sanatorium pod klepsydr* (*Sanatorium under the Sign of the Hourglass*). On first reading, they seem to tell of a young man's path to maturity, but experiences that should lead the author's *alter ego*, Joseph N., to greater understanding instead confirm his naivety and remoteness from truth. The universe first revealed to him by his wily Magus-like father Jacob, the "incorrigible improvisor," is one that has forms but no Form (Creation after the Fall?). Like his biblical forebear, Joseph remains trusting, innocent, and blessed by Providence.

Decomposition and decay are the main elements of a Schulz story, as the mannequin-like characters, the village, the plot, and the time materialize, merge, and melt away again. Though sequential in written form, the stories occur in parallel as alternative readings of the same elements in the same space. In the anti-world of the sanatorium run by Dr. Gothard, the clock is put back to postpone the father's imminent death so he can set up business one last time in that dimension. In another dimension the father's metamorphosis into a crab surprises no one in the family; indeed he is even served up for supper. Joseph's uncanny influence over reality is shown particularly in the story "Wiosna" [Spring], when he is shown a stamp album by his cousin Rudolf. The stamps' portraits and countries suggest to him a perilous adventure set in the romantic Mexico of the Emperor Maximilian, though its events seem to take place on the very edge of the town where Joseph lives. His passion for a Bianca, imprisoned by a wicked uncle, disintegrates into faithful duty as Joseph becomes a minister when a *coup d'état* is staged in her name. As the plot crumbles further, and the waxwork dummies of a travelling show get involved, Joseph is arrested and sacrificed for the cause.

The schizophrenic character of Joseph's many manifestations and experiences and the unstable nature of everything around him are balanced by Creation itself: it assures that each dimension is self-contained, and as declared by Joseph in ''Wiosna,'' ''it was a spring that took its text seriously.'' Here is the sense of Schulz's writing: not self-discovery, but discovery itself is the objective, the quest for the ''Authentic,'' for the ''Book,'' and thus God Himself. The multiple dimensions of Schulz's stories are the environments lent to facilitate or hinder that search. Thus Schulz gives no conclusive definitions, but a finite number of readings of Creation, expressed as highly metaphorically charged writing. Just as Jehovah's written Word is an approximation of Him, so too the stories are permutations of God's creativity. The final effect is magical, timeless, and intensely claustrophobic.

In effect, Schulz's worlds are a constantly shifting set of conversions of his adolescent memory. Runaway similes and metaphors create infinite numbers of unpredictable texts. Joseph's mission to isolate the ''Authentic,'' much like his father's definitive ''Grammar of Autumn,'' is closely linked to the Cabbalistic transliteration of the correspondences between physical objects, mental states, and Divine inspiration, but could equally be seen as a case history of sublimated hysteria. Yet his multi-dimensional world is not one of the struggle between Good and Evil—Jewish moralism plays no part at all—it is rather a complex metaphor for his own creativeness, and a repudiation of the bleak reality around him, the one in which he was shot by an SS-officer in 1942.

—Donald Pirie

SCIASCIA, Leonardo

Born: Racalmuto, Sicily, Italy, 8 January 1921. **Education:** Educated at the Istituto Magistrate ''IX Maggio'' [9th May], Caltanisetta, Sicily, 1935–38. **Family:** Married Maria Andronico in 1944, two daughters. **Career:** Clerk in Ucsea, organizing collection of wheat, barley, and oil, 1941–48; teacher, elementary school, Caltanisetta, 1949–57; writer and journalist from 1953; on attachment to the Department of Education, Rome, 1957–58; moved to Palermo, 1967, and taught there until 1970; contributor, *Il Corriere della Sera*, from 1969; independent councillor (on the Communist Party list), Palermo commune, 1975–77; elected as Radical Party Deputy to the European (subsequently given up) and Italian parliaments, 1979: member of the commission of enquiry into the murder of Aldo Moro, 1979–83; co-editor, with Alberto Moravia, *q.v.*, and Enzo Siciliano, *Nuovi Argomenti*, 1982. **Awards:** Pirandello prize, 1953; *Libera Stampa* prize, 1957; Prato prize, 1960; Crotone prize, 1956, 1961; Séguier prize, 1975; Foreign Book prize (France), 1976. **Died:** 20 November 1989.

PUBLICATIONS

Collection

Opere, edited by Claude Ambroise. 3 vols., 1987–91.

Fiction

Le parrocchie di Regalpetra. 1956; as *Salt in the Wound*, translated by Judith Green, 1969.

Gli zii di Sicilia. 1958; enlarged edition (includes ''L'antimonio''), 1961; as *Sicilian Uncles: Four Novellas*, translated by N.S. Thompson, 1986.

Il giorno della civetta. 1961; as *Mafia Vendetta*, translated by Archibald Colquhoun and Arthur Oliver, 1963; as *The Day of the Owl*, translated by Colquhoun and Oliver, with *Equal Danger*, 1989.

Il consiglio d'Egitto. 1963; as *The Council of Egypt*, translated by Adrienne Foulke, 1966; as *The Council of Egypt*, translated by Adrienne Foulke, 1998.

Morte dell'inquisitore. 1964; as *Death of the Inquisitor*, in *Salt in the Wound*, translated by Judith Green, 1969; also translated in *Death of an Inquisitor and Other Stories*, 1990.

A ciascuno il suo. 1966; as *A Man's Blessing*, translated by Adrienne Foulke, 1968; as *To Each His Own*, translated by Foulke, 1989.

Racconti siciliani. 1966.

Il contesto. 1971; edited by Tom O'Neill, 1986; as *Equal Danger*, translated by Adrienne Foulke, 1973, and with *The Day of the Owl*, 1989.

Eufrosina. 1973.

Il mare colore del vino. 1973; as *The Wine-Dark Sea*, translated by Avril Bardoni, 1985.

Todo modo. 1974; as *One Way or Another*, translated by Adrienne Foulke, 1977; also translated by Sacha Rabinovitch, 1989.

I pugnalatori. 1976.

Candido; ovvero un sogno fatto in Sicilia. 1977; as *Candido, or, A Dream Dreamed in Sicily*, translated by Adrienne Foulke, 1979.

Dalle parti degli infedeli. 1979.

La sentenza memorabile. 1982.

Storia della povera Rosetta. 1983.

Una commedia siciliana. 1983.

Occhio di capra. 1984.

Chronachette. 1985; as *Little Chronicles*, translated by Ian Thompson, 1990.

1912 + 1. 1986; as *1912 + 1*, translated by Sacha Rabinovitch, 1989.

La strega e il capitano. 1986; as *The Captain and the Witch*, translated by Ian Thompson, 1990.

Porte aperte. 1987; as *Open Doors*, translated by Marie Evans, in *The Knight and Death and Other Stories*, 1991.

Il cavaliere e la morte. 1988; as *The Knight and Death and Other Stories*, translated by Joseph Farrell and Marie Evans, 1991; as *Knight and Death: Three Novellas*, translated by Farrell and Evans, 1992.

Una storia semplice. 1989; as *A Straightforward Tale*, translated by Joseph Farrell, in *The Knight and Death and Other Stories*, 1991.

Death of an Inquisitor and Other Stories, translated by Ian Thompson. 1990.

Verse

Favole della dittatura. 1950.
La Sicilia, il suo cuore. 1952.
Cola Pesce. 1975.

Plays

L'onorevole. 1965.
Recitazione della controversia liparitana dedicata ad A.D. 1969.
I mafiosi, from a play by Giuseppe Rizzotto and Gaspare Mosca (produced 1972). In *L'onorevole, Recitazione della controversia liparitana, I mafiosi.* 1976.

Other

Pirandello e il pirandellismo. 1953.
Pirandello e la Sicilia. 1961.
Santo Marino. 1964.
Feste religiose in Sicilia, photographs by Fernando Scianna. 1965.
La corda pazza: Scrittori e cose della Sicilia. 1970.
Atti relativi alla morte di Raymond Roussel. 1971; as "Acts Relative to the Death of Raymond Roussel," in *Raymond Roussel: Life, Death and Works,* 1987.
Emilio Greco. 1971.
Jaki. 1975.
La scomparsa di Majorana. 1975; as *The Mystery of Majorana,* translated by Sacha Rabinovitch, with *The Moro Affair,* 1987.
Les siciliens, with Dominique Fernandez, photographs by Ferdinando Scianna. 1977; Italian edition, as *I siciliani,* translated by Maria Vittoria Malvano, 1977.
L'affaire Moro. 1978; as *The Moro Affair,* translated by Sacha Rabinovitch, with *The Mystery of Majorana,* 1987.
Nero su Nero. 1979.
La Sicilia come metafora: Intervista, with Marcelle Padovani. 1979; as *Sicily as Metaphor,* translated by James Marcus, 1994.
Il volto sulla maschera: Mosjoukine—Mattia Pascal. 1980.
Il teatro della memoria. 1981.
Conversazione in una stanza chiusa, with Davide Lajolo (interview). 1981.
Kermesse. 1982.
La contea di Modica. 1983.
Stendhal e la Sicilia. 1984.
Cruciverba. 1984.
Mediterraneo: Viaggio nelle isole (mainly photographs), with Enzo Ragazzini. 1984.
Per un ritratto dello scrittore da giovane. 1985.
Ignoto a me stesso: ritratti di scrittori da Edgar Allan Poe a Jorge Luis Borges, edited by Daniela Palazzoli. 1987.
Alfabeto pirandelliano. 1989.
Ora di Spagna, photographs by Ferdinando Scianna. 1989.
Editor, with Salvatore Guglielmino, *Narratori di Sicilia.* 1967.
Editor, *Catologo della mostra antologica dell'opera di Francesco Trombadori,* with others. 1976.
Editor, *Torre di guardia,* by Alberto Savinio. 1977.
Editor, with Giuliano Briganti, *Alberto Savinio: Pittura e letteratura.* 1979.
Editor, *Delle cose di Sicilia: Testi inediti o rari.* 1980.
Editor, *Opere,* by Vitaliano Brancati. 2 vols., 1987–92.

Translator, with Salvatore Girgenti, *La veglia a Benicarló,* by Manuel Azaña. 1967.
Translator, *Il procuratore della Giudea,* by Anatole France. 1979.
Translator, *Morte del sogno,* by Pedro Salinas. 1981.

*

Bibliography: "A Bibliography of the Mystery Writings of Leonardo Sciascia," in *Clues: A Journal of Detection,* Spring-Summer 1989.

Critical Studies: *Leonardo Sciascia* by Walter Mauro, 1970; *Leonardo Sciascia e la Sicilia* by Giovanna Ghetti Abruzzi, 1974; *Invito alla lettura di Sciascia* by Claude Ambroise, 1974, revised edition 1978; *Due scrittori siciliani* by Filippo Cilluffo, 1974; *La Sicilia di Sciascia* by Santi Correnti, 1977, enlarged edition, 1987; *Leonardo Sciascia: Introduzione e guida allo studio dell'opera sciasciana* by Luigi Cattanei, 1979; Sciascia Issue of *L'Arc,* 77, 1979; *Leonardo Sciascia 1956–1976: A Thematic and Structural Study* by Giovanna Jackson, 1981; "Sciascia," in *Writers and Society in Contemporary Italy* edited by Michael Caesar and Peter Hainsworth, 1984 and "Leonardo Sciascia," in *Association of Teachers of Italian Journal,* 52, 1988, both by Verina R. Jones; *Leonardo Sciascia: La verità, l'aspra verità* by Antonio Motta, 1985; *Pigliari di lingua: temi e forme della narrativa di Leonardo Sciascia* by Aldo Budriesi, 1986; "The Metaphysical Detective Novel and Sciascia's *Il contesto*: Parody or Tyranny of a Borrowed Form?" by Carol Lazzaro-Weiss, in *Quaderni d'Italianistica,* 8(1), 1987; *Leonardo Sciascia: Tecniche narrative e ideologia,* 1988, and *La fede nella scrittura: Leonardo Sciascia,* 1990, both by Onofrio Lo Dico; "Literal Insularity Versus Literary Universality: The Case of Sciascia" by Tom O'Neill, in *Literature and National Cultures* edited by Brian Edwards, 1988; "Of Valiant Knights and Labyrinths: Leonardo Sciascia's *Il cavaliere e la morte*" by Susan Briziarelli, in *Italica,* 68(1), 1991; *Sciascia: Scrittura e verità: Atti del convegno, Novembre/Dicembre 1990,* 1991; *Sciascia: La storia ed altro,* 1991; *La ragione di un intellettuale libero: Leonardo Sciascia* by Lucrezia Lorenzini, 1992; *Leonardo Sciascia* by Joseph Farrell, 1995.

*   *   *

In the 1967 preface to the reprint of his first work, *Le parrocchie di Regalpetra* (*Salt in the Wound*), a series of "essays" on various aspects of his native Racalmuto, Leonardo Sciascia claimed that it contained, in essence, all the themes that he would ever deal with:

> All my books in effect are simply one. A book on Sicily touching on the sore points of its past and present and which ends up taking on the shape of a story of an ongoing defeat of reason and of those individuals who were personally caught up in it and destroyed by it.

The claim is, up to a point, true. Bellodi, the protagonist of *Il giorno della civetta* (*The Day of the Owl*), Sciascia's first detective story (his preferred genre), "has played his part in a revolution and has seen law created by it. This law, the law of the Republic, which safeguarded liberty and justice, he served and enforced." In the end, though, he will be defeated, like a whole series of other, no less committed, protagonists—from the Jacobin lawyer Di Blasi in *Il consiglio d'Egitto* (*The Council of Egypt*), a historical novel set in late

915

18th-century Palermo (arguably his best work), to Laurana, the teacher-detective in *A ciascuno il suo* (*To Each His Own*), and Rogas, the investigator who "had principles, in a country where almost no one did," of *Il contesto* (*Equal Danger*).

The antagonist to the law safeguarding liberty and justice is the Mafia, and in the earlier realistic novels it is the historically recognizable criminal organization, involved in protection rackets in the building industry (in *The Day of the Owl*), and implicated politically at both local and national level (*To Each His Own*) which dominates. In the later works, however, where sober realism gives way to a more fantastic elaboration of themes (precisely because fact is often stranger than fiction), it is clear that the Mafia has become more a metaphor for something much more universal, "power anywhere in the world," as Sciascia defines it in an endnote to *Equal Danger*, which "in the impenetrable form of a concatenation that we can roughly term *mafioso*, works steadily greater degradation," and where we may recognize Kant's affirmation in his *Principles of Politics* that "the possession of power inevitably corrupts the free judgement of reason."

Liberty and justice, law ("a rational thing born of reason" notes Sciascia in *The Day of the Owl*), power and corruption (including that Kantian reason) are all concerns that underline the moral quality of Sciascia's work. But we should not allow them, important though they be, to blind us to the imaginative manner in which they find expression. "No flights of fantasy," Bellodi's superior had warned him; but Sicily, as the captain realized, "is all a realm of fantasy and what can anyone do there without imagination?" It is unbridled imagination that sustains Vella in his invention of an ancient Arabic chronicle (the Council of Egypt of that novel's title) which justifies baronial privilege and restores to the Kingdom of Naples all power over the island. And it is Di Blasi, prior to his beheading for having attempted to overturn just these privileges, who provides the gloss: "there is so much fraud in life," but, Vella is told, yours "has at least the merit of being a zestful one, and even, in one sense, . . . useful." And, adds the messenger, Di Blasi "admires your imagination."

Sciascia's work is replete with fraud, particularly of the written, imaginative kind. To Vella's historical fabrications can be added such others as the forged confession in *The Day of the Owl*, or the threatening letter composed of words cut from a copy of the Vatican daily newspaper with which *To Each His Own* opens. But, beyond these specific examples there is a broader concern with the nature of literature itself. The penultimate chapter of *The Council of Egypt* concludes:

> Because he felt that he could not and should not write all the true and profound things that stirred within him, Di Blasi began to write verses. The concept of poetry then prevalent held that the poet is free to lie. Today the concept of poetry no longer permits this, although perhaps poetry itself allows it still.

And early on in *Equal Danger*, Rogas becomes convinced "that it was not difficult, all told, to distinguish on dead papers, in dead words, truth from falsehood; and that any fact whatsoever, once fixed in written form, repeated the problem which scholars consider belongs only to art, to poetry." (The passage has been inexplicably omitted from the English translation.) Poetry and literature, truth and falsehood. This concern may in part explain why many of Sciascia's works—including *Morte dell'inquisitore* (*Death of an Inquisitor*), *La scomparsa di Majorana* (*The Mystery of Majorana*), on the disappearance in 1938 of a promising young nuclear physicist, and

L'affaire Moro (*The Moro Affair*) on the kidnapping and assassination of the Christian Democrat leader, Aldo Moro—may be classified as historical reconstructions of important events or intriguing cases. No less true, however is the degree to which writing and writers may be called upon to help unravel the "truth" as, for example, in the Majorana case with its frequent recourse to Pirandello, Shakespeare (Majorana's own favourite writers) and, especially, Stendhal (Sciascia's favourite).

George Steiner defines heresy as "unending re-reading and revaluation" (*Real Presences*), and Don Gaetano, the priestly protagonist of *Todo modo* (*One Way or Another*) who, like Stéphane Mallarmé, has read all the books, is also in this sense heretical. "Perhaps it's possible today," he asserts, "to rewrite all the books that have ever been written. . . . All of them. Except *Candide*." Don Gaetano's creator, Sciascia, was to do just that and rewrite *Candide*, in 1977—the ultimate heresy, but it confirmed an ever-growing belief on Sciascia's part that literature and truth were one. He used literature heretically, to examine reality in such a way that our orthodox view of it gave way to more sophisticated and consequently more illuminating perceptions.

—Tom O'Neill

SCRIBE, (Augustin) Eugène

Born: Paris, France, 24 December 1791. **Education:** Educated at the Collège de Sainte-Barbe and Lycée Napoléon, both Paris; studied law briefly. **Career:** Playwright from 1810; in a commercially successful career, went on to write more than 330 (and possibly as many as 400) works for the stage, including plays and *comédies-vaudevilles* for the Parisian boulevard theatres (especially the Gymnase, for which he was resident dramatist, 1821–31, and the Vaudeville) and later for the Comédie-Française, and libretti for operas, *opéras-comiques*, and ballets for the Paris Opéra and Opéra-Comique. His principal dramatic collaborators included Germain Delavigne, Henri Dupin, Mélesville, and E.-W. Legouvé, and he wrote libretti to the music of leading composers, including Auber, Donizetti, Boïeldieu, Gounod, Meyerbeer, Rossini, and Verdi. **Member:** Académie française, 1834. **Died:** 20 February 1861.

PUBLICATIONS

Collections

Oeuvres complètes. 76 vols., 1874–85; includes five series:
1. *Comédies-drames.* 9 vols.
2. *Comédies-vaudevilles.* 33 vols.
3. *Opéras; Ballets.* 6 vols.
4. *Opéras-comiques.* 20 vols.
5. *Proverbes; Nouvelles; Romans.* 8 vols.

Plays (selection)

The following list includes those plays and libretti that have been translated into English, and some collections published within the author's lifetime. Non-musical collaborators are not listed.

La Somnabule (produced 1819). 1821; translated as *The Somnabulist*, 1850.

Le Gastronome sans argent (produced 1821). 1821; as *A Race for Dinner*, adapted by J.T.G. Rodwell, 1829.

Michel et Christine (produced 1821). 1821; as *Love in Humble Life*, translated by J.H. Payne, 1850.

Le Vieux Garçon et la petite fille (produced 1822). 1822; translated as *The Popular Farce Called Old and Young*, 1822.

Le Menteur véridique (produced 1823). 1823; translated as *He Lies like Truth*, 1850.

Léocadie, music by Daniel Auber (produced 1824). 1824; as *Léocadia*, translated by Cavillini, 1835.

La Chatte métamorphosée en femme (produced 1827). 1827; translated as *The Woman That Was a Cat*, 1840.

Le Comte Ory, music by Rossini (produced 1828). 1828; as *The Count Ory*, translated anonymously, 1829.

La Muette de Portici, music by Daniel Auber (produced 1828). 1828; translated as *Mansaniello; or, The Dumb Girl of Portici*, 1850.

L'Enfant prodigue, music by Daniel Auber (produced 1830). 1850; translated as *Il Prodigo, The Prodigal*, 1851.

Robert-le-diable, music by Giacomo Meyerbeer (produced 1831). 1831; translated as *Robert-le-diable*, 1832.

Gustave III; ou, Le Bal masqué, music by Daniel Auber (produced 1833). 1833; translated as *Gustavus the Third; or, The Masked Ball*, adapted by J.R. Planché, 1833.

Le Chalet, music by Adolphe Adam. 1834; translated as *Betly: An Opera*, 1838.

Salvoisy; ou, L'Amoureux de la reine (produced 1834). 1834; as *Salvoisy; or, The Queen's Lover*, translated anonymously by Catherine Dove, 1834; as *The Queen's Champion*, translated by Catherine Dove, 1886.

La Frontière de Savoie (produced 1834). 1834; as *A Peculiar Position*, translated by J. R. Planché, 1837; also in *Camille and Other Plays*, edited by Stephen Sadler Stanton, 1957.

Théâtre complet. 24 vols., 1834–47.

La Juive, music by Jacques Halévy (produced 1835). 1835; as *The Jewess*, adapted by J.R. Planché, 1835; translated by Henri Drayton, 1854.

Le Cheval de bronze, music by Daniel Auber (produced 1835). 1835; as *Opera of the Bronze Horse*, adapted by A. Bunn, 1836.

Les Huguenots, music by Giacomo Meyerbeer (produced 1836). 1836; translated as *The Huguenots*, n.d.

Fra Diavalo; ou, L'Hôtellerie de Terracine, music by Daniel Auber. 1836; as *Fra Diavalo: A Comic Opera*, translated anonymously, 1854.

Le Domino noir, music by Daniel Auber. 1837; translated as *The Black Domino; or, A Night's Adventure*, 1837.

César; ou, Le Chien du château (produced 1837). 1837; translated as *Caesar: The Watchdog of the Castle*, 1886.

La Reine d'un jour, music by Adolphe Adam (produced 1839). 1839; as *Opera of A Queen for a Day*, adapted by J.T. Haines, 1841.

Les Martyres, music by Donizetti (produced 1842). 1840; translated as *The Martyrs*, 1852.

Le Verre d'eau; ou, Los Effets et les causes. 1840; as *A Glass of Water*, adapted by W.E. Suter, 1850; also translated by Robert Cornthwaite, 1995.

Oeuvres complètes. 5 vols., 1840–42.

Les Diamants de ta couronne, music by Daniel Auber (produced 1841). 1841; translated as *The Crown Diamonds*, 1844.

Une chaîne (produced 1841). 1841; as *In Honour Bound*, translated anonymously, 1885.

Dom Sébastien, roi de Portugal, music by Donizetti (produced 1843). 1843; translated as *Don Sebastiano: A Tragic Opera*, 1860.

La Part du diable, music by Daniel Auber (produced 1843). 1843; as *Asmodeus, the Little Demon*, translated by T. Archer, 1850.

La Sirène, music by Daniel Auber (produced 1844). 1844; as *The Syren*, translated and adapted by George Soane, 1849.

Haydée; ou, Le Secret, music by Daniel Auber (produced 1847). 1848; as *Haydee; or, The Secret*, translated and adapted by George Soane, 1848.

Le Prophète, music by Giacomo Meyerbeer (produced 1849). 1849; translated as *The Opera of the Prophet*, 1850.

Adrienne Lecouvreur (produced 1849). 1849; edited by Theodore Ely Hamilton, 1917; as *Adrienne Lecouvreur*, translated by Frederick A. Schwab, 1880; also translated by H. Herman, 1883.

Giralda; ou, La Nouvelle Psyché, music by Adolphe Adam (produced 1850). 1850; as *Giralda; or, Which Is My Husband?*, translated by Mrs. Davidson, 1850; as *Giralda; or, The Invisible Husband*, translated by H. Welstead, 1850.

La Dame de pique, music by Jacques Halévy (produced 1850). 1851; as *The Queen of Spades*, translated by Dion Boucicault, n.d.

Bataille des dames; ou, Un duel d'amour (produced 1851). 1851; as *The Ladies' Battle*, translated by Charles Reade, 1850; also translated by George B. Coale, 1887.

Zerline; ou, La Corbeille d'oranges, music by Daniel Auber (produced 1851). 1851; translated as *Zerlina*, 1851.

Marco Spada, music by Daniel Auber (produced 1852). 1851; as *Marco Spada*, translated by J.P. Simpson, 1850.

L'Africaine, music by Giacomo Myerbeer (produced 1851). 1865; translated as *L'Africaine*, 1866.

Oeuvres illustrées. 12 vols., 1853–55.

L'Étoile du nord, music by Giacomo Meyerbeer (produced 1854). 1854; translated as *The Star of the North*, 1855.

Les Doigts de fée (produced 1858). 1858; translated as *The World of Fashion*, 1860; translated as *Fairy Fingers*, in *Easy French Plays*, edited by C.W. Benton, 1901.

Fiction

La Maîtresse anonyme. 1840.

Maurice. 1845.

Piquillo Alliaga; ou, Los Maures sous Philippe III. 2 vols., 1847; as *The Victim of the Jesuits; or, Piquillo Alliaga: A Romance*, translated anonymously, 3 vols., 1848.

Le Filleul d'Amadis; ou, Les Amours d'une fée. 3 vols., 1858.

Les Yeux de ma tante. 6 vols., 1859.

Fleurette la bouquetière. 6 vols., 1861; as *Fleurette*, translated by F.P. Clark, 1886.

Noélie. 4 vols., 1862.

Other

Proverbes et nouvelles. 1840.

Historiettes et Proverbes. 1856.

*

Critical Studies: *Eugène Scribe and the French Theatre (1815–1860)* by N. Cole Arvin, 1924; *Eugène Scribe* by H. Hoop and R. Switzer,

1979; *Eugène Scribe and French Opera of the Nineteenth Century* by Karin Pendle, 1979; Eugène *Scribe* by Helen Koon, 1980.

* * *

There is a cruel irony in the fact that Rossini's cheerful light opera *Le Comte Ory* (*The Count Ory*) of 1828 is about the only example of Eugène Scribe's immense output of stage works of every sort that has survived in the repertory, and if it is still performed from time to time, that is certainly more a compliment to the ebullience of its music than to the dramatic qualities of its libretto. *The Count Ory* can, neverthe-less, tell us quite a lot about Scribe and his attitudes to writing. By 1828 Scribe already had to his credit some successes in both the theatre and the opera house, but that did not mean he was unwilling to undertake what really was little better than hackwork. During his Parisian period Rossini had tackled major themes in an innovative style with ambitious operas like *William Tell*, but *The Count Ory* was a reversion to an earlier, far less demanding style, and Scribe cannot be said to have put himself out unduly to provide a libretto, either. Though it is true that the manifestly implausible story of a 12th-century crusading nobleman's amorous adventures is entertaining, there is no great imagination here either in the theme, which in fact owes something to the late 18th-century French interest in more or less fictionalized medievalism, or in its treatment. On the other hand, though, the plot is so transparent that it never gets in the way of the musical development of the opera; there are plenty of "cues for song," whether from the principals or the chorus, and that is basically what Rossini was looking for. Scribe also gave him just the right sort of words to set. The verse of the libretto is simple and repetitive, full of clichés, and with no real indication of poetic strengths. As a result it does not read particularly well, but it is the sort of text that could easily be set to music and which would carry its meaning clearly even when sung against an orchestral background. Two final points about *The Count Ory*: first, that Scribe had no scruples about fashioning its libretto out of two little one-act plays of his from an earlier period and, second, that this was not his unaided work but rather the product of collaboration, with Charles Delestre-Poirson.

All this serves to give some impression of a writer with real talent and considerable versatility but perhaps with no very strong convic-tions, and who regarded writing for the stage as a skilled craft rather than as a means of self-expression. Though the 19th century is not normally considered to be one of the great periods of French drama, Parisian theatres were the centre of enormous, bustling activity from the time of the Revolution, which gave the managements far greater freedom than they had previously experienced. High society enjoyed going to the play just like the ordinary folk up in the gods, and the press dwelt no less on the beauties of the brilliantly lighted theatres than on the scandals that dogged the leading actresses of the day. Above all, in an age that produced few dramatic masterpieces, there was an insatiable demand for new plays, and, though many writers were astonishingly prolific and versatile, none could rival Scribe.

He began, often in collaboration, with *comédies-vaudevilles*, of which an important early example is *Une nuit de la Garde nationale* [A Night for the National Guard]. These ephemeral little one-act plays in prose, with a spice of topicality and opportunities for song, quite often to well-known tunes, provided him with a training in theatrical technique that was to stand him in good stead, particularly when he turned his hand to the writing of librettos for comic operas which, of course, also combined songs and spoken dialogue but

demanded rather fuller development. In a list of more than 80 comic opera librettos written over a period of some 50 years, it is *La Dame blanche* [The White Lady], with its fashionable setting in 18th-century Scotland, which is generally reckoned to be the masterpiece. It was written for Boïeldieu in 1825 and enjoyed great popularity for a long time. Many of the grand operas for which Scribe provided librettos were also highly successful throughout the 19th century. Among the most important are *La Muette de Portici* (*The Dumb Girl of Portici*), written for Auber; *Robert-le-diable, Les Huguenots, Le Prophète* (*The Opera of the Prophet*), and *L'Africaine* for Meyerbeer; *La Juive* (*The Jewess*) for Halévy; and *Los Vêpres siciliennes* [The Sicilian Vespers] for Verdi. In these librettos Scribe takes the blazing Romanticism of Victor Hugo's stage plays, such as *Hernani*, and transposes it into opera, providing rich opportunities for the expres-sion of the strongest imaginable personal, political, and religious emotions, in solos, ensembles, and choruses, in crisis situations and in historical settings of considerable splendour and magnificence.

Scribe also made highly significant contributions to the spoken theatre, and he is above all associated with the development of the "well-made play," such as *Le Verre d'eau* (*A Glass of Water*), with its highly significant subtitle "Or the Effects and Its Causes." *Bertrand et Raton*, set in Copenhagen, is among Scribe's most successful historical comedies, and *Adrienne Lecouvreur* is a roman-ticized account of the career of the great 18th-century actress that gave the Swiss-born star Rachel every opportunity to display her talents and her beauty. By the end of the 19th century Scribe had become a byword for plays that were deftly crafted, rather superficial theatrical entertainments, and a reaction set in. In his time, however, he had a great reputation, and historically he may be seen not only as one of the men who brought Romanticism into grand opera but also as the playwright who developed the theatrically weak "bourgeois drama" of the Enlightenment so that it could be employed effectively in the realist theatre of the late 19th century.

—Chistopher Smith

SEFERIS, George

Born: Giorgos Stylianou Seferiades in Smyrna (now Izmir), Turkey, 29 February 1900; emigrated to Athens in 1914. **Education:** Edu-cated at Protypon Classical Gymnasium, Athens; University of Ath-ens; the Sorbonne, Paris, law degree 1924; studied English in London, 1924–25. **Family:** Married Maria Zannos in 1941. **Career:** Entered Royal Greek Ministry of Foreign Affairs, 1926: vice-consul, later consul, in London, 1931–34; in Athens, 1934–36; consul, Korytsa, Albania, 1936–38; press officer, Athens, 1938–41; worked for Free Greek Government in Crete, 1941, South Africa, 1941–42, Egypt, 1942–44, and Italy, 1944; in Athens, 1944–48, Ankara, 1948–50, and London, 1951–52; Ambassador to Lebanon and Minister to Syria, Iraq, and Jordan, 1953–56; Ambassador to the United Nations, 1956–57, and to Great Britain, 1957–62; retired 1962. Full-time writer, from 1962. **Awards:** Kostis Palamas prize, 1947; Foyle poetry prize (UK), 1961; Nobel prize for literature, 1963. Litt. D.: Cam-bridge University, 1960; Oxford University, 1964; Princeton Univer-sity, New Jersey, 1965; D.Phil.: University of Salonica, 1964. Mem-ber, Institute for Advanced Study, Princeton, 1968; honorary member,

American Academy of Arts and Sciences, and American Academy, 1971. Knight Commander of Order of George I; Grand Cross of Order of Phoenix; Order of Holy Sepulchre; Grand Cross of the Cedar; Grand Cross of Order of Merit (Syria). **Died:** 20 September 1971.

PUBLICATIONS

Collection

Collected Poems 1924–1955 (bilingual edition), edited and translated by Edmund Keeley and Philip Sherrard. 1967; revised edition, 1981; as *Complete Poems*, edited and translated by Keeley and Sherrard, 1990.

Verse

Strophe [Turning Point]. 1931.
I sterna [The Cistern]. 1932.
Mythistorema. 1935; as *Mythistorima*, with *Gymnopaidia*, translated by Mary Cooper Walton, 1977.
Gymnopedia. 1936; as *Gymnopaidia*, with *Mythistorima*, translated by Mary Cooper Walton, 1977.
Imerologio katastromatos A,B,C [Logbook I, II, III]. 3 vols., 1940–55.
Tetradio gymnasmaton [Exercise Book]. 1940.
Poiemata I [Poems]. 1940.
Six Poems from the Greek of Sikelianos and Seferis, translated by Lawrence Durrell. 1946.
Kichli [The Thrush]. 1947.
The King of Asine and Other Poems, translated by Bernard Spencer, Nanos Valaoritis, and Lawrence Durrell. 1948.
Poiemata [Poems]. 1950; 13th edition, 1981.
Poems, translated by Rex Warner. 1960.
Delphoi. 1963; as *Delphi*, translated by Philip Sherrard, 1963.
Tria kryfa poiemata. 1966; as *Three Secret Poems*, translated by Walter Kaiser, 1969.
Tetradio gymnasmaton B [Exercise Book II]. 1976.

Fiction

Eksi nychtes sten Akropole [Six Nights on the Acropolis], edited by G.P. Savidis. 1974.

Other

Dokimes [Essays]. 1944; revised edition, 1962; edited by G.P. Savidis, 2 vols., 1974.
On the Greek Style: Selected Essays in Poetry and Hellenism, translated by Rex Warner and T. Frangopoulos. 1966.
Cheirographo Sop. '41 [Manuscript Sept. '41]. 1972.
Meres tou 1945–1951. 1973; as *A Poet's Journal: Days of 1945–1951*, translated by Athan Anagnostopoulos, 1974.
Politiko imerologio [Political Diary], edited by Alexandrou Xydes. 2 vols., 1979–86.
Metagraphes, edited by Giorges Giatromanolakes. 1980.
Atlelographia 1953–1971 (correspondence), with Adamnatios Diamantes. 1985.
Meres 20 Aprili 1951–4 Avgoustou 1956 (journal). 1986.
George Seferis to Henry Miller: Two Letters from Greece. 1990.

Translator, *T.S. Eliot* (selection). 1936; revised edition, as *The Waste Land and Other Poems*, 1949.
Translator, *Phoniko sten Ekklesia* [Murder in the Cathedral], by T.S. Eliot. 1963.
Translator, *Antigraphes* [Copies]. 1965.
Translator, *Asma asmaton* [Song of Songs]. 1965.
Translator, *E apokalypse tou Ioanne* [The Apocalypse of St. John]. 1966.

*

Critical Studies: "Seferis and the 'Mythical Method'," in *Comparative Literature Studies*, 6, 1969, and *A Conversation with George Seferis* (bilingual edition), 1982, both by Edmund Keeley; *George Seferis, 1900–1971* (by National Book League and British Council), 1975; *War in the Poetry of George Seferis* by C. Capri-Karka, 1986; *George Seferis* by Roderick Beaton, 1991; *Seferis and Friends* by George Thaniel, 1994.

* * *

It can be said with hindsight that George Seferis was the foremost of a generation of Greek poets and prose writers who in different ways introduced modernism into Greek letters, the so-called "Generation of the Thirties." His early career developed under the influence of French symbolism, but additional formative influences on him were an urgent awareness of the Greek cultural tradition stretching back to antiquity, and, from the end of 1931, the poetry and critical ideas of T.S. Eliot.

These three strands first come together in the integrated and highly innovative work, *Mythistorema* (*Mythistorima*); the title, which means "a novel," also alludes to the poem's main theme, the juxtaposition of ancient myth and contemporary history. In this sequence of 24 short poems Seferis attempts, through the mouthpieces of different, anonymous characters and through the evocation of their changing moods—heroic aspiration, frustrated love, fear, resignation—to come to terms as a modern Greek with the past tradition of his country, which he sees as both an inspiration and a burden. The poem alludes to the mythical voyage of the Argonauts in search of the Golden Fleece, a quest that Seferis sees repeated throughout history up to the present, and for the most part futile thanks to man's inadequacy and weakness.

Mythistorima portrays modern man, and more particularly the modern Greek, as cut off from the creative power that inspired the artistic achievements of the classical past, but weighed down by the burden of the relics it has left behind, represented by the worn statues and the "old stones." This theme continues to be prominent throughout his poetry of the 1930s and 1940s, culminating in the longer poem *Kichli* [The Thrush], in which he imagines a modern Odysseus striving to return, not to Ithaca, but to a symbolic home which he calls merely "the light."

New refinements and differences of emphasis appear in Seferis's collections of poems of the 1950s and 1960s, respectively *Imerologio katastromatos C* [Logbook III], based on his experience of Cyprus in 1953 and 1954, and *Tria kryfa poiemata* (*Three Secret Poems*), in which the poet retreats into a fragmented world, a world that "must burn / This noon when the sun is nailed / To the heart of the centifoliate rose." The poems of Seferis's last decade show a new pessimism, and an even sparser style that almost literally fades out into silence in the posthumously published late poems and fragments.

Seferis was not only a poet but also one of Greece's most lucid essayists and critics. Many of his essays on older figures in modern Greek literature (essays on Kalvos, Makriyannis, *Erotókritos*) have become classics and have helped to shape the contemporary perspective on modern Greek literary history, while others deal perceptively with the issues of tradition and modernism which also preoccupied him in his poetry. Poetry and essays alike are permeated by Seferis's deeply held humanist convictions.

Seferis was largely responsible for introducing modern English poetry to Greece, through his acclaimed translations of Eliot, Pound, and Yeats. He also translated the Apocalypse into modern Greek.

Before embarking on his career as a poet, he wrote a novel, *Eksi nychtes sten Akropole* [Six Nights on the Acropolis], which was substantially complete and published posthumously. In this novel, written chiefly in 1928 and reworked in 1954, Seferis first tried to work out many of the themes which came to dominate his poetry, but without the novelist's grasp of narration and character *Eksi nychtes* is a failure, though a remarkable literary experiment.

—Roderick Beaton

See the essay on *Mythistorima*.

SENDER (GARCÉS), Ramón J(osé)

Born: Chalamera de Cinca, Huesca, Aragón, Spain, 3 February 1902. **Education:** Educated at the Colegio de la Sagrada Familia, Reus, Tauste, Catalonia; Instituto de Segunda Enseñanza de Teruel, Alcañiz, to 1917; Instituto de Zaragoza, 1918–19; University of Madrid, Faculty of Philosophy and Letters, degree 1924. **Military Service:** Infantry officer, Spanish army in Morocco, 1923–25. **Family:** Married 1) Amparo Barayon in 1933 (executed 1936), one son and one daughter; 2) Florence Hall in 1943 (divorced 1963). **Career:** Worked as pharmacist during school years; editor, *El Sol*, Madrid, 1924–29; imprisoned for anti-monarchist activity, 1927; freelance writer and journalist, 1931–36, contributing to *Solidaridad, Obrera, La Libertad, El Socialista*, and other periodicals; lived in Paris, Berlin, and Moscow, 1933; active supporter of the Republic: National Council of Culture, and Alliance of Intellectuals for Defence of Democracy, 1930s, brigade commander and major general of staff, Republican army, 1936–37, and undertook speaking tour of the United States to win support for the Republic, 1938; founder, *La Voz de Madrid*, Paris, 1938; lived in Mexico, 1939–41; moved to the United States, 1942: naturalized 1946; translator and adaptor, Metro-Goldwyn-Mayer Inc., New York, 1943–44; professor of Spanish literature, Amherst College, Massachusetts, 1943–44, University of Denver, Colorado, 1946, and University of New Mexico, Albuquerque, 1947–63 (emeritus from 1963); subsequently lectured at Ohio State University, 1951, University of California, Los Angeles, 1963–64, University of Southern California, Los Angeles, 1964–72 (also writer in residence, 1968, and emeritus professor from 1972); resettled in Spain, 1976, and regained Spanish citizenship, 1980. **Awards:** National literature prize, 1935; Guggenheim fellowship, 1942; Fiction prize (Barcelona), 1967; Planeta prize, 1969. Honorary degrees: University of New Mexico; University of Southern California. Medal of Morocco and Military Cross of Merit, Spain c.1925; Cross of Isabel the Catholic, Spain, 1980. **Member:** North American Academy of the Spanish Language, 1974 (corresponding member from 1943), Spanish Confederated Societies (honorary), and board of advisers, Hispanic Society of America, all New York; Atheneum of Science, Literature and the Arts, Madrid, 1975; International Society of Arts and Sciences, Berne. **Died:** 15 January 1982.

PUBLICATIONS

Fiction

Imán. 1930; as *Earmarked for Hell*, translated by James Cleugh, 1934; as *Pro Patria*, translated by Cleugh, 1935.

O.P.: Orden público. 1931.

El verbo se hizo sexo: Teresa de Jesús. 1931; revised edition, as *Tres novetas teresianas*, 1967.

Siete domingos rojos. 1932; revised edition, as *Las Tres Sorores*, 1974; as *Seven Red Sundays*, translated by Sir Peter Chalmers Mitchell, 1936.

Viaje a la aldea del crimen. 1934.

La noche de las cien cabezas. 1934.

Míster Witt en el cantón. 1936; edited by José María Joves, 1987; as *Mr. Witt among the Rebels*, translated by Sir Peter Chalmers Mitchell, 1937.

El lugar del hombre. 1939; as *El lugar de un hombre*, 1958; as *A Man's Place*, translated by Oliver La Farge, 1940.

Proverbio de la muerte. 1939; revised edition, as *La esfera*, 1947; as *The Sphere*, translated by Felix Giovanelli, 1949.

Mexicayotl (stories). 1940.

Epitalamio del Prieto Trinidad. 1942; as *Dark Wedding*, translated by Eleanor Clark, 1943.

Crónica del alba. 1942; also in Volume 1 of *Crónica del alba* trilogy, 1963; as *Chronicle of Dawn*, translated by Willard R. Trask, 1944, also in *Before Noon*, 1957.

El rey y la reina. 1949; as *The King and the Queen*, translated by Mary Low, 1948.

El verdugo afable. 1952; as *The Affable Hangman*, translated by Florence Sender, 1954.

Mosén Millán. 1953; revised edition, as *Réquiem por un campesino español*, 1960; edited by Patricia MacDermott, 1991; as *Requiem for a Spanish Peasant*, translated by Elinor Randall, 1960.

Hipogrifo violento. 1954; also in Volume 1 of *Crónica del alba* trilogy, 1963; as *Violent Griffin*, in *Before Noon*, 1957.

Ariadna. 1955; as *Los cinco libros de Ariadna*, 1957.

Bizancio. 1956.

La quinta Julieta. 1957; also in Volume 1 of *Crónica del alba* trilogy, 1963; as *The Villa Julieta*, in *Before Noon*, 1957.

Before Noon (includes *Chronicle of Dawn; Violent Griffin; The Villa Julieta*), translated by Florence Sender and Willard R. Trask. 1957.

Emen hetan. 1958.

Los laureles de Anselmo. 1958.

El mancebo y los héroes. 1960; also in Volume 2 of *Crónica del alba* trilogy, 1963.

Novelas ejemplares de Cibola (stories). 1961; as *Tales of Cibola*, translated by Florence Sender and others, 1964.

La tesis de Nancy. 1962.

La luna de los perros. 1962.

Carolus Rex. 1963.

Los tontos de la Concepción. 1963.

Crónica del alba (trilogy). 1963–65:
   1) *Crónica del alba; Hipogrifo violento; La quinta Julieta.* 1963; as *Before Noon*, 1957.
   2) *El mancebo y los héroes; La onza de oro; Los niveles det existir.* 1963.
   3) *Los términos del presagio; La orilla donde los locos sonríen; La vida comienza ahora.* 1965.
La aventura equinocial de Lope de Aguirre, antiepopeya. 1964.
El bandido adolescente. 1965.
Cabrerizas Altas (stories). 1965.
La llave, y otras narraciones (stories). 1967.
La galinas de Cervantes, y otras narraciones parabólicas (stories). 1967.
Jubileo en et Zócalo: Retablo conmemorativo. 1967.
Las criaturas saturnianas. 1968.
El extraño señor Photynos, y otras novelas americanas (stories). 1968.
Novelas del otro jueves (stories). 1969.
En la vida de Ignacio Morel. 1969.
Nocturno de los 14. 1969.
Tánit. 1970.
Zu, el ángel anfibio. 1970.
Relatos frontizeros (stories). 1970.
La antesala. 1971.
El fugitivo. 1972.
Túpac Amaru. 1973.
Una virgen llama a tu puerta. 1973.
Nancy y el bato loco. 1974.
La mesa de las tres moiras. 1974.
Cronus y la señora con rabo. 1974.
Nancy, doctora en gitanería. 1974.
Arlene y la gaya ciencia. 1976.
La efemérides. 1976.
El mechudo y la Llorona. 1977.
El alarido de Yaurí. 1977.
Gloria y vejamen de Nancy. 1977.
El pez de oro. 1977.
Adela y yo. 1978.
El superviviente. 1978.
Solanar y lucernario aragonés. 2 vols., 1978–81.
La mirada inmóvil. 1979.
Ramú y los animales propicios. 1980.
Saga de los suburbios. 1980.
La muñeca en la vitrina: Bajo el signo de Virgo. 1980.
Una hoguera en la noche: Bajo el signo de Aries. 1980.
Orestíada de los pingüinos: Bajo el signo de Piscis. 1981.
La cisterna de Chichén-Itzá. 1981.
El oso malayo. 1981.
La kermesse de los alguaciles. 1982.
El jinete y la yegua: Bajo el signo de Capricornio. 1982.
Epílogo a Nancy: Bajo el signo de Tauro. 1982.
Hugues y el once negro. 1984.
Chandrío en la plaza de las Cortes. 1985.

Verse

Las imágenes migratorias. 1960.
Poesía y memorias bisiestas. 1974.
Libro armilar de poesía y memorias bisiestas. 1974.

Plays

El secreto. 1935; as *The Secret*, translated anonymously, in *One Act Play Magazine*, 1, 1937.
Hernán Cortés. 1940.
La llave. 1960; as *The Key*, translated anonymously, in *Kenyon Review*, 5, 1943.
El diantre. 1958.
Comedia del diantre y otras dos (includes *Los antofagastas* and *Donde crece la marihuana*). 1967.
Don Juan en la mancebía. 1968.

Other

Teatro de masas. 1932.
Casas viejas. 1933.
Carta de Moscú sobre el amor. 1934.
Proclamación de la sonrisa. 1934.
Madrid-Moscú. 1934.
Contraataque. 1938; as *Counter-Attack in Spain*, translated by Sir Peter Chalmers Mitchell, 1937; as *The War in Spain: A Personal Narrative*, translated by Mitchell, 1937.
Unamuno, Baroja, Valle-Inclán y Santayana (essays). 1955; revised edition, as *Examen de ingenios: Los noventayochos*, 1961.
Valle-Inclán y la dificultad de ta tragedia. 1965.
Ensayos sobre et infringimiento cristiano. 1967.
Tres ejemplos de amor y una teorí. 1969.
Ensayos del otro mundo. 1970.
Conversaciones con Ramón Sender, edited by Marcelino C. Peñuelas. 1970.
Páginas escogidas, edited by Marcelino C. Peñuelas. 1972.
El futuro comenzó ayer: Lecturas mosaicas. 1975.
Obra completa. 3 vols., 1976–81.
Porqué se suicidan las ballenas. 1979.
Luz zodiacal en el parque: Bajo el signo de Acuario. 1980.
Monte Odina. 1980.
Álbum de radiografías secretas. 1982.
Toque de queda. 1985.
Cabrerizas altas; Arabescos; Impresion del carnet de un soldado, edited by Vicente Moga Romero. 1990.
Editor, *Escrito en Cuba: Cinco poetas disidentes.* 1979.

*

Bibliography: *Ramón J. Sender: An Annotated Bibliography 1928–1974* by Charles L. King, 1976.

Critical Studies: *El escritor y su senda: Estudio crítico y literario sobre Ramón J. Sender* by J. Rivas, 1967; *Imán y la novela histórica de Sender*, 1971, and *La verdad de Ramón J. Sender*, 1982, both by F. Carrasquer; *La obra narrativa de Ramón J. Sender* by Marcelino C. Peñuelas, 1971; *Ramón J. Sender* (in English) by Charles L. King, 1974; *El anarquismo en las obras de Ramón J. Sender* by Michiko Nonoyama, 1979; *Ramón J. Sender en los años 1930–36: Sus ideas sobre la relación entre literatura y sociedad* by Patrick Collard, 1980; *Ramón J. Sender: In memoriam* edited by José Carlos Mainer, 1983; *Ramón J. Sender: El distanciamiento del exilio* by José Luis Castillo-Puche, 1985; *Adjusting to Reality: Philosophical Ideas in the Post-Civil War Novels of Ramón J. Sender* by Anthony M. Trippett, 1986; *Homenaje a Ramón J. Sender* edited by Mary S. Vásquez, 1987; *Réquiem por un campesino español* (critical guide, in English) by

Stephen Hart, 1990; *Politics and Philosophy in the Early Novels of Ramón J. Sender, 1930–1936: The Impossible Revolution* by Francis Lough, 1996.

* * *

Ramón J. Sender's life, as adventurous and filled with danger as any novel, produced works containing significant autobiographical substrata. A rebel from childhood, involved early and then often in politics and social protest, he saw military service in Morocco, inspiring his first novel, *Imán* (*Earmarked for Hell*, or *Pro Patria*), wherein a soldier's experience in Spain's disastrous African campaign expresses Sender's anti-war stance. Hundreds of articles favouring land reform (a major fictional theme) appeared in *La Libertad* [Liberty], *Solidaridad Obrera* [Workers' Solidarity], and other newspapers (1930–36), and he founded a war propaganda magazine, *La Voz de Madrid* [The Voice of Madrid], in Paris in 1938.

O.P.: Orden público [Law and Order] recounts experiences while its author was jailed in Madrid's Cárcel Modelo (Model Prison), for opposing oppressive governmental policies. *El verbo se hizo sexo* [The Word Was Made Sex], a novelized biography of St. Teresa, allegedly the work of Sender while a teenager, was rewritten as *Tres novelas teresianas* [Three Teresan Novellas], stories suggesting that erotic drive is sublimated as sanctity. *Siete domingos rojos* (*Seven Red Sundays*) probes the motives of Spanish revolutionaries—anarchists, communists, syndicalists, and socialists—examining seven Sundays of bloodshed. The leftist intellectual protagonist's love for a bourgeois girl, abandoned for the revolution, allegorically expresses Sender's opposition to the bourgeoisie. *Viaje a la aldea del crimen* [Trip to the Village of Crime] documents governmental repression of a failed peasant insurrection in the Andalusian village of Casas Viejas, while *La noche de las cien cabezas* [Night of a Hundred Heads], set in a Madrid cemetery one stormy night, applauds social unrest as 100 severed heads—representing Spain's corrupt society—evoke satiric commentary. The theme reappears in *Proverbio de la muerte* [Proverb of Death], and is redeveloped as *La esfera* (*The Sphere*), Sender's major symbolic, lyrical attempt at philosophical summation. *O.P.: Orden público*, *Viaje a la aldea del crimen*, and *La noche de las cien cabezas* became a testimonial trilogy entitled "Terms of Presage," whose themes reappear in *El verdugo afable* (*The Affable Hangman*).

Míster Witt en el cantón (*Mr. Witt among the Rebels*) won Spain's National literature prize and is among the few of Sender's novels with real plots. Sender's description of it, "the erotic consciousness of man and woman linked with the collective unconscious against the panorama of revolution," applies also to several other works. The struggle during the First Republic (1873), when Murcia attempted to gain independence, is a historical fact. Confusion, inept leadership, and rebel lack of discipline are viewed by an English Victorian gentleman-engineer: civilized, intelligent, and bookish, he believes in progress via science and order, but ambivalence regarding his wife's fidelity leads him to break with the revolutionaries.

Contraataque (*Counter-Attack in Spain*), a response to the Franco uprising, appeared first in English translation. *El lugar del hombre* (*A Man's Place*), set in an Aragonese village near Sender's childhood home, recounts an actual occurrence: a man allegedly murdered suddenly reappears 15 years after two workmen who "confessed" to the killing under torture were sentenced (in a political intrigue to discredit the labour movement).

Crónica del alba (*Chronicle of Dawn*), first of a nine-novel thinly fictionalized autobiography, traces the development of Sender's alter ego, Pepe Garcés, a Loyalist officer. The first book covers 11 childhood years; *Hipogrifo violento* (*Violent Griffin*) and *La quinta Julieta* (*The Villa Julieta*) treat life in boarding school; *El mancebo y los héroes* [The Young Man and the Heroes] shows the youth's first contact with class conflict; *La onza de oro* [The Ounce of Gold] presents an interlude with his wise peasant grandfather; in *Los niveles del existir* [Levels of Existence], Pepe works in a pharmacy during high school (as did Sender), reaching manhood in *Los términos del presagio* [Terms of Presage] and *La orilla donde los locos sonríen* [The Shore Where the Maniacs Smile], and entering the Civil War in *La vida comienza ahora* [Life Begins Now]. The narrator-protagonist, a prisoner in a French concentration camp while writing, wants only to die. Civil conflict fills *Los cinco libros de Ariadna* [The Five Books of Ariadne], which describes Soviet treachery on the Republican front during the Spanish Civil War.

Réquiem por un campesino español (*Requiem for a Spanish Peasant*), originally entitled *Mosén Millán*, is, artistically, among Sender's best achievements. The priest, Mosén Millán, recalls Paco (another alter ego), an idealized, Christlike socialist organizer executed by fascists after Mosén has betrayed him out of fear. *El rey y la reina* (*The King and the Queen*), a realistic allegory exuding metaphysical and symbolic implications, exhibits Sender's characteristic emphasis on humanity: a lower-class Andalusian gardener struggles to protect the beautiful duchess, hidden in an abandoned tower, from Republican militiamen during the Civil War, in this psychological study of class values.

Epitalamio del Prieto Trinidad (*Dark Wedding*) is wholly fanciful: the black boss of a Caribbean penal colony journeys to the mainland to marry an innocent girl and returns immediately to the island. Disturbed by the raucous reception, he kills two convicts and that night is murdered outside the bridal chamber. Two factions fight for power and the widow; she remains with her schoolteacher-rescuer to help the inmates, embodying Sender's faith in essential human goodness. Similarly fanciful is *Emen hetan* [Here We Are]: an 18th-century witches' sabbath on midsummer's eve suggests that Spain is the land of Satan, and facilitates a virulent attack on the Catholic Church. *Los laureles de Anselmo* [Anselm's Laurels] updates Calderón's baroque drama, *La vida es sueño* (*Life Is a Dream*), in a 20th-century American industrial metropolis. *La luna de los perros* [Moon of the Dogs], with nihilistic mood and criminal ambience presents a Spanish exile's trials during the German occupation of Paris in 1941: in the absence of conventional norms, his suicidal urges culminate in the gratuitous murder of his enigmatic lover. Sender's obsession with suicide dominates *Nocturno de los 14* [Nocturne for 14], whose first-person narrator discusses motives for suicide with 14 former acquaintances, all suicides.

Social protest, revolution, war, and death, generally based on personal experience, recur throughout Sender's more than 70 novels; but other topics do feature: *La tesis de Nancy* [Nancy's Thesis] parodies an American University student's encounter with Spanish culture and gypsies, satirizing postgraduate "research." *El bandido adolescente* [The Adolescent Bandit], retells the 1970s adventures of Billy the Kid in the only novel set in New Mexico, where Sender lived for 16 years; several tales in *Novelas ejemplares de Cíbola* (*Tales of Cibola*) also take place there. Other short-story collections reflecting exile experience include *Mexicayotl*, inspired by Mexican life and myth, and *El extraño señor Photynos, y otras novelas americanas* [The Strange Señor, Photynos, and Other American Novellas], five novellas with American settings. In *En la vida de Ignacio Morel* [In the Life of Ignacio Morel], another *alter ego* and contemporary Don Juan humorously recalls his life and loves while teaching in a Parisian school. *Zu, el ángel anfibio* [Zu, the Amphibious Angel] presents a rebel blue whale who challenges ancient cultural myths, discovers human evil, and eventually dies at the hands of whalers. In *Tánit*, a modern incarnation of Aphrodite becomes the bride of the narrator, Enrique, amid discussions of literature, drugs, love, and death. In *La antesala* [The Antechamber], a grotesque allegory set in Madrid toward the end of the Civil War, a teacher of retarded children discovers that life is but the antechamber of death. Sender also wrote historical novels, including *Bizancio* [Byzantium], *Los tontos de la Concepción* [The Idiots of Conception Mission] on Spanish missionaries in the American Southwest, *Carolus Rex* [King Charles], sympathetically depicting the unfortunate monarch Charles II, last of the Habsburgs, *La aventura equinoccial de Lope de Aguirre* [The Equinoctial Adventure of Lope de Aguirre], re-creating the ''treason'' of the allegedly mad Basque explorer of the Amazon, and *Las criaturas saturnianas* [Saturnine Creatures], which has as its protagonist a niece of Catherine the Great of Russia. Her travels constitute allegories of good and evil.

Always opinionated, sometimes arbitrary, and seldom polished, Sender's work varies from being the best of his generation to being merely trivial and propagandist. Developing a few fundamental concepts from many different angles, he pursues preoccupations with existential meaning, life and death, the enigma of individual and collective evil, and the individual need for dignity and ideals, as well as specific socio-political issues—land reform, injustice, revolution, war, and oppression. Sender's peculiar fusion of nearly photographic realism with the lyrical, fantastic, allegorical, and metaphysical lends originality and depth to his work, introducing the reader to a twilight land where his original quixotic vision carries conviction.

—Janet Pérez

SENECA

Born: Lucius Annaeus Seneca in Corduba (now Cordoba), Spain, c. 4 BC; second son of the writer and teacher of rhetoric Lucius Annaeus Seneca. Sent to Rome as an infant; placed in care of his aunt until the rest of the family could follow. **Education:** Studied grammar and rhetoric, then various schools of philosophy, in Rome. **Family:** Married Pompeia Paulina; one son (died AD 41). **Career:** Spent some time in Egypt for his health; returned to Rome, c. AD 31; elected financial administrator (*quaestor*) in AD 30s; exiled to Corsica for alleged adultery with Julia Livilla, sister of Caligula and niece of Claudius, AD 41–49; tutor to Nero, and designated judicial officer (*praetor*), AD 50; with Burrus, adviser and minister to Nero, AD 54–62: consul, AD 56; on Burrus' death in AD 62, he retired and withdrew from public life. Forced to commit suicide for supposed participation in Pisonian conspiracy. **Died:** AD 65.

PUBLICATIONS

Collections

Opera, edited by F. Haase. 1852; also edited by E. Hermes and others, 3 vols., 1898–1907, R. Peiper and G. Richter, 1902, and Fabricus

Serra, 19 vols., 1981–84; translated by J.W. Basore and others [Loeb Edition], 10 vols., 1917–72.

Plays

Agamemnon, edited by R.J. Tarrant. 1976; as *Agamemnon*, translated by John Studley (verse), 1566, and in *Seneca: His Tenne Tragedies*, 1581; also translated by Watson Bradshaw, in *The Ten Tragedies*, 1902; Ella Isabel Harris, in *Tragedies*, 1904; Frank Justus Miller, in *Tragedies*, 1907; David R. Slavitt, in *Tragedies*, vol. 1, 1992.

Hercules Furens, edited by Franco Caviglia. 1979; also edited by John G. Fitch, 1987; as *Hercules Furens*, translated by Jasper Heywood, 1561, and in *Seneca: His Tenne Tragedies*, 1581; also translated by Watson Bradshaw, in *The Ten Tragedies*, 1902; Frank Justus Miller, in *Tragedies*, 1907; as *Mad Hercules*, translated by Ella Isabel Harris, in *Tragedies*, 1904.

Hercules Oetaeus (probably not by Seneca), as *Hercules Oetaeus*, translated by John Studley, in *Seneca: His Tenne Tragedies*. 1581; also translated by Watson Bradshaw, in *The Ten Tragedies*, 1902; Frank Justus Miller, in *Tragedies*, 1907; as *Hercules on Oeta*, translated by Ella Isabel Harris, in *Tragedies*, 1904.

Medea, edited by C.D.N. Costa. 1973; as *Medea*, translated by John Studley (verse), 1566, and in *Seneca: His Tenne Tragedies*, 1581; also translated by Edward Sherburne (verse), in *Tragedies*, 1701; Ella Isabel Harris (verse), in *Two Tragedies of Seneca*, 1898, and in *Tragedies*, 1904; Watson Bradshaw, in *The Ten Tragedies*, 1902; Frank Justus Miller, in *Tragedies*, 1907; Moses Hadas, 1955; Frederick Ahl, in *Three Tragedies*, 1986; David R. Slavitt, in *Tragedies*, vol. 1, 1992; H.M. Hine, 2000.

Octavia (probably not by Seneca), edited (with commentary) by Lucile Yow Whitman. 1978; as *Octavia*, translated by Thomas Nuce, 1566, and in *Seneca: His Tenne Tragedies*, 1581; also translated by E.F. Watling, in *Four Tragedies and Octavia*, 1966.

Oedipus, edited by T.H. Sluiter. 1941; as *Oedipus*, translated by Alexander Nevile. 1563, and in *Seneca: His Tenne Tragedies*, 1581; also translated by Watson Bradshaw, in *The Ten Tragedies*, 1902; Ella Isabel Harris, in *Tragedies*, 1904; Frank Justus Miller, in *Tragedies*, 1907; Moses Hadas, 1956; E.F. Watling, in *Four Tragedies and Octavia*, 1966; translated and adapted by Ted Hughes, 1969; as *Oedipus Rex*, translated by Clarence W. Mendell (verse), in *Our Seneca*, 1941.

Phaedra (also called *Hippolytus*), edited by Pierre Grimal. 1965; also edited by Michael Coffey and Roland Mayer, 1990; as *Hippolytus*, translated by John Studley, in *Seneca: His Tenne Tragedies*, 1581; as *Hippolitus*, translated by E. Prestwich, 1651; as *Phaedra/Hippolitus*, translated by Edward Sherburne (verse), 1701; as *Phaedra*, translated by Watson Bradshaw, in *The Ten Tragedies*, 1902; also translated by Ella Isabel Harris, in *Tragedies*, 1904; Frank Justus Miller, in *Tragedies*, 1907; E.F. Watling, in *Four Tragedies and Octavia*, 1966; Frederick Ahl, in *Three Tragedies*, 1986; A.J. Boyle, 1987; David R. Slavitt, in *Tragedies*, vol. 1, 1992.

Phoenissae, edited by T. Hirschberg. 1989; as *Thebais*, translated by Thomas Newton, in *Seneca: His Tenne Tragedies*, 1581; as *Phoenissae*, translated by Watson Bradshaw, in *The Ten Tragedies*, 1902; also translated by Frank Justus Miller, in *Tragedies*, 1907; as *The Phoenician Women*, translated by Ella Isabel Harris, in *Tragedies*, 1904.

Thyestes, edited by Joost Daalder. 1982; also edited by R.J. Tarrant, 1985; as *Thyestes*, translated by Jasper Heywood, 1560, and in *Seneca: His Tenne Tragedies*, 1581; also translated by John Wright, 1674; Watson Bradshaw, in *The Ten Tragedies*, 1902; Ella Isabel Harris, in *Tragedies*, 1904; Frank Justus Miller, in *Tragedies*, 1907; Moses Hadas, 1957; E.F. Watling, in *Four Tragedies and Octavia*, 1966; Jane Elder, 1982; David R. Slavitt, in *Tragedies*, vol. 1, 1992; Caryl Churchill, 1995.

Troades, edited by Elaine Fantham. 1982; as *Troas*, translated by Jasper Heywood, 1559, and in *Seneca: His Tenne Tragedies*, 1581; also translated by J. Talbot, 1686; as *Troades*, translated by S. Pordage, 1660; also translated by Edward Sherburne, 1679, and in *Tragedies*, 1701; Frank Justus Miller, in *Tragedies*, 1907; as *The Daughters of Troy*, translated by Ella Isabel Harris (verse), in *Two Tragedies of Seneca*, 1898, and in *Tragedies*, 1904; as *Trojan Women*, translated by E.F. Watling, in *Four Tragedies and Octavia*, 1966; also translated by Frederick Ahl, in *Three Tragedies*, 1986; David R. Slavitt, in *Tragedies*, vol. 1, 1992; as *Seneca's Troades: Introduction, Text, Translation and Commentary* by A.J. Boyle, 1994.

Seneca: His Tenne Tragedies (includes *Hercules Furens; Thyestes; Troas; Oedipus; Medea; Hippolytus; Agamemnon; Hercules Oetaeus; Octavia; Thebais*), edited by Thomas Newton, translated by Newton, Jasper Heywood, Alexander Beville, John Studley, and Thomas Nuce. 1581, 2 vols., reprinted 1927, 1966.

Collections Out of Seneca's Works Touching Life and Death, translated in *Six Excellent Treatises*, edited by P. de Mornay. 1607.

Works, translated by Thomas Lodge. 1614.

Tragedies (includes *Medea; Phaedra/Hippolytus; Troades; The Rape of Helen* by Coluthus), translated by Edward Sherburne (verse). 1701.

Two Tragedies of Seneca (includes *The Daughters of Troy; Medea*), translated by Ella Isabel Harris. 1898.

The Ten Tragedies, translated by Watson Bradshaw. 1902.

Tragedies (includes *Mad Hercules; The Daughters of Troy; The Phoenician Women; Medea; Phaedra; Oedipus; Agamemnon; Thyestes; Hercules on Oeta; Octavia*), translated by Ella Isabel Harris. 1904.

Tragedies (includes *Oedipus; Phoenissae; Medea; Hercules Furens; Phaedra; or, Hippolytus; Hercules Oetaeus; Thyestes; Troades; Agamemnon; Octavia*), translated by Frank Justus Miller. 1907.

Selections, edited by R. Dinsdale Stocker. 1910.

[*Tragedies*], in *Complete Roman Drama*, edited by George Duckworth. 2 vols., 1942.

[*Tragedies*], edited by G. Viansino. 3 vols., 1965; also edited by G.C. Giardina, 2 vols., 1966.

Four Tragedies and Octavia (includes *Thyestes; Phaedra; The Trojan Women; Oedipus; Octavia*), translated by E.F. Watling. 1966.

Three Tragedies (includes *The Trojan Women; Medea; Phaedra*), translated by Frederick Ahl. 1986.

Tragoediae, edited by Otto Zwierlein. 1986.

Tragedies, vol. 1 (includes *Trojan Women; Thyestes; Phaedra; Medea; Agamemnon*), translated by David R. Slavitt. 1992.

Verse

Apocolocyntosis divi Claudii (possibly not by Seneca), edited by C.F. Russo. 1964; also edited by P.T. Eden (includes translation), 1984; as *Apocolocyntosis; or, A Mockery Upon the Death and Deification of Claudius Caesar*, translated by Roger L'Estrange, 1664; as

The Satire of Seneca on the Apotheosis of Claudius, translated by Allan P. Ball, 1902, as *Satire of the Deification of Claudius*, with *Selected Essays of Seneca*, 1908; as *Apocolocyntosis*, translated by W.H.D. Rouse, in *Petronius and Seneca*, 1913; also translated by J.P. Sullivan, 1966, with *Satyricon* by Petronius, 1977.

Other

Ad Lucilium epistulae morales, edited by L.D. Reynolds. 2 vols., 1965; as *Letters* [Loeb Edition; bilingual], edited and translated by R.M. Gummere, 3 vols., 1917–25; as *Morals*, translated by Roger L'Estrange, 1678; also translated by J.W. Basore [Loeb Edition; bilingual], 3 vols., 1928–35; selection of translations by Roger L'Estrange and Thomas Lodge, edited by Watson Clode, 1888; other selections as *The Epistles*, translated by T. Morell, 1786; as *Select Letters of Seneca*, translated by W.C. Summers, 1910; as *Seneca's Letters to Lucilius*, translated by E. Phillips Barker, 2 vols., 1932; as *Letters from a Stoic*, translated by Robin Campbell, 1969.

De beneficiis, edited by C. Hosius. 1914; as *Concerning Benefyting*, translated by A. Golding, 1578; as *On Benefits*, translated by Aubrey Stewart, 1887.

De clementia, edited by C. Hosius. 1914; translated as *Clemency*, 1653; also translated by Aubrey Stewart, in *Minor Dialogues*, 1899.

De providentia, as *Why Good Men Suffer Misfortunes, Seeing There Is a Divine Providence*, translated by Edward Sherburne. 1648; as *Providence*, translated by W.B. Langsdorf, with *Tranquillity of Mind*, 1900.

De tranquiltitate animi (late work), as *Tranquillity of Mind*, translated by W.B. Langsdorf, with *Providence*. 1900.

Dialogi, edited by E. Hermes and others. 3 vols., 1898–1907; also edited by L.D. Reynolds, 1977.

Epistolae ad Paulum (attributed), as *The Epistles of Paul the Apostle to Seneca with Seneca's to Paul*, in *The Apocryphal New Testament*, edited by W. Hone. 1820; also edited by C.W. Barlow, 1938.

Naturales quaestiones, edited by P. Oltramare. 1929; edited by Harry M. Hines (Book II; with commentary), 1981; as *Physical Science in the Time of Nero*, translated by John Clarke, 1910; as *Natural Questions* [Loeb Edition], translated by T.H. Corcoran, 2 vols., 1971–72.

Minor Dialogues, translated by Aubrey Stewart. 1899.

Moral Essays [Loeb Edition]. 3 vols., 1928–35.

Selected Prose (Latin text), edited by H. MacL. Currie. 2nd edition, 1980.

Seventeen Letters, translated by C.D.N. Costa. 1988.

Four Dialogues, translated by C.D.N. Costa. 1994.

Moral and Political Essays, edited and translated by John M. Cooper and J.F. Procopé. 1995.

Dialogues and Letters, edited and translated by C.D.N. Costa. 1997.

Seneca in English, edited by Don Share. 1998.

*

Bibliography: *Seneca: A Critical Bibliography 1900–1980: Scholarship on His Life, Thought, Prose and Influence* by Anna L. Motto and John R. Clark, 1989.

Critical Studies: *Seneca the Philosopher and His Modern Message* by R.M. Gummere, 1922; *Seneca and Elizabethan Tragedy* by F.L. Lucas, 1922; *Our Seneca* by C.W. Mendell, 1941; *Discourses upon*

Seneca the Tragedian by W. Cornwallis, 1952; *Anger in Juvenal and Seneca* by William S. Anderson, 1964; *The Medieval Tradition of Seneca's Letters* by L.D. Reynolds 1965; *Seneca Sourcebook*, 1971, and *Seneca*, 1973, both by Anna L. Motto, and *Senecan Tragedy*, 1988, and *Essays on Seneca*, 1993, both by Motto and John R. Clark; *Racine and Seneca* by Ronald W. Tobin, 1971; *Seneca* edited by C.D.N. Costa, 1974; *Seneca, a Philosopher in Politics* by Miriam Tamara Griffin, 1976; *Inlaboratus et Facilis: Aspects of Structure in Some Letters of Seneca* by B.L. Hijmans, 1976; *Post-Augustan Poetry from Seneca to Juvenal* by Harold E. Butler, 1977; *Seneca's Hercules Furens: Theme, Structure and Style* by Jo-Ann Shelton, 1978; *Seneca's Drama* by Norman T. Pratt, 1983; *Seneca: The Humanist at the Court of Nero* by Villy Sørenson, 1984; *Seneca's Daggered Stylus: Political Code in the Tragedies* by J. David Bishop, 1985; *The Mask of Power: Seneca's Tragedies and Imperial Rome* by Denis Henry, 1985; *Language and Desire in Seneca's Phaedra* by Charles Segal, 1986; *Seneca on the Stage* by Dana F. Sutton, 1986; *Seneca and Celestina* by Louise Fothergill-Payne, 1988; *Senecan Drama and Stoic Cosmology* by Thomas G. Rosenmeyer, 1989; *Shakespeare and Classical Tragedy: The Influence of Seneca* by Robert S. Miola, 1992; *Studies in the Text of Seneca's Naturales quaestiones* by Harry M. Hine, 1996; *Tragic Seneca: An Essay in the Theatrical Tradition* by A.J. Boyle, 1997; *Correspondence Between Paul and Seneca: A.D. 61–65* by Paul Berry, 1999.

* * *

Seneca's influence and importance have been enduring and twofold, as a thinker and as a stylist. Though he was by no means an original philosopher his prose works are a major source for the history of Stoicism as developed and modified at Rome. Most of these—the *Dialogi* (*Dialogues*)—are ethical treatises, strongly hortatory in tone and including traditional moralizing topics—the shortness of life, tranquillity of mind, the self-sufficiency of the wise man—and three "consolations" (addresses to afflicted individuals with conventional advice on coping with distress and bereavement). These treatises are not so much exercises in speculative philosophy as practical moral teaching, and though there are dull stretches in them the style overall is brilliant, and the arguments skilfully highlighted by anecdote and wit. The 124 letters of *Ad Lucilium epistulae morales* (*Letters to Lucilius*) have a similar aim of ethical instruction. Though ostensibly addressed to a younger friend in public life they are not genuine private letters but clearly look to a general readership. With their variety of tone and wide-ranging subject matter they have always been Seneca's most attractive and popular works, and were one of the most widely read classical texts in the Middle Ages. Another side of his omnivorous learning is seen in the seven books of *Naturales quaestiones* (*Natural Questions*), which consist largely of surveys and assessments of existing theories on natural phenomena, and are of considerable interest to the history of scientific speculation. The *Apocolocyntosis divi Claudii* (*Satire of the Deification of Claudius*) is an interesting literary survival: a moderately funny skit on the deification of the dead emperor Claudius, written in an early style of satire which mingled prose and verse.

Seneca's tragedies have a unique place in classical literature. Their themes are taken from Greek legend, and most have detectable links with surviving Greek tragedies, but the treatment is very different. They were almost certainly not written for full stage performance but recited or declaimed by a solo performer. Seneca is not interested in plots or character development but in exploring strongly opposed attitudes and the conflict of violent emotions. This is done usually in a succession of virtually self-contained scenes of dialogue or self-debating soliloquy, with little regard for dramatic continuity. The tragedies were enormously popular in the Renaissance and were the models for innumerable imitations in both Latin and vernacular languages in Italy, France, and England: tragedians in 16th-century England and 17th-century France were particularly indebted to them, and the influence of the Latin declamatory style can be traced in Shakespeare.

Both the plays and the prose works illustrate very markedly the rhetorical use of language and verbal ingenuity which was always to some extent characteristic of Latin literature, but which was brought to a high degree of refinement in the 1st century AD, and notably by Seneca himself. This brilliant, pointed, and strongly epigrammatic style was in strong contrast with Ciceronian Latin, and the popularity of Seneca's works in the Middle Ages and Renaissance led in turn to the fashion of imitating his prose style. Thus by the late 16th century, when Latin was still the language of learned communication, there was a reaction against Ciceronianism and the Senecan style became overwhelmingly popular.

—C.D.N. Costa

See the essays on *Oedipus* and *Thyestes*.

SHIGA Naoya

Born: Ishinomaki, Japan, 20 February 1883. **Education:** Attended school in Tokyo; Gakushuin (Peers' School), 1889–1906; Tokyo Imperial University, 1906–10 (does not graduate). **Family:** Married Sadako Kadenokoji, 1914; two sons, six daughters. **Career:** Disciple of the Christian writer and evangelist, Kanzo Uchimura, 1900–07; first serious conflict with his father when the latter forbade him from showing solidarity with miners poisoned at the Ashio Copper Mine, 1901; wrote first "fictional" story, *Nanohana to komusume* (*The Little Girl and the Rapeseed Flower*), 1904; wrote first diary-like, "autobiographical" story, *Aru asa* (*One Morning*), 1907; second major conflict with his father who opposed his proposed marriage to one of the family maids, 1907; with friend, the writer Saneatsu Mushanokoji, and other fellow Peers' School graduates who described themselves as "Tolstoyan humanists," founded the literary journal *Shirakaba* (*White Birch*) and published story, *Abashiri made* (*As Far As Abashiri*) in the first issue, 1910; began lifelong friendship with the great English potter, Bernard Leach, 1912; because of conflicts with his father, finally moved out of parents' house, 1912 (although, due to his wealthy father's continuing if intermittent support, Shiga never pursued any career other than writing); seriously injured when hit by a train, Tokyo, 1913; began period of "wandering" and "communing with nature" in a series of seaside towns, hotspring resorts, mountain and forest areas (Onomichi, Kinosaki, Matsue, Mt. Daisen, Mt. Akagi), and in the old capital, Kyoto; finally settled in Abiko, Chiba Prefecture, 1915–1922; became a protégé of the great Meiji writer, Soseki Natsume, but unable to keep his promise of completing his novel, *Tokito Kensaku* (later published as *A Dark Night's Passing*) for serialization in Soseki's newspaper, the *Asahi Shimbun*, 1913–1916; finally reconciled with his father, 1917; moved back to Kyoto, and he immersed himself in traditional Japanese culture, 1923; started an affair with a young Gion teahouse waitress and was shocked by the violence of his wife's reaction—the "last crisis" of his life; finally completed his major lifework, *An'ya Kōro* (*A Dark Night's Passing*), 1937; after this wrote very little fiction and contented himself with writing short lyrical essays and sketches that reflect the tranquility of his life in the bosom of nature and family. **Awards:** National Cultural award for Literature, Japan, 1949. **Died:** 21 October 1971.

PUBLICATIONS

Collections

Shiga Naoya Zenshū (*Collected Works of Naoya Shiga*). 17 vols., 1955–56.
Shiroi sen (*The White Line: Collected Sketches*). 1966.
Shiga Naoya Taiwa-shū (*Collected Conversations with Naoya Shiga*). 1969.
Shiga Naoya Zenshū (*Collected Works of Naoya Shiga*). 16 vols., 1973–74, 1984.
Shinpan Shiga Naoya Zenshū (*New Edition of the Collected Works of Naoya Shiga*). 22 vols., 1998–2001.
Shiga Naoya Zenshū Hokan (*Supplementary Volumes to the Collected Works of Naoya Shiga*). 6 vols., 2001–02.

Fiction

"Abashiri made." 1910; as "As Far As Abashiri," translated by Lane Dunlop, 1987.
"Kamisori." 1910; as "The Razor," translated by Lane Dunlop, 1987.
"Fusuma." 1911; as "The Paper Door," translated by Lane Dunlop, 1987.
"Haha no shi to atarashii haha." 1912.
"Kurōdiasu no nikki." 1912; as "The Diary of Claudius," translated by Roy Starrs, 1998.
Ōtsu Junkichi. 1912.
"Seibei to hyōtan." 1912; as "Seibei's Gourd's," translated by Ivan Morris, 1956.
"Han no hanzai." 1913; as "Han's Crime," translated by Ivan Morris, 1956.
"Akanishi Kakita." 1917; as "Akanishi Kakita," translated by Lane Dunlop, 1987.
"Wakai." 1917; as "Reconciliation," translated by Roy Starrs, 1998.
"Kinosaki nite." 1917; as "At Kinosaki," translated by Edward Seidensticker, 1956.
"Kozō no kamisama." 1919; as "The Shopboy's God," translated by Lane Dunlop, 1987.
"Takibi." 1920; as "Bonfire," translated by Roy Starrs, 1998.
Amagaeru. 1923; as *Rain Frogs*, translated by Lane Dunlop, 1987.
"Horibata no sumai." 1924; as "The House by the Moat," translated by Lane Dunlop, 1987.
"Yamashina no omoide." 1925; as "A Memory of Yamashina," translated by Lane Dunlop, 1987.
"Chijō." 1926; as "Infatuation," translated by Lane Dunlop, 1987.
"Kuniko." 1927; as "Kuniko," translated by Lane Dunlop, 1987.
An'ya Kōro. 1937; as *A Dark Night's Passing*, translated by Edwin McClellan, 1976.

"Hai-iro no tsuki." 1946; as "A Gray Moon," translated by Lane Dunlop, 1987.
Le Samourai (22 stories), translated by Marc Mécréant, 1970.
The Paper Door and Other Stories, translated by Lane Dunlop, 1987.
Selected Translations, translated by Roy Starrs, in *An Artless Art: The Zen Aesthetic of Shiga Naoya*. 1998.

*

Bibliography: *Nihon bungaku kenkyū shiryō sōsho: Shiga Naoya*, 1970; *Nihon bungaku kenkyū shiryō sōsho: Shiga Naoya 2*, 1978; *Shiga Naoya kenkyūshi* in *Shiga Naoya: Jiga no kiseki* by Ikeuchi Teruo, 1992.

Critical Studies: *Shiga Naoya no sakuhin* by Tanikawa Testsuzō, 1942; *Shiga Naoya no bungaku* by Sudō Matsuo, 1963; *Shiga Naoya ron* by Nakamura Mitsuo, 1966; *Shiga Naoya shiron* by Yasuoka Shōtarō, 1972; *Shiga Naoya* by Francis Mathy, 1974; *The Shiga Hero* by William Sibley, 1979; *The Rhetoric of Confession: Shishōsetsu in Early Twentieth-Century Japanese Fiction* by Edward Fowler, 1988; *Shiga Naoya* by Miyakoshi Tsutomu, 1991; *Shiga Naoya no ryōiki* by Ikeuchi Teruo, 1990; *Shiga Naoya* by Honda Shūgo, 1990; *Shiga Naoya runessansu* by Shinozawa Hideo, 1994; *Shiga Naoya* by Agawa Hiroyuki, 1994; *An Artless Art: The Zen Aesthetic of Shiga Naoya* by Roy Starrs, 1998.

* * *

Shiga Naoya is generally regarded as the leading practitioner of the *shishōsetsu* (literally, "I-novel"), the major genre of modern Japanese literary (as opposed to popular) fiction. As such, he was probably the most influential Japanese writer of the 20th century within his own country. This latter qualification is significant because Shiga never attained anything like the renown abroad that he enjoyed at home. No doubt this was because the *shishōsetsu* genre itself depends for its appeal largely on certain culture-specific factors such as the traditional Confucian privileging of "sincere confession" over "literary fabrication" and the intense interest that the Japanese reading public has in every last detail of a writer's life. More specifically, there is also the problem that much of the special quality of Shiga's celebrated "lyrical" prose style is lost in translation.

This is not to say that the *shishōsetsu* is uniquely Japanese in all its features. As an autobiographical or semi-autobiographical genre of fiction focused upon a single protagonist who is a thinly disguised alter ego of the author himself, it could be legitimately placed in a larger historical context and seen as a typical example of the world-wide "inward turn," or subjectification of fiction which occurred in the early 20th century as one of the main characteristics of modernism. In Europe at the same time, novelists such as Proust, Joyce, Lawrence and Woolf were developing strains of fiction that were comparable at least in this respect. Within the Japanese context, Shiga's introspective fiction marks him as a representative writer of the Taishō period (1912–26). This was a period during which a "second generation" of modern Japanese writers emerged who, in pronounced contrast to the engagé writers of the "first generation"—writers of the Meiji period (1868–1912) such as Mori Ōgai, Natsume Sōseki and Shimazaki Tōson—were almost completely uninterested

926

in the "state of the nation" and in larger social and political issues. Although the two other major Taishō writers, Akutagawa Ryūnosuke and Tanizaki Junichirō, did not write much autobiographical fiction, they were both aesthetes who shared Shiga's social/political disengagement. Shiga's main concern was his own spiritual and emotional life; he was interested in others only insofar as they impinged upon that life. As a writer he was determined "to mine what is in me." Thus his *shishōsetsu* focus on issues such as his difficult relationship with his father and other family members, his troubled marriage, and the early death of some of his children. Even more narrowly, they also focus on his problems as a writer such as his long struggles with writer's block. It could be argued, however, that what his work lacks in social breadth it makes up for in psychological, emotional and spiritual depth. What is true of the best lyrical poets is also true of this most lyrical of prose writers: he delves so deeply within that he reaches a level of the mind that is free of egotism—that is, in fact, impersonal and universal. Thus his inward-turning leads to a heightened, intuitive sensitivity, if not at first to other people, at least to the natural world. This may be seen clearly in perhaps his most celebrated short work, "Kinosaki nite"(At Kinosaki), written while Shiga was recovering from a serious injury: painfully aware of his own closeness to death, he is able to describe the deaths of three humble creatures, a bee, a rat, and a water lizard, with both a heartfelt sympathy and an almost surreal precision.

But the culmination of Shiga's art of *shishōsetsu* is a much longer work, the only novel-length work he wrote, *An'ya Kōro* (*A Dark Night's Passing*). In this work the themes of family conflict and mishap, the struggle of the writer with himself, and the achievement of a healing unity with nature, combine to form both the dialectical tension and the final resolution of the narrative. The central character, Kensaku Tokitō, is confronted by a seemingly irresolvable existential problem early in the novel: he discovers that the "dirty old man" who had always been presented to him as his grandfather is actually his father; he is the illegitimate offspring of an illicit, incestuous relationship. This initial shock to his ego is compounded by a series of further traumas and misfortunes, including the unfaithfulness of his wife and his long and recalcitrant writer's block. His struggle to recover from the resultant psychological turmoil drives him ultimately into the arms of nature, where he finds the only balm able to soothe his tortured spirit.

How can one account for the remarkable popularity of this work for much of the 20th century in Japan, for its almost cult-like status? There is, of course, the great appeal of the famous "Shiga style"— spare, precise, strongly rhythmical, and beautifully phrased, one of most highly praised styles in all of Japanese literature. But there is more to it than that: the novel also possesses what must be described as a kind of spiritual power. On one level, it could be regarded as a modern novelistic version of traditional East Asian wisdom literature, whether Buddhist, Daoist, Shinto or neo-Confucian, which teaches the overcoming of ego-based conflict through a self-transcendent mystical union with nature. Nature is to be understood here, in this monistic worldview, as not only "without" but also "within"—that is, as the beneficent ground of all being. It is exactly this natural state of grace that Kensaku experiences in the lyrical climax of the novel on Mount Daisen, and the final scene of the novel, in which he wordlessly expresses a new, unconditional love for and compassion towards his wife, proves the transformative power of this experience.

Generations of Japanese readers thus have found themselves profoundly moved by this simple (in the best sense of the word), almost archetypal story of one man's struggle through a dark night of the soul to a final spiritual and emotional liberation—which may occur (the novel is ambiguous about this) only on his deathbed.

In addition to his major achievement as the leading writer of autobiographical *shishōsetsu*, Shiga is also recognized as one of the masters of the modern Japanese short story—that is, of works of short, purely imaginary, "well-made" fiction in the traditional Western style. Modern Japanese literature is particularly rich in this genre (it is sometimes said that the Japanese genius is more suited to small than large-scale work) and Shiga stories such as "Han no hanzai" ("Han's Crime") and "Kamisori" ("The Razor") are undoubted masterpieces of compressed psychological fiction.

With more translations and critical studies of his work appearing in English and French in recent years, Shiga has at last begun to find a wider readership in the West. Whatever his reception internationally, however, as the leading 20th century practitioner of a genre that descends from the mainstream classical Japanese traditions of *nikki* (fictionalized diary) and *zuihitsu* (lyrical essay), his high place within the national literary canon seems likely to endure.

—Roy Starrs

SHIMAZAKI Haruki (Tōson)

Also known as Shimazaki Tōson and Tōson. **Born:** Magome, Japan, 25 March, 1872. **Education:** Tutored by father in Chinese classics; Misaka Elementary School, Magome, 1878–80; Taimei Elementary School, Tokyo 1881–86; further tutoring in Classical Chinese and English, Mita Eigakkō, Kyōritsu Gakkō, Tokyo, 1886–87; Meiji Gakuin, 1887–91; Tokyo Ongaku Gakkō,1898. **Family:** Married 1) Hata Fuyuko (died 1910) in 1899, four daughters, three of whom died in early childhood, and three sons; 2)Katō Shizuko in 1928. **Career:** Contributor to the journals *Jogaku Zasshi*, 1890–95 and *Bungakukai*, 1895–98; Instructor at Meiji Jogakkō 1892–93, 1894–95; English instructor, Tohoku Gakuin, Sendai, 1896–97; English instructor, Komoro Gijuku, Komoro, 1899–1905; Paris and Limoges, 1913–16; adjunct lecturer in Contemporary French Literature, Waseda University, 1916–17; Keiō University, 1917. Founder, editor and publisher of feminist journal *Shojochi*, 1922–23. Founding President, Japan PEN Club, 1935–36; Japanese representative, International PEN Congress, Buenos Aires, 1936; visited Brazil, Argentina, the United States, France, and Italy. **Died:** Oiso, Japan, 21 August 1943.

PUBLICATIONS

Collections

Tōson Zenshū. 12 vols., 1922.
Shimazaki Tōson Zenshū. 31 vols., 1956–57.
Tōson Zenshū. 18 vols., 1966–71.
Tōson Zenshū. 12 vols., 1981–83.

Poetry

Wakanashū. 1896.
Hitohabune. 1898.
Natsugusa. 1898.
Rakubaishū. 1901.
Tōsonshishū. 1912.

Fiction

Hakai. 1906; as *The Broken Commandment,* translated by Kenneth Strong, 1974.
Ryokuyōshū. 1907.
Haru. 1908.
Ie. 1911; as *The Family,* translated by Cecilia Segawa Seigle, 1976.
Chikumagawa no Suketchi. 1912; as *Chikuma River Sketchbooks* in *Chikuma River Sketches,* translated by William E. Naff, 1991.
Shokugo. 1912.
Osanaki Hi. 1912–13.
Asameshi. 1913.
Bifū. 1913.
Sakura no Mi no Jukusuru Toki. 1919.
Shinsei. 1919.
Arashi. 1927.
Yo-ake Mae. 1929–35; as *Before the Dawn,* translated by William E. Naff, 1987.

Essays

Shinkatamachi yori. 1909.
Nochi no Shinkatamachi yori. 1913.
Asakusadayori. 1924.
Haru o Machitsutsu. 1925.
Iiguradayori. 1926.
Shisei ni Arite. 1930.
San'in Miyage Sono Ta. 1929.
Momo no Shizuku. 1936.

Other

Megane (children). 1913.
Heiwa no Pari (travel). 1915.
Sensō to Pari (travel). 1915.
Umi e (travel). 1918.
Furusato (children). 1920.
Etoranzee (travel). 1922.
Osanaki Mono ni (children). 1922.
Osonamonogatari (children). 1924.
Chikaramochi (children). 1940.
Junrei (travel). 1940.

*

Bibliography: *Tōson Shoshi* by Itō Kazuo, 1973; *Shimazaki Tōson Jiten* by Itō Kazuo, revised edition, 1976.

Critical Studies: *Shimazaki Tōson Ron* by Kamei Katsuichirō, 1953; *Shimazaki Tōson,* edited by Hirano Ken, 1957; *Bungakukai to sono jidai (Bungakukai and its times),* 2 vols., by Sasabuchi Tomoichi, 1963; *Shimazaki Tōson Ron* by Miyoshi Yukio, 1966; *Two Japanese Novelists: Soseki and Tōson* by Edwin McClellan, 1969; *Shimazaki Tōson,* 3 vols., by Tanaka Tornijirō, 1977–78; *Shimazaki Tōson* by Togawa Shinsuke, 1980; *Hyōden Shimazaki Tōson* by Senuma Shigeki, 1981; *Tōson n o dōwa: sono ichi to keifu* by Hida Fumio, 1983; *Tōson bungaku josetsu* by Kenmochi Takehiko, 1985; *Tōson no Pari* by Kawamori Yoshizō, 1998; *Burakumin and Shimazaki Tōson's Hakai* by René Andersson, 2001.

*   *   *

Often called the creator of modern Japanese poetry, Shimazaki Tōson is even better known for autobiographical novels portraying half a century of Japanese life and for his essays and travel writings. Although he sometimes thought that his children's literature might have the best chance of surviving him, it is not widely read today.

Born into a family of post station keepers and headmen in a mountain village on the inland highway between Kyoto and Edo, Tōson was sent to Tokyo at an early age for education. He emerged with a command of English, a deep love of Shakespeare, Byron, and Wordsworth, and a tireless and wide-ranging intellectual curiosity.

Although frequently counted among the Japanese Naturalists, Tōson differed with them in many important respects. His breadth of vision ties at the root of any claims to greatness that might be made for him; he was not an imaginative writer nor was he, for all his contributions to modern literary Japanese, an outstanding stylist. A quest for connection, a struggle to define a place for himself in Japan and, increasingly as time went on, to define a place for Japan in the constantly-changing world civilization into which Japan had been thrust during his father's time defined his personal and professional life.

With *Wakanashū* [Young Herbs], constantly in print for more than a century, Tōson became the first Japanese poet to successfully blend European stance with Japanese theme, form, and diction. Both excitingly new and comfortably familiar, these poems, which bore a heavy imprint of English Romanticism and the Pre-Raphaelite Brotherhood, made him a national figure but left him poor. He soon turned to prose.

For all its buried autobiographical elements, Tōson's *Hakai (The Broken Commandment)* is the first literary treatment of Japanese outcasts, a subject about which there is still much denial in Japan. Here Tōson achieved the transparent and austere modern prose style that is his greatest stylistic legacy. *Commandment* occupies a position in the history of the modern Japanese novel comparable to that of *Herbs* in modern Japanese poetry.

Many of Tōson's earliest publications appeared in the literary journal *Bungaku Kai* [Literary World] the pioneering voice of Japanese Romanticism, to which he was one of the most important contributors. Those days are the subject of the autobiographical novel *Haru (Springtime,* allusion to Botticelli's *La Primavera)* that tells of the dreams and torments of the young mission-school graduates who would become so important in Japanese literary and intellectual life. The later *Sakura no Mi no Juku-suru Toki* [When the Cherries Ripen] steps back a few years to portray his college life at Meiji Gakuin, providing yet another documentation of defining experiences for Tōson's generation.

In spite of problems with that label, *Ie (The Family)* is often called the most outstanding product of Japanese Naturalism. A study of the decline of his own family and that of his sister's husband, it is an uncompromising presentation of family life in a time when traditional views of the institution were coining into conflict with the realities of life in Meiji Japan. It also demonstrates Tōson's lifelong preoccupation with family.

Following Fuyuko's death in childbirth, the usually puritanical Tōson drifted into a liaison with a niece who had come to help with the children. Her pregnancy precipitated his flight to France. During his three years there he observed and commented knowledgeably on French cultural life and the Japanese artistic community. Once back home he fell back into the affair with his niece. To force himself to break away, he began serial publication of a fictional account of his recent life that would become the novel *Shinsei* (*New Life*, allusion to Dante).

In spite of the awkwardness surrounding *Shinsei*, it has the artistic integrity and power to engage readers who know nothing of its background. About half of the action takes place on ships and in France. With the protagonist's return to Japan, the tone shades gradually from shame and self-disgust to a deeply-felt and moving contemplation, illuminated by reflections on the story of Abélard and Éloise, of the greatest, though utterly untenable, love of his life. Even though Tōson was their prime source of support, the publication of the novel finally forced the niece's family to intervene.

The 1920s were filled with living down the *Shinsei* scandal, the maturing of his children, the relocating of one son to his native Magome, his short-lived venture with the feminist journal *Shojochi* (*Virgin Soil*, allusion to Turgenev), his courtship and marriage to Katō Shizuko, his most faithful editorial assistant, and preparations for the writing of his masterpiece, *Yo-ake Mae* (*Before the Dawn*). A combination of official harassment with physical and financial exhaustion closed *Shojochi* after just ten issues.

The title story of *Arashi* [The Tempest], written when the author was around the age at which Shakespeare had written his play, sets the storms of his sons' adolescences against a background of growing social unrest. *Aru Onna no Shōgai* (*The Life of a Certain Woman*, after Maupassant's *Une Vie*), the most powerful story in the collection, was inspired by the ghastly marriage and the physical and mental decline and death of his eldest sister, the relative to whom he had always felt closest.

Following his marriage to Katō Shizuko, Tōson began serial publication of *Before the Dawn*. Defining the form in which this extraordinary era has passed into the national memory, it begins with Perry in 1853 and ends in 1886 with the death of the protagonist, closely modeled on Tōson's father. Its account of the turmoil, triumph, and tragedy of mid-19th-century Japan and of the disillusionment that the new age brought to so many of those who had worked hardest and sacrificed most to bring it into being give it claim to being the most important Japanese novel of the first half of the 20th century.

At the 1936 International PEN congress in Buenos Aires, Tōson represented Japan. He won the scheduling of the 1940 International Congress—later aborted by World War II—for a Tokyo then rapidly falling into international isolation. In *Junrei* [The Pilgrimage], Tōson tells of this trip, the return leg of which included visits to Brazil, the United States, and a France on the brink of World War II.

Although frequently approached by wartime authorities, Tōson pleaded advancing age and the press of writing commitments to stay clear of official involvement. Beneath the constraints imposed both by wartime public sentiment and official limits, the little that he then wrote about current affairs reveals an unbroken commitment to the humane values that had informed his entire life as well as deep misgivings about the course taken by Japan.

Tōson died of a stroke while at work on the third chapter of a projected final novel, *Tōhō no Mon* [The Gate to the East] that took its title from a painting by French muralist Pierre Puvis de Chavannes. It was apparently to be a continuation of *Dawn*, with which it shares many characters.

—William E. Naff

SHOLOKHOV, Mikhail (Aleksandrovich)

Born: Kruzhilin, Russia, 24 May 1905. **Education:** Educated at schools in Moscow, Boguchar, and Veshenskaia: formal education ended in 1918 because of the Civil War. **Military Service:** Served with Communist food requisitioning detachments, 1920–22. **Family:** Married Maria Petrovna Gromoslavskaia in 1923; four children. **Career:** Teacher, clerk, tax inspector, labourer, playwright, actor, journalist; war correspondent during World War II. Member of the Communist Party of the Soviet Union, 1932, of the Central Committee, 1961, of the Presidium of the 23rd to 26th Party Congresses, 1966–81. Elected deputy of the Supreme Soviet, 1937. Member of the Presidium, Union of Soviet Writers, 1934. **Awards:** Stalin prize, 1941; Lenin prize, 1960; Nobel prize for literature, 1965. Hero of Socialist Labour, 1967, 1980; Fadeev medal, 1974. LL.D.: University of St Andrews, Scotland, 1962; Ph.D.: University of Rostov, 1965; University of Leipzig, 1965. **Member:** Academy of Sciences, 1939. **Died:** 20 February 1984.

PUBLICATIONS

Collections

Sobranie sochinenii [Collected Works], edited by M.M. Sokolov. 8 vols., 1975.
Sobranie sochinenii [Collected Works], edited by M. Manokhinoi. 8 vols., 1980.
Collected Works, translated by Robert Daglish. 8 vols., 1984.

Fiction

Dvukhmuzhniaia [The Woman Who Had Two Husbands]. 1925.
Krasnogvardeitsy [Red Guards]. 1925.
Donskie rasskazy. 1926; as *Tales from the Don*, translated by H.C. Stevens, 1961.
Lazorevaia step. 1926; enlarged edition, 1931; as *The Azure Steppe*, translated in *Early Stories*, 1966.
Tikhii Don. 4 vols., 1928–40; complete edition, 4 vols., 1939–40; as *And Quiet Flows the Don* and *The Don Flows Home to the Sea*, translated by Stephen Garry, 2 vols., 1934–40; in a single volume

as *The Silent Don*, translated by Garry, 1941; as *Quiet Flows the Don: A Novel in Two Volumes*, translated by Robert Daglish, 1959, revised and edited by Brian Murphy, 1996.

Rasskazy [Stories]. 1931.

Podniataia tselina. 1932–60; (as a play 1940), revised edition, 1952; as *Virgin Soil Upturned* and *Harvest on the Don*, translated by Stephen Garry, 2 vols., 1935–60; as *Seeds of Tomorrow* and *Harvest on the Don*, translated by Garry and H.C. Stevens, 2 vols., 1935–61; as *Virgin Soil Upturned*, translated by Robert Daglish, 1980.

Nauka nenavisti. 1942; as *Hate*, translated anonymously, 1942; as *The Science of Hatred*, translated anonymously, 1943; as *A Lesson in Hatred*, translated by H.C. Stevens in *One Man's Destiny and Other Stories*, 1967.

Sud'ba cheloveka. 1957; as *The Fate of a Man*, translated by Robert Daglish, 1957, revised translation, 1962; also translated by Miriam Morton, in *Fierce and Gentle Warriors*, 1967; as *One Man's Destiny*, translated by H.C. Stevens, in *One Man's Destiny and Other Stories* . . . , 1967.

Rannie rasskazy [Early Stories]. 1961.

Zherebenok [Foal]. 1963.

Nakhalenok [Impudent Fellow]. 1965.

Nauka nenavisti; Oni srazhalis' za rodinu; Sud'ba cheloveka. 1971.

Early Stories (includes *The Birthmark; The Herdsman; The Bastard; The Azure Steppe; The Foal; Alien Blood*), translated by Robert Daglish and Elena Altshuler. 1966.

Fierce and Gentle Warriors (includes *The Colt; The Rascal; The Fate of a Man*), translated by Miriam Morton. 1967.

Rasskazy [Stories]. 1975.

Rodinka [Homeland] (stories). 1975.

Predsedatel' Revvoensoveta Respubliki [The Chairman of the Revolutionary War Council of the Republic] (stories). 1980.

Proza i publitsistika o voine [Prose about Publicists on War]. 1985.

Iz rannikh rasskazov [From Early Stories]. 1987.

The Fate of a Man and Early Stories. 1989.

Other

Kazaki [The Cossacks] (essay). 1941.

Na iuge [In the South] (essay). 1942.

Slovo o Rodine. 1948; as *One Man's Destiny and Other Stories, Articles, and Sketches 1923–1962*, translated by H.C. Stevens, 1967.

Svet i mrak [Light and Gloom] (essay). 1949.

Ne uiti palacham ot suda narodov! [The Executioners Cannot Escape the Verdict of the Nations] (articles). 1950.

Sobranie sochinenii [Collected Works], edited by K.V. Potanov. 8 vols., 1962.

Put'-dorozhen'ka [The Way and the Road] (for children). 1962.

Po veleniiu dushi. 1970; as *At the Bidding of the Heart: Essays, Sketches, Papers*, translated by Olga Shartse, 1973.

Rossiia v serdtse [Russia in the Heart] (stories and essays). 1975.

Zhivaia sila realizma [The Living Strength of Realism]. 1983.

Zemle nuzhny molodye ruki [The Earth Needs Young Hands]. 1983.

Sholokhov: Zhizn'. Tvorchestvo. Vospominaniia. Fotografii. Dokumenty [Sholokhov: Life, Work, Reminiscences, Photographs, Documents]. 1985.

*

Critical Studies: *Mikhail Sholokhov: A Critical Introduction* by D. Stewart, 1967; *Sholokhov* by C.G. Bearne, 1969; *Sholokhov: A Critical Appreciation* by L. Iakimenko, 1973; *Problems in the Literary Biography of Sholokhov* by Roy A. Medvedev, 1977; *Sholokhov and His Art* by Herman Ermolaev, 1982; *The Authorship of "The Quiet Don"* by Geir Kjestsaa and others, 1984; *Meetings with Sholokhov* by Anatoly Sofronov, 1985; *Sholokhov's Tikhii Don: A Commentary in 2 Volumes* by A.B. Murphy, V.P. Butt and H. Ermolaev, 1997.

* * *

In 1918–19 the Don area saw Reds succeed Whites and vice versa five times, each change being effected with increasing brutality. During the Civil War Mikhail Sholokhov's family lived in the heart of these conflicts. *Donskie rasskazy* (*Tales from the Don*) records the horrors as Sholokhov experienced them in his boyhood. At that time his faith in the righteousness of the Communist cause was still naive and the stories do not aspire to any wider perspective.

Sholokhov started writing *Tikhii Don* (*Quiet Flows the Don*) to counter the widespread view of the Cossacks as diehard counter-revolutionaries. The novel owes its loose construction to changes in the author's perception over the years when he was struggling to publish a more objective account. Books One and Two were serialized in the journal *Oktiabr'* [October] in 1928. Publication was suspended when the author approached the tricky subject of the Red army's conduct in the Don territory. In 1932 as *Oktiabr'* resumed publication, the editors tried to omit several of the most sensitive chapters. Sholokhov made his case with Stalin, firstly that the Cossack rebellion against the Communists was brought about by the Red army's mass execution of peaceful villagers, and secondly that the anti-Communist uprising had been on a much larger scale than Soviet historians had previously admitted. The Red Terror of 1919 remains a controversial issue: when many Cossacks accused the Communists of genocide. Both Stalin and Fadeev wanted the novel's central figure, Grigory Melekhov, to be converted to Communism, as Socialist Realism so often decreed. Sholokhov showed considerable courage by insisting he would prefer to leave the novel unfinished rather than distort it with an unconvincing "happy" ending.

Some critics found it hard to believe that a young and unsophisticated author could produce a novel with such a wide knowledge of history. It was rumoured in 1928 that he had plagiarized the text of some other author. Solzhenitsyn and others later attempted to lend substance to this accusation. Against them must be weighed Kjetsaa's computer-study comparing *Quiet Flows the Don* with Sholokhov's other work, besides some 2,000 pages of manuscript, authenticated as being in Sholokhov's own hand. Unless some solid evidence is produced to the contrary he must be considered the true author.

Both sides in the Civil War acknowledged that in its broad lines the work gives readers a true picture of this crucial turning point in Russia's history. Sholokhov's chief informant on the Don uprising was Ermakov, who had commanded a division of rebels in 1919. He was arrested and shot in 1927 without a proper trial. The author realized as he learnt from him that he represented many of the best features of the Cossacks. Ermakov naturally became the prototype for

Grigorii in Books Three and Four. The story concentrates on this central character, who retains a certain nobility even in the most degrading circumstances, while so many around him are brutalized by the endless killings. Grigorii's marriage is arranged in keeping with the patriarchal traditions of Cossack society. Breaking free from convention, his attachment to Aksinya develops from a purely carnal exploitation to become complete devotion for which he would sacrifice his life. Alongside his higher qualities Sholokhov keeps Grigorii within the bounds of credibility, not lacking in practical sense or earthy sensuality.

The author sets out lovingly the landscape of the steppes in painstakingly accurate images. There are many associations with folklore, and extended Homeric similes also lend an epic tone to the work. Notwithstanding the novel's great length the scenes of war and family life are presented with compelling vividness. Multitudinous individuals, both fictional and historical, are given distinct identity by their physical features or their mannerisms of speech. Critics were not slow to remark that in *Quiet Flows the Don* the Cossack characters are more memorable than the Communists. Stokman appears a rather conventional figure, as though each Soviet novel must include one idealistic Party agitator. But in reality the natives of the Don looked with amazement and incomprehension at Party functionaries sent by Moscow to govern their territory. For the Cossacks these were beings from an alien world coming to rob them of the land they had won in earlier centuries. In contrast Koshevoi's limitations are skilfully treated, with no false heroism, and his bitter experience leads directly to the blind ruthlessness with which he drives Grigorii from the village.

None of Sholokhov's other works is in the same class as *Quiet Flows the Don*. *Podniataia tselina* (*Virgin Soil Upturned*) is a propagandist account of the collectivization of agriculture. *Sud'ba cheloveka* (*The Fate of a Man*) has been the best known work by Sholokhov on the Great Patriotic War. The few published extracts of *Oni srazhalis' za rodinu* (*They Fought for Their Country*) gave hope that this might be a worthwhile account of the Russian front, but the novel was not completed.

In the 1960s Sholokhov's attacks on Pasternak, Iulii Daniel, and Andrei Siniavskii made him cordially detested by many of the Soviet intelligentsia.

—Brian Murphy

SIBURAPHA

Pseudonyms: Siburapha, Issarachon. **Born:** Kulap Saipradit in Bangkok, Thailand, 31 March 1905. **Education:** Attended Thepsirin School, 1915–23. **Family:** Married Chanid Princhanakon, 1935; one daughter, one son. **Career:** Worked as a teacher, translator, writer and editor for a number of magazines, 1923–28, including *Sena Su'ksa lae Phrae Witthayasat*; founded and edited the fortnightly *Suphapburut* literary magazine,1928; briefly edited several Bangkok daily papers before becoming editor of *Prachachat*, 1932; travelled to Japan to observe newspaper industry, 1936; edited *Prachamit-Suphapburut* newspaper, 1939; imprisoned for three months for criticising the government's alliance with Japan, 1942; President of the Thai Newspaper Association, 1945; travelled to Australia, 1947–48; Deputy Chairman of the Thai Peace Committee, opposing the war in Korea, 1952; arrested as part of a clamp-down on alleged communists and

sentenced to 20 years imprisonment, 1952; released from prison in a general amnesty, 1957; invited to Moscow for fortieth anniversary of the Revolution, 1957; invited to lead cultural delegation to Beijing, 1958; remained in China following military coup in Thailand in 1958. **Died:** 16 June 1974, in Beijing, China.

PUBLICATIONS

Fiction

Arai kan (short stories). 1926.
Wasana Manut (short stories). 1926.
Luk phuchai. 1928.
Prap phayot. 1928.
Phachon bap. 1928.
Hua chai pratthana. 1928.
Lok sanniwat. 1928.
Len kap Fai (short stories). 1929.
Man manut. 1930.
Saen rak saen khaen. 1930.
Songkhram chiwit. 1932.
Phuying ik baep nu'ng (*ru'ang thi nu'ng*) (short stories). 1933.
Thaeng Tho'ng (short stories). 1935.
Khang khu'n khang raem (short stories). 1935.
Sing thi chiwit to'ngkan. 1936.
Ko'n taeng ngan (short stories). 1937.
Pa nai chiwit. 1937.
Khang lang phap. 1937; as *Behind the Painting*, translated by David Smyth, 1990.
Chon kwa rao cha phop kan ik. 1950; as *Until We Meet Again*, translated by Scot Barmé, 1995.
No'p (short stories). 1938.
Nang Maew kap Sarika (short stories). 1941.
Sunthari (short stories). 1942.
Phuying ik baep nu'ng (*ru'ang thi so'ng*) (short stories). 1943.
Mae yo't Yuphadi (short stories). 1948.
Anuphap thi nu'a kwa ato'mik bo'm (short stories). 1949.
Kae thi phlat fung (short stories). 1949.
Yi Yuan Wa We Piyamit (short stories). 1949.
Nak Bun Chak Chantan (short stories). 1949.
Klap ma ha Mae (short stories). 1949.
Mahaburut kho'ng Chanthima (short stories). 1949.
Khao lu'ak lambarene nai sayam (short stories). 1949.
Khon phuak nan (short stories). 1950; as *Those Kind of People*, translated by David Smyth, 1990.
Kham khan rap (short stories). 1950.
Kho' raeng noi thoe (short stories). 1952; as *Lend Us a Hand*, translated by David Smyth, 1990.
Ai nu long thang (short stories). 1950.
Prakai mai nai duangta kho'ng khao (short stories). 1951.
Lung phrahm haeng ko loi (short stories). 1952.
Khao tu'n (short stories). 1952; as *The Awakening*, translated by David Smyth, 1990.
Lae pai khang na. 1955 (part 1); 1957 (part 2).

*

Critical Studies: *Kulap in Oz* by Scot Barmé, 1995; *Behind the Painting and Other Stories* by David Smyth, 1990.

*   *   *

Siburapha is one of the most important figures in the development of the novel in Thailand. His reputation is based on his early success as a popular novelist, and later, as one of the first Thai writers to use fiction to highlight social injustice. This later, political fiction, together with non-fictional works covering Marxism, Buddhism and the status of women, made him an icon of the Thai youth movement in the late 1960s, when much of his work was rediscovered.

Siburapha first rose to fame in the late 1920s at a time when the Thai reading public was tiring of novels translated from English and wanted something that was genuinely Thai. Within a short time he produced a succession of well-crafted, eloquently written romantic novels, which despite their frequent dependence on improbable coincidences, appeared fresh and unusual to audiences of the day.

Having made a name as a writer, Siburapha soon moved into political journalism, where his outspoken views on social injustice and the abuse of power often got him into trouble with newspaper owners and government alike. His epistolary novel *Songkhram chiwit* [The War of Life], was a major departure from his earlier romantic novels in its portrayal of the selfishness, vanity and corruption of the ruling élite and the lack of freedom of speech within the country. Siburapha himself became a victim of increasing government interference and curbs on press freedom and in 1936 he resigned from the editorship of *Prachachat* and accepted an invitation to visit Japan, which was to provide the setting for his stylistically most-accomplished novel, *Khang lang phap* (*Behind the Painting*). At one level, the novel is the tragic story of a beautiful woman from the minor royalty whose options in life are severely restricted by her status; at another, it is a confessional novel about a young man's infatuation with an older married woman and his subsequent awakening, after the death of her husband, to the frailty of his own romantic feelings; and at yet another level, according to some Thai critics, it symbolizes the decline of the traditional aristocracy and its replacement by a cold, calculating merchant class, symbolized by the narrator, a graduate in banking from Tokyo. The novel has been reprinted more than forty times, twice made into a film and translated into Chinese, Japanese and English.

By the late 1940s Siburapha was the most prominent of a number of writers to have been influenced by Marxist ideas on literature. From this time his fiction became essentially a means for highlighting social injustice and criticizing the government. In stories such as *Kho' raeng noi thoe* (*Lend Us a Hand*) and *Khon phuak nan* (*Those Kind of People*), the conflict between an arrogant, exploiting élite and an honest, hard-working underclass is portrayed in stark black and white terms. But to condemn these works for their simplistic portrayal of class relations and their lack of artistic merit is both to fail to understand the historical context in which they were written, and to recognise the author's courage and integrity. Two novels date from this period, *Chon kwa rao cha phop kan ik* (*Until We Meet Again*) and two volumes of the incomplete trilogy, *Lae pai khang na* [Look Forward]. The former, set in Australia, consists largely of conversations in which a naive Australian girl learns from a Thai student of the injustice in his country, while the latter sets out to provide a panoramic view of Thai history from the last days of the absolute monarchy in 1932.

Siburapha died in Beijing in 1974 without ever returning to his homeland. His later, "radical" fiction was frequently reprinted during the early 1970s and had a considerable influence on many young writers at the time. But while radical fiction lost its power with the increased political stability in the 1980s, Siburapha's reputation continued to grow with regular reprints of his earlier novels, frequent articles in newspapers and magazines about his life, the setting up of a Siburapha Foundation with an annual literary prize, and even a road in Bangkok named after him.

—David Smyth

SIENKIEWICZ, Henryk (Adam Aleksander Pius)

Born: Wola Okrzejska, Poland, 5 May 1846. **Education:** Educated at Warsaw Gymnasium, 1858–65; Polish University, Warsaw, 1866–71. **Family:** Married 1) Maria Szetkiewicz in 1881 (died 1885), one son and one daughter; 2) Maria Wołodkowicz in 1893 (marriage annulled 1895); 3) Maria Babska in 1904. **Career:** Journalist and freelance writer; co-owner and editor of the biweekly, *Niwa*, 1874; visited the United States to search for site for a California settlement, 1876–78; co-editor of the newspaper *Słowo* [The Word], 1882–87; founding member, Mianowski Foundation, 1882; co-founder and president, Literary Foundation, 1899, and Swiss Relief Committee for the War Victims in Poland, 1915. Given an estate by the Polish government at Oblegorek, near Kielce, 1900. **Awards:** Nobel prize for literature, 1905; Cracow Academy of Sciences gold medal, 1911. **Member:** Légion d'honneur (France), 1904, Imperial Academy of Arts and Letters, Serbian Academy of Arts and Letters, 1906, and Warsaw Scientific Association, 1907. **Died:** 15 November 1916.

PUBLICATIONS

Collections

Dzieła [Works], edited by Julian Krzyzanowski. 60 vols., 1948–55.
Pisma wybrane [Selected Works]. 1976–78.
The Little Trilogy, translated by Miroslaw Lipinski. 1995.

Fiction

Humoreski z teki Worszyłły [Humourous Stories from the Worszyllo's Portfolio]. 1872.
Stary sługa. 1875; translated as *The Old Servant*, 1897.
Na marne. 1876; as *In Vain*, translated by Jeremiah Curtin, 1899.
Hania. 1876; as *Hania*, translated by Jeremiah Curtin, 1897; also translated by Casimir Gonski, 1898; Casimir W. Dynicwicz, 1908; in part as *Let Us Follow Him*, translated by Curtin, 1897; also translated by Sigmund C. Slupski, 1897; Vatslaf A. Hlasko and Thomas H. Bullick, in *Let Us Follow Him, and Other Stories*, 1897.
Janko muzykant. 1880; as *Yanko the Musician*, translated by Jeremiah Curtin, in *Yanko the Musician and Other Stories*, 1893; as *Janko the Musician*, translated by Peter A. Ostafin, 1938.
Szkice węglem. 1880; as *Charcoal Sketches*, translated by Jeremiah Curtin, 1897; also translated by Adam Zamoyski, in *Charcoal Sketches and Other Tales*, 1990.

Za chlebem. 1880; as *After Bread*, translated by Vatslaf A. Hlasko and Thomas H. Bullick, 1897; as *For Daily Bread*, translated by Hlasko and Bullick, 1898; as *Peasants in Exile (For Daily Bread)*, translated by C. O'Conor-Eccles, 1898; as *Her Tragic Fate*, translated by J. Christian Bay, 1899; translated as *In the New Promised Land*, 1900.

Trilogy:

Ogniem i mieczem. 1884; as *With Fire and Sword*, translated by Jeremiah Curtin, 1890; also translated by Samuel A. Binion, 1898; W.S. Kuniczak, 1991.

Potop. 1886; as *The Deluge: An Historical Novel of Poland, Sweden, and Russia*, translated by Jeremiah Curtin, 1891; also translated by W.S. Kuniczak, 1991.

Pan Wołodyjowski. 3 vols., 1887–88; as *Pan Michael*, translated by Jeremiah Curtin, 1893; also translated by Samuel A. Binion, 1898; as *Fire in the Steppe*, translated by W.S. Kuniczak, 1992.

On the Sunny Shore, translated by Jeremiah Curtin. 1897; also translated by S.C. de Soissons, 1897; as *On the Bright Shore*, translated by Curtin, 1898.

Ta trzecia. 1889; as *The Third Woman*, translated by Nathan M. Babad, 1898; as *That Third Woman*, translated by Jeremiah Curtin, 1898.

Sielanka. 1889; as *Sielanka: A Forest Picture*, translated by Jeremiah Curtin, in *Sielanka: A Forest Picture, and Other Stories*, 1898.

Bez dogmatu. 1889; as *Without Dogma*, translated by Iza Young, 1893.

Yanko the Musician and Other Stories, translated by Jeremiah Curtin. 1893.

Lillian Morris, and Other Stories, translated by Jeremiah Curtin. 1894.

Rodzina Połanieckich. 1895; as *Children of the Soil*, translated by Jeremiah Curtin, 1895; as *The Irony of Life*, translated by Nathan M. Babad, 1900.

Quo vadis? 1896; as *Quo Vadis?: A Narrative of the Time of Nero*, translated by Jeremiah Curtin, 1896; also translated by Samuel A. Binion and S. Malevsky, 1897; William E. Smith, 1898; C.J. Hogarth, 1914; Stanley F. Conrad, 1992; W.S. Kuniczak, 1997.

For Daily Bread, and Other Stories, translated by Iza Young. 1896.

Na jasnym brzegu. 1897; as *In Monte Carlo*, translated by S.C. de Soissons, 1899.

Let Us Follow Him, and Other Stories, translated by Vatslaf Hlasko and Thomas H. Bullick. 1897.

Let Us Follow Him, and Other Stories (contents different from 1897 title of same name), translated by Sigmund C. Slupski and Iza Young. 1898.

Sielanka: A Forest Picture, and Other Stories, translated by Jeremiah Curtin. 1898.

So Runs the World: Stories, translated by S.C. de Soissons. 1898.

Tales, translated by S.C. de Soissons. 1899; edited by Monica M. Gardner, 1931.

Where Worlds Meet, translated by J. Christian Bay. 1899.

Krzyżacy. 4 vols., 1900; as *The Knights of the Cross*, translated by S.C. de Soissons, 1897; also translated by Samuel A. Binion, 1899; Jeremiah Curtin, 1900; B. Dahl, 1900; translated as *Danusia*, 1900; as *The Teutonic Knights*, translated by Alicia Tyszkiewicz, 1943, revised by Miroslav Lipinski, 1993.

Life and Death and Other Legends and Stories, translated by Jeremiah Curtin. 1904.

Na polu chwały. 1906; as *On the Field of Glory*, translated by Jeremiah Curtin, 1906; as *The Field of Glory*, translated by Henry Britoff, 1906; translated and edited by Miroslaw Lipinski, 2000.

Wiry. 1910; as *Whirlpools: A Novel of Modern Poland*, translated by Max A. Drezmal, 1910.

Legiony [The Legions] (unfinished). 1913–14.

Western Septet: Seven Stories of the American West, edited and translated by Marion Moore Coleman. 1973.

Charcoal Sketches and Other Tales (includes ''Charcoal Sketches''; ''Bartek the Conqueror''; ''On the Bright Shore''), translated by Adam Zamoyski. 1990.

Other

Listy z podróży do Ameryki. 2 vols., 1876–78; as *Portrait of America: Letters of Henryk Sienkiewicz*, edited and translated by Charles Morley, 1959.

Listy z Afryki [Letters from Africa]. 2 vols., 1891–92.

W pustyni i w puszczy (for children). 1911; as *In Desert and Wilderness*, translated by Max A. Drezmal, 1912; translated by Miroslaw Lipinski, 1994; as *Through the Desert*, translated by Mary Webb Artois, 1912.

Listy [Letters], edited by Julian Krzyzanowski and others. 1977–.

*

Critical Studies: *The Patriotic Novelist of Poland, Henryk Sienkiewicz* by Monica M. Gardner, 1926; *Bits of Table Talk on Pushkin, Mickiewicz, Goethe, Turgenev, and Sienkiewicz*, 1956, and *Henryk Sienkiewicz: A Retrospective Synthesis*, 1960, both by Wacław Lednicki; *Wanderers Twain: Modjeska and Sienkiewicz: A View from California* by Arthur Prudden and Marion Moore Coleman, 1964; *Henryk Sienkiewicz's American Resonance*, 1966, and *Henryk Sienkiewicz*, 1968, both by Mieczyslaw Giergielewicz; *The Trilogy Companion: A Reader's Guide to the Trilogy of Henryk Sienkiewicz* edited by Jerzy Krzyżanowski, 1991; *Linguistic Images of Emotions in Translation from Polish into Swedish: Henryk Sienkiewicz as a Case in Point* by Ewa Gruszczynska, 2001.

*   *   *

Henryk Sienkiewicz's historical novels, comprising his Trilogy— *Ogniem i mieczem* (*With Fire and Sword*), *Potop* (*The Deluge*), and *Pan Wołodyjowski* (*Pan Michael*)—and *Quo vadis?*, brought him celebrity in Poland and abroad. The historical novel had a special place in 19th-century Polish literature, when Poland was partitioned between Russia, Prussia, and Austro-Hungary, and was used by a number of novelists as a metaphor, in which the Polish reader could see contemporary reality ''masked'' by historical events. Too much can be made of this, of course: did Sienkiewicz intend the early Christians in *Quo vadis?* to represent the early socialists in 19th-century Russia? He never said so.

His popularity was due largely to his narrative power: from his early fiction, he reveals himself as a self-conscious literary artist, not merely a ''storyteller,'' stringing together striking incidents. He gained his effects from the manner in which he tells the tale: scenes are scrupulously dramatized for maximum effect, the various elements—dialogue, description, authorial comment, analysis—are balanced, and he used sophisticated literary devices such as "represented discourse" to produce dramatic presence. The dominant element in his narrative is the extended scene, following a character or group of characters intently for many pages at a time—a device frequently used by other major novelists, from Dickens to Tolstoi and Dostoevskii. The fact that all his novels were originally written as serials for Warsaw newspapers had an essential bearing on their structure: Sienkiewicz learned early on the necessity of careful planning in advance. His use of historical source materials for the Trilogy (the 17th century) and *Quo vadis?* (Rome under Nero) was scrupulous, and is reflected in his prose style.

When he turned to novels of psychological analysis (fashionable in Western Europe in the 1890s), Sienkiewicz was less successful, although both *Bez dogmatu* (*Without Dogma*) and *Rodzina Połanieckich* (*Children of the Soil*) are still of interest to literary people, as are the novels of Henry James, read not so much for what happens next, as "how the thing is done."

—David Welsh

SIKELIANOS, Angelos

Born: on island of Levkada, Greece, 15 March 1884. **Education:** Educated at Levkada Gymnasium, graduated 1900; studied law at the University of Athens, 1900. **Family:** Married 1) Eva Palmer in 1907 (dissolved 1940), one son; 2) Anna Karamani in 1940. **Career:** Attempted to revive the Delphic drama festivals, 1927–30. **Died:** 6 June 1951.

PUBLICATIONS

Collections

Thymele [Collected Plays], edited by G.P. Savidis. 3 vols., 1950–75.
Lyrikós vîos [Lyrical Life] (collected poems), edited by G.P. Savidis. 7 vols., 1965–69.
Pezos logos [Prose], edited by G.P. Savidis. 4 vols., 1978–83.

Verse

Alafroïkiotos [The Visionary]. 1909.
Prologos sti zoi [Prologue to Life]. 4 vols., 1915–17; 5th volume, 1947.
Mitir theou [Mother of God]. 1917–19.
The Delphic Word, translated by Alma Reed. 1928.
Ho dithyrambos tou Rhodou. 1934; as *The Dithyramb of the Rose*, translated by Frances Sikelianos, 1939.
Akritan Songs (bilingual edition), translated by Paul Nord. 1944.
Six Poems from the Greek of Sikelianos and Seferis, translated by Lawrence Durrell. 1946.
To Pascha ton Ellinon [Easter of the Greeks]. 1947.

Selected Poems, translated by Edmund Keeley and Philip Sherrard. 1979.

Plays

O Daidalos stin Criti [Daedalus in Crete]. 1943.
Sivylla [Sibyl]. 1944.
Ho Christos ste Rome [Christ at Rome]. 1946.

Other

Grammata sten Anna [Letters to Anna]. 1980.

*

Critical Study: *The Marble Threshing Floor* by Philip Sherrard, 1956.

* * *

Angelos Sikelianos was something very unusual in the 20th century—an uncompromising Romantic. This does not make him an anachronism: the world of his poetry was enhanced by what he knew of Einstein, and by 20th-century discoveries in archaeology and comparative mythology, as well as by the events through which he lived. But Sikelianos's larger-than-life personality, both in his life and his poetry, the boundless confidence with which he expounded his vision of a greater reality beyond the visible world, and the ponderous, sculpted rhetoric of his verse, seem almost incongruous in a poet who had fought in World War I, lived through the Greek defeat in Anatolia in 1922, with its disastrous repercussions for the Greek sense of identity, the political polarization of the 1930s, and then the Axis occupation of the early 1940s. In fact Sikelianos was the kind of visionary poet who might appear in any age; but the roots of his poetry lie in the final stage of Greek and European Romanticism in which he grew up.

The poem *Alafroïskiotos* [The Visionary] was written in 1907 and in many respects belongs to its time, with its "profound *logos*" (borrowed from the ancient dramatist Sophocles) that "We are but images and shadows." But the exultant lyricism of the poem, and the breathless rhythms of its free verse, reveal that even then Sikelianos was a poet with a voice very much his own. And it is this same voice, tempered but never deflected by the events of his times, that Sikelianos developed over the next 40 years. It is above all a lyrical voice, and it is appropriate that the title he later gave to his collected poems was *Lyrikós vîos* [Lyrical Life]. *Alafroïskiotos* anticipates the themes and mood of much that was to follow, in its celebration of the joy of life, of the unity of man with nature, and in weaving together myths from ancient Greece with modern folk legends and a rich evocation of the Greek landscape.

In later poems Sikelianos began to introduce a synthesis of Christian and pagan mythology, and also, in defiance of the trend among his contemporaries, moved steadily away from free verse to more formal verse patterns. After the long poems of the second decade of the century, we find Sikelianos in the 1920s writing some of his finest short lyrical poems. But to many readers his greatest achievement consists in the poems, written in a form of blank verse with long flowing periods, that began in 1935 with "Iera Odos" ("The Sacred Way"). In this poem a chance encounter with a gypsy and two performing bears, mother and child, on the sacred way that led in classical times from Athens to Eleusis, provides both a re-enactment of the ancient myth of Demeter and Persephone, and a symbol, in the bears brutally forced by their master to dance for a few pennies, of human exploitation and suffering.

Sikelianos had the conviction that poetry includes and unifies everything in the universe, and he linked it with the primitive capacity for myth-making, in opposition to science and rational philosophy. His ideas on the almost supernatural powers of poetry, as he saw it, and on myth, are expressed in his few prose works, which are vitiated by a diffuse and bombastic style. Sikelianos also wrote a number of verse dramas from which, however, the dramatic element is largely lacking. This is probably due to the very gift for synthesis, and a perception of the hidden sameness underlying opposites, that make him one of Europe's most remarkable lyric poets.

—Roderick Beaton

See the essay on "The Sacred Way."

SILONE, Ignazio

Born: Secondo Tranquilli in Pescina dei Marsi, Abruzzi, Italy, 1 May 1900. **Education:** Educated at Jesuit and other Catholic schools in Abruzzi and Rome. **Family:** Married Darina Laracy in 1944. **Career:** Secretary, Federation of Land Workers of the Abruzzi, 1917, and a leader of the Italian Socialist Youth Movement, 1917–21; member, Central Committee of Italian Communist Party, 1921–29, and editor of several party newspapers, including *L'Avanguardia*, Rome, *Il Lavoratore*, Trieste, 1921–22, and *L'Unità*; imprisoned in Spain, 1923; left Communist Party, 1930; worked in anti-fascist underground, and when warrants were issued against him by Fascist Special Tribunal left Italy to live in Switzerland, 1931–43: political secretary, Foreign Centre of the Italian Socialists, Zurich; member of the Executive Committee, Italian Socialist Party, 1941–47; editor, *Avanti*, a socialist daily paper, after World War II; founding president, Teatro del Popolo, 1945; Socialist Party Deputy, Italian Constituent Assembly, 1946–48; mainly a writer from 1950; co-editor, *Tempo Presente* magazine, Rome, 1956–68. President, Italian PEN Club, 1945–59; chair, Italian Committee for Cultural Freedom. **Awards:** Salento prize, 1957; Marzotto prize, 1965; Campiello prize, 1968; Jerusalem prize, 1969; Cino del Duca prize, 1971; Golden Pen prize, 1971; Keller prize, 1973. D.Litt.: Yale University, New Haven, Connecticut, 1965; University of Warwick; University of Toulouse, 1969. Commandeur, Légion d'honneur (France). **Died:** 22 August 1978.

PUBLICATIONS

Fiction

Fontamara. 1933; revised editions, 1949 and 1958; as *Fontamara*, translated by Eric Mosbacher and Gwenda David, 1934; also

translated by Michael Wharf, 1934; revised edition, translated by Harvey Fergusson II, 1960.
Un viaggio a Parigi (story). 1934.
Mr. Aristotle, translated by Samuel Putnam. 1935.
Pane e vino. 1937; revised edition, as *Vino e pane*, 1955; as *Bread and Wine*, translated by Eric Mosbacher and Gwenda David, 1936; revised edition, translated by Harvey Fergusson II, 1962.
Il seme sotto la neve. 1941 (in German translation); in Italian, 1945; as *The Seed beneath the Snow*, translated by Frances Frenaye, 1942; also translated by Harvey Fergusson II, 1965.
Una manciata di more. 1952; as *A Handful of Blackberries*, translated by Darina Tranquilli, 1953.
Il segreto di Luca. 1956; as *The Secret of Luca*, translated by Darina Tranquilli, 1959.
La volpe e le camelie. 1960; as *The Fox and the Camellias*, translated by Eric Mosbacher, 1961.
Severina, edited by Darina Tranquilli. 1982.

Plays

Ed egli si nascose, from his novel *Pane e vino*. 1944 (in German translation); in Italian, 1945; revised edition, 1966; as *And He Hid Himself*, translated by Darina Tranquilli, 1946; as *And He Did Hide Himself*, translated by Tranquilli, 1946.
L'avventura di un povero cristiano. 1968; as *The Story of a Humble Christian*, translated by William Weaver, 1970.

Other

Der Fascismus: Seine Entstehung und seine Entwicklung. 1934.
La scuola dei dittatori. 1938; as *The School for Dictators*, translated by Eric Mosbacher and Gwenda David, 1938; also translated by William Weaver, 1963.
Un dialogo difficile: Sono liberi gli scrittori russi?, with Ivan Anissimov. 1950; as *An Impossible Dialogue between Ivan Anissimov and Silone*, 1957.
Uscita di sicurezza. 1951; as *Emergency Exit*, translated by Darina Silone, 1968.
La scelta dei compagni. 1954.
Mi paso por el comunismo. 1959.
Per una legge sull'obiezione di coscienza, with others. 1962.
Paese dell'anima, edited by Maria Letizia Cassata. 1968.
Memoriale dal carcere svizzero, edited by Lamberto Mercuri. 1979.
Editor, *Mazzini.* 1939; translated as *The Living Thoughts of Mazzini*, edited by I. Silone, 1939.
Editor, *A trent'anni dal concordato.* 1959.

*

Critical Studies: *The God That Failed: Six Studies in Communism* edited by Richard Crossman, 1950; *Rehearsals of Discomposure: Alienation and Reconciliation in Modern Literature: Franz Kafka, Ignazio Silone, D.H. Lawrence, and T.S. Eliot* by Nathan A. Scott, 1952; *Ignazio Silone* (in Italian) by Ferdinando Virdia, 1967; *Ignazio Silone: Un amore religioso per la giustizia* by Alessandro Scurani, 1969; *The Politics of Ignazio Silone*, 1974; *Invito alla lettura di Ignazio Silone* by Carlo Annoni, 1974; *A Need to Testify: Portraits of*

Lauro de Bosis, Ruth Draper, Gaetano Salvemini, and Ignazio Silone by Iris Origo, 1983; *Ignazio Silone: Beyond the Tragic Vision* by Maria Nicolai Paynter, 2000.

* * *

Ignazio Silone's origins were humble and his early life was spent in active politics. His father was a day-labourer and his mother a weaver. He was left an orphan after the 1915 earthquake that destroyed large areas of central Abruzzi and his consciousness was first raised, as he describes in *Uscita di sicurezza* (*Emergency Exit*), by the misappropriation of relief funds. His first articles for *Avanti* in 1917 were on this subject.

Under Fascist rule, books by known communists and socialists were not published in Italy. Silone wrote his first and most famous novel, *Fontamara*, in Switzerland just after he left the Communist Party. It describes the plight of the peasants, the Abruzzese *cafoni*, struggling under the abuse that fascism had added to their eternal sufferings. The story of the rape and destruction of the village of Fontamara is told by three people, father, mother, and son, who have escaped and come to the author with their tale. Silone simply sets it down. This novel device may have been suggested to him by a Tolstoi tract, ''What's to Be Done,'' which describes Tolstoi in a similar situation after the 1905 revolution in Russia. Silone thus manages to communicate the immediacy of the peasants' plight, their limited knowledge of the world, and yet their clear understanding of what has been done to them. And he avoids the very real difficulty of trying to make peasants speak in ''standard'' Italian. The end of the novel describes the foundation of a newspaper at Fontamara called *Che fare* [What's to be done], a name that echoes the Russian revolutionary call of Chernyshevskii, Tolstoi, and Lenin. It rings through the ending of the novel challenging the tragic events of the plot. The sacrificial death of the hero, Berardo, in a Fascist prison in Rome may well parallel the death of Romolo, Silone's brother, at the hands of his jailers on Procida.

In *Pane e vino* (*Bread and Wine*)—later dramatized as *Ed egli si nascose* (*And He Hid Himself*)—and *Il seme sotto la neve* (*The Seed beneath the Snow*) a third-person narrator describes the clandestine wanderings of the returned political exile, Pietro Spina, who tries to raise the consciousness of the *cafoni* and to span the enormous gap between the official propaganda of the Left and the peasants' understanding. He is disguised as a priest, which emphasizes Silone's continual use of Christian symbolism, liturgy, and language. He frequently said that before socialism the only movement to have stirred the primeval consciousness of the Abruzzi was the 13th-century Franciscan movement. Both novels end with a sacrifice, and in *The Seed beneath the Snow*, Silone's favourite novel, the legendary Abruzzi figure of the dying Christ who is still on the Cross is likened to the suffering peasants.

Silone's post-war writing faces the problem of the individual at the mercy of political machines invented ostensibly for his good. *Una manciata di more* (*A Handful of Blackberries*) tackles post-war problems and the position of the ex-communists. *Il segreto di Luca* (*The Secret of Luca*) concerns the integrity of one *cafone* falsely imprisoned for murder. *La volpe e le camelie* (*The Fox and the Camellias*), the only work set outside the Abruzzi, in Switzerland, allows for some good in a Fascist character for the first time.

L'avventura di un povero cristiano (*The Story of a Humble Christian*) sees the 13th-century Pope Celestine V as an idealist who prefers to abdicate rather than compromise. *Severina* is a figure similarly committed to ''truth'' who falls against the background of the militancy of the 1960s. The message is still one of hope, however, despite all institutions that menace the integrity of the individual.

—Judy Rawson

See the essays on *Bread and Wine* and *Fontamara*.

SIMENON, Georges (Joseph Christian)

Pseudonyms: Georges Sim; Jean du Perry; Georges-Martin Georges; Christian Brulls; Gom Gut; Luc Dorsan; Jean Dorsage; Gaston Vialis; Jacques Dersonne; Georges d'Isly; Plick et Hock; Bobette; Germain d'Antibes; Jean Dossage; G. Violis. **Born:** Liège, Belgium, 13 February 1903. **Education:** Educated at convent nursery school, Liège, 1906–08; Institut St. André, 1908–14; Jesuit College of Saint-Louis, 1914–15; Collège St. Servais, Liège, to age 15. **Military Service:** Served in the Belgian cavalry, 1921–22; high commissioner for Belgian refugees in La Rochelle during World War II. **Family:** Married 1) Régine Renchon in 1923 (divorced 1950), one son; 2) Denise Ouimet in 1950 (marriage dissolved). **Career:** Apprenticed to a pastry chef and a bookseller, 1918–19; reporter and columnist, *Gazette de Liège*, 1919–21; secretary to the writers Henri Binet-Valmer, 1922–23, and the Marquis de Tracy, 1923–24; contracted to Eugène Merle to write novel while locked inside a glass cage, 1927; then freelance writer in Paris; contributor to *Détective* magazine, 1928. Travelled in Europe, 1929–30 and in Africa, 1932; threatened with deportation to concentration camp by Vichy authorities, 1942; lived in the United States and Canada after World War II, and in Switzerland after 1955. **Awards:** Mystery Writers of America Grand Master award, 1965. **Member:** Royal Academy of French Language and Literature (Belgium), 1953; member, Légion d'honneur. **Died:** 4 September 1989.

PUBLICATIONS

Fiction

Étoile de cinéma (as Georges d'Isly). 1925.
Volupteuses étreintes (as Plick et Hock). 1925.
Le Chéri de Tantine (as Plick et Plock). 1925.
Bobette et ses satyres (as Bobette). 1925.
Un petit poison (as Kim). 1928.
Hélas! (as Germain d'Antibes). 1929.
Des deux maîtresses (as Jean Dossage). 1929.
Trop belle pour elle! (as G. Violis). 1929.
Pietr-le-Letton. 1931; as *The Strange Case of Peter the Lett*, translated anonymously, 1933; as *The Case of Peter the Lett*, translated by Anthony Abbott, in *Inspector Maigret Investigates*, 1933; as *Maigret and the Enigmatic Lett*, translated by Daphne Woodward, 1963.

Au rendez-vous des Terre-Neuvas. 1931; as *The Sailor's Rendezvous*, translated by Margaret Ludwig, in *Maigret Keeps a Rendezvous*, 1940.

Le Charretier de "La Providence." 1931; as *The Crime at Lock 14*, with *The Shadow on the Courtyard*, 1934; in *The Triumph of Inspector Maigret*, 1934; as *Maigret Meets a Milord*, translated by Robert Baldick, 1963.

Le Chien jaune. 1931; as *A Face for a Clue*, translated by Geoffrey Sainsbury, in *The Patience of Maigret*, 1939, and with *A Crime in Holland*, 1952; as *Maigret and the Yellow Dog*, translated by Linda Asher, 1987.

La Danseuse du Gai-Moulin. 1931; as *At the Gai-Moulin*, translated by Geoffrey Sainsbury in *Maigret Abroad*, 1940, and with *A Battle of Nerves*, 1950.

M. Gallet décédé. 1931; as *The Death of Monsieur Gallet*, translated by Anthony Abbott, 1932; as *Maigret Stonewalled*, translated by Margaret Marshall, 1963.

La Nuit de carrefour. 1931; as *The Crossroad Murders*, translated by Anthony Abbott, in *Inspector Maigret Investigates*, 1933; as *Maigret at the Crossroads*, translated by Robert Baldick, 1963.

Le Pendu de Saint-Pholien. 1931; as *Maigret et Le Pendu de Saint-Pholien*, edited by Geoffrey Goodall, 1965; as *The Crime of Inspector Maigret*, translated by Anthony Abbott, *in Introducing Inspector Maigret*, 1933; as *Maigret and the Hundred Gibbets*, translated by Tony White, 1963.

Un crime en Hollande. 1931; as *A Crime in Holland*, translated by Geoffrey Sainsbury in *Maigret Abroad*, 1940, and with *A Face for a Clue*, 1963; as *Maigret in Holland*, translated by Geoffrey Sainsbury, 1993.

La Tête d'un homme. 1931; as *L'Homme de la Tour Eiffel*, 1950; as *A Battle of Nerves*, translated by Geoffrey Sainsbury, in *The Patience of Maigret*, 1939, and with *At The Gai-Moulin*, 1950.

Le Relais d'Alsace. 1931; as *The Man from Everywhere*, translated by Stuart Gilbert, in *Maigret and M. L'Abbé*, 1941, and with *Newhaven-Dieppe*, 1952.

L'Affaire Saint-Fiacre. 1932; as *The Saint-Fiacre Affair*, translated by Margaret Ludwig, in *Maigret Keeps a Rendezvous*, 1940; as *Maigret Goes Home*, translated by Robert Baldick, 1967.

Chez les Flammands. 1932; as *The Flemish Shop*, translated by Geoffrey Sainsbury, in *Maigret to the Rescue*, 1940.

Le Fou de Bergerac. 1932; as *The Madman of Bergerac*, translated by Geoffrey Sainsbury, in *Maigret Travels South*, 1940.

La Guinguette à deux sous. 1932; as *Guinguette by the Seine*, translated by Geoffrey Sainsbury, in *Maigret to the Rescue*, 1940.

Liberty Bar. 1932; as *Liberty Bar*, translated by Geoffrey Sainsbury, in *Maigret Travels South*, 1940.

L'Ombre chinoise. 1932; as *The Shadow in the Courtyard*, with *The Crime at Lock 14*, 1934; in *The Triumph of Inspector Maigret*, 1934; as *Maigret Mystified*, translated by Jean Stewart, 1965.

Le Port des brumes. 1932; as *Death of a Harbour Master*, translated by Stuart Gilbert, in *Maigret and M. L'Abbé*, 1941.

Le Passageur du "Polarlys." 1932; as *The Mystery of the "Polarlys"*, translated by Stuart Gilbert, in *In Two Latitudes*, 1942; as *Danger at Sea*, translated by Victor Kosta, in *On Land and Sea*, 1954.

Les Treize Mystères. 1932.

Les Treize Enigmes. 1932.

Les Treize Coupables. 1932.

L'Écluse no. 1. 1933; as *The Lock at Charenton*, translated by Margaret Ludwig, in *Maigret Sits It Out*, 1941.

L'Âne rouge. 1933; as *The Night-Club*, translated by Jean Stewart, 1979.

Le Coup de lune. 1933; as *Tropic Moon*, translated by Stuart Gilbert, in *In Two Latitudes*, 1942.

Les Fiançailles de M. Hire. 1933; as *Mr. Hire's Engagement*, translated by Daphne Woodward, in *The Sacrifice*, 1956.

Les Gens d'en face. 1933; as *The Window over the Way*, translated by Geoffrey Sainsbury, with *The Gendarme's Report*, 1951; as *Danger Ashore*, translated by Victor Kosta, in *On Land and Sea*, 1954; also translated by Robert Baldick, 1966.

Le Haut Mal. 1933; as *The Woman in the Grey House*, translated by Stuart Gilbert, in *Affairs of Destiny*, 1942.

Inspector Maigret Investigates (includes *La Nuit de carrefour* and *Pietr-le-Letton*), translated by Anthony Abbott. 1933.

Introducing Inspector Maigret (includes *M. Gallet décédé* and *Le Pendu de Saint-Pholien*), translated by Anthony Abbott. 1933.

La Maison du canal. 1933; as *The House by the Canal*, translated by Geoffrey Sainsbury, with *The Ostenders*, 1952.

L'Homme de Londres. 1934; as *Newhaven-Dieppe*, translated by Stuart Gilbert, in *Affairs of Destiny*, 1942.

Maigret. 1934; as *Maigret Returns*, translated by Margaret Ludwig, in *Maigret Sits It Out*, 1941.

Les Suicidés. 1934; as *One Way Out*, translated by Stuart Gilbert, in *Escape in Vain*, 1943.

Le Locataire. 1934; as *The Lodger*, translated by Stuart Gilbert, in *Escape in Vain*, 1943.

The Triumph of Inspector Maigret (includes *Le Charretier de la "Providence"* and *L'Ombre chinoise*). 1934.

Les Clients d'Avrenos. 1935.

Les Pitard. 1935; as *A Wife at Sea*, translated by Geoffrey Sainsbury, with *The Murderer*, 1949.

Quartier Nègre. 1935.

Les Demoiselles de Concarneau. 1936; as *The Breton Sisters*, translated by Stuart Gilbert, in *Havoc by Accident*, 1943.

L'Évadé. 1936; as *The Disintegration of J.P.G.*, translated by Geoffrey Sainsbury, 1937.

Long Cours. 1936; as *The Long Exile*, translated by Eileen Ellenbogen, 1982.

45° à l'ombre. 1936.

L'Assassin. 1937; as *The Murderer*, translated by Geoffrey Sainsbury, with *A Wife at Sea*, 1947.

Le Blanc à lunettes. 1937; as *Tatala*, translated by Stuart Gilbert, in *Havoc by Accident*, 1943.

Faubourg. 1937; as *Home Town*, translated by Stuart Gilbert, in *On the Danger Line*, 1944.

Le Testament Donadieu. 1973; as *The Shadow Falls*, translated by Stewart Gilbert, 1945; as *Donadieu's Will*, translated by Gilbert, 1991.

Les Sept Minutes (includes *Le Grand Langoustier, La Nuit des sept minutes*, and *L'Énigme de la "Marie Gallante"*). 1938.

Ceux de la soil. 1938.

Chemin sans issue. 1938; as *Blind Alley*, translated by Stuart Gilbert, in *Lost Moorings*, 1946; as *Blind Path*, translated by Gilbert, 1946.

Le Cheval blanc. 1938; as *The White Horse Inn*, translated by Norman Denny, 1980.

L'Homme qui regardait passer les trains. 1938; as *The Man Who Watched the Trains Go By,* translated by Stuart Gilbert, 1942.

La Marie du port. 1938; as *A Chit of a Girl,* translated by Geoffrey Sainsbury, 1949; as *The Girl in Waiting,* translated by Sainsbury, with *Justice,* 1957.

Monsieur La Souris. 1938; as *Monsieur La Souris,* translated by Geoffrey Sainsbury, with *Poisoned Relations,* 1950; as *The Mouse,* translated by Robert Baldick, 1966.

Les Rescapés du Télémaque. 1938; as *The Survivors,* translated by Stuart Gilbert, 1949, and with *Black Rain,* 1951.

Les Soeurs Lacroix. 1938; as *Poisoned Relations,* translated by Geoffrey Sainsbury, with *Monsieur La Souris,* 1950.

Le Suspect. 1938; as *The Green Thermos,* translated by Stuart Gilbert, in *On the Danger Line,* 1944.

Touriste de bananes. 1938; as *Banana Tourist,* translated by Stuart Gilbert, in *Lost Moorings,* 1946.

Les Trois Crimes de mes amis. 1938.

Le Bourgmestre de Furnes. 1939; as *The Bourgomaster of Furnes,* translated by Geoffrey Sainsbury, 1952.

Chez Krull. 1939; as *Chez Krull,* translated by Daphne Woodwood, in *A Sense of Guilt,* 1955.

The Patience of Maigret (includes *A Face For a Clue* and *A Battle of Nerves*), translated by Geoffrey Sainsbury. 1939.

Maigret Travels South (includes *The Madman of Bergerac* and *Liberty Bar*), translated by Geoffrey Sainsbury. 1940.

Les Inconnus dans la maison. 1940; as *Strangers in the House,* translated by Geoffrey Sainsbury, 1951; also translated by Robert Baldick, 1967.

Malempin. 1940; as *The Family Lie,* translated by Isabel Quigly, 1978.

Maigret to the Rescue (includes *The Flemish Shop* and *Guinguette by the Seine*), translated by Geoffrey Sainsbury. 1940.

Bergelon. 1941; as *The Delivery,* translated by Eileen Ellenbogen, 1981.

Cour d'assises. 1941; as *Justice,* translated by Geoffrey Sainsbury, with *The Girl in Waiting,* 1957.

Il pleut bergère. 1941; as *Black Rain,* translated by Geoffrey Sainsbury, with *The Survivors,* 1951.

La Maison des sept jeunes filles. 1941.

L'Outlaw. 1941; as *The Outlaw,* translated by Howard Curtis, 1986.

Le Voyageur de la Toussaint. 1941; as *Strange Inheritance,* translated by Geoffrey Sainsbury, 1950.

Maigret Sits It Out (includes *The Lock at Charenton* and *Maigret Returns*), translated by Margaret Ludwig. 1941.

Le Fils Cardinaud. 1942; as *Young Cardinaud,* translated by Richard Brain, in *The Sacrifice,* 1956.

Oncle Charles s'est enfermé. 1942; as *Uncle Charles Has Locked Himself In,* translated by Howard Curtis, 1987.

La Vérité sur Bébé Donge. 1942; as *The Trial of Bebe Donge,* translated by Geoffrey Sainsbury, 1952; as *I Take This Woman,* translated by Louise Varèse, in *Satan's Children,* 1953; as *The Truth About Bébé Donge,* translated by Varèse, 1992.

La Veuve couderc. 1942; as *Ticket of Leave,* translated by John Petrie, 1954; as *The Widow,* translated by Petrie, with *Magician,* 1955.

Maigret revient (includes *Cécile est mort; Les Caves du majestic; La Maison du juge*). 1942.

Les Dossiers de l'Agence O. 1943.

Le Petit Docteur. 1943; as *The Little Doctor,* translated by Jean Stewart, 1978.

Havoc by Accident (includes *The Breton Sisters* and *Tatala*), translated by Stuart Gilbert. 1943.

Escape in Vein (includes *One Way Out* and *The Lodger*), translated by Stuart Gilbert. 1943.

Les Nouvelles Enquêtes de Maigret. 1944.

La Rapport du gendarme. 1944; as *The Gendarme's Report,* translated by Geoffrey Sainsbury, with *The Window over the Way,* 1951.

Signé Picpus. 1944; as *To Any Lengths,* translated by Geoffrey Sainsbury, in *Maigret on Holiday,* 1950.

L'Inspecteur Cadavre. 1944; as *Maigret's Rival* translated by Helen Thompson, 1979.

On the Danger Line (includes *The Green Thermos* and *Home Town*), translated by Stuart Gilbert. 1944.

L'Aîné des ferchaux. 1945; as *The First Born,* translated by Geoffrey Sainsbury, 1947; as *Magnet of Doom,* translated by Sainsbury, 1948.

La Fenêtre des Rouet. 1945; as *Across the Street,* translated by John Petrie, 1954.

La Fuite de M. Monde. 1945; as *Monsieur Monde Vanishes,* translated by Jean Stewart, 1967.

Le Cercle des Mahé. 1946.

Les Noces de Poitiers. 1946; as *The Couple from Poitiers,* translated by Eileen Ellenbogen, 1985.

Trois Chambres à Manhattan. 1946; as *Three Beds in Manhattan,* translated by Lawrence G. Blochman, 1964.

Lost Moorings (includes *Banana Tourist* and *Blind Alley*), translated by Stuart Gilbert. 1946.

Au Bout du rouleau. 1947.

Le Clan des Ostendais. 1947; as *The Ostenders,* translated by Geoffrey Sainsbury, with *The House by the Canal,* 1952.

Lettre à mon juge. 1947; as *Act of Passion,* translated by Louise Varèse, 1952.

Le Passager clandestin. 1947; as *The Stowaway,* translated by Nigel Ryan, 1957.

Maigret et l'inspecteur malchanceux (includes *Le Client le plus obstiné du monde; Maigret et l'inspecteur malchanceux; On ne tue pas les pauvres types; Le Témoignage de l'enfant de choeur*). 1947.

Maigret à New York. 1947; as *Maigret in New York's Underworld,* translated by Adrienne Foulke, 1955; as *Inspector Maigret in New York's Underworld,* translated by Anthony Abbott, 1956.

Maigret se fâche, suivi de Le Pipe de Maigret. 1947; *Le Pipe de Maigret* as *Maigret's Pipe,* translated by Jean Stewart, 1978.

Maigret et son mort. 1948; as *Maigret's Special Murder,* translated by Jean Stewart, 1964; as *Maigret's Dead Man,* translated by Stewart, 1964.

Les Vacances de Maigret. 1948; as *Maigret on Holiday,* translated by Geoffrey Sainsbury, 1950; as *No Vacation for Maigret,* translated by Sainsbury, 1953; as *Maigret on Holiday,* translated by Jacqueline Baldick, 1970.

Le Bilan malétras. 1948; as *The Reckoning,* translated by Emily Read, 1984.

Le Destin des Matou. 1948; as *The Fate of the Malous,* translated by Denis George, 1962.

La Jument perdue. 1948.

La Neige était sale. 1948; as *The Snow Was Black*, translated by Louise Varèse, 1950; as *The Stain on the Snow*, translated by John Petrie, 1953.

Pedigree. 1948; as *Pedigree*, translated by Robert Baldick, 1962.

Maigret chez le coroner. 1949; as *Maigret and the Coroner*, translated by Francis Keene, 1980; as *Maigret at the Coroner's*, translated by Keene, 1980.

Maigret et la vieille dame. 1949; as *Maigret and the Old Lady*, translated by Robert Brain, 1958.

Mon ami Maigret. 1949; as *My Friend Maigret*, translated by Nigel Ryan, 1956.

La Première Enquête de Maigret, 1913. 1949; as *Maigret's First Case*, translated by Robert Brain, 1958.

Les Fantômes du chapelier. 1949; as *The Hatter's Ghost*, translated by Nigel Ryan, in *The Judge and the Hatter*, 1956; as *The Hatter's Phantom*, translated by Willard R. Trask, 1976.

Le Fond de la bouteille. 1949; as *The Bottom of the Bottle*, translated by Cornelia Schaeffer, in *Tidal Wave*, 1954.

Les Quatre Jours du pauvre homme. 1949; as *Four Days in a Lifetime*, translated by Louise Varèse, in *Satan's Children*, 1953.

L'Amie de Mne Maigret. 1950; as *Madame Maigret's Own Case*, translated by Helen Sebba, 1959; as *Madame Maigret's Friend*, translated by Sebba, 1960.

Les Petits Cochons sans queues. 1950.

L'Enterrement de Monsieur Bouvet. 1950; as *The Burial of Monsieur Bouvet*, translated by Eugene MacCown, in *Destinations*, 1955; as *Inquest on Bouvet*, translated by MacCown, 1958.

Les Volets verts. 1950; as *The Heart of a Man*, translated by Louise Varèse, 1951.

Un nouveau dans la ville. 1950.

Tante Jeanne. 1950; as *Aunt Jeanne*, translated by Geoffrey Sainsbury, 1953.

Le Temps d'Anaïs. 1951; as *The Girl in His Past*, translated by Louise Varèse, 1952.

Une vie comme neuve. 1951; as *A New Lease of Life*, translated by Joanna Richardson, 1963.

Un Noël de Maigret. 1951; as *Maigret's Christmas*, translated by Lawrence G. Blochman, 1959; also translated by Jean Stewart, 1976.

Maigret au picratt's. 1951; as *Maigret in Montmartre*, translated by Daphne Woodward, in *Maigret Right and Wrong*, 1954; as *Inspector Maigret and the Strangled Stripper*, translated by Cornelia Schaeffer, 1954.

Maigret en meuble. 1951; as *Maigret Takes a Room*, translated by Robert Brain, 1960; as *Maigret Rents a Room*, translated by Brain, 1961.

Maigret et la grande perche. 1951; as *Maigret and the Burglar's Wife*, translated by J. Maclaren-Ross, 1955; as *Inspector Maigret and the Burglar's Wife*, translated by Maclaren-Ross, 1956.

Les Mémoires de Maigret. 1951; as *Maigret's Memories*, translated by Jean Stewart, 1963; as *Maigret's Memoirs*, translated by Stewart, 1985.

Marie qui louche. 1951; as *The Girl with a Squint*, translated by Helen Thompson, 1978.

Omnibus Simenon. 10 vols., 1951–52.

Maigret, Lognon, et les gangsters. 1952; as *Maigret and the Killers*, translated by Louise Varèse, 1954; as *Maigret and the Gangsters*, translated by Varèse, 1974.

Le Revolver de Maigret. 1952; as *Maigret's Revolver*, translated by Nigel Ryan, 1956.

Les Frères Rico. 1952; as *The Brothers Rico*, translated by Ernest Pawel, in *Tidal Wave*, 1954, and in *Violent Ends*, 1954.

La Mort de Belle. 1952; as *Belle*, translated by Louise Varèse, in *Tidal Wave*, 1954, and in *Violent Ends*, 1954.

Antoine et Julie. 1953; as *The Magician*, translated by Helen Sebba, with *The Widow*, 1955.

L'Escalier de fer. 1953; as *The Iron Staircase*, translated by Eileen Ellenbogen, 1963.

Feux rouges. 1953; as *The Hitch-hiker*, translated by Norman Denny, in *Destinations*, 1955; as *Red Lights*, translated by Denny, in *Danger Ahead*, 1955.

Maigret et l'homme du banc. 1953; as *Maigret and the Man on the Bench*, translated by Eileen Ellenbogen, 1975; as *Maigret and the Man on the Boulevard*, translated by Ellenbogen, 1975.

Maigret a peur. 1953; as *Maigret Afraid*, translated by Margaret Duff, 1961.

Maigret se trompe. 1953; as *Maigret's Mistake*, translated by Alan Hodge, in *Maigret Right and Wrong*, 1954.

Satan's Children (includes *Four Days in a Lifetime* and *Take This Woman*), translated by Louise Varèse. 1953.

Le Bateau d'Émile. 1954.

Maigret à l'école. 1954; as *Maigret Goes to School*, translated by Daphne Woodward, 1957.

Maigret et la jeune morte. 1954; as *Maigret and the Young Girl*, translated by Daphne Woodward, 1955; as *Inspector Maigret and the Dead Girl*, translated by Woodward, 1955.

Crime impuni. 1954; as *Fugitive*, translated by Louise Varèse, 1955; as *Account Unsettled*, translated by Tony White, 1962.

Le Grand Bob. 1954; as *Big Bob*, translated by Eileen Lowe, 1969.

L'Horloger d'Everton. 1954; as *The Watchmaker of Everton*, translated by Norman Denny, in *Danger Ahead*, 1955, and with *Witnesses*, 1956.

Les Témoins. 1954; as *Witnesses*, translated by Moura Budberg, with *The Watchmaker of Everton*, 1956.

La Boule noire. 1955.

Maigret Right and Wrong (includes *Maigret in Montmartre* and *Maigret's Mistake*). 1954.

On Land and Sea (includes *Danger at Sea* and *Danger Ashore*), translated by Victor Kosta. 1954.

Maigret tend un piège. 1955; as *Maigret Sets a Trap*, translated by Daphne Woodward, 1965.

Maigret chez le ministre. 1954; as *Maigret and the Calame report*, translated by Moura Budberg, 1969; as *Maigret and the Minister*, translated by Budberg, 1969.

Maigret et le corps sans tête. 1955; as *Maigret and the Headless Corpse*, translated by Eileen Ellenbogen, 1967.

Les Complices. 1955; as *The Accomplices*, translated by Bernard Frechtman, with *The Blue Room*, 1964.

En cas de malheur. 1956; as *In Case of Emergency*, translated by Helen Sebba, 1958.

Le Petit Homme d'Arkhangelsk. 1957; as *The Little Man from Arkangel*, translated by Nigel Ryan, 1957.

Un échec de Maigret. 1956; as *Maigret's Failure*, translated by Daphne Woodward, 1962.

Maigret s'amuse. 1957; as *Maigret's Little Joke*, translated by Richard Brain, 1957; as *None of Maigret's Business*, translated by Brain, 1958.

Maigret voyage. 1957; as *Maigret and the Millionairess*, translated by Jean Stewart, 1974.

Le Fils. 1957; as *The Son*, translated by Daphne Woodward, 1958.

Le Nègre. 1957; as *The Negro*, translated by Helen Sebba, 1959.

Le Passage de la ligne. 1958.

Le Président. 1958; as *The Premier*, translated by Daphne Woodward, 1961.

Strip-Tease. 1958; as *Striptease*, translated by Richard Brain, 1959.

Dimanche. 1958; as *Sunday*, translated by Nigel Ryan, 1960.

Les Scrupules de Maigret. 1958; as *Maigret Has Scruples*, translated by Robert Eglesfield, 1959.

La Vieille. 1959; as *The Grandmother*, translated by Jean Stewart, 1978.

Une Confidence de Maigret. 1959; as *Maigret Has Doubts*, translated by Lyn Moir, 1968.

Maigret et les témoins recalcitrants. 1959; as *Maigret and the Reluctant Witnesses*, translated by Daphne Woodward, 1959.

The Short Cases of Inspector Maigret, translated by Lawrence G. Blochman. 1959.

Versus Inspector Maigret (includes *Maigret Has Scruples* and *Maigret and the Reluctant Witnesses*). 1960.

L'Ours en peluche. 1960; as *Teddy Bear*, translated by John Clay, 1971.

Le Veuf. 1960; as *The Widower*, translated by Robert Baldick, 1961.

Maigret aux assises. 1960; as *Maigret in Court*, translated by Robert Brain, 1961.

Maigret et les vieillards. 1960; as *Maigret in Society*, translated by Robert Eglesfield, 1962.

Betty. 1961; as *Betty*, translated by Alistair Hamilton, 1975.

Le Train. 1961; as *The Train*, translated by Robert Baldick, 1964.

Maigret et le voleur paraisseux. 1961; as *Maigret and the Lazy Burglar*, translated by Daphne Woodward, 1963.

Maigret et les braves gens. 1962; as *Maigret and the Black Sheep*, translated by Helen Thomson, 1976.

Maigret et le client du samedi. 1962; as *Maigret and the Saturday Caller*, translated by Tony White, 1964,

Les Autres. 1962; as *The House on Quai Notre Dame*, translated by Alistair Hamilton, 1975; as *The Others*, translated by Hamilton, 1975.

La Porte. 1962; as *The Door*, translated by Daphne Woodward, 1964.

Maigret et le clochard. 1963; as *Maigret and the Bum*, translated by Jean Stewart, 1973; as *Maigret and the Dosser*, translated by Stewart, 1973.

Lea Anneaux de Bicetre. 1963; as *The Patient*, translated by Jean Stewart, 1963; as *The Bells of Bicetre*, translated by Stewart, 1964.

La Colère de Maigret. 1963; as *Maigret Loses His Temper*, translated by Robert Eglesfield, 1965.

Le Rue aux trois poussins. 1963.

La Chambre bleue. 1964; as *The Blue Room*, translated by Eileen Ellenbogen, with *The Accomplices*, 1964.

L'Homme au petit chien. 1964; as *The Man with the Little Dog*, translated by Jean Stewart, 1965.

Maigret et le fantôme. 1964; as *Maigret and the Ghost*, translated by Eileen Ellenbogen, 1976; as *Maigret and the Apparition*, translated by Jean Stewart, 1976.

Maigret se défend. 1964; as *Maigret on the Defensive*, translated by Alistair Hamilton, 1966.

La Patience de Maigret. 1965; as *The Patience of Maigret*, translated by Alistair Hamilton, 1966; as *Maigret Bides His Time*, translated by Hamilton, 1985.

Le Petit Saint. 1965; as *The Little Saint*, translated by Bernard Frechtman, 1965.

Le Train de Venise. 1965; as *The Venice Train*, translated by Alistair Hamilton, 1974.

Les Enquêtes du Commissaire Maigret. 2 vols., 1966–67.

Le Confessionnel. 1966; as *The Confessional*, translated by Jean Stewart, 1967.

La Mort d'Auguste. 1966; as *The Old Man Dies*, translated by Bernard Frechtman, 1967.

Maigret et l'affaire Nahour. 1966; as *Maigret and the Nahour Case*, translated by Alistair Hamilton, 1967.

Le Voleur de Maigret. 1967; as *Maigret's Pickpocket*, translated by Nigel Ryan, 1968; as *Maigret and the Pickpocket*, translated by Ryan, 1989.

Le Chat. 1967; as *The Cat*, translated by Bernard Frechtman, 1967.

Le Déménagement. 1967; as *The Neighbours*, translated by Christopher Sinclair-Stevenson, 1968; as *The Move*, translated by Sinclair-Stevenson, 1968.

La Main. 1968; as *The Man on the Bench in the Barn*, translated by Moura Budberg, 1970.

La Prison. 1968; as *The Prison*, translated by Lyn Moir, 1969.

L'Ami d'enfance de Maigret. 1968; as *Maigret's Boyhood Friend*, translated by Eileen Ellenbogen, 1970.

Maigret à Vichy. 1968; as *Maigret Takes the Waters*, translated by Eileen Ellenbogen, 1969; as *Maigret in Vichy*, translated by Ellenbogen, 1969.

Maigret hésite. 1968; as *Maigret Hesitates*, translated by Lyn Moir, 1970.

Il y a encore des noisetiers. 1969.

Novembre. 1969; as *November*, translated by Jean Stewart, 1970.

Maigret et le tueur. 1969; as *Maigret and the Killer*, translated by Lyn Moir, 1971.

Le Riche Homme. 1970; as *The Rich Man*, translated by Jean Stewart, 1971.

La Folle de Maigret. 1970; as *Maigret and the Madwoman*, translated by Eileen Ellenbogen, 1972.

Maigret et le marchand de vin. 1970; as *Maigret and the Wine Merchant*, translated by Eileen Ellenbogen, 1971.

Le Cage de verre. 1971; as *The Glass Cage*, translated by Antonia White, 1973.

La Disparition d'Odile. 1971; as *The Disappearance of Odile*, translated by Lyn Moir, 1972.

Maigret et l'homme tout seul. 1971; as *Maigret and the Loner*, translated by Eileen Ellenbogen, 1975.

Maigret et l'indicateur. 1971; as *Maigret and the Informer*, translated by Lyn Moir, 1972; as *Maigret and the Flea*, translated by Moir, 1972.

Les Innocents. 1972; as *The Innocents*, translated by Eileen Ellenbogen, 1973.

Maigret et Monsieur Charles. 1972; as *Maigret and Monsieur Charles*, translated by Marianne A. Sinclair, 1973.

Complete Maigret Short Stories. 2 vols., 1976.

Maigret and the Toy Village, translated by Eileen Ellenbogen. 1978.

African Trio. 1979.

The Rules of the Game, translated by Howard Curtis. 1988.

Maigret on the Riviera, translated by Geoffrey Sainsbury. 1988.

Fiction as Georges Sim

Au Pont des arches. 1921.
Les Ridicules. 1921.
Les Larmes avant le bonheur. 1925.
Le Feu s'éteint. 1927.
Les Voleurs de navires. 1927.
Défense d'aimer. 1927.
Le Cercle de la soif. 1927.
Paris-L'est. 1927.
Un monsieur libidineux. 1927.
Les Coeurs perdus. 1928.
Le Secret des Lamas. 1928.
Les Maudits du Pacifique. 1928.
Le Monstre blanc de la terre de feu. 1928; as *L'Île de la désolation* (as
    Christian Brulls), 1933.
Miss Baby. 1928.
Le Semeur de larmes. 1928.
Le Roi des glaces. 1928.
Le Sous-Marin dans la forêt. 1928.
La Maison sans soleil. 1928.
Aimer l'amour. 1928.
Songes d'été. 1928.
Les Nains des cataractes. 1928.
Le Lac d'angoisse. 1928; as *Le Lac des esclaves* (as Christian Brulls),
    1933.
Le Sang des gitanes. 1928.
Chair de Beauté. 1928.
Les Mémoires d'un prostitué. 1929.
En robe de mariée. 1929.
La Panthère borgne. 1929.
La Fiancée aux mains de glace. 1929.
Les Bandits de Chicago. 1929.
L'Île des hommes roux. 1929.
Le Roi du Pacifique. 1929; as *Le Bateau d'or*, 1935.
Le Gorille-Roi. 1929.
Les Contrabandiers de l'alcool. 1929.
La Femme qui tue. 1929.
Destinées. 1929.
L'Île des maudits. 1929; as *Naufrage du "Pelican"*, 1933.
La Femme en deuil. 1929.
Le Chinois de San-Fransisco. 1930.
La Femme 47. 1930.
L'Homme qui tremble. 1930.
Mademoiselle Million. 1930; as *Les Ruses de l'amour*, 1954.
Nez d'argent. 1930; as *Le Paria des bois sauvages*, 1933.
L'Oeil de l'Utah. 1930.
Le Pêcheur de bouées. 1930.
Les Errants. 1931.
L'Homme à la cigarette. 1931.
L'Homme de proie. 1931.
Katia, acrobate. 1931.
La Maison de l'inquiétude. 1932.
L'Épave. 1932.
La Fiancée du diable. 1932.
Matricule 12. 1932.
La Femme rousse. 1933.
Le Château des sables rouges. 1933.
Deuxième bureau. 1933.
Le Yacht fantôme. 1933.

Fiction as Jean du Perry

Le Roman d'une dactylo. 1924.
À l'assaut d'un coeur. 1925.
Amour d'Afrique. 1925.
Amour d'exilée. 1925.
Ceux qu'on avait oubliés. . . 1925.
Entre deux haines. 1925.
La Fiancée fugitive. 1925.
L'Heureuse Fin. 1925.
L'Oiseau blessée. 1925.
Pour le sauver. 1925.
Pour qu'il soit heureux. 1925.
L'Orgueil d'aimer. 1926.
Celle qui est aimée. 1926.
Les Yeux qui ordonnent. 1926.
Que ma mère l'ignore!. 1926.
De la rue au bonheur. 1926.
Un péché de jeunesse. 1926.
Lili Tristesse. 1927.
Un tout petit coeur. 1927.
Le Fou d'amour. 1928.
Coeur exalté. 1928.
Trois coeurs dans la tempête. 1928.
Les Amants de la mansarde. 1928.
Un jour de soleil. 1928.
La Fille de l'autre. 1929.
L'Amour et l'argent. 1929.
Coeur de poupée. 1929.
Une femme a tué. 1929.
Deux Coeurs de femme. 1929.
L'Épave d'amour. 1929.
Le Mirage de Paris. 1929.
Celle qui passe. 1930.
Petite Exilée. 1930.
Les Amants du malheur. 1930.
La Femme ardente. 1930.
La Porte close. 1930.
La Poupée brisée. 1930.
Pauvre Amante!. 1931.
Le Rêve qui meurt. 1931.
Marie-Mystère. 1931.

Fiction as Georges-Martin Georges

L'Orgueil qui meurt. 1925.
Un soir de vertige. 1928.
Brin d'amour. 1928.
Les Coeurs vides. 1928.
Cabotine. . . 1928.
Aimer, mourir. 1928.
Voleuse d'amour. 1928.
Une ombre dans la nuit. 1929.
Nuit de Paris. 1929.
La Victime. 1929.
Un nid d'amour. 1930.
Bobette, mannequin. 1930.
La Puissance du souvenir. 1930.
Le Bonheur de Lili. 1930.
La Double vie. 1931.

Fiction as Christian Brulls

La Prêtresse des vaudoux. 1925.
Nox l'insaisissable. 1926.
Se Ma Tsien, le sacrificateur. 1926.
Le Désert du froid qui tue. 1928; as *Le Yacht fantôme* (as Georges Sim), 1933.
Mademoiselle X. 1928.
Annie, danseuse. 1928.
Dolorosa. 1928.
Les Adolescents passionnés. 1929.
L'Amant sans nom. 1929.
Un drame au Pôle Sud. 1929.
Les Pirates du Texas. 1929; as *La Chasse au whiskey*, 1934.
Captaine, S.O.S. 1929.
Jacques d'Antifer, roi des Îles du Vent. 1930; as *L'Héritier du corsair*, 1934.
L'Inconnue. 1930.
Train de nuit. 1930.
Pour venger son père. 1931.
La Maison de la haine. 1931.
La Maison des disparus. 1931.
Les Forçats de Paris. 1932.
La Figurante. 1932.
Fièvre. 1932.
L'Évasion. 1934.
L'Île empoisonnée. 1937.
Seut parmi les gorilles. 1937.

Fiction as Gom Gut

Un viol aux quat'z'arts. 1925.
Perversités frivoles. 1925.
Au grand 13. 1925.
Plaisirs charnels. 1925.
Aux vingt-huit négresses. 1925.
La Noce à Montmartre. 1925.
Liquettes au vent. 1926.
Une petite très sensuelle. 1926.
Orgies bourgeoises. 1926.
L'Homme aux douze étreintes. 1927.
Étreintes passionnées. 1927.
Une môme dessalée. 1927.
L'Amant fantôme. 1928.
L'Amour à Montparnasse. 1928.
Les Distractions d'Hélène. 1928.

Fiction as Luc Dorsan

Histoire d'un pantalon. 1926.
Nine violée. 1926.
Nochonnette. 1926.
Mémoires d'un vieux suiveur. 1926.
Nuit de noces, doubles noces, les noces ardentes. 1926.
La Pucelle de Benouville. 1927.
Une petite dessalée. 1928.
Un drôle de Coco. 1929.

Fiction as Jean Dorsage

L'Amour méconnu. 1928.
Celle qui revient. 1929.
Coeur de jeune fille. 1930.
Soeurette. 1930.
Les Chercheurs de bonheur. 1930.

Fiction as Gaston Vialis

Un petit corps blessé. 1928.
Haïr à force d'aimer. 1928.
Le parfum du passé. 1929.
Lili-sourire. 1930.
Folie d'un soir. 1930.
À me de jeune fille. 1931.

Fiction as Jacques Dersonne

Un seul baiser. . . 1928.
La Merveilleuse Aventure. 1929.
Les Étapes du mensonge. 1930.
Baisers mortels. 1930.
Victime de son fils. 1931.

Plays

Quartier nègre (produced 1936).
La Neige était sale, with Frédéric Dard, from the novel by Simenon (produced 1950). In *Oeuvres Libres 57*, 1951.
La Chambre (ballet), music by Georges Auric (produced 1955).

Other

Les Trois Crimes de mes amis. 1938.
Le Mauvais Étoile. 1938.
Je me souviens. . . 1945.
Long cours sur les rivières et canaux. 1952.
Le Roman de l'homme. 1960; as *The Novel of Man*, translated by Bernard Frechtman, 1964.
La Femme en France. 1960.
Entretiens avec Roger Stéphane. 1963.
Ma conviction profonde. 1963.
Oeuvres complètes, edited by Gilbert Sigaux. 72 vols., 1967–75.
Le Paris de Simenon. 1969; as *Simenon's Paris*, translated by Frederick Frank, 1970.
Quand j'étais vieux. 1970; as *When I Was Old*, translated by Helen Eustis, 1971,
Lettre à ma mère. 1974; as *Letter to My Mother*, translated by Ralph Manheim, 1976.
Un homme comme un autre. 1975.
Des traces de pos. 1975.
Vent du nord, vent du sud. 1976.
Les Petits Hommes. 1976.

Mes Apprentissages: À la découverte de la France, à la recherche de l'homme nu, edited by Francis Lacassin and Gilbert Sigaux. 2 vols., 1976.
De la cave au grenier. 1977.
À l'abri de notre arbre. 1977.
Un banc au soleil. 1977.
Tant que je suis vivant. 1978.
Vacances obligatoires. 1978.
La Main dans la main. 1978.
Au-delà de ma porte-fenêtre. 1979.
Point-virgule. 1979.
À quoi bon jurer?. 1979.
Je suis resté un enfant de choeur. 1979.
Le Prix d'un homme. 1980.
Le Roman de l'homme. 1980.
On dit que j'ai soixante-quinze ans. 1980.
Quand vient le froid. 1980.
Les Libertés qu'il nous reste. 1981.
La Femme endormie. 1981.
Jour et nuit. 1981.
Destinées. 1981.
Mémoires intimes. 1981; as *Intimate Memoirs*, translated by Harold J. Salemson, 1984.
L'Âge du roman. 1988.

*

Bibliography: *Simenon* by Bernard de Fallois, 1961; *Simenon: A Checklist of His "Maigret" and Other Mystery Novels and Short Stories in French and English Translations* by Trudee Young, 1976.

Critical Studies: *The Art of Simenon* by Thomas Narcejac, translated by Cynthia Rowland, 1952; "Simenon and Spillane: The Metaphysics of Murder for the Millions" by Charles J. Rolo, in *New World Writing*, 1952; "The Art of Fiction IX: Georges Simenon" by Carvel Collins in *Paris Review*, 9, 1955; *Simenon* by Bernard de Fallois, 1961, revised edition, 1971; *Simenon in Court* by John Raymond, 1968; *Multiplying Villainies* edited by R.E. Briney and F.M. Nevins, 1973; *Simenon* by Francis Lacassin and Gilbert Sigaux, 1973; *Georges Simenon* by Lucille Frackman Becker, 1977; *The Mystery of Georges Simenon: A Biography* by Fenton Bresler, 1983; *L'Univers de Simenon* (includes bibliography) by Maurice Piron, 1983; *Index des personnages de Georges Simenon* by Michel Lemoine, 1986; *Simenon: A Critical Biography* by Stanley G. Eskin, 1987; *Simenon: Biographie* by Pierre Assouline, 1992; *The Man Who Wasn't Maigret: A Portrait of Georges Simenon* by Patrick Marnham, 1992; *Georges Simenon Revisited* by Lucille F. Becker, 1999.

*   *   *

Although Georges Simenon is well known as the creator of the French detective Jules Maigret, he always wanted to write something more than just popular fiction. In 1918, after receiving sudden news that his father was mortally ill, Simenon, who wanted to go to medical school originally, changed his plans in favour of journalism. His ambition was to become a novelist. He made a name for himself in the newspaper industry and wrote a few potboilers before turning to detective stories. When asked about this experience years later, he explained that he began with the detective stories in order to gain some experience before going on to more difficult novels.

Simenon realized that the simplicity of mysteries is not their only virtue—they also sell well. The first Maigret novel, *Pietr-le-Letton* (*Maigret and the Enigmatic Lett*), was successful, and Simenon's publisher contracted him to write a few more. At the time, however, he had no thoughts of doing a series. For him, Maigret was both a breadwinner and a hindrance. A look at the chronology of the series reveals Simenon's difficulties. Maigret appeared in novels in two distinct blocks of time: from 1931–33, and from 1946–72. Simenon made two attempts to get rid of his famous detective before he succeeded.

The first attempt was made in 1933, after Simenon had completed 18 Maigret novels. He felt ready to proceed to a psychological novel without a famous central character who could overshadow the purpose of the work. His publisher reminded him that detective novelists are rarely successful in another field and often cannot do away with their detectives, citing the example of Arthur Conan Doyle's failed attempt to kill off Sherlock Holmes. These words were harsh, but apposite. Although Simenon did write a number of non-Maigret works, the Inspector did return. The novels with Maigret sold better than the novels without him, even when those in the latter category were made into films. Simenon himself admitted that he cared for Maigret. In his autobiographical work *Mémoires intimes* (*Intimate Memoirs*), he often calls the Inspector "good old Maigret." In this book, he also credits Maigret with his success as a writer, saying, "I owe him a great debt, because it was thanks to him that I ceased being an amateur and became a novelist."

However, Simenon was never able to put Maigret aside effectively and turn his attention solely to what he called "plain" novels. In 1973, when he stopped writing about his famous detective, he stopped writing novels altogether. He explained that he had become too engrossed in trying to understand characters; instead, he wanted to understand himself.

Although he could not stay away from detective fiction, Simenon managed to write both Maigrets and "plain" novels simultaneously. Altogether, he wrote well over 100 of each type. The "plain" novels are studies of the human mind which emphasize strong psychological themes.

The most powerful of these ideas is that all men are essentially alone. *Pedigree*, for example, relates the life experiences of Roger Mamelin. Roger moves through the turbulence of his life as a solitary figure, with no real support from others. Instead of reaching out for companionship, he rebels from it and turns to debauchery. After much restless wandering and soul-searching, Roger finds his place in the world when his father suffers a heart attack. This strong sense of solitude and inner conflict is apparent in the majority of Simenon's psychological works.

This physical and emotional solitude often creates in the character a strong desire to be noticed. Many of them resort to cheap sex or to alcohol. For example, Kees Popinga, the protagonist in *L'Homme qui regardait passer les trains* (*The Man Who Watched the Trains Go By*), enters the world of crime and consorts with thieves and prostitutes after murdering a woman. The descent into crime is a last-ditch cry for attention often found in these novels.

Companionship, especially through paternity, is another theme which is predominant throughout Simenon's works. *Pedigree* is an obvious illustration of this point. Roger sees a way out of his meaningless life after establishing a close understanding with his dying father. The father-son relationship figures prominently in many of Simenon's "plain" novels, providing a friend and mentor for the lonely protagonist. It is this filial connection that helps the character to gain self-awareness.

It is intriguing to note that the Maigret works, which Simenon saw as almost inconsequential in relation to the other novels, are themselves psychological studies, emphasizing the same themes as the other works. For example, Maigret is often portrayed as a solitary figure. Most of his ideas are revealed to the reader through the inner workings of his mind rather than through dialogue with other characters. Even in his home, Maigret seems to be isolated, and communicates only tersely with his wife. The characters he investigates are for the most part lonely people who are looking for companionship in sordid places. These characters resort to murder to make themselves known through revenge and violence against the indifferent world around them. Maigret, however, is sometimes able to find companionship when he befriends younger detectives in his department, often forming an almost paternal relationship with them. It is these friendships which help the investigations proceed as swiftly as they do and which make Maigret a complete man. Simenon may have felt limited by the restrictions imposed on him by the genre of detective fiction, but in reality, these restrictions did not prevent him from creating effective psychological studies in the Maigret novels.

—Lisa M. Ruch

SKÁRMETA, Antonio

Born: Antofagasta, Chile, 7 November 1940. **Education:** Studied literature and philosophy, University of Santiago, B.A. in philosophy, 1964; Columbia University, M.A. with a thesis on the Argentine writer Julio Cortázar, 1966. **Family:** Married; two children. **Career:** Taught philosophy and literature at the University of Santiago and also directed plays imported from Broadway, from 1967–73; moved to Argentina, 1973, and to Germany after a military coup overthrew Chilean president Salvador Allende. In exile he wrote and collaborated on many film and theater projects based on his work. In Berlin he taught scriptwriting at the German Academy of Film and Television. Visited Chile on occasion during the 1980s and taught at various American universities. Worked in TV and film, creating an award-winning program called "El Show de los Libros," upon return to Chile in 1989. Gained internationally reknown for his script for the Academy Award-wining film *Il Postino*, mid-1990s. Named Chile's ambassador to Germany, 2000. **Awards:** Casa de las Américas short story prize (Cuba) for *Desnudo en el tejado*, 1969; Boccaccio International prize for Literature (Italy) for *No pasó nada*, 1986; Chaplin prize for the best scriptwriter in Chilean television, 1998; Golden Book prize (Portugal) for *El cartero de Neruda*; Grinzane Cavour prize (Italy) for *La boda del poeta*, 2001; Adolf Grimme prize (Germany) for his film version of *Ardiente paciencia*, 1984; Prix Georges Sadoul (France) for his film version *Ardiente paciencia*, 1984; Order of Merit at the rank of Commander from the Italian Republic; Chevalier of the Order of Arts and Letters of France.

PUBLICATIONS

Collections

Watch Where the Wolf Is Going: Stories. 1991; translated by Donald L. Schmidt and Federico Cordovez.
Uno a uno: cuentos completos. 1996.

Fiction

El entusiasmo. 1967.
Desnudo en el tejado. 1969.
El ciclista de San Cristóbal. 1973.
Tiro libre. 1973.
Novios y solitarios. 1975.
Soñé que la nieve ardía. 1975; as *I Dreamt the Snow Was Burning*, translated by Malcolm Coad, 1985.
No pasó nada. 1980.
La insurrección. 1982; as *The Insurrection*, translated by Paula Sharp, 1983.
Ardiente paciencia. 1985; as *Burning Patience*, translated by K. Silver, 1987.
Match Ball. 1989; as *Love-Fifteen*, translated by Jonathan Tittler, 1996.
La composición. 1998; as *The Composition*, translated by Elisa Amado, 2000.
La boda del poeta. 1999; as *The Poet's Wedding*, translated by Susan Giersbach Rascón, 2002.
La chica del trombón. 2001.

*

Critical Studies: *Del cuerpo a la palabra: la narrativa de Antonio Skármeta* edited by Raúl Silva Cáceres, 1983; *Skármeta: la inteligencia de los sentidos* by Constanza Lira, 1985; *Skármeta, una narrativa de la liberación* by Monique Lemaitre, 1991; *Antonio Skármeta and the Post Boom* by Donald Shaw, 1994.

*　*　*

Antonio Skármeta is one of Chile's most important writers of the 20th century and is considered one of the most representative voices of the post-boom period in Spanish American literature. The so-called boom occurred in the 1960s, a time of great productivity and creativity in the Spanish American novel. During this decade, writers such as Julio Cortázar, Carlos Fuentes, Gabriel García Márquez, and José Donoso brought worldwide recognition to Spanish American letters with their highly experimental texts that exhibited a great deal of narrative fragmentation, linguistic innovation, and a generally pessimistic outlook on life. Sharing many traits of the avant-garde movements of the 1920s and 1930s (such as the incorporation of surrealism into literature), boom writers challenged the notion of the realistic psychological novel with its linear timeframe and narrative coherence. The protagonists of boom novels are often anti-heroes mired in an existential malaise. These novels tend to question the nature of reality by mixing reality with fantasy to create highly ambiguous texts that can be inaccessible to unsophisticated readers.

Skármeta typifies the post-boom by rejecting the fragmentation, experimentalism, and elitism of boom novels, which tend to appeal to a well-educated, upper-middle class readership. Skármeta's writings are much more preoccupied with reality than with fantasy or magical realism and also typify the new emphasis on youth and youth culture in the post-boom. During Skármeta's formative years, his vision of literature was much more influenced by the harsh social realities of Latin America than by esoteric philosophical schools or experimental aesthetics. Events such as the Cuban revolution of 1959, the emergence of the socialist movement in Chile, and the 1973 overthrow of Chilean president Salvador Allende all had much to do with Skármeta's development into a socially committed author. His writings display an explicit acceptance and celebration of life rather than the pessimistic questioning of reality (and, consequently, of literature itself) evident in the boom. Skármeta, along with other writers of his generation, emphasize the importance of a coherent and realistic plot as well as the need to present in literature matters of social justice that affect the lives of the common people of Latin America. This left-wing orientation of solidarity with the proletariat becomes even more prominent in Skármeta's writings after socialist Allende's downfall and his succession by General Augusto Pinochet. Skarmeta's writings in the mid-1970s and early 1980s are much more politically charged than his early texts, which are characterized by their lyricism and exuberant individualism.

Although he began as a short story writer, Skármeta is most well known for his novels, the first of which is titled *Soñé que la nieve ardía* (*I Dreamt the Snow Was Burning*). Skármeta began this book in Chile before the fall of the Allende government and finished it in exile in Argentina. The story focuses on the lives of a group of politically committed young Chileans just before the 1973 coup. The main character of the novel is Arturo, a young soccer player who undergoes an ideological transformation into a left-wing activist. Although the novel has been criticized for being a bit too black-and-white in its depiction of highly idealized characters and its romantic vision of the Allende regime, *Soñé...* nevertheless represents an important step away from boom literature with its humor and straightforward human appeal.

Skármeta's second novel, *No pasó nada* [Nothing Happened], focuses on the theme of exile. Its main character and narrator is Lucho, a Chilean teenager living with his refugee family in Berlin shortly after the coup that overthrew Allende. The book presents a new take on the exile experience by viewing the situation through the eyes of a young man who doesn't really understand why he and his family have been forced to leave their homeland. Furthermore, the story takes on a more universal appeal by transcending South American politics through the parallel plot of Lucho's sexual coming-of-age.

La insurrección (*The Insurrection*) continues Skármeta's series of novels based on political events in Latin America during the 1970s. This novel has its origins in a film script written by Skármeta after he visited Nicaragua shortly after the triumph of the 1979 Sandinista revolution. The story has what could be described as a collective protagonist, the residents of a small neighborhood in the Nicaraguan city of León, who band together to help topple the cruel Somoza dictatorship. In this novel Skármeta once again champions the ideals of solidarity among the oppressed masses of Latin America and the importance of subordinating individualistic concerns to the greater common good.

Ardiente paciencia (*Burning Patience*) is by far Skármeta's most popular novel. Originally published in 1985, the highly successful adaptation of this novel to the big screen in 1994 (as *Il Postino*) made the book an international success. The story, full of humor and written in Skármeta's intensely poetic style, revolves around the exploits of Mario Jiménez, a working-class Chilean teenager who learns about poetry, politics and love thanks to his relationship with Nobel laureate Pablo Neruda, Chile's greatest poet for whom Mario works as a letter carrier. *Burning Patience* is similar to *No pasó nada* in that both are essentially bildungsromans (coming-of-age novels) told within the context of political strife. In addition to helping Mario become a budding writer, Neruda also oversees his protégé's amorous conquest of the beautiful Beatriz. Due to his relationship with the leftist Neruda, the young man is eventually detained and presumably assassinated in the wake of the 1973 military coup. Despite its rather tragic ending, this novel, like all of Skármeta's writing, is essentially a celebration of life, as is suggested by its title, an excerpt from Neruda's Nobel acceptance speech in which he affirmed that "only with an ardent patience shall we conquer the splendid city that will give light, justice and dignity to all men."

—Stephen J. Clark

SŁOWACKI, Juliusz

Born: Krzemieniec, Poland, 4 September 1809. **Education:** Educated at home, schools in Krzemieniec and Wilno (Vilnius), and the University of Wilno (1825–28, law degree). **Career:** Employed in administrative and diplomatic offices in Warsaw, 1829–31. Left for Dresden, then traveled as a diplomatic envoy to Paris, London, and back to Paris, 1831–32. Lived in Geneva, 1833–36, and later traveled in Italy, Greece, Egypt, and Palestine. Settled in Paris, 1838, where he spent the rest of his life, supported by money inherited from his father. Made a trip to Poznań, then to Wrocław, where he met with his mother, 1848. **Died:** 3 April 1849.

PUBLICATIONS

Collections

Dzieła wszystkie, edited by Juliusz Kleiner and Władysław Floryan. 17 vols., 1952–56.
Dzieła, edited by Julian Krzyżanowski. 14 vols., 1952, also 1959.
Korespondencja, edited by Eugeniusz Sawrymowicz. 2 vols., 1962–63.
Ja Orfeusz. Liryki i fragmenty z lat 1836–1849, edited by Marian Bizan. 1974; 1978.

Verse

Poezje. 2 vols., 1832.
Poezje. 1833.
Anhelli. 1838; as *Anhelli*, translated by Dorothea Prall Radin, 1930, also 1979.
Trzy poemata. Ojciec zadżumionych, W Szwajcarii, Wacław. 1839; as *The Father of the Plague-Stricken at El-Arish*, translated by J.P. Wachowski, in *Free Poland*, 1915; also as *The Father of the Plague-Stricken in El Arish*, translated by William J. Rose, in *Juliusz Słowacki*, 1951; as *In Switzerland*, translated by Kenneth Mackenzie, 1953; also translated by George Gomori and Keith Bosley, in *Comparative Criticism*, 1984.
Beniowski. I–V. 1841.
Król-Duch. I. 1847.
Do Autora Trzech Psalmów. 1848.

Genezis z Ducha. 1866; as *Genesis from the Spirit*, translated by Kazimierz Chodkiewicz, 1966.

This Fateful Power, edited and translated by Michael J. Mikoś. 1999.

Plays

Maria Stuart. 1832; as *Mary Stuart*, translated by Arthur P. Coleman and Marion M. Coleman, 1937.

Kordian. 1834.

Balladyna. 1839; translated by Marion M. Coleman with Walter Twardowski, 1960.

Mazepa. 1840; as *Mazeppa*, translated by Carlton F. Wells and Cecilia D. Wells, 1929; also translated by Marion M. Coleman, 1966.

Lilla Weneda. 1840.

Złota Czaszka. 1866.

Fantazy. 1866; translated by Harold B. Segel, in *Polish Romantic Drama*, 1977.

Ksiadz Marek. 1843.

Sen srebrny Salomei. 1844.

Samuel Zborowski. 1901.

Zawisza Czarny. 1909.

Other

Do emigracji o potrzebie idei. 1846

*

Bibliography: *Juliusz Słowacki* by Halina Gacowa, in *Nowy Korbut*, vol. 11, 2000.

Critical Studies: *Juliusz Słowacki: Dzieje twórczości*, 4 vols., by Juliusz Kleiner, 1923–28, 1958; *Szkice o dramatach Słowackiego* by Edward Csató, 1960; *Kalendarz życia i twórczości Juliusza Słowackiego* edited by Eugeniusz Sawrymowicz with Stanisław Makowski and Zbigniew Sudolski, 1960; *Słowacki na scenach polskich* edited by Tadeusz Sivert and Tadeusz Pacewicz, 1963; *Dziedzictwo Słowackiego w poezji polskiej ostatniego półwiecza, 1918–1968* by Marian Tatara, 1973; *Spadkobiercy Króla Ducha. O recepcji filozofii Słowackiego w światopoglądzie polskiego modernizmu* by Halina Floryńska, 1976; *Liryka w pełni romantyczna: studia i szkice o wierszach Słowackiego* by Czesław Zgorzelski, 1981; *Juliusz Słowacki* by Stanisław Makowski, 1987; *Słowacki. Opowieść biograficzna* by Zbigniew Sudolski, 1996; *Juliusz Słowacki* by Małgorzata Kamela in *Polski Słownik Biograficzny*, 1999; *Słowacki*, 2nd edition, by Alina Kowalczykowa, 1999.

*   *   *

A leading Romantic poet, playwright, and epistolographer, Juliusz Słowacki was a creator of a mystical doctrine and a precursor of the Symbolist poets. He grew up in the intellectual milieu of Wilno, where his father, Euzebiusz Słowacki, was a professor of rhetoric and poetry at Wilno University. Four years after his father's death in 1814, Słowacki's mother, Salomea, married August Bécu, a doctor and professor of pathology and hygiene, who died when struck by lightning in 1824. Słowacki studied law and after graduating went to Warsaw, the center of intellectual and political activity. He made his literary debut with Romantic tales in verse: *Hugo, The Monk, Jan Bielecki*, and *The Arab*; and two historical dramas, *Mindowe* and *Mary Stuart*; deriving inspiration from Shakespeare, Byron, Scott,

and Mickiewicz. Drawn to the cause of national independence that led to the November Uprising of 1830, Słowacki wrote a series of patriotic poems, among them *Hymn* and *Ode to Freedom*, which gained great popularity in Poland and allowed him to claim the title of the bard of the revolution. When the uprising was nearly suppressed, Słowacki left Poland and went to Paris, where he published two volumes of his works.

Throughout his life Słowacki lived in the shadow of Adam Mickiewicz, a celebrated compatriot and poet. Mickiewicz's critical comment about Słowacki's early poetry (''an edifice of beautiful architecture, like a lofty church—but there is no God in that church'') and his presentation of Doctor Bécu, Słowacki's stepfather, as a collaborator in *Forefathers' Eve, III* deeply hurt the younger poet. Słowacki moved to Geneva and during the next four years developed an aesthetic program, which contained his ideas on poetry and on the role of literature in national history, pertaining especially to the current predicament of the partitioned Poland. While Mickiewicz saw Poland resurrected like Christ and saved by heroic actions of her sons, Słowacki implied in his play *Kordian* (published in 1834) that the fall was caused by the sins of her people and that heroic intentions of the protagonists were nothing more than noble dreams, doomed to failure in the moment of trial. Similarly, in contrast to Mickiewicz's *Books of the Polish Nation and of the Polish Pilgrimage*, in which the author called upon his countrymen to carry the light of a new spirituality across Europe, Słowacki's long poem *Anhelli* (published in 1838) showed the earthly hell of the Polish exiles in Siberia, who were doomed to die, but destined to pass their faith in Poland's rebirth to future generations. Thus, Mickiewicz and Słowacki articulated two programs: the first, of the messianic and heroic will to struggle; the other, of reaching to the core of Polish religion and tradition in order to restore national independence, a task left not to helpless émigrés but to the Poles in their homeland. These two distinct plans evolved into major premises in Polish debates on the future of the country during over a century of its subjugation and subsequent occupations.

Many of Słowacki's lyrical masterpieces which date from the period of his travels present the sinuous grace of his language and evocative imagery. Some examples of this style are his nostalgic *Hymn*, a poignant *My Testament*, a love poem *In Switzerland*, his reflective and provocative message to his compatriots entitled *Agamemnon's Tomb*, and several moving poems addressed to his mother. In *The Father of the Plague-Stricken in El Arish* and *Wacław*, two poems inspired by Dante and Byron, Słowacki depicted infernal suffering and death of the protagonists.

Misunderstood and viewed with disfavor by the émigré critics, Słowacki responded with an autobiographical poem, *Beniowski*. The five books of this poetic tour de force offered inspired images; heartfelt confessions; bold polemics with critics, including Mickiewicz; and profound insights into literary, political, and spiritual matters. When his friend Zygmunt Krasiński condemned revolutionary movements in his *Psalms of the Future*, especially the bloody attacks of Galician peasants against landowners in 1846, Słowacki responded with the zeal of a youthful revolutionary, calling for the liberation of Poland in his poem *To the Author of Three Psalms*. In 1848, he organized a confederacy and left with a group of friends for Poznań in Great Poland to take part in the local uprising, but was expelled by the police after nearly a month and did not witness its fall.

Słowacki was a prolific and innovative playwright who laid the foundations of modern Polish drama. In his plays *Balladyna, Mazepa, Lilla Weneda, Zawisza the Black, The Golden Skull, Father Mark*, and *The Silver Dream of Salomea*, written between 1834 and 1845, he returned to the important people and events in Poland's national life, while in his most popular play, *Fantazy*, he mocked the Romantic pose and shallowness of Polish aristocrats. Free from censorship and conventional rules of the theatre, as none of his plays was staged in Poland in his lifetime, he experimented by combining tragic themes with satire, irony, and grotesque, displaying the provocative power of his imagination and language.

In 1842, Słowacki fell under the spell of Andrzej Towiański, a notorious mystic and religious reformer, but over a year later he broke with him and his circle and embarked on a solitary religious and philosophical quest, manifested in his short lyrics, such as *A Fiery Angel—Angel at My Left Side* and *When the First Cocks Sing unto the Master* as well as in his poetic treatise *Genesis from the Spirit* (1844) and the book of legends entitled *King-Spirit* (1845–49). Conjuring up powerful spirits reincarnated in the bodies of Polish historical leaders, Słowacki envisioned a union of the earthly and supernatural worlds that would determine national destiny in its ascendance towards eternity.

Słowacki was seriously ill for a longtime and lived a lonely existence, documented in his voluminous correspondence. His letters, particularly to his mother, a moving testimonial of filial love, recorded the progress of his creative and emotional life, especially in his final years. He was buried at Montmartre Cemetery in Paris, but in 1927 his body was exhumed, brought to Poland, and laid to rest side by side with Mickiewicz in the crypt of the royal castle of Wawel in Cracow, "to be equal to the kings."

—Michael J. Mikoś

SÖDERGRAN, Edith (Irene)

Born: St. Petersburg, Russia, 4 April 1892. Grew up in Raivola, on the Karelian Isthmus; father died of tuberculosis, 1907. **Education:** Educated at the Deutsche Hauptschule zu Sankt-Petri (German girls' school), St. Petersburg, 1902–08. **Career:** Diagnosed with tuberculosis, 1908, and stayed in tuberculosis sanatoria in Nummela, 1909–11, and Davos-Dorf, Switzerland, 1912–14; returned to Raivola, 1914. Wrote first in German, then in Swedish. **Died:** 24 June 1923.

PUBLICATIONS

Collections

Samlade dikter, edited by Gunnar Tideström. 1949.
Dikter 1907–1909, edited by Olof Enckell. 2 vols., 1961.
Collected Poems, translated by Martin S. Allwood. 1980.
Complete Poems, translated by David McDuff. 1984,
Samlade skrifter 1: Dikter och aforismer, edited by Holger Lillqvist. 1990.

Verse

Dikter. 1916; as *Poems*, translated by Martin S. Allwood, in *Collected Poems*, 1980; also translated by David McDuff, in *Complete Poems*, 1984.
Septemberlyran. 1918; as *The September Lyre*, translated by Martin S. Allwood, in *Collected Poems*, 1980; also translated by David McDuff, in *Complete Poems*, 1984.

Rosenaltaret. 1919; as *The Rose Altar*, translated by Martin S. Allwood, in *Collected Poems*, 1980; also translated by David McDuff, in *Complete Poems*, 1984.
Framtidens skugga. 1920; as *The Shadow of the Future*, translated by Martin S. Allwood, in *Collected Poems*, 1980; also translated by David McDuff, in *Complete Poems*, 1984.
Landet sore icke är. 1925; as *The Land That Is Not*, translated by Martin S. Allwood, in *Collected Poems*, 1980; also translated by David McDuff, in *Complete Poems*, 1984.
Love and Solitude, Selected Poems, 1916–1923, translated by Stina Katchadourian. 1981; revised edition, 1985; 2nd revised edition, 1992.
Poems, translated by Gounil Brown. 1990.

Other

Brokiga iakttagelser (aphorisms). 1919; as *Motley Observations*, translated by David McDuff, in *Complete Poems*, 1984.
Ediths brev: brev från Edith Södergran till Hagar Olsson [Edith's Letters: Letters from Edith Södergran to Hagar Olsson], edited by Hagar Olsson, 1955; selection in *Books from Finland*, translated by David McDuff. 26(2), 1992.
Poet Who Created Herself: The Complete Letters of Edith Södergran to Hagar Olsson with Hagar Olsson's Commentary and the Complete Letters of Edith Södergran to Elmer Diktonius, translated and edited by Silvester Mazzarella. 2001.

*

Critical Studies: "Edith Södergran's *Wallensteinprofil*," in *Scandinavian Studies*, edited by Carl F. Bayerschmidt and Erik J. Friis, 1965, "A Life on the Edge," in *Books from Finland*, 17(3), 1983, and *Edith Södergran: Modernist Poet in Finland*, 1984, all by George C. Schoolfield; *Edith Södergran* by Loup de Fages, 1970; "Edith Södergran: A Pioneer of Finland-Swedish Modernism" by Gladys Hird, in *Books from Finland*, 12(1), 1978; *Edith Södergran, a Changing Image: Looking for a New Perspective on the Work of the Finnish Avant-Garde Poet* by Petra Broomans, Adriaan van der Hoeven and Jytte Kronig, 1992.

* * *

Edith Södergran was one of the first modernist poets, not only in Scandinavia but also in Europe. With Gunnar Björling (1887–1960) and Elmer Diktonius (1896–1961) she was a pioneer of Finland-Swedish avant-gardism in poetry. Like them, she drew on foreign sources for some of her inspiration. In her case, however, this is complicated by the fact that because of her mixed cultural and linguistic background (her education at a German girls' school in St. Petersburg and subsequent stays at a tuberculosis sanatorium in Davos-Dorf, Switzerland, were the principal factors in this regard), she never managed completely to adapt to any one specific literary tradition. Essentially cosmopolitan, her work contains elements of both German expressionism (Heym, Stadler, and Dauthendey) and Russian Futurism (Severianin and Maiakovskii), yet it is written for the most part in a Finnish Swedish which, paradoxically, has a curiously archaic ring, derived in part from her mother's rural speech idiom. The result is a poetry of metalanguage, an utterance that, while it undeniably reflects the twin landscapes of the Karelian Isthmus and mountainous Davos, is not really fixed on any geo-linguistic point but travels freely in the realm of the absolute, speaking of the ultimate realities of flesh, disintegration, spirit, death, and rebirth in tones that at times recall Nietzsche, at others Lichtenberg, Rimbaud, or Vilhelm Ekelund.

The poems of Södergran's first collection, *Dikter* (*Poems*), in many ways represent a development of the styles and techniques she had already elaborated in the 225 poems contained in the "*Vaxdukshäftet*" or "oil-cloth notebook" she wrote between the ages of 14 and 16. There are the romantic motifs of pale autumn lakes and moonlit evenings, but there is also the presence of startlingly expressionistic imagery and colouration: "Violet dusks I bear within me from my origins... "; "In hell no one speaks, but everyone screams, / there tears are not tears and all sorrows are without strength. . . ."

In *Septemberlyran* (*The September Lyre*) Södergran confronted both her own physical and psychic instability and the chaos of the new world that was being formed quite literally on her doorstep. Raivola, the small settlement where she and her mother lived, was situated on the frontier between Finland and Russia, on the railway line that connected Helsinki with St. Petersburg, and the military operations that accompanied the onset of civil war were never far in the background. The poems Södergran wrote at this time reflect a sense of change and transformation, and also one of danger: "Guard your boat from superhuman currents, / from the whirlpool abyss of madness . . . ."

In her short foreword to *The September Lyre*, the poet declared that she had "discovered her dimensions," adding: "It does not become me to make myself less than I am." This last statement, which inevitably drew accusations of megalomania from the small-minded (and male) Finland-Swedish critical establishment, none the less points the way to an understanding of Södergran's achievement. For she really did perceive a correspondence between her own visions of disintegration and rebirth and the cataclysms that were taking place in the world around her, and this correspondence can be seen as an objective fact. Like some of the other Modernist poets of her age, she represented a part of events that lay far beyond literature.

The collection *Rosenaltaret* (*The Rose Altar*), which appeared in 1919, displays another important element of Södergran's poetic world: her mysticism, which was largely influenced by the writings and teachings of Rudolf Steiner, and a belief that "the Kingdom of God is beginning":

Not Christ's
wasting empire,
but higher, brighter
human forms
come to the altar
bearing forth their gratitude
celestially scented,
overwhelming the senses.

This collection also contains the poems Södergran wrote to her "sister," the writer and critic Hagar Olsson, who had defended the poet from the worst of the attacks that appeared in the Finland-Swedish press following the publication of *The September Lyre*. These poems are best read in conjunction with Olsson's volume *Ediths brev* [Edith's Letters], which provides a fascinating account of the friendship between the two women against the background of war and revolution.

In the poems of *Framtidens skugga* (*The Shadow of the Future*), written during the painful latter stages of her terminal illness, there is a sense of giving up; the struggle for material existence is abandoned and the poet's soul is freed. The victory is not achieved at once; there are seemingly overwhelming doubts to be overcome. The soul often seems unreal: "I do not believe in seeming and soul, / the game of games is so foreign to me." Physical suffering intensifies her sensation of her own body's grossness and helplessness, yet even this grossness and animality becomes transformed into a redeeming force, the power of Eros.

The posthumous collection *Landet som icke är* (*The Land That Is Not*) contains poems from nearly all periods of Södergran's activity as a poet, and it too explores the power of Eros, though more in connection with a rediscovery of childhood: "My childhood's trees stand rejoicing around me; O human! / and the grass bids me welcome from foreign lands."

An assessment of Södergran's poetry should not overlook her contribution to the peculiarly Finland-Swedish literary tradition of aphorisms. Her collection of these, *Brokiga iakttagelser* (*Motley Observations*), is considered to have been influential on subsequent generations of both Finland-Swedish and Swedish poets.

In general, Edith Södergran may be seen as one of the great 20th-century European literary innovators. Although her work is "Nordic," it is sufficiently international to bear comparison with the work of poets such as Else Lasker-Schüler, Gabriele D'Annunzio, and Paul Claudel.

—David McDuff

SOKOLOV, Sasha

Born: Alexander Vsevolodovich Sokolov in Ottawa, Ontario, Canada, 6 November 1943. **Education:** Educated at the Military Institute of Foreign Languages, Moscow, 1962–65; Moscow University, B.A. in journalism 1971. **Family:** Married; one daughter. **Career:** Staff writer, *Novorossiiskii rabochii* [The Novorossiisk Worker], 1967, *Kolkhoznaia pravda* [Kolkhoz Truth], Morky, 1967–68, *Literaturnaia Rossiia* [Literary Russia], Moscow, 1969–71, *Studencheskii meridian* [The Student Meridian], summers 1970–71, and *Leninskaia pravda* [Leninist Truth], Georgievsk, 1974; went on hunger strike to obtain exit visa from Soviet authorities following ban on his marriage; emigrated to Canada, 1976; writer-in-residence and instructor in Russian, Grand Valley State College, Allendale, Michigan, from 1977; returned to Russia, 1989–90. Lives in Russia and Greece.

PUBLICATIONS

Fiction

Shkola dlia durakov. 1976; as *A School for Fools*, translated by Carl R. Proffer, 1977.
Mezhdu sobakoi i volkom [Between Dog and Wolf]. 1980.
Palisandriia. 1985; as *Astrophobia*, translated by Michael Henry Heim. 1989.

*

Bibliography: in *Canadian-American Slavic Studies*, 21(3–4), 1987.

Critical Studies: "A Structural Analysis of Sasha Sokolov's *School for Fools*: A Paradigmatic Novel," in *Fiction and Drama in Eastern and Southeastern Europe: Evolution and Experiment in the Postwar Period* edited by H. Birnbaum and T. Eekman, 1980; "Sasha Sokolov's *Palisandrija*," in *Slavic and East European Journal*, 30, 1986, "Sasha Sokolov's Twilight Cosmos: Themes and Motifs," in *Slavic Review*, 45, 1986, "Sasha Sokolov: The New Russian Avant-Garde," in *Critique: Studies in Modern Fiction*, 30, 1989, and "The Galoshes Manifesto: A Motif in the Novels of Sasha Sokolov," in *Oxford Slavonic Papers*, 22, 1989, all by D. Barton Johnson; "Sasha Sokolov's *Palisandriia*: History and Myth" by Olga Matich, in *Russian Review*, 45, 1986; Sokolov issue of *Canadian-American Slavic Studies*, 21(3–4), 1987; "Incarnations of the Hero Archetype in *School for Fools*" by C. Simmons, in *The Supernatural in Slavic and Baltic Literature: Essays in Honor of Victor Terras*, 1989; "Aberration or the Future: The Avant-Garde Novels of Sasha Sokolov" by Arnold McMillin, in *From Pushkin to Palisandriia: Essays on the Russian Novel in Honor of Richard Freeborn* edited by McMillin, 1990; *Their Fathers' Voice: Vassily Aksyonov, Venedikt Erofeev, Eduard Limonov, and Sasha Sokolov* by Cynthia Simmons, 1993.

*   *   *

Sasha Sokolov is widely regarded as one of the most outstanding Russian prose writers of today. Each of his novels reveals an almost completely different aspect of his talent. In the first, *Shkola dlia durakov* (*A School for Fools*), he shows most clearly the influence of Nabokov, in depicting with delicate grace the confused yet poetic world of a schizophrenic youth in a special school near Moscow. Recalling his life some two years earlier, the 20-year-old hero/narrator reveals his thoughts and aspirations via a stream of consciousness, sometimes in dialogue with his *alter ego*, sometimes reflective, and sometimes imaginative. The main themes arising from this subtle and sensitive mind's rambling discourse are: the boundaries between madness and sanity; adolescent cravings (identity, status, and sex); the selectivity of memory that characterizes madness, and related to it, the elusiveness of conventional time—the absence of conventional chronology, like the blurred differences between life and death, is both a thematic element and at the same time a fundamental structural element. Close attention is demanded of the reader wishing to disentangle every strand, but the lyrical atmosphere and the narrator's whimsical charm are always evident, and the complexity never seems forced. *A School for Fools* is a psychological and stylistic *tour de force* which may well prove to be Sokolov's masterpiece.

His second novel, *Mezhdu sobakoi i volkom* [Between Dog and Wolf], has been described by the leading Sokolov scholar D. Barton Johnson as "a quantum leap, leaving behind many . . . readers." The thin and sometimes unclear line between reality and fantasy of *A School for Fools* is here completely lost. Written in a mixture of poetry and prose, the novel is set in a godforsaken part of the Upper Volga region where crippled, deranged, and deformed people lead lives of physical squalor and spiritual emptiness. The story, which appears to retell the Oedipus legend in an obscure and grotesque form, is of adventures, jealousy, revenge, love, murder, and other extremes of behaviour. But with the boundary between life and death being eroded, causality reduced to the point of disappearance, and time erratic and unpredictable, it requires close reading and considerable detective work to unravel a text whose complexity appears to have defied all translators. An important part of the book comprises

discursive, barely literate letters to the public prosecutor by the (probably dead) hero Il'ia and 37 poems by his son (and, possibly, murderer) Iakov, mainly comprising parodies of the great early 19th-century classics, Pushkin, Lermontov, and Gogol'.

As always with Sokolov, language and style are paramount, philosophical and moral ideas minimal. In this he is an untypical Russian writer, but his mastery of native, uncorrupted, almost folkloric Central Russian vocabulary and style for the main narration, the half-literate passion of the letters, and the parodic verse all reveal a dark but powerful and original talent. Critical rapture has been modified, but the Leningrad *samizdat* journal *Chasy* acclaimed *Mezhdu sobakoi i volkom* "the best prose of 1981."

Sokolov's third novel, *Palisandriia* (*Astrophobia*), unlike its two predecessors, does have an overt plot, but its purpose seems to be to link a series of wild and colourful episodes rather than to pursue a credible or consistent story or, indeed, to develop a strong idea. Ostensibly produced in the year 2757 by a biographer-cum-editor, it consists of the picaresque memoirs of Palisandr Dal'berg, a grand-nephew of Beriia and great-grandson of Rasputin, who is heir apparent to the throne of Russia during Brezhnev's reign. His life comprises a series of erotic and political adventures, as the narrator, an oversexed hermaphrodite, bald, seven-fingered, and cross-eyed, rampages around the Kremlin, Moscow, and later Europe, indulging his necrophiliac passions (induced by rape as a child) and pursuing a successful career as a bisexual prostitute, pornographer, and Nobel prize-winning advocate of hermaphrodite rights, before collecting together the graves of all exiled Russians and returning home to assume his rightful place on the throne of Russia.

Highly referential like all Sokolov's works, *Astrophobia* is a comic, picaresque extravaganza parodying many aspects of Soviet and, particularly, émigré life and literature, especially the historical and memoir genres epitomized by Solzhenitsyn. Other parodied literary forms include science fiction, political treatises, detective novels, and, above all, erotic or pornographic novels, although in the latter category self-parody is so endemic that Sokolov may simply be joining a murky stream into which several other émigrés have dived. The style of Palisandr's memoirs is quasi-chivalric and, for all the novel's elaborate and perverted sex, virtually free of vulgarisms. In English, however, the multilayered references to Russian literature and politics presented in an absurd and grotesquely fantastic setting may provide an obstacle to full appreciation. Sokolov's stories and poems are less considerable, and it is on the three novels, in particular the first, that his high reputation rests.

—Arnold McMillin

See the essay on *A School for Fools*.

SOLZHENITSYN, Aleksandr (Isaevich)

Born: Kislovodsk, Russia, 11 December 1918. **Education:** Educated at school in Rostov-on-Don; University of Rostov, 1936–41, degree in mathematics and physics 1941; correspondence course in philology, Moscow University, 1939–41. **Military Service:** Served in the Soviet army, 1941–45: captain; decorated twice; arrested and stripped of rank, 1945. **Family:** Married 1) Natalia Alekseevna Reshetovskaia in 1940 (divorced 1950, remarried in 1957, divorced 1972), three sons; 2) Natalia Svetlova in 1973, one stepson. **Career:** Physics teacher, secondary school, Morozovsk, 1941; sentenced to eight years imprisonment for anti-Soviet agitation, 1945: in prisons in Moscow, 1945–50, and labour camp in Kazakhstan, 1950–53; released from prison, and exiled to Kok-Terek, Siberia: mathematics teacher, 1953–56; released from exile, 1956, and settled in Riazan', 1957, as teacher, then full-time writer; unable to publish from 1966; charged with treason and expelled from USSR, 1974; lived in Zurich, 1974–76, and in Cavendish, Vermont, 1976–94; reinstated to Union of Soviet Writers, 1989; Soviet citizenship restored, 1990; treason charges formally removed, 1991; returned to Russia, 1994. **Awards:** Foreign book prize (France), 1969; Nobel prize for literature, 1970; Templeton prize, 1983. D.Litt.: Harvard University, Cambridge, Massachusetts, 1978. **Member:** American Academy of Arts and Sciences, 1969; Honorary fellow, Hoover Institution on War, Revolution, and Peace, 1975.

PUBLICATIONS

Fiction

Odin den' Ivana Denisovicha. 1962; as *One Day in the Life of Ivan Denisovich,* translated by Ralph Parker, 1963; also translated by Max Hayward and Ronald Hingley, 1963; Bela Von Block, 1963; Gillon R. Aitken, 1971, revised edition, 1978; Harry T. Willetts, 1990.

Dlia pol'zy dela. 1963; as *For the Good of the Cause,* translated by David Floyd and Max Hayward, 1964.

Sluchai na stantsii Krechetovka; Matrenin dvor [An Incident at Krechetovka Station; Matriona's House]. 1963; as *We Never Make Mistakes,* translated by Paul W. Blackstock, 1963.

Etudy i krokhotnye rasskazy. 1964; as *Stories and Prose Poems,* translated by Michael Glenny, 1971; as *Prose Poems,* translated by Glenny, 1971; as *Matryona's House and Other Stories,* translated by Glenny, 1975.

V kruge pervom. 1968; restored complete edition, 1978; as *The First Circle,* translated by Thomas P. Whitney, 1968; also translated by Michael Guybon, 1968; Max Hayward, Manya Harari, and Michael Glenny, 1988.

Rakovyi korpus. 1968; as *Cancer Ward,* translated by Nicholas Bethell and David Burg, 2 vols., 1968–69; as *The Cancer Ward,* translated by Rebecca Frank, 1968.

Six Etudes, translated by James G. Walker. 1971.

Avgust chetyrnadtsatogo. 1971; as *August 1914,* translated by Michael Glenny, 1972; enlarged version, as *Krasnoe koleso 1,* 1983; revised edition, as part of *Krasnoe koleso,* 1983–86.

Krasnoe koleso: povestvovan'e v otmerennykh srokakh [The Red Wheel]:

> *Uzel 1: Avgust chetyrnadtsatogo.* 2 vols., 1983; as *The Red Wheel: A Narrative in Discrete Periods of Time,* translated by Harry T. Willetts, 1989.
> *Uzel 2: Oktiabr' shestnadtsatogo.* 2 vols., 1984.
> *Uzel 3: Mart semnadtsatogo.* 2 vols., 1986.
> *Uzel 4: Aprel' semnadtsatogo.* 1991.

Rasskazy [Stories]. 1990.

Plays

Olen' i shalashovka. 1968; as *The Love-Girl and the Innocent,* translated by Nicholas Bethell and David Burg, 1969; as *Respublika truda,* in *Sobranie sochinenii,* 1981.

Svecha na vetru. 1968; as *Candle in the Wind,* translated by Keith Armes and Arthur Hudgins, 1973; as *Svet, koroty, v tebe,* 1981.

Pir podebitelei. 1981; as *Victory Celebrations* (produced 1990), translated by Helen Rapp and Nancy Thomas, 1983.

Plenniki. 1981; as *Prisoners,* translated by Helen Rapp and Nancy Thomas, 1983.

P'esy i kinostsenarii (plays and film scripts). 1981.

Verse

Prusskie nochi: Poema napisannaia v lagere v 1950. 1974; as *Prussian Nights,* translated by Robert Conquest, 1977.

Other

Les Droits de l'écrivain. 1969.

Sobranie sochinenii [Collected Works]. 6 vols., 1969–70.

Nobelevskaia lektsiia po literature. 1972; as *Nobel Lecture,* edited and translated by F.D. Reeve, 1972; translated as *One Word of Truth,* 1972.

Arkhipelag Gulag: 1918–1956. 3 vols., 1973–76; as *The Gulag Archipelago,* translated by Thomas P. Whitney, 3 vols., 1974–78; abridged edition in one volume, edited by Edward Ericson, Jr., translated by Whitney and Harry T. Willetts, 1985.

Iz-pod glyb, with others. 1974; as *From under the Rubble,* translated by A.M. Brock and others, 1975.

Mir i nasilie [Peace and Violence]. 1974.

Pis'mo vozhdiam Sovetskogo soiuza. 1974; as *Letter to the Soviet Leaders,* translated by Hilary Sternberg, 1974.

Solzhenitsyn, the Voice of Freedom (two speeches). 1975.

Bodalsia telenok s dubom (autobiography). 1975; as *The Oak and the Calf,* translated by Harry T. Willetts, 1980.

Lenin v Tsiurikhe. 1975; as *Lenin in Zurich,* translated by Harry T. Willetts, 1976.

Detente: Prospects for Democracy and Dictatorship. 1975.

America, We Beg You to Interfere (speeches). 1975.

Amerikanskie rechi [American Discourse]. 1975.

Warning to the Western World (interview). 1976.

A World Split Apart (address), translated by Irina Alberti and Alexis Klimoff. 1978.

Sobranie sochinenii [Collected Works]. 1978–.

Alexander Solzhenitsyn Speaks to the West (speeches), edited by Alexis Klimoff, translated by Harris L. Coulter and Nataly Martin. 1978.

The Mortal Danger: How Misconceptions about Russia Imperil the West, translated by Alexis Klimoff and Michael Nicholson. 1980.

East and West (miscellany). 1980.

Issledovaniia noveishei russkoi istorii. 1980–.

Publitsistika: Stat'i i rechi (articles and speeches). 1981.

Kak nam obustroit' Rossiiu. 1990; as *Rebuilding Russia: Toward Some Formulations,* translated by Alexis Klimoff, 1991.

Les Invisibles. 1992.

Nashi pliuralisty: Otryvok iz vtorogo toma "Ocherkov literaturnoi zhizni" (Mai 1982). 1992.

Invisible Allies, translated by Alexis Klimoff and Michael Nicholson. 1995.

The Russian Question: At the End of the Twentieth Century, translated and annotated by Yermolai Solzhenitsyn. 1995.

Editor, *Russkii slovar' iazykovogo rasshireniia.* 1990.

*

Bibliography: *Alexander Solzhenitsyn: An International Bibliography of Writings by and about Him* by Donald M. Fiene, 1973.

Critical Studies: *Alexander Solzhenitsyn* by Georg Lukács, 1970; *Alexander Solzhenitsyn: The Major Novels* by Abraham Rothberg, 1971; *Alexander Solzhenitsyn* by David Burg and George Feifer, 1973; *Alexander Solzhenitsyn: Critical Essays and Documentary Materials* edited by John B. Dunlop and others, 1973, revised edition, 1975; *Alexander Solzhenitsyn* by Christopher Moody, 1973, revised edition, 1976; *Alexander Solzhenitsyn: A Collection of Critical Essays* edited by Kathryn Feuer, 1976; *Solzhenitsyn: Politics and Form* by Francis Barker, 1977; *The Politics of Solzhenitsyn* by Stephen Carter, 1977; *Alexander Solzhenitsyn* by Steven Allaback, 1978; *Solzhenitsyn and the Secret Circle* by Olga Andreyev Carlisle, 1978; *Solzhenitsyn and Dostoevsky: A Study in the Polyphonic Novel* by Vladislav Krasnov, 1980; *Solzhenitsyn, Tvardovsky and "Novy mir"* by Vladimir Lakshin, 1980; *Solzhenitsyn: The Moral Vision* by Edward E. Ericson, 1982; *Alexander Solzhenitsyn's Traditional Imagination* by James Curtis, 1984; *Solzhenitsyn* by Georges Nivat, 1984; *Alexander Solzhenitsyn: A Biography* by Michael Scammell, 1984; *Alexander Solzhenitsyn in Exile: Critical Essays and Documentary Material* edited by John B. Dunlop, Richard S. Haugh, and Michael Nicholson, 1985; *Alexander Solzhenitsyn: Myth and Reality* by A. Flegon, 1986; *Solzhenitsyn and the Modern World* by Edward E. Ericson, Jr., 1993; *The Solzhenitsyn Files: Secret Soviet Documents Reveal One Man's Fight Against the Monolith*, edited with introduction by Michael Scammell, translated by Catherine A. Fitzpatrick, 1995; *Solzhenitsyn's One Day in the Life of Ivan Denisovich* by Robert Porter, 1997; *Solzhenitsyn: A Soul in Exile* by Joseph Pearce, 1999.

* * *

Aleksandr Solzhenitsyn's literary ambitions were already manifested in 1937 when he conceived the idea of creating a long novel about the Russian Revolution and wrote several chapters of it. At that time Solzhenitsyn believed in Leninism, approving of the October Revolution. His experience in Soviet prisons and forced labour camps made him change his political orientation, and he took upon himself the messianic task of exposing the brutality, the mendacity, and the illegitimacy of the Communist rule in Russia.

Odin den' Ivana Denisovicha (*One Day in the Life of Ivan Denisovich*), called a novel in the West but really a short story, was his first published work. Written tersely and effectively, it presents a Soviet camp through the eyes of a peasant prisoner who manages to preserve his integrity in dehumanizing conditions. The story came out only because Khrushchev considered it useful for his anti-Stalin campaign. This fact facilitated the publication of *Sluchai na stantsii Krechetovka* [An Incident at Krechetovka Station], *Matrenin dvor* [Matriona's House], and *Dlia pol'zy dela* (*For the Good of the Cause*). The first story demonstrates how a young lieutenant is corrupted by the intense propaganda of vigilance designed to justify domestic repression. In the second story Solzhenitsyn draws an impressive portrait of a kind and unselfish peasant woman, a type of the righteous person that forms Russia's moral foundation. The third story, showing a callous bureaucratic disregard for ordinary Soviet citizens, lacks depth and poignancy.

Solzhenitsyn's last work to be published before his exile from the USSR was the short story "Zakhar the Pouch," concerned with the preservation of historic monuments. No Soviet publisher could be found for "Pravaia kist" ("The Right Hand"), "Kak zhal" ("What a Pity"), "The Easter Procession," and some 15 poems in prose—tiny masterpieces containing Solzhenitsyn's philosophical observations.

The novels *V kruge pervom* (*The First Circle*) and *Rakovyi korpus* (*Cancer Ward*) draw much upon Solzhenitsyn's personal experiences—the one upon his life in a special prison for scientists and the other upon his stay in a cancer clinic. In both novels Solzhenitsyn raises questions of human destiny, morality, freedom, happiness, love, death, faith, social injustice, and the political purges. Man is seen in non-materialist terms as a repository of the image of eternity who must guide himself by his own conscience. The full 96-chapter version of *The First Circle*, published for the first time in Russian in 1978, has a stronger political colouration than its 87-chapter version, which was translated into many languages.

As in all of Solzhenitsyn's fiction, the action in both novels takes place within a very brief period of time. The characters are well individualized. In transmitting different viewpoints, Solzhenitsyn relies heavily on heated dialogues, enhancing their dynamism by the use of short interrogative and exclamatory sentences and by references to the characters' gestures, eyes, tones of voice, and facial expressions. Solzhenitsyn is fond of refreshing the Russian literary language with racy folk locutions, sayings, and proverbs. The novels are rich in metaphors, notably *Cancer Ward*, in which the animal imagery takes on symbolic significance. At the end of the novels the reader is left in the dark about the ultimate fate of the characters. But this does not matter much for Solzhenitsyn. What counts is the moral behaviour of a character at the critical point in his life, where he reveals his true value.

Avgust chetyrnadtsatogo (*August 1914*) was the first published "knot" in the novel cycle *Krasnoe koleso* (*The Red Wheel*), which includes *Oktiabr' shestnadtsatogo, Mart semnadtsatogo*, and *Aprel' semnadtsatogo*, and depicts the history of the Russian Revolution by focusing on its crucial events. In *August 1914* such an event is the defeat of the Russian troops in East Prussia, which, in Solzhenitsyn's view, was the first in a series of military disasters that eventually led to the revolution. Solzhenitsyn equates the revolution with the senseless destruction of Russia, whose salvation lay in a gradual socioeconomic evolution with the emphasis on individual morality.

Outside the imaginative literature Solzhenitsyn's unique achievement is *Arkhipelag Gulag* (*The Gulag Archipelago*), a comprehensive picture of the Soviet penal system from its inception to the mid-1960s. Resorting to metaphors and irony, Solzhenitsyn tells the story of arrests, interrogations, executions, camps, and exile. He rejects the principle of survival at any price. Moral decline caused by materialism and the appeasement of the Soviet Union by the West are the dominant themes of his speeches and journalistic writings. His literary autobiography, *Bodalsia telenok s dubom* (*The Oak and the Calf*), is essential for an understanding of his personality.

—Herman Ermolaev

See the essays on *Cancer Ward* and *One Day in the Life of Ivan Denisovich*.

SOPHOCLES

Born: Colonus, near Athens, c. 496 BC. **Family:** Married Nicostrate, one son (Iophon, the tragedian); also had one son by his concubine

Theoris. **Career:** Actor in his early plays; 122 titles known (though some may be subtitles). Acquainted with the historian Herodotus *q.v.*, to whom he wrote a poem (since lost). Served as imperial treasurer, 443–42 BC; elected general twice, the first time in 440 BC when he assisted Pericles in suppressing the Samian revolt, and later with Nicias; advisory commissioner for recovery after defeat at Syracuse, 413 BC. Also served as priest of the hero Halon(?), a cult associated with that of Asclepius (for which he was honoured after his death), and founded a literary club. **Awards:** Won his first playwriting prize in 468 BC: won a total of 18 victories at the City Dionysia, and six at the Lenaea. **Died:** in late 406 BC.

PUBLICATIONS

Collections

Plays and Fragments, edited by Lewis Campbell. 2 vols., 1871; revised edition, 1969.

The Plays and Fragments (bilingual edition; with commentary; prose), translated by Richard C. Jebb. 7 vols., 1883–96; revised edition, edited by Moses Hadas, 1967.

[*Plays*], edited by A.C. Pearson. 1924; also edited by A. Dain, 1955–58, R.D. Dawe, 2 vols., 1975–79, and Hugh Lloyd-Jones and N.G. Wilson [Loeb Edition], 1990, revised edition, 2 vols., 1994; as *The Tragedies*, translated by George Adams. 2 vols., 1729; also translated by Thomas Francklin, 2 vols., 1759; R. Potter (verse), 1788; T. Dale (verse), 2 vols., 1824; E.H. Plumptre, 2 vols., 1865; Theodore A. Buckley, 1877; Lewis Campbell (verse), 1883; Robert Whitelaw (verse), 1883; George Young (verse), 1888; Edward P. Coleridge, 1893; Arthur S. Way, 1909–14; F. Storr [Loeb Edition; bilingual], 2 vols., 1912–13; E.F. Watling (verse), 1947–53; David Grene, Robert Fitzgerald, Elizabeth Wyckoff, John Moore, and Michael Jameson, in *Complete Greek Tragedies*, edited by Grene, 2 vols., 1954–57.

Sophocles, edited and translated by Hugh Lloyd-Jones. 1994–1996.

Sophocles, edited by David R. Slavitt and Palmer Bovie. 1998.

Four Dramas of Maturity, edited by Michael Ewans. 1999.

Three Dramas of Old Age: Elektra, Philoktetes, Oidipous at Kolonos with Trackers and Other Selected Fragments, edited by Michael Ewans, translated by Michael Ewans, Graham Ley and Gregory McCart. 2000.

Plays

Ajax (produced before 441 BC?). Edited by W.B. Stanford, 1963; as *Ajax*, translated by George Rotallero, with *Antigone* and *Electra*, 1550; also translated by Jackson and N. Rowe (verse), 1714; Lewis Campbell (verse), 1876; Richard C. Jebb, 1882; E.D.A. Morshead, 1895; J.H. Haydon, 1896; R.C. Trevelyan, 1919; Lennox James Morison, 1951; John Moore, in *Complete Greek Tragedies*, 1957; Theodore H. Banks, in *Four Plays*, 1966; Robert Cannon, in *Plays Two*, 1990; as *Aias*, translated by George Burges, 1849; translated by A.F. Garvie, 1998; translated by James Kerr, 2001.

Antigone (produced c. 441 BC?). Edited by Andrew Brown (includes translation), 1986; as *Antigone*, translated by George Adams, in *The Tragedies*, 1729; also translated by T.W.C. Edwards, 1824; R. Mongan, 1881; John S. Phillimore, 1902; Elizabeth Wyckoff, in *Complete Greek Tragedies*, 1954; Theodore H. Banks, in *Three*

Theban Plays, 1956; Paul Roche, in *The Oedipus Plays*, 1958; H.D.F. Kitto, in *Three Tragedies*, 1962; Richard Emil Braun, 1973; Joan V. O'Brien (with commentary), 1978; Kenneth McLeish, 1979; Robert Fagles, in *The Three Theban Plays*, 1982; Stephen Spender, 1985; Don Taylor, in *Plays One: The Theban Plays*, 1986; C.A. Trypanis, in *The Three Theban Plays*, 1986; D.W. Myatt, 1990; translated and adapted by Timberlake Wertenbaker, in *The Thebans*, 1992; as *The Riot Act*, adapted by Tom Paulin, 1985; translated by Brendan Kennelly, 1996; translated by Nicholas Rudall, 1998; translated by Declan Donnellan, 1999; translated by Paul Woodruff, 2001.

Oedipus Tyrannus (produced after 430 BC). Edited by M.L. Earle, 1900; as *Oedipus, King of Thebes*, translated by Mr. Theobald, 1715; also translated by G.S. Clarke (prose), 1790; translated as *Oedipus Tyrannus*, 1759; also translated by J. Prendergast (prose; bilingual edition), 1839; John S. Phillimore, 1902; as *King Oedipus*, translated by T.W.C Edwards, 1823; also translated by E.F. Watling, in *Plays*, vol. 1, 1947; C.A. Trypanis, in *The Three Theban Plays*, 1986; as *Oedipus the King*, translated by David Grene, in *Three Greek Tragedies*, 1942, and in *Complete Greek Tragedies*, 1954; also translated by Theodore H. Banks, in *Three Theban Plays*, 1956; Paul Roche, in *The Oedipus Plays*, 1958; H.D.F. Kitto, in *Three Tragedies*, 1962; T. Gould, 1970; Philip Vellacott, 1971; Anthony Burgess, 1972; Stephen Berg and Diskin Clay, 1978; Luci Berkowitz and Theodore F. Brunner, 1980; Robert Fagles, in *The Three Theban Plays*, 1982; Don Taylor, in *Plays One: The Theban Plays*, 1986; Christopher Stace, 1987; D.W. Myatt (with commentary), 1991; as *Oedipus Rex*, translated by Dudley Fitts and Robert Fitzgerald, 1949; also translated by Albert Cook, 1957; Stephen Spender, 1985; as *Oedipus Tyrannos*, translated and adapted by Timberlake Wertenbaker, in *The Thebans*, 1992; as *Oedipus the King*, translated by Nicholas Rudall, 2000; as *Oedipus Tyrannus*, translated by Peter Meineck and Paul Woodruff, 2000.

Trachiniae (produced c. 430–420 BC). Edited and translated by P.E. Easterling, 1982; also edited and translated by Malcolm Davies (with commentary), 1991; as *Trachiniae*, translated by George Adams, in *The Tragedies*, 1729; also translated by D. Spillan, 1831; J.A. Prout, 1904; E.S. Barlow, 1938; as *The Trachinian Maidens*, translated by Hugo Sharpley (verse), 1909; as *The Wife of Heracles*, translated by Gilbert Murray (verse), 1947; translated as *The Wife of Hercules*, 1948; also translated by Lennox James Morison, 1951; as *Women of Trachis*, translated by E.F. Watling, in *Electra and Other Plays*, 1953; also translated by Ezra Pound, 1955; Michael Jameson, in *Complete Greek Tragedies*, 1957; Theodore H. Banks, in *Four Plays*, 1966; R. Torrance, 1966; C.K. Williams and Gregory W. Dickerson, 1978; J. Michael Walton, in *Plays Two*, 1990.

Electra (produced 418–410 BC?). Edited by J.H. Kells, 1973; edited by William Merritt Sale III (with commentary), 1973, and Jan Coenraad Kamerbeek, 1974; as *Elektra* (bilingual edition), edited and translated by J. Thompson and B.J. Hayes, 1894; as *Electra*, translated by Christopher Wase (verse), 1649; also translated (prose) 1714; E.D.A. Morshead, 1895; E.F. Watling, in *Electra and Other Plays*, 1953; David Grene, in *Complete Greek Tragedies*, 1957; H.D.F. Kitto, in *Three Tragedies*, 1962; Theodore H. Banks, in *Four Plays*, 1966; Kenneth McLeish, 1979, and in *Plays Two*, 1990; translated and adapted by Ezra Pound and Rudd Fleming, edited by Richard Reid, 1989; translated by Nicholas

Rudall, 1993; translated by Frank McGuiness, 1997; translated by Anne Carson, 2001.

Philoctetes (produced 409 BC). Edited by T.B.L. Webster (with commentary), 1970; edited and translated by R.G. Ussher, 1990; as *Philoctetes*, translated by George Adams, in *The Tragedies*, 1729; also translated by T.W.C. Edwards (prose), 1829; Kathleen Freeman, 1948; E.F. Watling, in *Electra and Other Plays*, 1953; David Grene, in *Complete Greek Tragedies*, 1957; Theodore H. Banks, in *Four Plays*, 1966; R. Torrance, 1966; Douglas Brown, 1969; Kenneth McLeish, 1979, and in *Plays Two*, 1990; E. Bowen, 1991; as *The Cure at Troy*, adapted by Seanus Heaney, 1990; commentary by Jan Coenraad Kamerbeek, 1980.

Oedipus Coloneus (produced posthumously 401 BC). Edited by Richard C. Jebb, 1900; as *Oedipus Coloneus*, translated by George Adams, in *The Tragedies*, 1729; translated as *Oedipus at Colonus* (prose), 1841; also translated by Edward P. Coleridge, 1892; A.C. Auchmuty, 1894; Alexander Harvey, 1925; Robert Fitzgerald, 1941, and in *Complete Greek Tragedies*, 1954; R.C. Trevelyan, 1946; Gilbert Murray, 1948; J.T. Sheppard (verse; bilingual edition), 1949; Theodore H. Banks, in *Three Theban Plays*, 1956; Paul Roche, in *The Oedipus Plays*, 1958; Francis A. Evelyn, 1960; Lindell Williams Hubbell, 1978; Robert Fagles, in *The Three Theban Plays*, 1982; Stephen Spender, 1985; Don Taylor, in *Plays One: The Theban Plays*, 1986; C.A. Trypanis, in *The Three Theban Plays*, 1986; Christopher Stace, 1987; translated and adapted by Timberlake Wertenbaker, in *The Thebans*, 1992; translated by Nicholas Rudall, 2001; as *Oedipus Colonus*, translated by John P. Phillimore, in *Plays*, 1902; as *Oidipous at Kolonus*, translated by Charles H. Hitchcock, 1931.

Ichneutae [Trackers] (fragment of satyr play), as *Ichneutae*, translated by Richard Johnson Walker. 1919; as *The Searching Satyrs*, translated by Roger Lancelyn Green, 1946.

Plays (includes *Oedipus Tyrannus; Oedipus Colonus; Antigone*), edited and translated by John S. Phillimore. 1902.

Electra and Other Plays (includes *Philoctetes; Women of Trachis; Electra*), translated by E.F. Watling. 1953.

Three Theban Plays (includes *Oedipus the King; Oedipus at Colonus; Antigone*), translated by Theodore H. Banks. 1956.

The Oedipus Plays (includes *Oedipus the King; Oedipus at Colonus; Antigone*), translated by Paul Roche. 1958.

Three Tragedies (includes *Antigone; Oedipus the King; Electra*), translated by H.D.F. Kitto (verse). 1962.

Four Plays (includes *Ajax; Electra; Philoctetes; Women of Trachis*), translated by Theodore H. Banks. 1966.

Papyrus Fragments, edited by Richard Carden. 1974.

[Fragments] (including *Ichneutae*), edited by S. Radt. 1977.

Electra; Antigone; Philoctetes, translated by Kenneth McLeish. 1979.

The Three Theban Plays (includes *Oedipus the King; Oedipus at Colonus; Antigone*), translated by Robert Fagles. 1982.

Plays One: The Theban Plays (includes *Oedipus the King; Oedipus at Colonus; Antigone*), translated by Don Taylor. 1986.

The Three Theban Plays (includes *Antigone; Oedipus the King; Oedipus at Colonus*), translated by C.A. Trypanis. 1986.

Plays Two (includes *Electra; Philoctetes; Ajax; Women of Trachis*), edited by J. Michael Walton, translated by Walton, Kenneth McLeish, and Robert Cannon. 1990.

The Thebans (includes *Oedipus Tyrannos; Oedipus at Colonus; Antigone*), translated and adapted by Timberlake Wertenbaker. 1992.

*

Critical Studies: *An Introduction to Sophocles* by T.B.L. Webster, 1936; *Sophoclean Tragedy* by C.M. Bowra, 1944; *The Style of Sophocles* by F.R. Earp, 1944; *The Imagery of Sophocles' Antigone* by R.F. Goheen, 1951; *Religion and Drama in Oedipus at Colonus* by I.M. Linforth, 1951; *Sophocles the Dramatist* by A.J.A. Waldock, 1951; *Sophocles: A Study of Heroic Humanism* by C.H. Whitman, 1951; *Sophocles and Greek Pessimism* by J. Opstelten, translated by J. Ross, 1952; *Sophocles and Pericles* by V. Ehrenberg, 1954; *Sophocles the Playwright* by S.M. Adams, 1957; *A Study of Sophoclean Drama* by G.M. Kirkwood, 1958; *Sophocles, Dramatist and Philosopher*, 1958, and *Poiesis: Structure and Thought*, 1966, both by H.D.F. Kitto; *Shakespeare, Sophocles: Dramatic Themes and Modes* by M.H. Shackford, 1960; *Oedipus Rex: A Mirror for Greek Drama* edited by Albert Cook, 1963; *Aeschylus and Sophocles: Their Work and Influence* by J.T. Sheppard, 1963; *The Heroic Temper: Studies in Sophoclean Tragedy* by B.M.W. Knox, 1964; *Notes on Sophocles' Oedipus the King, Oedipus at Colonus and Antigone* by Robert J. Milch, 1965; *The Plays of Sophocles* by W. Walter, 1966; *Sophocles: A Collection of Critical Essays* edited by T.M. Woodard, 1966; *The Light and the Darkness: Studies in the Dramatic Poetry of Sophocles* by H. Musurillo, 1967; *Language and Thought in Sophocles* by A.A. Long, 1968; *Sophocles: A Reading* by G.H. Gellie, 1972; *Sophocles* by Siegfried Melchinger, translated by David Store, 1974; *The Madness of Antigone* by Gerald F. Else, 1976; *Sophocles* by Karl Reinhardt, translated by Hazel and David Harvey, 1979; *The Iambic Trimeter in Aeschylus and Sophocles: A Study in Metrical Form* by Seth L. Schein, 1979; *The Chorus in Sophocles' Tragedies* by R.W.B. Burton, 1980; *Sophocles: An Interpretation* by R.P. Winnington-Ingram, 1980; *Tragedy and Civilization: An Interpretation of Sophocles* by Charles Segal, 1981; *The Plays of Sophocles* by Valdis Leinieks, 1982; *The Syntax of Sophocles* by A.C. Moorhouse, 1982; *Vision and Stagecraft in Sophocles* by David Seale, 1982; *Sophocles' Oedipus and the Tale of the Theatre* by Franco Tonelli, 1983; *Sophocles* by R.G.A. Buxton, 1984; *The Lost Sophocles* by Akiko Kiso, 1984; *Antigones: The Antigone Myth in Western Literature, Art and Thought* by George Steiner, 1984; *The Sophoclean Chorus: A Study of Character and Function* by G.P. Gardiner, 1987; *Tragic Ambiguity: Anthropology, Philosophy and Sophocles' Antigone* by T.C.W. Oudemans, 1987; *Genre and Meaning in Sophocles' Ajax* by Joe Park Poe, 1987; *Sophocles: Antigone and Oedipus the King: A Companion to the Penguin Translation of Robert Fagles* by John Wilkins, 1987; *Prophesying Tragedy: Sign and Voice in Sophocles' Theban Plays* by Rebecca W. Bushnell, 1988; *Helping Friends and Harming Enemies: A Study in Sophocles and Greek Ethics* by Mary Whitlock Blundell, 1989; *Horizontal Resonance as a Principle of Composition in the Plays of Sophocles* by James Daly, 1990; *Sophoclea: Studies on the Text of Sophocles* by Hugh Lloyd-Jones and N.G. Wilson, 1990; *The Plays of Sophocles: A Companion to the University of Chicago Press Translations* by James C. Hogan, 1991; *The Thematic Sophocles* by Richard Minadeo, 1994; *Sophocles' Tragic World: Divinity, Nature, Society* by Charles Segal, 1995; *The Seal of Orestes: Self-reference and Authority in Sophocles' Electra* by Ann G. Batchelder, 1995; *The Theatre of Apollo: Divine Justice and Sophocles' Oedipus the King* by R. Drew Griffith, 1996; *Theatrical Space and Historical Place in Sophocles' Oedipus at Colonus* by Lowell Edmunds, 1996; *What Really Goes on in Sophocles' Theban Plays* by Charles B. Daniels and Sam Scully, 1996; *Sophocles: Second Thoughts* by Hugh Lloyd-Jones and Nigel G. Wilson, 1997;

The Hero and the City: An Interpretation of Sophocles' Oedipus at Colonus by Joseph P. Wilson, 1997; *Oedipus: The Meaning of a Masculine Life* by Thomas Van Nortwick, 1998; *Recapturing Sophocles' Antigone* by William Blake Tyrrell and Larry J. Bennett, 1998; *Electra and the Empty Urn: Metatheater and Role Playing in Sophocles* by Mark Ringer, 1998; *Readings on Antigone*, edited by Don Nardo, 1999; *Sacred Transgressions: A Reading of Sophocles' Antigone* by Seth Benardete, 1999; *Sophocles Revisited: Essays Presented to Sir Hugh Lloyd-Jones*, edited by Jasper Griffin, 1999; *Allegory and the Tragic Chorus in Sophocles' Oedipus at Colonus* by Roger Travis, 1999; *Telling Tragedy: Narrative Technique in Aeschylus, Sophocles and Euripides* by Barbara Goward, 1999; *Sophocles' Use of Psychological Terminology: Old and New* by Shirley Darcus Sullivan, 1999; *Exchange and the Maiden: Marriage in Sophoclean Tragedy* by Kirk Ormand, 1999; *Oedipus Tyrannus: Tragic Heroism and the Limits of Knowledge* by Charles Segal, 2001; *The Psyche on Stage: Individuation Motifs in Shakespeare and Sophocles* by Edward F. Edinger, edited by Sheila Dickman Zarrow, 2001.

* * *

Very little of Sophocles' large output survives, and only his last two plays can be dated with certainty. We are not in a position to trace stylistic or ideological development in his work. Since the seven tragedies we possess display a considerable unity of theme and style, it is possible that their composition may not have spanned a very long period.

Sophocles began his dramatic career in competition with Aeschylus. For most of his life, however, his most distinguished rival was his younger contemporary, Euripides, whom he briefly survived. Antiquity often treats these playwrights as polar opposites and modern criticism has tended to follow suit. The pious, traditional, "Homeric," conservative craftsman, Sophocles, is set against the free-thinking, materialistic, artistic innovator, Euripides. This contrast is not wholly convincing when applied to stagecraft since a strong case can be made for regarding Sophocles as at least as daring in some aspects of dramatic technique as Euripides. Even regarding ideology and belief it requires considerable qualification (in any case not many would now accept the traditional picture of Euripides as committed rationalist). Euripides allows the world of 5th-century Athens and the advanced thought of his time to intrude anachronistically into his plays, but Sophocles' restraint in this matter need not imply a lack of interest in or total alienation from the time in which he lived. It may be questioned whether either of the tragedians' apparent criticism of the Olympian gods is anything more than effective articulation of the feelings of characters reacting to exceptional and terrible sufferings, but it should be pointed out in any case that there are occasions in Sophocles when complaints about the divine dispensation are voiced which are just as strong as those to be found in the plays of Euripides. *Trachiniae* (*Women of Trachis*), a play which has seen the destruction of the great hero and benefactor of mankind, Heracles, brought about unwittingly by his long-suffering wife, ends with the chorus's bitter assertion "and nothing of what has happened is not [the work] of Zeus."

Sophoclean "heroism" has been the subject of much study in modern times and, although some critics have attacked the approach to his work by way of "the hero," it cannot be denied that the recalcitrant, isolated individual at odds with the world in which he lives is a prominent feature of the seven tragedies. Heracles, Ajax, Antigone, Electra, Philoctetes, and Oedipus are alike in that they operate on a level different from their more comfortable and less demanding fellows. Sometimes we can actually observe Sophocles changing the details of a particular heroic legend in order to enhance the isolation and suffering of the central character of the play. It happens that the treatment of the story of the return of Orestes and the avenging of Agamemnon is extant in the plays of all three tragedians. Where Sophocles is seen to differ from the other two in his *Electra*, almost all the divergences are calculated to make the heroine more isolated and her condition more pitiable. She is given a sister Chrysothemis—a replica of Antigone's timid sister Ismene—whose pusillanimity serves to make Electra even more alone and helpless. In the other versions brother and sister are reunited before the intrigue against their enemies is set in motion and in Euripides' play Electra takes an active part in it. In Sophocles' play she is excluded. Her final desolation comes when she is confronted by her disguised brother (whom she does not recognize until he reveals himself to her) carrying an urn supposed to contain the ashes of the dead Orestes.

We also happen to know how Aeschylus and Euripides treated the story of the Greeks' embassy to the great archer Philoctetes who at the beginning of their campaign against Troy had been deposited by them on the island of Lemnos after a snake-bite had rendered his presence among them physically repellent. Sophocles' reshaping of the legend in his *Philoctetes* is radical. Lemnos is transformed into a desert island and Philoctetes becomes a virtual Robinson Crusoe. Instructed by the villainous Odysseus, Philoctetes' mortal enemy, the young Neoptolemus, son of the great Achilles, deceitfully ingratiates himself with Philoctetes and wins possession of the famous bow without which it is prophesied the Greeks will never take Troy. When Philoctetes realizes he has been betrayed (the betrayal is redeemed since Neoptolemus, temperamentally and by heredity a stranger to deceit, eventually breaks with Odysseus and returns the bow) his despair and sense of isolation are all the greater because, thinking that after ten solitary years he had found a true friend, he has been cruelly deceived.

In late antiquity and during the middle ages the three Sophoclean tragedies most read and studied were *Ajax*, *Oedipus Tyrannus* (*Oedipus the King*), and *Electra*. In the modern era attention has concentrated perhaps most upon two plays, *Antigone* and *Oedipus the King*.

For many the attraction of *Antigone* is the conflict between the rebellious heroine and her uncle Creon. Antigone goes against his decree and buries her traitor brother, justifying her action by appeal to the "unwritten laws" which are not man's laws. The conflict has been seen as a kind of clash between two sorts of right, the right of the individual against the right of the state, the demands of conscience opposed to the constraints of legitimate authority. However that may be, the issue is settled decisively in favour of Antigone. Total calamity befalls Creon and his family. That does not, however, save Antigone from death. The second half of the play arouses less enthusiasm than the first as it is hard to feel moved by the downfall of a man as undistinguished as Creon.

Oedipus the King, regarded as the model tragedy by Aristotle, has certainly become the most famous of all Greek tragedies. When real events are compared to "a Greek tragedy" it is almost always this play which lurks behind the comparison. In fact there are many respects in which the play is not at all typical of its genre. The investigative nature of the plot with the hero as detective eventually uncovering his own identity and at the same time the terrible crimes he has unknowingly committed is unique. Devastating in its effect and constantly fascinating (by reason of the myth it retells) as the play is, it would be a pity if it were to eclipse all other Sophoclean tragedies, particularly the two great plays of Sophocles' final years, *Philoctetes* and *Oedipus Coloneus* (*Oedipus at Colonus*).

Oedipus at Colonus contains some of Sophocles' finest choral poetry, odes which evoke the beauties of the Athenian landscape and reflect with extreme pessimism on the afflictions of man's existence and the burdens of old age. Oedipus about to confront his final destiny, now a blind beggar attended only by his daughters, abandoned by the sons he hates, arrives in the Athenian suburb of Colonus where Apollo has told him he will end his life. Another oracle makes him the object of pursuit by warring parties. Whoever has him on his side will win the coming battle for Thebes. An attempted kidnap by the Thebans is thwarted by the Athenian king Theseus. Eventually Oedipus answers a sign from heaven and walks unaided into the sacred grove where he is to meet his end. The account of his disappearance is one of the most remarkable and enthralling passages in all Greek tragedy. Although the play brings an end for Oedipus, general harmony and resolution of conflict are not attained. One son, dismissed with a father's curse, has departed to certain death. He will kill his brother and be killed by him. The curse is not retracted, and Oedipus leaves the world implacable and irreconcilable. His faithful daughters have nothing but ill to contemplate in the future.

It is something of a paradox, though perhaps only an apparent one, that Sophocles, renowned throughout his life for piety and serenity of temperament and praised by critics for the harmony and moderation of his creations, was capable of writing such emotionally disturbing and harrowing plays. Whatever Aristotle said about the matter, it is Sophocles, not Euripides, who seems to the modern reader the "most tragic" of the three tragedians if we define "tragic" with reference to the ability to depict human suffering at its harshest and human emotions at their most deep.

—David M. Bain

See the essays on *Ajax*, *Antigone*, *Electra*, *Oedipus at Colonus*, *Oedipus the King*, *Philoctetes*, and *Women of Trachis*.

SOR JUANA INÉS DE LA CRUZ

See JUANA INÉS DE LA CRUZ, Sor

STAËL, Madame de

Born: Anne-Louise-Germaine Necker in Paris, France, 22 April 1766. **Family:** Married 1) Baron Eric-Magnus de Staël von Holstein in 1786 (separated 1798), two sons and one daughter; 2) John Rocca in 1816, one son; two sons by Count Louis de Narbonne, with whom she had an affair, 1788–93. **Career:** Set up her own salon which became a powerful political and intellectual centre; emigrated to England during the revolution, 1793; settled at Coppet on Lake Geneva; visited Paris, 1795, and 1797; repeatedly exiled by Napoleon; travelled widely to Italy, Austria, Germany, Russia, Sweden and England, with various travelling companions including August W. Schlegel, Benjamin Constant, and Simonde de Sismondi; returned to

Paris after Napoleon's defeat, 1814. Major precursor of Romanticism and of modern criticism. **Died:** 14 July 1817.

PUBLICATIONS

Collections

Oeuvres complètes, edited by Auguste-Louis de Staël. 17 vols., 1820–21.
Oeuvres inédites. 3 vols., 1830–36.
Oeuvres complètes. 2 vols., 1836.
Oeuvres. 1838.
Oeuvres complètes. 3 vols., 1861.
L'Oeuvre imprimée de Mme Germaine de Staël, edited by F.-C. Lonchamp. 1949.
An Extraordinary Woman: Selected Writings of Germaine de Staël, translated by Vivian Folkenflik. 1987.

Fiction

Jane Grey. 1790.
Mirza (stories). 1795.
Delphine. 4 vols., 1802; edited by Claudine Hermann, 1981; as *Delphine*, translated anonymously, 5 vols., 1803; translated with introduction by Avriel H. Goldberger, 1995.
Corinne; ou, L'Italie. 3 vols., 1807; edited by Claudine Hermann, 1979, and Simone Balayé, 1966; as *Corinne; or, Italy*, translated by Isabel Hill, 1883; translated by Avriel H. Goldberger, 1987; also translated by John Isbell, 1998.
Zulma (stories). 1794.

Plays

Sophie; ou, Les Sentiments secrets. 1790.

Other

Lettres sur les ouvrages et le caractère de Jean-Jacques Rousseau. 1788; revised edition, 1789.
Réflexions sur le procès de la reine. 1793.
Recueil de morceaux détachés. 1795.
Réflexions sur la paix. 1795; edited by C. Cordié, 1945.
De l'influence des passions sur le bonheur des individus et des nations. 1796; edited by Tournier, 1979; as *A Treatise on the Influence of the Passions upon the Happiness of Individuals and Nations*, translated anonymously, 1798.
Essai sur les fictions. 1796; edited by Tournier, 1979.
De la littérature considérée dans ses rapports avec les institutions sociales. 2 vols., 1800; edited by Paul van Tieghem, 1959; as *A Treatise on Ancient and Modern Literature*, translated anonymously, 1803; as *The Influence of Literature upon Society*, translated anonymously, 1812.
Du caractère de M. Necker et de sa vie privée. 1804.
Mémoires sur la vie privée de mon père. 1804.
De l'Allemagne. 3 vols., 1813; edited by H.W. Eve, 1906, Jean de Pange, 5 vols., 1958–60, and by Simone Balayé, 2 vols., 1968.
Réflexions sur le suicide. 1813; as *Reflections on Suicide*, translated anonymously, 1813.

Considerations sur la Révolution française. 3 vols., 1818; edited by Jacques Godechot, 1983.

Dix années d'exil. 1821; edited by Simone Balayé, 1966, and Margaret Crosland, 1968; as *Ten Years of Exile*, translated by Doris Beik, 1972; also translated by Avriel H. Goldberger, 2000.

Essais dramatiques. 1821.

Lettres inédites de Mme. de Staël à Henri Meister. 1903.

Seize lettres inédites. 1913.

Lettres de Mme. de Staël à Benjamin Constant, edited by Mme. de Nolde. 1928.

Lettres inédites à Juste Constant de Rebecque 1795–1812. 1937.

Lettres inédites à Madame Odier. 1940.

Benjamin Constant et Mme. de Staël: Lettres à un ami. 1949.

Lettres de Mme. de Staël à Juliette Récamier, edited by E. Beau de Loménie. 1952.

Lettres de Mme. de Staël à Ribbing, edited by Simone Balayé. 1960.

Lettres inédites à Louis de Narbonne, edited by Béatrice Jasinski. 1960.

Madame de Staël et le duc de Wellington: correspondance inédite 1815–1817, edited by Victor de Pange. 1962; as *The Unpublished Correspondence of Madame de Staël and the Duke of Wellington,* translated by Harold Kurtz, 1965.

Correspondance générale, edited by Béatrice Jasinski. 7 vols., 1962–78.

Madame de Staël on Politics, Literature, and National Character, translated by Morroe Berger. 1964.

De Staël-Du Pont Letters, edited and translated by James F. Marshall. 1968.

Choix de lettres de Madame de Staël 1766–1817, edited by Georges Solovieff. 1970.

Correspondance inédite 1786–1817, edited by Robert de Luppé. 1970.

Des circonstances actuelles qui peuvent terminer la révolution et des principes qui doivent fonder la république en France, edited by Lucia Omacini. 1979.

Lettres de Mme. de Staël à Pedro de Souza, edited by Béatrix d'Andlau. 1979.

Le plus beau de toutes les fêtes (correspondence with Elizabeth Harvey, Duchess of Devonshire), edited by Victor de Pange. 1980.

Correspondances Suédoises de Germaine de Staël (1812–1816), edited by Norman King. 1988.

Selected Correspondence, translated and edited by Kathleen Jameson-Cemper. 2000.

*

Bibliography: *Bibliographie des oeuvres de Madame de Staël* by P. Schazmann, 1938; *L'Oeuvre imprimé de Mme de Staël* by F.C. Lonchamp, 1949.

Critical Studies: *The Passionate Exiles: Madame de Staël and Madame Récamier* by Maurice Levaillant, translated by Malcolm Barnes, 1958; *Mistress to an Age: A Life of Madame de Staël* by J. Christopher Herold, 1958; *Madame de Staël and Freedom Today* by Roberta J. Forsberg and H. C. Nixon, 1963; *Germaine: A Portrait of Madame de Staël* by Wayne Andrews, 1964; *Madame de Staël* by Helen B. Posgate, 1968; *Madame de Staël et la Révolution française: Politique, philosophie, littérature* by G.E. Gwynne, 1969; *Les Idées littéraires de Madame de Staël et l'héritage des Lumiéres* by Robert de Luppé, 1969; *La Jeunesse Mme. de Staël* by Béatrix d'Andlau, 1970; *Les Carnets de voyage de Madame de Staël contribution à la*

genèse des ses oeuvres, 1971, and *Madame de Staël: Lumières et liberté,* 1979, both edited by Simone Balayé; *Madame de Staël et Henri Heine: Les Deux Allemagnes* by Eve Sourain, 1974; *Madame de Staël, Novelist: The Emergence of the Artist as Woman* by Madelyn Gutwirth, 1978; *Benjamin Constant, Madame de Staël et le Groupe de Coppet* edited by Étienne Hofmann, 1980; *Mme. de Staël* by Ghislain de Diesbach, 1983; *Madame de Staël* (in English) by Renée Winegarten, 1985; *The Noise of Words and the Voice of Conscience: The Literary Existence of Germanine de Staël* by Charlotte Hogsett, 1987; *Fictions féminines: Madame de Staël et les voix de la Sibylle* by Marie-Claire Vallois, 1987; *Germaine de Staël: Crossing the Borders* edited by Madelyn Gutwirth, Avriel Goldberger, and Karyna Szumerlo, 1991; *The Birth of European Romanticism: Truth and Propaganda in Staël's De l'Allemagne, 1810–1813* by John Claiborne Isbell, 1994; *Germaine de Staël Revisited* by Gretchen Rous Besser, 1994; *Madame de Staël et les Français* by Simone Balayé, 1996; *Lord Byron and Madame de Staël: Born for Opposition* by Joanne Wilkes, 1999; *The Novel's Seductions: Staël's Corinne in Critical Inquiry,* edited by Karyna Szmurlo, 1999; *(Un)Manly Citizens: Jean-Jacques Rousseau's and Germaine de Staël's Subversive Women* by Lori Jo Marso, 1999; *Madame de Staël: Delphine and Corinne* by Angelica Gooden, 2000.

*   *   *

In her own lifetime Madame Germaine de Staël was a celebrated, if controversial, figure on the European political, literary, and cultural scene thanks to her widely read and influential theoretical works, her two popular novels, and her tireless political activism and powerful, high-profile personality. Her repute could not be completely eclipsed after her death because of the pivotal role she played in the transition from Enlightenment to Romanticism. However, a continued prurient curiosity (more often than not tinged by chauvinistic hostility) about the unconventional aspects of her personal (especially sexual) life, precipitated a marked decline in her literary stature, and her works remained largely unread until the remarkable resurgence of interest in her ideas and writings fostered by 20th-century feminist critics.

A spiritual "daughter" of the Enlightenment, she remained a loyal follower of the *philosophes* and especially of Rousseau, to whom she devoted her first published essay *Lettres sur les ouvrages et le caractère de Jean-Jacques Rousseau* [Letters on the Writings and Character of Jean-Jacques Rousseau]. She warmly welcomed the Revolution, but as a passionate libertarian with a special fondness for the English language, the English constitutional monarch, and English social institutions, she recoiled before the revolutionary excesses and endeavoured to promote reasonableness, moderation, and humaneness in her *Réflexions sur le procès de la reine* [Reflections on the Trial of the Queen] and *Réflexions sur la paix* [Reflections on Peace].

Generally acknowledged as the "mother" of Romanticism, Staël set forth a new aesthetic of enthusiasm and unrestricted emotional expression in her essay *De l'influence des passions sur le bonheur des individus et des nations* (*A Treatise on the Influence of the Passions upon the Happiness of Individuals and Nations*). A staunch believer in the notion of social betterment and progress and in the perfectability of humankind, she is keenly concerned with the interaction of culture and political institutions, and *De la littérature considérée dans ses rapports avec les institutions sociales* (*The Influence of Literature upon Society*) brilliantly demonstrates that sociology and literature are inextricably intertwined. She also laid down the basic elements of comparative cultural studies in her doctrine of the classical Mediterranean and Southern tradition that is in harmony with a serene, sunny, natural environment, versus the romantic Northern tradition that seeks to escape from the hostile and forbidding surroundings in the realm of the imagination and the ineffable, mysterious sublime. The immensely influential book in which she compared French and German cultures, *De l'Allemagne* [On Germany], Napoleon ordered to be destroyed.

Staël was, of course, deeply and personally involved in what has been characterized as the "woman question," especially with the difficult condition of womanhood in general, and the tragic destiny of the superior woman in particular. She was convinced that all attempts on the part of woman to escape from the narrow sphere in which both nature and society have imprisoned her are doomed to failure in contemporary society. Those exceptional women who, like herself, heedlessly defy this law of nature and rule of society sacrifice all chances of achieving personal happiness. Her hope was that future enlightened legislators would give more serious attention to the education of women and would enact laws designed to protect and guarantee their rightful place in society.

Staël's two autobiographically-inspired novels, *Delphine* and *Corinne*, specifically deal with this question in compelling terms, for they show how women's legitimate aspirations to personal happiness and artistic creativity are cruelly thwarted by the oppressive forces of the hypocritical and traditionalistic society. *Corinne*, in particular, presents an eloquent and moving plea on behalf of the woman of genius, and as such it became a paradigmatic model and a source of inspiration, directly or indirectly, for such notable women as Jane Austen, Elizabeth Barrett Browning, George Sand, Harriet Beecher, Margaret Fuller, and Charlotte Brontë.

—Gita May

STAMPA, Gaspara

Born: Padua, Venetian Republic, c. 1524. After death of her father, moved with family to Venice, 1535. **Education:** Studied classical languages, singing, and music. **Career:** Probably lived the life of a "cortigiana onesta" (kept mistress or society courtesan), and held a prominent place in the literary and musical life of Venice: member (under the name Anassilla) of the salon Academy of the Pellegrini; lived under the protection of Count Collaltino di Collalto, 1549–51 (who inspired all her verse), and had later relationships with Bartolomeo Zen and Giovanni Andrea Viscolo. **Died:** 1554.

PUBLICATIONS

Verse

Rime, edited by Cassandra Stampa. 1554; revised edition, 1738; also edited by Pia Mestica Chiapetti, 1877; as *Rime di Gaspara Stampa e di Veronica Franco*, edited by Abdelkader Salza, 1913; Gustavo Rodolfo Ceriello, 1954; Maria Bellonci, 1976; selections translated by William Reynes, in *Gaspara Stampa*, by Eugene Benson, 1881; selections also in: *Gaspara Stampa*, translated by Sally Purcell, 1984, *Three Women Poets: Renaissance and Baroque*,

edited by Frank J. Warnke, 1986, and *Women Writers of the Renaissance and Reformation*, edited by Katharina M. Wilson, 1987.

Selected Poems, edited and translated by Laura Anna Stortoni and Mary Prentice Lillie. 1994.

*

Critical Studies: *Due poetesse italiane nel secolo decimosesto* by Luisa Caprile, 1902; *Gaspara Stampa* by Eugenio Donadoni, 1919; *Gaspara Stampa, donna e poetessa* by Giovanni Cesareo, 1920; "Gaspara Stampa: The Ambiguities of Martyrdom" by Justine Vitiello, in *Modern Language Notes*, 90, 1975; *Gaspara Stampa*, 1982, and "Male Canon/Female Poet: The Petrarchism of Gaspara Stampa," in *Interpreting the Italian Renaissance: Literary Perspectives* edited by Antonio Toscana, 1991, both by Fiora Bassanese; "Gaspara Stampa: Aphrodite's Priestess, Love's Martyr" by Frank Warnke, in *Women Writers of the Renaissance and Reformation* edited by Katharina M. Wilson, 1987; *Love's Remedies: Recantation and Renaissance Lyric Poetry* by Patricia Berrahou Phillippy, 1995.

* * *

Frank Warnke has described Gaspara Stampa as "the greatest woman poet of the Italian Renaissance," and certainly the power of her passionate love poetry to her unfaithful lover Collaltino has been cited by generations of later poets as an example of the poetic heights that a combination of pain and talent can reach. The strength of the voice that claimed:

> If, abject and vile woman though
> I be, I still carry such a noble flame,
> why should I not give just a tiny part
> of it to the world, with humour and with style?

reflects an authenticity that transcends the skilful crafting of her Petrarchan inspired style. That authenticity is combined with a strong assertion of independence, despite the subject matter of much of her poetry which focuses on the pain she feels at being neglected by her lover, and a sense of self-deprecatory humour. So in her "Chi vuol conoscer, donne, il mio signore," she describes her lover's physical appearance, his golden hair and gentle bearing in classic, conventional terms, but then adds that although perfect in all things "he is, (alas, for me!) somewhat despicable in love."

Stampa's independence, her public acknowledgement in verse of an intensely sexual passion and her fame as writer and singer in the Venetian salons of the 16th century gave cause for concern to critics in earlier periods which could not reconcile such open behaviour with models of feminine decency. There has been a great deal of debate about whether Stampa was a courtesan (*cortigiana*) and, if so, precisely what that meant, with some critics offering a compromise suggestion that regards her as an "honest courtesan." It seems fruitless to continue this kind of outmoded debate, but it is worth noting because of the impact the discussion of her morals has had on editions and on critical studies of her works. Moreover, fictionalized versions of Stampa's life inspired both plays and novels in the post-Romantic period, when her work was rediscovered by a new generation of readers who admired poetry that expressed extreme states of emotion.

Stampa was heavily influenced by Petrarch, as were all the poets of her day, but she used Petrarchan lyric conventions in her own way. Her poems tell the story of her love for Collaltino, the years of requited love, his absences, her pain at being apart, the gradual disintegration of the relationship through jealousy, neglect, and separation, the possibility of new love mitigated by memories of the past (though in fact she did fall in love again, and versions of her life story which see her as perpetually grieving for a lost love belong to the realm of fiction). Just as Vittoria Colonna used the loss of her husband as an inspirational source for her writing, and Petrarch used his love for the unattainable Laura as his inspiration, so Stampa used her unfaithful lover as the central focus for her poetry. But whereas Petrarch's verse expresses his resignation and acceptance of love's suffering as a means of attaining a higher goal in the world to come, Stampa's poetry is firmly in the present. "idatemi il cor, empio tiranno" ("Give me back my heart, unfeeling tyrant") she demands in one poem, asking herself in another poem: "Fool, what am I saying? Why go like this?" She uses rhetorical questions, direct statements, and assertions frequently, stylistic devices that give her poems a sense of immediacy, as does her playing with tenses and use of repetition:

> I burned, I wept, I sang; I weep, I burn and sing
> I shall weep, burn, sing forever
>
> (until Death, Time or Fortune wear away
> the poetry, fire and weeping in my mind and eyes and heart.)

The imagery of fire runs throughout Stampa's poetry. "Amor m'ha fatto tal ch'io vivo in foco" ("Love has made me so that I live in fire") runs one of her most famous lines, and she rejoices in the imagery of burning, seeing herself as a phoenix, the mythical creature that is consumed and regenerated by fire. That a woman of her period should choose such masculine imagery as fire is striking in itself, and that she should choose to assert herself by actively desiring fire is a further example of her independent spirit and individual voice. She writes about earthly passions, and for her love and desire are not stepping stones to higher things, but rather reminders of the power of physicality. "Down here, the infinite is given to me / as long as I can know my lover's mine," she writes, in a poem that proclaims her refusal to envy heavenly angels. Stampa used the metaphysical poetry of the Petrarchan tradition along with the idealism of neoplatonism, but transformed them into texts that surprise us with their lack of self-restraint and direct appeal to the senses. One of her typical poems proclaims the savagery of love and exults in the sado-masochistic response to that savagery:

> Tear me to pieces, Love, torment me,
> Take away the one I most want by my side,
> Take away too with him, cruel and disloyal
> All my peace, and all my satisfaction,
> Make me melancholy and joyful all at once
> Give me deaths in a single blow,
> Make me an unhappy example to my sex,
> And yet I don't regret I chose to follow you.

This poem exemplifies Stampa's style: assertive, uninhibited and yet carefully crafted, an excellent example of Renaissance wit written from a female point of view. This aspect of her writing is the feature that is most striking to modern readers: despite her anguish she does not give up, she does not write out of resignation but out of a sense of continuous struggle. She retains a sense of humour even when writing about her weariness and endless weeping.

During her lifetime, only three of her sonnets were published. After her premature death, her sister Cassandra edited her poems, which appeared in 1554. The poems were not a success, and Stampa's work effectively disappeared from view until a descendant of her unfaithful lover reissued them in 1738. The timing of that publication, fuelled by the sentimental account of her life offered by the editor, revived interest in her writing, and subsequent fascination with her life and works made her a heroine of Italian Romanticism in the 19th century. Today, feminist scholarship provides an alternative way of reading her works, enabling us to hear her strong, clear voice unhindered by prejudice.

—Susan Bassnett

STENDHAL

Pseudonym for Marie-Henri Beyle. **Born:** Grenoble, France, 23 January 1783. **Education:** Educated by tutors at home, and at École Centrale, Grenoble, 1796–99. **Military Service:** Served as a clerk in the war office, then in French Army in Italy, 1800: 2nd lieutenant of dragoons; invalided to Paris, 1801; resigned, 1802. **Career:** Lived in Paris, 1802–06; civil servant: provisional deputy, deputy, and intendant to Commissariat of Wars at Brunswick, Vienna, and Hungary, 1806–09; commissioner for Council of State and Inspector of Crown Furnishings and Buildings, Paris, 1810; courier to Napoleon in Russia, 1812–13; administrator in Silesia and Dauphiné; left government service, 1814; lived in Milan, 1814–21, and in Paris, doing much freelance journalism for French and English papers, 1821–30; French Consul, Trieste, 1830–31, and Civitavecchia, from 1831; in Paris on extended leave, 1836–39, and on sick leave from 1841. **Died:** 23 March 1842.

PUBLICATIONS

Collections

Oeuvres completes (incomplete). 34 vols., 1914–40.
Oeuvres complètes. 79 vols., 1927–37.
[Works] (Pléiade edition), edited by Henri Martineau and Victor Del Litto. 6 vols., 1952–68.
Oeuvres complètes, edited by Victor Del Litto and Ernest Abravanel. 18 vols., 1960–62; new edition, 50 vols., 1972–74.
Oeuvres intimes, edited by Victor Del Litto. 2 vols., 1981–82.

Fiction

Armance; ou, Quelques Scènes d'un salon de Paris en 1827. 1827; as *Armance*, translated by C.K. Scott Moncrieff, 1928; also translated by Gilbert and Suzanne Sale, 1960.
Le Rouge et le noir: Chronique du XIXe siècle. 1830; as *Red and Black*, translated by E.P. Robins, 1898; also translated by Charles

Tergie, 1900; as *The Red and the Black*, translated by Horace B. Samuel, 1913; also translated by C.K. Scott Moncrieff, 1926, Joan Charles, 1949(?), Robert M. Adams, 1969, Lloyd C. Parks, 1970, and Catherine Slater, 1991; as *Scarlet and Black*, translated by Scott Moncrieff, 1927; also translated by Margaret R.B. Shaw, 1953.

La Chartreuse de Parme. 1839; as *La Chartreuse de Parme*, translated by E.P. Robins, 1895; as *The Chartreuse of Parma*, translated by Lady Mary Loyd, 1901, revised by Robert Cantwell, 1955; as *The Charterhouse of Parma*, translated by C.K. Scott Moncrieff, 1925; also translated by Margaret R.B. Shaw, 1958; Lowell Bair, 1960; Margaret Mauldon, 1997; Richard Howard, 1999.

L'Abbesse de Castro (includes *Vittoria Accoramboni* and *Les Cenci*). 1839; as *The Abbess of Castro, and Other Tales* (includes *The Duchess of Palliano* and *Vanina Vanini*), translated by C.K. Scott Moncrieff, 1926, enlarged edition, as *The Shorter Novels of Stendhal* (includes *Armance*), translated by Scott Moncrieff, 1946.

Nouvelles inédites. 1855.

Chroniques italiennes. 1855; edited by Michel Mohrt, 1964, Roland Beyer, 1964, and Robert André, 1986.

Lucien Leuwen. In *Nouvelles inédites*, 1855; published separately, 1894; edited by Claude Roy, 1960; as *Lucien Leuwen: The Green Huntsman* [and] *The Telegraph*, translated by Louise Varèse, 2 vols., 1950; also translated by H.L.R. Edwards, 2 vols., 1951, revised by Robin Buss, 1991.

Lamiel, edited by Casimir Stryienski. 1889, and by Victor Del Litto, 1971; as *Lamiel*, translated by Jacques Le Clerq, 1929; also translated by T.W. Earp, 1951.

Féder. In *Romans et nouvelles*, 1928; as *Féder; or, The Moneyed Husband*, translated by H.L.R. Edwards, 1960.

Le Rose et le vert; Mina de Vanghel. In *Romans et nouvelles*, 1928; in *Le Rose et le vert, Mina de Vanghel, et autres nouvelles*, 1982; as *The Pink and the Green; Mina de Vanghel*, translated by Richard Howard, 1988.

Romans et nouvelles, edited by Henri Martineau. 2 vols., 1928.

Le Rose et le vert, Mina de Vanghel, et autres nouvelles, edited by Victor Del Litto. 1982.

Other

Lettres écrites de Vienne . . . sur . . . Haydn, . . . Mozart et . . . Métastase. 1814; as *Vies de Haydn, de Mozart, et de Métastase*, 1817; as *The Life of Haydn; The Life of Mozart; Observations on Metastasio*, translated by L.A.C. Bombet, 1817; as *The Lives of Haydn and Mozart*, translated by Bombet, 1818.

Histoire de la peinture en Italie. 1817.

Rome, Naples, et Florence en 1817. 1817, revised edition, 1826; as *Rome, Naples, and Florence*, 1818; also translated by Richard Coe, 1959.

De l'amour. 1822; as *On Love*, translated by Philip Sidney Woolf and Cecil N. Sidney Woolf, 1914; also translated by Vyvyan Beresford Holland, 1926; as *Love*, translated by Gilbert and Suzanne Sale, 1957.

Racine et Shakespeare. 2 vols., 1823–25; as *Racine and Shakespeare*, translated by Guy Daniels, 1962.

La Vie de Rossini. 1823; as *The Memoirs of Rossini*, 1824; as *Life of Rossini*, translated by Richard Coe, 1970.

Promenades dans Rome. 1829; as *A Roman Journal*, edited and translated by Haakon Chevalier, 1957.

Mémoires d'un touriste. 2 vols., 1838, revised and enlarged edition, 1854; part as *Voyage dans le midi de la France*, in *Oeuvres complètes*, 1929; selection, as *Memoirs of a Tourist*, translated by Allan Seager, 1962; as *Travels in the South of France*, translated by Elisabeth Abbott, 1970.

Vie de Napoléon. In *Oeuvres complètes*, 1876; published separately, edited by Michel Wassiltchikov, 1969; translated as *A Life of Napoleon*, 1956.

Vie de Henry Brulard, edited by Casimir Stryienski. 1890, revised edition, edited by Henry Debraye, 2 vols., 1913; also edited by Henri Martineau, 1953, and Beatrice Didier, 1978; as *The Life of Henry Brulard*, translated by Catherine Alison Phillips, 1925; also translated by Jean Stewart and B.C.J.G. Knight, 1958; John Sturrock, 1995.

Souvenirs d'égotisme, edited by Casimir Stryienski. 1892; also edited by Henri Martineau, 1927; as *Memoirs of an Egotist*, translated by T.W. Earp, 1949; also translated by David Ellis, 1975; as *Memoirs of Egotism*, translated by Hannah and Matthew Josephson, 1949.

Journal, edited by Henry Debraye and Louis Royer. 5 vols., 1923–34; also edited by Henri Martineau, 5 vols., 1937; selection, as *The Private Diaries of Stendhal*, edited and translated by Robert Sage, 1954; selection, as *The Private Journals of Stendhal*, edited and translated by Francis Carmody, 1954.

To the Happy Few (selected letters), edited by Emmanuel Boudot-Lamotte and translated by Norman Cameron. 1952.

En marge des manuscrits de Stendhal, edited by Victor Del Litto. 1955.

Feuillets inédits (journal of 1837–38), edited by Marcel A. Ruff. 1957.

Selected Journalism from the English Reviews, edited by Geoffrey Strickland. 1959.

Correspondance (3 vols. of Pléiade edition), edited by Henri Martineau and Victor Del Litto. 3 vols., 1962–68.

Du Romantisme dans les arts, edited by Henri Martineau. 1966.

Stendhal and the Arts, edited by David Wakefield. 1973.

Voyages en Italie, edited by Victor Del Litto. 1973.

Chroniques pour l'Angleterre: Contributions à la presse britannique (bilingual edition), edited by K.G. McWatters, translated (into French) by R. Dénier. 2 vols., 1980–82.

Voyages en France, edited by Victor Del Litto. 1992.

*

Bibliography: *Bibliographie stendhalienne 1938–1946* by Victor Del Litto, 1948 (and supplements).

Critical Studies: *Stendhal: Notes on a Novelist* by Robert Martin Adams, 1959; *Stendhal: A Collection of Critical Essays* edited by Victor Brombert, 1962, and *Stendhal: Fiction and the Themes of Freedom* by Brombert, 1968; *Stendhal: A Study of His Novels* by F.W.J. Hemmings, 1964; *The Masked Citadel: The Significance of the Title of Stendhal's Chartreuse de Parme*, 1968, and *The Romantic Prison*, 1978, both by Herbert Morris; *Stendhal* by Marcel M. Gutwirth, 1971; *Stendhal: The Background of the Novels* by Margaret G. Tillett, 1971; *Stendhal* by Michael Wood, 1971; *The Unhappy Few: A Psychological Study of the Novels of Stendhal* by Gilbert D. Chaitin, 1972; *Stendhal: Le Rouge et le Noir* by John Mitchell, 1973; *Stendhal* by Joanna Richardson, 1974; *The Education of a Novelist* by Geoffrey Strickland, 1974; *Stendhal and England* by Keith Gordon

McWatters, 1976; *Stendhal and the Age of Napoleon* by Gita May, 1977; *Stendhal: A Biography* by Robert Alter, 1979; *Speaking of Stendhal* by Storm Jameson, 1979; *La Poétique de Stendhal*, 1983, and *Le Héros fourbe chez Stendhal*, 1987, both by Michel Crouzet; *Stendhal: La Chartreuse de Parme* by Alison Finch, 1983; *The Narrative Matrix: Stendhal's Le Rouge et le noir* by Carol A. Mossman, 1984; *Stendhal and Romantic Esthetics* by Emile Talbot, 1985; *Stendhal's Paper Mirror: Patterns of Self-Consciousness in His Novels* by James T. Day, 1987; *The Stendhal Bicentennial Papers* edited by Avriel H. Goldberger, 1987; *Reading Realism in Stendhal* by Ann Jefferson, 1988; *Stendhal's Violin: A Novelist and His Reader* by Roger Pearson, 1988; *Stendhal: The Red and the Black* by Stirling Haig, 1989; *Stendhal*, edited with introduction by Harold Bloom, 1989; *Stendhal Revisited* by Emile J. Talbot, 1993; *Stendhal* (biography) by Jonathan Keates, 1994; *Metamorphoses of Passion and the Heroic in French Literature: Corneille, Stendhal, Claudel* by Moya Longstaffe, 1999; *Function of Gift Exchange in Stendhal and Balzac* by Doreen Thesen, 2000.

* * *

Stendhal belongs to that small and privileged group of writers whose modernity has grown with the passage of time. An eminently self-conscious and self-critical author, he nevertheless did not consider art above and apart from the business of living. He expected and demanded a relation of art to life.

Stendhal's position among French Romantics is crucial by virtue of several factors. His life span embraced an era marked by swift and momentous changes, ranging from the French Revolution through the Empire, Bourbon Restoration, and July Monarchy. He maintained strong intellectual, ideological, and aesthetic ties with the 18th century, especially the Enlightenment and the French Revolution, which he considered the logical extension of the principles and ideals set forth by the *philosophes*. This commitment to the political and intellectual ideals of the 18th century is attested repeatedly by Stendhal's steadfast devotion to libertarian principles and by the hostility and scorn he heaped upon Restoration and Orleanist France.

Non-conformist by temperamental inclination as well as by ideological conviction (for he remained deeply convinced that marginality is the fate of any writer or artist sincerely committed to his calling), Stendhal nevertheless had strong opinions that he was always prepared to defend at great personal risk. Unlike Flaubert, he accepted eagerly the challenges and even absurdities of life and did not regard his calling as a writer as a sufficient reason for retiring to the isolation of an ivory tower. Yet, even in the most heated moments of personal involvement, enthusiasm, or physical danger, something always held him back from total commitment.

Intellectual clear-sightedness, a sense of humour and of the grotesque, a healthy scepticism in the 18th-century tradition which his contemporaries only too willingly identified with outright cynicism prevented Stendhal from becoming the docile follower of a cause, no matter how compelling. Unquestioning admiration was not his forte. In this respect, as in so many others, he remains the supreme individualist. Hence his sense of alienation and growing estrangement from his contemporaries.

Nothing was more alien to Stendhal's temperament than a fixed, rigid course and set ways. The variegated and colourful pattern of his own life and career amply testify to his openness of mind and heart: the precociously rebellious and lonely boy of Grenoble, the bookish and solitary young philosopher, the enthusiastic yet solitary dragoon of Milan, the passionate and quixotic lover, the fearless soldier and ambitious administrator closely involved in Napoleon's campaigns across Europe, the avid theatre-goer and witty conversationalist, the incisive and provocative critic, the tirelessly inquisitive traveller and tourist, and, finally, the disillusioned yet tenderhearted diplomat belatedly and reluctantly turned novelist.

Stendhal's apprenticeship as a novelist was a long and roundabout one, and he came to it almost by accident and afterthought. Yet having at last come to the realization that writing fiction was his true calling, he turned to it with immense zest and enthusiasm. But because he would frequently use actual events and cases, as in *Le Rouge et le noir* (*Scarlet and Black*), or historical sources, as in the *La Chartreuse de Parme* (*The Charterhouse of Parma*), he has been accused of lacking the powers of invention and imagination.

If it is true that Stendhal is not, like Balzac, the creator of a host of fictional characters, and that his main protagonists either reflect aspects of himself or of the men and women who had made a strong impact upon him, his originality and creativity lie elsewhere. Always fascinated with cases exemplifying the conflict between the energetic, strong-willed individual and social institutions, Stendhal came to the realization that contemporary France, as well as Italian folk history, mores, and legends, could provide him with stunning insights into human behaviour under unusual stress. If Julien Sorel, the hero of *Scarlet and Black*, is, like his real-life counterpart, a social misfit endowed with a lively intelligence but soon embittered by life, he embodies, more than anything else, the conflict between passionate impulsiveness and opportunistic hypocrisy.

Fabrice del Dongo, the hero of *The Charterhouse of Parma*, is much more open to the tender, gentle feelings of life than the sombre, ambitious, and calculating Julien Sorel. The Italian background confers on *The Charterhouse of Parma* a particularly poetic and lyrical aura, and the presence of mountains, lakes, and high towers adds special colour to the narrative. But these external features are not merely meant to introduce a note of exoticism for its own sake; they are the symbols of Stendhal's inner ideal landscape. The prison theme, present in both novels, is also an integral part of this symbolic language of sacrifice and exaltation through suffering and love.

If Fabrice is Stendhal's fictional projection of his young, idealistic self, Count Mosca, minister and man of experience and of the world, is Fabrice's dramatic counterpart. He might well be, as has been suggested, a recreation of Stendhal, the mature, disillusioned, yet still generous man.

In *Scarlet and Black*, two dissimilar yet complementary feminine figures vie for the hero's affections. Mme. de Rênal and Mathilde de La Mole may be envisioned as two facets of the feminine dilemma: compliance and tenderness on the part of Mme. de Rênal, and rebellion as well as headstrong action on the part of Mathilde de La Mole. Similarly, in *The Charterhouse of Parma* the touching and innocent young Clélia Conti contrasts with the fiery, knowledgeable, and wilful Duchess Sanseverina. All Stendhalian heroines are strongly individualized and have the capacity to seek and define their own identity and to assert their will and freedom of choice as individuals. Lamiel, the main protagonist of Stendhal's last and unfinished novel by that name, is perhaps the most striking example of Stendhal's willingness to endow a female character with those qualities of boldness and recklessness generally reserved for heroes.

Stendhal's interest in the novel and in autobiography developed simultaneously; and this is no mere accident. But the relationship between autobiography and fiction is never a simple linear one with Stendhal. Having reached his fifties and faced with his own mortality, Stendhal embarked upon *Vie de Henry Brulard* (*The Life of Henry Brulard*), which was to retrace his spiritual development more fully than his other autobiographical essays and furnish some sort of an answer to a question that had long haunted him: "What kind of a man have I been?"

The Life of Henry Brulard was never finished. But if it does not go beyond the author's 17th year, it offers us a world of intimate details revealing the circumstances of his early life, but more importantly his reaction to the big and small events that contributed to shaping his mental and emotional outlook. It combines tenderness and humour, sincerity and reticence, candour and discretion, but while it evidently owes much of its inspiration to Rousseau's *Confessions*, it resolutely rejects self-justification. There is always an element of self-depreca-tory humour and irony in Stendhal's most solemn declarations.

Stendhal's loyalty to the ideals of the Enlightenment produced among his contemporaries the mistaken impression that he was not moving with the times. He emerged from the revolutionary era with his faith in its accomplishments wholly intact, and his desolation after Waterloo knew no bounds, especially when he saw legitimist France foster a narrow conformism and hypocrisy in many ways even more repressive than the Old Regime.

Stendhal's youthful admiration for Bonaparte and his nostalgic cult of Napoleon after Waterloo can best be understood in light of his lifelong belief in the spirit of adventure and in his willingness to take risks, to gamble on uncertain stakes. When he undertook to write, not to please his contemporaries but in order to appeal to future yet unborn generations of readers, he could hope only that posterity would vindicate his daring act of faith. His tentative expectation was fulfilled beyond his fondest dreams, for the "happy few" for whom he wrote have multiplied into a vast reading public, and teams of scholars and critics scrutinize his every printed word and scrap of manuscript.

—Gita May

See the essays on *The Charterhouse of Parma* and *Scarlet and Black*.

STERNHEIM, Carl

Born: Leipzig, Germany, 1 April 1878. **Education:** Educated at Gymnasium, Berlin; universities of Munich, Göttingen, Leipzig, and Berlin, 1897–1901. **Family:** Married 1) Eugenie Hauth in 1900 (divorced 1905), one son; 2) Thea Bauer in 1907 (divorced 1927), one daughter and one son; 3) the actress Pamela Wedekind (daughter of the writer Frank Wedekind, *q.v.*) in 1930 (divorced 1934). **Career:** Freelance writer; lived in Munich 1903; travelled in Italy 1905–06; suffered a nervous breakdown in 1920 and had recurring breakdowns and intermittent spells in hospital throughout his life; co-editor of the journal *Hyperion*, 1908 (resigned 1912); lived in Brussels, 1912–13 and 1917, Harzburg, 1914, Königstein, 1916, Switzerland, 1918–22, Dresden, 1923 and settled in Brussels, 1930. His works were banned by the Nazi regime. **Died:** 3 November 1942.

PUBLICATIONS

Collections

Aus dem bürgerlichen Heldenleben, edited by Friedrich Eisenlohr. 2 vols., 1947; further 2 volumes as *Das dramatische Werk*, 1948.
Gesammelte Werke, edited by Fritz Hofmann. 6 vols., 1963–68.
Gesamtwerk, edited by Wilhelm Emrich. 10 vols., 1963–76.

Plays

Der Heiland. 1898.
Judas Ischarioth. 1901.
Auf Krugdorf (produced 1902). 1902.
Vom König und der Königin (as *Die Königin* produced 1929). 1905.
Ulrich und Brigitte. 1907.
Don Juan (produced 1910). 1909.
Die Hose (as *Der Reise* produced 1911). 1911; translated as *A Pair of Drawers*, in *Translation*, (6–9), 1927; as *The Underpants*, translated by Eric Bentley, in *Modern Theatre 6*, edited by Bentley, 1960; as *The Bloomers*, translated by M.A. McHaffie, in *Scenes from the Heroic Life of the Middle Classes*, edited by J.M. Ritchie, 1970.
Die Kassette (produced 1911). 1912; as *The Strongbox*, translated by Maurice Edwards and Valerie Reich, in *An Anthology of German Expressionist Drama*, edited by Walter H. Sokel, 1963.
Bürger Schippel (produced 1913). 1913; as *Paul Schippel Esq.*, translated by M.A.L. Brown, in *Scenes from the Heroic Life of the Middle Classes*, edited by J.M. Ritchie, 1970.
Der Kandidat, from the play by Flaubert (produced 1915). 1914.
Der Snob (produced 1914). 1914; as *A Place in the World*, translated by Barrett H. Clark and Winifred Katzin, in *Eight European Plays*, edited by Katzin, 1927; as *The Snob*, translated by Eric Bentley, in *From the Modern Repertoire*, 1949; also translated by J.M. Ritchie and J.D. Stowell, in *Scenes from the Heroic Life of the Middle Classes*, edited by Ritchie, 1970; Marion Andre, 1984.
1913 (produced 1919). 1915; translated as *1913* by J.M. Ritchie, in *Scenes from the Heroic Life of the Middle Classes*, edited by Ritchie, 1970.
Das leidende Weib, from a play by F.M. Klinger (produced 1916). 1915.
Der Scharmante (produced 1915). 1915.
Der Geizige, from a play by Molière (produced 1917). 1916.
Tabula rasa (produced 1919). 1916.
Perleberg (produced 1917).
Die Marquise von Arcis, from a play by Diderot. 1918; as *The Mask of Virtue*, translated by Ashley Dukes, in *Famous Plays of 1935*, 1935.
Der entfesselte Zeitgenosse (produced 1921). 1920.
Manon Lescaut, from the novel by Abbé Prévost (produced 1921). 1921.
Der Nebbich (produced 1922). 1922.
Der Abenteurer. 1922.

Das Fossil (produced 1923). In *Die Aktion*, vol. 13, 1925; as *The Fossil*, translated by J.M. Ritchie, in *Scenes from the Heroic Life of the Middle Classes*, edited by Ritchie, 1970.

Oskar Wilde. 1925.

Die Schule von Uznach; oder, Neue Sachlichkeit (produced 1926). 1926.

Die Väter; oder, Knock Out. 1928.

John Pierpont Morgan (produced 1930). 1930.

Aut Caesar aut nihil. 1930.

Scenes from the Heroic Life of the Middle Classes: Five Plays (includes *The Bloomers; Paul Schippel Esq.; The Snob; 1913; The Fossil*), edited by J.M. Ritchie. 1970.

Fiction

Busekow. 1914; as *Busekow*, translated by Eugene Jolas, in *Transition*, 1, 1927.

Napoleon (stories). 1915.

Meta. 1916.

Schuhlin. 1916.

Die drei Erzählungen. 1916.

Mädchen (stories). 1917; revised edition, 1926.

Posinsky. 1917.

Chronik von des zwanzigsten Jahrhunderts Beginn (stories). 2 vols., 1918.

Ulrike. 1918.

Vier Novellen: Neue Folge der Chronik vom Beginn des zwanzigsten Jahrhunderts. 1918. 1918.

Europa. 2 vols., 1919–20.

Fairfax. 1921; as *Fairfax*, translated by Alfred B. Kuttner, 1923.

Libussa, des Kaisers Leibross. 1922.

Verse

Fanale!. 1901.

Other

Prosa. 1918.

Die Deutsche Revolution. 1919.

Berlin; oder, Juste milieu (essays). 1920.

Tasso; oder, Kunst des Juste milieu: Ein Wink für die Jugend (essays). 1921.

Gauguin und van Gogh (essays). 1924.

Lutetia. Berichte über europäische Politik, Kunst und Volksleben 1926 (essays). 1926.

Kleiner Katechismus für das Jahr 1930–31. 1930.

Vorkriegseuropa im Gleichnis meines Lebens (autobiography). 1936.

*

Bibliography: *Sternheim-Compendium: Carl Sternheim: Werke, Weg, Wirkung* by Rudolf Billetta, 1975.

Critical Studies: *Über Wedekind, Sternheim und das Theater* by Franz Blei, 1915; *Carl Sternheim* by Hellmuth Karasek, 1965; *Carl Sternheim: Weltvorstellung und Kunstprinzipien* by Wolfgang Wendler, 1966, and *Carl Sternheim: Materialienbuch*, 1980, edited by Wendler; *Carl Sternheims Dramen. Zur Textanalyse, Ideologiekritik und Rezeptionsgeschichte* edited by J. Schönert, 1975; *Die Bürgerkomödien* *Carl Sternheims* by Winfried Freund, 1976; *Das expressionistische Drama: Cart Sternheim und Georg Kaiser* by Manfred Durzak, 1978; *Geschichtsbewusstsein, Satire, Zensur; eine Studie zu Carl Sternheim* by Karl Deiritz, 1979; *Carl Sternheim* by Manfred Linke, 1979; *Idiom der Entstellung: Auffaltung des Satirischen in Carl Sternheims "Aus dem bürgerlichen Heldenleben"* by Eckehard Czucka, 1982; *Carl Sternheim* by Burghard Dedner, 1982; *Carl Sternheim: A Critical Study* by Rhys W. Williams, 1982; *Über die Wahrheit und über die Lüge des radikalen, antibürgerlichen Individualismus: Eine Studie zum erzählerischen und essayistischen Werk Carl Sternheims* by Bernhard Budde, 1983; *German Molière Revival and the Comedies of Hugo von Hofmannsthal and Carl Sternheim* by Dugald S. Sturges, 1993.

* * *

After inauspicious literary beginnings Carl Sternheim achieved a breakthrough to a new and distinctive comic form with *Die Hose* (*The Bloomers*). The impetus for his new comic mode derived from a productive misreading of Molière's comedy *George Dandin*. For Sternheim, Dandin is a hero: having attempted to assimilate to a higher social class through marriage, Dandin recognizes the error of his ambition. Molière, Sternheim insists, was motivated by a desire to preserve the vitality of his own bourgeois class by ridiculing its attempts to seek assimilation to the aristocracy. Sternheim sides with the central comic character, seeing his obsession, not as held up to ridicule, but as an exaggeration of qualities (such as brutal realism) which are essential to his survival. Small wonder, then, that Sternheim reserved his highest praise for Molière's Alceste, whose misanthropic rejection of prevailing social values Sternheim views as highly positive. In a post-Nietzschean world the refusal to conform to the "mentality of the herd" becomes positively heroic. Idiosyncratic as his interpretation of Molière is, it supplies Sternheim with a blueprint for his own comedies.

Theobald Maske in *The Bloomers* was the first of a long line of "bourgeois heroes." His behaviour is dominated by his concern with his position as a minor civil servant. When his wife, Luise, loses her knickers in public, he fears that the extraordinary incident will draw attention to him and threaten his secure position and the pension which awaits him. The incident is witnessed by two bystanders, the would-be poet Scarron and the Wagnerian barber Mandelstam. Both apply to rent the vacant room in Theobald's flat, hoping that they may seduce Luise, who is aided and abetted in her romantic dreams by Fraulein Deuter. An audience nurtured on French classical comedy would have no difficulty in recognizing the comic constellation. Theobald, with his obsessive fear of scandal and his brutal materialism, has all the rigidity of character of Molière's central comic figures and seems destined to be cuckolded. The comedy, however, confounds the expectations of Scarron and Mandelstam (and those of the audience). Far from being defeated by the comic action, Theobald's obsessive realism triumphs over the delusions of the ideology-ridden minor characters. While in Molière's comedy the central comic figure is defeated and society "pragmatically free" (Northrop Frye) at the end of the play, in Sternheim's brand of comedy it is society, represented by all the minor characters, which is defeated and the "bourgeois hero" who is pragmatically free. The audience finds itself laughing not *at* Theobald, but *with* Theobald at the minor characters who constitute society. The laughter which it had originally directed at Theobald proves to be misplaced; the audience is forced to concede that it has been laughing at itself, at its own cultural assumptions, and it is this which constitutes the shock of recognition which Sternheim's comedies provide.

In his three subsequent comedies, *Die Kassette* (*The Strongbox*), *Bürger Schippel* (*Paul Schippel Esq.*), and *Der Snob* (*The Snob*), Sternheim once again adapts Molière's comedies for his own ends. *The Strongbox* offers a reworking of *L'Avare* (*The Miser*): in Molière's comedy Harpagon fails in his attempt to impose his rigid order on the other characters, while in *The Strongbox* it is materialism, in the shape of the cash box, which prevails, drawing all the characters into its orbit. In *Paul Schippel Esq.* Sternheim takes a most unlikely candidate for acceptance into the bourgeoisie and demonstrates his rapid assimilation. In this function Schippel is a typical Sternheim hero: dynamic and vital, he serves to expose the intellectual feebleness of an ideology-ridden society. But Schippel is also a comic figure: he can curse the bourgeoisie with one breath and willingly prostitute his talent as a singer with the next. The ambiguity is characteristic of Sternheim's comic manner. Schippel's vitality and materialism unmask bourgeois pretensions and ensure his success, but he is sidetracked into a world of make-believe. Self-delusion in French classical comedy points away from society, but in Sternheim's world it is bourgeois society which is deluded and hence Schippel's self-delusion leads to his social integration. In *The Snob*, Sternheim produces a modern version of *Le Bourgeois Gentilhomme* (*Would-Be Gentleman*): like Monsieur Jourdain, Christian Maske is obsessed with the outward trappings of aristocratic life. But if he retains the comic features of the social climber, his efforts (unlike Monsieur Jourdain's) are crowned with success as he pensions off his now dispensable mistress and marries Count Palen's daughter. The audience, expecting to laugh at Christian's expense, finds that it is he who has the last laugh. Bourgeois society (including that represented by the audience's values) is no match for the ruthless dynamism of Sternheim's hero.

The outbreak of World War I marked a turning point in Sternheim's fortunes. He was widely regarded as an opponent of the war and his work was banned from performance. He responded by adapting the work of others: a play by Flaubert, another by the 18th-century German writer, F.M. Klinger, Molière's *The Miser*, Prévost's *Marion Lescaut*, a Maupassant story, and material found in the work of Diderot. That French literature, in the main, supplied the models was in itself a provocative political act on Sternheim's part at a time of unprecedented jingoistic nationalism. He also adapted his "bourgeois hero" to the changed situation, producing a series of plays championing a radical individualism which finds expression in a wholesale rejection of European society. While the pre-war heroes could fulfil themselves in and through society, characters such as Ständer in the political play *Tabula rasa* (1916), turn their backs on Europe and contemplate regression to a primitive idyll set in the South Seas. Sternheim's post-war work: *Der entfesselte Zeitgenosse* [The Contemporary Unleashed], *Der Nebbich, Das Fossil* (*The Fossil*), *Oskar Wilde*, and *Die Schule von Uznach* [The School of Uznach], never reached the level of his pre-war work. While he is best known as a dramatist, Sternheim also published short stories, collected under the title *Chronik von des zwanzigsten Jahrhunderts Beginn*, a novel, *Europa*, and an autobiography, *Vorkriegseuropa im Gleichnis meines Lebens*. The linguistic distortion and the density of his prose style, derived from his theory that language should be pared down to essentials in order to grasp a hidden "essence," render Sternheim's

prose works, especially in their later reworked editions, difficult to access.

Comedy traditionally dealt with aberrations from current social norms; Sternheim's brand of comedy operates in a world in which social norms are portrayed as spurious. For Sternheim, social conventions merely mask materialistic power struggles; linguistic conventions have petrified into cliché. He presents society not from the perspective of social normality, but from that of the outsider. Aberrations from the norm are seen as heroic, and only incidentally comic; they constitute a kind of perverse ideal, measured against which society is shown to be enfeebled and debilitated. A comic vision which takes as its starting-point an individualistic and misanthropic materialism is calculated to challenge the received ideas and values of an audience familiar with the cultural tradition. It is this socio-critical reversal of traditional comedy which constitutes Sternheim's startling originality.

—Rhys W. Williams

STIFTER, Adalbert

Born: Oberplan, Bohemia, Austria (now Horní Planá, Czech Republic), 23 October 1805. **Education:** Educated at village school; Benedictine monastery school, Kremsmünster, 1818–26; studied law at University of Vienna, 1828–30. **Family:** Married Amalia Mohaupt in 1837. **Career:** Tutor and painter, editor, *Der Wiener Bote*, 1849–50; school inspector, Vienna, 1850, and in Linz, 1851–65; art critic, *Linzer Zeitung*, 1852–57. Curator of Monuments for Upper Austria, 1853, vice-president, Linzer Kunstverein. Order of Franz Joseph, 1854; Ritterkreuz des Weissen Falkenordens, 1867. **Died:** (suicide) 28 January 1868.

PUBLICATIONS

Collections

Sämtliche Werke, edited by August Sauer. 25 vols., 1904–79.
Werke, edited by Gustav Wilhelm. 5 vols., 1926.
Gesammelte Werke, edited by Max Stefl. 6 vols., 1939.
Werke, edited by Magda Gerken and Josef Thanner. 5 vols., 1949–61.
Werke, edited by Max Stefl. 9 vols., 1950–60.
Werke und Briefe, edited by Alfred Doppler and Wolfgang Frühwald. 1978–.

Fiction

Studien (stories). 6 vols., 1844–50; enlarged edition, 1855.
Pictures of Rural Life in Austria and Hungary, translated by Mary Norman. 3 vols., 1850.
Pictures of Life, translated by Mary Howitt. 1852.
Der Hagelstolz. 1852; as *The Recluse*, translated by David Luke, 1968.
Bunte Steine: Ein Festgeschenk (stories). 1853.

Der Nachsommer. 1857; as *Indian Summer*, translated by Wendell Freye, 1985.

Witiko. 1865–67; translated by Wendell Frye, 1999.

The Heather Village, translated by C.C. Machlev. 1868.

Erzählungen, edited by Johannes Aprent. 2 vols., 1869.

Der Watdsteig (in English). 1942.

The Condor. 1946.

Die Mappe meines Urgrossvaters (final version). 1946.

Erzählungen in der Urfassung, edited by Max Stefl. 3 vols., 1950–52.

Limestone and Other Stories, translated by David Luke. 1968.

Brigitta (includes *Abdias; Limestone; The Forest Path*), translated by Helen Watanabe-O'Kelly. 1990.

Other

Briefe, edited by Johannes Aprent. 3 vols., 1869.

Stifter: Sein Leben in Selbstzeugnissen, Briefen, und Berichten, edited by Karl Privat. 1946.

Jugendbriefe (1822–1839) edited by Gustav Wilhelm. 1954.

Leben und Werk in Briefen und Dokumenten, edited by K.G. Fischer. 1962.

Briefwechsel, edited by Josef Buchowiecki. 1965.

Editor, with Johannes Aprent, *Lesebuch zur Förderung humaner Bildung*. 1854.

*

Bibliography: *Adalbert Stifter: Bibliographie* by Eduard Eisenmeier, 3 vols., 1964–78.

Critical Studies: *Stifter: A Critical Study* by E.A. Blackall, 1948; *Natural Science in the Work of Stifter* by W.E. Umbach, 1950; *The Marble Statue as Idea: Collected Essays on Stifter's "Der Nachsommer"* by Christine O. Sjögren, 1972; *Stifter* by Margaret Gump, 1974; *Stifter Heute* edited by Johann Lachinger, Alexander Stillmark, and Martin Swales. 1984; *Adalbert Stifter: A Critical Study* by Martin and Erika Swales, 1984; *Adalbert Stifter. Sein Leben und Werk* by P.A. Schoenborn, 1992; *Goethe as Cultural Icon: Intertextual Encounters with Stifter and Fontane* by Nancy Birch Wagner, 1994; *Adalbert Stifter's Late Prose: The Mania for Moderation* by Helena Ragg-Kirkby, 2000.

* * *

The publication of Adalbert Stifter's narrative prose, consisting of some 30 stories and novellas and three novels, broadly coincides with the end of the Biedermeier era and extends into the so-called poetic realism of the 1850s and 1860s. The temper of Austrian Biedermeier culture was, on the surface of things, moderate, contemplative, and reverential towards traditional values, and this is ostensibly reflected in the restrained, measured prose of this meticulous stylist. However, it was also an age of repression and censorship under the Metternich System which ended in the March Revolution of 1848. At a submerged level, Stifter's language also expresses profound existential tensions and conflicts which he attempts to resolve through formal mastery in an act of the artistic will. The subjects of his fiction are set very largely within the landscapes of his native Bohemia and the characters he draws subtly interact with their rural environment in a manner greatly reminiscent of Wordsworth, though it is unlikely that he had ever read the latter. In his earlier works there are, if at all, some

literary echoes of Walter Scott, Fenimore Cooper, and Jean Paul. Like Wordsworth, Stifter was a lifelong "worshipper of nature" and his name is likewise synonymous, in German literature, with the sensuous and symbolic representation of nature as a power and a presence. His masterly descriptions of forest and mountain scenery early gained him the reputation of being a painter in words (he was, in fact, also a gifted landscape painter and a pioneering educationalist).

From his earliest stories ("Das Haidedorf" ["The Village on the Heath"], "Der Hochwald" ["The Hochwald"]) the unusual prominence ascribed to nature's awe-inspiring presence makes the role of humanity appear almost subordinate; yet man is treated in relation to images of nature and a subtle parallelism of meaning is insinuated largely through symbolic suggestion but also by means of juxtaposition and contrast. The trials and griefs of fallible humanity are set beside the flawless model of a natural order which expresses constancy, innocence, and beauty. Yet the proximity of the sublime to the terrible, of beauty to pain, repeatedly asserts itself. Though he largely suppresses overt depiction of violent passions and the darker aspects of life, Stifter often achieves an increased intensity by narrative devices which exploit concealment and intimation. These secrecies of his style demand an especially attentive and receptive reader.

Underlying his descriptions of even the smallest detail of a world minutely explored and fastidiously recorded is the grandeur of a universal design. It was never Stifter's purpose to conceal or ignore the disturbing conflicts of existence—ever and again he allows them to shatter the calm of "normality" with eruptive force—rather, he hoped to introduce a reversal of the conventional view of what is perceived as "great" and "little." In his famous preface to the cycle of stories entitled *Bunte Steine* [Coloured Stones], he attempted to set forth his controversial aesthetic creed. This radical revaluation of common perceptions of the ordinary and the extraordinary brings a qualitative, instead of a merely quantitative, understanding to bear on constancy and change in natural and human existence. The scientific cum moral principle ("the Gentle Law") which Stifter proposes as a universal sustaining idea, with its aura of sublimity, has given rise to much critical dispute and misunderstanding. It appears as no accident that this thought-provoking preface, written at a time when rival claims of religion and science were sharply dividing, should represent a brave attempt to reconcile a moral with a broadly scientific worldview by pointing to a higher uniting principle.

From his *Studien* [Studies] onwards, the attention Stifter lavishes on objects, whether natural or domestic, conveys an almost obsessional interest which dignifies "things" with ontological import. (His influence on Rilke and Kafka has not gone unnoticed.) The human figures he draws are not so much psychologically explored as externally observed and intricately related to their physical environment. An heir to the legacy of Weimar classicism and dedicated to the humanist ideals of enlightenment and self-cultivation, Stiffter wrote his first novel *Der Nachsommer* (*Indian Summer*) in a form derivative of the German novel of education. However, he possessed a highly individual sense of the novel form and of its symbolic potential. In limiting the focus onto the timeless, idyllic setting, devoid of blemishes and marked off from the busy world of commerce and institutions, he created a more perfect alternative for the good and simple life. Yet here too he presents, in transfiguring light, the archetypal heart-break situation recurrent in his oeuvre: the love that fails in youth but finds propitiation and fulfilment in maturity. Stifter's second novel *Witiko* (which took him 15 years to write) takes the form of a vast prose epic set in medieval times; it is an original and ambitious attempt to depict the founding of a society on premises of morality and justice. In his third, unfinished novel, *Die Mappe meines Urgrossvaters*, Stifter offers the moving story of a country doctor who attains self-mastery and wholeness through the dire trials of renunciation, bereavement, and service to others. A masterpiece of controlled economic style, it contains some of his most assured and memorable writing. In his late style, Stifter developed an austere simplicity of expression, a stylized manner which is defiantly contrary to contemporary European realism. His mature fiction puzzled and alienated his readership increasingly and it fell to Nietzsche to alert the literary world to his importance.

—Alexander Stillmark

See the essays on ''Abdias,'' *Indian Summer*, and ''Rock Crystal.''

STORM, (Hans) Theodor (Woldsen)

Born: Husum, Schleswig-Holstein, Germany, 14 September 1817. **Education:** Educated at local schools and the Gymnasium, Lübeck; studied law at Kiel University, 1837–42. **Family:** Married 1) Constanze Esmarch in 1846 (died 1865), seven children; 2) Dorothea Jensen in 1866, one child. **Career:** Set up legal practice in Husum, 1843–53; forced into exile in Potsdam in 1853 after the Danish occupation; assignment, Prussian civil service, Potsdam, 1853–56; magistrate, Heiligenstadt, 1856; chief legal and administration officer, 1864 and chief judge, 1874, Husum. **Died:** 4 July 1888.

PUBLICATIONS

Collections

Gedichte, edited by Hans Heitmann. 1943.
Sämtliche Werke, edited by Peter Goldammer. 4 vols., 1956; 4th edition, 1982.
Werke, edited by Gottfried Honnefelder. 2 vols., 1975.
Sämtliche Werke, edited by Karl Ernst Laage and Dieter Lohmeier. 4 vols., 1987–88.
Hans and Heinz Kirch; with, Immensee; and, Journey to a Hallig, translated by Denis Jackson and Anja Nauck. 1999.

Fiction

Immensee. 1851; as *Immensee*, translated by Helene Clark, 1863; also translated by Irma Ann Heath, 1902; Charles C. Bubb, 1909; C.W. Bell, 1919; Matthew Taylor Mellon, 1937; E.W. Triess, 1941; Ronald Taylor, 1966; J.M. Ritchie, 1969; as *Immen Lake*, translated by M. Briton, 1881.
Im Sonnenschein. 1854.
Ein grünes Blatt (stories). 1855.
Hinzelmeier. 1857.
Auf dem Staatshof. 1859.
In der Sommer-Mondnacht (stories). 1860.
Drei Novellen. 1861.
Im Schloss. 1863.
Auf der Universität. 1863; as *Lenore*, 1865.
Zwei Weihnachtsidyllen (stories). 1865.

Drei Märchen. 1866; as *Geschichten aus der Tonne*, 2nd edition, 1873.
Eine Malerarbeit. 1867.
Von Jenseit des Meeres. 1867.
In St. Jürgen. 1868.
Zerstreute Kapitel. 1873.
Pole Poppenspäler and *Waldwinkel*. 1875.
Viola tricolor. 1874; as *Viola Tricolor*, translated by Bayard Quincy Morgan, 1956.
Ein stiller Musikant. 1875.
Psyche. 1876.
Gesammelte Schriften. 10 vols., 1877–89.
Aquis submersus. 1877; as *Aquis Submersus*, translated by James Millar, 1910; as *Beneath the Flood*, translated by Geoffrey Skelton, 1962.
Renate. 1878; as *Renate*, translated by James Millar, 1909.
Carsten Curator. 1878; as *Carsten Curator*, translated by Frieda M. Voigt, 1956.
Eekenhof and *Im Brauer-Hause*. 1880; *Eekenhof*, translated by James Millar, 1905.
Zur Wald-und-Wasserfreude. 1880.
Die Söhne des Senators and *Der Herr Etatsrath*. 1881; *Die Söhne des Senators*; as *The Senator's Sons*, translated by E.M. Huggard, 1947.
Hans und Heinz Kirch. 1883.
Schweigen. 1883.
Zwei Novellen. 1883.
Zur Chronik von Grieshuus. 1884; as *A Chapter in the History of Grieshuus*, translated by James Millar, 1905.
Ein Fest auf Haderslevhuus and *John Riew'*. 1885. *Ein Fest auf Haderslevhuus*; as *A Festival at Haderslevhuss*, translated by James Millar, 1909.
Vor Zeiten 1886.
Bötjer Basch. 1887.
Ein Doppelgänger. 1887.
Bei kleinen Leuten (stories). 1887.
Ein Bekenntnis. 1887.
Der Schimmelreiter. 1888; numerous translations including as *The Rider on the White Horse*, 1915; as *The White Horseman*, translated by Geoffrey Skelton, 1962; as *The White Horse Rider*, translated by Stella Humphries, 1966; as *The Dykemaster*, translated by Denis Jackson, 1996.
Es waren zwei Königskinder. 1888.
Little Hobbin, translated by Anthea Bell. 1995.

Verse

Liederbuch dreier Freunde. 1843.
Gedichte. 1852; revised edition, 1856.

Other

Der Briefwechsel zwischen Theodor Storm und Gottfried Keller, edited by Albert Köster. 1904.
Briefe an Friedrich Eggers, edited by Hans Wolfgang Seidel. 1911.
Briefe, edited by Gertrud Storm. 4 vols., 1915–17.
Briefwechsel zwischen Theodor Storm und Eduard Mörike, edited by Hanns Wolfgang Rath. 1919.
Theodor Storms Briefe an seinen Freund Georg Lorenzen 1876 bis 1882, edited by C. Höfer. 1923.

Blätter der Freundschaft. Aus dem Briefwechsel zwischen Theodor Storm und Ludwig Pietsch, edited by V. Pauls. 1939; revised edition, 1943.

Storm als Erzieher. Seine Briefe an Ada Christen, edited by O. Katann. 1948.

Garten meiner Jugend (autobiography), edited by Frank Schnass. 1950.

Der Weg wie weit (autobiography), edited by Frank Schnass. 1951.

Bittersüsser Lebenstrank (autobiography), edited by Frank Schnass. 1952.

Der Briefwechsel zwischen Theodor Storm und Gottfried Keller, edited by Peter Goldammer. 1960.

Briefwechsel mit Theodor Mommsen, edited by H.E. Teitge. 1966.

Theodor Storm und Iwan Turgenjew. Persönlichkeit und literarische Beziehungen, Einflüsse, Briefe, Bilder, edited by K.E. Laage. 1967.

Theodor Storm—Emil Kuh, Briefwechsel, edited by E. Streitfeld. 1985.

Editor, *Deutsche Liebeslieder seit Johann Christian Guenther: Eine Codification.* 1859.

Editor, *Hausbuch aus deutschen Dichtern seit Claudius: Eine kritische Anthologie.* 1870.

*

Bibliography: *Theodor Storm-Bibliographie* by H.E. Teitge, 1967.

Critical Studies: *Studies in Theodor Storm* by Elmer O. Wooley, 1943; *Theodor Storm's Craft of Fiction: The Torment of a Narrator* by Clifford A. Bernd, 1963; *Theodor Storm's Novellen: Essays on Literary Technique* by E. Allen McCormick, 1964; *The Theme of Loneliness in Theodor Storm's Novellen* by Lloyd W. Wedberg, 1964; *Techniques of Solipsism: A Study of Theodor Storm's Narrative Fiction* by Terence J. Rogers, 1970; *Theodor Storm. Die zeitkritische Dimension seiner Novellen* by Ingrid Schuster, 1971; *Sound and Sense in the Poetry of Theodor Storm: A Phonological-Statistical Study* by Alan B. Galt, 1973; *Theodor Storm* by Tilo Alt, 1973; *Theodor Storm: Studies in Ambivalence: Symbol and Myth in His Narrative Fiction* by David Artiss, 1978; *Theodor Storm: Der Schimmelreiter* by M.G. Ward, 1988; *Der Schimmelreiter* by A.D. White, 1988; *Theodor Storm* edited by Patricia M. Boswell, 1989; *Storm in Schleswig und Holstein* by Dietmat Albrecht, 1991; *Theodor Storm: The Life and Works of a Democratic Humanitarian* by David A. Jackson, 1992; *Theodor Storm* by Roger Paulin, 1992; *Theory and Patterns of Tragedy in the Later Novellen of Theodor Storm* by Barbara Burns, 1996.

* * *

Theodor Storm is associated particularly with the period of poetic realism in German literature, with a certain regionalism stemming from his fond depiction of his homeland of Schleswig-Holstein, and perhaps most importantly with an intricate skill in composing stories of human failure and disaster which illustrate the tragic imperfection of life in universal terms. As well as the novellas for which he is best known, Storm's work also includes a fine collection of poetry and a few fairytales which proved less successful.

Written largely in the early period of his literary activity, Storm's poetry furnishes considerable insight into the loves and preoccupations of the man. Poems such as "Die Stadt" [The Town] and "Meeresstrand" [Shoreline] reveal an individual deeply rooted in his native area, whose descriptions are pervaded with a sense of belonging and encapsulate the bleak beauty of this northern coastal landscape. Perhaps not surprisingly for a man so strongly attached to his homeland, the threat imposed by the invaders during the Dano-Prussian War prompted from Storm a series of patriotic outpourings. His political verse, however, concentrates less on the detail of historical events than on the violation of that which was synonymous with his very identity, and as such these poems retain a timeless validity. Inspired as they were by the love of two women, Constanze Esmarch and Dorothea Jensen, Storm regarded his love poems as among his most significant achievements. The poems for his first wife Constanze, on whose devotion and companionship he heavily relied, are tender pieces expressing the depth of his affection for her, while those relating to his brief affair with Dorothea are quite different, displaying the passionate, physical side of his nature and employing a choice of vocabulary and imagery which made them rather explicit for their time and social context. In the few poems of Storm's later years the themes of loneliness, transience, and death, already present earlier, are intensified. Profoundly shaken by Constanze's death in 1865, he composed a cycle of poems entitled "Tiefe Schatten" [Deep Shadows] in which he conveys the pain of one who is spiritually lost, who has felt obliged on rational grounds to give up his hope of immortality, and yet is comfortless without it. The great strength of Storm's poetry lies in its honesty and its accessibility. He succeeds admirably in achieving his aim, namely to focus on individual events of personal experience, and through these to express truths that apply to all humanity.

Storm's early novellas grew by his own admission from his lyrics, and display a strong element of late-Romantic sentimentality. *Immensee* typifies the young writer as a master of delicate tones, skilled in evoking idyllic natural settings and bittersweet memories. Storm's talents, however, extended beyond this popular style of rather self-indulgent escapism, for even in the relatively early novellas *Auf dem Staatshof* [At the Manor], 1859, and *Im Schloss* [In the Castle], 1863, we find him already beginning to explore important 19th-century issues such as the power of heredity, the conflict between science and religion, and the decline of the nobility.

Storm's interest in the fantastic, together with his knowledge of local folklore and folksongs is manifest throughout his work, but especially in his fairytales. Of the five tales only one "Die Regentrude" [The Rain Maiden], can truly be called a fairytale achieving a successful fusion of the real and the fantastic. The others might better be described as allegories that explore sometimes disturbing aspects of human nature, but which lack a conventional happy ending and produce no sense of moral satisfaction that wrongs have been righted. Storm did not return to this genre after 1866, but his fascination for the weird and supernatural persisted, and found expression in a number of later novellas, notably in *Zur Chronik von Grieshuus* (*A Chapter in the History of Grieshuus*) and *Der Schimmelreiter* (*The White Horseman*).

It was in the early 1870s that Storm began to strike a deeper note in his work, employing more objective language and leaving behind much of his former inclination towards poetic embellishment. Storm's later novellas portray the lonely struggle of the common man, resulting from class prejudice, superstition, social stigma, his genetic inheritance, and at times his personal guilt. The characters are much less resigned and passive than before, and pit themselves with fortitude against their fate—the supreme example of this being found in the figure of Hauke Haien in *The White Horseman*—even if ultimately their effort is in vain. Often the issues which motivate the catastrophes in Storm's tragic novellas emanate directly from his own private world. His eldest son Hans died young as an alcoholic, and Storm agonized at the sight of his child being destroyed by seemingly hereditary and uncontrollable powers. The novella *Carsten Curator*, draws most heavily on this experience, and the theme of heredity recurs frequently throughout his work. Moreover, in his professional capacity as lawyer and judge, Storm was a perceptive observer of human behaviour and his indignation at the evils of class distinction and intolerance and his compassion for the plight of the victimized are conveyed in many tragic tales, including *Aquis submersus* (*Beneath the Flood*) and *Ein Doppelgänger*.

There is a progression in Storm's work, which begins with the elegiac features typical of the Biedermeier age or of early poetic realism, and ends up conveying a sombre mood of destruction and death that becomes widespread towards the end of the century in German thought and literature. Despite his pessimistic streak, however, Storm remained ever true to his conception of the poetic and insisted on the need for some spark of hope in literature as in life itself. Consequently some of his most devastating tales are placed within a positive, even idyllic framework, which produces a distancing effect, thus muting the tragedy and reaffirming the writer's determination not to give way to unmitigated despair.

—B. Burns

See the essays on *Immensee* and *The White Horseman*.

STRINDBERG, August

Born: Stockholm, Sweden, 22 January 1849. **Education:** Educated at Uppsala University, 1867, 1870–72, no degree. **Family:** Married 1) Baroness Siri von Essen in 1877 (divorced 1891), three children; 2) Frida Uhl in 1893 (divorced 1897), one daughter; 3) Harriet Bosse in 1901 (divorced 1904), one daughter. **Career:** Teacher, tutor, actor, and journalist; trained as telegraph clerk, 1873; assistant librarian, Royal Library, Stockholm, 1874–79; centre of a group of radical writers in 1880s; tried for blasphemy, but acquitted, 1884; lived in France, Switzerland, Bavaria, and Denmark, 1883–89; opened an experimental theatre in Copenhagen, 1889 (closed same year); lived in Berlin, 1892–94, Paris, 1894–96, Lund, 1896–99, and Stockholm, after 1899; suffered his "Inferno" crisis, 1894–97: stayed in a mental clinic in Ystad, Sweden, 1895, 1896; founder, Intima Teatern [Intimate Theatre], Stockholm, 1907 (closed 1910). Also a painter. **Died:** 14 May 1912.

PUBLICATIONS

Collections

Samlade skrifter [Collected Writings], edited by John Landqvist. 55 vols., 1912–20; supplemented with *Samlade otryckta skrifter* [Collected Unpublished Writings], 2 vols., 1918–19.
Plays, translated by Edith and Warner Öland. 4 vols., 1912–14.
Plays, translated by Edwin Björkman. 7 vols., 1912–16.
Plays, translated by C.D. Locock, E. Classen, and others. 4 vols., 1929–39.
Skrifter [Writings], edited by Gunnar Brandell. 14 vols., 1945–46.

The Washington Strindberg, edited and translated by Walter Johnson. 12 vols., 1955–83.
Dramer, edited by Carl R. Smedmark. 3 vols., 1962–.
Plays, translated by Michael Meyer. 2 vols., 1964 (US edition published in one volume, 1973); revised edition, 1975; selections as *Plays*, 3 vols., 1976–91.
Samlade verk [Collected Works], edited by Lars Dahlbäck and others. 1980–.
Selected Essays by August Strindberg, selected, edited and translated by Michael Robinson. 1996.
Strindberg—Other Sides: Seven Plays, translated and introduced by Joe Martin. 1997.
Three Chamber Plays, translated by Inga-Stina Ewbank. 1997.
Miss Julie and Other Plays, translated with an introduction and notes by Michael Robinson. 1998.
The Father; Lady Julie; Playing with Fire, translated by Eivor Martinus. 1998.

Plays

I Rom [In Rome] (produced 1870). 1870.
Hermione. 1871.
Den fredlöse (produced 1871). 1881; as *The Outlaw*, translated by Edwin Björkman, in *Plays*, 1912.
Gillets hemlighet [The Secret of the Guild] (produced 1880). 1880.
Mäster Olof (prose version; produced 1881). 1881; revised version (verse, produced 1890), 1878; as *Master Olof*, translated by Edwin Björkman, 1915; also translated by C.D. Locock, in *Master Olof and Other Plays*, 1931; Walter Johnson, in *The Washington Strindberg*, vol. 6, 1959; Evert Sprinchorn, in *Selected Plays*, 1986.
Anno fyrtioåtta [Anno Forty-Eight]. 1881.
Lycko-Pers resa (produced 1883). 1882; as *Lucky Pehr*, translated by Edwin Björkman, in *Plays*, 1912; as *Lucky Peter's Travels*, translated by E. Classen, in *Lucky Peter's Travels and Other Plays*, 1930; as *Lucky Per's Journey*, translated by Arvid Paulson, in *Eight Expressionist Plays*, 1965.
Herr Bengts husfru [Mr. Bengt's Wife] (produced 1882). 1882.
Kamraterna (produced 1905). 1886; as *Comrades*, translated by Edith and Warner Öland, in *Plays*, 1912; also translated by Edwin Björkman, in *Plays*, 1913; Horace B. Samuel, in *Plays*, 1914; Arvid Paulson, in *Seven Plays*, 1960.
Fadren (produced 1887). 1887; as *The Father*, translated by N. Erichsen, 1899, and in *Eight Famous Plays*, 1949; also translated by C.D. Locock, in *Lucky Peter's Travels and Other Plays*, 1930; Elizabeth Sprigge, in *Six Plays*, 1955; Peter Watts, in *Three Plays*, 1958; Arvid Paulson, in *Seven Plays*, 1960; Valborg Anderson, 1964; Walter Johnson, in *The Washington Strindberg*, vol. 7, 1970; Harry G. Carlson, in *Five Plays*, 1983; Evert Sprinchorn, in *Selected Plays*, 1986; adapted by John Osborne, with Ibsen's *Hedda Gabler*, 1989.
Fröken Julie (produced 1889). 1888; as *Julie*, translated by Arthur Swan, 1911; as *Countess Julia*, translated by Charles Recht, 1912; as *Miss Julia*, translated by Edwin Björkman, in *Plays*, 1913, and in *Eight Famous Plays*, 1949; Peter Watts, in *Three Plays*, 1958; as *Miss Julie*, translated by Horace B. Samuel, in *Plays*, 1914; also translated by Elizabeth Sprigge, in *Six Plays*, 1955; Arvid Paulson, in *Seven Plays*, 1960; Evert Sprinchorn, in *Selected Plays and Prose*, 1964; F.R. Southerington, in *Three Experimental Plays*, 1975;

Harry G. Carlson, in *Five Plays*, 1983; Peter Hogg and Helen Cooper, 1992; Truda Stockenstrom, 1996; as *Lady Julie*, translated by C.D. Locock, in *Lucky Peter's Travels and Other Plays*, 1930; Walter Johnson, in *The Washington Strindberg*, vol. 7, 1970; as *After Miss Julie: A Version of Strindberg's Miss Julie* by Patrick Marber, 1996.

Paria (produced 1889). 1890; as *Pariah*, translated by Edwin Björkman, in *Plays*, 1912; also translated by Edith and Warner Öland, in *Plays*, 1912; Walter Johnson, in *The Washington Strindberg*, vol. 12, 1983; Eivor Martinus, in *Three One-Act Plays*, 1987; as *Paria*, translated by Horace B. Samuel, in *Plays*, 1914.

Den starkare (produced 1889). 1890; as *The Stronger*, translated by Francis J. Ziegler, 1906; also translated by Edwin Björkman, in *Plays*, 1912, and in *Eight Famous Plays*, 1949; Charles Wangel, in *Ten-Minute Plays*, edited by P. Loving, 1923; Elizabeth Sprigge, in *Six Plays*, 1955; Arvid Paulson, in *Seven Plays*, 1960; Walter Johnson, in *The Washington Strindberg*, vol. 7, 1970; F.R. Southerington, in *Three Experimental Plays*, 1975; Evert Sprinchorn, in *Selected Plays*, 1986; as *The Stronger Woman*, translated by Horace B. Samuel, in *Plays*, 1914.

Hemsöborna [The Natives of Hemsö], from his own novel (produced 1889).

Fordringsägare (produced 1889). 1890; as *The Creditor*, translated by Francis J. Ziegler, 1910; also translated by Mary Harned, 1911; Horace B. Samuel, 1914; as *Creditors*, translated by Edwin Björkman, in *Plays*, 1913; also translated by Horace B. Samuel, in *Plays*, 1914; Elizabeth Sprigge, in *Five Plays*, 1960; Walter Johnson, in *The Washington Strindberg*, vol. 7, 1970; Evert Sprinchorn, in *Selected Plays*, 1986.

Samum (produced 1890). 1890; as *Simoom*, translated by Francis J. Ziegler, 1905; also translated by Edwin Björkman, in *Plays*, 1913; as *Simoon*, translated by Mary Harned, in *Three One-Act Plays*, 1906; also translated by Horace B. Samuel, in *Plays*, 1914; Walter Johnson, in *The Washington Strindberg*, vol. 12, 1983.

Bandet (produced 1902). 1892; as *The Link*, translated by Edwin Björkman, in *Plays*, 1912, and in *Eight Famous Plays*, 1949; as *The Bond*, translated by Elizabeth Sprigge and C. Napier, in *Lucky Peter's Travels and Other Plays*, 1930; also translated by Arvid Paulson, in *Seven Plays*, 1960; Walter Johnson, in *The Washington Strindberg*, vol. 7, 1970.

Leka med elden (produced 1893). 1892; as *Playing with Fire*, translated by E. Classen, in *Lucky Peter's Travels and Other Plays*, 1930; also translated by Walter Johnson, in *The Washington Strindberg*, vol. 12, 1983; and Evert Sprinchorn, in *Selected Plays*, 1986.

Debet ock kredit (produced 1893). 1892; as *Debit and Credit*, translated by Mary Harned, in *Three One-Act Plays*, 1906; also translated by Edwin Björkman, in *Plays*, 1913; Walter Johnson, in *The Washington Strindberg*, vol. 12, 1983.

Moderskärlek (produced 1894). 1892; as *Motherlove*, translated by Francis J. Ziegler, 1910; as *Motherly Love*, translated by Horace B. Samuel, in *Plays*, 1914; also translated in *Miss Julie and Other Plays*, 1918; Eivor Martinus, in *Three One-Act Plays*, 1987; as *Mother Love*, translated by Walter Johnson, in *The Washington Strindberg*, vol. 12, 1983.

Första varningen (produced 1893). 1892; as *The First Warning*, translated by Edwin Björkman, in *Plays*, 1916; also translated by Walter Johnson, in *The Washington Strindberg*, vol. 12, 1983; Eivor Martinus, in *Three One-Act Plays*, 1987.

Inför döden (produced 1893). 1892; as *Facing Death*, translated by Velma Swanston Howard, 1907; also translated by Olive M. Johnson, 1911; Edith and Warner Öland, in *Plays*, 1912; Walter Johnson, in *The Washington Strindberg*, vol. 12, 1983.

Advent (produced 1915). 1898; as *Advent*, translated by Edwin Björkman, in *Plays*, 1913; also translated by Claud Field, 1914; Walter Johnson, in *Dramas of Testimony*, 1975, and in *The Washington Strindberg*, vol. 9, 1976.

Folkungasagen (produced 1901). 1899; as *The Saga of the Folkungs*, translated by C.D. Locock, in *Master Olof and Other Plays*, 1931; also translated by Walter Johnson, in *The Washington Strindberg*, vol. 5, 1959.

Gustav Vasa (produced 1899). 1899; as *Gustavus Vasa*, translated by Edwin Björkman, in *Plays*, 1916, and in *Eight Famous Plays*, 1949; also translated by C.D. Locock, in *Master Olof and Other Plays*, 1931; as *Gustav Vasa*, translated by Walter Johnson, in *The Washington Strindberg*, vol. 6, 1959.

Erik XIV (produced 1899). 1899; as *Erik XIV*, translated by Joan Bulman, in *Master Olof and Other Plays*, 1931; also translated by Walter Johnson, in *The Washington Strindberg*, vol. 6, 1959.

Brott och brott (produced 1900). 1899; as *There Are Crimes and Crimes*, translated by Edwin Björkman, 1912, and in *Eight Famous Plays*, 1949; also translated by Walter Johnson, in *The Washington Strindberg*, vol. 9, 1976; as *Crimes and Crimes*, translated by Elizabeth Sprigge, in *Five Plays*, 1960; also translated by Arvid Paulson, in *Seven Plays*, 1960; Evert Sprinchorn, in *The Genius of the Scandinavian Theater*, 1964.

Till Damaskus (trilogy) (produced 1900–24). 1900–04; edited by G. Lindström, 1964; as *To Damascus*, translated by Harriet Middleship, 1913; also translated by Sam E. Davidson, 1933; Graham Rawson, 1939; Evert Sprinchorn, in *The Genius of the Scandinavian Theater*, 1964; Arvid Paulson, in *Eight Expressionist Plays*, 1965; Walter Johnson, in *The Washington Strindberg*, vol. 10, 1979.

Påsk (produced 1901). 1900; as *Easter*, translated by Velma Swanston Howard, in *Easter and Stories*, 1912; also translated by Edith and Warner Öland, in *Plays*, 1912; E. Classen, in *Easter and Other Plays*, 1929; Elizabeth Sprigge, 1949; Peter Watts, in *Three Plays*, 1958; Arvid Paulson, in *Seven Plays*, 1960; Walter Johnson, in *The Washington Strindberg*, vol. 4, 1976.

Gustav Adolf (produced 1903). 1900; as *Gustav Adolf*, translated by Edwin Björkman, in *Plays*, 1912; also translated by Walter Johnson, in *The Washington Strindberg*, vol. 3, 1957.

Svanevit (produced 1908). 1901; as *Swanwhite*, translated by Francis J. Ziegler, 1909; also translated by Edith and Warner Öland, 1914; Elizabeth Sprigge, in *Five Plays*, 1960; Walter Johnson, in *The Washington Strindberg*, vol. 11, 1981.

Karl XII (produced 1905). 1901; as *Charles XII*, translated by Walter Johnson, in *The Washington Strindberg*, vol. 1, 1955.

Dödsdansen (produced 1905). 1901; as *The Dance of Death*, translated by Edwin Björkman, in *Plays*, 1912, and in *Eight Famous Plays*, 1949; also translated by C.D. Locock, in *Easter and Other Plays*, 1929; Elizabeth Sprigge, in *Five Plays*, 1960; Walter Johnson, in *The Washington Strindberg*, vol. 9, 1976; Suzane Grossman, 1981; Harry G. Carlson, in *Five Plays*, 1983; Evert Sprinchorn, in *Selected Plays*, 1986.

Engelbrekt (produced 1901). 1901; translated as *Engelbrekt*, 1955; also translated by Walter Johnson, in *The Washington Strindberg*, vol. 5, 1959.

Midsommar (produced 1901). 1901.

Kronbruden (produced 1906). 1902; as *The Bridal Crown*, translated by Edwin Björkman, in *Plays*, 1912; as *The Virgin Bride*, translated by Michael Meyer, in *Plays*, 1975; as *The Crownbride*, translated by Walter Johnson, in *The Washington Strindberg*, vol. 11, 1981.

Gustav III (produced 1916). 1902; as *Gustav III*, translated by Walter Johnson, in *The Washington Strindberg*, vol. 1, 1955.

Ett drömspel (produced 1907). 1902; as *The Dream Play*, translated by Edwin Björkman, in *Plays*, 1912; also translated by Elizabeth Sprigge, in *Six Plays*, 1955; as *A Dream Play*, translated by C.D. Locock, in *Easter and Other Plays*, 1929; also translated by Evert Sprinchorn, in *Selected Plays and Prose*, 1964; Arvid Paulson, in *Eight Expressionist Plays*, 1965; Walter Johnson, in *The Washington Strindberg*, vol. 8, 1973; F.R. Southerington, in *Three Experimental Plays*, 1975; Harry G. Carlson, in *Five Plays*, 1983.

Näktergalen i Wittenberg (produced 1914). 1903; as *The Nightingale of Wittenberg*, translated by Arvid Paulson, in *World Historical Plays*, 1970.

Himmelrikets nycklar, in *Samlede dramatiska arbeten*. 1903–04; as *The Keys of Heaven*, translated by Arvid Paulson, in *Eight Expressionist Plays*, 1965.

Kristina (produced 1908). 1904; as *Queen Christina*, translated by Walter Johnson, in *The Washington Strindberg*, vol. 1, 1955.

Three One-Act Plays, translated by Mary Harned (includes *Simoon; Debit and Credit; The Outcast*, latter from novel of Ola Hansson). 1906.

Spöksonaten (produced 1908). 1907; edited by G. Lindström, 1963; as *The Spook Sonata*, translated by Edwin Björkman, in *Plays*, 1916, and in *Eight Famous Plays*, 1949; as *The Ghost Sonata*, translated by E. Palmstierna and J.B. Fagan, in *Easter and Other Plays*, 1929; also translated by Elizabeth Sprigge, in *Six Plays*, 1955; Evert Sprinchorn, in *The Chamber Plays*, 1962, revised edition, 1981; Michael Meyer, in *Plays*, 1964, revised edition, 1982; Arvid Paulson, in *Eight Expressionist Plays*, 1965; Walter Johnson, in *The Washington Strindberg*, vol. 8, 1973; Harry G. Carlson, in *Five Plays*, 1983; Eivor Martinus, in *Chamber Plays*, 1991.

Oväder (produced 1907). 1907; as *The Storm*, translated by Edwin Björkman, in *Plays*, 1912; as *Storm Weather*, translated by Seabury Quinn, Jr. and Kenneth Petersen, in *The Chamber Plays*, 1962, revised edition, 1981; as *Stormy Weather*, translated by Walter Johnson, in *The Washington Strindberg*, vol. 8, 1973; as *Thunder in the Air*, translated by Eivor Martinus, in *Chamber Plays*, 1991.

Brända tomten (produced 1907). 1907; as *After the Fire*, translated by Edwin Björkman, in *Plays*, 1913; also translated by Eivor Martinus, in *Chamber Plays*, 1991; as *The Burned House*, translated by Seabury Quinn, Jr., in *The Chamber Plays*, 1962, revised edition, 1981; as *The House That Burned*, translated by Walter Johnson, in *The Washington Strindberg*, vol. 8, 1973.

Pelikanen (produced 1907). 1907; as *The Pelican*, translated by Edwin Björkman, in *Plays*, 1916; also translated by Evert Springhorn, in *The Chamber Plays*, 1962, revised edition, 1981; Walter Johnson, in *The Washington Strindberg*, vol. 8, 1973; Eivor Martinus, in *Chamber Plays*, 1991.

Abu Casems tofflor [Abu Casem's Slippers] (produced 1908). 1908.

Siste riddaren (produced 1908). 1908; as *The Last of the Knights*, translated by Walter Johnson, in *The Washington Strindberg*, vol. 2, 1956.

Riksföreståndaren (produced 1911). 1908; as *The Regent*, translated by Walter Johnson, in *The Washington Strindberg*, vol. 2, 1956.

Bjälbo-Jarlen (produced 1909). 1908; as *Earl Birger of Bjälbo*, translated by Walter Johnson, in *The Washington Strindberg*, vol. 2, 1956.

Svarta handsken (produced 1909). 1909; as *The Black Glove*, translated by Edwin Björkman, in *Plays*, 1916; also translated by Eivor Martinus, in *Chamber Plays*, 1991.

Stora landsvägen (produced 1910). 1909; as *The Great Highway*, translated by Arvid Paulson, in *Modern Scandinavian Plays*, 1954, and in *Eight Expressionist Plays*, 1965; also translated by Elizabeth Sprigge, in *Five Plays*, 1960; Walter Johnson, in *The Washington Strindberg*, vol. 11, 1981.

Plays (includes *The Stronger Woman; Motherly Love; Paria; Simoon; Comrades; Miss Julie; Creditors*), translated by Horace B. Samuel. 1914.

Genom öknar till arvland; eller, Moses (produced 1922). In *Samlade otryckta skrifter*, 1918–19; as *Moses*, translated by Edwin Björkman, in *Plays*, 1916; as *Through Deserts to Ancestral Lands*, translated by Arvid Paulson, in *World Historical Plays*, 1970.

Toten-Insel, in *Samlade skriften*. 1918; translated as *Isle of the Dead*, in *Modern Drama*, 3, 1962.

Miss Julie and Other Plays (includes *Miss Julie; The Creditor; The Stronger Woman; Motherly Love; Paria; Simoon*). 1918.

Hellas; eller, Sokrates (produced 1922). In *Samlade otryckta skrifter*, 1918–19; as *Hellas*, translated by Arvid Paulson, in *World Historical Plays*, 1970.

Lammet och vilddjuret; eller, Kristus (produced 1922). In *Samlade otryckta skrifter*, 1918–19; as *The Lamb and the Beast*, translated by Arvid Paulson, in *World Historical Plays*, 1970.

Easter and Other Plays (includes *Easter; Dance of Death; A Dream Play; Ghost Sonata*), translated by E. Classen, C.D. Locock, E. Palmstierna, and J.B. Fagan. 1929.

Lucky Peter's Travels and Other Plays (includes *Lucky Peter's Travels; The Father; Lady Julie; The Bond; Playing with Fire*), translated by E. Classen, C.D. Locock, and C. Napier. 1930.

Master Olof and Other Plays (includes *Master Olof; The Saga of the Folkungs; Gustavus Vasa; Erik XIV*), translated by C.D. Locock and Joan Bulman. 1931.

Eight Famous Plays (includes *The Link; The Father; Miss Julia; The Stronger; There Are Crimes and Crimes; Gustavus Vasa; The Dance of Death; The Spook Sonata*), translated by Edwin Björkman and N. Erichsen. 1949, reprinted as *Eight Best Plays*, 1979.

Six Plays (includes *The Father; Miss Julie; The Stronger; Easter; Dream Play; The Ghost Sonata*), translated by Elizabeth Sprigge. 1955.

Three Plays (includes *The Father; Miss Julie; Easter*), translated by Peter Watts. 1958.

Miss Julie and Other Plays (includes *Miss Julie; Creditors; The Ghost Sonata; The Stronger*), translated and adapted by Max Faber. 1960.

Five Plays (includes *Creditors; Crimes and Crimes; Swanwhite; Dance of Death; The Great Highway*), translated by Elizabeth Sprigge. 1960.

Seven Plays (includes *Comrades; The Father; Miss Julie; The Stronger; The Bond; Crimes and Crimes; Easter*), translated by Arvid Paulson. 1960.

The Chamber Plays (includes *Storm Weather; The Burned House; The Ghost Sonata; The Pelican*), translated by Evert Sprinchorn, Seabury Quinn, Jr., and Kenneth Petersen. 1962; revised edition, 1981.

Twelve Plays (includes text of *Six Plays*, 1955, *Five Plays*, 1960, with *The Bond*), translated by Elizabeth Sprigge. 1963.

Eight Expressionist Plays (includes *Lucky Per's Journey*; *To Damascus I–III*; *A Dream Play*; *The Great Highway*; *The Keys of Heaven*; *The Ghost Sonata*), translated by Arvid Paulson. 1965.

Strindberg's One-Act Plays, translated by Arvid Paulson. 1969.

World Historical Plays (includes *The Nightingale of Wittenberg*; *Through Deserts to Ancestral Lands*; *Hellas*; *The Lamb and the Beast*), translated by Arvid Paulson. 1970.

Three Experimental Plays (includes *Miss Julie*; *The Stronger*; *A Dream Play*), translated by F.R. Southerington. 1975.

Five Plays (includes *The Father*; *Miss Julie*; *Dance of Death*; *A Dream Play*; *Ghost Sonata*), translated by Harry G. Carlson. 1983.

Selected Plays (includes *Master Olof*; *The Father*; *The Stronger*; *The Creditor*; *Playing with Fire*; *The Dance of Death*), translated by Evert Sprinchorn. 1986.

Three One-Act Plays: Motherly Love; Pariah; The First Warning, translated by Eivor Martinus. 1987.

Chamber Plays (includes *Thunder in the Air*; *After the Fire*; *Ghost Sonata*; *Pelican*; *Black Glove*), translated by Eivor Martinus. 1991.

Fiction

Röda rummet. 1879; as *The Red Room*, translated by Ellie Schleussner, 1913.

Svenska öden och äventyr [Swedish Fates and Adventures]. 2 vols., 1883–90.

Giftas. 2 vols., 1884–86; as *Married: 20 Stories of Married Life*, translated by Ellie Schleussner, 1913; complete version, as *Getting Married*, translated by Mary Sandbach, 1972.

Hemsöborna. 1887; as *The People of Hemsö*, translated by Elspeth Harley Schubert, 1959; as *The Natives of Hemsö*, translated by Arvid Paulson, 1967.

Skärkarlsliv [Life in the Skerries]. 1888.

Tschandala (in Danish). 1889.

I havsbandet. 1890; as *By the Open Sea*, translated by Ellie Schleussner, 1913; also translated by Mary Sandbach, 1984; as *On the Seaboard*, translated by Elizabeth Clarke Westergren, 1913.

Fagervik och Skamsund. 1902; translated as *Fair Haven and Foul Strand*, 1914.

Sagor. 1903; as *Tales*, translated by L.J. Potts, 1930.

Gotiska rummen [The Gothic Rooms]. 1903.

Historiska miniatyrer. 1905; as *Historical Miniatures*, translated by Claud Field, 1913.

Svarta fanor [Black Banners]. 1907.

Taklagsöl. 1907; as *The Roofing Ceremony*, with *The Silver Lake*, translated by David Mel Paul and Margareta Paul, 1987.

Syndabocken. 1907; as *The Scapegoat*, translated by Arvid Paulson, 1967.

In Midsummer Days, and Other Tales, translated by Ellie Schleussner. 1913.

The German Lieutenant, and Other Stories, translated by Claud Field. 1915.

Stories and Poems (bilingual edition), edited by Joseph E.A. Alexis. 1924.

Verse

Dikter [Poems]. 1883.

Other

Svenska folket [The Swedish People]. 2 vols., 1880–82.

Det nya riket [The New Kingdom]. 1882.

Utopier i verkligheten [Utopias in Reality]. 1884.

Likt och olikt [This and That]. 2 vols., 1884.

Tjänstekvinnans son. 4 vols., 1886–87; as *The Growth of a Soul*, translated by Claud Field, 1913; in part as *The Son of a Servant*, translated by Field, 1913; also translated by Evert Sprinchorn, 1967.

Blomster målningar och djurstycken [Flower Pictures and Animal Pieces]. 1888.

Le Plaidoyer d'un fou. 1895; as *En dåres försvarstal*, 1914; as *The Confession of a Fool*, translated by Ellie Schleussner, 1912; as *A Madman's Defense*, edited by Evert Sprinchorn, translated by Schleussner, 1968; as *A Madman's Manifesto*, translated by Anthony Swerling, 1968.

Inferno. 1897; as *Inferno*, translated by Claud Field, 1912; also translated by Evert Sprinchorn, in *Inferno, Alone, and Other Writings*, 1968; part translated by Robert Brustein, in *Selected Plays and Prose*, 1964.

Legender. 1898; translated as *Legends: Autobiographical Sketches*, 1912.

Ensam. 1903; as *Alone*, translated by Evert Sprinchorn, in *Inferno, Alone, and Other Writings*, 1968.

Hövdingaminnen [Memories of Leaders]. 1906.

En blå bok. 4 vols., 1907–12; in part as *Zones of the Spirit*, translated by Claud Field, 1913.

Öppna brev till Intima Teatern. 1908; as *Open Letters to the Intimate Theater*, translated by Walter Johnson, 1959; as *Letters to the Intimate Theatre*, edited by Johnson, 1967.

Tal till svenska nationen [Speeches to the Swedish Nation]. 1910.

Gamla Stockholm [Old Stockholm], with Claës Lundin. 1912.

Easter and Stories (miscellany). 1912.

Brev till Harriet Bosse. 1923; as *Letters of Strindberg to Harriet Bosse*, edited and translated by Arvid Paulson, 1959.

Brev [Letters], edited by Torsten Eklund and Björn Meidal. 1948–.

Vivisektioner (essays), edited by Torsten Eklund. 1958.

Brev till min dotter Kerstin [Letters to My Daughter Kerstin], edited by Karin Boye and A[ring]ke Thulstrup. 1961.

Ur ockulta dagboken, edited by Torsten Eklund. 1963; complete version, 1977; in part as *From an Occult Diary*, translated by Mary Sandbach, 1965.

Selected Plays and Prose (includes *The Father*; *Miss Julie*; selection from *Inferno*; *A Dream Play*), edited by Robert Brustein and translated by Brustein, Evert Sprinchorn, and N. Erichsen. 1964.

Klostret. 1966; as *The Cloister*, edited by C.G. Bjurström, translated by Mary Sandbach, 1969.

Inferno, Alone, and Other Writings, translated by Evert Sprinchorn. 1968.

Letters 1892–1912, edited and translated by Michael Robinson. 2 vols., 1992.

*

Bibliography: ''Strindberg's Reception in England and America'' by Esther H. Rapp, in *Scandinavian Studies*, 23, 1951, supplemented by Jackson R. Bryer in *Modern Drama*, 5, 1962, and Birgitta Steene in *Structures of Influence: A Comparative Approach to Strindberg* edited by Marilyn Johns Blackwell, 1981; *Illustrerad svensk litteraturhistoria 4* by Sven Rinman, 1967; *August Strindberg* by Paul Fritz, 1979.

Critical Studies: *Strindberg the Man* by Carl Gustaf Uddgren, 1920; *August Strindberg: A Psychoanalytic Study with Special Reference to the Oedipus Complex* by Axel Johan Uppvall, 1920; *Strindberg: An Introduction to His Life and Work* by Brita Mortensen and Brian W. Downs, 1949; *The Strange Life of August Strindberg* by Elizabeth Sprigge, 1949; *Strindberg's Naturalistic Theatre* by B.G. Madsen, 1962; *Strindberg and the Historical Drama*, 1963, and *Strindberg*, 1976, both by Walter Johnson; *Essays on Strindberg* edited by Carl. R. Smedmark, 1966, and *Strindberg and Modern Theatre* edited by Smedmark, 1975; *The Novels of Strindberg* by Eric O. Johannesson, 1968; *August Strindberg* by Martin Lamm, 1971; *Strindberg: A Collection of Critical Essays* edited by Otto Reinert, 1971; *Strindberg's Impact in France 1920–1960* by Anthony Swerling, 1971; *August Strindberg* (English text) by Gunnar Ollén, 1972; *The Greatest Fire: A Study of Strindberg* by Birgitta Steene, 1973, 2nd revised edition as *August Strindberg: An Introduction to His Major Works*, 1982, and *Strindberg and History*, edited by Steene, 1992; *Strindberg in Inferno* by Gunnar Brandell, 1974; *The Social and Religious Plays of Strindberg* by John Ward, 1980; *Structures of Influence: A Comparative Approach to August Strindberg* by Marilyn Johns Blackwell, 1981; *Strindberg and Shakespeare: Shakespeare's Influence on Strindberg's Historical Drama* by Joan Bulman, 1982; *Strindberg* by George A. Campbell, 1982; *Strindberg and the Poetry of Myth* by Harry G. Carlson, 1982; *Strindberg as Dramatist* by Evert Sprinchorn, 1982; *Strindbergian Drama: Themes and Structure* by Egil Törnqvist, 1982, and *Strindberg's Miss Julie: A Play and Its Transpositions* by Törnqvist and Barry Jacobs, 1988; *August Strindberg* by Olof Lagercrantz, 1983; *Strindberg on Stage: Report from the Symposium in Stockholm, May 18–22, 1981* edited by Donald K. Weaver, 1983; *August Strindberg* by Margery Morgan, 1985; *Strindberg: A Biography*, 1985, and *File on Strindberg*, 1986, both by Michael Meyer; *Strindberg and Autobiography: Writing and Reading a Life* by Michael Robinson, 1986, and *Strindberg and Genre* edited by Robinson, 1991; *Strindberg and the Intimate Theatre* by Inga-Stina Ewbank, 1988; *Strindberg's Dramaturgy* edited by Göran Stockenström, 1988; *Harriet Bosse, Strindberg's Muse and Interpreter* by Carla Waal, 1990; *Out of Inferno: Strindberg's Reawakening as an Artist* by Harry G. Carlson, 1996; *Strindberg, Ibsen and Bergman: Essays on Scandinavian Film and Drama Offered to Egil Törnqvist on the Occasion of this 65th Brithday*, edited by Harry Perridon, 1998; *Theatrical and Narrative Space: Studies in Ibsen, Strindberg and J.P. Jacobsen* by Erik Østerud, 1998; *Strindberg: The Moscow Papers*, edited by Michael Robinson, 1998; *Questioning the Father: From Darwin to Zola, Ibsen, Strindberg, and Hardy* by Ross Shideler, 1999; *Expressionism and Modernism: New Approaches to August Strindberg*, edited by Michael Robinson and Sven Hakon Rossel, 1999; *Ibsen, Strindberg and the Intimate Theatre: Studies in TV Presentation* by Egil Törnqvist, 1999; *The Psychology of the Grotesque in August Strindberg's "The Ghost Sonata"* by Terry John Converse, 1999; *Stella Adler on Ibsen, Strindberg, and Chekhov* by Stella Adler, edited by Barry Paris, 1999; *Strindberg and the Five Senses: Studies in Strindberg's Chamber Plays* by Hans-Göran Ekman, 2000; *Strindberg's The Ghost Sonata: From Text to Performance* by Egil Törnqvist, 2000; *Strindberg and Love* by Eivor Martinus, 2001.

*   *   *

August Strindberg's achievement as an immensely productive dramatist, poet, novelist, essayist, painter, historian, autobiographer, and speculator in the natural sciences, alchemy, and linguistics is so various as almost to preclude summary. His international reputation, however, undoubtedly rests upon his plays. Strindberg experimented with many theatrical forms, fairytale comedy in *Lycko-Pers resa* (*Lucky Peter's Travels*), the folkplay in *Kronbruden* (*The Virgin Bride*), and, beginning with his first major work, *Mäster Olof* (*Master Olof*), from 1872, the history play, in a cycle of 12 history plays which represent the most important contribution to the genre since Shakespeare. Indeed, *Gustav Vasa, Erik XIV, Karl XII* (*Charles XII*), and *Kristina* (*Queen Christina*) combine a Shakespearean response to the sweep and detail of history with an acute and personal insight into historical characters, but they have been unduly neglected abroad because their material is taken from Swedish history.

This is certainly not the case with the two sets of plays that Strindberg wrote with his sights already trained on the theatres of France and Germany, two countries where, after his attack on Swedish society in the satirical pamphlet *Det nya riket* [The New Kingdom] in 1882, and his trial for blasphemy arising from the collection of stories *Giftas* (*Getting Married*) in 1884, he was to spend several important years of his life. The first set consists of the naturalist plays which Strindberg wrote between 1887 and 1892 as if in response to Zola's plea for someone to abandon the contrived formula of the contemporary well-made play and "put a man of flesh and bones on the stage, taken from reality scientifically analysed, and described without one lie." Building upon extensive reading in current psychology and cultivating a remarkable propensity for self-analysis that he owed in part to his pietist upbringing, Strindberg developed an intense and concentrated form for the portrayal on stage of what he called "the harsh, cynical and heartless drama that life presents." At the heart of this drama is an elemental struggle between man and woman, which he explores tragically in *Fadren* (*The Father*) and *Fröken Julie* (*Miss Julie*) and sardonically in *Fordringsägare* (*Creditors*). Conflict, however, is no longer physical but what Strindberg termed a "battle of the brains" in which one character seeks through suggestion to impose his or her will upon another. His ideas are outlined in the volume of essays, *Vivisektioner* [Vivisections], whose title implies the kind of analysis to which the naturalist writer aspired, and the preface to *Miss Julie*, which is the major theoretical statement of theatrical naturalism, where Strindberg describes his characters as not only the products of environmental and inherited forces but also as "split and vacillating . . . agglomerations of past and present cultures, scraps from books and newspapers, fragments of humanity, torn shreds of once-fine clothing that has become rags, in just the way that a human soul is patched together."

Miss Julie itself may not fully realize Strindberg's intentions, but in his next major group of plays, begun after an interval of six years, he effected a radical break with prevailing dramatic conventions and produced the key works in the development of theatrical modernism. In *Till Damaskus* (*To Damascus*), a sequence of three plays in which Strindberg projected his inner life through the figure of his protagonist, The Unknown, the picture-frame stage of the naturalists, with its abundance of realistic detail, gives way to the interior stage of the mind, a landscape through which The Unknown journeys as he delves into the past and encounters characters who are either aspects of his own personality or the product of his anxious imagination. In *Ett drömspel* (*A Dream Play*), meanwhile, which is generally regarded as

Strindberg's major achievement, he sought "to imitate the inconsequent yet transparently logical shape of a dream" where time and place do not exist and everything is possible and probable. The similarity of Strindberg's concerns with those of his contemporary, Sigmund Freud, have often, and rightly, been observed, but the dramatic presentation of life as a dream and the world as a stage also occurs in earlier drama, for example in Shakespeare, Calderón, and Henrik Ibsen's *Peer Gynt*. Nevertheless, *A Dream Play* initiated a succession of metatheatrical plays and marks the transition from a drama centred on plot and character to a theme-centred drama. In their use of concrete theatrical images enlisting all the resources of the stage, and in their apparently fluid structure, these plays are often easier to comprehend in terms of music, an affinity Strindberg underlined by calling his last important collection of plays, the Chamber Plays—*Oväder* (*The Storm*), *Brända tomten* (*The Burned House*), *Spöksonaten* (*The Ghost Sonata*), and *Pelikanen* (*The Pelican*)—written in 1907, his "last sonatas."

That Strindberg could make this remarkable transition from naturalism to modernism was largely a consequence of what is known as his "Inferno crisis." This was a period of acute mental suffering which verged on psychological breakdown, during which he was largely unproductive as an imaginative writer. Between 1892 and 1898 he spent much time on scientific studies which, in accord with the spirit of *fin de siècle* Paris where he lived for long periods, gravitated towards alchemy and magic. Behind his apparently aimless experiments, however, lay the need to renew himself by the discovery of fresh ways of seeing and apprehending both the visible and invisible world. At a time when Freud was similarly engaged on the self-analysis which led to *The Interpretation of Dreams* (1900), Strindberg also sought and found access to the unconscious life of the mind, employing techniques, outlined in the essay "The New Arts; or, The Role of Chance in Artistic Creation," which anticipate surrealism, and which he first applied in his paintings. A friend of Paul Gauguin and Edvard Munch, Strindberg was a considerable artist, and the way in which he approaches a non-representational art in his paintings marks a parallel development to his move away from plot and character in drama.

A partial account of these years is provided by the autobiographical novel *Inferno*, and his *Ur Ockulta dagboken* (*From an Occult Diary*), two in a sequence of autobiographical works which Strindberg saw as the core of his life's work. Employing various narrative techniques he traces the stages of an existence during which, both in life and literature, he experimented in a Kierkegaardian manner with a succession of different points of view, including an anarchism penetrated by the thought of Rousseau, an uneasy accommodation with Darwinism, atheism, Nietzschean individualism, and, after 1896, the discovery of a fruitful perspective for his writing in a personal syncretic religion that owed much to the Swedish scientist and mystic Emanuel Swedenborg (1688–1772). In *Tjänstekvinnans son* (*The Son of a Servant*), which stresses his lifelong identification with his mother, a former servant girl and waitress, rather than with his middle-class father, he undertook a naturalist investigation into his childhood and youth. This is followed by *En dåres försvarstal* (*A Madman's Defense*), first published as *Le Plaidoyer d'un fou*, the savage and exuberant vivisection of the first of his three turbulent marriages, *Klostret* (*The Cloister*), *Inferno*, *Legender* (*Legends*), and finally *Ensam* (*Alone*), an evocative portrayal of loneliness and the artistic process. Strindberg wished these works to be published as a single book, together with the *From an Occult Diary* and his letters,

an unwieldy project since the letters alone (and Strindberg was a formidable correspondent) fill over 18 volumes.

Inevitably the problem of subjectivity is one that Strindberg's work frequently raises. He regarded his life as literary capital and can often be discovered provoking experience in order to obtain material for further books. The real point, however, is not whether it is possible to correlate what is known of his life with the matter of his writing, but the transformation this material undergoes as it is turned into literature to enter into a complex set of relationships with all his other works. And if Strindberg appears to lack both imagination and humour, the reproach is belied by yet another portion of his work, again little known abroad—his novels and stories. *Röda rummet* (*The Red Room*), for example, with which he first made his reputation in Sweden, is an iridescent novel of Stockholm life, by turns comic, pathetic, and satiric, in which the influences of Charles Dickens and Honoré de Balzac are adroitly balanced. The humour of *Hemsöborna* (*The Natives of Hemsö*) is rich, even ribald, and like its successor, *I havsbandet* (*By the Open Sea*), it demonstrates Strindberg's passionate feeling for nature, particularly the landscape of the Stockholm archipelago. *Getting Married* is amusing as well as acerbic in its treatment of women. *Taklagsöl* (*The Roofing Ceremony*) is a finely judged experiment in the stream-of-consciousness technique. *Gotiska rummen* [The Gothic Rooms] and *Svarta fanor* [Black Banners] are both lively as well as bitter attacks on contemporary society. In all these books, as well as in his many essays on natural history, his historical studies *Gamla Stockholm* [Old Stockholm] and *Svenska folket* [The Swedish People], his historical fiction, and the political polemics in which he was engaged at the end of his life, Strindberg displays a multi-faceted response to experience which is consistently invigorated by a virtuoso command of his native language.

—Michael Robinson

See the essays on *The Ghost Sonata* and *Miss Julie*.

STURLUSON, Snorri

Born: on estate of Hvamm, Iceland, in 1179. Grew up in the cultivated household of Jón Loptsson at Oddi, 1181–97. **Family:** Married Herdís Bersadóttir in 1199 (separated 1206 or 1207); had children by several other women. **Career:** Lived in Reykholt after his separation from his wife, and became leading chieftain in Iceland; served as Law-Speaker of the Althing, 1215–18, 1222–31; visited Norway and Sweden, 1218—20, and made a later visit to Norway under political threat, 1237–39. Collector of earlier court poetry. **Died:** Murdered by political rival, 23 September 1241.

PUBLICATIONS

Works

Heimskringla [The Orb of the World], edited by Bjarni Aalbjarnarson, in *Íslensk fornrit*, vols. 26–28. 1941–51; as *Heimskringla: Chronicle of the Kings of Norway*, translated by Samuel Laing, 3 vols., 1844, revised by Peter Foote, as *Heimskringla: Sagas of the Norse Kings*, 1961; as *The Stories of the Kings of Norway, Called The Round World*, translated by William Morris and Eiríkr Magnússon, 4 vols., 1893–1905; as *Heimskringla: History of the Kings of*

Norway, translated by Lee M. Hollander, 1964; as *Heimskringla: The Lives of the Norse Kings*, edited by Erling Monsen, translated by Monsen and A.H. Smith, 1932; part as *King Harald's Saga*, translated by Magnus Magnusson and Hermann Pálsson, 1966.

Edda (prose), edited by Finnur Jónsson. 1900; revised edition, 1931; translated by G.W. Dasent, 1842; also translated by Arthur G. Brodeur, 1916; Jean I. Young, 1954; Anthony Faulkes, 1987.

*

Bibliography: in *Islandica*, 1908–.

Critical Studies: *Snorri Sturluson* (in Icelandic) by Sigurur Nordal, 1920, revised edition, 1973; *The Meaning of Snorri's Categories* by Arthur G. Brodeur, 1952; *Origins of Icelandic Literature* by G. Turville-Petre, 1953; *The Icelandic Saga* by Peter Hallberg, 1956; *Gods and Myths of Northern Europe* by H.R. Ellis Davidson, 1964; *Snorri Sturluson* by Marlene Ciklamini, 1978; *Skáldskaparmál: Snorri Sturluson's ars poetica and Medieval Theories of Language* by Margaret Clunies Ross, 1987.

*   *   *

Snorri Sturluson lived during the great age of saga-writing in Iceland, the 13th century; and his name has survived where the names of most other saga-writers have long been forgotten. He was a child of his time, combining a love of learning and intellectual pursuits with greed for wealth and power, and participation in the political machinations of the power struggle between Iceland and Norway, which at first brought him royal patronage, but finally a violent end. However, it is for his historical and imaginative writings, composed during the period 1222–35, that he is now remembered, and still read in Scandinavia as is no other medieval writer.

Snorri's major achievement as a historical writer is *Heimskringla* [The Orb of the World], a history of the kings of Norway from the earliest days (based on semi-mythical tales) to 1177. It is actually a collection of 17 sagas, of which one—the saga of King Olaf the Saint—dominates over all the others. Although Olaf ruled for only 15 years, his saga takes up one-third of the work; the Christian warrior-king was a figure who fascinated Snorri, and there is evidence that his saga was written first and then incorporated into the longer work. Snorri was a painstaking and meticulous historian, who used all the available source material, including written histories, earlier sagas, verbal reports, and scaldic poetry, in order to arrive at as accurate a version as possible of past events. He was, however, not merely a scientific recorder; his aim was rather to give a personal interpretation of events, to reconstruct the past. History was in his view formed by great men—a view with which many modern historians would disagree; yet his skilful reconstructions of the lives of the kings, combining fact with imagination and inventiveness, bring the atmosphere of the age vividly before us.

The other work which Snorri is known to have composed, the prose *Edda*, gave full scope to his creative literary talents. It fulfils several aims, but its most important function is as a preserver of literary and mythological tradition. It contains a mythology of the old Norse gods and the heathen world-view, ostensibly as an aid to poets who needed to know the origins of the myths from which scaldic poetry drew its images—material which was in danger of being forgotten in the new Christian era. But is is also clearly a story that Snorri relishes telling; his enthusiasm for the myths turns the textbook into a lively and humorous re-creation. The *Edda* further records and

gives examples of all the different forms of scaldic verse, of which it provides an invaluable collection; and it explains and exemplifies the use of poetic imagery in scaldic verse. Thus in several areas it has preserved material that would otherwise have been lost.

In addition to these two works, Snorri wrote other poems, mainly to wealthy patrons; and there is a large body of scholarly opinion which attributes to him the authorship of *Egil's Saga*, the life-story of the poet Egil Skalla-Grímsson.

—Janet Garton

See the essays on "The prose *Edda*" and *The Saga of King Óláf the Saint*.

SU DONGPO

See SU SHI

SU SHI

Also known as Su Zizhan (courtesy name); Su Dongpo [Su Tung-p'o] (pen name). **Born:** Meishan, Sichuan province, China, 8 January 1037. **Family:** Married in 1054; took Zhao Yun as mistress 1074. **Career:** Passed final civil-service examinations, 1057; government official from 1060, with the courtesy name Su Zizhan; obtained judicial post in the capital city Bianliang (now Kaifeng), 1069; demoted to provincial posts for opposing reforms in 1071, jailed in 1079 and banished to Huangzhou until 1084, where he farmed land and took the pen name Su Dongpo in 1082; recalled to the capital, 1086; appointed governor of Hangzhou prefecture, 1089; other official posts, 1091–97; second banishment, to Huizhou, 1094, then to Hainan Island, 1097: pardoned in 1100. Wrote more than 2,000 poems and more than 300 lyric pieces. Also active as essayist, calligrapher, and painter. Posthumously honoured as Wenzhong in 1235; tablets in his name removed from Confucian institutions in 1845. Earliest compilation of his work, 1097–1100, and there were three more editions during the 12th century. **Died:** in 1101.

PUBLICATIONS

Collection

Su Shi wenji [The Collected Writings of Su Shi], edited by Kong Fanli. 1986.

Verse

Su Wenzhonggong quanji [Complete Works of Su, Honoured as Wenzhong]. 1534.
Dongpo ji zhu [Works of Dongpo]. 27 vols., 1656.
[Works], edited by Shao Changhenh, from the version edited by Shi Yuanzhi. 1699.
[Works], edited by Zha Shenxing. 1761.
[Works: Composite Edition], edited by Feng Yingliu. 1793.

Su Wenzhonggong shi bianzhu jicheng (works; includes the *zongan* commentary), edited by Wang Wen'gao. 1822, reprinted, 1967; revised as *Su Shi shi ji* [Collected Poetry], 1982.

Dongpo ji [Works of Dongpo]. 40 vols., 1909.

Sibu congkan. 1929.

Dongpo yuefu jian [Dongpo's Lyrics], edited by Long Muxun. 1936.

Sibu beiyao. 1936.

Selections from the Works of Su Tung-p'o, translated by Cyril D. Le Gros Clark. 1931.

The Prose-Poetry of Su Tung-p'o, translated by Cyril D. Le Gros Clark. 1935, reprinted 1964.

Chinese Lyrics, translated by Ch'u Ta-kao. 1937.

The White Pony (includes poems by Su Shi), translated by R. Payne. 1947.

Su Tung-p'o: Selections from a Sung Dynasty Poet, translated by Burton Watson. 1965.

Zeng bu zu ben Shi Gu zhu Su Shi, edited by Zheng Qian and Yan Yiping (from the Qing Dynasty reconstruction of the 13th-century texts compiled by Shi Yanzhi). 1980.

Su Dong-po: A New Translation, translated by Xu Yuanzhang. 1982.

So Tōba shishū, edited by Ogawa Tamaki and Yamamoto Kazuyoshi. 4 vols., 1983–86.

Su Shi shi xuan [Selected Poems of Su Shi], edited by Xu Ji. 1986.

Other

Jiazheng jingjin Dongpo wenji shilue [Annotated Selection of Prose by Dongpo], edited by Lang Ye. 1957.

*

Critical Studies: ''The Works of Su Tung-p'o'' by J.C. Ferguson, in *China Journal*, 12, 1930; *The Gay Genius: The Life and Times of Su Tung-p'o* by Lin Yutang, 1948; ''Su Tung-p'o'' in *An Introduction to Sung Poetry* by K. Yoshikawa, translated by Burton Watson, 1967; *The Chinese Literation Painting: Su Shih (1037–1101) to Tung Ch'i-Ch'ang (1555–1636)* by S. Bush, 1971; *Major Lyricists of the Northern Sung* by J.J.Y. Liu, 1974; *Nature and Self: A Study of the Poetry of Su Dongpo with Comparisons to the Poetry of William Wordsworth* by Vincent Yang, 1989; ''Su Shih and Culture,'' in *Sung Dynasty Uses of the I Ching*, 1990, and *''This Culture of Ours'': Intellectual Transitions in T'ang and Sung China*, 1992, both by Peter K. Bol; *The Road to East Slope: The Development of Su Shi's Poetic Voice* by Michael A. Fuller, 1990; *Word, Image and Deed in the Life of Su Shi* by Ronald E. Egan, 1994; *Mount Lu Revisited* by Beata Grant, 1994; *The Concept of the Relationship Between Painting and Poetry* by Yuheng Bao, 1999.

*   *   *

Su Shi is one of the greatest men of letters in China's 2,000-year cultural tradition. He was the best poet of the Song dynasty (960–1279) and a powerful prose stylist in an age of great writers. He provided prestige and theoretical justification for an emergent style that came to dominate literati painting for the next 800 years. Su Shi also was an effective local administrator and rose to high government office. He dabbled in Daoist herbal lore and wrote commentaries on the Confucian classics. For Su Shi, writing well was an important part of coming to know the world. Literariness and rhetoric were crucial for

an adequate representation of a world of complex, constantly unfolding patterns of transformation. As he explains:

> My writing is like a spring of ten thousand gallons; it does not choose its path as it goes out. On level land it flows smoothly and quickly, and a thousand miles a day is not difficult. When it comes to turns and breaks over mountains and stones, it follows the object to describe the form, and it cannot be known. That which can be known is that it always travels where it ought to travel, and it always stops where it ought to stop. It is like this, and for all else, I too cannot know.

(quoted by Fuller, in *The Road to East Slope*, p. 85)

The written text becomes an object record of where one has been, what one has encountered, and in the end, who one is. Despite Su Shi's great talents and posthumous fame, however, he fought a losing battle as he attempted to find a significant role for aesthetic activity in the larger Chinese intellectual culture. Soon after his death, *dao xue* (or Neo-Confucian) moral philosophy rose to prominence, and the aesthetic was reduced to mere subjective colouration of experience that was dangerously distracting or, at best, just ephemeral. (See Peter Bol's discussion of Su Shi in *This Culture of Ours*, pp. 254–99). In this new climate, poetry became just words nicely arranged on a page, and Su Shi became just a poet.

Unlike the textual corpora for many Chinese writers, enough of Su Shi's writings remain and are datable for us to trace his intellectual and aesthetic development. His most important early work seems polarized about the problem of subjectivity. The political and historical essays Su Shi submitted in 1061 for an imperial examination confront the issue of partiality in forming government policy. In seeming contradiction, his earliest poetry has a strong inward turn. The ''Song of the Stone Drums,'' a bravura performance piece, for example, is Su Shi's account of a set of ancient rocks inscribed with commemorative poems. The ''Song'' recreates an imagined history for the Drums to convey Su Shi's impression of standing before the prehistoric relics. The poem's bold imagery and the twists and turns in its organization explicitly reveal the wilfully shaping hand of the young poet.

Su Shi's writings during his service as vice-prefect of Hangzhou, a major cultural centre in south China, show an enlargement of perspective. Strongly opposed to the reform regime then in power, Su Shi wrote a series of bitingly sarcastic poems to criticize the impact of the new policies. Among the most famous of these are ''Mountain Village, five quatrains'' and ''Jesting with Ziyou.'' In Hangzhou, Su Shi also began to explore the art of writing *ci*, a popular form of song lyric with prosodic requirements and thematic conventions very different from the more usual *shi* poetry. Su Shi quickly developed a distinctive ''unbridled'' style of *ci* through which he wrote about topics previously reserved for *shi*. (Some of his contemporaries objected to this transformation of the song genre, and the debate continues down to the present day). Some of Su Shi's best early *ci* are ''Twentieth Day of the First Month of Yimao (1075), Recording a Dream,'' written to mourn his wife, and ''Mid-Autumn, Bingchen (1076),'' written for his brother. After Hangzhou, Su Shi served as prefect in a series of smaller cities, and during this period, his fame as a poet, lyricist, and prose stylist continued to spread. The ''Account of the Terrace of Transcendence'' written to celebrate the restoration of a small park while Su Shi served as prefect of Mizhou, suggests the allure of his prose style. The account, interpreting the new name for the park, addresses the weighty issue of transcendence and explains the broader meaning of the park's rebuilding in the context of the history and folk traditions of the region. The skill with which Su Shi combines the two themes—and thereby significantly recasts the notion of transcendence—reveals both the breadth of Su Shi's sensibility and his stylistic mastery.

Su Shi's satiric verses eventually irritated the politically embattled regime, and they decided to set an example by arresting him for insulting the Emperor. Su Shi was duly convicted and exiled to the small city of Huangzhou on the Yangzi River, where he bided his time reflecting, writing, and cultivating a small farm called Dongpo ("East Slope"). Exile brought many previous trends in Su Shi's thinking and writing to full maturity. Indeed, "Su Dongpo" ("Su of East Slope")—the name that he took for himself in Huangzhou—has come to stand for the persona developed through the writings in exile and is the name by which he is primarily known in both China and Japan. His compositions in Huangzhou reveal a "firm, philosophic, yet jovial poise of spirit" (Fuller, p. 251). The series "Eight Poems on East Slope," for instance, celebrates the first crop harvested from the abandoned fields at East Slope and—with a very light hand—interprets the process of cultivation within the larger norms of Chinese civilization. Su Shi also finished his commentary on the *Yi jing* ("The Classic of Change") in Huangzhou to give a systematic account of his position in the ever more inescapable metaphysical debates of the late 11th century. (See Peter Bol, "Su Shih and Culture," in *Sung Dynasty Uses of the I Ching*.) Three of Su Shi's most famous literary pieces—two prose poems on Red Cliff and a *ci*, "Cherishing the Old at Red Cliff"—were written at Huangzhou. The breath of perspective and boldness of imagination and composition mark these works as quintessential "Su of East Slope."

Su Shi set the pattern for many aspects of literati identity in late imperial China. Yet the enduring popularity of "Su of East Slope" has strangely erased much of the complexity, richness, and seriousness of purpose that lies behind the persona.

—Michael A. Fuller

SU Tong

Also known as Tong Zhong Gui and Tong Zhonggui. **Born:** Suzhou, People's Republic of China, 21 January 1963 (some sources give 23 January). **Education:** Suzhou public schools; Beijing Normal University, B.D., 1984. **Family:** Married Wei Hong in 1987; one child. **Career:** Worked briefly as a schoolteacher in Nanjing after 1983; editor of Zhongshan literary magazine in Jiangsu, 1986–92; full-time novelist and short-story writer from the mid-1980s; literary seminar on his works was convened in Beijing, 1987; writer-in-residence, University of Iowa International Writing Program, 2001–. Lives in Nanjing, China.

PUBLICATIONS

Collections

Su Tong xiao shuo jing pin. 1993.
Su Tong san wen. 2000.

Fiction

Qi qie Cheng qun. 1990; as *Raise the Red Lantern: Three Novellas*, translated by Michael S. Duke, 1993; includes: *Da hong deng long gao gao gua* (*Wives and Concubines*), *1934 nien ti t'ao wang* (*1934 Escapes*), and *Ying su chih chia* (*Opium Family*).
Mi. 1991; as *Rice*, translated by Howard Goldblatt, 1995.
Hong Fen. 1991.
Nan fang di duo luo. 1991.
Hun yin chi ching. 1993.
Shao nien hsieh. 1993.
Shih chieh liang ts'e. 1993.
Hou gong. 1994.
Mo tai ai ch'ing. 1994.
Pu sa man. 1999.

*

Critical Studies: "Walking Toward the World: A Turning Point in Contemporary Chinese Fiction" by Michael S. Duke, in *World Literature Today*, Summer 1991; "Su Tong: Young Teller of Old Tales" by Wei Liming, in *Beijing Review*, 12 April 1993; "Rice" by Richard Bernstein, in *New York Times*, 13 November 1995.

* * *

Since the late 1980s, Su Tong has emerged as one of contemporary China's most celebrated fiction writers, with a critically acclaimed portfolio of short stories, novellas, and novels, some of which have been translated into English and other languages. His life and career parallels a convulsive time in the history of modern China. Su Tong was born as Tong Zhonggui in 1963, not long before Mao Zedong launched the Great Proletarian Cultural Revolution that demanded greater intellectual conformity to the nation's socialist ideology. Born in the southern Chinese city of Suzhou, Su Tong enrolled in the Chinese department of Beijing Normal University in 1980, after graduating from secondary school in his hometown. After graduation, he took a teaching position in the city of Nanjing, the old southern capital of China, where he still resides. While in Nanjing, he began writing professionally and joined the editorial staff of *Zhongshan*, a literary magazine that was publishing the works of younger writers with diverse opinions about Chinese society. Among the writers he admires is William Faulkner, the U.S. novelist and Nobel prize winner famous for his portrayals of life in the American South in the early 20th century.

Mao had died in 1976, and over the next decade China had adopted more liberal economic and diplomatic policies, though dissident literature and civil liberties were still tightly controlled. Nevertheless, younger writers like Su Tong and his peers were able to express themselves more freely, without the need to adhere to the strict ideological purity demanded of the previous generation. The stories that Su Tong began publishing from the mid-1980s did not need to idealize the noble proletariat or indict the corruption of capitalism. Instead, he began to drew on older Chinese traditions as well as Western sources to create a detached, apolitical, individualist literature that expressed his own sense of ethics and aesthetics. His characters are portrayed realistically, warts and all, as they live vulnerable lives beleaguered by superstition, irrationality, or passion. His dysfunctional characters are so caught up in greed, sexual obsession, ambition, and sheer survival that they have little luxury for intellectual or ideological pursuits. Even in the narratives set during the Cultural Revolution and its aftermath, like "The Brothers Shu," a short story, or *The North Part of Town*, a novel, there is little overt political commentary. Instead, Su Tong focuses his attention on such issues as family conflict or misdirected youth. The short story "Escape" chronicles the tragic life of a peasant who finally dies after a life of trying to escape society's strictures, such as abandoning his wife or deserting his military obligations.

For Su Tong, the family saga offers a fertile expressive milieu for his fiction. In one sense, this can be seen as a conservative attribute that attests to the author's rootedness in a more traditional (pre-Mao) China in which Confucian values predominated. Still, Su Tong does not idealize these earlier models, and he does not refrain from portraying them as dysfunctional or scandal-ridden.

One of Su Tong's best-known works, especially in the West, is *Qi qie Cheng qun* (*Raise the Red Lantern*), a compilation of three "family saga" novellas published in English in 1993. The titles of the three novellas underscore the author's refusal to idealize the traditional family: *Da hong deng long gao gao gua* (*Wives and Concubines*), *1934 nien ti t'ao wang* (*1934 Escapes*), and *Ying su chih chia* (*Opium Family* or *Poppy Family*). In the second of these, for example, Su Tong traces the rise and fall of an inbred clan in Maple Village, where intrigue and rivalry are far more prominent than adherence to ethical values. In this, as in his other works, Su Tong employs often graphic symbols to dramatize the depravity of the family; here, it is a jade jar containing semen that spills and causes a plague in the town. In *Opium Family*, its patriarch sells his daughter to an old man, and she is later raped by a peasant who becomes a Communist leader. This novella can be seen as a veiled critique of the Communist era, in which traditional family ties were abruptly replaced by a revolutionary ethos.

Su Tong's novel, *Mi* (*Rice*), which appeared in English in 1995, is set in the 1930s, when China was besieged by chaos, famine, and foreign invasion. Once again, Su Tong downplays direct political commentary in favor of his focus on the depravity and greed of its central character, Five Dragons. Su Tong uses rice, the staple food of China and a traditional symbol of prosperity, as the unifying metaphor of the novel, but he often describes it being used in a negative fashion, as when it is used during the sexual violation of a woman, the suffocation of a child, or the desecration of a corpse.

Reviewing this novel for the *New York Times*, Richard Bernstein wrote that Su Tong had emerged as one of a group of younger Chinese writers who no longer felt compelled to write the kind of "good-news-only literature" that was favored during the Mao Zedong era. By choosing themes and situations that were bawdy and profane by Communist standards, Su Tong argues for a literature of realism that indicts its characters by standards that transcend narrower ideological aims.

—Edward Moran

See the essay on *Rice*.

SU ZIZHAN

See SU SHI

SUETONIUS

Born: Gaius Suetonius Tranquillus in Rome, c. AD 69. **Career:** Began a military career, then practised law in Rome; secretary at the court of Hadrian: dismissed AD 121–22. **Died:** AD 160.

PUBLICATIONS

Collections

[Works], edited by Maximilian Ihm. 1907–08; translated by J.C. Rolfe [Loeb Edition], 2 vols., 1914.

Works

De vita Caesarum, edited by C.L. Roth, 1858; also edited by Giorgio Brugnoli, 1960–; as *History of the Twelve Caesars*, translated by Philemon Holland, 1606, reprinted 1899; as *Caesars—From Galba to Domitian*, translated by G.W. Mooney, 1930; as *The Twelve Caesars*, translated by Robert Graves, 1957, revised by Michael Grant, 1979; as *Lives of the Caesars*, translated with introduction and notes by Catharine Edwards, 2000; individual lives: *Augustus*, edited by E.S. Shuckburgh, 1896, M. Adams, 1939, M.A. Levi, 1951, and J.M. Carter, 1982; *Caligula*, edited by J.A. Maurer, 1949; *Claudius*, edited by H. Smilda, 1896, and J. Mottershead, 1986; as *Divvs Clavdivs*, edited by Donna W. Hurley, 2001; *Galba, Otho, Vitellius*, edited by C.L. Murison, 1992, and edited and translated by David Shotter, 1993; *Julius*, edited by H.E. Butler and M. Cary, 1927; *Nero*, edited by G.H. Warmington, 1977; *Tiberius*, edited by J.H. Rietra, 1927, and M.J. du Four, 1941; *Tiberius*, edited by Hugh Lindsay, 1995; *Titus*, edited by H. Price, 1919; *Vespasian*, edited by A.W. Braithwaite, 1927; *Vespasian*, edited by Brian W. Jones, 2000; *Domitian*, edited by B. Jones, 1996.

De grammaticis et rhetoribus, edited by R.P. Robinson. 1925; translated and edited by Robert A. Kaster, 1995; as *The Grammarians; The Rhetoricians*, edited by C.L. Roth, 1871; as *Lives of the Grammarians*, translated by Alexander Thomson, 1796.

*

Critical Studies: *Sueton und die antike Biographie* by W. Steidle, 1951; *Index to Suetonius* by A.A. Ḥoward and C.N. Jackson, 1963; *The Ancient Historians* by M. Grant, 1970; *Suetonius: The Scholar and His Caesars* by Andrew Wallace-Hadrill, 1983; *The Arts of Suetonius* by Richard C. Lounsbury, 1987; *An Historical and Historiographical Commentary on Suetonius' Life of C. Caligula* by Donna W. Hurley, 1993; *Suetonius' Life of Caligula: A Commentary* by D. Wardle, 1994.

*   *   *

"So much for Caligula the Emperor; the rest of this history must needs deal with Caligula the monster." So writes Suetonius at the start of the 22nd chapter (out of 60) of the book devoted to this particular ruler in his *De vita Caesarum* (*The Twelve Caesars*). There can be no doubt that what many readers have looked for in this work is scandalous, even hair-raising detail about the appalling private lives of such as Caligula, Tiberius, and, of course, Nero. If ever proof were

needed that the greater the power a man possesses, the more it can corrupt him, it can be found here in abundance in accounts of arbitrary cruelty, unbridled lust, and attempts to revive flagging passions by novel vices. Suetonius does not provide details about such matters simply in passing; there is some evidence that he occasionally preferred the more shocking anecdote to the version of events more flattering to the memory of the emperor about whom he was writing. Like some of his readers, he appears to have relished the seamy side of the imperial image.

Suetonius is, however, not merely of interest to those in search of the sensational. By no means all of his works have come down to posterity, but his biographical writings do contain, inextricably mixed with a good deal of what must be accounted mere apocryphal anecdote, nuggets of information concerning personalities in the 1st century AD about whom we should otherwise know very little indeed. Large sections of his *De viris illustribus* [Famous Men] have been lost. The section on *The Rhetoricians* provides, however, not only an account of the rise of rhetoric in Rome, but also, albeit in summary form, facts about some of the practitioners of this highly influential art. *The Grammarians* likewise offers some account of the literature teachers of the period. Also by Suetonius are a number of brief lives of certain major poets, such as Virgil, Horace, and Terence. The scantiness of these accounts is quite infuriating, and sometimes there is gossip where more substantial information would be welcome. All the same, we should know far less about these writers if we did not have what Suetonius chose to tell us. Much the same point may justly be made about *The Twelve Caesars*, even if it has to be observed that Suetonius might generally be regarded as a less important source of historical details, were it not for the fact that the *Annals* by Tacitus, his near contemporary and a more insightful historian, were not available.

Born into a good family but declining to follow his father's example and embark on a military career, Suetonius soon decided that he was also ill-suited to legal work. Instead he found employment in the imperial household. What his first duties were under Trajan has yet to be explained with precision, but he next became director of the imperial library and was then promoted, significantly, to the important post of correspondence secretary to the demanding and discriminating Hadrian who, however, dismissed him for some slight to the empress. Employment at the very centre of public affairs and ready access to existing records gave Suetonius great advantages when he turned from writing on Roman antiquities and the natural sciences to presenting portraits of the 12 emperors from Julius Caesar onwards. In this fascinating sequence the greatest emphasis naturally falls on Caesar, Augustus, Tiberius, Caligula, Claudius, and Nero, who were the more striking personalities and in any case ruled longer than the next six emperors, but there is also a suspicion that Suetonius was less well-placed to consult written sources about their reigns.

Suetonius had no ambition to write history as such. In Roman times this implied not only a strong chronological pattern but also a high degree of stylistic polish. His *The Twelve Caesars* stands rather in the biographical tradition, and even within that it is noteworthy that Suetonius has no time for the deeply rooted ancient fashion for eulogy. Starting with his subject's ancestry and early life, Suetonius moves on rapidly to a survey of his public career. Next comes a description of his physical appearance and finally an account of his private life. Background information is largely taken for granted, but we do, on the other hand, receive a most vivid account of the personality in question. Some of the detail may indeed be scabrous, but Suetonius also possesses the true biographer's ability for allowing

us to share in his subject's innermost feelings. The account of Nero's last moments, for instance, has often been admired for its vividness and understanding of human emotions.

As a stylist Suetonius is not generally considered to merit a high place among Latin writers, for he lacks both the elegance of the Ciceronian manner and the lapidary pregnancy of the mordant Tacitus. He does not interlard his biographies with grand speeches any more than he goes out of his way to coin flashing epigrams. His language is, in fact, of a piece with his storytelling: plain, clear, and easily grasped. It comes as something of a surprise to learn from one of the letters of Pliny the Younger that Suetonius fussed over his writings and had to be persuaded to stop revising them and make them available at last to the reading public.

—Christopher Smith

SŪRDĀS

Also known as Sūr Dās. **Born:** into a Brahmin (priestly caste) family in Sīhī, probably in Uttar Pradesh, India, probably late 15th century (1478 or c. 1530 have been suggested). Either born or became blind. **Career:** At age of eight, accompanied parents on pilgrimage to Mathura, and was left in care of guardian. Joined the Kṛṣṇbhakti movement founded by Vallabhāchārya, becoming an ascetic on the banks of the Yamuna river, 1509–10. Traditionally said to have composed 1 million songs in praise of Kṛṣṇ, which he sang in the temple of Śrīnāth. Reputed to be the author of five works, of which two are only known by their titles (*Nal Damayantī* and *Vyahala*). **Died:** Late 16th/early 17th century (1570, 1583, and 1610 have been suggested).

PUBLICATIONS

Works

Sūrasāgara [Ocean of Sūrdās], edited by R.K. Dāsa. 1908; also edited by Dāsa and others, 1936, and Jagannath Das and N.D. Vājepeyī, 2 vols., 1948–50; as *Bhramaragītasāra*, edited by R.C. Śūkla and V.P. Miśra, 1953; as *Sūradāsa aur unkā bhramaragīta*, edited by D.D. Gupta, 1963; as *Sūrasāgara satika*, edited by Horadeva Bāharī and Rājendra Kumāra (critical edition, with modern Hindi), 4 vols., 1974–; as *Sūr Sāgar*, edited by Jagannāthdās Ratnākar, 1976; *The Padas of Surdas* (manuscript facsimile), edited by Gopal Narayan, 1982; selections in: *Surdas*, translated by U. Nielson, 1982, *Sūrdās: Poet Singer Saint*, translated by John Stratton Hawley, 1984; *Divine Sports of Krishna: Poems of Sūr Dāsa*, translated by A.J. Alston (includes 295 verses), 1993; as *The Poems of Sūradāsa* by Krishna P. Bahadur, 1999.

*

Critical Studies: *Poems to the Child-God: Structures and Strategies in the Poetry of Sūrdās* by Kenneth E. Bryant, 1978; *Surdas: Poetry and Personality* by S.N. Srivastava, 1978; *Krishna the Butter Thief*, 1983, and *Sūrdās: Poet Singer, Saint*, 1984, both by John Stratton

Hawley; *Sūrdāsa: A Critical Study of His Life and Work* by K.C. Sharma, K.C. Yadav and Pushpendra Sharma, 1997.

* * *

One of the greatest *bhakti* (devotional) poets in Hindi (he wrote in a dialect of Hindi called Brajbhāṣā, the language of Braj—a region of Uttar Pradesh, formerly called United Provinces), Sūrdās was born into a Brahmin family, in a village between Mathura and Agra in western Uttar Pradesh. Little is known of his life, except that he was blind, although whether he was born blind is uncertain. He was a follower of the southern Indian reformer Vallabhāchārya, founder and exponent of the movement called *Kṛṣṇabhakti* (devotion to Kṛṣṇa), and dedicated numerous poems (*padas*) to Kṛṣṇa, who was regarded as the personification of the Supreme, just as Rāma is so regarded by the other great *bhakti* poet, Tulsīdās. Whereas Tulsīdās's Rāma embodies heroism and perfection even from childhood, Sūrdās's Kṛṣṇa, although divine by nature, acts and behaves like any other child, until he grows up and becomes the champion of virtue, moral perfection, and personal purity and morality.

It is while probing into the psychology of Kṛṣṇa as a child, and at the same time representing him as an incarnation of the Supreme, that Sūrdās reaches the poetically charged meeting between the human and divine, between innocence and experience, between what is linguistically simple, ingenuous, and childlike, and what constitutes the subtly symbolic and allegorical vein running through the language in which Sūrdās conveys the feelings of the devotees and the lovers of Kṛṣṇa.

Although there are two other works attributed to Sūrdās (*Sūrsārāvalī* and *Sāhitya Laharī*), it is chiefly by virtue of his voluminous collections of lyric poems that Sūrdās ranks with Kabīr, Tulsīdās, and Mīra Bāī, as one of the greatest *bhakti* poets. The principal themes of his poetry, apart from the various phases and episodes in the life of Kṛṣṇa seen in a dual capacity (god and child), are love, pangs of separation, nostalgia and longing for reunion with the beloved, and hankering after the heart-rending as well as heart-soothing melodies of Kṛṣṇa's flute.

Love of Kṛṣṇa, on the part of his female admirers, the so-called "gopīs" (milkmaids) and especially Rādhā, is depicted in emotional and subjective terms, and is often a veil for the aspiration to something higher: the Supreme Being Himself. That is why the accents through which it is expressed are often those of a passionately felt prayer. In one of the most poignant lyrics Rādhā, personifying female love at its most intense, bemoans her sense of separation from her beloved Gopāla (another name for Kṛṣṇa), and the disastrous consequences it has had both on her and on the world around her:

In Gopāl's absence
these groves and thickets
have turned into my enemies.
Once so cool and refreshing,
the creepers have turned into flames.
The Yamuna flows in vain,
and in vain do the birds sing,
the bees hum, or the lotuses bloom. . .

The burning intensity of Rādhā's love for Śyām (yet another name for Kṛṣṇa) is such that the more she tries to hide it, the more difficult it becomes to do so:

"Rādhā!," a friend of hers tells her,
"you are hiding your love from me."
"Who is Śyām? Is he dark/or fair? Where does he live?
Whose son is he?
Is he old or young
or is he just a child?"
"O look! how Rādhā pretends.
She's asking me what Śyām is like!"

Rādhā's jealousy of another woman—for, like a bee, Śyām goes from one flower to another—makes both her love for him and her devotion to him even greater and more intense:

O black bee,
why do you want to taste me?
I am not that yellow jasmine
you spent the night with,
having spent the day with me.
Take your fragrant body to the night lily.
Your face, your body, your limbs,
they shine differently with different women.
It irks you that I'm devoted to you,
but for me separation from you
is a mountain I cannot climb,
and each day finds me
weaker still.

Another dimension to such love and devotion is the one where the poet turns to Kṛṣṇa for his own salvation, and, using a very ingenious piece of logic, begs forgiveness for his sins:

My Master,
please don't take note of my faults.
You are the one who looks upon everyone
with the same eye; hence save me.
One piece of iron is used
in a place of worship, another in a butcher's shop;
but the gilder doesn't differentiate
between them and he covers them
both with pure gold . . . hence save me or you will break
your own promise to help your devotees.

This is the promise Kṛṣṇa makes to his devotees in another well-known poem by Sūrdās:

I belong to my devotees
and they to me. Listen to me, Arjuna,
this is my promise
which can never be broken.
Wherever my devotees are in trouble,
I run barefoot to help them,
abandoning all sense of shame.
. . . Those who are his enemies
are my enemies too. That's why
I am driving your chariot. If you win
I win too; and your
defeat is also my defeat.

The most popular poems by Sūrdās, however, are those where Kṛṣṇa, a child, talks to his mother Yashodā (also called Jasumati), and she to him, while each, caught up in the web of emotions of love and affection, forgets the divine aspect of the child's personality:

> "O mother, my elder brother Dāū
> teases me a lot.
> He tells me that you didn't give me birth,
> just bought me. That's why
> I don't go out to play.
> He keeps asking me:
> Who's your father, your mother?
> Why are you dark, when they
> both are fair? Encouraged by him
> all the cowherds clap their hands
> and mock at me
> You never punish Dāū only me."
> Seeing Kṛṣṇa's angry face,
> Jasumati is secretly amused.
> And she reassures him: "Listen, Kṛṣṇa, Dāū has been a
>   naughty boy since his birth.
> I swear by all I cherish
> that I am your mother, and you my son."

Against the background of religious, devotional, and philosophical thought and sentiment, Sūrdās's songs throb with a lyric fervour and intensity in dealing with such themes as the love of Rādhā and Kṛṣṇa, Yashoda's love for her unique son Kṛṣṇa, and the passion of love which the "gopīs," Rādhā included, feel for one who is both unattainable and unforgettable. Last, but not least, is the poet's own rapturous devotion to the multi-dimensional, multi-faceted figure of Kṛṣṇa: child, lover, guru, exemplar of human perfection, and embodiment of the Supreme.

—G. Singh

SVEVO, Italo

Born: Ettore Aron Schmitz in Trieste (then part of Austro-Hungarian Empire), 19 December 1861. **Education:** Educated at Jewish schools in Trieste to 1873; Brüsselische Handels-und Erziehunginstitut, Segnitz-am-Main, 1873–78; Istituto Superiore Commerciale Revoltella, Trieste, 1878–80. **Family:** Married Livia Veneziani in 1896, one daughter. **Career:** Clerk, Trieste branch of Unionbank of Vienna, 1880–99; instructor in French and German commercial correspondence, Istituto Superiore Commerciale Revoltella, 1893–1900; partner in Ditta Veneziani (his wife's family's manufacturing firm), from 1899. Took English lessons from James Joyce in Trieste, from 1907. **Died:** 13 September 1928.

PUBLICATIONS

Collections

Opere di Italo Svevo, edited by Bruno Maier. 1954.
Opera omnia, edited by Bruno Maier. 4 vols., 1966–69.
The Works. 5 vols., 1967–80.
Edizione critica delle opere di Italo Svevo, edited by Bruno Maier. 1985–.

Fiction

Una vita. 1892; as *A Life*, translated by Archibald Colquhoun, 1963.
Senilità. 1898; as *As a Man Grows Older*, translated by Beryl de Zoete, 1932; as *Emilio's Carnival*, translated by Beth Archer Brombert, 2001.
La coscienza di Zeno. 1923; as *Confessions of Zeno*, translated by Beryl de Zoete, 1930; as *Zeno's Conscience*, translated by Dalya M. Sachs, 2001.
The Hoax, translated by Beryl de Zoete. 1929.
La novella del buon vecchio e della bella fanciulla. 1930; as *The Nice Old Man and the Pretty Girl and Other Stories*, translated by L. Collison-Morley, 1930.
Corto viaggio sentimentale e altri racconti inediti, edited by Umbro Apollonio. 1949; as *Short Sentimental Journey and Other Stories*, translated by Beryl de Zoete and others, 1967.
The Further Confessions of Zeno, translated by Ben Johnson and P.N. Furbank. 1969.
Il vegliando. 1987.

Plays

Terzetta spezzato (produced 1927). In *Commedie*, 1960.
Commedie (includes *Terzetta spezzato; Un marito; L'avventura di Maria; Una commedia inedita; La verità; Inferiorità; Le ire di Giuliano; Le teorie del conte Alberto; Il ladro in casa; Primo del ballo; Atto unico; Con la penna d'oro; La rigenerazione*), edited by Umbro Apollonio. 1960.
Un marito (produced 1961). In *Commedie*, 1960.
L'avventura di Maria (produced 1966). In *Commedie*, 1960.
Una commedia inedita, La verità Inferiorità (produced 1967). In *Commedie*, 1960.

Other

James Joyce (lecture), translated by Stanislaus Joyce. 1950.
Corrispondenza con Valéry Larbaud, Benjamin Crémieux e Marie Anne Comnene. 1953.
Saggi e pagine sparse, edited by Umbro Apollonio. 1954.
Diario per la fidanzata, edited by Bruno Maier and Anita Pittoni. 1962.
Lettere alla moglie, edited by Anita Pittoni. 1963.
Lettere: Eugenio Montale—Svevo. 1966.
Saba, Svevo, Comisso: Lettere inedite, edited by Mario Sutor. 1968.
Carteggio con gli scritti di Montale su Svevo, edited by Giorgio Zampa. 1976.
Carteggio con James Joyce, Valery Larbaud, Benjamin Cremieux, Marie Anne Comnene, Eugenio Montale, Valerio Jahier, edited by Bruno Maier. 1978.
Scritti su Joyce, edited by Giancarlo Mazzacurati. 1986.

*

Bibliography: by Bruno Maier, in *Opera omnia*, 2, 1969; "Criticism of Italo Svevo: A Selected Checklist" by J.W. Van Voorhis, in *Modern Fiction Studies*, 18, 1972; *An Annotated Bibliography on the Theatre of Italo Svevo* by Beno Weiss, 1974.

Critical Studies: *Italo Svevo: The Man and the Writer* by P.N. Furbank, 1966; *Essays on Italo Svevo* edited by Thomas F. Staley, 1969; *Italo Svevo: A Critical Introduction*, 1974, and *Italo Svevo and* *the European Novel*, 1977, both by Brian Moloney; *Italo Svevo* by Naomi Lebowitz, 1978; *Italo Svevo, The Writer from Trieste: Reflections on His Background and His Work* by Charles C. Russell, 1978; *Italo Svevo* by Beno Weiss, 1987; *Italo Svevo: A Double Life* by John Gatt-Rutter, 1988; *Memoir of Italo Svevo* by Livia Veneziana Svevo, translated by Isabel Quigly, 1989; *Origin and Identity: Essays on Svevo and Trieste* by Elizabeth Schächter, 2000.

* * *

The first Italian novelist who tackled such typical 20th-century themes as psychoanalysis and investigation into the self-obsessed modern anti-hero, Italo Svevo makes telling use of autobiography in order to depict the problems faced by his anti-heroes. His experience as a clerk in his father's bank in Trieste provided him with the raw material for his first interesting, though artistically uneven novel, *Una vita* (*A Life*). The protagonist, Alfonso Nitti, is an inept young man unable to come to grips with the reality around him that does not match his grandiose dreams. This inability leads to an increasingly irreconcilable hiatus between his meaningless existence and his lofty aspirations, as a result of which he commits suicide.

Svevo's second novel, *Senilità* (*As a Man Grows Older*), has as protagonist Emilio Brentani, a rather older version of Alfonso Nitti, who in spite of a minor literary success, finds himself at the age of 35 essentially a failure in art as well as in life. His senility is depicted as a psychological condition which, as in the case of Alfonso Nitti, prevents him from coming to terms with the reality of everyday life. His abortive attempt at self-fulfilment through a relationship with an exuberantly sexual working-class girl, Angiolina, serves merely to bring out his basic inability to cope with the most vital aspects of human experience. He ultimately renounces life and takes refuge in a self-contained dream world of his own making in which even the memory of his sister, neglected by Emilio in life and abandoned by him on her death (she dies of alcoholism), becomes distorted and merges with his idealized memory of Angiolina.

Svevo's reputation as a major Italian novelist was secured with *La coscienza di Zeno* (*Confessions of Zeno*), the novel of his maturity. Zeno Cosini, the protagonist, is an older and wiser Brentani who has come to terms with his basic ineptitude and lack of direction in life. With the help of psychoanalysis he has learned to diagnose his own weakness and "sickness" and to face the challenges of the "healthy" everyday life of the generally corrupt and unthinking bourgeoisie of which he is a member. Thus he can look forward to a relatively comfortable old age—the reward of an almost Darwinian struggle to survive. The originality of Svevo's view of the survival of the fittest lies in the fact that his anti-hero Zeno, although to all intents and purposes a perfect example of a vacillating, weak-willed, inept man, survives and prospers precisely because of his ability to cope with his shortcomings, and even to exploit them to his own advantage. His account of his efforts to overcome his fear of illness (deriving, according to him, from his addiction to cigarettes), his sense of guilt (for having desired the death of his father and for his infidelity to his wife), his feelings of jealousy (provoked by the manifestly virile behaviour of his initially successful brother-in-law) are recounted and analysed with an unfailing sense of humour and irony which elicit from the reader something like the indulgent sympathy one shows to a naughty but endearing child. It is, perhaps, a mark of Svevo's originality that he was long neglected in Italy as a writer. Part of the reason for this neglect was undoubtedly his rather unstylistic Italian;

and part was because of the fact that his anti-heroes were too far removed from the cult and ideal of the superman that a writer like D'Annunzio had done so much to propogate in Fascist Italy.

—Gabrielle Barfoot

See the essay on *Confessions of Zeno*.

SZYMBORSKA, Wisława

Born: Bnin, Poland, 2 July 1923. **Education:** Educated at a private school of the Ursulan Sisters, Kraków, 1935–39; Jagiellonian University, Kraków, 1945–48. **Family:** Married Adam Włodek in 1948 (divorced in 1954); companion of Kornel Filipowicz from the 1970s (died in 1990). **Career:** Assistant editor in publishing houses 1948–53; editor of the poetry section in Kraków-based *Życie Literackie*, 1953–68, and member of its Editorial Board until 1976. **Awards:** Goethe prize, 1991; Herder prize, 1995; Honorary Doctor of Letters, University of Poznań, 1995; Polish PEN Club prize, 1996; Nobel prize for Literature, 1996.

PUBLICATIONS

Poetry

Dlatego żyjemy. 1952.
Pytania zadawane sobie. 1954.
Wołanie do Yeti. 1957.
Sól. 1962.
Sto pociech. 1967.
Wszelki wypadek. 1972.
Poezje. 1977.
Wielka liczba. 1977.
Sounds, Feelings, Thoughts: Seventy Poems, translated by Magnus J. Krynski and Robert A. Maguire. 1981.
Ludzie na moście. 1986; as *People on a Bridge: Poems*, translated by Adam Czerniawski, 1990.
Koniec i początek. 1993.
Widok z ziarnkiem piasku. 1996; as *View with a Grain of Sand: Selected Poems*, translated by Stanisław Barańczak and Claire Cavanagh, 1995.
Nothing Twice: Selected Poems, edited and translated by Stanisław Barańczak and Claire Cavanagh. 1997.
Poems, New and Collected, 1957–1997, translated by Stanisław Barańczak and Claire Cavanagh. 1998.
Wiersze wybrane. 2000.
Miracle Fair: Selected Poems of Wislawa Szymborska, translated by Joanna Trzeciak. 2001.

Prose

Lektury nadobowiązkowe. 1973.
Lektury nadobowiązkowe, cz.2. 1981.
Nonrequired Reading: prose pieces, translated by Clare Cavanagh. 2002.

Other

Życie na poczekaniu: Lekcja Literatury z Jerzym Kwiatkowskim i Marianem Stalą. 1996.

*

Bibliography: *Pamiątkowe rupiecie, przyjaciele i sny Wisławy Szymborskiej* by Anna Bikont and Joanna Szczęsna, 1997.

Critical Studies: *Świat ze wszystkich stron świata: O Wisławie Szymborskiej* by Stanisław Balbus, 1996; *Szymborska: Szkice* by Edward Balcerzan and others, 1996; *Tak lekko było nic o tym nie wiedzieć. . . : Szymborska i świat* by Małgorzata Baranowska, 1996; "Wisława Szymborska: Rapturous Skeptic" by Edward Hirsh, in *Responsive Reading* by Edward Hirsh, 1999; "Mozartian Joy: The Poetry of Wisława Szymborska," in *The Mature Laurel: Essays on Modern Polish Poetry* edited by Adam Czerniawski, 1991.

* * *

Wisława Szymborska is Poland's foremost contemporary woman poet. In 1996, at the age of 73, she was awarded the Nobel prize for Literature. The fact that some of her poems, such as "Nothing Twice" (1957) and "Cat in an Empty Apartment" (1993), have achieved almost a cult status illustrates the high esteem in which her poetry is held among Polish readers. Szymborska's entire published oeuvre consists of about 200 poems, which in itself makes the high recognition she has received remarkable. Another remarkable feature about her popularity in Poland is the fact that Szymborska does not perform any of the roles traditionally associated in Polish literature with poets; she is neither a bard nor a teacher, she is not a blessed or a chosen one, she does not regard herself as superior to her readers, and does not assume that she knows and understands more than they do. Her poetic persona does not resemble the platonic or demonic lover or, at the other extreme, of the patriotic mother—roles typically reserved for women writers by the same tradition. Although it would be easy to argue that being a woman plays a central role in her poetry, Szymborska is not, strictly speaking, a feminist; her concerns are not with women's issues specifically but with human beings in general, who for her do not divide primarily along gender lines. Nevertheless, her poetry does elevate the private and domestic spheres of life that are traditionally associated with women to the level of truly important topics.

The first two volumes of Szymborska's poems, written according to Socialist Realist precepts, *Dlatego żyjemy* [That What We Live For] and *Pytania zadawane sobie* [Questions Put To Myself], have not yet been widely accepted by critics and some have even declared her third volume, *Wołanie do Yeti* [Calling Out To Yeti] to be her real literary debut. Citing her lack of political, social, and literary maturity as an explanation of the weaknesses of her early poems, they overlook the fact that the world of politics and social responsibilities is not what makes Szymborska's poetry interesting or original. Despite her attempts to stay close to contemporary events, such poems as "Vietnam" or "Written in a Hotel" (in *Sto prociech* [No End of Fun]) are not among her best poetic achievements. It is only in her 1993 volume *Koniec i poczatek* [The End and The Beginning] that Szymborska found her own poetic approach to social, ideological, and political themes by viewing them from the perspective of small, domestic issues.

Szymborska's poetic work focuses on common, everyday happenings and things. She is (as Malgorzata Baranowska observed) a master of rediscovering everyday reality and expanding its treatment in poetry. Central to her poetry are humanity and the human being, seen from a variety of often unusual perspectives. The narrator of Szymborska's poems speaks in a quiet tone and asks questions instead of providing answers or proffering advice. But it is not so much her poetic voice as the perspective she brings that sets her poetry apart from the work of other poets. One of her favorite devices is to view human affairs from a nonhuman perspective to reveal, ironically, what people are really like. As she writes in "No End of Fun":

> With that ring in his nose, with that toga, that sweater,
> He's no end of fun, for all you say.
> Poor little beggar.
> A human, if ever we saw one.

The skeptical, ironic, and questioning tone disappears, however, when Szymborska writes about women, such as the mothers in "Born" and "Pieta," or the teenage girl she once was in "Laughter" or "A Moment in Troy." Interestingly, when describing herself as *"one first person sing., temporarily / declined in human form,"* Szymborska's poetic persona seems to remember and comprise all previous biological stages of existence, as when she confesses in "A Speech at the Lost-And-Found":

> *I'm not even sure exactly where I left my claws,*
> *Who got my fur coat, who's living in my shell.*

As a woman, however, she is also a cultural construct-not only visiting Troy, understanding Lot's wife, or being a Cassandra-but aware of the role of art in the perception of female body. In "Rubens' Women," referring to the absence in his paintings, of "skinny sisters" who have been "exiled by style," she writes:

> The thirteenth century would have given them golden haloes.
> The twentieth, silver screens.
> The seventeenth, alas, holds nothing for the unvoluptuous.

Her poems, with their penchant for paradox, are devoted not only to what is, but also to what isn't, to what happened and to what did not happen. "My nonarrival in the city of N. / took place on the dot," she writes in the beginning of "The Railroad Station," only to add later: "The railroad station in the city of N. / passed its exam / in objective existence." However, the mere fact of existence is less important for Szymborska than the presence of human attributes, especially feelings. That is why in her poem "Museum" the idea of struggle is a synonym for the life of both humans and objects, and why the poem "Wrong Number" ends with the observation "He lives, so he errs." Years later, mourning the man she loved in her "Parting with a View," Szymborska wrote:

> There is one thing I won't agree to:
> my own return.
> The privilege of presence—
> I give it up.

Szymborska does not struggle against reality, does not attempt to mould it to her own purposes by the use of cultural or poetic clichés, and does not wax sentimental. "True Love," as she put it "couldn't populate the planet in a million years." In the "Family Album" she notes that "No one in this family has ever died of love." This

981

acceptance of reality leads Szymborska to eschew the patriotic role of poetry. In ''The End and the Beginning'' she writes:

Those who knew
what all this was about
must make way for those
who know little.
And less than that.
And at last nothing less than nothing.

Instead of fulfilling traditional roles, her poetry is an appreciation of the miracle of everyday things. She highlights what we all take for granted by using and contrasting different perspectives, by deconstructing cultural images and comparing them with a commonsensical point of view, by using—as in ''Hitler's First Photograph,''—a cliché and a point in time that, though perfectly normal and justified, collide with readers' knowledge of Hitler's role in history. Perspectives that seem to surprise readers in her poems are in fact often points of view we all share but seldom put in words. Szymborska's poetry, in which words are not meant to create new meanings but to follow thoughts and points of view with care, makes a consistent statement that everyday, unimportant, non-heroic reality, which belonged to women through ages and cultures, is not only fascinating and refreshing but also fully deserving of poetic recognition.

—Bożena Karwowska

T

TACITUS

Born: Publius (or Gaius) Cornelius Tacitus, perhaps in Gaul, c. AD 56. **Education:** Studied law in Rome. **Family:** Married the daughter of Agricola, AD 77. **Career:** Entered public life under Vespasian, c. AD 69–79; financial administrator (*quaestor*), AD 81, judicial officer (*praetor*), AD 88, consul, AD 97; prosecuted Marius Priscus for extortion, AD 100; proconsul of Asia, c. AD 112–13. **Died:** AD 116 or later.

PUBLICATIONS

Collections

Works, translated by Thomas Gordon. 2 vols., 1728–31; selection as *The Reign of Tiberius* [six *Annals*]; *Germany; Agricola*, edited by A. Galton, 1890.

Works, translated by Arthur Murphy. 4 vols., 1793; selection as *Historical Works*, edited by E.H. Blakeney, translated by Arthur Murphy, 2 vols., 1908.

Opera, edited by A.J. Valpy. 3 vols., 1834.

Opera minora [Loeb Edition], edited and translated by W. Peterson and M. Hutton. 1914; revised by Michael Winterbottom, E.H. Warmington, and R.M. Ogilvie, 1970; as *Minor Works*, translated by W.H. Fyfe, 1908.

Complete Works. 1942.

[*Works*; Loeb Edition]. 5 vols., 1970–81.

Works

Annales, edited by H. Furneaux (with commentary). 2 vols., 1896; also edited by E. Koestermann, 4 vols., 1963–68, H. Heubner, 1983, and S. Borzsák and Kenneth Wellesley, 1986–92; Books I–II edited by F.R.D. Goodyear, 2 vols., 1972–81, Book III–IV by Ronald Martin and A.J. Woodman, 1989–96, and Book XIV by E.C. Woodcock, 1992; as *Annals*, translated by Henry Savile and R. Grenewey, 1598; also translated by John Dryden, W. Higden, and others, with *History*, 3 vols., 1698; A.J. Church and W.J. Brodribb, 1877; G.C. Ramsay, 1904; J. Jackson [Loeb Edition; Books IV–VI, XI–XII, XIII–XVI], 3 vols., 1931–37; Michael Grant, 1952, revised edition, 1989; D.R. Dudley, 1966; D.C.A. Shorter, 1989 (Book IV); selection as *Empires and Emperors*, translated by Graham I.F. Tingay, 1983.

De origine et situ Germanorum, edited by J.G.C. Anderson (with commentary). 1938; also edited by Michael Winterbottom, 1973, A. Önnerfors, 1983, and A.A. Lund, 1988; as *Description of Germany*, translated by R. Grenewey, in *Annals*, 1598; as *A Treatise on the Situation, Manners and Inhabitants of Germany*, translated by John Aikin, 1777; as *Dissertation on the Manners of the Germans*, translated by N.S. Smith, with *Life of Agricola*, 1821; as *Germany*, translated by H. Owgan, with *Agricola*, 1851; also translated by A.J. Church and W.J. Brodribb, with *Agricola*, 1868; Herbert W. Benario, with *Agricola* and *Dialogue on Orators*, 1967, revised edition, 1991; as *Germania*, translated by R.B.

Townshend, with *Agricola*, 1894; also translated by E.A. Wells, revised by W.H. Forbes, with *Agricola*, 1901; W. Hamilton Fyfe, with *Agricola* and *Dialogus*, 1908; Maurice Hutton [Loeb Edition], with *Agricola* and *Dialogus*, 1914; William Peterson, with *Agricola* and *Dialogus*, 1914; H. Mattingly, revised by S.A. Handford, with *Agricola*, 1970; commentary by J.H. Sleeman, 1914; *Germania*, translated by J.B. Rives, 1999.

De vita Iulii Agricolae, edited by R.M. Ogilvie. 1973; also edited by J. Delz, 1983; as *Agricola*, translated by Henry Savile, 1591; also translated by H. Owgan, with *Germany*, 1851; A.J. Church and W.J. Brodribb, with *Germany*, 1868; R.B. Townshend, with *Germania*, 1894; E.A. Wells, revised by W.H. Forbes, with *Germania*, 1901; Anthony R. Birley, with *Germany*, 1999; W. Hamilton Fyfe, with *Germania* and *Dialogus*, 1908; Maurice Hutton [Loeb Edition], with *Germania* and *Dialogus*, 1914; William Peterson, with *Germania* and *Dialogus*, 1914; G.J. Acheson, 1938; Herbert W. Benario, with *Germany* and *Dialogue on Orators*, 1967, revised edition, 1991; H. Mattingly, revised by S.A. Handford, with *Germania*, 1970; as *Life of Agricola*, translated by John Aikin, 1777; also translated by N.S. Smith, with *Dissertation on the Manners of the Germans*, 1821; *Selections*, edited by D.E. Soulsby, 1973; commentary by J.H. Sleeman, 1914.

Dialogus de oratoribus, edited by R. Güngerich (with commentary). 1980; also edited by Michael Winterbottom, 1973, H. Heubner, 1983, and as *Dialogus*, translated by W. Hamilton Fyfe, with *Agricola* and *Germania*, 1908; Maurice Hutton [Loeb Edition], with *Agricola* and *Germania*, 1914; William Peterson, with *Agricola* and *Germania*, 1914; as *Dialogue on Orators*, translated by Herbert W. Benario, with *Germany* and *Agricola*, 1967, revised edition, 1991; also translated by Michael Winterbottom, 1972; commentary by W. Peterson, 1893.

Historiae, edited by H. Heubner. 1978; also edited by Kenneth Wellesley, 1989; as *Histories*, translated by Henry Savile, 1591; as *History*, translated by John Dryden, W. Higden, and others, with *Annals*, 1698; also translated by W.H. Fyfe, 1912; G.C. Ramsay, 1915; C.H. Moore [Loeb Edition; Books I–V], 1925–31; Kenneth Wellesley, 1964, revised edition, 1991; selection as *The Year of the Four Emperors*, edited by P.V. Jones, 1974; commentaries by W.A. Spooner, 1891, and G.E.F. Chilver, 1979, revised by G.B. Townend, 1985.

*

Bibliography: *Aufstieg und Niedergang der römischen Welt* edited by W. Haase and H. Temporini, 1990–91.

Critical Studies: *The Annals of Tacitus* by B. Walker, 1952; *Tacitus, the Man and His Work* by Clarence W. Mendell, 1957; *Tacitus*, 1958, and *Ten Studies in Tacitus*, 1970, both by Ronald Syme; *The Annals of Tacitus* by B. Walker, 1960; *Religion and Philosophy in the Histories of Tacitus* by Russell T. Scott, 1968; *Tacitus* edited by T.A. Dorey, 1969; *The World of Tacitus* by D.R. Dudley, 1969; *Tacitus* by F.R.D. Goodyear, 1970; *An Introduction to Tacitus* by Herbert W. Benario, 1975; *Tacitus in Renaissance Political Thought* by Kenneth C.

Schellhase, 1976; *Tradition and Theme in the Annals of Tacitus* by Judith Ginsburg, 1981; *Tacitus* by Ronald Martin, 1981; *Narrative Cause in the Annals of Tacitus* by Harold Y. McCulloch, 1984; *Tacitus and the Tacitean Tradition* edited by T.J. Luce and A.J. Woodman, 1993; *Tacitus* by Ronald Mellor, 1993; *Tacitus: The Classical Heritage*, edited by Ronald Mellor, 1995; *Tacitus the Sententious Historian: A Sociology of Rhetoric in Annales 1–6* by Patrick Sinclair, 1995; *Latin Historians* by C.S. Kraus and A.J. Woodman, 1997; *Tacitus Reviewed* by A.J. Woodman, 1998; *Ordering Anarchy: Armies and Leaders in Tacitus' Histories* by Rhiannon Ash, 1999; *Tacitus' Fragment 2: The Anti-Roman Movement of the Christiani and the Nazoreans* by Eric Laupot, 2000; *Irony and Misreading in the Annals of Tacitus* by Ellen O'Gorman, 2000.

*   *   *

Tacitus began his literary career with the appearance in AD 98 of *De vita Iulii Agricolae* (*Agricola*), a biography of his father-in-law, Julius Agricola, who governed Britain between AD 78 and 84. He capitalized on ancient literary convention, which dictated that biography should be eulogistic, by contrasting the work's eponymous hero with the evil emperor Domitian, thus throwing the former's virtues into greater relief. In his next work, *De origine et situ Germanorum* (*Germany*), circulated in the same year, Tacitus again took advantage of literary tradition. Ethnographical works had always included discussion of the morality of races and peoples, and Tacitus suggested that the more primitive Germans displayed qualities which were lacking from the more advanced society of contemporary Rome. Such disillusionment with Roman politics in general, and with emperors in particular, emerges also in Tacitus' work on the decline of oratory, *Dialogus de oratoribus* (*Dialogue on Orators*), and blossoms forth in the two principal works for which he is most famous.

The *Historiae* (*Histories*), covering the years AD 69–96, and the *Annales* (*Annals*), covering the years AD 14–68, together amounted to 30 volumes, of which more than half are now lost. This ambitious treatment of the emperors of the 1st century AD from Tiberius to Domitian was composed on a large scale and in the annalistic manner, thereby recalling the outstanding history of the Republic, that of Livy (c. 59 BC–c. AD 17), whom Tacitus clearly wished to rival. But whereas Livy had portrayed the republic in largely sympathetic terms and in the fullness and elegance of a Ciceronian style, Tacitus chose to present the early Empire in dissenting terms and in the abbreviated and disjointed style of Sallust (c. 86–35 BC). Tacitus' choice of Sallust as his chief stylistic inspiration is likely to have represented a radical departure from his immediate predecessors since most 1st-century AD historians seem, despite the almost total loss of their works, to have emulated Livy's style rather than Sallust's. Moreover, since Sallust charted the disintegration of society at the end of the Republic, Tacitus' adoption of his style suggests also an affinity of subject matter: the crises of the new autocracy are presented as the crises of the dying republic, and the new emperors and their henchmen appear as reincarnations of the villains of the past.

On account of his dissenting attitude Tacitus has been praised as an anti-imperialist by the opponents or victims of dictatorship, and as a forerunner of modern historiography by those who confuse cynicism with criticism. The reality is perhaps somewhat different. In his writing Tacitus reveals not only an admiration for Sallust which is itself idiosyncratic, but also an almost obsessive aversion to the normal conventions of language and style: he is the writer who literally refused to call a spade a spade ("the things with which earth is carried and turf cut out," *Annals* I). This characteristic is so pervasive that we may legitimately infer Tacitus was a dissenter by nature rather than by conviction. Indeed, he himself prospered and held high office under the political system which his writings so vigorously attack. But none of this is to deny him his superb merits as a dramatic storyteller. Ancient historiography was aimed primarily at entertaining its readers, as Tacitus himself was naturally well aware (*Histories* I); his typically perverse claim that the *Annals* do not meet this requirement (*Annals* IV) has been rightly disbelieved by generations of readers, for whom his works describe everything that was wrong about the Roman Empire.

—A.J. Woodman

See the essay on *Annals*.

TAGORE, Rabindranath

Also known as Ravīndranātha Thākura. **Born:** Calcutta, India, 7 May 1861. **Education:** Educated privately, and at Bengal Academy, Calcutta, and University College, London, (1878–80). **Family:** Married Mrinalinidebi in 1884 (died 1902); one son and one daughter. **Career:** Managed family estates at Shileida, from 1885; editor, *Balak*, 1885; founder, 1889, and editor, 1894, literary journal *Sādhanā*; established the Santiniketan school in Bolpur, Bengal, 1901, intended to combine Eastern and Western forms of education: school developed into the international University Visva-Bharti [Universal Voice], 1918; editor, *Bāngadarsham*, 1901–06; travelled to England, 1912; contributor, *Sabuj Patra*, from 1914; toured Japan and America, 1916, Europe, 1920–21 and 1926, China, Japan, and South America, 1922, and South-East Asia, 1927; Hibbert lecturer, Oxford University, 1930, and Professor of Bengali, University of Calcutta, 1932. Also a painter: exhibitions in Moscow, Berlin, Munich, Paris, and New York. Wrote in Bengali, and translated many of his own works into English. Elected vice-president, Bengali Academy of Letters, 1894. **Awards:** Nobel prize for literature, 1913. D.Lit.: University of Calcutta; Hindu University, Benares; University of Dacca; Osmania University, Hyderabad. D.Litt.: Oxford University. Knighted 1915: resigned knighthood in 1919 as protest against British policies in the Punjab. **Died:** 30 July 1941.

PUBLICATIONS (ENGLISH EDITIONS, WITH SELECTED BENGALI TITLES)

Collections

A Tagore Reader, edited by Amiya Chakravarty. 1961.

Two Buddhist Plays: The Court Dancer and Chandalika, transcreated by Shyamasree Devi. 1993.

The English Writings of Rabindranath Tagore, edited by Sisir Kumar Das. 1994.

The Heart of God: Prayers, selected and edited by Herbert F. Vetter. 1997.

Rabindranath Tagore: An Anthology, edited by Krishna Dutta and Andrew Robinson. 1997.

A Hundred Devotional Songs of Tagore, translated by Mohit Chakrabarti. 1999.

On the Shores of Eternity: Poems from Tagore on Immortality and Beyond: New English Versions by Deepak Chopra. 1999.

Fiction

Bauthakuranir Hat. 1883.

Rajarshi. 1887.

Binodini. 1903; translated by Krishna Kripalani, 1959.

Nankadubi. 1906; translated as *The Wreck*, 1921.

Gorā. 1910; as *Gora*, translated by Tagore, 1924.

Glimpses of Bengal Life (stories). 1913.

Ghare-Baire. 1914; as *The Home and the World*, translated by Surendranath Tagore, 1919, reprinted 1985.

The Hungry Stones and Other Stories, translated by C.F. Andrews and others. 1916.

Mashi and Other Stories. 1918.

The Parrot's Training and Other Stories. 1918.

The Runaway and Other Stories, edited by Somnath Maitra. 1919, reprinted 1959.

Broken Ties and Other Stories. 1925.

Shesher Kabita. 1929; as *Farewell My Friend*, translated by Krishna Kripalani, 1946.

Dui Bon. 1933; as *Two Sisters*, translated by Krishna Kripalani, 1943.

Malancha. 1934; as *The Garden*, translated by Krishna Kripalani, 1946.

Char Adhya. 1934; as *Four Chapters*, translated by Surendranath Tagore, 1950.

More Stories from Tagore. 1951.

Chaturanga, translated by Asok Mitra. 1963; also translated by Kaiser Haq, 1993.

Lipika, translated by Indu Dutt. 1969; also translated by Aurobindo Bose, 1977.

The Broken Nest, translated by Mary Lago and Supriya Sen. 1971.

Selected Short Stories, translated by Mary Lago and Krishna Dutta. 1990.

Verse

Sandhya Sangit [Evening Songs]. 1880.

Mānasi [The Mind's Embodiment]. 1890.

Sōnār Tari. 1895; as *The Golden Boat*, translated by Chabani Bhattarcharya, 1932.

Gītānjali. 1909; as *Song Offerings*, translated by Tagore, 1913; as *Gitanjali: A Collection of Prose Translations Made by the Author from the Original Bengali*, with introduction by W.B. Yeats, 1997.

The Gardener. 1913.

The Crescent Moon: Child-Poems. 1913.

Bālāka [Flight of Wild Cranes]. 1914.

Fruit-Gathering. 1916.

Lover's Gift, and Crossing. 1918.

The Fugitive and Other Poems. 1921.

Poems. 1922.

Fireflies. 1928.

Fifteen Poems. 1928.

Sheaves: Poems and Songs, edited and translated by Nagendranath Gupta. 1929.

The Child. 1931.

Prantik [Borderland]. 1937.

Poems, edited by Krishna Kripalani. 1942.

A Flight of Swans, translated by Aurobindo Bose. 1955.

Syamali, translated by Sheila Chatterjee. 1955.

The Herald of Spring, translated by Aurobindo Bose. 1957.

Wings of Death: The Last Poems, translated by Aurobindo Bose. 1960.

Devouring Love, translated by Shakuntala Sastri. 1961.

A Bunch of Poems, translated by Monika Varma. 1966.

One Hundred and One. 1967.

Last Poems, translated by Shyamasree Devi and P. Lal. 1972.

Later Poems, translated by Aurobindo Bose. 1974.

Selected Poems, translated by William Radice. 1985.

I Won't Let You Go: Selected Poems, translated by Ketaki Kushavi Dyson. 1991.

Plays

Vālmīki Pratibha [The Genius of Vālmīki]. 1881.

Visarjana. 1890; as *Sacrifice*, translated by Kshitish Chandra Sen, in *Sacrifice and Other Plays*. 1917.

Chitrāngada [Beauty]. 1892; translated as *Chitra*, 1914.

Raja. 1910; translated as *The King of the Dark Chamber*, 1914.

Daghar (produced 1913). 1912; as *The Post Office*, translated by Devabrata Mukerjee, 1914; translated by Krishna Dutta and Andrew Robinson, 1996.

Malini (produced 1915). As *Malini*, translated by Kshitish Chandra Sen, in *Sacrifice and Other Plays*, 1917.

The Cycle of Spring. 1916.

Prakrtir Parisodh. As *Sanyasi; or, The Ascetic*, translated by Kshitish Chandra Sen, in *Sacrifice and Other Plays*, 1917.

Raja o Rani. As *The King and the Queen*, translated by Kshitish Chandra Sen, in *Sacrifice and Other Plays*, 1917.

Sacrifice and Other Plays (includes *Sacrifice; Malini; Sanyasi; or, The Ascetic; The King and the Queen*), translated by Kshitish Chandra Sen. 1917.

The Fugitive. 1918.

The Mother's Prayer (produced 1920). 1919.

Sardotsava (produced in English, 1920). Translated as *Autumn Festival*, 1920.

Vidhay-abhisap (produced in English, 1920). Translated as *The Farewell Curse*, 1920; as *The Curse at Farewell*, translated by Edward Thompson, 1924.

The Deserted Mother (produced 1920).

The Sinner (produced 1920).

Suttee (produced 1920).

Trial by Luck (produced 1921).

Raktu-Karabi. Translated as *Red Oleanders*, 1925.

Worship of the Dancing Girl (produced 1925).

Natir Puja. 1926; as *Natir Puja*, translated by Marjorie Sykes, in *Three Plays*, 1950.

Sapmochan. 1930.

Kana and Kunti. In *Collected Poems and Plays*, 1936.

Muktadhara (produced 1959). In *Three Plays*, translated by Marjorie Sykes, 1950.

Three Plays (includes *Muktadhara; Natir Puja; Candalika*), translated by Marjorie Sykes. 1950.

Sesher Rashtri. As *The Housewarming*, translated by Mary Lago and Tarun Gupta, in *The Housewarming and Other Selected Writings*, edited by Amiya Chakravarty, 1965.

Karmaphal. As *Consequences*, translated by Mary Lago and Tarun Gupta, in *The Housewarming and Other Selected Writings*, edited by Amiya Chakravarty, 1965.

Other

Sadhana: The Realisation of Life. 1913.

Stray Birds (aphorisms). 1916.

My Reminiscences, translated by Surendranath Tagore. 1917.

Letters. 1917.

Nationalism (lectures). 1917.

Personality: Lectures Delivered in America. 1917.

Greater India (lectures). 1921.

Thought Relics. 1921.

Creative Unity. 1922.

The Visvabharati, with C.F. Andrews. 1923.

Letters from Abroad, edited by C.F. Andrews. 1924; revised edition, as *Letters to a Friend*, 1928.

Talks in China. 1925.

Lectures and Addresses, edited by Anthony X. Soares. 1928.

City and Village. 1928.

Rashiar Chithi. 1931; as *Letters from Russia*, translated by Sasadhar Sinha, 1960.

The Religion of Man (lectures). 1931.

Collected Poems and Plays. 1936.

Man (lectures). 1937.

My Boyhood Days. 1940.

Eighty Years, and Selections. 1941.

Crisis in Civilisation. 1941.

A Tagore Testament. 1953.

Our Universe, translated by Indu Dutt. 1958.

Letters from Russia, translated by Sasadhar Sinha. 1960.

Tagore, Pioneer in Education: Essays and Exchanges Between Tagore and L.K. Elmhirst. 1961.

A Visit to Japan, translated by Shakuntala Shastri. 1961.

Towards Universal Man. 1961.

On Art and Aesthetics, edited by Pritwish Neogy. 1961.

The Diary of a Westward Voyage. 1962.

The Centre of Indian Culture. 1962.

On Rural Reconstruction. 1962.

The Cooperative Principle. 1963.

Boundless Sky (miscellany). 1964.

The Housewarming and Other Selected Writings, edited by Amiya Chakravarty, translated by Mary Lago and Tarun Gupta. 1965.

Imperfect Encounter: Letters of William Rothenstein and Tagore 1912–1941. 1972.

Collected Essays, edited by Mary Lago and Ronald Warwick. 1989.

The Mahatma and the Poet: Letters and Debates Between Gandhi and Tagore, 1915–1941, edited by Sabyasachi Bhattacharya. 1997.

Selected Letters of Rabindranath Tagore, edited by Krishna Dutta and Andrew Robinson. 1997.

*

Bibliography: *Tagore: A Bibliography* by Katherine Henn, 1985; *Rabindranath Tagore: A Bibliography* by Martin Kämpchen, 1991.

Critical Studies: *Rabindranath Tagore: His Life and Work*, 1921, and *Rabindranath Tagore, Poet and Dramatist*, 1948, reprinted 1991, both by E.J. Thompson; *Rabindranath Tagore* by Marjorie Sykes, 1943; *Tagore, Poet and Thinker* by Mohinimohana Battarcharya, 1961; *Tagore: A Biography* by Krishna Kripalani, 1962, revised edition 1971; *The Lute and the Plough: A Life of Tagore* by G.D. Khanotkar, 1963; *Rabindranath's Poetry* by Dattatuaya Muley, 1964; *Rabindranath* by Sati Ghosh, 1966; *The Volcano: Some Comments on the Development of Tagore's Aesthetic Theories*, 1968, and *The Humanism of Tagore*, 1979, both by Mulk Raj Anand; *Tagore: His Mind and Art* by Birendra C. Chakravorty, 1971; *Poet and Plowman* by L.K. Elmhirst, 1975; *The Poetry of Tagore* by S.B. Mukherji, 1977; *Tagore* by Mary Lago, 1978, *Rabindranath Tagore: A Celebration of His Life and Work* (essays) by Lago and others, 1986, and *Tagore: Perspectives in Time* edited by Lago and Ronald Warwick, 1989; *Folklore and Nationalism in Rabindranath Tagore* by Abu Saeed Zahunal Haque, 1981; *Tagore the Novelist* by G.V. Raj, 1983; *Tagore: His Imagery and Ideas* by Ajai Singh, 1984; *Tagore* by Sisirkumar Ghose, 1986; *Tagore: A Critical Introduction* by K.R. Srinivasa Iyengar, 1986; *Perspectives on Tagore*, 1986, and *Essays on Rabindranath Tagore*, 1987, both edited by T.R. Sharma; *In Your Blossoming Flower-Garden: Tagore and Victoria Ocampo* by K.K. Dyson, 1988; *The Art of Rabindranath Tagore* by Andrew Robinson, 1989, and *Purabi: A Miscellany in Memory of Rabindranath Tagore* edited by Robinson and Krishna Dutta, 1991; *Tagore and Flowers* by P.K. Ghosh, G.N. Bhattacharya, and S. Mandal, 1993; *Social Thought of Rabindranath Tagore: A Historical Analysis* by Tapati Dasgupta, 1993; *Religious Philosophy of Tagore and Radhakrishnan: A Comparative and Analytical Study* by Harendra Prasad Sinha, 1993; *Tagore and Education for Social Change* by Mohit Chakrabarti, 1993; *Alien Homage: Edward Thompson and Rabindranath Tagore* by E.P. Thompson, 1993; *Tagore, Indian Film and Film Music* by Nirupama Sheth and Ajita Sheth, 1994; *Vedanta and Tagore* by B.C. Mukherji, 1994; *Rabindranath Tagore: The Myriad-minded Man* by Krishna Dutta and Andrew Robinson, 1995; *The Saint and the Singer: Reflections on Gandhi and Tagore* by V.S. Naravane, 1995; *Modernism and Tagore* by Abu Sayeed Ayyub, translated by Amitava Ray, 1995; *Rabindranath Tagore: A Quest* by Mohit Chakrabarti, 1995; *Rabindranath Tagore and Modern Sensibility* by Bhabatosh Chatterjee, 1996; *Tagoreana in the Modern Review*, compiled by Supriya Roy, 1998; *Rabindranath Tagore in Germany: Four Responses to a Cultural Icon* by Martin Kämpchen, 1999; *Art and Aesthetics of Rabindra Nath Tagore* by S.K. Nandi, 1999; *Imagining Tagore: Rabindranath and the British Press, 1912–1941*, compiled and edited by Kalyan Kundu, Sakti Bhattacharya and Kalyan Sircar, 2000; *Rabindranath Tagore and His Medical World* by Asoke K. Bagchi, 2000.

* * *

Rabindranath Tagore, Indian poet, playwright, novelist, short-story writer, essayist, and philosopher wrote mostly in his mother tongue Bengali, but also in English. He founded at Santiniketan an international university, Vishva Bharati, which was to be a bridge between the cultures of the East and the West, and whose motto is: "where the whole world forms its single nest." A patriot to the core— "I shall be born in India again and again, with all the poverty, misery and wretchedness"—Tagore sided with England on the eve of World War II in 1939, declaring that "no Indian can wish England to lose the war she is fighting for the sake of liberty."

Although a versatile writer, painter, and musician, Tagore was essentially a lyric poet and as the author of *Gītānjali* (*Song Offerings*) he acquired international fame. W.B. Yeats said of *Song Offerings* that it was a work of supreme culture which had stirred his blood as nothing had for years. Ezra Pound regarded Tagore as "an artist pure and simple, an author whose voice has almost as many nuances as one can expect from Voltaire and whose sense of humour is as delicate as that of any poet living in Paris.'' He was also struck by what he calls ''a saner stillness'' in Tagore's poetry as well as by ''its subtle underflow.''

The songs in *Song Offerings*, the poet's colloquies with God, seek to define and at the same time to transcend the dichotomy between ''I'' and ''Thou,'' or the Vaishnava duality between the divine and the human, between the contemplator and the contemplated. Like Kabir, Tagore brings to a most intimately personal realization of God a musical as well as a lyrical skill, an imagery at once realistic and evocative, and a wealth of symbols and concepts from the most disparate faiths and philosophies.

''Thou hast made me endless, such is thy pleasure,'' he tells God the Lover and the Master, ''This frail vessel thou emptiest again and again, and fillest it with fresh life.'' Desire and inspiration, joy and dedication merge into one another, and the music so born is both prayer and poetry, ecstasy and confession: ''When thou commandest me to sing it seems that my heart would break with pride; and I look at thy face, and tears come to my eyes.'' The joy of singing makes the poet forget himself and ''I . . . call thee friend who art my Lord.'' Poetic and artistic technique burns itself out at the altar of a devotion that knows no pride and has a rhythm and a music all its own. But the real song that the poet wants to sing remains unsung and the poet spends his days in ''stringing and mastering my instrument.'' There is that silent communion with his lord and lover to sustain and inspire him, and he feels that the object of his adoration is ''on every side,'' ''in everything'' and ''at every moment.'' However, even though every moment seems to be ripe for the meeting between the poet and his lover, it never really takes place; for that would indeed be the end of his quest and yearning, the soul and substance of his song. But such is the intensity of his yearning that it turns what is intangible into something concrete and fully realized. It is, in fact, this interplay between the tangible and the intangible, which enables the poet to express ''the-life-throb of ages dancing in my blood,'' as well as to retrieve something from what is perpetually threatening to dissolve and to give it a new meaning and a new rhythm. Thus even death ceases to be a challenge, and the poet is eager to ''dive down into the depth of the ocean of forms,'' ''to die into the deathless.''

If *Song Offerings* is Tagore's masterpiece and his most characteristic book, it is because none of his subsequent volumes of poetry— *The Gardener, The Crescent Moon, Fruit-Gathering, The Fugitive and Other Poems*, for instance, or even the posthumously published poems *Wings of Death*—achieves the kind of freshness and subtlety of creative inspiration, together with technical mastery, of this book; nor do they add anything to the poetic and mystical philosophy so superbly expressed in *Song Offerings*.

Among Tagore's more important plays are *Chitrāngada* (*Chitra*), *Daghar* (*The Post Office*), *Raja* (*The King of the Dark Chamber*), *The Cycle of Spring*, and *Raktu-Karabi* (*Red Oleanders*)—all of which centre upon the conflict between the vital urge represented by the human personality, and the impersonal and mechanical force represented by industrialization, with the ultimate triumph of personality. Among Tagore's novels, *Gorā* and *Ghare-Baire* (*The Home and the World*) are the best known. Both are novels with a political and social background. As a short-story writer too Tagore was a pioneer in Bengali literature and he published several collections of short stories—*The Hungry Stones and Other Stories, Mashi and Other*

Stories, Broken Ties and Other Stories, and *The Runaway and Other Stories*. Tagore's short stories are studies in psychology or impressionistic sketches depicting the village life in East Bengal. Some of Tagore's best known short stories from these volumes are ''Kabuliwala,'' ''Home-Coming,'' ''Number One,'' and ''Laboratory.''

Of his literary, political, and philosophical essays the ones most worthy of note are *Sadhana, Nationalism, Personality, Creative Unity, The Religion of Man*, and *Crisis in Civilisation*. A celebrated article of Tagore's is entitled ''The Call of Truth'' (March 1921); it is addressed to Gandhi and sums up Tagore's political creed. While hailing Gandhi as ''the wielder of that rod which can awaken India in Truth and Love,'' Tagore criticized his campaign for non-co-operation, which included a call to the nation to spin and weave their own clothes and to burn foreign cloth. ''What irony of fate,'' Tagore wrote in a letter from Chicago, ''that I should be preaching co-operation of cultures between East and West on this side of the sea just at the moment when the doctrine of non-co-operation is preached on the other side!''

Gandhi rebutted his arguments and defended non-co-operation as a ''protest against an unwitting and unwilling participation in evil, a struggle against compulsory co-operation, against one-sided combination, against the armed imposition of modern methods of exploitation masquerading under the name of civilization.'' For all his optimistic faith and idealism—he described pessimism as ''a form of mental dipsomania'' and never suffered from it himself—Tagore ultimately accepted Gandhi's views about exploitation. For, shortly before his death, he wrote: ''I look around and see famished bodies crying for bread. I have seen women in villages dig up ground for a few drops of drinking water, for wells are even more scarce in Indian villages than schools.''

Tagore travelled practically all over the world and met most of the eminent writers, thinkers, and artists of his day. A few months before his death, the University of Oxford conferred upon him the honorary degree of Doctor of Letters.

—G. Singh

TANG Xianzu

Also known as Tang Hsien-tsu. **Born:** Linchuan, Jiangxi, China, 24 September 1550. **Education:** Completed highest imperial examination in the mandarin system, 1584. **Career:** Held various government offices, 1584–98, including that of secretary under the Board of Ceremonies at Nanjing, from which he was demoted after writing a memorial that displeased the authorities; afterwards becoming a district magistrate; then devoting him self to writing full-time and supervising productions of his dramatic works. Known as the author of ''legends,'' or dramatic pieces for Kunqu opera based on old historical sources and traditions. Notable among them are *The Four Dreams at Linchuan*, also known as *The Four Dreams at Yu Ming Tang*. One of them is his masterpiece, the libretto *Mudan Ting* (*The Peony Pavilion*), based on a short story from the Song (Sung) dynasty; its music dates from 1792. Also wrote poems and essays. **Died:** 29 July 1616 in Linchuan, Jiangxi, China.

PUBLICATIONS

Plays

Lin chuan ssu meng; as *The Four Dreams at Linchuan*. 1598.
Mudan Ting; as *The Peony Pavilion* (one of the plays in *The Four Dreams at Linchuan*), translated by Cyril Birch. 1980.

*

Critical Studies: "'Alienation-effect' for Whom?: Brecht's (Mis)interpretation of the Classical Chinese Theatre" by Min Tian, in *Asian Theatre Journal*, vol. 14, no. 2, Fall 1997.

*   *   *

China's most significant dramatist and poet in the later Ming dynasty (1368–1644), Tang Xianzu was a master of the chuan-qi style that was prominent during this period. Translated as "accounts of remarkable things," the chuan-qi plays are often long, complex works with intricate plots and subplots, such as *Mudan Ting* (*The Peony Pavilion*), Tang Xianzu's most celebrated work.

Tang Xianzu, whose dates nearly parallel those of William Shakespeare in the West, was born in Linchuan, China in 1560 and by the age of 24 had passed the highest examinations, enabling him to enter government service under the mandarin system of scholar-officials. He served as the secretary of the Board of Ceremonies in Nanjing before being demoted in a disagreement involving an article he had written. After serving as a district magistrate for a time, he soon devoted himself full-time to writing. *The Peony Pavilion* is the most prominent of the four plays he wrote, which are collectively known as *Lin-chuan's Four Dreams* (Lin-chuan is the name by which Tang Xianzu's studio is known).

As did Shakespeare, Tang Xianzu often based his dramas on familiar folk tales or historical incidents that he would embellish for the stage, creating a cast of colorful characters to enliven the script, which alternated dramatic and comic scenes with serious as well as ribald elements. For example, in his introduction to *The Peony Pavilion*, Tang Xianzu describes in detail how the story is a composite of several events in earlier Chinese history, commenting "I changed them a bit and elaborated them." His engaging portrayals of characters from every rank in society have also earned his work comparisons with the Baroque opera style that was then emerging in Europe. His characters often engaged in complex wordplay, another element that gives evidence of the author's firm grasp of the Chinese language. Still, he remains modest about his accomplishments, writing in the same introduction that "I am not someone of comprehensive knowledge, and I must always investigate matters to consider whether they are rational." Even so, Tang Xianzu admits that "the feeling of love" may overpower rationality, and he proves himself a master of a style that combines fantastical dream sequences with familiar historical accounts.

—Edward Moran

See the essay on *The Peony Pavilion*.

TANIZAKI Jun'ichiro

Born: Tokyo, Japan, 24 July 1886. **Education:** Educated at Tokyo Imperial University, 1908–10. **Family:** Married 1) Chiyoko Ishikawa in 1915 (divorced 1930); 2) Furukawa Tomiko in 1931 (divorced); 3) Nezu Matsuko in 1935. **Career:** Lived in Yokohama and Tokyo; moved to Kausai, near Osaka, after Tokyo earthquake in 1923. Travelled in China, 1918. **Awards:** Mainichi prize, 1947; Asahi culture prize, 1949; Imperial cultural medal, 1949. **Member:** Japan Academy of Arts, 1957; honorary member, American Academy, 1964. **Died:** 30 July 1965.

PUBLICATIONS

Collections

Zenshū [Collected Works]. 28 vols., 1966–70.
The Reed Cutter and Captain Shigemoto's Mother: Two Novellas, translated by Anthony H. Chambers. 1994.

Fiction

Shisei (includes plays). 1911; as *The Tattooer*, translated by Howard Hibbett, in *Seven Japanese Tales*, 1963.
Akuma [Demon]. 1913.
Osai to Minosuke [Osai and Minosuke]. 1915.
Otsuya-goroshi. 1915; as *A Spring-Time Case*, translated by Zenchi Iwado, 1927.
Ningyō no nageki [Mermaid's Grief]. 1917.
Kin to gin [Gold and Silver]. 1918.
Kami to hito no aida [Between God and Man]. 1924.
Chijin no ai [A Fool's Love]. 1925; as *Naomi*, translated by Anthony H. Chambers, 1985.
Kōjin [Shark-Man]. 1926.
Tade kuu mushi. 1928; as *Some Prefer Nettles*, translated by Edward G. Seidensticker, 1955.
Manji [Buddhist Swastika]. 1931; as *Quicksand*, translated by Howard Hibbett, 1994.
Mōmoku monogatari [A Blind Man's Tale]. 1932.
Ashikari. 1933; as *Ashikari*, translated by Roy Humpherson and Hajime Okita, with *The Story of Shunkin*, 1936; as *The Reed Cutter*, translated by Anthony H. Chambers, with *Captain Shigemoto's Mother*, 1994.
Shunkin shō. 1933; as *The Story of Shunkin*, translated by Roy Humpherson and Hajime Okita, with *Ashikari*, 1936; as *A Portrait of Shunkin*, translated by Howard Hibbett, in *Seven Japanese Tales*, 1963.
Bushuko hiwa. 1935; as *The Secret History of the Lord of Musashi*, translated by Anthony H. Chambers, with *Arrowroot*, 1982.
Yoshino kuzu. 1937; as *Arrowroot*, translated by Anthony H. Chambers, with *The Secret History of the Lord of Musashi*, 1982.
Neko to shōzō to futari no onna. 1937; as *Cat, a Man and Two Women*, translated by Paul McCarthy, 1990.
Sasameyuki. 1948; as *The Makioka Sisters*, translated by Edward G. Seidensticker, 1957.
Rangiku monogatari [Story of Tangled Chrysanthemums]. 1949.

Shōshō Shigemoto no haha. 1950; as *Captain Shigemoto's Mother*, translated by Anthony H. Chambers, with *The Reed Cutter*, 1994.
Hyōfū. 1950.
Kagi. 1956; as *The Key*, translated by Howard Hibbett, 1960.
Yume no ukihashi [Floating Bridge of Dreams]. 1960.
Fūten rojin nikki. 1962; as *Diary of a Mad Old Man*, translated by Howard Hibbett, in *Seven Japanese Tales*, 1963.
Seven Japanese Tales, translated by Howard Hibbett. 1963.
Kokumin no bungaku. 1964.
Hagi no hana [Bush Clover Flower]. 1973.
Shisei, Shonen (stories). 1974.

Plays

Hosshoji monogatari [Story of Hosso Temple] (produced 1915).
Aisureba koso [If Indeed One Loves]. 1921.
Okuni to Gohei [Okuni and Gohei] (produced 1922).
Mandorin wo hiko otoko [The Man with the Mandolin]. 1925.
Byakko-no-yu, as *The White Fox*, translated by Haruo Endo and Eric S. Bell, in *Eminent Authors of Contemporary Japan*, edited by Bell and E. Ukai. 1930.
Shinzei [Lord Shinzei]. 1949.

Other

Zenshū [Collected Works]. 12 vols., 1930; and later editions.
In'ei raisan (essay). 1933; as *In Praise of Shadows*, translated by Thomas J. Harper and Edward G. Seidensticker, 1977.
Setsuyo zuihitsu (essays). 1935.
Bunshō tokuhon [On Language Style]. 1936.
Kyō no yume: Ōsaka no yume (addresses, essays, and lectures). 1950.
Selected Works (in Japanese). 1953.
Yosho-jidai. 1957; as *Childhood Years: A Memoir*, translated by Paul McCarthy, 1988.
Tōsei shika modoki. 1961.
Setsugoan yawa [Reminiscences]. 1968.
Editor, *Kokumin no bungaku* (Japanese literature collections). 18 vols., 1963–65.
Translator (into modern Japanese), *Genji monogatari*, by Murasaki Shikibu. 26 vols., 1939–41.

*

Critical Studies: *The Search for Authenticity in Modern Japanese Literature* by Hisaaki Yamanouchi, 1978; *The Moon in the Water: Understanding Tanizaki, Kawabata, and Mishima* by Gwenn Boardman Petersen, 1979; *Three Modern Novelists: Sōseki, Tanizaki, Kawabata* by Van C. Gessel, 1993; *The Secret Window: Ideal Worlds in Tanizaki's Fiction* by Anthony H. Chambers, 1994; *A Tanizaki Feast: An International Symposium in Venice*, edited by Adriana Boscaro and Anthony H. Chambers, 1998; *Tanizaki in Western Languages: A Bibliography of Translations and Studies* by Adriana Boscaro, 2000.

* * *

Tanizaki Jun'ichiro is better regarded as a narrative artist or storyteller than as a novelist—narrative artistry is a broader, more basic, even primitive skill. He was a born narrator, remarkable for his spontaneity and versatility, and many of his writings do not conform to the general concept of or rules for the "modern novel." He could be both realistic and fabulous at the same time, so factually detailed in his description of the daily lives of his characters, and yet so unconventional, so fantastic in his plots and themes.

Tanizaki made a brilliant literary debut in 1910 with *Shisei* (*The Tattooer*), in which a beautiful but modest girl is turned into a different personality by being tattooed. Young Tanizaki was intensely interested in *fin de siècle* Western aestheticism, but this story revealed his own style. Mishima Yukio was an ardent admirer of Tanizaki, and they obviously had much in common. They were committed aesthetes, and pursued and developed an ideal of a beauty highly coloured with sensuality. Each could be called both modern and classical, being susceptible to Western literature and yet well versed in traditional Japanese literature. Both were, at least when young, flamboyant personalities, notorious "bad boys" of the rather closed literary world of Japan, and their behaviour and lifestyles often shocked conservative readers. However, Tanizaki turned out to be more consistent as an aesthete, keeping himself aloof from politics throughout his long literary career of more than a half century, a stormy period for modern Japan.

In the early 1930s there was a sudden upsurge of "proletarian literature" in Japan and many established writers turned "left." Tanizaki's *Tade kuu mushi* (*Some Prefer Nettles*) suffered from the hostility of leftist critics, being condemned as "bourgeois, decadent, reactionary." But his next novel, *Manji* (*Quicksand*), was even more decadent, dealing with lesbian characters and promiscuity. Literary concession or conformity was out of the question for him, and it was not Tanizaki but the "proletarian" writers who were soon submerged. He proved as bold and challenging in his technique of narration, though he was neither avant-garde nor experimental. His literary innovations were accomplished far more subtly. In *Some Prefer Nettles*, he managed to keep a delicate balance between the psychosexual analysis of domestic crisis and the theme of the central character's cultural conversion from West to East. *Quicksand* is another triumph with its subtle blend of female confessions in Osaka dialect, badly written letters, and town gossip.

Tanizaki was one of the few Japanese writers who passed through the turbulent war years almost unscathed. Of course, there was a censorship problem, and *Sasameyuki* (*The Makioka Sisters*), serialized in a literary magazine, was stopped by the militaristic censors. But he continued to write consistently, and this novel of manners was completed three years after the war. Having successfully preserved the prewar mores and nuances of an upper-middle-class family in Osaka, he struck readers as a master of the art of survival.

Tanizaki proved himself a marvellous impersonator in narrative. He liked to use the first-person voice, which seemed apparently naïve, but the range of adopted voices was very wide and rich in variety. The narrator in *Chijin no ai* (*Naomi*) is a middle-aged engineer who falls in love with a very young girl (anticipating Nabokov's *Lolita*), and tries hard to "educate" her into his "ideal woman," a highly Westernized type both in dress and manner. He is too successful: the girl becomes independent, and begins to tease and even tyrannize him. The whole story can be taken as an allegory, or even a moral lesson, concerning the folly of hasty Westernization, but the confessional voice of the protagonist provides a curious mixture of bitter self-mockery and sensual intoxication—he is both grieved and satisfied with the reversal of his plan. This masochistic element is discernible in many of Tanizaki's stories, and probably rooted deeply in his personality. First-person narration is also used in "Story of a Blind Masseur," in which the blind protagonist reminisces about the attractive ladies whom he had adored and massaged.

Kagi (*The Key*) and *Fūten rojin nikki* (*Diary of a Mad Old Man*) are minor masterpieces from Tanizaki's last period, with the dotage and ecstasy of old age as common themes. They support the claim that Tanizaki be counted among the narrative masters of this century.

—Shoichi Saeki

See the essay on *Some Prefer Nettles*.

TAO QIAN

Also known as T'ao Ch'ien and Tao Yuanming. **Born:** Into a poor family, in what is now Jiangxi province, China, 365 AD. **Career:** Became a government official in 393; held other minor posts, but retired to become a farmer in 405. About 120 poems are extant. **Died:** 427.

PUBLICATIONS

Collections

Tao Yuanming ji [Works], edited by Wang Yao. 1956; edited by Yang Yong, 1971.
Gleanings from T'ao Yuan-ming (Prose and Poetry), translated by Roland C. Fang. 1980.
Tao Yuanming ji [Works], edited by Lu Qinli. 1979.
T'ao Yuan-ming: His Works and Their Meaning, translated by A.R. Davis. 2 vols., 1983.
Selected Poems, translated by Gladys Yang and Yang Xianyi. 1993.

Verse

Jingjie xiansheng ji (poetic works), edited by Tao Fu. 1883; revised edition, 1936; edited by Ku Chi, 1968.
T'ao the Hermit: Sixty Poems, translated by William Acker. 1952.
The Poems, translated by Lily Pao-hu Chang and Marjorie Sinclair. 1953.
The Poetry, translated by James Robert Hightower. 1970.
Selected Poems, translated by David Hinton. 1993.

Other

Taohua yuan ji [Tale of the Peach-Blossom Spring]. N.d.
Wu liu xiansheng zhuan [The Gentleman of the Five Willows], N.d.

*

Critical Studies: *The Poetry of T'ao Ch'ien*, commentary and annotations by James Robert Hightower, 1970; *T'ao Yuanming: His Works and their Meaning* (commentary) by A.R. Davis, 2 vols., 1983; *Tao Qian and the Chinese Poetic Tradition: The Quest for Cultural Identity* by Charles Yimtze Kwong, 1994.

* * *

Like much of Chinese lyricism, Tao's poetry is an expression of personal thoughts, feelings and experiences. It is thus important to remember that China's most celebrated nature poet and hermit was also an ardent visionary forced by political and social ills to choose eremitism for the last 20 years of his life. Charting a lifelong quest for a personal and cultural identity, his work reveals a dialectic search for a social and natural ideal informed by Daoism and Confucianism, as they form an alternating existential current charging him with antipodal sentiments and impelling his shifting perspective on the cosmic principles directing his destiny. More importantly, these visions constitute a thematic macrostructure and a stylistic underpinning of his art, which stands in unity with his life and ideals. As the poet returned to an intrigue-free world of nature with his social aspirations frustrated but never extinguished, his writings, like the famous "Yin jiu" [Drinking Wine] poems, continued to reflect the contrasting hues and intermingled tones of an artistic world that included not only portraits of nature, but also a poignant response to history, mortality and time.

Tao is best known for his "farmstead poetry" (*tianyuan shi*), which has often been called "pastoral." Certainly some of his poems—especially those from the earlier years after his permanent withdrawal, like "Guiqulai ci" ("Return Home")—sing of the peacefulness of country dwelling, the harmony of domestic life, and of a return to nature that is also a return to the natural Way (*Dao*) and original human nature. Yet even these poems are far from being pastoral in that they are not conventional fabrications but born of husbandry experience; showing a balanced appreciation of the freedom and vulnerability of rural existence—from the delights of work and familial contentment to material privation and plaintive reflection, or even simple scenes—they are complete with the inclemencies of rusticity and a broad range of moods, featuring not aesthetic shepherds but real farmers worried about their crops. Besides, free from the rhetorical ambiguity in pastoral verse of a precious presentation of simplicity, Tao's farmstead poetry is marked by plain, lucid language and a directly expressed voice. While objects like hills, birds, fish, pines and chrysanthemums are more readily identifiable as images, the line between image and object is often hard to draw where his language expresses quotidian experience, for it represents both the poet's diction and the rustic's life. Vibrant with a conversational vitality and immediacy sharply different from contemporary stylistic sophistication and verbal embellishment, his "farmer's words" (against which criticism has been levied) blend life and art into a crystalline beauty without heavy adornment. Both the concerns of his livelihood—concerns that constitute what, until then, was assumed to be "unfitting" content for literati verse, and the "inelegant" language of such concerns, which infuses his style—mark the literary and cultural originality of a poetry that records the totality of heartfelt experience.

At the same time, the combination of Tao's earthy life and visionary sensibility means that his writings are at once symbolically charged and empirically rooted, wherein human and transcendental levels of meaning are intermingled. One finds his lyric voice imbuing all forms (poetic and narrative) and subjects (natural, historical, autobiographical, mythical, and fictional) that serve as his expressive medium, resulting in cross-fertilization among formal and generic types and an extension of the ambit of Chinese lyricism. Yet this symbolism is essentially not the coinage of elaborate exertion and self-conscious design but the lyrical outgrowth of an inner vision, spontaneously projected on, and authenticated by, its perceived objects as they constitute a permanent and universal macrostructure of values validating the truth of his convictions. Such visionary transfiguration of a fundamental realism produces an organic unity between the realistic and ideal, the subjective and objective, the finite and infinite, and the spiritual and material. It is what underlies the work of the first great Chinese poet of the mundane and humble, as he conveys the daily moods and concerns of ordinary rural life with a refreshing and resonant simplicity. Tao is the first to link successfully, in poetry, a natural symbolism to a cosmic frame of reference, and the first, therefore, to realize fully the potential that structure holds for lyric expression. If his poetry comes across with an unobtrusive symbolic force, it is not only because he speaks what he sees in nature but because nature embodies the substance that allows him to speak thus.

In the final analysis, the simplicity and seemingly effortless ease of Tao's poetry are artistic attributes reflective of his own nature and determined by his ideals, its appeal lying in a unity between existential and aesthetic values. Poetry, for Tao, became witness and companion to his life, the sustaining mainstay of his idealism, and the fortifying inspiration that enabled him at times to attain a spiritual-aesthetic transcendence of his shattering historical reality. But beyond all this, poetry became a substitute fulfilment for his social responsibility as a literatus, a means of illuminating the natural and moral path amid his reclusion, and a way of preserving cultural ideals at a time when they seemed all but lost.

Virtually isolated in the political and artistic ethos of the day, Tao was largely left in oblivion for three centuries after his death before being recognized by the High Tang poets, and it was another three centuries before he was fully appreciated by the Song writers. It was at an unnoticed point that the Chinese lyric vision of nature came to maturity.

—Charles Kwong

TAO YUANMING

See TAO QIAN

TASSO, Torquato

Born: Sorrento, territory of Naples, 11 March 1544; son of the poet Bernardo Tasso. **Education:** Educated at a Jesuit school in Naples; at Court of Urbino with his father, 1557–60; studied law at University of Padua, 1560–62, and in Bologna, 1562–64; joined Accademia degli Eterei (under Scipione Gonzaga), Padua, 1564–65. **Career:** In household of Cardinal Luigi d'Este, Ferrara, 1565–70, and Paris, 1570–71; in Duke Alfonso d'Este's household, 1572–78; fearful of persecution, fled to Sorrento, 1577, and on to Rome, Mantua, Padua, and Venice, returning to Ferrara for medical treatment, 1579; confined as insane to hospital of Sant'Anna, 1579–86; released into care of Duke of Mantua, and spent remaining years wandering through Italy, to Naples, Rome, Florence, and Mantua; granted pension by Pope Clement VIII, 1595. **Died:** 25 April 1595.

PUBLICATIONS

Collections

Opere, edited by Luigi Bonfigli. 3 vols., 1934–36.
Opere, edited by Bruno Maier. 1963.

Verse

Rinaldo. 1562; edited by Luigi Bonfigli, 1936, and by Michael Sherberg, 1990; as *Rinaldo*, translated by John Hoole, 1792.
Gerusalemme liberata. 1580 (as *Il Goffredo*); complete version, 1581; revised edition, 1581; edited by G. Casoni, 1625, S. Barbato, 1628, and by Lanfranco Caretti, in *Tutte le poesie*, 1957: as *Godfrey of Bouillon: The Recovery of Jerusalem*, translated by Edward Fairfax, 1600, edited by Kathleen M. Lea and T.M. Gang, 1981; as *Tasso's Jerusalem*, translated by Henry Brooke, 1738; as *Delivery of Jerusalem*, translated by P. Doyne, 1761; several translations as *Jerusalem Delivered*, including by John Hoole, 1763, Jeremiah H. Wiffen, 1826, J.R. Broadhead, 1837, Alexander Cunningham Robertson, 1853, Charles Lesingham Smith, 1874, John Kingston James, 1884, Joseph Tusiani, 1970, and Ralph Nash, 1987; translated by Anthony M. Esolen, 2000.
Gerusalemme conquistata. 1593; edited by Luigi Bonfigli, 1934.
Le sette giornate del mondo creato. 1607; edited by Giorgio Petrocchi, 1951; as *Creation of the World*, translated by Joseph Tusiani, 1982.
Tasso's Sonnets, translated by Charles Chorley. 1866.
Opere minori in versi, edited by Angelo Solerti. 3 vols., 1891–95.
Rime, edited by Angelo Solerti. 3 vols., 1898–1902.
Later Work of Torquato Tasso, translated by Henry Cloriston. 1907.

Plays

Aminta (produced 1573). 1581; edited by B.T. Sozzi, 1957, and by C.E.J. Griffiths, 1972; in *The Countess of Pembroke's Ivychurch*, translated by Abraham Fraunce, 1591; as *Aminta*, translation attributed to John Reynolds, 1628; also translated by John Dancer, 1660, P.B. Du Bois, 1726, William Ayre, 1737, Percival Stockdale, 1770, Ernest Grillo, 1924, and Louis E. Lord, 1931; as *Amyntas*, translated by Leigh Hunt, 1820, and Frederic Whitmore, 1900; translated by Pastor Fido in *Three Renaissance Pastorals: Tasso-Guarini-Daniel*, edited and annotated by Elizabeth Story Donno, 1993.
Il Re Torrismondo. 1586; edited by Bartolo T. Sozzi, in *Opere* 2, 1956; as *King Torrismondo*, translated by Maria Pastore Passaro, 1997.
Intrighi d'amore (produced 1598). 1604; edited by Enrico Malato, 1976.

Other

Rime e prose. 1581.
Discorsi dell'arte poetica (lecture). 1587; revised version, as *Discorsi del poema eroico*, 1594; both versions edited by Luigi Poma, 1964; as *Discourses on the Heroic Poem*, translated by Mariella Cavalchini and Irene Samuel, 1973.
Lettere, edited by Cesare Guasti. 5 vols., 1852–55.
Prose diverse, edited by Cesare Guasti. 2 vols., 1875.
Tales from Tasso, translated by G. Grinnell Milne. 1909.
Dialoghi, edited by Ezio Raimondi. 3 vols., 1958; as *Tasso's Dialogues: A Selection, with Discourse on the Art of the Dialogue*, edited and translated by Carnes Lord and Dain A. Trafton (bilingual edition), 1982.
Prose, edited by E. Mazzali. 1959.

*

Bibliography: *Bibliografia analitica tassiana* by A. Tortoreto and J.G. Fucilla, 1935; "Nuovi studii su Torquato Tasso: Bibliografia analitica 1931–1945" by A. Tortoreto, in *Aevum*, 20, 1946; in *Studi tassiani*, from 1952; "Rassegna di studi tassiani 1970–1980" by B. Basile, in *Letter italiane*, July-September 1981.

Critical Studies: *Tasso and His Times* by William Boulting, 1907; *From Virgil to Milton* by C.M. Bowra, 1945; *Interpretazione del Tasso* by Giovanni Getto, 1951, revised edition, 1967; *Studi sul Tasso*, 1954, and *Nuovi studi sul Tasso*, 1963, both by B.T. Sozzi; *Ariosto e Tasso* by Lanfranco Caretti, 1961; *Tasso: A Study of the Poet and of His Contribution to English Literature* by C.P. Brand, 1965; *Il manierismo del Tasso e altri studi* by F. Ulivi, 1966; *Prospettive sul Tasso* by F. Bruni, 1969; *Torquato Tasso* by W. Moretti, 1973; *The Textual Problems of Tasso's "Gerusalemme conquistata"* by Anthony Oldcorn, 1976; *Torquato Tasso: Epos, parola, scena* by C. Varese, 1976; *Tasso* by G. Baldassarri, 1979; *Torquato Tasso: L'uomo, il poeta, il cortigiano* by F. Pittorru, 1982; *Ad nubes—The Horation Ode of Torquato Tasso* by Hannu Riikonen, 1982; *Trials of Desire: Renaissance Defenses of Poetry* by Margaret W. Ferguson, 1983; *The Genesis of Tasso's Narrative Theory: English Translations of the Early Poetics and a Comparative Study of their Significance* by Lawrence F. Rhu, 1993; *Rinaldo: Character and Intertext in Ariosto and Tasso* by Michael Sherberg, 1993; *Tasso (Torquato Tasso)* by Goethe, translated by Robert David MacDonald, 1994; *Musical-dramatic Productions Derived from Ariosto and Tasso in the City of Paris, 1600–1800* by Charles Townsend Downey, 1998; *The Epic Rhetoric of Tasso: Theory and Practice* by Maggie Günsberg, 1998; *Armida and Rinaldo in Eighteenth-Century Vienna: Context, Content, and Tonal Coding in Viennese Italian Reform Operas, 1761–1782* by Susanne E. Dunlap, 1999; *Renaissance Transactions: Ariosto and Tasso*, edited by Valeria Finucci, 1999.

* * *

Although best known for his epic poem *Gerusalemme liberata* (*Jerusalem Delivered*), Torquato Tasso was a typical man of his age in that he wrote important works in virtually all of the literary genres practised in Italy during the late Renaissance. Like his father Bernardo, who was also a poet of some prominence, Tasso spent most of his adult life as a courtier. It was in this capacity that he wrote the lyric, religious, and occasional verse, epic poetry, plays, dialogues, letters, and literary criticism that poured from his pen throughout a productive but unhappy life. Though clearly not the misunderstood, persecuted, and consequently mad poet his 19th-century admirers thought him, Tasso was certainly neurotic, in today's terms, and in certain periods of his life severely unbalanced. Indeed, there were times when his extreme susceptibility and the fears of persecution that plagued him for much of his adulthood led him to behaviour so politically injudicious that his worried patron had him placed in protective custody and eventually imprisoned. Tasso was a man of great learning and sophistication who at the same time was emotionally torn by doubts of his own worth and orthodoxy. Misgivings of this sort help explain his sometimes aberrant behaviour and were behind his incessant request that his religious views be examined by the Inquisition. They were also responsible for his insistence that the text of his poem be scrutinized by the leading literary arbiters of the day for traces of possible offence to linguistic, literary, or moral propriety.

The tensions and contradictions that made Tasso's life a legend even in his own time give his poetry its unmistakable aura of high drama and intensity. In the *Jerusalem Delivered*, discipline and indulgence, piety and sensuality, jealousy and magnanimity, hope and disillusionment, love and solitude, cowardice and valour, calculation and ingenuousness, history and invention, theatricality and simplicity, the epic and the lyric all combine in an impassioned poetic texture that is unique in the tradition of chivalric epic. In this work, Tasso's characters excite admiration not so much for their virtues or heroic accomplishments as for their capacities for intense feeling. Some of the most celebrated moments in the poem—the combat of Tancredi and Clorinda, for example, or the episode of Erminia and the shepherds—find their true dynamic in a barely repressed eroticism pulsing beneath an ostensibly heroic or idyllic surface. Partly from temperament, partly because of the uncertainties of the age in which he lived, Tasso was acutely aware of the fragility of virtue, the evanescence of even the best of human emotions, and the potential insidiousness of an imperfectly understood natural environment. The importance allotted to magic in his poem is indicative of his belief in the fundamental mysteriousness of life and the universe in which the human drama unfolds. Tasso is a poet of desire rather than satisfaction, and his best writing is characterized by anxiety and melancholy, a longing for liberation from the contingencies to which the human condition is subject.

Jerusalem Delivered is an epic poem in 20 cantos of *ottava rima*. Much of its action concerns the fall of Jerusalem in 1099 to Godfrey of Boulogne and his European allies during the First Crusade. Unlike the previous chivalrous epics written for the Ferrarese court by Boiardo and Ariosto, Tasso's poem is an overtly serious work, stoutly Christian and explicitly moralistic, and deeply concerned from its inception with such theoretical matters as the relation of truth to invention and the problem of historical authenticity. Its subject-matter, a protracted military contest between Christians and Muslims, was not without contemporary significance in a time of continuing struggle between the Italian states and the Ottoman Empire for commercial domination of the eastern Mediterranean. Moreover, the themes of loyalty and treachery and the conflicting claims of public and private obligation, so important for Renaissance epic in general, were still pertinent to the court ethos and interstate political rivalry characteristic of the age in which Tasso lived. In the poem, the blood and gore of antique epic (the "aspra tragedia dello stato umano," as Tasso called it) are mitigated by idyllic and lyric passages which derive more from Petrarch and the Greek and Latin elegiac and erotic poets than from Homer or Tasso's own sometimes rough-hewn epic forbears. The women of Tasso's poetry, in particular, and the love interests they give rise to provide a more complex foil to the traditional military skirmishing and bravado, in part because all of Tasso's characters are more fully realized and psychologically developed than those of his predecessors.

Second in importance to Tasso's epic poetry are his plays. They too come at the end of a long and glorious Ferrarese tradition. There are three of these: *Aminta*, a pastoral; *Il Re Torrismondo* (*King Torrismondo*), a tragedy on the Aristotelian-Sophoclean model; and *Intrighi d'amore*, a comedy whose authorship has only recently been securely attributed to Tasso. Of the three, the most important and influential is the *Aminta*. An apparently naïve story of a shepherd in love with a reluctant nymph, this "woodland fable" was first produced in 1573 for the delectation of the Ferrarese court, many of whose members are alluded to or depicted in it. The play is permeated by a kind of Counter-Reformation *Weltschmerz* that gives it its special sweetness; its charm derives in part from Tasso's indulgent smile at the simplicity of his rustic characters and the impossible world of innocence and fantasy they inhabit.

Tasso wrote over 1,500 occasional poems or *rime* on a very wide variety of subjects. In addition to the sonnets, ballads, *canzoni*, and *sestine* of tradition, these include a large number of madrigals, a relatively new form that was particularly well-suited to his sensual and musical poetic imagination. In these lyrics one finds not the chaste introspection of Petrarch, but rather an unabashed though sometimes bittersweet delight in amorous attraction and the physical world.

Tasso's prose works include letters, dialogues, and literary discourses. These last are elegant examples of the neo-Aristotelian theory of the day and deal primarily with epic poetry; first composed in the late 1560s and published as the *Discorsi dell'arte poetica* [Discourses on the Art of Poetry], they were then reworked and expanded and in 1594 republished as the *Discorsi del poema eroico* (*Discourses on the Heroic Poem*). The *Dialoghi* (*Dialogues*) are part of a long Renaissance tradition and treat such fashionable subjects as nobility, courtesy, jealousy, dignity, and piety. The letters, especially those from confinement, are often extremely moving. Generally lucid and elegant, Tasso's prose works are considered by many to be among the most accomplished that the century produced. Tasso also wrote devotional verse, especially at the end of his life, including *Le sette giornate del mondo creato* (*Creation of the World*), which was known and admired by John Milton.

Tasso belongs to the end of the Renaissance, a time when many were inclined to agree with Dafne's remark in the *Aminta*, "Il mondo invecchia, / E invecchiando intristisce" ("the world grows old and growing old grows sad"). His personal inquietude and problematic character both mark his own peculiar genius and herald a succeeding age that would quickly claim him as the dawn of a new, baroque era.

—Charles Klopp

See the essays on *Aminta* and *Jerusalem Delivered*.

TAWFIQ AL-HAKIM

Born: Husay Tawfiq Ismail Ahmad al-Hakim in Alexandria, Egypt, 9 October 1898. **Education:** Educated at Damanhur infant school; Muhammad Ali Secondary School, Cairo, until 1921; law school at University of Cairo, 1921–25; the Sorbonne, Paris, 1925–28. **Family:** Married in 1944 (wife died 1977); one son (died 1978) and one daughter. **Career:** Apprentice public prosecutor, Alexandria, 1928–29, then public prosecutor in small towns, 1929–34; director of Investigation Bureau, Ministry of Education, 1934–39; director of social guidance, Ministry of Social Affairs, 1939–43; then full-time writer: associated with the newspapers *Akhbar al-Yawm* and *Al-Ahram*; director general of Egyptian National Library, 1951–56; member of the Egyptian Higher Council of Arts, Literature, and Social Sciences, 1956–59, and from 1960. Egyptian representative, Unesco, Paris, 1959–60. President, Nadi al-Qissa, 1974. **Awards:** State literature prize, 1961. Awarded Cordon of the Republic, 1958. **Member:** Academy of the Arabic Language, 1954. **Died:** 26 July 1987.

PUBLICATIONS

Collections

In the Tavern of Life and Other Stories, translated by William Maynard Hutchins. 1998.

Plays

Ahl al-Kahf. 1933; translated as *The People of the Cave*, 1989.
Shahrazad. 1934; as *Shahrazad*, translated by William M. Hutchins, in *Plays, Prefaces, and Postscripts*, 1981.
Muhammad. 1936; as *Muhammed*, translated by Ibrahim Hassan el-Mongy, 1964, revised by Ahmad Kamal Metwalli, 1985.
Nahr al-Junun, in *Masrahiyat* [Plays]. 1937; translated as *The River of Madness*, in *Islamic Literature*, 1963.
Masrahiyat [Plays]. 2 vols., 1937.
Praksa, aw Mushkilāt al-Hukm [Praksa, the Difficult Business of Ruling]. 1939.
Nashid al-Anshad [The Song of Songs]. 1940.
Sulayman at-Hakīm. 1941; as *The Wisdom of Solomon*, translated by William M. Hutchins, in *Plays, Prefaces, and Postscripts*, 1981.
Pygmalion. 1942.
Shajarāt al-Hukm [The Rulership Tree]. 1945.
Al-Malik Udib. 1949; as *King Oedipus*, translated by William M. Hutchins, in *Plays, Prefaces, and Postscripts*, 1981.
Masrah at-Mujtama' [The Theatre of Society] (collection). 1950.
Al-Aydi al-Na'ima. 1954; as *Tender Hands*, translated by William M. Hutchins, in *Plays, Prefaces, and Postscripts*, 1981.
Isis. 1955.
Al-Masrah al-Munawwa' [The Diverse Theatre] (collection). 1956.
As-Safqa [The Deal]. 1956.
Rihla ila al-Ghad [Voyage of Tomorrow]. 1957; as *Al-'ālam al-Majhul* [The Unknown World], 1973; as *Voyage to Tomorrow*, translated by William M. Hutchins, in *Plays, Prefaces, and Postscripts*, 1981.
La'bat al-Mawt [Death Game]. 1957.
Ashwāk al-Salāam [The Thorns of Peace]. 1957.
Al-Sultan al-Ha'ir. 1960; as *The Sultan's Dilemma*, translated by Denys Johnson-Davies, in *Fate of a Cockroach*, 1973; also translated by F. Abdel Wahab, in *Modern Egyptian Drama*, 1974; with *The Song of Death*, in *Arabic Writing Today—The Drama*, edited by M. Manzalaoui, 1977.
Ya Tali' al-Shajara. 1962; as *The Tree Climber*, translated by Denys Johnson-Davies, 1966.
Al-Ta'am li-Kull Fam. 1963; as *Samira wa Hamdi*, 1973; as *Food for the Millions*, translated by William M. Hutchins, in *Plays, Prefaces, and Postscripts*, 1981.
Rihlat al-Rabi' wa-l-Kharif [Spring and Autumn Journeys] (includes verse). 1964; as *Ma'a al-Zamān* [Over the Years], 1973.
Shams al-Nahar. 1965; as *Shams wa Qamar*, 1973; as *Princess Sunshine*, translated by William M. Hutchins, in *Plays, Prefaces, and Postscripts*, 1981.
Al-Warta. 1966; as *Incrimination*, translated by William M. Hutchins, in *Plays, Prefaces and Postscripts*, 1981.
Bank al-Qalaq [Anxiety Bank]. 1966.
Masir Sarsar. 1966; as *Fate of a Cockroach*, translated by Denys Johnson-Davies, 1973.
Majlis al-'Adl [Council of Justice]. 1972.
Al-hubb [Love] (collection). 1973.

Fate of a Cockroach (includes *Fate of a Cockroach; The Song of Death; The Sultan's Dilemma; Not a Thing out of Place*), translated by Denys Johnson-Davies. 1973.

Al-Dunyā Riwaya Hazaliya. 1974; as *The World Is a Comedy*, translated by Riad Habib Youssef, with *A Conversation with the Planet Earth*, 1985.

Al-Hamir [Donkeys]. 1975.

Ashad al-Sa'ada al-Zawjiya [Happily Married] (collection). 1981.

Imsik Harami [Catch a Thief]. 1981.

Ah . . . Law 'Arafa al-Shabāb [Oh . . . If Only Youth Knew]. 1981.

'Imar Mu'allim Kanduz [The Building of Master Kanduz] (collection). 1981.

Plays, Prefaces, and Postscripts (includes *Shahrazad; The Wisdom of Solomon; King Oedipus; Tender Hands; Voyage to Tomorrow; Food for the Millions; Princess Sunshine*), translated by William M. Hutchins. 2 vols., 1981–84.

Fiction

Awdat al-Ruh [Return of the Spirit]. 1933.

Ahl al-Fann [Artistes]. 1934.

Al-Qasr al-Mashur [The Enchanted Castle], with Taha Husayn. 1936.

Yawmyyat Na'ib fi al-Aryaf. 1937; as *The Maze of Justice*, translated by Abba S. Eban, 1947.

Tārikh Hayāt Ma'ida [Biography of a Stomach]. 1938; as *Malik al-Tufayliyin* [King of the Moochers], 1946; as *Ash'ab, Amir al-Tufayliyin* [Ash'ab, Prince of the Moochers], 1963.

'Usfur min al-Sharq. 1938; as *Bird of the East*, translated by Bayley Winder, 1966.

'Ahd al-Shaytān [Pact with Satan]. 1938; as *Madrasat al-Shaytān* [Satan's School], 1955.

Raqisat al-Ma'bad [The Temple Dancer]. 1939.

Al-Ribāt al-Muqaddas [The Sacred Bond]. 1944.

Qisās [Stories]. 2 vols., 1949.

'Adala wa Fann [Justice and Art]. 1953; as *Ann wa'l-Qanun wal'Fann* [The Law, Art, and I], 1973.

Arini Allah [Show Me God]. 1953.

Min Dhikrayāt al-Fann wa't-Qada' [Memories of Art and Justice]. 1953.

Madrasa al-Mughaffalin [School for Fools]. 1953.

Laylat at-Zifāf [Wedding Night]. 1966.

Al-Amira al-Bayda aw Bayad al-Nahar [Snow White]. 1978.

Other

Tahta Shams al-Fikr [By the Light of the Sun of Thought]. 1938.

Himar al-Hakim [Al-Hakim's Ass]. 1940.

Sultan al-Zalam [The Reign of Darkness]. 1941.

Taht al-Misbh al-Akhdar [By the Light of the Green Lamp]. 1941.

Min al-Burj al-'Aji [From the Ivory Tower]. 1941.

Zahrat al-'Umr [The Flower of Life]. 1943.

Himari Qala li [My Donkey Told Me]. 1945.

Fann al-Adab [The Art of Literature]. 1952.

'Asā al-Hākim [Al-Hakim's Staff]. 1954.

Ta'ammulat fi al-Siyasa [Reflections on Politics]. 1954.

Al-Ta'āduliya [The Art of Balance]. 1955.

Adab al-Haycāt [The Literature of Life]. 1959.

Sijn al-'Umr. 1964; as *The Prison of Life*, translated by Pierre Cachia, 1992.

Qalibuna al-Masrahi [Our Theatrical Form]. 1967.

Qult . . . dhat Yawm [I Said . . . One Day]. 1970.

Tawfiq al-Hakim yatahaddath [Tawfiq al-Hakim Discusses]. 1971.

Thawrat al-Shabāb [Revolt of the Young]. 1971.

Ahadith ma'a Tawfiq al-Hakim min sana 1951–1971 [Conversations with Tawfiq al-Hakim], edited by Salah Tahir. 1971.

Rahib bayna Nisa' [A Monk among Women]. 1972.

Rihla bayna 'Asrayn [Journey Between Two Ages]. 1972.

Himari wa'Asaya wa'l-Akharun [My Donkey and Stick and the Others]. 1972.

Hadith ma'a al-Kawtab. 1974; as *A Conversation with the Planet Earth*, translated by Riad Habib Youssef, with *The World Is a Comedy*, 1985.

'Awdat al-Wa'y. 1974; as *The Return of Consciousness*, translated by Bayley Winder, 1985.

Safahāt min al-Tārikh al-Adabi min Waqi' Rasa'il wa-Watha'iq [Pages from Literary History: Selected Letters and Documents]. 1975.

Bayn al-Fikr wa'l-Fann [Between Thought and Art]. 1976.

Ta'ām al-Fann wa'l-Ruh wa'l-Aql [Food for Art, Spirit, and Intellect]. 1977.

Malamih Dakhiliya [Inner Features]. 1982.

Equilibrium and Islam. 1983.

*

Critical Studies: *Tawfiq al-Hakim* by I. Adham and I. Nagi, 1945; *Studies in the Arab Theatre and Cinema* by J. Landau, 1958; *Tawfiq al-Hakim and the West* by Gilbert Tutunji, 1966; *Drama and Society in Contemporary Egypt* by A. Ismail, 1967; ''Un Dramaturge égyptien: Tawfiq al-Hakîm et l'avantgarde'' by Nada Tomiche, in *Revu de littérature comparée*, 45, 1971; *The Modern Egyptian Novel* by H. Kilpatrick, 1974; *Arabic Writing Today—The Drama* (includes translations) by M. Manzalaoui, 1977; ''Philosophical Themes in Tawfiq al-Hakim's Drama,'' in *Journal of Arabic Literature*, 8, 1977, *From the Ivory Tower: A Critical Study of Tawfiq al-Hakim*, 1987, and ''Tawfiq al-Hakim (1898–1987): Leading Playwright of the Arab World,'' in *Theater Three*, 6, 1989, all by Paul Starkey; *Mort— résurrection: Une Lecture de Tawfiq al-Hakîm* by J. Fontaine, 1978; *Tawfiq al Hakim: Playwright of Egypt* by Richard Long, 1979; ''Idealism and Ideology: The Case of Tawfiq al-Hakim'' by Pierre Cachia, in *Journal of the American Oriental Society*, 100, 1980; *Modern Arabic Drama in Egypt* by M.M. Badawi, 1988; ''The Treatment of Greek Drama by Tawfiq al-Hakim'' by Mahmoud al-Shetawi, in *World Literature Today*, 63, 1989.

* * *

Tawfiq al-Hakim is widely regarded both as the founder of the modern Egyptian theatre, and as a major contributor to the development of the modern Arabic novel.

Though he had already written some plays in colloquial Arabic for the popular theatre while studying in Cairo, it was al-Hakim's stay in France between 1925 and 1928 that played the major role in determining the course of his future literary career. In Paris he fell under the spell of avant-garde authors such as Shaw, Maeterlinck, and Pirandello, and it is these writers' influence that is apparent in the ''intellectual'' plays for which al-Hakim is best known.

The first of these dramas, *Ahl al-Kahf* (*The People of the Cave*), related the Qur'ānic story of the sleepers of Ephesus to the contemporary situation of Egypt, as the country woke from a long period of stagnation to face the challenges of the 20th century. The Pirandellian confusion between fantasy and reality apparent there was carried further in *Shahrazad*, in which the heroine of *The Thousand and One Nights* is presented as the embodiment of a "mysterious woman," whose nature is interpreted by the other main characters each according to his own disposition, but whose true nature remains elusive to the end of the play. Meanwhile, al-Hakim had already produced his first novel, *Awdat al-Ruh* [Return of the Spirit], a work set at the time of the 1919 uprising against British rule. This work, characterized by a vision of the Egyptian peasant as the direct descendant of his Pharaonic forebears, marked the beginning of a new realistic trend in the Arabic novel, and was much admired by, among others, Nasser.

The series of "intellectual" dramas begun with *The People of the Cave* and *Shahrazad* was continued with *Pygmalion*—partly inspired by Shaw's play of the same title—and *Al-Malik Udib* (*King Oedipus*), an attempt, according to the author, to rework the legend of Oedipus in accordance with Islamic beliefs, eliminating the concept of fate. Though these plays have apparently little direct relevance to contemporary Egyptian society, elsewhere al-Hakim's treatment of his themes is clearly intended to relate to the Egypt of the day. *Sulayman al-Hakīm* (*The Wisdom of Solomon*), for example, discusses the relationship between wisdom and power, using stories from the Qur'ān and *The Thousand and One Nights*; *Isis* takes as its main theme the question of whether the end justifies the means; and in *Al-Sultan al-Ha'ir* (*The Sultan's Dilemma*)—a play set in Mameluke Egypt—al-Hakim discusses a question which he regarded as crucial for the world, and the Egypt, of the 1960s: should the country seek to resolve its problems by the application of law, or by force?

In addition to these "intellectual" plays, al-Hakim composed, between 1945 and 1950, a series of short plays on Egyptian social themes—of widely varying quality—which were later collected and published in book form.

Unlike most Egyptian writers of his generation, al-Hakim had not allowed himself to become identified with any particular political party in the inter-war years. This attitude of detachment stood him in good stead with the new regime which came to power in 1952, and in the following years he received a number of honours and official appointments. His attitude towards the new regime was expressed in the play *Al-Aydi al-Na'ima* (*Tender Hands*), the main theme of which is the need for reconciliation between the various classes of Egyptian society. Meanwhile, he had continued to produce a stream of essays and articles in the Egyptian press, in addition to three more major novels, including *Yawmiyyat Na'ib fi al-Aryaf* (*The Maze of Justice*), the work regarded by some as his masterpiece. This work, in diary form, and based on al-Hakim's own experiences as a rural prosecutor, presents a damning picture of corruption in Egyptian rural society, highlighting the gulf between the mentality of the Egyptian *fellah* and that of the European-style legal system imposed on him.

Two main trends can be seen in al-Hakim's work during the post-1952 period. Firstly, his major works are for the most part all plays; secondly, his work shows a new enthusiasm for technical experiment, largely, though not exclusively, inspired by developments in contemporary Western theatre. The first, and most successful, of these experimental plays—*Ya Tali'al-Shajara* (*The Tree Climber*)—shows the influence of the "theatre of absurd," with which al-Hakim had become acquainted on a recent visit to Paris; while *Al-Ta'am li-Kull*

Fam (*Food for the Millions*), for example, seems to have been influenced by Brecht.

By the end of his life, al-Hakim had become almost a national institution in his native Egypt. The range of themes and influences evident in his work, however, makes an overall evaluation difficult; and his work is further marked by an inconsistency both of quality and of outlook. On the one hand, his use of language is characterized by an admirable simplicity of style; on the other, much of his work is marred by a tendency to quasi-philosophical rambling at the expense of artistic unity. Many of his plays lack dramatic qualities, and were—on his own admission—intended to be read rather than acted. The best of them, however, have an appeal far beyond the Arab world, and assure him of a lasting place in the history of modern Arabic literature.

—Paul Starkey

TÉLLEZ, Gabriel

See TIRSO DE MOLINA

TERENCE

Born: Publius Terentius Afer, probably in North Africa, c. 190 BC. **Family:** Had a daughter. **Career:** Possibly a freed slave in household of Terentius Lucanus; his plays were produced in the 160s BC, and came to be admired by Cicero and Horace. **Died:** c. 159 BC.

PUBLICATIONS

Collections

Terence in English: Fabulae (bilingual edition), translated by Richard Bernard. 1598.
[Plays], edited by S.G. Ashmore (as *Comedies*). 1908; also edited by J. Marouzeau, 2 vols., 1947–56; as *Comoediae*, edited by Robert Kauer and Wallace M. Lindsay, revised by O. Skutsch, 1958, and R. Ranzato and R. Cantarella, 1971–; as *Comedies* (bilingual edition), translated by Charles Hode, 1633; also translated by Laurence Echard and others, 1694, edited by Robert Graves as *The Comedies of Terence*, 1962; also translated by Thomas Cooke (bilingual edition), 1734; S. Patrick (prose), 2 vols., 1745; "Mr." Gordon (prose), 1752; George Colman the Elder (verse), 1765; John Benson Rose, 1870; Henry Thomas Riley (prose), 1883; William Ritchie, 1927; F. Perry, 1929; Frank O. Copley, 1967; Betty Radice, 1976; as *Terence* [Loeb Edition], translated by John Sargeaunt, 2 vols., 1912; translations in *Complete Roman Drama* (translations), edited by George Duckworth, 1942; as *Complete Comedies*, edited by Smith Palmer Boyle and translated by Bovie, Constance Carrier, and Douglass Parker, 1974.

Plays

Andria (produced 166 BC). Edited (with commentary) by G.P. Shipp, 1960; translated as *Andria*, c. 1520, reprinted as *That Girl from Andros: An Early Sixteenth-Century Translation*, edited by Meg Twycross, 1987; also translated by Maurice Kyffin, 1588; T.

Newman (verse), with *Eunuch*, 1627, reprinted 1931; William Gardiner, 1821; St. George and R.A. Stock, 1891; translated as *The Andrian*, 1777; also translated by Henry C. Englefield, 1814; W.R. Goodluck (prose), 1820; J.A. Phillips, 1836; as *The Lady of Andros*, translated by John Sargeaunt, in *Terence* [Loeb Edition], 1912; as *The Woman from Andros*, translated by Alexander Harvey, 1925; as *The Woman of Andros*, translated by Frank O. Copley, 1949; as *The Girl from Andros*, translated by Smith Palmer Bovie, in *Complete Comedies*, 1974.

Eunuchus (produced 161 BC). Edited by P. Fabia, 1895; as *Eunuchus*, translated in *Terence in English*, 1598; also translated by Dr. Webbe (bilingual edition), 1629; William Gardiner, 1821; as *The Eunuch*, translated by T. Newman (verse), with *Andria*, 1627; also translated by John Sargeaunt, in *Terence* [Loeb Edition], 1912; Betty Radice, in *The Brothers and Other Plays*, 1965; Frank O. Copley, 1967; Douglass Parker, 1970; commentary by John Barsby, with *Phormio* and *The Brothers*, 1991.

Heauton timorumenos (produced 163 BC). Edited by K.I. Lietzmann, 2 vols., 1974; as *Heauton timorumenos*, translated in *Terence in English*, 1598; as *Heautontimorumenos*, translated by "a member of the University of Oxford" (prose), with *Adelphi*, 1777; also translated by J.A. Phillips, 1836; as *Heauton timorumenos*, translated by W.H. Girdlestone, 1869; also translated by St. George and R.A. Stock, 1891; as *The Self-Tormentor*, translated by E.S. Shuckburgh, 1878; also translated by Frederick William Ricord, 1883; John Sargeaunt, in *Terence* [Loeb Edition], 1912; Alexander Harvey, 1925; A.J. Brothers (bilingual edition), 1988.

Hecyra (produced 165 BC). Edited by T.F. Carney (with commentary), 1968; edited and translated by Stanley Ireland (bilingual edition), 1989; as *Hecyra*, translated by Richard Bernard, in *Terence in English*, 1598; also translated by J.A. Phillips, 1836; as *The Mother-in-Law*, translated by John Sargeaunt, in *Terence* [Loeb Edition], 1912; as *Her Husband's Mother*, translated by Constance Carrier, in *Complete Comedies*, 1974.

Phormio (produced 161 BC). Edited by Ronald H. Martin, 1959, C. Coury, 1982; as *Phormio*, translated in *Terence in English*, 1598; also translated by John Henry Newman, 1864; Aubrey Stewart, 1879; St. George and R.A. Stock, 1891; M.H. Morgan (prose), 1894; Barrett H. Clark, 1909; John Sargeaunt, in *Terence* [Loeb Edition], 1912; Betty Radice, in *Phormio and Other Plays*, 1967; Frank O. Copley, 1967; Douglass Parker, 1970; commentary by John Barsby, with *The Eunuch* and *The Brothers*, 1991.

Adelphoe also known as *Adelphi* (produced 160 BC). Edited by P. Fabia, 1892, K. Dziatzko and R. Kauer, 1903, Ronald H. Martin, 1976; as *Adelphoe*, translated in *Terence in English*, 1598; as *Adelphi*, translated (verse), 1774; also translated by "a member of the University of Oxford" (prose), with *Heautontimorumenos*, 1777; Dr. Giles (bilingual edition), 1858; St. George and R.A. Stock, 1891; as *The Brothers*, translated by Alexander Harvey, 1925; also translated by Betty Radice, in *The Brothers and Other Plays*, 1965; Frank O. Copley, 1967; Constance Carrier, in *Complete Comedies*, 1974; A.S. Gratwick (bilingual edition), 1987; commentary by John Barsby, with *The Eunuch* and *Phormio*, 1991.

Flowers For Latin Speaking (selection), edited and translated by Nicholas Udall. 1533.

Andria; Heauton timorumenos; Phormio; Adelphi, translated by St. George and R.A. Stock. 1891.

The Brothers and Other Plays, translated by Betty Radice. 1965.

Phormio and Other Plays, translated by Betty Radice. 1967.

*

Bibliography: *Bibliografia terenziana (1470–1983)* by G. Cupaiuolo, 1984.

Critical Studies: *The Art of Terence*, 1923, and *Plautus and Terence*, 1965, both by G. Norwood; *The Syntax of Terence* by J.T. Allardice, 1929; *The Prosody of Terence* by W.A. Laidlaw, 1938; *The Nature of Roman Comedy* by George Duckworth, 1952; *Menander, Plautus, and Terence* by W.G. Arnott, 1968; *Roman Comedy* by Kenneth McLeish, 1976; *Roman Comedy* by David Konstan, 1983; *Terence* by W.E. Forehand, 1985; *The New Comedy of Greece and Rome* by R.L. Hunter, 1985; *The Comic Theatre of Greece and Rome* by F.H. Sandbach, 1985; *Understanding Terence* by Sander M. Goldberg, 1986; *Studies in the Textual Tradition of Terence* by John N. Grant, 1986; *The Roman Theatre and Its Audience* by Richard C. Beacham, 1991; *Ancient Comedy: The War of the Generations* by Dana F. Sutton, 1993; *Shakespeare and Classical Comedy: The Influence of Plautus and Terence* by Robert S. Miola, 1994; *Anglo-Saxon Gestures and the Roman Stage* by C.R. Dodwell, 2000.

*   *   *

The plays of Terence read like close adaptations of Greek New Comedy, an effect both innovative and deceptive. The innovation lies in Terence's rebellion against the popular aesthetic standards of his time. Where traditional Roman comedy, well represented to us in the plays of Plautus, delighted in the broad effects of stock characterizations and situations, elaborate songs, and extravagant, highly stylized diction, Terence sought instead to reproduce the more subtle effects of the later Greek comedy. He based four of his six plays upon works of Menander, the most literary of the Greek dramatists, and two upon Apollodorus of Carystos, himself said to have been one of Menander's greatest admirers. The result was a set of Latin plays with more sophisticated characterizations, a more sedate and elegant diction, and a more refined humour than Roman audiences had previously witnessed. The plays are also deceptive, however, because they are not in fact faithful copies of Greek models. Terence made many changes which affect both the structure and the meaning of his plays. He avoided, for example, the expository divine prologues of Greek drama, which meant that his audiences lack the foreknowledge that would enable them to feel superior to his characters. Not only does the dramatic action then depend entirely on human agents and human motives, but the audience tends to see the action that unfolds as the characters see it. Terence also borrowed elements freely from one Greek play to enrich the action of another, a process modern scholars call *contaminatio*. His *Eunuchus* (*The Eunuch*), for example, which is based on a play of that name by Menander, nevertheless features a slave and parasite borrowed from a second play called *The Flatterer*. In *Adelphoe* (*The Brothers*), a slapstick scene from Diphilus is woven into a Menandrean plot. A second set of lovers enters *Andria* (*The Girl from Andros*) by way of Menander's *Perinthian Girl*. While these additions certainly enliven (and sometimes complicate) the stage action, their contributions to meaning are equally significant.

Terence's need to change the significance of his dramatic actions is rooted in the most striking difference between him and Menander, which is a change in their moral vision. Menander treats human frailties with great sympathy. His characters learn from their mistakes, and we are meant to share in that process of growth. Terence is the consummate ironist. In his plays, a correct course of action is not always easy to see, a character's virtue is not easily defined, and suitable rewards for them are thus more difficult to imagine. He is as likely to deny knowledge to characters at the end of a play as to share it among them, and the process of recognition does not necessarily lead to moral improvement. All the characters in *The Eunuch*, for example, are shown to be as self-serving as the imported soldier and parasite; the slapstick scene in *The Brothers* helps balance the absurdity of the country brothers with the equally absurd arrogance of the city dwellers. The characters who win our sympathy in *Hecyra* (*The Mother-in-Law*) are excluded from the play's conclusion, and their legitimate concerns are simply ignored. In retrospect, we can see that Terence's wry view of human capabilities has more in common with the later Roman genres of satire and elegy than with his Greek dramatic predecessors.

The Romans themselves, however, were slow to appreciate Terence, and they never fully recognized his comic genius. The stage life of his plays was much briefer than that of Plautus' plays. Four of the six are theatrically brilliant—*The Eunuch* in fact commanded an unusual encore performance and a record fee—but none went on to achieve the status of stage classic that many Plautine plays attained. Two attempts to perform *The Mother-in-Law* failed in Terence's own lifetime, and after his death successors reverted to the broader, more traditional style of Plautus. Enduring fame came to him only later, and it came through reading rather than seeing his plays. In the 1st century BC, by which time original stage comedy at Rome was all but dead, Terence took on a new life. Both Cicero and Caesar praise his style; Cicero quotes him often to illustrate moral arguments in his forensic speeches and cites him in rhetorical works as an example of correct Latin usage. By the 4th century AD grammarians had produced copiously annotated editions of his plays, and Terence acquired a fame second only to Virgil's. The 10th-century nun Hrotswitha of Gandersheim claimed him as the stylistic model for her own martyr plays, and the Latin comedies themselves were never forgotten. Many manuscripts, some with beautiful illustrations, survive. During the 15th and 16th centuries the plays were widely studied and translated and became a seminal influence on Renaissance, and thus modern, comedy.

—Sander M. Goldberg

See the essays on *The Brothers*, *The Eunuch*, and *Phormio*.

THEOCRITUS

Born: Probably born in Syracuse, Sicily, c. 300 BC. **Career:** Little is known about his life. Associated with the poetic circle on Cos under Philetas' patronage, and active in Alexandria under the patronage of Ptolemy II Philadelphus in the 270s BC.

PUBLICATIONS

Verse

Sixe Idyllia. 1588, reprinted 1922.
The Idylliums, translated by Thomas Creech, with *Eclogues*. 1654; also translated by Francis Fawkes, 1767; as *The Idylls*, translated

by J. Banks and J.M. Chapman, 1853; also translated by J.H. Hallard, 1894; A.S. Way, in *Theocritus, Bion and Moschus*, 1913; R.C. Trevelyan, 1925; Jack Lindsay, 1929; W.D.P. Hill, 1959; Robert Wells, 1988; as *Theocritus: A Selection: Idylls 1, 3, 4, 6, 7, 10, 11 and 13*, edited by Richard Hunter, 1999.
Translations Out of Theocritus, translated by John Dryden, in *Miscellany Poems*. 1692.
The Encomium of Ptolemy (Idyll XVII), translated by William Dodd, in *The Hymns of Callimachus*. 1755.
Idyllia, Epigrams and Fragments of Theocritus [and others], translated by Richard Polwhele. 1786.
[*Idylls, Epigrams, and Epitaphs*], translated by C.S. Calverley. 1869.
[*Idylls and Epigrams*], translated by Andrew Lang (prose), in *Theocritus, Bion and Moschus*. 1889; also translated by Anthony Holden, in *Greek Pastoral Poetry*, 1974.
Sicilian Idyls [sic] (Idylls I–XIII), translated by Marion Mills Miller. 1900.
The Festival of Adonis (Idyll XV), edited and translated by E.H. Blakeney. 1933.
[*Verse*], edited by A.S.F. Gow (includes translation). 2 vols., 1950.
Selected Poems, edited by K.J. Dover. 1971; translated by J.M. Edmonds, in *The Greek Bucolic Poets*, 1912; also translated by Anna Rist, 1978; Thelma Sargent, 1982; Daryl Hine, 1982.

*

Critical Studies: *Theocritus' Coan Pastorals: A Poetry Book* by Gilbert Lawall, 1967; *The Green Cabinet: Theocritus and the European Pastoral Lyric* by Thomas G. Rosenmeyer, 1969; *Theocritus at Court* by Frederick T. Griffiths, 1979; *Poetry and Myth in Ancient Pastoral: Essays on Theocritus and Virgil* by Charles Segal, 1981; *Studies in Theocritus and Other Hellenistic Poets* by Heather White, 1981; *Before Pastoral: Theocritus and the Ancient Tradition of Bucolic Poetry* by David M. Halperin, 1983; *Theocritus' Pastoral Analogies: The Formation of a Genre* by Kathryn J. Gutzwiller, 1991; *Pastoral and the Poetics of Self-contradiction: Thocritus to Marvell* by Judith Haber, 1994; *Theocritus's Urban Mimes: Mobility, Gender, and Patronage* by Joan B. Burton, 1995; *Theocritus and the Archaeology of Greek Poetry* by Richard Hunter, 1996; *Theocritus: Dioscuri (Idyll 22)*, translated by Alexander Sens, 1997; *The Pipes of Pan: Intertextuality and Literary Fiction in the Pastoral Tradition from Theocritus to Milton* by Thomas K. Hubbard, 1998; *The Epigrams Ascribed to Theocritus: A Method of Approach* by Laura Rossi, 2001.

* * *

Theocritus wrote most of the poems for which we remember him in Alexandria, the capital of Hellenistic Egypt, during the second quarter of the 3rd century BC. His work—like that of Callimachus of Cyrene and Apollonius of Rhodes, Theocritus' contemporaries and fellow Alexandrians—owes its heightened consciousness of poetic artifice and almost painful awareness of the overshadowing presence of accumulated literary, tradition to the temper of the post-classical, pre-Roman era in which it was composed. In an age whose sophistication made it difficult for writers to treat personal experience with a sense of immediacy, Theocritus strives to recover for poetry a measure of freshness and emotional power. He accomplishes his purpose without extravagant displays of feeling or explicit literary polemics; rather, his best effects are typically achieved through a complex combination of irony, allusiveness, detachment, wit, tonal control, and subtle manipulation of lexical and linguistic nuance.

Theocritus' reputation rests chiefly upon ten of the 30 preserved poems, commonly called *Idylls* (though few are in fact idyllic), which antiquity has transmitted to us under his name together with two dozen epigrams and a few fragments. The poems numbered I and III–XI in the conventional arrangement (VIII and IX are probably spurious) furnished the model for the major portion of Virgil's *Eclogues* and so became in time the ultimate if indirect source of the European pastoral tradition. Although the pastoral *Idylls* exploit many of the literary conventions familiar to us from later pastoral poetry in order to express the outlook or set of attitudes we currently recognize as distinctive to the pastoral genre, it is not certain that Theocritus considered them a separate subgroup within his larger *oeuvre* or conceived his own invention, which he termed bucolic poetry, according to the same criteria we use to define pastoral. At any rate, poems I and III–XI contain rustic dialogues and serenades which celebrate, with pointed naïvety, the enamoured Cyclops, the sorrows of Daphnis, and other piquant, faintly absurd subjects from the lives and loves of Greek herdsmen. Adapting a technique previously employed by Homer in *The Odyssey*'s rural interludes, by Euripides in certain choral odes, and by Plato in the *Phaedrus*, Theocritus transforms his country settings by means of an aesthetic illusion and thereby creates a landscape halfway between the sensuous descriptions of the classical poets and the sentimental metaphors of the Romantics. Within such a landscape at once realistic and artificial, distant and familiar, the cultivated reader and the passionate shepherd are equally at home. Their encounter is one of the triumphs of Hellenistic poetry.

Although the pastoral *Idylls* include some minor masterpieces (I, VII, XI), the majority of Theocritus' best works are to be found outside the pastoral corpus (II, XIII, XVI, XXIV; also of considerable interest are XII, XIV, XV, and XXII). They feature unsentimental tales of love, impertinent reworkings of mythological episodes, and humorous scenes of daily life among housewives or mercenaries. With the exception of *Idylls* XXVIII–XXXI, composed in Aeolic dialect and in lyric meters, all of Theocritus' genuine *Idylls* are set in dactylic hexameter, the form of versification used by Homer, Hesiod, and the Greek epicists for heroic or didactic poetry. If there is unity in the works of Theocritus as they have come down to us, perhaps it can be found in a shared programme of epic revisionism spanning both the pastoral and non-pastoral works and utilizing a variety of artistic strategies to a common end. Theocritus replaces princes with paupers, tragic sympathy with comic irony, and heroic themes with erotic ones, thereby reversing traditional epic society, tone, and subject matter. In this way he was able to prolong and to renew the life of the Greek epic.

—David M. Halperin

See the essays on "Idyll I," "Idyll IV," and "Idyll VII."

THEOPHRASTUS

Born: Eresus, on the island of Lesbos, c. 370 BC. **Education:** Studied in Athens under Aristotle, *q.v..* **Career:** Travelled with Aristotle to Macedonia and Athens, 335 BC; on Aristotle's retirement, succeeded him as head of the Lyceum, 322 BC. **Died:** c. 287 BC.

PUBLICATIONS

Collections

[Works], edited by J.G. Schneider (Greek and Latin text). 5 vols., 1818–21; also edited by Friedrich Wimmer (Greek text with Latin notes), 2 vols., 1854–62.
Major Fragments, edited by D. Eicholz. 1994–.

Works

Characteres (Greek and Latin text), edited by Hermann Diels. 1909; also edited by O. Navarre, 1920, and O. Immisch, 1923; as *The Characters*, edited by R.G. Ussher (with commentary), 1960, revised edition, 1993; edited and translated by J.M. Edmonds [Loeb Edition], 1929, and Jeffrey Ruslen, I.C. Cunningham, and A.D. Knox, 1929; translated by John Healey, 1616, reprinted 1899; also translated by R.C. Jebb, 1870, revised by J.E. Sandys, 1909; Jean Stewart, 1970.
De igne, as *On Fire*, translated by A. Gercke. 1896.
De lapidibus, as *On Stones*, edited and translated by Earle R. Caley and John F.C. Richards. 1956; as *History of Stones*; translated by John Hill, 1746; as *On Stones*, translated by D. Eichholz, 1965.
De sensu, as *Theophrastus and the Greek Physiological Psychology Before Aristotle*, translated by G.M. Stratton. 1917, as *On Sense Perception*, 1927.
De signis pluviarum, ventorum, tempestatis et serenitatis, in *Minor Works on Odours and Weather Signs*, with *Enquiry into Plants* [Loeb Edition], edited and translated by Arthur Hort. 1916; as *On Winds and on Weather Signs*, translated by J.G. Wood, 1894.
De ventis, edited and translated by Victor Coutant and Val L. Eichenlaub. 1975.
Historiam plantarum, edited by Friedrich Wimmer. 1842, revised edition, 1854; as *Enquiry into Plants*, with *Minor Works on Odours and Weather Signs* [Loeb Edition], edited and translated by Arthur Hort, 1916; as *The Calendar of Flora*, translated by Bishop Stillingfleet, 1761; as *The Causes of Plants, Book I*, translated by R.E. Dengler, 1927; as *De causis plantarum* [Loeb Edition], translated by Benedict Einarson and George K.K. Link, 3 vols., 1976–90.
Metaphysica, as *The Metaphysics*, translated by W.D. Ross and F.H. Forbes. 1929.
Meteorologica (fragments; German text). 1918.
Rhetorica (fragments), edited by Augustus Mayer. 1910.
Doctrines of Natural Philosophy, edited by H. Diels. 1879.
On Piety, edited by W. Potscher. 1964.

*

Critical Studies: *Theophrastus of Eresus: Sources for His Life, Writings, Thought and Influence* edited and translated by William W. Fortenbaugh and others, 1992; *Theophrastus on Theories of Perception, Argument and Purpose in De sensibus* by Han Baltussen, 1993; *Theophrastus of Eresus: Commentary, Volume 3.1* by R.W. Sharples, 1998; *Lucretius and the Transformation of Greek Wisdom* by David Sedley, 1998; *Theophrastus: Reappraising the Sources*, edited by Johannes M. van Ophuijsen and Marlein van Raalte, 1998;

Theophrastus against the Presocratics and Plato: Peripatetic Dialectic in the De sensibus by H. Baltussen, 2000.

* * *

Theophrastus owes his place in literary history to two things: his authorship of the unique and fascinating series of 30 short sketches of different types of personality known as the *Characteres* (*The Characters*); and his position at the head of the Peripatetic School of philosophers (from the verb *peripatein*, the habit of giving lectures whilst walking to and fro) or Lyceum, during its period of greatest activity, size, and influence, from 323–22 BC, when he succeeded his teacher Aristotle (who had left Athens for Chalcis and died shortly afterwards) until his own death c. 287 BC. Like his teacher, he was not a native of Athens, although he seems to have spent most of his life there, but hailed from the relative backwater of Eresus, a city of Lesbos. The main source for his life and work is the brief account by the historian of philosophy Diogenes Laertius, a writer probably of the 3rd century AD, who gathered together a short biography, a couple of telling anecdotes and witty remarks (*chreiai*), the text of his will, an extract from a letter, and a bibliography of his works. This *oeuvre* amounted to more than 200 titles, covering logic, metaphysics, zoology (*Of Animals Reputed to Be Envious, On the Diversity of Sounds Made by Animals of the Same Species*), psychology and physiology (*On Odours, On Suffocation, On Perspiration*), meteorology and geology (*On the Eruption of Sicily*), as well as botany, ethics, religion, politics, economics, rhetoric, poetics, music, and the history of philosophy. What survives today is but a tiny fraction of what was known to Diogenes: *Historiam plantarum* (*Enquiry into Plants* in nine books, and *The Causes of Plants* in six books), *Characters*, extracts and epitomes of the scientific treatises, the *Metaphysica* (*The Metaphysics*), and fragments preserved by other authors.

Because Theophrastus' *oeuvre* covers such a wide range of subjects, and because the surviving remnant is such a small proportion of the whole, it is difficult to generalize about his production. But it is generally agreed that Theophrastus continued the work of Aristotle more or less in Aristotle's spirit, although the master's strong instinctive tendency to systematize, to divide things into neat hierarchical taxonomies, was more restrained in his pupil, who seems to have been happy simply to collect as many varieties of any particular thing as he could. His approach is altogether more concrete and more empirical, less speculative and less synthetic than Aristotle's. These qualities are manifest in the most substantial of his extant treatises, his works on plants, which can be seen as the inauguration of the science of botany, in as much as they treat the variety and physiology of plants for the first time as a subject worthy of scholarly interest in its own right, instead of only taking into account their medicinal properties and the uses that could be made of them.

As can be seen from his bibliography, Theophrastus wrote on poetry, comedy, and (probably) historiography. His influence on literary history has been made much of in the past. Scholars writing earlier this century tended to lay at the door of Theophrastus and his school everything that they thought was wrong or decadent about the Hellenistic age. The comments of Sir William Tarn, the great historian of the period, on Hellenistic historiography were typical:

The Peripatetic influence on history proper was to become thoroughly bad; they created or fixed that doctrine of Fortune which gained such vogue, and from their diligence in collecting every scrap of everything sprang the so prevalent habit of mixing up truth and legend without discrimination, a habit which quickly enough became nothing but a passion for scandal.

But this picture of all-pervading, all-contaminating influence is difficult to justify from what the fragments tell us of Theophrastus' own production. As far as his own literary qualities are concerned, although his surviving works are not particularly distinguished, he was praised as a stylist in antiquity. His original name was said to have been Tyrtamos, but was changed to Theophrastus by Aristotle, who was impressed by his "graceful style" (*thespesion phraseos*). His work on rhetoric seems to have been used by later critics, but little can be said with certainty about it. What is agreed is that he emphasized four virtues above all others, *hellenismos* (Greekness, grammatical correctness), *sapheneia* (clarity), *prepon* (what is appropriate or relevant), and *kataskeue* (ornamentation). What is more doubtful is that he was the first to distinguish three styles of composition: full, plain, and middle, thus initiating a tripartite taxonomy that was to enjoy a long life in succeeding rhetorical treatises.

Nowadays scholars tend to play down the role of Theophrastus and his school as the dominating influence on every aspect of the intellectual life of the era, but if the Peripatetics now seem less important, it is also the case that there is less to blame them for.

—James N. Davidson

See the essay on *Characters*.

THUCYDIDES

Born: c. 460 BC. **Career:** Owned property in Thrace. Plague victim in Athens, 430–27 BC; elected military magistrate (*strategos*) in 424 BC with task of protecting the Thracian coast, but lost Athenian colony of Amphipolis to the Spartans, was condemned in his absence, and went into exile until the end of the Peloponnesian War, 404 BC. Xenophon and others attempted to complete his unfinished works. **Died:** c. 399 BC.

PUBLICATIONS

Works

[History], edited by H. Stuart Jones, revised by Enoch Powell. 2 vols., 1942; also edited by Jacqueline de Romilly and others, 1953–72, and E.C. Marchant, T. Wiedemann, and others, 1978–89; translated by Thomas Nicolls, 1550; also translated by S.T. Bloomfield, 3 vols., 1829; as *The History of the Peloponnesian War*, translated by William Smith, 2 vols., 1753; also translated by Henry Dale, 1848; Thomas Arnold, 2 vols., 1848–49; Richard Crawley, 1874; Henry Owgan, 1884; C.F. Smith [Loeb Edition], 4 vols., 1919–23 (Books I–IV revised 1928–30); translated in part by Thomas Hobbes, 1629, as *Eight Books of the Peloponnesian War*, edited by David Grene, 1959; Benjamin Jowett, 2 vols., 1881; R.W. Livingstone, 1943; Rex Warner, 1954, revised edition, 1972; P.J. Rhodes (Book II), 1988; J.S. Rusten (Book II),

1989; *The Best of Thucydides* (extracts), edited and translated by M.G. Dickson, 1991; commentaries by A.W. Gomme, A. Andrewes, and K.J. Dover, 5 vols., 1945–81, and Simon Hornblower, vol. 1, 1991; as *On Justice, Power and Human Nature: The Essence of Thucydides' History of the Peloponnesian War*, edited and translated by Paul Woodruff, 1993; as *The Landmark Thucydides: A Comprehensive Guide to the Peloponnesian War*, edited by Robert B. Strassler, 1996; as *History IV.1–V.24*, edited with translation and commentary by P.J. Rhodes, 1998; as *The Peloponnesian War*, translated by Steven Lattimore, 1998.

*

Critical Studies: *Thucydides and the History of His Age* by George B. Grundy, 1911; *Thucydides and the Science of History* by Charles N. Cochrane, 1929; *Thucydides*, 1942, and *Three Essays on Thucydides*, 1967, both by John H. Finley, Jr.; *Man in His Pride: A Study in the Political Philosophy of Thucydides and Plato* by David Grene, 1950; *Thucydides and His History* by F.E. Adcock, 1963; *Thucydides and Athenian Imperialism* by Jacqueline de Romilly, translated by Philip Thody, 1963; *Poiesis* by H.D.F. Kitto, 1966; *Individuals in Thucydides*, 1968, and *Studies in Thucydides and Greek History*, 1989, both by H.D. Westlake; *Thucydides on the Nature of Power* by A.G. Woodhead, 1970; *Thucydides* by K.J. Dover, 1973; *Thucydides, The Artful Reporter*, 1973, and *Past and Process in Herodotus and Thucydides*, 1982, both by Virginia J. Hunter; *The Speeches in Thucydides: A Collection of Original Studies and a Bibliography* edited by Philip A. Stadter, 1973; *Chance and Intelligence in Thucydides* by Lowell Edmunds, 1975; *Pylos 425 BC: A Historical and Topographical Study of Thucydides' Account of the Campaign* edited by J.B. Wilson, 1979; *The Necessities of War: A Study of Thucydides' Pessimism* by Peter R. Pouncey, 1980; *The Experience of Thucydides* by D. Proctor, 1980; *The Human Thing: The Speeches and Principles of Thucydides' History* by M. Cogan, 1981; *Thucydides and Religion* by Nanno Marinatos, 1981; *Logos and Ergon in Thucydides* by A.M. Parry, 1981; *The Structure of Thucydides' History* by H.R. Rawlings III, 1981; *Thucydides and the Tradition of Funeral Speeches at Athens* by John E. Ziolkowski, 1981; *Collected Essays* by Colin Macleod, 1983; *Thucydides* by Simon Hornblower, 1984; *Athens and Corcyra: Strategy and Tactics in the Peloponnesian War* by John Wilson, 1987; *Anagkē in Thucydides* by M. Ostwald, 1988; *Rhetoric in Classical Historiography* by A.J. Woodman, 1988; *Power and Preparedness in Thucydides* by June W. Allison, 1989; *The Ambition to Rule: Alcibiades and the Politics of Imperialism in Thucydides* by Steven Forde, 1989; *Thucydides VI and VII: A Companion to the Penguin Translation of Rex Warner* by N.K. Rutter, 1989; *Love of Glory and the Common Good: Aspects of the Political Thought of Thucydides* by M. Palmer, 1992; *Money, Expense, and Naval Power in Thucydides' History 1–5.24* by Lisa Kallet-Marx, 1993; *Thucydides, Hobbes, and the Interpretation of Realism* by Laurie M. Johnson, 1993; *The Humanity of Thucydides* by Clifford Orwin, 1994; *The Blinded Eye: Thucydides and the New Written Word* by Gregory Crane, 1996; *Word and Concept in Thucydides* by June W. Allison, 1997; *Thucydides and the Peloponnesian War* by George Cawkwell, 1997; *Thucydides: Narrative and Explanation* by Tim Rood, 1998; *Thucydides and the Ancient Simplicity: The Limits of Political Realism* by Gregory Crane, 1998; *Ethics in Thucydides: The Ancient Simplicity* by Mary Frances Williams, 1998; *Thucydides' Theory of International Relations: A Lasting Possession*, edited by Lowell S. Gustafson, 2000; *Speaking the Same Language: Speech and Audience in Thucydides' Spartan Debates* by Paula Debnar, 2001; *Money and the Corrosion of Power in Thucydides: The Sicilian Expedition and Its Aftermath* by Lisa Kallet, 2001; *Thucydides and Internal War* by Jonathan J. Price, 2001.

* * *

Thucydides' plan was to write the history of the Peloponnesian War between Athens and Sparta (431–04 BC), but his narrative breaks off at VIII.109 in the year 411 BC and it is generally agreed that substantial parts of the extant work are unfinished. His history has nevertheless been immensely influential.

Thucydides states (I.1.1) that he began writing in the expectation that the war would be a great one and more worthy of record than any in the past. This statement will have raised eyebrows among his contemporaries, who would not only have remembered the wars with Persia and Herodotus' recent account of them but would also have regarded with reverence the presentation of the Trojan War given by Homer in *The Iliad*. Yet it was Thucydides' intention precisely to challenge his predecessors, and Homer in particular. The whole of his preface is devoted to an elaborate depreciation of earlier history (I.1–21.1), especially of the Trojan War (I.9–11), and a corresponding magnification of his own subject (I.21.2, 23.1–3). Moreover, it is clear from I.23.1–3, which constitutes a beautifully written programme for the work as a whole, that Thucydides saw his own war principally in terms of the sufferings it entailed (and which were "without parallel over a similar period") and of the disasters it brought (and among which he mentions an unprecedented number of sacked cities, refugees, deaths, earthquakes, droughts, famines—and also "that which caused very great damage and significant destruction: the plague"). As we know from the beginnings of *The Iliad* and *The Odyssey*, this is the perspective of epic poetry, in which war and its attendant sufferings are the staple ingredients.

The greatest disaster was that which overtook Thucydides' native city, Athens; the greatest sufferings those which afflicted her inhabitants. Thucydides' treatment of both is analogous to that of a tragic poet, as a classic section of Book II demonstrates. In the famous Funeral Speech early in that book (34–46), the leading Athenian, Pericles, is made to describe the city as an oasis of sunlight and civilization, his fellow citizens as models of virtue and culture. No sooner has he finished speaking (or so it seems) than the plague strikes Athens. The symptoms are described in all their medical detail (49–50), and the consequent collapse of morale gives rise to the kind of *peripeteia* (reversal) associated with Greek tragedy: Thucydides relates (51–3) the vices to which the citizens now succumbed in place of the virtues which Pericles had previously been made to catalogue. The effect is all the more dramatic because Thucydides characteristically makes no personal comment but appears to let the events speak for themselves; in fact, he has imposed a structure on the narrative which brings the plague into dramatic contrast with all that has gone before. The relationship of speech to action, the suggestion that reality is different from appearances and from the protestations of men, the transition from joy to despair, the combination of the inflated and the understated—all these are typical of Thucydides' technique and are used with almost equal effectiveness throughout his work.

Thucydides is traditionally seen as little different from a modern historian; uniquely among ancient historians, he took the trouble to acquire multiple sources of evidence, evaluated them with painstaking care, and from them compiled a narrative which is unrivalled in its accuracy and objectivity. Unfortunately, through lack of comparative material, we are almost always unable to check Thucydides' statements; so the traditional view of his achievement rests almost entirely on the magisterial assurance of his narrative and on the unverifiable assumption that he consistently adhered to the methodology which he famously outlines in Book I (22). His ancient readers saw him quite differently. According to Plutarch in *Morals* (*Moralia* , 347 a-c) he "is always struggling for vivid representation, eager to turn his readers into eyewitnesses and to engender in them the emotional disturbances actually experienced by the real eyewitnesses"; and to Dionysius of Halicarnassus (*On Thucydides*, 15) he "sometimes makes the sufferings appear so cruel, so terrible, so piteous, as to leave no room for historians or poets to surpass him." With their references to emotional disturbances and emulation by poets, these verdicts would have pleased the historian who employed tragic techniques in his ambition to rival the work of Homer.

—A.J. Woodman

TIBILLUS, Albius

Born: Between 55 and 48 BC into a family of equestrian rank. **Military Service:** May have served as a soldier, probably under the direct command of Messalla Corvinus, his literary patron. **Career:** Horace, *q.v.*, who seems to have been his friend, implies (*Epistles* I. 4) that he retained a country estate at Pedum in Latium. **Died:** 19 or 18 BC.

PUBLICATIONS

Works

[Works], edited by J.P. Postgate. 1894; also edited by K.F. Smith (with commentary), 1913, and F.W. Lenz, 1959, revised by G.K. Galinsky, 1971; edited and translated by J.P. Postgate, in *Catullus, Tibullus and Pervigilium Veneris* [Loeb Edition; bilingual], 1914; translated by T.C. Williams, 1905; also translated by A.S. Way, 1936; Philip Dunlop, 1972; A.G. Lee (bilingual edition), 1990; commentaries by M.C.J. Putnam, 1973, and Paul Murgatroyd, 1980, 1994; as *Delia and Nemesis: The Elegies of Albius Tibullus*, translated by George W. Shea, 1998.

*

Bibliography: *À propos du Corpus Tibullianum: un siècle de philologie latine classique* by A. Cartault, 1906; *A Bibliography to the Corpus Tibullianum* by Hermann Harrauer, 1971; "The *Corpus Tibullianum* (1974–80)" by H. Dettmer, in *Aufstieg und Niedergang der römischen Welt*, II, 30, 3, 1983.

Critical Studies: *Latin Elegiac Verse: A Study of the Metrical Usages of Tibullus, Propertius, and Ovid* by Maurice Plautnauer, 1951; *The Latin Love Elegy* (with some translations) by G. Luck, 1969; *Haec mihi fingebam: Tibullus in His World* by D.F. Bright, 1978; *Tibullus: A Hellenistic Poet at Rome* by Francis Cairns, 1979; *The Latin Love Poets from Catullus to Horace* (with some translations) by R.O.A.M. Lyne, 1980; *Tibullus the Elegist: A Critical Survey* by Robert A. Ball, 1983.

* * *

Albius Tibullus is one of three surviving major writers of the personal love elegy (the others are Propertius and Ovid, in his *Amores*). This type of poetry, which enjoyed its brief flowering in the principate of Augustus (31 BC–AD 14) and was at odds with much of his ideology, is characterized by its metre, the elegiac couplet (a longer and a shorter line alternating, each conforming to a basically fixed rhythmical pattern), and by its principal subject, ostensibly its author's own troubled love for a named woman of uncertain social status, whom he cannot ultimately possess. Scholars debate endlessly whether the love affair as presented was real or fictitious, but most probably a blend of experience and invention is what the poet offers.

Tibullus' elegies, written some time in the 20s BC, comprise two books (a third has been transmitted under his name, but is not by him; the three are collectively known as the *Corpus Tibullianum*). Book I (of ten poems) features his love for a woman called Delia; Book II (of six poems) for one called Nemesis. Why the choice of these names, both invented? "Delia" (claimed by Apuleius in Apology 10 to conceal a real woman named Plania) most readily brings to mind "Delian" Apollo, so-called after his cult on the island of Delos, where he was allegedly born. This seems in itself appropriate enough, given that Apollo was the god of poetry, but it does not produce a satisfying symbolic pairing with Nemesis, which in Greek means "retribution." Possibly "Delia" is intended to suggest light and joy through the associations of Apollo and his Delos-born sister, Artemis-Diana, with sun and moon respectively, while "Nemesis," as the name of the daughter of Night in Hesiod's *Theogony*, is meant to evoke darkness and sorrow. For, whether Tibullus conceives of two different women in Books I and II, or is merely showing us two different sides of the same woman, it is evident that in much of his Delia-book he clings to the possibility, however remote, of his love being reciprocated, but in his Nemesis-book concentrates on the grim prospect of suffering and rejection.

Tibullus' personal vision of the ideal life pervades his poetry. Repudiating the urban luxury and glory conventionally won by a commerce or warfare, he repeatedly expresses his longing to live as a simple farmer of modest means in the countryside, piously respectful of its traditional moral values and an enthusiastic participant in its religious festivals. However, he needs an obliging mistress for his happiness to be complete, and he is in love with a city sophisticate who does not share his outlook. In Book I he is, from time to time, able to resolve this impasse through pleasant fantasy: Delia tending him on his deathbed and piously grieving at his funeral; Delia virtuously whiling away the time in his absence overseas with the housewifely task of spinning; and, most fancifully of all, Delia joining him as a working partner on the longed-for farm. Fulfilment in love, however, is never more than a dream which, during the course of Book I, becomes overshadowed by Tibullus' insecurity and disillusion. His trust in Venus and commendation of magic avail him nothing; his gentle instruction of Delia in the art of deception backfires on him; she is unfaithful and remains under the influence of control of others—her official partner, a rich rival lover, a crafty procuress, and her mother. The rustic ideal survives to the last poem of the book, but it no longer includes Delia; rather Tibullus at this stage recognizes love as a threat to his vision of peace and serenity. In Book II the threat has become a reality. Frequently depicting his love as a form of voluntary slavery, Tibullus now sees the countryside as the setting for the incessant toil and degradation he would be prepared to suffer to retain the love of the cruel and haughty Nemesis. Willingly, too, he would plunder the sanctuaries of Venus to provide her with the gifts she demands and even sell his ancestral estates. Love for the grasping woman of the city has now both destroyed Tibullus' rural idyll and corrupted his own moral standards; his relationship with Nemesis is beyond redemption even by Hope "which springs eternal."

Tibullus' attachment to his patron M. Valerius Messalla Corvinus, general, orator, and man of letters, presents him with another conflict to be resolved. He has to reconcile his respect and affection for Messalla himself with his own emphatic distaste for the military route to distinction (this amounts to a rejection of the lifestyle encouraged by Augustus, but Tibullus, uniquely among the elegists, never mentions the Princeps directly). Accordingly, he gives his patron a place in his visions of rural contentment: Messalla is envisaged as a fêted guest (waited on by Delia!) in the poet's humble home and honoured at a country festival almost like a rustic divinity himself. Furthermore, each book contains one ambitiously complex elegy which specifically celebrates the achievements of Messalla and his family, associating them with peace, benefaction, and continuance of ancient Roman tradition: in Book I it marks Messalla's triumph over the Gallic Aquitani in 27 BC, and Book II the installation of his son Messallinus as a *quindecimvir* (one of 15 priestly officials who looked after the sacred Sibylline books).

The emergent picture of Tibullus so far is one of a gentle, wistful lover; sentimental, superstitious, and apparently naïve, yet on occasion possessed of a more formal voice. It is, however, incomplete, for three poems in Book I present a very different character. In one Tibullus reports the lecherous scarecrow-god Priapus' advice on how to win and keep the love of a young boy, surprising the reader at the end with the revelation that these precepts, which he passed on to a third party, have proved of no use to him, Tibullus, in his own affair with one Marathus. Another is a lively dramatic monologue in which Tibullus confronts the said Marathus and his unobliging girlfriend Pholoe, for whom Marathus has deserted him; he consoles and counsels the distraught boy and reprimands the haughty girl, again only gradually unfolding the complete situation. In another poem, he dismisses Marathus as a lover, now regretting his involvement with one who has transferred his affections to a richer and older man. From these poems we discover firstly that Tibullus, alone among the extant Latin elegists, has a literary interest in homosexual love, which was at least as common as the heterosexual kind in the erotic elegiacs of his Greek predecessors (e.g., the poems on boy-love attributed to Theognis and the Hellenistic epigrams in Book XII of the *Greek Anthology*); secondly, that he is capable of a humorously detached attitude towards amatory affairs (the ironic pathos of his portrayal of the love-crossed Marathus warns against too solemn a reading of his own alleged sufferings at the hands of women); and thirdly, that although his general preference is for discursive elegies whose connections of thought are subtle rather than obvious, he has the ability to structure tightly when it suits him.

Modern scholars have often been puzzled by the ancient critics' high opinion of Tibullus (Quintilian judges him "the most polished and elegant" of the elegists). Of the lucidity of his style and the smoothness of his metrication there is no question, but his linguistic usage is unadventurous and his learning unparaded. Mythological allusions, in particular, are few, but scrutiny reveals creative use of Homeric and Virgilian epic, of Callimachus, and, most extensively, the pastoral poetic tradition. On the whole, however, Tibullus' work is notable for its very lack of showiness and idiosyncrasy, and even

the most strenuous efforts to defend his reputation on positive grounds (e.g., the monographs of Bright and Cairns) have only limited success. Perhaps it is simply to be accepted that the ancients set more store by sheer restraint than we would expect.

—Joan Booth

TIECK, (Johann) Ludwig

Born: Berlin, Germany, 31 May 1773. **Education:** Educated at the Gymnasium, Berlin, 1782–92; studied theology and philology, Halle University, 1792; transferred to the University of Göttingen, 1792, studied English literature and philosophy. **Family:** Married Amalie Alberti in 1798 (died 1837); two daughters. **Career:** Suffered from bouts of depression in the 1790s, a condition which was to remain with him throughout his life. Travelled to Nuremberg with Wilhelm Heinrich Wackenroder in 1793. Worked for the publisher, Christoph Friedrich Nicolai, Berlin, 1794–97; contributor to the rationalist literary journal *Straussfedern*, 1795–98; associated with the writers Friedrich and August Wilhelm q.v., Dorothea and Caroline Schlegel, Friedrich Schleiermacher and Novalis q.v., and the philosophers Friedrich Wilhelm Joseph Schelling and Johann Gottlieb Fichte and others, known as the Jena Romantics; health deteriorated and suffered crippling bouts of rheumatism and periods of severe depression; travelled frequently between Hamburg, Berlin, and Dresden in search of full-time work, 1800–02; lived at Ziebingen, near Frankfurt, 1802–10; travelled extensively despite failing health, 1811–17; visited England in 1817 and met Samuel Taylor Coleridge; dramaturg (literary historian and editor), Dresden theatre, 1819, later applied to Wilhelm IV for an appointment at the Prussian theatres; dramaturg and stage director, Berlin, from 1841. **Died:** 28 April 1853.

PUBLICATIONS

Collections

Werke, edited by Marianne Thalmann. 4 vols., 1963–66.
Werke, edited by Peter Plett. 1967.
Schriften, edited by Manfred Frank. 1985–.
Schriften, edited Achim Hölter. 1991.

Fiction

Abdallah. 1795.
Peter Lebrecht: Eine Geschichte ohne Abentheuerlichkeiten. 1795–96.
William Lovell. 1795–96.
Die sieben Weiber des Blaubart. 1797.
Volksmärchen. 1797.
Franz Sternbalds Wanderungen. 1798.
Romantische Dichtungen. 1799–1800.
Das Ungeheuer und der verzauberte Wald: Ein musikalisches Märchen in vier Aufzügen. 1800.
Phantasus: Eine Sammlung von Märchen, Erzählungen, Schauspielen und Novellen. 3 vols., 1812–16; as *Tales from the Phantas*, translated by Julius Hare and others, 1848.
Die Gemälde. 1822.

Novellen. 7 vols., 1823–28; enlarged edition as *Gesammelte Novellen*,
14 vols., 1835–42.

Die Verlobung. 1823.

Der Geheimnissvolle (stories). 1823.

Die Gemälde. 1822; as *The Pictures*, translated by G. Cunningham, in
Foreign Tales and Traditions, 1829.

Musikalische Leiden und Freuden. 1824.

Die Reisenden. 1824.

Pietro von Abano; oder, Petrus Apone. 1825; translated as "Pietro of
Abano," in *Blackwoods Magazine*, 46, 1839.

Die Gesellschaft auf dem Lande. 1825.

Der Aufruhr in den Cevennen. 1826; as *The Rebellion in the Cevennes*,
translated by Madame Burette, 1845.

*Der Alte vom Berge, und die Gesellschaft auf dem Lande: zwei
Novellen.* 1828; *Der Alte vom Berge*; as *The Old Man of the
Mountain*, translated by J.C. Hare, 1831.

Schriften. 28 vols., 1828–54.

Novellenkranz. 5 vols., 1831–35.

Der Schutzgeist. 1835.

Der junge Tischlermeister. 1836.

Wunderlichkeiten. 1837.

Die Klausenburg. 1837.

Des Lebens Überfluss. 1839.

Vittoria Accorombona. 1840; as *The Roman Matron; or, Vittoria
Accorombona*, 1845.

Plays

Alla-Moddin. 1790–91.

Der Abschied. 1792.

Ritter Blaubart (produced 1835). 1797.

Der gestiefelte Kater (produced 1844). 1797; as *Puss in Boots*,
translated by Lillie Winter, in *The German Classics of the Nineteenth and Twentieth Centuries*, vol. 4, edited by Kuno Francke
and W.G. Howard, 1914; also translated by Gerald Gillespie,
1974.

Ein Schurke über den andern; oder, die Fuchsprelle. 1798.

Die verkehrte Welt. 1798.

Prinz Zerbino; oder, Die Reise nach dem guten Geschmack. 1799.

Leben und Tod der Heiligen Genoveva. 1800.

Kaiser Octavianus. 1804.

Die Sommernacht: Eine Jugenddichtung (fragment). 1851; as *The
Midsummer Night; or, Shakespeare and the Fairies*, translated by
Mary C. Rumsey, 1854.

Verse

Almansur. 1798.

Gedichte. 3 vols., 1821–23.

Gedichte. 1841.

Other

Herzensergiessungen eines kunstliebenden Klosterbruders, with Wilhelm Heinrich Wackenroder. 1797; as *Outpourings from the
Heart of an Art-Loving Friar*, translated by Edward Mornin, 1975.

Sämmtliche Werke. 12 vols., 1799.

Phantasien über die Kunst, für Freunde der Kunst, with Wilhelm
Heinrich Wackenroder. 1799; as "Fantasies on Art for Friends of

Arts" translated by Mary Hurst Shubert, in *Confessions and
Fantasies*, 1971.

Sämmtliche Werke. 30 vols., 1817–24.

Dramaturgische Blätter. 3 vols., 1826–52.

Kritische Schriften. 4 vols., 1848–52.

Tieck and Solger: The Complete Correspondence, edited by Percy
Matenko. 1933.

Letters of Ludwig Tieck Hitherto Unpublished 1792–1853, edited by
Edwin H. Zeydel and others. 1937.

Editor, *Volksmärchen.* 3 vols., 1797.

Editor, *Minnelieder aus dem Schwäbischen Zeitalter.* 1803.

Editor, *Frauendienst; oder, Geschichte und Liebe des Ritters und
Sängers*, by Ulrich von Lichtenstein. 1812.

Editor, *Deutsches Theater.* 2 vols., 1817.

Editor, *Hinterlassene Schriften*, by Heinrich Kleist. 1821.

Editor, *Shakespeare's Vorschule.* 1823–29.

Editor, *Gesammelte Schriften*, by Heinrich Kleist. 1826.

Editor, *Schriften und Briefwechsel*, by Karl Ferdinand Solger. 1826.

Editor, *Gesammelte Schriften*, by J.M.R. Lenz. 1828.

Editor, *Die Insel Felsenburg; oder, wunderliche Fata einiger Seefahrer:
Eine Geschichte aus dem Anfange des achtzehnten Jahrhunderts*,
by Johann Gottfried Schnabel. 6 vols., 1828.

Editor, *Evremont*, by Sophie Bernhardi. 1836.

Editor, *Gesammelte Schriften*, by Novalis. 5th edition, 1837.

Editor, *König Sebastian.* 1839.

Editor, *Gesammelte Novellen*, by F. Berthold. 1842.

Editor, *Gedichte*, by Karl Förster, 1843.

Editor, *Älteste Liedersammlung*, by Goethe. 1844.

Editor, with Eduard von Bülow, *Novalis Schriften: Dritter Theil.*
1846.

Editor and translator, *Alt-Englisches Theater; oder, Supplement zum
Shakespear.* 2 vols., 1811.

Translator, *Der Sturm: Ein Schauspiel*, by Shakespeare. 1796.

Translator, *Leben und Thaten des scharfsinnigen Edlen Don Quixote
von La Manchu*, by Cervantes. 1799–1800.

Translator, *Dramatische Werke*, by Shakespeare. 1826–33.

Translator, *Leben und Begebenheiten des Escudero Marcus Obregon;
oder, Autobiographie des Spanischen Dichters Vicente Espinel.*
1827.

Translator, *Vier Schauspiele.* 1836.

Translator, *Mucedorus; ein englisches Drama aus Shakespeares Zeit.*
1893.

*

Critical Studies: *Ludwig Tieck: Erinnerungen aus dem Leben des
Dichters nach dessen mündlichen und schriftlichen Mitteilungen* by
Rudolf Köpke, 2 vols., 1855, revised edition, 1970; *Ludwig Tieck:
The German Romanticist—A Critical Study* by Edwin H. Zeydel,
1935, 2nd edition, 1971; *Ludwig Tieck and America* by Percy C.
Matenko, 1954; *Ludwig Tieck: From Gothic to Romantic* by James
Trainer, 1964; *Ludwig Tiecks späte Novellen: Grundlage und Technik
des Wunderbaren* by Roll Stamm, 1973; *Renaissance and Romanti-
cism: Tieck's Conception of Cultural Decline as Portrayed in His
Vittoria Accorombona* by Christiane E. Keck, 1976; *Ludwig Tieck:
Wege der Forschung* edited by Wulf Segebrecht, 1976; *The Motif of
"Fate" in the Works of Ludwig Tieck* by Alan Corkhill, 1978;
Reality's Dark Dream: The Narrative Fiction of Ludwig Tieck by
William J. Lillyman, 1978; *The Boundless Present: Space and Time*

in the Literary Fairy Tales of Novalis and Tieck by Gordon Birrell, 1979; Das Frauenbild im Jugendwerk von Ludwig Tieck als Mosaikstein zu seiner Weltanschauung by Sonia Fritz-Grandjean, 1980; König der Romantik: Das Leben des Dichters Ludwig Tieck in Briefen, Selbstzeugnissen und Berichten by Klaus Günzel, 1981; Ludwig Tieck: A Literary Biography by Roger Paulin, 1985; The Crises of "Language and Dead Signs" in Ludwig Tieck's Prose Fiction by William Crisman, 1996; In Praise of Nonsense: Kant and Bluebeard by Winfried Menninghaus, translated by Henry Pickford, 1999.

* * *

The long life of Ludwig Tieck was rich in literary accomplishments and renown. From one of the earliest German Romantic poets, playwrights, and novelists he developed into one of the earliest realists. He was a genuine scholar of Elizabethan language and literature, playing both creative and organizing roles in one of the greatest feats of translation in world literature, the German Shakespeare. Though less of a Spanish scholar, he produced a translation of Cervantes's *Don Quixote* that long remained standard. He was a serious scholar of Sir Walter Scott, who provided the inspiration for the historical novel in Germany, and Tieck himself wrote one of the finest examples of historical fiction towards the end of his career. A craftsman of the novella form, he made a seminal contribution to its theory which was an enduring preoccupation of German literary study. He rescued the works of writers cut off early in life: Jakob Michael Reinhold Lenz, Novalis, and Heinrich von Kleist. He edited chapbooks and medieval *Minnelieder* and made transcriptions of heroic epics and the *Nibelungenlied* that were used for philological editions. For 20 years he directed the court theatre in Dresden, making a name for himself as a talented dramatic elocutionist, then held a similar position in Berlin. After the death of Goethe in 1832, he filled the position of representative living German writer in the world at large. All this he achieved while struggling out of impoverished origins and coping with severe emotional and, later, physical infirmities.

One would suppose that a writer with such a career would loom large in the literary patrimony of his nation. But this has not really been the case. Something went awry with Tieck's reputation even during his own lifetime, so that it did not remain proportionate to his achievements and his objective importance in the history of literature, although there has been some renewed and more fitting attention to him in recent times. Much of the most important work on him has been accomplished by scholars in Britain and America, suggesting that he somehow, certainly unwittingly and involuntarily, fell out of his own national context. There are a number of possible reasons for this. In his middle age the quality of his writing became quite uneven as he struggled to earn money with his pen. He became so committed to Goethean equilibrium and so hostile to extremes that he seemed to be an enemy of any dissidence and of the imagination itself. A fanatical adherent of the autonomy of art and poesy, he combated the politicization of literature in the 1830s with rude satire, drawing fierce counter-attacks from Heinrich Heine and the liberal Young German writers. Although the occasionally encountered view that his reputation was undermined by Heine and the Young Germans overestimates their influence on public opinion, he did not help himself by the appearance he sometimes gave of choleric conservatism and allegiance to the ruling order. More problematically, to many, then and later, he seemed in some way unserious, his evolving career a meretricious following of fashions without philosophical profundity.

It is likely that there lies in such intuitions something rightly discerned but insensitively evaluated. It was an embarrassment to Tieck that he was celebrated as the "King of Romanticism" long after he had parted company with the movement, and it may be that he was a disguised subversive even in his high Romantic phase, carrying subliminal traces of the Enlightenment spirit and rationalism from which he had come originally. Even in the paradigmatically Romantic work he composed with Wilhelm Heinrich Wackenroder, *Herzensergiessungen eines kunstliebenden Klosterbruders* (*Outpourings from the Heart of an Art-Loving Friar*), Tieck's contributions (in so far as we can infer which these are) question the total dissolution of the self in the religion of art. The novel *William Lovell* reads almost as a parody of Goethe's *The Sufferings of Young Werther*; while we continue to maintain a sympathy with Werther despite all his self-indulgence and blindness, Lovell becomes increasingly repugnant in his amoral egotism. The unfinished *Franz Sternbalds Wanderungen* deconstructs the artist novel before that Romantic genre properly took shape: Sternbald's artistic sensibilities are so delicate and elevated that he can rarely manage anything so mundane as actual painting, while all his artistic friends assure him that art is craft and labour.

Tieck's most famous comedy, *Der gestiefelte Kater* (*Puss in Boots*), where the actors and the audience get into quarrels with one another, is as much a modern unmasking of dramatic illusion as a Romantic attack on the aesthetically oblivious. His art fairytales are more like nightmares than the veridical, divinatory dreams of, say, Novalis. The element of nature in them is deeply ambiguous if not actually alien and hostile. They are frustratingly resistant to explication—literary equivalents of the graphics of M.C. Escher. Tieck's anti-Romantic turn might be understood as an intensification of a scepticism that was present from the outset. His last novella is a mischievous spoof of '*Waldeinsamkeit* [Forest Solitude], the neologism that he himself had introduced in his enduringly famous "Blond Eckbert" and that had in his own time degenerated into a cliché of sub-Romantic sentimentality. Amid much that is undistinguished in his later writing there are moments that challenge expectations and convention. This is especially true of the late historical novel, *Vittoria Accorombona*, with its grim portrayal of Renaissance culture and the transformation of the "White Devil" from John Webster's gory Elizabethan drama into a talented, courageous, and majestic woman. Conservative though Tieck may have been politically, he was uncommonly emancipated in sexual matters, both in his personal life and in his writing, a point that has not been fully appreciated.

Thus, for all he has been studied, Tieck remains in some ways a writer yet to be discovered, and new respect for his intelligence and artistic acumen as well as for his service to the cause of literature may be in the offing.

—Jeffrey L. Sammons

TIRSO DE MOLINA

Born: Gabriel Téllez in Madrid, Spain, in 1580 or 1581(?). **Education:** Educated at the universities of Alcalá and Guadalajara. **Career:** Entered the Order of Mercy (also known as the Mercedarian Order), 1601: novitiate, then friar: probably in Toledo, 1605–15; in Santo

Domingo, Hispaniola (now Dominican Republic, West Indies), 1616–18; based in Madrid, 1621–25; the Council of Castille opposed his playwriting in 1625, was forbidden to write further secular plays, and was banished to the remote friary at Trujillo, where he was prior, 1626–29; official chronicler of the Order, c. 1632; in Barcelona, Madrid, and Toledo during the 1630s; another controversy about his plays and banished again, to Soria, 1640; Prior of the Sofia friary, 1645–47; in Almazán, 1647–48. The majority of his plays written before 1625; possibly the author of as many as 300–400. **Died:** 1648.

PUBLICATIONS

Collections

Comedias escogidas. 1826–34.
Teatro escogido (includes 36 *comedias*). 1848.
Comedias (includes 45 *comedias*), edited by E. Cotarelo y Mori. 2 vols., 1906–07.
Obras dramáticas completas, edited by Blanca de los Ríos. 3 vols., 1946–58, revised edition, 4 vols., 1989.

Plays (selection: modern editions or plays translated into English)

Antona García, edited by Margaret Wilson. 1957.
El burlador de Sevilla, edited by G.E. Wade. 1969; also edited by Alfredo Rodríguez López-Vázquez, 1987; as *The Love Rogue*, translated by Harry Kemp, 1923; as *The Trickster of Seville and the Guest of Stone*, translated by Roy Campbell, in *Masterpieces of the Golden Age*, edited by Angel Flores, 1957; as *The Trickster of Seville*, in *The Classic Theatre*, edited by Eric Bentley, 1959; as *The Rogue of Seville*, translated by Robert O'Brien, in *Spanish Drama*, edited by Angel Flores, 1962; as *The Playboy of Seville*, translated by Walter Starkie, in *The Theatre of Don Juan*, edited by Oscar Mandel, 1963; as *The Joker of Seville*, translated by Derek Walcott, 1979; as *The Trickster of Seville and the Guest of Stone* (bilingual edition), translated by Gwynne Edwards, 1986.
El castigo del penseque; as *The Opportunity*. 1640.
El condenado por desconfiado, edited by Daniel Rogers. 1974; as *Damned for Despair*, edited and translated by Nicholas G. Round (bilingual edition), 1986; also translated by Laurence Boswell and Deidre McKenna, 1992.
Don Gil de las calzas verdes, edited by Everett W. Hesse and Charles J. Moolick. 1971; as *Don Gil of the Green Breeches*, edited and translated by G.G. Minter, 1991; also translated by Laurence Boswell and Deidre McKenna, 1992.
Marta la piadosa, edited by Elvira E. García. 1972.
El melancílico, edited by Jacomé Delgado Varela. 1967.
Por el sótano y el torno, edited by A. Zamora Vicente. 1949.
Privar contra su gusto, edited by Battista J. Galassi. 1971.
La prudencia en la mujer, edited by R.R. MacCurdy. 1965; as *Prudence in Women*, in *The Genius of the Spanish Theatre*, edited by Robert O'Brien, 1964.
La Santa Juana, edited by A. del Campo. 1948.
La venganza de Tamar, edited by A.K.G. Paterson. 1969; as *Tamar's Revenge*, edited and translated by John Lyon (bilingual edition), 1988; as *The Rape of Tamar*, translated and adapted by Paul Whitworth, 1998.
La villana de Vallecas, edited by Sherman W. Brown. 1948.

Fiction

El bandolero, edited by Luis Carlos Viada y Lluch. 1915.

Verse

Acto de contrición. 1630.
Poesías líricas, edited by Ernesto Jareño. 1969.

Other

Los cigarrales de Toledo (miscellany). 1621; edited by Victor Said Armesto, 1913; in part as *Three Husbands Hoaxed*, translated by Ilsa Barea, 1955.
Comedias, edited by Francisco de Ávila. 5 vols., 1627–36.
Deleitar aprovechando. 1635.
Una obra inédita [La vida de la santa Madre doña María de Cervellón], edited by M. Menéndez y Pelayo. 1908.
Historia general de la Orden de Nuesra Señora de las Mercedes, edited by Manuel Penedo Rey. 2 vols., 1974.

*

Bibliography: *An Annotated, Analytical Bibliography of Tirso de Molina Studies 1627–1977* edited by Vern G. Williamsen and Walter Poesse, 1979.

Critical Studies: *Tirso de Molina: Studies in Dramatic Realism* by Ivy L. McClelland, 1948; *The Situational Drama of Tirso de Molina* by Ion T. Agheana, 1972; *Studies in Tirso: The Dramatist and His Contemporaries 1620–26* by Ruth Lee Kennedy, 1974; *Tirso de Molina and the Drama of the Counter Reformation* by Henry W. Sullivan, 1976; *Tirso de Molina: El burlador de Sevilla* by Daniel Rogers, 1977; *Tirso de Molina* by M. Wilson, 1977; *Religious Imagery in the Theatre of Tirso de Molina* by A.N. Hughes, 1984; *Tirso's Don Juan: The Metamorphosis of a Theme* (proceedings of a conference held 1985) edited by Josep M. Sola-Solé and George E. Gingras, 1988; *Irony and Theatricality in Tirso de Molina* by Jane Albrecht, 1994; *Tirso de Molina: His Originality Then and Now*, edited by Henry W. Sullivan and Raúl A. Galoppe, 1996.

* * *

Tirso de Molina is the pseudonym of the Mercedarian priest and Spanish Golden-Age playwright Fray Gabriel Téllez. Best known to posterity as the creator of the defiant seducer Don Juan Tenorio (or Don Giovanni), Tirso wrote 80-odd extant, full-length dramas and one-act allegories which place him, with Lope de Vega and Calderón, in the forefront of Spanish Classical drama. He was more aggressive and intelligent in his defence of the *comedia nueva* (''new drama'') than his master Lope, however, and in prose miscellanies such as *Los cigarrales de Toledo* [Toledo's Country Houses] he justified his non-classical methods by using arguments derived from mimesis and pragmatic didacticism *against* the neo-Aristotelians, as well as by advancing revolutionary theories of his own invoking the freedom of the artistic will and expressiveness in the act of creation.

After priestly ordainment in 1601, Tirso began writing for the Madrid theatres (1605–10). He produced his comic masterpiece *Don Gil de las calzas verdes* (*Don Gil of the Green Breeches*) in 1615. This uses his favourite device of the resolute heroine who, dressed as a man, pursues the fickle lover who has seduced and abandoned her. The heroine's successful wooing of the rival woman gives an erotic and perversely tantalizing effect to the 20 or so works built around this situation. Tirso presents striking female characters of a different kind in his *El amor médico* [Medical Love], where Jerónima, in an anticipation of modern feminism, adopts male attire to pursue her lover and her career as a doctor. The heroine of *Marta la piadosa* [Martha the Devout] is an early, but engaging, stage hypocrite, who feigns a religious vocation in order to avoid an arranged marriage and to receive her lover under her father's roof. The eponymous heroines of *Antona Garcia* and *La gallega Mari-Hernández* [Mari-Hernández the Galician] embody another favourite type: the virile superwoman or *mujer hombruna*. Tirso's uncanny insight into male and female psychology and his championing of women over the tyrannies and conventions of the male-dominated Spanish society of his time helped to make him the greatest dramatist of character in the Golden Age.

Tirso also wrote a number of fine Old-Testament plays, such as *La mujer que manda en casa* [The Woman Who Rules in the House], treating the career of the orgiastic, power-driven and bloody Queen Jezabel, and *La mejor espigadera* [The Best Gleaner], a moving, insightful account of the lives of Ruth and Naomi, and Ruth's ambiguous stance towards marriage and her destiny. His Old-Testament masterpiece, *La venganza de Tamar* (*Tamar's Revenge*), is a gripping tragedy concerning Amnon's incestuous rape of his halfsister, and the dynastic chaos this unleashes in the House of David. Tirso dealt with medieval Spanish history in *La prudencia en la mujer* (*Prudence in Women*), the finest chronicle-drama of the Golden Age, where Queen María de Molina saves her bloodline by her astute political wisdom. Tirso also contributed a vivid historical trilogy on his near-contemporaries, the Pizarros, conquerors of Peru.

Tirso displayed great gifts of social and political satire—*El vergonzoso en palacio* [The Timid Man in the Palace]; *Tanto es lo de más como lo de menos* [So Much the More, So Much the Less]—which eventually led to his official suppression (1625) under the régime of Philip IV's first minister, Olivares. But he reserved his greatest genius for two theological plays: one of them, *El condenado por desconfiado* (*Damned for Despair*), treating the theme of free-will and predestination in paradoxical fashion. The other was his ultimate masterpiece, *El burlador de Sevilla* (*The Trickster of Seville*), and the first Don Juan play. The flippant libertine and homicide Don Juan is dragged into Hell by the stone Comendador not for his social misconduct, but for his defiance of the day of reckoning with God. Tirso also wrote a didactic miscellany in prose, *Deleitar aprovechando* [To Delight while Profiting], and a bulky History of the Mercedarian Order (MS, 1637–39). He resembles Molière in his arresting felicity of rhyme, as well as in the creation of comic lead parts; his stress on butts and wits, and the rigid predictability of his gullible personages, places him closer to Ben Jonson. Tirso is well loved in Germany and Austria, and his Don Juan has become a property of the western tradition. However, he died in obscurity at Almazán (Soria) in 1648.

—Henry W. Sullivan

See the essay on *The Trickster of Seville*.

TOER, Pramoedya Ananta

Following the reform of the spelling of Indonesian in 1972, his name is sometimes spelled Pramudya Ananta Tur; this form is not preferred by the author. **Born:** Blora, East Java, 6 February 1925. **Education:**

Studied in his father's nationalist (Budi Utomo) school, 1929–39; Radio Vakschool (Radio Technician's School), Surabaya, 1940–41. **Military Service:** 1945–46, Press officer, Badan Keamanan Rakyat (a civil defence unit), before transferring to the Siliwangi Division of the Indonesian Army: promoted to Second Lieutenant. **Family:** Married 1) Arfah Iljas, 1950, two children; 2) Maemunah Thamrin, 1955, six children. **Career:** After graduating from Radio Technician's School, returned to Blora to provide for his family by working as a petty trader, rather than serve in the Dutch military reserve. Following his mother's death in May 1942, he left for Jakarta where he worked in the Japanese-run Domei Press Agency, followed various courses, including short-hand, made the acquaintance of various political leaders, and became interested in literature. Left Domei in May 1945, and Jakarta in June 1945, eventually joining the army of the new Republic of Indonesia (proclaimed 17 August 1945), as a press officer. Following the reorganisation of the army in 1946, joined the Voice of Free Indonesia and was arrested by Dutch marines on 2 July 1947: held as a prisoner of war until the end of the Indonesian Revolution against the Dutch, at the end of December 1949. While in prison, wrote various short stories and the novel *Perburuan* (*The Fugitive*) which were smuggled out and published. After he was released from prison, worked briefly for the Indonesian government literary agency, Balai Pustaka in May 1950, before establishing his own literary agency, Duta, in 1951. In 1953, visited the Netherlands as a guest of the *Stichting Culturele Samenwerking* (Foundation for Cultural Cooperation), but was disappointed by Dutch materialism. In October 1956, visited People's Republic of China, and thereafter became increasingly identified with the Indonesian Communist Party (PKI) and its literary organisation Lekra (Lembaga Kebudayaan Rakyat), although never formally becoming a member of the party. Following the Coup of the 30 September 1965, which was blamed on the PKI, was arrested and imprisoned in various centres, eventually being sent to the island of Buru in Eastern Indonesia after August 1969. Was finally released in December 1979. Lives in Jakarta Timur, Indonesia. **Awards:** Pustaka award for *Perburuan* (*The Fugitive*), 1951; Badan Musyawarah Kebudayaan Nasional award for *cerita dari Blora*; Honorary Life Membership, International PEN, Australian Centre 1982; Honorary Membership, PEN Centre, Sweden, 1982; Honorary Membership, PEN Center, United States, 1988; Freedom to Write award, PEN America, 1988; Honorary Membership, Deutschsweizereiches PEN, Switzerland, 1989; The Fund for Free Expression award, New York, 1989; International PEN English Centre award, 1992; Stichting Wertheim award, Netherlands, 1995; Ramon Magsaysay award, Philippines, 1995; Chancellor's Distinguished Honor award, University of California, Berkeley, 1999; Honorary Doctorate: University of Michigan, Ann Arbor, 1999; Chevalier de l'Ordre des Arts et des Lettres, Republic de France, 2000; Fukuoka Asian Culture Grand prize, Fukuoka, Japan, 2000.

PUBLICATIONS

Fiction

Kranji Bekasi Jatuh. 1947.
Perburuan. 1950; as *The Fugitive*, translated by Harry Aveling, 1975; translated by Willem Samuels, 1990.
Percikan Revolusi (short stories). 1950.
Subuh (short stories). 1950.
Mereka yang Dilumpuhkan. 1951.

Bukan Pasarmalam. 1951; as *It's Not An All Night Fair* by C.W. Watson, 1973, reprinted 2001; as "No Night Market" in *A Heap of Ashes*, translated by Harry Aveling, 1975.

Cerita dari Blora. 1952; three stories, "Lonely Paradise," "The Birth," and "The Vanquished," in *A Heap of Ashes*, translated by Harry Aveling, 1975.

Keluarga Gerilya. 1950.

Gulat di Jakarta. 1953.

Midah Si Manis Bergigi Emas. 1954.

Korupsi. 1954.

Cerita Calon Arang. 1957.

Cerita dari Jakarta. 1957; as "Tales from Djakarta," various translators, introduced by B. R. O'G. Anderson, reprinted 2000.

Suatu Peristiwa di Banten Selatan. 1958.

Orang-orang Baru dari Banten Selatan. 1959.

Bumi Manusia. 1980; as *This Earth of Mankind*, translated by Max Lane, 1982.

Anak Semua Bangsa. 1980: as *Child of All Nations*, translated by Max Lane, 1984.

Jejak Langkah. 1985; as *Footsteps*, translated by Max Lane, 1990.

Gadis Pantai. 1987; as *The Girl from the Coast*, translated by Harry Aveling, 1991.

Rumah Kaca. 1988; as *House of Glass*, translated by Max Lane, 1992.

Arus Balik. 1995.

Arok Dedes. 1999.

Mangir. 1999.

Larasati: Sebuah Roman Revolusi. 2000.

Other

Hoakiau di Indonesia. 1960.

Panggil Aku Kartini Saja. 1962.

Sang Pemula. 1985.

Nyanyi sunyi Seorang Bisu. vol 1: 1995; vol. 2: 1997.

Editor, *Tempo Doeloe.* 1982.

Editor, *Hikayat Siti Mariah.* 1987.

Editor, *Memoar Oei Tjoe Tat.* 1995.

Editor, *Kronik Revolusi Indonesia.* 1999.

*

Critical Studies: *Pramoedya Ananta Toer dan Karya Seninya* by Bahrum Rangkuti, 1963; "Pramudya Ananta Tur: The Writer as Outsider," *Cultural Options and the Role of Tradition* by A.H. Johns, 1979; "Pramudya Ananta Tur: The Writer as Outsider" in *Cultural Options and the Role of Tradition* by A.H. Johns, 1979; *Social Commitment in Literature and the Arts: The Indonesian "Institute of People's Culture"* by Keith Foulcher, 1986; "The Early Fiction of Pramoedya Ananta Toer, 1946–1949" and "Literature, Cultural Politics, and the Indonesian Revolution," both by Keith Foulcher, in *Text/Politics in Island Southeast Asia*, ed. D.M. Roskies, 1993; *Pramoedya Ananta Toer: De Verbeelding van Indonesie* by A. Teeuw, 1993; *Pramoedya Ananta Toer: Selected Early Works 1949–1952* by Nur'ainy Ali, 1999.

*   *   *

Pramoedya Ananta Toer is generally considered Indonesia's most important modern prose writer. His writings display a deep commitment to his nation's struggle for independence. As a consequence,

however, he has served extensive periods as a political prisoner of conscience under the Dutch, briefly under Sukarno and extensively under the regime of President Suharto.

Pramoedya began writing in 1946, while Indonesia was still struggling for its Independence from Dutch colonialism. His early works dealt with the Indonesian Revolution (1945–49), sometimes with his own rural background, and sometimes with both. A good example of his early work is "Dia yang Menyerah" ("She Who Surrendered"), first published in 1950. The story is set in Pramoedya's own village, Blora, and deals with the fortunes of a family similar to his own during the 1940s. The family is divided in its political allegiances: between the nationalism of the new Republic of Indonesia, the radical politics of the Communist Party, and a self-defensive indifference determined only to survive the horrors of war. Each change of regime (from the Japanese Occupation, to the announcement of the Republic, and challenges to the Republic) brings widespread suffering, more intense poverty, and savage loss of life.

Pramoedya describes these changes with a relentless, brutal realism. His descriptions are further tempered by a dark pessimism about the willingness of Indonesian society to commit itself to any ultimately positive national vision. At the end of the novelette, high offices in the government are taken by cynical, ambitious individuals, who "live proudly in a castle in the sky somewhere above our small unimportant town." This same sense of despair pervades "No Night Market," published a year later. This novelette marks the death of Pramoedya's father, who had been a strong nationalist. "Politics killed him . . . , "an anonymous figure states, "He fell sick with despair at how things were. He couldn't stand to see so much confusion. And its consequences. Those who had led the people fought among themselves for power and glory, like clowns, the pirates of fate."

In his quest for a more positive orientation, Pramoedya became increasingly associated with Lekra, the mass literary movement of the Indonesian Communist Party, after the mid-1950s. *Gadis Pantai* (*The Girl from the Coast*), published originally as a serial between 1962–64, is the story of a young girl of fourteen, who is married to a religious aristocrat in a small coastal town in North Java. Pramoedya uses the story to contrast the earthy honesty of her oppressed fishing village with the luxurious hypocrisy of the city elite. The book is set at the beginning of the 20th century and its major theme is struggle. "Serve the land," the Girl is told by her guardian. "The land gives you food and drink. The kings, the lords and the regents have sold this sacred land to the Dutch. The fight against the kings, the lords and the regents has only just begun. It will take more than one generation . . . Until you defeat the aristocracy, you will never be able to defeat the Dutch. It may take many generations. But we must start now."

Pramoedya was arrested for his leftist tendencies after the army came to power following the "abortive communist coup" of 30 September 1965. He was held in various camps and not allowed to write until the early 1970s. Gradually he began to set down the stories he had been telling his fellow prisoners. *The Buru Quartet*, as these four novels are sometimes called (after the island of Buru where he was held), are also historical. Like *The Girl from the Coast*, they explore the rise of the early nationalist movement at the beginning of the 20th century. The most famous is, perhaps, the first: *Bumi Manusia* (*This Earth of Mankind*). The novel is based on the life an early nationalist and journalist, Tirto Adhi Soerjo. Although the story is in some ways melodramatic, it traces the growing awareness of a young Indonesian that the colonial government under which he lives in ruthlessly exploitative and greedy, despite its claims of an "ethical mission'' to bring Indonesians ''from darkness to the light.'' Like *She Who Surrendered* and *The Girl from the Coast*, the struggle of the main protagonist of *This Earth of Mankind* also seems to fail, but it is intended as a constant source of encouragement for those who come after. With the final removal of Suharto from power in 1998 after 32 years of rule, Pramoedya has been increasingly recognised, both within Indonesia and abroad, as one of his nation's greatest spokesmen for full political independence in the face of tyranny.

—Harry Aveling

See the essay on *The Fugitive*.

TOLLER, Ernst

Born: Samotschin, Germany (now Szamocin, Poland), 1 December 1893. **Education:** Educated at the Realgymnasium, Bromberg, from 1906; studied law at the University of Grenoble, France, 1912–14; University of Munich, 1914–17; University of Heidelberg, 1917–18. **Military Service:** Served in the army during World War I; suffered a mental breakdown, invalided out, 1916. **Family:** Married the actress Christiane Grautoff in 1935 (separated 1938). **Career:** Co-organized a munitions workers' strike, Munich, 1918, arrested and subsequently convicted of treason, spent three months in a military prison and pronounced unfit for military service; became active in anti-war politics, associated with the Communist government in Bavaria, 1918; candidate for the newly formed USPD (Independent Social Democratic Party of Germany), Bavaria, 1919, and chairman, USPD 1919; section commander of the Red army during the events of the Bavarian uprising, resigned because of political differences; after the collapse of the Bavarian revolution, arrested and sentenced to five years imprisonment, 1919–24, during which time he wrote most of his plays; lectured and lobbied widely, in Europe, the Soviet Union, and the United States in the 1920s and 1930s on anti-fascist causes; exiled from Germany in 1933, his works burnt and banned; fled to Switzerland, France, and then England, 1933–35; travelled to Portugal and Spain, 1936; moved to the United States in 1936; screenwriter, Metro-Goldwyn-Mayer, 1936–38; activist for pro-Republican intervention in the Spanish Civil War, lobbying in the United States, France, England, and Sweden, 1938. **Died:** (suicide) 22 May 1939.

PUBLICATIONS

Collections

Ausgewählte Schriften. 1959.
Prosa, Briefe, Dramen, Gedichte. 1961.
Gesammelte Werke, edited by John M. Spalek and Wolfgang Frühwald. 5 vols., 1978.

Plays

Die Wandlung: Das Ringen eines Menschen (produced 1919). 1919; as *Transfiguration*, translated by Edward Crankshaw, in *Seven Plays*, 1935.
Masse-Mensch (produced 1920). 1921; as *Masses and Man*, translated by Vera Mendel, 1923; as *Man and the Masses*, translated by Louis Untermeyer, 1924.

Die Maschinenstürmer (produced 1922). 1922; as *The Machine-Wreckers*, translated by Ashley Dukes, 1923.
Der deutsche Hinkemann (produced 1923). 1923; as *Hinkemann*, 1924; as *Brokenbrow*, translated by Vera Mendel, 1926.
Der entfesselte Wotan (produced 1924). 1923.
Die Rache des verhöhnten Liebhabers; odor, Frauenlist und Männerlist (puppetshow). 1925.
Hoppla, wir leben! (produced 1927). 1927; as *Hoppla!*, translated by Herman Ould, 1928.
Feuer aus den Kesseln (produced 1930). 1930; as *Draw the Fires!*, translated by Edward Crankshaw, 1934, and in *Seven Plays*, 1935.
Wunder in Amerika, with Hermann Kesten (produced 1934). 1931; as *Mary Baker Eddy; or, Miracle in America*, translated by Edward Crankshaw, in *Seven Plays*, 1935.
Die blinde Göttin. 1933; as *The Blind Goddess*, translated by Edward Crankshaw, 1934.
Seven Plays, translated by Edward Crankshaw. 1935.
Nie wieder Friede!. 1936; as *No More Peace! A Thoughtful Comedy*, translated by Edward Crankshaw, 1937.
Pastor Hall. 1938; as *Pastor Hall*, translated by Stephen Spender and Hugh Hunt, 1939.
Berlin—letzte Ausgabe! (radio play). In *Frühe sozialistische Hörspiele*, edited by Stefan Bodo Würffel, 1982.

Verse

Der Tag des Proletariats. 1920.
Gedichte der Gefangenen: Ein Sonettenkreis. 1921.
Vormorgen. 1924.
Weltliche Passion. 1934.

Other

Das Schwalbenbuch. 1924; as *The Swallow Book*, translated by Ashley Dukes, 1924.
Deutsche Revolution. 1925.
Justiz. 1927.
Quer Durch: Reisebilder und Reden. 1930; translated in part as *Which World Which Way?* by Hermon Ould, 1931.
Nationalsozialismus (radio broadcast). 1930.
Eine Jugend in Deutschland (autobiography). 1933; as *I Was a German*, translated by Edward Crankshaw, 1934.
Briefe aus dem Gefängnis. 1935; as *Letters from Prison* (includes *The Swallow Book*), translated by R. Ellis Roberts, 1936; as *Look Through the Bars*, 1937.

*

Bibliography: *Ernst Toller and His Critics: A Bibliography* by J.M. Spalek, 1968.

Critical Studies: *Ernst Toller: Product of Two Revolutions*, 1941, and *Ernst Toller and His Ideology*, 1945, both by W.A. Willibrand; *Ernst Toller* by Tankred Dorst, 1968; *Ernst Toller* by Malcolm Pittock, 1979; *Anarchism in the Drama of Ernst Toller: The Realm of Necessity and the Realm of Freedom* by Michael Ossar, 1980; *Ernst Toller in Selbstzeugnissen und Bilddokumenten* by Wolfgang Rothe, 1983; *German Expressionist Drama: Ernst Toller and Georg Kaiser* by Renate Benson, 1984; *Revolutionary Socialism in the Work of*

Ernst Toller, 1986, and *He Was a German: A Biography of Ernst Toller*, 1990, both by Richard Dove; *Ernst Toller und die Weimarer Republik, 1918–1933* by Andreas Lixl, 1986; *Weimar Germany and the Limits of Political Art: A Study of the Work of Georg Grosz and Ernst Toller* by Martin Kane, 1987; *The Plays of Ernst Toller: A Revaluation* by Cecil Davies, 1996.

* * *

"Placing Toller's fiasco as a revolutionary within the narrative of the failed German Revolution enhances the symbolism of his case, but also blurs the particularities of his concern as a writer and a public figure." Trommler's recent appraisal of the legendary Expressionist dramatist and left-wing leader of the Bavarian Räterepublik, Ernst Toller, focuses on the contradictions within his personality and of his reception since his suicide in a New York hotel in 1939, and mirrors these within his major works. From the biographical accounts of the Munich episode (given compelling but critical dramatic form in Tankred Dorst's *Toller* in 1968) Ernst Toller appears as an idealist appeaser; however, the subtitle of his first play, *Das Ringen eines Menschen* [The Struggle of a Man], records better the underlying tone of Toller's life and work. Dealing with Toller's experiences in the war, it is revolutionary in its autobiographical and historical background. Toller's personal nationalist fervour became pacifist commitment in a moment of vision celebrated in this play and is here developed into disillusionment in a chronicle of revolution. Friedrich's passion in *Die Wandlung* (*Transfiguration*) represents the compelling sense of responsibility that Toller felt throughout his life as a writer.

On this discrepancy between fantasy and reality both he and his central characters came asunder. Yet, as he realized, dramatic form emphasizes such discrepancies to the detriment of the expression of the greater ideals of progress and the brotherhood of man. His attempts to reconcile ideal vision with self-destructive reality are the reason for the declamatory, rhetorical style of his early dramas. *Transfiguration*, finished in March 1918 and first performed in October 1919, is a typical "O-Mensch" work in six tableaux, castigating and commiserating, a form of spiritual pamphleteering aiming at revolution to bring a form of utopia where man could be free from social misery caused above all by war. Despite scenes depicting soldiers and workers who have lost their dignity, it is a drama of hope rather than a politically thought-out programme.

Far more persuasive is *Masse-Mensch* (*Masses and Man*)—his most interesting drama. Set during wartime, it shows a workers' committee deciding to strike to enforce peace and secure a fair society. Sonja Irene, wife of a disapproving bourgeois, has joined the committee and finds her strike call disputed by an anonymous opponent who insists that the utopia of lasting peace and social justice can only come through violent revolution. She is unable to prevent violence and the subsequent shooting of an enemy soldier. She is captured in the ensuing battle, refuses help from her husband and from her anonymous former opponent because she would have to kill a warden to escape, and is executed. This reveals, in Richard Dove's words, "the strong vein of determinism increasingly evident in Toller's work." The play is written as a vision containing "real" and "dream" scenes in which the banality of real-life situations is contrasted with the utopia of a new society to come. The problems of the political resolve needed for mass action are examined dialectically through the central character, who is portrayed both as a real-life person and as an abstract figure. All the central oppositions remain unresolved, with the reality of revolution in conflict with noble ideals

expressed in abstract argument. Moral principle is set against revolutionary expediency, and expressed in a clash between ethical socialism and applied Marxism. The individual here has to show the way, the mass can only achieve ethical freedom through an act of limited violence. Despite many Expressionist features, the involvement with political argument lifts the play beyond propaganda and ideology. The central figure becomes a "new woman" and combines a hard-headed understanding of her companions with a vision for the future.

Toller's growing objectivization is seen in *Die Maschinenstürmer* (*The Machine-Wreckers*) by his use of historical material (the Luddite movement in 1815) and rejection of Expressionist language and form. Early capitalism is shown as an exploitative system reducing weavers to starvation even before the new machines arrive that will put many of them out of work. Lord Byron's sympathetic speech on behalf of the weavers in the House of Lords is met with derisive laughter, and the stage is set for a punitive strike to destroy the machines. Jimmy Cobbett tries to persuade the weavers to work for political change through a nascent trade union but is killed by the machine wreckers. In exhorting them to settle their differences and join a mass Labour movement Cobbett foreshadows 20th-century developments within an early 19th-century situation. His attack on inner and outer divisions make him both outcast and messiah, and his emotionalism overwhelms the underlying dramatic conflict with an oratorical style that no longer convinces because it is overdone.

The effusive lyricism of this play is effectively channelled in more muted tones in the lyrical cycle *Das Schwalbenbuch* (*The Swallow Book*), where Toller admires the naïve innocence of two swallows nesting near his prison cell, in contrast with the complex so-called civilized yet brutal behaviour of man in society.

Der deutsche Hinkemann (*Brokenbrow*), written 1921–22 and first performed in September 1923, symbolizes the tragedy and cynical sense of betrayal in post-war Germany felt by a soldier returning home. He becomes a laughing-stock because his sexual organ has been shot away, and he is reduced to the macabre fairground act of biting the throats of rats and mice. He suffers the injustices of both meaningless war and forgetful man. His revolt is grotesque and time-bound, restricted and ineffective, but no less heartfelt than those of Toller's earlier, less realistic figures.

Hoppla, wir leben! (*Hoppla!*), in five acts, is equally pessimistic in its portrayal of a former revolutionary who, having spent eight years in an asylum, discovers when he comes back into society the corruption of industrialists, bankers, and politicians. He is wrongly arrested for the murder of a minister and hangs himself, unable to cope with the madness of the world. This is a prime example of political theatre unmasking some of the worst injustices of the Weimar Republic. Karl Thomas's early optimism is shattered by the ridicule of all he meets. In an earlier four-act version of the play he is kept in an asylum (to which he has voluntarily returned) but his psychiatrist as an enemy of the state. The expanded version staged by Erwin Piscator in 1927 using several simultaneous stages became a turning-point in theatre history.

Toller gave an early warning of the dangers of fascism in *Der entfesselte Wotan* [Wotan Unchained], a pessimistic comedy about a little man with delusions of grandeur published in 1923 and first performed in Moscow in 1924. The satiric tone enables Toller to provide a social and psychological analysis of a would-be saviour of Germany and Europe who on being arrested announces that he will write his memoirs in prison. Seen as a light-hearted attack on megalomania, the play however warns the public not to laugh too soon, and viewed with hindsight, with an explicit later version, was an open attack in Berlin in 1926 of Nazi methods and aims. Also often wrongly overlooked is *Feuer aus den Kesseln* (*Draw the Fires!*), dealing with the German naval mutiny in Kiel in 1917. First performed in 1930, it is a neglected example of early documentary drama, to be placed alongside works by Paquet, Pliever, Mehring, and Wolf. The central figure gives way here to a collective of five sailors as victims of class conflict at a court martial.

Toller's later years were torn by spiritual suffering and frustration over the unwillingness of the democratic world to stop Hitler. He had been deeply indebted to Gustav Landauer's "Aufruf zum Sozialismus" [Call to Socialism] and to Kurt Eisner's thinking. Their personal fate and that of their political ideals made him distrust party allegiances and remain an independent revolutionary socialist. It has been suggested that Toller's commitment ceased and his talent dried up after 1924, yet his over 200 speeches, lectures, and broadcasts given in exile bear witness to growing, despairing involvement in the struggle against fascism. This is mirrored in his drama *Pastor Hall*, written in 1938 and based on the real-life figure of Martin Niemöller, his opposition to the Nazi régime as a Protestant pastor, and his trial and eventual imprisonment in a concentration camp. The combination of realist and symbolist features to depict the conquest of fear is unsuccessful mainly because Toller makes his central figure die of a heart attack, or in a second version preach a final sermon. Despite the relevance of Toller's confessional works that move from early attempts to cope with the guilt of nationalist fervour, though social criticisms and political warnings, his works as an exiled politician after 1933 was perhaps best summed up by Christopher Isherwood in an ironic phrase: "He was in the process of becoming a respectable institution."

—Brian Keith-Smith

TOLSTAYA (LEBEDEVA), Tatyana (Nikitichna)

Also known as Tat'iana Tolstaia and Tat'jana Tolstaja. **Born:** Leningrad, 3 May 1951, granddaughter of Aleksei Nikolaevich Tolstoi and Nataliia Vasil'evna Krandievskaia; great-grandniece of Lev Tolstoi. **Education:** Degree in philology (Language and Literature) from Leningrad State University, 1968–74. **Family:** Married Andrei Lebedev, 1974; two sons. **Career:** Junior editor of Eastern Literature Division of Nauka (Science) publishing house in Moscow, 1974–83; writer in residence, University of Virigina, Richmond, 1988; senior lecturer in Russian literature, University of Texas at Austin, 1989; writer in residence, Texas Tech University in Lubbock, 1990; teacher of creative writing and Russian literature, Skidmore College, Sarasota Springs, New York, until 2001. Lives in Moscow, Russia. **Awards:** Triumph award, 2001; finalist for the Booker prize, 2001.

PUBLICATIONS

Collections

Na zolotom kryl'tse sideli (short stories). 1987; as *On the Golden Porch*, translated by Antonina W. Bouis, 1989.
Sleepwalker in a Fog (selections), translated by Jamey Gambrell. 1992.

Three stories/Tri rasskaza, selections in Russian with a glossary by S. Dalton-Brown, 1996.
Liubish'—ne liubish': rasskazy. 1997.
Sestry: sbornik, with Nataliia Nikitichna Tolstaia. 1998.
Reka Okkervil': rasskazy. 1999.
Noch': rasskazy. 2001.

Fiction

Kys': roman. 2001.

*

Critical Studies: "Tatiana Tolstaya" by Elena Patrusheva, in *Soviet Literature*, vol. 2, no. 467, 1987; "Poeziia grusti" by Fazil' Iskander, in *Literaturnaia Gazeta*, vol. 35, no. 5153, 1987; "Mechty i fantomy" by M. Zolotonosov, in *Literaturnoe Obozrenie*, vol. 4, 1987; "Rastochitel'nost' talanta" by I. Grekova, in *Novyi Mir*, vol. 1, 1988; "Tat'iana Tolstaia's 'Dome of Many-Colored Glass': The World Refracted through Multiple Perspectives" by Helena Goscilo, in *Slavic Review*, vol. 47, no. 2, 1988; "'Golos letiashchii v kupol'" by Karen Stepanian, in *Voprosy Literatury*, vol. 2, 1988; "Tolstajan Love as Surface Text" by Helena Goscilo, in *Slavic & East European Journal*, vol. 34, no. 1, 1990; "Zhenskaia proza and the New Generation of Women Writers" by K. A. Simmons, in *Slovo*, vol. 3, no. 1, 1990; "Tolstoian Times: Transversals and Transfers" by Helena Goscilo, in *New Directions in Soviet Literature*, edited by Sheelagh Duffy Graham, 1992; "Perspective in Tatyana Tolstaya's Wonderland of Art" by Helena Goscilo, in *World Literature Today*, vol. 67, no. 1, 1993; "Interview with Tatyana Tolstaya" by Tamara Alagova and Nina Efimov, translated by Michael A. Aguirre, in *World Literature Today*, vol. 67, no. 1, 1993; *Fruits of Her Plume: Essays on Contemporary Russian Women's Culture*, edited by Helena Goscilo, 1993; "Tatyana Tolstaya" by Elisabeth Rich, in *South Central Bulletin*, vol. 12, nos. 3–4, 1995; "Violence in the Garden: A Work by Tolstaja in Kleinian Perspective" by Daniel Rancour-Laferriere, Vera Loseva, and Alexsej Lunkov, in *Slavic & East European Journal*, vol. 39, no. 4, 1995; *The Explosive World of Tatyana N. Tolstaya's Fiction* by Helena Goscilo, 1996; "V minus pervom i minus zerkale: Tat'iana Tolstaia, Viktor Erofeev—akhmatoviana i arkhetipy" by A.K. Zholkovskii, in *Literaturnoe Obozrenie*, vol. 6, no. 253, 1995; "Motiv igry v proizvedeniiakh L. Petrushevskoi i T. Tolstoi" by Nina Efimova, in *Vestnik Moskovskogo Universiteta*, Seriia 9, Filologiia 3, 1998; "Female Space in Contemporary Russian Women's Writing: Tat'jana Tolstaja's 'Ogon' i Pyl'" by Teresa Polowy, in *Critical Essays on the Prose and Poetry of Modern Slavic Women*, edited by N.A. Efimov, C.D. Tomei, and R.L. Chapple, 1998; "Tat'iana Tolstaia" by Sophie T. Wisnewska, in *Russian Women Writers, II*, edited by C.D. Tomei, 1999; "The Seduction of the Story: Flight and 'Fall' in Tolstaya's 'Heavenly Flame'" by Catharine Theimer Nepomnyashchy, in *Twentieth-Century Russian Literature*, edited by K.L. Ryan and B. P. Scherr, 2000; "Pushkin s malen'koi bukvy" by Ol'ga Slavnikova, in *Novyi Mir*, vol. 3, no. 911, 2001.

*   *   *

In her status as a contemporary woman writer in Russia, Tatyana Tolstaya is second only to Russia's beloved storyteller Liudmila

Petrushevskaia. In January 1983, while recuperating from an illness, Tolstaya began to write stories "accidentally." Her first story was published in the Russian journal *Avrora* in August of the same year. Described as "heiress to Russia's literary aristocracy," Tolstaya has published in the literary journals *Oktiabr'* [October], *Znamia* [Banner], *Novyi mir* [New World], and *The New York Review of Books*. Her writing has been compared to Russian prose of the 1920s, including that of Bulgakov, Grin, and Nabokov, as well as to German expressionism. With other representatives of Russian's *drugaia*, or "different," literature, Petrushevskaia, S. Kaledin, Evgenii Popov, Venedikt Erofeev, and V. Narbikova, Tolstaya borrows freely from canonical tradition while injecting a post-modern sense of fantasy into her plots. Best known for short stories, Tolstaya has now turned to longer forms with her first novel *Kys'*. Despite her stated fear of the internet, Tolstaya followed the example of other Russian writers, notably V. Pelevin and S. Kaledin, by publishing her dystopic novel at a Web site (http://www.lib.ru/PROZA/TOLSTAYA/kys.txt). She is currently writing another novel while overseeing the translation of *Kys'*.

Helena Goscilo, the foremost scholar of Tolstaya's work, has noted the important role color and smell play in Tolstaya's atmosphere; her texts are dense with allusive sensual details. One word that appears again and again in interpretations of Tolstaya's work is "kaleidoscopic," referring especially to her treatment of childhood impressions. Tolstaya has said that life is interesting only in the mind, where the ordinary is transformed by fantasy. Imagination thus gives beauty to life; life in the mind seems real because it is a gestalt of one's perceptions of the universe and its possibilities. Yet Tolstaya's characters show ambivalence toward their fantasy lives. Her protagonists share the flaw of trying to make what they imagine real by forcing reality to fit. Illusion is important to these characters, but they are not satisfied with temporary escapism. They want permanent refuge from everything that is ugly and dreary in life, and a fantasy alone is not enough to sustain them. Their ultimate goal is to make the imagined real, but its eventual disintegration brings disillusionment. In a manner reminiscent of Nabokov, Tolstaya fulfills her role as puppet-master with relish as she reveals the tawdry props behind her characters' dreams.

The competition between what is real and what is imagined is especially well-demonstrated in the story "The Fakir." The "fakir," Filin (whose name refers to a mythological bird) charms the young woman Galya with his worldly mystique; she imagines him to be all-powerful, able to transform the ugliness of reality into something beautiful. But Filin's power, like imagination's, is limited. His power to create a beautiful world for Galya goes only as far as his apartment. Galya comes into Filin's apartment, admires the Wedgwood, envies his sophistication—and then she must go home to her dismal apartment on the outskirts of Moscow. Filin's tasseled robe, snuffboxes, and china are magical talismans fending off the tiresome world outside. When Galya tries to escape ordinary life, she is pulled down by worldly details. Filin, however, has the trappings of luxury—he seems wonderful—and Galya believes in him until those trappings are snatched away. Then her fantasy is unrecognizable in the real man, the sublet apartment, and the borrowed robe. Galya feels that Filin has unfairly abused her trust, but by the same token, he has exposed her to the only luxury that she will ever experience. She and Filin are conspirators in a game of make-believe, although Galya does not realize that she is playing. Her sense of betrayal, of moral outrage against Filin, is expressed by many of Tolstaya's characters in other works. It stems from a conviction that life is not fair, that fate is withholding the glittering stuff of dreams in real life.

In "Rendezvous with a Bird," the child Petya is similarly seduced by a quasi-imaginary being and brutally disenchanted at the end. The child, in the beginning, is not yet convinced that dreams do not come true and that fate is brutal. Again Tolstaya shows the conspiracy of the one imagining with the one imagined. Petya's neighbor, Tamila, is self-consciously exotic. She lives in a fantastic way, surrounded by magical objects and legend: a toad ring, without which she will turn into powder, a dragon robe "retained from her captivity," the egg of a mythical bird, the Alkonost, and even Chinese roses in her garden. Unlike other people, Tamila eats only chocolates and drinks "panacea" from a black bottle. Petya wants to escape from the hateful Uncle Borya, from rice kasha, from his grandfather's illness: Tamila presents a means of escape. For Petya, the ultimate betrayal is Tamila's affair with Borya. At the moment of this discovery, Petya realizes that everything of Tamila's is a fraud—the ring, the robe, the enchanted garden, and Tamila herself. Not only is Grandfather dead, but the lake, the forest, and the entire world seem dead, too. The eternal anguish in the Alkonost's egg then symbolizes disillusionment and a longing for a fantasy world which will never be real.

In "Okkervil River," the dream is inspired by a woman's music instead of by the woman. The fantasy takes on a life of its own in the same way that art has a life of its own once it leaves the hands of its creator. A voice, captured on records, "rises from the depths, spreads its wings, shooting up over the world." Yet as soon as Simeonov embarks on his quest for Vera, the voice behind the recording, the fantasy is undermined. Simeonov takes Vera chrysanthemums and a cake, offerings to his imagined Vera Vasilevna. If it were still a dream, the flowers would be fresh and beautiful and the cake would not have a fingerprint on it. Unfortunately, real life is full of irritating, worldly, sordid details. Thus the flowers, instead of an offering to Simeonov's goddess, become funeral flowers for her bier. Vera's 'death'—the death of the imaginary Vera Vasilevna whom Simeonov had created so lovingly in his mind—is Simeonov's disillusionment. Instead of realizing the fantasy, Simeonov has destroyed it; his recognition of the reality has made it impossible to continue the dream.

In Tolstaya's stories, the discovery of the schism between illusion and reality is portrayed as the death of the imagination and of part of the protagonist's psyche. Simultaneous with this death is a realization that the beloved's magical accessories are tawdry and fake. Thus not only the beloved but everything associated with him or her is discredited. The protagonists' desire to make fantasy real burdens it with mundane details, with the weight of reality, and the fantasy is destroyed. The qualities of imagination are often related to birds and images of flight; nowhere is this more disturbingly demonstrated than in the story "Serafim," in which the hero envisions himself as a pure, heavenly being, only to be revealed as a loathsome reptile from Russian folklore. Tolstaya's protagonists try to escape the earthly bonds that hold them to soar over the workaday world into the realm of beauty and impossibility. Illusion only maintains its freedom in the imagination—otherwise the dream hardens into real life and loses its magic.

—Natalie Smith

TOLSTOI, (Count) Lev (Nikolaevich)

Also known as Leo Tolstoy. **Born:** At Iasnaia Poliana, near Tula, Russia, 28 August 1828. **Education:** Educated at home, in Moscow,

1837–41, and in Kazan, 1841–44; Kazan University, 1844–47, no degree. **Family:** Married Sof'ia Andreevna Bers in 1862; 13 children (three died in infancy); also had one illegitimate son. **Career:** Landowner on his inherited estate, 1847–48; in Moscow, 1848–51; visited his brother's military unit in Caucasus, and joined artillery battery as noncommissioned officer, 1851–54, then transferred to a unit near Bucharest, 1854, and, as sub-lieutenant, in Sevastopol, 1854–55: resigned as lieutenant, 1855; travelled to France, Switzerland, and Germany; landowner on his Iasnaia estate: set up school, and edited the school journal *Iasnaia Poliana*, 1862–63 (and member of local educational committee, 1870s); disseminated his social and religious views widely in last decades of his life; excommunicated from Orthodox Church in 1901 because of these views. As a result of censorship, many of his works were first published abroad. **Died:** 7 November 1910.

PUBLICATIONS

Collections

Complete Works, edited and translated by Leo Weiner. 24 vols., 1904–05.

Polnoe sobranie sochinenii [Complete Works], edited by V. Chertkov and others. 90 vols., 1928–58; reprinted 1992.

Centenary Edition (in English), edited by Aylmer Maude, translated by Aylmer and Louise Maude. 21 vols., 1928–37.

Izbrannye povesti i rasskazy [Selected Novels and Stories]. 1945–50.

Sobranie khudozhestvennykh proizvedenii [Collected Artistic Works], edited by N.K. Gudzii. 1948.

Sobranie sochinenii [Collected Works], edited by N.N. Akopova. 20 vols., 1960–65.

Izbrannye proizvedeniia [Selected Works], edited by M. Kondrat'ev. 2 vols., 1964.

The Portable Tolstoy, translated by Aylmer and Louise Maude, and George L. Kline. 1978.

Sobranie sochinenii [Collected Works], edited by M.B. Khrapchenko. 22 vols., 1978–86.

Sobranie sochinenii [Collected Works], edited by S.A. Makashina. 12 vols., 1980–87.

Dramaticheskie proizvedenie, 1864–1910 [Dramatical Works 1864–1910]. 1983.

Izbrannye proizvedeniia [Selected Works], edited by K.N. Lomunov. 1986.

Izbrannye sochineniia [Selected Works], edited by G.I. Belen'kii. 3 vols., 1988.

P'esy [Plays]. 1988.

Izbrannye filosofskie proizvedeniia [Selected Philosophical Works], edited by N.P. Semykin. 1992.

How Much Land Does a Man Need?: and Other Stories, translated by Ronald Wilks. 1993.

Tolstoy: Plays, translated by Marvin Kantor with Tanya Tulchinsky. 1994.

The Kreutzer Sonata and Other Stories, translated by Louise and Aylmer Maude and J.D. Duff. 1997.

An Anthology of Tolstoy's Spiritual Economics by Kenneth C. Wenzer. 1997.

Divine and Human, and Other Stories, translated by Gordon Spence. 2000.

Fiction

Sevastopolskie rasskazy. 1855–56; as *Sevastopol*, translated by Isabel F. Hapgood, 1887; as *The Sebastopol Sketches*, translated by David McDuff, 1986.

Semeinoe schast'e. 1859; translated as *Katia*, 1887; as *Family Happiness*, translated by Nathan Haskell Dole, 1888; as *My Husband and I*, 1888; as *The Romance of Marriage*, translated by Alexina Loranger, 1890.

Kazaki. 1863; as *The Cossacks*, translated by Eugene Schuyler, 1878.

Voina i mir. 1863–69; as *War and Peace*, translated by Clara Bell, 1886; numerous subsequent translations including by Louise and Aylmer Maude, 3 vols., 1922–23, Constance Garnett, 1925, Rosemary Edmonds, 1957, and Helen Edmundson, 1996.

Anna Karenina. 1875–77; as *Anna Karenina*, translated by Nathan Haskell Dole, 1886; numerous subsequent translations including by Constance Garnett, 1901, Rosemary Edmonds, 1954, Joel Carmichael, 1960, and Margaret Wettlin, 1978; Helen Edmundson, 1994.

Kreitserova sonata. 1891; as *The Kreutzer Sonata*, translated by Benjamin R. Tucker, 1890.

Khoziain i rabotnik. 1895; as *Master and Man*, translated by S. Rapoport and John C. Kenworthy, 1895; also translated by A. Hulme, 1897.

Voskresenie. 1899; as *Resurrection*, translated by Vera Traill, 1899; also translated by Louise Maude, 1899.

Khadzhi-Murat. 1904; as *Hadji Murat*, translated by Paul Foote, in *Master and Man and Other Stories*, 1977.

Rasskazy o zhivotnykh [Stories about Animals]. 1932.

Dlia samykh malen'kikh [For the Smallest]. 1936.

Akula: rasskazy [Akula: Stories]. 1938.

Dva tovarishcha [Two Comrades]. 1940.

Voennye rasskazy [Military Stories]. 1944.

Bul'ka. 1947.

Rasskazy dlia detei [Stories for Children]. 1948.

Dva gusara—Metel' [Two Hussars—A Storm]. 1948.

Devochka i griby [A Little Girl and Mushrooms]. 1957.

Rasskazy o prirode [Stories about Nature]. 1961.

Smert' Ivana Il'icha, edited by Michael Beresford. 1966; as *The Death of Ivan Ilyich*, translated by Rosemary Edmonds, 1960; also translated by Lynn Solotaroff, 1981; as *The Death of Ivan Illych*, translated by Louise and Aylmer Maude, in *The Raid and Other Stories*, 1982.

Master and Man and Other Stories (includes *Father Sergius*; *Master and Man*; *Hadji Murat*), translated by Paul Foote. 1977.

Basni, skazki, rasskazy; Kavkazskii plennik [Fables, Tales, Stories; A Captive in the Caucusus]. 1978.

Povesti i rasskazy [The Stories]. 1978.

The Raid and Other Stories (includes ''The Raid''; ''Sevastopol in May 1855''; ''Two Hussars''; ''Albert''; ''What Men Live By''; ''Master and Man''; ''How Much Does a Man Need?''; ''The Death of Ivan Illych''; ''The Three Hermits''), translated by Louise and Aylmer Maude. 1982.

Tolstoy's Short Fiction: Revised Translations, Backgrounds and Sources, Criticism, edited and revised translations by Michael R. Katz. 1991.

How Much Land Do You Need? and Other Stories, translated by Ronald Wilks. 1993.

Plays

Nigilist (produced 1863). In *Polnoe sobranie sochinenii*, 1928; as *The Nihilists*, in *Stories and Dramas*, 1926.

Pervyi vinokur; ili, kak chertenok Kraiushku zasluzhil (produced 1886). 1886(?); as *The First Distiller*, in *Plays*, 1903; also translated by Nathan Haskell Dole, in *Dramatic Works*, 1923.

Vlast' t'my (produced 1888). 1887; as *The Dominion of Darkness*, 1888; as *The Power of Darkness*, translated by G.R. Noyes and George Z. Patrick, in *Plays*, 1903.

Plody prosveshcheniia (produced 1889). 1889; as *The Fruits of Enlightenment*, translated by E.J. Dillon, 1891; also translated by Michael Frayn, 1979; as *The Fruits of Culture*, translated by Dillon, 1891.

Zhivoi trup (produced 1911). 1911(?); as *The Living Corpse*, translated by Mrs. E.M. Evarts, 1912; as *The Live Corpse*, translated by Louise Maude, 1919; also translated by Nathan Haskell Dole, in *Dramatic Works*, 1923.

Other

Detstvo, Otrochestvo, Iunost'. 3 vols., 1852–57; as *Childhood, Boyhood, Youth*, translated by Isabel F. Hapgood, 1886; also translated by Rosemary Edmonds, 1962, and by C.J. Hogarth, 1991; as *Childhood, Adolescence and Youth*, translated by Constantine Popoff, 1890; as *Childhood, Adolescence, Youth*, translated by Fainna Solasko, 1981.

Azbuka [An ABC Book]. 1872; revised edition, 1875.

Ispoved'. 1884; edited by A.D.P. Briggs, 1994; as *A Confession*, 1885; also translated by Jane Kentish, in *A Confession and Other Religious Writings*, 1987.

V chem moia vera? 1884; as *My Religion*, translated by Huntington Smith, 1885; as *What I Believe*, translated by Constantine Popoff, 1885.

In Pursuit of Happiness (essays), translated by Mrs. Aline Delano. 1887.

Tak chtozhe nam delat'? 1902; as *What to Do?*, translated by Isabel F. Hapgood, 1887; uncensored edition, 1888.

The Long Exile and Other Stories for Children, translated by Nathan Haskell Dole. 1888.

O zhizni. 1888; uncensored edition, 1891; as *Life*, translated by Isabel F. Hapgood, 1888; as *On Life*, translated by Mabel and Agnes Cook, 1902.

The Physiology of War, translated by Huntington Smith. 1889.

Gospel Stories, translated by Nathan Haskell Dole. 1890.

Kritika dogmaticheskogo bogosloviia [An Examination of Dogmatic Theology]. 1891.

Soedinenie i perevod chetyrekh evangelii. 3 vols., 1892–94; as *The Four Gospels Harmonized and Translated*, 1895–96; shortened version, 1890; as *The Gospel in Brief*, 1896; also translated by Isabel Hapgood, 1997.

Tsarstvo Bozhe vnutri vas. 2 vols., 1893–94; as *The Kingdom of God Is Within You*, translated by Constance Garnett, 2 vols., 1894.

Pis'ma o Genre Dzhorzhe [Letters on Henry George]. 1897.

Kristianskoe uchenie. 1898; as *The Christian Teaching*, translated by Vladimir Tchertkoff, 1898.

Chto takoe iskusstvo? 1898; as *What Is Art?*, translated by Charles Johnston, 1898; translated by Aylmer Maude, 1930; also translated by Richard Pevear and Larissa Volokhansky, 1995.

Rabstvo nashego vremeni. 1900; as *The Slavery of Our Times*, translated by Aylmer Maude, 1900.

Essays and Letters, translated by Aylmer Maude. 1903.

Christianity and Patriotism, translated by Paul Borger and others. 1905; also translated by Constance Garnett, 1922.

End of the Age; The Crisis in Russia, translated by V. Tchertkhoff and I.F. Mayo. 1906.

The Russian Revolution, translated by Aylmer Maude. 1907.

The Hanging Czar, translated by Louise and Aylmer Maude. 1908.

Social Evils and Their Remedy, edited by Helen Chrouschoff Matheson. 1915.

Tolstoy on Art, translated by Aylmer Maude. 1924.

Sevastopol'skie ocherki [Sevastopol Essays]. 1932.

On Life and Essays on Religion, translated by Aylmer Maude. 1934.

Dnevniki i zapisnye knizhki 1910 goda [Diaries and Notebooks of 1910]. 1935.

The Kingdom of God and Peace Essays, translated by Aylmer Maude. 1936.

Rukopisi, perepiska i dokumenty [Manuscripts, Correspondence and Documents]. 1937.

Recollections and Essays, translated by Aylmer Maude. 1937.

Russkaia kniga dlia chteniia [A Russian Book for Reading]. 1946.

Pedagogicheskie sochineniia [Pedagogical Works]. 1948.

Essays from Tula, translated by Evgeny Lamport. 1948.

Proizvedeniia o Kavkaze [Works about the Caucusus]. 1950.

Za chto? [What For?]. 1957.

Perepiska s russkimi pisateliami [Correspondence with Russian Writers]. 1962.

Stat'i i materialy [Articles and Materials]. 1966.

Neizbezhnyi perevorot; as *The Inevitable Revolution*, translated by Ronald Sampson. 1975.

Letters, edited by R.F. Christian. 2 vols., 1978.

Novaia azbuka [A New ABC Book]. 1978; as *Stories for My Children*, translated by James Riordan, 1988.

Tolstoy on Education: Tolstoy's Educational Writings 1861–62, edited by Alan Pinch and Michael Armstrong, translated by Pinch. 1982.

Ne mogu molchat' [I Cannot Be Silent]. 1985.

Diaries, edited and translated by R.F. Christian. 2 vols., 1985.

The Lion and the Puppy and Other Stories (for children). 1986.

A Confession and Other Religious Writings, translated by Jane Kentish. 1987.

The Lion and the Honeycomb: The Religious Writings of Tolstoy, edited by A.N. Wilson, translated by Robert Chandler. 1987.

Schast'e, kotoroe menia ozhidaet. . . [Happiness Which Awaits Me . . .] (stories, diaries, and letters). 1988.

Dnevnik molodosti L.N. Tolstogo [The Diary of the Young L.N. Tolstoi]. 1988.

Pora opomnit'sia! [It's Time to Remember!]. 1989.

I Cannot Be Silent: Selection from Tolstoy's Non-Fiction, edited by W. Gareth Jones. 1989.

Perepiska L.N. Tolstogo s sestroi i brat'iami [Tolstoi's Correspondence with His Sister and Brothers]. 1990.

Ia veriu [I Believe]. 1990.

Uchenie Khrista, izlozhennoe dlia detei [The Teachings of Jesus for Children]. 1990.

Evangelii dlia detei [The Gospels for Children]. 1991.

Krug chteniia [A Circle of Reading]. 2 vols., 1991; as *A Calendar of Wisdom: Daily Thoughts to Nourish the Soul*, translated by Peter Sekirin, 1997.

Mysli mudrykh liudei na kazhdyi den' [The Everyday Thoughts of Ordinary People]. 1991.

Evangelii Tolstogo [Tolstoi's Gospels]. 1992.

Leo Tolstoy—Peter Verigin: Correspondence, translated by John Woodsworth. 1995.

*

Bibliography: "Tolstoy Studies in Great Britain: A Bibliographical Survey" by Garth M. Terry, in *New Essays on Tolstoy* by Malcolm Jones, 1978; *Leo Tolstoy: An Annotated Bibliography of English-Language Sources to 1978* by David R. Egan, 1979.

Critical Studies: *The Life of Tolstoy* by Aylmer Maude, 2 vols., 1930; *Leo Tolstoy*, 1946, *Introduction to Tolstoy's Writings*, 1968, and *Tolstoy*, 1973, all by Ernest H. Simmons; *The Hedgehog and the Fox: An Essay on Tolstoy's View of History* by Isaiah Berlin, 1953; *Tolstoy or Dostoevsky* by George Steiner, 1959; *Tolstoy's "War and Peace,"* 1962, and *Tolstoy: A Critical Introduction*, 1969, both by R.F. Christian; *Tolstoy and the Novel* by John Bayley, 1966; *Leo Tolstoy: A Collection of Critical Essays* edited by Ralph E. Matlaw, 1967; *Tolstoy* by Henri Troyat, translated by Nancy Leroux, 1970; *Leo Tolstoy: A Critical Anthology* edited by Henry Gifford, 1971, and *Tolstoy* by Gifford, 1982; *Tolstoy and Chekhov* by Logan Spiers, 1971; *The Young Tolstoi*, translated by Gary Kern, 1972, *Tolstoi in the Sixties*, translated by Duffield White, 1982, and *Tolstoi in the Seventies*, translated by Albert Kaspin, 1982, all by Boris Eikhenbaum; *Tolstoy: The Making of a Novelist* by Edward Crankshaw, 1974; *Tolstoy: The Comprehensive Vision* by E.B. Greenwood, 1975; *The Architecture of Anna Karenina* by E. Stenbock-Fermor, 1975; *Tolstoy: A Life of My Father* by Aleksandra Tolstaia, 1975; *Tolstoy, the Rebel* by Leo Hecht, 1976; *Tolstoy* by T.G.S. Cain, 1977; *From Achilles to Christ: The Myth of the Hero in Tolstoy's War and Peace* by Laura Jepsen, 1978; *New Essays on Tolstoy* by Malcolm Jones, 1978; *Tolstoy: The Critical Heritage* edited by A.V. Knowles, 1978; *Tolstoy's Major Fiction*, 1978, and *Leo Nikolayevich Tolstoy: Life, Work, and Criticism*, 1985, both by Edward Wasiolek, and *Critical Essays on Tolstoy* edited by Wasiolek, 1986; *Lev Tolstoy* by Viktor Shklovskii (in English), 1978; *Tolstoy in London* by Victor Lucas, 1979; *Tolstoy in Pre-Revolutionary Russian Criticism* by Boris Sorokin, 1979; *The Structure of Anna Karenina* by Sydney Schultze, 1982; *Tolstoy and the Russians: Reflections on a Relationship* by Alexander Fodor, 1984; *Tolstoy's What Is Art?* by T.J. Diffey, 1985; *Leo Tolstoy* edited by Harold Bloom, 1986; *Leo Tolstoy* by William W. Rowe, 1986; *Lev and Sonya* by Louise Smolunchowski, 1987; *Leo Tolstoy: Anna Karenina* by Anthony Thorlby, 1987; *The Unsaid Anna Karenina* by Judith M. Armstrong, 1988; *Essays on L.N. Tolstoj's Dramatic Art* by Andrew Donskov, 1988; *Hidden in Plain View: Narrative and Creative Potentials in War and Peace* by Gary Saul Marson, 1988; *Tolstoy: A Biography* by A.N. Wilson, 1988; *Reflecting on Anna Karenina* by Mary Evans, 1989; *Tolstoy, Resident and Stranger: A Study in Fiction and Theology* by Richard F. Gustafson, 1989; *Narrative and Anti-Narrative Structures in Lev Tolstoj's Early Works* by Eric de Haard, 1989; *In the Shade of the*

Giant: Essays on Tolstoy edited by Hugh McLean, 1989; *Essays on Leo Tolstoy* edited by T.R. Sharma, 1989; *The Influence of Tolstoy on Readers of His Works* by Gareth Williams, 1991; *Tolstoy, the Philosopher* by David Redfearn, 1992; *Tolstoy's Art and Thought, 1847–1900* by Donna Trussing Orwin, 1993; *A Karenina Companion* by C.J.G. Turner, 1993; *Tolstoy's Pierre Bezukhov: A Psychoanalytic Study* by Daniel Rancour-Laferriere, 1993; *A Signature on a Portrait: Highlights of Tolstoy's Thought* by Michael L. Levin, 1994; *Love and Hatred: The Troubled Marriage of Leo and Sonya Tolstoy*, 1994; *Tolstoi and Britain*, edited by W. Gareth Jones, 1995; *Tolstoy's Childhood* by Gareth Williams, 1995; *Anna Karenina: Backrounds and Sources Criticism*, translation revised by George Gibian, 1995; *Tolstoy and the Genesis of "War and Peace"* by Kathryn B. Feuer, 1996; *L.N. Tolstoy and D.H. Lawrence: Cross-Currents and Influence* by Dorthe G.A. Engelhardt, 1996; *Tolstoy, Woman, and Death: A Study of War and Peace and Anna Karenina* by David Holbrook, 1997; *Leo Tolstoy* by John Bayley, 1997; *Leo Tolstoy* by Dragan Milivojevic, 1998; *Tolstoy's Phoenix: From Method to Meaning in War and Peace* by George R. Clay, 1998; *Tolstoy on the Couch: Misogyny, Masochism, and the Absent Mother* by Daniel Rancour-Laferriere, 1998; *Creating and Recovering Experience: Repetition in Tolstoy* by Natasha Sankovitch, 1998; *Saviour or Superman?: Old and New Essays on Tolstoy and Dostoevsky* by Frank Seeley, 1999; *Tolstoy's The Death of Ivan Ilich: A Critical Companion*, edited by Gary R. Jahn, 1999; *Tolstoy on Aesthetics: What Is Art?* by H.O. Mounce, 2001.

* * *

The name of Lev Tolstoi is indissolubly linked to Russian literature and the great tradition of the prose novel. Yet these associations, if taken alone, diminish the standing of this unique figure. Tolstoi, the creed of Tolstoianism, and the legend of the man were among the principal intellectual and spiritual influences in Russia during the last four decades of the 19th century.

From the beginning Tolstoi's literature was never just fiction. His experiences of childhood and youth, military adventure and war, education and landowning, foreign travel, courtship and marriage, history and philosophy, religion and art, the fear of death and the love of life are transformed into a uniquely personal body of literature. Tolstoi's search for moral codes and values, the discipline to hold himself to them and a new, simple, "real" vision of the Christian faith, all this is played out as a national and even cosmic experience on the broad Russian canvas of his writings. This striving for a presumed "truth," the whole, unified system of being he desired is pursued through works dominated almost exclusively by the only two social groups he really knew, the aristocracy to which he belonged and the peasantry who belonged to him, and his kind. Rarely do the inconveniently modern faces of the middle classes and the urban poor, so illuminated by Dostoevskii, intrude into Tolstoi's attempt to recapture a "natural" world.

Tolstoi's early series of autobiographical works, *Detstvo, Otrochestvo, Iunost'* (*Childhood, Boyhood, Youth*), establishes his interest in the loss and retrieval of innocence and the life of the family. Other essential lines of development are laid down by his military stories, including his Caucasian tales, such as "Nabeg" ("The Raid") and "ubka lesa" ("The Wood Felling"), and the grimmer

Sevastopolskie rasskazy (*The Sebastopol Sketches*). The tensions and contradictions within Tolstoi's practice and beliefs are revealed in the interplay between spontaneous comradeship and conflict on the one hand, and loneliness, sadness, and death on the other. The Caucasian stories also initiate that Rousseauesque confrontation between "civilized" men (the Russian military) and the natural men (the Caucasian tribespeople) which Tolstoi was to continue in *Kazaki* (*The Cossacks*) and *Khadzhi-Murat* (*Hadji Murat*) and which manifested itself elsewhere in his work in the oppositions between town and country, Petersburg and Moscow, Europe and Russia, the rulers and the people, Church dogma and popular faith. In the distinctly unromantic *Sebastopol* Tolstoi grasps the bitterness of war with pitiless documentary detail: here war is folly, an insane, drab routine of destruction and butchery, and death no gallant moment, but an inexorable process of disintegration through violence and fear.

Between 1856 and 1863 Tolstoi's educational work on his estate at Iasnaia Poliana, his European travels, his courtships and marriage provided the rest of the background for *Voina i mir* (*War and Peace*). This is Tolstoi's extraordinary attempt to capture the wholeness of life in his "comprehensive vision" of the fates of the Rostov and Bolkonskii families and the Russia which they represent, in the period of the Napoleonic Wars. In the fiction, the historical documentary, and the philosophy of history that is *War and Peace* Tolstoi pursues his truth: the truth of real life for Natasha Rostov, the truth of the meaning of life for the "God-seekers" Pierre Bezukhov and Andrei Bolkonskii, the truth of traditional Russia and the truth of historical reality, in which "great men" are found to be merely appearances and history is seen to move under the impetus of an impossibly complex network of causes.

Whereas in *War and Peace* the newly married Tolstoi had seen the constancy of the family as a unifying force in society and the gradual willing surrender of the individual's freedom to that greater whole as the true course, the unfolding of *Anna Karenina* reflects very different experiences. Heroic, historical Russia gives way to the contemporary scene. The family, important though it is as an abstract concept, remains just that: everywhere it is incomplete, displaced, or disrupted. The society of *Anna Karenina* is one of alienated and restless individuals, frustrated by and yet dependent on the conventions of a duplicitous society. The ordeal of the doomed Anna, who forsakes a sterile marriage for the transient happiness of a passionate liaison, is paralleled by the attempts of Levin, Tolstoi's autobiographical representative, to find both happiness and meaning within the bounds of lawful existence. While Anna gradually loses self-mastery, Levin gradually acquires it. Anna's surrender to the flesh, her disruption of her family and the fated course of her life, and, finally, her desire to retain the good opinion of society draw her down to death; while Levin's gradual submission to the natural rhythms of life, his creation of a family, and his measured disregard for the opinion of society raise him to life.

In his remaining years Tolstoi sought certainties with a furious, self-imposed rigour. To do so, he purged himself, rejected his past, sundered his family, and gave himself away to his Tolstoian followers and a demanding humanity. The route towards the demystification of Christianity, its reduction to simple, childlike yet meaningful precepts such as those revealed to Pierre Bezukhov and Levin, is described in *Ispoved'* (*A Confession*). While Tolstoi's devotion to life as the medium of discovery is evinced in his quietly appalling picture of

illness and death in *Smert' Ivana Il'icha* (*The Death of Ivan Ilyich*), his desire for a moral revolution in sexual relations results in works such as "Otets Sergii" ("Father Serge"), "D'iavol" ("The Devil"), and *Kreitserova sonata* (*The Kreutzer Sonata*). Two fictional evocations of moral transformation, the short novel *Khoziain i rabotnik* (*Master and Man*) and the novel *Voskresenie* (*Resurrection*), together with two daunting dramas of good and evil, *Vlast' t'my* (*The Dominion of Darkness*) and *Plody prosveshcheniia* (*The Fruits of Enlightenment*), are also of note in this period, which is otherwise characterized by the extensive essay *Chto takoe iskusstvo?* (*What Is Art?*), an articulate rejection of all art that is not accessible to the people and of positive moral purpose.

Even as Tolstoi devoted himself to the Tolstoian cause, scriptural revision, and the writing of simple fables, he could not exorcize his artistic gift. That gift is fundamentally simple. It is that of the pre-eminent realist, the ability to articulate for us our unformed feelings and perceptions of life with such accuracy and reality that we are held entranced. At the same time, this realism, whether in the fleeting detail of a character's facial expression or the abiding evocation of a natural scene, is never an end in itself for Tolstoi. Harnessed to sweeping narrative command and relentless moral scrutiny, it promotes the natural, positive movement of life entailed in Tolstoi's reflection that "Pitiful are those who do not seek, or who think that they have found."

—Christopher R. Pike

See the essays on *Anna Karenina*, *The Death of Ivan Ilyich*, *The Kreutzer Sonata*, and *War and Peace*.

TOMASI DI LAMPEDUSA, Giuseppe

See LAMPEDUSA, Giuseppe Tomasi di

TORGA, Miguel

Pseudonym for Adolfo Correia da Rocha. **Born:** São Martinho da Anta, Trás-os-Montes, Portugal, 12 August 1907; lived in Brazil, 1920–25. **Education:** Educated at Seminário de Lamego, 1918–19; University of Coimbra, 1925–33, degree in medicine, 1933. **Career:** Doctor, in São Martinho da Anta, Vila Nova de Miranda do Corvo, Leiria, and, since 1940, in Coimbra; travelled frequently in Europe, from 1953; visited Brazil, 1954, and Angola and Mozambique, 1973. Contributor, *Presença*, from 1930; co-founder, with Branquinho da Fonseca, *Sinal*, 1930; adopted pseudonym Miguel Torga, 1936; co-founder, with Albano Nogueira, *Manifesto*, 1936 (five issues). **Awards:** Montaigne prize; Morgado de Mateus prize; Almeida Garrett prize; *Diário de Notícias* prize, 1969; Biennial International Grand prize for poetry (Belgium), 1976; International Association of Directors medal, 1978; Camões prize, 1989; Association of Portuguese Writers Vide Literária prize, 1992; Foreign Correspondents prize, 1992. **Died:** Coimbra, Portugal, 17 January 1995.

PUBLICATIONS

Verse

Ansiedade (as Adolfo Correia da Rocha). 1928.
Rampa. 1930.
Tributo. 1931.
Abismo. 1932.
O outro livro de Job. 1936.
Lamentação. 1943.
Libertação. 1944.
Odes. 1946; revised edition, 1977.
Nihil sibi. 1948.
Cântico do homem. 1950.
Alguns poemas ibéricos. 1952.
Penas do purgatório. 1954.
Orfeu rebelde. 1958; revised edition, 1970.
Câmara ardente. 1962.
Poemas ibéricos. 1965.
Antologia poética. 1981; revised edition, 1985.
Miguel Torga (selection), edited by David Mourão-Ferreira. 1988.

Fiction

Pão Ázimo (stories). 1931.
A criação do mundo: Os dois primeiros dias. 1937; revised edition, 1981; as *The Creation of the World: The First Day and the Second Day*, translated by Ivana Rangel-Carlsen, 1996.
O terceiro dia da criação do mundo. 1938; revised edition, 1970.
O quarto dia da criação do mundo. 1939; revised edition, 1971.
Bichos. 1940; revised edition, 1970; as *Farrusco the Blackbird and Other Stories*, translated by Denis Brass, 1950.
Montanha: Contos. 1941; enlarged edition, as *Contos da Montanha*, 1982.
Rua: Contos. 1942; revised edition, 1967.
O senhor Ventura. 1943.
Novos contos da Montanha. 1944; revised editions, 1975, 1980.
Vindima. 1945; revised edition, 1971.
Pedras Lavradas (stories). 1951; revised edition, 1958.
Open Sesame and Other Stories, translated by Denis Brass. 1960.
The Death Penalty, translated anonymously. 1967.
O quinto dia da criação do mundo. 1974.
O sexto dia da criação do mundo. 1981.
Tales from the Mountain, translated by Ivana Carlsen. 1991.
Tales and More Tales from the Mountain, translated by Ivana Rangel-Carlsen. 1995.

Plays

Teatro: Terra firme; Mar. 1941.
Mar (produced 1946). In *Teatro*, 1941; published separately, 1958, revised edition, 1983.
Terra firme (produced 1947). In *Teatro*, 1941; published separately, 1947, revised edition, 1977.
Sinfonia. 1947.
O Paraíso. 1949.

Other

A terceira voz. 1934.

Diário 1–15. 1941–90; vol. 1 revised, 1967; vol. 5 revised, 1974; vol. 6 revised, 1960; vol. 7 revised, 1961.
Um reino maravilhoso: Trás-os-Montes. 1941.
O Porto. 1944.
Portugal (travel writing). 1950; revised edition, 1967.
Traço de união (travel writing). 1955; revised edition, 1969.
Fogo preso. 1976.
Lavrador de palavras e ideias. 1978.
Trás-os-Montes, illustrated by Georges Dussaud. 1984.
Camões. 1987.

*

Bibliography: *Ensaio bibliográfico de Miguel Torga* by Maria de Lurdes Gouveia, 1979; *Miguel Torga: Ensaio biobibliofotográfico* by José de Melo, 1983.

Critical Studies: *Sá Carneiro, José Régio, Miguel Torga: Três atitudes perante a vida* by Castro Gil, 1949; *Humanist Despair in Miguel Torga* by Eduardo Lourenço, translated from the Portuguese, 1955; "Miguel Torga: A New Portuguese Poet" in *Dublin Review*, 229, 1955, and "The Art and Poetry of Miguel Torga" in *Sillages*, 2, 1973, both by Denis Brass; *Homenagem a Miguel Torga* edited by Frederico de Moura, 1959; *O Drama de Miguel Torga* by Armindo Augusto, 1960; *Cinco personalidades literárias* by Óscar Lopes, 1961; *Casticismo e humanidade em Miguel Torga* by Jacinto do Prado Coelho, 1976; *Sete meditações sobre Miguel Torga* by Fernão de Magalhães Gonçalves, 1977; *Vestígios de Miguel Torga* by Frederico de Moura, 1977; *O Espaço autobiográfico em Miguel Torga* by Clara Crabbé Rocha, 1977; "The Portuguese Revolution Seen Through the Eyes of Three Contemporary Writers" by Alice Clemente, in *Proceedings of the Fourth National Portuguese Conference*, 1979; *Miguel Torga: Poeta Ibérico* by Jesús Herrero, 1979; *Estudio orientado dos Bichos de Miguel Torga* by Lino Moreira da Silva, 1980; "Madwomen, Whores and Torga: Desecrating the Canon?" by Maria Manuel Lisboa, in *Portuguese Studies*, 7, 1991; *Estudos Torguianos* by António Arnaut, 1993; *Aqui, neste lugar e nesta hora: Actas do Primeiro Congresso Internacional sobre Miguel Torga*, 1994.

* * *

Miguel Torga, the *doyen* of Portuguese letters, and Portuguese candidate for the Nobel prize, has shown over almost 60 years a consistency of courage and artistic purpose rarely equalled among his national contemporaries. This has led him into clashes with authorities duing the Salazar period, and he did his stint in prison. His early experience in a seminary, from which he fled to Brazil as a poor peasant boy to eke out an existence as a menial on a coffee estate, has marked his writing. He has rejected his childhood Catholicism but retained the imagery. With the Revolution of 1974 he achieved almost guru status with the new socialist government, and published his political writings under the title *Fogo preso* [Shackled Fire]. His fame rests, however, on a substantial corpus of poetry, and on his several collections of short stories which have been acclaimed as some of the finest in the language. "Torga found himself with a twofold problem. On the one hand he wanted to find real living types, that, while keeping the peninsular fire of their own condition, would have a universal message, and at the same time remain Portuguese. On the other hand he had to create a style that could interpret this message in the drama and dynamism of our own times. And so he took the language to pieces and built it anew, taking in idioms and vocabulary of his own region, charged with dramatic content. And so, his is the short sentence and the significant word. An approach to cine technique'' (introduction by Denis Brass to *Farrusco the Blackbird*).

The key to his work is his intense, even sensual, relationship with his birthplace in Trás-os-Montes. His anguish is that the people there, for whom he wrote in the first place, are, many of them, illiterate, and cannot appreciate his work. Torga is a passionate traveller in his own and other countries; many journeys are recorded in the *Diário*. He recognizes the importance of the sea for the history and the economy of his country, and in his *Poemas ibéricos* [Iberian Poems] he addresses the peninsular explorers who set out to till the sea against an uncertain harvest. The sea is also the title of one of his theatre pieces, *Mar* [Sea], where he treats a favourite theme of the prodigal, the man who is lost in a shipwreck, or who goes overseas abandoning his family, and who may or may not return. Torga sees himself as a kind of smuggler on the frontier between two worlds: Agarez, his birthplace, and the rest. Agarez symbolizes the whole Iberian peninsula. He set out to explore that other world—Europe—but he always returned to "my peninsular night." He is very conscious of his mission as a peninsular writer. His world, he says, finishes only at the Pyrenees, that great barrier that saves his Don Quixote from the temptations of the *Folies Bergères*.

Torga has the "uncontaminated vision" of the countryman and the hunter. Hunting is his recreation, and it informs several of his stories. He is a practising doctor, and his observation has been helped by his experience in the consulting room. He sees a link between the healing mission of the doctor, the priest, and the poet, all intent on saving or praising life, a mission wonderfully portrayed in the short story *O senhor Ventura*. The poet's alternating moods of hope and despair find utterance in the two longer poems *Lamentação* and *Libertação*. His poet's faith and optimism are boldly proclaimed in the title poem of the collection *Orfeu rebelde* [Orpheus in Revolt].

—Denis Brass

TRAKL, Georg

Born: Salzburg, Austria, 3 February 1887. **Education:** Educated at Catholic school, Salzburg; Gymnasium, Salzburg, 1899–1905; apprenticeship at pharmacy in Salzburg, 1905–08; University of Salzburg, 1908–10, graduated as pharmacist. **Military Service:** Military service in Vienna, 1910–11, 1914. **Career:** Pharmacist in Salzburg, 1911, and several short stints as military pharmacist and other military jobs; regular contributor to *Der Brenner*, 1912–14. **Died:** 7 November 1914.

PUBLICATIONS

Collections

Gesamtausgabe, edited by Wolfgang Schneditz. 3 vols., 1938–49.
Dichtungen und Briefe, edited by Walther Killy and Hans Szklenar. 2 vols., 1969.

Werke, Entwürfe, Briefe, edited by Hans-Georg Kemper and Frank Rainer Max. 1984.
Die Dichtungen, edited by Walther Killy. 1989.
Dark Seasons: A Selection of Poems, translated by Robin Skelton. 1994.
Poems and Prose, translated with introduction by Alexander Stillmark. 2001.

Verse

Gedichte. 1913.
Sebastian im Traum. 1915.
Die Dichtungen, edited by Karl Röck. 1918.
Aus goldenem Kelch: Die Jugenddichtungen, edited by Erhard Buschbeck. 1939.
Decline: Twelve Poems, translated by Michael Hamburger. 1952.
Twenty Poems (bilingual edition), translated by James Wright and Robert Bly. 1961.
Selected Poems, edited by Christopher Middleton, translated by Robert Grenier and others. 1968.
Poems, translated by Lucia Getsi. 1973.
Georg Trakl in the Red Forest, translated by Johannes Kaebitzsch. 1973.
Autumn Sonata: Selected Poems, translated by Daniel Simko. 1989.

Other

Erinnerungen an Trakl: Zeugnisse und Briefe, edited by Ludwig von Ficker. 1926; 3rd edition, 1966.
Georg Trakl: A Profile (poetry and letters), edited by Frank Graziano. 1984.

*

Bibliography: *Trakl-Bibliographie*, 1956, and *Neue Trakl Bibliographie*, 1983, both by W. Ritzer.

Critical Studies: *Manshape That Shone: An Interpretation of Trakl* by Timothy J. Casey, 1964; *Trakl* by Herbert Lindenberger, 1971; *Dimensions of Style and Meaning in the Language of Trakl and Rilke* by Joseph P. Colbert, 1974; *Trakl* by Maire Jaanus Kurrik, 1974; *The Poet's Madness: A Reading of Georg Trakl* by Francis Michael Sharp, 1981; *Georg Trakl's Poetry: Toward a Union of Opposites* by Richard Detsch, 1983; *Internationales Georg Trakl Symposium* edited by Joseph P. Strelka, 1984; *The Blossoming Thorn: Georg Trakl's Poetry of Atonement* by Erasmo Leiva-Merikakis, 1987; *The Dark Flutes of Fall: Critical Essays on Georg Trakl*, 1991, and *The Mirror and the Word: Modernism, Literary Theory and Georg Trakl*, 1993, both by Eric B. Williams; *Postcards from Trakl* by John Yau and Bill Jensen, 1994; *Webern and the Lyric Impulse: Songs and Fragments on Poems of Georg Trakl* by Anne C. Shreffler, 1994.

* * *

The poet Georg Trakl was a dedicated perfectionist for whom the craft of poetry meant striving for absolute truth of expression, purity, and precision of language. His relatively small and cohesive *oeuvre* is remarkable for the extant number of variant versions of the poems. Though Rimbaud, Verlaine, and Baudelaire variously influenced his development and he showed a partial affinity with German Expressionism, Trakl early established a pronounced personal style. This is distinguished by great linguistic concentration, recurrent patterns in diction and imagery, individual use of colour symbolism, and a fine lyricism, which set him apart as a distinctive new voice in poetry. Like Hölderlin, to whom he owes something of his elliptical conciseness and hymnic intensity, Trakl was essentially a visionary poet in whom the inner vision, the image-making faculty, takes precedence over the mimetic function of creative imagination.

His early poetry is written in rhyming and mellifluous verse which still owes much to *fin de siècle* influence. In one sense, it represents a development out of decadence in its rejection of the classical ideal of beauty, its preoccupation with disease, corruption, death, and the aesthetic of the ugly. (Trakl wrote in 1910: "one does well to resist perfect beauty.") In another, it wholly overcomes art for art's sake and fashions necessary connections between the aesthetic and the moral, an existential aspect which owes much to the idealistic influence of Dostoevskii and Tolstoi. The persistent religious registers of his poetic language also owe something to this moral orientation as well as to a highly individualized use of traditional Biblical and devotional vocabulary.

In Trakl the melancholy and elegiac moods predominate, and his poetry heralds the calamity of World War I. The principal subject of this poetry is a darkened world of pain, death, and decay in which man is the passive suffering victim. The poet's self is repeatedly projected into mythical poetic personas (Elis, Sebastian, Helian, Kaspar Hauser) who represent pure vessels of violated humanity, yet not without an ethereal strength and some redemptive significance. In Trakl's treatment, established religious imagery (for example in "De Profundis," "Ein Winterabend," "Abendländisches Lied") is fragmented, inverted or distorted and projected into startling combinations which produce new resonances and meanings.

The privacy of Trakl's poetic language derives from the solitariness of his self-centred world which is nonetheless registered in deeply sensuous terms. His poems achieve their vividness because the urgency of meaning, however complex or suggestive, unerringly finds its objective correlative in glowing images. Though his poetic language appears, on early acquaintance, to consist of autonomous meanings and to have a hermetic quality, the repeated verbal patterns, poetic ciphers, symbols, and distinctive tonalities combine into a coherent vision of life. His supreme economy of verbal means is largely a result of the conscious aim to achieve a high degree of objectivism in composition, to evolve a mode of lyrical utterance which depends upon a wholly impersonal form. The effect produced, however, is that of a personal tone of great intimacy. A sparseness and simplicity of diction result which render the full stress of subjective experience. Strong incantatory elements and energetic rhythms constantly assert themselves in Trakl's language and these serve both to counterbalance and to heighten the tragic tone.

A letter to a friend (26 June 1913) sums up the sense of guilt, self-loathing, and despair which filled so much of the poet's life:

Too little love, too little justice and mercy, and always too little love; all too much hardness, arrogance, and all manner of criminality—that's me. I'm certain I only avoid evil out of weakness and cowardice and thereby only abuse my wickedness. I long for the day when the soul shall cease to wish or be able to live in this wretched body polluted with melancholy, when it shall quit this laughable form made of muck and rottenness, which is all too faithful a reflection of a godless, cursed century.

Little more than a year later Trakl found release from this dark world through an overdose of cocaine.

—Alexander Stillmark

See the essay on "Grodek."

TRIFONOV, Iurii (Valentinovich)

Born: Moscow, Russia, 28 August 1925. Grew up with his grandmother after the arrest of his father, 1937, and the exile of his mother. **Education:** Educated at school in Tashkent (where he had been evacuated), 1941–42; studied creative writing at the Gor'kii Literary Institute, 1944–49. **Career:** Rejected for the armed services on account of poor eyesight, and worked in an aircraft factory, 1942–44. Travelled to Turkmenistan in 1953, and several times 1956–63; sports correspondent and commentator, at Olympic Games and other events in Hungary, Spain, Italy, and Austria, during the 1950s and early 1960s. **Awards:** Stalin prize, 1950; Badge of Honour, 1975. **Member:** RSFSR Writers' Union, 1965–70. **Died:** 28 March 1981.

PUBLICATIONS

Collection

Sobranie sochinenii [Collected Works], edited by S.A. Baruzdin. 4 vols., 1985–87.

Fiction

Studenty. 1951; as *Students*, translated by I. Litvinova and Margaret Wettlin, 1953.
Pod solntsem [Under the Sun] (stories). 1959.
V kontse sezona [At the End of the Season]. 1961.
Utolenie zhazhdy. 1963; as *Thirst Acquenched*, translated by Ralph Parker, in *Soviet Literature*, 1, 1964.
Kostry i dozhd' [The Campfire and Rain]. 1964.
Otblesk kostra [The Gleam of a Campfire]. 1966.
Kepka s bol'shim kozyr'kom [A Cap with a Big Peak]. 1969.
Rasskazy i povesti [Stories and Novels]. 1971.
Dolgoe proshchanie. 1973; translated as *The Long Goodbye*, in *The Long Goodbye: Three Novellas*, 1978.
Neterpenie. 1973; revised edition, 1974; as *The Impatient Ones*, translated by Robert Daglish, 1978.
Drugaia zhizn'. 1976; as *Another Life*, with *The House on the Embankment*, translated by Michael Glenny, 1983, and issued separately, 1985.
Obmen, in *Povesti*. 1978; as *Obmen/Exchange*, edited by Robert Russell, 1990; translated as *The Exchange*, in *The Long Goodbye: Three Novellas*, 1978.
Dom na naberezhnoi, in *Povesti*. 1978; translated as *The House on the Embankment*, with *Another Life*, translated by Michael Glenny, 1983, and issued separately, 1985.
Predvaritel'nye itogi, in *Povesti*. 1978; translated as *Taking Stock*, in *The Long Goodbye: Three Novellas*, 1978.
Povesti [Stories] (includes *Obmen; Predvaritel'nye itogi; Dolgoe proshchanie; Drugania zhizn'; Dom na naberezhnoi*). 1978.

The Long Goodbye: Three Novellas (includes *The Exchange; The Long Goodbye; Taking Stock*), translated by Helen P. Burlingame and Ellendea Proffer. 1978.

Starik. 1979; as *The Old Man*, translated by Jacqueline Edwards and Mitchell Schneider, 1984.

The House on the Embankment and Another Life, translated by Michael Glenny. 1983.

Vechnye temy [Eternal Themes]. 1984.

Moskovskie povesti [Moscow Stories]. 1988.

Vremia i mesto [Time and Place]. 1988.

Ischeznovenie (includes *Otblesk kostra; Starik; Ischeznovenie*). 1988; *Ischeznovenie* as *Disappearance*, translated by David Lowe, 1991.

Plays

Zalog uspekha [Promise of Success] (produced 1953).

Utolenie zhazhady [Thirst Satisfied], with A. Morov (produced 1964).

Obmen, from his own story (produced 1977). 1977; as *The Exchange*, translated by Michael Frayn, 1990.

Dom na naberezhnoi [House on the Embankment], from his own story (produced 1980). In *Teatr pisatelia*, 1982.

Beskonechnye igry, in *Teatr pisatelia*. 1982; edited by A.P. Shitov, 1989.

Teatr pisatelia: Tri povesti dlia teatra [Theatre of a Writer: Three Stories for the Theatre] (includes *Beskonechnye igry; Obmen; Dom na naberezhnoi*). 1982.

Screenplays: *Khokkeisty* [Hockey Players], 1964.

Other

Fakely nad Flaminio: Rasskazy i ocherki (stories and essays). 1965.

Igry v sumerkakh [Games in the Twilight] (stories and essays). 1970.

Prodolzhitel'nye uroki: Ocherki [Continuous Lessons] (essays). 1975.

Izbrannye proizvedeniia [Selected Works], edited by A. Turkov. 2 vols., 1978.

Kak slovo nashe otzovetsia. . . [How Our Word is Sown. . .]. 1985.

Iadro pravdy [The Kernel of Truth] (articles, interviews, essays). 1987.

Beskonechnye igry, o sporte, o vremeni, o sebe (articles and sports commentary). 1989.

*

Critical Studies: "Iurii Trifonov and the Ethics of Contemporary Soviet City Life," in *Canadian Slavonic Papers*, 19(3), 1977, "The New Dimensions of Time and Place in Iurii Trifonov's Prose of the 1980s," in *Canadian Slavonic Papers*, 27(2), 1985, and *Soviet Literature in the 1970s: Artistic Diversity and Ideological Conformity*, n.d., all by N.N. Schneidman; *The Soviet Novel: History as Ritual* by Katerina Clark, 1981; "Jurij Trifonov's *House on the Embankment:* Narration and Meaning" by Sigrid McLaughlin, in *Slavic and East European Journal*, 26(4), 1982; "Trifonov: The Historian as Artist" by Edward Brown, in *Soviet Society and Culture: Essays in Honor of Vera S. Dunham* edited by Terry L. Thompson and Richard Sheldon, 1988; "Time, History, and the Individual in the Works of Yury Trifonov," in *Modern Language Quarterly*, 83(2), 1988, and

Iurii Trifonov, 1992, both by David C. Gillespie; *Trifonov and the Drama of the Russian Intelligentsia*, by Carolina Maëgd-Soep, 1990; *Yuri Trifonov's The Moscow Cycle* by Colin Partridge, 1990; *Yury Trifonov: A Critical Study* by Nina Kolesnikoff, 1991; *Invented Truth: Soviet Reality and the Literary Imagination of Iurii Trifonov* by Josephine Woll, 1991; *Iurii Trifonov: Unity through Time* by David Gillespie, 1992.

*   *   *

During the final decade of his life Iurii Trifonov was widely regarded as one of Russia's finest prose writers. He emerged from relative obscurity through a series of stories and novellas from the late 1960s and early 1970s, in which he depicted a spiritual malaise within the urban middle and upper classes that had grown up in the shadow of Stalinism. Particularly important in this regard is his "Moscow cycle," which originally consisted of the novellas *Obmen* (*The Exchange*), *Predvaritel'nye itogi* (*Taking Stock*), and *Dolgoe proshchanie* (*The Long Goodbye*), but which most would extend to include the majority of his subsequent novels as well. While the three novellas are not overtly political, they offer an implicit critique of Soviet society by showing an entire generation of people who no longer believe, or are even interested, in revolutionary ideals. Their lives are totally occupied with efforts to achieve success, but they have discovered that neither acclaim from their peers nor material possessions provide satisfaction.

In his novels Trifonov generally combined portrayals of society with investigations into the past events that formed his characters. *Starik* (*The Old Man*) veers between a contemporary effort to obtain a dacha and the memories of an incident during the Civil War. A questionable action in the past haunts the present and throws into relief the materialism that has come to replace revolutionary idealism; by suggesting that this idealism may have been tainted in the first place, Trifonov implicitly blames the past for the ills of the present. The work is based on an event described in a novel written at the beginning of his mature period, *Otblesk kostra* [The Gleam of a Campfire], an account of Trifonov's father, Valentin, and his role in the revolution and its aftermath. Although inspired by actual documents and memoirs, *Otblesk kostra* is less a conventional biography than an attempt on the part of the narrator to understand several key moments of his father's life. Trifonov's interest in the biography of revolutionaries can also be seen in *Neterpenie* (*The Impatient Ones*), a portrayal of Andrei Zheliabov, who, as a member of the People's Will party, conspired to assassinate Aleksandr II in 1881. Although a historical novel, the work offers parallels with Trifonov's own day and it too contains what some have seen as a delicate undercutting of certain Bolshevik ideals—a task carried out more openly in the later novel *The Old Man*.

Trifonov's writing did not so much broaden as deepen. As with *The Old Man,* he would return to situations and topics that he had treated earlier, trying to gain a deeper understanding of his characters, of recent Russian history, and ultimately both of his father, a revolutionary hero who perished in Stalin's purges, and of himself. Thus in *Dom na naberezhnoi* (*The House on the Embankment*) he in part retells the story of *Studenty* (*Students*), his first novel, which dealt with academic life during the post-war years. *Students* was awarded a Stalin prize and brought Trifonov early renown, but in the later work he judges his characters differently and presents the moral dilemmas of those involved far more subtly. *Vremia i mesto* [Time and Place], like *The House on the Embankment,* moves between 1937 and the time of Trifonov's actual work on the novel. In *Vremia i mesto,* though, the main figure, who is in turn writing an autobiographical novel, is clearly based on Trifonov himself—the self examination takes place on several levels. And in his final work, *Ischeznovenie (Disappearance),* Trifonov presents a fictionalized account of his father's arrest and the effect that it had on him as a child.

Trifonov's talents are seen first of all in the subtleties of his narrative technique, which distinguishes each of the works in his Moscow cycle. Thus *Drugaia zhizn' (Another Life)* is told from the viewpoint of Ol'ga, the widow of a historian who was basically a failure in life and died in his early forties. Typically for Trifonov, Ol'ga's thoughts are presented in almost a stream-of-consciousness manner, with pieces of at first disconnected and seemingly random information being placed before the reader. Only as the story unfolds do the links emerge, and then it becomes clear that the author's sympathies are more with the deceased husband, who, while he was not a success within a society where intrigue and moral compromise are the norm, possessed a passion for the truth and an appreciation for the manner in which the past affects the present. In most of his later novels Trifonov employs two or more perspectives from which the action is viewed; thus *The House on the Embankment* switches among a first-person narrator, a third-person narration about a figure with whom the narrator shared childhood experiences, and then an authorial voice.

Trifonov's narrative technique is intimately related to his thematic concerns. He wants to show that knowledge of the past is an elusive thing, that one person's memory of an event may be genuinely quite different from that of another, and construction of the "truth" may be a difficult or impossible task. At the very least, no one individual's reconstruction of events can embody their full complexity. Yet the works, taken as a whole, do not shrink from moral concerns. Those people unwilling to take a stand, who either lack values or do not defend the ones they possess, are ultimately condemned. Thus an artist in *Another Life,* genuinely talented in his youth and personally acquainted with famous Western artists, had come back to the USSR and become "re-educated." From then on he was to paint almost nothing of value. In *Vremia i mesto* an author who rewrote a major novel to make it more acceptable (and who appears to have acted less than honourably when his fellows were arrested during the purges) is eventually driven to suicide (not unlike the real-life writer Aleksandr Fadeev).

Trifonov's chief concerns are perhaps summed up by the title of the last book he completed: time and place. Many of his works leap back and forth between eras, showing how past and present are inevitably intertwined, how memory comes to serve as conscience. The characters are linked to place in an equally complex way: they are often characterized by the manner in which they relate to dachas, apartments, and the move from one setting to another. Trifonov is a master not just of showing the large-scale physical settings of his characters, but of imparting striking significance to the smallest details of their everyday lives.

Most importantly, though, Trifonov served as a spokesman for his generation. During the Brezhnev years, when most writers were too timid to examine the Stalinist legacy, he pushed back the limits of what was permissible within Soviet literature. But he did not just treat once forbidden topics; his works are notable most of all for their honesty, an honesty that does not allow for easy judgements. People do not necessarily fit into easy categories: apparent victims could be the victimizers if given the chance, and villains may turn out to be weak once the situation changes. Those whose outlooks were formed during the revolution find themselves ill-equipped for life afterwards, while their descendants, those of Trifonov's age, have compromised all too often. Perhaps his greatest achievement, then, was to chronicle the moral void sensed by many of his contemporaries who no longer believed in the exemplars of the past and could find no heroes in the present.

—Barry P. Scherr

TROYES, Chrétien de

See CHRÉTIEN DE TROYES

TSUSHIMA Yuko

Also known by the pen names Yuzuko Aki (1967) and Yuko Ashi (1968). **Born:** Satoko Tsushima in Mitaka, Tokyo, 30 March 1947; daughter of writer Osamu Dazai (Shuji Tsushima). **Education:** Attended Oiwake Primary School of Tokyo Gakugei University, 1953–59; Shirayuri Gakuen, 1959–65 (Junior High School, 1959–62; High School, 1962–65); Shirayuri Women's College, 1965–69; B.A. in English literature; attended Master's program in Graduate School of Meiji University, 1969–70. **Family:** Married Yoneyama in 1970 (divorced 1976); one daughter, one son. **Career:** Member and contributor to *Bungei Shuto,* 1966–69; worked for Hoso Bangumi Center (Center for Broadcast Programs) and quit for marriage, 1970; frequent contributor to *Bungei, Mita Bungaku, Gunzo, Bungakukai,* and other major literary journals, from 1969; published collected stories and original works as books, from 1971; lecturer of modern Japanese literature at Institut National des Langues et Civilisations Orientales, Université de Paris, 1991–92. **Awards:** Tamura Toshiko award for literature, 1976; Izumi Kyoka award for fantastic literature, 1977; Joryu Bungaku award for women's literature, 1978; Noma literature award for young writers, 1979; Kawabata Yasunari award for literature, 1983; Yomiuri literature award, 1987; Tanizaki Jun'ichiro award for literature, Noma literature award, 1998.

PUBLICATIONS

Collections

Shanikusai (includes *Rekuiemu, Aozora,* and *Shanikusai*). 1971.
Doji no kage (includes *Kitsune o haramu, Yurikago,* and *Doji no kage*). 1973.
Mugura no haha (includes *Mugura no haha* and five other stories). 1975.
Kusa no fushido (includes *Kusa no fushido, Hana wo maku,* and *Onibi*). 1977.
Yorokobi no shima (includes *Shateki, Kusamura,* and eight other stories). 1978.
Hikari no ryobun (includes *Hikari no ryobun* and 11 other stories). 1979.
Suifu (includes *Suifu, Tatokai,* and three other stories). 1982.

Danmari ichi (includes *Numa, Danmari ichi*, and nine other stories). 1984.

Oma monogatari [Stories of Encounters with the Uncanny] (includes *Fusehime, Kikumushi*, and three other stories). 1984.

Mahiru e (includes *Mahiru e* and two other stories). 1988.

Yume no kiroku (includes *Hoyo, Hikari kagayaku itten o*, and eight other stories). 1988.

Kusamura—jisen tanpenshu (includes *Kusamura, Kuchu buranko*, and nine other stories). 1989.

Fiction

"Rekuiem—inu to otona no tameni" [Requiem—for Dogs and Adults]. 1969.

"Shanikusai" [Carnival]. 1971.

"Yurikago" [The Cradle]. 1971.

"Kitsune o haramu" [Becoming Pregnant with a Fox]. 1972.

"Doji no kage" [The Shadow of a Child]. 1973.

"Ikimono no atsumaru ie" [The House Where Living Things Gather]. 1973.

"Yukuefumei." 1973; as "Missing," translated by Geraldine Harcourt in *The Shooting Gallery*, 1988.

"Mugura no haha" [Mother in the Bush]. 1974.

"Hatsujoki." 1974; as "A Sensitive Season," translated by Geraldine Harcourt in *The Shooting Gallery*, 1988.

"Shateki." 1975; as "The Shooting Gallery," translated by Geraldine Harcourt in *The Shooting Gallery*, 1988.

"Kusamura." 1976; as "Clearing the Thickets," translated by Geraldine Harcourt in *The Shooting Gallery*, 1988.

"Kusa no fushido." 1977; as "A Bed of Grass," translated by Yukiko Tanaka and Elizabeth Hanson in *This Kind of Woman: Ten Stories by Japanese Women Writers, 1960–76*, 1982.

"Hana o maku." 1977; as "To Scatter Flower Petals," translated by Lora Sharnoff in *Japan Quarterly* 27(2), 1980; also as "Scattering Flowers," translated by Phyllis I. Lyons in *Longman Anthology of World Literature by Women 1875–1975*, 1989.

"Yorokobi no shima." 1977; as "Island of Joy," translated by Lora Sharnoff in *Japan Quarterly* 27(2), 1980.

"Minamikaze." 1978; as "South Wind" translated by Geraldine Harcourt in *The Shooting Gallery*, 1988.

Choji. 1978; as *Child of Fortune*, translated by Geraldine Harcourt, 1983.

Hikari no ryobun [The Domain of Light]. 1978.

Moeru kaze [Burning Wind]. 1980.

Yama o hashiru onna. 1980; as *Woman Running in the Mountains*, translated by Geraldine Harcourt, 1991.

"Numa." 1981; as "The Marsh," translated by Yukiko Tanaka in *Unmapped Territories: New Women's Fiction from Japan*, 1991.

Suifu [Water City]. 1982.

"Danmari ichi." 1982; as "Silent Traders," translated by Geraldine Harcourt in *The Shooting Gallery*, 1988.

Hi no kawa no hotori de [At the River of Fire]. 1983.

"Kikumushi." 1983; as "Chrysanthemum Beetle," translated by Geraldine Harcourt in *The Shooting Gallery*, 1988.

"Hoyo." 1985; as "An Embrace," translated by Geraldine Harcourt in *The Shooting Gallery*, 1988.

Yoru no hikari ni owarete [Chased by the Light of the Night]. 1986.

Hikari kagayaku itten o [The Shining Point of Light]. 1988.

Kaze yo, sora kakeru kaze yo [Wind, O Wind Running in the Sky]. 1995.

Hi no yama—yamazaruki [The Mountain of Fire—The Record of Mountain Monkeys]. 2 vols., 1996–97.

Warai ookami [The Laughing Wolf]. 2000.

Other

Tomei kukan ga mieru toki [When One Sees Transparent Space] (essays). 1977.

Yoru no ti pati [A Tea Party at Night] (essays). 1979.

Tsushima Yuko shi ni kiku [An Interview with Yuko Tsushima], in *Subaru*. December 1979.

Watashi no jikan [My Time] (essays). 1982.

Taidan: Sozoryoku to joseiteki na mono (dialogues with Kenzaburo Oe, on the imaginary and the feminine). 1985.

Hon no naka no shojo tachi [Girls in Books] (essays). 1989.

Kyaria to kazoku (dialogues with Margaret Drabble, on career and family). Iwanami Booklet series, vol. 163, 1990.

Ise monogatari, Tosa nikki—koten no tabi 2 (guide to classic Japanese literature). 1990; revised as *Ise monogatari, Tosa nikki o tabi shiyo—koten o aruku 2*, 1998.

Izumi Kyoka (guide to Kyoka Izumi). Gunzo nihon no sakka series, vol. 5, 1992.

Ani no yume, watashi no inochi [The Dream of Brother, My Life] (essays). 1999.

Translator, with Nobuko Fukui, *Ai no jidai* (*Kaerestesorg*), by Kristen Bjornkjaer. 1990.

Editor & Translator, *Tombent, tombent, les gouttes d'argent—Chants du peuple ainou* (Collection of the Ainu epic, translated in cooperation with graduate students of Université de Paris). 1995.

Editor, *Jerashi: nihon no meizuihitsu* [Jealousy: Best Japanese Essays]. 1997.

*

Critical Studies: "Onna ni tsuite" [About Women] by Kojin Karatani, in *Han-bungakuron* [Anti-Literary Theory], 1979; "Tsushima Yuko ron" [On Tsushima Yuko] by Yoichi Komori, in *Kokubungaku kaishaku to kansho* 33(10), 1988; "The Politics of Miscegenation: The Discourse of Fantasy in 'Fusehime' by Yuko Tsushima" by Livia Monnet, in *Japan Forum* 5(1), 1993; "*Connaissance delicieuse*, or the Science of Jealousy: Tsushima Yuko's 'The Chrysanthemum Beetle'" by Livia Monnet, in *The Woman's Hand: Gender and Theory in Japanese Women's Writing*, edited by Paul Gordon Schalow & Janet A. Walker, 1996; "When Seeing Is Not Believing: Tsushima Yuko's 'Hikarikagayaku itten o'" by Van C. Gessel, in *Currents in Japanese Culture*, edited by Amy Vladeck Heinrich, 1997; "The Reality of Pregnancy and Motherhood for Women: Tsushima Yuko's *Choji* and Margaret Drabble's *The Millstone*" by Yoshiko Enomoto, in *Comparative Literature Studies* 35(2), 1998.

*   *   *

Tsushima Yuko has been a leading force in women's literature in Japan since the end of World War II. Surrounded by the literary tradition of modern Japan, which was largely dominated by male authors, Japanese women writers have ardently sought their voices to pursue their own livelihoods and writing styles against social expectations and literary standards. After the rise of women's fiction that dramatized the social and cultural changes of women's status in the

1920s and 1930s, represented by Kanoko Okamoto, Fumiko Hayashi, and Hirabayashi Taiko, women's writing was somewhat dormant until the emergence of the younger generation in the 1960s led by writers such as Taeko Kono, Minako Oba, and Yuko Tsushima. Their writings unhesitatingly express female experience of sexuality, desire, and motherhood, reframing literature as a site of protest or as a point of departure for changes in both society and literary tradition.

Tsushima's career as a writer began at age 20, when she started regularly sending manuscripts of her short stories to literary journals. Her sophisticated writing style and subtlety in observation of people's lives soon caught special attention from major literary journals as well. Although she has published some novels, she is best known for her autobiographical slice-of-life short stories like "Kusa no fushido" ("A Bed of Grass") and "Danmari ichi" ("Silent Traders"). She has also shown her comprehensive knowledge of classic Japanese literature and folktales by intertwining mythic elements with contemporary settings in her writing. While her stories show strong influences from Japanese literary tradition, especially of women writers like Kanoko Okamoto, she has employed a number of ideas and images from Western writers of fantastic fiction as well, such as Edgar Allan Poe and William Faulkner, in addition to Dr. Faustus and Walküre (Valkyrie), from whom she obtained inspirations to begin writing at the earliest stage of her career.

Born as the second daughter of Osamu Dazai, one of the most acclaimed writers of modern Japanese literature, she grew up with the curse of being "a child of the genius," compounded with the tragic family issues of her father's suicide (1948) and her brother's death (1960). Tsushima's childhood memories of her brother become the central images in many of her works, in which he appears as an innocent "chieokure" (retarded) figure who sometimes develops incestuous relationship with his protective sister (the author's persona). Her brother's character sometimes overlaps with the image of her physically disabled son who died very young. Throughout her writing career, Tsushima's biographical elements are closely reflected in the recurrent theme of the family. She challenges the existing ideas of family by sketching lives at the margin of society, such as unwed pregnant women, ambivalent mother-daughter relationships, children with physical/mental disabilities, and ethnic minorities. The various forms of family relationships explored in Tsushima's works bluntly reject modern Japan's patriarchal models of the biological family.

Tsushima's autobiographical writing is often discussed in relation to the tradition of shishosetsu or watakushi shosetsu (known as I-Novel in English), which is the autobiographical novel that established the nucleus of the 20th-century Japanese literature. Unlike the male-dominant shishosetsu that emphasized such literary factors as realism and truthful confession of personal matters, however, Tsushima's writings present "reality and dream as attributes of the one and the same dimension" ("An Interview with Tsushima Yuko," 1979). Her writings also blur various borders of our conceptual categories such as space and time, by juxtaposing the past and the present (e.g., "I" as a daughter and as a mother), or by inverting the public and the private (e.g., inside and outside the family). One of the most important effects of these techniques is that her stories do not provide the reader any definitive meaning, message, or conclusion after reading. Her stories rather leave the reader with the impression that the author "neither engages in, nor refuses, but hangs 'meanings' in air" (Kojin Karatani, "Onna ni tsuite," 1979). This "hanging of meaning" may indicate the author's wish to write without limiting words to a certain interpretation, just as her independent female characters represent her wish to live life free from the boundaries of convention.

Tsushima is still considered as one of Japan's most important writers. She is productively writing fiction and essays, as well as actively participating in literary events, symposiums, and political movements such as bridging projects for Korean, Chinese, and Japanese women's literature. However, after more contemporary women writers, such as Banana Yoshimoto and Amy Yamada, opened space for casual pop narrative in the 1990s, Tsushima's writings may appear too literary or too serious to today's readers. As women's lives and social obligations quickly change in contemporary Japan, as represented by the increasing rates of unwed mothers and divorces, Tsushima's concerns are also shifting toward a more diachronic perspective of different generations of women and of Japan's history since its defeat in 1945. It is important to remember that Tsushima's fiction does not only mirror the norms and limits of Japanese society, but also tries to find new narratives that can produce social change. For Tsushima, imagination and fantasy are the driving forces to revisit the ideas of reality and history, and this is one of the reasons that makes her a representative writer of contemporary Japanese literature.

—Kumiko Sato

TSVETAEVA, Marina (Ivanovna)

Born: Moscow, Russia, 26 September 1892. **Education:** Educated at schools in Switzerland and Germany, and at the Sorbonne, Paris. **Family:** Married Sergei Efron in 1912 (executed 1939); two daughters and one son. **Career:** Emigrated in 1922 to Berlin, then Prague and Paris; returned to the USSR in 1939, but ostracized and unable to publish. **Died:** (suicide) 31 August 1941.

PUBLICATIONS

Collections

Izbrannoe [Selection], edited by V. Orlov. 1961; revised edition, as *Izbrannye proizvedeniia* [Selected Works], 1965.
Izbrannaia proza v dvukh tomakh 1917–1937 [Selected Prose], edited by Alexander Sumerkin. 1979.
Stikhotvoreniia i poemy [Poetry and Narrative Verse], edited by A.A. Saakiants. 1980.
Stikhotvoreniia i poemy v piati tomakh [Poetry and Narrative Verse], edited by Alexander Sumerkin and Viktoria Schweitzer. 5 vols., 1980–93.
Sochineniia [Works], edited by A.A. Saakiants. 2 vols., 1980.
Teatr [Theatre], edited by A.A. Saakiants. 1988.
Sobranie sochinenii, poem i dramaticheskikh proizvedenii [Collected Works, Poetry, and Dramatic Works], edited by A.A. Saakiants. 3 vols., 1990.
Captive Spirit: Selected Prose, edited and translated by J. Marin King. 1994.
Poem of the End: Selected Narrative and Lyrical Poetry, translated by Nina Kossman with Andrew Newcomb. 1998.

Verse

Vechernii al'bom [Evening Album]. 1910.
Volshebnyi fonar' [Magic Lantern]. 1912.
Iz dvukh knig [From Two Books] (selections). 1913.
Versty [Mileposts]. 1921.
Versty, Vypusk I [Mileposts: Book One]. 1922.
Razluka [Separation]. 1922.
Stikhi k Bloku [Poems to Blok]. 1922.
Tsar'-devitsa [Tsar-Maiden]. 1922.
Remeslo [Craft]. 1923.
Psikheia [Psyche]. 1923.
Molodets [The Swain]. 1924.
Posle Rossii. 1928; as *After Russia* (bilingual edition), translated by Michael M. Nayden, 1992.
Lebedinyi stan. 1957; as *The Demesne of the Swan,* edited and translated by Robin Kemball, 1980.
Prosto serdtse [Simply the Heart]. 1967.
Stikhotvoreniia i poemy [Poetry and Narrative Verse]. 1979.
Selected Poems, translated by Elaine Feinstein. 1971; revised editions, 1981, 1986.
Stikhotvoreniia [Poetry]. 1983.
Three Russian Women Poets (with Anna Akhmatova and Bella Akhmadulina), edited and translated by Mary Maddock. 1983.
Stikhotvoreniia. Izbrannaia lirika 1908–1939 [Poetry. Selected Lyrics]. 1986.
Poemy; Stikhotvoreniia [Narrative Verse; Poetry]. 1987.
Selected Poems, translated by David McDuff. 1987.
Stikhi i poemy [Poems and Narrative Verse]. 1988.
In the Inmost Hour of the Soul, translated by Nina Kossman. 1989.
V polemike s vekom [Polemics with the Century]. 1991.
Sivilla [Seville]. 1991.
The Ratcatcher: A Lyrical Satire, translated by Angela Livingstone. 1999.

Plays

Konets Kazanovy [Casanova's End]. 1922.

Other

Proza [Prose]. 1953.
Proza [Prose]. 1969.
Pis'ma k Anne Teskovoi [Letters to Anna Teskovoi], edited by V. Morkovin. 1969.
Pis'ma k raznym litsam [Letters to Various Persons]. 1969.
Neizdannye pis'ma [Unpublished Letters], edited by Gleb and Nikita Struve. 1972.
Marina Cvetaeva, Boris Pasternak, Rainer Maria Rilke: Lettere 1926, edited by Yevgeny Pasternak, Yelena Pasternak, and Konstantin M. Azadovsky. 1980; as *Letters, Summer 1926: Correspondence Between Boris Pasternak, Marina Tsvetaeva and Rainer Maria Rilke,* translated by Margaret Wettlin and Walter Arndt, 1985.
'Poklonis' Moskvy. . . [Worship Moscow. . .] (poetry, prose, diaries, letters). 1989.
Prosa, edited by A.A. Saakiants. 1989.
Avtobiograficheskaia proza [Autobiographical Prose]. 1991.
Gde otstypaetsia liubov' . . . [Where Love Renounces. . .]. 1991.
Poemy. Dramaticheskie proizvedeniia [Narrative Verse. Dramatic Works]. 1992.

Vospominaniia [Reminiscences], edited by L.A. Mnukhin and L.M. Turchinskii. 1992.
Art in the Light of Conscience: Eight Essays on Poetry, translated by Angela Livingston. 1992.
Earthly Signs, translated and edited by Jamey Gambrell. 2002.

*

Bibliography: *Bibliographie des oeuvres de Tsvetayeva* by Tatiana Gladkova and Lev Mnukhin, 1982.

Critical Studies: *Cvetaeva: Her Life and Art,* 1966, and *Tsvetaeva: The Woman, Her World and Her Poetry,* 1985, both by Simon Karlinsky; *Cvetaeva: Studien und Materialien* edited by Horst Lampl and Aage A. Hansen-Löve, 1981; ''A Poet and Prose'' and ''Footnote to a Poem,'' both by Iosif Brodskii, in *Less than One,* 1986; *The Life of Marina Tsvetayeva* by Elaine Feinstein, 1987; *Terrible Perfection: Women and Russian Literature* by Barbara Heldt, 1987; *A Life through Poetry: Marina Tsvetaeva's Lyric Diary* by Jane A. Taubman, 1989; *Marina Tsvetayeva: A Critical Biography* by Maria Razumovsky, 1990; *Tsvetaeva* by Viktoria Schweitzer, translated by Robert Chandler, H.T. Willers, and Peter Norman, 1993; *Marina Tsvetaeva: Poetics of Appropriation* by Michael Markin, 1994; *Tsvetaeva's Orphic Journeys in the Worlds of the Word* by Olga Peters Hasty, 1996; *Russian Psyche: The Poetic Mind of Marina Tsvetaeva* by Alyssa W. Dinega, 2001.

*   *   *

Marina Tsvetaeva, who was called ''the most Russian of poets,'' ''a poet's poet,'' and ''a poet of sacrifice,'' died virtually forgotten: nobody attended her funeral and the location of her grave is not known. Today she enjoys international fame and respect. Her life was a tragedy; but her work is a triumph. Her reputation has gone ''beyond and above'' her fellow poets, including many of the most outstanding. Her poetry offers in many ways the culmination of modern poetry's concern with language. With her, language assumes an importance far greater than we might ever have imagined: she marks its concern with the creation and maintenance of existential orders. Tsvetaeva's poetry plays a part in what constitutes an enormous intellectual challenge for the reader: ''The rediscovery of the pun,'' i.e., the rediscovery of the vital interconnections of language and reality, that we find in Shakespeare. Her mystical belief in the power of poetry was expressed in one of her earliest poems, dated 1913:

Thrown carelessly about the dusty shelves of bookshops,
Untouched, then, now, by any reader's thumb,
My poems, stored deep like wines of precious vintage,
I know their time will come.

Throughout her life she was forced to speak not only across space, but also across time. It took so long for her to be accepted as among the great, not only because of her life and her character, but because of the very nature of her poetry. Her first collection of verse, privately printed, was noticed only by fellow poets. Her next two books of lyrics had mixed reviews, although Pasternak praised her ''tremendous, uniquely powerful language.'' Both in Russia and in exile she had failed to find a reading public. As she said: ''For those on the Right it [her poetry] is Left in form. For those on the Left it is Right in content.'' Her loyalty to all the ''old oaths'' was out of fashion in post-revolutionary Russia. Outcast by fellow émigrés, she proclaimed the absolute, unsullied concepts of honour, duty, and justice: ''I have two foes in the world, twins inextricably interrelated—the hunger of the hungry and the glut of the glutted.'' This ''calvinistic spirit of personal responsibility,'' as Brodskii called it, is felt in all her works. ''A single one—from everyone—for everyone—against everyone,'' she stated her place in life and in poetry. An aesthetic rebel, Tsvetaeva was striving all her life towards ''boundlessness'' (*bezmernost'*) that became one of the major themes of her poetry as well as its principle.

Her ethics are in many ways determined by her aesthetics. Her massive self-confidence was based on her idealistic cult of the Poet: ''. . . there are not poets, there is one single poet, one and the same from the beginning of creation to the end.'' A keen, poetic, and fertile intelligence is revealed in Tsvetaeva's innovative treatment of language and in her profound meditation on time and the tragedy of human existence. She demonstrated that language itself is interested in tragic content: by using dactylic rhymes, for instance, she created an intonation of lament. With her, the density of the sentence is often achieved by omission of the verbs ''compensated by a brilliant and characteristic use of inflection, especially dative and instrumental case endings, a tactic beyond the scope of any translator,'' as John Bayley has written. Forceful alliteration and internal rhymes allow her to expand the formal and semantic possibilities of the end-rhyme. She was a master of enjambment, a device she used to attack ''the most inhumanely senseless of words: se-pa-ration.'' This insane, unnatural state of being was, in fact, her fate. Separated from her country, from her family, from her readers, she wrote shortly before her suicide, ''I don't want to die. I want not to be'':

I refuse to be. In the mad house of inhuman.
I refuse to live. With the wolves
of the market place. I refuse to howl . . . .

She saw even death in linguistic terms, ''tot svet . . . ne bez—a vse—iazychen'' [the other world is not without language, it is multilingual]. There is a constant awareness of the power of language to shape and explode perception of the world. She commemorated all her love affairs, real and imaginary, in her poetry. Again and again, language takes her to such heights and with such speed that neither experience nor imagination can compete with it. She had written the finest love poems ever addressed to a man. All her lovers, even those ''who can stand the sunlight,'' wither under Tsvetaeva's gaze. Her ''emotional superiority'' was equal to her linguistic capacity to surprise. In her numerous letters, in her brilliant prose, and in theoretical essays she displayed the same degree of dependence on language as in her poetry. She did an enormous service to Russian poetry by creating a new linguistic space. She influenced a whole new generation of poets, including Brodskii, who has written the most penetrating appreciation of her poetry and prose.

—Valentina Polukhina

TULSĪDĀS, Gosvami

Born: Probably into a Brahmin (priestly caste) family in Soron or Rājāpur, Uttar Pradesh, India, 11 August 1532 (some sources suggest 1497, 1526, or 1543). Mother died in infancy, and he was brought up by Bābā Narharidās, who took him to Benares. **Education:** Accepted as disciple by scholar Śeṣ Sanātan. **Family:** Married Ratnāvalī; one son. **Career:** After Sanatan's death, returned to Rājāpur, where he preached the devotional songs (*bhakti*) of Rām; travelled widely across northern India, and may have met Sūrdās, *q.v.*, and Mīrā Bāī, *q.v.* A relatively small number of the works attributed to him thought genuine. **Died:** 30 June 1623.

PUBLICATIONS

Collections

Granthāvalī [Complete Works], edited by R.C. Śukla and others. 1923–37(?); revised edition, 4 vols., 1973–77.
The Complete Works of Gosvami Tulsidas, translated by S.P. Bahadur. 6 vols., 1978–80.

Verse (principal works)

Rāmacaritamānas. As *Rāmcharita Mānasa,* edited by Pandit Rāmajasana, 1861; Hindi edition, 1889; also edited by S.S. Dās, 1917 (abridged) and 1922, V.A. Tripāthī 1937; as *Rāmacaritamānas,* edited by S.N. Chaube, 1948; as *The Ramayana/ Rācāritmanāas,* edited by A.G. Atkins (bilingual edition), 3 vols., 1954; as *The Ramayana of Tulasī Dāsa,* translated by F.S. Growse, 4 vols., 1877–81, revised edition, 1978; as *The Ramayana of Tulsi Das,* translated by J.M. Macfie, 1930; as *The Book of Ram: The Bible of India,* translated by Hari Prasad Shastri, 1935; as *The Holy Lake of the Acts of Rāma,* translated by W. Douglas P. Hill, 1952; as *The Gospel of Love: An English Rendering of Tulasi's Shri Rama Charita Manasa (The Spiritual Lake of Rama's Pastime),* translated by Chandan Lal Dhody, 1987; as *Tulsidasa's Shriramacharitamanasa,* edited and translated by R.C. Prasad, 1988; as *Shri Ramcharitamanasa,* translated by G.B. Kanungo and Leela Kanungo, 2000.
Kavitāvalī [or *Kavitta Rāmāyana*], edited by V.P. Misra, 1948; also edited by C.S. Shastri, 1964; as *Kavitāvalī* translated by F.Raymond Allchin. 1964.
Vinayapatrikā edited by B.S. Bhaṭṭa (Hindi and Braj), 1925; also edited by G. Gupta (Hindi and Braj), 1936, M. Mālavīya, 1936, H.P. Dwevedi (Hindi and Braj), 1944, A. Śaraṇa (Hindi and Braj), 4 vols., 1947–66, D.N. Dvivedī, 2nd edition, 1962, R.N. Sarmā, 1963, and Viyogī Hari, 1965; as *The Petition to Ram,* translated by F.Raymond Allchin, 1966.

Other

The Sayings of Tulsidas, edited and translated by Lalo Kannoo Mal. 1923.

*

Critical Studies: *The Ramayana of Tulsidas* by J.M. Macfie (includes translations), 1930; *Étude sur les sources et la composition du Rāmāyana de Tulsīdās* by C. Vaudeville, 1955; *A Comparative Study of Kamba Ramayanam and Tulasi Ramayan* by S. Shankar Raju Naidu, 1971; ''The View from the Ghats: Traditional Exigesis of a Hindu Epic,'' in *Journal of Asian Studies,* 48, 1989, and *The Life of a Text: Performing the Ramcaritmanas of Tulsidas,* both by Philip Lutgendorf, 1991; *Many Rāmāyanas: The Diversity of a Narrative Tradition in South Asia* edited by Paula Richman, 1991; *Shri Rama: The Man and His Mission* by G.N. Das, 1998; *Tulasidasa: A Bibliography* by Sudha Verma, 1998; *Protocol in Sri Ramcharitmanas* by Devi Dayal Aggarwal, 1998; *Rama: The Lord of Decorum* by Rajendra Arun, 2000.

* * *

Tulsīdās is the most celebrated poet of modern India. His *Rāmacaritamānas* is one of the most influential works for the Hindus of northern India and is known not only in India but throughout the world. Much of what has come down to us about Tulsīdās's life and the way in which he became a devotee of the god-hero Rāma depends on unreliable tradition, and attempts to link his name to the *bhakti* movement, which advocated the supreme value of the worship of Rāma. Like his predecessor Kabīr, Tulsīdās owes much of his inspiration to the monotheistic devotion of the Vaiṣṇavite sects, who worshipped the god Kṛṣṇa, a form of worship that had long been popular. Tulsīdās's aim, however, was to group the vital forces in Hinduism about the theme of Rāma and make it a living faith. His is the role of a unifier, and he did not hesitate to make use of the previous, sometimes rival, doctrines, such as Krishnaism.

The works attributed to Tulsīdās are numerous, but among them only 12 are considered to have been written by him. Most of them deal with the story of Rāma and have the object of popularizing his worship. They have, therefore, an edifying purpose. The story of Rāma, the great hero who was an incarnation of Viṣṇu, had been told long before by the Sanskrit poet Vālmīkī, who probably lived in the 4th century BC. The story exerted a profound influence on later poets. A brief survey of Tulsīdās's works will illustrate the sources of inspiration of the poet and the religious aim of his literary production.

The Gītāvalī is a series of stanzas on the life of Rāma, adapted for singing. The *Kavitta Rāmāyana,* the *Rāmājnā-praśnāvalī* the *Jānakī Manāgala,* the *Rāmalalānahachū,* and the *Baravai Rāmāyana,* as well as several others that are probably spurious, retell the story of Rāma focusing on some event essential to the legend of the hero. The *Vinayapatrikā (The Petition to Ram)* is a collection of petitions addressed to various deities, rivers, sacred places, and the heroes and heroine of the *Rāmāyana* of Vālmīki. The *Kṛṣṇa Gītāvalī* is a collection of songs in honour of the god Kṛṣṇa. The *Vairāgya-sandīpinī* is a didactic treatise which deals with the qualities of the true saint and the peace of mind (*śānti*) he enjoys. Special mention should be made of the *Rāmasatasai,* which contains a systematic exposition of Tulsīdās's religious beliefs. The poem is divided into seven sargas in which the poet teaches: the doctrine of faith (*bhakti*), central to his work; the path of self-knowledge (*ātmabodha*); the law of action (*karma*); and the doctrine of knowledge (*jñāna*). There is also a description of the essence of Rāma (*Rāmarasa*) in a number of cryptic riddles.

The great masterpiece of Tulsīdās is, however, the *Rāmacaritamānas*—translated as *The Holy Lake* [i.e. the quintessence] *of the Acts of Rāma*—and generally known as the *Rāmāyana* of Tulsā. It follows freely the course of the story of the *Rāmāyana* of Vālmīki, although the writer has also drawn on other Sanskrit sources besides Vālmīki. However, the spirit of Tulsīdās's poem is very different from that of Vālmīki. *The Holy Lake* exalts Rāma as the supreme Lord above all the other divinities of the Hindu pantheon, and the events narrated are examples of truth and fidelity. The message of the poem is made clear throughout the book: salvation comes only through absolute faith in Rāma, The chief merit of Tulsīdās's work lies in the fact that it brought a new message of salvation to the average Hindu, oppressed by the strict tenets of traditional Hinduism which advocated the doctrine of reincarnation

and the impossibility of the uneducated people ever attaining the knowledge of the Absolute Truth.

In order to be understood by everybody, Tulsīdās used the vernacular in his poem, a fact that provoked the ire of the most traditional pandits, who despised his work as a concession to the uneducated masses. The poem is written in the Avadhi dialect of Hindi, although the influence of other dialects, especially Braj, is also evident. Tulsīdās makes use of a simple and vigorous language, which abounds in colloquialisms. We also find descriptive passages of great beauty in which the poet displays his skill in the use of Sanskrit metres and rhymes. These virtues have earned him his fame as the creator of modern Hindi.

The impetus that this work gave to vernacular literature was extremely important. However, *The Holy Lake* owes its success not so much to its language as to the spiritual message it conveys. It speaks with a human voice to pious Hindus who find their inspiration and example, as well as their means to salvation, in the figure of Rāma. This means is devotion (*bhakti*), evident in all of Rāma's deeds; everything else is illusion (*māyā*). The last verses of the seventh book of *The Holy Lake* illustrate the message of hope and liberation that the work conveys:

> Those who plunge with faith into this Holy Lake of Rāma's Acts, a lake of merit, sin-destroying, ever blessing the soul and granting faith and wisdom, which by its pure, clear waters full of love washes away the filth of ignorance and illusion, are not scorched by the burning rays of the sun of birth and death.

> (translated by W.D.P. Hill)

Tulsīdās wrote his work at a time in which Hindus felt the need to escape the oppressive intellectualism of Brahmanic philosophy. At the same time, they were aware of the presence of an external threat to their religious beliefs—Muslim power. In these circumstances it is almost logical that Tulsīdās's work, which proposes devotion towards a personal god who loves and sympathizes with his devotees, exerted a profound influence on the Hindu masses. *The Holy Lake* has influenced Hindu spiritual life to such an extent that it has been rightly called the Bible of the Hindu people of northern India.

—Ana M. Ranero

TURGENEV, Ivan (Sergeevich)

Born: Orel, Russia, 28 October 1818, **Education:** Educated at home; briefly at Armenian Institute and Weidenhammer's boarding school in Moscow; University of Moscow, 1833–34; University of St. Petersburg, 1834–37; University of Berlin, 1838–41; completed master's exam in St. Petersburg, 1842. **Career:** Civil servant in Ministry of the Interior, 1843–45; then mainly interested in country pursuits, especially hunting; went to France with the singer Pauline Viardot and her husband, 1845–46, and again in 1847–50; exiled to his country estate for a "faulty" obituary of Gogol', *q.v.,* 1852–53; in Western Europe again for long spells after 1856, often in Baden-Baden after 1863, and in Paris with the Viardots, 1871–83. Corresponding member, Imperial Academy of Sciences, 1860. Doctor of Civil Laws: Oxford University. 1879. **Died:** 3 September 1883.

PUBLICATIONS

Collections

Novels and Stories, translated by Isabel F. Hapgood. 16 vols., 1903–04.
Novels, translated by Constance Garnett. 15 vols., 1894–99.
Plays, translated by M.S. Mandell. 1924.
Polnoe sobranie sochinenii i pisem [Complete Works and Letters]. 28 vols., 1960–68.
Polnoe sobranie sochinenii i pisem [Complete Works and Letters], edited by M.P. Alekseev. 30 vols., 1978.
Sochineniia [Works]. 2 vols., 1980.
Izbrannye sochineniia [Selected Works], edited by V.R. Shcherbina. 1987.
First Love, and Other Stories, translated by Isaiah Berlin and Leonard Schapiro. 1994.
The Essential Turgenev, edited by Elizabeth Cheresh Allen. 1994.
First Love; and, The Diary of a Superfluous Man, translated by Constance Garnett. 1995.

Fiction

Zapiski okhotnika. 1852; as *Russian Life in the Interior,* translated by James D. Meiklejohn, 1855; as *Annals of a Sportsman,* translated by Franklin Pierce Abbott, 1885; as *A Sportsman's Sketches,* translated by Constance Garnett, 1932; as *Sketches from a Hunter's Album,* translated by Richard Freeborn, 1967, complete edition, 1990; as *A Sportman's Notebook,* translated by Charles and Natasha Hepburn, 1992.
Povesti i rasskazy [Tales and Stories]. 1856.
Rudin. 1856; edited by Galina Stilman, 1955; as *Dmitri Roudine,* 1873; as *Rudin,* translated by Richard Freeborn, 1975; also translated by Kathleen Cook, with *A Nest of the Gentry,* 1985.
Asia. 1858; as *Annouchka,* translated by Franklin Pierce Abbott, 1884.
Dvorianskoe gnezdo. 1859; as *A Nest of Gentlefolk,* 1869; as *Lisa,* 1872; as *A House of Gentlefolk,* translated by Constance Garnett, 1897; as *A Nest of the Gentry,* translated by Bernard Isaacs, 1947, also translated by Kathleen Cook, with *Rudin,* 1985; as *A Nest of Hereditary Legislators,* translated by Franz Davidovitch Davies, 1913; as *Home of the Gentry,* translated by Richard Freeborn, 1970.
Pervaia liubov'. 1860; as *First Love,* 1884; also translated by Isaiah Berlin, 1950.
Nakanune. 1860; as *On the Eve,* translated by C.E. Turner, 1871; also translated by Isabel F. Hapgood, 1903.
Ottsy i deti. 1862; as *Fathers and Sons,* translated by Eugene Schuyler, 1867; numerous subsequent translations including by Barbara Makanowitzky, 1959, Rosemary Edmonds, 1965, Ralph E. Matlaw, 1989, Richard Freeborn, 1991, and Michael R. Katz, 1994; as *Fathers and Children,* translated by Avril Pyman, 1991; translated by Constance Garnett, 1998.
Dym. 1867; translated as *Smoke,* 1868.
Neschastnaia. 1869; as *An Unfortunate Woman,* translated by Henry Gersoni, 1886; as *The Unfortunate One,* translated by A.R. Thompson, 1888.
Stepnoi Korol' Lir. 1870; as *A Lear of the Steppe,* with *Spring Floods,* 1874.

Veshnie vody. 1872; as *Spring Floods,* with *A Lear of the Steppe,* 1874; as *The Torrents of Spring,* translated by David Magarshack, 1959; as *Spring Torrents,* translated by Leonard Shapiro, 1972.
Nov'. 1877; as *Virgin Soil,* translated by T.S. Perry, 1877; also translated by Constance Garnett, 1896.
Klara Milich. 1883.
The Brigadier and Other Stories, translated by Moura Budberg. 1962.
Youth and Age (includes "Bunin and Baburin"; "The Inn"; "The Watch"), translated by Marion Mainwaring. 1968.
Love and Death: Six Stories (includes "The Diary of a Superfluous Man"; "Mumu"; "Asya"; "First Love"; "King Lear of the Steppes"; "The Song of Triumphant Love"), translated by Richard Freeborn. 1983; as *First Love and Other Stories,* translated by Freeborn, 1989.
The Diary of a Superfluous Man, translated by David Patterson. 1984.

Plays

Neostorozhnost' [Carelessness], in *Otechestvenye zapiski* [Notes of the Fatherland]. 1843.
Bezdenezh'e (produced 1852). 1846; as *The Poor Gentleman,* translated by Constance Garnett, in *Three Famous Plays,* 1934.
Gde tonko, tam i rvetsia (produced 1851). 1848; as *Where It's Thin, There It Tears,* translated by M.S. Mandell, in *Plays,* 1924.
Zavtrak s predvoditelia [Lunch with the Marshal of the Nobility] (produced 1849). 1856.
Kholostiak (produced 1849). 1849; as *The Bachelor,* translated by M.S. Mandell, in *Plays,* 1924.
Razgovor na bolshoi doroge (produced 1850). 1851; as *A Conversation on the Highway,* translated by M.S. Mandell, in *Plays,* 1924.
Provintsialka (produced 1851). 1851; as *The Provincial Lady,* translated by M.S. Mandell, in *Plays,* 1924; as *A Provincial Lady,* translated by Constance Garnett, in *Three Famous Plays,* 1934.
Mesiats v derevne (produced 1872). In *Sobranie sochinenii,* 1869; as *A Month in the Country,* translated by M.S. Mandell, in *Plays,* 1924; also translated by Emlyn Williams, 1943; Ariadne Nicolaeff, 1976; Isaiah Berlin, 1981; Richard Freeborn, 1991.
Nakhlebnik (produced 1862). 1857; as *The Family Charge,* translated by M.S. Mandell, in *Plays,* 1924.
Vecher v Sorrente (produced 1882). 1891; as *An Evening in Sorrento,* translated by M.S. Mandell, in *Plays,* 1924.

Verse

Parasha. 1843.
Razgovor [The Conversation]. 1845.
Andrei. 1846.
Pomeshchik [The Landowner]. 1846.
Senilia. 1878; as *Stikhotvoreniia v proze,* 1882; translated as *Poems in Prose,* 1883; as *Senilia: Poems in Prose,* translated by S.J. Macmullan, 1890; bilingual edition, 1951.

Other

Sobranie sochinenii [Complete Works]. 5 vols., 1860–61, and later editions.
Literaturnye i zhiteiskie vospominaniia. 1874; revised edition, 1880; as *Literary Reminiscences and Autobiographical Fragments,* translated by David Magarshack, 1958.
Nouvelle correspondance inédite, edited by A. Zviguilsky. 2 vols., 1971–72.

Lettres inédites à Pauline Viardot et à sa famille, edited by A. Zviguilsky. 1972.

I.S. Turgenev: Voprosy biografii i tvorchestva [I.S. Turgenev: Questions of Biography and Creation]. 1982.

Letters (selection), edited by A.V. Knowles. 1983.

Letters (selection), edited by David Lowe. 2 vols., 1983.

Flaubert and Turgenev: A Friendship in Letters: The Complete Correspondence, edited and translated by Barbara Beaumont. 1985.

Ivan Turgenev and Britain, edited by Patrick Waddington. 1995.

Turgenev and Pavlovsky: A Friendship and a Correspondence, presented by Patrick Waddington. 1998.

*

Bibliography: *Turgenev in English: A Checklist of Works by and about Him* by Rissa Yachnin and David H. Stam, 1962; *A Bibliography of Writings by and about Turgenev Published in Great Britain Up to 1900* by Patrick Waddington, 1985; *Turgenev: A Bibliography of Books 1843–1982 by and about Ivan Turgenev: With a Checklist of Canadian Library Holdings* by Nicholas G. Zekulin, 1985.

Critical Studies: *Turgenev: The Man, His Art, and His Age* by Avrahm Yarmolinsky, 1926, 2nd edition, 1959; *Turgenev: The Novelist's Novelist: A Study* by Richard Freeborn, 1960; *Turgenev: The Portrait Game* edited by Marion Mainwaring, 1973; *Hamlet and Don Quixote: Turgenev's Ambivalent Vision* by Eva Kagan-Kans, 1975; *The Clement Vision: Poetic Realism in Turgenev and James* by Dale E. Peterson, 1976; *The Gentle Barbarian: The Life and Work of Turgenev* by V.S. Pritchett, 1977; *Turgenev: His Life and Times* by Leonard Schapiro, 1978; *Dialogue in Turgenev's Novels: Speech-introductory Devices* by Ludmila Hellgren, 1980; *Turgenev's Russia: From "Notes of a Hunter" to "Fathers and Sons"* by Victor Ripp, 1980; *Turgenev's Early Works: From Character Sketches to a Novel* by Walter Smyrniw, 1980; *Turgenev and England, 1980, and Turgenev and George Sand: An Improbable Entente,* 1981, both by Patrick Waddington; *Turgenev's Fathers and Sons* by David Allan Lowe, 1983; *Ivan Turgenev* by A.V. Knowles, 1988; *Turgenev: A Biography* by Henri Troyat, 1988; *Worlds Within Worlds: The Novels of Turgenev* by Jane T. Costlow, 1990; *Metaphysical Conflict: A Study of the Major Novels of Ivan Turgenev* by James B. Woodward, 1990; *Turgenev: A Reading of His Fiction* by Frank Friedeberg Seeley, 1991; *Beyond Realism: Turgenev's Poetics of Secular Salvation* by Elizabeth Cheresh Allen, 1992; *Turgenev and the Context of English Literature 1850–1900* by Glyn Turton, 1992; *Turgenev's Fathers and Sons* by James Woodward, 1996; *Character in the Short Prose of Ivan Sergeevic Turgenev* by Sander Brouwer, 1996; *Vicissitudes of Genre in the Russian Novel: Turgenev's "Fathers and Sons," Chernyshevsky's "What is to be Done?," Dostoevsky's "Demons," Gorky's "Mother"* by Russell Scott Valentino, 2001.

* * *

Ivan Turgenev is indisputably in the pantheon of 19th-century Russian literature, but he stands apart from many of the other authors, and especially from his two great contemporaries, Tolstoi and Dostoevskii. He had little taste for confronting the ultimate questions of life, for wrestling with philosophical issues as they visited themselves on the Slavic soul—indeed he doubted that an abstraction like "Slavic soul" was meaningful. The scope of Turgenev's works is narrow, often confined to the cares of a small group of gentry gathered on a remote estate, and his style was geared to capture the half-spoken phrase and the tremor of emotion. He was a miniaturist; but a miniaturist who produced some of the most politically telling fiction of the century.

It took some time for Turgenev to find his distinctive voice. He began his career arguing with German Romanticism, whose influences he had felt during his years as a student at the University of Berlin. His early works, notably the long story "Andrei Kolosov," were attempts to deflate Romantic pretensions, but they were partially contaminated by the disease they attacked. In these early works, Turgenev's language is occasionally pompous and his sense of character vague.

With the *Zapiski okhotnika* (*A Sportsman's Notebook*) cycle, Turgenev hit his stride. Begun almost off-handedly as a favour to some friends who needed material to fill their journal, it comprised 22 sketches when it was published to great acclaim in 1852. The sketches relate the events that befall a nobleman from Orel as he wanders through the countryside. With the creation of this character—much like himself, yet slightly distanced—Turgenev found the means to control his tendency toward high-flown sentiments. Though there are many descriptions about the futility of life and the indifference of nature, the overall effect is bracing, the view of a man coolly contemplating the social landscape of mid-19th-century Russia.

The sense of control is most evident in Turgenev's treatment of the peasantry, which in fact represented an innovation in the Russian tradition. Previously, peasants were treated as stock characters or aspects of an undifferentiated mass, the *narod*. From the first paragraph of the first sketch, "Khor and Kalinych," where the traits of the peasants of one district are contrasted with those of another, Turgenev shows that the peasantry was variegated and individualized. Obviously deeply felt, this perspective also fitted into the programme of the group with which Turgenev was allied, the Westernizers, who argued that the self-conscious individual was the most important element of a society, on all its levels. As Turgenev himself put it, "Let me be an atom, but my own matter; I do not want salvation but truth, and I expect it from reason not grace."

Whether or not *A Sportsman's Notebook* was instrumental in Aleksandr II's decision to abolish serfdom (and Turgenev always believed it was), there is no question that it was a key part of the quickening political atmosphere. It was a tenet of the times, however, that only the novel could adequately capture social reality, and in the early 1850s Turgenev turned to that genre. His first, never-completed effort, entitled *Two Generations*, served mainly to show how unsuited his temperament was for complicated plot construction and psychological development.

He solved many of these technical problems in *Rudin*. Though essentially composed of one incident with an extended preamble and epilogue, and set among a small group of gentry on their provincial estate, the book has novelistic scope because the concerns of the characters parallel the nation's concerns. Most of all this applies to the treatment of the eponymous hero (based in part on Turgenev's old friend the anarchist Mikhail Bakunin). The question asked of Rudin—can he match his idealistic phrases with action?—was a question that many educated Russians in the 1850s asked themselves.

In his next two novels, *Dvorianskoe gnezdo* (*Home of the Gentry*) and *Nakanune* (*On the Eve*), Turgenev continued his investigation of the moral life of the nation. Though these works confirmed his status as the pre-eminent author of the period, the themes he chose also made him a likely target of criticism, especially from the group of radical critics who were at that time acquiring new influence. Men like Chernyshevskii and Dobroliubov, both of whom served on the leading journal *Sovremennik* [The Contemporary], agreed that the questions the novels raised were pertinent, but they insisted that Turgenev was too restrained, too moderate in his answers. The tone of this quarrel is summed up by Dobroliubov's review of *On the Eve*. Significantly entitled ''When Will the Real Day Come?,'' it drew out all the revolutionary implications of the novel, as well as several that were not there.

Such instances tended to strengthen a side of Turgenev that had always despised politics. He wrote numerous works, such as ''Faust'' (1856) and ''Journey to the Forest'' (1857), stories that announce the omnipotence of transcendental, ahistorical forces. As it happens, this view of the world also accounts for one of Turgenev's masterpieces, *Pervaia liubov'* (*First Love*). This story, which was his own favourite, is one of the great accounts of the universal relations between father and son. But for all his reservations about politics, Turgenev never ignored the subject for very long, and was capable of remarkable perspicacity and broadness of vision. Thus, though he intensely disagreed with the utilitarian ethics of the radicals, he showed a remarkable understanding for their political programme, even to the extent of sympathetically comparing it with his own liberalism. He defined this contrast in his landmark essay ''Don Quixote and Hamlet'' (1860), in which he posited two political personalities: one jousts singlemindedly at windmills, ignoring adverse odds, the other understands these odds so acutely that even the first step toward action seems not worth taking. Turgenev saw the heroism and shortcomings of each type.

His most notable acknowledgement of the radical position, however, was the creation of the character Bazarov, in *Ottsy i deti* (*Fathers and Sons*). Written just as the emancipation of the serfs was becoming a reality, the novel underscores the extreme handicaps confronting a progressive political movement in mid-19th-century Russia. Bazarov, who has grown up watching the rumblings of a generation committed to the spiritual and idealistic aspects of man, puts his faith in science and reason, even though that means totally ignoring many of the humanistic values that the ''fathers'' embraced.

Turgenev shows the historical logic of Bazarov's position; but he also depicts its fatal flaw, the inability to comprehend emotion. Indeed, at the climax of the novel, Bazarov, the powerful representative of radical politics, is brought low by unrequited love.

The novel provoked a maelstrom of controversy. To conservatives, it appeared an apotheosis of radicalism; to radicals, it was a calumny against one of their kind. In fact, Bazarov is so richly depicted that no simple political definition is possible. Some years later, Turgenev announced that he sympathized with most of Bazarov's views, but this afterthought did not quiet the dispute, which indeed continues to this day.

The reaction to *Fathers and Sons* proved a turning point for Turgenev. Though he had spent much of his adult life abroad, in order to be near his great love, Pauline Viardot, he now settled himself even more firmly in Europe, first in Baden-Baden and then in the estate he purchased jointly with Viardot and her husband in Bougival, outside Paris. He returned to Russia only rarely thereafter, and when he did felt out of touch with the direction of events there—even though it was his Bazarov that had inspired some of the more radical members of the political opposition.

Turgenev's work also became distant from Russia's problems. Two later novels, *Dym* (*Smoke*) and *Nov'* (*Virgin Soil*), both suffer from a caricaturing of the radical mentality, a striking flaw in view of Turgenev's earlier ability to depict sympathetically political types he disagreed with. A more compelling strain in Turgenev's later work is a philosophical pessimism derived from Schopenhauer. This melancholic mood, which is on display in *Senilia* (*Poems in Prose*), prompted some powerful writing, though still not comparable to his early work. In fact, the greatest achievement of the final two decades of his life was the introduction of Russian culture to Europe, through translations he made or through the medium of the many literary friends he acquired abroad.

—Nancy Kanach Fehsenfeld

See the essays on *Fathers and Sons*, *First Love*, and *A Month in the Country*.

U

UNAMUNO (Y JUGO), Miguel de

Born: Bilbao, Spain, 29 September 1864. **Education:** Educated at Colegio de San Nicolás, and Instituto Vizcaíno, both Bilbao; University of Madrid, 1880–84, Ph.D. 1884. **Family:** Married Concepción Lizárraga Ecénarro in 1891; nine children. **Career:** Professor of Greek, 1891–1924, 1930–34, and rector, 1901–14, 1934–36, University of Salamanca. Exiled to Canary Islands for criticism of Primo de Rivera government, 1924, then lived in Paris, 1924, and Hendaye, 1925–30; under house arrest for criticism of Franco government, 1936. **Award:** Cross of the Order of Alfonso XII, 1905. **Died:** 31 December 1936.

PUBLICATIONS

Collections

Obras completas, edited by Manuel García Blanco. 16 vols., 1966–71.
Selected Works, edited by Anthony Kerrigan and others. 1967.
Poesía completa, edited by Ana Suárez Miramón. 4 vols., 1987–89.

Fiction

Paz en la guerra. 1897; as *Peace in War*, translated by Allen Lacy, Martin Nozick, and Anthony Kerrigan, 1983.
Amor y pedagogía. 1902.
El espejo de la muerte. 1913.
Niebla. 1914; as *Mist*, translated by Warner Fite, 1929.
Abel Sánchez: Una historia de pasión. 1917; edited by Luciano González Egido, 1987; as *Abel Sanchez*, translated 1947.
Tulio Montalbán y Julio Macedo. 1920.
Tres novelas ejemplares y un prólogo. 1920; as *Three Exemplary Novels* (includes *Marquis of Lumbria*; *Two Mothers*; *Nothing Less Than a Man*), translated by Angel Flores, 1930.
La tía Tula. 1921.
San Manuel Bueno, mártir y tres historias más. 1933; edited by C.A. Longhurst, 1984; as *San Manuel Bueno*, translated by Mario J. and María Elena de Valdés, 1973.
Abel Sanchez and Other Stories, translated by Anthony Kerrigan. 1956.
Dos Novelas Cortas, edited by A. Galip Ulsoy and Warren R, Devries. 1975.

Plays

La Venda, La princesa, Doña Lambra. 1913.
Fedra. 1924.
Sombras de sueño. 1931.
El otro. 1932; as *The Others*, in *Selected Works*, 1976.
Raquel. 1933.
El hermano Juan o El mundo es teatro. 1934.
La esfinge. 1934.
Teatro completo, edited by Manuel García Blanco. 1959.

Verse

Poesías. 1907.
Rosario de sonetos líricos. 1911.

El Cristo de Velázquez. 1920; as *The Christ of Velazquez*, translated by Eleanor L. Turnbull, 1951.
Rimas de dentro. 1923.
Teresa. 1923.
De Fuerteventura a París. 1925.
Romancero del destierro. 1928.
Poems, translated by Eleanor L. Turnbull. 1952.
Cancionero: Diario poético. 1953.
Cincuenta poesías inéditas, edited by Manuel García Blanco. 1958.
Last Poems, translated by Edita Mas-López. 1974.
Poemas de los pueblos de España (selection), edited by Manuel García Blanco. 1975.
[*Poems*], edited by Julio López. 1985.

Other

De la enseñanza superior en España. 1899.
Tres ensayos. 1900.
En torno al casticismo. 1902.
Paisajes. 1902.
De mi país. 1903.
Vida de Don Quijote y Sancho. 1905; as *The Life of Don Quixote and Sancho*, translated by Homer P. Earle, 1927.
Recuerdos de niñez y de mocedad. 1908.
Mi religión y otros ensayos breves. 1910; as *Perplexities and Paradoxes*, translated by S. Gross, 1945.
Por tierras de Portugal y de España (articles). 1911.
Soliloquios y conversaciones. 1911.
Contra esto y aquello. 1912.
El porvenir de España, with Angel Ganivet. 1912.
Del sentimiento trágico de la vida en los hombres y en los pueblos. 1913; as *The Tragic Sense of Life in Men and in Peoples*, translated by J.E. Crawford Flitch, 1921; as *The Tragic Sense of Life in Men and Nations*, in *Selected Works*, 1967.
Ensayos. 8 vols., 1916–18; revised edition, 2 vols., 1942.
Andanzas y visiones españolas (articles). 1922.
La agonía del cristianismo. 1925; as *The Agony of Christianity*, translated by Pierre Loving (from the French), 1928; also translated by Kurt F. Reinhardt, 1960.
Essays and Soliloquies (selection), translated by J.E. Crawford Flitch. 1925.
Cómo se hace una novela. 1927; as *How to Make a Novel*, in *Selected Works*, 1976.
Dos artículos y dos discursos. 1930.
Ensayos y sentencias de Unamuno, edited by Wilfred A. Beardsley. 1932.
La ciudad de Henoc: Comentario 1933. 1941.
Paisajes del alma. 1944.
Prosa Diversa, edited by Joan Gili. 1946.
Algunas consideraciones sobre la literatura hispanoamericana. 1947.
Madrid. 1950.
Mi Salamanca. 1950.
Epistolario (letters), with Juan Maragall. 1951; revised edition, 1976.
Correspondencia entre Unamuno y Vaz Ferreira (letters). 1957.
Autodiálogos. 1959.
Pensamiento político, edited by Elías Díaz. 1965.

Diario íntimo, edited by P. Félix García. 1970; translated in part by Anthony Kerrigan, Allen Lacy, and Martin Nozick, in *The Private World*, 1984.

Epistolario, with Alonso Quesada, edited by Lázaro Santana. 1970.

Cartas 1903–1933 (letters between Unamuno and Luis de Zulueta), edited by Carmen de Zulueta. 1972.

The Agony of Christianity and Essays on Faith, edited by Anthony Kerrigan and Martin Nozick, translated by Kerrigan. 1974.

Escritos socialistas. 1976.

Unamuno "agitador de espíritus" y Giner: Correspondencia inédita, edited by D. Gómez Molleda. 1976.

Artículos olvidados sobre España y la primera guerra mundial, edited by Christopher Cobb. 1976.

Gramática y glosario del Poema del Cid, edited by Barbara D. Huntley and Pilar Liria. 1977.

The Private World: Selections from the Diario íntimo and Selected Letters 1890–1936, translated by Anthony Kerrigan, Allen Lacy, and Martin Nozick. 1984.

Azorín-Unamuno, cartas y escritos complementarios, edited by Laureano Robles. 1990.

Epistolario inédito, edited by Laureano Robles. 2 vols., 1991.

Translator, *Ética de las prisiones, Exceso de legislación, De las leyes en general*, by Herbert Spencer. 3 vols., 1895.

Translator, *Historia de la economía política*, by J.K. Ingram. 1895(?).

Translator, *Historia de las literaturas castellana y portuguesa*, by Ferdinand J. Wolf. 2 vols., 1895–96.

*

Bibliography: *An Unamuno Source Book: A Catalogue of Readings and Acquisitions: with an Introductory Essay on Unamuno's Dialectical Enquiry* by Mario James Valdés, 1973; *Bibliografía crítica de Unamuno 1888–1975* by Pelayo H. Fernández, 1976.

Critical Studies: *Unamuno* by John B. Trende, 1951; *Unamuno* by Arturo Barea, translated by Ilsa Barea, 1952; *Unamuno: A Philosophy of Tragedy* by José Ferrater-Mora, 1962; *The Lone Heretic: A Biography of Unamuno* by Margaret Thomas Rudd, 1963; *Death in the Literature of Unamuno* by Mario J. Valdés, 1964; *The Victorious Expression: A Study of Four Contemporary Spanish Poets: Miguel de Unamuno, Antonio Machado, Juan Ramón Jiménez, Federico García Lorca* by Howard T. Young, 1964; *Miguel de Unamuno* by Julián Marías, translated by Frances M. López-Marillas, 1966; *Unamuno: An Existential View of Self and Society* by Paul Ilie, 1967; *Miguel de Unamuno: The Rhetoric of Existence* by Allen Lacy, 1967; *Unamuno, Creator and Creation* edited by José Rubia Barcia and M.A. Zeitlin, 1967; *Unamuno* by Martin Nozick, 1971; *Unamuno Novelist: A European Perspective* by R.E. Batchelor, 1972; *Reason Aflame: Unamuno and the Heroic Will* by Victor Ouimette, 1974; *Unamuno: Abel Sánchez* by Nicholas G. Round, 1974, and *Re-reading Unamuno*, 1989, edited by Round; *Unamuno's Webs of Fatality* by David G. Turner, 1974; *Miguel de Unamuno: The Contrary Self* by Frances Wyers, 1976; *Miguel de Unamuno: San Manuel Bueno, Mártir* by John Butt, 1981; *Unamuno: Niebla* by Paul R. Olson, 1984; *The Tragic Pursuit of Being: Unamuno and Sartre* by Robert Richmond Ellis, 1988; *The Legend of Herostratus: Existential Envy in Rousseau and Unamuno* by Gregory L. Ulmer, 1989; *Elusive Self: Archetypal Approaches to the Novels of Miguel de Unamuno* edited by Gayana Jurkevich, 1991; *Intra-historia in Miguel de Unamuno's Novels: A Continual Presence* by Peggy W. Watson, 1993; *Uncovering the Mind: Unamuno, the Unknown, and the Vicissitudes of Self* by Alison Sinclair, 2001.

*   *   *

Miguel de Unamuno strove very consciously to be the voice and conscience of Spain for his generation, to give form to a timeless and metaphysical "Spanishness" that he felt as part of his flesh and bone. The Basque, educated in Madrid, found the roots of his life in the ancient university town of Salamanca as professor of Greek and Romance philology, later as rector of the university. His academic profession served as a secure base for Unamuno, as did his marriage and the family it produced. Yet his unquiet spirit drove him to incessant travel throughout the peninsula in his attempt to know Spain in its most intimate historical, linguistic, and geographical detail. His travels are recorded in two collections of short articles, *Por tierras de Portugal y de España* [Through the Lands of Portugal and of Spain] and *Andanzas y visiones españolas* [Spanish Adventures and Fantasies]. Their language is not that of the Baedeker, but a subjective, often intellectual, reaction to provincial cities and towns, rivers, mountains, and plains. Indeed, Unamuno lacked the painter's eye for colour and detail; everywhere he finds literary and historical associations. A stripped cork-oak brings to his mind the martyrdom of St. Bartholomew; a group of shepherds he encounters are the very ones Don Quixote engaged in his "eternal discourse"; Trujillo is the cradle of the conquistadores; Avila, of course, is St. Teresa.

Unamuno is one of the most difficult writers to classify in a generation of extreme individualists—the Generation of 1898. This loosely defined group included poets, novelists, playwrights, and essayists of outstanding quality. Unamuno wrote in all of these forms, but in one field he was unique: he was the only theologian of the literary group. He was a troubled, anguished, declamative doubter whose quest for God was basic to all of his mature work. Like Pascal and Kierkegaard, whose writing he knew and revered, the Basque could accept no religious panaceas or compromises. Following a religious crisis in 1897, he was deeply shaken to an agonizing awareness of his own mortality and the horrendous void of non-being. He could no longer accept the traditional comforts of Catholic doctrine nor accommodate himself to the facile, intellectualized atheism of some rationalist currents. He read widely in contemporary Protestant theologians, but was not looking for answers; he was looking for the core questions that would serve him to find his own answers, his personal faith that could never be enshrined in doctrine or dogma. Years later this desperate search would be externalized in his great philosophical analysis, *Del sentimiento trágico de la vida en los hombres y en los pueblos* (*The Tragic Sense of Life in Men and in Peoples*). Faith was never a serene gift to Unamuno. It had to be constantly re-examined, explored, doubted, denied, and re-vindicated. This is the sense of a second treatise, *La agonía del cristianismo* (*The Agony of Christianity*).

Unamuno had written an early historical, loosely autobiographical novel, *Paz en la guerra* (*Peace in War*), dealing with the impact of the Carlist wars on Bilbao, where he had spent his childhood. He did not repeat this exercise of writing within the typical framework of 19th-century historical fiction. He sought a totally different approach, a more reduced and intimate way of creating fictional beings and examining their reactions to life. His first *nivola*—as he baptized this new form—was *Niebla* (*Mist*); it is one of his most widely translated and universally admired creations. Augusto Pérez, a rich young man of no talent, no convictions, and no overriding interests, wanders through life as a series of relationships grow around him. He decides to be in love, and when the girl he has chosen, a piano teacher who detests music, dupes him and runs off with her lover, Augusto determines to kill himself. First, however, he wants to discuss his decision with Unamuno, and he makes the journey to Salamanca to consult the sage. Unamuno informs Augusto that suicide is impossible for him, since Augusto is merely a character in a novel that Unamuno is writing. The author tells his creation that he will, indeed, kill him in the novel. Now, Augusto, threatened with death from outside himself, wants desperately to live. He begs for his life, but the author rather testily replies that he can't carry Augusto about with him indefinitely. Augusto points out that Unamuno, too, will die, that God will run out of ideas for him, and he, too, will return to nothingness, as will the readers as well. Unamuno is obdurate with the death sentence and Augusto, terribly shaken, returns to Madrid, orders an almost endless meal, and dies that night of a heart attack induced by over-eating.

The situation of the character appealing to his author, of confrontation between creator and created, broke totally with 19th-century novelistic procedure and provided Unamuno with a means to examine his own existence as well as his creative instinct. His next novel, *Abel Sánchez*, is a chilling study of envy and hatred: the Cain/Abel theme that obsessed Unamuno and was later given theatrical form in his play *El otro* (*The Others*). Between 1898 and 1929 Unamuno wrote half a dozen short plays. All are muddled and undramatic, serving as clumsy vehicles for the ideas he had already examined more effectively in his essays and novels.

The political dimension of Unamuno's thought parallels his religious quest. He was outspoken in the extreme on questions of government. An early attraction to socialism and the nascent workers' movements in Spain, along with wide reading in the social philosophy of the late 19th century, especially German, inspired him for a while in the 1890s, but was soon rejected. He quickly came to feel that the progressive doctrines of a workers' state were fundamentally deceptive and served only to mask the true problems of Man's existence in the world. As he found no panaceas in organized religion, he found none in organized or organizational politics. His severe criticism of the Spanish monarchy and the ineptitude of its ministers during World War I grew ever more volatile with the disaster of Spain's African policy and the dictatorship of Primo de Rivera in the 1920s, and led finally to his exile from 1924 to 1930. The establishment of the Republic in 1931 restored Unamuno to the rectorship of the university of Salamanca, but the chaotic politics of Spanish liberalism pleased him no more than the repressive regime of Alfonso XIII. He continued to criticize both left and right of the new government in the most acerbic tones, a Socratic gadfly in every area of public faith.

It was perhaps primarily as a poet that Unamuno sought the immortality of literary fame. His production was voluminous, from the early *Poesías* [Poems] to the *Romancero del destierro* [Ballads of Exile] and a posthumous collection, *Cancionero* [Songs]. His major work of poetry is the massive *El Cristo de Velázquez* (*The Christ of Velázquez*), a long and complex meditation on the figure of the crucified Christ painted by the Spanish baroque master. This fervent Christology has all the thunder and bombast of evangelical certainty, but with the peculiar and personal insight of Unamuno, of "religious, not theological faith, free of dogma." As a poet, Unamuno lacked tone and sensibility; he had little ear for the rhythms and subtleties of verse. As he resorts to declamation and repetition in his essays, so he does in his poetry, rejecting the refinements of language and the sensuality of metaphor typical of Modernism, the movement that had

influenced both the poetry and the prose of many of his contemporaries. In his frequently tortured lines, Unamuno gives us little music, little that might be called lyric beauty. He tries to open our eyes to see his own despairing vision of reality, and this severe honesty gives unmatched force and intensity of spirit to the best of his work.

One short novel that may stand as a recapitulation of Unamuno's thought and style, perhaps his last *nivola*, is *San Manuel Bueno*. Revealed here is the tragedy of a village priest who is denied the gift—or the blindfold—of faith. His life is spent in the martyrdom of leading a village of simple folk in a faith that he cannot personally accept, in the "pious fraud" of giving temporal peace and the hope of eternal life to those who must never feel the agony of Christian doubt. The author raises the question, Does faith make the martyr, or does the martyr, in his own heroic act, make the faith?

Unamuno had very real shortcomings as a poet, novelist, and dramatist, yet through all his work the originality of his mind and the sincerity and magnitude of his philosophic and religious quest elevate the text and smooth the sometimes bellicose harshness of his language, often as gritty as the clay of the Castilian highlands he so loved.

—James Russell Stamm

See the essay on *The Christ of Velazquez* and *Mist*.

UNDSET, Sigrid

Born: Kalundborg, Denmark, 20 May 1882; brought up in Oslo, Norway. **Education:** Educated at Commercial College, Oslo, graduated 1898. **Family:** Married the painter Anders C. Svarstad in 1912 (marriage annulled 1924); two sons and one daughter. **Career:** Worked in office of electrical firm, Oslo, 1899–1909; then writer; converted to Catholicism, 1925; lived in the United States during World War II. **Awards:** Nobel prize for literature, 1928. Honorary degrees: Rollins College, Winter Park, Florida, 1942; Smith College, Northampton, Massachusetts, 1943. Grand Cross of Order of St. Olav, 1947. **Died:** 10 June 1949.

PUBLICATIONS

Collections

Middelalder-romaner [Historical Novels]. 10 vols., 1959.
Romaner og fortellinger fra nutiden [Contemporary Novels and Stories]. 10 vols., 1964–65.
The Unknown Sigrid Undset: Jenny and Other Works, translated by Tiina Nunnally. 2001.

Fiction

Fru Marta Oulie [Mrs. Martha Oulie]. 1907.
Den lykkelige alder [The Happy Age]. 1908.
Fortællingen om Viga-Ljot og Vigdis. 1909; as *Gunnar's Daughter*, translated by Arthur G. Chater, 1936.
Jenny. 1911; as *Jenny*, translated by W. Emmé, 1920.
Fattige skjæbner [Miserable Fates]. 1912.
Vaaren [Spring]. 1914.

Splinten av troldspeilet. 1917; as *Images in a Mirror*, translated by Arthur G. Chater, 1938.

De kloke jomfruer [The Wise Virgins]. 1918.

Kristin Lavransdatter, translated by Charles Archer and J.S. Scott. 1930.

> *Kransen.* 1920; as *The Garland*, translated by Charles Archer and J.S. Scott, 1922; as *The Bridal Wreath*, translated by Archer and Scott, 1923; as *The Wreath*, translated with introduction by Tiina Nunnally, 1997.
>
> *Husfrue.* 1922; as *The Mistress of Husaby*, translated by Charles Archer, 1925.
>
> *Korset.* 1922; as *The Cross*, translated by Charles Archer, 1927.

Olav Audunssøn i Hestviken. 2 vols., 1925; *Olav Audunssøn og hans børn*, 2 vols., 1927; entire text, as *The Master of Hestviken* (includes *The Axe*; *The Snake Pit*; *In the Wilderness*; *The Son Avenger*), translated by Arthur G. Chater, 4 vols., 1928–30; single-volume edition, 1934.

Gymnadenia. 1929; as *The Wild Orchid*, translated by Arthur G. Chater, 1931.

Den brændende busk. 1930; as *The Burning Bush*, translated by Arthur G. Chater, 1932.

Ida Elisabeth. 1932; as *Ida Elisabeth*, translated by Arthur G. Chater, 1933.

Elleve år. 1934; as *The Longest Years*, translated by Arthur G. Chater, 1935.

Den trofaste hustru. 1936; as *The Faithful Wife*, translated by Arthur G. Chater, 1937.

Madame Dorthea. 1939; as *Madame Dorothea*, translated by Arthur G. Chater, 1941.

Verse

Ungdom [Youth]. 1910.

Plays

Østenfor sol og vestenfor maane [East of the Sun and West of the Moon]. 1960.

Other

Fortællinger om Kong Artur og ridderne av Det runde Bord [Tales of King Arthur and the Knights of the Round Table]. 1915.

Tre søstre [Three Sisters]. 1917.

Et kvindesynspunkt [A Woman's Point of View]. 1919.

Katolsk propaganda [Catholic Propaganda]. 1927.

Etapper. 2 vols., 1929–33; as *Stages on the Road*, translated by Arthur G. Chater, 1934.

Hellig Olav, Norges Konge [St. Olav, King of Norway]. 1930.

Christmas and Twelfth Night: Reflections, translated by E.C. Ramsden. 1932.

Fortschritt, Rasse, Religion (written in German). 1935.

Norske helgener. 1937; as *Saga of Saints*, translated by E.C. Ramsden, 1934.

Selvportretter og landskapsbilleder. 1938; as *Men, Women, and Places*, translated by Arthur G. Chater, 1939.

Tilbake til fremtiden. 1945; as *Return to the Future*, translated by Henriette K. Naeseth, 1942.

Lykkelige dager—. 1947; as *Happy Times in Norway*, translated by Joran Birkeland, 1943.

Die Saga von Vilmund Vidutan und seinen Gefährten (written in German), translated as *Sigurd and His Brave Companions, a Tale of Medieval Norway.* 1943.

Caterina av Siena. 1951; as *Catherine of Siena*, translated by Kate Austin-Lund, 1954.

Artikler og taler fra krigstiden [Articles and Speeches from the War]. 1952.

Steen Steensen Blicher. 1957; as *Diary of a Parish Clerk*, translated by Alexander Fenton, 1976.

I grålysningen [At Dawn]. 1968.

*

Bibliography: *Sigrid Undset bibliografi* by Ida Packness, in *Norsk Bibliografisk Bibliotek*, 1963; *Sigrid Undset in America: An Annotated Bibliography and Research Guide* by Marie Maman, 2000.

Critical Studies: *Three Ways of Modern Man* by Harry Slochower, 1937; *Six Scandinavian Novelists: Lie, Jacobsen, Heidenstam, Selma Lagerlöf, Hamsun, Sigrid Undset* by Alrik Gustafson, 1940; *Sigrid Undset: A Study in Christian Realism* by A.H. Winsnes, translated by P.G. Foote, 1953; *Sigrid Undset* by Carl F. Bayerschmidt, 1970; *Sigrid Undset: Chronicles of Norway* by Mitzi Brunsdale, 1988; *Vertical Man: The Human Being in the Catholic Novels of Graham Greene, Sigrid Undset and George Bernanos* by J.C. Whitehouse, 1990; *Kristin: A Reading* by Andrew Lytle, 1992; *Redefining Integrity: The Portrayal of Women in the Contemporary Novels of Sigrid Undset* by Elisabeth Solbakken, 1992; *Sigrid Undset on Saints and Sinners: New Translations and Studies*, edited with introduction by Deal W. Hudson, 1993; *Paradigms and Paradoxes in the Life and Letters of Sigrid Undset* by Sister Margaret Dunn, 1994.

* * *

Thirst for knowledge and wide reading, particularly in the fields of history and archaeology, disposed Sigrid Undset early in life to a career as a researcher into and chronicler of past ages. Coming from an academic background, she used her intimate knowledge of Norwegian history as a foundation for number of medieval historical novels, of which the most successful were the trilogy *Kristin Lavransdatter*, set in the 14th century, and the novels about Olav Audunssøn, from the 13th century.

Kristin Lavransdatter is usually classed as Undset's finest achievement. It is the story of a young girl, Kristin, and her development through maturity, marriage, and motherhood, to old age and death, the whole set against a panoramic backdrop of medieval Norway, involving the political jockeyings between the Scandinavian kingdoms, and the struggles between an emergent Christianity and a still tenacious paganism. The illusion of realism is sustained by a wealth of detail about the minutiae of daily life; yet the greatest strength of the trilogy lies in the timeless and sympathetic portrayal of the central character. Kristin, as a young woman, is torn between submission to the patriarchal tradition and the desire to follow the dictates of her own heart; she chooses the latter, but pays a heavy price of guilt and self-recrimination throughout her life.

Not all of Undset's fiction is historical; in fact the majority of her novels and short stories deal with contemporary society. She was herself forced to earn her own living while a young woman, and many of the women in her novels and stories are modern working girls, faced with the dilemmas created by the clash between newly-won independence and traditional expectations. The central characters of

Fattige skjæbner [Miserable Fates] are low-paid workers who suffer from both physical and emotional deprivation, finding that the struggle to survive takes all their strength. The eponymous heroine of *Jenny* is an artist who stakes her life on fulfilment both in art and in love, and is defeated—but because of forces within herself rather than social or moral pressures. Undset's relationship with women's liberation was always an ambivalent one; her heroines have ambition and ability which demand to be realized, and yet many of them, like Marta in *Fru Marta Oulie* [Mrs. Martha Oulie], conclude with the insight that home, husband, and family represent the ultimate goal of female self-fulfilment.

Religious themes are central to many of Undset's novels, particularly her medieval ones. In 1925 she became a Catholic, yet she was never a dogmatic one; on religious as on many other matters she kept an open mind. In the political crisis of the 1930s, however, she took a determined stand, speaking out and writing against Nazism from the start. With the outbreak of the war she had to flee to the United States, and her career in fiction came to an abrupt end in the middle of a planned series of books; but she continued writing essays and memoirs until the end of her life.

—Janet Garton

See the essay on *Kristin Lavransdatter*.

UNGARETTI, Giuseppe

Born: Alexandria, Egypt, 10 February 1888. **Education:** Educated at École Suisse Jacot, Alexandria, until 1905; Collège de France, Paris, 1912; the Sorbonne, Paris. **Military Service:** Served in the Italian army infantry, 1915–18. **Family:** Married Anne Jeanne Dupoix in 1920 (died 1958); one daughter and one son. **Career:** Paris correspondent, *Popolo d'Italia*, 1919–20; journalist, Ministry of Foreign Affairs, Rome, 1921–30; travel writer, *Gazzetta del Popolo*, Turin, 1931–35; joint managing editor, *Mesures*, Paris, 1935–36; professor of Italian literature, University of São Paulo, Brazil, 1936–42; professor of modern Italian literature, University of Rome, 1942–59. Visiting professor, Columbia University, New York, 1964; lecturer, Harvard University, Cambridge, Massachusetts, 1968. President, European Community of Writers, 1962–63. **Awards:** Premio del Gonfaloniere, 1932; Premio Roma, 1949; International Grand prize for poetry, 1956; Etna-Taormina International prize, 1967; Neustadt International prize, 1970. Chevalier, Légion d'honneur (France); Honorary fellow, Modern Language Association (United States). **Member:** Bavarian Academy. **Died:** 1/2 June 1970.

PUBLICATIONS

Verse

Il porto sepolto. 1916.
La Guerre (in French). 1919.
Allegria di naufragi. 1919; revised edition, as *L'Allegria*, 1931; edited by Annalisa Cima, 1967.
Sentimento del tempo. 1933.
La vita d'un uomo. 1942–69:
    L'allegria. 1942.
    Sentimento del tempo. 1943.

Poesie disperse. 1945.
Il dolore (1937–1946). 1947.
La terra promessa. 1954.
Un grido e paesaggi. 1954.
Il taccuino del vecchio. 1961.
Tutte le poesie, edited by Leone Piccione. 1969; revised edition, 1972.
Frammenti per la terra promessa. 1945.
Derniers jours 1919, edited by Enrico Falqui. 1947.
La terra promessa. 1950.
Gridasti: Soffoco. . . 1951.
Un grido e paesaggi. 1952.
The Promised Land and Other Poems: An Anthology of Four Contemporary Poets, edited by Sergio Pacifici. 1957.
Life of a Man, edited and translated by Allen Mandelbaum. 1958; revised edition, as *Selected Poems*, 1975.
Il taccuino del vecchio. 1960.
Quattro poesie. 1960.
75° compleanno: Il taccuino del vecchio, Apocalissi. 1963.
Poesie, edited by Elio Felippo Accrocca. 1964.
Apocalissi e sedici traduzioni. 1965.
Morte delle stagioni, edited by Leone Piccioni. 1967.
Dialogo, with Bruna Bianco. 1968.
Croazia segreta. 1969.
L'impietrito e il velluto. 1970.
Selected Poems, edited and translated by Patrick Creagh. 1971.
Major Selection of the Poetry of Giuseppe Ungaretti, translated by Diego Bastianutti. 1997.
Giuseppe Ungaretti: Selected Poems, translated by Andrew Frisardi. 2002.

Other

Piccola Roma. 1944.
La vita d'un uomo (translations):
    40 Sonetti di Shakespeare. 1946.
    Da Góngora e da Mallarmé. 1948.
    Fedra di Jean Racine (includes critical study). 1950.
    Visioni di William Blake. 1965.
Il povero nella città (essays). 1949.
Pittori italiani contemporanei. 1950.
La vita d'un uomo (prose):
    Il deserto e dopo: Prose di viaggio e saggi. 1961.
    Saggi e interventi, edited by Mario Discono and Luciano Rebay. 1974.
Viaggetto in Etruria. 1965.
Il carso mon è piú un inferno, edited by Vanni Scheiwiller. 1966.
Innocence et mémoire. 1969.
Propos improvisés, with J. Amrouche. 1972.
Lettere a un fenomenologo. 1972.
Lettere dal fronte a Gherardo Marone (1916–1918), edited by Armando Marone. 1978.
Lettere a Sofizi, 1917–1930, edited by Paola Montefoschi and Leoni Piccioni. 1981.
Lettere a Giovanni Papini, 1915–1948, edited by Maria Antonietta Terzoli. 1988.
Editor, with David Lajolo, *I poeti scelti.* 1949.
Editor, *Le voci tragiche di Guido Gonzato.* 1952.
Translator, *Traduzioni.* 1936.
Translator, *XXII Sonetti di Shakespeare.* 1944.

Translator, *L'Après-midi et le monologue d'un faune*, by Mallarmé. 1947.
Translator, *Finestra del caos*, by Murilo Mendes. 1961.
Translator, *Visioni di William Blake* (selection). 1965.
Translator, *Anabase*, by Saint-John Perse. 1967 (trilingual edition, with English translation by T.S. Eliot).
Translator, *Cinque poesie di Vinicius de Moraes.* 1969.

*

Critical Studies: *Ungaretti* by Glauco Cambon, 1967; *Three Modern Italian Poets: Saba, Ungaretti, Montale* by Joseph Cary, 1969; "Ungaretti Issue" of *Books Abroad 44*, 1970; *Ungaretti Poet and Critic* by Frederic J. Jones, 1977.

* * *

Together with Montale, Giuseppe Ungaretti is regarded as the most important modern Italian poet. This, however, does not mean that there is any fundamental affinity between the two, nor, for that matter, any comparison in terms of their influence. Montale's has no doubt been a greater and more enduring influence than that of Ungaretti. But it was Ungaretti who, with his first volume of poems, *Il porto sepolto* [The Buried Harbour], which came out nine years before Montale's *Ossi di seppia* (*Cuttlefish Bones*), signalled a crucial and creatively important reaction against D'Annunzianism and made the kind of impact that only a major poet could have made. Pinpointing what was original in his poetry, the Italian critic Francesco Flora characterized it as hermetic, thereby indicating the succinct, epigrammatic, and impressionistically graphic character of Ungaretti's lyricism and particularly of his poetic imagery. In fact, in Ungaretti's best and most characteristic lyrics imagery and sentiment, moral intensity and artistic self-control, verbal economy and evocative richness are so interfused as to form a closely-knit pattern that serves as its own objective correlative. Another characteristic of Ungaretti's poetry, which he shares with Saba, is his habit of taking the depth and tumult of a personal sentiment as a sufficient guarantee that even a simple and unelaborated linguistic transcription of it can stand by itself as poetry. Thus what is subjective about Ungaretti's lyricism is rooted in what one might call psychological innocence or naive psychologism.

The volumes *Allegria di naufragi, Sentimento del tempo* [The Feeling of Time], and *Il dolore* [Pain] represent Ungaretti's art and technique at their best—an art in which, by discarding the use of punctuation, traditional syntax, and metre, and by introducing the pauses or the so-called "spazi bianchi" (blank spaces), Ungaretti not only forges the accents and idiom of modern poetry, but also achieves a peculiar kind of unity and autonomy that reminds one of Imagistic poetry. In the poems dealing with the theme of his brother's and his son's deaths—the most poignantly personal Ungaretti ever wrote—while giving vent to his sense of bereavement, he shows a degree of self-control and moral maturity that determined the form and structure as well as the style and imagery of his best poetry. In such poems each and every detail—a memory, an image, or an association—serves to transmute the pain of a personal tragedy into something objective and impersonal and mould it into the sharply chiselled contours of art. From the anguished yet ennobling intensity of personal tragedy Ungaretti derived a strength, and—more importantly—a relentless austerity of form and diction, which enabled him to deal with the explosive force of emotion with impressive mastery over

the imaginative resources of the language as well as over his own experience.

Ungaretti subsequently published other volumes of poetry in which the theme of bereavement gives way to the theme of love—love which, "mentre arrivo vicino al gran silenzio" ("while I approach the great silence"), reasserts its hold on the poet and makes him experience all its frenzy, and all its grandeur and cruelty once more. For under the duress of the race against time and of the relentless tug-of-war between age and desire, reason and emotion, the poet finds himself in the grip of what Thomas Hardy called "the strongest passion known to humanity" which shakes "this fragile frame at eve / With throbbings of noontide."

—G. Singh

See the essay on "Sirens."

d'URFÉ, Honoré

Born: 1567(?); baptized 11 February 1567. **Education:** Educated at the collège des Jesuites, Tournon, 1577–83. **Family:** Married Diane de Châteaumorand in 1600. **Career:** Lieutenant general of Forez government, appointed by the Duke of Nemours, 1594; governor of Forez, 1595. Arrested by royalists and imprisoned briefly in Montbrison, 1595. Supporter of the Ligue and after its defeat retired to the territories of the Duke of Savoy. **Died:** (in the course of military operations between Savoy and Genoa) 1625.

PUBLICATIONS

Fiction

L'Astrée. Part I, 1607; part II, 1610; part III, 1619; part IV, 1627; *La Conclusion et dernière partie d'Astrèe* (completed by Balthazar Baro), 1628; edited by Hugues Vaganay. 5 vols., 1925–28, Maurice Magendie, 1928; Gérard Genette, 1964; Maxime Gaume, 1981; as *The History of Astrea: The First Part*, translated anonymously, 1620; as *Astrea: Part One*, translated with introduction by Steven Rendall, 1995.
Les Tristes Amours de Floridon. 1628.

Verse

Le Sireine. 2nd edition, 1606; enlarged edition, 1618; edited by Marcos, 1979.
La Sylvanire; ou, La Morte-vive. 1627.

Other

La Triomphante Entrée de la tres illustre Dame Madame Madeleine de la Rochefoucauld. 1583; edited by Maxime Gaume, 1976.
Les Épîtres morales. 3 vols., 1598–1608.

*

Bibliography: *Recherches bibliographiques sur le Roman d'Astrée* by A.J. Bernard, 1839.

Critical Studies: *La Vie et les oeuvres d'Honoré d'Urfé* by O.-C. Reure, 1910; *L'Astrée: Ses origines, son importance dans la formation de la littérature classique* by Henri Bochet, 1923; *Aesthetics and Art in the Astrée of Honoré d'Urfé* by Mary C. MacMahon, 1925; *Du nouveau sur L'Astrée* by Maurice Magendie, 1927; *Un paradis désespéré: L'Amour et l'illusion dans "L'Astrée"* by Jacques Ehrmann, 1963; *Les Inspirations et les sources de l'oeuvre d'Honoré d'Urfé* by Maxime Gaume, 1977; *The Character under the Mask: Disguise and Identity in "L'Astrée,"* 1980, and *The Pastoral Masquerade: Disguise and Identity in "L' Astrée,"* 1992, both by Laurence A. Gregorio; *The Golden World of the Pastoral: A Comparative Study of Sidney's "New Arcadia" and d'Urfé's "L'Astrée"* by Myriam Y. Jehenson, 1981; *Honoré d'Urfé* by Louise K. Horowitz, 1984; *L'Astrée et Polexandre: Du roman pastoral au roman héroïque* by Madeleine Bertaud, 1986; *Une esthétique nouvelle: Honoré d'Urfé, correcteur de l'Astrée (1607–1625)* by Anne Sancier-Chateau, 1995; *Subjectivity and the Signs of Love: Discourse, Desire, and the Emergence of Modernity in Honoré d'Urfé's L'Astrée* by James M. Hembree, 1997; *Forgotten Virgo: Humanism and Absolutism in Honoré d'Urfé's "l'Astrée"* by Kathleen Wine, 2000; *Narrative Transformations from L'Astrée to Le berger extravagant* by Leonard Hinds, 2001.

* * *

Honoré d'Urfé is remembered chiefly for *L'Astrée*, which marked the true beginning of the French novel. It is a work in the pastoral tradition, published in five parts between 1607 and 1627: the fifth and last section was published by d'Urfé's secretary, Balthazar Baro, after the author's death.

The novel is set in 5th-century Forez, in the area of the River Lignon, where d'Urfé had spent his childhood. The love between the shepherd Céladon and the shepherdess Astrée is troubled by jealousy and Astrée banishes him from her presence. In despair, he jumps into the river and is carried away. He is rescued by three nymphs, who fall in love with him. He remains faithful to Astrée and, respecting her command never to return unless summoned, withdraws into the forest to build a temple dedicated to her. Helped by a druid, he finally approaches her disguised as a girl. Reminded of her lover, Astrée befriends "Alexis" and talks of her remorse, but Céladon still refuses to reveal his identity. After further adventures, Baro's concluding section finally unites the lovers in eternal bliss.

This outline is the framework for a 5,000-page novel of some complexity. In addition to Astreé and Céladon, there are scores of lesser characters and some 50 sub-plots ingeniously interwoven. D'Urfé describes an idyllic woodland setting peopled by sensitive and well-educated shepherds and shepherdesses who spend their time telling stories, writing poetry, discussing problems of the heart, and organizing platonic but accident-prone love affairs.

Like his predecessor, Montemayor, d'Urfé does not hide the fact that his characters are shepherds in name only: the way they exchange visits, indulge in leisurely conversations about feelings, and never directly involve themselves in manual work clearly evokes the life of the rural gentry of his day. Even the nymphs are not mythological figures, but represent the nobility of the Court. To a 17th-century reader therefore, *L'Astrée* did not have the air of unreality that makes it difficult for modern readers: on the contrary, the contemporary social hierarchy is scrupulously respected. An even clearer sign that the novel is not really just about shepherds is the amount of heroic activity that it contains: on top of the pastoral convention, d'Urfé has grafted a novel of romantic adventure containing numberless duels, battles, escapes, disguises, and enchantments. These episodes are far more numerous than in the Spanish models.

But the unifying factor is love. Every conceivable shade of feeling is developed and analyzed, from falling in love to jealousy, from shyness to rejection. Without being an abstraction, each character embodies some kind of amorous sentiment: from the true lovers Astrée and Céladon to the mystic Silvandre, the faithless Hylas, and the perfidious Sémire. Many of the sub-plots examine some aspect of love and differing viewpoints are vigorously debated. Behind the pastoral fiction, *L'Astrée* is already a *roman d'analyse*.

It also demonstrates that the rationalism associated with Corneille had already made an impression at the beginning of the new century. Love may be central to our lives, but it also involves judgement. Running through *L'Astrée* is the Aristotelian notion that love is linked to merit: "It is difficult to love a person one does not admire . . . [Love] is an act of will which extends only to what the understanding deems to be good." Moreover, love tends to be associated with heroism. The plight of lovers simultaneously separated and drawn together by their notion of "gloire," famously explored in *Le Cid*, is already a prominent feature of *L'Astrée*. If Céladon had not felt honour-bound to wait for Astrée to end his banishment, the novel would have been rather shorter! Like Corneille's heroes, these lovers lucidly analyze their feelings and never let passion take over. Where heart and head conflict, reason invariably triumphs, through a fierce exercise of will: when Eudoxe chooses to reject the man she loves because he is of too lowly a rank, we read that "she resolved to remain mistress of her will."

To a modern reader, the work is undeniably flawed: it is too long, the narrative pace is slow, there are too many digressions, too much depends on chance, and the interminable conversations resemble exercises in subtlety. But these defects are those of the pastoral convention. In the 17th century, the novel had a colossal impact. It was hugely popular and the publication of each volume was a literary event. The notion of pure love had a great influence on the development of the *précieux* salons and, indirectly, on classicism itself. The precision of the setting, vague as it seems today, was something new in the novel. Its themes and stories proved a rich source of inspiration to later novelists and playwrights. As well as prefiguring aspects of Cornelian psychology, the novel's profound analysis of the human heart anticipates Racine. The simple clarity of d'Urfé's style, a clear reaction against the contrived metaphors of his contemporaries Nervèze and Des Escuteaux, entitles him to be considered one of the initiators of classical prose. And, a century later, it drew tears from Rousseau, the precursor of Romanticism.

—David Shaw

V

VALENZUELA, Luisa

Born: Buenos Aires, Argentina, 26 November 1938. **Education:** Attended Belgrano Girls' School; Colegio Nacional Vicente Lopez, Buenos Aires; University of Buenos Aires, B.A. **Family:** Married Theodore Marjak in 1958 (divorced, 1964); one daughter. **Career:** Lived in Paris, 1958–61; assistant editor of Sunday supplement, *La Nacion*; Buenos Aires, 1964–69; freelance journalist in the United States, Europe and Mexico, 1970–73; and Buenos Aires, 1973–79; writer-in-residence, Columbia University, New York, 1980–83; Visiting Professor, New York University, 1984–89; Fellow, New York Institute for the Humanities. Lived in New York, Buenos, and Teopoztlan, Mexico, 1978–89; returned to Buenos Aires, 1989. Visiting Professor, Escorial for Madrid's Universidad Complutense, 1993. Visiting Professor, California Arts Institute, Los Angeles, 1995. **Awards:** Fondo Nacional de las Artes award 1966 and 1973; Insituto Nacional de Cinematografia award, 1973; Fulbright fellowship, 1969–70; Guggenheim fellowship,1983; Honorary Degree in Humane Letters from Know College (Illinois), 1991; Honored by the 15th Puterbaugh Conference on World Literature at the University of Oklahoma, 1995.

PUBLICATIONS

Fiction

Hay que sonreir. 1966; as *Clara: Thirteen Short Stories and a Novel*, translated by Hortense Carpentier, and J. Jorge Castello, 1976; with selections from *Los hereticos*, also translated as *Clara* by Andrea G Labinger, 2000.
Los hereticos (short stories). 1967.
El gato eficaz. 1972.
Aqui pasan cosas raras. 1975; as *Strange Things Happen Here: Twenty-Six Stories and a Novel*, translated by Helen Lane, 1979.
Como en la Guerra. 1977; as *He Who Searches*, translated by Helen Lane, 1979, 1986.
Libro que no muerde (short stories, essays). 1980.
Cambio de armas (short stories). 1982; as *Other Weapons*, translated by Deborah Bonner, 1985.
Donde viven las aguilas (short stories). 1983; as *Up Among the Eagles*, translated by Hortense Carpentier, in *Open Door*, 1988.
Cola de lagartija: El brujo hormiga roja senor del Tacuru. 1983; as *The Lizard's Tail*, translated by Gregory Rabassa, 1983.
Realidad nacional desde la cama. 1990; as *Bedside Manners*, translated by Margaret Jull Costa, 1995.
Novela negra con argentinos. 1990; as *Black Novel (with Argentines)*, translated by Toby Talbot. 1992.
Simetrias (short stories). 1993; as *Symmetries*, translated by Margaret Jull Costa, 1998.
Travesia. 2001.

Other

Peligrosos Palabras (essays). 2001.

Bibliography: "Selected Bibliography (Luisa Valenzuela)" by David Draper Clark, in *World Literature Today*, vol. 69, no. 4.

Critical Studies: "I Was Always a Bit of a Rebel" by Jane Katz, in *Artists in Exile*, 1983; *Reflections/Refractions: Reading Luisa Valenzuela* by Sharon Magnarelli,1988; "Luisa Valenzuela" by Marie-Lise Gazarian Gautier, in *Interviews with Latin American Writers*, 1989; *Poetica de transgresion en la novelistica de Luisa Valenzuela* by Juanamaria Cordones-Cook, 1991; "Writing with the Body" by Luisa Valenzuela, in *The Writer on Her Work*, vol. 2, 1991; "Appropriating the Master's Weapons: Luisa Valenzuela" by Debra A. Castillo, in *Talking Back: Toward a Latin American Feminist Literary Criticism*, 1992; "Luisa Valenzuela habla sobre Novela negra con argentinos y Realidad nacional desde la cama," in *Letras Femeninas*, vol. 18, 1992; *El silencio que habla: Aproximacion a la obra de Luisa Valenzuela* by Nelly Z. Martinez, 1994; "Journey to Luisa Valenzuela's Land of Fear" by Fernando Ainsa, in *World Literature Today*, vol. 69, no. 4, 1995; "The New Novel/A New Novel: Spider's Webs and Detectives in Luisa Valenzuela's Black Novel (with Argentines)" by Sharon Magnarelli, in *Studies in 20th Century Literature*, vol. 19, Winter, 1995; *La palabra en vilo: narrativa de Luisa Valenzuela*, edited by Gwendolyn Diaz and Maria Ines Lagos, 1996.

*   *   *

Luisa Valenzuela is known as one of the most prominent contemporary women authors from Latin America. Most of her novels and short story collections have been translated into English and published in North America. Her work, with its mixture of the fantastic and the real, has been characterized as belonging to that Latin American school of writing called magic realism. Valenzuela considers her prose as critical and revolutionary, as a form of "writing with the body" and thus has brought a decidedly feminist perspective to Hispanic American literature.

Valenzuela was drawn toward literature from a very early age. Her mother, Luisa Mercedes Levinson, was a well- known writer and Luisa was personally acquainted with such famous Latin American writers as Jorge Luis Borges and Julio Cortazar, who became influences on her work. From her early reading of Jack London, Somerset Maugham, Grahame Greene, and William Faulkner she would learn narrative techniques that she would later incorporate into her prose style. Foreign authors such as Raymond Radiguet and Sigmund Freud would inspire her to shape many of her novels with elements of the erotic and with psychoanalytic concepts.

While working as a young journalist in her native Argentina, Valenzuela published her first story at the age of 18, and two years later she published her first novel, *Hay que sonreir (Clara)*, which she wrote in Paris from 1959–61 during her marriage to a French sailor. Less experimental than her later fiction, the work nonetheless demonstrates her early feminist concerns since it describes the brutal exploitation and sordid life of a young prostitute living in Buenos Aires. As Valenzuela traveled widely her writing began to target more boldly the diverse aspects of society, its institutions, customs and taboos. Above all, she strove to expose the abuses of poverty, hunger, humiliation and exploitative relationships. *El gato eficaz* [Cat-O-Nine-Deaths] was begun in 1969 in the United States while she was a Fulbright scholar and was confronted by the shock of New York City. The novel reflects Valenzuela's desire to change her literary voice at this point in her career. The work criticizes modern love and marriage through a form of surrealistic writing that uses a teasing narrative tone and has no consistently recognizable theme or plot. It is with this novel that experimental techniques such as shifting points of view, extensive use of metaphors and word play become her trademarks.

After a return trip to Buenos Aires in 1975 where she observed the onset of the new repressive political regime, Valenzuela wrote a collection of short stories, *Aqui pasan cosas raras* (*Strange Things Happen Here*), which described the absurdity and horror of everyday life in Argentina. The narrative focus of these vignettes reveals a shift in tone from Valenzuela's previous use of humor and playfulness. The author instead stresses the paranoia, horror and violence of existence through associations of meanings and bizarre physical contiguities. This is exemplified in the title story which traces the misadventures of two characters who find in the city streets abandoned objects which eventually become obsessive burdens for them. In the late 1970s, Valenzuela's writing became even more strongly shaped by the events in Argentina that were propelled by a military government that was committed to the "dirty war" which caused the persecution, torture and the disappearance of thousands of people. She became particularly conscious of the idea of literature as a danger when she wrote *Como en la Guerra* (*He Who Searches*), for parts of the novel were cut by censors in Argentina, because scenes of torture were depicted. The novel's elusive plot uses as its point of departure a case history of psychoanalysis that also involves revolutionary terrorism, repression and torture that can be read as an allegory of Argentina's political regime.

Cola de lagartija (*The Lizard's Tale*), published in 1983, is considered Valenzuela's most interesting and effective artistic protest against the regime's horrendous political violence. The key player is a wizard who represents Lopez Rega, Argentina's minister of Welfare during Peron's government and that of his third wife, Isabel. On the other side are those Argentineans opposed to the terror, particularly in the form of the author's own persona, named Luisa Valenzuela. The historical reality of the text which depicts how the magician plots his dreams of omnipotence works within the realms of myth and metaphor. These demonstrate how the character of the writer, Valenzuela, uses her skill as a storyteller to rewrite language which can counteract and eventually overthrow the brutal power of the evil politician's sorcery. Valenzuela has often tied her criticism of Argentina's politics to trenchant criticism of the fate of women in such a society. The five narratives about male/female relationships in *Cambio de armas* (*Other Weapons*) examine the difficulties of maintaining personal ties in politically stressful times. The author's capacity as a storyteller also helped her to incorporate elements of mythology and ritual into the realistic settings of other Latin American locales that shape the collection of tales, *Donde viven las aguilas* (*Up Among the Eagles*). These stories are characterized by the author's love and respect for Latin American rituals and symbols. They also reflect her skill at reinventing myths, a narrative technique that shapes much of her fiction and symbolizes the way people in modern times recover the ability to integrate their lives.

In 1989 Valenzuela returned to Buenos Aires to complete a novel she had begun in New York, *Novela negra con argentinos* (*Black Novel [with Argentines]*). The work is written like a crime novel and depicts the fate of an Argentinean exile who seeks political asylum in New York and commits the same horror he was trying to escape. The author uses the meaningless murder as a metaphor for the horrors of the dirty war perpetrated by the Argentinean military. Valenzuea's shock on her return to a post-junta Argentina was reflected in another novel published in 1990, *Realidad nacional desde la cama* (*Bedside Manners*). The work is an absurdist political allegory that reminds readers about the ongoing threat of right-wing militarism in the country.

Although Valenzuela has at times been criticized for using self-indulgent prose and hyperbolic attempts at virtuosity, she has generally been praised for producing some of the most daring, innovative and important works of modern Latin American fiction. Her novels and story collections are continually reissued in new editions and translations; she carries the banner for free thought and speech through extensive lecturing and efforts on behalf of human rights organizations. The link between freedom and self-expression is inevitable, or as she so ardently states in "Writing with the Body," ". . . writing is an exercise of liberty."

—Diana Chlebek

VALÉRY, (Ambroise) Paul (Toussaint Jules)

Born: Cette (now Sète), France, 30 October 1871. **Education:** Educated at a school in Sète to 1884, and a lycée in Montpellier, 1884; University of Montpellier, licence in law 1892. **Military Service:** 1889–90. **Family:** Married Jeannie Gobillard in 1900, three children. **Career:** Worked for the War Office, 1897–99; private secretary to Édouard Lebey, director of the press association Agence Havas, Paris, 1900–22; editor, with Valéry Larbaud and Léon-Paul Fargue, *Commerce* literary review, 1924–32; administrator, Centre Universitaire Mediterranéen, Nice, from 1933; held Chair of Poetics, Collège de France, Paris, 1937–45. **Awards:** Honorary Doctorate: Oxford University. Chevalier, 1923, Officer, 1926, and Commander, 1931, Légion d'honneur. **Member:** Académie française. **Died:** 20 July 1945.

PUBLICATIONS

Collections

Collected Works, edited by Jackson Mathews. 15 vols., 1956–75.
Oeuvres, edited by Jean Hytier. 2 vols., 1957–60.

Verse (includes prose poems)

La Jeune Parque. 1917; edited by Octave Nadal, 1957.
Album de vers anciens 1890–1900. 1920.
Charmes; ou, Poèmes. 1922.
Poésies. 1933, enlarged edition, 1942.
Paraboles. 1935.
Mélange (includes prose). 1941.
L'Ange. 1946.
Agathe; ou, La Sainte du sommeil. 1956.
Paul Valéry: An Anthology, edited and translated by James R. Lawler. 1977.

Plays

Amphion: Mélodrame, music by Arthur Honegger (produced 1931). 1931.

Sémiramis: Mélodrame, music by Arthur Honegger (produced 1934). 1934.

Mon Faust (produced 1962). 1946.

Other

La Soirée avec Monsieur Teste. 1919, revised edition, as *Monsieur Teste 1*, 946; as *An Evening with Mr. Teste*, translated by Ronald Davis, 1925; also translated by Merton Gould, 1936; as *Monsieur Teste*, translated by Jackson Mathews, 1947.

Introduction à la méthode de Léonard de Vinci. 1919; as *Introduction to the Method of Leonardo da Vinci*, translated by Thomas McGreevy, 1929.

Eupalinos; ou, L'Architecte; L'Âme et la danse. 1923; as *Eupalinos; or, The Architect*, translated by William McCausland, 1932; as *Dance and the Soul*, translated by Dorothy Bussy, 1951.

Fragments sur Mallarmé. 1924.

Une conquête méthodique. 1924.

Variété 1–5. 5 vols., 1924–44; first 2 vols., as *Variety*, translated by Malcolm Cowley and William Aspenwall Bradley, 1927–38.

Durtal. 1925.

Études et fragments sur le rêve. 1925.

Le Retour de Hollande: Descartes et Rembrandt. 1926.

Petit Recueil de paroles de circonstance. 1926.

De la diction des vers. 1926.

Propos sur l'intelligence. 1926.

Analecta. 1926.

Rhumbs. 1926.

Quinze lettres à Pierre Lous (1916–17). 1926.

Autre Rhumbs. 1927.

Maîtres et amis. 1927.

Quatre lettres sur Nietzsche. 1927.

Essai sur Stendhal. 1927.

Lettre à Madame C . . . 1928.

Poésie: Essais sur la poétique et le poète. 1928.

Variation sur une "Pensée." 1930.

Propos sur la poésie. 1930.

Cahiers B. 1930; as *Notebooks*, translated by Paul Gifford, 2001.

Littérature. 1930.

Oeuvres. 12 vols., 1931–50.

Discours de l'histoire. 1932.

Choses tues. 1932.

Moralités. 1932.

Discours en l'honneur de Goethe. 1932.

Calepin d'un poète: Essais sur la poétique et le poète. 1933.

L'Idée fixe. 1934.

Pièces sur l' art. 1934.

Suite. 1934.

Hommage à Albert Thibaudet. 1936.

Villon et Verlaine. 1937.

L'Homme et la coquille. 1937; as *Sea Shells*, translated by Ralph Manheim, 1998.

Technique au service de la pensée. 1938.

Discours aux chirurgiens. 1938.

Introduction à la poétique. 1938.

Degas, Danse, Dessin. 1938; as *Degas, Dance, Drawing*, translated by Helen Burlin, 1948.

Existence du symbolisme. 1939.

Conférences. 1939.

Tel quel. 2 vols., 1941–43.

Mauvaises pensées et autres. 1942.

Eupalinos ou l'architecte; L'Âme et la danse; Dialogue de l'arbre. 1944.

Au sujet de Nerval. 1944.

Regards sur le monde actuel et autre essais. 1945; as *Reflections on the World Today*, translated by Francis Scarfe, 1948.

Henri Bergson. 1945.

Mon Faust: Ébauches. 1946.

Souvenirs poétiques. 1947.

Vues. 1948.

Écrits divers sur Stéphane Mallarmé. 1950.

Histoires brisées. 1950.

Selected Writings, translated by Denis Devlin. 1950.

Lettres à quelques-uns. 1952.

Correspondance 1890–1942, with André Gide, edited by Robert Mallet. 1955; as *Self-Portrait: The Gide/Valéry Letters*, translated by Jean Guicharnaud, 1966.

Correspondance 1887–1933, with Gustave Fourment, edited by Octave Nadal. 1957.

Cahiers. 29 vols., 1957–61.

Cahiers 1894–1914, edited by Nicole Celeyrette-Pietri and Judith Robinson-Valéry. 2 vols., 1989.

Translator, *Les Bucoliques*, by Virgil. 1953.

*

Bibliography: *Bibliographie des oeuvres de Valéry 1895–1925* by Ronald Davis and Raoul Simonson, 1926.

Critical Studies: *Valéry* by Theodora Bosanquet, 1935; *Valéry* by Elizabeth Sewell, 1952; *The Art of Valéry* by Francis Scarfe, 1954; *The Universal Self: A Study of Paul Valéry* by Agnes Ethel Mackay, 1961; *Valéry* by Henry Grubbs, 1968; *Worlds Apart: Structural Parallels in the Poetry of Paul Valéry, Saint-John Perse, Benjamin Peret, and René Char* by Elizabeth R. Jackson, 1976; *The Devil in Thomas Mann's "Doktor Faust" and Paul Valéry's "Mon Faust"* by Lucie Pfaff, 1976; *The Figure of Faust in Valéry and Goethe: An Exegesis of "Mon Faust"* by Kurt Weinburg, 1976; *Valéry* by Charles Gammons Whiting, 1978; *Figures of Transformation: Rilke and the Example of Valéry* by Richard Cox, 1979; *The Rhetoric of Valéry's Prose Aubades* by Ursula Franklin, 1979; *Corbière, Mallarmé, Valéry: Preservations and Commentary* by Robert L. Mitchell, 1981; *Valéry and the Poetry of Voice* by Christine M. Crow, 1982; *Valéry's "Album de vers anciens": A Past Transfigured* by Suzanne Nash, 1983; *Paul Valéry and Music: A Study of the Techniques of Composition in Valéry's Poetry* by Brian Stimpson, 1984; *Poetic Principles and Practice: Occasional Papers on Baudelaire, Mallarmé and Valéry* by Lloyd Austin, 1987; *Narrative Transgression and the Foregrounding of Language in Selected Prose Works of Poe, Valéry and Hofmannstahl* by Leroy T. Day, 1988; *Paul Valéry: Philosophical Reflections* by William Kluback, 1988; *Valéry and Poe: A Literary Legacy* by Lois Davis Vine, 1992; *Paul Valéry Revisited* by Walter C. Putnam, 1995; *Reading Paul Valéry: Universe in Mind*, edited by Paul Gifford, 1998; *Wittgenstein, Kraus, and Valéry: A Paradigm for Poetic Rhyme and Reason* by Luis Miguel Isava, 2002.

* * *

After 20 years of solitude and study (1897–1917), Paul Valéry broke his silence in 1917 with a 500-line poem, "La Jeune Parque" [The Young Fate]. His early poems were collected in *Album de vers anciens* (*Album of Early Verse*), and in 1922 his major collection, *Charmes* [Charms], appeared; this contains "Le Cimetière marin" ("The Graveyard by the Sea"), "Fragments du Narcisse" ("Fragments of the Narcissus"), "Ebauche d'un serpent" ("Silhouette of a Serpent"), "Palme" ("Palm"), and other poems. *Charmes* (meaning "incantations" or "poems") placed Valéry in company with the purest of the French poets—with Mallarmé, in particular, and with Chénier, La Fontaine, and Racine.

After *Charmes*, Valéry wrote two Platonic dialogues: *L'Âme et la danse* (*Dance and the Soul*), a meditation on the movement of a dancer that transforms her from an ordinary woman into a supernatural being; and *Eupalinos; ou, L'Architecte* (*Eupalinos; or, The Architect*), a discussion on the genius of the architect and, more generally, any artist who is able to create out of his chosen materials a masterpiece. In a series of five volumes of collected essays, *Variété* (*Variety*), Valéry discussed several problems of his age and analyzed various literary problems, especially those related to poets with whom he felt close affinity: Mallarmé, Verlaine, Baudelaire, Poe, La Fontaine.

For Valéry, the poet is the artist who does not stifle any of his inner voices or any of the hidden desires of his nature. His particular vocation forces him to translate and interpret those voices and desires. To do this, he must remain lucid and fully rational. He is not a man inspired by the Muse, but one who must cultivate a universal intelligence and thus not close himself off from any reality. "La Jeune Parque" describes the successive stages of consciousness in a young girl as she moves from sleep to a full awakening. "La Pythie" [The Pythoness] is the oracle, convulsed before she can deliver herself of the divine message (or the poem). In composing sonnets like "L'Abeille" ("The Bee"), "Les Grenades" ("Pomegranates") or odes like "Aurore" ("Dawn") or the long poems "Le Cimetière marin" and "La Jeune Parque," Valéry accepted all the discipline of the classical style, all the demanding rules of vocabulary, rhythm, and rhyme. He used metaphors, alliteration, and harmonious effects to sustain the mystery and the enchantment of the poem.

Charmes is the last landmark of French symbolism. From the time of its publication until his death, Valéry was an almost official representative of his country's culture. In today's language Valéry's mind and attitude would be called that of a *contestataire*. He decried any doctrine that named literature something sacred and, like his master Mallarmé, pointed out the discrepancy between the thought of a man and the words in which he tries to express the thought. The composition of a poem interrupts and distorts the purity of the inner dialogue the poet carries on with himself.

Valéry ushered in a movement in French literature in which the poem was preferred to the poet, the study of poetics preferred to the study of the poem, and a literary work studied in its relationship to the general power of language. He treated poetry as something comparable to architecture and music. All three of these arts were for Valéry the offspring of the science of numbers. Almost in spite of himself, his work was expressed in words, in poetry, and in accord with that "inspiration" (a word he disliked) that the contemplation of the sea offered him.

"Le Cimetière marin," not his greatest poem perhaps, but the one that has received the greatest attention, restored the forgotten resources of the decasyllabic line of French poetry. The long poem is a monologue in which the poet's voice speaks of the most basic and constant themes of his emotional and intellectual life associated with the sea and the sunlight as it strikes certain parts of the land bordering on the Mediterranean.

No thinker has considered this age with greater perspicacity and penetration than Valéry. And no thinker has demolished it more thoroughly. His fame has been built upon fragments—poems, aphorisms, dialogues, brief essays. He was the supreme example of a writer indifferent to his public, detached from any need to please his public. The actual "subjects" of his pages are varied: the beauty of a shell, the prose of Bossuet, the method of Stendhal. He tells us that *le moi pur* is unique and monotonous. Yet it is the deepest note of existence that dominates all the "varieties" of existence. To hear this note clearly was the goal and the ecstasy of Valéry's intellectual search.

With each essay, with each fragment of prose writing and each poem, Valéry extended the hegemony of his thought over most of the intellectual problems facing man today. But the subtlety and suppleness of his writing were such that he never reached, nor wished to reach, the creation of a philosophical system.

It has often been claimed that all of French literature, more than other national literatures, is of a social origin. It seems to come into its own under the stimulation of debate, in an atmosphere of worldliness and *mondanité*. Valéry was for many years, and particularly during the decade of the 1930s, looked upon as an esoteric poet, as a difficult thinker who never left the realm of abstractions, and hence as a writer who stood apart from the central tradition of French letters. But he was in reality a fervent observer of humanity and a man who always strove to express himself in the most meaningful and the most "social" way. The conquest of *le moi pur* led Valéry through a labyrinth of human experience and human sentiment, from the seeming indifference of Monsieur Teste to the tenderness of the character Lust in the posthumously published volume, *Mon Faust*. Our entire historical period is in his work—the gravest problems that worry us and the oldest myths that enchant us.

—Wallace Fowlie

See the essay on "Le Cimetière marin" and "La Jeune Parque."

VALLE-INCLÁN, Ramón (Mariá) del

Born: Ramón José Simón del Valle y Peña in Villanueva de Arosa, Galicia, Spain, 28 October 1866. **Education:** Studied law at the University of Santiago de Compostela, 1887–90, no degree. **Family:** Married Josefina Blanco in 1907 (divorced 1932); six children. **Career:** Journalist in Madrid, 1890, and in Mexico and Cuba, 1892–93; returned to Galicia, 1893; settled in Madrid, 1895, and frequented artistic circles; stage debut as actor, 1898; left arm amputated after a fight, 1899; regular contributor to the periodical *El Imparcial*; toured Spain and South America with his wife's acting company, 1910; unsuccessful political candidacy, 1910; visited Western Front as war correspondent, 1916; professor of ethics, Madrid School of Fine Arts, from 1916; visited Mexico, Cuba, and New York, 1921; period of illness, followed by convalescence in a sanatorium, 1923–24;

imprisoned for two weeks under the dictatorship of Primo de Rivera; unsuccessful Republican candidate for parliament, 1931; director, Spanish Academy of Fine Arts, Rome, 1934–35. Elected President of the Atheneum, Madrid, 1932. **Died:** 5 January 1936.

PUBLICATIONS

Collections

Obras completas. 11 vols., 1944.
Obras completas. 2 vols., 1954.
Savage Acts: Four Plays, translated by Robert Lima. 1993.
Three Plays, translated by Maria M. Delgado. 1993.
Obras selectas, prologue by Julián Marías. 1998.

Plays

Cenizas (produced 1899). 1899; revised version, as *El yermo de las almas,* 1908.
Aguila de blasón (produced 1960). 1907.
El marqués de Bradomín (produced 1906). 1907.
Romance de lobos (produced 1960). 1908; as *Wolves! Wolves!,* translated by C.B. Lander, 1957.
Cuento de abril (produced 1910). 1909.
Farsa de la cabeza del dragón (produced 1910). 1914; as *The Dragon's Head,* translated by May Heywood Broun, in *Poet Lore Plays 2,* 1919.
Voces de gesta (produced 1912). 1911.
La marquesa Rosalinda (produced 1912). 1913; edited by Leda Schiavo, 1992.
El embrujado (produced 1931). 1914.
Divinas palabras (produced 1920). 1920; edited by Luis Iglesias Feijoo, 1991; as *Divine Words,* translated by Trader Faulkner, 1977; also translated by María Delgado, in *Plays 1,* 1993.
Luces de Bohemia (produced in French, 1963). In *España,* July-October 1920; revised version, 1924; as *Bohemian Lights,* translated by Anthony N. Zahareas and Gerald Gillespie, 1976; translated by María Delgado, in *Plays 1,* 1993; as *Lights of Bohemia,* translated by John Lyon, 1993.
Farsa y licencia de la reina castiza (produced 1922). 1922.
Cara de plata (produced 1960). 1923; edited by Antón Risco, 1992; as *Silver Face,* translated by Maria Delgado, in *Plays 1,* 1993.
La rosa de papel (produced 1924). With *La cabeza del bautista,* 1924.
La cabeza del bautista (produced 1924). With *La rosa de papel,* 1924; as *The Head of the Baptist,* translated by Robert Lima, in *Savage Acts,* 1993.
Sacrilegio (produced 1924). 1927; as *Sacrilege,* translated by Robert Lima, in *Savage Acts,* 1993.
Los cuernos de Don Friolera (produced 1925). 1925; as *The Grotesque Farce of Mr Punch the Cuckold,* translated by Dominic Keown and Robin Warner, 1991.
Las galas del difunto. 1926.
Ligazón (produced 1926).
Retablo de la avaricia, la lujuria y la muerte. 1927.
La hija del capitán. 1927.
Martes de carnaval (includes *Las galas del difunto; Los cuernos de Don Friolera; La hija del capitán*). 1930; edited by Ricardo Senabre, 1990.

Teatro selecto (includes *Romance de lobos; Tablado de marionetas: La enamorada del rey, La cabeza del dragón, La reina castiza; Divinas palabras*), edited by Anthony N. Zahareas. 1969.
Plays 1 (includes *Divine Words; Bohemian Lights; Silver Face*), translated by María Delgado. 1993.
Savage Acts: Four Plays (includes *Blood Pact; The Head of the Baptist; Sacrilege*), translated by Robert Lima. 1993.

Fiction

Femeninas: Seis historias amorosas (stories). 1895.
Epitalamio. 1897.
Sonata de otoño. 1902; as *Sonata of Autumn,* in *The Pleasant Memoirs of the Marquis de Bradomín,* 1924; as *Autumn and Winter Sonatas: The Memoirs of the Marquis of Bradomín,* translated by Margaret Jull Costa, 1998.
Corte de amor (stories). 1903.
Sonata de estío. 1903; as *Sonata of Summer,* in *The Pleasant Memoirs of the Marquis de Bradomín,* 1924.
Jardín umbrío (stories and dialogues). 1903; enlarged edition, as *Jardín novelesco,* 1905.
Alma española. 1903.
Sonata de primavera. 1904; as *Sonata of Spring,* in *The Pleasant Memoirs of the Marquis de Bradomín,* 1924; as *Spring and Summer Sonatas: The Memoirs of the Marquis of Bradomín,* translated by Margaret Jull Costa, 1997.
Flor de santidad. 1904.
Sonata de invierno. 1905; as *Sonata of Winter,* in *The Pleasant Memoirs of the Marquis de Bradomín,* 1924.
Historias pervesas (stories). 1907; enlarged edition, as *Historias de amor,* 1909.
La guerra carlista. 1909; edited by María José Alonso Seoane, 1979.
　Los cruzados de la causa. 1908.
　El resplendor de la hoguera. 1909.
　Gerifaltes de antaño. 1909.
Cofre de sándalo (stories). 1909.
Mi hermana Antonia (story). 1918; as "My Sister Antonia," translated by Harriet de Onís, in *Spanish Stories and Tales,* edited by de Onís, 1954; also translated by Anita Vollard, in *Great Spanish Short Stories,* 1962; William E. Colford, in *Classic Tales from Modern Spain,* edited by Colford, 1964.
The Pleasant Memoirs of the Marquis de Bradomin: Four Sonatas, translated by May Heywood Broun and Thomas Walsh. 1924.
Tirano Banderas: novelà de tierra caliente. 1926; edited by Alonso Zamora Vicente, 1978; as *The Tyrant: A Novel of Warm Lands,* translated by Margarita Pavitt, 1929.
La Corte de los Milagros. 1927.
Viva mi dueño. 1928.
Flores de almendro. 1936.
El trueno dorado. 1936; edited by G. Fabra Barreiro. 1975.
Baza de espadas. 1958.
Novelas inmortales (selection). 1985.

Verse

Aromas de leyenda. 1907.
La pipa de Kif. 1919.
El pasajero. 1920.
Claves líricas (includes *Aromas; El pasajero; La pipa de kif*). 1930.

Other

Las mieles del rosal (stories, plays, poems). 1910.
Opera omnia. 26 vols., 1913–30.
La lámpara maravillosa. 1916; as *The Lamp of Marvels*, translated by
    Robert Lima, 1986.
La media noche. 1917.
Cuentos, estética y poemas. 1919.
Antología, edited by Florentino M. Turner. 1963.
Antología, edited by Rafael Conte. 1966.
Un Valle-Inclán olvidado: Entrevistas y conferencias, edited by Dru
    Dougherty. 1983.
Artículos completos y otras páginas olvidadas, edited by Javier
    Serrano Alonso. 1987.
Obras selectas. 1989.
Colaboraciones periodísticas. 1992.

*

Bibliography: *A Bibliography and Iconography of Valle-Inclán* by
José Rubia Barcía, 1960; *An Annotated Bibliography of Ramón del
Valle-Inclán* by Robert Lima, 1972.

Critical Studies: *Vida y literatura de Valle-Inclán* by M. Fernández,
1943; *La vida altiva de Valle-Inclán* by F. Madrid, 1943; *Don Ramón
María del Valle-Inclán* by R. Gómez de la Serna, 1944; *Las Sonatas
de Ramón del Valle-Inclán: Contribución al estudio de la prosa* by
Alonso Zamora Vicente, 1951; *La elaboración artística en Tirano
Banderas*, 1957, *De Sonata de otoño al esperpento: Aspectos del arte
de Valle-Inclán*, 1968, and *El ocultismo en Valle-Inclán*, 1974, all by
Emma S. Speratti Piñero; *Valle-Inclán y la dificultad de la tragedia*
by Ramón J. Sender, 1965; *Las guerras carlistas y el reinado
isabelino en la obra de Ramón del Valle-Inclán* by María D. Lado,
1966; *La estética de Valle-Inclán en los esperpentos y en El ruedo
ibérico* by A. Risco, 1966; *La idea de la sociedad en Valle-Inclán* by
José Gómez Marín, 1967; *El arte dramático de Valle-Inclán: Del
decadentismo al expresionismo*, 1967, and *La poesía de Valle-Inclán:
Del simbolismo al expresionismo*, 1973, both by Emilio González
López; *Valle-Inclán Centennial Studies* by Ricardo Gullón, 1968;
Valle-Inclán by Francisco Umbral, 1968; *Ramón del Valle-Inclán: An
Appraisal of His Life and Works* edited by Anthony N. Zahareas,
1968; *El Valle-Inclán que yo conocí y otros ensayos* by Francisco
Pina, 1969; *Valle-Inclán: Tres estudios* by Francisco Ynduráin, 1969;
*Visión del esperpento: Teoría y práctica en los esperpentos de Valle-
Inclán* by Rodolfo Cardona and Anthony N. Zahareas, 1970; *Valle-
Inclán: Introducción a su obra* by Manuel Bermejo Marcos, 1971;
Valle-Inclán: Tirano Banderas, 1971, and *Valle-Inclán* (in English),
1973, both by Verity Smith; *Valle-Inclán: Anatomía de un teatro
problemático* by Sumner M. Greenfield, 1972; *Ramón María del
Valle-Inclán: La política, la cultura, el realismo y el pueblo*, 1972,
and *Valle-Inclán: Cronología y documentos*, 1978, both by Juan
Antonio Hormigón; *Ramón del Valle-Inclán*, 1972, and *Valle-Inclán:
The Theatre of His Life*, 1988, both by Robert Lima; *Ramón del Valle-
Inclán: Vida y milagros* by Mariano Tudela, 1972; *Dominant Themes
in the Sonatas* by Rosco N. Tolman, 1973; *Valle-Inclán y la plástica:
Estudios literarios* by Eva Llorens, 1975; *The Primitive Themes in
Valle-Inclán* by R. Spoto, 1976; *Semiología de las comedias bárbaras*
by Joaquina Canoa Galiana, 1977; *Valle-Inclán y el Novecientos*,

1977, and *América en Valle-Inclán*, 1984, both by Obdulia Guerrero;
Valle-Inclán: Su ambigüedad modernista by María E. Pérez, 1977; *El
demiurgo y su mundo: Hacia un nuevo enfoque da la obra de Valle-
Inclán* by Antonio Risco, 1977; *Ruido ibérico: A Popular View of
Revolution* by A. Sinclair, 1977; *Valle-Inclán: Materia y forma del
esperpento* by Hebe N. Capanella, 1980; *Valle-Inclán, agnóstico y
vanguardista (La lámpara maravillosa)* by Humberto Antonio
Maldonado Marcías, 1980; *Time and History in Valle-Inclán's His-
torical Novels and Tirano Banderas* by Peggy Lynne Tucker, 1980;
La anunciación de Valle-Inclán by Valentín Paz-Andrade, 1981; *La
Galicia decimonónica en las "Comedias bárbaras" de Valle-Inclán*
by María del Carmen Porrúa, 1983; *Ramón del Valle-Inclán* by José
Servera Baño, 1983; *The Theatre of Valle-Inclán* by John E. Lyon,
1984; *Epica y tragedia en la obra de Valle-Inclán* by Clara Luisa
Barbeito, 1985; *Dramatists in Perspective: Spanish Theatre in the
Twentieth Century* by Gwynne Edwards, 1985; *Valle-Inclán: Las
comedias bárbaras* by Lourdes Ramos-Kuethe, 1985; *La crueldad y
el horror en el teatro de Valle-Inclán* by Juan C. Esturo Velarde,
1985; *Valle-Inclán y la Segunda República* by Dru Dougherty, 1986;
Genio y virtuosismo de Valle-Inclán edited by Claire J. Paolini, 1986,
*Valle-Inclán's Modernism: Use and Abuse of Religious and Mystical
Symbolism*, 1986, and *Valle-Inclán: Nueva valoración de su obra:
Estudios críticos en el cincuentenario de su muerte*, 1988, both by
Paolini; *Valle-Inclán: Cronología, escritos dispersos, epistolaria*,
1987, and *Quimera, Cántico: Busca y rebusca de Valle-Inclán*, 1989,
both edited by Juan Antonio Hormigón; *Ramón María del Valle-
Inclán: El escritor y la crítica* edited by Ricardo Domenech, 1988;
Valle-Inclán (1866–1936): Creación y lenguaje edited by J.M. García
de la Torre, 1988; *Valle-Inclán y su mundo: Ideología y forma
narrativa* by Roberta L. Salper, 1988, and *Ramón María del Valle-
Inclán: Questions of Gender* edited by Salper and Carol Maier, 1994;
Ramón del Valle-Inclán edited by Harald Wentzlaff-Eggebert, 1988;
El expresionismo en Valle-Inclán by Carlos Jeréz Farrán, 1989; *La
ficción breve de Valle-Inclán* by Luis González del Valle, 1990; *La
musa funambulesca de Valle-Inclán: Poética de la carnavalación* by
Iris M. Zavala, 1990; *Spanish Reactions to the Anglo-Irish Revival in
the Early Twentieth Century: The Stone by the Elixir* by Jean
Andrews, 1991; *Summa Vallein daniana*, edited by Gabriele, 1992;
Ramón María del Valle-Inclán: Questions of Gender edited by Carol
Maier and Roberta L. Solper, 1994; *Valle-Inclán and the Theater:
Innovation in La cabeza del dragón, El Embrujado, and La Marquesa
Rosalinda*, 1994; *Beyond the Glitter: The Language of Gems in
Modernista Writers Rubén Darío, Ramón del Valle-Inclán, and José
Asunción Silva* by Rosemary C. LoDato, 1999; *The Esperpento
Tradition in the Works of Ramon del Valle-Inclan and Luis Bunuel* by
Diane M. Almeida, 2000.

* * *

Author of novels, plays, short stories, essays, and poetry, Ramón
del Valle-Inclán features prominently among Spain's most profoundly innovative dramatists and is almost unquestionably the most
significant writer for Spanish theatre since Calderón. A genius long
unrecognized because his radical originality was decades ahead of his
time for Spain (morally, aesthetically, and with regard to existing
theatrical technology), Valle-Inclán suffered critical neglect because
the Franco regime included him among prohibited authors; his works

could not be performed for a quarter of a century, nor critical studies published.

A flamboyant Bohemian who created eccentric and contradictory legends about himself, Valle-Inclán so fictionalized his early life in his "autobiography," *Alma española* [Spanish Soul] that little if any reliable content remains. Cultivating outlandish appearance with outrageous behaviour, he was known for his wit, arrogance, and his contempt for conformity, bourgeois values, establishment religion, politics, literature, and other institutions. During the Republic, he became director of Spain's Academy of Fine Arts in Rome, but terminal illness forced him to return to Galicia.

Valle-Inclán's politics and aesthetics both underwent revolutionary change. A Carlist (conversative, aristocratic, possibly even reactionary) in his youth, he moved ever further left, attacking the monarchy and the military establishment, for which he was imprisoned several times by the Primo de Rivera dictatorship. In the period of unrest preceding the outbreak of the Civil War, aged and dying, he volunteered his services to the Republic. His youthful *modernista* aesthetics (combining symbolism, Parnassian, and decadent elements, exotic settings, refined eroticism, and idealization of times past)—art for art's sake—evolved to social and political commitment, espousal of populist causes, and a negative, grotesque, distorted portrayal of reality. Critics divide his production into three main periods: youthful modernism, refinement and artificiality (1895–1912); transition and experimentation (1912–23); and the Expressionist *esperpento*, as he called his final negative manner in fiction and theatre (1924–36), with its absurd caricatures of "classical heroes and values seen via a concave mirror." Reworking and republishing his works in varying forms and with different titles over the years, he complicated attempts to date and clarify his artistic evolution, even provoking accusations of plagiarism.

Valle-Inclán's least significant impact was on poetry. Evolving thematically and stylistically from early *modernista* pieces in *Aromas de leyenda* [Legendary Aromas], to something resembling Antonio Machado's critical vision of Spanish landscape and types as seen in Valle-Inclán's *El pasajero* [The Traveller] (written over several years) and the playful, iconoclastic, bizarre caricatures of *La pipa de Kif* [The Hashish Pipe], his poems were republished in 1930 under the title *Claves líricas* [Lyrical Keys]. His long interest in and practice of the occult, flirtations with Rosacrucianism, theosophy, and other esoteric cults, culminated in *La lámpara maravillosa* (*The Lamp of Marvels*) which also expounds his theoretical and mystic views of language, literature, and aesthetics.

Valle-Inclán's first narrative successes came with the short-story collections *Femeninas: Seis historias amorosas* [Femininities: Six Erotic Tales], *Epitalamio* [Nuptial Chant], and *Corte de amor* [Court of Love], likewise distinctly erotic, anticipating the style and themes of his most successful novels, the four *Sonatas*, named for the four seasons and representing corresponding stages in the narrator's life. The Marquis of Bradomin, self-described "ugly, Catholic, and sentimental" Don Juan, recounts his scandalous life (considered pornographic by conservative readers) with irony, humour, and cynicism. Reissued jointly as *The Pleasant Memoirs of the Marquis of Bradomín* in 1924, the four decadent, sensuous novellas and Valle-Inclán's numerous other erotic works led some critics to view him as an unqualified misogynist. Contemporary scholars, however, believe that his work attempts to surmount gender constraints. The short stories of *Jardín*

umbrío [Shady Garden] and the novella *Flor de santidad* [Flower of Sanctity], both set in millennial, timeless Galicia, examine witchcraft, superstition, primitive emotions, and mysterious or supernatural occurrences without abandoning eroticism. *Aguila de blasón* [Heraldic Eagle], *Romance de lobos* (*Wolves! Wolves!*), and *Cara de plata* (*Silver Face*), three long works in dialogue or theatrical form subtitled *comedias bárbaras* (barbarous comedies), present another ageing Don Juan and putative *alter ego* of Valle-Inclán, Don Juan Manuel Montenegro, a Galician aristocrat who develops a social conscience and is murdered by his sons. Linked by the common protagonist, but published out of sequence, the series culminates with *Wolves! Wolves!*, a powerful dramatic achievement, which contains echoes of *King Lear*. Valle-Inclán's transitional novels, *Los cruzados de la causa* [Crusaders of the Cause], *El resplendor de la hoguera* [The Bonfire's Glare], and *Gerifaltes de antaño* [Gerfalcons of Yore], a cycle on the 19th-century Carlist wars, anticipate the *esperpento*, whose narrative variants include *Tirano Banderas: novelà de tierra caliente* (*The Tyrant: A Novel of Warm Lands*), *La Corte de los milagros* [Court of Miracles], and *Viva mi dueño* [Long Live My Lord]. Spanish politics are ridiculed mercilessly, especially what Valle-Inclán views as the 19th-century origins of incompetence, venality, stupidity, and posturing in the monarchy, as are varied contemporary problems, including a corrupt diplomatic corps and uninformed international policy.

Valle-Inclán's highly theatrical dramatic works shocked most theatregoers of his day. Modernist aesthetics dominated his first play, *Cenizas* [Ashes], revised as *El yermo de las almas* [The Desert of Souls]. *Farsa de la cabeza del dragón* (*The Dragon's Head*), a humorous fairytale farce, abounds in magic and anachronisms (Valle-Inclán often deliberately sought atemporal or non-temporal effects). Among several verse plays are the modernist *Cuento de abril* [April Tale] and *La marquesa Rosalinda*, both of them gallant, artificial, and aristocratic; the violent, tragic *Voces de gesta* [Epic Voices] about a Galician shepherdess raped and blinded by a Carlist captain who later murders their child, for which she beheads him and *Divinas palabras* (*Divine Words*), a dark, critical vision of rural Galicia anticipating the *esperpento*. The latter, Valle-Inclán's crowning dramatic creations, comprise both full-length and one-act pieces, among which the best-known include *Luces de Bohemia* (*Bohemian Lights*), *Los cuernos de Don Friolera* (*The Grotesque Farce of Mr. Punch the Cuckold*), *Las galas del difunto* [The Finery of the Deceased], and *La hija del capitán* [The Captain's Daughter], the last seized by the dictatorship for its sarcastic treatment of the military and government. A collection of dramatic *esperpentos* treating humanity's vices and basest emotions, collectively entitled *Retablo de la avaricia, la lujuria y la muerte* [Altarpiece of Avarice, Lust, and Death] includes *El embrujado* [The Bewitched]; two puppet plays, *La rosa de papel* [Paper Rose] and *La cabeza del bautista* (*The Head of the Baptist*); and two "autos" or sacramental mystery plays for silhouettes, *Ligazón* [Liaison] and *Sacrilegio* (*Sacrilege*), several of them exemplifying Valle-Inclán's efforts at liberating his theatre from the constraints of time. *Farsa y licencia de la reina castiza* [Farce of the Legitimate Queen] bitingly satirizes Queen Isabel II and her court (also caricatured in the novel, *La Corte de los milagros*). Perhaps only in his enduring dislike of Isabel II—whose "illegal" enthronement provoked the Carlist wars—does Valle-Inclán retain in later works any trace of his early reactionary, aristocratic Carlism.

Post-Franco abolition of the censorship has spurred rediscovery of Valle-Inclán's theatre and critical re-evaluation of his work, resulting in an outpouring of articles, monographs, and translations. Still controversial, he constitutes the single most influential precedent for Spanish dramatists from early 20th century hence.

—Janet Pérez

VALLEJO, César (Abraham)

Born: Santiago de Chuco, Peru, 16 March 1892. **Education:** Educated at a secondary school in Huamachuco, 1905–08; Trujillo University, 1910–11, 1913–17, B.A. 1915, also law degree; studied medicine in Lima, 1911. **Family:** Married Georgette Phillipart. **Career:** Worked in his father's notary office, in mine offices, as a tutor, and in an estate accounts office; taught at Centro Escolar de Verones and Colegio Nacional de San Juan while at Trujillo University; lived in Lima, 1917–23: teacher at Colegio Barrós, 1918–19, and another school, 1920; involved in political riot at Santiago de Chuco and imprisoned, 1920–21; teacher, Colegio Guadalupe, 1921–23; lived in Europe after 1923; secretary, Iberoamerican press agency, 1925; freelance writer: founder, with Juan Larrea, *Favorables-Paris-Poema* (two issues), 1926; visited Russia several times; expelled from France and lived in Spain, 1930–32; lived in Paris from 1932; helped publish *Nuestra España* during Spanish Civil War. **Died:** 15 April 1938.

PUBLICATIONS

Collections

Obra poética completa, edited by Georgette de Vallejo. 1968.
Novelas y cuentos completos. 1970.
Obras completas. 3 vols., 1973–74.
The Complete Posthumous Poetry, translated by Clayton Eshleman and José Rubia Barcia (bilingual edition). 1978.
Poesía completa, edited by Juan Larrea. 1978.
Teatro completo, edited by Enrique Ballón Aguirre. 1979.

Verse

Los heraldos negros. 1919.
Trilce. 1922; as *Trilce*, translated by David Smith, 1973; also translated by Rebecca Seiferie, 1992.
Poemas humanos, edited by Georgette Vallejo. 1939; as *Human Poems*, translated by Clayton Eshleman, 1969.
España, aparta de mí este cáliz. 1940; as *Spain, Take This Cup from Me*, translated by Clayton Eshleman, 1974.
Twenty Poems, translated by Robert Bly, James Wright, and John Knoepfle. 1962.
An Anthology (in Spanish), edited by James Higgins. 1970.
Neruda and Vallejo: Selected Poems, translated by Robert Bly, James Wright, and John Knoepfle. 1971.
Selected Poems, edited by Gordon Brotherston and Ed Dorn. 1976.
Palms and Guitar, translated by J.C.R. Green. 1982.
Selection, translated by James Higgins (bilingual edition). 1987.

Fiction

Escalas melografiadas. 1923.
Fabla salvaje. 1923.
El tungsteno. 1931; as *Tungsten*, translated by R. Mezey, 1988.

Other

Rusia en 1931. 1931.
El romanticismo en la poesía castellana. 1954.
Reflexiones al pie del Kremlin. 1959.
Aula Vallejo 1–3. 1959–67.
Artículos olvidados, edited by Luis Alberto Sánchez. 1960.
Rusia ante el segundo plan quinquenal. 1965.
Literatura y arte. 1966.
Desde Europa, edited by Jorge Puccinelli. 1969.
Cartas a Pablo Abril. 1971.
Autopsy on Surrealism, translated by R. Schaaf. 1986.
The Mayakovsky Case, translated by R. Schaaf. 1986.
Translator, *L'Élévation*, by Henri Barbusse. 1931.

*

Critical Studies: *Aproximaciones a Vallejo* edited by Angel Flores, 2 vols., 1971; *Vallejo: Héroe y mártir indo-hispano*, 1973, and *Vallejo y el surrealismo*, 1976, both by Juan Larrea; *Vallejo* edited by Julio Ortega, 1975; *César Vallejo: The Dialectics of Poetry and Silence* by Jean Franco, 1976; *César Vallejo* by Eduardo Neale-Silva, 1976; *Wounded Fiction: Modern Poetry and Deconstruction* by Joseph Adamson, 1988.

* * *

A man of a profound and complex sensibility who could not express himself in the commonly accepted patterns of poetic communication, César Vallejo transformed the Spanish lyrical language so dramatically that his works have had a definite influence on contemporary poetry. The intensity of his feelings finds expression in a simple but highly concentrated style in which everyday language, and the extremely personal images of his own views on the world, create a very effective tension supported by the broken rhythm of free verse.

When reading Vallejo's poetry it is important to take into consideration his being a *mestizo* from the Peruvian Andes. His outlook on life was greatly affected by his early formation in the traditionally Catholic and economically poor circumstances of his boyhood. Although early in his life he ceased to be a practising Catholic, he was imbued by religious values and made constant use of religious images and references in his poetry. Most of his life he suffered from poverty and from a feeling of bereavement as he confronted a world characterized by human injustice.

Suffering is a main motif in Vallejo's writing. At the beginning it is mainly a self-centred preoccupation as he encounters the injustices of Peruvian society, and longs for the lost world of the Andes, the family, and his religious beliefs. His first two books of verse, both published in Peru before he left for Europe, deal with this personal anguish. The first one, *Los heraldos negros* [The Black Heralds], is very much a continuation of Latin American modernism. *Trilce*, on the contrary, represents a break with tradition and constitutes one of the best examples in Spanish of contemporary vanguardist poetry. A very difficult book because of its peculiar syntax and hermetic images, *Trilce* is the result of Vallejo's desperate effort to express his very painful and complex intimate feelings and emotions.

The poems he wrote in Europe are much more influenced by his political views, and they are the result of his involvement in political activity as a left-wing writer. Thus *Poemas humanos* (*Human Poems*) and *España, aparta de mí este cáliz* (*Spain, Take This Cup from Me*), both published posthumously, are concerned mostly with social matters, and with the political developments of socialism in the world. Suffering has become now a communal feeling and the poet develops a new language which, in spite of retaining many peculiarly personal elements, is highly communicative. The colloquialisms and common expressions used by Vallejo in all of his books have in these two a more direct effect in making the poem an expression of the common man, of the basic needs and dreams of the working classes. The poet has made of his own suffering a redeeming force, taking upon himself the duty to save the poor and the defenceless. As such, Vallejo became one of the first writers to develop in Spanish a politically committed lyric poetry. The rest of his literary works seem much less valuable than his poems.

—Santiago Daydi-Tolson

See the essays on "Considerando en frio" and "The Eternal Dice."

VARGAS LLOSA, (Jorge) Mario (Pedro)

Born: Arequipa, Peru, 28 March 1936. Grew up in Cochabamba, Bolivia, 1937–45, Piura, Peru, 1945–46, then in Lima. **Education:** Educated at Leoneio Prado Military Academy, Lima, 1950–52; Colegio Nacional San Miguel de Piura, 1952; University of San Marcos, Lima, degree in literature and law, 1957; University of Madrid, 1957–59, Ph.D. 1959. **Family:** Married 1) Julia Urquidi in 1955 (divorced 1963); 2) Patricia Llosa in 1965, two sons and one daughter. **Career:** Journalist, *La industria*, Piura, c. 1952; co-editor, *Cuadernos de Conversación*, 1957, and *Literatura*, 1958; journalist, Radio Panamericana and *La Crónica*, both in Lima; after university study, moved to Paris, 1959; Spanish teacher, journalist, Agence-France-Presse, and broadcaster, Radio Télévision Française, early 1960s; visited Peru, 1964; contributing editor, *Casa de las Américas*, Havana, 1965; contributor, *Caretas*, Lima, 1966; lecturer or visiting professor, Queen Mary College and King's College, University of London, 1966–68, University of Washington, Seattle, 1968, University of Puerto Rico, Río Piedras, 1969, Columbia University, New York, 1975, University of Jerusalem, 1976, Cambridge University, 1977, in Japan, 1980, Florida International University, Miami, 1991, and Wissenschaftskolleg, Berlin, 1991–92. Fredemo (Democratic Front) candidate in Peruvian presidential elections, 1990. Fellow, Woodrow Wilson Center, Smithsonian Institute, Washington, DC, 1979–80; Scottish Arts Council Neil Gunn International fellow, 1986. Lives in Lima. **Awards:** Leopoldo Alas prize, 1959; Biblioteca Breve prize (Spain), 1962; Rómulo Gallegos prize (Venezuela), 1967; National Critics' prize (Spain), 1967; National prize, 1967; *La Vanguardia* Godó Llallana prize (Spain), 1979; Critics' Annual prize

for theatre (Argentina), 1981; Instituto Italo Latinoamericano Iila prize (Italy), 1982; Ritz Paris Hemingway award, 1985; Prince of Asturias prize (Spain), 1986; Cervantes prize for literature, 1994; Jerusalem prize, 1995; National Book Critics Circle award for criticism, 1997; PEN/Nabokov award, 2002.

PUBLICATIONS

Fiction

Los jefes (stories). 1959; in *The Cubs and Other Stories*, 1979.
La ciudad y los perros. 1963; as *The Time of the Hero*, translated by Lysander Kemp, 1966.
La casa verde. 1966; as *The Green House*, translated by Gregory Rabassa, 1968.
Los cachorros. 1967; as "The Cubs," in *The Cubs and Other Stories*, 1979.
Conversación en La Catedral. 1969; as *Conversation in The Cathedral*, translated by Gregory Rabassa, 1975.
Obras escogidas. 1973.
Pantaléon y las visitadoras. 1973; as *Captain Pantoja and the Special Services*, translated by Gregory Kolovakos and Ronald Christ, 1978.
La tía Julia y el escribidor. 1977; as *Aunt Julia and the Scriptwriter*, translated by Helen Lane, 1982. *The Cubs and Other Stories*, translated by Gregory Kolovakos and Ronald Christ, 1979.
La guerra del fin del mundo. 1981; as *The War of the End of the World*, translated by Helen Lane, 1984.
Historia de Mayta. 1984; as *The Real Life of Alejandro Mayta*, translated by Alfred MacAdam, 1986.
¿Quien mató a Palomino Molero?. 1986; as *Who Killed Palomino Molero?*, translated by Alfred MacAdam, 1987.
El hablador. 1987; as *The Storyteller*, translated by Helen Lane, 1989.
Elogio de la madrastra. 1988; as *In Praise of the Stepmother*, translated by Helen Lane, 1990.
El pez en el agua. 1993; as *A Fish in the Water*, translated by Helen Lane, 1994.
Lituma en los Andes. 1993; as *Death in the Andes*, translated by Edith Grossman, 1996.
Making Waves, edited and translated by John King, 1996.
Obra reunida, Narrativa breva (short stories). 1999.
La Fiesta del Chivo. 2000; as *The Feast of the Goat,* translated by Edith Grossman, 2001.

Plays

La huida del Inca (produced 1952).
La señorita de Tacna (produced 1981). 1981; as *The Young Lady from Tacna*, translated by David Graham-Young, in *Three Plays*, 1990.
Kathie y el hipopótamo (produced 1983). 1983; as *Kathie and the Hippopotamus*, translated by David Graham-Young, in *Three Plays*, 1990.
La Chunga (produced in English, 1986). 1986; as *La Chunga*, translated by David Graham-Young, in *Three Plays*, 1990.
Three Plays (includes *The Young Lady from Tacna; Kathie and the Hippopotamus; La Chunga*), translated by David Graham-Young. 1990.

Other

La novela en América Latina; diálogo, with Gabriel García Márquez. 1968.

La literatura en la revolución y revolución en la literatura, with Julio Cortázar and Oscar Collazos. 1970.

Historia secreta de una novela. 1971.

Gabriel García Márquez: Historia de un deicidio. 1971.

La novela y el problema de la expresión literaria en Perú. 1974.

La orgía perpetua: Flaubert y Madame Bovary. 1975; as *The Perpetual Orgy: Flaubert and Madame Bovary*, translated by Helen R. Lane, 1986.

José María Arguedas: Entre sapos y halcones. 1978.

La utopía arcaica. 1978.

Art, Authenticity and Latin American Culture. 1981.

Entre Sartre y Camus. 1981.

Contra vientro y marea (1962–1982). 3 vols., 1983–90.

La cultura de la libertad, la libertad de la cultura. 1985.

Diálogo sobre la novela latinoamericana, with Gabriel García Márquez. 1988.

Sobre la vida y la política (interview), with Ricardo A. Setti. 1989.

A Writer's Reality (lectures in English). 1990; Spanish edition, as *La verdad de las mentiras: ensayos sobre literatura*, 1990.

Letra de batalla por Tirant lo Blanc. 1991.

Questions of Conquest and Culture. 1993.

Literature and Freedom. 1994.

Desafíos a la Libertad. 1994.

Ojos bonitos, cuadros feos. 1996.

Los cuadernos de don Rigoberto. 1997; as *The Notebooks of Don Rigoberto*, translated by Edith Grossman, 1998.

Una historia no oficial. 1997.

Cartas a un joven Novelista. 1997.

Guide to the Perfect Latin American Idiot, with Plinio Apuleyo Mendoza and Carlos Alberto Montaner. 2000.

El lenguaje de la pasion. 2001.

Editor, with Gordon Brotherston, *Seven Stories from Spanish America.* 1968.

*

Bibliography: Mario Vargas Llosa' in *Peruvian Literature: A Bibliography of Secondary Sources* by David William Foster, 1981.

Critical Studies: *Mario Vargas Llosa y la literatura en el Perú de hoy*, 1969, and *Vargas Llosa y sus técnicas desconcertantes*, 1974, both by Rosa Boldori; *Mario Vargas Llosa's Pursuit of the Total Novel* by Luis Alfonso Diez, 1970; *Homenaje a Mario Vargas Llosa* edited by Helmy F. Giacoman and José Miguel Oviedo, 1972; *La narrativa de Vargas Llosa, acercamiento estilístico* by José Luis Martín, 1974; *Mario Vargas Llosa: La invención de una realidad* by José Miguel Oviedo, 1977; *Mario Vargas Llosa, desarticulador de realidades: Una introducción a sus obras* by Wolfgang A. Lutching, 1978; *Mario Vargas Llosa: A Collection of Critical Essays* edited by Charles Rossman and Alan Warren Friedman, 1978; *Literary Analysis: Reflections on Vargas Llosa's The Green House* by M.J. Fenwick, 1981; *From Lima to Laticia: The Peruvian Novels of Mario Vargas Llosa* by Marvin A. Lewis, 1983; *Novel Lives: The Fictional Autobiographies of Guillermo Cabrera Infante and Mario Vargas Llosa* by

Rosemary Geisdorfer Feal, 1986; *Mario Vargas Llosa* by Raymond Leslie Williams, 1986; *My Life with Mario Vargas Llosa* by Julia Urquidi Illanes, translated by C.R. Perricone, 1988; *Understanding Mario Vargas Llosa* by Sara Castro-Klarén, 1989; *A Marxist Reading of Fuentes, Vargas Llosa and Puig* by Victor Manuel Durtin, 1993; *Vargas Llosa among the Postmodernists* by M. Keith Booker, 1994; *The War at the End of Democracy: Mario Vargas Llosa vs Alberto Fujimori* by Jeff Daeschner, 1993; *Temptation of the Word: The Novels of Mario Vargas Llosa* by Efraín Kristal, 1998; *A Storyteller: Mario Vargas Llosa between Civilization and Barbarism* by Braulio Munoz, 2000.

* * *

Of the writers associated with "the Boom" in Latin American literature in the 1960s, Mario Vargas Llosa was the youngest and the principal Peruvian. Attentive to the lessons of European and Anglo-American modernism, Vargas Llosa fused the panoramic realism characteristic of the 19th-century novel with the dynamic techniques found in the 20th-century novel: multiple points of view; interior monologues and internalized dialogues; suspended identifications of characters; montage effects; discontinuous, fragmented, and intertwined narrative lines. His themes echo his narrative experiments. A promise of freedom, exhilarating and tantalizing, ends with disillusion as those established in power re-impose their authority by violence, or as those devoid of power adopt and accept more tacit but no less forceful social constraints. In his more recent fiction, the power of storytelling subverts such constraints without denying their power over reality. Not surprisingly, in an increasingly extensive body of criticism, Vargas Llosa speaks eloquently for the view that fictions repair reality and make it possible to "endure the burden of life."

From his first published work, a collection of short stories spare in style and dramatic in construction, *Los jefes* [The Bosses], to his masterwork, *Conversación en La Catedral* (*Conversation in The Cathedral*), Vargas Llosa's fiction pursues a trajectory of increasing narrative complexity. His more recent fiction and plays exploit the same devices, but more simply, and, with the notable exception of *La guerra del fin del mundo* (*The War of the End of the World*), more briefly. While the latter, based on Euclides da Cunha's *Rebellion in the Backlands* (1902), shares the totalizing impulse of Vargas Llosa's earlier fiction, the later works usually isolate specific social, political, or amorous conflicts intertwined with a literary problem or puzzle. Plot has become the explicit vehicle for the difficulty of representation, the impossibility of historical accuracy, the deceptiveness of any single statement or perspective, the false certainties imposed by the irresistible necessity of choice. In addition, his most recent fiction dramatizes the relation between autobiography and art that has long been a theme of his criticism, relative both to his own work, as in *Historia secreta de una novela* [The Secret History of a Novel], and to the work of others, as in *Gabriel García Márquez: Historia de un deicidio*.

His first novel, *La ciudad y los perros* (*The Time of the Hero*), set in Lima's Colegio Militar Leoncio Prado, where Vargas Llosa had been a student, was doubly distinguished by a Spanish literary prize and a public burning in the school's courtyard. Using the school as a claustrophobic microcosm of Peruvian society, the novel explores the brutalizing effects of the military discipline of the school and the codes of honour the students impose on themselves. His second novel, *La casa verde* (*The Green House*), extended the opposition between city and school geographically to an opposition between the green "freedom" of the Amazonian jungle and the dusty constraints of Piura. A temporal contrast compounds the physical contrast, with both locations possessed of a mythic past invaded and altered by the present, an effect achieved by the shuffling of five interconnected narratives taking place over a 40-year span. In *Conversation in The Cathedral*, Vargas Llosa returned to Lima, and, still intercutting narrative lines, elaborated an unwinding circular structure affined to the detective story. Masterly in its narrative coherence, the novel ranges through social, sexual, and political corruption at all levels during the Odria regime of the 1950s, with the unaccountable murder of a prostitute as the absent centre on which the narrative turns.

The autobiographical element, submerged source material in his earlier fiction, made its way to the surface in the comic novel *La tía Julia y el escribidor* (*Aunt Julia and the Scriptwriter*). Not political corruption but the paradoxes of daily life, love, and writing play into and against one another as Vargas Llosa intercuts "Maritos" courtship of his own Aunt Julia and the extravagant, but socially representative soap operas of the scriptwriter Pedro Camacho. (The real life Aunt Julia, Vargas Llosa's first wife, has written a reply to that novel.) In *El hablador* (*The Storyteller*), Vargas Llosa moves beyond the inclusion of bits of biography (recognizable principally to those who know him) to include references to his earlier work (recognizable to all who read him). The practice makes explicit the uncertain, shimmering relation between reality and fiction, as one passes into the other, changing form and status as it goes, and putting into question the status of the fiction.

Descending from the meditative structure of *Conversation in The Cathedral*, later works such as *The Storyteller* and *Historia de Mayta* (*The Real Life of Alejandro Mayta*) address particular political and economic problems through the medium of a narrator juggling obscure and contradictory evidence to construct an account of a man, hero or fool, who resisted the powers of the present. *The Real Life of Alejandro Mayta* reconstructs an earlier, failed terrorist episode in a Peru still struggling with the Sendero Luminoso armed opposition group, while *The Storyteller* weighs, without resolving, the conflicting claims of traditional Amazonian cultures and modernization. In each, the narrator's activities provide the matrix within which others act and multiple meanings and alternatives proliferate. The strength of such texts is the equal play they give to the processes of narrative and to the ongoing, still unsolved political choices that will, in spite of fiction, be resolved in one unsatisfactory way or another.

Doing without the foregrounded narrator, other fiction uses the more dramatic narrative shuffling of *The Green House*, though it abandons temporal shifts for simple linearity. *Elogio de la madrastra* (*In Praise of the Stepmother*), a comic novel significantly more wicked than *Aunt Julia and the Scriptwriter* or *Pantaléon y las visitadoras* (*Captain Pantoja and the Special Services*), introduces paintings, reproduced as plates in the text, to complicate the levels of reality and systems of interpretation the reader encounters. Somewhat oddly, Vargas Llosa's plays incorporate the meditating narrator instead of proceeding by purely dramatic means. In *La señorita de Tacna* (*The Young Lady from Tacna*), the grandson Belisario writes as the young lady and her family age and decay; in *Kathie y el hipopótamo* (*Kathie and the Hippopotamus*), the characters invent and act multiple roles.

Vargas Llosa is engagingly frank about the deficiencies of life and the consequent demands he places on literature for order, excitement, erotic and imaginative stimulation. As he puts it in *La orgía perpetua* (*The Perpetual Orgy*), *Madame Bovary* endures partly for its exploitation of violence, sex, and melodrama. Vargas Llosa's own project is a literature that agitates, stirs up, and questions as it explores the fissures between life as it is lived, life as it is reconstructed by memory and desire, and the mysterious alchemy of art that uses and transforms those materials. To achieve it, he engages the disasters of reality as subject-matter (corruption sexual and political; violence sexual and political, religious and historical) through a literary technique that implicates the reader, struggling to connect narrative strands, puzzling over juxtapositions, laughing aloud at the surprises produced by those juxtapositions, startled and horrified at the springing of a sudden narrative trap. As in life, both reader and writer are trapped in a downward spiral, but the text between them enlivens, distracts, and gives form and value to the journey.

—Regina Janes

VEGA CARPIO, Lope (Félix) de

Born: Madrid, Spain, 25 November 1562. **Education:** Educated at Jesuit Imperial College, 1574–75; Universidad Complutense, 1577. **Family:** Married 1) Isabel de Urbina in 1588 (died 1595); 2) Juana de Guarda c. 1602, several children; also had children by Micaela de Luján and Marta de Nevares, and another illegitimate son. **Career:** Went to Madrid after leaving university: writer and traveller; patronized by Marqués de Las Navas, 1583–87, and Marqués de Malpica; love affair with Elena Osorio led to accusations of libel, and jail and exile from Castile; joined the Spanish Armada against England in 1588; then lived in Valencia and Toledo; secretary to the Duke of Alba, 1590–95; in household of Marqués de Sarría, 1598–1600; secretary and counsellor to the Duke of Sessa from 1605; also "familiar of the Inquisition," 1608, and prosecutor of Apostolic Chamber; lived in Madrid after 1610; ordained priest, 1614. **Award:** Order of Malta, 1627. **Died:** 27 August 1635.

PUBLICATIONS

Collections

Las Comedias. 29 vols., 1604–45(?).
Fiestas del Santísimo Sacramento. 1644.
Colección de las obras sueltas así en prosa, como en verso, edited by F. Cerdá y Rico. 21 vols., 1776–79.
Obras, edited by M. Menéndez y Pelayo. 15 vols., 1890–1913; revised edition, edited by E. Cotarelo y Mori, 13 vols., 1916–30.
Poemas, edited by L. Guarner. 1935.
Epistolario, edited by Agustín González de Amezúa. 4 vols., 1935–43.
Obras escogidas, edited by F.C. Sainz de Robles. 3 vols., 1946–55.
Cartas completas, edited by Ángel Rosenblatt. 2 vols., 1948.

Fuente ovejuna: The Knight from Olmedo; Punishment without Revenge, translated by Gwynne Edwards. 1999.

Plays (selection: mainly modern editions or plays translated into English)

El acero de Madrid, edited by Jean Lemartinel and others. 1971.

Las almenas de toro, edited by Thomas E. Case. 1971.

Amar sin saber a quién, edited by Carmen Bravo-Villasante. 1967.

El amor desatinado, edited by J. García Morales. 1968.

El amor enamorado, edited by J.B. Wooldridge. 1978.

El arauco domado, edited by A. de Lezama. 1953.

Barlaán y Josafat, edited by José F. Montesinos. 1935.

Las bizarrías de Belisa, edited by Alonso Zamora Vicente (with *El Villano en su rincón*). 1963.

El Brasil restituido, edited by José Maria Viqueira Barreiro. 1950.

Las burlas veras, edited by S.L.M. Rosenberg. 1912.

El caballero de Olmedo, edited by Francisco Rico. 1970; also edited as *The Knight of Olmedo*, by W.F. King (in English), 1972; as *The Knight from Olmedo*, translated by Jill Booty, in *Five Plays*, 1961; as *The Gentleman from Olmedo*, translated by David Johnston, 1992.

El cardenal de Belén, edited by Elisa Aragone. 1957.

Carlos V en Francia, edited by Arnold G. Reichenberger. 1962.

Castelvines y Monteses. Adapted as *Romeo and Juliet*, 1770; as *Castelvins and Monteses*, translated by Cynthia Rodriguez-Badendyck, 1998.

El castigo del discreto, edited by William L. Fichter. 1925.

El castigo sin venganza, edited by A.D. Kossoff. 1970; also edited by José María Díez Borque, 1987; as *Justice Without Revenge*, translated by Jill Booty, in *Five Plays*, 1961; also translated by Charles Davis, 1991; as *Lost in a Mirror*, translated by Adrian Mitchell, 1989.

Lo cierto por lo dudoso, as *A Certainty for a Doubt*, translated by John Garrett Underhill, in *Four Plays*. 1936.

La corona de Hungría, edited by R.W. Tyler. 1972.

La corona merecida, edited by José F. Montesinos. 1923.

El cuerdo loco, edited by José F. Montesinos. 1922.

La dama boba, edited by E.R. Hesse (with *Fuenteovejuna*). 1964; as *The Lady Nit-Wit*, translated by William I. Oliver, 1958.

El desdén vengado, edited by M.M. Harlan. 1930.

La desdichada Estefanía, edited by J.H. Arjona. 1967.

Dineros son calidad, edited by Klaus Wagner. 1966.

El doctor simple, as *Doctors All*, translated and adapted by Moritz Adolf Jagendorf. 1937.

El duque de Viseo, edited by F. Ruiz Ramón. 1966.

Los embustes de Celauro, edited by Joaquín de Entrambasaguas. 1942.

La estrella de Sevilla, edited by William M. Whitley and Robert Roland Anderson. 1971; as *The Star of Castile*, translated by Henry Thomas, 1950.

Las ferias de Madrid, edited by Alva V. Ebersole (with *La victoria de la honra*). 1977.

La fianza satisfecha, edited by William M. Whitley and Robert Roland Anderson. 1971; as *A Bond Honoured*, translated by John Osborne, 1966.

Lo fingido verdadero/Acting is Believing, translated by Michael D. McGaha. 1987.

Fuenteovejuna, edited by E.R. Hesse (with *La dama boba*). 1964; also edited by Victor Dixon (with translation), 1989; as *Fuente Ovejuna*, translated by John Garrett Underhill, in *Four Plays*, 1936; also translated by Jill Booty, in *Five Plays*, 1961; and by William E. Colford, 1969; as *All Citizens Are Soldiers*, translated and adapted by Ruth Fainlight and Alan Sillitoe, 1969; as *Fuenteovejuna*, translated by Alberto Romo, 1987; also translated by Adrian Mitchell, 1989.

El galán de la Membrilla, edited by Diego Marín and Evelyn Rugg. 1962.

Lo que hay que fiar del mundo, edited by A.L. Gasparetti. 1931.

El Marqués de las Navas, edited by José F. Montesinos. 1925. *El mayordomo de la duquesa de Amalfi*, as *The Duchess of Amalfi's Steward*, translated by Cynthia Rodriguez-Badenyck. 1985.

El mejor alcalde, el rey, as *The King, the Greatest Alcalde*, translated by John Garrett Underhill, in *Four Plays*. 1936.

El mejor mozo de España, edited by W.T. McCready. 1967; as *The Best Boy in Spain*, translated by David Gitlitz, 1999.

Los melindres de Belisa, edited by Henriette C. Barrau. 1933.

La moza de cántaro, edited by C. Gonzalez Echegaray. 1968.

La noche de San Juan, edited by H. Serís. 1935.

La nueva victoria de don Gonzalo de Córdoba, edited by Henryk Ziomek. 1962.

El nuevo mundo descubierto pot Cristóbal Colón, edited by J. Martinel and Charles Minguet. 1980; as *The Discovery of the New World by Christopher Columbus*, translated by Frieda Fligelman, 1950.

Las paces de los reyes y Judía de Toledo, edited by James A. Castañeda. 1962.

El padre engañado, as *The Father Outwitted*. 1805.

El palacio confuso, edited by Charles Henry Stevens. 1939.

Pedro Carbonero, edited by José F. Montesinos. 1929.

Peribáñez y el comendador de Ocaña, edited by J.M. Ruano and J.E. Varey. 1980; also edited by J.M. Lloyd (in English), 1990; as *Peribanez*, translated by Eva R. Price, 1936; also translated by Jill Booty, in *Five Plays*, 1961; as *The Commander of Ocaña*, translated by Booty, 1958; as *Peribáñez and the Comendador of Ocaña*, translated by Walter Starkie, in *Eight Spanish Plays of the Golden Age*, 1964; translated by James Lloyd (bilingual edition, with commentary), 1990; as *Peribañez and the Comendador of Ocaña,*, translated by Nick Drake, 1998.

El perro del hortelano, edited by Victor Dixon. 1981; as *The Gardener's Dog*, translated by John Garrett Underhill, in *Four Plays*, 1936; as *The Dog in the Manger*, translated by Jill Booty, in *Five Plays*, 1961.

El piadoso aragonés, edited by James N. Greer. 1951.

El príncipe despeñado, edited by Henry H. Hoge. 1955.

La prueba de los amigos, edited by L.B. Simpson. 1934.

Los Ramírez de Arellano, edited by Diana Ramírez de Arellano. 1954.

El remedio en la desdicha, edited by J.W. Barker. 1931.

Santiago el verde, edited by Jean Lemartinel and others. 1974.

El sembar en buena tierra, edited by William L. Fichter. 1944.

Servir a señor discreto, edited by F. Weber de Kurlat. 1975.

La siega, edited by José Fradejas Lebrero. 1958.

El sufrimiento premiado, edited by Victor Dixon. 1967.

El villano en su rincón, edited by Alonso Zamora Vicente (with *Las bizarrías de Belisa*). 1963; as *The King and the Farmer*, translated by Cecily Radford, 1948.

La victoria de la honra, edited by Alva V. Ebersole (with *Las ferias de Madrid*). 1977.

Ya anda la de Mazagatos, edited by S.G. Morley. 1924.

Four Plays (includes *A Certainty for a Doubt; The King, the Greatest Alcalde; The Gardener's Dog; Fuente Ovejuna*), translated by John Garrett Underhill. 1936.

Five Plays (includes *Fuente Ovejuna; Justice Without Revenge; The Dog in the Manger; Peribáñez; The Knight of Olmedo*), edited by R.D.F. Pring-Mill, translated by Jill Booty. 1961.

Locos de Valencia; as *Madness in Valencia*, version by David Johnston. 1998.

Verse

La Dragontea. 1598.

Isidro: Poema castellano. 1599.

La hermosura de Angélica, con otras diversas rimas. 1602.

Rimas. 1604.

La Jerusalém conquistada. 1609; edited by Joaquín de Entrambasaguas, 3 vols., 1951–54.

Arte nuevo de hacer comedias en este tiempo. 1609.

Rimas sacras. 1614; edited by Luis Guarner (with *Romancero espiritual*), 1949.

Triunfo de la fe en los reinos del Japón. 1618; edited by J.S. Cummins, 1965.

La Filomena con otras diversas rimas, prosas, y versos. 1621.

La Circe, con otras rimas y prosas. 1624; edited by Charles V. Aubrun and Manuel Muñoz Cortés, 1962.

Romancero espiritual. 1624; edited by Luis Guarner, 1941.

Triunfos divinos con otras rimas sacras. 1625.

Corona trágica: Vida y muerte de la Serenísima Reina de Escocia María Estuarda. 1627.

Laurel de Apolo, con otras rimas. 1630. *Amarilis: Égloga.* 1633.

Rimas humanas y divinas del licenciado Tomé de Burguillos. 1634.

La Gatomaquia. 1807; edited by Agustín del Campo, 1948.

Ultimos amores. 1876.

Sonetos, edited by Manuel Arce. 1960.

Fiction

La Arcadia: Prosas y verso. 1598; edited by Edwin S. Morby, 1975.

El peregrino en su patria. 1604; edited by M.A. Peyton, 1971; translated as *The Pilgrime of Casteele*, 1621; as *The Pilgrim; or, The Stranger in His Own Country*, translated by George de Montemajor (abridged version), 1738.

Pastores de Belén: prosas y versos divinos. 1612.

La Dorotea: Acción en prosa. 1632; edited by Edwin S. Morby, 1958; as *La Dorotea*, translated by A.S. Trueblood and Edwin Honig, 1985.

Other

Fiestas de Denia al Rey Católico Felipe III. 1599.

Iusta poética y alabanzas iustas. 1620.

Epistolario, edited by Agustín González de Amezúa. 4 vols., 1935–43.

Cartas completas, edited by Ángel Rosenblatt. 2 vols., 1948.

Translator, *Soliloquios amorosos de un alma a Dios.* 1626; edited by María Antonia Sanz Cuadrado, 1948.

*

Bibliography: *The Chronology of the Lope de Vega Comedias* by S. Griswold Morley and Courtney Bruerton, 1940, addenda in *Hispanic Review*, 15, 1947; *Ensayo de una bibliografía de las obras y artículos sobre la vida y escritos de Lope de Vega Carpio*, 1955, and supplement *Lope de Vega: Nuevos estudios*, 1961, both by I. Simón Díaz and J. de José Prades; *Bibliografía de las comedias históricas de Lope de Vega* by Robert B. Brown, 1958; *Lope de Vega Studies 1937–1962* by Jack H. Parker and Arthur M. Fox, 1964; *Bibliografía del teatro de Lope de Vega* by María Cruz Pérez y Pérez, 1973.

Critical Studies: *Lope de Vega and the Spanish Drama* by James Fitzmaurice-Kelly, 1902, new edition, 1982; *The Dramatic Art of Lope de Vega* by R. Schevill, 1918; *The ''Romancero'' in the Chronicle-Legend Plays of Lope de Vega* by Jerome Aaron Moore, 1940; *The Internal Line-Structure of Thirty Autograph Plays of Lope de Vega* by Walter Poesse, 1949; *Physical Aspects of the Spanish Stage in the Time of Lope de Vega* by Ruth Lundelius, 1961; *Lope de Vega* by Francis C. Hayes, 1967; *The Metamorphosis of Lope de Vega's King Pedro* by Frances Exum, 1974; *Lope de Vega: El Caballero de Olmedo* by Jack W. Sage, 1974; *Experience and Artistic Expression in Lope de Vega: The Making of La Dorotea* by A.S. Trueblood, 1974; *Songs in the Plays of Lope de Vega: A Study of Their Dramatic Function* by Gustavo Umpierre, 1975; *The Honor Plays of Lope de Vega* by Donald R. Larson, 1977; *Studies in Honor of Everett W. Hesse* edited by William C. McCrary and José A. Madrigal, 1981; *Boccaccio's Novelle in the Plays of Lope de Vega* by Nancy D'Antuono, 1984; *A Reconsideration of Lope de Vega's Honor Plays* by Alix Zuckerman-Ingber, 1984; *Lope de Vega: Fuenteovejuna* by J.B. Hall, 1985; *Honor Conflicts and the Role of the Imagination in Selected Plays of John Fletcher and Lope de Vega* by Margaret R. Hicks, 1990; *Refiguring the Hero: From Peasant to Noble in Lope de Vega and Calderón* by Dian Fox, 1991; *Feminism and the Honor Plays of Lope de Vega* by Yvonne Yarbro, 1994; *Feminism and the Honor Plays of Lope de Vega* by Yvonne Yarbro-Bejarano, 1994; *Lope de Vega and the commedia de santos* by Robert R. Morrison, 2000; *Playing the King: Lope de Vega and the Limits of Conformity* by Melveena McKendrick, 2000; *Pilgrimage to Patronage: Lope de Vega and Court of Philip III, 1598–1621* by Elizabeth R. Wright, 2001.

* * *

Lope de Vega Carpio fashioned the *comedia*, the distinctive drama that prevailed in the popular theatres (the *corrales de comedias*) of 17th-century Spain. His copious output gave contemporaries and successors such as Tirso de Molina, Ruiz de Alarcón, and Calderón de la Barca influential models for the *arte nuevo*, the ''new art,'' of dramatic composition. But Lope's literary activity went beyond the theatre. His poetic works are varied and prolific, even by the standards of his own times. His prose writings are substantial and represent a wide range of genres (the picaresque excluded). He acted as ''secretario de señor'' to several noble masters. For these activities as much as for the social figure he cut (he was a skilled dancer) and his love life, the man was a legend in his own time. Lope's complex self and rich experience stand at the centre of much of his literary activity. His youthful affair with Elena Osorio, of scandalous consequence, took on many guises in the ensuing years, eventually to reach an elegant synthesis of mature wisdom, regretful melancholy, and compassionate humour in a last major work (*La Dorotea*) by the then septuagenarian writer; from many points of view, this is the most remarkable piece of fiction of its century, inside and outside Spain. The intricate weaving of experience and fiction over a great span of years that culminates in *La Dorotea* is traced in the masterful study by

A.S. Trueblood. As one literary persona replaces another in this process, Lope's sincerity ceases to be a clear-cut issue. Even his memorable confession, "I was born into two extremes, to love and to hate; I have never had a middle way," is adapted from a verse by Publius Sirus. The interaction between life and poeisis is often signalled in his works by familiar pseudonyms (Belardo, Fernando, Dorotea, Amarilis). But not always: Lope's major contribution to the pastoral, *La Arcadia*, though ostensibly recording the loves of his patron the Duke of Alba, must owe its pessimism and suffering (unusual even for pastoral) to its author's own emotional mood. By way of contrast, Lope's great poem on personal tribulation, "Huerto deshecho," the central image of which—the poet's garden laid waste by storm—has often been related to the abduction of the poet's daughter, appeals simultaneously to our own humanity and for our intellectual engagement on several levels; the biographical circumstances add little to our enjoyment. Lope could stand above the traditions of poetry, while yet absorbing them; in *Rimas humanas y divinas del licenciado Tomé de Burguillos* [Rhymes Human and Divine by the Licentiate Tomé de Burguillos], the eponymous sonneteer, in hapless love with a washerwoman, turns Petrarchism to warm mockery; in *La Gatomaquia* [The Cat-War], an epic battle between Madrid cats, Lope genially sends up the devices of his own poetry.

Lope claimed to have written a total of 1,500 plays; a modest third survive, including Corpus Christi playlets and palace plays. The temptation to see his theatre as carelessly composed should be resisted. His art was born of and made for a popular theatre. He recognized that his true capital as a dramatist lay in his audience. That is the burden of his single excursion into dramatic aesthetics, the *Arte nuevo de hacer comedias en este tiempo* [The New Art of Playmaking in Our Own Time], an apologia for a type of play that defied rules for dramatic excellence revered in academic circles; "the art of plays and poetry," Lope claimed, "is the invention of the princes among poets, for great minds are not bound by rules." His theatre mirrors life, without forfeiting imagination and fantasy. Its issues can range from the values and customs of gentrified Madrid—e.g., *La dama boba* (*The Lady Nit-Wit*), an urban satire with an elegant peripety that turns its heroine from *boba* to *discreta*—to deep issues concerning the individual and social order. His theatre contains generic subgroups. *Fuenteovejuna, Peribáñez y el comendador de Ocaña* (*Peribáñez and the Comendador of Ocaña*), *El mejor alcalde, el rey* (*The King, the Greatest Alcalde*), and *El villano en su rincón* (*The King and the Farmer*) have a common interest in the peasant. They combine a rich poetical evocation of authentic, rural existence with a rigorous, even realistic analysis of conflict in society. Lope was fascinated by how passion can disrupt social order. The privileged maintainers of order (typically a *comendador*, a local lord) betray the values that give their social role credence and purpose. Lope has been disparaged as an "idealist" in his view of society, especially for ending social conflict with the "restoration of harmony." Yet he has a realistic sense that a community seeks, after suffering, deliverance into a new order (not a restored one) that can contain turbulence in a way that a past system of authority could not. These plays are complex compositions. They draw local events and national events into one coherent dramatic structure. What happens at the level of a village community is sensed as being part of the great forces at work in a nation's evolution. The passage from an old and flawed order to a new and whole one is willed by those who are ruled as much as by their rulers. They are history

plays, their plots frequently drawn from chronicles and ballads. Yet they engage with contemporary issues concerning the sovereign state that much exercised political philosophers of Lope's time and the previous century as they applied themselves to defining the moral identity of a modern state. How centralized monarchy is based on a divinely entrusted and just exercise of power and how hierarchy is justified in terms of morally informed relationships between its lowly and privileged are key issues in these plays. Lope was a brilliant apologist for the centralized Habsburg authority under which he and his audience lived, and his theatre can be seen as an epic celebration of their common values. Yet he was not afraid of confronting the violence and disorientation caused when social restraints are broken; witness the fury of the womenfolk of *Fuenteovejuna* who hold aloft the severed head of their *comendador*, or the lethal rage of Peribáñez in defence of his wife Casilda. *The King and the Farmer* deals with these issues in a comic vein; the humorously presented rivalry between countryside and court is resolved in a solemn, even sacramental banquet at which the king invites the peasant to partake of the species of power with his ruler.

In another sub-group, that has plays such as *El perro del hortelano* (*The Gardener's Dog*), *Arminda celosa* [Jealous Arminda], *Las burlas de amor* [The Mockery of Love] and *El secretario de sí mismo* [To Be One's Own Secretary], Lope explores another area of social turbulence, caused by the social climber who confuses established roles. In *El mayordomo de la duquesa de Amalfi* (*The Duchess of Amalfi's Steward*), he adapts for a similar end, but in sombre key, the well-known tale from Bandello. And in another adaptation from Bandello's *novelle*, he offers his most disturbed tragic vision of passion and disorder, *El castigo sin venganza* (*Justice without Revenge*); there, the Duke of Ferrara, driven by a lethal combination of pride and sexual humiliation, wreaks vengeance on his bastard son and adulteress duchess in a double murder that he chillingly justifies as an act of divine and human justice. It may be wondered why the same Bandello tale that provided Shakespeare with the plot of *Romeo and Juliet* should end happily in Lope's version, *Castelvines y Monteses*; but the lovers' cheeky trouncing of the rival elders together with the casual appearance of a Fernando and a Dorotea in the last act are a reminder not only of Lope's sympathy for the young and distrust of the old, but also of the imperious influence exerted by his youthful love for Elena Osorio. In *El caballero de Olmedo* (*The Knight from Olmedo*), however, Lope confronts the tragedy of youth, and in an intensely lyrical play offers his moving account of romantic love, jealousy, and death.

—Alan K.G. Paterson

See the essays on *Fuenteovejuna*, *Justice without Revenge*, *Peribáñez and the Comendador of Ocaña*.

VERGA, Giovanni

Born: Catania, Sicily, 2 September 1840. **Education:** Educated at home, and privately, 1851–60; studied law at University of Catania, 1860–65. **Career:** Lived in Florence, 1865–70, and Milan, 1870–85; then returned to Catania. Made a senator, 1920. **Died:** 27 January 1922.

PUBLICATIONS

Collections

Le Opere, edited by Lina and Vito Perroni. 2 vols., 1945.
Opere, edited by Luigi Russo. 1955.
Tutte il teatro (includes *Cavalleria rusticana*; *In portineria*; *La lupa*; *La caccia al lupo*; *La caccia alla volpe*; *Rose caduche*; *Dal tuo al mio*; *Dopo*), edited by Natale Tedesco. 1980.
Cavalleria Rusticana and Other Stories, translated with introduction by G.H. McWilliam. 1999.

Fiction

I carbonari della montagna. 4 vols., 1861–62.
Una peccatrice. 1867; as *A Mortal Sin*, translated with introduction by Iain Halliday, 1995.
Storia di una capinera. 1873; as *Sparrow: The Story of a Songbird*, translated by Christine Donougher, 1994; as *Sparrow*, translated by Lucy Gordan and Frances Frenaye, 1997.
Eva. 1874.
Nedda. 1874; translated as *Nedda*, 1888.
Tigre reale. 1875.
Eros. 1875.
Primavera ed altri racconti. 1876.
Vita dei campi. 1880; as *Cavalleria Rusticana and Other Tales of Sicilian Peasant Life*, translated by A. Strettell, 1893; as *Under the Shadow of Etna*, translated by N.H. Dole, 1896; as *Cavalleria Rusticana and Other Stories*, translated by D.H. Lawrence, 1928, new edition, 1987.
I vinti:
  I Malavoglia. 1881; as *The House by the Medlar Tree*, translated by M.A. Craig, 1890; also translated by Eric Mosbacher, 1950; Raymond Rosenthal, 1964; L. Landry, 1991.
  Mastro-don Gesualdo. 1889; edited by Carla Riccardi, 1979; as *Master Don Gesualdo*, translated by M.A. Craig, 1893, and by Giovanni Cecchetti, 1979; as *Mastro-Don Gesualdo*, translated by D.H. Lawrence, 1923.
Il marito di Elena. 1882.
Novelle rusticane. 1882; as *Little Novels of Sicily*, translated by D.H. Lawrence, 1925, reprinted as *Short Sicilian Novels*, 1984; as *Sicilian Stories/Novelle siciliane: A Dual-language Book*, edited and translated by Stanley Appelbaum, 2001.
Per le vie. 1883.
Drammi intimi. 1884.
Vagabondaggio. 1887.
I ricordi del Capitano d'Arce. 1891.
Don Candeloro e c.ⁱ. 1894.
The She-Wolf and Other Stories, translated by Giovanni Cecchetti. 1958.

Plays

Cavalleria rusticana, from his own story (produced 1884). 1884.
La lupa; In portineria, from his own stories. 1896.
La caccia al lupo; La caccia alla volpe. 1902.
Dal tuo al mio. 1906.
Teatro (includes *Cavalleria rusticana*; *La lupa*; *In portineria*; *La caccia al lupo*; *La caccia alla volpe*). 1912.

The Wolf-Hunt, in *Plays of the Italian Theatre*, edited by Isaac Goldberg. 1921.
Rose caduche, in *Maschere 1*. 1929.

Other

Lettere a suo traduttore (correspondence with Édouard Rod), edited by Fredi Chiappelli. 1954.
Lettere a Dina (correspondence with Dina Castellazzi di Sordevolo), edited by Gino Raya. 1962.
Lettere a Luigi Capuana, edited by Gino Raya. 1975.
Lettere sparse, edited by Giovanna Finocchiaro Chimirri. 1980.

*

Bibliography: *Un secolo di bibliografia verghiana* by Gino Raya, 1960; revised edition, as *Bibliografia verghiana*, 1972.

Critical Studies: *Giovanni Verga* by Thomas G. Bergin, 1931; *Verga's Milanese Tales* by Olga Ragusa, 1964; *Giovanni Verga: A Great Writer and His World* by Alfred Alexander, 1972; *Language in Verga's Early Novels* by Nicholas Patruno, 1977; *Giovanni Verga* by Giovanni Cecchetti, 1978; *The Narrative of Realism and Myth: Verga, Lawrence, Faulkner, Pavese* by Gregory L. Lucente, 1981; *The Aspiration toward a Lost Natural Harmony in the Work of Three Italian Writers: Leopardi, Verga and Moravia* by Foscarina Alexander, 1990.

*   *   *

Giovanni Verga, along with his fellow Sicilian Luigi Capuana, was one of the founding fathers of the Italian realist movement known as *verismo*. Although Verga began his literary career writing elegantly stylized novels of romance, illicit desire, and adventure, both the interests and the manner of presentation of his narratives changed markedly with the appearance in the mid-1870s of his first work in the new realist mode, *Nedda* (subtitled "A Sicilian Sketch"). Verga's subsequent literary output was substantial, including various plays and a large number of short stories, but his literary reputation rests predominantly on four works published in the 1880s, including two collections of stories, *Vita dei campi* (*Cavalleria Rusticana and Other Stories*) and *Novelle rusticane* (*Little Novels of Sicily*), and two novels, *I Malavoglia* (*The House by the Medlar Tree*), and *Mastro-don Gesualdo* (*Master Don Gesualdo*), all of which are masterpieces of realist prose.

In common with such other authors writing in the age of Darwin as Dickens, Zola, and Galdós, Verga focused on the day-to-day events and struggles of human society, and especially on those of the lower classes. Verga's narratives concentrated, moreover, on the customs and characteristics of the region he knew best, Sicily. However, because the everyday language of the Sicilian populace is a regional dialect quite different from Italian, Verga was faced with a particularly intricate linguistic problem. To solve it, he transposed the locutions, rhythms, and syntax peculiar to the dialect into standard Italian both in dialogue and in descriptive passages. At the same time, he made extensive use of free indirect discourse, in which the distinctions between the narrator and the characters are blurred to such an extent that the work of art, in Verga's own words in the introduction to the story "Gramigna's Mistress," seems "to have made itself.'' The dual effects of Verga's linguistic mastery are, therefore, immediacy and objectivity. Since Verga's narrative is told from what appears in part to be the perspectives of the characters themselves, furthermore, his stories seem to bear the stamp of authenticity in their very narration, as though the world created by the fiction were indeed ''real.''

These characteristics are shared by all of Verga's realist narratives, even though their characters and subject matter vary considerably. *Nedda* is the story of a young farm worker whose child (fathered by Janu, who has died of malaria) is born out of wedlock. When Nedda refuses to give up her baby, she is ostracized, and the child dies of starvation shortly thereafter. Although Nedda suffers from her situation, she does not seem finally to understand it. If there is to be understanding, therefore, it must come from the reader. This sort of implicit appeal to the reader is typical of Verga's works, and it accounts both for the power of their starkly objective presentation and for the surprisingly consistent sympathy that they elicit for the plight of their protagonists.

Among the short stories of *Vita dei campi* (*Cavalleria Rusticana and Other Stories*) and *Little Novels of Sicily*, four in particular deserve special mention. ''Cavalleria Rusticana'' is the story of temptation, jealousy, and violence amid Sicily's rural peasantry that furnished the characters and plot for Mascagni's opera of the same name. ''The She-Wolf'' uses a distinctive mixture of realistic effects and mythic background to portray the superhuman powers and sexual enticements of its title character. ''Rosso Malpelo'' describes the unconscionable conditions of child labour in the period of Sicily's incipient industrialization, and it shows the local populace's pathetically uncomprehending view of its own role in contributing to such conditions. ''Property'' tells the story of the vast holdings of the successful and avaricious proprietor, Mazzarò, and of his fetishistic obsession with what he owns. Indeed, his obsession is so strong that even at his death he is unwilling to leave his belongings behind, as he goes about his courtyard killing the animals like a madman, screaming, ''oba mia, vientene con me!'' (''My property, come with me!'').

Verga's first full novel in the realist mode, *The House by the Medlar Tree*, is the story of the Malavoglia family of Aci Trezza, a fishing village not far from Catania. Padron 'Ntoni, the head of the family, contracts to use his boat, the *Provvidenza*, to transport a cargo of lupins to be sold on the mainland. When the *Provvidenza* goes down in stormy seas off the Sicilian coast, the family not only loses several of its members but also forfeits the familial house by the medlar tree because of failure to repay the sum borrowed to make the contract. Even more clearly than the short story ''Property,'' *The House by the Medlar Tree* demonstrates Verga's condemnation of the economic system then on the rise in Italy, which brought with it, in his view, the destruction of the social order of the family and the end of the old codes of honour and labour that the family had always sustained.

Master Don Gesualdo carries Verga's critique a step further by concentrating on the main character's economic and social advancement from ''Mastro,'' or ''Journeyman,'' to ''Don,'' or ''Lord.'' Master Don Gesualdo uses both his wits and an advantageous marriage to gain fabulous wealth. But his social and economic success is matched by the nearly total deterioration of his emotional life, until at the end of the novel, in a scene reminiscent of the conclusion of Balzac's *Père Goriot*, Gesualdo suffers the agonies of the deathbed completely alone, with only the uncaring servants to notice his passing. These two novels were planned originally as the first and second books in a five-part series entitled *I vinti*, or ''The

Defeated,'' which was to move up the social scale until it reached the Sicilian aristocracy, Verga's own class. It is probably impossible to establish beyond doubt whether Verga stopped with *Master Don Gesualdo* because his inspiration failed him, because of unresolvable stylistic problems, or because his view of Italian historical development was simply too pessimistic to permit him to continue. What is certain, however, is that before Verga gave up on the rest of the cycle, he had created several of the most memorable and most enduring narratives in all of 19th-century European literature.

—Gregory L. Lucente

See the essays on *The House by the Medlar Tree* and *Master Don Gesualdo*.

VERLAINE, Paul (-Marie)

Born: Metz, France, 30 March 1844. **Education:** Educated at Institution Landry, Paris; Lycée Bonaparte (now Condorcet), Paris, 1855–62, baccalauréat, 1862; École de Droit, Paris, 1862–63. **Family:** Married Mathilde Mauté in 1870 (judicially separated 1874, divorced 1884), one son. **Career:** Clerk for insurance company, 1864, 1872, and at the Hôtel de Ville, Paris, 1864–71; had romantic relationship with Arthur Rimbaud, q.v., in France, Belgium, and England, 1871–73: shot Rimbaud in Brussels and served term in Petits-Carmes prison, Brussels, and in Mons, 1873–75; teacher, Stickney, Lincolnshire, 1875–76; St. Aloysius' School, Bournemouth, 1876–77, Collège Notre-Dame, Rethel, France, 1877–79, and Solent School, Lymington, Hampshire, 1879; made two attempts at farming in north-eastern France, then returned to Paris; served short prison term for threatening his mother, 1884; hospitalized for much of the time from 1886. **Died:** 8 January 1896.

PUBLICATIONS

Collections

Oeuvres complètes, edited by Léon Vernier. 1899.
Oeuvres complètes, edited by H. de Bouillane de Lacoste and Jacques Borel. 2 vols., 1959–60.
Oeuvres poétiques complètes, Oeuvres en prose complètes, edited by Jacques Borel. 2 vols., 1962–72.
Oeuvres poétiques, edited by Jacques Robichez. 1969.
Oeuvres poétiques complètes, edited by Yves-Alain Faure. 1992.
One Hundred and One Poems by Paul Verlaine: A Bilingual Edition, translated by Norman R. Shapiro. 1999.
Selected Poems, translated with introduction by Martin Sorrell. 1999.

Verse

Poèmes saturniens. 1866.
Les Amies. 1868.
Fêtes galantes. 1869; as *Gallant Parties*, translated by Arthur Clark Kennedy, 1912.
La Bonne Chanson. 1870.

Romances sans paroles. 1874; edited by D. Hillery, 1976; as *Romances without Words*, translated by Arthur C. Kennedy, 1921.

Sagesse. 1881, revised edition, 1889; edited by C. Chadwick, 1973.

Jadis et naguère. 1884.

Amour. 1888.

Parallèlement. 1889.

Dédicaces. 1890, revised edition, 1894.

Femmes. 1890.

Bonheur. 1891.

Chansons pour elle. 1891; as *Chansons pour elle*, translated anonymously, 1926.

Choix de poésies. 1891.

Liturgies intimes. 1892.

Élégies. 1893.

Odes en son honneur. 1893.

Dans les limbes. 1894.

Épigrammes. 1894.

Poems, translated by Gertrude Hall. 1895.

Invectives. 1896.

Chair. 1896.

Hombres. 1903/1904; edited by Hubert Juin, 1977.

Biblio-sonnets. 1913.

Forty Poems, translated by Roland Gant and Claude Apcher. 1948.

Selected Poems, translated by C.F. MacIntyre. 1948.

The Sky above the Roof: Fifty-six Poems, translated by Brian Hill. 1957.

Selected Poems, translated by Joanna Richardson. 1974.

Femmes/Hombres, edited and translated by William Packard and John D. Mitchell. 1977; edited by Jean-Paul Corsetti and Jean-Pierre Giusto, 1990; as *Women, Men* translated by Alistair Elliot, 1979; as *Women and Men: Erotic Works*, translated by Alan Stone, 1985.

Other

Les Poètes maudits. 1884, revised edition, 1888.

Mémoires d'un veuf. 1886.

Louise Leclercq (short stories and play, *Madame Aubin*). 1886.

Mes hôpitaux. 1891.

Mes prisons. 1893.

Confessions. 1895; as *Confessions of a Poet*, translated by Joanna Richardson, 1950.

Correspondance, edited by A. van Bever. 3 vols., 1922–29.

Lettres inédites à Cazals, edited by Georges Zayed. 1957.

Lettres inédites à Charles Morice, edited by Georges Zayed. 1964.

Lettres inédites à divers correspondants, edited by Georges Zayed. 1976.

Editor, *Illuminations*, by Arthur Rimbaud. 1886.

Editor, *Poésies complètes*, by Arthur Rimbaud. 1895.

*

Critical Studies: *The Art of Paul Verlaine* by Antoine Adam, 1963; *Verlaine: A Study in Parallels* by Alfred E. Carter, 1969; *Verlaine* by Joanna Richardson, 1971; *Verlaine* by C. Chadwick, 1973; *Verlaine and the Decadence 1882–1890* by Phillip Stephan, 1974; *Paul Verlaine: A Centenary Tribute*, translated by Allen Prowle, 1976; *Verlaine: Fixing an Image* by David Hillery, 1988.

* * *

"Verlaine," wrote the French critic Jules Lemaître in 1889, "c'est un enfant, seulement cet enfant a une musique dans l'âme." Ten years later the English critic Arthur Symons made the same points when he talked of Verlaine's "simplicity of language which is the direct outcome of a simplicity of temperament" and contended that some of his poems "go as far as verse can go to become pure music." Verlaine himself, in his "Art poétique" of 1874, recognized that his genius did indeed lie in simplicity and musicality. "De la musique avant toute chose," he commanded in the poem's opening line and he went on to condemn eloquence and to plead instead for a certain casual quality that had been lacking in French poetry up to that time.

In point of fact it was only during the ten years from 1865 to 1875 that Verlaine's poetry achieved this simplicity and musicality. Before 1865, as a young poet barely 20 years old, he imitated the classical grandeur of the Parnassian poets who were then in vogue, preaching the virtue of industry rather than inspiration and claiming that poetry is analogous not to music but to sculpture in that it must be slowly and carefully shaped. It was he who formulated one of the best known statements of the Parnassian doctrine when, in the prologue to his first volume of verse, *Poèmes saturniens* [Saturnian Poems] in 1866, he asked: "Est-elle en marbre ou non, la Vénus de Milo?" Not surprisingly the volume often practises what it preaches: in, for example, a description of a portrait of Caesar Borgia and an account of the death of Philippe II, both of them in sonorous 12-syllable alexandrines richly rhymed. But in the same volume there are, in contrast, a number of poems such as "Soleils couchants," "Chanson d'automne," and "Le Rossignol" which have an intimate rather than an oratorical note, achieved through the use of short lines rather than alexandrines, and lines with an uneven number of syllables creating an unstable rhythm, plus extensive enjambment in which one line frequently runs into the next, thus further disturbing any fixed rhythmic pattern, and weak rather than rich rhymes so that the verse is not too far removed from everyday prose. These are poems of an intensely personal kind inspired by Verlaine's emotional problems and their hesitant, murmuring rhythms are matched by the blurred, ill-defined landscapes he uses to symbolize his vague feelings of unhappiness—setting suns, waning moons, falling leaves, weeping willows, misty horizons.

His second volume of poetry, *Fêtes galantes* (*Gallant Parties*), in 1869, may appear to mark a backward step in his development in so far as it is the transposition into poetry of paintings by Watteau and other 18th-century artists of life during the Regency. But behind the façade of costumed figures, "quasi tristes sous leurs déguisements fantasques" can be perceived the lonely, moody figure of the "poète saturnien" himself still searching for the "femme inconnue, et que j'aime, et qui m'aime," of whom he had written in his first volume. Not only does *Gallant Parties*, despite its 18th-century setting, thus continue the note of personal sadness that had made its appearance in *Poèmes saturniens*, it also continues the trend noted in the earlier poems as regards imagery and versification. Verlaine is more than ever the poet of twilight and moonlight, of autumn leaves and fading flowers, and he is more than ever the poet of short lines with weak rhymes and a fluid rhythm.

His third volume of verse, *La Bonne Chanson* [The Good Song], does however, save for one or two poems, mark a backward step in the development of his poetry. His forthcoming marriage in August 1870 made life seem less gloomy and the future more stable. The vague melancholy and inexplicable sadness of the earlier volumes is there-fore replaced by a joyful certainty, the blurred imagery by sunlit scenes, and changing, hesitant rhythms by firm and measured lines. But despite the solemn promises made in *La Bonne Chanson*, before the marriage was much more than a year old Verlaine found himself once more in that state of emotional uncertainty that seems to have been essential for the flowering of his poetic genius. The arrival in Paris in September 1871 of Arthur Rimbaud meant that Verlaine fell increasingly under his spell over the course of the next two years and in his fourth volume, *Romances sans paroles* (*Romances without Words*), whose very title suggests that it is the music of the lines that matters more than their meaning, there is the same note of indecision, reflected in the same kind of twilit scenes and uncertain rhythms as in *Poèmes saturniens* and *Gallant Parties*.

Perhaps predictably, Verlaine's relationship with Rimbaud lasted scarcely longer than his marriage had done and it ended in a violent quarrel in July 1873 as a consequence of which he was sentenced to two years imprisonment. The devastating effect of these two related events plunged him even deeper into gloom and despondency and in such poems as "Je ne sais pourquoi," "Un grand sommeil noir," "L'espoir luit," and "Le ciel est, par-dessus le toit," written in the last half of 1873 and later incorporated into *Sagesse* [Wisdom], the simple vocabulary, the uncomplicated syntax, the undeveloped im-ages, the tenuous rhymes, and the intimate rhythms transcribe his distress with telling directness.

Verlaine had one final supreme emotional crisis in his life when, after his wife rejected his attempt at reconciliation, he turned instead towards God for comfort and consolation. The initial ardour of his conversion in 1874 inspired some of his finest poems, such as "Mon Dieu m'a dit: Men fils, il faut m'aimer," "Bon chevalier masqué qui chevauche en silence," and "Les faux beaux jours ont lui tout le jour, ma pauvre âme" ("Poor soul, the false fair lights that shone all day"). But all too soon, as in *La Bonne Chanson*, his new found optimism and stability led him to lapse into wordy platitudes and to adopt the more composed kind of style that makes so many of the poems of *Sagesse* as disappointing as the vast majority of those in *La Bonne Chanson*.

The remainder of Verlaine's considerable output, after this crucial decade from 1865 to 1875, is equally disappointing. Lacking any further emotional impulse to write but driven to do so by the necessity to earn a living, he simply used up old poems that he had not thought worthy of publication at an earlier stage and then lapsed permanently into a verbose, descriptive, platitudinous style that renders 15 of his 20 volumes of verse virtually unreadable. But, despite this long, sad decline over the last 20 years of his life, Verlaine remains for posterity the poet who, in his first five volumes of poetry, displayed in a number of memorable poems his unique gift for subtly conveying the infinite sadness of things.

—C. Chadwick

See the essays on "L'Angoisse," "Art Poétique," and "Il pleure dans mon coeur . . . ."

VERNE, Jules (-Gabriel)

Born: Nantes, France, 8 February 1828. **Education:** Educated at Institut de Mme. Sambin, 1833; École Saint-Stanislas; Saint-Donatien seminary; the lycée, Nantes, from 1841, baccalauréat, 1846; studied law in Paris, 1847–49, licence in law, 1849. **Family:** Married Honorine de Viane in 1857, one son. **Career:** Secretary, Théâtre lyrique, 1852. Travelled in England and Scotland, 1859, and New York, 1867. Suffered a series of attacks of facial paralysis. Elected to Academy of Amiens, 1872; elected councillor, Amiens, 1888 (re-elected 1892, 1896, 1900). **Award:** Officer, Légion d'honneur, 1892. **Member:** Geography Society. **Died:** 24 March 1905.

PUBLICATIONS

Collections

Works, edited by Charles F. Horne. 1911.
Novels, edited by H.C. Harwood. 1929.
The Omnibus Jules Verne. 1951.
The Fitzroy Edition of Jules Verne, edited by I.O. Evans. 1958.
Jules Verne: Anthologie, edited by François Raymond. 1986.
Poésies inédites, edited by Christian Robin. 1989.
The Complete Twenty Thousand Leagues Under the Sea, translated by J. Mickel. 1992.
The Eternal Adam and Other Stories, edited by Peter Costello. 1999.

Fiction

Cinq semaines en ballon (for children). 1863; as *Five Weeks in a Balloon*, translated by William Lackland, 1870; also translated by Arthur Chambers, 1926; I.O. Evans, 1958.
Voyage au centre de la terre. 1864; as *Journey to the Centre of the Earth*, 1872; also translated by Frederick Malleson, 1876; H.E. Palmer, 1938; Willis T. Bradley, 1956; I.O. Evans, 1961; Robert Baldick, 1965; William Butcher, 1992.
Les Aventures du capitaine Hatteras. 2 vols., 1864–1866:
  Les Anglais au pôle nord. 1864; as *English at the North Pole*, 1874; as *At the North Pole*, translated by I.O. Evans, 1961.
  Le Désert de glace. 1866; as *The Field of Ice*, 1876; as *Field of Ice*, edited and translated by Grace Lloyd Williams, 1931; as *The Ice Desert*, also translated by Lloyd Williams, 1937; as *The Wilderness of Ice*, translated by I.O. Evans, 1961.
De la terre á la lune. 1865; edited (as *From Earth to Moon*) by P.F.R. Bashford, 1930; Michael West, 1950; William Meiklejohn, 1960; J. Reynolds, 1962; as *From the Earth to the Moon; Passage Direct in 97 Hours and 20 Minutes*, translated by J.K. Hoyt, 1869; as *From the Earth to the Moon Direct in 97 Hours 20 Minutes; A Trip Around It*, translated by Louis Mercier and Eleanor C. King, 1873; as *The American Gun Club*, translated by Mercier and King, 1874; as *The Baltimore Gun Club*, translated by Edward Roth, 1874; as *From the Earth to the Moon Direct, with Round the Moon*, translated by T.H. Linklator, 1877; also translated by Lowell Bair, 1967; Jacqueline and Robert Baldick, 1970; as *From the Earth to the Moon*, translated by Edward Roth, 1895; also translated by I.O. Evans, 1958.
Les Enfants du capitaine Grant. 3 vols., 1867–68; as *Voyage Round the World*, 1876–77; as *The Mysterious Document*, 1876; as *Captain Grant's Children*, translated by I.O. Evans, 1961.
Autour de la lune. 1870; translated by Louis Mercier and Eleanor C. King, in *From the Earth to the Moon Direct in 97 Hours 20 Minutes; A Trip Around It*, 1873; as *All Around the Moon*, translated by Edward Roth, 1876; as *Round the Moon*, with *From*

the Earth to the Moon Direct, translated by T.H. Linklator, 1877; Lowell Bair, 1967; Jacqueline and Robert Baldick, 1970.

Vingt mille lieues sous les mers. 1870; as *Twenty Thousand Leagues under the Sea*, translated by Henry Frith, 1873; also translated by I.O. Evans, 1960; Anthony Bonner, 1962; Walter James Miller, 1965; William Butcher, 1998.

Une ville flottante. 1871; as *A Floating City*, with *The Blockade Runners*, 1874; also translated by Henry Frith, 1876.

Aventures de trois Russes et de trois Anglais. 1872; as *Meridiana: The Adventures of Three Englishmen and Three Russians in South Africa*, translated by Ellen Frewer, 1873; also translated by H. Frith, 1887.

Une fantaisie du docteur Ox. 1872; as *Dr Ox's Experiment and Other Stories*, translated by George M. Towle, 1874; also translated by I.O. Evans, 1964; as *From the Clouds to the Mountains*, translated by A.L Alger, 1874; as *A Winter in the Ice, and Other Stories*, translated by Towle, 1881.

Les Voyages extraordinaires (includes *Autour de la lune; De La Terre à la lune*). 1872.

Le Pays des fourrures. 2 vols., 1873; as *The Fur Country* (includes *The Sun in Eclipse* and *Through the Bering Strait*), translated by N. D'Anvers, 1873.

Le Tour du monde en quatre-vingt jours. 1873; edited by L.A. Barbé, 1899; as *Around the World in Eighty Days*, translated by G.M. Towle, 1874; also translated by Louis Mercier, 1962; K.E. Lichtenecker, 1965; Irene R. Gibbons, 1965; I.O. Evans, 1967; Jacqueline and Robert Baldick, 1968.

Un drame dans les airs. 1874; edited by J.G. Lloyd Jones, 1899.

L'Île mystérieuse (includes *Les Naufrages de l'air; L'Abandonné; Le Secret de l'île*). 3 vols., 1873; as *The Mysterious Island* (includes *Shipwrecked in the Air; The Abandoned; The Secret of the Island*), translated by W.H.G. Kingston, 3 vols., 1875; also translated by I.O. Evans, 1959; Lowell Bair, 1970; vol. 1 also published as *Wrecked in the Air*, 1875, and *Dropped from the Clouds*, 1909, both translated by Kingston.

Le Chancellor. 1875; as *The Survivors of the Chancellor*, translated by Ellen Frewer, 1875; as *The Chancellor*, translated by I.O. Evans, 1965.

Michel Strogoff. 2 vols., 1876; as *Michel Strogoff, the Courier of the Czar*, 2 vols., translated by W.H.G. Kingston, 1876–77; as *Michael Strogoff*, translated by I.O. Evans, 1959.

A Winter Amid the Ice, and Other Stories. 1876.

Hector Servadac. 2 vols., 1877; as *To the Sun? Off On a Comet!*, translated by Edward Roth, 1878; as *Hector Servadac*, translated by Ellen Frewer, 1878; also translated by I.O. Evans, 2 vols., 1965 (includes *Homeward Bound* and *Anomalous Phenomena*).

Les Indes noires. 1877; as *The Child of the Cavern*, translated by W.H.G. Kingston, 1877; as *Black Diamonds*, translated by I.O. Evans, 1961.

Un Capitaine de quinze ans. 2 vols., 1878; as *Dick Sands, the Boy Captain*, translated by Ellen Frewer, 1879.

Les Cinq Cents Millions de la Bégum. 1879; as *The Begum's Fortune*, translated by W.H.G. Kingston, 1880; also translated by I.O. Evans, 1958.

Les Révoltés de la Bounty. 1879; as *The Mutineers of the Bounty*, 1880.

Les Tribulations d'un Chinois en Chine. 1879; as *The Tribulations of a Chinaman*, translated by Ellen Frewer, 1880; as *The Adventures of a Chinaman*, translated by Virginia Champlin, 1889; as *The*

Tribulations of a Chinese Gentleman, translated by I.O. Evans, 1963.

La Maison à vapeur. 2 vols., 1880; as *The Steam House*, translated by W.H.G. Kingston, 1881; also translated by I.O. Evans, 2 vols., 1959 (includes *The Demon of Cawnpore* and *Tigers and Traitors*).

La Jangada. 2 vols., 1881; as *The Giant Raft*, translated by W.J. Gordon, 1883; also translated by I.O. Evans, 2 vols., 1967 (includes *Down the Amazon* and *The Cryptogram*).

L'École des Robinsons. 1882; as *Godfrey Morgan: A Californian Mystery*, translated by W.J. Gordon, 1883; as *The School for Crusoes*, translated by I.O. Evans, 1966.

Le Rayon vert. 1882; as *The Green Ray*, translated by M. de Hauteville, 1883; also translated by I.O. Evans, 1965.

Kéraban le têtu. 2 vols., 1883; as *Keraban the Inflexible*, 2 vols., 1884–1885.

L'Archipel en feu. 1884; as *The Archipelago on Fire*, 1886.

L'Étoile du sud. 1884; as *The Vanished Diamond: A Tale of South Africa*, 1885; as *The Southern Star Mystery*, translated by I.O. Evans, 1966.

L'Épave du Cynthia. 1885; as *Salvage from the Cynthia*, translated by I.O. Evans, 1964.

Mathias Sandorf. 3 vols., 1885; translated as *Mathias Sandorf*, 1886.

Robur le Conquérant. 1886; as *The Clipper of the Clouds*, 1887; edited by I.O. Evans, 1963.

Un billet de loterie. 1886; as *The Lottery Ticket: A Tale of Tellemarken*, 1887.

Le Chemin de France. 1887; as *Flight to France*, 1888; also translated by I.O. Evans, 1966.

Nord contre Sud. 2 vols., 1887; as *North against South: A Tale of the American Civil War*, 1888; as *North against South* (includes *Burbank the Northerner* and *Texar the Southerner*), translated by I.O. Evans, 2 vols., 1963.

Deux ans de vacances; ou, un pensionnat de Robinsons. 2 vols., 1888; as *Two Years' Holiday*, 1889; also translated by I.O. Evans, 2 vols., 1964 (includes *Adrift in the Pacific* and *Second Year Ashore*); as *Two Years' Vacation*, 1891; as *A Long Vacation*, translated by Olga Marx, 1967.

Famille sans nom. 2 vols., 1889; as *A Family without a Name*, 1889; also translated by I.O. Evans, 2 vols., 1963 (includes *Leader of the Resistance* and *Into the Abyss*).

Sans dessus dessous. 1889; as *The Purchase of the North Pole*, 1891; edited by I.O. Evans, 1966.

César Cascabel. 2 vols., 1890; translated as *Cesar Cascabel*, 1891; as *Cesar Cascabal* (includes *The Travelling Circus* and *The Show on Ice*), translated by I.O. Evans, 1966.

Mistress Branican. 2 vols., 1891; as *Mistress Branican*, translated by A. Estoclet, 1892.

Le Château des Carpathes. 1892; as *Castle of the Carpathians*, 1893; as *Carpathian Castle*, translated by I.O. Evans, 1963.

Claudius Bombarnac. 1892; translated as *Claudius Bombarnac*, 1894.

P'tit Bonhomme. 2 vols., 1893; as *Foundling Mick*, 1892.

Mirifiques Aventures de maître Antifer. 2 vols., 1894; as *Captain Antifer*, 1895.

L'Île à hélice. 2 vols., 1895; as *The Floating Island*, translated by William J. Gordon, 1896; as *Propeller Island*, translated by I.O. Evans, 1961.

Clovis Dardentor. 1896; translated as *Clovis Dardentor*, 1897.

Face au drapeau. 1896; as *For the Flag*, translated by Mrs. C. Hoey, 1897; also translated by I.O. Evans, 1961.

Le Sphinx des glaces. 2 vols., 1897; as *An Antarctic Mystery*, translated by Mrs. C. Hoey, 1898; as *The Sphinx of the Ice Fields*, translated by I.O. Evans, in *The Mystery of Arthur Gordon Pym*, 1960.

Le Superbe Orénoque. 2 vols., 1898.

Le Testament d'un excentrique. 2 vols., 1899; as *The Will of an Eccentric*, 1900.

Seconde Patrie. 2 vols., 1900; as *Their Island Home; and, Castaways of the Flag: The Final Adventures of the Swiss Family Robinson*, translated by Cranstoun Metcalfe, 1923.

Les Histoires de Jean-Marie Cabidoulin. 1901.

Le Serpent de mer. 1901; as *The Sea Serpent*, translated by I.O. Evans, 1967.

Le Village aérien. 1901; as *Village in the Treetops*, translated by I.O. Evans, 1964.

Les Frères Kip. 2 vols., 1902.

Bourses de voyage. 2 vols., 1903.

Un drame en Livonie. 1904; as *A Drama in Livonia*, edited and translated by I.O. Evans, 1967.

Maître du monde. 1904; as *Master of the World*, 1914; also translated by I.O. Evans, 1962.

L'Invasion de la mer. 1905; as *Invasion of the Sea*, translated by Edward Baxter, 2001.

Le Phare du bout du monde. 1905; as *The Lighthouse at the End of the World*, translated by Cranstoun Metcalf, 1923.

Le Volcan d'or. 2 vols., 1906; as *The Golden Volcano* (includes *The Claim on Forty Mite Greek* and *Flood and Flame*), translated by I.O. Evans, 2 vols., 1963.

L'Agence Thompson. 2 vols., 1907; as *The Thompson Travel Agency* (includes *Package Holiday* and *End of the Journey*), translated by I.O. Evans, 2 vols., 1965.

La Chasse au météore. 1908; as *The Chase of the Golden Meteor*, translated by Frederick Lawton, 1909; as *The Hunt for the Meteor*, edited and translated by I.O. Evans, 1965.

Le Pilote du Danube. 1908; as *The Danube Pilot*, translated by I.O. Evans, 1967.

Les Naufragés du Jonathan. 2 vols., 1909; as *The Survivors of the Jonathan* (includes *The Masterless Man* and *The Unwilling Dictator*), translated by I.O. Evans, 1962.

Hier et demain (includes stories). 1910.

Le Secret de Wilhelm Storitz. 1910; as *The Secret of Wilhelm Storitz*, translated by I.O. Evans, 1963.

L'Étonnante Aventure de la mission Barsac. 2 vols., 1919; as *Into the Niger Bend and City in the Sahara*, translated by I.O. Evans, 1960.

Yesterday and Tomorrow (includes stories), translated by I.O. Evans. 1965.

En Magellanie. 1987.

Le Beau Danube jaune. 1988.

Paris in the Twentieth Century, translated by Richard Howard. 1996.

Plays

Le Colin Maillard, with Michel Carré, (opera libretto, produced 1853). 1847.

Les Pailles rompues (produced 1850). 1850.

Les Compagnons de la Marjolaine, with Michel Carré. 1855.

Monsieur de Chimpanzé, with Michel Carré (produced 1858). 1858.

L'Auberge des Ardennes, with Michel Carré (produced 1860). 1860.

Onze jours de siège, with Charles Wallut (produced 1861). 1861.

Un neveu d'Amerique; ou, Les Deux Frontignac, with Edouard Cadol and Charles Wallut (produced 1873). 1873.

Le Tour du monde en quatre-vingt jours, with Adolphe d'Ennery (produced 1874). 1874.

Les Enfants du capitaine Grant, with Adolphe d'Ennery (produced 1878). 1881.

Michel Strogoff, with Adolphe d'Ennery (produced 1880). 1881; as *Michael Strogoff*, screenplay by Thomas Roberdeau, 1995.

Un voyage à travers l'impossible, with Adolphe d'Ennery (produced 1882). 1881.

Kéraban le têtu (produced 1883). 1883.

Mathias Sandorf, with William Busnach and Georges Mauren (produced 1887). 1885.

Other

Le Comte de Chanteleine: Épisode de la révolution. 1864.

Géographie illustrée de la France et de ses colonies, with Théophile Lavallée. 1867–68; edited by M. Dubail, 1876.

Histoire des grands voyages et des grands voyageurs, with Gabriel Marcel. 1870–73; as *Celebrated Travels and Travellers*, 3 vols., translated by Dora Leigh and N. D'Anvers, 1879–81.

Découverte de la terre. 1878–80.

*

Bibliography: *Jules Verne: A Primary and Secondary Bibliography* by Edward J. Gallagher and others, 1980.

Critical Studies: *Jules Verne: The Biography of an Imagination* by G.H. Waltz, 1943; *Jules Verne* by Catherine O. Peare, 1961; *The Man Who Invented the Future* by F. Born, 1964; *Jules Verne and His Work* by I.O. Evans, 1965; *Jules Verne: Portrait of a Prophet* by R. Freedman, 1965; *Jules Verne* (in English) by B. Beeker, 1966; *The Political and Social Ideas of Jules Verne* by J. Chesneaux, translated by Thomas Wirkeley, 1972; *Jules Verne* by Jean Jules-Verne, 1976; *Jules Verne: Inventor of Science Fiction* by Peter Costello, 1978; *Jules Verne* by Oliver Dumas, 1988; *The Mask of the Prophet* by Andrew Martin, 1990; *Verne's Journey to the Centre of the Self* by William Butcher, 1991; *Jules Verne: An Exploratory Biography* by Herbert R. Lottman, 1996; *The Jules Verne Encyclopedia* by Brian Taves and Stephen Michaluk, Jr., 1996; *Jules Verne on Film: A Filmography of the Cinematic Adaptations of His Works, 1902 Through 1997* by Thomas C. Renzi, 1998; *Jules Verne: Narratives of Modernity*, edited by Edmund J. Smyth, 2000.

* * *

Jules Verne wrote novels that captured the essence of the mid- to late-19th century in more ways than were perhaps apparent to the youngsters who were their first enthusiastic readers, not only in France, but throughout Europe. It was the heroic age of engineering, as was evident, more than in anything else, in a revolution in transport that seemed to surmount new challenges every succeeding decade, drastically cutting the time of journeys that had previously taken weeks and even months. Express trains thundered through tunnels and over great steel bridges to link in hours cities that formerly had always seemed distant, and great steamers crossed oceans at scarcely credible speeds as they safely navigated through latitudes that until shortly before had been the terror of sailing ships. There seemed no limit to what might be achieved, and Verne knew the art of creating a thrill by extending the bounds of the possible without ever quite lapsing into fantastic implausibility. Though trained as a lawyer rather than as an engineer or a physicist, he assiduously collected scientific information and used it skilfully in his fiction. Those who wished to do so could easily persuade themselves that reading his novels provided some tincture of scientific instruction, just as the journeys on which he sent his heroes might be said to provide some insights into the geography of distant lands and the people who inhabited them, though Verne had not travelled very extensively. What counted was the sustained seriousness with which Verne creates his stories. It serves as a warrant for complete surrender to the excitement of his fiction.

Verne's *oeuvre* takes his readers from one end of the globe to the other: around the world in 80 days; to the jungles of India; to the Russian Steppes; to the icy wastes of the North Pole with Captain Hatteras. Not even that is enough for Verne, and he goes 20,000 leagues under the sea in a marvellous submarine with a mysterious commander; down to even greater depths on a journey to the centre of the earth; and, with the aid of a super-cannon, shoots right up to the moon. The narrative moves as fast as the huge variety of vehicles that are pressed into service by his heroes, and bizarre experiences, exciting adventures, and hair's-breadth escapes from dire peril follow on one another's heels at top speed.

In all this, there is little time for in-depth characterization, and Verne adds to the impression of a certain superficiality when he is not only content with heroes who are merely amusing national stereotypes, but also presents the natives of various lands with no more than a couple of conventional traits. Social distinctions are an inherent part of his world, and servants are often comic types. For the most part, Verne depicts a male society, with well-to-do heroes who can afford to indulge their scientific dreams. Women do not figure very significantly, and when they do appear, he does not develop their roles; it is as if he were afraid they might exert charms that would be altogether too disruptive, especially when they come from exotic backgrounds.

Verne first glimpsed the romance of travel at Nantes, the seaport where he was born, but his life was largely that of a French *petit-bourgeois* who, rather than buckle down to the law, set out to make a living with his pen, first in the theatre, then by providing the publisher Jules Hetzel with copious amounts of fiction, year in and year out. Hetzel's object was to satisfy the demand for morally improving literature for young people in France, and he objected whenever Verne showed any tendency to treat politically or socially sensitive topics in a way that might cause annoyance to conservative parents or the clergy.

Hugely popular in the late-19th century and the earlier decades of the 20th, Verne's fiction lost some of its power to hold the attention of young people as science moved on far beyond even his most daring imaginings, and as eyebrows were raised at his male-dominated Euro-centrism. The myth, however, of Vernian adventure has remained widespread, even if Captain Nemo and Phineas Fogg are invariably seen nowadays as rather amusingly eccentric representatives of a bygone age.

Verne's loss of favour among the young has, however, been more than balanced by a rising tide of scholarly interest in his work. It has been examined as a paradigm of children's literature, with illustration playing its part alongside the letterpress. The influence on Verne of Edgar Allan Poe is taken as a clue to an uneasy Romantic imagination that seeks what are essentially eternal spiritual values in natural phenomena, despite all the modern scientific trappings. It is argued too that Verne's work demands respect not simply as a presentation of 19th-century science that is all the more interesting because it is complemented with some remarkable prophecies of what was to come, but also because there was a complex and pained psyche half-concealed beneath the exciting stories whose apparent optimism was increasingly undercut as Verne's career developed and he suffered certain personal misfortunes.

Modern critics have discovered many new and exciting facets to Verne's work, even if some might suspect that among their reasons for seeking them has been a desire to reveal hidden depths in a body of work that had traditionally been disparaged as being sub-literary. The criticism can, however, be appreciated for its acumen in its own right, without interfering with the reader's ability to enjoy Verne's stories simply as ripping yarns.

—Christopher Smith

See the essay on *Around the World in Eighty Days*.

VESAAS, Tarjei

Born: On Vesaas, the family farm, in Vinje parish in the province of Telemark, Norway, 20 August 1897. **Education:** Completed elementary school in 1912, attended Voss Folk High School (folkehøjskole) 1917–18. **Military Service:** Seven months of compulsory military service from 1918–1919. **Family:** Married the poet Halldis Moren in 1934; one son and one daughter. **Career:** Writer, from 1920s. **Awards:** Venice prize, 1953; Nordic Council Literary prize, 1963. **Died:** 15 March 1970.

PUBLICATIONS

Collections

Tarjei Vesaas: Huset og fuglen; Texter og bilete, 1919–1969, edited by Walter Baumgartner. 1971.
30 Poems, selected and translated by Kenneth G. Chapman. 1971.
Through Naked Branches. Selected Poems of Tarjei Vesaas, translated and edited by Roger Greenwald. 2000.
Beyond the Moment: One Hundred and One Selected Poems, translated by Anthony Barnett with Anne K. Stenersen and others. 2001.

Fiction

Dei svarte hestane. 1928.
Klokka i haugen. 1929.
Sandeltreet. 1933.
Det store spelet. 1934; as *The Great Cycle*, translated by Elizabeth Rokkan, 1967.
Kvinnor ropar heim. 1935.
Kimen. 1940; as *The Seed*, translated by Kenneth G. Chapman, 1964.
Huset i mørkret. 1945; as *The House in the Dark*, translated by Elizabeth Rokkan, 1976.

Bleikeplassen. 1946; as *The Bleaching Yard*, translated by Elizabeth Rokkan, 1981.

Vindane. 1952.

Vårnatt. 1954; as *Spring Night*, translated by Kenneth G. Chapman, 1964.

Fuglane. 1957; as *The Birds*, translated by Torbjörn Stöverud and Michael Barnes, 1968.

Brannen. 1961.

Is-slottet. 1963; as *The Ice Palace*, translated by Elizabeth Rokkan, 1966.

Bruene. 1966; as *The Bridges*, translated by Elizabeth Rokkan, 1969.

Båten om kvelden. 1968; as *The Boat in the Evening*, translated by Elizabeth Rokkan, 1971.

Verse

Kjeldene. 1946.

Leiken og lynet. 1947.

Lykka for ferdesmenn. 1949.

Løynde elders land. 1953; as *Land of Hidden Fires*, translated by Fritz König and Jerry Crisp, 1973.

Ver ny, vår draum. 1956.

Liv ved straumen. 1970.

Plays

Guds bustader. Spel i tre skrift. 1925.

Ultimatum. Spel i fyra akter. 1934.

Morgonvinden, 1947.

*

Critical Studies: *Tarjei Vesaas* by Kenneth G. Chapman, 1970; *Tarjei Vesaas: Eine ästhetische biographie* by Walter Baumgartner, 1976; *Child of the Earth. Tarjei Vesaas and Scandinavian Primitivism* by Frode Hermundsgård, 1989; *Løynde land. Ei bok om Tarjei Vesaas* by Olav Vesaas, 1995.

* * *

Tarjei Vesaas is one of the most important Norwegian writers of the 20th century. Vesaas grew up and lived most of his life in the Telemark region of Norway. Norway has two official written languages, *bokmål* (literally "book language," mostly used in urban areas) and *nynorsk* ("New Norwegian," a form of the language developed from a number of rural dialects). Although most Norwegian writers have written in *bokmål*, Vesaas wrote his works in *nynorsk*. He is one of the foremost representatives of modernist trends in 20th century Norwegian literature, as well as one of the most experimental fiction writers of his time. Among the most important themes of Vesaas's works, which are set almost exclusively in rural environments, is the need for human beings to find their place within the patterns of nature or within *livsstrømmen* (the flow of life). Related to this is the importance the author places on intuition for understanding and connecting with the world around us.

Over a 50 year period, Vesaas published 23 novels, four collections of short stories, six collections of poetry, and several plays. While clearly a "modernist" writer, it is otherwise difficult to categorize Vesaas within any particular literary school or movement. It would also be a mistake to label him as either a "rural" or a "provincial" author. Many of his works deal with the spiritual world of children, or with individuals with a child-like capacity for experience. As Kenneth Chapman observes, "Vesaas has, to a greater degree than most people, perhaps even than most writers, preserved the native poetic ability displayed by children."

After publishing two novels and a play by age 28, a government grant allowed him to travel for two years on the European continent. Much of his time was spent in European cities until his marriage in 1934, when he returned to live in his native province. Vesaas's early novels and stories are for the most part realistic, with an emphasis on themes of responsibility and redemption. In his first mature novel, *Det svarte hestene* [The Black Horses], the recurrence of a single image (in this case, a black horse) throughout the book hints at later developments in Vesaas's approach to fiction.

After publishing 11 books, Vesaas had his first major success with *Det store spelet* (*The Great Cycle*). *The Great Cycle* tells the story of Per Bufast, who, as the first-born son (or *odelsgut*) in a rural family, is destined to take over the family farm, and his struggle to come to terms with this responsibility. A sequel, *Kvinnor ropar heim* [The Woman Call: Come Home] continues themes taken up in *The Great Cycle* with the focus on female characters and on Per as an adult. Vesaas would soon abandon realistic fiction (especially the broadly-conceived epic novel) and begin to develop a more evocative, lyrical type of novel.

While in Vesaas's early works the cycles of nature are central, his works take a more pessimistic turn after 1940. Of the four short, allegorical novels written during World War II (and the German occupation of Norway which began in 1940), three were not published until after the war ended in 1945. All four of these novels have a markedly dramatic quality. *Kimen* (*The Seed*) and *Bleikeplassen* (*The Bleaching Yard*) are both studies of the sources of human violence as well as expressions of faith in the power of redemption. *Huset i mørkret* (*The House in Dark*) is an allegory based on the Norwegian resistance movement, but the moral issues depicted in the book (loyalty, commitment, the use of violence to combat evil) are of general concern.

Although he had previously written and published a few poems, Vesaas did not publish his first collection of poems until 1946, at the age of 49. Themes and images from his novels and short stories appear in his poetry as well, while in his later fiction lyrical elements often play an important role. In his first poetry collection, Vesaas used traditional forms, many of which are reminiscent of Norwegian folk songs, while in later collections free verse forms predominate.

In terms of either theme or style, it is difficult to separate Vesaas's prose and poetry. One notable feature is a marked recurrence of motifs and images. The images are often simple (a snake, a boat) and may be repeated throughout a novel or poem. Kenneth Chapman writes that "One of the most characteristic features of Vesaas's writing is his tendency to assign unexpected qualities to objects and things in the world." Vesaas also makes frequent use of ellipsis, which can place great demands on the reader. The open style of Vesaas's later works invites the reader to make her own associations. As he wrote in an essay, "The reader must be allowed to open his own secret rooms."

Vesaas's acknowledged masterpiece is *Fuglane* (*The Birds*), one of several books dealing with individuals who are isolated from society or who, for whatever reason, are unable to develop psychologically or emotionally. In *The Birds*, Mattis is a man of about 40 who lives with his sister, Hege. Although Mattis is unable to communicate with other people, including his sister, he has a special relationship with birds. "He would have liked to have started using bird language for good—to have gone back home to Hege and never spoken in any other way."

Vesaas's subsequent novels, such as *Brannen* [The Fire], are less realistic and more lyrical. *Is-slottet* (*The Ice Palace*), one of Vesaas's most challenging works, is a simple story about two young girls. Shortly after the girls become friends, one of the girls disappears while exploring an ice formation which has formed over a nearby river. Vesaas's final book, *Båten om kvelden* (*The Boat in the Evening*) is his most associative work, abandoning realistic plot altogether.

When Tarjei Vesaas died in 1970, he was one of the few Norwegian writers with an international reputation. Although there are few critical studies of Vesaas's work in English, a generous selection of his novels and poems has been translated into English. Several of Vesaas's novels have been made into films, including a Polish version of *Fuglane* (*The Birds*) made in 1967 as well as Norwegian productions of *Dei svarte hestene*, *Kimen*, *Vårnatt* (*Spring Night*), *Brannen* and *Is-slottet*.

—Paul Norlen

VESTDIJK, Simon

Born: Harlingen, The Netherlands, 17 October 1898. **Education:** Educated in Amsterdam; studied music, 1926, and medicine, 1927. **Family:** Married. **Career:** Practised briefly as ship's doctor; full-time writer from 1929. Interred at St. Michielgestel during World War II: gave lectures to fellow prisoners. Co-editor, with Menno ter Braak, of the magazine *Forum*, 1934–35. **Awards:** P.C. Hooft prize, 1950; Grand prize of Dutch letters, 1971. **Died:** 23 March 1971.

PUBLICATIONS

Collection

Werken [Complete Works]. 1977–.

Fiction

De oubliette [The Dungeon]. 1933.
Anton Wachterromans [The Anton Wachter Novels]. 8 vols., 1934–60.
    Terug tot Ina Damman [Back to Ina Damman]. 1934.
    Sint Sebastiaan [St. Sebastian]. 1939.
    Surrogaten voor Mark Tuinstra [Surrogates for Mark Tuinstra]. 1940.
    De andere school [The Other School]. 1948.
    De beker van de main [The Cup of Love]. 1957.
    De vrije vogel en zijn kooien [The Free Bird and Its Cages]. 1958.
    De rimpels van Esther Ornstein [The Wrinkles of Esther Ornstein]. 1959.
    De laatste kans [The Last Chance]. 1960.

Else Böhler, Duits dienstmeisje [Else Böhler, German Servant Girl]. 1935.
De dood betrapt [Death Caught in the Act]. 1935.
De bruine vriend. 1935; translated by M.C. Duyvendale, in *New Writing, Red Dust*, 1973.
Heden ik, morgen gij [Me Today, You Tomorrow], with H. Marsman. 1936.
Het vijfde zegel [The Fifth Seal]. 1937.
Meneer Visser's hellevaart [Mr. Visser's Descent into Hell]. 1938.
De nadagen van Pilatus [The Latter Days of Pilatus]. 1938.
Narcissus op vrijersvoeten [Narcissus Courting]. 1938.
De verdwenen horlogemaker. 1939; as *The Watchmaker Vanishes*, translated by J. May in *Harvest of the Lowlands*, 1945.
De zwarte ruiter [The Black Rider]. 1940.
Rumeiland. 1940; as *Rum Island*, translated by Brian K. Bowes, 1963.
Aktaion onder de sterren [Actaeon under the Stars]. 1941.
De vuuraanbidders [The Fire Worshippers]. 1947.
De overnachting [Staying Overnight], with J. van Schaik-Willing. 1947.
Stomme getuigen [Mute Witnesses]. 1947; one story, "Gummivingers," as "ubber Fingers," translated by Jo May, in *Best of Modern European Literature*, 1945.
Puriteinen en piraten [Puritans and Pirates]. 1947.
Iersche nachten [Irish Nights]. 1948.
De redding van Fré Bolderhey [The Salvation of Fré Bolderhey]. 1948.
Pastorale 1943 [Pastoral Interlude 1943]. 1948.
Bevrijdingsfeest [Liberation Celebrations]. 1949.
De kellner en de levenden [The Steward and the Living]. 1949.
Avontuur met Titia [Adventure with Titia], with H. van Eyk. 1949.
De fantasia en andere verhalen [Fantasy and Other Stories]. 1949.
De koperen tuin. 1950; as *The Garden Where the Brass Band Played*, translated by A. Brotherton, 1965.
De dokter en het lichte meisje [The Doctor and the Loose Woman]. 1951.
De vijf roeiers [The Five Rowers]. 1951.
Ivoren wachters [Ivory Watchmen]. 1951.
Op afbetaling [On Account]. 1952.
De verminkte Apollo [The Maimed Apollo]. 1952.
De schandalen [The Scandals]. 1953.
Het glinsterend pantser [The Shining Armour]. 1956.
Open boek [Open Book]. 1957.
De arme Heinrich [Poor Heinrich]. 1958.
De ziener [The Seer]. 1959.
Een moderne Antonius [A Modern Antonius]. 1960.
Een Alpenroman [A Novel of the Alps]. 1961.
De filosoof en de sluipmoordenaar [The Philosopher and the Assassin]. 1961.
De held van Temesa [The Hero of Temesa]. 1962.
Het genadeschot [The Lethal Shot]. 1964.
Bericht uit het hiernamaals [Report from the Hereafter]. 1964.
Juffrouw Lot [Miss Fate]. 1965.
Zo de ouden zongen. . . [As the Old Ones Sang]. 1965.
De onmogelijke moord [The Impossible Murder]. 1965.
Het spook en de schaduw [The Ghost and the Shadow]. 1966.
De leeuw en zijn huid [The Lion and Its Hide]. 1967.
Een huisbewaarder [The Caretaker]. 1967.

Het schandaal der blauwbaarden [The Scandal of the Bluebeards].
   1968.
De hotelier doet niet meer mee [The Landlord Is No Longer in the
   Running]. 1968.
De filmheld en het gidsmeisje [The Movie Star and the Girl Guide].
   1968.
Vijf vadem diep [Five Fathoms Deep]. 1969.
Het verboden bacchanaal [The Forbidden Bacchanal]. 1969.
Het proces van meester Eckhart [The Trial of Master Eckhart]. 1970.
Kind tussen vier vrouwen [Child among Four Women]. 1972.
De persconferentie [The Press Conference] (unfinished). 1974.
De grenslijnen uitgewist [Borderlines Effaced] (stories). 1984.

Verse

Verzen [Verses]. 1932.
Berijmd palet [Rhymed Palette]. 1933.
Vrouwendienst [Service of Women]. 1934.
Kind van stad en land [Child of Town and Country]. 1936.
Fabels met kleurkrijt. 1938; excerpts as *Fables in Coloured Chalk*,
   translated by J. Holmes, in *Delta*, 10, 1956.
Klimmende legenden [Climbing Legends]. 1940.
Water in zicht [Water in Sight]. 1940.
Simplicia. 1941.
De vliegende hollander [The Flying Dutchman]. 1941.
Mnemosyne in de bergen [Mnemosyne in the Mountains]. 1946.
Thanatos aan banden [Thanatos Bound]. 1948.
Gestelsche liederen [Songs of Gestel]. 1949.
Rembrandt en de engelen [Rembrandt and the Angels]. 1956.

Other

Kunstenaar en oorlogspsychologie [Artist and War Psychology].
   1937.
Rilke als barokkunstenaar [Rilke as Baroque Artist]. 1938.
Lier en lancet [Lyre and Lancet]. 1939.
Strijd en vlucht op papier [Battle and Flight on Paper]. 1939.
Albert Verwey en de idee [Albert Verwey and the Idea]. 1940.
Muiterij tegen het etmaal [Mutiny Against the 24-Hour Day]. 2 vols.,
   1942–47.
Het schuldprobleem bij Dostojewski [The Guilt Problem in
   Dostoevskii]. 1945.
De Poolse ruiter [The Polish Rider]. 1946.
Het eeuwige telaat [The Eternal Too Late]. 1947.
De toekomst der religie [The Future of Religion]. 1947.
Astrologie en wetenschap [Astrology and Science]. 1949.
De glanzende kiemcel [The Shining Germ Cell]. 1950.
Swordplay, Wordplay, with A. Roland Holst. 1950.
Essays in duodecimo. 1952.
Zuiverende kroniek [Purifying Chronicle]. 1956.
Het eerste en het laatste [The First and the Last]. 1956.
Keurtroepen van Euterpe [Elite Troops of Euterpe]. 1957.
Merlijn (libretto), music by Willem Pijper. 1957.
Marionettenspel met de dood [Puppet Play with Death], with S.
   Dresden. 1957.
Kunst en droom [Art and Dream]. 1958.
Her kastje van Oma [Granny's Little Cupboard]. 1958.
De dubbele weegschaal [The Double Balance]. 1960.
Voor en na de explosie [Before and After the Explosion]. 1960.
Muziek in blik [Music in Sight]. 1960.

Gustav Mahler. Over de structuur van zijn symfonisch oeuvre [The
   Structure of Mahler's Symphonies]. 1960.
Gestalten tegenover mij [Figures Facing Me] (autobiographical es-
   says). 1961.
De symfonieën van Jean Sibelius [The Symphonies of Jean Sibelius].
   1962.
Hoe schrijft men over muziek [How One Writes on Music]. 1963.
De zieke mens in de romanliteratuur [The Diseased Person in the
   Novel]. 1964.
De leugen is onze moeder [The Lie Is Our Mother]. 1965.
De symfonieën van Anton Bruckner [The Symphonies of Anton
   Bruckner]. 1966.
Brieven uit de oorlogsjaren ann Theun de Vries [War Letters to Theun
   de Vries]. 1967.
Gallische facetten [Gallic Facets]. 1968.
Het wezen van de angst [The Nature of Fear] (unfinished university
   thesis). 1970.
Translator, *Fantastische vertellingen*, by Edgar Allan Poe. 1941.
Translator, *Gedichten*, by Emily Dickinson. 1939.
Translator, *Avonturen van Sherlock Holmes*, by Arthur Conan Doyle.
   1946.
Translator, *Nieuwe avonturen van Sherlock Holmes*, by Arthur Conan
   Doyle. 1948.
Translator, *De hond van de Baskervilles*, by Arthur Conan Doyle.
   1948.

*

Critical Studies: *De duivelskunstenaar* by Menno ter Braak, 1943;
Over Simon Vestdijk by M. Nord, 1948; *Simon Vestdijk en Lahringen*,
1958, and *In gesprek met Simon Vestdijk*, 1967, both by N. Gregoor;
Het fragmentarisch huis by J. Starink, 1964; *Handdruk en handgemeen,
leesavonturen met Simon Vestdijk* by A. Wadman, 1965; *De chaos en
de volheid* by R.A. Cornets de Groot, 1966; *Tweemaal Vestdijk* by
Hella S. Haase, 1970; *Simon Vestdijk en de kerkgeschiedenis* by J.
Kamphuis, 1973; *Over de "Koperen tuin" van Vestdijk* by J. Pop,
1976; *Meester en Leerling. In de voetsporen van Simon Vestdijk* by
W.A.M. de Moor, 1978; *Over de Griekse romans van Simon Vestdijk*
by R. Th. de Paardt, 1979; *Over "Terug naar Ina Damman" en de
andere Anton Wachter romans van Simon Vestdijk* by R. Marres,
1981; *De toverbron. Simon Vestdijk en de geschiedenis* by P.
Kralt, 1988.

*   *   *

Simon Vestdijk is one of the most prolific and versatile writers the
Netherlands has ever produced. This impressive productivity attracted attention in the first assessment of Vestdijk's work, *De
duivelskunstenaar* [The Devil's Artist], by Menno ter Braak, written
nine years after the first novel, *Terug tot Ina Damman* [Back to Ina
Damman], had appeared. Ter Braak's title, together with the poet A.
Roland Holst's line, "Oh thou that writes faster than God can read,"
sums up the contemporary view of Vestdijk.

Vestdijk was one of the few major writers in the Netherlands to be
active before, during, and after World War II. If his extensive *oeuvre*
is surveyed chronologically, it is possible to discern some patterns.

All but one volume of poetry, *Rembrandt en de engelen* [Rembrandt and the Angels], was published in the 1930s and 1940s. During this same period, the short stories and roughly equal numbers of historical and non-historical novels appeared in print. The final 20 years' output was dominated by non-historical novels. There was also a steady stream of non-fiction running through his entire productive period of some 40 years.

Vestdijk became associated with the literary journal *Forum* in 1931 at a time when leading members of the *Forum* group, like Menno ter Braak and E. du Perron, were outspoken about the threat to democracy posed by totalitarianism, particularly National Socialism. Their unequivocal political stance led them to an equally unequivocal literary stance: that a writer's integrity and the way it was revealed in his work was paramount. Emphasis on literary form, which had been the focus of innovation since roughly 1915, was rejected. Vestdijk's early autobiographical fiction was completely in tune with this new mood. The first such novel, *Kind tussen vier vrouwen* [Child among Four Women], was too subjective for the literary establishment and was only published posthumously. It was reworked into a series of eight novels, the *Anton Wachterromans* [The Anton Wachter Novels], published between 1934 and 1960. The acknowledged influence is Proust, but the worlds of small-town Dutch life and Amsterdam landladies are an ironic transformation of the Proustian settings. The novels contain the essence of Vestdijk's fiction: detailed exploration of the individual self, emphasizing sexuality, fear, isolation, and alienation.

Rather than forming a web of distinct themes, Vestdijk's novels can be viewed as a whole that is more than the sum of the individual works: it amounts to an investigation of what it is to be human through an exploration of the self and an application of the insights thus gained to all conditions of humanity. The focus is on the struggle of individuals to live with themselves and with their fellow human beings.

For example, the treatment of sexuality in all the novels reveals an almost programmatic approach to this subject. Almost every aspect of sexuality imaginable is portrayed somewhere in the *oeuvre*, including some which readers have found disturbing. There is no moral content, just a laying bare of humanity at its most vulnerable and most laughable. This gives rise to moments of comedy, such as when the French teacher and her pupil in *De ziener* [The Seer] become aware of the figure of Leroy, the voyeur and visionary of the title, perched in a tree outside her bedroom window. Typically, the humour is multi-layered, for this farcical climax is simultaneously a romantic climax for the couple and an anti-climax for both Leroy and the reader, who are denied the gratification of witnessing sexual activity. If there is a "moral" message in such novels, it is to remind the reader that he or she is no different from those portrayed.

The use of humour and irony as counterweights to a portrait of humanity stripped of illusions foreshadowed post-war developments in Dutch literature when a new generation of writers such as Gerard Reve and Willem Frederik Hermans depicted the atmosphere of gloom and disillusionment in Dutch society with bizarre or sardonic humour.

The historical novels show Vestdijk's skill at exploiting adventure, colour, and outlandish settings. Eighteenth-century Jamaica; the painter El Greco; an encounter between Voltaire and the assassin of the Swedish king; an eternal triangle of Caligula, Pontius Pilate, and Mary Magdalen are subjects in the historical novels, *Rumeiland* (*Rum*

Island), *Het vijfde zegel* [The Fifth Seal], *De filosoof en de sluipmoordenaar* [The Philosopher and the Assassin], and *De nadagen van Pilatus* [The Latter Days of Pilate], respectively.

There is another dimension to the historical fiction, best illustrated by *Het vijfde zegel* and *De nadagen van Pilatus*. Both portray an abuse of power and disregard for human values: in El Greco's Spain it emanates from the Inquisition, and in Pilate's Rome it resides in the crazed figure of Caligula. Both novels deal with the persecution of Jews, the use of history to justify a political position, and the manipulation of the masses through the use of spectacle, offering a chilling picture of what was already a reality in Germany.

World War II—a major preoccupation in Dutch post-war literature—is given more direct expression in *Pastorale 1943* [Pastoral Interlude 1943], *Bevrijdingsfeest* [Liberation Celebrations], both unflattering portraits of the Dutch Resistance, and in *Het genadeschot* [The Lethal Shot], which is about living with memories of the war.

Vestdijk produced an astonishing range and volume of writing. The literary work includes poetry, short stories, and autobiographical, historical, and non-historical novels, as well as translations of fiction. Other prose ranges over psychology, religion, philosophy, music, and European and American literature. Add to these a thesis on the nature of fear, *Het wezen van de angst* [The Nature of Fear], a treatise on "the future of religion," *De toekomst der religie*, and another on astrology and science, *Astrologie en wetenschap*, and one has the sense of an unbridled enquiring mind and an unlimited urge to communicate.

—Jane Fenoulhet

VIAN, Boris

Pseudomyns: Bison Ravi, Hugo Hachebuisson, and Vernon Sullivan. **Born:** Ville-d'Avray, France, 10 March 1920. **Education:** Educated at Lycée de Sèvres; Lyceé Condorcet; Lycée Hoche, baccalauréats, 1935 and 1937; L'École centrale des Arts et Manufactures, Angoulême, 1939–42, diploma in engineering, 1942. **Family:** Married 1) Michelle Léglise in 1941 (divorced 1952), one son and one daughter; 2) Ursula Kubler in 1954. **Career:** Engineer, AFNOR, 1942–46, invented a rubber wheel, 1943; learned jazz trumpet, joined Abadie orchestra, 1942; reviewer, *Combat* and *Jazz-Hot*, 1946; artistic director for jazz division of Philips, record company, 1955; freelance writer, under pseudonyms, Bison Ravi and Hugo Hachebuisson, also published under the name Vernon Sullivan; toured as singer and recording artist, 1954–59. **Died:** 23 June 1959.

PUBLICATIONS

Collections

Théâtre. 2 vols., 1965–71.
Textes et chansons. 1966.
Chroniques de jazz, edited by Lucien Malson. 1967.
Chansons et poèmes. 1967.
Théâtre inédit. 1970.
Romans, poèmes, nouvelles et théâtre. 1978.

Opéras (includes *Le Marquis de Lejanes; Fiesta; Lily Strasa; Arne Sakmussem; Le Mercenaire*), edited by Noël Arnaud. 1982.

Fiction

Vercoquin et le plancton. 1946.
J'irai cracher sur vos tombes (as Vernon Sullivan). 1946; as *I Shall Spit on Your Graves*, translated by Vian and Milton Rosenthal, 1948.
L'Écume des jours. 1947; as *Froth on the Daydream*, translated by Stanley Chapman, 1967, as *Mood Indigo*, translated by John Sturrock, 1968.
L'Automne à Pékin. 1947.
Les Morts ont tous la même peau (as Vernon Sullivan). 1947.
Le Loup-garou (stories). 1947.
Et on tuera tous les affreux (as Vernon Sullivan). 1948.
Les Fourmis (stories). 1949.
Les Poissons morts. 1949.
L'Herbe rouge. 1950.
L'Arrache-coeur. 1953; as *Heartsnatcher*, translated by Stanley Chapman, 1968.
Elles se rendent pas compte (as Vernon Sullivan). 1953.
Les Lurettes fourrées (stories). 1962.
Trouble dans les Andains. 1966.
Le Ratichon baigneur (stories). 1981.
Blues for a Black Cat and Other Stories, translated by Julia Older. 1992.

Verse

Barnum's Digest (collection). 1948.
Cantilènes en gelée. 1949.
Je voudrais pas crever. 1962.
Cent sonnets, edited by Noël Arnaud. 1984.

Plays

L'Équarrissage pour tous (produced 1950). 1948; with *Le Dernier des métiers*; as *Knackery for All*, translated by Marc Estrin, in *Plays for a New Theatre*, 2, 1966; as *The Knacker's ABC*, translated by Simon Watson Taylor, 1968.
Le Chevalier de neige, music by Georges Delerue (produced 1953). 1953.
Les Bâtisseurs d'empire (produced 1959). 1959; as *The Empire Builders*, translated by Simon Watson Taylor, in *Plays of the Year*, 1961–62.
Fiesta, music by Darius Milhaud (opera libretto; produced 1958). In *Opéras*, 1982.
Le Goûter des généraux. 1962; as *The Generals' Tea Party*, translated by Simon Watson Taylor, 1967.
Petits spectacles. 1977.

Screenplays: *Rencontres*, 1941; *Un homme comme les autres*, 1941; *Le Devin*, 1941; *La Photo envoyée*, 1941; *La Semeuse d'amour*, 1941; *Notre terre ici-bas*, 1942; *Notre Faust; ou, Le Vélo-taxi*, 1942; *Trop sérieux s'abstenir*, 1942; *Histoire naturelle; ou, Le Marché noir*, 1945; *Zoneilles*, 1947; *Marie-toi*, 1950–53; *Avant-projet de scénario*,

with Pierre Kast, 1953; *Le Cow-Boy de Normandie*, with Pierre Kast, 1953; *Le Baron annibal*, with Pierre Kast, 1954; *L'Auto-stoppeur*, with Pierre Kast, 1955; *Tous les péchés de la terre; ou, L'Accident*, with Pierre Kast, 1956; *Rue des Ravissantes*, with Pierre Kast, 1957; *Fiesta*, 1958; *De quoi je me mêle*, with Pierre Kast, 1958; *Strip-tease*, 1958; *Faites-moi chanter*, 1958; *J'irai cracher sur vos tombes*, 1959.

Other

Livre d'or. 1940.
Les Aventures de A. 1957.
En avant la Zizique . . . et par ici les gros sous. 1958.
En verve (selection). 1970.
Chroniques de jazz. 1971; revised edition, 1986.
Chroniques du menteur. 1974.
Derrière la zizique (articles). 1976.
Cinéma. Science-fiction. 1978.
Mémoire concernant le calcul numérique de Dieu par les méthodes simples et fausses. 1979.
Écrits pornographiques, edited by Noël Arnaud. 1980.
Écrits sur jazz. 1981; as *Roundabout Close to Midnight: The Jazz Writings of Boris Vian*, translated by Mike Zwerin, 1988.
Autres écrits sur le jazz. 2 vols., 1981–82.
La Belle Époque (articles). 1982.
Chansons. 1984.
Autres écrits sur le jazz, edited by Claude Raueil. 2 vols., 1981–82.
Translator, *Mademoiselle Julie*, by Strindberg. 1952.
Translator, *Le Monde des A*, by Alfred E. van Vogt. 1953.
Translator, *Là-bas près de la rivière*, by Richard Wright. 1957.
Translator, *L'Homme au bras d'or*, by Nelson Algren. 1955.
Translator, *Les Femmes s'en balancent*, by Peter Cheyney. 1949.

*

Critical Studies: *Boris Vian* (in French) by David Noakes, 1964; *Boris Vian* by Jean Clouzet, 1966; *Boris Vian: Essai d'interprétation et de documentation* by Michel Rybalka, 1969; *Les Vies parallèles de Boris Vian* by Noël Arnaud, 1970; *"L'Écume des jours" analyse critique* by Michel Gauthier, 1973; *Boris Vian* by Alfred Cismaru, 1974; *Les Vies post-humes de Boris Vian* by Michel Fauré, 1975; *Lecture plurielle de "L'Écume des jours"* by Alain Costes, 1979; *Boris Vian* by Philippe Boggio, 1993; *Boris Vian: L'écume des jours* by David Meakin, 1996; *The Flight of the Angels: Intertextuality in Four Novels of Boris Vian* by Alistair Charles Rolls, 1999.

* * *

Boris Vian's dramatically short career started immediately after World War II and ended with a heart attack in 1959. Diagnosed with a heart condition at the age of 12, Vian was to lead an extremely active and unconventional life, which has been one reason for his uninterrupted popularity among successive generations of French teenagers. Jazz, pacifism, and pataphysics were the three passions of this controversial engineer.

Hearing Duke Ellington play live in 1937 was a momentous experience which sealed Vian's love for the trumpet, an instrument he went on to play all his life. Another offshoot of his passion for jazz music was his interest in American culture in general and Afro-American culture in particular which led him to invent Vernon

Sullivan. Under this pseudonym, Vian published a series of violent and sexually explicit thrillers. The Sullivan novels have a strongly parodic element about them. Aimed at a readership fascinated by Faulkner, Steinbeck, Caldwell and others, they poke fun at the fashion for lurid tales of racial hatred and sexual aberration so prominent in post-war France. The first of these novels, *J'irai cracher sur vos tombes* (*I Shall Spit on Your Graves*), was written to save a publisher friend from bankruptcy, and was indeed an instant bestseller. It brought Vian a lot of money, a lawsuit, and a scandalous reputation.

His involvement with music and musicians also led him to compose songs which he often performed himself. "The Deserter," banned at the time of the Algerian crisis, is easily Vian's most famous single text. However this moving cry for peace should not be allowed to overshadow Vian's fine output of serious and less serious songs such as "J'suis snob" [I'm a Snob] or "Bourrée de complexes" [Bundle of Nerves], hilarious caricatures of the Saint-German-des-Prés élite.

The poems which Vian did not set to music are not regarded as highly, though at least the autobiographical title poem of the collection *Je voudrais pas crever* [I Don't Want to Kick the Bucket] ranks among his finest texts.

Pacifism is also a main theme in Vian's theatre. The issue is addressed in two plays, *L'Équarrissage pour tous* (*The Knacker's ABC*) and *Le Goûter des généraux* (*The Generals' Tea Party*). The first of these is a *pièce à thèse* suffering from all the weakness of the *théâtre engagé* of the time. The second one enjoyed excellent reviews when it was first produced after Vian's death. It is about a group of generals who are told by the President that they should start a war to solve the crisis of over-production from which the country is suffering.

However, Vian's most successful work as a dramatist is his absurd play *Les Bâtisseurs d'empire* (*The Empire Builders*). Closer to Beckett and Ionesco than any of Vian's other plays, *The Empire Builders* has Father, Mother, and Daughter Zénobie hounded by the Noise, a mysterious foe whose existence the parents persistently deny. Equally mysterious is the character (or anti-character) of the Schmürtz, who has no identity but is everybody's scapegoat. The plot unfolds a typical Vian nightmare of shrinking rooms, diminishing possessions, and vanishing people.

Nearly everything Vian wrote evinces an irresistible humour largely based on puns and fantastic situations. In the teeth of the Sartrian call for a *littérature engagée*, Vian successfully held his ground as an independent creator free to use his favourite weapon, laughter, against new and old creeds alike. Logically enough, then, the only organized group he joined was the anti-establishment College of Pataphysicians founded in 1948. A brainchild of Alfred Jarry, Pataphysics could be defined as the science of satire and hoax.

There is much humour of a poetic kind in the four novels on which Vian's fame mostly rests. *L'Herbe rouge* [Red Grass] contains few facts of an autobiographical nature, but provides many insights into Vian's thoughts on his childhood and marriage. It tells the story of Wolf's attempt at building a time-machine. The disastrous result is that instead of travelling towards the future, Wolf journeys endlessly through his past and eventually commits suicide.

L'Automne à Pékin [Autumn in Peking] also takes place in an imaginary country, sterile Exopotamie. This desert is rather densely populated by a set of intriguing characters: ruthless entrepreneur Amadis, demented Doctor Mangemanche, blasphemous Abbé Petitjean,

and the wise archaeologist Athanagore Porphyrogénète among others, most of whom are somehow involved in the nonsensical business of building a railway line through the only hotel in the whole of Exopotamie. The sadder part of the story revolves around the two young engineer friends, Anne and Angel, who are rivals in love.

Angel is also the name of the father in *L'Arrache-coeur* (*Heartsnatcher*), turned down by Gallimard in 1951. The blow was such that Vian never tried to write a full-length novel again. *Heartsnatcher* concentrates on two characters, the morbidly loving mother Clémentine and her lodger, unemployed psychoanalyst Jacquemort. Clémentine gradually shuts out anything that might come between her three sons and herself: first their father, then the trees, the whole garden, and finally life itself. The chronicle of Clémentine's growing maternal passion is frightening and masterly. Jacquemort is an onlooker in this drama, just as he is in the cruel goings-on in the village where children, old people, and animals are constantly tortured.

Vian's undisputed masterpiece, *L'Écume des jours* (*Froth on the Daydream*), is one of his earliest books. Like *L'Herbe rouge*, it tells of two ill-fated couples who are eventually destroyed by monomania and illness. Chick is in love with Alise, but he is even more enamoured of the writer Jean-Sol Partre whose books and personal objects he avidly collects. Alise has no choice but to kill Partre in a doomed attempt to save her fiancé from ruin. On the other hand their friends Colin and Chloé are blissfully happy until a flower starts growing in Chloé's lung. All the young man's sacrifices are in vain and Chloé dies. Few novels capture as this one does the unbearable anguish that accompanies an incurable disease. As the world around Chloé becomes ever smaller and darker, her pet mouse surrenders to despair and begs for her friend the cat to kill her.

Vian, who would have been sent to the front in 1939 had it not been for his heart ailment, was a rebel with a cause. He brought to the manichean literary scene of post-war France true iconoclasm and true *joie de vivre* in the face of death.

—Pascale Voilley

VICENTE, Gil

Born: Possibly in the province of Beira or the town of Guimarães, Portugal, c. 1465. **Family:** Married 1) Branca Bezerra c. 1484–86 (died c. 1514), two sons; 2) Melicia Rodrigues c. 1517, one son and two daughters. **Career:** Dramatist and actor for Portuguese court, 1502–36: wrote plays in both Spanish and Portuguese; probably a goldsmith by trade; worked on the manufacture of the Belém monstrance, 1503–06; in the service of D. Leonor (widow of D. João II) and her brother D. Manuel I, by 1509; appointed inspector and contractor for gold at three important religious houses, 1509; elected goldsmiths' company representative for the Guild of Twenty-Four, 1512; elected as one of four guildsmen on the city council, Lisbon; appointed *mestre da balança* at the royal mint, 1513; sold office, 1517; defended New Christians of Santarém from violence following Lisbon earthquake, 1531; probably in Évora at the time of his death. **Died:** c. 1536.

PUBLICATIONS

Collections

Copilaçam de todalas obras. 1562; edited by Maria Leonor Carvalhão Buescu, 2 vols., 1983.

Obras, edited by Mendes de Remédios. 3 vols., 1907–14.

Obras completas, edited by Marques Braga. 6 vols., 1942–44.

Obras completas, edited by Álvaro Júlio da Costa Pimpão. 1956; revised edition, 1979.

Obras dramáticas castellanas, edited by Thomas R. Hart. 1962.

Obras completas, edited by Reis Brasil. 3 vols., 1966–70.

Plays (selection: modern editions, smaller collections, and plays translated into English)

Auto da Alma, as *The Soul's Journey,* edited and translated by Aubrey F.G. Bell, in *Four Plays.* 1920; edited by Reis Brasil, 1956, Manuel dos Santos Alves, 1964, and by Maria Idalina Resina Rodrigues, 1980.

Os autos das barcas, edited by Luiz Francisco Rebello. 1975; also edited by Armando López Castro, 1987; as *The Ship of Hell,* translated by A.F. Gerald (ie. Aubrey F.G. Bell), 1929.

Auto da Barca do Inferno, edited by I.S. Révah. 1951.

Auto da Barca do Purgatório, edited by Maria da Conceição Gonçalves. 1970.

Auto da Barca da Glória, edited by Paulo Quintela. 1956.

Auto da Cananeia, edited by Agostinho de Campos. 1938.

Auto da Feira, edited by Luís F. Lindley Cintra. 1989.

Auto da Índia, edited by Thomas R. Hart, in *Farces and Festival Plays.* 1972; as *The Sailor's Wife,* in *Early Spanish Plays,* edited by Robert O'Brien, 1964.

Auto da Lusitânia, edited by Segismundo Spina, in *Obra-sprimas do teatro vicentino.* 1970.

Auto de São Martinho, edited by Sebastião Pestana. 1985.

Auto da Sibila Cassandra, as *Cassandra the Sibyl,* in *Early Spanish Plays,* edited by Robert O'Brien. 1964; as *Sibyl Cassandra: A Christmas Play with the Insanity and Sanctity of Five Centuries Past,* translated by Cheryl Folkins McGinniss, 2000.

Auto das Ciganas, edited by Thomas R. Hart, in *Obras dramáticas castellanas.* 1962.

Auto de Deus Padre e justiça e misericórdia (attributed to Vicente), edited by I.S. Révah, in *Deux "autos" méconnus.* 1948.

Auto de Mofina Mendes, edited by Segismundo Spina, in *Obras-primas do teatro vicentino.* 1970.

Auto dos reis magos, edited by Sebastião Pestana. 1979; as *Three Wise Men,* in *Early Spanish Plays,* edited by Robert O'Brien, 1964.

Auto pastoril castelhano, edited by Sebastião Pestana. 1978.

Breve sumário da história de Deus, edited by João de Almeida Lucas. 1943.

Comédia de Rubena, edited by Giuseppe Tavani. 1965.

Comédia do viúvo, edited by Alonso Zamora Vicente. 1962; as *The Widower's Comedy,* in *Early Spanish Plays,* edited by Robert O'Brien, 1964.

Comédia sobre a divisa da cidade de Coimbra, edited by Daniel Rangel-Guerrero. 1980.

Côrtes de Júpiter, edited by Thomas R. Hart, in *Farces and Festival Plays.* 1972.

Exortação da guerra, as *Exhortation to War,* edited and translated by Aubrey F.G. Bell, in *Four Plays.* 1920.

Farsa de Inês Pereira, edited by Albano Monteiro Soares. 1975.

Farsa dos almocreves, as *The Carriers,* edited and translated by Aubrey F.G. Bell, in *Four Plays.* 1920; edited by Segismundo Spina, in *Obras-primas do teatro vicentino,* 1970.

Farsa dos físicos, edited by Alberto da Rocha Brito. 1946.

Floresta de enganos, edited by C.C. Stathatos. 1972.

Frágua de Amor, edited by Thomas R. Hart, in *Farces and Festival Plays.* 1972.

O Juiz da Beira, edited by Maria de Lourdes Saraiva, in *Sátiras sociais.* 1975.

Obra da geração, (attributed to Vicente), edited by I.S. Révah, in *Deux "autos méconnus."* 1948.

Quem tem farelos?, edited by Ernesto de Campos de Andrada. 1938; also edited by Vanda Anastácio, 1985; as *The Serenade,* in *Early Spanish Plays,* edited by Robert O'Brien, 1964.

Romagem de agravados, edited by Paul Teyssier. 1975.

Tragicomédia de Amadis de Gaula, edited by T.P. Waldron. 1959.

Tragicomédia de Dom Duardos, edited by Thomas R. Hart, in *Obras dramáticas castellanas.* 1962; as *Don Duardos,* translated by Mary Borelli, 1976.

Tragicomédia pastoril da Serra da Estrela, as *Pastoral Tragicomedy of the Serra da Estrella,* edited and translated by Aubrey F.G. Bell, in *Four Plays.* 1920; edited by Júlio da Costa Pimpão, 1963.

O triunfo do inverno, edited by Thomas R. Hart, in *Farces and Festival Plays.* 1972.

O velho da horta, edited by João de Almeida Lucas. 1943.

Four Plays (includes *The Soul's Journey; Exhortation to War; The Carriers; Pastoral Tragicomedy of the Serra da Estrella*), translated by Aubrey F.G. Bell. 1920.

Early Spanish Plays (includes *The Sailor's Wife; Cassandra the Sibyl; Three Wise Men; The Widower's Comedy; The Serenade*), edited by Robert O'Brien. 1964.

Farces and Festival Plays, edited by Thomas R. Hart. 1972.

Three Discovery Plays, edited and translated by Anthony Lappin. 1997.

Verse

Lyrics (bilingual edition), edited and translated by Aubrey F.G. Bell. 1914.

Pranto de Maria Parda, edited by Sebastião Pestana. 1975.

*

Bibliography: *Bibliografia vicentina* by Luísa Maria de Castro e Azevedo, 1942; *A Gil Vicente Bibliography (1940–1975)* by Constantine C. Stathatos, 1980, supplement, 1982.

Critical Studies: *Gil Vicente* by Aubrey F.G. Bell, 1921; *The Play of the Sibyl Cassandra* by Georgiana G. King, 1921; *The Court Theatre of Gil Vicente* by Laurence Keates, 1962; *Gil Vicente* by Jack Horace Parker, 1967; *The Farces of Gil Vicente: A Study in the Stylistics of Satire* by Hope Hamilton-Faria, 1976; *Gil Vicente: Cassandra and Don Duardos* by Thomas R. Hart, 1981; *The Concept of Allegory and Gil Vicente's Auto da Alma* by Janet E. Carter, 1982; *Gil Vicente and* *the Development of the Comedia* by René Pedro Garay, 1988; *Carnival Stage: Vicentine Comedy within the Serio-Comic Mode* by José I. Suárez, 1993.

* * *

From 1502 to 1536, Gil Vicente served as purveyor of entertainment for the Portuguese royal court under two successive sovereigns, Manuel I and John III. In that capacity, he composed plays expressly designed to celebrate specific occasions in the life of the Court. Writing to order does not seem to have stifled his creative genius, especially since his patrons encouraged artistic endeavours.

His dramatic production, as we know it today, consists of 44 plays, 15 of which are entirely in his native Portuguese, 11 in Spanish, and the remaining 18 in both languages. His Spanish has its own idiosyncrasies and is typical of one who had never been in Spain. His mastery of it was not such that would allow him to delineate some of the delightful types which appear in his Portuguese plays. With few exceptions, Vicente's plays were compiled and published for the first time posthumously in 1562. Unfortunately, the text of this edition is corrupt, a fact which has been attributed primarily to the incompetence of his son and editor Luís.

In his work Vicente blended the most diverse and unpredictable ingredients, so that a good portion of it defies categorization under a single genre. Of the several attempts to classify his plays in terms of content, the most widely accepted is that of T.P. Waldron, who, in his edition of *Tragicomédia de Amadis de Gaula*, has devised the following categories: 1) early plays in the rustic style of Juan del Encina's *églogas*; 2) moralities; 3) farces; 4) allegorical fantasies; 5) romantic comedies.

A distinctive feature of Vicente's career as a dramatist is that he tends to be cyclic: he takes up a certain theme and then abandons it, only to come back to it later on. The motif of the lecherous old man, for instance, which first appeared in the *Velho da horta* [Old Man of the Orchard], reappears in the *Comédia de Rubena* [Play of Rubena] and, once again, in his last play, *Floresta de enganos* [Forest of Deceits]. Since he keeps experimenting with new possibilities, there is no clear pattern of development in his work.

Several of Vicente's plays are characterized by a lack of dramatic unity, as we understand it today. The fact, however, that his pieces were composed on command to form integral parts of court festivals may account for their structure. In all likelihood, theatricality was the playwright's main concern. A play like *Quem tem farelos?* (*The Serenade*) may not be dramatically significant but it is eminently theatrical.

Vicente's work is permeated by a profound lyricism, which has exerted a considerable influence on even 20th-century poets (e.g., Federico García Lorca and Rafael Alberti) and reaches a climax in the *Tragicomédia de Dom Duardos*, one of the finest poetic dramas in Hispanic literature. Apart from this overall lyricism, all his plays are veritable mines of songs, whether his own compositions or borrowed from popular tradition. As a rule, they are well integrated into the dramatic action, as is the case with the *Auto da Sibila Cassandra* (*Cassandra the Sibyl*) which abounds in delightful songs (the most frequently translated and anthologized).

In general, Vicente's plays are plays of character rather than intrigue. In this respect, they are more akin to those of Molière than

those of the Spanish Golden Age. Although types (the peasant, the negro, the Jew, the gypsy, the fool, the braggart, the corrupt judge, the impoverished squire, the maid, etc.), some of his characters are so well drawn that they become three-dimensional. This is particularly true of female characters in farces as well as serious plays: Constança and Inês, the unfaithful wives of the *Auto da Índia* (*The Sailor's Wife*) and *Farsa de Inês Pereira* [The Farce of Inês Pereira], respectively, the presumptuous Cassandra, of *Cassandra the Sibyl*, who expects to become the mother of God. Even though the plays are crowded with figures from literary tradition, the Bible, and the classical pantheon and mythology, it is Vicente's contemporary Portuguese society which supplied most of his characters.

As a believer in a well-structured society, he was disturbed by the rampant social abuse and the decline of mores and reacted forcefully against them, not only in his farces and comedies but also in his allegorical plays. The principal butts of his satire were the two major parasitic classes, the nobility and the clergy. Noblemen, judges, and clerics are ridiculed in the trilogy of *Os autos das barcas* (*The Ship of Hell*), the *Frágua de Amor* [Forge of Love], and the *Floresta de enganos*. No member of the clerical hierarchy was immune to his caustic wit, although it was the friar who was ridiculed most vehemently for his improper conduct and his absurd aspirations, like Frei Narciso in the *Romagem de agravados* [Pilgrimage of the Aggrieved]. In his anti-clericalism, Vicente sounds very much like Erasmus, but it is generally agreed that he was not influenced by him.

Considering that he had no access to an established literary dramatic tradition on which to rely, Vicente succeeded admirably in shaping Portuguese theatre and in creating a poetic cosmos that delighted his audience and can still delight his reader. The prominent place he occupies in Peninsular literature is well deserved, as is the critical attention accorded him.

—C.C. Stathatos

See the essay on *Auto da Barca do Inferno, Auto da Barca do Purgatório, Auto da Barca da Glória,* and *Farsa de Inês Pereira.*

VIGNY, Alfred de

Born: Loches, France, 27 March 1797. **Education:** Educated at Institution Hix, 1807–11; Lycée Bonaparte (now Lycée Condorcet), Paris, 1811–14. **Military Service:** Sub-lieutenant, 1st Regiment of Gendarmes du Roi, 1814–15; in 5th Regiment, Garde Royale, 1816; captain in 55th Regiment of the Line, 1823–27 (frequently on leave after 1822); commander of a National Guard battalion, 1830. **Family:** Married Lydia Bunbury in 1825 (died 1862). **Award:** Chevalier, Légion d'honneur, 1833. **Member:** Académie française, 1845: director, October-December 1849. **Died:** 16 September 1863.

Publications

Collections

Oeuvres complètes, edited by F. Baldensperger. 7 vols., 1914–35.
Oeuvres complètes, edited by F. Baldensperger. 2 vols., 1948.

Verse

Poèmes. 1822.
Éloa; ou, La Soeur des anges. 1824.
Poèmes antiques et modernes. 1826, enlarged edition, 1829, revised edition, 1837; edited by E. Estève, 1931.
Les Destinées, edited by Louis Ratisbonne. 1864; also edited by V.L. Saulnier, 1947, and Paul Viallaneix, 1983.

Plays

Le More de Venise, from *Othello* by Shakespeare (produced 1829). With *Le Marchand de Venise*, 1839.
La Maréchale d'Ancre (produced 1831).
Quitte pour la peur (produced 1833).
Chatterton (produced 1835). 1835; edited by L. Petroni, 1962, and by A.H. Diverres, 1967; translated as *Chatterton*, 1847; also translated by Philip A. Fulvi, 1990.
Le Marchand de Venise, from *The Merchant of Venice* by Shakespeare. With *Le More de Venise*, 1839, revised version, as *Shylock* (produced 1905), in *Oeuvres complètes*, 1914–35.

Fiction

Cinq-Mars. 1825; as *Cinq-Mars*, translated by William Hazlitt, 1847; as *The Conspiracy*, translated by W. Bellingham, 1851; as *The Conspirators*, translated by Hazlitt, 1877; as *The Spider and the Fly*, translated by Madge Pemberton, 1925.
Stello; ou, Les Diables bleus. 1832; as *Stello; or, A Session with Doctor Noir*, translated by Irving Massey, 1963.
Servitude et grandeur militaires (stories). 1835; as *Military Servitude and Grandeur*, translated by Frances Wilson Huard, 1919; as *The Military Necessity*, translated by Humphrey Hare, 1953; as *The Military Condition*, translated by Marguerite Barnett, 1964; as *Servitude and Grandeur of Arms*, translated with introduction by Roger Gard, 1996.
Daphné. 1912.

Other

Journal d'un poète, edited by Louis Ratisbonne. 1867.
Correspondance 1816–1863, edited by Emma Sakellaridès. 1905.
Correspondance, edited by Léon Séché. 2 vols., 1913.
Lettres inédites d'Alfred de Vigny au Marquis et à la Marquise de la Grange (1827–1861), edited by Albert de Luppé. 1914.
Mémoires inédites, fragments, et projets, edited by Jean Sangnier. 1958.

*

Critical Studies: *Alfred de Vigny: La Vie et l'oeuvre* by E. Dupuy, 1915; *La Pensée religieuse et morale d'Alfred de Vigny* by G. Bonnefoy, 1946; *L'Imagination de Vigny* by F. Germain, 1961; *Alfred de Vigny* by James Doolittle, 1967; *Les Destinées d'un style* by J.P. Saint-Gérand, 1979; *Vigny, Chatterton* by Robin Buss, 1984; *Alfred de Vigny: Sous le masque de fer* by Nicole Casanova, 1990; *The Novels of Alfred de Vigny: A Study of Their Form and Composition* by Elaine K. Shwimer, 1991.

* * *

Alfred de Vigny was the most philosophically minded and the most pessimistic of the French Romantic poets, and the one whose works have perhaps remained the most readable in the 20th century. Indeed, his vision of humanity as condemned to inexplicable physical suffering in an absurd and godless world has strong similarities with the world view of Albert Camus, and his poem "Le Mont des Oliviers" ("The Agony in the Garden") could well be read as a commentary on certain chapters of Camus's *La Peste* (*The Plague*). His view that the poet, like all men of genius, can never be understood or appreciated by ordinary people nevertheless strikes a more dated note, though it may have contributed to Vigny's early recognition of Charles Baudelaire as the greatest and most original of all French lyric poets. Some of Vigny's own poems, especially "La Maison du Berger" ("The Shepherd's Hut"), have a Baudelairean touch to their poetic rhythm, though the extent of Vigny's achievement and appeal in a different direction can be judged from the fact that he was the first non-classical French author to be included on the syllabus at Eton. The high strain of stoic morality which informs the closing stanza of "La Mort du Loup" ("The Death of the Wolf") is certainly assimilable within the tradition that gave rise to Henry Newbolt's "Vitae Lampada" ("Play-up, Play-up, and Play the Game"), and Vigny was very fond of England. He was married to an English woman, Lydia Bunbury, who was unfortunately unable to have children to carry on the family name, and who became a lifelong invalid. Vigny, true to his principles and to the genuine affection he felt for her, cared for her devotedly, though he found consolation with the actress Marie Dorval. He was disappointed when she left him for, *inter alia*, George Sand, and wrote a very bad poem called "La Colère de Samson" ("The Anger of Samson"). Marie Dorval had, however, added considerably to Vigny's reputation as a dramatist by sliding to her death down a banister in the appalling drama *Chatterton*. Vigny shared the desire of other Romantics such as Victor Hugo to revolutionize the French theatre, often by following what they thought of as the example of Shakespeare.

Vigny's best work of fiction, *Servitude et grandeur militaires* (*Military Servitude and Grandeur*), presents the soldier as the model of stoic self-denial in modern society, and has considerable value as an account of certain aspects of French society in the early 19th century. His historical novel, *Cinq-Mars* (*The Spider and the Fly*), is an indictment of Richelieu's policy of domesticating the hereditary nobility to make way for the absolutism of Louis XIV, and Vigny's sense of personal isolation was heightened by his awareness that the aristocracy to which he was so conscious of belonging had no further role to play in contemporary society. His pessimism was thus social as well as religious and metaphysical, and he also differed from the majority of the Romantic poets, in France as well as in England, in totally rejecting the "Pathetic Fallacy" and seeing Nature not so much as hostile but as indifferent to man. The reactionary nature of his political views revealed itself towards the end of his life when he showed himself ready to collaborate with the government of Napoleon III in providing information on anyone in his area holding political views unpopular with the government.

—Philip Thody

See the essays on *Chatterton*, *Military Servitude and Grandeur*, and "Moses."

VILLON, François

Born: François de Montcorbier in Paris, France, c. 1430; adopted when very young by Guillaume de Villon. **Education:** Educated at the University of Paris, baccalauréat 1449, M.A. 1452. **Career:** Fled Paris after killing a priest in a brawl, 1455; pardoned six months later, but then involved in a theft and again left Paris; led a wandering life in the provinces and was imprisoned at Meung-sur-Loire, 1461; probably returned to Paris, but condemned to death for involvement in a street brawl, 1462: sentence commuted to ten-year banishment, after which the record ends. Villon's works—about 3,000 lines—were first published in 1489.

PUBLICATIONS

Collections

The Complete Works, edited and translated by J.U. Nicholson. 2 vols., 1928.
Complete Works, edited and translated by Anthony Bonner. 1960.
Complete Poems, edited by John Fox, translated by Beram Saklatvala. 1968.
François Villon: Complete Poems, translated and edited by Barbara N. Sargent-Baur. 1994.

Verse

I Laugh through Tears: The Ballades, translated by G.P. Cuttino. 1955.
The Poems, translated by Galway Kinnell. 1965; revised edition, 1977.
The Legacy and Other Poems, translated by Peter Dale. 1971; revised edition, as *The Legacy, The Testament, and Other Poems*, 1973; as *Selected Poems*, 1978.
La Testament Villon, edited by Jean Rychner and Albert Henry. 2 vols., 1974.
Les Lais Villon et les poèmes variés, edited by Jean Rychner and Albert Henry. 2 vols., 1977.
Poésies, edited by Jean Dufournet. 1992.

*

Bibliography: *François Villon: A Bibliography* by Robert D. Peckham, 1990.

Critical Studies: *Villon: A Documented Survey* by D.B. Wyndham Lewis, 1928; *Lexique de la langue de Villon* by A. Burger, 1957; *The Poetry of Villon* by John Fox, 1962; *Recherches sur le Testament de Villon* by Jean Dufournet, 2 vols., 1971–73; *Villon: Un Testament ambigu* by Pierre Demarolle, 1973; *Français Villon* by Jean Favier, 1982; *The Otherness Within: Gnostic Readings in Marcel Proust, Flannery O'Connor, and Villon* by Jefferson Humphries, 1983; *Villon: Poems* by John Fox, 1984; *The Quest for Equivalence: On Translating Villon* by Margaret Jennifer Kewley Draskau, 1986; *Villon and His Reader* by David A. Fein, 1989; *Brothers of Dragons:*
"Job Dolens" and François Villon by Barbara Nelson Sargent-Baur, 1990; *Villon's Last Will: Language and Authority in the Testament* by Tony Hunt, 1996; *François Villon Revisted* by David A. Fein, 1997; *Danse Macabre: François Villon: Poetry and Murder in Medieval France* by Aubrey Burl, 2000.

* * *

Swinburne called François Villon the last medieval and first modern poet but, although there is a kernel of truth in this, he was in fact neither. Villon was very much a man of his time and, for that matter, place. His works were so firmly rooted in the France—in the Paris even—of the 1450s and 1460s that much of their meaning had become obscure by the time they were first printed in 1489.

For Villon's work is topical in the extreme, and he wrote not for posterity but for a small audience who might not only understand but also be prompted into helping him. He is not above a certain obsequiousness (notably towards the King of France, Louis XI), and most of the targets of his jibes had skeletons in their closets which the present-day reader can only guess at but which were probably more or less open secrets. His major work, *The Testament*, is an anthology probably collected and revised some time between his release from prison in October 1461 and the following summer. Its function was to amuse, dazzle, flatter, and move, and also to signal his continued existence and myriad talents to an audience of friends and potential patrons. A false impression can be gained of his work as a whole by wrenching the more accessible parts of *The Testament* from their context. Nevertheless it is these anthology pieces which have earned him his reputation and inspired dozens of imitators and translators (from Rossetti to Lowell). The deservedly famous "Ballade des dames du temps jadis" ("Ballade of the Ladies of Time Past") is a disquisition on time and its treachery to women, the harshness of the sentiments wonderfully softened by the haunting refrain which likens the passing of beauty to the melting of last year's snows. What is sometimes overlooked, though, is that it is part of a verse triptych describing the inevitability of death and the vanity of human wishes. He fatalistically remarks that this world is but illusion and points out—not without a hint of grim satisfaction perhaps—that even princes are ruled by death.

Critical opinion has learned not to take the author at face value and it is now widely agreed that poems such as the prayer on his mother's behalf to the Virgin are less altruistic than they might at first appear. This ballade's refrain, "In this faith I wish to live and die," should not necessarily be taken as proof of Villon's repentance or religious sincerity. By the same token, the ballade to "Fat Margot" does not represent so much a slice of the poet's life as a very successful literary exercise in the tradition of the *sotte chanson*, in which the traditions of courtly poetry were deliberately turned on their head.

Not all Villon's compositions could be fitted into the framework of *The Testament*. Among them are two of his finest poems: in the "Débat" or dialogue with his heart he publicly examines his conscience and (predictably?) regrets the errors of his ways, and in the magnificent ballade about the hanged criminals among whom he seems to count himself by implication he graphically describes the rotting corpses on the Paris gibbet and makes a plea for absolution.

Villon has become known almost as much for his life—about which we know little, despite the fantasizings of later poets and critics—as for his work, but as a writer he has become the archetypal outsider, the spokesman for the misfit and the failure, the poet of lost love and lost youth, bemoaning the power of Fortune over men's lives and our impotence in the face of Time. His frequent obscenities and scurrilous jokes are a useful antidote to over-seriousness, and the cup of strong red wine which he downs at the end of his fictitious *Testament* is both an act of poetic bravado and a form of courage.

—Michael Freeman

See the essays on "Ballade des dames du temps jadis" and "Ballade des Pendus."

VIRAHSAWMY, Dev

Born: Mauritius, 16 March 1942. **Education:** Attended school in Mauritius, 1948–62; University of Edinburgh, 1963–67. **Family:** Married Loga Virahsawmy; two daughters. **Career:** Active in politics, 1966–87; elected Member of Parliament, 1970; Lecturer, Mauritius Institute of Education, 1982–92; private tutoring, from 1992. Lives in Mairitius. **Awards:** Winner, Concours théâtral Inter-Africain, Radio France International, 1981.

PUBLICATIONS

Plays

Li. 1976; trilingual edition, 1979; as *The Prisoner of Conscience*, translated by Ramesh Ramdoyal, 1982.
Linconsing Finalay. 1978.
Bef dâ disab. 1979.

Dropadi: Teks pu en trazi-komedi mizikal baze lor Mahabharata. 1982.
Zeneral Makbef. 1982.
Tâtin Madok. 1983.
Doktèr Nipat. 1983.
Profesèr Madli. 1984.
Krishna. 1984.
ABS Lemanifik. 1985.
Toufann, enn fâtezi â trwa ak. 1991; as *Toufann, a Mauritian Fantasy*, translated by Nisha and Michael Walling, 1999.
Hamlet 2. 1995.
Galileo Gonaz [The Life of Galileo]. 1996.
Doktèr Hamlet. 1997.
Mamzel Zann. 2000.
Sir Toby. 1998.
Ti-Marie. 2000.
Ziliet ek so Romeo. 2001.

Translations

Zozef ek so palto larkansiel [Joseph and the Amazing Technicolour Dreamcoat], with Gérard Sullivan. 1983.
Zil Sezar [Julius Caesar]. Completed in 1986, published in 1999.
Enn ta senn dan vid [Much Ado About Nothing]. Serialized 1994, published 1995.
Trazedji Makbess [Macbeth]. 1997.
Les Miserables, with Gérard Sullivan. 1998.
Tartchif Frodèr [Le Tartuffe]. 1999.
Zistoir Ti-Prins [Le Petit prince]. 2001.

Poetry

Disik salé. Written in prison, 1972, published 1976.
Lafimé dâ lizie. 1976.
Trip séré lagorz amaré. 1980.
Mo rapel. 1980.
Lôbraz lavi: soley feneâ. 1981.
Poem pu zâfâ. 1983.
Twa ek mwa. 1984.
Zwazo Samarel Pelmel. 1987–88.
Kaysé ba. 1991.
The walls: an operatic poem. 1984; revised 1999.
Nwar, nwar, nwar do mama. 1986.
Lalang peyna lezo. 1991.
Petal ek pikan, parsi-parla. 1996.
Trazedi Sir Kutta-Gram: en badinaz futâ. 1980; revised as *Trazedi Sir Kouta-Gram 001: Enn badinaz foutan—relouke*, 2001.
Latchizann pou letan lapli. 1997.
Enn diya dan divan. 1999.
Lintelizans Yonik. 2000.
Kantik. 2001.
Pa Vre. 2001.

Other

Zozo mâyok: en komedi mizikal pu zâfâ morisiê (for children). 1980.
Les lapo kabri gazuyé (for children). 1980.
Mersi Mama. 1980.
Zistwar Bisma (for children). 1983.
Chanda Mama. 1984.
Testaman enn Metchiss. 1999.
Jericho. 2000.
Jamouna-Ganga-Devi. 2001.
Vignet, Kameo ek lezot badinaz. 2002.
Dayri Enn Fouka. 2002.
Souiv larout ziska . . . . 2002.

*

Critical Studies: *La littérature mauricienne d'expression creole: essai d'analyse socio-culturelle* by Vicram Ramharai, 1990; "Dev Virahsawmy" by Edith Hallberg, in *notre librairie*, vol. 114, 1993; "Creole voice in Mauritius: Redefining a linguistic and cultural diglossia through theatre" by Roshni Mooneeram, in *International Journal of Francophone Studies*, vol. 2, 1999; *Rencontres*, edited by Danielle Tranquille and Soorya Nirsimloo-Gayan, 2000; "'Translating' *The Tempest*: Dev Virahsawmy's *Toufann*, Cultural Creolization, and the Rise of Mauritian Kreol" by Shawkat M. Toorawa, in *African Theatre: Playwrights & Politics*, edited by Martin Banham et al., 2000. *Creative Writing in Mauritian Creole: The Emergence of a Literary Language and Its Contribution to Standardization* by Roshni Mooneeram, 2001.

* * *

Dev Virahsawmy is the leading Creole (Kreol) language writer in the Indian Ocean island of Mauritius. There are only a few such writers (the playwright Henri Favory, the poets Sedley Richard Assonne and Vidya Golam, and the novelist Lindsay Collen), but Virahsawmy is the dean of them all, having opted for Kreol (he prefers the name Morisien) as a literary language since 1967, upon his return from the University of Edinburgh. Since then he has been a tireless champion of Kreol, through his plays, translations, adaptations, songs, stories, and poetry, and interviews. The themes of his literary work have consistently been freedom, hybridity, and women's liberation and empowerment; and his agenda has been to make Kreol the national language and to elevate it to the status of a world language.

When Mauritius became an independent nation in 1968, Virahsawmy saw politics as one way to bring these themes and this agenda into the public arena. He was elected Member of Parliament in 1970, but was later imprisoned for what were regarded as radical political (and linguistic) views. It was in prison that he wrote his first collection of poems, *Disik Salé* [Salty sugar], and about a prisoner that he wrote *Li* [The Prisoner of Conscience], which went on to win an international Francophone drama prize and bring Virahsawmy worldwide attention. But it was locally that he wanted to make an impact.

Virahsawmy wrote a play a year in the 1980s as he attempted to create a written Kreol. Most of Virahsawmy's early work is self-published under the imprint Boukié Banané using a Kreol orthography he developed himself. In the 1990s he adopted the orthography developed by the Kreol adult literacy organization Ledikasyon Pu Travayer (Education for the Workers), and in mid-1999, reached an agreement with the Catholic Church in Mauritius regarding a standardized orthography—the latter had been using a different one for vernacular Bibles. Virahsawmy's last work using the orthography he pioneered is *Testaman enn Metchiss* [Mestizo Manifesto], a mixture of poetry, translation (including "Dover Beach," "The Love Song of J. Alfred Prufrock," and "To Byzantium"), and linguistic excursuses on Kreol.

Virahsawmy has a particular fascination for Shakespeare, one which goes beyond mere influence or bardolatry. His last four plays and half of his translations have recourse to Shakespeare, the adroitly translated 1994 *Enn Ta Senn Dan Vid* (*Much Ado About Nothing*), for example, and the 1998 *Sir Toby* (cf. *Twelfth Night*). As Vicram Ramharai has put it, this is an integral part of Virahsawmy's quest for a truly Mauritian culture. Nowhere is this clearer than in his 1991 play, *Toufann* [Tempest], a supremely creative reworking of several Shakespearean plays. Virahsawmy himself has said, according to *Rencontres*:

I've translated Molière, Shakespeare, and right now I'm translating fairy tales of the Brothers Grimm because I am convinced that such a project follows the logic of cultural creolization (*métissage*). Our culture is necessarily linked to a world culture. It's a way for me to share this heritage with all of humanity. This helps to build bridges between peoples, between the past and the present, between different cultures . . . Translations can build bridges between the Tower of Babel's different rooms.

As this sentiment reveals, Virahsawmy draws inspiration from a wide range of literatures, literary traditions, and musical traditions of the world. He has reworked and mined Brecht, Tim Rice and Andrew Lloyd Webber, as well as The Mahabharat. Mauritius itself is, of course, not forgotten. The poetry collections *Kaysé Ba* [What's up?], *Nwar, nwar, nwar do mama* [Black, dude!—Black and beautiful], and *Enn diyaa dan divan* [A lamp in the wind] draw specifically from local Bhojpuri, Creole, and Hindu song and folklore.

Virahsawmy's works in progress now appear on his webpage. These include, in particular, new forays by him into prose (begun

already in *Testaman*); short stories, in *Vignet, Kameo ek lezot badinaz* [Stories, cameos and other pleasantries], *Dayri Enn Fouka* [Diary of a dolt]; and a novel, *Souiv Larout Ziska* [Follow the road to. . .].

Dev Virahsawmy has almost single-handedly created a Mauritian Kreol literary tradition, and without respite, but with wit, aplomb, and an unmatched turn of phrase.

—Shawkat M. Toorawa

VIRGIL

Born: Publius Vergilius Maro in Andes, near Mantua, northern Italy, 15 October 70 BC. **Education:** Educated at Cremona and Milan, then Rome, where he studied rhetoric and was influenced by Catullus, *q.v.*, and Naples, where he studied philosophy. **Career:** Associated with C. Asinius Pollio, then with the patron Maecenas, to whom he recommended his friend Horace, *q.v.*, c. 39 BC. Apart from one appearance as an advocate, took no part in public life, though he had the friendship of many important men. **Died:** 20 September 19 BC.

PUBLICATIONS

Collections

[Works], edited by John Conington and H. Nettleship, revised by F. Haverfield. 3 vols., 1893–98, reprinted 1963; also edited by R.A.B. Mynors, 1969, R.D. Williams, 3 vols., 1972–79, and M. Geymonat, 1973; translated by John Ogilby, 1649; also translated by John Dryden, 1697; Richard, Earl of Lauderdale, 1700; Joseph Trapp, 1731; Christopher Pitt, Joseph Warton, and others, 4 vols., 1763; Robert Andrews, 1766; Charles Rann Kennedy, 2 vols., 1849; J. Davidson, 1850; George B. Wheeler, 1853; Robert C. Singleton, 1855; James Lonsdale and Samuel Lee, 1871; John Augustine Wilstack, 2 vols., 1884; A. Hamilton Bryce, 1894; John Jackson, 1908; James Rhoades, 1921; H. Rushton Fairclough [Loeb Edition], 2 vols., 1930, revised edition, 2 vols., 1988; John W. Mackail, 1934; C. Day Lewis, 3 vols., 1940–63; as *Virgil in English*, edited by K.W. Gransden, 1996.

Verse

Aeneis, edited by T.E. Page. 2 vols., 1894–1900; reprinted 1938–40; also edited by J.W. Mackail, 1930, R.D. Williams, 2 vols., 1972–73, D.A.S. John and A.F. Turberfield (Books I–VI), 1985, and C.J. Fordyce (Books VII–VIII), 1985; as *The Aeneid*, translated by Gavin Douglas, 1553; also translated by Thomas Phaer and Thomas Twyne, 1573, edited by Steven Lally, 1987; Richard Stanyhurst (Books I–VI), 1582; John Vicars (Books I–XII), 1632; John Dryden, in [Works], 1697, edited by Robin Sowerby, 1986, Howard Clarke, 1989; Henry Owgan, 1853; H. R. Fairclough, 1916; Rolfe Humphries, 1951; C. Day Lewis, 1952; Kevin Guinagh, 1953; W.F. Jackson Knight, 1956; Michael Oakley, 1957; Patric Dickinson, 1961; T.H. Delabere May, 1961; L.R. Lind, 1963; Frank O. Copley, 1965; W.F. Jackson Knight, 1969; Allen Mandelbaum, 1971; Robert Fitzgerald, 1983; C.H. Sisson, 1986; David West, 1990; *Selections from the Aeneid*, translated by Graham Tingay, 1984; as *Book IX*, edited by Philip Hardie, 1994; Edward McCrorie, 1995; edited by R. H. Jordan, 1999.

Eclogae [Eclogues or Bucolics or Pastorals], edited by Robert Coleman. 1977; also edited by Guy Lee (bilingual edition), 1980, R.D. Williams, with *Georgics*, 1980, H.E. Gould, 1983, Richard F. Thomas (with commentary), 2 vols., 1988, and R.A.B. Mynors, 1990; as *Eclogues*, translated by Francis Wrangham, 1830; also translated by Henry Owgan, 1853; E.V. Rieu (prose), 1949; Geoffrey Johnson, 1960; C. Day Lewis, 1963; W. Berg, in *Early Virgil*, 1974; A.J. Boyle, 1976; Paul Joel Alpers, in *The Singer of the Eclogues*, 1979; John Campbell-Kease, 1979; David R. Slavitt, with *Georgics*, 1990; commentary by Wendell V. Clausen, 1994; Barbara Hughes Fowler, 1997; David Ferry, 1999.

Georgica, edited by W. Richter. 1957; also edited by R.D. Williams, with *Eclogues*, 1980, Richard R. Thomas, 2 vols., 1988, and R.A.B. Mynors (with commentary), 1990; as *Georgics*, translated by William Sotheby, 1830; also translated by Henry Owgan, 1853; C. Day Lewis, 1940; Smith P. Bovie, 1956; Nigel Lambourne, 1969; Robert Wells, 1982; L.P. Wilkinson, 1982; David R. Slavitt, with *Eclogues*, 1990; Kristina Chew, 2002.

*

Bibliography: *Virgil Bibliography* edited by R.G. Austin, with supplement edited by R.D. Williams, 1978; *A Bibliography of Venetian Editions of Virgil, 1470–1599* edited by Craig Kallendorf, 1991.

Critical Studies: *The Allegory of the Aeneid* by D.L. Drew, 1927; *The Development of Virgil's Art* by Henry W. Prescott, 1927; *Virgil* by George E. Woodberry, 1930; *The Magical Art of Virgil* by E.K. Rand, 1931; *Virgil, Father of the West* by Theodore Haecker, translated by A.W. Wheen, 1934; *Roman Vergil* by W.F. Jackson Knight, 1944; *Structural Patterns and Proportions in Virgil's Aeneid: A Study in Mathematical Composition* by George E. Duckworth, 1962; *The Art of Virgil* by Viktor Pöschl, 1962; *Virgil: A Study in Civilized Poetry* by Brooks Otis, 1963; *The Poetry of the Aeneid*, 1965, *Virgil's Pastoral Art*, 1970, and *Virgil's Poem of the Earth*, 1979, all by Michael C.J. Putnam; *Appendix Virgiliana* edited by Wendell V. Clausen and others, 1966, and *Virgil's Aeneid and the Tradition of Hellenistic Poetry* by Clausen, 1987; *Virgil: A Collection of Critical Essays* edited by Steele Commager, 1966; *Notes on Virgil's Aeneid* by Robert J. Milch, 1966; *Virgil's Aeneid: A Critical Description* by Kenneth Quinn, 1968; *The Art of the Aeneid* by William S. Anderson, 1969; *Introduction to Virgil's Aeneid* by W.A. Camps, 1969; *Virgil* edited by D.R. Dudley, 1969; *The Georgics of Virgil* by L.P. Wilkinson, 1969; *Patterns of Action in the Aeneid: An Interpretation of Virgil's Epic Similes* by Roger A. Hornsby, 1970; *Vergil's Italy* by A.G. McKay, 1970; *The Speeches in Vergil's Aeneid* by Gilbert A. Highet, 1972; *Forms of Glory: Structure and Sense in Virgil's Aeneid* by John W. Hunt, 1973; *The Altar and the City: A Reading of Vergil's Aeneid* by Mario A. DiCesare, 1974; *Virgil's Eclogues: Landscapes of Experience* by Eleanor W. Leach, 1974; *Method for Reading Virgil's Hexameters* by G. Nussbaum, 1974; *Pivotal Catalogues in the Aeneid* by W.P. Basson, 1975; *Darkness Visible: A Study of Virgil's Aeneid* by W.R. Johnson, 1976; *The Living Universe: Gods and Men in Virgil's Aeneid* by Agathe Thornton, 1976; *Half-Lines and Repetitions in Virgil* by John Sparrow, 1977; *Fathers and Sons in Virgil's Aeneid*, 1978, and *Death and Rebirth in Virgil's Arcadia*, 1989, both by M. Owen Lee; *Patterns of Time in Virgil* by Sara Mack, 1978; *The Design of Virgil's Bucolics* by John Van Sickle, 1978; *The Singer of the Eclogues: A Study of Virgilian Pastoral*, by Paul Joel Alpers, 1979; *Narrative and Simile from the Georgics in the Aeneid* by Ward

W. Briggs, 1980; *Vergil's Agricultural Golden Age: A Study of the Georgics* by Patricia A. Johnston, 1980; *Virgil's Georgics: A New Interpretation* by Gary B. Miles, 1980; *The Dido Episode and the Aeneid: Roman Social and Political Values in the Epic* by Richard C. Monti, 1981; *Poetry and Myth in Ancient Pastoral: Essays on Theocritus and Virgil* by Charles Segal, 1981; *Formular Language and Poetic Design in the Aeneid* by Walter Moskalew, 1982; *Virgil: His Poetry Through the Ages* by R.D. Williams and Thomas S. Pattie, 1982, and *Virgil's Aeneid* by Williams, 1985; *A Reading of Vergil's Georgics* by James Seaton, 1983; *Technique and Ideas in the Aeneid* by Gordon Williams, 1983; *The Effects of Divine Manifestation on the Reader's Perspective in Vergil's Aeneid* by Elizabeth Block, 1984; *The Language of Virgil: An Introduction to the Poetry of the Aeneid* by Daniel H. Garrison, 1984; *Virgil's Iliad: An Essay on Epic Narrative*, 1984, and *Virgil: The Aeneid*, 1990, both by K.W. Grandsen; *Virgil and His Influence: Bimillennial Studies* edited by C. Martindale, 1984; *The Aeneid: Notes* by Robin Sowerby, 1984; *Virgil at 2000: Commemorative Essays on the Poet and His Influence* edited by John D. Bernard and Paul T. Alessi, 1986; *The Chaonian Dove: Studies in the Eclogues, Georgics and Aeneid of Virgil* by A.J. Boyle, 1986; *Virgil* by Jasper Griffin, 1986; *Virgil in a Cultural Tradition: Essays to Celebrate the Bimillennium* edited by Janet Hamilton, 1986; *Virgil's Aeneid: Cosmos and Imperium* by Colin Hardie, 1986; *Further Voices in Virgil's Aeneid*, 1987, and *Words and the Poet: Characteristic Techniques of Style in Vergil's Aeneid*, 1989, both by R.O.A.M. Lyne; *Burial Places of Memory: Epic Underworlds in Virgil, Dante and Milton* by Ronald R. Macdonald, 1987; *Virgil's Elements: Physics and Poetry in the Georgics* by David O. Ross, 1987; *Pastoral and Ideology: Virgil to Valéry* by Annabel M. Patterson, 1988; *Meminisse iuvabit: Selections from the Proceedings of the Virgil Society* edited by F. Robertson, 1988; *Virgil's Augustan Epic* by Francis Cairns, 1989; *Vigour of Prophecy: A Study of Virgil's Aeneid* by Elisabeth Henry, 1989; *In Praise of Aeneas: Virgil and Epideictic Rhetoric in the Early Italian Renaissance* by Craig Kallendorf, 1989; *The Poet's Truth: A Study of the Poet in Virgil's Georgics* by Christine G. Perkell, 1989; *Public and Private in Virgil's Aeneid* by Susan Ford Wiltshire, 1989; *Virgil and "The Tempest": The Politics of Imitation* by Donna B. Hamilton, 1990; *Oxford Readings in Virgil's Aeneid* by Stephen J. Harrison, 1990; *Labor and Fortuna in Virgil's Aeneid* by Susan Scheinberg Kristol, 1990; *Virgil* edited by Ian McAuslan and Peter Walcot, 1990; *Death and the Optimist: Prophecy in Virgil's Aeneid* by James J. O'Hara, 1990; *Vergil's Georgics and the Traditions of Ancient Epic: The Art of Allusion in Literary History* by Joseph Farrell, 1991; *Virgil* by David R. Slavitt, 1991; *Classical Epic: Homer and Virgil* by Richard Jenkyns, 1992; *The Two Worlds of the Poet: New Perspectives on Vergil* edited by Robert M. Wilhelm and Howard Jones, 1992; *The Choice of Achilles: The Ideology of Figure in the Epic* by Susanne Lindgren Wofford, 1992; *The Epic Successors of Virgil: A Study in the Dynamics of Tradition* by Philip Hardie, 1993; *Virgil's Epic Technique* by Richard Henize, 1993; *Virgil and the Moderns* by Theodore Ziolkowski, 1993; *The Specter of Dido: Spenser and Virgilian Epic* by John Watkins, 1995; *Divine Purpose and Heroic Response in Homer and Virgil: The Political Plan of Zeus* by John Alvis, 1995; *Virgil in Medieval England: Figuring the Aeneid from the Twelfth Century to Chaucer* by Christopher Baswell, 1995; *Virgil's Aeneid: Interpretation and Influence* by Michael C.J. Putnam, 1995; *The Criticism of Didactic Poetry: Essays on Lucretius, Virgil, and Ovid* by Alexander Dalzell, 1996; *Virgil as Orpheus: A Study of the Georgics* by M. Owen Lee, 1996; *Virgil's Aeneid: Semantic*

Relations and Proper Names by Michael Paschalis, 1997; *The Cambridge Companion to Virgil*, edited by Charles Martindale, 1997; *Poetic Allusion and Poetic Embrace in Ovid and Virgil* by R.A. Smith, 1997; *Virgil's Experience: Nature and History: Times, Names, and Places* by Richard Jenkyns, 1998; *Virgil: His Life and Times* by Peter Levi, 1998; *Virgil's Epic Designs: Ekphrasis in the Aeneid* by Michael C.J. Putnam, 1998; *Virgil* by Philip Hardie, 1998; *Vergil's Aeneid: Augustan Epic and Political Context*, edited by Hans-Peter Stahl, 1998; *Aeneas Takes the Metro: The Presence of Virgil in Twentieth-Century French Literature* by Fiona Cox, 1999; *Patterns of Redemption in Virgil's Georgics* by Llewelyn Morgan, 1999; *Reading Vergil's Aeneid: An Interpretive Guide*, edited by Christine Perkell, 1999; *Reading Virgil and His Texts: Studies in Intertextuality* by Richard F. Thomas, 1999; *Virgil: Critical Assessments of Classical Authors*, edited by Philip Hardie, 1999; *Virgil and the Myth of Venice: Books and Readers in the Italian Renaissance* by Craig Kallendorf, 1999; *Virgil on the Nature of Things: The Georgics, Lucretius, and the Didactic Tradition* by Monica R. Gale, 2000; *Language in Virgil's Eclogues* by Michael Lipka, 2001; *Poets and Critics Read Vergil*, edited by Sarah Spence, 2001; *Virgil's Aeneid: Decorum, Allusion, and Ideology* by Wendell Clausen, 2002.

*   *   *

The reputation of Virgil's poetry and the meaning ascribed to it have varied greatly through the ages. He was highly respected during his own lifetime. *Aeneis* (*The Aeneid*), appeared posthumously and contrary to his dying wishes, quickly established itself as the Romans' national epic. Later generations of school teachers praised his rhetorical accomplishment. During the Middle Ages, a change in the spelling of his name from *Vergilius* to *Virgilius* reflected his role for some as master of the occult with his magic wand (*virga*); for others that same change underlined his role as the pagan of virginal purity who foresaw the birth of Christ. Dante cast Virgil as his guide in the *Inferno*; Milton chose *The Aeneid* as the model for *Paradise Lost*; Addison honoured his *Georgics* as "the best poem by the best poet." But with the 19th century Virgil's reputation suffered a decline. His poetry was thought to lack the spontaneity that was rather naïvely attributed to his Greek models: Theocritus for the *Eclogues*, Hesiod for the *Georgics*, and Homer for *The Aeneid*. His great epic was regarded as a rather mannered celebration of the Augustan Principate and Roman imperialism.

Modern interest in Virgil, particularly since the 1950s, may be seen partly as a reaction against 19th-century assessments of his works. Stylistic and thematic studies have sought to establish the full measure to which Virgil transformed the raw material of his Greek sources in accordance with a vision distinctively Roman and distinctively his own. In particular, his relation to the Augustan regime has come into question. Early debates about whether Virgil was pro- or anti-Augustan have generally given way to more nuanced attempts to discover the depth of Virgil's ambivalence and the subtlety of his judgements both about the course of Roman politics in his own age and about the human condition itself.

Not surprisingly for one who began writing in the midst of civil war and died before the Augustan Principate could be felt to have attained stability, the problems of achieving order and of coping with disorder are close to the surface of all Virgil's works and thematically at their core. Throughout his life Virgil explored those problems on two levels, the political and the psychological. In his earliest works those two themes are developed as complementary parallels. The first eclogue introduces shepherds who represent the innumerable Italians caught up by forces vastly beyond their power to control or even adequately comprehend during the Roman civil wars. Against that harsh reality Virgil contrasts the modest satisfactions of a way of life in jeopardy and the longed-for escape of a Golden Age. He also shows the disturbing power of human passion, whether in the self-dramatizing laments of a young lovesick shepherd, in the madness of an unrequited lover, even in the melancholy of one of his own fellow-poets whose longing for an absent lover finds no solace in the countryside and its divinities.

The *Georgics*, leaving behind interest in an ideal of pastoral ease, turns instead to the national myth of the Roman Republic, an ideal of rustic life as the austere school of Roman excellence. The poem juxtaposes the fruitful orderliness of this and other idealized versions of rustic life with contrasting scenes of urban decadence and civil war. Such disorders are now viewed as analogous to disorder inherent in nature itself: Virgil introduces the civil wars as a kind of storm accompanied by heavenly signs, just as other storms; description of the wars parallels description of a plague against which all efforts are helpless. Human passion is presented as actually part of an elemental vitality that operates in all creatures. Comparing humans and animals, Virgil observes that "love is the same for all." In animals it is the necessary basis for procreation, but also a dangerous force that leads to violence; in the moving story of Orpheus and Eurydice that dominates the poem's conclusion it is the force that inspires Orpheus to brave Hades and win permission for his wife's return to the living, but it is also the force that compels him to look back at her as they approach the upper world and so to violate the one condition on which her return depended.

In *The Aeneid* Virgil contrasts the high promise of Augustus' new Golden Age, which is presented as the final goal of Roman civilization, with the terrible suffering and sense of personal loss that must be experienced in the pursuit of that goal. Here, for the first time, he shows a close interrelation between the two types of disorder that were complementary themes in his previous works: political disorder emanates from the passions of individuals. The desperate rage of Dido, queen of Carthage, when she is abandoned by Aeneas, and her curse against his descendants through eternity prepare for the fierce and protracted rivalry between Carthage and Rome; the resentment of the Latin hero, Turnus, when Aeneas usurps both his bride and his political position, gives rise to bitter warfare that implicates all of Italy—warfare that anticipates later wars between Rome and her Italian allies and the civil wars of Virgil's own age.

True to the underlying vision of man and nature developed in the *Georgics*, Virgil continues to present violent disorder as inherent in the very order of nature itself. *The Aeneid* begins with the wrath of the goddess Juno, jealous and quick to anger, who sets herself against the Trojans; Dido compromises her personal and political integrity under the influence of a love that has been arranged through the intrigues of Juno and Venus; Turnus is attacked by Juno's agents, who enter secretly into his breast and drive him mad; the poem ends with Juno and Jupiter reaching an accommodation: no people will honour Juno more than the Romans. The characters of *The Aeneid* are at the mercy of overpowering forces—the gods, Roman destiny, their own passions—whose influence on themselves they perceive only occasionally and then only fleetingly and imperfectly, and whose meaning is never certain and clear: when the destiny of Rome is laid out before Aeneas by his father in the Underworld and again on a shield made for him by Vulcan, the hero responds with awe but without full understanding.

Of the many qualities that have impressed Virgil's readers, the richness of his language, the vividness of his narrative, the magnitude of the events he describes, two perhaps deserve special attention. The first is the range of his human sympathies. Without losing sight of values to which we should aspire and by which we must be measured, Virgil none the less refrains from making simple judgements. In his vision we are all subject to the same forces of nature; none of us is capable of resisting their influence. In the *Eclogues* and *Georgics* he acknowledges explicitly his own susceptibility to *amor*. In *The Aeneid*, Dido and Turnus, the unwitting agents of opposition to Roman destiny, are as much the victims of the divine powers arrayed against Aeneas and his followers as are those heroes of Roman destiny themselves. In the final books of *The Aeneid*, Turnus achieves a kind of nobility, despite his madness, while Aeneas becomes increasingly a victim of his passions until he, too, acts not from a sense of mission, but "inflamed with rage."

Related to this complexity of viewpoint is a second distinguishing characteristic, Virgil's restraint. He interprets events from the perspective of the shepherd or the farmer or, in *The Aeneid*, of a hero who is by disposition modest in his aspirations, moderate in his behaviour. It is in the intimate, often mundane details of private existence that Virgil locates the ultimate measure of significance and value. And it is in terms of those details that he is able to acknowledge both the powerlessness of humankind to resist the pervasive forces of disorder in nature, society, and the individual, and simultaneously the awesome capacity to persist in the face of uncertainty, repeatedly to start anew in the face of disaster. Virgil conveys both respect for the cost that such continual effort requires and also a conviction that the effort is necessary.

—Gary B. Miles

See the essays on *The Aeneid* and *Georgics*.

VITTORINI, Elio

Born: Syracuse, Sicily, 23 July 1908. **Education:** After five years at secondary school, attended a technical school to study accounting; left after three years without a certificate. **Career:** Worked in a road-building gang, Gorizia, 1925; proofreader and journalist, Florence, 1929–35; proofreader for *La Nazione*, Florence, 1930, and taught himself English; translator and editor for Bompiani, Einaudi, and Mondadori publishers, Milan, from 1936. At outbreak of World War II opposed the Mussolini regime, and joined an underground movement in Milan. In the early 1940s his work was suppressed; imprisoned by the Fascists, 1943; founded the periodicals *Il politecnico*, 1945–47, and *Il menabò*, 1959–67; founding editor of the "I gettoni" series, 1951, and the "Nuovo politecnico" series, 1965, both for Einaudi, and of the "Nuovi scrittori stranieri" series, 1964, for Mondadori. **Awards:** Salento prize, 1956. **Died:** 12/13 February 1966.

PUBLICATIONS

Collection

Le opere narrative, edited by Maria Certi. 2 vols., 1974.

Fiction

Piccola borghesia. 1931.

Nei Morlacchi—Viaggio in Sardegna. 1936; as *Sardegna come un 'infanzia*, 1952.

Conversazione in Sicilia. 1938–39; edited by Giovanni Falaschi, 1975; as *Conversation in Sicily*, translated by Wilfrid David, 1948; also translated by Alane Salierno Mason, 2000; as *In Sicily*, translated by David, 1949.

Nome e lagrime. 1941.

Uomini e no. 1945; edited by Edoardo Esposito, 1977; as *Men and Not Men*, 1987.

Il garofano rosso. 1948; as *The Red Carnation*, translated by Anthony Bower, 1952.

Il sempione strizza l'occhio al Fréjus. 1949; as *The Twilight of the Elephant*, translated by Cinna Brescia, 1951; as *Tune for an Elephant*, translated by Eric Mosbacher, 1955.

Le donne di Messina. 1949; revised edition, 1964; as *Women of Messina*, translated by Francis Frenaye and Frances Keene, 1973.

Erica e i suoi fratelli; La garibaldina. 1956; as *The Dark and the Light: Erica and La Garibaldina*, translated by Frances Keene, 1960.

Women on the Road: Three Short Novels (includes *Women on the Road; Erica; La Garibaldina*), translated by Frances Keene and Bernard Wall. 1961.

Le città del mondo (unfinished). 1969.

Nome e lagrime e altri racconti, edited by Raffaella Rodondi. 1972.

Vittorini Omnibus (includes *In Sicily; The Twilight of the Elephant; La Garibaldina*). 1973.

Plays

Le città del mondo: Una sceneggiatura (screenplay). 1975.

Other

La tragica vicenda di Carlo III, with Giansiro Ferrata. 1939; as *Sangue a Parma*, 1967.

Guttuso. 1942.

Diario in pubblico 1929–1956. 1957; revised edition, 1970.

Storia di Renato Guttuso e nota congiunta sulla pittura contemporanea. 1960.

Le due tensioni: Appunti per una ideologia della letterature, edited by Dante Isella. 1967.

Vittorini: Progettazione e letteratura, edited by Italo Calvino. 1968.

Editor, with Enrico Falqui, *Scrittori nuovi*. 1930.

Editor, *Teatro spagnolo*. 1941.

Editor, *Americana*. 1942.

Editor, *Orlando Furioso*, by Ariosto. 1950.

Editor, *Commedie*, by Goldoni. 1952.

Translator, *Il purosangue*, by D.H. Lawrence. 1933.

Translator, *La vergine e lo zingaro*, by D.H. Lawrence. 1935.

Translator, *Il serpente piumato*, by D.H. Lawrence. 1935.

Translator, with Delfino Cinelli, *Racconti e arabeschi*, by Edgar Allan Poe. 1936.

Translator, with Delfino Cinelli, *Gordon Pym e altre storie*, by Edgar Allan Poe. 1937.

Translator, *Luce d'agosto*, by William Faulkner. 1939.

Translator, *Il mietitore di Dodder*, by T.F. Powys. 1939.

Translator, *Pian della Tortilla*, by John Steinbeck. 1939.

Translator, *Che ve se sembra dell'America?*, by William Saroyan. 1940.

Translator, *La peste di Londra*, by Daniel Defoe. 1940.

Translator, *I pascoli del cielo*, by John Steinbeck. 1940.

Translator, *Piccolo campo*, by Erskine Caldwell. 1940.

Translator, *Il cammino nella polvere*, by John Fante. 1941.

Translator, *Nozze di sangue*, by Federico García Lorca, in *Teatro spagnolo*. 1942.

Translator, *Pagine di viaggio*, by D.H. Lawrence. 1942.

Translator, *Tito Andronico*, by William Shakespeare, in *Teatro*. 1943.

Translator, *Il potere e la gloria*, by Graham Greene. 1945.

*

Critical Studies: *Three Italian Novelists: Moravia, Pavese, Vittorini* by Donald W. Heiney, 1968; *Vittorini* (in Italian) by Sandro Briosi, 1970; *Vittorini* (in Italian) by Folco Zanobini, 1974; *Guida a Vittorini* by Sergio Pautasso, 1977; *Vittorini* by Felice Rappazzo, 1996; *Elio Vittorini: The Writer and the Written* by Guido Bonsaver, 2000.

* * *

Elio Vittorini's origins were humble. His father was a Sicilian station master. He ran away to the north, and in Milan and Florence turned himself into a powerful intellectual who for the rest of his life was ready to take his stand in the area where literature and politics overlap. The stories of *Piccola borghesia* [Petty Bourgeoisie] turn a sharp eye on the middle classes under fascism. *Viaggio in Sardegna* [Travels in Sardinia] combines the factual with childhood memories and was written in the spirit of the Florentine magazine *Solaria*, for which he worked as a proofreader. It was in this capacity that he "discovered" Pavese's early poetry. In 1933–34 *Solaria* published the first eight instalments of *Il garofano rosso* (*The Red Carnation*), which portrays the attitudes of adolescents to fascism in the early 1930s. Censorship intervened and the book did not appear in full until 1948 when a very important preface described how in both *The Red Carnation* and *Conversazione in Sicilia* (*Conversation in Sicily*) Vittorini had invented a new style that would incorporate into "poetry" (in the sense of creative writing) the essay material that had accrued to the genre of the novel during the last century.

Having learned English by reading *Robinson Crusoe*, Vittorini had gone on to translate Poe, Faulkner, Steinbeck, and Saroyan. He read Hemingway and became friendly with him. From Saroyan and Hemingway he picked up and perfected a style based on rhythm and repetition which went a long way to achieving his ambitions for the novel. *Conversation in Sicily*, first published in *Letteratura* (the successor to *Solaria*) in 1938–39, is his most famous work. It describes a journey back to his childhood roots by an autobiographical, near-Dantesque, figure who is trying to make positive sense of his past and his present. Contemporary reality is superimposed on the past in symbolical and even allegorical terms. For instance much importance is given to food: the bitter oranges of returning fruit pickers, his mother's herring, and the childhood memories of melons—a basic reality and yet symbolic of poverty, oppression, and resilience. The language used to re-create this experience is lyrical but sometimes unorthodox, and yet through the rhythmic repetition of certain key phrases such as "reale due volte" (twice real) and "l'in più d'ora" (the extra now) the theme is raised to the level of the universal.

Speaking of poetry in his post-war magazine *Il politecnico* in 1945, Vittorini said, "Poetry is poetry because it does not stay bound to its origins and if it is born of sorrow it can be linked to all sorrow."

Il politecnico was his contribution to the polemics of the culture of the left after the war. The final struggle of the Milan Resistance is depicted in *Uomini e no* (*Men and Not Men*); the social problems of the immediate post-war period are the subject of *Il sempione strizza l'occhio al Fréjus* (*Tune for an Elephant*) with the apotheosis of the Vittorinian worker-grandfather figure as the elephant preparing himself for death. *Erica e i suoi fratelli; La garibaldina* (*The Dark and the Light: Erica and La Garibaldina*), written in 1936 and published 20 years later, deals with women's suffering when the heroine is forced into prostitution in order to buy food. *Le donne di Messina* (*Women of Messina*), *La Garibaldina*, and *Le città del mondo* (which was never finished) all return to Sicily with some hope of renewal despite inertia. During the 1950s and 1960s Vittorini presided over the later period of neorealism, discovering Sciascia, Cassola, and Fenoglio, while rejecting Lampedusa's *Il Gattopardo* (*The Leopard*) as too old-fashioned. The journal *Il menabò* (on which Calvino also worked) was meant to tackle the new problems of industrialization.

Vittorini's greatest contributions are his raising of the consciousness of his readers and his work as cultural impresario for Italian letters during the mid-20th century.

—Judy Rawson

See the essay on *Conversations in Sicily*.

VOLTAIRE

Born: François-Marie Arouet in Paris, France, February or November 1694. **Education:** Educated at Collège Louis-le-Grand, Paris, 1704–11; studied law, 1711–13. **Career:** Articled by his father to a lawyer, 1714; arrested and exiled from Paris for 5 months, 1716, and imprisoned in the Bastille, 1717–18, for satiric writings; quarrel with the Chevalier de Rohan-Chabot led to another term in the Bastille and departure for England, 1726–28; retired to Château de Cirey with Madame Du Châtelet, 1734–40 (she died 1749); Courtier with Frederick of Prussia, Berlin, 1750–53; lived in Colmar, 1753–54, at Les Délices, near Geneva, 1755–59, and at Ferney, 1759–78; visited Paris and received triumphant welcome, 1778. **Member:** Royal Society (London); Royal Society of Edinburgh, 1745; Académie française, 1746; Academy of St. Petersburg, 1746; Royal Historiographer of France, 1745–50; and Gentleman of the Bedchamber, 1746. **Died:** 30 May 1778.

PUBLICATIONS

Collections

Oeuvres complètes [Kehl Edition]. 70 vols., 1785–89.
Oeuvres complètes, edited by L. Moland. 52 vols., 1877–85.
Works. 1901–03.
Complete Works (includes *Correspondence*, 51 vols., 1968–77), edited by Theodore Besterman and others. 1968–.

Romans et contes, edited by Frédéric Deloffre and Jacques van den Heuvel. 2 vols., 1978.
Political Writings, edited and translated by David Williams. 1994.

Fiction

Zadig; ou, La Destinée. 1748; edited by G. Ascoli and J. Fabre, 1962; as *Zadig; or, The Book of Fate*, translated anonymously, 1775; also translated by Francis Ashmore, 1782; Robert Bruce Boswell, 1907; and H.I. Woolf and Wilfred Jackson, 1929; as *Zadig*, translated by John Butt, with *L'Ingénu*, 1978.

Micromégas. 1752; edited by Ira O. Wade, 1950; translated as *Micromegas*, 1753; also translated by W. Fleming, 1989.

Songe de Platon. 1756; edited by Jacques van den Heuvel, in *Complete Works*, 17, 1991.

Candide; ou, L'Optimisme. 1759; edited by René Pomeau, in *Complete Works*, 48, 1980; translated as *Candid*, 1759; as *Candide*, translated by Lowell Bair, 1959; also translated by Richard Aldington, 1985; and Roger Pearson, in *Candide and Other Stories*, 1990; as *Candide; or, Optimism*, edited and translated by Robert M. Adams, 1966, reprinted 1990; as *Candide*, edited with introduction and notes by Haydn Mason, 1995; translated and edited by Daniel Gordon, 1999.

L'Ingénu. 1767; edited by W.R. Jones, 1957; as *Le Huron; ou, L'Ingénu*, 1767; as *The Pupil of Nature*, translated by Thomas Smollett, 1771; as *The Sincere Huron*, translated by Francis Ashmore, 1786; as *L'Ingénu*, translated by John Butt, with *Zadig*, 1978.

La Princesse de Babylone. 1768; translated as *The Princess of Babylon*, 1927.

L'Homme aux quarante écus. 1768; edited by N. Kotta, 1966; as *The Man of Forty Crowns*, translated anonymously, 1768.

Les Lettres d'Amabed. 1769.

Le Taureau blanc. 1774; edited by René Pomeau, 1957; as *The White Bull*, translated by Jeremy Bentham, 1774; also translated by C.E. Vulliamy, 1929.

Histoire de Jenni; ou, Le Sage et l'athée. 1775; as *Young James; or, The Sage and the Atheist*, translated anonymously, 1776.

Zadig and Other Stories, edited by Haydn T. Mason. 1971.

Candide and Other Stories (includes "Candide"; "Micromegas"; "Zadig"; "The Ingenu"; "The White Bull"), translated by Roger Pearson. 1990.

Plays

Oedipe (produced 1718). 1719; as *Oedipus*, in *Works*, 1901–03, and in *Seven Plays*, 1988.

Artémire (produced 1720). Fragments published in *Oeuvres*, 1, 1784.

Mariamne (produced 1724; as *Hérode et Mariamne*, produced 1725). 1725.

L'Indiscret (produced 1725). 1725.

Brutus (produced 1730). 1731.

Ériphile (produced 1732). 1732.

Zaïre (produced 1732). 1733; edited by E. Jacobs, 1975; translated as *Zara*, 1736; as *Zaïra*, translated by Charles B. Burrell, 1873.

Les Originaux (produced 1732). In *Oeuvres*, 9, 1820.

Adélaïde du Guesclin (produced 1734). In *Oeuvres*, 6, 1745; edited by M. Cartwright, in *Complete Works*, 10, 1985.

La Mort de César (produced 1735). 1736; edited by A.-M. Rousseau, 1964, also edited by D.J. Fletcher, in *Complete Works*, 8, 1988.

Alzire; ou, Les Américains (produced 1736). 1736; edited by T.E.D. Braun, in *Complete Works*, 14, 1989; translated as *Alzira*, 1736; as *Alzire*, in *Works*, 1901–03, and in *Seven Plays*, 1988.

L'Enfant prodigue (produced 1736). 1738.

L'Échange (produced 1736, revised version, as *Quand est-ce qu'on me marie?*, produced 1761). 1761; as *Le Comte de Boursoufle*, in *Oeuvres*, 7, 1819; edited by C. Duckworth, in *Complete Works*, 14, 1989.

Zulime (produced 1740). 1761.

Mahomet (produced 1741). 1742; as *Le Fanatisme; ou, Mahomet le prophète*, 1743; as *Mohamet the Imposter*, 1744; as *Mohamet the Prophet*, in *The Drama*, 8, edited by A. Bates, 1903–04.

Mérope (produced 1743). 1744; edited by J.R. Vrooman and J. Godden, in *Complete Works*, 17, 1991; translated as *Merope*, 1744; also translated by E.R. Sahiar, 1909.

La Princesse de Navarre, music by Rameau (produced 1745). 1745.

Le Temple de la Gloire, music by Rameau (produced 1745). 1745.

La Prude; ou, La Gardeuse de cassette, from *The Plain-Dealer* by Wycherley (produced 1747). In *Oeuvres*, 8, 1748.

Sémiramis (produced 1748). 1749; translated as *Semiramis*, 1760.

Nanine (produced 1749). 1749; translated as *Nanine*, in *Eighteenth-Century French Plays*, edited by C.D. Brenner and N.A. Goodyear, 1927.

Oreste (produced 1750). 1750; as *Orestes*, in *Works*, 1901–03, and in *Seven Plays*, 1988.

Catilina; ou, Rome sauvée (produced 1750). 1752; as *Rome Preserved*, translated anonymously, 1760.

Le Duc de Foix (produced 1752). 1752; as *Amélie; ou, Le Duc de Foix*, in *Collection complète des oeuvres*, 11, 1756; edited by M. Cartwright, in *Complete Works*, 10, 1985.

L'Orphelin de la Chine (produced 1755). 1755; as *The Orphan of China*, translated anonymously, 1756.

Saül. 1755; as *Saul*, translated by Oliver Martext, 1820.

La Femme qui a raison (produced 1758). 1759.

Socrate. 1759; translated as *Socrates*, 1760; also translated by Oliver H.G. Leigh, 1903.

Tancrède (produced 1759). 1760; translated as *Almida*, 1771.

L'Écossaise (produced 1760). 1760; edited by C. Duckworth, in *Complete Works*, 50, 1986; as *The Coffee House*, translated anonymously, 1760; as *The Highland Girl*, translated by W.G. Collingwood, 1910.

Le Droit du seigneur (as *L'Écueil du sage*, produced 1762). 1763; edited by W.D. Howarth, in *Complete Works*, 50, 1986; as *L'Écueil du sage*, 1764.

Olympie (produced 1764). 1763; as *Olympia*, in *Works*, 1901–03, and in *Seven Plays*, 1988.

Octave et le jeune Pompée; ou, Le Triumvirat (produced 1764). 1766.

Les Scythes (produced 1767). 1767.

Charlot; ou, La Comtesse de Givri (produced 1767). 1767.

Les Guèbres; ou, La Tolérance. 1769.

Sophonisbe (produced 1774). 1770.

Le Dépositaire (produced 1772). 1772.

Les Lois de Minos; ou, Astérie. 1773.

Don Pèdre. 1775.

Agathocle (produced 1777). In *Oeuvres*, 6, 1784.

Irène (produced 1778). 1779. *Le Duc d'Alençon; ou, Les Frères ennemis*, edited by M.L. Dubois. 1821.

L'Envieux. 1834.

Seven Plays (includes *Oedipus; Alzire; Orestes; Olympia; Merope; Zaïre; Caesar*), translated by William F. Fleming, 1988.

Verse

La Ligue; ou, Henri le Grand: Poème epique. 1723; as *La Henriade*, 1728; edited by O.R. Taylor, in *Complete Works*, 2, 1970; as *Henriade*, translated by Thomas Smollett, 1732.

Le Temple du Goût. 1733, revised edition, as *Le Temple de l'amitié et le temple du goût*, 1733; as *The Temple of Taste*, translated anonymously, 1734.

Discours en vers sur l'homme. 1738; edited by H.T. Mason, in *Complete Works*, 17, 1991.

La Pucelle d'Orléans. 1755; enlarged edition, 1762, 1780; edited by J. Vercruysse, in *Complete Works*, 7, 1970; as *La Pucelle; or, The Maid of Orleans*, translated anonymously, 2 vols., 1785–86.

Poème sur le désastre de Lisbonne. 1756.

Poème sur la loi naturelle. 1756.

Précis de l'Ecclésiaste en vers. 1759.

La Cantique des cantiques en vers. 1759.

Contes de Guillaume Vadé. 1764.

La Guerre civile de Genève. 1767; edited by J. Renwick, in *Complete Works*, 63A, 1990; as *The Civil War of Geneva*, translated by T. Teres, 1769.

Épîtres, satires, contes, odes, et pièces fugitives. 1771.

Poèmes, épîtres, et autres poésies. 1777.

Other

Essai sur les guerres civiles de France. 1729; as *Essay upon the Civil Wars in France*, translated anonymously, 1727.

Histoire de Charles XII, roi de Suède. 2 vols., 1731; as *The History of Charles XII, King of Sweden*, translated by Antonia White, 1976; as *Lion of the North: Charles XII of Sweden*, translated by M.F.O. Jenkins, 1981.

Lettres écrites de Londres sur les Anglais. 1734; as *Lettres philosophiques*, 1734; edited by G. Lanson and A.-M. Rousseau, 1964; as *Letters Concerning the English Nation*, 1733; as *Letters on England*, translated by Leonard Tancock, 1980.

Eléments de la philosophie de Newton. 1738; as *The Elements of Newton's Philosophy*, translated by John Hanna, 1738.

Essai sur la nature du feu. 1739; edited by W.A. Smeaton and R.L. Walters, in *Complete Works*, 17, 1991.

Oeuvres. 8 vols., 1739 (and many later editions).

Histoire de la guerre de mil sept cent quarante et un. 2 vols., 1745; as *The History of the War of Seventeen Hundred and Forty One*, translated anonymously, 1756.

Le Siècle de Louis XIV. 2 vols., 1751; *Supplément*, 1753; as *The Age of Louis XIV*, 2 vols., 1752, revised edition, 1753; also translated by J.H. Brumfitt, 1966.

Annales de l'Empire depuis Charlemagne. 2 vols., 1753; as *Annals of the Empire from the Reign of Charlemagne*, 1781.

Essai sur l'histoire générale et sur les moeurs et l'esprit des nations. 7 vols., 1756, revised edition, 8 vols., 1761–63; as *The General History and State of Europe*, translated by Sir Timothy Waldo, 1754; as *An Essay on Universal History*, translated by Mr Nugent, 1759.

Histoire de l'empire de Russie sous Pierre le Grand. 2 vols., 1759–63; as *The History of the Russian Empire under Peter the Great*, translated by J. Johnson, 1763.

Anecdotes sur Fréron. 1761; edited by J. Balcou, in *Complete Works*, 50, 1986.

Appel à toutes les nations de l'Europe. 1761.

Traité sur la tolérance. 1763; as *A Treatise of Religious Tolerance*, translated anonymously, 1764.

Dictionnaire philosophique portratif. 1764, revised edition, 1765 (and later editions): revisions include *La Raison par Alphabet*, 2 vols., 1769, and *Questions sur l'Encyclopédie*, 9 vols., 1770–72; as *The Philosophical Dictionary for the Pocket*, translated 1765; as *Philosophical Dictionary*, translated by H.I. Woolf, 1945; also edited and translated by Theodore Besterman, 1971; *Oeuvres alphabétiques I*, edited by J. Vercruysse and others, in *Complete Works*, 33, 1987.

La Philosophie de l'histoire. 1765; edited by J.H. Brumfitt, in *Complete Works*, 59, 1969.

Collection des lettres sur les miracles. 1765; 20 letters also published separately, 1765.

Le Philosophe ignorant. 1766; edited by J.L. Carr, 1965, also edited by R. Mortier, in *Complete Works*, 62, 1987; as *The Ignorant Philosopher*, translated by David Williams, 1767.

Commentaire sur le livre des délits et des peines. 1766.

André Destouches à Siam. 1766; edited by J. Renwick, in *Complete Works*, 62, 1987.

Les Questions de Zapata. 1766; edited by J. Marchand, in *Complete Works*, 62, 1987.

La Défense de mon oncle. 1767; edited by J.-M. Moureaux, in *Complete Works*, 64, 1984.

Anecdotes sur Bélisaire. 1767; edited by J. Renwick, in *Complete Works*, 63A, 1990.

Les Honnêtetés littéraires. 1767.

Examen important de milord Bolingbroke. 1767; edited by R. Mortier, in *Complete Works*, 62, 1987.

Lettres sur Rabelais. 1767.

Homélies prononcées à Londres en 1765. 1767; edited by J. Marchand, in *Complete Works*, 62, 1987, also edited by U. Kölving, and J.-M. Moureaux, in *Complete Works*, 63A, 1990; *Cinquième homélie*, 1769.

Le Dîner du comte de Boulainvilliers. 1767.

Essai historique et critique sur les dissensions des Églises de Pologne. 1767; edited by D. Beauvoir and E. Rostworowski, in *Complete Works*, 63A, 1990.

Les Singularités de la nature. 1768.

L'ABC. 1768.

Histoire du Parlement de Paris. 2 vols., 1769.

Collection d'anciens évangiles; ou, Monument du premier siècle du christianisme. 1769.

Dieu et les hommes: Oeuvre théologique, mais raisonnable. 1769.

Précis du siècle de Louis XV. 2 vols., 1769; as *The Age of Louis XV*, translated anonymously, 2 vols., 1774.

Fragments sur l'Inde. 1773; enlarged edition, with *Fragments d'histoire générale, et sur la France*, 1774; as *Fragments Relating to the Late Revolutions in India*, 1774; as *Fragments on India*, translated by Freda Bedi, 1937.

Commentaire historique sur les oeuvres de l'auteur de la Henriade (autobiography). 1776; as *Historical Memoirs of the Author of the Henriade*, 1777.

La Bible enfin expliquée. 2 vols., 1776.

Dialogues d'Évhémère. 1777.

Commentaire sur L'Esprit des Lois de Montesquieu. 1778.

Prix de la justice et de l'humanité. 1778.

Traité de métaphysique. 1784; edited by H. Temple Petterson, 1937, also edited by W.H. Barber, in *Complete Works*, 14, 1989.

Oeuvres historiques, edited by René Pomeau. 1957.

The Portable Voltaire, edited by Ben Ray Redman. 1968; enlarged edition, 1977.

Notebooks, edited by Theodore Besterman, in *Complete Works*, 81–82. 1968.

Editor, *Anti-Machiavel; ou, Essais critiques sur Le Prince de Machiavel*, by Frederick II. 1740.

Editor, *Testament de Jean Meslier*. 1762.

Editor, *Théâtre de Pierre Corneille avec des commentaires*. 12 vols., 1764; *Commentaires*, edited by D. Williams, in *Complete Works* 53–55, 1974–75.

Editor, *Journal de la cour de Louis XIV*, by the Marquis de Dangeau. 1769.

Editor, *Les Souvenirs de Mme de Caylus*. 1770.

Editor, *Éloge et pensées de Pascal*. 1778.

Translator, *Jules César*, by Shakespeare, in *Théâtre de Pierre Corneille 2*. 1764.

Translator, *L'Héraclius espagnol; ou, Dans cette vie tout est verité et tout mensonge*, by Calderón. In *Théâtre de Pierre Corneille 5*, 1764.

*

Bibliography: *Voltaire: Bibliographie de ses oeuvres* by Georges Bengesco, 4 vols., 1882–90 (index by Jean Malcolm, 1953); *A Century of Voltaire Study: Bibliography of Writings on Voltaire 1825–1926* by Mary Margaret Barr, 1929; supplements in *Modern Language Notes*, 1933, 1941.

Critical Studies: *Voltaire Historian* by J.H. Brumfitt, 1958; *Voltaire's Politics: The Poet as Realist* by Peter Gay, 1959; *Voltaire and "Candide,"* 1959, and *The Intellectual Development of Voltaire*, 1969, both by Ira O. Wade; *Voltaire* by V.W. Topazio, 1967; *Voltaire dans ses contes* by Jacques van den Heuvel, 1967; *Le Religion de Voltaire* by R. Pomeau, 1969; *Voltaire and the Century of Light* by A.O. Aldridge, 1975; *Voltaire*, 1975, and *Voltaire: A Biography*, 1981, both by Haydn Mason; *Voltaire and the French Academy* by Karlis Racevskis, 1975; *Voltaire's Comic Theatre: Composition, Conflict and Critics* by Lilian Willens, 1975; *Voltaire* by Theodore Besterman, 1976; *Voltaire and the Form of the Novel* by Douglas A. Bonneville, 1976; *Voltaire* by John Edward Hearsey, 1976; *Voltaire on War and Peace* by Henry Meyer, 1976; *Voltaire's Russia: Window on the East* by Carolyn Wilberger, 1976; *Voltaire and English Literature: A Study of English Literary Influences on Voltaire* by Ahmad Gunny, 1979; *Voltaire and Protestantism* by Graham Gargett, 1980; *Voltaire: Notes* by Colin Niven, 1980; *Voltaire* by Wayne Andrews, 1981; *Voltaire and the Eucharist* by William H. Trapnell, 1981; *Voltaire en son temps* by R. Pomeau and others, 5 vols., 1985–94; *Voltaire and His World: Studies Presented to W.H. Barber* edited by R.J. Howells and others, 1985; *Reading Voltaire's Contes: A Semiotics of Philosophical Narration* by Carol Sherman, 1985; *Voltaire: An Intellectual Biography* by A.J. Ayer, 1986; *Voltaire's Binary Masterpiece: L'Ingénu Reconsidered* by John S. Clouston, 1986; *Voltaire and Tragedy* by Eva Jacobs, 1987; *The Art of Voltaire's Theatre: An Exploration of Possibility* by Marie A. Wellington, 1988; *The Illustrated Editions of Candide: The Interpretation of a Classic: An Examination and Checklist* by Peter Tucker, 1993; *The Fables of Reason: A Study of Voltaire's "Contes philosophiques"* by Roger Pearson, 1993; *Pour encourager les autres: Studies for the Tercentenary of Voltaire's Birth, 1694–1994*, edited by Haydn Mason, 1994; *Voltaire: Candide* by David Williams, 1997; *Voltaire and the Theatre of the Eighteenth Century* by Marvin Carlson, 1998; *Voltaire Revisited* by Bettina L. Knapp, 2000.

* * *

Voltaire was the universal genius of the French Enlightenment: dramatist, poet, philosopher, scientist, novelist, moralist, satirist, polemicist, historian, letter-writer. He established his credentials in the literary world at an early age, laying claim to pre-eminence in two of the most exalted domains of letters: tragedy and the epic. His very first play, *Oedipe* (*Oedipus*), 1718, on a theme where he rivalled Sophocles and Corneille, was an immediate success, placing him at once in the front rank of tragic dramatists. His epic poem *La Ligue* (later called *La Henriade*) triumphed likewise, bringing heroic verse back into fashion. But this early brilliance was checked by the quarrel with the chevalier de Rohan that led to his years in England. From them emerged on his return the *Lettres philosophiques* (*Letters on England*) which, based on the superior example of English life, worked out a programme for a whole civilization, where the French might learn to use experimental enquiry, avoid matters of faith in science and philosophy, encourage trade, literature, and the arts.

The scandal caused by these letters forced him into retreat at Cirey, where began the career of unremitting hard work that was to characterize the rest of his life. Poetry, plays, *contes*, historical and philosophical works poured forth: like the *Traité de métaphysique* (written 1734–37; published 1784), the tragedy *Zaïre* (*Zara*), the worldly poems "Le Mondain" and "Défense du Mondain" (1736–37), and most notably of all the *Eléments de la philosophie de Newton* (*The Elements of Newton's Philosophy*), where a popular account of the great Englishman's thought becomes a major vehicle in spreading enlightenment. By contrast, the 1740s were less prolific, but they include his first-published important *conte*, *Zadig*, where the problem of evil is evoked, without any reassuring answers being found. After the fiasco of his stay at Frederick the Great's court, Voltaire eventually found an ever-precarious but growing stability in and later near Geneva. Shock at the catastrophic earthquake in Lisbon led within weeks to the *Poème sur le désastre de Lisbonne* (*Poem on the Disaster of Lisbon*), an anguished exploration of the meaning of such suffering. In *Candide*, the same theme is revisited, but in a more profound form and expanded into an attack on philosophical Optimism and, through it, all philosophical systems that claim falsely to justify the presence of evil in the world. It is, however, by its style above all that *Candide* is superior to the poem about Lisbon. Brilliantly ironic where the latter is but sombre, satirical of human pretensions and malice alike, expressing at the same time both a horror of evil and an unquenchable vitality, it conveys a unique tone that makes it Voltaire's masterpiece. Every illusion is betrayed, even the belief (held by the Manichean Martin) that everything is evil. The human lot is not to make sense of the universe, nor yet to abandon hope and commit suicide; it is to survive, to work, to put together a few fragments as a flimsy structure against total despair. Experience is a better teacher than metaphysical systems: "il faut cultiver notre jardin." That final phrase appears to represent a counsel of positive endeavour and courage.

Such a spirit animates the multitudinous writings of the Ferney years (1759–78), in which Voltaire makes an all-out assault on manmade injustice. Crusades in real life on behalf of persecuted victims like Calas, Sirven, and La Barre find their literary counterpart in such works as the *Traité sur la tolérance* (*A Treatise of Religious Tolerance*), the *Dictionnaire philosophique portratif* (*Philosophical Dictionary*), *contes* like *L'Ingénu*, and innumerable pamphlets, dialogues, satires, and sermons. *L'Ingénu* seeks to heighten the reader's awareness of the reality of persecution in France, whether the target be Protestants or Jansenists or innocent maidens, by a sentimental tale that makes the injustices all the more horrible for being viewed through the reactions of the simple and natural hero who gives the story its title. More polemically, the *Examen important de milord Bolingbroke* is a comprehensive attack on the follies of the Christian faith, first as found in the Old and New Testaments and then as seen in the history of the Catholic Church; the tone is one of high indignation at the massacres and barbarities that absurdities of dogma have caused ever since the time of Christ. Everything about Christianity is false: founder, scriptures, doctrines, morality. Enlightened men should quit Catholicism and turn to the only true religion, deism, which consists simply of worshipping God and being just to one's fellowmen.

How to represent fairly in a thousand words a man whose extant works alone run to 15 million of them? The scale of Voltaire's prestige overwhelms all attempts to convey comprehensively his writings as his life. For 60 years he dominated the French intellectual and literary world. The greatest tragedian and epic-writer of his day, he has come since then to be seen as an unparalleled *conteur philosophique*. His historical works, especially *Le Siècle de Louis XIV* (*The Age of Louis XIV*) and the universal *Essai sur l'histoire générale et sur les moeurs et l'esprit des nations* (*An Essay on Universal History*), are major items in the development of historiography as the study of civilization. Latterly, now that his correspondence is at last available in the great Besterman edition, containing some 17,000 surviving letters by him with some 1,200 correspondents and on a vast range of subjects, it is becoming apparent that here too is a literary masterpiece. His comprehensive commitment to secular values in the defence of intellectual and judicial freedom, arrayed against a Church-dominated society, allied to his love of classical ideals—reason and lucidity—expressed in brilliant irony and wit, assure him a dominance in the history of French literature that is unlikely ever to be surpassed.

—Haydn Mason

See the essays on *Candide, Philosophical Dictionary, Poem on the Disaster of Lisbon, Zadig.*

VONDEL, Joost van den

Born: Cologne, Germany, 17 November 1587. Son of Antwerp Anabaptists forced to leave their native city because of their religious convictions; moved to Amsterdam in 1597. **Family:** Married Maeyken de Wolff in 1610 (died 1635); two sons (second son died in infancy in 1632) and two daughters (died 1633 and 1675). **Career:** Worked as a stocking merchant; often fined for views expressed in his plays; thereafter wrote satirical poems about magistrates and clergy; member of *Her wit lavendel*, 1606, then joined d'Eglantier; opened the new theatre in Amsterdam, staging *Gysbrecht van Aemstel*, 1637; converted to Catholicism, 1641; given laurels by painters and poets of the city, 1653; financial problems increased when, at the age of 70, he was obliged to pay off debts incurred by his son. **Died:** 1679.

PUBLICATIONS

Collections

De werken [Works], edited by J. van Lennep. 12 vols., 1855–69; revised by J.H.W. Unger, 30 vols., 1889–94.
De werken [Works], edited by J.M.F. Sterck, H.W.E. Moiler, and C.R. de Klerk. 10 vols., 1927–37.
De volledige werken [The Complete Works], edited by H.C. Diferee. 7 vols., 1929–34.
Volledige dichtwerken en oorspronkelijk proza [Complete Poems and Original Prose], edited by A. Verwey. 1937.

Verse

Den gulden winckel der konstlievende Nederlanders [The Gilt Shop of Art-Loving Dutchmen]. 1613.
Vorstelijcke warande der dieren [Royal Park of Animals]. 1617.
Het lof der zee-vaert. 1623; edited by M. Spies, 1987; as *In Praise of Navigation*, translated by Peter Skrine, in *Dutch Crossing*, 13, 1981.
De vervoering van Grol [The Rapture of Grol]. 1627.
Rommelpot van 't Hanekot. 1627.
Roskam. 1630; as *Curry-Comb*, translated by Paul Vincent, in *Dutch Crossing*, 32, 1987.
Harpoen [Harpoon]. 1630.
Een otter in 't bolwerk [An Otter in the Stronghold]. 1630.
Decretum horribile. 1631.
Geuse-vesper. 1631.
Inwying der doorluchtige Schoole t'Amsterdam [Inauguration of the Illustrious School in Amsterdam]. 1632; edited by S. Albrecht, 1982.
Lyckklaght ann het vrouekoor, over het verlies van mijn ega [Funerary Lament for Female Choir, Concerning the Loss of My Wife]. 1635.
Brieven der Heilige Maeghden, Martelaaressen [Letters of the Holy Virgins, Martyrs]. 1642.
Aen de Beurs van Amsterdam [To the Stock Exchange of Amsterdam]. 1643.
Verspreide gedichten [Various Poems]. 1644.
Altaergeheimnissen [Altar Secrets]. 1645.
Eeuwgety der heilige Stede. 1645.
Poezij. 1650; selected poems translated by Agnes Budd and others, in *Dutch Crossing*, 8, 1979.
Inwydinghe van 't Stadhuis t'Amsterdam [Inauguration of the Town Hall in Amsterdam]. 1655.
Het stockske van Johan van Oldenbarnevelt. 1657.
Zeemagazijn. 1658.
Wildzang [Wild Song]. 1660.
Johannes de Boetgezant. 1662.
Bespiegelingen van Godt en godtsdienst [Reflections on God and Religion]. 1662.
De Heerlijkheit der Kercke [The Glory of the Church]. 1663.
Uitvaert van Maria van den Vondel [The Funeral of Maria van den Vondel]. 1668.

Plays

Het pascha (produced 1610). 1612.
Hierusalem verwoest [Jerusalem Destroyed]. 1620.
Palamedes. 1625.

Gysbreght van Aemstel (produced 1637). 1637; translated by Kristiaan P. Aercke, 1991.

Maeghden [Virgins]. 1639.

Gebroeders, Joseph in Dothan en Joseph in Egypten [Brothers]. 1640, reprinted 1983; *Joseph in Dothan* edited by A.M. Verstraeten and J. Salsmans, 1943.

Peter en Pauwels. 1641.

Maria Stuart. 1646; as *Mary Stuart, or, Tortured Majesty*, translated with introduction and notes by Kristiaan P. Aercke, 1996.

Leeuwendalers. 1647.

Salomon. 1648.

Lucifer. 1654; as *Lucifer*, translated by L. van Noppen, 1917; also translated by W. Kirkconnell, 1952; Noel Clark, 1990.

Salmoneus. 1657.

Jeptha. 1659.

Koning David in ballingschap [King David in Exile]. 1660.

Koning David herstelt [King David Recovers]. 1660.

Samson. 1660; as *Samson*, translated by W. Kirkconnell, 1964.

Adonias. 1661.

De Batavische gebroeders [The Batavian Brothers]. 1663.

Faeton. 1663.

Adam in ballingschap. 1664; as *Adam*, translated by W. Kirkconnell, 1952.

Zungchin. 1667.

Noah, of Ondergang der eerste Weerelt [Noah, or the Destruction of the First World]. 1667.

Other

Verscheiden werken [Various Works]. 1639–56.

Aenleidinge ter Nederduytsche dichtkunste. 1650; as *Introduction to Dutch Poetry*, translated by Lesley Gilbert and Theo Hermans, in *Dutch Crossing*, 29, 1986.

Toneelschilt. 1661.

Translator, *Hecuba*, by Seneca. 1626.

Translator, *Sofompaneas, of Joseph in't hof*, by Grotius. 1635.

Translator, *Heldinnebrieven*, by Ovid. 1646.

Translator, *Virgilius Maro* [Works]. 1646.

Translator, *Horatius Flaccus lierzangen* (in prose), by Horace. 1653.

Translator, *Koning Davids harpzangen* (Psalms of David). 1657.

Translator, *Koning Edipus*, by Sophocles. 1660.

Translator, *Elektra*, by Sophocles. 1661.

Translator, *Hyppolytus*, by Seneca. 1661.

Translator, *Iphigenia in Taurin*, by Euripides. 1666.

Translator, *Feniciaensche of Gebroeders van Thebe*, by Euripides. 1668.

Translator, *Herkules in Trachin*, by Sophocles. 1668.

Translator, *Herscheppinghen*, by Ovid. 1671.

*

Critical Studies: *Joost van den Vondel* by A. Baumgarten, 1882; *Studiën over Vondel* by G. Segers, 1896; *Vondelstudies* by P. Maximilianus, 1968; *Vondel bij gelegenheid* edited by K. Porteman and L. Roose, 1979; "Vondel, a Prophet in His Own Country" by P. King, in *Dutch Crossing*, 11, 1980; *Vondel* edited by M. Geesink and A. Boosers, 1987; *Het treurspel spant de kroon* by K. Langvik-Johannessen, 1987; *Vondel* edited by Marijke Spies and others, 1987; *Jetzt geh ich an den Rhein* edited by H. Vekemans and H. van Uffelen, 1987.

* * *

Religion played a predominant role in Joost van den Vondel's life, politics being the second in importance. The son of Anabaptists, a sect that was considered less than acceptable even by moderate Calvinists, Vondel converted to Catholicism in 1641, thus moving from a position to the extreme left of Calvinism to one to its extreme right. It was no wonder that his contemporaries did not understand him, and that he continued to write didactic and apologetic poems to justify his conduct. Vondel also wrote what seems to us an immense amount of public poetry, celebrating anything from the birth of an heir to the house of Orange to the Amsterdam Stock Exchange. Not all his public poetry was laudatory, however. Vondel was feared by many influential contemporaries for his sharp, satirical pen. He was quick to attack whatever wrongs he detected in the government of the city in which he lived, in his country as a whole, and in the Calvinist establishment that was trying to dominate it after the Netherlands had gained independence from Spain. Later he was to attack Calvinism on theological grounds, and to glorify the Roman Catholic faith which he had embraced in early middle age.

Vondel also wrote private poetry that is still considered moving: on the deaths of his children and his wife; on events that marked the lives of his friends; or on his own state of mind, tossed back and forth between anguish and surrender to faith. Vondel's place in Dutch literature does not, however, rest primarily on his poetry. Rather, he is remembered as both the greatest, and probably the most ineffectual, playwright of his time. During the first half of his career, his plays were modelled on those of Seneca; during the second half, under the influence of his friends Hugo Grotius and Gerardus Johannes Vossius, he tried to emulate Sophocles. In Amsterdam his plays were regularly produced, and sometimes forbidden, but they generally failed to achieve popular success. Large audiences flocked to productions of the plays written by Jan Vos and his followers, unfettered by any Aristotelian rules, and modelled after the English and Spanish theatre of the day. Vondel lashed out against this competition in the prefaces to many of his plays and, since many more of his prefaces have survived than have similar texts produced by the school of Vos, the mistaken assumption arose that Vondel was the most popular playwright of his time.

Vondel has become, however, the most respected dramatist *manqué* in Dutch literature which, with the possible exception of Herman Heijermans in the 19th century, has produced very little viable drama since Vondel's death. The recurrent theme of Vondel's later tragedies is what he called "*staetzucht.*" During his lifetime, he had seen the King of Spain deposed in the Netherlands, and had vivid memories of his parents' wanderings through Europe in search of a place to live where they could worship as they pleased. "*Staetzucht*" became to Vondel the epitome of all that threatened the complicated legal construction called a "state," designed to ensure a modest degree of individual liberty, and always, seemingly, at the mercy of those scheming to overthrow it, who will, like Lucifer, not hesitate to drag thousands along in their wake. Vondel's earlier tragedies, with a nod to the non-Aristotelian competition, included the odd gory description designed to titillate the audience. However, the tragedies of Vondel's maturity were modelled on Sophocles, dependent for their success on the sheer power of their poetic language and the way in which they presented and tried to resolve philosophical and theological problems.

Vondel was not only a poet and playwright; he also attempted to be a theologian, and succeeded in being a literary theorist. When newly converted, Vondel made what use he could of the popular genre of the didactic poem to propagate his Catholic views, albeit with limited success. The mature Vondel brought out an edition of his collected poems in 1650 (*Poezij*) and prefaced it with what has remained one of the most influential statements ever on Dutch poetics. He also tried his hand at the other required poetic genre of his time—the epic. For some years he worked on an epic based on the life of the emperor Constantine, the "Constantiniade," but finally gave up and burned the manuscript. However, with *Johannes de Boetgezant* he successfully introduced the biblical epic into Dutch literature.

Eventually the Bible was to prove Vondel's greatest challenge. Convinced of the superiority of the Roman Catholic religion, Vondel saw it as one of his tasks to prove that superiority also on the literary level, by showing that tragedies based on the Bible, the superior text, would of necessity have to be better than tragedies (Sophocles', for instance, or Euripides') based on mere Greek (or, in Seneca's case, Roman) mythology. It might be argued that Vondel's desire to prove the superiority of his new-found religion did little to bring his literary talent to maximum fruition. No critic has ever doubted Vondel's superior craftsmanship, nor the heights to which his creative genius was occasionally able to rise. Many critics, however, have pointed out that his obedience to rules, whether religious, political, or literary, was at the expense of excellence. The fact that Vondel is generally regarded as the national poet of the Netherlands testifies to the ironic poetic justice history occasionally metes out.

—André Lefevere

VÖRÖSMARTY, Mihály

Born: Kápolnásnyék, Hungary, 1 December 1800. **Education:** Educated at Cistercian school in Székesfehérvár and Piarist school in Pest, 1811–17; University of Pest 1817–20. **Family:** Married Laura Csajághy in 1843. **Career:** Tutor to Perczel family during early 1820s; full-time writer from 1826; became regular member of Academy in 1830; co-founder of Kisfaludy Társaság, 1836; co-founder of journals *Atheneum* and *Figyelmező* [Monitor], 1837; took active part in 1848 Revolution; parliamentary deputy, then high court judge, 1848–49; after Hungary's War of Independence forced to hide to avoid persecution, 1849–50; retired to family village in 1853. **Awards:** Academy prize 1833, 1834, 1839, 1842. **Died:** 19 November 1855.

PUBLICATIONS

Collections

Minden munkái [Complete Works], edited by Pál Gyulai. 12 vols., 1861–64.
Kiadatlan költeményei [Unpublished Poetry], edited by Frigyes Brisits. 1926.
Összes drámai művei [Complete Dramatic Works], edited by Károly Horváth and Dezső Tóth. 1955.
Összes művei [Complete Works], edited by Károly Horváth and Dezső Tóth. 18 vols., 1960–65.

Verse

Zalán futása [The Flight of Zalán]. 1825.
A két szomszédvár [Two Neighbouring Castles]. 1832.
Munkái [Works]. 3 vols., 1833.
Újabb munkái [Recent Works]. 4 vols., 1840.
Minden munkái [Complete Works]. 10 vols., 1845–48.
Három rege [Three Tales]. 1851.

Plays

Salamon király [King Solomon]. 1827.
A bújdosók [The Exiled]. 1830.
Csongor és Tünde [Csongor and Tünde] (produced 1879). 1831.
Vérnász [Blood Wedding] (produced 1834). 1834.
Árpád ébredése [The Wake of Árpád] (produced 1837). 1837.
Marót bán [Ban Marót] (produced 1838). 1838.
Czillei és a Hunyadiak [Czillei and the Hunyadis] (produced 1844). 1845.

Other

Translator, *Arabian Nights*. 11 vols., 1829–33.
Translator, *King Lear*, by Shakespeare. 1856.
Translator, *Julius Caesar*, by Shakespeare. 1864.

*

Bibliography: *A Vörösmarty-irodalom repertóriuma, 1825–1899* [The Repertory of Vörösmarty's Works], in *Vörösmarty emlékkönyve*, 1900; *A Magyar Tudományos Akadémia Vörösmarty-kéziratainak jegyzéke* [List of Vörösmarty Manuscripts Held by the Hungarian Academy of Sciences], 1928; *Hungarian Authors: A Bibliographical Handbook* by Albert Tezla, 1970; *A magyar irodalomtörténet bibliográfiája, 1772–1849* by György Kókay, 1975.

Critical Studies:: "Vörösmarty Mihály" by Mihály Babits, in *Irodalmi problémák*, 1917; *Vörösmarty tanulmányok* [Essays on Vörösmarty] by Antal Szerb, in *Minerva*, 1930; *Vörösmarty Mihály* by Dezső Tóth, 1957; "Mihály Vörömarty" by D. Mervyn Jones, in *Five Hungarian Writers*, 1966; *Vörösmarty drámái* by János Horváth, 1969.

* * *

Mihály Vörösmarty was the best and most influential poet of Hungarian romanticism. He excelled in the field of both epic and lyrical poetry and also wrote plays, at least one of which is regarded as a Hungarian classic. Born into an impoverished noble family, the young Vörösmarty earned his living by private teaching and it was during the first half of the 1820s, when he was employed as instructor to the children of the Perczel family, that he took to writing poetry and historical plays. He scored his first success with the long epic poem *Zalán futása* [The Flight of Zalán], which dealt with an episode of the conquest of Hungary by the Hungarian tribes in the 9th century AD: with the Hungarian Árpád's victory over the Bulgarian leader, Zalán, and the latter's flight to Belgrade. Apart from an account of historical events, based on a story by "Anonymus," a Hungarian chronicler, this epic has other sub-plots such as the love story of Ete, a young

Hungarian warrior, and the beautiful Hajna, as well as a parallel action to fighting on earth in heaven, where Hadúr, the God of Hungarians, defeats his arch-enemy Ármány (''Intrigue,'' a name based on the Zoroastrian deity Ahriman). *Zalán futása* is in flowing hexameters (which sound natural in Hungarian) and contains descriptive passages of great beauty, attesting to Vörösmarty's mastery of the language. The foreword to the epic, with its evocation of the glories of Hungarian past, stands as an important literary contribution to the awakening of Hungarian national awareness which ushered in the Age of Reform, the age of Széchenyi, and Lajos Kossuth.

Between 1825 and 1832 Vörösmarty wrote several other epic poems, of which ''Cserhalom'' and ''Eger'' deal with heroic episodes of Hungarian history, whereas ''Tündérvölgy'' [The Valley of the Fairies] and the unfinished ''Délsziget'' [Island of the South] are tales immersed in a timeless and exotic world of Romantic imagination. Not unlike Aleksandr Pushkin and Adam Mickiewicz, Vörösmarty also used bold Oriental imagery in most of these shorter epics, which enchanted the reader with their supple and expressive language and wide range of sentiments. The last of these epics, *A két szomszédvár* [Two Neighbouring Castles], the story of a 13th-century family feud, is a tale of vendetta-duplicating gothic horrors. In 1831 Vörösmarty wrote a poetic drama, *Csongor és Tünde* [Csongor and Tünde], which is now regarded as his best play. He based the plot on an old Hungarian fairy story: Csongor is a young ''seeker of happiness'' who falls in love with the fairy maiden Tünde but is prevented from uniting with her by the intrigues of the wicked witch Mirigy. Csongor, during his adventures, has a Sancho Panza-like companion, Balga, whose lover is Tünde's fairy attendant, Ilma. The latter represent an often comic realism which is contrasted with Csongor's dreamy idealism. The play, although it ultimately vindicates the power of love, is pessimistic in its outlook. Man's search for happiness in society is futile and his ''cosmic'' prospects are bleak. ''Love'' is, in fact, escapism from man's philosophical dilemmas, for which there is no apparent solution.

As a lyrical poet, Vörösmarty wrote both private and public verse. His ''Szózat'' [Appeal], a dramatic survey of Hungarian history, ends with a passionate assertion of patriotism. The short ''A Guttenberg-albumba'' [For a Book in Honour of Gutenberg] celebrates the invention of printing and expresses the hope in mankind's progress: ''When light spreads from the West to the East, when the heart / Knowing of sacrifice, ennobles the mind'' (translated by Clive Wilmer and George Gömöri), but the meditations in ''Gondolatok a könyvtárban'' [Thoughts in a Library] are already full of doubts about mankind's capacity to reform. Vörösmarty's fears about the precariousness of progress became acute in ''Az emberek'' [Mankind], a poem written after the peasant revolt of Galicia where the gap between social issues and the cause of national independence had become painfully obvious. However, before 1848, Vörösmarty was active both in politics and in cultural life, working for the cause of reform: during the War of Independence in 1848–49 he was first parliamentary deputy and then High Court Judge. The defeat of the national cause, however, and the brutal retaliation that followed left an indelible imprint on his mind. In the last six years of his life he wrote very few poems, although two are extremely powerful: ''Előszó'' [Prelude], with its apocalyptic, cosmic images, showing the earth ''turned grey'' after the catastrophe, and ''A vén cigány'' [The Old Gypsy Fiddler], the poet's monologue to a gypsy fiddler which in its seven stanzas displays a wide range of emotions, from rage and despair, verging on madness, to the hope of a better, peaceful life in which ''a Noah's Ark will arrive / to enclose in it a new world.'' While this imagery projects the possibility of a new beginning after a cataclysm, Vörösmarty's internal drama reflects the state of many European minds after the failure of the revolutionary and reformist movements of 1848–49.

—George Gömöri

WALTHER VON DER VOGELWEIDE

Born: Austria, possibly in the Tyrol, probably about 1170. **Career:** Active at the ducal court in Vienna and influenced there by Reinmar, before 1198; worked in numerous princely courts of southern and central Germany in the next 20 years; mentioned in the household accounts of Bishop Wolfger of Passau in 1203; sought the patronage of Emperor Frederick II after 1212 and received a grant of land near Würzburg a few years later; last datable poem c. 1227. **Died:** c. 1230.

PUBLICATIONS

Verse

I Saw the World: Sixty Poems from Walther von der Vogelweide, translated by Ian G. Colvin. 1938.
Poems, translated by Edwin H. Zeydel and Bayard Quincy Morgan. 1952.
Gedichte, edited by P. Wapnewski, with modern German translations. 1962.
Die Gedichte, edited by K. Lachmann, revised by Hugo Kuhn. 1965.
Die Lieder, edited by Friedrich Maurer. 2 vols., 1967–74.

*

Bibliography: *Bibliographie zu Walther von der Vogelweide* by Manfred Scholz, 1969; *Walther von der Vogelweide* by K.H. Halbach, 1973.

Critical Studies: *Walther von der Vogelweide* by George F. Jones, 1968; *Walther von der Vogelweide: Eine Einführung* edited by Gerhard Hahn, 1986; *Walther von der Vogelweide: Höfische Idealität und konkrete Erfahrung* by Theodor Nolte, 1991; *Walther van der Vogelweide für Anfänger* by Hermann Reichert, 1992; *Walther von der Vogelweide in Oesterreich* by J.E. Wackernell, 1996.

* * *

Walther von der Vogelweide still holds the leading position among medieval German lyric poets which contemporaries accorded him—both for his original development of the *Minnesang* (courtly love lyric), and for his striking *Spruchdichtung* (songs of social commentary), two genres with distinct formal and thematic criteria. As poetic interpreter of the social scene Walther von der Vogelweide was not merely the first but the greatest German, if not indeed medieval, political poet. His career spanned the four decades from the 1190s to the 1220s. In the 19th century Walther von der Vogelweide came at times to be idealized as mythical spokesman for the German concept of the Reich, and it is only in recent decades that his poetry, in both genres, and his personality have together been better apprehended as dialectic reflection of tensions between ethical ideality and social reality.

Walther von der Vogelweide's love poetry ranges from juvenilia, somewhat laboured in style and strongly imitative, to superbly crafted lyrics which bestow upon traditional themes and motifs startling simplicity and spontaneity. *Minnesang* derived largely from French *trouvère* lyric; the poet extols the courtly lady in a love which ennobles him although—or rather because—it lacks the prospect of consummation. The genre involves speculation about the nature of love and the emotions of the lovers, in a kaleidoscope of stock motifs and epithets. Faced with conventional treatments of emotional aesthetic experiences Walther von der Vogelweide rooted himself strongly in social reality and transcended the vacuum in which love lyric seemed to be practised. Proceeding from ethical and emotional potential of males and females, he evolved a stimulating, critical, personal ideal: the girl of humble station embodying the purest type of womanly grace. Here Walther von der Vogelweide broke with Reinmar, the mentor of his youth in Vienna, and irony and role playing contribute to elements of parody in his love poetry, which posits new gender roles. Interaction with his audience is a notable feature of Walther von der Vogelweide's love poems, and reciprocity plays a major part; so, also, does humour, and above all direct, frank self-assertion, qualities central to his political poetry, too. *Minnesang* seems to have been the prerogative of members of the courtly community, or at least of resident poets, and Walther von der Vogelweide's practice of this genre as a professional poet may have led to role conflict. Walther von der Vogelweide's lyric embraces the range of the Troubadours, then, but also that of the Latin Wandering Scholars, to whom he shows close affinities.

Walther von der Vogelweide was active as political poet in the troubled decades of German affairs after the accession of Pope Innocent III and the death of Henry VI. In the struggle between Staufen and Welf for the Imperial crown after 1198 he worked for various royal and princely patrons including the monarchs Philipp, Otto, and Frederick. His propaganda poems reflect the conflicts which the need for patronage imposed, and his frequent changes of patron invite the charge of opportunism. In fact, it is clear that Walther von der Vogelweide campaigned consistently for the unity and stability of Germany, seeing the prestige of an acknowledged emperor as the best guarantor of peace at home and as the sole effective check on papal power without and princely pretension within. Walther von der Vogelweide's political poems constitute in effect the inauguration of the genre of *Spruchdichtung*, for previous verses in this sphere were slight, maxims on proverbial themes. His poems contain pregnant theoretical statements on the nature and duties of kingship, couched in striking and vigorous language, with powerful imagery: the imperial crown occurs repeatedly as embodiment of the ideal of the Empire; the monarch is frequently extolled in Christological or Trinitarian terms. As overriding goal Walther von der Vogelweide posits the order embodied in God's creation. German disorder he contrasts to the ordered ranks of the animal kingdoms; papal interference in the sphere of the monarchy he repudiates as abuse of the pope's very blessing in the imperial coronation. There has been much debate as to the relationship between the single strophes and the thematic cycles of songs set to a common melody; in each case the strophe must be seen in its concrete performance before a critical courtly patron and public. In a host of religious and didactic poems

Walther von der Vogelweide appeals for ordered balance in individual conduct (*mâze*), and stresses the manly virtues of *triuwe* ("keeping faith with others") and *staete* ("steadfastness"). One of his best-known songs (formerly called the "elegy") begins with the powerful evocation of the sense of loss and alienation of an old man returning to the landscape of his youth and finally reveals itself to be a recruiting song for a Crusade sponsored by the emperor.

Perhaps Walther von der Vogelweide's most startling facet is his enormous self-assertion: while showing solidarity with professional itinerant poets he distances himself from inferior entertainers; despite the precarious position held by a travelling poet he claims for himself the respect and social integration which his powerful art justified, the right to "walk upright like a crane," to be accepted by the courtly public as "brother." On occasion he expresses gratitude for gifts that honour him; at times he is prepared to break with a patron rather than forego due recognition. His poetic fortune can be detected in both love lyric and political song, and he was wont in both genres to see crises in his own life in connection with the crises of German society. Repeatedly he addresses himself directly to princes, pope, and emperors alike; on occasion he adopts the biblical prophet's pose as *"penseur"*; once he even claims the title of *vrônebote* ("messenger of the Lord"). For his expressive enrichment of the fledgeling genres of love lyric and political verse in Germany Walther von der Vogelweide stands justified in his high poetic claim.

—Lewis Jillings

WEDEKIND, (Benjamin) Frank(lin)

Born: Hanover, Germany, 24 July 1864. Brought up in Switzerland. **Education:** Educated at Gemeindeknabenschule and Bezirksschule, Lenzburg; Kantonsschule, Aarau; universities of Lausanne, 1884, Munich, 1884–85, and Zurich, 1888. **Family:** Married the actress Tilly Newes (died 1917); two daughters. **Career:** Worked in advertising, 1866–68, secretary with a circus, 1888; journalist and actor: performed in several of his own plays; visited Paris, London, Zurich, Berlin; lived mainly in Munich. **Died:** 9 March 1918.

PUBLICATIONS

Collections

Gesammelte Werke, edited by A. Kutscher and R. Friedenthal. 9 vols., 1912–21.
Ausgewählte Werke, edited by Fritz Strich. 5 vols., 1924.
Prosa, Dramen, Verse, edited by Hans-Georg Maier. 2 vols., 1954–60.
Werke, edited by Manfred Hahn. 3 vols., 1969.
Plays: One, translated by Edward Bond and Elisabeth Bond-Pablé. 1993.

Plays

Der Schnellmaler (produced 1916). 1889.

Kinder und Narren. 1891; revised version, as *Die junge Welt* (produced 1908), 1897.
Frühlings Erwachen (produced 1906). 1891; as *The Awakening of Spring*, translated by Francis J. Ziegler, 1909; as *Spring's Awakening*, translated by S.A. Eliot, in *Tragedies of Sex*, 1923; also translated by Frances Fawcett and Stephen Spender, in *Five Tragedies of Sex*, 1952; Eric Bentley, in *The Modern Theatre*, 6, 1960; as *Spring Awakening*, translated by Tom Osborn, 1969; Edward Bond, 1980; Ted Hughes, 1995.
Lulu. 1913; as *The Lulu Plays*, translated by C.R. Mueller, 1967; as *Lulu*, 1971; translated by Wes Williams, version by Nicholas Wright, 2001.
   Der Erdgeist (produced 1898). 1895; as *Erdgeist*, translated by S.A. Eliot, 1914; as *Earth-Spirit*, translated by Eliot, in *Tragedies of Sex*, 1923; also translated by Frances Fawcett and Stephen Spender, in *Five Tragedies of Sex*, 1952.
   Die Büchse der Pandora (produced 1904). 1904; as *Pandora's Box*, 1918; also translated by Frances Fawcett and Stephen Spender, in *Five Tragedies of Sex*, 1952; as *Frank Wedekind's The First Lulu*, translated by Eric Bentley, 1994.
Der Kammersänger (produced 1899). 1899; as *Heart of a Tenor*, 1913; as *The Tenor*, translated by André Tridon, 1921.
Der Liebestrank (produced 1900). 1899.
Der Marquis von Keith (produced 1901). 1901; edited by Wolfgang Hartwig, 1965; as *The Marquis of Keith*, translated by Beatrice Gottlieb, in *From the Modern Repertoire* 2, edited by Eric Bentley, 1957; also translated by C.R. Mueller, in *The Modern Theatre*, edited by R.W. Corrigan, 1964.
So ist das Leben (produced 1902). 1902; as *König Nicolo*, 1911; as *Such Is Life*, translated by Francis J. Ziegler, 1912.
Die Kaiserin von Neufundland (pantomime; produced 1902).
Hidalla; oder, Sein und Haben (produced 1905). 1904; as *Karl Hetmann, der Zwergriese*, in *Gesammelte Werke*, 1913.
Totentanz (produced 1906). 1906; as *Tod und Teufel*, 1909; as *Death and Devil*, translated by Frances Fawcett and Stephen Spender, in *Five Tragedies of Sex*, 1952.
Musik (produced 1908). 1908.
Die Zensur (produced 1909). 1908.
Oaha (produced 1911). 1908; as *Till Eulenspiegel*, 1916.
Der Stein der Weisen (produced 1911). 1909.
In allen Sätteln gerecht. 1910.
Mit allen Hunden gehetzt. 1910.
In allen Wassern gewaschen. 1910.
Schloss Wetterstein (produced 1917). 1912; as *Castle Wetterstein*, translated by Frances Fawcett and Stephen Spender, in *Five Tragedies of Sex*, 1952.
Franziska (produced 1912). 1912.
Simson; oder, Scham und Eifersucht (produced 1914). 1914.
Bismarck (produced 1926). 1916.
Überfürchtenichts (produced 1919). 1917.
Herakles (produced 1919). 1917.
Das Sonnen Spektrum (produced 1922). As *The Solar Spectrum*, translated by D. Faehl and E. Vaughn, in *Tulane Drama Review*, (4), 1959.
Tragedies of Sex (includes *Spring's Awakening*; *Earth-Spirit*; *Pandora's Box*; *Damnation!*), translated by S.A. Eliot. 1923.
Ein Genussmensch, edited by Fritz Strich. 1924.

Five Tragedies of Sex (includes *Earth-Spirit*; *Pandora's Box*; *Castle Wetterstein*; *Death and the Devil*; *Spring's Awakening*), translated by Frances Fawcett and Stephen Spender. 1952; as *The Lulu Plays and Other Sex Tragedies*, 1972.

Fiction

Die Fürstin Russalka. 1897.
Mine-Haha; oder, Über die körperliche Erziehung der jungen Mädchen. 1901.
Feuerwerk. 1905.

Verse

Lautenlieder. 1920.
Ich hab meine Tante geschlachtet: Lautenlieder und "Simplizissimus"-Gedichte, edited by Manfred Hahn. 1967.

Other

Schauspielkunst: Ein Glossarium. 1910.
Gesammelte Briefe, edited by Fritz Strich. 2 vols., 1924.
Selbstdarstellung, edited by Willi Reich. 1954.
Der vermummte Herr: Briefe 1881—1917, edited by Wolfdietrich Rasch. 1967.
Die Tagebücher: Ein erotisches Leben, edited by Gerhard Hay. 1986; as *Diary of an Erotic Life*, translated by W.E. Yuill, 1990.

*

Bibliography: *Frank Wedekind* by A. Kutscher, 3 vols., 1922–31.

Critical Studies: *Frank Wedekind* by Sol Gittlemann, 1955; *Wedekind, Leben und Werk* by Arthur Kutscher, 2nd edition, 1964; *Frank Wedekind und das Theater*, 1964, and *Frank Wedekind in Selbstzeugnissen und Bilddokumenten*, 1974, both by Günter Seehaus; *Frank Wedekind* by Alan Best, 1975; *Der Theaterdichter Frank Wedekind* by H.J. Irmer, 1975; *Frank Wedekind* by Hartmut Vinçon, 1986; *The Sexual Circus: Wedekind's Theatre of Subversion* by Elizabeth Boa, 1987; *Hauptmann, Wedekind and Schnitzler* by Peter Skrine, 1989; *The Ironic Dissident: Frank Wedekind in the View of His Critics* by Ward B. Lewis, 1997; *Modernism and Masculinity: Mann, Wedekind, Kandinsky Through World War I* by Gerald N. Izenberg, 2000.

* * *

Few writers have ever aroused as much controversy as did Frank Wedekind during the Wilhelmine era in Germany. Celebrated in literary circles, he held views and used methods of expressing them that were bound—and often calculated—to antagonize the establishment and shock the general public. As a result he was frequently censored and banned on grounds of obscenity, immorality, and subversiveness; on one occasion, having circulated some sarcastic verses about the Kaiser, he was imprisoned for *lèse-majesté*. In his private life—which was marked by youthful conflicts with his wealthy father, an early affair with Strindberg's estranged wife Frida, quarrels with professional associates, and a stormy marriage to the actress Tilly Newes—he combined a disregard for conventional behaviour with a desire for upperclass respectability.

In his plays, stories, and essays, as well as his satirical sketches, poems, and ballads—many of which he published in the magazine *Simplizissimus* or sang in the cabaret "Die elf Scharfrichter" [The Eleven Executioners] in Munich—Wedekind violently attacked the moral, spiritual, and political beliefs of the bourgeoisie, and particularly what he considered its perniciously hypocritical attitude to sex. Inspired by Nietzsche's denunciation of the prevailing ethical standards and sharing some of Freud's insights, he set out to liberate primitive irrational instinct from the constraints of rational civilization. It was with these ideas in mind that Dürrenmatt described him as an "extreme moralist" and Brecht claimed that "he belonged with Tolstoi and Strindberg among the great educators of the new Europe," while Thomas Mann in a double-edged compliment called his writings "profoundly questionable and shimmering with infinite cunning."

Best known as a playwright, Wedekind disowned both the classical tradition and contemporary naturalism. The actor and writer Friedrich Kayssler in particular congratulated him: "You have strangled the naturalist beast of verisimilitude and brought the element of playfulness to the stage." Drawing on various types of popular entertainment—circus, funfair, pantomime, vaudeville, grand-guignol—he replaced the "closed" form, which dominated the mainstream theatre, with "open" structures involving disjointed episodic actions, puppet-like characters moved by their creator's idiosyncrasies regardless of psychological or circumstantial motivation, and distorted dialogues incongruously combining polished rhetorical and poetic devices with raw colloquialisms, evoking a sense of non-communication, and displaying a savagely cynical wit. Set in a murky demi-monde of bohemians, adventurers, prostitutes, deviants, and criminals, culminating in sadomasochistic sexual excesses and death by murder or suicide, mixing melodrama and slapstick, swinging between passion and provocation, revelling in lurid sensations and steeped in black humour, his grotesque tragicomedies are outstanding examples of "non-Aristotelian" drama. Influenced by Lenz, Büchner, and Grabbe, he became in his turn a decisive influence on Expressionism, Dadaism, the epic theatre of Brecht, and the theatres of cruelty and the absurd. Of his performers he demanded a harshly stylized technique of acting, which he himself demonstrated by appearing, according to Brecht, in a variety of roles as an "ugly, brutal, dangerous" figure with a "metallic, hard, dry voice nobody could forget." His approach as author, director, and actor is epitomized by a statement in the reflections entitled "Schauspielkunst": "I really believe that for 20 years our literary theatre has been, firstly, far too little theatre and, secondly, far too literary. I believe that for 20 years the literary theatre has provided far too little pleasure and far too little entertainment." His own plays, by contrast, are carefully designed to offer pleasure and entertainment of a theatrical rather than literary kind.

Wedekind's most successful plays include *Der Kammersänger* (*The Tenor*), *So ist das Leben* (*Such Is Life*), and *Hidalla; oder, Sein und Haben* (also known as *Karl Hetmann, der Zwergriese* [Karl Hetmann, the Dwarf-Giant]), all of which dramatize, ironically and more or less autobiographically, the plight of imaginative nonconformists in a degenerate middleclass environment that they reject and that rejects them. He himself regarded *Der Marquis von Keith* (*The Marquis of Keith*), in which the schemes of "a Don Quijote of hedonism and a Don Quijote of morality" are equally thwarted by their external circumstances and their inner contradictions, as his "artistically most mature and intellectually most substantial piece" and the title hero as "the best part I have written." However, his masterpieces are two tragicomedies concerned primarily with sexual themes. The first, *Frühlings Erwachen* (*Spring Awakening*), juxtaposes the sympathetic portrayal of teenagers in the throes of adolescence—some of whom die while others emerge into a life of pleasure—with vicious caricatures of prudish or authoritatian parents and teachers. Claiming to have drawn on "personal experiences or experiences of my schoolfellows," and rebutting accusations of "pure pornography" and "dryest didacticism" alike, Wedekind stresses the "carefree humour" of the much-invoked "children's tragedy." The second, comprising *Der Erdgeist* (*Earth-Spirit*) and *Die Büchse der Pandora* (*Pandora's Box*)—also famous as Alban Berg's opera *Lulu* and G.W. Pabst's film *Pandora's Box*—chronicles the escapades of a demonic vamp, praised in the prologue as "a true animal, a wild beautiful animal," who ruins a succession of bizarre lovers before she is reduced to a cheap streetwalker and killed by Jack the Ripper. Wedekind argues that he wanted to "exclude all those concepts which are logically untenable, for example, love, fidelity, gratitude" in order to demonstrate the defeat of "human consciousness" by the "human unconscious." In both works Wedekind glorifies his concept of uninhibited natural impulses, pitted against a repressed and repressive society bent on corrupting and destroying them. His rare comments on his own works, including those quoted above, are found in the jottings entitled "Was ich mir dabei dachte."

It is debatable whether Wedekind reverses the accepted social and aesthetic norms in order to indulge in his notorious "Satanism" or to make an oblique case for a genuine morality. What is certain is that he will long be remembered as the author of some remarkably original plays and as one of the great innovators of European drama.

—Ladislaus Löb

See the essays on *The Lulu Plays* and *Spring Awakening*.

WEISS, Peter (Ulrich)

Born: Nowawes (now Neubabelsberg), Germany, 8 November 1916; naturalized Swedish citizen, 1945. **Education:** Educated at Volksschule and Gymnasium, Bremen-Horn; private art lessons, 1932; Rackow-Handelsschule, Berlin, 1933; Polytechnic School of Photography, London, 1935; Kunstakademie, Prague, 1937–38; guest student, Art Academy, Stockholm, 1942. **Family:** Married the artist and designer Gunilla Palmstierna in 1964; one son (adopted) and one daughter. **Career:** Painter, writer, and film producer; moved with his family to London, 1934, then to Czechoslovakia, lived in Sweden, after 1939; draftsman and designer for his father's textile business, 1939–42; solo exhibitions of his paintings, Sweden, 1941–46; Berlin correspondent, *Stockholms-Tidningen*, 1947; joined the Swedish Experimental Film Studio, 1952; travelled to North Vietnam, 1968; travelled to writers' congress, Moscow, 1974; retrospective art exhibition toured Europe, 1976. Wrote in both Swedish and German. **Awards:** Veillon prize (with Italo Calvino), 1963; Lessing prize (Hamburg), 1965; Heinrich Mann prize (East Berlin), 1966; Tony award (United States), 1966; New York Drama Critics Circle award, 1966; Carl Albert Anderson prize (Stockholm), 1967; Thomas Dehler prize, 1978. Cologne literature prize, 1981; Büchner prize, 1982; City of Bremen prize, 1982; Swedish Theatre Critics' prize, 1982; De Nios prize, 1982. Honorary doctorates: Wilhelm Peck University, Rostock, 1982; Philips University, Marburg, 1982. **Died:** 10 May 1982.

PUBLICATIONS

Plays

Der Turm (broadcast 1949; produced on stage 1950). 1963; as *The Tower*, translated by Michael Benedict and George Wellwarth, 1967.

Die Versicherung (produced 1971). 1952.

Ein Traumspiel, from a play by Strindberg. 1963.

Nacht mit Gästen (produced 1963). 1963; as *Night with Guests*, 1968.

Die Verfolgung und Ermordung Jean Paul Marats, dargestellt durch die Schauspielgruppe des Hospizes zu Charenton unter Anleitung des Herrn de Sade (produced 1964). 1964; as *The Persecution and Assassination of Jean-Paul Marat as Performed by the Inmates of the Asylum of Charenton under the Direction of the Marquis de Sade*, translated by Geoffrey Skelton, adapted by Adrian Mitchell, 1965; usually known by its abbreviated title, *Marat/Sade*, in both English and German.

Die Ermittlung: Oratorium in elf Gesängen (produced 1965). 1965; as *The Investigation: Oratorio in Eleven Cantos*, translated by Alexander Gross, 1966; also translated by Jon Swan and Ulu Grosbard, 1966.

Gesang vom lusitanischen Popanz (produced 1967). 1968; as *Song of the Lusitanian Bogey*, translated by Lee Baxandall, in *Two Plays*, 1970.

Diskurs über die Vorgeschichte und den Verlauf des lang andauernden Befreiungskrieges in Viet Nam als Beispiel für die Notwendigkeit des bewaffneten Kampfes der Unterdrückten gegen ihre Unterdrücker, sowie über die Versuche der Vereinigten Staaten von Amerika, die Grundlagen der Revolution zu vernichten (produced 1968). 1967; as *Discourse on the Progress of the Prolonged War of Liberation in Viet Nam*, translated by Geoffrey Skelton, in *Two Plays*, 1970.

Wie dem Herrn Mockinpott das Leiden ausgetrieben wird (produced 1968). In *Dramen*, 1968; as *How Mr. Mockinpott Was Cured of His Sufferings*, translated by Christopher Holmes, in *Contemporary German Theatre*, edited by Michael Roloff, 1972.

Dramen. 2 vols., 1968.

Trotzki im Exil (produced 1970). 1970; as *Trotsky in Exile*, translated by Geoffrey Skelton, 1971.

Hölderlin (produced 1971). 1971.

Der Prozess, from the novel by Kafka (produced 1975).

Stücke. 2 vols., 1976–77.

Der Vater, from a play by Strindberg. In *August Strindberg: Drei Stücke*, 1981.

Fräulein Julie, from a play by Strindberg. In *August Strindberg: Drei Stücke*, 1981.

Der neue Prozess (produced 1982). As *The New Trial*, translated with introduction by James Rolleston and Kai Evers, 2001.

Marat/Sade; The Investigation; and The Shadow of the Coachman's Body, edited by Robert Cohen. 1998.

Radio Plays: *Der Turm*, 1949.

Fiction

Duellen (in Swedish). 1953.

Der Schatten des Körpers des Kutschers. 1960; as *The Shadow of the Coachman's Body*, translated by E.B. Garside and Rosemarie

Waldrop, in *Bodies and Shadows*, 1970; also translated by S.M. Cupitt, in *The Conversation of the Three Walkers and the Shadow of the Coachman's Body*, 1972.

Abschied von den Eltern. 1961; as *The Leavetaking*, translated by Christopher Levenson, 1962.

Fluchtpunkt. 1962; as *Vanishing Point*, translated by Christopher Levenson, 1966.

Das Gespräch der drei Gehenden. 1963; as *Conversations of the Three Wayfarers*, translated by E.B. Garside and Rosemarie Waldrop, in *Bodies and Shadows*, 1970; as *The Conversation of the Three Walkers*, translated by S.M. Cupitt, in *The Conversation of the Three Walkers and the Shadow of the Coachman's Body*, 1972. *Exile* (includes *The Leavetaking* and *Vanishing Point*). 1968.

Die Ästhetik des Widerstandes. 3 vols., 1975–81.

Verse

Frän ö till ö [From Island to Island] (in Swedish). 1947.
De besegrade [The Vanquished] (in Swedish). 1948.

Other

Dokument I. 1949.
Avantgardefilm. 1956.
10 Arbeitspunkte eines Autors in der geteilten Welt. 1965.
Notizen zum kulturellen Leben der Demokratischen Republik Viet Nam. 1968; as *Notes on the Cultural Life of the Democratic Republic of Vietnam,* 1970.
Das Material und die Modelle: Notizen zum dokumentarischen Theater. 1968.
Rapporte. 2 vols., 1968–71.
Aufsätze, Journale, Arbeitspunkte: Schriften zu Kunst und Literatur, edited by Manfred Haiduk. 1979.
Der Maler Peter Weiss: Bilder, Zeichnungen, Collagen, Filme. 1980.
Notizbücher 1971–1980. 2 vols., 1981.

*

Critical Studies: *Peter Weiss: A Search for Affinities* by Ian Hilton, 1970; *Dialog und Mord: Eine Interpretation des Marat/Sade von Peter Weiss* by Brigitte Keller-Schumacher, 1973; *Von Dante zu Hölderlin: Traditionswall und Engagement in Werk von Peter Weiss* by Wolfgang Kehn, 1975; *Peter Weiss* by Otto F. Best, 1976; *Der Dramatiker Peter Weiss* by Manfred Haiduk, 1977; *The Theme of Alienation in the Prose of Weiss* by Kathleen A. Vance, 1981; *Peter Weiss* by Heinrich Vormweg, 1981; *Peter Weiss* edited by Rainer Gerlach, 1984, and *Peter Weiss im Gespräch* edited by Gerlach and Matthias Richter, 1986; *The Mother in the Work and Life of Peter Weiss* by Åsa Eldh, 1990; *Ästhetik, Revolte, Widerstand: zum literarischen Werk von Peter Weiss* by Thomas Hocke, 1990; *Understanding Peter Weiss* by Robert Cohen, 1993.

* * *

When Bertolt Brecht died in East Berlin in 1956, Peter Weiss was already 40. His own unexpected death in 1982 at the age of 65 robbed the world of the legitimate successor to the great Marxist dramatist from whom, Weiss had said, he had learned "clarity . . . , the necessity of making clear the social question in a play."

"Change the world, it needs it," Brecht had demanded; Weiss likewise believed that it was absolutely necessary "to write with the point of trying to influence or change society," and in his last novel, *Die Ästhetik des Widerstandes* [The Aesthetics of Resistance] he wrote that "we should never be in a position to change our situation as long as we remained prisoners of our incompleteness (*Halbheit*) and our alienation."

Brecht died in a country which he believed was at least *trying* to bring about the changes for which he yearned; Weiss, a German writer, but resident in Stockholm since 1939, could claim that he had seen changes in Western society—the anti-authoritarian students' revolts of 1968 and the advance in the cause of feminism, for example—which might just herald the dawn of that juster, socialist society.

The three prose works—the "micro-novel" *Der Schatten des Körpers des Kutschers* (*The Shadow of the Coachman's Body*), *Abschied von den Eltern* (*The Leavetaking*), and *Fluchtpunkt* (*Vanishing Point*), the last two in particular describing in autobiographical manner a young man's search for an identity—brought Weiss international recognition in the early 1960s. His move from writing novels to writing for the stage began with the premiere in 1964 of his best-known play, usually shortened to *Marat/Sade*, a famous example of "total theatre" in Artaud's then modish "theatre-of-cruelty" style.

The imagined confrontation of the individualist, authoritarian Marquis de Sade with the demagogic, revolutionary Marat, set against the background of the frightening, obscene gyrations of the demented inmates, was Weiss's attempt to show why society must be changed. Murat's "socialist" solution was mirrored in the next important plays—*Die Ermittlung* (*The Investigation*) and *The Viet Nam Discourse*—which coincided with the growing anti-American trend in world opinion, in particular of the younger generation. *The Investigation*, a documentary play based on the transcripts of the Auschwitz Concentration Camp trials, castigated the world of the students' fathers who had "permitted" these atrocities, while the Vietnam play fuelled that discontent at the massive United States involvement in a war against what was termed a "peasant population." (The angry critical reception of his next plays, *Trotzki im Exil* [*Trotsky in Exile*] and *Hölderlin*, led to Weiss's first serious heart attack.)

His last important work, the three-volume novel *Die Ästhetik des Widerstandes* [The Aesthetics of Resistance], which dealt with the important international crises and wars during Weiss's lifetime, shows the progressive (and, for Weiss, depressing) de-humanization of mankind to which "resistance" must be offered.

This gifted literary artist, painter, and film-buff made a major contribution to European culture and has an honoured place among those European intellectuals who have sought to make the world a better place to live in.

—Kenneth S. Whitton

See the essays on *The Investigation* and *Marat/Sade*.

WEÖRES, Sándor

Born: Szombathely, Hungary, 22 June 1913. **Education:** Educated at elementary schools in Pápa and Csönge; high school in Szombathely, Győr, and Sopron; University of Pécs, Ph.D. in philosophy 1939.

Family: Married the poet Amy Károlyi in 1947. **Career:** Visited the Far East in 1937; librarian in Pécs, Székesfehérvár, and Budapest, 1941–50; co-editor of *Sorsunk* [Our Destiny]; travelled in Italy, 1947–48; freelance writer from 1950; visited China in 1959 and England several times in the 1960s. **Awards:** Baumgarten prize, 1935 and 1936; Kossuth prize, 1970; Austrian State prize for European literature, 1974. **Died:** 22 January 1989.

PUBLICATIONS

Verse

Hideg van [It Is Cold]. 1934.
A kő és az ember [Stone and Man]. 1935.
A teremtés dícsérete [In Praise of Creation]. 1938.
Theomachia. 1941.
Medúza [Medusa]. 1943.
Elysium. 1946.
Gyümölcskosár [A Basket of Fruit]. 1946.
A szerelem ábécéje [The Alphabet of Love]. 1946.
A fogak tornáca [The Colonnade of Teeth]. 1947.
A hallgatás tornya [The Tower of Silence]. 1956.
A lélek idézése [The Evocation of Spirit]. 1958.
Tűzkút [Well of Fire]. 1964.
Merülő Saturnus [Saturn Sinking]. 1968.
Selected Poems, with Ferenc Juhász, translated by Edwin Morgan and David Wevill. 1970.
Psyché: Egy hajdani költőnő írásai [Psyche: Writings of a Poetess of Yore]. 1972.
Áthallások [Subconscious Influences]. 1973.
Tizenegy szimfónia [11 Symphonies]. 1973.
111 vers [111 Poems]. 1974.
Harmincöt vers [35 Poems]. 1978.
Ének a határtalanról [Song about the Infinite]. 1980.
Posta messziről. 1984.
Kútbanéző. 1987.
Eternal Moment: Selected Poems, edited by Miklós Vajna, various translators. 1988.
A sebzett föld éneke. 1989.

Plays

Hold és Sárkány [The Moon and the Dragon]. 1967.
A kétfejű fenevad [The Double-Headed Beast]. 1982.
Színjátétok. 1983.

Other

A vers születése [The Birth of the Poem] (thesis). 1939.
Bolond Istók [Stevie Crackpot]. 1943.
A teljesség felé. Gondolatok [Toward Totality: Thoughts]. 1945.
Bóbita [Tufty] (verse for children). 1955.
Zimzizim (verse for children). 1969.
Fairy Spring (in Hungarian; for children). 1970.
Egybegyűjtött írások [Collected Writings]. 2 vols., 1970; revised edition, 3 vols., 1975; 2nd revised edition, 4 vols., 1981.
Ha a világ rigó lenne (verse for children). 1973; as *If All the World Were a Blackbird*, translated by Alexander Fenton, 1985.
ÁBC (verse for children). 1974.
Egybegyűjtött műfordítások [Collected Translations]. 3 vols., 1976.
Egyedül mindenkivel [Interviews with Weöres]. 1993.

Editor, *Három veréb hat szemmel* [Three Sparrows with Six Eyes] (verse anthology). 1977.
Translator, *Po Csü Ji versei* [Poems of Bo Juyi]. 1952.
Translator, *Csü Juan versei* [Poems of Qu Yuan]. 1954.
Translator, *A tigrisbőrös lovag* [Knight Dressed in a Tiger Skin], by S. Rustaveli. 1954.
Translator, *Az út és az Erény Könyve*, by Lao Zi. 1958.
Translator, *A léek idézése* [Evocation of Spirit]. 1958.
Translator, *A megszabaditott Prometheus* [Prometheus Unbound], by Percy Bysshe Shelley. 1961.
Translator, *Stéphane Mallarmé költeményei* [Poems]. 1964.
Translator, *Ostromlott derű* [Besieged Cheerfulness], by Vasko Popa. 1968.
Translator, with G. Kerényi, *Micsoda szerencse* [What Luck!], by M. Bialoszewski. 1974.
Translator, *Fehér hajnalok* [White Dawns] by Kocsa Racin. 1978.
Translator, *Te titok-virág: Válogatott versek* [You, Flower of Mystery: Selected Poems], by Oton Zupačič. 1978.
Translator, *Tita Govinda.* 1982.

*

Critical Studies: "Weöres Issue" of *Magyar Műhely*, 2, 1964; "Conversation with Weöres" by László Cs. Szabó, in *TriQuarterly*, Spring 1967; "Weöres: Unity in Diversity" by George Gömöri, in *Books Abroad*, 43, 1969; introduction to *Eternal Moment* by M. Vajda, 1988; as *Form and Philosophy in Sándor Weöres' Poetry* by Susanna Fahlström, 1999.

*   *   *

Sándor Weöres was the leading poet of the third *Nyugat* generation and one of the most versatile and talented Hungarian poets of his age. His extraordinary talent became apparent in his early youth; he was still in his teens when his poems were first printed in the review *Nyugat*. At the time Weöres still lived in the Transdanubian village of Csönge, but as his parents came from the landowning class he attended grammar school in town. With his secondary education completed, Weöres studied aesthetics and philosophy at the University of Pécs and it was here that he obtained a doctorate with the thesis *A vers születése* [The Birth of the Poem] in 1939.

While on the one hand Weöres is clearly a *poeta doctus*, his great mimetic talent enabled him to play-act with much skill, writing grave philosophical poems alongside jocular, folksy ones and produce nursery rhymes, the linguistic and rhythmic quality of which is excellent. In the 1930s Weöres travelled widely, visiting distant countries in the East such as India. He discovered Eastern philosophy and studied ancient myths and civilizations, interests which were reflected in some of the longer poems of the collection *A teremtés dícsérete* [In Praise of Creation] which won Weöres much critical acclaim. The myth of the struggle of Kronos and Zeus is the theme of the poetic oratory *Theomachia*, ending with the older god's castration and downfall. Weöres's interest in the great myths of mankind is profound and productive from a poetic point of view: creation, death, and resurrection are more real to him than mass culture or sweeping political programmes. This explains certain "gnomic" utterances in such "anthropological" poems as "De Profundis," "Tryptych," and "A fogak tornáca" ("The Colonnade of Teeth"), as well as deep scepticism of salvationist political ideologies (as in "Fresco from the 20th Century"). These poems and the collection of prose gnomes and axioms in *A teljesség felé* [Towards Totality], in which Weöres advocated individual self-perfection rather than radical social reforms or revolution, earned him much hostility amongst Marxist critics. At any rate, Weöres saw himself as a poet-educator who, through widening the scope of poetic investigation into the unknown, could help contemporary man "to rearrange . . . his closed, finite, existential Ego into an open, social, cosmic, infinite one" (introduction to *Egybegyűjtött írások*).

Weöres's ambition as a poet is to embrace all aspects of human existence; hence his interest in poetry for children and his play-acting as a woman. In the 1940s Weöres wrote the cycle "Rongyszőnyeg" [Rag-Rug] which includes—apart from straightforward nursery rhymes—invented folksongs, humorous epigrams, and unusual metric experiments. Several collections of verse for children followed, such as *Bóbita* [Tufty] and *Ha a világ rigó lenne* (*If All the World Were a Blackbird*), which established Weöres as an undisputed master of light, entertaining verse. Many of Weöres's nursery rhymes hid sexual symbolism, yet when he first wrote an outspoken, but beautiful, poetic tale of physical love (the "Fairy Spring" cycle) it shocked conservative readers. Weöres scored a triumph of play-acting with the volume *Psyché: Egy hajdani költőnő írásai* [Psyche: Writings of a Poetess of Yore] in which he captured not only the spirit of early 19th-century Hungarian poetry, but achieved a "feat of psychological transvestism" (Miklós Vajda) as well. Weöres's Psyche is a talented and passionate young woman whose emotions, griefs, and joys shine through the self-imposed constraints of Biedermeier form.

For a poet given to so much play-acting it would be strange not to write plays, and, indeed, Weöres tried his hand at this genre. *Hold és Sárkány* [The Moon and the Dragon] comprises two plays with mythical characters, whereas *A kétfejű fenevad* [The Double-Headed Beast] is a blistering parody of the political situation in late 17th-century Hungary, newly liberated from Turkish occupation. Weöres was an accomplished translator into Hungarian, and his translations (apart from those done from most Western languages) also include Sanskrit, Chinese, and Georgian poems.

—George Gömöri

WERFEL, Franz

Born: Prague, Bohemia (now Czech Republic) 10 September 1890.
Education: Educated at Prague Gymnasium, until 1908; University of Prague, 1909–10; University of Leipzig; University of Hamburg.
Military Service: Served as a volunteer in the Austrian army, 1911–12 and on the Russian Front during World War I. **Family:** Married in 1918 (name of first wife not known); 2) Alma Mahler, widow of the composer Gustav Mahler, in 1929. **Career:** Reader for Kurt Wolft, publishers, Leipzig, 1912–14; co-founder of the expressionist periodical *Der Jüngste Tag*, 1913–21; freelance writer, Vienna, from 1917; member, literary section, Prussian Academy of the Arts, 1926; travelled to Italy, Capri, Locarno, and Ischl during the 1920s, visited Palestine, 1925; emigrated to France, 1938, to Spain, 1940, and emigrated with Heinrich Mann to the United States. **Awards:** Grillparzer prize, 1926. **Died:** 26 August 1945.

PUBLICATIONS

Collections

Gedichte aus den Jahren 1908–1945, edited by Ernst Gottlieb and Felix Guggenheim. 1946.
Gesammelte Werke, edited by Adolf D. Klarmann. 14 vols., 1948–75.

Plays

Die Versuchung. 1913.
Die Troerinnen, adaptation of the play by Euripides (produced 1916). 1915.
Der Gerichtstag. 1919.
Der Mittagsgöttin. 1919.
Der Besuch aus dem Elysium (produced 1920). 1920.
Spiegelmensch (produced 1921). 1920.
Bocksgesang (produced 1922). 1921; as *Goat Song*, translated by Ruth Langner, 1926.
Schweiger (produced 1923). 1922.
Juarez und Maximilian. Dramatische Historie in 3 Phasen und 13 Bildern. 1924; as *Juarez and Maximilian: A Dramatic History in Three Phases and Thirteen Pictures*, translated by Ruth Langner, 1926.
Paulus unter den Juden (produced 1926). 1926; as *Paul among the Jews*, translated by Paul P. Levertoff, 1928.
Das Reich Gottes in Böhmen. 1930.
Der Weg der Verheissung, music by Kurt Weill (produced 1937). 1935; as *The Eternal Road*, translated by Ludwig Lewisohn, 1936.
In einer Nacht. 1937.
Jacobowsky und der Oberst (produced 1944). 1944; as *Jacobowsky and the Colonel*, translated by Gustave O. Arlt, 1944.

Fiction

Der Dschin. 1919.
Nicht der Mörder: Der Ermordete ist schuldig. 1920.
Spielhof. 1920.
Arien. 1921.
Verdi, Roman der Oper. 1924; as *Verdi: A Novel of the Opera*, translated by Helen Jessiman, 1925.
Der Tod des Kleinbürgers (stories). 1927; as *The Man Who Conquered Death*, translated by Clifton P. Fadiman and William A. Drake, 1927; as *The Death of a Poor Man*, 1927.
Geheimnis eines Menschen (stories). 1927.
Der Abituriententag: Die Geschichte einer Jugendschuld. 1928; as *Class Reunion*, translated by Whittaker Chambers, 1929.
Barbara; oder, Die Frömmigkeit. 1929; as *The Pure in Heart*, translated by Geoffrey Dunlop, 1931; as *The Hidden Child*, 1931.
Kleine Verhältnisse. 1931.
Die Geschwister von Neapel. 1931; as *The Pascarella Family*, translated by Dorothy F. Tait-Price, 1932.
Die vierzig Tage des Musa Dagh. 1933; as *The Forty Days of Musa Dagh*, translated by Geoffrey Dunlop, 1934; as *The Forty Days*, 1934.
Höret die Stimme. 1937; as *Hearken unto the Voice*, translated by Moray Firth, 1938; as *Jeremias*, 1956.
Twilight of a World (collection), translated by H.T. Lowe-Porter. 1937.
Erzählungen aus zwei Welten, edited by Adolf D. Klarmann. 3 vols., 1938–39.

Der veruntreute Himmel: Die Geschichte einer Magd. 1939; as *Embezzled Heaven*, translated by Moray Firth, 1940.
Eine blassblaue Frauenschrift. 1941.
Das Lied von Bernadette. 1941; as *The Song of Bernadette*, translated by Ludwig Lewisohn, 1942.
Die wahre Geschichte vom Wiederhergestelltlen. 1942.
Stern der Ungeborenen. 1946; as *Star of the Unborn*, translated by Gustave O. Arlt, 1946.

Verse

Der Weltfreund. 1911.
Wir sind. 1913.
Einander. 1915.
Gesänge aus den drei Reichen. 1917.
Beschwörungen. 1923.
Gedichte. 1927.
Neue Gedichte. 1928.
Schlaf und Erwachen. 1935.
Gedichte aus dreissig Jahren. 1939.
Poems, translated by Edith Abercrombie Snow. 1945.

Other

Gesammelte Werke. 8 vols., 1927–36.
Realismus und Innerlichkeit (essays). 1931.
Können wir ohne Gottesglauben leben? (essays). 1932.
Reden und Schriften. 1932.
Von der reinsten Glückseligkeit des Menschen. 1938.
Zwischen Oben und Unten (essays). 1946; as *Between Heaven and Earth*, translated by Maxim Newmark, 1947.
Das Franz Werfel Buch, edited by Peter Stephan Jungk. 1986.
Editor, *Briefe*, by Giuseppe Verdi. 1926; as *Verdi: The Man in His Letters*, translated by Edward Downes, 1942.
Translator, *Simone Boccanegra*, by Giuseppe Verdi and F.M. Piave. 1929.
Translator, *Don Carlos.* 1932.
Translator, *Die Macht des Schicksals*, by Giuseppe Verdi and F.M. Piave. 1950.

*

Bibliography: "Franz Werfel: A Bibliography of Works and Criticism" by David L. Pell, in *West Virginia University Philological Papers*, (18), 1971.

Critical Studies: *Franz Werfel 1890–1945* edited by Lore B. Foltin, 1961; "Prodigal Sons in Werfel's Fiction," in *Germanic Review*, (15), 1965, and "The Failure of Political Activism in Werfel's Plays," in *Symposium*, (22), 1968, both by Henry A. Lea; *Franz Werfel* by Leopold Zahn, 1966; *Franz Werfel* by Lore B. Foltin, 1972; *Franz Werfel: The Faith of an Exile, from Prague to Beverly Hills* by Lionel B. Steiman, 1985; *Franz Werfel: Eine Lebensgeschichte* by Peter Stephan Jungk, 1987; *Franz Werfel: An Austrian Writer Reassessed* edited by Lothar Huber, 1988; *Franz Werfel in Exile* edited by Wolfgang Nehring and Hans Waggener, 1992; *Understanding Franz Werfel* by Hans Wagener, 1993; *Franz Werfel and the Critics* by Jennifer E. Michaels, 1994; *Jewish-German Identity in the Orientalist Literature of Else Lasker-Schüler, Friedrich Wolf, and*

Franz Werfel by Donna K. Heizer, 1996; *The Culturally Complex Individual: Franz Werfel's Reflections on Minority Identity and Historical Depiction in The Forty Days of Musa Dagh* by Rachel Kirby, 1999.

*   *   *

Franz Werfel achieved literary fame in his early twenties with a number of volumes of poetry that appeared in quick succession, *Der Weltfreund* [The World Friend], *Wir sind* [We Are], and *Einander* [One Another]. In the famous anthology of Expressionist verse edited by Kurt Pinthus, *Menschheitsdämmerung* (1918), Werfel is represented by more poems than any other writer. His was a powerful new voice and within the movement of Expressionism it constituted an antidote to the apostles of doom and decay, with whom he nevertheless shared a spirit of rebellion against the moral inertia of the age, the alienation and isolation of the individual.

His poetry is a hymnic celebration of life, whether in individual figures like that of "An old woman walking" or in the most general terms, as in that of "the beautiful radiant human being." Out of stagnation and materialism he salvages essential qualities of humanity, above all compassion and brotherly love, convinced to the end of his life of the "invincibility of the terms of a good person."

He is not one of the truly experimental poets, often making use of rhyme and even of the sonnet form. But his idiom is modern in the sense that he mixes together the most diverse elements, profound insights with trivialities, high pathos with colloquialisms. His message is presented emphatically and with an enthusiasm that seeks to sweep the reader along with it. Never showing any clear commitment to specific political aims, his poetry remained concerned with personal and existential themes and a mode of pious contemplation of the world.

During the 1920s the emphasis of Werfel's writing shifted to drama and fiction. In the dramatic field, having started with an adaptation of Euripides' *The Trojan Women* he wrote *Spiegelmensch* [Mirrorman], a drama on a grand scale, full of literary echoes, including allusions to *Faust, Peer Gynt*, and *Parsival*, and combining them with typical Expressionist themes. Bursting with exuberance and linguistic invention, it is a late and self-conscious product of Expressionism characterized by an epic structure and use of distancing techniques, an uneasy fluctuation between tragedy and comedy, and the blending of a quest for redemption with contemporary satire.

Bocksgesang (*Goat Song*) shows how the irrational in the shape of the monstrous goat man fascinates the masses and, inspiring hope for redemption, can be used to dominate them. The theme of leadership at a time of political upheaval links these plays with the drama *Schweiger*, and his other plays of the 1920s. *Juarez und Maximilian* presents the tragedy of the idealist Habsburg prince who was made emperor of Mexico. With this and *Das Reich Gottes in Böhmen* [The Kingdom of God in Bohemia], he turned to historical subjects which in their combination of intimacy and colourful mass scenes suited the new production techniques of directors like Max Reinhardt. *Paulus unter den Juden* (*Paul among the Jews*) deals with that moment in history when Christianity separated from Judaism; Werfel addresses himself to the task of opening up a dialogue between the two religions, a concern which was at the centre of much of the thinking of a writer who felt variously attracted to the one or the other.

In *Der Weg der Verheissung* (*The Eternal Road*), he attempted no less than a dramatization of the history of the Jewish people through the ages. With music by Kurt Weill, and produced by Max Reinhardt, it was a truly monumental enterprise. Performed at the Manhattan Opera House at great expense, it was successful with the public but had to be abandoned because it made heavy losses. His last play, *Jacobowsky und der Oberst* (*Jacobowsky and the Colonel*), reflects the experiences of his escape from the Nazis during the fall of France. This "comedy of a tragedy," about a character who, with his Jewish wisdom, through ingenuity, and not without the help of miracles, steers the nationalist Polish officer through a beleaguered France, is a true star-vehicle and was indeed made into an award-winning film as *Me and the Colonel* with Danny Kaye and Curt Jürgens.

Werfel's first major work of fiction, the novella *Nicht der Mörder: Der Ermordete ist schuldig* [Not the Murderer], is a psychological study of the relationship between father and son, individual and authority (a central theme for Expressionism), and presents a reversal of conventional moral viewpoints. Other short fictional works include the novelle *Der Tod des Kleinbürgers* (*The Man Who Conquered Death*), a memorable depiction of the milieu of the petit bourgeois, set in the Vienna of the post-war period, and evoking memories of the glories of a bygone age.

His first bestseller was a novel on the subject of music: *Verdi, Roman der Oper* (*Verdi: A Novel of the Opera*). Not a true biography but the "legend" of a genius, it includes a fictional encounter between Verdi and Wagner, the great antipodes of opera in the second half of the 19th century. *Barbara; oder, Die Frömmigkeit* (*The Pure in Heart*) excels in vivid evocation of the turbulent times at the end of World War I in Vienna. Strongly autobiographical, it gives credible portraits of many of Werfel's fellow writers who shared the view that they ought to take an active part in forming a new society. Cured of his belief in activism, the protagonist, under the influence of his former nurse, Barbara, finds his solution in a pious acceptance of his role in society, serving as a doctor. Two journeys to the Middle East provided the stimulus for *Die vierzig Tage des Musa Dagh* (*The Forty Days of Musa Dagh*), about the persecution of the Armenians in the Turkish empire. The novel focuses on a community of Armenians who decide to resist deportation (which would have meant certain ignoble death) and defend themselves successfully on the hill fortress of Musa Dagh until they are rescued by the French navy. By a strange irony this prophetic book, which foreshadowed the fate of Werfel's own Jewish people, was published in the year Hitler came to power.

Like the plays, his fiction clearly demonstrates Werfel's double interest in Judaism and Christianity. *Höret die Stimme* (*Hearken unto the Voice* or *Jeremias*) focuses on Judaism, while *Der veruntreute Himmel* (*Embezzled Heaven*), deals with a humorous aspect of the Christian faith and was followed by the bestselling novel about the Catholic saint of Lourdes, Bernadette Soubirous, *Das Lied von Bernadette* (*The Song of Bernadette*), where Werfel keeps through the personae of his characters a sensitive balance between belief and scepticism. This work made him a hero of American Catholics, when he had already proved himself a champion of the Armenians and had obviously shown a strong allegiance to his Jewish roots.

In his last novel, *Stern der Ungeborenen* (*Star of the Unborn*), Werfel makes his own near-death experience the starting point for an exploration of the future of humanity. Looking 100,000 years ahead, he finds on the one hand the greatest refinement in the "astromental" world, while on the other hand violence and aggression are only barely suppressed and eventually break loose. Unjustly neglected, this novel deserves to be given its proper place among the great utopian novels of the century. Like the best of his works, it is full of a deep humanity, a delightful humour, and an inexhaustible wealth of invention.

—Lothar Huber

WIELAND, Christoph Martin

Born: Oberholzheim, near Biberach, Germany, 5 September 1733. **Education:** Educated at Klosterbergen, near Magdeburg, 1747–48; educated privately by Johann Wilhelm Baumer, professor of medicine, chemistry, and philosophy, 1748–49; enrolled at the University of Erfurt, 1749. **Family:** Engaged to Sophie Gutermann (later Sophie La Roche) in 1750, broken off 1753; married Dorothea von Hillenbrand in 1765 (died 1801); 14 children (two deceased in infancy). **Career:** Returned to Oberholzheim, 1750; began a course in jurisprudence, Tübingen, 1950, concentrated on his poetry rather than law; lived as the guest of the scholar J.J. Bodmer in Zurich, 1952–54; private tutor, Zurich and Berne, 1754–60; senator and acting town clerk, Biberach, 1760; professor of philosophy, Erfurt University, 1769–72; private tutor to Dowager Duchess Anna Amalia of Sachsen-Weimar's sons, 1772–74; founding editor, with Friedrich Heinrich and Georg Jacobi, *Der Teutsche Merkur*, 1773; co-founder, *Allgemeine Literaturzeitung*, Jena, 1784; editor, *Der Neue Teutsche Merkur*, 1790–96. **Awards:** Legion of Merit (France), 1808; Cross of Saint Anna, (Russia), 1808. **Member:** Order of Freemasons, 1809, and Prussian Academy of Science, Berlin, 1786. **Died:** 20 January 1813.

PUBLICATIONS

Collections

Sämtliche Werke, edited by Heinrich Duntzer. 40 vols., 1867–79.
Gesammelte Schriften, edited by Bernhard Seuffert, Hans Werner Seiffert, and others. 23 vols., 1909–.
Werke, edited by Fritz Martini and Hans Werner Seiffert. 5 vols., 1964–68.
Politische Schriften. 1988.

Verse

Lobgesang auf die Liebe. 1751.
Die Natur der Dinge. 1752; revised edition, 1753.
Zwölf moralische Briefe in Versen. 1752.
Anti-Ovid; oder, die Kunst zu lieben. 1752.
Briefe von Vestorbenen an hinterlassene Freunde. 1753.
Der geprüfte Abraham. 1753; as *The Trial of Abraham*, 1764.
Hymnen: Von dem Verfasser des gepryften Abrahams. 1754.
Erinnerungen an eine Freundin. 1754
Ode auf die Auferstehung Jesu. 1754.
Ode auf die Geburt des Erlösers. 1754.
Ode zum dankbaren Andenken eines Erlauchten und Verdienstvollen Staatsmanns in der Republick Zürich. 1757.
Cyrus (fragment). 1759.
Poetische Schriften. 1762; revised edition, 1770.
Der Sieg der Natur über die Schwärmerey; oder, Die Abenteuer des Don Sylvio von Rosalva. 1764; as *Der neue Amadis*, 1771; as *Reason Triumphant over Fancy, Exemplified in the Singular*

Adventures of Don Sylvio de Rosalva, 1773; as *The Adventures of Don Sylvio de Rosalva*, 1904.
Musarion; oder, Die Philosophie der Grazien. 1768; revised edition, 1769.
Idris und Zenide. 1768.
Die Grazien. 1770; as *The Graces: A Classical Allegory*, translated by Sarah Taylor Austin, 1823.
Der verklagte Amor. 1774.
An Psyche. 1774.
Neueste Gedichte vom Jahre 1770–1777. 1777–79.
Auserlesene Gedichte. 1784–87.
Der Stein der Weisen; oder, Sylvester und Rosene. 1791.

Fiction

Erzählungen. 1752.
Sympathien. 1756; as *The Sympathy of Souls*, translated by F.A. Winzer, 1787.
Sammlung einiger prosaischen Schriften. 1758; as *Sammlung prosaischer Schriften*, 1763–64; as *Prosaiche Schriften*, 1771–72.
Araspes und Panthea: Eine moralische Geschichte in einer Reyhe von Unterredungen. 1760; as "Araspes and Panthea; or, the Effects of Love," translated by John Richardson, in *Dialogues from the German of C. M. Wieland*, 1775.
Komische Erzählungen. 1765.
Die Geschichte des Agathon. 1766–67; as *Agathon*, 1773; as *The History of Agathon*, translated by John Richardson, 1773.
Die Geschichte des Prinzen Biribinkers. 1769.
Beyträge zur Geheimen Geschichte des menschlichen Verstandes und Herzens: Aus den Archiven der Natur gezogen. 1770.
Combabus. 1770.
Sokrates mainomenos; oder, die Dialogen des Diogenes yon Sinope. 1770; as *Nachlass des Diogenes von Sinope: Gedanken über eine alte Aufschrift*, 1822; translated as *Socrates Out of His Senses; or, Dialogues of Diogenes of Sinope*, 1771.
Kleine Schriften. 1772.
Der goldne Spiegel; oder, die Könige von Scheschian. 1772.
Die Abderiten: Eine sehr wahrscheinliche Geschichte. 1774; revised edition as *Geschichte der Abderiten*, 1781; as *The Republic of Fools: Being the History of the State and People of Abdera in Thrace*, translated by Henry Christmas, 1861; as *History of the Abderites*, translated by Max Dufner, 1993.
Geron, der Adelich. 1777.
Oberon. 1780; as *Oberon*, translated by William Sotheby, 1798; also translated by John Quincy Adams, 1940.
Clelia und Sinibald: Eine Legende aus dem zwölften Jahrhundert. 1784.
Kleinere prosaische Schriften. 2 vols., 1785–86.
Vermischte Erzahlungen. 1791.
Geheime Geschichte des Philosophen Peregrinus Proteus. 1791; as *Private History of Peregrinus Proteus, the Philosopher*, translated by William Tooke, 1796; translated in part as *Confessions in Elysium; or, The Adventures of a Platonic Philosopher*, by John Battersby Elgington, 1804. *Agathodämon*, 1799.
Aristipp und einige seiner Zeitgenossen. 1800.
Menander und Glycerion. 1803.
Krates und Hipparchia. 1804; as *Crates and Hipparchia: A Tale in a Series of Letters*, translated by Charles Richard Coke, 1823.
Das Hexameron von Rosenhain. 1805.

Plays

Lady Johanna Gray. 1758.
Clementina von Poretta. 1760.
Aurora (libretto; produced 1772). 1772.
Alceste, from the play by Euripides (libretto; produced 1772). 1773.
Die Wahl des Hercules. 1774.

Other

Gebet eines Deisten: Veranlasst durch das Gebet eines Freygeistes. 1753.
Gebet eines Christen: Von dem Verfasser des Gebets eines Deisten. 1753.
Abhandlung von den Schönheiten des Epischen Gedichts Der Noah. 1753.
Ankündigung einer Dunciade für die Deutschen. 1755.
Betrachtungen: Über den Menschen nebst einer allegorischen Geschichte der menschlichen Seele. 1755.
Fragmente in der erzählenden Dichtart von verschiedenem Innhalte, with J.J. Bodmer. 1755.
Hymnen auf die Allgegenwart und Gerechtigkeit Gottes. 1756.
Empfindungen eines Christen. 1757.
Auf das Bildniss des Königs von Preussen von Herrn Wille. 1758.
Gedanken über eine alte Auffschrift. 1772.
Gedanken von der Freyheit über Gegenstände des Glaubens zu philosophieren. 1789.
Neue Götter-Gespräche. 1791; as *Dialogues of the Gods*, translated by William Taylor, 1795.
Sämmtliche Werke, Ausgabe letzter Hand. 45 vols., 1794–1811; revised edition by H. Radspieler, 14 vols., 1984.
Euthanasia: Drei Gespräche über das Leben nach dern Tode. 1805.
Über das Fortleben in Andenken der Nachwelt. 1812.
Auswahl denkwürdiger Briefe von C.M. Wieland, edited by Ludwig Wieland. 2 vols., 1815.
Ausgewählte Briefe von C.M. Wieland an verschiedene Freunde in den Jahren 1751 (correspondence), edited by Heinrich Gessner. 4 vols., 1815–16.
Briefe an Sophie von la Roche, nebst einern Schreiben yon Gellert und Lavater, edited by Franz Horn. 1820.
Aus Klassischer Zeit: Weiland und Reinhold (correspondence), edited by Robert Keil. 1885.
Briefwechsel, edited by Hans Werner Seiffert. 5 vols., 1963–83.
Editor, *Geschichte des Fräuleins von Sternheim*, by Sophie von La Roche. 2 vols., 1771.
Editor, with others, *Dschinnistan; oder, Auserlesene Feenund Geister-Märchen, theils neu erfunden, theils neu übersetzt und urngearbeitet*. 3 vols., 1786–89.
Editor, *Von der natürlichen Moral*, by Johann Heinrich Meister. 1789.
Editor, with Johann Wilhelm von Archenholtz, *Historischer Calender für Damen für das Jahr 1790*. 1790.
Editor, *Das attische Museum*. 4 vols., 1796–1804.
Editor, with Goethe, *Taschenbuch auf das Jahr 1804*. 1803.
Editor, *Erzählungen und Dialogen*, by Ludwig Wieland. 2 vols., 1803–05.
Editor, *Die deutschen Volksmährchen*, by Johann Karl August Musiäus. 5 vols., 1804–05.
Editor, with Johann Jakob Hottinger and Friedrich Jacobs, *Das neue attische Museum*. 3 vols., 1805–11.
Editor, *Melusinens Sommer-Abende*, by Sophie von La Roche. 1806.

Editor, *Des blinden Flötenspielers Leben und Meinungen*, by Friedrich Ludwig Dulon. 2 vols., 1807–08.

Translator, *Theatralische Werke*, by William Shakespeare. 8 vols., 1762–66.

Translator, *Briefe, aus dem Lateinischen übersetzt und mit Historischen Einleitungen und auch nöthigen Erläuterungen versehen*, by Horace. 2 vols., 1782.

Translator, *Satyren, aus dem Lateinischen abersetzt und mit Einleitungen und erläuternden Anmerkungen versehen*, by Horace. 2 vols., 1786.

Translator, *Sämmtliche Werke*, by Lucian. 6 vols., 1788–89.

Translator, *Sämmtliche Briefe, übersetzt und erläutert*, by Cicero. 4 vols., 1808–12.

*

Bibliography: *Bibliographie der Wieland-Übersetzungen* by Julius Steinberger, 1930; *Wieland-Bibliographie* by Gottfried Günther and Heidi Zeilinger, 1983.

Critical Studies: *Wieland and Shaftesbury* by Charles Elson, 1913, 2nd edition, 1966; *Wieland* by Friedrich Sengel, 1949; *Christoph Martin Wieland (1733–1813): A Literary Biography* by Derek M. Van Abbé, 1961; *The Enchanted Forest* by Werner Beyer, 1963; *C.M. Wielands Entwicklungsbegriff und die Geschichte des Agathon* by Wolfram Buddecke, 1966; *Christoph Martin Wieland as the Originator of the Modern Travesty in German Literature* by Charlotte Craig, 1970; *Phantasie und Erfahrung: Studien zur Erzähtpoetik Christoph Martin Wielands* by Klaus Oettinger, 1970; *Wielands Verhältnis zu Ariost und Tasso* by Hans Tribolet, 1970; *Wielands späte Romane: Untersuchungen zur Erzählweise und zur erzählten Wirklichkeit* by Jan-Dirk Müller, 1971; *Wieland* by Cornelius Sommer, 1971; *Zeitgenössische Persiflagen auf C.M. Wieland und seine Schriften* by Manfred A. Poitzsch, 1972; *Der skeptische Bürger: Wielands Schrifien zur Französischen Revolution* by Bernd Weyergraf, 1972; *Perspectives and Points of View: The Early Works of Wieland and their Background* by Lieselotte E. Kurth-Voigt, 1974; *Musarion and Wieland's Concept of Genre* by Herbert Rowland, 1975; *Christoph Martin Wieland* by John A. McCarthy, 1979; *A Method of Stylistic Analysis Exemplified on C.M. Wieland's Geschichte des Agathon* by Rebecca E. Schrader, 1980; *The Reader in the Novels of C.M. Wieland* by Richard G. Rogan, 1981; *Christoph Martin Wieland* edited by Hansjörg Schelle, 1981; *The Narrative Strategy of Wieland's Don Sylvio von Rosalva* by Daniel W. Wilson, 1981; *Christoph Martin Wieland: Nordamerikanische Forschungsbeiträge zur 250. Wiederkehr seines Geburtstages*, by Hansjörg Schelle, 1983; *Horace's Epistles, Wieland and the Reader: A Three-Way Relationship* by Jane Veronica Curran, 1995; *Noble Lies, Slant Truths, Necessary Angels: Aspects of Fictionality in the Novels of Christoph Martin Wieland* by Ellis Shookman, 1997.

* * *

Christoph Martin Wieland belongs to the age of Enlightenment in German literature. He is regarded, furthermore, as the representative of all the major trends of the age of Enlightenment and beings an un-German and Latin element into German literature: a poet who gained stature primarily for his novels, verse narratives, and translations. Wieland achieved his unique position after embracing the influence of a variety of foreign authors: he was one of the most open-minded writers of the day, who knew how to turn diverse styles of European

literature to his own particular style. From Cervantes he took over the theme of experience dispelling self-deception. Shakespeare and Fielding in their different ways attracted him because they portrayed reality with unswerving truth, while Sterne and Voltaire influenced him to look at human nature with ironic detachment. He adopted Shaftesbury's ideal of the virtuoso and the concept of moral grace. These influences formed the basis of Wieland's idea of personal culture or *Bildung*.

His early work, *Zwölf moralische Briefe in Versen* [Twelve Moral Letters in Verse], composed in alexandrines, was in keeping with the 18th-century didactic style. This style, however, was changed when he wrote the *Komische Erzählungen* [Comic Stories], which are four satirical verse tales on mythological subjects. Wieland demonstrated a conversion from the extremes of "Pythagorean" other-worldliness and cynical materialism to a balanced acceptance of life's sensual pleasures in *Musarion; oder, Die Philosophie der Grazien* [Mussarion; or, the Philosophy of the Graces]. It is the story of a Greek youth who foolishly sought happiness in philosophy rather than in a woman's love.

Wieland's next works, *Idris und Zenide* and *Der neue Amadis* [The New Amadis], demonstrate Wieland's skill in the free use of complex thematic material wholly imaginative in character, and his adept and individual use of traditional verse forms, particularly the *ottava rima*. In *Der neue Amadis* Wieland imitates Cervantes's *Don Quixote*, and uses autobiographical narrative to show how, early in his life, he departed from all the religious feelings and fervour which his acquaintance with Bodmer and Klopstock had aroused in him. Like Amadis or Don Silvio, Wieland prefers to become a man of the world, elegant, witty, graceful, and sceptical, a poet especially influenced by hedonism. In the novel, Don Silvio believes in the existence of fairies and goes into the world to discover them. His adventures are described with great charm. One of the important elements is the language of the work, a language which Wieland acquired through his studies of the Romance languages and literatures.

Die Geschichte des Agathon (*The History of Agathon*) established Wieland's fame as an enlightened writer. It is considered one of the great German novels of the 18th century, but, like so much of Wieland's work, the novel has a Greek background. Yet his conceptions of antiquity never advanced far beyond the somewhat superficial views in vogue before Winckelmann. His Greek novels are Greek only in costume and scenery and sometimes fail even at that level; in other aspects they are saturated with the rationalism of the 18th-century. Agathon, a beautiful Athenian youth, who has been brought up in the tenets of Plato's philosophy, is carried off by pirates to Smyrna, where the Epicurean, Hippas, endeavours to convert him to materialism. It is in essence a novel of apprenticeship or Bildungsroman, in which the aesthetic rather than the religious education of the young hero is emphasized. Fine psychological analyses of Agathon and the ideal Danae, two lovable Greek Epicureans of the 4th century BC have here replaced the many external events that had hitherto usually formed the substance of the German novel. The background of this Greek seeker of a philosophy of life is utterly different from the Romantic and medieval tone which had prevailed in *Parzival*.

Wieland edited and published the review *Der teutsche Merkur*, from 1773 to 1789. Modelled on the famous *Mercure de France*, this was practically the first modern review devoted to *belles-lettres* in Germany, and helped to mould public opinion and taste in Germany and Austria. Most of Wieland's own literary work from 1773 onward first appeared in its pages, and its critical and political articles show how carefully he followed the progress of events in Europe. Wieland first published the novel *Die Abderiten* (*The Republic of Fools*), in

Der teutsche Merkur. It is principally a satire on German provincial life of his time. Under the guise of an attack upon the often ridiculed burghers of the ancient Greek city of Abdera, Wieland good-naturedly pokes fun at the philistinism and narrow morality of the people of the town of Biberach, where he, the elegant cosmopolitan, had spent a few boring and unhappy years. The inhabitants of ancient Abdera are famous for their excessive stupidity: for example, they build a beautiful fountain, but neglect to furnish it with water, and they purchase a Venus by Praxiteles, but place it on so high a pedestal that no one can see it. In this novel, Wieland has already lost his concise style and inclines to long and unwieldy sentences.

Oberon is a colourful medieval fairytale about the king of the elves, relating how he helped Huon of Bordeaux perform wondrous deeds in the Orient. In this novel Wieland replaced the dull sobriety of the age of Gottschied with his own beautiful language, smooth rhymes, and a colourful imagination, even though fairytales were just another aspect of life in which Wieland did not believe. The influence of Shakespeare's *A Midsummer Night's Dream* and of Ariosto's *Orlando Furioso* is clearly seen in this epic novel. Because of his wit and scepticism, Wieland has often been called the German Ariosto or the German Voltaire.

Although Wieland devoted his life to writing, he was not one of those authors who wrote for posterity. The great bulk of his work was of his time and for his time, and he did not consciously strive to become a great writer. Yet Wieland provides a characteristic and indispensable element in German literature.

—Brigittte Edith Zapp Archibald

WIESEL, Elie

Born: Eliezar Wiesel, in Sighet, Hungary (now Romania), 30 September 1928. **Education:** Educated in the local Jewish day school (Heder) in Sighet; studied philosophy, French literature, and psychology at the University of Paris (Sorbonne). **Family:** Married Marion Erster Rose in 1969, one son. **Career:** Deported and imprisoned in German Nazi concentration camps, beginning 3 June 1944; liberated by the American Third Army in Buchenwald, 11 April 1945; worked in Paris, 1945–55, mainly as a journalist for a Franco-Jewish magazine and for a major Tel Aviv newspaper; foreign correspondent at various times for *Yedioth Ahronoth*, Tel Aviv, Israel, *L'Arche*, Paris, France, and *Jewish Daily Forward*, New York City, 1949–; City College of the City University of New York, New York City, distinguished professor, 1972–76; Boston University, Boston, Massachusetts, Andrew Mellon professor in the humanities, 1976–, professor of Philosophy, 1988–; Whitney Humanities Center, Yale University, New Haven, Connecticut, Henry Luce visiting scholar in Humanities and Social Thought, 1982–83; Florida International University, Miami, distinguished visiting professor of literature and philosophy, 1982. Chair, United States President's Commission on the Holocaust, 1979–80, U.S. Holocaust Memorial Council, 1980–86. **Awards:** Hundreds of decorations and prizes throughout the world, especially in the United States, France, and Israel; including: the Nobel prize for Peace, 1986; Grand Officer of the French Legion of Honor, 1985; Congressional Gold medal presented by President Ronald Reagan, 1985; Presidential Medal of Freedom presented by President Bill Clinton, 1992; literary awards include Prix Goncourt, Grand Prix de Litterature, Prix Rivarol, National Jewish Book Council award, and Prix Medicis.

PUBLICATIONS

Fiction

Un di velt hat geshwigen (And the World Was Silent) (in Yiddish). 1956; abridged and translated into French as *La Nuit.* 1958; as *Night*, translated by Stella Rodway, 1960.

L'Aube. 1960; as *Dawn*, translated by Anne Borchardt, 1961.

Le Jour. 1961; as *The Accident*, translated by Anne Borchardt. 1962.

La Ville de la chance. 1962; as *The Town beyond the Wall*, translated by Steven Becker, 1964.

Le Mendiant de Jerusalem. 1968; as *A Beggar in Jerusalem*, translated by Lily Edelman and Elie Wiesel, 1970.

Le Serment de Kolvillag. 1973; as *The Oath*, translated by Marion Wiesel, 1973.

Le Testament d'un Juif assassine. 1980; as *The Testament*, translated by Marion Wiesel, 1981.

Le Cinquieme Fils. 1985; as *The Fifth Son*, translated by Marion Wiesel, 1985.

The Night Trilogy: Night, Dawn, and The Accident. 1987.

Le Crepuscule au loin. 1987; as *Twilight*, translated by Marion Wiesel, 1988.

Les Juges. 1999.

Jewish and Biblical Work

Les Juifs du silence. 1966; as *The Jews of Silence: A Personal Report on the Jews of the Soviet Union*, translated from the Hebrew by Neal Kozodoy, 1968.

Les Chants des Morts. 1966; as *Legends of Our Time*, translated by Steven Donadio, 1968.

Entre deux soleils. 1970; as *One Generation After*, translated by Lily Edelman and Elie Wiesel, 1970.

Celebration Hassidique: Portraits et Legendes, as *Souls on Fire: Portraits and Legends of Hasidic Masters* translated by Marion Wiesel. 1972.

Celebration biblique: portraits et legends. 1975; as *Messengers of God: Biblical Portraits and Legends*, translated by Marion Wiesel, 1976.

Un Juif aujourd'hui. 1977; as *A Jew Today*, translated by Marion Wiesel, 1978.

Four Hasidic Masters and Their Struggle Against Melancholy. 1978.

Five Biblical Portraits. 1981.

Contre la melancolie: Celebration Hassidique II. 1981; as *Somewhere a Master: Further Hasidic Portraits and Legends*, translated by Marion Wiesel, 1982.

The Golem: The Story of a Legend as Told by Elie Wiesel. 1983.

Job ou Dieu dans la tempete. 1986.

The Six Days of Destruction, with Albert Friedlander. 1988.

Celebration talmudique. 1991.

Celebrations, portraits et legendes. 1994.

La Haggadah de Paque. 1995.

Celebration prophetique. 1998.

Le Golem. 1998.

Essays and Collections

Paroles d'etranger. 1982.
Signes d'exode. 1985.
Against Silence: The Voice and Vision of Elie Wiesel, Vols. I–II–III, in collaboration with Irving Abrahamson. 1985.
Discours d'Oslo. 1987; (Nobel Laureate Address translated by Wiesel from English version).
From the Kingdom of Memory: Reminiscences. 1990.
D'ou viens-tu?. 2001.

Memoirs

Tous les fleuves vont a la mer: Memoires. 1994; as *All Rivers Run to the Sea: Memoirs*, translated by Marion Wiesel, 1995.
Et la mer n'est pas remplie: Memoires 2. 1996; as *And the Sea is Never Full*, translated by Marion Wiesel, 1999.

Plays

Zalmen ou la folie de Dieu. 1968; as *Zalmen, or The Madness of God*, translated and adapted for the stage by Nathan Edelman and Marion Wiesel, 1974.
Ani Maamin: Un Chant perdu et retrouve. 1973; as *Ani Maamin: A Song Lost and Found Again*, bilingual edition in French and English, with translation by Marion Wiesel, 1973.
Le Proces de Shamgorod (tel qu'il se deroula le 25 fevrier 1649). 1979; as *The Trial of God (as it was held on February 25, 1649, in Shamgorod)*, translated by Marion Wiesel, 1979.

Other

"The Holocaust as Literary Imagination," in *Dimensions of the Holocaust: Lectures at Northwestern University*. 1977.
Job ou Dieu dans la tempete, in collaboration with Rabbi Josy Eisenberg. 1986.
Elie Wiesel—Qui etes-vous?, with Brigitte-Fanny Cohen. 1987.
Le Mal et l'exil. 1988; as *Evil and Exile*, translated by John Rothschild and Jody Gladding, 2000.
Se taire est impossible (dialogue with Jorge Semprun). 1995.
Memoires a deux voix (dialogue with President Francois Mitterrand). 1995; as *Memoir in Two Voices*, translated by Richard Seaver and Timothy Bent, 1996.

*

Critical Studies: *Elie Wiesel: The Holocaust and the Literary Imagination* by Lawrence Langer, 1975; *Conversations with Elie Wiesel* by Harry James Cargas, 1976; *Responses to Elie Wiesel: Critical Essays by Major Jewish and Christian Scholars* by Harry James Cargas, 1978; *Confronting the Holocaust: The Impact of Elie Wiesel*, edited by Alvin Rosenfeld and Irving Greenbert, 1979; *The Vision of the Void: Theological Reflections on the Works of Elie Wiesel* by Michael Berenbaum, 1979; *A Consuming Fire: Encounters with Elie Wiesel* by John K. Roth, 1979; *Elie Wiesel* by Ted Estess, 1980; *Le rire dans l'univers tragique d'Elie Wiesel* by Joe Friedman, 1981; *Legacy of Night: The Literary Universe of Elie Wiesel* by Ellen S. Fine, 1982; *Elie Wiesel: Witness for Life* by Ellen Norman Stern, 1982; *Elie Wiesel: Messenger to All Humanity* by Robert McAffee Brown, 1989; *Elie Wiesel: Between Memory and Hope*, by Carol Rittner, R.S.M., editor, 1990; *Elie Wiesel: pelerin de la memoire* by Michael de Saint Cheron, 1994; *Elie Wiesel's Secretive Texts* by Colin Davis 1994; *Silence in the Novels of Elie Wiesel* by Simon P. Sibelman, 1995; *Elie Wiesel: En Hommage* edited by Ariane Kalfa and Michael de Saint Cheron, 1998; *The Worlds of Elie Wiesel* by Jack Kolbert, 2001.

* * *

Many regard Elie Wiesel as the voice and conscience of the Jewish people and their tragic situation during the Holocaust of World War II. Incontestably the Holocaust forms the epicenter of his lifelong literary production. Despite the fact that this traumatic moment dominates his personal life and literary career, ironically in only a relatively small portion of his prodigious oeuvre does this author deal directly and descriptively with the tragedy itself. But the reverberations of what he saw and suffered in four concentration camps insinuate themselves into the very architecture of his texts. Whether he alludes to the Holocaust or whether he chooses to circumvent it, Wiesel almost always depicts the destinies of the victims as well as their survivors. His memories of the atrocities loom over his writing like an ominous and terrifying cloud. In numerous works he dissects the causes of the Holocaust such as recurrent anti-Semitism, racial and religious persecution, discrimination, hatred, prejudice, indifference to the plight of the downtrodden, ethnic intolerance. In a substantial number of his books he also deals with Jewish themes, including the exploits of the ancient prophets, medieval rabbis, Hasidic personalities, heroes and heroines from the Biblical legends and tales.

Following his release from the death camp at Buchenwald, Wiesel could not immediately muster the inner courage to describe his own personal tribulations during the Holocaust. The rational nature of rhetoric seemed to contradict the irrationality of what he had witnessed in the camps. For ten years he remained silent. Finally, with the memories and scars of his experiences in the death camps exploding within his soul, he no longer could remain silent and produced his first great book: *La Nuit* (*Night*). He truly believed that unless his memories could transmute themselves into concrete form, humanity might eventually forget the most monstrous human tragedy in the history of the world.

Although, in the overarching reaches of Wiesel's cumulative literature there exists a coherent philosophy of humanitarianism, his readers must assemble that philosophy by themselves as they scan the fragmentary pronouncements, aphorisms and maxims pregnant with Wieselean thought dispersed throughout this writer's many texts. Wiesel's is a philosophy that celebrates the sacredness of human life (a paradoxical phenomenon in the case off someone who had witnessed so many mass killings). In his philosophy he wages war on indifference to evil, on our all too facile tendency to forget painful memories, and on our natural tendency to be suspicious of people who differ from our ambient culture in their cultural, ethnic, racial, national and religious makeup. While exalting the basic tenets of his own Jewish faith and the impressive achievements of the Jewish people, he calls for dialogue and understanding between people of all religious faiths and national allegiances.

More than just a prominent writer; he is a recognized educator, religious authority, internationally sought-after speaker, a respected thinker, and an esteemed colleague who rubs elbows with heads of state, religious leaders, academicians, media personalities, and ordinary people from around the world. The head of the Nobel Peace prize Committee called him ''a messenger to Mankind.''

—Jack Kolbert

WITKACY

See WITKIEWICZ, Stanislaw

WITKIEWICZ, Stanisław (Ignacy)

Pseudonym: Witkacy. **Born:** Warsaw, Poland, 24 February 1885; son of the writer and painter Stanisław Witkiewicz (used pseudonym to distinguish himself from his father). **Education:** Educated at secondary school, Lvov, to 1903; Academy of Fine Arts, Cracow, 1905–06, and in Italy, France, and Germany. **Military Service:** Served in the Tsarist forces in Russia during World War I: wounded 1915; elected political commissar by his regiment, 1917. **Family:** Married Jadwiga Unrug in 1923. **Career:** Accompanied the anthropologist Bronisław Malinowski on an anthropological expedition to Australia, 1914; painter from 1918: individual show, Cracow, 1967; Founder, Formist Theatre, an amateur group, Zakopane, 1925–27; in later years wrote mainly philosophical works; lived in Zakopane and Warsaw, 1930–39; fled east after the German and Soviet occupations of Poland, 1939. **Died:** (suicide) 18 September 1939.

PUBLICATIONS

Collections

Dramaty [Plays], edited by Konstanty Puzyna. 2 vols., 1962; revised edition, 1972.

Dzieła wybrane [Selected Works] (includes reprints from the 1972 edition of *Dramaty*). 5 vols., 1985.

A Witkacy Reader: The Life and Works of Stanisław Ignacy Witkiewicz, edited and translated by Daniel Gerould. 1987.

Selected Writings, translated by Daniel Gerould. 1988.

The Mother and Other Unsavory Plays: Including the Shoemaker[s] and They, edited and translated by Daniel Gerould and C.S. Durer. 1993.

Plays

Pragmatyści (produced 1921). In *Dramaty,* 1962; as *The Pragmatists,* in *Tropical Madness: Four Plays,* translated by Daniel and Eleanor Gerould, 1972.

Tumor Mózgowicz (produced 1921). In *Dramaty,* 1962; as *Tumor Brainowicz,* translated by Daniel Gerould, in *The Beelzebub Sonata,* 1977.

W małym dworku [In a Small Country House] (produced 1923). 1921; with *Szewcy,* 1948.

Kurka wodna (produced 1922). In *Dramaty,* 1962; as *The Water Hen,* in *The Madman and the Nun and Other Plays,* translated by Daniel Gerould and C.S. Durer, 1968.

Wariat i zakonnica; czyli, Nie ma złego, coby na jeszcze gorsze nie wyszło (produced 1924). In *Dramaty,* 1962; as *The Madman and the Nun,* in *The Madman and the Nun and Other Plays,* translated by Daniel Gerould and C.S. Durer, 1968.

Nowe Wyzwolenie (produced 1925). In *Dramaty,* 1962; translated as *The New Deliverance,* 1974.

Sonata Belzebuba; cyzli, Prawdziwe zdarzenie w Mordowarze (produced 1966). 1925; in *Dramaty,* 1962; as *The Beelzebub Sonata,* translated by Daniel Gerould, 1977.

Jan Maciej Karol Wścieklica [Jan Maciej Karol Hellcat] (produced 1925). In *Dramaty,* 1962.

Mister Price; czyli, Bzik tropikalny, with Eugenia Dunin-Borkowska (produced 1926). In *Dramaty,* 1962; as *Mr. Price; or, Tropical Madness,* in *Tropical Madness: Four Plays,* translated by Daniel and Eleanor Gerould, 1972.

Persy Zwierżontkowskaja [Persy Bestialskaya] (produced 1927).

Metafizyka dwugłowego cielęcia (produced 1928). In *Dramaty,* 1962; as *Metaphysics of a Two-Headed Calf,* in *Tropical Madness: Four Plays,* translated by Daniel and Eleanor Gerould, 1972.

Mtwa; czyli, Hyrkaniczny światopogld (produced 1933). In *Dramaty,* 1962; as *The Cuttlefish,* translated by Daniel and Eleanor Gerould, in *Treasury of the Theatre 2,* edited by Bernard F. Dukore and John Gassner, 1969, and in *Twentieth-Century Polish Theatre,* edited by Bohdan Drozdowski, 1979.

Straszliwy wychowawca [The Frightful Tutor] (produced 1935).

Szewcy (produced 1957). With *W małym dworku,* 1948; as *The Shoemakers,* in *The Madman and the Nun and Other Plays,* translated by Daniel Gerould and C.S. Durer, 1968.

Maciej Korbowa i Bellatrix [Maciej Korbowa and Bellatrix]. In *Dramaty,* 1962.

Niepodległość trójktów [The Independence of Triangles] (produced 1988). In *Dramaty,* 1962.

Oni (produced 1963). In *Dramaty,* 1962; as *They,* in *The Madman and the Nun and Other Plays,* translated by Daniel Gerould and C.S. Durer, 1968.

Matka (produced 1964). In *Dramaty,* 1962; as *The Mother,* in *The Madman and the Nun and Other Plays,* translated by Daniel Gerould and C.S. Durer, 1968.

Szalona lokomotywa (produced 1965). In *Dramaty,* 1962; as *The Crazy Locomotive,* in *The Madman and the Nun and Other Plays,* translated by Daniel Gerould and C.S. Durer, 1968.

Gyubal Wahazar; czyli, Na przełęczach absurdu (produced 1966). In *Dramaty,* 1962; as *Gyubal Wahazar; or, Along the Cliffs of the Absurd,* in *Tropical Madness: Four Plays,* translated by Daniel and Eleanor Gerould, 1972.

Bezimienne dzielo (produced 1967). In *Dramaty,* 1962; as *The Anonymous Work,* translated by Daniel and Eleanor Gerould, in *Twentieth-Century Polish Avant-Garde Drama,* edited by Daniel Gerould, 1977.

Nadobnisie i koczkodany; czyli, Zielona pigułka (produced 1967). In *Dramaty,* 1962; as *Dainty Shapes and Hairy Apes,* translated by Daniel Gerould, in *The Beelzebub Sonata,* 1977.

Janulka, córka Fizdejki [Janulka, Daughter of Fizdejko] (produced 1974). In *Dramaty,* 1962.

Karaluchy [Cockroaches] (produced 1966).

Menażeria; cyzli, Wybryk słonia [Menagerie; or, The Elephant's Escapades] (produced 1966).

Księżniczka Magdalena; cyzli, Natrętny ksiźe [Princess Magdalena; or, The Importunate Princess] (produced 1966).

The Madman and the Nun and Other Plays (includes *The Madman and the Nun*; *The Water Hen*; *The Crazy Locomotive*; *The Mother*; *They*; *The Shoemakers*), edited and translated by Daniel Gerould and C.S. Durer. 1968.

Odważna księżniczka [The Courageous Princess] (produced 1970).

Biedny chłopiec [The Poor Boy] (produced 1970).

Tropical Madness: Four Plays (includes *The Pragmatists*; *Mr. Price; or Tropical Madness*; *Gyubal Wahazar; or, Along the Cliffs of the Absurd*; *Metaphysics of a Two-Headed Calf*), translated by Daniel and Eleanor Gerould. 1972.

Panna Tutli-Putli [Miss Tootli-Pootli] (produced 1975). 1974.

The Beelzebub Sonata (includes *The Beelzebub Sonata*; *Dainty Shapes and Hairy Apes*; *Tumor Brainowicz*; and non-dramatic writings) translated by Daniel Gerould. 1977.

Fiction

Pożegnanie jesieni [Farewell to Autumn]. 1927.

Nienasycenie. 1930; as *Insatiability*, translated by Louis Iribarne, 1977, revised version, 1996.

Jedyne wyjście [The Only Way Out], edited by Tomasz Jodelka-Burzecki. 1968.

622 Upadki Bunga; czyli, Demoniczna Kobieta [622 Downfalls of Bungo; or, The Demonic Woman]. 1972.

Other

Nowe formy w malarstwie i wynikjace std nieporozumienia [New Forms in Painting and the Resulting Misunderstandings]. 1919.

Teatr: Wstęp do teorii czystej formy w teatrze [Theatre: Introduction to the Theory of Pure Form in the Theatre]. 1923; as *Czysta forma w teatrze*, edited by J. Degler, 1977.

Nikotyna, alkohol, kokaina, peyotl, morfina, eter [Nicotine, Alcohol, Cocaine, Peyote, Morphine, Ether]. 1932.

Pojęcia i twierdzenia implikowane przez pojecie istnienia [The Concepts and Principles Implied by the Concept of Existence]. 1935.

Pisma filozoficzne i estetyczne [Philosophical and Aesthetic Writings], edited by J. Leszczyński. 2 vols., 1974–76.

Bez kompromisu: Pisma krytyczne i publicystyczne [No Compromise: Critical and Journalistic Writings], edited by J. Degler. 1976.

Poza rzeczywistości [Outside Reality]. 1977.

Marzenia improduktywne: Dywagacja metafizyczna [Improductive Daydreams: Metaphysical Palaver]. 1977.

Zagadnienie psychofizyczne [A Psychophysical Problem], edited by B. Michalski. 1978.

Listy do Bronisława Malinowskiego [Letters to Bronisław Malinowski]. 1981.

*

Bibliography: "Theatre Checklist No. 6: Stanisław Ignacy Witkiewicz," in *Theatrefacts*, 2(2), 1975.

Critical Studies: *Witkiewicz: Aux sources d'un théâtre nouveau* by Alain von Crugten, 1971; Witkiewicz issue of *Polish Review*, 18, 1973; *Witkacy: Stanisław Ignacy Witkiewicz as an Imaginative Writer* by Daniel Gerould, 1981; *Stanisław Witkiewicz* by Tymon Terlecki, 1983; *Witkacy the Painter* by Irena Jakimowicz, 1987; *Revolutionaries in the Theatre: Meyerhold, Brecht, and Witkiewicz* by Christine Kiebuzinska, 1988; *Witkacy: S.I. Witkiewicz: Life and Work* by Anna Micinska, 1990.

*   *   *

Stanisław Witkiewicz (also known as Witkacy) was an artist with many skills: in his lifetime his reputation as a painter easily superseded his literary fame, and within the domain of literature he cultivated three such different fields as the theatre, the novel, and art criticism. All his literary works to some extent illustrated his philosophical and aesthetic theories which were first expounded in *Nowe formy w malarstwie* [New Forms in Painting] and in *Teatr: Wstęp do teorii czystej formy w teatrze* [Theatre: Introduction to the Theory of Pure Form in the Theatre]. According to Witkiewicz nothing can be asserted about Being except that it predicates "particular existences" and that these "monads" experience the strangeness of separate existence. It is only through metaphysical feelings that the mystery of the Universe can be grasped, and the significance of art lies in its unique capacity (with the decline of religious feeling) to induce "metaphysical thrills." In art Witkiewicz was an advocate of Pure Form ("The form of the work of art is its only essential content") but he realized that it was attainable only in music and perhaps in painting, so in the theatre he suggested bold deformations and illogical, irrational, purely "scenic" constructions. Though for a while he was associated with the Formists, a group of painters and poets in Cracow, Witkiewiez's aesthetic views differed from those of the so-called "Cracow Vanguard" showing more affinity with such similarly lonely precursors of the modern theatre as Antonin Artaud.

Most of Witkiewicz's plays were written in the 1920s though his best political satire, *Szewcy* (*The Shoemakers*), dates from 1931–34. His plays do not fit into traditional categories: they are grotesque and eclectic mixtures of sex, philosophy, politics, and art in which sudden outbursts of private passion alternate with lengthy expositions of new creeds and ideologies. The characters, as Miłosz puts it in his *The History of Polish Literature*, are mainly "madmen, misfits and maniacs" moving in a cosmopolitan upperclass and intellectual milieu; they usually include a tyrannical leader, a disillusioned Artist or Philosopher, and a Demonic Woman who all undergo shattering changes during the play, even death (often reversed) or moral degradation. Some of Witkiewicz's plays can be read as parables on history and society. In *The Shoemakers*, for example, we witness the fall of the *ancien régime* and the victory of the shoemakers' revolution which is then followed by the murder of Sajetan Tempe, their leader, by the shoemakers themselves and by the imposition of military and bureaucratic rule upon the people, with the gigantic figure of the Hyperworkoid (Hiper-Robociarz) serving as a convenient façade.

Witkiewicz's plays achieved popularity only after 1956, when with the advent of the theatre of the absurd and the theatre of cruelty his dramatized fantasies struck the public as thoroughly modern. As for his novels only two of these were published in his lifetime and of these *Nienasycenie* (*Insatiability*) was the more ambitious. It is an anti-utopian novel on one level, evoking the image of a decadent and semi-fascistic Polish state of the future ruled by a popular dictator, a Poland which is a buffer-zone between the superficially communistic states of the West and the radical Communist Chinese who have by now taken over Russia. On another level, it is a novel of adventure, the story of a young hero's initiation in sex, art, drugs, and politics. *Insatiability* ends with the collapse of Western civilization—the

Chinese take over Poland without war, thanks to the widespread use of the drug *Murti-Bing*, not unlike Aldous Huxley's *soma*. In fact, Witkiewicz experimented with drugs many years before Huxley and described his experiences in *Nikotyna, alkohol, kokaina, peyotl, motfina, eter* [Nicotine, Alcohol, Cocaine, Peyote, Morphine, Ether].

Insatiability makes interesting though difficult reading; although Witkiewicz often parodied the style of the Modernist writers of "Young Poland," his own roots lie in art nouveau and his style suffers from an excess of metaphors and adjectives. Storytelling is often interrupted by digressions and debates on the merits of modern philosophical theories, while important political events are told in small print in the form of "information bulletins." The style of *Insatiability* can be described as "psycho-expressionistic"—it represents an expressionism with much psychological insight but sometimes steering perilously close to psychotic phenomena. Witkiewicz's fear of a collectivized, mechanized, herd-like society turning its back on art for the sake of advanced technology is well-nigh prophetic; according to his English translator, Louis Iribarne, Witkiewicz's main concern was "the threat posed to human consciousness by a process that is beyond man's capacity to control."

—George Gömöri

WOLF, Christa

Born: Landsberg an der Warthe, Germany (now Gorzow, Poland), 18 March 1929. **Education:** Educated at schools in Landsberg, Schwerin, and Bad Frankenhausen, graduated 1949; universities of Jena and Leipzig, 1949–53, diploma 1953. **Family:** Married Gerhard Wolf in 1951; two daughters. **Career:** Secretary to the mayor of Gammelin, 1945–46; worked as technical assistant, East German Writers' Union, 1953–59; editor, *Neue deutsche Literatur*, 1958–59; reader for Mitteldeutscher Verlag, Halle, 1959–62, and Verlag Neues Leben, Berlin; resident writer in a freight car manufacturing company, 1959–62; freelance writer since 1962. Member of the German Communist Party, from 1949 (resigned 1989); candidate member of central committee, SED, 1963–67. Lives in Berlin, Germany. **Awards:** Heinrich Mann prize, 1963; National prize, 1964; Raabe prize, 1972; Fontane prize, 1972; City of Bremen prize, 1978; Büchner prize, 1980; Schiller prize, 1983. **Member:** Academy of Arts, Berlin.

PUBLICATIONS

Fiction

Moskauer Novelle. 1961.
Der geteilte Himmel. 1963; as *Divided Heaven*, translated by Joan Becker, 1965.
Nachdenken über Christa T. 1968; as *The Quest for Christa T.*, translated by Christopher Middleton, 1970.
Till Eulenspiegel. Erzählung für den Film. 1972.
Unter den Linden: Drei unwahrscheinliche Geschichten. 1974.
Kindheitsmuster. 1976; as *A Model Childhood*, translated by Ursula Molinaro and Hedwig Rappolt, 1980.
Kein Ort, Nirgends. 1979; as *No Place on Earth*, translated by Jan van Heurck, 1982.
Gesammelte Erzählungen. 1980.

Kassandra. 1983; as *Cassandra: A Novel and Four Essays*, translated by Jan Van Heurck, 1984.
Störfall: Nachrichten eines Tages. 1987; as *Accident: A Day's News*, translated by Heike Schwarzbauer and Rick Takvorian, 1989.
Sommerstück. 1989.
Was bleibt: Erzählung. 1990.
What Remains and Other Stories, translated by Heike Schwarzbauer and Rick Takvorian. 1993.
Painting from Phantoms: Selected Writings, 1990–1994, translated and annotated by Jan Van Heurck. 1997.
Selected Prose and Drama, with Ingeborg Bachmann, edited by Patricia A. Herminghouse. 1998.
Medea: A Modern Retelling, translated by John Cullen. 1998.

Verse

Das Leben der Schildkröten in Frankfurt am Main: ein Prosagedicht. 1989.

Other

Lesen und Schreiben: Aufsätze und Prosastücke. 1972; revised edition, 1981; as *The Reader and the Writer*, translated by Joan Becker, 1977.
Fortgesetzter Versuch: Aufsätze, Gespräche, Essays. 1979.
Voraussetzungen einer Erzählung; Kassandra. 1983.
Ins Ungebundene gehet eine sehnsucht: Gesprächsraum Romantik, with Gerhard Wolf. 1985.
Die Dimension des Autors: Essays und Aufsätze, Reden und Gespräche, 1959–1985. 2 vols., 1986; selection published as *The Fourth Dimension: Interviews with Christa Wolf*, 1988; as *The Author's Dimension: Selected Essays*, translated by Jan Van Heurck, edited by Alexander Stephan, 1993.
Ansprachen. 1988.
Essays of Christa Wolf. 1990.
Reden im Herbst. 1990.
Editor, with Gerhard Wolf, *Wir, unsere Zeit.* 1959.
Editor, *In diesen Jahren: Deutsche Erzähler der Gegenwart.* 1959.
Editor, *Proben junger Erzähler. Ausgewählte deutsche Prosa.* 1959.
Editor, *Glauben an Irdisches*, by Anna Seghers. 1969.
Editor, *Der Schatten eines Traumes*, by Karoline von Günderrode. 1979.
Editor, *Die Günderrode*, by Bettina von Arnim. 1981.
Editor, *Ausgewählte Erzählungen*, by Anna Seghers. 1983.

*

Bibliography: *Christa Wolf. Ein Arbeitsbuch: Studien-Dokumente-Bibliographie* by Agela Drescher, 1989.

Critical Studies: *Christa Wolf* by Alexander Stephan, 1976; *Materialienbuch* edited by Klaus Sauer, 1979; *Women Writers—The Divided Self: Analysis of Novels by Christa Wolf, Ingeborg Bachmann, Doris Lessing and Others* by Inta Ezergailis, 1982; *The Death of Socialist Realism in the Novels of Christa Wolf* by George Bühler, 1984; *Wolf. Darstellung-Deutung-Diskussion* edited by Manfred Jurgensen, 1984; *Christa Wolf. Text + Kritik* edited by Heinz Ludwig Arnold, 3rd edition, 1985; *Erinnerte Zukunft. 11 Studien zum Werk Christa Wolfs* edited by Wolfram Mauser, 1985; *Christa Wolf* by Sonja Hilzinger, 1986; *Tradition, Art and Society: Christa Wolf's*

Prose by Colin E. Smith, 1987; *Christa Wolf's Utopian Vision: From Marxism to Feminism* by Anna K. Kuhn, 1988; *Difficulties of Saying "I": The Narrator as Protagonist in Christa Wolf's Kindheitsmuster and Uwe Johnson's Jahrestage* by Robert K. Shirer, 1988; *Responses to Christa Wolf* edited by Marilyn Sibley Fries, 1989; *Christa Wolf: Literature and the Conscience of History* by Myran N. Love, 1991; *Understanding Christa Wolf: Returning Home to a Foreign Land* by Margit Resch, 1997; *Christa Wolf* by Gail Finney, 1999.

*   *   *

Internationally acknowledged by the late 1980s as the German Democratic Republic's most prominent literary figurehead, as well as one of the foremost women writers in German, Christa Wolf established her reputation in GDR letters in the 1960s and early 1970s on the basis of her critical engagement with the rigid structures of the Communist regime and her position in the vanguard of formal and stylistic innovation in GDR prose writing.

Having worked as a literary critic and editor from 1955, she made her creative literary debut in 1961 with *Moskauer Novelle* [Moscow Novella], a tale of renounced love between a GDR doctor and a Soviet translator which Wolf herself would later dismiss as naive and dogmatic. Her second work, *Der geteilte Himmel* (*Divided Heaven*), another story of ill-fated love, this time between an idealistic young student and a cynical chemist who ultimately leaves for the West, created a critical stir on its publication in 1963 with its (for the time) remarkably differentiated critique of GDR society.

But it was with the short story "Juninachmittag" [June Afternoon], and her major novel *Nachdenken über Christa T.* (*The Quest for Christa T.*), that Wolf found her characteristic style, a style she would later term "subjective authenticity." The term implied a challenge to the ruling party's claim to an objective overview of the processes of history, and with it Wolf sought to validate subjective experience, using her own authentic experience as the basis for literary treatments intended paradigmatically to disclose disorders in society as a means of promoting their redress. She thus broke with the conventions of officially sanctioned Socialist Realism with its formally conservative agitprop didacticism, adopting instead techniques associated with Western modernism—self-conscious narration, shifting narrative perspectives—in order to create a probing, questioning prose which draws the reader into its process of reflection. *The Quest for Christa T.* narrates the attempt to write the life of a dead friend, in the course of which the narrator finds herself confronting her own political past; it is ultimately an affirmation of the dynamism and imaginativeness embodied by Christa T. in a society seen as promoting conformism. It and the essay written to accompany it, "The Reader and the Writer," became pivotal texts in the development of GDR literature.

There followed a lengthy autobiographically-based project examining Wolf's childhood and upbringing under Nazism, *Kindheitsmuster* (*A Model Childhood*). The three intertwined narrative levels combine the recollections of youth, the account of a 1971 journey to the narrator's hometown, now in Poland, and a commentary on the writing of the novel. Although focusing on Germany's past—and it is perhaps the most compelling account by any German writer of everyday life in the Third Reich—its central question concerns the present: "How did we become what we are today?" The basic premise of *A Model Childhood* is that patterns of behaviour learned by Wolf's generation as children under Nazism continue to inform their contemporary political behaviour.

In 1976 the singer Wolf Biermann was expelled from the GDR and as one of the first signatories of the protest Wolf fell foul of the Communist authorities; the subsequent period of backlash during which many writers left the GDR shattered her hitherto fundamental faith in the GDR's socialist project, and the works that followed were marked by a new sense of cultural pessimism. *Kein Ort, Nirgends* (*No Place on Earth*) is an imaginary encounter between the Romantic poets Heinrich von Kleist and Karoline Günderode, visionaries who found "no place" in the society of their day. *Kassandra* (*Cassandra*) is a "re-vision" of the classical legend of Troy in which the seer Cassandra frees herself from her loyalty to the ruling hierarchy in Troy and predicts the downfall of her society. Both can be read as allegories of Wolf's own situation, but they also address broader cultural issues which inform her work of the 1980s: the exclusion of women from cultural agency, the inherent militarism and aggression of Western culture, the exclusive rationalism of the technocratic age as symptomatic of subjective alienation. With these works and the complex of essays surrounding them, Wolf stepped decisively into the arena of feminist debate.

The critique of the self-destructive rationalism and technocracy of modern culture returned as the central theme of *Störfall: Nachrichten eines Tages* (*Accident: A Day's News*), published as a literary response to the 1986 nuclear reactor explosion at Chernobyl. This work also marked a return to Wolf's earlier "subjectively authentic" style: the literary treatment of authentic experience in which the writing process becomes a process of reflection. The same is true of *Sommerstück* [Summer Piece], a wistful Chekhovian account of a summer among friends in the late 1970s after the Biermann expulsion, and the controversial *Was bleibt* [What Remains] of 1990.

Wolf's participation in the events of 1989 made it clear that, while she had distanced herself from the ruling regime, she nevertheless continued to cherish the hope of a reformed democratic socialism in an independent East German state. She greeted reunification with misgivings. Moreover, the publication of *Was bleibt*, the account of the day in the life of a writer under surveillance by the State Security police, written in 1979 when she herself was under surveillance and revised for publication only after the fall of the Berlin Wall, made her the focus of bitter personal attacks in the Western press. She was accused of having propped up the Communist regime by her continued presence as a prestigious intellectual figure and by her failure to speak out unequivocally against it, of having enjoyed the privileges of her position, and now of trying to number herself *post factum* amongst the victims. A more sympathetic reading sees in *Was bleibt* a characteristically sensitive, if self-accusatory analysis of the effects of surveillance and of the psychological mechanisms of the totalitarian state.

Despite the controversy lately surrounding her, Wolf remains a major writer in post-1945 German literature, an essayist and editor of note, as well as novelist and cultural commentator.

—Georgina Paul

WOLFRAM VON ESCHENBACH

Fl. 1195–1220. **Born:** Near Anspach, in Bavaria. **Career:** Possibly in the service of the counts of Wertheim, and of the Landgrave Hermann of Thuringia at Wartburg.

PUBLICATIONS

Collections

[Works], edited by Karl Lachmann, 1833, revised by Eduard Hartl. 1952.
[Works], edited by Albert Leitzmann, revised edition. 3 vols., 1933–48.

Verse

Parzival, und Titurel, edited by Karl Bartsch, revised by Marta Marti. 3 vols., 1929–35; *Parzival* translated by Jessie L. Weston, 2 vols., 1894; also translated by Edwin H. Zeydel, 1951; Helen M. Mustard and Charles E. Passage, 1961; A.T. Hatto, 1980; translated in part by Margaret F. Richey, as *Schionatulander and Sigune*, 1960.
Die Lyrik, edited by Peter Wapnewski. 1972.
Willehalm, edited by Hedwig Heger. 1978; also edited by Werner Schröder, 1978; as *Willehalm*, translated by Charles E. Passage, 1977; also translated by Marion E. Gibbs and Sidney M. Johnson, 1984.
Titurel and the Songs, edited and translated by Marion E. Gibbs and Sidney M. Johnson. 1988.

*

Bibliography: *Bibliographie zu Wolfram von Eschenbach* by Willy Krogmann and Ulrich Pretzel, 1963, revised edition, 1968.

Critical Studies: *Studies of Wolfram von Eschenbach* by Margaret F. Richey, 1957; *An Introduction to Wolfram's "Parzifal"* by Hugh Sacker, 1963; *Wolfram's "Parzifal"* by H.J. Wiegand, edited by Ursula Joffman, 1969; *Rennewart in Wolfram's "Willehalm": A Study of Wolfram von Eschenbach and His Sources* by C.J. Lofmark, 1972; *Wolfram von Eschenbach* by James F. Poag, 1972; *Wolfram's Parzifal: An Attempt at a Total Evaluation* by Henry Kratz, 1973; *Wolfram and His Audience: Study of the Themes of Quest and of Recognition of Kinship Identity* by Stephen C. Harroff, 1974; *The Use of Imagery in Wolfram's Parzifal: A Distributional Study* by Patricia L. Kutzner, 1975; *Narrative Art in Wolfram's "Willehalm"* by Marion E. Gibbs, 1976; *Approaches to Wolfram von Eschenbach: Five Essays* by D.H. Green, 1978; *The Influence of Biblical Terminology and Thought on Wolfram's Parzifal* by David Duckworth, 1980; *Wolfram von Eschenbach's Couples* by Siegfried Richard Christoph, 1981; *The Art of Narration in Wolfram's Parzifal and Albrecht's Jüngerer Titurel* by Linda B. Parshall, 1981; *The Art of Recognition in Wolfram's Parzifal* by D.H. Green, 1982; *Wolfram's Parzifal: On the Genesis of Its Poetry* by Marianne Wynn, 1984; *Commentary on the Soltane and Jeschute Episodes in Book III of Wolfram von Eschenbach's Parzival* by David N. Yeandle, 1984; *Narrator and Audience Roles in Wolfram's Parzifal* by Robert Lee Bradley, 1988; *Studien zu Wolfram von Eschenbach* edited by Kurt Gärtner and Joachim Heinzele, 1989; *Symbols of the Grail Quest: A Consideration of Parzifal by Wolfram von Esenbach* by Ian Forrester Roberts, 1990; *Vivianz: An Analysis of the Martyr Figure in Wolfram von Eschenbach's "Willehalm" and in His Old French Source Material* by John Greenfield, 1991; *Romancing the Grail: Genre, Science, and Quest in Wolfram's Parzival* by Arthur Groos, 1995; *Illuminating the Epic: The Kassel Willehalm Codex and the Landgraves of Hesse in the Early Fourteenth Century* by Joan A. Holladay, 1996; *A Companion to Wolfram's Parzival*, edited by Will Hasty, 1999.

* * *

Wolfram von Eschenbach is best known for his epic poems, but eight short poems composed by him have also been preserved. These display great lyricism, passion, and control. They are also notable for certain features of striking originality such as his praise of marital love.

His only completed epic is *Parzival* (25,000 lines), loosely based on a similar epic by Chrétien de Troyes. Through very many connected and unconnected episodes the hero progresses from a state of complete innocence and naïvety brought about by his secluded infancy to a state of readiness to be Grail King. He is the epitome of the Knight in the service of ladies, humanity, and God.

The Holy Grail is a central feature of this poem, and Wolfram's conception of the Grail bears close similarities in its gnosticism to the Cathar heresy which prevailed in the area of the Pyrenees at the beginning of the 13th century. Wolfram himself tells us that he was supplied with additional material by one Kyot, who has been, albeit problematically, identified with Guiot of Provence. Moreover, Wolfram displays a genuine ethical and religious seriousness which is not in any conventional ecclesiastical tradition.

Parzival is a very rich development of the material which he took from his basic sources, and shows signs of constant re-editing over the period (1200–10 approximately), in which it was composed, with immense elaboration of detail.

Parzival's progress is illustrated in the very numerous incidents of the epic. He first follows the advice of others in obtaining the trappings of chivalry, such as knightly weapons and tactful avoidance of being over-inquisitive. He later discovers that it is necessary to transcend formal etiquette when the dictates of humanity require this. A knight who serves humanity and is at one with God will sense when it is right to show sympathetic interest in another's suffering despite the rules enjoining discretion. The rules of chivalry are in these scenes depicted as a guide to those who seek to serve humanity and God, but not as the epitome of such service.

An excellent example of the unceasing development of his ideas is given by the *Titurel* fragments (c. 1210–20). In this, characters associated with *Parzival* recur in a work dealing with a search. In these fragments Wolfram's mastery of form combines magnificently with immense profundity of feeling in a work of striking maturity. *Parzival* and *Willehalm* are in rhyming couplets, but *Titurel* is composed in complex strophes.

Willehalm (14,000 lines; from c. 1210–12) is unfinished and is again the work of a mature writer displaying a sure mastery of form. The central pillars of the work are the two battles of Aliscans against the Saracens. One of these battles results in the tragic death of the model knight Vivianz. In the other the mighty hero Renewart plays a notable part in the successful quest for revenge.

Wolfram is an unconventional and strikingly confident poet with strong powers of imagination and humour. He displays a genuine piety and belief in the possibility of a direct knowledge of God by man. Realistic detail suffuses the idealistic knightly world, and his characters are brought lovingly to life. Even in his own lifetime, the richness of his language was the subject of comment (albeit unfavourable comment by Gottfried von Strassburg). He himself showed an awareness that his love of detail (foreign words are an example) was human or antiquarian rather than scholarly. It may be true that his love of detail, the sheer mass of his work, its depth and richness, the eccentricities and difficulties of his style, conspire occasionally to give an impression of excessive weight. Yet this is a minor misgiving when placed beside Wolfram's truly monumental achievements. When material of such richness and complexity is contained with sure control in works of masterly form which are suffused throughout with life and interest, the resulting impact is unambiguously great literature of the very first rank.

—G.P. Cubbin

See the essays on *Parzival*, *Titurel*, and *Willehalm*.

WYSPIAŃSKI, Stanisław (Mateusz Ignacy)

Born: Cracow, Poland (then part of the Austrian Empire), 15 January 1869. **Education:** Educated at College of St. Anne, Cracow, 1879–87; Academy of Fine Arts and Jagiellonian University, Cracow, from 1887. **Career:** Painter and draftsman from late 1880s; created the stained-glass windows for the Franciscan Church, Cracow, 1895; co-editor of *Życie* [Life] from 1898; stage designer and director from 1898; physical breakdown, caused by syphilis, 1903; worked on renovation of the royal castle in Cracow, 1903–05, and other art and interior design projects; elected alderman of Cracow, 1905; second physical breakdown, 1906: bedridden at his home in Wegrzce, 1906–07. **Died:** 28 November 1907.

PUBLICATIONS

Collections

Dzieła [Works], edited by Adam Chmiel, Tadesuz Sinko, and Leon Płoszewski. 8 vols., 1924–32.
Dzieła zebrane [Collected Works], edited by Leon Płoszewski and others. 16 vols., 1958–71.

Plays

Legenda I (produced 1905). 1897.
Warszawianka [Song of Warsaw] (produced 1898). In Z*Życie*, 45, 1898; in book form, 1901.
Meleager (produced 1908). 1898; as *Meleager*, translated by Florence Noyes and George Rapall Noyes, 1933.
Lelewel (produced 1899). 1899.
Kltwa [The Curse] (produced 1909). In Z*Życie*, 15–16, 1899; in book form, 1901.
Protesilas i Laodamia (produced 1903). In *Przegld Polski*, 34, 1899; in book form, 1901; translated as *Protesilaus and Laodamia*, in *Slavonic Review*, 11, 1933.
Legion (produced 1911). 1900.
Wesele (produced 1901). 1901; as *The Wedding*, translated by F. Sobieniowski and H. Pearson, 1933; also translated by Gerard T. Kapolka, 1990; as *The Wedding: A Drama in Three Acts*, translated by Noel Clark, 1998.

Bolesław Śmiały [Bolesław the Bold] (produced 1903). 1902 (first complete edition); revised version, 1903.
Achilleis [Achilles] (produced 1925). 1903.
Wyzwolenie [Deliverance] (produced 1903). 1903.
Noc listopadowa [November Night] (produced 1908). 1904.
Legenda II [A Legend II] (produced 1905). 1904.
Akropolis [Acropolis] (produced in part, 1916; produced in full, 1926). 1904.
Śmierć Ofelji [The Death of Ophelia] (fragment; produced 1909). In *Nowa Reforma*, 114, 1906; in book form, in *Dzieła*, vol. 6, 1932.
Zaïre, from the play by Voltaire (incomplete), in *Nowa Reforma*. May 1906.
Skałka [The Rock] (produced 1957). 1906.
Cyd, from a play by Pierre Corneille (produced 1907). In *Nowa Reforma*, June 1906; in book form, 1907.
Powrót Odysa (produced 1917). 1907; as *The Return of Odysseus*, translated by Howard Clarke, 1966.
Sędziowie [The Judges] (produced 1907). 1907.
Samuel Zborowski [Samuel Zborowski] (fragment), parts in *Nowa Reforma*, 593 (supplement). 1907; all fragments in *Dzieła*, vol. 6, 1932.
Jadwiga [Jadwiga] (fragment; produced 1914). In *Przegld Powszechny*, February 1908; in book form, in *Dzieła*, vol. 6, 1932.
Królowa polskiej korony [The Queen of the Polish Crown] (produced 1919). In *Czas*, 61, 1908; in book form, in *Dzieła*, vol. 1, 1924.
Piastowicze [The Descendants of the Piasts] (fragment), in *Krytyka*. November 1909; in book form, in *Dzieła*, vol. 6, 1932.
Juliusz II [Juliusz II] (fragment; produced 1911). In *Dzieła*, vol. 8, 1932.
Ajas [Ajax] (fragment), in *Sztuka*. January 1913; in book form, in *Dzieła*, vol. 6, 1932.
Zygmunt August (fragments; parts produced 1915). 1930 (first complete edition).
Daniel (produced 1927). In *Dzieła*, vol. 1, 1924.
Batory pod Pskowem [Batory at Pskov], in *Dzieła*, vol. 1. 1924.
Weimar (fragment; produced 1932). In *Dzieła*, vol. 6, 1932.
Król Kazimierz Jagiellonczyk [King Casimir the Jagellonian], in *Dzieła*, vol. 6. 1932.
Mż [The Husband], in *Dzieła*, vol. 6. 1932.
Feakowie [The Phaeacians], in *Dzieła*, vol. 6. 1932.
Rudera [The Ruin] (fragment), in *Dzieła*, vol. 6. 1932.

Verse

Kazimierz Wielki [Casimir the Great], in *Czas*, 148–152. 1900; in book form, 1901.
Henryk Pobozny, in *Kuryer Warsawski*, 98. 1903; in book form, in *Dzieła*, vol. 7, 1932.
Hymn Veni Creator, in *Nowa Reforma*, 125. 1906; in book form, in *Dzieła*, vol. 7, 1932.
Wernyhora (fragments), parts in *Lamus*, 1. 1908–09; all fragments in *Dzieła*, vol. 7, 1932.
Święty Stanisław, in *Pamietnik literacki*, 1–2. 1908; in book form, in *Dzieła*, vol. 7, 1932.

Other

Dzieła, vol. 8 (includes writings on theatre, his study of Shakespeare's *Hamlet*, and his *mise en scène* for *Dzaidy* by Adam Mickiewicz). 1932.
Listy do Stanisława Lacka [Letters to Stanisław Lack]. 1957.

Listy do Lucjana Rydla [Letters to Lucjan Rydel], edited by Leon Płoszewski and Maria Rydlowa. 2 vols., 1979.

*

Bibliography: *Monografia bibliograficzna III–IV: Teatr Wyspiańskiego* by Maria Stokowa, 1968.

Critical Studies: "Stanisław Wyspiański" by Stefan Srebrny, in *Slavonic Review*, 2, 1923; "Stanisław Wyspiański" by W. Borowy, in *Slavonic Review*, 11, 1933; *Heinrich von Kleist und Stanisław Wyspiański: Ein Vergleich der Tragik in ihren Dramen* by B. Rosenthal, 1938; *Le Dramaturge Stanisław Wyspiański* by Claude Backvis, 1952; "Stanisław Wyspiański and the Poetics of Symbolist Drama," in *Polish Review*, 15(4), 1970, "The Greatness and Ill Fortune of Stanisław Wyspiański," in *Antemurale*, 14, 1970, "Wyspiański in Two Perspectives," in *Antemurale*, 15, 1971, and *Stanisław Wyspiański* (in English), 1983, all by Tymon Terlecki; "Stanisław Wyspiański and Symbolist Drama: The Work of Art as *Dramatis Persona*" by Nina Taylor, in *Slavonic and East European Review*, 66, 1988.

*   *   *

Stanisław Wyspiański was a highly versatile artist. As one of the leading representatives of art nouveau in Poland, he made a name in painting and applied arts. He also composed several historical poems, called rhapsodies, such as *Kazimierz Wielki* [Casimir the Great] and *Bolesław Śmiały* [Bolesław the Bold], while his scarce but remarkable lyrical poetry struck a very private tone and was not destined for publication.

In the history of Polish literature, however, Wyspiański is best known as one of the leading dramatists, who, in a broader cultural context, was also a great reformer of national theatre. The deep interest in the theatre, dominant in his later years, had its roots in Polish Romantic plays, Wagner's operas, seen in Germany, and Greek drama. During his long sojourn in Paris, Wyspiański systematically visited the Comédie-Française and the Théâtre Libre, and was particularly impressed by the production of Sophocles' *Oedipus Tyrannus* (*Oedipus the King*). Combining Romantic and Wagnerian traditions, he developed the idea of "monumental theatre," engaging numerous actors and cumulating diverse stage effects. His study of Shakespeare's *Hamlet* contains general remarks which pioneered interest in the theatre as a category distinct from literary texts due to its extra-verbal effects.

Wyspiański's dramatic output includes plays in verse based on Greek mythology, Polish history, and contemporary events. Their techniques encompass ancient tragedy, Romantic drama, and modern symbolism. Although he maintained the patriotic commitment of the Romantics, his modern "intellectual dramas" seek out truth by unmasking human role-playing. Consequently, in the book about *Hamlet*, Wyspiański placed drama within much the broader *theatrum mundi*, granting it the role of symbolic expression for the general structure of the world.

Warszawianka [Song of Warsaw], a one-act play about the November Uprising, is the initial attempt at his artistic and intellectual pursuits. Its theatrical appeal involves not only dialogues, but also music, visual effects, and pantomime, to deliver the foremost attack against the enactment of a "patriotic theatre" in real life. The army officers and agitated young women, who exalt the beauty of heroic death and in their lofty rhetoric create the atmosphere of inescapable

fate, are contrasted with the simplicity of a speechless episode, where an old soldier, straight from a battlefield, hands over a sad message, salutes, and leaves. *Kltwa* [The Curse], set in a contemporary Galician village afflicted by a drought (allegedly caused by sins of the parish priest), conveys another portrayal of self-imposed tragic fate. It combines Greek-style drama with a contemporary understanding of destiny, guilt, and responsibility in an interesting attempt to bring ancient tragedy back to life.

Calamity generated by self-deception found its finest expression in *Wesele* (*The Wedding*), Wyspiański's most popular work. It has its origins in an authentic marriage between a popular Cracow poet and a peasant girl, but in its artistic shape the play blends together a realistic, factual report and Symbolist dramatic poetry. The rapid succession of dialogues and events at the wedding party is subsequently elevated by the appearance of phantom guests representing the human characters' hidden fears and desires. The idea of national unity, which the marriage between a gentleman and an uneducated village girl was supposed to demonstrate, appears to be an illusion. Another fallacy is a call for national uprising, provoked by Wernyhora, the symbolic impersonation of Polish romantic bards. The last episode is dominated by the "Chochol," that is, by an animated bundle of straw brought to life by the power of poetic imagination. In an amazing pantomime the wedding guests follow his tunes in a state of trance which makes clear the dangers of artistic illusions and national mythology in a vision unsurpassed in Polish literature.

Accusations against the supremacy of art in Polish thinking are carried on in *Wyzwolenie* [Deliverance], Wyspiański's most avant-garde and complex play. This theatre within a theatre is a plotless poetic drama which blurs demarcations between stage rehearsals, national symbols, and an external political situation. The events portrayed apparently take place in the Municipal Theatre in Cracow, where a play about contemporary Poland is rehearsed, but their transparent structure exceeds those limits and refers directly to the real country. Theatre eventually turns into a symbol of Poland, where disingenuous rhetoric and role-playing keep the nation in the state of inertia. *Akropolis* [Acropolis] is another experimental play or dramatic poem, conceived as an imaginary animation of works of art in Wawel Cathedral. During one night old statues engage in conversation, while human figures step down from tapestries to recreate scenes from the Holy Bible and the Trojan war, thus activating an extraordinary concoction in time and space. This allows Wyspiański to outline his general idea of human response to pressures coming from God and the outer world.

Noc listopadowa [November Night] portrays the first hours of the November Uprising, following Polish Romantic drama in its loose, disjointed form. It brings to life the statues of the Greek gods in a Warsaw park in order to enhance the events represented and to lend them a more general dimension by drawing an analogy with the Eleusinian myth of rebirth. The historical events of the November night form a sequence, encompassing major heroes and the most important developments. Wyspiański seems to believe that Polish society had not been ready to fight for independence because of its shortlived enthusiasm ("a fire of straw") and reckless operations. Nonetheless, the patriotic spirit of those days has survived to encourage future generations.

Sędziowie [The Judges] elevates a common crime, actually committed in Galicia, into a universal tragedy where only the death of an innocent secures genuine justice. Wyspiański's "Greek dramas," such as *Achilleis* [Achilles] and *Powrót Odysa* (*The Return of Odysseus*), are mostly reinterpretations of Homeric epic, and concern human fate along with its moral horizons. Wyspiański's theatre anticipated 20th-century developments in Poland, while the idea of ''roles'' and ''masks'' in Polish society has influenced many modern writers, including Jerzy Andrzejewski and Sławomir Mrożek, and filmmakers such as Andrzej Wajda.

—Stanisław Eile

X-Y

XENOPHON

Born: Athens, c. 431 or 428–27 BC. **Family:** Married to Philesia; two sons. **Career:** Associated with the Socratics as a young man; served in Athenian cavalry in latter stages of Peloponnesian War; left Athens in 410 BC, and joined the army of the Persian prince Cyrus in Asia Minor in his unsuccessful attempt to gain the Persian throne; after the failure of the expedition, Xenophon was elected general by the army, and led the army from Persia to the Greek city of Trapezus (now Trabzon) on the Black Sea, 400 BC; hired out the army to a Thracian prince in present-day Bulgaria and to Spartan generals in Asia Minor, 399 BC; probably formally exiled from Athens in 399 BC; served with the Spartan forces under general Agesilaus in war with Persia, 396–94 BC, and the Corinthian War against Athens, 394 BC; lived in Sparta, then granted an estate at Scillus, near Olympia: served as local representative (*proxenos*); forced to leave Scillus for Corinth, 371 BC; his Athenian exile was rescinded, c. 368 BC, when Athens and Sparta became allies against Thebes, and he probably returned to Athens, c. 366 BC. **Died:** c. 354 BC.

PUBLICATIONS

Collections

[Works], edited by E.C. Marchant. 5 vols., 1900–21; translated by Carleton L. Brownson and others [Loeb Edition], 7 vols., 1914–68.
Opuscula [Small Works], edited by G. Pierleoni. 1937.
The Shorter Socratic Writings: Apology of Socrates to the Jury, Oeconomicus, and Symposium: Translations, with Interpretive Essays and Notes, edited by Robert C. Bartlett. 1996.
Hiero the Tyrant and Other Treatises, translated by Robin Waterfield. 1997.

Works

Anabasis, edited by Carl Hude, revised by J. Peters. 1972; as *The History*, translated by John Bingham, 1623; as *The Ascent of Cyrus*, translated by John Hawkey, 1738; as *The Expedition of Cyrus*, translated by Edward Spelman, 2 vols., 1740; as *Anabasis*, translated by N.S. Smith (bilingual edition), 1824; also translated by J.S. Watson, 1854; Thomas Clark, 1859 (bilingual edition); George B. Wheeler, 1866; M.W. Mather and J.W. Hewitt (Books I–IV), 1985; as *The March of the Ten Thousand*, translated by H.G. Dakyns, 1901; translated as *The Persian Expedition*, 1929; also translated by Rex Warner, 1949; as *The March Upcountry*, translated by W.H.D. Rouse, 1947.
Apologia, as *Defence of Socrates*, translated by Sarah Fielding, with *Memoirs of Socrates*. 1762; as *Socrates' Defence to the Jury*, translated by O.J. Todd, 1922; as *Socrates' Defence before the Jury*, translated by A.S. Benjamin, 1965.
Cyropaedia, edited by W. Genoll. 1968; as *Cyropaedia*, translated by Philemon Holland, 1632; also translated by Maurice Ashley, 1728; J.S. Watson and Henry Dale, 1855; Roscoe Mongan, 1865; as *The Institution and Life of Cyrus the Great*, translated by

Francis Digby and John Norris, 1685; translated as *The Story of Cyrus*, 1900; as *The Education of Cyrus*, translated by M.W. Barker (Books I–VI), 1560; H.G. Dakyns, 1914; also translated by Walter Miller [Loeb Edition], 2 vols., 1914.
De magistri equitum officio, as *The Art of Horsemanship*, edited by Morris H. Morgan. 1893; translated by E.C. Marchant (bilingual edition), 1951; translated as *Rules for the Choice, Management and Training of Horses*, 1802.
De Republica Atheniensium, as *The Constitution of the Athenians*, edited by Hartvig Frisch (with translation). 1942; translated by E.C. Marchant and G.W. Bowersock, with *Scripta minora*, 1967; as *Defence of the Athenian Democracy*, translated by Henry J. Pye, 1794; as *An Athenian Critic of Athenian Democracy*, translated by Francis Brooks, 1912; as *The Old Oligarch*, translated by James A. Petch, 1926.
De Republica Lacedaemoniorum [Spartan Constitution], as *A Discourse upon Improving the Revenue of the States of Athens*, translated by Waker Moyle. 1697; as *Republica Lacedaemoniorum*, translated by J.M. Moore, in *Aristotle and Xenophon on Democracy and Oligarchy*, 1975.
Hellenica, edited by Carl Hude. 1969; also edited by Gisela Strasburger, 1970; as *History of the Affairs of Greece*, translated by John Newman, 1685; also translated by William Smith, 1770; as *Hellenics*, translated by J.S. Watson and Henry Dale, 1855; as *Hellenica* [Loeb Edition], translated by Carleton L. Brownson (Books I–VII), 2 vols., 1918–21; also translated by Peter Krentz (Books I–II), 1989; as *History of My Times*, translated by Rex Warner, 1966; selections as *The Fall of Athens*, edited by T. Horn, 1978.
Hiero, translated as *Hiero*. 1713; also translated by Richard Graves, 1793; Leo Strauss, in *On Tyranny*, 1948; revised edition, 1963.
Memorabilia, edited by Carl Hude. 1969; as *Memorable Things of Socrates*, translated by Edward Bysshe, 1712; as *Memoirs of Socrates*, translated by Sarah Fielding, with *Defence of Socrates*, 1762; also translated by Edward Levien, 1872; as *Memorabilia*, translated by J.W. Underwood (Books I and II; bilingual edition), 1845; also translated by George B. Wheeler, 1852; Edward Brine (Book IV), 1856; J.A. Giles, 1857; E.C. Marchant [Loeb Edition], with *Oeconomicus*, 1923; translated as *The Life and Death of Socrates*, 1923; as *Recollections of Socrates*, translated by A.S. Benjamin, 1965; as *Memoirs of Socrates*, translated by H. Tredennick, 1970, and in *Conversations of Socrates*, translated by Tredennick, edited by Robin Waterfield, 1990; as *Memorabilia*, translated by Amy L. Bonnette, 1994.
Oeconomicus, as *Treatise of Household*, translated by Gentian Hervet. 1532; as *The Science of Good Husbandry*, translated by Richard Bradley, 1727; as *The Economist*, translated by Alexander D.O. Wedderburn and W. Gershom Collingwood, 1876; as *Oeconomicus* [Loeb Edition], translated by E.C. Marchant, with *Memorabilia*, 1923; also translated by Carries Lord, in *Xenophon's Socratic Discourse: An Interpretation of the "Oeconomicus"* by Leo Strauss, 1970; as *Xenophon, Oeconomicus: A Social and Historical Commentary*, translated by Sarah B. Pomeroy, 1994.
Symposium, as *The Banquet*, translated by James Welwood. 1710; also translated by O.J. Todd, 1922; as *Symposium*, translated by H.

Tredennick, 1970, and in *Conversations of Socrates*, translated by Tredennick, edited by Robin Waterfield, 1990.

Minor Works, translated by Sarah Fielding, James Welwood, and Richard Bradley. 1813; also translated by J.S. Watson, 1857; as *Scripta minora* [Loeb Edition], translated by E.C. Marchant and G.W. Bowersock, with *Constitution of the Athenians*, 1967.

Xenophon and Arrian: On Hunting, edited and translated by A.A. Phillips and M.M. Willcock. 1999.

*

Bibliography: *Bibliography of Editions, Translations and Commentary on Xenophon's Socratic Writings* by Donald Morrison, 1987.

Critical Studies: *On Tyranny: An Interpretation of Xenophon's Hiero*, 1948, revised edition, 1963, *Xenophon's Socratic Discourse: An Interpretation of the "Oeconomicus,"* 1970, and *Xenophon's Socrates*, 1972, all by Leo Strauss; *The Ten Thousand: A Study of Social Organization and Action in Xenophon's Anabasis* by Gerald B. Nussbaum, 1967; *Military Theory and Practice in the Age of Xenophon*, 1970, and *Xenophon*, 1974, both by J.K. Anderson; *Xenophon and Thucydides* by E.M. Soulis, 1972; *Aristotle and Xenophon on Democracy and Oligarchy* by J.M. Moore, 1975; *Xenophon the Athenian* by W.E. Higgins, 1977; *Xenophon: "Persian Expedition"* by J. Antrich and Stephen Usher, 1978; *Xenophon* by Rainer Nickel, 1979; *Xenophon* by John Kinlich Anderson, 1981; *Friendship of the Barbarians: Xenophon and the Persian Empire* by Stephen W. Hirsch, 1985; *The Character of Xenophon's "Hellenica"* by Vivienne Gray, 1989; *Xenophon's Imperial Fiction: On "The Education of Cyrus"* by James Tatum, 1989; *Xenophon's Cyropaedia: Style, Genre, and Literary Technique* by Deborah Levine Gera, 1993; *The Failings of Empire: A Reading of Xenophon Hellenica 2.3.11–7.5.27* by Christopher Tulpin, 1993; *The Ten Thousand in Thrace: An Archeological and Historical Commentary on Xenophon's Anabasis, Books VI.iii–vi–VII* by Jan P. Stronk, 1995; *Xenophon and the History of His Times* by John Dillery, 1995; *Xenophon of Ephesus: His Compositional Technique and the Birth of the Novel* by James N. O'Sullivan, 1995; *The Framing of Socrates: The Literary Interpretation of Xenophon's Memorabilia* by Vivienne J. Gray, 1998; *Xenophon's Prince: Republic and Empire in the Cyropaedia* by Christopher Nadon, 2001.

*   *   *

Xenophon's distinguished military career fitted him to deal with practical details rather than with philosophical abstractions or broad historical questions. His *Memorabilia* (*Memoirs of Socrates*) consist of short conversations in which Socrates, while constantly reminding his hearers of their duty to the city and its gods, instructs them on such matters as the qualifications of a speaker in the Assembly, the duties of a general or of a cavalry officer, and even table manners. These conversations recall the openings of some of the Platonic dialogues, but break off at the point where Plato's Socrates begins to develop some abstract question, such as the nature of justice or the aims of education. Even when, in the *Oeconomicus* (*The Economist*), Xenophon does make Socrates discuss a matter at some length, the subject is practical—the detailed management of a rich man's house and estate—and the "Socratic method" of cross-examination is turned upon its inventor, not in order to elicit abstract principles but to show that the science of agriculture is based on common-sense observations that are within the power of the average townsman. The work is of great interest to the social historian rather than to the philosopher.

To what extent Xenophon's Socrates resembles the historical man is debated. Xenophon certainly used the "Socratic dialogue" as a vehicle for his own opinions; he put into Socrates' mouth, in *The Economist*, an account of the younger Cyrus which he could not possibly have heard Socrates utter, and which is based on facts reported in his own *Anabasis* (*The Persian Expedition*); and offered in his *Apologia* (*Socrates' Defence Before the Jury*) a defence of Socrates which is unlikely to bear any resemblance to the philosopher's own speech in court. But there is insufficient reason to doubt Xenophon's testimony in *The Persian Expedition* that he was sufficiently close to Socrates to rely on his advice. Socrates may be supposed to have known young men whom he considered capable of moral improve meat, though not of metaphysics. Recent attempts to read profound subtleties into Xenophon's philosophy have demonstrated their authors' own intellectual ability, rather than Xenophon's.

Xenophon's chief historical work, the *Hellenica* (*History of My Times*), picks up the story of the Peloponnesian War where the unfinished history of Thucydides breaks off in 411 BC, covers the end of the war and its aftermath down to the restoration of democracy in 403 BC, neglects the next four years, during much of which Xenophon was campaigning in Asia, and resumes as a somewhat rambling chronicle ending with the battle of Mantinea in 362 BC. It reports vividly a number of events which Xenophon may have witnessed or heard described by eyewitnesses, but lacks Thucydides' power of analysis and ability to draw general conclusions. Its supposed Spartan bias seems to reflect the one-sidedness of Xenophon's sources rather than intentional prejudice.

In *The Persian Expedition* Xenophon's abilities as a first-hand reporter are shown at their best. It is a pity that most students first come to this brilliant and exciting narrative when their knowledge of Greek only allows them to struggle slowly through its opening chapters. The clarity and purity of Xenophon's style make his work an excellent textbook.

The Cyropaedia (*The Education of Cyrus*), a historical romance based on the career of the founder of the Persian empire, sums up Xenophon's practical and moral teachings, and was formerly regarded as his masterpiece. It continued to influence political thought until the 18th century, but is now little read.

Of Xenophon's instructional handbooks, *De magistri equitum officio* (*The Art of Horsemanship*) retains its freshness, and something of practical value, to the present day.

—J.K. Anderson

XIAO Hong

Pseudonyms: Xiao Hong [Hsiao Hung], Qiao Yin [Ch'iao Yin]. **Born:** Zhang Naiying in Hulan, Heilongjiang, China, 1 June 1911. **Education:** Attended Harbin First Girl's Middle School and Beijing Women's Normal University High School; did not finish. **Family:** Married Xiao Jun, 1932 (common-law); and Duanmu Hongliang, 1938; no children. **Career:** Full-time writer and member of Lu Xun's inner circle of artists and intellectuals. **Member:** Chinese Writers' Anti-Aggression Association, 1938. **Died:** 22 January 1942, in Hong Kong of respiratory failure and complications from ill-conceived surgery. Her remains were buried in Repulse Bay, but were recovered in 1958 and returned to China and buried in the city of Guangdong

(Canton). Her restored childhood house in Hulan, Heilongjiang is now a provincial museum.

PUBLICATIONS

Collections

Bashe [Trudging]. 1933. Joint collection of stories by Qiao Yin [Xiao Hong] and San Lang [Xiao Jun].
Xiao Hong xuanji [Selected Works of Xiao Hong]. 1958.
Xiaocheng sanyue [Spring in a Small Town] (short stories). 1961.
Selected Stories of Xiao Hong, translated by Howard Goldblatt. 1982.
Xiao Hong quanji [Complete Works of Xiao Hong]. 2 vols. 2000.

Fiction

Shengsi chang. 1935; as *The Field of Life and Death*, translated by Howard Goldblatt, 1979; revised, 2002.
Qiao [The Bridge] (short stories). 1936.
Niuche shang [On the Oxcart] (short stories). 1937.
Kuangye de huhan [A Cry in the Wilderness] (short stories). 1940.
Ma Bole. 1940.
Hulanhe zhuan. 1940; as *Tales of Hulan River*, translated by Howard Goldblatt, 1979; revised, 2002.
Mao Bole. 1941.

Other

Shangshi jie (autobiographical essays). 1936, as *Market Street: A Chinese Woman in Harbin*, translated by Howard Goldblatt, 1986.
"Huiyi Lu Xun xiansheng." 1939, as "A Remembrance of Lu Xun," translated by Howard Goldblatt. 1981.
Minzu hun [Soul of the People] (mime play). 1940.

*

Bibliography: *Hsiao Hung* by Howard Goldblatt, 1976; *Xiao Hong*. 1990.

Critical Studies: *Hsiao Hung* by Howard Goldblatt, 1976; "Xiao Hong and Her Novel *Tales of Hulan River*" by Tsau Shuying, in *Women and Literature in China*, 1985; "Women and Sexuality in Xiao Hong's *Sheng Sichang*," by Simone Cros-Moréa, in *Women and Literature in China*, 1985; "Life as Art: Xiao Hong and Autobiography" by Howard Goldblatt, in *Women and Literature in China*, 1985; "Xiao Hong's Vague Expectations—A Study in Feminine Writing" by Ruth Keen, in *Women and Literature in China*, 1985; *Xiao Hong xinzhuan* (A New Biography of Xiao Hong) by Ge Haowen (Howard Goldblatt), 1991; "The Female Body and Nationalist Discourse: The Field of Life and Death Revisited" by Lydia Liu, in *Scattered Hegemonies*, edited by Grewal and Kaplan, 1994; *Xiao Hong zhuan* (A Biography of Xiao Hong) by Ji Hongzhen, 2000.

* * *

Few writers from the Republican era in China (1911–49) have been as widely praised or egregiously misunderstood, as frequently emulated or variously labeled, as Xiao Hong, whose writing career spanned less than a decade, but who furthered the development of the novel in ways that came to be acknowledged only decades after her death. Born into a landlord family in Northeastern China (Manchuria), she was caught up in the war of resistance against Japan, living a life of deprivation, abuse, and constant flight from the reaches of battle for virtually all her adult life. Unlike most of her contemporaries, she seldom wrote about Japanese aggression in a corpus of fiction that can be described as deeply autobiographical, feminine, lyrical, and path-breaking.

Xiao Hong's first novel, *Shengsi chang* (*The Field of Life and Death*), has been heralded by Chinese critics as one of the most important examples of anti-Japanese fiction. Yet that is not the dominant theme. Rather, the novel is primarily a grim and powerful portrait of the lives of Manchurian peasants. The effect of the work on contemporary readers was anger, pity, and a sense of outrage, not only against outside forces that so demeaned and brutalized the villagers, but also against the fatalistic, passive, and conservative mentality of the peasants themselves. The publication of *The Field of Life and Death* gained for its author instant fame, owing in part to her descriptions of a part of China little known south of the Great Wall. What is most remarkable about this novel, which opens with stark scenes of domestic conflict that center on a young female protagonist, is the wrenching shift in tone and perspective two-thirds of the way through the work: Suddenly, war comes to rural Manchuria, and darkly cinematic scenes replete with animal imagery and coarse language are replaced by hearsay and musings on the future of the village.

After leaving, and writing about, her homeland in the northeast, Xiao Hong spent the remaining years of her life as a vagabond, one step ahead of Japanese military incursions on the Chinese mainland. She spent three years in Shanghai in close contact with her patron, Lu Xun, the most important cultural figure of his age, except for several months in Japan as a refugee from an oppressive relationship with her common-law husband, the Northeast Chinese novelist, Xiao Jun. She then went to the Chinese interior before traveling with her new husband, another Northeast Chinese novelist named Duammu Hongliang, to Hong Kong, where she spent the last two years of her life. She died in hospital shortly after Hong Kong fell to the Japanese. During the years between Shanghai and Hong Kong, Xiao Hong was relatively quiescent as a writer, devoting most of her creative energies to moving out of harm's way, which scarred her physically, and dealing with the break-up of one romantic relationship and the beginning of another, which took a heavy toll on her emotionally. She did, however, manage to write several stories set in the various war zones and many short, generally patriotic, essays that did little to advance her reputation as a novelist, but answered the "call of the times." The highlight of this period is her long, and extremely personal, reminiscence of her patron, Lu Xun, "A Remembrance of Lu Xun," which humanizes this cultural giant, who died in 1937, in ways no one else has managed since.

In 1940, Xiao Hong flew from the wartime capital of Chongqing to Hong Kong, where she would write or complete three novels: her signature work, *Hulanhe zhuan* (*Tales of Hulan River*), an autobiographical novel that set a standard sought but not reached in the sixty years that followed, and a two-part comic satire, *Ma Bole*, that earned for its author unalloyed enmity by contemporary critics who continued to demand war-based patriotic fiction. Remembered by readers of the day as the author of the earlier "anti-Japanese" novel, she would be heralded by later generations as the creator of literary masterpieces—those published in Hong Kong—that have stood the test of time as have few others by her contemporaries.

The eponymous protagonist of *Ma Bole* mocks the patriotism of his era and trivializes the war raging around him as he follows the route taken by his author in the years leading up to her arrival in Hong Kong; he drifts along the perimeter of wartime China, a self-serving and self-deluding, though not self-supporting, maverick from society. A true anti-hero, he has few redeeming qualities as a human being, though his despicability makes him, if not a model representative of humanity, at least a lively and engaging fictional character. He is a raucous, pathetic, cunning, and hapless bundle of paradoxes for whom every place he finds himself is the worst of all possible worlds. In a period when humor and satire scarcely existed in China, *Ma Bole* stands as a monument to Xiao Hong's creative genius, and is a lacerating view of the worst aspects of Chinese society by a novelist who was herself victimized by many of those same aspects.

If the tone of *Ma Bole* is ironic, detached, and censorious, that of *Tales of Hulan River* is lyrical, personal, and nostalgic. Set in the author's hometown in the early years of the new Republic, the novel brilliantly evokes quotidian domestic images through the eyes of the narrator, investing the narrative with childlike innocence and unmediated observations of place, people, and a way of life. This is accomplished through simple yet poetic language and revealing descriptions of ordinary events. Xiao Hong's genius in capturing detail and nuance with camera-like clarity and perspective makes this autobiographical novel appeal to the reader's visual as well as verbal senses. The early chapters—often ironic glimpses of life in small-town northeastern China—form, in the words of one of Xiao Hong's contemporaries, a "genre painting," and lead to increasingly personal and intimate recreations of the author's family and the tenants who shared her childhood compound. There is in these final chapters a mixture of outrage and sadness—the tragic story of a child bride who suffers unimaginable abuse—and hope, in the tale of a peasant who is determined to survive, perhaps even thrive, in the face of harsh material and social conditions. As fiction and as memoir, *Tales of Hulan River* not only capped the career of a writer who barely lived into her thirties but remains, more than half a century later, one of the most frequently read and most influential novels from the first half of the 20th century in China. It and its predecessors have established Xiao Hong as a national treasure.

—Howard Goldblatt

YEHOSHUA, A(vraham) B(en)

Born: Jerusalem, British Mandated Palestine (now Israel), 9 December 1936. **Education:** Educated at the Gymnasium; graduated from the Hebrew University, Jerusalem, B.A. in literature and philosophy. **Military Service:** Served in the parachutist unit. **Family:** Married psychologist Rivka Kirsminski, 1960; three children. **Career:** Taught high school, 1961–63; educator in Paris and general secretary of the World Union of Jewish Students, 1963–67; Dean of Students at the University of Haifa, 1967–72; senior lecturer of world literature, University of Haifa, since 1972; eight months in the University of Iowa's writers' program; visiting faculty member, Harvard University, 1977, University of Chicago, 1988 and 1997, and Princeton University, 1992. **Awards:** Brenner prize, 1983; Alterman prize, 1986; Bialik prize, 1988; American prize, 1990 and 1993; Israeli Booker prize, 1991; and Israel prize, 1995.

PUBLICATIONS

Collections

Mot ha-zaken: sipurim [Death of the Old Man]. 1962.
Mul ha-Ye'arot [Facing the Forests]. 1968.
Sheloshah yamim ve-yeled. 1968; as *Three Days and a Child,* translated by Miriam Arad, 1970.
Bi-tehilat kayits—1970. 1972; as *Early in the Summer of 1970,* translated by Miriam Arad and Pauline Shrier, 1977.
The Continuing Silence of a Poet: Collected Stories, a collection of stories previously translated by Miriam Arad, Pauline Shrier, Marsha Pomerantz, and Philip Simpson. 1988.

Novels

Hasmme'ahev. 1977; as *The Lover,* translated by Philip Simpson, 1978.
Gerushim me'uharim. 1982; as *A Late Divorce,* translated by Hillel Halkin, 1984.
Molkho. 1987; as *Five Seasons,* translated by Hillel Halkin, 1989.
Mar Mani. 1989; as *Mr. Mani,* translated by Hillel Halkin, 1992.
HaShivah me-Hodu. 1994; as *Open Heart,* translated by Dalya Bilu, 1996.
Masa el tom ha-elef. 1997; as *Journey to the End of the Millennium,* translated by Nicholas de Lange, 1999.

Plays

Mai-erev, lailah ve-shahar. 1969; as *A Night in May,* translated by Miriam Arad, 1974.
Possessions, in Modern Israeli Drama in Translation, edited by Michael Carasik. 1993.

Other

Bi-zekhut ha-normaliyut. 1980; as *Between Right and Right,* translated by Arnold Schwartz, 1981.
Ha-Kir veha-har [The Wall and the Mountain]. 1989.
Kohah ha-nora shel ashmah ketanah: ha-heksher ha-musari shel ha-tekst ha-sifruti. 1998; as *The Terrible Power of a Minor Guilt: Literary Essays,* translated by Ora Cummings, 2000.

*

Bibliography: *A.B. Yehoshua—Bibliography 1955–1979* by Joseph Yerushalmi, 1980.

Critical Studies: "Affirmative Structure in A.B. Yehoshua's *The Lover*" by Gilead Morahg in *Hebrew Studies* 1979–80; *Israeli Mythogynies: Women in Contemporary Hebrew Fiction* by Esther Fuchs, 1987; "Facing the Wilderness: God and Country in the Fiction of A.B. Yehoshua" by Gilead Morahg in *Prooftexts,* vol. 8, no. 3, 1988; "A Symbolic Psyche: The Structure of Meaning in A.B. Yehoshua's 'Flood Tide'," by Gilead Morahg in *Hebrew Studies,* vol. 29, 1988; *Voices of Israel: Essays on and Interviews with Yehuda Amichai, A.B. Yehoshua, T. Carmi, Aharon Appelfeld, and Amos Oz* by Joseph Cohen, 1990; "The Womb of Culture: Fictions of Identity and Their Undoing in Yehoshua's *Mr. Mani*" by Anne Golomb Hoffman in *Prooftexts,* vol. 12, no. 3, 1992; *Facing the Fires;*

Conversations with A.B. Yehoshua by Bernard Horn, 1997; "The Shoah, the Akeda, and the Conversations in A.B. Yehoshua's *Mr. Mani*" by Bernard Horn in *Symposium*, vol. 53, no. 3, 1999; "Testing Tolerance: Cultural Diversity and National Unity in A.B. Yehoshua's *A Journey to the End of the Millennium*" by Gilead Morahg in *Prooftexts*, vol. 19, no. 3, 1999; "The Plot of Suicide in A.B. Yehoshua and Leo Tolstoy" by Bernard Horn in *European Legacy*, vol. 6, no. 5, 2001; *Translating Israel: Contemporary Hebrew Literature and Its Reception in America* by Alan L. Mintz, 2001.

* * *

A.B. Yehoshua is unquestionably one of Israel's greatest fiction writers. All six of his novels have proven to be bestsellers in Israel; his two most popular novels in Israel have been *HaShivah me-Hodu* (*Open Heart*) and *Mar Mani* (*Mr. Mani*), with the former being his most successful commercially. In the United States, *Mr. Mani* has proven to be quite successful. Yehoshua's success in Israel can be measured by the sales of his novel *Open Heart*. According to Bernard Horn in his book *Facing the Fires*, *Open Heart* "sold more than a hundred thousand copies, one sale for every fifty inhabitants of the country." Yehoshua's novels provide complex and insightful psychological characterizations. Although Yehoshua admits that he has been influenced by many great writers such as S.Y. Agnon and Fyodor Dostoevsky, the one writer in particular who has influenced him is William Faulkner. Yehoshua has written six novels, short stories, plays, political essays, and works of literary criticism. Because of the popularity of his works of fiction, several of them have been transformed by others into plays and movies.

One of Yehoshua's best stories is "The Yatir Evening Express." In this story, people in this barren and sparsely inhabited town feel neglected and bored so they conspire to provide their lives with meaning. Although they admire the fast Yatir Evening Express Train, they decide to cause it to crash into an abyss so that they will feel important and needed—not ignored and insignificant—because the train swiftly glides past them on a daily basis. Some of the characters express shock when they discover the plan, yet they subsequently indicate that the purposeful destruction intrigues and excites them. The narrator illustrates the self-centered nature of the townspeople, for he knows that it is wrong to help cause the train to crash, yet his lust for Ziva, feelings that he realizes are unrequited, supersedes his conscience. He willingly aids Ziva in her quest to destroy the train and the lives of many of the passengers, in exchange for a sexual encounter with her. Ziva is motivated to destroy the train by curiosity and boredom. As the story concludes, old Arditi, the stationmaster is made the town's scapegoat, further indicating the callous nature of Ziva. The townspeople, being desperate to call their existence to the attention of others, create a disaster to affirm, and call attention to, their existence and to put themselves on the map. This violence employed to maintain and reaffirm their existence is not surprising in the fiction of a man whose country is constantly fighting for its existence. The cruelty and indifference to human life exhibited by the townspeople in "The Yatir Evening Express" might remind readers of similar destructive and violent behavior in "Death of the Old Man," in which people in an apartment building, tired of an old Jew in their building even though he is still quite active, decide to murder him, burying him alive.

In *Hasmme'ahev* (*The Lover*), Yehoshua demonstrates his penchant for merging realism with the absurd, portraying characters that are individualistic yet universal. In this best-selling novel, a man

(Adam) decides to find a lover for his wife, Asya, and for his daughter, Dafi. Adam feels impotent in his marriage, which has disintegrated; he hopes to find a man who will stimulate his wife sexually. The man (Gabriel) that he chooses, however, gets sent to the front during the Yom Kippur War and later deserts. Adam chooses Gabriel because of the unusual car he drives—a 1947 Morris. Gabriel has come to Israel to receive his grandmother Veducha's inheritance upon her death. The novel manifests Yehoshua's interest in psychological fiction, for instance, in Adam's motives for supplying his wife and daughter with lovers. As with much of Yehoshua's fiction, there is a historical backdrop—in this case, the 1973 Yom Kippur War. There is also a political aspect to the novel. Joseph Cohen asserts that Gabriel's aging grandmother symbolizes "Zionism, a once youthful pioneering spirit, now drifting into decline. Her 1947 Morris is the symbol of the 1948 War of Independence and the resulting freedom it brought to the Jews in Israel."

Mr. Mani is also, in some respects, an historical novel. Yehoshua traces the history of the Mani family during significant historical events that shaped world history. For instance, in the second of the five conversations of which the novel consists, a Nazi soldier (Egon Bruner) describes his desertion from the army, which occurred in part because he has lost his glasses. Against the backdrop of World War II, and thus the Holocaust, Egon Bruner, taking a walk with his patriotic grandmother in Crete in 1944, tells her how he came across the Mani family and took the grandfather (Yosef Mani) prisoner. After Mani dies, Bruner realizes that the family is Jewish and subsequently becomes obsessed with them. He considers arresting Yosef Mani's son, Efrayim, but for quite some time decides not to capture the son because Efrayim informs him that he has renounced his Judaism. The novel manifests the obsession of the Mani family—in fact, obsession is a word that applies to many of Yehoshua's characters. Yehoshua's great popularity as an author derives in part from his brilliant psychological characterizations.

—Eric Sterling

See the essay on *Mr. Mani*.

YOSANO Akiko

Also known as Ōtori Akiko. **Born:** Hō (also read Ōtori) Shō in Sakai, Osaka-fu (then Sakai Prefecture), 7 December 1878. **Education:** Shukuin Elementary School 1884–88; Sakai Girls's School, where she studied ethics, Japanese and sewing, 1888–92; Sakai Girls' School Supplementary Course, where she studied sewing and home economics, 1892–94. During elementary school years and before, she studied traditional Japanese dance, koto, samisen, tea ceremony, and Chinese classics for short periods with private teachers. Mostly self-educated: a serious reader from the age of six, by her late teens had read most of the major and minor works of classical and contemporary Japanese history and literature, including *Genji Monogatari* (*The Tale of Genji*), as well as the T'ang Chinese poets, and (in translation) the Old Testament and some of the essays of Leo Tolstoy. **Family:** Married Yosano Tekkan (Hiroshi) in 1901 (died 1935); gave birth to thirteen children, of whom six girls and five boys lived to maturity. **Career:** Worked in the Surugaya, the family store, which manufactured and sold traditional sweets; from childhood, and by her late teens played the central role in its management in place of her parents; first poem (a tanka) published, 1895; after publishing in local and regional literary magazines, joined Yosano Hiroshi's New Poetry Society and contributed tanka, new-style verse, and prose to its magazine *Myōjō* (Morning Star), 1900–08, and then again when it was revived, 1921–27; ran away to Tokyo and published her first volume of poetry, 1901; published first volume of essays, 1911; supporting member, The Bluestocking Association, and contributor to its magazine, *Seitō* (Bluestocking), 1911–15; involved in launching and editing of at least three other literary magazines (*Subaru, Tokihagi, Tōhaku*). Longterm involvement with *Genji Monogatari* (*The Tale of Genji*): lectured on it, 1909, under salary from Kobayashi Tenmin (Masaharu), prepared annotated edition of it (prior to publication destroyed in the Great Kanto Earthquake), 1909–23, translated it into modern Japanese twice, 1911–12, 1932–38. Traveled to Europe, 1912; debated motherhood with Hiratsuka Raichō and others in open letters, 1918; helped establish and taught, then became Head of Girls' Division, at Bunka Gakuin school in Tokyo, 1921–40; General Editor, with Hiroshi and Masamune Hakuchō, *Nihon Koten Zenshū* (Complete Japanese Classics), 1925–28; traveled to China, 1928; attack of angina pectoris, 1934; cerebral hemorrhage, followed by partial paralysis, 1940. **Died:** Tokyo, 29 May 1942.

PUBLICATIONS

Collections

Teihon Yosano Akiko Zenshū [The Definitive Complete Works of Yosano Akiko]. 20 vols., 1979–81.
Yosano Akiko Hyōron Chosakushū [Yosano Akiko: Collected essays and Criticism]. 22 vols., 2001–02.

Verse

Midaregami [Tangled Hair]. 1901.
Saōgi [The Little Fan]. 1904.
Dokugusa [Poison Grass], with Yosano Hiroshi. 1904.
Koigoromo [Robe of Love], with Yamakawa Tomiko and Masuda Masako. 1905.
Maihime [The Dancing Girl]. 1906.
Yume no Hana [Dream Flowers]. 1906.
Tokonatsu [Eternal Summer]. 1908.
Saohime [Princess Sao]. 1909.
Shundeishū [Spring Mud]. 1911.
Seigaiha [Blue Waves on the Sea]. 1912.
Natsu yori Aki e [From Summer into Autumn]. 1914.
Sakurasō [Cherry Blossom Grass]. 1915.
Shuyōshū [Vermillion Leaves]. 1916.
Maigoromo [The Dancing Robe]. 1916.
Akiko Shinshū [Akiko Anew]. 1917.
Hi no Tori [The Firebird]. 1919.
Taiyo to Bara [The Sun and Roses]. 1921.
Kusa no Yume [Grass Dreams]. 1922.
Ryūsei no Michi [The Meteor's Path]. 1924.
Rurikō [Lapis Light]. 1925.
Kokoro no Enkei [Perspectives of the Heart]. 1928.
Kirishima no Uta [Poems from Kirishima], with Yosano Hiroshi. 1929.
Akiko Shihen Zenshū [Akiko: The Complete Longer Poems]. 1929.
Hakuōshū [White Cherry Blossoms], edited by Hirano Banri. 1942.

Essays

Ichigū yori [From One Corner]. 1911.
Zakkichō [A Miscellany Book]. 1915.
Hito oyobi Onna to shite [As a Person and a Woman]. 1916.
Watakushira Nani wo motomuru ka [What Shall We Seek?]. 1917.
Ai, Risei oyobi Yūki [Love, Reason, and Courage]. 1917.
Wakaki Tomo e [To a Young Friend]. 1918.
Shintō Zassō [Heart Weeds]. 1919.
Gekidō no naka wo yuku [Passing through Turmoil]. 1919.
Nyonin Sōzō [The Creation of Women]. 1920.
Ningen Reihai [The Worship of the Human]. 1921.
Ai no Sōsaku [The Creation of Love]. 1923.
Suna ni Kaku [Writing on Sand]. 1925.
Hikaru Kumo [Shining Clouds]. 1928.
Gaitō ni Okuru [Message to the Streets]. 1931.
Yūshōsha to nare [Become a Victor]. 1934.

Fiction

Kumo no Iroiro [Varieties of Clouds]. 1912.
Akarumi e [To the Light]. 1916.

Other

Otogibanashi Shōnen Shōjo [Fairy tales: Young Boys and Girls] (for children). 1910.
Shin'yaku Genji Monogatari [The Tale of Genji Newly Translated]. 4 vols., 1912–13.
Parii yori [From Paris], with Yosano Hiroshi. 1914.
Yattsu no yoru [Eight Nights] (for children). 1914.
Uta no Tsukuriyō [The Making of Poems] (poetic critcism). 1915.
Watakushi no oitachi [My childhood]. 1915.
Tanka Sanbyaku Kō [Lectures on 300 Tanka] (poetic critcism). 1916.
Akiko Kawa [Akiko on Poetry] (poetic critcism). 1919.
Itte mairimasu [See You Later] (for children). 1919.
Mammōyuki, with Yosano Hiroshi. 1930. As *Travels in Manchuria and Mongolia*, part translated by Joshua Fogel, 2001.
Shin-shin'yaku Genji Monogatari [The Tale of Genji: Newly Translated Again]. 6 vols., 1938–39.

*

Bibliography: "Chosaku Mokuroku" and "Sankō Bunken," in *Teihon Yosano Akiko Zenshū*, vol. 8, 1981; "Yosano Akiko kenkyūshi tenbō" by Irie Haruyuki, in *Gunzō Nihon no Sakka 6: Yosano Akiko*, 1992; "Yosano Akiko Botsugo Gojūnen no Kenkyū Tenbō" by Kōuchi Nobuko, in *Shōwa Bungaku Kenkyū*, vol. 26, 1993; "Yosano Akiko Botsugo Gojūnen Ikō no Kenkyū Dōkō (1993–1998)" by Kōuchi Nobuko, in *Kokubungaku: Kaishaku to Kyōzai no Kenkyū*, vol. 44, 1999.

Critical Studies: *Tangled Hair: Modern Japanese Poets Series* by Sakanishi Shio, 1935; *Zenshaku Midaregami Kenkyū* [Tangled Hair: A complete commentary and study] by Satake Kazuhiko, 1957; *Tangled Hair: Selected Tanka from Midaregami* by Sanford Goldstein and Shinoda Seishi, 1971; "Young Akiko: The Literary Debut of Yosano Akiko" by Edwin Cranston, in *Literature East & West* 18, 1974; *Hyōden Yosano Tekkan Akiko* [The lives of Yosano Tekkan and Akiko] by Itsumi Kumi, 1975; "Yosano Akiko" by Makoto Ueda in *Modern Japanese Poets and the Nature of Literature*, 1983; Yosano Akiko by Shinma Shin'ichi, 1986; *Yama no Ugoku Hi Kitaru Hyōden*

Yosano Akiko [The day the mountains move will come: The life of Yosano Akiko] by Yamamoto Chie, 1986; "Yosano Akiko: Return to the Female" by Janine Beichman, in *Japan Quarterly*, 37, 1990; *Journal of the Association of Teachers of Japanese* Special Issue, Yosano Akiko (1878–1942), 25, 1991; "Yosano Akiko and the Taishō Debate over the 'New Woman'" by Laurel Rasplica Rodd, in *Recreating Japanese Women, 1600–1945*, edited by Gail Lee Bernstein, 1991; *Shin Midaregami Zenshaku* [Tangled Hair: A new complete commentary] by Itsumi Kumi, 1996; "Yosano Akiko on Poetic Inspiration" by Laurel Rasplica Rodd, in *The Distant Isle: Studies and Translations of Japanese Literature in Honor of Robert H. Brower*, ed. Thomas Hare, Robert Borgen, and Sharalyn Orbaugh, 1996; *Modern Japanese Tanka: An Anthology* by Makoto Ueda, 1996; *River of Stars: Selected Poems of Yosano Akiko* by Keiko Matsui Gibson and Sam Hamill, 1997; "Yosano Akiko in Heaven and Earth" by Janine Beichman in *Currents*, 1997; "The Clash of Traditions: New Style Poetry and the Waka Tradition in Yosano Akiko's 'Midaregami' (1901)" by Leith Morton, in *The Renewal of Song: Renovation in Lyric Conception and Practice*, 2000; *Yosano Akiko and The Tale of Genji*, by G.G. Rowley, 2000; *Yosano Akiko: Poète de la passion et figure de proue du féminisme japonais* by Claire Dodane, 2000; *Embracing the Firebird: Yosano Akiko and the Birth of the Female Voice in Modern Japanese Poetry* by Janine Beichman, 2002.

* * *

Yosano Akiko is the pre-eminent female poet of modern Japan. The emergence of the female voice in modern Japanese poetry coincided with her first collection of tanka poems, *Midaregami* [Tangled Hair], which brought romanticism to traditional poetry with a tempestuous force and passion found in no other work of the period. A sensation at the time, it has become one of the undisputed classics of modern Japanese poetry.

Paradoxically, there would have been no strong female voice had Akiko not undone the straitjacket of gender, for the "feminine" woman avoided expression of her own feelings. Akiko instinctively realized this early on in her career and deliberately decided "to write as if I were a man." This daring decision was the origin of the shamanic tone that characterized some of the most effective poems in her first collections, and her own characterization of them later on as having "transcended the sexes." Some of the most compelling poems of the early collections are in the voice of beings who express passionate love in a kind of disembodied, unearthly tone, like the "star that once within night's velvet whispered all the words of love" but is "now a mortal in the world below." Her femaleness is suggested by her "swirling hair," but nothing else about her seems human, and her tone has an imperiousness that was foreign to the idea of femininity in 1901, the year the collection was published.

Akiko's early poetry centered around passionate love, youth, and art itself; subsidiary themes were more realistic, focusing on childhood and descriptions of nature. As she matured, her attention also turned to politics and about social issues, particularly those relating to women and feminism. Among her most famous longer poems are "Kimi Shinitamō koto nakare" [Thou Shalt Not Die] and "Yama no ugoku hi kitaru" [The Day the Mountains Move Has Come]. The former, written for her brother, who was a soldier during the Russo-Japanese War, was bitterly attacked at the time as a pacifist poem (and, after World War II, praised for the same reason). Akiko denied the accusation in "Hirakibumi" [Open letter], an essay which is an

eloquent statement of the independence of art and the artist's responsibility to express emotion without regard to the political implications. "Yama no ugoku hi kitaru," which Akiko contributed to the premier issue of *Seitō* (*Bluestocking*), Japan's first feminist literary journal, was a prophetic celebration of the resurgence of women in Japanese life. Today it is almost an anthem of the Japanese feminist movement and is known worldwide as well.

In Akiko's middle years, three themes came to the fore: the ambiguities of marital love, childbirth and the emotions surrounding it, and the sublime ecstasy of artistic creation. These themes grew out of her own experience of being married for over thirty years and giving birth to thirteen children and, at the same time, continuing to write poetry on a daily basis throughout her life, for, as she once said, "My poems are my diary." By this, she did not mean a literal diary of day-to-day events but a record of her thoughts, feelings, fantasies and dreams, her total response to life itself. Many of the poems of her middle age probably do reflect feelings about the reality of her life, particularly her marriage, but others are notation for imagined selves.

Among the most original and powerful of Akiko's poems and prose works are those on birth. As Akiko in her twenties had broken the taboo on speaking about physical love, so in her thirties she broke the taboo on speaking of the act of birth. She developed her own image of birth as a journey to death and back, with the birth-giver compared to a warrior. She challenged the traditional attitude that the woman should bear her pain in silence. She expressed with searing honesty the anger and fear that the birthing woman could feel, as well as her joy. Perhaps it was the spirit behind these poems that made Akiko say that in her poetry after 1911, "I returned to the female."

The transcendent figures that populate the world of Akiko's poetry began with the star-woman whose declaration of her heavenly origins opened *Midaregami*. When they reappeared in the poetry of her middle age and later, they often seemed to be metaphoric portraits of the artist. This tanka from *Hi no Tori* (*The Firebird*) can be read as a celestial vision of the world of the imagination where the poet roams: "Half-horse, half-human, / on me / red rains of coral fall, / blue showers / of lapis lazuli (mizukara wa / hanjin hanba / furu mono wa / sango no ame to / hekiruri no ame). In other poems Akiko envisioned the world of the imagination as a sea, and the poet as a swimmer within it. Thus, from *Akiko Shihen Zenshū* [Akiko: The Complete Longer Poems], "Because my songs are brief, / People think I hoarded words. / I have spared nothing in my songs. / There is nothing I can add. / Unlike a fish, my soul swims without gills. / I sing on one breath."

After Akiko's death, her disciple Hirano Banri collected the poetry she had written in the last nine years of her life. *Hakuōshū* [White Cherry Blossoms] contains over 2,300 tanka poems, and is the largest of all her tanka collections. Its most famous poems are those of mourning and remembrance for her husband Hiroshi, which are among the most moving expressions of marital love in the Japanese language.

For many years, there was a strong tendency for even her greatest admirers to essentialize her as "the poet of passion" (*jonetsu no kajin*) and to emphasize *Midaregami* and "Kimi Shinitamō koto nakare" above all else. Since both works were written before she was twenty-five, the result was that the last forty years of her long career were virtually ignored, as were her evolution through three distinct historical periods—the nation-building of Meiji (1868–1912), the liberalism of Taishō (1912–26), and the militarism of early Shōwa (1926–42). In addition, her contributions as a leading social critic, essayist, educator, and translator of classical Japanese literature into the modern vernacular, not to mention her travel diaries, fiction, and stories for children, were almost entirely forgotten. In the 1980s, however, a resurgence of feminism and the development of women's studies led to renewed interest in her work and her reputation today has now been restored. What remains is to explore in detail the riches of Yosano Akiko's collected works and make them better known both in Japan and abroad.

—Janine Beichman

YOURCENAR, Marguerite

Born: Marguerite Antoinette Jeanne Marie Ghislaine de Crayencour, in Brussels, Belgium, 8 June 1903; moved to the United States, 1939; dual French-American nationality. **Education:** Educated privately in France. **Career:** Part-time lecturer in comparative literature, Sarah Lawrence College, Bronxsville, New York, 1939–49. **Awards:** Fémina-Vacaresco prize, 1951; Académie française award, 1952; Newspaper Guild of New York award, 1955; Combat prize, 1963; Fémina prize, 1968; Monaco grand prize, 1972; National Grand prize for letters (France), 1974; Académie françise grand prize, 1977; Erasmus prize (Amsterdam), 1983; National Arts Club medal, 1986. Honorary degrees: Smith College, Northampton, Massachusetts, 1961; Bowdoin College, Brunswick, Maine, 1968; Colby College, Waterville, Maine, 1972; Harvard University, Cambridge, Massachusetts, 1981. Officer, Légion d'honneur. **Member:** Foreign member, Royal Belgian Academy, 1971; American Academy; Académie française, 1981 (first woman elected). **Died:** 18 December 1987.

PUBLICATIONS

Collection

Oeuvres romanesques. 1982.

Fiction

Alexis; ou, Le Traité du vain combat. 1929; revised edition, 1952; as *Alexis,* translated by Yourcenar and Waiter Kaiser, 1984.
La Nouvelle Eurydice. 1931.
La Mort conduit l'attelage. 1934.
Denier du rêve. 1934; revised edition, 1959; as *A Coin in Nine Hands,* translated by Yourcenar and Doff Katz, 1982.
Nouvelles orientales (stories). 1938; revised edition, 1963; enlarged edition, 1978; as *Oriental Tales,* translated by Yourcenar and Alberto Manguel, 1985.
Le Coup de grâce. 1939; revised edition, 1953; as *Coup de grâce,* translated by Yourcenar and Grace Frick, 1957.
Mémoires d'Hadrien. 1951; as *Memoirs of Hadrian,* translated by Yourcenar and Grace Frick, 1954.
L'Oeuvre au noir. 1968; as *The Abyss,* translated by Yourcenar and Grace Frick, 1976.
Anna, soror. 1981; as *Anna, Soror,* translated by Walter Kaiser, 1987; with *An Obscure Man* and *A Lovely Morning,* 1992.
Comme l'eau qui coule (stories). 1982; as *Two Lives and a Dream,* translated by Walter Kaiser, 1987.

Un homme obscur—Une belle matinée. 1985; translated as *An Obscure Man* and *A Lovely Morning,* with *Anna, Soror,* 1992.
Conte bleu; Le Premier Soir; Maléfice. 1993.

Plays

Électre; ou, La Chute des masques. 1954; as *Electra,* translated by Yourcenar and Dori Katz, in *Plays,* 1984.
Le Mystère d'Alceste, suivi de Qui n'a pas son Minotaure?. 1963; as *To Each His Minotaur,* translated by Yourcenar and Dori Katz, in *Plays,* 1984.
Théâtre (includes *Rendre à César; La Petite Sirène; Le Dialogue dans le Marécage; Électre; ou, La Chute des masques; Le Mystère d'Alceste; Qui n'a pas son Minataure?*). 2 vols., 1971.
Le dialogue dans le marécage: Pièce en un acte. 1971.
Plays. 1984.

Verse

Le Jardin des chimères. 1921.
Les Dieux ne sont pas morts. 1922.
Feux (prose poems). 1936; as *Fires,* translated by Yourcenar and Dori Katz, 1981.
Les Charités d'Alcippe et autres poèmes. 1956; revised and enlarged, 1984; as *The Alms of Alcippe,* translated by Edith R. Farrell, 1982.

Other

Pindare. 1932.
Les Songes et les sorts. 1938; as *Dreams and Destinies,* translated by Donald Flanell Friedman, 1999.
Comment Wang-Fô fut sauvé (for children). 1952.
L'Écrivan devant l'Histoire. 1954.
Préface à la Gita-Govinda. 1958.
Sous bénéfice d'inventaire. 1962; as *The Dark Brain of Piranesi and Other Essays,* translated by Richard Howard, 1984.
Discours de réception de Marguerite Yourcenar à l'Académie Royale belge. 1971.
Entretiens radiophoniques, with Patrick de Rosbo. 1972.
Le Labyrinthe du monde (autobiography). 3 vols., 1974–88. *Souvenirs pieux.* 1974; as *Dear Departed,* translated by Maria Louise Ascher, 1992. *Archives du nord.* 1977; as *How Many Years,* translated by Maria Louise Ascher, 1995. *Quoi? L'Éternité.* 1988.
Les Yeux ouverts: Entretiens avec Matthieu Galey. 1980; as *With Open Eyes: Conversations with Matthieu Galey,* translated by Arthur Goldhammer, 1984.
Mishima; ou, La Vision du vide. 1981; as *Mishima: A Vision of the Void,* translated by Yourcenar and Alberto Manguel, 1986, with afterword by Donald Richie, 2001.
Discours de réception à L'Académie française de Mme. M. Yourcenar et résponse de M.J. D'Ormesson. 1981.
Notre Dame des Hirondelles (for children). 1982.
Le Temps, ce grand sculpteur (essays). 1983; as *That Mighty Sculptor, Time,* translated by Yourcenar and Walter Kaiser, 1992.
En Pèlerin et en étranger (essays). 1990.
Le Tour de la prison (on travel). 1991.
Editor, *Le Cheval noir à tête blanche.* 1985.
Editor, *La Voix des choses,* photographs by Jerry Wilson. 1987.
Editor and Translator, *Fleuve profond, sombre rivière: Les "Negro spirituals."* 1964.

Editor and Translator, *La Couronne et la lyre: Poèmes traduits du grec*. 1979.

Translator, *Les Vagues*, by Virginia Woolf. 1937.

Translator, *Ce que savait Maisie*, by Henry James. 1947.

Translator, with Constantin Dimaras, *Présentation critique de Constantine Cavafy 1863–1933*. 1958.

Translator, *Présentation critique d'Hortense Flexner*. 1969.

Translator, *Le Coin des "Amen,"* by James Baldwin. 1983.

Translator, with Jun Shiragi, *Cinq Nô modernes*, by Yukio Mishima. 1984.

Translator, *Blues and Gospels*. 1984.

*

Critical Studies: *Marguerite Yourcenar* by Jean Blot, 1971, revised edition, 1980; *La Création romanesque dans l'oeuvre de Marguerite Yourcenar* by Michel Constanty, 1981; *Zenon; ou, Le Thème de l'alchimie dans l'oeuvre au noir de Marguerite Yourcenar* by Geneviève Spencer-Noël, 1981; *Marguerite Yourcenar in Counterpoint* by C. Frederick Farrell Jr., and Edith R. Farrell, 1983; *The Yourcenar Collection* by Robert R. Nunn and Edward J. Geary, 1984; *Marguerite Yourcenar* by Pierre Horn, 1985; *Marguerite Yourcenar: Qui êtes-vous?* by Georges Jacquemin, 1985, revised edition, 1989; *Marguerite Yourcenar: Sagesse et mystique* by Madeleine Boussuges, 1987; *Marguerite Yourcenar: A Readers' Guide* by Georgia Hooks Shurr, 1987; *L'Expression du temps dans l'oeuvre romanesque et autobiographique du Marguerite Yourcenar* by Christiane Papadopoulos, 1988; *Le "Don sombre": Le Thème de la mort dans quatre romans de Marguerite Yourcenar* by Kajsa Andersson, 1989; *En mémoire d'une souveraine: Marguerite Yourcenar* by Yvon Bernier, 1990; *From Vision to Violence: Sacrifice in the Works of Marguerite Yourcenar* by Joan E. Howard, 1992, and *Marguerite Yourcenar: Inventing a Life* by Josyane Savignean, translated by Howard, 1993; *Petite Plaisance: Marguerite Yourcenar, 1903–1987* by Yvon Bernier, 1994; *Marguerite Yourcenar: Reading the Visual* by Nigel Saint, 2000; *The Troubling Play of Gender: The Phaedra Dramas of Tsvetaeva, Yourcenar, and H.D.* by Maria Stadter Fox, 2001.

* * *

Marguerite Yourcenar's contribution to 20th-century French literature reflects both her classical upbringing and her extensive travels. Although she declared that her work was separate from the philosophical and literary trends of Paris, her election to the Académie française in 1980 inevitably drew her into mainstream debates. As the first woman to enter the hitherto male bastion of French literati, she was accused of having a male style of writing. Certainly her protagonists are nearly all male, but some of the androgynous descriptions found in the early works, such as *Le Coup de grâce, Denier du rêve* (*A Coin in Nine Hands*), and *Mémoirs d'Hadrien* (*Memoirs of Hadrian*), suggest that Yourcenar is more interested in the human condition in general than particularly female concerns.

Feeling the need to experiment with literary genres throughout a rich and productive career, she wrote récits, short stories, historical novels, poetry, drama, critical essays, travel accounts, and an autobiography of a sort. Both the range and the preoccupations of all her writing indicate her self-consciousness as a writer. Her development as a writer is particularly chaotic given her constant attempts to rewrite both the works themselves and their prefaces.

The scope of Yourcenar's production is such that it is impossible to cover all her work, ranging from essays on time to analyses of dreams, from translations of Virginia Woolf and Henry James to a study of Yukio Mishima. However, mention will be made of what are considered to be her most significant works.

Alexis was described by Yourcenar as the "first portrait of a voice." Its legacy was the portrait of the Emperor Hadrian's voice in the much lauded *Memoirs of Hadrian*. *Alexis* is an epistolary novel in which Alexis announces his imminent departure to his wife, Monique, and explains a growing awareness of his homosexual desires. *A Coin in Nine Hands* was to follow. Rewritten several times, it is a denunciation of fascism in 1930s Rome and intuits a shrewd awareness of the political drama of the time. The story incorporates residuals of myth by presenting recurrent patterns of tragic human experience. Marcella, the revolutionary, seeks retribution on an all-powerful dictator but fails in her mission and is shot dead. *Feux* (*Fires*), written as short stories in poetic prose, is based on the writer's early experiences of love. Yourcenar's attraction to homosexual men seems to have resulted in a preoccupation with the torment of forbidden or unreciprocated love in this work. Myth plays an important role in *Fires*, as it does in the *Nouvelles orientales* (*Oriental Tales*), where she reinterprets various Eastern, modern Greek, and Slavonic legends. Some of her versions have been illustrated and published as children's stories. The common themes of war, homosexuality, thwarted love, and the universal patterns of man's behaviour found in the works thus far are also reflected in *Le Coup de grâce*. Published in 1939, it anticipates World War II and recounts the story of a love triangle in which Sophie loves Eric and Eric loves Sophie's brother Conrad. The relationships are complex, and motivation remains ambiguous even with the coup de grâce at the end of the novel when Eric shoots Sophie as a traitor. Yourcenar wrote little during the war and her next venture was theatre. Her two volumes of theatre reflect the widespread interest shown in myth by French playwrights in the 1940s and 1950s, who imposed on the ancient myths new and more relevant meanings for modern man.

Yourcenar's writing, however, is largely too prosaic to be tenable as theatre. Her greatness as a writer is found in the historical novels of the post-war period that she sometimes referred to as her "Human Trilogy." These three complementary works, *Memoirs of Hadrian, L'Oeuvre au noir* (*The Abyss*), and *Un homme obscur* (*An Obscure Man*), illustrate how three different human types come to terms with themselves and the world around them. Hadrian, Roman emperor, man of peace, and patron of the arts, struggles to understand the human condition and represent it. Zeno, the protagonist of *The Abyss*, an alchemist, doctor, and philosopher, is on a quest for ultimate knowledge, represented symbolically in the gold of the alchemical experiment. Finally Nathanaël in *An Obscure Man* represents a man "virtually uneducated" who, after a series of adventures, dies a wild animal's death and is finally reconciled with the natural cycle of things. Each of these works is a contemplation of both life and death. As a trilogy they bring together opposing facets of the universal human condition.

It is this obsession with man's origin and final destination that is represented in Yourcenar's spurious autobiography—a trilogy collectively entitled *Le Labyrinthe du monde* [The Labyrinth of the World]. For the most part the three works, *Souvenirs pieux* (*Dear Departed*), *Archives du nord* [Archives of the North], and *Quoi? L'Éternité* [What? Eternity], are an account of her family history up until the time of her birth, on both the maternal and paternal sides. They do not deal at all with her adult life. The reappearance of Hadrian and Zeno in what purports to be a factual, historical account unites Yourcenar's literary creations with her extended historical family. *Quoi? L'Éternité* remained unfinished at the writer's death and some critics claim that this was because Yourcenar could not continue indefinitely postponing her account of self.

Nevertheless, it is of interest to note that while Yourcenar tells us very little about her private life, virtually her entire literary output is an egocentric testimony to her life experience, her aspirations, and her thinking. While her writing stands as an admirable and fascinating experiment with styles and literary genre, she remains best known as an historical writer who bestows modern significance on our antecedents.

—Sally A. White-Wallis

See the essay on *Memoirs of Hadrian*.

Z

ZAMIATIN, Evgenii (Ivanovich)

Also known as Yevgeniy Zamyatin. **Born:** Lebedian', Russia, 20 January 1884. **Education:** Educated at Progymnasium, Lebedian', 1892–96; gymnasium in Voronezh 1896–1902; studied naval engineering at St. Petersburg Polytechnic Institute, 1902–08; arrested and exiled for student political activity, 1906 and 1911. **Career:** Naval engineer, 1908–11, and lecturer from 1911, St. Petersburg Polytechnic Institute; supervised the construction of ice-breakers in Britain, 1916–17; associated with the literary group, Serapionovii brat'ia [Serapion Brothers], from 1921; tutor, *Dora Iskusstva* [House of the Arts], 1921; editor, *Sovremennyi zapad* [Contemporary West], 1922–24, and *Russkii Sovremennik* [Russian Contemporary], 1924; editor, with Kornei Chukovskii, English section of World Literature series; victimized from the late 1920s, and removed from the leadership of Soviet Writers Union; left Soviet Union, 1931; settled in Paris, 1932. **Died:** 10 March 1937.

PUBLICATIONS

Collections

Povesti i rasskazy [Tales and Stories]. 1969.
Sochineniia [Works]. 4 vols., 1970–88.
Povesti. Rasskazy [Tales. Stories]. 1986.
Sochineniia [Collection], edited by T.V. Gromov. 1988.
Izbrannye proizvedeniia [Selected Works], edited by A.Iu. Galushkin. 1989.
Izbrannye proizvedeniia [Selected Works], edited by E. Skorosnelova. 1990.
Izbrannye proizvedeniia [Selected Works], edited by O. Mikhailov. 2 vols., 1990.

Fiction

Uezdnoe. 1916; as *A Provincial Tale*, 1978.
Ostrovitiane. 1922; title story translated as "The Islanders," in *Russian Literature Triquarterly*, 2, 1972.
Bol'shim detiam skazki [Fairy Tales for Grown-up Children]. 1922.
Na kulichkakh [At the World's End]. 1923; as *A Godforsaken Hole*, translated by Walker Foard, 1988.
My: Roman. 1952; as *We*, translated by Gregory Zilboorg, 1924; also translated by Bernard Guilbert Guerney, 1970; Mirra Ginsburg, 1972; Clarence Brown, 1993; edited by Andrew Barratt, 1994.
Rasskaz o samom glavnom [Story about the Most Important Thing]. 1924.
Nechestivye rasskazy [Impious Stories]. 1927.
Zhitie Blokhi ot dnia chudesnogo ee rozhdeniia... [The Life of a Flea from the Day of Its Miraculous Birth...]. 1929.
Navodnenie [The Flood]. 1930.
Bich Bozhii (unfinished). 1939.

The Dragon: Fifteen Stories, edited and translated by Mirra Ginsburg. 1967; as *The Dragon and Other Stories*, translated by Ginsburg, 1975.
"Mamai," translated by Neil Cornwell, in *Stand*, 4. 1976.
The Islanders and Fishers of Men, translated by Sophie Fuller and Julian Sacchi. 1984.

Plays

Ogni sviatogo Dominika [The Fires of St. Dominic]. 1922.
Blokha [The Flea] (produced 1925). 1926.
Obshchestvo pochotnykh zvonarei [The Society of Honorable Bellringers] (produced 1925). 1926.
Sensatsiia, from the play *The Front Page* by Ben Hecht and Charles MacArthur (produced 1930).

Screenplays: *Severnaia liubov'* [Northern Love], 1928; *Les Bas-Fonds* [The Lower Depths], 1936.

Other

Robert Mayer. 1922.
Gerbert Uells. 1922; as Herbert Wells, 1978.
Sobranie sochinenii [Collected Works]. 4 vols., 1929.
Litsa [Faces]. 1955; as *A Soviet Heretic: Essays*, edited and translated by Mirra Ginsburg, 1970.

*

Critical Studies: *Zamyatin: A Soviet Heretic* by David J. Richards, 1962; *The Life and Works of Evgeny Zamjatin* by Alex M. Shane (includes bibliography), 1968; *Evgenii Zamiatin: An Interpretative Study* by Christopher Collins, 1973; "Literature and Revolution in *We*" by Robert Russell, in *Slavonic and East European Review*, 1973; *Brave New World, 1984, and We: An Essay on Anti-Utopia* by Edward J. Brown, 1976; "The Imagination and the 'I' in Zamjatin's *We*" by Gary Rosenshield, in *Slavic and East European Journal*, 1979; *Three Russian Writers and the Irrational: Zamyatin, Pil'nyak, and Bulgakov* by T.R.N. Edwards, 1982; "Adam and the Ark of Ice: Man and Revolution in Zamyatin's *The Cave*," in *Irish Slavonic Studies*, (4), 1983, "Evolution as Collusion: The Heretic and the Slave in Zamyatin's *My*," in *Slavonic and East European Review*, 1984, and "The X-Factor in Zamyatin's *We*," in *Modern Language Review*, 1985, all by Andrew Barratt; *Zamyatin's "We": A Collection of Critical Essays* (includes bibliography) edited by Garry Kern, 1988.

*   *   *

Evgenii Zamiatin published his first short story as early as 1908, but the best known of his early works was *Uezdnoe* (*A Provincial Tale*), which illustrates many of the features of his "neo-realist" innovative style (elements of the grotesque, distortive imagery, satire, primitivism, and distinctive characterization and linguistic effects). He saw this development in literature as a dialectical synthesis of the two dominant trends of the turn of the century—symbolism and naturalism—which would superimpose the stylistic flights of the one upon the materialist base of the other. He developed in his stories systems of imagery which at times almost dominated the narrative, as in ''Mamai'' and ''Peshchera'' (''The Cave''), and are a prominent feature of his only completed novel, *My* (*We*). His sojourn in England produced two satirical depictions of bourgeois English life: ''Ostrovitiane'' (''The Islanders''), set in the north-east, and ''Lovets chelovekov'' (''Fishers of Men''), set in London. Zamiatin turned again to satire and renewed experimentation, and to the theatre, in his work of the 1920s. His later stories, notably ''Navodnenie'' (''The Flood''), achieved a greater structural unity in a style which may best be described as mature primitivism. Zamiatin himself remarked: ''all the complexities through which I passed turned out to be necessary in order to achieve simplicity.''

Returning to Russia between the two revolutions of 1917, Zamiatin, a convinced revolutionary, proceeded to question the direction of the revolution from the standpoint of his philosophy of heresy (a kind of renegade Marxism): there must always be ''a voice in the wilderness'' inveighing against the status quo, in order to maintain a dialectical progression of history that recognizes no final revolution. These views, expressed in a number of pungent stories and essays and in the futuristic novel *We*, aroused the antipathy of the new Soviet literary establishment, who did not take kindly, either, to his concern for the future of literature. *We* was denounced as ''a malicious pamphlet'' and was not published in the Soviet Union until 1988. Branded an ''inner émigré'' by Trotskii, Zamiatin was hounded from Soviet literature after the ''Pil'niak—Zamiatin affair'' of 1929 (see Vera Reck's account in her book *Boris Pil'niak*, 1975).

We, Zamiatin's best-known work, depicts an apparently unsuccessful uprising against a totalitarian, glass-enclosed city-state of the distant future. Built on extreme mathematical and collectivist principles, ''The Single [or ''One''] State,'' having reduced its populace to the status of ''numbers,'' determines to eradicate all remaining individuality by imposing an operation of ''fantasiectomy,'' to remove the imagination. Narrated in diary form, *We* shows Zamiatin's innovative style at its most developed (notably its image systems built on mathematical terminology and colour symbolism), as well as providing an imaginative psychological view of a virtually alien society. It is also the principal fictional statement of his philosophical preoccupations: the role of the heretic, inevitable conflict with the stagnation and philistinism of whatever the status quo, and the cosmic struggle between energy and entropy. Influenced stylistically by Andrei Belyi, in its promotion of the irrational by Dostoevskii, and in its futurism by H.G. Wells, *We* can be read as: a prophetic warning against tyranny (of whatever complexion), an unusually advanced work of science fiction (for 1920); and a penetrating study of alienation and schizophrenia. Its assumed influence upon Huxley's *Brave New World* (1932) is probably erroneous; Orwell, however, acknowledged its impact on *1984* (1949). There are also parallels to be seen with near-contemporaneous works by Karel Čapek and Georg Kaiser, and with Fritz Lang's film *Metropolis*.

Zamiatin was a leading figure of Russian modernism and an important influence on the prose of the 1920s. However, until the

glasnost' period, he was far better known in the West than in the Soviet Union where, unlike most of his disgraced contemporaries, he remained totally unpublished and rarely discussed until 1988.

—Neil Cornwell

See the essay on *We*.

ZEAMI

Also known as Kanze Saburō or Kanze Zeami Motokiyo. **Born:** Yuzaki Saemon Tayu Motokiyo in Yamada (now Sakurai City, Nara Prefecture), Japan, 1363. **Family:** Had one daughter and two sons. **Career:** Received theatrical training from his father, Kannami Kiyotsugu, the originator of Nō drama, and inherited leadership of the Kanze School of Nō from him. Given the name Zeami by his patron, Shogun Ashikaga Yoshimitsu; following death of Yoshimitsu, 1408, his performing career declined; gave over leadership of Kanze theatre to his son, Motomasa, 1422; chief musician to Shogun Ashikaga Yoshimochi, 1424; banished to Sado Island, northern Japan (reasons unknown). Between 79 and 145 Nō plays have been attributed to him. **Died:** c. 8 August 1443.

PUBLICATIONS

Collections

The Nō Plays of Japan (includes *Atsumori; Kagekiyo; Ukai; Aya no Tsuzami; Aoi no Ue; Kantan; Hakurakuten*), translated by Arthur Waley. 1921.
Tōchū Zeami Nijūsanbushū (includes 23 plays), edited by Kazuma Kawase. 1945.
Japanese Noh Drama: Ten Plays (includes *Takasago; Tamura; Sanemori; Kiyotsune; Tōboku; Izutsu; Tadanori; Yuya; Kantan; Aoi no Ue; Kagekiyo; Yamamba*), translated by Nippon Gakujutsu Shinkōkai [Japanese Classics Translation Committee]. 1955.
Zeami Jūrokubushū Hyōshaku (includes 16 plays), edited by Asaji Nose. 1962.
Twenty Plays of the Nō Theatre (includes *Komachi at Sekidera; The Brocade Tree; Semimaru; The Deserted Crone; Lady Han; The Reed Cutter*), translated by Donald Keene. 1970.
Masterworks of the Nō Theater (includes *Nonomiya; Izutsu; Atsumori; Tadanori; Matsukaze; Higaki; Obasute; Saigyōzakura; Nue; Taema; Tōru*), translated by Kenneth Yamada. 1989.
Japanese Nō Drama (includes *Atsumori; Hanjo; Izutsu; Kinuta; Kureba; Matsukaze; Nonomiya; Saigyō-zakura; Semimaru; Tadanori; Tagasogo; Yamamba; Yashimai*; and plays by other authors), translated by Royall Tyler. 1992.

Plays (selected published translations, in order of the five play-categories of Nō)

1. Waki/kami Nō (God Plays):

Hakurakuten, translated by Arthur Waley, in *The Nō Plays of Japan*. 1921.
Kureba, translated by Royall Tyler, in *Japanese Nō Drama*. 1992.

Oimatsu, as *The Old Pine Tree*, translated by Makoto Ueda, in *"The Old Pine Tree" and Other Noh Plays*. 1962.

Takasogo, translated in *Japanese Noh Drama: Ten Plays*. 1955; also translated by Royall Tyler, in *Japanese Nō Drama*, 1992.

2. Shura Nō (Man Plays, or Warrior Plays):

Atsumori, translated by Arthur Waley, in *The Nō Plays of Japan*. 1921.

Kiyotsune, translated in *Japanese Noh Drama: Ten Plays*. 1955.

Sanemori, translated in *Japanese Noh Drama: Ten Plays*. 1955.

Tadanori, translated in *Japanese Noh Drama: Ten Plays*. 1955.

Tamura, translated in *Japanese Noh Drama: Ten Plays*. 1955.

Tōboku, translated in *Japanese Noh Drama: Ten Plays*. 1955.

Yashima, as *The Battle of Yashima*, translated by Makoto Ueda, in *"The Old Pine Tree" and Other Noh Plays*. 1962; as *Yashima*, translated by Royall Tyler, in *Japanese Nō Drama*, 1992.

3. Kazura Nō (Woman Plays; or Wig Plays):

Higaki, as *The Woman Within the Cyprus Fence*, translated by Makoto Ueda, in *"The Old Pine Tree" and Other Noh Plays*. 1962; as *Higaki*, translated by Kenneth Yamada, in *Masterworks of the Nō Theater*, 1989.

Izutsu, translated in *Japanese Noh Drama*. 1955; also translated by Kenneth Yamada, in *Masterworks of the Nō Theater*, 1989; as *Izuttóu: The Well-Cradle*, translated by Royall Tyler, in *Japanese Nō Drama*, 1992.

Kakitsubata, translated as *Kakitsubata (The Iris)*, in *Twelve Plays of the Noh and Kyōgen Theaters*, translated by Monica Bethe, Karen Brazell, and Philip J. Gabriel. 1988.

Matsukaze, translated in *Japanese Noh Drama: Ten Plays*. 1955; also translated by Kenneth Yamada, in *Masterworks of the Nō Theater*, 1989; as *Pining Wind*, translated by Royall Tyler, in *Japanese Nō Drama*, 1992.

Nonomiya, translated by Kenneth Yamada, in *Masterworks of the Nō Theater*. 1989; as *The Wildwood Shrine*, translated by Royall Tyler, in *Japanese Nō Drama*, 1992.

Obasute, as *The Deserted Crone*, translated by Donald Keene, in *Twenty Plays of the Nō Theatre*. 1970; as *Obasute*, translated by Kenneth Yamada, in *Masterworks of the Nō Theater*, 1989.

Saigyō-zakura, translated as *Saigyō and the Cherry Tree*, in *Twelve Plays of the Noh and Kyōgen Theaters*, translated by Monica Bethe, Karen Brazell, and Philip J. Gabriel. 1988; as *Saigyōzakura*, translated by Kenneth Yamada, in *Masterworks of the Nō Theater*, 1989; as *Saigyō's Cherry Tree*, translated by Royall Tyler, in *Japanese Nō Drama*, 1992.

Sekidera Komachi, as *Komachi at Sekidera*, translated by Donald Keene, in *Twenty Plays of the Nō Theater*. 1970; also translated by Royall Tyler, in *Japanese Nō Drama*, 1992.

Unoha, as *Unoha (Cormorant Plumes)*, in *Twelve Plays of the Noh and Kyōgen Theaters*, translated by Monica Bethe, Karen Brazell, and Philip J. Gabriel. 1988.

Yuya, translated in *Japanese Noh Drama: Ten Plays*. 1955.

4. Zatsu Nō (Miscellaneous Plays; Madman, Obsession, Present-Life Plays):

Anoi-no-Ue, translated by Arthur Waley, in *The Nō Plays of Japan*. 1921; also translated in *Japanese Noh Drama: Ten Plays*, 1955.

Ashikari, as *The Reed Cutter*, translated by Donald Keene, in *Twenty Plays of the Nō Theatre*. 1970. *Aya no Tsuzumi*, translated by Arthur Waley, in *The Nō Plays of Japan*. 1921.

Hanjo, as *Lady Han*, translated by Donald Keene, in *Twenty Plays of the Nō Theatre*. 1970; also translated by Royall Tyler, in *Japanese Nō Drama*, 1992.

Kagekiyo, translated by Arthur Waley, in *The Nō Plays of Japan*. 1921; also translated in *Japanese Noh Drama: Ten Plays*, 1955.

Kantan, translated by Arthur Waley, in *The Nō Plays of Japan*. 1921: also translated in *Japanese Noh Drama: Ten Plays*, 1955.

Kinuta, as *The Falling Block*, translated by Royall Tyler, in *Japanese Nō Drama*. 1992.

Mitsuyama, as *Jinen the Preacher*, translated by Makoto Ueda, in *"The Old Pine Tree" and Other Noh Plays*. 1962.

Nishikigi, as *The Brocade Tree*, translated by Donald Keene, in *Twenty Plays of the Nō Theatre*. 1970.

Semimaru, translated by Donald Keene, in *Twenty Plays of the Nō Theatre*. 1970; also translated by Royall Tyler, in *Japanese Nō Drama*, 1992.

5. Kiri Nō (Concluding or Demon Plays):

Nue, translated by Kenneth Yamada, in *Masterworks of the Nō Theater*. 1989.

Suma Genji, translated as *The Tale of Genji*. 1976.

Taema, translated in *Monumenta Nipponica*, 25(3–4). 1970; also translated by Kenneth Yamada, in *Masterworks of the Nō Theater*, 1989.

Tōru, translated by Kenneth Yamada, in *Masterworks of the Nō Theater*. 1989.

Ukai, translated by Arthur Waley, in *The Nō Plays of Japan*. 1921.

Yamamba, translated in *Japanese Noh Drama: Ten Plays*. 1955; also translated by Royall Tyler, in *Japanese Nō Drama*, 1992.

Other

Kadensho, or The Flower Book, translated by Nobori Asaji. 1975; as *The Fushikaden*, translated by Shohei Shimada, 1975.

On the Art of Nō Drama: The Major Treatises of Zeami, translated by J. Thomas Rimer and Yamazaki Masakazu. 1984.

Sarugaku dangi, as *Zeami's Talks on Sarugaku*, translated by Erika de Poorter. 1986.

*

Critical Studies: *Zeami and His Theories on Noh* by Nogami Toyoichiro, 1955; *Early Nō Drama: Its Background, Character and Development 1300–1450* by P.G. O'Neill, 1958; *La Tradition secrète du no* by R. Sieffert, 1960; *Nō: The Classical Drama of Japan* by Donald Keene, 1966; *Ze-Ami and His Theories of Noh Drama* by Masaru Sekine, 1985; *Zeami's Style: The Noh Plays of Zeami Motokiyo* by Thomas Blenman Hare, 1986; "Aristotle's Poetics and Zeami's Teachings on Style" by Megumi Sata, in *Asian Theatre Journal*, 6(1), 1989; *The Artistry of Aeschylus and Zeami: A Comparative Study of Greek Tragedy and Nō* by Mac J. Smethurst, 1989.

*   *   *

The significance of Zeami's contributions to the foundation of the Nō theatre as we know it today is manifold. He was a superb performer who was respected and admired by both aristocrats and the general public.

He wisely realized the enormous advantage of demonstrating his talents as a performer by writing plays for himself, and he proved the validity of his concept through the many masterpieces he wrote.

Beyond these extraordinary contributions as an artist, he was the foremost theorist of Nō theatre and its educator, a fact that was amply demonstrated by the famous 23 treatises he left, some as a secret record of a tradition to be transmitted to his successors and the rest to be left for his colleagues. The remarkable quality of his insight into the art of Nō theatre, as contained in his writings, ranges from how to write an effective play to how to train a professional performer starting at the age of seven, and it provides the reader with perceptions as valuable to Nō theatre as Aristotle's *Poetics* was to Greek tragedy, with his subtle discussion of acting as sophisticated as Stanislavskii's advice to actors.

The first treatise Zeami wrote was *Fūshi Kaden*, commonly known as *Kadensho* (*The Flower Book*), dated 1402. This work deals primarily with the innumerable problems a performer faces in obtaining the acknowledgement of the world and in maintaining such fame once he gains it. He analyses the concept of *hana*, a flower that is the life of art in Nō theatre by which the art itself is illuminated. A flower is something which is capable of charming the audience. *The Flower Book* explains how one can make such a flower bloom.

By Zeami's own admission, *The Flower Book* was a collection of precepts learned from his father Kannami, who was known as a great master of *monomane* (imitation). He is credited with being a playwright of such plays as *Jinen-koji*, which requires of the main actor an ability to dance several popular dance forms within the play. Zeami's greatness is indicated by the fact that he mastered all the skills required to be a competent performer and saw the importance of entertaining the Shogun Yoshimitsu and his court with ever fresh attractions in Nō, which he provided in order to survive and prosper well into the future.

Zeami saw the enormous potential in the concept of *yūgen* as the aesthetic backbone of his art. The concept was practised first in religion as something deep and unfathomable, and later in *waka*, the court poetry in the early 12th-century poetics by Fujiwara Shunzei, as the highest ideal of poetic expression: the feeling which stimulates an image of life's tranquil loneliness as revealed in the truth of nature. The same term was used in the mid-15th century by Shōtetsu, a Zen monk, to mean an infinitely rich and nuanced feeling of grace in ethereal beauty. Shōtetsu posed a rhetorical question: "Could it be possible to explain the style of *yūgen* as the feeling you obtain by seeing four or five finely dressed court ladies who are viewing cherry blossoms in full bloom at the courtyard of the South Wing [of the palace]?" This same sentiment of *yūgen* is discussed by Zeami in his *Nōsakusho* [Treatise on Playwriting]. Thus we may refer to Zeami's *yūgen* as the beauty of elegance. By providing such a refined touch of beauty through a mythical aura, instead of simply relying on the power of imitation, Zeami succeeded in elevating the artistic status of Nō to an entertainment form which satisfied the tastes of the Shogun and his court.

His awareness of the requirements of Nō theatre was well expressed in other works, throughout which he emphasized the significance of *buka nikyoku* (dance and song), two fundamental elements of Nō. In the 600-year span of Nō theatre, no other contributor has ranked with Zeami, a genius whose talent was so deeply and widely applied that it covered all aspects of the form. His plays are still performed regularly, and his theories are often consulted in judging the appropriateness of the contemporary practice of Nō theatre.

—Andrew T. Tsubaki

ZOLA, Émile

Born: Paris, France, 2 April 1840, of Italian father; naturalized French citizen, 1862. **Education:** Educated at Collège d'Aix; Lycée Bourbon, Aix; Lycée Saint-Louis, Paris, 1858–59. **Family:** Married Alexandrine-Gabrielle Meley in 1870; had two children by Jeanne Rozerot. **Career:** Worked briefly as a clerk in the Excise Office; worked in the dispatch office, then in sales promotion, Hachette, publishers, Paris, 1862–66; art critic (as "Claude"), *L'Événement* newspaper, 1866; staff member, *Le Globe* and *L'Événement Illustré*, 1868, and staff member or contributor to other papers until 1900; made accusations of false trial during the Dreyfus affair: tried and convicted of libel, 1898: in England, 1898–99. **Died:** 29 September 1902.

PUBLICATIONS

Collections

Oeuvres complètes, edited by Eugène Fasquelle and Maurice Le Blond. 50 vols., 1927–29.
Oeuvres complètes, edited by Henri Mitterand. 15 vols., 1966–69.
The Dreyfus Affair: J'accuse and Other Writings, translated by Eleanor Levieux. 1996.

Fiction

Contes à Ninon. 1864; as *Stories for Ninon*, translated by Ernest A. Vizetelly, 1895.
La Confession de Claude. 1865; as *Claude's Confession*, translated by George D. Cox, 1888.
Le Voeu d'une morte. 1866; as *A Dead Woman's Wish*, translated by Count de Soissons, 1902.
Les Mystères de Marseille. 1867; as *The Mysteries of Marseilles*, translated by Myron A. Cooney, 1885; as *The Flower Girls of Marseilles*, translated by George D. Cox, 1888.
Thérèse Raquin. 1867; as *Thérèse Raquin*, translated by Edward Vizetelly, 1887; also translated by Philip G. Downs, 1955; Lee Marcourt, 1959; Willard R. Trask, 1960; Leonard Tancock, 1962; Andrew Rothwell, 1992; Brian Nelson, 1993; as *Theresa*, translated by Vizetelly, 1952.
Madeleine Férat. 1868; as *Madeleine Férat*, translated by John Stirling, 1888; as *Shame*, translated by Alec Brown, 1954; as *Fatal Intimacy*, translated by Brown, 1964.
Les Rougon-Macquart, edited by Henri Mitterand. 5 vols., 1960–67:
  1. *La Fortune des Rougon*. 1871; as *The Fortune of the Rougons*, translated anonymously, 1886.
  2. *La Curée*. 1872; as *The Rush for the Spoil*, translated anonymously, 1886; as *The Kill*, translated by Alexander Teixeira de Mattos, 1895.

3. *Le Ventre de Paris*. 1873; as *La Belle Lisa; or, The Paris Market Girls*, translated by John Stirling, 1882; as *The Fat and the Thin*, translated by Ernest A. Vizetelly, 1888; as *Savage Paris*, translated by David Hughes and Marie-Jacqueline Mason, 1955.

4. *La Conquête de Plassans*. 1874; as *The Conquest of Plassans*, translated by Ernest A. Vizetelly, 1887; as *A Priest in the House*, translated by Brian Rhys, 1957.

5. *La Faute de l'Abbé Mouret*. 1875; as *Abbé Mouret's Transgression*, translated by John Stirling, 1886; as *The Sin of the Abbé Mouret*, translated by M. Smyth, 1904; as *The Abbé Mouret's Sin*, translated by Alec Brown, 1957.

6. *Son Excellence Eugène Rougon*. 1876; as *Clorinda; or, The Rise and Reign of His Excellency Eugégne Rougon*, translated by John Stirling, 1880; as *His Excellency Eugène Rougon*, translated by Ernest A. Vizetelly, 1886; as *His Excellency*, translated by Alec Brown, 1958.

7. *L'Assommoir*. 1877; as *L'Assommoir*, translated by John Stirling, 1879; also translated by Arthur Symons, 1895, and by Leonard Tancock, 1970; as *Gervaise*, translated by Edward Binsse, 1879; as *The Dram-Shop*, translated by Ernest A. Vizetelly, 1897; as *Drink*, translated by S.S. Fitzgerald, 1903; as *The Gin Palace*, translated by Alec Brown, 1952.

8. *Une Page d'amour*. 1878; as *Hélène: A Love Episode*, translated by Mary Neal Sherwood, 1878; as *A Page of Love*, translated by T.F. Rogerson, 1897; as *A Love Affair*, translated by Jean Stewart, 1957.

9. *Nana*. 1880; as *Nana*, translated by Ernest A. Vizetelly, 1884; also translated by Lowell Bair, 1962; George Holden, 1972; Douglas Parmée, 1992.

10. *Pot-Bouille*. 1882; as *Piping Hot!*, translated anonymously, 1885; as *Pot-Bouille*, translated by Mary Neal Sherwood, 1895; as *Lesson in Love*, translated by George Moore, 1953; as *Restless House*, translated by Percy Pinkerton, 1953; as *Pot Luck (Pot-bouille)*, translated by Brian Nelson, 1999.

11. *Au bonheur des dames*. 1883; edited by Henri Mitterand, 1980; as *Shop Girls of Paris*, translated by Mary Neal Sherwood, 1883; as *The Ladies' Paradise*, translated by John Stirling, 1883; as *Ladies' Delight*, translated by April Fitzlyon, 1957.

12. *La Joie de vivre*. 1884; as *How Jolly Life Is!*, translated anonymously, 1886; as *The Joy of Life*, translated by Ernest A. Vizetelly, 1901; as *Zest for Life*, translated by Jean Stewart, 1955.

13. *Germinal*. 1885; as *Germinal*, translated anonymously, 1885; numerous subsequent translations including by Havelock Ellis, 1894, and by Leonard Tancock, 1954.

14. *L'Oeuvre*. 1886; as *The Masterpiece*, translated by G.D. Cox, 1886; also translated by Katherine Woods, 1946; as *His Masterpiece*, translated by Albert Vandam, 1886; also translated by Ernest A. Vizetelly, 1902; Thomas Walton, 1930.

15. *La Terre*. 1887; edited by Henri Mitterand, 1980; as *The Soil*, translated anonymously, 1888; as *La Terre*, translated by Ernest Dowson, 1895; as *Earth*, translated by Ann Lindsay, 1954, and by Margaret Crosland, 1962; as *The Earth*, translated by Douglas Parmée, 1980.

16. *Le Rêve*. 1888; as *The Dream*, translated anonymously, 1893; as *A Dream of Love*, translated by Eliza Chase, 1912.

17. *La Bête humaine*. 1890; as *The Human Beast*, translated by G.D. Cox, 1891(?); as *The Monomaniac*, translated by Ernest

A. Vizetelly, 1901; as *The Beast in Man*, translated by Alec Brown, 1958; as *La Bête Humaine*, translated by Leonard Tancock, 1977; also translated by Roger Pearson, 1996.

18. *L'Argent*. 1891; as *Money*, translated by Benjamin R. Tucker, 1894; also translated by Ernest A. Vizetelly, 1894.

19. *La Débâcle*. 1892; as *The Downfall*, translated by Ernest A. Vizetelly, 1892; as *The Debacle*, translated by John Hands, 1968; also translated by Leonard Tancock, 1972.

20. *Le Docteur Pascal*. 1893; as *Doctor Pascal*, translated by Ernest A. Vizetelly, 1893; also translated by Vladimir Keen, 1957.

Nouveaux contes à Ninon. 1874.

Le Capitaine Burle. 1882.

Naïs Micoulin. 1884.

A Soldier's Honour (stories). 1888.

The Attack on the Mill (stories), translated by E.P. Robins. 1892; also translated by Douglas Parmée, 1984.

Les Trois villes:

    Lourdes. 1894; as *Lourdes*, translated by Ernest A. Vizetelly, 1894.

    Rome. 1896; as *Rome*, translated by Ernest A. Vizetelly, 1896.

    Paris. 1898; as *Paris*, translated by Ernest A. Vizetelly, 1898.

Les Quatres Évangiles (incomplete):

    Fécondité. 1899; as *Fruitfulness*, translated by Ernest A. Vizetelly, 1900.

    Travail. 1901; as *Labor*, translated anonymously, 1901; as *Work*, translated by Ernest A. Vizetelly, 1901.

    Vérité. 1903; as *Truth*, translated by Ernest A. Vizetelly, 1903.

Madame Sourdis. 1929.

Stories. 1935.

Plays

Les Mystères de Marseille, with Marius Roux (produced 1867).

Thérèse Raquin, from his own novel (produced 1873). 1873; as *Thérèse Raquin*, translated by Kathleen Boutall, in *From the Modern Repertoire*, edited by Eric Bentley, 1956.

Les Héritiers Rabourdin, from a play by Jonson (produced 1874). 1874; as *The Heirs of Rabourdin*, translated by Alexander Teixeira de Mattos, 1893.

Le Bouton de Rose (produced 1878). In *Théâtre*, 1878.

Nana, with William Busnach, from the novel by Zola (produced 1881). In *Trois pièces*, 1885.

Pot-Bouille, with William Busnach, from the novel by Zola (produced 1883). In *Trois pièces*, 1885; as *Restless House*, translated by Percy Pinkerton, 1953.

Le Ventre de Paris, with William Busnach, from the novel by Zola (produced 1887); translated by Ernst A. Vizetelly, 1993.

Renée, from his novel *La Curée* (produced 1887). 1887.

Germinal, with William Busnach, from the novel by Zola (produced 1888).

Madeleine (produced 1889). In *Oeuvres complètes*, 1927–29.

Le Rêve, music by Alfred Bruneau (produced 1891).

L'Attaque du Moulin, music by Alfred Bruneau (produced 1893).

Messidor, music by Alfred Bruneau (produced 1897). 1897.

L'Ouragan, music by Alfred Bruneau (produced 1901). 1901.

L'Enfant-roi, music by Alfred Bruneau (produced 1905). 1905.

Sylvanire; ou, Paris en amour (libretto; produced 1924). In *Poèmes lyriques*, 1921.

Poèmes lyriques (opera libretti; includes *Messidor*; *L'Ouragan*; *L'Enfant-Roi*; *Lazare*; *Violaine la chevelue*; *Sylvanire*). 1921.

Other

Mes haines. 1866; as *My Hatreds* translated by Patomba Paves-Yashinsky and Jack Yashinsky, 1991.

Le Roman expérimental. 1880.

Les Romanciers naturalistes. 1881.

Documents littéraires. 1881.

Le Naturalisme au théâtre. 1881.

Nos auteurs dramatiques. 1881.

Une campagne. 1882.

The Experimental Novel and Other Essays, translated by Belle M. Sherman. 1893.

Nouvelle campagne. 1897.

La Vérité en marche. 1901.

Letters to J. Van Santen Kolff, edited by Robert J. Niess. 1940.

La République en marche: Chroniques parlementaires, edited by Jacques Kayser. 2 vols., 1956.

Mes voyages: Lourdes, Rome: Journaux inédits, edited by René Ternois. 1958.

Salons (art criticism), edited by F.W.J. Hemmings and Robert J. Niess. 1959.

Lettres inédites à Henry Céard, edited by A.J. Salvan. 1959.

Vingt messages inédits de Zola à Céard, edited by A.J. Salvan. 1961.

L'Atelier de Zola: Textes de journaux 1865–1870, edited by Martin Kanes. 1963.

Lettres de Paris (articles from *Vestnik Europy*), edited by P.A. Duncan and Vera Erdely. 1963.

Correspondance, edited by B.H. Bakker. 1978–.

*

Bibliography: *Zola, Journaliste: Bibliographie chronologique et analytique* by Henri Mitterand and Halina Suwala, 2 vols., 1968–72; *Émile Zola: A Selective Analytical Bibliography* by Brian Nelson, 1982.

Critical Studies: *Zola: An Introductory Study of His Novels* by Angus Wilson, 1952; *Zola* by Marc Bernard, 1960; *Zola's "Son Excellence Eugène Rougon"* by Richard B. Grant, 1960; *Zola's "Germinal": A Critical and Historical Study*, 1962, and *Zola*, 1967, both by Elliott M. Grant; *Zola and the Theatre* by Lawson A. Carter, 1963; *Zola Before the "Rougon-Macquart"* by John C. Lapp, 1964; *Zola*, 1966, and *The Life and Times of Émile Zola*, 1977, both by F.W.J. Hemmings; *Zola, Cézanne, and Manet: A Study of "L'Oeuvre"* by Robert J. Niess, 1968; *Zola* by Philip Walker, 1968; *Through Those Living Pillars: Man and Nature in the Works of Émile Zola* by Winston Hewitt, 1974; *Garden of Zola: Émile Zola and His Novels for English Readers* by Graham King, 1978; *Zola* by Joanna Richardson, 1978; *Zola and the Bourgeoisie: A Study of Themes and Techniques in "Les Rougon-Macquart"* by Brian Nelson, 1983; *Émile Zola* by Philip Walker, 1985; *Émile Zola: A Bourgeois Rebel* by Alan Schom, 1987; *Models of Power: Politics and Economics in Zola's Rougon-Macquart* by David F. Bell, 1988; *Zola and the Craft of Fiction* by Terry Keefe and Robert Lethbridge, 1990; *L'Assommoir* by David Baguley, 1992; *The Visual Novel: Émile Zola and the Art of His Times* by William J. Berg, 1993; *Politics and Narratives of Birth Gynocolonization from Rousseau to Zola* by Carol A. Mossman,

1993; *Émile Zola Centenary Colloquium 1893–1993: London, 23–25 September 1993*, edited by Patrick Pollard, 1995; *Zola: A Life* by Frederick Brown, 1995; *To Kill a Text: The Dialogic Fiction of Hugo, Dickens, and Zola* by Ilinca Zarifopol-Johnston, 1995; *Emile Zola: Germinal* by Colin Smethurst, 1996; *Messiah or Antichrist?: A Study of the Messianic Myth in the Work of Zola* by Anthony John Evenhuis, 1998; *Emile Zola: La curée* by Susan Harrow, 1998; *Questioning the Father: From Darwin to Zola, Ibsen, Strindberg, and Hardy* by Ross Shideler, 1999.

*   *   *

With the death of Victor Hugo in 1885, Émile Zola became the dominant literary figure in France. That year saw the publication of *Germinal*, generally recognized as his masterpiece, but he had already achieved fame, indeed notoriety, by some 20 novels, including *L'Assommoir* and *Nana*.

At the centre of Zola's work stands the 20-volume cycle of novels entitled *Les Rougon-Macquart*, which contains all his best work. It represents an attempt to "study" the effects of hereditary flaws (neurosis, alcoholism, violence) and various environments on the members of two families during the Second Empire (1851–70).

Zola developed an aesthetic that combined Hugo's epic breadth and imaginative power with Balzac's stress on the material setting and Flaubert's relative detachment and objectivity. In order to emphasize its originality, he dubbed it "Naturalism" and underlined its supposedly scientific character. This strategy was successful in drawing attention to his work, but it was ultimately to mislead many critics into neglecting the poetic and Romantic character of much of his output. In the epic treatment of crowd scenes such as the miners' rampage in *Germinal*, and the mythical atmosphere that transforms key scenes of novels like *Nana*, Zola succeeded brilliantly in creating a world that owed much to tendencies quite foreign to the scientific pretentions of Naturalism. Zola's greatest works owe little or nothing to the Naturalist theories he propagated in his volumes of criticism.

Sex is a central element in Zola's novels, and this undoubtedly helped to make them bestsellers because at that period such a topic was considered scandalous. But his treatment of sex was no cynical exploitation, for he saw in it a dark but magnificent force of almost mystical character on which man was dependent not only for reproduction but for all creativity.

Although he became wealthy from the sale of his novels, Zola never forgot the poverty of his youth, and he remained a convinced democrat and socialist all his life, with a deep sympathy for the lower classes—workers (*L'Assommoir*), miners (*Germinal*), peasants (*La Terre* [*The Earth*])—which he specialized in portraying, and a bitter contempt for the corruption and cynicism of the bourgeoisie, which he castigated in vitriolic portraits in *La Curée* (*The Kill*), *Son Excellence Eugène Rougon* (*His Excellency Eugène Rougon*), *L'Argent* (*Money*).

Zola was a classmate and particular friend of Paul Cézanne, and wrote much art criticism supporting the struggle of Édouard Manet and Impressionists like Claude Monet to develop and impose a revolutionary new style and vision in painting. Manet thanked him with a now well-known portrait.

In 1898, Zola's scandalous anti-establishment reputation (he was rejected by the Académie française 31 times) took on a new dimension when he wrote an open letter to the President of France denouncing the racism that had led to the framing of Dreyfus, a Jewish army man, as a spy by fellow officers. For his role in this affair, Zola was convicted and forced to flee the country until the courts recognized the truth of his accusations and released Dreyfus from Devil's Island.

—Patrick Brady

See the essays on *L'Assommoir*, *The Earth*, and *Germinal*.

ZOSHCHENKO, Mikhail Mikhailovich

Born: Poltava, Russia, 10 August 1895. **Education:** Graduated from high school in St. Petersburg, 1913; studied law at St. Petersburg University 1913–15. **Military Service:** Volunteered in the Tsarist army, promoted to officer: injured, gassed; volunteered in the Red Army 1917–21. **Career:** Pursued many professions: railroad ticket agent, border guard, telephone operator, instructor in rabbit and poultry raising, militiaman, census taker, carpenter, shoemaker, typist clerk, professional gambler; freelance writer from 1930s. **Died:** Leningrad, 22 July 1958.

PUBLICATIONS

Collections

Izbrannoe. 1933, 1981, 1982, 1983.
Rasskazy. 1933, 1971, 1974, 1979, 1988.
Povesti i rasskazy. 1952.
Sobranie sochinenii v trekh tomakh. 1986–87.
Sobranie sochinenii v 5-ti tomakh. 1993–94.

Fiction

Rasskazy Nazara Il'icha gospodina Sinebrukhova. 1922.
Uvazhaemye grazhdane. 1926.
Nervnye liudi. 1927; as *Nervous People and Other Satires*, translated by Maria Gordon and Hugh McLean, 1963.
O chem pel solovei: Sentimental'nye povesti. 1927.
Siren' tsvetyot. 1929.
Lichnaia zhizn'. 1933.
Vozvrashchennaia molodost'. 1933, as *Youth Restored*, translated by Joel Stern, 1984.
Golubaia kniga. 1934–35.
Russia Laughs. 1935.
Istoriia odnoi zhizni. 1935.
The Woman Who Could Not Read and Other Tales, translated by Elisaveta Fen. 1940.
The Wonderful Dog and Other Tales, translated by Elisaveta Fen. 1942.
Pered voskhodom solntsa. 1943–72; as *Before Sunrise*, translated by Gary Kern, 1974.
Scenes from the Bathhouse and Other Stories of Communist Russia, translated by Sidney Monas. 1961.
A Man Is Not a Flea, translated by Serge Shiskoff. 1989.
The Galosh and Other Stories, translated by Jeremy Hicks. 2000.

*

Critical Studies: "The Tragedy of a Soviet Satirist, or, the Case of Zoshchenko" by Rebecca A. Domar, in *Through the Glass of Soviet Literature*, 1953; "Zoshchenko's 'Adventures of a Monkey' as an Allegory" by Vasa D. Mihailovich, in *Satire Newsletter*; "Introduction to M. Zoshchenko" by Sidney Monas, in *Scenes from the Bathhouse*, 1962; "Mikhail Zoshchenko: The Condemned Humorist" by Marc Slonim, in *Soviet Russian Literature*, 1964; "Introduction to M. Zoshchenko" by Hugh McLean, in *Nervous People and Other Satires*, 1965; "Zoshchenko's Psychological Interests" by Vera Von Wiren-Garczynski, in *Slavic and East European Journal*, 1967; "Mikhail Zoshchenko and the Problem of skaz" by Irwin R. Titunik, in *California Slavic Studies*, 1971.

* * *

Mikhail Zoshchenko is known almost exclusively as a writer of satirical short stories. Perhaps his greatest achievement is making his brand of humor and satire unmistakably his. In hundreds of four-to-six-page sketches he would touch on a seemingly unimportant event that, upon further scrutiny, turns out to be rather important for the characters involved. Zoshchenko showed an infallible understanding of human habits and foibles. He saw humor in almost every situation, even though it is clear that life is not always as funny as it may seem. In fact, his characters are using humor as a safety valve necessary to escape or mitigate the dangers and rigors of the new political and cultural climate in Russia in the first decade after the revolution, when Zoshchenko wrote most of his stories. It was a period of relative freedom; writers were tolerated in expressing themselves. When this period was replaced by much stricter, suffocating controls of literary activity in the 1930s and 1940s, Zoshchenko's output came to a trickle. He turned to writing autobiographical fiction in which he attempted a psychological explanation of his experiences and those of his compatriots.

The political system forcing people to think and behave in a prescribed way is Zoshchenko's prime target of satire. His characters come from the lower middle classes, common folks, workers, managers, clerks, small business entrepreneurs, artists, intelligentsia, frustrated wives, unrequited lovers and, more sparsely, peasants. Many of them are small bureaucrats forced into their behavior by the omnipresent political system, who are trying to survive by pleasing the powers-that-be. Even though such stories tend to suffer now from being passé, they are nevertheless a gold mine for students of that historical period and they are, above all, a pleasure to read.

Satire of the political system is not the only object of satire, however. Zoshchenko is often critical of the people themselves. Granted, many of their foibles are engendered by the unfair system, but others are the result of their own weaknesses. In perhaps his best story, "Adventures of a Monkey," a monkey escapes from the zoo, is adopted by a boy, but then returns to the zoo because he finds living among human beings worse than living in a zoo. In criticizing the foibles of his characters, Zoshchenko points at a moral laxness that had allowed the political system to impose itself on people in the first place. The rampant dishonesty, cheating, bribery and hypocrisy, for example, are not mandated by the system. Also, infidelity demonstrates a lack of marital morality, while cowardice stems from a personal weakness. To be sure, Zoshchenko allows for mitigating circumstances for such behavior. One is the persisting discrepancy between the ideal and the real, between the official facade and reality, and between appearance and substance. He sees another explanation in the perennial clash between an individual and the society. Yet another reason for such behavior he sees in untenable living conditions (several people sharing the same room, for example). Zoshchenko also allows for the imperfection of human nature, manifested in self-centeredness, insensitivity toward other fellow human beings, greed, and vanity, to mention a few. All these possible explanations bring up the age-old question of chicken and egg. The truth may be found in both. Be that as it may, with his stories Zoshchenko underscores the essence of the problem, formulated by one of his characters: "I've always been of the opinion that respect for individuals, praise and esteem produce exceptional results. Many personalities unfold because of this, just like roses at daybreak."

Zoshchenko has an uncanny gift for reproducing the language of his characters. In trying to outwit or impress the authorities, they use outlandish concoctions of bureaucrats in order to sound sophisticated while, in reality, they are parvenus conforming to behavior they neither want nor understand. In their peculiar speech the reader gets the impression that the author does not always mean what he says and does not always say what he means. This, of course, is Zoshchenko's one way of protecting himself from the suspicious authorities. His predilection for the absurd and grotesque is another safety valve, while at the same time adding a colorful, Chaplinesque flavor to his stories.

Some of Zoshchenko's stories are simply humorous without any pretense of deeper meaning, or parodies of other literary pieces, or stories showing the Russian's veneration of everything foreign. They all contribute to a multicolored mosaic of genuine human character traits, of human emotions and failings, of lessons about life for those who need or seek them, and of plain enjoyment for connoisseurs of good literature. All this makes Zoshchenko one of the most popular and esteemed among Russian writers.

—Vasa D. Mihailovich

ZRÍNYI, Count Miklós

Born: Ozaly or Csáktornya (now Čakovec, Croatia), 1 May 1620. **Education:** Educated in Graz, 1630, Vienna, 1634, and Nagyszombat, 1635. **Family:** Married 1) Euzébia Draskovics in 1646 (died 1651); 2) Zsófia Lőbl in 1652. **Career:** Visited Rome, Naples, Florence, and Venice in 1636; withdrew to family estate in Csáktornya and devoted his energies to political questions and military activity, from 1637; family estates were continually subject to devastations by the Turks; initiated partisan warfare against the Turkish occupying forces, 1639. Appointed general, 1646, and viceroy of Croatia, 1647, by Ferdinand III; fought numerous successful campaigns against the Turks but efforts were constantly hampered by the court in Vienna. **Died:** 18 November 1664, killed by a wild boar while hunting.

PUBLICATIONS

Collections

Minden munkáji [Complete Works], edited by Ferenc Kazinczy. 1817.

Összes művei [Complete Works], edited by Tibor Klaniczay and Csaba Csapodi. 1958.

Verse

Adriai tengernek Syrénája [The Siren of the Adriatic Sea] (includes *Szigeti veszedelem* [The Peril of Sziget]). 1651.

Other

Az török áfium ellen való orvosság [An Antidote to the Turkish Opium], edited by Zoltán Ferenczi. 1901.
Tábori kis tracta... [Treatise on Camp Organization...] (includes *Tábori kis tracta; Mátyás király életéről való elmélkedések; Az török áfium ellen való orvosság*), edited by Tibor Klaniczay. 1983.

*

Bibliography: *Hungarian Authors: A Bibliographical Handbook* by Albert Tezla, 1970; *A magyar irodalomtörténet bibliográfiája 1772-ig* by Béla Stoll, Imre Varga, and Sándor V. Kovács, 1972.

Critical Studies: "Zrínyi és Tasso" by János Arany, in *Budapesti Szemle*, 1859; *Zrínyi* by Károly Széchy, 5 vols., 1896–1902; "Zrínyi Miklós verselése" by Géza Képes, in *Irodalomtudományi Közlemények*, 1961; *Zrínyi Miklós* by Tibor Klaniczay, revised enlarged edition, 1964; *Zrínyi Miklós és kora* [Miklós Zrínyi and his Age] by Géza Perjés, 1965; "Miklós Zrínyi" by D. Mervyn Jones, in *Five Hungarian Writers*, 1966.

*   *   *

Miklós Zrínyi's poem *Szigeti veszedelem* [The Peril of Sziget] is of major importance because it combines the qualities of "authentic" and "literary" epic. With the Turks only 40 kilometres away, Zrínyi tells how his great-grandfather defied the army under Suleiman the Magnificent besieging Szigetvár in 1566 and finally led his men out to die gallantly. The poet converts military defeat into moral victory by giving his epic a religious framework; the Hungarians are victorious before God. They are superb soldiers, yet humble; the numerically stronger Turkish enemy is arrogant and overconfident; hence the initial Hungarian successes.

As regards the "literary" aspect, Zrínyi's epic is firmly in the classical tradition, with a definite shape and in particular, episodes reflecting his familiarity with Homer, Virgil, Tasso, and Marino, but without any loss of authenticity. The title of his collected poems, *Adriai tengernek Syrénája* [The Siren of the Adriatic Sea], was suggested by Marino's calling himself "Siren of the Tyrrhenian Sea." The other poems in the collection, though overburdened with classical allusions, clearly show the poet learning his art. In the epic, the heroism and spiritual strength far outweigh the stylistic inelegance. In the preface to the collection Zrínyi says he "had no time" to correct his work, though much thought has obviously gone into the construction of the epic to make an aesthetically satisfying whole.

All Zrínyi's prose works except the purely practical *Tábori kis tracta* [Treatise on Camp Organization] (written 1648; unfinished) appear today as important contributions to early Hungarian prose, though they remained unknown until the 19th century. In the preface to *Vitéz hadnagy* [The Gallant General] (written 1650–52) Zrínyi says "I have taken pains to write good Hungarian"; the style has a direct vigour and conciseness.

Vitéz hadnagy is a collection of discourses, aphorisms, and centuriae, of which the last remained unfinished. They are a collection of miscellaneous observations based on 17th-century Italian models; the aphorisms are comments on passages of Tacitus. Zrínyi describes the centuriae in his preface as "a mixture of what I have seen, heard and read"; many of the military precepts in the whole work have already been illustrated by the action of the epic. Zrínyi was particularly exercised by Fortune; his own motto "Sors bona, nihil aliud" (Good fortune, nothing else [is what I want]). Fortune limits, but does not offset, the extent to which people make their own destiny.

The Mátyás király életéről való elmélkedések [Thoughts on the Life of King Mátyás] were written "for my own amusement" in a fortnight during the winter of 1656–57. Zrínyi was thinking about the ideal ruler to achieve an independent united Hungary free from religious persecution and class oppression (there had been an understandable peasant revolt in Croatia in 1653). The great Renaissance King Mátyás (Matthias Corvinus) was a natural choice of subject; Zrínyi's admiration for his hero is not uncritical, especially about Mátyás's receptivity to rash advice, nor does he mention the King's patronage of the arts. The total achievement "would be useless to compress into a short essay." Being about a particular individual, the work marks a step towards artistic unity, though it is constructed in sections on particular episodes, and depicts the ideal of a soldier-statesman.

Az török áfium ellen való orvosság [An Antidote to the Turkish Opium] was written in 1660–61 against the background of the Turkish capture of Nagyvárad (now Oradea in Romania) in 1660 and devastation of Transylvania, coming on top of an order to Zrínyi to stop operations already started. Zrínyi argues forcefully that Hungary must have a standing army of men well equipped, clothed, fed, and paid. Any foreign help in the present emergency will be forthcoming if Hungary is seen to be relying on her own strength, but is not a substitute for self-help. This is Zrínyi's Philippic, most of it written as if for delivery, with a power anticipated only occasionally in *Mátyás király életéről való elmélkedések*, in which Zrínyi was communing with himself. The argument gives *Az török áfium ellen való orvosság* a logical unity analogous to that of the epic.

Zrínyi is an outstanding example of a man of letters who was also a man of action, like Sir Walter Raleigh and Sir Philip Sidney. His pen and his sword were equally formidable instruments.

—D. Mervyn Jones

ZUCKMAYER, Carl

Born: Nackenheim, Germany, 27 December 1896. **Education:** Educated at the Gymnasium, Mainz, 1903–14; studied biology at the University of Heidelberg, 1918–20. **Military Service:** Volunteer with the German army in France, 1914–18: lieutenant. **Family:** Married 1) Annemarie Gans in 1920 (divorced 1921); 2) the actress Alice Frank in 1925, two daughters (one adopted). **Career:** Voluntary worker and freelance writer, Berlin, 1920; visited Norway and Lapland, 1920–22; director, Stadttheater, Kiel, 1922–23; worked for Max Reinhardt, Berlin, 1923–25 and with Bertolt Brecht, 1924; plays banned by the Nazi regime; lived in Austria, 1925–38; moved to Switzerland after the German annexation of Austria; emigrated to the United States, 1939; worked briefly as a scriptwriter in Hollywood;

lecturer, Piscator's Dramatic Workshop, New School for Social Research, New York, 1941; farmer, Barnard, Vermont, 1941–46; returned to Germany as cultural adviser for the American Military Administration, 1946; divided his time between homes in the United States and Europe, 1947–58; settled in Saas-Feé, Switzerland, 1958; gave up American citizenship. **Awards:** Kleist prize, 1926; Büchner prize, 1929; Heidelberg Festival prize, 1929; Goethe prize, 1952; Vienna Culture prize, 1955. Great Order of Merit of the Federal Republic of Germany, with Star, 1955. **Died:** 18 January 1977.

PUBLICATIONS

Plays

Kreuzweg (produced 1920). 1921.
Eunuch, from a play by Terence (produced 1923).
Pankraz erwacht; oder, die Hinterwälder (produced 1925). 1978.
Kiktahan; oder, Die Hinterwälder (produced 1925). 1925.
Der fröhliche Weinberg (produced 1925). 1925.
Schinderhannes (produced 1927). 1927.
Rivalen (produced 1928). 1929.
Katharina Knie (produced 1928). 1929.
Kakadu-Kakada (for children; produced 1929). 1929.
Der Hauptmann von Köpenick (produced 1931). 1930; as *The Captain of Köpenick*, translated by David Portmann, 1932.
Kat, with Heinz Hilpert, from a novel by Ernest Hemingway (produced 1931).
Der Schelm von Bergen (produced 1934). 1934.
Ulla Winblad; oder, Musik und Leben des Carl Michael Bellman (produced as *Bellmann* 1938). 1938; revised version (produced 1953), 1953.
Somewhere in France (produced 1941).
Des Teufels General (produced 1946). 1946; as *The Devil's General*, translated by Robert Gore Browne, 1953; also translated by Ingrid G. and William F. Gilbert, in *Masters of Modern Drama*, edited by Haskell M. Block and Robert G. Shedd, 1962.
Die deutschen Dramen. 1947.
Barbara Blomberg (produced 1949). 1949.
Der Gesang im Feuerofen (produced 1950). 1950.
Herbert Engelmann, completion of the play by Hauptmann (produced 1952). 1952.
Das kalte Licht (produced 1955). 1955.
Dramen. 1960.
Die Uhr schlägt eins (produced 1961). 1961.
Der Kranichtanz (produced 1967). In *Die neue Rundschau*, 74(4), 1961.
Mainzer Umzug, music by Paul Hindemith (produced 1962). 1962.
Das Leben des Horace A. W. Tabor (produced 1964). 1964.
Der Rattenfänger (produced 1975). 1975.

Screenplays: *Quälender Nacht*, 1925; *Der blaue Engel*, 1930; *Escape Me Never*, 1935; *Rembrandt*, 1936; *De Mayerling à Sarajevo*, 1940; *Die Jungfrau auf dem Dach*, 1953.

Fiction

Ein Bauer aus dem Taunus und andere Geschichten (stories). 1927.
Die Affenhochzeit. 1932; as *Monkey Wedding*, translated by F.A. Beaumont, in *Argosy*, (23), 1938.
Eine Liebesgeschichte. 1934; as *Love Story*, translated by F.A. Beaumont, in *Argosy*, (22), 1937.

Salwàre; oder, die Magdalena von Bozen. 1936; as *The Moons Ride Over*, translated by Moray Firth, 1937; as *The Moon in the South*, translated by Firth, 1937.
Ein Sommer in Österreich. 1937.
Herr über Leben und Tod. 1938.
Der Seelenbräu. 1945.
Die Erzählungen. 1952.
Engele von Löwen. 1955.
Die Fastnachtsbeichte. 1959; as *Carnival Confession*, translated by John and Necke Mander, 1961.
Erzählungen. 1960.
Geschichten aus vierzig Jahren. 1963.
Auf einem Weg im Frühling. 1970.

Verse

Der Baum. 1926.
Gedichte 1916–1948. 1948.
Gedichte. 1960.

Other

Pro Domo (essay). 1938.
Second Wind (autobiography), translated by Elizabeth Reynolds Hapgood. 1940.
Carlo Mierendorff: Porträt eines deutschen Sozialisten. 1947.
Die Brüder Grimm: Ein deutscher Beitrag zur Humanität. 1948.
Die langen Wege. 1952.
Ein Blick auf den Rhein, with others. 1957.
Ein Weg zu Schiller. 1959.
Gesammelte Werke. 4 vols., 1960.
Ein voller Erdentag; Festrede zu Gerhart Hauptmann hundertstem Geburtstag. 1962.
Als wärs ein Stück von mir (autobiography). 1966; as *A Part of Myself*, translated by Richard and Clara Winston, 1970.
Scholar zwischen gestern und morgen. Ein Vortrag. 1967.
Memento zum zwanzigsten Juli 1969. 1969.
Über die musiche Bestimmung des Menschen, Rede zur Eröffnung der Salzburger Festspiele (essay), edited by Max Kaindl-Hönig. 1970.
Carl Zuckmayer in Mainz (address), translated by Walter Heist. 1970.
Werkausgabe 1920–1975. 10 vols., 1976.
Späte Freundschaft: Carl Zuckmayer, Karl Barth in Briefen, edited by Hinrich Stoevesandt. 1977; as *A Late Friendship: The Letters of Karl Barth and Carl Zuckmayer*, translated by Geoffrey W. Bromiley, 1982.

*

Bibliography: *Carl Zuckmayer: Eine Bibliographie* by Ludwig Emanuel Reindl, 1962; Arnold John Jacobius, 1971.

Critical Studies: *Motive und Dramaturgie im Schauspiel Carl Zuckmayers* by Arnold J. Jacobius, 1971; *Carl Zuckmayer* by Arnold Bauer, 1976; *Der Hauptmann von Köpenick: Erläuterungen und Dokumente* edited by Hartmut Schieble, 1977; *The Central Women Figures in Carl Zuckmayer's Dramas* by Ausma Balinkin, 1978; *Ohne Glanz und Gloria: Die Geschichte des Hauptmanns von Köpenick* by Winifried Löschburg, 1978; *Carl Zuckmayer* by Siegfried Mews, 1981; *Carl Zuckmayer, ''Der Hauptmann von Köpenick'': Interpretation und Materialien* by Hans Gehrke, 1983; *Carl Zuckmayer* by

Hans Waggener, 1983; *Carl Zuckmayer Criticism: Tracing Endangered Fame* by Hans Wagener, 1995.

* * *

Carl Zuckmayer is chiefly known as a playwright who produced stage hits in the 1920s and then again immediately after World War II. Yet Zuckmayer's total work is fairly extensive and includes drama, prose, lyric poetry, adaptations for the stage, and film scripts—among them *Der blaue Engel* (*The Blue Angel*).

Zuckmayer's early plays, the expressionist *Kreuzweg* [Crossroads] and the experimental *Pankraz erwacht* [Pankraz Awakens], achieved neither critical nor popular success. The playwright then turned to the folk-play in the vein of the New Objectivity. In contrast to Expressionism, the New Objectivity of the 1920s concentrated on the here and now and a factual style of representation; it dispensed with the feverish atmosphere of Expressionist lays, their anti-bourgeois sentiments, and their predilection for revolutions and wars as the harbingers of a better future.

The hugely successful *Der fröhliche Weinberg* [The Merry Vineyard] was Zuckmayer's first play in the new mode. It is firmly rooted in the playwright's native soil, the wine-growing Rhine region, and adopts characteristics of the region's people and their dialect. The play's uncomplicated plot, its employment of time-honoured comedic devices, and its earthy humour conform to the tradition of the folk-play. Above all, the play exudes an unbridled zest for life and displays a conciliatory attitude that tends to minimize existing social barriers and humorously de-emphasize the disquieting right-wing views expressed by one character. In the play's conventional happy ending, which features no less than four engagements, all complications are resolved.

The following two dramas from the late 1920s are also in the tradition of the folk-play and take place in the playwright's home region. *Schinderhannes* is named after protagonist Johannes (Hannes) Wilhelm Bückler, a kind of German Robin Hood of the late 1700s. Although Zuckmayer portrays Schinderhannes as a friend of the people, the outlaw is not primarily motivated by social compassion or the attainment of political goals: he simply follows his natural inclination for showing off his strength and prowess. Schinderhannes's execution cannot prevent the triumph of the life force, symbolized in Schinderhannes's surviving child. *Katharina Knie* features a courageous and determined heroine who returns to the family circus and assumes its directorship after the death of her father. The conflict between two antithetical modes of existence, the artists' and the middleclasses' ways of life, is not fully developed, and the play suffers from a heavy dose of sentimentality.

Zuckmayer's best-known play, *Der Hauptmann von Köpenick* (*The Captain of Köpenick*), is based on a historical incident, the impersonation of a captain by the ex-convict and unemployed cobbler Wilhelm Voigt in 1906. Voigt's theft of the city's municipal funds in the town of Köpenick (then outside the city limits of Berlin) was widely interpreted as an indictment of German-Prussian militarism and the reverence for uniform in imperial Germany. But Zuckmayer's criticism of a social system that attributes exaggerated importance to the military is muted. There are no real villains in the play, and most of the representatives of the system appear in a sympathetic light. In fairytale-like fashion the captain's uniform assumes a life of its own and displays magical powers that seem to absolve its wearers from responsibility for their acts. The non-antagonistic ending—Voigt bursts out laughing when he sees himself for the first time in the captain's uniform—confirms the play's status as "metaphysical" theatre. Its thrust is not directed against specific political institutions or specific individuals functioning in a social context; rather, it takes issue with the system's underlying abstract ideas and general principles.

Zuckmayer's involuntary exile from Germany during the Nazi period—first in Austria and, after the *Anschluss* of 1938, in the United States—seriously affected his creativity and severely curtailed his publishing opportunities. Since plays were difficult to stage, Zuckmayer primarily wrote prose fiction and film scripts. But during his World War II exile in remote Vermont, he created what was to become his most controversial play, *Des Teufels General* (*The Devil's General*). An ambitious attempt to offer an explanation for many Germans' backing of Hitler, the play was intensely debated in post-war Germany owing to Zuckmayer's portrayal of a great number of characters with a wide range of views on Nazism—from outright opposition to whole-hearted and unequivocal support. The protagonist, Nazi general Harras, solves his moral dilemma of being both an opponent of Hitler and his servant by submitting to "divine judgement." He flies a defective aeroplane in which he crashes and is killed. Harras's death does not answer the question of how to combat the demonic forces of evil; hence the message of the play remains ambivalent. Despite Zuckmayer's ultimately placating stance towards Harras and his wavering attitude towards the chief representative of the anti-Nazi resistance, the drama played a vital role in Germany's coming to terms with the Nazi past, the so-called *Vergangenheitsbewältigung*.

None of Zuckmayer's subsequent dramas struck as responsive a chord as *The Devil's General*. Plays such as *Der Gesang im Fueurofen* [The Song of the Fiery Furnace], which deals with the theme of resistance and betrayal, and *Das kalte Licht* [Cold Light], which is loosely based on the story of atomic spy Klaus Fuchs, treat political and topical issues related to World War II and the Cold War—albeit in humanitarian and individualistic rather than political terms. However, Zuckmayer's autobiography, *Als wärs ein Stück von mir* (*A Part of Myself*), was enthusiastically received, and its publication in 1966 confirmed his position as "the grand old man of German letters." "Portrait of an Epoch," the subtitle of the abridged English translation, provides an indication of the range that Zuckmayer's personal history encompasses—from the turn of the century to the 1950s and beyond. One of the significant themes of the autobiography is that of friendship; friendship is the bedrock of Zuckmayer's humanitarian vision and optimistic outlook on life.

Presumably, Zuckmayer's comparatively limited reception in the English-speaking world is attributable to the fact that he is a quintessentially German author whose best plays address incisive moments in 20th-century German history. As a contemporary fully attuned to the problems of his times, the playwright manages in some of his plays to transcend mere topicality and to provide in masterfully realistic and nonideological fashion insights into the dilemmas human beings in our century were confronted with.

—Siegfried Mews

Blood was lying in shadow right near the front door. He'd suggested I try and pick off any dogs with the roverpak first, if I could. That would allow him to operate freely.

That was the least of my worries.

I'd wanted to hole up in another room, one with only a single entrance, but I had no way of knowing if the rovers were already in the building, so I did the best I could with what I had.

Everything was quiet. Even that Quilla June. It'd taken me valuable minutes to convince her she'd damned well better hole up and not make any noise; she was better off with me than with twenty of *them.* "If you ever wanna see your mommy and daddy again," I warned her. After that she didn't give me no trouble, packing her in with mats.

Quiet.

Then I heard two things, both at the same time. From back in the swimming pool I heard boots crunching plaster. Very soft. And from one side of the front door, I heard a tinkle of metal striking wood. So they were going to try a yoke. Well, I was ready.

Quiet again.

I sighted the Browning on the door to the pool room. It was still open from when I'd come through. Figure him at maybe five-ten, and drop the sights a foot and a half, and I'd catch him in the chest. I'd learned long ago you don't try for the head. Go for the widest part of the body: the chest and stomach. The trunk.

Suddenly, outside, I heard a dog bark, and part of the darkness near the front door detached itself and moved inside the gym. Directly opposite Blood. I didn't move the Browning.

The rover at the front door moved a step along the wall, away from Blood. Then he cocked back his arm and threw something—a rock, a piece of metal, something—across the room to draw fire. I didn't move the Browning.

When the thing he'd thrown hit the floor, two rovers jumped out of the swimming pool door, one on either side of it, rifles down, ready to spray. Before they could open up, I'd squeezed off the first shot, tracked across and put a second shot into the other one. They both went down.

Dead hits, right in the heart. Bang, they were down, neither one moved.

The mother by the door turned to split, and Blood was on him. Just like that, out of the darkness, riiiip!

Blood leaped, right over the crossbar of the guy's rifle held at ready, and sank his fangs into the rover's throat. The guy screamed, and Blood dropped, carrying a piece of the guy with him. The guy was making awful bubbling sounds and went down on one knee. I put a slug into his head, and he fell forward.

It went quiet again.

Not bad. Not bad atall atall. Three takeouts and they still didn't know our positions. Blood had fallen back into the murk by the entrance. He didn't say a thing, but I knew what he was thinking: maybe that was three out of seventeen, or three out of twenty, or twenty-two. No way of knowing; we could be faced-off in here for a week and never know if we'd gotten them all, or some, or none. They could go and get poured full again, and I'd find myself run out of slugs and no food and that girl, that Quilla June, crying and making me divide my attention, and daylight—and they'd be still laying out there, waiting till we got hungry enough to do something dumb, or till we ran out of slugs; and then they'd cloud up and rain all over us.

A rover came dashing straight through the front door at top speed, took a leap, hit on his shoulders, rolled, came up going in a different direction, and snapped off three rounds into different corners of the room before I could track him with the Browning. By that time he was close enough under me where I didn't have to waste a .22 slug. I picked up the .45 without a sound and blew the back off his head. Slug went in neat, came out and took most of his hair with it. He fell right down.

"Blood! The rifle!"

Came out of the shadows, grabbed it up in his mouth and dragged it over to the pile of wrestling mats in the far corner. I saw an arm poke out from the mass of mats, and a hand grabbed the rifle, dragged it inside. Well, it was at least safe there, till I needed it. Brave little bastard: he scuttled over to the dead rover and started worrying the

HARLAN ELLISON
A BOY AND HIS DOG

ammo bandolier off his body. It took him a while; he could have been picked off from the doorway or outside one of the windows, but he did it. Brave little bastard. I had to remember to get him something good to eat when we got out of this. I smiled, up there in the darkness: if we got out of this, I wouldn't have to worry about getting him something tender. It was lying all over the floor of that gymnasium.

Just as Blood was dragging the bandolier back into the shadows, two of them tried it with their dogs. They came through a ground floor window, one after another, hitting and rolling and going in opposite directions, as the dogs—a mother-ugly akita, big as a house, and a Doberman bitch the color of a turd—shot through the front door and split in the unoccupied two directions. I caught one of the dogs, the akita, with the .45, and it went down thrashing. The Doberman was all over Blood.

But firing, I'd given away my position. One of the rovers fired from the hip and .30-06 soft-nosed slugs spanged off the girders around me. I dropped the automatic, and it started to slip off the girder as I reached for the Browning. I made a grab for the .45 and that was the only thing saved me. I fell forward to clutch at it, it slipped away and hit the gym floor with a crash, and the rover fired at where I'd been. But I was flat on the girder, arm dangling, and the crash startled him. He fired at the sound, and right at that instant I heard another shot from a Winchester, and the other rover, who'd made it safe into the shadows, fell forward holding a big pumping hole in his chest. That Quilla June had shot him, from behind the mats.

I didn't even have time to figure out what the fuck was happening. . .Blood was rolling around with the Doberman and the sounds they were making were awful. . .the rover with the .30-06 chipped off another shot and hit the muzzle of the Browning, protruding over the side of the girder, and wham it was gone, falling down. I was naked up there without clout, and the sonofabitch was hanging back in shadow waiting for me.

Another shot from the Winchester, and the rover fired right into the mats. She ducked back behind, and I knew I couldn't count on her for anything more. But I didn't need it; in that second, while he was focused on her, I grabbed the climbing rope, flipped myself over the girder, and howling like a burnpit-screamer, went sliding down, feeling the rope cutting my palms. I got down far enough to swing, and kicked off. I swung back and forth, whipping my body three different ways each time, swinging out and over, way over, each time. The sonofabitch kept firing, trying to track a trajectory, but I kept spinning out of his line of fire. Then he was empty, and I kicked back as hard as I could, and came zooming in toward his corner of shadows, and let loose all at once and went ass-over-end into the corner, and there he was, and I went right into him and he spanged off the wall, and I was on top of him, digging my thumbs into his eyesockets. He was screaming and the dogs were screaming and that girl was screaming and I pounded the motherfucker's head against the floor till he stopped moving, then I grabbed up the empty .30-06 and whipped his head till I knew he wasn't gonna give me no more aggravation.

Then I found the .45 and shot the Doberman.

Blood got up and shook himself off. He was cut up bad. "Thanks," he mumbled, and went over to lie down in the shadows, to lick himself off.

I went and found that Quilla June, and she was crying. About all the guys we'd killed. Mostly about the one *she'd* killed. I couldn't get her to stop bawling so I cracked her across the face and told her she'd saved my life, and that helped some.

Blood came dragassing over. "How're we going to get out of this, Albert?"

"Let me think."

I thought and knew it was hopeless. No matter how many we got, there'd be more. And it was a matter of *macho* now. Their honor.

"How about a fire?" Blood suggested.

"Get away while it's burning?" I shook my head. "They'll have the place staked-out all around. No good."

"What if we don't leave? What if we burn up with it?"

I looked at him. Brave. . .and smart as hell.

HARLAN ELLISON
A BOY AND HIS DOG

V

We gathered all the lumber and mats and scaling ladders and vaulting boxes and benches and anything else that would burn, and piled the garbage against a wooden divider at one end of the gym. Quilla June found a can of kerosene in a storeroom, and we set fire to the whole damn pile. Then we followed Blood to the place he'd found for us. The boiler room way down under the YMCA. We all climbed into the empty boiler, and dogged down the door, leaving a release vent open for air. We had one mat in there with us, and all the ammo we could carry, and the extra rifles and sidearms the rovers'd had on them.

"Can you catch anything?" I asked Blood.

"A little. Not much. I'm reading one guy. The building's burning good."

"You be able to tell when they split?"

"Maybe. *If* they split."

I settled back. Quilla June was shaking from all that had happened. "Just take it easy," I told her. "By morning the place'll be down around our ears, and they'll go through the rubble and find a lot of dead meat, and maybe they won't look too hard for a chick's body. And everything'll be all right. . .if we don't get choked off in here."

She smiled, very thin, and tried to look brave. She was okay, that one. She closed her eyes and settled back on the mat and tried to sleep. I was beat. I closed my eyes, too.

"Can you handle it?" I asked Blood.

"I suppose. You better sleep."

I nodded, eyes still closed, and fell on my side. I was out before I could think about it.

When I came back, I found the girl, that Quilla June, snuggled up under my armpit, her arm around my waist, dead asleep. I could hardly breathe. It was like a furnace; hell, it *was* a furnace. I reached out a hand and the wall of the boiler was so damned hot I couldn't touch it. Blood was up on the mattress with us. That mat had been the only thing'd kept us from being singed good. He was asleep, head buried in his paws. She was asleep, still naked.

I put a hand on her tit. It was warm. She stirred and cuddled into me closer. I got a hard-on.

Managed to get my pants off, and rolled on top of her. She woke up fast when she felt me pry her legs apart, but it was too late by then. "Don't. . .*stop*. . .what are you doing. . .no, don't. . ."

But she was half-asleep, and weak, and I don't think she really wanted to fight me anyhow.

She cried when I broke her, of course, but after that it was okay. There was blood all over the wrestling mat. And Blood just kept sleeping.

It was really different. Usually, when I'd get Blood to track something down for me, it'd be grab it and punch it and pork it and get away fast before something bad could happen. But when she came, she rose up off the mat, and hugged me around the back so hard I thought she'd crack my ribs, and then she settled back down slow slow slow, like I do when I'm doing leg-lifts in the makeshift gym I rigged in the auto wrecking yard. And her eyes were closed, and she was relaxed-looking. And happy. I could tell.

We did it a lot of times, and after a while it was her idea, but I didn't say no. And then we lay out side-by-side and talked.

She asked me about how it was with Blood, and I told her how the skirmisher dogs had gotten telepathic, and how they'd lost the ability to hunt food for themselves, so the solos and roverpaks had to do it for them, and how dogs like Blood were good at finding chicks for solos like me. She didn't say anything to that.

I asked her about what it was like where she lived, in one of the downunders.

"It's nice. But it's always very quiet. Everyone is very polite to everyone else. It's just a small town."

"Which one you live in?"

"Topeka. It's real close to here."

"Yeah, I know. The access dropshaft is only about half a mile from here. I went out there once, to take a look around."

HARLAN ELLISON
A BOY AND HIS DOG

"Have you ever been in a downunder?"

"No. But I don't guess I want to be, either."

"Why? It's very nice. You'd like it."

"Shit."

"That's very crude."

"*I'm* very crude."

"Not all the time."

I was getting mad. "Listen, you ass, what's the matter with you? I grabbed you and pushed you around, I raped you half a dozen times, so what's so good about me, huh? What's the matter with you, don't you even have enough smarts to know when somebody's—"

She was smiling at me. "I didn't mind. I liked doing it. Want to do it again?"

I was really shocked. I moved away from her. "What the hell is wrong with you? Don't you know that a chick from a downunder like you can be really mauled by solos? Don't you know chicks get warnings from their parents in the downunders, 'Don't cumup, you'll get snagged by them dirty, hairy, slobbering solos!' Don't you know that?"

She put her hand on my leg and started moving it up, the fingertips just brushing my thigh. I got another hard-on. "My parents never said that about solos," she said. Then she pulled me over her again, and kissed me, and I couldn't stop from getting in her again.

God, it just went on like that for hours. After a while Blood turned around and said, "I'm not going to keep pretending I'm asleep. I'm hungry. And I'm hurt."

I tossed her off me—she was on top by this time—and examined him. The Doberman had taken a good chunk out of his right ear, and there was a rip right down his muzzle, and blood-matted fur on one side. He was a mess, "Jesus, man, you're a mess," I said.

"You're no fucking rose garden yourself, Albert!" he snapped. I pulled my hand back.

"Can we get out of here?" I asked him.

He cast around, and then shook his head. "I can't get any readings. Must be a pile of rubble on top of this boiler. I'll have to go out and scout."

We kicked that around for a while, and finally decided if the building was razed, and had cooled a little, the roverpak would have gone through the ashes by now. The fact that they hadn't tried the boiler indicated that we were probably buried pretty good. Either that, or the building was still smoldering overhead. In which case, they'd still be out there, waiting to sift the remains.

"Think you can handle it, the condition you're in?"

"I guess I'll *have* to, won't I?" Blood said. He was really surly. "I mean, what with you busy coitusing your brains out, there won't be much left for staying alive, will there?"

I sensed real trouble with him. He didn't like Quilla June. I moved around him and undogged the boiler hatch. It wouldn't open. So I braced my back against the side, and jacked my legs up, and gave it a slow, steady shove.

Whatever had fallen against it from outside resisted for a minute, then started to give, then tumbled away with a crash. I pushed the door open all the way, and looked out. The upper floors had fallen in on the basement, but by the time they'd given, they'd been mostly cinder and lightweight rubble. Everything was smoking out there. I could see daylight through the smoke.

I slipped out, burning my hands on the outside lip of the hatch. Blood followed. He started to pick his way through the debris. I could see that the boiler had been almost completely covered by the gunk that had dropped from above. Chances were good the roverpak had taken a fast look, figured we'd been fried, and moved on. But I wanted Blood to run a recon anyway. He started off, but I called him back. He came.

"What is it?"

I looked down at him. "I'll tell you what it is, man. You're acting very shitty."

"Sue me."

"Goddammit, dog, what's got your ass up?"

"Her. That nit chick you've got in there."

"So what? Big deal. . .I've had chicks before."

HARLAN ELLISON
A BOY AND HIS DOG

"Yeah, but never any that hung on like this one. I warn you, Albert, she's going to make trouble."

"Don't be dumb!" He didn't reply. Just looked at me with anger and then limped off to check out the scene. I crawled back inside and dogged the hatch. She wanted to make it again. I said I didn't want to; Blood had brought me down. I was bugged. And I didn't know which one to be pissed off at.

But God she was pretty.

She kind of pouted and settled back with her arms wrapped around her. "Tell me some more about the downunder," I said.

At first she was cranky, wouldn't say much, but after a while she opened up and started talking freely. I was learning a lot. I figured I could use it some time, maybe.

There were only a couple of hundred downunders in what was left of the United States and Canada. They'd been sunk on the sites of wells or mines or other kinds of deep holes. Some of them, out in the west, were in natural cave formations. They went way down, maybe two to five miles. They were like big caissons, stood on end. And the people who'd settled them were squares of the worst kind. Southern Baptists, Fundamentalists, lawanorder goofs, real middle-class squares with no taste for the wild life. And they'd gone back to a kind of life that hadn't existed for a hundred and fifty years. They'd gotten the last of the scientists to do the work, invent the how and why, and then they'd run them out. They didn't want any progress, they didn't want any dissent, they didn't want anything that would make waves. They'd had enough of that. The best time in the world had been just before the First War, and they figured if they could keep it like that, they could live quiet lives and survive. Shit! I'd go nuts in one of the downunders.

Quilla June smiled, and snuggled up again, and this time I didn't turn her off. She started touching me again, down there and all over, and then she said, "Vic?"

"Uh-huh."

"Have you ever been in love?"

259

"What?"

"In love? Have you ever been in love with a girl?"

"Well, I damn well guess I haven't!"

"Do you know what love is?"

"Sure. I guess I do."

"But if you've never been in love. . .?"

"Don't be dumb. I mean, I've never had a bullet in the head, and I know I wouldn't like it."

"You don't know what love is, I'll bet."

"Well, if it means living in a downunder, I guess I just don't wanna find out." We didn't go on with the conversation much after that. She pulled me down and we did it again. And when it was over, I heard Blood scratching at the boiler. I opened the hatch, and he was standing out there. "All clear," he said.

"You sure?"

"Yeah, yeah, I'm sure. Put your pants on," he said it with a sneer in the tone, "and come on out here. We have to talk some stuff."

I looked at him, and he wasn't kidding. I got my jeans and sneakers on, and climbed down out of the boiler.

He trotted ahead of me, away from the boiler over some blacksoot beams, and outside the gym. It was down. Looked like a rotted stump tooth.

"Now what's lumbering you?" I asked him.

He scampered up on a chunk of concrete till he was almost nose level with me.

"You're going dumb on me, Vic."

I knew he was serious. No Albert shit, straight Vic. "How so?"

"Last night, man. We could have cut out of there and left her for them. *That* would have been smart."

"I wanted her."

"Yeah, I know. That's what I'm talking about. It's today now, not last night. You've had her about a half a hundred times. Why're we hanging around?"

"I want some more."

HARLAN ELLISON
A BOY AND HIS DOG

Then he got angry. "Yeah, well, listen, chum. . .I want a few things myself. I want something to eat, and I want to get rid of this pain in my side, and I want away from this turf. Maybe they *don't* give up this easy."

"Take it easy. We can handle all that. Don't mean she can't go with us."

"*Doesn't* mean," he corrected me. "And so *that's* the new story. Now we travel three, is that right?"

I was getting really uptight myself. "You're starting to sound like a damn poodle!"

"And you're starting to sound like a boxer."

I hauled back to crack him one. He didn't move. I dropped the hand. I'd never hit Blood. I didn't want to start now.

"Sorry," he said, softly.

"That's okay."

But we weren't looking at each other.

"Vic, man, you've got a responsibility to me, you know."

"You don't have to tell me that."

"Well, I guess maybe I do. Maybe I have to remind you of some stuff. Like the time that burnpit-screamer came up out of the street and made a grab for you."

I shuddered. The motherfucker'd been green. Righteous stone green, glowing like fungus. My gut heaved, just thinking.

"And I went for him, right?"

I nodded. Right, mutt, right.

"And I could have been burned bad, and died, and that would've been all of it for me, right or wrong, isn't that true?" I nodded again. I was getting pissed off proper. I didn't like being made to feel guilty. It was a fifty-fifty with Blood and me. He knew that. "But I did it, right?" I remembered the way the green thing had screamed. Christ, it was all ooze and eyelashes.

"Okay, okay, don't hanger me."

"*Harangue*, not hanger."

"Well, WHATEVER!" I shouted. "Just knock off the crap, or we can forget the whole fucking arrangement!"

Then Blood blew. "Well, maybe we *should*, you simple *dumb putz!*"

"What's a *putz*, you little turd. . .is that something bad. . .yeah, it must be. . .you watch your fucking mouth, son of a bitch; or I'll kick your ass!"

We sat there and didn't talk for fifteen minutes. Neither one of us knew which way to go.

Finally, I backed off a little. I talked soft and I talked slow. I was about up to here with him, but told him I was going to do right by him, like I always had, and he threatened me, saying I'd damned well better because there were a couple of very hip solos making it around the city, and they'd be delighted to have a sharp tail-scent like him. I told him I didn't like being threatened, and he'd better watch his fucking step or I'd break his leg. He got furious and stalked off. I said screw you and went back to the boiler to take it out on that Quilla June again.

But when I stuck my head inside the boiler, she was waiting, with a pistol one of the dead rovers had supplied. She hit me good and solid over the right eye with it, and I fell straight forward across the hatch, and was out cold.

VI

"I told you she was no good." He watched me as I swabbed out the cut with disinfectant from my kit, and painted the gash with iodine. He smirked when I flinched.

I put away the stuff, and rummaged around in the boiler, gathering up all the spare ammo I could carry, and ditching the Browning in favor of the heavier .30-06. Then I found something that must've slipped out of her clothes.

It was a little metal plate, about three inches long and an inch-and-a-half high. It had a whole string of numbers on it, and there were holes in it, in random patterns. "What's this?" I asked Blood.

He looked at it, sniffed it.

HARLAN ELLISON
A BOY AND HIS DOG

"Must be an identity card of some kind. Maybe it's what she used to get out of the downunder."

That made my mind up.

I jammed it in a pocket and started out. Toward the access dropshaft.

"Where the hell are you going?" Blood yelled after me.

"Come on back, you'll get killed out there!

"I'm hungry, dammit! I'm wounded!

"Albert, you sonofabitch! Come back here!"

I kept right on walking. I was gonna find that bitch and brain her. Even if I had to go downunder to find her.

It took me an hour to walk to the access dropshaft leading down to Topeka. I thought I saw Blood following, but hanging back a ways. I didn't give a damn. I was mad.

Then, there it was. A tall, straight, featureless pillar of shining black metal. It was maybe twenty feet in diameter, perfectly flat on top, disappearing straight into the ground. It was a cap, that was all. I walked straight up to it, and fished around in my pocket for that metal card. Then something was tugging at my right pants leg.

"Listen, you moron, you can't go down there!"

I kicked him off, but he came right back.

"Listen to me!"

I turned around and stared at him.

Blood sat down; the powder puffed up around him. "Albert. . ."

"My name is Vic, you little eggsucker."

"Okay, okay, no fooling around. Vic." His tone softened. "Vic. Come on, man." He was trying to get through to me. I was really boiling, but he was trying to make sense. I shrugged, and crouched down beside him.

"Listen, man," Blood said, "this chick has bent you way out of shape. You *know* you can't go down there. It's all square and settled, and they know everyone; they hate solos. Enough roverpaks have raided downunder, and raped their women, and stolen their food, they'll have defenses set up. They'll *kill* you, Vic!"

"What the hell do you care? You're always saying you'd be better off without me." He sagged at that.

"Vic, we've been together almost three years. Good and bad. But this can be the worst. I'm scared, man. Scared you won't come back. And I'm hungry, and I'll have to go find some dude who'll take me on. . .and you know most solos are in paks now, I'll be low mutt. I'm not that young any more. And I'm hurt pretty bad."

I could dig it. He was talking sense. But all I could think of was how that bitch, that Quilla June, had rapped me. And then there were images of her soft tits, and the way she made little sounds when I was in her, and I shook my head, and knew I had to go get even.

"I got to do it, Blood. *I got to.*"

He breathed deep and sagged a little more. He knew it was useless. "You don't even see what she's done to you, Vic. That metal card, it's too easy, as if she *wanted* you to follow."

I got up. "I'll try to get back quick. Will you wait. . .?"

He was silent a long while, and I waited. Finally, he said, "For a while. Maybe I'll be here, maybe not."

I understood. I turned around and started walking around the pillar of black metal. Finally I found a slot in the pillar, and slipped the metal card into it. There was a soft humming sound, then a section of the pillar dilated. I hadn't even seen the lines of the sections. A circle opened and I took a step through. I turned and there was Blood, watching me. We looked at each other, all the while that pillar was humming.

"So long, Vic."

"Take care of yourself, Blood."

"Hurry back."

"Do my best."

"Yeah. Right."

Then I turned around and stepped inside. The access portal irised closed behind me.

HARLAN ELLISON
A BOY AND HIS DOG

VII

I should have known. I should have suspected. Sure, every once in a while a chick came up to see what it was like on the surface, what had happened to the cities; sure, it happened. Why, I'd believed her when she'd told me, cuddled up beside me in that steaming boiler, that she'd wanted to see what it was like when a girl did it with a guy, that all the flicks she'd seen in Topeka were sweet and solid and dull, and the girls in her school'd talked about beaver flicks, and one of them had a little eight-page comic book and she'd read it with wide eyes. . .sure, I'd believed her. It was logical. I should have suspected something when she left that metal I.D. plate behind. It was too easy. Blood'd tried to tell me. Dumb? Yeah!

The second that access iris swirled closed behind me, the humming got louder, and some cool light grew in the walls. Wall. It was a circular compartment with only two sides to the wall: *inside* and *outside*. The wall pulsed up light and the humming got louder, and the deckplate I was standing on dilated just the way the outside port had done. But I was standing there, like a mouse in a cartoon, and as long as I didn't look down I was cool, I wouldn't fall.

Then I started settling. Dropped through the floor, the iris closed overhead, I was dropping down the tube, picking up speed but not too much, just dropping steadily. Now I knew what a dropshaft was.

Down and down I went and every once in a while I'd see something like 10 LEV or ANTIPOLL 55 or BREEDER-CON or PUMP SE 6 on the wall, faintly I could make out the sectioning of an iris. . .but I never stopped dropping.

Finally, I dropped all the way to the bottom, and there was TO-PEKA CITY LIMITS POP. 22,860 on the wall, and I settled down without any strain, bending a little from the knees to cushion the impact, but even that wasn't much.

I used the metal plate again, and the iris—a much bigger one this time—swirled open, and I got my first look at a downunder.

It stretched away in front of me, twenty miles to the dim shining

265

horizon of tin can metal where the wall behind me curved and curved and curved till it made one smooth, encircling circuit and came back around around around to where I stood, staring at it. I was down at the bottom of a big metal tube that stretched up to a ceiling an eighth of a mile overhead, twenty miles across. And in the bottom of that tin can, someone had built a town that looked for all the world like a photo out of one of the water-logged books in the library on the surface. I'd seen a town like this in the books. Just like this. Neat little houses, and curvy little streets, and trimmed lawns, and a business section and everything else that a Topeka would have.

Except a sun, except birds, except clouds, except rain, except snow, except cold, except wind, except ants, except dirt, except mountains, except oceans, except big fields of grain, except stars, except the moon, except forests, except animals running wild, except. . .

Except freedom.

They were canned down here, like dead fish. Canned.

I felt my throat tighten up. I wanted to get out. Out! I started to tremble, my hands were cold and there was sweat on my forehead. This had been insane, coming down here. I had to get out. *Out!*

I turned around to get back in the dropshaft, and then it grabbed me.

That bitch Quilla June! I shoulda suspected!

The thing was low, and green, and boxlike, and had cables with mittens on the ends instead of arms, and it rolled on tracks, and it grabbed me.

It hoisted me up on its square flat top, holding me with them mittens on the cables, and I couldn't move, except to try kicking at the big glass eye in the front, but it didn't do any good. It didn't bust. The thing was only about four feet high, and my sneakers almost reached the ground, but not quite, and it started moving off into Topeka, hauling me along with it.

People were all over the place. Sitting in rockers on their front porches, raking their lawns, hanging around the gas station, sticking pennies in gumball machines, painting a white stripe down the middle

HARLAN ELLISON
A BOY AND HIS DOG

of the road, selling newspapers on a corner, listening to an oompah band on a shell in a park, playing hopscotch and pussy-in-the-corner, polishing a fire engine, sitting on benches reading, washing windows, pruning bushes, tipping hats to ladies, collecting milk bottles in wire carrying-racks, grooming horses, throwing a stick for a dog to retrieve, diving into a communal swimming pool, chalking vegetable prices on a slate outside a grocery, walking hand-in-hand with a girl, all of them watching me go past on that metal motherfucker.

I could hear Blood speaking, saying just what he'd said before I'd entered the dropshaft: *It's all square and settled and they know everyone; they hate solos. Enough roverpaks have raided downunders, and raped their women and stolen their food, they'll have defenses set up. They'll kill you, Vic!*

Thanks, mutt.

Goodbye.

VII

The green box tracked through the business section and turned in at a shopfront with the words BETTER BUSINESS BUREAU on the window. It rolled right inside the open door, and there were half a dozen men and old men and very old men in there, waiting for me. Also a couple of women. The green box stopped.

One of them came over and took the metal plate out of my hand. He looked at it, then turned around and gave it to the oldest of the old men, a withered toad wearing baggy pants and a green eyeshade and garters that held up the sleeves of his striped shirt. "Quilla June, Lew," the guy said to the old man. Lew took the metal plate and put it in the top left drawer of a rolltop desk. "Better take his guns, Aaron," the old coot said. And the guy who'd taken the plate cleaned me.

"Let him loose, Aaron," Lew said.

Aaron stepped around the back of the green box and something clicked, and the cable-mittens sucked back inside the box, and I got down off the thing. My arms were numb where the box had held me. I rubbed one, then the other, and I glared at them.

267

"Now, boy. . ." Lew started.

"Suck wind, asshole!"

The women blanched. The men tightened their faces.

"I told you it wouldn't work," another of the old men said to Lew.

"Bad business, this," said one of the younger ones.

Lew leaned forward in his straight-back chair and pointed a crumbled finger at me. "Boy, you better be nice."

"I hope all your fuckin' children are hare-lipped!"

"This is no good, Lew!" another man said.

"Guttersnipe," a woman with a beak snapped.

Lew stared at me. His mouth was a nasty little black line. I knew the sonofabitch didn't have a tooth in his crummy head that wasn't rotten and smelly. He stared at me with vicious little eyes. God, he was ugly, like a toad ready to snaffle a fly off the wall with his tongue. He was getting set to say something I wouldn't like. "Aaron, maybe you'd better put the sentry back on him." Aaron moved to the green box.

"Okay, hold it," I said, holding up my hand.

Aaron stopped, looked at Lew, who nodded. Then Lew leaned real far forward again, and aimed that bird-claw at me. "You ready to behave yourself, son?"

"Yeah, I guess."

"You'd better be dang sure."

"Okay. I'm *dang* sure. Also *fuckin'* sure!"

"And you'll watch your mouth."

I didn't reply. Old coot.

"You're a bit of an experiment for us, boy. We tried to get one of you down here other ways. Sent up some good folks to capture one of you little scuts, but they never came back. Figgered it was best to lure you down to us."

I sneered. That Quilla June. I'd take care of her!

One of the women, a little younger than Bird-Beak, came forward and looked into my face. "Lew, you'll never get this one to cow-tow. He's a filthy little killer. Look at those eyes."

"How'd you like the barrel of a rifle jammed up your ass, bitch?"

HARLAN ELLISON
A BOY AND HIS DOG

She jumped back. Lew was angry again. "Sorry," I said real quickly, "I don't like bein' called names. *Macho*, y'know?"

He settled back and snapped at the woman. "Mez, leave him alone. I'm tryin' to talk a bit of sense here. You're only making it worse."

Mez went back and sat with the others. Some Better Business Bureau these creeps were!

"As I was saying, boy: you're an experiment for us. We've been down here in Topeka close to thirty years. It's nice down here. Quiet, orderly, nice people, who respect each other, no crime, respect for the elders, and just all around a good place to live. We're growin' and we're prosperin'."

I waited.

"But, well, we find now that some of our folks can't have no more babies, and the women that do, they have mostly girls. We need some men. Certain special kind of men."

I started laughing. This was too good to be true. They wanted me for stud service. I couldn't stop laughing.

"Crude!" one of the women said, scowling.

"This's awkward enough for us, boy, don't make it no harder." Lew was embarrassed.

Here I'd spent most of Blood's and my time aboveground hunting up tail, and down here they wanted me to service the local ladyfolk. I sat down on the floor and laughed till tears ran down my cheeks.

Finally, I got up and said, "Sure. Okay. But if I do, there's a couple of things *I* want."

Lew looked at me close.

"The first thing I want is that Quilla June. I'm gonna fuck her blind, and then I'm gonna bang her on the head the way she did me!"

They huddled for a while, then came out and Lew said, "We can't tolerate any violence down here, but I s'pose Quilla June's as good a place to start as any. She's capable, isn't she, Ira?"

A skinny, yellow-skinned man nodded. He didn't look happy about it. Quilla June's old man, I bet.

"Well, let's get started," I said. "Line 'em up." I started to unzip my jeans.

The women screamed, the men grabbed me, and they hustled me

off to a boarding house where they gave me a room, and they said I should get to know Topeka a little bit before I went to work because it was, uh, er, well, awkward, and they had to get the folks in town to accept what was going to have to be done. . .on the assumption, I suppose, that if I worked out okay they'd import a few more young bulls from aboveground and turn us loose.

So I spent some time in Topeka, getting to know the folks, seeing what they did, how they lived.

It was nice, real nice.

They rocked in rockers on the front porches, they raked their lawns, they hung around the gas station, they stuck pennies in gumball machines, they painted white stripes down the middle of the road, they sold newspapers on the corners, they listened to oompah bands in a shell in the park, they played hopscotch and pussy-in-the-corner, they polished fire engines, they sat on benches reading, they washed windows and pruned bushes, they tipped their hats to ladies, they collected milk bottles in wire carrying-racks, they groomed horses and threw sticks for their dogs to retrieve, they dove into the communal swimming pool, they chalked vegetable prices on a slate outside the grocery, they walked hand-in-hand with some of the ugliest chicks I've ever seen, *and they bored the ass offa me.*

Inside a week I was ready to scream.

I could feel that tin can closing in on me.

I could feel the weight of the earth over me.

They ate artificial shit: artificial peas and fake meat and make-believe chicken and ersatz corn and bogus bread, and it all tasted like chalk and dust to me.

Polite? Christ, you could puke from the lying, hypocritical crap they called civility. Hello Mr. This and Hello Mrs. That. And how are you? And how is little Janie? And how is business? Are you going to the sodality meeting Thursday? And I started gibbering in my room at the boarding house.

The clean, sweet, neat, lovely way they lived was enough to kill a guy. No wonder the men couldn't get it up and make babies that had balls instead of slots.

HARLAN ELLISON
A BOY AND HIS DOG

The first few days, everyone watched me like I was about to explode and cover their nice whitewashed fences with shit. But after a while, they got used to seeing me. Lew took me over to the Mercantile, and got me fitted out with a pair of bib overalls and a shirt that any solo could've spotted a mile away. That Mez, that dippy bitch who'd called me a killer, she started hanging around, finally said she wanted to cut my hair, make me look civilized. But I was hip to where she was at. Wasn't a bit of the mother in her.

"What'sa'matter, cunt," I pinned her. "Your old man isn't taking care of you?"

She tried to stick her fist in her mouth, and I laughed like a loon. "Go chop off *his* balls, baby. My hair stays the way it is." She cut and run. Gone like she had a diesel tail-pipe.

It went on like that for a while. Me just walking around, them coming and feeding me, keeping all their young meat out of my way till they got the town stacked-away for what was coming with me.

Jugged like that, my mind wasn't right for a while. I got all claustrophobed, clutched, went and sat under the porch in the dark at the rooming house. Then that passed, and I got piss-mean, snapped at them, then surly, then quiet, then just mud dull. Quiet.

Finally, I started getting hip to the possibilities of getting out of there. It began with me remembering the poodle I'd fed Blood one time. It had to come from a downunder. And it couldn't have got up through the dropshaft. So that meant there were other ways out.

They gave me pretty much the run of the town, as long as I kept my manners around me and didn't try anything sudden. That green sentry box was always somewhere nearby.

So I found the way out. Nothing so spectacular; it just had to be there, and I found it.

Then I found out where they kept my weapons, and I was ready. Almost.

It was a week to the day when Aaron and Lew and Ira came to get me. I was pretty goofy by that time. I was sitting out on the back porch of the boarding house, smoking a corncob pipe with my shirt off, catching some sun. Except there wasn't no sun. Goofy.

They came around the house. "Morning, Vic," Lew greeted me. He was hobbling along with a cane, the old fart. Aaron gave me a big smile. The kind you'd give a big black bull about to stuff his meat into a good breed cow. Ira had a look that you could chip off and use in your furnace.

"Well, howdy, Lew. Mornin', Aaron, Ira."

Lew seemed right pleased by that.

Oh, you lousy bastards, just you wait!

"You 'bout ready to go meet your first lady?"

"Ready as I'll ever be, Lew," I said, and got up.

"Cool smoke, ain't it?" Aaron said.

I took the corncob out of my mouth. "Pure *dee*-light." I smiled. I hadn't even lit the fucking thing.

They walked me over to Marigold Street and as we came up on a little house with yellow shutters and a white picket fence, Lew said, "This's Ira's house. Quilla June is his daughter."

"Well, land sakes," I said, wide-eyed.

Ira's lean jaw muscles jumped.

We went inside.

Quilla June was sitting on the settee with her mother, an older version of her, pulled thin as a withered muscle. "Miz Holmes," I said and made a little curtsey. She smiled. Strained, but smiled.

Quilla June sat with her feet right together, and her hands folded in her lap. There was a ribbon in her hair. It was blue.

Matched her eyes.

Something went thump in my gut.

"Quilla June," I said.

She looked up. "Mornin', Vic."

HARLAN ELLISON
A BOY AND HIS DOG

Then everyone sort of stood around looking awkward, and finally Ira began yapping and yipping about get in the bedroom and get this unnatural filth over with so they could go to Church and pray the Good Lord wouldn't Strike All Of Them Dead with a bolt of lightning in the ass, or some crap like that.

So I put out my hand, and Quilla June reached for it without looking up, and we went in the back, into a small bedroom, and she stood there with her head down.

"You didn't tell 'em, did you?" I asked.

She shook her head.

And suddenly, I didn't want to kill her at all. I wanted to hold her. Very tight. So I did. And she was crying into my chest, and making little fists beating on my back, and then she was looking up at me and running her words all together: "Oh, Vic, I'm sorry, so sorry, I didn't mean to, I had to, I was sent out to, I was so scared, and I love you, and now they've got you down here, and it isn't dirty, is it, it isn't the way my Poppa says it is, is it?"

I held her and kissed her and told her it was okay, and then I asked her if she wanted to come away with me, and she said yes yes yes she really did. So I told her I might have to hurt her Poppa to get away, and she got a look in her eyes that I knew real well.

For all her propriety, Quilla June Holmes didn't much like her prayer-shouting Poppa.

I asked her if she had anything heavy, like a candlestick or a club, and she said no. So I went rummaging around in that back bedroom and found a pair of her Poppa's socks in a bureau drawer. I pulled the big brass balls off the headboard of the bed and dropped them into the sock. I hefted it. Oh. Yeah.

She stared at me with big eyes. "What're you going to do?"

"You want to get out of here?"

She nodded.

"Then just stand back behind the door. No, wait a minute. I got a better idea. Get on the bed."

She lay down on the bed. "Okay," I said, "now pull up your skirt,

273

pull off your pants, and spread out." She gave me a look of pure horror. "Do it," I said. "If you want out."

So she did it, and I rearranged her so her knees were bent and her legs open at the thighs, and I stood to one side of the door, and whispered to her, "Call your Poppa. Just him."

She hesitated a long moment, then she called out in a voice she didn't have to fake, "Poppa! Poppa, come here, please!" Then she clamped her eyes shut tight.

Ira Holmes came through the door, took one look at his secret desire, his mouth dropped open, I kicked the door closed behind him and walloped him as hard as I could. He squished a little, and spattered the bedspread, and went very down.

She opened her eyes when she heard the thunk! and when the stuff spattered her legs, she leaned over and puked on the floor. I knew she wouldn't be much good to me in getting Aaron into the room, so I opened the door, stuck my head around, looked worried, and said, "Aaron, would you come here a minute, please?" He looked at Lew, who was rapping with Mrs. Holmes about what was going on in the back bedroom, and when Lew nodded him on, he came into the room. He took a look at Quilla June's naked bush, at the blood on the wall and bedspread, at Ira on the floor, and opened his mouth to yell just as I whacked him. It took two more to get him down, and then I had to kick him in the chest to put him away. Quilla June was still puking.

I grabbed her by the arm and swung her up off the bed. At least she was being quiet about it, but man, did she stink.

"Come on!"

She tried to pull back, but I held on and opened the bedroom door. As I pulled her out, Lew stood up, leaning on his cane. I kicked the cane out from under the old fart and down he went in a heap. Mrs. Holmes was staring at us, wondering where her old man was. "He's back in there," I said, heading for the front door. "The Good Lord got him in the head."

Then we were out in the street, Quilla June stinking along behind me, dry-heaving and bawling and probably wondering what had hap-

HARLAN ELLISON
A BOY AND HIS DOG

pened to her underpants.

They kept my weapons in a locked case at the Better Business Bureau, and we detoured around by my boarding house where I pulled the crowbar I'd swiped from the gas station out from under the back porch. Then we cut across behind the Grange and into the business section, and straight into the BBB. There was a clerk who tried to stop me, and I split his gourd with the crowbar. Then I pried the latch off the cabinet in Lew's office and got the .30-06 and my .45 and all the ammo, and my spike and my knife and my kit, and loaded up. By that time Quilla June was able to make some sense.

"Where we gonna go, where we gonna go, oh Poppa Poppa Popp. . .!"

"Hey, listen, Quilla June, Poppa me no Poppas. You said you wanted to be with me. . .well, I'm goin'! *Up*, baby, and if you wanna go with me, you better stick close."

She was too scared to object.

I stepped out the front of the shopfront, and there was that green box sentry, coming on like a whippet. It had its cables out, and the mittens were gone. It had hooks.

I dropped to one knee, wrapped the sling of the .30-06 around my forearm, sighted clean, and fired dead at the big eye in the front. One shot, spang!

Hit that eye, the thing exploded in a shower of sparks, and the green box swerved and went through the front window of The Mill End Shoppe, screeching and crying and showering the place with flames and sparks. Nice.

I turned around to grab Quilla June, but she was gone. I looked off down the street, and here came all the vigilantes, Lew hobbling along with his cane like some kind of weird grasshopper.

And right then the shots started. Big, booming sounds. The .45 I'd given Quilla June. I looked up, and on the porch around the second floor, there she was, the automatic down on the railing like a pro, sighting into that mob and snapping off shots like maybe Wild Bill Elliott in a '40s Republic flick.

But dumb! Mother dumb! Wasting time on that, when we had to get away.

I found the outside staircase going up there, and took it three steps at a time. She was smiling and laughing, and every time she'd pick one of those boobs out of the pack her little tonguetip would peek out of the corner of her mouth, and her eyes would get all slick and wet and wham! down the boob would go.

She was really into it.

Just as I reached her, she sighted down on her scrawny mother. I slammed the back of her head, and she missed the shot, and the old lady did a little dance-step and kept coming. Quilla June whipped her head around at me, and there was kill in her eyes. "You made me miss." The voice gave me a chill.

I took the .45 away from her. Dumb. Wasting ammunition like that.

Dragging her behind me, I circled the building, found a shed out back, dropped down onto it, and had her follow. She was scared at first, but I said, "Chick can shoot her old lady as easy as you do shouldn't be worried about a drop this small." She got out on the ledge, other side of the railing and held on. "Don't worry," I said, "you won't wet your pants. You haven't got any."

She laughed, like a bird, and dropped. I caught her, we slid down the shed door, and took a second to see if that mob was hard on us. Nowhere in sight.

I grabbed Quilla June by the arm and started off toward the south end of Topeka. It was the closest exit I'd found in my wandering, and we made it in about fifteen minutes, panting and weak as kittens.

And there it was.

A big air-intake duct.

I pried off the clamps with the crowbar, and we climbed up inside. There were ladders going up. There had to be. It figured. Repairs. Keep it clean. Had to be. We started climbing.

It took a long, long time.

Quilla June kept asking me, from down behind me, whenever she got too tired to climb, "Vic, do you love me?" I kept saying yes. Not only because I meant it. It helped her keep climbing.

HARLAN ELLISON
A BOY AND HIS DOG

X

We came up a mile from the access dropshaft. I shot off the filter covers and the hatch bolts, and we climbed out. They should have known better down there. You don't fuck around with Jimmy Cagney.

They never had a chance.

Quilla June was exhausted. I didn't blame her. But I didn't want to spend the night out in the open; there were things out there I didn't like to think about meeting even in daylight. It was getting on toward dusk.

We walked toward the access dropshaft.

Blood was waiting.

He looked weak. But he'd waited.

I stooped down and lifted his head. He opened his eyes, and very softly he said, "Hey."

I smiled at him. Jesus, it was good to see him. "We made it back, man."

He tried to get up, but he couldn't. The wounds on him were in ugly shape. "Have you eaten?" I asked.

"No. Grabbed a lizard yesterday. . .or maybe it was day before. I'm hungry, Vic."

Quilla June came up then, and Blood saw her. He closed his eyes. "We'd better hurry, Vic," she said. "Please. They might come up from the dropshaft."

I tried to lift Blood. He was dead weight. "Listen, Blood, I'll leg it into the city and get some food. I'll come back quick. You just wait here."

"Don't go in there, Vic," he said. "I did a recon the day after you went down. They found out we weren't fried in that gym. I don't know how. Maybe mutts smelled our track. I've been keeping watch, and they haven't tried to come out after us. I don't blame them. You don't know what it's like out here at night, man. . .you don't know. . ."

He shivered.

"Take it easy, Blood."

277

"But they've got us marked lousy in the city, Vic. We can't go back there. We'll have to make it someplace else."

That put it on a different stick. We couldn't go back, and with Blood in that condition we couldn't go forward. And I knew, good as I was solo, I couldn't make it without him. And there wasn't anything out here to eat. He had to have food at once, and some medical care. I had to do something. Something good, something fast.

"Vic!" Quilla June's voice was high and whining. "Come *on*! He'll be all right. We have to hurry!"

I looked up at her. The sun was sinking into the darkness. Blood trembled in my arms.

She got a pouty look on her face. "If you love me, you'll come *on*!"

I couldn't make it alone out there without him. I knew it. If I loved her. She asked me, in the boiler, do you know what love is?

It was a small fire, not nearly big enough for any roverpak to spot from the outskirts of the city. No smoke. And after Blood had eaten his fill, I carried him to the air-duct a mile away, and we spent the night inside on a little ledge. I held him all night. He slept good. In the morning, I fixed him up pretty good. He'd make it; he was strong.

He ate again. There was plenty left from the night before. I didn't eat. I wasn't hungry.

We started off across the blast wasteland that morning. We'd find another city, and make it.

We had to move slow because Blood was still limping. It took a long time before I stopped hearing her calling in my head. Asking me, asking me: *do you know what love is?*

Sure I know.

A boy loves his dog.

—*Los Angeles, 1968-69*

HARLAN ELLISON
A BOY AND HIS DOG